PENSION AND EMPLOYEE BENEFITS

CODE•ERISA•REGULATIONS

As of January 1, 2018
Volume 2

ERISA Law and Regulations
Related Laws
Proposed Regulations

Wolters Kluwer Editorial Staff Publication

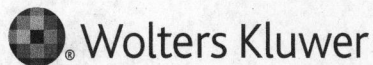

Portfolio Managing Editor . . . . Barbara O'Dell

Editor . . . . Elizabeth Pope

Production Editor . . . . Carmen Kane

This publication is designed to provide accurate and authoritative information in regard to the subject matter covered. It is sold with the understanding that the publisher is not engaged in rendering legal, accounting or other professional service. If legal advice or other expert assistance is required, the services of a competent professional person should be sought.

Compiled from

PENSION PLAN GUIDE

As of January 1, 2018

ISBN 978-1-4548-9564-0

2700 Lake Cook Road
Riverwoods, IL 60015
866 529-6600
www.WoltersKluwerLR.com

Printed in the United States of America

Table of Contents

VOLUME TWO

Post-2000 Benefits-Related Provisions of Selected Post-2000 Public Laws (Non-Code, Non-ERISA)

Note: See Public Law/Code and ERISA Locator Table on p. 86 for provisions amending Code or ERISA

VOLUME ONE

Finding List
Employee Retirement Income Security Act of 1974
(ERISA)
P.L. 93-406

Note: Employee Retirement Income Security Act of 1974, Title II (Secs. 1001 to 2008) made amendments to Internal Revenue Code provisions. These amendments are incorporated in place in the Internal Revenue Code provisions in Volume I.

Title I: Protection of Employee Benefit Rights

Title II: Amendments to the Internal Revenue Code Relating to Retirement Plans

[Note: Title II amendments to the Internal Revenue Code, encompassing ERISA Secs. 1011—2008, are incorporated in place in the Internal Revenue Code provisions in Volume I.]

Title III: Jurisdiction, Administration, Enforcement; Joint Pension Task Force, Etc.

Title IV: Plan Termination Insurance

Finding List
Veterans' Employment and Training Service Regulations

Finding List
Employee Benefits Security Administration (formerly Pension and Welfare Benefits Administration) Regulations

Finding List
Joint Board for the Enrollment of
Actuaries Regulations

Finding List
Pension Benefit Guaranty Corporation Regulations

Subpart A—Single-Employer Plans Covered by Title IV

Subpart B—Defined Contribution Plans

Subpart C—Certain Defined Benefit Plans Not Covered by Title IV

Finding List
Department of Justice Regulations

Procedures Governing Applications for Certificates of Exemption Under the Employee Retirement Income Security of Act of 1974

Finding List
Age Discrimination in Employment Act of 1967
P.L. 90-202

Finding List
Age Discrimination in Employment Regulations
(Equal Employment Opportunity Commission—DOL)

Finding List
Criminal Code

Reproduced at the paragraphs noted below are selected benefits-related portions of the U.S. Criminal Code.

Finding List
Fair Labor Standards Act

Excerpts from the Fair Labor Standards Act are reproduced below, including benefits-related changes made in 2010 by the Affordable Care Act (P.L. 111-148/111-152).

Act Sec.	Par. (¶)	Act Sec.	Par. (¶)
206 Minimum wage	16,301	**218B** Notice to employees	16,301
207 Maximum hours	16,301	**218C** Protections for employees	16,301
218A Automatic enrollment for employees of large employers	16,301		

Finding List
National Credit Union Administration Regulations

Reproduced at the paragraphs noted below are selected regulations issued by the National Credit Union Administration.

Act Sec.	Par. (¶)	Act Sec.	Par. (¶)
701.19 Benefits for Employees of Federal Credit Unions	16,401	**721.3(m)** Trustee or custodial services	16,401F
701.19(a) General authority	16,401	**724.1** Federal credit unions acting as trustees and custodians of certain tax-advantaged savings plans	16,402
701.19(b) Plan trustees and custodians	16,401	**724.2** Self-directed plans	16,402A
701.19(c) Investment authority	16,401	**724.3** Appointment of successor trustee or custodian	16,402B
701.19(d) Defined benefit plans	16,401	**745.9-1** IRA/Keogh accounts	16,403
701.19(e) Liability insurance	16,401	**745.9-2** Pass-through share insurance	16,403A
701.19(f) Definitions	16,401	Appendix to Part 745—Examples of Insurance Coverage Afforded Accounts in Credit Unions Insured by the National Credit Union Share Insurance Fund	16,404
701.35 Share, share draft and share certificate accounts	16,401A		
721.3 What categories of activities are preapproved as incidental powers necessary or requisite to carry on a credit union's business?	16,401F		

Finding List
Public Health Service Act
P.L. 78-410

Excerpts from the Public Health Service Act, including benefits-related changes made in 2010 by the Affordable Care Act (P.L. 111-148/111-152) are reproduced at ¶16,421.

Finding List
Uniformed Services Employment and Reemployment Rights Act of 1994
P.L. 103-353

Reproduced at the paragraphs noted below are benefits-related portions of the Uniformed Services Employment and Reemployment Rights Act of 1994.

Act Sec.	Par. (¶)	Act Sec.	Par. (¶)
4317 Health plans	16,452	**4318** Employee pension benefit plans	16,453

Finding List
Economic Growth and Tax Relief Reconciliation Act of 2001
P.L. 107-16

Finding List
Bankruptcy Abuse Prevention and Consumer Protection Act of 2005

P.L. 109-08

Reproduced at the paragraphs noted below are excerpts from the Bankruptcy Abuse Prevention and Consumer Protection Act of 2005 that pertain to pensions and employee benefits.

Finding List
Katrina Emergency Tax Relief Act

P.L. 109-73

Reproduced at the paragraphs noted below are excerpts from the Katrina Emergency Tax Relief Act that pertain to pensions and employee benefits.

Finding List
Pension Protection Act of 2006
P.L. 109-280

Reproduced at the paragraphs noted below are sections of the Pension Protection Act pertaining to pensions and employee benefits that did not amend any sections of the Internal Revenue Code or any sections of the Employee Retirement Income Security Act of 1974 (ERISA).

Finding List
Genetic Information Nondiscrimination Act of 2008

P.L. 110-233

Finding List
Heartland, Habitat, Harvest, and Horticulture Act of 2008

P.L. 110-246

Finding List
Emergency Economic Stabilization Act of 2008

P.L. 110-343

Finding List
Worker, Retiree, and Employer Recovery Act of 2008

P.L. 110-458

Reproduced at the paragraphs noted below are section of the Worker, Retiree and Employer Recovery Act of 2008 that did not amend any section of the Internal Revenue Code of 1986 or any sections of the Employee Retiree Income Security Act of 1974 (ERISA).

Finding List
American Recovery and Reinvestment Act of 2009

P.L. 111-5

Reproduced at the paragraphs noted below are sections of the American Recovery and Reinvestment Act of 2009 pertaining to pensions and employee benefits that did not amend any sections of the Internal Revenue Code or any sections of the Employee Retirement Income Security Act of 1974 (ERISA).

Finding List
FAA Modernization and Reform Act of 2012
P.L. 112-95

Reproduced at the paragraphs noted below are sections of the FAA Modernization and Reform Act of 2012, pertaining to rollovers of amounts received in airline carrier bankruptcies, that did not amend the Internal Revenue Code or ERISA.

Finding List
Moving Ahead For Progress in the 21st Century Act

P.L. 112-141

Reproduced at the paragraphs noted below are sections of the Moving Ahead for Progress in the 21st Century Act, pertaining to pensions and employee benefits, that did not amend the Internal Revenue Code or ERISA.

Act Sec.	Par. (¶)
40231 Pension Benefit Guaranty Corporation governance improvement	**16,474A**
40231(f) Study regarding governance structures	**16,474A**
40233 Quality control procedures for the Pension Benefit Guaranty Corporation	**16,474B**

Act Sec.	Par. (¶)
40233(a) Annual peer review of insurance modeling systems	**16,474B**
40233(b) Policies and procedures relating to the policy, research, and analysis department	**16,474B**
40233(c) Report relating to OIG recommendations	**16,474B**

Finding List
Cooperative and Small Employer Charity Pension Flexibility Act

P.L. 113-97

Reproduced at the paragraphs noted below are provisions of the Cooperative and Small Employer Charity Pension Flexibility Act, pertaining to pensions and employee benefits, that did not amend the Internal Revenue Code or ERISA.

Act Sec.	Par. (¶)
103 Elections	**16,475A**
105 Sponsor Education and Assistance	**16,475B**

Finding List
Consolidated and Further Continuing Appropriations Act, 2015
P.L. 113-235

Reproduced at the paragraphs noted below are provisions of the Consolidated and Further Continuing Appropriations Act, 2015, pertaining to pensions and employee benefits, that did not amend the Internal Revenue Code or ERISA.

Finding List
Disaster Tax Relief and Airport and Airway Extension Act of 2017
P.L. 115-63

Reproduced below are excerpts from the Disaster Tax Relief and Airport and Airway Extension Act of 2017 (P.L. 115-63) that pertains to pensions and employee benefits.

Finding List
ERISA Reorganization Plan

List of IRS Proposed Regulations

Following is a list of proposed regulations relating to employee benefits issued by the Internal Revenue Service. The listing is by Internal Revenue Code section.

Title 26—Internal Revenue Code of 1986

1986 Code Sec.	Regs. Section	Date Proposed [1]	Date Adopted [2]	Paragraph (¶) [3]
36B	1.36B-0—1.36B-5	8/17/11	5/23/12 T.D. 9590	20,262X; 23,284
	1.36B-0—1.36B-3	5/3/13	12/18/15 T.D. 9745	20,263N; 23,321
	1.36B-0—1.36B-3	7/8/16	12/19/16 T.D. 9804	20,264M; 23,329
	1.36B-0	7/2/13	5/7/14 T.D. 9663	20,263O; 11,112F-1
	1.36B-5	7/2/13	5/7/14 T.D. 9663	20,263O; 11,112F-6
	1.36B-5	7/8/16	12/19/16 T.D. 9804	20,264M; 11,112F-6
	1.36B-6	5/3/13	12/18/15 T.D. 9745	20,263N; 11,112F-7
	1.36B-6	9/1/15	12/18/15 T.D. 9745	20,264E; 11,112F-7
45R	1.45R-0—1.45R-5	8/26/13	6/30/14 T.D. 9672	20,263P; 23,303
61	1.61-2	7/9/02	9/17/03 T.D. 9092	20,260M; 23,214
	1.61-2T	12/23/85 T.D. 8063	7/6/89 T.D. 8256	11,172A
	1.61-16	3/3/78	. . . .	20,159
	1.61-21(d)(3)	10/9/92		20,159B
	1.61-21(k)	5/20/91	1/16/92 T.D. 8389	11,176
	1.61-22	7/9/02	9/17/03 T.D. 9092	20,260M; 23,214
		5/9/03	. . . .	20,260T
62	1.62-1(c)(13)	7/14/81	. . . .	20,137B
	1.62-1T(c)(2)	12/17/90	. . . .	20,184
	1.62-1T(f)	12/17/90	. . . .	20,184
	1.62-2	9/30/98	1/26/00 T.D. 8864	11,182
	1.62-2(e)(2)	11/12/02	. . . .	20,260Q
72	1.72-4	4/30/75	. . . .	20,121
	1.72-4	withdrawn 1/13/87	. . . .	20,150A
	1.72-4—1.72-7	3/24/86	12/16/86 T.D. 8115	11,194—11,197
	1.72-9	3/24/86	12/16/86 T.D. 8115	11,199
	1.72-11	3/24/86	12/16/86 T.D. 8115	11,201
	1.72-13	4/30/75	. . . .	20,121
	1.72-15	withdrawn 1/13/87	. . . .	20,150A
	1.72-15	8/20/07	5/12/14 T.D. 9665	20,262C; 11,205
	1.72-17A	12/21/95	7/31/00 T.D. 8894	20,210
	1.72(e)-1T	2/4/86	. . . .	20,137Y; 11,209
	1.72(p)	12/21/95	7/31/00 T.D. 8894	20,210
	1.72(p)-1	1/2/98	7/31/00 T.D. 8894	20,230
	1.72(p)-1	7/31/00	12/3/02 T.D. 9021	23,199; 11,210
	1.72(p)-1	7/14/05	10/20/06 T.D. 9294	20,261O; 11,210
79	1.79-0	10/7/82	10/6/83 T.D. 7917	11,230A
	1.79-1	10/7/82	12/6/83	11,231
	1.79-1(d)(3)	2/17/04	8/29/05 T.D. 9223	11,231
	1.79-1(d)(7)	7/7/83	T.D. 7924	11,231
	1.79-1(g)	withdrawn 1/13/87	. . . .	20,150D
	1.79-3(d)(2)	7/7/83	12/6/83 T.D. 7924	11,233

[1] Date published in the *Federal Register*.

[2] Date filed with the *Federal Register*.

[3] Location of text in Pension Plan Guide.

1986 Code Sec.	Regs. Section	Date Proposed[1]	Date Adopted[2]	Paragraph (¶)[3]
		1/13/99	5/28/99 T.D. 8821	20,240
83	1.79-4T	2/4/86	. . . .	20,137Y; 11,234
	1.83-1	[Draft]	. . . .	20,108A
		7/9/02	9/17/03 T.D. 9092	20,260M; 23,214
	1.83-2	7/17/15	7/26/16 T.D. 9779	20,264C; 11,242
	1.83-3	11/16/83	8/5/85 T.D. 8042	11,243
		7/9/02	9/17/03 T.D. 9092	20,260M; 23,214
	1.83-3	5/30/12	2/26/14 T.D. 9659	20,263E; 11,243
	1.83-3(e)	2/17/04	8/29/05 T.D. 9223	11,243
	1.83-6	12/5/94	T.D. 8599	11,246
		12/5/94	. . . .	20,203
		7/9/02	9/17/03 T.D. 9092	20,260M; 23,214
		5/9/03	9/17/03 T.D. 9092	20,260T; 23,214
	1.83-7	7/2/03	. . . .	20,260X
89	1.89(a)-1	repealed P.L. 101-140 11/8/89	. . . .	20,118I
	1.89(k)-1	repealed P.L. 101-140 11/8/89	. . . .	20,118I
101	1.101-1(a)(2)	12/24/80	9/23/82 T.D. 7836	11,251 20,121
	1.101-2	4/30/75	. . . .	11,252
	1.101-2	12/24/80	9/23/82 T.D. 7836	
	1.101-2	10/31/83	5/10/84 T.D. 7955	11,252
	1.101-2(e)(1) and (2)	11/2/92	6/9/94 T.D. 8540	23,117; 11,252
	1.101-7T	9/21/87	11/17/89 T.D. 8272	11,256D
104	1.104-1	withdrawn 1/13/87	. . . .	20,150A
105	1.105-1	withdrawn 1/13/87		20,150A
	1.105-2	withdrawn 1/13/87		20,150A
	1.105-4	withdrawn 1/13/87		20,150A
	1.105-4	8/20/07	5/12/14 T.D. 9665	20,262C; 11,274
	1.105-6	8/20/07	5/12/14 T.D. 9665	20,262C; 11,276
	1.105-7—1.105-10	withdrawn 1/13/87	. . . .	20,150A
	1.105-11(f)	2/28/83		20,137G
	7.105-1	withdrawn 1/13/87		20,150A
	7.105-2	withdrawn 1/13/87	. . . .	20,150A
106	1.106-1	withdrawn 1/13/87		20,111
	1.106-1	6/15/87	2/2/99 T.D. 8812	20,149A
	1.106-1	8/20/07	5/12/14 T.D. 9665	20,262C; 11,281
	1.106-6	withdrawn 1/13/87	. . . .	20,150A
120	1.120-1	4/29/80		20,164A
	1.120-2	5/13/71		20,164A
125	1.125-0	8/6/07		20,262B
	1.125-1	withdrawn	. . . .	20,137Q
	1.125-1	withdrawn	. . . .	20,137R
	1.125-1	withdrawn	. . . .	20,118I
	1.125-1	withdrawn	. . . .	20,227
	1.125-1	withdrawn	. . . .	20,247
	1.125-1	1/10/2001	. . . .	20,258
	1.125-1	8/6/2007	. . . .	20,262B
	1.125-2	withdrawn	. . . .	20,118I
	1.125-2	withdrawn	. . . .	20,227
	1.125-2	8/6/07	. . . .	20,262B
	1.125-2T	2/4/86	. . . .	20,137Y; 11,288C
	1.125-3	12/21/95	10/17/01 T.D. 8966	20,211; 11,288B-45
	1.125-4	withdrawn	. . . .	20,247

1986 Code Sec.	Regs. Section	Date Proposed [1]	Date Adopted [2]	Paragraph (¶) [3]
	1.125-4T	11/7/97	. . . .	20,227; 11,288E
	1.125-5—1.125-7	8/6/07	. . . .	20,262B
127	1.127-1—1.127-2	11/23/81	7/5/83 T.D. 7898	11,289A—11,289B
132	1.132-1T—8T	12/23/85 T.D. 8063	7/6/86 T.D. 8256	11,289N-1 to N-8
	1.132-5	9/25/91	12/29/92	20,186
	1.132-6	5/20/91	1/16/92 T.D. 8389	11,289O-6
	1.132-9	1/27/2000	10/20/06 T.D. 9294	20,245; 11,289O-9
152	1.152-4	5/2/07	T.D. 9408	20,261X; 11,295D
162	1.162-10T	2/4/86	. . . .	20,137Y; 11,304A
	1.162-25T	1/7/85	. . . .	20,137S; 11,306
	1.162-25T	11/6/85	. . . .	20,137V; 11,306
	1.162-25T	withdrawn	. . . .	20,137W; 11,306
	1.162(k)-1	8/25/05		20,261R
	1.162-26	6/15/87	2/2/99 T.D. 8812	20,149A; 23,152
162(m)	1.162-27	12/20/93	12/20/95 T.D. 8650	20,201; 11,307
	1.162-27	12/02/94	12/20/95 T.D. 8650	20,202; 11,307
	1.162-27	6/24/11	3/31/15 T.D. 9716	20,262W; 11,307
	1.162-31	4/2/13	9/23/14 T.D. 9694	20,263M; 11,307G
	1.162-31	6/10/16		20,264J
219	1.219-1(b)	11/23/81	. . . .	20,137B
	1.219-1(d)	7/14/81	. . . .	20,137B
	1.219-1(e)	7/14/81	. . . .	20,137B
	1.219-2	7/14/81	. . . .	20,137B
	1.219-3	7/14/81	. . . .	20,137B
	1.219(a)-1—1.219(a)-6	1/23/84		20,137O
220	1.220-1(a)	7/14/81	. . . .	20,137B
274	1.274-3	12/16/82	9/19/88 T.D. 8230	11,357
	1.274-5	9/30/98	1/26/2000 T.D. 8864	11,357B
	1.274-5(j) and (m)	11/12/02		20,260Q
	1.274-5T	3/25/97	. . . .	20,222
	1.274-5T	2/20/85	. . . .	20,137T; 11,357G
	1.274-5T	11/6/85 partially withdrawn	. . . .	20,137V; 11,357G
	1.274-5T	12/23/85 T.D. 8063	. . . .	20,137W; 11,357G
	1.274-6T	2/20/85	. . . .	20,137T; 11,357H
	1.274-6T	11/6/85 T.D. 8061	. . . .	20,137V; 11,357H
	1.274-6T	12/23/85		20,137W; 11,357H
	1.274-8	1/9/89 T.D. 8063		20,118G
280F	1.280F-3T	11/6/85 T.D. 8061	. . . .	20,137V
	1.280F-6T	2/20/85	. . . .	20,137T
	1.280F-6T	11/6/85		20,137V
280G	1.280G-1	5/5/89	2/20/02 amended	20,178; 20,260G
	1.280G-1	2/20/02	8/4/03 T.D. 9083	20,260G; 23,213
401	1.401-1(b)(1)(ii)	8/20/07	5/12/14 T.D. 9665	20,262C; 11,701
	1.401-3(e)	11/15/88	. . . . T.D. 8061	20,166A
	1.401-4(c)(1)	1/26/82	1/9/84 T.D. 7934	11,704
	1.401-4(c)(7)(i)— 1.401-4(c)(7)(vi)	1/26/82	1/9/84 T.D. 7934	11,704
	1.401-4(d)(1)-(2)	8/10/92	. . . .	20,188
	1.401(a)-1	7/27/87	. . . .	20,163B
		11/10/04	. . . .	20,261G
		1/27/16	. . . .	20,264G
	1.401(a)-1(b)(1)(i)	11/10/04	5/22/07 T.D. 9325	20,261G; 23,247 11,715
	1.401(a)-1(b)(2)—(4)	11/10/04	5/22/07 T.D. 9325	20,261G; 23,247 11,715
	1.401(a)-2(b)	5/31/05	4/5/07 T.D. 9319	11,716
	1.401(a)-3	3/11/83	7/22/02	20,137I
		11/10/04	. . . .	20,261G
	1.401(a)-4, A-1(a)(1)	5/10/90	. . . .	20,121A
		12/3/90	. . . .	20,183

1986 Code Sec.	Regs. Section	Date Proposed [1]	Date Adopted [2]	Paragraph (¶) [3]
	1.401(a)-4, A-2(b)(4)(i)	5/10/90	. . . .	20,121A
	1.401(a)-4, A-6	8/10/92	. . . .	20,188
	1.401(a)-11	10/27/82	. . . .	20,137D
	1.401(a)-11T	7/19/85	. . . .	20,138A; 20,138B
	1.401(a)-13(g)(4)(ii)	10/9/08	. . . .	20,262R
	1.401(a)-13T	7/19/85	. . . .	20,138B
	1.401(a)-18	3/24/86	. . . .	20,118F
	1.401(a)-20	1/28/05	3/24/06 T.D. 9256	20,261L; 11,720F
	1.401(a)-20	10/9/08	. . . .	20,262R
	1.401(a)-21	7/14/05	10/20/06 T.D. 9294	20,261O; 11,720Z-18
	1.401(a)-50	11/17/81	12/1/82 T.D. 7859	11,720V
	1.401(a)(4)-0	1/29/16	. . . .	20,264H
	1.401(a)(4)-0—1.401(a)(4)-13	1/12/93	9/3/93 T.D. 8485	11,720W-14
		8/10/92	T.D. 8360	
	1.401(a)(4)-8	10/6/00	6/29/01 T.D. 8954	20,250; 23,183
	1.401(a)(4)-8—1.401(a)(4)-9	1/29/16	. . . .	20,264H
	1.401(a)(4)-9	10/6/00	6/29/01 T.D. 8954	20,250; 23,183
	1.401(a)(4)-12	8/10/92	. . . .	20,188
		4/21/93	. . . .	20,195
		4/21/93	. . . .	20,196
	1.401(a)(4)-12—1.401(a)(4)-13	1/29/16	. . . .	20,264H
		8/10/92	. . . .	20,188
	1.401(a)(5)-1	5/10/90	9/19/91 T.D. 8359	11,720X
		8/10/92	. . . .	20,188
	1.401(a)(9)	5/31/05	. . . .	20,261N
	1.401(a)(9)-0	1/17/01	. . . .	20,260C
	1.401(a)(9)-1	7/27/87	. . . .	20,163B
		12/30/97	. . . .	20,162B
		1/17/01	. . . .	20,260C
		7/10/08	9/8/09 T.D. 9459	20,262M; 23,261
	1.401(a)(9)-2	7/27/87	. . . .	20,163B
		1/17/01	. . . .	20,260C
	1.401(a)(9)-3	1/17/01	. . . .	20,260C
	1.401(a)(9)-4	1/17/01	. . . .	20,260C
	1.401(a)(9)-5	1/17/01	. . . .	20,260C
	1.401(a)(9)-5	5/31/05	4/5/07 T.D. 9319	11,720Y-5
	1.401(a)(9)-5	2/3/12	7/2/14 T.D. 9673	20,263A; 11,720Y-5
	1.401(a)(9)-6	1/17/01	6/15/04 T.D. 9130	20,260C; 11,720Y-6
	1.401(a)(9)-6	7/10/08	9/8/09 T.D. 9459	20,262M; 23,261
	1.401(a)(9)-6	2/13/12	7/2/14 T.D. 9673	20,263A; 11,720Y-6
	1.401(a)(9)-7	1/17/01	. . . .	20,260C
	1.401(a)(9)-8	1/17/01	6/15/04 T.D. 9130	20,260C; 11,720Y-8
	1.401(a)(17)-1	5/10/90	9/19/91 T.D. 8362	11,720Z
		8/10/92	. . . .	20,188
		12/30/93	6-23-94 T.D. 8547	11,720Z-11
	1.401(a)(26)-0	5/10/90	12/4/91 T.D. 8375	11,720Z-31—11,720Z-40
	1.401(a)(26)-1—1.401(a)(26)-3	withdrawn	. . . .	20,118H
	1.401(a)(26)-1(d)(1)(i)	5/18/89	12/4/91 T.D. 8375	11,720Z-32
	1.401(a)(26)-1(d)(2)(iv)	5/18/89	12/4/91 T.D. 8375	11,720Z-33
	1.401(a)(26)-2	2/1/91	12/4/91 T.D. 8375	11,720Z-34
	1.401(a)(26)-3(b)(8)	5/18/89	12/4/91 T.D. 8375	11,720Z-37
	1.401(a)(26)-6	2/1/91	12/4/91 T.D. 8375	11,720Z-39
	1.401(a)(26)-8(b)(4)	5/18/89	12/4/91 T.D. 8375	11,720Z-39
	1.401(a)(26)-8(b)(5)	5/18/89	12/4/91 T.D. 8375	11,720Z-39
	1.401(a)(26)-8(b)(6)	5/18/89	12/4/91 T.D. 8375	11,720Z-39
	1.401(a)(26)-9	8/10/92	. . . .	20,188
	1.401(a)(31)-1	9/19/96	4/21/2000	11,720Z-50

1986 Code Sec.	Regs. Section	Date Proposed [1]	Date Adopted [2]	Paragraph (¶) [3]
		12/17/98	T.D. 8880 4/21/2000	11,720Z
	1.401(a)(35)-1	1/3/08	T.D. 8880 5/19/2010	T.D. 9484
	1.401(b)-1	3/15/83	12/28/84	20,137H; 11,721
		8/1/97	2/4/00	20,226; 11,721
			T.D. 8871	
	1.401(b)-1T	8/1/97	2/4/00	20,226; 11,722
			T.D. 8871	
	1.401(j)-1—1.401(j)-6	3/24/86	. . . .	20,118F
		4/21/93	. . . .	20,197
	1.401(k)-0	1/26/06	4/30/07	11,731F
			T.D. 9324	
	1.401(k)-0	11/8/07	2/24/09	20,262E; 23,260
			T.D. 9447	
	1.401(k)-0	5/18/09	11/15/13	20,262T
			T.D. 9641	
	1.401(k)-0—1.401(k)-6	7/17/03	. . . .	20,261
			T.D. 8357	
	1.401(k)-1	5/10/90	8/15/91	11,731
			T.D. 8357	
		8/10/92	. . . .	20,188
	1.401(k)-1	11/8/07	2/24/09	20,262E; 23,260
			T.D. 9447	
	1.401(k)-1	1/18/17	. . . .	20,264Q
	1.401(k)-1(e)	5/31/05	. . . .	20,261N
	1.401(k)-1(e)(8)	5/31/05	4/5/07	11,731G
			T.D. 9319	
	1.401(k)-1(f)	3/2/05	. . . .	20,261M
		1/26/06	4/30/07	11,731G
			T.D. 9324	
	1.401(k)-1(g)(11)(iii)(A)	1/4/93	. . . .	20,192
	1.401(k)-1(g)(11)(iii)(D)(2)	1/4/93	. . . .	20,192
	1.401(k)-2	3/2/05	. . . .	20,261M
	1.401(k)-2	11/8/07	2/24/09	20,262E; 23,260
			T.D. 9447	
	1.401(k)-3	3/2/05	10/20/06	11,731I
			T.D. 9294	
	1.401(k)-3	11/8/07	2/24/09	20,262E; 23,260
			T.D. 9447	
	1.401(k)-3(e)(4)(ii)	5/18/09	11/15/13	20,262T
			T.D. 9641	
	1.401(k)-3(g)	5/18/09	. . . .	20,262T
	1.401(k)-6	3/2/05	. . . .	20,261M
	1.401(k)-6	11/8/07	2/24/09	20,262E; 23,260
			T.D. 9447	
	1.401(k)-6	1/18/17	. . . .	20,264Q
	1.401(l)-1—1.401(l)-6	5/10/90	9/19/91	11,731P—11,731P-6
			T.D. 8359	
		8/10/92	. . . .	20,188
		4/21/93	9/3/93	11,731Q
			T.D. 8486	
	1.401(m)-0—1.401(m)-2	5/10/90	8/15/91	11,732—11,732B
			T.D. 8357	
		8/10/92	. . . .	20,188
	1.401(m)-0	11/8/07	2/24/09	20,262E; 23,260
			T.D. 9447	
	1.401(m)-0	5/18/09	11/15/13	20,262T
			T.D. 9641	
	1.401(m)-1	11/8/07	2/24/09	20,262E; 23,260
			T.D. 9447	
	1.401(m)-1	1/18/17	. . . .	20,264Q
	1.401(m)-2	3/2/05	. . . .	20,261M
	1.401(m)-2	11/8/07	2/24/09	20,262E; 23,260
			T.D. 9447	
	1.401(m)-3	11/8/07	2/24/09	20,262E; 23,260
			T.D. 9447	
	1.401(m)-3(f)(4)(ii)	5/18/09	11/15/13	20,262T
			T.D. 9641	
	1.401(m)-3(h)	5/18/09	11/15/13	20,262T
			T.D. 9641	
	1.401(m)-5	1/18/17	. . . .	20,264Q
402	1.402(a)-1	4/30/75	. . . .	20,121
		8/10/92	. . . .	20,188
		2/17/04	8/29/05	11,751
			T.D. 9223	
	1.402(a)-1	8/20/07	5/12/14	20,262C; 11,751
			T.D. 9665	
	1.402(a)-1(a)-9, 1.402(e)-2(d)(iii)	5/31/79	. . . .	20,146A
	1.402(a)-1(d)	11/10/81	. . . .	20,142C
	1.402(a)(5)-1T	2/4/86		20,137Y; 11,751A
	1.402(b)-1	11/16/04	7/26/07	20,261H; 23,251

1986 Code Sec.	Regs. Section	Date Proposed [1]	Date Adopted [2]	Paragraph (¶) [3]
	1.402(c)-2	10/21/92	T.D. 9340 9/15/95	20,189; 11,753-10
	1.402(c)-2	9/19/96	T.D. 8619 4/21/2000	11,753-10
	1.402(c)-2	5/31/05	T.D. 8880 4/5/07	20,261N; 11,753-10
	1.402(c)-2	8/20/07	T.D. 9319 5/12/14	20,262C; 11,753-10
	1.402(c)-2	11/8/07	T.D. 9665 2/24/09	20,262E; 23,260
	1.402(e)-2, 1.402(e)-3	4/30/75	T.D. 9447	20,121
	1.402(e)-14	10/9/08	. . . .	20,262R
	1.402(f)-1	12/18/98	2/8/00	11,775-2
	1.402(f)-1	7/14/05	10/20/06	20,261O; 11,755-2
	1.402(f)-1T	7/19/85	T.D. 9294	20,138A
	1.402(f)-2T	withdrawn		20,189; 11,755-2F
	1.402(g)-0—	8/8/88	8/8/91	11,755-3—11,755-4
	1.402(g)-1	1/26/06	4/30/07	20,261W; 11,755-4
	1.402(g)(3)-1	11/16/04	T.D. 9324 7/26/07	23,251; 11,755A
402A	1.402A-1	1/26/06	4/30/07	20,261W; 11,799A-1
		11/16/04	T.D. 9324 7/26/07	23,251; 11,799A-1
	1.402A-1	9/19/14	5/18/16	20,263Z; 11,799A-1
	1.402A-2	1/26/06	T.D. 9769 4/30/07	20,261W; 11,799A-2
403	1.403(a)-1(g)	8/20/07	T.D. 9324 5/12/14	20,262C; 11,801
	1.403(a)-1—1.403(a)-2	4/30/75	T.D. 9665	20,121
	1.403(a)-2(e)(3)(ii)	5/31/79	9/23/82	20,146A
	1.403(b)-1(d)	12/24/80	T.D. 7836	11,803
	1.403(b)-1(d)(4)(iv)	3/24/86	12/16/86	11,803
	1.403(b)-1(h)	withdrawn 1/13/87	T.D. 8115	20,160
	1.403(b)-1(h)	withdrawn 1/13/87	. . . .	20,174
	1.403(b)-2	7/27/87	. . . .	20,163B
		10/21/92	9/15/95	20,189; 11,803-10
		1/17/01	T.D. 8619	20,260C
		1/26/06	. . . .	20,261W
	1.403(b)-3	5/31/05	. . . .	20,261N
		1/26/06	. . . .	20,261W
	1.403(b)-0—1.403(b)11	11/16/04	7/26/07	23,251; 11,802M; 11,803; 11,803-10; 11,803-11; 11,803-12; 11,803-13; 11,803-14; 11,803-15; 11,803-16; 11,803-17; 11,803-18; 11,803-19
	1.403(b)-5	1/26/06	T.D. 9340	20,261W
	1.403(b)-6	2/3/12	7/2/14	20,263A; 11,803-14
	1.403(b)-6(g)	8/20/07	T.D. 9673 5/12/14	20,262C; 11,803-14
	1.403(b)-6(e)	7/10/08	T.D. 9665 9/8/09	20,262M; 23,261
	1.403(b)-7	1/26/06	T.D. 9459	20,261W
404	1.404(a)-1T	2/4/86	. . . .	20,137Y; 11,851A
	1.404(a)(8)-1T	2/4/86	. . . .	20,137Y; 11,859A
	1.404(b)-1T	2/4/86	. . . .	20,137Y; 11,865A
	1.404(d)-1T	2/4/86	. . . .	20,137Y; 11,867
	1.404(g)-1	5/20/85	5/1/86	11,869A
	1.404(h)-1	7/14/81		20,137B
	1.404(k)-1T	2/4/86	. . . .	20,137Y; 11,870
	1.404(k)-2	8/25/05		20,261R
	1.404(k)-3	8/25/05		20,261R
404A	1.404A.1—1.404A-7	5/7/93	. . . .	20,162A
	1.404A-1—1.404A-6	withdrawn 5/7/93	. . . .	20,163A
408	1.408-2(b)	1/23/84	. . . .	20,137O
	1.408-2(c)(3)	7/14/81	. . . .	20,137B
	1.408-2(e)(8)	7/22/04	6/18/07	12,054
	1.408-3(b)(2)	. . . .	T.D. 9331	20,137O
	1.408-4	7/14/81	. . . .	20,137B
		7/23/02	5/5/03	20,260O; 12,056
	1.408-5	11/16/84	. . . .	20,118B

1986 Code Sec.	Regs. Section	Date Proposed [1]	Date Adopted [2]	Paragraph (¶) [3]
	1.408-6(b)	7/14/81	. . . .	20,137B
	1.408-8	7/27/87		20,163B
	1.408-8	1/17/01	. . . .	20,260C
	1.408-8	2/3/12	7/2/14 T.D. 9673	20,263A; 12,060
	1.408-7—1.408-9	7/14/81		20,137B
	1.408-10	1/23/84	. . . .	20,137O
	1.408-11	7/23/02	5/5/03	20,260O; 12,063
	1.408(q)-1	5/20/03	7/22/04	20,260U; 12,070
408A	1.408A-2	8/31/98	2/3/99	20,233
	1.408A-4	8/31/98	2/3/99	20,233
	1.408A-4, Q&A-14	8/22/05	7/20/08	20,261Q
	1.408A-5	8/31/98	2/3/99	20,233
		7/23/02	5/5/03	20,260O; 12,097A-5
	1.408A-6	2/3/12	7/2/14 T.D. 9673	20,263A; 12,097A-6
	1.408A-7	8/31/98	2/3/99	20,233
	1.408A-10	1/26/06	4/30/07 T.D. 9324	20,261W; 12,097A-10
409	1.409-1	7/14/81	. . . .	20,137B
	1.409-1(b)(2)	1/23/84		20,137O
	1.409(a)(9)-1 A-2(d)	7/10/08		20,262M
	1.409(a)(9)-6 Q & A-16	7/10/08		20,262M
	1.409(p)-1	7/21/03		20,261A
	1.409(p)-1	12/17/04	. . . .	20,261I
409A	1.409A-1—1.409A-6	10/4/05	4/17/07	12,147A—12,147G
	1.409A-1—1.409A-4	6/22/16	. . . .	20,264L
	1.409A-4	12/08/08	. . . .	20,262S
	1.409A-6	6/22/16	. . . .	20,264L
410	1.410(a)-3T	1/6/88	. . . .	20,165C
	1.410(a)-4A	4/11/88		20,149C
	1.410(a)-5T	7/19/85		20,138B
	1.410(a)-7T	7/19/85	. . . .	20,138B
	1.410(a)-8T	1/6/88	. . . .	20,165C
	1.410(a)-9T			
	1.410(b)-0—1.410(b)-10	1/6/88	. . . .	20,165C
		5/18/89	9/19/91	12,163—12,163J
		8/10/92	. . . .	20,188
	1.410(b)-0	4/21/93	9/1/93 T.D. 8487	12,165
	1.410(b)-0	9/7/93	6/23/94 T.D. 8548	12,165
	1.410(b)-1(a)	5/18/89	9/19/91	12,163A
	1.410(b)-2	4/21/93	9/1/93 T.D. 8487	12,165
	1.410(b)-2(b)(1)	5/10/90	9/19/91	12,163B
	1.410(b)-2(b)(6)	5/10/90	9/19/91	12,163B
	1.410(b)-2(b)(7)	5/10/90	9/19/91	12,163B
	1.410(b)-2(b)(8)	5/10/90	9/19/91	12,163B
	1.410(b)-2(c)(2)(ii)(C)	5/10/90	9/19/91	12,163B
	1.410(b)-3	4/21/93	9/1/93 T.D. 8487	12,165
	1.410(b)-5	9/14/90	9/19/91	12,163E
	1.410(b)-5	4/21/93	. . . .	12,165
	1.410(b)-5(a)	5/18/89	9/19/91	12,163E
	1.410(b)-5(b)	5/18/89	9/19/91	12,163E
	1.410(b)-5(c)	5/18/89	9/19/91	12,163E
	1.410(b)-5(d)	5/10/90	9/19/91	12,163E
	1.410(b)-5(e)	5/10/90	T.D. 8363	12,163E
	1.410(b)-6	2/1/91	. . . .	20,110
	1.410(b)-6	4/21/93	9/1/93 T.D. 8487	12,165
	1.410(b)-6(b)(1)	5/10/90	T.D. 8363	12,163F
	1.410(b)-6(b)(2)	5/10/90	T.D. 8363	12,163F
	1.410(b)-7	9/14/90	T.D. 8363	12,163G
	1.410(b)-7	2/1/91	. . . .	20,110A
	1.410(b)-7	4/21/93	9/1/93 T.D. 8487	12,165
	1.410(b)-7	9/7/93	. . . .	20,198
	1.410(b)-9	2/1/91	. . . .	20,110A
	1.410(b)-9	4/21/93	9/1/93 T.D. 8487	12,165
	1.410(b)-9(g)	5/10/90	T.D. 8363	12,163I
	1.410(b)-10	4/21/93	9/1/93 T.D. 8487	12,165
	1.410(b)-10(a)	5/10/90	T.D. 8363	12,163J
	1.410(b)-10(d)	5/10/90	T.D. 8363	12,163J
		12/3/90	T.D. 8363	12,163J
411	1.411(a)	1/6/88	. . . .	20,165C
	1.411(a)-1	4/11/88	. . . .	20,149C
	1.411(a)-4	11/8/07	2/24/09 T.D. 9447	20,262E; 23,260

1986 Code Sec.	Regs. Section	Date Proposed [1]	Date Adopted [2]	Paragraph (¶) [3]
	1.411(a)-7	4/11/88	. . . .	20,149C
	1.411(a)-7	12/21/98	. . . .	20,239
	1.411(a)-11	10/9/08	. . . .	20,262R
	1.411(a)-11	12/21/98	2/8/00	12,219D
	1.411(a)-11	7/14/05	10/20/06 T.D. 9294	20,261O; 12,219D
	1.411(a)-11	7/19/85	T.D. 8219 12/18/98	12,219D 20,238
	1.411(a)-11	9/22/95	T.D. 8796 12/17/98	20,207
	1.411(a)(13)-1	12/28/07	10/19/10 T.D. 9505	20,262F; 12,220
	1.411(a)(13)-1	10/19/10	9/19/14 T.D. 9693	20,262V; 12,220
	1.411(b)-1	6/18/08	. . . .	20,262L
	1.411(b)-1	10/19/10	9/19/14 T.D. 9693	20,262V; 12,223
	1.411(b)-2	4/11/88	. . . .	20,149C
	1.411(b)(5)-1	12/28/07	10/19/10 T.D. 9505	20,262F; 12,224
	1.411(b)(5)-1	10/19/10	9/19/14 T.D. 9693	20,262V; 12,224
	1.411(b)(5)-1	9/19/14	11/16/15 T.D. 9743	20,263Y; 12,224
	1.411(c)-1	4/11/88	. . . .	20,149C
	1.411(c)-1	12/22/95	. . . .	20,212
	1.411(d)-1(a)—1.411(d)-1(c)	4/9/80	. . . .	20,172
	1.411(d)-1(c)(2)	6/12/80	. . . .	20,165B
	1.411(d)-1(d)	4/9/80 withdrawn 6/12/80	. . . .	20,165B
	1.411(d)	7/19/85	8/22/88 T.D. 8219	20,138B
	1.411(d)-3	3/24/04	8/12/05 T.D. 9219	12,231
	1.411(d)-3	3/21/08	11/24/09 T.D. 9472	20,262J; 23,267
	1.411(d)-3(a)(3)	8/12/05	8/9/06 T.D. 9280	20,261P; 12,231
	1.411(d)-3(a)(4)	8/12/05	8/9/06 T.D. 9280	20,261P; 12,231
	1.411(d)-3(b)(4)	8/12/05	8/9/06 T.D. 9280	20,261P; 12,231
	1.411(d)-3(f)	8/12/05	8/9/06 T.D. 9280	20,261P; 12,231
	1.411(d)-3(h)	8/12/05	8/9/06 T.D. 9280	20,261P; 12,231
	1.411(d)-3(j)(3)	8/12/05	8/9/06 T.D. 9280	20,261P; 12,231
	1.411(d)-3(j)(4)	8/12/05	8/9/06 T.D. 9280	20,261P; 12,231
	1.411(d)-4	1/30/86 3/29/00	7/11/88	12,233 20,248
			T.D. 8212	
		7/2/97	6/5/98 T.D. 8769	20,225
		9/4/98 T.D. 8781	9/4/98 T.D. 8781	20,234; 23,142
	1.411(d)-4, A-1(b)	5/10/90	. . . .	20,121C
	1.411(d)-4, A-1(b)(1)	12/3/90		20,183
	1.411(d)-4, Q&A-2(b)	6/21/12	11/8/12 T.D. 9601	20,263F; 12,233
	1.411(d)-4, Q&A-2(e)	7/8/03	. . . .	20,260Y
	1.411(d)-4, Q&A-12	11/10/04	5/22/07 T.D. 9325	20,261G; 23,247 12,233
	1.411(d)-6	12/15/95 4/23/02	12/4/98	T.D. 8795 20,260I
412	1.412(a)-1	12/1/82	. . . .	20,137E
	1.412(b)-1—1.412(b)-4	12/1/82	. . . .	20,137E
	1.412(c)(2)-2	12/1/82	. . . .	20,137E
	1.412(c)(1)	10/22/90	10/21/93 T.D. 8494	20,182
	1.412(c)(4)-1—1.412(c)(10)-1	12/1/82	. . . .	20,137E
	1.412(g)-1	12/1/82	. . . .	20,137E
	1.412(l)(7)-1	12/2/05	. . . .	20,261V
413	1.413-1(f)	12/1/82	. . . .	20,137E
	1.413-1(g)	12/1/82	. . . .	20,137E
	1.413-2(e)	12/1/82	. . . .	20,137E
	1.413-2(f)	12/1/82	. . . .	20,137E
414	1.414(b)-1	11/5/75	3/1/88	12,353

1986 Code Sec.	Regs. Section	Date Proposed [1]	Date Adopted [2]	Paragraph (¶) [3]
	1.414(c)-1—1.414(c)-5	11/5/75	T.D. 8179 3/1/88	12,354—12,358
			T.D. 8179	
	1.414(c)-2(b)(2)	11/2/92	. . . .	20,190
	1.414(c)-2(c)(1)	11/16/83	3/1/88	12,355
			T.D. 8179	
	1.414(c)-2(e)	11/16/83	3/1/88	12,355
			T.D. 8179	
	1.414(c)-4(b)(3)	11/2/92	6/9/94	23,895F
			T.D. 8540	
	1.414(c)-5	11/16/04	7/26/07	23,251; 12,358
			T.D. 9340	
	1.414(d)-1 [advance]	11/8/11	. . . .	20,262Z
	1.414(d)-1(g) [advance]	11/8/11	. . . .	20,263
	1.414(m)-1—1.414(m)-4	2/28/83	. . . .	20,137G
	1.414(m)-5	8/27/87	. . . .	20,149B
	1.414(m)-6	8/27/87	. . . .	20,149B
	1.414(n)-1-1.414(n)-4	8/27/87	. . . .	20,149B
	1.414(o)-1	8/27/87	. . . .	20,149B
	1.414(q)	2/19/88	. . . .	20,165D
			T.D. 8173	
		8/8/88	. . . .	20,138C
	1.414(q)	2/1/91	. . . .	20,163B
	1.414(r)-0—1.414(r)-3	9/7/93	6/23/94	20,198
			T.D. 8548	
	1.414(r)-0—1.414(r)-11	2/1/91	. . . .	20,110A
		8/10/92	. . . .	20,188
	1.414(r)-5—1.414(r)-8	9/7/93	6/23/94	12,364F-11—12,364F-19
			T.D. 8548	
	1.414(r)-11	9/7/93	6/23/94	12,364F-22
			T.D. 8548	
	1.414(s)-1	5/10/90	9/19/91	12,364G
			T.D. 8361	
		8/10/92	. . . .	20,188
			T.D. 8301	
		4/21/93	9/2/93	12,364K
			T.D. 8488	
	1.414(v)-1	10/23/01	7/8/03	20,260E; 24,507E; 11,755-5; 12,364N
			T.D. 9072	
	1.414(w)-1	11/8/07	2/24/09	20,262E; 23,260
			T.D. 9447	
	11.414(c)-2	10/31/83	5/10/84	12,365
			T.D. 7955	
	11.414(c)-2(c)(1)	11/16/83	. . . .	20,137M
	11.414(c)-2(e)	11/16/83	5/10/84	20,137M
			T.D. 7955	
	11.414(c)-4	10/31/83	. . . .	12,365
	11.414(c)-5(e)	11/16/83	. . . .	20,137M
415	1.415-1	1/23/84	4/5/07	20,137O
	1.415(a)-1	5/31/05	4/5/07	20,261N; 23,244; 12,422
			T.D. 9319	
	1.415(b)-1	5/31/05	4/5/07	20,261N; 23,244; 12,423
			T.D. 9319	
	1.415(b)-2	5/31/05	4/5/07	20,261N; 23,244; 12,424
			T.D. 9319	
	1.415(c)-1	5/31/05	4/5/07	20,261N; 23,244; 12,425
			T.D. 9319	
	1.415(c)-2	5/31/05	4/5/07	20,261N; 23,244; 12,426
	1.415(c)-2	11/15/13	. . . .	20,263T
			T.D. 9319	
	1.415(d)-1	5/31/05	4/5/07	20,261N; 23,244; 12,427
			T.D. 9319	
	1.415(f)-1	5/31/05	4/5/07	20,261N; 23,244; 12,429
			T.D. 9319	
	1.415(g)-1	5/31/05	4/5/07	20,261N; 23,244; 12,430
			T.D. 9319	
	1.415(j)-1	5/31/05	4/5/07	20,261N; 23,244; 12,433
			T.D. 9319	
	1.415-2	1/23/84	. . . .	20,137O
	1.415-2	5/10/90	9/19/91	12,402
			T.D. 8361	
			T.D. 8301	
	1.415-6	8/8/88	8/8/91	12,406
	1.415-6(b)	1/23/84	. . . .	20,137O
	1.415-7(c)(2)	1/23/84	. . . .	20,137O
	1.415-8(c)	2/28/83	. . . .	20,137G
	1.415-8(i)	7/14/81	. . . .	20,137B
416	1.416-1	3/15/83	12/28/84	20,137H
			T.D. 7997	
		8/8/88	8/8/91	12,503
		5/31/05	4/5/07	

1986 Code Sec.	Regs. Section	Date Proposed [1]	Date Adopted [2]	Paragraph (¶) [3]
417	1.417(a)(3)-1	1/28/05	T.D. 9319 3/24/06	20,261L; 12,551
	1.417(a)(3)-1	7/14/05	T.D. 9256 10/20/06	20,261O; 12,551
	1.417(e)	7/19/85	T.D. 9294	
	1.417(e)	4/5/95	T.D. 8219 4/3/98	20,207
	1.417(e)	9/22/95	T.D. 8768 12/18/98	20,207; 12,556
	1.417(e)-1	12/21/98	T.D. 8796 7/18/00	20,239; 12,556
	1.417(e)-1	1/17/01	T.D. 8891 7/16/03	20,260B; 12,556
	1.417(e)-1	10/9/08	T.D. 9076	20,262R
	1.417(e)-1	2/3/12	9/9/16	20,263B; 12,556
	1.417(e)-1	11/25/16	T.D. 9783	20,264O
419	1.419	2/4/86	. . . .	20,137Y
419A	1.419A	2/4/86	. . . .	20,137Y
	1.419A	7/3/85	. . . .	20,118D
	1.419A(f)(6)-1	7/11/02	7/17/03	20,260N; 23,211
420	1.420-1	1/5/01	T.D. 9079 6/19/01	13,031
421	1.421-1	7/29/08	11/17/09	20,262Q; 23,265
	1.421-7—1.421-8	2/7/84	T.D. 9471 withdrawn 6/9/03	20,150E
	1.421-1—1.421-2	6/9/03	8/3/04	20,260W; 23,220
422	1.422-1—1.422-5	6/9/03	T.D. 9144 8/3/04	20,260W; 23,220
	1.422-2	7/29/08	T.D. 9144 11/17/09	20,262Q; 23,265
	1.422-5	7/29/08	T.D. 9471 11/17/09	20,262Q; 23,265
422A	1.422A-1—1.422A-3	2/7/84	T.D. 9471 withdrawn 6/9/03	20,150E
423	1.423-1—1.423-2	6/9/03	8/3/04	20,260W; 23,220
	1.423-1	7/29/08	T.D. 9144 11/17/09	20,262Q; 23,265
	1.423-2	7/29/08	T.D. 9471 11/17/09	20,262Q; 23,265
424	1.424-1	6/9/03	T.D. 9471 8/3/04	20,260W; 23,220
425	1.425-1	2/7/84	T.D. 9144 withdrawn 6/9/03	20,150E
	1.425-1(e)(5)(i)	11/14/01	withdrawn 7/1/05	20,260F
430	1.430(a)-1	4/15/08	9/9/15	20,262K; 13,151L-2
	1.430(d)-1	12/31/07	T.D. 9732 10/15/09	20,262G; 23,264
	1.430(f)-1	8/31/07	T.D. 9467 10/15/09	20,262D; 23,264
	1.430(g)-1	12/31/07	T.D. 9467 10/15/09	20,262G; 23,264
	1.430(h)(2)-1	12/31/07	T.D. 9467 10/15/09	20,262G; 23,264
	1.430(h)(3)-1	5/29/07	T.D. 9467 T.D. 9419	20,261Y; 13,151L-20
	1.430(h)(3)-1	12/29/16	T.D. 9419 10/5/17	20,264P
	1.430(h)(3)-2	5/29/07	T.D. 9826 T.D. 9419	20,261Y; 13,151L-22
	1.430(h)(3)-2	12/29/16	T.D. 9419 10/5/17	20,264P
	1.430(i)-1	12/31/07	T.D. 9826 10/15/09	20,262G; 23,264
	1.430(j)-1	4/15/08	T.D. 9467 9/9/15	20,262K; 13,151L-32
431	1.431(c)(6)-1	5/29/07	T.D. 9732 T.D. 9419	20,261Y; 23,322; 13,151M-15
	1.431(c)(6)-1	12/29/16	10/5/17	20,264P
432	1.432(a)-1	3/18/08	T.D. 9826	20,262I
	1.432(b)-1	3/18/08	. . . .	20,262I
	1.432(e)(9)-1	6/19/15	4/28/16	20,264B; 13,151N-1
	1.432(e)(9)-1	2/11/16	T.D. 9765 5/5/16	20,264I; 13,151N-1
433	1.433(h)(3)-1	12/29/16	T.D. 9767 10/5/17	20,264P
436	1.436-1	8/31/07	T.D. 9826 10/15/09	20,262D; 23,264
457	1.457-1—1.457-4	12/24/80	T.D. 9467 9/23/82	13,154—13,154C

1986 Code Sec.	Regs. Section	Date Proposed[1]	Date Adopted[2]	Paragraph (¶)[3]
	1.457-1—1.457-12	5/8/02	7/11/03	13,154; 13,154A; 13,154B; 13,154C; 13,154C-1; 13,154C-2; 13,154C-3; 13,154C-4; 13,154C-5; 13,154C-6; 13,154C-7; 13,154C-8
			T.D. 7836	
	1.457-1—1.45	6/22/16	. . . .	20,264K
	1.457-4	5/31/05	4/15/07	20,261N; 13,154C
			T.D. 9319	
	1.457-4	6/22/16	. . . .	20,264K
	1.457-5	5/31/05	4/15/07	20,261N; 13,154C-1
			T.D. 9319	
	1.457-6	5/31/05	4/15/07	20,261N; 13,154C-2
			T.D. 9319	
	1.457-6—1.457-7	6/22/16	. . . .	20,264K
	1.457-9—1.457-13	6/22/16	. . . .	20,264K
	1.457-10	5/31/05	4/15/07	20,261N; 13,154C-6
			T.D. 9319	
501	1.501(a)-1(e)	11/17/81	12/1/82	13,161
			T.D. 7859	
	1.501(c)(5)-1	12/21/95	7/29/97	20,213
			T.D. 8726	
	1.501(c)(9)-2(a)(1)	8/7/92	. . . .	20,187
	1.501(c)(9)-2(d)	8/7/92	. . . .	20,187
	1.501(c)(9)-2(d)	8/7/92	. . . .	20,187
	1.501(c)(20)-1	4/29/80	. . . .	20,164A
503	1.503(a)-1	11/22/99	. . . .	20,244
505	1.505(c)-1T	2/4/86	. . . .	20,137Y; 13,194
	1.512(a)-1	1/22/93	withdrawn	20,194
817	1.817-5	9/15/86	3/1/89	13,312B
	1.817-5(f)(3)	7/31/07	3/7/08	20,262A; 13,312B
			T.D. 9385	
817A	1.817A-0—1.817A-2	6/3/02	5/7/03	20,260L; 13,313A
			T.D. 9058	
1042	1.1042-1T	2/4/86	. . . .	20,137Y; 13,383
	1.1042-1T	7/10/03	. . . .	20,260Z
1402	1.1402(a)-2	1/13/97	. . . .	20,221
	1.1042(a)-18	7/9/02	9/17/03	20,260M; 23,208
			T.D. 9092	
1441	1.1441-1	4/22/96	10/6/97	20,216
			T.D. 8734	
	1.1441-2	7/12/76	removed 4/22/96	20,143
	1.1441-2	4/22/96	10/6/97	20,216
			T.D. 8734	
	1.1441-4(b)(1)(ii)	4/26/96	10/6/97	20,216
			T.D. 8734	
	1.1441-4(d)	4/26/96	10/6/97	20,216
			T.D. 8734	
2039	20.2039-2(c)	1/23/84	. . . .	20,137O
	20.2039-2(c)(1)	11/2/92	6/9/94	23,117; 13,498A
			T.D. 8540	
	20.2039-4(d) and (e)	9/27/83	5/11/84	13,502B
			T.D. 7956	
	20.2039-4(h)	1/23/84	. . . .	20,137O
	20.2039-1T	2/4/86	. . . .	20,137Y; 13,502D
	20.2039-5(c)(1) and (2)	11/2/92	6/9/94	23,117; 13,502
			T.D. 8540	
2517	25.2517-1(c)	1/23/84	. . . .	20,137O
3121	31.3121(a)-1(k)	11/14/01	withdrawn 7/1/05	20,260F
	31.3121(a)-1T	1/7/85	. . . .	20,137S; 13,530A
		T.D. 8004		
	31.3121(a)(5)-1(d)	7/14/81		20,137B
	31.3121(a)(5)-2	11/16/04	. . . .	20,261H
	31.3121(a)(18)-1	11/23/81	7/5/83	13,534M
			T.D. 7898	
	31.3121(v)(2)-1	1/25/96	. . . .	20,214
	31.3121(v)(2)-1(g)	12/24/97		20,229
	32.1	6/30/82	. . . .	20,142H
3306	31.3306(b)-1(1)	11/14/01	withdrawn 7/1/05	20,260F
	31.3306(b)(5)-1(d)	7/14/81	. . . .	20,137B
	31.3306(r)(2)-1	1/25/96		20,215
	31.3306(r)(2)-1	12/24/97	. . . .	20,229
3401	31.3401(a)-1	2/12/82	4/22/83	13,551
			T.D. 7888	
	31.3401(a)-1T	1/7/85		20,137S; 13,551A
	31.3401(a)-1(b)(15)	11/14/01	withdrawn 7/1/05	20,260F
		T.D. 8004		
	31.3401(a)(18)-1	11/23/81	7/5/83	13,553G
			T.D. 7898	
3405	31.3405(c)-1	10/21/92	9/15/95	20,189; 13,566-10

1986 Code Sec.	Regs. Section	Date Proposed [1]	Date Adopted [2]	Paragraph (¶) [3]
	35.3405-1	12/28/98	T.D. 8619 2/8/00	13,566-50
	35.3405-1	7/14/05	10/20/06 T.D. 9294	20,261O; 13,566-50
3501	31.3501(a)-1T	1/7/85	. . . .	20,137S; 13,576
4375	46.4375-1	4/17/12	T.D. 8004 12/6/12 T.D. 9602	20,263C; 13,578A-1
4376	46.4376-1	4/17/12	12/6/12 T.D. 9602	20,263C; 13,578F-1
4377	46.4377-1	4/17/12	12/6/12 T.D. 9602	20,263C; 13,578K-1
	46.4377-1	6/10/16	. . . .	20,264J
4941	53.4941(e)-1	2/13/84	5/1/86 T.D. 8084	13,584
4965	53.4965-1	7/6/07	7/6/10 T.D. 9492	20,262; 23,274
	53.4965-2	7/6/07	7/6/10 T.D. 9492	20,262; 23,274
	53.4965-3	7/6/07	7/6/10 T.D. 9492	20,262; 23,274
	53.4965-4	7/6/07	7/6/10 T.D. 9492	20,262; 23,274
	53.4965-5	7/6/07	7/6/10 T.D. 9492	20,262; 23,274
	53.4965-6	7/6/07	7/6/10 T.D. 9492	20,262; 23,274
	53.4965-7	7/6/07	7/6/10 T.D. 9492	20,262; 23,274
	53.4965-8	7/6/07	7/6/10 T.D. 9492	20,262; 23,274
	53.4965-9	7/6/07	7/6/10 T.D. 9492	20,262; 23,274
4971	54.4971-1	12/1/82	. . . .	20,137E
	54.4971-1(c), 54.4971-1(d)	2/13/84	5/1/86 T.D. 8084	13,600D
	54.4971(c)-1	4/15/08	9/9/15 T.D. 9732	20,262K; 13,600I
	54.4971-2	12/1/82	. . . .	20,137E
	54.4971-3	12/1/82	. . . .	20,137E
4973	54.4973-1	7/14/81	. . . .	20,137B
4974	54.4974-1(d)	7/14/81	. . . .	20,137B
	54.4974-2	7/27/87	. . . .	20,163B
		1/17/01	. . . .	20,260C
4975	54.4975-1	5/1/86 T.D. 8084	. . . .	13,642
	141.4975-13	2/13/84	5/1/86 T.D. 8084	13,648
4976	54.4976-1T	2/4/86	. . . .	20,137Y; 13,648C
4977	54.4977-1T	1/7/85 T.D. 8004	. . . .	20,137S; 13,648E
4978	54.4978-1T	2/4/86	. . . .	20,137Y; 13,648G
4979	54.4979-0	8/8/88	8/8/91	13,648K
	54.4979-1	8/8/88	8/8/91	13,648K-1
	54.4979-1	11/8/07	2/24/09 T.D. 9447	20,262E; 23,260
4980B	54.4980B-0	7/16/08	9/8/09 T.D. 9457	20,262N; 13,648W-5
	54.4980B-1	1/7/98	2/2/99 T.D. 8812	20,231; 13,648W-6
	54.4980B-2	7/16/08	9/8/09 T.D. 9457	20,262N; 13,648W-7
	54.4980B-9	2/3/99	. . . .	20,241
	54.4980B-10	2/3/99	. . . .	20,241
4980D	54.4980D-1	7/16/08	9/8/09 T.D. 9457	20,262N; 13,648W-55
4980F	54.4980F-1	4/23/02	. . . .	20,260I
	54.4980F-1	3/24/04	8/12/05 T.D. 9219	13,648W-87
	54.4980F-1	7/14/05	10/20/06 T.D. 9294	20,261O; 13,648W-87
	54.4980F-1	3/21/08	. . . .	20,262J
4980G	54.4980G-0	8/26/05	7/31/06 T.D. 9277	20,261S; 13,648W-100
	54.4980G-0	6/1/07	4/17/08 T.D. 9393	20,261Z; 13,648W-100
	54.4980G-1	8/26/05	7/31/06 T.D. 9277	20,261S; 13,648W-101
	54.4980G-1	7/16/08	9/8/09 T.D. 9457	20,262N; 13,648W-101
	54.4980G-2	8/26/05	7/31/06 T.D. 9277	20,261S; 13,648W-102

64   List of IRS Proposed Regulations

1986 Code Sec.	Regs. Section	Date Proposed [1]	Date Adopted [2]	Paragraph (¶) [3]
	54.4980G-3	8/26/05	7/31/06 T.D. 9277	20,261S; 13,648W-103
	54.4980G-3	7/16/08	9/8/09 T.D. 9457	20,262N; 13,648W-103
	54.4980G-4	8/26/05	7/31/06 T.D. 9277	20,261S; 13,648W-104
	54.4980G-4	6/1/07	4/17/08 T.D. 9393	20,261Z; 13,648W-104
	54.4980G-4	7/16/08	9/8/09 T.D. 9457	20,262N; 13,648W-104
	54.4980G-5	8/26/05	7/31/06 T.D. 9277	20,261S; 13,648W-105
	54.4980G-6	7/16/08	9/8/09 T.D. 9457	20,262N; 13,648W-106
	54.4980G-7	7/16/08	9/8/09 T.D. 9457	20,262N; 13,648W-107
4980H	54.4980H-0	1/2/13	2/12/14 T.D. 9655	20,263I; 13,648W-142
	54.4980H-1	1/2/13	2/12/14 T.D. 9655	20,263I; 13,648W-143
	54.4980H-2	1/2/13	2/12/14 T.D. 9655	20,263I; 13,648W-144
	54.4980H-3	1/2/13	2/12/14 T.D. 9655	20,263I; 13,648W-145
	54.4980H-4	1/2/13	2/12/14 T.D. 9655	20,263I; 13,648W-146
	54.4980H-5	1/2/13	2/12/14 T.D. 9655	20,263I; 13,648W-147
	54.4980H-6	1/2/13	2/12/14 T.D. 9655	20,263I; 13,648W-148
4981	54.4981A-1T	12/10/87	. . . .	20,177; 13,648T
5000A	1.5000A-0	2/1/13	8/30/13 T.D. 9632	20,263J; 13,648Z-55
	1.5000A-0	1/27/14	11/26/14 T.D. 9705	20,263V; 13,648Z-55
	1.5000A-1	2/1/13	8/30/13 T.D. 9632	20,263J; 13,648Z-56
	1.5000A-2	2/1/13	8/30/13 T.D. 9632	20,263J; 13,648Z-57
	1.5000A-2	1/27/14	11/26/14 T.D. 9705	20,263V; 13,648Z-57
	1.5000A-2	6/10/16	. . . .	20,264J
	1.5000A-3	2/1/13	8/30/13 T.D. 9632	20,263J; 13,648Z-58
	1.5000A-3	1/27/14	11/26/14 T.D. 9705	20,263V; 13,648Z-58
	1.5000A-3	7/8/16	12/19/16 T.D. 9804	20,264M; 13,648Z-58
	1.5000A-4	2/1/13	8/30/13 T.D. 9632	20,263J; 13,648Z-59
	1.5000A-4	1/27/14	11/26/14 T.D. 9705	20,263V; 13,648Z-59
	1.5000A-5	2/1/13	8/30/13 T.D. 9632	20,263J; 13,648Z-60
	1.5000A-5	7/8/16	. . . .	20,264M
6011	54.6011-1	7/6/07	7/6/10 T.D. 9492	20,262; 23,274
	54.6011-1T	4/3/87 T.D. 8133	. . . .	13,649B
	301.6011-2	9/18/85	3/20/86 T.D. 8081	13,649D
	54.6011-2	7/16/08	9/8/09 T.D. 9457	20,262N; 13,649C
	301.6011-2	7/8/16	. . . . T.D. 9804	20,264M; 13,649D
	301.6011-2T	10/10/86		
	1.6011-8	8/17/11	5/23/12 T.D. 9590	20,262X; 23,284
	1.6011-8	5/3/13	12/18/15 T.D. 9745	20,263N; 13,649E-15
	1.6011-8	7/8/16	12/19/16 T.D. 9804	20,264M; 13,649E-15
	31.6011(a)-4	10/16/95	. . . .	20,208
	301.6011(g)-1	7/6/07	7/6/10 T.D. 9492	20,262; 23,274
6033	1.6033-2(a)(2)(i)	8/26/80		13,662
	1.6033-4		11/13/07 T.D. 9363	13,662A; 13,663
	301.6033-4T	1/12/05	. . . .	20,261K
	301.6033-4	. . . .	11/13/07 T.D. 9363	13,663A
	1.6033-5	7/6/07	7/6/10	20,262; 23,274

1986 Code Sec.	Regs. Section	Date Proposed [1]	Date Adopted [2]	Paragraph (¶) [3]
	301.6033-5	7/6/07	T.D. 9492 7/6/10	20,262; 23,274
6039	1.6039-1—1.6039-2	2/7/84	T.D. 9492 6/9/03 withdrawn	20,150E; 20,260W
		6/9/03	8/3/04	20,260W; 23,220
		7/16/08	T.D. 9144 11/17/09	20,260O; 23,266
6041	1.6041-1	4/26/96	T.D. 9470 10/6/97	20,216
	1.6041-6	1/27/00	T.D. 8734 8/18/00	13,683
6047	1.6047-1(a)(6)	1/27/00	T.D. 8895 8/18/00	13,691
	1.6047-2	2/3/12	T.D. 8895 7/2/14	20,263A; 13,691B
6051	31.6051-1	9/20/17	T.D. 9673	20,264R
	31.6051-3	5/1/81	3/15/82	13,711
6052	31.6051-3	9/20/17	T.D. 7813	20,264R
	1.6052-1(b)(ii)	1/27/00	8/18/00	13,721
6055	1.6052-2	9/20/17	T.D. 8895	20,264R
	1.6055-1	9/9/13	3/10/14	20,263R; 13,724A
	1.6055-1	8/2/16	T.D. 9660	20,264N
	1.6055-2	9/9/13	3/10/14	20,263R; 13,724B
6056	1.6055-2	6/10/16	T.D. 9660	20,264J
	301.6056-1	9/9/13	3/10/14	20,263S; 13,729A
	301.6056-2	9/9/13	T.D. 9661 3/10/14	20,263S; 13,729A
6057	301.6056-2	6/10/16	T.D. 9661	20,264J
	301.6057-1	6/21/12		20,263G
	301.6057-2	6/21/12	. . . .	20,263G
	301.6057-3	8/30/13	9/29/14	20,263Q; 13,735
6058	301.6058-2	8/30/13	T.D. 9695 9/29/14	20,263Q; 13,746
6059	301.6059-1	7/8/80	T.D. 9695 11/23/81	13,750B
	301.6059-2	8/30/13	9/29/14	20,263Q; 13,750G
6081	1.6081-5	11/7/05	T.D. 9695 7/1/08	20,261U; 13,755D
	1.6081-8	8/13/15	T.D. 9407	20,264D
	1.6081-11	11/7/05	7/1/08	20,261U; 13,755L
	1.6081-11	6/21/12	T.D. 9407	20,263G
6104	301.6104(a)-1—301.6104(a)-6	12/30/80	11/5/82	13,771—13,776
6109	301.6109-1	6/8/95	T.D. 7845 5/23/96	13,782
	301.6109-1	4/26/96	T.D. 8671 10/6/97	20,216
6302	31.6302-1(e)	11/4/93	T.D. 8734 12/22/93	20,199
	31.6302-3(b)	11/4/93	T.D. 8504 12/22/93	20,199
	31.6302-4(a)-(d)	11/4/93	T.D. 8504 12/22/93	20,199
6652	301.6652-4	1/23/84	T.D. 8504	20,137O
6692	301.6692-1	5/2/84	11/23/81	13,845
6693	301.6693-1	7/8/80	T.D. 7798	20,137B
7122	301.7122-1	7/21/99	. . . .	20,243
7508A	301.7508A-1	7/15/08	T.D. 9294 1/15/09	20,262P; 13,919M
7701	301.7701-1	5/13/96	T.D. 9443 12/17/96	20,217
	301.7701-2	10/27/80	. . . .	20,150C
	301.7701-2	7/22/92	5/13/93	13,922
	301.7701-2	1/2/13	T.D. 8475 2/12/14	20,263I; 13,922
	301.7701-4(c)	5/2/84	T.D. 9655 3/21/86	13,924
	301.7701-5	6/5/97	2/1/99	13,925
	301.7701-7	6/5/97	2/1/99	13,927
	301.7701-7	10/12/00	8/9/01	20,251; 13,927
	301.7701-17T	2/4/86	T.D. 8962 1/29/85	20,137Y; 13,934

1986 Code Sec.	Regs. Section	Date Proposed [1]	Date Adopted [2]	Paragraph (¶) [3]
	301.7701-18	10/23/15	T.D. 8073 9/2/16	20,264F; 13,935
7872	1.7872-15	7/9/02	T.D. 9785 9/17/03	20,260M; 23,259
9801	54.9801-1—54.9801-6	3/21/13	T.D. 9443 2/24/14	20,263L; 23,295
	54.9801-1T	4/8/97	T.D. 9656 12/30/04	20,223
		12/22/97	2/2/10 Withdrawn	20,228; 20,262U
	54.9801-2	6/10/16	10/31/16	20,264J; 13,968Q-12
	54.9801-2T	4/8/97	T.D. 9791 12/30/04	20,223
		12/22/97	2/2/10 Withdrawn	20,228; 20,262U
	54.9801-3T	4/8/97	12/30/04	20,223
	54.9801-4	12/30/04	. . . .	20,261J
	54.9801-4T	12/30/04	12/30/04	20,223
		12/22/97	2/2/10 Withdrawn	20,228; 20,262U
	54.9801-5	12/30/04	. . . .	20,261J
	54.9801-5T	4/8/97	12/30/04	20,223
		12/22/97	2/2/10 Withdrawn	20,228; 20,262U
	54.9801-6	12/30/04	. . . .	20,261J
	54.9801-6T	4/8/97	12/30/04	20,223
	54.9801-7	12/30/04	. . . .	20,261J
9802	54.9802-1	1/8/01	12/13/06	20,255; 13,968R-3
	54.9802-1	11/26/12	T.D. 9298 6/3/13	20,263H; 13,968R-3
	54.9802-1	3/21/13	T.D. 9620 2/24/14	20,263L; 13,968R-3
	54.9802-1T	4/8/97	T.D. 9656	20,223
	54.9802-2	1/8/01	12/13/06	20,254; 13,968R-4
9811	54.9811-1	10/26/98	T.D. 9299 10/20/08	20,236
9812	54.9812-1T	12/27/97	T.D. 9427 2/2/10 Withdrawn	20,228; 20,262U
	54.9812-1T	2/2/10	11/13/13	20,262U; 13,968U-12
9815	54.9815-2705	11/26/12	T.D. 9640 6/3/13	20,263H; 13,968V-20H
	54.9815-2708	3/21/13	T.D. 9620 2/24/14	20,263L; 13,968V-20K
	54.9815-2708	2/24/14	T.D. 9656 6/25/14	20,263W; 13,968V-20K
	54.9815-2711	6/10/16	T.D. 9671 10/31/16	20,264J; 13,968V-20NA
	54.9815-2713	2/6/13	T.D. 9791 7/2/13	20,263K; 13,968V-20PA
	54.9815-2713A	2/6/13	T.D. 9624 7/2/13	20,263K; 13,968V-20PB
	54.9815-2713A	8/27/14	T.D. 9624 7/14/15	20,263X; 13,968V-20PB
	54.9815-2715	8/22/11	T.D. 9726 2/14/12	20,262Y; 13,968V-20R
	54.9815-2715	12/30/14	T.D. 9575 6/16/15	20,264A; 13,968V-20R
9831	54.9831-1	12/30/04	T.D. 9724	20,261J
	54.9831-1	3/21/13	2/24/14	20,263L; 13,968W-10
	54.9831-1	12/24/13	T.D. 9656 10/1/14	20,263U; 13,968W-10
	54.9831-1	12/23/14	T.D. 9697 3/18/15	20,264; 13,968W-10
	54.9831-1	6/10/16	T.D. 9714 10/31/16	20,264J; 13,968W-10
	54.9831-1T	12/22/97	T.D. 9791 2/2/10 Withdrawn	20,228; 20,262U
9833	54.9833-1	6/10/16	10/31/16	20,264J; 13,968Y-10
	54.9833-1T	12/22/97	T.D. 9791 2/2/10 Withdrawn	20,228; 20,262U

List of Proposed Regs. for Department of Labor/Other Agencies

Following is a list of proposed regulations relating to employee benefits issued by the Labor Department's Employee Benefits Security Administration (formerly the Pension and Welfare Benefit Administration), Pension Benefit Guaranty Corporations and other selected agencies. The listing is by ERISA section.

Title 29—Employee Benefits Security Administration—Labor

ERISA Sec.	Regs. Section	Date Proposed[1]	Date Adopted[2]	Paragraph (¶)[3]
3	2510.3-2	1/27/81	11/4/81	14,132
	2510.3-2	11/18/15	8/30/16	20,539B; 14,132
	2510.3-2	8/30/16	12/20/16	20,539G; 14,132
	2510.3-18	5/17/88	. . . .	20,531E
	2510.3-21	4/20/15	4/8/16	20,538Z; 14,138A
	2510.3-21	3/2/17	4/7/17	20,539I; 14,138A
	2510.3-37	11/7/75		14,139
	2510.3-38	12/9/03	8/24/04	20,534O
	2510.3-40(a)	8/1/95	. . . .	20,533H
	2510.3-40(a)—(h)	10/27/00		20,534E
	2510.3-40	10/27/00	4/9/03	14,139C
	2510.3-101	1/8/85	11/12/86	14,139M
	2510.3-101(i)	2/15/85	11/12/86	14,139M
	2510.3-102	12/20/95	8/7/96	14,139N
	2510.3-102	2/29/08	1/14/10	20,537I; 14,139N
	2510.3-102(b)	3/27/97	11/24/97	14,139N
101	2520.101-2	2/11/00	4/9/03	14,212; 14,212A
	2520.101-2	12/6/11	3/1/13	20,538E; 14,212
	2520.101-4	11/18/10	2/2/15	20,538; 14,214
	2520.101-5	9/14/07	3/2/10	14,215
	2520.101-5	11/18/10	2/2/15	20,538; 14,215
	Appendix A to 2520.101-5	11/18/10	2/2/15	20,538; 14,215A
	Appendix B to 2520.101-5	11/18/10	2/2/15	20,538; 14,215B
	2520.101-10	9/14/07	3/2/10	14,216
102	2520.102-1	8/5/99	. . . .	20,534A
	2520.102-3(d)	8/28/98	11/21/00	14,223
	2520.102-3(j)	8/28/98	11/21/00	14,223
	2520.102-3(l)	8/28/98	11/21/00	14,223
	2520.102-3(m)(3)	8/28/98	11/21/00	14,223
	2520.102-3(o)	8/28/98	11/21/00	14,223
	2520.102-3(s)	8/28/98	11/21/00	14,223
	2520.102-3(t)(2)	8/28/98	11/21/00	14,223
	2520.102-4	8/5/99	. . . .	20,534A
	2520.102-5	8/28/98	11/21/00	14,225
103	2520.103-1	1/2/87		14,231A
	2520.103-1	12/10/98	4/19/00	20,533X
	2520.103-1	12/6/11	3/1/13	20,538E; 14,231A
	2520.103-1—2520.103-4	7/21/16	. . . .	20,539F
	2520.103-1(a)	8/5/99		20,534A
	2520.103-1(b)	1/24/85	11/12/86	14,231A
	2520.103-1(e)	12/30/80	12/10/81	14,231A
	2520.103-1(f)	8/30/05	. . . .	20,534Y
	2520.103-2	1/2/87		14,231B
	2520.103-2	12/10/98	4/19/00	20,533X
	2520.103-2(b)	3/27/97		20,533O
	2520.103-2(c)	8/30/05		20,534Y
	2520.103-3	12/10/98	4/19/00	20,533X
	2520.103-4	12/10/98	4/19/00	20,533X
	2520.103-5	12/10/98	4/19/00	20,533X
	2520.103-5(a), (c)	8/5/99	. . . .	20,534A
	2520.103-6	4/3/96	6/28/96	14,231F
	2520.103-6	12/10/98	4/19/00	20,533X
	2520.103-6	7/21/16	. . . .	20,539F
	2520.103-7	4/3/96	6/28/96	14,231G
	2520.103-8	7/21/16		20,539F
	2520.103-9	12/10/98	4/19/00	20,533X
	2520.103-9(d)	8/30/05	. . . .	20,534Y
	2520.103-10	1/2/87		14,231J
	2520.103-10	7/21/16		20,539F
	2520.103-11	12/10/98	4/19/00	20,533X
	2520.103-12	12/10/98	4/19/00	20,533X
	2520.103-12(a)	8/5/99	. . . .	20,534A
	2520.103-12(a)—(e)	1/24/85	11/12/86	14,231L
	2520.103-12(f)	8/30/05		20,534Y
	2520.103-13	3/10/05	4/21/06	20,534W; 14,231M
	2520.103-13	12/12/12		20,538H
104	2520.101-4	2/4/05	1/11/06	20,534T; 24,244
	2520.104-2	4/3/96	6/28/96	14,244
	2520.104-3	4/3/96	6/28/96	14,245
	2520.104-4	1/27/05		20,534T
	2520.104-4(a)	8/5/99	. . . .	20,534A
	2520.104-5	4/3/96	6/28/96	14,246

[1] Date published in the *Federal Register*.
[2] Date filed with the *Federal Register*.
[3] Location of text in Pension Plan Guide.

ERISA Sec.	Regs. Section	Date Proposed[1]	Date Adopted[2]	Paragraph (¶)[3]
	2520.104-6	4/3/96	6/28/96	14,246A
	2520.104-20	12/6/11	3/1/13	20,538E; 14,247
	2520.104-20	7/21/16	. . . .	20,539F
	2520.104-20(a), (c)	8/5/99	. . . .	20,534A
	2520.104-21	12/10/98	4/19/00	20,533X
	2520.104-21(a), (c)	8/5/99	. . . .	20,534A
	2520.104-22	1/2/87	. . . .	14,247B
	2520.104-22(c)	9/30/14	. . . .	20,538U
	2520.104-23	1/2/87	. . . .	14,247C
	2520.104-23(b)(2)	8/5/99	. . . .	20,534A
	2520.104-23(c)	9/30/14	. . . .	20,538U
	2520.104-24(b)	8/5/99	. . . .	20,534A
	2520.104-25	8/5/99	. . . .	20,534A
	2520.104-26	7/21/16	. . . .	20,539F
	2520.104-26(a)	8/5/99	. . . .	20,534A
	2520.104-27(a)	8/5/99	. . . .	20,534A
	2520.104-28	4/3/96	6/28/96	14,247H
	2520.104-41	1/2/87	. . . .	14,247U
	2520.104-41	12/1/99	10/19/00	14,247U
	2520.104-41	12/10/98	4/19/00	20,533X
	2520.104-41	12/6/11	3/1/13	20,538E; 14,247U
	2520.104-41(b)	8/5/99	. . . .	20,534A
	2520.104-42	7/21/16	. . . .	20,539F
	2520.104-43	12/10/98	4/19/00	20,533X
	2520.104-43(a)	8/5/99	. . . .	20,534A
	2520.104-44	12/10/98	4/19/00	20,533X
	2520.104-44(d)	8/5/99	. . . .	20,534A
	2520.104-45	4/3/96	6/28/96	14,247Y
	2520.104-46	1/2/87	. . . .	14,247Z
	2520.104-46	12/1/99	10/19/00	14,247Z
	2520.104-46	12/10/98	4/19/00	20,533X
	2520.104-46	11/18/10	2/2/15	20,538; 14,247Z
104(a)	2520.104a-2	8/5/99	. . . .	20,534A
	2520.104a-2	8/30/05	. . . .	20,534Y
	2520.104a-3	1/2/87	. . . .	14,248B
	2520.104a-3	8/5/99	. . . .	20,534A
	2520.104a-4	1/2/87	. . . .	14,248C
	2520.104a-4	8/5/99	. . . .	20,534A
	2520.104a-5(a)	8/5/99	. . . .	20,534A
	2520.104a-7	8/5/99	. . . .	20,534A
	2520.104a-8	8/5/99	1-7-02	20,534B; 14,248G
104(b)	2520.104b-1	1/28/99	. . . .	20,533Y
	2520.104b-1(3)	8/5/99	. . . .	20,534A
	2520.104b-2	4/3/96	6/28/96	14,249A
	2520.104b-3(a), (d), (e)	8/28/98	11/21/00	14,249B
	2520.104b-3(f), (g)	8/5/99	. . . .	20,534A
	2520.104b-4	4/3/96	6/28/96	14,249C
	2520.104b-5	4/3/96	6/28/96	14,249D
	2520.104a-2	. . . .	11/16/07	14,248A
	2520.104b-10	. . . .	11/16/07	14,249H
	2520.104b-10	1/6/81	7/20/82	14,249H
	2520.104b-10	12/10/98	4/19/00	20,533X
	2520.104b-10	11/18/10	2/2/15	20,538; 14,249H
	2520.104b-10	7/21/16	. . . .	20,539F
	2520.104b-12	4/3/96	6/28/96	14,249K
	2520.104b-30	9/14/07	3/2/10	14,249Z
	2520.104-44	. . . .	11/16/07	14,247X
	2520.104-46	. . . .	11/16/07	14,247Z
105	2520.105-1	8/1/80	. . . .	20,519L
	2520.105-1 [advance]	5/8/13	. . . .	20,538L
	2520.105-2	8/1/80	. . . .	20,519L
	2520.105-3	8/8/80	. . . .	20,526L
107	2520.107-1	1/28/99	. . . .	20,533Y
203	2530.203-3	8/31/81	12/1/81	14,433
	2530.203-3	1/27/81		20,525B
209	2530.209-1-2530.209-2	8/1/80	. . . .	20,519L
209(b)	2570.100-209b-1	4/18/97	7/29/97	20,533P
211	2509.76-2	4/3/96	6/28/96	14,521
	2509.76-3	4/3/96	6/28/96	14,522
305	2540.305-1	3/25/08	. . . .	20,537L
401(b)	2530.209-3	8/8/80	. . . .	20,526L
	2550.401b-1(a)—(d)	8/28/79		20,509
401(c)	2550.401c-1	12/22/97	1/5/00	20,533S
403	2510.3-102	12/20/95	8/6/96	14,139N
403(a)	2550.403a-1	8/28/79	5/13/82	14,733
403(b)	2550.403b-1	8/28/79	5/13/82	14,734
404(a)	2550.404a-2	3/2/04	9/28/04	14,742A
	2550.404a-3	3/10/05	2/5/07	20,534W; 14,742B
	2550.404a-3	12/12/12	. . . .	20,538H
	2550.404a-4	9/12/07		20,537B
	2550.404a-5	7/23/08	10/20/2010	20,537O; 14,742D
	2550.404a-5	11/30/10	10/20/2010	20,537O; 14,742D

ERISA Sec.	Regs. Section	Date Proposed[1]	Date Adopted[2]	Paragraph (¶)[3]
	2550.404a-5	9/27/06	. . . .	20,538A
	2550.404a-5	6/1/11	7/19/11	20,538C; 14,742D
404(c)	2550.404c-1	7/23/08	10/20/2010	20,537O; 14,744
	2550.404c-1	3/13/91	10/9/92	14,744
	2550.404c-5	9/27/06		20,538A
	2509.96-1	4/20/15	4/8/16	20,538Z; 14,746C
407(a)	2550.407a-3	4/3/96	6/28/96	14,771B
	2550.407a-4	4/3/96	6/28/96	14,771C
	2550.407c-3	4/3/96	6/28/96	14,775
408(a)	2570.30—2570.51	6/28/88	8/10/90	20,531F
	2570.30—2570.52	8/30/10	10/27/11	20,537Y; 14,789B-5
408(b)	2550.408b-1	1/22/88	7/19/89	14,781
	2550.408b-2	6/1/11	7/19/11	20,538C; 14,782
	2550.408b-2	12/13/07	7/16/10; 2/3/12	20,537F; 14,782
	2550.408b-2	3/12/14	. . . .	20,538Q
408(g)	2550.408g-1	3/2/10	10/25/11	20,537V; 24,306
	2550.408g-2	3/2/10	10/25/11	20,537V; 24,306
412	2580.412-45—2580.412-48	8/19/87		20,530D
414	2509.75-1	4/3/96	6/28/96	14,875
	2509.75-2	4/3/96	6/28/96	14,876
	2509.75-5	12/9/03	8/24/04	20,534O
	2509.75-7	4/3/96	6/28/96	14,881
414(b)	2550.414b-1	4/3/96	6/28/96	14,841
414(c)	2550.414c-1	4/3/96	6/28/96	14,844A
	2550.414c-2	4/3/96	6/28/96	14,844B
	2550.414c-3	4/3/96	6/28/96	14,845
	2550.414c-4	4/3/96	6/28/96	14,845A
502(c)(1)	2570.100	4/18/97	7/29/97	20,533P
502(c)(2)	2560.502c-2	10/17/88	6/26/89	14,925A
	2570.60—2570.71	10/17/88	6/26/89	14,928B
	2570.100	4/18/97	7/29/97	20,533P
	2570.502c-1	4/18/97	7/29/97	20,533P
	2570.502c-2	4/18/97	7/29/97	20,533P
	2560.502c-2(a)	8/5/99	. . . .	20,534A
502(c)(3)	2570.100	4/18/97	7/29/97	20,533P
	2570.502c-3	4/18/97	7/29/97	20,533P
502(c)(4)	2560.502c-4	12/19/07	1/2/09	20,537G; 14,925C
502(c)(6)	2560.502c-6	8/5/99	1/7/02	20,534B; 14,925E
	2570.110	8/5/99	1/7/02	20,534B; 14,928Q
502(c)(7)	2578.1	3/10/05	2/15/07	20,534W; 14,929S
	2578.1	12/12/12	. . . .	20,538H
502(c)(8)	2560.502c-8	9/4/09	2/26/10	20,537T; 24,289
502(i)	2560.502i-1	8/27/86	9/23/89	14,926
	2570.1—2570.12	8/27/86	9/23/89	14,928
	2570.150—2570.159	10/27/00	4/9/03	20,534F; 24,229
502(l)	2560.502l-1	withdrawn 6/20/90	. . . .	20,532F
503	2560.503-1	8/28/98	11/21/00	14,931
	2560.503-1	11/18/15	12/19/16	20,539A; 14,931
	2560.503-1	10/12/17	. . . .	20,539J
521	2560.521-1—2560.521-4	12/6/11	3/1/13	20,538F; 24,313
	2571.1—2571.12	12/6/11	3/1/13	20,538F; 24,313
606	2590.606-1	5/28/03	5/26/04	20,534M; 15,046B-1
	2590.606-1	5/7/14	. . . .	20,538S
	2590.606-2	5/28/03	5/26/04	20,534M; 15,046B-3
	2590.606-3	5/28/03	5/26/04	20,534M; 15,046B-4
	2590.606-4	5/28/03	5/26/04	20,534M; 15,046B-5
	2590.606-4	5/7/14	. . . .	20,538S
609	2590.609-2	11/15/99	12/27/00	20,534C; 15,047I
701	2590.701-1—2590.701-7	3/21/13	2/24/14	20,538J; 24,318
	2590.701-2	6/10/16	10/31/16	20,539E; 15,049J
	2590.701-4—2590.701-8	12/30/04	. . . .	20,534S
702	2590.702	1/8/01	12/13/06	20,534H; 15,050A-1
	2590.702	11/26/12	6/3/13	20,538G; 15,050A-1
	2590.702	3/21/13	2/24/14	20,538J; 15,050A-1
712	2590.712	12/22/97	2/27/07	20,228; 15,050K-1
715	2590.715-2705	11/26/12	6/3/13	20,538G; 15,050R-50H
	2590.715-2708	3/21/13	2/24/14	20,538J; 15,050R-50K
	2590.715-2708	2/24/14	6/25/14	20,538P; 15,050R-50K
	2590.715-2711	6/10/16	10/31/16	20,539E; 15,050R-50NA
	2590.715-2713	2/6/13	7/2/13	20,538I; 15,050R-50PA
	2590.715-2713A	2/6/13	7/2/13	20,538I; 15,050R-50PB
	2590.715-2713A	8/27/14	7/14/15	20,538T; 15,050R-50PB
	2590.715-2715	8/22/11	2/14/12	20,262Y; 15,050R-50RR
	2590.715-2715	12/30/14	6/16/15	20,538W; 15,050R-50RR
	2590.715-2715A	7/21/16	. . . .	20,539F
	2590.715-2717	7/21/16		20,539F
731	2590.731	3/21/13	2/24/14	20,538J; 15,051A-1
732	2590.732	12/30/04	. . . .	20,534S
	2590.732	3/21/13	2/24/14	20,538J; 15,051B-1
	2590.732	12/24/13	10/1/14	20,538N; 15,051B-1
	2590.732	12/23/14	3/18/15	20,538V; 15,051B-1

ERISA Sec.	Regs. Section	Date Proposed[1]	Date Adopted[2]	Paragraph (¶)[3]
	2590.732	6/10/16	10/31/16	20,539E; 15,051B-1
	2590.736	6/10/16	10/31/16	20,539E; 15,051E-1

Title 29—Pension Benefit Guaranty Corporation—Labor

ERISA Sec.	Regs. Section	Date Proposed [1]	Date Adopted [2]	Paragraph (¶) [3]
. . . .	4000.1—4000.5	2/14/03	. . . .	20,534L
	4000.3—4000.4	12/28/04	3/9/05	20,534R; 24,239
	4000.3	3/9/05	6/1/06	20,534V; 15,302A
	4000.3	4/3/13	9/11/15	20,538K; 15,302A
	4000.3	7/23/13	3/11/14	20,538M; 15,302A
	4000.3	4/3/15	9/17/15	20,538Y; 15,302A
	4000.11—4000.15	2/14/03	. . . .	20,534L
	4000.21—4000.32	2/14/03	. . . .	20,534L
	4000.23	12/28/04	3/9/05	20,534R; 15,302U
	4000.23	3/9/05	. . . .	20,534V
	4000.29	12/28/04	. . . .	20,534R
	4000.41	9/20/16	. . . .	20,539H
	4000.41—4000.43	2/14/03	. . . .	20,534L
	4000.51—4000.54	2/14/03	. . . .	20,534L
	4000.53	4/3/13	9/11/15	20,538K; 15,302YY
4001	2612.2	3/14/97	11/6/97	20,533N
	4001.1	9/20/16	. . . .	20,539H
	4001.2	3/19/08	12/30/08	15,315A
	4001.2	7/1/08	6/14/11	20,537N; 15,315A
	4001.2	3/30/09	6/08/09	20,537R; 24,282
	4001.2	7/29/09	11/17/09	20,537S; 24,284
	4001.2	11/23/09	. . . .	20,537U
	4001.2	10/31/11	. . . .	20,538D
	4001.2	4/2/14	11/25/14	20,538R; 15,315A
	4001.2	9/20/16	. . . .	20,539H
4002	2603.2	4/23/87	8/14/87	15,322
	2603.8	4/23/87	8/14/87	15,322
	2603.21	4/23/87	8/14/87	15,322
	2603.32	4/23/87	8/14/87	15,322
	2603.36	4/23/87	8/14/87	15,322
	2606.1—2606.2	12/14/92	6/30/93	15,325
	2609.1—2609.6	5/20/94	5/20/94	20,533F
	2612.1—2612.3	12/14/92	6/30/93	15,315
	4002.2	7/29/09	. . . .	20,537S
	4002.11	7/29/09	. . . .	20,537S
4003	4003.1	1/12/01	4/16/12	20,534I; 24,311
	4003.1	10/18/07	7/3/08	20,537D; 15,331
	4003.1	9/20/16	. . . .	20,539H
	4003.2	10/18/07	7/3/08	20,537D; 15,331A
	4003.4	10/18/07	7/3/08	20,537D; 15,331C
	4003.9	2/14/03	. . . .	20,534L
	4003.10	2/14/03	. . . .	20,534L
	4003.33	2/14/03	. . . .	20,534L
	4003.33	10/18/07	7/3/08	20,537D; 15,333B
	4003.35	10/18/07	7/3/08	20,537D; 15,333D
	4003.53	2/14/03	. . . .	20,534L
	4003.53	10/18/07	7/3/08	20,537D; 15,334B
	4003.54	10/18/07	7/3/08	20,537D; 15,334C
	4003.58	10/18/07	7/3/08	20,537D; 15,334G
	4003.60	10/18/07	7/3/08	20,537D; 15,334I
	4003.61	3/27/02	7/22/02	15,334J
4006	2610.5	3/14/97	11/6/97	20,533N
	4006.2—4006.6	5/31/07	3/21/08	20,537A; 24,266
	4006.2—4006.5	7/23/13	3/11/14	20,538M; 24,319
	4006.7	7/23/13	3/11/14	20,538M; 15,361F
4007	2603.51—2603.55	4/23/87	8/14/87	15,322
	2603.52	8/18/86	10/2/86	15,322
	2606.1—2606.45	5/18/83	. . . .	20,525H
	2610.1—2610.2	4/10/92	. . . .	20,533B
	2610.1—2610.11	10/5/88	7/10/89	15,371—15,371J
	2610.4—2610.5	4/10/92	. . . .	20,533B
	2610.8	4/10/92	. . . .	20,533B
	2610.10	12/17/96	7/9/97	15,371I
	2610.21—2610.25	4/10/92	. . . .	20,533B
	2610.21—2610.26	10/5/88	7/10/89	15,371K—15,371P
	2610.25	4/10/92	12/14/98	15,371J
	2610.31	4/10/92	. . . .	20,533B
	2610.31—2610.34			
	4007.2—4007.3	5/31/07	3/21/08	20,537A; 24,266
	4007.2—4007.3	7/23/13	3/11/14	20,538M; 24,319
	4007.3	2/14/03	. . . .	20,534L
	4007.3	2/20/07	. . . .	20,537
	4007.3—4007.4	3/9/05	6/1/06	20,534V; 24,247
	4007.5	2/14/03	. . . .	20,534L

ERISA Sec.	Regs. Section	Date Proposed [1]	Date Adopted [2]	Paragraph (¶) [3]
	4007.6	2/14/03	. . . .	20,534L
	4007.7—4007.10	2/20/07	. . . .	20,537
	4007.8	4/27/99	11/26/99	15,371G
		1/12/01	11/17/06	20,534I; 15,371G
	4007.8	7/23/13	1/3/14 and 3/11/14	20,538M; 15,371G
	4007.8	4/28/16	9/23/16	20,539C; 15,371G
	4007.10	2/14/03	. . . .	20,534L
	4007.10—4007.11	5/31/07	3/21/08	20,537A; 24,266
	4007.11	7/23/13	1/3/14 and 3/11/14	20,538M; 15,371J
	4007.12—4007.13	7/23/13	3/11/14	20,538M; 24,319
	4007.12—4007.13	2/20/07	. . . .	20,537
	Appendix to Part 4007	7/23/13	3/11/14	20,538M; 15,373
4010	2628.1—2628.10	7/6/95	. . . .	20,532H
		10/5/88	7/10/89	15,371Q—15,371V
	2610.33—2610.34	4/10/92	. . . .	20,533B
	4010.1—4010.10	2/20/08	3/16/09	20,537H; 24,279
	4010.2	7/27/15	3/23/16	20,539; 15,396A
	4010.3—4010.9	12/28/04	3/9/05	20,534R
				15,396B—15,396H
	4010.4	7/27/15	3/23/16	20,539; 15,396C
	4010.8	7/27/15	3/23/16	20,539; 15,396G
	4010.10	2/14/03	. . . .	20,534L
	4010.11—4010.13	2/20/08	3/16/09	20,537H; 24,279
	4010.11	7/27/15	3/23/16	20,539; 15,396J
4022	Appendix A	4/30/98	7/15/98	15,401K
	2610.2—2610.3	1/9/85	3/28/85	15,371A; 15,371B
	2610.5—2610.6	1/9/85	3/28/85	15,371D; 15,371E
	2610.9	1/9/85	3/28/85	15,371H
	2623.1—2623.2	12/14/92	6/30/93	15,429G-15; 15,429G-16
				15,429G-19; 15,429G-20;
	2623.5—2623.7	12/14/92	6/30/93	15,429G-21
	2623.61	3/14/97	11/6/97	20,533N
	2623.81—2623.82	12/18/97	. . . .	20,533R
	2648.1—2648.9	11/14/84	. . . .	20,531C
	2670.4	6/13/83	. . . .	20,526R
	4022.2	7/1/08	6/14/11	20,537N; 15,421A
	4022.2	3/11/11	5/6/14	15,421A
	4022.2	10/31/11	. . . .	20,538D
	4022.3	7/1/08	6/14/11	20,537N; 15,421B
	4022.4	12/26/00	4/8/02	20,534G; 24,219
	4022.4	7/1/08	6/14/11	20,537N; 15,421C
	4022.6	12/26/00	4/8/02	20,534G; 24,219
	4022.6	7/1/08	6/14/11	20,537N; 15,421E
	4022.7	4/30/98	7/15/98	15,421F
	4022.7	12/26/00	4/8/02	20,534G; 24,219
	4022.7	4/2/14	11/25/14	20,538R; 15,421F
	4022.8	12/26/00	4/8/02	20,534G; 24,219
	4022.8	4/2/14	11/25/14	20,538R; 15,421G
	4022.9	12/26/00	4/8/02	20,534G; 24,219
	4022.9	2/14/03	. . . .	20,534L
	4022.11	7/27/09	11/17/09	20,537S; 24,284
	4022.21	12/26/00	4/8/02	20,534G; 24,219
	4022.21	7/1/08	6/14/11	20,537N; 15,422
	4022.22	7/1/08	6/14/11	20,537N; 15,422A
	4022.22	4/2/14	11/25/14	20,538R; 15,422A
	4022.23	7/1/08	6/14/11	20,537N; 15,422B
	4022.24	7/1/08	6/14/11	20,537N; 15,422C
	4022.24	3/11/11	5/6/14	15,422C
	4022.24	4/2/14	11/25/14	20,538R; 15,422C
	4022.25	12/26/00	4/8/02	20,534G; 24,219
	4022.25	7/1/08	6/14/11	20,537N; 15,422D
	4022.27	3/11/11	5/6/14	15,422F
	4022.51	7/1/08	6/14/11	20,537N; 15,422D
	4022.61	7/1/08	6/14/11	20,537N; 15,423
	4022.62	7/1/08	6/14/11	20,537N; 15,423A
	4022.62	3/11/11	5/6/14	15,423A
	4022.63	7/1/08	6/14/11	20,537N; 15,423B
	4022.81-4022.83	12/18/97	5/28/98	15,424-15,424B
	4022.81	12/26/00	4/8/02	20,534G; 24,219
	4022.82	7/1/08	6/14/11	20,537N; 15,424A
	4022.83	10/26/98	3/15/2000	15,424C—15,424F
	4022.91	12/26/00	4/8/02	20,534G; 24,219
	4022.92	12/26/00	4/8/02	20,534G; 24,219
	4022.93	12/26/00	4/8/02	20,534G; 24,219
	4022.94	12/26/00	4/8/02	20,534G; 24,219
	4022.95	12/26/00	4/8/02	20,534G; 24,219
	4022.120	10/31/11	. . . .	20,538D
	4022.121	10/31/11	. . . .	20,538D
	4022.122	10/31/11	. . . .	20,538D
	4022.123	10/31/11	. . . .	20,538D
4022A	2613.2	12/12/86	12/14/87	15,422
	2613.8	12/12/86	12/14/87	15,428
	2623.1—2623.2	10/31/83	1/28/85	20,519P

ERISA Sec.	Regs. Section	Date Proposed [1]	Date Adopted [2]	Paragraph (¶) [3]
	2623.5—2623.8	10/31/83	1/28/85	20,519P
	2623.11—2623.13	10/31/83	1/28/85	20,519P
	2690.1—2690.5	2/1/83	. . . .	20,525D
4022B	4022B.1	12/26/00	4/8/02	20,534G; 24,219
				15,441—15,446C; 15,446O—
4041	2616.1—2616.18	9/2/87	12/11/92	15,446W
	2616.4	12/14/92	6/30/93	15,444
	2616.1—2616.8	3/14/97	11/6/97	20,533N
	2616.41—2616.50	3/14/97	11/6/97	20,533N
				15,447—15,447I; 15,447T—
	2617.1—2617.18	9/2/87	12/11/92	15,448
	2617.21—2617.31	3/14/97	11/6/97	20,533N
	2691.1—2691.7	2/1/83	. . . .	20,525D
	2692.1—2692.4	2/1/83	. . . .	20,525D
	2693.1—2693.9	2/1/83	. . . .	20,525D
	2694.1—2694.7	2/1/83	. . . .	20,525D
	2695.1—2695.2	2/1/83	. . . .	20,525D
	2604.1—2604.6	7/24/79	1/26/83	15,323
	2617.4	12/12/86	12/14/87	15,447C
	2617.12—2617.14	11/2/84	7/31/85	15,447K; 15,447M
	2617.23	11/2/84	7/31/85	15,447V
	2617.40—2617.43	11/15/91	. . . .	20,533A
	4041.2	10/31/11	. . . .	20,538D
	4041.3	2/14/03	. . . .	20,534L
	4041.5	2/14/03	. . . .	20,534L
	4041.28	10/31/11	. . . .	20,538D
	4000.28	9/20/16	. . . .	20,539H
	4041.42	12/18/97	5/28/98	15,440J-1
	4041.42	10/31/11	. . . .	20,538D
	4041.51	12/05/07	. . . .	20,537E
4041A	4041A.3	2/14/03	. . . .	20,534L
	4041A.11	4/3/15	9/17/15	20,538Y; 15,449J
	4041A.24	1/29/14	5/28/14	20,538O; 15,449O
	4041A.25	4/3/15	9/17/15	20,538Y; 15,449P
	4041A.42	9/20/16	. . . .	20,539H
	4041A.43	4/30/98	7/15/98	15,449U
4042	4042.1—4042.5	5/12/07	. . . .	20,537E
4043	2615.1	8/17/83	5/29/84	15,461
	2615.1—2615.2	12/14/92	6/30/93	15,461; 15,461A
	2615.4	8/17/83	5/29/84	15,461C
	2615.13	8/17/83	5/29/84	15,463B
	2615.14	8/17/83	5/29/84	15,463C
		12/14/92	6/30/93	15,463C
	2615.16	8/17/83	5/29/84	15,464
	4043.5—4043.7	2/14/03	. . . .	20,534L
	4043.1—4043.81	4/3/13	9/11/15	20,538K; 24,332
	4043.1—4043.6	11/23/09	. . . .	20,537U
	4043.23	11/23/09	. . . .	20,537U
	4043.25—4043.27	11/23/09	. . . .	20,537U
	4043.291—4043.37	11/23/09	. . . .	20,537U
	4043.61—4043.70	11/23/09	. . . .	20,537U
	4043.81	11/23/09	. . . .	20,537U
4044	2620.1—2620.3	5/8/85	. . . .	20,519R
	2620.5—2620.8	5/8/85	. . . .	20,519R
	2620.10—2620.16	5/8/85	. . . .	20,519R
	2670.4	7/7/86	7/10/89	15,715A
	2675.1—2675.44	7/7/86	7/10/89	15,715Z
	4044.2(b)	12/26/00	4/8/02	20,534G; 24,219
	4044.2	7/1/08	6/14/11	20,537N; 15,471A
	4044.2	10/31/11	. . . .	20,538D
	4044.10	7/1/08	6/14/11	20,537N; 15,472
	4044.12	4/2/14	11/25/14	20,538R; 15,472B
	4044.13	12/26/00	4/8/02	20,534G; 24,219
	4044.13	7/1/08	6/14/11	20,537N; 15,472C
	4044.14	7/1/08	6/14/11	20,537N; 15,472D
	4044.52	4/30/98	7/15/98	15,475A
	4044.52	10/31/11	. . . .	20,538D
	4044.54	4/30/98	7/15/98	15,475C
	4044.76	10/31/11	. . . .	20,538D
4047	4047.4	7/23/13	3/11/14	20,538M; 15,501C
4050	2606.1	8/24/95	11/30/95	15,325
	2606.51	8/24/95	11/30/95	15,325
	2616.2	8/24/95	11/30/95	15,442
	2616.7	8/24/95	11/30/95	15,446A
	2616.29	8/24/95	11/30/95	15,446W
	2617.2	8/24/95	11/30/95	15,447A
	2617.8	8/24/95	11/30/95	15,447G
	2617.28	8/24/95	11/30/95	15,448
	2629.1—2629.12	3/14/97	11/6/97	20,533N
	2629.1—2629.13	8/24/95	11/30/95	15,530A—15,530O
	4022.7	10/26/98	. . . .	20,533W
	4044.52	10/26/98	. . . .	20,533W
	4044.53	10/26/98	. . . .	20,533W

ERISA Sec.	Regs. Section	Date Proposed [1]	Date Adopted [2]	Paragraph (¶) [3]
		3/14/05	. . . .	20,534X
	4044.54	10/26/98	. . . .	20,533W
	4050.2	4/30/98	7/15/98	15,530B
	4050.2	12/18/98	5/28/98	15,530B
	4050.2	10/26/98		20,533W
	4050.5	4/30/98	7/15/98	15,530E
	4050.6	2/14/03	. . . .	20,534L
	4050.101—4050.107	9/20/16	. . . .	20,539H
	4050.201—4050.207	9/20/16	. . . .	20,539H
	4050.301—4050.307	9/20/16	. . . .	20,539H
	4050.401—4050.407	9/20/16	. . . .	20,539H
	Appendix A	4/30/98	7/15/98	15,530M
4062	2618.1—2618.17	10/2/80	10/7/81	15,472—15,473F
	2618.30—2618.32	10/2/80	10/7/81	15,473T—15,473V
	2611.1	4/18/77	. . . .	20,533
	2611.2	4/18/77	. . . .	20,533
	2611.5	4/18/77	. . . .	20,533
	2611.6	4/18/77	. . . .	20,533
	2611.7	4/18/77	. . . .	20,533
	2611.10	4/18/77	. . . .	20,533
	2611.11	4/18/77	. . . .	20,533
	2611.12	4/18/77	. . . .	20,533
	2611.13	4/18/77	. . . .	20,533
	2622.1—2622.4	12/14/92	6/30/93	15,623—15,623C
	2622.6—2622.8	12/14/92	6/30/93	15,623E—15,623G
	4062.9	2/14/03	. . . .	20,534L
	4062.10	2/14/03	. . . .	20,534L
	4062.1—4062.35	8/10/10	. . . .	20,537X
4071	4071.1	1/12/01	. . . .	20,534I
	4071.4	1/12/01	. . . .	20,534I
4201	2619.3	3/25/86	. . . .	20,532A
		1/19/93	. . . .	20,533E
	2640.8	10/6/87	. . . .	20,520C
4203	4203.4	2/14/03	. . . .	20,534L
4204	2619.25	3/25/86	. . . .	20,532A
		1/19/93	. . . .	20,533E
	2619.26	12/12/86	12/14/87	15,620I
	2619.42—2619.44	3/25/86	. . . .	20,532A
	2619.46—2619.48	3/25/86	. . . .	20,532A
	2619.42—2619.48	1/19/93	. . . .	20,533E
	2640.3	7/7/83	8/26/85	15,663C
	2611.14	4/18/77	. . . .	20,533
	4204.11	2/14/03	. . . .	20,534L
	4204.12	4/3/13	9/11/15	20,538K; 15,668C
	4204.12	11/23/09	. . . .	20,537U
	4204.21	2/14/03	. . . .	20,534L
4206	2649.1—2649.8	10/6/87	12/15/92	20,520C
	4206.7	4/3/13	9/11/15	20,538K; 15,670G
	4206.7	11/23/09	12/15/92	20,527U
4207	2640.6	3/5/84	. . . .	20,525K
	2640.7	11/14/84	. . . .	20,531C
	2643.1	2/14/83	5/30/84	15,668A
	2643.2	2/14/83	5/30/84	15,668B
	2640.6	6/5/87	12/15/92	20,530C
	2647.1—2647.8	3/5/84	3/24/86	15,663F; 15,671A—15,671H
	2647.1	10/23/92	3/1/94	15,671A
	2647.2	10/23/92	3/1/94	15,671B
	2647.9	10/23/92	3/1/94	15,671I
	4207.10	2/14/03	. . . .	20,534L
	4207.11	2/14/03	. . . .	20,534L
4208	2646.1—2646.8	6/5/87	. . . .	20,530C
	4208.9	2/14/03	. . . .	20,534L
	4208.10	2/14/03	. . . .	20,534L
4211	2640.4	11/9/87	12/15/92	15,663D
	2642.1	9/9/85	10/23/87	15,678
	2642.1	11/9/87	12/15/92	15,678
	2642.2	9/9/85	10/23/87	15,678A
	2642.5—2642.7	9/9/85	10/23/87	15,678B—15,678D
	2642.11—2642.14	9/9/85	10/23/87	15,678E—15,678H
	2642.21—2642.27	11/9/87	12/15/92	15,678O—15,678U
	4211.2	11/9/87	12/15/92	15,678O—15,678U
	4211.2	3/19/08	12/30/08	15,678A
	4211.4	3/19/08	12/30/08	15,678B-5
	4211.12	3/19/08	12/30/08	15,678D
	4211.22	2/14/03	. . . .	20,534L
4219	2643.10—2643.13	2/14/83	5/30/84	15,668J—15,668M
	2676.1—2676.31	9/19/85	3/24/86	15,687D—15,687V
	4219.1	3/19/08	12/30/08	15,687
	4219.12	3/19/08	12/30/08	15,687A
	4219.15	3/19/08	12/30/08	15,687F
	4219.17	2/14/03	. . . .	20,534L
	4219.19	2/14/03	. . . .	20,534L
4220	4220.3	2/14/03	. . . .	20,534L

ERISA Sec.	Regs. Section	Date Proposed [1]	Date Adopted [2]	Paragraph (¶) [3]
4221	4221.4	2/14/03	. . . .	20,534L
	4221.6	2/14/03	. . . .	20,534L
	4221.12	2/14/03	. . . .	20,534L
	4221.13	2/14/03	. . . .	20,534L
	4221.14	2/14/03	. . . .	20,534L
4225	2648.1—2648.10	11/14/84	3/24/86	15,696A—15,696J
4231	2644.1—2644.4	2/14/83	5/30/84	15,687—15,687C
	4231.1—4231.10	5/1/97	5/1/98	15,700A—15,700J
	4231.1—4231.18	6/6/16	. . . .	20,539D
	4231.2	4/3/13	9/11/15	20,538K; 15,700B
	4231.2	11/23/09	. . . .	20,537U
	4231.6	4/3/13	9/11/15	20,538K; 15,700F
	4231.6	11/23/09	. . . .	20,537U
	4231.8	2/14/03	. . . .	20,534L
	4231.8	1/29/14	5/28/14	20,538O; 15,700H
4234	2641.1—2641.12	7/7/83	8/26/85	15,689A—15,689L
4245	4245.3—4245.8	2/14/03	. . . .	20,534L
4281	2670.3	12/22/81	12/1/83	15,718D-1
	4281.13—4281.15	4/30/98	7/15/98	15,715G-15,715I
	4281.3	2/14/03	. . . .	20,534L
	4281.3	4/3/15	9/17/15	20,538Y; 15,715C
	4281.32	2/14/03	. . . .	20,534L
	4281.43	2/14/03	. . . .	20,534L
	4281.43	4/3/15	9/17/15	20,538Y; 15,715R
	4281.43	1/29/14	5/28/14	20,538O; 15,715R
	4281.44	1/29/14	5/28/14	20,538O; 15,715S
	4281.45	2/14/03	. . . .	20,534L
	4281.46	1/29/14	5/28/14	20,538O; 15,715U
	4281.47	1/29/14	5/28/14	20,538O; 15,715V
	4281.47	4/3/15	9/17/15	20,538Y; 15,715V
4402	4902.9	4/2/01	6/14/01	20,534J; 24,215
Rehabili-	2672.1—2672.8	12/22/81	12/1/83	15,700A—15,700H
tation	2675.1—2675.8	6/13/83	7/31//85	15,715A—15,715H
Act	2676.13	1/19/93	. . . .	20,533E
of	2676.16	1/19/93	. . . .	20,533E
1973,	2608.101—2608.170	8/28/84	6/20/86	15,326
§ 504				
4901	4901.2	3/30/09	6/8/09	20,537R; 24,282
	4901.6	2/14/03	. . . .	20,534L
	4901.11	2/14/03	. . . .	20,534L
	4901.11	3/30/09	6/8/09	20,537R; 24,282
	4901.15	2/14/03	. . . .	20,534L
	4901.33	2/14/03	. . . .	20,534L
4902	4902.1	3/30/09	6/8/09	20,537R; 24,282
	4902.2	3/30/09	6/8/09	20,537R; 24,282
	4902.3	2/14/03	. . . .	20,534L
	4902.3	3/30/09	6/8/09	20,537R; 24,282
	4902.4	3/30/09	6/8/09	20,537R; 24,282
	4902.5—4902.7	2/14/03	. . . .	20,534L
	4902.6—4902.7	3/30/09	6/8/09	20,537R; 24,282
	4902.9—4902.12	3/30/09	6/8/09	20,537R; 24,282
4903	4903.1—4903.22	7/22/10	11/5/10	20,537W; 24,299
	4903.2	2/14/03	. . . .	20,534L
	4903.2	2/14/03	. . . .	20,534L
	4903.24	2/14/03	. . . .	20,534L
4907	4907.170	2/14/03	. . . .	20,534L

Title 29—Family and Medical Leave Act—Labor

Act Sec.	Regs. Section	Date Proposed [1]	Date Adopted [2]	Paragraph (¶) [3]
	825.300—825.311	2/11/08	11/17/08	20,537J; 24,275
	825.400—825.404	2/11/08	11/17/08	20,537J; 24,275
	825.500	2/11/08	11/17/08	20,537J; 24,275
	825.600—825.604	2/11/08	11/17/08	20,537J; 24,275
	825.700—825.702	2/11/08	11/17/08	20,537J; 24,275
	825.800	2/11/08	11/17/08	20,537J; 24,275

Veterans' Employment and Training Service

Regs. Section	Date Proposed [1]	Date Adopted [2]	Paragraph (¶) [3]
1002.1—1002.314	9/20/04	9/20/04	20,534Q; 24,242

U.S. Code-ERISA Locator Table

The Employee Retirement Income Security Act of 1974 (ERISA) is codified at 29 U.S.C. § 1001, *et seq.* Provided below are the Act's section names and the conversion of the U.S. Code sections to ERISA sections.

Recent Public Law Code and ERISA Locator Table

Listed below is the location of significant benefits-related amendments to the Internal Revenue Code and ERISA made by selected laws enacted after 2000. Public Law numbers are listed in chronological order. (The Internal Revenue Code is located in Volume 1. ERISA is located in Volume 2.)

P.L. No.	Name	Enactment Date	Paragraph
107-16	Economic Growth and Tax Relief Reconciliation Act	June 7, 2001	11,050; 11,100; 11,113; 11,114; 11,118; 11,118A; 11,180; 11,190; 11,289; 11,289M; 11,293; 11,294A; 11,330; 11,334A; 11,700; 11,750; 11,799A; 11,800; 11,850; 12,050; 12,130; 12,200; 12,350; 12,400; 12,500; 13,153; 13,160; 13,193; 13,239A; 13,550; 13,566; 13,610; 13,620; 13,640; 13,648M; 13,648W-87; 13,655; 13,690; 13,710; 13,850; 13,919L; 13,920; 13,968U-10; 14,140; 14,430; 14,440; 14,620; 14,740; 14,780
107-134	Victims of Terrorism Tax Relief Act	January 23, 2002	11,250; 11,260; 13,919L; 15,043H; 15,320
107-147	Job Creation and Worker Assistance Act	March 9, 2002	11,050; 11,100; 11,109; 11,113; 11,118; 11,118A; 11,293; 11,294A; 11,334; 11,358F; 11,700; 11,750; 11,800; 11,850; 12,050; 12,130; 12,350; 12,400; 12,500; 12,550; 13,153; 13,239A; 13,648W-70; 13,968U-8; 14,140; 14,440; 14,450; 14,620; 14,740; 15,360
107-204	Sarbanes-Oxley Act	July 30, 2002	14,910; 14,920
107-210	Andean Trade Preference Act	August 6, 2002	13,648W; 15,045T
108-173	Medicare Prescription Drug, Improvement and Modernization Act of 2003	December 8, 2003	11,180; 11,280; 11,288A; 11,334; 11,335; 13,540; 13,620; 13,640; 13,648W-92; 13,681; 13,850
108-218	Pension Funding Equity Act of 2004	April 10, 2004	11,850; 12,400; 13,030; 13,160; 14,730; 14,210; 14,620; 14,780; 14,920; 15,360; 15,689
108-311	Working Families Tax Relief Act of 2004	October 4, 2004	11,050; 11,100; 11,109; 11,190; 11,270; 11,283; 11,289H; 11,289M; 11,294; 11,294A; 11,295; 11,326; 11,334; 11,700; 11,800; 12,050; 12,200; 12,350; 12,400; 12,500; 13,239A; 13,610; 13,620; 13,648F; 13,920; 13,943; 13,968U-8; 14,430; 15,050K; 15,360
108-357	American Jobs Creation Act of 2004	October 22, 2004	11,113; 11,114; 11,180; 11,190; 11,240; 11,293; 11,300; 11,330; 11,334A; 12,145; 13,030; 13,100; 13,130; 13,160; 13,480; 13,490; 13,495; 13,530; 13,540; 13,550; 13,640; 13,640; 13,710; 13,919U; 13,920; 13,920; 14,210; 14,730; 14,780
109-135	Gulf Opportunity Zone Act of 2005	December 21, 2005	11,050; 11,100; 11,109; 11,113; 11,114; 11,180; 11,295; 11,335; 11,359; 11,800; 12,400; 13,160; 13,239A; 13,473; 13,474; 13,475; 13,640; 13,648W-50; 14,620
109-151	[Extension of Mental Health Parity Act]	December 30, 2005	13,968U-8; 15,050K
109-171	Deficit Reduction Act of 2005	February 8, 2006	15,360
109-222	Tax Increase Prevention and Reconciliation Act of 2005	May 17, 2006	12,097; 13,598; 13,660; 13,800
109-227	Heroes Earned Retirement Opportunities Act	May 29, 2006	11,330

P.L. No.	Name	Enactment Date	Paragraph
109-280	Pension Protection Act of 2006	August 17, 2006	11,109; 11,113; 11,114; 11,118; 11,190; 11,250; 11,289M; 11,330; 11,700; 11,750; 11,799A; 11,800; 11,850; 11,899A; 12,050; 12,097; 12,130; 12,145; 12,150; 12,200; 12,250; 12,350; 12,400; 12,500; 12,550; 12,850; 13,030; 13,151L; 13,151M; 13,151N; 13,153; 13,160; 13,193; 13,239A; 13,530; 13,550; 13,566; 13,600; 13,610; 13,620; 13,640; 13,648J; 13,648M; 13,648P; 13,648W-75; 13,648W-87; 13,660; 13,678; 13,690; 13,706; 13,710; 13,750; 13,800; 13,850; 13,920; 13,943; 14,130; 14,140; 14,210; 14,230; 14,240; 14,250; 14,430; 14,440; 14,450; 14,460; 14,470; 14,490; 14,500; 14,610; 14,620; 14,630; 14,640; 14,650; 14,655; 14,657; 14,660; 14,730; 14,740; 14,770; 14,780; 14,820; 14,920; 15,000; 15,010; 15,040; 15,310; 15,320; 15,330; 15,360; 15,370; 15,380; 15,395; 15,400; 15,410; 15,420; 15,440; 15,450; 15,460; 15,470; 15,530; 15,620; 15,662U; 15,669; 15,675; 15,676; 15,689; 15,696; 15,709; 15,713
109-432	Tax Relief and Health Care Act of 2006	December 20, 2006	11,113; 11,180; 11,280; 11,334; 11,334A; 11,335; 12,050; 13,648W-92; 13,968U-8; 15,050K
110-28	U.S. Troop Readiness, Veterans' Care, Katrina Recovery, and Iraq Accountability Appropriations Act of 2007	May 25, 2007	12,350; 13,030; 13,480; 13,780; 13,919U; 14,130
110-172	Tax Technical Corrections Act of 2007	December 29, 2007	11,050; 11,113; 11,288A; 11,750; 12,050; 13,598
110-233	Genetic Information Nondiscrimination Act of 2008	May 21, 2008	13,968R; 13,968X; 14,920; 15,050A; 15,051C
110-245	Heroes Earnings Assistance and Relief Tax Act of 2008	June 17, 2008	11,113; 11,190; 11,288A; 11,330; 11,800; 11,850; 12,350; 13,239A; 13,334; 13,530; 13,540; 13,550; 13,920; 13,968U-8; 15,050K
110-343	Emergency Economic Stabilization Act of 2008	October 3, 2008	11,100; 11,109; 11,113; 11,180; 11,289M; 11,300; 11,334A; 11,358P; 12,050; 13,154C-50; 13,660; 13,919L; 13,968U-8; 15,050K
110-458	Worker, Retiree and Employer Recovery Act of 2008	December 23, 2008	11,190; 11,270; 11,700; 11,750; 11,850; 12,097; 12,145; 12,200; 12,250; 12,350; 12,400; 12,550; 13,030; 13,151L; 13,151N; 13,530; 13,600; 13,640; 13,648P; 14,130; 14,210; 14,230; 14,231A; 14,240; 14,430; 14,440; 14,450; 14,460; 14,490; 14,500; 14,620; 14,630; 14,650; 14,740; 14,780; 14,920; 15,360; 15,395; 15,410; 15,440; 15,450; 15,470; 15,530; 15,662U; 15,689
111-3	Children's Health Insurance Program Reauthorization Act of 2009	February 4, 2009	13,968Q; 14,220; 14,920; 15,049H
111-5	American Recovery and Reinvestment Act of 2009	February 17, 2009	11,289Y; 13,787M; 13,857M; 15,045F; 15,049H
111-148	Patient Protection and Affordable Care Act (including amendments made by the Health Care and Education Reconciliation Act of 2010 (P.L. 111-152)	March 23, 2010	11,112J; 11,119; 11,270; 11,280; 11,288A; 11,289Z; 11,300; 11,326; 11,334; 11,335; 11,700; 13,160; 13,480; 13,578; 13,578F; 13,58K; 13,648W-140; 13,648W-170; 13,648Z-50; 13,660; 13,680; 13,724; 13,724; 13,920; 13,968V-20B; 14,210; 14,910; 14,940; 15,043K; 15,043N; 15,043Q; 15,050R-50
111-240	Small Business Jobs Act of 2010	September 27, 2010	11,113; 11,190; 11,300; 11,799A; 13,858; 13,859
111-312	Tax Relief, Unemployment Insurance Reauthorization, and Job Creation Act of 2010	December 17, 2010	11,180; 11,289M; 11,334A; 12,050; 13,655
111-344	Omnibus Trade Act of 2010	December 29, 2010	11,112C; 13,919T; 13,968Q; 13,648W; 15,045F; 15,049H
112-9	Comprehensive 1099 Taxpayer Protection and Repayment of Exchange Subsidy Overpayments Act of 2011	April 14, 2011	11,112F; 13,680
112-141	Moving Ahead for Progress in the 21st Century Act	July 6, 2012	11,190; 11,850; 12,550; 13,030; 14,210; 14,450; 14,630; 14,730; 14,780; 15,320; 15,339; 15,350; 15,360; 15,395; 15,720
112-240	American Taxpayer Relief Act	January 2, 2013	11,107; 11,109; 11,180; 11,289M; 11,290; 11,750; 12,050
113-67	Bipartisan Budget Act of 2013	December 26, 2013	15,360

P.L. No.	Name	Enactment Date	Paragraph
113-97	Cooperative and Small Employer Charity Pension Flexibility Act	April 7, 2014	11,700; 11,850; 12,250; 12,300; 12,350; 13,030; 13,151N-5; 13,600; 13,750; 14,210, 14230; 14,440; 14,460; 14,500; 14,620; 14,656; 14,920; 15,330; 15,395; 15,662U; 16,475
113-128	Workforce Innovation and Opportunity Act	July 22, 2014	13,919T
113-159	Highway and Transportation Funding Act of 2014	August 8, 2014	13,151L; 13,151O; 14,210; 14,460; 14,630
113-235	Consolidated and Further Continuing Appropriations Act, 2015	December 16, 2014	12,200; 12,353; 12,600; 12,650; 12,700; 12,750; 12,800; 12,850; 13,151M; 13,151N; 14,210; 14,440; 14,500; 14,640; 14,650; 14,920; 15,310; 15,330; 15,350; 15,360; 15,429H; 15,686; 15,700; 15,703; 15,706; 15,708; 15,709; 15,710; 14,712; 15,713; 16,476
113-295	Tax Increase Prevention Act of 2014	December 19, 2014	11,113; 11,180; 11,190; 11,270; 11,280; 11,283; 11,288A; 11,289M; 11,330; 11,358F; 11,700; 11,750; 11,799A; 12,050; 12,350; 12,550; 13,130; 13,151M; 13,151O; 13,153; 13,160; 13,180; 13,334; 13,490; 13,530; 13,540; 13,598; 13,620; 13,649; 13,674; 13,800; 13,850; 13,859; 13,919U; 13,920; 13,968R; 14,450; 14,460; 14,630; 14,640
114-41	Surface Transportation and Veterans Health Care Choice Improvement Act of 2015	July 31, 2015	14,210; 14,730; 14,780
114-74	Bipartisan Budget Act of 2015	November 2, 2015	13,151L; 14,210; 14,630; 15,360
114-113	Consolidated Appropriations Act, 2016	December 18, 2015	11,180; 11,190; 11,270; 11,281G; 11,289M; 12,050; 12,350.033; 13,780
115-97	Tax Cuts and Jobs Act	December 22, 2017	11,107; 11,109; 1,112F; 11,113; 11,119; 11,122; 11,170; 11,180; 11,240; 11,250; 11,288A; 11,289M; 11,289Q; 11,290; 11,295; 11,300; 11,326; 11,330; 11,334; 11,335; 11,355; 11,358F; 11,750; 13,153; 13,313; 13,334; 13,566; 13,648W-170; 13,648Z-50; 13,660; 13,690; 13,710; 13,800; 13,859; 13,920

Employee Retirement Income Security Act of 1974 (ERISA) (Pension Reform Act of 1974)
P.L. 93-406
88 United States Statutes at Large 829
Signed by the President
September 2, 1974

>>>→ *Note: ERISA Sec. 1 reproduced below is the official full text of the Employee Retirement Income Security Act of 1974. ERISA Sec. 1 is not codified in the United States Code.*

[¶ 14,110]
SHORT TITLE AND TABLE OF CONTENTS

Act Sec. 1. This Act may be cited as the "Employee Retirement Income Security Act of 1974".

TABLE OF CONTENTS

TITLE I—PROTECTION OF EMPLOYEE BENEFIT RIGHTS

Subtitle A—General Provisions

[¶ 14,120]
FINDINGS AND DECLARATION OF POLICY

Act Sec. 2.(a) BENEFIT PLANS AS AFFECTING INTERSTATE COMMERCE AND THE FEDERAL TAXING POWER.—The Congress finds that the growth in size, scope, and numbers of employee benefit plans in recent years has been rapid and substantial; that the operational scope and economic impact of such plans is increasingly interstate; that the continued well-being and security of millions of employees and their dependents are directly affected by these plans; that they are affected with a national public interest; that they have become an important factor affecting the stability of employment and the successful development of industrial relations; that they have become an important factor in commerce because of the interstate character of their activities, and of the activities of their participants, and the employers, employee organizations, and other entities by which they are established or maintained; that a large volume of the activities of such plans is carried on by means of the mails and instrumentalities of interstate commerce; that owing to the lack of employee information and adequate safeguards concerning their operation, it is desirable in the interests of employees and their beneficiaries, and to provide for the general welfare and the free flow of commerce, that disclosure be made and safeguards be provided with respect to the establishment, operation, and administration of such plans; that they substantially affect the revenues of the United States because they are afforded preferential Federal tax treatment; that despite the enormous growth in such plans many employees with long years of employment are losing anticipated retirement benefits owing to the lack of vesting provisions in such plans; that owing to the inadequacy of current minimum standards, the soundness and stability of plans with respect to adequate funds to pay promised benefits may be endangered; that owing to the termination of plans before requisite funds have been accumulated, employees and their beneficiaries have been deprived of anticipated benefits; and that it is therefore desirable in the interests of employees and their beneficiaries, for the protection of the revenue of the United States, and to provide for the free flow of commerce, that minimum standards be provided assuring the equitable character of such plans and their financial soundness.

Act Sec. 2. (b) PROTECTION OF INTERSTATE COMMERCE AND BENEFICIARIES BY REQUIRING DISCLOSURE AND REPORTING, SETTING STANDARDS OF CONDUCT, ETC., FOR FIDUCIARIES.—It is hereby declared to be the policy of this Act to protect interstate commerce and the interests of participants in employee benefit plans and their beneficiaries, by requiring the disclosure and reporting to participants and beneficiaries of financial and other information with respect thereto, by establishing standards of conduct, responsibility, and obligation for fiduciaries of employee benefit plans, and by providing for appropriate remedies, sanctions, and ready access to the Federal courts.

Act Sec. 2. (c) PROTECTION OF INTERSTATE COMMERCE, THE FEDERAL TAXING POWER, AND BENEFICIARIES BY VESTING OF ACCRUED BENEFITS, SETTING MINIMUM STANDARDS OF FUNDING, REQUIRING TERMINATION INSURANCE.—It is hereby further declared to be the policy of this Act to protect interstate commerce, the Federal taxing power, and the interests of participants in private pension plans and their beneficiaries by improving the equitable character and the soundness of such plans by requiring them to vest the accrued benefits of employees with significant periods of service, to meet minimum standards of funding, and by requiring plan termination insurance.

[¶ 14,130]
DEFINITIONS

Act Sec. 3. For purposes of this title:

(1) The terms "employee welfare benefit plan" and "welfare plan" mean any plan, fund, or program which was heretofore or is hereafter established or maintained by an employer or by an employee organization, or by both, to the extent that such plan, fund, or program was established or is maintained for the purpose of providing for its participants or their beneficiaries, through the purchase of insurance or otherwise, (A) medical, surgical, or hospital care or benefits, or benefits in the event of sickness, accident, disability, death or unemployment, or vacation benefits, apprenticeship or other training programs, or day care centers, scholarship funds, or prepaid legal services, or (B) any benefit described in section 302(c) of the Labor Management Relations Act, 1947 (other than pensions on retirement or death, and insurance to provide such pensions).

(2)(A) Except as provided in subparagraph (B), the terms "employee pension benefit plan" and "pension plan" mean any plan, fund, or program which was heretofore or is hereafter established or maintained by an employer or by an employee organization, or by both, to the extent that by its express terms or as a result of surrounding circumstances such plan, fund, or program—

(i) provides retirement income to employees, or

(ii) results in a deferral of income by employees for periods extending to the termination of covered employment or beyond,

regardless of the method of calculating the contributions made to the plan, the method of calculating the benefits under the plan or the method of distributing benefits from the plan. A distribution from a plan, fund, or program shall not be treated as made in a form other than retirement income or as a distribution prior to termination of covered employment solely because such distribution is made to an employee who has attained age 62 and who is not separated from employment at the time of such distribution.

(B) The Secretary may by regulation prescribe rules consistent with the standards and purposes of this Act providing one or more exempt categories under which—

(i) severance pay arrangements, and

(ii) supplemental retirement income payments, under which the pension benefits of retirees or their beneficiaries are supplemented to take into account some portion or all of the increases in the cost of living (as determined by the Secretary of Labor) since retirement,

shall, for purposes of this title, be treated as welfare plans rather than pension plans. In the case of any arrangement or payment a principal effect of which is the evasion of the standards or purposes of this Act applicable to pension plans, such arrangement or payment shall be treated as a pension plan. An applicable voluntary early retirement incentive plan (as defined in section 457(e)(11)(D)(ii) of the Internal Revenue Code of 1986) making payment or supplements described in section 457(e)(11)(D)(i) of such Code, and an applicable employment retention plan (as defined in section 457(f)(4)(C) of such

Code) making payment of benefits described in section 457(f)(4)(A) of such Code, shall, for purposes of this title, be treated as a welfare plan (and not a pension plan) with respect to such payments and supplements.

(3) The term "employee benefit plan" or "plan" means an employee welfare benefit plan or an employee pension benefit plan or a plan which is both an employee welfare benefit plan and an employee pension benefit plan.

(4) The term "employee organization" means any labor union or any organization of any kind, or any agency or employee representation committee, association, group, or plan, in which employees participate and which exists for the purpose, in whole or in part, of dealing with employers concerning an employee benefit plan, or other matters incidental to employment relationships; or any employees' beneficiary association organized for the purpose in whole or in part, of establishing such a plan.

(5) The term "employer" means any person acting directly as an employer, or indirectly in the interest of an employer, in relation to an employee benefit plan; and includes a group or association of employers acting for an employer in such capacity.

(6) The term "employee" means any individual employed by an employer.

(7) The term "participant" means any employee or former employee of an employer, or any member or former member of an employee organization, who is or may become eligible to receive a benefit of any type from an employee benefit plan which covers employees of such employer or members of such organization, or whose beneficiaries may be eligible to receive any such benefit.

(8) The term "beneficiary" means a person designated by a participant, or by the terms of an employee benefit plan, who is or may become entitled to a benefit thereunder.

(9) The term "person" means an individual, partnership, joint venture, corporation, mutual company, joint-stock company, trust, estate, unincorporated organization, association, or employee organization.

(10) The term "State" includes any State of the United States, the District of Columbia, Puerto Rico, the Virgin Islands, American Samoa, Guam, Wake Island, and the Canal Zone. The term "United States" when used in the geographic sense means the States and the Outer Continental Shelf lands defined in the Outer Continental Shelf Lands Act (43 U.S.C. 1331-1343).

(11) The term "commerce" means trade, traffic, commerce, transportation, or communication between any State and any place outside thereof.

(12) The term "industry or activity affecting commerce" means any activity, business, or industry in commerce or in which a labor dispute would hinder or obstruct commerce or the free flow of commerce, and includes any activity or industry "affecting commerce" within the meaning of the Labor Management Relations Act, 1947, or the Railway Labor Act.

(13) The term "Secretary" means the Secretary of Labor.

(14) The term "party in interest" means, as to an employee benefit plan—

    (A) any fiduciary (including, but not limited to, any administrator, officer, trustee, or custodian), counsel, or employee of such employee benefit plan;

    (B) a person providing services to such plan;

    (C) an employer any of whose employees are covered by such plan;

    (D) an employee organization any of whose members are covered by such plan;

    (E) an owner, direct or indirect, of 50 percent or more of—

        (i) the combined voting power of all classes of stock entitled to vote or the total value of shares of all classes of stock of a corporation,

        (ii) the capital interest or the profits interest of a partnership, or

        (iii) the beneficial interest of a trust or unincorporated enterprise,

which is an employer or an employee organization described in subparagraph (C) or (D);

    (F) a relative (as defined in paragraph (15)) of any individual described in subparagraph (A), (B), (C), or (E);

    (G) a corporation, partnership, or trust or estate of which (or in which) 50 percent or more of—

        (i) the combined voting power of all classes of stock entitled to vote or the total value of shares of all classes of stock of such corporation,

        (ii) the capital interest or profits interest of such partnership, or

        (iii) the beneficial interest of such trust or estate,

is owned directly or indirectly, or held by persons described in subparagraph (A), (B), (C), (D), or (E);

    (H) an employee, officer, director (or an individual having powers or responsibilities similar to those of officers or directors), or a 10 percent or more shareholder directly or indirectly, of a person described in subparagraph (B), (C), (D), (E), or (G), or of the employee benefit plan; or

    (I) a 10 percent or more (directly or indirectly in capital or profits) partner or joint venturer of a person described in subparagraph (B), (C), (D), (E), or (G).

The Secretary, after consultation and coordination with the Secretary of the Treasury, may by regulation prescribe a percentage lower than 50 percent of subparagraphs (E) and (G) and lower than 10 percent for subparagraph (H) or (I). The Secretary may prescribe regulations for determining the ownership (direct or indirect) of profits and beneficial interests, and the manner in which indirect stockholdings are taken into account. Any person who is a party in interest with respect to a plan to which a trust described in section 501(c)(22) of the Internal Revenue Code of 1986 is permitted to make payments under section 4223 shall be treated as a party in interest with respect to such trust.

(15) The term "relative" means a spouse, ancestor, lineal descendant, or spouse of a lineal descendant.

(16)(A) The term "administrator" means—

        (i) the person specifically so designated by the terms of the instrument under which the plan is operated;

        (ii) if an administrator is not so designated, the plan sponsor; or

        (iii) in the case of a plan for which an administrator is not designated and a plan sponsor cannot be identified, such other person as the Secretary may by regulation prescribe.

    (B) The term "plan sponsor" means (i) the employer in the case of an employee benefit plan established or maintained by a single employer, (ii) the employee organization in the case of a plan established or maintained by an employee organization, or (iii) in the case of a plan established or maintained by two or more employers or jointly by one or more employers and one or more employee organizations, the association, committee, joint board of trustees, or other similar group of representatives of the parties who establish or maintain the plan.

(17) The term "separate account" means an account established or maintained by an insurance company under which income, gains, and losses, whether or not realized, from assets allocated to such account, are, in accordance with the applicable contract, credited to or charged against such account without regard to other income, gains, or losses of the insurance company.

(18) The term "adequate consideration" when used in part 4 of subtitle B means (A) in the case of a security for which there is a generally recognized market, either (i) the price of the security prevailing on a national securities exchange which is registered under section 6 of the Securities Exchange Act of 1934, or (ii) if the security is not traded on such a national securities exchange, a price not less favorable to the plan than the offering price for the security as established by the current bid and asked prices quoted by persons independent of the issuer and of any party in interest; and (B) in the case of an asset other than a security for which there is a generally recognized market, the fair market value of the asset as determined in good faith by the trustee or named fiduciary pursuant to the terms of the plan and in accordance with regulations promulgated by the Secretary.

(19) The term "nonforfeitable" when used with respect to a pension benefit or right means a claim obtained by a participant or his beneficiary to that part of an immediate or deferred benefit under a pension plan which arises from the participant's service, which is unconditional, and which is legally enforceable against

the plan. For purposes of this paragraph, a right to an accrued benefit derived from employer contributions shall not be treated as forfeitable merely because the plan contains a provision described in section 203(a)(3).

(20) The term "security" has the same meaning as such term has under section 2(1) of the Securities Act of 1933 (15 U.S.C. 77b(1)).

(21)(A) Except as otherwise provided in subparagraph (B), a person is a fiduciary with respect to a plan to the extent (i) he exercises any discretionary authority or discretionary control respecting management of such plan or exercises any authority or control respecting management or disposition of its assets, (ii) he renders investment advice for a fee or other compensation, direct or indirect, with respect to any moneys or other property of such plan, or has any authority or responsibility to do so, or (iii) he has any discretionary authority or discretionary responsibility in the administration of such plan. Such term includes any person designated under section 405(c)(1)(B).

(B) If any money or other property of an employee benefit plan is invested in securities issued by an investment company registered under the Investment Company Act of 1940, such investment shall not by itself cause such investment company or such investment company's investment adviser or principal underwriter to be deemed to be a fiduciary or a party in interest as those terms are defined in this title, except insofar as such investment company or its investment adviser or principal underwriter acts in connection with an employee benefit plan covering employees of the investment company, the investment adviser, or its principal underwriter. Nothing contained in this subparagraph shall limit the duties imposed on such investment company, investment adviser, or principal underwriter by any other law.

(22) The term "normal retirement benefit" means the greater of the early retirement benefit under the plan, or the benefit under the plan commencing at normal retirement age. The normal retirement benefit shall be determined without regard to—

(A) medical benefits, and

(B) disability benefits not in excess of the qualified disability benefit.

For purposes of this paragraph, a qualified disability benefit is a disability benefit provided by a plan which does not exceed the benefit which would be provided for the participant if he separated from the service at normal retirement age. For purposes of this paragraph, the early retirement benefit under a plan shall be determined without regard to any benefit under the plan which the Secretary of the Treasury finds to be a benefit described in section 204(b)(1)(G).

(23) The term "accrued benefit" means—

(A) in the case of a defined benefit plan, the individual's accrued benefit determined under the plan and, except as provided in section 204(c)(3), expressed in the form of an annual benefit commencing at normal retirement age, or

(B) in the case of a plan which is an individual account plan, the balance of the individual's account.

The accrued benefit of an employee shall not be less than the amount determined under section 204(c)(2)(B) with respect to the employee's accumulated contribution.

(24) The term "normal retirement age" means the earlier of—

(A) the time a plan participant attains normal retirement age under the plan, or

(B) the later of—

(i) the time a plan participant attains age 65, or

(ii) the 5th anniversary of the time a plan participant commenced participation in the plan.

(25) The term "vested liabilities" means the present value of the immediate or deferred benefits available at normal retirement age for participants and their beneficiaries which are nonforfeitable.

(26) The term "current value" means fair market value where available and otherwise the fair value as determined in good faith by a trustee or a named fiduciary (as defined in section 402(a)(2)) pursuant to the terms of the plan and in accordance with regulations of the Secretary, assuming an orderly liquidation at the time of such determination.

(27) The term "present value", with respect to a liability, means the value adjusted to reflect anticipated events. Such adjustments shall conform to such regulations as the Secretary of the Treasury may prescribe.

(28) The term "normal service cost" or "normal cost" means the annual cost of future pension benefits and administrative expenses assigned, under an actuarial cost method, to years subsequent to a particular valuation date of a pension plan. The Secretary of the Treasury may prescribe regulations to carry out this paragraph.

(29) The term "accrued liability" means the excess of the present value, as of a particular valuation date of a pension plan, of the projected future benefit costs and administrative expenses for all plan participants and beneficiaries over the present value of future contributions for the normal cost of all applicable plan participants and beneficiaries. The Secretary of the Treasury may prescribe regulations to carry out this paragraph.

(30) The term "unfunded accrued liability" means the excess of the accrued liability, under an actuarial cost method which so provides, over the present value of the assets of a pension plan. The Secretary of the Treasury may prescribe regulations to carry out this paragraph.

(31) The term "advance funding actuarial cost method" or "actuarial cost method" means a recognized actuarial technique utilized for establishing the amount and incidence of the annual actuarial cost of pension plan benefits and expenses. Acceptable actuarial cost methods shall include the accrued benefit cost method (unit credit method), the entry age normal cost method, the individual level premium cost method, the aggregate cost method, the attained age normal cost method, and the frozen initial liability cost method. The terminal funding cost method and the current funding (pay-as-you-go) cost method are not acceptable actuarial cost methods. The Secretary of the Treasury shall issue regulations to further define acceptable actuarial cost methods.

(32) The term "governmental plan" means a plan established or maintained for its employees by the Government of the United States, by the government of any State or political subdivision thereof, or by any agency or instrumentality of any of the foregoing. The term "governmental plan" also includes any plan to which the Railroad Retirement Act of 1935 or 1937 applies, and which is financed by contributions required under that Act and any plan of an international organization which is exempt from taxation under the provisions of the International Organizations Immunities Act (59 Stat. 669). The term "governmental plan" includes a plan which is established and maintained by an Indian tribal government (as defined in section 7701(a)(40) of the Internal Revenue Code of 1986), a subdivision of an Indian tribal government (determined in accordance with section 7871(d) of such Code), or an agency or instrumentality of either, and all of the participants of which are employees of such entity substantially all of whose services as such an employee are in the performance of essential governmental functions but not in the performance of commercial activities (whether or not an essential government function).

(33)(A) The term "church plan" means a plan established and maintained (to the extent required in clause (ii) of subparagraph (B)) for its employees (or their beneficiaries) by a church or by a convention or association of churches which is exempt from tax under section 501 of the Internal Revenue Code of 1986.

(B) The term "church plan" does not include a plan—

(i) which is established and maintained primarily for the benefit of employees (or their beneficiaries) of such church or convention or association of churches who are employed in connection with one or more unrelated trades or businesses (within the meaning of section 513 of the Internal Revenue Code of 1986), or

(ii) if less than substantially all of the individuals included in the plan are individuals described in subparagraph (A) or in clause (ii) of subparagraph (C) (or their beneficiaries).

(C) For purposes of this paragraph—

(i) A plan established and maintained for its employees (or their beneficiaries) by a church or by a convention or association of churches includes a plan maintained by an organization, whether a civil law corporation or otherwise, the principal purpose or function of which is the administration or funding of a plan or program for the provision of retirement benefits or welfare benefits, or both, for the employees of a church or a convention or association of churches, if such organization is controlled by or associated with a church or a convention or association of churches.

(ii) The term employee of a church or a convention or association of churches includes—

(I) a duly ordained, commissioned, or licensed minister of a church in the exercise of his ministry, regardless of the source of his compensation;

(II) an employee of an organization, whether a civil law corporation or otherwise, which is exempt from tax under section 501 of the Internal Revenue Code of 1986 and which is controlled by or associated with a church or a convention or association of churches; and

(III) an individual described in clause (v).

(iii) A church or a convention or association of churches which is exempt from tax under section 501 of the Internal Revenue Code of 1986 shall be deemed the employer of any individual included as an employee under clause (ii).

(iv) An organization, whether a civil law corporation or otherwise, is associated with a church or a convention or association of churches if it shares common religious bonds and convictions with that church or convention or association of churches.

(v) If an employee who is included in a church plan separates from the service of a church or a convention or association of churches or an organization, whether a civil law corporation or otherwise, which is exempt from tax under section 501 of the Internal Revenue Code of 1986 and which is controlled by or associated with a church or a convention or association of churches, the church plan shall not fail to meet the requirements of this paragraph merely because the plan—

(I) retains the employee's accrued benefit or account for the payment of benefits to the employee or his beneficiaries pursuant to the terms of the plan; or

(II) receives contributions on the employee's behalf after the employee's separation from such service, but only for a period of 5 years after such separation, unless the employee is disabled (within the meaning of the disability provisions of the church plan or, if there are no such provisions in the church plan, within the meaning of section 72(m)(7) of the Internal Revenue Code of 1986) at the time of such separation from service.

(D)(i) If a plan established and maintained for its employees (or their beneficiaries) by a church or by a convention or association of churches which is exempt from tax under section 501 of the Internal Revenue Code of 1986 fails to meet one or more of the requirements of this paragraph and corrects its failure to meet such requirements within the correction period, the plan shall be deemed to meet the requirements of this paragraph for the year in which the correction was made and for all prior years.

(ii) If a correction is not made within the correction period, the plan shall be deemed not to meet the requirements of this paragraph beginning with the date on which the earliest failure to meet one or more of such requirements occurred.

(iii) For purposes of this subparagraph, the term "correction period" means—

(I) the period ending 270 days after the date of mailing by the Secretary of the Treasury of a notice of default with respect to the plan's failure to meet one or more of the requirements of this paragraph; or

(II) any period set by a court of competent jurisdiction after a final determination that the plan fails to meet such requirements, or, if the court does not specify such period, any reasonable period determined by the Secretary of the Treasury on the basis of all the facts and circumstances, but in any event not less than 270 days after the determination has become final; or

(III) any additional period which the Secretary of the Treasury determines is reasonable or necessary for the correction of the default,

whichever has the latest ending date.

⫸→ *CCH NOTE—: The following public law clarifies the definition of church plans under ERISA Sec. 3(33).*

P.L. 106-244

CHURCH PLAN PARITY AND ENTANGLEMENT PROTECTION ACT

SECTION 1. PURPOSE

The purpose of this Act is only to clarify the application to a church plan that is a welfare plan of State insurance laws that require or solely relate to licensing, solvency, insolvency, or the status of such plan as a single employer plan.

SECTION 2. CLARIFICATION OF CHURCH WELFARE PLAN STATUS UNDER STATE INSURANCE LAW.

(a) In General. For purposes of determining the status of a church plan that is a welfare plan under provisions of a State insurance law described in subsection (b), such a church plan (and any trust under such plan) shall be deemed to be a plan sponsored by a single employer that reimburses costs from general church assets, or purchases insurance coverage with general church assets, or both.

(b) State Insurance Law. A State insurance law described in this subsection is a law that—

(1) requires a church plan, or an organization described in section 414(e)(3)(A) of the Internal Revenue Code of 1986 and section 3(33)(C)(i) of the Employee Retirement Income Security Act of 1974 (29 U.S.C. 1002(33)(C)(i)) to the extent that it is administering or funding such a plan, to be licensed; or

(2) relates solely to the solvency or insolvency of a church plan (including participation in State guaranty funds and associations).

(c) Definitions. For purposes of this section:

(1) Church plan. The term "church plan" has the meaning given such term by section 414(e) of the Internal Revenue Code of 1986 and section 3(33) of the Employee Retirement Income Security Act of 1974 (29 U.S.C. 1002(33)).

(2) Reimburses costs from general church assets. The term "reimburses costs from general church assets" means engaging in an activity that is not the spreading of risk solely for the purposes of the provisions of State insurance laws described in subsection (b).

(3) Welfare plan. The term "welfare plan"—

(A) means any church plan to the extent that such plan provides medical, surgical, or hospital care or benefits, or benefits in the event of sickness, accident, disability, death or unemployment, or vacation benefits, apprenticeship or other training programs, or day care centers, scholarship funds, or prepaid legal services; and

(B) does not include any entity, such as a health insurance issuer described in section 9832(b)(2) of the Internal Revenue Code of 1986 or a health maintenance organization described in section 9832(b)(3) of such Code, or any other organization that does business with the church plan or organization sponsoring or maintaining such a plan.

(d) Enforcement Authority. Notwithstanding any other provision of this section, for purposes of enforcing provisions of State insurance laws that apply to a church plan that is a welfare plan, the church plan shall be subject to State enforcement as if the church plan were an insurer licensed by the State.

(e) Application of Section. Except as provided in subsection (d), the application of this section is limited to determining the status of a church plan that is a welfare plan under the provisions of State insurance laws described in subsection (b). This section shall not otherwise be construed to recharacterize the status, or modify or affect the rights, of any plan participant or beneficiary, including participants or beneficiaries who make plan contributions.

(34) The term "individual account plan" or "defined contribution plan" means a pension plan which provides for an individual account for each participant and for benefits based solely upon the amount contributed to the participant's account, and any income, expenses, gains and losses, and any forfeitures of accounts of other participants which may be allocated to such participant's account.

(35) The term "defined benefit plan" means a pension plan other than an individual account plan; except that a pension plan which is not an individual account plan and which provides a benefit derived from employer contributions which is based partly on the balance of the separate account of a participant—

(A) for the purposes of section 202, shall be treated as an individual account plan, and

(B) for the purposes of paragraph (23) of this section and section 204, shall be treated as an individual account plan to the extent benefits are based upon the separate account of a participant and as a defined benefit plan with respect to the remaining portion of benefits under the plan.

(36) The term "excess benefit plan" means a plan maintained by an employer solely for the purpose of providing benefits for certain employees in excess of the limitations on contributions and benefits imposed by section 415 of the Internal Revenue Code of 1986 on plans to which that section applies, without regard to whether the plan is funded. To the extent that a separable part of a plan (as determined by the Secretary of Labor) maintained by an employer is maintained for such purpose, that part shall be treated as a separate plan which is an excess benefit plan.

(37)(A) The term "multiemployer plan" means a plan—

(i) to which more than one employer is required to contribute,

(ii) which is maintained pursuant to one or more collective bargaining agreements between one or more employee organizations and more than one employer, and

(iii) which satisfies such other requirements as the Secretary may prescribe by regulation.

(B) For purposes of this paragraph, all trades or businesses (whether or not incorporated) which are under common control within the meaning of section 4001(b)(1) are considered a single employer.

(C) Notwithstanding subparagraph (A), a plan is a multiemployer plan on and after its termination date if the plan was a multiemployer plan under this paragraph for the plan year preceding its termination date.

(D) For purposes of this title, notwithstanding the preceding provisions of this paragraph, for any plan year which began before the date of the enactment of the Multiemployer Pension Plan Amendments Act of 1980, the term "multiemployer plan" means a plan described in section 3(37) of this Act as in effect immediately before such date.

(E) Within one year after the date of the enactment of the Multiemployer Pension Plan Amendments Act of 1980, a multiemployer plan may irrevocably elect, pursuant to procedures established by the corporation and subject to the provisions of sections 4403(b) and (c), that the plan shall not be treated as a multiemployer plan for all puposes under this Act or the Internal Revenue Code of 1954 if for each of the last 3 plan years ending prior to the effective date of the Multiemployer Pension Plan Amendments Act of 1980—

(i) the plan was not a multiemployer plan because the plan was not a plan described in section 3(37)(A)(iii) of this Act and section 414(f)(1)(C) of the Internal Revenue Code of 1954 (as such provisions were in effect on the day before the date of the enactment of the Multiemployer Pension Plan Amendments Act of 1980); and

(ii) the plan had been identified as a plan that was not a multiemployer plan in substantially all its filings with the corporation, the Secretary of Labor and the Secretary of the Treasury.

(F)(i) For purposes of this title a qualified football coaches plan—

(I) shall be treated as a multiemployer plan to the extent not inconsistent with the purposes of this subparagraph; and

(II) notwithstanding section 401(k)(4)(B) of the Internal Revenue Code of 1986, may include a qualified cash and deferred arrangement.

(ii) For purposes of this subparagraph, the term "qualified football coaches plan" means any defined contribution plan which is established and maintained by an organization—

(I) which is described in section 501(c) of such Code;

(II) the membership of which consists entirely of individuals who primarily coach football as full-time employees of 4-year colleges or universities described in section 170(b)(1)(A)(ii) of such Code; and

(III) which was in existence on September 18, 1986.

(G)(i) Within 1 year after the enactment of the Pension Protection Act of 2006—

(I) an election under subparagraph (E) may be revoked, pursuant to procedures prescribed by the Pension Benefit Guaranty Corporation, if, for each of the 3 plan years prior to the date of the enactment of that Act, the plan would have been a multiemployer plan but for the election under subparagraph (E), and

(II) a plan that meets the criteria in clauses (i) and (ii) of subparagraph (A) of this paragraph or that is described in clause (vi) may, pursuant to procedures prescribed by the Pension Benefit Guaranty Corporation, elect to be a multiemployer plan, if—

(aa) for each of the 3 plan years immediately preceding the first plan year for which the election under this paragraph is effective with respect to the plan, the plan has met those criteria or is so described,

(bb) substantially all of the plan's employer contributions for each of those plan years were made or required to be made by organizations that were exempt from tax under section 501 of the Internal Revenue Code of 1986, and

(cc) the plan was established prior to September 2, 1974.

(ii) An election under this subparagraph shall be effective for all purposes under this Act and under the Internal Revenue Code of 1986, starting with any plan year beginning on or after January 1, 1999, and ending before January 1, 2008, as designated by the plan in the election made under clause (i)(II).

(iii) Once made, an election under this subparagraph shall be irrevocable, except that a plan described in clause (i)(II) shall cease to be a multiemployer plan as of the plan year beginning immediately after the first plan year for which the majority of its employer contributions were made or required to be made by organizations that were not exempt from tax under section 501 of the Internal Revenue Code of 1986.

(iv) The fact that a plan makes an election under clause (i)(II) does not imply that the plan was not a multiemployer plan prior to the date of the election or would not be a multiemployer plan without regard to the election.

(v)(I) No later than 30 days before an election is made under this subparagraph, the plan administrator shall provide notice of the pending election to each plan participant and beneficiary, each labor organization representing such participants or beneficiaries, and each employer that has an obligation to contribute to the plan, describing the principal differences between the guarantee programs under title IV and the benefit restrictions under this title for single employer and multiemployer plans, along with such other information as the plan administrator chooses to include.

(II) Within 180 days after the date of enactment of the Pension Protection Act of 2006, the Secretary shall prescribe a model notice under this clause.

(III) A plan administrator's failure to provide the notice required under this subparagraph shall be treated for purposes of section 502(c)(2) as a failure or refusal by the plan administrator to file the annual report required to be filed with the Secretary under section 101(b)(1).

(vi) A plan is described in this clause if it is a plan sponsored by an organization which is described in section 501(c)(5) of the Internal Revenue Code of 1986 and exempt from tax under section 501(a) of such Code and which was established in Chicago, Illinois, on August 12, 1881.

(vii) For purposes of this Act and the Internal Revenue Code of 1986, a plan making an election under this subparagraph shall be treated as maintained pursuant to a collective bargaining agreement if a collective bargaining agreement, expressly or otherwise, provides for or permits employer contributions to the plan by one or more employers that are signatory to such agreement, or participation in the plan by one or more employees of an employer that is signatory to such agreement, regardless of whether the plan was created, established, or maintained for such employees by virtue of another document that is not a collective bargaining agreement.

(38) The term "investment manager" means any fiduciary (other than a trustee or named fiduciary, as defined in section 402(a)(2))—

(A) who has the power to manage, acquire, or dispose of any asset of a plan;

(B) who (i) is registered as an investment adviser under the Investment Advisers Act of 1940; (ii) is not registered as an investment adviser under such Act by reason of paragraph (1) of section 203A(a) of such Act, is registered as an investment adviser under the laws of the State (referred to in such paragraph (1)) in which it maintains its principal office and place of business, and, at the time the fiduciary last filed the registration form most recently filed by the fiduciary with such State in order to maintain the fiduciary's registration under the laws of such State, also filed a copy of such form with the Secretary; (iii) is a bank, as defined in that Act; or (iv) is an insurance company qualified to perform services described in subparagraph (A) under the laws of more than one State; and

(C) has acknowledged in writing that he is a fiduciary with respect to the plan.

(39) The terms "plan year" and "fiscal year of the plan" mean, with respect to a plan, the calendar, policy, or fiscal year on which the records of the plan are kept.

(40)(A) The term "multiple employer welfare arrangement" means an employee welfare benefit plan, or any other arrangement (other than an employee welfare benefit plan), which is established or maintained for the purpose of offering or providing any benefit described in paragraph (1) to the employees of two or more employers (including one or more self-employed individuals), or to their beneficiaries, except that such term does not include any such plan or other arrangement which is established or maintained—

(i) under or pursuant to one or more agreements which the Secretary finds to be collective bargaining agreements,

(ii) by a rural electric cooperative, or

(iii) by a rural telephone cooperative association.

(B) For purposes of this paragraph—

(i) two or more trades or businesses, whether or not incorporated, shall be deemed a single employer if such trades or businesses are within the same control group,

(ii) the term "control group" means a group of trades or businesses under common control,

(iii) the determination of whether a trade or business is under "common control" with another trade or business shall be determined under regulations of the Secretary applying principles similar to the principles applied in determining whether employees of two or more trades or businesses are treated as employed by a single employer under section 4001(b), except that, for purposes of this paragraph, common control shall not be based on an interest of less than 25 percent,

(iv) the term "rural electric cooperative" means—

(I) any organization which is exempt from tax under section 501(a) of the Internal Revenue Code of 1986 and which is engaged primarily in providing electric service on a mutual or cooperative basis, and

(II) any organization described in paragraph (4) or (6) of section 501(c) of the Internal Revenue Code of 1986 which is exempt from tax under section 501(a) of such Code and at least 80 percent of the members of which are organizations described in subclause (I), and

(v) the term "rural telephone cooperative association" means an organization described in paragraph (4) or (6) of section 501(c) of the Internal Revenue Code of 1986 which is exempt from tax under section 501(a) of such Code and at least 80 percent of the members of which are organizations engaged primarily in providing telephone service to rural areas of the United States on a mutual, cooperative, or other basis.

(41) SINGLE-EMPLOYER PLAN. The term "single-employer plan" means an employee benefit plan other than a multiemployer plan.

(41) [*]The term "single-employer plan" means a plan which is not a multiemployer plan.

(42) the term "plan assets" means plan assets as defined by such regulations as the Secretary may prescribe, except that under such regulations the assets of any entity shall not be treated as plan assets if, immediately after the most recent acquisition of any equity interest in the entity, less than 25 percent of the total value of each class of equity interest in the entity is held by benefit plan investors. For purposes of determinations pursuant to this paragraph, the value of any equity interest held by a person (other than such a benefit plan investor) who has discretionary authority or control with respect to the assets of the entity or any person who provides investment advice for a fee (direct or indirect) with respect to such assets, or any affiliate of such a person, shall be disregarded for purposes of calculating the 25 percent threshold. An entity shall be considered to hold plan assets only to the extent of the percentage of the equity interest held by benefit plan investors. For purposes of this paragraph, the term "benefit plan investor" means an employee benefit plan subject to part 4, any plan to which section 4975 of the Internal Revenue Code of 1986 applies, and any entity whose underlying assets include plan assets by reason of a plan's investment in such entity.

Amendments

P.L. 110-458, § 111(c)(1):

Amended ERISA Sec. 3(37)(G)(ii), (iii), and (v)(I) by striking "paragraph" each place it appears and inserting "subparagraph".

The above amendments take effect as if included in the provisions of the 2006 Act to which the amendment relate [i.e., § 1106 of P.L. 109-280—CCH]. For the effective date of § 1106, see below.

P.L. 110-458, § 111(c)(2):

Amended ERISA Sec. 3(37)(G)(iii) by striking "subclause (i)(II)" and inserting "clause (i)(II)".

The above amendment takes effect as if included in the provisions of the 2006 Act to which the amendment relate [i.e., § 1106 of P.L. 109-280—CCH]. For the effective date of § 1106, see below.

P.L. 110-458, § 111(c)(3):

Amended ERISA Sec. 3(37)(G)(v)(II) by striking "subparagraph" and inserting "clause".

The above amendment takes effect as if included in the provisions of the 2006 Act to which the amendment relate [i.e., § 1106 of P.L. 109-280—CCH]. For the effective date of § 1106, see below.

P.L. 110-458, § 111(c)(4):

Amended ERISA Sec. 3(37)(G)(v)(III) by striking "section 101(b)(4)" and inserting "section 101(b)(1)".

The above amendment takes effect as if included in the provisions of the 2006 Act to which the amendment relate [i.e., § 1106 of P.L. 109-280—CCH]. For the effective date of § 1106, see below.

P.L. 110-28, § 6611(a)(1)(A):

Amended ERISA Sec. 3(37)(G)(i)(II)(aa) by striking "for each of the 3 plan years immediately before the date of the enactment of the Pension Protection Act of 2006," and inserting "for each of the 3 plan years immediately preceding the first plan year for which the election under this paragraph is effective with respect to the plan,".

The above amendment takes effect as if included in section 1106 of the Pension Protection Act of 2006. For the effective date of section 1106, see below.

P.L. 110-28, § 6611(a)(1)(B):

Amended ERISA Sec. 3(37)(G)(ii), by striking "starting with the first plan year ending after the date of the enactment of the Pension Protection Act of 2006" and

inserting "starting with any plan year beginning on or after January 1, 1999, and ending before January 1, 2008, as designated by the plan in the election made under clause (i)(II)".

The above amendment takes effect as if included in section 1106 of the Pension Protection Act of 2006. For the effective date of section 1106, see below.

P.L. 110-28, § 6611(a)(1)(C):

Amended ERISA Sec. 3(37)(G), by adding at the end clause (vii) to read as above.

The above amendment takes effect as if included in section 1106 of the Pension Protection Act of 2006. For the effective date of section 1106, see below.

P.L. 110-28, § 6611(b)(1):

Amended ERISA Sec. 3(37)(G)(vi) by striking "if it is a plan—"and all that follows and inserting the following: "if it is a plan sponsored by an organization which is described in section 501(c)(5) of the Internal Revenue Code of 1986 and exempt from tax under section 501(a) of such Code and which was established in Chicago, Illinois, on August 12, 1881.".

The above amendment takes effect as if included in section 1106 of the Pension Protection Act of 2006. For the effective date of section 1106, see below.

P.L. 109-280, § 611(f):

Amended ERISA Sec. 3 by adding a new paragraph (42) to read as above.

The above amendment applies to transactions occurring after the date of the enactment (August 17, 2006).

P.L. 109-280, § 905(a):

Amended ERISA Sec. 3(2)(A) by adding at the end a new sentence.

The above amendment applies to distributions in plan years beginning after December 31, 2006.

P.L. 109-280, § 906(a)(2)(A):

Amended ERISA Sec. 3(32) by adding at the end a new sentence.

The above amendment applies to any year beginning on or after the date of the enactment (August 17, 2006).

P.L. 109-280, § 1104(c):

Amended ERISA Sec. 3(2)(B) by adding at the end a new sentence.

The above amendment applies to plan years ending after the date of the enactment (August 17, 2006).

P.L. 109-280, § 1106(a):

Amended ERISA Sec. 3(37) by adding new subparagraph (G) to read as above.

No specific effective date is provided by the Act. The provision is, therefore, considered effective on the date of the enactment (August 17, 2006).

P.L. 105-72, §1(a):

Amended ERISA Sec. 3(38)(B) by redesignating clauses (ii) and (iii) as clauses (iii) and (iv), respectively; and by striking "who is" and all that followed through clause (i) and inserting clauses (i) and (ii) to read as above, effective July 8, 1997.

Prior to amendment (as effective from 10/11/96 to 10/10/98, as changed by P.L. 104-290, §308(b)(1)), the section read:

"(B) who is (i) registered as an investment adviser under the Investment Advisers Act of 1940 or under the laws of any State; (ii) is a bank, as defined in that Act; or (iii) is an insurance company qualified to perform services described in subparagraph (A) under the laws of more than one State; and".

Prior to amendment (as effective beginning 10/11/98, following expiration of P.L. 104-290 changes under §308(b)(2)), the section read:

"(B) who is (i) registered as an investment adviser under the Investment Advisers Act of 1940; (ii) is a bank, as defined in that Act; or (iii) is an insurance company qualified to perform services described in subparagraph (A) under the laws of more than one State; and".

The above amendments are effective July 8, 1997. For a special rule, see Act Sec. 1(c), reproduced below.

Act Sec. 1(c) provides:

(c) Effective Date.—The amendments made by subsection (a) shall take effect on July 8, 1997, except that the requirement of section 3(38)(B)(ii) of the Employee Retirement Income Security Act of 1974 (as amended by this Act) for filing with the Secretary of Labor of a copy of a registration form which has been filed with a State before the date of the enactment of this Act, or is to be filed with a State during the 1-year period beginning with such date, shall be treated as satisfied upon the filing of such a copy with the Secretary at any time during such 1-year period. This section shall supersede section 308(b) of the National Securities Markets Improvement Act of 1996 (and the amendment made thereby).

P.L. 104-290, §308(b)(1):

Amended ERISA Sec. 3(38) by adding "or under the laws of any State" after "1940".

The above amendment is effective on the date of enactment of this Act. For a special rule, see Act Sec. 308(b)(2), reproduced below.

Act Sec. 308(b)(2) provides:

The amendment made by paragraph (1) shall cease to be effective 2 years after the date of enactment of this Act.

P.L. 102-89, §2:

Amended ERISA Sec. 3(40) by striking "or" at the end of subparagraph (A)(i); by striking "cooperative." in subparagraph (A)(ii) and adding "cooperative, or"; by adding a new subparagraph (iii) in paragraph (A) to read as above; by striking "and" at the end of subparagraph (B)(iii); by striking "subclause (I)." in subparagraph (B)(iv)(II) and adding "subclause (I), and"; and by adding a new subclause (v) at the end of subparagraph (B) to read as above, effective on the date of enactment.

P.L. 101-508, §12001(b)(2)(C):

Amended ERISA Sec. 3 by adding a new paragraph (41) to read as above effective for reversions occurring after September 30, 1990 except for the provisions of Act. Sec. 12003(b). [* Paragraph (41) was previously enacted in P.L. 101-239—CCH.]

SEC. 12003. EFFECTIVE DATE.

* * *

(b) EXCEPTION.—The amendments made by this subtitle shall not apply to any reversion after September 30, 1990, if—

(1) in the case of plans subject to title IV of the Employee Retirement Income Security Act of 1974, a notice of intent to terminate under such title was provided to participants (or if no participants, to the Pension Benefit Guaranty Corporation) before October 1, 1990,

(2) in the case of plans subject to title I (and not to title IV) of such Act, a notice of intent to reduce future accruals under section 204(h) of such Act was provided to participants in connection with the termination before October 1, 1990,

(3) in the case of plans not subject to title I or IV of such Act, a request for a determination letter with respect to the termination was filed with the Secretary of the Treasury or the Secretary's delegate before October 1, 1990, or

(4) in the case of plans not subject to title I or IV of such Act and having only 1 participant, a resolution terminating the plan was adopted by the employer before October 1, 1990.

P.L. 101-239, §7871(b)(2):

Amended ERISA Sec. 3(24)(B) to read as above, effective for plan years beginning on or after January 1, 1988 and for service performed on or after that date. Prior to amendment, Sec. 3(24)(B) read as follows:

(B) the latest of—

(i) the time a plan participant attains age 65,

(ii) in the case of a plan participant who commences participation in the plan within 5 years before attaining normal retirement age under the plan, the 5th anniversary of the time the plan participant commences participation in the plan, or

(iii) in the case of a plan participant not described in clause (ii), the 10th anniversary of the time the plan participant commences participation in the plan.

P.L. 101-239, §7881(m)(2)(D):

Amended ERISA Sec. 3(23) by adding a new flush sentence to read as above effective December 22, 1987.

P.L. 101-239, §7893(a):

Amended ERISA Sec. 3(37)(B) by striking "section 4001(c)(1)" and inserting "section 4001(b)(1)" effective April 7, 1986.

P.L. 101-239, §7894(a)(1)(A):

Amended ERISA Sec. 3(33)(D)(iii) by inserting "of the Treasury" after "Secretary" each place it appears effective as if included in P.L. 96-364, §407.

P.L. 101-239, §7894(a)(2):

Amended ERISA Sec. 3(37)(F) in clause (i)(II) by striking "such Code" and inserting "the Internal Revenue Code of 1986;" in clause (ii)(I) by inserting "of such Code" after "section 501(c);" and in clause (ii)(II) by inserting "of such Code" after "section 170(b)(1)(A)(ii)" effective as if included in P.L. 100-202, §136.

P.L. 101-239, §7894(a)(3):

Amended ERISA Sec. 3(39) by inserting a comma after "mean" and by inserting "the" before "calendar" effective September 2, 1986.

P.L. 101-239, §7894(a)(4):

Amended ERISA Sec. 3 by adding a new paragraph (41) to read as above effective September 2, 1986.

P.L. 101-239, §7891(a)(1):

Titles I, III, and IV of ERISA (other than sections 3(37)(E), 301(a)(7), and 308, the last sentence of section 408(d), and sections 414(c), 4001(a)(3)(ii), and 4303) are each amended by striking "Internal Revenue Code of 1954" each place it appears and inserting "Internal Revenue Code of 1986" effective April 7, 1986.

P.L. 100-202, §136:

Amended ERISA Sec. 3(37) by adding subparagraph (F) to read as above.

P.L. 99-514, §1897(u)(3):

Repealed section 11016 of P.L. 99-272, effective on April 7, 1986.

P.L. 99-509, §9203(b)(1):

Amended ERISA Sec. 3(24)(B) to read as above, effective with respect to plan years beginning on or after January 1, 1988 and only with respect to service performed on or after such date. See also §9204(c) at ¶14,440 (amendment notes). Prior to amendment, Sec. 3(24)(B) read as follows:

(24) The term "normal retirement age" means the earlier of—

* * *

(B) the later of—

(i) the time a plan participant attains age 65, or

(ii) the 10th anniversary of the time a plan participant commenced participation in the plan.

.P.L. 99-272:

Act Sec. 11016(c)(1) amended ERISA Sec. 3(37)(A) by inserting "pension" before "plan" effective on April 7, 1986.

.P.L. 97-473:

Added paragraph (40), effective January 14, 1983.

P.L. 96-364; §§302(a), 305, 407(a), and 409:

Amended Sec. 3(2) by adding "(A) Except as provided in subparagraph (B), the", by renumbering subsections (A) and (B) as (i) and (ii) and by adding new subparagraph (B), effective September 26, 1980.

Amended Sec. 3(14) by adding the last sentence to read as above, effective April 29, 1980.

Amended Sec. 3(33) to read as above, effective January 1, 1974. Prior to amendment, the section read:

"(33)(A) The term 'church plan' means (i) a plan established and maintained for its employees by a church or by a convention or association of churches which is exempt from tax under section 501 of the Internal Revenue Code of 1954, or (ii) a plan described in subparagraph (C).

(B) The term 'church plan' (notwithstanding the provisions of subparagraph (A)) does not include a plan—

(i) which is established and maintained primarily for the benefit of employees (or their beneficiaries) of such church or convention or association of churches who are employed in connection with one or more unrelated trades or businesses (within the meaning of section 513 of the Internal Revenue Code of 1954), or

(ii) which is a plan maintained by more than one employer, if one or more of the employers in the plan is not a church (or a convention or association of churches) which is exempt from tax under section 501 of the Internal Revenue Code of 1954.

(C) Notwithstanding the provisions of subparagraph (B)(ii), a plan in existence on January 1, 1974, shall be treated as a 'church plan' if it is established and maintained by a church or convention or association of churches for its employees and employees of one or more agencies of such church (or convention or association) for the employees of such church (or convention or association) and the employees of one or more agencies of such church (or convention or association), and if such church (or convention or association) and each such agency is exempt from tax under section 501 of the Internal Revenue Code of 1954. The first sentence of this subparagraph shall not apply to any plan maintained for employees of an agency with respect to which the plan was not maintained on January 1, 1974. The first sentence of this subparagraph shall not apply with respect to any plan for any plan year beginning after December 31, 1982."

Amended Sec. 3(37) to read as above generally effective for plan years beginning on or after September 26, 1980. Prior to amendment, the section read:

"(37)(A) The term 'multiemployer plan' means a plan—

(i) to which more than one employer is required to contribute,

(ii) which is maintained pursuant to one or more collective-bargaining agreements between an employee organization and more than one employer,

(iii) under which the amount of contributions made under the plan for a plan year by each employer making such contributions is less than 50 percent of the aggregate amount of contributions made under the plan for that plan year by all employers making such contributions,

(iv) under which benefits are payable with respect to each participant without regard to the cessation of contributions by the employer who had employed that participant except to the extent that such benefits accrued as a result of service with the employer before such employer was required to contribute to such plan, and

(v) which satisfies such other requirements as the Secretary may by regulations prescribe.

(B) For purposes of this paragraph—

(i) if a plan is a multiemployer plan within the meaning of subparagraph (A) for any plan year, clause (iii) of subparagraph (A) shall be applied by substituting '75 percent' for '50 percent' for each subsequent plan year until the first plan year following a plan year in which the plan had one employer who made contributions of 75 percent or more of the aggregate amount of contributions made under the plan for that plan year by all employers making such contributions, and

(ii) all corporations which are members of a controlled group of corporations (within the meaning of section 1563(a) of the Internal Revenue Code of 1954, determined without regard to section 1563(e)(3)(C) of such Code) shall be deemed to be one employer. Effective September 26, 1980, except that the prior law definition will contiinue for plan years beginning before enactment."

Regulations

The following regulations were adopted by FR Doc. 75-21470 under "Title 29—Labor; Chapter XXV—Office of Employee Benefits Security; Part 2510—Definitions of Terms used in Subchapters C, D, E, F, and G of this Chapter." The regulations were published in the Federal Register of August 15, 1975, and are effective August 15, 1975. Reg. § 2510.3-16 was added on July 2, 2013 by 78 FR 39869. Reg. § 2510.3-16 was amended on July 14, 2015 (80 FR 41317). Reg. § 2510.3-2 was amended on August 30, 2016 (81 FR 59464). Reg. § 2510.3-2 was amended on December 20, 2016 (81 FR 92639). Reg. § 2510.3-2 was amended on June 28, 2017 (82 FR 29236) to remove changes made on August 30, 2016 and December 20, 2016 pertaining to an ERISA safe harbor for state payroll deduction IRA programs. The removal of the changes is effective June 28, 2017.

[¶ 14,131]

§ 2510.3-1. **Employee welfare benefit plan.** (a) *General.* (1) The purpose of this section is to clarify the definition of the terms "employee welfare benefit plan" and "welfare plan" for purposes of Title I of the Act and this chapter by identifying certain practices which do not constitute employee welfare benefit plans for those purposes. In addition, the practices listed in this section do not constitute employee pension benefit plans within the meaning of section 3(2) of the Act, and, therefore, do not constitute employee benefit plans within the meaning of section 3(3). Since under section 4(a) of the Act, only employee benefit plans within the meaning of section 3(3) are subject to Title I of the Act, the practices listed in this section are not subject to Title I.

(2) The terms "employee welfare benefit plan" and "welfare plan" are defined in section 3(1) of the Act to include plans providing "(i) medical, surgical, or hospital care or benefits, or benefits in the event of sickness, accident, disability, death or unemployment, or vacation benefits, apprenticeship or other training programs, or day care centers, scholarship funds, or prepaid legal services, or (ii) any benefit described in section 302(c) of the Labor Management Relations Act, 1947 (other than pensions on retirement or death, and insurance to provide such pensions)." Under this definition only plans which provide benefits described in section 3(1)(A) of the Act or in section 302(c) of the Labor-Management Relations Act 1947 (hereinafter "the LMRA") (other than pensions on retirement or death) constitute welfare plans. For example, a system of payroll deductions by an employer for deposit in savings accounts owned by its employees is not an employee welfare benefit plan within the meaning of section 3(1) of the Act because it does not provide benefits described in section 3(1)(A) of the Act or section 302(c) of the LMRA. (In addition, if each employee has the right to withdraw the balance in his or her account at any time, such a payroll savings plan does not meet the requirements for a pension plan set forth in section 3(2) of the Act and, therefore, is not an employee benefit plan within the meaning of section 3(3) of the Act).

(3) Section 302(c) of the LMRA lists exceptions to the restrictions contained in subsections (a) and (b) of that section on payments and loans made by an employer to individuals and groups representing employees of the employer. Of these exceptions, only those contained in paragraphs (5), (6), (7) and (8) describe benefits provided through employee benefit plans. Moreover, only paragraph (6) describes benefits not described in section 3(1)(A) of the Act. The benefits described in section 302(c)(6) of the LMRA but not in section 3(1)(A) of the Act are "* * * holiday, severance or similar benefits". Thus, the effect of section 3(1)(B) of the Act is to include within the definition of "welfare plan" those plans which provide holiday and severance benefits, and benefits which are similar (for example, benefits which are in substance severance benefits, although not so characterized).

(4) Some of the practices listed in this section as excluded from the definition of "welfare plan" or mentioned as examples of general categories of excluded practices are inserted in response to questions received by the Department of Labor and, in the Department's judgment, do not represent borderline cases under the definition in section 3(1) of the Act. Therefore, this section should not be read as implicitly indicating the Department's views on the possible scope of section 3(1).

(b) *Payroll practices.* For purposes of Title I of the Act and this chapter, the terms "employee welfare benefit plan" and "welfare plan" shall not include—

(1) Payment by an employer of compensation on account of work performed by an employee, including compensation at a rate in excess of the normal rate of compensation on account of performance of duties under other than ordinary circumstances, such as—

(i) Overtime pay,

(ii) Shift premiums,

(iii) Holiday premiums,

(iv) Weekend premiums;

(2) Payment of an employee's normal compensation, out of the employer's general assets, on account of periods of time during which the employee is physically or mentally unable to perform his or her duties, or is otherwise absent for medical reasons (such as pregnancy, a physical examination or psychiatric treatment); and

(3) Payment of compensation, out of the employer's general assets, on account of periods of time during which the employee, although physically and mentally able to perform his or her duties and not absent for medical reasons (such as pregnancy, a physical examination or psychiatric treatment) performs no duties; for example—

(i) Payment of compensation while an employee is on vacation or absent on a holiday, including payment of premiums to induce employees to take vacations at a time favorable to the employer for business reasons,

(ii) Payment of compensation to an employee who is absent while on active military duty,

(iii) Payment of compensation while an employee is absent for the purpose of serving as a juror or testifying in official proceedings,

(iv) Payment of compensation on account of periods of time during which an employee performs little or no productive work while engaged in training (whether or not subsidized in whole or in part by Federal, State or local government funds), and

(v) Payment of compensation to an employee who is relieved of duties while on sabbatical leave or while pursuing further education.

(c) *On-premises facilities.* For purposes of Title I of the Act and this chapter, the terms "employee welfare benefit plan" and "welfare plan" shall not include—

(1) The maintenance on the premises of an employer or of an employee organization of recreation, dining or other facilities (other than day care centers) for use by employees or members; and

(2) The maintenance on the premises of an employer of facilities for the treatment of minor injuries or illness or rendering first aid in case of accidents occurring during working hours.

(d) *Holiday gifts.* For purposes of Title I of the Act and this chapter the terms "employee welfare benefit plan" and "welfare plan" shall not include the distribution of gifts such as turkeys or hams by an employer to employees at Christmas and other holiday seasons.

(e) *Sales to employees.* For purposes of Title I of the Act and this chapter, the terms "employee welfare benefit plan" and "welfare plan" shall not include the sale by an employer to employees of an employer, whether or not at prevailing market prices, of articles or commodities of the kind which the employer offers for sale in the regular course of business.

(f) *Hiring halls.* For purposes of Title I of the Act and this chapter, the terms "employee welfare benefit plan" and "welfare plan" shall not include the maintenance by one or more employers, employee organizations, or both, of a hiring hall facility.

(g) *Remembrance funds.* For purposes of Title I of the Act and this chapter, the terms "employee welfare benefit plan" and "welfare plan" shall not include a program under which contributions are made to provide remembrances such as flowers, an obituary notice in a newspaper or a small gift on occasions such as the sickness, hospitalization, death or termination of employment of employees, or members of an employee organization, or members of their families.

(h) *Strike funds.* For purposes of Title I of the Act and this chapter, the terms "employee welfare benefit plan" and "welfare plan" shall not include a fund maintained by an employee organization to provide payments to its members during strikes and for related purposes.

(i) *Industry advancement programs.* For purposes of Title I of the Act and this chapter, the terms "employee welfare benefit plan" and "welfare plan" shall not include a program maintained by an employer or group or association of employers, which has no employee participants and does not provide benefits to employees or their dependents, regardless of whether the program serves as a conduit through which funds or other assets are channelled to employee benefit plans covered under Title I of the Act.

(j) *Certain group or group-type insurance programs.* For purposes of Title I of the Act and this chapter, the terms "employee welfare benefit plan" and "welfare plan" shall not include a group or group-type insurance program offered by an insurer to employees or members of an employee organization, under which

(1) no contributions are made by an employer or employee organization;

(2) participation in the program is completely voluntary for employees or members;

(3) the sole functions of the employer or employee organization with respect to the program are, without endorsing the program, to permit the insurer to publicize the program to employees or members, to collect premiums through payroll deductions or dues checkoffs and to remit them to the insurer; and

(4) the employer or employee organization receives no consideration in the form of cash or otherwise in connection with the program, other than reasonable compensation, excluding any profit, for administrative services actually rendered in connection with payroll deductions or dues checkoffs.

(k) *Unfunded scholarship programs.* For purposes of Title I of the Act and this chapter, the terms "employee welfare benefit plan" and "welfare plan" shall not include a scholarship program, including a tuition and education expense refund program, under which payments are made solely from the general assets of an employer or employee organization.

[¶ 14,132]

§ 2510.3-2. **Employee pension benefit plan.** (a) *General.* This section clarifies the limits of the defined terms "employee pension benefit plan" and "pension plan" for purposes of Title I of the Act and this chapter by identifying certain specific plans, funds and programs which do not constitute employee pension benefit plans for those purposes. To the extent that these plans, funds and programs constitute employee welfare benefit plans within the meaning of section 3(1) of the Act and § 2510.3–1, they will be covered under Title I; however, they will not be subject to parts 2 and 3 of Title I of the Act. [Revised August 30, 2016 (81 FR 59464) and June 28, 2017 (82 FR 29236).]

(b) *Severance pay plans.* (1) For purposes of Title I of the Act and this chapter, an arrangement shall not be deemed to constitute an employee pension benefit plan or pension plan solely by reason of the payment of severance benefits on account of the termination of an employee's service, provided that:

(i) Such payments are not contingent, directly or indirectly, upon the employee's retiring;

(ii) The total amount of such payments does not exceed the equivalent of twice the employee's annual compensation during the year immediately preceding the termination of his service; and

(iii) All such payments to any employee are completed,

(A) In the case of an employee whose service is terminated in connection with a limited program of terminations, within the later of 24 months after the termination of the employee's service, or 24 months after the employee reaches normal retirement age; and

(B) In the case of all other employees, within 24 months after the termination of the employee's service.

(2) For purposes of this paragraph (b),

(i) "Annual compensation" means the total of all compensation, including wages, salary, and any other benefit of monetary value, whether paid in the form of cash or otherwise, which was paid as consideration for the employee's service during the year, or which would have been so paid at the employee's usual rate of compensation if the employee had worked a full year.

(ii) "Limited program of terminations" means a program of terminations:

(A) Which, when begun, was scheduled to be completed upon a date certain or upon the occurrence of one or more specified events;

(B) Under which the number, percentage or class or classes of employees whose services are to be terminated is specified in advance; and

(C) Which is described in a written document which is available to the Secretary upon request, and which contains information sufficient to demonstrate that the conditions set forth in subclauses (A) and (B) of this clause (ii) have been met. [Amended February 23, 1979, by FR Doc. 79-5812.]

(c) *Bonus program.* For purposes of Title I of the Act and this chapter, the terms "employee pension benefit plan" and "pension plan" shall not include payments made by an employer to some or all of its employees as bonuses for work performed, unless such payments are systematically deferred to the termination of covered employment or beyond, or so as to provide retirement income to employees.

(d) *Individual Retirement Accounts.* (1) For purposes of Title I of the Act and this chapter, the terms "employee pension benefit plan" and "pension plan" shall not include an individual retirement account described in section 408(a) of the Code, an individual retirement annuity described in section 408(b) of the Internal Revenue Code of 1954 (hereinafter "the Code") and an individual retirement bond described in section 409 of the Code, provided that—

(i) no contributions are made by the employer or employee association;

(ii) participation is completely voluntary for employees or members;

(iii) the sole involvement of the employer or employee organization is without endorsement to permit the sponsor to publicize the program to employees or members, to collect contributions through payroll deductions or dues checkoffs and to remit them to the sponsor; and

(iv) the employer or employee organization receives no consideration in the form of cash or otherwise, other than reasonable compensation for services actually rendered in connection with payroll deductions or dues checkoffs.

(e) *Gratuitous payments to pre-Act retirees.* For purposes of Title I of the Act and this chapter the terms "employee pension benefit plan" and "pension plan" shall not include voluntary, gratuitous payments by an employer to former employees who separated from the service of the employer if:

(1) payments are made out of the general assets of the employer,

(2) former employees separated from the service of the employer prior to September 2, 1974,

(3) payments made to such employees commenced prior to September 2, 1974, and

(4) each former employee receiving such payments is notified annually that the payments are gratuitous and do not constitute a pension plan.

(f) *Tax sheltered annuities.* For the purpose of Title I of the Act and this chapter, a program for the purchase of an annuity contract or the establishment of a custodial account described in section 403(b) of the Internal Revenue Code of 1954 (the Code), pursuant to salary reduction agreements or agreements to forego an increase in salary, which meets the requirements of 26 CFR § 1.403(b)-1(b)(3) shall not be "established or maintained by an employer" as that phrase is used in the definition of the terms "employee pension benefit plan" and "pension plan" if

(1) participation is completely voluntary for employees;

(2) all rights under the annuity contract or custodial account are enforceable solely by the employee, by a beneficiary of such employee, or by any authorized representative of such employee or beneficiary;

(3) the sole involvement of the employer, other than pursuant to paragraph (f)(2) above, is limited to any of the following:

(i) permitting annuity contractors (which term shall include any agent or broker who offers annuity contracts or who makes available custodial accounts within the meaning of section 403(b)(7) of the Code) to publicize their products to employees,

(ii) requesting information concerning proposed funding media, products or annuity contractors;

(iii) summarizing or otherwise compiling the information provided with respect to the proposed funding media or products which are made available, or the annuity contractors whose services are provided, in order to facilitate review and analysis by the employees;

(iv) collecting annuity or custodial account considerations as required by salary reduction agreements or by agreements to forego salary increases, remitting such considerations to annuity contractors and maintaining records of such considerations;

(v) holding in the employer's name one or more group annuity contracts covering its employees;

(vi) before February 7, 1978, to have limited the funding media or products available to employees, or the annuity contractors who could approach employees, to those which, in the judgment of the employer, afforded employees appropriate investment opportunities; or

(vii) after February 6, 1978, limiting the funding media or products available to employees, or the annuity contractors who may approach employees, to a number and selection which is designed to afford employees a reasonable choice in light of all relevant circumstances. Relevant circumstances may include, but would not necessarily be limited to, the following types of factors:

(A) the number of employees affected,

(B) the number of contractors who have indicated interest in approaching employees,

(C) the variety of available products,

(D) the terms of the available arrangements,

(E) the administrative burdens and costs to the employer, and

(F) the possible interference with employee performance resulting from direct solicitation by contractors; and

(4) the employer receives no direct or indirect consideration or compensation in cash or otherwise other than reasonable compensation to cover expenses properly and actually incurred by such employer in the performance of the employer's duties pursuant to the salary reduction agreements or agreements to forego salary increases described in this paragraph (f) above.

[Reg. § 2510.3-2(f) was published in the Federal Register of April 20, 1979, effective retroactively from January 1, 1975.]

(g) *Supplemental payment plans.* (1) *General rule.* Generally, an arrangement by which a payment is made by an employer to supplement retirement income is a pension plan. Supplemental payments made on or after September 26, 1980, shall be treated as being made

under a welfare plan rather than a pension plan for purposes of Title I of the Act if all of the following conditions are met:

(i) Payment is made for the purpose of supplementing the pension benefits of a participant or his or her beneficiary out of:

(A) the general assets of the employer, or

(B) a separate trust fund established and maintained solely for that purpose.

(ii) The amount payable under the supplemental payment plan to a participant or his or her beneficiary with respect to a month does not exceed the payee's supplemental payment factor ("SPF," as defined in paragraph (g)(3)(i) of this section) for that month, provided however, that unpaid monthly amounts may be cumulated and paid in subsequent months to the participant or his or her beneficiary.

(iii) The payment is not made before the last day of the month with respect to which it is computed.

(2) *Safe harbor for arrangements concerning pre-1977 retirees.* (i) Notwithstanding paragraph (g)(1) of this section, effective January 1, 1975 an arrangement by which a payment is made by an employer to supplement the retirement income of a former employee who separated from the service of the employer prior to January 1, 1977 shall be deemed not to have been made under an employee benefit plan if all of the following conditions are met:

(A) The employer is not obligated to make the payment or similar payments for more than twelve months at a time.

(B) The payment is made out of the general assets of the employer.

(C) The former employee is notified in writing at least once each year in which a payment is made that the payments are not part of an employee benefit plan subject to the protections of the Act.

(D) The former employee is notified in writing at least once each year in which a payment is made of the extent of the employer's obligation, if any, to continue the payments.

(ii) A person who receives a payment on account of his or her relationship to a former employee who retired prior to January 1, 1977 is considered to be a former employee for purposes of this paragraph (g)(2).

(3) *Definitions and special rules.* For purposes of this paragraph (g)—

(i) The term "supplemental payment factor" (SPF) is, for any particular month, the product of: (A) The individual's pension benefit amount (as defined in paragraph (g)(3)(ii) of this section), and (B) the cost of living increase (as defined in paragraph (g)(3)(v) of this section) for that month.

(ii)(A) The term "pension benefit amount" (PBA) means, with regard to a retiree, the amount of pension benefits payable, in the form of the annuity chosen by the retiree, for the first full month that he or she is in pay status under a pension plan (as defined in paragraph (g)(3)(iii) of this section) sponsored by his or her employer or under a multiemployer plan in which his or her employer participates. If the retiree has received a lump-sum distribution from the plan, the PBA for the retiree shall be determined as follows:

(1) If the plan provides an annuity option at the time of the distribution, the PBA shall be computed as if the distribution had been applied on that date to the purchase from the plan of a level straight annuity for the life of the participant if the participant was unmarried at the time of the distribution or a joint and survivor annuity if the participant was married at the time of distribution.

(2) If the plan does not provide an annuity option at the time of the distribution, the PBA shall be computed as if the distribution had been applied on that date to the purchase from an insurance company qualified to do business in a State of a commercially available level straight annuity for the life of the participant if the participant was then single, or a joint and survivor annuity if the participant was then married, based upon the assumption that the participant and beneficiary are standard mortality risks.

(B) If the retiree has received from the plan a series of distributions which do not constitute a lump-sum distribution or an annuity, the PBA for the retiree shall be determined with respect to each distribution according to paragraph (g)(3)(ii)(A) above, or in accordance with a reasonably equivalent method.

(C) The term PBA, with regard to the beneficiary of a plan participant, means: (*1*) The amount of pension benefits, payable in the form of a survivor annuity to the beneficiary, for the first full month that he or she begins to receive the survivor annuity, reduced by: (*2*) Any increases which have been incorporated as part of the survivor annuity under the plan since the participant entered pay status or, if the participant died before the commencement of pension benefits, since the participant's date of death.

(D) Where a plan participant has commenced to receive his or her pension benefits in the form of a straight-life annuity, or another form of an annuity that does not continue after the participant's death in the form of a survivor annuity, no beneficiary of the participant will have a PBA.

(iii) The term "pension plan" means, for purposes of this paragraph (g), a pension plan as defined in section 3(2) of the Act, but not including a plan described in section 4(b), 201(2), or 301(a)(3) of the Act. The term also does not include an arrangement meeting all the conditions of paragraph (g)(1) or (g)(2) of this section or of an arrangement described in §2510.3-2(e). In the case of a controlled group of corporations within the meaning of section 407(d)(5) of the Act, all pension plans sponsored by members of the group shall be considered to be one pension plan.

(iv) The term "employer" means, for purposes of paragraph (g) of this section, the former employer making the supplemental payment. In the case of a controlled group of corporations within the meaning of section 407(d)(7) of the Act, all members of the controlled group shall be considered to be one employer for purposes of this paragraph (g).

(v) The term "cost of living increase" (CLI) means, as to any month, a percentage equal to the following fraction:

$$\frac{a-b}{b}$$

where a = the CPIU for the month for which a payment is being computed, and b = the CPIU for the first full month the retiree was in pay status. Where the CLI is calculated for the beneficiary of a plan participant, "b" continues to be equal to the CPIU for the first full month the retiree was in pay status. If, however, the participant dies before the commencement of pension benefits, "b" is equal to the CPIU for the first full month the survivor is in pay status.

(vi) The term "CPIU" means the U.S. City Average All Items Consumer Price Index for all Urban Consumers, published by the U.S. Department of Labor, Bureau of Labor Statistics. Data concerning the CPIU for a particular period can be obtained from the U.S. Department of Labor, Bureau of Labor Statistics, Division of Consumer Prices and Price Indexes, Washington, D.C. 20212.

(vii) Where an employer does not pay to a retiree the full amount of the supplemental payments which would be permitted under paragraph (g)(1) of this section, any unpaid amounts may be cumulated and paid in subsequent months to either the retiree or the beneficiary of the retiree. The beneficiary need not be the recipient of a survivor annuity in order to be paid these cumulated supplemental payments.

(4) *Examples*. The following examples illustrate how this paragraph (g) works. As referred to in these examples, the CPIU's for July through November of 1980 are as follows:

July 1980: 247.8

August 1980: 249.4

September 1980: 251.7

October 1980: 253.9

November 1980: 256.2

Example (1)(a). E is an employer. R received monthly benefits of $600 under a straight-life annuity under E's defined benefit pension plan after R retired from E and entered pay status on July 1, 1980. The amount that E may pay to R as supplemental payments under a welfare rather than pension plan with respect to the months of July through September of 1980 is computed as follows:

SPF for July 1980

$$\text{SPF} = \frac{a-b}{b} \times \text{PBA}$$

$$= \frac{247.8 - 247.8}{247.8} \times \$600 = \$0.00$$

SPF for August 1980

$$\text{SPF} = \frac{249.4 - 247.8}{247.8} \times \$600 = \$3.87$$

SPF for September 1980

$$\text{SPF} = \frac{251.7 - 247.8}{247.8} \times \$600 = \$9.44$$

Total = $ 0.00
            3.87
            9.44
            —————
           $13.31

No supplemental payment may be made to R as a welfare plan payment with respect to July 1980, the month of retirement. The $3.87 that may be paid with respect to August 1980 may be paid at any time after August 31, 1980. The $9.44 that may be paid with respect to September 1980 may be paid at any time after September 30, 1980.

Example (1)(b). S is the beneficiary of R. Because R received pension benefits under a straight-life annuity, S will receive no survivor annuity from E after R's death. S thus will have no PBA after R's death and will not be eligible to receive any supplemental payments from E based on S's PBA. To the extent, however, that R did not receive supplemental payments from E to the maximum limit allowable under paragraph (g)(1), any amounts not paid to R may be cumulated and paid to S after R's death.

Example (2)(a). E is an employer. Q received monthly benefits of $500 in the form of a joint and survivor annuity under E's defined benefit pension plan since retirement from E on July 1, 1980. The amount that E may pay to Q as welfare rather than pension plan payments with respect to the months of July through September of 1980 is computed as follows:

SPF for July 1980

$$\text{SPF} = \frac{249.4 - 247.8}{247.8} \times \$500 = \$0.00$$

SPF for August 1980

$$\text{SPF} = \frac{249.4 - 247.8}{247.8} \times \$500 = \$3.23$$

SPF for September 1980

$$\text{SPF} = \frac{251.7 - 247.8}{247.8} \times \$500 = \$7.87$$

Total = $0.00
            3.23
            7.87
            —————
           $11.10

No supplemental payment may be made as a welfare plan payment with respect to July 1980, the month of retirement. The $3.23 that may be paid with respect to August 1980 may be paid at any time after August 31, 1980. The $7.87 that may be paid with respect to September 1980 may be paid at any time after September 30, 1980.

Example (2)(b). Q dies on October 15, 1980 without having received any supplemental payments from E. T is the beneficiary of Q. E pays T a survivor's annuity of $300 beginning in November of 1980. The amount payable to T as a survivor annuity under the plan has not been increased since Q began to receive pension benefits. Thus, T's PBA is $300. The amount that E may pay to T as welfare rather than pension plan payments with respect to the months of July through November 1980 is computed as follows:

SPF for July 1980 = $0.00

SPF for August 1980 = $3.23

SPF for September 1980 = $7.87

SPF for October 1980

$$SPF = \frac{a - b}{b} \times PBA$$

$$= \frac{253.9 - 247.8}{247.8} \times \$500$$

$$= \$12.31$$

(Note that T's "b" is equal to Q's "b".)

SPF for November 1980

$$SPF = \frac{256.2 - 247.8}{247.8} \times \$300 = \$10.17$$

Total that may be paid to T:

The maximum E may pay T with respect to the months of July through November 1980 as welfare rather than pension plan payments is the sum of those months' SPFs, which is $33.58.

Example (3). Assume the same facts as in Example (1)(a), except that R elected to receive a lump-sum distribution rather than a straight-life annuity. If R is unmarried on July 1, 1980, R's PBA is $600 for the remainder of R's life. If R is married to S on July 1, 1980, the PBAs of R and S are based on the annuity that would have been paid under an election to receive a joint and survivor annuity. See paragraph (g)(3)(ii)(A)(*1*) of this section.

[Added November 4, 1982, by FR Doc. 82-30403 (47 FR 50237).]

[¶ 14,133]

§ 2510.3-3. **Employee benefit plan.** (a) *General.* This section clarifies the definition in section 3(3) of the term "employee benefit plan" for purposes of Title I of the Act and this chapter. It states a general principle which can be applied to a large class of plans to determine whether they constitute employee benefit plans within the meaning of section 3(3) of the Act. Under section 4(a) of the Act, only employee benefit plans within the meaning of section 3(3) are subject to Title I.

(b) *Plans without employees.* For purposes of Title I of the Act and this chapter, the term "employee benefit plan" shall not include any plan, fund or program, other than an apprenticeship or other training program, under which no employees are participants covered under the plan, as defined in paragraph (d) of this section. For example, a so-called "Keogh" or "H.R. 10" plan under which only partners or only a sole proprietor are participants covered under the plan will not be covered under Title I. However, a Keogh plan under which one or more common law employees in addition to the self-employed individuals are participants covered under the plan, will be covered under Title I. Similarly, partnership buyout agreements described in section 736 of the Internal Revenue Code of 1954 will not be subject to Title I.

(c) *Employees.* For purposes of this section:

(1) An individual and his or her spouse shall not be deemed to be employees with respect to a trade or business, whether incorporated or unincorporated, which is wholly owned by the individual or by the individual and his or her spouse, and

(2) A partner in a partnership and his or her spouse shall not be deemed to be employees with respect to the partnership.

(d) *Participant covered under the plan.* (1)(i) An individual becomes a participant covered under an employee welfare benefit plan on the earlier of—

(A) the date designated by the plan as the date on which the individual begins participation in the plan;

(B) the date on which the individual becomes eligible under the plan for a benefit subject only to occurrence of the contingency for which the benefit is provided; or

(C) the date on which the individual makes a contribution to the plan, whether voluntary or mandatory.

(ii) An individual becomes a participant covered under an employee pension plan—

(A) in the case of a plan which provides for employee contributions or defines participation to include employees who have not yet retired, on the earlier of—

(*1*) the date on which the individual makes a contribution, whether voluntary or mandatory, or

(*2*) the date designated by the plan as the date on which the individual has satisfied the plan's age and service requirements for participation, and

(B) in the case of a plan which does not provide for employee contributions and does not define participation to include employees who have not yet retired, the date on which the individual completes the first year of employment which may be taken into account in determining—

(*1*) whether the individual is entitled to benefits under the plan, or

(*2*) the amount of benefits to which the individual is entitled,

whichever results in earlier participation.

(2)(i) An individual is not a participant covered under an employee welfare plan on the earliest date on which the individual—

(A) is ineligible to receive any benefit under the plan even if the contingency for which such benefit is provided should occur, and

(B) is not designated by the plan as a participant.

(ii) An individual is not a participant covered under an employee pension plan or a beneficiary receiving benefits under an employee pension plan if—

(A) the entire benefit rights of the individual—

(*1*) are fully guaranteed by an insurance company, insurance service or insurance organization licensed to do business in a State, and are legally enforceable by the sole choice of the individual against the insurance company, insurance service or insurance organization; and

(*2*) a contract, policy or certificate describing the benefits to which the individual is entitled under the plan has been issued to the individual; or

(B) the individual has received from the plan a lump-sum distribution or a series of distributions of cash or other property which represents the balance of his or her credit under the plan.

(3)(i) In the case of an employee pension benefit plan, an individual who, under the terms of the plan, has incurred a one-year break in service after having become a participant covered under the plan, and who has acquired no vested right to a benefit before such break in service is not a participant covered under the plan until the individual has completed a year of service after returning to employment covered by the plan.

(ii) For purposes of paragraph (d)(3)(i) of this section, in the case of an employee pension benefit plan which is subject to section 203 of the Act the term "year of service" shall have the same meaning as in section 203(b)(2)(A) of the Act and any regulations issued under the Act and the term "one-year break in service" shall have the same meaning as in section 203(b)(3)(A) of the Act and any regulations issued under the Act.

[¶ 14,136H]

§ 2510.3-16. **Definition of "plan administrator."**

(a) *In general.* The term "plan administrator" or "administrator" means the person specifically so designated by the terms of the instrument under which the plan is operated. If an administrator is not so designated, the plan administrator is the plan sponsor, as defined in section 3(16)(B) of ERISA.

(b) In the case of a self-insured group health plan established or maintained by an eligible organization, as defined in § 2590.715–2713A(a) of this chapter, if the eligible organization provides a copy of the self-certification of its objection to administering or funding any contraceptive benefits in accordance with § 2590.715–2713A(b)(1)(ii) of this chapter to a third party administrator, the self-certification shall be an instrument under which the plan is operated, shall be treated as a designation of the third party administrator as the plan administrator under section 3(16) of ERISA for any contraceptive services required to be covered under § 2590.715–2713(a)(1)(iv) of this chapter to which the eligible organization objects on religious grounds, and shall supersede any earlier designation. If, instead, the eligible organization notifies the Secretary of Health and Human Services of its objection to administering or funding any contraceptive benefits in accordance with § 2590.715–2713A(b)(1)(ii) of this chapter, the Department of Labor, working with the Department of Health and Human Services, shall separately provide notification to each third party administrator that such third party administrator shall be the plan administrator under section 3(16) of ERISA for any contraceptive services required to be covered under § 2590.715–2713(a)(1)(iv) of this chapter to which the eligible organization objects on religious grounds, with 51100 respect to benefits for contraceptive services that the third party administrator would otherwise manage. Such notification from the Department of Labor shall be an instrument under which the plan is operated and shall supersede any earlier designation. [Amended 7/14/15 by 80 FR 41317.]

(c) A third party administrator that becomes a plan administrator pursuant to this section shall be responsible for—

(1) Complying with section 2713 of the Public Health Service Act (42 U.S.C. 300gg-13) (as incorporated into section 715 of ERISA) and § 2590.715–2713 of this chapter with respect to coverage of contraceptive services. To the extent the plan contracts with different third party administrators for different classifications of benefits (such as prescription drug benefits versus inpatient and outpatient benefits), each third party administrator is responsible for providing contraceptive coverage that complies with section 2713 of the Public Health Service Act (as incorporated into section 715 of ERISA) and § 2590.715–2713 of this chapter with respect to the classification or classifications of benefits subject to its contract.

(2) Establishing and operating a procedure for determining such claims for contraceptive services in accordance with § 2560.503–1 of this chapter.

(3) Complying with disclosure and other requirements applicable to group health plans under Title I of ERISA with respect to such benefits. [Amended 7/14/15 by 80 FR 41317.]

[Added on 7/2/2013 by 78 FR 39869. Amended 7/14/2015 by 80 FR 41317.]

Interim Final Regulations

Reg. § 2510.3-16 was adopted and published in the *Federal Register* on August 27, 2014 by 79 FR 51092. Reg. § 2510.3-16 was finalized on July 14, 2015 (80 FR 41317). See ¶ 14,136H for the final version of the regulations.

[¶ 14,136HH]

§ 2510.3-16. **Definition of "plan administrator." [Finalized on 7/14/2015 (80 FR 41317). See ¶ 14,136H for the final version of the regulations.]**

[Added 8/27/2014 by 79 FR 51092. Finalized 7/14/2015 by 80 FR 41317.]

Regulations

Reg. § 2510.3-21 was filed with the *Federal Register* on October 28, 1975 and published on October 31, 1975 (40 FR 50843). Reg. § 2510.3-21 was revised on April 8, 2016 (81 FR 20945). The revised regulation is at ¶ 14,138A. The revised Reg. § 2510.3-21 was amended by adding subsection (j) on April 8, 2016 (81 FR 20945). The revised Reg. § 2510.3-21 was amended on April 7, 2017 (82 Fr 16902) to extend the applicability date to June 9, 2017.

»»→ Caution: Revised Reg. § 2510.3-21 at ¶ 14,138A is effective June 7, 2016 and applicable June 9, 2017. Until the revised regulations become applicable, the existing Reg. § 2510.3-21 below applies.

[¶ 14,138]

§ 2510.3-21 **Definition of "Fiduciary".** (a) **[Reserved]**

(b) **[Reserved]**

(c) *Investment advice.* (1) A person shall be deemed to be rendering "investment advice" to an employee benefit plan, within the meaning of section 3(21)(A)(ii) of the Employee Retirement Income Security Act of 1974 (the Act) and this paragraph, only if:

(i) Such person renders advice to the plan as to the value of securities or other property, or makes recommendations as to the advisability of investing in, purchasing, or selling securities or other property; and

(ii) Such person either directly or indirectly (e.g., through or together with any affiliate)—

(A) has discretionary authority or control, whether or not pursuant to agreement, arrangement or understanding, with respect to purchasing or selling securities or other property for the plan; or

(B) renders any advice described in paragraph (c)(1)(i) of this section on a regular basis to the plan pursuant to a mutual agreement, arrangement or understanding, written or otherwise, between such person and the plan or a fiduciary with respect to the plan, that such services will serve as a primary basis for investment decisions with respect to plan assets, and that such person will render individualized investment advice to the plan based on the particular needs of the plan regarding such matters as, among other things, investment policies or strategy, overall portfolio composition, or diversification of plan investments.

(2) A person who is a fiduciary with respect to a plan by reason of rendering investment advice (as defined in paragraph (c)(1) of this section) for a fee or other compensation, direct or indirect, with respect to any moneys or other property of such plan, or having any authority or responsibility to do so, shall not be deemed to be a fiduciary regarding any assets of the plan with respect to which such person does not have any discretionary authority, discretionary control or discretionary responsibility, does not exercise any authority or control, does not render investment advice (as defined in paragraph (c)(1) of this section) for a fee or other compensation, and does not have any authority or responsibility to render such investment advice, provided that nothing in this paragraph shall be deemed to:

(i) Exempt such person from the provisions of section 405(a) of the Act concerning liability for fiduciary breaches by other fiduciaries with respect to any assets of the plan; or

(ii) Exclude such person from the definition of the term "party in interest" (as set forth in section 3(14)(B) of the Act) with respect to any assets of the plan.

(d) *Execution of securities transactions.* (1) A person who is a broker or dealer registered under the Securities Exchange Act of 1934, a reporting dealer who makes primary markets in securities of the United States Government or of an agency of the United States Government and reports daily to the Federal Reserve Bank of New York its positions with respect to such securities and borrowings thereon, or a bank supervised by the United States or a State, shall not be deemed to be a fiduciary, within the meaning of section 3(21)(A) of the Act, with respect to an employee benefit plan solely because such person exe-

»»→ *Caution: Revised Reg. § 2510.3-21 at ¶ 14,138A is effective June 7, 2016 and applicable June 9, 2017. Until the revised regulations become applicable, the existing Reg. § 2510.3-21 below applies.*

cutes transactions for the purchase or sale of securities on behalf of such plan in the ordinary course of its business as a broker, dealer, or bank, pursuant to instructions of a fiduciary with respect to such plan, if:

(i) Neither the fiduciary nor any affiliate of such fiduciary is such broker, dealer, or bank; and

(ii) The instructions specify (A) the security to be purchased or sold, (B) a price range within which such security is to be purchased or sold, or, if such security is issued by an open-end investment company registered under the Investment Company Act of 1940 (15 U.S.C. 80a-1, et seq.), a price which is determined in accordance with Rule 22c-1 under the Investment Company Act of 1940 (17 CFR 270.22c-1), (C) a time span during which such security may be purchased or sold (not to exceed five business days), and (D) the minimum or maximum quantity of such security which may be purchased or sold within such price range, or, in the case of a security issued by an open-end investment company registered under the Investment Company Act of 1940, the minimum or maximum quantity of such security which may be purchased or sold, or the value of such security in dollar amount which may be purchased or sold, at the price referred to in paragraph (d)(1)(ii)(B) of this section.

(2) A person who is a broker-dealer, reporting dealer, or bank which is a fiduciary with respect to an employee benefit plan solely by reason of the possession or exercise of discretionary authority or discretionary control in the management of the plan or the management or disposition of plan assets in connection with the execution of a transaction or transactions for the purchase or sale of securities on behalf of such plan which fails to comply with the provisions of paragraph (d)(1) of this section, shall not be deemed to be a fiduciary

regarding any assets of the plan with respect to which such broker-dealer, reporting dealer or bank does not have any discretionary authority, discretionary control or discretionary responsibility, does not exercise any authority or control, does not render investment advice (as defined in paragraph (c)(1) of this section) for a fee or other compensation, and does not have any authority or responsibility to render such investment advice, provided that nothing in this paragraph shall be deemed to:

(i) Exempt such broker-dealer, reporting dealer, or bank from the provisions of section 405(a) of the Act concerning liability for fiduciary breaches by other fiduciaries with respect to any assets of the plan; or

(ii) Exclude such broker-dealer, reporting dealer, or bank from the definition of the term "party in interest" (as set forth in section 3(14)(B) of the Act) with respect to any assets of the plan.

(e) *Affiliate and control.* (1) For purposes of paragraphs (c) and (d) of this section, an "affiliate" of a person shall include:

(i) Any person directly or indirectly, through one or more intermediaries, controlling, controlled by, or under common control with such person;

(ii) Any officer, director, partner, employee or relative (as defined in section 3(15) of the Act) of such person; and

(iii) Any corporation or partnership of which such person is an officer, director or partner.

(2) For purposes of this paragraph, the term "control" means the power to exercise a controlling influence over the management or policies of a person other than an individual. [§ 2510.3-21 was filed with the Federal Register on October 28, 1975.]

»»→ *Caution: Revised Reg. § 2510.3-21 at ¶ 14,138A is effective June 7, 2016 and applicable June 9, 2017. Until the revised regulations become applicable, the existing Reg. § 2510.3-21 at ¶ 14,138 applies.*

[¶ 14,138A]

§ 2510.3-21 **Definition of "Fiduciary".** (a) *Investment advice.* For purposes of section 3(21)(A)(ii) of the Employee Retirement Income Security Act of 1974 (Act) and section 4975(e)(3)(B) of the Internal Revenue Code (Code), except as provided in paragraph (c) of this section, a person shall be deemed to be rendering investment advice with respect to moneys or other property of a plan or IRA described in paragraph (g)(6) of this section if—

(1) Such person provides to a plan, plan fiduciary, plan participant or beneficiary, IRA, or IRA owner the following types of advice for a fee or other compensation, direct or indirect:

(i) A recommendation as to the advisability of acquiring, holding, disposing of, or exchanging, securities or other investment property, or a recommendation as to how securities or other investment property should be invested after the securities or other investment property are rolled over, transferred, or distributed from the plan or IRA;

(ii) A recommendation as to the management of securities or other investment property, including, among other things, recommendations on investment policies or strategies, portfolio composition, selection of other persons to provide investment advice or investment management services, selection of investment account arrangements (*e.g.,* brokerage versus advisory); or recommendations with respect to rollovers, transfers, or distributions from a plan or IRA, including whether, in what amount, in what form, and to what destination such a rollover, transfer, or distribution should be made; and

(2) With respect to the investment advice described in paragraph (a)(1) of this section, the recommendation is made either directly or indirectly (*e.g.,* through or together with any affiliate) by a person who:

(i) Represents or acknowledges that it is acting as a fiduciary within the meaning of the Act or the Code;

(ii) Renders the advice pursuant to a written or verbal agreement, arrangement, or understanding that the advice is based on the particular investment needs of the advice recipient; or

(iii) Directs the advice to a specific advice recipient or recipients regarding the advisability of a particular investment or manage-

ment decision with respect to securities or other investment property of the plan or IRA.

(b)(1) For purposes of this section, "recommendation" means a communication that, based on its content, context, and presentation, would reasonably be viewed as a suggestion that the advice recipient engage in or refrain from taking a particular course of action. The determination of whether a "recommendation" has been made is an objective rather than subjective inquiry. In addition, the more individually tailored the communication is to a specific advice recipient or recipients about, for example, a security, investment property, or investment strategy, the more likely the communication will be viewed as a recommendation. Providing a selective list of securities to a particular advice recipient as appropriate for that investor would be a recommendation as to the advisability of acquiring securities even if no recommendation is made with respect to any one security. Furthermore, a series of actions, directly or indirectly (*e.g.,* through or together with any affiliate), that may not constitute a recommendation when viewed individually may amount to a recommendation when considered in the aggregate. It also makes no difference whether the communication was initiated by a person or a computer software program.

(2) The provision of services or the furnishing or making available of information and materials in conformance with paragraphs (b)(2)(i) through (iv) of this section is not a "recommendation" for purposes of this section. Determinations as to whether any activity not described in this paragraph (b)(2) constitutes a recommendation must be made by reference to the criteria set forth in paragraph (b)(1) of this section.

(i) *Platform providers.* Marketing or making available to a plan fiduciary of a plan, without regard to the individualized needs of the plan, its participants, or beneficiaries a platform or similar mechanism from which a plan fiduciary may select or monitor investment alternatives, including qualified default investment alternatives, into which plan participants or beneficiaries may direct the investment of assets held in, or contributed to, their individual accounts, provided the plan fiduciary is independent of the person who markets or makes available the platform or similar mechanism, and the person discloses in writing to the plan fiduciary that the person is not undertaking to provide impartial investment advice or to give advice in a fiduciary capacity. A plan participant or beneficiary or relative of either shall not be considered a plan fiduciary for purposes of this paragraph.

(ii) *Selection and monitoring assistance.* In connection with the activities described in paragraph (b)(2)(i) of this section with respect to a plan,

(A) Identifying investment alternatives that meet objective criteria specified by the plan fiduciary (*e.g.,* stated parameters concerning expense ratios, size of fund, type of asset, or credit quality), provided that the person identifying the investment alternatives discloses in writing whether the person has a financial interest in any of the identified investment alternatives, and if so the precise nature of such interest;

(B) In response to a request for information, request for proposal, or similar solicitation by or on behalf of the plan, identifying a limited or sample set of investment alternatives based on only the size of the employer or plan, the current investment alternatives designated under the plan, or both, provided that the response is in writing and discloses whether the person identifying the limited or sample set of investment alternatives has a financial interest in any of the alternatives, and if so the precise nature of such interest; or

(C) Providing objective financial data and comparisons with independent benchmarks to the plan fiduciary.

(iii) *General Communications.* Furnishing or making available to a plan, plan fiduciary, plan participant or beneficiary, IRA, or IRA owner general communications that a reasonable person would not view as an investment recommendation, including general circulation newsletters, commentary in publicly broadcast talk shows, remarks and presentations in widely attended speeches and conferences, research or news reports prepared for general distribution, general marketing materials, general market data, including data on market performance, market indices, or trading volumes, price quotes, performance reports, or prospectuses.

(iv) *Investment Education.* Furnishing or making available any of the following categories of investment-related information and materials described in paragraphs (b)(2)(iv)(A) through (D) of this section to a plan, plan fiduciary, plan participant or beneficiary, IRA, or IRA owner irrespective of who provides or makes available the information and materials (*e.g.,* plan sponsor, fiduciary or service provider), the frequency with which the information and materials are provided, the form in which the information and materials are provided (*e.g.,* on an individual or group basis, in writing or orally, or via call center, video or computer software), or whether an identified category of information and materials is furnished or made available alone or in combination with other categories of information and materials, provided that the information and materials do not include (standing alone or in combination with other materials) recommendations with respect to specific investment products or specific plan or IRA alternatives, or recommendations with respect to investment or management of a particular security or securities or other investment property, except as noted in paragraphs (b)(2)(iv)(C)(*4*) and (b)(2)(iv)(D)(*6*) of this section.

(A) *Plan information.* Information and materials that, without reference to the appropriateness of any individual investment alternative or any individual benefit distribution option for the plan or IRA, or a particular plan participant or beneficiary or IRA owner, describe the terms or operation of the plan or IRA, inform a plan fiduciary, plan participant, beneficiary, or IRA owner about the benefits of plan or IRA participation, the benefits of increasing plan or IRA contributions, the impact of preretirement withdrawals on retirement income, retirement income needs, varying forms of distributions, including rollovers, annuitization and other forms of lifetime income payment options (*e.g.,* immediate annuity, deferred annuity, or incremental purchase of deferred annuity), advantages, disadvantages and risks of different forms of distributions, or describe product features, investor rights and obligations, fee and expense information, applicable trading restrictions, investment objectives and philosophies, risk and return characteristics, historical return information, or related prospectuses of investment alternatives available under the plan or IRA.

(B) *General financial, investment, and retirement information.* Information and materials on financial, investment, and retirement matters that do not address specific investment products, specific plan or IRA investment alternatives or distribution options available to the plan or IRA or to plan participants, beneficiaries, and IRA owners, or specific investment alternatives or services offered outside the plan or IRA, and inform the plan fiduciary, plan participant or beneficiary, or IRA owner about:

(1) General financial and investment concepts, such as risk and return, diversification, dollar cost averaging, compounded return, and tax deferred investment;

(2) Historic differences in rates of return between different asset classes (*e.g.,* equities, bonds, or cash) based on standard market indices;

(3) Effects of fees and expenses on rates of return;

(4) Effects of inflation;

(5) Estimating future retirement income needs;

(6) Determining investment time horizons;

(7) Assessing risk tolerance;

(8) Retirement-related risks (*e.g.,* longevity risks, market/interest rates, inflation, health care and other expenses); and

(9) General methods and strategies for managing assets in retirement (*e.g.,* systematic withdrawal payments, annuitization, guaranteed minimum withdrawal benefits), including those offered outside the plan or IRA.

(C) *Asset allocation models.* Information and materials (*e.g.,* pie charts, graphs, or case studies) that provide a plan fiduciary, plan participant or beneficiary, or IRA owner with models of asset allocation portfolios of hypothetical individuals with different time horizons (which may extend beyond an individual's retirement date) and risk profiles, where—

(1) Such models are based on generally accepted investment theories that take into account the historic returns of different asset classes (*e.g.,* equities, bonds, or cash) over defined periods of time;

(2) All material facts and assumptions on which such models are based (*e.g.,* retirement ages, life expectancies, income levels, financial resources, replacement income ratios, inflation rates, and rates of return) accompany the models;

(3) The asset allocation models are accompanied by a statement indicating that, in applying particular asset allocation models to their individual situations, plan participants, beneficiaries, or IRA owners should consider their other assets, income, and investments (*e.g.,* equity in a home, Social Security benefits, individual retirement plan investments, savings accounts, and interests in other qualified and non-qualified plans) in addition to their interests in the plan or IRA, to the extent those items are not taken into account in the model or estimate; and

(4) The models do not include or identify any specific investment product or investment alternative available under the plan or IRA, except that solely with respect to a plan, asset allocation models may identify a specific investment alternative available under the plan if it is a designated investment alternative within the meaning of 29 CFR 2550.404a-5(h)(4) under the plan subject to oversight by a plan fiduciary independent from the person who developed or markets the investment alternative and the model:

(i) Identifies all the other designated investment alternatives available under the plan that have similar risk and return characteristics, if any; and

(ii) is accompanied by a statement indicating that those other designated investment alternatives have similar risk and return characteristics and identifying where information on those investment alternatives may be obtained, including information described in paragraph (b)(2)(iv)(A) of this section and, if applicable, paragraph (d) of 29 CFR 2550.404a-5.

Reg. §2510.3-21(b)(2)(iv)(C)(4)(ii)   ¶14,138A

(D) *Interactive investment materials.* Questionnaires, worksheets, software, and similar materials that provide a plan fiduciary, plan participant or beneficiary, or IRA owner the means to: Estimate future retirement income needs and assess the impact of different asset allocations on retirement income; evaluate distribution options, products, or vehicles by providing information under paragraphs (b)(2)(iv)(A) and (B) of this section; or estimate a retirement income stream that could be generated by an actual or hypothetical account balance, where—

(1) Such materials are based on generally accepted investment theories that take into account the historic returns of different asset classes (*e.g.*, equities, bonds, or cash) over defined periods of time;

(2) There is an objective correlation between the asset allocations generated by the materials and the information and data supplied by the plan participant, beneficiary or IRA owner;

(3) There is an objective correlation between the income stream generated by the materials and the information and data supplied by the plan participant, beneficiary, or IRA owner;

(4) All material facts and assumptions (*e.g.*, retirement ages, life expectancies, income levels, financial resources, replacement income ratios, inflation rates, rates of return and other features, and rates specific to income annuities or systematic withdrawal plans) that may affect a plan participant's, beneficiary's, or IRA owner's assessment of the different asset allocations or different income streams accompany the materials or are specified by the plan participant, beneficiary, or IRA owner;

(5) The materials either take into account other assets, income and investments (*e.g.*, equity in a home, Social Security benefits, individual retirement plan investments, savings accounts, and interests in other qualified and non-qualified plans) or are accompanied by a statement indicating that, in applying particular asset allocations to their individual situations, or in assessing the adequacy of an estimated income stream, plan participants, beneficiaries, or IRA owners should consider their other assets, income, and investments in addition to their interests in the plan or IRA; and

(6) The materials do not include or identify any specific investment alternative or distribution option available under the plan or IRA, unless such alternative or option is specified by the plan participant, beneficiary, or IRA owner, or it is a designated investment alternative within the meaning of 29 CFR 2550.404a-5(h)(4) under a plan subject to oversight by a plan fiduciary independent from the person who developed or markets the investment alternative and the materials:

(i) Identify all the other designated investment alternatives available under the plan that have similar risk and return characteristics, if any; and

(ii) Are accompanied by a statement indicating that those other designated investment alternatives have similar risk and return characteristics and identifying where information on those investment alternatives may be obtained; including information described in paragraph (b)(2)(iv)(A) of this section and, if applicable, paragraph (d) of 29 CFR 2550.404a-5;

(c) Except for persons who represent or acknowledge that they are acting as a fiduciary within the meaning of the Act or the Code, a person shall not be deemed to be a fiduciary within the meaning of section 3(21)(A)(ii) of the Act or section 4975(e)(3)(B) of the Code solely because of the activities set forth in paragraphs (c)(1), (2), and (3) of this section.

(1) *Transactions with independent fiduciaries with financial expertise.* The provision of any advice by a person (including the provision of asset allocation models or other financial analysis tools) to a fiduciary of the plan or IRA (including a fiduciary to an investment contract, product, or entity that holds plan assets as determined pursuant to sections 3(42) and 401 of the Act and 29 CFR 2510.3-101) who is independent of the person providing the advice with respect to an arm's length sale, purchase, loan, exchange, or other transaction related to the investment of securities or other investment property, if, prior to

entering into the transaction the person providing the advice satisfies the requirements of this paragraph (c)(1).

(i) The person knows or reasonably believes that the independent fiduciary of the plan or IRA is:

(A) A bank as defined in section 202 of the Investment Advisers Act of 1940 or similar institution that is regulated and supervised and subject to periodic examination by a State or Federal agency;

(B) An insurance carrier which is qualified under the laws of more than one state to perform the services of managing, acquiring or disposing of assets of a plan;

(C) An investment adviser registered under the Investment Advisers Act of 1940 or, if not registered an as investment adviser under the Investment Advisers Act by reason of paragraph (1) of section 203A of such Act, is registered as an investment adviser under the laws of the State (referred to in such paragraph (1)) in which it maintains its principal office and place of business;

(D) A broker-dealer registered under the Securities Exchange Act of 1934; or

(E) Any independent fiduciary that holds, or has under management or control, total assets of at least $50 million (the person may rely on written representations from the plan or independent fiduciary to satisfy this paragraph (c)(1)(i));

(ii) The person knows or reasonably believes that the independent fiduciary of the plan or IRA is capable of evaluating investment risks independently, both in general and with regard to particular transactions and investment strategies (the person may rely on written representations from the plan or independent fiduciary to satisfy this paragraph (c)(1)(ii));

(iii) The person fairly informs the independent fiduciary that the person is not undertaking to provide impartial investment advice, or to give advice in a fiduciary capacity, in connection with the transaction and fairly informs the independent fiduciary of the existence and nature of the person's financial interests in the transaction;

(iv) The person knows or reasonably believes that the independent fiduciary of the plan or IRA is a fiduciary under ERISA or the Code, or both, with respect to the transaction and is responsible for exercising independent judgment in evaluating the transaction (the person may rely on written representations from the plan or independent fiduciary to satisfy this paragraph (c)(1)(iv)); and

(v) The person does not receive a fee or other compensation directly from the plan, plan fiduciary, plan participant or beneficiary, IRA, or IRA owner for the provision of investment advice (as opposed to other services) in connection with the transaction.

(2) *Swap and security-based swap transactions.* The provision of any advice to an employee benefit plan (as described in section 3(3) of the Act) by a person who is a swap dealer, security-based swap dealer, major swap participant, major security-based swap participant, or a swap clearing firm in connection with a swap or security-based swap, as defined in section 1a of the Commodity Exchange Act (7 U.S.C. 1a) and section 3(a) of the Securities Exchange Act of 1934 (15 U.S.C. 78c(a)) if—

(i) The employee benefit plan is represented by a fiduciary under ERISA independent of the person;

(ii) In the case of a swap dealer or security-based swap dealer, the person is not acting as an advisor to the employee benefit plan (within the meaning of section 4s(h) of the Commodity Exchange Act or section 15F(h) of the Securities Exchange Act of 1934) in connection with the transaction;

(iii) The person does not receive a fee or other compensation directly from the plan or plan fiduciary for the provision of investment advice (as opposed to other services) in connection with the transaction; and

(iv) In advance of providing any recommendations with respect to the transaction, or series of transactions, the person obtains a written representation from the independent fiduciary that the independent fiduciary understands that the person is not undertaking to provide impartial investment advice, or to give advice in a fiduciary

»»→ *Caution: Revised Reg. §2510.3-21 at ¶ 14,138A is effective June 7, 2016 and applicable June 9, 2017. Until the revised regulations become applicable, the existing Reg. §2510.3-21 at ¶ 14,138 applies.*

capacity, in connection with the transaction and that the independent fiduciary is exercising independent judgment in evaluating the recommendation.

(3) *Employees.*

(i) In his or her capacity as an employee of the plan sponsor of a plan, as an employee of an affiliate of such plan sponsor, as an employee of an employee benefit plan, as an employee of an employee organization, or as an employee of a plan fiduciary, the person provides advice to a plan fiduciary, or to an employee (other than in his or her capacity as a participant or beneficiary of an employee benefit plan) or independent contractor of such plan sponsor, affiliate, or employee benefit plan, provided the person receives no fee or other compensation, direct or indirect, in connection with the advice beyond the employee's normal compensation for work performed for the employer; or

(ii) In his or her capacity as an employee of the plan sponsor of a plan, or as an employee of an affiliate of such plan sponsor, the person provides advice to another employee of the plan sponsor in his or her capacity as a participant or beneficiary of the plan, provided the person's job responsibilities do not involve the provision of investment advice or investment recommendations, the person is not registered or licensed under federal or state securities or insurance law, the advice he or she provides does not require the person to be registered or licensed under federal or state securities or insurance laws, and the person receives no fee or other compensation, direct or indirect, in connection with the advice beyond the employee's normal compensation for work performed for the employer.

(d) *Scope of fiduciary duty—investment advice.* A person who is a fiduciary with respect to a plan or IRA by reason of rendering investment advice (as defined in paragraph (a) of this section) for a fee or other compensation, direct or indirect, with respect to any securities or other investment property of such plan or IRA, or having any authority or responsibility to do so, shall not be deemed to be a fiduciary regarding any assets of the plan or IRA with respect to which such person does not have any discretionary authority, discretionary control or discretionary responsibility, does not exercise any authority or control, does not render investment advice (as described in paragraph (a)(1) of this section) for a fee or other compensation, and does not have any authority or responsibility to render such investment advice, provided that nothing in this paragraph shall be deemed to:

(1) Exempt such person from the provisions of section 405(a) of the Act concerning liability for fiduciary breaches by other fiduciaries with respect to any assets of the plan; or

(2) Exclude such person from the definition of the term "party in interest" (as set forth in section 3(14)(B) of the Act) or "disqualified person" (as set forth in section 4975(e)(2) of the Code) with respect to any assets of the employee benefit plan or IRA.

(e) *Execution of securities transactions.*

(1) A person who is a broker or dealer registered under the Securities Exchange Act of 1934, a reporting dealer who makes primary markets in securities of the United States Government or of an agency of the United States Government and reports daily to the Federal Reserve Bank of New York its positions with respect to such securities and borrowings thereon, or a bank supervised by the United States or a State, shall not be deemed to be a fiduciary, within the meaning of section 3(21)(A) of the Act or section 4975(e)(3)(B) of the Code, with respect to a plan or IRA solely because such person executes transactions for the purchase or sale of securities on behalf of such plan in the ordinary course of its business as a broker, dealer, or bank, pursuant to instructions of a fiduciary with respect to such plan or IRA, if:

(i) Neither the fiduciary nor any affiliate of such fiduciary is such broker, dealer, or bank; and

(ii) The instructions specify:

(A) The security to be purchased or sold;

(B) A price range within which such security is to be purchased or sold, or, if such security is issued by an open-end

investment company registered under the Investment Company Act of 1940 (15 U.S.C. 80a-1, *et seq.*), a price which is determined in accordance with Rule 22c1 under the Investment Company Act of 1940 (17 CFR 270.22c1);

(C) A time span during which such security may be purchased or sold (not to exceed five business days); and

(D) The minimum or maximum quantity of such security which may be purchased or sold within such price range, or, in the case of a security issued by an open-end investment company registered under the Investment Company Act of 1940, the minimum or maximum quantity of such security which may be purchased or sold, or the value of such security in dollar amount which may be purchased or sold, at the price referred to in paragraph (e)(1)(ii)(B) of this section.

(2) A person who is a broker-dealer, reporting dealer, or bank which is a fiduciary with respect to a plan or IRA solely by reason of the possession or exercise of discretionary authority or discretionary control in the management of the plan or IRA, or the management or disposition of plan or IRA assets in connection with the execution of a transaction or transactions for the purchase or sale of securities on behalf of such plan or IRA which fails to comply with the provisions of paragraph (e)(1) of this section, shall not be deemed to be a fiduciary regarding any assets of the plan or IRA with respect to which such broker-dealer, reporting dealer or bank does not have any discretionary authority, discretionary control or discretionary responsibility, does not exercise any authority or control, does not render investment advice (as defined in paragraph (a) of this section) for a fee or other compensation, and does not have any authority or responsibility to render such investment advice, provided that nothing in this paragraph shall be deemed to:

(i) Exempt such broker-dealer, reporting dealer, or bank from the provisions of section 405(a) of the Act concerning liability for fiduciary breaches by other fiduciaries with respect to any assets of the plan; or

(ii) Exclude such broker-dealer, reporting dealer, or bank from the definition of the term "party in interest" (as set forth in section 3(14)(B) of the Act) or "disqualified person" (as set forth in section 4975(e)(2) of the Code) with respect to any assets of the plan or IRA.

(f) *Internal Revenue Code.* Section 4975(e)(3) of the Code contains provisions parallel to section 3(21)(A) of the Act which define the term "fiduciary" for purposes of the prohibited transaction provisions in Code section 4975. Effective December 31, 1978, section 102 of the Reorganization Plan No. 4 of 1978, 5 U.S.C. App. 237 transferred the authority of the Secretary of the Treasury to promulgate regulations of the type published herein to the Secretary of Labor. All references herein to section 3(21)(A) of the Act should be read to include reference to the parallel provisions of section 4975(e)(3) of the Code. Furthermore, the provisions of this section shall apply for purposes of the application of Code section 4975 with respect to any plan, including any IRA, described in Code section 4975(e)(1).

(g) *Definitions.* For purposes of this section—

(1) The term "affiliate" means any person directly or indirectly, through one or more intermediaries, controlling, controlled by, or under common control with such person; any officer, director, partner, employee, or relative (as defined in paragraph (g)(8) of this section) of such person; and any corporation or partnership of which such person is an officer, director, or partner.

(2) The term "control," for purposes of paragraph (g)(1) of this section, means the power to exercise a controlling influence over the management or policies of a person other than an individual.

(3) The term "fee or other compensation, direct or indirect" means, for purposes of this section and section 3(21)(A)(ii) of the Act, any explicit fee or compensation for the advice received by the person (or by an affiliate) from any source, and any other fee or compensation received from any source in connection with or as a result of the purchase or sale of a security or the provision of investment advice services, including, though not limited to, commissions, loads, finder's fees, revenue sharing payments, shareholder servicing fees, marketing

>>>→ *Caution: Revised Reg. § 2510.3-21 at ¶ 14,138A is effective June 7, 2016 and applicable June 9, 2017. Until the revised regulations become applicable, the existing Reg. § 2510.3-21 at ¶ 14,138 applies.*

or distribution fees, underwriting compensation, payments to brokerage firms in return for shelf space, recruitment compensation paid in connection with transfers of accounts to a registered representative's new broker-dealer firm, gifts and gratuities, and expense reimbursements. A fee or compensation is paid "in connection with or as a result of" such transaction or service if the fee or compensation would not have been paid but for the transaction or service or if eligibility for or the amount of the fee or compensation is based in whole or in part on the transaction or service.

(4) The term "investment property" does not include health insurance policies, disability insurance policies, term life insurance policies, and other property to the extent the policies or property do not contain an investment component.

(5) The term "IRA owner" means, with respect to an IRA, either the person who is the owner of the IRA or the person for whose benefit the IRA was established.

(6)(i) The term "plan" means any employee benefit plan described in section 3(3) of the Act and any plan described in section 4975(e)(1)(A) of the Code, and

(ii) The term "IRA" means any account or annuity described in Code section 4975(e)(1)(B) through (F), including, for example, an individual retirement account described in section 408(a) of the Code and a health savings account described in section 223(d) of the Code.

(7) The term "plan fiduciary" means a person described in section (3)(21)(A) of the Act and 4975(e)(3) of the Code. For purposes

of this section, a participant or beneficiary of the plan or a relative of either is not a "plan fiduciary" with respect to the plan, and the IRA owner or a relative is not a "plan fiduciary" with respect to the IRA.

(8) The term "relative" means a person described in section 3(15) of the Act and section 4975(e)(6) of the Code or a brother, a sister, or a spouse of a brother or sister.

(9) The term "plan participant" or "participant" means, for a plan described in section 3(3) of the Act, a person described in section 3(7) of the Act.

(h) *Effective and applicability dates*

(1) *Effective date.* This section is effective on June 7, 2016.

(2) *Applicability date.* Paragraphs (a), (b), (c), (d), (f), and (g) of this section apply June 9, 2017. [Amended 4/7/2017 by 82 FR 16902.]

(3) Until the applicability date under this paragraph (h), the prior regulation under the Act and the Code (as it appeared in the July 1, 2015 edition of 29 CFR part 2510 and the April 1, 2015 edition of 26 CFR part 54) applies.

(i) *Continued applicability of State law regulating insurance, banking, or securities.* Nothing in this part shall be construed to affect or modify the provisions of section 514 of Title I of the Act, including the savings clause in section 514(b)(2)(A) for state laws that regulate insurance, banking, or securities.

>>>→ *Caution: Reg. § 2510.3-21(j) is effective June 7, 2016 and applicable until June 9, 2017.*

(j) *Temporarily applicable provisions.*

(1) During the period between June 7, 2016 and June 9, 2017, this paragraph (j) shall apply. [Amended 4/7/2017 by 82 FR 16902.]

(i) A person shall be deemed to be rendering "investment advice" to an employee benefit plan, within the meaning of section 3(21)(A)(ii) of the Act, section 4975(e)(3)(B) of the Code and this paragraph (j), only if:

(A) Such person renders advice to the plan as to the value of securities or other property, or makes recommendation as to the advisability of investing in, purchasing, or selling securities or other property; and

(B) Such person either directly or indirectly (*e.g.*, through or together with any affiliate)—

(1) Has discretionary authority or control, whether or not pursuant to agreement, arrangement or understanding, with respect to purchasing or selling securities or other property for the plan; or

(2) Renders any advice described in paragraph (j)(1)(i) of this section on a regular basis to the plan pursuant to a mutual agreement, arrangement or understanding, written or otherwise, between such person and the plan or a fiduciary with respect to the plan, that such services will serve as a primary basis for investment deci-

sions with respect to plan assets, and that such person will render individualized investment advice to the plan based on the particular needs of the plan regarding such matters as, among other things, investment policies or strategy, overall portfolio composition, or diversification of plan investments.

(2) *Affiliate and control.*

(i) For purposes of paragraph (j) of this section, an "affiliate" of a person shall include:

(A) Any person directly or indirectly, through one or more intermediaries, controlling, controlled by, or under common control with such person;

(B) Any officer, director, partner, employee or relative (as defined in section 3(15) of the Act) of such person; and

(C) Any corporation or partnership of which such person is an officer, director or partner.

(ii) For purposes of this paragraph (j), the term "control" means the power to exercise a controlling influence over the management or policies of a person other than an individual.

(3) *Expiration date.* This paragraph (j) expires on June 9, 2017. [Added April 8, 2016 by 81 FR 20945. Amended 4/7/2017 by 82 FR 16902.]

Regulations

Reg. § 2510.3-37 was adopted by FR Doc. 75-30032 under "Title 29—Labor; Chapter XXV—Employee Benefits Security, Office of Department of Labor; Part 2510—Definitions of Terms used in Subchapters C, D, E, F and G of this Chapter." The regulation was published in the *Federal Register* on November 7, 1975, filed November 6, 1975, and effective November 6, 1975 (40 FR 52008). Reg. § 2510.3-101 was added by 51 FR 41280, effective March 13, 1987, and amended by 51 FR 47226, December 31, 1986. Reg. § 2510.3-102 was adopted by 53 FR 17628, May 17, 1988, and amended by 61 FR 41220 on August 7, 1996, effective February 3, 1997. Reg. § 2510.3-102 was further amended by FR Doc. 97-30961, filed with the *Federal Register* on November 24, 1997, published in the *Federal Register* on November 25, 1997, and effective on November 25, 1997 (62 FR 62934). Reg. § 2510.3-40 was added on April 9, 2003 (68 FR 17471). Reg. § 2510.3-38 was added on August 24, 2004 (69 FR 52119). Reg. § 2510-102(a), (b), (c), and (f) were amended January 14, 2010 (75 FR 2068).

[¶ 14,139]

§ 2510.3-37 **Multiemployer plan.** (a) *General.* Section 3(37) of the Act contains in subparagraph (a)(i)-(iv) a number of criteria which an employee benefit plan must meet in order to be a multiemployer plan under the Act. Section 3(37) also provides that the Secretary may prescribe by regulation other requirements in addition to those contained in subparagraph (a)(i)-(iv). The purpose of this regulation is to establish such requirements.

(b) *Plans in existence before the effective date.* (1) A plan in existence before September 2, 1974, will be considered a multiemployer plan if it satisfies the requirements of section 3(37)(A)(i)-(iv) of the Act.

(2) For purposes of this section, a plan is considered to be in existence if:

(i)(A) The plan was reduced to writing and adopted by the participating employers and the employee organization (including, in the case of a corporate employer, formal approval by an employer's board of directors or shareholders, if required), even though no amounts had been contributed under the plan, and

    (B) The plan has not been terminated; or

    (ii)(A) There was a legally enforceable agreement to establish such a plan signed by the employers and the employee organization, and

    (B) The contributions to be made to the plan were set forth in the agreement.

    (iii) If a plan was in existence within the meaning of paragraph (b)(i) or (ii) of this section, any other plan with which such existing plan is merged or consolidated shall also be considered to be in existence.

    (c) *Plans not in existence before the effective date.* In addition to the provisions of section 3(37)(A)(i)-(iv) of the Act, a multiemployer plan established on or after September 2, 1974, must meet the requirement that it was established for a substantial business purpose. A substantial business purpose includes the interest of a labor organization in securing an employee benefit plan for its members. The following factors are relevant in determining whether a substantial business purpose existed for the establishment of a plan; any single factor may be sufficient to constitute a substantial business purpose:

    (1) The extent to which the plan is maintained by a substantial number of unaffiliated contributing employers and covers a substantial portion of the trade, craft or industry in terms of employees or a substantial number of the employees in the trade, craft or industry in a locality or geographic area;

    (2) The extent to which the plan provides benefits more closely related to years of service within the trade, craft or industry rather than with an employer, reflecting the fact that an employee's relationship with an employer maintaining the plan is generally short-term although service in the trade, craft or industry is generally long-term;

    (3) The extent to which collective bargaining takes place on matters other than employee benefit plans between the employee organization and the employers maintaining the plan; and

    (4) The extent to which the administrative burden and expense of providing benefits through single employer plans would be greater than through a multiemployer plan.

[Adopted by FR Doc. 75-30032, effective November 6, 1975 (40 FR 52008).]

[¶ 14,139A]

§ 2510.3-38 **Filing requirements for State registered investment advisers to be investment managers.** (a) *General.* Section 3(38) of the Act sets forth the criteria for a fiduciary to be an investment manager for purposes of section 405 of the Act. Subparagraph (B)(ii) of section 3(38) of the Act provides that, in the case of a fiduciary who is not registered under the Investment Advisers Act of 1940 by reason of paragraph (1) of section 203A(a) of such Act, the fiduciary must be registered as an investment adviser under the laws of the State in which it maintains its principal office and place of business, and, at the time the fiduciary files registration forms with such State to maintain the fiduciary's registration under the laws of such State, also files a copy of such forms with the Secretary of Labor. The purpose of this section is to set forth the exclusive means for investment advisers to satisfy the filing obligation with the Secretary described in subparagraph (B)(ii) of section 3(38) of the Act.

    (b) *Filing Requirement.* To satisfy the filing requirement with the Secretary in section 3(38)(B)(ii) of the Act, a fiduciary must be registered as an investment adviser with the State in which it maintains its principal office and place of business and file through the Investment Adviser Registration Depository (IARD), in accordance with applicable IARD requirements, the information required to be registered and maintain the fiduciary's registration as an investment adviser in such State. Submitting to the Secretary investment adviser registration forms filed with a State does not constitute compliance with the filing requirement in section 3(38)(B)(ii) of the Act.

    (c) *Definitions.* For purposes of this section, the term "Investment Adviser Registration Depository" or "IARD" means the centralized electronic depository described in 17 CFR 275.203-1.

    (d) *Cross Reference.* Information for investment advisers on how to file through the IARD is available on the Securities and Exchange Commission website at "http://www.sec.gov/iard."

[¶ 14,139C]

§ 2510.3-40 **Plans Established or Maintained Under or Pursuant to Collective Bargaining Agreements Under Section 3(40)(A) of ERISA.** (a) *Scope and purpose.* Section 3(40)(A) of the Employee Retirement Income Security Act of 1974 (ERISA) provides that the term "multiple employer welfare arrangement" (MEWA) does not include an employee welfare benefit plan that is established or maintained under or pursuant to one or more agreements that the Secretary of Labor (the Secretary) finds to be collective bargaining agreements. This section sets forth criteria that represent a finding by the Secretary whether an arrangement is an employee welfare benefit plan established or maintained under or pursuant to one or more collective bargaining agreements. A plan is established or maintained under or pursuant to collective bargaining if it meets the criteria in this section. However, even if an entity meets the criteria in this section, it will not be an employee welfare benefit plan established or maintained under or pursuant to a collective bargaining agreement if it comes within the exclusions in the section. Nothing in or pursuant to this section shall constitute a finding for any purpose other than the exception for plans established or maintained under or pursuant to one or more collective bargaining agreements under section 3(40) of ERISA. In a particular case where there is an attempt to assert state jurisdiction or the application of state law with respect to a plan or other arrangement that allegedly is covered under Title I of ERISA, the Secretary has set forth a procedure for obtaining individualized findings at 29 CFR part 2570, subpart H.

    (b) *General criteria.* The Secretary finds, for purposes of section 3(40) of ERISA, that an employee welfare benefit plan is "established or maintained under or pursuant to one or more agreements which the Secretary finds to be collective bargaining agreements" for any plan year in which the plan meets the criteria set forth in paragraphs (b)(1), (2), (3), and (4) of this section, and is not excluded under paragraph (c) of this section.

    (1) The entity is an employee welfare benefit plan within the meaning of section 3(1) of ERISA.

    (2) At least 85% of the participants in the plan are:

    (i) Individuals employed under one or more agreements meeting the criteria of paragraph (b)(3) of this section, under which contributions are made to the plan, or pursuant to which coverage under the plan is provided;

    (ii) Retirees who either participated in the plan at least five of the last 10 years preceding their retirement, or

    (A) Are receiving benefits as participants under a multiemployer pension benefit plan that is maintained under the same agreements referred to in paragraph (b)(3) of this section, and

    (B) Have at least five years of service or the equivalent under that multiemployer pension benefit plan;

    (iii) Participants on extended coverage under the plan pursuant to the requirements of a statute or court or administrative agency decision, including but not limited to the continuation coverage requirements of the Consolidated Omnibus Budget Reconciliation Act of 1985, sections 601-609, 29 U.S.C. 1169, the Family and Medical Leave Act, 29 U.S.C. 2601 et seq., the Uniformed Services Employment and Reemployment Rights Act of 1994, 38 U.S.C. 4301 et seq., or the National Labor Relations Act, 29 U.S.C. 158(a)(5);

    (iv) Participants who were active participants and whose coverage is otherwise extended under the terms of the plan, including but not limited to extension by reason of self-payment, hour bank, long or short-term disability, furlough, or temporary unemployment, provided that the charge to the individual for such extended coverage is no more than the applicable premium under section 604 of the Act;

    (v) Participants whose coverage under the plan is maintained pursuant to a reciprocal agreement with one or more other employee welfare benefit plans that are established or maintained under or pursuant to one or more collective bargaining agreements and that are multiemployer plans;

    (vi) Individuals employed by:

(A) An employee organization that sponsors, jointly sponsors, or is represented on the association, committee, joint board of trustees, or other similar group of representatives of the parties who sponsor the plan;

(B) The plan or associated trust fund;

(C) Other employee benefit plans or trust funds to which contributions are made pursuant to the same agreement described in paragraph (b)(3) of this section; or

(D) An employer association that is the authorized employer representative that actually engaged in the collective bargaining that led to the agreement that references the plan as described in paragraph (b)(3) of this section;

(vii) Individuals who were employed under an agreement described in paragraph (b)(3) of this section, provided that they are employed by one or more employers that are parties to an agreement described in paragraph (b)(3) and are covered under the plan on terms that are generally no more favorable than those that apply to similarly situated individuals described in paragraph (b)(2)(i) of this section;

(viii) Individuals (other than individuals described in paragraph (b)(2)(i) of this section) who are employed by employers that are bound by the terms of an agreement described in paragraph (b)(3) of this section and that employ personnel covered by such agreement, and who are covered under the plan on terms that are generally no more favorable than those that apply to such covered personnel. For this purpose, such individuals in excess of 10% of the total population of participants in the plan are disregarded;

(ix) Individuals who are, or were for a period of at least three years, employed under one or more agreements between or among one or more "carriers" (including "carriers by air") and one or more "representatives" of employees for collective bargaining purposes and as defined by the Railway Labor Act, 45 U.S.C. 151 et seq., providing for such individuals' current or subsequent participation in the plan, or providing for contributions to be made to the plan by such carriers; or

(x) Individuals who are licensed marine pilots operating in United States ports as a state-regulated enterprise and are covered under an employee welfare benefit plan that meets the definition of a qualified merchant marine plan, as defined in section 415(b)(2)(F) of the Internal Revenue Code (26 U.S.C.).

(3) The plan is incorporated or referenced in a written agreement between one or more employers and one or more employee organizations, which agreement, itself or together with other agreements among the same parties:

(i) Is the product of a bona fide collective bargaining relationship between the employers and the employee organization(s);

(ii) Identifies employers and employee organization(s) that are parties to and bound by the agreement;

(iii) Identifies the personnel, job classifications, and/or work jurisdiction covered by the agreement;

(iv) Provides for terms and conditions of employment in addition to coverage under, or contributions to, the plan; and

(v) Is not unilaterally terminable or automatically terminated solely for non-payment of benefits under, or contributions to, the plan.

(4) For purposes of paragraph (b)(3)(i) of this section, the following factors, among others, are to be considered in determining the existence of a bona fide collective bargaining relationship. In any proceeding initiated under 29 CFR part 2570 subpart H, the existence of a bona fide collective bargaining relationship under paragraph (b)(3)(i) shall be presumed where at least four of the factors set out in paragraphs (b)(4)(i) through (viii) of this section are established. In such a proceeding, the Secretary may also consider whether other objective or subjective indicia of actual collective bargaining and representation are present as set out in paragraph (b)(4)(ix) of this section.

(i) The agreement referred to in paragraph (b)(3) of this section provides for contributions to a labor-management trust fund structured according to section 302(c)(5), (6), (7), (8), or (9) of the Taft-Hartley Act, 29 U.S.C. 186(c)(5), (6), (7), (8) or (9), or to a plan lawfully negotiated under the Railway Labor Act;

(ii) The agreement referred to in paragraph (b)(3) of this section requires contributions by substantially all of the participating employers to a multiemployer pension plan that is structured in accordance with section 401 of the Internal Revenue Code (26 U.S.C.) and is either structured in accordance with section 302(c)(5) of the Taft-Hartley Act, 29 U.S.C. 186(c)(5), or is lawfully negotiated under the Railway Labor Act, and substantially all of the active participants covered by the employee welfare benefit plan are also eligible to become participants in that pension plan;

(iii) The predominant employee organization that is a party to the agreement referred to in paragraph (b)(3) of this section has maintained a series of agreements incorporating or referencing the plan since before January 1, 1983;

(iv) The predominant employee organization that is a party to the agreement referred to in paragraph (b)(3) of this section has been a national or international union, or a federation of national and international unions, or has been affiliated with such a union or federation, since before January 1, 1983;

(v) A court, government agency, or other third-party adjudicatory tribunal has determined, in a contested or adversary proceeding, or in a government-supervised election, that the predominant employee organization that is a party to the agreement described in paragraph (b)(3) of this section is the lawfully recognized or designated collective bargaining representative with respect to one or more bargaining units of personnel covered by such agreement;

(vi) Employers who are parties to the agreement described in paragraph (b)(3) of this section pay at least 75% of the premiums or contributions required for the coverage of active participants under the plan or, in the case of a retiree-only plan, the employers pay at least 75% of the premiums or contributions required for the coverage of the retirees. For this purpose, coverage under the plan for dental or vision care, coverage for excepted benefits under 29 CFR 2590.732(b), and amounts paid by participants and beneficiaries as co-payments or deductibles in accordance with the terms of the plan are disregarded;

(vii) The predominant employee organization that is a party to the agreement described in paragraph (b)(3) of this section provides, sponsors, or jointly sponsors a hiring hall(s) and/or a state-certified apprenticeship program(s) that provides services that are available to substantially all active participants covered by the plan;

(viii) The agreement described in paragraph (b)(3) of this section has been determined to be a bona fide collective bargaining agreement for purposes of establishing the prevailing practices with respect to wages and supplements in a locality, pursuant to a prevailing wage statute of any state or the District of Columbia.

(ix) There are other objective or subjective indicia of actual collective bargaining and representation, such as that arm's-length negotiations occurred between the parties to the agreement described in paragraph (b)(3) of this section; that the predominant employee organization that is party to such agreement actively represents employees covered by such agreement with respect to grievances, disputes, or other matters involving employment terms and conditions other than coverage under, or contributions to, the employee welfare benefit plan; that there is a geographic, occupational, trade, organizing, or other rationale for the employers and bargaining units covered by such agreement; that there is a connection between such agreement and the participation, if any, of self-employed individuals in the employee welfare benefit plan established or maintained under or pursuant to such agreement.

(c) *Exclusions.* An employee welfare benefit plan shall not be deemed to be "established or maintained under or pursuant to one or more agreements which the Secretary finds to be collective bargaining agreements" for any plan year in which:

(1) The plan is self-funded or partially self-funded and is marketed to employers or sole proprietors

(i) By one or more insurance producers as defined in paragraph (d) of this section;

(ii) By an individual who is disqualified from, or ineligible for, or has failed to obtain, a license to serve as an insurance producer to the extent that the individual engages in an activity for which such license is required; or

(iii) By individuals (other than individuals described in paragraphs (c)(1)(i) and (ii) of this section) who are paid on a commission-type basis to market the plan.

(iv) For the purposes of this paragraph (c)(1):

(A) "Marketing" does not include administering the plan, consulting with plan sponsors, counseling on benefit design or coverage, or explaining the terms of coverage available under the plan to employees or union members;

(B) "Marketing" does include the marketing of union membership that carries with it plan participation by virtue of such membership, except for membership in unions representing insurance producers themselves;

(2) The agreement under which the plan is established or maintained is a scheme, plan, stratagem, or artifice of evasion, a principal intent of which is to evade compliance with state law and regulations applicable to insurance; or

(3) There is fraud, forgery, or willful misrepresentation as to the factors relied on to demonstrate that the plan satisfies the criteria set forth in paragraph (b) of this section.

(d) *Definitions.* (1) Active participant means a participant who is not retired and who is not on extended coverage under paragraphs (b)(2)(iii) or (b)(2)(iv) of this section.

(2) Agreement means the contract embodying the terms and conditions mutually agreed upon between or among the parties to such agreement. Where the singular is used in this section, the plural is automatically included.

(3) Individual employed means any natural person who furnishes services to another person or entity in the capacity of an employee under common law, without regard to any specialized definitions or interpretations of the terms "employee," "employer," or "employed" under federal or state statutes other than ERISA.

(4) Insurance producer means an agent, broker, consultant, or producer who is an individual, entity, or sole proprietor that is licensed under the laws of the state to sell, solicit, or negotiate insurance.

(5) Predominant employee organization means, where more than one employee organization is a party to an agreement, either the organization representing the plurality of individuals employed under such agreement, or organizations that in combination represent the majority of such individuals.

(e) *Examples.* The operation of the provisions of this section may be illustrated by the following examples.

Example 1. Plan A has 500 participants, in the following 4 categories of participants under paragraph (b)(2) of this section:

Categories of participants	Total number	Nexus group	Non-nexus
1. Individuals working under CBAs	335 (67%)	335 (67%)	0
2. Retirees	50 (10%)	50 (10%)	0
3. "Special Class"—Non-CBA, non-CBA-alumni	100 (20%)	50 (10%)	50 (10%)
4. Non-nexus participants	15 (3%)	0	15 (3%)
Total	500 (100%)	435 (87%)	65 (13%)

In determining whether at least 85% of Plan A's participant population is made up of individuals with the required nexus to the collective bargaining agreement as required by paragraph (b)(2) of this section, the Plan may count as part of the nexus group only 50 (10% of the total plan population) of the 100 individuals described in paragraph (b)(2)(viii) of this section. That is because the number of individuals meeting the category of individuals in paragraph (b)(2)(viii) exceeds 10% of the total participant population by 50 individuals. The paragraph specifies that of those individuals who would otherwise be deemed to be nexus individuals because they are the type of individuals described in paragraph (b)(2)(viii), the number in excess of 10% of the total plan population may not be counted in the nexus group. Here, 50 of the 100 individuals employed by signatory employers, but not covered by the collective bargaining agreement, are counted as nexus individuals and 50 are not counted as nexus individuals. Nonetheless, the Plan satisfies the 85% criterion under paragraph (b)(2) because a total of 435 (335 individuals covered by the collective bargaining agreement, plus 50 retirees, plus 50 individuals employed by signatory employers), or 87%, of the 500 participants in Plan A are individuals who may be counted as nexus participants under paragraph (b)(2). Beneficiaries (e.g., spouses, dependent children, etc.) are not counted to determine whether the 85% test has been met.

Example 2. (i) International Union MG and its Local Unions have represented people working primarily in a particular industry for over 60 years. Since 1950, most of their collective bargaining agreements have called for those workers to be covered by the National MG Health and Welfare Plan. During that time, the number of union-represented workers in the industry, and the number of active participants in the National MG Health and Welfare Plan, first grew and then declined. New Locals were formed and later were shut down. Despite these fluctuations, the National MG Health and Welfare Plan meets the factors described in paragraphs (b)(4)(iii) and (iv) of this section, as the plan has been in existence pursuant to collective bargaining agreements to which the International Union and its affiliates have been parties since before January 1, 1983.

(ii) Assume the same facts, except that on January 1, 1999, International Union MG merged with International Union RE to form International Union MRGE. MRGE and its Locals now represent the active participants in the National MG Health and Welfare Plan and in the National RE Health and Welfare Plan, which, for 45 years, had been maintained under collective bargaining agreements negotiated by International Union RE and its Locals. Since International Union MRGE is the continuation of, and successor to, the MG and RE unions, the two plans continue to meet the factors in paragraphs (b)(4)(iii) and (iv) of this section. This also would be true if the two plans were merged.

(iii) Assume the same facts as in paragraphs (i) and (ii) of this Example. In addition to maintaining the health and welfare plans described in those paragraphs, International Union MG also maintained the National MG Pension Plan and International Union RE maintained the National RE Pension Plan. When the unions merged and the health and welfare plans were merged, National MG Pension Plan and National RE Pension Plan were merged to form National MRGE Pension Plan. When the unions merged, the employees and retirees covered under the pre-merger plans continued to be covered under the post-merger plans pursuant to the collective bargaining agreements and also were given credit in the post-merger plans for their years of service and coverage in the pre-merger plans. Retirees who originally were covered under the pre-merger plans and continue to be covered under the post-merger plans based on their past service and coverage would be considered to be "retirees" for purposes of 2550.3-40(b)(2)(ii). Likewise, bargaining unit alumni who were covered under the pre-merger plans and continued to be covered under the post-merger plans based on their past service and coverage and their continued employment with employers that are parties to an agreement described in paragraph (b)(3) of this section would be considered to be bargaining unit alumni for purposes of 2550.3-40(b)(2)(vii).

Example 3. Assume the same facts as in paragraph (ii) of Example 2 with respect to International Union MG. However, in 1997, one of its Locals and the employers with which it negotiates agree to set up a new multiemployer health and welfare plan that only covers the individuals represented by that Local Union. That plan would not meet the factor in paragraph (b)(4)(iii) of this section, as it has not been incorporated or referenced in collective bargaining agreements since before January 1, 1983.

Example 4. (i) Pursuant to a collective bargaining agreement between various employers and Local 2000, the employers contribute $2 per hour to the Fund for every hour that a covered employee works under the agreement. The covered employees are automatically entitled to health and disability coverage from the Fund for every calendar quarter the employees have 300 hours of additional covered service in the preceding quarter. The employees do not need to make any additional contributions for their own coverage, but must pay $250 per month if they want health coverage for their dependent spouse and children. Because the employer payments cover 100% of the required contributions for the employees' own coverage, the Local 2000 Employers Health and Welfare Fund meets the "75% employer payment" factor under paragraph (b)(4)(vi) of this section.

(ii) Assume, however, that the negotiated employer contribution rate was $1 per hour, and the employees could only obtain health coverage for themselves if they also elected to contribute $1 per hour, paid on a pre-tax basis through salary reduction. The Fund would not meet the 75% employer payment factor, even though the employees' contributions are treated as employer contributions for tax purposes. Under ERISA, and therefore under this section, elective salary reduction contributions are treated as employee contributions. The outcome would be the same if a uniform employee contribution rate applied to all employees, whether they had individual or family coverage, so that the $1 per hour employee contribution qualified an employee for his or her own coverage and, if he or she had dependents, dependent coverage as well.

Example 5. Arthur is a licensed insurance broker, one of whose clients is Multiemployer Fund M, a partially self-funded plan. Arthur takes bids from insurance companies on behalf of Fund M for the insured portion of its coverage, helps the trustees to evaluate the bids, and places the Fund's health insurance coverage with the carrier that is selected. Arthur also assists the trustees of Fund M in preparing material to explain the plan and its benefits to the participants, as well as in monitoring the insurance company's performance under the contract. At the Trustees' request, Arthur meets with a group of employers with which the union is negotiating for their employees' coverage under Fund M, and he explains the cost structure and benefits that Fund M provides. Arthur is not engaged in marketing within the meaning of paragraph (c)(1) of this section, so the fact that he provides these administrative services and sells insurance to the Fund itself does not affect the plan's status as a plan established or maintained under or pursuant to a collective bargaining agreement. This is the case whether or how he is compensated.

Example 6. Assume the same facts as Example 5, except that Arthur has a group of clients who are unrelated to the employers bound by the collective bargaining agreement, whose employees would not be "nexus group" members, and whose insurance carrier has withdrawn from the market in their locality. He persuades the client group to retain him to find them other coverage. The client group has no relationship with the labor union that represents the participants in Fund M. However, Arthur offers them coverage under Fund M and persuades the Fund's Trustees to allow the client group to join Fund M in order to broaden Fund M's contribution base. Arthur's activities in obtaining coverage for the unrelated group under Fund M constitutes marketing through an insurance producer; Fund M is a MEWA under paragraph (c)(1) of this section.

Example 7. Union A represents thousands of construction workers in a three-state geographic region. For many years, Union A has maintained a standard written collective bargaining agreement with several hundred large and small building contractors, covering wages, hours, and other terms and conditions of employment for all work performed in Union A's geographic territory. The terms of those agreements are negotiated every three years between Union A and a multiemployer Association, which signs on behalf of those employers who have delegated their bargaining authority to the Association. Hundreds of other employersincluding both local and traveling contractorshave chosen to become bound to the terms of Union A's standard area agreement for various periods of time and in various ways, such as by signing short-form binders or "me too" agreements, executing a single job or project labor agreement, or entering into a subcontracting arrangement with a signatory employer. All of these employ individuals represented by Union A and contribute to Plan A, a self-insured multiemployer health and welfare plan established and maintained under Union A's standard area agreement. During the past year, the trustees of Plan A have brought lawsuits against several signatory employers seeking contributions allegedly owed, but not paid to the trust. In defending that litigation, a number of employers have sworn that they never intended to operate as union contractors, that their employees want nothing to do with Union A, that Union A procured their assent to the collective bargaining agreement solely by threats and fraudulent misrepresentations, and that Union A has failed

to file certain reports required by the Labor Management Reporting and Disclosure Act. In at least one instance, a petition for a decertification election has been filed with the National Labor Relations Board. In this example, Plan A meets the criteria for a regulatory finding under this section that it is a multiemployer plan established and maintained under or pursuant to one or more collective bargaining agreements, assuming that its participant population satisfies the 85% test of paragraph (b)(2) of this section and that none of the disqualifying factors in paragraph (c) of this section is present. Plan A's status for the purpose of this section is not affected by the fact that some of the employers who deal with Union A have challenged Union A's conduct, or have disputed under labor statutes and legal doctrines other than ERISA section 3(40) the validity and enforceability of their putative contract with Union A, regardless of the outcome of those disputes.

Example 8. Assume the same facts as Example 7. Plan A's benefits consultant recently entered into an arrangement with the Medical Consortium, a newly formed organization of health care providers, which allows the Plan to offer a broader range of health services to Plan A's participants while achieving cost savings to the Plan and to participants. Union A, Plan A, and Plan A's consultant each have added a page to their Web sites publicizing the new arrangement with the Medical Consortium. Concurrently, Medical Consortium's Web site prominently publicizes its recent affiliation with Plan A and the innovative services it makes available to the Plan's participants. Union A has mailed out informational packets to its members describing the benefit enhancements and encouraging election of family coverage. Union A has also begun distributing similar material to workers on hundreds of non-union construction job sites within its geographic territory. In this example, Plan A remains a plan established and maintained under or pursuant to one or more collective bargaining agreements under section 3(40) of ERISA. Neither Plan A's relationship with a new organization of health care providers, nor the use of various media to publicize Plan A's attractive benefits throughout the area served by Union A, alters Plan A's status for purpose of this section.

Example 9. Assume the same facts as in Example 7. Union A undertakes an area-wide organizing campaign among the employees of all the health care providers who belong to the Medical Consortium. When soliciting individual employees to sign up as union members, Union A distributes Plan A's information materials and promises to bargain for the same coverage. At the same time, when appealing to the employers in the Medical Consortium for voluntary recognition, Union A promises to publicize the Consortium's status as a group of unionized health care service providers. Union A eventually succeeds in obtaining recognition based on its majority status among the employees working for Medical Consortium employers. The Consortium, acting on behalf of its employer members, negotiates a collective bargaining agreement with Union A that provides terms and conditions of employment, including coverage under Plan A. In this example, Plan A still meets the criteria for a regulatory finding that it is collectively bargained under section 3(40) of ERISA. Union A's recruitment and representation of a new occupational category of workers unrelated to the construction trade, its promotion of attractive health benefits to achieve organizing success, and the Plan's resultant growth, do not take Plan A outside the regulatory finding.

Example 10. Assume the same facts as in Example 7. The Medical Consortium, a newly formed organization, approaches Plan A with a proposal to make money for Plan A and Union A by enrolling a large group of employers, their employees, and self-employed individuals affiliated with the Medical Consortium. The Medical Consortium obtains employers' signatures on a generic document bearing Union A's name, labeled "collective bargaining agreement," which provides for health coverage under Plan A and compliance with wage and hour statutes, as well as other employment laws. Employees of signatory employers sign enrollment documents for Plan A and are issued membership cards in Union A; their membership dues are regularly checked off along with their monthly payments for health coverage. Self-employed individuals similarly receive union membership cards and make monthly payments, which are divided between Plan A and the Union. Aside from health coverage matters, these new participants have little or no contact with Union A. The new participants enrolled through the Consortium amount to 18% of the population of Plan A during the current Plan Year. In this example, Plan A now fails to meet the criteria in paragraphs (b)(2) and (b)(3) of this section, because more than 15% of its participants are individuals who are not employed under agreements that are the product of a bona fide collective bargaining relationship and who do not fall within any of the other nexus categories set forth in paragraph (b)(2) of this section. Moreover, even if the number of additional participants enrolled through the Medical Consortium, together with any other participants who did not fall within any of the nexus categories, did not exceed 15% of the total participant population under the plan, the circumstances in this example would trigger the disqualification of paragraph (c)(2) of this section, because Plan A now is being maintained under a substantial number of agreements that are a "scheme, plan, stratagem or artifice of evasion" intended primarily to evade compliance with state laws and regulations pertaining to insurance. In either case, the consequence of adding the participants through the Medical Consortium is that Plan A is now a MEWA for purposes of section 3(40) of ERISA and is not exempt from state regulation by virtue of ERISA.

(f) *Cross-reference.* See 29 CFR part 2570, subpart H for procedural rules relating to proceedings seeking an Administrative Law Judge finding by the Secretary under section 3(40) of ERISA.

(g) *Effect of proceeding seeking Administrative Law Judge Section 3(40) Finding.*

(1) An Administrative Law Judge finding issued pursuant to the procedures in 29 CFR part 2570, subpart H will constitute a finding whether the entity in that proceeding is an employee welfare benefit plan established or maintained under or pursuant to an agreement that the Secretary finds to be a collective bargaining agreement for purposes of section 3(40) of ERISA.

(2) Nothing in this section or in 29 CFR part 2570, subpart H is intended to provide the basis for a stay or delay of a state administrative or court proceeding or enforcement of a subpoena.

[¶ 14,139M]

§ 2510.3-101 **Definition of "plan assets"—plan investments.** (a) *In general.* (1) This section describes what constitutes assets of a plan with respect to a plan's investment in another entity for purposes of Subtitle A, and Parts 1 and 4 of Subtitle B, of Title I of the Act and section 4975 of the Internal Revenue Code. Paragraph (a)(2) of this section contains a general rule relating to plan investments. Paragraphs (b) through (f) of this section define certain terms that are used in the application of the general rule. Paragraph (g) of this section describes how the rules in this section are to be applied when a plan owns property jointly with others or where it acquires an equity interest whose value relates solely to identified assets of an issuer. Paragraph (h) of this section contains special rules relating to particular kinds of plan investments. Paragraph (i) describes the assets that a plan acquires when it purchases certain guaranteed mortgage certificates. Paragraph (j) of this section contains examples illustrating the operation of this section. The effective date of this section is set forth in paragraph (k) of this section.

(2) Generally, when a plan invests in another entity, the plan's assets include its investment, but do not, solely by reason of such investment, include any of the underlying assets of the entity. However, in the case of a plan's investment in an equity interest of an entity that is neither a publicly-offered security nor a security issued by an investment company registered under the Investment Company Act of 1940 its assets include both the equity interest and an undivided interest in each of the underlying assets of the entity, unless it is established that—

(i) The entity is an operating company, or

(ii) Equity participation in the entity by benefit plan investors is not significant.

Therefore, any person who exercises authority or control respecting the management or disposition of such underlying assets, and any person who provides investment advice with respect to such assets for a fee (direct or indirect), is a fiduciary of the investing plan.

(b) *"Equity interests" and "publicly-offered securities".* (1) The term "equity interest" means any interest in an entity other than an instrument that is treated as indebtedness under applicable local law and which has no substantial equity features. A profits interest in a partnership, an undivided ownership interest in property and a beneficial interest in a trust are equity interests.

(2) A "publicly-offered security" is a security that is freely transferrable, part of a class of securities that is widely held and either—

(i) Part of a class of securities registered under section 12(b) or 12(g) of the Securities Exchange Act of 1934, or

(ii) Sold to the plan as part of an offering of securities to the public pursuant to an effective registration statement under the Securities Act of 1933 and the class of securities of which such security is a part is registered under the Securities Exchange Act of 1934 within 120 days (or such later time as may be allowed by the Securities and Exchange Commission) after the end of the fiscal year of the issuer during which the offering of such securities to the public occurred.

(3) For purposes of paragraph (b)(2) of this section, a class of securities is "widely-held" only if it is a class of securities that is owned by 100 or more investors independent of the issuer and of one another. A class of securities will not fail to be widely-held solely because subsequent to the initial offering the number of independent investors falls below 100 as a result of events beyond the control of the issuer.

(4) For purposes of paragraph (b)(2) of this section, whether a security is "freely transferable" is a factual question to be determined on the basis of all relevant facts and circumstances. If a security is part of an offering in which the minimum investment is $10,000 or less, however, the following factors ordinarily will not, alone or in combination, affect a finding that such securities are freely transferable:

(i) Any requirement that not less than a minimum number of shares or units of such security be transferred or assigned by any investor, provided that such requirement does not prevent transfer of all of the then remaining shares or units held by an investor;

(ii) Any prohibition against transfer or assignment of such security or rights in respect thereof to an ineligible or unsuitable investor;

(iii) Any restriction on, or prohibition against, any transfer or assignment which would either result in a termination or reclassification of the entity for federal or state tax purposes or which would violate any state or federal statute, regulation, court order, judicial decree, or rule of law;

(iv) Any requirement that reasonable transfer or administrative fee be paid in connection with a transfer or assignment;

(v) Any requirement that advance notice of a transfer or assignment be given to the entity and any requirement regarding execution of documentation evidencing such transfer or assignment (including documentation setting forth representations from either or both of the transferor or transferee as to compliance with any restriction or requirement described in this paragraph (b)(4) of this section or requiring compliance with the entity's governing instruments);

(vi) Any restriction on substitution of an assignee as a limited partner of a partnership, including a general partner consent requirement, provided that the economic benefits of ownership of the assignee may be transferred or assigned without regard to such restriction or consent (other than compliance with any other restriction described in this paragraph (b)(4)) of this section;

(vii) Any administrative procedure which establishes an effective date, or an event, such as the completion of the offering, prior to which a transfer or assignment will not be effective; and

(viii) Any limitation or restriction on transfer or assignment which is not created or imposed by the issuer or any person acting for or on behalf of such issuer.

(c) *"Operating company".* (1) An "operating company" is an entity that is primarily engaged, directly or through a majority owned subsidiary or subsidiaries, in the production or sale of a product or service other than the investment of capital. The term "operating company" includes an entity which is not described in the preceding sentence, but which is a "venture capital operating company" described in paragraph (d) or a "real estate operating company" described in paragraph (e).

(d) *"Venture capital operating company".* (1) An entity is a "venture capital operating company" for the period beginning on an initial valuation date described in paragraph (d)(5)(i) and ending on the last day of the first "annual valuation period" described in paragraph (d)(5)(ii) (in the case of an entity that is not a venture capital operating company immediately before the determination) or for the 12 month period following the expiration of an "annual valuation period" described in paragraph (d)(5)(ii) (in the case of an entity that is a venture capital operating company immediately before the determination) if—

(i) On such initial valuation date, or at any time within such annual valuation period, at least 50 percent of its assets (other than short-term investments pending long-term commitment or distribution to investors), valued at cost, are invested in venture capital investments described in paragraph (d)(3)(i) or derivative investments described in paragraph (d)(4); and

(ii) During such 12 month period (or during the period beginning on the initial valuation date and ending on the last day of the first annual valuation period), the entity, in the ordinary course of its business, actually exercises management rights of the kind described in paragraph (d)(3)(ii) with respect to one or more of the operating companies in which it invests.

(2)(i) A venture capital operating company described in paragraph (d)(1) shall continue to be treated as a venture capital operating company during the "distribution period" described in paragraph (d)(2)(ii). An entity shall not be treated as a venture capital operating company at any time after the end of the distribution period.

(ii) The "distribution period" referred to in paragraph (d)(2)(i) begins on a date established by a venture capital operating company that occurs after the first date on which the venture capital operating company has distributed to investors the proceeds of at least 50 percent of the highest amount of investments (other than short-term investments made pending long-term commitment or distribution to investors) outstanding at any time from the date it commenced business (determined on the basis of the cost of such investments) and ends on the earlier of—

(A) The date on which the company makes a "new portfolio investment", or

(B) The expiration of 10 years from the beginning of the distribution period.

(iii) For purposes of paragraph (d)(2)(ii)(A), a "new portfolio investment" is an investment other than—

(A) An investment in an entity in which the venture capital operating company had an outstanding venture capital investment at the beginning of the distribution period which has continued to be outstanding at all times during the distribution period, or

(B) A short-term investment pending long-term commitment or distribution to investors.

(3)(i) For purposes of this paragraph (d) a "venture capital investment" is an investment in an operating company (other than a venture capital operating company) as to which the investor has or obtains management rights.

(ii) The term "management rights" means contractual rights directly between the investor and an operating company to substantially participate in, or substantially influence the conduct of, the management of the operating company.

(4)(i) An investment is a "derivative investment" for purposes of this paragraph (d) if it is—

(A) A venture capital investment as to which the investor's management rights have ceased in connection with a public offering of securities of the operating company to which the investment relates, or

(B) An investment that is acquired by a venture capital operating company in the ordinary course of its business in exchange for an existing venture capital investment in connection with:

(1) A public offering of securities of the operating company to which the existing venture capital investment relates, or

(2) A merger or reorganization of the operating company to which the existing venture capital investment relates, provided that such merger or reorganization is made for independent business reasons unrelated to extinguishing management rights.

(ii) An investment ceases to be a derivative investment on the later of:

(A) 10 years from the date of the acquisition of the original venture capital investment to which the derivative investment relates, or

(B) 30 months from the date on which the investment becomes a derivative investment.

(5) For purposes of this paragraph (d) and paragraph (e)—

(i) An "initial valuation date" is the later of—

(A) Any date designated by the company within the 12-month period ending with the effective date of this section, or

(B) The first date on which an entity makes an investment that is not a short-term investment of funds pending long-term commitment.

(ii) An "annual valuation period" is a preestablished annual period, not exceeding 90 days in duration, which begins no later than the anniversary date of an entity's initial valuation date. An annual valuation period, once established, may not be changed except for good cause unrelated to a determination under this paragraph (d) or paragraph (e).

(e) *"Real estate operating company"*. An entity is a "real estate operating company" for the period beginning on an initial valuation date described in paragraph (d)(5)(i) and ending on the last day of the first "annual valuation period" described in paragraph (d)(5)(ii) (in the case of an entity that is not a real estate operating company immediately before the determination) or for the 12-month period following the expiration of an annual valuation period described in paragraph (d)(5)(ii) (in the case of an entity that is a real estate operating company immediately before the determination) if:

(1) On such initial valuation date, or on any date within such annual valuation period, at least 50 percent of its assets, valued at cost (other than short-term investments pending long-term commitment or distribution to investors), are invested in real estate which is managed or developed and with respect to which such entity has the right to substantially participate directly in the management or development activities; and

(2) During such 12-month period (or during the period beginning on the initial valuation date and ending on the last day of the first annual valuation period) such entity in the ordinary course of its business is engaged directly in real estate management or development activities. [Corrected by 51 FR 47226 on December 31, 1986.]

(f) *Participation by benefit plan investors*. (1) Equity participation in an entity by benefit plan investors is "significant" on any date if, immediately after the most recent acquisition of any equity interest in the entity, 25 percent or more of the value of any class of equity interests in the entity is held by benefit plan investors (as defined in paragraph (f)(2)). For purposes of determinations pursuant to this paragraph (f), the value of any equity interests held by a person (other than a benefit plan investor) who has discretionary authority or control with respect to the assets of the entity or any person who provides investment advice for a fee (direct or indirect) with respect to such assets, or any affiliate of such a person, shall be disregarded.

(2) A "benefit plan investor" is any of the following—

(i) Any employee benefit plan (as defined in section 3(3) of the Act), whether or not it is subject to the provisions of Title I of the Act,

(ii) Any plan described in section 4975(e)(1) of the Internal Revenue Code,

(iii) Any entity whose underlying assets include plan assets by reason of a plan's investment in the entity.

(3) An "affiliate" of a person includes any person, directly or indirectly, through one or more intermediaries, controlling, controlled by, or under common control with the person. For purposes of this paragraph (f)(3), "control", with respect to a person other than an individual, means the power to exercise a controlling influence over the management or policies of such person.

(g) *Joint ownership*. For purposes of this section, where a plan jointly owns property with others, or where the value of a plan's equity interest in an entity relates solely to identified property of the entity, such property shall be treated as the sole property of a separate entity.

(h) *Specific rules relating to plan investments*. Notwithstanding any other provision of this section—

(1) Except where the entity is an investment company registered under the Investment Company Act of 1940, when a plan acquires or holds an interest in any of the following entities its assets include its

investment and an undivided interest in each of the underlying assets of the entity:

(i) A group trust which is exempt from taxation under section 501(a) of the Internal Revenue Code pursuant to the principles of Rev. Rul. 81-100, 1981-1 C.B. 326,

(ii) A common or collective trust fund of a bank,

(iii) A separate account of an insurance company, other than a separate account that is maintained solely in connection with fixed contractual obligations of the insurance company under which the amounts payable, or credited, to the plan and to any participant or beneficiary of the plan (including an annuitant) are not affected in any manner by the investment performance of the separate account.

(2) When a plan acquires or holds an interest in any entity (other than an insurance company licensed to do business in a State) which is established or maintained for the purpose of offering or providing any benefit described in section 3(1) or section 3(2) of the Act to participants or beneficiaries of the investing plan, its assets will include its investment and an undivided interest in the underlying assets of that entity.

(3) When a plan or a related group of plans owns all of the outstanding equity interests (other than director's qualifying shares) in an entity, its assets include those equity interests and all of the underlying assets of the entity. This paragraph (h)(3) does not apply, however, where all of the outstanding equity interests in an entity are qualifying employer securities described in section 407(d)(5) of the Act, owned by one or more eligible individual account plan(s) (as defined in section 407(d)(3) of the Act) maintained by the same employer, provided that substantially all of the participants in the plan(s) are, or have been, employed by the issuer of such securities or by members of a group of affiliated corporations (as determined under section 407(d)(7) of the Act) of which the issuer is a member.

(4) For purposes of paragraph (h)(3), a "related group" of employee benefit plans consists of every group of two or more employee benefit plans—

(i) Each of which receives 10 percent or more of its aggregate contributions from the same employer or from members of the same controlled group of corporations (as determined under section 1563(a) of the Internal Revenue Code, without regard to section 1563(a)(4) thereof); or

(ii) Each of which is either maintained by, or maintained pursuant to a collective bargaining agreement negotiated by, the same employee organization or affiliated employee organizations. For purposes of this paragraph, an "affiliate" of an employee organization means any person controlling, controlled by, or under common control with such organization, and includes any organization chartered by the same parent body, or governed by the same constitution and bylaws, or having the relation of parent and subordinate.

(i) *Governmental mortgage pools.* (1) Where a plan acquires a guaranteed governmental mortgage pool certificate, as defined in paragraph (i)(2), the plan's assets include the certificate and all of its rights with respect to such certificate under applicable law, but do not, solely by reason of the plan's holding of such certificate, include any of the mortgages underlying such certificate.

(2) A "guaranteed governmental mortgage pool certificate" is a certificate backed by, or evidencing an interest in, specified mortgages or participation interests therein and with respect to which interest and principal payable pursuant to the certificate is guaranteed by the United States or an agency or instrumentality thereof. The term "guaranteed governmental mortgage pool certificate" includes a mortgage pool certificate with respect to which interest and principal payment pursuant to the certificate is guaranteed by:

(i) The Government National Mortgage Association;

(ii) The Federal Home Loan Mortgage Corporation; or

(iii) The Federal National Mortgage Association.

(j) *Examples.* The principles of this section are illustrated by the following examples:

(1) A plan, P, acquires debentures issued by a corporation, T, pursuant to a private offering. T is engaged primarily in investing and reinvesting in precious metals on behalf of its shareholders, all of which are benefit plan investors. By its terms, the debenture is convert-

ible to common stock of T at P's option. At the time of P's acquisition of the debentures, the conversion feature is incidental to T's obligation to pay interest and principal. Although T is not an operating company, P's assets do not include an interest in the underlying assets of T because P has not acquired an *equity* interest in T. However, if P exercises its option to convert the debentures to common stock, it will have acquired an equity interest in T at that time and (assuming that the common stock is not a publicly-offered security and that there has been no change in the composition of the other equity investors in T) P's assets would then include an undivided interest in the underlying assets of T.

(2) A plan, P, acquires a limited partnership interest in a limited partnership, U, which is established and maintained by A, a general partner in U. U has only one class of limited partnership interests. U is engaged in the business of investing and reinvesting in securities. Limited partnership interests in U are offered privately pursuant to an exemption from the registration requirements of the Securities Act of 1933. P acquires 15 percent of the value of all the outstanding limited partnership interests in U, and, at the time of P's investment, a governmental plan owns 15 percent of the value of those interests. U is not an operating company because it is engaged primarily in the investment of capital. In addition, equity participation by benefit plan investors is significant because immediately after P's investment such investors hold more than 25 percent of the limited partnership interests in U. Accordingly, P's assets include an undivided interest in the underlying assets of U, and A is a fiduciary of P with respect to such assets by reason of its discretionary authority and control over U's assets. Although the governmental plan's investment is taken into account for purposes of determining whether equity participation by benefit plan investors is significant, nothing in this section imposes fiduciary obligations on A with respect to that plan.

(3) Assume the same facts as in paragraph (j)(2), except that P acquires only 5 percent of the value of all the outstanding limited partnership interests in U, and that benefit plan investors in the aggregate hold only 10 percent of the value of the limited partnership interests in U. Under these facts, there is no significant equity participation by benefit plan investors in U, and, accordingly, P's assets include its limited partnership interest in U, but do not include any of the underlying assets of U. Thus, A would not be a fiduciary of P by reason of P's investment.

(4) Assume the same facts as in paragraph (j)(3) and that the aggregate value of the outstanding limited partnership interests in U is $10,000 (and that the value of the interests held by benefit plan investors is thus $1000). Also assume that an affiliate of A owns limited partnership interests in U having a value of $6500. The value of the limited partnership interests held by A's affiliate are disregarded for purposes of determining whether there is significant equity participation in U by benefit plan investors. Thus, the percentage of the aggregate value of the limited partnership interests held by benefit plan investors in U for purposes of such a determination is approximately 28.6% ($1000/$3500). Therefore there is significant benefit plan investment in T.

(5) A plan, P, invests in a limited partnership, V, pursuant to a private offering. There is significant equity participation by benefit plan investors in V. V acquires equity positions in the companies in which it invests, and, in connection with these investments, V negotiates terms that give it the right to participate in or influence the management of those companies. Some of these investments are in publicly-offered securities and some are in securities acquired in private offerings. During its most recent valuation period, more than 50 percent of V's assets, valued at cost, consisted of investments with respect to which V obtained management rights of the kind described above. V's managers routinely consult informally with, and advise, the management of only one portfolio company with respect to which it has management rights, although it devotes substantial resources to its consultations with that company. With respect to the other portfolio companies, V relies on the managers of other entities to consult with and advise the companies' management. V is a venture capital operating company and therefore P has acquired its limited partnership investment, but has not acquired an interest in any of the underlying assets of V. Thus, none of the managers of V would be fiduciaries with respect to P solely by reason of its investment. In this situation, the mere fact that V does not participate in or influence the management of all its portfolio compa-

nies does not affect its characterization as a venture capital operating company.

(6) Assume the same facts as in paragraph (j)(5) and the following additional facts: V invests in debt securities as well as equity securities of its portfolio companies. In some cases V makes debt investments in companies in which it also has an equity investment; in other cases V only invests in debt instruments of the portfolio company. V's debt investments are acquired pursuant to private offerings and V negotiates covenants that give it the right to substantially participate in or to substantially influence the conduct of the management of the companies issuing the obligations. These covenants give V more significant rights with respect to the portfolio companies' management than the covenants ordinarily found in debt instruments of established, creditworthy companies that are purchased privately by institutional investors. V routinely consults with and advises the management of its portfolio companies. The mere fact that V's investments in portfolio companies are debt, rather than equity, will not cause V to fail to be a venture capital operating company, provided it actually obtains the right to substantially participate in or influence the conduct of the management of its portfolio companies and provided that in the ordinary course of its business it actually exercises those rights.

(7) A plan, P, invests (pursuant to a private offering) in a limited partnership, W, that is engaged primarily in investing and reinvesting assets in equity positions in real property. The properties acquired by W are subject to long-term leases under which substantially all management and maintenance activities with respect to the property are the responsibility of the lessee. W is not engaged in the management or development of real estate merely because it assumes the risks of ownership of income-producing real property, and W is not a real estate operating company. If there is significant equity participation in W by benefit plan investors, P will be considered to have acquired an undivided interest in each of the underlying assets of W.

(8) Assume the same facts as in paragraph (j)(7) except that W owns several shopping centers in which individual stores are leased for relatively short periods to various merchants (rather than owning properties subject to long-term leases under which substantially all management and maintenance activities are the responsibility of the lessee). W retains independent contractors to manage the shopping center properties. These independent contractors negotiate individual leases, maintain the common areas and conduct maintenance activities with respect to the properties. W has the responsibility to supervise and the authority to terminate the independent contractors. During its most recent valuation period more than 50 percent of W's assets, valued at cost, are invested in such properties. W is a real estate operating company. The fact that W does not have its own employees who engage in day-to-day management and development activities is only one factor in determining whether it is actively managing or developing real estate. Thus, P's assets include its interest in W, but do not include any of the underlying assets of W.

(9) A plan, P, acquires a limited partnership interest in X pursuant to a private offering. There is significant equity participation in X by benefit plan investors. X is engaged in the business of making "convertible loans" which are structured as follows: X lends a specified percentage of the cost of acquiring real property to a borrower who provides the remaining capital needed to make the acquisition. This loan is secured by a mortgage on the property. Under the terms of the loan, X is entitled to receive a fixed rate of interest payable out of the initial cash flow from the property and is also entitled to that portion of any additional cash flow which is equal to the percentage of the acquisition cost that is financed by its loan. Simultaneously with the making of the loan, the borrower also gives X an option to purchase an interest in the property for the original principal amount of the loan at the expiration of its initial term. X's percentage interest in the property, if it exercises this option, would be equal to the percentage of the acquisition cost of the property which is financed by its loan. The parties to the transaction contemplate that the option ordinarily will be exercised at the expiration of the loan term if the property has appreciated in value. X and the borrower also agree that, if the option is exercised, they will form a limited partnership to hold the property. X negotiates loan terms which give it rights to substantially influence, or to substantially participate in, the management of the property which is acquired with the proceeds of the loan. These loan terms give X significantly greater rights to participate in the management of the

property than it would obtain under a conventional mortgage loan. In addition, under the terms of the loan, X and the borrower ratably share any capital expenditures relating to the property. During its most recent valuation period, more than 50 percent of the value of X's assets valued at cost consisted of real estate investment of the kind described above. X, in the ordinary course of its business, routinely exercises its management rights and frequently consults with and advises the borrower and the property manager. Under these facts, X is a real estate operating company. Thus, P's assets include its interest in X, but do not include any of the underlying assets of X.

(10) In a private transaction, a plan, P, acquires a 30 percent participation in a debt instrument that is held by a bank. Since the value of the participation certificate relates solely to the debt instrument, that debt instrument is, under paragraph (g), treated as the sole asset of a separate entity. Equity participation in that entity by benefit plan investors is significant since the value of the plan's participation exceeds 25 percent of the value of the instrument. In addition, the hypothetical entity is not an operating company because it is primarily engaged in the investment of capital (*i.e.,* holding the debt instrument). Thus, P's assets include the participation and an undivided interest in the debt instrument, and the bank is a fiduciary of P to the extent it has discretionary authority or control over the debt instrument.

(11) In a private transaction, a plan, P, acquires 30% of the value of class equity securities issued by an operating company, Y. These securities provide that dividends shall be paid solely out of earnings attributable to certain tracts of undeveloped land that are held by Y for investment. Under paragraph (g), the property is treated as the sole asset of a separate entity. Thus, even though Y is an operating company, the hypothetical entity whose sole assets are the undeveloped tracts of land is not an operating company. Accordingly, P is considered to have acquired an undivided interest in the tracts of land held by Y. Thus, Y would be a fiduciary of P to the extent it exercises discretionary authority or control over such property.

(12) A medical benefit plan, P, acquires a beneficial interest in a trust, Z, that is not an insurance company licensed to do business in a State. Under this arrangement, Z will provide the benefits to the participants and beneficiaries of P that are promised under the terms of the plan. Under paragraph (h)(2), P's assets include its beneficial interest in Z and an undivided interest in each of its underlying assets. Thus, persons with discretionary authority or control over the assets of Z would be fiduciaries of P.

(k) *Effective date and transitional rules.* (1) In general, this section is effective for purposes of identifying the assets of a plan on or after March 13, 1987. Except as a defense, this section shall not apply to investments in an entity in existence on March 13, 1987, if no plan subject to Title I of the Act or plan described in section 4975(e)(1) of the Code (other than a plan described in section 4975(g)(2) or 4975(g)(3)) acquires an interest in the entity from an issuer or underwriter at any time on or after March 13, 1987 except pursuant to a contract binding on the plan in effect on March 13, 1987 with an issuer or underwriter to acquire an interest in the entity.

(2) Notwithstanding paragraph (k)(1), this section shall not, except as a defense, apply to a real estate entity described in section 11018(a) of Pub. L. 99-272.

[Added by 51 FR 41280 on November 13, 1986, effective Mar. 13, 1987.]

[¶ 14,139N]

§ 2510.3-102 **Definition of "plan assets"—participant contributions.** (a)(1) *General rule.* For purposes of subtitle A and parts 1 and 4 of subtitle B of title I of ERISA and section 4975 of the Internal Revenue Code only (but without any implication for and may not be relied upon to bar criminal prosecutions under 18 U.S.C. 664), the assets of the plan include amounts (other than union dues) that a participant or beneficiary pays to an employer, or amounts that a participant has withheld from his wages by an employer, for contribution or repayment of a participant loan to the plan, as of the earliest date on which such contributions or repayments can reasonably be segregated from the employer's general assets. [Amended January 14, 2010 by 75 FR 2068.]

(2) *Safe harbor.* (i) For purposes of paragraph (a)(1) of this section, in the case of a plan with fewer than 100 participants at the

beginning of the plan year, any amount deposited with such plan not later than the 7th business day following the day on which such amount is received by the employer (in the case of amounts that a participant or beneficiary pays to an employer), or the 7th business day following the day on which such amount would otherwise have been payable to the participant in cash (in the case of amounts withheld by an employer from a participant's wages), shall be deemed to be contributed or repaid to such plan on the earliest date on which such contributions or participant loan repayments can reasonably be segregated from the employer's general assets.

(ii) This paragraph (a)(2) sets forth an optional alternative method of compliance with the rule set forth in paragraph (a)(1) of this section. This paragraph (a)(2) does not establish the exclusive means by which participant contribution or participant loan repayment amounts shall be considered to be contributed or repaid to a plan by the earliest date on which such contributions or repayments can reasonably be segregated from the employer's general assets. [Added January 14, 2010 by 75 FR 2068.]

(b) *Maximum time period for pension benefit plans.* (1) Except as provided in paragraph (b)(2) of this section, with respect to an employee pension benefit plan as defined in section 3(2) of ERISA, in no event shall the date determined pursuant to paragraph (a)(1) of this section occur later than the 15th business day of the month following the month in which the participant contribution or participant loan repayment amounts are received by the employer (in the case of amounts that a participant or beneficiary pays to an employer) or the 15th business day of the month following the month in which such amounts would otherwise have been payable to the participant in cash (in the case of amounts withheld by an employer from a participant's wages).

(2) With respect to a SIMPLE plan that involves SIMPLE IRAs (*i.e.,* Simple Retirement Accounts, as described in section 408(p) of the Internal Revenue Code), in no event shall the date determined pursuant to paragraph (a)(1) of this section occur later than the 30th calendar day following the month in which the participant contribution amounts would otherwise have been payable to the participant in cash. [Amended by 62 FR 62934 on November 25, 1997, effective immediately.] [Amended January 14, 2010 by 75 FR 2068.]

(c) *Maximum time period for welfare benefit plans.* With respect to an employee welfare benefit plan as defined in section 3(1) of ERISA, in no event shall the date determined pursuant to paragraph (a)(1) of this section occur later than 90 days from the date on which the participant contribution amounts are received by the employer (in the case of amounts that a participant or beneficiary pays to an employer) or the date on which such amounts would otherwise have been payable to the participant in cash (in the case of amounts withheld by an employer from a participant's wages). [Amended January 14, 2010 by 75 FR 2068.]

(d) *Extension of maximum time period for pension plans.* (1) With respect to participant contributions received or withheld by the employer in a single month, the maximum time period provided under paragraph (b) of this section shall be extended for an additional 10 business days for an employer who—

(i) Provides a true and accurate written notice, distributed in a manner reasonably designed to reach all the plan participants within 5 business days after the end of such extension period, stating—

(A) That the employer elected to take such extension for that month;

(B) That the affected contributions have been transmitted to the plan; and

(C) With particularity, the reasons why the employer cannot reasonably segregate the participant contributions within the time period described in paragraph (b) of this section;

(ii) Prior to such extension period, obtains a performance bond or irrevocable letter of credit in favor of the plan and in an amount of not less than the total amount of participant contributions received or withheld by the employer in the previous month; and

(iii) Within 5 business days after the end of such extension period, provides a copy of the notice required under paragraph (d)(1)(i) of this section to the Secretary, along with a certification that

such notice was provided to the participants and that the bond or letter of credit required under paragraph (d)(1)(ii) of this section was obtained.

(2) The performance bond or irrevocable letter of credit required in paragraph (d)(1)(ii) of this section shall be guaranteed by a bank or similar institution that is supervised by the Federal government or a State government and shall remain in effect for 3 months after the month in which the extension expires.

(3)(i) An employer may not elect an extension under this paragraph (d) more than twice in any plan year unless the employer pays to the plan an amount representing interest on the participant contributions that were subject to all the extensions within such plan year.

(ii) The amount representing interest in paragraph (d)(3)(i) of this section shall be the greater of—

(A) The amount that otherwise would have been earned on the participant contributions from the date on which such contributions were paid to, or withheld by, the employer until such money is transmitted to the plan had such contributions been invested during such period in the investment alternative available under plan which had the highest rate of return; or

(B) Interest at a rate equal to the underpayment rate defined in section 6621(a)(2) of the Internal Revenue Code from the date on which such contributions were paid to, or withheld by, the employer until such money is fully restored to the plan.

(e) *Definition.* For purposes of this section, the term *business day* means any day other than a Saturday, Sunday or any day designated as a holiday by the Federal Government.

(f) *Examples.* The requirements of this section are illustrated by the following examples:

(1) Employer A sponsors a 401(k) plan. There are 30 participants in the 401(k) plan. A has one payroll period for its employees and uses an outside payroll processing service to pay employee wages and process deductions. A has established a system under which the payroll processing service provides payroll deduction information to A within 1 business day after the issuance of paychecks. A checks this information for accuracy within 5 business days and then forwards the withheld employee contributions to the plan. The amount of the total withheld employee contributions is deposited with the trust that is maintained under the plan on the 7th business day following the date on which the employees are paid. Under the safe harbor in paragraph (a)(2) of this section, when the participant contributions are deposited with the plan on the 7th business day following a pay date, the participant contributions are deemed to be contributed to the plan on the earliest date on which such contributions can reasonably be segregated from A's general assets. [Amended January 14, 2010 by 75 FR 2068.]

(2) Employer B is a large national corporation which sponsors a 401(k) plan with 600 participants. B has several payroll centers and uses an outside payroll processing service to pay employee wages and process deductions. Each payroll center has a different pay period. Each center maintains separate accounts on its books for purposes of accounting for that center's payroll deductions and provides the outside payroll processor the data necessary to prepare employee paychecks and process deductions. The payroll processing service issues the employees' paychecks and deducts all payroll taxes and elective employee deductions. The payroll processing service forwards the employee payroll deduction data to B on the date of issuance of paychecks. B checks this data for accuracy and transmits this data along with the employee 401(k) deferral funds to the plan's investment firm within 3 business days. The plan's investment firm deposits the employee 401(k) deferral funds into the plan on the day received from B. The assets of B's 401(k) plan would include the participant contributions no later than 3 business days after the issuance of paychecks. [Amended January 14, 2010 by 75 FR 2068.]

(3) Employer C sponsors a self-insured contributory group health plan with 90 participants. Several former employees have elected, pursuant to the provisions of ERISA section 602, 29 U.S.C. 1162, to pay C for continuation of their coverage under the plan. These checks arrive at various times during the month and are deposited in the employer's general account at bank Z. Under paragraphs (a) and (c) of this section, the assets of the plan include the former employees'

payments as soon after the checks have cleared the bank as C could reasonably be expected to segregate the payments from its general assets, but in no event later than 90 days after the date on which the former employees' participant contributions are received by C. If, however, C deposits the former employees' payments with the plan no later than the 7th business day following the day on which they are received by C, the former employees' participant contributions will be deemed to be contributed to the plan on the earliest date on which such contributions can reasonably be segregated from C's general assets. [Amended January 14, 2010 by 75 FR 2068.]

(4) Employer Y is a medium-sized company which maintains a self-insured contributory group health plan. Several former employees have elected, pursuant to the provisions of ERISA section 602, 29 U.S.C. 1162, to pay Y for continuation of their coverage under the plan. These checks arrive at various times during the month and are deposited in the employer's general account at bank Z. Under paragraphs (a) and (b) of this section, the assets of the plan include the former employees' payments as soon after the checks have cleared the bank as Y could reasonably be expected to segregate the payments from its general assets, but in no event later than the 90 days after a participant or beneficiary, including a former employee, pays to an employer, or has withheld from his wages by an employer, money for contribution to the plan.

(g) *Effective date.* This section is effective February 3, 1997.

(h) *Applicability date for collectively-bargained plans.* (1) Paragraph (b) of this section applies to collectively-bargained plans no sooner that the later of—

(i) February 3, 1997; or

(ii) The first day of the plan year that begins after the expiration of the last to expire of any applicable bargaining agreement in effect on August 7, 1996.

(2) Until paragraph (b) of this section applies to a collectively-bargained plan, paragraph (c) of this section shall apply to such plan as if such plan were an employee welfare benefit plan.

(i) *Optional postponement of applicability.* (1) The application of paragraph (b) of this section (g) shall be postponed for up to an additional 90 days beyond the effective date described in paragraph (g) of this section for an employer who, prior to February 3, 1997—

(i) Provides a true and accurate written notice, distributed in a manner designed to reach all the plan participants before the end of February 3, 1997, stating—

(A) That the employer elected to postpone such applicability;

(B) The date that the postponement will expire; and

(C) With particularity the reasons why the employer cannot reasonably segregate the participant contributions within the time period described in paragraph (b) of this section, by February 3, 1997;

(ii) Obtains a performance bond or irrevocable letter of credit in favor of the plan and in an amount of not less than the total amount of participant contributions received or withheld by the employer in the previous 3 months;

(iii) Provides a copy of the notice required under paragraph (i)(1)(i) of this section to the Secretary, along with a certification that such notice was provided to the participants and that the bond or letter of credit required under paragraph (i)(1)(ii) of this section was obtained; and

(iv) For each month during which such postponement is in effect, provides a true and accurate written notice to the plan participants indicating the date on which the participant contributions received or withheld by the employer during such month were transmitted to the plan.

(2) The notice required in paragraph (i)(1)(iv) of this section shall be distributed in a manner reasonably designed to reach all the plan participants within 10 days after transmission of the affected participant contributions.

(3) The bond or letter of credit required under paragraph (i)(1)(ii) shall be guaranteed by a bank or similar institution that is supervised by the Federal government or a State government and shall remain in effect for 3 months after the month in which the postponement expires.

(4) During the period of any postponement of applicability with respect to a plan under this paragraph (i), paragraph (c) of this section shall apply to such plan as if such plan were an employee welfare benefit plan.

[Adopted by 53 FR 17628, May 17, 1988, amended by 61 FR 41220 on August 7, 1996, effective February 3, 1997, amended by 62 FR 62934 on November 24, 1997, effective on November 25, 1997. Amended by 75 FR 2068 on January 14, 2010, effective on January 14, 2010.]

[¶ 14,140]
COVERAGE

Act Sec. 4. (a) IN GENERAL.—Except as provided in subsection (b) or (c) and in sections 201, 301, and 401, this title shall apply to any employee benefit plan if it is established or maintained—

(1) by any employer engaged in commerce or in any industry or activity affecting commerce; or

(2) by any employee organization or organizations representing employees engaged in commerce or in any industry or activity affecting commerce; or

(3) by both.

Act Sec. 4. (b) EXCEPTIONS FOR CERTAIN PLANS.—The provisions of this title shall not apply to any employee benefit plan if—

(1) such plan is a governmental plan (as defined in section 3(32));

(2) such plan is a church plan (as defined in section 3(33)) with respect to which no election has been made under section 410(d) of the Internal Revenue Code of 1986;

(3) such plan is maintained solely for the purpose of complying with applicable workmen's compensation laws or unemployment compensation or disability insurance laws;

(4) such plan is maintained outside of the United States primarily for the benefit of persons substantially all of whom are nonresident aliens; or

(5) such plan is an excess benefit plan (as defined in section 3(36)) and is unfunded.

The provisions of part 7 of subtitle B shall not apply to a health insurance issuer (as defined in section 706(b)(2)) solely by reason of health insurance coverage (as defined in section 706(b)(1) provided by such issuer in connection with a group health plan (as defined in section 706(a)(1)) if the provisions of this title do not apply to such group health plan.

Act Sec. 4. (c) VOLUNTARY EMPLOYEE CONTRIBUTIONS TO ACCOUNTS AND ANNUITIES.— If a pension plan allows an employee to elect to make voluntary employee contributions to accounts and annuities as provided in section 408(q) of the Internal Revenue Code of 1986, such accounts and annuities (and contributions thereto) shall not be treated as part of such plan (or as a separate pension plan) for purposes of any provision of this title other than section 403(c), 404, or 405 (relating to exclusive benefit, and fiduciary and co-fiduciary responsibilities) and part 5 (relating to administration and enforcement). Such provisions shall apply to such accounts and annuities in a manner similar to their application to a simplified employee pension under section 408(k) of the Internal Revenue Code of 1986.

Amendments

P.L. 109-280, §811:

SEC. 811. PENSIONS AND INDIVIDUAL RETIREMENT ARRANGEMENT PROVISIONS OF ECONOMIC GROWTH AND TAX RELIEF RECONCILIATION ACT OF 2001 MADE PERMANENT.

Title IX of the Economic Growth and Tax Relief Reconciliation Act of 2001 [P.L. 107-16] shall not apply to the provisions of, and amendments made by, subtitles A through F of title VI [§§601-666]of such Act (relating to pension and individual retirement arrangement provisions).

P.L. 107-147, §411(i)(2):

Amended ERISA Sec. 4(c) by inserting "and part 5 (relating to administration and enforcement" before the period at the end and by adding a new sentence at the end to read as above.

The above amendment is effective for plan years beginning after December 31, 2002, subject to sunset after 2010 under P.L. 107-16, Sec. 901.

P.L. 107-16, §602(b)(1):

Amended ERISA Sec. 4 by adding at the end a new subsection (c) to read as above.

The above amendment is effective for plan years beginning after December 31, 2002 subject to the sunset after 2010 under P.L. 107-16, Sec. 901 [but see P.L. 109-280, §811, above].

P.L. 107-16, §602(b)(2):

Amended ERISA Sec. 4(a) by inserting "or (c)" after "subsection (b)".

The above amendment is effective for plan years beginning after December 31, 2002 subject to the sunset after 2010 under P.L. 107-16, Sec. 901 [but see P.L. 109-280, §811, above].

P.L. 104-191, §101(d):

Amended ERISA Sec. 4(b) by adding at the end, after and below paragraph (5), a new sentence to read as above.

The above amendment generally applies with respect to group health plans for plan years beginning after June 30, 1997. For special rules, see Act Sec. 101(g)(2)- (5), reproduced below.

Act Sec. 101(g)(2)-(5) reads as follows:

(g) EFFECTIVE DATES.—

(1) IN GENERAL.—Except as provided in this section, this section (and the amendments made by this section) shall apply with respect to group health plans for plan years beginning after June 30, 1997.

(2) DETERMINATION OF CREDITABLE COVERAGE.—

(A) PERIOD OF COVERAGE.—

(i) IN GENERAL.—Subject to clause (ii), no period before July 1, 1996, shall be taken into account under part 7 of subtitle B of title I of the Employee Retirement Income Security Act of 1974 (as added by this section) in determining creditable coverage.

(ii) SPECIAL RULE FOR CERTAIN PERIODS.—The Secretary of Labor, consistent with section 104, shall provide for a process whereby individuals who need to establish creditable coverage for periods before July 1, 1996, and who would have such coverage credited but for clause (i) may be given credit for creditable coverage for such periods through the presentation of documents or other means.

(B) CERTIFICATIONS, ETC.—

(i) IN GENERAL.—Subject to clauses (ii) and (iii), subsection (e) of section 701 of the Employee Retirement Income Security Act of 1974 (as added by this section) shall apply to events occurring after June 30, 1996.

(ii) NO CERTIFICATION REQUIRED TO BE PROVIDED BEFORE JUNE 1, 1997.—In no case is a certification required to be provided under such subsection before June 1, 1997.

(iii) CERTIFICATION ONLY ON WRITTEN REQUEST FOR EVENTS OCCURRING BEFORE OCTOBER 1, 1996.—In the case of an event occurring after June 30, 1996, and before October 1, 1996, a certification is not required to be provided under such subsection unless an individual (with respect to whom the certification is otherwise required to be made) requests such certification in writing.

(C) TRANSITIONAL RULE.—In the case of an individual who seeks to establish creditable coverage for any period for which certification is not required because it relates to an event occurring before June 30, 1996—

(i) the individual may present other credible evidence of such coverage in order to establish the period of creditable coverage; and

(ii) a group health plan and a health insurance issuer shall not be subject to any penalty or enforcement action with respect to the plan's or issuer's crediting (or not crediting) such coverage if the plan or issuer has sought to comply in good faith with the applicable requirements under the amendments made by this section.

(3) SPECIAL RULE FOR COLLECTIVE BARGAINING AGREEMENTS.—Except as provided in paragraph (2), in the case of a group health plan maintained pursuant to one or more collective bargaining agreements between employee representatives and one or more employers ratified before the date of the enactment of this Act, part 7 of subtitle B of title I of Employee Retirement Income Security Act of 1974 (other than section 701(e) thereof) shall not apply to plan years beginning before the later of—

(A) the date on which the last of the collective bargaining agreements relating to the plan terminates (determined without regard to any extension thereof agreed to after the date of the enactment of this Act), or

(B) July 1, 1997.

For purposes of subparagraph (A), any plan amendment made pursuant to a collective bargaining agreement relating to the plan which amends the plan solely to conform to any requirement of such part shall not be treated as a termination of such collective bargaining agreement.

(4) TIMELY REGULATIONS.—The Secretary of Labor, consistent with section 104, shall first issue by not later than April 1, 1997, such regulations as may be necessary to carry out the amendments made by this section.

(5) LIMITATION ON ACTIONS.—No enforcement action shall be taken, pursuant to the amendments made by this section, against a group health plan or health insurance issuer with respect to a violation of a requirement imposed by such amendments before January 1, 1998, or, if later, the date of issuance of regulations referred to in paragraph (4), if the plan or issuer has sought to comply in good faith with such requirements.

Subtitle B—Regulatory Provisions

Part 1—Reporting and Disclosure

»»→ *Caution: Interpretive Bulletins Relating to Reporting and Disclosure are reproduced beginning at ¶ 14,370.—CCH.*

[¶ 14,210]
DUTY OF DISCLOSURE AND REPORTING

Act Sec. 101.(a) SUMMARY PLAN DESCRIPTION AND INFORMATION TO BE FURNISHED TO PARTICIPANTS AND BENEFICIARIES. The administrator of each employee benefit plan shall cause to be furnished in accordance with section 104(b) to each participant covered under the plan and to each beneficiary who is receiving benefits under the plan—

(1) a summary plan description described in section 102(a)(1); and

(2) the information described in subsection (f) and sections 104(b)(3) and 105(a) and (c).

Act Sec. 101. (b) REPORTS TO BE FILED WITH SECRETARY OF LABOR. The administrator shall, in accordance with section 104(a), file with the Secretary—

(1) the annual report containing the information required by section 103; and

(2) terminal and supplementary reports as required by subsection (c) of this section.

Act Sec. 101.(c)(1) TERMINAL AND SUPPLEMENTARY REPORTS. Each administrator of an employee pension benefit plan which is winding up its affairs (without regard to the number of participants remaining in the plan) shall, in accordance with regulations prescribed by the Secretary, file such terminal reports as the Secretary may consider necessary. A copy of such report shall also be filed with the Pension Benefit Guaranty Corporation.

(2) The Secretary may require terminal reports to be filed with regard to any employee welfare benefit plan which is winding up its affairs in accordance with regulations promulgated by the Secretary.

(3) The Secretary may require that a plan described in paragraph (1) or (2) file a supplementary or terminal report with the annual report in the year such plan is terminated and that a copy of such supplementary or terminal report in the case of a plan described in paragraph (1) be also filed with the Pension Benefit Guaranty Corporation.

Act Sec. 101. (d) NOTICE OF FAILURE TO MEET MINIMUM FUNDING STANDARDS.—

(1) IN GENERAL. If an employer maintaining a plan other than a multiemployer plan fails to make a required installment or other payment required to meet the minimum funding standard under section 302 to a plan before the 60th day following the due date for such installment or other payment, the employer shall notify each participant and beneficiary (including an alternate payee as defined in section 206(d)(3)(K)) of such plan of such failure. Such notice shall be made at such time and in such manner as the Secretary may prescribe.

(2) SUBSECTION NOT TO APPLY IF WAIVER PENDING. This subsection shall not apply to any failure if the employer has filed a waiver request under section 303 or 306 with respect to the plan year to which the required installment relates, except that if the waiver request is denied, notice under paragraph (1) shall be provided within 60 days after the date of such denial.

(3) DEFINITIONS. For purposes of this subsection, the terms "required installment" and "due date" have the same meanings given such terms by section 303(j) or 306(f), whichever is applicable.

Act Sec. 101. (e) Notice of Transfer of Excess Pension Assets to Health Benefits Accounts.—

(1) Notice to Participants. Not later than 60 days before the date of a qualified transfer by an employee pension benefit plan of excess pension assets to a health benefits account or applicable life insurance account, the administrator of the plan shall notify (in such manner as the Secretary may prescribe) each participant and beneficiary under the plan of such transfer. Such notice shall include information with respect to the amount of excess pension assets, the portion to be transferred, the amount of health benefits liabilities or applicable life insurance benefit liabilities expected to be provided with the assets transferred, and the amount of pension benefits of the participant which will be nonforfeitable immediately after the transfer.

(2) Notice to Secretaries, Administrator, and Employee Organizations.—

(A) In General. Not later than 60 days before the date of any qualified transfer by an employee pension benefit plan of excess pension assets to a health benefits account or applicable life insurance account, the employer maintaining the plan from which the transfer is made shall provide the Secretary, the Secretary of the Treasury, the administrator, and each employee organization representing participants in the plan a written notice of such transfer. A copy of any such notice shall be available for inspection in the principal office of the administrator.

(B) Information relating to transfer. Such notice shall identify the plan from which the transfer is made, the amount of the transfer, a detailed accounting of assets projected to be held by the plan immediately before and immediately after the transfer, and the current liabilities under the plan at the time of the transfer.

(C) Authority for additional reporting requirements. The Secretary may prescribe such additional reporting requirements as may be necessary to carry out the purposes of this section.

(3) Definitions. For purposes of paragraph (1), any term used in such paragraph which is also used in section 420 of the Internal Revenue Code of 1986 (as in effect on the date of the enactment of the Surface Transportation and Veterans Health Care Choice Improvement Act of 2015) shall have the same meaning as when used in such section.

Act Sec. 101. (f) Defined benefit plan funding notices.—

(1) In General. The administrator of a defined benefit plan to which title IV applies shall for each plan year provide a plan funding notice to the Pension Benefit Guaranty Corporation, to each plan participant and beneficiary, to each labor organization representing such participants or beneficiaries, and, in the case of a multiemployer plan, to each employer that has an obligation to contribute to the plan.

(2) Information Contained in notices.—

(A) Identifying information. Each notice required under paragraph (1) shall contain identifying information, including the name of the plan, the address and phone number of the plan administrator and the plan's principal administrative officer, each plan sponsor's employer identification number, and the plan number of the plan.

(B) Specific information. A plan funding notice under paragraph (1) shall include—

(i)(I) in the case of a single-employer plan, a statement as to whether the plan's funding target attainment percentage (as defined in section 303(d)(2)) for the plan year to which the notice relates, and for the 2 preceding plan years, is at least 100 percent (and, if not, the actual percentages), or

(II) in the case of a multiemployer plan, a statement as to whether the plan's funded percentage (as defined in section 305(i)) for the plan year to which the notice relates, and for the 2 preceding plan years, is at least 100 percent (and, if not, the actual percentages),

(ii)(I) in the case of a single-employer plan, a statement of —

(aa) the total assets (separately stating the prefunding balance and the funding standard carryover balance) and liabilities of the plan, determined in the same manner as under section 303, for the plan year to which the notice relates and for the 2 preceding plan years, as reported in the annual report for each such plan year, and

(bb) the value of the plan's assets and liabilities for the plan year to which the notice relates as of the last day of the plan year to which the notice relates determined using the asset valuation under subclause (II) of section 4006(a)(3)(E)(iii) and the interest rate under section 4006(a)(3)(E)(iv), and

(II) in the case of a multiemployer plan, a statement, for the plan year to which the notice relates and the preceding 2 plan years, of the value of the plan assets (determined both in the same manner as under section 304 and under the rules of subclause (I)(bb)) and the value of the plan liabilities (determined in the same manner as under section 304 except that the method specified in section 305(i)(8) shall be used),

(iii) a statement of the number of participants who are—

(I) retired or separated from service and are receiving benefits,

(II) retired or separated participants entitled to future benefits, and

(III) active participants under the plan,

(iv) a statement setting forth the funding policy of the plan and the asset allocation of investments under the plan (expressed as percentages of total assets) as of the end of the plan year to which the notice relates,

(v) in the case of a multiemployer plan, whether the plan was in critical or endangered status under section 305 for such plan year and, if so—

(I) a statement describing how a person may obtain a copy of the plan's funding improvement or rehabilitation plan, as appropriate, adopted under section 305 and the actuarial and financial data that demonstrate any action taken by the plan toward fiscal improvement, and

(II) a summary of any funding improvement plan, rehabilitation plan, or modification thereof adopted under section 305 during the plan year to which the notice relates,

(vi) in the case of a multiemployer plan, whether the plan was in critical and declining status under section 305 for such plan year and, if so—

(I) the projected date of insolvency;

(II) a clear statement that such insolvency may result in benefit reductions; and

(III) a statement describing whether the plan sponsor has taken legally permitted actions to prevent insolvency.

(vii) in the case of any plan amendment, scheduled benefit increase or reduction, or other known event taking effect in the current plan year and having a material effect on plan liabilities or assets for the year (as defined in regulations by the Secretary), an explanation of the amendment, schedule increase or reduction, or event, and a projection to the end of such plan year of the effect of the amendment, scheduled increase or reduction, or event on plan liabilities,

(viii)(I) in the case of a single-employer plan, a summary of the rules governing termination of single-employer plans under subtitle C of title IV, or

(II) in the case of a multiemployer plan, a summary of the rules governing reorganization or insolvency, including the limitations on benefit payments,

(ix) a general description of the benefits under the plan which are eligible to be guaranteed by the Pension Benefit Guaranty Corporation, along with an explanation of the limitations on the guarantee and the circumstances under which such limitations apply,

(x) a statement that a person may obtain a copy of the annual report of the plan filed under section 104(a) upon request, through the Internet website of the Department of Labor, or through an Intranet website maintained by the applicable plan sponsor (or plan administrator on behalf of the plan sponsor), and

(xi) if applicable, a statement that each contributing sponsor, and each member of the contributing sponsor's controlled group, of the single-employer plan was required to provide the information under section 4010 for the plan year to which the notice relates.

(C) OTHER INFORMATION. —Each notice under paragraph (1) shall include—

(i) in the case of a multiemployer plan, a statement that the plan administrator shall provide, upon written request, to any labor organization representing plan participants and beneficiaries and any employer that has an obligation to contribute to the plan, a copy of the annual report filed with the Secretary under section 104(a), and

(ii) any additional information which the plan administrator elects to include to the extent not inconsistent with regulations prescribed by the Secretary.

(D) EFFECT OF SEGMENT RATE STABILIZATION ON PLAN FUNDING.—

(i) IN GENERAL. In the case of a single-employer plan for an applicable plan year, each notice under paragraph (1) shall include—

(I) a statement that the MAP-21, the Highway and Transportation Funding Act of 2014, and the Bipartisan Budget Act of 2015 modified the method for determining the interest rates used to determine the actuarial value of benefits earned under the plan, providing for a 25-year average of interest rates to be taken into account in addition to a 2-year average,

(II) a statement that, as a result of the MAP-21, the Highway and Transportation Funding Act of 2014, and the Bipartisan Budget Act of 2015, the plan sponsor may contribute less money to the plan when interest rates are at historical lows, and

(III) a table which shows (determined both with and without regard to section 303(h)(2)(C)(iv)) the funding target attainment percentage (as defined in section 303(d)(2)), the funding shortfall (as defined in section 303(c)(4)), and the minimum required contribution (as determined under section 303), for the applicable plan year and each of the 2 preceding plan years.

(ii) APPLICABLE PLAN YEAR. For purposes of this subparagraph, the term 'applicable plan year' means any plan year beginning after December 31, 2011, and before January 1, 2023, for which—

(I) the funding target (as defined in section 303(d)(2)) is less than 95 percent of such funding target determined without regard to section 303(h)(2)(C)(iv),

(II) the plan has a funding shortfall (as defined in section 303(c)(4) and determined without regard to section 303(h)(2)(C)(iv)) greater than $500,000, and

(III) the plan had 50 or more participants on any day during the preceding plan year. For purposes of any determination under subclause (III), the aggregation rule under the last sentence of section 303(g)(2)(B) shall apply.

(iii) SPECIAL RULE FOR PLAN YEARS BEGINNING BEFORE 2012. —In the case of a preceding plan year referred to in clause (i)(III) which begins before January 1, 2012, the information described in such clause shall be provided only without regard to section 303(h)(2)(C)(iv).

(E) EFFECT OF CSEC PLAN RULES ON PLAN FUNDING. In the case of a CSEC plan, each notice under paragraph (1) shall include—

(i) a statement that different rules apply to CSEC plans than apply to single-employer plans,

(ii) for the first 2 plan years beginning after December 31, 2013, a statement that, as a result of changes in the law made by the Cooperative and Small Employer Charity Pension Flexibility Act, the contributions to the plan may have changed, and

(iii) in the case of a CSEC plan that is in funding restoration status for the plan year, a statement that the plan is in funding restoration status for such plan year.

A copy of the statement required under clause (iii) shall be provided to the Secretary, the Secretary of the Treasury, and the Director of the Pension Benefit Guaranty Corporation.

(3) TIME FOR PROVIDING NOTICE.—

(A) IN GENERAL. —Any notice under paragraph (1) shall be provided not later than 120 days after the end of the plan year to which the notice relates.

(B) EXCEPTION FOR SMALL PLANS. —In the case of a small plan (as such term is used under section 303(g)(2)(B)) any notice under paragraph (1) shall be provided upon filing of the annual report under section 104(a).

(4) FORM AND MANNER. Any notice under paragraph (1)—

(A) shall be provided in a form and manner prescribed in regulations of the Secretary,

(B) shall be written in a manner so as to be understood by the average plan participant, and

(C) may be provided in written, electronic, or other appropriate form to the extent such form is reasonably accessible to persons to whom the notice is required to be provided.

Act Sec. 101. (g) REPORTING BY CERTAIN ARRANGEMENTS. The Secretary shall, by regulation, require multiple employer welfare arrangements providing benefits consisting of medical care (within the meaning of section 733(a)(2)) which are not group health plans to register with the Secretary prior to operating in a State and may, by regulation, require such multiple employer welfare arrangements to report, not more frequently than annually, in such form and such manner as the Secretary may require for the purpose of determining the extent to which the requirements of part 7 are being carried out in connection with such benefits.

Act Sec. 101. (h) SIMPLE RETIREMENT ACCOUNTS.—

(1) NO EMPLOYER REPORTS. Except as provided in this subsection, no report shall be required under this section by an employer maintaining a qualified salary reduction arrangement under section 408(p) of the Internal Revenue Code of 1986.

(2) SUMMARY DESCRIPTION. The trustee of any simple retirement account established pursuant to a qualified salary reduction arrangement under section 408(p) of such Code shall provide to the employer maintaining the arrangement each year a description containing the following information:

(A) The name and address of the employer and the trustee.

(B) The requirements for eligibility for participation.

(C) The benefits provided with respect to the arrangement.

(D) The time and method of making elections with respect to the arrangement.

(E) The procedures for, and effects of, withdrawals (including rollovers) from the arrangement.

(3) EMPLOYEE NOTIFICATION. The employer shall notify each employee immediately before the period for which an election described in section 408(p)(5)(C) of such Code may be made of the employee's opportunity to make such election. Such notice shall include a copy of the description described in paragraph (2).

Act Sec. 101. (i) NOTICE OF BLACKOUT PERIODS TO PARTICIPANT OR BENEFICIARY UNDER INDIVIDUAL ACCOUNT PLAN—

(1) DUTIES OF PLAN ADMINISTRATOR. In advance of the commencement of any blackout period with respect to an individual account plan, the plan administrator shall notify the plan participants and beneficiaries who are affected by such action in accordance with this subsection.

(2) NOTICE REQUIREMENTS—

(A) IN GENERAL. The notices described in paragraph (1) shall be written in a manner calculated to be understood by the average plan participant and shall include—

(i) the reasons for the blackout period,

(ii) an identification of the investments and other rights affected,

(iii) the expected beginning date and length of the blackout period,

(iv) in the case of investments affected, a statement that the participant or beneficiary should evaluate the appropriateness of their current investment decisions in light of their inability to direct or diversify assets credited to their accounts during the blackout period, and

(v) such other matters as the Secretary may require by regulation.

(B) NOTICE TO PARTICIPANTS AND BENEFICIARIES. Except as otherwise provided in this subsection, notices described in paragraph (1) shall be furnished to all participants and beneficiaries under the plan to whom the blackout period applies at least 30 days in advance of the blackout period.

(C) EXCEPTION TO 30-DAY NOTICE REQUIREMENT. In any case in which—

(i) a deferral of the blackout period would violate the requirements of subparagraph (A) or (B) of section 404(a)(1), and a fiduciary of the plan reasonably so determines in writing, or

(ii) the inability to provide the 30-day advance notice is due to events that were unforeseeable or circumstances beyond the reasonable control of the plan administrator, and a fiduciary of the plan reasonably so determines in writing, subparagraph (B) shall not apply, and the notice shall be furnished to all participants and beneficiaries under the plan to whom the blackout period applies as soon as reasonably possible under the circumstances unless such a notice in advance of the termination of the blackout period is impracticable.

(D) WRITTEN NOTICE. The notice required to be provided under this subsection shall be in writing, except that such notice may be in electronic or other form to the extent that such form is reasonably accessible to the recipient.

(E) NOTICE TO ISSUERS OF EMPLOYER SECURITIES SUBJECT TO BLACKOUT PERIOD. In the case of any blackout period in connection with an individual account plan, the plan administrator shall provide timely notice of such blackout period to the issuer of any employer securities subject to such blackout period.

(3) EXCEPTION FOR BLACKOUT PERIODS WITH LIMITED APPLICABILITY. In any case in which the blackout period applies only to 1 or more participants or beneficiaries in connection with a merger, acquisition, divestiture, or similar transaction involving the plan or plan sponsor and occurs solely in connection with becoming or ceasing to be a participant or beneficiary under the plan by reason of such merger, acquisition, divestiture, or transaction, the requirement of this subsection that the notice be provided to all participants and beneficiaries shall be treated as met if the notice required under paragraph (1) is provided to such participants or beneficiaries to whom the blackout period applies as soon as reasonably practicable.

(4) CHANGES IN LENGTH OF BLACKOUT PERIOD. If, following the furnishing of the notice pursuant to this subsection, there is a change in the beginning date or length of the blackout period (specified in such notice pursuant to paragraph (2)(A)(iii)), the administrator shall provide affected participants and beneficiaries notice of the change as soon as reasonably practicable. In relation to the extended blackout period, such notice shall meet the requirements of paragraph (2)(D) and shall specify any material change in the matters referred to in clauses (i) through (v) of paragraph (2)(A).

(5) REGULATORY EXCEPTIONS. The Secretary may provide by regulation for additional exceptions to the requirements of this subsection which the Secretary determines are in the interests of participants and beneficiaries.

(6) GUIDANCE AND MODEL NOTICES. The Secretary shall issue guidance and model notices which meet the requirements of this subsection.

(7) BLACKOUT PERIOD. For purposes of this subsection—

(A) IN GENERAL. The term 'blackout period' means, in connection with an individual account plan, any period for which any ability of participants or beneficiaries under the plan, which is otherwise available under the terms of such plan, to direct or diversify assets credited to their accounts, to obtain loans from the plan, or to obtain distributions from the plan is temporarily suspended, limited, or restricted, if such suspension, limitation, or restriction is for any period of more than 3 consecutive business days.

(B) EXCLUSIONS. The term 'blackout period' does not include a suspension, limitation, or restriction—

(i) which occurs by reason of the application of the securities laws (as defined in section 3(a)(47) of the Securities Exchange Act of 1934),

(ii) which is a change to the plan which provides for a regularly scheduled suspension, limitation, or restriction which is disclosed to participants or beneficiaries through any summary of material modifications, any materials describing specific investment alternatives under the plan, or any changes thereto, or

(iii) which applies only to 1 or more individuals, each of whom is the participant, an alternate payee (as defined in section 206(d)(3)(K)), or any other beneficiary pursuant to a qualified domestic relations order (as defined in section 206(d)(3)(B)(i)).

(8) INDIVIDUAL ACCOUNT PLAN—

(A) IN GENERAL. For purposes of this subsection, the term 'individual account plan' shall have the meaning provided such term in section 3(34), except that such term shall not include a one-participant retirement plan.

(B) ONE-PARTICIPANT RETIREMENT PLAN. For purposes of subparagraph (A), the term 'one-participant retirement plan' means a retirement plan that on the first day of the plan year—

(i) covered only one individual (or the individual and the individual's spouse) and the individual (or the individual and the individual's spouse) owned 100 percent of the plan sponsor (whether or not incorporated), or

(ii) covered only one or more partners (or partners and their spouses) in the plan sponsor.

Act Sec. 101. (j) NOTICE OF FUNDING-BASED LIMITATION ON CERTAIN FORMS OF DISTRIBUTION. —The plan administrator of a single-employer plan shall provide a written notice to plan participants and beneficiaries within 30 days—

(1) after the plan has become subject to a restriction described in paragraph (1) or (3) of section 206(g),

(2) in the case of a plan to which section 206(g)(4) applies, after the valuation date for the plan year described in section 206(g)(4)(A) for which the plan's adjusted funding target attainment percentage for the plan year is less than 60 percent (or, if earlier, the date such percentage is deemed to be less than 60 percent under section 206(g)(7)), and

(3) at such other time as may be determined by the Secretary of the Treasury.

The notice required to be provided under this subsection shall be in writing, except that such notice may be in electronic or other form to the extent that such form is reasonably accessible to the recipient. The Secretary of the Treasury, in consultation with the Secretary, shall have the authority to prescribe rules applicable to the notices required under this subsection.

Act Sec. 101. (k) MULTIEMPLOYER PLAN INFORMATION MADE AVAILABLE ON REQUEST.—

(1) IN GENERAL.—Each administrator of a defined benefit plan that is a multiemployer plan shall, upon written request, furnish to any plan participant or beneficiary, employee representative, or any employer that has an obligation to contribute to the plan a copy of—

(A) the current plan document (including any amendments thereto),

(B) the latest summary plan description of the plan,

(C) the current trust agreement (including any amendments thereto), or any other instrument or agreement under which the plan is established or operated,

(D) in the case of a request by an employer, any participation agreement with respect to the plan for such employer that relates to the employer's plan participation during the current or any of the 5 immediately preceding plan years,

(E) the annual report filed under section 104 for any plan year,

(F) the plan funding notice provided under subsection (f) for any plan year,

(G) any periodic actuarial report (including any sensitivity testing) received by the plan for any plan year which has been in the plan's possession for at least 30 days,

(H) any quarterly, semi-annual, or annual financial report prepared for the plan by any plan investment manager or advisor or other fiduciary which has been in the plan's possession for at least 30 days,

(I) audited financial statements of the plan for any plan year,

(J) any application filed with the Secretary of the Treasury requesting an extension under section 304(d) of this Act or section 431(d) of the Internal Revenue Code of 1986 and the determination of such Secretary pursuant to such application, and

(K) in the case of a plan which was in critical or endangered status under section 305 for a plan year, the latest funding improvement or rehabilitation plan, and the contribution schedules applicable with respect to such funding improvement or rehabilitation plan (other than a contribution schedule applicable to a specific employer).

(2) COMPLIANCE.—Information required to be provided under paragraph (1)—

(A) shall be provided to the requesting participant, beneficiary, or employer within 30 days after the request in a form and manner prescribed in regulations of the Secretary,

(B) may be provided in written, electronic, or other appropriate form to the extent such form is reasonably accessible to persons to whom the information is required to be provided, and

(C) shall not—

(i) include any individually identifiable information regarding any plan participant, beneficiary, employee, fiduciary, or contributing employer, or

(ii) reveal any proprietary information regarding the plan, any contributing employer, or entity providing services to the plan.

Subparagraph (C)(i) shall not apply to individually identifiable information with respect to any plan investment manager or adviser, or with respect to any other person (other than an employee of the plan) preparing a financial report required to be included under paragraph (1)(B).

(3) LIMITATIONS.—In no case shall a participant, beneficiary, employee representative, or employer be entitled under this subsection to receive more than one copy of any document described in paragraph (1) during any one 12-month period, or, in the case of any document described in subparagraph (E), (F), (G), (H) or (I) of paragraph (1), a copy of any such document that as of the date on which the request is received by the administrator, has been in the administrator's possession for 6 years or more. If the administrator provides a copy of a document described in paragraph (1) to any person upon request, the administrator shall be considered as having met any obligation the administrator may have under any other provision of this title to furnish a copy of the same document to such person upon request. The administrator may make a reasonable charge to cover copying, mailing, and other costs of furnishing copies of information pursuant to paragraph (1). The Secretary may by regulations prescribe the maximum amount which will constitute a reasonable charge under the preceding sentence.

Act Sec. 101. (l) NOTICE OF POTENTIAL WITHDRAWAL LIABILITY.—

(1) IN GENERAL.—The plan sponsor or administrator of a multiemployer plan shall, upon written request, furnish to any employer who has an obligation to contribute to the plan a notice of—

(A) the estimated amount which would be the amount of such employer's withdrawal liability under part 1 of subtitle E of title IV if such employer withdrew on the last day of the plan year preceding the date of the request, and

(B) an explanation of how such estimated liability amount was determined, including the actuarial assumptions and methods used to determine the value of the plan liabilities and assets, the data regarding employer contributions, unfunded vested benefits, annual changes in the plan's unfunded vested benefits, and the application of any relevant limitations on the estimated withdrawal liability.

For purposes of subparagraph (B), the term 'employer contribution' means, in connection with a participant, a contribution made by an employer as an employer of such participant.

(2) COMPLIANCE.—Any notice required to be provided under paragraph (1)—

(A) shall be provided in a form and manner prescribed in regulations of the Secretary to the requesting employer within—

(i) 180 days after the request, or

(ii) subject to regulations of the Secretary, such longer time as may be necessary in the case of a plan that determines withdrawal liability based on any method described under paragraph (4) or (5) of section 4211(c); and

(B) may be provided in written, electronic, or other appropriate form to the extent such form is reasonably accessible to employers to whom the information is required to be provided.

(3) LIMITATIONS.—In no case shall an employer be entitled under this subsection to receive more than one notice described in paragraph (1) during any one 12-month period. The person required to provide such notice may make a reasonable charge to cover copying, mailing, and other costs of furnishing such notice pursuant to paragraph (1). The Secretary may by regulations prescribe the maximum amount which will constitute a reasonable charge under the preceding sentence.

Act Sec. 101. (m) NOTICE OF RIGHT TO DIVEST. —Not later than 30 days before the first date on which an applicable individual of an applicable individual account plan is eligible to exercise the right under section 204(j) to direct the proceeds from the divestment of employer securities with respect to any type of contribution, the administrator shall provide to such individual a notice—

(1) setting forth such right under such section, and

(2) describing the importance of diversifying the investment of retirement account assets.

The notice required by this subsection shall be written in a manner calculated to be understood by the average plan participant and may be delivered in written, electronic, or other appropriate form to the extent that such form is reasonably accessible to the recipient.

Act Sec. 101. (n) CROSS REFERENCE. For regulations relating to coordination of reports to the Secretaries of Labor and the Treasury, see section 3004.

Amendments

P.L. 114-74, § 504(b)(2)(A):

Amended ERISA Sec. 101(f)(2)(D) in clause (i) by striking "and the Highway and Transportation Funding Act of 2014" both places it appears and inserting ", the Highway and Transportation Funding Act of 2014, and the Bipartisan Budget Act of 2015" and in clause (ii) by striking "2020" and inserting "2023".

Prior to the amendment, ERISA Sec. 101(f)(2)(D) read as follows:

(D) EFFECT OF SEGMENT RATE STABILIZATION ON PLAN FUNDING—

(i) IN GENERAL In the case of a single-employer plan for an applicable plan year, each notice under paragraph (1) shall include—

(I) a statement that the MAP-21 and the Highway and Transportation Funding Act of 2014 modified the method for determining the interest rates used to determine the actuarial value of benefits earned under the plan, providing for a 25-year average of interest rates to be taken into account in addition to a 2-year average,

(II) a statement that, as a result of the MAP-21 and the Highway and Transportation Funding Act of 2014, the plan sponsor may contribute less money to the plan when interest rates are at historical lows, and

(III) a table which shows (determined both with and without regard to section 303(h)(2)(C)(iv)) the funding target attainment percentage (as defined in section 303(d)(2)), the funding shortfall (as defined in section 303(c)(4)), and the minimum required contribution (as determined under section 303), for the applicable plan year and each of the 2 preceding plan years.

(ii) APPLICABLE PLAN YEAR For purposes of this subparagraph, the term 'applicable plan year' means any plan year beginning after December 31, 2011, and before January 1, 2020, for which—

(I) the funding target (as defined in section 303(d)(2)) is less than 95 percent of such funding target determined without regard to section 303(h)(2)(C)(iv),

(II) the plan has a funding shortfall (as defined in section 303(c)(4) and determined without regard to section 303(h)(2)(C)(iv)) greater than $500,000, and

(III) the plan had 50 or more participants on any day during the preceding plan year. For purposes of any determination under subclause (III), the aggregation rule under the last sentence of section 303(g)(2)(B) shall apply.

(iii) SPECIAL RULE FOR PLAN YEARS BEGINNING BEFORE 2012 —In the case of a preceding plan year referred to in clause (i)(III) which begins before January 1, 2012, the information described in such clause shall be provided only without regard to section 303(h)(2)(C)(iv).

The above amendment shall apply to plan years beginning after December 31, 2015.

P.L. 114-74, § 504(b)(2)(B) provides:

(B) Statements

The Secretary of Labor shall modify the statements required under subclauses (I) and (II) of section 101(f)(2)(D)(i) of such Act to conform to the amendments made by this section.

P.L. 114-41, § 2007(b)(1):

Amended ERISA Sec. 101(e)(3) by striking "MAP-21" and inserting "Surface Transportation and Veterans Health Care Choice Improvement Act of 2015".

The above amendments take effect on July 31, 2015.

P.L. 113-235, § 111(a), Div. O:

Amended ERISA Sec. 101(k)(1) to read as above.

Prior to amendment, ERISA Sec. 101(k)(1) read as follows:

(1) IN GENERAL.—Each administrator of a multiemployer plan shall, upon written request, furnish to any plan participant or beneficiary, employee representative, or any employer that has an obligation to contribute to the plan—

(A) a copy of any periodic actuarial report (including any sensitivity testing) received by the plan for any plan year which has been in the plan's possession for at least 30 days,

(B) a copy of any quarterly, semi-annual, or annual financial report prepared for the plan by any plan investment manager or advisor or other fiduciary which has been in the plan's possession for at least 30 days, and

(C) a copy of any application filed with the Secretary of the Treasury requesting an extension under section 304 of this Act or section 431(d) of the Internal Revenue Code of 1986 and the determination of such Secretary pursuant to such application.

The above amendment applies with respect to plan years beginning after December 31, 2014.

P.L. 113-235, § 111(b), Div. O:

Amended ERISA Sec. 101(k)(3) by striking the first sentence and inserting a new sentence to read as above.

Prior to amendment, ERISA Sec. 101(k)(3) read as follows:

In no case shall a participant, beneficiary, or employer be entitled under this subsection to receive more than one copy of any report or application described in paragraph (1) during any one 12-month period. The administrator may make a reasonable charge to cover copying, mailing, and other costs of furnishing copies of information pursuant to paragraph (1). The Secretary may by regulations prescribe the maximum amount which will constitute a reasonable charge under the preceding sentence.

The above amendment applies with respect to plan years beginning after December 31, 2014.

P.L. 113-235, § 201(a)(4)(A)-(B), Div. O:

Amended ERISA Sec. 101(f)(2)(B) by redesignating clauses (vi) through (x) as clauses (vii) through (xi), respectively, and by inserting a new clause (vi) to read as above.

The above amendments take effect on December 16, 2014.

P.L. 113-159, § 2003(b)(2)(A):

Amended ERISA Sec.101(f)(2)(D) in clause (i) by inserting "and the Highway and Transportation Funding Act of 2014" after "MAP–21" both places it appears, and in clause (ii) by striking "2015" and inserting "2020".

The above amendments shall apply with respect to plan years beginning after December 31, 2012.

P.L. 113-159, § 2003(b)(2)(B) provides:

(B) STATEMENTS.—The Secretary of Labor shall modify the statements required under subclauses (I) and (II) of section 101(f)(2)(D)(i) of such Act to conform to the amendments made by this section.

The above amendments shall apply with respect to plan years beginning after December 31, 2012.

P.L. 113-159, § 2003(e)(2) provides:

(2) ELECTIONS.—A plan sponsor may elect not to have the amendments made by subsections (a), (b), and (d) apply to any plan year beginning before January 1, 2014, either (as specified in the election)—

(A) for all purposes for which such amendments apply, or

(B) solely for purposes of determining the adjusted funding target attainment percentage under sections 436 of the Internal Revenue Code of 1986 and 206(g) of the Employee Retirement Income Security Act of 1974 (29 U.S.C. 1054(g)) for such plan year.

A plan shall not be treated as failing to meet the requirements of section 204(g) of such Act and section 411(d)(6) of such Code solely by reason of an election under this paragraph.

P.L. 113-97, § 104(a)(1):

Amended ERISA Sec. 101(f)(2) by adding at the end a new subparagraph (E) to read as above.

Effective for years beginning after 12-31-2013.

P.L. 113-97, § 104(a)(2) provides:

(2) Model notice.–The Secretary of Labor may modify the model notice required to be published under section 501(c) of the Pension Protection Act of 2006 to include the information described in section 101(f)(2)(E) of the Employee Retirement Income Security Act of 1974, as added by this subsection.

P.L. 113-97, § 104(b)(1):

Amended ERISA Sec. 101(d)(2) by striking "303" and inserting "303 or 306".

Effective for years beginning after 12-31-2013.

P.L. 113-97, § 104(b)(2):

Amended ERISA Sec. 101(d)(3) by by striking "303(j)" and inserting "303(j) or 306(f), whichever is applicable".

Effective for years beginning after 12-31-2013.

P.L. 112-141, § 40211(b)(2)(A):

Amended ERISA Sec. 101(f)(2) by adding at the end new subparagraph (D) to read as above.

For effective date, see P.L. 112-141, § 40211(c), below.

P.L. 112-141, § 40211(b)(2)(B), provides:

(B) MODEL NOTICE.—The Secretary of Labor shall modify the model notice required to be published under section 501(c) of the Pension Protection Act of 2006 to prominently include the information described in section 101(f)(2)(D) of the Employee Retirement Income Security Act of 1974, as added by this paragraph.

For effective date, see P.L. 112-141, § 40211(c), below.

P.L. 112-141, § 40211(c):

(c) EFFECTIVE DATE.—

(1) IN GENERAL.—The amendments made by this section shall apply with respect to plan years beginning after December 31, 2011.

(2) RULES WITH RESPECT TO ELECTIONS.—

(A) ADJUSTED FUNDING TARGET ATTAINMENT PERCENTAGE.—A plan sponsor may elect not to have the amendments made by this section apply to any plan year beginning before January 1, 2013, either (as specified in the election)—

(i) for all purposes for which such amendments apply, or

(ii) solely for purposes of determining the adjusted funding target attainment percentage under sections 436 of the Internal Revenue Code of 1986 and 206(g) of the Employee Retirement Income Security Act of 1974 for such plan year.

A plan shall not be treated as failing to meet the requirements of sections 204(g) of such Act and 411(d)(6) of such Code solely by reason of an election under this paragraph.

(B) OPT OUT OF EXISTING ELECTIONS.—If, on the date of the enactment of this Act, an election is in effect with respect to any plan under sections 303(h)((2)(D)(ii) of the Employee Retirement Income Security Act of 1974 and 430(h)((2)(D)(ii) of the Internal Revenue Code of 1986, then, notwithstanding the last sentence of each such section, the plan sponsor may revoke such election without the consent of the Secretary of the Treasury. The plan sponsor may make such revocation at any time before the date which is 1 year after such date of enactment and such revocation shall be effective for the 1st plan year to which the amendments made by this section apply and all subsequent plan years. Nothing in this subparagraph shall preclude a plan sponsor from making a subsequent election in accordance with such sections.

P.L. 112-141, §40241(b)(1):

Amended ERISA Sec. 101(e)(3) by striking "Pension Protection Act of 2006" and inserting "MAP-21". For effective date, see P.L. 112-141, §40241(c), below.

P.L. 112-141, §40241(c), provides:

(c) EFFECTIVE DATE.—The amendments made by this Act [section]shall take effect on the date of the enactment of this Act [July 6, 2012].

P.L. 112-141, §40242(e)(14)(A) and (B):

Amended ERISA Sec. 101(e)(1) and (2) by inserting "or applicable life insurance account" after "health benefits account" each place that it appears, and in ERISA Sec. 101(e)(1) by inserting "or applicable life insurance benefit liabilities" after "health benefits liabilities".

For effective date, see P.L. 112-141, §40241(h)(1), below.

P.L. 112-141, §40242(h), provides:

(h) EFFECTIVE DATE.—

(1) IN GENERAL.—The amendments made by this section shall apply to transfers made after the date of the enactment of this Act [July 6, 2012].

* * *

P.L. 111-148, §6606:

Amended ERISA Sec. 101(g) by striking "Secretary may" and inserting "Secretary shall" and by inserting "to register with the Secretary prior to operating in a State and may, by regulation, require such multiple employer welfare arrangements" after "not group health plans".

The above amendment is effective on the date of enactment (March 23, 2010).

P.L. 110-458, §101(c)(1)(A)(i):

Amended ERISA Sec. 101(j)(2) by striking "section 206(g)(4)(B)" and inserting "section 206(g)(4)(A)".

The above amendment takes effect as if included in the provisions of the 2006 Act to which the amendment relates. For effective date, see P.L. 109-280, §103(c), below.

P.L. 110-458, §101(c)(1)(A)(ii):

Amended ERISA Sec. 101(j) by adding at the end the following:

The Secretary of the Treasury, in consultation with the Secretary, shall have the authority to prescribe rules applicable to the notices required under this subsection.

The above amendment takes effect as if included in the provisions of the 2006 Act to which the amendment relates. For effective date, see P.L. 109-280, §103(c), below.

P.L. 110-458, §105(a)(1):

Amended ERISA Sec. 101(f)(2)(B)(ii)(I)(aa) by striking "for which the latest annual report filed under section 104(a) was filed" and inserting "to which the notice relates".

The above amendment takes effect as if included in the provisions of the 2006 Act to which the amendment relates. For effective date, see P.L. 109-280, §501(d), below.

P.L. 110-458, §105(a)(2):

Amended ERISA Sec. 101(f)(2)(B)(ii) by striking subclause (II) and inserting subclause (II) to read as above. Prior to the amendment, ERISA Sec. 101(f)(2)(B)(ii)(II) read as follows:

(II) in the case of a multiemployer plan, a statement of the value of the plan's assets and liabilities for the plan year to which the notice relates as the last day of such plan year and the preceding 2 plan years,

The above amendment takes effect as if included in the provisions of the 2006 Act to which the amendment relates. For effective date, see P.L. 109-280, §501(d), below.

P.L. 110-458, §105(b)(1):

Amended ERISA Sec. 101(k)(2) by filing at the end the following new flush sentence:

Subparagraph (C)(i) shall not apply to individually identifiable information with respect to any plan investment manager or advisor, or with respect to any other person (other than an employee of the plan) preparing a financial report required to be included under paragraph (1)(B).

The above amendment takes effect as if included in the provisions of the 2006 Act to which the amendment relates [effective with respect to plan years beginning after December 31, 2007.—CCH].

P.L. 110-458, §105(g):

Amended ERISA Sec. 101(i)(8)(B) to read as above. Prior to amendment ERISA Sec. 101(i)(8)(B) read as follows:

(B) ONE-PARTICIPANT RETIREMENT PLAN. For purposes of subparagraph (A), the term 'one-participant retirement plan' means a retirement plan that—

(i) on the first day of the plan year—

(I) covered only one individual (or the individual and the individual's spouse) and the individual (or the individual and the individual's spouse) owned 100 percent of the plan sponsor (whether or not incorporated), or

(II) covered only one or more partners (or partners and their spouses) in the plan sponsor, and

(ii) does not cover a business that leases employees.

The above amendments take effect as if included in the provisions of the 2006 Act to which the amendment relates. [The amendments take effect as if included in the provisions of section 306 of P.L. 107-204 (116 Stat. 745 et seq.). The effective date of section 306 of the Sarbanes-Oxley Act (P.L. 107-204) is January 26, 2003.—CCH]

P.L. 109-280, § 103(b)(1)(A-(B):

Amended ERISA Sec. 101(j)-(k) by redesignating subsection (j) as subsection (k) and inserting after subsection (i) subsection (j) to read as above.

For effective dates, see P.L. 109-280, § 103(c) below.

P.L. 109-280, § 103(c):

103(c) EFFECTIVE DATES.—

103(c)(1) IN GENERAL.—

The amendments made by this section shall apply to plan years beginning after December 31, 2007.

103(c)(2) COLLECTIVE BARGAINING EXCEPTION.—

In the case of a plan maintained pursuant to 1 or more collective bargaining agreements between employee representatives and 1 or more employers ratified before January 1, 2008, the amendments made by this section shall not apply to plan years beginning before the earlier of—

103(c)(2)(A) the later of —

103(c)(2)(A)(i) the date on which the last collective bargaining agreement relating to the plan terminates (determined without regard to any extension thereof agreed to after the date of the enactment of this Act), or

103(c)(2)(A)(ii) the first day of the first plan year to which the amendments made by this subsection would (but for this subparagraph) apply, or

103(c)(2)(B) January 1, 2010.

For purposes of subparagraph (A)(i), any plan amendment made pursuant to a collective bargaining agreement relating to the plan which amends the plan solely to conform to any requirement added by this section shall not be treated as a termination of such collective bargaining agreement.

P.L. 109-280, § 107(a)(1):

Amended ERISA Sec. 101(d)(3), by striking "section 302(e)" and inserting "section 303(j)".

The above amendment applies to plan years beginning after 2007.

P.L. 109-280, § 107(a)(11):

Amended ERISA Sec. 101(e)(3), by striking "American Jobs Creation Act of 2004" and inserting "Pension Protection Act of 2006".

The above amendment applies to plan years beginning after 2007.

P.L. 109-280, § 501(a):

Amended ERISA Sec. 101(f) to read as above.

Prior to amendment, ERISA Sec. 101(f) read as follows:

(f) MULTIEMPLOYER DEFINED BENEFIT PLAN FUNDING NOTICES.—

(1) IN GENERAL.—The administrator of a defined benefit plan which is a multiemployer plan shall for each plan year provide a plan funding notice to each plan participant and beneficiary, to each labor organization representing such participants or beneficiaries, to each employer that has an obligation to contribute under the plan, and to the Pension Benefit Guaranty Corporation.

(2) INFORMATION CONTAINED IN NOTICES.—

(A) IDENTIFYING INFORMATION.—Each notice required under paragraph (1) shall contain identifying information, including the name of the plan, the address and phone number of the plan administrator and the plan's principal administrative officer, each plan sponsor's employer identification number, and the plan number of the plan.

(B) SPECIFIC INFORMATION.—A plan funding notice under paragraph (1) shall include—

(i) a statement as to whether the plan's funded current liability percentage (as defined in section 302(d)(8)(B)) for the plan year to which the notice relates is at least 100 percent (and, if not, the actual percentage);

(ii) a statement of the value of the plan's assets, the amount of benefit payments, and the ratio of the assets to the payments for the plan year to which the notice relates;

(iii) a summary of the rules governing insolvent multiemployer plans, including the limitations on benefit payments and any potential benefit reductions and suspensions (and the potential effects of such limitations, reductions, and suspensions on the plan); and

(iv) a general description of the benefits under the plan which are eligible to be guaranteed by the Pension Benefit Guaranty Corporation, along with an explanation of the limitations on the guarantee and the circumstances under which such limitations apply.

(C) OTHER INFORMATION.—Each notice under paragraph (1) shall include any additional information which the plan administrator elects to include to the extent not inconsistent with regulations prescribed by the Secretary.

(3) TIME FOR PROVIDING NOTICE.—Any notice under paragraph (1) shall be provided no later than two months after the deadline (including extensions) for filing the annual report for the plan year to which the notice relates.

(4) FORM AND MANNER.—Any notice under paragraph (1)—

(A) shall be provided in a form and manner prescribed in regulations of the Secretary,

(B) shall be written in a manner so as to be understood by the average plan participant, and

(C) may be provided in written, electronic, or other appropriate form to the extent such form is reasonably accessible to persons to whom the notice is required to be provided.

For effective dates, see P.L. 109-280 below.

P.L. 109-280, § 501(d):

501(d) EFFECTIVE DATE.—

501(d)(1) IN GENERAL.—

The amendments made by this section shall apply to plan years beginning after December 31, 2007, except that the amendment made by subsection (b) shall apply to plan years beginning after December 31, 2006.

501(d)(2) TRANSITION RULE.—

Any requirement under section 101(f) of the Employee Retirement Income Security Act of 1974 (as amended by this section) to report the funding target attainment percentage or funded percentage of a plan with respect to any plan year beginning before January 1, 2008, shall be treated as met if the plan reports—

501(d)(2)(A) in the case of a plan year beginning in 2006, the funded current liability percentage (as defined in section 302(d)(8) of such Act) of the plan for such plan year, and

501(d)(2)(B) in the case of a plan year beginning in 2007, the funding target attainment percentage or funded percentage as determined using such methods of estimation as the Secretary of the Treasury may provide.

P.L. 109-280, § 502(a)(1)(A)-(B):

Amended ERISA Sec. 101, as previously amended by Act Sec. 103(b)(1)(A)-(B), by redesignating subsection (k) as subsection (l); and by inserting after subsection (j) a new subsection (k) to read as above. Prior to amendment, subsection (k) read as follows:

(k) For regulations relating to coordination of reports to the **Secretaries of Labor and the Treasury**, see section 3004.

The above amendment applies to plan years beginning after December 31, 2007.

P. L. 109-280, § 502(b)(1)(A)-(B):

Amended ERISA Sec. 101, as previously amended by Act Sec. 502(a)(1)(A)-(B), by redesignating subsection (l) as subsection (m), and by inserting after subsection (k) a new subsection (l) to read as above. Prior to amendment, subsection (l) read as follows:

(l) For regulations relating to coordination of reports to the Secretaries of Labor and the Treasury, see section 3004.

The above amendment applies to plan years beginning after December 31, 2007.

P.L. 109-280, § 503(c)(2):

Amended ERISA Sec. 101(a)(2) by inserting "subsection (f) and" before "sections 104(b)(3) and 105(a) and (c)".

The above amendment applies to plan years beginning after December 31, 2007.

P.L. 109-280, § 507(a):

Amended ERISA Sec. 101, as previously amended by P.L. 109-280, by redesignating subsection (m) as subsection (n) and by inserting after subsection (l) a new subsection (m) to read as above. Prior to amendment, subsection (m) read as follows:

For regulations relating to coordination of reports to the Secretaries of Labor and the Treasury, see section 3004.

For effective dates, see P.L. 109-280, § 507(d) below.

507(d) EFFECTIVE DATES.—

507(d)(1) IN GENERAL.—

The amendments made by this section shall apply to plan years beginning after December 31, 2006.

507(d)(2) TRANSITION RULE.—

If notice under section 101(m) of the Employee Retirement Income Security Act of 1974 (as added by this section) would otherwise be required to be provided before the 90th day after the date of the enactment of this Act, such notice shall not be required to be provided until such 90th day.

P.L. 109-280, § 509(a):

Amended ERISA Sec. 101(i)(8)(B) by striking clauses (i) through (iv), by redesignating clause (v) as clause (ii), and by inserting before clause (ii), as so redesignated, a new clause (i), to read as above. Prior to amendment, Sec. 101(i)(8)(B) read as follows:

(B) ONE-PARTICIPANT PLAN.—For purposes of subparagraph (A), the term "one-participant retirement plan" means a retirement plan that—

(i) on the first day of the plan year —

(I) covered only the employer (and the employer's spouse) and the employer owned the entire business (whether or not incorporated), or

(II) covered only one or more partners (and their spouses) in a business partnership (including partners in an S or C corporation (as defined in section 1361(a) of the Internal Revenue Code of 1986)),

(ii) meets the minimum coverage requirements of section 410(b) of the Internal Revenue Code of 1986 (as in effect on the date of the enactment of this paragraph)

without being combined with any other plan of the business that covers the employees of the business,

(iii) does not provide benefits to anyone except the employer (and the employer's spouse) or the partners (and their spouses),

(iv) does not cover a business that is a member of an affiliated service group, a controlled group of corporations, or a group of businesses under common control, and

(v) does not cover a business that leases employees.

The amendments above shall take effect as if included in the provisions of section 306 of P.L. 107-204 (116 Stat. 745 et seq.). [The effective date of section 306 of the Sarbanes-Oxley Act (P.L. 107-204) is January 26, 2003.]

P.L. 108-357, § 709(a)(1):

Act. Sec. 709(a)(1) amended ERISA Sec. 101(e)(3) by striking "Pension Funding Equity Act of 2004" and inserting "American Jobs Creation Act of 2004."

P.L. 108-218, § 204(b):

Act. Sec. 204(b) amended ERISA Sec. 101(e)(3) by replacing "Tax Relief Extension Act of 1999" with "Pension Funding Equity Act of 2004."

P.L. 108-218, § 103(a):

Act Sec. 103(a) amended ERISA Sec. 101 by inserting after subsection (e), subsection (f) to read as above. The amendment applies to plan years beginning after December 31, 2004.

Act Sec. 103 provides:

(c) Regulations and Model Notice.—The Secretary of Labor shall, not later than 1 year after the date of the enactment of this Act, issue regulations (including a model notice) necessary to implement the amendments made by this section.

P.L. 107-204, § 306(b)(1):

Act. Sec. 306(b)(1) amended ERISA Sec. 101 by redesignating the second subsection (h) as subsection (j) and inserting after the first subsection (h), subsection (i) to read as above.

P.L. 107-204, § 306(c):

Act. Sec. 306(c) EFFECTIVE DATE-The provisions of this section (including the amendments made thereby) shall take effect 180 days after the date of the enactment of this Act. Good faith compliance with the requirements of such provisions in advance of the issuance of applicable regulations thereunder shall be treated as compliance with such provisions.

P.L. 106-170, § 535(a)(2)(A):

Act Sec. 535(a)(2)(A) amended ERISA Sec. 101(e)(3) by striking "January 1, 1995" and inserting "the date of the enactment of the Tax Relief Extension Act of 1999".

The above amendment applies to qualified transfers occurring after December 17, 1999.

P.L. 105-200, § 402(h)(1):

Repealed ERISA Sec. 101(f). Prior to repeal, ERISA Sec. 101(f) read as follows:

Act Sec. 101. (f) INFORMATION NECESSARY TO COMPLY WITH MEDICARE AND MEDICAID COVERAGE DATA BANK REQUIREMENTS.—

(1) PROVISION OF INFORMATION BY GROUP HEALTH PLAN UPON REQUEST OF EMPLOYER.—

(A) IN GENERAL.—An employer shall comply with the applicable requirements of section 1144 of the Social Security Act (as added by section 13581 of the Omnibus Budget Reconciliation Act of 1993). Upon the request of an employer maintaining a group health plan, any plan sponsor, plan administrator, insurer, third-party administrator, or other person who maintains under the plan the information necessary to enable the employer to comply with the applicable requirements of section 1144 of the Social Security Act shall, in such form and manner as may be prescribed in regulations of the Secretary (in consultation with the Secretary of Health and Human Services), provide such information (not inconsistent with paragraph (2))—

(i) in the case of a request by an employer described in subparagraph (B) and a plan that is not a multiemployer plan or a component of an arrangement described in subparagraph (C), to the Medicare and Medicaid Coverage Data Bank;

(ii) in the case of a plan that is a multiemployer plan or is a component of an arrangement described in subparagraph (C), to the employer or to such Data Bank, at the option of the plan; and

(iii) in any other case, to the employer or to such Data Bank, at the option of the employer.

(B) EMPLOYER DESCRIBED.—An employer is described in this subparagraph for any calendar year if such employer normally employed fewer than 50 employees on a typical business day during such calendar year.

(C) ARRANGEMENT DESCRIBED.—An arrangement described in this subparagraph is any arrangement in which two or more employers contribute for the purpose of providing group health plan coverage for employees.

(2) INFORMATION NOT REQUIRED TO BE PROVIDED.—Any plan sponsor, plan administrator, insurer, third-party administrator, or other person described in paragraph (1)(A) (other than the employer) that maintains the information under the plan shall not provide to an employer in order to satisfy the requirements of section 1144 of the Social Security Act, and shall not provide to the Data Bank under such section, information that pertains in any way to—

(A) the health status of a participant, or of the participant's spouse, dependent child, or other beneficiary,

(B) the cost of coverage provided to any participant or beneficiary, or

(C) any limitations on such coverage specific to any participant or beneficiary.

(3) REGULATIONS.—The Secretary may, in consultation with the Secretary of Health and Human Service, prescribe such regulations as are necessary to carry out this subsection.

The above repeal is effective as if included in P.L. 104-226 (October 2, 1996).

P.L. 105-34, § 1503(a):

Amended ERISA Sec. 101(b) by striking paragraphs (1), (2), and three and redesignating paragraphs (4) and (5) as (1) and (2), respectively. Prior to amendment, the three paragraphs read as follows:

(1) the summary plan description described in section 102(a)(1);

(2) a plan description containing the matter required in section 102(b);

(3) modifications and changes referred to in section 102(a)(2).

The above amendment is effective August 5, 1997.

P.L. 104-204, § 603(b)(3)(B):

Amended ERISA Sec. 101(g) by striking "section 706(a)(2)" and inserting "section 733(a)(2)".

The above amendment applies to group health plans for plan years beginning on or after January 1, 1998.

P.L. 104-191, § 101(e)(1):

Amended ERISA Sec. 101 by redesignating subsection (g) as subsection (h) and by inserting after subsection (f) the new subsection (g) to read as above.

The above amendments generally apply with respect to group health plans for plan years beginning after June 30, 1997. For special rules, see Act Sec. 101(g)(2)- (5), reproduced below.

Act Sec. 101(g)(2)-(5) reads as follows:

(g) EFFECTIVE DATES.—

(1) IN GENERAL.—Except as provided in this section, this section (and the amendments made by this section) shall apply with respect to group health plans for plan years beginning after June 30, 1997.

(2) DETERMINATION OF CREDITABLE COVERAGE.—

(A) PERIOD OF COVERAGE.—

(i) IN GENERAL.—Subject to clause (ii), no period before July 1, 1996, shall be taken into account under part 7 of subtitle B of title I of the Employee Retirement Income Security Act of 1974 (as added by this section) in determining creditable coverage.

(ii) SPECIAL RULE FOR CERTAIN PERIODS.—The Secretary of Labor, consistent with section 104, shall provide for a process whereby individuals who need to establish creditable coverage for periods before July 1, 1996, and who would have such coverage credited but for clause (i) may be given credit for creditable coverage for such periods through the presentation of documents or other means.

(B) CERTIFICATIONS, ETC.—

(i) IN GENERAL.—Subject to clauses (ii) and (iii), subsection (e) of section 701 of the Employee Retirement Income Security Act of 1974 (as added by this section) shall apply to events occurring after June 30, 1996.

(ii) NO CERTIFICATION REQUIRED TO BE PROVIDED BEFORE JUNE 1, 1997.—In no case is a certification required to be provided under such subsection before June 1, 1997.

(iii) CERTIFICATION ONLY ON WRITTEN REQUEST FOR EVENTS OCCURRING BEFORE OCTOBER 1, 1996.—In the case of an event occurring after June 30, 1996, and before October 1, 1996, a certification is not required to be provided under such subsection unless an individual (with respect to whom the certification is otherwise required to be made) requests such certification in writing.

(C) TRANSITIONAL RULE.—In the case of an individual who seeks to establish creditable coverage for any period for which certification is not required because it relates to an event occurring before June 30, 1996—

(i) the individual may present other credible evidence of such coverage in order to establish the period of creditable coverage; and

(ii) a group health plan and a health insurance issuer shall not be subject to any penalty or enforcement action with respect to the plan's or issuer's crediting (or not crediting) such coverage if the plan or issuer has sought to comply in good faith with the applicable requirements under the amendments made by this section.

(3) SPECIAL RULE FOR COLLECTIVE BARGAINING AGREEMENTS.—Except as provided in paragraph (2), in the case of a group health plan maintained pursuant to one or more collective bargaining agreements between employee representatives and one or more employers ratified before the date of the enactment of this Act, part 7 of subtitle B of title I of Employee Retirement Income Security Act of 1974 (other than section 701(e) thereof) shall not apply to plan years beginning before the later of—

(A) the date on which the last of the collective bargaining agreements relating to the plan terminates (determined without regard to any extension thereof agreed to after the date of the enactment of this Act), or

(B) July 1, 1997.

For purposes of subparagraph (A), any plan amendment made pursuant to a collective bargaining agreement relating to the plan which amends the plan solely to conform to any requirement of such part shall not be treated as a termination of such collective bargaining agreement.

(4) TIMELY REGULATIONS.—The Secretary of Labor, consistent with section 104, shall first issue by not later than April 1, 1997, such regulations as may be necessary to carry out the amendments made by this section.

(5) LIMITATION ON ACTIONS.—No enforcement action shall be taken, pursuant to the amendments made by this section, against a group health plan or health insurance issuer with respect to a violation of a requirement imposed by such amendments before January 1, 1998, or, if later, the date of issuance of regulations referred to in paragraph (4), if the plan or issuer has sought to comply in good faith with such requirements.

P.L. 104-188, § 1421(d)(1):

Amended ERISA Sec. 101 by redesignating subsection (g) as subsection (h) and by inserting after subsection (f) the new subsection (g) to read as above.

The above amendments apply to tax years beginning after December 31, 1996.

P.L. 103-66, § 4301(b)(1):

Amended ERISA Sec. 101 by redesignating subsection (f) as subsection (g) and by inserting after subsection (e) the new subsection (f) to read as above.

The above amendments are effective on August 10, 1993. Any plan amendment required to be made by Act Sec. 4301 need not be made before the first plan year beginning on or after January 1, 1994 if: (1) the plan is operated in accordance with Act Sec. 4301 during the period after August 9, 1993 and before such first plan year; and (2) the amendment applies retroactively to this period. A plan will not be treated as failing to be operated in accordance with plan provisions merely because it operates in accordance with the effective date requirements.

P.L. 101-508, Sec. 12012(d)(1):

Amended ERISA Sec. 101 by redesignating subsection (e) as subsection (f) and adding new subsection (e) to read as above effective for qualified transfers under Code Sec. 420 made after November 5, 1990.

P.L. 101-239, § 7881(b)(5)(A):

Amended ERISA Sec. 101(d)(1) by striking "an employer of a plan" and inserting "an employer maintaining a plan" effective for plan years beginning after December 31, 1987.

P.L. 101-239, § 7881(b)(5)(C):

Amended P.L. 100-203, § 9304(d) by striking "Section" and inserting "Effective with respect to plan years beginning after December 31, 1987, section" effective for plan years beginning after December 31, 1987.

P.L. 101-239, § 7894(b)(1):

Amended the heading for part 1 of subtitle B of title I of ERISA by striking "Part I" and inserting "Part 1" effective September 2, 1974.

P.L. 101-239, § 7894(b)(2):

Amended ERISA Sec. 101(a)(2) by striking "section" and inserting "sections" effective September 2, 1974.

P.L. 100-203, § 9304(d):

Amended ERISA Sec. 101 by redesignating subsection (d) as (e) and adding new subsection (d) to read as above, effective for plan years beginning after December 31, 1987.

Regulations

Reg. § 2520.101-1 was published in the *Federal Register* on April 23, 1976 (41 FR 16957). Interim Reg. § 2520.101-2 was published in the *Federal Register* on February 11, 2000 (65 FR 7152), and was effective April 11, 2000. Final Reg. § 2520.101-2 was published in the *Federal Register* on April 9, 2003 (68 FR 17493), and is effective January 1, 2004. Interim Reg. § 2520.101-3 was published in the *Federal Register* on October 21, 2002 (67 FR 64765) and was effective January 26, 2003. Reg. § 2520.101-3 was revised and finalized on January 24, 2003 (68 FR 3715). Reg. § 2520.101-4 was added on January 11, 2006 (71 FR 1904). Reg. § 2520.101-5 was added and reserved and Reg. § 2520.101-6 was added on March 2, 2010 (75 FR 9334). Reg. § 2520.101-2 was amended on March 1, 2013 (78 FR 13781), effective April 1, 2013. Reg. § 2520.101-4 was removed and reserved on February 2, 2015 (80 FR 5625). Text was added to Reg. § 2520.101-5, Appendix A to Reg. § 2520.101-5 was added, and Appendix B to Reg. § 2520.101-5 was added on February 2, 2015 (80 FR 5625).

Subpart A—General Reporting and Disclosure Requirements

[¶ 14,211]

§ 2520.101-1 **Duty of reporting and disclosure.** The procedures for implementing the plan administrator's duty of reporting to the Secretary of Labor and disclosing information to participants and beneficiaries are located in Subparts D, E, and F of this part [see Finding Lists in Volume 1—CCH].

[¶ 14,212]

§ 2520.101-2 **Filing by Multiple Employer Welfare Arrangements and Certain Other Related Entities.**

(a) *Basis and scope.* Section 101(g) of the Employee Retirement Income Security Act (ERISA), as amended by the Patient Protection and Affordable Care Act, requires the Secretary of Labor (the Secretary) to establish, by regulation, a requirement that multiple employer welfare arrangements (MEWAs) providing benefits that consist of medical care (as described in paragraph (b)(6) of this section), which are not group health plans, to register with the Secretary prior to operating in a State. Section 101(g) also permits the Secretary to require, by regulation, such MEWAs to report, not more frequently than annually, in such form and manner as the Secretary may require, for the purpose of determining the extent to which the requirements of part 7 of subtitle B of title I of ERISA (part 7) are being carried out in connection with such benefits. Section 734 of ERISA provides that the Secretary may promulgate such regulations as may be necessary or appropriate to carry out the provisions of part 7. This section sets out requirements for reporting by MEWAs that provide benefits that consist of medical care and by certain entities that claim not to be a MEWA solely due to the exception in section 3(40)(A)(i) of ERISA (referred to in this section as Entities Claiming Exception or ECEs). The reporting requirements apply regardless of whether the MEWA or ECE is a group health plan.

(b) *Definitions.* As used in this section, the following definitions apply:

(1) *Administrator* means. (i) The person specifically so designated by the terms of the instrument under which the MEWA or ECE is operated;

(ii) If the MEWA or ECE is a group health plan and the administrator is not so designated, the plan sponsor (as defined in section 3(16)(B) of ERISA); or

(iii) In the case of a MEWA or ECE for which an administrator is not designated and a plan sponsor cannot be identified, jointly and severally, the person or persons actually responsible (whether or not so designated under the terms of the instrument under which the MEWA or ECE is operated) for the control, disposition, or management of the cash or property received by or contributed to the MEWA or ECE, irrespective of whether such control, disposition, or management is exercised directly by such person or persons or indirectly through an agent, custodian, or trustee designated by such person or persons.

(2) *Entity Claiming Exception (ECE)* means an entity that claims it is not a MEWA on the basis that the entity is established or maintained pursuant to one or more agreements that the Secretary finds to be collective bargaining agreements within the meaning of section 3(40)(A)(i) of ERISA and § 2510.3-40.

(3) *Excepted benefits* means *excepted benefits* within the meaning of section 733(c) of ERISA and § 2590.701-2 of this chapter.

(4) *Group health plan* means a *group health plan* within the meaning of section 733(a) of ERISA and § 2590.701-2 of this chapter.

(5) *Health insurance issuer* means a *health insurance issuer* within the meaning of section 733(b)(2) of ERISA and § 2590.701-2 of this chapter.

(6) *Medical care* means *medical care* within the meaning of section 733(a)(2) of ERISA and § 2590.701-2 of this chapter.

(7) *Multiple employer welfare arrangement (MEWA)* means a *multiple employer welfare arrangement* within the meaning of section 3(40) of ERISA.

(8) *Operating* means any activity including but not limited to marketing, soliciting, providing, or offering to provide benefits consisting of *medical care.*

(9) *Origination* means, with regard to an ECE, the occurrence of any of the following events (an ECE is considered to have been *originated* only when an event described below occurs)—

(i) The ECE begins operating with regard to the employees of two or more employers (including one or more self-employed individuals);

(ii) The ECE begins operating following a merger with another ECE (unless all of the ECEs that participate in the merger previously were last originated at least three years prior to the merger); or

(iii) The number of employees receiving coverage for medical care under the ECE is at least 50 percent greater than the number of such employees on the last day of the previous calendar year (unless the increase is due to a merger with another ECE under which all ECEs that participate in the merger were last originated at least three years prior to the merger).

(10) *Reporting or to report* means to file the Form M-1 as required pursuant to sections 101(g) of ERISA; § 2520.101-2; or the instructions to the Form M-1.

(11) *Special filing event* means, with regard to an ECE—

(i) The ECE begins knowingly operating in any additional State or States that were not indicated on a previous report filed pursuant to paragraph (e)(1)(i) or (f)(2)(i) of this section; or

(ii) The ECE experiences a material change as defined in the Form M-1 instructions.

(12) *State* means *State* within the meaning of § 2590.701-2 of this chapter.

(c) *Persons required to report.* (1) *General rule.* Except as provided in paragraph (c)(2) of this section, the following persons are required to report under this section:

(i) The administrator of a MEWA regardless of whether the entity is a group health plan; and

(ii) The administrator of an ECE during the three-year period following an event described in paragraph (b)(9) of this section.

(2) *Exceptions.* (i) Nothing in this paragraph (c) shall be construed to require reporting under this section by the administrator of a MEWA or ECE described under this paragraph (c)(2)(i).

(A) A MEWA or ECE licensed or authorized to operate as a health insurance issuer in every State in which it offers or provides coverage for medical care to employees;

(B) A MEWA or ECE that provides coverage that consists solely of excepted benefits, which are not subject to ERISA part 7. If the MEWA or ECE provides coverage that consists of both excepted benefits and other benefits for medical care that are not excepted benefits, the administrator of the MEWA or ECE is required to report under this section;

(C) A MEWA or ECE that is a group health plan not subject to ERISA, including a governmental plan, church plan, or a plan maintained solely for the purpose of complying with workmen's compensation laws, within the meaning of sections 4(b)(1), 4(b)(2), or 4(b)(3) of ERISA, respectively; or

(D) A MEWA or ECE that provides coverage only through group health plans that are not covered by ERISA, including governmental plans, church plans, or plans maintained solely for the purpose of complying with workmen's compensation laws within the meaning of sections 4(b)(1), 4(b)(2), or 4(b)(3) of ERISA, respectively (or other arrangements not covered by ERISA, such as health insurance coverage offered to individuals other than in connection with a group health plan, known as individual market coverage).

(ii) Nothing in this paragraph (c) shall be construed to require reporting under this section by the administrator of an entity that would not constitute a MEWA or ECE *but for* the following circumstances under this paragraph (c)(2)(ii).

(A) The entity provides coverage to the employees of two or more trades or businesses that share a common control interest of at least 25 percent at any time during the plan year, applying principles similar to the principles of section 414(c) of the Internal Revenue Code;

(B) The entity provides coverage to the employees of two or more employers due to a change in control of businesses (such as a merger or acquisition) that occurs for a purpose other than avoiding Form M-1 filing and is temporary in nature. For purposes of this paragraph, "temporary" means the MEWA or ECE does not extend beyond the end of the plan year following the plan year in which the change in control occurs; or

(C) The entity provides coverage to persons (excluding spouses and dependents) who are not employees or former employees of the plan sponsor, such as non-employee members of the board of directors or independent contractors, and the number of such persons who are not employees or former employees does not exceed one percent of the total number of employees or former employees covered under the arrangement, determined as of the last day of the year to be reported or, determined as of the 60th day following the date the MEWA or ECE began operating in a manner such that a filing is required pursuant to paragraph (e)(1)(i), (2), or (3) of this section.

(3) *Examples.* The rules of this paragraph (c) are illustrated by the following examples:

Example 1. (i) *Facts.* MEWA *A* begins operating by offering coverage to the employees of two or more employers on August 1, 2013. MEWA *A* is licensed or authorized to operate as a health insurance issuer in every State in which it offers coverage for medical care to employees.

(ii) *Conclusion.* In this *Example 1,* the administrator of MEWA *A* is not required to report via Form M-1. MEWA *A* meets the exception to the filing requirement in paragraph (c)(2)(i)(A) of this section because it is licensed or authorized to operate as a health insurance issuer in every State in which it offers coverage for medical care to employees.

Example 2. (i) *Facts.* Company *B* maintains a group health plan that provides benefits for medical care for its employees (and their dependents). Company *B* establishes a joint venture in which it has a 25 percent stock ownership interest, determined by applying the principles similar to the principles under section 414(c) of the Internal Revenue Code, and transfers some of its employees to the joint venture. Company *B* continues to cover these transferred employees under its group health plan.

(ii) *Conclusion.* In this *Example 2,* the administrator is not required to file the Form M-1 because Company *B's* group health plan meets the exception to the filing requirement in paragraph (c)(2)(ii)(A) of this section. This is because Company *B's* group health plan would not constitute a MEWA but for the fact that it provides coverage to two or more trades or businesses that share a common control interest of at least 25 percent.

Example 3. (i) *Facts.* Company *C* maintains a group health plan that provides benefits for medical care for its employees. The plan year of Company *C's* group health plan is the fiscal year for Company *C,* which is October 1st—September 30th. Therefore, October 1, 2012—September 30, 2013 is the 2013 plan year. Company *C* decides to sell a portion of its business, Division *Z,* to Company *D.* Company *C* signs an agreement with Company *D* under which Division *Z* will be transferred to Company *D,* effective September 30, 2013. The change in control of Division *Z* therefore occurs on September 30, 2013. Under the terms of the agreement, Company *C* agrees to continue covering all of the employees that formerly worked for Division *Z* under its group health plan until Company *D* has established a new group health plan to cover these employees. Under the terms of the agreement, it is anticipated that Company *C* will not be required to cover the employees of Division *Z* under its group health plan beyond the end of the 2014 plan year, which is the plan year following the plan year in which the change in control of Division *Z* occurred.

(ii) *Conclusion.* In this *Example 3,* the administrator of Company *C's* group health plan is not required to report via the Form M-1 on March 1, 2014 for fiscal year 2013 because it is subject to the exception to the filing requirement in paragraph (c)(2)(ii)(B) of this section for an entity that would not constitute a MEWA but for the fact that it is created by a change in control of businesses that occurs for a purpose other than to avoid filing the Form M-1 and is temporary in nature. Under the exception, "temporary" means the MEWA does not extend beyond the end of the plan year following the plan year in which the change in control occurs. The administrator is not required to file the 2013 Form M-1 annual report because it is anticipated that Company *C* will not be required to cover the employees of Division *Z* under its group health plan beyond the end of the 2014 plan year, which is the plan year following the plan year in which the change in control of businesses occurred.

Example 4. (i) *Facts.* Company *E* maintains a group health plan that provides benefits for medical care for its employees (and their dependents) as well as certain independent contractors who are self-employed individuals. The plan is therefore a MEWA. The administrator of Company *E's* group health plan uses calendar year data to report for purposes of the Form M-1. The administrator of Company *E's* group health plan determines that the number of independent contractors covered under the group health plan as of the last day of calendar year 2013 is less than one percent of the total number of employees and former employees covered under the plan determined as of the last day of calendar year 2013.

(ii) *Conclusion.* In this *Example 4,* the administrator of Company *E's* group health plan is not required to report via the Form M-1 for calendar year 2013 (a filing that is otherwise due by March 1, 2014) because it is subject to the exception to the filing requirement provided in paragraph (c)(2)(ii)(C) of this section for entities that cover a very small number of persons who are not employees or former employees of the plan sponsor.

(d) *Information to be reported.* (1) Any reporting required by this section shall consist of a completed copy of the Form M-1 Report for Multiple Employer Welfare Arrangements (MEWAs) and Certain Entities Claiming Exception (ECEs) (Form M-1) and any additional statements required pursuant to the instructions for the Form M-1.

(2) *Rejected filings.* The Secretary may reject any filing under this section if the Secretary determines that the filing is incomplete, in accordance with § 2560.502c-5 of this chapter.

(3) If the Secretary rejects a filing under paragraph (d)(2) of this section, and if a revised filing satisfactory to the Secretary is not submitted within 45 days after the notice of rejection, the Secretary may bring a civil action for such relief as may be appropriate (including penalties under section 502(c)(5) of ERISA and § 2560.502c-5 of this chapter).

(e) *Origination, registration, and other non-annual reporting requirements and timing.* (1) *General rule for ECEs.* (i) Except as provided in paragraph (e)(1)(ii) of this section, and subject to the limitations established by paragraph (c)(1)(ii) of this section, when an ECE experiences an event described in paragraphs (b)(9) or (b)(11) of this section, the administrator of the ECE shall file Form M-1 by the 30th day following the date of the event.

(ii) *Exception.* Paragraph (e)(1)(i) of this section does not apply to ECEs that experience an origination as described in paragraph (b)(9)(i) of this section. Such entities are required, subject to the limitations established by paragraph (c)(1)(ii) of this section, to file the Form M-1 30 days prior to the date of the event.

(2) *General rule for MEWAs.* (i) *In general.* Except as provided in paragraph (e)(2)(ii) of this section, the administrator of the MEWA is required to register with the Secretary by filing the Form M-1 30 days prior to operating in any State.

(ii) *Exception.* Paragraph (e)(2)(i) of this section does not apply to MEWAs that, prior to the effective date of this section, were already in operation in a State (or States). Such entities are required to submit an annual filing pursuant to annual reporting rules described in paragraph (f)(2)(i) of this section for that State (or those States).

(3) *Special rule requiring MEWAs to make additional filings.* Subsequent to registering with the Secretary pursuant to paragraph (e)(2)(i) of this section, the administrator of a MEWA shall file the Form M-1:

(i) Within 30 days of knowingly operating in any additional State or States that were not indicated on a previous report filed pursuant to paragraph (e)(2)(i) or (f)(2)(i) of this section;

(ii) Within 30 days of the MEWA operating with regard to the employees of an additional employer (or employers, including one or more self-employed individuals) after a merger with another MEWA;

(iii) Within 30 days of the date the number of employees receiving coverage for medical care under the MEWA is at least 50 percent greater than the number of such employees on the last day of the previous calendar year; or

(iv) Within 30 days of experiencing a material change as defined in the Form M-1 instructions.

(4) *Anti-abuse rule.* If a MEWA or ECE neither offers nor provides benefits consisting of medical care within a State during the calendar year immediately following the year in which a filing is made by the ECE pursuant to paragraph (e)(1) of this section (due to an event described in paragraph (b)(9)(i) or (b)(11)(i) of this section) or a filing is made by the MEWA pursuant to paragraph (e)(2) or (3) of this section, with respect to operating in such State, such filing will be considered to have lapsed.

(5) *Multiple filings not required in certain circumstances.* If multiple filings are required under this paragraph (e), a single filing will satisfy this section so long as the filing is timely for each required filing.

(6) *Extensions.* (i) An extension may be granted for filing a report required by paragraph (e)(1), (2), or (3) of this section if the administrator complies with the extension procedure prescribed in the instructions to the Form M-1.

(ii) If the filing deadline set forth in this paragraph (e) is a Saturday, Sunday, or federal holiday, the form must be filed no later than the next business day.

(f) *Annual reporting requirements and timing.* (1) *Period for which reporting is required.* A completed copy of the Form M-1 is required to be filed for each calendar year during all or part of which the MEWA is operating and for each of the three calendar years following an origination during all or part of which the ECE is operating.

(2) *Filing deadline.* (i) *General March 1 filing due date for annual filings.* Except as provided in paragraph (f)(2)(ii) of this section, a completed copy of the Form M-1 is required to be filed on or before each March 1 that follows a period for which reporting is required (as described in paragraph (f)(1) of this section).

(ii) *Exception.* Paragraph (f)(2)(i) of this section does not apply to ECEs and MEWAs if, between October 1 and December 31, the entity is required to make a filing pursuant to paragraph (e)(1), (2), or (3) of this section and makes that filing timely.

(3) *Extensions.* (i) An extension may be granted for filing a report required by paragraph (f)(2)(i) of this section if the administrator complies with the extension procedure prescribed in the instructions to the Form M-1.

(ii) If the filing deadline set forth in this paragraph (f) is a Saturday, Sunday, or federal holiday, the form must be filed no later than the next business day.

(4) *Examples.* The rules of paragraphs (e) and (f) of this section are illustrated by the following examples:

Example 1. (i) *Facts.* MEWA *A* began offering coverage for medical care to the employees of two or more employers on July 1, 2003 (and continues to offer such coverage). MEWA *A* has satisfied all filing requirements to date.

(ii) *Conclusion.* In this *Example 1,* the administrator of MEWA *A* must continue to file a timely completed Form M-1 annual report each year, but the administrator is not required to register with the Secretary because MEWA *A* meets the exception to the registration requirement in paragraph (e)(2)(ii) of this section and has not experienced any event described in paragraph (e)(3) that would require registering with the Secretary.

Example 2. (i) *Facts.* On August 25, 2013, MEWA *B* is operating in State *P* and has made all appropriate filings related to those operations. On December 22, 2013 one of the employers that participates in MEWA *B* is awarded a new contract in State *Q*. The employer adds an office in State *Q* and the employees there are eligible to access its group health plan.

(ii) *Conclusion.* In this *Example 2,* the administrator of MEWA *B* must report the addition of State *Q* by filing the Form M-1 within 30 days *of knowing that it is operating in State* Q.

Example 3. (i) *Facts.* As of July 1, 2013, MEWA *C* is preparing to operate in States *Y* and *Z*. MEWA *C* is not licensed or authorized to operate as a health insurance issuer in any State and does not meet any of the other exceptions set forth in paragraph (c)(2) of this section.

(ii) *Conclusion.* In this *Example 3,* the administrator of MEWA *C* is required to register with the Secretary by filing a completed Form M-1 30 days prior to operating in States *Y* or *Z*. The administrator of MEWA *C* must also report by filing the Form M-1 annually by every March 1 thereafter.

Example 4. (i) *Facts.* As of July 28, 2013, MEWA *D* is operating in States *V* and *W*. MEWA *D* has satisfied the requirements of (e)(2) and, if applicable, (e)(3) with respect to those States. MEWA *D* is not licensed or authorized to operate as a health insurance issuer in any State and does not meet any of the other exceptions set forth in (c)(2) of this section. On August 5, 2013 MEWA *D* knowingly begins operating in State *X*.

(ii) *Conclusion.* In this *Example 4,* the administrator of MEWA *D* is required to make an additional registration filing with the Secretary by September 4, 2013 (within 30 days of knowingly operating in State *X*). Additionally, the administrator of MEWA *D* must continue to file the Form M-1 annually by every March 1 thereafter.

Example 5. (i) *Facts.* ECE *A* began offering coverage for medical care to the employees of two or more employers on January 1, 2007 and ECE *A* has not been involved in any mergers or experienced any other origination as described in paragraph (b)(9) of this section.

(ii) *Conclusion.* In this *Example 5,* ECE *A* was originated on January 1, 2007 and has not been originated since then. Therefore, the administrator of ECE *A* is not required to file a 2012 Form M-1 because the last time the ECE *A* was originated was January 1, 2007 which is more than three years prior. Further, the ECE has satisfied its reporting requirements by making three timely annual filings after its origination.

Example 6. (i) *Facts.* ECE *B* wants to begin offering coverage for medical care to the employees of two or more employers on July 1, 2013.

(ii) *Conclusion.* In this *Example 6,* the administrator of ECE *B* must file a completed Form M-1 on or before June 1, 2013 (which is 30 days prior to the origination date). In addition, the administrator of ECE *B* must file an updated copy of the Form M-1 by March 1, 2014 because the last date ECE *B* was originated was July 1, 2013 (which is less than three years prior to the March 1, 2014 due date). Furthermore, the administrator of ECE *B* must file the Form M-1 by March 1, 2015 and again by March 1, 2016 (because July 1, 2013 is less than three years prior to March 1, 2015 and March 1, 2016, respectively). However, if ECE *B* is not involved in any mergers and does not experience any other origination as described in paragraph (b)(9) of this section, there would not be a new origination date and no Form M-1 is required to be filed after March 1, 2016.

Example 7. (i) *Facts.* ECE *D*, which currently operates in State *A* and is still within the three-year window following its origination and the timely filing related thereto, is making preparations to operate in State *B* beginning on November 1, 2013.

(ii) *Conclusion.* In this *Example 7,* by operating in State *B*, ECE *D* experiences a special event within the three-year window following its origination and must make a filing by December 2, 2013.

Example 8. (i) *Facts.* Same facts as *Example 7*. ECE *D* satisfied its special filing requirement but is unsure about its annual filing requirements.

(ii) *Conclusion.* ECE *D* is exempt from the next annual filing due March 1, 2014 pursuant to the filing deadline exception under (f)(2)(ii) of this section. However, ECE *D* must continue making annual filings for the remainder of the three years following its origination.

Example 9. (i) *Facts.* MEWA *E* begins distributing marketing materials on August 31, 2013.

(ii) *Conclusion.* In this *Example 8,* because MEWA *E* began operating on August 31, 2013, the administrator of MEWA *E* must register with the Secretary by filing a completed Form M-1 on or before August 1, 2013 (30 days prior to operating in any State). In addition, the administrator of MEWA *E* must file the Form M-1 annually by every March 1 thereafter.

Example 10. (i) *Facts.* Same facts as *Example 9,* but MEWA *E* registers on or before August 1, 2013 by filing a Form M-1 indicating it will begin operating in every State. However, in the calendar year immediately following the filing, MEWA *E* only offered or provided benefits consisting of medical care to participants in State *Z*.

(ii) *Conclusion.* In this Example 10, the registration for all States (other than State *Z*) have lapsed under (e)(4) because MEWA *E* only offered or provided benefits consisting of medical care to participants in State *Z* in the calendar year immediately following the filing. If subsequently, MEWA *E* begins offering or providing benefits consisting of medical care to participants in any additional State (or States), it must make a new registration filing pursuant to (e)(3) of this section.

(g) *Electronic filing.* A completed Form M-1 is filed with the Secretary by submitting it electronically as prescribed in the instructions to the Form M-1.

(h) *Penalties.* (1) *Civil penalties and procedures.* For information on civil penalties under section 502(c)(5) of ERISA for persons who fail to file the information required under this section, see § 2560.502c-5 of this chapter. For information relating to administrative hearings and appeals in connection with the assessment of civil penalties under section 502(c)(5) of ERISA, see §§ 2570.90 through 2570.101 of this chapter.

(2) *Criminal penalties and procedures.* For information on criminal penalties under section 519 of ERISA for persons who knowingly make false statements or false representation of fact with regards to the information required under this section, see section 501(b) of ERISA.

(3) *Cease and desist and summary seizure orders.* For information on the Secretary's authority to issue a cease and desist or summary seizure order under section 521 of ERISA, see § 2560.521.

[Added by EBSA on April 9, 2003 by 68 FR 17493. Revised by EBSA on March 1, 2013 (78 FR 13781).]

[¶ 14,213]

§ 2520.101-3 **Notice of blackout periods under individual account plans.**

(a) *In general.* In accordance with section 101(i) of the Act, the administrator of an individual account plan, within the meaning of paragraph (d)(2) of this section, shall provide notice of any blackout period, within the meaning of paragraph (d)(1) of this section, to all participants and beneficiaries whose rights under the plan will be temporarily suspended, limited, or restricted by the blackout period (the "affected participants and beneficiaries") and to issuers of employer securities subject to such blackout period in accordance with this section.

(b) *Notice to participants and beneficiaries.* (1) *Content.* The notice required by paragraph (a) of this section shall be written in a manner calculated to be understood by the average plan participant and shall include—

(i) The reasons for the blackout period;

(ii) A description of the rights otherwise available to participants and beneficiaries under the plan that will be temporarily suspended, limited or restricted by the blackout period (e.g., right to direct or diversify assets in individual accounts, right to obtain loans from the plan, right to obtain distributions from the plan), including identification of any investments subject to the blackout period;

(iii) The length of the blackout period by reference to:

(A) The expected beginning date and ending date of the blackout period; or

(B) The calendar week during which the blackout period is expected to begin and end, provided that during such weeks information as to whether the blackout period has begun or ended is readily available, without charge, to affected participants and beneficiaries, such as via a toll-free number or access to a specific web site, and the notice describes how to access the information;

(iv) In the case of investments affected, a statement that the participant or beneficiary should evaluate the appropriateness of their current investment decisions in light of their inability to direct or diversify assets in their accounts during the blackout period (a notice that includes the advisory statement contained in paragraph 4. of the model notice in paragraph (e)(2) of this section will satisfy this requirement);

(v) In any case in which the notice required by paragraph (a) of this section is not furnished at least 30 days in advance of the last date on which affected participants and beneficiaries could exercise affected rights immediately before the commencement of the blackout period, except for a notice furnished pursuant to paragraph (b)(2)(ii)(C) of this section:

(A) A statement that Federal law generally requires that notice be furnished to affected participants and beneficiaries at least 30 days in advance of the last date on which participants and beneficiaries

could exercise the affected rights immediately before the commencement of a blackout period (a notice that includes the statement contained in paragraph 5. of the model notice in paragraph (e)(2) of this section will satisfy this requirement), and

(B) An explanation of the reasons why at least 30 days advance notice could not be furnished; and

(vi) The name, address and telephone number of the plan administrator or other contact responsible for answering questions about the blackout period.

(2) *Timing.* (i) The notice described in paragraph (a) of this section shall be furnished to all affected participants and beneficiaries at least 30 days, but not more than 60 days, in advance of the last date on which such participants and beneficiaries could exercise the affected rights immediately before the commencement of any blackout period.

(ii) The requirement to give at least 30 days advance notice contained in paragraph (b)(2)(i) of this section shall not apply in any case in which—

(A) A deferral of the blackout period in order to comply with paragraph (b)(2)(i) of this section would result in a violation of the requirements of section 404(a)(1)(A) or (B) of the Act, and a fiduciary of the plan reasonably so determines in writing;

(B) The inability to provide the advance notice of a blackout period is due to events that were unforeseeable or circumstances beyond the reasonable control of the plan administrator, and a fiduciary of the plan reasonably so determines in writing; or

(C) The blackout period applies only to one or more participants or beneficiaries solely in connection with their becoming, or ceasing to be, participants or beneficiaries of the plan as a result of a merger, acquisition, divestiture, or similar transaction involving the plan or plan sponsor.

(iii) In any case in which paragraph (b)(2)(ii) of this section applies, the administrator shall furnish the notice described in paragraph (a) of this section to all affected participants and beneficiaries as soon as reasonably possible under the circumstances, unless such notice in advance of the termination of the blackout period is impracticable.

(iv) Determinations under paragraph (b)(2)(ii)(A) and (B) of this section must be dated and signed by the fiduciary.

(3) *Form and manner of furnishing notice.* The notice required by paragraph (a) of this section shall be in writing and furnished to affected participants and beneficiaries in any manner consistent with the requirements of Sec. 2520.104b-1 of this chapter, including paragraph (c) of that section relating to the use of electronic media.

(4) *Changes in length of blackout period.* If, following the furnishing of a notice pursuant to this section, there is a change in the length of the blackout period (specified in such notice pursuant to paragraph (b)(1)(iii) of this section), the administrator shall furnish all affected participants and beneficiaries an updated notice explaining the reasons for the change and identifying all material changes in the information contained in the prior notice. Such notice shall be furnished to all affected participants and beneficiaries as soon as reasonably possible, unless such notice in advance of the termination of the blackout period is impracticable.

(c) *Notice to issuer of employer securities.* (1) The notice required by paragraph (a) of this section shall be furnished to the issuer of any employer securities held by the plan and subject to the blackout period. Such notice shall contain the information described in paragraph (b)(1)(i), (ii), (iii) and (vi) of this section and shall be furnished in accordance with the time frames prescribed in paragraph (b)(2) of this section. In the event of a change in the length of the blackout period specified in such notice, the plan administrator shall furnish an updated notice to the issuer in accordance with the requirements of paragraph (b)(4) of this section.

(2) For purposes of this section, notice to the agent for service of legal process for the issuer shall constitute notice to the issuer, unless the issuer has provided the plan administrator with the name of another person for service of notice, in which case the plan administrator shall furnish notice to such person. Such notice shall be in writing, except that the notice may be in electronic or other form to the extent

the person to whom notice must be furnished consents to receive the notice in such form.

(3) If the issuer designates the plan administrator as the person for service of notice pursuant to paragraph (c)(2) of this section, the issuer shall be deemed to have been furnished notice on the same date as notice is furnished to affected participants and beneficiaries pursuant to paragraph (b) of this section.

(d) *Definitions.* For purposes of this section—

(1) *Blackout period*—

(i) *General.* The term "blackout period" means, in connection with an individual account plan, any period for which any ability of participants or beneficiaries under the plan, which is otherwise available under the terms of such plan, to direct or diversify assets credited to their accounts, to obtain loans from the plan, or to obtain distributions from the plan is temporarily suspended, limited, or restricted, if such suspension, limitation, or restriction is for any period of more than three consecutive business days.

(ii) *Exclusions.* The term "blackout period" does not include a suspension, limitation, or restriction—

(A) Which occurs by reason of the application of the securities laws (as defined in section 3(a)(47) of the Securities Exchange Act of 1934);

(B) Which is a regularly scheduled suspension, limitation, or restriction under the plan (or change thereto), provided that such suspension, limitation or restriction (or change) has been disclosed to affected plan participants and beneficiaries through the summary plan description, a summary of material modifications, materials describing specific investment alternatives under the plan and limits thereon or any changes thereto, participation or enrollment forms, or any other documents and instruments pursuant to which the plan is established or operated that have been furnished to such participants and beneficiaries;

(C) Which occurs by reason of a qualified domestic relations order or by reason of a pending determination (by the plan administrator, by a court of competent jurisdiction or otherwise) whether a domestic relations order filed (or reasonably anticipated to be filed) with the plan is a qualified order within the meaning of section 206(d)(3)(B)(i) of the Act; or

(D) Which occurs by reason of an act or a failure to act on the part of an individual participant or by reason of an action or claim by a party unrelated to the plan involving the account of an individual participant.

(2) *Individual account plan.* The term "individual account plan" shall have the meaning provided such term in section 3(34) of the Act, except that such term shall not include a "one-participant retirement plan" within the meaning of paragraph (d)(3) of this section.

(3) *One-participant retirement plan.* The term "one-participant retirement plan" means a one-participant retirement plan as defined in section 101(i)(8)(B) of the Act.

(4) *Issuer.* The term "issuer" means an issuer as defined in section 3 of the Securities Exchange Act of 1934 (15 U.S.C. 78c), the securities of which are registered under section 12 of the Securities Exchange Act of 1934, or that is required to file reports under section 15(d) of the Securities Exchange Act of 1934, or files or has filed a registration statement that has not yet become effective under the Securities Act of 1933 (15 U.S.C. 77a et seq.), and that it has not withdrawn.

(5) *Calendar week.* For purposes of paragraph (b)(1)(iii)(B), the term "calendar week" means a seven day period beginning on Sunday and ending on Saturday.

(e) *Model notice.* (1) *General.* The model notice set forth in paragraph (e)(2) of this section is intended to assist plan administrators in discharging their notice obligations under this section. Use of the model notice is not mandatory. However, a notice that uses the statements provided in paragraphs 4. and 5.(A) of the model notice will be deemed to satisfy the notice content requirements of paragraph

(b)(1)(iv) and (b)(1)(v)(A), respectively, of this section. With regard to all other information required by paragraph (b)(1) of this section, compliance with the notice content requirements will depend on the facts and circumstances pertaining to the particular blackout period and plan.

(2) *Form and content of model notice.*

Important Notice Concerning Your Rights

Under The [Enter Name of Individual Account Plan]

[Enter date of notice]

1. This notice is to inform you that the [enter name of plan]will be [enter reasons for blackout period, as appropriate: changing investment options, changing recordkeepers, etc.].

2. As a result of these changes, you temporarily will be unable to [enter as appropriate: direct or diversify investments in your individual accounts (if only specific investments are subject to the blackout, those investments should be specifically identified), obtain a loan from the plan, or obtain a distribution from the plan]. This period, during which you will be unable to exercise these rights otherwise available under the plan, is called a "blackout period." Whether or not you are planning retirement in the near future, we encourage you to carefully consider how this blackout period may affect your retirement planning, as well as your overall financial plan.

3. The blackout period for the plan [enter the following as appropriate: is expected to begin on [enter date] and end [enter date]/ is expected to begin during the week of [enter date] and end during the week of [enter date]. During these weeks, you can determine whether the blackout period has started or ended by [enter instructions for use toll-free number or accessing web site].

4. [In the case of investments affected by the blackout period, add the following: During blackout period you will be unable to direct or diversify the assets held in your plan account. For this reason, it is very important that you review and consider the appropriateness of your current investments in light of your inability to direct or diversify those investments during the blackout period. For your long-term retirement security, you should give careful consideration to the importance of a well-balanced and diversified investment portfolio, taking into account all your assets, income and investments.] [If the plan permits investments in individual securities, add the following: You should be aware that there is a risk to holding substantial portions of your assets in the securities of any one company, as individual securities tend to have wider price swings, up and down, in short periods of time, than investments in diversified funds. Stocks that have wide price swings might have a large loss during the blackout period, and you would not be able to direct the sale of such stocks from your account during the blackout period.]

5. [If timely notice cannot be provided (see paragraph (b)(1)(v) of this section) enter: (A) Federal law generally requires that you be furnished notice of a blackout period at least 30 days in advance of the last date on which you could exercise your affected rights immediately before the commencement of any blackout period in order to provide you with sufficient time to consider the effect of the blackout period on your retirement and financial plans. (B) [Enter explanation of reasons for inability to furnish 30 days advance notice.]]

6. If you have any questions concerning this notice, you should contact [enter name, address and telephone number of the plan administrator or other contact responsible for answering questions about the blackout period].

(f) *Effective date.* This section shall be effective and shall apply to any blackout period commencing on or after January 26, 2003. For the period January 26, 2003 to February 25, 2003, plan administrators shall furnish notice as soon as reasonably possible.

[Reg. §2520.101-3 was added by FR Doc. 02-26522, interim regulations, published in the *Federal Register* October 21, 2002, effective January 26, 2003 (67 FR 64765). Reg. §2520.101-3 was revised and finalized on January 24, 2003 (68 FR 3715).]

[¶ 14,214]

§2520.101-4 Annual funding notice for multiemployer defined benefit pension plans.

[Removed and reserved.]

[Reg. § 2520.101-4 was added on January 11, 2006 (71 FR 1904). Removed and reserved on February 2, 2015 (80 FR 5625).]

>>>→ *Caution: EBSA Reg. § 2520.101-5 and appendices are applicable to notices for plan years beginning on or after January 1, 2015.*

[¶ 14,215]

§ 2520.101-5 Annual funding notice for defined benefit pension plans.

(a) *In general.* (1) Except as provided in paragraphs (a)(2) and (3) of this section, pursuant to section 101(f) of the Act, the administrator of a defined benefit plan to which title IV of the Act applies shall furnish annually to each person specified in paragraph (f) of this section a funding notice that conforms to the requirements of this section.

(2) A plan administrator shall not be required to furnish a funding notice—

(i) In the case of a multiemployer plan, for a plan year if the due date for such notice is on or after the earlier of:

(A) The date the plan complies with the insolvency notice requirements of section 4245(e) or 4281(d)(3) of the Act and regulations thereunder; or

(B) The date the plan has distributed assets in satisfaction of all nonforfeitable benefits under the plan pursuant to section 4041A of the Act and the regulations thereunder.

(ii) In the case of a single-employer plan, for a plan year if the due date for the funding notice is on or after the date:

(A) The Pension Benefit Guaranty Corporation is appointed as trustee of the plan pursuant to section 4042 of the Act;

(B) The plan has distributed assets in satisfaction of all benefit liabilities in a distress termination pursuant to section 4041(c)(3)(B)(i) of the Act or of all guaranteed benefits in a distress termination pursuant to section 4041(c)(3)(B)(ii) of the Act; or

(C) The plan administrator filed a standard termination notice with the Pension Benefit Guaranty Corporation pursuant to 29 CFR 4041.25, provided that the proposed termination date is on or before the due date of the funding notice and a final distribution of assets in satisfaction of all benefit liabilities proceeds in accordance with section 4041(b) of the Act.

(3) In the case of a merger or consolidation of two or more plans—

(i) The plan administrator of a non-successor plan shall not be required to furnish a funding notice for the plan year in which the merger or consolidation occurred; and

(ii) The funding notice of the successor plan, for the plan year in which the merger or consolidation occurred, must, in addition to the requirements of paragraph (b) of this section, contain a general explanation, including the effective date, of the merger or consolidation and an identification of each plan (*e.g.*, name and plan number) involved in the merger or consolidation.

(b) *Content of notice.* A funding notice shall include the following information:

(1) *Identifying information.* The name of the plan, the name, address, and phone number of the plan administrator and the plan's principal administrative officer (if different than the plan administrator), each plan sponsor's name and employer identification number, and the plan number.

(2) *Funding percentage.* (i) *Single-employer plans.* For single-employer plans, a statement as to whether the plan's funding target attainment percentage (as defined in section 303(d)(2) of the Act) for the notice year, and for each of the two preceding plan years, is at least 100 percent (and, if not, the actual percentages).

(ii) *Multiemployer plans.* For multiemployer plans, a statement as to whether the plan's funded percentage (as defined in section 305(i) of the Act) for the notice year, and for each of the two preceding plan years, is at least 100 percent (and, if not, the actual percentages).

(3) *Assets and liabilities.* (i) *Single-employer plans.* For single-employer plans—

(A) A statement of the total assets (separately stating the prefunding balance and the funding standard carryover balance) and liabilities of the plan, determined in the same manner as under section 303 of the Act, as of the valuation date of the notice year and for each of the two preceding plan years, as reported in the annual report filed under section 104 of the Act for each such preceding plan year, and

(B) A statement of the value of the plan's assets and liabilities determined as of the last day of the notice year. For purposes of this statement, the value of the plan's assets is the fair market value of plan assets. Plan liabilities are equal to the present value of benefits accrued through the last day of the notice year determined in the same manner as liabilities are calculated under section 303 of the Act (including actuarial assumptions and methods), but using the interest rate under section 4006(a)(3)(E)(iv) of the Act in effect for the last month of the notice year.

(ii) *Multiemployer plans.* For multiemployer plans—

(A) A statement of the value of the plan's assets (determined in the same manner as under section 304(c)(2) of the Act) and liabilities (determined in the same manner as under section 305(i)(8) of the Act, using reasonable actuarial assumptions as required under section 304(c)(3) of the Act) as of the valuation date of the notice year and each of the two preceding plan years, and

(B) A statement of the fair market value of plan assets as of the last day of the notice year, and as of the last day of each of the two preceding plan years as reported in the annual report filed under section 104(a) of the Act for each such preceding plan year.

(iii) *Contributions receivable.* For purposes of determining the fair market value of plan assets as of the last day of the notice year under paragraphs (b)(3)(i)(B) and (b)(3)(ii)(B) of this section, the plan administrator may, but is not required to, include contributions made after the notice year and before the notice is furnished to recipients, but only to the extent such contributions are treated for funding purposes as having been made on account of the notice year under section 303(g)(4) of the Act, in the case of a single-employer plan, or under section 304(c)(8) of the Act, in the case of a multiemployer plan.

(4) *Demographic information.* A statement of the number of participants and beneficiaries who, as of the valuation date of the notice year, are: Retired or separated from service and receiving benefits; retired or separated from service and entitled to future benefits (but currently not receiving benefits); or active participants under the plan. The statement shall indicate the number of participants and beneficiaries in each category and the sum of all such participants and beneficiaries. The terms "active" and "retired or separated" shall have the same meaning given to those terms in instructions to the annual report filed under section 104(a) of the Act.

(5) *Funding policy.* A statement setting forth—

(i) The funding policy of the plan;

(ii) The asset allocation of investments under the plan (expressed as percentages of total assets) as of the end of the notice year; and

(iii) A general description of any investment policy of the plan as it relates to the funding policy in paragraph (b)(5)(i) of this section and the asset allocation of investments under paragraph (b)(5)(ii) of this section.

(6) *Endangered, critical, or critical and declining status.* In the case of a multiemployer plan, a statement whether the plan was in endangered, critical, or critical and declining status under section 305 of the Act for the notice year and, if so—

(i) A statement describing how a person may obtain a copy of the plan's funding improvement plan or rehabilitation plan, as appropriate, adopted under section 305 of the Act and the actuarial and financial data that demonstrate any action taken by the plan toward fiscal improvement;

(ii) A summary of the plan's funding improvement plan or rehabilitation plan, including any update or modification of such funding improvement or rehabilitation plan adopted under section 305 of the Act during the notice year; and

(iii) In the case of a multiemployer plan in critical and declining status:

(A) The projected date of insolvency;

(B) A clear statement that such insolvency may result in benefit reductions; and

(C) A statement describing whether the plan sponsor has taken legally permitted actions to prevent insolvency.

(7) *Events having a material effect on liabilities or assets.* Subject to paragraph (g) of this section, in the case of any plan amendment, scheduled benefit increase or reduction, or other known event taking effect in the current plan year and having a material effect on plan liabilities or assets for the year, an explanation of the amendment, scheduled benefit increase or reduction, or event, and a projection to the end of such plan year of the effect of the amendment, scheduled benefit increase or reduction, or event on plan liabilities.

(8) *Rules on termination or insolvency.* (i) *Single-employer plans.* In the case of a single-employer plan, a summary of the rules governing termination of single-employer plans under subtitle C of title IV of the Act.

(ii) *Multiemployer plans.* In the case of a multiemployer plan, a summary of the rules governing insolvency, including the limitations on benefit payments.

(9) *PBGC guarantees.* A general description of the benefits under the plan which are eligible to be guaranteed by the Pension Benefit Guaranty Corporation, along with an explanation of the limitations on the guarantee and the circumstances under which such limitations apply.

(10) *Annual report information.* A statement that a person entitled to notice under paragraph (f) of this section may obtain a copy of the annual report of the plan filed under section 104(a) of the Act upon request, through the Internet Web site of the Department of Labor, or through any Intranet Web site maintained by the applicable plan sponsor (or plan administrator on behalf of the plan sponsor).

(11) *Information disclosed to PBGC.* In the case of a single-employer plan, if applicable, a statement that the contributing sponsor of the plan or a member of the contributing sponsor's controlled group was required to provide information under section 4010 of the Act for the information year ending in the notice year (see 29 CFR 4010.5).

(12) *Additional information.* Any additional information that the plan administrator elects to include, provided that such information is necessary or helpful to understanding the mandatory information in the notice, or is otherwise permitted by law.

(c) *Style and format of notice.* Funding notices shall be written in a manner that is consistent with the style and format requirements of § 2520.102-2 of this chapter.

(d) *When to furnish notice.* (1) Except as provided in paragraph (d)(2) of this section, a funding notice shall be provided not later than 120 days after the end of the notice year.

(2) In the case of a small plan, a funding notice shall be provided not later than the earlier of the date on which the annual report is filed under section 104(a) of the Act or the latest date the annual report must be filed under that section (including extensions). For this purpose, a single-employer plan is a small plan if it meets the exception in section 303(g)(2)(B) of the Act, and a multiemployer plan is a small plan if it had 100 or fewer participants on each day during the plan year preceding the notice year.

(e) *Manner of furnishing notice.* (1) [Reserved.]

(2) A funding notice must be furnished to the Pension Benefit Guaranty Corporation in a manner consistent with the requirements of part 4000 of title IV of the Act. The date that the notice is furnished to the Pension Benefit Guaranty Corporation is determined consistent with that part.

(f) *Persons entitled to notice.* Persons entitled to a funding notice under this section are:

(1) Each participant covered under the plan on the last day of the notice year;

(2) Each beneficiary receiving benefits under the plan on the last day of the notice year;

(3) Each alternate payee under the plan on the last day of the notice year;

(4) Each labor organization representing participants under the plan on the last day of the notice year;

(5) In the case of a multiemployer plan, each employer that, as of the last day of the notice year, is a party to the collective bargaining agreement(s) pursuant to which the plan is maintained or who otherwise may be subject to withdrawal liability pursuant to section 4203 of the Act; and

(6) The Pension Benefit Guaranty Corporation.

(g) *Special rules and definitions for material effect disclosures.* (1) The term "current plan year" means the plan year after the notice year. Thus, for example, if the notice year is January 1, 2017 through December 31, 2017, then the current plan year would be January 1, 2018 through December 31, 2018.

(2) An event described in paragraph (b)(7) of this section is recognized as "taking effect" in the current plan year if the effect of the event is taken into account for the first time for funding under section 430 or 431 of the Internal Revenue Code, as applicable, in such year.

(3) An event described in paragraph (b)(7) of this section has a "material effect" if it results, or is projected to result, in an increase or decrease of five percent or more in the value of assets or liabilities from the valuation date of the notice year. For this measurement, calculate assets and liabilities in the same manner as under paragraph (b)(2) of this section.

(4) An event described in paragraph (b)(7) of this section has a "material effect" if, in the judgment of the plan's enrolled actuary, the effect of the event is considered material for purposes of the plan's funding status under section 430 or 431, as applicable, of the Internal Revenue Code, without regard to paragraph (g)(3) of this section.

(5) An event described in paragraph (b)(7) of this section is "known" only if it is known by the plan administrator prior to 120 days before the due date of the notice. Thus, if an event otherwise described in paragraph (b)(7) first becomes known to a plan administrator 120 days or less before the due date of a notice, the plan administrator is not required to explain, or project the effect of, the event in that notice.

(6) The term "other known event" includes, but is not limited to, an extension of coverage under the existing terms of the plan to a new group of employees; a plan merger, consolidation, or spinoff pursuant to regulations under section 414(l) of the Internal Revenue Code; or, a shutdown of any facility, plant, store, or such other similar corporate event that creates immediate eligibility for benefits that would not otherwise be immediately payable for participants separating from service. The term does not include market fluctuations.

(7) With respect to events described in paragraph (g)(4) of this section, the plan administrator may, instead of projecting the effect on plan liabilities to the end of the current plan year, include an explanation why the event is considered material by the enrolled actuary.

(8) *Example.* The following example illustrates the special rules and definitions of paragraph (g) of this section: Plan Y is a single-employer calendar year plan. Company X, the sponsor of Plan Y, adopts an amendment on June 1, 2017, offering a subsidized early retirement benefit to participants age 50 or older who retire on or after September 1, 2017 and before March 1, 2018. The amendment increases the liabilities of Plan Y by an amount greater than 5% of the value of Plan Y's liabilities on January 1, 2017. Company X does not make an election under Code section 412(d)(2) to accelerate recognition of the event for funding. The amendment is taken into account for the first time under section 430 of the Code as of the January 1, 2018 valuation date. Therefore, the amendment is recognized as taking effect under the final rule in 2018. Since the amendment adopted on June 1, 2017, is known more than 120 days prior to the April 30, 2018 due date of the 2017 funding notice, the amendment must be disclosed in the 2017

funding notice under paragraph (b)(7) of the final regulations as a material effect event taking effect in 2018 (*i.e.*, the current plan year).

(h) *Model notices.* (1) The appendices to this section contain a model notice for single-employer plans and a model notice for multiemployer plans. These models are intended to assist plan administrators in discharging their notice obligations under this section. Use of a model notice is not mandatory. However, subject to paragraph (h)(2) of this section, use of a model notice will be deemed to satisfy the requirements of paragraphs (b)(1) through (b)(11) and paragraph (c) of this section.

(2) To the extent a plan administrator elects to include in a model notice information described in paragraph (b)(12) of this section, such additional information must be consistent with the style and format requirements in paragraph (c) of this section.

(i) *Notice year.* For purposes of this section, the term "notice year" means the plan year to which the notice relates. For example, for a calendar year plan that must furnish its 2010 funding notice no later than the 120th day of 2011, the "notice year" is the 2010 plan year.

(j) *Alternative method of compliance for furnishing notice to PBGC for certain single-employer plans.* Notwithstanding any other provision of this section, the plan administrator of a single-employer plan is not required to furnish a notice to the Pension Benefit Guaranty Corporation annually if, based on the data described in paragraph (b)(3)(i)(A) of this section for the notice year, plan liabilities do not exceed total plan assets by more than $50 million, provided that the plan administrator furnishes the latest available funding notice to the Pension Benefit Guaranty Corporation within 30 days of a written request.

(k) *Alternative method of compliance for multiemployer plans terminated by mass withdrawal.* (1) Notwithstanding any other provision of this section, for plan years beginning after the date specified in section 4041A(b)(2) of the Act, an alternative method of compliance is available in the case of a multiemployer plan that terminates as a result of the withdrawal of every employer from the plan or the cessation of the obligation of all employers to contribute under the plan, as described in section 4041A(a)(2) of the Act. Under this alternative method, the plan administrator shall furnish annually to each person described in paragraph (f)(1) through (3) of this section a notice that complies with paragraphs (c), (d), (e), and (k)(2) of this section.

(2) The notice includes:

(i) A statement of the fair market value of the plan's assets as of the last day of the notice year, and as of the last day of each of the two preceding plan years as reported in the annual report filed under section 104(a) of the Act for each such preceding plan year;

(ii) A statement of the amount of benefit payments made during the notice year and each of the two preceding plan years;

(iii) If a notice has not already been furnished pursuant to 29 CFR 4281.32, a statement that benefits may be reduced pursuant to section 4281(c) of the Act and a summary of the rules governing such reductions;

(iv) A summary of the rules governing insolvency, including the limitations on benefit payments, pursuant to paragraph (b)(8)(ii) of this section;

(v) The information described in paragraphs (b)(1), (b)(9), and (b)(10) of this section; and

(vi) Any additional information that the plan administrator elects to include, subject to the requirements of paragraph (b)(12) of this section.

(l) *Alternative method of compliance for Internal Revenue Code section 412(e)(3) plans.* (1) Notwithstanding any other provision of this section, an alternative method of compliance is available in the case of an insurance contract plan described in section 412(e)(3) of the Internal Revenue Code of 1986. Under this alternative method, the plan administrator shall furnish annually to each person described in paragraph (f) of this section a notice that complies with paragraphs (c), (d), (e), and (l)(2) of this section.

(2) The notice includes:

(i) An explanation that the plan is funded exclusively by an insurance contract or contracts, that such contract or contracts provide for the benefit payments to participants and beneficiaries, that such benefit payments are guaranteed by a licensed insurance company or companies, and the name of the insurance company or companies;

(ii) A statement whether, as of the last day of the notice year, there were any delinquent premiums and, if so, the amount and date of the delinquency and the effect on the plan and on participants and beneficiaries in the event of a policy lapse;

(iii) The information described in paragraph (b)(1), (b)(9), and (b)(10) of this section; and

(iv) Any additional information that the plan administrator elects to include, provided that such information meets the standard in paragraph (b)(12) of this section.

(m) *CSEC plans. [Reserved].*

[Added by 75 FR 9334, 3/2/10. Text added 2/2/2015 (80 FR 5625).]

>>>→ *Caution: EBSA Reg. § 2520.101-5 and appendices are applicable to notices for plan years beginning on or after January 1, 2015.*

[¶ 14,215A]

Appendix A to § 2520.101-5—Single-Employer Plan Model Annual Funding Notice.

COVER PAGE

PAPERWORK BURDEN DISCLOSURE NOTICE
OMB Control Number 1210-0126; expires 04/17/2017

Behind this cover page is a model notice that may be used to satisfy the mandatory disclosure requirements set forth in 29 CFR 2520.101-5. The model notice is a collection of information instrument subject to the Paperwork Reduction Act. Use of the model notice to meet the disclosure requirements is optional. You may also develop your own notice, provided it contains all of the information required by 29 CFR 2520.101-5. The Department of Labor estimates that it will take an average of approximately 21 hours for plan administrators to complete the model. You may send comments on this collection of information, including suggestions for reducing burden to: US Department of Labor, Policy and Research, Attention: PRA Officer, 200 Constitution Avenue, NW, Room N-5718, Washington, DC 20210. The disclosure requirements in 29 CFR 2520.101-5, referenced above, are also a collection of information under the PRA. The public is not required to respond to a collection of information unless it displays a currently valid OMB control number.

DO NOT INCLUDE THIS PAPERWORK REDUCTION ACT BANNER IN NOTICES TO
PARTICIPANTS AND BENEFICIAIRES

ANNUAL FUNDING NOTICE
For
[insert name of single-employer pension plan]

<u>Introduction</u>

This notice includes important information about the funding status of your single-employer pension plan (the "Plan"). It also includes general information about the benefit payments guaranteed by the Pension Benefit Guaranty Corporation ("PBGC"), a federal insurance agency. All traditional pension plans (called "defined benefit pension plans") must provide this notice every year regardless of their funding status. This notice does not mean that the Plan is terminating. It is provided for informational purposes and you are not required to respond in any way. This notice is required by federal law. This notice is for the plan year beginning *[insert beginning date]* and ending *[insert ending date]* ("Plan Year").

<u>How Well Funded Is Your Plan</u>

The law requires the administrator of the Plan to tell you how well the Plan is funded, using a measure called the "funding target attainment percentage." The Plan divides its Net Plan Assets by Plan Liabilities to get this percentage. In general, the higher the percentage, the better funded the plan. The Plan's Funding Target Attainment Percentage for the Plan Year and each of the two preceding plan years is shown in the chart below. The chart also shows you how the percentage was calculated.

Funding Target Attainment Percentage			
	[insert Plan Year, e.g., 2015]	[insert plan year preceding Plan Year, e.g., 2014]	[insert plan year 2 years preceding Plan year, e.g., 2013]
1. Valuation Date	[insert date]	[insert date]	[insert date]
2. Plan Assets			
a. Total Plan Assets	[insert amount]	[insert amount]	[insert amount]
b. Funding Standard Carryover Balance	[insert amount]	[insert amount]	[insert amount]
c. Prefunding Balance	[insert amount]	[insert amount]	[insert amount]
d. Net Plan Assets (a) – (b) – (c) = (d)	[insert amount]	[insert amount]	[insert amount]

3. Plan Liabilities	[insert amount]	[insert amount]	[insert amount]
4. At-Risk Liabilities	[insert amount]	[insert amount]	[insert amount]
5. Funding Target Attainment Percentage (2d)/(3)	**[insert percentage]**	**[insert percentage]**	**[insert percentage]**

{Instructions: Report Valuation Date entries in accordance with section 303(g)(2) of ERISA. Report Total Plan Assets in accordance with section 303(g)(3) of ERISA. Report credit balances (i.e., funding standard carryover balance and prefunding balance) in accordance with section 303(f) of ERISA. Report Net Plan Assets, Plan Liabilities (i.e., funding target), and Funding Target Attainment Percentage in accordance with section 303(d)(2) of ERISA. The amount reported as "Plan Liabilities" should be the funding target determined without regard to at-risk assumptions, even if the plan is in at-risk status. At-Risk Liabilities are determined under section 303(i) of ERISA (taking into account section 303(i)(5) of ERISA). Report At-Risk Liabilities for any year covered by this chart in which the plan was in "at-risk" status within the meaning of section 303(i) of ERISA, only if At-Risk Liabilities are greater than Plan Liabilities; otherwise delete the entire row designated as number 4. Round off all amounts in this chart to the nearest dollar.}

Plan Assets and Credit Balances

The chart above shows certain "credit balances" called the Funding Standard Carryover Balance and Prefunding Balance. A plan might have a credit balance, for example, if in a prior year an employer contributed money to the plan above the minimum level required by law. Generally, an employer may credit the excess money toward the minimum level of contributions required by law that it must make in future years. Plans must subtract these credit balances from Total Plan Assets to calculate their Funding Target Attainment Percentage.

{Instructions: Include the preceding discussion, entitled Plan Assets and Credit Balances, only where such balances exist.}

Plan Liabilities

Plan Liabilities in line 3 of the chart above is an estimate of the amount of assets the Plan needs on the Valuation Date to pay for promised benefits under the Plan.

At-Risk Liabilities

The law considers a plan to be in "at risk" status if its funding target attainment percentage for the prior plan year was below a legal threshold. The sponsor of an at-risk plan must make certain assumptions and contribute more money to that plan. For example, plans in "at-risk" status must assume that all workers eligible to retire in the next 10 years will do so as soon as they can, and that they will take their distribution in whatever form would create the highest cost to the plan, without regard to whether those workers actually do so. The additional contributions that result from "at-risk" status may then remove a plan from this status. The Plan was in "at-risk" status in [*enter year or years covered by the chart above*]. The At-Risk Liabilities row in the chart above shows the increased liabilities resulting from "at-risk" status.

{Instructions: Include the preceding discussion, entitled At-Risk Liabilities, only in the case of a plan required to report At-Risk Liabilities. Delete the entire row designated as number 4 in the chart above if the At-Risk Liabilities discussion is not included in the notice.}

Year-End Assets and Liabilities

The asset values in the chart above are measured as of the first day of the Plan Year. They also are "actuarial values." Actuarial values differ from market values in that they do not fluctuate daily based on changes in the stock or other markets. Actuarial values smooth out those fluctuations and can allow for more predictable levels of future contributions. Despite the fluctuations, market values tend to show a clearer picture of a plan's funded status at a given point in time. As of [*enter the last day of the Plan Year*], the fair market value of the Plan's assets was [*enter amount*]. On this same date, the Plan's liabilities, determined using market rates, were [*enter amount*].

{Instructions: Insert the fair market value of the plan's assets as of the last day of the plan year. You may include contributions made after the end of the plan year to which the notice relates and before the date the notice is timely furnished but only if such contributions are attributable to such plan year for funding purposes. A plan's liabilities as of the last day of the plan year are equal to the present value, as of the last day of the plan year, of benefits accrued as of that same date. With the exception of the interest rate assumption, the present value should be determined using assumptions used to determine the funding target under section 303. The interest rate assumption is the rate provided under section 4006(a)(3)(E)(iv), but using the last month of the year to which the notice relates rather than the month preceding the first month of the year to which the notice relates. If, consistent with section 303(g)(2) of ERISA, the plan's valuation date is not the first day of the plan year, make appropriate modifications to the preceding paragraph, e.g., replace "first day of" with "valuation date for."}

{Instructions: If, pursuant to section 303(g)(3) of ERISA, the value of the plan's assets in the chart above is fair market value, include the paragraph below rather than the paragraph above, but otherwise follow the instructions above.}

The asset values in the chart above are measured as of the first day of the Plan Year. As of [*enter the last day of the Plan Year*], the fair market value of the Plan's assets was [*enter amount*]. On this same date, the Plan's liabilities, determined using market rates, were [*enter amount*].

Participant Information

The total number of participants and beneficiaries covered by the Plan on the Valuation Date was [*insert number*]. Of this number, [*insert number*] were current employees, [*insert number*] were retired and receiving benefits, and [*insert number*] were retired or no longer working for the employer and have a right to future benefits.

Funding & Investment Policies

Every pension plan must have a procedure to establish a funding policy for plan objectives. A funding policy relates to how much money is needed to pay promised benefits. The funding policy of the Plan is [*insert a summary statement of the Plan's funding policy*].

Pension plans also have investment policies. These generally are written guidelines or general instructions for making investment management decisions. The investment policy of the Plan is [*insert a summary statement of the Plan's investment policy*].

Under the investment policy, the Plan's assets were allocated among the following categories of investments, as of the end of the Plan Year. These allocations are percentages of total assets:

{Instructions: Insert and complete either Alternative 1 or Alternative 2, below.}

Alternative 1:

Asset Allocations	Percentage
1. Cash (interest bearing and non-interest bearing)	_____
2. U.S. Government securities	_____
3. Corporate debt instruments (other than employer securities):	
Preferred	_____
All other	_____
4. Corporate stocks (other than employer securities):	
Preferred	_____
Common	_____
5. Partnership/joint venture interests	_____
6. Real estate (other than employer real property)	_____
7. Loans (other than to participants)	_____
8. Participant loans	_____
9. Value of interest in common/collective trusts	_____
10. Value of interest in pooled separate accounts	_____
11. Value of interest in master trust investment accounts	_____
12. Value of interest in 103-12 investment entities	_____
13. Value of interest in registered investment companies (e.g., mutual funds)	_____
14. Value of funds held in insurance co. general account (unallocated contracts)	_____
15. Employer-related investments:	
Employer Securities	_____
Employer real property	_____
16. Buildings and other property used in plan operation	_____
17. Other	_____

For information about the Plan's investment in any of the following types of investments – common/collective trusts, pooled separate accounts, master trust investment accounts, or 103-12 investment entities – contact [*insert the name, telephone number, email address or mailing address of the plan administrator or designated representative*].

{*Instructions: Percentages must total 100%. If a plan holds an interest in one or more of the direct filing entities (DFEs) noted above, i.e., MTIAs, CCTs, PSAs, or 103-12IEs and the administrator does not break out the DFE's investments among the other asset classes, immediately following the asset allocation chart include the paragraph above informing recipients how to obtain more information regarding the plan's DFE investments (e.g., the plan's Schedule D and/or the DFE's Schedule H). If a plan does not hold an interest in a DFE or the plan administrator breaks out the investments of all DFEs among the other asset classes, do not include the above paragraph. If the administrator knows the actual asset allocation of an MTIA, the MTIA entry (line 11) should not be competed and the investments of the MTIA should be reflected in the relevant asset classes.*}

Alternative 2

Asset Allocations	Percentage:
Stocks	_____
Investment grade debt instruments	_____
High-yield debt instruments	_____
Real estate	_____
Other	_____

{*Instructions: Percentages must total 100%. Follow the instructions for the latest Schedule R to Form 5500 to allocate investments to one of the above asset classes.*}

Events Having a Material Effect on Assets or Liabilities

By law this notice must contain a written explanation of new events that have a material effect on plan liabilities or assets. This is because such events can significantly impact the funding condition of a plan. For the plan year beginning on [*insert the first day of the current plan year (i.e., the year after the notice year)*] and ending on [*insert the last day of the current plan year*], the Plan expects the following events to have such an effect: [*Insert explanation of any plan amendment, scheduled benefit increase or reduction, or other known event taking effect in the current plan year and having a material effect on plan liabilities or assets for the current plan year, as well as a projection to the end of the current plan of the effect of the amendment, scheduled increase or reduction, or event on plan liabilities*].

{*Instructions: Include the preceding discussion, entitled Events having a Material Effect on Assets or Liabilities, only if and to the extent applicable.*}

Right to Request a Copy of the Annual Report

Pension plans must file annual reports with the US Department of Labor. The report is called the "Form 5500." These reports contain financial and other information. You may obtain an electronic copy of your Plan's annual report by going to www.efast.dol.gov and using the search tool. Annual reports also are available from the US Department of Labor, Employee Benefits Security Administration's Public Disclosure Room at 200 Constitution Avenue, NW, Room N-1513, Washington, DC 20210, or by calling 202.693.8673. Or you may obtain a copy of the Plan's annual report by making a written request to the plan administrator: [*If the plan's annual report is available on an Intranet website maintained by the plan sponsor (or plan administrator on behalf of the plan sponsor), modify the preceding sentence to include a statement that the annual report also may be obtained through that website and include the website address.*] Annual reports do not contain personal information, such as the amount of your accrued benefits. You may contact your plan administrator if you want information about your accrued benefits. Your plan administrator is identified below under "Where To Get More Information."

Summary of Rules Governing Termination of Single-Employer Plans

If a plan terminates, there are specific termination rules that must be followed under federal law. A summary of these rules follows.

There are two ways an employer can terminate its pension plan. First, the employer can end a plan in a "standard termination" but only after showing the PBGC that such plan has enough money to pay all benefits owed to participants. Under a standard termination, a plan must either purchase an annuity from an insurance company (which will provide you with periodic retirement benefits, such as monthly for life or for a set period of time when you retire) or, if the plan allows, issue one lump-sum payment that covers your entire benefit. Your plan administrator must give you advance notice that identifies the insurance company (or companies) selected to provide the annuity. The PBGC's guarantee ends upon the purchase of an annuity or payment of the lump-sum. If the plan purchases an annuity for you from an insurance company and that company becomes unable to pay, the applicable state guaranty association guarantees the annuity to the extent authorized by that state's law.

Second, if the plan is not fully-funded, the employer may apply for a distress termination. To do so, however, the employer must be in financial distress and prove to a bankruptcy court or to the PBGC that the employer cannot remain in business unless the plan is terminated. If the application is granted, the PBGC will take over the plan as trustee and pay plan benefits, up to the legal limits, using plan assets and PBGC guarantee funds.

Under certain circumstances, the PBGC may take action on its own to end a pension plan. Most terminations initiated by the PBGC occur when the PBGC determines that plan termination is needed to protect the interests of plan participants or of the PBGC insurance program. The PBGC can do so if, for example, a plan does not have enough money to pay benefits currently due.

Benefit Payments Guaranteed by the PBGC

When the PBGC takes over a plan, it pays pension benefits through its insurance program. Only benefits that you have earned a right to receive and that cannot be forfeited (called vested benefits) are guaranteed. Most participants and beneficiaries receive all of the pension benefits they would have received under their plan, but some people may lose certain benefits that are not guaranteed.

The amount of benefits that PBGC guarantees is determined as of the plan termination date. However, if a plan terminates during a plan sponsor's bankruptcy, then the amount guaranteed is determined as of the date the sponsor entered bankruptcy.

The PBGC maximum benefit guarantee is set by law and is updated each calendar year. For a plan with a termination date or sponsor bankruptcy date, as applicable in [*insert current calendar year*], the maximum guarantee is [*insert amount from PBGC web site, www.pbgc.gov, applicable for the current calendar year*] per month, or [*insert amount from PBGC web site, www.pbgc.gov, applicable for the current calendar year*] per year, for a benefit paid to a 65-year-old retiree with no survivor benefit. If a plan terminates during a plan sponsor's bankruptcy, the maximum guarantee is fixed as of the calendar year in which the sponsor entered bankruptcy. The maximum guarantee is lower for an individual who begins receiving benefits from PBGC before age 65 reflecting the fact that younger retirees are expected to receive more monthly pension checks over their lifetimes. [*If the plan does not provide for commencement of benefits before age 65, you may omit this sentence.*] Similarly, the maximum guarantee is higher for an individual who starts receiving benefits from PBGC after age 65. The maximum guarantee by age can be found on PBGC's website, www.pbgc.gov. The guaranteed amount is also reduced if a benefit will be provided to a survivor of the plan participant.

The PBGC guarantees "basic benefits" earned before a plan is terminated, which include [*Include the following guarantees that apply to benefits available under the plan.*]:

- pension benefits at normal retirement age;
- most early retirement benefits;
- annuity benefits for survivors of plan participants; and
- disability benefits for a disability that occurred before the date the plan terminated or the date the sponsor entered bankruptcy, as applicable.

¶ 14,215A   Reg. §2520.101-5

The PBGC does not guarantee certain types of benefits [*Include the following guarantee limits that apply to the benefits available under the plan*.]:

- The PBGC does not guarantee benefits for which you do not have a vested right, usually because you have not worked enough years for the company.

- The PBGC does not guarantee benefits for which you have not met all age, service, or other requirements.

- Benefit increases and new benefits that have been in place for less than one year are not guaranteed. Those that have been in place for less than five years are only partly guaranteed.

- Early retirement payments that are greater than payments at normal retirement age may not be guaranteed. For example, a supplemental benefit that stops when you become eligible for Social Security may not be guaranteed.

- Benefits other than pension benefits, such as health insurance, life insurance, death benefits, vacation pay, or severance pay, are not guaranteed.

- The PBGC generally does not pay lump sums exceeding $5,000.

In some circumstances, participants and beneficiaries still may receive some benefits that are not guaranteed. This depends on how much money the terminated plan has and how much the PBGC recovers from employers for plan underfunding.

For additional general information about the PBGC and the pension insurance program guarantees, go to the "General FAQs about PBGC" on PBGC's website at www.pbgc.gov/generalfaqs. Please contact your employer or plan administrator for specific information about your pension plan or pension benefit. PBGC does not have that information. See "Where to Get More Information About Your Plan," below.

<u>Corporate and Actuarial Information on File with PBGC</u>

A plan sponsor must provide the PBGC with financial information about itself and actuarial information about the plan under certain circumstances, such as when the funding target attainment percentage of the plan (or any other pension plan sponsored by a member of the sponsor's controlled group) falls below 80 percent (other triggers may also apply). The sponsor of the Plan, [*enter name of plan sponsor*] or a member of its controlled group, was subject to this requirement to provide corporate financial information and plan actuarial information to the PBGC. The PBGC uses this information for monitoring and other purposes.

{Instructions: Insert the preceding paragraph entitled "Corporate and Actuarial Information on File with PBGC" only if a reporting under section 4010 of ERISA was required for the information year ending in the Plan Year. Modify the preceding paragraph, as appropriate, if the plan sponsor is the sole member of its controlled group.

<u>Where to Get More Information</u>

For more information about this notice, you may contact [*enter name of plan administrator and if applicable, principal administrative officer*], at [*enter phone number and address and insert email address if appropriate*]. For identification purposes, the official plan number is [*enter plan number*] and the plan sponsor's name and employer identification number or "EIN" are [*enter name and EIN of plan sponsor*].

[Added 2/2/2015 (80 FR 5625).]

⋙→ *Caution: EBSA Reg. § 2520.101-5 and appendices are applicable to notices for plan years beginning on or after January 1, 2015.*

[¶ 14,215B]
Appendix B to § 2520.101-5—Multiemployer Plan Model Annual Funding Notice.

COVER PAGE

PAPERWORK BURDEN DISCLOSURE NOTICE
OMB Control Number 1210-0126; expires 04/17/2017

Behind this cover page is a model notice that may be used to satisfy the mandatory disclosure requirements set forth in 29 CFR 2520.101-5. The model notice is a collection of information instrument subject to the Paperwork Reduction Act. Use of the model notice to meet the disclosure requirements is optional. You may also develop your own notice, provided it contains all of the information required by 29 CFR 2520.101-5. The Department of Labor estimates that it will take an average of approximately 21 hours for plan administrators to complete the model. You may send comments on this collection of information, including suggestions for reducing burden to: US Department of Labor, Policy and Research, Attention: PRA Officer, 200 Constitution Avenue, NW, Room N-5718, Washington, DC 20210. The disclosure requirements in 29 CFR 2520.101-5, referenced above, are also a collection of information under the PRA. The public is not required to respond to a collection of information unless it displays a currently valid OMB control number.

DO NOT INCLUDE THIS PAPERWORK REDUCTION ACT BANNER IN NOTICES TO PARTICIPANTS AND BENEFICIAIRES

ANNUAL FUNDING NOTICE

For
[insert name of multiemployer pension plan]

Introduction

This notice includes important information about the funding status of your multiemployer pension plan (the "Plan"). It also includes general information about the benefit payments guaranteed by the Pension Benefit Guaranty Corporation ("PBGC"), a federal insurance agency. All traditional pension plans (called "defined benefit pension plans") must provide this notice every year regardless of their funding status. This notice does not mean that the Plan is terminating. It is provided for informational purposes and you are not required to respond in any way. This notice is required by federal law. This notice is for the plan year beginning *[insert beginning date]* and ending *[insert ending date]* ("Plan Year").

How Well Funded Is Your Plan

The law requires the administrator of the Plan to tell you how well the Plan is funded, using a measure called the "funded percentage." The Plan divides its assets by its liabilities on the Valuation Date for the plan year to get this percentage. In general, the higher the percentage, the better funded the plan. The Plan's funded percentage for the Plan Year and each of the two preceding plan years is shown in the chart below. The chart also states the value of the Plan's assets and liabilities for the same period.

Funded Percentage			
	[insert Plan Year, e.g., 2015]	[insert plan year preceding Plan Year, e.g., 2014]	[insert plan year 2 years preceding Plan Year, e.g., 2013]
Valuation Date	[insert date]	[insert date]	[insert date]
Funded Percentage	[insert percentage]	[insert percentage]	[insert percentage]

	[insert amount]	[insert amount]	[insert amount]
Value of Assets			
Value of Liabilities	[insert amount]	[insert amount]	[insert amount]

{Instructions: The plan's "funded percentage" is equal to a fraction, the numerator of which is the actuarial value of the plan's assets (determined in the same manner as under section 304(c)(2) of ERISA) and the denominator of which is the accrued liability of the plan (under section 305(i)(8) of ERISA, using reasonable actuarial assumptions as required under section 304(c)(3) of ERISA). Report the value of the plan's assets and liabilities in the same manner as under section 304 of ERISA (but determining the plan's liabilities under section 305(i)(8) of ERISA, using reasonable actuarial assumptions as required under section 304(c)(3) of ERISA) as of the plan's valuation date for the plan year. Round off all amounts in this chart to the nearest dollar.}

Year-End Fair Market Value of Assets

The asset values in the chart above are measured as of the Valuation Date. They also are "actuarial values." Actuarial values differ from market values in that they do not fluctuate daily based on changes in the stock or other markets. Actuarial values smooth out those fluctuations and can allow for more predictable levels of future contributions. Despite the fluctuations, market values tend to show a clearer picture of a plan's funded status at a given point in time. The asset values in the chart below are market values and are measured on the last day of the Plan Year. The chart also includes the year-end market value of the Plan's assets for each of the two preceding plan years.

	[insert last day of Plan Year, e.g., 2015]	[insert last day of plan year preceding Plan Year, e.g., 2014]	[insert last day of plan year 2 years preceding Plan Year, e.g., 2013]
Fair Market Value of Assets	[insert amount]	[insert amount]	[insert amount]

{Instructions: Insert the fair market value of the plan's assets as of the last day of the plan year. You may include contributions made after the end of the plan year to which the notice relates and before the date the notice is timely furnished but only if such contributions are attributable to such plan year for funding purposes. For each of the two preceding plan years, you may use the fair market value of assets on the last day of the plan year as reported in the annual report for such plan year.}

Endangered, Critical, or Critical and Declining Status

Under federal pension law, a plan generally is in "endangered" status if its funded percentage is less than 80 percent. A plan is in "critical" status if the funded percentage is less than 65 percent (other factors may also apply). A plan is in "critical and declining" status if it is in critical status and is projected to become insolvent (run out of money to pay benefits) within 15 years (or within 20 years if a special rule applies). If a pension plan enters endangered status, the trustees of the plan are required to adopt a funding improvement plan. Similarly, if a pension plan enters critical status or critical and declining status, the trustees of the plan are required to adopt a rehabilitation plan. Funding improvement and rehabilitation plans establish steps and benchmarks for pension plans to improve their funding status over a specified period of time. The plan sponsor of a plan in critical and declining status may apply for approval to amend the plan to reduce current and future payment obligations to participants and beneficiaries.

{Instructions: Select and complete the appropriate option below.}

{Option one}
The Plan was not in endangered, critical, or critical and declining status in the Plan Year.

{Option two}
The Plan was in [*insert "endangered" or "critical"*] status in the Plan Year ending [*insert last day of Plan Year*] because [*insert summary description of why plan was in this status based on statutory factors*]. In an effort to improve the Plan's funding situation, the trustees adopted [*insert summary of the plan's funding improvement or rehabilitation plan, including when adopted and expected duration, and a description of any modification or update to the plan adopted during the plan year to which the notice relates*]. You may get a copy of the Plan's [*insert "funding improvement plan" or "rehabilitation plan"*], any update to such plan and the actuarial and financial data that demonstrate any action taken by the Plan toward fiscal improvement. You may get this information by contacting the plan administrator. [*If applicable, insert:* "Or you may obtain this information at [*insert Intranet address of plan sponsor (or plan administrator on behalf of the plan sponsor)*].]

{Option three}
The Plan was in critical and declining status in the Plan Year ending [*insert last day of Plan Year*] because [*insert summary description of why plan was in this status based on statutory factors*]. The Plan is projected to be insolvent in the [*insert plan year*] Plan Year. Such insolvency may result in benefit reductions. In an effort to improve the Plan's funding situation, the trustees adopted a rehabilitation plan on [*insert date*]. The rehabilitation plan [*Insert a summary of the plan's rehabilitation plan, including expected duration and a description of any modification or update to the plan adopted during the plan year to which the notice relates*]. [*Insert the following if applicable*: The plan sponsor has taken the following legally permitted actions to prevent insolvency: [*Insert explanation of actions*]." You may get a copy of the Plan's rehabilitation plan, any update to such plan and the actuarial and financial data that demonstrate any action taken by the Plan toward fiscal improvement. You may get this information by contacting the plan administrator. [*If applicable, insert:* "Or you may obtain this information at [*insert Intranet address of plan sponsor (or plan administrator on behalf of the plan sponsor)*].]

If the Plan is in endangered, critical, or critical and declining status for the plan year ending [*insert the last day of the plan year following the Plan Year*], separate notification of that status has or will be provided.

<u>Participant Information</u>

The total number of participants and beneficiaries covered by the Plan on the valuation date was [*insert number*]. Of this number, [*insert number*] were current employees, [*insert number*] were retired and receiving benefits, and [*insert number*] were retired or no longer working for the employer and have a right to future benefits.

Funding & Investment Policies

Every pension plan must have a procedure to establish a funding policy for plan objectives. A funding policy relates to how much money is needed to pay promised benefits. The funding policy of the Plan is [*insert a summary statement of the Plan's funding policy*].

Pension plans also have investment policies. These generally are written guidelines or general instructions for making investment management decisions. The investment policy of the Plan is [*insert a summary statement of the Plan's investment policy*].

Under the Plan's investment policy, the Plan's assets were allocated among the following categories of investments, as of the end of the Plan Year. These allocations are percentages of total assets:

{*Instructions: Insert and complete either Alternative 1 or Alternative 2, below.*}

Alternative 1:

Asset Allocations	Percentage
1. Cash (Interest bearing and non-interest bearing)	_____
2. U.S. Government securities	_____
3. Corporate debt instruments (other than employer securities):	
Preferred	_____
All other	_____
4. Corporate stocks (other than employer securities):	
Preferred	_____
Common	_____
5. Partnership/joint venture interests	_____
6. Real estate (other than employer real property)	_____
7. Loans (other than to participants)	_____
8. Participant loans	_____
9. Value of interest in common/collective trusts	_____
10. Value of interest in pooled separate accounts	_____
11. Value of interest in 103-12 investment entities	_____
12. Value of interest in registered investment companies (e.g., mutual funds)	_____
13. Value of funds held in insurance co. general account (unallocated contracts)	_____
14. Employer-related investments:	
Employer Securities	_____
Employer real property	_____
15. Buildings and other property used in plan operation	_____
16. Other	_____

For information about the Plan's investment in any of the following types of investments– common/collective trusts, pooled separate accounts, or 103-12 investment entities – contact [*insert the name, telephone number, email address or mailing address of the plan administrator or designated representative*].

{Instructions: Percentages must total 100%. If a plan holds an interest in one or more of the direct filing entities (DFEs) noted above, i.e., CCTs, PSAs, or 103-12IEs and the administrator does not break out the DFE's investments among the other asset classes, immediately following the asset allocation chart include the paragraph above informing recipients how to obtain more information regarding the plan's DFE investments (e.g., the plan's Schedule D and/or the DFE's Schedule H). If a plan does not hold an interest in a DFE or the administrator breaks out the investments of all DFEs among the other asset classes, do not include the above paragraph.

Alternative 2

Asset Allocations	Percentage:
Stocks	_____
Investment grade debt instruments	_____
High-yield debt instruments	_____
Real estate	_____
Other	_____

{Instructions: Percentages must total 100%. Follow the instructions in the latest Schedule R to Form 5500 to allocate investments to one of the above asset classes.

Events Having a Material Effect on Assets or Liabilities

By law this notice must contain a written explanation of new events that have a material effect on plan liabilities or assets. This is because such events can significantly impact the funding condition of a plan. For the plan year beginning on [*insert the first day of the current plan year (i.e., the year after the notice year)*] and ending on [*insert the last day of the current plan year*], the Plan expects the following events to have such an effect: [*Insert explanation of any plan amendment, scheduled benefit increase or reduction, or other known event taking effect in the current plan year and having a material effect on plan liabilities or assets for the current plan year, as well as a projection to the end of the current plan of the effect of the amendment, scheduled increase or reduction, or event on plan liabilities*].

{Instructions: Include the preceding discussion, entitled Events having a Material Effect on Assets or Liabilities, only if and to the extent applicable.}

Right to Request a Copy of the Annual Report

Pension plans must file annual reports with the US Department of Labor. The report is called the "Form 5500." These reports contain financial and other information. You may obtain an electronic copy of your Plan's annual report by going to www.efast.dol.gov and using the search tool. Annual reports also are available from the US Department of Labor, Employee Benefits Security Administration's Public Disclosure Room at 200 Constitution Avenue, NW, Room N-1513, Washington, DC 20210, or by calling 202.693.8673. Or you may obtain a copy of the Plan's annual report by making a written request to the plan administrator. [*If the plan's annual report is available on an Intranet website maintained by the plan sponsor (or plan administrator on behalf of the plan sponsor), modify the preceding sentence to include a statement that the annual report also may be obtained through that website and include the website address.*] Annual reports do not contain personal information, such as the amount of your accrued benefit. You may contact your plan administrator if you want information about your accrued benefits.   Your plan administrator is identified below under "Where To Get More Information."

Summary of Rules Governing Insolvent Plans

Federal law has a number of special rules that apply to financially troubled multiemployer plans that become insolvent, either as ongoing plans or plans terminated by mass withdrawal. The plan administrator is required by law to include a summary of these rules in the annual funding notice. A plan is insolvent for a plan year if its available financial resources are not sufficient to pay benefits when due for that plan year. An insolvent plan must reduce benefit payments to the highest level that can be paid from the plan's available resources. If such resources are not enough to pay benefits at the level specified by law (see Benefit Payments Guaranteed by the PBGC, below), the plan must apply to the PBGC for financial assistance. The PBGC will loan the plan the amount necessary to pay benefits at the guaranteed level. Reduced benefits may be restored if the plan's financial condition improves.

A plan that becomes insolvent must provide prompt notice of its status to participants and beneficiaries, contributing employers, labor unions representing participants, and PBGC. In addition, participants and beneficiaries also must receive information regarding whether, and how, their benefits will be reduced or affected, including loss of a lump sum option.

Benefit Payments Guaranteed by the PBGC

The maximum benefit that the PBGC guarantees is set by law. Only benefits that you have earned a right to receive and that cannot be forfeited (called vested benefits) are guaranteed. There are separate insurance programs with different benefit guarantees and other provisions for single-employer plans and multiemployer plans. Your Plan is covered by PBGC's multiemployer program. Specifically, the PBGC guarantees a monthly benefit payment equal to 100 percent of the first $11 of the Plan's monthly benefit accrual rate, plus 75 percent of the next $33 of the accrual rate, times each year of credited service. The PBGC's maximum guarantee, therefore, is $35.75 per month times a participant's years of credited service.

Example 1: If a participant with 10 years of credited service has an accrued monthly benefit of $600, the accrual rate for purposes of determining the PBGC guarantee would be determined by dividing the monthly benefit by the participant's years of service ($600/10), which equals $60. The guaranteed amount for a $60 monthly accrual rate is equal to the sum of $11 plus $24.75 (.75 x $33), or $35.75. Thus, the participant's guaranteed monthly benefit is $357.50 ($35.75 x 10).

Example 2: If the participant in Example 1 has an accrued monthly benefit of $200, the accrual rate for purposes of determining the guarantee would be $20 (or $200/10). The guaranteed amount for a $20 monthly accrual rate is equal to the sum of $11 plus $6.75 (.75 x $9), or $17.75. Thus, the participant's guaranteed monthly benefit would be $177.50 ($17.75 x 10).

The PBGC guarantees pension benefits payable at normal retirement age and some early retirement benefits. In addition, the PBGC guarantees qualified preretirement survivor benefits (which are preretirement death benefits payable to the surviving spouse of a participant who dies before starting to receive benefit payments). In calculating a person's monthly payment, the PBGC will disregard any benefit increases that were made under a plan within 60 months before the earlier of the plan's termination or insolvency (or benefits that were in effect for less than 60 months at the time of termination or insolvency). Similarly, the PBGC does not guarantee benefits above the normal retirement benefit, disability benefits not in pay status, or non-pension benefits, such as health insurance, life insurance, death benefits, vacation pay, or severance pay.

For additional information about the PBGC and the pension insurance program guarantees, go to the Multiemployer Page on PBGC's website at www.pbgc.gov/multiemployer. Please contact your employer or plan administrator for specific information about your pension plan or pension benefit. PBGC does not have that information. See "Where to Get More Information About Your Plan," below.

Where to Get More Information

For more information about this notice, you may contact [*enter name of plan administrator and if applicable, principal administrative officer*], at [*enter phone number and address and insert email address if appropriate*]. For identification purposes, the official plan number is [*enter plan number*] and the plan sponsor's name and employer identification number or "EIN" is [*enter name and EIN of plan sponsor*].

[Added 2/2/2015 (80 FR 5625).]

[¶ 14,216]

§ 2520.101-6 **Multiemployer Pension Plan Information Made Available on Request.**

(a) *In general.* For purposes of compliance with the requirements of section 101(k) of the Employee Retirement Income Security Act of 1974, as amended (the Act), 29 U.S.C. 1001, *et. seq.*, the administrator of a multiemployer pension plan shall, in accordance with the requirements of this section, furnish copies of reports and applications described in paragraph (c) of this section to plan participants, beneficiaries, employee representatives and contributing employers, described in paragraph (e) of this section.

(b) *Obligation to furnish.* (1) Except as provided in paragraph (d) of this section, the administrator of a multiemployer pension plan shall, not later than 30 days after receipt of a written request for a report(s) or application(s) described in paragraph (c) of this section from a plan participant, beneficiary, employee representative or contributing employer described in paragraph (e) of this section, furnish the requested document or documents to the requester.

(2) The plan administrator shall furnish reports and applications pursuant to paragraph (b)(1) of this section in a manner consistent with the requirements of 29 CFR 2520.104b-1, including paragraph (c) of that section relating to the use of electronic media.

(3) The plan administrator may impose a reasonable charge to cover the costs of furnishing documents pursuant to this section, but in no event may such charge exceed—

(i) The lesser of: (A) the actual cost to the plan for the least expensive means of acceptable reproduction of the document(s) or (B) 25 cents per page; plus

(ii) The cost of mailing or delivery of the document.

(c) *Documents to be furnished.* For purposes of paragraph (a) of this section, and subject to paragraph (d) of this section, a plan participant, beneficiary, employee representative or contributing employer described in paragraph (e) of this section, shall be entitled to request and receive a copy of any:

(1) Periodic actuarial report. For this purpose the term "periodic actuarial report" means any—

(i) Actuarial report prepared by an actuary of the plan and received by the plan at regularly scheduled, recurring intervals; and

(ii) Study, test (including a sensitivity test), document, analysis or other information (whether or not called a "report") received by the plan from an actuary of the plan that depicts alternative funding scenarios based on a range of alternative actuarial assumptions, whether or not such information is received by the plan at regularly scheduled, recurring intervals.

(2) Quarterly, semi-annual, or annual financial report prepared for the plan by any plan investment manager or advisor (without regard to whether such advisor is a fiduciary within the meaning of section 3(21) of the Act) or other fiduciary; and

(3) Application filed with the Secretary of the Treasury requesting an extension under section 304 of the Act or section 431(d) of the Internal Revenue Code of 1986 and the determination of such Secretary pursuant to such application.

(d) *Limitations and exceptions.* For purposes of this section, reports and applications (and related determinations) required to be disclosed under this section shall not include:

(1) Any report or application that was furnished to the requester within the 12- month period immediately preceding the date on which the request is received by the plan;

(2) Any report or application that, as of the date on which the request is received by the plan, has been in the plan's possession for 6 years or more;

(3) Any report described in paragraph (c)(1) and (c)(2) of this section that, as of the date on which the request is received by the plan, has not been in the plan's possession for at least 30 days; except that, if the plan administrator elects not to furnish any such document, the administrator shall furnish a notice, not later than 30 days after the date on which request is received by the plan, informing the requester of the existence of the document and the earliest date on which the document can be furnished by the plan.

(4) Any information or data which served as the basis for any report or application described in paragraph (c) of this section, although nothing herein shall limit any other right that a person may have to review or obtain such information under the Act; or

(5)(i) Any information within a report or application that the plan administrator reasonably determines to be either:

(A) individually identifiable information with respect to any plan participant, beneficiary, employee, fiduciary, or contributing employer, except that such limitation shall not apply to an investment manager, adviser, or other person (other than an employee of the plan) preparing a financial report described in paragraph (c)(2) of this section; or

(B) proprietary information regarding the plan, any contributing employer, or entity providing services to the plan.

(ii) For purposes of paragraph (d)(5)(i)(B) of this section, the term "proprietary information" means trade secrets and other non-public information (e.g., processes, procedures, formulas, methodologies, techniques, strategies) that, if disclosed by the plan, may cause, or increase a reasonable risk of, financial harm to the plan, a contributing employer, or entity providing services to the plan.

(iii) The plan administrator may treat information relating to a contributing employer or entity providing services to the plan as other than proprietary if the contributing employer or service provider has not identified such information as proprietary.

(iv) A plan administrator shall inform the requester if the plan administrator withholds any information described in paragraph (d)(5)(i) of this section from a report or application requested under paragraph (b) of this section.

(e) *Persons entitled to request documents.* For purposes of this section, a plan participant, beneficiary, employee representative or contributing employer entitled to request and receive reports and applications includes:

(1) Any participant within the meaning of section 3(7) of the Act;

(2) Any beneficiary receiving benefits under the plan;

(3) Any labor organization representing participants under the plan;

(4) Any employer that is a party to the collective bargaining agreement(s) pursuant to which the plan is maintained or who otherwise may be subject to withdrawal liability pursuant to section 4203 of the Act. [Added by FR 9334, 3/2/10.]

[¶ 14,220]
SUMMARY PLAN DESCRIPTION

Act Sec. 102. (a) A summary plan description of any employee benefit plan shall be furnished to participants and beneficiaries as provided in section 104(b). The summary plan description shall include the information described in subsection (b), shall be written in a manner calculated to be understood by the average plan participant, and shall be sufficiently accurate and comprehensive to reasonably apprise such participants and beneficiaries of their rights and obligations under the plan. A summary of any material modification in the terms of the plan and any change in the information required under subsection (b) shall be written in a manner calculated to be understood by the average plan participant and shall be furnished in accordance with section 104(b)(1).

Act Sec. 102. (b) The summary plan description shall contain the following information: The name and type of administration of the plan; in the case of a group health plan (as defined in section 733(a)(1)), whether a health insurance issuer (as defined in section 733(b)(2)) is responsible for the financing or administration (including payment of claims) of the plan and (if so) the name and address of such issuer; the name and address of the person designated as agent for the service of legal process, if such person is not the administrator; the name and address of the administrator; names, titles, and addresses of any trustee or trustees (if they are persons different from the administrator); a description of the relevant provisions of any applicable collective bargaining agreement; the plan's requirements respecting eligibility for participation and benefits; a description of the provisions providing for nonforfeitable pension benefits; circumstances which may result in disqualification, ineligibility, or denial or loss of benefits; the source of financing of the plan and the identity of any organization through which benefits are provided; the date of the end of the plan year and whether the records of the plan are kept on a calendar, policy, or fiscal year basis; the procedures to be followed in presenting claims for benefits under the plan including the office at the Department of Labor through which participants and beneficiaries may seek assistance or information regarding their rights under this Act and the Health Insurance Portability and Accountability Act of 1996 with respect to health benefits that are offered through a group health plan (as defined in section 733(a)(1), the remedies available under the plan for the redress of claims which are denied in whole or in part (including procedures required under section 503 of this Act), and if the employer so elects for purposes of complying with section 701(f)(3)(B)(i), the model notice applicable to the State in which the participants and beneficiaries reside.

Amendments

P.L. 111-3, § 311(b)(1)(B):

Amended ERISA Sec. 102(b) by striking "and the remedies" and inserting ", the remedies"; and by inserting before the period ", and if the employer so elects for purposes of complying with section 701(f)(3)(B)(i), the model notice applicable to the State in which the participants and beneficiaries reside". For the **effective** date, see Act Sec. 3, below.

P.L. 111-3, § 3, provides:

SEC. 3. GENERAL EFFECTIVE DATE; EXCEPTION FOR STATE LEGISLATION; CONTINGENT EFFECTIVE DATE; RELIANCE ON LAW.

(a) GENERAL EFFECTIVE DATE.—Unless otherwise provided in this Act, subject to subsections (b) through (d), this Act (and the amendments made by this Act) shall take effect on April 1, 2009, and shall apply to child health assistance and medical assistance provided on or after that date.

(b) EXCEPTION FOR STATE LEGISLATION.—In the case of a State plan under title XIX or State child health plan under XXI of the Social Security Act, which the Secretary of Health and Human Services determines requires State legislation in order for the respective plan to meet one or more additional requirements imposed by amendments made by this Act, the respective plan shall not be regarded as failing to comply with the requirements of such title solely on the basis of its failure to meet such an additional requirement before the first day of the first calendar quarter beginning after the close of the first regular session of the State legislature that begins after the date of enactment of this Act. For purposes of the previous sentence, in the case of a State that has a 2-year legislative session, each year of the session shall be considered to be a separate regular session of the State legislature.

(c) COORDINATION OF CHIP FUNDING FOR FISCAL YEAR 2009.—Notwithstanding any other provision of law, insofar as funds have been appropriated under section 2104(a)(11), 2104(k), or 2104(l) of the Social Security Act, as amended by section 201 of Public Law 110-173, to provide allotments to States under CHIP for fiscal year 2009—

(1) any amounts that are so appropriated that are not so allotted and obligated before April 1, 2009 are rescinded; and

(2) any amount provided for CHIP allotments to a State under this Act (and the amendments made by this Act) for such fiscal year shall be reduced by the amount of such appropriations so allotted and obligated before such date.

(d) RELIANCE ON LAW.—With respect to amendments made by this Act (other than title VII) that become effective as of a date—

(1) such amendments are effective as of such date whether or not regulations implementing such amendments have been issued; and

(2) Federal financial participation for medical assistance or child health assistance furnished under title XIX or XXI, respectively, of the Social Security Act on or after such

date by a State in good faith reliance on such amendments before the date of promulgation of final regulations, if any, to carry out such amendments (or before the date of guidance, if any, regarding the implementation of such amendments) shall not be denied on the basis of the State's failure to comply with such regulations or guidance.

P.L. 105-34, § 1503(b)(1):

Amended ERISA Sec. 102(a) by striking paragraph (2) and by striking (a)(1) and inserting (a). Prior to amendment, ERISA Sec. 102(a)(2) read as follows:

(2) A plan description (containing the information required by subsection (b)) of any employee benefit plan shall be prepared on forms prescribed by the Secretary, and shall be filed with the Secretary as required by section 104(a)(1). Any material modification in the terms of the plan and any change in the information described in subsection (b) shall be filed in accordance with section 104(a)(1)(D).

P.L. 105-34, § 1503(b)(2):

Amended ERISA Sec. 102 by striking "PLAN DESCRIPTION AND" in the heading and ERISA Sec. 102(b) by striking "The plan description and summary plan description shall contain" and inserting "The summary plan description shall contain."

The above amendments are effective August 5, 1997.

P.L. 104-204, § 603(b)(3)(C):

Amended ERISA Sec. 102(b) by striking "section 706(a)(1)" each place it appears and inserting "section 733(a)(1)" and by striking "section 706(b)(2)" and inserting "section 733(b)(2)".

The above amendment applies to group health plans for plan years beginning on or after January 1, 1998.

The above amendments are effective August 5, 1997.

P.L. 104-191, § 101(c)(2):

Amended ERISA Sec. 102(b) by inserting "in the case of a group health plan (as defined in section 706(a)(1)), whether a health insurance issuer (as defined in section 706(b)(2)) is responsible for the financing or administration (including payment of claims) of the plan and (if so) the name and address of such issuer;" after "type of administration of the plan" and by inserting "including the office at the Department of Labor through which participants and beneficiaries may seek assistance or information regarding their rights under this Act and the Health Insurance Portability and Accountability Act of 1996 with respect to health benefits that are offered through a group health plan (as defined in section 706(a)(1)" after "benefits under the plan".

The above amendments generally apply with respect to group health plans for plan years beginning after June 30, 1997. For special rules, see Act Sec. 101(g)(2)-(5), reproduced below.

Act Sec. 101(g)(2)-(5) reads as follows:

(g) EFFECTIVE DATES.—

(1) IN GENERAL.—Except as provided in this section, this section (and the amendments made by this section) shall apply with respect to group health plans for plan years beginning after June 30, 1997.

(2) DETERMINATION OF CREDITABLE COVERAGE.—

(A) PERIOD OF COVERAGE.—

(i) IN GENERAL.—Subject to clause (ii), no period before July 1, 1996, shall be taken into account under part 7 of subtitle B of title I of the Employee Retirement Income Security Act of 1974 (as added by this section) in determining creditable coverage.

(ii) SPECIAL RULE FOR CERTAIN PERIODS.—The Secretary of Labor, consistent with section 104, shall provide for a process whereby individuals who need to establish creditable coverage for periods before July 1, 1996, and who would have such coverage credited but for clause (i) may be given credit for creditable coverage for such periods through the presentation of documents or other means.

(B) CERTIFICATIONS, ETC.—

(i) IN GENERAL.—Subject to clauses (ii) and (iii), subsection (e) of section 701 of the Employee Retirement Income Security Act of 1974 (as added by this section) shall apply to events occurring after June 30, 1996.

(ii) NO CERTIFICATION REQUIRED TO BE PROVIDED BEFORE JUNE 1, 1997.—In no case is a certification required to be provided under such subsection before June 1, 1997.

(iii) CERTIFICATION ONLY ON WRITTEN REQUEST FOR EVENTS OCCURRING BEFORE OCTOBER 1, 1996.—In the case of an event occurring after June 30, 1996, and before October 1, 1996, a certification is not required to be provided under such subsection unless an individual (with respect to whom the certification is otherwise required to be made) requests such certification in writing.

(C) TRANSITIONAL RULE.—In the case of an individual who seeks to establish creditable coverage for any period for which certification is not required because it relates to an event occurring before June 30, 1996—

(i) the individual may present other credible evidence of such coverage in order to establish the period of creditable coverage; and

(ii) a group health plan and a health insurance issuer shall not be subject to any penalty or enforcement action with respect to the plan's or issuer's crediting (or not crediting) such coverage if the plan or issuer has sought to comply in good faith with the applicable requirements under the amendments made by this section.

(3) SPECIAL RULE FOR COLLECTIVE BARGAINING AGREEMENTS.—Except as provided in paragraph (2), in the case of a group health plan maintained pursuant to one or more collective bargaining agreements between employee representatives and one or more employers ratified before the date of the enactment of this Act, part 7 of subtitle B of title I of Employee Retirement Income Security Act of 1974 (other than section 701(e) thereof) shall not apply to plan years beginning before the later of—

(A) the date on which the last of the collective bargaining agreements relating to the plan terminates (determined without regard to any extension thereof agreed to after the date of the enactment of this Act), or

(B) July 1, 1997.

For purposes of subparagraph (A), any plan amendment made pursuant to a collective bargaining agreement relating to the plan which amends the plan solely to conform to any requirement of such part shall not be treated as a termination of such collective bargaining agreement.

(4) TIMELY REGULATIONS.—The Secretary of Labor, consistent with section 104, shall first issue by not later than April 1, 1997, such regulations as may be necessary to carry out the amendments made by this section.

(5) LIMITATION ON ACTIONS.—No enforcement action shall be taken, pursuant to the amendments made by this section, against a group health plan or health insurance issuer with respect to a violation of a requirement imposed by such amendments before January 1, 1998, or, if later, the date of issuance of regulations referred to in paragraph (4), if the plan or issuer has sought to comply in good faith with such requirements.

Regulations

Reg. § 2520.102-1 was adopted by FR Doc. 76-11859 (41 FR 16957) under "Title 29—Labor; Chapter XXV—Office of Employee Benefits Security; Subchapter C—Reporting and Disclosure Under the Employee Retirement Income Security Act of 1974; Part 2520—Rules and Regulations for Reporting and Disclosure." The regulation was filed with the *Federal Register* on April 22, 1976, and published in the *Federal Register* on April 23, 1976. Reg. §§ 2520.102-2 through 2520.102-4 were adopted by FR Doc. 77-7637, filed with the *Federal Register* on March 11, 1977, and published in the *Federal Register* on March 15, 1977 (42 FR 14266). Reg. § 2520.102-3(m) and 2520.102-3(t) are interim as well as proposed regulations. The regulations are effective March 15, 1977. Reg. § 2520.102-3 was amended by FR Doc. 20810, filed with the *Federal Register* on July 18, 1977, published in the *Federal Register* on July 19, 1977, effective July 19, 1977 (42 FR 37178). Reg. § 2520.102-5 was added by FR Doc. 81-2105, filed with the *Federal Register* on January 19, 1981, published in the *Federal Register* on January 21, 1981, effective February 20, 1981 (46 FR 5882). Reg. § 2520.102-3(q) was amended, § 2520.102-3(u) and (v) were amended, § 2520.104b-1(c) was added, § 2520.104b-3(a) was amended, § 2520.104b-3(d) and § 2520.104b-3(e) were added by FR Doc. 97-8173, interim regulations, filed with the *Federal Register* on April 1, 1997, published in the *Federal Register* on April 8, 1997, effective June 1, 1997 (62 FR 16979). Reg. § 2520.102-3 was officially corrected on June 10, 1997 (62 FR 31690). Reg. § 2520.102-3 was amended, effective June 1, 1997 (62 FR 36205). Reg. § 2520.102-3(u) was amended, effective September 9, 1998 (63 FR 48371). Reg. §§ 2520.102-3 (d), (j), (l), (m)(3), (o), (q), (s), (t)(2) and (u) were amended effective January 20, 2001 and published in the *Federal Register* on November 21, 2000 (65 FR 70225). Reg. § 2520.102-3(m)(4) was added effective January 20, 2001 and published in the *Federal Register* on November 21, 2000 (65 FR 70225). Reg. § 2520.102-5 was removed effective January 20, 2001 and published in the *Federal Register* on November 21, 2000 (65 FR 70225). Reg. §§ 2520.104b-3 (a), (d) and (e) were amended effective January 20, 2001 and published in the *Federal Register* on November 21, 2000 (65 FR 70225). ERISA Reg. Sec. 2520.102-1 was removed and reserved by 67 FR 771 and published in the *Federal Register* on January 7, 2002. ERISA Reg. Sec. 2520.102-4 was revised by 67 FR 771 and published in the *Federal Register* on January 7, 2002.

Subpart B—Contents of Plan Description and Summary Plan Description

[¶ 14,221]

§ 2520.102-1 **Plan description**. Reserved. [67 FR 771, 1/7/02].

[¶ 14,222]

§ 2520.102-2 **Style and format of summary plan description**. (a) *Method of presentation*. The summary plan description shall be written in a manner calculated to be understood by the average plan participant and shall be sufficiently comprehensive to apprise the plan's participants and beneficiaries of their rights and obligations under the plan. In fulfilling these requirements, the plan administrator shall exercise considered judgment and discretion by taking into account such factors as the level of comprehension and education of typical participants in the plan and the complexity of the terms of the plan. Consideration of these factors will usually require the limitation or elimination of technical jargon and of long, complex sentences, the use of clarifying examples and illustrations, the use of clear cross-references and a table of contents.

(b) *General format*. The format of the summary plan description must not have the effect of misleading, misinforming or failing to inform participants and beneficiaries. Any description of exceptions, limitations, reductions, and other restrictions of plan benefits shall not be minimized, rendered obscure, or otherwise made to appear unimportant. Such exceptions, limitations, reductions, or restrictions of plan benefits shall be described or summarized in a manner not less prominent than the style, captions, printing type, and prominence used to describe or summarize plan benefits. The advantages and disadvantages of the plan shall be presented without either exaggerating the benefits or minimizing the limitations. The description or summary of restrictive plan provisions need not be disclosed in the summary plan description in close conjunction with the description or summary of benefits, provided that adjacent to the benefit description the page on which the restrictions are described is noted.

(c) *Foreign languages*. In the case of either—

(1) A plan that covers fewer than 100 participants at the beginning of a plan year, and in which 25 percent or more of all plan participants are literate only in the same non-English language, or

(2) A plan which covers 100 or more participants at the beginning of the plan year, and in which the lesser of: (i) 500 or more participants, or (ii) 10% or more of all plan participants are literate only in the same non-English language, so that a summary plan description in English would fail to inform these participants adequately of their rights and obligations under the plan, the plan administrator for such plan shall provide these participants with an English-language summary plan description which prominently displays a notice, in the non-English language common to these participants, offering them assistance. The assistance provided need not involve written materials, but shall be given in the non-English language common to these participants and shall be calculated to provide them with a reasonable opportunity to become informed as to their rights and obligations under the plan. The notice offering assistance contained in the summary plan description shall clearly set forth in the non-English language common to such participants the procedures they must follow in order to obtain such assistance.

Example. Employer A maintains a pension plan which covers 1000 participants. At the beginning of a plan year five hundred of Employer A's covered employees are literate only in Spanish, 101 are literate only in Vietnamese, and the remaining 399 are literate in English. Each of the 1000 employees receives a summary plan description in English, containing an assistance notice in both Spanish and Vietnamese stating the following:

This booklet contains a summary in English of your plan rights and benefits under Employer A Pension Plan. If you have difficulty understanding any part of this booklet, contact Mr. John Doe, the plan administrator, at his office in Room 123, 456 Main St., Anywhere City, State 20001. Office hours are from 8:30 A.M. to 5:00 P.M. Monday through Friday. You may also call the plan administrator's office at 202 555-2345 for assistance. [Added by 42 FR 14266, effective March 15, 1977.]

[¶ 14,223]

§ 2520.102-3 **Contents of summary plan description.** Section 102 of the Act specifies information that must be included in the summary plan description. The summary plan description must accurately reflect the contents of the plans as of a date not earlier than 120 days prior to the date such summary plan description is disclosed. The following information shall be included in the summary plan description of both employee welfare benefit plans and employee pension benefit plans, except as stated otherwise in subsection (j) through (n):

(a) The name of the plan, and, if different, the name by which the plan is commonly known by its participants and beneficiaries;

(b) The name and address of—

(1) In the case of a single employer plan, the employer whose employees are covered by the plan,

(2) In the case of a plan maintained by an employee organization for its members, the employee organization that maintains the plan,

(3) In the case of a collectively-bargained plan established or maintained by one or more employers and one or more employee organizations, the association, committee, joint board of trustees, parent, or most significant employer of a group of employers all of which contribute to the same plan, or other similar representative of the parties who established or maintain the plan, as well as:

(i) A statement that a complete list of the employers and employee organizations sponsoring the plan may be obtained by participants and beneficiaries upon written request to the plan administrator, and is available for examination by participants and beneficiaries, as required by § § 2520.104b-1 and 2520.104b-30, or,

(ii) A statement that participants and beneficiaries may receive from the plan administrator, upon written request, information as to whether a particular employer or employee organization is a sponsor of the plan and, if the employer or employee organization is a plan sponsor, the sponsor's address.

(4) In the case of a plan established or maintained by two or more employers, the association, committee, joint board of trustees, parent, or most significant employer of a group of employers all of which contribute to the same plan, or other similar representative of the parties who established or maintain the plan, as well as:

(i) A statement that a complete list of the employers sponsoring the plan may be obtained by participants and beneficiaries upon written request to the plan administrator, and is available for examination by participants and beneficiaries, as required by § § 2520.104b-1 and 2520.104b-30, or,

(ii) A statement that participants and beneficiaries may receive from the plan administrator, upon written request, information as to whether a particular employer is a sponsor of the plan and, if the employer is a plan sponsor, the sponsor's address. [Amended by 42 FR 37178, effective July 19, 1977.]

(c) The employer identification number (EIN) assigned by the Internal Revenue Service to the plan sponsor and the plan number assigned by the plan sponsor. (For further detailed explanation, see the instructions to the plan description Form EBS-1 and "Identification Numbers Under ERISA" (Publ. 1004), published jointly by DOL, IRS, and PBGC);

(d) The type of pension or welfare plan, e.g. pension plans—defined benefit, defined contribution, 401(k), cash balance, money purchase, profit sharing, ERISA section 404(c) plan, etc., and for welfare plans—group health plans, disability, pre-paid legal services, etc. [Amended 11/21/00 by 65 FR 70225. Corrected by PWBA on 7/2/01, 66 FR 34994. Corrected by PWBA on 7/11/01, 66 FR 36368.]

(e) The type of administration of the plan, *e.g.,* contract administration, insurer administration, etc.;

(f) The name, business address, and business telephone number of the plan administrator as that term is defined by section 3(16) of the Act;

(g) The name of the person designated as agent for service of legal process, and the address at which process may be served on such person, and in addition, a statement that service of legal process may be made upon a plan trustee or the plan administrator;

(h) The name, title, and address of the principal place of business of each trustee of the plan;

(i) If a plan is maintained pursuant to one or more collective bargaining agreements, a statement that the plan is so maintained, and that a copy of any such agreement may be obtained by participants and beneficiaries upon written request to the plan administrator, and is available for examination by participants and beneficiaries, as required by § § 2520.104b-1 and 2520.104b-30. For the purpose of this paragraph, a plan is maintained pursuant to a collective bargaining agreement if such agreement controls any duties, rights or benefits under the plan, even though such agreement has been superseded in part for other purposes;

(j) The plan's requirements respecting eligibility for participation and for benefits. The summary plan description shall describe the plan's provisions relating to eligibility to participate in the plan and the information identified in paragraphs (j)(1), (2) and (3) of this section, as appropriate. [Amended 11/21/00 by 65 FR 70225.]

(1) For employee pension benefit plans, it shall also include a statement describing the plan's normal retirement age, as that term is defined in section 3(24) of the Act, and a statement describing any other conditions which must be met before a participant will be eligible to receive benefits. Such plan benefits shall be described or summarized. In addition, the summary plan description shall include a description of the procedures governing qualified domestic relations order (QDRO) determinations or a statement indicating that participants and beneficiaries can obtain, without charge, a copy of such procedures from the plan administrator. [Amended 11/21/00 by 65 FR 70225.]

(2) For employee welfare benefit plans, it shall also include a statement of the conditions pertaining to eligibility to receive benefits, and a description or summary of the benefits. In the case of a welfare plan providing extensive schedules of benefits (a group health plan, for example), only a general description of such benefits is required if reference is made to detailed schedules of benefits which are available without cost to any participant or beneficiary who so requests. In addition, the summary plan description shall include a description of the procedures governing qualified medical child support order (QMCSO) determinations or a statement indicating that participants and beneficiaries can obtain, without charge, a copy of such procedures from the plan administrator. [Amended 11/21/00 by 65 FR 70225.]

(3) For employee welfare benefit plans that are group health plans, as defined in section 733(a)(1) of the Act, the summary plan description shall include a description of: any cost-sharing provisions, including premiums, deductibles, coinsurance, and copayment amounts for which the participant or beneficiary will be responsible; any annual or lifetime caps or other limits on benefits under the plan; the extent to which preventive services are covered under the plan; whether, and under what circumstances, existing and new drugs are covered under the plan; whether, and under what circumstances, coverage is provided for medical tests, devices and procedures; provisions governing the use of network providers, the composition of the provider network, and whether, and under what circumstances, coverage is provided for out-of-network services; any conditions or limits on the selection of primary care providers or providers of speciality medical care; any conditions or limits applicable to obtaining emergency medical care; and any provisions requiring preauthorizations or utilization review as a condition to obtaining a benefit or service under the plan. In the case of plans with provider networks, the listing of providers may

be furnished as a separate document that accompanies the plan's SPD, provided that the summary plan description contains a general description of the provider network and provided further that the SPD contains a statement that provider lists are furnished automatically, without charge, as a separate document. [Added 11/21/00 by 65 FR 70225. Corrected by PWBA on 7/2/01, 66 FR 34994. Corrected by PWBA on 7/11/01, 66 FR 36368.]

(k) In the case of an employee pension benefit plan, a statement describing any joint and survivor benefits provided under the plan, including any requirement that an election be made as a condition to select or reject the joint and survivor annuity;

(l) For both pension and welfare benefit plans, a statement clearly identifying circumstances which may result in disqualification, ineligibility, or denial, loss, forfeiture, suspension, offset, reduction, or recovery (e.g., by exercise of subrogation or reimbursement rights) of any benefits that a participant or beneficiary might otherwise reasonably expect the plan to provide on the basis of the description of benefits required by paragraphs (j) and (k) of this section. In addition to other required information, plans must include a summary of any plan provisions governing the authority of the plan sponsors or others to terminate the plan or amend or eliminate benefits under the plan and the circumstances, if any, under which the plan may be terminated or benefits may be amended or eliminated; a summary of any plan provisions governing the benefits, rights and obligations of participants and beneficiaries under the plan on termination of the plan or amendment or elimination of benefits under the plan, including, in the case of an employee pension benefit plan, a summary of any provisions relating to the accrual and the vesting of pension benefits under the plan upon termination; and a summary of any plan provisions governing the allocation and disposition of assets of the plan upon termination. Plans also shall include a summary of any provisions that may result in the imposition of a fee or charge on a participant or beneficiary, or on an individual account thereof, the payment of which is a condition to the receipt of benefits under the plan. The foregoing summaries shall be disclosed in accordance with the requirements under 29 CFR 2520.102-2(b). [Amended 11/21/00 by 65 FR 70225.]

(m) For an employee pension benefit plan the following information:

(1) if the benefits of the plan are not insured under Title IV of the Act, a statement of this fact, and the reason for the lack of insurance; and

(2) if the benefits of the plan are insured under Title IV of the Act, a statement of this fact, a summary of the pension benefit guaranty provisions of Title IV, and a statement indicating that further information on the provisions of Title IV can be obtained from the plan administrator or the Pension Benefit Guaranty Corporation. The address of the PBGC shall be provided.

(3) A summary plan description for a single-employer plan will be deemed to comply with paragraph (m)(2) of this section if it includes the following statement:

Your pension benefits under this plan are insured by the Pension Benefit Guaranty Corporation (PBGC), a federal insurance agency. If the plan terminates (ends) without enough money to pay all benefits, the PBGC will step in to pay pension benefits. Most people receive all of the pension benefits they would have received under their plan, but some people may lose certain benefits.

The PBGC guarantee generally covers: (1) Normal and early retirement benefits; (2) disability benefits if you become disabled before the plan terminates; and (3) certain benefits for your survivors.

The PBGC guarantee generally does not cover: (1) Benefits greater than the maximum guaranteed amount set by law for the year in which the plan terminates; (2) some or all of benefit increases and new benefits based on plan provisions that have been in place for fewer than 5 years at the time the plan terminates; (3) benefits that are not vested because you have not worked long enough for the company; (4) benefits for which you have not met all of the requirements at the time the plan terminates; (5) certain early retirement payments (such as supplemental benefits that stop when you become eligible for Social Security) that result in an early retirement monthly benefit greater than your monthly benefit at the plan's normal retirement age; and (6) nonpension benefits, such as health insurance, life insurance, certain death benefits, vacation pay, and severance pay.

Even if certain of your benefits are not guaranteed, you still may receive some of those benefits from the PBGC depending on how much money your plan has and on how much the PBGC collects from employers.

For more information about the PBGC and the benefits it guarantees, ask your plan administrator or contact the PBGC's Technical Assistance Division, 1200 K Street N.W., Suite 930, Washington, D.C. 20005-4026 or call 202-326-4000 (not a toll-free number). TTY/TDD users may call the federal relay service toll-free at 1-800-877-8339 and ask to be connected to 202-326-4000. Additional information about the PBGC's pension insurance program is available through the PBGC's website on the Internet at http://www.pbgc.gov. [Added by 42 FR 37178, effective July 19, 1977. Amended 11/21/00 by 65 FR 70225.]

(4) A summary plan description for a multiemployer plan will be deemed to comply with paragraph (m)(2) of this section if it includes the following statement:

Your pension benefits under this multiemployer plan are insured by the Pension Benefit Guaranty Corporation (PBGC), a federal insurance agency. A multiemployer plan is a collectively bargained pension arrangement involving two or more unrelated employers, usually in a common industry.

Under the multiemployer plan program, the PBGC provides financial assistance through loans to plans that are insolvent. A multiemployer plan is considered insolvent if the plan is unable to pay benefits (at least equal to the PBGC's guaranteed benefit limit) when due.

The maximum benefit that the PBGC guarantees is set by law. Under the multiemployer program, the PBGC guarantee equals a participant's years of service multiplied by (1) 100% of the first $5 of the monthly benefit accrual rate and (2) 75% of the next $15. The PBGC's maximum guarantee limit is $16.25 per month times a participant's years of service. For example, the maximum annual guarantee for a retiree with 30 years of service would be $5,850.

The PBGC guarantee generally covers: (1) Normal and early retirement benefits; (2) disability benefits if you become disabled before the plan becomes insolvent; and (3) certain benefits for your survivors.

The PBGC guarantee generally does not cover: (1) Benefits greater than the maximum guaranteed amount set by law; (2) benefit increases and new benefits based on plan provisions that have been in place for fewer than 5 years at the earlier of: (i) The date the plan terminates or (ii) the time the plan becomes insolvent; (3) benefits that are not vested because you have not worked long enough; (4) benefits for which you have not met all of the requirements at the time the plan becomes insolvent; and (5) nonpension benefits, such as health insurance, life insurance, certain death benefits, vacation pay, and severance pay.

For more information about the PBGC and the benefits it guarantees, ask your plan administrator or contact the PBGC's Technical Assistance Division, 1200 K Street, N.W., Suite 930, Washington, D.C. 20005-4026 or call 202-326-4000 (not a toll-free number). TTY/TDD users may call the federal relay service toll-free at 1-800-877-8339 and ask to be connected to 202-326-4000. Additional information about the PBGC's pension insurance program is available through the PBGC's website on the Internet at http://www.pbgc.gov. [Added 11/21/00 by 65 FR 70225.]

(n) In the case of an employee pension benefit plan, a description and explanation of the plan provisions for determining years of service for eligibility to participate, vesting, and breaks in service, and years of participation for benefit accrual. The description shall state the service required to accrue full benefits and the manner in which accrual of benefits is prorated for employees failing to complete full service for a year.

(o) In the case of a group health plan, within the meaning of section 607(1) of the Act, subject to the continuation coverage provisions of Part 6 of Title I of ERISA, a description of the rights and obligations of participants and beneficiaries with respect to continuation coverage, including, among other things, information concerning qualifying events and qualified beneficiaries, premiums, notice and election requirements and procedures, and duration of coverage. [Amended 11/21/00 by 65 FR 70225.]

(p) The sources of contributions to the plan—for example, employer, employee organization, employees—and the method by which the amount of contribution is calculated. Defined benefit pension plans may state without further explanation that the contribution is actuarially determined.

(q) The identity of any funding medium used for the accumulation of assets through which benefits are provided. The summary plan description shall identify any insurance company, trust fund, or any other institution, organization, or entity which maintains a fund on behalf of the plan or through which the plan is funded or benefits are provided. If a health insurance issuer, within the meaning of section 733(b)(2) of the Act, is responsible, in whole or in part, for the financing or administration of a group health plan, the summary plan description shall indicate the name and address of the issuer, whether and to what extent benefits under the plan are guaranteed under a contract or policy of insurance issued by the issuer, and the nature of any administrative services (e.g., payment of claims) provided by the issuer. [Amended by 62 FR 16979, effective June 1, 1997. Amended 11/21/00 by 65 FR 70225.]

(r) The date of the end of the year for purposes of maintaining the plan's fiscal records;

(s) The procedures governing claims for benefits (including procedures for obtaining preauthorizations, approvals, or utilization review decisions in the case of group health plan services or benefits, and procedures for filing claim forms, providing notifications of benefit determinations, and reviewing denied claims in the case of any plan), applicable time limits, and remedies available under the plan for the redress of claims which are denied in whole or in part (including procedures required under section 503 of Title I of the Act). The plan's claims procedures may be furnished as a separate document that accompanies the plan's SPD, provided that the document satisfies the style and format requirements of 29 CFR 2520.102-2 and, provided further that the SPD contains a statement that the plan's claims procedures are furnished automatically, without charge, as a separate document. [Amended 11/21/00 by 65 FR 70225.]

(t)(1) The statement of ERISA rights authorized by section 104(c) of the Act, containing the items of information applicable to the plan included in the model statement of subparagraph (2) of this paragraph. Items which are not applicable to the plan are not required to be included. The statement may contain explanatory and descriptive provisions in addition to those prescribed in paragraph (t)(2) of this section. However, the style and format of the statement must not have the effect of misleading, misinforming or failing to inform participants and beneficiaries of a plan. All such information shall be written in a manner calculated to be understood by the average plan participant, taking into account factors such as the level of comprehension and education of typical participants in the plan and the complexity of the items required under this subparagraph to be included in the statement. Inaccurate, incomprehensible or misleading explanatory material will fail to meet the requirements of this section. The statement of ERISA rights (the model statement or a statement prepared by the plan), must appear as one consolidated statement. If a plan finds it desirable to make additional mention of certain rights elsewhere in the summary plan description, it may do so. The summary plan description may state that the statement of ERISA rights is required by federal law and regulation.

(2) A summary plan description will be deemed to comply with the requirements of paragraph (t)(1) of this section if it includes the following statement; items of information which are not applicable to a particular plan should be deleted:

As a participant in (name of plan) you are entitled to certain rights and protections under the Employee Retirement Income Security Act of 1974 (ERISA). ERISA provides that all plan participants shall be entitled to:

Receive Information About Your Plan and Benefits

Examine, without charge, at the plan administrator's office and at other specified locations, such as worksites and union halls, all documents governing the plan, including insurance contracts and collective bargaining agreements, and a copy of the latest annual report (Form 5500 Series) filed by the plan with the U.S. Department of Labor and available at the Public Disclosure Room of the Employee Benefits Security Administration. [EBSA technical correction, 68 FR 16399 (April 3, 2003).]

Obtain, upon written request to the plan administrator, copies of documents governing the operation of the plan, including insurance contracts and collective bargaining agreements, and copies of the latest annual report (Form 5500 Series) and updated summary plan description. The administrator may make a reasonable charge for the copies.

Receive a summary of the plan's annual financial report. The plan administrator is required by law to furnish each participant with a copy of this summary annual report.

Obtain a statement telling you whether you have a right to receive a pension at normal retirement age (age * * *) and if so, what your benefits would be at normal retirement age if you stop working under the plan now. If you do not have a right to a pension, the statement will tell you how many more years you have to work to get a right to a pension. This statement must be requested in writing and is not required to be given more than once every twelve (12) months. The plan must provide the statement free of charge.

Continue Group Health Plan Coverage

Continue health care coverage for yourself, spouse or dependents if there is a loss of coverage under the plan as a result of a qualifying event. You or your dependents may have to pay for such coverage. Review this summary plan description and the documents governing the plan on the rules governing your COBRA continuation coverage rights.

Reduction or elimination of exclusionary periods of coverage for preexisting conditions under your group health plan, if you have creditable coverage from another plan. You should be provided a certificate of creditable coverage, free of charge, from your group health plan or health insurance issuer when you lose coverage under the plan, when you become entitled to elect COBRA continuation coverage, when your COBRA continuation coverage ceases, if you request it before losing coverage, or if you request it up to 24 months after losing coverage. Without evidence of creditable coverage, you may be subject to a preexisting condition exclusion for 12 months (18 months for late enrollees) after your enrollment date in your coverage.

Prudent Actions by Plan Fiduciaries

In addition to creating rights for plan participants ERISA imposes duties upon the people who are responsible for the operation of the employee benefit plan. The people who operate your plan, called "fiduciaries" of the plan, have a duty to do so prudently and in the interest of you and other plan participants and beneficiaries. No one, including your employer, your union, or any other person, may fire you or otherwise discriminate against you in any way to prevent you from obtaining a (pension, welfare) benefit or exercising your rights under ERISA.

Enforce Your Rights

If your claim for a (pension, welfare) benefit is denied or ignored, in whole or in part, you have a right to know why this was done, to obtain copies of documents relating to the decision without charge, and to appeal any denial, all within certain time schedules.

Under ERISA, there are steps you can take to enforce the above rights. For instance, if you request a copy of plan documents or the latest annual report from the plan and do not receive them within 30 days, you may file suit in a Federal court. In such a case, the court may require the plan administrator to provide the materials and pay you up to $110 a day until you receive the materials, unless the materials were not sent because of reasons beyond the control of the administrator. If you have a claim for benefits which is denied or ignored, in whole or in part, you may file suit in a state or Federal court. In addition, if you disagree with the plan's decision or lack thereof concerning the qualified status of a domestic relations order or a medical child support order, you may file suit in Federal court. If it should happen that plan fiduciaries misuse the plan's money, or if you are discriminated against for asserting your rights, you may seek assistance from the U.S. Department of Labor, or you may file suit in a Federal court. The court will decide who should pay court costs and legal fees. If you are successful the court may order the person you have sued to pay these costs and fees. If you lose, the court may order you to pay these costs and fees, for example, if it finds your claim is frivolous.

Assistance with Your Questions

If you have any questions about your plan, you should contact the plan administrator. If you have any questions about this statement or about your rights under ERISA, or if you need assistance in obtaining documents from the plan administrator, you should contact the nearest office of the Employee Benefits Security Administration, U.S. Department of Labor, listed in your telephone directory or the Division of Technical Assistance and Inquiries, Employee Benefits Security Administration, U.S. Department of Labor, 200 Constitution Avenue N.W., Washington, D.C. 20210. You may also obtain certain publications about your rights and responsibilities under ERISA by calling the publications hotline of the Employee Benefits Security Administration. [Amended by 62 FR 16979, effective June 1, 1997. Amended 11/21/00 by 65 FR 70225. EBSA technical correction, 68 FR 16399 (April 3, 2003).]

(u)(1) For a group health plan, as defined in section 733(a)(1) of the Act, that provides maternity or newborn infant coverage, a statement describing any requirements under federal or state law applicable to the plan, and any health insurance coverage offered under the plan, relating to hospital length of stay in connection with childbirth for the mother or newborn child. If federal law applies in some areas in which the plan operates and state law applies in other areas, the statement should describe the different areas and the federal or state law requirements applicable in each.

(2) In the case of a group health plan subject to section 720 of the Act, the summary plan description will be deemed to have complied with paragraph (u)(1) of this section relating to the required description of federal law requirements if it includes the following statement in the summary plan description:

Group health plans and health insurance issuers generally may not, under Federal law, restrict benefits for any hospital length of stay in connection with childbirth for the mother or newborn child to less than 48 hours following a vaginal delivery, or less than 96 hours following a cesarean section. However, Federal law generally does not prohibit the mother's or newborn's attending provider, after consulting with the mother, from discharging the mother or her newborn earlier than 48 hours (or 96 hours as applicable). In any case, plans and issuers may not, under Federal law, require that a provider obtain authorization from the plan or the insurance issuer for prescribing a length of stay not in excess of 48 hours (or 96 hours). [Added by 63 FR 48371 effective September 9, 1998. Amended 11/21/00 by 65 FR 70225.]

(v) *Applicability dates.* [Added by 42 FR 37178, effective July 19, 1977. Amended by 62 FR 16979, effective June 1, 1997. Corrected June 10, 1997, by 62 FR 31690. Amended by 62 FR 36205, effective June 1, 1997. Removed 11/21/00 by 65 FR 70225.]

[¶ 14,224]

§ 2520.102-4 **Option for different summary plan descriptions**. In some cases an employee benefit plan may provide different benefits for various classes of participants and beneficiaries. For example, a plan amendment altering benefits may apply to only those participants who are employees of an employer when the amendment is adopted and to employees who later become participants, but not to participants who no longer are employees when the amendment is adopted. (See § 2520.104b-4.) Similarly, a plan may provide for different benefits for participants employed at different plants of the employer, or for different classes of participants in the same plant. In such cases the plan administrator may fulfill the requirement to furnish a summary plan description to participants covered under the plan and beneficiaries receiving benefits under the plan by furnishing to each member of each class of participants and beneficiaries a copy of a summary plan description appropriate to that class. Each summary plan description so prepared shall follow the style and format prescribed in § 2520.102-2, and shall contain all information which is required to be contained in the summary plan description under § 2520.102-3. It may omit information which is not applicable to the class of participants or beneficiaries to which it is furnished. It should also clearly identify on the first page of the text the class of participants and beneficiaries for which it has been prepared and the plan's coverage of other classes. If the classes which the employee benefit plan covers are too numerous to be listed adequately on the first page of the text of the summary plan description, they may be listed elsewhere in the text so long as the first page of the text contains a reference to the page or pages in the text which contain this information. Revised by 67 FR 771, effective March 8, 2002. [Added by 42 FR 14266, effective March 15, 1977.]

[¶ 14,225]

§ 2520.102-5 **Limited exemption with respect to summary plan descriptions of welfare plans providing benefits through a qualified health maintenance organization**. [Added by 46 FR 5882, originally scheduled to be effective February 20, 1981. However, the effective date was delayed under the President's regulation freeze until March 30, 1981 (46 FR 11253). Removed 11/21/00 by 65 FR 70225.]

[¶ 14,230]
ANNUAL REPORTS

Act Sec. 103.(a) PUBLICATION AND FILING.—

(1)(A) An annual report shall be published with respect to every employee benefit plan to which this part applies. Such report shall be filed with the Secretary in accordance with section 104(a), and shall be made available and furnished to participants in accordance with section 104(b).

(B) The annual report shall include the information described in subsections (b) and (c) and where applicable subsections (d), (e), and (f) and shall also include—

(i) a financial statement and opinion, as required by paragraph (3) of this subsection, and

(ii) an actuarial statement and opinion, as required by paragraph (4) of this subsection.

(2) If some or all of the information necessary to enable the administrator to comply with the requirements of this title is maintained by—

(A) an insurance carrier or other organization which provides some or all of the benefits under the plan, or holds assets of the plan in a separate account,

(B) a bank or similar institution which holds some or all of the assets of the plan in a common or collective trust or a separate trust, or custodial account, or

(C) a plan sponsor as defined in section 3(16)(B),

such carrier, organization, bank, institution, or plan sponsor shall transmit and certify the accuracy of such information to the administrator within 120 days after the end of the plan year (or such other date as may be prescribed under regulations of the Secretary).

(3)(A) Except as provided in subparagraph (C), the administrator of an employee benefit plan shall engage, on behalf of all plan participants, an independent qualified public accountant, who shall conduct such an examination of any financial statements of the plan, and of other books and records of the plan, as the accountant may deem necessary to enable the accountant to form an opinion as to whether the financial statements and schedules required to be included in the annual report by subsection (b) of this section are presented fairly in conformity with generally accepted accounting principles applied on a basis consistent with that of the preceding year. Such examination shall be conducted in accordance with generally accepted auditing standards, and shall involve such tests of the books and records of the plan as are considered necessary by the independent qualified public accountant. The independent qualified public accountant shall also offer his opinion as to whether the separate schedules specified in subsection (b)(3) of this section and the summary material required under section 104(b)(3) present fairly, and in all material respects the information contained therein when considered in conjunction with the financial statements taken as a whole. The opinion by the independent qualified public accountant shall be made a part of the annual report. In a case where a plan is not required to file an annual report, the requirements of this paragraph shall not apply. In a case where by reason of section 104(a)(2) a plan is required only to file a simplified annual report, the Secretary may waive the requirements of this paragraph.

(B) In offering his opinion under this section the accountant may rely on the correctness of any actuarial matter certified to by an enrolled actuary, if he so states his reliance.

(C) The opinion required by subparagraph (A) need not be expressed as to any statements required by subsection (b)(3)(G) prepared by a bank or similar institution or insurance carrier regulated and supervised and subject to periodic examination by a State or Federal agency if such statements are certified by the bank, similar institution, or insurance carrier as accurate and are made a part of the annual report.

(D) For purposes of this title, the term "qualified public accountant" means—

(i) a person who is a certified public accountant, certified by a regulatory authority of a State;

(ii) a person who is a licensed public accountant, licensed by a regulatory authority of a State; or

(iii) a person certified by the Secretary as a qualified public accountant in accordance with regulations published by him for a person who practices in States where there is no certification or licensing procedure for accountants.

(4)(A) The administrator of an employee pension benefit plan subject to the reporting requirement of subsection (d) of this section shall engage, on behalf of all plan participants, an enrolled actuary who shall be responsible for the preparation of the materials comprising the actuarial statement required under subsection (d) of this section. In a case where a plan is not required to file an annual report, the requirement of this paragraph shall not apply, and, in a case where by reason of section 104(a)(2), a plan is required only to file a simplified report, the Secretary may waive the requirement of this paragraph.

(B) The enrolled actuary shall utilize such assumptions and techniques as are necessary to enable him to form an opinion as to whether the contents of the matters reported under subsection (d) of this section—

(i) are in the aggregate reasonably related to the experience of the plan and to reasonable expectations; and

(ii) represent his best estimate of anticipated experience under the plan. The opinion by the enrolled actuary shall be made with respect to, and shall be made a part of, each annual report.

(C) For purposes of this title, the term "enrolled actuary" means an actuary enrolled under subtitle C of title III of this Act.

(D) In making a certification under this section the enrolled actuary may rely on the correctness of any accounting matter under section 103(b) as to which any qualified public accountant has expressed an opinion, if he so states his reliance.

Act Sec. 103. (b) FINANCIAL STATEMENT.—An annual report under this section shall include a financial statement containing the following information:

(1) With respect to an employee welfare benefit plan: a statement of assets and liabilities; a statement of changes in fund balance; and a statement of changes in financial position. In the notes to financial statements, disclosures concerning the following items shall be considered by the accountant: a description of the plan including any significant changes in the plan made during the period and the impact of such changes on benefits; a description of material lease commitments, other commitments, and contingent liabilities; a description of agreements and transactions with persons known to be parties in interest; a general description of priorities upon termination of the plan; information concerning whether or not a tax ruling or determination letter has been obtained; and any other matters necessary to fully and fairly present the financial statements of the plan.

(2) With respect to an employee pension benefit plan: a statement of assets and liabilities, and a statement of changes in net assets available for plan benefits which shall include details of revenues and expenses and other changes aggregated by general source and application. In the notes to financial statements, disclosures concerning the following items shall be considered by the accountant: a description of the plan including any significant changes in the plan made during the period and the impact of such changes on benefits; the funding policy (including policy with respect to prior service cost), and any changes in such policies during the year; a description of any significant changes in plan benefits made during the period; a description of material lease commitments, other commitments, and contingent liabilities; a description of agreements and transactions with persons known to be parties in interest; a general description of priorities upon termination of the plan; information concerning whether or not a tax ruling or determination letter has been obtained; and any other matters necessary to fully and fairly present the financial statements of such pension plan.

(3) With respect to all employee benefit plans, the statement required under paragraph (1) or (2) shall have attached the following information in separate schedules:

(A) a statement of the assets and liabilities of the plan aggregated by categories and valued at their current value, and the same data displayed in comparative form for the end of the previous fiscal year of the plan;

(B) a statement of receipts and disbursements during the preceding twelve-month period aggregated by general sources and applications;

(C) a schedule of all assets held for investment purposes aggregated and identified by issuer, borrower, or lessor, or similar party to the transaction (including a notation as to whether such party is known to be a party in interest), maturity date, rate of interest, collateral, par or maturity value, cost, and current value;

(D) a schedule of each transaction involving a person known to be party in interest, the identity of such party in interest and his relationship or that of any other party in interest to the plan, a description of each asset to which the transaction relates; the purchase or selling price in case of a sale or purchase, the rental in case of a lease, or the interest rate and maturity date in case of a loan; expenses incurred in connection with the transaction; the cost of the asset, the current value of the asset, and the net gain (or loss) on each transaction;

(E) a schedule of all loans or fixed income obligations which were in default as of the close of the plan's fiscal year or were classified during the year as uncollectable and the following information with respect to each loan on such schedule (including a notation as to whether parties involved are known to be parties in interest): the original principal amount of the loan, the amount of principal and interest received during the reporting year, the unpaid balance, the identity and address of the obligor, a detailed description of the loan (including date of making and maturity, interest rate, the type and value of collateral, and other material terms), the amount of principal and interest overdue (if any) and an explanation thereof;

(F) a list of all leases which were in default or were classified during the year as uncollectable; and the following information with respect to each lease on such schedule (including a notation as to whether parties involved are known to be parties in interest): the type of property leased (and, in the case of fixed assets such as land, buildings, leasehold, and so forth, the location of the property), the identity of the lessor or lessee from or to whom the plan is leasing, the relationship of such lessors and lessees, if any, to the plan, the employer, employee organization, or any other party in interest, the terms of the lease regarding rent, taxes, insurance, repairs, expenses, and renewal options; the date the leased property was purchased and its cost, the date the property was leased and its approximate value at such date, the gross rental receipts during the reporting period, expenses paid for the leased property during the reporting period, the net receipts from the lease, the amounts in arrears, and a statement as to what steps have been taken to collect amounts due or otherwise remedy the default;

(G) if some or all of the assets of a plan or plans are held in a common or collective trust maintained by a bank or similar institution or in a separate account maintained by an insurance carrier or a separate trust maintained by a bank as trustee, the report shall include the most recent annual statement of assets and liabilities of such common or collective trust, and in the case of a separate account or a separate trust, such other information as is required by the administrator in order to comply with this subsection; and

(H) a schedule of each reportable transaction, the name of each party to the transaction (except that, in the case of an acquisition or sale of a security on the market, the report need not identify the person from whom the security was acquired or to whom it was sold) and a description of each asset to which the transaction applies; the purchase or selling price in case of a sale or purchase, the rental in case of a lease, or the interest rate and maturity date in case of a loan; expenses incurred in connection with the transaction; the cost of the asset, the current value of the asset, and the net gain (or loss) on each transaction. For purposes of the preceding sentence, the term "reportable transaction" means a transaction to which the plan is a party if such transaction is—

(i) a transaction involving an amount in excess of 3 percent of the current value of the assets of the plan;

(ii) any transaction (other than a transaction respecting a security) which is part of a series of transactions with or in conjunction with a person in a plan year, if the aggregate amount of such transaction exceeds 3 percent of the current value of the assets of the plan;

(iii) a transaction which is part of a series of transactions respecting one or more securities of the same issuer, if the aggregate amount of such transactions in the plan year exceeds 3 percent of the current value of the assets of the plan; or

(iv) a transaction with or in conjunction with a person respecting a security, if any other transaction with or in conjunction with such person in the plan year respecting a security is required to be reported by reason of clause (i).

(4) The Secretary may, by regulation, relieve any plan from filing a copy of a statement of assets and liabilities (or other information) described in paragraph (3)(G) if such statement and other information is filed with the Secretary by the bank or insurance carrier which maintains the common or collective trust or separate account.

Act Sec. 103. (c) INFORMATION TO BE FURNISHED BY ADMINISTRATOR.—The administrator shall furnish as a part of a report under this section the following information:

(1) The number of employees covered by the plan.

(2) The name and address of each fiduciary.

(3) Except in the case of a person whose compensation is minimal (determined under regulations of the Secretary) and who performs solely ministerial duties (determined under such regulations), the name of each person (including but not limited to, any consultant, broker, trustee, accountant, insurance carrier, actuary, administrator, investment manager, or custodian who rendered services to the plan or who had transactions with the plan) who received directly or indirectly compensation from the plan during the preceding year for services rendered to the plan or its participants, the amount of such compensation, the nature of his services to the plan or its participants, his relationship to the employer of the employees covered by the plan, or the employee organization, and any other office, position, or employment he holds with any party in interest.

(4) An explanation of the reason for any change in appointment of trustee, accountant, insurance carrier, enrolled actuary, administrator, investment manager, or custodian.

(5) Such financial and actuarial information including but not limited to the material described in subsections (b) and (d) of this section as the Secretary may find necessary or appropriate.

Act Sec. 103. (d) ACTUARIAL STATEMENT.—With respect to an employee pension benefit plan (other than (A) a profit sharing, savings, or other plan, which is an individual account plan, (B) a plan described in section 301(b), or (C) a plan described both in section 4021(b) and in paragraph (1), (2), (3), (4), (5), (6), or (7) of section 301(a)) an annual report under this section for a plan year shall include a complete actuarial statement applicable to the plan year which shall include the following:

(1) The date of the plan year, and the date of the actuarial valuation applicable to the plan year for which the report is filed.

(2) The date and amount of the contribution (or contributions) received by the plan for the plan year for which the report is filed and contributions for prior plan years not previously reported.

(3) The following information applicable to the plan year for which the report is filed: the normal costs or target normal costs, the accrued liabilities or funding target, an identification of benefits not included in the calculation; a statement of the other facts and actuarial assumptions and methods used to determine costs, and a justification for any change in actuarial assumptions or cost methods; and the minimum contribution required under section 302.

(4) The number of participants and beneficiaries, both retired and nonretired, covered by the plan.

(5) The current value of the assets accumulated in the plan, and the present value of the assets of the plan used by the actuary in any computation of the amount of contributions to the plan required under section 302 and a statement explaining the basis of such valuation of present value of assets.

(6) Information required in regulations of the Pension Benefit Guaranty Corporation with respect to:

(A) the current value of the assets of the plan,

(B) the present value of all nonforfeitable benefits for participants and beneficiaries receiving payments under the plan,

(C) the present value of all nonforfeitable benefits for all other participants and beneficiaries,

(D) the present value of all accrued benefits which are not nonforfeitable (including a separate accounting of such benefits which are benefit commitments, as defined in section 4001(a)(16)), and

(E) the actuarial assumptions and techniques used in determining the values described in subparagraphs (A) through (D).

(7) A certification of the contribution necessary to reduce the minimum required contribution determined under section 303, or the accumulated funding deficiency determined under section 304, to zero.

(8) A statement by the enrolled actuary—

(A) that to the best of his knowledge the report is complete and accurate, and determined under section 304,

(B) the applicable requirements of sections 303(h), 304(c)(3), and 306(c)(3) (relating to reasonable actuarial assumptions and methods) have been complied with.

(9) A copy of the opinion required by subsection (a)(4).

(10) A statement by the actuary which discloses—

(A) any event which the actuary has not taken into account, and

(B) any trend which, for purposes of the actuarial assumptions used, was not assumed to continue in the future,

but only if, to the best of the actuary's knowledge, such event or trend may require a material increase in plan costs or required contribution rates.

(11) If the current value of the assets of the plan is less than 70 percent of—

(A) in the case of a single-employer plan, the funding target (as defined in section 303(d)(1)) of the plan, or

(B) in the case of a multiemployer plan, the current liability (as defined in section 304(c)(6)(D)) under the plan,

the percentage which such value is of the amount described in subparagraph (A) or (B).

(12) A statement explaining the actuarial assumptions and methods used in projecting future retirements and forms of benefit distributions under the plan.

(13) Such other information regarding the plan as the Secretary may by regulation require.

(14) Such other information as may be necessary to fully and fairly disclose the actuarial position of the plan.

Such actuary shall make an actuarial valuation of the plan for every third plan year, unless he determines that a more frequent valuation is necessary to support his opinion under subsection (a)(4) of this section.

Act Sec. 103. (e) STATEMENT FROM INSURANCE COMPANY, INSURANCE SERVICE, OR OTHER SIMILAR ORGANIZATIONS WHICH SELL OR GUARANTEE PLAN BENEFITS.—If some or all of the benefits under the plan are purchased from and guaranteed by an insurance company, insurance service, or other similar organization, a report under this section shall include a statement from such insurance company, service, or other similar organization covering the plan year and enumerating—

(1) the premium rate for subscription charge and the total premium or subscription charges paid to each such carrier, insurance service, or other similar organization and the approximate number of persons covered by each class of such benefits; and

(2) the total amount of premiums received, the approximate number of persons covered by each class of benefits, and the total claims paid by such company, service, or other organization; dividends or retroactive rate adjustments, commissions, and administrative service or other fees or other specific acquisition costs paid by such company, service, or other organization; any amounts held to provide benefits after retirement; the remainder of such premiums; and the names and addresses of the brokers, agents, or other persons to whom commissions or fees were paid, the amount paid to each, and for what purpose. If any such company, service, or other organization does not maintain separate experience records covering the specific groups it serves, the report shall include in lieu of the information required by the foregoing provisions of this paragraph (A) a statement as to the basis of its premium rate or subscription charge, the total amount of premiums or subscription charges received from the plan, and a copy of the financial report of the company, service

or other organization and (B) if such company, service, or organization incurs specific costs in connection with the acquisition or retention of any particular plan or plans, a detailed statement of such costs.

Act Sec. 103. (f) Additional information with respect to defined benefit plans.—

(1) Liabilities under 2 or more plans.—

(A) In general.—In any case in which any liabilities to participants or their beneficiaries under a defined benefit plan as of the end of a plan year consist (in whole or in part) of liabilities to such participants and beneficiaries under 2 or more pension plans as of immediately before such plan year, an annual report under this section for such plan year shall include the funded percentage of each of such 2 or more pension plans as of the last day of such plan year and the funded percentage of the plan with respect to which the annual report is filed as of the last day of such plan year.

(B) Funded percentage.—For purposes of this paragraph, the term "funded percentage"—

(i) in the case of a single-employer plan, means the funding target attainment percentage, as defined in section 303(d)(2), and

(ii) in the case of a multiemployer plan, has the meaning given such term in section 305(i)(2).

(2) Additional information for multiemployer plans.—With respect to any defined benefit plan which is a multiemployer plan, an annual report under this section for a plan year shall include, in addition to the information required under paragraph (1), the following, as of the end of the plan year to which the report relates:

(A) The number of employers obligated to contribute to the plan.

(B) A list of the employers that contributed more than 5 percent of the total contributions to the plan during such plan year.

(C) The number of participants under the plan on whose behalf no contributions were made by an employer as an employer of the participant for such plan year and for each of the 2 preceding plan years.

(D) The ratios of—

(i) the number of participants under the plan on whose behalf no employer had an obligation to make an employer contribution during the plan year, to

(ii) the number of participants under the plan on whose behalf no employer had an obligation to make an employer contribution during each of the 2 preceding plan years.

(E) Whether the plan received an amortization extension under section 304(d) of this Act or section 431(d) of the Internal Revenue Code of 1986 for such plan year and, if so, the amount of the difference between the minimum required contribution for the year and the minimum required contribution which would have been required without regard to the extension, and the period of such extension.

(F) Whether the plan used the shortfall funding method (as such term is used in section 305) for such plan year and, if so, the amount of the difference between the minimum required contribution for the year and the minimum required contribution which would have been required without regard to the use of such method, and the period of use of such method.

(G) Whether the plan was in critical or endangered status under section 305 for such plan year, and if so, a summary of any funding improvement or rehabilitation plan (or modification thereto) adopted during the plan year, and the funded percentage of the plan.

(H) The number of employers that withdrew from the plan during the preceding plan year and the aggregate amount of withdrawal liability assessed, or estimated to be assessed, against such withdrawn employers.

(I) In the case of a multiemployer plan that has merged with another plan or to which assets and liabilities have been transferred, the actuarial valuation of the assets and liabilities of each affected plan during the year preceding the effective date of the merger or transfer, based upon the most recent data available as of the day before the first day of the plan year, or other valuation method performed under standards and procedures as the Secretary may prescribe by regulation.

Act Sec. 103. (g) Additional Information With Respect to Multiple Employer Plans.—With respect to any multiple employer plan, an annual report under this section for a plan year shall include a list of participating employers and a good faith estimate of the percentage of total contributions made by such participating employers during the plan year.

Amendments

P.L. 113-97, § 102(b)(5):

Amended ERISA Sec. 103(d)(8)(B) by striking "303(h) and 304(c)(3)" and inserting "303(h), 304(c)(3), and 306(c)(3)".

Effective for years beginning after 12-31-2013.

P.L. 113-97, § 104(c):

Amended ERISA Sec. 103 by adding at the end a new subsection (g) to read as above.

Effective for years beginning after 12-31-2013.

P.L. 110-458, § 101(d)(1)(A)(i):

Amended ERISA Sec. 103(d)(3) by striking "the normal costs, the accrued liabilities" and inserting "the normal costs or target normal costs, the accrued liabilities or funding target".

The above amendment takes effect as if included in the provisions of the 2006 Act to which the amendment relates [effective with respect to plan years beginning after 2007.—CCH]

P.L. 110-458, § 101(d)(1)(A)(ii):

Amended ERISA Sec. 103(d) by striking paragraph (7) and inserting paragraph (7) to read as above. Prior to amendment, ERISA Sec. 103(d)(7) read as follows:

(7) A certification of the contribution necessary to reduce the accumulated funding deficiency to zero.

The above amendment takes effect as if included in the provisions of the 2006 Act to which the amendment relates [effective with respect to plan years beginning after 2007.—CCH]

P.L. 109-280, § 107(a)(2):

Amended ERISA Sec. 103(d)(8)(B) by striking "the requirements of section 302(e)(3)" and inserting "the applicable requirements of sections 303(b) and 304(c)(3)".

The above amendment applies to plan years beginning after 2007.

P.L. 109-280, § 107(a)(3):

Amended ERISA Sec. 103(d)(11) by striking the prior paragraph (11) and inserting a new paragraph (11) to read as above.

Prior to amendment, ERISA Sec. 103(d)(11) read as follows:

(11) If the current value of the assets of the plan is less than 70 percent of the current liability under the plan (within the meaning of section 302(d)(7)), the percentage which such value is of such liability.

The above amendment applies to plan years beginning after 2007.

P.L. 109-280, § 503(a)(1)(A):

Amended ERISA Sec. 103(a)(1)(B) by striking "subsections (d) and (e)" and inserting "subsections (d), (e) and (f)".

The above amendment applies to plan years beginning after December 31, 2007.

P.L. 109-280, § 503(a)(1)(B):

Amended ERISA Sec. 103 by adding a new subsection (f) to read as above.

The above amendment applies to plan years beginning after December 31, 2007.

P.L. 109-280, § 503(b)(1) and (2):

Amended ERISA Sec. 103(d) by redesignating paragraphs (12) and (13) as paragraphs (13) and (14), respectively, and by adding a new paragraph (12) to read as above.

The above amendment applies to plan years beginning after December 31, 2007.

P.L. 101-239, § 7881(j)(1):

Amended ERISA Sec. 103(d)(11) by striking "60 percent" and inserting "70 percent" and by striking "such percentage" and inserting "the percentage which such value is of such liability" effective with respect to reports required to be filed after December 31, 1987.

P.L. 100-203, § 9342(a)(1):

Amended ERISA Sec. 103(d) by redesignating paragraphs (11) and (12) as paragraphs (12) and (13), respectively, and by inserting paragraph (11) to read as above, effective with respect to reports required to be filed after December 31, 1987.

P.L. 99-272, § 11016(b)(1):

Amended ERISA Sec. 103(d)(6) to read as above, effective on April 7, 1986.

Prior to the amendment, ERISA Sec. 103(d)(6) read as follows:

(6) The present value of all of the plan's liabilities for nonforfeitable pension benefits allocated by the termination priority categories as set forth in section 4044 of this Act, and the actuarial assumptions used in these computations. The Secretary shall establish regulations defining (for purposes of this section) "termination priority categories" and acceptable methods, including approximate methods, for allocating the plan's liabilities to such termination priority categories.

P.L. 96-364, §307:

Added new subsection 103(d)(10) to read as above and renumbered old subsections 103(d)(10) and (11) to be 103(11) and (12), respectively, effective September 26, 1980.

Regulations

The following regulations on annual reporting requirements were adopted, effective generally for plan years beginning in 1977, by FR Doc. 78-6073 under "Title 29—Labor," "Chapter XXV—Pension and Welfare Benefit Programs, Department of Labor," "Part 2520—Rules and Regulations for Reporting and Disclosure." The regulations were filed with the Federal Register on March 9, 1978, and published in the Federal Register on March 10, 1978 (41 FR 10130). Reg. §§2520.103-1—2520.103-6 and §§2520.103-9—2520.103-12 were amended by 65 FR 21067 and published in the *Federal Register* on April 19, 2000 (65 FR 21067). Reg. Sec. 2520.103-13 was added on April 21, 2006 (71 FR 20820); effective May 22, 2006. Reg. §§ 2520.103-1, 2520.103-2, 2520.103-9, and 2520.103-12 were amended on July 21, 2006 (71 FR 41359); effective September 19, 2006. Reg. Sec. 2520.103-1 was revised on November 16, 2007 (72 FR 64710), effective January 15, 2008. Reg. §2520.103-1 was amended on March 1, 2013 (78 FR 13781), effective April 1, 2013.

Subpart C—Annual Report Requirements

[¶ 14,231A]

§ 2520.103-1 **Contents of the annual report.** (a) *In general.* The administrator of a plan required to file an annual report in accordance with section 104(a)(1) of the Act shall include with the annual report the information prescribed in paragraph (a)(1) of this section or in the simplified report, limited exemption or alternative method of compliance described in paragraph (a)(2) of this section. [Amended by EBSA on March 1, 2013 (78 FR 13781).]

(1) The annual report shall contain the information prescribed in section 103 of the Act.

(2) Under the authority of subsections 104(a)(2), 104(a)(3) and 110 of the Act, and section 1103(b) of the Pension Protection Act of 2006, a simplified report, limited exemption or alternative method of compliance is prescribed for employee welfare and pension benefit plans, as applicable. A plan filing a simplified report or electing the limited exemption or alternative method of compliance shall file an annual report containing the information prescribed in paragraph (b) or paragraph (c) of this section, as applicable, and shall furnish a summary annual report as prescribed in § 2520.104b-10.

(b) *Contents of the annual report for plans with 100 or more participants electing the limited exemption or alternative method of compliance.* Except as provided in paragraph (d) and paragraph (f) of this section and in §§2520.103-2 and 2520.104-44, the annual report of an employee benefit plan covering 100 or more participants at the beginning of the plan year which elects the limited exemption or alternative method of compliance described in paragraph (a)(2) of this section shall include: [Amended by EBSA on March 1, 2013 (78 FR 13781).]

(1) A Form 5500 "Annual Return/Report of Employee Benefit Plan" and any statements or schedules required to be attached to the form, completed in accordance with the instructions for the form, including Schedule A (Insurance Information), Schedule SB (Single-Employer Defined Benefit Plan Actuarial Information), Schedule MB (Multiemployer Defined Benefit Plan and Certain Money Purchase Plan Actuarial Information), Schedule C (Service Provider Information), Schedule D (DFE/Participating Plan Information), Schedule G (Financial Transaction Schedules), Schedule H (Financial Information), Schedule R (Retirement Plan Information), and other financial schedules described in Sec. 2520.103-10. See the instructions for this form.

(2) Separate financial statements (in addition to the information required by paragraph (b)(1) of this section), if such financial statements are prepared in order for the independent qualified public accountant to form the opinion required by section 103(a)(3)(A) of the Act and §2520.103-1(b)(5). These statements shall include the following:

(i) A statement of assets and liabilities at current value presented in comparative form for the beginning and end of the year. The statement of plan assets and liabilities shall include the assets and liabilities required to be reported on Form 5500; however, the assets and liabilities may be aggregated into categories in a manner other than that used on Form 5500. [Amended on March 1, 1989 by 54 FR 8624; amended on April 19, 2000 by 65 FR 21080.]

(ii) Separate or combined statements of plan income and expenses and of changes in net assets which include the categories of income, expense, and changes in assets required to be reported on the Form 5500; however, the income, expense, and changes in net assets

may be aggregated into categories in a manner other than that used on Form 5500. [Amended on March 1, 1989 by 54 FR 8624.]

(3) Notes to the financial statements described in paragraphs (b)(1) or (2) of this section which contain a description of the accounting principles and practices reflected in the financial statements and, if applicable, variances from generally accepted accounting principles; a description of the plan, including any significant changes in the plan made during the period and the impact of such changes on benefits; the funding policy (including policy with respect to prior service cost) and any changes in such policy from the prior year, a description of material lease commitments, other commitments, and contingent liabilities; a description of agreements and transactions with persons known to be parties in interest; a general description of priorities upon termination of the plan; information concerning whether or not a tax ruling or determination letter has been obtained; an explanation of the differences, if any, between the information contained in the separate financial statements and the assets, liabilities, income, expenses and changes in net assets as required to be reported on the Form 5500, and any other matters necessary to fully and fairly present the financial condition of the plan. [Amended on March 1, 1989 by 54 FR 8624.]

(4) In the case of a plan, some or all of the assets of which are held in a pooled separate account maintained by an insurance company, or a common or collective trust maintained by a bank or similar institution, a copy of the annual statement of assets and liabilities of such account or trust for the fiscal year of the account or trust which ends with or within the plan year for which the annual report is made as required to be furnished to the administrator by such account or trust under §2520.103-5(c). Although the statement of assets and liabilities referred to in §2520.103-5(c) shall be considered part of the plan's annual report, such statement of assets and liabilities need not be filed with the plan's annual report. See §§2520.103-3 and 2520.103-4 for reporting requirements for plans some or all of the assets of which are held in a pooled separate account maintained by an insurance company, or a common or collective trust maintained by a bank or similar institution. [Amended April 19, 2000 by 65 FR 21080.]

(5) A report of an independent qualified public accountant.

(i) *Technical requirements.* The accountant's report—

(A) Shall be dated;

(B) Shall be signed manually;

(C) Shall indicate the city and state where issued; and

(D) Shall identify without detailed enumeration the financial statements and schedules covered by the report.

(ii) *Representations as to the audit.* The accountant's report—

(A) Shall state whether the audit was made in accordance with generally accepted auditing standards; and

(B) Shall designate any auditing procedures deemed necessary by the accountant under the circumstances of the particular case which have been omitted, and the reasons for their omission. Authority for the omission of certain procedures which independent accountants might ordinarily employ in the course of an audit made for the purpose of expressing the opinions required by paragraph (b)(5)(iii) of this section is contained in §§2520.103-8 and 2520.103-12. [Amended by 51 FR 41285 on Nov. 13, 1986; amended on March 1, 1989 by 54 FR 8624.]

(iii) *Opinion to be expressed.* The accountant's report shall state clearly:

(A) The opinion of the accountant in respect of the financial statements and schedules covered by the report and the accounting principles and practices reflected therein; and

(B) The opinion of the accountant as to the consistency of the application of the accounting principles with the application of such principles in the preceding year or as to any changes in such principles which have a material effect on the financial statements.

(iv) *Exceptions.* Any matters to which the accountant takes exception shall be clearly identified, the exception thereto specifically and clearly stated, and, to the extent practicable, the effect of the matters to which the accountant takes exception on the related financial statements given. The matters to which the accountant takes exception shall be further identified as (A) those that are the result of DOL regulations, and (B) all others.

(c) *Contents of the annual report for plans with fewer than 100 participants.*

(1) Except as provided in paragraph (c)(2), paragraph (d) and paragraph (f) of this section, and in §§2520.104-43, 2520.104a-6, and 2520.104-44, the annual report of an employee benefit plan that covers fewer than 100 participants at the beginning of the plan year shall include a Form 5500 "Annual Return/Report of Employee Benefit Plan" and any statements or schedules required to be attached to the form, completed in accordance with the instructions for the form, including Schedule A (Insurance Information), Schedule SB (Single Employer Defined Benefit Plan Actuarial Information), Schedule MB (Multiemployer Defined Benefit Plan and Certain Money Purchase Plan Actuarial Information), Schedule D (DFE/Participating Plan Information), Schedule I (Financial Information—Small Plan), and Schedule R (Retirement Plan Information). See the instructions for this form. [Amended by EBSA on March 1, 2013 (78 FR 13781).]

(2)(i) The annual report of an employee benefit plan that covers fewer than 100 participants at the beginning of the plan year and that meets the conditions in paragraph (c)(2)(ii) of this section with respect to a plan year may, as an alternative to the requirements of paragraph (c)(1) of this section, meet its annual reporting requirements by filing the Form 5500-SF "Short Form Annual Return/Report of Small Employee Benefit Plan" and any statements or schedules required to be attached to the form, including Schedule SB (Single Employer Defined Benefit Plan Actuarial Information) and Schedule MB (Multiemployer Defined Benefit Plan and Certain Money Purchase Plan Actuarial Information), completed in accordance with the instructions for the form. See the instructions for this form.

(ii) A plan meets the conditions in this paragraph (c)(2)(ii) with respect to the year if the plan:

(A) Does not hold any employer securities at any time during the year;

(B) Satisfies the audit waiver conditions in §§ 2520.104-46(b)(1)(i)(A)(1), (b)(1)(i)(B) and (b)(1)(i)(C);

(C) Had at all times during the plan year 100 percent of the plan's assets held for investment purposes invested in assets that have a readily determinable fair market value. For purposes of this section, the following shall be treated as assets that have a readily determinable fair market value: shares issued by an investment company registered under the Investment Company Act of 1940; investment and annuity contracts issued by any insurance company, qualified to do business under the laws of a State, that provides valuation information at least annually to the plan administrator; bank investment contracts issued by a bank or similar financial institution, as defined in § 2550.408b-4(c) of this chapter, that provides valuation information at least annually to the plan administrator; securities (except employer securities) traded on a public exchange; government securities issued by the United States or by a State; cash or cash equivalents held by a bank or similar financial institution, as defined in § 2550.408b-4(c) of this chapter, by an insurance company, qualified to do business under the law of a State, by an organization registered as a broker-dealer under the Securities Exchange Act of 1934, or by any other organization authorized to act as a trustee for individual retirement accounts under section 408 of the Internal Revenue Code; and any loan meeting the requirements of section 408(b)(1) of the Act and the regulations issued thereunder; [Amended by EBSA on March 1, 2013 (78 FR 13781).]

(D) Is not a multiemployer plan; and [Amended by EBSA on March 1, 2013 (78 FR 13781).]

(E) Is not a plan subject to the Form M-1 requirements under §2520.101-2 (Filing by Multiple Employer Welfare Arrangements and Certain Other Related Entities). [Added by EBSA on March 1, 2013 (78 FR 13781).]

(d) *Special rule.* If a plan has between 80 and 120 participants (inclusive) as of the beginning of the plan year, the plan administrator may elect to file the same category of annual report (i.e., the annual report for plans with 100 or more participants under paragraph (b) of this section or the annual report for plans with fewer than 100 participants under paragraph (c) of this section) that was filed for the previous plan year. [Added on July 29, 1980 by 45 FR 51446; amended on March 1, 1989 by 54 FR 8624; amended April 19, 2000 by FR 65 21080.]

(e) *Plans which participate in a master trust.* The plan administrator of a plan which participates in a master trust shall file an annual report on Form 5500 in accordance with the instructions for the form relating to master trusts and master trust investment accounts. For purposes of annual reporting, a master trust is a trust for which a regulated financial institution serves as trustee or custodian (regardless of whether such institution exercises discretionary authority or control respecting the management of assets held in the trust) and in which assets of more than one plan sponsored by a single employer or by a group of employers under common control are held. For purpose of this paragraph, a regulated financial institution is a bank, trust company, or similar financial institution regulated, supervised, and subject to periodic examination by a State or Federal agency. Common control is determined on the basis of all relevant facts and circumstances (whether or not such employers are incorporated). [Added on December 10, 1981, by 46 FR 61074; amended on March 1, 1989 by 54 FR 8624; amended April 19, 2000 by FR 65 21080.]

(f) *Plans subject to the Form M-1 filing requirements under § 2520.101-2.* The annual report of an employee welfare benefit plan that is subject to the Form M-1 requirements under § 2520.101-2 (Filing by Multiple Employer Welfare Arrangements and Certain Other Related Entities) during the plan year shall also include any statements or information required by the instructions to the Form 5500 relating to compliance with the Form M-1 filing requirements under § 2520.101-2. [Added by EBSA on March 1, 2013 (78 FR 13781).]

(g) *Electronic filing.* See § 2520.104a-2 and the instructions for the Form 5500 "Annual Return/Report of Employee Benefit Plan" for electronic filing requirements. The plan administrator must maintain an original copy, with all required signatures, as part of the plan's records. [Amended July 21, 2006 by 71 FR 41368 and November 16, 2007 by 72 FR 64710. Redesignated by EBSA on March 1, 2013 (78 FR 13781).]

[¶ 14,231B]

§2520.103-2 **Contents of the annual report for a group insurance arrangement.** (a) *General.* (1) A trust or other entity described in § 2520.104-43(b) that files an annual report for purposes of § 2520.104-43 shall include in such report the items set forth in paragraph (b) of this section.

(b) *Contents.* (1) A Form 5500 "Annual Return/Report of Employee Benefit Plan" and any statements or schedules required to be attached to the form, completed in accordance with the instructions for the form, including Schedule A (Insurance Information), Schedule C (Service Provider Information), Schedule D (DFE/Participating Plan Information), Schedule G (Financial Transaction Schedules), Schedule H (Financial Information), and the other financial schedules described in § 2520.103-10. See the instructions for this form. [Amended on March 1, 1989 by 54 FR 8624; amended April 19, 2000 by 65 FR 21080.]

(2) Separate financial statements (in addition to the information required by paragraph (b)(1) of this section), if such financial statements are prepared in order for the independent qualified public accountant to form the opinion required by section 103(a)(3)(A) of the Act and §2520.103-2(b)(5). These financial statements shall include the following:

(i) A statement of all trust assets and liabilities at current value presented in comparative form for the beginning and end of the year. The statement of trust assets and liabilities shall include the assets and liabilities required to be reported on the Form 5500; however, the assets and liabilities may be aggregated into categories in a manner other than that used on Form 5500. [Amended on March 1, 1989 by 54 FR 8624; amended April 19, 2000 by 65 FR 21080.]

(ii) Separate or combined statements of all trust income and expenses and changes in net assets which includes the categories of income, expense, and changes in assets required to be reported on the Form 5500; however, the income, expense, and changes in assets may be aggregated into categories in a manner other than that used on Form 5500. [Amended on March 1, 1989 by 54 FR 8624.]

(3) Notes to the financial statements described in paragraphs (b)(1) or (2) of this section which contain a description of the accounting principles and practices reflected in the financial statements and, if applicable, variances from generally accepted accounting principles; a description of the group insurance arrangement including any significant changes in the group insurance arrangement made during the period and the impact of such changes on benefits; a description of material lease commitments, other commitments, and contingent liabilities; a description of agreements and transactions with persons known to be parties in interest; a general description of priorities upon termination of the plan; an explanation of the differences, if any, between the information contained in the separate financial statements and the assets, liabilities, income, expenses and changes in net assets as required to be reported on the Form 5500; and any other matters necessary to fully and fairly present the financial condition of the plan. [Amended on March 1, 1989 by 54 FR 8624.]

(4) In the case of a group insurance arrangement some or all of the assets of which are held in a pooled separate account maintained by an insurance carrier, or in a common or collective trust maintained by a bank, trust company or similar institution, a copy of the annual statement of assets and liabilities of such account or trust for the fiscal year of the account or trust which ends with or within the plan year for which the annual report is made as required to be furnished by such account or trust under §2520.103-5(c). Although the statement of assets and liabilities referred to in §2520.103-5(c) shall be considered part of the group insurance arrangement's annual report, such statement of assets and liabilities need not be filed with its annual report. See §§2520.103-3 and 2520.103-4 for reporting requirements for plans some or all of the assets of which are held in a pooled separate account maintained by an insurance company, or a common or collective trust maintained by a bank or similar institution, and see §2520.104-43(b)(2) for when the terms "group insurance arrangement" or "trust or other entity" shall be, respectively, used in place of the terms "plan" and "plan administrator." [Amended April 19, 2000 by 65 FR 21080.]

(5) A report of an independent qualified public accountant.

(i) *Technical requirements.* The accountant's report—

(A) Shall be dated;

(B) Shall be signed manually;

(C) Shall indicate the city and State where issued; and

(D) Shall identify without detailed enumeration the financial statements and schedules covered by the report.

(ii) *Representations as to the audit.* The accountant's report—

(A) Shall state whether the audit was made in accordance with generally accepted auditing standards; and

(B) Shall designate any auditing procedures deemed necessary by the accountant under the circumstances of the particular case, which have been omitted, and the reasons for their omission. Authority for the omission of certain procedures which independent accountants might ordinarily employ in the course of an audit made for the purpose of expressing the opinions required by paragraph (b)(5)(iii) of this section is contained in §2520.103-8.

(iii) *Opinion to be expressed.* The accountant's report shall state clearly:

(A) The opinion of the accountant in respect of the financial statements and schedules covered by the report and the accounting principles and practices reflected therein; and

(B) The opinion of the accountant as to the consistency of the application of the accounting principles with the application of such

principles in the preceding year, or as to any changes in such principles which have a material effect on the financial statements.

(iv) *Exceptions.* Any matters to which the accountant takes exception shall be clearly identified, the exception thereto specifically and clearly stated, and, to the extent practicable, the effect of the matters to which the accountant takes exception on the related financial statements given. The matters to which the accountant takes exception shall be further identified as to (a) those that are the result of DOL regulations and (b) all others. [Added March 9, 1978, by 43 F.R. 10130.]

(c) *Electronic filing.* See §2520.104a-2 and the instructions for the Form 5500 "Annual Return/Report of Employee Benefit Plan" for electronic filing requirements. The trust or other entity described in §2520.104-43(b) filing under this section must maintain an original copy, with all required signatures, as part of its records. [Amended July 21, 2006 by 71 FR 41368.]

[¶ 14,231C]

§2520.103-3 **Exemption from certain annual reporting requirements for assets held in a common or collective trust.** (a) *General.* Under the authority of sections 103(b)(3)(G), 103(b)(4), 104(a)(2)(B), 104(a)(3), 110 and 505 of the Act, a plan whose assets are held in whole or in part in a common or collective trust maintained by a bank, trust company, or similar institution which meets the requirements of paragraph (b) of this section shall include as part of the annual report required to be filed under §§2520.104a-5 or 2520.104a-6 the information described in paragraph (c) of this section. Such plan is not required to include in its annual report information concerning the individual transactions of the common or collective trust. This exemption has no application to assets not held in such trusts. [Amended April 19, 2000 by 65 FR 21081.]

(b) *Application.* This provision applies only to a plan some or all of the assets of which are held in a common or collective trust maintained by a bank, trust company, or similar institution regulated and supervised and subject to periodic examination by a State or Federal agency. For purposes of this section, (1) a common or collective trust is a trust which consists of the assets of two or more participating entities and is maintained for the collective investment and reinvestment of assets contributed thereto, and (2) plans maintained by a single employer or by the members of a controlled group of corporations, as defined in section 1563(a) of the Internal Revenue Code of 1954, shall be deemed to be a single participating entity.

(c) *Contents.* (1) A plan which meets the requirements of paragraph (b) of this section, and which invests in a common or collective trust that files a Form 5500 report in accordance with §2520.103-9, shall include in its annual report: information required by the instructions to Schedule H (Financial Information) or Schedule I (Financial Information—Small Plan) about the current value of and net investment gain or loss relating to the units of participation in the common or collective trust held by the plan; identifying information about the common or collective trust including its name, employer identification number, and any other information required by the instructions to the Schedule D (DFE/Participating Plan Information); and such other information as is required in the separate statements and schedules of the annual report about the value of the plan's units of participation in the common or collective trust and transactions involving the acquisition and disposition by the plan of units of participation in the common or collective trust. [Amended April 18, 2000 by 65 FR 21081.]

(2) A plan which meets the requirements of paragraph (b) of this section, and which invests in a common or collective trust that does not file a Form 5500 report in accordance with §2520.103-9, shall include in its annual report: information required by the instructions to Schedule H (Financial Information) or Schedule I (Financial Information—Small Plan) about the current value of the plan's allocable portion of the underlying assets and liabilities of the common or collective trust and the net investment gain or loss relating to the units of participation in the common or collective trust held by the plan; identifying information about the common or collective trust including its name, employer identification number, and any other information required by the instructions to the Schedule D (DFE/Participating Plan Information); and such other information as is required in the separate statements

and schedules of the annual report about the value of the plan's units of participation in the common or collective trust and transactions involving the acquisition and disposition by the plan of units of participation in the common or collective trust. [Added March 9, 1978, by 43 FR 10130; amended April 19, 2000 by 65 FR 21081.]

[¶ 14,231D]

§ 2520.103-4 **Exemption from certain annual reporting requirements for assets held in an insurance company pooled separate account.** (a) *General.* Under the authority of sections 103(b)(3)(G), 103(b)(4), 104(a)(2)(B), 104(a)(3), 110 and 505 of the Act, a plan whose assets are held in whole or in part in a pooled separate account of an insurance carrier which meets the requirements of paragraph (b) of this section shall include as part of the annual report required to be filed under § 2520.104a-5 or § 2520.104a-6 the information described in paragraph (c) of this section. Such plan is not required to include in its annual report information concerning the individual transactions of the pooled separate account. This exemption has no application to assets not held in such a pooled separate account. [Amended April 19, 2000 by 65 FR 21081.]

(b) *Application.* This provision applies only to a plan some or all of the assets of which are held in a pooled separate account of an insurance carrier regulated and supervised and subject to periodic examination by a State agency. For purposes of this section, (1) a pooled separate account is an account which consists of the assets of two or more participating entities and is maintained for the collective investment and reinvestment of assets contributed thereto, and (2) plans maintained by a single employer or by members of a controlled group of corporations, as defined in section 1563(a) of the Internal Revenue Code of 1954, shall be deemed to be a single participating entity.

(c) *Contents.* (1) A plan which meets the requirements of paragraph (b) of this section, and which invests in a pooled separate account that files a Form 5500 report in accordance with § 2520.103-9, shall include in its annual report: information required by the instructions to Schedule H (Financial Information) or Schedule I (Financial Information—Small Plan) about the current value of, and net investment gain or loss relating to, the units of participation in the pooled separate account held by the plan; identifying information about the pooled separate account including its name, employer identification number, and any other information required by the instructions to the Schedule D (DFE/Participating Plan Information); and such other information as is required in the separate statements and schedules of the annual report about the value of the plan's units of participation in the pooled separate accounts and transactions involving the acquisition and disposition by the plan of units of participation in the pooled separate account. [Amended on April 19, 2000 by 65 FR 21081.]

(2) A plan which meets the requirements of paragraph (b) of this section, and which invests in a pooled separate account that does not file a Form 5500 report in accordance with § 2520.103-9, shall include in its annual report: information required by the instructions to Schedule H (Financial Information) or Schedule I (Financial Information—Small Plan) about the current value of the plan's allocable portion of the underlying assets and liabilities of the pooled separate account and the net investment gain or loss relating to the units of participation in the pooled separate account held by the plan; identifying information about the pooled separate account including its name, employer identification number, and any other information required by the instructions to the Schedule D (DFE/Participating Plan Information); and such other information as is required in the separate statements and schedules of the annual report about the value of the plan's units of participation in the pooled separate account and transactions involving the acquisition and disposition by the plan of units of participation in the pooled separate account.[Added March 9, 1978, by 43 FR 10130; amended April 19, 2000 by 65 FR 21081.]

[¶ 14,231E]

§ 2520.103-5 **Transmittal and certification of information to plan administrator for annual reporting purposes.** (a) *General.* In accordance with section 103(a)(2) of the Act, an insurance carrier or other organization which provides benefits under the plan or holds plan assets, a bank or similar institution which holds plan assets, or a plan

sponsor shall transmit and certify such information as needed by the administrator to file the annual report under section 104(a)(1) of the Act and § 2520.104a-5 or § 2520.104a-6:

(1) Within 9 months after the close of the plan year which begins in 1975 or September 30, 1976, whichever is later, and

(2) Within 120 days after the close of any plan year which begins after December 31, 1975.

(b) *Application.* This requirement applies with respect to—

(1) An insurance carrier or other organization which:

(i) Provides from its general asset account funds for the payment of benefits under a plan, or

(ii) Holds assets of a plan in a separate account;

(2) A bank, trust company, or similar institution which holds assets of a plan in a common or collective trust, separate trust, or custodial account; and

(3) A plan sponsor as defined in section 3(16)(B) of the Act.

(c) *Contents.* The information required to be provided to the administrator shall include—

(1) In the case of an insurance carrier or other organization which:

(i) Provides funds from its general asset account for the payment of benefits under a plan, upon request of the plan administrator, such information as is contained within the ordinary business records of the insurance carrier or other organization and is needed by the plan administrator to comply with the requirements of section 104(a)(1) of the Act and § 2520.104a-5 or § 2520.104a-6;

(ii) Holds assets of a plan in a pooled separate account and files a Form 5500 report pursuant to § 2520.103-9 for the participating plan's plan year—

(A) A copy of the annual statement of assets and liabilities of the separate account for the fiscal year of such account ending with or within the plan year for which the participating plan's annual report is made,

(B) A statement of the value of the plan's units of participation in the separate account,

(C) The Employer Identification Number (EIN) of the separate account, entity number required for purposes of completing the Form 5500 and any other identifying number assigned by the insurance carrier to the separate account,

(D) A statement that a filing pursuant to § 2520.103-9(c) will be made for the separate account (for its fiscal year ending with or within the participating plan's plan year) on or before the filing due date for such account in accordance with the Form 5500 instructions, and

(E) Upon request of the plan administrator, any other information that can be obtained from the ordinary business records of the insurance carrier and that is needed by the plan administrator to comply with the requirements of section 104(a)(1) of the Act and § 2520.104a-5 or § 2520.104a-6; [Amended April 19, 2000 by 65 FR 21081.]

(iii) Holds assets of a plan in a pooled separate account and does not file a Form 5500 report pursuant to § 2520.103-9 for the participating plan's plan year—

(A) A copy of the annual statement of assets and liabilities of the separate account for the fiscal year of such account that ends with or within the plan year for which the participating plan's annual report is made,

(B) A statement of the value of the plan's units of participation in the separate account,

(C) The EIN of the separate account and any other identifying number assigned by the insurance carrier to the separate account,

(D) A statement that a filing pursuant to § 2520.103-9(c) will not be made for the separate account for its fiscal year ending with or within the participating plan's plan year, and

(E) Upon request of the plan administrator, any other information that can be obtained from the ordinary business records of the insurance carrier and that is needed by the plan administrator to comply with the requirements of section 104(a)(1) of the Act and § 2520.104a-5 or § 2520.104a-6. [Added April 19, 2000 by 65 FR 21081.]

(iv) Holds assets of a plan in a separate account which is not exempted from certain reporting requirements under § 2520.103-4, a listing of all transactions of the separate account and, upon request of the plan administrator, such information as is contained within the ordinary business records of the insurance carrier and is needed by the plan administrator to comply with the requirements of section 104(a)(1) of the Act and § 2520.104a-5 or § 2520.104a-6. [Amended April 19, 2000 by 65 FR 21081.]

(2) In the case of a bank, trust company, or similar institution holding assets of a plan—

(i) In a common or collective trust that files a Form 5500 report pursuant to § 2520.103-9 for the participating plan's plan year—

(A) A copy of the annual statement of assets and liabilities of the common or collective trust for the fiscal year of such trust ending with or within the plan year for which the participating plan's annual report is made,

(B) A statement of the value of the plan's units of participation in the common or collective trust,

(C) The EIN of the common or collective trust, entity number assigned for purposes of completing the Form 5500 and any other identifying number assigned by the bank, trust company, or similar institution,

(D) A statement that a filing pursuant to § 2520.103-9(c) will be made for the common or collective trust (for its fiscal year ending with or within the participating plan's plan year) on or before the filing due date for such trust in accordance with the Form 5500 instructions, and

(E) Upon request of the plan administrator, any other information that can be obtained from the ordinary business records of the bank, trust company or similar institution and that is needed by the plan administrator to comply with the requirements of section 104(a)(1) of the Act and § § 2520.104a-5 or 2520.104a-6. [Amended April 19, 2000 by 65 FR 21082.]

(ii) In a common or collective trust that does not file a Form 5500 report pursuant to § 2520.103-9 for the participating plan's plan year—

(A) A copy of the annual statement of assets and liabilities of the common or collective trust for the fiscal year of such account that ends with or within the plan year for which the participating plan's annual report is made,

(B) A statement of the value of the plan's units of participation in the common or collective trust,

(C) The EIN of the common or collective trust and any other identifying number assigned by the bank, trust company or similar institution,

(D) A statement that a filing pursuant to § 2520.103-9(c) will not be made for the common or collective trust for its fiscal year ending with or within the participating plan's plan year, and

(E) Upon request of the plan administrator, any other information that can be obtained from the ordinary business records of the bank, trust company or similar institution and that is needed by the plan administrator to comply with the requirements of section 104(a)(1) of the Act and § § 2520.104a-5 or 2520.104a-6. [Added April 19, 2000 by 65 FR 21082.]

(iii) In a trust which is not exempted from certain reporting requirements under § 2520.103-3, a listing of all transactions of the separate trust and, upon request of the the plan administrator, such information as is contained within the ordinary business records of the bank, trust company, or similar institution and is needed by the plan administrator to comply with the requirements of section 104(a)(1) of the Act and § 2520.104a-5. [Amended April 19, 2000 by 65 FR 21082.]

(iv) In a custodial account, upon request of the plan administrator, such information as is contained within the ordinary business records of the bank, trust company, or similar institution and is needed by the plan administrator to comply with the requirements of section 104(a)(1) of the Act and § 2520.104a-5 or § 2520.104a-6. [Amended April 19, 2000 by 65 FR 21082.]

(3) In the case of a plan sponsor, a listing of all transactions directly or indirectly involving plan assets engaged in by the plan sponsor and such information as is needed by the plan administrator to comply with the requirements of section 104(a)(1) of the Act and § 2520.104a-5 or § 2520.104a-6.

(d) *Certification.* (1) An insurance carrier or other organization, a bank, trust company, or similar institution, or plan sponsor, as described in paragraph (b) of this section, shall certify to the accuracy and completeness of the information described in paragraph (c) of this section by a written declaration which is signed by a person authorized to represent the insurance carrier, bank, or plan sponsor. Such certification will serve as a written assurance of the truth of the facts stated therein.

(2) *Example of Certification.* The XYZ Bank (Insurance Carrier) hereby certifies that the foregoing statement furnished pursuant to 29 CFR 2520.103-5(c) is complete and accurate. [Added March 9, 1978, by 43 FR 10130.]

[¶ 14,231F]

§ 2520.103-6 **Definition of reportable transaction for Annual Return/Report.** (a) *General.* General. For purposes of preparing the schedule of reportable transactions described in § 2520.103-10(b)(6), and subject to the exceptions provided in § § 2520.103-3, 2520.103-4 and 2520.103-12, with respect to individual transactions by a common or collective trust, pooled separate account, or a 103-12 investment entity, a reportable transaction includes any transaction or series of transactions described in paragraph (c) of this section. [Corrected April 4, 1978, by 43 FR 14009; amended April 19, 2000 by 65 FR 21082.]

(b) *Definitions.* (1)(i) Except as provided in paragraphs (c)(2) and (d)(1)(vi) of this section (relating to assets acquired or disposed of during the plan year), "current value" shall mean the current value, as defined in section 3(26) of the Act, of plan assets as of the beginning of the plan year, or the end of the previous plan year. [Amended July 1, 1996 by 61 FR 33847.]

(ii) Except as provided in paragraphs (c)(2) and (d)(1)(vi) of this section (relating to assets acquired or disposed of during the plan year), with respect to schedules of reportable transactions for the initial plan year of a plan, "current value" shall mean the current value, as defined in section 3(26) of the Act, of plan assets at the end of a plan's initial plan year. [Amended April 19, 2000 by 65 FR 21082.]

(2)(i) A "transaction with respect to securities" is any purchase, sale, or exchange of securities. A transaction with respect to securities for purposes of this section occurs on either the trade date or settlement date of a purchase, sale, or exchange of securities; either the trade date or settlement date must be used consistently during the plan year for the purposes of this section. For the purposes of this section, except as provided in paragraph (b)(2)(ii) of this section, "securities" includes a unit of participation in a common or collective trust or a pooled separate account.

(ii) Solely for purposes of paragraph (c)(1)(iv) of this section, the term "securities", as it applies to any transaction involving a bank or insurance company regulated by a Federal or State agency, an investment company registered under the Investment Company Act of 1940, or a broker-dealer registered under the Securities Exchange Act of 1934, shall not include:

(A) Debt obligations of the United States or any United States agency with a maturity of not more than one year;

(B) Debt obligations of the United States or any United States agency with a maturity of more than one year if purchased or sold, under a repurchase agreement having a term of less than 91 days;

(C) Interests issued by a company registered under the Investment Company Act of 1940;

(D) Bank certificates of deposit with a maturity of not more than one year;

(E) Commercial paper with a maturity of not more than nine months if it is ranked in the highest rating category for commercial paper by at least two nationally recognized statistical rating services and is issued by a company required to file reports under section 13 of the Securities Exchange Act of 1934;

(F) Participations in a bank common or collective trust;

(G) Participations in an insurance company pooled separate account;

(3)(i) Except as provided by paragraph (b)(3)(ii) of this section, a transaction is "with or in conjunction with a person" for purposes of this section if that person benefits from, executes, facilitates, participates, promotes, or solicits a transaction or part of a transaction involving plan assets.

(ii) Solely for the purposes of paragraph (c)(1)(iv) of this section, a transaction shall not be considered "with or in conjunction with a person" if:

(A) That person is a broker-dealer registered under the Securities Exchange Act of 1934;

(B) The transaction involves the purchase or sale of securities listed on a national securities exchange registered under section 6 of the Securities Exchange Act of 1934 or quoted on NASDAQ; and

(C) The broker-dealer does not purchase or sell securities involved in the transaction for its own account or the account of an affiliated person.

(c) *Application.* (1) Except as provided in paragraph (c)(4) of this section, this provision applies to—

(i) A transaction within the plan year, with respect to any plan asset, involving an amount in excess of 3 percent of the current value of plan assets;

(ii) Any series of transactions (other than transactions with respect to securities) within the plan year with or in conjunction with the same person which, when aggregated, regardless of the category of asset and the gain or loss on any transation, involves an amount in excess of 3 percent of the current value of plan assets;

(iii) Any transaction within the plan year involving securities of the same issue if within the plan year any series of transactions with respect to such securities, when aggregated, involves an amount in excess of 3 percent of the current value of plan assets; and

(iv) Any transaction within the plan year with respect to securities with or in conjunction with a person if any prior or subsequent single transaction within the plan year with such person with respect to securities exceeds 3 percent of the current value of plan assets.

(2) For purposes of determining whether any 3 percent transactions occur, the "current value" of an asset acquired or disposed of during the plan year is the current value, as defined in section 3(26) of the Act, at the time of acquisition or disposition of such asset.

(3) Plans whose assets are held in whole or in part in a common or collective trust or a pooled separate account, as provided in §§ 2520.103-3 and 2520.103-4, and which satisfy the requirements of those sections, are not required to prepare schedules of reportable transactions with respect to the individual transactions of the common or collective trust or pooled separate account.

(4) For plan years beginning on or after January 1, 1988, 5 percent shall be substituted for 3 percent in paragraphs (c)(1) and (2) of this section for purposes of determining whether a transaction or series of transactions constitutes a reportable transaction under this section. [Amended on March 1, 1989 by 54 FR 8624.]

(d) *Contents.* (1) The schedule of transactions shall include the following information as to each transaction or series of transactions:

(i) The name of each party, except that in the case of a transaction or series of transactions involving a purchase or sale of a security on the market, the schedule need not include the person from whom it was purchased or to whom it was sold. A purchase or sale on the market is a purchase or sale of a security through a registered broker-dealer acting as a broker under the Securities Exchange Act of 1934;

(ii) A brief description of each asset;

(iii) The purchase or selling price in the case of a purchase or sale, the rental in the case of a lease, and the amount of principal, interest rate, payment schedule (e.g., fully amortized, partly amortized with balloon) and maturity date in the case of a loan;

(iv) Expenses incurred, including, but not limited to, any fees or commissions;

(v) The cost of any asset;

(vi) The current value of any asset acquired or disposed of at the time of acquisition or disposition; and

(vii) The net gain or loss.

(2) The schedule of transactions with respect to a series of transactions described in subparagraph (c)(1)(iii) may include the following information for each issue in lieu of the information prescribed in paragraphs (d)(1)(i)—(vii):

(i) The total number of purchases of such securities made by the plan within the plan year;

(ii) The total number of sales of such securities made by the plan within the plan year;

(iii) The total dollar value of such purchases;

(iv) The total dollar value of such sales;

(v) The net gain or loss as a result of these transactions.

(e) *Examples.* These examples are effective for reporting for plan years beginning on or after January 1, 1988.

(1) At the beginning of the plan year, XYZ plan has 10 percent of the current value of its plan assets invested in ABC common stock. Halfway through the plan year, XYZ purchases ABC common stock in a single transaction in an amount equal to 6 percent of the current value of plan assets. At about this time, XYZ plan also purchases a commercial development property in an amount equal to 8 percent of the current value of plan assets. Under paragraph (c)(1)(i) of this section, the 6 percent stock transaction is a reportable transaction for the plan year because it exceeds 5 percent of the current value of plan assets. The 8 percent land transaction is also reportable under paragraph (c)(1)(i) of this section because it exceeds 5 percent of the current value of plan assets.

(2) During the plan year, AAA plan purchases a commercial lot from ZZZ corporation at a cost equal to 2 percent of the current value of the plan assets. Two months later, AAA plan loans ZZZ corporation an amount of money equal to 3.5 percent of the current value of plan assets. Under the provisions of paragraph (c)(1)(ii) of this section, the plan has engaged in a reportable series of transactions with or in conjunction with the same person, ZZZ corporation, which when aggregated involves 5.5 percent of plan assets.

(3) During the plan year NMN plan sells to OPO corporation a commercial property that represents 3.5 percent of the current value of plan assets. OPO simultaneously executes a note and mortgage on the purchased property to NMN which represents 3 percent of the current value of plan assets. Under the provisions of paragraph (c)(1)(ii) of this section, NMN has engaged in a reportable series of transactions with or in conjunction with the same person, OPO corporation, consisting of a simultaneous sale of property and a loan, which, when aggregated, involves 6.5 percent of the current value of plan assets.

(4) At the beginning of the plan year, ABC plan has 10 percent of the current value of plan assets invested equally in a combination of XYZ Corporation common stock and XYZ preferred stock. One month into the plan year, ABC sells some of its XYZ common stock in an amount equal to 2 percent of the current value of plan assets.

(i) Six weeks later the plan sells XYZ preferred stock in an amount equal to 4 percent of the current value of plan assets. A reportable series of transactions has not occurred because only transactions involving securities of the same issue are to be aggregated under paragraph (c)(1)(iii) of this section.

(ii) Two weeks later when the ABC plan purchases XYZ common stock in an amount equal to 3.5 percent of the current value of plan assets, a reportable series of transactions under (c)(1)(iii) of this section has occurred. The sale of XYZ common stock worth 2 percent of plan assets and the purchase of XYZ common stock worth 3.5 percent of plan assets aggregate to exceed 5 percent of the total value of plan assets.

(5) At the beginning of the plan year, Plan X purchases through broker-dealer Y common stock of Able Industries in an amount equal to 6 percent of plan assets. The common stock of Able Industries is not listed on any national securities exchange or quoted on NASDAQ. This purchase is a reportable transaction under paragraph (c)(1)(i) of this section. Three months later, Plan X purchases short term debt obligations of Charley Company through broker-dealer Y in the amount of 0.2

percent of plan assets. This purchase is also a reportable transaction under the provisions of paragraph (c)(1)(iv) of this section.

(6) At the beginning of the plan year, Plan X purchases from Bank B certificates of deposit having a 180 day maturity in an amount equal to 6 percent of plan assets. Bank B is a national bank regulated by the Comptroller of the Currency. This purchase is a reportable transaction under paragraph (c)(1)(i) of this section. Three months later, Plan X purchases through Bank B 91-day Treasury bills in the amount of 0.2 percent of plan assets. This purchase is not a reportable transaction under paragraph (c)(1)(iv) of this section because the purchase of the Treasury bills as well as the purchase of the certificates of deposit are not considered to involve a security under the definition of "securities" in paragraph (b)(2)(ii) of this section. [Corrected April 4, 1978, by 43 FR 14009; amended on March 1, 1989 by 54 FR 8624.]

(7) At the beginning of the plan year, Plan X purchases through broker-dealer Y common stock of Able Industries, a New York Stock Exchange listed security, in an amount equal to 6 percent of plan assets. This purchase is a reportable transaction under paragraph (c)(1)(i) of this section. Three months later, Plan X purchases through broker-dealer Y, acting as agent, common stock of Baker Corporation, also a New York Stock Exchange listed security, in an amount equal to 0.2 percent of plan assets. This latter purchase is not a reportable transaction under paragraph (c)(1)(iv) of this section because it is not a transaction "with or in conjunction with a person" pursuant to paragraph (b)(3)(ii) of this section. [Added March 9, 1978, by 43 FR 10130; amended on March 1, 1989 by 54 FR 8624.]

(f) *Special rule for certain participant-directed transactions*. Participant or beneficiary directed transactions under an individual account plan shall not be taken into account under paragraph (c)(1) of this section for purposes of preparing the schedule of reportable transactions described in this section. For purposes of this section only, a transaction will be considered directed by a participant or beneficiary if it has been authorized by such participant or beneficiary. [Added April 19, 2000 by 65 FR 21082.]

[¶ 14,231G]

§ 2520.103-7 **Special accounting rules for plans filing the initial (1975) annual report**. [Officially removed by 61 FR 33847, 7/1/96.]

[¶ 14,231H]

§ 2520.103-8 **Limitation on scope of accountant's examination**. (a) *General*. Under the authority of section 103(a)(3)(C) of the Act, the examination and report of an independent qualified public accountant need not extend to any statement or information prepared and certified by a bank or similar institution or insurance carrier. A plan, trust or other entity which meets the requirements of paragraph (b) of this section is not required to have covered by the accountant's examination or report any of the information described in paragraph (c) of this section.

(b) *Application*. This section applies to any plan, trust or other entity some or all of the assets of which are held by a bank or similar institution or insurance carrier which is regulated and supervised and subject to periodic examination by a State or Federal agency.

(c) *Excluded information*. Any statements or information certified to by a bank or similar institution or insurance carrier described in paragraph (b) of this section, provided that the statements or information regarding assets so held are prepared and certified to by the bank or insurance carrier in accordance with § 2520.103-5. [Added March 9, 1978 by 43 FR 10130.]

[¶ 14,231I]

§ 2520.103-9 **Direct filing for bank or insurance carrier trusts and accounts**. (a) *General*. Under the authority of sections 103(b)(4), 104(a)(3), 110 and 505 of the Act, an employee benefit plan, some or all of the assets of which are held in a common or collective trust or a pooled separate account described in section 103(b)(3)(G) of the Act and §§ 2520.103-3 and 2520.103-4, is relieved from including in its annual report information about the current value of the plan's allocable portion of assets and liabilities of the common or collective trust or pooled separate account and information concerning the individual transactions of the common or collective trust or pooled separate account, provided that the plan meets the requirements of paragraph (b) of this section, and, provided further, that the bank or insurance carrier which holds the plan's assets meets the requirements of paragraph (c) of this section. [Amended April 19, 2000 by 65 FR 21802.]

(b) *Application*. A plan whose assets are held in a common or collective trust or a pooled separate account described in section 103(b)(3)(G) of the Act and §§ 2520.103-3 and 2520.103-4, provided the plan administrator, on or before the end of the plan year, provides the bank or insurance carrier which maintains the common or collective trust or pooled separate account with the plan number, and name and Employer Identification Number of the plan sponsor as will be reported on the plan's annual report. [Amended April 19, 2000 by 65 FR 21802.]

(c) *Separate filing by common or collective trusts and pooled separate accounts*. The bank or insurance carrier which maintains the common or collective trust or pooled separate account in which assets of the plan are held shall file, in accordance with the instructions for the form, a completed Form 5500 "Annual Return/Report of Employee Benefit Plan" and any statements or schedules required to be attached to the form for the common or collective trust or pooled separate account, including Schedule D (DFE/Participating Plan Information) and Schedule H (Financial Information). See the instructions for this form. The information reported shall be for the fiscal year of such trust or account ending with or within the plan year for which the annual report of the plan is made. [Added March 9, 1978, by 43 FR 10130; corrected April 4, 1978, by 43 FR 14009; amended July 29, 1980 by 45 FR 51446; amended April 19, 2000 by 65 FR 21083.]

(d) *Electronic filing*. See § 2520.104a-2 and the instructions for the Form 5500 "Annual Return/Report of Employee Benefit Plan" for electronic filing requirements. The bank or insurance company which maintains the common or collective trust or pooled separate account must maintain an original copy, with all required signatures, as part of its records. [Amended July 21, 2006 by 71 FR 41368.]

[¶ 14,231J]

§ 2520.103-10 **Annual Report Financial Schedules**. (a) *General*. The administrator of a plan filing an annual report pursuant to § 2520.103-1(a)(2) or the report for a group insurance arrangement pursuant to § 2520.103-2 shall, as provided in the instructions to the Form 5500 "Annual Return/Report of Employee Benefit Plan," include as part of the annual report the separate financial schedules described in paragraph (b) of this section. [Amended April 19, 2000 by 65 FR 21803].

(b) *Schedules*. (1) Assets held for investment.

(i) A schedule of all assets held for investment purposes at the end of the plan year (see § 2520.103-11) with assets aggregated and identified by:

(A) Identity of issue, borrower, lessor or similar party to the transaction (including a notation as to whether such party is known to be a party in interest);

(B) Description of investment including maturity date, rate of interest, collateral, par, or maturity value;

(C) Cost; and

(D) Current value, and, in the case of a loan, the payment schedule.

(ii) Except as provided in the Form 5500 and the instructions thereto, in the case of assets or investment interests of two or more plans maintained in one trust, all entries on the schedule of assets held for investment purposes that relate to the trust shall be completed by including the plan's allocable portion of the trust. [Amended April 19, 2000 by 65 FR 21803].

(2) *Assets acquired and disposed within the plan year*. (i) A schedule of all assets acquired and disposed of within the plan year (see § 2520.103-11) with assets aggregated and identified by:

(A) Identity of issue, borrower, issuer or similar party;

(B) Descriptions of investment including maturity date, rate of interest, collateral, par, or maturity value;

(C) Cost of acquisitions; and

(D) Proceeds of dispositions.

Reg. § 2520.103-10(b)(2)(i)(D)   ¶ 14,231J

(ii) Except as provided in the Form 5500 and the instructions thereto, in the case of assets or investment interests of two or more plans maintained in one trust, all entries on the schedule of assets held for investment purposes that relate to the trust shall be completed by including the plan's allocable portion of the trust. [Amended April 19, 2000 by 65 FR 21803].

(3) *Party in interest transactions.* A schedule of each transaction involving a person known to be a party in interest except do not include:

(i) A transaction to which a statutory exemption under part 4 of title I applies;

(ii) A transaction to which an administrative exemption under section 408(a) of the Act applies; or

(iii) A transaction to which the exemptions of section 4975(c) or 4975(d) of the Internal Revenue Code (Title 26 of the United States Code) applies. [Amended April 19, 2000 by 65 FR 21803].

(4) *Obligations in default.* A schedule of all loans or fixed income obligations which were in default as of the end of the plan year or were classified during the year as uncollectible. [Amended April 19, 2000 by 65 FR 21803].

(5) *Leases in default.* A schedule of all leases which were in default or were classified during the year as uncollectible. [Amended April 19, 2000 by 65 FR 21803].

(6) *Reportable transactions.* A schedule of all reportable transactions as defined in § 2520.103-6. [Amended on March 1, 1989 by 54 FR 8624; amended Apri 19, 2000 by 65 FR 21083.]

(c) *Format requirements for certain schedules.* See the instructions to the Form 5500 "Annual Return/Report of Employee Benefit Plan" as to the format requirement for the schedules referred to in paragraphs (b)(1), (b)(2) or (b)(6) of this section. [Added April 19, 2000 by 65 FR 21803].

[¶ 14,231K]

§ 2520.103-11 **Assets held for investment purposes.** (a) *General.* For purposes of preparing the schedule of assets held for investment purposes described in § 2520.103-10(b)(1) and (2), assets held for investment purposes include those assets described in paragraph (b) of this section. [Amended April 19, 2000 by 65 FR 21083.]

(b) *Definitions.* (1) Assets held for investment purposes shall include:

(i) Any investment asset held by the plan on the last day of the plan year; and

(ii) Any investment asset which was purchased at any time during the plan year and was sold at any time before the last day of the plan year, except as provided by paragraphs (b)(2) and (b)(3) of this section.

(2) Assets held for investment purposes shall not include any investment which was not held by the plan on the last day of the plan year for which the annual report is filed if that investment falls within any of the following categories:

(i) Debt obligations of the United States or any agency of the United States;

(ii) Interests issued by a company registered under the Investment Company Act of 1940;

(iii) Bank certificates of deposit with a maturity of not more than one year;

(iv) Commercial paper with a maturity of not more than nine months if it is ranked in the highest rating category by at least two nationally recognized statistical rating services and is issued by a company required to file reports with the Securities and Exchange Commission under section 13 of the Securities Exchange Act of 1934;

(v) Participations in a bank common or collective trust;

(vi) Participations in an insurance company pooled separate account;

(vii) Securities purchased from a person registered as a broker-dealer under the Securities Exchange Act of 1934 and listed on a national securities exchange registered under section 6 of the Securities Exchange Act of 1934 or quoted on NASDAQ;

(3) Assets held for investment purposes shall not include any investment which was not held by the plan on the last day of the plan year for which the annual report is filed if that investment is reported on the annual report of that same plan in any of the following:

(i) The schedule of each transaction involving a person known to be a party in interest required by section 103(b)(3)(D) of the Act and § 2520.103-10(b)(3);

(ii) The schedule of loans or fixed income obligations in default required by section 103(b)(3)(E) of the Act and § 2520.103-10(b)(4);

(iii) The schedule of leases in default or classified as uncollectible required by section 103(b)(3)(F) of the Act and § 2520.103-10(b)(5); or

(iv) The schedule of reportable transactions required by section 103(b)(3)(H) of the Act and § 2520.103-10(b)(6).

(c) *Examples.* (1) On February 1, 1977, plan N purchases an interest in registered investment company F (fund F). Fund F is not a party in interest with respect to plan N. On November 1, 1977, plan N sells this interest in fund F and purchases 1,000 shares of stock S, which the plan holds for the rest of the plan year. Plan N mustinclude in its schedule of assets held for investment purposes the 1,000 shares of stock S under paragraph (b)(1) of this section, but need not include the interest in fund F because of Paragraph (b)(2)(ii) of this section.

(2) On February 1, 1977, plan N purchases a parcel of real estate from Mr. M, who is not a party in interest with respect to plan N. On November 1, 1977, plan N sells the parcel of real estate for cash to Mr. X, who is not a party in interest with respect to plan N. Plan N uses the cash from this transaction to purchase a 1-year certificate of deposit in bank B, which it holds until maturity in 1978. Plan N must include in its schedule of assets held for investment purposes the 1-year certificate of deposit in bank B under paragraph (b)(1)(i) of this section, and must also include the parcel of real estate under paragraph (b)(1)(ii) of this section.

(d) *Special rule for certain participant-directed transactions.* Cost information may be omitted from the schedule of assets held for investment purposes for assets described in paragraphs (b)(1)(i) and (b)(1)(ii) of this section only with respect to participant or beneficiary directed transactions under an individual account plan. For purposes of this section only, a transaction will be considered directed by a participant or beneficiary if it has been authorized by such participant or beneficiary. [Added April 19, 2000 by 65 FR 21083.]

[¶ 14,231L]

§ 2520.103-12 **Limited exemption and alternative method of compliance for annual reporting of investments in certain entities.** (a) This section prescribes an exemption from and alternative method of compliance with the annual reporting requirements of Part 1 of Title I of ERISA for employee benefit plans whose assets are invested in certain entities described in paragraph (c). A plan utilizing this method of reporting shall include as part of its annual report the current value of its investment or units of participation in the entity in the manner prescribed by the Return/Report Form and the instructions thereto. The plan is not required to include in its annual report any information regarding the underlying assets or individual transactions of the entity, provided the information described in paragraph (b) regarding the entity is reported directly to the Department on behalf of the plan administrator on or before the filing due date for the entity in accordance with the instructions to the Form 5500 Annual Return/ Report. The information described in paragraph (b), however, shall be considered as part of the annual report for purposes of the requirements of section 104(a)(1) of the Act and § § 2520.104a-5 and 2520.104a-6. [Amended April 19, 2000 by 65 FR 21083.]

(b) The following information must be filed regarding the entity described in paragraph (c) of this section:

(1) A Form 5500 "Annual Return/Report of Employee Benefit Plan" and any statements or schedules required to be attached to the form for such entity, completed in accordance with the instructions for the form, including Schedule A (Insurance Information), Schedule C (Service Provider Information), Schedule D (DFE/Participating Plan Information), Schedule G (Financial Transaction Schedules), Schedule H (Financial Information), and the schedules described in

§ 2520.103-10(b)(1) and (b)(2). See the instructions for this form. The information reported shall be for the fiscal year of such entity ending with or within the plan year for which the annual report of the plan is made.

(2) A report of an independent qualified public accountant regarding the financial statements and schedules described in paragraph (b)(1) of this section which meets the requirements of § 2520.103-1(b)(5). [Amended April 19, 2000 by 65 FR 21084.]

(c) This method of reporting is available to any employee benefit plan which has invested in an entity the assets of which are deemed to include plan assets under § 2510.3-101, provided the entity holds the assets of two or more plans which are not members of a "related group" of employee benefit plans as that term is defined in paragraph (e) of this section. The method of reporting is not available for investments in an insurance company pooled separate account or a common or collective trust maintained by a bank, trust company, or similar institution.

(d) The examination and report of an independent qualified public accountant required by § 2520.103-1 for a plan utilizing the method of reporting described in this section need not extend to any information concerning an entity which is reported directly to the Department under paragraph (b) of this section.

(e) A "related group" of employee benefit plans consists of every group of two or more employee benefit plans—

(1) Each of which receives 10 percent or more of its aggregate contributions from the same employer or from members of the same controlled group of corporations (as determined under section 1563(a) of the Internal Revenue Code, without regard to section 1563(a)(4) thereof); or

(2) Each of which is either maintained by, or maintained pursuant to a collective bargaining agreement negotiated by, the same employee organization or affiliated employee organizations. For purposes of this paragraph, an "affiliate" of an employee organization means any person controlling, controlled by, or under common control with such organization, and includes any organization chartered by the same parent body, or governed by the same constitution and bylaws, or having the relation of parent and subordinate. [Added by 51 FR 41285 on November 13, 1986]

(f) *Electronic filing.* See § 2520.104a-2 and the instructions for the Form 5500 "Annual Return/Report of Employee Benefit Plan" for electronic filing requirements. The entity described in paragraph (c) of this section must maintain an original copy, with all required signatures, as part of its records. [Amended July 21, 2006 by 71 FR 41368.]

[¶ 14,231M]

§ 2520.103-13 **Special terminal report for abandoned plans**. (a) *General.* The terminal report required to be filed by the qualified

termination administrator pursuant to § 2578.1(d)(2)(viii) of this chapter shall consist of the items set forth in paragraph (b) of this section. Such report shall be filed in accordance with the method of filing set forth in paragraph (c) of this section and at the time set forth in paragraph (d) of this section.

(b) *Contents.* The terminal report described in paragraph (a) of this section shall contain:

(1) Identification information concerning the qualified termination administrator and the plan being terminated.

(2) The total assets of the plan as of the date the plan was deemed terminated under § 2578.1(c) of this chapter, prior to any reduction for termination expenses and distributions to participants and beneficiaries.

(3) The total termination expenses paid by the plan and a separate schedule identifying each service provider and amount received, itemized by expense.

(4) The total distributions made pursuant to § 2578.1(d)(2)(vii) of this chapter and a statement regarding whether any such distributions were transfers under § 2578.1(d)(2)(vii)(B) of this chapter.

(5) The identification, fair market value and method of valuation of any assets with respect to which there is no readily ascertainable fair market value.

(c) *Method of filing.* The terminal report described in paragraph (a) shall be filed:

(1) On the most recent Form 5500 available as of the date the qualified termination administrator satisfies the requirements in § 2578.1(d)(2)(i) through § 2578.1(d)(2)(vii) of this chapter; and

(2) In accordance with the Form's instructions pertaining to terminal reports of qualified termination administrators.

(d) *When to file.* The qualified termination administrator shall file the terminal report described in paragraph (a) within two months after the end of the month in which the qualified termination administrator satisfies the requirements in § 2578.1(d)(2)(i) through § 2578.1(d)(2)(vii) of this chapter.

(e) *Limitation.* (1) Except as provided in this section, no report shall be required to be filed by the qualified termination administrator under part 1 of title I of ERISA for a plan being terminated pursuant to § 2578.1 of this chapter.

(2) Filing of a report under this section by the qualified termination administrator shall not relieve any other person from any obligation under part 1 of title I of ERISA.

[Added by 71 FR 20820, April 21, 2006; effective May 22, 2006.]

[¶ 14,232—14,234b **Reserved.** Temporary and proposed Reg. §§ 2520.104-41—2520.104-46, 2520.104a-5, 2520.104a-6, 2520.104b-10—2520.104b-12 formerly appeared at the above paragraphs. Sections 2520.104b-10—2520.104b-12 are at ¶ 14,249I—14,249K. Final regulations for the other sections have been adopted and are at ¶ 14,247U—14,247Z, 14,248D, and 14,248E.]

[¶ 14,240]
FILING WITH SECRETARY AND FURNISHING INFORMATION TO PARTICIPANTS AND CERTAIN EMPLOYERS

Act Sec. 104. (a) FILING OF ANNUAL REPORT WITH SECRETARY.—

(1) The administrator of any employee benefit plan subject to this part shall file with the Secretary the annual report for a plan year within 210 days after the close of such year (or within such time as may be required by regulations promulgated by the Secretary in order to reduce duplicative filing). The Secretary shall make copies of such annual reports available for inspection in the public document room of the Department of Labor.

(2)(A) With respect to annual reports required to be filed with the Secretary under this part, he may by regulation prescribe simplified annual reports for any pension plan which covers less than 100 participants.

(B) Nothing contained in this paragraph shall preclude the Secretary from requiring any information or data from any such plan to which this part applies where he finds such data or information is necessary to carry out the purposes of this title nor shall the Secretary be precluded from revoking provisions for simplified reports for any such plan if he finds it necessary to do so in order to carry out the objectives of this title.

(3) The Secretary may by regulation exempt any welfare benefit plan from all or part of the reporting and disclosure requirements of this title, or may provide for simplified reporting and disclosure if he finds that such requirements are inappropriate as applied to welfare benefit plans.

(4) The Secretary may reject any filing under this section—

(A) if he determines that such filing is incomplete for purposes of this part; or

(B) if he determines that there is any material qualification by an accountant or actuary contained in an opinion submitted pursuant to section 103(a)(3)(A) or section 103(a)(4)(B).

(5) If the Secretary rejects a filing of a report under paragraph (4) and if a revised filing satisfactory to the Secretary is not submitted within 45 days after the Secretary makes his determination under paragraph (4) to reject the filing, and if the Secretary deems it in the best interest of the participants, he may take any one or more of the following actions—

    (A) retain an independent qualified public accountant (as defined in section 103(a)(3)(D)) on behalf of the participants to perform an audit,

    (B) retain an enrolled acutary (as defined in section 103(a)(4)(C) of this Act) on behalf of the plan participants, to prepare an actuarial statement,

    (C) bring a civil action for such legal or equitable relief as may be appropriate to enforce the provisions of this part, or

    (D) take any other action authorized by this title.

The administrator shall permit such accountant or actuary to inspect whatever books and records of the plan are necessary for such audit. The plan shall be liable to the Secretary for the expenses for such audit or report, and the Secretary may bring an action against the plan in any court of competent jurisdiction to recover such expenses.

(6) The administrator of any employee benefit plan subject to this part shall furnish to the Secretary, upon request, any documents relating to the employee benefit plan, including but not limited to, the latest summary plan description (including any summaries of plan changes not contained in the summary plan description), and the bargaining agreement, trust agreement, contract, or other instrument under which the plan is established or operated.

Act Sec. 104. (b) PUBLICATION OF SUMMARY PLAN DESCRIPTION AND ANNUAL REPORT TO PARTICIPANTS AND BENEFICIARIES OF PLAN.—Publication of the summary plan descriptions and annual reports shall be made to participants and beneficiaries of the particular plan as follows:

(1) The administrator shall furnish to each participant, and each beneficiary receiving benefits under the plan, a copy of the summary, plan description, and all modifications and changes referred to in section 102(a)—

    (A) within 90 days after he becomes a participant, or (in the case of a beneficiary) within 90 days after he first receives benefits, or

    (B) if later, within 120 days after the plan becomes subject to this part.

The administrator shall furnish to each participant, and each beneficiary receiving benefits under the plan, every fifth year after the plan becomes subject to this part an updated summary plan description described in section 102 which integrates all plan amendments made within such five-year period, except that in a case where no amendments have been made to a plan during such five-year period this sentence shall not apply. Notwithstanding the foregoing, the administrator shall furnish to each participant, and to each beneficiary receiving benefits under the plan, the summary plan description described in section 102 every tenth year after the plan becomes subject to this part. If there is a modification or change described in section 102(a) (other than a material reduction in covered services or benefits provided in the case of a group health plan (as defined in section 733(a)(1)), a summary description of such modification or change shall be furnished not later than 210 days after the end of the plan year in which the change is adopted to each participant, and to each beneficiary who is receiving benefits under the plan. If there is a modification or change described in section 102(a) that is a material reduction in covered services or benefits provided under a group health plan (as defined in section 733(a)(1)), a summary description of such modification or change shall be furnished to participants and beneficiaries not later than 60 days after the date of the adoption of the modification or change. In the alternative, the plan sponsors may provide such description at regular intervals of not more than 90 days. The Secretary shall issue regulation within 180 days after the date of enactment of the Health Insurance Portability and Accountability Act of 1996, providing alternative mechanisms to delivery by mail through which group health plans (as so defined) may notify participants and beneficiaries of material reductions in covered services or benefits.

(2) The administrator shall make copies of the latest updated summary plan description and the latest annual report and the bargaining agreement, trust agreement, contract, or other instruments under which the plan was established or is operated available for examination by any plan participant or beneficiary in the principal office of the administrator and in such other places as may be necessary to make available all pertinent information to all participants (including such places as the Secretary may prescribe by regulations).

(3) Within 210 days after the close of the fiscal year of the plan, the administrator (other than an administrator of a defined benefit plan to which the requirements of section 101(f) applies) shall furnish to each participant, and to each beneficiary receiving benefits under the plan, a copy of the statements and schedules, for such fiscal year, described in subparagraphs (A) and (B) of section 103(b)(3) and such other material (including the percentage determined under section 103(d)(11)) as is necessary to fairly summarize the latest annual report.

(4) The administrator shall, upon written request of any participant or beneficiary, furnish a copy of the latest updated summary plan description, and the latest annual report, any terminal report, the bargaining agreement, trust agreement, contract, or other instruments under which the plan is established or operated. The administrator may make a reasonable charge to cover the cost of furnishing such complete copies. The Secretary may by regulation prescribe the maximum amount which will constitute a reasonable charge under the preceding sentence.

(5) Identification and basic plan information and actuarial information included in the annual report for any plan year shall be filed with the Secretary in an electronic format which accommodates display on the Internet, in accordance with regulations which shall be prescribed by the Secretary. The Secretary shall provide for display of such information included in the annual report, within 90 days after the date of the filing of the annual report, on an Internet website maintained by the Secretary and other appropriate media. Such information shall also be displayed on any Intranet website maintained by the plan administrator (or by the plan administrator on behalf of the plan sponsor) for the purpose of communicating with employees and not the public, in accordance with regulations which shall be prescribed by the Secretary.

Act Sec. 104. (c) STATEMENT OF RIGHTS.—The Secretary may by regulation require that the administrator of any employee benefit plan furnish to each participant and to each beneficiary receiving benefits under the plan a statement of the rights of participants and beneficiaries under this title.

(d) FURNISHING SUMMARY PLAN INFORMATION TO EMPLOYERS AND EMPLOYEES REPRESENTATIVES OF MULTIEMPLOYER PLANS.—

(1) IN GENERAL. With respect to a multiemployer plan subject to this section, within 30 days after the due date under subsection (a)(1) for the filing of the annual report for the fiscal year of the plan, the administrators shall furnish to each employee organization and to each employer with an obligation to contribute to the plan a report that contains—

    (A) a description of the contribution schedules and benefit formulas under the plan, and any modification to such schedules and formulas, during such plan year;

    (B) the number of employers obligated to contribute to the plan;

    (C) a list of the employers that contributed more than 5 percent of the total contributions to the plan during such plan year;

    (D) the number of participants under the plan on whose behalf no contributions were made by an employer as an employer of the participant for such plan year and for each of the 2 preceding plan years;

    (E) whether the plan was in critical or endangered status under section 305 for such plan year and, if so, include—

        (i) a list of the actions taken by the plan to improve its funding status; and

        (ii) a statement describing how a person may obtain a copy of the plan's funding improvement or rehabilitation plan, as applicable, adopted under section 305 and the actuarial and financial data that demonstrate any action taken by the plan toward fiscal improvement;

    (F) the number of employers that withdrew from the plan during the preceding plan year and the aggregate amount of withdrawal liability assessed, or estimated to be assessed, against such withdrawn employers, as reported on the annual report for the plan year to which the report under this subsection relates;

    (G) in the case of a multiemployer plan that has merged with another plan or to which assets and liabilities have been transferred, the actuarial valuation of the assets and liabilities of each affected plan during the year preceding the effective date of the merger or transfer, based upon the most recent data available as of the day before the first day of the plan year, or other valuation method performed under standards and procedures as the Secretary may prescribe by regulation;

    (H) a description as to whether the plan—

(i) sought or received an amortization extension under section 304(d) of this Act or section 431(d) of the Internal Revenue Code of 1986 for such plan year; or

(ii) used the shortfall funding method (as such term is used in section 305) for such plan year; and

(I) notification of the right under this section of the recipient to a copy of the annual report filed with the Secretary under subsection (a), summary plan description, summary of any material modification of the plan, upon written request, but that—

(i) in no case shall a recipient be entitled to receive more than one copy of any such document described during any one 12-month period; and

(ii) the administrator may make a reasonable charge to cover copying, mailing, and other costs of furnishing copies of information pursuant to this subparagraph.

(2) EFFECT OF SUBSECTION. Nothing in this subsection waives any other provision under this title requiring plan administrators to provide, upon request, information to employers that have an obligation to contribute under the plan.

(e) CROSS REFERENCES.—

For regulations respecting coordination of reports to the Secretaries of Labor and the Treasury, see section 3004.

Amendments

P.L. 110-458, Sec. 105(c)(1)(A)(i) and (ii):

Amended ERISA Sec. 104(b)(3) by striking "section 103(f)" and inserting "section 101(f)", and by striking "the administrators" and inserting "the administrator".

The above amendments take effect as if included in the provisions of the 2006 Act to which the amendments relate [effective with respect to plan years beginning after December 31, 2007.—CCH].

P.L. 110-458, Sec. 105(c)(1)(B):

Amended ERISA Sec. 104(d)(1)(E)(ii) by inserting "funding" after "plan's".

The above amendment takes effect as if included in the provisions of the 2006 Act to which the amendment relates [effective with respect to plan years beginning after December 31, 2007.—CCH].

P.L. 109-280, Sec. 503(c)(1):

Amended ERISA Sec. 104 (b)(3) by adding a parenthetical after "the administrator."

The above amendment applies to plan years beginning after December 31, 2007.

P.L. 104-204, Sec. 603(b)(3)(D):

Amended ERISA Sec. 104(b)(1) by striking "section 706(a)(1)" each place it appears and inserting "section 733(a)(1)".

The above amendment applies to plan years beginning after December 31, 2007.

P.L. 109-280, Sec. 503(d)(1):

Amended the heading of ERISA Sec. 104 by striking "participants" and inserting "participants and certain employers."

The above amendment applies to plan years beginning after December 31, 2007.

P.L. 109-280, Sec. 503(d)(2) and (3):

Amended ERISA Sec. 104 by redesignating subsection (d) as subsection (e); and adding new subsection (d) to read as above.

Prior to amendment, ERISA Sec. 105(d) read as follows:

(d) CROSS REFERENCES.—

For regulations respecting coordination of reports to the Secretaries of Labor and the Treasury, see section 3004.

The above amendment applies to plan years beginning after December 31, 2007.

P.L. 109-280, Sec. 504(a):

Amended ERISA Sec. 104(b) by adding a new subparagraph (5) to read as above.

The above amendment applies to plan years beginning after December 31, 2007.

P.L. 105-34, § 1503(c)(1):

Amended ERISA Sec. 104(a)(1) to read as above. Previously, the paragraph read as follows:

Act Sec. 104. (a)(1) The administrator of any employee benefit plan subject to this part shall file with the Secretary—

(A) the annual report for a plan year within 210 days after the close of such year (or within such time as may be required by regulations promulgated by the Secretary in order to reduce duplicative filing);

(B) the plan description within 120 days after such plan becomes subject to this part and an updated plan description, no more frequently than once every 5 years, as the Secretary may require;

(C) a copy of the summary plan description at the time such summary plan description is required to be furnished to participants and beneficiaries pursuant to subsection (b)(1)(B) of this section; and

(D) modifications and changes referred to in section 102(a)(2) within 60 days after such modification or change is adopted or occurs, as the case may be.

The Secretary shall make copies of such plan descriptions, summary plan descriptions, and annual reports available for inspection in the public document room of the Department of Labor. The administrator shall also furnish to the Secretary, upon request, any documents relating to the employee benefit plan, including but not limited to the bargaining agreement, trust agreement, contract, or other instrument under which the plan is established or operated.

P.L. 105-34, § 1503(c)(2):

Added ERISA Sec. 104(a)(6) to read as above.

The above amendment is effective August 5, 1997.

P.L. 105-34, § 1503(d)(1):

Amended ERISA Sec. 104(b)(1) by striking "section 102(a)(1)" each place it appears and inserting "section 102(a)."

The above amendment is effective August 5, 1997.

P.L. 105-34, § 1503(d)(2):

Amended ERISA Sec. 104(b)(2) by striking "the plan description and" and inserting "the latest updated summary plan description and."

The above amendment is effective August 5, 1997.

P.L. 105-34, § 1503(d)(3):

Amended ERISA Sec. 104(b)(4) by striking "the plan description."

The above amendment is effective August 5, 1997.

P.L. 104-191, § 101(c)(1):

Amended ERISA Sec. 104(b)(1) by striking "102(a)(1)," and inserting "102(a)(1) (other than a material reduction in covered services or benefits provided in the case of a group health plan (as defined in section 706(a)(1)),"; and adding at the end three new sentences to read as above.

The above amendments generally apply with respect to group health plans for plan years beginning after June 30, 1997. For special rules, see Act Sec. 101(g)(2)-(5), reproduced below.

Act Sec. 101(g)(2)-(5) reads as follows:

(g) EFFECTIVE DATES.—

(1) IN GENERAL.—Except as provided in this section, this section (and the amendments made by this section) shall apply with respect to group health plans for plan years beginning after June 30, 1997.

(2) DETERMINATION OF CREDITABLE COVERAGE.—

(A) PERIOD OF COVERAGE.—

(i) IN GENERAL.—Subject to clause (ii), no period before July 1, 1996, shall be taken into account under part 7 of subtitle B of title I of the Employee Retirement Income Security Act of 1974 (as added by this section) in determining creditable coverage.

(ii) SPECIAL RULE FOR CERTAIN PERIODS.—The Secretary of Labor, consistent with section 104, shall provide for a process whereby individuals who need to establish creditable coverage for periods before July 1, 1996, and who would have such coverage credited but for clause (i) may be given credit for creditable coverage for such periods through the presentation of documents or other means.

(B) CERTIFICATIONS, ETC.—

(i) IN GENERAL.—Subject to clauses (ii) and (iii), subsection (e) of section 701 of the Employee Retirement Income Security Act of 1974 (as added by this section) shall apply to events occurring after June 30, 1996.

(ii) NO CERTIFICATION REQUIRED TO BE PROVIDED BEFORE JUNE 1, 1997.—In no case is a certification required to be provided under such subsection before June 1, 1997.

(iii) CERTIFICATION ONLY ON WRITTEN REQUEST FOR EVENTS OCCURRING BEFORE OCTOBER 1, 1996.—In the case of an event occurring after June 30, 1996, and before October 1, 1996, a certification is not required to be provided under such subsection unless an individual (with respect to whom the certification is otherwise required to be made) requests such certification in writing.

(C) TRANSITIONAL RULE.—In the case of an individual who seeks to establish creditable coverage for any period for which certification is not required because it relates to an event occurring before June 30, 1996—

(i) the individual may present other credible evidence of such coverage in order to establish the period of creditable coverage; and

(ii) a group health plan and a health insurance issuer shall not be subject to any penalty or enforcement action with respect to the plan's or issuer's crediting (or not crediting) such coverage if the plan or issuer has sought to comply in good faith with the applicable requirements under the amendments made by this section.

(3) SPECIAL RULE FOR COLLECTIVE BARGAINING AGREEMENTS.—Except as provided in paragraph (2), in the case of a group health plan maintained pursuant to one or more collective bargaining agreements between employee representatives and one or more employers ratified before the date of the enactment of this Act, part 7 of subtitle B of title I of Employee Retirement Income Security Act of 1974 (other than section 701(e) thereof) shall not apply to plan years beginning before the later of—

(A) the date on which the last of the collective bargaining agreements relating to the plan terminates (determined without regard to any extension thereof agreed to after the date of the enactment of this Act), or

(B) July 1, 1997.

For purposes of subparagraph (A), any plan amendment made pursuant to a collective bargaining agreement relating to the plan which amends the plan solely to conform to any requirement of such part shall not be treated as a termination of such collective bargaining agreement.

(4) Timely Regulations.—The Secretary of Labor, consistent with section 104, shall first issue by not later than April 1, 1997, such regulations as may be necessary to carry out the amendments made by this section.

(5) Limitation on Actions.—No enforcement action shall be taken, pursuant to the amendments made by this section, against a group health plan or health insurance issuer with respect to a violation of a requirement imposed by such amendments before January 1, 1998, or, if later, the date of issuance of regulations referred to in paragraph (4), if the plan or issuer has sought to comply in good faith with such requirements.

P.L. 101-239, §7894(b)(3):

Amended ERISA Sec. 104(a)(5)(B) by striking the period and inserting a comma, effective September 2, 1974.

P.L. 101-239, §7894(b)(4):

Amended ERISA Sec. 104(b)(1) by striking the comma after "summary" effective September 2, 1974.

P.L. 100-203, §9342(a)(2):

Amended ERISA Sec. 104(b)(3) by striking out "such other material" and inserting "such other material (including the precentage determined under section 103(d)(11)" instead, effective December 17, 1987 for reports required to be filed after December 31, 1987.

P.L. 99-272, §11016(b)(2):

Amended ERISA Sec. 104(a)(2)(A) by striking out the second sentence, effective on April 7, 1986.

Prior to amendment, the second sentence read:

In addition, and without limiting the foregoing sentence, the Secretary may waive or modify the requirements of section 103(d)(6) in such cases or categories of cases as to which he finds that (i) the interests of the plan participants are not harmed thereby and (ii) the expense of compliance with the specific requirements of section 103(d)(6) is not justified by the needs of the participants, the Pension Benefit Guaranty Corporation, and the Department of Labor for some portion or all of the information otherwise required under section 103(d)(6).

Regulations

Reg. §2520.104-3 was adopted by FR Doc. 75-11656 under "Title 29—Labor; Chapter XXV—Office of Employee Benefits Security; Part 2520—Rules and Regulations for Reporting and Disclosure." The regulation was filed with the Federal Register on April 30, 1975, and published in the Federal Register on May 5, 1975. Reg. §2520.104-3 was amended and Reg. §§2520.104-2, and 2520.104-20—2520.104-25 were adopted by FR Doc. 75-21470, effective August 15, 1975, and published in the Federal Register on August 15, 1975. Reg. §§2520.104-1, 2520.104-5, 2520.104-6, 2520.104a-1, 2520.104a-2, 2520.104a-4, 2520.104b-1, 2520.104b-5 and 2520.104b-30 were adopted by FR Doc. 76-11859 (41 FR 16957) filed with the Federal Register on April 22, 1976, published in the Federal Register of April 23, 1976, and effective April 23, 1976. Reg. §§2520.104-4, 2520.104-26, 2520.104-27, 2520.104a-3, 2520.104b-2, 2520.104b-3, and 2520.104b-4 were adopted by FR Doc. 77-7637, filed with the Federal Register on March 11, 1977, and published in the Federal Register and effective on March 15, 1977 (42 FR 14266). Reg. §§2520.104-26, 2520.104-27, 2520.104b-(2)(d)(2), 2520.104b-2(e)(2), and 2520.104b-2(f) are interim as well as proposed regulations. Reg. §§2520.104-5 and 2520.104-6 were amended by FR Doc. 77-7464 (42 FR 14280), published in the Federal Register of March 15, 1977, and effective March 15, 1977. The following sections or portions of sections, previously published as interim rules on March 15, 1977, were made final by FR Doc. 20810 (42 FR 37178), effective July 19, 1977: §§2520.104-26, 2520.104-27, and 2520.104b-2. At the same time, the following sections were adopted as interim rules: §§2520.104-5, 2520.104-6, 2520.104-28, 2520.104a-5, 2520.104b-2(a)(3), and 2520.104b-4. Reg. §§2520.104-41—2520.104-46, 2520.104a-5, and 2520.104a-6, were adopted by 41 FR 10130, effective generally for plan years beginning 1977 and thereafter. Reg. §§2520.104-20, 2520.104-21, and 2520.104a-4 were amended at the same time. Reg. §2520.104b-10 was adopted by 44 FR 19400, published on April 3, 1979. The following interim rules were made final by FR Doc. 80-6528 (45 FR 14029), effective April 3, 1980; Reg. §2520.104-5, 2520.104-6, 2520.104-28, 2520.104a-7, 2520.104b-2(a)(3), and 2520.104b-4. Reg. §2520.104-48 was adopted by 45 FR 24866 and published on April 11, 1980. Reg. §2520.104-49 was adopted by 46 FR 1261 and published in the Federal Register on January 6, 1981. Reg. §2520.104-50 was adopted by 46 FR 1265 and published in the Federal Register on January 6, 1981. Reg. §§2520.104-23(b)(2)(ii) and 2520.104-44(b)(1)(ii) were amended by 46 FR 5882 and published in the *Federal Register* on January 21, 1981. Reg. §§2520.104-2, 2520.104-3, 2520.104-5, 2520.104-6, 2520.104-28, and 2520.104-45 were removed and reserved by 61 FR 33847 on July 1, 1996. Reg. §§2520.104b-1 and 2520.104b-3 were amended by 62 FR 36205, effective June 1, 1997, and published in the *Federal Register* on July 7, 1997. Reg. §§2520.104-20, 2520.104-41, 2520.104-43, 2520.104-44, 2520.104-46 and 2520.104(b)-10 were amended by 65 FR 21067 and published in the *Federal Register* on April 19, 2000. Reg §§2520.104-41 and 2520.104-46 were amended by 65 FR 62957 and published in the *Federal Register* on October 19, 2000. ERISA Reg. Secs. 2520.104-4, 2520.104-20, 2520.104-21, 2520.104-26, 2520.104-27, and 2520.104b-2 were revised effective March 8, 2002 and published in the *Federal Register* on January 7, 2002 (67 FR 771). ERISA Reg. Secs. 2520.104-23, 2520.104-24, 2520.104-25, 2520.104-43, 2520.104-44, 2520.104a-5, 2520.104b-1, and 2520.104b-3 were amended effective March 8, 2002 and published in the *Federal Register* on January 7, 2002 (67 FR 771). ERISA Reg. Secs. 2520.104a-2, 2520.104a-3, 2520.104a-4, and 2520.104a-7 were removed and reserved effective March 8, 2002 (67 FR 771, 1/7/02). Reg. §2520.104b-1 was amended by the PWBA on April 9, 2003 by 67 FR 17264. Reg. §2520.104a-8 was added on January 7, 2002 (67 FR 777). Reg. §§2520.104-22, 2520.104-23, and 2530.104b-10 were amended by EBSA on April 3, 2003 by 68 FR 16399. Reg. Sec. 2520.104a-2 was added on July 21, 2006 (71 FR 41359); effective September 19, 2006. Reg. Sec. 2520.104-44, Reg. Sec. 2520.104-46, Reg. Sec. 2520.104a-2 and Reg. Sec. 2520.104b-10 were amended November 16, 2007 (72 FR 64710) effective January 15, 2008. Reg. §§2520.104-20 and 2520.104-41 were amended on March 1, 2013 (78 FR 13781), effective April 1, 2013. Reg. Sec. 2520.104-46 and Reg. Sec. 2520.104b-10 were amended February 2, 2015 (80 FR 5625).

Subpart D—Provisions Applicable to Both Reporting and Disclosure Requirements

[¶ 14,243]

§2520.104-1 **General**. The administrator of an employee benefit plan covered by Part 1 of Title I of the Act must file reports and additional information with the Secretary of Labor, and disclose reports, statements, and documents to plan participants and to beneficiaries receiving benefits from the plan. The regulations contained in this Subpart are applicable to both the reporting and disclosure requirements of Part 1 of Title I of the Act. Regulations concerning only a plan administrator's duty of reporting to the Secretary of Labor are set forth in Subpart E of this part, and those applicable only to the duty of disclosure to participants and beneficiaries are set forth in Subpart F of this part. [Added by 41 FR 16957, effective April 23, 1976.]

[¶ 14,244]

§2520.104-2 **Postponing effective date of annual reporting requirements and extending WPPDA reporting requirements**. [Removed and reserved by 61 FR 33847 on 7/1/96.]

[¶ 14,245]

§2520.104-3 **Deferral of certain initial reporting and disclosure requirements**. [Removed and reserved by 61 FR 33847 on 7/1/96.]

[¶ 14,245A]

§2520.104-4 **Alternative method of compliance for certain successor pension plans**. (a) *General*. Under the authority of section 110 of the Act, this section sets forth an alternative method of compliance for certain successor pension plans in which some participants and beneficiaries not only have their rights set out in the plan, but also retain eligibility for certain benefits under the terms of a former plan which has been merged into the successor. This section is applicable only to plan mergers which occur after the issuance by the successor plan of the initial summary plan description under the Act. Under the alternative method, the plan administrator of the successor plan is not required to describe relevant provisions of merged plans in summary plan descriptions of the successor plan furnished after the merger to that class of participants and beneficiaries still affected by the terms of the merged plans. Revised by 67 FR 771, effective March 8, 2002. [Amended by 42 F.R. 37178, effective July 19, 1977.]

(b) *Scope and application*. This alternative method of compliance is available only if:

(1) The plan administrator of the successor plan furnishes to the participants covered under the merged plan and beneficiaries receiving pension benefits under the merged plan within 90 days after the effective date of the merger—

(i) A copy of the most recent summary plan description of the successor plan;

(ii) A copy of any summaries of material modifications to the successor plan not incorporated in the most recent summary plan description; and

(iii) A separate statement containing a brief description of the merger; a description of the provisions of, and benefits provided by, the merged and successor plans which are applicable to the participants and beneficiaries of the merged plan; and a notice that copies of the merged and successor plan documents, as well as the plan merger documents (including the portions of any corporate merger documents which describe or control the plan merger), are available for inspection and that copies may be obtained upon written request for a duplication charge (pursuant to § 2520.104b-30); and

(2) After the merger, the plan administrator, in all subsequent summary plan descriptions furnished pursuant to § 2520.104b-2(a)—

(i) Clearly and conspicuously identifies the class of participants and beneficiaries affected by the provisions of the merged plan, and

(ii) States that the documents described in paragraph (b)(1) of this section are available for inspection and that copies may be obtained upon written request for a duplication charge (pursuant to § 2520.104(b)-30). [Added by 42 F.R. 14266, effective March 15, 1977, and amended by 42 FR 37178, effective July 19, 1977.]

[¶ 14,246]

§ 2520.104-5 **Deferral of certain reporting and disclosure requirements relating to the summary plan description for welfare plans**. [Removed and reserved by 61 FR 33847 on 7/1/96.]

[¶ 14,246A]

§ 2520.104-6 **Deferral of certain reporting and disclosure requirements relating to the summary plan description for pension plans**. [Removed and reserved by 61 FR 33847 on 7/1/96.]

[¶ 14,247]

§ 2520.104-20 **Limited exemption for certain small welfare plans**. (a) *Scope*. Under the authority of section 104(a)(3) of the Act, the administrator of any employee welfare benefit plan which covers fewer than 100 participants at the beginning of the plan year and which meets the requirements of paragraph (b) of this section is exempted from certain reporting and disclosure provisions of the Act. Specifically, the administrator of such plan is not required to file with the Secretary an annual or terminal report. In addition, the administrator of a plan exempted under this section—

(1) Is not required to furnish participants covered under the plan and beneficiaries receiving benefits under the plan with statements of the plan's assets and liabilities and receipts and disbursements and a summary of the annual report required by section 104(b)(3) of the Act;

(2) Is not required to furnish upon written request of any participant or beneficiary a copy of the annual report and any terminal report, as required by section 104(b)(4) of the Act;

(3) Is not required to make copies of the annual report available for examination by any participant or beneficiary in the principal office of the administrator and such other places as may be necessary, as required by section 104(b)(2) of the Act. [Revised by 67 FR 771, effective March 8, 2002.]

(b) *Application*. This exemption applies only to welfare benefit plans—

(1) Which have fewer than 100 participants at the beginning of the plan year;

(2)(i) For which benefits are paid as needed solely from the general assets of the employer or employee organization maintaining the plan, or

(ii) The benefits of which are provided exclusively through insurance contracts or policies issued by an insurance company or similar organization which is qualified to do business in any State or through a qualified health maintenance organization as defined in section 1310(d) of the Public Health Service Act, as amended, 42 U.S.C. § 300e-9(d), the premiums for which are paid directly by the employer or employee organization from its general assets or partly from its general assets and partly from contributions by its employees or mem-

bers, *Provided,* that contributions by participants are forwarded by the employer or employee organization within three months of receipt, or [Amended by 46 FR 5882, originally scheduled to be effective February 20, 1981. However, the effective date was delayed under the President's regulation freeze until March 30, 1981 (46 FR 11253).]

(iii) Both; [Amended by EBSA on March 1, 2013 (78 FR 13781).]

(3) for which, in the case of an insured plan—

(i) Refunds, to which contributing participants are entitled, are returned to them within three months of receipt by the employer or employee organization, and

(ii) Contributing participants are informed upon entry into the plan of the provisions of the plan concerning the allocation of refunds; and [Amended by EBSA on March 1, 2013 (78 FR 13781).]

(4) Which are not subject to the Form M-1 requirements under § 2520.101-2 (Filing by Multiple Employer Welfare Arrangements and Certain Other Related Entities). [Added by EBSA on March 1, 2013 (78 FR 13781).]

(c) *Limitations*. This exemption does not exempt the administrator of an employee benefit plan from any other requirement of title I of the Act, including the provisions which require that plan administrators furnish copies of the summary plan description to participants and beneficiaries (section 104(b)(1)) and furnish certain documents to the Secretary of Labor upon request (section 104(a)(6)), and which authorize the Secretary of Labor to collect information and data from employee benefit plans for research and analysis (section 513). [Revised by 67 FR 771, effective March 8, 2002.]

(d) *Examples*. (1) A welfare plan has 75 participants at the beginning of the plan year and 105 participants at the end of the plan year. Plan benefits are fully insured and premiums are paid directly to the insurance company by the employer pursuant to an insurance contract purchased with premium payments derived half from the general assets of the employer and half from employee contributions (which the employer forwards within three months of receipt). Refunds to the plan are paid to participating employees within three months of receipt as provided in the plan and as described to each participant upon entering the plan. The plan appoints the employer as its plan administrator. The employer, as plan administrator, provides summary plan descriptions to participants and beneficiaries. He also makes copies of certain plan documents available at the plan's principal office and such other places as necessary to give participants reasonable access to them. The exemption provided by § 2520.104-20 applies even though the plan has more than 100 participants by the end of the plan year, because it had fewer than 100 participants at the beginning of the plan year and otherwise satisfied the conditions of the exemption.

(2) A welfare plan is established and maintained in the same way as the plan described in example (1), except that a trade association which sponsors the plan is the holder of the insurance contract. Since the plan still sends the premium payments directly to the insurance company, the exemption applies, as in example (1). [Amended March 9, 1978, by 43 F.R. 10130.]

[¶ 14,247A]

§ 2520.104-21 **Limited exemption for certain group insurance arrangements**. (a) *Scope*. Under the authority of section 104(a)(3) of the Act, the administrator of any employee welfare benefit plan which covers fewer than 100 participants at the beginning of the plan year and which meets the requirements of paragraph (b) of this section is exempted from certain reporting and disclosure provisions of the Act. Specifically, the administrator of such plan is not required to file with the Secretary a terminal report or furnish upon written request of any participant or beneficiary a copy of any terminal report as required by section 104 (b) (4) of the Act. [Revised by 67 FR 771, effective March 8, 2002.]

(b) *Application*. This exemption applies only to welfare plans, each of which has fewer than 100 participants at the beginning of the plan year and which are part of a group insurance arrangement if such arrangement:

(1) Provides benefits to the employees of two or more unaffiliated employers, but not in connection with a multiemployer plan as

defined in section 3(37) of the Act and any regulations prescribed under the Act concerning section 3(37);

(2) Fully insures one or more welfare plans of each participating employer through insurance contracts purchased solely by the employers or purchased partly by the employers and partly by their participating employees, with all benefit payments made by the insurance company: *Provided,* That—

(i) Contributions by participating employees are forwarded by the employers within three months of receipt,

(ii) Refunds, to which contributing participants are entitled, are returned to them within three months of receipt, and

(iii) Contributing participants are informed upon entry into the plan of the provisions of the plan concerning the allocation of refunds; and

(3) Uses a trust (or other entity such as a trade association) as the holder of the insurance contracts and uses a trust as the conduit for payment of premiums to the insurance company. [Amended April 19, 2000 by 65 FR 21084.]

(c) *Limitations.* This exemption does not exempt the administrator of an employee benefit plan from any other requirement of title I of the Act, including the provisions which require that plan administrators furnish copies of the summary plan description to participants and beneficiaries (section 104(b)(1)), file an annual report with the Secretary of Labor (section 104(a)(1)) and furnish certain documents to the Secretary of Labor upon request (section 104(a)(6)), and authorize the Secretary of Labor to collect information and data from employee benefit plans for research and analysis (section 513). [Revised by 67 FR 771, effective March 8, 2002.]

(d) *Examples.* (1) A welfare plan has 25 participants at the beginning of the plan year. It is part of a group insurance arrangement of a trade association which provides benefits to employees of two or more unaffiliated employers, but not in connection with a multiemployer plan as defined in the Act. Plan benefits are fully insured pursuant to insurance contracts purchased with premium payments derived half from employee contributions (which the employer forwards within three months of receipt) and half from the general assets of each participating employer. Refunds to the plan are paid to participating employees within three months of receipt as provided in the plan and as described to each participant upon entering the plan. The trade association holds the insurance contracts. A trust acts as a conduit for payments, receiving premium payments from participating employers and paying the insurance company. The plan appoints the trade association as its plan administrator. The association, as plan administrator, provides summary plan descriptions to participants and beneficiaries, enlisting the help of participating employers in carrying out this distribution. The plan administrator also makes copies of certain plan documents available to the plan's principal office and such other places as necessary to give participants reasonable access to them. The plan administrator files with the Secretary an annual report covering activities of the plan, as required by the Act and such regulations as the Secretary may issue. The exemption provided by this section applies because the conditions of paragraph (b) have been satisfied. [Amended April 19, 2000 by 65 FR 21084.]

(2) Assume the same facts as paragraph (d)(1) of this section except that the premium payments for the insurance company are paid from the trust to an independent insurance brokerage firm acting as the agent of the insurance company. The trade association is the holder of the insurance contract. The plan appoints an officer of the participating employer as the plan administrator. The officer, as plan administrator, performs the same reporting and disclosure functions as the administrator in paragraph (d)(1) of this section, enlisting the help of the association in providing summary plan descriptions and necessary information. The exemption provided by this section applies. [Amended April 19, 2000 by 65 FR 21084.]

(3) The facts are the same as paragraph (d)(1) of this section except the welfare plan has 125 participants at the beginning of the plan year. The exemption provided by this section does not apply because the plan had 100 or more participants at the beginning of the plan year. See, however, § 2520.104-43. [Amended April 19, 2000 by 65 FR 21084.]

(4) The facts are the same as paragraph (d)(2) of this section except the welfare plan has 125 participants. The exemption provided by this section does not apply because the plan had 100 or more participants at the beginning of the plan year. See, however, § 2520.104-43. [Amended March 9, 1978, by 41 F.R. 10130; amended April 19, 2000 by 65 FR 21084.]

(e) *Applicability date.* For purposes of paragraph (b)(3) of this section, the arrangement may continue to use an entity (such as a trade association) as the conduit for the payment of insurance premiums to the insurance company for reporting years of the arrangement beginning before January 1, 2001. [Added April 19, 2000 by 65 FR 21084.]

[¶ 14,247B]

§ 2520.104-22 **Exemption from reporting and disclosure requirements for apprenticeship and training plans.** (a) An employee welfare benefit plan that provides exclusively apprenticeship training benefits or other training benefits or that provides exclusively apprenticeship and training benefits shall not be required to meet any requirement of Part 1 of the Act, provided that the administrator of such plan: (1) has filed with the Secretary the notice described in paragraph (b) of this section; (2) takes steps reasonably designed to ensure that the information required to be contained in such notice is disclosed to employees of employers contributing to the plan who may be eligible to enroll in any course of study sponsored or established by the plan; and (3) makes such notice available to such employees upon request.

(b) The notice referred to in paragraph (a) of this section shall contain accurate information concerning: (1) the name of the plan; (2) the Employer Identification Number (EIN) of the plan sponsor; (3) the name of the plan administrator; (4) the name and location of an office or person from whom an interested individual can obtain: [i] a description of any existing or anticipated future course of study sponsored or established by the plan, including any prerequisites for enrolling in such course; and [ii] a description of the procedure by which to enroll in such course. [Amended March 10, 1980, by 45 FR 15527.]

(c) *Filing Address.* The notice referred to in paragraph (a) of this section shall be filed with the Secretary of Labor by mailing it to: Apprenticeship and Training Plan Exemption, Employee Benefits Security Administration, Room N-1513, U.S. Department of Labor, 200 Constitution Avenue NW., Washington, DC 20210, or by delivering it during normal working hours to the Employee Benefits Security Administration, Room N-1513, U.S. Department of Labor, 200 Constitution Avenue NW., Washington, DC. [Amended on March 1, 1989 by 54 FR 8624. Amended by EBSA on April 3, 2003 by 68 FR 16399.]

[¶ 14,247C]

§ 2520.104-23 **Alternative method of compliance for pension plans for certain selected employees.** (a) *Purpose and scope.* (1) This section contains an alternative method of compliance with the reporting and disclosure requirements of Part 1 of Title I of the Employee Retirement Income Security Act of 1974 for unfunded or insured pension plans maintained by an employer for a select group of management or highly compensated employees, pursuant to the authority of the Secretary of Labor under section 110 of the Act (88 Stat. 851).

(2) Under section 110 of the Act, the Secretary is authorized to prescribe an alternative method for satisfying any requirement of Part 1 of Title I of the Act with respect to any pension plans, or class of pension plans, subject to such requirement.

(b) *Filing obligation.* Under the authority of section 110 of the Act, an alternative form of compliance with the reporting and disclosure requirements of Part 1 of the Act is provided for certain pension plans for a select group of management or highly compensated employees. The administrator of a pension plan described in paragraph (d) shall be deemed to satisfy the reporting and disclosure provisions of Part 1 of Title I of the Act by—

(1) Filing a statement with the Secretary of Labor that includes the name and address of the employer, the employer identification number (EIN) assigned by the Internal Revenue Service, a declaration that the employer maintains a plan or plans primarily for the purpose of providing deferred compensation for a select group of management or highly compensated employees, and a statement of the number of such plans and the number of employees in each, and

(2) Providing plan documents, if any, to the Secretary upon request as required by section 104(a)(6) of the Act. Only one statement need be filed for each employer maintaining one or more of the plans described in paragraph (d) of this section. For plans in existence on May 4, 1975, the statement shall be filed on or before August 31, 1975. For a plan to which Part 1 of Title I of the Act becomes applicable after May 4, 1975, the statement shall be filed within 120 days after the plan becomes subject to Part 1. [Revised by 67 FR 771, effective March 8, 2002.]

(c) *Filing Address*. Statements may be filed with the Secretary of Labor by mailing them addressed to: Top Hat Plan Exemption, Employee Benefits Security Administration, Room N-1513, U.S. Department of Labor, 200 Constitution Avenue NW., Washington, DC 20210, or by delivering it during normal working hours to the Employee Benefits Security Administration, Room N-1513, U.S. Department of Labor, 200 Constitution Avenue NW., Washington, D.C. [Amended on March 1, 1989 by 54 FR 8624. Amended by EBSA on April 3, 2003 by 68 FR 16399.]

(d) *Application*. The alternative form of compliance described in paragraph (b) of this section is available only to employee pension benefit plans—

(1) Which are maintained by an employer primarily for the purpose of providing deferred compensation for a select group of management or highly compensated employees, and

(2) For which benefits (i) are paid as needed solely from the general assets of the employer, (ii) are provided exclusively through insurance contracts or policies, the premiums for which are paid directly by the employer from its general assets, issued by an insurance company or similar organization which is qualified to do business in any State, or (iii) both. [Amended by EBSA on April 3, 2003 by 68 FR 16399.]

[¶ 14,247D]

§ 2520.104-24 **Exemption for welfare plans for certain selected employees.** (a) *Purpose and scope*. (1) This section, under the authority of section 104(a)(3) of the Employee Retirement Income Security Act of 1974, exempts unfunded or insured welfare plans maintained by an employer for the purpose of providing benefits for a select group of management or highly compensated employees from the reporting and disclosure provisions of Part 1 of Title I of the Act, except for the requirement to provide plan documents to the Secretary of Labor upon request under section 104(a)(1) of the Act.

(2) Under section 104(a)(3) of the Act, the Secretary is authorized to exempt by regulation any welfare benefit plan from all or part of the reporting and disclosure requirements of Title I of the Act.

(b) *Exemption*. Under the authority of section 104(a)(3) of the Act, each employee welfare benefit plan described in paragraph (c) of this section is exempted from the reporting and disclosure provisions of Part 1 of Title I of the Act, except for providing plan documents to the Secretary of Labor upon request as required by section 104(a)(6). [Revised by 67 FR 771, effective March 8, 2002.]

(c) *Application*. This exemption is available only to employee welfare benefit plans:

(1) Which are maintained by an employer primarily for the purpose of providing benefits for a select group of management or highly compensated employees, and

(2) For which benefits (i) are paid as needed solely from the general assets of the employer, (ii) are provided exclusively through insurance contracts or policies, the premiums for which are paid directly by the employer from its general assets, issued by an insurance company or similar organization which is qualified to do business in any State, or (iii) both.

[¶ 14,247E]

§ 2520.104-25 **Exemption from reporting and disclosure for day care centers.** Under the authority of section 104(a)(3) of the Act, day care centers are exempted from the reporting and disclosure provisions of Part 1 of Title I of the Act, except for providing plan documents to the Secretary upon request as required under section 104(a)(6) of the Act. [Revised by 67 FR 771, effective March 8, 2002.]

[¶ 14,247F]

§ 2520.104-26 **Limited exemption for certain unfunded dues financed welfare plans maintained by employee organizations.** (a) *Scope*. Under the authority of section 104(a)(3) of the Act, a welfare benefit plan that meets the requirements of paragraph (b) of this section is exempted from the provisions of the Act that require filing with the Secretary an annual report and furnishing a summary annual report to participants and beneficiaries. Such plans may use a simplified method of reporting and disclosure to comply with the requirement to furnish a summary plan description to participants and beneficiaries, as follows:

(1) In lieu of filing an annual report with the Secretary or distibuting a summary annual report, a filing is made of Report Form LM-2 or LM-3, pursuant to the Labor-Management Reporting and Disclosure Act (LMRDA) and regulations thereunder, and

(2) In lieu of a summary plan description, the employee organization constitution or by-laws may be furnished in accordance with Sec. 2520.104b-2 to participants and beneficiaries together with any supplement to such document necessary to meet the requirements of Secs. 2520.102-2 and 2520.102-3. [Revised by 67 FR 771, 3/8/02.]

(b) *Application*. This exemption is available only to welfare benefit plans maintained by an employee organization, as that term is defined in section 3(4) of the Act, paid for out of the employee organization's assets, which are derived wholly or partly from membership dues, and which cover employee organization members and their beneficiaries.

(c) *Limitations*. This exemption does not exempt the administrator from any other requirement of Part 1 of Title I of the Act. [Added by 42 FR 37178, effective July 19, 1977.]

[¶ 14,247G]

§ 2520.104-27 **Alternative method of compliance for certain unfunded dues financed pension plans maintained by employee organizations.** (a) *Scope*. Under the authority of section 110 of the Act, a pension benefit plan that meets the requirements of paragraph (b) of this section is exempted from the provisions of the Act that require filing with the Secretary an annual report and furnishing a summary annual report to participants and beneficiaries receiving benefits. Such plans may use a simplified method of reporting and disclosure to comply with the requirement to furnish a summary plan description to participants and beneficiaries receiving benefits, as follows:

(1) In lieu of filing an annual report with the Secretary or distributing a summary annual report, a filing is made of Report Form LM-2 or LM-3, pursuant to the Labor-Management Reporting and Disclosure Act (LMRDA) and regulations thereunder, and

(2) In lieu of a summary plan description, the employee organization constitution or bylaws may be furnished in accordance with Sec. 2520.104b-2 to participants and beneficiaries together with any supplement to such document necessary to meet the requirements of Secs. 2520.102-2 and 2520.102-3. [Revised by 67 FR 771, 3/8/02.]

(b) *Application*. This exemption is available only to pension benefit plans maintained by an employee organization, as that term is defined in section 3(4) of the Act, paid for out of the employee organization's general assets, which are derived wholly or partly from membership dues, and which cover employee organization members and their beneficiaries.

(c) *Limitations*. This exemption does not exempt the administrator from any other requirement of Part 1 of Title I of the Act. [Added by 42 FR 37178, effective July 19, 1977.]

[¶ 14,247H]

§ 2520.104-28 **Extension of time for filing and disclosure of the initial summary plan description.** [Removed and reserved by 61 FR 33847 on 7/1/96.]

[¶ 14,247U]

§ 2520.104-41 **Simplified annual reporting requirements for plans with fewer than 100 participants.** (a) *General*. (1) Under the authority of section 104(a)(2)(A), the Secretary of Labor may prescribe simplified annual reporting for employee pension benefit plans with fewer than 100 participants.

(2) Under the authority of section 104(a)(3), the Secretary of Labor may provide a limited exemption for any employee welfare benefit plan with respect to certain annual reporting requirements.

(b) *Application.* The administrator of an employee pension or welfare benefit plan which covers fewer than 100 participants at the beginning of the plan year and the administrator of an employee pension or welfare benefit plan described in §2520.103-1(d) may file the simplified annual report described in paragraph (c) of this section in lieu of the annual report described in §2520.103-1(b). [Corrected April 4, 1978, by 43 FR 14010. Amended July 29, 1980 by 45 FR 51446; amended April 19, 2000 by 65 FR 21084.]

(c) *Contents.* The administrator of an employee pension or welfare benefit plan described in paragraph (b) of this section shall file, in the manner described in §2520.104a-5, a completed Form 5500 "Annual Return/Report of Employee Benefit Plan" including, if applicable, the information described in §2520.103-1(f) or, to the extent eligible, a completed Form 5500-SF "Short Form Annual Return/Report of Small Employee Benefit Plan," and any required schedules or statements prescribed by the instructions to the applicable form, and, unless waived by §2520.104-44 or §2520.104-46, a report of an independent qualified public accountant meeting the requirements of §2520.103-1(b). [Amended March 1, 1989 by 54 FR 8624; amended July 29, 1980 by 45 FR 51446; amended April 19, 2000 by 65 FR 21084; amended October 19, 2000 by 65 FR 62957; amended March 1, 2013 by 78 FR 13781.]

[¶ 14,247V]

§2520.104-42 **Waiver of certain actuarial information in the annual report.** Under the authority of §104(a)(2)(A) of ERISA, the requirement of section 103(d)(6) of ERISA that the annual report include as part of the actuarial statement (Schedule B) the present value of all of the plan's liabilities for nonforfeitable pension benefits allocated by termination priority categories, as set forth in section 4044 of Title IV of ERISA, and the actuarial assumptions used in these computations, is waived. [Amended January 23, 1979, by 44 FR 5440.]

[¶ 14,247W]

§2520.104-43 **Exemption from annual reporting requirement for certain group insurance arrangements.** (a) *General.* Under the authority of section 104(a)(3) of the Act, the administrator of an employee welfare benefit plan which meets the requirements of paragraph (b) of this section is not required to file an annual report with the Secretary of Labor as required by section 104(a)(1) of the Act. [Revised by 67 FR 771, effective Match 8, 2002.]

(b) *Application.* (1) This exemption applies only to a welfare plan for a plan year in which (i) such plan meets the requirements of §2520.104-21, except the requirement that the plan cover fewer than 100 participants at the beginning of the plan year, and (ii) an annual report containing the items set forth in §2520.103-2 has been filed with the Secretary of Labor in accordance with §§2520.104a-6 by the trust or other entity which is the holder of the group insurance contracts by which plan benefits are provided. [Amended April 19, 2000 by 65 FR 21084.]

(2) For purposes of this section, the terms "group insurance arrangement" or "trust or other entity" shall be used in place of the terms "plan" and "plan administrator," as applicable, in §§2520.103-3, 2520.103-4, 2520.103-6, 2520.103-8, 2520.103-9 and 2520.103-10. [Amended April 19, 2000 by 65 FR 21084.]

(c) *Limitation.* This provision does not exempt the administrator of an employee benefit plan which meets the requirements of paragraph (b) from furnishing a copy of a summary annual report to participants and beneficiaries of the plan, as required by section 104(b)(3) of the Act. [Added March 9, 1978, by 43 F.R. 10130.]

[¶ 14,247X]

§2520.104-44 **Limited exemption and alternative method of compliance for annual reporting by unfunded plans and by certain insured plans.** (a) *General.* (1) Under the authority of section 104(a)(3) of the Act, the Secretary of Labor may exempt an employee welfare benefit plan from any or all of the reporting and disclosure requirements of Title I. An employee welfare benefit plan which meets

the requirements of paragraph (b)(1) of this section is not required to comply with the annual reporting requirements described in paragraph (c) of this section. [Amended July 29, 1980 by 45 FR 51446.]

(2) Under the authority of section 110 of the Act, an alternative method of compliance is prescribed for certain employee pension benefit plans subject to Part 1, Title I of the Act. An employee pension benefit plan which meets the requirements of paragraph (b)(2) or (b)(3) of this section is not required to comply with the annual reporting requirements described in paragraph (c) of this section. [Amended April 19, 2000 by 65 FR 21085.]

(b) *Application.* This section applies only to:

(1) An employee welfare benefit plan under the terms of which benefits are to be paid—

(i) Solely from the general assets of the employer or employee organization maintaining the plan;

(ii) The benefits of which are provided exclusively through insurance contracts or policies issued by an insurance company or similar organization which is qualified to do business in any State or through a qualified health maintenance organization as defined in section 1310(d) of the Public Health Service Act, as amended, 42 U.S.C. §300e-9(d), the premiums for which are paid directly by the employer or employee organization from its general assets or partly from its general assets and partly from contributions by its employees or members, provided that any plan assets held by such an insurance company are held solely in the general account of such company or organization, contributions by participants are forwarded by the employer or employee organization within three months of receipt and, in the case of a plan that provides for the return of refunds to contributing participants, such refunds are returned to them within three months of receipt by the employer or employee organization, or [Amended by 46 FR 5882, originally scheduled to be effective February 20, 1981. However, the effective date was delayed under the President's regulation freeze until March 30, 1981 (46 FR 11253).]

(iii) Partly in the manner specified in paragraph (b)(1)(i) of this section and partly in the manner specified in paragraph (b)(1)(ii) of this section; and

(2) A pension benefit plan the benefits of which are provided exclusively through allocated insurance contracts or policies which are issued by, and pursuant to the specific terms of such contracts or policies benefit payments are fully guaranteed by an insurance company or similar organization which is qualified to do business in any State, and the premiums for which are paid directly by the employer or employee organization from its general assets or partly from its general assets and partly from contributions by its employees or members: Provided, That contributions by participants are forwarded by the employer or employee organization to the insurance company or organization within three months of receipt and, in the case of a plan that provides for the return of refunds to contributing participants, such refunds are returned to them within three months of receipt by the employer or employee organization.

(c) *Contents.* An employee benefit plan described in paragraph (b) of this section is exempt from complying with the following annual reporting requirements:

(1) Completing certain items of the annual report relating to financial information and transactions entered into by the plan as described in the instructions to the Form 5500 "Annual Return/Report of Employee Benefit Plan" and accompanying schedules; [Amended July 29, 1980 by 45 FR 51446; amended April 19, 2000 by 65 FR 21085.]

(2) Engaging an independent qualified public accountant pursuant to section 103(a)(3)(A) of the Act and §2520.103-1(b) to conduct an examination of the financial statements and schedules of the plan; and

(3) Including in the annual report a report of an independent qualified public accountant concerning the financial statements and schedules required to be a part of the annual report pursuant to section 103(b) of the Act and §2520.103-1(b).

(d) *Limitation.* This section does not exempt any plan from filing an annual report form with the Secretary in accordance with section 104(a)(1) of the Act and §2520.104a-5. [Revised by 67 FR 771, effective Match 8, 2002.]

(e) *Example*. A welfare plan which is funded entirely with insurance contracts and which meets all the requirements of exemption under § 2520.104-20 except that it covers 100 or more participants at the beginning of the plan year is not exempt from the annual reporting requirements under § 2520.104-20, but is exempt from certain reporting requirements under § 2520.104-44. Under the latter section, such a welfare plan should file Form 5500, including Schedule A "Insurance Information." However, the plan is not required to engage an independent qualified public accountant and need not complete certain items on Form 5500. [Added March 9, 1978, by 43 FR 10130 and amended by 45 FR 51446 on July 29, 1980 and by 72 FR 64710 on November 16, 2007.]

[¶ 14,247Y]

§ 2520.104-45 **Temporary exemption from reporting insurance fees and commissions for insured plans with fewer than 100 participants**. [Removed and reserved by 61 FR 33847 on 7/1/96.]

[¶ 14,247Z]

§ 2520.104-46 **Waiver of examination and report of an independent qualified public accountant for employee benefit plans with fewer than 100 participants**. (a) *General*. (1) Under the authority of section 103(a)(3)(A) of the Act, the Secretary may waive the requirements of section 103(a)(3)(A) in the case of a plan for which simplified annual reporting has been prescribed in accordance with section 104(a)(2) of the Act.

(2) Under the authority of section 104(a)(3) of the Act the Secretary may exempt any employee welfare benefit plan from certain annual reporting requirements.

(b) *Application*. (1)(i) The administrator of an employee pension benefit plan for which simplified annual reporting has been prescribed in accordance with section 104(a)(2)(A) of the Act and Sec. 2520.104-41 is not required to comply with the annual reporting requirements described in paragraph (c) of this section, provided that with respect to each plan year for which the waiver is claimed—

(A)(1) At least 95 percent of the assets of the plan constitute qualifying plan assets within the meaning of paragraph (b)(1)(ii) of this section, or

(2) Any person who handles assets of the plan that do not constitute qualifying plan assets is bonded in accordance with the requirements of section 412 of the Act and the regulations issued thereunder, except that the amount of the bond shall not be less than the value of such assets;

(B) The summary annual report (described in § 2520.104b–10) or, in the case of plans subject to section 101(f) of the Act, the annual funding notice (described in § 2520.101–5), includes, in addition to any other required information: [Amended 2/2/2015 (80 FR 5625).]

(1) Except for qualifying plan assets described in paragraph (b)(1)(ii)(A), (B) and (F) of this section, the name of each regulated financial institution holding (or issuing) qualifying plan assets and the amount of such assets reported by the institution as of the end of the plan year;

(2) The name of the surety company issuing the bond, if the plan has more than 5% of its assets in non-qualifying plan assets;

(3) A notice indicating that participants and beneficiaries may, upon request and without charge, examine, or receive copies of, evidence of the required bond and statements received from the regulated financial institutions describing the qualifying plan assets; and

(4) A notice stating that participants and beneficiaries should contact the Regional Office of the U.S. Department of Labor's Employee Benefits Security Administration if they are unable to examine or obtain copies of the regulated financial institution statements or evidence of the required bond, if applicable; and [EBSA technical correction, 68 FR 16399 (April 3, 2003).]

(C) in response to a request from any participant or beneficiary, the administrator, without charge to the participant or beneficiary, makes available for examination, or upon request furnishes copies of, each regulated financial institution statement and evidence of any bond required by paragraph (b)(1)(i)(A)(2).

(ii) For purposes of paragraph (b)(1), the term "qualifying plan assets" means:

(A) Qualifying employer securities, as defined in section 407(d)(5) of the Act and the regulations issued thereunder;

(B) Any loan meeting the requirements of section 408(b)(1) of the Act and the regulations issued thereunder;

(C) Any assets held by any of the following institutions:

(1) A bank or similar financial institution as defined in Sec. 2550.408b-4(c);

(2) An insurance company qualified to do business under the laws of a state;

(3) An organization registered as a broker-dealer under the Securities Exchange Act of 1934; or

(4) Any other organization authorized to act as a trustee for individual retirement accounts under section 408 of the Internal Revenue Code.

(D) Shares issued by an investment company registered under the Investment Company Act of 1940;

(E) Investment and annuity contracts issued by any insurance company qualified to do business under the laws of a state; and,

(F) In the case of an individual account plan, any assets in the individual account of a participant or beneficiary over which the participant or beneficiary has the opportunity to exercise control and with respect to which the participant or beneficiary is furnished, at least annually, a statement from a regulated financial institution referred to in paragraphs (b)(1)(ii)(C), (D) or (E) of this section describing the assets held (or issued) by such institution and the amount of such assets.

(iii)(A) For purposes of this paragraph (b)(1), the determination of the percentage of all plan assets consisting of qualifying plan assets with respect to a given plan year shall be made in the same manner as the amount of the bond is determined pursuant to Secs. 2580.412-11, 2580.412-14, and 2580.412-15.

(B) *Examples*. Plan A, which reports on a calendar year basis, has total assets of $600,000 as of the end of the 1999 plan year. Plan A's assets, as of the end of year, include: investments in various bank, insurance company and mutual fund products of $520,000; investments in qualifying employer securities of $40,000; participant loans, meeting the requirements of ERISA section 408(b)(1), totaling $20,000; and a $20,000 investment in a real estate limited partnership. Because the only asset of the plan that does not constitute a "qualifying plan asset" is the $20,000 real estate investment and that investment represents less than 5% of the plan's total assets, no bond would be required under the proposal as a condition for the waiver for the 2000 plan year. By contrast, Plan B also has total assets of $600,000 as of the end of the 1999 plan year, of which $558,000 constitutes "qualifying plan assets" and $42,000 constitutes non-qualifying plan assets. Because 7%—more than 5%—of Plan B's assets do not constitute "qualifying plan assets," Plan B, as a condition to electing the waiver for the 2000 plan year, must ensure that it has a fidelity bond in an amount equal to at least $42,000 covering persons handling non-qualifying plan assets. Inasmuch as compliance with section 412 requires the amount of bonds to be not less than 10% of the amount of all the plan's funds or other property handled, the bond acquired for section 412 purposes may be adequate to cover the non-qualifying plan assets without an increase (i.e., if the amount of the bond determined to be needed for the relevant persons for section 412 purposes is at least $42,000). As demonstrated by the foregoing example, where a plan has more than 5% of its assets in non-qualifying plan assets, the bond required by the proposal is for the total amount of the non-qualifying plan assets, not just the amount in excess of 5%. [Added March 9, 1978, by 43 FR 10130. Amended October 19, 2000 by 65 FR 62957.]

(2) The administrator of an employee welfare benefit plan that covers fewer than 100 participants at the beginning of the plan year is not required to comply with annual reporting requirements described in paragraph (c) of this section.

(c) *Waiver*. The administrator of a plan described in paragraph (b)(1) or (2) of this section is not required to:

(1) Engage an independent qualified public accountant to conduct an examination of the financial statements of the plan;

(2) Include within the annual report the financial statements and schedules prescribed in section 103(b) of the Act and §§ 2520.103-1, 2520.103-2, and 2520.103-10; and

(3) Include within the annual report a report of an independent qualified public accountant as prescribed in section 103(a)(3)(A) of the Act and § 2520.103-1.

(d) *Limitations.* (1) The waiver described in this section does not affect the obligation of a plan described in paragraph (b)(1) or (2) of this section to file a Form 5500 "Annual Return/Report of Employee Benefit Plan," including any required schedules or statements prescribed by the instructions to the form. See Sec. 2520.104-41. [Amended April 19, 2000 by 65 FR 21085 and October 19, 2000 by 65 FR 62957.]

(2) For purposes of this section, an employee pension benefit plan for which simplified annual reporting has been prescribed includes an employee pension benefit plan which elects to file a Form 5500 as a small plan pursuant to Sec. 2520.103-1(d) with respect to the plan year for which the waiver is claimed. See Sec. 2520.104-41. [Corrected April 4, 1978 by 43 FR 14010; amended July 29, 1980 by 45 FR 51446; amended March 1, 1989 by 54 FR 8624; amended October 19, 2000 by 65 FR 62957.]

(3) For purposes of this section, an employee welfare benefit plan that covers fewer than 100 participants at the beginning of the plan year includes an employee welfare benefit plan which elects to file a Form 5500 as a small plan pursuant to Sec. 2520.103-1(d) with respect to the plan year for which the waiver is claimed. See Sec. 2520.104-41.

(4) A plan that elects to file a Form 5500 as a large plan pursuant to Sec. 2520.103-1(d) may not claim a waiver under this section. [Amended October 19, 2000 by 65 FR 62957.]

(e) *Model notice.* The appendix to this section contains model language for inclusion in the summary annual report to assist plan administrators in complying with the requirements of paragraph (b)(1)(i)(B) of this section to avail themselves of the waiver of examination and report of the independent qualified public accountant for employee benefit plans with fewer than 100 participants. Use of the model language is not mandatory. In order to use the model language in the plan's summary annual report, administrators must, in addition to any other information required to be in the summary annual report, select among alternative language and add relevant information where appropriate in the model language. Items of information that are not applicable to a particular plan may be deleted. Use of the model language, appropriately modified and supplemented, will be deemed to satisfy the notice content requirements of paragraph (b)(1)(i)(B) of this section.

Appendix to § 2520.104-46 - Model Summary Annual Report Notice (Plan Administrators Will Need to Modify the Model to Omit Information That Is Not Applicable to the Plan)

The U.S. Department of Labor's regulations require that an independent qualified public accountant audit the plan's financial statements unless certain conditions are met for the audit requirement to be waived. This plan met the audit waiver conditions for the plan year beginning (insert year) and therefore has not had an audit performed. Instead, the following information is provided to assist you in verifying that the assets reported on the (Form 5500 or Form 5500-SF - select as applicable) were actually held by the plan.

At the end of the (insert year) plan year, the plan had (include separate entries for each regulated financial institution holding or issuing qualifying plan assets):

[Set forth amounts and names of institutions as applicable where indicated]

[(insert $ amount) in assets held by (insert name of bank)],

[(insert $ amount) in securities held by (insert name of registered broker-dealer)],

[(insert $ amount) in shares issued by (insert name of registered investment company)],

[(insert $ amount) in investment or annuity contract issued by (insert name of insurance company)].

The plan receives year-end statements from these regulated financial institutions that confirm the above information. [Insert as applicable - The remainder of the plan's assets were (1) qualifying

employer securities, (2) loans to participants, (3) held in individual participant accounts with investments directed by participants and beneficiaries and with account statements from regulated financial institutions furnished to the participant or beneficiary at least annually, or (4) other assets covered by a fidelity bond at least equal to the value of the assets and issued by an approved surety company.]

Plan participants and beneficiaries have a right, on request and free of charge, to get copies of the financial institution year-end statements and evidence of the fidelity bond. If you want to examine or get copies of the financial institution year-end statements or evidence of the fidelity bond, please contact [insert mailing address and any other available way to request copies such as e-mail and phone number].

If you are unable to obtain or examine copies of the regulated financial institution statements or evidence of the fidelity bond, you may contact the regional office of the U.S. Department of Labor's Employee Benefits Security Administration (EBSA) for assistance by calling toll-free 1.866.444.EBSA (3272). A listing of EBSA regional offices can be found at http://www.dol.gov/ebsa.

General information regarding the audit waiver conditions applicable to the plan can be found on the U.S. Department of Labor Web site at http://www.dol.gov/ebsa under the heading "Frequently Asked Questions." [Amended November 16, 2007 (72 FR 64710).]

[¶ 14,247ZA]

§ 2520.104-47 **Limited exemption and alternative method of compliance for filing of insurance company financial reports**. An administrator of an employee benefit plan to which section 103(e)(2) of the Act applies shall be deemed in compliance with the requirement to include with its annual report a copy of the financial report of the insurance company, insurance service or similar organization, provided that the administrator files a copy of such report within 45 days of receipt of a written request for such report by the Secretary of Labor. [Added by 45 FR 14034, effective March 4, 1980.]

[¶ 14,247ZB]

§ 2520.104-48 **Alternative Method of Compliance for Model Simplified Employee Pensions—IRS Form 5305-SEP**. Under the authority of section 110 of the Act the provisions of this section are prescribed as an alternative method of compliance with the reporting and disclosure requirements set forth in Part 1 of Title I of the Employee Retirement Income Security Act of 1974 in the case of a simplified employee pension (SEP) described in section 408(k) of the Internal Revenue Code of 1954 as amended (the Code) that is created by use without modification of Internal Revenue Service (IRS) Form *5305-SEP*.

(a) At the time an employee becomes eligible to participate in the SEP (whether at the creation of the SEP or thereafter), the administrator of the SEP (generally the employer establishing and maintaining the SEP) shall furnish the employee with a copy of the completed and unmodified IRS Form *5305-SEP* used to create the SEP, including (1) the completed Contribution Agreement, (2) the General Information and Guidelines, and (3) the Questions and Answers.

(b) Following the end of each calendar year the administrator of the SEP shall notify each participant in the SEP in writing of any employer contributions made under the Contribution Agreement to the participant's individual retirement account or individual retirement annuity (IRA) for that year.

(c) If the employer establishing and maintaining the SEP selects, recommends, or in any other way influences employees to choose a particular IRA or type of IRA into which contributions under the SEP will be made, and if that IRA is subject to restrictions on a participant's ability to withdraw funds (other than restrictions imposed by the Code that apply to all IRAs), the administrator of the SEP shall give to each employee, in writing, within 90 days of the adoption of this regulation or at the time such employee becomes eligible to participate in the SEP, whichever is later, a clear explanation of those restrictions and a statement to the effect that other IRAs, into which rollovers or employee contributions may be made, may not be subject to such restrictions. [Added by 45 FR 24866, adopted and effective April 8, 1980.]

[¶ 14,247ZC]

§ 2520.104-49 **Alternative method of compliance for certain simplified employee pensions**. Under the authority of section 110 of the

Act, the provisions of this section are prescribed as an alternative method of compliance with the reporting and disclosure requirements set forth in Part 1 of Title I of the Act for a simplified employee pension (SEP) described in section 408(k) of the Internal Revenue Code of 1954 as amended, except for (1) a SEP that is created by proper use of Internal Revenue Service Form *5305-SEP,* or (2) a SEP in connection with which the employer who establishes or maintains the SEP selects, recommends or influences its employees to choose the IRAs into which employer contributions will be made and those IRAs are subjectto provisions that prohibit withdrawal of funds by participants for any period of time.

(a) At the time an employee becomes eligible to participate in the SEP (whether at the creation of the SEP or thereafter) or up to 90 days after the effective date of this regulation, whichever is later, the administrator of the SEP (generally the employer establishing or maintaining the SEP) shall furnish the employee in writing with:

(1) Specific information concerning the SEP, including:

(i) The requirements for employee participation in the SEP,

(ii) The formula to be used to allocate employer contributions made under the SEP to each participant's individual retirement account or annuity (IRA).

(iii) The name or title of the individual who is designated by the employer to provide additional information to participants concerning the SEP, and

(iv) If the employer who establishes or maintains the SEP selects, recommends or substantially influences its employees to choose the IRAs into which employer contributions under the SEP will be made, a clear explanation of the terms of those IRAs, such as the rate(s) of return and any restrictions on a participant's ability to roll over or withdraw funds from the IRAs, including restrictions that allow rollovers or withdrawals but reduce earnings of the IRAs or impose other penalties.

(2) General information concerning SEPs and IRAs, including a clear explanation of:

(i) What a SEP is and how it operates,

(ii) The statutory provisions prohibiting discrimination in favor of highly compensated employees.

(iii) A participant's right to receive contributions under a SEP-and the allowable sources of contributions to a SEP-related IRA (SEP-IRA),

(iv) The statutory limits on contributions to SEP-IRAs,

(v) The consequences of excess contributions to a SEP-IRA and how to avoid excess contributions,

(vi) A participant's rights with respect to contributions made under a SEP to his or her IRA(s),

(vii) How a participant must treat contributions to a SEP-IRA for tax purposes,

(viii) The statutory provisions concerning withdrawal of funds from a SEP-IRA and the consequences of a premature withdrawal, and

(ix) A participant's ability to roll over or transfer funds from a SEP-IRA to another IRA, SEP-IRA, or retirement bond, and how such a rollover or transfer may be effected without causing adverse tax consequences.

(3) A statement to the effect that:

(i) IRAs other than the IRA(s) into which employer contributions will be made under the SEP may provide different rates of return and may have different terms concerning, among other things, transfers and withdrawals of funds from the IRA(s),

(ii) In the event a participant is entitled to make a contribution or rollover to an IRA, such contribution or rollover can be made to an IRA other than the one into which employer contributions under the SEP are to be made, and

(iii) Depending on the terms of the IRA into which employer contributions are made, a participant may be able to make rollovers or transfers of funds from that IRA to another IRA.

(4) A description of the disclosure required by the Internal Revenue Service to be made to individuals for whose benefit an IRA is established by the financial institution or other person who sponsors the IRA(s) into which contributions will be made under the SEP.

(5) A statement that, in addition to the information provided to an employee at the time he or she becomes eligible to participate in a SEP, the administrator of the SEP must furnish each participant:

(i) Within 30 days of the effective date of any amendment to the terms of the SEP, a copy of the amendment and a clear written explanation of its effects, and

(ii) No later than the later of:

(A) January 31 of the year following the year for which a contribution is made,

(B) 30 days after a contribution is made, or

(C) 30 days after the effective date of this regulation written notification of any employer contributions made under the SEP to that participant's IRA(s).

(6) In the case of a SEP that provides for integration with Social Security.

(i) A statement that Social Security taxes paid by the employer on account of a participant will be considered as an employer contribution under the SEP to a participant's SEP-IRA for purposes of determining the amount contributed to the SEP-IRA(s) of a participant by the employer pursuant to the allocation formula,

(ii) A description of the effect that integration with Social Security would have on employer contributions under a SEP, and

(iii) The integration formula, which may constitute part of the allocation formula required by paragraph (a)(1)(ii) of this section.

(b)(1) The requirements of paragraphs (a)(1)(i), (a)(1)(ii), (a)(1)(iii) and (a)(6)(i) of this regulation may be met by furnishing the SEP agreement to participants, provided that the SEP agreement is written in a manner reasonably calculated to be understood by the average plan participant.

(2) The requirements of paragraph (a)(1)(iv) of this regulation may be met through disclosure materials furnished by the financial institution in which the participant's IRA is maintained, provided the materials contain the information specified in such paragraph.

(c) No later than the later of:

(1) January 31 of the year following the year for which a contribution is made,

(2) 30 days after a contribution is made, or

(3) 30 days after the effective date of this regulation the administrator of the SEP shall notify a participant in the SEP in writing of any employer contributions made under the SEP to the participant's IRA(s).

(d) Within 30 days of the effective date of any amendment to the terms of the SEP, the administrator shall furnish each participant a copy of the amendment and a clear explanation in writing of its effect. [Adopted by 46 FR 1261, originally scheduled to be effective February 6, 1981. However, the effective date was delayed under the President's regulation freeze at least until March 30, 1981 (46 FR 10465).]

[¶ 14,247ZD]

§ 2520.104-50 **Short plan years, deferral of accountant's examination and report**. (a) *Definition of "short plan year".* For purposes of this section, a short plan year is a plan year, as defined in section 3(39) of the Act, of seven or fewer months' duration, which occurs in the event that—(1) a plan is established or commences operations; (2) a plan is merged or consolidated with another plan or plans; (3) a plan is terminated; or (4) the annual date on which the plan year begins is changed.

(b) *Deferral of accountant's report.* A plan administrator is not required to include the report of an independent qualified public accountant in the annual report for the first of two consecutive plan years, one of which is a short plan year, provided that the following conditions are satisfied:

(1) The annual report for the first of the two consecutive plan years shall include:

(i) Financial statements and accompanying schedules prepared in conformity with the requirements of section 103(b) of the Act and regulations promulgated thereunder;

(ii) An explanation why one of the two plan years is of seven or fewer months' duration; and

(iii) A statement that the annual report for the immediately following plan year will include a report of an independent qualified public accountant with respect to the financial statements and accompanying schedules for both of the two plan years.

(2) The annual report for the second of the two consecutive plan years shall include:

(i) Financial statements and accompanying schedules prepared in conformity with section 103(b) of the Act and regulations promulgated thereunder with respect to both plan years;

(ii) A report of an independent qualified public accountant with respect to the financial statements and accompanying schedules for both plan years; and

(iii) A statement identifying any material differences between the unaudited financial information relating to, and contained in the annual report for, the first of the two consecutive plan years and the audited financial information relating to that plan year contained in the annual report for the immediately following plan year.

(c) *Accountant's examination and report.* The examination by the accountant which serves as the basis for the portion of his report relating to the first of the two consecutive plan years may be conducted at the same time as the examination which serves as the basis for the portion of his report relating to the immediately following plan year. The report of the accountant shall be prepared in conformity with section 103(a)(3)(A) of the Act and regulations thereunder. [Adopted December 30, 1980 by 46 FR 1265, effective December 29, 1980.]

Subpart E—Reporting Requirements

[¶ 14,248]

§2520.104a-1 **Filing with the Secretary of Labor.** (a) *General reporting requirements.* Part 1 of Title I of the Act requires that the administrator of an employee benefit plan subject to the provisions of Part 1 file with the Secretary of Labor certain reports and additional documents. Each report filed shall accurately and comprehensively detail the information required. Where a form is prescribed, the reports shall be filed on that form. The Secretary may reject any incomplete filing. Reports and documents shall be filed as specified in this part.

(b) *Exemption for certain welfare plans.* See §§ 2520.104-20, 2520.104-21, 2520.104-22, 2520.104-24, and 2520.104-25.

(c) *Alternative method of compliance for pension plans for certain selected employees.* See § 2520.104-23. [Added by 41 FR 16957, effective April 23, 1976.]

[¶ 14,248A]

§2520.104a-2 **Electronic filing of annual reports.** (a) Any annual report (including any accompanying statements or schedules) filed with the Secretary under part 1 of title I of the Act for any plan year (reporting year, in the case of common or collective trusts, pooled separate accounts, and similar non-plan entities) beginning on or after January 1, 2009, shall be filed electronically in accordance with the instructions applicable to such report, and such other guidance as the Secretary may provide. [Amended November 16, 2007 (72 FR 64710).]

(b) Nothing in paragraph (a) of this section is intended to alter or affect the duties of any person to retain records or to disclose information to participants, beneficiaries, or the Secretary. [Added July 21, 2006 by 71 FR 41368.]

[¶ 14,248B]

§2520.104a-3 **Summary plan description.** [Reserved.] [67 FR 771, 1/7/02.]

[¶ 14,248C]

§2520.104a-4 **Material modifications to the plan and changes in plan description information.** [Reserved.][67 FR 771, 1/7/02.]

[¶ 14,248D]

§2520.104a-5 **Annual reporting filing requirements.** (a) *Filing obligation.* Except as provided in §2520.104a-6, the administrator of an employee benefit plan required to file an annual report pursuant to

section 104(a)(1) of the Act shall file an annual report containing the items prescribed in §2520.103-1 within:

(1) [Removed and reserved by 67 FR 771, 1/7/02.]

(2) Seven months after the close of any plan year which begins after December 31, 1975, unless extended. See "When to file" instructions of the appropriate annual Return/Report Form. [Corrected April 4, 1978, by 43 FR 14010.]

(b) *Where to file.* The annual report described in §2520.103-1 shall be filed in accordance with and at the address provided in the instructions to the Annual Return/Report Form. [Added March 9, 1978, by 43 FR 10130. Revised by 67 FR 771, effective March 8, 2002.]

[¶ 14,248E]

§2520.104a-6 **Annual reporting for plans which are part of a group insurance arrangement.** (a) *General.* A trust or other entity described in §2520.104-43(b) that files an annual report in accordance with the terms of subsections (b) and (c) shall be deemed to have filed such report in accordance with §2520.104a-6 for purposes of §2520.104-43.

(b) *Date of filing.* The annual report shall be filed within:

(1) Eleven and one-half months after the close of the fiscal year of the trust or other entity described in §2520.104-43 which begins in 1975 or December 15, 1977, whichever is later; and

(2) Seven months after the close of the fiscal year of the trust or other entity which begins after December 31, 1975, unless extended. See "When to file" instructions of the appropriate Annual Return/Report Form. [Corrected April 4, 1978, by 43 FR 14010.]

(c) *Where to file.* The annual report prescribed in §2520.103-2 shall be filed in accordance with and at the address provided in the instructions to the Annual Return/Report Form. [Added March 9, 1978, by 43 FR 10130.]

[¶ 14,248F]

§2520.104a-7 **Summary of material modifications.** [Reserved.] [67 FR 771, 1/7/02.]

[¶ 14,248G]

§2520.104a-8 **Requirement to furnish documents to the Secretary of Labor on request.** (a) *In general.* (1) Under section 104(a)(6) of the Act, the administrator of an employee benefit plan subject to the provisions of part 1 of title I of the Act is required to furnish to the Secretary, upon request, any documents relating to the employee benefit plan. For purposes of section 104(a)(6) of the Act, the administrator of an employee benefit plan shall furnish to the Secretary, upon service of a written request, a copy of:

(i) The latest updated summary plan description (including any summaries of material modifications to the plan or changes in the information required to be included in the summary plan description); and

(ii) Any other document described in section 104(b)(4) of the Act with respect to which a participant or beneficiary has requested, in writing, a copy from the plan administrator and which the administrator has failed or refused to furnish to the participant or beneficiary.

(2) Multiple requests for document(s). Multiple requests under this section for the same or similar document or documents shall be considered separate requests for purposes of §2560.502c-6(a).

(b) For purposes of this section, a participant or beneficiary will include any individual who is:

(1) A participant or beneficiary within the meaning of ERISA sections 3(7) and 3(8), respectively;

(2) An alternate payee under a qualified domestic relations order (see ERISA section 206(d)(3)(K)) or prospective alternate payee (spouses, former spouses, children or other dependents);

(3) A qualified beneficiary under COBRA (see ERISA section 607(3)) or prospective qualified beneficiary (spouse or dependent child);

(4) An alternate recipient under a qualified medical child support order (see ERISA section 609(a)(2)(C)) or a prospective alternate recipient; or

(5) A representative of any of the foregoing.

(c) *Service of request.* Requests under this section shall be served in accordance with § 2560.502c-6(i).

(d) *Furnishing documents.* A document shall be deemed to be furnished to the Secretary on the date the document is received by the Department of Labor at the address specified in the request; or, if a document is delivered by certified mail, the date on which the document is mailed to the Department of Labor at the address specified in the request.

Subpart F—Disclosure Requirements

[¶ 14,249]

§ 2520.104b-1 **Disclosure.** (a) *General disclosure requirements.* The administrator of an employee benefit plan covered by Title I of the Act must disclose certain material, including reports, statements, notices, and other documents, to participants, beneficiaries and other specified individuals. Disclosure under Title I of the Act generally takes three forms. First, the plan administrator must, by direct operation of law, furnish certain material to all participants covered under the plan and beneficiaries receiving benefits under the plan (other than beneficiaries under a welfare plan) at stated times or if certain events occur. Second, the plan administrator must furnish certain material to individual participants and beneficiaries upon their request. Third, the plan administrator must make certain material available to participants and beneficiaries for inspection at reasonable times and places.

(b) *Fulfilling the disclosure obligation.* (1) Except as provided in paragraph (e) of this section, where certain material, including reports, statements, notices and other documents, is required under Title I of the Act, or regulations issued thereunder, to be furnished either by direct operation of law or on individual request, the plan administrator shall use measures reasonably calculated to ensure actual receipt of the material by plan participants, beneficiaries and other specified individuals. Material which is required to be furnished to all participants covered under the plan and beneficiaries receiving benefits under the plan (other than beneficiaries under a welfare plan) must be sent by a method or methods of delivery likely to result in full distribution. For example in-hand delivery to an employee at his or her worksite is acceptable. However, in no case is it acceptable merely to place copies of the material in a location frequented by participants. It is also acceptable to furnish such material as a special insert in a periodical distributed to employees such as a union newspaper or a company publication if the distribution list for the periodical is comprehensive and up-to-date and a prominent notice on the front page of the periodical advises readers that the issue contains an insert with important information about rights under the plan and the Act which should be read and retained for future reference. If some participants and beneficiaries are not on the mailing list, a periodical must be used in conjunction with other methods of distribution such that the methods taken together are reasonably calculated to ensure actual receipt.

Material distributed through the mail may be sent by first, second, or third-class mail. However, distribution by second or third-class mail is acceptable only if return and forwarding postage is guaranteed and address correction is requested. Any material sent by second or third-class mail which is returned with an address correction shall be sent again by first-class mail or personally delivered to the participant at his or her worksite.

(2) For purposes of section 104(b)(4) of the Act, materials furnished upon written request shall be mailed to an address provided by the requesting participant or beneficiary or personally delivered to the participant or beneficiary.

(3) For purposes of section 104(b)(2) of the Act, where certain documents are required to be made available for examination by participants and beneficiaries in the principal office of the plan administrator and in such other places as may be necessary to make available all pertinent information to all participants and beneficiaries, disclosure shall be made pursuant to the provisions of this paragraph.

Such documents must be current, readily accessible, and clearly identified, and copies must be available in sufficient number to accommodate the expected volume of inquiries. Plan administrators shall make copies of the latest annual report, and the bargaining agreement, trust agreement, contract, or other instruments under which the plan is established or operated available at all times in their principal offices. They are not required to maintain these plan documents at all times at each employer establishment or union hall or office as described in paragraphs (b)(3)(i), (ii), and (iii) of this section, but the documents must be made available at any such location within ten calendar days following the day on which a request for disclosure at that location is made.

Plan administrators shall make plan documents available at the appropriate employer establishment or union meeting hall or office within the required ten day period when a request is made directly to the plan administrator or through a procedure establishing reasonable rules governing the making of requests for examination of plan documents. If a plan administrator prescribes such a procedure and communicates it to plan participants and beneficiaries, a plan administrator will not be required to comply with a request made in a manner which does not conform to the established procedure. In order to comply with the requirements of this section, a procedure for making requests to examine plan documents must permit requests to be made in a reasonably convenient manner both directly to the plan administrator and at each employer establishment, or union meeting hall or office where documents must be made available in accordance with this paragraph. If no such reasonable procedure is established, a good faith effort by a participant or beneficiary to request examination of plan documents will be deemed a request to the plan administrator for purposes of this paragraph.

(i) In the case of a plan not maintained according to a collective bargaining agreement, including a plan maintained by a single employer with more than one establishment, a multiple employer plan, and a plan maintained by a controlled group of corporations (within the meaning of § 1563(a) of the Internal Revenue Code of 1954 (the Code), determined without regard to § 1563(a)(4) and (e)(3)(C) of the Code), documents shall be made available for examination in the principal office of the employer and at each employer establishment in which at least 50 participants covered under a plan are customarily working. "Establishment" means a single physical location where business is conducted or where services or industrial operations are performed. Where employees are engaged in activities which are physically dispersed, such as agriculture, construction, transportation, and communications, the "establishment" shall be the place to which employees report each day. When employees do not usually work at, or report to, a single establishment—for example, traveling salesmen, technicians, and engineers—the establishment shall be the location from which the employees customarily carry out their activities—for example the field office of an engineering firm servicing at least 50 participants covered under the plan.

(ii) In the case of a plan maintained solely by an employee organization, the plan administrator shall take measures to ensure that documents are available for examination at the meeting hall or office of each union local in which there are at least 50 participants covered under the plan. Such measures shall include distributing copies of the documents to each union local in which there are at least 50 participants covered under the plan.

(iii) In the case of a plan maintained according to a collective bargaining agreement, including a collectively bargained single employer plan with more than one establishment, a collectively bargained multiple employer plan, and a multiemployer plan which meets the definition of section 3(37) of the Act, § 2510.3-37 of this chapter, and section 414(b) of the Internal Revenue Code of 1954 and 26 CFR § 1.414(f) (40 CFR 43034), documents shall be made available for examination in the principal office of the employee organization and at each employer establishment in which at least 50 participants covered under the plan are customarily working. In employment situations where employees do not usually work at, or report to, a single establishment, the plan administrator shall take measures to ensure that plan documents are available for examination at the meeting hall or office of each union local in which there are at least 50 participants covered under the plan. [Revised by 67 FR 771, effective March 8, 2002. Revised by 67 FR 17263, April 9, 2002]

(c) *Disclosure through electronic media.* (1) Except as otherwise provided by applicable law, rule or regulation, the administrator of an employee benefit plan furnishing documents through electronic media is deemed to satisfy the requirements of paragraph (b)(1) of this section with respect to an individual described in paragraph (c)(2) if:

(i) The administrator takes appropriate and necessary measures reasonably calculated to ensure that the system for furnishing documents—

(A) Results in actual receipt of transmitted information (e.g., using return-receipt or notice of undelivered electronic mail features, conducting periodic reviews or surveys to confirm receipt of the transmitted information); and

(B) Protects the confidentiality of personal information relating to the individual's accounts and benefits (e.g., incorporating into the system measures designed to preclude unauthorized receipt of or access to such information by individuals other than the individual for whom the information is intended);

(ii) The electronically delivered documents are prepared and furnished in a manner that is consistent with the style, format and content requirements applicable to the particular document;

(iii) Notice is provided to each participant, beneficiary or other individual, in electronic or non-electronic form, at the time a document is furnished electronically, that apprises the individual of the significance of the document when it is not otherwise reasonably evident as transmitted (e.g., the attached document describes changes in the benefits provided by your plan) and of the right to request and obtain a paper version of such document; and

(iv) Upon request, the participant, beneficiary or other individual is furnished a paper version of the electronically furnished documents.

(2) Paragraph (c)(1) shall only apply with respect to the following individuals:

(i) A participant who—

(A) Has the ability to effectively access documents furnished in electronic form at any location where the participant is reasonably expected to perform his or her duties as an employee; and

(B) With respect to whom access to the employer's or plan sponsor's electronic information system is an integral part of those duties; or

(ii) A participant, beneficiary or any other person entitled to documents under Title I of the Act or regulations issued thereunder (including, but not limited to, an "alternate payee" within the meaning of section 206(d)(3) of the Act and a "qualified beneficiary" within the meaning of section 607(3) of the Act) who—

(A) Except as provided in paragraph (c)(2)(ii)(B) of this section, has affirmatively consented, in electronic or non-electronic form, to receiving documents through electronic media and has not withdrawn such consent;

(B) In the case of documents to be furnished through the Internet or other electronic communication network, has affirmatively consented or confirmed consent electronically, in a manner that reasonably demonstrates the individual's ability to access information in the electronic form that will be used to provide the information that is the subject of the consent, and has provided an address for the receipt of electronically furnished documents;

(C) Prior to consenting, is provided, in electronic or non-electronic form, a clear and conspicuous statement indicating:

(1) The types of documents to which the consent would apply;

(2) That consent can be withdrawn at any time without charge;

(3) The procedures for withdrawing consent and for updating the participant's, beneficiary's or other individual's address for receipt of electronically furnished documents or other information;

(4) The right to request and obtain a paper version of an electronically furnished document, including whether the paper version will be provided free of charge; and

(5) Any hardware and software requirements for accessing and retaining the documents; and

(D) Following consent, if a change in hardware or software requirements needed to access or retain electronic documents creates a material risk that the individual will be unable to access or retain electronically furnished documents:

(1) Is provided with a statement of the revised hardware or software requirements for access to and retention of electronically furnished documents;

(2) Is given the right to withdraw consent without charge and without the imposition of any condition or consequence that was not disclosed at the time of the initial consent; and

(3) Again consents, in accordance with the requirements of paragraph (c)(2)(ii)(A) or paragraph (c)(2)(ii)(B) of this section, as applicable, to the receipt of documents through electronic media.

This paragraph (c) applies on or after June 1, 1997. [Added by 62 FR 16979, April 8, 1997.] [Revised by 67 FR 17263, April 9, 2002.]

(d) *Participant and beneficiary status for purposes of sections 101(a) and 104(b)(1) of the Act and Subpart F of this part.*—See §§ 2510.3-3(d)(1), 2510.3-3(d)(2), and 2520.3-3(d)(3) of this chapter. (Approved by the Office of Management and Budget under control number 1210-0039.) [Added by 41 FR 16957, effective April 23, 1976. Amended by 62 FR 36205, effective June 1, 1997.]

(e) *Limitations.* This section does not apply to disclosures required under provisions of part 2 and part 3 of the Act over which the Secretary of the Treasury has interpretative and regulatory authority pursuant to Reorganization Plan No. 4 of 1978.

[Added by 67 FR 17263, April 9, 2002.]

[¶ 14,249A]

§ 2520.104b-2 **Summary plan description**. (a) *Obligation to furnish.* Under the authority of sections 104(b)(1) and 104(c) of the Act, the plan administrator of an employee benefit plan subject to the provisions of Part 1 of Title I shall furnish a copy of the summary plan description and a statement of ERISA rights as provided in § 2520.102-3(t), to each participant covered under the plan (as defined in § 2510.3-(d)), and each beneficiary receiving benefits under a pension plan on or before the later of:

(1) The date which is 90 days after the employee becomes a participant, or (in the case of a beneficiary receiving benefits under a pension plan) within 90 days after he or she first receives benefits, except as provided in § 2520.104b-4(a), or,

(2) Within 120 days after the plan becomes subject to Part 1 of Title I.

(3)(i) A plan becomes subject to Part 1 of Title I on the first day on which an employee is credited with an hour of service under § 2530.200b-2 or § 2530.200b-3. Where a plan is made prospectively effective to take effect after a certain date or after a condition is satisfied, the day upon which the plan becomes subject to Part 1 of Title I is the day after such date or condition is satisfied. Where a plan is adopted with a retroactive effective date, the 120 day period begins on the day after the plan is adopted. Where a plan is made retroactively effective dependent on a condition, the day on which the plan becomes subject to Part 1 of Title I is the day after the day on which the condition is satisfied. Where a plan is made retroactively effective subject to a contingency which may or may not occur in the future, the day on which the plan becomes subject to Part 1, Title I is the day after the day on which the contingency occurs.

(ii) *Examples*: Company A is negotiating the purchase of Company B. On September 1, 1978, as part of the negotiations, Company A adopts a pension plan covering the employees of Company B, contingent on the successful conclusion of its negotiations to purchase Company B. The plan provides that it shall take effect on the first day of the calendar year in which the purchase is concluded. On February 1, 1979, the negotiations conclude with Company A's purchase of Company B. The plan therefore becomes effective on February 1, 1979, retroactive to January 1, 1979. The summary plan description must be filed and disclosed no later than 120 days after February 1, 1979. [Amended by 42 FR 37178, effective July 19, 1977; amended and finalized by 45 FR 14029, effective April 3, 1980.]

(b) *Periods for furnishing updated summary plan description.* (1) For purposes of the requirement to furnish the updated summary plan description to each participant and each beneficiary receiving benefits under the plan (other than beneficiaries receiving benefits under a welfare plan) required by section 104(b)(1) of the Act, the administrator of an employee benefit plan shall furnish such updated summary plan description no later than 210 days following the end of the plan year within which occurs the later of—

(i) November 16, 1983, or

(ii) Five years after the last date a change in the information required to be disclosed by section 102 or 29 CFR 2520.102-3 would have been reflected in the most recently distributed summary plan description (or updated summary plan description), as described in section 102 of the Act.

(2) In the case of a plan to which no amendments have been made between the end of the time period covered by the last distributed summary plan description (or updated summary plan description), described in section 102 of the Act, and the next occurring applicable date described in paragraph (b)(1)(i) or (ii) of this section, for purposes of the requirement to furnish the updated summary plan description to each participant, and to each beneficiary receiving benefits under the plan (other than beneficiaries receiving benefits under a welfare plan), required by section 104(b)(1) of the Act, the administrator of an employee benefit plan shall furnish such updated summary plan description no later than 210 days following the end of the plan year within which occurs ten years after the last date a change in the information required to be disclosed by section 102 or 29 CFR 2520.102-3 would have beend reflected in the most recently distributed summary plan description (or updated summary plan description), as described in action 102 of the Act. [Paragraph (b) was amended on July 1, 1996 by 61 FR 33847.]

(c) *Alternative ERISA Notice requirements.* [Officially removed and reserved by 61 FR 33847 on 7/1/96.]

(d) *Use of form EBS-1 as summary plan description.* [Officially removed and reserved by 61 FR 33847 on 7/1/96.]

(e) *Disclosure obligation for plans which filed and disclosed by May 30, 1976 in reliance upon regulations of the Department.* [Officially removed and reserved by 61 FR 33847 on 7/1/96.]

(f) *Disclosure obligation for all other plans which previously disclosed the summary plan description.* [Officially removed and reserved by 61 FR 33847 on 7/1/96.]

(g) *Terminated plans.* (1) If, on or before the date by which a plan is required to furnish a summary plan description or updated summary plan description to participants and pension plan beneficiaries under this section, the plan has terminated within the meaning of paragraph (g)(2) of this section, the administrator of such plan is not required to furnish to participants covered under the plan or to beneficiaries receiving benefits under the plan a summary plan description.

(2) For purposes of this section, a plan shall be considered terminated if:

(i) in the case of an employee pension benefit plan, all distributions to participants and beneficiaries have been completed; and

(ii) in the case of an employee welfare benefit plan, no claims can be incurred which will result in a liability of the plan to pay benefits. A claim is incurred upon the occurrence of the event or condition from which the claim arises (whether or not discovered). [Revised by 67 FR 771, effective March 8, 2002.]

(h) *Alternative requirements for plans subject to the alternative ERISA Notice requirements.* [Officially removed and reserved by 61 FR 33847 on 7/1/96.]

(i) *Style and format of the summary plan description.* See §2520.102-2.

(j) *Contents of the summary plan description.* See §2520.102-3.

(k) *Option for different summary plan descriptions.* See §2520.102-4, §2520.104-26, and §2520.104-27.

(l) *Employee benefit plan—participant covered under a plan.* See §2510.3-3(d). [Added by 42 FR 14266, effective March 15, 1977; and amended by 42 FR 37178, effective July 19, 1977.]

§2520.104b-3 **Summary of material modifications to the plan and changes in the information required to be included in the summary plan description.** (a) The administrator of an employee benefit plan subject to the provisions of Part 1 of Title I of the Act shall, in accordance with §2520.104b-1(b), furnish a summary description of any material modification to the plan and any change in the information required by section 102(b) of the Act and §2520.102-3 of these regulations to be included in the summary plan description to each participant covered under the plan and each beneficiary receiving benefits under the plan. Except as provided in paragragh (d) of this section, the plan administrator shall furnish this summary, written in a manner calculated to be understood by the average plan participant, not later than 210 days after the close of the plan year in which the modification or change was adopted. This disclosure date is not affected by retroactive application to a prior plan year of an amendment which makes a material modification to the plan; a modification does not occur before it is adopted. For example, a calendar year plan adopts a modification in April 1978. The modification, by its terms, applies retroactively to the 1977 plan year. A summary description of the material modification is furnished on or before July 29, 1979. A plan which adopts an amendment which makes a material modification to the plan which takes effect on a date in the future must disclose a summary of that modification within 210 days after the close of the plan year in which the modification or change is adopted. Under the authority of sections 104(a)(3) and 110 of the Act, a summary description of a material modification or change is not required to be disclosed if it is rescinded or otherwise does not take effect. For example, a calendar year plan adopts a modification in June 1978. The modification, by its terms, becomes effective beginning in plan year 1979. Before the beginning of plan year 1979, the prospective modification is withdrawn. No summary of the material modification is required to be disclosed. [Amended 11/21/00 by 65 FR 70225.]

(b) The summary of material modifications to the plan or changes in information required to be included in the summary plan description need not be furnished separately if the changes or modifications are described in a timely summary plan description. For example, a calendar year plan adopts a material modification on June 3, 1976. The modification is incorporated in a summary plan description furnished on July 15, 1977. No separate summary of the material modification is furnished. The plan adopts another material modification September 15, 1977. A separate summary of the modification is furnished on or before July 29, 1978.

(c) The copy of the summary plan description furnished in accordance with §§2520.104b-2(a)(1)(i) and 2520.104b-4 shall be accompanied by all summaries of material modifications or changes in information required to be included in the summary plan description which have not been incorporated into that summary plan description.

(d) *Special rule for group health plans.* (1) *General.* Except as provided in paragraph (d)(2) of this section, the administrator of a group health plan, as defined in section 733(a)(1) of the Act, shall furnish to each participant covered under the plan a summary, written in a manner calculated to be understood by the average plan participant, of any modification to the plan or change in the information required to be included in the summary plan description, within the meaning of paragraph (a) of this section, that is a material reduction in covered services or benefits not later than 60 days after the date of adoption of the modification or change.

(2) *90-day alternative rule.* The administrator of a group health plan shall not be required to furnish a summary of any material reduction in covered services or benefits within the 60-day period described in paragraph (d)(1) of this section to any participant covered under the plan who would reasonably be expected to be furnished such summary in connection with a system of communication maintained by the plan sponsor or administrator, with respect to which plan participants are provided information concerning their plan, including modifications and changes thereto, at regular intervals of not more than 90 days and such communication otherwise meets the disclosure requirements of 29 CFR 2520.104b-1.

(3) *"Material reduction".* (i) For purposes of this paragraph (d), a "material reduction in covered services or benefits" means any modi-

fication to the plan or change in the information required to be included in the summary plan description that, independently or in conjunction with other contemporaneous modifications or changes, would be considered by the average plan participant to be an important reduction in covered services or benefits under the plan.

(ii) A "reduction in covered services or benefits" generally would include any plan modification or change that: eliminates benefits payable under the plan; reduces benefits payable under the plan, including a reduction that occurs as a result of a change in formulas, methodologies or schedules that serve as the basis for making benefit determinations; increases premiums, deductibles, coinsurance, copayments, or other amounts to be paid by a participant or beneficiary; reduces the service area covered by a health maintenance organization; establishes new conditions or requirements (e.g., preauthorization requirements) to obtaining services or benefits under the plan. [Added by 62 FR 16979, April 8, 1997. Amended 11/21/00 by 65 FR 70225. Corrected by PWBA on 7/2/01, 66 FR 34994.]

(e) *Applicability date.* Paragraph (d) of this section is applicable as of the first day of the first plan year beginning after June 30, 1997. [Added by 62 FR 16979, April 8, 1997. Amended 11/21/00 by 65 FR 70225.]

(f) *Alternative requirements for plans subject to alternative ERISA Notice requirements.* Reserved. [67 FR 771, 1/7/02.]

(g) *Filing obligation for all other plans which previously filed and disclosed the summary plan description.* Reserved. [67 FR 771, 1/7/02.]

[¶ 14,249C]

§ 2520.104b-4 Alternative methods of compliance for furnishing the summary plan description and summaries of material modifications of a pension plan to a retired participant, a separated participant with vested benefits, and a beneficiary receiving benefits. Under the authority of section 110 of the Act, in the case of an employee pension benefit plan—

(a) *Summary plan descriptions.* A plan administrator will be deemed to satisfy the requirements of section 104(b)(1) of the Act and § 2520.104b-2(a) to furnish a copy of the initial summary plan description to a retired participant, a beneficiary receiving benefits, or a separated participant with vested benefits ("vested separated participant") if, no earlier than the date stated in subparagraph (4) of this paragraph.

(1) In the case of a retired participant or a beneficiary receiving benefits, a document is furnished which—

(i) Meets the requirements of § § 2520.102-2 and 2520.102-3 except paragraphs (b)(3), (b)(4), (j), (k), (l), (n), (o), and (p);

(ii) Contains a statement that the benefit payment presently being received by the retired participant or beneficiary receiving benefits will continue in the same amount and for the period provided in the mode of settlement selected at retirement, and will not be changed except as described in subparagraph (iii); and

(iii) Contains a statement describing any plan provision under which the present benefit payment may be reduced, changed, terminated, forfeited, or suspended;

(2) In the case of a vested separated participant, a document is furnished which—

(i) Meets the requirements of § § 2520.102-2 and 2520.102-3 except paragraphs (b)(3), (b)(4), (j), (l), (n), (o), (p), and (r);

(ii)(A) If at or after separation, a separated vested participant was furnished a statement of the dollar amount of the vested benefit or the method of computation of the benefit, includes a statement that the dollar amount of the vested benefit was previously furnished and that a copy of the previously furnished statement of the dollar amount of such vested benefit or method of computation of the benefit may be obtained from the plan upon request;

(B) If the vested separate participant was not furnished a statement of the dollar amount of the vested benefit or the method of computation of the benefit, the plan furnishes either a statement of the dollar amount of the vested benefit, or a statement of the formula used to determine the dollar amount of the vested benefit;

(iii) Includes a statement of the form in which the benefits will be paid and duration of the payment period or a description of the optional modes of payment available under the plan; and

(iv) Includes a statement describing any plan provision under which a benefit may be reduced, changed, terminated, forfeited, or suspended; or

(3)(i) Such retired participant, vested separated participant, or beneficiary receiving benefits was furnished with a copy of a document which—

(A) Satisfies the requirements of section 102(a)(1) of the Act and § 2520.102-2 (relating to the style and format of the summary plan description) and § 2520.102-3 (relating to the content of the summary plan description);

(B) Describes the rights and obligations under the plan of such retired participant, vested separated participant, or beneficiary receiving benefits as of the date stated in subparagraph (4);

(ii) In the case of a person who retired, became a beneficiary, or separated with vested benefits before November 16, 1977, a document will be deemed to comply with the requirements of subparagraph (i) if the document omitted only information described in one or more of the provisions of § 2520.102-3 listed below, provided that a supplement containing such information, which meets the requirements of § 2520.102-2, is furnished to the retired participant, vested separated participant, or beneficiary receiving benefits by November 16, 1977.

(A) Employer identification number (EIN), as required by § 2520.102-3(c);

(B) Type of administration, as required by § 2520.102-3(e):

(C) Name of agent for service of legal process, as required by § 2520.102-3(g);

(D) Names and addresses of trustees, as required by § 2520.102-3(h);

(E) Statement regarding plan termination insurance as required by § 2520.102-3(m);

(F) Date of the end of the fiscal year, as required by § 2520.102-3(r); or

(G) Statement of ERISA rights, as required by § 2520.102-3(t).

(4) For purposes of this paragraph the dates are: for a vested separated participant, the date of separation; for a beneficiary, the date on which payment of benefits commences; and for a retired participant, the date of retirement.

(b) *Updated summary plan descriptions.* A copy of an updated summary plan description need not be furnished as prescribed in section 104(b)(1) of the Act and § 2520.104b-2(b) to a retired participant, vested separated participant, or a beneficiary receiving benefits if—

(1)(i) On or after the date stated in subparagraph (ii), the retired participant, vested separated participant, or beneficiary is furnished with a copy of the most recent summary plan description and a copy of any summaries of material modifications not incorporated in such summary plan description;

(ii) For purposes of subparagraph (i) the dates are: for a retired participant, the date of retirement; for a vested separated participant, the date of separation; and for a beneficiary, the date on which payment of benefits commences;

(2) No later than the date on which an updated summary plan description is furnished to participants and beneficiaries as prescribed by section 104(b)(1) of the Act and § 2520.104b-2(b), a retired participant, vested separated participant, or beneficiary receiving benefits is furnished a notice containing the following:

(i) A statement that the benefit rights of such retired participant, vested separated participant, or beneficiary receiving benefits are set forth in the earlier summary plan description and any subsequently furnished summaries of material modifications (see paragraph (c)), and

(ii) A statement that such retired participant, vested separated participant, or beneficiary receiving benefits may obtain a copy of the earlier summary plan description and summaries of material modifications described in subparagraph (i), and the updated summary plan description, without charge, upon request, from the plan administrator; and

(3) The plan administrator furnishes a copy of the documents described in subparagraph (2)(ii) to such retired participant, vested separated participant or beneficiary, without charge, upon request.

(c) *Summary of material modifications or changes.* A summary description of a material modification to the plan or a change in the information required to be included in the summary plan description need not be furnished to a retired participant, a vested separated participant or a beneficiary receiving benefits under the plan, within the time prescribed in section 104(b)(1) of the Act and § 2520.104b-3 for furnishing summary descriptions of such modifications and changes, if the material modification or change in no way affects such retired participant's, vested separated participant's, or beneficiary's rights under the plan. For example, a change in trustees is information which such a person may need to know in order to make inquiries about his or her rights expeditiously, and hence must be furnished. On the other hand, a modification in benefits under the plan to which such retired participant, vested separated participant, or beneficiary had not at any time been entitled (and would not in the future be entitled) would not affect his or her rights and hence need not be furnished. If such retired participant, vested separated participant, or beneficiay requests a copy of a summary description of a material modification or a change which was not furnished, the plan administrator shall furnish the copy, without charge.

(d) *Special rule for a plan which has previously furnished a summary plan description.* [Officially removed and reserved by 61 FR 33847 on 7/1/96.]

[¶ 14,249D]

§ 2520.104b-5 **ERISA Notice**. [Officially removed and reserved by 61 FR 33847 on 7/1/96.]

[¶ 14,249H]

§ 2520.104b-10 **Summary Annual Report**. (a) *Obligation to furnish.* Except as otherwise provided in paragraphs (g) of this section, the administrator of any employee benefit plan shall furnish annually to each participant of such plan and to each beneficiary receiving benefits under such plan (other than beneficiaries under a welfare plan) a summary annual report conforming to the requirements of this section. Such furnishing of the summary annual report shall take place in accordance with the requirements of § 2520.104b-1 of this part.

[Amended on July 20, 1982, by 47 FR 31871.]

(b) [Amended on July 20, 1982, by 47 FR 31871; reserved April 19, 2000 by 65 FR 21085.][REMOVED and RESERVED on April 19, 2000 by 65 FR 21805.]

(c) *When to furnish.* Except as otherwise provided in this paragraph (c), the summary annual report required by paragraph (a) of this section shall be furnished within nine months after the close of the plan year. [Amended on April 19, 2000 by 65 FR 21805.]

(1) In the case of a welfare plan described in § 2520.104-43 of this part, such furnishing shall take place within 9 months after the close of the fiscal year of the trust or other entity which files the annual report under § 2520.104a-6 of this part.

(2) When an extension of time in which to file an annual report has been granted by the Internal Revenue Service, such furnishing shall take place within 2 months after the close of the period for which the extension was granted.

[Amended on July 20, 1982, by 47 FR 31871.]

(d) *Contents, style and format.* Except as otherwise provided in this paragraph (d), the summary annual report furnished to participants and beneficiaries of an employee pension benefit plan pursuant to this section shall consist of a completed copy of the form prescribed in subparagraph (3) of this paragraph (d), and the summary annual report furnished to participants and beneficiaries of an employee welfare benefit plan pursuant to this section shall consist of a completed copy of the form prescribed in subparagraph (4) of this paragraph (d). The information used to complete the form shall be based upon information contained in the most recent annual report of the plan which is required to be filed in accordance with section 104(a)(1) of the Act.

(1) Any portion of the forms set forth in this paragraph (d) which is not applicable to the plan to which the summary annual report relates, or which would require information which is not required to be reported on the annual report of that plan, may be omitted.

(2) Where the plan administrator determines that additional explanation of any information furnished pursuant to this paragraph (d) is necessary to fairly summarize the annual report, such explanation shall be set forth following the completed form required by this paragraph (d) and shall be headed, "Additional Explanation."

(3) *Form for Summary Annual Report Relating to Pension Plans.*

Summary Annual Report for (name of plan)

This is a summary of the annual report for (name of plan and EIN) for (period covered by this report). The annual report has been filed with the Employee Benefits Security Administration, as required under the Employee Retirement Income Security Act of 1974 (ERISA). [Corrected by DOL, 65 FR 35568, June 5, 2000. Amended by EBSA, 68 FR 16399, April 3, 2003.]

Basic Financial Statement

Benefits under the plan are provided by (indicate funding arrangements). Plan expenses were ($). These expenses included ($) in administrative expenses and ($) in benefits paid to participants and beneficiaries, and ($) in other expenses. A total of (   ) persons were participants in or beneficiaries of the plan at the end of the plan year, although not all of these persons had yet earned the right to receive benefits. [Amended on April 19, 2000 by 65 FR 21805.]

[If the plan is funded other than solely by allocated insurance contracts:]

The value of plan assets, after subtracting liabilities of the plan, was ($) as of (the end of the plan year), compared to ($) as of (the beginning of the plan year). During the plan year the plan experienced an (increase) (decrease) in its net assets of ($). This (increase) (decrease) includes unrealized appreciation or depeciation in the value of plan assets; that is, the difference between the value of the plan's assets at the end of the year and the value of the assets at the beginning of the year or the cost of assets acquired during the year. The plan had total income of ($), including employer contributions of ($), employee contributions of ($), (gains) (losses) of ($), from the sale of assets, and earnings from investments of ($).

[If any funds are used to purchase allocated insurance contracts:]

The plan has (a) contract(s) with (name of insurance carrier(s)) which allocate(s) funds toward (state whether individual policies, group deferred annuities or other). The total premiums paid for the plan year ending (date) were ($).

[Officially corrected May 31, 1979, and published in the *Federal Register* of June 1, 1979 (44 FR 31640).]

Minimum Funding Standards

[If the plan is a defined benefit plan:]

An actuary's statement shows that (enough money was contributed to the plan to keep it funded in accordance with the minimum funding standards of ERISA) (not enough money was contributed to the plan to keep it funded in accordance with the minimum funding standards of ERISA. The amount of the deficit was $).

[If the plan is a defined contribution plan covered by funding requirements:]

(Enough money was contributed to the plan to keep it funded in accordance with the minimum funding standards of ERISA) (Not enough money was contributed to the plan to keep it funded in accordance with the minimum funding standards of ERISA. The amount of the deficit was $).

Your Rights to Additional Information

You have the right to receive a copy of the full annual report, or any part thereof, on request. The items listed below are included in that report: [*Note*—list only those items which are actually included in the latest annual report]

1. an accountant's report; [Amended on April 19, 2000 by 65 FR 21805.]

2. financial information and information on payments to service providers; [Amended on April 19, 2000 by 65 FR 21805.]

3. assets held for investment; [Amended on April 19, 2000 by 65 FR 21805.]

4. fiduciary information, including non-exempt transactions between the plan and parties-in-interest (that is, persons who have certain relationships with the plan); [Amended on April 19, 2000 by 65 FR 21805.]

5. loans or other obligations in default or classified as uncollectible; [Amended on April 19, 2000 by 65 FR 21805.]

6. leases in default or classified as uncollectible; [Amended on April 19, 2000 by 65 FR 21805.]

7. transactions in excess of 5 percent of the plan assets; [Amended on April 19, 2000 by 65 FR 21805.]

8. insurance information including sales commissions paid by insurance carriers; [Amended on April 19, 2000 by 65 FR 21805.]

9. information regarding any common or collective trusts, pooled separate accounts; master trusts or 103-12 investment entities in which the plan participates, and [Added on April 19, 2000 by 65 FR 21805.]

10. actuarial information regarding the funding of the plan.

To obtain a copy of the full annual report, or any part thereof, write or call the office of (name), who is (state title: e.g., the plan administrator), (business address and telephone number). The charge to cover copying costs will be ($) for the full annual report, or ($) per page for any part thereof. [Added on April 19, 2000 by 65 FR 21805.]

You also have the right to receive from the plan administrator, on request and at no charge, a statement of the assets and liabilities of the plan and accompanying notes, or a statement of income and expenses of the plan and accompanying notes, or both. If you request a copy of the full annual report from the plan administrator, these two statements and accompanying notes will be included as part of that report. The charge to cover copying costs given above does not include a charge for the copying of these portions of the report because these portions are furnished without charge.

You also have the legally protected right to examine the annual report at the main office of the plan (address   ), (at any other location where the report is available for examination), and at the U.S. Department of Labor in Washington, D.C., or to obtain a copy from the U.S. Department of Labor upon payment of copying costs. Requests to the Department should be addressed to: Public Disclosure Room, Room N-1513, Employee Benefits Security Administration, U.S. Department of Labor, 200 Constitution Avenue, N.W., Washington, D.C. 20210. [Corrected by DOL, 65 FR 35568, June 5, 2000. Amended by EBSA, 68 FR 16399, April 3, 2003.]

(4) *Form for Summary Annual Report Relating to Welfare Plans*

Summary Annual Report for (name of plan)

This is a summary of the annual report of the (name of plan, EIN and type of welfare plan) for (period covered by this report). The annual report has been filed with the Employee Benefits Security Administration as required under the Employee Retirement Income Security Act of 1974 (ERISA).[Corrected by DOL, 65 FR 35568, June 5, 2000. Amended by EBSA, 68 FR 16399, April 3, 2003.]

[If any benefits under the plan are provided on an uninsured basis:]

(Name of sponsor) has committed itself to pay (all, certain) (state type of) claims incurred under the terms of the plan.

[If any of the funds are used to purchase insurance contracts:]

Insurance Information

The plan has (a) contract(s) with (name of insurance carrier(s) to pay (all, certain) (state type of) claims incurred under the terms of the plan. The total premiums paid for the plan year ending (date   ) were ($).

[If applicable add:]

Because (it is a) (they are) so called "experience-rated" contract(s), the premium costs are affected by, among other things, the number and size of claims. Of the total insurance premiums paid for the plan year ending (date), the premiums paid under such "experience-rated" contract(s) were ($) and the total of all benefit claims paid under the(se) experience-rated contract(s) during the plan year was ($).

[If any funds of the plan are held in trust or in a separately maintained fund:]

Basic Financial Statement

The value of plan assets, after subtracting liabilities of the plan, was ($) as of (the end of plan year), compared to ($) as of (the beginning of the plan year). During the plan year the plan experienced an (increase) (decrease) in its net assets of ($). This (increase) (decrease) includes unrealized appreciation or depreciation in the value of plan assets; that is, the difference between the value of the plan's assets at the end of the year and the value of the assets at the beginning of the year or the cost of assets acquired during the year. During the plan year, the plan had total income of ($) including employer contributions of ($), employee contributions of ($), realized (gains) (losses) of ($) from the sale of assets, and earnings from investments of ($).

Plan expenses were ($). These expenses included ($) in administrative expenses, ($) in benefits paid to participants and beneficiaries, and ($) in other expenses.

[Officially corrected on May 31, 1979, and published in the *Federal Register* of June 1, 1979 (44 FR 31640).]

Your Rights to Additional Information

You have the right to receive a copy of the full annual report, or any part thereof, on request. The items listed below are included in that report: [Note—list only those items which are actually included in the latest annual report]

1. an accountant's report; [Amended on April 19, 2000 by 65 FR 21805.]

2. financial information and information on payments to service providers; [Amended on April 19, 2000 by 65 FR 21805.]

3. assets held for investment; [Amended on April 19, 2000 by 65 FR 21805.]

4. fiduciary information, including non-exempt transactions between the plan and parties-in-interest (that is, persons who have certain relationships with the plan); [Amended on April 19, 2000 by 65 FR 21805.]

5. loans or other obligations in default or classified as uncollectible; [Amended on April 19, 2000 by 65 FR 21805.]

6. leases in default or classified as uncollectible; [Amended on April 19, 2000 by 65 FR 21805.]

7. transactions in excess of 5 percent of the plan assets; [Amended on April 19, 2000 by 65 FR 21805.]

8. insurance information including sales commissions paid by insurance carriers; and [Added on April 19, 2000 by 65 FR 21805.]

9. information regarding any common or collective trusts, pooled separate accounts, master trusts or 103-12 investment entities in which the plan participates. [Added on April 19, 2000 by 65 FR 21805.]

To obtain a copy of the full annual report, or any part thereof, write or call the office of (name), who is (state title: e.g., the plan administrator), (business address and telephone number). The charge to cover copying costs will be ($) for the full annual report, or ($) per page for any part thereof.

You also have the right to receive from the plan administrator, on request and at no charge, a statement of the assets and liabilities of the plan and accompanying notes, or a statement of income and expenses of the plan and accompanying notes, or both. If you request a copy of the full annual report from the plan administrator, these two statements and accompanying notes will be included as part of that report. The charge to cover copying costs given above does not include a charge for the copying of these portions of the report because these portions are furnished without charge.

You also have the legally protected right to examine the annual report at the main office of the plan (address), (at any other location where the report is available for examination), and at the U.S. Department of Labor in Washington, D.C. or to obtain a copy from the U.S. Department of Labor upon payment of copying costs. Requests to the Department should be addressed to: Public Disclosure Room, Room N1513, Employee Benefits Security Administration, U.S. Department of Labor, 200 Constitution Avenue, N.W., Washington, D.C. 20210. [Amended April 19, 2000 by 65 FR 21085. Amended by EBSA, 68 FR 16399, April 3, 2003.]

(e) *Foreign languages.* In the case of either—

(1) A plan which covers fewer than 100 participants at the beginning of a plan year in which 25 percent or more of all plan participants are literate only in the same non-English language; or

(2) A plan which covers 100 or more participants in which 500 or more participants or 10 percent or more of all plan participants, whichever is less, are literate only in the same non-English language—

The plan administrator for such plan shall provide these participants with an English-language summary annual report which prominently displays a notice, in the non-English language common to these participants, offering them assistance. The assistance provided need not involve written materials, but shall be given in the non-English language common to these participants. The notice offering assistance

Sec. 2520.104b-10 Summary Annual Report.

shall clearly set forth any procedures participants must follow to obtain such assistance.

[Amended on July 20, 1982, by 47 FR 31871; amended April 19, 2000 by 65 FR 21085.]

(f) *Furnishing of additional documents to participants and beneficiaries.* A plan administrator shall promptly comply with any request by a participant or beneficiary for additional documents made in accordance with the procedures or rights described in paragraph (d) of this section.

[Amended on July 20, 1982, by 47 FR 31871; amended April 19, 2000 by 65 FR 21085.]

(g) *Exemptions.* Notwithstanding the provisions of this section, a summary annual report is not required to be furnished with respect to the following:

(1) A totally unfunded welfare plan described in 29 CFR 2520.104-44(b)(1)(i); [Added by 44 FR 19400, effective June 5, 1979.]

(2) A welfare plan which meets the requirements of 29 CFR 2520.104-20(b); [Added by 44 FR 19400.]

(3) An apprenticeship or other training plan which meets the requirements of 29 CFR 2520.104-22; [Added by 44 FR 19400.]

(4) A pension plan for selected employees which meets the requirements of 29 CFR 2520.104-23; [Added by 44 FR 19400.]

(5) A welfare plan for selected employees which meets the requirements of 29 CFR 2520.104-24; [Added by 44 FR 19400.]

(6) A day care center referred to in 29 CFR 2520.104-25; [Added by 44 FR 19400.]

(7) A dues financed welfare plan which meets the requirements of 29 CFR 2520.104-26; [Added by 44 FR 19400 and amended 2/2/2015 (80 FR 5625).]

(8) A dues financed pension plan which meets the requirements of 29 CFR 2520.104-27; and [Added by 44 FR 19400 and amended 2/2/2015 (80 FR 5625).]

(9) A plan to which title IV of the Act applies. [Added 2/2/2015 (80 FR 5625).]

* * *

Appendix to § 2520.104b-10 - The Summary Annual Report (SAR) Under ERISA: A Cross-Reference to the Annual Report

SAR Item	Form 5500 Large Plan Filer Line Items	Form 5500 Small Plan Filer Line Items	Form 5500-SF Filer Line Items
A. PENSION PLAN			
1. Funding arrangement	Form 5500-9a	Same	Not applicable
2. Total plan expenses	Sch. H - 2j	Sch. I-2j	Line 8h
3. Administrative expenses	Sch. H - 2i(5)	Sch. I - 2h	Line 8f
4. Benefits paid	Sch. H - 2e(4)	Sch. I - 2e	Line 8d
5. Other expenses	Sch. H - Subtract the sum of 2e(4) & 2i(5) from 2j	Sch. I - 2i	Line 8g
6. Total participants	Form 5500 - 6f	Same	Line 5b
7. Value of plan assets (net):			
a. End of plan year	Sch. H - 11 [Col. (b)]	Sch. I - 1c [Col. (b)]	Line 7c [Col. (b)]
b. Beginning of plan year	Sch. H - 11 [Col. (a)]	Sch. I - 1c [Col. (a)]	Line 7c [Col. (a)]
8. Change in net assets	Sch. H - Subtract 11 [Col. (a)] from 11 [Col. (b)]	Sch. I - Subtract 1c [Col. (a) from Col. (b)]	Line 7c - Subtract Col. (a) from Col. (b)
9. Total income	Sch. H - 2d	Sch. I - 2d	Line 8c
a. Employer contributions	Sch. H - 2a(1)(A) & 2a(2) if applicable	Sch. I - 2a(1) & 2b if applicable	Line 8a(1) if applicable
b. Employee contributions	Sch. H - 2a(1)(B) & 2a(2) if applicable	Sch. I - 2a(2) & 2b if applicable	Line 8a(2) & 8a(3) if applicable
c. Gains (losses) from sale of assets	Sch. H - 2b(4)(C)	Not applicable	Not applicable
d. Earnings from investments	Sch. H - Subtract the sum of 2a(3), 2b(4)(C) and 2c from 2d	Sch. I -2c	Line 8b
10. Total insurance premiums	Total of all Schs. A - 6b	Total of all Schs. A - 6b	Not applicable
11. Unpaid minimum required contribution (S-E plans) or Funding deficiency (ME plans):			
a. S-E Defined benefit plans	Sch. SB-39	Same	Same
b. ME Defined benefit plans	Sch. MB-10	Same	Not applicable
c. Defined contribution plans	Sch. R - 6c, if more than zero	Same	Line 12d
B. WELFARE PLAN			
1. Name of insurance carrier	All Schs. A - 1(a)	Same	Not applicable
2. Total (experience rated and non-experienced rated) insurance premiums	All Schs. A - Sum of 9a(1) and 10a	Same	Not applicable
3. Experience rated premiums	All Schs. A - 9a(1)	Same	Not applicable
4. Experience rated claims	All Schs. A-9b(4)	Same	Not applicable
5. Value of plan assets (net):			
a. End of plan year	Sch. H - 11 [Col. (b)]	Sch. I - 1c [Col. (b)]	Line 7c [Col. (b)]
b. Beginning of plan year	Sch. H - 11 [Col. (a)]	Sch. I-1c [Col. (a)]	Line 7c [Col. (a)]
6. Change in net assets	Sch. H - Subtract 11 [Col. (a)] from 11 [Col. (b)]	Sch. I - Subtract 1c [Col. (a)] from 1c [Col. (b)]	Line 7c - Subtract [Col. (a)] from 7c [Col. (b)]
7. Total income	Sch. H - 2d	Sch. I - 2d	Line 8c
a. Employer contributions	Sch. H - 2a(1)(A) & 2a(2) if applicable	Sch. I - 2a(1) & 2b if applicable	Line 8a(1) if applicable
b. Employee contributions	Sch. H - 2a(1)(B) & 2a(2) if applicable	Sch. I - 2a(2) & 2b if applicable	Line 8a(2) if applicable
c. Gains (losses) from sale of assets.	Sch. H - 2b(4)(C)	Not applicable	Not applicable
d. Earnings from investments	Sch. H - Subtract the sum of 2a(3), 2b(4)(C) and 2c from 2d	Sch. I - 2c	Line 8b
8. Total plan expenses	Sch. H - 2j	Sch. I-2j	Line 8h
9. Administrative expenses	Sch. H - 2i(5)	Sch. I - 2h	Line 8f
10. Benefits paid	Sch. H - 2e(4)	Sch. I - 2e	Line 8d
11. Other expenses	Sch. H - Subtract the sum of 2e(4) & 2i(5) from 2j	Sch. I-2i	Line 8g

[44 FR 19403, April 3, 1979, as amended by 44 FR 31640, June 1, 1979, by 47 FR 31871 on July 20, 1982, and by 54 FR 8624 on March 1, 1989; amended April 19, 2000 by 65 FR 21085; amended April 3, 2003 by 68 FR 16399; amended November 16, 2007 (72 FR 64710).]

Temporary Regulations

The temporary and proposed Reg. § 2520.104b-12 was filed with the *Federal Register* on February 9, 1977, and published in the *Federal Register* on February 11, 1977. It is effective upon publication in the *Federal Register*.

[¶ 14,249K]

§ 2520.104b-12 Summary Annual Report for 1975 Plan Year— Optional Method of Distribution for Certain Multiemployer Plans. [Removed and reserved by 61 FR 33847 on 7/1/96.]

Regulations

Reg. § 2520.104b-30 was added by 41 FR 16957, effective April 23, 1976, and amended by 75 FR 9334, effective April 1, 2010.

[¶ 14,249Z]

§ 2520.104b-30 Charges for documents. (a) *Application.* The plan administrator of an employee benefit plan may impose a reasonable charge to cover the cost of furnishing to participants and beneficiaries upon their written request as required under section 104(b)(4) of the Act, copies of the following information, statements or documents: The latest updated summary plan description, and the latest annual report, any terminal report, the bargaining agreement, trust agreement, contract, or other instruments under which the plan is established or operated. Except where explicitly permitted under the Act, no charge may be assessed for furnishing information, statements or documents as required by other provisions of the Act, which include, in part 1 of title I, sections 104(b)(1), (2), (3) and (c) and 105(a) and (c). [Amended 3/2/10 by 75 FR 9334.]

(b) *Reasonableness.* The charge assessed by the plan administrator to cover the costs of furnishing documents is reasonable if it is equal to the actual cost per page to the plan for the least expensive means of acceptable reproduction, but in no event may such charge exceed 25 cents per page. For example, if a plan printed a large number of pamphlets at $1.00 per 50-page pamphlet, the actual cost of reproduction for the entire pamphlet ($1.00) would be equal to 2 cents per page. If only one page of such a pamphlet were requested, the actual cost of providing that page from the printed copy would be $1.00, since the copy would no longer be complete. In such a case, the least expensive means of acceptable reproduction would be individually reproducing the page requested at a charge of no more than 25 cents. On the other hand, if six pages of the same plan document were requested and each page cost 20 cents to be reproduced, the actual cost of providing those pages would be $1.20. In such a case, if a printed copy is available, the least expensive means of acceptable reproduction would be to use pages from the printed copy at a charge of no more than $1.00. No other charge for furnishing documents, such as handling or postage charges, will be deemed reasonable. The plan administrator shall provide information to a plan participant or beneficiary, upon request, about the charge that would be made to provide a copy of material described in this paragraph. [Added by 41 FR 16957, effective April 23, 1976.]

[¶ 14,250]
REPORTING OF PARTICIPANT'S BENEFIT RIGHTS

Act Sec. 105.(a) REQUIREMENTS TO PROVIDE PENSION BENEFIT STATEMENTS.—

(1) REQUIREMENTS.—

(A) INDIVIDUAL ACCOUNT PLAN. —The administrator of an individual account plan (other than a one-participant retirement plan described in section 101(i)(8)(B)) shall furnish a pension benefit statement—

(i) at least once each calendar quarter to a participant or beneficiary who has the right to direct the investment of assets in his or her account under the plan,

(ii) at least once each calendar year to a participant or beneficiary who has his or her own account under the plan but does not have the right to direct the investment of assets in that account, and

(iii) upon written request to a plan beneficiary not described in clause (i) or (ii).

(B) DEFINED BENEFIT PLAN. —The administrator of a defined benefit plan (other than a one-participant retirement plan described in section 101(i)(8)(B)) shall furnish a pension benefit statement—

(i) at least once every 3 years to each participant with a nonforfeitable accrued benefit and who is employed by the employer maintaining the plan at the time the statement is to be furnished, and

(ii) to a participant or beneficiary of the plan upon written request.

Information furnished under clause (i) to a participant may be based on reasonable estimates determined under regulations prescribed by the Secretary, in consultation with the Pension Benefit Guaranty Corporation.

(2) STATEMENTS.—

(A) IN GENERAL. —A pension benefit statement under paragraph (1)—

(i) shall indicate, on the basis of the latest available information—

(I) the total benefits accrued, and

(II) the nonforfeitable pension benefits, if any, which have accrued, or the earliest date on which benefits will become nonforfeitable,

(ii) shall include an explanation of any permitted disparity under section 401(l) of the Internal Revenue Code of 1986 or any floor-offset arrangement that may be applied in determining any accrued benefits described in clause (i),

(iii) shall be written in a manner calculated to be understood by the average plan participant, and

(iv) may be delivered in written, electronic, or other appropriate form to the extent such form is reasonably accessible to the participant or beneficiary.

(B) ADDITIONAL INFORMATION. In the case of an individual account plan, any pension benefit statement under clause (i) or (ii) of paragraph (1)(A) shall include—

(i) the value of each investment to which assets in the individual account have been allocated, determined as of the most recent valuation date under the plan, including the value of any assets held in the form of employer securities, without regard to whether such securities were contributed by the plan sponsor or acquired at the direction of the plan or of the participant or beneficiary, and

(ii) in the case of a pension benefit statement under paragraph (1)(A)(i)—

(I) an explanation of any limitations or restrictions on any right of the participant or beneficiary under the plan to direct an investment,

(II) an explanation, written in a manner calculated to be understood by the average plan participant, of the importance, for the long-term retirement security of participants and beneficiaries, of a well-balanced and diversified investment portfolio, including a statement of the risk that holding more than 20 percent of a portfolio in the security of one entity (such as employer securities) may not be adequately diversified, and

(III) a notice directing the participant or beneficiary to the Internet website of the Department of Labor for sources of information on individual investing and diversification.

(C) ALTERNATIVE NOTICE. —The requirements of subparagraph (A)(i)(II) are met if, at least annually and in accordance with requirements of the Secretary, the plan—

(i) updates the information described in such paragraph which is provided in the pension benefit statement, or

(ii) provides in a separate statement such information as is necessary to enable a participant or beneficiary to determine their nonforfeitable vested benefits.

(3) DEFINED BENEFIT PLANS.—

(A) ALTERNATIVE NOTICE. —In the case of a defined benefit plan, the requirements of paragraph (1)(B)(i) shall be treated as met with respect to a participant if at least once each year the administrator provides to the participant notice of the availability of the pension benefit statement and the ways in which the participant may obtain such statement. Such notice may be delivered in written, electronic, or other appropriate form to the extent such form is reasonably accessible to the participant.

(B) YEARS IN WHICH NO BENEFITS ACCRUE. —The Secretary may provide that years in which no employee or former employee benefits (within the meaning of section 410(b) of the Internal Revenue Code of 1986) under the plan need not be taken into account in determining the 3-year period under paragraph (1)(B)(i).

Act Sec. 105. (b) LIMITATION ON NUMBER OF STATEMENTS.—In no case shall a participant or beneficiary of a plan be entitled to more than 1 statement described in subparagraph (A)(iii) or (B)(ii) of subsection (a)(1), whichever is applicable, in any 12-month period.

Act Sec. 105. (c) INDIVIDUAL STATEMENT FURNISHED BY ADMINISTRATOR TO PARTICIPANTS SETTING FORTH INFORMATION IN ADMINISTRATOR'S INTERNAL REVENUE REGISTRATION STATEMENT AND NOTIFICATION OF FORFEITABLE BENEFITS.—Each administrator required to register under section 6057 of the Internal Revenue Code of 1986 shall, before the expiration of the time prescribed for such registration, furnish to each participant described in subsection (a)(2)(C) of such section, an individual statement setting forth the information with respect to such participant required to be contained in the registration statement required by section 6057(a)(2) of such Code. Such statement shall also include a notice to the participant of any benefits which are forfeitable if the participant dies before a certain date.

Amendments

P.L. 109-280, Sec. 508(a)(1):

Amended ERISA Sec.105(a) to read as above. For the effective date, see Act Sec. 508(c), below.

Prior to amendment, ERISA Sec. 105(a) read as follows:

(a) STATEMENT FURNISHED BY ADMINISTRATOR TO PARTICIPANTS AND BENEFICIARIES—Each administrator of an employee pension benefit plan shall furnish to any plan participant or beneficiary who so requests in writing, a statement indicating, on the basis of the latest available information—

(1) the total benefits accrued, and

(2) the nonforfeitable pension benefits, if any, which have accrued, or the earliest date on which benefits will become nonforfeitable.

P.L. 109-280, Sec. 508(a)(2)(A):

Amended ERISA Sec. 105 by striking subsection (d). For the effective date, see Act Sec. 508(c), below.

Prior to repeal, ERISA Sec. 105(d) read as follows:

(d) PLANS TO WHICH MORE THAN ONE UNAFFILIATED EMPLOYER IS REQUIRED TO CONTRIBUTE; REGULATIONS–Subsection (a) of this section shall apply to a plan to which more than one unaffiliated employer is required to contribute only to the extent provided in regulations prescribed by the Secretary in coordination with the Secretary of the Treasury.

P.L. 109-280, Sec. 508(a)(2)(B):

Amended ERISA Sec. 105(b) to read as above. For the effective date, see Act Sec. 508(c), below.

Prior to amendment, ERISA Sec. 105(b) read as follows:

(b) ONE-PER-YEAR LIMIT ON REPORTS. In no case shall a participant or beneficiary be entitled under this section to receive more than one report described in subsection (a) during any one 12-month period.

P.L. 109-280, Sec. 508(c):

(c) EFFECTIVE DATE.—

(1) IN GENERAL.—The amendments made by this section shall apply to plan years beginning after December 31, 2006.

(2) SPECIAL RULES FOR COLLECTIVELY BARGAINED AGREEMENTS.—In the case of a plan maintained pursuant to 1 or more collective bargaining agreements

between employee representatives and 1 or more employers ratified on or before the date of the enactment of this Act, paragraph (1) shall be applied to benefits pursuant to, and individuals covered by, any such agreement by substituting for "December 31, 2006" the earlier of—

(A) the later of—

(i) December 31, 2007, or

(ii) the date on which the last of such collective bargaining agreements terminates (determined without regard to any extension thereof after such date of enactment), or

(B) December 31, 2008.

P.L. 101-239, §7891(a)(1):

Titles I, III, and IV of ERISA (other than sections 3(37)(E), 301(a)(7), and 308, the last sentence of section 408(d), and sections 414(c), 4001(a)(3)(ii), and 4303) are each amended by striking "Internal Revenue Code of 1954" each place it appears and inserting "Internal Revenue Code of 1986," effective October 22, 1986.

P.L. 101-239, §7894(b)(5):

Amended ERISA Sec. 105(b) by striking "12 month" and inserting "12-month," effective September 2, 1974.

P.L. 98-397, §106

Act Sec. 106 amended ERISA Sec. 105(c) by adding the last sentence at the end thereof.

The above amendment applies to plan years beginning after December 31, 1984.

However, Act Sec. 302(b) provides:

(b) Special Rule for Collective Bargaining Agreements.—In the case of a plan maintained pursuant to 1 or more collective bargaining agreements between employee representatives and 1 or more employers ratified before the date of enactment of this Act, except as provided in subsection (d) or section 303, the amendments made by this Act shall not apply to plan years beginning before the earlier of—(1) the date on which the last of the collective bargaining agreements relating to the plan terminates (determined without regard to any extension thereof agreed to after the date of the enactment of this Act), or

(2) January 1, 1987.

For purposes of paragraph (1), any plan amendment made pursuant to a collective bargaining agreement relating to the plan which amends the plan solely to conform to any requirement added by title I or II shall not be treated as a termination of such collective bargaining agreement.

[¶14,260]
REPORTS MADE PUBLIC INFORMATION

Act Sec. 106.(a) Except as provided in subsection (b), the contents of the annual reports, statements, and other documents filed with the Secretary pursuant to this part shall be public information and the Secretary shall make any such information and data available for inspection in the public document room of the Department of Labor. The Secretary may use the information and data for statistical and research purposes, and compile and publish such studies, analyses, reports, and surveys based thereon as he may deem appropriate.

Act Sec. 106. (b) Information described in sections 105(a) and 105(c) with respect to a participant may be disclosed only to the extent that information respecting that participant's benefits under title II of the Social Security Act may be disclosed under such Act.

Amendment

P.L. 105-34, §1503(d)(4):

Amended ERISA Sec. 106(a) by striking "descriptions," effective August 5, 1997.

P.L. 101-239, §7894(b)(6):

Amended ERISA Sec. 106(b) by striking "section" and inserting "sections" effective September 2, 1974.

[¶ 14,270]
RETENTION OF RECORDS

Act Sec. 107. Every person subject to a requirement to file any report (including the documents described in subparagraphs (E) through (I) of section 101(k)) or to certify any information therefor under this title or who would be subject to such a requirement but for an exemption or simplified reporting requirement under section 104(a)(2) or (3) of this title shall maintain a copy of such report and records on the matters of which disclosure is required which will provide in sufficient detail the necessary basic information and data from which the documents thus required may be verified, explained, or clarified, and checked for accuracy and completeness, and shall include vouchers, worksheets, receipts, and applicable resolutions, and shall keep such records available for examination for a period of not less than six years after the filing date of the documents based on the information which they contain, or six years after the date on which such documents would have been filed but for an exemption or simplified reporting requirement under section 104(a)(2) or (3).

Amendment

P.L. 113-235, § 111(c)(1)-(2), Div. O:

Amended ERISA Sec. 107 by inserting "(including the documents described in subparagraphs (E) through (I) of section 101(k))" after "file any report" and by inserting "a copy of such report and" after "shall maintain".

The above amendments apply to plan years beginning after December 31, 2014.

P.L. 105-34, § 1503(d)(5):

Amended ERISA Sec. 107 by striking "description or" effective August 5, 1997.

Regulations

The following regulations under Code Section 107 were adopted under document number RIN 1210-AA71 under the title "Final Rules Relating to Use of Electronic Communication and Recordkeeping Technologies by Employee Pension and Welfare Benefit Plans". The regulation was filed with the Federal Register on April 8, 2002 and published on April 9, 2002 (67 FR 17264).

[¶ 14,270B]
Subpart G - Recordkeeping Requirements

Sec. 2520.107-1 Use of electronic media for maintenance and retention of records.—(a) *Scope and purpose.* Sections 107 and 209 of the Employee Retirement Income Security Act of 1974, as amended (ERISA), contain certain requirements relating to the maintenance of records for reporting and disclosure purposes and for determining the pension benefits to which participants and beneficiaries are or may become entitled. This section provides standards applicable to both pension and welfare plans concerning the use of electronic media for the maintenance and retention of records required to be kept under sections 107 and 209 of ERISA.

(b) *General requirements.* The record maintenance and retention requirements of sections 107 and 209 of ERISA are satisfied when using electronic media if: (1) The electronic recordkeeping system has reasonable controls to ensure the integrity, accuracy, authenticity and reliability of the records kept in electronic form;

(2) The electronic records are maintained in reasonable order and in a safe and accessible place, and in such manner as they may be readily inspected or examined (for example, the recordkeeping system should be capable of indexing, retaining, preserving, retrieving and reproducing the electronic records);

(3) The electronic records are readily convertible into legible and readable paper copy as may be needed to satisfy reporting and disclosure requirements or any other obligation under Title I of ERISA;

(4) The electronic recordkeeping system is not subject, in whole or in part, to any agreement or restriction that would, directly or indi-

rectly, compromise or limit a person's ability to comply with any reporting and disclosure requirement or any other obligation under Title I of ERISA; and

(5) Adequate records management practices are established and implemented (for example, following procedures for labeling of electronically maintained or retained records, providing a secure storage environment, creating back-up electronic copies and selecting an off-site storage location, observing a quality assurance program evidenced by regular evaluations of the electronic recordkeeping system including periodic checks of electronically maintained or retained records, and retaining paper copies of records that cannot be clearly, accurately or completely transferred to an electronic recordkeeping system).

(c) *Legibility and readability.* All electronic records must exhibit a high degree of legibility and readability when displayed on a video display terminal or other method of electronic transmission and when reproduced in paper form. The term "legibility" means the observer must be able to identify all letters and numerals positively and quickly to the exclusion of all other letters or numerals. The term "readability" means that the observer must be able to recognize a group of letters or numerals as words or complete numbers.

(d) *Disposal of original paper records.* Original paper records may be disposed of any time after they are transferred to an electronic recordkeeping system that complies with the requirements of this section, except such original records may not be discarded if the electronic record would not constitute a duplicate or substitute record under the terms of the plan and applicable federal or state law. [Added by 67 FR 17264, effective October 9, 2002.]

[¶ 14,280]
RELIANCE ON ADMINISTRATIVE INTERPRETATIONS

Act Sec. 108. In any criminal proceeding under section 501 based on any act or omission in alleged violation of this part or section 412, no person shall be subject to any liability or punishment for or on account of the failure of such person to

(1) comply with this part or section 412, if he pleads and proves that the act or omission complained of was in good faith, in conformity with, and in reliance on any regulation or written ruling of the Secretary, or

(2) publish and file any information required by any provision of this part if he pleads and proves that he published and filed such information in good faith, and in conformity with any regulation or written ruling of the Secretary issued under this part regarding the filing of such reports. Such a defense, if established, shall be a bar to the action or proceeding, nonwithstanding that

(A) after such act or omission, such interpretation or opinion is modified or rescinded or is determined by judicial authority to be invalid or of no legal effect, or

(B) after publishing or filing the annual reports and other reports required by this title, such publication or filing is determined by judicial authority not to be in conformity with the requirements of this part.

Amendment

P.L. 105-34, § 1503(d)(6):

Amended ERISA Sec. 108(2)(B) by striking "plan description, annual reports," and inserting "annual reports" effective August 5, 1997.

P.L. 101-239, § 7894(b)(7):

Amended ERISA Sec. 108 by striking "act of ommission" and inserting "act or omission" effective September 2, 1974.

[¶ 14,290]
FORMS

Act Sec. 109. (a) INFORMATION REQUIRED ON FORMS.—Except as provided in subsection (b) of this section, the Secretary may require that any information required under this title to be submitted to him, including but not limited to the information required to be filed by the administrator pursuant to section 103(b)(3) and (c), must be submitted on such forms as he may prescribe.

Act Sec. 109. (b) Information not required on forms.—The financial statement and opinion required to be prepared by an independent qualified public accountant pursuant to section 103(a)(3)(A), the actuarial statement required to be prepared by an enrolled actuary pursuant to section 103(a)(4)(A) and the summary plan description required by section 102(a) shall not be required to be submitted on forms.

Act Sec. 109. (c) Format and content of summary plan description, annual report, etc., required to be furnished to plan participants and beneficiaries.—The Secretary may prescribe the format and content of the summary plan description, the summary of the annual report described in section 104(b)(3) and any other report, statements or documents (other than the bargaining agreement, trust agreement, contract, or other instrument under which the plan is established or operated), which are required to be furnished or made available to plan participants and beneficiaries receiving benefits under the plan.

[¶ 14,300]
ALTERNATIVE METHODS OF COMPLIANCE

Act Sec. 110. (a) The Secretary on his own motion or after having received the petition of an administrator may prescribe an alternative method for satisfying any requirement of this part with respect to any pension plan, or class of pension plans, subject to such requirement if he determines—

(1) that the use of such alternative method is consistent with the purposes of this title and that it provides adequate disclosure to the participants and beneficiaries in the plan, and adequate reporting to the Secretary.

(2) that the application of such requirement of this part would—

(A) increase the costs to the plan, or

(B) impose unreasonable administrative burdens with respect to the operation of the plan, having regard to the particular characteristics of the plan or the type of plan involved; and

(3) that the application of this part would be adverse to the interests of plan participants in the aggregate.

Act Sec. 110. (b) An alternative method may be prescribed under subsection (a) by regulation or otherwise. If an alternative method is prescribed other than by regulation, the Secretary shall provide notice and an opportunity for interested persons to present their views, and shall publish in the Federal Register the provisions of such alternative method.

[¶ 14,310]
REPEAL AND EFFECTIVE DATE

Act Sec. 111. (a)(1) The Welfare and Pension Plans Disclosure Act is repealed except that such Act shall continue to apply to any conduct and events which occurred before the effective date of this part.

(2)(A) Section 664 of title 18, United States Code, is amended by striking out "any such plan subject to the provisions of the Welfare and Pension Plans Disclosure Act" and inserting in lieu thereof "any employee benefit plan subject to any provision of title I of the Employee Retirement Income Security Act of 1974".

(B)(i) Section 1027 of such title 18 is amended by striking out "Welfare and Pension Plans Disclosure Act" and inserting in lieu thereof "title I of the Employee Retirement Income Security Act of 1974", and by striking out "Act" each place it appears and inserting in lieu thereof "title".

(ii) The heading for such section is amended by striking out "welfare and pension plans disclosure act" and inserting in lieu thereof "employee retirement income security act of 1974".

(iii) The table of sections of chapter 47 of such title 18 is amended by striking out "Welfare and Pension Plans Disclosure Act" in the item relating to section 1027 and inserting in lieu thereof "Employee Retirement Income Security Act of 1974".

(C) Section 1954 of such title 18 is amended by striking out "any plan subject to the provisions of the Welfare and Pension Plans Disclosure Act as amended" and inserting in lieu thereof "any employee welfare benefit plan or employee pension benefit plan, respectively, subject to any provision of title I of the Employee Retirement Income Security Act of 1974"; and by striking out "sections 3(3) and 5(b)(1) and (2) of the Welfare and Pension Plans Disclosure Act, as amended" and inserting in lieu thereof "sections 3(4) and (3)(16) of the Employee Retirement Income Security Act of 1974".

(D) Section 211 of the Labor-Management Reporting and Disclosure Act of 1959 (29 U.S.C. 441) is amended by striking out "Welfare and Pension Plans Disclosure Act" and inserting in lieu thereof "Employee Retirement Income Security Act of 1974".

Act Sec. 111. (b)(1) Except as provided in paragraph (2), this part (including the amendments and repeals made by subsection (a)) shall take effect on January 1, 1975.

(2) In the case of a plan which has a plan year which begins before January 1, 1975, and ends after December 31, 1974, the Secretary may postpone by regulation the effective date of the repeal of any provision of the Welfare and Pension Plans Disclosure Act (and of any amendment made by subsection (a)(2)) and the effective date of any provision of this part, until the beginning of the first plan year of such plan which begins after January 1, 1975.

Act Sec. 111. (c) The provisions of this title authorizing the Secretary to promulgate regulations shall take effect on the date of enactment of this Act.

Act Sec. 111. (d) Subsections (b) and (c) shall not apply with respect to amendments made to this part in provisions enacted after the date of the enactment of this Act.

Amendment

P.L. 101-239, § 7894(h)(1):

Amended ERISA Sec. 111 by adding new subsection (d) to read as above effective September 2, 1974.

Interpretive Bulletins

Interpretive Bulletin ERISA IB RD 75-1 was adopted by FR Doc. 75-31318 under "Title 29—Labor; Chapter XXV—Office of Employee Benefits Security; Part 2556—Interpretive Bulletins Relating to Reporting and Disclosure." The bulletin was published in the Rules and Regulations section of the Federal Register on November 20, 1975 (40 FR 53998). The bulletin was filed with the Federal Register on November 19, 1975. The notice on the addition of a new Part 2556, "Interpretive Bulletins Relating to Reporting and Disclosure" to Title 29 of the Code of Federal Regulations was published in the Federal Register of November 20, 1975 (40 FR 53998). ERISA IB RD 75-1 was redesignated as Reg. § 2509.75-9 under "Part 2509—Interpretive Bulletins Relating to the Employee Retirement Income Security Act of 1974" by FR Doc. 76-966 (41 FR 1906), filed with the Federal Register on January 12, 1976, and published in the Federal Register of January 13, 1976.

Regulations

[¶ 14,370]

§ 2509.75-9 **Independence of Accountant Retained by Employee Benefit Plan**. The Department of Labor today announced guidelines for determining when a qualified public accountant is independent for purposes of auditing and rendering an opinion on the financial information required to be included in the annual report filed with the Department.

Section 103(a)(3)(A) requires that the accountant retained by an employee benefit plan be "independent" for purposes of examining plan financial information and rendering an opinion on the financial statements and schedules required to be contained in the annual report.

Under the authority of section 103(a)(3)(A) the Department of Labor will not recognize any person as an independent qualified public accountant who is in fact not independent with respect to the employee benefit plan upon which that account renders an opinion in the annual report filed with the Department of Labor. For example, an accountant will not be considered independent with respect to a plan if:

(1) During the period of professional engagement to examine the financial statements being reported, at the date of the opinion, or during the period covered by the financial statements, the accountant or his or her firm or a member thereof had, or was committed to acquire, any direct financial interest or any material indirect financial interest in such plan, or the plan sponsor, as that term is defined in section 3(16)(B) of the Act.

(2) During the period of professional engagement to examine the financial statements being reported, at the date of the opinion, or during the period covered by the financial statements, the accountant, his or her firm or a member thereof was connected as a promoter, underwriter, investment advisor, voting trustee, director, officer, or employee of the plan or plan sponsor except that a firm will not be deemed not independent in regard to a particular plan if a former officer or employee of such plan or plan sponsor is employed by the firm and such individual has completely diassociated himself from the plan or plan sponsor and does not participate in auditing financial statements of the plan covering any period of his or her employment by the plan or plan sponsor. For the purpose of this bulletin the term "member" means all partners or shareholder employees in the firm and all professional employees participating in the audit or located in an office of the firm participating in a significant portion of the audit;

(3) An accountant or a member of an accounting firm maintains financial records for the employee benefit plan.

However, an independent qualified public accountant may permissably engage in or have members of his or her firm engage in certain activities which will not have the effect of removing recognition of his or her independence. For example, (1) an accountant will not fail to be recognized as independent if at or during the period of his or her professional engagement with the employee benefit plan the accountant or his or her firm is retained or engaged on a professional basis by the plan sponsor, as that term is defined in section 3(16)(B) of the Act. However, to retain recognition of independence under such circumstances the accountant must not violate the prohibitions against recognition of independence established under paragraphs (1), (2) or (3) of this interpretive bulletin: (2) the rendering of services by an actuary associated with an accountant or accounting firm shall not impair the accountant's or accounting firm's independence. However, it should be noted that the rendering of services to a plan by an actuary and accountant employed by the same firm may constitute a prohibited transaction under section 406(a)(1)(C) of the Act. The rendering of such multiple services to a plan by a firm will be the subject of a later interpretive bulletin that will be issued by the Department of Labor.

In determining whether an accountant or accounting firm is not, in fact, independent with respect to a particular plan, the Department of Labor will give appropriate consideration to all relevant circumstances, including evidence bearing on all relationships between the accountant or accounting firm and that of the plan sponsor or any affiliate thereof, and will not confine itself to the relationships existing in connection with the filing of annual reports with the Department of Labor.

Further interpretive bulletins may be issued by the Department of Labor concerning the question of independence of an accountant retained by an employee benefit plan. [Amended by 40 FR 59728, filed with the Federal Register December 29, 1975, and published in the Federal Register December 30, 1975.]

Part 2—Participation and Vesting

[¶ 14,410]
COVERAGE

Act Sec. 201. This part shall apply to any employee benefit plan described in section 4(a) (and not exempted under section 4(b)) other than—

(1) an employee welfare benefit plan;

(2) a plan which is unfunded and is maintained by an employer primarily for the purpose of providing deferred compensation for a select group of management or highly compensated employees;

(3)(A) a plan established and maintained by a society, order, or association described in section 501(c)(8) or (9) of the Internal Revenue Code of 1986, if no part of the contributions to or under such plan are made by employers of participants in such plan, or

(B) a trust described in section 501(c)(18) of such Code;

(4) a plan which is established and maintained by a labor organization described in section 501(c)(5) of the Internal Revenue Code of 1986 and which does not at any time after the date of enactment of this Act provide for employer contributions;

(5) any agreement providing payments to a retired partner or a deceased partner's successor in interest, as described in section 736 of the Internal Revenue Code of 1986;

(6) an individual retirement account or annuity described in section 408 of the Internal Revenue Code of 1954, or a retirement bond described in section 409 of the Internal Revenue Code of 1954 (as effective for obligations issued before January 1, 1984);

(7) an excess benefit plan; or

(8) any plan, fund or program under which an employer, all of whose stock is directly or indirectly owned by employees, former employees or their beneficiaries proposes through an unfunded arrangement to compensate retired employees for benefits which were forfeited by such employees under a pension plan maintained by a former employer prior to the date such pension plan became subject to this Act.

Amendments

P.L. 101-239, §7894(c)(1):

Amended ERISA Sec. 201, in pargraph 6, by striking "or" at the end; in paragraph (7) by striking "plan." and inserting "plan; or;" and in paragraph (8), by striking "Any" and inserting "any" effective as if included in P.L. 96-364, §411.

P.L. 101-239, §7894(c)(11):

Amended ERISA Sec. 201(6) by striking "section 409 of such Code" and inserting "section 409 of the Internal Revenue Code of 1954 (as effective for obligations issued before January 1, 1984)" effective as if included in P.L. 98-369, §491(b).

P.L. 101-239, §7891(a)(1):

Titles I, III, and IV of ERISA (other than sections 3(37)(E), 301(a)(7), and 308, the last sentence of section 408(d), and sections 414(c), 4001(a)(3)(ii), and 4303) are each amended by striking "Internal Revenue Code of 1954" each place it appears and inserting "Internal Revenue Code of 1986" effective October 22, 1986.

P.L. 96-364, §411(a):

Added new section 201(8), effective September 26, 1980.

Regulations

The following regulations were adopted under "Title 29—Labor," "Chapter XXV—Pension and Welfare Benefit Programs, Department of Labor," "Subchapter C—Minimum Standards for Employee Pension Benefit Plans Under the Employee Retirement Income Security Act of 1974," "Part 2530—Rules and Regulations for Minimum Standards for Employee Pension Benefit Plans." The regulations were filed with the Federal Register on December 23, 1976, and published in the Federal Register of December 28, 1976 (41 FR 56462).

Subpart A—Scope and General Provisions

§ 2530.200a Scope.

[¶ 14,411]

§ 2530.200a-1 **Relationship of the Act and Internal Revenue Code of 1954.**

(a) Part 2 of Title I of the Employee Retirement Income Security Act of 1974 (hereinafter referred to as "the Act") contains minimum standards that a plan which is an employee pension benefit plan within the meaning of section 3(2) of the Act and which is covered under Part 2 must satisfy. (For a general explanation of the coverage of Part 2, see § 2530.201-1.) Substantially identical requirements are imposed by Subchapter D of Chapter 1 of Subtitle A of the Internal Revenue Code of 1954 (hereinafter referred to as "the Code") for plans seeking qualification for certain tax benefits under the Code. In general, the Code provisions apply to "qualified" pension, profitsharing, and stock bonus plans described in section 401(a) of the Code, annuity plans described in section 403(a) of the Code and bond purchase plans described in section 405(a) of the Code. The standards contained in Title I of the Act generally apply to both "non-qualified" and "qualified" employee pension benefit plans. The standards contained in the Act, and the related Code provisions, are "minimum" standards. In general, more liberal plan provisions (in terms of the benefit to be derived by the employee) are not prohibited.

(b) For a definition of the term "employee pension benefit plan", see section 3(2) of the Act and § 2510.3-2.

(c) For a statement of the coverage of Part 2 of Title I of the Act, see sections 4 and 201 of the Act and §§ 2510.3-2, 2510.3-3, 2530.201-1 and 2530.201-2.

[¶ 14,411A]

§ 2530.200a-2 **Treasury regulations for purposes of the Act.**

Regulations prescibed by the Secretary of the Treasury or his delegate under sections 410 and 411 of the Code (relating to minimum standards for participation and vesting) shall apply for purposes of sections 202 through 204 of the Act. Thus, except for those provisions (such as the definition of an hour of service or a year of service) for which authority to prescribe regulations is specifically delegated to the Secretary of Labor, regulations prescribed by the Secretary of the Treasury shall also be used to implement the related provisions contained in the Act. Those regulations specify the credit that must be given to an employee for years of service and years of participation completed by the employee. The allocation of regulatory jurisdiction between the Secretary of the Treasury or his delegate and the Secretary of Labor is governed by Titles I through III of the Act. *See* section 3002 of the Act (88 Stat. 996).

[¶ 14,411B]

§ 2530.200a-3 **Labor regulations for purposes of the Internal Revenue Code of 1954.**

The Secretary of Labor is specifically authorized to prescribe certain regulations (generally relating to hour of service, year of service, break in service, year of participation and special rules for seasonal and maritime industries) applicable to both Title I of the Act and sections 410 and 411 of the Code. These regulations are contained in this Subpart (A) and Subpart (B) of this part (2530) and must be integrated with regulations prescribed by the Secretary of the Treasury or his delegate under section 410 of the Code (relating to minimum participation standards), 411(a) of the Code (relating to minimum vesting standards) and 411(b) of the Code (relating to benefit accrual requirements). The allocation of regulatory jurisdiction between the Secretary of Labor and the Secretary of the Treasury or his delegate is governed by Titles I through III of the Act. *See* section 3002 of the Act (88 Stat. 996).

[¶ 14,412]

§ 2530.200b-1 **Computation periods.**

(a) *General.* Under sections 202, 203 and 204 of the Act and sections 410 and 411 of the Code, an employee's statutory entitlements with regard to participation, vesting and benefit accrual are generally determined by reference to years of service and years of participation completed by the employee and one-year breaks in service incurred by

the employee. The units used for determining an employee's credit towards statutory participation, vesting and benefit accrual entitlements are in turn defined in terms of the number of hours of service credited to the employee during a specified period—in general, a twelve-consecutive-month period—referred to herein as a "computation period". A plan must designate eligibility computation periods pursuant to § 2530.202-2 and vesting computation periods pursuant to § 2530.203-2, and, under certain circumstances, a defined benefit plan must designate accrual computation periods pursuant to § 2530.204-2. An employee who is credited with 1000 hours of service during an eligibility computation period must generally be credited with a year of service for purposes of section 202 of the Act and section 410 of the Code (relating to minimum participation standards). An employee who is credited with 1000 hours of service during a vesting computation period must generally be credited with a year of service for purposes of section 203 of the Act and 411(a) of the Code (relating to minimum vesting standards). An employee who completes 1000 hours of service during an accrual computation period must, under certain circumstances, be credited with at least a partial year of participation for purposes of section 204 of the Act and section 411(b) of the Code (relating to benefit accrual requirements). With respect to benefit accrual, however, the plan may not be required to credit an employee with a full year of participation and, therefore, full accrual for such year of participation unless the employee is credited with the number of hours of service or other permissible units of credit prescribed under the plan for crediting of a full year of participation (*see* § 2530.204-2 (c) and (d)). It should be noted that under some of the equivalencies which a plan may use under § 2530.200b-3 to determine the number of units of service to be credited to an employee in a computation period, an employee must be credited with a year of service or partial year of participation if the employee is credited with a number of units of service which is less than 1000 in a computation period. *See also* § 2530.200b-9, relating to elapsed time.

(b) *Rules generally applicable to computation periods.* In general, employment at the beginning or the end of an applicable computation period or on any particular date during the computation period is not determinative of whether the employee is credited with a year of service or a partial year of participation, or incurs a break in service, for the computation period. Rather, these determinations generally must be made solely with reference to the number of hours (or other units of service) which are credited to the employee during the applicable computation period. For example, an employee who is credited with 1000 hours of service during any portion of a vesting computation period must be credited with a year of service for that computation period regardless of whether the employee is employed by the employer on the first or the last day of the computation period. It should be noted, however, that in certain circumstances, a plan may provide that certain consequences follow from an employee's failure to be employed on a particular date. For example, under section 202(a)(4) of the Act and section 410(a)(4) of the Code, a plan may provide that an individual otherwise entitled to commence participation in the plan on a specified date does not commence participation on that date if he or she was separated from the service before that date. Similarly, under section 204(b)(1) of the Act and section 411(b)(1) of the Code, a plan which is not a defined benefit plan is not subject to section 204 (b)(1) and (b)(3) of the Act and section 411 (b)(1) and (b)(3) of the Code. Such a plan, therefore, may provide that an individual who has been a participant in the plan, but who has separated from service before the date on which the employer's contributions to the plan or forfeitures are allocated among participant's accounts or before the last day of the vesting computation period, does not share in the allocation of such contributions or forfeitures even though the individual is credited with 1000 or more hours of service for the applicable vesting computation period. Under certain circumstances, however, such a plan provision may result in discrimination prohibited under section 401(a)(4) of the Code. *See* Revenue Ruling 76-250, I.R.B 1976-27.

[¶ 14,412A]

§ 2530.200b-2 **Hour of service.**

(a) *General rule.* An hour of service which must, as a minimum, be counted for the purposes of determining a year of service, a year of participation for benefit accrual, a break in service and employment commencement date (or reemployment commencement date) under sections 202, 203 and 204 of the Act and sections 410 and 411 of the Code, is an hour of service as defined in paragraphs (a) (1), (2) and (3) of this section. The employer may round up hours at the end of a computation period or more frequently.

(1) An hour of service is each hour for which an employee is paid, or entitled to payment, for the performance of duties for the employer during the applicable computation period.

(2) An hour of service is each hour for which an employee is paid, or entitled to payment, by the employer on account of a period of time during which no duties are performed (irrespective of whether the employment relationship has terminated) due to vacation, holiday, illness, incapacity (including disability), layoff, jury duty, military duty or leave of absence. Notwithstanding the preceding sentence,

(i) No more than 501 hours of service are required to be credited under this paragraph (a) (2) to an employee on account of any single continuous period during which the employee performs no duties (whether or not such period occurs in a single computation period);

(ii) An hour for which an employee is directly or indirectly paid, or entitled to payment, on account of a period during which no duties are performed is not required to be credited to the employee if such payment is made or due under a plan maintained solely for the purpose of complying with applicable workmen's compensation, or unemployment compensation or disability insurance laws; and

(iii) Hours of service are not required to be credited for a payment which solely reimburses an employee for medical or medically related expenses incurred by the employee.

For purposes of this paragraph (a) (2), a payment shall be deemed to be made by or due from an employer regardless of whether such payment is made by or due from the employer directly, or indirectly through, among others, a trust fund, or insurer, to which the employer contributes or pays premiums and regardless of whether contributions made or due to the trust fund, insurer or other entity are for the benefit of particular employees or are on behalf of a group of employees in the aggregate.

(3) An hour of service is each hour for which back pay, irrespective of mitigation of damages, is either awarded or agreed to by the employer. The same hours of service shall not be credited both under paragraph (a) (1) or paragraph (a) (2), as the case may be, and under this paragraph (a) (3). Thus, for example, an employee who receives a back pay award following a determination that he or she was paid at an unlawful rate for hours of service previously credited will not be entitled to additional credit for the same hours of service. Crediting of hours of service for back pay awarded or agreed to with respect to periods described in paragraph (a) (2) shall be subject to the limitations set forth in that paragraph. For example, no more than 501 hours of service are required to be credited for payments of back pay, to the extent that such back pay is agreed to or awarded for a period of time during which an employee did not or would not have performed duties.

(b) *Special rule for determining hours of service for reasons other than the performance of duties.* In the case of a payment which is made or due on account of a period during which an employee peforms no duties, and which results in the crediting of hours of service under paragraph (a) (2) of this section, or in the case of an award or agreement for back pay, to the extent that such award or agreement is made with respect to a period described in paragraph (a) (2) of this section, the number of hours of service to be credited shall be determined as follows:

(1) *Payments calculated on the basis of units of time.* (i) Except as provided in paragraph (b) (3) of this section, in the case of a payment made or due which is calculated on the basis of units of time, such as hours, days, weeks or months, the number of hours of service to be credited shall be the number of regularly scheduled working hours included in the units of time on the basis of which the payment is calculated. For purposes of the preceding sentence, in the case of an employee without a regular work schedule, a plan may provide for the calculation of the number of hours to be credited on the basis of a 40-hour workweek or an 8-hour workday, or may provide for such calculation on any reasonable basis which reflects the average hours worked by the employee, or by other employees in the same job

classification, over a representative period of time, provided that the basis so used is consistently applied with respect to all employees within the same job classifications, reasonably defined. Thus, for example, a plan may not use a 40-hour workweek as a basis for calculating the number of hours of service to be credited for periods of paid absences for one employee while using an average based on hours worked over a representative period of time as a basis for such calculation for another, similarly situated employee.

(ii) *Examples.* The following examples illustrate the rules in paragraph (b) (1) of this section without regard to paragraphs (b) (2) and (3).

(A) Employee A was paid for 6 hours of sick leave at his normal hourly rate. The payment was therefore calculated on the basis of units of time (hours). A must, therefore, be credited with 6 hours of service for the 6 hours of sick leave.

(B) Employee B was paid his normal weekly salary for 2 weeks of vacation. The payment was therefore calculated on the basis of units of time (weeks). B is scheduled to work 37 ½ hours per week (although from time to time working overtime). B must, therefore, be credited with 75 hours of service for the vacation (37 ½ hours per week multiplied by 2 weeks).

(C) Employee C spent 3 weeks on a paid vacation. C's salary is established at an annual rate but is paid on a bi-weekly basis. The amount of salary payments attributable to be paid vacation was calculated on the basis of units of time (weeks). C has no regular work schedule but works at least 50 hours per week. The plan provides for the calculation of hours of service to be credited to employees in C's situation for periods of paid absences on the basis of a 40-hour workweek. C must, therefore, be credited with 120 hours of service for the vacation (3 weeks multiplied by 40 hours per week).

(D) Employee D spent 2 weeks on vacation, for which he was paid $150. Although D has no regular work schedule, the $150 payment was established on the assumption that an employee in D's position works an average of 30 hours per week at a rate of $2.50 per hour. The payment of $150 was therefore calculated on the basis of units of time (weeks). The plan provides for the calculation of hours of service to be credited to employees in D's situation for periods of paid absences on the basis of the average number of hours worked by an employee over a period of 6 months. D's employer's records show that D worked an average of 28 hours per week for a 6-month period. D must, therefore, be credited with 56 hours of service for the vacation (28 hours per week multiplied by 2 weeks).

(E) Employee E is regularly scheduled to work a 40-hour week. During a computation period E is incapacitated as a result of injury for a period of 11 weeks. Under the sick leave policy of E's employer E is paid his normal weekly salary for the first 8 weeks of his incapacity. After 8 weeks the employer ceases to pay E's normal salary but, under a disability insurance program maintained by the employer, E receives payments equal to 65% of his normal weekly salary for the remaining 3 weeks during which E is incapacitated. For the period during which he is incapacitated, therefore, E receives credit for 440 hours of service (11 weeks multiplied by 40 hours per week) regardless of the fact that payments to E for the last 3 weeks of the period during which he was incapacitated were made in amounts less than E's normal compensation.

(2) *Payments not calculated on the basis of units of time.* (i) Except as provided in paragraph (b) (3) of this section, in the case of a payment made or due, which is not calculated on the basis of units of time, the number of hours of service to be credited shall be equal to the amount of the payment divided by the employee's most recent hourly rate of compensation (as determined under paragraph (b) (2) (ii) of this section) before the period during which no duties are performed.

(ii) For purposes of paragraph (b) (2) (i) of this section an employee's hourly rate of compensation shall be determined as follows:

(A) In the case of an employee whose compensation is determined on the basis of an hourly rate, such hourly rate shall be the employee's most recent hourly rate of compensation.

(B) In the case of an employee whose compensation is determined on the basis of a fixed rate for specified periods of time (other than hours) such as days, weeks or months, the employee's

Reg. §2530.200b-2(b)(2)(ii)(B)   ¶14,412A

hourly rate of compensation shall be the employee's most recent rate of compensation for a specified period of time (other than an hour), divided by the number of hours regularly scheduled for the performance of duties during such period of time. For purposes of the preceding sentence, in the case of an employee without a regular work schedule, the plan may provide for the calculation of the employee's hourly rate of compensation on the basis of a 40-hour workweek, an 8-hour workday, or may provide for such calculation on any reasonable basis which reflects the average hours worked by the employee over a representative period of time, provided that the basis so used is consistently applied with respect to all employees within the same job classifications, reasonably defined.

(C) In the case of an employee whose compensation is not determined on the basis of a fixed rate for specified periods of time, the employee's hourly rate of compensation shall be the lowest hourly rate of compensation paid to employees in the same job classification as that of the employee or, if no employees in the same job classification have an hourly rate, the minimum wage as established from time to time under section 6(a)(1) of the Fair Labor Standards Act of 1938, as amended.

(iii) *Examples.* The following examples illustrate the rules in paragraph (b)(2) of this section without regard to paragraphs (b)(1) and (3).

(A) As a result of an injury, an employee is incapacitated for 5 weeks. A lump sum payment of $500 is made to the employee with respect to the injury under a disability insurance plan maintained by the employee's employer. At the time of the injury, the employee's rate of pay was $3.00 per hour. The employee must, therefore, be credited with 167 hours of service ($500 divided by $3.00 per hour).

(B) Same facts as in Example (A), above, except that at the time of the injury, the employee's rate of pay was $160 per week and the employee has a regular work schedule of 40 hours per week. The employee's hourly rate of compensation is, therefore, $4.00 per hour ($160 per week divided by 40 hours per week) and the employee must be credited with 125 hours of service for the period of absence ($500 divided by $4.00 per hour).

(C) An employee is paid at an hourly rate of $3.00 per hour and works a regular schedule of 40 hours per week. The employee is disabled for 26 weeks during a computation period. For the first 12 weeks of disability, the employee is paid his normal weekly earnings of $120 per week by the employer. Thereupon, a lump-sum disability payment of $1000 is made to the employee under a disability insurance plan maintained by the employer. Under paragraph (a)(3)(i) of this section, the employee is credited with 501 hours of service for the period of disability (lesser of 501 hours—the maximum number of hours required to be credited for a period of absence—or the sum of 12 weeks multiplied by 40 hours per week plus $1000 divided by $3.00 per hour).

(3) *Rule against double credit.* (i) Notwithstanding paragraphs (b)(1) and (2) of this section, an employee is not required to be credited on account of a period during which no duties are performed with a number of hours of service which is greater than the number of hours regularly scheduled for the performance of duties during such period. For purposes of applying the preceding sentence in the case of an employee without a regular work schedule, a plan may provide for the calculation of the number of hours of service to be credited to the employee for a period during which no duties are performed on the basis of a 40-hour workweek or an 8-hour workday, or may provide for such calculation on any reasonable basis which reflects the average hours worked by the employee, or by other employees in the same job classification, over a representative period of time, provided that the basis so used is consistently applied with respect to all employees within the same job classifications, reasonably defined.

(ii) *Examples.* (A) Employee A has a regular 40-hour workweek. Each year Employee A is entitled to pay for a two-week vacation, in addition to receiving normal wages for all hours worked, regardless of whether A actually takes a vacation and regardless of the duration of his vacation. The vacation payments are, therefore, calculated on the basis of units of time (weeks). In computation period I, A takes no vacation but receives vacation pay. A is entitled to no credit for hours of service for the vacation payment made in computation period I because

the payment was not made on account of a period during which no duties were performed. In computation period II, A takes a vacation of one week in duration, although receiving pay for a two-week vacation. A is entitled to be credited with 40 hours of service for his one-week vacation in computation period II even though paid for two weeks of vacation. In computation period III, A takes a vacation for a period lasting more than 2 weeks. A is entitled to be credited with 80 hours of service for his vacation in computation period III (40 hours per week multiplied by 2 weeks) even though the vacation lasted more than 2 weeks.

(B) Employee B has no regular work schedule. As a result of an injury, B is incapacitated for 1 day. A lump-sum payment of $500 is made to A with respect to the injury under an insurance program maintained by the employer. A pension plan maintained by the employer provides for the calculation of the number of hours of service to be credited to an employee without a regular work schedule on the basis of an 8-hour day. A is therefore required to be credited with no more than 8 hours for the day during which he was incapacitated, even though A's rate of pay immediately before the injury was $3.00 per hour.

(c) *Crediting of hours of service to computation periods.* (1) Except as provided in paragraph (c)(4) of this section, hours of service described in paragraph (a)(1) of this section shall be credited to the computation period in which the duties are performed.

(2) Except as provided in paragraph (c)(4) of this section, hours of service described in paragraph (a)(2) of this section shall be credited as follows:

(i) Hours of service credited to an employee on account of a payment which is calculated on the basis of units of time, such as hours, days, weeks or months, shall be credited to the computation period or computation periods in which the period during which no duties are performed occurs, beginning with the first unit of time to which the payment relates.

(ii) Hours of service credited to an employee by reason of a payment which is not calculated on the basis of units of time shall be credited to the computation period in which the period during which no duties are performed occurs, or if the period during which no duties are performed extends beyond one computation period, such hours of service shall be allocated between not more than the first two computation periods on any reasonable basis which is consistently applied with respect to all employees within the same job classifications, reasonably defined.

(3) Except as provided in paragraph (c)(4) of this section, hours of service described in paragraph (a)(3) of this section shall be credited to the computation period or periods to which the award or agreement for back pay pertains, rather than to the computation period in which the award, agreement or payment is made.

(4) In the case of hours of service to be credited to an employee in connection with a period of no more than 31 days which extends beyond one computation period, all such hours of service may be credited to the first computation period or the second computation period. Crediting of hours of service under this subparagraph must be done consistently with respect to all employees within the same job classifications, reasonably defined.

(5) *Examples.* The following examples are intended to illustrate paragraph (c)(4) of this section.

(i) An employer maintaining a plan pays employees on a bi-weekly basis. The plan designates the calendar year as the vesting computation period. The employer adopts the practice of crediting hours of service for the performance of duties during a bi-weekly payroll period to the vesting computation period in which the payroll period ends. Thus, when a payroll period ends on January 7, 1978, all hours of service to be credited to employees for the performance of duties during that payroll period are credited to the vesting computation period beginning on January 1, 1978. This practice is consistent with paragraph (c)(4) of this section, even though some hours of service credited to the computation period beginning on January 1, 1978, are attributable to duties performed during the previous vesting computation period.

(ii) An employer maintains a sick leave policy under which an employee is entitled to a certain number of hours of sick leave each year, on account of which the employee is paid his or her normal rate of compensation. An employee with a work schedule of 8 hours per day, 5 days per week, is sick from December 26, 1977 through January 4, 1978. Under the employer's sick leave policy, the employee is entitled to compensation for the entire period. A plan maintained by the employer establishes a calendar-year vesting computation period. The period from December 26, 1977 through December 31, 1977 includes 5 working days; the period from January 1, 1978 through January 4, 1978 includes 3 working days. Unless the plan adopts the alternative method for crediting service under paragraph (c)(4) of this section (illustrated in Example (iii), below) for the period of paid sick leave, the plan, pursuant to paragraph (c)(2)(i) of this section, must credit the employee with 40 hours of service in the 1977 vesting computation period (5 days multiplied by 8 hours per day) and 24 hours of service in the 1978 vesting computation period (3 days multiplied by 8 hours per day).

(iii) Same facts as in Example (ii), above, except that the plan adopts the practice of crediting hours of service for sick leave and other periods of compensated absences to the vesting computation period in which the employer's bi-weekly payroll period ends. The employee returns to work on January 5, 1978 and works for 2 days. For the 2-week payroll period ending on January 8, 1978, the employee may be credited with 80 hours of service in the 1978 vesting computation period (64 hours of service for the paid sick leave and 16 hours of service for the 2 days during which duties were performed).

(d) *Other Federal law.* Nothing in this section shall be construed to alter, amend, modify, invalidate, impair or supersede any law of the United States or any rule or regulation issued under any such law. Thus, for example, nothing in this section shall be construed as denying an employee credit for an "hour of service" if credit is required by separate federal law. Furthermore, the nature and extent of such credit shall be determined under such law.

(e) *Additional examples.* (1) During a computation period, an employee was paid for working 38 ¼ hours a week for 45 weeks. During the remaining 7 weeks of the computation period the employee was not employed by this employer. The employee completed 1,721 ¼ hours of service (45 weeks worked multiplied by 38 ¼ hours per week). The employer may also round up hours at the end of the computation period or more frequently. Thus, this employee could be credited with 1,722 hours of service (or, if the employer rounded up at the end of each week, 39 hours of service per week, resulting in credit for 1,755 hours of service).

(2) During a computation period, an employee was paid for a workweek of 40 hours per week for 40 weeks and, including overtime, for working 50 hours per week for 8 weeks. The employee completed 2,000 hours of service (40 weeks multiplied by 40 hours per week, plus 8 weeks worked multiplied by 50 hours per week).

(3) During a computation period, an employee was paid for working 2 regularly scheduled 40-hour weeks and then became disabled. The employee was disabled through the remainder of the computation period and the following computation period. Throughout the period of disability, payments were made to the employee as follows: for the first month of a period of disability, the employer continued to pay the employee the employee's normal compensation at the same rate as before the disability occurred; thereupon, under the employer's disability insurance policy, payments were made to the employee in amounts equal to 80 percent of the employee's compensation before the disability. For the first computation period the employee is credited with 80 hours of service for the performance of duties (2 weeks multiplied by 40 hours per week) and 501 hours of service for the period of disability (the lesser of 501 hours of service or 50 weeks multiplied by 40 hours per week), or a total of 581 hours of service; for the second computation period the employee is credited with no hours of service because, under paragraph (a)(2)(i) of this section, the maximum of 501 hours of service has been credited for the period of disability in the first computation period.

(4) An employee has a regularly scheduled 5-day, 40-hour week. During a computation period the employee works for the first week, spends the second week on a paid vacation, returns to work for an hour and is then disabled for the remainder of the computation period. Payments under a disability plan maintained by the employer

are made to the employee on account of the period of disability. The employee is credited with 582 hours of service for the computation period (40 hours for the period of paid vacation; 41 hours for the performance of duties; 501 hours for the period of disability).

(5) Same facts as in Example (4), above, except that the employee's period of disability begins before the employee returns from vacation to the performance of duties. The employee is credited with only 541 hours of service, because the paid vacation and the disability together constitute a single, continuous period during which no duties were performed and, therefore, under paragraph (a)(2)(i) of this section, no more than 501 hours of service are required to be credited for such period.

(6) During a computation period, an employee worked 40 hours a week for the first 2 weeks. The employee then began serving on active duty in the Armed Forces of the United States, which service occupied the remaining 50 weeks of the computation period. The employee would be credited with 80 hours (2 weeks worked multiplied by 40 hours) plus such credit as may be prescribed by separate Federal laws relating to military service. The nature and extent of the credit that the employee receives upon his return and the purpose for which such credit is given, e.g., the percentage of his or her accrued benefits derived from employer contributions which are nonforfeitable (or vested), will depend upon the interpretation of the federal law governing veterans' reemployment rights.

(f) *Plan document.* A plan which credits service on the basis of hours of service must state in the plan document the definition of hours of service set forth in paragraph (a) of this section, but is not required to state the rules set forth in paragraphs (b) and (c) of this section if they are incorporated by reference.

[¶ 14,412B]

§ 2530.200b-3 **Determination of service to be credited to employees.**

(a) *General rule.* For the purpose of determining the hours of service which must be credited to an employee for a computation period, a plan shall determine hours of service from records of hours worked and hours for which payment is made or due or shall use an equivalency permitted under paragraphs (d), (e) or (f) of this section to determine hours of service. Any records may be used to determine hours of service to be credited to employees under a plan, even though such records are maintained for other purposes, provided that they accurately reflect the actual number of hours of service with which an employee is required to be credited under § 2530.200b-2(a). Payroll records, for example, may provide sufficiently accurate data to serve as a basis for determining hours of service. If, however, existing records do not accurately reflect the actual number of hours of service with which an employee is entitled to be credited, a plan must either develop and maintain adequate records or use one of the permitted equivalencies. A plan may in any case credit hours of service under any method which results in the crediting of no less than the actual number of hours of service required to be credited under § 2530.200b-2(a) to each employee in a computation period, even though such method may result in the crediting of hours of service in excess of the number of hours required to be credited under § 2530.200b-2. A plan is not required to prescribe in its documents which records are to be used to determine hours of service.

(b) *Determination of pre-effective date hours of service.* To the extent that a plan is required to determine hours of service completed before the effective date of Part 2 of Title I of the Act (see section 211 of the Act), the plan may use whatever records may be reasonably accessible to it and may make whatever calculations are necessary to determine the approximate number of hours of service completed before such effective date. For example, if a plan or an employer maintaining a plan has, or has access to, only the records of compensation of employees for the period before the effective date, it may derive the pre-effective date hours of service by using the hourly rate for the period or the hours customarily worked. If accessible records are insufficient to make an approximation of the number of pre-effective date hours of service for a particular employee or group of employees, the plan may make a reasonable estimate of the hours of service completed by such employee or employees during the particular period. For example, if records are available with respect to some employees, the plan may estimate the hours of other employees in the same job classification based on these records. A plan may use any of the equivalencies permitted under this section, or the elapsed time method of crediting service permitted under this section, or the elapsed time method of crediting service permitted under § 2530.200b-9, to determine hours of service completed before the effective date of Part 2 of Title I of the Act.

(c) *Use of equivalencies for determining service to be credited to employees.* (1) The equivalencies permitted under paragraphs (d), (e) and (f) of this section are methods of determining service to be credited to employees during computation periods which are alternatives to the general rule for determining hours of service set forth in paragraph (a) of this section. The equivalencies are designed to enable a plan to determine the amount of service to be credited to an employee in a computation period on the basis of records which do not accurately reflect the actual number of hours of service required to be credited to the employee under § 2530.200b-2(a). However, the equivalencies may be used even if such records are maintained. Any equivalency used by a plan must be set forth in the document under which the plan is maintained.

(2) A plan may use different methods of crediting service, including equivalencies permitted under paragraphs (d), (e) and (f) of this section and the method of crediting service under the general rule set forth in § 2530.200b-2(a), for different classifications of employees covered under the plan or for different purposes, provided that such classifications are reasonable and are consistently applied. Thus, for example, a plan may provide that part-time employees are credited under the general method of crediting service set forth in § 2530.200b-2 and full-time employees are credited under a permissible equivalency. A classification, however, will not be deemed to be reasonable or consistently applied if such classification is designed with an intent to preclude an employee or employees from attaining statutory entitlement with respect to eligibility to participate, vesting or benefit accrual. For example, a classification applied so that any employee credited with less than 1,000 hours of service during a given 12-consecutive-month period would be considered part-time and subject to the general method of crediting service rather than an equivalency would not be reasonable.

(3) Notwithstanding paragraphs (c) (1) and (2) of this section, the use of a permissible equivalency for some, but not all, purposes or the use of a permissible equivalency for some, but not all, employees may, under certain circumstances, result in discrimination prohibited under section 401(a) of the Code, even though it is permitted under this section.

(d) *Equivalencies based on working time.* (1) *Hours worked.* A plan may determine service to be credited to an employee on the basis of hours worked, as defined in paragraph (d)(3)(i) of this section, if 870 hours worked are treated as equivalent to 1,000 hours of service and 435 hours worked are treated as equivalent to 500 hours of service.

(2) *Regular time hours.* A plan may determine service to be credited to an employee on the basis of regular time hours, as defined in paragraph (d)(3)(ii) of this section, if 750 regular time hours are treated as equivalent to 1,000 hours of service and 375 regular time hours are treated as equivalent to 500 hours of service.

(3) For purposes of this section:

(i) The term "hours worked" shall mean hours of service described in § 2530.200b-2(a)(1), hours for which back pay, irrespective of mitigation of damages, is awarded or agreed to by an employer, to the extent that such award or agreement is intended to compensate an employee for periods during which the employee would have been engaged in the performance of duties for the employer.

(ii) The term "regular time hours" shall mean hours worked, except hours for which a premium rate is paid because such hours are in excees of the maximum workweek applicable to an employee under section 7(a) of the Fair Labor Standards Act of 1938, as amended, or because such hours are in excess of a bona fide standard workweek or workday.

(4) A plan determining service to be credited to an employee on the basis of hours worked or regular time hours shall credit hours worked or regular time hours, as the case may be, to computation periods in accordance with the rules for crediting hours of service to computation periods set forth in § 2520.200b-2(c).

(5) *Examples.* (i) A defined benefit plan uses the equivalency based on hours worked permitted under paragrph (d) (1) of this section. The plan uses the same 12-consecutive-month period for the vesting and accrual computation periods. The plan credits a participant with each hour for which the participant is paid, or entitled to payment, for the performance of duties for the employer during a computation period (as well as each hour for which back pay is awarded or agreed to). During a vesting/accrual computation period Participant A is credited with 870 hours worked. A is credited with a year of service for purposes of vesting for the computation period and with at least a partial year of participation for purposes of accrual, as if A had been credited with 1000 hours of service during the computation period. During the same computation period Participant B is credited with 436 hours of service. B is not credited with a year of service for purposes of vesting or a partial year of participation for purposes of accrual for the computation period, but does not incur a one-year break in service for the computation period, as if B had been credited with 501 hours of service during the computation period.

(ii) A plan uses the equivalency based on regular time hours permitted under paragraph (d) (2) of this section. During a computation period a participant works 370 regular time hours and 20 overtime hours. The participant incurs a one-year break in service for the computation period because he has not been credited with 375 regular hours in the computation period.

(e) *Equivalencies based on periods of employment.* (1) Except as provided in paragraphs (e) (4) and (6) of this section, a plan may determine the number of hours of service to be credited to employees in a computation period on the following bases:

(i) On the basis of days of employment, if an employee is credited with 10 hours of service for each day for which the employee would be required to be credited with at least one hour of service under § 2530.200b-2;

(ii) On the basis of weeks of employment, if an employee is credited with 45 hours of service for each week for which the employee would be required to be credited with at least one hour of service under § 2530.200b-2;

(iii) On the basis of semi-monthly payroll periods, if an employee is credited with 95 hours of service for each semi-monthly payroll period for which the employee would be required to be credited with at least one hour of service under § 2530.200b-2; or

(iv) On the basis of months of employment, if an employee is credited with 190 hours of service for each month for which the employee would be required to be credited with at least one hour of service under § 2530.200b-2.

(2) Except as provided in paragraphs (e) (4) and (6) of this section, a plan may determine the number of hours of service to be credited to employees in a computation period on the basis of shifts if an employee is credited with the number of hours included in a shift for each shift for which the employee would be required to be credited with at least one hour of service under § 2530.200b-2. If a plan uses the equivalency based on shifts permitted under this paragraph, the times of the beginning and end of each shift used as a basis for the determination of service shall be set forth in a document referred to in the plan.

(3) *Examples.* The following examples illustrate the application of paragraphs (e) (1) and (2) of this section:

(i) A plan uses the equivalency based on weeks of employment permitted under paragraph (e)(1)(ii) of this section. An employee works for one hour on the first workday of a week and then takes leave without pay for the entire remainder of the week. The plan must credit the employee with 45 hours of service for the week.

(ii) A plan uses the equivalency based on weeks of employment permitted under paragraph (e)(1)(ii) of this section. An employee spends a week on vacation with pay. The plan must credit the employee with 45 hours of service for the week.

(iii) A plan uses the equivalency based on weeks of employment permitted under paragraph (e)(1)(ii) of this section. An employee spends two days of a week on vacation with pay and the remainder of the week on leave without pay. The plan must credit the employee with 45 hours of service for the week.

(iv) A plan uses the equivalency based on weeks of employment permitted under paragraph (e)(1)(ii) of this section. An employee spends the entire week on leave without pay. The plan is not required to credit the employee with any hours of service for the week because no payment was made to the employee for the week of leave and, therefore, under § 2530.200b-2 no hours of service would be credited to the employee for the week of leave.

(v) The workday of an employer maintaining a plan is scheduled in shifts. Ordinarily, each shift is 6 hours in duration. At certain times, however, the employer schedules 8-hour shifts in order to meet increased demand. Such shifts are described in a collective bargaining agreement referred to in the plan documents. The plan must credit an employee with 6 hours of service for each 6-hour shift for which the employee would be credited with one hour of service under § 2530.200b-2; and with 8 hours of service for each such 8-hour shift.

(vi) An employer's workday is divided into three 8-hour shifts, each employee generally working 5 shifts per week. A plan maintained by the employer uses the equivalency based on shifts permitted under paragraph (e)(2) of this section. An employee is on vacation with pay for 2 weeks, during which, in the ordinary course of his work schedule, he would have worked 10 shifts. The employee must be credited with 80 hours of service for the vacation (10 shifts multiplied by 8 hours per shift).

(vii) An employer's workday is divided into 3 8-hour shifts, each employee generally working 1 shift per workday. A plan maintained by the employer uses the equivalency based on shifts permitted under paragraph (e)(2) of this section. On a certain day, an employee works his normal 8-hour shift and an hour during the following shift. In addition to 8 hours service for the first shift, the employee must be credited with 8 hours of service for the following shift, since he would be entitled to be credited with at least one hour of service for the second shift under § 2530.200b-2.

(viii) A plan uses the equivalency based on days permitted under paragraph (e)(1)(i) of this section. During a computation period an employee spends 2 weeks on vacation with pay. In the ordinary course of the employee's regular work schedule, the employee would be engaged in the performance of duties for 10 days during the 2-week vacation period. Under § 2530.200b-2, the employee would be credited with at least one hour of service for each of the 10 days during the 2-week vacation for which the employee would ordinarily be engaged in the performance of duties. Under paragraph (e)(4) of this section, the employee is credited with 100 hours of service for the 2-week vacation (10 days multiplied by 10 hours of service per day).

(4) For purposes of this paragraph, in the case of a payment described in § 2530.20b-2(b)(2) (relating to payments not calculated on the basis of units of time), a plan using an equivalency based on units of time permitted under this paragraph shall credit the employee with the number or hours of service determined under subparagraph (2) of § 2530.200b-2(b), and, to the extent applicable, paragraph (e)(3) of § 2530.200b-2(b), containing the rule against double crediting, of § 2530.200b-2(b). For example, if an employee with a regular work schedule of 40 hours per week paid at a rate of $3.00 per hour is incapacitated for a period of 4 weeks and receives a lump sum payment of $500 for his incapacity, the employee must be credited with 160 hours of service for the period of incapacity, regardless of whether the plan uses an equivalency permitted under this paragraph (see example at § 2530.200b-2(b)(2)(iii)(A)). If, however, the employee is incapacitated for only 3 weeks, under § 2530.200b-2(b)(3) the employee is not required to be credited with more than 120 hours of service (lesser of 167 hours of service determined under the preceding sentence or 3 weeks multiplied by 40 hours per week).

(5) For purposes of this paragraph, in the case of a payment to an employee calculated on the basis of units of time which are greater than the periods of employment used by a plan as a basis for determining service to be credited to the employee under this paragraph, the plan shall credit the employee with the number of periods of employment which, in the course of the employees' regular work schedule, would be included in the unit or units of time on the basis of which the payment is calculated. For example, a plan uses the equivalency based on days permitted under paragraph (e)(1)(i) of this section. During a

computation period an employee spends 2 weeks on vacation with pay. In the ordinary course of the employee's regular work schedule, the employee would be engaged in the performance of duties for 10 days during the 2-week vacation period. Under § 2530.200b-2, the employee would be credited with at least one hour of service for each of the 10 days off during the 2-week vacation for which the employee would ordinarily be engaged in the performance of duties. Under this subparagraph the employee is credited with 100 hours of service for the 2-week vacation (10 days multiplied by 10 hours of service per day). If, however, the employee, although paid for a 2-week vacation, spends only one week on vacation, under § 2530.200b-2(b)(3) the employee is not required to be credited with more than 50 hours of service (5 days multiplied by 10 hours per day).

(6) For purposes of this paragraph, in the case of periods of time used as a basis for determining service to be credited to an employee which extend into two computation periods, the plan may credit all hours of service (or other units of service) credited for such a period to the first computation period or the second computation period, or may allocate such hours of service (or other units of service) between the two computation periods on a pro rata basis. Crediting of service under this subparagraph must be done consistently with respect to all employees within the same job classifications, reasonably defined.

(7) A plan may combine an equivalency based on working time permitted under paragraph (d) of this section (i.e., hours worked or regular time hours) with an equivalency based on periods of employment permitted under this paragraph if the following conditions are met:

(i) The plan credits an employee with the number of hours worked or regular time hours, as the case may be, equal to the number of hours of service which would be credited to the employee under paragraphs (e)(1) and (2) of this section, for each period of employment for which the employee would be credited with one hour worked or one regular time hour; and

(ii) The plan treats hours worked and regular time hours in the manner prescribed under paragraphs (d)(1) and (d)(2) of this section.

(8) *Example.* The following example illustrates the application of paragraph (e)(7) of this section. A plan uses the equivalency based on weeks of employment permitted under paragraph (e)(1)(ii) of this section in conjunction with the equivalency based on hours worked permitted under paragraph (d)(1) of this section, as provided in paragraph (e)(7) of this section. During a vesting computation period an employee is paid for the performance of duties for at least 1 hour in each of the first 20 weeks of the computation period and spends the next 2 weeks on a paid vacation. The employee thereupon terminates employment performing no further duties for the employer, and receiving no further compensation in the computation period. The employee is therefore credited with 900 hours worked for the vesting computation period (20 weeks multiplied by 45 hours per week), receiving no credit for the two weeks of paid vacation. The employee is credited with a year of service for the vesting computation period because he has been credited with more than 870 hours for the computation period.

(f) *Equivalencies based on earnings.* (1) In the case of an employee whose compensation is determined on the basis of an hourly rate, a plan may determine the number of hours to be credited the employee in a computation period on the basis of earnings, if:

(i) The employee is credited with the number of hours equal to the total of the employee's earnings from time to time during the computation period divided by the employee's hourly rate as in effect at such times during the computation period, or equal to the employee's total earnings for the performance of duties during the computation period divided by the employee's lowest hourly rate of compensation during the computation period, or by the lowest hourly rate of compensation payable to an employee in the same, or a similar, job classification, reasonably defined; and

(ii) 870 hours credited under paragraph (f)(1)(i) of this section are treated as equivalent to 1,000 hours of service, and 435 hours credited under paragraph (f)(1)(i) of this section are treated as equivalent to 500 hours of service.

Reg. § 2530.200b-3(f)(1)(ii)   ¶ 14,412B

For purposes of this paragraph (f)(1), a plan may divide earnings at premium rates for overtime by the employee's hourly rate for overtime, rather than the regular time hourly rate.

(2) In the case of an employee whose compensation is determined on a basis other than an hourly rate, a plan may determine the number of hours to be credited to the employee in a computation period on the basis of earnings if:

(i) The employee is credited with the number of hours equal to the employee's total earnings for the performance of duties during the computation period divided by the employee's lowest hourly rate of compensation during the computation period, determined under paragraph (f)(3) of this section; and

(ii) 750 hours credited under paragraph (f)(2)(i) of this section are treated as equivalent to 1,000 hours of service, and 375 hours credited under paragraph (f)(2)(i) of this section are treated as equivalent to 500 hours of service.

(3) For purposes of paragraph (f)(2) of this section, an employee's hourly rate of compensation shall be determined as follows:

(i) In the case of an employee whose compensation is determined on the basis of a fixed rate for a specified period of time (other than an hour) such as a day, week or month, the employee's hourly rate of compensation shall be the employee's lowest rate of compensation during a computation period for such specified period of time divided by the number of hours regularly scheduled for the performance of duties during such period of time. For purposes of the preceding sentence, in the case of an employee without a regular work schedule, the plan may provide for the calculation of the employee's hourly rate of compensation on the basis of a 40-hour workweek or an 8-hour workday, or may provide for such calculation on any reasonable basis which reflects the average hours worked by the employee over a representative period of time, provided that the basis so used is consistently applied to all employees within the same job classifications, reasonably defined.

(ii) In the case of an employee whose compensation is not determined on the basis of a fixed rate for a specified period of time, the employee's hourly rate of compensation shall be the lowest hourly rate of compensation payable to employees in the same job classification as the employee, or, if no employees in the same job classification have an hourly rate, the minimum wage as established from time to time under section 6(a)(1) of the Fair Labor Standards Act of 1938, as amended.

(4) Examples. (i) In a particular job classification employees' wages range from $3.00 per hour to $4.00 per hour. To determine the number of hours to be credited to an employee in that job classification who is compensated at a rate of $4.00 per hour, a plan may divide the employee's total earnings during the computation period for the performance of duties either by $3.00 per hour (the lowest hourly rate of compensation in the job classification) or by $4.00 per hour (the employee's own hourly rate of compensation).

(ii) An hourly employee's total earnings for the performance of duties during a vesting computation period amount to $4,350. During that calendar year, the employee's lowest hourly rate of compensation was $5.00 per hour. The plan may determine the number of hours to be credited to the employee for that vesting computation period by dividing $4,350 by $5.00 per hour. The employee is credited with 870 hours for the vesting computation period and is, therefore, credited with a year of service for purposes of vesting.

(iii) During the first 3 months of a vesting computation period an hourly employee is paid at a rate of $3.00 per hour and earns $675 for the performance of duties; during the next 6 months, the employee is paid at a rate of $3.50 per hour and earns $1,575 for the performance of duties; during the final 3 months the employee is paid at a rate of $3.60 per hour and earns $810 for the performance of duties. The plan may determine the number of hours to be credited to the employee in the computation period under the equivalency set forth in paragraph (f)(1) of this section either (A) by dividing the employee's earnings for each period during which the employee was paid at a separate rate ($675 divided by $3.00 per hour equals 225 hours; $1,575 divided by $3.50 per hour equals 450 hours; $810 divided by $3.60 per hour equals 225 hours) and adding the hours so obtained (900 hours), or (B) by dividing the employee's total compensation for the vesting

computation period by the employee's lowest hourly rate during the computation period ($3,020 divided by $3.00 per hour equals 1,009 ⅔ hours). The plan may also divide the employee's total compensation during the computation period by the lowest hourly rate payable to an employee in the same, or a similar, job classification.

(iv) During a plan's computation period an hourly employee's total earnings for the performance of duties consist of $7,500 at a basic rate of $5.00 per hour and $750 at an overtime rate of $7.50 per hour for hours worked in excess of 40 in a week. If the plan uses the equivalency permitted under paragraph (f)(1) of this section, the plan may adjust for the overtime rate in calculating the number of hours to be credited to the employee. Thus, the plan may calculate the number of hours to be credited to the employee by adding the employee's earnings at the basic rate divided by the basic rate and the employee's earnings at the overtime rate divided by the overtime rate ($7,500 divided by $5.00 per hour, plus $750 divided by $7.50 per hour, or 1,500 hours plus 100 hours), resulting in credit for 1,600 hours for the computation period.

(v) During a plan's vesting computation period an employee's lowest weekly rate of compensation is $400 per week. The employee has a regular work schedule of 40 hours per week. The employee's lowest hourly rate during the vesting computation period is, therefore, $10 per hour ($400 per week divided by 40 hours per week). During the vesting computation period, the employee receives a total of $7,500 for the performance of duties. The plan determines the number of regular time hours to be credited to the employee for the computation period by dividing $7,500 by $10 per hour. The employee is credited with 750 hours for the computation period and is, therefore, credited with a year of service for purposes of vesting.

[¶ 14,412C]
§ 2530.200b-4 One-year break in service.

(a) Computation period. (1) Under sections 202(b) and 203(b)(3) of the Act and sections 410(a)(5) and 411(a)(6) of the Code, a plan may provide that an employee incurs a one-year break in service for a computation period or periods if the employee fails to complete more than 500 hours of service or, in the case of any maritime industry, 62 days of service in such period or periods.

(2) For purposes of section 202(b) of the Act and section 410(a)(5) of the Code, relating to one-year breaks in service for eligibility to participate, in determining whether an employee incurs a one-year break in service, a plan shall use the eligibility computation period designated under § 2530.202-2(b) for measuring years of service after the initial eligibility computation period.

(3) For purposes of section 203(b)(3) of the Act and section 411(a)(6) of the Code, relating to breaks in service for purposes of vesting, in determining whether an employee incurs a one-year break in service, a plan shall use the vesting computation period designated under § 2530.203-2(a).

(4) For rules regarding service which is not required to be taken into account for purposes of benefit accrual, see § 2530.204-1(b)(1).

(b) Service following a break in service. (1) For purposes of section 202(b)(3) of the Act and section 410(a)(5)(C) of the Code (relating to completion of a year of service for eligibility to participate after a one-year break in service), the following rules shall be applied in measuring completion of a year of service upon an employee's return after a one-year break in service:

(i) In the case of a plan which, after the initial eligibility computation period, measures years of service for purposes of eligibility to participate on the basis of eligibility computation periods beginning on anniversaries of an employee's employment commencement date, as permitted under § 2530.202-2(b)(1), the plan shall use the 12-consecutive-month period beginning on an employee's reemployment commencement date (as defined in paragraph (b)(1)(iii) and (iv) of this section) and, where necessary, subsequent 12-consecutive-month periods beginning on anniversaries of the reemployment commencement date.

(ii) In the case of a plan which, after the initial eligibility computation period, measures years of service for eligibility to participate on the basis of plan years beginning with the plan year which includes the first anniversary of the initial eligibility computation period, as permitted under § 2530.202-2(b)(2), the plan shall use the 12-consecutive-month period beginning on an employee's reemployment commencement date (as defined in paragraph (b)(1)(iii) and (iv) of this section) and, where necessary, plan years beginning with the plan year which includes the first anniversary of the employee's reemployment commencement date.

(iii) Except as provided in paragraph (b)(1)(iv) of this section, an employee's reemployment commencement date shall be the first day on which the employee is entitled to be credited with an hour of service described in § 2530.200b-2(a)(1) after the first eligibility computation period in which the employee incurs a one-year break in service following an eligibility computation period in which the employee is credited with more than 500 hours of service.

(iv) In the case of an employee who is credited with no hours of service in an eligibility computation period beginning after the employee's reemployment commencement date established under subparagraph (b)(1)(iii) of this section, the employee shall be treated as having a new reemployment commencement date as of the first day on which the employee is entitled to be credited with an hour of service described in § 2530.200b-2(a)(1) after such eligibility computation period.

(2) For purposes of section 203(b)(3)(B) of the Act and section 411(a)(6)(B) of the Code (relating to the completion of a year of service for vesting following a one-year break in service), in measuring completion of a year of service upon an employee's return after a one-year break in service, a plan shall use the vesting computation period designated under § 2530.203-2. In the case of a plan which designates a separate vesting computation period for each employee (rather than one vesting computation period for all employees), when an employee who has incurred a one-year break in service later completes an initial hour of service, the plan may change the employee's vesting computation period to a 12-consecutive-month period beginning on the day on which such initial hour of service is completed, provided that the plan follows the rules for changing the vesting computation period set forth in § 2530.203-2(c)(1). Specifically, such a plan must ensure that as a result of the change of the vesting computation period of an employee who has incurred a one-year break in service to the 12-month period beginning on the first day on which the employee later completes an initial hour of service, the employee's vested percentage of the accrued benefit derived from employer contributions will not be less on any date after the change than such nonforfeitable percentage would be in the absence of the change. As under § 2530.203-2(c)(i), the plan will be deemed to satisfy the requirement of that paragraph if, in the case of an employee who has incurred a one-year break in service, the vesting computation period beginning on the day on which the employee completes an hour of service after the one-year break in service begins before the end of the last vesting computation period established before the change of vesting computation periods and, if the employee is credited with 1000 hours of service in both such vesting computation periods, the employee is credited with 2 years of service for purposes of vesting.

(3) For purposes of section 203(b)(3)(B) of the Act and section 411(a)(6)(B) of the Code (relating to the completion of a year of service for vesting following a one-year break in service), in measuring completion of a year of service upon an employee's return after a one-year break in service, a plan shall use the vesting computation period designated under § 2530.203-2. In the case of a plan which designates a separate vesting computation period for each employee (rather than one vesting computation period for all employees), when an employee who has incurred a one-year break in service later completes an initial hour of service, the plan may change the employee's vesting computation period to a 12-consecutive-month period beginning on the day on which such initial hour of service is completed, provided that the plan follows the rules for changing the vesting computation period set forth in § 2530.203-2(c)(1).

(4) *Examples.* (i) Employer X maintains a pension plan. The plan uses a calendar year vesting computation period and plan year. As conditions for participation, the plan requires that an employee of X complete one year of service and attain age 25, and, in accordance with § 2530.202-2(b)(2), provides that after the initial eligibility computation period, plan years will be used as eligibility computation periods,

beginning with the plan year which includes the first anniversary of an employee's employment commencement date. Thus, under paragraph (a)(2) of this section, the plan must use plan years in measuring one-year breaks in service for eligibility to participate. The plan provides that an employee acquires a nonforfeitable right to 100 percent of the accrued benefit derived from employer contributions upon completion of 10 years of service. Under the plan, for purposes of vesting, years of service completed before an employee attains age 22 are not taken into account. The plan also provides that if an employee has incurred a one-year break in service, in computing the employee's period of service for eligibility to participate, years of service before such break will not be taken into account until the employee has completed a year of service with X after the employee's return. The plan further provides that in the case of an employee who has no vested right to an accrued benefit derived from employer contributions, years of service for purposes of eligibility to participate or vesting before a one-year break in service for eligibility or vesting (as the case may be) shall not be required to be taken into account if the number of consecutive one-year breaks in service equals or exceeds the aggregate number of such years of service before such consecutive one-year breaks in service.

(A) Employee A commences employment with X on January 1, 1976 at age 30 and completes a year of service for eligibility to participate and vesting in both the 1976 and 1977 computation periods. A becomes a participant in the plan on January 1, 1977. A terminates employment with X on November 3, 1977, after completing 1000 hours of service; completes no hours of service in 1978, incurring a one-year break in service; and is reemployed by X on June 1, 1979. A completes 800 hours of service during the remainder of 1979 and 600 hours of service from January 1, 1980 through May 31, 1980. Under paragraph (b)(1)(iii) of this section, A's reemployment commencement date is June 1, 1979. By June 1, 1980, A has completed a year of service during the eligibility computation period following his return, and receives credit for his pre-break service to the extent required under section 202 of the Act and section 410 of the Code and the regulations thereunder. The plan is not, however, required to credit A with a year of service for vesting during 1979 because he failed to complete 1,000 hours of service during that vesting computation period. If A completes 400 or more hours of service from June 1, 1980 to December 31, 1980, then A will be credited with one year of service for vesting purposes for the 1980 vesting computation period.

(B) Employee B was born on February 22, 1955 and commenced employment with Employer X on July 1, 1975. B is credited with a year of service for eligibility to participate in the plan for the eligibility computation period beginning on his employment commencement date (July 1, 1975) and a year of service for eligibility and vesting for the 1976 and 1977 plan years. As of the end of the 1977 plan year, B is credited with 3 years of service for purposes of eligibility to participate, but only one year of service for purposes of vesting. Not having attained age 25, however, B is not admitted to participation in the plan upon completion of his first year of service with X. In the 1978 plan year, B fails to be credited with 500 hours of service, thereby incurring a one-year break in service. As a result of B's one-year break in service in the 1978 plan year, the year of service for vesting which was earlier credited to B for the 1977 plan year is disregarded because the one-year break in service equals the one year of service credited to B before the one-year break in service. After the end of the 1978 plan year, B does not perform an hour of service with X until February 3, 1979. February 3, 1979, therefore, is B's reemployment commencement date under paragraph (b)(1)(i) of this section. B fails to be credited with 1000 hours of service in the first eligibility computation period beginning on February 3, 1979, and also for the vesting computation period beginning January 1, 1979. Because, in accordance with § 2530.202-2(b)(2), the plan provides that after the initial eligibility computation period, plan years will be used as eligibility computation periods, under paragraph (b)(1)(ii) of this section the plan must provide that, in measuring completion of a year of service for eligibility to participate after a one-year break in service, plan years beginning with the plan year which includes an employee's reemployment commencement date will be used. B is credited with 1000 hours of service for the plan year beginning on January 1, 1980 and is therefore credited with a year of service for the 1980 plan year. Under section 202(b)(3) of the Act and section 410(a)(5)(C) of the Code, as a consequence of B's completion of a year of service in the 1980 plan year, B's service before his one-year break in service in the 1978 plan year must be taken into account for eligibility purposes. As conditions of participation, the plan requires that an employee attain age 25 and complete one year of service. Upon his completion of a year of service for the 1980 plan year, B is deemed to have met the plan's participation requirements as of February 22, 1980, his twenty-fifth birthday, because the year of service completed by B in B's eligibility computation period beginning on January 1, 1976 is taken into account for eligibility purposes.

(ii) Employer Y maintains a defined benefit pension plan. The plan provides that an employee acquires a nonforfeitable right to 100 percent of the employee's accrued benefit derived from employer contributions upon completion of 10 years of service. As conditions for participation, the plan requires that an employee of Y complete one year of service and provides that if an employee has incurred a one-year break in service, in computing the employee's period of service for eligibility to participate, years of service before such break will not be taken into account until the employee has completed a year of service with Y after the employee's return. In accordance with § 2530.202-2(b)(1), the plan provides that after the initial eligibility computation period, eligibility computation periods beginning on anniversaries of an employee's employment commencement date will be used. Thus, under paragraph (a)(1) of this section, the plan must use computation periods beginning on anniversaries of the employee's employment commencement date in measuring one-year breaks in service. Employee C's employment commencement date with Y is February 1, 1975. C is credited with a year of service for eligibility to participate in the eligibility computation period beginning on C's employment commencement date and meets the plan's eligibility requirements as of February 1, 1976. In accordance with the provisions of the plan, C commences participation in the plan as of July 1, 1976. C is thereafter credited with a year of service for eligibility to participate in each of the eligibility computation periods beginning on anniversaries of C's employment commencement date (February 1) in 1976, 1977, 1978 and 1979. Thus, as of February 1, 1980, C is credited with 5 years of service for eligibility to participate. In the eligibility computation period beginning on February 1, 1980, C fails to be credited with more than 500 hours of service and therefore incurs a one-year break in service. In the eligibility computation period beginning on February 1, 1981, C is not credited with an hour of service for the performance of duties until March 1, 1981. Under paragraph (b)(1)(iii) of this section, March 1, 1981 is C's reemployment commencement date. C terminates employment with Y on May 1, 1981 and fails to be credited with 1000 hours of service in the 12-consecutive-month period beginning on March 1, 1981, or with more than 500 hours of service in the eligibility computation period beginning on February 1, 1981, thereby incurring a second one-year break in service for eligibility to participate. C is credited with no hours of service in the eligibility computation period beginning on February 1, 1982, thereby incurring a third one-year break in service for eligibility to participate, and is likewise credited with no hours of service in the 12-consecutive-month period beginning on March 1, 1982, the anniversary of B's reemployment commencement date. Under paragraph (b)(1)(iv) of this section, C must therefore be treated as having a new reemployment commencement date as of the first day following the close of the eligibility computation period beginning on February 1, 1982. On January 1, 1984 (before the end of the eligibility computation period beginning February 1, 1983) C is rehired by Y and is credited with an hour of service for the performance of duties. C is therefore treated as having a new reemployment commencement date of January 1, 1984. C fails to be credited with more than 500 hours of service in the eligibility computation period beginning on February 1, 1983, thereby incurring a fourth one-year break in service, and fails to be credited with 1000 hours of service in the 12-consecutive-month period beginning on March 1, 1983, the anniversary of C's original reemployment commencement date. However, in the 12-consecutive-month period beginning on January 1, 1984, C is credited with 1000 hours of service, thus meeting the plan's requirement that an employee who has incurred a one-year break in service for eligibility to participate must complete a year of service upon the employee's return in order for years of service before the one-year break in service to be taken into account for purposes of eligibility. Because C's years of service completed before C's first one-year break in service must be taken into account under section 202(b) of the Act and section 410(b)(5) of the Code for purposes of eligibility to partici-

pate, under § 2530.204-2(a)(2) the period beginning on July 1, 1976 (the earliest date on which C was a participant) and extending until January 31, 1980 (the last day before C's first one-year break in service) must be taken into account for purposes of benefit accrual.

(c) *Prior service for eligibility to participate.* For rules relating to computing service preceding a break in service for the purpose of eligibility to participate in the plan, *see* § 2530.202-2(c).

(d) *Prior service for vesting.* For rules relating to computing service preceding a break in service for the purpose of credit toward vesting, see § 2530.203-2(d).

[¶ 14,412D]
§ 2530.200b-5 **Seasonal industries.** [Reserved.]

[¶ 14,412E]
§ 2530.200b-6 **Maritime industry.**

(a) *General.* Sections 202(a)(3)(D), 203(b)(2)(D) and 204(b)(3)(E) of the Act and sections 410(a)(3)(D) and 411 (a)(5)(D) and (b)(3)(E) of the Code contain special provisions applicable to the maritime industry. In general, those provisions permit statutory standards otherwise expressed in terms of 1,000 hours of service to be applied to employees in the maritime industry as if such standards were expressed in terms of 125 days of service. A plan covering employees in the maritime industry may nevertheless credit service to such employees on the basis of hours of service, as prescribed in § 2530.200b-2, including the use of any equivalency permitted under § 2530.200b-3, or may credit service to such employees on the basis of elapsed time, as permitted under § 2530.200b-9.

(b) *Definition.* For purposes of sections 202, 203, and 204 of the Act and sections 410 and 411 of the Code, the maritime industry is that industry in which employees perform duties on board commercial, exploratory, service or other vessels moving on the high seas, inland waterways, Great Lakes, coastal zones, harbors and noncontiguous areas, or on offshore ports, platforms or other similar sites.

(c) *Computation periods.* For employees in the maritime industry, computation periods shall be established as for employees in any other industry.

(d) *Year of service.* To the extent that a plan covers employees engaged in the maritime industry, and credits service for such employees on the basis of days of service, such employees who are credited with 125 days of service in the applicable computation period must be credited with a year of service. In the case of a plan covering both employees engaged in the maritime industry and employees not engaged in the maritime industry, service of employees not engaged in the maritime industry shall not be determined on the basis of days of service.

(e) *Year of participation for benefit accrual.* A plan covering employees engaged in the maritime industry may determine such an employee's period of service for purposes of benefit accrual on any basis permitted under § 2530.204-2 and § 2530.204-3. For purposes of § 2530.204-2(c) (relating to partial years of participation), in the case of an employee engaged in the maritime industry who is credited by the plan on the basis of days of service and whose service is not less than 125 days of service during an accrual computation period, the calculation of such employee's period of service for purposes of benefit accrual shall be treated as not made on a reasonable and consistent basis if service during such computation period is not taken into account. Thus, the employee must be credited with at least a partial year of participation (but not necessarily a full year of participation) for that accrual computation period, in accordance with § 2530.204-2(c).

(f) *Employment commencement date.* For purposes of § 2530.200b-4 (relating to breaks in service) and § 2530.202-2 (relating to eligibility computation periods):

(1) The employment commencement date of an employee engaged in the maritime industry who is credited by the plan on the basis of days of service shall be the first day for which the employee is entitled to be credited with a day of service described in § 2530.200b-7(a)(1).

(2)(i) Except as provided in paragraph (f)(2)(ii) of this section, the reemployment commencement date of an employee engaged in the maritime industry shall be the first day for which the employee is entitled to be credited with a day of service described in § 2530.200b-7(a)(1) after the first eligibility computation period in which the employee incurs a one-year break in service following an eligibility computation period in which the employee is credited with more than 62 days of service.

(ii) In the case of an employee engaged in the maritime industry who is credited with no hours of service in an eligibility computation period beginning after the employee's reemployment commencement date established under paragraph (f)(2)(i) of this section, the employee shall be treated as having a new reemployment commencement date as of the first day for which the employee is entitled to be credited with a day of service described in § 2530.200b-7(a)(1) after such eligibility computation period.

[¶ 14,412F]

§ 2530.200b-7 **Day of service for employees in the maritime industry**.

(a) *General rule*. A day of service in the maritime industry which must, as a minimum, be counted for the purposes of determining a year of service, a year of participation for benefit accrual, a break in service and an employment commencement date (or reemployment commencement date) under sections 202, 203 and 204 of the Act and sections 410 and 411 of the Code by a plan that credits service by days of service rather than hours of service (as prescribed in § 2530.200b-2, or under equivalencies permitted under § 2530.200b-3) or elapsed time (as permitted under § 2530.200b-9), is a day of service as defined in paragraphs (a) (1), (2) and (3) of this section.

(1) A day of service is each day for which an employee is paid, or entitled to payment for the performance of duties for the employer during the applicable computation period.

(2) A day of service is each day for which an employee is paid, or entitled to payment, by the employer on account of a period of time during which no duties are performed (irrespective of whether the employment relationship has terminated) due to vacation, holiday, illness, incapacity (including disability), layoff, jury duty, military duty or leave of absence. Notwithstanding the preceding sentence;

(i) No more than 63 days of service are required to be credited under this paragraph (a)(2) to an employee on account of any single continuous period during which the employee performs no duties (whether or not such period occurs in a single computation period);

(ii) A day for which an employee is directly or indirectly paid, or entitled to payment, on account of a period during which no duties are performed is not required to be credited to the employee if such payment is made or due under a plan maintained solely for the purpose of complying with applicable workmen's compensation (including maintenance and care), or unemployment compensation or disability insurance laws; and

(iii) Days of service are not required to be credited for a payment which solely reimburses an employee for medical or medically related expenses incurred by the employee.

For purposes of this paragraph (a)(2), a payment shall be deemed to be made by or due from an employer regardless of whether such payment is made by or due from the employer directly, or indirectly through, among others, a trust, fund, or insurer, to which the employer contributes or pays premiums, and regardless of whether contributions made or due to the trust, fund, insurer or other entity are for the benefit of particular employees or are made on behalf of a group of employees in the aggregate.

(3) A day of service is each day for which back pay, irrespective of mitigation of damages, has been either awarded or agreed to by the employer. Days of service shall not be credited both under paragraph (a)(1) or paragraph (a)(2), as the case may be, and under this subparagraph. Thus, for example, an employee who receives a back pay award following a determination that he or she was paid at an unlawful rate for days of service previously credited will not be entitled to additional credit for the same days of service. Crediting of days of service for back pay awarded or agreed to with respect to periods described in paragraph (a)(2) shall be subject to the limitations set forth in that paragraph. For example, no more than 63 days of service are required to be credited for payments of back pay, to the extent that such back pay is agreed to or awarded for a period of time during which an employee did not or would not have performed duties.

(b) *Special rule for determining days of service for reasons other than the performance of duties*. In the case of a payment which is made or due on account of a period during which an employee performs no duties, and which results in the crediting of days of service under paragraph (a)(3) of this section, or, in the case of an award or agreement for back pay, to the extent that such award or agreement is made with respect to a period described in paragraph (a)(2) of this section, the number of days of service to be credited shall be determined as follows:

(1) *Payments calculated on the basis of units of time*. In the case of a payment made or due which is calculated on the basis of units of time, such as days, weeks or months, the number of days of service to be credited shall be the number of regularly scheduled working days included in the units of time on the basis of which the payment is calculated. For purposes of the preceding sentence, in the case of an employee without a regular work schedule, a plan may provide for the calculation of the number of days of service to be credited on the basis of a 5-day workweek, or may provide for such calculation on any reasonable basis which reflects the average days worked by the employee, or by other employees in the same job classification, over a representative period of time, provided that the basis so used is consistently applied with respect to all employees within the same job classifications, reasonably defined.

(2) *Payments not calculated on the basis of units of time*. Except as provided in paragraph (b)(3) of this section, in the case of a payment made or due, which is not calculated on the basis of units of time, the number of days of service to be credited shall be equal to the amount of the payment divided by the employee's most recent daily rate of compensation before the period during which no duties are performed.

(3) *Rule against double credit*. Notwithstanding paragraphs (b)(1) and (2) of this section, an employee is not required to be credited on account of a period during which no duties are performed with a number of days of service which is greater than the number of days regularly scheduled for the performance of duties during such period. For purposes of the preceding sentence, in the case of an employee without a regular work schedule, a plan may provide for the calculation of the number of days of service to be credited to the employee for a period during which no duties are performed on the basis of a 5-day workweek, or may provide for such calculation on any reasonable basis which reflects the average hours worked by the employee, or by other employees in the same job classification, over a representative period of time, provided that the basis so used is consistently applied with respect to all employees in the same job classifications, reasonably defined.

(c) *Crediting of days of service to computation periods*. (1) Except as provided in paragraph (c)(4) of this section, days of service described in paragraph (a)(1) of this section shall be credited to the computation period in which the duties are performed.

(2) Except as provided in paragraph (c)(4) of this section, days of service described in paragraph (a)(2) of this section shall be credited as follows:

(i) Days of service credited to an employee on account of a payment which is calculated on the basis of units of time, such as days, weeks or months, shall be credited to the computation period or computation periods in which the period during which no duties are performed occurs, beginning with the first unit of time to which the payment relates.

(ii) Days of service credited to an employee by reason of a payment which is not calculated on the basis of units of time shall be credited to the computation period in which the period during which no duties are performed occurs, or if the period during which no duties are performed extends beyond one computation period, such hours of service shall be allocated between not more than the first two computation periods on any reasonable basis which is consistently applied with respect to all employees within the same job classifications, reasonably defined.

(3) Except as provided in paragraph (c)(4) of this section, days of service described in paragraph (a)(3) of this section shall be credited to the computation period or periods to which the award or agreement for back pay pertains, rather than to the computation period in which the award, agreement or payment is made.

(4) In the case of days of service to be credited to an employee in connection with a period of no more than 31 days which extends beyond one computation period, all such days of service may be credited to the first computation period or the second computation period. Crediting of days of service under this subparagraph must be done consistently with respect to all employees with the same job classifications, reasonably defined.

(d) *Other federal law*. Nothing in this section shall be construed to alter, amend, modify, invalidate, impair or supersede any law of the United States or any rule or regulation issued under any such law. Thus, for example, nothing in this section shall be construed as denying an employee credit for a day of service if credit is required by separate federal law. Furthermore, the nature and extent of such credit shall be determined under such law.

(e) *Nondaily employees*. For maritime employees whose compensation is not determined on the basis of certain amounts for each day worked during a given period, service shall be credited on the basis of hours of service as determined in accordance with § 2530.200b-2(a) (including use of any equivalency permitted under § 2530.200b-3) or on the basis of elapsed time, as permitted under § 2530.200b-9.

(f) *Plan document*. A plan which credits service on the basis of days of service must state in the plan document the definition of days of service set forth in paragraph (a) of this section, but is not required to state the rules set forth in paragraph (b) and (c) if they are incorporated by reference.

[¶ 14,412G]

§ 2530.200b-8 **Determination of days of service to be credited to maritime employees**.

(a) *General rule*. For the purpose of determining the days of service which must be credited to an employee for a computation period, a plan shall determine days of service from records of days worked and days for which payment is made or due. Any records may be used to determine days of service to be credited to employees under a plan, even though such records are maintained for other purposes, provided that they accurately reflect the actual number of days of service with which an employee is required to be credited under § 2530.200b-7(a). Payroll records, for example, may provide sufficiently accurate data to serve as a basis for determining days of service. If, however, existing records do not accurately reflect the actual number of days of service with which an employee is entitled to be credited, a plan must develop and maintain adequate records. A plan may in any case credit days of service under any method which results in the crediting of no less than the actual number of days of service required to be credited under § 2530.200b-7(a) to each employee in a computation period, even though such method may result in the crediting of days of service in excess of the number of days required to be credited under § 2530.200b-7(a). A plan is not required to prescribe in its documents which records are to be used to determine days of service.

(b) *Determination of pre-effective date days of service*. To the extent that a plan is required to determine days of service completed before the effective date of Part 2 of Title I of the Act (*see* section 211 of the Act), the plan may use whatever records may be reasonably accessible to it and may make whatever calculations are necessary to determine the approximate number of hours of service completed before such effective date. For example, if a plan or an employer maintaining the plan has, or has access to, only the records of compensation of employees for the period before the effective date, it may derive the pre-effective date days of service by using the daily rate for the period or the days customarily worked. If accessible records are insufficient to make an approximation of the number of pre-effective date days of service for a particular employee or group of employees, the plan may make a reasonable estimate of the days of service completed by such

employee or employees during the particular period. For example, if records are available with respect to some employees, the plan may estimate the days of service of other employees in the same job classification based on these records. A plan may use the elapsed time method prescribed under § 2530.200b-9 to determine days of service completed before the effective date of Part 2 of Title I of the Act.

>>>→ *Caution: The following regulation was formerly temporary and proposed. It has since been amended, finalized and redesignated as IRS Reg. § 1.410(a)-7 at ¶ 12,162 because of the ERISA Reorganization Plan which transferred jurisdiction of this subject matter to the IRS. The regulation below was subsequently deleted by the DOL from its regulations (45 FR 40987). It is retained here in its temporary and proposed form for historical purposes.*

[¶ 14,413]

§ 2530.200b-9 **Elapsed time**.

(a) *General*. (1) *Introduction to elapsed time method of crediting service*. (i) § 2530.200b-2 sets forth the general method of crediting service for an employee. The general method is based upon the actual counting of hours of service during the applicable 12-consecutive-month computation period. The equivalencies set forth in § 2530.200b-3 are also methods for crediting hours of service during computation periods. Under the general method and the equivalencies, an employee receives a year's credit (in units of years of service or years of participation) for a computation period during which the employee is credited with a specified number of hours of service. In general, an employee's statutory entitlement with respect to eligibility to participate, vesting and benefit accrual is determined by totalling the number of years' credit to which an employee is entitled.

(ii) Under the alternative method set forth in this section, by contrast, an employee's statutory entitlement with respect to eligibility to participate, vesting and benefit accrual is not based upon the actual completion of a specified number of hours of service during a 12-consecutive-month period. Instead, such entitlement is determined generally with reference to the total period of time which elapses while the employee is employed (i.e., while the employment relationship exists) with the employer or employers maintaining the plan. The alternative method set forth in this section is designed to enable a plan to lessen the administrative burdens associated with the maintenance of records of an employee's hours of service by permitting each employee to be credited with his or her total period of service with the employer or employers maintaining the plan, irrespective of the actual hours of service completed in any 12-consecutive-month period.

(2) *Overview of the operation of the elapsed time method*. (i) Under the elapsed time method of crediting service, a plan is generally required to take into account the period of time which elapses while the employee is employed (i.e., while the employment relationship exists) with the employer or employers maintaining the plan, regardless of the actual number of hours he or she completes during such period. Under this alternative method of crediting service, an employee's service is required to be taken into account for purposes of eligibility to participate and vesting as of the date he or she first performs an hour of service within the meaning of § 2530.200b-2(a)(1) for the employer or employers maintaining the plan. Service is required to be taken into account for the period of time from the date the employee first performs such an hour of service until the date he or she severs from service with the employer or employers maintaining the plan.

(ii) The date the employee severs from service is the earlier of the date the employee quits, is discharged, retires or dies, or the first anniversary of the date the employee is absent from service for any other reason (e.g., disability, vacation, leave of absence, layoff, etc.). Thus, for example, if an employee quits, the severance from service date is the date the employee quits. On the other hand, if an employee is granted a leave of absence (and if no intervening event occurs), the severance from service date will occur one year after the date the employee was first absent on leave, and this one year of absence is required to be taken into account as service for the employer or employers maintaining the plan. Because the severance from service date occurs on the earlier of two possible dates (i.e., quit, discharge, retirement or death *or* the first anniversary of an absence from service for any other reason), a quit, discharge, retirement or death within the year after the beginning of an absence for any other reason results in an immediate severance from service. Thus, for example, if an employee dies at the end of a four-week absence resulting from illness, the severance from service date is the date of death, rather than the first anniversary date of the first day of absence for illness.

(iii) In addition, for purposes of eligibility to participate and vesting under the elapsed time method of crediting service, an employee who has severed from service by reason of a quit, discharge or retirement may be entitled to have a period of time of 12 months or less taken into account by the employer or employers maintaining the plan if the employee returns to service within a certain period of time and performs an hour of service within the meaning of § 2530.200b-2(a)(1). In general, the period of time during which the employee must return to service begins on the date the employee severs from service as a result of a quit, discharge or retirement and ends on the first anniversary of such date. However, if the employee is absent for any other reason (e.g., layoff) and then quits, is discharged or retires, the period of time during which the employee may return and receive credit begins on the severance from service date and ends one year after the first day of absence (e.g., first day of layoff). As a result of the operation of these rules, a severance from service (e.g., a quit), or an absence (e.g., layoff) followed by a severance from service, never results in a period of time of more than one year being required to be taken into account after an employee severs from service or is absent from service.

(iv) For purposes of benefit accrual under the elapsed time method of crediting service, an employee is entitled to have his or her service taken into account from the date he or she begins to participate in the plan until the severance from service date. Periods of severance under any circumstances are not required to be taken into account. For example, a participant who is discharged on December 14, 1980 and rehired on October 14, 1981 is not required to be credited with the 10 month period of severance for benefit accrual purposes.

(3) *Overview of certain concepts relating to the elapsed time method.* (i) *General.* The rules with respect to the elapsed time method of crediting service are based on certain concepts which are defined in paragraph (b) of this section. These concepts are applied in the substantive rules contained in paragraphs (c), (d), (e), (f) and (g) of this section. The purpose of this subparagraph is to summarize these concepts.

(ii) *Employment commencement date.* (A) A concept which is necessary in order to credit service accurately under any service crediting method is the establishment of a starting point for crediting service. The employment commencement date, which is the date on which an employee first performs an hour of service within the meaning of § 2530.200b-2(a)(1) for the employer or employers maintaining the plan, is used throughout Part 2530 to establish the date upon which an employee must begin to receive credit for certain purposes (e.g. eligibility to participate and vesting).

(B) In order to credit accurately an employee's total service with an employer or employers maintaining the plan, a plan also may provide for an "adjusted" employment commencement date (i.e., a recalculation of the employment commencement date to reflect non-creditable periods of severance) or a reemployment commencement date as defined in paragraph (b)(3) of this section. Fundamentally, all three concepts rely upon the performance of an hour of service to provide a starting point for crediting service. One purpose of these three concepts is to enable plans to satisfy the requirements of this section in a variety of ways.

(C) The fundamental rule with respect to these concepts is that any plan provision is permissible so long as it satisfies the minimum standards. Thus, for example, although the rules of this section provide that credit must begin on the employment commencement date, a plan is permitted to "adjust" the employment commencement date to reflect periods of time for which service is not required to be credited. Similarly, a plan may wish to credit service under the elapsed time method as discrete periods of service and provide for a reemployment commencement date. Certain plans may wish to provide for both

concepts, although it is not a requirement of this section that plans so provide.

(iii) *Severance from service date.* Another fundamental concept of the elapsed time method of crediting service is the severance from service date, which is defined as the earlier of the date on which an employee quits, retires, is discharged or dies, or the first anniversary of the first date of absence for any other reason. One purpose of the severance from service date is to provide the endpoint for crediting service under the elapsed time method. As a general proposition, service is credited from the employment commencement date (i.e., the starting point) until the severance from service date (i.e., the endpoint). A complementary purpose of the severance from service date is to establish the starting point for measuring a period of severance from service in order to determine a "break in service" (see paragraph (a)(3)(v) of this section). A third purpose of such date is to establish the starting point for measuring the period of time which may be required to be taken into account under the service spanning rules (see paragraph (a)(3)(vi) of this section).

(iv) *Period of service.* A third elapsed time concept is the use of the "period of service" rather than the "year of service" in determining service to be taken into account for purposes of eligibility to participate, vesting and benefit accrual. For purposes of eligibility to participate and vesting, the period of service runs from the employment commencement date or reemployment commencement date until the severance from service date. For purposes of benefit accrual, a period of service runs from the date that a participant commences participation under the plan until the severance from service date. Because the endpoint of the period of service is marked by the severance from service date, an employee is credited with the period of time which runs during any absence from service (other than for reasons of a quit, retirement, discharge or death) which is 12 months or less. Thus, for example, a three week absence for vacation is taken into account as part of a period of service and does not trigger a severance from service date.

(v) *Period of severance.* A period of severance begins on the severance from service date and ends when an employee returns to service with the employer or employers maintaining the plan. The purpose of the period of severance is to apply the statutory "break in service" rules to an elapsed time method of crediting service.

(vi) *Service spanning.* Under the elapsed time method of crediting service, a plan is required to credit periods of service and, under the service spanning rules, certain periods of severance of 12 months or less for purposes of eligibility to participate and vesting. Under the first service spanning rule, if an employee severs from service as a result of quit, discharge or retirement and then returns to service within 12 months, the period of severance is required to be taken into account. However, a situation may arise in which an employee is absent from service for any reason other than quit, discharge, retirement or death and during the absence a quit, discharge or retirement occurs. The second service spanning rule provides in that set of circumstances that a plan is required to take into account the period of time between the severance from service date (i.e., the date of quit, discharge or retirement) and the first anniversary of the date on which the employee was first absent, if the employee returns to service on or before such first anniversary date.

(4) *Scope.* (i) Except for certain provisions for which the Secretary of Labor has been specifically authorized to prescribe regulations, regulations prescribed by the Secretary of the Treasury under sections 410 and 411 of the Code shall, pursuant to section 3002(c) of the Act, implement the counterpart provisions of sections 202, 203 and 204 of the Act. Certain provisions for which the Secretary of Labor has been authorized to prescribe regulations relate to the methods for computing service to be credited to an employee, such as the calculation of an hour of service, year of service, year of participation and breaks in service, and such concepts are implemented in Part 2530. Accordingly, because elapsed time represents an alternative method of crediting service, this alternative method is set forth in Part 2530.

(ii) In order to clarify and illustrate the elapsed time method of crediting service, this section restates certain statutory provisions for which the Secretary of the Treasury has been authorized to prescribe regulations. In certain instances, as a result of the nature of the elapsed time method of crediting service, it has been necessary in this section to recast these concepts in a mode consistent with and solely for the purpose of using the elapsed time method. Thus, for example, due to the lack of computation periods under the elapsed time method of crediting service, a plan using elapsed time may disregard service for vesting purposes prior to the date an employee attains the age of 22, while under the general rule under section 203(b)(1)(A) of the Act, 411(a)(4)(A) of the Code and Treasury Department regulations under section 411(a) of the Code, contained in 26 CFR, a plan may disregard service for vesting computation periods prior to the vesting computation period during which an employee attains the age of 22. Except as otherwise expressly provided in this section, the rules applicable to the general methods of crediting service are also applicable to the elapsed time method of crediting service.

(5) *Application of elapsed time method to sections 202, 203 or 204 of the Act and sections 410 and 411 of the Code.* (i) The substantive rules for crediting service under the elapsed time method with respect to eligibility to participate are contained in paragraph (c), the rules with respect to vesting are contained in paragraph (d), and the rules with respect to benefit accrual are contained in paragraph (e). The format of the rules is designed to enable a plan to use the elapsed time method of crediting service either for all purposes or for any one or combination of purposes under Part 2 of Title I of the Act and the counterpart provisions of the Code. Thus, for example, a plan may credit service for eligibility to participate purposes by the use of the general method of crediting service set forth in § 2530.200b-2 or by the use of any of the equivalencies set forth in § 2530.200b-3, while the plan may credit service for vesting and benefit accrual purposes by the use of the elapsed time method of crediting service.

(ii) A plan using the elapsed time method of crediting service for one or more classifications of employees covered under the plan may use the general method of crediting service set forth in § 2530.200b-2 or any of the equivalencies set forth in § 2530.200b-3 for other classifications of employees, provided that such classifications are reasonable and are consistently applied. Thus, for example, a plan may provide that part-time employees are credited under the general method of crediting service set forth in § 2530.200b-2 and full-time employees are credited under the elapsed time method. A classification, however, will not be deemed to be reasonable or consistently applied if such classification is designed with an intent to preclude an employee or employees from attaining his or her statutory entitlement with respect to eligibility to participate, vesting or benefit accrual. For example, a classification applied so that any employee credited with less than 1,000 hours of service during a given 12-consecutive-month period would be considered part-time and subject to the general method of crediting service rather than the elapsed time method would not be reasonable.

(iii) Notwithstanding paragraph (a) (5) i) and (ii) of this section, the use of the elapsed time method for some purposes or the use of the elapsed time method for some employees may, under certain circumstances result in discrimination prohibited under section 401(a)(4) of the Code, even though the use of the elapsed time method for such purposes and for such employees is permitted under this section.

(b) *Definitions.* (1) *Employment commencement date.* For purposes of this section, the term "employment commencement date" shall mean the date on which the employee first performs an hour of service within the meaning of § 2530.200b-2(a)(1) for the employer or employers maintaining the plan.

(2) *Severance from service date.* For purposes of this section, a "severance from service" shall occur on the earlier of—

(i) The date on which an employee quits, retires, is discharged or dies; or

(ii) The first anniversary of the first date of a period in which an employee remains absent from service (with or without pay) with the employer or employers maintaining the plan for any reason other than quit, retirement, discharge or death, such as vacation, holiday, sickness, disability, leave of absence or layoff.

(3) *Reemployment commencement date.* For purposes of this section, the term "reemployment commencement date" shall mean the first date, following a period of severance from service which is not required to take into account under the service spanning rules in paragraphs (c)(2)(iii) and (d)(1)(iii) of this section, on which the employee performs an hour of service within the meaning of paragraph § 2530.200b-2(a)(1) for the employer or employers maintaining the plan.

(4) *Participation commencement date.* For purposes of this section, the term "participation commencement date" shall mean the date a participant first commences participation under the plan.

(5) *Period of severance.* For purposes of this section, the term "period of severance" shall mean the period of time commencing on the severance from service date and ending on the date on which the employee again performs an hour of service within the meaning of § 2530.200b-2(a)(1) for an employer or employers maintaining the plan.

(6) *Period of service.* (i) *General rule.* For purposes of this section, the term "period of service" shall mean a period of service commencing on the employee's employment commencement date or reemployment commencement date, whichever is applicable, and ending on the severance from service date.

(ii) *Aggregation rule.* Unless a plan provides in some manner for an "adjusted" employment commencement date or similar method of consolidating periods of service, periods of service shall be aggregated unless such periods may be disregarded under section 202(b) or 203(b) of the Act and section 410(a)(5) or 411(a)(4) of the Code.

(iii) *Other federal law.* Nothing in this section shall be construed to alter, amend, modify, invalidate, impair or supersede any law of the United States or any rule or regulation issued under any such law. Thus, for example, nothing in this section shall be construed as denying an employee credit for a "period of service" if credit is required by separate federal law. Furthermore, the nature and extent of such credit shall be determined under such law.

(c) *Eligibility to participate.* (1) *General rule.* For purposes of section 202(a)(1)(A) of the Act and section 410(a)(1)(A) of the Code, a plan generally may not require as a condition of participation in the plan that an employee complete a period of service with the employer or employers maintaining the plan extending beyond the later of—

(i) The date on which the employee attains the age of 25; or

(ii) The date on which the employee completes a one-year period of service.

See regulations, relating to eligibility to participate rules (section 410(a) of the Code), prescribed by the Secretary of the Treasury in 26 CFR.

(2) *Determination of one-year period of service.* (i) For purposes of determining the date on which an employee satisfies the service requirement for initial eligibility to participate under the plan, a plan, using the elapsed time method of crediting service, shall provide that an employee who completes the 1-year period of service requirement on the first anniversary of his employment commencement date satisfies the minimum service requirement as of such date. In the case of an employee who fails to complete a one-year period of service on the first anniversary of his employment commencement date, a plan which does not contain a provision permitted by section 202(b)(4) of the Act and section 410(a)(5)(D) of the Code (rule of parity) shall provide for the aggregation of periods of service so that a one-year period of service shall be completed as of the date the employee completes 12 months of service (30 days are deemed to be a month in the case of the aggregation of fractional months) or 365 days of service.

(ii) For purposes of section 202(a)(1)(B)(i) of the Act and section 410(a)(1)(B)(i) of the Code, a "3-year period of service" shall be deemed to be "3 years of service."

(iii) *Service spanning rules.* In determining a 1-year period of service for purposes of initial eligibility to participate and a period of service for purposes of retention of eligibility to participate, in addition to taking into account an employee's period of service, a plan shall take into account the following periods of severance—

(A) If an employee severs from service by reason of a quit, discharge or retirement and the employee then performs an hour of service within the meaning of §2530.200b-2(a)(1) within 12 months of the severance from service date, the plan is required to take into account the period of severance; and

(B) Notwithstanding paragraph (c)(2)((iii)(A) of this section, if an employee severs from service by reason of a quit, discharge or retirement during an absence from service of 12 months or less for any reason other than a quit, discharge, retirement or death, and then performs an hour of service within the meaning of §2530.200b-2(a)(1) within 12 months of the date on which the employee was first absent from service, the plan is required to take into account the period of severance.

(iv) For purposes of determining an employee's retention of eligibility to participate in the plan, a plan shall take into account an employee's entire period of service unless certain periods of service may be disregarded under section 202(b) of the Act and section 410(a)(5) of the Code.

(v) *Example.* Employee W, age 31, completed 6 months of service and was laid off. After 2 months of layoff, W quit. Five months later, W returned to service. For purposes of eligibility to participate, W was required to be credited with 13 months of service (8 months of service and 5 months of severance). If, on the other hand, W had not returned to service within the first 10 months of severance (i.e., within 12 months after the first day of layoff), W would be required to be credited with eight months of service.

(3) *Entry date requirements.* (i) *General rule.* For purposes of section 202(a)(4) of the Act and section 410(a)(4) of the Code, it is necessary for a plan to provide that any employee who has satisfied the minimum age and service requirements, and who is otherwise entitled to participate in the plan, commences participation in the plan no later than the earlier of—

(A) The first day of the first plan year beginning after the date on which such employee satisfied such requirements, or

(B) The date six months after the date on which he satisfied such requirements, unless such employee was separated from service before the date referred to in subparagraph (A) or (B), whichever is applicable.

(ii) *Separation from service.* (A) *Definition.* For purposes of this section, the term "separated from service" includes a severance from service or an absence from service for any reason other than a quit, discharge, retirement or death, regardless of the duration of such absence. Accordingly, if an employee is laid off for a period of six weeks, the employee shall be deemed to be "separated from service" during such period for purposes of the entry date requirements.

(B) *Application.* A period of severance which is taken into account under the service spanning rules in paragraph (c)(2)(iii) of this section or an absence of 12 months or less may result in an employee satisfying the plan's minimum service requirement during such period of time. In addition, once an employee satisfies the plan's minimum service requirement, either before or during such period of time, such period of time may contain an entry date applicable to such employee. In the case of an employee whose period of severance is taken into account and such period contains an entry date applicable to the employee, he or she shall be made a participant in the plan (if otherwise eligible) no later than the date on which he or she ended the period of severance. In the case of an employee whose period of absence contains an entry date applicable to such employee, he or she, no later than the date such absence ended, shall be made a participant in the plan (if otherwise eligible) as of the first applicable entry date which occurred during such absence from service.

(iii) *Examples.* For purposes of the following examples, assume that the plan provides for a minimum age requirement of 25 and a minimum service requirement of one year, and provides for semiannual entry dates.

(A) Employee A, age 35, worked for 10 months in a job classification covered under the plan, became disabled for nine consecutive months and then returned to service. During the period of absence, A completed a 1-year period of service and passed a semi-

annual entry date after satisfying the minimum service requirement. Accordingly, the plan is required to make A a participant no later than his return to service effective as of the applicable entry date.

(B) Employee B, after satisfying the minimum age and service requirements, quit work before the next semi-annual entry date, and then returned to service before incurring a 1-year period of severance, but after such semi-annual entry date. Employee B is entitled to become a participant immediately upon his return to service effective as of the date of his return.

See regulations, relating to eligibility to participate rules (Section 410(a) of the Code), prescribed by the Secretary of the Treasury in 26 CFR.

(4) *Break in service.* For purposes of applying the break in service rules under sections 202(b) (2) and (3) of the Act and sections 410(a)(5) (B) and (C) of the Code, the term "1-year period of severance" shall be substituted for the term "1-year break in service." A 1-year period of severance shall be determined on the basis of a 12-consecutive-month period beginning on the severance from service date and ending on the first anniversary of such date provided that the employee during such 12-consecutive-month period does not perform an hour of service within the meaning of §2530.200b-2(a)(1) for the employer or employers maintaining the plan.

(5) *One-year hold-out.* (i) *General rule.* (A) For purposes of section 202(b)(3) of the Act and section 410(a)(5)(C) of the Code, in determining the period of service of an employee who has incurred a 1-year period of severance, a plan may disregard the employee's period of service before such period of severance until the employee completes a 1-year period of service after such period of severance.

(B) *Example.* Assume that a plan provides for a minimum service requirement of 1 year and provides for semi-annual entry dates, but does not contain the provisions permitted by section 202(b)(4) of the Act and section 410(a)(5)(D) of the Code (relating to the rule of parity). Employee G, age 40, completed a seven-month period of service, quit and then returned to service 15 months later, thereby incurring a 1-year period of severance. After working four months, G was laid off for nine months and then returned to work again. Although the plan may hold employee G out from participation in the plan until the completion of a 1-year period of service after the 1-year (or greater) period of severance, once the 1-year hold-out is completed the plan is required to provide the employee with such statutory entitlement as arose during the 1-year hold-out. Accordingly, employee G satisfied the 1-year of service requirement as of the first month of layoff, and G is entitled to become a participant in the plan immediately upon his return to service after the nine month layoff effective as of the first applicable entry date occurring after the date on which he satisfied the 1-year of service requirement (i.e., the first applicable entry date after the first month of layoff).

See regulations, relating to eligibility to participate rules (Section 410(a) of the Code), prescribed by the Secretary of the Treasury in 26 CFR.

(6) *Rule of parity.* (i) *General rule.* For purposes of section 202(b)(4) of the Act and section 410(a)(5)(D) of the Code, in the case of a participant who does not have any nonforfeitable right under the plan to his accrued benefit derived from employer contributions and who incurs a 1-year period of severance, a plan, in determining an employee's period of service for purposes of section 202(a)(1) of the Act and section 410(a)(1) of the Code, may disregard his period of service if his latest period of severance equals or exceeds his prior period of service, whether or not consecutive, completed before such period of severance.

(ii) In determining whether a completely nonvested employee's service may be disregarded under the rule of parity, a plan is not permitted to apply the rule until the employee incurs a 1-year period of severance. Accordingly, a plan may not disregard a period of service of less than one year until an employee has incurred a period of severance of at least one year.

(iii) *Example.* Assume that a plan provides for a minimum service requirement of one year and provides for the rule of parity. An employee works for three months, quits and then is rehired 10 months later. Such employee is entitled to receive 13 months of credit for purposes of eligibility to participate and vesting (see service spanning rules). Although the period of severance exceeded the period of service, the three months of service may not be disregarded because no 1-year period of severance occurred.

See regulations, relating to eligibility to participate rules (Section 410(a) of the Code), prescribed by the Secretary of the Treasury in 26 CFR.

(d) *Vesting.* (1) *General rule.* (i) For purposes of section 203(a)(2) of the Act and section 411(a)(2) of the Code, relating to vesting in accrued benefits derived from employer contributions, a plan, which determines service to be taken in account on the basis of elapsed time, shall provide that an employee is credited with a number of years of service equal to at least the number of whole years of the employee's period of service, whether or not such periods of service were completed consecutively.

(ii) In order to determine the number of whole years of an employee's period of service, a plan shall provide that nonsuccessive periods of service must be aggregated and that less than whole year periods of service (whether or not consecutive) must be aggregated on the basis that 12 months of service (30 days are deemed to be a month in the case of the aggregation of fractional months) or 365 days of service equal a whole year of service.

(iii) *Service spanning rules.* In determining a participant's period of service for vesting purposes, a plan shall take into account the following periods of severance—

(A) If an employee severs from service by reason of a quit, discharge or retirement and the employee then performs an hour of service within the meaning of §2530.200b-2(a)(1) within 12 months of the severance from service date, the plan is required to take into account the period of severance; and

(B) Notwithstanding subparagraph (d)(1)((iii)(A) of this section, if an employee severs from service by reason of a quit, discharge or retirement during an absence from service of 12 months or less for any reason other than a quit, discharge, retirement or death, and then performs an hour of service within the meaning of §2530.200b-2(a)(1) within 12 months of the date on which the employee was first absent from service, the plan is required to take into account the period of severance.

(iv) For purposes of determining an employee's nonforfeitable percentage of accrued benefits derived from employer contributions, a plan, after calculating an employee's period of service in the manner prescribed in this paragraph, may disregard any remaining less than whole year, 12-month or 365-day period of service. Thus, for example, if a plan provides for the statutory five to fifteen year graded vesting, an employee with a period (or periods) of service which yield 5 whole year periods of service and an additional 321-day period of service is twenty-five percent vested in his or her employer-derived accrued benefits (based solely on the 5 whole year periods of service).

(2) *Service which may be disregarded.* (i) For purposes of section 203(b)(1) of the Act and section 411(a)(4) of the Code, in determining the nonforfeitable percentage of an employee's right to his or her accrued benefits derived from employer contributions, all of an employee's period or periods of service with an employer or employers maintaining the plan shall be taken into account unless such service may be disregarded under paragraph (d)(2)(ii) of this section.

(ii) For purposes of paragraph (d)(2)(i) of this section, the following periods of service may be disregarded—

(A) The period of service completed by an employee before the date on which he attains age 22;

(B) In the case of a plan which requires mandatory employee contributions, the period of service which falls within the period of time to which a particular employee contribution relates if the employee had the opportunity to make a contribution for such period of time and failed to do so;

(C) The period of service during any period for which the employer did not maintain the plan or a predecessor plan;

(D) The period of service which is not required to be taken into account by reason of a period of severance which constitutes a break in service within the meaning of paragraph (d)(4) of this section;

(E) The period of service completed by an employee prior to January 1, 1971, unless the employee completes a period of service of at least 3 years at any time after December 31, 1970; and

(F) The period of service completed before the first plan year for which this section applies to the plan, if such service would have been disregarded under the plan rules relating to breaks in service.

See regulations, relating to service which may be disregarded (Section 411(a) of the Code), prescribed by the Secretary of the Treasury in 26 CFR.

(3) *Seasonal industry.* (Reserved.)

(4) *Break in service.* For purposes of applying the break in service rules, the term "1-year period of severance" shall be substituted for the term "1-year break in service." A 1-year period of severance shall be a 12-consecutive-month period beginning on the severance from service date and ending on the first anniversary of such date, provided that the employee during such 12-consecutive-month period fails to perform an hour of service within the meaning of §2530.200b-2(a)(1) for an employer or employers maintaining the plan.

(5) *One-year hold-out.* For purposes of section 203(b)(3)(B) of the Act and section 411(a)(6)(B) of the Code, in determining the nonforfeitable percentage of the right to accrued benefits derived from employer contributions of an employee who has incurred a 1-year period of severance, the period of service completed before such period of severance is not required to be taken into account until the employee has completed a 1-year period of service after his return to service.

See regulations, relating to vesting rules (Section 411(a) of the Code), prescribed by the Secretary of the Treasury under 26 CFR.

(6) *Vesting in pre-break accruals.* For purposes of section 203(b)(3)(C) of the Act and section 411(a)(6)(C) of the Code, a "1-year period of severance" shall be deemed to constitute a "1-year break in service."

See regulations, relating to vesting rules (Section 411(a) of the Code), prescribed by the Secretary of the Treasury under 26 CFR.

(7) *Rule of parity.* (i) *General rule.* For purposes of section 203(b)(3)(D) of the Act and section 411(a)(6)(D) of the Code, in the case of an employee who is a nonvested participant in employer-derived benefits at the time he incurs a 1-year period of severance, the period of service completed by such participant before such period of severance is not required to be taken into account for purposes of determining the vested percentage of his or her right to employer-derived benefits if at such time the consecutive period of severance equals or exceeds his prior period of service, whether or not consecutive, completed before such period of severance.

See regulations, relating to vesting rules (Section 411(a) of the Code), prescribed by the Secretary of Treasury under 26 CFR.

(e) *Benefit accrual.* (1) For purposes of section 204 of the Act and section 411(b) of the Code, a plan may provide that a participant's service with an employer or employers maintaining the plan be determined on the basis of the participant's total period of service beginning on the participation commencement date and ending on the severance from service date.

(2) Under section 204(b)(3)(A) of the Act and section 411(b)(3)(A) of the Code, a defined benefit pension plan may determine an employee's service for purposes of benefit accrual on any basis which is reasonable and consistent and which takes into account all service during the employee's participation in the plan which is included in a period of service required to be taken into account under section 202(b) of the Act and section 410(a) of the Code (relating to service which must be taken into account for purposes of determining an employee's eligibility to participate). A plan which provides for the determination of an employee's service with an employer or employers maintaining the plan on the basis permitted under paragraph (e)(1) of this section will be deemed to meet the requirements of section 204(b)(3)(A) of the Act and section 411(b)(3)(A) of the Code, provided that the plan meets the requirements of §2530.204-3, relating to plans which determine an employee's service for purposes of benefit accrual on a basis other than computation periods. Specifically, under

§ 2530.204-3, it must be possible to provide that, despite the fact that benefit accrual under such a plan is not based on computation periods, the plan's provisions meet at least one of the three benefit accrual rules of section 204(b)(1) of the Act and section 411(b)(1) of the Code under all circumstances. Further, § 2530.204-3 prohibits such a plan from disregarding service under section 204(b)(3)(C) of the Act and section 411(b)(3)(C) of the Code (which would otherwise permit a plan to disregard service performed by an employee during a computation period in which the employee is credited with less than 1,000 hours).

See regulations, relating to benefit accrual rules (Section 411(b) of the Code), prescribed by the Secretary of the Treasury under 26 CFR.

(f) *Transfers between methods of crediting service.* (1) *Single plan.* A plan may provide that an employee's service for purposes of eligibility to participate, vesting or benefit accrual shall be determined on the basis of computation periods under the general method set forth in § 2530.200b-1 for certain classes of employees but under the alternative method permitted under this section for other classes of employees if the plan provides as follows—

(i) In the case of an employee who transfers from a class of employees whose service is determined on the basis of computation periods to a class of employees whose service is determined on the alternative basis permitted under this section, the employee shall receive credit, as of the date of the transfer, for a period of service consisting of—

(A) A number of years equal to the number of years of service credited to the employee before the computation period during which the transfer occurs; and

(B) The greater of (1) the period of time beginning on the first day of the computation period during which the transfer occurs and ending on the date of such transfer or (2) the service taken into account under the computation periods method as of the date of the transfer.

If the period of service for which an employee receives credit under this paragraph (f)(1)(i) consists of the total of the periods of service determined under paragraph (f)(1)(i)(A) plus paragraph (f)(1)(i)(B)(1) of this section, the employee shall receive credit for service subsequent to the transfer commencing on the date the transfer occurs. If such period of service consists of the total of the amounts of service determined under paragraph (f)(1)(i)(A) plus paragraph (f)(1)(i)(B)(2) of this section, the employee shall receive credit for service subsequent to the transfer commencing on the day after the last day of the computation during which the transfer occurred.

(1) *Single plan.* A plan may provide that an employee's service for purposes of eligibility to participate, vesting or benefit accrual shall be determined on the basis of computation periods under the general method set forth in § 2530.200b-1 for certain classes of employees but under the alternative method permitted under this section for other classes of employees if the plan provides as follows—

(ii) In the case of an employee who transfers from a class of employees whose service is determined on the alternative basis permitted under this section to a class of employees whose service is determined on the basis of computation periods—

(A) The employee shall receive credit, as of the date of the transfer, for a number of years of service equal to the number of 1-year periods of service credited to the employee as of the date of the transfer, and

(B) The employee shall receive credit in the computation period which includes the date of the transfer, for a number of hours of service determined by applying one of the equivalencies set forth in § 2530.200b-4(e)(1) to any fractional part of a year credited to the employee under this section as of the date of the transfer. Such equivalency shall be set forth in the plan and shall apply to all similarly situated employees.

(2) *More than one plan.* In the case of an employee who transfers from a plan using either the general method of determining service on the basis of computation periods set forth in § 2530.200b-1 or the method of determining service permitted under this section to a plan using the other method of determining service, all service required to be credited under the plan to which the employee transfers shall be determined under the method of determining service used by such plan. Accordingly, to the extent that service credited to the employee under the plan from which he or she transfers must also be credited to the employee under the plan to which he or she transfers, such service must be redetermined under the latter plan.

(g) *Amendments to change method of crediting service.* A plan may be amended to change the method of crediting service for any purpose or for any class of employees between the general method set forth in § 2530.200b-1 and the method permitted under this section, if such amendment contains provisions under which each employee with respect to whom the method of crediting service is changed is treated in the same manner as an employee who transfers from one class of employees to another under paragraph (f)(1) of this section.

[¶ 14,414]

§ 2530.201-1 **Coverage; general**.

Coverage of the provisions of Part 2 of Title I of the Act is determined under a multiple step process. First, the plan must be an employee benefit plan as defined under section 3(3) of the Act and § 2510.3-3. (See also the definitions of employee welfare benefit plan, section 3(1) of the Act and § 2510.3-1 and employee pension benefit plan, section 3(2) of the Act and § 2510.3-2.) Second, the employee benefit plan must be subject to Title I of the Act. Coverage for Title I is specified in section 4 of the Act. Third, section 201 of the Act specifies the employee benefit plans subject to Title I which are not subject to the minimum standards of Part 2 of Title I of the Act. Section 2530.201-2 specifies the employee benefit plans subject to Title I of the Act which are exempted from coverage under Part 2 of Title I of the Act and this Part (2530).

[¶ 14,415]

§ 2530.201-2 **Plans covered by part 2530**.

This part (2530) shall apply to any employee benefit plan described in section 4(a) of the Act (and not exempted under section 4(b)) other than—

(a) An employee welfare benefit plan as defined in section 3(1) of the Act and § 2510.3-1;

(b) A plan which is unfunded and is maintained by an employer primarily for the purpose of providing deferred compensation for a select group of management or highly compensated employees;

(1) (Reserved.)

(2) (Reserved.)

(c) A plan established and maintained by a society, order, or association described in section 501(c)(8) or (9) of the Code, if no part of the contributions to or under such plan are made by employers of participants in such plan;

(d) A trust described in section 501(c)(18) of the Code:

(e) A plan which is established and maintained by a labor organization described in section 501(c)(5) of the Code and which does not at any time after the date of enactment of the Act provide for employer contributions;

(f) An agreement providing payments to a retired partner or a deceased partner's successor in interest, as described in section 736 of the Code;

(g) An individual retirement account or annuity described in section 408 of the Code, or a retirement bond described in section 409 of the Code;

(h) An excess benefit plan as described in section 3(36) of the Act.

[¶ 14,420]
MINIMUM PARTICIPATION STANDARDS

Act Sec. 202.(a)(1)(A) No pension plan may require, as a condition of participation in the plan, that an employee complete a period of service with the employer or employers maintaining the plan extending beyond the later of the following dates—

(i) the date on which the employee attains the age of 21; or

(ii) the date on which he completes 1 year of service.

(B)(i) In the case of any plan which provides that after not more than 2 years of service each participant has a right to 100 percent of his accrued benefit under the plan which is nonforfeitable at the time such benefit accrues, clause (ii) of subparagraph (A) shall be applied by substituting "2 years of service" for "1 year of service".

(ii) In the case of any plan maintained exclusively for employees of an educational organization (as defined in section 170(b)(1)(A)(ii) of the Internal Revenue Code of 1986) by an employer which is exempt from tax under section 501(a) of such Code, which provides that each participant having at least 1 year of service has a right to 100 percent of his accrued benefit under the plan which is nonforfeitable at the time such benefit accrues, clause (i) of subparagraph (A) shall be applied by substituting "26" for "21". This clause shall not apply to any plan to which clause (i) applies.

(2) No pension plan may exclude from participation (on the basis of age) employees who have attained a specified age.

(3)(A) For purposes of this section, the term "year of service" means a 12-month period during which the employee has not less than 1,000 hours of service. For purposes of this paragraph, computation of any 12-month period shall be made with reference to the date on which the employee's employment commenced, except that, in accordance with regulations prescribed by the Secretary, such computation may be made by reference to the first day of a plan year in the case of an employee who does not complete 1,000 hours of service during the 12-month period beginning on the date his employment commenced.

(B) In the case of any seasonal industry where the customary period of employment is less than 1,000 hours during a calendar year, the term "year of service" shall be such period as may be determined under regulations prescribed by the Secretary.

(C) For purposes of this section, the term "hour of service" means a time of service determined under regulations prescribed by the Secretary.

(D) For purposes of this section, in the case of any maritime industry, 125 days of service shall be treated as 1,000 hours of service. The Secretary may prescribe regulations to carry out the purposes of this subparagraph.

(4) A plan shall be treated as not meeting the requirements of paragraph (1) unless it provides that any employee who has satisfied the minimum age and service requirements specified in such paragraph, and who is otherwise entitled to participate in the plan, commences participation in the plan no later than the earlier of—

(A) the first day of the first plan year beginning after the date on which such employee satisfied such requirements, or

(B) the date 6 months after the date on which he satisfied such requirements, unless such employee was separated from the service before the date referred to in subparagraph (A) or (B), whichever is applicable.

Act Sec. 202.(b)(1) Except as otherwise provided in paragraphs (2), (3), and (4), all years of service with the employer or employers maintaining the plan shall be taken into account in computing the period of service for purposes of subsection (a)(1).

(2) In the case of any employee who has any 1-year break in service (as defined in section 203(b)(3)(A)) under a plan to which the service requirements of clause (i) of subsection (a)(1)(B) apply, if such employee has not satisfied such requirements, service before such break shall not be required to be taken into account.

(3) In computing an employee's period of service for purposes of subsection (a)(1) in the case of any participant who has any 1-year break in service (as defined in section 203(b)(3)(A)), service before such break shall not be required to be taken into account under the plan until he has completed a year of service (as defined in subsection (a)(3)) after his return.

(4)(A) For purposes of paragraph (1), in the case of a nonvested participant, years of service with the employer or employers maintaining the plan before any period of consecutive 1-year breaks in service shall not be required to be taken into account in computing the period of service if the number of consecutive 1-year breaks in service within such period equals or exceeds the greater of—

(i) 5, or

(ii) the aggregated number of years of service before such period.

(B) If any years of service are not required to be taken into account by reason of a period of breaks in service to which subparagraph (A) applies, such years of service shall not be taken into account in applying subparagraph (A) to a subsequent period of breaks in service.

(C) For purposes of subparagraph (A), the term "nonvested participant" means a participant who does not have any nonforfeitable right under the plan to an accrued benefit derived from employer contributions.

(5)(A) In the case of each individual who is absent from work for any period—

(i) by reason of the pregnancy of the individual,

(ii) by reason of the birth of a child of the individual,

(iii) by reason of the placement of a child with the individual in connection with the adoption of such child by such individual, or

(iv) for purposes of caring for such child for a period beginning immediately following such birth or placement,

the plan shall treat as hours of service, solely for purposes of determining under this subsection whether a 1-year break in service (as defined in section 203(b)(3)(A)) has occurred, the hours described in subparagraph (B).

(B) The hours described in this subparagraph are—

(i) the hours of service which otherwise would normally have been credited to such individual but for such absence, or

(ii) in any case in which the plan is unable to determine the hours described in clause (i), 8 hours of service per day of such absence,

except that the total number of hours treated as hours of service under this subparagraph by reason of any such pregnancy or placement shall not exceed 501 hours.

(C) The hours described in subparagraph (B) shall be treated as hours of service as provided in this paragraph—

(i) only in the year in which the absence from work begins, if a participant would be prevented from incurring a 1-year break in service in such year solely because the period of absence is treated as hours of service as provided in subparagraph (A); or

(ii) in any other case, in the immediately following year.

(D) For purposes of this paragraph, the term "year" means the period used in computations pursuant to section 202(a)(3)(A).

(E) A plan may provide that no credit will be given pursuant to this paragraph unless the individual furnishes to the plan administrator such timely information as the plan may reasonably require to establish—

(i) that the absence from work is for reasons referred to in subparagraph (A), and

(ii) the number of days for which there was such an absence.

Amendments

P.L. 101-239, § 7891(a)(1):

Titles I, III, and IV of ERISA (other than sections 3(37)(E), 301(a)(7), and 308, the last sentence of section 408(d), and sections 414(c), 4001(a)(3)(ii), and 4303) are each amended by striking "Internal Revenue Code of 1954" each place it appears and inserting "Internal Revenue Code of 1986" effective October 22, 1986.

P.L. 101-239, § 7892(a):

Amended ERISA Sec. 202(a)(2) by striking out the comma.

P.L. 101-239, § 7894(c)(2)(A):

Amended ERISA Sec. 202(a)(1)(B)(ii) by striking "institution" and inserting "organization" effective September 2, 1974.

P.L. 101-239, § 7894(c)(2)(B):

Amended ERISA Sec. 202(b)(2) by striking "the plan" and inserting "a plan" effective September 2, 1974.

P.L. 99-514, § 1113(d)(3):

Amended ERISA Sec. 202(a)(1)(B)(1) by striking out "3 years" and substituting "2 years" instead, effective for plan years beginning after 1988, but subject to the special rules of Act Sec. 1113(e)[(f)](2) and (3), which provide:

(2) SPECIAL RULE FOR COLLECTIVE BARGAINING AGREEMENTS.—In the case of a plan maintained pursuant to 1 or more collective bargaining agreements between employee representatives and 1 or more employers ratified before March 1, 1986, the amendments made by this section shall not apply to employees covered by any such agreement in plan years beginning before the earlier of—

(A) the later of—

(i) January 1, 1989, or

(ii) the date on which the last of such collective bargaining agreements terminates (determined without regard to any extension thereof after February 28, 1986), or

(B) January 1, 1991.

(3) PARTICIPATION REQUIRED.—The amendments made by this section shall not apply to any employee who does not have 1 hour of service in any plan year to which the amendments made by this section apply.

P.L. 99-509; § 9203(a)(1):

Amended ERISA Sec. 202(a)(2) by striking out "unless" and all that followed and inserting a period. This amendment is effective with respect to plan years beginning on or after January 1, 1988 and only with respect to service performed on or after such date. See also § 9204(c) at ¶ 14,440 (amendment notes). Prior to amendment, Sec. (a)(2) read as follows:

(2) No pension plan may exclude from participation (on the basis of age) employees who have attained a specified age, unless—

(A) the plan is a—

(i) defined benefit plan, or

(ii) target benefit plan (as defined under regulations prescribed by the Secretary of the Treasury), and

(B) such employees begin employment with the employer after they have attained a specified age which is not more than 5 years before the normal retirement age under the plan.

P.L. 98-397, § 102:

Act Sec. 102(a)(1) amended ERISA Sec. 202(a)(1)(A)(i) by striking out "25" and inserting in lieu thereof "21."

Act Sec. 102(a)(2) amended ERISA Sec. 202(a)(1)(B)(ii) by striking out "'30' for '25'" and inserting in lieu thereof "'26' for '21'."

Act Sec. 102(d)(1) amended ERISA Sec. 202(b)(4) by striking out the prior law and replacing it with new paragraph (4). Prior to amendment, ERISA Sec. 202(b)(4) read as follows:

(4) In the case of an employee who does not have any nonforfeitable right to an accrued benefit derived from employer contributions, years of service with the employer or employers maintaining the plan before a break in service shall not be required to be taken into account in computing the period of service for purposes of subsection (a)(1) if the number of consecutive 1-year breaks in service equals or exceeds the aggregate number of such years of service before such break. Such aggregate number of years of service before such break shall be deemed not to include any years of service not required to be taken into account under this paragraph by reason of any prior break in service.

Act Sec. 102(e) amended ERISA Sec. 202(b) by adding at the end thereof a new paragraph (5) to read as above.

The above amendments are generally effective for plan years beginning after December 31, 1984. However, Act Sec. 303(a)(1) and (2) provide the following:

SEC. 303. TRANSITIONAL RULES.

(a) Amendments Relating to Vesting Rules; Breaks in Service; Maternity or Paternity Leave.—

(1) Minimum Age for Vesting.—The amendments made by sections 102(b) and 202(b) shall apply in the case of participants who have at least 1 hour of service under the plan on or after the first day of the first plan year of which the amendments made by this Act apply.

(2) Break in Service Rules.—If, as of the day before the first day of the first plan year to which the amendments made by this Act apply, section 202(a) or (b) or 203(b) of the Employee Retirement Income Security Act of 1974 or section 410(a) or 411(a) of the Internal Revenue Code of 1954 (as in effect on the day before the date of the enactment of this Act) would not require any service to be taken into account, nothing in the amendments made by subsections (c) and (d) of section 102 of this Act and subsections (c) and (d) of section 202 of this Act shall be construed as requiring such service to be taken into account under such section 202(a) or (b), 203(b), 410(a), or 411(a); as the case may be.

Also, see Act Sec. 302(b) for a special rule for collective bargaining agreements at ¶ 14,250.09.

Regulations

The following regulations were adopted under "Title 29—Labor," "Chapter XXV—Pension and Welfare Benefit Programs, Department of Labor," "Subchapter C—Minimum Standards for Employee Pension Benefit Plans Under the Employee Retirement Income Security Act of 1974," "Part 2530—Rules and Regulations for Minimum Standards for Employee Pension Benefit Plans." The regulations were filed with the Federal Register on December 23, 1976, and published in the Federal Register of December 28, 1976 (41 FR 56462).

Subpart B—Participation, Vesting and Benefit Accrual

[¶ 14,421]

§ 2530.202-1 **Eligibility to participate; general**.

(a) Section 202 of the Act and section 410 of the Code contain minimum participation standards relating to certain employee pension benefit plans. In general, an employee pension benefit plan may not require, as a condition of participation in the plan, that an employee complete a period of service with the employer or employers maintaining the plan in excess of limits established by section 202 of the Act and section 410 of the Code and the regulations issued thereunder. Service for this purpose is measured in units of years of service. Section 2530.202-2 sets forth rules relating to the computation periods which a plan must use to determine whether an employee has completed a year of service for purposes of eligibility to participate ("eligibility computation periods").

(b) For rules relating to service with the employer or employers maintaining the plan, see § 2530.210.

[¶ 14,422]

§ 2530.202-2 **Eligibility computation period.**

(a) *Initial eligibility computation period.* For purposes of section 202(a)(1)(A)(ii) of the Act and section 410(a)(1)(A)(ii) of the Code, the initial eligibility computation period the plan must use is the 12-consecutive-month-period beginning on the employment commencement date. An employee's employment commencement date is the first day for which the employee is entitled to be credited with an hour of service described in § 2530.200b-2(a)(1) for an employer maintaining the plan. (For establishment of a reemployment commencement date following a break in service, see § 2530.200b-4(b)(1)(iii) and (iv)).

(b) *Eligibility computation periods after the initial eligibility computation period.* In measuring years of service for purposes of eligibility to participate after the initial eligibility computation period, a plan may adopt either of the following alternatives:

(1) A plan may designate 12-consecutive-month periods beginning on the first anniversary of an employee's employment commencement date and succeeding anniversaries thereof as the eligibility computation period after the initial eligibility computation period; or

(2) A plan may designate plan years beginning with the plan year which includes the first anniversary of an employee's employment commencement date as the eligibility computation period after the initial eligibility computation period (without regard to whether the employee is entitled to be credited with 1000 hours of service during such period), provided that an employee who is credited with 1000 hours of service in both the initial eligibility computation period and the plan year which includes the first anniversary of the employee's employment commencement date is credited with two years of service for purposes of eligibility to participate.

(c) *Service prior to a break in service.* For purposes of applying section 202(b)(4) of the Act and section 410(a)(5)(D) of the Code (relating to years of service completed prior to a break in service for purposes of eligibility to participate), the computation periods used by a plan in determining years of service before such break shall be the eligibility computation periods established in accordance with paragraphs (a) and (b) of this section.

(d) *Plans with three-year 100 percent vesting.* A plan which, under 202(a)(1)(B)(i) of the Act and section 410a(1)(B)(i) of the Code, requires more than one year of service for eligibility to participate in the plan shall use an initial eligibility computation period established under paragraph (a) of this section and eligibility computation periods designated in accordance with paragraph (b) of this section. Thus, for the eligibility computation period after the initial eligibility computation period, such a plan may designate either eligibility computation periods beginning on anniversaries of an employee's employment commencement date or plan years beginning with the plan year which includes the anniversary of the first day of the initial eligibility computation period.

(e) *Alternative eligibility computation period.* The following rule is designed primarily for a plan using a recordkeeping system which does not permit the plan to identify an employee's employment commencement date (or, in the case of an employee who has incurred a one-year break in service, the employee's reemployment computation date), but which does permit the plan to identify a period of no more than 31 days during which the employee's employment commencement date (or reemployment commencement date) occurred.

(1) A plan may be an initial eligibility computation period (or initial computation period for measuring completion of a year of service upon an employee's return after a one-year break in service) beginning on the first day of a period of no more than 31 days during which an employee's employment commencement date (or reemployment commencement date) occurs and ending on the anniversary of the last day of such period.

(2) If a plan uses an initial eligibility computation period (or initial computation period for measuring completion of a year of service upon an employee's return after a one-year break in service) permitted under paragraph (e)(1) of this section, the plan shall use the following computation periods after the initial computation period:

(i) If the plan does not use plan years for computation periods after the initial computation period, the plan shall use computation periods beginning on anniversaries of the first day of the initial computation period and ending on anniversaries of the last day of the initial computation period, and including a period of at least 12 consecutive months.

(ii) If the plan uses plan years for computation periods after the initial computation period, the plan shall use plan years beginning with the plan year which includes the anniversary of the first day of the initial computation period.

(3) For purposes of determining an employee's commencement of participation under section 202(a)(4) of the Act and section 410(a)(4) of the Code, regardless of whether an eligibility computation period permitted under this paragraph includes a period longer than 12 consecutive months, an employee who completes 1000 hours of service in such eligibility computation period shall be treated as having satisfied the plan's service requirement for eligibility to participate as of the last day of the 12-consecutive-month period beginning on the first day of such eligibility computation period. In the case of a plan described in section 202(a)(1)(B)(i) of the Act and section 410(a)(1)(B)(i) of the Code, the requirement of the preceding sentence shall apply only with respect to the last year of service required under the plan for eligibility to participate.

(4) *Example.* A plan maintained by Employer X obtains records from X which indicate the number of hours worked by an employee during a monthly payroll period. The records do not, however, break down the number of hours worked by an employee by days. Thus, after a new employee has begun employment with X it is impossible for the plan to ascertain the employee's employment commencement date from the records furnished by X (although it is possible for the plan to determine the month during which an employee's employment commencement date occurred). For administrative convenience, in conjunction with the equivalency based on hours worked permitted under § 2530.200b-3(d)(1), and with the method of crediting hours of service to computation periods set forth in § 2530.200b-2(c)(4), the plan uses the alternative initial eligibility computation period permitted under this paragraph. The plan provides that an employee's initial eligibility computation period shall be the period beginning on the first day of the first monthly payroll period for which the employee is entitled to credit for the performance of duties and ending on the last day of the monthly payroll period which includes the anniversary of the last day of the initial monthly payroll period. This condition ensures that the initial eligibility computation period will include the 12-consecutive-month period beginning on the employee's employment commencement date and ending on the day before the anniversary of the employee's employment commencement date. If, however, an employee completes the plan's requirement of one year of service for eligibility to participate (i.e., completion of 870 hours worked in an eligibility computation period) in the initial eligibility computation period, the plan provides that the employee is deemed to have satisfied the plan's service requirements for eligibility to participate as of the day before the anniversary of the first day of the initial eligibility computation period. This provision ensures that no employee who has in fact completed 1000 hours of service in the 12-consecutive-month period beginning on the employee's employment commencement date will be admitted to participation later than the date specified under section 202(a)(4) of the Act and section 410(a)(4) of the Code. For example, in the case of an employee who begins employment in January, 1977, the employee's initial eligibility computation period begins on January 1, 1977 and ends on January 31, 1978. If the employee completes 879 hours worked in the initial eligibility computation period, the employee is treated as having met the plan's service requirements for eligibility to participate as of December 31, 1977. If the plan provides for semi-annual entry dates of January 1 and July 1, and the employee has met any eligibility requirements of the plan other than the minimum service requirements as of December 31, 1977, the plan must provide that the employee commences participation as of January 1, 1978.

[¶ 14,430]
MINIMUM VESTING STANDARDS

Act Sec. 203.(a) NONFORFEITABILITY REQUIREMENTS.—Each pension plan shall provide that an employee's right to his normal retirement benefit is nonforfeitable upon the attainment of normal retirement age and in addition shall satisfy the requirements of paragraphs (1) and (2) of this subsection.

(1) A plan satisfies the requirements of this paragraph if an employee's rights in his accrued benefit derived from his own contributions are nonforfeitable.

(2)(A)(i) In the case of a defined benefit plan, a plan satisfies the requirements of this paragraph if it satisfies the requirements of clause (ii) or (iii).

(ii) A plan satisfies the requirements of this clause if an employee who has completed at least 5 years of service has a nonforfeitable right to 100 percent of the employee's accrued benefit derived from employer contributions.

(iii) A plan satisfies the requirements of this clause if an employee has a nonforfeitable right to a percentage of the employee's accrued benefit derived from employer contributions determined under the following table:

Years of service:	The nonforfeitable percentage is:
3	20
4	40
5	60
6	80
7 or more	100

(B)(i) In the case of an individual account plan, a plan satisfies the requirements of this paragraph if it satisfies the requirements of clause (ii) or (iii).

(ii) A plan satisfies the requirements of this clause if an employee who has completed at least 3 years of service has a nonforfeitable right to 100 percent of the employee's accrued benefit derived from employer contributions.

(iii) A plan satisfies the requirements of this clause if an employee has a nonforfeitable right to a percentage of the employee's accrued benefit derived from employer contributions determined under the following table:

Years of service:	The nonforfeitable percentage is:
2	20
3	40
4	60
5	80
6 or more	100

(3)(A) A right to an accrued benefit derived from employer contributions shall not be treated as forfeitable solely because the plan provides that it is not payable if the participant dies (except in the case of a survivor annuity which is payable as provided in section 205).

(B) A right to an accrued benefit derived from employer contributions shall not be treated as forfeitable solely because the plan provides that the payment of benefits is suspended for such period as the employee is employed, subsequent to the commencement of payment of such benefits—

(i) in the case of a plan other than a multiemployer plan, by an employer who maintains the plan under which such benefits were being paid; and

(ii) in the case of a multiemployer plan, in the same industry, in the same trade or craft, and the same geographic area covered by the plan, as when such benefits commenced.

The Secretary shall prescribe such regulations as may be necessary to carry out the purposes of this subparagraph, including regulations with respect to the meaning of the term "employed".

(C) A right to an accrued benefit derived from employer contributions shall not be treated as forfeitable solely because plan amendments may be given retroactive application as provided in section 302(d)(2).

(D)(i) A right to an accrued benefit derived from employer contributions shall not be treated as forfeitable solely because the plan provides that, in the case of a participant who does not have a nonforfeitable right to at least 50 percent of his accrued benefit derived from employer contributions, such accrued benefit may be forfeited on account of the withdrawal by the participant of any amount attributable to the benefit derived from mandatory contributions (as defined in the last sentence of section 204(c)(2)(C)) made by such participant.

(ii) Clause (i) shall not apply to a plan unless the plan provides that any accrued benefit forfeited under a plan provision described in such clause shall be restored upon repayment by the participant of the full amount of the withdrawal described in such clause plus, in the case of a defined benefit plan, interest. Such interest shall be computed on such amount at the rate determined for purposes of section 204(c)(2)(C) (if such subsection applies) on the date of such repayment (computed annually from the date of such withdrawal). The plan provision required under this clause may provide that such repayment must be made (I) in the case of a withdrawal on account of separation from service, before the earlier of 5 years after the first date on which the participant is subsequently re-employed by the employer, or the close of the first period of 5 consecutive 1-year breaks in service commencing after the withdrawal; or (II) in the case of any other withdrawal, 5 years after the date of the withdrawal.

(iii) In the case of accrued benefits derived from employer contributions which accrued before the date of the enactment of this Act, a right to such accrued benefit derived from employer contributions shall not be treated as forfeitable solely because the plan provides that an amount of such accrued benefit may be forfeited on account of the withdrawal by the participant of an amount attributable to the benefit derived from mandatory contributions, made by such participant before the date of the enactment of this Act if such amount forfeited is proportional to such amount withdrawn. This clause shall not apply to any plan to which any mandatory contribution is made after the date of the enactment of this Act. The Secretary of the Treasury shall prescribe such regulations as may be necessary to carry out the purposes of this clause.

(iv) For purposes of this subparagraph, in the case of any class-year plan, a withdrawal of employee contributions shall be treated as a withdrawal of such contributions on a plan year by plan year basis in succeeding order of time.

(v) CROSS REFERENCE. For nonforfeitability where the employee has a nonforfeitable right to at least 50 percent of his accrued benefit, see section 206(c).

(E)(i) A right to an accrued benefit derived from employer contributions under a multiemployer plan shall not be treated as forfeitable solely because the plan provides that benefits accrued as a result of service with the participant's employer before the employer had an obligation to contribute under the plan may not be payable if the employer ceases contributions to the multiemployer plan.

(ii) A participant's right to an accrued benefit derived from employer contributions under a multiemployer plan shall not be treated as forfeitable solely because—

(I) the plan is amended to reduce benefits under section 4244A or 4281, or

(II) benefit payments under the plan may be suspended under section 4245 or 4281.

(F) A matching contribution (within the meaning of section 401(m) of the Internal Revenue Code of 1986) shall not be treated as forfeitable merely because such contribution is forfeitable if the contribution to which the matching contribution relates is treated as an excess contribution under section 401(k)(8)(B) of such Code, an excess deferral under section 402(g)(2)(A) of such Code, an erroneous automatic contribution under section 414(w) of such Code, or an excess aggregate contribution under section 401(m)(6)(B) of such Code.

Act Sec. 203.(b)(1) COMPUTATION OF PERIOD OF SERVICE.—In computing the period of service under the plan for purposes of determining the nonforfeitable percentage under subsection (a)(2), all of an employee's years of service with the employer or employers maintaining the plan shall be taken into account, except that the following may be disregarded:

(A) years of service before age 18,

(B) years of service during a period for which the employee declined to contribute to a plan requiring employee contributions;

(C) years of service with an employer during any period for which the employer did not maintain the plan or a predecessor plan, defined by the Secretary of the Treasury;

(D) service not required to be taken into account under paragraph (3);

(E) years of service before January 1, 1971, unless the employee has had at least 3 years of service after December 31, 1970;

(F) years of service before this part first applies to the plan if such service would have been disregarded under the rules of the plan with regard to breaks in service, as in effect on the applicable date; and

(G) in the case of a multiemployer plan, years of service—

(i) with an employer after—

(I) a complete withdrawal of such employer from the plan (within the meaning of section 4203); or

(II) to the extent permitted by regulations prescribed by the Secretary of the Treasury, a partial withdrawal described in section 4205(b)(2)(A)(i) in connection with the decertification of the collective bargaining representative; and

(ii) with any employer under the plan after the termination date of the plan under section 4048.

(2)(A) For purposes of this section, except as provided in subparagraph (C), the term "year of service" means a calendar year, plan year, or other 12-consecutive-month period designated by the plan (and not prohibited under regulations prescribed by the Secretary) during which the participant has completed 1,000 hours of service.

(B) For purposes of this section, the term "hour of service" has the meaning provided by section 202(a)(3)(C).

(C) In the case of any seasonal industry where the customary period of employment is less than 1,000 hours during a calendar year, the term "year of service" shall be such period as determined under regulations of the Secretary.

(D) For purposes of this section, in the case of any maritime industry, 125 days of service shall be treated as 1,000 hours of service. The Secretary may prescribe regulations to carry out the purposes of this subparagraph.

(3)(A) For purposes of this paragraph, the term "1-year break in service" means a calendar year, plan year, or other 12-consecutive-month period designated by the plan (and not prohibited under regulations prescribed by the Secretary) during which the participant has not completed more than 500 hours of service.

(B) For purposes of paragraph (1), in the case of any employee who has any 1-year break in service, years of service before such break shall not be required to be taken into account until he has completed a year of service after his return.

(C) For purposes of paragraph (1), in the case of any participant in an individual account plan or an insured defined benefit plan which satisfies the requirements of subsection 204(b)(1)(F) who has 5 consecutive 1-year breaks in service, years of service after such 5-year period shall not be required to be taken into account for purposes of determining the nonforfeitable precentage of his accrued benefit derived from employer contributions which accrued before such 5-year period.

(D)(i) For purposes of paragraph (1), in the case of a nonvested participant, years of service with the employer or employers maintaining the plan before any period of consecutive 1-year breaks in service shall not be required to be taken into account if the number of consecutive 1-year breaks in service within such period equals or exceeds the greater of—

(I) 5, or

(II) the aggregate number of years of service before such period.

(ii) If any years of service are not required to be taken into account by reason of a period of breaks in service to which clause (i) applies, such years of service shall not be taken into account in applying clause (i) to a subsequent period of breaks in service.

(iii) For purposes of clause (i), the term "nonvested participant" means a participant who does not have any nonforfeitable right under the plan to an accrued benefit derived from employer contributions.

(E)(i) In the case of each individual who is absent from work for any period—

(I) by reason of the pregnancy of the individual,

(II) by reason of the birth of a child of the individual,

(III) by reason of the placement of a child with the individual in connection with the adoption of such child by such individual, or

(IV) for purposes of caring for such child for a period beginning immediately following such birth or placement,

the plan shall treat as hours of service, solely for purposes of determining under this paragraph whether a 1-year break in service has occurred, the hours described in clause (ii).

(ii) The hours described in this clause are—

(I) the hours of service which otherwise would normally have been credited to such individual but for such absence, or

(II) in any case in which the plan is unable to determine the hours described in subclause (I), 8 hours of service per day of absence,

except that the total number of hours treated as hours of service under this clause by reason of pregnancy or placement shall not exceed 501 hours.

(iii) The hours described in clause (ii) shall be treated as hours of service as provided in this subparagraph—

(I) only in the year in which the absence from work begins, if a participant would be prevented from incurring a 1-year break in service in such year solely because the period of absence is treated as hours of service as provided in clause (i); or

(II) in any other case, in the immediately following year.

(iv) For purposes of this subparagraph, the term "year" means the period used in computations pursuant to paragraph (2).

(v) A plan may provide that no credit will be given pursuant to this subparagraph unless the individual furnishes to the plan administrator such timely information as the plan may reasonably require to establish—

(I) that the absence from work is for reasons referred to in clause (i), and

(II) the number of days for which there was such an absence.

(4) Cross references.—

(A) For definitions of "accrued benefit" and "normal retirement age", see sections 3 (23) and (24).

(B) For effect of certain cash out distributions, see section 204(d)(1).

Act Sec. 203. (c)(1)(A) Plan amendments altering vesting schedule.—A plan amendment changing any vesting schedule under the plan shall be treated as not satisfying the requirements of subsection (a)(2) if the nonforfeitable percentage of the accrued benefit derived from employer contributions (determined as of the later of the date such amendment is adopted, or the date such amendment becomes effective) of any employee who is a participant in the plan is less than such nonforfeitable percentage computed under the plan without regard to such amendment.

(B) A plan amendment changing any vesting schedule under the plan shall be treated as not satisfying the requirements of subsection (a)(2) unless each participant having not less than 3 years of service is permitted to elect, within a reasonable period after adoption of such amendment, to have his nonforfeitable percentage computed under the plan without regard to such amendment.

(2) Subsection (a) shall not apply to benefits which may not be provided for designated employees in the event of early termination of the plan under provisions of the plan adopted pursuant to regulations prescribed by the Secretary of the Treasury to preclude the discrimination prohibited by section 401(a)(4) of the Internal Revenue Code of 1986.

(3)(A) The requirements of subsection (a)(2) shall be treated as satisfied in the case of a class-year plan if such plan provides that 100 percent of each employee's right to or derived from the contributions of the employer on the employee's behalf with respect to any plan year is nonforfeitable not later than when such participant was performing services for the employer as of the close of each of 5 plan years (whether or not consecutive) after the plan year for which the contributions were made.

(B) For purposes of subparagraph (A) if—

(i) any contributions are made on behalf of a participant with respect to any plan year, and

(ii) before such participant meets the requirements of subparagraph (A), such participant was not performing services for the employer as of the close of each of any 5 consecutive plan years after such plan year,

then the plan may provide that the participant forfeits any right to or derived from the contributions made with respect to such plan year.

(C) For purposes of this part, the term "class year plan" means a profit-sharing, stock bonus, or money purchase plan which provides for the separate nonforfeitability of employees' rights to or derived from the contributions for each plan year.

Act Sec. 203. (d) Nonforfeitable benefits after lesser period and in greater amounts than required.—A pension plan may allow for nonforfeitable benefits after a lesser period and in greater amounts than are required by this part.

Act Sec. 203. (e)(1) Consent for distribution; present value; covered distributions.—If the present value of any nonforfeitable benefit with respect to a participant in a plan exceeds $5,000, the plan shall provide that such benefit may not be immediately distributed without the consent of the participant.

(2) For purposes of paragraph (1), the present value shall be calculated in accordance with section 205(g)(3).

(3) This subsection shall not apply to any distribution of dividends to which section 404(k) of the Internal Revenue Code of 1986 applies.

(4) A plan shall not fail to meet the requirements of this subsection if, under the terms of the plan, the present value of the nonforfeitable accrued benefit is determined without regard to that portion of such benefit which is attributable to rollover contributions (and earnings allocable thereto). For purposes of this subparagraph, the term "rollover contributions" means any rollover contribution under sections 402(c), 403(a)(4), 403(b)(8), 408(d)(3)(A)(ii), and 457(e)(16) of the Internal Revenue Code of 1986.

Act Sec. 203. (f) SPECIAL RULES FOR PLANS COMPUTING ACCRUED BENEFITS BY REFERENCE TO HYPOTHETICAL ACCOUNT BALANCE OR EQUIVALENT AMOUNTS.—

(1) IN GENERAL. An applicable defined benefit plan shall not be treated as failing to meet—

(A) subject to paragraph (2), the requirements of subsection (a)(2), or

(B) the requirements of section 204(c) or 205(g), or the requirements of subsection (e), with respect to accrued benefits derived from employer contributions,

solely because the present value of the accrued benefit (or any portion thereof) of any participant is, under the terms of the plan, equal to the amount expressed as the balance in the hypothetical account described in paragraph (3) or as an accumulated percentage of the participant's final average compensation.

(2) 3-YEAR VESTING. In the case of an applicable defined benefit plan, such plan shall be treated as meeting the requirements of subsection (a)(2) only if an employee who has completed at least 3 years of service has a nonforfeitable right to 100 percent of the employee's accrued benefit derived from employer contributions.

(3) APPLICABLE DEFINED BENEFIT PLAN AND RELATED RULES. For purposes of this subsection —

(A) IN GENERAL. The term "applicable defined benefit plan" means a defined benefit plan under which the accrued benefit (or any portion thereof) is calculated as the balance of a hypothetical account maintained for the participant or as an accumulated percentage of the participant's final average compensation.

(B) REGULATIONS TO INCLUDE SIMILAR PLANS. The Secretary of the Treasury shall issue regulations which include in the definition of an applicable defined benefit plan any defined benefit plan (or any portion of such a plan) which has an effect similar to an applicable defined benefit plan.

Amendments

P.L. 110-458, §107(a)(1):

Amended ERISA Sec. 203(f)(1)(B) to read as above. Prior to amendment, ERISA Sec. 203(f)(1)(B) read as follows:

(B) the requirements of section 204(c) or section 205(g) with respect to contributions other than employee contributions,

The above amendment takes effect as if included in the provisions of the 2006 Act to which the amendment relates. For effective date, see P.L. 109-280, §701(e), below.

P.L. 109-280, § 107(a)(4):

Amended ERISA Sec. 203(a)(3)(C) by striking "section 302(c)(8)" and inserting "section 302(d)(2)".

The above amendment applies to plan years beginning after 2007.

P.L. 109-280, § 701(a)(2):

Amended ERISA Sec. 203 by adding new subsection (f) to read as above.

See P.L. 109-280, §701(e) below for effective date.

P.L. 109-280, §701(e) provides as follows:

(e) EFFECTIVE DATE.—

701(e)(1) IN GENERAL.—

The amendments made by this section shall apply to periods beginning on or after June 29, 2005.

701(e)(2) PRESENT VALUE OF ACCRUED BENEFIT.—

The amendments made by subsections (a)(2) and (b)(2) shall apply to distributions made after the date of the enactment of this Act.

701(e)(3) VESTING AND INTEREST CREDIT REQUIREMENTS.—

In the case of a plan in existence on June 29, 2005, the requirements of clause (i) of section 411(b)(5)(B) of the Internal Revenue Code of 1986, clause (i) of section 204(b)(5)(B) of the Employee Retirement Income Security Act of 1974, and clause (i) of section 4(i)(10)(B) of the Age Discrimination in Employment Act of 1967 (as added by this Act) and the requirements of 203(f)(2) of the Employee Retirement Income Security Act of 1974 and section 411(a)(13)(B) of the Internal Revenue Code of 1986 (as so added) shall, for purposes of applying the amendments made by subsections (a) and (b), apply to years beginning after December 31, 2007, unless the plan sponsor elects the application of such requirements for any period after June 29, 2005, and before the first year beginning after December 31, 2007.

701(e)(4) SPECIAL RULE FOR COLLECTIVELY BARGAINED PLANS.—

In the case of a plan maintained pursuant to 1 or more collective bargaining agreements between employee representatives and 1 or more employers ratified on or before the date of the enactment of this Act, the requirements described in paragraph (3) shall, for purposes of applying the amendments made by subsections (a) and (b), not apply to plan years beginning before—

701(e)(4)(A) the earlier of —

701(e)(4)(A)(i) the date on which the last of such collective bargaining agreements terminates (determined without regard to any extension thereof on or after such date of enactment), or

701(e)(4)(A)(ii) January 1, 2008, or

701(e)(4)(B) January 1, 2010.

701(e)(5) CONVERSIONS.—

The requirements of clause (ii) of section 411(b)(5)(B) of the Internal Revenue Code of 1986, clause (ii) of section 204(b)(5)(B) of the Employee Retirement Income Security Act of 1974, and clause (ii) of section 4(i)(10)(B) of the Age Discrimination in Employment Act of 1967 (as added by this Act), shall apply to plan amendments adopted after, and taking effect after, June 29, 2005, except that the plan sponsor may elect to have such amendments apply to plan amendments adopted before, and taking effect after, such date.

P.L. 109-280, § 902(d)(2)(E):

Amended ERISA Sec. 203(a)(3)(F) by inserting "an erroneous automatic contribution under section 414(w) of such Code," after "402(g)(2)(A) of such Code,".

The above amendment applies to plan years beginning after December 31, 2007.

P.L. 109-280, § 904(b)(1):

Amended ERISA Sec. 203(a)(2) to read as above.

Prior to amendment, ERISA Sec. 203(a)(2) read as follows:

(2) Except as provided in paragraph (4), a plan satisfies the requirements of this paragraph if it satisfies the requirements of subparagraph (A) or (B).

(A) A plan satisfies the requirements of this subparagraph if an employee who has completed at least 5 years of service has a nonforfeitable right to 100 percent of the employee's accrued benefit derived from employer contributions.

(B) A plan satisfies the requirements of this subparagraph if an employee has a nonforfeitable right to a percentage of the employee's accrued benefit derived from employer contributions determined under the following table:

Years of service:	The Nonforfeitable percentage is:
3	20
4	40
5	60
6	80
7 or more	100

See P.L. 109-280, §904(c) below for effective date.

P.L. 109-280, § 904(b)(2):

Amended ERISA Sec. 203(a) by striking paragraph (4).

Prior to repeal, ERISA Sec. 203(a)(4) read as follows:

(4) In the case of matching contributions (as defined in section 401(m)(4)(A) of the Internal Revenue Code of 1986), paragraph (2) shall be applied –

(A) by substituting "3 years" for "5 years" in subparagraph (A), and

(B) by substituting the following table for the table contained in subparagraph (B):

Years of service:	The Nonforfeitable percentage is:
2	20
3	40
4	60
5	80
6 or more	100

See P.L. 109-280, §904(c) below for effective date.

P.L. 109-280, §904(c) provides as follows:

904(c) EFFECTIVE DATES

904(c)(1) IN GENERAL. —Except as provided in paragraphs (2) and (4), the amendments made by this section shall apply to contributions for plan years beginning after December 31, 2006.

904(c)(2) COLLECTIVE BARGAINING AGREEMENTS. —In the case of a plan maintained pursuant to one or more collective bargaining agreements between employee representatives and one or more employers ratified before the date of the enactment of this Act, the amendments made by this section shall not apply to contributions on behalf of employees covered by any such agreement for plan years beginning before the earlier of —

904(c)(2)(A) the later of —

904(c)(2)(A)(i) the date on which the last of such collective bargaining agreements terminates (determined without regard to any extension thereof on or after such date of the enactment); or

904(c)(2)(A)(ii) January 1, 2007; or

904(c)(2)(B) January 1, 2009.

904(c)(3) SERVICE REQUIRED.—With respect to any plan, the amendments made by this section shall not apply to any employee before the date that such employee has 1 hour of service under such plan in any plan year to which the amendments made by this section apply.

904(c)(4) SPECIAL RULE FOR STOCK OWNERSHIP PLANS.—Notwithstanding paragraph (1) or (2), in the case of an employee stock ownership plan (as defined in section 4975(e)(7) of the Internal Revenue Code of 1986) which had outstanding on September 26, 2005, a loan incurred for the purpose of acquiring qualifying employer securities (as defined in section 4975(e)(8) of such Code), the amendments made by this section shall not apply to any plan year beginning before the earlier of —

904(c)(4)(A) the date on which the loan is fully repaid, or

904(c)(4)(B) the date on which the loan was, as of September 26, 2005, scheduled to be fully repaid.

P.L. 108-311, §408(b)(8):

Amended ERISA §203(b)(4) by adding "or more" after "6" in the last line of the table.

P.L. 107-16, §633(b)(1):

Act Sec. 633(b)(1) amended ERISA Sec. 203(a)(2) by striking "A plan" and inserting "Except as provided in paragraph (4), a plan".

P.L. 107-16, §633(b)(2):

Act Sec. 633(b)(2) amended ERISA Sec. 203(a) by adding subsection (4) at the end to read as above.

P.L. 107-16, §633(c):

Act Sec. 633(c) governs the effective date of the above amendments:

"(c) EFFECTIVE DATES.—

(1) IN GENERAL.—Except as provided in paragraph (2), the amendments made by this section shall apply to contributions for plan years beginning after December 31, 2001.

(2) COLLECTIVE BARGAINING AGREEMENTS.—In the case of a plan maintained pursuant to one or more collective bargaining agreements between employee representatives and one or more employers ratified by the date of the enactment of this Act, the amendments made by this section shall not apply to contributions on behalf of employees covered by any such agreement for plan years beginning before the earlier of—

(A) the later of—

(i) the date on which the last of such collective bargaining agreements terminates (determined without regard to any extension thereof on or after such date of the enactment); or

(ii) January 1, 2002; or

(B) January 1, 2006.

(3) SERVICE REQUIRED.—With respect to any plan, the amendments made by this section shall not apply to any employee before the date that such employee has 1 hour of service under such plan in any plan year to which the amendments made by this section apply."

P.L. 107-16, §648(a)(2):

Act Sec. 648(a)(2) amended ERISA Sec. 203(e) by adding subsection (4) at the end to read as above.

The above amendment applies to distributions after December 31, 2001.

P.L. 105-34, §1071(b)(1):

Act Sec. 1071(b)(1) amended ERISA Sec. 203(e)(1) by striking "$3,500" and inserting "$5,000".

The above amendment is effective for plan years beginning after August 5, 1997.

P.L. 104-188, §1442(b):

Act Sec. 1442(b) amended ERISA Sec. 203(a)(2) by striking "subparagraph (A), (B), or (C)" and inserting "subparagraph (A) or (B)"; and by striking subparagraph (C). Prior to amendment, ERISA Sec. 203(a)(2)(C) read as follows:

(C) A plan satisfies the requirements of this subparagraph if—

(i) the plan is a multiemployer plan (within the meaning of section 3(37)), and

(ii) under the plan—

(I) an employee who is covered pursuant to a collective bargaining agreement described in section 3(37)(A)(ii) and who has completed at least 10 years of service has a nonforfeitable right to 100 percent of the employee's accrued benefit derived from employer contributions, and

(II) the requirements of subparagraph (A) or (B) are met with respect to employees not described in subclause (I).

The above amendments apply to plan years beginning on or after the earlier of:

(1) the later of—

(A) January 1, 1997, or

(B) the date on which the last of the collective bargaining agreements pursuant to which the plan is maintained terminates (determined without regard to any extension thereof after the date of the enactment of this Act), or

(2) January 1, 1999.

Such amendments shall not apply to any individual who does not have more than 1 hour of service under the plan on or after the 1st day of the 1st plan year to which such amendments apply.

P.L. 103-465, §767(c)(1):

Act Sec. 767(c)(1) amended ERISA Sec. 203(e)(2) to read as above. Prior to amendment, ERISA Sec. 203(e)(2) read as follows:

(2)(A) For purposes of paragraph (1), the present value shall be calculated—

(i) by using an interest rate no greater than the applicable interest rate if the vested accrued benefit (using such rate) is not in excess of $25,000, and

(ii) by using an interest rate no greater than 120 percent of the applicable interest rate if the vested accrued benefit exceeds $25,000 (as determined under clause (i)).

In no event shall the present value determined under subclause (II) be less than $25,000.

(B) For purposes of subparagraph (A), the term "applicable interest rate" means the interest rate which would be used (as of the date of the distribution) by the Pension Benefit Guaranty Corporation for purposes of determining the present value of a lump-sum distribution on plan termination.

The above amendment applies to plan years and limitation years beginning after December 31, 1994, except that an employer may elect to treat the amendments made by this section as being effective on or after December 8, 1994. For special rules, see Act Sec. 767(e)(2)-(3), below.

Act Sec. 767(e)(2)-(3) provides:

(2) No REDUCTION IN ACCRUED BENEFITS.—A participant's accrued benefit shall not be considered to be reduced in violation of section 411(d)(6) of the Internal Revenue Code of 1986 or section 204(g) of the Employee Retirement Income Security Act of 1974 merely because (A) the benefit is determined in accordance with section 417(e)(3)(A) of such Code, as amended by this Act, or section 205(g)(3) of the Employee Retirement Income Security Act of 1974, as amended by this Act or (B) the plan applies section 415(b)(2)(E) of such Code, as amended by this Act.

(3) SECTION 415.

(A) NO REDUCTION REQUIRED.—An accrued benefit shall not be required to be reduced below the accrued benefit as of the last day of the last plan year beginning before January 1, 1995, merely because of the amendments made by subsection (b).

(B) TIMING OF PLAN AMENDMENT.—A plan that operates in accordance with the amendments made by subsection (b) shall not be treated as failing to satisfy section 401(a) of the Internal Revenue Code of 1986 or as not being operated in accordance with the provisions of the plan until such date as the Secretary of the Treasury provides merely because the plan has not been amended to include the amendments made by subsection (b).

P.L. 101-239, §7861(a)(1):

Amended ERISA Sec. 203(a)(2) by striking "following" the first place it appears and by striking "414(f)(1)(B)" in subparagraph (C)(ii)(I) and inserting "3(37)(A)(ii)".

P.L. 101-239, §7861(a)(2):

Amended P.L. 99-514, §1113(e)(3) by striking "Section 202(B)(i)" and inserting "Section 202(a)(1)(B)(i)".

P.L. 101-239, §7861(a)(3):

Redesignated the second subsection (e) of P.L. 99-514, §1113 as subsection (f).

P.L. 101-239, §7861(a)(4):

Added a new paragraph (4) to P.L. 99-514, §1113(f).

P.L. 101-239, §7861(a)(5)(B):

Amended ERISA Sec. 203(a)(3) by adding a new subparagraph (F) to read as above.

P.L. 101-239, §7861(a)(6)(B):

Amended ERISA Sec. 203(b)(1)(A) to read as above. Prior to amendment, ERISA Sec. 203(b)(1)(A) read as follows:

(A) years of service before age 18, except that in the case of a plan which does not satisfy subparagraph (A) or (B) of subsection (a)(2), the plan may not disregard any such year of service during which the employee was a participant;

P.L. 101-239, §7862(d)(5) and (10):

Amended ERISA Sec. 203(e)(1) to read as above. Previously the subsection read as follows:

(e)(1) If the present value of any vested accrued benefit exceeds $3,500, a pension plan shall provide that such benefit may not be immediately distributed without the consent of the participant.

The above amendments are effective October 22, 1986.

P.L. 101-239, §7891(a)(1):

Titles I, III, and IV of ERISA (other than sections 3(37)(E), 301(a)(7), and 308, the last sentence of section 408(d), and sections 414(c), 4001(a)(3)(ii), and 4303) are each amended by striking "Internal Revenue Code of 1954" each place it appears and inserting "Internal Revenue Code of 1986" effective October 22, 1986.

P.L. 101-239, §7891(b)(2):

Amended ERISA Sec. 203(e)(2)(B) by striking "APPLICABLE INTEREST RATE.—" effective October 22, 1986.

P.L. 101-239, §7894(c)(3):

Amended ERISA Sec. 203(a)(3)(D)(v) by striking "**nonforfeitably**" and inserting "**nonforfeitability**" effective September 2, 1974.

P.L. 99-514, §1113(d)(4)(A):

Amended ERISA Sec. 203(c)(1)(B) by striking out "5 years" and inserting "3 years" instead.

P.L. 99-514, §1113(e)(1):

Amended paragraph 2 to read as above in section 203(a). Prior to amendment, paragraph (2) read as follows:

(2) A plan satisfies the requirement of this paragraph if it satisfies the requirements of subparagraph (A), (B), or (C).

(A) A plan satisfies the requirements of this subparagraph if an employee who has at least 10 years of service has a nonforfeitable right to 100 percent of his accrued benefit derived from employer contributions.

(B) A plan satisfies the requirements of this subparagraph if an employee who has completed at least 5 years of service has a nonforfeitable right to a percentage of his accrued benefit derived from employer contributions which percentage is not less than the percentage determined under the following table:

Years of service:	Nonforfeitable percentage
5	25
6	30

If years of service equal or exceed—	
5	
6	
7	
8	
9	
10	

(ii) Notwithstanding clause (i), a plan shall not be treated as satisfying the requirements of this subparagraph unless any participant who has completed at least 10 years of service has a nonforfeitable right to not less than 50 percent of his accrued benefit derived from employer contributions and to not less than an additional 10 percent for each additional year of service thereafter.

P.L. 99-514, §1113(e)(2):

Struck out paragraph (3), section 203(c). Prior to its repeal, paragraph (3) read as follows:

Act Sec. 203. (c) * * *

(3) The requirements of subsection (a)(2) shall be deemed to be satisfied in the case of a class year plan if such plan provides that 100 percent of each employee's right to or derived from the contributions of the employer on his behalf with respect to any plan year are nonforfeitable not later than the end of the 5th plan year following the plan year for which such contributions were made. For purposes of this part, the term "class year plan" means a profit sharing, stock bonus, or money purchase plan which provides for the separate nonforfeitability of employees' rights to or derived from the contributions for each plan year.

P.L. 99-514, §1113(f):

Section (f) provides as follows:

(f) EFFECTIVE DATES.—

(1) IN GENERAL.—Except as provided in paragraph (2), the amendments made by this section shall apply to plan years beginning after December 31, 1988.

(2) SPECIAL RULE FOR COLLECTIVE BARGAINING AGREEMENTS.—In the case of a plan maintained pursuant to 1 or more collective bargaining agreements between employee representatives and 1 or more employers ratified before March 1, 1986, the amendments made by this section shall not apply to employees covered by any such agreement in plan years beginning before the earlier of—

(A) the later of—

(i) January 1, 1989, or

(ii) the date on which the last of such collective bargaining agreements terminates (determined without regard to any extension thereof after February 28, 1986), or

(B) January 1, 1991.

(3) PARTICIPATION REQUIRED.—The amendments made by this section shall not apply to any employee who does not have 1 hour of service in any plan year to which the amendments made by this section apply.

(4) REPEAL OF CLASS YEAR VESTING.—If a plan amendment repealing class year vesting is adopted after October 22, 1986, such amendment shall not apply to any employee for the 1st plan year to which the amendments made by subsections (b) and (e)(2) apply (and any subsequent plan year) of—

(A) such plan amendment would reduce the nonforfeitable right of such employee for such year, and

(B) such employee has at least 1 hour of service before the adoption of such plan amendment and after the beginning of such 1st plan year.

This paragraph shall not apply to an employee who has 5 consecutive 1-year breaks in service (as defined in section 411(a)(6)(A) of the Internal Revenue Code of 1986) which include the 1st day of the 1st plan year to which the amendments made by subsection (b) and (e)(2) apply. A plan shall not be treated as failing to meet the requirements of section 401(a)(26) of such Code by reason of complying with the provisions of this paragraph.

Years of service:	Nonforfeitable percentage
7	35
8	40
9	45
10	50
11	60
12	70
13	80
14	90
15 or more	100

(C)(1) A plan satisfies the requirements of this subparagraph if a participant who is not separated from the service, who has completed at least 5 years of service, and with respect to whom the sum of his age and years of service equals or exceeds 45, has a nonforfeitable right to a percentage of his accrued benefit derived from employer contributions determined under the following table:

and sum of age and service equals or exceeds—	then the nonforfeitable percentage is—
45	50
47	60
49	70
51	80
53	90
55	100

P.L. 99-514, §1139(c)(1):

Amended ERISA Sec. 203(e)(2) to read as above. Prior to amendment, ERISA Sec. 203(e)(2) read as follows:

(2) For purposes of paragraph (1), the present value shall be calculated by using an interest rate not greater than the interest rate which would be used (as of the date of the distribution) by the Pension Benefit Guaranty Corporation for purposes of determining the present value of a lump-sum distribution on plan termination.

The above amendment applies to distributions in plan years beginning after December 31, 1984, except that such amendments shall not apply to any distributions in plan years beginning after December 31, 1984, and before January 1, 1987, if such distributions were made in accordance with the requirements of the regulations issued under the Retirement Equity Act of 1984. However, for a special rule, see Act Sec. 1139(d)(2) below.

Act Sec. 1139(d)(2) provides:

(2) Reduction in Accrued Benefits.—

(A) In General.—If a plan—

(i) adopts a plan amendment before the close of the first plan year beginning on or before January 1, 1989, which provides for the calculation of the present value of the accrued benefit in the manner provided by the amendments made by this section, and

(ii) the plan reduces the accrued benefits for any plan year to which such plan amendment applies in accordance with such plan amendment,

such reduction shall not be treated as a violation of section 411(d)(6) of the Internal Revenue Code of 1986 or section 204(g) of the Employee Retirement Income Security Act of 1974 (29 U.S.C. 1054(g)).

(B) Special Rule.—In the case of a plan maintained by a corporation incorporated on April 11, 1934, which is headquartered in Tarrant County, Texas—

(i) such a plan may be amended to remove the option of an employee to receive a lump sum distribution (within the meaning of section 402(e)(5) of such Code) if such amendment—

(I) is adopted within 1 year of the date of the enactment of this Act, and

(II) is not effective until 2 years after the employees are notified of such amendment, and

(ii) the present value of any vested accrued benefit of such plan determined during the 3-year period beginning on the date of the enactment of this Act shall be determined under the applicable interest rate (within the meaning of section 411(a)(11)(B)(ii) of such Code), except that if such value (as so determined) exceeds $50,000, then the value of any excess over $50,000 shall be determined by using the interest rate specified in the plan as of August 16, 1986.

P.L. 99-514, §1898(a)(1)(B):

Amended ERISA Sec. 203(c)(3) to read as above. The amendment is to take effect according to the provision of Act Sec. 1898(a)(1)(C) which provides:

(C) EFFECTIVE DATE.—The amendments made by this paragraph shall apply to contributions made for plan years beginning after the date of the enactment of this Act; except that, in the case of a plan described in section 302(b) of the Retirement Equity Act of 1984, such amendments shall not apply to any plan year to which the amendments made by such Act do not apply by reason of such section 302(b).

P.L. 99-514, §1898(a)(4)(B)(i):

Amended ERISA Sec. 203(a)(3)(D)(ii), last sentence, to read as above. This amendment is effective for plan years beginning after 1984. Prior to amendment, the last sentence read as follows:

In the case of a defined contribution plan the plan provision required under this clause may provide that such repayment must be made before the participant has any 1-year break in service commencing after the withdrawal.

P.L. 99-514, § 1898(d)(1)(B):

Amended ERISA Sec. 203(e)(1) to read as above. This amendment is effective for plan years beginning after 1984. Prior to amendment, paragraph (1) read as follows:

Act Sec. 203. (e)(1) If the present value of any accrued benefit exceeds $3,500, such benefit shall not be treated as nonforfeitable if the plan provides that the present value of such benefit could be immediately distributed without the consent of the participant.

P.L. 99-514, § 1898(d)(2)(B):

Amended ERISA Sec. 203(e)(3) to read as above, effective for distributions made after 1984.

P.L. 98-397, §§ 102 and 105:

Act Sec. 102(b) amended ERISA Sec. 203(b)(1)(A) by striking out "22" and inserting "18" in its place.

For the effective date of the above amendment, see Act Sec. 303(a)(1) which is reproduced in the amendment notes to ERISA Sec. 202 at ¶ 102.

Act Sec. 102(c) amended ERISA Sec. 203(b)(3)(C): (1) by striking out "any 1-year break in service" and inserting in lieu thereof "5 consecutive 1-year breaks in service", and (2) by striking out "such break" each place it appeared and inserting in lieu thereof "such 5-year period".

Act Sec. 102(d)(2) amended ERISA Sec. 203(b)(3)(D) by striking out the prior law and replacing it with new subparagraph (D). Prior to amendment, ERISA Sec. 203(b)(3)(D) read as follows:

(D) For purposes of paragraph (1), in the case of a participant who, under the plan, does not have any nonforfeitable right to an accrued benefit derived from employer contributions, years of service before any 1-year break in service shall not be required to be taken into account if the number of consecutive 1-year breaks in service equals or exceeds the aggregate number of such years of service prior to such break. Such aggregate number of years of service before such break shall be deemed not to include any years of service not required to be taken into account under this subparagraph by reason of any prior break in service.

Act Sec. 102(e)(2) amended ERISA Sec. 203(b)(3) by adding at the end thereof new subparagraph (E) to read as above.

Act Sec. 105(a) added new ERISA Sec. 203(e) to read as above.

The above amendments generally are effective for plan years beginning after December 31, 1984.

However, Act Secs. 303(a)(3) and (b) provide:

(a)(3) Maternity or Paternity Leave.—The amendments made by sections 102(e) and 202(e) shall apply in the case of absences from work which begin on or after the first day of the first plan year to which the amendments made by this Act apply.

(b) Special Rule for Amendments Relating to Maternity or Paternity Absences.—If a plan is administered in a manner which would meet the amendments made by sections 102(e) and 202(e) (relating to certain maternity or paternity absences not treated as breaks in service), such plan need not be amended to meet such requirements until the earlier of—

(1) the date on which such plan is first otherwise amended after the date of the enactment of this Act, or

(2) the beginning of the first plan year beginning after December 31, 1986.

Also, see Act Sec. 302(b) for a special rule for collecting bargaining agreements at ¶ 14,250.09.

P.L. 96-364, § 303:

Added new subsections 203(a)(3)(E) and 203(b)(1)(G), effective September 26, 1980.

Regulations

The following regulations were adopted on December 23, 1976, and were published in the Federal Register of December 28, 1976 (41 FR 56462). Reg. § 2530.203-3 was adopted on January 26, 1981, and was published in the Federal Register of January 27, 1981 (46 FR 8894). The regulation was due to take effect on May 27, 1981, but the effective date was delayed until final amendments to the regulation were adopted. The amendments were adopted on December 1, 1981 (46 FR 59243), and, accordingly, the regulation is effective January 1, 1982.

[¶ 14,431]

§ 2530.203-1 **Vesting; general.**

(a) Section 203 of the Act and section 411(a) of the Code contain minimum vesting standards relating to certain employee pension benefit plans. In general, a pension plan subject to section 203 of the Act or section 411(a) of the Code must meet certain requirements relating to an employee's nonforfeitable ("vested") right to his or her normal retirement benefit. One of these requirements specifies that an employee's accrued benefit derived from employer contributions must be vested in accordance with certain schedules. The schedules (or alternative minimum vesting standards) are generally based on the employee's number of years of service with the employer or employers maintaining the plan. Section 2530.203-2 sets forth rules relating to the computation periods used to determine whether an employee has completed a year of service for vesting purposes ("vesting computation periods").

(b) For rules relating to service with the employer or employers maintaining the plan, *see* § 2530.210.

[¶ 14,432]

§ 2530.203-2 **Vesting computation period.** (a) *Designation of vesting computation periods.* Except as provided in paragraph (b) of this section, a plan may designate any 12-consecutive-month period as the vesting computation period. The period so designated must apply equally to all participants. This requirement may be satisfied even though the actual 12-consecutive-month periods are not the same for all employees (e.g., if the designated vesting computation period is the 12-consecutive-month period beginning on an employee's employment commencement date and anniversaries of that date). The plan is prohibited, however, from using any period that would result in artificial postponement of vesting credit, such as a period measured by anniversaries of the date four months following the employment commencement date.

(b) *Plans with 3-year 100 percent vesting.* For rules regarding when a participant has a nonforfeitable right to his accrued benefit, see section 202(a)(1)(B)(i) of the Act and 410(a)(1)(B)(i) of the Code and regulations issued thereunder.

(c) *Amendments to change the vesting computation period.* (1) A plan may be amended to change the vesting computation period to a different 12-consecutive-month period provided that as a result of such change no employee's vested percentage of the accrued benefit derived from employer contributions is less on any date after such change than such vested percentage would be in the absence of such change. A plan amendment changing the vesting computation period shall be deemed to comply with the requirements of this subparagraph if the first vesting computation period established under such amendment begins before the last day of the preceding vesting computation period and an employee who is credited with 1,000 hours of service in both the vesting computation period under the plan before the amendment and the first vesting computation period under the plan as amended is credited with 2 years of service for those vesting computation periods. For example, a plan which has been using a calendar year vesting computation period is amended to provide for a July 1—June 30 vesting computation period starting in 1977. Employees who complete more than 1,000 hours of service in both of the 12-month periods extending from January 1, 1977 to December 31, 1977 and from July 1, 1977 to June 30, 1978 are advanced two years on the plan's vesting schedule. The plan is deemed to meet the requirements of this subparagraph.

(2) For additional requirements pertaining to changes in the vesting schedule, see section 203(c)(1) of the Act and section 411(a)(10) of the Code and the regulations issued thereunder.

(d) *Service preceding a break in service.* For purposes of applying section 203(b)(3)(D) of the Act and section 411(a)(6)(D) of the Code (relating to counting years of service before a break in service for vesting purposes), the computation periods used by the plan in computing years of service before such break must be the vesting computation periods. (For application of the break in service rules, see section 203(b)(3)(D) and section 411(a)(6)(D) of the Code and regulations issued thereunder.)

[¶ 14,433]

§ 2530.203-3 **Suspension of pension benefits upon reemployment of retirees.** (a) *General.* Section 203(a)(3)(B) of the Act provides that the right to the employer-derived portion of an accrued pension benefit shall not be treated as forfeitable solely because an employee pension benefit plan provides that the payment of benefits is suspended during certain periods of reemployment which occur subsequent to the commencement of payment of such benefits. This section sets forth the circumstances and conditions under which such benefit payments may be suspended. A plan may provide for the suspension of pension benefits which commence prior to the attainment of normal retirement age, or for the suspension of that portion of pension benefits which exceeds the normal retirement benefit, or both, for any reemployment and without regard to the provisions of section 203(a)(3)(B) and this regulation to the extent (but only to the extent) that suspension of such benefits does not affect a retiree's entitlement to normal retirement benefits payable after attainment of normal retirement age, or the actuarial equivalent thereof.

(b) *Suspension rules.* (1) *General rule.* A plan may provide for the permanent withholding of an amount which does not exceed the suspendible amount of an employee's accrued benefit for each calendar month, or for each four or five week payroll period ending in a calendar month, during which an employee is employed in "section 203(a)(3)(B) service" as described in § 2530.203-3(c).

[Amended by F.R. Doc. 81-34837 on December 1, 1981 (46 FR 59243)]

(2) *Resumption of payments.* If benefit payments have been suspended pursuant to paragraph (b)(1) of this section, payments shall resume no later than the first day of the third calendar month after the calendar month in which the employee ceases to be employed in section 203(a)(3)(B) service: *Provided,* That the employee has complied with any reasonable procedure adopted by the plan for notifying the plan that he has ceased such employment. The initial payment upon resumption shall include the payment scheduled to occur in the calendar month when payments resume and any amounts withheld during the period between the cessation of employment and the resumption of payments, less any amounts which are subject to offset.

(3) *Offset rules.* A plan which provides for the permanent withholding of benefits may deduct from benefit payments to be made by the plan payments previously made by the plan during those calendar months or pay periods in which the employee was employed in section 203(a)(3)(B) service, *Provided,* That such deduction or offset does not exceed in any one month 25 percent of that month's total benefit payment which would have been due but for the offset (excluding the initial payment described in paragraph (b)(2) of this section, which may be subject to offset without limitation).

[Amended by F.R. Doc. 81-34837 on December 1, 1981 (46 FR 59243)]

(4) *Notification.* No payment shall be withheld by a plan pursuant to this section unless the plan notifies the employee by personal delivery or first class mail during the first calendar month or payroll period in which the plan withholds payments that his benefits are suspended. Such notification shall contain a description of the specific reasons why benefit payments are being suspended, a general description of the plan provisions relating to the suspension of payments, a copy of such provisions, and a statement to the effect that applicable Department of Labor regulations may be found in § 2530.203-3 of the Code of Federal Regulations. In addition, the suspension notification shall inform the employee of the plan's procedure for affording a review of the suspension of benefits. Requests for such reviews may be considered in accordance with the claims procedure adopted by the plan pursuant to section 503 of the Act and applicable regulations. In the case of a plan which requires the filing of a benefit resumption notice as a condition precedent to the resumption of benefits, the suspension notification shall also describe the procedure for filing such notice and include the forms (if any) which must be filed. Furthermore, if a plan intends to offset any suspendible amounts actually paid during the periods of employment in section 203(a)(3)(B) service, the notification shall identify specifically the periods of employment, the suspendible amounts which are subject to offset, and the manner in which the plan intends to offset such suspendible amounts. Where the plan's summary plan description (SPD) contains information which is substantially the same as information required by this subparagraph (4), the suspension notification may refer the employee to relevant pages of the SPD for information as to a particular item, provided the employee is informed how to obtain a copy of the SPD, or relevant pages thereof, and provided requests for referenced information are honored within a reasonable period of time, not to exceed 30 days.

[Amended by F.R. Doc. 81-34837 on December 1, 1981 (46 FR 59243)]

(5) *Verification.* A plan may provide that an employee must notify the plan of any employment. A plan may request from an employee access to reasonable information for the purpose of verifying such employment. Furthermore, a plan may provide that an employee must, at such time and with such frequency as may be reasonable, as a condition to receiving future benefit payments, either certify that he is unemployed or provide factual information sufficient to establish that any employment does not constitute section 203(a)(3)(B) service if specifically requested by the plan administrator. Once an employee has furnished the required certification or information, the plan must forward, at the next regularly scheduled time for payment of benefits, all payments which had been withheld pursuant to this subparagraph (5) except to the extent that payments may be withheld and offset pursuant to other provisions of this regulation.

(6) *Status determination.* If a plan provides for benefits suspension, the plan shall adopt a procedure, and so inform employees, whereunder an employee may request, and the plan administrator in a reasonable amount of time will render, a determination of whether specific contemplated employment will be section 203(a)(3)(B) service for purposes of plan provisions concerning suspension of benefits. Requests for status determinations may be considered in accordance with the claims procedure adopted by the plan pursuant to section 503 of the Act and applicable regulations.

(7) *Presumptions.* (i) A plan which has adopted verification requirements described in paragraph (b)(5) of this section, and which complies with the notice requirements set forth in paragraph (b)(7)(ii) of this section may provide that whenever the plan fiduciaries become aware that a retiree is employed in section 203(a)(3)(B) service and the retiree has not complied with the plan's reporting requirements with regard to that employment, the plan fiduciaries may, unless it is unreasonable under the circumstances to do so, act on the basis of a rebuttable presumption that the retiree had worked a period exceeding the plan's minimum number of hours for that month. In addition, a plan covering persons employed in the building trades which has adopted verification requirements described in paragraph (b)(5) of this section and which complies with the notice requirements set forth in paragraph (b)(7)(ii) of this section may provide that whenever the plan fiduciaries become aware that a retiree is employed in section 203(a)(3)(B) service at a construction site and the retiree has not complied with the plan's reporting requirements with regard to that employment, then the plan fiduciaries may, unless it is unreasonable under the circumstances to do so, act on the basis of a rebuttable presumption that the retiree engaged in such employment for the same employer in work at that site for so long before the work in question as that same employer performed that work at that construction site.

(ii) A plan which provides for a presumption described in paragraph (b)(7)(i) of this section may employ such presumption only if the following requirements are met. The plan must describe its employment verification requirements and the nature and effect of such presumption in the plan's summary plan description and in any communication to plan participants which relates to such verification requirements (for example, employment reporting reminders or forms), and retirees must be furnished such disclosure, whether through receipt of the above communications or by special distribution, at least once every 12 months.

(c) *Section 202(a)(3)(B) Service.* (1) *Plans other than multiemployer plans.* In the case of a plan other than a multiemployer plan, as defined in section 3(37) of the Act, the employment of an employee, subsequent to the time the payment of benefits commenced or would have commenced if the employee had not remained in or returned to employment, results in section 203(a)(3)(B) service during a calendar month, or during a four or five week payroll period ending in a calendar month, if the employee, in such month or payroll period,

Completes 40 or more hours of service (as defined in 29 CFR 2530.200b-2(a)(1) and (2)) for an employer which maintains the plan, including employers described in § 2530.210(d) and (e), as of the time that the payment of benefits commenced or would have commenced if the employee had not remained in or returned to employment; or

Receives from such employer payment for any such hours of service performed on each of 8 or more days (or separate work shifts) in such month or payroll period, *Provided,* That the plan has not for any purpose determined or used the actual number of hours of service which would be required to be credited to the employee under § 2530.200b-(2)(a).

[Amended by F.R. Doc. 81-34837 on December 1, 1981 (46 FR 59243)]

(2) *Multiemployer plans.* In the case of a multiemployer plan, as defined in section 3(37) of the Act, the employment of an employee subsequent to the time the payment of benefits commenced or would have commenced if the employee had not remained in or returned to employment results in section 203(a)(3)(B) service during a calendar month, or during a four or five week payroll period ending in a calendar month, if the employee, in such month or payroll period:

—Completes 40 or more hours of service (as defined in §2530.200b-2(a)(1) and 2)); or

—Receives payment for any such hours of service performed on each of 8 or more days (or separate work shifts) in such month or payroll period, *Provided,* That the plan has not for any purpose determined or used the actual number of hours of service which would be required to be credited to the employee under §2530.200b-2(a); in

—An industry in which employees covered by the plan were employed and accrued benefits under the plan as a result of such employment at the time that the payment of benefits commenced or would have commenced if the employee had not remained in or returned to employment, and

—A trade or craft in which the employee was employed at any time under the plan, and

—The geographic area covered by the plan at the time that the payment of benefits commenced or would have commenced if the employee had not remained in or returned to employment.

[Amended by F.R. Doc. 81-34837 on December 1, 1981 (46 FR 59243)]

(i) *Industry.* The term "industry" means the business activities of the types engaged in by any employers maintaining the plan.

• *Example.* One of the employers contributing to a multiemployer plan engages in heavy construction, another in textile manufacturing, and another in communications. Employee E began his career as an employee of an employer engaged in heavy construction. Later E was employed by an employer in communications. With both employers, E accrued benefits under the plan. If E retires and then becomes reemployed in the same trade or craft and in the same geographic area, employment by E in either heavy construction, communications or textile manufacturing, whether or not with an employer who contributes to the plan or in a self-employed capacity, may be considered by the plan to be employment in the same industry, assuming that employees covered by the plan were accruing benefits as a result of employment in these industries at the time E commenced receiving benefits. This is true even though E did not previously accrue benefits as a result of employment with an employer engaged in textile manufacturing because other employees covered by the plan were employed in that industry and were accruing benefits under the plan as a result of such employment at the time when benefit payments to E commenced or would have commenced if E had not returned to employment.

(ii) *Trade or craft.* A trade or craft is (A) a skill or skills, learned during a significant period of training or practice, which is applicable in occupations in some industry, (B) a skill or skills relating to selling, retailing, managerial, clerical or professional occupations, or (C) supervisory activities relating to a skill or skills described in (A) or (B) of this paragraph (c)(2)(ii). For purposes of this paragraph (c)(2)(ii), the determination whether a particular job classification, job description or industrial occupation constitutes or is included in a trade or craft shall be based upon the facts and circumstances of each case. Factors which may be examined include whether there is a customary and substantial period of practical, on-the-job training or a period of related supplementary instruction. Notwithstanding any other factor, the registration of an apprenticeship program with the Bureau of Apprenticeship and Training of the Employment Training Administration of the U.S. Department of Labor is sufficient for the conclusion that

a skill or skills which is the subject of the apprenticeship program constitutes a trade or craft.

• *Example.* Participation in a multiemployer plan is limited solely to electricians. Electrician E retired and then became reemployed as a foreman of electricians. Because a "trade or craft" includes related supervisory activities, E remains within his trade or craft for purposes of this section.

(iii) *Geographic area covered by the plan.* (A) With the exception of a plan covering employees in a maritime industry, the "geographic area covered by the plan" consists of any state or any province of Canada in which contributions were made or were required to be made by or on behalf of an employer and the remainder of any Standard Metropolitan Statistical Area (SMSA) which falls in part within such state, determined as of the time that the payment of benefits commenced or would have commenced if the employee had not returned to employment.

• *Example.* A multiemployer plan covers plumbers in Pennsylvania. All contributing employers have always been located within Pennsylvania. Accordingly, the "geographic area covered by the plan" consists of Pennsylvania and any SMSAs which fall in part within Pennsylvania. Thus, for example, in the case of the Philadelphia SMSA, Burlington, Camden and Gloucester Counties in New Jersey are within the "geographic area covered by the plan".

(B) [Reserved—for definition of the geographic area covered by a plan that covers employees in a maritime industry.]

For purposes of this paragraph (c)(2)(iii), contributions shall not include amounts contributed: after December 31, 1978 by or on behalf of an employer where no contributions were made by or on behalf of that employer before that date, if the primary purpose of such contribution is to allow for the suspension of plan benefits in a geographic area not otherwise covered by the plan; or with respect to isolated projects performed in states where plan participants were not otherwise employed.

(3) *Employment in a maritime industry.* For plans covering employees employed in a maritime industry, as defined in §2530.200b-6, the standard of "five or more days of service, as defined in §2530.200b-7(a)(1)" shall be used in lieu of the standard "40 or more hours of sservice", for purposes of determining whether an employee is employed in section 203(a)(3)(B) service.

(d) *Suspendable amount.* (1) *Life annuity.* In the case of benefits payable periodically on a monthly basis for as long as a life (or lives) continues, such as a straight life annuity or a qualified joint and survivor annuity, a plan may provide that an amount not greater than the portion of a monthly benefit payment derived from employer contributions may be withheld permanently for a calendar month, or for a four or five week payroll period ending in a calendar month, in which the employee is employed in section 203(a)(3)(B) service.

(2) *Other benefit forms.* In the case of benefits payable in a form other than the form described in paragraph (d)(1) of this section, a plan may provide for the permanent withholding of an amount of the employer-derived portion of benefit payments for a calendar month, or for a four or five week payroll period ending in a calendar month, in which the employee is employed in section 203(a)(3)(B) service, not exceeding the lesser of—

(i) The amount of benefits which would have been payable to the employee if he had been receiving monthly benefits under the plan since actual retirement based on a single life annuity commencing at actual retirement age; or

(ii) The actual amount paid or scheduled to be paid to the employee for such month. Payments which are scheduled to be paid less frequently than monthly may be converted to monthly payments for purposes of this paragraph (d)(2)(ii).

[Amended by F.R. Doc. 81-34847 on December 1, 1981 (46 FR 59243)]

[¶ 14,440]
BENEFIT ACCRUAL REQUIREMENTS

Act Sec. 204.(a) SATISFACTION OF REQUIREMENTS BY PENSION PLANS.—Each pension plan shall satisfy the requirements of subsection (b)(3), and—

(1) in the case of a defined benefit plan, shall satisfy the requirements of subsection (b)(1); and

(2) in the case of a defined contribution plan, shall satisfy the requirements of subsection (b)(2).

Act Sec. 204.(b)(1)(A) ENUMERATION OF PLAN REQUIREMENTS.—A defined benefit plan satisfies the requirements of this paragraph if the accrued benefit to which each participant is entitled upon his separation from the service is not less than—

(i) 3 percent of the normal retirement benefit to which he would be entitled at the normal retirement age if he commenced participation at the earliest possible entry age under the plan and served continuously until the earlier of age 65 or the normal retirement age specified under the plan, multiplied by

(ii) the number of years (not in excess of 33 ⅓) of his participation in the plan.

In the case of a plan providing retirement benefits based on compensation during any period, the normal retirement benefit to which a participant would be entitled shall be determined as if he continued to earn annually the average rate of compensation which he earned during consecutive years of service, not in excess of 10, for which his compensation was the highest. For purposes of this subparagraph, social security benefits and all other relevant factors used to compute benefits shall be treated as remaining constant as of the current year for all years after such current year.

(B) A defined benefit plan satisfies the requirements of this paragraph for a particular plan year if under the plan the accrued benefit payable at the normal retirement age is equal to the normal retirement benefit and the annual rate at which any individual who is or could be a participant can accrue the retirement benefits payable at normal retirement age under the plan for any later plan year is not more than 133 ⅓ percent of the annual rate at which he can accrue benefits for any plan year beginning on or after such particular plan year and before such later plan year. For purposes of this subparagraph—

(i) any amendment to the plan which is in effect for the current year shall be treated as in effect for all other plan years;

(ii) any change in an accrual rate which does not apply to any individual who is or could be a participant in the current year shall be disregarded;

(iii) the fact that benefits under the plan may be payable to certain employees before normal retirement age shall be disregarded; and

(iv) social security benefits and all other relevant factors used to compute benefits shall be treated as remaining constant as of the current year for all years after the current year.

(C) A defined benefit plan satisfies the requirements of this paragraph if the accrued benefit to which any participant is entitled upon his separation from the service is not less than a fraction of the annual benefit commencing at normal retirement age to which he would be entitled under the plan as in effect on the date of his separation if he continued to earn annually until normal retirement age the same rate of compensation upon which his normal retirement benefit would be computed under the plan, determined as if he had attained normal retirement age on the date any such determination is made (but taking into account no more than the 10 years of service immediately preceding his separation from service). Such fraction shall be a fraction, not exceeding 1, the numerator of which is the total number of his years of participation in the plan (as of the date of his separation from the service) and the denominator of which is the total number of years he would have participated in the plan if he separated from the service at the normal retirement age. For purposes of this subparagraph, social security benefits and all other relevant factors used to compute benefits shall be treated as remaining constant as of the current year for all years after such current year.

(D) Subparagraphs (A), (B), and (C) shall not apply with respect to years of participation before the first plan year to which this section applies but a defined benefit plan satisfies the requirement of this subparagraph with respect to such years of participation only if the accrued benefit of any participant with respect to such years of participation is not less than the greater of—

(i) his accrued benefit determined under the plan, as in effect from time to time prior to the date of the enactment of this Act, or

(ii) an accrued benefit which is not less than one-half of the accrued benefit to which such participant would have been entitled if subparagraph (A), (B), or (C) applied with respect to such years of participation.

(E) Notwithstanding subparagraphs (A), (B), and (C) of this paragraph, a plan shall not be treated as not satisfying the requirements of this paragraph solely because the accrual of benefits under the plan does not become effective until the employee has two continuous years of service. For purposes of this subparagraph, the term "years of service" has the meaning provided by section 202(a)(3)(A).

(F) Notwithstanding subparagraphs (A), (B), and (C), a defined benefit plan satisfies the requirements of this paragraph if such plan—

(i) is funded exclusively by the purchase of insurance contracts, and

(ii) satisfies the requirements of paragraphs (2) and (3) of section 301(b) (relating to certain insurance contract plans),

but only if an employee's accrued benefit as of any applicable date is not less than the cash surrender value his insurance contracts would have on such applicable date if the requirements of paragraphs (4), (5), and (6) of section 301(b) were satisfied.

(G) Notwithstanding the preceding subparagraphs, a defined benefit plan shall be treated as not satisfying the requirements of this paragraph if the participant's accrued benefit is reduced on account of any increase in his age or service. The preceding sentence shall not apply to benefits under the plan commencing before benefits payable under title II of the Social Security Act which benefits under the plan—

(i) do not exceed such social security benefits, and

(ii) terminate when such social security benefits commence.

(H)(i) Notwithstanding the preceding subparagraphs, a defined benefit plan shall be treated as not satisfying the requirements of this paragraph if, under the plan, an employee's benefit accrual is ceased, or the rate of an employee's benefit accrual is reduced, because of the attainment of any age.

(ii) A plan shall not be treated as failing to meet the requirements of this subparagraph solely because the plan imposes (without regard to age) a limitation on the amount of benefits that the plan provides or a limitation on the number of years of service or years of participation which are taken into account for purposes of determining benefit accrual under the plan.

(iii) In the case of any employee who, as of the end of any plan year under a defined benefit plan, has attained normal retirement age under such plan—

(I) if distribution of benefits under such plan with respect to such employee has commenced as of the end of such plan year, then any requirement of this subparagraph for continued accrual of benefits under such plan with respect to such employee during such plan year shall be treated as satisfied to the extent of the actuarial equivalent of in-service distribution of benefits, and

(II) if distribution of benefits under such plan with respect to such employee has not commenced as of the end of such year in accordance with section 206(a)(3), and the payment of benefits under such plan with respect to such employee is not suspended during such plan year pursuant to section 203(a)(3)(B), then any requirement of this subparagraph for continued accrual of benefits under such plan with respect to such employee during such plan year shall be treated as satisfied to the extent of any adjustment in the benefit payable under the plan during such plan year attributable to the delay in the distribution of benefits after the attainment of normal retirement age.

The preceding provisions of this clause shall apply in accordance with regulations of the Secretary of the Treasury. Such regulations may provide for the application of the preceding provisions of this clause, in the case of any such employee, with respect to any period of time within a plan year.

(iv) Clause (i) shall not apply with respect to any employee who is a highly compensated employee (within the meaning of section 414(q) of the Internal Revenue Code of 1986) to the extent provided in regulations prescribed by the Secretary of the Treasury for purposes of precluding discrimination in favor of highly compensated employees within the meaning of subchapter D of chapter 1 of the Internal Revenue Code of 1986.

(v) A plan shall not be treated as failing to meet the requirements of clause (i) solely because the subsidized portion of any early retirement benefit is disregarded in determining benefit accruals.

(vi) Any regulations prescribed by the Secretary of the Treasury pursuant to clause (v) of section 411(b)(1)(H) of the Internal Revenue Code of 1986 shall apply with respect to the requirements of this subparagraph in the same manner and to the same extent as such regulations apply with respect to the requirement of such section 411(b)(1)(H).

(2)(A) A defined contribution plan satisfies the requirements of this paragraph if, under the plan, allocations to the employee's account are not ceased, and the rate at which amounts are allocated to the employee's account is not reduced, because of the attainment of any age.

(B) A plan shall not be treated as failing to meet the requirements of subparagraph (A) solely because the subsidized portion of any early retirement benefit is disregarded in determining benefit accruals.

(C) Any regulations prescribed by the Secretary of the Treasury pursuant to subparagraphs (B) and (C) of section 411(b)(2) of the Internal Revenue Code of 1986 shall apply with respect to the requirements of this paragraph in the same manner and to the same extent as such regulations apply with respect to the requirements of such section 411(b)(2).

(3) A plan satisfies the requirements of this paragraph if—

(A) in the case of a defined benefit plan, the plan requires separate accounting for the portion of each employee's accrued benefit derived from any voluntary employee contributions permitted under the plan; and

(B) in the case of any plan which is not a defined benefit plan, the plan requires separate accounting for each employee's accrued benefit.

(4)(A) For purposes of determining an employee's accrued benefit, the term "year of participation" means a period of service (beginning at the earliest date on which the employee is a participant in the plan and which is included in a period of service required to be taken into account under section 202(b), determined without regard to section 202(b)(5)) as determined under regulations prescribed by the Secretary which provide for the calculation of such period on any reasonable and consistent basis.

(B) For purposes of this paragraph, except as provided in subparagraph (C), in the case of any employee whose customary employment is less than full time, the calculation of such employee's service on any basis which provides less than a ratable portion of the accrued benefit to which he would be entitled under the plan if his customary employment were full time shall not be treated as made on a reasonable and consistent basis.

(C) For purposes of this paragraph, in the case of an employee whose service is less than 1,000 hours during any calendar year, plan year or other 12-consecutive-month period designated by the plan (and not prohibited under regulations prescribed by the Secretary), the calculation of his period of service shall not be treated as not made on a reasonable and consistent basis merely because such service is not taken into account.

(D) In the case of any seasonal industry where the customary period of employment is less than 1,000 hours during a calendar year, the term "year of participation" shall be such period as determined under regulations prescribed by the Secretary.

(E) For purposes of this subsection in the case of any maritime industry, 125 days of service shall be treated as a year of participation. The Secretary may prescribe regulations to carry out the purposes of this subparagraph.

(5) Special rules relating to age.—

(A) Comparison to similarly situated younger individual.—

(i) In general. —A plan shall not be treated as failing to meet the requirements of paragraph (1)(H)(i) if a participant's accrued benefit, as determined as of any date under the terms of the plan, would be equal to or greater than that of any similarly situated, younger individual who is or could be a participant.

(ii) Similarly situated. —For purposes of this subparagraph, a participant is similarly situated to any other individual if such participant is identical to such other individual in every respect (including period of service, compensation, position, date of hire, work history, and any other respect) except for age.

(iii) Disregard of subsidized early retirement benefits. —In determining the accrued benefit as of any date for purposes of this subparagraph, the subsidized portion of any early retirement benefit or retirement-type subsidy shall be disregarded.

(iv) Accrued benefit. —For purposes of this subparagraph, the accrued benefit may, under the terms of the plan, be expressed as an annuity payable at normal retirement age, the balance of a hypothetical account, or the current value of the accumulated percentage of the employee's final average compensation.

(B) Applicable defined benefit plans.—

(i) Interest credits.—

(I) In general. —An applicable defined benefit plan shall be treated as failing to meet the requirements of paragraph (1)(H) unless the terms of the plan provide that any interest credit (or an equivalent amount) for any plan year shall be at a rate which is not greater than a market rate of return. A plan shall not be treated as failing to meet the requirements of this subclause merely because the plan provides for a reasonable minimum guaranteed rate of return or for a rate of return that is equal to the greater of a fixed or variable rate of return.

(II) Preservation of capital. —An applicable defined benefit plan shall be treated as failing to meet the requirements of paragraph (1)(H) unless the plan provides that an interest credit (or equivalent amount) of less than zero shall in no event result in the account balance or similar amount being less than the aggregate amount of contributions credited to the account.

(III) Market rate of return. —The Secretary of the Treasury may provide by regulation for rules governing the calculation of a market rate of return for purposes of subclause (I) and for permissible methods of crediting interest to the account (including fixed or variable interest rates) resulting in effective rates of return meeting the requirements of subclause (I).

(ii) Special rule for plan conversions. —If, after June 29, 2005, an applicable plan amendment is adopted, the plan shall be treated as failing to meet the requirements of paragraph (1)(H) unless the requirements of clause (iii) are met with respect to each individual who was a participant in the plan immediately before the adoption of the amendment.

(iii) Rate of benefit accrual. —Subject to clause (iv), the requirements of this clause are met with respect to any participant if the accrued benefit of the participant under the terms of the plan as in effect after the amendment is not less than the sum of—

(I) the participant's accrued benefit for years of service before the effective date of the amendment, determined under the terms of the plan as in effect before the amendment, plus

(II) the participant's accrued benefit for years of service after the effective date of the amendment, determined under the terms of the plan as in effect after the amendment.

(iv) Special rules for early retirement subsidies. —For purposes of clause (iii)(I), the plan shall credit the accumulation account or similar amount with the amount of any early retirement benefit or retirement-type subsidy for the plan year in which the participant retires if, as of such time, the participant has met the age, years of service, and other requirements under the plan for entitlement to such benefit or subsidy.

(v) Applicable plan amendment. —For purposes of this subparagraph—

(I) In general. —The term "applicable plan amendment" means an amendment to a defined benefit plan which has the effect of converting the plan to an applicable defined benefit plan.

(II) Special rule for coordinated benefits. —If the benefits of 2 or more defined benefit plans established or maintained by an employer are coordinated in such a manner as to have the effect of the adoption of an amendment described in subclause (I), the sponsor of the defined benefit plan or plans providing for such coordination shall be treated as having adopted such a plan amendment as of the date such coordination begins.

(III) MULTIPLE AMENDMENTS. —The Secretary of the Treasury shall issue regulations to prevent the avoidance of the purposes of this subparagraph through the use of 2 or more plan amendments rather than a single amendment.

(IV) APPLICABLE DEFINED BENEFIT PLAN. —For purposes of this subparagraph, the term "applicable defined benefit plan" has the meaning given such term by section 203(f)(3).

(vi) TERMINATION REQUIREMENTS. —An applicable defined benefit plan shall not be treated as meeting the requirements of clause (i) unless the plan provides that, upon the termination of the plan—

(I) if the interest credit rate (or an equivalent amount) under the plan is a variable rate, the rate of interest used to determine accrued benefits under the plan shall be equal to the average of the rates of interest used under the plan during the 5-year period ending on the termination date, and

(II) the interest rate and mortality table used to determine the amount of any benefit under the plan payable in the form of an annuity payable at normal retirement age shall be the rate and table specified under the plan for such purpose as of the termination date, except that if such interest rate is a variable rate, the interest rate shall be determined under the rules of subclause (I).

(C) CERTAIN OFFSETS PERMITTED. —A plan shall not be treated as failing to meet the requirements of paragraph (1)(H)(i) solely because the plan provides offsets against benefits under the plan to the extent such offsets are otherwise allowable in applying the requirements of section 401(a) of the Internal Revenue Code of 1986.

(D) PERMITTED DISPARITIES IN PLAN CONTRIBUTIONS OR BENEFITS. —A plan shall not be treated as failing to meet the requirements of paragraph (1)(H) solely because the plan provides a disparity in contributions or benefits with respect to which the requirements of section 401(l) of the Internal Revenue Code of 1986 are met.

(E) INDEXING PERMITTED.—

(i) IN GENERAL. —A plan shall not be treated as failing to meet the requirements of paragraph (1)(H) solely because the plan provides for indexing of accrued benefits under the plan.

(ii) PROTECTION AGAINST LOSS. —Except in the case of any benefit provided in the form of a variable annuity, clause (i) shall not apply with respect to any indexing which results in an accrued benefit less than the accrued benefit determined without regard to such indexing.

(iii) INDEXING. —For purposes of this subparagraph, the term "indexing" means, in connection with an accrued benefit, the periodic adjustment of the accrued benefit by means of the application of a recognized investment index or methodology.

(F) EARLY RETIREMENT BENEFIT OR RETIREMENT-TYPE SUBSIDY. —For purposes of this paragraph, the terms "early retirement benefit" and "retirement-type subsidy" have the meaning given such terms in subsection (g)(2)(A).

(G) BENEFIT ACCRUED TO DATE. —For purposes of this paragraph, any reference to the accrued benefit shall be a reference to such benefit accrued to date.

Act. Sec. 204.(c)(1) EMPLOYEE'S ACCRUED BENEFITS DERIVED FROM EMPLOYER AND EMPLOYEE CONTRIBUTIONS.—For purposes of this section and section 203 an employee's accrued benefit derived from employer contributions as of any applicable date is the excess (if any) of the accrued benefit for such employee as of such applicable date over the accrued benefit derived from contributions made by such employee as of such date.

(2)(A) In the case of a plan other than a defined benefit plan, the accrued benefit derived from contributions made by an employee as of any applicable date is—

(i) except as provided in clause (ii), the balance of the employee's separate account consisting only of his contributions and the income, expenses, gains, and losses attributable thereto, or

(ii) if a separate account is not maintained with respect to an employee's contributions under such a plan, the amount which bears the same ratio to his total accrued benefit as the total amount of the employee's contributions (less withdrawals) bears to the sum of such contributions and the contributions made on his behalf by the employer (less withdrawals).

(B) DEFINED BENEFIT PLANS. In the case of a defined benefit plan, the accrued benefit derived from contributions made by an employee as of any applicable date is the amount equal to the employee's accumulated contributions expressed as an annual benefit commencing at normal retirement age, using an interest rate which would be used under the plan under section 205(g)(3) (as of the determination date).

(C) For purposes of this subsection, the term "accumulted contributions" means the total of—

(i) all mandatory contributions made by the employee,

(ii) interest (if any) under the plan to the end of the last plan year to which section 203(a)(2) does not apply (by reason of the applicable effective date) and

(iii) interest on the sum of the amounts determined under clauses (i) and (ii) compounded annually—

(I) at the rate of 120 percent of the Federal midterm rate (as in effect under section 1274 of the Internal Revenue Code of 1986 for the 1st month of a plan year for the period beginning with the 1st plan year to which subsection (a)(2) applies by reason of the applicable effective date) and ending with the date on which the determination is being made, and

(II) at the interest rate which would be used under the plan under section 205(g)(3) (as of the determination date) for the period beginning with the determination date and ending on the date on which the employee attains normal retirement age.

For purposes of this subparagraph, the term "mandatory contributions" means amounts contributed to the plan by the employee which are required as a condition of employment, as a condition of participation in such plan, or as a condition of obtaining benefits under the plan attributable to employer contributions.

(D) The Secretary of the Treasury is authorized to adjust by regulation the conversion factor described in subparagraph (B) from time to time as he may deem necessary. No such adjustment shall be effective for a plan year beginning before the expiration of 1 year after such adjustment is determined and published.

(3) For purposes of this section, in the case of any defined benefit plan, if an employee's accrued benefit is to be determined as an amount other than an annual benefit commencing at normal retirement age, or if the accrued benefit derived from contributions made by an employee is to be determined with respect to a benefit other than an annual benefit in the form of a single life annuity (without ancillary benefits) commencing at normal retirement age, the employee's accrued benefit, or the accrued benefits derived from contributions made by an employee, as the case may be, shall be the actuarial equivalent of such benefit or amount determined under paragraph (1) or (2).

(4) In the case of a defined benefit plan which permits voluntary employee contributions, the portion of an employee's accrued benefit derived from such contributions shall be treated as an accrued benefit derived from employee contributions under a plan other than a defined benefit plan.

Act Sec. 204. (d) EMPLOYEE SERVICE WHICH MAY BE DISREGARDED IN DETERMINING EMPLOYEE'S ACCRUED BENEFITS UNDER PLAN.—Notwithstanding section 203(b)(1), for purposes of determining the employee's accrued benefit under the plan, the plan may disregard service performed by the employee with respect to which he has received—

(1) a distribution of the present value of his entire nonforfeitable benefit if such distribution was in an amount (not more than $5,000) perrmitted under regulations prescribed by the Secretary of the Treasury, or

(2) a distribution of the present value of his nonforfeitable benefit attributable to such service which he elected to receive.

Paragraph (1) shall apply only if such distribution was made on termination of the employee's participation in the plan. Paragraph (2) shall apply only if such distribution was made on termination of the employee's participation in the plan or under such other circumstances as may be provided under regulations prescribed by the Secretary of the Treasury.

Act Sec. 204. (e) OPPORTUNITY TO REPAY FULL AMOUNT OF DISTRIBUTIONS WHICH HAVE BEEN REDUCED THROUGH DISREGARDED EMPLOYEE SERVICE.—For purposes of determining the employee's accrued benefit, the plan shall not disregard service as provided in subsection (d) unless the plan provides an opportunity for the participant to repay the full amount of a distribution described in subsection (d) with, in the case of a defined benefit plan, interest at the rate determined for purposes of subsection (c)(2)(C) and provides that upon such repayment the employee's accrued benefit shall be recomputed by taking into account service so disregarded. This subsection shall apply only in the case of a participant who—

(1) received such a distribution in any plan year to which this section applies, which distribution was less than the present value of his accrued benefit,

(2) resumes employment covered under the plan, and

(3) repays the full amount of such distribution with, in the case of a defined benefit plan, interest at the rate determined for purposes of subsection (c)(2)(C).

The plan provision required under this subsection may provide that such repayment must be made (A) in the case of a withdrawal on account of separation from service, before the earlier of 5 years after the first date on which the participant is subsequently re-employed by the employer, or the close of the first period of 5 consecutive 1-year breaks in service commencing after the withdrawal; or (B) in the case of any other withdrawal, 5 years after the date of the withdrawal.

Act Sec. 204. (f) EMPLOYER TREATED AS MAINTAINING A PLAN.—For the purposes of this part, an employer shall be treated as maintaining a plan if any employee of such employer accrues benefits under such plan by reason of service with such employer.

Act Sec. 204. (g)(1) DECREASE OF ACCRUED BENEFITS THROUGH AMENDMENT OF PLAN.—The accrued benefit of a participant under a plan may not be decreased by an amendment of the plan, other than an amendment described in section 302(d)(2) or section 4281.

(2) For purposes of paragraph (1), a plan amendment which has the effect of—

(A) eliminating or reducing an early retirement benefit or a retirement-type subsidy (as defined in regulations), or

(B) eliminating an optional form of benefit,

with respect to benefits attributable to service before the amendment shall be treated as reducing accrued benefits. In the case of a retirement-type subsidy, the preceding sentence shall apply only with respect to a participant who satisfies (either before or after the amendment) the preamendment conditions for the subsidy. The Secretary of the Treasury shall by regulations provide that this paragraph shall not apply to any plan amendment which reduces or eliminates benefits or subsidies which create significant burdens or complexities for the plan and plan participants, unless such amendment adversely affects the rights of any participant in a more than de minimis manner. The Secretary of the Treasury may by regulations provide that this subparagraph shall not apply to a plan amendment described in subparagraph (B) (other than a plan amendment having an effect described in subparagraph (A)).

(3) For purposes of this subsection, any—

(A) tax credit employee stock ownership plan (as defined in section 409(a) of the Internal Revenue Code of 1986), or

(B) employee stock ownership plan (as defined in section 4975(e)(7) of such Code),

shall not be treated as failing to meet the requirements of this subsection merely because it modifies distribution options in a nondiscriminatory manner.

(4)(A) A defined contribution plan (in this subparagraph referred to as the "transferee plan") shall not be treated as failing to meet the requirements of this subsection merely because the transferee plan does not provide some or all of the forms of distribution previously available under another defined contribution plan (in this subparagraph referred to as the "transferor plan") to the extent that—

(i) the forms of distribution previously available under the transferor plan applied to the account of a participant or beneficiary under the transferor plan that was transferred from the transferor plan to the transferee plan pursuant to a direct transfer rather than pursuant to a distribution from the transferor plan;

(ii) the terms of both the transferor plan and the transferee plan authorize the transfer described in clause (i);

(iii) the transfer described in clause (i) was made pursuant to a voluntary election by the participant or beneficiary whose account was transferred to the transferee plan;

(iv) the election described in clause (iii) was made after the participant or beneficiary received a notice describing the consequences of making the election; and

(v) the transferee plan allows the participant or beneficiary described in clause (iii) to receive any distribution to which the participant or beneficiary is entitled under the transferee plan in the form of a single sum distribution.

(B) Subparagraph (A) shall apply to plan mergers and other transactions having the effect of a direct transfer, including consolidations of benefits attributable to different employers within a multiple employer plan.

(5) Except to the extent provided in regulations promulgated by the Secretary of the Treasury, a defined contribution plan shall not be treated as failing to meet the requirements of this subsection merely because of the elimination of a form of distribution previously available thereunder. This paragraph shall not apply to the elimination of a form of distribution with respect to any participant unless—

(A) a single sum payment is available to such participant at the same time or times as the form of distribution being eliminated; and

(B) such single sum payment is based on the same or greater portion of the participant's account as the form of distribution being eliminated.

Act Sec. 204. (h)(1) NOTICE OF SIGNIFICANT REDUCTION IN BENEFIT ACCRUALS.—An applicable pension plan may not be amended so as to provide for a significant reduction in the rate of future benefit accrual unless the plan administrator provides the notice described in paragraph (2) to each applicable individual (and to each employee organization representing applicable individuals and to each employer who has an obligation to contribute to the plan).

(2) The notice required by paragraph (1) shall be written in a manner calculated to be understood by the average plan participant and shall provide sufficient information (as determined in accordance with regulations prescribed by the Secretary of the Treasury) to allow applicable individuals to understand the effect of the plan amendment. The Secretary of the Treasury may provide a simplified form of notice for, or exempt from any notice requirement, a plan—

(A) which has fewer than 100 participants who have accrued a benefit under the plan, or

(B) which offers participants the option to choose between the new benefit formula and the old benefit formula.

(3) Except as provided in regulations prescribed by the Secretary of the Treasury, the notice required by paragraph (1) shall be provided within a reasonable time before the effective date of the plan amendment.

(4) Any notice under paragraph (1) may be provided to a person designated, in writing, by the person to which it would otherwise be provided.

(5) A plan shall not be treated as failing to meet the requirements of paragraph (1) merely because notice is provided before the adoption of the plan amendment if no material modification of the amendment occurs before the amendment is adopted.

(6)(A) In the case of any egregious failure to meet any requirement of this subsection with respect to any plan amendment, the provisions of the applicable pension plan shall be applied as if such plan amendment entitled all applicable individuals to the greater of—

(i) the benefits to which they would have been entitled without regard to such amendment, or

(ii) the benefits under the plan with regard to such amendment.

(B) For purposes of subparagraph (A), there is an egregious failure to meet the requirements of this subsection if such failure is within the control of the plan sponsor and is—

(i) an intentional failure (including any failure to promptly provide the required notice or information after the plan administrator discovers an unintentional failure to meet the requirements of this subsection),

(ii) a failure to provide most of the individuals with most of the information they are entitled to receive under this subsection, or

(iii) a failure which is determined to be egregious under regulations prescribed by the Secretary of the Treasury.

(7) The Secretary of the Treasury may by regulations allow any notice under this subsection to be provided by using new technologies.

(8) For purposes of this subsection—

(A) The term "applicable individual" means, with respect to any plan amendment—

(i) each participant in the plan; and

(ii) any beneficiary who is an alternate payee (within the meaning of section 206(d)(3)(K)) under an applicable qualified domestic relations order (within the meaning of section 206(d)(3)(B)(i)),

whose rate of future benefit accrual under the plan may reasonably be expected to be significantly reduced by such plan amendment.

(B) The term "applicable pension plan" means—

(i) any defined benefit plan; or

(ii) an individual account plan which is subject to the funding standards of section 412 of the Internal Revenue Code of 1986.

(9) For purposes of this subsection, a plan amendment which eliminates or reduces any early retirement benefit or retirement-type subsidy (within the meaning of subsection (g)(2)(A)) shall be treated as having the effect of reducing the rate of future benefit accrual.

Act Sec. 204.(i)(1) PROHIBITION ON BENEFIT INCREASES WHERE PLAN SPONSOR IS IN BANKRUPTCY.—In the case of a plan described in paragraph (3) which is maintained by an employer that is a debtor in a case under title 11, United States Code, or similar Federal or State law, no amendment of the plan which increases the liabilities of the plan by reason of—

(A) any increase in benefits,

(B) any change in the accrual of benefits, or

(C) any change in the rate at which benefits become nonforfeitable under the plan,

with respect to employees of the debtor, shall be effective prior to the effective date of such employers' plan of reorganization.

(2) Paragraph (1) shall not apply to any plan amendment that—

(A) the Secretary of the Treasury determines to be reasonable and that provides for only de minimis increases in the liabilities of the plan with respect to employees of the debtor,

(B) only repeals an amendment described in section 302(d)(2),

(C) is required as a condition of qualification under part I of subchapter D of chapter 1 of the Internal Revenue Code of 1986, or

(D) was adopted prior to, or pursuant to a collective bargaining agreement entered into prior to, the date on which the employer became a debtor in a case under title 11, United States Code, or similar Federal or State law.

(3) This subsection shall apply only to plans (other than multiemployer plans or CSEC plans) covered under section 4021 of this Act for which the funding target attainment percentage (as defined in section 303(d)(2)) is less than 100 percent after taking into account the effect of the amendment.

(4) For purposes of this subsection, the term "employer" has the meaning set forth in section 302(b)(1), without regard to section 302(b)(2).

Act Sec. 204. (j) DIVERSIFICATION REQUIREMENTS FOR CERTAIN INDIVIDUAL ACCOUNT PLANS.—

(1) IN GENERAL.—An applicable individual account plan shall meet the diversification requirements of paragraphs (2), (3), and (4).

(2) EMPLOYEE CONTRIBUTIONS AND ELECTIVE DEFERRALS INVESTED IN EMPLOYER SECURITIES.—In the case of the portion of an applicable individual's account attributable to employee contributions and elective deferrals which is invested in employer securities, a plan meets the requirements of this paragraph if the applicable individual may elect to direct the plan to divest any such securities and to reinvest an equivalent amount in other investment options meeting the requirements of paragraph (4).

(3) EMPLOYER CONTRIBUTIONS INVESTED IN EMPLOYER SECURITIES.—In the case of the portion of the account attributable to employer contributions other than elective deferrals which is invested in employer securities, a plan meets the requirements of this paragraph if each applicable individual who—

(A) is a participant who has completed at least 3 years of service, or

(B) is a beneficiary of a participant described in subparagraph (A) or of a deceased participant,

may elect to direct the plan to divest any such securities and to reinvest an equivalent amount in other investment options meeting the requirements of paragraph (4).

(4) INVESTMENT OPTIONS.—

(A) IN GENERAL.—The requirements of this paragraph are met if the plan offers not less than 3 investment options, other than employer securities, to which an applicable individual may direct the proceeds from the divestment of employer securities pursuant to this subsection, each of which is diversified and has materially different risk and return characteristics.

(B) TREATMENT OF CERTAIN RESTRICTIONS AND CONDITIONS.—

(i) TIME FOR MAKING INVESTMENT CHOICES.—A plan shall not be treated as failing to meet the requirements of this paragraph merely because the plan limits the time for divestment and reinvestment to periodic, reasonable opportunities occurring no less frequently than quarterly.

(ii) CERTAIN RESTRICTIONS AND CONDITIONS NOT ALLOWED.—Except as provided in regulations, a plan shall not meet the requirements of this paragraph if the plan imposes restrictions or conditions with respect to the investment of employer securities which are not imposed on the investment of other assets of the plan. This subparagraph shall not apply to any restrictions or conditions imposed by reason of the application of securities laws.

(5) APPLICABLE INDIVIDUAL ACCOUNT PLAN.—For purposes of this subsection—

(A) IN GENERAL.—The term "applicable individual account plan" means any individual account plan (as defined in section 3(34)) which holds any publicly traded employer securities.

(B) EXCEPTION FOR CERTAIN ESOPS.—Such term does not include an employee stock ownership plan if—.

(i) there are no contributions to such plan (or earnings thereunder) which are held within such plan and are subject to subsection (k) or (m) of section 401 of the Internal Revenue Code of 1986, and

(ii) such plan is a separate plan (for purposes of section 414(l) of such Code) with respect to any other defined benefit plan or individual account plan maintained by the same employer or employers.

(C) EXCEPTION FOR ONE PARTICIPANT PLANS. —Such term shall not include a one-participant retirement plan (as defined in section 101(i)(8)(B)).

(D) CERTAIN PLANS TREATED AS HOLDING PUBLICLY TRADED EMPLOYER SECURITIES.—

(i) IN GENERAL. —Except as provided in regulations or in clause (ii), a plan holding employer securities which are not publicly traded employer securities shall be treated as holding publicly traded employer securities if any employer corporation, or any member of a controlled group of corporations which includes such employer corporation, has issued a class of stock which is a publicly traded employer security.

(ii) EXCEPTION FOR CERTAIN CONTROLLED GROUPS WITH PUBLICLY TRADED SECURITIES. —Clause (i) shall not apply to a plan if—

(I) no employer corporation, or parent corporation of an employer corporation, has issued any publicly traded employer security, and

(II) no employer corporation, or parent corporation of an employer corporation, has issued any special class of stock which grants particular rights to, or bears particular risks for, the holder or issuer with respect to any corporation described in clause (i) which has issued any publicly traded employer security.

(iii) DEFINITIONS. —For purposes of this subparagraph, the term—

(I) "controlled group of corporations" has the meaning given such term by section 1563(a) of the Internal Revenue Code of 1986, except that "50 percent" shall be substituted for "80 percent" each place it appears,

(II) "employer corporation" means a corporation which is an employer maintaining the plan, and

(III) "parent corporation" has the meaning given such term by section 424(e) of such Code.

(6) OTHER DEFINITIONS. —For purposes of this paragraph—

(A) APPLICABLE INDIVIDUAL. —The term "applicable individual" means—

(i) any participant in the plan, and

(ii) any beneficiary who has an account under the plan with respect to which the beneficiary is entitled to exercise the rights of a participant.

(B) ELECTIVE DEFERRAL. —The term "elective deferral" means an employer contribution described in section 402(g)(3)(A) of the Internal Revenue Code of 1986.

(C) EMPLOYER SECURITY. —The term "employer security" has the meaning given such term by section 407(d)(1).

(D) EMPLOYEE-STOCK OWNERSHIP PLAN. —The term "employee stock ownership plan" has the meaning given such term by section 4975(e)(7) of such Code.

(E) PUBLICLY TRADED EMPLOYER SECURITIES. —The term "publicly traded employer securities" means employer securities which are readily tradable on an established securities market.

(F) YEAR OF SERVICE. —The term "year of service" has the meaning given such term by section 203(b)(2).

(7) TRANSITION RULE FOR SECURITIES ATTRIBUTABLE TO EMPLOYER CONTRIBUTIONS.—

(A) RULES PHASED IN OVER 3 YEARS.—

(i) IN GENERAL. —In the case of the portion of an account to which paragraph (3) applies and which consists of employer securities acquired in a plan year beginning before January 1, 2007, paragraph (3) shall only apply to the applicable percentage of such securities. This subparagraph shall be applied separately with respect to each class of securities.

(ii) EXCEPTION FOR CERTAIN PARTICIPANTS AGED 55 OR OVER. —Clause (i) shall not apply to an applicable individual who is a participant who has attained age 55 and completed at least 3 years of service before the first plan year beginning after December 31, 2005.

(B) APPLICABLE PERCENTAGE. —For purposes of subparagraph (A), the applicable percentage shall be determined as follows:

Plan year to which paragraph (3) applies:	The applicable percentage is:
1st	33
2d	66
3d	100

Act Sec. 204 (k) SPECIAL RULE FOR DETERMINING NORMAL RETIREMENT AGE FOR CERTAIN EXISTING DEFINED BENEFIT PLANS.—

(1) IN GENERAL. —Notwithstanding section 3(24), an applicable plan shall not be treated as failing to meet any requirement of this title, or as failing to have a uniform normal retirement age for purposes of this title, solely because the plan provides for a normal retirement age described in paragraph (2).

(2) APPLICABLE PLAN. —For purposes of this subsection—

(A) IN GENERAL. —The term 'applicable plan' means a defined benefit plan the terms of which, on or before December 8, 2014, provided for a normal retirement age which is the earlier of—

(i) an age otherwise permitted under section 3(24), or

(ii) the age at which a participant completes the number of years (not less than 30 years) of benefit accrual service specified by the plan.

A plan shall not fail to be treated as an applicable plan solely because the normal retirement age described in the preceding sentence only applied to certain participants or only applied to employees of certain employers in the case of a plan maintained by more than 1 employer.

(B) EXPANDED APPLICATION. —Subject to subparagraph (C), if, after December 8, 2014, an applicable plan is amended to expand the application of the normal retirement age described in subparagraph (A) to additional participants or to employees of additional employers maintaining the plan, such plan shall also be treated as an applicable plan with respect to such participants or employees.

(C) LIMITATION ON EXPANDED APPLICATION. —A defined benefit plan shall be an applicable plan only with respect to an individual who—

(i) is a participant in the plan on or before January 1, 2017, or

(ii) is an employee at any time on or before January 1, 2017, of any employer maintaining the plan, and who becomes a participant in such plan after such date.

Act Sec. 204. (l) CROSS REFERENCE.—

For special rules relating to plan provisions adopted to preclude discrimination see section 203(c)(2).

Amendments

P.L. 113-235, § 2(a), Div. P:

Amended ERISA Sec. 204 by redesignating subsection (k) as subsection (l) and by inserting after subsection (j) a new subsection (k) to read as above.

The amendment applies to all periods before, on, and after the date of enactment (December 16, 2014).

P.L. 113-97, § 102(b)(4):

Amended ERISA Sec. 204(i)(3) by striking "multiemployer plans" and inserting "multiemployer plans or CSEC plans".

Effective for years beginning after 12-31-2013.

P.L. 110-458, § 107(a)(2)(A):

Amended ERISA Sec. 204(b)(5)(A)(iii) by striking "clause" and inserting "subparagraph".

The above amendment takes effect as if included in the provisions of the 2006 Act to which the amendment relates. For effective date, see P.L. 109-280, § 701(e), below.

P.L. 110-458, § 107(a)(2)(B):

Amended ERISA Sec. 204(b)(5)(C) by inserting "otherwise" before "allowable".

The above amendment takes effect as if included in the provisions of the 2006 Act to which the amendment relates. For effective date, see P.L. 109-280, § 701(e), below.

P.L. 110-458, § 107(a)(3):

Amended ERISA Sec. 204(b)(5)(B)(i)(II) to read as above. Prior to amendment, ERISA Sec. 204(b)(5)(B)(i)(II) read as follows:

(II) PRESERVATION OF CAPITAL.—An interest credit (or an equivalent amount) of less than zero shall in no event result in the account balance or similar amount being less than the aggregate amount of contributions credited to the account.

The above amendment takes effect as if included in the provisions of the 2006 Act to which the amendment relates. For effective date, see P.L. 109-280, § 701(e), below.

P.L. 109-280, § 811, provides:

SEC. 811. PENSIONS AND INDIVIDUAL RETIREMENT ARRANGEMENT PROVISIONS OF ECONOMIC GROWTH AND TAX RELIEF RECONCILIATION ACT OF 2001 MADE PERMANENT.

Title IX of the Economic Growth and Tax Relief Reconciliation Act of 2001 [P.L. 107-16] shall not apply to the provisions of, and amendments made by, subtitles A through F of title VI [§§ 601-666] of such Act (relating to pension and individual retirement arrangement provisions).

P.L. 109-280, § 107(a)(5):

Amended ERISA Sec. 204(g)(1) by striking "section 302(c)(8)" and inserting "section 302(d)(2)".

The above amendment applies to plan years beginning after 2007.

P.L. 109-280, § 107(a)(6):

Amended ERISA Sec. 204(i)(2)(B) by striking "section 302(c)(8)" and inserting "section 302(d)(2)".

The above amendment applies to plan years beginning after 2007.

P.L. 109-280, § 107(a)(7):

Amended ERISA Sec. 204(i)(3) by striking "funded current liability percentage (within the meaning of section 302(d)(8) of this Act)" and inserting "funding target attainment percentage (as defined in section 303(d)(2))".

The above amendment applies to plan years beginning after 2007.

P.L. 109-280, § 107(a)(8):

Amended ERISA Sec. 204(i)(4) by striking "section 302(c)(11)(A), without regard to section 302(c)(11)(B)" and inserting "section 302(b)(1), without regard to section 302(b)(2)".

The above amendment applies to plan years beginning after 2007.

P.L. 109-280, § 502(c)(1):

Amended ERISA Sec. 204(h)(1) by inserting at the end before the period the following: "and to each employer who has an obligation to contribute to the plan.".

The above amendment applies to plan years beginning after December 31, 2007.

P.L. 109-280, § 701(a)(1):

Amended ERISA Sec. 204(b) by adding at the end new subsection (5) to read as above.

See P.L. 109-280, § 701(e) below for effective date.

P.L. 109-280, § 701(e) provides as follows:

(e) EFFECTIVE DATE.—

701(e)(1) IN GENERAL.—

The amendments made by this section shall apply to periods beginning on or after June 29, 2005.

701(e)(2) PRESENT VALUE OF ACCRUED BENEFIT.—

The amendments made by subsections (a)(2) and (b)(2) shall apply to distributions made after the date of the enactment of this Act.

701(e)(3) VESTING AND INTEREST CREDIT REQUIREMENTS.—

In the case of a plan in existence on June 29, 2005, the requirements of clause (i) of section 411(b)(5)(B) of the Internal Revenue Code of 1986, clause (i) of section

204(b)(5)(B) of the Employee Retirement Income Security Act of 1974, and clause (i) of section 4(i)(10)(B) of the Age Discrimination in Employment Act of 1967 (as added by this Act) and the requirements of 203(f)(2) of the Employee Retirement Income Security Act of 1974 and section 411(a)(13)(B) of the Internal Revenue Code of 1986 (as so added) shall, for purposes of applying the amendments made by subsections (a) and (b), apply to years beginning after December 31, 2007, unless the plan sponsor elects the application of such requirements for any period after June 29, 2005, and before the first year beginning after December 31, 2007.

701(e)(4) SPECIAL RULE FOR COLLECTIVELY BARGAINED PLANS.—

In the case of a plan maintained pursuant to 1 or more collective bargaining agreements between employee representatives and 1 or more employers ratified on or before the date of the enactment of this Act, the requirements described in paragraph (3) shall, for purposes of applying the amendments made by subsections (a) and (b), not apply to plan years beginning before—

701(e)(4)(A) the earlier of—

701(e)(4)(A)(i) the date on which the last of such collective bargaining agreements terminates (determined without regard to any extension thereof on or after such date of enactment), or

701(e)(4)(A)(ii) January 1, 2008, or

701(e)(4)(B) January 1, 2010.

701(e)(5) CONVERSIONS.—

The requirements of clause (ii) of section 411(b)(5)(B) of the Internal Revenue Code of 1986, clause (ii) of section 204(b)(5)(B) of the Employee Retirement Income Security Act of 1974, and clause (ii) of section 4(i)(10)(B) of the Age Discrimination in Employment Act of 1967 (as added by this Act), shall apply to plan amendments adopted after, and taking effect after, June 29, 2005, except that the plan sponsor may elect to have such amendments apply to plan amendments adopted before, and taking effect after, such date.

P.L. 109-280, § 901(b)(1):

Amended ERISA Sec. 204 by redesignating subsection (j) as subsection (k) and by inserting after subsection (i) a new subsection (j) to read as above.

See P.L. 109-280, § 901(c) below for effective date.

P.L. 109-280, § 901(c) provides as follows:

(c) EFFECTIVE DATES.—

901(c)(1) IN GENERAL.—Except as provided in paragraphs (2) and (3), the amendments made by this section shall apply to plan years beginning after December 31, 2006.

901(c)(2) SPECIAL RULE FOR COLLECTIVELY BARGAINED AGREEMENTS.—In the case of a plan maintained pursuant to 1 or more collective bargaining agreements between employee representatives and 1 or more employers ratified on or before the date of the enactment of this Act, paragraph (1) shall be applied to benefits pursuant to, and individuals covered by, any such agreement by substituting for "December 31, 2006" the earlier of—

901(c)(2)(A) the later of—

901(c)(2)(A)(i) December 31, 2007, or

901(c)(2)(A)(ii) the date on which the last of such collective bargaining agreements terminates (determined without regard to any extension thereof after such date of enactment), or

901(c)(2)(B) December 31, 2008.

901(c)(3) SPECIAL RULE FOR CERTAIN EMPLOYER SECURITIES HELD IN AN ESOP.—

901(c)(3)(A) IN GENERAL.—In the case of employer securities to which this paragraph applies, the amendments made by this section shall apply to plan years beginning after the earlier of—

901(c)(3)(A)(i) December 31, 2007, or

901(c)(3)(A)(ii) the first date on which the fair market value of such securities exceeds the guaranteed minimum value described in subparagraph (B)(ii).

901(c)(3)(B) APPLICABLE SECURITIES.—This paragraph shall apply to employer securities which are attributable to employer contributions other than elective deferrals, and which, on September 17, 2003—

901(c)(3)(B)(i) consist of preferred stock, and

901(c)(3)(B)(ii) are within an employee stock ownership plan (as defined in section 4975(e)(7) of the Internal Revenue Code of 1986), the terms of which provide that the value of the securities cannot be less than the guaranteed minimum value specified by the plan on such date.

901(c)(3)(C) COORDINATION WITH TRANSITION RULE.—In applying section 401(a)(35)(H) of the Internal Revenue Code of 1986 and section 204(j)(7) of the Employee Retirement Income Security Act of 1974 (as added by this section) to employer securities to which this paragraph applies, the applicable percentage shall be determined without regard to this paragraph.

P.L. 107-147, § 411(u)(2):

Act Sec. 411(u)(2) amended ERISA Sec. 204(h)(9) by striking the word "significantly" each time it appears.

The above amendment is effective for years beginning after December 31, 2001, subject to sunset after 2010 under P.L. 107-16, Sec. 901. [But see P.L. 109-280, § 811, above.]

P.L. 107-16, § 645(a)(2):

Act Sec. 645(a)(2) amended ERISA Sec. 204(g) by adding subsections (4) and (5) to read as above.

The above amendment is effective for years beginning after December 31, 2001; subject to sunset after 2010 under P.L. 107-16, Sec. 901. [But see P.L. 109-280, § 811, above.]

P.L. 107-16, § 645(b)(2):

Act Sec. 645(b)(2) amended ERISA Sec. 204(g)(2) by inserting after the second sentence the following: "The Secretary of the Treasury shall by regulations provide that this paragraph shall not apply to any plan amendment which reduces or eliminates benefits or subsidies which create significant burdens or complexities for the plan and plan participants, unless such amendment adversely affects the rights of any participant in a more than de minimis manner." [But see P.L. 109-280, § 811, above.]

P.L. 107-16, § 659(b):

Act Sec. 659(b) amended ERISA Sec. 204(h) to read as above. Previously, paragraph 204(h) read as follows:

"(h)(1) A plan described in paragraph (2) may not be amended so as to provide for a significant reduction in the rate of future benefit accrual, unless, after adoption of the plan amendment and not less than 15 days before the effective date of the plan amendment, the plan administrator provides a written notice, setting forth the plan amendment and its effective date, to—

(A) each participant in the plan,

(B) each beneficiary who is an alternate payee (within the meaning of section 206(d)(3)(K)) under an applicable qualified domestic relations order (within the meaning of section 206(d)(3)(B)(i)), and

(C) each employee organization representing participants in the plan, except that such notice shall instead be provided to a person designated, in writing, to receive such notice on behalf of any person referred to in paragraph (A), (B), or (C).

(2) A plan is described in this paragraph if such plan is—

(A) a defined benefit plan, or

(B) an individual account plan which is subject to the funding standards of section 302."

P.L. 107-16, § 659(c):

Act Sec. 659(c) provides the following effective dates:

"(c) EFFECTIVE DATES.—

(1) IN GENERAL.—The amendments made by this section shall apply to plan amendments taking effect on or after the date of the enactment of this Act.

(2) TRANSITION.—Until such time as the Secretary of the Treasury issues regulations under sections 4980F(e)(2) and (3) of the Internal Revenue Code of 1986, and section 204(h) of the Employee Retirement Income Security Act of 1974, as added by the amendments made by this section, a plan shall be treated as meeting the requirements of such sections if it makes a good faith effort to comply with such requirements.

(3) SPECIAL NOTICE RULE.—

(A) IN GENERAL.—The period for providing any notice required by the amendments made by this section shall not end before the date which is 3 months after the date of the enactment of this Act.

(B) REASONABLE NOTICE.—The amendments made by this section shall not apply to any plan amendment taking effect on or after the date of the enactment of this Act if, before April 25, 2001, notice was provided to participants and beneficiaries adversely affected by the plan amendment (or their representatives) which was reasonably expected to notify them of the nature and effective date of the plan amendment."

P.L. 105-34, § 1071(b)(2):

Act Sec. 1071(b)(2) amended ERISA Sec. 204(d)(1) by striking "$3,500" and inserting "$5,000".

The above amendment is effective for plan years beginning after August 5, 1997.

P.L. 103-465, § 766(a):

Act Sec. 766(a) amended ERISA Sec. 204 by redesignating subsection (i) as (j) and inserting after subsection (h) subsection (i), to read as above.

The above amendments apply to plan amendments adopted on or after December 8, 1994.

P.L. 101-239, § 7862(b)(2):

Amended ERISA Sec. 204(h)(2) by adjusting the left-hand margin of the material preceding subparagraph (A) effective October 22, 1986.

P.L. 101-239, § 7871(a)(1):

Amended ERISA Sec. 204(b)(2) by striking subparagraph (B) and by redesignating subparagraphs (C) and (D) as subparagraphs (B) and (C), respectively. Previously, subparagraph (B) read as follows:

(B) Subparagraph (A) shall not apply with respect to any employee who is a highly compensated employee (within the meaning of section 414(q) of the Internal Revenue Code of 1986) to the extent provided in regulations prescribed by the Secretary of the Treasury for purposes of precluding discrimination in favor of highly compensated employees within the meaning of subchapter D of chapter 1 of the Internal Revenue Code of 1986.

P.L. 101-239, § 7871(a)(3):

Amended ERISA Sec. 204(b)(2)(C), as redesignated by § 7863(a)(1) above, by striking "(C) and (D)" and inserting "(B) and (C)."

P.L. 101-239, § 7881(m)(2)(A):

Amended ERISA Sec. 204(c)(2)(C)(iii) to read as above. Previously, subparagraph (iii) read as follows:

(iii) interest on the sum of the amounts determined under clauses (i) and (ii) compounded annually at the rate of 120 percent of the Federal mid-term rate (as in effect under section 1274 of the Internal Revenue Code of 1986 for the 1st month of a plan year) from the beginning of the first plan year to which section 203(a)(2) applies (by reason of the applicable effective date) to the date upon which the employee would attain normal retirement age.

P.L. 101-239, § 7881(m)(2)(B):

Amended ERISA Sec. 204(c)(2)(B) to read as above. Previously, paragraph (B) read as follows:

(B)(i) In the case of a defined benefit plan providing an annual benefit in the form of a single life annuity (without ancillary benefits) commencing at normal retirement age, the accrued benefit derived from contributions made by an employee as of any applicable date is the annual benefit equal to the employee's accumulated contributions multiplied by the appropriate conversion factor.

(ii) For purposes of clause (i), the term "appropriate conversion factor" means the factor necessary to convert an amount equal to the accumulated contributions to a single annuity (without ancillary benefits) commencing at normal retirement age and shall be 10 percent for a normal retirement age of 65 years. For other normal retirement ages the conversion factor shall be determined in accordance with regulations prescribed by the Secretary of the Treasury or his delegate.

P.L. 101-239, § 7881(m)(2)(C):

Amended ERISA Sec. 204(c)(2) by striking subparagraph (E). Previously subparagraph (E) read as follows:

(E) The accrued benefit derived from employee contributions shall not exceed the greater of—

(i) the employee's accrued benefit under the plan, or

(ii) the accrued benefit derived from employee contributions determined as though the amounts calculated under clauses (ii) and (iii) of subparagraph (C) were zero.

The above amendments are effective October 21, 1986.

P.L. 101-239, § 7891(a)(1):

Titles I, III, and IV of ERISA (other than sections 3(37)(E), 301(a)(7), and 308, the last sentence of section 408(d), and sections 414(c), 4001(a)(3)(ii), and 4303) are each amended by striking "Internal Revenue Code of 1954" each place it appears and inserting "Internal Revenue Code of 1986."

P.L. 101-239, § 7894(c)(4):

Amended ERISA Sec. 204(b)(1)(A) in the last sentence by striking "suparagraph" and inserting "subparagraph."

P.L. 101-239, § 7894(c)(5):

Amended ERISA Sec. 204(b)(1)(E) in the last sentence by striking "years" and inserting "year."

P.L. 101-239, § 7894(c)(6):

Amended ERISA Sec. 204(d) to remove the indentation of the term "paragraph" the first place it appeared in the matter following paragraph (2).

The above amendments are effective October 22, 1986.

P.L. 100-203, § 9346(a)(1):

Amended ERISA Sec. 204(c)(2)(C)(iii) by striking "5 percent per annum" and inserting "120 percent of the Federal mid-term rate (as in effect under section 1274 of the Internal Revenue Code of 1986 for the 1st month of a plan year)" instead.

P.L. 100-203, § 9346(a)(2):

Amended ERISA Sec. 204(c)(2)(D) by striking ", the rate of interest described in clause (iii) of subparagraph (C), or both,"; and by striking the second sentence.

P.L. 99-514, § 1113(e)(4)(B):

Amended ERISA Sec. 204(i) to read as above. Prior to amendment, section (i) read as follows:

(i) Cross Reference.

For special rules relating to class year plans and plan provisions adopted to preclude discrimination, see sections 203(c)(2) and (3).

For effective dates, see Act Sec. 1113(e) in amendment notes under ERISA Sec. 203.

P.L. 99-514, § 1879(u)(1):

Amended ERISA Sec. 204(h) by striking out "single-employer plan" and inserting in lieu thereof "plan described in paragraph (2)"; by redesignating paragraphs (1), (2), and (3) as subparagraphs (A), (B), and (C), respectively; by striking out "paragraph (1), (2), or (3)" and inserting in lieu thereof "subparagraph (A), (B), or (C)"; by inserting "(1)" after "(h)"; and by adding paragraph (2) to read as above.

P.L. 99-514, § 1879(u)(4):

Act Sec. 1879(u)(4) provides as follows:

(4) EFFECTIVE DATE.—

(A) GENERAL RULE.—Except as provided in subparagraph (B), the preceding provisions of this subsection shall be effective as if such provisions were included in the enactment of the Single-Employer Pension Plan Amendments Act of 1986.

(B) SPECIAL RULE.—Subparagraph (B) of section 204(h)(2) of the Employee Retirement Income Security Act of 1974 (as amended by paragraph (1)) shall apply only with respect to plan amendments adopted on or after the date of the enactment of this Act.

P.L. 99-514, § 1898(a)(4)(B)(ii):

Amended ERISA Sec. 204(e), last sentence to read as above, effective for plan years beginning after 1984. Prior to amendment, the last sentence read as follows:

In the case of a defined contribution plan, the plan provision required under this subsection may provide that such repayment must be made before the participant has 5 consecutive 1-year breaks in service commencing after such withdrawal.

P.L. 99-514, § 1898(f)(1):

Added ERISA Sec. 204(g)(3) to read as above, effective for years beginning after 1984.

P.L. 99-514, §1898(f)(2):

Amended ERISA Sec. 204(g)(1) by striking out "section 302(c)(8)" and inserting "section 302(c)(8) or 4281" instead, effective for plan years beginning after 1984.

P.L. 99-509, §9202(a)(1):

Amended ERISA Sec. 204(a) to read as above. Prior to amendment, Sec. 204(a) read as follows:

Act Sec. 204. (a) Each pension plan shall satisfy the requirements of subsection (b)(2), and in the case of a defined benefit plan shall also satisfy the requirements of subsection (b)(1).

This amendment is effective with respect to plan years beginning on or after January 1, 1988 and only with respect to employees who have 1 hour of service in any plan year to which the amendment applies.

P.L. 99-509, §9204(a)(3) and (c):

Secs. 9204(a)(3) and (c) provide as follows:

(b)(2) SPECIAL RULES FOR COLLECTIVELY BARGAINED PLANS.—In the case of a plan maintained pursuant to 1 or more collective bargaining agreements between employee representatives and 1 or more employers ratified before March 1, 1986, paragraph (1) shall be applied to benefits pursuant to, and individuals covered by, any such agreement by substituting for "January 1, 1988" the date of the commencement of the first plan year beginning on or after the earlier of—

(A) the later of—

(i) January 1, 1988, or

(ii) the date on which the last of such collective bargaining agreements terminate (determined without regard to any extension thereof after February 28, 1986), or

(B) January 1, 1990.

* * *

(c) PLAN AMENDMENTS.—If any amendment made by this subtitle requires an amendment to any plan, such plan amendment shall not be required to be made before the first plan year beginning on or after January 1, 1989, if—

(1) during the period after such amendment takes effect and before such first plan year, the plan is operated in accordance with the requirements of such amendment, and

(2) such plan amendment applies retroactively to the period after such amendment takes effect and such first plan year.

A pension plan shall not be treated as failing to provide definitely determinable benefits or contributions, or to be operated in accordance with the provisions of the plan, merely because it operates in accordance with this subsection.

P.L. 99-509, §9202(a)(2):

Amended ERISA Sec. 204(b)(1) by adding a new subparagraph (H) to read as above.

This amendment is effective with respect to plan years beginning on or after January 1, 1988 and only with respect to, employees who have 1 hour of service in any plan year to which the amendment applies.

P.L. 99-509, §9202(a)(3):

Amended ERISA Sec. 204(b) by redesignating paragraphs (2) and (3) as paragraphs (3) and (4), respectively, and adding a new paragraph (2) to read as above.

This amendment is effective with respect to plan years beginning on or after January 1, 1988 and only with respect to employees who have 1 hour of service in any plan year to which the amendment applies.

P.L. 99-272:

Act Sec. 11006(a) amended ERISA Sec. 204 by redesignating section (h) as section (i) and by adding a new section (h) to read as above, effective for plan amendments adopted on or after January 1, 1986. Act Sec. 11006(b) also contains the following provisions:

". . . except that, in the case of plan amendments adopted on or after January 1, 1986, and on or before the date of the enactment of this Act, the requirements of section 204(h) of the Employee Retirement Income Security Act of 1974 (as added by this section) shall be treated as met if the written notice required under such section 204(h) is provided before 60 days after the date of the enactment of this Act."

P.L. 98-397, §§102, 105 and 301:

Act Sec. 102(e)(3) amended ERISA Sec. 204(b)(3)(A) by inserting ", determined without regard to section 202(b)(5)" after "section 202(b)."

For the effective date of the above amendment, see Act Sec. 303(b), which appears in the amendment notes for ERISA Sec. 203 at ¶ 103.

Act Sec. 102(f) amended ERISA Sec. 204(e) by striking out "any 1-year break in service" and inserting in lieu thereof "5 consecutive 1-year breaks in service."

Act. Sec. 105(b) amended ERISA Sec. 204(d)(1) by striking out "$1,750" and inserting in lieu thereof "$3,500."

The above amendments apply to plan years beginning after December 31, 1984.

Act Sec. 301(a)(2) amended ERISA Sec. 204(g) by striking out the prior law and replacing it with new subsection (g) to read as above. Prior to amendment, ERISA Sec. 204(g) read as follows:

(g) The accrued benefit of a participant under a plan may not be decreased by an amendment of the plan, other than an amendment described in section 302(c)(8).

The above amendment applies to plan amendments made after July 30, 1984 but a special rule under Act Sec. 302(d)(2) also provides:

(2) Special Rule for Collective Bargaining Agreements.—In the case of a plan maintained pursuant to 1 or more collective bargaining agreements entered into before January 1, 1985, which are—

(A) between employee representatives and 1 or more employers, and

(B) successor agreements to 1 or more collective bargaining agreements which terminate after July 30, 1984, and before January 1, 1985, the amendments made by section 301 shall not apply to plan amendments adopted before April 1, 1985, pursuant to such successor agreements (without regard to any modification or reopening after December 31, 1984).

Regulations

The following regulations were adopted under "Title 29—Labor," "Chapter XXV—Pension and Welfare Benefit Programs, Department of Labor," "Subchapter C—Minimum Standards for Employee Pension Benefit Plans Under the Employee Retirement Income Security Act of 1974," "Part 2530—Rules and Regulations for Minimum Standards for Employee Pension Benefit Plans." The regulations were filed with the Federal Register on December 23, 1976, and published in the Federal Register of December 28, 1976 (41 FR 56462).

[¶ 14,441]
§ 2530.204-1 Year of participation for benefit accrual.

(a) *General.* Section 204(b)(1) of the Act and section 411(b)(1) of the Code contain certain requirements relating to benefit accrual under a defined benefit pension plan. Some of these requirements are based on the number of years of participation included in an employee's period of service. Paragraph (b) of this section relates to service which must be taken into account in determining an employee's period of service for purposes of benefit accrual. Section 2530.204-2 sets forth rules relating to the computation periods to be used in measuring years of participation for benefit accrual ("accrual computation periods").

(b) *Service which may be disregarded for purposes of benefit accrual.* (1) In calculating an employee's period of service for purposes of benefit accrual under a defined benefit pension plan, section 204(b)(3) of the Act and section 411(b)(3) of the Code permit the following service to be disregarded: service before an employee first becomes a participant in the plan; service which is not required to be taken into account under section 202(b) of the Act and section 410(b)(5) of the Code (relating to one-year breaks in service for purposes of eligibility to participate); and service which is not required to be taken into account under section 204(b)(3)(C) of the Act and section 411(b)(3)(C) of the Code (relating to 12-consecutive-month periods during which an employee's service is less than 1000 hours). In addition, in calculating an employee's period of service for purposes of benefit accrual, a defined benefit plan shall not be required to take into account service before the conclusion of a series of consecutive 1-year breaks in service occurs which permits a plan to disregard prior service

under section 203(b)(3)(D) of the Act and section 411(a)(6)(D) of the Code.

(2) *Example.* The following example illustrates paragraph (b)(1) of this section. A plan has a calendar year vesting and accrual computation period and, under § 2530.202-2(a) and (b)(1), uses eligibility computation periods beginning on an employee's employment commencement date and anniversaries thereof. The plan provides that an employee who has at least 10 years of service has a vested right to 100 percent of his accrued benefit derived from employer contributions. The plan provides that an employee who is credited with at least 1,000 hours of service in a calendar year accrual computation period is credited with at least partial year of participation for purposes of benefit accrual. An employee whose birthday is October 16, 1956, begins employment with an employer maintaining the plan on January 1, 1977. Under § 2530.202-2(a)(1), January 1, 1977 is the employee's employment commencement date and the calendar year 1977 is the employee's initial eligibility computation period. The employee completes at least 1,000 hours of service in each of the calendar years from 1977 through 1981. On January 1, 1982 the employee is admitted to participation in the plan, having met the plan's age requirement (25 years) and service requirement (one year of service) for eligibility to participate. In 1982, the employee is credited with the number of hours of service required for a full year of participation (i.e., more than 1,000 hours of service). Under § 2530.202-2(c), for purposes of applying section 202(b)(4) of the Act and section 410(a)(5)(D) of the Code (relating to years of service completed before a break in service for purposes of eligibility to participate), eligibility computation periods beginning on the employee's employment commencement date and anniversaries thereof are used under the plan to measure service prior to a break in

service (in addition, under §2530.200b-4(a)(2), the same eligibility computation periods are used in measuring one-year breaks in service for purposes of eligibility to participate). Thus, as of January 1, 1983, the employee is credited with six years of service for purposes of eligibility to participate and is credited with one year of participation. In accordance with section 203(b)(1)(A) of the Act and section 411(a)(4)(A) of the Code, the plan provides that years of service completed before age 22 are disregarded for purposes of vesting. As of January 1, 1983, therefore, the employee is credited with four years of service for purposes of vesting. In 1983 the employee terminates employment with the employer, incurrinng one-year breaks in service in each of the calendar years from 1983 through 1986. As of December 31, 1986, the employee's consecutive one-year breaks in service equal the employee's four years of service for vesting before such breaks. Under section 203(b)(3)(D) of the Act and section 410(a)(5)(D) of the Code and the terms of the plan, the four years of service for vesting completed by the employee before his four consecutive one-year breaks in service are not taken into account for purposes of vesting. Under paragraph (b)(1) of this section, therefore, in calculating the employee's period of service for purposes of benefit accrual, the plan may disregard the year of participation completed by the employee before his four consecutive one-year breaks in service for vesting, because the four consecutive one-year breaks in service equal the four years of service credited to the employee for vesting. The employee is re-employed by the employer on January 1, 1987 completing an hour of service on that date. Under §2530.-200b-4(b)(1), therefore, January 1, 1987 is the employee's reemployment commencement date. In 1987, the employee completes the number of hours of service required for a full year of participation (i.e., more than 1,000 hours of service). For 1987, therefore, the employee is credited with a year of service for purposes of eligibility to participate and vesting, and with a year of participation. As of December 31, 1987, the employee is credited with one year of service for purposes of vesting, since service before the employee's four consecutive one-year breaks in service—including the year of service completed in 1982—is not taken into account. Because under paragraph (b)(1) of this section, the year of participation credited to the employee for 1982 is not required to be taken into account for purposes of benefit accrual, the employee is credited with one year of participation as of December 31, 1987.

[¶ 14,442]

§2530.204-2   Accrual computation period.

(a) *Designation of accrual computation periods.* A plan may designate any 12-consecutive-month period as the accrual computation period except that the period so designated must apply equally to all participants. This requirement may be satisfied even though the actual time periods are not the same for all participants. For example, the accrual computation period may be designated as the vesting computation period, the plan year, or the 12-consecutive-month period beginning on either of two semi-annual dates designated for entry to participation under a plan.

(b) *Participation prior to effective date.* For purposes of applying the accrual rules of section 204(b)(1)(D) of the Act and section 411(b)(1)(D) of the Code (relating to accrual requirements for defined benefit plans for periods prior to the effective date of those sections), all service from the date of participation in the plan, as determined in accordance with applicable plan provisions, shall be taken into account in determining an employee's period of service. When the plan documents do not provide a definite means for determining the date of commencement of participation, the date of commencement of employment covered under the plan during the period that the employer maintained the plan shall be presumed to be the date of commencement of participation in the plan. The plan may rebut this presumption by demonstrating from circumstances surrounding the operation of the plan, such as the date of commencement of mandatory employee contributions, that participation actually began on a later date.

(c) *Partial year of participation.* (1) Under section 204(b)(3)(C) of the Act and section 411(b)(3)(C) of the Code, in calculating an employee's period of service for purposes of benefit accrual, a plan is not required to take into account a 12-consecutive-month period during which the employee's service is less than 1000 hours of service. In measuring an employee's service for purposes of section 204(b)(3)(C)

of the Act and section 411(b)(3)(C) of the Code, a plan shall use the accrual computation period designated under paragraph (a) of this section. Under section 204(b)(3)(B) of the Act and section 411(b)(3)(B) of the Code, in the case of an employee whose service is not less than 1,000 hours of service during an accrual computation period, the calculation of such employee's period of service will not be treated as made on a reasonable and consistent basis unless service during such computation period is taken into account. To the extent that the employee's service during the accrual computation period is less than the service required under the plan for a full year of participation, the employee must be credited with a partial year of participation equivalent to no less than a ratable portion of a full year of participation.

(2) For purposes of calculating the portion of a full year of participation to be credited to an employee whose service during a computation period is not less than 1,000 hours of service but is less than service required for a full year of participation in the plan, the plan may credit the employee with a greater portion of a full year of participation than a ratable portion, or may credit an employee with a full year of participation even though the employee's service is less than the service required for a full year of participation, provided that such crediting is reasonable and is consistent for all employees within the same job classifications, reasonably established.

(3) In the case of an employee who commences participation in a plan (or recommences participation in the plan upon the employee's return after one or more 1-year breaks in service) on a date other than the first day of an applicable accrual computation period, all hours of service required to be credited to the employee during the entire accrual computation period, including hours of service credited to the employee for the portion of the computation period before the date on which the employee commences (or recommences) participation, shall be taken into account in determining whether the employee has 1,000 or more hours of service for purposes of section 204(b)(3)(C) of the Act and section 411(b)(3)(C) of the Code. If such employee's service is not less than 1,000 hours in such accrual computation period, the employee must be credited with a partial year of participation which is equivalent to no less than a ratable portion of a full year of participation for service credited to the employee for the portion of the computation period after the date of commencement (or recommencement) of participation.

(4) *Examples.* The following are examples of reasonable and consistent methods for crediting partial years of participation:

(i) A plan requires 2,000 hours of service for a full year of participation. An employee who is credited during a computation period with no less than 1,000 hours of service but less than 2,000 hours of service is credited with a partial year of participation equal to a portion of a full year of participation determined by dividing the number of hours of service credited to the employee by 2,000.

(ii) A plan requires 2,000 hours of service for a full year of participation. The plan credits service in an accrual computation period in accordance with the following table:

Hours of service credited:	Percentage of full year of participation credited
1000	50
1001 to 1200	60
1201 to 1400	70
1401 to 1600	80
1601 to 1800	90
1801 and above	100

Under this method of crediting partial years of participation, each employee who is credited with not less than 1,000 hours of service is credited with at least a ratable portion of a full year of participation.

(iii) A plan provides that each employee who is credited with at least 1,000 hours of service in an accrual computation period must receive credit for at least a partial year of participation for that computation period. For full accrual, however, the plan requires that an employee must be credited with a specified number of hours worked; employees who meet the 1,000 hours of service requirement but who are not credited with the specified number of hours worked required for a full year of participation are credited with a partial year of participation on a pro rata basis. For example, if the plan requires 1,500 hours worked for full accrual, an employee with 1,500 hours worked would be credited with full accrual, but an employee with 1,000 hours worked and 500 other hours of service would be credited with ⅔ of full accrual. The plan's method of crediting service for accrual purposes is consistent with the requirements of this paragraph. It should be noted, however, that use of hours worked as a basis for prorating benefit accrual may result in discrimination prohibited under section 401(a)(4) of the Code.

(iv) Employee A is employed on June 1, 1980 in service covered by a plan with a calendar year accrual computation period, and which requires 1,800 hours of service for a full accrual. Employee A completes 500 hours from June 1, 1980 to December 31, 1980, and completes 100 hours per month in each month during 1981. A is admitted to participation on July 1, 1981. A is credited with 1,200 hours of service for the accrual computation period beginning January 1, 1981. Under the rules set forth in paragraph (c)(3) of this section, A is required to be credited with not less than one-third of a full accrual (600 hours divided by 1,800 hours).

(d) *Prohibited double proration.* (1) In the case of a defined benefit plan that (i) defines benefits on a basis which has the effect of prorating benefits to reflect less than full-time employment or less than maximum compensation and (ii) does not adjust less-than-full-time service to reflect the equivalent of full-time hours or compensation (as the case may be), the plan may not further prorate benefit accrual under section 204(b)(3)(B) of the Act and section 411(b)(3)(B) of the Code by crediting less than full years of participation, as would otherwise be permitted under paragraph (c) of this section. These plans must credit, except when service may be disregarded under section 204(b)(3)(C) of the Act and section 411(b)(3)(C) of the Code (relating to less than 1000 hours of service), less-than-full-time employees with a full year of participation for the purpose of accrual of benefits.

(2) *Examples.* (i) A plan's defined benefit formula provides that the annual retirement benefit shall be 2 percent of the average compensation in all years of participation multiplied by the number of years of participation. Employee A is a full-time employee who has completed 2,000 hours during each of 20 accrual computation periods. A's average hourly rate was $5 an hour. Thus, A's average compensation for each year during participation in the plan is $10,000 ($5 per hour multiplied by 2,000 hours). If the plan states that a full year of participation is 2,000 hours, then A's annual retirement benefits, if he retired at that time, would be $4,000 ($10,000 per year of compensation × .02 × 20 years of participation). Employee B, however, is a part-time employee who completes 1,000 hours of service during each of 20 accrual computation periods. Like A, B's average hourly rate is $5 per hour. B's average compensation is $5,000 ($5 per hour multiplied by 1,000 hours). Thus, the plan's benefit formula, by basing benefits on an employee's average compensation in all years of participation, in effect prorates benefits to reflect the fact that during B's participation in the plan, he has earned less than the maximum compensation that a full-time employee paid at the same rate could earn during the same period of participation in the plan. Under the rule of subparagraph (1), therefore, the plan is not permitted to prorate B's years of participation to reflect B's less than full-time employment throughout his participation in the plan. Therefore, B's annual retirement benefit would be $2,000 ($5,000 average compensation × .02 × 20 years of participation). (If double proration were permitted, then B's total years of participation would be only 10 since he would be credited with only one-half of a year of participation during each of the accrual computation periods (1,000/2,000). Thus, B's annual retirement benefit would be $1,000—i.e., $5,000 average compensation × .02 × 10 years of participation.)

(ii) If the plan adjusts the average compensation during plan participation to reflect full compensation, then the plan may prorate years of participation. Thus, the average full annual compensation for B would be $10,000 rather than the $5,000 actually paid. Employee B's annual retirement benefit would then be $2,000 ($10,000 average full compensation × .02 × 10 years of participation).

(e) *Amendments to change accrual computation periods.* (1) A plan may be amended to change the accrual computation period to a differ-

ent 12-consecutive-month period, provided that the period between the end of the last accrual computation period under the plan as in effect before such amendment and the beginning of the first accrual computation period under the plan as amended is treated as a partial accrual computation period in accordance with the rules set forth in subparagraph (2) of this paragraph.

(2) In the case of a partial accrual computation period, the following rules shall apply:

(i) A plan having a minimum service requirement expressed in hours of service (or other units of service) for benefit accrual in a full accrual computation period (as permitted under section 204(b)(3)(B) of the Act and section 411(b)(3)(B) of the Code) may apply a minimum service requirement for benefit accrual in a full accrual computation period, multiplied by the ratio of the length of the partial accrual computation period to a full year.

(ii) In the case of a participant who meets a plan's minimum service requirement for benefit accrual in a partial accrual computation period (as permitted under subparagraph (2)(i) of this paragraph), the plan shall credit the participant with at least a partial year of participation for purposes of benefit accrual. Credit for a partial accrual computation period shall be determined in accordance with paragraphs (c) and (d) of this section.

(3) *Example.* Effective October 1, 1977, a plan is amended to change the accrual computation period from the 12-consecutive-month period beginning on January 1 to the 12-consecutive-month period beginning on October 1. The period from January 1, 1977 to September 30, 1977 must be treated as a partial accrual computation period. The plan has a requirement that a participant must be credited with 1,000 hours of service in an accrual computation period in order to be credited with a year of participation for purposes of benefit accrual. For the partial accrual computation period the plan may require a participant to be credited with 750 hours of service in the partial accrual computation period in order to receive credit for purposes of benefit accrual (1,000 hours of service multiplied by the ratio of 9 months to 12 months). To the extent permitted under paragraph (d) of this section, the plan may prorate accrual credit on whatever basis the plan uses to prorate accrual credit for employees whose service is 1,000 hours of service or more but less than service required for full accrual in a full accrual computation period.

[¶ 14,443]
§ 2530.204-3 **Alternative computation methods for benefit accrual.**

(a) *General.* Under section 204(b)(3)(A) of the Act and section 411(b)(3)(A) of the Code, a defined benefit pension plan may determine an employee's service for purposes of benefit accrual on the basis of accrual computation periods, as specified in § 2530.204-2, or on any other basis which is reasonable and consistent and which takes into account all covered service during the employee's participation in the plan which is included in a period of service required to be taken into account under section 202(b) of the Act and section 410(a)(5) of the Code. If, however, a plan determines an employee's service for purposes of benefit accrual on a basis other than computation periods, it must be possible to prove that, despite the fact that benefit accrual under the plan is not based on computation periods, the plan's provisions meet at least one of the three benefit accrual rules of section 204(b)(1) of the Act and section 411(b)(1) of the Code under all circumstances. Further, a plan which does not provide for benefit accrual on the basis of computation periods may not disregard service under section 204(b)(3)(C) of the Act and section 411(b)(3)(C) of the Code.

(b) *Examples.* The following are examples of methods of determining an employee's period of service for purposes of benefit accrual under which an employee's period of service is not determined on the basis of computation periods but which may be used by a plan provided that the requirements of paragraph (a) of this section are met:

(1) *Career Compensation.* A defined benefit formula based on a percentage of compensation earned in a participant's career or during participation, with no variance depending on hours completed in given periods.

(2) *Credited Hours.* A defined benefit formula pursuant to which an employee is credited with a specified amount of accrual for each hour of service (or hour worked or regular time hour) completed by the employee during his or her career.

(3) *Elapsed Time.* See § 2530.200b-9 (e).

[¶ 14,444]

§ 2530.204-4 **Deferral of Benefit Accrual.** For purposes of section 204(b)(1)(E) of the Act and section 411(b)(1)(E) of the Code (which permit deferral of benefit accrual until an employee has two continuous years of service), an employee shall be credited with a year of service for each computation period in which he or she completes 1,000 hours of service. The computation period shall be the eligibility computation period designated in accordance with § 2530.202-2.

[¶ 14,450]
REQUIREMENT OF JOINT AND SURVIVOR ANNUITY AND PRERETIREMENT SURVIVOR ANNUITY

Act Sec. 205. (a) REQUIRED CONTENTS FOR APPLICABLE PLANS.—Each pension plan to which this section applies shall provide that

(1) in the case of a vested participant who does not die before the annuity starting date, the accrued benefit payable to such participant shall be provided in the form of a qualified joint and survivor annuity, and

(2) in the case of a vested participant who dies before the annuity starting date and who has a surviving spouse, a qualified preretirement survivor annuity shall be provided to the surviving spouse of such participant.

Act Sec. 205. (b)(1) APPLICABLE PLANS.—This section shall apply to—

(A) any defined benefit plan,

(B) any individual account plan which is subject to the funding standards of section 302, and

(C) any participant under any other individual account plan unless—

(i) such plan provides that the participant's nonforfeitable accrued benefit (reduced by any security interest held by the plan by reason of a loan outstanding to such participant) is payable in full, on the death of the participant, to the participant's surviving spouse (or, if there is no surviving spouse or the surviving spouse consents in the manner required under subsection (c)(2), to a designated beneficiary),

(ii) such participant does not elect the payment of benefits in the form of a life annuity, and

(iii) with respect to such participant, such plan is not a direct or indirect transferee (in a transfer after December 31, 1984) of a plan which is described in subparagraph (A) or (B) or to which this clause applied with respect to the participant.

Clause (iii) of subparagraph (C) shall apply only with respect to the transferred assets (and income therefrom) if the plan separately accounts for such assets and any income therefrom.

(2)(A) In the case of—

(i) a tax credit employee stock ownership plan (as defined in section 409(a) of the Internal Revenue Code of 1986), or

(ii) an employee stock ownership plan (as defined in section 4975(e)(7) of such Code),

subsection (a) shall not apply to that portion of the employee's accrued benefit to which the requirements of section 409(h) of such Code apply.

(B) Subparagraph (A) shall not apply with respect to any participant unless the requirements of clause (i), (ii), and (iii) of paragraph (1)(C) are met with respect to such participant.

(3) This section shall not apply to a plan which the Secretary of the Treasury or his delegate has determined is a plan described in section 404(c) of the Internal Revenue Code of 1986 (or a continuation thereof) in which participation is substantially limited to individuals who, before January 1, 1976, ceased employment covered by the plan.

(4) A plan shall not be treated as failing to meet the requirements of paragraph (1)(C) or (2) merely because the plan provides that benefits will not be payable to the surviving spouse of the participant unless the participant and such spouse had been married throughout the 1-year period ending on the earlier of the participant's annuity starting date or the date of the participant's death.

Act Sec. 205. (c)(1) PLANS MEETING REQUIREMENTS OF SECTION.—A plan meets the requirements of this section only if—

(A) under the plan, each participant—

(i) may elect at any time during the applicable election period to waive the qualified joint and survivor annuity form of benefit or the qualified preretirement survivor annuity form of benefit (or both),

(ii) if the participant elects a waiver under clause (i), may elect the qualified optional survivor annuity at any time during the applicable election period, and

(iii) may revoke any such election at any time during the applicable election period, and

(B) the plan meets the requirements of paragraphs (2), (3), and (4).

(2) Each plan shall provide that an election under paragraph (1)(A)(i) shall not take effect unless—

(A)(i) the spouse of the participant consents in writing to such election, (ii) such election designates a beneficiary (or a form of benefits) which may not be changed without spousal consent (or the consent of the spouse expressly permits designations by the participant without any requirement of further consent by the spouse), and (iii) the spouse's consent acknowledges the effect of such election and is witnessed by a plan representative or a notary public, or

(B) it is established to the satisfaction of a plan representative that the consent required under subparagraph (A) may not be obtained because there is no spouse, because the spouse cannot be located, or because of such other circumstances as the Secretary of the Treasury may by regulations prescribe.

Any consent by a spouse (or establishment that the consent of a spouse may not be obtained) under the preceding sentence shall be effective only with respect to such spouse.

(3)(A) Each plan shall provide to each participant, within a reasonable period of time before the annuity starting date (and consistent with such regulations as the Secretary of the Treasury may prescribe) a written explanation of—

(i) the terms and conditions of the qualified joint and survivor annuity and of the qualified optional survivor annuity,

(ii) the participant's right to make, and the effect of, an election under paragraph (1) to waive the joint and survivor annuity form of benefit,

(iii) the rights of the participant's spouse under paragraph (2), and

(iv) the right to make, and the effect of, a revocation of an election under paragraph (1).

(B)(i) Each plan shall provide to each participant, within the applicable period with respect to such participant (and consistent with such regulations as the Secretary may prescribe), a written explanation with respect to the qualified preretirement survivor annuity comparable to that required under subparagraph (A).

(ii) For purposes of clause (i), the term "applicable period" means, with respect to a participant, whichever of the following periods ends last:

(I) The period beginning with the first day of the plan year in which the participant attains age 32 and ending with the close of the plan year preceding the plan year in which the participant attains age 35.

(II) A reasonable period after the individual becomes a participant.

(III) A reasonable period ending after paragraph (5) ceases to apply to the participant.

(IV) A reasonable period ending after section 205 applies to the participant.

In the case of a participant who separates from service before attaining age 35, the applicable period shall be a reasonable period after separation.

(4) Each plan shall provide that, if this section applies to a participant when part or all of the participant's accrued benefit is to be used as security for a loan, no portion of the participant's accrued benefit may be used as security for such loan unless—

(A) the spouse of the participant (if any) consents in writing to such use during the 90-day period ending on the date on which the loan is to be so secured, and

(B) requirements comparable to the requirements of paragraph (2) are met with respect to such consent.

(5)(A) The requirements of this subsection shall not apply with respect to the qualified joint and survivor annuity form of benefit or the qualified preretirement survivor annuity form of benefit, as the case may be, if such benefit may not be waived or another beneficiary selected and if the plan fully subsidizes the costs of such benefit.

(B) For purposes of subparagraph (A), a plan fully subsidizes the costs of a benefit if under the plan the failure to waive such benefit by a participant would not result in a decrease in any plan benefits with respect to such participant and would not result in increased contributions from such participant.

(6) If a plan fiduciary acts in accordance with part 4 of this subtitle in—

(A) relying on a consent or revocation referred to in paragraph (1)(A), or

(B) making a determination under paragraph (2),

then such consent, revocation, or determination shall be treated as valid for purposes of discharging the plan from liability to the extent of payments made pursuant to such Act.

(7) For purposes of this subsection, the term "applicable election period" means—

(A) in the case of an election to waive the qualified joint and survivor annuity form of benefit, the 180-day period ending on the annuity starting date, or

(B) in the case of an election to waive the qualified preretirement survivor annuity, the period which begins on the first day of the plan year in which the participant attains age 35 and ends on the date of the participant's death.

In the case of a participant who is separated from service, the applicable election period under subparagraph (B) with respect to benefits accrued before the date of such separation from service shall not begin later than such date.

(8) Notwithstanding any other provision of this subsection—

(A)(i) A plan may provide the written explanation described in paragraph (3)(A) after the annuity starting date. In any case to which this subparagraph applies, the applicable election period under paragraph (7) shall not end before the 30th day after the date on which such explanation is provided.

(ii) The Secretary of the Treasury may by regulations limit the application of clause (i), except that such regulations may not limit the period of time by which the annuity starting date precedes the provision of the written explanation other than by providing that the annuity starting date may not be earlier than termination of employment.

(B) A plan may permit a participant to elect (with any applicable spousal consent) to waive any requirement that the written explanation be provided at least 30 days before the annuity starting date (or to waive the 30-day requirement under subparagraph (A)) if the distribution commences more than 7 days after such explanation is provided.

Act Sec. 205. (d)(1) "Qualified joint and survivor annuity" defined.—For purposes of this section, the term "qualified joint and survivor annuity" means an annuity—

(A) for the life of the participant with a survivor annuity for the life of the spouse which is not less than 50 percent of (and is not greater than 100 percent of) the amount of the annuity which is payable during the joint lives of the participant and the spouse, and

(B) which is the actuarial equivalent of a single annuity for the life of the participant.

Such term also includes any annuity in a form having the effect of an annuity described in the preceding sentence.

(2)(A) For purposes of this section, the term "qualified optional survivor annuity" means an annuity—

(i) for the life of the participant with a survivor annuity for the life of the spouse which is equal to the applicable percentage of the amount of the annuity which is payable during the joint lives of the participant and the spouse, and

(ii) which is the actuarial equivalent of a single annuity for the life of the participant.

Such term also includes any annuity in a form having the effect of an annuity described in the preceding sentence.

(B)(i) For purposes of subparagraph (A), if the survivor annuity percentage—

(I) is less than 75 percent, the applicable percentage is 75 percent, and

(II) is greater than or equal to 75 percent, the applicable percentage is 50 percent.

(ii) For purposes of clause (i), the term "survivor annuity percentage" means the percentage which the survivor annuity under the plan's qualified joint and survivor annuity bears to the annuity payable during the joint lives of the participant and the spouse.

Act Sec. 205. (e) "Qualified preretirement survivor annuity" defined.—For purposes of this section—

(1) Except as provided in paragraph (2), the term "qualified preretirement survivor annuity" means a survivor annuity for the life of the surviving spouse of the participant if—

(A) the payments to the surviving spouse under such annuity are not less than the amounts which would be payable as a survivor annuity under the qualified joint and survivor annuity under the plan (or the actuarial equivalent thereof) if—

(i) in the case of a participant who dies after the date on which the participant attained the earliest retirement age, such participant had retired with an immediate qualified joint and survivor annuity on the day before the participant's date of death, or

(ii) in the case of a participant who dies on or before the date on which the participant would have attained the earliest retirement age, such participant had—

(I) separated from service on the date of death,

(II) survived to the earliest retirement age,

(III) retired with an immediate qualified joint and survivor annuity at the earliest retirement age, and

(IV) died on the day after the day on which such participant would have attained the earliest retirement age, and

(B) under the plan, the earliest period for which the surviving spouse may receive a payment under such annuity is not later than the month in which the participant would have attained the earliest retirement age under the plan.

In the case of an individual who separated from service before the date of such individual's death, subparagraph (a)(ii)(I) shall not apply.

(2) In the case of any individual account plan or participant described in subparagraph (B) or (C) of subsection (b)(1), the term "qualified preretirement survivor annuity" means an annuity for the life of the surviving spouse the actuarial equivalent of which is not less than 50 percent of the portion of the account balance of the participant (as of the date of death) to which the participant had a nonforfeitable right (within the meaning of section 203).

(3) For purposes of paragraphs (1) and (2), any security interest held by the plan by reason of a loan outstanding to the participant shall be taken into account in determining the amount of the qualified preretirement survivor annuity.

Act Sec. 205. (f) (1) MARRIAGE REQUIREMENTS FOR PLAN.—Except as provided in paragraph (2), a plan may provide that a qualified joint and survivor annuity (or a qualified preretirement survivor annuity) will not be provided unless the participant and spouse had been married throughout the 1-year period ending on the earlier of—

    (A) the participant's annuity starting date, or

    (B) the date of the participant's death.

  (2) For purposes of paragraph (1), if—

    (A) a participant marries within 1 year before the annuity starting date, and

    (B) the participant and the participant's spouse in such marriage have been married for at least a 1-year period ending on or before the date of the participant's death,

such participant and such spouse shall be treated as having been married throughout the 1-year period ending on the participant's annuity starting date.

Act Sec. 205. (g) (1) DISTRIBUTION OF PRESENT VALUE OF ANNUITY; WRITTEN CONSENT; DETERMINATION OF PRESENT VALUE.—A plan may provide that the present value of a qualified joint and survivor annuity or a qualified preretirement survivor annuity will be immediately distributed if such value does not exceed the amount that can be distributed without the participant's consent under section 203(e). No distribution may be made under the preceding sentence after the annuity starting date unless the participant and the spouse of the participant (or where the participant has died, the surviving spouse) consent in writing to such distribution.

  (2) If—

    (A) the present value of the qualified joint and survivor annuity or the qualified preretirement survivor annuity exceeds the amount that can be distributed without the participant's consent under section 203(e), and

    (B) the participant and the spouse of the participant (or where the participant has died, the surviving spouse) consent in writing to the distribution,

the plan may immediately distribute the present value of such annuity.

  (3)(A) For purposes of paragraphs (1) and (2), the present value shall not be less than the present value calculated by using the applicable mortality table and the applicable interest rate.

    (B) For purposes of subparagraph (A)—

      (i) The term 'applicable mortality table' means a mortality table, modified as appropriate by the Secretary of the Treasury, based on the mortality table specified for the plan year under subparagraph (A) of section 303(h)(3) (without regard to subparagraph (C) or (D) of such section).

      (ii) The term 'applicable interest rate' means the adjusted first, second, and third segment rates applied under rules similar to the rules of section 303(h)(2)(C) (determined by not taking into account any adjustment under clause (iv) thereof) for the month before the date of the distribution or such other time as the Secretary of the Treasury may by regulations prescribe.

      (iii) For purposes of clause (ii), the adjusted first, second, and third segment rates are the first, second, and third segment rates which would be determined under section 303(h)(2)(C) (determined by not taking into account any adjustment under clause (iv) thereof) if section 303(h)(2)(D) were applied by substituting the average yields for the month described in clause (ii) for the average yields for the 24-month period described in such section.

Act Sec. 205. (h) DEFINITIONS.—For purposes of this section—

  (1) The term "vested participant" means any participant who has a nonforfeitable right (within the meaning of section 3(19)) to any portion of such participant's accrued benefit.

  (2)(A) The term "annuity starting date" means—

      (i) the first day of the first period for which an amount is paid as an annuity, or

      (ii) in the case of a benefit not payable in the form of an annuity, the first day on which all events have occurred which entitle the participant to such benefit.

    (B) For purposes of subparagraph (A), the first day of the first period for which a benefit is to be received by reason of disability shall be treated as the annuity starting date only if such benefit is not an auxiliary benefit.

  (3) The term "earliest retirement age" means the earliest date on which, under the plan, the participant could elect to receive retirement benefits.

Act Sec. 205. (i) INCREASED COSTS FROM PROVIDING ANNUITY.—A plan may take into account in any equitable manner (as determined by the Secretary of the Treasury) any increased costs resulting from providing a qualified joint or survivor annuity or a qualified preretirement survivor annuity.

Act Sec. 205. (j) USE OF PARTICIPANT'S ACCRUED BENEFIT AS SECURITY FOR LOAN AS NOT PREVENTING DISTRIBUTION.—If the use of any participant's accrued benefit (or any portion thereof) as security for a loan meets the requirements of subsection (c)(4), nothing in this section shall prevent any distribution required by reason of a failure to comply with the terms of such loan.

Act Sec. 205. (k) SPOUSAL CONSENT.—No consent of a spouse shall be effective for purposes of subsection (g)(1) or (g)(2) (as the case may be) unless requirements comparable to the requirements for spousal consent to an election under subsection (c)(1)(A) are met.

Act Sec. 205. (l) REGULATIONS; CONSULTATION OF SECRETARY OF THE TREASURY WITH SECRETARY OF LABOR.—In prescribing regulations under this section, the Secretary of the Treasury shall consult with the Secretary of Labor.

Amendments

P.L. 113-295, § 221(a)(57)(B)(ii), Div. A:

Amended ERISA Sec. 205(g)(3)(B)(iii) by striking clauses (II) and (III), by striking "if—" and all that follows through "section 303(h)(2)(D)" and inserting "if section 303(h)(2)(D)" and by striking "described in such section," and inserting "described in such section.".

Prior to amendment, ERISA Sec. 205(g)(3)(B)(iii)(II) and (III) read as follows:

(II) section 303(h)(2)(G)(i)(II) were applied by substituting 'section 205(g)(3)(A)(ii)(II)' for 'section 302(b)(5)(B)(ii)(II)', and

(III) the applicable percentage under section 303(h)(2)(G) were determined in accordance with the following table:

In the case of plan years beginning in:	The applicable percentage is:
2008	20 percent
2009	40 percent
2010	60 percent
2011	80 percent.

The above amendments shall take effect on the date of enactment of this Act [December 19, 2014.-CCH]. For a special rule, see Act Sec. 221(b)(2), Div. A, below.

P. L. 113-295, § 221(b)(2), Div. A, provides:

(2) Savings provision.—If—

(A) any provision amended or repealed by the amendments made by this section applied to—

  (i) any transaction occurring before the date of the enactment of this Act,

  (ii) any property acquired before such date of enactment, or

  (iii) any item of income, loss, deduction, or credit taken into account before such date of enactment, and

(B) the treatment of such transaction, property, or item under such provision would (without regard to the amendments or repeals made by this section) affect the liability for tax for periods ending after date of enactment, nothing in the amendments or repeals made by this section shall be construed to affect the treatment of such transaction, property, or item for purposes of determining liability for tax for periods ending after such date of enactment.

P.L. 112-141, § 40211(b)(3)(B):

Amended ERISA Sec. 205(g)(3)(B)(ii) and (iii) by striking "section 303(h)(2)(C)" and inserting "section 303(h)(2)(C) (determined by not taking into account any adjustment under clause (iv) thereof)".

For effective date, see P.L. 112-141, § 40211(c), below.

P.L. 112-141, § 40211(c):

(c) EFFECTIVE DATE.—

(1) IN GENERAL.—The amendments made by this section shall apply with respect to plan years beginning after December 31, 2011.

(2) RULES WITH RESPECT TO ELECTIONS.—

(A) ADJUSTED FUNDING TARGET ATTAINMENT PERCENTAGE.—A plan sponsor may elect not to have the amendments made by this section apply to any plan year beginning before January 1, 2013, either (as specified in the election)—

(i) for all purposes for which such amendments apply, or

(ii) solely for purposes of determining the adjusted funding target attainment percentage under sections 436 of the Internal Revenue Code of 1986 and 206(g) of the Employee Retirement Income Security Act of 1974 for such plan year.

A plan shall not be treated as failing to meet the requirements of sections 204(g) of such Act and 411(d)(6) of such Code solely by reason of an election under this paragraph.

(B) OPT OUT OF EXISTING ELECTIONS.—If, on the date of the enactment of this Act, an election is in effect with respect to any plan under sections 303(h)((2)(D)(ii) of the Employee Retirement Income Security Act of 1974 and 430(h)((2)(D)(ii) of the Internal Revenue Code of 1986, then, notwithstanding the last sentence of each such section, the plan sponsor may revoke such election without the consent of the Secretary of the Treasury. The plan sponsor may make such revocation at any time before the date which is 1 year after such date of enactment and such revocation shall be effective for the 1st plan year to which the amendments made by this section apply and all subsequent plan years. Nothing in this subparagraph shall preclude a plan sponsor from making a subsequent election in accordance with such sections.

P.L. 110-458, § 103(b)(1):

Amended ERISA Sec. 205(g)(3)(B)(iii)(II) by striking "section 205(g)(3)(B)(iii)(II)" and inserting "section 205(g)(3)(A)(ii)(II)".

The above amendment takes effect as if included in the provisions of the 2006 Act to which the amendment relates [effective with respect to plan years beginning after December 31, 2007.—CCH]

P.L. 109-280, § 302(a):

Amended ERISA Sec. 205(g)(3) to read as above.

Prior to amendment, ERISA Sec. 205(g)(3) read as follows:

(3) DETERMINATION OF PRESENT VALUE. –

(A) IN GENERAL. –

(i) PRESENT VALUE. Except as provided in subparagraph (B), for purposes of paragraphs (1) and (2), the present value shall not be less than the present value calculated by using the applicable mortality table and the applicable interest rate.

(ii) DEFINITIONS. For purposes of clause (i) –

(I) APPLICABLE MORTALITY TABLE. The term "applicable mortality table" means the table prescribed by the Secretary of the Treasury. Such table shall be based on the prevailing commissioners' standard table (described in section 807(d)(5)(A) of the Internal Revenue Code of 1986) used to determine reserves for group annuity contracts issued on the date as of which present value is being determined (without regard to any other subparagraph of section 807(d)(5) of such Code).

(II) APPLICABLE INTEREST RATE. The term "applicable interest rate" means the annual rate of interest on 30-year Treasury securities for the month before the date of distribution or such other time as the Secretary of the Treasury may by regulations prescribe.

(B) EXCEPTION. In the case of a distribution from a plan that was adopted and in effect prior to the date of the enactment of the Retirement Protection Act of 1994, the present value of any distribution made before the earlier of—

(i) the later of when a plan amendment applying subparagraph (A) is adopted or made effective, or

(ii) the first day of the first plan year beginning after December 31, 1999,

shall be calculated, for purposes of paragraphs (1) and (2), using the interest rate determined under the regulations of the Pension Benefit Guaranty Corporation for determining the present value of a lump sum distribution on plan termination that were in effect on September 1, 1993, and using the provision of the plan as in effect on the day before such date of enactment; but only if such provisions of the plan met the requirements of section 205(g)(3) as in effect on the date before such date of enactment.

The above amendment is effective for plan years beginning after December 31, 2007.

P.L. 109-280, § 1004(b)(1)(A)-(C):

Amended ERISA Sec. (c)(1)(A) by striking the word "and" and replacing it with a comma in clause (i), by redesignating clause (ii) as clause (iii), and by inserting the following after clause (i): "(ii) if the participant elects a waiver under clause (i), may elect the qualified optional survivor annuity at any time during the applicable election period, and"

See below for effective dates.

P.L. 109-280, § 1004(b)(2)(A)-(C):

Amended ERISA Sec. 205(d) by inserting "(1)" after "(d)", by redesignating paragraphs (1) and (2) as subparagraphs (A) and (B), respectively, and by adding new subsection 205(d)(2) to read as above.

P.L. 109-280, § 1004(b)(3):

Amended ERISA Sec. 205(c)(3)(A)(i) by inserting "and of the qualified optional survivor annuity" after the word "annuity."

P.L. 109-280, § 1004(c) provides as follows:

(c) EFFECTIVE DATES.—

(1) IN GENERAL.—

The amendments made by this section shall apply to plan years beginning after December 31, 2007.

(2) SPECIAL RULE FOR COLLECTIVELY BARGAINED PLANS.—

In the case of a plan maintained pursuant to 1 or more collective bargaining agreements between employee representatives and 1 or more employers ratified on or before the date of the enactment of this Act, the amendments made by this section shall not apply to plan years beginning before the earlier of —

(A) the later of —

(i) January 1, 2008, or

(ii) the date on which the last collective bargaining agreement related to the plan terminates (determined without regard to any extension thereof after the date of enactment of this Act), or

(B) January 1, 2009.

P.L. 109-280, § 1102(a)(2)(A):

Amended ERISA Sec. 205(c)(7)(A) by striking "90-day" and inserting "180-day" in its place.

The above amendment is effective for years beginning after December 31, 2006.

P.L. 107-147, § 411(r)(2):

Act Sec. 411(r)(2)(A) amended ERISA Sec. 205(g)(1) by striking "exceed the dollar limit under section 203(e)(1)" and inserting "exceed the amount that can be distributed without the participant's consent under section 203(e)."

Act Sec. 411(r)(2)(B) amended ERISA Sec. 205(g)(2)(A) by striking "exceeds the dollar limit under section 203(e)(1)" and inserting "exceeds the amount that can be distributed without the participant's consent under section 203(e)."

P.L. 105-34, § 1601(d)(5):

Act Sec. 1601(d)(5) amended ERISA Sec. 205(c)(8)(A)(ii) by striking "Secretary" and inserting "Secretary of the Treasury".

The above amendment is effective with respect to plan years beginning after December 31, 1996.

P.L. 105-34, § 1071(g)(1):

Act Sec. 1071(g)(1) amended ERISA Sec. 205(g)(1) by striking "$3,500" and inserting "$5,000".

P.L. 105-34, § 1071(g)(2):

Act Sec. 1071(g)(2) amended ERISA Sec. 205(g)(2) by striking "$3,500" and inserting "$5,000".

The above amendments are effective for plan years beginning after August 5, 1997.

P.L. 104-188, § 1451(b):

Act Sec. 1451(b) amended ERISA Sec. 205(c) by adding at the end the new paragraph (8) to read as above.

The above amendment applies to plan years beginning after December 31, 1996.

P.L. 103-465, § 767(c)(2):

Act Sec. 767(c)(2) amended ERISA Sec. 205(g)(3) to read as above. Prior to amendment, ERISA Sec. 205(g)(3) read as follows:

(3)(A) For purposes of paragraphs (1) and (2), the present value shall be calculated—

(i) by using an interest rate no greater than the applicable interest rate if the vested accrued benefit (using such rate) is not in excess of $25,000, and

(ii) by using an interest rate no greater than 120 percent of the applicable interest rate if the vested accrued benefit exceeds $25,000 (as determined under clause (i)).

In no event shall the present value determined under subclause (II) be less than $25,000.

(B) For purposes of subparagraph (A), the term "applicable interest rate" means the interest rate which would be used (as of the date of the distribution) by the Pension Benefit Guaranty Corporation for purposes of determining the present value of a lump sum distribution on plan termination.

The above amendment applies to plan years and limitation years beginning after December 31, 1994, except that an employer may elect to treat the amendments made by this section as being effective on or after December 8, 1994. For special rules, see Act Sec. 767(e)(2)-(3), following ERISA Sec. 203(e).

P.L. 101-239, § 7862(d)(1)(B):

Amended ERISA Sec. 205(c)(3)(B)(ii) by striking clause (V) and inserting a new flush sentence to read as above effective for plan years beginning after 1984. Previously, clause (V) read as follows:

(V) A reasonable period after separation from service in case of a participant who separates before attaining age 35.

P.L. 101-239, § 7862(d)(3):

Amended ERISA Sec. 205(h) in paragraph (1), by striking "the term" and inserting "The term", and by striking "benefit," and inserting "benefit."; and in paragraph (3), by striking "the term" and inserting "The term", effective for plan years beginning after 1984.

P.L. 101-239, § 7862(d)(6):

Amended ERISA Sec. 205(c)(3)(B)(ii) by striking "401(a)(11)" and inserting "205" effective for plan years beginning after 1984.

P.L. 101-239, § 7862(d)(8):

Amended ERISA Sec. 205(e)(2) by striking "nonforfeitable accrued benefit" and inserting "nonforfeitable right (within the meaning of section 203)" effective for plan years beginning after 1984.

P.L. 101-239, § 7862(d)(9)(B):

Redesignated paragraph (3) of ERISA Sec. 205(b) (as added by P.L. 99-514, § 1898(b)(14)(B)) as paragraph (4) effective for plan years beginning after 1984.

P.L. 101-239, § 7891(e):

Amended ERISA Sec. 205(h) by striking "the term" and inserting "The term" and by striking "benefit," and inserting "benefit." in paragraph (1) and by striking "the term" and inserting "The term" in paragraph (3) effective October 22, 1986.

P.L. 101-239, § 7894(c)(7):

Amended ERISA Sec. 205(c)(6) by striking "act" and inserting "Act" effective September 2, 1974.

P.L. 99-514, § 1139(c)(2):

Amended paragraph (3) of Sec. 205(g) to read as above. Prior to amendment, paragraph (3) read as follows:

Act Sec. 205(g).

* * *

(3) For purposes of paragraphs (1) and (2), the present value of a qualified joint and survivor annuity or a qualified preretirement survivor annuity shall be determined as of the date of the distribution and by using an interest rate not greater than the interest rate which would be used (as of the date of the distribution) by the Pension Benefit Guaranty Corporation for purposes of determining the present value of a lump-sum distribution on plan termination.

P.L. 99-514, § 1139(d):

Act Sec. 1139(d) provides as follows:

(d) EFFECTIVE DATE.—

(1) IN GENERAL.—The amendments made by this section shall apply to distributions in plan years beginning after December 31, 1984, except that such amendments shall not apply to any distributions in plan years beginning after December 31, 1984, and before January 1, 1987, if such distributions were made in accordance with the requirements of the regulations issued under the Retirement Equity Act of 1984.

(2) Reduction in Accrued Benefits.—

(A) IN GENERAL.—If a plan—

(i) adopts a plan amendment before the close of the first plan year beginning on or before January 1, 1989, which provides for the calculation of the present value of the accrued benefits in the manner provided by the amendments made by this section, and

(ii) the plan reduces the accrued benefits for any plan year to which such plan amendment applies in accordance with such plan amendment,

such reduction shall not be treated as a violation of section 411(d)(6) of the Internal Revenue Code of 1986 or section 204(g) of the Employee Retirement Income Security Act of 1974 (29 U.S.C. 1054(g)).

(B) SPECIAL RULE.—In the case of a plan maintained by a corporation incorporated on April 11, 1934, which is headquartered in Tarrant County, Texas—

(i) such plan may be amended to remove the option of an employee to receive a lump-sum distribution (within the meaning of section 402(e)(5) of such Code) if such amendment—

(I) is adopted within 1 year of the date of the enactment of this Act, and

(II) is not effective until 2 years after the employees are notified of such amendment, and

(ii) the present value of any vested accrued benefit of such plan determined during the 3-year period beginning on the date of the enactment of this Act shall be determined under the applicable interest rate (within the meaning of section 411(a)(11)(B)(ii) of such Code), except that if such value (as so determined) exceeds $50,000, then the value of any excess over $50,000 shall be determined by using the interest rate specified in the plan as of August 16, 1986.

P.L. 99-514, § 1145(b):

Amended ERISA Sec. 205(b) by adding a new paragraph (3) to read as above, effective for taxable years beginning after 1984.

P.L. 99-514, § 1898(b)(1)(B):

Amended ERISA Sec. 205(e)(1) by adding a new sentence at the end to read as above, effective for plan years beginning after 1984.

P.L. 99-514, § 1898(b)(2)(B)(i):

Amended ERISA Sec. 205(b)(1)(C)(iii) by striking out "a transferee" and inserting "a direct or indirect transferee (in a transfer after December 31, 1984)" instead, effective for plan years beginning after 1984.

P.L. 99-514, § 1898(b)(2)(B)(ii):

Amended ERISA Sec. 205(b)(1) by adding a new sentence at the end to read as above, effective for plan years beginning after 1984.

P.L. 99-514, § 1898(b)(3)(B):

Amended ERISA Sec. 205(a)(1) by striking out "who retires under the plan" and inserting "who does not die before the annuity starting date" instead, effective for plan years beginning after 1984.

P.L. 99-514, § 1898(b)(4)(B)(i):

Amended ERISA Sec. 205(c)(1)(B) by striking "paragraphs (2) and (3)" and inserting "paragraphs (2), (3), and (4)" instead.

P.L. 99-514, § 1898(b)(4)(B)(ii):

Amended ERISA Sec. 205(c) by redesignating paragraphs (4), (5), and (6) as (5), (6), and (7), respectively and by adding a new paragraph (4) to read as above.

P.L. 99-514, § 1898(b)(4)(C):

Subsection (C) provides as follows:

(C) Effective dates.—

(i) The amendments made by this paragraph shall apply with respect to loans made after August 18, 1985.

(ii) In the case of any loan which was made on or before August 18, 1985, and which is secured by a portion of the participant's accrued benefit, nothing in the amendments made by sections 103 and 203 of the Retirement Equity Act of 1984 shall prevent any distribution required by reason of a failure to comply with the terms of such loan.

(iii) For purposes of this subparagraph, any loan which is revised, extended, renewed, or renegotiated after August 18, 1985, shall be treated as made after August 18, 1985.

P.L. 99-514, § 1898(b)(5)(B):

Amended ERISA Sec. 205(c)(3)(B) to read as above, effective for plan years beginning after 1984. Prior to amendment, subparagraph (B) read as follows:

(B) Each plan shall provide to each participant, within the period beginning with the first day of the plan year in which the participant attains age 32 and ending with the close of the plan year preceding the plan year in which the participant attains age 35 (and consistent with such regulations as the Secretary of the Treasury may prescribe), a written explanation with respect to the qualified preretirement survivor annuity comparable to that required under subparagraph (A).

P.L. 99-514, § 1898(b)(6)(B):

Amended ERISA Sec. 205(c)(2)(A) to read as above, effective for plan years beginning after 1984. Prior to amendment, subparagraph (A) read as follows:

(A) the spouse of the participant consents in writing to such election, and the spouse's consent acknowledges the effect of such election and is witnessed by a plan representative or a notary public, or

P.L. 99-514, § 1898(b)(7)(B):

Amended ERISA Sec. 205(b)(1)(C) by striking out "the participant's nonforfeitable accrued benefit" and inserting "the participant's nonforfeitable accrued benefit (reduced by any security interest held by the plan by reason of a loan outstanding to such participant)" instead, effective for plan years beginning after 1984.

P.L. 99-514, § 1898(b)(8)(B):

Amended ERISA Sec. 205(h)(1) by striking out "the accrued benefit derived from employer contributions" and inserting "such participant's accrued benefit" instead, effective for plan years beginning after 1984.

P.L. 99-514, § 1898(b)(9)(B)(i):

Amended ERISA Sec. 205(e)(2) by striking "the account balance of the participant as of the date of death" and inserting "the portion of the account balance of the participant (as of the date of death) to which the participant had a nonforfeitable accrued benefit" instead, effective for plan years beginning after 1984.

P.L. 99-514, § 1898(b)(9)(B)(ii):

Added ERISA Sec. 205(e)(3) to read as above, effective for plan years beginning after 1984.

P.L. 99-514, § 1898(b)(10)(B):

Redesignated ERISA Sec. 205(k) as (l) and added new subsection (k) to read as above, effective for plan years beginning after 1984.

P.L. 99-514, § 1898(b)(11)(B):

Amended ERISA Sec. 205(c)(5)(A) by striking "if the plan" and inserting "if such benefit may not be waived or another beneficiary selected and if the plan" instead, effective for plan years beginning after 1984.

P.L. 99-514, § 1898(b)(12)(B):

Amended ERISA Sec. 205(h)(2) to read as above, effective for plan years beginning after 1984. Prior to amendment, paragraph (2) read as follows:

Act Sec. 205. (h) For purposes of this section—

* * *

(2) the term "annuity starting date" means the first day of the first period for which an amount is received as an annuity (whether by reason of retirement or disability), and

P.L. 99-514, § 1898(b)(13)(B):

Amended ERISA Sec. 205(b)(1)(C)(i) by striking out "subsection (c)(2)(A)" and inserting "subsection (c)(2)" instead, effective for plan years beginning after 1984.

P.L. 99-514, § 1898(b)(14)(B):

Added ERISA Sec. 205(b)(3) to read as above, effective for plan years beginning after 1984.

P.L. 98-397, § 103:

Act Sec. 103 amended ERISA Sec. 205 by striking out the prior law and replacing it with new section 205. Prior to amendment, ERISA Sec. 205 read as follows:

(a) If a pension plan provides for the payment of benefits in the form of an annuity, such plan shall provide for the payment of annuity benefits in a form having the effect of a qualified joint and survivor annuity.

(b) In the case of a plan which provides for the payment of benefits before the normal retirement age as defined in section 3(24), the plan is not required to provide for the payment of annuity benefits in a form having the effect of a qualfied joint and survivor annuity during the period beginning on the date on which the employee enters into the plan as a participant and ending on the later of—

(1) the date the employee reaches the earliest retirement age, or

(2) the first day of the 120th month beginning before the date on which the employee reaches normal retirement age.

(c)(1) A plan described in subsection (b) does not meet the requirements of subsection (a) unless, under the plan, a participant has a reasonable period in which he may elect the qualified joint and survivor annuity form with respect to the period beginning on the date on which the period described in subsection (b) ends and ending on the date on which he reaches normal retirement age if he continues his employment during that period.

(2) A plan does not meet the requirements of this subsection unless, in the case of such election, the payments under the survivor annuity are not less than the payments which would have been made under the joint annuity to which the participant would have been entitled if he had made an election under this subsection immediately prior to his retirement and if his retirement had occurred on the date immediately preceding the date of his death and within the period within which an election can be made.

(d) A plan shall not be treated as not satisfying the requirements of this section solely because the spouse of the participant is not entitled to receive a survivor annuity (whether or not an election has been made under subsection (c)) unless the participant and his spouse have been married throughout the 1-year period ending on the date of such participant's death.

(e) A plan shall not be treated as satisfying the requirements of this section unless, under the plan, each participant has a reasonable period (as prescribed by the Secretary of the Treasury by regulations) before the annuity starting date during which he may elect in writing (after having received a written explanation of the terms and conditions of the joint and survivor annuity and the effect of an election under this subsection) not to take such joint and survivor annuity.

(f) A plan shall not be treated as not satisfying the requirements of this section solely because, under the plan there is a provision that any election under subsection (c) or (e), and any revocation of any such election, does not become effective (or ceases to be effective) if the participant dies within a period (not in excess of 2 years) beginning on the date of such election or revocation, as the case may be. The preceding sentence does not apply unless the plan provision described in the preceding sentence also provides that such an election or revocation will be given effect in any case in which—

(1) the participant dies from accidental causes,

(2) a failure to give effect to the election or revocation would deprive the participant's survivor of a survivor annuity, and

(3) such election or revocation is made before such accident occurred.

(g) For purposes of this section:

(1) The term "annuity starting date" means the first day of the first period for which an amount is received as an annuity (whether by reason of retirement or by reason or disability).

(2) The term "earliest retirement age" means the earliest date on which, under the plan, the participant could elect to receive retirement benefits.

(3) The term "qualified joint and survivor annuity" means an annuity for the life of the participant with a survivor annuity for the life of his spouse which is not less than one-half or, or greater than, the amount of the annuity payable during the joint lives of the participant and his spouse and which is the actuarial equivalent of a single annuity for the life of the participant.

(h) For the purposes of this section, a plan may take into account in any equitable fashion (as determined by the Secretary of the Treasury) any increased costs resulting from providing joint and survivor annuity benefits under an election made under subsection (c).

(i) This section shall apply only if—

(1) the annuity starting date did not occur before the effective date of this section, and

(2) the participant was an active participant in the plan on or after such effective date.

Generally, the above amendment is effective for plan years beginning after December 31, 1984. However, Act Secs. 303(c) and (e) provide:

(c) Requirement of Joint and Survivor Annuity and Preretirement Survivor Annuity.—

(1) Requirement That Participant Have at Least 1 Hour of Service or Paid Leave on or After Date of Enactment.—The amendments made by sections 103 and 203 shall apply only in the case of participants who have at least 1 hour of service under the plan on or after the date of the enactment of this Act or have at least 1 hour of paid leave on or after such date of enactment.

(2) Requirement That Preretirement Survivor Annuity Be Provided in Case of Certain Participants Dying on or After Date of Enactment.—In the case of any participant—

(A) who has at least 1 hour of service under the plan on or after the date of the enactment of this Act or has at least 1 hour of paid leave on or after such date of enactment.

(B) who dies before the annuity starting date, and

(C) who dies on or after the date of the enactment of this Act and before the first day of the first plan year to which the amendments made by this Act apply.

the amendments made by sections 103 and 203 shall be treated as in effect as of the time of such participant's death.

(3) Spousal Consent Required for Certain Elections After Date of Enactment.—Any election after December 31, 1984, and before the first day of the first plan year to which the amendments made by this Act apply not to take a joint and survivor annuity shall not be effective unless the requirements of section 205(c)(2) of the Employee Retirement Income Security Act of 1974 (as amended by section 103 of this Act) and section 417(a)(2) of the Internal Revenue Code of 1954 (as added by section 203 of this Act) are met with respect to such election.

(e) Treatment of Certain Participants Who Separate From Service Before Date of Enactment.—

(1) Joint and Survivor Annuity Provisions of Employee Retirement Income Security Act of 1974 Apply to Certain Participants.—If—

(A) a participant had at least 1 hour of service under the plan on or after September 2, 1974.

(B) section 205 of the Employee Retirement Income Security Act of 1974 and section 401(a)(11) of the Internal Revenue Code of 1954 (as in effect on the day before the date of the enactment of this Act) would not (but for this paragraph) apply to such participant,

(C) the amendments made by section 103 and 203 of this Act do not apply to such participant, and

(D) as of the date of the enactment of this Act, the participant's annuity starting date has not occurred and the participant is alive,

then such participant may elect to have section 205 of the Employee Retirement Income Security Act of 1974 and section 401(a)(11) of the Internal Revenue Code of 1954 (as in effect on the day before the date of the enactment of this Act) apply.

(2) Treatment of Certain Participants Who Perform Service on or After January 1, 1976.—If—

(A) a participant had at least 1 hour of service in the first plan year beginning on or after January 1, 1976,

(B) the amendments made by sections 103 and 203 would not (but for this paragraph) apply to such participant,

(C) when such participant separated from service, such participant had at least 10 years of service under the plan and had a nonforfeitable right to all (or any portion) of such participant's accrued benefit derived from employer contributions, and

(D) as of the date of the enactment of this Act, such participant's annuity starting date has not occurred and such participant is alive, then such participant may elect to have the qualified preretirement survivor annuity requirements of the amendments made by sections 103 and 203 apply.

Also, see Act Sec. 303(b) for a special rule for collective bargaining agreements at ¶ 14,250.09.

[¶ 14,460]
OTHER PROVISIONS RELATING TO FORM AND PAYMENT OF BENEFITS

Act Sec. 206. (a) COMMENCEMENT DATE FOR PAYMENT OF BENEFITS.—Each pension plan shall provide that unless the participant otherwise elects, the payment of benefits under the plan to the participant shall begin not later than the 60th day after the latest of the close of the plan year in which—

(1) occurs the date on which the participant attains the earlier of age 65 or the normal retirement age specified under the plan,

(2) occurs the 10th anniversary of the year in which the participant commenced participation in the plan, or

(3) the participant terminates his service with the employer.

In the case of a plan which provides for the payment of an early retirement benefit, such plan shall provide that a participant who satisfied the service requirements for such early retirement benefit, but separated from the service (with any nonforfeitable right to an accrued benefit) before satisfying the age requirement for such early retirement benefit, is entitled upon satisfaction of such age requirement to receive a benefit not less than the benefit to which he would be entitled at the normal retirement age, actuarially reduced under regulations prescribed by the Secretary of the Treasury.

Act Sec. 206. (b) DECREASE IN PLAN BENEFITS BY REASON OF INCREASES IN BENEFIT LEVELS UNDER SOCIAL SECURITY ACT OR RAILROAD RETIREMENT ACT OF 1937.—If—

(1) a participant or beneficiary is receiving benefits under a pension plan, or

(2) a participant is separated from the service and has nonforfeitable rights to benefits,

a plan may not decrease benefits of such a participant by reason of any increase in the benefit levels payable under title II of the Social Security Act or the Railroad Retirement Act of 1937, or any increase in the wage base under such title II, if such increase takes place after the date of the enactment of this Act or (if later) the earlier of the date of first entitlement of such benefits or the date of such separation.

Act Sec. 206. (c) FORFEITURE OF ACCRUED BENEFITS DERIVED FROM EMPLOYER CONTRIBUTIONS.—No pension plan may provide that any part of a participant's accrued benefit derived from employer contributions (whether or not otherwise nonforfeitable) is forfeitable solely because of withdrawal by such participant of any amount attributable to the benefit derived from contributions made by such participant. The preceding sentence shall not apply (1) to the accrued benefit of any participant unless, at the time of such withdrawal, such participant has a nonforfeitable right to at least 50 percent of such accrued benefit, or (2) to the extent that an accrued benefit is permitted to be forefeited in accordance with section 203(a)(3)(D)(iii).

Act Sec. 206. (d)(1) ASSIGNMENT OR ALIENATION OF PLAN BENEFITS.—Each pension plan shall provide that benefits provided under the plan may not be assigned or alienated.

(2) For the purposes of paragraph (1) of this subsection, there shall not be taken into account any voluntary and revocable assignment of not to exceed 10 percent of any benefit payment, or of any irrevocable assignment or alienation of benefits executed before the date of enactment of this Act. The preceding

sentence shall not apply to any assignment or alienation made for the purposes of defraying plan administration costs. For purposes of this paragraph a loan made to a participant or beneficiary shall not be treated as an assignment or alienation if such loan is secured by the participant's accrued nonforfeitable benefit and is exempt from the tax imposed by section 4975 of the Internal Revenue Code of 1986 (relating to tax on prohibited transactions) by reason of section 4975(d)(1) of such Code.

(3)(A) Paragraph (1) shall apply to the creation, assignment, or recognition of a right to any benefit payable with respect to a participant pursuant to a domestic relations order, except that paragraph (1) shall not apply if the order is determined to be a qualified domestic relations order. Each pension plan shall provide for the payment of benefits in accordance with the applicable requirements of any qualified domestic relations order.

(B) For purposes of this paragraph—

(i) the term "qualified domestic relations order" means a domestic relations order—

(I) which creates or recognizes the existence of an alternate payee's right to, or assigns to an alternative payee the right to, receive all or a portion of the benefits payable with respect to a participant under a plan, and

(II) with respect to which the requirements of subparagraphs (C) and (D) are met, and

(ii) the term "domestic relations order" means any judgment, decree, or order (including approval of a property settlement agreement) which—

(I) relates to the provisions of child support, alimony payments, or marital property rights to a spouse, former spouse, child, or other dependent of a participant, and

(II) is made pursuant to a State domestic relations law (including a community property law).

(C) A domestic relations order meets the requirements of this subparagraph only if such order clearly specifies—

(i) the name and the last known mailing address (if any) of the participant and the name and mailing address of each alternate payee covered by the order,

(ii) the amount or percentage of the participant's benefits to be paid by the plan to each such alternate payee, or the manner in which such amount or percentage is to be determined,

(iii) the number of payments or period to which such order applies, and

(iv) each plan to which such order applies.

(D) A domestic relations order meets the requirements of this subparagraph only if such order—

(i) does not require a plan to provide any type or form of benefits, or any option, not otherwise provided under the plan,

(ii) does not require the plan to provide increased benefits (determined on the basis of actuarial value), and

(iii) does not require the payment of benefits to an alternate payee which are required to be paid to another alternate payee under another order previously determined to be a qualified domestic relations order.

(E)(i) A domestic relations order shall not be treated as failing to meet the requirements of clause (i) of subparagraph (D) solely because such order requires that payment of benefits be made to an alternate payee—

(I) in the case of any payment before a participant has separated from service, on or after the date on which the participant attains (or would have attained) the earliest retirement age,

(II) as if the participant had retired on the date on which such payment is to begin under such order (but taking into account only the present value of benefits actually accrued and not taking into account the value of any employer subsidy for early retirement), and

(III) in any form in which such benefits may be paid under the plan to the participant (other than in the form of a joint and survivor annuity with respect to the alternate payee and his or her subsequent spouse).

For purposes of subclause (II), the interest rate assumption used in determining the present value shall be the interest rate specified in the plan or, if no rate is specified, 5 percent.

(ii) For purposes of this subparagraph, the term 'earliest retirement age' means the earlier of—

(I) the date on which the participant is entitled to a distribution under the plan, or

(II) the later of the date of the participant attains age 50 or the earliest date on which the participant could begin receiving under the plan if the participant separated from service.

(F) To the extent provided in any qualified domestic relations order—

(i) the former spouse of a participant shall be treated as a surviving spouse of such participant for purposes of section 205 (and any spouse of the participant shall not be treated as a spouse of the participant for such purposes), and

(ii) if married for at least 1 year, the surviving former spouse shall be treated as meeting the requirements of section 205(f).

(G)(i) In the case of any domestic relations order received by a plan—

(I) the plan administrator shall promptly notify the participant and each alternate payee of the receipt of such order and the plan's procedures for determining the qualified status of domestic relations orders, and

(II) within a reasonable period after receipt of such order, the plan administrator shall determine whether such order is a qualified domestic relations order and notify the participant and each alternate payee of such determination.

(ii) Each plan shall establish reasonable procedures to determine the qualified status of domestic relations orders and to administer distributions under such qualified orders.

Such procedures—

(I) shall be in writing,

(II) shall provide for the notification of each person specified in a domestic relations order as entitled to payment of benefits under the plan (at the address included in the domestic relations order) of such procedures promptly upon receipt by the plan of the domestic relations order, and

(III) shall permit an alternate payee to designate a representative for receipt of copies of notices that are sent to the alternate payee with respect to a domestic relations order.

(H)(i) During any period in which the issue of whether a domestic relations order is a qualified domestic relations order is being determined (by the plan administrator, by a court of competent jurisdiction, or otherwise), the plan administrator shall separately account for the amounts (hereinafter in this subparagraph referred to as the "segregated amounts") which would have been payable to the alternate payee during such period if the order had been determined to be a qualified domestic relations order.

(ii) If within the 18-month period described in clause (c) the order (or modification thereof) is determined to be a qualified domestic relations order, the plan administrator shall pay the segregated amounts (including any interest thereon) to the person or persons entitled thereto.

(iii) If within the 18-month period described in clause (v)—

(I) it is determined that the order is not a qualified domestic relations order, or

(II) the issue as to whether such order is a qualified domestic relations order is not resolved,

then the plan administrator shall pay the segregated amounts (including any interest thereon) to the person or persons who would have been entitled to such amounts if there had been no order.

(iv) Any determination that an order is a qualified domestic relations order which is made after the close of the 18-month period described in clause (v) shall be applied prospectively only.

(v) For purposes of this subparagraph, the 18-month period described in this clause is the 18-month period beginning with the date on which the first payment would be required to be made under the domestic relations order.

(I) If a plan fiduciary acts in accordance with part 4 of this subtitle in—

(i) treating a domestic relations order as being (or not being) a qualified domestic relations order, or

(ii) taking action under subparagraph (H),

then the plan's obligation to the participant and each alternate payee shall be discharged to the extent of any payment made pursuant to such Act.

(J) A person who is an alternate payee under a qualified domestic relations order shall be considered for purposes of any provision of this Act a beneficiary under the plan. Nothing in the preceding sentence shall permit a requirement under section 4001 of the payment of more than 1 premium with respect to a participant for any period.

(K) The term "alternate payee" means any spouse, former spouse, child, or other dependent of a participant who is recognized by a domestic relations order as having a right to receive all, or a portion of, the benefits payable under a plan with respect to such participant.

(L) This paragraph shall not apply to any plan to which paragraph (1) does not apply.

(M) Payment of benefits by a pension plan in accordance with the applicable requirements of a qualified domestic relations order shall not be treated as garnishment for purposes of section 303(a) of the Consumer Credit Protection Act.

(N) In prescribing regulations under this paragraph, the Secretary shall consult with the Secretary of the Treasury.

(4) Paragraph (1) shall not apply to any offset of a participant's benefits provided under an employee pension benefit plan against an amount that the participant is ordered or required to pay to the plan if—

(A) the order or requirement to pay arises—

(i) under a judgment of conviction for a crime involving such plan,

(ii) under a civil judgment (including a consent order or decree) entered by a court in an action brought in connection with a violation (or alleged violation) of part 4 of this subtitle, or

(iii) pursuant to a settlement agreement between the Secretary and the participant, or a settlement agreement between the Pension Benefit Guaranty Corporation and the participant, in connection with a violation (or alleged violation) of part 4 of this subtitle by a fiduciary or any other person,

(B) the judgment, order, decree, or settlement agreement expressly provides for the offset of all or part of the amount ordered or required to be paid to the plan against the participant's benefits provided under the plan, and

(C) in a case in which the survivor annuity requirements of section 205 apply with respect to distributions from the plan to the participant, if the participant has a spouse at the time at which the offset is to be made—

(i) either—

(I) such spouse has consented in writing to such offset and such consent is witnessed by a notary public or representative of the plan (or it is established to the satisfaction of a plan representative that such consent may not be obtained by reason of circumstances described in section 205(c)(2)(B)), or

(II) an election to waive the right of the spouse to a qualified joint and survivor annuity or a qualified preretirement survivor annuity is in effect in accordance with the requirements of section 205(c),

(ii) such spouse is ordered or required in such judgment, order, decree, or settlement to pay an amount to the plan in connection with a violation of part 4 of this subtitle, or

(iii) in such judgment, order, decree, or settlement, such spouse retains the right to receive the survivor annuity under a qualified joint and survivor annuity provided pursuant to section 205(a)(1) and under a qualified preretirement survivor annuity provided pursuant to section 205(a)(2), determined in accordance with paragraph (5).

A plan shall not be treated as failing to meet the requirements of section 205 solely by reason of an offset under this paragraph.

(5)(A) The survivor annuity described in paragraph (4)(C)(iii) shall be determined as if—

(i) the participant terminated employment on the date of the offset,

(ii) there was no offset,

(iii) the plan permitted commencement of benefits only on or after normal retirement age,

(iv) the plan provided only the minimum-required qualified joint and survivor annuity, and

(v) the amount of the qualified preretirement survivor annuity under the plan is equal to the amount of the survivor annuity payable under the minimum-required qualified joint and survivor annuity.

(B) For purposes of this paragraph, the term "minimum-required qualified joint and survivor annuity" means the qualified joint and survivor annuity which is the actuarial equivalent of the participant's accrued benefit (within the meaning of section 3(23)) and under which the survivor annuity is 50 percent of the amount of the annuity which is payable during the joint lives of the participant and the spouse.

(e) LIMITATION ON DISTRIBUTIONS OTHER THAN LIFE ANNUITIES PAID BY THE PLAN.—

(1) IN GENERAL. Notwithstanding any other provision of this part, the fiduciary of a pension plan that is subject to the additional funding requirements of section 303(j)(4) shall not permit a prohibited payment to be made from a plan during a period in which such plan has a liquidity shortfall (as defined in section 303(j)(4)(E)(i)).

(2) PROHIBITED PAYMENT. For purposes of paragraph (1), the term "prohibited payment" means—

(A) any payment, in excess of the monthly amount paid under a single life annuity (plus any social security supplements described in the last sentence of section 204(b)(1)(G)), to a participant or beneficiary whose annuity starting date (as defined in section 205(h)(2)), that occurs during the period referred to in paragraph (1),

(B) any payment for the purchase of an irrevocable commitment from an insurer to pay benefits, and

(C) any other payment specified by the Secretary of the Treasury by regulations.

(3) PERIOD OF SHORTFALL. For purposes of this subsection, a plan has a liquidity shortfall during the period that there is an underpayment of an installment under section 303(j)(3) by reason of section 303(j)(4)(A).

(4) COORDINATION WITH OTHER PROVISIONS. Compliance with this subsection shall not constitute a violation of any other provision of this Act.

(f) MISSING PARTICIPANTS IN TERMINATED PLANS. In the case of a plan covered by section 4050, upon termination of the plan, benefits of missing participants shall be treated in accordance with section 4050.

(g) FUNDING-BASED LIMITS ON BENEFITS AND BENEFIT ACCRUALS UNDER SINGLE-EMPLOYER PLANS.—

(1) FUNDING-BASED LIMITATION ON SHUTDOWN BENEFITS AND OTHER UNPREDICTABLE CONTINGENT EVENT BENEFITS UNDER SINGLE-EMPLOYER PLANS.—

(A) IN GENERAL. If a participant of a defined benefit plan which is a single-employer plan is entitled to an unpredictable contingent event benefit payable with respect to any event occurring during any plan year, the plan shall provide that such benefit may not be provided if the adjusted funding target attainment percentage for such plan year —

(i) is less than 60 percent, or

(ii) would be less than 60 percent taking into account such occurrence.

(B) EXEMPTION. Subparagraph (A) shall cease to apply with respect to any plan year, effective as of the first day of the plan year, upon payment by the plan sponsor of a contribution (in addition to any minimum required contribution under section 303) equal to —

(i) in the case of subparagraph (A)(i), the amount of the increase in the funding target of the plan (under section 303) for the plan year attributable to the occurrence referred to in subparagraph (A), and

(ii) in the case of subparagraph (A)(ii), the amount sufficient to result in an adjusted funding target attainment percentage of 60 percent.

(C) UNPREDICTABLE CONTINGENT EVENT BENEFIT. For purposes of this paragraph, the term "unpredictable contingent event benefit" means any benefit payable solely by reason of —

(i) a plant shutdown (or similar event, as determined by the Secretary of the Treasury), or

(ii) an event other than the attainment of any age, performance of any service, receipt or derivation of any compensation, or occurrence of death or disability.

(2) LIMITATIONS ON PLAN AMENDMENTS INCREASING LIABILITY FOR BENEFITS.—

(A) IN GENERAL. No amendment to a defined benefit plan which is a single-employer plan which has the effect of increasing liabilities of the plan by reason of increases in benefits, establishment of new benefits, changing the rate of benefit accrual, or changing the rate at which benefits become nonforfeitable may take effect during any plan year if the adjusted funding target attainment percentage for such plan year is —

(i) less than 80 percent, or

(ii) would be less than 80 percent taking into account such amendment.

(B) EXEMPTION. Subparagraph (A) shall cease to apply with respect to any plan year, effective as of the first day of the plan year (or if later, the effective date of the amendment), upon payment by the plan sponsor of a contribution (in addition to any minimum required contribution under section 303) equal to —

(i) in the case of subparagraph (A)(i), the amount of the increase in the funding target of the plan (under section 303) for the plan year attributable to the amendment, and

(ii) in the case of subparagraph (A)(ii), the amount sufficient to result in an adjusted funding target attainment percentage of 80 percent.

(C) EXCEPTION FOR CERTAIN BENEFIT INCREASES. Subparagraph (A) shall not apply to any amendment which provides for an increase in benefits under a formula which is not based on a participant's compensation, but only if the rate of such increase is not in excess of the contemporaneous rate of increase in average wages of participants covered by the amendment.

(3) LIMITATIONS ON ACCELERATED BENEFIT DISTRIBUTIONS.—

(A) FUNDING PERCENTAGE LESS THAN 60 PERCENT. A defined benefit plan which is a single-employer plan shall provide that, in any case in which the plan's adjusted funding target attainment percentage for a plan year is less than 60 percent, the plan may not pay any prohibited payment after the valuation date for the plan year.

(B) BANKRUPTCY. A defined benefit plan which is a single-employer plan shall provide that, during any period in which the plan sponsor is a debtor in a case under title 11, United States Code, or similar Federal or State law, the plan may not pay any prohibited payment. The preceding sentence shall not apply on or after the date on which the enrolled actuary of the plan certifies that the adjusted funding target attainment percentage of such plan (determined by not taking into account any adjustment of segment rates under section 303(h)(2)(C)(iv)) is not less than 100 percent.

(C) LIMITED PAYMENT IF PERCENTAGE AT LEAST 60 PERCENT BUT LESS THAN 80 PERCENT.—

(i) IN GENERAL. A defined benefit plan which is a single-employer plan shall provide that, in any case in which the plan's adjusted funding target attainment percentage for a plan year is 60 percent or greater but less than 80 percent, the plan may not pay any prohibited payment after the valuation date for the plan year to the extent the amount of the payment exceeds the lesser of—

(I) 50 percent of the amount of the payment which could be made without regard to this subsection, or

(II) the present value (determined under guidance prescribed by the Pension Benefit Guaranty Corporation, using the interest and mortality assumptions under section 205(g)) of the maximum guarantee with respect to the participant under section 4022.

(ii) ONE-TIME APPLICATION.—

(I) IN GENERAL. The plan shall also provide that only 1 prohibited payment meeting the requirements of clause (i) may be made with respect to any participant during any period of consecutive plan years to which the limitations under either subparagraph (A) or (B) or this subparagraph applies.

(II) TREATMENT OF BENEFICIARIES. For purposes of this clause, a participant and any beneficiary on his behalf (including an alternate payee, as defined in section 206(d)(3)(K)) shall be treated as 1 participant. If the accrued benefit of a participant is allocated to such an alternate payee and 1 or more other persons, the amount under clause (i) shall be allocated among such persons in the same manner as the accrued benefit is allocated unless the qualified domestic relations order (as defined in section 206(d)(3)(B)(i)) provides otherwise.

(D) EXCEPTION. This paragraph shall not apply to any plan for any plan year if the terms of such plan (as in effect for the period beginning on September 1, 2005, and ending with such plan year) provide for no benefit accruals with respect to any participant during such period.

(E) PROHIBITED PAYMENT. For purpose of this paragraph, the term "prohibited payment" means —

(i) any payment, in excess of the monthly amount paid under a single life annuity (plus any social security supplements described in the last sentence of section 204(b)(1)(G)), to a participant or beneficiary whose annuity starting date (as defined in section 205(h)(2)) occurs during any period a limitation under subparagraph (A) or (B) is in effect,

(ii) any payment for the purchase of an irrevocable commitment from an insurer to pay benefits, and

(iii) any other payment specified by the Secretary of the Treasury by regulations.

Such term shall not include the payment of a benefit which under section 203(e) may be immediately distributed without the consent of the participant.

(4) LIMITATION ON BENEFIT ACCRUALS FOR PLANS WITH SEVERE FUNDING SHORTFALLS.—

(A) IN GENERAL. A defined benefit plan which is a single-employer plan shall provide that, in any case in which the plan's adjusted funding target attainment percentage for a plan year is less than 60 percent, benefit accruals under the plan shall cease as of the valuation date for the plan year.

(B) EXEMPTION. Subparagraph (A) shall cease to apply with respect to any plan year, effective as of the first day of the plan year, upon payment by the plan sponsor of a contribution (in addition to any minimum required contribution under section 303) equal to the amount sufficient to result in an adjusted funding target attainment percentage of 60 percent.

(5) RULES RELATING TO CONTRIBUTIONS REQUIRED TO AVOID BENEFIT LIMITATIONS.—

(A) SECURITY MAY BE PROVIDED.—

(i) IN GENERAL. For purposes of this subsection, the adjusted funding target attainment percentage shall be determined by treating as an asset of the plan any security provided by a plan sponsor in a form meeting the requirements of clause (ii).

(ii) FORM OF SECURITY. The security required under clause (i) shall consist of —

(I) a bond issued by a corporate surety company that is an acceptable surety for purposes of section 412 of this Act,

(II) cash, or United States obligations which mature in 3 years or less, held in escrow by a bank or similar financial institution, or

(III) such other form of security as is satisfactory to the Secretary of the Treasury and the parties involved.

(iii) ENFORCEMENT. Any security provided under clause (i) may be perfected and enforced at any time after the earlier of —

(I) the date on which the plan terminates,

(II) if there is a failure to make a payment of the minimum required contribution for any plan year beginning after the security is provided, the due date for the payment under section 303(j), or

(III) if the adjusted funding target attainment percentage is less than 60 percent for a consecutive period of 7 years, the valuation date for the last year in the period.

(iv) RELEASE OF SECURITY. The security shall be released (and any amounts thereunder shall be refunded together with any interest accrued thereon) at such time as the Secretary of the Treasury may prescribe in regulations, including regulations for partial releases of the security by reason of increases in the adjusted funding target attainment percentage.

(B) PREFUNDING BALANCE OR FUNDING STANDARD CARRYOVER BALANCE MAY NOT BE USED. No prefunding balance or funding standard carryover balance under section 303(f) may be used under paragraph (1), (2), or (4) to satisfy any payment an employer may make under any such paragraph to avoid or terminate the application of any limitation under such paragraph.

(C) DEEMED REDUCTION OF FUNDING BALANCES. (i) IN GENERAL. Subject to clause (iii), in any case in which a benefit limitation under paragraph (1), (2), (3), or (4) would (but for this subparagraph and determined without regard to paragraph (1)(B), (2)(B), or (4)(B)) apply to such plan for the plan year, the plan sponsor of such plan shall be treated for purposes of this Act as having made an election under section 303(f) to reduce the prefunding balance or funding standard carryover balance by such amount as is necessary for such benefit limitation to not apply to the plan for such plan year.

(ii) EXCEPTION FOR INSUFFICIENT FUNDING BALANCES. Clause (i) shall not apply with respect to a benefit limitation for any plan year if the application of clause (i) would not result in the benefit limitation not applying for such plan year.

(iii) RESTRICTIONS OF CERTAIN RULES TO COLLECTIVELY BARGAINED PLANS. With respect to any benefit limitation under paragraph (1), (2), or (4), clause (i) shall only apply in the case of a plan maintained pursuant to 1 or more collective bargaining agreements between employee representatives and 1 or more employers.

(6) NEW PLANS. Paragraphs (1), (2) and (4) shall not apply to a plan for the first 5 plan years of the plan. For purposes of this paragraph, the reference in this paragraph to a plan shall include a reference to any predecessor plan.

(7) PRESUMED UNDERFUNDING FOR PURPOSES OF BENEFIT LIMITATIONS.—

(A) PRESUMPTION OF CONTINUED UNDERFUNDING. In any case in which a benefit limitation under paragraph (1), (2), (3), or (4) has been applied to a plan with respect to the plan year preceding the current plan year, the adjusted funding target attainment percentage of the plan for the current plan year shall be presumed to be equal to the adjusted funding target attainment percentage of the plan for the preceding plan year until the enrolled actuary of the plan certifies the actual adjusted funding target attainment percentage of the plan for the current plan year.

(B) PRESUMPTION OF UNDERFUNDING AFTER 10TH MONTH. In any case in which no certification of the adjusted funding target attainment percentage for the current plan year is made with respect to the plan before the first day of the 10th month of such year, for purposes of paragraphs (1), (2), (3), and (4), such first day shall be deemed, for purposes of such paragraph, to be the valuation date of the plan for the current plan year and the plan's adjusted funding target attainment percentage shall be conclusively presumed to be less than 60 percent as of such first day.

(C) PRESUMPTION OF UNDERFUNDING AFTER 4TH MONTH FOR NEARLY UNDERFUNDED PLANS. In any case in which—

(i) a benefit limitation under paragraph (1), (2), (3), or (4) did not apply to a plan with respect to the plan year preceding the current plan year, but the adjusted funding target attainment percentage of the plan for such preceding plan year was not more than 10 percentage points greater than the percentage which would have caused such paragraph to apply to the plan with respect to such preceding plan year, and

(ii) as of the first day of the 4th month of the current plan year, the enrolled actuary of the plan has not certified the actual adjusted funding target attainment percentage of the plan for the current plan year,

until the enrolled actuary so certifies, such first day shall be deemed, for purposes of such paragraph, to be the valuation date of the plan for the current plan year and the adjusted funding target attainment percentage of the plan as of such first day shall, for purposes of such paragraph, be presumed to be equal to 10 percentage points less than the adjusted funding target attainment percentage of the plan for such preceding plan year.

(8) TREATMENT OF PLAN AS OF CLOSE OF PROHIBITED OR CESSATION PERIOD. For purposes of applying this part—

(A) OPERATION OF PLAN AFTER PERIOD. Unless the plan provides otherwise, payments and accruals will resume effective as of the day following the close of the period for which any limitation of payment or accrual of benefits under paragraph (3) or (4) applies.

(B) TREATMENT OF AFFECTED BENEFITS. Nothing in this paragraph shall be construed as affecting the plan's treatment of benefits which would have been paid or accrued but for this subsection.

(9) TERMS RELATING TO FUNDING TARGET ATTAINMENT PERCENTAGE. For purposes of this subsection—

(A) IN GENERAL. The term "funding target attainment percentage" has the same meaning given such term by section 303(d)(2).

(B) ADJUSTED FUNDING TARGET ATTAINMENT PERCENTAGE. The term "adjusted funding target attainment percentage" means the funding target attainment percentage which is determined under subparagraph (A) by increasing each of the amounts under subparagraphs (A) and (B) of section

303(d)(2) by the aggregate amount of purchases of annuities for employees other than highly compensated employees (as defined in section 414(q) of the Internal Revenue Code of 1986) which were made by the plan during the preceding 2 plan years

(C) APPLICATION TO PLANS WHICH ARE FULLY FUNDED WITHOUT REGARD TO REDUCTIONS FOR FUNDING BALANCES.—

In the case of a plan for any plan year, if the funding target attainment percentage is 100 percent or more (determined without regard to the reduction in the value of assets under section 303(f)(4)), the funding target attainment percentage for purposes of subparagraphs (A) and (B) shall be determined without regard to such reduction.

(10) SECRETARIAL AUTHORITY FOR PLANS WITH ALTERNATE VALUATION DATE. In the case of a plan which has designated a valuation date other than the first day of the plan year, the Secretary of the Treasury may prescribe rules for the application of this subsection which are necessary to reflect the alternate valuation date.

(12) CSEC PLANS. This subsection shall not apply to a CSEC plan (as defined in section 210(f)).

Amendments

P.L. 113-295, §221(a)(57)(E)(ii), Div. A:

Amended ERISA Sec. 206(g)(9)(C) by striking clauses (ii) and (iii) and by striking "(i) In general.—". Prior to being stricken, ERISA Sec. 206(g)(9)(C)(ii) and (iii) read as follows:

(ii) Transition rule.—Clause (i) shall be applied to plan years beginning after 2007 and before 2011 by substituting for "100 percent" the applicable percentage determined in accordance with the following table:

In the case of a plan year beginning in calendar year	The applicable percentage is—
2008	92
2009	94
2010	96 .

(iii) Limitation.—Clause (ii) shall not apply with respect to any plan year beginning after 2008 unless the funding target attainment percentage (determined without regard to the reduction in the value of assets under section 303(f)(4)) of the plan for each preceding plan year beginning after 2007 was not less than the applicable percentage with respect to such preceding plan year determined under clause (ii).

The above amendments shall take effect on the date of enactment of this Act [December 19, 2014.-CCH.]. For a special rule, see Act Sec. 221(b)(2), Div. A, below.

P.L. 113-295, §221(b)(2), Div. A, provides:

(2) Savings provision.—If—

(A) any provision amended or repealed by the amendments made by this section applied to—

(i) any transaction occurring before the date of the enactment of this Act,

(ii) any property acquired before such date of enactment, or

(iii) any item of income, loss, deduction, or credit taken into account before such date of enactment, and

(B) the treatment of such transaction, property, or item under such provision would (without regard to the amendments or repeals made by this section) affect the liability for tax for periods ending after date of enactment, nothing in the amendments or repeals made by this section shall be construed to affect the treatment of such transaction, property, or item for purposes of determining liability for tax for periods ending after such date of enactment.

P.L. 113-295, §221(a)(57)(F)(ii), Div. A:

Amended ERISA Sec. 206(g)(9) by striking subparagraph (D). Prior to being stricken, ERISA Sec. 206(g)(9)(D) read as follows:

(D) Special rule for certain years.—Solely for purposes of any applicable provision—

(i) In general.—For plan years beginning on or after October 1, 2008, and before October 1, 2010, the adjusted funding target attainment percentage of a plan shall be the greater of—

(I) such percentage, as determined without regard to this subparagraph, or

(II) the adjusted funding target attainment percentage for such plan for the plan year beginning after October 1, 2007, and before October 1, 2008, as determined under rules prescribed by the Secretary of the Treasury.

(ii) Special rule.—In the case of a plan for which the valuation date is not the first day of the plan year—

(I) clause (i) shall apply to plan years beginning after December 31, 2007, and before January 1, 2010, and

(II) clause (i)(II) shall apply based on the last plan year beginning before November 1, 2007, as determined under rules prescribed by the Secretary of the Treasury.

(iii) Applicable provision.—For purposes of this subparagraph, the term 'applicable provision' means—

(I) paragraph (3), but only for purposes of applying such paragraph to a payment which, as determined under rules prescribed by the Secretary of the Treasury, is a payment under a social security leveling option which accelerates payments under the plan before, and reduces payments after, a participant starts receiving social security benefits in order to provide substantially similar aggregate payments both before and after such benefits are received, and

(II) paragraph (4).

The above amendments shall take effect on the date of enactment of this Act [December 19, 2014.-CCH.]. For a special rule, see Act Sec. 221(b)(2), Div. A, below.

P.L. 113-295, §221(b)(2), Div. A, provides:

(2) Savings provision.—If—

(A) any provision amended or repealed by the amendments made by this section applied to—

(i) any transaction occurring before the date of the enactment of this Act,

(ii) any property acquired before such date of enactment, or

(iii) any item of income, loss, deduction, or credit taken into account before such date of enactment, and

(B) the treatment of such transaction, property, or item under such provision would (without regard to the amendments or repeals made by this section) affect the liability for tax for periods ending after date of enactment, nothing in the amendments or repeals made by this section shall be construed to affect the treatment of such transaction, property, or item for purposes of determining liability for tax for periods ending after such date of enactment.

P.L. 113-295, §221(a)(57)(G)(ii), Div. A:

Amended ERISA Sec. 206(g) by striking paragraph (11). Prior to being stricken, ERISA Sec. 206(g)(11) read as follows:

(11) Special rule for 2008.—For purposes of this subsection, in the case of plan years beginning in 2008, the funding target attainment percentage for the preceding plan year may be determined using such methods of estimation as the Secretary of the Treasury may provide.

The above amendment shall take effect on the date of enactment of this Act [December 19, 2014.-CCH.]. For a special rule, see Act Sec. 221(b)(2), Div. A, below.

P.L. 113-295, §221(b)(2), Div. A, provides:

(2) Savings provision.—If—

(A) any provision amended or repealed by the amendments made by this section applied to—

(i) any transaction occurring before the date of the enactment of this Act,

(ii) any property acquired before such date of enactment, or

(iii) any item of income, loss, deduction, or credit taken into account before such date of enactment, and

(B) the treatment of such transaction, property, or item under such provision would (without regard to the amendments or repeals made by this section) affect the liability for tax for periods ending after date of enactment, nothing in the amendments or repeals made by this section shall be construed to affect the treatment of such transaction, property, or item for purposes of determining liability for tax for periods ending after such date of enactment.

P.L. 113-159, §2003(c)(2):

Amended the second sentence of ERISA Sec. 206(g)(3)(B) by striking "of such plan" and inserting "of such plan (determined by not taking into account any adjustment of segment rates under section 303(h)(2)(C)(iv))".

For the effective date, see Act Sec. 2003(c)(3)-(4), below.

P.L. 113-159, §2003(c)(3) provides:

(3) EFFECTIVE DATE.—

(A) IN GENERAL.—Except as provided in subparagraph (B), the amendments made by this subsection shall apply to plan years beginning after December 31, 2014.

(B) COLLECTIVELY BARGAINED PLANS.—In the case of a plan maintained pursuant to 1 or more collective bargaining agreements, the amendments made by this subsection shall apply to plan years beginning after December 31, 2015.

(4) PROVISIONS RELATING TO PLAN AMENDMENTS.—

(A) IN GENERAL.—If this paragraph applies to any amendment to any plan or annuity contract, such plan or contract shall be treated as being operated in accordance with the terms of the plan during the period described in subparagraph (B)(ii).

(B) AMENDMENTS TO WHICH PARAGRAPH APPLIES.—

(i) In general.—This paragraph shall apply to any amendment to any plan or annuity contract which is made—

(I) pursuant to the amendments made by this subsection, or pursuant to any regulation issued by the Secretary of the Treasury or the Secretary of Labor under any provision as so amended, and

(II) on or before the last day of the first plan year beginning on or after January 1, 2016, or such later date as the Secretary of the Treasury may prescribe.

(ii) CONDITIONS.—This subsection shall not apply to any amendment unless, during the period—

(I) beginning on the date that the amendments made by this subsection or the regulation described in clause (i)(I) takes effect (or in the case of a plan or contract amendment not required by such amendments or such regulation, the effective date specified by the plan), and

(II) ending on the date described in clause (i)(II) (or, if earlier, the date the plan or contract amendment is adopted), the plan or contract is operated as if such plan or contract amendment were in effect, and such plan or contract amendment applies retroactively for such period.

(C) ANTI-CUTBACK RELIEF.—A plan shall not be treated as failing to meet the requirements of section 204(g) of the Employee Retirement Income Security Act of

1974 (29 U.S.C. 1054(g)) and section 411(d)(6) of the Internal Revenue Code of 1986 solely by reason of a plan amendment to which this paragraph applies.

P.L. 113-97, §102(b)(3):

Amended ERISA Sec. 206(g) by adding at the end a new paragraph (12) to read as above.

Effective for years beginning after 12-31-2013.

P.L. 111-192, §203(a)(1):

Amended ERISA Sec. 206(g)(9) by adding new subparagraph (D) to read as above.

Except as provided below, the above amendment applies to plan years beginning on or after October 1, 2008. In the case of a plan for which the valuation date is not the first day of the plan year, the above amendment applies to plan years beginning after December 31, 2007.

P.L. 111-192, §203(b) provides:

INTERACTION WITH WRERA RULE.—Section 203 of the Worker, Retiree, and Employer Recovery Act of 2008 shall apply to a plan for any plan year in lieu of the amendments made by this section applying to sections 206(g)(4) of the Employee Retirement Income Security Act of 1974 and 436(e) of the Internal Revenue Code of 1986 only to the extent that such section produces a higher adjusted funding target attainment percentage for such plan for such year.

P.L. 110-458, §101(c)(1)(B):

Amended ERISA Sec. 206(g)(1)(B)(ii) by striking "a funding" and inserting "an adjusted funding".

The above amendment takes effect as if included in the provisions of the 2006 Act to which the amendment relates. For effective date, see P.L. 109-280, §103(c), below.

P.L. 110-458, §101(c)(1)(C):

Amended the heading for ERISA Sec. 206(g)(1)(C) by inserting "BENEFIT" after "EVENT".

The above amendment takes effect as if included in the provisions of the 2006 Act to which the amendment relates. For effective date, see P.L. 109-280, §103(c), below.

P.L. 110-458, §101(c)(1)(D):

Amended ERISA Sec. 206(g)(3)(E) by adding at the end the following new flush sentence:

Such term shall not include the payment of a benefit which under section 203(e) may be immediately distributed without the consent of the participant.

The above amendment takes effect as if included in the provisions of the 2006 Act to which the amendment relates. For effective date, see P.L. 109-280, §103(c), below.

P.L. 110-458, §101(c)(1)(E):

Amended ERISA Sec. 206(g)(5)(A)(iv) by inserting "adjusted" before "funding".

The above amendment takes effect as if included in the provisions of the 2006 Act to which the amendment relates. For effective date, see P.L. 109-280, §103(c), below.

P.L. 110-458, §101(c)(1)(F)(i):

Amended ERISA Sec. 206(g)(9)(C)(i) by striking "without regard to this subparagraph and".

The above amendment takes effect as if included in the provisions of the 2006 Act to which the amendment relates. For effective date, see P.L. 109-280, §103(c), below.

P.L. 110-458, §101(c)(1)(F)(ii)(I):

Amended ERISA Sec. 206(g)(9)(C)(iii) by striking "without regard to this subparagraph" and inserting "without regard to the reduction in the value of assets under section 303(f)(4)".

The above amendment takes effect as if included in the provisions of the 2006 Act to which the amendment relates. For effective date, see P.L. 109-280, §103(c), below.

P.L. 110-458, §101(c)(1)(F)(ii)(II):

Amended ERISA Sec. 206(g)(9)(C)(iii) by inserting "beginning" before "after" each place it appears.

The above amendments take effect as if included in the provisions of the 2006 Act to which the amendment relates. For effective date, see P.L. 109-280, §103(c), below.

P.L. 110-458, §101(c)(1)(G):

Amended ERISA Sec. 206(g) by redesignating paragraph (10) as paragraph (11) and by inserting after paragraph (9) a new paragraph (10) to read as above.

The above amendments take effect as if included in the provisions of the 2006 Act to which the amendment relates. For effective date, see P.L. 109-280, §103(c), below.

P.L. 109-280, §103(a):

Amended ERISA Sec. 206, by adding new paragraph (g) to read as above.

For effective dates, see §103(c) below.

P.L. 109-280, §103(c):

103(c) EFFECTIVE DATES.—

103(c)(1) IN GENERAL.—The amendments made by this section shall apply to plan years beginning after December 31, 2007.

103(c)(2) COLLECTIVE BARGAINING EXCEPTION.—In the case of a plan maintained pursuant to 1 or more collective bargaining agreements between employee

representatives and 1 or more employers ratified before January 1, 2008, the amendments made by this section shall not apply to plan years beginning before the earlier of—

103(c)(2)(A) the later of—

103(c)(2)(A)(i) the date on which the last collective bargaining agreement relating to the plan terminates (determined without regard to any extension thereof agreed to after the date of the enactment of this Act), or

103(c)(2)(A)(ii) the first day of the first plan year to which the amendments made by this subsection would (but for this subparagraph) apply, or

103(c)(2)(B) January 1, 2010.

For purposes of subparagraph (A)(i), any plan amendment made pursuant to a collective bargaining agreement relating to the plan which amends the plan solely to conform to any requirement added by this section shall not be treated as a termination of such collective bargaining agreement.

P.L. 109-280, §107(a)(9):

Amended ERISA Sec. 206(e)(1), by striking "section 302(d)" and inserting "section 303(j)(4)", and by striking "section 302(e)(5)" and inserting "section 303(j)(4)(E)(i)".

The above amendment applies to plan years beginning after 2007.

P.L. 109-280, §107(a)(10):

Amended ERISA Sec. 206(e)(3), by striking "section 302(e) by reason of paragraph (5)(A) thereof" and inserting "section 303(j)(3) by reason of section 303(j)(4)(A)".

The above amendment applies to plan years beginning after 2007.

P.L. 109-280, §410(b)(1)-(2):

Amended ERISA Sec. 206(f), by striking "title IV" and inserting "section 4050"; and by striking "the plan shall provide that,".

The above amendment applies to distributions made after final regulations implementing ERISA Secs. 4050(c) and 4050(d) are prescribed.

P.L. 105-34, §1502(a):

Act Sec. 1502(a) amended ERISA Sec. 206(d) by adding paragraphs (4) and (5) to read as above.

The above amendment applies to judgments, orders, and decrees issued, and settlement agreements entered into, on or after August 5, 1997.

P.L. 103-465, §761(a)(9)(B)(i):

Act Sec. 761(a)(9)(B)(i) amended ERISA Sec. 206 by adding subsection (e) to read as above.

The above amendment applies to plan years beginning after December 31, 1994.

P.L. 103-465, §776(c)(2):

Act Sec. 776(c)(2) amended ERISA Sec. 206 by adding subsection (f) to read as above.

The above amendment is effective with respect to distributions that occur in plan years commencing after final regulations implementing these provisions are prescribed by the Pension Benefit Guaranty Corporation.

P.L. 101-239, §7894(c)(8):

Amended ERISA Sec. 206(a)(1) by inserting "occurs" after "(1)," effective September 2, 1974.

P.L. 101-239, §7894(c)(9):

Amended ERISA Sec. 206(d)(3)(I) by striking "act" and inserting "Act," effective as if included in P.L. 98-397, §104.

P.L. 99-514, §1898(c)(2)(B)(i):

Amended ERISA Sec. 206(d)(3)(H)(i) by striking out "shall segregate in a separate account in the plan or in an escrow account the amounts" and inserted "shall separately account for the amounts (hereinafter in this subparagraph referred to as the 'segregated amounts')" instead, effective January 1, 1985.

P.L. 99-514, §1898(c)(2)(B)(ii):

Amended ERISA Sec. 206(d)(3)(h)(ii) by striking out "18-months" and inserting "the 18-month period described in clause (c)" and by striking out "plus any interest" and inserting "including any interest" instead, effective January 1, 1985.

P.L. 99-514, §1898(c)(2)(B)(iii):

Amended ERISA Sec. 206(d)(3)(H)(iii) by striking out "18-months" and inserting "the 18-month period described in clause (v)" and by striking out "plus any interest" and inserting "including any interest" instead, effective January 1, 1985.

P.L. 99-514, §1898(c)(2)(B)(iv):

Amended ERISA Sec. 206(d)(3)(H)(iv) by striking out "the 18-month period" and inserting "the 18-month period described in clause (v)" instead, effective January 1, 1985.

P.L. 99-514, §1898(c)(2)(B)(v):

Added ERISA Sec. 206(d)(3)(H)(v) to read as above, effective January 1, 1985.

P.L. 99-514, §1898(c)(4)(B):

Amended ERISA Sec. 206(d)(3) by redesignating subparagraph (L) as (N) and by inserting a new subparagraph (L) to read as above, effective January 1, 1985.

P.L. 99-514, §1898(c)(5):

Added new ERISA Sec. 206(d)(3)(M) to read as above, effective January 1, 1985.

P.L. 99-514, §1898(c)(6)(B):

Amended ERISA Sec. 206(d)(3)(F)(i) by striking out "section 205" and inserting "section 205 (and any spouse of the participant shall not be treated as a spouse of the participant for such purposes)" instead, effective January 1, 1985.

Amended ERISA Sec. 206(d)(3)(F)(ii) by striking out "the former spouse" and inserting "the surviving former spouse" instead, effective January 1, 1985.

Amended ERISA Sec. 206(d)(3)(G)(i)(I) by striking out "any other alternate payee" and inserting "each alternate payee" instead, effective January 1, 1985.

Amended ERISA Sec. 206(d)(3)(E) by striking out "In the case of any payment before a participant has separated from service, a" in clause (i) and inserting "A" and by inserting "in the case of any payment before a participant has separated from service," before "on or" in subclause (I), effective January 1, 1985.

Amended ERISA Sec. 206(d)(3)(E)(ii) to read as above, effective January 1, 1985. Prior to amendment, clause (ii) read as follows:

(ii) For purposes of this subparagraph, the term "earliest retirement age" has the meaning given such term by section 205(h)(3), except that in the case of any individual

account plan, the earliest retirement age shall be the date which is 10 years before the normal retirement age.

P.L. 98-397, § 104:

Act Sec. 104(a) amended ERISA Sec. 206(d) by adding a new paragraph (3) to read as above.

The above amendment is to take effect as provided by Act Sec. 303(d) which follows:

(d) Amendments Relating to Assignments in Divorce, Etc., Proceedings.—The amendments made by sections 104 and 204 shall take effect on January 1, 1985, except that in the case of a domestic relations order entered before such date, the plan administrator—

(1) shall treat such order as a qualified domestic relations order if such administrator is paying benefits pursuant to such order on such date, and

(2) may treat any other such order entered before such date as a qualified domestic relations order even if such order does not meet the requirements of such amendments.

Regulations

The following final regulation was published in the Federal Register on June 10, 2010 (75 FR 32846). Interim final rules were published on March 7, 2007 (72 FR 10070).

[¶ 14,465]

§ 2530.206 Time and order of issuance of domestic relations orders.

(a) *Scope.*. This section implements section 1001 of the Pension Protection Act of 2006 by clarifying certain timing issues with respect to domestic relations orders and qualified domestic relations orders under the Employee Retirement Income Security Act of 1974, as amended (ERISA), 29 U.S.C. 1001 *et seq.* The examples herein illustrate the application of this section in certain circumstances. This section also applies in circumstances not described in the examples.

(b) *Subsequent domestic relations orders.*. (1) Subject to paragraph (d)(1) of this section, a domestic relations order shall not fail to be treated as a qualified domestic relations order solely because the order is issued after, or revises, another domestic relations order or qualified domestic relations order.

(2) The rule described in paragraph (b)(1) of this section is illustrated by the following examples:

Example (1). Subsequent domestic relations order between the same parties. Participant and Spouse divorce, and the administrator of Participant's 401(k) plan receives a domestic relations order. The administrator determines that the order is a QDRO. The QDRO allocates a portion of Participant's benefits to Spouse as the alternate payee. Subsequently, before benefit payments have commenced, Participant and Spouse seek and receive a second domestic relations order. The second order reduces the portion of Participant's benefits that Spouse was to receive under the QDRO. The second order does not fail to be treated as a QDRO solely because the second order is issued after, and reduces the prior assignment contained in, the first order. The result would be the same if the order were instead to increase the prior assignment contained in the first order.

Example (2). Subsequent domestic relations order between different parties. Participant and Spouse 1 divorce and the administrator of Participant's 401(k) plan receives a domestic relations order. The administrator determines that the order is a QDRO. The QDRO allocates a portion of Participant's benefits to Spouse 1 as the alternate payee. Participant marries Spouse 2, and then they divorce. Participant's 401(k) plan administrator subsequently receives a domestic relations order pertaining to Spouse 2. The order assigns to Spouse 2 a portion of Participant's 401(k) benefits not already allocated to Spouse 1. The second order does not fail to be a QDRO solely because the second order is issued after the plan administrator has determined that an earlier order pertaining to Spouse 1 is a QDRO.

(c) *Timing.*. (1) Subject to paragraph (d)(1) of this section, a domestic relations order shall not fail to be treated as a qualified domestic relations order solely because of the time at which it is issued.

(2) The rule described in paragraph (c)(1) of this section is illustrated by the following examples:

Example (1). Orders issued after death. Participant and Spouse divorce, and the administrator of Participant's plan receives a domestic relations order, but the administrator finds the order deficient and determines that it is not a QDRO. Shortly thereafter, Participant dies while actively employed. A second domestic relations order correcting the defects in the first order is subsequently submitted to the plan. The

second order does not fail to be treated as a QDRO solely because it is issued after the death of the Participant. The result would be the same even if no order had been issued before the Participant's death, in other words, the order issued after death were the only order.

Example (2). Orders issued after divorce. Participant and Spouse divorce. As a result, Spouse no longer meets the definition of "surviving spouse" under the terms of the plan. Subsequently, the plan administrator receives a domestic relations order requiring that Spouse be treated as the Participant's surviving spouse for purposes of receiving a death benefit payable under the terms of the plan only to a participant's surviving spouse. The order does not fail to be treated as a QDRO solely because, at the time it is issued, Spouse no longer meets the definition of a "surviving spouse" under the terms of the plan.

Example (3). Orders issued after annuity starting date. Participant retires and begins receipt of benefits in the form of a straight life annuity, equal to $1,000 per month, and with respect to which Spouse has consented to the waiver of the surviving spousal rights provided under the plan and section 205 of ERISA. Subsequent to the commencement of benefits (in other words, subsequent to the annuity starting date as defined in section 205(h)(2) of ERISA and as further explained in 26 CFR 1.401(a)-20, Q&A-10(b)), Participant and Spouse divorce and present the plan with a domestic relations order requiring 50 percent ($500) of Participant's future monthly annuity payments under the plan to be paid instead to Spouse, as an alternate payee (so that monthly payments of $500 are to be made to Spouse during Participant's lifetime). Pursuant to paragraph (c)(1) of this section, the order does not fail to be a QDRO solely because it is issued after the annuity starting date. If the order instead had required payments to Spouse for the lifetime of Spouse, this would constitute a reannuitization with a new annuity starting date, rather than merely allocating to Spouse a part of the determined annuity payments due to Participant, so that the order, while not failing to be a QDRO because of the timing of the order, would fail to meet the requirements of section 206(d)(3)(D)(i) of ERISA (unless the plan otherwise permits such a change after the participant's annuity starting date). See 29 CFR 2530.206(d)(2), Example (4).

(d) *Requirements and protections.*. (1) Any domestic relations order described in this section shall be a qualified domestic relations order only if the order satisfies the same requirements and protections that apply under section 206(d)(3) of ERISA.

(2) The rule described in paragraph (d)(1) of this section is illustrated by the following examples:

Example (1). Type or form of benefit. Participant and Spouse divorce, and their divorce decree provides that the parties will prepare a domestic relations order assigning 50 percent of Participant's benefits under a 401(k) plan to Spouse to be paid in monthly installments over a 10-year period. Shortly thereafter, Participant dies while actively employed. A domestic relations order consistent with the divorce decree is subsequently submitted to the 401(k) plan; however, the plan does not provide for 10-year installment payments of the type described in the order. Pursuant to paragraph (c)(1) of this section, the order does not fail to be treated as a QDRO solely because it is issued after the death of Participant, but the order would fail to be a QDRO under section 206(d)(3)(D)(i) and paragraph (d)(1) of this section because the order requires the plan to provide a type or form of benefit, or any option, not otherwise provided under the plan.

Example (2). Segregation of payable benefits. Participant and Spouse divorce, and the administrator of Participant's plan receives a domestic relations order under which Spouse would begin to receive benefits immediately if the order is determined to be a QDRO. The plan administrator separately accounts for the amounts covered by the domestic relations order as is required under section 206(d)(3)(H)(v) of ERISA. The plan administrator finds the order deficient and determines that it is not a QDRO. Subsequently, after the expiration of the segregation period pertaining to that order, the plan administrator receives a second domestic relations order relating to the same parties under which Spouse would begin to receive benefits immediately if the second order is determined to be a QDRO. Notwithstanding the expiration of the first segregation period, the amounts covered by the second order must be separately accounted for by the plan administrator for an 18-month period, in accordance with section 206(d)(3)(H) of ERISA and paragraph (d)(1) of this section.

Example (3). Previously assigned benefits. Participant and Spouse 1 divorce, and the administrator of Participant's 401(k) plan receives a domestic relations order. The administrator determines that the order is a QDRO. The QDRO assigns a portion of Participant's benefits to Spouse 1 as the alternate payee. Participant marries Spouse 2, and then they divorce. Participant's 401(k) plan administrator subsequently receives a domestic relations order pertaining to Spouse 2. The order assigns to Spouse 2 a portion of Participant's 401(k) benefits already assigned to Spouse 1. The second order does not fail to be treated as a QDRO solely because the second order is issued after the plan admin-

istrator has determined that an earlier order pertaining to Spouse 1 is a QDRO. The second order, however, would fail to be a QDRO under section 206(d)(3)(D)(iii) and paragraph (d)(1) of this section because it assigns to Spouse 2 all or a portion of Participant's benefits that are already assigned to Spouse 1 by the prior QDRO.

Example (4). Type or form of benefit. Participant retires and commences benefit payments in the form of a straight life annuity based on the life of Participant, with respect to which Spouse consents to the waiver of the surviving spousal rights provided under the plan and section 205 of ERISA. Participant and Spouse divorce after the annuity starting date and present the plan with a domestic relations order that eliminates the straight life annuity based on Participant's life and provides for Spouse, as alternate payee, to receive all future benefits in the form of a straight life annuity based on the life of Spouse. The plan does not allow reannuitization with a new annuity starting date, as defined in section 205(h)(2) of ERISA (and as further explained in 26 CFR 1.401(a)-20, Q&A-10(b)). Pursuant to paragraph (c)(1) of this section, the order does not fail to be a QDRO solely because it is issued after the annuity starting date, but the order would fail to be a QDRO under section 206(d)(3)(D)(i) and paragraph (d)(1) of this section because the order requires the plan to provide a type or form of benefit, or any option, not otherwise provided under the plan. However, the order would not fail to be a QDRO under section 206(d)(3)(D)(i) and paragraph (d)(1) of this section if instead it were to require all of Participant's future payments under the plan to be paid instead to Spouse, as an alternate payee (so that payments that would otherwise be paid to the Participant during the Participant's lifetime are instead to be made to the Spouse during the Participant's lifetime). [Added 6/10/10 by 75 FR 32846.]

[¶ 14,470]
ERISA Sec. 207—Repealed

TEMPORARY VARIANCES FROM CERTAIN VESTING REQUIREMENTS

Act Sec. 207. Amendment

P.L. 109-280, § 107(d):

Amended ERISA by repealing ERISA Sec. 207.

Prior to the repeal, ERISA Sec. 207 read as follows:

In the case of any plan maintained on January 1, 1974, if, not later than 2 years after the date of enactment of this Act, the administrator petitions the Secretary, the Secretary may prescribe an alternate method which shall be treated as satisfying the requirements of section 203(a)(2) or 204(b)(1) (other than subparagraph (D) thereof) or both for a period of not more than 4 years. The Secretary may prescribe such alternate method only when he finds that—

(1) the application of such requirements would increase the costs of the plan to such an extent that there would result a substantial risk to the voluntary continuation of the

plan or a substantial curtailment of benefit levels or the levels of employees' compensation,

(2) the application of such requirement or discontinuance of the plan would be adverse to the interests of plan participants in the aggregate, and

(3) a waiver or extension of time granted under section 303 or 304 of this Act would be inadequate.

In the case of any plan with respect to which an alternate method has been prescribed under the preceding provisions of this subsection for a period of not more than 4 years, if, not later than 1 year before the expiration of such period, the administrator petitions the Secretary for an extension of such alternate method, and the Secretary makes the findings required by the preceding sentence, such alternate method may be extended for not more than 3 years.

The above amendment is effective for plan years beginning after 2007.

[¶ 14,480]
MERGERS AND CONSOLIDATIONS OF PLANS OR TRANSFERS OF PLAN ASSETS

Act Sec. 208. A pension plan may not merge or consolidate with, or transfer its assets or liabilities to, any other plan after the date of the enactment of this Act, unless each participant in the plan would (if the plan then terminated) receive a benefit immediately after the merger, consolidation, or transfer which is equal to or greater than the benefit he would have been entitled to receive immediately before the merger, consolidation, or transfer (if the plan had then terminated). The preceding sentence shall not apply to any transaction to the extent that participants either before or after the transaction are covered under a multiemployer plan to which title IV of this Act applies.

Amendment

P.L. 96-364, § 402(b)(1):

Amended Sec. 208, effective September 26, 1980, by striking out the last sentence which read "This paragraph shall apply in the case of a multiemployer plan only to the

extent determined by the Pension Benefit Guaranty Corporation" and inserting the new last sentence to read as above.

[¶ 14,490]
RECORDKEEPING AND REPORTING REQUIREMENTS

Act Sec. 209.(a)(1) Except as provided by paragraph (2) every employer shall, in accordance with such regulations as the Secretary may prescribe, maintain records with respect to each of his employees sufficient to determine the benefits due or which may become due to such employees. The plan administrator shall make a report, in such manner and at such time as may be provided in regulations prescribed by the Secretary, to each employee who is a participant under the plan and who—

(A) requests such report, in such manner and at such time as may be provided in such regulations,

(B) terminates his service with the employer, or

(C) has a 1-year break in service (as defined in section 203(b)(3)(A)).

The employer shall furnish to the plan administrator the information necessary for the administrator to make the reports required by the preceding sentence. Not more than one report shall be required under subparagraph (A) in any 12-month period. Not more than one report shall be required under subparagraph (C) with respect to consecutive 1-year breaks in service. The report required under this paragraph shall be in the same form, and contain the same information, as periodic benefit statements under section 105(a).

(2) If more than one employer adopts a plan, each such employer shall furnish to the plan administrator the information necessary for the administrator to maintain the records, and make the reports, required by paragraph (1). Such administrator shall maintain the records, and make the reports, required by paragraph (1).

Act Sec. 209. (b) If any person who is required, under subsection (a), to furnish information or maintain records for any plan year fails to comply with such requirement, he shall pay to the Secretary a civil penalty of $10 for each employee with respect to whom such failure occurs, unless it is shown that such failure is due to reasonable cause.

Amendments

P.L. 110-458, §105(f)(1)(A) and (B):

Amended ERISA Sec. 209(a)(1) by striking "regulations prescribed by the Secretary" and inserting "such regulations as the Secretary may prescribe", and by striking the last sentence and inserting a new last sentence to read as above.

The above amendments take effect as if included in the provisions of the 2006 Act to which the amendments relate. For effective date, see P.L. 109-280, §508(c), below.

P.L. 110-458, §105(f)(2):

Amended ERISA Sec. 209(a)(2) by striking paragraph (2) and inserting a new paragraph (2) to read as above. Prior to amendment, ERISA Sec. 209(a)(2) read as follows:

(2) If more than one employer adopts a plan, each such employer shall, in accordance with regulations prescribed by the Secretary, furnish to the plan administrator the information necessary for the administrator to maintain the records and make the reports required by paragraph (1). Such administrator shall maintain the records and, to the extent provided under regulations prescribed by the Secretary, make the reports, required by paragraph (1).

The above amendment takes effect as if included in the provisions of the 2006 Act to which the amendments relate. For effective date, see P.L. 109-280, §508(c), below.

P.L. 109-280, Sec. 508(c):

508(c) EFFECTIVE DATE.—

508(c)(1) IN GENERAL.—

The amendments made by this section shall apply to plan years beginning after December 31, 2006.

508(c)(2) SPECIAL RULES FOR COLLECTIVELY BARGAINED AGREEMENTS.—

In the case of a plan maintained pursuant to 1 or more collective bargaining agreements between employee representatives and 1 or more employers ratified on or before the date of the enactment of this Act, paragraph (1) shall be applied to benefits pursuant to, and individuals covered by, any such agreement by substituting for "December 31, 2006" the earlier of —

508(c)(1)(A) the later of—

508(c)(1)(A)(i) December 31, 2007, or

508(c)(1)(A)(ii) the date on which the last of such collective bargaining agreements terminates (determined without regard to any extension thereof after such date of enactment), or

508(c)(1)(B) December 31, 2008.

[¶ 14,500]

PLANS MAINTAINED BY MORE THAN ONE EMPLOYER, PREDECESSOR PLANS, AND EMPLOYER GROUPS

Act Sec. 210. (a) PLAN MAINTAINED BY MORE THAN ONE EMPLOYER.—Notwithstanding any other provision of this part or part 3, the following provisions of this subsection shall apply to a plan maintained by more than one employer:

(a)(1) Section 202 shall be applied as if all employees of each of the employers were employed by a single employer.

(a)(2) Sections 203 and 204 shall be applied as if all such employers constituted a single employer, except that the application of any rules with respect to breaks in service shall be made under regulations prescribed by the Secretary.

(a)(3) The minimum funding standard provided by section 302 shall be determined as if all participants in the plan were employed by a single employer.

Act Sec. 210. (b) MAINTENANCE OF PLAN OF PREDECESSOR EMPLOYER.—For purposes of this part and part 3—

(b)(1) in any case in which the employer maintains a plan of a predecessor employer, service for such predecessor shall be treated as service for the employer, and

(b)(2) in any case in which the employer maintains a plan which is not the plan maintained by a predecessor employer, service for such predecessor shall, to the extent provided in regulations prescribed by the Secretary of the Treasury, be treated as service for the employer.

Act Sec. 210. (c) PLAN MAINTAINED BY CONTROLLED GROUP OF CORPORATIONS.—For purposes of sections 202, 203, and 204, all employees of all corporations which are members of a controlled group of corporations (within the meaning of section 1563(a) of the Internal Revenue Code of 1986, determined without regard to section 1563(a)(4) and (e)(3)(C) of such Code) shall be treated as employed by a single employer. With respect to a plan adopted by more than one such corporation, the minimum funding standard of section 302 shall be determined as if all such employers were a single employer, and allocated to each employer in accordance with regulations prescribed by the Secretary of the Treasury.

Act Sec. 210. (d) PLAN OF TRADES OR BUSINESSES UNDER COMMON CONTROL.—For purposes of sections 202, 203, and 204, under regulations prescribed by the Secretary of the Treasury, all employees of trades or businesses (whether or not incorporated) which are under common control shall be treated as employed by a single employer. The regulations prescribed under this subsection shall be based on principles similar to the principles which apply in the case of subsection (c).

Act Sec. 210. (e) SPECIAL RULES FOR ELIGIBLE COMBINED DEFINED BENEFIT PLANS AND QUALIFIED CASH OR DEFERRED ARRANGEMENTS.—

(e)(1) GENERAL RULE. —Except as provided in this subsection, this Act shall be applied to any defined benefit plan or applicable individual account plan which are part of an eligible combined plan in the same manner as if each such plan were not a part of the eligible combined plan. In the case of a termination of the defined benefit plan and the applicable defined contribution plan forming part of an eligible combined plan, the plan administrator shall terminate each such plan separately.

(e)(2) ELIGIBLE COMBINED PLAN. —For purposes of this subsection—

(A) IN GENERAL. —The term "eligible combined plan" means a plan—

(i) which is maintained by an employer which, at the time the plan is established, is a small employer,

(ii) which consists of a defined benefit plan and an applicable individual account plan each of which qualifies under section 401(a) of the Internal Revenue Code of 1986,

(iii) the assets of which are held in a single trust forming part of the plan and are clearly identified and allocated to the defined benefit plan and the applicable individual account plan to the extent necessary for the separate application of this Act under paragraph (1), and

(iv) with respect to which the benefit, contribution, vesting, and nondiscrimination requirements of subparagraphs (B), (C), (D), (E), and (F) are met.

For purposes of this subparagraph, the term "small employer" has the meaning given such term by section 4980D(d)(2) of the Internal Revenue Code of 1986, except that such section shall be applied by substituting "500" for "50" each place it appears.

(B) BENEFIT REQUIREMENTS.—

(i) IN GENERAL. —The benefit requirements of this subparagraph are met with respect to the defined benefit plan forming part of the eligible combined plan if the accrued benefit of each participant derived from employer contributions, when expressed as an annual retirement benefit, is not less than the applicable percentage of the participant's final average pay. For purposes of this clause, final average pay shall be determined using the period of consecutive years (not exceeding 5) during which the participant had the greatest aggregate compensation from the employer.

(ii) APPLICABLE PERCENTAGE. —For purposes of clause (i), the applicable percentage is the lesser of—

(I) 1 percent multiplied by the number of years of service with the employer, or

(II) 20 percent.

(iii) SPECIAL RULE FOR APPLICABLE DEFINED BENEFIT PLANS. —If the defined benefit plan under clause (i) is an applicable defined benefit plan as defined in section 203(f)(3)(B) which meets the interest credit requirements of section 204(b)(5)(B)(i), the plan shall be treated as meeting the requirements of clause (i) with respect to any plan year if each participant receives pay credit for the year which is not less than the percentage of compensation determined in accordance with the following table:

If the participant's age as of the beginning of the year is—	The percentage is—
30 or less	2
Over 30 but less than 40	4
40 or over but less than 50	6
50 or over	8.

(iv) YEARS OF SERVICE. —For purposes of this subparagraph, years of service shall be determined under the rules of paragraphs (1), (2), and (3) of section 203(b), except that the plan may not disregard any year of service because of a participant making, or failing to make, any elective deferral with respect to the qualified cash or deferred arrangement to which subparagraph (C) applies.

(C) CONTRIBUTION REQUIREMENTS.—

(i) IN GENERAL. —The contribution requirements of this subparagraph with respect to any applicable individual account plan forming part of an eligible combined plan are met if —

(I) the qualified cash or deferred arrangement included in such plan constitutes an automatic contribution arrangement, and

(II) the employer is required to make matching contributions on behalf of each employee eligible to participate in the arrangement in an amount equal to 50 percent of the elective contributions of the employee to the extent such elective contributions do not exceed 4 percent of compensation.

Rules similar to the rules of clauses (ii) and (iii) of section 401(k)(12)(B) of the Internal Revenue Code of 1986 shall apply for purposes of this clause.

(ii) NONELECTIVE CONTRIBUTIONS. —An applicable individual account plan shall not be treated as failing to meet the requirements of clause (i) because the employer makes nonelective contributions under the plan but such contributions shall not be taken into account in determining whether the requirements of clause (i)(II) are met.

(D) VESTING REQUIREMENTS. —The vesting requirements of this subparagraph are met if—

(i) in the case of a defined benefit plan forming part of an eligible combined plan an employee who has completed at least 3 years of service has a nonforfeitable right to 100 percent of the employee's accrued benefit under the plan derived from employer contributions, and

(ii) in the case of an applicable individual account plan forming part of eligible combined plan—

(I) an employee has a nonforfeitable right to any matching contribution made under the qualified cash or deferred arrangement included in such plan by an employer with respect to any elective contribution, including matching contributions in excess of the contributions required under subparagraph (C)(i)(II), and

(II) an employee who has completed at least 3 years of service has a nonforfeitable right to 100 percent of the employee's accrued benefit derived under the arrangement from nonelective contributions of the employer.

For purposes of this subparagraph, the rules of section 203 shall apply to the extent not inconsistent with this subparagraph.

(E) UNIFORM PROVISION OF CONTRIBUTIONS AND BENEFITS. —In the case of a defined benefit plan or applicable individual account plan forming part of an eligible combined plan, the requirements of this subparagraph are met if all contributions and benefits under each such plan, and all rights and features under each such plan, must be provided uniformly to all participants.

(F) REQUIREMENTS MUST BE MET WITHOUT TAKING INTO ACCOUNT SOCIAL SECURITY AND SIMILAR CONTRIBUTIONS AND BENEFITS OR OTHER PLANS.—

(i) IN GENERAL. —The requirements of this subparagraph are met if the requirements of clauses (ii) and (iii) are met.

(ii) SOCIAL SECURITY AND SIMILAR CONTRIBUTIONS. —The requirements of this clause are met if—

(I) the requirements of subparagraphs (B) and (C) are met without regard to section 401(l) of the Internal Revenue Code of 1986, and

(II) the requirements of sections 401(a)(4) and 410(b) of the Internal Revenue Code of 1986 are met with respect to both the applicable defined contribution plan and defined benefit plan forming part of an eligible combined plan without regard to section 401(l) of the Internal Revenue Code of 1986.

(iii) OTHER PLANS AND ARRANGEMENTS. —The requirements of this clause are met if the applicable defined contribution plan and defined benefit plan forming part of an eligible combined plan meet the requirements of sections 401(a)(4) and 410(b) of the Internal Revenue Code of 1986 without being combined with any other plan.

(e)(3) AUTOMATIC CONTRIBUTION ARRANGEMENT. —For purposes of this subsection—

(A) IN GENERAL. —A qualified cash or deferred arrangement shall be treated as an automatic contribution arrangement if the arrangement—

(i) provides that each employee eligible to participate in the arrangement is treated as having elected to have the employer make elective contributions in an amount equal to 4 percent of the employee's compensation unless the employee specifically elects not to have such contributions made or to have such contributions made at a different rate, and

(ii) meets the notice requirements under subparagraph (B).

(B) NOTICE REQUIREMENTS.—

(i) IN GENERAL. —The requirements of this subparagraph are met if the requirements of clauses (ii) and (iii) are met.

(ii) REASONABLE PERIOD TO MAKE ELECTION. —The requirements of this clause are met if each employee to whom subparagraph (A)(i) applies —

(I) receives a notice explaining the employee's right under the arrangement to elect not to have elective contributions made on the employee's behalf or to have the contributions made at a different rate, and

(II) has a reasonable period of time after receipt of such notice and before the first elective contribution is made to make such election.

(iii) ANNUAL NOTICE OF RIGHTS AND OBLIGATIONS. —The requirements of this clause are met if each employee eligible to participate in the arrangement is, within a reasonable period before any year, given notice of the employee's rights and obligations under the arrangement.

The requirements of this subparagraph shall not be treated as met unless the requirements of clauses (i) and (ii) of section 401(k)(12)(D) of the Internal Revenue Code of 1986 are met with respect to the notices described in clauses (ii) and (iii) of this subparagraph.

(4) COORDINATION WITH OTHER REQUIREMENTS.—

(A) TREATMENT OF SEPARATE PLANS. —The except clause in section 3(35) shall not apply to an eligible combined plan.

(B) REPORTING. —An eligible combined plan shall be treated as a single plan for purposes of section 103.

(5) APPLICABLE INDIVIDUAL ACCOUNT PLAN. —For purposes of this subsection—

(A) IN GENERAL. —The term "applicable individual account plan" means an individual account plan which includes a qualified cash or deferred arrangement.

(B) QUALIFIED CASH OR DEFERRED ARRANGEMENT. —The term "qualified cash or deferred arrangement" has the meaning given such term by section 401(k)(2) of the Internal Revenue Code of 1986.

Act Sec. 210. (f) COOPERATIVE AND SMALL EMPLOYER CHARITY PENSION PLANS.—

(1) IN GENERAL. For purposes of this title, except as provided in this subsection, a CSEC plan is an employee pension benefit plan (other than a multiemployer plan) that is a defined benefit plan—

(A) to which section 104 of the Pension Protection Act of 2006 applies, without regard to—

(i) section 104(a)(2) of such Act;

(ii) the amendments to such section 104 by section 202(b) of the Preservation of Access to Care for Medicare Beneficiaries and Pension Relief Act of 2010; and

(iii) paragraph (3)(B);

(B) that, as of June 25, 2010, was maintained by more than one employer and all of the employers were organizations described in section 501(c)(3) of the Internal Revenue Code of 1986; or

(C) that, as of June 25, 2010, was maintained by an employer—

(i) described in section 501(c)(3) of such Code,

(ii) chartered under part B of subtitle II of title 36, United States Code,

(iii) with employees in at least 40 States, and

(iv) whose primary exempt purpose is to provide services with respect to children.

(2) AGGREGATION. All employers that are treated as a single employer under subsection (b) or (c) of section 414 of the Internal Revenue Code of 1986 shall be treated as a single employer for purposes of determining if a plan was maintained by more than one employer under subparagraph (B) and (C) of paragraph (1).

(3) ELECTION.

(A) IN GENERAL. If a plan falls within the definition of a CSEC plan under this subsection (without regard to this paragraph), such plan shall be a CSEC plan unless the plan sponsor elects not later than the close of the first plan year of the plan beginning after December 31, 2013, not to be treated as a CSEC plan. An election under the preceding sentence shall take effect for such plan year and, once made, may be revoked only with the consent of the Secretary of the Treasury.

(B) SPECIAL RULE. If a plan described in subparagraph (A) is treated as a CSEC plan, section 104 of the Pension Protection Act of 2006, as amended by the Preservation of Access to Care for Medicare Beneficiaries and Pension Relief Act of 2010, shall cease to apply to such plan as of the first date as of which such plan is treated as a CSEC plan.

Amendments

P.L. 113-235, §3(a)(1), Div. P:

Amended ERISA Sec. 210(f)(1) by striking "or" at the end of subparagraph (A), by striking the period at the end of subparagraph (B) and inserting "; or" and by inserting after subparagraph (B) a new subparagraph (C) to read as above.

The above amendment shall take effect as if included in the amendments made by the Cooperative and Small Employer Charity Pension Flexibility Act (29 U.S.C. 401 note) [effective for years beginning after 12-31-2013.—CCH].

P.L. 113-235, §3(a)(2), Div. P:

Amended ERISA Sec. 210(f)(2) by striking "paragraph (1)(B)" and inserting "subparagraph (B) and (C) of paragraph (1)".

The above amendment shall take effect as if included in the amendments made by the Cooperative and Small Employer Charity Pension Flexibility Act (29 U.S.C. 401 note) [effective for years beginning after 12-31-2013.—CCH].

P.L. 113-97, §101:

Amended ERISA Sec. 210 by adding at the end a new subsection (f) to read as above.

Effective for years beginning after 12-31-2013.

P.L. 113-97, §103(a):

Amended ERISA Sec. 210(f), as added by Act Sec. 101 above, by adding at the end a new paragraph (3) to read as above.

Effective as of the date of enactment of this Act.

P.L. 110-458, §109(c)(2)(A):

Amended ERISA Sec. 210(e)(1) by adding at the end the following new sentence:

In the case of a termination of the defined benefit plan and the applicable defined contribution plan forming part of an eligible combined plan, the plan administrator shall terminate each such plan separately.

The above amendment takes effect as if included in the provisions of the 2006 Act to which the amendment relates [effective with respect to plan years beginning after December 31, 2009.—CCH].

P.L. 110-458, §109(c)(2)(B):

Amended ERISA Sec. 210(e) by striking paragraph (3) and by redesignating paragraphs (4), (5), and (6) as paragraphs (3), (4), and (5), respectively. Prior to the amendment, ERISA Sec. 210(e)(3) read as follows:

(3) NONDISCRIMINATION REQUIREMENTS FOR QUALIFIED CASH OR DEFERRED ARRANGEMENT.—

(A) IN GENERAL.—A qualified cash or deferred arrangement which is included in an applicable individual account plan forming part of an eligible combined plan shall be treated as meeting the requirements of section 401(k)(3)(A)(ii) of the Internal Revenue Code of 1986 if the requirements of paragraph (2) are met with respect to such arrangement.

(B) MATCHING CONTRIBUTIONS. —In applying section 401(m)(11) of such Code to any matching contribution with respect to a contribution to which paragraph (2)(C) applies, the contribution requirement of paragraph (2)(C) and the notice requirements of paragraph (5)(B) shall be substituted for the requirements otherwise applicable under clauses (i) and (ii) of section 401(m)(11)(A) of such Code.

The above amendments take effect as if included in the provisions of the 2006 Act to which the amendment relates [effective with respect to plan years beginning after December 31, 2009.—CCH].

P.L. 109-280, §903(b)(1):

Amended ERISA Sec. 210 by adding new subsection (e) to read as above.

The above amendment applies to plan years beginning after December 31, 2009.

P.L. 109-280, §903(b)(2)(A):

Amended ERISA Sec. 210 by amending the heading to read as follows: "Sec. 210 Multiple Employer Plans and Other Special Rules".

The above amendment applies to plan years beginning after December 31, 2009.

P.L. 101-239, §7894(c)(10):

Amended ERISA Sec. 210(c) by striking "such code" and inserting "such Code" effective September 2, 1974.

P.L. 101-239, §7891(a)(1):

Titles I, III, and IV of ERISA (other than sections 3(37)(E), 301(a)(7), and 308, the last sentence of section 408(d), and sections 414(c), 4001(a)(3)(ii), and 4303) are each amended by striking "Internal Revenue Code of 1954" each place it appears and inserting "Internal Revenue Code of 1986" effective October 22, 1986.

Regulations

The following regulations were adopted under "Title 29—Labor," "Chapter XXV—Pension and Welfare Benefit Programs, Department of Labor," "Subchapter C—Minimum Standards for Employee Pension Benefit Plans Under the Employee Retirement Income Security Act of 1974," "Part 2530—Rules and Regulations for Minimum Standards for Employee Pension Benefit Plans." The regulations were filed with the Federal Register on December 23, 1976, and published in the Federal Register of December 28, 1976 (41 FR 56462).

Subpart D—Plan Administration as Related to Benefits

[¶ 14,501]

§ 2530.210 Employer or employers maintaining the plan.

(a) *General statutory provisions.* (1) *Eligibility to participate and vesting.* Except as otherwise provided in sections 202(b) or 203(b)(1) of the Act and sections 410(a)(5), 411(a)(5) and 411(a)(6) of the Code, all years of service with the employer or employers maintaining the plan shall be taken into account for purposes of section 202 of the Act and section 410 of the Code (relating to minimum eligibility standards) and section 203 of the Act and section 411(a) of the Code (relating to minimum vesting standards).

(2) *Accrual of benefits.* Except as otherwise provided in section 202(b) of the Act and section 410(a)(5) of the Code, all years of participation under the plan must be taken into account for purposes of section 204 of the Act and section 411(b) of the Code (relating to benefit accrual). Section 204(b) of the Act and 411(b) of the Code require only that periods of actual participation in the plan (e.g., covered service) be taken into account for purposes of benefit accrual.

(b) *General rules concerning service to be credited under this section.* Section 210 of the Act and sections 413(c), 414(b) and 414(c) of the Code provide rules applicable to sections 202, 203, and 204 of the Act and sections 410, 411(a) and 411(b) of the Code for purposes of determining who is an "employer or employers maintaining the plan" and, accordingly, what service is required to be taken into account in the case of a plan maintained by more than one employer. Paragraphs (c) through (e) of this section set forth the rules for determining service required to be taken into account in the case of a plan or plans maintained by multiple employers, controlled groups of corporations and trades or businesses under common control. Note throughout that every mention of multiple employer plans includes multiemployer plans. *See* § 2530.210(c)(3). Paragraph (f) of this section sets forth special break-in-service rules for such plans. Paragraph (g) of this section applies the break-in-service rules of sections 202(b)(4) and 203(b)(3)(D) of the Act and sections 410(a)(5)(D) and 411(a)(6)(D) of the Code (rule of parity) to such plans.

(c) *Multiple employer plans.* (1) *Eligibility to participate and vesting.* A multiple employer plan shall be treated as if all maintaining employers constitute a single employer so long as an employee is employed in either covered service or contiguous noncovered service. Accordingly, except as referred to in paragraph (a)(1) and provided in paragraph (f) of this section, in determining an employee's service for eligibility to participate and vesting purposes, all covered service with an employer or employers maintaining the plan and all contiguous noncovered service with an employer or employers maintaining the plan shall be taken into account. Thus, for example, if an employee in service covered under a multiple employer plan leaves covered service with one employer maintaining the plan and is employed immediately thereafter in covered service with another employer maintaining the plan, the plan is required to credit all hours of service with both employers for purposes of participation and vesting. If an employee moves from contiguous noncovered to covered service, or from covered service to contiguous noncovered service, with the same employer, the plan is required to credit all hours of service with such employer for purposes of eligibility to participate and vesting.

(2) *Benefit accrual.* A multiple employer plan shall be treated as if all maintaining employers constitute a single employer so long as an employee is employed in covered service. Accordingly, except as referred to in paragraph (a)(2) and provided in paragraph (f) of this section, in determining a participant's service for benefit accrual purposes, all covered service with an employer or employers maintaining the plan shall be taken into account.

(3) *Definitions.* (i) For purposes of this section, the term "multiple employer plan" shall mean a multiemployer plan as defined in section 3(37) of the Act and section 414(f) of the Code or a multiple employer plan within the meaning of sections 413 (b) and (c) of the Code and the regulations issued thereunder. Notwithstanding the preceding sentence, a plan maintained solely by members of the same controlled group of corporations within the meaning of paragraph (d) of this section or by trades or businesses which are under the common control of one person or group of persons within the meaning of paragraph (e) of this section shall not be deemed to be a multiple employer plan for purposes of this section, and such plan is required to apply the rules under this section which are applicable to controlled groups of corporations or commonly controlled trades or businesses respectively.

(ii) For purposes of this section, the term "covered service" shall mean service with an employer or employers maintaining the plan within a job classification or class of employees covered under the plan.

(iii) For purposes of this section the term "noncovered service" shall mean service with an employer or employers maintaining the plan which is not covered service.

(iv)(A) *General.* For purposes of this section noncovered service shall be deemed "contiguous" if (1) the noncovered service precedes or follows covered service and (2) no quit, discharge or retirement occurs between such covered service and noncovered service.

(B) *Exception.* Notwithstanding the preceding paragraph, in the case of a controlled group of corporations within the meaning of paragraph (d) of this section or trades or businesses which are under the common control of one person or group of persons within the meaning of paragraph (e) of this section, any transfer of an employee from one member of the controlled group to another member or from one trade or business under common control to another trade or business under the common control of the same person or group of persons shall result in the period of noncovered service which immediately precedes or follows such transfer being deemed "noncontiguous" for purposes of paragraph (c) of this section.

Diagram No. 1. **(Multiple Employer Plan.)**

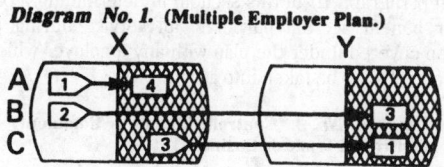

Assume for purposes of diagram No. 1 that X and Y are both employers who are required to contribute to a multiple employer plan and that neither employer maintains any other plan. Covered service is represented by the shaded segments of the diagram. After completing 1 year of noncovered service, employee A immediately enters covered service with X and completes 4 years of covered service. For purposes of eligibility to participate and vesting, the plan is required to credit employee A with 5 years of service with employer X because his period of service with X includes a period of covered service and a period of contiguous noncovered service. On the other hand, employee B, immediately after completing 2 years of noncovered service with X, enters covered service with Y. Because B quit employment with X, his period of noncovered service with X is not contiguous and, therefore, is not required to be taken into account. In the case of employee C, the plan is required to take into account all service with employers X and Y because employee C is employed in covered service with both employers.

Diagram No. 2. (Multiple Employer Plan—Noncovered Service.)

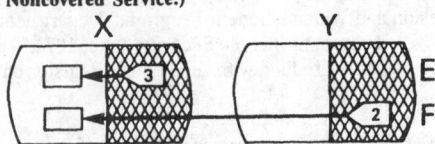

The multiple employer plan rules with respect to noncovered service are illustrated in diagram No. 2. Assume that X and Y are both employers who are required to contribute to a multiple employer plan and that neither employer maintains any other plan. Covered service is represented by the shaded segments of the diagram. Employee E completed 3 years of service with employer X in covered service and then immediately entered noncovered service with X. Because E's noncovered service is contiguous, the plan is required to take into account all service with X for purposes of eligibility to participate and vesting under the multiple employer plan. Employee F does not continue to receive credit; F quit the employment of Y and entered noncovered service with X.

(d) *Controlled groups of corporations.* (1) With respect to a plan maintained by one or more members of a controlled group of corporations (within the meaning of section 1563(a) of the Code, determined without regard to section 1563 (a)(4) and (e)(3)(C)), all employees of such corporations shall be treated as employed by a single employer.

(2) Accordingly, except as referred to in paragraph (a)(1) and provided in paragraph (f) of this section, in determining an employee's service for eligibility to participate and vesting purposes, all service with any employer which is a member of the controlled group of corporations shall be taken into account. Except as referred to in paragraph (a)(2) and provided in paragraph (f) of this section, in determining a participant's service for benefit accrual purposes, all service during periods of participation covered under the plan with any employer which is a member of the controlled group of corporations shall be taken into account.

(e) *Commonly controlled trades or businesses.* With respect to a plan maintained only by one or more trades or businesses (whether or not incorporated) which are under common control within the meaning of section 414(c) of the Code and the regulations issued thereunder, all employees of such trades or businesses shall be treated as employed by a single employer. Accordingly, except as referred to in paragraph (a)(1) and provided in paragraph (f) of this section, in determining an employee's service for eligibility to participate and vesting purposes, all service with any employer which is under common control shall be taken into account. Except as referred to in paragraph (a)(2) and provided in paragraph (f) of this section, in determining a participant's service for benefit accrual purposes, all service during periods of participation covered under the plan with any employer which is under common control shall be taken into account.

Diagram No. 3. (Controlled Group or Commonly Controlled Trade or Business.)

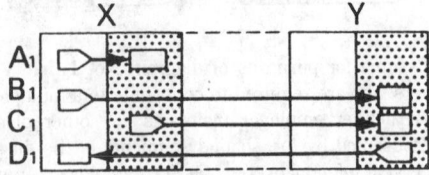

Assume for purposes of diagram No. 3 that X and Y are either members of the same controlled group of corporations or trades or businesses which are under the same common control. The dotted segments of the diagram represent plan coverage under plans separately maintained by X and Y. Neither employer maintains any other plans. Because A1, B1, C1, and D1 have their service with X and Y treated as if X and Y were a single employer, the plans are required to take into account all service with X and Y for eligibility to participate and vesting purposes.

(f) *Special break in service rules.* (1) In addition to service which may be disregarded under the statutory provisions referred to in

paragraph (a) of this section, a multiple employer plan may disregard noncontiguous noncovered service.

(2) In the case of a plan maintained solely by one or more members of a controlled group of corporations or one or more trades or businesses which are under common control, if one of the maintaining employers is also a participating employer in a multiple employer plan which includes other employers which are not members of the controlled group or commonly controlled trades or businesses, service with such other employer maintaining the multiple employer plan may be disregarded by the controlled group or commonly controlled plan.

Diagram No. 4. (Break in Service Rules.)

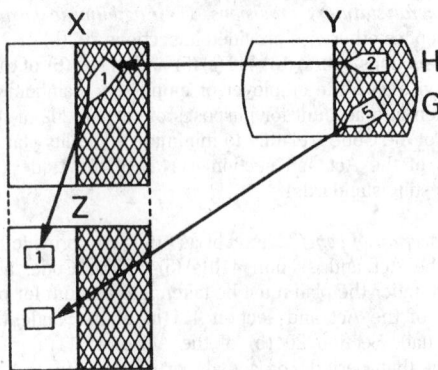

Diagram No. 4 illustrates the break in service rules of paragraph (f) of this section. Assume for purposes of diagram no. 4 that employer Z is controlled by employer X but employer Y's only relation to X and Z is that X, Y and Z are required to contribute to a multiple employer plan. The multiple employer plan, represented by the shaded segments of the diagram, provides for 100% vesting after 10 years. X, Y and Z maintain no other plans.

Employee G completed 5 years of covered service with employer Y, and then moved to noncovered service with employer Z. G's noncovered service is noncontiguous (see employee F in diagram No. 2 above), and such service may be disregarded for purposes of the multiple employer plan under the rule in paragraph (f)(1).

Employee H completed 2 years of covered service with employer Y and then entered covered service with employer X for 1 year. The multiple employer plan is required to credit H with 3 years of service. H then entered noncovered service with employer Z. H's noncovered service is noncontiguous (see employee F in diagram No. 2 above), and such service may be disregarded for purposes of the multiple employer plan under the rule in paragraph (f)(1).

(g) *Rule of parity.* For purposes of sections 202(b)(4) and 203(b)(3)(D) of the Act and sections 410(a)(5)(D) and 411(a)(6)(D) of the Code, in the case of an employee who is a nonvested participant in employer-derived accrued benefits at the time he incurs a 1-year break in service, years of service completed by such employee before such break are not required to be taken into account if at such time he incurs consecutive 1-year breaks in service which equal or exceed the aggregate number of years of service before such breaks. This is so even though the period of noncontiguous noncovered service with an employer or employers maintaining the plan may subsequently be deemed contiguous as the result of the employee entering covered service with the same employer maintaining the plan and, consequently, such plan may be required to credit such service.

Diagram No. 5. (Rule of Parity.)

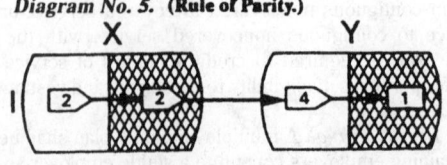

Assume for purposes of diagram No. 5 that X and Y are both employers who are required to contribute to a multiple employer plan which contains a provision applying the rule of parity. Covered service is represented by the shaded segments of the diagram. The plan has 100% vesting after ten years. X and Y maintain no other plan.

The multiple employer plan credited employee I with 4 years of service with X when he quit employment with X and entered noncovered service with Y. As a result of 4 years of noncontiguous noncovered service with Y, employee I incurred 4 consecutive 1-year breaks in service, so that the multiple employer plan may disregard his prior service (i.e., the 4 years of service with X).

When employee I entered covered service with Y (as a "new employee"), his 4 years of noncontiguous service with Y became contiguous for purposes of the multiple employer plan. Consequently, after 1 year of covered service with Y, the plan is required to credit employee I with 5 years of service.

(h) *Example.* Under section 203(b)(1)(C) of the Act and section 411(a)(4)(C) of the Code, service with an employer prior to such employer's adoption of the plan need not be taken into account. The following example demonstrates that this rule applies even if an employee is employed in contiguous noncovered service. The example is applicable to any plan subject to the rules of this section. However, for purposes of clarity, the example assumes that X and Y are required to contribute to a multiple employer plan.

Assume that employee D completed 3 years of covered service with employer Y as of the date X adopts the plan. Immediately after X's adoption of the plan D left covered service with Y and D entered covered service with X. His prior covered service with Y is required to be counted, and D remains a participant.

On the other hand, if D had entered service with X anytime prior to X's adoption of the plan and subsequently was covered by the plan when X adopted it, his prior service with Y must also be counted, unless such service may be disregarded under the break in service rules because the period of service with X before X's adoption of the plan was equal to or greater than his prior service with Y. For example, if X adopted the plan three years after D began employment with X, and consequently after D had incurred 3 consecutive 1-year breaks in service, his prior service with Y could be disregarded.

(i) *Comprehensive diagram.* (No. 6)

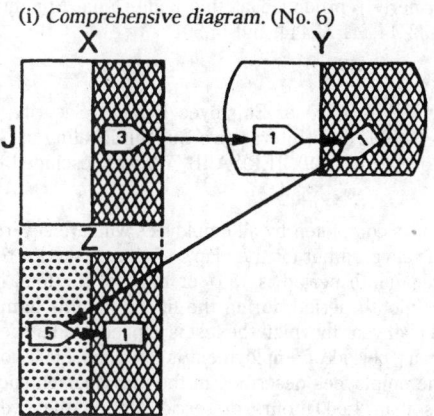

Assume for purposes of diagram No. 6 that employer Z is controlled by employer X within the meaning of paragraph (d) but employer Y's only relation to X and Z is that X, Y and Z are required to contribute to a multiple employer plan. The shaded segments represent coverage under the multiple employer plan which contains a provision applying the rule of parity. The dotted segment represents a separate plan maintained by Z. Both plans have 100% vesting after 10 years.

Employee J completed 3 years of service with employer X in covered service with the multiple employer plan. J then entered noncovered service with Y and remained with Y for 1 year, and thereby incurred a 1-year break in service under the multiple employer plan. J then entered covered service with Y, thereby causing the noncovered service with Y to become contiguous. Covered service with X and contiguous noncovered and covered service with Y must be taken into account for purposes of the multiple employer plan; accordingly, that plan is required to credit J with a total of 5 years of service.

J then left service with Y and entered noncovered service (with respect to the multiple employer plan) with Z. J remained in noncovered service with Z (with respect to the multiple employer plan) for 5 years and thereby incurred 5 consecutive 1-year breaks in service for purposes of the multiple employer plan. Consequently, the prior service with X and Y may be disregarded for purposes of the multiple employer plan.

J then entered covered service under the multiple employer plan with Z and completed 1 year of service. Because the 5 years of noncovered service with Z is contiguous with the 1 year of covered service, the multiple employer plan is now required to credit J with 6 years of service for purposes of eligibility to participate and vesting.

For purposes of Z's controlled group plan (i.e., dotted segment), employee J is entitled to receive credit for 9 years of service. The 3 years of service with X, a member of the controlled group, may not be disregarded under the rule of parity because J incurred only 2 consecutive 1-year breaks in service while employed with Y. When J entered service with Z covered under Z's controlled group plan, the 3 years of service with X were still required to be credited by the controlled group plan. In addition, J must receive credit for the 5 years of service with Z covered under the controlled group plan. Finally, when J moved to service with Z covered under the multiple employer plan the controlled group plan was required to credit J with an additional year of service.

[¶ 14,510]
EFFECTIVE DATES

Act Sec. 211.(a) Except as otherwise provided in this section, this part shall apply in the case of plan years beginning after the date of the enactment of this Act.

Act Sec. 211.(b)(1) Except as otherwise provided in subsection (d), sections 205, 206(d), and 208 shall apply with respect to plan years beginning after December 31, 1975.

(2) Except as otherwise provided in subsections (c) and (d) in the case of a plan in existence on January 1, 1974, this part shall apply in the case of plan years beginning after December 31, 1975.

Act Sec. 211.(c)(1) In the case of a plan maintained on January 1, 1974, pursuant to one or more agreements which the Secretary finds to be collective bargaining agreements between employee organizations and one or more employers, no plan shall be treated as not meeting the requirements of sections 204 and 205 solely by reason of a supplementary or special plan provision (within the meaning of paragraph (2)) for any plan year before the year which begins after the earlier of—

(A) the date on which the last of such agreements relating to the plan terminates (determined without regard to any extension thereof agreed to after the date of the enactment of this Act), or

(B) December 31, 1980.

For purposes of subparagraph (A) and section 307(c), any plan amendment made pursuant to a collective bargaining agreement relating to the plan which amends the plan solely to conform to any requirement contained in this Act or the Internal Revenue Code of 1986 shall not be treated as a termination of such collective bargaining agreement. This paragraph shall not apply unless the Secretary determines that the participation and vesting rules in effect on the date of enactment of this Act are not less favorable to participants, in the aggregate, than the rules provided under sections 202, 203, and 204.

(2) For purposes of paragraph (1), the term "supplementary or special plan provision" means any plan provision which—

(A) provides supplementary benefits, not in excess of one-third of the basic benefit, in the form of an annuity for the life of the participant, or

(B) provides that, under a contractual agreement based on medical evidence as to the effects of working in an adverse environment for an extended period of time, a participant having 25 years of service is to be treated as having 30 years of service.

(3) This subsection shall apply with respect to a plan if (and only if) the application of this subsection results in a later effective date for this part than the effective date required by subsection (b).

Act Sec. 211. (d) If the administrator of a plan elects under section 1017(d) of this Act to make applicable to a plan year and to all subsequent plan years the provisions of the Internal Revenue Code of 1986 relating to participation, vesting, funding, and form of benefit, this part shall apply to the first plan year to which such election applies and to all subsequent plan years.

Act Sec. 211. (e)(1) No pension plan to which section 202 applies may make effective any plan amendment with respect to breaks in service (which amendment is made or becomes effective after January 1, 1974, and before the date on which section 202 first becomes effective with respect to such plan) which provides that any employee's participation in the plan would commence at any date later than the later of—

(A) the date on which his participation would commence under the break in service rules of section 202(b), or

(B) the date on which his participation would commence under the plan as in effect on January 1, 1974.

(2) No pension plan to which section 203 applies may make effective any plan amendment with respect to breaks in service (which amendment is made or becomes effective after January 1, 1974, and before the date on which section 203 first becomes effective with respect to such plan) if such amendment provides that the nonforfeitable benefit derived from employer contributions to which any employee would be entitled is less than the lesser of the nonforfeitable benefit derived from employer contributions to which he would be entitled under—

(A) the break in service rules of section 202(b)(3), or

(B) the plan as in effect on January 1, 1974.

Subparagraph (B) shall not apply if the break in service rules under the plan would have been in violation of any law or rule of law in effect on January 1, 1974.

Act Sec. 211. (f) The preceding provisions of this section shall not apply with respect to amendments made to this part in provisions enacted after the date of the enactment of this Act.

Amendments

P.L. 99-272:

Act Sec. 11015(a)(1)(B) amended ERISA Sec. 211(c)(1) by striking out "306(c)" and inserting "307(c)" in its place, effective with respect to applications for waivers, extensions and modifications filed on or after April 7, 1986.

P.L. 101-239, § 7891(a)(1):

Titles I, III, and IV of ERISA (other than sections 3(37)(E), 301(a)(7), and 308, the last sentence of section 408(d), and sections 414(c), 4001(a)(3)(ii), and 4303) are each amended by striking "Internal Revenue Code of 1954" each place it appears and inserting "Internal Revenue Code of 1986" effective October 22, 1986.

P.L. 101-239, § 7894(h)(2):

Amended ERISA Sec. 211 by adding new subsection (f) to read as above effective September 2, 1974.

[¶ 14,515] Reserved. Temporary regulations on Minimum Standards for Employee Pension Benefit Plans Under the Employee Retirement Income Security Act of 1974, effective under the Special Reliance Procedure, were formerly reproduced at this point. Final Minimum Standard Regulations have been adopted. They appear at ¶ 14,411-14,415, 14,421, 14,422, 14,431, 14,432, 14,441-14,444, and 14,501.

Regulations

Interpretive Bulletin ERISA IB 76-1 was adopted under "Title 29—Labor; Chapter XXV—Office of Employee Benefits Security; Part 2509—Interpretive Bulletins Relating to the Employee Retirement Income Security Act of 1974—§ 2509.76-1" [Interpretive Bulletin Relating to Guidelines on Seasonal Industries]. The Bulletin was filed with the Federal Register on January 21, 1976 41 (FR 3289). [ERISA IB 76-1 was rescinded by ERISA IB 76-2, Reg. § 2509.76-2, at ¶ 14,521.]

[¶ 14,520]

§ 2509.76-1 **Interpretive bulletin relating to guidelines on seasonal industries.** [*] On January 16, 1976, the Department of Labor issued an interpretive bulletin, designated ERISA IB 76-1, establishing guidelines on seasonal industries under the Employee Retirement Income Security Act of 1974 (the Act). The guidelines enable employee pension benefit plans to comply with the Act until regulations can be issued under sections 202(a)(3)(B), 203(b)(2)(C) and 204(b)(3)(D) of the Act. Plans may rely on these guidelines, as provided in ERISA IB 75-10 and TIR-1415 (November 5, 1975), for computing service to be credited to employees in seasonal industries.

The Act makes special provision for a "seasonal" industry where the "customary period of employment" is less than 1,000 hours of service during a year. The provisions of the Act concerning participation, vesting and benefit accrual are applicable to plans, rather than to industries. It is therefore necessary to provide guidance for plans in an industry with customary annual employment of less than 1,000 hours for purposes of applying the special provision.

The guidelines establish two tests to determine whether a plan covers employees in a seasonal industry. First, a seasonality percentage test is used to measure peaking of hours of service, in order to limit seasonality to those business activities with at least one concentrated period of employment during a year. This is a primary characteristic of seasonality. Under this test, the seasonality percentage is met where the total hours completed by all employees who are covered by a plan, or would be covered but for the plan's minimum service requirements, in any three-month period is 150% or more of the total hours in any other three-month period during the fifteen months immediately preceding the plan year to which the test is applied. Under the second test, the customary period of employment is less than 1,000 hours if 50% or more of the employees described in the previous sentence have completed less than 1,000 hours of service during the twelve calendar months immediately preceding the plan year under consideration. If the plan meets these two tests for seasonality, the plan covers employees in a seasonal industry, and all employees who are covered or would be covered by the plan must be credited for participation, vesting and benefit accrual for the plan year on the basis of a 500 hour standard rather than the normal 1,000 hour standard.

Paragraph (b) sets forth in detail the first test for determining whether a plan covers employees in a seasonal industry and provides that a plan must meet the seasonality percentage test measured in units of thirteen overlapping three-month periods during the fifteen calendar months immediately preceding the plan year. By spanning a fifteen-month period, the seasonality percentage test insures measurement of all annual peaks. If only a twelve-month period were used, a plan year might begin in the midst of an annual peak period, and the highest three-month period actually occurring each year would not be measured under the test. The fifteen-month period covers all three-consecutive-month combinations during a year.

---

[*] § 2509.76-1 was rescinded by § 2509.76-2.

Paragraph (c) allows the exclusion of certain periods from the seasonality percentage test in the situation where a catastrophic event, unrelated to the business activities of the employer maintaining the plan, restricts operations for a significant period of time.

The guidelines follow:

Guidelines on seasonal industries.

(a) *General rule.* A plan covers employees in a seasonal industry for a plan year if—

(1) the hours of service of all employees covered by the plan (or who would be covered by the plan if they satisfied the minimum service requirements set by the plan as a condition for eligibility to participate) meet the seasonality percentage test set forth in paragraph (b) and

(2) Fifty percent or more of the employees described in paragraph (1) have less than 1,000 hours of service in the twelve calendar months immediately preceding the plan year to which this rule is being applied.

(b) *Seasonality percentage test* is a test by which hours of service are measured in each of thirteen different three-month periods that occur during the fifteen calendar months immediately preceding the plan year to which this rule is being applied. If the total hours of service completed by all employees described in paragraph (a)(1) within any one such three-month period is 150% or more of the total hours completed by all such employees in any other such three-month period, then the plan meets the seasonality percentage test. For example, assume that the total hours of service for all employees described in paragraph (a)(1) are as shown below for each of the three-month periods in the 15-month period. The plan is on a calendar year basis.

(1)	Oct.-Dec.	1974	7,500
(2)	Nov.-Jan.	1975	8,000
(3)	Dec.-Feb.	1975	8,000
(4)	Jan.-Mar.	1975	7,000
(5)	Feb.-Apr.	1975	6,500
(6)	Mar.-May	1975	6,500
(7)	Apr.-June	1975	8,000
(8)	May-July	1975	9,500
(9)	June-Aug.	1975	9,000
(10)	July-Sept.	1975	7,500
(11)	Aug.-Oct.	1975	6,000
(12)	Sept.-Nov.	1975	6,500
(13)	Oct.-Dec.	1975	7,500

The plan meets the seasonality percentage test in the 15-month period because the total hours in either period 8 or period 9 are equal to or more than 150% of the total hours in period 11. Therefore the plan meets the test of paragraph (a)(1) for the 1976 plan year.

(c) *Limitation on the use of the seasonality percentage test.* A plan is not required to include in the seasonality percentage test any period which contains a calendar month during which 50% or more of the employees described in paragraph (a)(1) were unable to complete an hour of service for 15 or more days as a result of a rare, atypical and nonrecurring event rather than the seasonal nature of employment. For the purposes of this paragraph, any fire, flood, explosion, earthquake or other event which is not a normal occurrence in the operations of a seasonal industry shall be deemed a rare, atypical and nonrecurring event.

If a plan—

(1) Excludes a three-month period or periods from the seasonality percentage test for the reasons set forth in this paragraph; and

(2) Fails to meet the seasonality percentage test for the plan year to which the test (measured now by less than thirteen three-month periods) is applied, seasonality shall be determined by applying the tests of seasonality set forth in paragraph (a) to the prior plan year.

(d) *Year of service.* An employee in a seasonal industry completes a year of service for the purposes of vesting and eligibility to participate if the employee completes 500 or more hours of service (or, in the case of a seasonal maritime industry, 62 or more days of service) in the respective computation periods beginning with or within the plan year for which the industry is determined to be seasonal.

(e) *Year of participation.* (1) An employee in a seasonal industry completes at least a partial year of participation for the purposes of benefit accrual if the employee completes 500 or more hours of service (or, in the case of a seasonal maritime industry, 62 or more days of service) in an accrual computation period beginning with or within the plan year for which the industry is determined to be seasonal.

(2) When partial years of participation are computed under § 2530.204-2(c), the number 500 will be substituted for the number 1,000 in determining the largest number of hours that a plan may require during the period for an employee to obtain credit for a partial year of participation for the purposes of benefit accrual. All other calculations shall remain the same.

(f) *Breaks in service.* For purposes of sections 202(b), 203(b)(3) and 204(b)(3)(A) of the Act and sections 410(a)(5), 411(a)(6) and 411(b)(3)(A) of the Code, a plan may charge an employee in a seasonal industry with a break in service for a computation period beginning with or within the plan year for which the industry is determined to be seasonal if the employee fails to complete more than 250 hours of service or, in the case of any seasonal maritime industry, 31 days of service in such period. All other rules relating to breaks in service, such as use of certain computation periods, are the same for employees in seasonal industries as for employees in other industries.

>>>→ *Caution: Regulation § 2509.76-2 was officially removed by 61 FR 33847 on July 1, 1996.*

[¶ 14,521]

§ 2509.76-2 **Interpretive bulletin rescinding guidelines on seasonal industries.** The Department of Labor has determined that the guidelines on seasonal industries, ERISA IB 76-1 published at 41 F.R. 3290 on January 22, 1976, should be rescinded. The Department will issue guidelines or a regulation on seasonal industries in the future.

In consideration of the foregoing, the guidelines on seasonal industries published in the *Federal Register* at 41 FR 3290 on January 22, 1976, and issued as ERISA IB 76-1 are hereby rescinded. (Added February 19, 1976, by 41 F.R. 7749.)

>>>→ *Caution: Regulation § 2509.76-3 was officially removed by 61 FR 33847 on July 1, 1996.*

[¶ 14,522]

§ 2509.76-3 **Interpretive bulletin withdrawing definition of seasonal industries from ERISA guidelines.** (a) The Department of Labor, with the concurrence of the Internal Revenue Service, has determined that the definition of seasonal industries should be withdrawn from the ERISA Guidelines. See TIR No. 1415 (November 5, 1975) and ERISA IB 75-10 (published November 5, 1975, originally numbered IB MS-75-1).

(b) On January 22, 1976, the Department of Labor issued guidelines on seasonal industries in ERISA IB 76-1, published at 41 FR 3290. In consideration of comments relating to the adverse impact of the guidelines on seasonal industries upon plans in industries which are generally recognized as nonseasonal, the Department, on February 20, 1976, issued an interpretive bulletin rescinding such guidelines. See ERISA IB 76-2 published at 41 FR 7749.

(c) The definition of seasonal industries is currently part of the ERISA Guidelines. For employers who wish to adopt new plans or amend existing plans to take advantage of the Special Reliance Procedure contained in TIR No. 1416 released on November 5, 1975, the ERISA Guidelines provide a fixed body of law for such purposes. In consideration of the need for employers who wish to take advantage of the Special Reliance Procedure to act promptly, and in view of the time delays which may be involved in formulating a revised definition of seasonal industries, the Department intends to withdraw the definition of seasonal industries from the schedule of documents comprising the ERISA Guidelines.

(d) The Employee Retirement Income Security Act of 1974 (ERISA) and relevant portions of the Internal Revenue Code of 1954 (the Code) provide that in the case of any seasonal industry where the customary period of employment is less than 1,000 hours during a calendar year, the term "year of service", for eligibility purposes, shall be such period as may be determined under regulations prescribed by the Secretary of Labor. ERISA § 202(a)(3)(B) and § 410(a)(3)(B) of the Code. Similar provisions apply to a year of service for vesting purposes and a year of participation for benefit accrual purposes. ERISA §§ 203(b)(2)(C) and 204(b)(3)(D) and Code §§ 411(a)(5)(C) and 411(b)(3)(D). Presently, there is no published guidance concerning the definition of a seasonal industry with a customary period of employment of less than 1,000 hours during a calendar year nor any special rules concerning the definition of a year of service or a year of participation in such industry. In the absence of regulations issued by the Secretary defining seasonal industries, the general standards for determining a year of service for eligibility to participate and vesting purposes, and a year of participation for benefit accrual purposes, apply to all plans.

(e) In consideration of the foregoing, the definition of seasonal industries is hereby withdrawn from the ERISA Guidelines. (Added June 21, 1976, by 41 F.R. 24999.)

Part 3—Funding

[¶ 14,610]
COVERAGE

Act Sec. 301.(a) PLANS EXCEPTED FROM APPLICABILITY OF THIS PART.—This part shall apply to any employee pension benefit plan described in section 4(a), (and not exempted under section 4(b)), other than—

(1) an employee welfare benefit plan;

(2) an insurance contract plan described in subsection (b);

(3) a plan which is unfunded and is maintained by an employer primarily for the purpose of providing deferred compensation for a select group of management or highly compensated employees;

(4)(A) a plan which is established and maintained by a society, order, or association described in section 501(c)(8) or (9) of the Internal Revenue Code of 1986, if no part of the contributions to or under such plan are made by employers of participants in such plan; or

(B) a trust described in section 501(c)(18) of such Code;

(5) a plan which has not at any time after the date of enactment of this Act provided for employer contributions;

(6) an agreement providing payments to a retired partner or deceased partner or a deceased partner's successor in interest as described in section 736 of the Internal Revenue Code of 1986;

(7) an individual retirement account or annuity as described in section 408 of the Internal Revenue Code of 1954 or a retirement bond described in section 409 of the Internal Revenue Code of 1954 (as effective for obligations issued before January 1, 1984);

(8) an individual account plan (other than a money purchase plan) and a defined benefit plan to the extent it is treated as an individual account plan (other than a money purchase plan) under section 3(35)(B) of this title;

(9) an excess benefit plan; or

(10) any plan, fund or program under which an employer, all of whose stock is directly or indirectly owned by employees, former employees or their beneficiaries, proposes through an unfunded arrangement to compensate retired employees for benefits which were forfeited by such employees under a pension plan maintained by a former employer prior to the date such pension plan became subject to this Act.

Act Sec. 301. (b) "INSURANCE CONTRACT PLAN" DEFINED.—For the purposes of paragraph (2) of subsection (a) a plan is an "insurance contract plan" if—

(1) the plan is funded exclusively by the purchase of individual insurance contracts,

(2) such contracts provide for level annual premium payments to be paid extending not later than the retirement age for each individual participating in the plan, and commencing with the date the individual became a participant in the plan (or, in the case of an increase in benefits, commencing at the time such increase becomes effective),

(3) benefits provided by the plan are equal to the benefits provided under each contract at normal retirement age under the plan and are guaranteed by an insurance carrier (licensed under the laws of a State to do business with the plan) to the extent premiums have been paid,

(4) premiums payable for the plan year, and all prior plan years under such contracts have been paid before lapse or there is reinstatement of the policy,

(5) no rights under such contracts have been subject to a security interest at any time during the plan year, and

(6) no policy loans are outstanding at any time during the plan year.

A plan funded exclusively by the purchase of group insurance contracts which is determined under regulations prescribed by the Secretary of the Treasury to have the same characteristics as contracts described in the preceding sentence shall be treated as a plan described in this subsection.

Act Sec. 301. (c) APPLICABILITY OF THIS PART TO TERMINATED MULTIEMPLOYER PLANS.—This part applies, with respect to a terminated multiemployer plan to which section 4021 applies, until the last day of the plan year in which the plan terminates, within the meaning of section 4041A(a)(2).

Amendments

P.L. 109-280, § 201(c)(1):

Amended ERISA Sec. 301 by striking subsection (d).

Prior to repeal, ERISA Sec. 301(d) read as follows:

(d) FINANCIAL ASSISTANCE FROM PENSION BENEFIT GUARANTY CORPORATION.—Any amount of any financial assistance from the Pension Benefit Guaranty Corporation to any plan, and any repayment of such amount, shall be taken into account under this section in such manner as determined by the Secretary of the Treasury.

The above amendment applies to plan years beginning after 2007.

P.L. 101-239, § 7891(a)(1):

Titles I, III, and IV of ERISA (other than sections 3(37)(E), 301(a)(7), and 308, the last sentence of section 408(d), and sections 414(c), 4001(a)(3)(ii), and 4303) are each amended by striking "Internal Revenue Code of 1954" each place it appears and inserting "Internal Revenue Code of 1986" effective October 22, 1986.

P.L. 101-239, § 7894(d)(1):

Amended ERISA Sec. 301, in paragraph (8), by striking "or" at the end; in paragraph (9), by striking "plan." and inserting "plan; or;" and, in paragraph (10), by striking "Any" and inserting "any" effective as if included in P.L. 96-364, § 411.

P.L. 101-239, § 7894(d)(4):

Amended ERISA Sec. 301(a)(7) by striking "section 409 of such Code" and inserting "section 409 of the Internal Revenue Code of 1954 (as effective for obligations issued before January 1, 1984)" effective as if included in P.L. 98-369, § 491(b).

P.L. 96-364, §§ 304(a) and 411(b):

Added new section 301(a)(10) and new sections 301(c) and (d), effective September 26, 1980.

[¶ 14,620]
MINIMUM FUNDING STANDARDS

Act Sec. 302.(a) REQUIREMENT TO MEET MINIMUM FUNDING STANDARD.—

(1) IN GENERAL. A plan to which this part applies shall satisfy the minimum funding standard applicable to the plan for any plan year.

(2) MINIMUM FUNDING STANDARD. For purposes of paragraph (1), a plan shall be treated as satisfying the minimum funding standard for a plan year if —

(A) in the case of a defined benefit plan which is a single-employer plan (other than a CSEC plan), the employer makes contributions to or under the plan for the plan year which, in the aggregate, are not less than the minimum required contribution determined under section 303 for the plan for the plan year,

(B) in the case of a money purchase plan which is a single-employer plan, the employer makes contributions to or under the plan for the plan year which are required under the terms of the plan,

(C) in the case of a multiemployer plan, the employers make contributions to or under the plan for any plan year which, in the aggregate, are sufficient to ensure that the plan does not have an accumulated funding deficiency under section 304 as of the end of the plan year, and

(D) in the case of a CSEC plan, the employers make contributions to or under the plan for any plan year which, in the aggregate, are sufficient to ensure that the plan does not have an accumulated funding deficiency under sec tion 306 as of the end of the plan year.

(b) LIABILITY FOR CONTRIBUTIONS.—

(1) IN GENERAL. Except as provided in paragraph (2), the amount of any contribution required by this section (including any required installments under paragraphs (3) and (4) of section 303(j) or under section 306(f)) shall be paid by the employer responsible for making contributions to or under the plan.

(2) JOINT AND SEVERAL LIABILITY WHERE EMPLOYER MEMBER OF CONTROLLED GROUP. If the employer referred to in paragraph (1) is a member of a controlled group, each member of such group shall be jointly and severally liable for payment of such contributions.

(3) MULTIEMPLOYER PLANS IN CRITICAL STATUS. Paragraph (1) shall not apply in the case of a multiemployer plan for any plan year in which the plan is in critical status pursuant to section 305. This paragraph shall only apply if the plan sponsor adopts a rehabilitation plan in accordance with section 305(e) and complies with the terms of such rehabilitation plan (and any updates or modifications of the plan).

(c) VARIANCE FROM MINIMUM FUNDING STANDARDS.—

(1) WAIVER IN CASE OF BUSINESS HARDSHIP.—

(A) IN GENERAL. If —

(i) an employer is (or in the case of a multiemployer plan or a CSEC plan, 10 percent or more of the number of employers contributing to or under the plan are) unable to satisfy the minimum funding standard for a plan year without temporary substantial business hardship (substantial business hardship in the case of a multiemployer plan), and

(ii) application of the standard would be adverse to the interests of plan participants in the aggregate,

the Secretary of the Treasury may, subject to subparagraph (C), waive the requirements of subsection (a) for such year with respect to all or any portion of the minimum funding standard. The Secretary of the Treasury shall not waive the minimum funding standard with respect to a plan for more than 3 of any 15 (5 of any 15 in the case of a multiemployer plan) consecutive plan years.

(B) EFFECTS OF WAIVER. If a waiver is granted under subparagraph (A) for any plan year—

(i) in the case of a single-employer plan (other than a CSEC plan), the minimum required contribution under section 303 for the plan year shall be reduced by the amount of the waived funding deficiency and such amount shall be amortized as required under section 303(e),

(ii) in the case of a multiemployer plan, the funding standard account shall be credited under section 304(b)(3)(C) with the amount of the waived funding deficiency and such amount shall be amortized as required under section 304(b)(2)(C), and

(iii) in the case of a CSEC plan, the funding standard account shall be credited under section 306(b)(3)(C) with the amount of the waived funding deficiency and such amount shall be amortized as required under section 306(b)(2)(C).

(C) WAIVER OF AMORTIZED PORTION NOT ALLOWED. The Secretary of the Treasury may not waive under subparagraph (A) any portion of the minimum funding standard under subsection (a) for a plan year which is attributable to any waived funding deficiency for any preceding plan year.

(2) DETERMINATION OF BUSINESS HARDSHIP. For purposes of this subsection, the factors taken into account in determining temporary substantial business hardship (substantial business hardship in the case of a multiemployer plan) shall include (but shall not be limited to) whether or not—

(A) the employer is operating at an economic loss,

(B) there is substantial unemployment or underemployment in the trade or business and in the industry concerned,

(C) the sales and profits of the industry concerned are depressed or declining, and

(D) it is reasonable to expect that the plan will be continued only if the waiver is granted.

(3) WAIVED FUNDING DEFICIENCY. For purposes of this part, the term 'waived funding deficiency' means the portion of the minimum funding standard under subsection (a) (determined without regard to the waiver) for a plan year waived by the Secretary of the Treasury and not satisfied by employer contributions.

(4) SECURITY FOR WAIVERS FOR SINGLE-EMPLOYER PLANS, CONSULTATIONS—

(A) SECURITY MAY BE REQUIRED—

(i) IN GENERAL. Except as provided in subparagraph (C), the Secretary of the Treasury may require an employer maintaining a defined benefit plan which is a single-employer plan (within the meaning of section 4001(a)(15)) to provide security to such plan as a condition for granting or modifying a waiver under paragraph (1) or for granting an extension under section 306(d).

(ii) SPECIAL RULES. Any security provided under clause (i) may be perfected and enforced only by the Pension Benefit Guaranty Corporation, or at the direction of the Corporation, by a contributing sponsor (within the meaning of section 4001(a)(13)), or a member of such sponsor's controlled group (within the meaning of section 4001(a)(14)).

(B) CONSULTATION WITH THE PENSION BENEFIT GUARANTY CORPORATION. —Except as provided in subparagraph (c), the Secretary of the Treasury shall, before granting or modifying a waiver under this subsection or an extension under 306(d) with respect to a plan described in subparagraph (A)(i)—

(i) provide the Pension Benefit Guaranty Corporation with —

(I) notice of the completed application for any waiver, modification, or extension and

(II) an opportunity to comment on such application within 30 days after receipt of such notice, and

(ii) consider —

(I) any comments of the Corporation under clause (i)(II), and

(II) any views of any employee organization (within the meaning of section 3(4)) representing participants in the plan which are submitted in writing to the Secretary of the Treasury in connection with such application.

Information provided to the Corporation under this subparagraph shall be considered tax return information and subject to the safeguarding and reporting requirements of section 6103(p) of the Internal Revenue Code of 1986.

(C) EXCEPTION FOR CERTAIN WAIVERS OR EXTENSIONS.—

(i) IN GENERAL. The preceding provisions of this paragraph shall not apply to any plan with respect to which the sum of—

(I) the aggregate unpaid minimum required contributions for the plan year and all preceding plan years, or the accumulated funding deficiency under section 306, whichever is applicable,

(II) the present value of all waiver amortization installments determined for the plan year and succeeding plan years under section 303(e)(2) or 306(b)(2)(C), is less than $1,000,000.

(III) the total amounts not paid by reason of an extension in effect under section 306(d),

(ii) TREATMENT OF WAIVERS OR EXTENSIONS FOR WHICH APPLICATIONS ARE PENDING. The amount described in clause (i)(I) shall include any increase in such amount which would result if all applications for waivers or extensions with respect to the minimum funding standard under this subsection which are pending with respect to such plan were denied.

(iii) UNPAID MINIMUM REQUIRED CONTRIBUTION. For purposes of this subparagraph —

(I) IN GENERAL. The term 'unpaid minimum required contribution' means, with respect to any plan year, any minimum required contribution under section 303 for the plan year which is not paid on or before the due date (as determined under section 303(j)(1)) for the plan year.

(II) ORDERING RULE. For purposes of subclause (I), any payment to or under a plan for any plan year shall be allocated first to unpaid minimum required contributions for all preceding plan years on a first-in, first-out basis and then to the minimum required contribution under section 303 for the plan year.

(5) SPECIAL RULES FOR SINGLE-EMPLOYER PLANS.—

(A) APPLICATION MUST BE SUBMITTED BEFORE DATE 2 ½ MONTHS AFTER CLOSE. —In the case of a single-employer plan, no waiver may be granted under this subsection with respect to any plan for any plan year unless an application therefor is submitted to the Secretary of the Treasury not later than the 15th day of the 3rd month beginning after the close of such plan year.

(B) SPECIAL RULE IF EMPLOYER IS MEMBER OF CONTROLLED GROUP. In the case of a single-employer plan, if an employer is a member of a controlled group, the temporary substantial business hardship requirements of paragraph (1) shall be treated as met only if such requirements are met —

(i) with respect to such employer, and

(ii) with respect to the controlled group of which such employer is a member (determined by treating all members of such group as a single employer).

The Secretary of the Treasury may provide that an analysis of a trade or business or industry of a member need not be conducted if such Secretary determines such analysis is not necessary because the taking into account of such member would not significantly affect the determination under this paragraph.

(6) ADVANCE NOTICE.—

(A) IN GENERAL. The Secretary of the Treasury shall, before granting a waiver under this subsection, require each applicant to provide evidence satisfactory to such Secretary that the applicant has provided notice of the filing of the application for such waiver to each affected party (as defined in section 4001(a)(21)). Such notice shall include a description of the extent to which the plan is funded for benefits which are guaranteed under title IV and for benefit liabilities.

(B) CONSIDERATION OF RELEVANT INFORMATION. The Secretary of the Treasury shall consider any relevant information provided by a person to whom notice was given under subparagraph (A).

(7) RESTRICTION ON PLAN AMENDMENTS.—

(A) IN GENERAL. No amendment of a plan which increases the liabilities of the plan by reason of any increase in benefits, any change in the accrual of benefits, or any change in the rate at which benefits become nonforfeitable under the plan shall be adopted if a waiver under this subsection or an extension of time under section 304(d) or section 306(d) is in effect with respect to the plan, or if a plan amendment described in subsection (d)(2) which reduces the accrued benefit of any participant has been made at any time in the preceding 12 months (24 months in the case of a multiemployer plan). If a plan is amended in violation of the preceding sentence, any such waiver, or extension of time, shall not apply to any plan year ending on or after the date on which such amendment is adopted.

(B) EXCEPTION. Subparagraph (A) shall not apply to any plan amendment which —

(i) the Secretary of the Treasury determines to be reasonable and which provides for only de minimis increases in the liabilities of the plan,

(ii) only repeals an amendment described in subsection (d)(2), or

(iii) is required as a condition of qualification under part I of subchapter D of chapter 1 of the Internal Revenue Code of 1986.

(8) CROSS REFERENCE. For corresponding duties of the Secretary of the Treasury with regard to implementation of the Internal Revenue Code of 1986, see section 412(c) of such Code.

(d) MISCELLANEOUS RULES.—

(1) CHANGE IN METHOD OR YEAR. If the funding method or a plan year for a plan is changed, the change shall take effect only if approved by the Secretary of the Treasury.

(2) CERTAIN RETROACTIVE PLAN AMENDMENTS. For purposes of this section, any amendment applying to a plan year which —

(A) is adopted after the close of such plan year but no later than 21/2 months after the close of the plan year (or, in the case of a multiemployer plan, no later than 2 years after the close of such plan year),

(B) does not reduce the accrued benefit of any participant determined as of the beginning of the first plan year to which the amendment applies, and

(C) does not reduce the accrued benefit of any participant determined as of the time of adoption except to the extent required by the circumstances,

shall, at the election of the plan administrator, be deemed to have been made on the first day of such plan year. No amendment described in this paragraph which reduces the accrued benefits of any participant shall take effect unless the plan administrator files a notice with the Secretary of the Treasury notifying him of such amendment and such Secretary has approved such amendment, or within 90 days after the date on which such notice was filed, failed to disapprove such amendment. No amendment described in this subsection shall be approved by the Secretary of the Treasury unless such Secretary determines that such amendment is necessary because of a temporary substantial business hardship (as determined under subsection (c)(2)) or a substantial business hardship (as so determined) in the case of a multiemployer plan and that a waiver under subsection (c) (or, in the case of a multiemployer plan or a CSEC plan, any extension of the amortization period under section 304(d) or section 306(d)) is unavailable or inadequate.

(3) CONTROLLED GROUP. For purposes of this section, the term 'controlled group' means any group treated as a single employer under subsection (b), (c), (m), or (o) of section 414 of the Internal Revenue Code of 1986.

Amendments

P.L. 113-97, § 102(b)(1):

Amended ERISA Sec. 302(a)(2) by striking "and" at the end of subparagraph (B), by striking the period at the end of subparagraph (c) and inserting ", and" and by inserting at the end subparagraph (D) to read as above.

Effective for years beginning after 12-31-2013.

P.L. 113-97, § 102(b)(2)(A):

Amended ERISA Sec. 302 by striking "multiemployer plan" in the first place it appears in clause (i) of subsection (c)(1)(A) and the last place it appears in paragraph (2) of subsection (d) and inserting "multiemployer plan or a CSEC plan."

Effective for years beginning after 12-31-2013.

P.L. 113-97, § 102(b)(2)(B):

Amended ERISA Sec. 302 by striking "303(j)" in paragraph (1) of subsection (b) and inserting "303(j) or under section 306(f)".

Effective for years beginning after 12-31-2013.

P.L. 113-97, § 102(b)(2)(C):

Amended ERISA Sec. 302(c)(1)(B) by striking "and" at the end of clause (i), by striking the period at the end of clause (ii) and inserting "and" and by inserting clause (iii) to read as above.

Effective for years beginning after 12-31-2013.

P.L. 113-97, § 102(b)(2)(D):

Amended ERISA Sec. 302(c)(4)(A)(i) by striking "under paragraph (1)" and inserting "under paragraph (1) or for granting an extension under section 306(d)".

Effective for years beginning after 12-31-2013.

P.L. 113-97, § 102(b)(2)(E):

Amended ERISA Sec. 302(c)(4)(B) by striking "waiver under this subsection" and inserting "waiver under this subsection or an extension under 306(d)".

Effective for years beginning after 12-31-2013.

P.L. 113-97, § 102(b)(2)(F):

Amended ERISA Sec. 302(c)(4)(B)(i)(I) by striking "waiver or modification" and inserting "waiver, modification, or extension".

Effective for years beginning after 12-31-2013.

P.L. 113-97, § 102(b)(2)(G):

Amended ERISA Sec. 302 by striking "waivers" in the heading of subsection (c)(4)(C) and of clause (ii) of subsection (c)(4)(C) and inserting "waivers or extensions".

Effective for years beginning after 12-31-2013.

P.L. 113-97, § 102(b)(2)(H):

Amended ERISA Sec. 302(c)(7)(A) and 302(d)(2) by striking "section 304(d)" and inserting "section 304(d) or section 306(d)".

Effective for years beginning after 12-31-2013.

P.L. 113-97, § 102(b)(2)(I):

Amended ERISA Sec. 302(c)(4)(C)(i)(I) by striking "and" and adding "or the accumulated funding deficiency under section 306, whichever is applicable,".

Effective for years beginning after 12-31-2013.

P.L. 113-97, § 102(b)(2)(J):

Amended ERISA Sec. 302(c)(4)(C)(i)(II) by striking "303(e)(2)" and inserting "303(e)(2) or 306(b)(2)(C)".

Effective for years beginning after 12-31-2013.

P.L. 113-97, § 102(b)(2)(K):

Amended ERISA Sec. 302(c)(4)(C)(i) by adding subclause (III) to read as above.

Effective for years beginning after 12-31-2013.

P.L. 113-97, § 102(b)(2)(L):

Amended ERISA Sec. 302(c)(4)(C)(ii) by striking "for waivers of" and inserting "for waivers or extensions with respect to".

Effective for years beginning after 12-31-2013.

P.L. 113-97, § 102(b)(2)(M):

Amended ERISA Sec. 302(a)(2)(A) and 302(c)(1(B)(i) by striking "single-employer plan" and inserting "single-employer plan (other than a CSEC plan)".

Effective for years beginning after 12-31-2013.

P.L. 110-458, § 101(a)(1)(A):

Amended ERISA Sec. 302(c)(1)(A)(i) by striking "the plan is" and inserting "the plan are".

The above amendment takes effect as if included in the provisions of the 2006 Act to which the amendment relates. For effective date, see P.L. 109-280, § 202(f), below.

P.L. 110-458, § 101(a)(1)(B):

Amended ERISA Sec. 302(c)(7)(A) by inserting "which reduces the accrued benefit of any participant" after "subsection (d)(2)".

The above amendment takes effect as if included in the provisions of the 2006 Act to which the amendment relates. For effective date, see P.L. 109-280, § 202(f), below.

P.L. 110-458, § 101(a)(1)(C):

Amended ERISA Sec. 302(d)(1) by striking ", the valuation date,".

The above amendment takes effect as if included in the provisions of the 2006 Act to which the amendment relates. For effective date, see P.L. 109-280, § 202(f), below.

P.L. 110-458, § 102(b)(1)(A):

Amended ERISA Sec. 302(b)(3) by striking "the plan adopts" and inserting "the plan sponsor adopts".

The above amendment takes effect as if included in the provisions of the 2006 Act to which the amendment relates. For effective date, see P.L. 109-280, § 202(f), below.

Amendments

P. L. 109-280, § 811, provides:

Sec. 811. PENSION AND INDIVIDUAL RETIREMENT ARRANGEMENT PROVISIONS OF ECONOMIC GROWTH AND TAX RELIEF RECONCILIATION ACT OF 2001 MADE PERMANENT.

Title IX of the Economic Growth and Tax Reconciliation Act of 2001 [P. L. 107-16] shall not apply to the provisions of, and amendments made by, subtitles A through F of title VI [§§ 601-666] of such Act (relating to pension and individual retirement arrangement provisions).

P. L. 109-280, § 101(a):

Repealed ERISA Sec. 302.

Prior to repeal, ERISA Sec. 302 read as follows:

(a)(1) AVOIDANCE OF ACCUMULATED FUNDING DEFICIENCY.—Every employee pension benefit plan subject to this part shall satisfy the minimum funding standard (or the alternative minimum funding standard under section 305) for any plan year to which this part applies. A plan to which this part applies shall have satisfied the minimum funding standard for such plan for a plan year if as of the end of such plan year the plan does not have an accumulated funding deficiency.

(a)(2) For the purposes of this part, the term "accumulated funding deficiency" means for any plan the excess of the total charges to the funding standard account for all plan years (beginning with the first plan year to which this part applies) over the total credits to such account for such years or, if less, the excess of the total charges to the alternative minimum funding standard account for such plan years over the total credits to such account for such years.

(a)(3) In any plan year in which a multiemployer plan is in reorganization, the accumulated funding deficiency of the plan shall be determined under section 4243.

(b)(1) FUNDING STANDARD ACCOUNT.—Each plan to which this part applies shall establish and maintain a funding standard account. Such account shall be credited and charged solely as provided in this section.

(b)(2) For a plan year, the funding standard account shall be charged with the sum of—

(b)(2)(A) the normal cost of the plan for the plan year,

(b)(2)(B) the amounts necessary to amortize in equal annual installments (until fully amortized)—

(b)(2)(B)(i) in the case of a plan in existence on January 1, 1974, the unfunded past service liability under the plan on the first day of the first plan year to which this part applies, over a period of 40 plan years,

(b)(2)(B)(ii) in the case of a plan which comes into existence after January 1, 1974, the unfunded past service liability under the plan on the first day of the first plan year to which this part applies, over a period of 30 plan years,

(b)(2)(B)(iii) separately, with respect to each plan year, the net increase (if any) in unfunded past service liability under the plan arising from plan amendments adopted in such year, over a period of 30 plan years,

(b)(2)(B)(iv) separately, with respect to each plan year, the net experience loss (if any) under the plan, over a period of 5 plan years (15 plan years in the case of a multiemployer plan), and

(b)(2)(B)(v) separately, with respect to each plan year, the net loss (if any) resulting from changes in actuarial assumptions used under the plan, over a period of 10 plan years (30 plan years in the case of a multiemployer plan),

(b)(2)(C) the amount necessary to amortize each waived funding deficiency (within the meaning of section 303(c)) for each prior plan year in equal annual installments (until fully amortized) over a period of 5 plan years (15 plan years in the case of a multiemployer plan),

(b)(2)(D) the amount necessary to amortize in equal annual installments (until fully amortized) over a period of 5 plan years any amount credited to the funding standard account under paragraph (3)(D), and

(b)(2)(E) the amount necessary to amortize in equal annual installments (until fully amortized) over a period of 20 years the contributions which would be required to be made under the plan but for the provisions of subsection (c)(7)(A)(i)(I).

(b)(3) For a plan year, the funding standard account shall be credited with the sum of—

(b)(3)(A) the amount considered contributed by the employer to or under the plan for the plan year,

(b)(3)(B) the amount necessary to amortize in equal annual installments (until fully amortized)—

(b)(3)(B)(i) separately, with respect to each plan year, the net decrease (if any) in unfunded past service liability under the plan arising from plan amendments adopted in such year, over a period of 30 plan years,

(b)(3)(B)(ii) separately, with respect to each plan year, the net experience (if any) under the plan, over a period of 5 plan years (15 plan years in the case of a multiemployer plan), and

(b)(3)(B)(iii) separately, with respect to each plan year, the net gain (if any) resulting from changes in actuarial assumptions used under the plan, over a period of 10 plan years (30 plan years in the case of a multiemployer plan), (b)(3)(C) the amount of the waived funding deficiency (within the meaning of section 303(c)) for the plan year, and

(b)(3)(D) in the case of a plan year for which the accumulated funding deficiency is determined under the funding standard account if such plan year follows a plan year for which such deficiency was determined under the alternative minimum funding standard, the excess (if any) of any debit balance in the funding standard account (determined without regard to this subparagraph) over any debit balance in the alternative minimum funding standard account.

(b)(4) Under regulations prescribed by the Secretary of the Treasury, amounts required to be amortized under paragraph (2) or paragraph (3), as the case may be—

(b)(4)(A) may be combined into one amount under such paragraph to be amortized over a period determined on the basis of the remaining amortization period for all items entering into such combined amount, and

(b)(4)(B) may be offset against amounts required to be amortized under the other such paragraph, with the resulting amount to be amortized over a period determined on the basis of the remaining amortization periods for all items entering into whichever of the two amounts being offset is the greater.

(b)(5) INTEREST.—

(b)(5)(A) IN GENERAL. The funding standard account (and items therein) shall be charged or credited (as determined under regulations prescribed by the Secretary of the Treasury) with interest at the appropriate rate consistent with the rate or rates of interest used under the plan to determine costs.

(b)(5)(B) REQUIRED CHANGE OF INTEREST RATE. For purposes of determining a plan's current liability and for purposes of determining a plan's required contribution under section 302(d) for any plan year—

(b)(5)(B)(i) IN GENERAL. If any rate of interest used under the plan to determine cost is not within the permissible range, the plan shall establish a new rate of interest within the permissible range.

(b)(5)(B)(ii) PERMISSIBLE RANGE. For purposes of this subparagraph—

(b)(5)(B)(ii)(I) IN GENERAL. Except as provided in subclause (II) or (III), the term "permissible range" means a rate of interest which is not more than 10 percent above, and not more than 10 percent below, the weighted average of the rates of interest on 30-year Treasury securities during the 4-year period ending on the last day before the beginning of the plan year.

(b)(5)(B)(ii)(II) SPECIAL RULE FOR YEARS 2004, 2005, 2006, AND 2007. In the case of plan years beginning after December 31, 2003, and before January 1, 2008, the term 'permissible range' means a rate of interest which is not above, and not more than 10 percent below, the weighted average of the rates of interest on amounts invested conservatively in long-term investment grade corporate bonds during the 4-year period ending on the last day before the beginning of the plan year. Such rates shall be determined by the Secretary of the Treasury on the basis of 2 or more indices that are selected periodically by the Secretary of the Treasury and that are in the top 3 quality levels available. The Secretary of the Treasury shall make the permissible range, and the indices and methodology used to determine the average rate, publicly available.

(b)(5)(B)(ii)(III) SECRETARIAL AUTHORITY. If the Secretary finds that the lowest rate of interest permissible under subclause (I) or (II) is unreasonably high, the Secretary may prescribe a lower rate of interest, except that such rate may not be less than 80 percent of the average rate determined under such subclause.

(b)(5)(B)(iii) ASSUMPTIONS. Notwithstanding subsection (c)(3)(A)(i), the interest rate used under the plan shall be—

(b)(5)(B)(iii)(I) determined without taking into account the experience of the plan and reasonable expectations, but

(b)(5)(B)(iii)(II) consistent with the assumptions which reflect the purchase rates which would be used by insurance companies to satisfy the liabilities under the plan.

(b)(6) In the case of a plan which, immediately before the date of the enactment of the Multiemployer Pension Plan Amendments Act of 1980, was a multiemployer plan (within the meaning of section 3(37) as in effect immediately before such date)—

(b)(6)(A) any amount described in paragraph (2)(B)(ii), (2)(B)(iii), or (3)(B)(i) of this subsection which arose in a plan year beginning before such date shall be amortized in equal annual installments (until fully amortized) over 40 plan years beginning with the plan year in which the amount arose;

(b)(6)(B) any amount described in paragraph (2)(B)(iv) or (3)(B)(ii) of this subsection which arose in a plan year beginning before such date shall be amortized in equal annual installments (until fully amortized) over 20 plan years, beginning with the plan year in which the amount arose;

(b)(6)(C) any change in past service liability which arises during the period of 3 plan years beginning on or after such date, and results from a plan amendment adopted before such date, shall be amortized in equal annual installments (until fully amortized) over 40 plan years, beginning with the plan year in which the change arises; and

(b)(6)(D) any change in past service liability which arises during the period of 2 plan years beginning on or after such date, and results from the changing of a group of participants from one benefit level to another benefit level under a schedule of plan benefits which—

(b)(6)(D)(i) was adopted before such date, and

(b)(6)(D)(ii) was effective for any plan participant before the beginning of the first plan year beginning on or after such date,

shall be amortized in equal annual installments (until fully amortized) over 40 plan years, beginning with the plan year in which the increase arises.

(b)(7) For purposes of this part—

(b)(7)(A) Any amount received by a multiemployer plan in payment of all or part of an employer's withdrawal liability under part 1 of subtitle E of title IV shall be considered an amount contributed by the employer to or under the plan. The Secretary of the Treasury may prescribe by regulation additional charges and credits to a multiemployer plan's funding standard account to the extent necessary to prevent withdrawal liability payments from being unduly reflected as advance funding for plan liabilities.

(b)(7)(B) If a plan is not in reorganization in the plan year but was in reorganization in the immediately preceding plan year, any balance in the funding standard account at the close of such immediately preceding plan year—

(b)(7)(B)(i) shall be eliminated by an offsetting credit or charge (as the case may be), but

(b)(7)(B)(ii) shall be taken into account in subsequent plan years by being amortized in equal annual installments (until fully amortized) over 30 plan years.

The preceding sentence shall not apply to the extent of any accumulated funding deficiency under section 418B(a) of the Internal Revenue Code of 1986 as of the end of the last plan year that the plan was in reorganization.

(b)(7)(C) Any amount paid by a plan during a plan year to the Pension Benefit Guaranty Corporation pursuant to section 4222 or to a fund exempt under section 501(c)(22) of such Code pursuant to section 4223 shall reduce the amount of contributions considered received by the plan for the plan year.

(b)(7)(D) Any amount paid by an employer pending a final determination of the employer's withdrawal liability under part 1 of subtitle E of title IV and subsequently refunded to the employer by the plan shall be charged to the funding standard account in accordance with regulations prescribed by the Secretary.

(b)(7)(E) For purposes of the full funding limitation under subsection (c)(7), unless otherwise provided by the plan, the accrued liability under a multiemployer plan shall not include benefits which are not nonforfeitable under the plan after the termination of the plan (taking into consideration section 411(d)(3) of the Internal Revenue Code of 1986).

(b)(7)(F) ELECTION FOR DEFERRAL OF CHARGE FOR PORTION OF NET EXPERIENCE LOSS

(b)(7)(F)(i) IN GENERAL. With respect to the net experience loss of an eligible multiemployer plan for the first plan year beginning after December 31, 2001, the plan sponsor may elect to defer up to 80 percent of the amount otherwise required to be charged under paragraph (2)(B)(iv) for any plan year beginning after June 30, 2003, and before July 1, 2005, to any plan year selected by the plan from either of the 2 immediately succeeding plan years.

(b)(7)(F)(ii) INTEREST. For the plan year to which a charge is deferred pursuant to an election under clause (i), the funding standard account shall be charged with interest on the deferred charge for the period of deferral at the rate determined under section 304(a) for multiemployer plans.

(b)(7)(F)(iii) RESTRICTIONS ON BENEFIT INCREASES. No amendment which increases the liabilities of the plan by reason of any increase in benefits, any change in the accrual of benefits, or any change in the rate at which benefits become nonforfeitable under the plan shall be adopted during any period for which a charge is deferred pursuant to an election under clause (i), unless—

(b)(7)(F)(iii)(I) the plan's enrolled actuary certifies (in such form and manner prescribed by the Secretary of the Treasury) that the amendment provides for an increase in annual contributions which will exceed the increase in annual charges to the funding standard account attributable to such amendment, or

(b)(7)(F)(iii)(II) the amendment is required by a collective bargaining agreement which is in effect on the date of enactment of this subparagraph.

If a plan is amended during any such plan year in violation of the preceding sentence, any election under this paragraph shall not apply to any such plan year ending on or after the date on which such amendment is adopted.

(b)(7)(F)(iv) ELIGIBLE MULTIEMPLOYER PLAN. For purposes of this subparagraph, the term 'eligible multiemployer plan' means a multiemployer plan—

(b)(7)(F)(iv)(I) which had a net investment loss for the first plan year beginning after December 31, 2001, of at least 10 percent of the average fair market value of the plan assets during the plan year, and

(b)(7)(F)(iv)(II) with respect to which the plan's enrolled actuary certifies (not taking into account the application of this subparagraph), on the basis of the acutuarial assumptions used for the last plan year ending before the date of the enactment of this subparagraph, that the plan is projected to have an accumulated funding deficiency (within the meaning of subsection (a)(2)) for any plan year beginning after June 30, 2003, and before July 1, 2006.

For purposes of subclause (I), a plan's net investment loss shall be determined on the basis of the actual loss and not under any actuarial method used under subsection (c)(2).

(b)(7)(F)(v) EXCEPTION TO TREATMENT OF ELIGIBLE MULTIEMPLOYER PLAN. In no event shall a plan be treated as an eligible multiemployer plan under clause (iv) if—

(b)(7)(F)(v)(I) for any taxable year beginning during the 10-year period preceding the first plan year for which an election is made under clause (i), any employer required to contribute to the plan failed to timely pay any excise tax imposed under section 4971 of the Internal Revenue Code of 1986 with respect to the plan,

(b)(7)(F)(v)(II) for any plan year beginning after June 30, 1993, and before the first plan year for which an election is made under clause (i), the average contribution required to be made by all employers to the plan does not exceed 10 cents per hour or no employer is required to make contributions to the plan, or

(b)(7)(F)(v)(III) with respect to any of the plan years beginning after June 30, 1993, and before the first plan year for which an election is made under clause (i), a waiver was granted under section 303 of this Act or section 412(d) of the Internal Revenue Code of 1986 with respect to the plan or an extension of an amortization period was granted under section 304 of this Act or section 412(e) of such Code with respect to the plan.

(b)(7)(F)(vi) NOTICE. If a plan sponsor makes an election under this subparagraph or section 412(b)(7)(F) of the Internal Revenue Code of 1986 for any plan year, the plan administrator shall provide, within 30 days of filing the election for such year, written notice of the election to participants and beneficiaries, to each labor organization representing such participants or beneficiaries, to each employer that has an obligation to contribute under the plan, and to the Pension Benefit Guaranty Corporation. Such notice shall include with respect to any election the amount of any charge to be deferred and the period of the deferral. Such notice shall also include the maximum guaranteed monthly benefits which the Pension Benefit Guaranty Corporation would pay if the plan terminated while underfunded.

(b)(7)(F)(vii) ELECTION. An election under this subparagraph shall be made at such time and in such manner as the Secretary of the Treasury may prescribe.

(c)(1) For purposes of this part, normal costs, accrued liability, past service liabilities, and experience gains and losses shall be determined under the funding method used to determine costs under the plan.

(c)(2)(A) For purposes of this part, the value of the plan's assets shall be determined on the basis of any reasonable actuarial method of valuation which takes into account fair market value and which is permitted under regulations prescribed by the Secretary of the Treasury.

(c)(2)(B) For purposes of this part, the value of a bond or other evidence of indebtedness which is not in default as to principal or interest may, at the election of the plan administrator, be determined on an amortized basis running from initial cost at purchase to par value at maturity or earliest call date. Any election under this subparagraph shall be made at such time and in such manner as the Secretary of the Treasury shall by regulations provide, shall apply to all such evidences of indebtedness, and may be revoked only with the consent of the Secretary of the Treasury. In the case of a plan other than a multiemployer plan, this subparagraph shall not apply, but the Secretary of the Treasury may by regulations provide that the value of any dedicated bond portfolio of such plan shall be determined by using the interest rate under subsection (b)(5).

(c)(3) For purposes of this section, all costs, liabilities, rates of interest, and other factors under the plan shall be determined on the basis of actuarial assumptions and methods—

(c)(3)(A) in the case of—

(c)(3)(A)(i) a plan other than a multiemployer plan, each of which is reasonable (taking into account the experience of the plan and reasonable expectations) or which, in the aggregate, result in a total contribution equivalent to that which would be determined if each such assumption and method were reasonable, or

(c)(3)(A)(ii) a multiemployer plan, which, in the aggregate, are reasonable (taking into account the experiences of the plan and reasonable expectations), and

(c)(3)(B) which, in combination, offer the actuary's best estimate of anticipated experience under the plan.

(c)(4) For purposes of this section, if—

(c)(4)(A) a change in benefits under the Social Security Act or in other retirement benefits created under Federal or State law, or

(c)(4)(B) a change in the definition of the term "wages" under section 3121 of the Internal Revenue Code of 1954, or a change in the amount of such wages taken into account under regulations prescribed for purposes of section 401(a)(5) of the Internal Revenue Code of 1986,

results in an increase or decrease in accrued liability under a plan, such increase or decrease shall be treated as an experience loss or gain.

(c)(5)(A) IN GENERAL. If the funding method for a plan is changed, the new funding method shall become the funding method used to determine costs and liabilities under the plan only if the change is approved by the Secretary of the Treasury. If the plan year for a plan is changed, the new plan year shall become the plan year for the plan only if the change is approved by the Secretary of the Treasury.

(c)(5)(B) APPROVAL REQUIRED FOR CERTAIN CHANGES IN ASSUMPTIONS BY CERTAIN SINGLE-EMPLOYER PLANS SUBJECT TO ADDITIONAL FUNDING REQUIREMENT.

(c)(5)(B)(i) IN GENERAL. No actuarial assumption (other than the assumptions described in subsection (d)(7)(C)) used to determine the current liability for a plan to which this subparagraph applies may be changed without the approval of the Secretary of the Treasury.

(c)(5)(B)(ii) PLANS TO WHICH SUBPARAGRAPH APPLIES. This subparagraph shall apply to a plan only if—

(c)(5)(B)(ii)(I) the plan is a defined benefit plan (other than a multiemployer plan) to which title IV applies;

(c)(5)(B)(ii)(II) the aggregate unfunded vested benefits as of the close of the preceding plan year (as determined under section 4006(a)(3)(E)(iii)) of such plan and all other plans maintained by the contributing sponsors (as defined in section 4001(a)(13)) and members of such sponsors' controlled groups (as defined in section 4001(a)(14)) which are covered by title IV (disregarding plans with no unfunded vested benefits) exceed $50,000,000; and

(c)(5)(B)(ii)(III) the change in assumptions (determined after taking into account any changes in interest rate and mortality table) results in a decrease in the unfunded current liability of the plan for the current plan year that exceeds $50,000,000, or that exceeds $5,000,000 and that is 5 percent or more of the current liability of the plan before such change.

(c)(6) If, as of the close of a plan year, a plan would (without regard to this paragraph) have an accumulated funding deficiency (determined without regard to the alternative minimum funding standard account permitted under section 305) in excess of the full funding limitation—

(c)(6)(A) the funding standard account shall be credited with the amount of such excess, and

(c)(6)(B) all amounts described in paragraphs (2)(B), (C), and (D) and (3)(B) of subsection (b) which are required to be amortized shall be considered fully amortized for purposes of such paragraphs.

(c)(7) FULL-FUNDING LIMITATION.

(c)(7)(A) IN GENERAL. For purposes of paragraph (6), the term "full-funding limitation" means the excess (if any) of—

(c)(7)(A)(i) the lesser of (I) in the case of plan years beginning before January 1, 2004, the applicable percentage of current liability (including the expected increase in current liability due to benefits accruing during the plan year), or (II) the accrued liability (including normal cost) under the plan (determined under the entry age normal funding method if such accrued liability cannot be directly calculated under the funding method used for the plan), over

(c)(7)(A)(ii) the lesser of—

(c)(7)(A)(ii)(I) the fair market value of the plan's assets, or

(c)(7)(A)(ii)(II) the value of such assets determined under paragraph (2).

(c)(7)(B) CURRENT LIABILITY. For purposes of subparagraph (D) and subclause (I) of subparagraph (A)(i), the term "current liability" has the meaning given such term by subsection (d)(7) (without regard to subparagraphs (C) and (D) thereof) and using the rate of interest used under subsection (b)(5)(B).

(c)(7)(C) SPECIAL RULE FOR PARAGRAPH (6)(B). For purposes of paragraph (6)(B), subparagraph (A)(i) shall be applied without regard to subclause (I) thereof.

(c)(7)(D) REGULATORY AUTHORITY. The Secretary of the Treasury may by regulations provide—

(c)(7)(D)(i) for adjustments to the percentage contained in subparagraph (A)(i) to take into account the respective ages or lengths of service of the participants and

(c)(7)(D)(ii) alternative methods based on factors other than current liability for the determination of the amount taken into account under subparagraph (A)(i).

(c)(7)(E) MINIMUM AMOUNT.

(c)(7)(E)(i) IN GENERAL. In no event shall the full-funding limitation determined under subparagraph (A) be less than the excess (if any) of—

(c)(7)(E)(i)(I) 90 percent of the current liability of the plan (including the expected increase in current liability due to benefits accruing during the plan year), over

(c)(7)(E)(i)(II) the value of the plan's assets determined under paragraph (2).

(c)(7)(E)(ii) CURRENT LIABILITY; ASSETS. For purposes of clause (i)—

(c)(7)(E)(ii)(I) the term "current liability" has the meaning given such term by subsection (d)(7) (without regard to subparagraph (D) thereof), and

(c)(7)(E)(ii)(II) assets shall not be reduced by any credit balance in the funding standard account.

(c)(7)(F) APPLICABLE PERCENTAGE. For purposes of subparagraph (A)(i)(I), the applicable percentage shall be determined in accordance with the following table:

"In the case of any plan year beginning in—	The applicable percentage is—
2002	165
2003	170.

(c)(8) For purposes of this part, any amendment applying to a plan year which—

(c)(8)(A) is adopted after the close of such plan year but no later than 2 ½ months after the close of the plan year (or, in the case of a multiemployer plan, no later than 2 years after the close of such plan year),

(c)(8)(B) does not reduce the accrued benefit of any participant determined as of the beginning of the first plan year to which the amendment applies, and

(c)(8)(C) does not reduce the accrued benefit of any participant determined as of the time of adoption except to the extent required by the circumstances,

shall, at the election of the plan administrator, be deemed to have been made on the first day of such plan year. No amendment described in this paragraph which reduces the accrued benefits of any participant shall take effect unless the plan administrator files a notice with the Secretary notifying him of such amendment and the Secretary has approved such amendment or, within 90 days after the date on which such notice was filed, failed to disapprove such amendment. No amendment described in this subsection shall be approved by the Secretary unless he determines that such amendment is necessary because of a substantial business hardship (as determined under section 303(b)) and that waiver under section 303(a) is unavailable or inadequate.

(c)(9)(A) For purposes of this part, a determination of experience gains and losses and a valuation of the plan's liability shall be made not less frequently than once every year, except that such determination shall be made more frequently to the extent required in particular cases under regulations prescribed by the Secretary of the Treasury.

(c)(9)(B)(i) Except as provided in clause (ii), the valuation referred to in subparagraph (A) shall be made as of a date within the plan year to which the valuation refers or within one month prior to the beginning of such year.

(c)(9)(B)(ii) The valuation referred to in subparagraph (A) may be made as of a date within the plan year prior to the year to which the valuation refers if, as of such date, the value of the assets of the plan are not less than 100 percent of the plan's current liability (as defined in paragraph (7)(B)).

(c)(9)(B)(iii) Information under clause (ii) shall, in accordance with regulations, be actuarially adjusted to reflect significant differences in participants.

(c)(9)(B)(iv) A change in funding method to use a prior year valuation, as provided in clause (ii), may not be made unless as of the valuation date within the prior plan year, the value of the assets of the plan are not less than 125 percent of the plan's current liability (as defined in paragraph (7)(B)).

(c)(10) For purposes of this section—

(c)(10)(A) In the case of a defined benefit plan other than a multiemployer plan, any contributions for a plan year made by an employer during the period—

(c)(10)(A)(i) beginning on the day after the last day of such plan year, and

(c)(10)(A)(ii) ending on the date which is 8 ½ months after the close of the plan year, shall be deemed to have been made on such last day.

(c)(10)(B) In the case of a plan not described in subparagraph (A), any contributions for a plan year made by an employer after the last day of such plan year, but not later than two and one-half months after such day, shall be deemed to have been made on such last day. For purposes of this subparagraph, such two and one-half month period may be extended for not more than six months under regulations prescribed by the Secretary of the Treasury.

(c)(11) LIABILITY FOR CONTRIBUTIONS.

(c)(11)(A) IN GENERAL. Except as provided in subparagraph (B), the amount of any contribution required by this section and any required installments under subsection

(e) shall be paid by the employer responsible for contributing to or under the plan the amount described in subsection (b)(3)(A).

(c)(11)(B) JOINT AND SEVERAL LIABILITY WHERE EMPLOYER MEMBER OF CONTROLLED GROUP.

(c)(11)(B)(i) IN GENERAL. In the case of a plan other than a multiemployer plan, if the employer referred to in subparagraph (A) is a member of a controlled group, each member of such group shall be jointly and severally liable for payment of such contribution or required installment.

(c)(11)(B)(ii) CONTROLLED GROUP. For purposes of clause (i), the term "controlled group" means any group treated as a single employer under subsection (b), (c), (m), or (o) of section 414 of the Internal Revenue Code of 1986.

(c)(12) ANTICIPATION OF BENEFIT INCREASES EFFECTIVE IN THE FUTURE. In determining projected benefits, the funding method of a collectively bargained plan described in section 413(a) of the Internal Revenue Code of 1986 (other than a multiemployer plan) shall anticipate benefit increases scheduled to take effect during the term of the collective bargaining agreement applicable to the plan.

(d) ADDITIONAL FUNDING REQUIREMENTS FOR PLANS WHICH ARE NOT MULTIEMPLOYER PLANS.

(d)(1) IN GENERAL. In the case of a defined benefit plan (other than a multiemployer plan) to which this subsection applies under paragraph (9) for any plan year, the amount charged to the funding standard account for such plan year shall be increased by the sum of—

(d)(1)(A) the excess (if any) of—

(d)(1)(A)(i) the deficit reduction contribution determined under paragraph (2) for such plan year, over

(d)(1)(A)(ii) the sum of the charges for such plan year under subsection (b)(2), reduced by the sum of the credits for such plan year under subparagraph (B) of subsection (b)(3), plus

(d)(1)(B) the unpredictable contingent event amount (if any) for such plan year.

Such increase shall not exceed the amount which, after taking into account charges (other than the additional charge under this subsection) and credits under subsection (b), is necessary to increase the funded current liability percentage (taking into account the expected increase in current liability due to benefits accruing during the plan year) to 100 percent.

(d)(2) DEFICIT REDUCTION CONTRIBUTION. For purposes of paragraph (1), the deficit reduction contribution determined under this paragraph for any plan year is the sum of—

(d)(2)(A) the unfunded old liability amount,

(d)(2)(B) the unfunded new liability amount,

(d)(2)(C) the expected increase in current liability due to benefits accruing during the plan year, and

(d)(2)(D) the aggregate of the unfunded mortality increase amounts.

(d)(3) UNFUNDED OLD LIABILITY AMOUNT. For purposes of this subsection—

(d)(3)(A) IN GENERAL. The unfunded old liability amount with respect to any plan year for any plan year is the amount necessary to amortize the unfunded old liability under the plan in equal annual installments over a period of 18 plan years (beginning with the 1st plan year beginning after December 31, 1988).

(d)(3)(B) UNFUNDED OLD LIABILITY. The term "unfunded old liability" means the unfunded current liability of the plan as of the beginning of the 1st plan year beginning after December 31, 1987 (determined without regard to any plan amendment increasing liabilities adopted after October 16, 1987).

(d)(3)(C) SPECIAL RULES FOR BENEFIT INCREASES UNDER EXISTING COLLECTIVE BARGAINING AGREEMENTS.

(d)(3)(C)(i) IN GENERAL. In the case of a plan maintained pursuant to 1 or more collective bargaining agreements between employee representatives and the employer ratified before October 17, 1987, the unfunded old liability amount with respect to such plan for any plan year shall be increased by the amount necessary to amortize the unfunded existing benefit increase liability in equal annual installments over a period of 18 plan years beginning with—

(d)(3)(C)(i)(I) the plan year in which the benefit increase with respect to such liability occurs, or

(d)(3)(C)(i)(II) if the taxpayer elects, the 1st plan year beginning after December 31, 1988.

(d)(3)(C)(ii) UNFUNDED EXISTING BENEFIT INCREASE LIABILITIES. For purposes of clause (i), the unfunded existing benefit increase liability means, with respect to any benefit increase under the agreements described in clause (i) which takes effect during or after the 1st plan year beginning after December 31, 1987, the unfunded current liability determined—

(d)(3)(C)(ii)(I) by taking into account only liabilities attributable to such benefit increase, and

(d)(3)(C)(ii)(II) by reducing (but not below zero) the amount determined under paragraph (8)(A)(ii) by the current liability determined without regard to such benefit increase.

(d)(3)(C)(iii) EXTENSIONS, MODIFICATIONS, ETC. NOT TAKEN INTO ACCOUNT. For purposes of this subparagraph, any extension, amendment, or other modification of an agreement after October 16, 1987, shall not be taken into account.

(d)(3)(D) SPECIAL RULE FOR REQUIRED CHANGES IN ACTUARIAL ASSUMPTIONS.

(d)(3)(D)(i) IN GENERAL. The unfunded old liability amount with respect to any plan for any plan year shall be increased by the amount necessary to amortize the amount of additional unfunded old liability under the plan in equal annual installments over a period of 12 plan years (beginning with the first plan year beginning after December 31, 1994).

(d)(3)(D)(ii) ADDITIONAL UNFUNDED OLD LIABILITY. For purposes of clause (i), the term "additional unfunded old liability" means the amount (if any) by which—

(d)(3)(D)(ii)(I) the current liability of the plan as of the beginning of the first plan year beginning after December 31, 1994, valued using the assumptions required by paragraph (7)(C) as in effect for plan years beginning after December 31, 1994, exceeds

(d)(3)(D)(ii)(II) the current liability of the plan as of the beginning of such first plan year, valued using the same assumptions used under subclause (I) (other than the assumptions required by paragraph (7)(C)), using the prior interest rate, and using such mortality assumptions as were used to determine current liability for the first plan year beginning after December 31, 1992.

(d)(3)(D)(iii) For purposes of clause (ii), the term 'prior interest rate' means the rate of interest that is the same percentage of the weighted average under subsection (b)(5)(B)(ii)(I) PRIOR INTEREST RATE. for the first plan year beginning after December 31, 1994, as the rate of interest used by the plan to determine current liability for the first plan year beginning after December 31, 1992, is of the weighted average under subsection (b)(5)(B)(ii)(I) for such first plan year beginning after December 31, 1992.

(d)(3)(E) OPTIONAL RULE FOR ADDITIONAL UNFUNDED OLD LIABILITY.

(d)(3)(E)(i) IN GENERAL. If an employer makes an election under clause (ii), the additional unfunded old liability for purposes of subparagraph (D) shall be the amount (if any) by which—

(d)(3)(E)(i)(I) the unfunded current liability of the plan as of the beginning of the first plan year beginning after December 31, 1994, valued using the assumptions required by paragraph (7)(C) as in effect for plan years beginning after December 31, 1994, exceeds

(d)(3)(E)(i)(II) the unamortized portion of the unfunded old liability under the plan as of the beginning of the first plan year beginning after December 31, 1994.

(d)(3)(E)(ii) ELECTION.

(d)(3)(E)(ii)(I) An employer may irrevocably elect to apply the provisions of this subparagraph as of the beginning of the first plan year beginning after December 31, 1994.

(d)(3)(E)(ii)(II) If an election is made under this clause, the increase under paragraph (1) for any plan year beginning after December 31, 1994, and before January 1, 2002, to which this subsection applies (without regard to this subclause) shall not be less than the increase that would be required under paragraph (1) if the provisions of this title as in effect for the last plan year beginning before January 1, 1995, had remained in effect.

(d)(4) UNFUNDED NEW LIABILITY AMOUNT. For purposes of this subsection—

(d)(4)(A) IN GENERAL. The unfunded new liability amount with respect to any plan for any plan year is the applicable percentage of the unfunded new liability.

(d)(4)(B) UNFUNDED NEW LIABILITY. The term "unfunded new liability" means the unfunded current liability of the plan for the plan year determined without regard to—

(d)(4)(B)(i) the unamortized portion of the unfunded old liability, the unamortized portion of the additional unfunded old liability, the unamortized portion of each unfunded mortality increase, and the unamortized portion of the unfunded existing benefit increase liability, and

(d)(4)(B)(ii) the liability with respect to any unpredictable contingent event benefits (without regard to whether the event has occurred).

(d)(4)(C) APPLICABLE PERCENTAGE. The term "applicable percentage" means, with respect to any plan year, 30 percent, reduced by the products of—

(d)(4)(C)(i) .40 multiplied by

(d)(4)(C)(ii) the number of percentage points (if any) by which the funded current liability percentage exceeds 60 percent.

(d)(5) UNPREDICTABLE CONTINGENT EVENT AMOUNT.

(d)(5)(A) IN GENERAL. The unpredictable contingent event amount with respect to a plan for any plan year is an amount equal to the greatest of—

(d)(5)(A)(i) the applicable percentage of the product of—

(d)(5)(A)(i)(I) 100 percent, reduced (but not below zero) by the funded current liability percentage for the plan year, multiplied by

(d)(5)(A)(i)(II) the amount of unpredictable contingent event benefits paid during the plan year, including (except as provided by the Secretary of the Treasury) any payment for the purchase of an annuity contract for a participant or beneficiary with respect to such benefits, or

(d)(5)(A)(ii) the amount which would be determined for the plan year if the unpredictable contingent event benefit liabilities were amortized in equal annual installments over 7 plan years (beginning with the plan year in which such event occurs), or

(d)(5)(A)(iii) the additional amount that would be determined under paragraph (4)(A) if the unpredictable contingent event benefit liabilities were included in unfunded new liability notwithstanding paragraph (4)(B)(ii).

(d)(5)(B) APPLICABLE PERCENTAGE.

In the case of plan years beginning in:	The applicable percentage is:
1989 and 1990	5
1991	10
1992	15
1993	20
1994	30
1995	40
1996	50
1997	60
1998	70
1999	80

In the case of plan years beginning in:	The applicable percentage is:
2000	90
2001 and thereafter	100

(d)(5)(C) PARAGRAPH NOT TO APPLY TO EXISTING BENEFITS. This paragraph shall not apply to unpredictable contingent event benefits (and liabilities attributable thereto) for which the event occurred before the first plan year beginning after December 31, 1988.

(d)(5)(D) SPECIAL RULE FOR FIRST YEAR OF AMORTIZATION. Unless the employer elects otherwise, the amount determined under subparagraph (A) for the plan year in which the event occurs shall be equal to 150 percent of the amount determined under subparagraph (A)(i). The amount under subparagraph (A)(ii) for subsequent plan years in the amortization period shall be adjusted in the manner provided by the Secretary of the Treasury to reflect the application of this subparagraph.

(d)(5)(E) The present value of the amounts described in subparagraph (A) with respect to any one event shall not exceed the unpredictable contingent event benefit liabilities attributable to that event.

(d)(6) SPECIAL RULES FOR SMALL PLANS.

(d)(6)(A) PLANS WITH 100 OR FEWER PARTICIPANTS. This subsection shall not apply to any plan for any plan year if on each day during the preceding plan year such plan had no more than 100 participants.

(d)(6)(B) In the case of a plan to which subparagraph (A) does not apply and which on each day during the preceding plan year had no more than 150 participants, the amount of the increase under paragraph (1) for such plan year shall be equal to the product of—

(d)(6)(B)(i) such increase determined without regard to this subparagraph, multiplied by

(d)(6)(B)(ii) 2 percent for the highest number of participants in excess of 100 on any such day.

(d)(6)(C) For purposes of this paragraph, all defined benefit plans maintained by the same employer (or any member of such employer's controlled group) shall be treated as 1 plan, but only liabilities of such employer or member shall be taken into account.

(d)(7) CURRENT LIABILITY. For purposes of this subsection—

(d)(7)(A) IN GENERAL. The term "current liability" means all liabilities to participants and their beneficiaries under the plan.

(d)(7)(B) TREATMENT OF UNPREDICTABLE CONTINGENT EVENT BENEFITS.

(d)(7)(B)(i) IN GENERAL. For purposes of subparagraph (A), any unpredictable contingent event benefit shall not be taken into account until the event on which the benefit is contingent occurs.

(d)(7)(B)(ii) UNPREDICTABLE CONTINGENT EVENT BENEFIT. The term "unpredictable contingent event benefit" means any benefit contingent on an event other than—

(d)(7)(B)(ii)(I) age, service compensation, death or disability, or

(d)(7)(B)(ii)(II) an event which is reasonably and reliably predictable (as determined by the Secretary of the Treasury).

(d)(7)(C) INTEREST RATE AND MORTALITY ASSUMPTIONS USED. Effective for plan year beginning after December 31, 1994—

(d)(7)(C)(i) INTEREST RATE.

(d)(7)(C)(i)(I) IN GENERAL. The rate of interest used to determine current liability under this subsection shall be the rate of interest used under subsection (b)(5), except that the highest rate in the permissible range under subparagraph (B)(ii) thereof shall not exceed the specified percentage under subclause (II) of the weighted average referred to in such subparagraph.

(d)(7)(C)(i)(II) SPECIFIED PERCENTAGE. For purposes of subclause (I), the specified percentage shall be determined as follows:

In the case of plan years beginning in calendar year:	The specified percentage is:
1995	109
1996	108
1997	107
1998	106
1999 and thereafter	105

(d)(7)(C)(i)(III) SPECIAL RULE FOR 2002 AND 2003. For a plan year beginning in 2002 or 2003, notwithstanding subclause (I), in the case that the rate of interest used under subsection (b)(5) exceeds the highest rate permitted under subclause (I), the rate of interest used to determine current liability under this subsection may exceed the rate of interest otherwise permitted under subclause (I); except that such rate of interest shall not exceed 120 percent of the weighted average referred to in subsection (b)(5)(B)(ii).

(d)(7)(C)(i)(IV) SPECIAL RULE FOR 2004, 2005, 2006, AND 2007. For plan years beginning in 2004, 2005, 2006, or 2007, notwithstanding subclause (I), the rate of interest used to determine current liability under this subsection shall be the rate of interest under subsection (b)(5).

(d)(7)(C)(ii) MORTALITY TABLES.

(d)(7)(C)(ii)(I) COMMISSIONERS' STANDARD TABLE. In the case of plan years beginning before the first plan year to which the first tables prescribed under subclause (II) apply, the mortality table used in determining current liability under this subsection shall be the table prescribed by the Secretary of the Treasury which is based on the prevailing commissioners' standard table (described in section 807(d)(5)(A) of the Internal Revenue Code of 1986) used to determine reserves for group annuity contracts issued on January 1, 1993.

(d)(7)(C)(ii)(II) SECRETARIAL AUTHORITY. The Secretary of the Treasury may by regulation prescribe for plan years beginning after December 31, 1999, mortality tables to be used in determining current liability under this subsection. Such tables shall be based

upon the actual experience of pension plans and projected trends in such experience. In prescribing such tables, the Secretary of the Treasury shall take into account results of available independent studies of mortality of individuals covered by pension plans.

(d)(7)(C)(ii)(III) PERIODIC REVIEW. The Secretary of the Treasury shall periodically (at least every 5 years) review any tables in effect under this subsection and shall, to the extent the Secretary determines necessary, by regulation update the tables to reflect the actual experience of pension plans and projected trends in such experience.

(d)(7)(C)(iii) SEPARATE MORTALITY TABLES FOR THE DISABLED. Notwithstanding clause (ii)—

(d)(7)(C)(iii)(I) IN GENERAL. In the case of plan years beginning after December 31, 1995, the Secretary of the Treasury shall establish mortality tables which may be used (in lieu of the tables under clause (ii)) to determine current liability under this subsection for individuals who are entitled to benefits under the plan on account of disability. Such Secretary shall establish separate tables for individuals whose disabilities occur in plan years beginning before January 1, 1995, and for individuals whose disabilities occur in plan years beginning on or after such date.

(d)(7)(C)(iii)(II) SPECIAL RULE FOR DISABILITIES OCCURRING AFTER 1994. In the case of disabilities occurring in plan years beginning after December 31, 1994, the tables under subclause (I) shall apply only with respect to individuals described in such subclause who are disabled within the meaning of title II of the Social Security Act and the regulations thereunder.

(d)(7)(C)(iii)(III) PLAN YEARS BEGINNING IN 1995. In the case of any plan year beginning in 1995, a plan may use its own mortality assumptions for individuals who are entitled to benefits under the plan on account of disability.

(d)(7)(C)(iii)(IV) SPECIAL RULE FOR 2004 AND 2005. For plan years beginning in 2004 or 2005, notwithstanding subclause (I), the rate of interest used to determine current liability under this subsection shall be the rate of interest under subsection (b)(5).

(d)(7)(D) CERTAIN SERVICE DISREGARDED.

(d)(7)(D)(i) IN GENERAL. In the case of a participant to whom this subparagraph applies, only the applicable percentage of the years of service before such individual became a participant shall be taken into account in computing the current liability of the plan.

(d)(7)(D)(ii) APPLICABLE PERCENTAGE. For purposes of this subparagraph, the applicable percentage shall be determined as follows:

If the years of participation are:	The applicable percentage is:
1	20
2	40
3	60
4	80
5 or more	100.

(d)(7)(D)(iii) PARTICIPANTS TO WHOM SUBPRARGRAPH APPLIES. This subparagraph shall apply to any participant who, at the time of becoming a participant—

(d)(7)(D)(iii)(I) has not accrued any other benefit under any defined benefit plan (whether or not terminated) maintained by the employer or a member of the same controlled group of which the employer is a member,

(d)(7)(D)(iii)(II) who first becomes a participant under the plan in a plan year beginning after December 31, 1987, and

(d)(7)(D)(iii)(III) has years of service greater than the minimum years of service necessary for eligibility to participate in the plan.

(d)(7)(D)(iv) ELECTION. An employer may elect not to have this subparagraph apply. Such an election, once made, may be revoked only with the consent of the Secretary of the Treasury.

(d)(8) OTHER DEFINITIONS. For purposes of this subsection—

(d)(8)(A) UNFUNDED CURRENT LIABILITY. The term "unfunded current liability" means, with respect to any plan year, the excess (if any) of—

(d)(8)(A)(i) the current liability under the plan, over

(d)(8)(A)(ii) value of the plan's assets determined under subsection (c)(2).

(d)(8)(B) FUNDED CURRENT LIABILITY PERCENTAGE. The term "funded current liability percentage" means, with respect to any plan year, the percentage which—

(d)(8)(B)(i) the amount determined under subparagraph (A)(ii), is of

(d)(8)(B)(ii) the current liability under the plan.

(d)(8)(C) CONTROLLED GROUP. The term "controlled group" means any group treated as a single employer under subsection (b), (c), (m), and (o) of section 414 of the Internal Revenue Code of 1986.

(d)(8)(D) ADJUSTMENTS TO PREVENT OMISSIONS AND DUPLICATIONS. The Secretary of the Treasury shall provide such adjustments in the unfunded old liability amount, the unfunded new liability amount, the unpredictable contingent event amount, the current payment amount, and any other charges or credits under this section as are necessary to avoid duplication or omission of any factors in the determination of such amounts, charges, or credits.

(d)(8)(E) DEDUCTION FOR CREDIT BALANCES. For purposes of this subsection, the amount determined under subparagraph (A)(ii) shall be reduced by any credit balance in the funding standard account. The Secretary of the Treasury may provide for such reduction for purposes of any other provision which references this subsection.

(d)(9) APPLICABILITY OF SUBSECTION.

(d)(9)(A) IN GENERAL. Except as provided in paragraph (6)(A), this subsection shall apply to a plan for any plan year if its funded current liability percentage for such year is less than 90 percent.

(d)(9)(B) EXCEPTION FOR CERTAIN PLANS AT LEAST 80 PERCENT FUNDED. Subparagraph (A) shall not apply to a plan for a plan year if—

(d)(9)(B)(i) the funded current liability percentage for the plan year is at least 80 percent, and

(d)(9)(B)(ii) such percentage for each of the 2 immediately preceding plan years (or each of the 2d and 3d immediately preceding plan years) is at least 90 percent.

(d)(9)(C) FUNDED CURRENT LIABILITY PERCENTAGE. For purposes of subparagraphs (A) and (B), the term "funded current liability percentage" has the meaning given such term by paragraph (8)(B), except that such percentage shall be determined for any plan year—

(d)(9)(C)(i) without regard to paragraph (8)(E), and

(d)(9)(C)(ii) by using the rate of interest which is the highest rate allowable for the plan year under paragraph (7)(C).

(d)(9)(D) TRANSITION RULES. For purposes of this paragraph:

(d)(9)(D)(i) FUNDED PERCENTAGE FOR YEARS BEFORE 1995. The funded current liability percentage for any plan year beginning before January 1, 1995, shall be treated as not less than 90 percent only if for such plan year the plan met one of the following requirements (as in effect for such year):

(d)(9)(D)(i)(I) The full-funding limitation under subsection (c)(7) for the plan was zero.

(d)(9)(D)(i)(II) The plan had no additional funding requirement under this subsection (or would have had no such requirement if its funded current liability percentage had been determined under subparagraph (C)).

(d)(9)(D)(i)(III) The plan's additional funding requirement under this subsection did not exceed the lesser of 0.5 percent of current liability or $5,000,000.

(d)(9)(D)(ii) SPECIAL RULE FOR 1995 AND 1996. For purposes of determining whether subparagraph (B) applies to any plan year beginning in 1995 or 1996, a plan shall be treated as meeting the requirements of subparagraph (B)(ii) if the plan met the requirements of clause (i) of this subparagraph for any two of the plan years beginning in 1992, 1993, and 1994 (whether or not consecutive).

(d)(10) UNFUNDED MORTALITY INCREASE AMOUNT.

(d)(10)(A) IN GENERAL. The unfunded mortality increase amount with respect to each unfunded mortality increase is the amount necessary to amortize such increase in equal annual installments over a period of 10 plan years (beginning with the first plan year for which a plan uses any new mortality table issued under paragraph (7)(C)(ii)(II) or (III)).

(d)(10)(B) UNFUNDED MORTALITY INCREASE. For purposes of subparagraph (A), the term "unfunded mortality increase" means an amount equal to the excess of—

(d)(10)(B)(i) the current liability of the plan for the first plan year for which a plan uses any new mortality table issued under paragraph (7)(C)(ii)(II) or (III), over

(d)(10)(B)(ii) the current liability of the plan for such plan year which would have been determined if the mortality table in effect for the preceding plan year had been used.

(d)(11) PHASE-IN OF INCREASES IN FUNDING REQUIRED BY RETIREMENT PROTECTION ACT OF 1994.

(d)(11)(A) IN GENERAL. For any applicable plan year, at the election of the employer, the increase under paragraph (1) shall not exceed the greater of—

(d)(11)(A)(i) the increase that would be required under paragraph (1) if the provisions of this title as in effect for plan years beginning before January 1, 1995, had remained in effect, or

(d)(11)(A)(ii) the amount which, after taking into account charges (other than the additional charge under this subsection) and credits under subsection (b), is necessary to increase the funded current liability percentage (taking into account the expected increase in current liability due to benefits accruing during the plan year) for the applicable plan year to a percentage equal to the sum of the initial funded current liability percentage of the plan plus the applicable number of percentage points for such applicable plan year.

(d)(11)(B) APPLICABLE NUMBER OF PERCENTAGE POINTS.

(d)(11)(B)(i) INITIAL FUNDED CURRENT LIABILITY PERCENTAGE OF 75 PERCENT OR LESS. Except as provided in clause (ii), for plans with an initial funded current liability percentage of 75 percent or less, the applicable number of percentage points for the applicable plan year is:

In the case of applicable plan years beginning in:	The applicable number of percentage points is:
1995	3
1996	6
1997	9
1998	12
1999	15
2000	19
2001	24

(d)(11)(B)(ii) OTHER CASES. In the case of a plan to which this clause applies, the applicable number of percentage points for any such applicable plan year is the sum of—

(d)(11)(B)(ii)(I) 2 percentage points;

(d)(11)(B)(ii)(II) the applicable number of percentage points (if any) under this clause for the preceding applicable plan year;

(d)(11)(B)(ii)(III) the product of .10 multiplied by the excess (if any) of (a) 85 percentage points over (b) the sum of the initial funded current liability percentage and the number determined under subclause (II);

(d)(11)(B)(ii)(IV) for applicable plan years beginning in 2000, 1 percentage point; and

(d)(11)(B)(ii)(V) for applicable plan years beginning in 2001, 2 percentage points.

(d)(11)(B)(iii) PLANS TO WHICH CLAUSE (ii) APPLIES.

(d)(11)(B)(iii)(I) IN GENERAL. Clause (ii) shall apply to a plan for an applicable plan year if the initial funded current liability percentage of such plan is more than 75 percent.

(d)(11)(B)(iii)(II) PLANS INITIALLY UNDER CLAUSE. (i) In the case of a plan which (but for this subclause) has an initial funded current liability percentage of 75 percent or less, clause (ii) (and not clause (i)) shall apply to such plan with respect to applicable plan years beginning after the first applicable plan year for which the sum of the initial funded current liability percentage and the applicable number of percentage points (determined under clause (i)) exceeds 75 percent. For purposes of applying clause (ii) to such a plan, the initial funded current liability percentage of such plan shall be treated as being the sum referred to in the preceding sentence.

(d)(11)(C) DEFINITIONS

(d)(11)(C)(i) The term "applicable plan year" means a plan year beginning after December 31, 1994, and before January 1, 2002.

(d)(11)(C)(ii) The term "initial funded current liability percentage" means the funded current liability percentage as of the first day of the first plan year beginning after December 31, 1994.

(d)(12) ELECTION FOR CERTAIN PLANS.

(d)(12)(A) IN GENERAL. In the case of a defined benefit plan established and maintained by an applicable employer, if this subsection did not apply to the plan for the plan year beginning in 2000 (determined without regard to paragraph (6)), then, at the election of the employer, the increased amount under paragraph (1) for any applicable plan year shall be the greater of—

(d)(12)(A)(i) 20 percent of the increased amount under paragraph (1) determined without regard to this paragraph, or

(d)(12)(A)(ii) the increased amount which would be determined under paragraph (1) if the deficit reduction contribution under paragraph (2) for the applicable plan year were determined without regard to subparagraphs (A), (B), and (D) of paragraph (2).

(d)(12)(B) RESTRICTIONS ON BENEFIT INCREASES. No amendment which increases the liabilities of the plan by reason of any increase in benefits, any change in the accrual of benefits, or any change in the rate at which benefits become nonforfeitable under the plan shall be adopted during any applicable plan year, unless—

(d)(12)(B)(i) the plan's enrolled actuary certifies (in such form and manner prescribed by the Secretary of the Treasury) that the amendment provides for an increase in annual contributions which will exceed the increase in annual charges to the funding standard account attributable to such amendment, or

(d)(12)(B)(ii) the amendment is required by a collective bargaining agreement which is in effect on the date of enactment of this subparagraph.

If a plan is amended during any applicable plan year in violation of the preceding sentence, any election under this paragraph shall not apply to any applicable plan year ending on or after the date on which such amendment is adopted.

(d)(12)(C) APPLICABLE EMPLOYER. For purposes of this paragraph, the term 'applicable employer' means an employer which is—

(d)(12)(C)(i) a commercial passenger airline,

(d)(12)(C)(ii) primarily engaged in the production or manufacture of a steel mill product or the processing of iron ore pellets, or

(d)(12)(C)(iii) an organization described in section 501(c)(5) of the Internal Revenue Code of 1986 and which established the plan to which this paragraph applies on June 30, 1955.

(d)(12)(D) APPLICABLE PLAN YEAR. For purposes of this paragraph—

(d)(12)(D)(i) IN GENERAL. The term 'applicable plan year' means any plan year beginning after December 27, 2003, and before December 28, 2005, for which the employer elects the application of this paragraph.

(d)(12)(D)(ii) LIMITATION ON NUMBER OF YEARS WHICH MAY BE ELECTED. An election may not be made under this paragraph with respect to more than 2 plan years.

(d)(12)(E) NOTICE REQUIREMENTS FOR PLANS ELECTING ALTERNATIVE DEFICIT REDUCTION CONTRIBUTIONS

(d)(12)(E)(i) IN GENERAL. If an employer elects an alternative deficit reduction contribution under this paragraph and section 412(l)(12) of the Internal Revenue Code of 1986 for any year, the employer shall provide, within 30 days of filing the election for such year, written notice of the election to participants and beneficiaries and to the Pension Benefit Guaranty Corporation.

(d)(12)(E)(ii) NOTICE TO PARTICIPANTS AND BENEFICIARIES. The notice under clause (i) to participants and beneficiaries shall include with respect to any election—

(d)(12)(E)(ii)(I) the due date of the alternative deficit reduction contribution and the amount by which such contribution was reduced from the amount which would have been owed if the election were not made, and

(d)(12)(E)(ii)(II) a description of the benefits under the plan which are eligible to be guaranteed by the Pension Benefit Guaranty Corporation and an explanation of the limitations on the guarantee and the circumstances under which such limitations apply, including the maximum guaranteed monthly benefits which the Pension Benefit Guaranty Corporation would pay if the plan terminated while underfunded.

(d)(12)(E)(iii) NOTICE TO PBGC. The notice under clause (i) to the Pension Benefit Guaranty Corporation shall include—

(d)(12)(E)(iii)(I) the information described in clause (ii)(I),

(d)(12)(E)(iii)(II) the number of years it will take to restore the plan to full funding if the employer only makes the required contributions, and

(d)(12)(E)(iii)(III) information as to how the amount by which the plan is underfunded compares with the capitalization of the employer making the election.

(d)(12)(F) ELECTION. An election under this paragraph shall be made at such time and in such manner as the Secretary of the Treasury may prescribe..

(e) QUARTERLY CONTRIBUTIONS REQUIRED.

(e)(1) IN GENERAL. If a defined benefit plan (other than a multiemployer plan) which has a funded current liability percentage (as defined in subsection (d)(8)) for the preceding plan year of less than 100 percent fails to pay the full amount of a required installment for *the plan year*, then the rate of interest charged to the funding standard account under subsection (b)(5) with respect to the amount of the underpayment for the period of the underpayment shall be equal to the greater of—

(e)(1)(A) 175 percent of the Federal mid-term rate (as in effect under section 1274 of the Internal Revenue Code of 1986 for the 1st month of such plan year), or

(e)(1)(B) the rate of interest used under the plan in determining costs (including adjustments under subsection (b)(5)(B)).

(e)(2) AMOUNT OF UNDERPAYMENT, PERIOD OF UNDERPAYMENT. For purposes of paragraph (1)—

(e)(2)(A) AMOUNT. The amount of the underpayment shall be the excess of—

(e)(2)(A)(i) the required installment, over

(e)(2)(A)(ii) the amount (if any) of the installment contributed to or under the plan on or before the due date for the installment.

(e)(2)(B) PERIOD OF UNDERPAYMENT. The period for which any interest is charged under this subsection with respect to any portion of the underpayment shall run from the due date for the installment to the date on which such portion is contributed to or under the plan (determined without regard to subsection (c)(10)).

(e)(2)(C) For purposes of subparagraph (A)(ii), contributions shall be credited against unpaid required installments in the order in which such installments are required to be paid.

(e)(3) NUMBER OF REQUIRED INSTALLMENTS: DUE DATES. For purposes of this subsection—

(e)(3)(A) PAYABLE IN 4 INSTALLMENTS. There shall be 4 required installments for each plan year.

(e)(3)(B) TIME FOR PAYMENT OF INSTALLMENTS.

In the case of the following required installments:	The due date is:
1st	April 15
2nd	July 15
3rd	October 15
4th	January 15 of the following year

(e)(4) AMOUNT OF REQUIRED INSTALLMENT. For purposes of this subsection—

(e)(4)(A) IN GENERAL. The amount of any required installment shall be the applicable percentage of the required annual payment.

(e)(4)(B) REQUIRED ANNUAL PAYMENT. For purposes of subparagraph (A), the term "required annual payment" means the lesser of—

(e)(4)(B)(i) 90 percent of the amount required to be contributed to or under the plan by the employer for the plan year under section 412 of the Internal Revenue Code of 1986 (without regard to any waiver under subsection (d) thereof), or

(e)(4)(B)(ii) 100 percent of the amount so required for the preceding plan year. Clause (ii) shall not apply if the preceding plan year was not a year of 12 months.

(e)(4)(C) APPLICABLE PERCENTAGE. For purposes of subparagraph (A), the applicable percentage shall be determined in accordance with the following table:

For plan years beginning in:	The applicable percentage is:
1989	6.25
1990	12.50
1991	18.75
1992 and thereafter	25.00

(e)(4)(D) SPECIAL RULES FOR UNPREDICTABLE CONTINGENT EVENT BENEFITS. In the case of a plan to which subsection (d) applies for any calendar year and which has any unpredictable contingent event benefit liabilities—

(e)(4)(D)(i) LIABILITIES NOT TAKEN INTO ACCOUNT. Such liabilities shall not be taken into account in computing the required annual payment under subparagraph (B).

(e)(4)(D)(ii) INCREASE IN INSTALLMENTS. Each required installment shall be increased by the greatest of—

(e)(4)(D)(ii)(I) the unfunded percentage of the amount of benefits described in subsection (d)(5)(A)(i) paid during the 3-month period preceding the month in which the due date for such installment occurs,

(e)(4)(D)(ii)(II) 25 percent of the amount determined under subsection (d)(5)(A)(ii) for the plan year, or

(e)(4)(D)(ii)(III) 25 percent of the amount determined under subsection (d)(5)(A)(iii) for the plan year.

(e)(4)(D)(iii) UNFUNDED PERCENTAGE. For purposes of clause (ii)(I), the term "unfunded percentage" means the percentage determined under subsection (d)(5)(A)(i)(I) for the plan year.

(e)(4)(D)(iv) LIMITATION ON INCREASE. In no event shall the increases under clause (ii) exceed the amount necessary to increase the funded current liability percentage (within the meaning of subsection (d)(8)(B)) for the plan year to 100 percent.

(e)(5) LIQUIDITY REQUIREMENT.

(e)(5)(A) IN GENERAL. A plan to which this paragraph applies shall be treated as failing to pay the full amount of any required installment to the extent that the value of the liquid assets paid in such installment is less than the liquidity shortfall (whether or not such liquidity shortfall exceeds the amount of such installment required to be paid but for this paragraph).

(e)(5)(B) PLANS TO WHICH PARAGRAPH APPLIES. This paragraph shall apply to a defined benefit plan (other than a multiemployer plan or a plan described in subsection (d)(6)(A)) which—

(e)(5)(B)(i) is required to pay installments under this subsection for a plan year, and

(e)(5)(B)(ii) has a liquidity shortfall for any quarter during such plan year.

(e)(5)(C) PERIOD OF UNDERPAYMENT. For purposes of paragraph (1), any portion of an installment that is treated as not paid under subparagraph (A) shall continue to be treated as unpaid until the close of the quarter in which the due date for such installment occurs.

(e)(5)(D) LIMITATION ON INCREASE. If the amount of any required installment is increased by reason of subparagraph (A), in no event shall such increase exceed the amount which, when added to prior installments for the plan year, is necessary to increase the funded current liability percentage (taking into account the expected increase in current liability due to benefits accruing during the plan year) to 100 percent.

(e)(5)(E) DEFINITIONS. For purposes of this paragraph—

(e)(5)(E)(i) LIQUIDITY SHORTFALL. The term "liquidity shortfall" means, with respect to any required installment, an amount equal to the excess (as of the last day of the quarter for which such installment is made) of the base amount with respect to such quarter over the value (as of such last day) of the plan's liquid assets.

(e)(5)(E)(ii) BASE AMOUNT.

(e)(5)(E)(ii)(I) IN GENERAL. The term "base amount" means, with respect to any quarter, an amount equal to 3 times the sum of the adjusted disbursements from the plan for the 12 months ending on the last day of such quarter.

(e)(5)(E)(ii)(II) SPECIAL RULE. If the amount determined under subclause (I) exceeds an amount equal to 2 times the sum of the adjusted disbursements from the plan for the 36 months ending on the last day of the quarter and an enrolled actuary certifies to the satisfaction of the Secretary of the Treasury that such excess is the result of nonrecurring circumstances, the base amount with respect to such quarter shall be determined without regard to amounts related to those nonrecurring circumstances.

(e)(5)(E)(iii) DISBURSEMENTS FROM THE PLAN. The term "disbursements from the plan" means all disbursements from the trust, including purchases of annuities, payments of single sums and other benefits, and administrative expenses.

(e)(5)(E)(iv) ADJUSTED DISBURSEMENTS. The term "adjusted disbursements" means disbursements from the plan reduced by the product of—

(e)(5)(E)(iv)(I) the plan's funded current liability percentage (as defined in subsection (d)(8)) for the plan year, and

(e)(5)(E)(iv)(II) the sum of the purchases of annuities, payments of single sums, and such other disbursements as the Secretary of the Treasury shall provide in regulations.

(e)(5)(E)(v) LIQUID ASSETS. The term "liquid assets" means cash, marketable securities and such other assets as specified by the Secretary of the Treasury in regulations.

(e)(5)(E)(vi) QUARTER. The term "quarter" means, with respect to any required installment, the 3-month period preceding the month in which the due date for such installment occurs.

(e)(5)(F) REGULATIONS. The Secretary of the Treasury may prescribe such regulations as are necessary to carry out this paragraph.

(e)(6) FISCAL YEARS AND SHORT YEARS.

(e)(6)(A) FISCAL YEARS. In applying this subsection to a plan year beginning on any date other than January 1, there shall be substituted for the months specified in this subsection, the months which correspond thereto.

(e)(6)(B) SHORT PLAN YEAR. This section shall be applied to plan years of less than 12 months in accordance with regulations prescribed by the Secretary of the Treasury.

(e)(7) SPECIAL RULE FOR 2002.—In any case in which the interest rate used to determine current liability is determined under subsection (d)(7)(C)(i)(III), for purposes of applying paragraphs (1) and (4)(B)(ii) for plan years beginning in 2002, the current liability for the preceding plan year shall be redetermined using 120 percent as the specified percentage determined under subsection (d)(7)(C)(i)(II).

(f) IMPOSITION OF LIEN WHERE FAILURE TO MAKE REQUIRED CONTRIBUTIONS.

(f)(1) IN GENERAL. In the case of a plan *covered under section 4021 of this Act* if—

(f)(1)(A) any person fails to make a required installment under subsection (e) or any other payment required under this section before the due date for such installment or other payment, and

(f)(1)(B) the unpaid balance of such installment or other payment (including interest), when added to the aggregate unpaid balance of all preceding such installments or other payments for which payment was not made before the due date (including interest), exceeds $1,000,000,

then there shall be a lien in favor of the plan in the amount determined under paragraph (3) upon all property and rights to property, whether real or personal, belonging to such person and any other person who is a member of the same controlled group of which such person is a member.

(f)(2) PLANS TO WHICH SUBSECTION APPLIES. This subsection shall apply to a defined benefit plan (other than a multiemployer plan) for any plan year for which the funded current liability percentage (within the meaning of subsection (d)(8)(B)) of such plan is less than 100 percent.

(f)(3) AMOUNT OF LIEN. For purposes of paragraph (1), the amount of the lien shall be equal to the aggregate unpaid balance of required installments and other payments required under this section (including interest)—

(f)(3)(A) for plan years beginning after 1987, and

(f)(3)(B) for which payment has not been made before the due date.

(f)(4) NOTICE OF FAILURE; LIEN.

(f)(4)(A) NOTICE OF FAILURE. A person committing a failure described in paragraph (1) shall notify the Pension Benefit Guaranty Corporation of such failure within 10 days of the due date for the required installment or other payment.

(f)(4)(B) PERIOD OF LIEN. The lien imposed by paragraph (1) shall arise on the due date for the required installment or other payment and shall continue until the last day of the first plan year in which the plan ceases to be described in paragraph (1)(B). Such lien shall continue to run without regard to whether such plan continues to be described in paragraph (2) during the period referred to in the preceding sentence.

(f)(4)(C) CERTAIN RULES TO APPLY. Any amount with respect to which a lien is imposed under paragraph (1) shall be treated as taxes due and owing the United States and rules similar to the rules of subsections (c), (d), and (e) of section 4068 shall apply with respect to a lien imposed by subsection (a) and the amount with respect to such lien.

(f)(5) ENFORCEMENT. Any lien created under paragraph (1) may be perfected and enforced only by the Pension Benefit Guaranty Corporation, or at the direction of the Pension Benefit Guaranty Corporation, by the contributing sponsor (or any member of the controlled group of the contributing sponsor).

(f)(6) DEFINITIONS. For purposes of this subsection—

(f)(6)(A) DUE DATE; REQUIRED INSTALLMENT. The term "due date" and "required installment" have the meanings given such terms by subsection (e), except that in the case of a payment other than a required installment, the due date shall be the date such payment is required to be made under this section.

(f)(6)(B) CONTROLLED GROUP. The term "controlled group" means any group treated under subsections (b), (c), (m), and (o) of section 414 of the Internal Revenue Code of 1986.

(g) QUALIFIED TRANSFERS TO HEALTH BENEFIT ACCOUNTS. For purposes of this section, in the case of a qualified transfer (as defined in section 420 of the Internal Revenue Code of 1986)—

(g)(1) any assets transferred in a plan year on or before the valuation date for such year (and any income allocable thereto) shall, for purposes of subsection (c)(7), be treated as assets in the plan as of the valuation date for such year, and

(g)(2) the plan shall be treated as having a net experience loss under subsection (b)(2)(B)(iv) in an amount equal to the amount of such transfer (reduced by any amounts transferred back to the plan under section 420(c)(1)(B) of such Code) and for which amortization charges begin for the first plan year after the plan year in which such transfer occurs, except that such subsection shall be applied to such amount by substituting "10 plan years" for "5 plan years".

(h) CROSS REFERENCE. For alternative amortization method for certain multiemployer plans see section 1013(d) of this Act.

The above amendment applies to plan years beginning after 2007.

P. L. 109-280, § 101(b):

Amended Part 3 of subtitle B of title I of ERISA (as amended by Act Sec. 101(a)) by inserting after section 301, the new section 302.

P. L. 109-280, § 202(d):

Amended ERISA Sec. 302(b), as amended by this Act, by adding paragraph (3) to read as above:

For effective date, see P.L. 109-280, § 202(f), below.

P.L. 109-280, § 202(f):

202(f) EFFECTIVE DATES.—

202(f)(1) IN GENERAL.—

The amendments made by this section shall apply with respect to plan years beginning after 2007.

202(f)(2) SPECIAL RULE FOR CERTAIN NOTICES.—

In any case in which a plan's actuary certifies that it is reasonably expected that a multiemployer plan will be in critical status under section 305(b)(3) of the Employee Retirement Income Security Act of 1974, as added by this section, with respect to the first plan year beginning after 2007, the notice required under subparagraph (D) of such section may be provided at any time after the date of enactment, so long as it is provided on or before the last date for providing the notice under such subparagraph.

202(f)(3) SPECIAL RULE FOR CERTAIN RESTORED BENEFITS.—

In the case of a multiemployer plan—

202(f)(3)(A) with respect to which benefits were reduced pursuant to a plan amendment adopted on or after January 1, 2002, and before June 30, 2005, and

202(f)(3)(B) which, pursuant to the plan document, the trust agreement, or a formal written communication from the plan sponsor to participants provided before June 30, 2005, provided for the restoration of such benefits,

the amendments made by this section shall not apply to such benefit restorations to the extent that any restriction on the providing or accrual of such benefits would otherwise apply by reason of such amendments.

P. L. 109-280, § 301(a)(1)(A):

Amended ERISA Sec. 302(b)(5)(B)(ii)(II) by striking "2006" and inserting "2008."

The above amendment is effective on the date of enactment (August 17, 2006).

P. L. 109-280, § 301(a)(1)(B):

Amended ERISA Sec. 302(b)(5)(B)(ii)(II) by striking "AND 2005" in the heading and inserting , "2005, 2006, AND 2007".

The above amendment is effective on the date of enactment (August 17, 2006).

P. L. 109-280, § 301(a)(2)(A):

Amended ERISA Sec 302(d)(7)(c)(i)(IV) by striking "or 2005" and inserting ", 2005, 2006, or 2007.".

The above amendment is effective on the date of enactment (August 17, 2006).

P. L. 109-280, § 301(a)(2)(B):

Amended ERISA Sec 302(d)(7)(c)(i)(IV) by striking "AND 2005" in the heading and inserting ", 2005, 2006, AND 2007.".

The above amendment is effective on the date of enactment (August 17, 2006).

P.L. 109-135, § 412:

Amended ERISA Sec. 302(e)(4)(B)(i) by striking "subsection (c)" and inserting "subsection (d)".

P.L. 108-218, § 104(a):

Amended ERISA Sec. 302(b)(7) by adding sub paragraph F.

P.L. 108-218, § 102(a):

Amended ERISA Sec. 302(d) by adding paragraph 12.

Act Sec. 102 provides:

(c) Effect of Election.

An election under section 302(d)(12) of the Employee Retirement Income Security Act of 1974 or section 412(l)(12) of the Internal Revenue Code of 1986 (as added by this section) with respect to a plan shall not invalidate any obligation (pursuant to a collective bargaining agreement in effect on the date of the election) to provide benefits, to change the accrual of benefits, or to change the rate at which benefits become nonforfeitable under the plan.

(d) Penalty for Failing To Provide Notice.

Section 502(c)(3) of the Employee Retirement Income Security Act of 1974 (29 U.S.C. 1132(c)(3)) is amended by inserting "or who fails to meet the requirements of section 302(d)(12)(E) with respect to any person" after "101(e)(2) with respect to any person".

P.L. 108-218, § 101(a):

Amended ERISA Sec. 302(b)(5)(B) by redesignating and amending subclause II as subclause III and by adding new subclause II to read as above.

Amended ERISA Sec. 302(d)(7)(C) by adding to the end of clause (i) a new subclause (IV) to read as above.

Amended ERISA Sec. 302(e) to read as above.

Act Sec. 101 provides:

(c) Provisions Relating to Plan Amendments.

(1) In general.—

If this subsection applies to any plan or annuity contract amendment—

(A) such plan or contract shall be treated as being operated in accordance with the terms of the plan or contract during the period described in paragraph (2)(B)(i), and

(B) except as provided by the Secretary of the Treasury, such plan shall not fail to meet the requirements of section 411(d)(6) of the Internal Revenue Code of 1986 and section 204(g) of the Employee Retirement Income Security Act of 1974 by reason of such amendment.

(2) Amendments to which section applies.—

(A) In general. This subsection shall apply to any amendment to any plan or annuity contract which is made—

(i) pursuant to any amendment made by this section, and

(ii) on or before the last day of the first plan year beginning on or after January 1, 2006.

(B) Conditions.—

This subsection shall not apply to any plan or annuity contract amendment unless—

(i) during the period beginning on the date the amendment described in subparagraph (A)(i) takes effect and ending on the date described in subparagraph (A)(ii) (or, if earlier, the date the plan or contract amendment is adopted), the plan or contract is operated as if such plan or contract amendment were in effect; and

(ii) such plan or contract amendment applies retroactively for such period.

(d) Effective Dates.—

(1) In general.

Except as provided in paragraphs (2) and (3), the amendments made by this section shall apply to plan years beginning after December 31, 2003.

(2) Lookback rules.

For purposes of applying subsections (d)(9)(B)(ii) and (e)(1) of section 302 of the Employee Retirement Income Security Act of 1974 and subsections (l)(9)(B)(ii) and (m)(1) of section 412 of the Internal Revenue Code of 1986 to plan years beginning after December 31, 2003, the amendments made by this section may be applied as if such amendments had been in effect for all prior plan years. The Secretary of the Treasury may prescribe simplified assumptions which may be used in applying the amendments made by this section to such prior plan years.

(3) Transition rule for Section 415 limitation.

In the case of any participant or beneficiary receiving a distribution after December 31, 2003 and before January 1, 2005, the amount payable under any form of benefit subject to section 417(e)(3) of the Internal Revenue Code of 1986 and subject to adjustment under section 415(b)(2)(B) of such Code shall not, solely by reason of the amendment made by subsection (b)(4), be less than the amount that would have been so payable had the amount payable been determined using the applicable interest rate in effect as of the last day of the last plan year beginning before January 1, 2004.

P.L. 107-147, § 405(b):

Act Sec. 405(b)(1) amended ERISA Sec. 302(d)(7)(C)(i) by adding subclause III to read as above.

Act Sec. 405(b(2) amended ERISA Sec. 302(e) by adding paragraph (7) to read as above.

P.L. 107-147, § 411(v)(2):

Act Sec. 411(v)(2) amended ERISA Sec. 302(c)(9)(B)(ii) by striking "125 percent" and inserting "100 percent" and by adding clause iv to read as above.

The above amendment applies to plan years beginning after December 31, 2001, subject to sunset after 2010 under P.L. 107-16, Sec. 901.

P.L. 107-16, §651(b)(1):

Act Sec. 651(b)(1) amended ERISA Sec. 302(c)(7) by striking "the applicable percentage" in subparagraph (A)(i)(I) and inserting "in the case of plan years beginning before January 1, 2004, the applicable percentage".

P.L. 107-16, §651(b)(2):

Act Sec. 651(b)(2) amended ERISA Sec. 302(c)(7) by amending subparagraph (F) to read as follows:

"(F) APPLICABLE PERCENTAGE.—For purposes of subparagraph (A)(i)(I), the applicable percentage shall be determined in accordance with the following table:

"In the case of any plan year beginning in—	The applicable percentage is—
2002	165
2003	170 ."

Prior to amendment, ERISA Sec. 302(c)(7)(F) read as follows:

"(F) APPLICABLE PERCENTAGE.—For purposes of subparagraph (A)(i)(I), the applicable percentage shall be determined in accordance with the following table:

In the case of any plan year beginning in—	The applicable percentage is—
1999 or 2000	155
2001 or 2002	160
2003 or 2004	165
2005 and succeeding years	170 ."

P.L. 107-16, §661(b):

Act Sec. 661(b) amended ERISA Sec. 302(c)(9) by inserting "(A)" after "(9)", and by adding at the end the following:

"(B)(i) Except as provided in clause (ii), the valuation referred to in subparagraph (A) shall be made as of a date within the plan year to which the valuation refers or within one month prior to the beginning of such year.

"(ii) The valuation referred to in subparagraph (A) may be made as of a date within the plan year prior to the year to which the valuation refers if, as of such date, the value of the assets of the plan are not less than 125 percent of the plan's current liability (as defined in paragraph (7)(B)).

"(iii) Information under clause (ii) shall, in accordance with regulations, be actuarially adjusted to reflect significant differences in participants.".

The above amendments apply to plan years beginning after December 31, 2001 subject to sunset after 2010 under P.L. 107-16, Sec. 901.

P.L. 105-34, §1521(b)(A):

Act Sec. 1521(b)(A) amended ERISA Sec. 302(c)(7) by striking "150 percent" in subparagraph (A)(i)(I) and inserting "the applicable percentage;" and by adding subparagraph (F) to read as above.

P.L. 105-34, §1521(c)(2):

Act Sec. 1521(c)(2) amended ERISA Sec. 302(b)(2) by striking "and" at the end of subparagraph (b)(2)(C) and deleting the period at the end of (b)(2)(D) and inserting ", and" at the end of (b)(2)(D) and by adding subparagraph (b)(2)(E) to read as above.

P.L. 105-34, §1521(c)(3):

Act Sec. 1521(c)(3)(B) amended ERISA Sec. 302(c)(7)(D) by adding "and" at the end of clause (i), by striking ", and" at the end of clause (ii) and inserting a period, and by striking clause (iii). Prior to amendment, clause (iii) read as follows:

(iii) for the treatment under this section of contributions which would be required to be made under the plan but for the provisions of subparagraph (A)(i)(I).

The above amendments apply to plan years beginning after December 31, 1998. But see Act Sec. 1521(d)(2) below for a special rule.

P.L. 105-34, §1521(d)(2):

(2) SPECIAL RULE FOR UNAMORTIZED BALANCES UNDER EXISTING LAW.—The unamortized balance (as of the close of the plan year preceding the plan's first year beginning in 1999) of any amortization base established under section 412(c)(7)(D)(iii) of such Code and section 302(c)(7)(D)(iii) of such Act (as repealed by subsection (c)(3)) for any plan year beginning before 1999 shall be amortized in equal annual installments (until fully amortized) over a period of years equal to the excess of—

(A) 20 years, over

(B) the number of years since the amortization base was established.

P.L. 105-34, §1604(b)(2):

Act Sec. 1604(b)(2) amended ERISA Sec. 302(e)(5)(E)(ii) by striking "clause (i)" and inserting "subclause (I)."

The above amendment applies to plan years beginning after December 31, 1994.

P.L. 103-465, §761(a)(1)(A):

Act Sec. 761(a)(1)(A) amended ERISA Sec. 302(d)(1) by striking "which has an unfunded current liability" and inserting "to which this subsection applies under paragraph (9)".

P.L. 103-465, §761(a)(1)(B):

Act Sec. 761(a)(1)(B) amended ERISA Sec. 302(d) by adding paragraph (9) to read as above.

P.L. 103-465, §761(a)(2)(A):

Act Sec. 761(a)(2)(A) amended ERISA Sec. 302(d)(1)(A)(ii) to read as above. Prior to amendment, ERISA Sec. 302(d)(1)(A)(ii) read as follows:

(ii) the sum of the charges for such plan year under subparagraph (B) (other than clauses (iv) and (v) thereof), (C), and (D) of subsection (b)(2), reduced by the sum of the credits for such plan year under subparagraph (B)(i) of subsection (b)(3), plus

P.L. 103-465, §761(a)(2)(B):

Act Sec. 761(a)(2)(B) amended the last sentence of ERISA Sec. 302(d)(1) to read as above. Prior to amendment, the last sentence of ERISA Sec. 302(d)(1) read as follows:

Such increase shall not exceed the amount necessary to increase the funded current liability percentage to 100 percent.

P.L. 103-465, §761(a)(3):

Act Sec. 761(a)(3) amended ERISA Sec. 302(d)(2) by striking "plus" at the end of subparagraph (A); by striking the period at the end of subparagraph (B) and inserting ", plus"; and by adding at the end subparagraph (C) to read as above.

P.L. 103-465, §761(a)(4)(A):

Act Sec. 761(a)(4)(A) amended ERISA Sec. 302(d)(3) by adding subparagraphs (D) and (E) to read as above.

P.L. 103-465, §761(a)(4)(B):

Act Sec. 761(a)(4)(B) amended ERISA Sec. 302(d)(4)(B)(i) by inserting ", the unamortized portion of the additional unfunded old liability," after "old liability".

P.L. 103-465, §761(a)(5):

Act Sec. 761(a)(5) amended ERISA Sec. 302(d)(4)(C) by striking ".25" and inserting ".40", and by striking "35" and inserting "60".

P.L. 103-465, §761(a)(6)(A):

Act Sec. 761(a)(6)(A) amended ERISA Sec. 302(d)(5)(A) by striking "greater of" and inserting "greatest of" before clause (i); by striking "or" at the end of clause (i); by striking the period at the end of clause (ii) and inserting ", or"; and by adding after clause (ii) a new clause (iii) to read as above.

P.L. 103-465, §761(a)(6)(B):

Act Sec. 761(a)(6)(B) amended ERISA Sec. 302(d)(5) by adding subparagraph (E) to read as above.

P.L. 103-465, §761(a)(6)(C):

Act Sec. 761(a)(6)(C) amended ERISA Sec. 302(e)(4)(D)(ii) by striking "greater of" and inserting "greatest of" before subclause (I); by striking "or" at the end of subclause (I); by striking the period at the end of subclause (II) and inserting ", or"; and by adding subclause (III) to read as above.

P.L. 103-465, §761(a)(7)(A):

Act Sec. 761(a)(7)(A) amended ERISA Sec. 302(d)(7)(C) to read as above. Prior to amendment, ERISA Sec. 302(d)(7)(C) read as follows:

(C) Interest Rates Used.—The rate of interest used to determine current liability shall be the rate of interest used under subsection (b)(5).

P.L. 103-465, §761(a)(7)(B)(i):

Act Sec. 761(a)(7)(B)(i) amended ERISA Sec. 302(d)(2), as amended by Act Sec. 761(a)(3), by striking "plus" at the end of subparagraph (B); by striking the period at the end of subparagraph (C), and inserting ", and"; and by adding subparagraph (D) to read as above.

P.L. 103-465, §761(a)(7)(B)(ii):

Act Sec. 761(a)(7)(B)(ii) amended ERISA Sec. 302(d), as amended by Act Sec. 761(a)(1), by adding paragraph (10) to read as above.

P.L. 103-465, §761(a)(7)(B)(iii):

Act Sec. 761(a)(7)(B)(iii) amended ERISA Sec. 302(d)(4)(B)(i), as amended by Act. Sec. 761(a)(4)(B), by inserting "the unamortized portion of each unfunded mortality increase," after "additional unfunded old liability".

P.L. 103-465, §761(a)(8):

Act Sec. 761(a)(8) amended ERISA Sec. 302(d), as amended by Act Sec. 761(a)(7), by adding paragraph (11) to read as above.

The above amendments apply to plan years beginning after December 31, 1994.

P.L. 103-465, §761(a)(9)(A):

Act Sec. 761(a)(9)(A) amended ERISA Sec. 302(e) by redesignating paragraph (5) as paragraph (6) and by inserting new paragraph (5) to read as above.

The above amendments apply to plan years beginning after December 31, 1994.

P.L. 103-465, §764(a):

Act Sec. 764(a) amended ERISA Sec. 302(e)(1) by inserting "which has a funded current liability percentage (as defined in subsection (d)(8)) for the preceding plan year of less than 100 percent" before "fails", and by striking "any plan year" and inserting "the plan year".

The above amendment applies to plan years beginning after December 8, 1994.

P.L. 103-465, §768(b)(1):

Act Sec. 768(b)(1) amended ERISA Sec. 302(f)(1) by striking "to which this section applies" and inserting "covered under section 4021 of this Act".

P.L. 103-465, §768(b)(2):

Act Sec. 768(b)(2) amended ERISA Sec. 302(f)(3) to read as above. Prior to amendment, ERISA Sec. 302(f)(3) read as follows:

(3) AMOUNT OF LIEN.—For purposes of paragraph (1), the amount of the lien shall be equal to the lesser of—

(A) the amount by which the unpaid balances described in paragraph (1)(B) (including interest) exceed $1,000,000, or

(B) the aggregate unpaid balance of required installments and other payments required under this section (including interest)—

(i) for plan years beginning after 1987, and

(ii) for which payment has not been made before the due date.

P.L. 103-465, § 768(b)(3):

Act Sec. 768(b)(3) amended ERISA Sec. 302(f)(4)(B) by striking "60th day following the" preceding "due date for the required installment".

The above amendments are effective for installments and other payments required under section 412 of the Internal Revenue Code of 1986 or under part 3 of subtitle B of the Employee Retirement Income Security Act of 1974 that become due on or after December 8, 1994.

P.L. 103-465, § 769(a) & (b):

Act Sec. 769(a) & (b) provide:

ACT SEC. 769. SPECIAL FUNDING RULES FOR CERTAIN PLANS.

(a) FUNDING RULES NOT TO APPLY TO CERTAIN PLANS.—Any changes made by this Act to section 412 of the Internal Revenue Code of 1986 or to part 3 of subtitle B of title I of the Employee Retirement Income Security Act of 1974 shall not apply to—

(1) a plan which is, on the date of enactment of this Act, subject to a restoration payment schedule order issued by the Pension Benefit Guaranty Corporation that meets the requirements of section 1.412(c)(1)-3 of the Treasury Regulations, or

(2) a plan established by an affected air carrier (as defined under section 4001(a)(14)(C)(ii)(I) of such Act) and assumed by a new plan Sponsor pursuant to the terms of a written agreement with the Pension Benefit Guaranty Corporation dated January 5, 1993, and approved by the United States Bankruptcy Court for the District of Delaware on December 30, 1992.

(b) CHANGE IN ACTUARIAL METHOD.—Any amortization installments for bases established under section 412(b) of the Internal Revenue Code of 1986 and section 302(b) of the Employee Retirement Income Security Act of 1974 for plan years beginning after December 31, 1987, and before January 1, 1993, by reason of nonelective changes under the frozen entry age actuarial cost method shall not be included in the calculation of offsets under section 412(l)(1)(A)(ii) of such Code and section 302(d)(1)(A)(ii) of such Act for the 1st 5 plan years beginning after December 31, 1994.

The above provisions are effective December 8, 1994.

P.L. 103-465, § 761(a)(10):

Act Sec. 761(a)(10) amended ERISA Sec. 302(c)(7) by inserting "(including the expected increase in current liability due to benefits accruing during the plan year)" after "current liability" in clause (i), and adding subparagraph (E) to read as above.

Act Sec. 761(a)(10)(C) amended ERISA Sec. 302(c)(7)(B) to read as above. Prior to amendment, it read as follows: "CURRENT LIABILITY.—For purposes of paragraphs (A) and (D), the term 'current liability' has the meaning given such term by subsection (d)(7) (without regard to subparagraph (D) thereof)."

The above amendments apply to plan years beginning after December 31, 1994.

P.L. 103-465, § 762(a):

Act Sec. 762(a) amended ERISA Sec. 302(c)(5) by striking "If the funding method" and inserting the following: "(A) IN GENERAL.—If the funding method", and by adding subparagraph (B) to read as above.

The above amendments apply to changes in assumptions for plan years beginning after October 28, 1993. For special rules, see Act Sec. 762(b)(2), below.

Act Sec. 762(b)(2) provides:

(2) CERTAIN CHANGES CEASE TO BE EFFECTIVE.—In the case of changes in assumptions for plan years beginning after December 31, 1992, and on or before October 28, 1993, such changes shall cease to be effective for plan years beginning after December 31, 1994, if—

(A) such change would have required the approval of the Secretary of the Treasury had such amendment applied to such change, and

(B) such change is not so approved.

P.L. 103-465, § 763(a):

Act Sec. 763(a) amended ERISA Sec. 302(c) by adding subparagraph (12) to read as above.

The above amendment shall apply to plan years beginning after December 31, 1994, with respect to collective bargaining agreements in effect on or after January 1, 1995.

P.L. 101-508, Sec. 12012(c):

Amended ERISA Sec. 302 by redesignating subsection (g) as subsection (h) and adding new subsection (g) to read as above effective for qualified transfers under Code Sec. 420 made after November 5, 1990.

P.L. 101-508, Sec. 12012(c):

Amended ERISA Sec. 302 by redesignating subsection (g) as subsection (h) effective for qualified transfers under Code Sec. 420 made after November 5, 1990.

P.L. 101-239, § 7881(a)(1)(B):

Amended ERISA Sec. 302(d)(3)(C)(ii)(II) by inserting "(but not below zero)" after "reducing."

P.L. 101-239, § 7881(a)(2)(B):

Amended ERISA Sec. 302(d)(4)(B)(i) by inserting "and the unamortized portion of the unfunded existing benefit increase liability" after "liability."

P.L. 101-239, § 7881(a)(3)(B):

Amended ERISA Sec. 302(d)(5)(C) by striking "October 17, 1987" and inserting "the first plan year beginning after December 31, 1988."

P.L. 101-239, § 7881(a)(4)(B):

Amended ERISA Sec. 302(d)(7)(D) by striking "and" at the end of clause (iii)(I) and by striking the period at the end of clause (iii)(II) and inserting, "and" and by adding new subclause (IV) at the end of clause (iii) and also by adding a new clause (iv) to read as above.

P.L. 101-239, § 7881(a)(5)(B):

Amended ERISA Sec. 302(d)(8) by striking "reduced by any credit balance in the funding standard account" in subparagraph (A)(ii) and by adding a new subparagraph (E).

The above amendments are effective for plan years beginning after December 31, 1988.

P.L. 101-239, § 7881(a)(6)(B):

Amended ERISA Sec. 302(c)(9) by striking "three years" and inserting "year."

P.L. 101-239, § 7881(b)(1)(B):

Amended ERISA Sec. 302(c)(10)(A) by inserting "defined benefit" before "plan other."

P.L. 101-239, § 7881(b)(2)(B):

Amended ERISA Sec. 302(c)(10)(B) by striking "multiemployer plan" and inserting "plan not described in subparagraph (A)."

P.L. 101-239, § 7881(b)(3)(B):

Amended ERISA Sec. 302(e)(1) by inserting "defined benefit" before "plan (other."

P.L. 101-239, § 7881(b)(4)(B):

Amended ERISA Sec. 302(e)(4)(D) to read as above. Prior to amendment, subparagraph (D) read as follows:

(D) Special Rules for Unpredictable Contingent Event Benefits.—In the case of a plan with any unpredictable contingent event benefit liabilities—

(i) such liabilities shall not be taken into account in computing the required annual payment under subparagraph (B), and

(ii) each required installment shall be increased by the greater of—

(I) the amount of benefits described in subsection (d)(5)(A)(i) paid during the 3-month period preceding the month in which the due date for such installment occurs, or

(II) 25 percent of the amount determined under subsection (d)(5)(A)(ii) for the plan year.

P.L. 101-239, § 7881(b)(6)(B)(i):

Amended ERISA Sec. 302(e)(1)(B) to read as above. Prior to amendment, subparagraph (B) read as follows:

(B) the rate under subsection (b)(5).

The above amendments are effective for plan years beginning after December 31, 1988.

P.L. 101-239, § 7881(d)(1)(B):

Amended ERISA Sec. 302(b)(5)(B)(iii) by striking "for purposes of this section and for purposes of determining current liability."

P.L. 101-239, § 7881(d)(2)(A):

Amended ERISA Sec. 302(b)(5)(B) by adding new material after the heading and before clause (i) to read as above.

P.L. 101-239, § 7881(d)(2)(B):

Amended ERISA Sec. 302(b)(5) by striking material following the heading and preceding subparagraph (A). Prior to being stricken, the material read as follows:

For purposes of determining a plan's current liability and for purposes of determining a plan's required contribution under section 412(l) for any plan year—

P.L. 101-239, § 7881(d)(2)(C):

Amended ERISA Sec. 302(b)(5)(B)(ii)(I) by striking "average weight" and inserting "the weighted average of the rates."

P.L. 101-239, § 7881(d)(3):

Amended P.L. 100-203, § 9307(f) to read as below.

The above amendments are effective for years beginning after December 31, 1987.

P.L. 101-239, § 7891(a)(1):

Titles I, III, and IV of ERISA (other than sections 3(37)(E), 301(a)(7), and 308, the last sentence of section 408(d), and sections 414(c), 4001(a)(3)(ii), and 4303) are each amended by striking "Internal Revenue Code of 1954" each place it appears and inserting "Internal Revenue Code of 1986" effective October 22, 1986.

P.L. 101-239, §7894(d)(2):

Amended ERISA Sec. 302(b)(3)(B)(ii), by striking the period and inserting a comma, effective September 2, 1974.

P.L. 101-239, §7894(d)(5):

Amended ERISA Sec. 302(c)(6) by striking "subsection (g)" and inserting "section 305."

The above amendments are effective for plan years beginning after December 31, 1987.

P.L. 100-203, §9301(b):

Amended ERISA Sec. 302(c)(7) to read as above, effective for years beginning after December 31, 1987. Prior to amendment, ERISA Sec. 302(c)(7) read as follows:

(7) For purposes of paragraph (6), the term "full funding limitation" means the excess (if any) of—

(A) the accrued liability (including normal cost) under the plan (determined under the entry age normal funding method if such accrued liability cannot be directly calculated under the funding method used for the plan), over

(B) the lesser of the fair market value of the plan's assets or the value of such assets determined under paragraph (2).

P.L. 100-203, §9303(d)(2):

Amended ERISA Sec. 302(c)(2)(B) by adding a new sentence at the end to read as above, effective for years beginning after December 31, 1987.

P.L. 100-203, §9304(a)(2):

Amended ERISA Sec. 302(c)(10) to read as above, effective for plan years beginning after December 31, 1987. Prior to amendment, ERISA Sec. 302(c)(10) read as follows:

(10) For purposes of this part, any contributions for a plan year made by an employer after the last day of such plan year, but not later than 2 ½ months after such day, shall be deemed to have been made on such last day. For purposes of this paragraph, such 2 ½ month period may be extended for not more than 6 months under regulations prescribed by the Secretary of the Treasury.

P.L. 100-203, §9303(b)(1):

Amended ERISA Sec. 302 by adding subsection (d) to read as above, effective for plan years beginning after December 31, 1988.

P.L. 100-203, §9304(b)(2):

Amended ERISA Sec. 302 by adding subsection (e) to read as above, effective for plan years beginning after 1988.

P.L. 100-203, §9304:

ERISA Sec. 302(d) was redesignated as subsection (e), which was redesignated as subsection (f), which was redesignated as subsection (g).

P.L. 100-203, §9307(a)(2)(A):

Amended ERISA Sec. 302(b)(2)(B)(iv), (2)(C) and (3)(B)(ii) by striking out "15 plan years" and inserting in lieu thereof "5 plan years (15 plan years in the case of a multiemployer plan)", effective for years beginning after December 31, 1987.

P.L. 100-203, §9307(a)(2)(B):

Amended ERISA Sec. 302(b)(2)(B)(iv) and (3)(B)(iii) by striking out "30 plan years" and inserting in lieu thereof "10 plan years (30 plan years in the case of a multiemployer plan)", effective for years beginning after December 31, 1987.

P.L. 100-203, §9307(b)(2):

Amended ERISA Sec. 302(c)(3) to read as above, effective for years beginning after December 31, 1987. Prior to amendment, ERISA Sec. 302(c)(3) read as follows:

(3) For purposes of this part, all costs, liabilities, rates of interest, and other factors under the plan shall be determined on the basis of actuarial assumptions and methods which, in the aggregate, are reasonable (taking into account the experience of the plan and reasonable expectations) and which, in combination, offer the actuary's best estimate of anticipated experience under the plan.

P.L. 100-203, §9307(e)(2):

Amended ERISA Sec. 302(b)(5) to read as above, effective for years beginning after December 31, 1987. Prior to amendment, ERISA Sec. 302(b)(5) read as follows:

(5) The funding standard account (and items therein) shall be charged or credited (as determined under regulations prescribed by the Secretary of the Treasury) with

interest at the appropriate rate consistent with the rate or rates of interest used under the plan to determine costs.

P.L. 100-203, §9307(f):

(f) EFFECTIVE DATE.—

(1) IN GENERAL.—Except as provided in paragraph (2), the amendments made by this section shall apply to years beginning after December 31, 1987.

(2) AMORTIZATION OF GAINS AND LOSSES.—Sections 412(b)(2)(B)(iv) and 412(b)(3)(B)(ii) of the Internal Revenue Code of 1986 and sections 302(b)(2)(B)(iv) and 302(b)(3)(B)(ii) of the Employee Retirement Income Security Act of 1974 (as amended by paragraphs (1)(A) and (2)(A) of subsection (a)) shall apply to gains and losses established in years beginning after December 31, 1987. For purposes of the preceding sentence, any gain or loss determined by a valuation occurring as of January 1, 1988, shall be treated as established in years beginning before 1988, or at the election of the employer, shall be amortized in accordance with Internal Revenue Service Notice 89-52.

P.L. 100-203, §9405(b)(2):

Amended ERISA Sec. 302(c) by adding paragraph (11) to read as above, effective for plan years beginning after December 31, 1987.

P.L. 100-203, §9304(e)(2):

Amended ERISA Sec. 302 by adding subsection (f) to read as above, effective for plan years beginning after December 31, 1987.

P.L. 96-364, §304:

Amended subsections 302(b)(2) and (3) to read as above and added new subsections 302(a)(3) and 302(b)(6) and (7), effective September 26, 1980.

Prior to being amended, subsections 302(b)(2) and (3) read:

"(2) For a plan year, the funding standard account shall be charged with the sum of—

(A) the normal cost of the plan for the plan year,

(B) the amounts necessary to amortize in equal annual installments (until fully amortized)—

(i) in the case of a plan in existence on January 1, 1974, the unfunded past service liability under the plan on the first day of the first plan year to which this part applies, over a period of 40 plan years,

(ii) in the case of a plan which comes into existence after January 1, 1974, the unfunded past service liability under the plan on the first day of the first plan year to which this part applies, over a period of 30 plan years (40 plan years in the case of a multiemployer plan),

(iii) separately, with respect to each plan year, the net increase (if any) in unfunded past service liability under the plan arising from plan amendments adopted in such year, over a period of 30 plan years (40 plan years in the case of a multiemployer plan),

(iv) separately, with respect to each plan year, the net experience loss (if any) under the plan, over a period of 15 plan years (20 plan years in the case of a multiemployer plan), and

(v) separately, with respect to each plan year, the net loss (if any) resulting from changes in actuarial assumptions used under the plan, over a period of 30 plan years,

(C) the amount necessary to amortize each waived funding deficiency (within the meaning of section 303(c)) for each prior plan year in equal annual installments (until fully amortized) over a period of 15 plan years, and

(D) the amount necessary to amortize in equal annual installments (until fully amortized) over a period of 5 plan years any amount credited to the funding standard account under paragraph (3)(D).

(3) For a plan year, the funding standard account shall be credited with the sum of—

(A) the amount considered contributed by the employer to or under the plan for the plan year,

(B) the amount necessary to amortize in equal annual installments (until fully amortized)—

(i) separately, with respect to each plan year, the net decrease (if any) in unfunded past service liability under the plan arising from plan amendments adopted in such year, over a period of 30 plan years (40 plan years in the case of a multiemployer plan),

(ii) separately, with respect to each plan year, the net experience gain (if any) under the plan, over a period of 15 plan years (20 plan years in the case of a multiemployer plan), and * * *"

[¶ 14,630]
MINIMUM FUNDING STANDARDS FOR SINGLE-EMPLOYER DEFINED BENEFIT PENSION PLANS

Act Sec. 303.(a) MINIMUM REQUIRED CONTRIBUTION. —For purposes of this section and section 302(a)(2)(A), except as provided in subsection (f), the term 'minimum required contribution' means, with respect to any plan year of a single-employer plan—

(1) in any case in which the value of plan assets of the plan (as reduced under subsection (f)(4)(B)) is less than the funding target of the plan for the plan year, the sum of—

(A) the target normal cost of the plan for the plan year,

(B) the shortfall amortization charge (if any) for the plan for the plan year determined under subsection (c), and

(C) the waiver amortization charge (if any) for the plan for the plan year as determined under subsection (e); or

(2) in any case in which the value of plan assets of the plan (as reduced under subsection (f)(4)(B)) equals or exceeds the funding target of the plan for the plan year, the target normal cost of the plan for the plan year reduced (but not below zero) by such excess.

Act Sec. 303. (b) TARGET NORMAL COST. —For purposes of this section:

(1) IN GENERAL. —Except as provided in subsection (i)(2) with respect to plans in at-risk status, the term 'target normal cost' means, for any plan year, the excess of —

(A) the sum of —

(i) the present value of all benefits which are expected to accrue or to be earned under the plan during the plan year, plus

(ii) the amount of plan-related expenses expected to be paid from plan assets during the plan year, over

(B) the amount of mandatory employee contributions expected to be made during the plan year.

(2) SPECIAL RULE FOR INCREASE IN COMPENSATION. —For purposes of this subsection, if any benefit attributable to services performed in a preceding plan year is increased by reason of any increase in compensation during the current plan year, the increase in such benefit shall be treated as having accrued during the current plan year.

Act Sec. 303. (c) SHORTFALL AMORTIZATION CHARGE.—

(1) IN GENERAL. —For purposes of this section, the shortfall amortization charge for a plan for any plan year is the aggregate total (not less than zero) of the shortfall amortization installments for such plan year with respect to any shortfall amortization base which has not been fully amortized under this subsection.

(2) SHORTFALL AMORTIZATION INSTALLMENT. —For purposes of paragraph (1)—

(A) DETERMINATION. —The shortfall amortization installments are the amounts necessary to amortize the shortfall amortization base of the plan for any plan year in level annual installments over the 7-plan-year period beginning with such plan year.

(B) SHORTFALL INSTALLMENT. —The shortfall amortization installment for any plan year in the 7-plan-year period under subparagraph (A) with respect to any shortfall amortization base is the annual installment determined under subparagraph (A) for that year for that base.

(C) SEGMENT RATES. —In determining any shortfall amortization installment under this paragraph, the plan sponsor shall use the segment rates determined under subparagraph (C) of subsection (h)(2), applied under rules similar to the rules of subparagraph (B) of subsection (h)(2).

(D) SPECIAL ELECTION FOR ELIGIBLE PLAN YEARS. (i) IN GENERAL. —If a plan sponsor elects to apply this subparagraph with respect to the shortfall amortization base of a plan for any eligible plan year (in this subparagraph and paragraph (7) referred to as an 'election year'), then, notwithstanding subparagraphs (A) and (B)—

(I) the shortfall amortization installments with respect to such base shall be determined under clause (ii) or (iii), whichever is specified in the election, and

(II) the shortfall amortization installment for any plan year in the 9-plan-year period described in clause (ii) or the 15-plan-year period described in clause (iii), respectively, with respect to such shortfall amortization base is the annual installment determined under the applicable clause for that year for that base.

(ii) 2 PLUS 7 AMORTIZATION SCHEDULE. —The shortfall amortization installments determined under this clause are—

(I) in the case of the first 2 plan years in the 9-plan-year period beginning with the election year, interest on the shortfall amortization base of the plan for the election year (determined using the effective interest rate for the plan for the election year), and

(II) in the case of the last 7 plan years in such 9-plan-year period, the amounts necessary to amortize the remaining balance of the shortfall amortization base of the plan for the election year in level annual installments over such last 7 plan years (using the segment rates under subparagraph (C) for the election year).

(iii) 15-YEAR AMORTIZATION. —The shortfall amortization installments determined under this subparagraph are the amounts necessary to amortize the shortfall amortization base of the plan for the election year in level annual installments over the 15-plan-year period beginning with the election year (using the segment rates under subparagraph (C) for the election year).

(iv) ELECTION—

(I) IN GENERAL. —The plan sponsor of a plan may elect to have this subparagraph apply to not more than 2 eligible plan years with respect to the plan, except that in the case of a plan described in section 106 of the Pension Protection Act of 2006, the plan sponsor may only elect to have this subparagraph apply to a plan year beginning in 2011.

(II) AMORTIZATION SCHEDULE. —Such election shall specify whether the amortization schedule under clause (ii) or (iii) shall apply to an election year, except that if a plan sponsor elects to have this subparagraph apply to 2 eligible plan years, the plan sponsor must elect the same schedule for both years.

(III) OTHER RULES. —Such election shall be made at such time, and in such form and manner, as shall be prescribed by the Secretary of the Treasury, and may be revoked only with the consent of the Secretary of the Treasury. The Secretary of the Treasury shall, before granting a revocation request, provide the Pension Benefit Guaranty Corporation an opportunity to comment on the conditions applicable to the treatment of any portion of the election year shortfall amortization base that remains unamortized as of the revocation date.

(v) ELIGIBLE PLAN YEAR. —For purposes of this subparagraph, the term 'eligible plan year' means any plan year beginning in 2008, 2009, 2010, or 2011, except that a plan year shall only be treated as an eligible plan year if the due date under subsection (j)(1) for the payment of the minimum required contribution for such plan year occurs on or after the date of the enactment of this subparagraph.

(vi) REPORTING. —A plan sponsor of a plan who makes an election under clause (i) shall—

(I) give notice of the election to participants and beneficiaries of the plan, and

(II) inform the Pension Benefit Guaranty Corporation of such election in such form and manner as the Director of the Pension Benefit Guaranty Corporation may prescribe.

(vii) INCREASES IN REQUIRED INSTALLMENTS IN CERTAIN CASES. —For increases in required contributions in cases of excess compensation or extraordinary dividends or stock redemptions, see paragraph (7).

(3) SHORTFALL AMORTIZATION BASE. —For purposes of this section, the shortfall amortization base of a plan for a plan year is—

(A) the funding shortfall of such plan for such plan year, minus

(B) the present value (determined using the segment rates determined under subparagraph (C) of subsection (h)(2), applied under rules similar to the rules of subparagraph (B) of subsection (h)(2)) of the aggregate total of the shortfall amortization installments and waiver amortization installments which have been determined for such plan year and any succeeding plan year with respect to the shortfall amortization bases and waiver amortization bases of the plan for any plan year preceding such plan year.

(4) FUNDING SHORTFALL. —For purposes of this section, the funding shortfall of a plan for any plan year is the excess (if any) of—

(A) the funding target of the plan for the plan year, over

(B) the value of plan assets of the plan (as reduced under subsection (f)(4)(B)) for the plan year which are held by the plan on the valuation date.

(5) EXEMPTION FROM NEW SHORTFALL AMORTIZATION BASE.—

In any case in which the value of plan assets of the plan (as reduced under subsection (f)(4)(A)) is equal to or greater than the funding target of the plan for the plan year, the shortfall amortization base of the plan for such plan year shall be zero.

(6) EARLY DEEMED AMORTIZATION UPON ATTAINMENT OF FUNDING TARGET. —In any case in which the funding shortfall of a plan for a plan year is zero, for purposes of determining the shortfall amortization charge for such plan year and succeeding plan years, the shortfall amortization bases for all preceding plan years (and all shortfall amortization installments determined with respect to such bases) shall be reduced to zero.

(7) INCREASES IN ALTERNATE REQUIRED INSTALLMENTS IN CASES OF EXCESS COMPENSATION OR EXTRAORDINARY DIVIDENDS OR STOCK REDEMPTIONS.—

(A) IN GENERAL. —If there is an installment acceleration amount with respect to a plan for any plan year in the restriction period with respect to an election year under paragraph (2)(D), then the shortfall amortization installment otherwise determined and payable under such paragraph for such plan year shall, subject to the limitation under subparagraph (B), be increased by such amount.

(B) TOTAL INSTALLMENTS LIMITED TO SHORTFALL BASE. —Subject to rules prescribed by the Secretary of the Treasury, if a shortfall amortization installment with respect to any shortfall amortization base for an election year is required to be increased for any plan year under subparagraph (A)—

(i) such increase shall not result in the amount of such installment exceeding the present value of such installment and all succeeding installments with respect to such base (determined without regard to such increase but after application of clause (ii)), and

(ii) subsequent shortfall amortization installments with respect to such base shall, in reverse order of the otherwise required installments, be reduced to the extent necessary to limit the present value of such subsequent shortfall amortization installments (after application of this paragraph) to the present value of the remaining unamortized shortfall amortization base.

(C) INSTALLMENT ACCELERATION AMOUNT. —For purposes of this paragraph—

(i) IN GENERAL. —The term 'installment acceleration amount' means, with respect to any plan year in a restriction period with respect to an election year, the sum of—

(I) the aggregate amount of excess employee compensation determined under subparagraph (D) with respect to all employees for the plan year, plus

(II) the aggregate amount of extraordinary dividends and redemptions determined under subparagraph (E) for the plan year.

(ii) ANNUAL LIMITATION. —The installment acceleration amount for any plan year shall not exceed the excess (if any) of—

(I) the sum of the shortfall amortization installments for the plan year and all preceding plan years in the amortization period elected under paragraph (2)(D) with respect to the shortfall amortization base with respect to an election year, determined without regard to paragraph (2)(D) and this paragraph, over

(II) the sum of the shortfall amortization installments for such plan year and all such preceding plan years, determined after application of paragraph (2)(D) (and in the case of any preceding plan year, after application of this paragraph).

(iii) CARRYOVER OF EXCESS INSTALLMENT ACCELERATION AMOUNTS.—

(I) IN GENERAL. —If the installment acceleration amount for any plan year (determined without regard to clause (ii)) exceeds the limitation under clause (ii), then, subject to subclause (II), such excess shall be treated as an installment acceleration amount with respect to the succeeding plan year.

(II) CAP TO APPLY. —If any amount treated as an installment acceleration amount under subclause (I) or this subclause with respect any succeeding plan year, when added to other installment acceleration amounts (determined without regard to clause (ii)) with respect to the plan year, exceeds the limitation under clause (ii), the portion of such amount representing such excess shall be treated as an installment acceleration amount with respect to the next succeeding plan year.

(III) LIMITATION ON YEARS TO WHICH AMOUNTS CARRIED FOR. —No amount shall be carried under subclause (I) or (II) to a plan year which begins after the first plan year following the last plan year in the restriction period (or after the second plan year following such last plan year in the case of an election year with respect to which 15-year amortization was elected under paragraph (2)(D)).

(IV) ORDERING RULES. —For purposes of applying subclause (II), installment acceleration amounts for the plan year (determined without regard to any carryover under this clause) shall be applied first against the limitation under clause (ii) and then carryovers to such plan year shall be applied against such limitation on a first-in, first-out basis.

(D) EXCESS EMPLOYEE COMPENSATION. —For purposes of this paragraph—

(i) IN GENERAL. —The term 'excess employee compensation' means, with respect to any employee for any plan year, the excess (if any) of—

(I) the aggregate amount includible in income under chapter 1 of the Internal Revenue Code of 1986 for remuneration during the calendar year in which such plan year begins for services performed by the employee for the plan sponsor (whether or not performed during such calendar year), over

(II) $1,000,000.

(ii) AMOUNTS SET ASIDE FOR NONQUALIFIED DEFERRED COMPENSATION. —If during any calendar year assets are set aside or reserved (directly or indirectly) in a trust (or other arrangement as determined by the Secretary of the Treasury), or transferred to such a trust or other arrangement, by a plan sponsor for purposes of paying deferred compensation of an employee under a nonqualified deferred compensation plan (as defined in section 409A of such Code) of the plan sponsor, then, for purposes of clause (i), the amount of such assets shall be treated as remuneration of the employee includible in income for the calendar year unless such amount is otherwise includible in income for such year. An amount to which the preceding sentence applies shall not be taken into account under this paragraph for any subsequent calendar year.

(iii) ONLY REMUNERATION FOR CERTAIN POST-2009 SERVICES COUNTED. —Remuneration shall be taken into account under clause (i) only to the extent attributable to services performed by the employee for the plan sponsor after February 28, 2010.

(iv) EXCEPTION FOR CERTAIN EQUITY PAYMENTS.—

(I) IN GENERAL. —There shall not be taken into account under clause (i)(I) any amount includible in income with respect to the granting after February 28, 2010, of service recipient stock (within the meaning of section 409A of the Internal Revenue Code of 1986) that, upon such grant, is subject to a substantial risk of forfeiture (as defined under section 83(c)(1) of such Code) for at least 5 years from the date of such grant.

(II) SECRETARIAL AUTHORITY. —The Secretary of the Treasury may by regulation provide for the application of this clause in the case of a person other than a corporation.

(v) OTHER EXCEPTIONS. —The following amounts includible in income shall not be taken into account under clause (i)(I):

(I) COMMISSIONS. —Any remuneration payable on a commission basis solely on account of income directly generated by the individual performance of the individual to whom such remuneration is payable.

(II) CERTAIN PAYMENTS UNDER EXISTING CONTRACTS. —Any remuneration consisting of nonqualified deferred compensation, restricted stock, stock options, or stock appreciation rights payable or granted under a written binding contract that was in effect on March 1, 2010, and which was not modified in any material respect before such remuneration is paid.

(vi) SELF-EMPLOYED INDIVIDUAL TREATED AS EMPLOYEE. —The term 'employee' includes, with respect to a calendar year, a self-employed individual who is treated as an employee under section 401(c) of such Code for the taxable year ending during such calendar year, and the term 'compensation' shall include earned income of such individual with respect to such self–employment.

(vii) INDEXING OF AMOUNT. —In the case of any calendar year beginning after 2010, the dollar amount under clause (i)(II) shall be increased by an amount equal to—

(I) such dollar amount, multiplied by

(II) the cost-of-living adjustment determined under section 1(f)(3) of such Code for the calendar year, determined by substituting 'calendar year 2009' for 'calendar year 1992' in subparagraph (B) thereof.

If the amount of any increase under clause (i) is not a multiple of $1,000, such increase shall be rounded to the next lowest multiple of $1,000.

(E) EXTRAORDINARY DIVIDENDS AND REDEMPTIONS.—

(i) IN GENERAL. —The amount determined under this subparagraph for any plan year is the excess (if any) of the sum of the dividends declared during the plan year by the plan sponsor plus the aggregate amount paid for the redemption of stock of the plan sponsor redeemed during the plan year over the greater of—

(I) the adjusted net income (within the meaning of section 4043) of the plan sponsor for the preceding plan year, determined without regard to any reduction by reason of interest, taxes, depreciation, or amortization, or

(II) in the case of a plan sponsor that determined and declared dividends in the same manner for at least 5 consecutive years immediately preceding such plan year, the aggregate amount of dividends determined and declared for such plan year using such manner.

(ii) ONLY CERTAIN POST-2009 DIVIDENDS AND REDEMPTIONS COUNTED. —For purposes of clause (i), there shall only be taken into account dividends declared, and redemptions occurring, after February 28, 2010.

(iii) EXCEPTION FOR INTRA-GROUP DIVIDENDS. —Dividends paid by one member of a controlled group (as defined in section 302(d)(3)) to another member of such group shall not be taken into account under clause (i).

(iv) EXCEPTION FOR CERTAIN REDEMPTIONS. —Redemptions that are made pursuant to a plan maintained with respect to employees, or that are made on account of the death, disability, or termination of employment of an employee or shareholder, shall not be taken into account under clause (i).

(v) EXCEPTION FOR CERTAIN PREFERRED STOCK.—

(I) IN GENERAL. —Dividends and redemptions with respect to applicable preferred stock shall not be taken into account under clause (i) to the extent that dividends accrue with respect to such stock at a specified rate in all events and without regard to the plan sponsor's income, and interest accrues on any unpaid dividends with respect to such stock.

(II) APPLICABLE PREFERRED STOCK. —For purposes of subclause (I), the term 'applicable preferred stock' means preferred stock which was issued before March 1, 2010 (or which was issued after such date and is held by an employee benefit plan subject to the provisions of this title).

(F) OTHER DEFINITIONS AND RULES. —For purposes of this paragraph—

(i) PLAN SPONSOR. —The term 'plan sponsor' includes any member of the plan sponsor's controlled group (as defined in section 302(d)(3)).

(ii) RESTRICTION PERIOD. —The term 'restriction period' means, with respect to any election year—

(I) except as provided in subclause (II), the 3-year period beginning with the election year (or, if later, the first plan year beginning after December 31, 2009), and

(II) if the plan sponsor elects 15-year amortization for the shortfall amortization base for the election year, the 5-year period beginning with the election year (or, if later, the first plan year beginning after December 31, 2009).

(iii) ELECTIONS FOR MULTIPLE PLANS. —If a plan sponsor makes elections under paragraph (2)(D) with respect to 2 or more plans, the Secretary of the Treasury shall provide rules for the application of this paragraph to such plans, including rules for the ratable allocation of any installment acceleration amount among such plans on the basis of each plan's relative reduction in the plan's shortfall amortization installment for the first plan year in the amortization period described in subparagraph (A) (determined without regard to this paragraph).

(iv) MERGERS AND ACQUISITIONS. —The Secretary of the Treasury shall prescribe rules for the application of paragraph (2)(D) and this paragraph in any case where there is a merger or acquisition involving a plan sponsor making the election under paragraph (2)(D).

Act Sec. 303. (d) RULES RELATING TO FUNDING TARGET. —For purposes of this section—

(1) FUNDING TARGET. —Except as provided in subsection (i)(1) with respect to plans in at-risk status, the funding target of a plan for a plan year is the present value of all benefits accrued or earned under the plan as of the beginning of the plan year.

(2) FUNDING TARGET ATTAINMENT PERCENTAGE. —The 'funding target attainment percentage' of a plan for a plan year is the ratio (expressed as a percentage) which—

(A) the value of plan assets for the plan year (as reduced under subsection (f)(4)(B)), bears to

(B) the funding target of the plan for the plan year (determined without regard to subsection (i)(1)).

Act Sec. 303. (e) WAIVER AMORTIZATION CHARGE.—

(1) DETERMINATION OF WAIVER AMORTIZATION CHARGE. —The waiver amortization charge (if any) for a plan for any plan year is the aggregate total of the waiver amortization installments for such plan year with respect to the waiver amortization bases for each of the 5 preceding plan years.

(2) WAIVER AMORTIZATION INSTALLMENT. —For purposes of paragraph (1)—

(A) DETERMINATION. —The waiver amortization installments are the amounts necessary to amortize the waiver amortization base of the plan for any plan year in level annual installments over a period of 5 plan years beginning with the succeeding plan year.

(B) WAIVER INSTALLMENT. —The waiver amortization installment for any plan year in the 5-year period under subparagraph (A) with respect to any waiver amortization base is the annual installment determined under subparagraph (A) for that year for that base.

(3) INTEREST RATE. —In determining any waiver amortization installment under this subsection, the plan sponsor shall use the segment rates determined under subparagraph (C) of subsection (h)(2), applied under rules similar to the rules of subparagraph (B) of subsection (h)(2).

(4) WAIVER AMORTIZATION BASE. —The waiver amortization base of a plan for a plan year is the amount of the waived funding deficiency (if any) for such plan year under section 302(c).

(5) EARLY DEEMED AMORTIZATION UPON ATTAINMENT OF FUNDING TARGET. —In any case in which the funding shortfall of a plan for a plan year is zero, for purposes of determining the waiver amortization charge for such plan year and succeeding plan years, the waiver amortization bases for all preceding plan years (and all waiver amortization installments determined with respect to such bases) shall be reduced to zero.

Act Sec. 303. (f) REDUCTION OF MINIMUM REQUIRED CONTRIBUTION BY PREFUNDING BALANCE AND FUNDING STANDARD CARRYOVER BALANCE.—

(1) ELECTION TO MAINTAIN BALANCES.—

(A) PREFUNDING BALANCE. —The plan sponsor of a single-employer plan may elect to maintain a prefunding balance.

(B) FUNDING STANDARD CARRYOVER BALANCE.—

(i) IN GENERAL. —In the case of a single-employer plan described in clause (ii), the plan sponsor may elect to maintain a funding standard carryover balance, until such balance is reduced to zero.

(ii) PLANS MAINTAINING FUNDING STANDARD ACCOUNT IN 2007. —A plan is described in this clause if the plan—

(I) was in effect for a plan year beginning in 2007, and

(II) had a positive balance in the funding standard account under section 302(b) as in effect for such plan year and determined as of the end of such plan year.

(2) APPLICATION OF BALANCES. —A prefunding balance and a funding standard carryover balance maintained pursuant to this paragraph—

(A) shall be available for crediting against the minimum required contribution, pursuant to an election under paragraph (3),

(B) shall be applied as a reduction in the amount treated as the value of plan assets for purposes of this section, to the extent provided in paragraph (4), and

(C) may be reduced at any time, pursuant to an election under paragraph (5).

(3) ELECTION TO APPLY BALANCES AGAINST MINIMUM REQUIRED CONTRIBUTION.—

(A) IN GENERAL. —Except as provided in subparagraphs (B) and (C), in the case of any plan year in which the plan sponsor elects to credit against the minimum required contribution for the current plan year all or a portion of the prefunding balance or the funding standard carryover balance for the current plan year (not in excess of such minimum required contribution), the minimum required contribution for the plan year shall be reduced as of the first day of the plan year by the amount so credited by the plan sponsor. For purposes of the preceding sentence, the minimum required contribution shall be determined after taking into account any waiver under section 302(c).

(B) COORDINATION WITH FUNDING STANDARD CARRYOVER BALANCE. —To the extent that any plan has a funding standard carryover balance greater than zero, no amount of the prefunding balance of such plan may be credited under this paragraph in reducing the minimum required contribution.

(C) LIMITATION FOR UNDERFUNDED PLANS. —The preceding provisions of this paragraph shall not apply for any plan year if the ratio (expressed as a percentage) which—

(i) the value of plan assets for the preceding plan year (as reduced under paragraph (4)(C)), bears to

(ii) the funding target of the plan for the preceding plan year (determined without regard to subsection (i)(1)),

is less than 80 percent. In the case of plan years beginning in 2008, the ratio under this subparagraph may be determined using such methods of estimation as the Secretary of the Treasury may prescribe.

(D) SPECIAL RULE FOR CERTAIN YEARS OF PLANS MAINTAINED BY CHARITIES.—

(i) IN GENERAL. —For purposes of applying subparagraph (C) for plan years beginning after August 31, 2009, and before September 1, 2011, the ratio determined under such subparagraph for the preceding plan year shall be the greater of—

(I) such ratio, as determined without regard to this subparagraph, or

(II) the ratio for such plan for the plan year beginning after August 31, 2007, and before September 1, 2008, as determined under rules prescribed by the Secretary of the Treasury.

(ii) SPECIAL RULE. —In the case of a plan for which the valuation date is not the first day of the plan year—

(I) clause (i) shall apply to plan years beginning after December 31, 2008, and before January 1, 2011, and

(II) clause (i)(II) shall apply based on the last plan year beginning before September 1, 2007, as determined under rules prescribed by the Secretary of the Treasury.

(iii) LIMITATION TO CHARITIES. —This subparagraph shall not apply to any plan unless such plan is maintained exclusively by one or more organizations described in section 501(c)(3) of the Internal Revenue Code of 1986.

(4) EFFECT OF BALANCES ON AMOUNTS TREATED AS VALUE OF PLAN ASSETS. —In the case of any plan maintaining a prefunding balance or a funding standard carryover balance pursuant to this subsection, the amount treated as the value of plan assets shall be deemed to be such amount, reduced as provided in the following subparagraphs:

(A) APPLICABILITY OF SHORTFALL AMORTIZATION BASE. —For purposes of subsection (c)(5), the value of plan assets is deemed to be such amount, reduced by the amount of the prefunding balance, but only if an election under paragraph (3) applying any portion of the prefunding balance in reducing the minimum required contribution is in effect for the plan year.

(B) DETERMINATION OF EXCESS ASSETS, FUNDING SHORTFALL, AND FUNDING TARGET ATTAINMENT PERCENTAGE.—

(i) IN GENERAL. —For purposes of subsections (a), (c)(4)(B), and (d)(2)(A), the value of plan assets is deemed to be such amount, reduced by the amount of the prefunding balance and the funding standard carryover balance.

(ii) SPECIAL RULE FOR CERTAIN BINDING AGREEMENTS WITH PBGC. —For purposes of subsection (c)(4)(B), the value of plan assets shall not be deemed to be reduced for a plan year by the amount of the specified balance if, with respect to such balance, there is in effect for a plan year a binding written agreement with the Pension Benefit Guaranty Corporation which provides that such balance is not available to reduce the minimum required contribution for the plan year. For purposes of the preceding sentence, the term 'specified balance' means the prefunding balance or the funding standard carryover balance, as the case may be.

(C) AVAILABILITY OF BALANCES IN PLAN YEAR FOR CREDITING AGAINST MINIMUM REQUIRED CONTRIBUTION. —For purposes of paragraph (3)(C)(i) of this subsection, the value of plan assets is deemed to be such amount, reduced by the amount of the prefunding balance.

(5) ELECTION TO REDUCE BALANCE PRIOR TO DETERMINATIONS OF VALUE OF PLAN ASSETS AND CREDITING AGAINST MINIMUM REQUIRED CONTRIBUTION.—

(A) IN GENERAL. —The plan sponsor may elect to reduce by any amount the balance of the prefunding balance and the funding standard carryover balance for any plan year (but not below zero). Such reduction shall be effective prior to any determination of the value of plan assets for such plan year under this section and application of the balance in reducing the minimum required contribution for such plan for such plan year pursuant to an election under paragraph (2).

(B) COORDINATION BETWEEN PREFUNDING BALANCE AND FUNDING STANDARD CARRYOVER BALANCE. —To the extent that any plan has a funding standard carryover balance greater than zero, no election may be made under subparagraph (A) with respect to the prefunding balance.

(6) PREFUNDING BALANCE.—

(A) IN GENERAL. —A prefunding balance maintained by a plan shall consist of a beginning balance of zero, increased and decreased to the extent provided in subparagraphs (B) and (C), and adjusted further as provided in paragraph (8).

(B) INCREASES.—

(i) IN GENERAL. —As of the first day of each plan year beginning after 2008, the prefunding balance of a plan shall be increased by the amount elected by the plan sponsor for the plan year. Such amount shall not exceed the excess (if any) of—

(I) the aggregate total of employer contributions to the plan for the preceding plan year, over—

(II) the minimum required contribution for such preceding plan year.

(ii) ADJUSTMENTS FOR INTEREST. —Any excess contributions under clause (i) shall be properly adjusted for interest accruing for the periods between the first day of the current plan year and the dates on which the excess contributions were made, determined by using the effective interest rate for the preceding plan year and by treating contributions as being first used to satisfy the minimum required contribution.

(iii) CERTAIN CONTRIBUTIONS NECESSARY TO AVOID BENEFIT LIMITATIONS DISREGARDED. —The excess described in clause (i) with respect to any preceding plan year shall be reduced (but not below zero) by the amount of contributions an employer would be required to make under paragraph (1), (2), or (4) of section 206(g) to avoid a benefit limitation which would otherwise be imposed under such paragraph for the preceding plan year. Any contribution which may be taken into account in satisfying the requirements of more than 1 of such paragraphs shall be taken into account only once for purposes of this clause.

(C) DECREASE. —The prefunding balance of a plan shall be decreased (but not below zero) by—

(i) as of the first day of each plan year after 2008, the amount of such balance credited under paragraph (2) (if any) in reducing the minimum required contribution of the plan for the preceding plan year, and

(ii) as of the time specified in paragraph (5))(A), any reduction in such balance elected under paragraph (5).

(7) FUNDING STANDARD CARRYOVER BALANCE.—

(A) IN GENERAL. —A funding standard carryover balance maintained by a plan shall consist of a beginning balance determined under subparagraph (B), decreased to the extent provided in subparagraph (C), and adjusted further as provided in paragraph (8).

(B) BEGINNING BALANCE. —The beginning balance of the funding standard carryover balance shall be the positive balance described in paragraph (1)(B)(ii)(II).

(C) DECREASES. —The funding standard carryover balance of a plan shall be decreased (but not below zero) by—

(i) as of the first day of each plan year after 2008, the amount of such balance credited under paragraph (2) (if any) in reducing the minimum required contribution of the plan for the preceding plan year, and

(ii) as of the time specified in paragraph (5))(A), any reduction in such balance elected under paragraph (5).

(8) ADJUSTMENTS FOR INVESTMENT EXPERIENCE. —In determining the prefunding balance or the funding standard carryover balance of a plan as of the first day of the plan year, the plan sponsor shall, in accordance with regulations prescribed by the Secretary of the Treasury, adjust such balance to reflect the rate of return on plan assets for the preceding plan year. Notwithstanding subsection (g)(3), such rate of return shall be determined on the basis of fair market value and shall properly take into account, in accordance with such regulations, all contributions, distributions, and other plan payments made during such period.

(9) ELECTIONS. —Elections under this subsection shall be made at such times, and in such form and manner, as shall be prescribed in regulations of the Secretary of the Treasury.

Act Sec. 303. (g) VALUATION OF PLAN ASSETS AND LIABILITIES.—

(1) TIMING OF DETERMINATIONS. —Except as otherwise provided under this subsection, all determinations under this section for a plan year shall be made as of the valuation date of the plan for such plan year.

(2) VALUATION DATE. —For purposes of this section—

(A) IN GENERAL. —Except as provided in subparagraph (B), the valuation date of a plan for any plan year shall be the first day of the plan year.

(B) EXCEPTION FOR SMALL PLANS. —If, on each day during the preceding plan year, a plan had 100 or fewer participants, the plan may designate any day during the plan year as its valuation date for such plan year and succeeding plan years. For purposes of this subparagraph, all defined benefit plans which are single-employer plans and are maintained by the same employer (or any member of such employer's controlled group) shall be treated as 1 plan, but only participants with respect to such employer or member shall be taken into account.

(C) APPLICATION OF CERTAIN RULES IN DETERMINATION OF PLAN SIZE. —For purposes of this paragraph—

(i) PLANS NOT IN EXISTENCE IN PRECEDING YEAR. —In the case of the first plan year of any plan, subparagraph (B) shall apply to such plan by taking into account the number of participants that the plan is reasonably expected to have on days during such first plan year.

(ii) PREDECESSORS. —Any reference in subparagraph (B) to an employer shall include a reference to any predecessor of such employer.

(3) DETERMINATION OF VALUE OF PLAN ASSETS. —For purposes of this section—

(A) IN GENERAL. —Except as provided in subparagraph (B), the value of plan assets shall be the fair market value of the assets.

(B) AVERAGING ALLOWED. —A plan may determine the value of plan assets on the basis of the averaging of fair market values, but only if such method—

    (i) is permitted under regulations prescribed by the Secretary of the Treasury,

    (ii) does not provide for averaging of such values over more than the period beginning on the last day of the 25th month preceding the month in which the valuation date occurs and ending on the valuation date (or a similar period in the case of a valuation date which is not the 1st day of a month), and

    (iii) does not result in a determination of the value of plan assets which, at any time, is lower than 90 percent or greater than 110 percent of the fair market value of such assets at such time.

Any such averaging shall be adjusted for contributions, distributions, and expected earnings (as determined by the plan's actuary on the basis of an assumed earnings rate specified by the actuary but not in excess of the third segment rate applicable under subsection (h)(2)(C)(iii)), as specified by the Secretary of the Treasury.

(4) ACCOUNTING FOR CONTRIBUTION RECEIPTS. —For purposes of determining the value of assets under paragraph (3)—

    (A) PRIOR YEAR CONTRIBUTIONS. —If—

    (i) an employer makes any contribution to the plan after the valuation date for the plan year in which the contribution is made, and

    (ii) the contribution is for a preceding plan year,

the contribution shall be taken into account as an asset of the plan as of the valuation date, except that in the case of any plan year beginning after 2008, only the present value (determined as of the valuation date) of such contribution may be taken into account. For purposes of the preceding sentence, present value shall be determined using the effective interest rate for the preceding plan year to which the contribution is properly allocable.

    (B) SPECIAL RULE FOR CURRENT YEAR CONTRIBUTIONS MADE BEFORE VALUATION DATE. —If any contributions for any plan year are made to or under the plan during the plan year but before the valuation date for the plan year, the assets of the plan as of the valuation date shall not include—

    (i) such contributions, and

    (ii) interest on such contributions for the period between the date of the contributions and the valuation date, determined by using the effective interest rate for the plan year.

Act Sec. 303. (h) ACTUARIAL ASSUMPTIONS AND METHODS.—

(1) IN GENERAL. —Subject to this subsection, the determination of any present value or other computation under this section shall be made on the basis of actuarial assumptions and methods—

    (A) each of which is reasonable (taking into account the experience of the plan and reasonable expectations), and

    (B) which, in combination, offer the actuary's best estimate of anticipated experience under the plan.

(2) INTEREST RATES.—

    (A) EFFECTIVE INTEREST RATE. —For purposes of this section, the term 'effective interest rate' means, with respect to any plan for any plan year, the single rate of interest which, if used to determine the present value of the plan's accrued or earned benefits referred to in subsection (d)(1), would result in an amount equal to the funding target of the plan for such plan year.

    (B) INTEREST RATES FOR DETERMINING FUNDING TARGET. —For purposes of determining the funding target and normal cost of a plan for any plan year, the interest rate used in determining the present value of the benefits of the plan shall be—

    (i) in the case of benefits reasonably determined to be payable during the 5-year period beginning on the valuation date for the plan year, the first segment rate with respect to the applicable month,

    (ii) in the case of benefits reasonably determined to be payable during the 15-year period beginning at the end of the period described in clause (i), the second segment rate with respect to the applicable month, and

    (iii) in the case of benefits reasonably determined to be payable after the period described in clause (ii), the third segment rate with respect to the applicable month.

    (C) SEGMENT RATES. —For purposes of this paragraph—

    (i) FIRST SEGMENT RATE. —The term 'first segment rate' means, with respect to any month, the single rate of interest which shall be determined by the Secretary of the Treasury for such month on the basis of the corporate bond yield curve for such month, taking into account only that portion of such yield curve which is based on bonds maturing during the 5-year period commencing with such month.

    (ii) SECOND SEGMENT RATE. —The term 'second segment rate' means, with respect to any month, the single rate of interest which shall be determined by the Secretary of the Treasury for such month on the basis of the corporate bond yield curve for such month, taking into account only that portion of such yield curve which is based on bonds maturing during the 15-year period beginning at the end of the period described in clause (i).

    (iii) THIRD SEGMENT RATE. —The term 'third segment rate' means, with respect to any month, the single rate of interest which shall be determined by the Secretary of the Treasury for such month on the basis of the corporate bond yield curve for such month, taking into account only that portion of such yield curve which is based on bonds maturing during periods beginning after the period described in clause (ii).

    (iv) SEGMENT RATE STABILIZATION.—

    (I) IN GENERAL. If a segment rate described in clause (i), (ii), or (iii) with respect to any applicable month (determined without regard to this clause) is less than the applicable minimum percentage, or more than the applicable maximum percentage, of the average of the segment rates described in such clause for years in the 25-year period ending with September 30 of the calendar year preceding the calendar year in which the plan year begins, then the segment rate described in such clause with respect to the applicable month shall be equal to the applicable minimum percentage or the applicable maximum percentage of such average, whichever is closest. The Secretary of the Treasury shall determine such average on an annual basis and may prescribe equivalent rates for years in any such 25-year period for which the rates described in any such clause are not available.

    (II) APPLICABLE MINIMUM PERCENTAGE; APPLICABLE MAXIMUM PERCENTAGE. For purposes of subclause (I), the applicable minimum percentage and the applicable maximum percentage for a plan year beginning in a calendar year shall be determined in accordance with the following table:

If the calendar year is:	The applicable minimum percentage is:	The applicable maximum percentage is:
2012, 2013, 2014, 2015, 2016, 2017, 2018, 2019, or 2020.	90%	110%
2021	85%	115%
2022	80%	120%
2023	75%	125%
After 2023	70%	130%.

(D) CORPORATE BOND YIELD CURVE. —For purposes of this paragraph—

(i) IN GENERAL. —The term 'corporate bond yield curve' means, with respect to any month, a yield curve which is prescribed by the Secretary of the Treasury for such month and which reflects the average, for the 24-month period ending with the month preceding such month, of monthly yields on investment grade corporate bonds with varying maturities and that are in the top 3 quality levels available.

(ii) ELECTION TO USE YIELD CURVE. —Solely for purposes of determining the minimum required contribution under this section, the plan sponsor may, in lieu of the segment rates determined under subparagraph (C), elect to use interest rates under the corporate bond yield curve. For purposes of the preceding sentence such curve shall be determined without regard to the 24-month averaging described in clause (i). Such election, once made, may be revoked only with the consent of the Secretary of the Treasury.

(E) APPLICABLE MONTH. —For purposes of this paragraph, the term 'applicable month' means, with respect to any plan for any plan year, the month which includes the valuation date of such plan for such plan year or, at the election of the plan sponsor, any of the 4 months which precede such month. Any election made under this subparagraph shall apply to the plan year for which the election is made and all succeeding plan years, unless the election is revoked with the consent of the Secretary of the Treasury.

(F) PUBLICATION REQUIREMENTS. —The Secretary of the Treasury shall publish for each month the corporate bond yield curve (and the corporate bond yield curve reflecting the modification described in section 205(g)(3)(B)(iii)(I) for such month), and each of the rates determined under subparagraph (C) and the averages determined under subparagraph (C)(iv) for such month. The Secretary of the Treasury shall also publish a description of the methodology used to determine such yield curve and such rates which is sufficiently detailed to enable plans to make reasonable projections regarding the yield curve and such rates for future months based on the plan's projection of future interest rates.

(3) MORTALITY TABLES.—

(A) IN GENERAL. —Except as provided in subparagraph (C) or (D), the Secretary of the Treasury shall by regulation prescribe mortality tables to be used in determining any present value or making any computation under this section. Such tables shall be based on the actual experience of pension plans and projected trends in such experience. In prescribing such tables, the Secretary of the Treasury shall take into account results of available independent studies of mortality of individuals covered by pension plans.

(B) PERIODIC REVISION. —The Secretary of the Treasury shall (at least every 10 years) make revisions in any table in effect under subparagraph (A) to reflect the actual experience of pension plans and projected trends in such experience.

(C) SUBSTITUTE MORTALITY TABLE.—

(i) IN GENERAL. —Upon request by the plan sponsor and approval by the Secretary of the Treasury, a mortality table which meets the requirements of clause (iii) shall be used in determining any present value or making any computation under this section during the period of consecutive plan years (not to exceed 10) specified in the request.

(ii) EARLY TERMINATION OF PERIOD. —Notwithstanding clause (i), a mortality table described in clause (i) shall cease to be in effect as of the earliest of—

(I) the date on which there is a significant change in the participants in the plan by reason of a plan spinoff or merger or otherwise, or

(II) the date on which the plan actuary determines that such table does not meet the requirements of clause (iii).

(iii) REQUIREMENTS. —A mortality table meets the requirements of this clause if—

(I) there is a sufficient number of plan participants, and the pension plans have been maintained for a sufficient period of time, to have credible information necessary for purposes of subclause (II), and

(II) such table reflects the actual experience of the pension plans maintained by the sponsor and projected trends in general mortality experience.

(iv) ALL PLANS IN CONTROLLED GROUP MUST USE SEPARATE TABLE. —Except as provided by the Secretary of the Treasury, a plan sponsor may not use a mortality table under this subparagraph for any plan maintained by the plan sponsor unless—

(I) a separate mortality table is established and used under this subparagraph for each other plan maintained by the plan sponsor and if the plan sponsor is a member of a controlled group, each member of the controlled group, and

(II) the requirements of clause (iii) are met separately with respect to the table so established for each such plan, determined by only taking into account the participants of such plan, the time such plan has been in existence, and the actual experience of such plan.

(v) DEADLINE FOR SUBMISSION AND DISPOSITION OF APPLICATION.—

(I) SUBMISSION. —The plan sponsor shall submit a mortality table to the Secretary of the Treasury for approval under this subparagraph at least 7 months before the 1st day of the period described in clause (i).

(II) DISPOSITION. —Any mortality table submitted to the Secretary of the Treasury for approval under this subparagraph shall be treated as in effect as of the 1st day of the period described in clause (i) unless the Secretary of the Treasury, during the 180-day period beginning on the date of such submission, disapproves of such table and provides the reasons that such table fails to meet the requirements of clause (iii). The 180-day period shall be extended upon mutual agreement of the Secretary of the Treasury and the plan sponsor.

(D) SEPARATE MORTALITY TABLES FOR THE DISABLED. —Notwithstanding subparagraph (A)—

(i) IN GENERAL. —The Secretary of the Treasury shall establish mortality tables which may be used (in lieu of the tables under subparagraph (A)) under this subsection for individuals who are entitled to benefits under the plan on account of disability. The Secretary of the Treasury shall establish separate tables for individuals whose disabilities occur in plan years beginning before January 1, 1995, and for individuals whose disabilities occur in plan years beginning on or after such date.

(ii) SPECIAL RULE FOR DISABILITIES OCCURRING AFTER 1994. —In the case of disabilities occurring in plan years beginning after December 31, 1994, the tables under clause (i) shall apply only with respect to individuals described in such subclause who are disabled within the meaning of title II of the Social Security Act and the regulations thereunder.

(iii) PERIODIC REVISION. —The Secretary of the Treasury shall (at least every 10 years) make revisions in any table in effect under clause (i) to reflect the actual experience of pension plans and projected trends in such experience.

(4) PROBABILITY OF BENEFIT PAYMENTS IN THE FORM OF LUMP SUMS OR OTHER OPTIONAL FORMS. —For purposes of determining any present value or making any computation under this section, there shall be taken into account—

(A) the probability that future benefit payments under the plan will be made in the form of optional forms of benefits provided under the plan (including lump sum distributions, determined on the basis of the plan's experience and other related assumptions), and

(B) any difference in the present value of such future benefit payments resulting from the use of actuarial assumptions, in determining benefit payments in any such optional form of benefits, which are different from those specified in this subsection.

(5) APPROVAL OF LARGE CHANGES IN ACTUARIAL ASSUMPTIONS.—

(A) IN GENERAL. —No actuarial assumption used to determine the funding target for a plan to which this paragraph applies may be changed without the approval of the Secretary of the Treasury.

(B) PLANS TO WHICH PARAGRAPH APPLIES. —This paragraph shall apply to a plan only if—

(i) the plan is a single-employer plan to which title IV applies,

(ii) the aggregate unfunded vested benefits as of the close of the preceding plan year (as determined under section 4006(a)(3)(E)(iii)) of such plan and all other plans maintained by the contributing sponsors (as defined in section 4001(a)(13)) and members of such sponsors' controlled groups (as defined in section 4001(a)(14)) which are covered by title IV (disregarding plans with no unfunded vested benefits) exceed $50,000,000, and

(iii) the change in assumptions (determined after taking into account any changes in interest rate and mortality table) results in a decrease in the funding shortfall of the plan for the current plan year that exceeds $50,000,000, or that exceeds $5,000,000 and that is 5 percent or more of the funding target of the plan before such change.

Act Sec. 303. (i) SPECIAL RULES FOR AT-RISK PLANS.—

(1) FUNDING TARGET FOR PLANS IN AT-RISK STATUS.—

(A) IN GENERAL. —In the case of a plan which is in at-risk status for a plan year, the funding target of the plan for the plan year shall be equal to the sum of—

(i) the present value of all benefits accrued or earned under the plan as of the beginning of the plan year, as determined by using the additional actuarial assumptions described in subparagraph (B), and

(ii) in the case of a plan which also has been in at-risk status for at least 2 of the 4 preceding plan years, a loading factor determined under subparagraph (C).

(B) ADDITIONAL ACTUARIAL ASSUMPTIONS. —The actuarial assumptions described in this subparagraph are as follows:

(i) All employees who are not otherwise assumed to retire as of the valuation date but who will be eligible to elect benefits during the plan year and the 10 succeeding plan years shall be assumed to retire at the earliest retirement date under the plan but not before the end of the plan year for which the at-risk funding target and at-risk target normal cost are being determined.

(ii) All employees shall be assumed to elect the retirement benefit available under the plan at the assumed retirement age (determined after application of clause (i)) which would result in the highest present value of benefits.

(C) LOADING FACTOR. —The loading factor applied with respect to a plan under this paragraph for any plan year is the sum of—

(i) $700, times the number of participants in the plan, plus

(ii) 4 percent of the funding target (determined without regard to this paragraph) of the plan for the plan year.

(2) TARGET NORMAL COST OF AT-RISK PLANS. —In the case of a plan which is in at-risk status for a plan year, the target normal cost of the plan for such plan year shall be equal to the sum of —

(A) the present value of all benefits which are expected to accrue or be earned under the plan during the plan year, determined using the additional actuarial assumptions described in paragraph (1)(B), plus

(B) in the case of a plan which also has been in at-risk status for at least 2 of the 4 preceding plan years, a loading factor equal to 4 percent of the target normal cost (determined without regard to this paragraph) of the plan for the plan year.

(2) TARGET NORMAL COST OF AT-RISK PLANS. —In the case of a plan which is in at-risk status for a plan year, the target normal cost of the plan for such plan year shall be equal to the sum of—

(A) the excess of —

(i) the sum of —

(I) the present value of all benefits which are expected to accrue or to be earned under the plan during the plan year, determined using the additional actuarial assumptions described in paragraph (1)(B), plus

(II) the amount of plan-related expenses expected to be paid from plan assets during the plan year, over

(ii) the amount of mandatory employee contributions expected to be made during the plan year, plus

(B) in the case of a plan which also has been in at-risk status for at least 2 of the 4 preceding plan years, a loading factor equal to 4 percent of the amount determined under subsection (b)(1)(A)(i) with respect to the plan for the plan year.

(3) MINIMUM AMOUNT. —In no event shall—

(A) the at-risk funding target be less than the funding target, as determined without regard to this subsection, or

(B) the at-risk target normal cost be less than the target normal cost, as determined without regard to this subsection.

(4) DETERMINATION OF AT-RISK STATUS. —For purposes of this subsection—

(A) IN GENERAL. —A plan is in at-risk status for a plan year if—

(i) the funding target attainment percentage for the preceding plan year (determined under this section without regard to this subsection) is less than 80 percent, and

(ii) the funding target attainment percentage for the preceding plan year (determined under this section by using the additional actuarial assumptions described in paragraph (1)(B) in computing the funding target) is less than 70 percent.

(B) TRANSITION RULE. —In the case of plan years beginning in 2008, 2009, and 2010, subparagraph (A)(i) shall be applied by substituting the following percentages for '80 percent':

    (i) 65 percent in the case of 2008.

    (ii) 70 percent in the case of 2009.

    (iii) 75 percent in the case of 2010.

In the case of plan years beginning in 2008, the funding target attainment percentage for the preceding plan year under subparagraph (A) may be determined using such methods of estimation as the Secretary of the Treasury may provide.

(C) SPECIAL RULE FOR EMPLOYEES OFFERED EARLY RETIREMENT IN 2006.—

    (i) IN GENERAL. —For purposes of subparagraph (A)(ii), the additional actuarial assumptions described in paragraph (1)(B) shall not be taken into account with respect to any employee if—

       (I) such employee is employed by a specified automobile manufacturer,

       (II) such employee is offered a substantial amount of additional cash compensation, substantially enhanced retirement benefits under the plan, or materially reduced employment duties on the condition that by a specified date (not later than December 31, 2010) the employee retires (as defined under the terms of the plan),

       (III) such offer is made during 2006 and pursuant to a bona fide retirement incentive program and requires, by the terms of the offer, that such offer can be accepted not later than a specified date (not later than December 31, 2006), and

       (IV) such employee does not elect to accept such offer before the specified date on which the offer expires.

    (ii) SPECIFIED AUTOMOBILE MANUFACTURER. —For purposes of clause (i), the term 'specified automobile manufacturer' means—

       (I) any manufacturer of automobiles, and

       (II) any manufacturer of automobile parts which supplies such parts directly to a manufacturer of automobiles and which, after a transaction or series of transactions ending in 1999, ceased to be a member of a controlled group which included such manufacturer of automobiles.

(5) TRANSITION BETWEEN APPLICABLE FUNDING TARGETS AND BETWEEN APPLICABLE TARGET NORMAL COSTS.—

    (A) IN GENERAL. —In any case in which a plan which is in at-risk status for a plan year has been in such status for a consecutive period of fewer than 5 plan years, the applicable amount of the funding target and of the target normal cost shall be, in lieu of the amount determined without regard to this paragraph, the sum of—

       (i) the amount determined under this section without regard to this subsection, plus

       (ii) the transition percentage for such plan year of the excess of the amount determined under this subsection (without regard to this paragraph) over the amount determined under this section without regard to this subsection.

    (B) TRANSITION PERCENTAGE. —For purposes of subparagraph (A), the transition percentage shall be determined in accordance with the following table:

If the consecutive number of years (including the plan year) the plan is in at-risk status is—	The transition percentage is—
1	20
2	40
3	60
4	80.

    (C) YEARS BEFORE EFFECTIVE DATE. —For purposes of this paragraph, plan years beginning before 2008 shall not be taken into account.

(6) SMALL PLAN EXCEPTION. —If, on each day during the preceding plan year, a plan had 500 or fewer participants, the plan shall not be treated as in at-risk status for the plan year. For purposes of this paragraph, all defined benefit plans (other than multiemployer plans) maintained by the same employer (or any member of such employer's controlled group) shall be treated as 1 plan, but only participants with respect to such employer or member shall be taken into account and the rules of subsection (g)(2)(C) shall apply.

Act Sec. 303. (j) PAYMENT OF MINIMUM REQUIRED CONTRIBUTIONS.—

(1) IN GENERAL. —For purposes of this section, the due date for any payment of any minimum required contribution for any plan year shall be 8 ½ months after the close of the plan year.

(2) INTEREST. —Any payment required under paragraph (1) for a plan year that is made on a date other than the valuation date for such plan year shall be adjusted for interest accruing for the period between the valuation date and the payment date, at the effective rate of interest for the plan for such plan year.

(3) ACCELERATED QUARTERLY CONTRIBUTION SCHEDULE FOR UNDERFUNDED PLANS.—

    (A) FAILURE TO TIMELY MAKE REQUIRED INSTALLMENT. —In any case in which the plan has a funding shortfall for the preceding plan year, the employer maintaining the plan shall make the required installments under this paragraph and if the employer fails to pay the full amount of a required installment for the plan year, then the amount of interest charged under paragraph (2) on the underpayment for the period of underpayment shall be determined by using a rate of interest equal to the rate otherwise used under paragraph (2) plus 5 percentage points. In the case of plan years beginning in 2008, the funding shortfall for the preceding plan year may be determined using such methods of estimation as the Secretary of the Treasury may provide.

    (B) AMOUNT OF UNDERPAYMENT, PERIOD OF UNDERPAYMENT. —For purposes of subparagraph (A)—

       (i) AMOUNT. —The amount of the underpayment shall be the excess of—

          (I) the required installment, over

          (II) the amount (if any) of the installment contributed to or under the plan on or before the due date for the installment.

       (ii) PERIOD OF UNDERPAYMENT. —The period for which any interest is charged under this paragraph with respect to any portion of the underpayment shall run from the due date for the installment to the date on which such portion is contributed to or under the plan.

       (iii) ORDER OF CREDITING CONTRIBUTIONS. —For purposes of clause (i)(II), contributions shall be credited against unpaid required installments in the order in which such installments are required to be paid.

    (C) NUMBER OF REQUIRED INSTALLMENTS; DUE DATES. —For purposes of this paragraph—

(i) PAYABLE IN 4 INSTALLMENTS. —There shall be 4 required installments for each plan year.

(ii) TIME FOR PAYMENT OF INSTALLMENTS. —The due dates for required installments are set forth in the following table:

In the case of the following required installment:	The due date is:
1st	April 15
2nd	July 15
3rd	October 15
4th	January 15 of the following year.

(D) AMOUNT OF REQUIRED INSTALLMENT. —For purposes of this paragraph—

(i) IN GENERAL. —The amount of any required installment shall be 25 percent of the required annual payment.

(ii) REQUIRED ANNUAL PAYMENT. —For purposes of clause (i), the term 'required annual payment' means the lesser of—

(I) 90 percent of the minimum required contribution (determined without regard to this subsection) to the plan for the plan year under this section, or

(II) 100 percent of the minimum required contribution (determined without regard to this subsection or to any waiver under section 302(c)) to the plan for the preceding plan year.

Subclause (II) shall not apply if the preceding plan year referred to in such clause was not a year of 12 months.

(E) FISCAL YEARS, SHORT YEARS, AND YEARS WITH ALTERNATE VALUATION DATE.—

(i) FISCAL YEARS. —In applying this paragraph to a plan year beginning on any date other than January 1, there shall be substituted for the months specified in this paragraph, the months which correspond thereto.

(ii) SHORT PLAN YEAR. —This subparagraph shall be applied to plan years of less than 12 months in accordance with regulations prescribed by the Secretary of the Treasury.

(iii) PLAN WITH ALTERNATE VALUATION DATE. —The Secretary of the Treasury shall prescribe regulations for the application of this paragraph in the case of a plan which has a valuation date other than the first day of the plan year.

(F) QUARTERLY CONTRIBUTIONS NOT TO INCLUDE CERTAIN INCREASED CONTRIBUTIONS. —Subparagraph (D) shall be applied without regard to any increase under subsection (c)(7).

(4) LIQUIDITY REQUIREMENT IN CONNECTION WITH QUARTERLY CONTRIBUTIONS.—

(A) IN GENERAL. —A plan to which this paragraph applies shall be treated as failing to pay the full amount of any required installment under paragraph (3) to the extent that the value of the liquid assets paid in such installment is less than the liquidity shortfall (whether or not such liquidity shortfall exceeds the amount of such installment required to be paid but for this paragraph).

(B) PLANS TO WHICH PARAGRAPH APPLIES. —This paragraph shall apply to a plan (other than a plan described in subsection (g)(2)(B)) which—

(i) is required to pay installments under paragraph (3) for a plan year, and

(ii) has a liquidity shortfall for any quarter during such plan year.

(C) PERIOD OF UNDERPAYMENT. —For purposes of paragraph (3)(A), any portion of an installment that is treated as not paid under subparagraph (A) shall continue to be treated as unpaid until the close of the quarter in which the due date for such installment occurs.

(D) LIMITATION ON INCREASE. —If the amount of any required installment is increased by reason of subparagraph (A), in no event shall such increase exceed the amount which, when added to prior installments for the plan year, is necessary to increase the funding target attainment percentage of the plan for the plan year (taking into account the expected increase in funding target due to benefits accruing or earned during the plan year) to 100 percent.

(E) DEFINITIONS. —For purposes of this paragraph—

(i) LIQUIDITY SHORTFALL. —The term 'liquidity shortfall' means, with respect to any required installment, an amount equal to the excess (as of the last day of the quarter for which such installment is made) of—

(I) the base amount with respect to such quarter, over

(II) the value (as of such last day) of the plan's liquid assets.

(ii) BASE AMOUNT.—

(I) IN GENERAL. —The term 'base amount' means, with respect to any quarter, an amount equal to 3 times the sum of the adjusted disbursements from the plan for the 12 months ending on the last day of such quarter.

(II) SPECIAL RULE. —If the amount determined under subclause (I) exceeds an amount equal to 2 times the sum of the adjusted disbursements from the plan for the 36 months ending on the last day of the quarter and an enrolled actuary certifies to the satisfaction of the Secretary of the Treasury that such excess is the result of nonrecurring circumstances, the base amount with respect to such quarter shall be determined without regard to amounts related to those nonrecurring circumstances.

(iii) DISBURSEMENTS FROM THE PLAN. —The term 'disbursements from the plan' means all disbursements from the trust, including purchases of annuities, payments of single sums and other benefits, and administrative expenses.

(iv) ADJUSTED DISBURSEMENTS. —The term 'adjusted disbursements' means disbursements from the plan reduced by the product of—

(I) the plan's funding target attainment percentage for the plan year, and

(II) the sum of the purchases of annuities, payments of single sums, and such other disbursements as the Secretary of the Treasury shall provide in regulations.

(v) LIQUID ASSETS. —The term 'liquid assets' means cash, marketable securities, and such other assets as specified by the Secretary of the Treasury in regulations.

(vi) QUARTER. —The term 'quarter' means, with respect to any required installment, the 3-month period preceding the month in which the due date for such installment occurs.

(F) REGULATIONS. —The Secretary of the Treasury may prescribe such regulations as are necessary to carry out this paragraph.

Act Sec. 303. (k) IMPOSITION OF LIEN WHERE FAILURE TO MAKE REQUIRED CONTRIBUTIONS.—

(1) IN GENERAL. —In the case of a plan to which this subsection applies (as provided under paragraph (2)), if—

(A) any person fails to make a contribution payment required by section 302 and this section before the due date for such payment, and

(B) the unpaid balance of such payment (including interest), when added to the aggregate unpaid balance of all preceding such payments for which payment was not made before the due date (including interest), exceeds $1,000,000,

then there shall be a lien in favor of the plan in the amount determined under paragraph (3) upon all property and rights to property, whether real or personal, belonging to such person and any other person who is a member of the same controlled group of which such person is a member.

(2) PLANS TO WHICH SUBSECTION APPLIES. —This subsection shall apply to a single-employer plan covered under section 4021 for any plan year for which the funding target attainment percentage (as defined in subsection (d)(2)) of such plan is less than 100 percent.

(3) AMOUNT OF LIEN. —For purposes of paragraph (1), the amount of the lien shall be equal to the aggregate unpaid balance of contribution payments required under this section and section 302 for which payment has not been made before the due date.

(4) NOTICE OF FAILURE; LIEN.—

(A) NOTICE OF FAILURE. —A person committing a failure described in paragraph (1) shall notify the Pension Benefit Guaranty Corporation of such failure within 10 days of the due date for the required contribution payment.

(B) PERIOD OF LIEN. —The lien imposed by paragraph (1) shall arise on the due date for the required contribution payment and shall continue until the last day of the first plan year in which the plan ceases to be described in paragraph (1)(B). Such lien shall continue to run without regard to whether such plan continues to be described in paragraph (2) during the period referred to in the preceding sentence.

(C) CERTAIN RULES TO APPLY. —Any amount with respect to which a lien is imposed under paragraph (1) shall be treated as taxes due and owing the United States and rules similar to the rules of subsections (c), (d), and (e) of section 4068 shall apply with respect to a lien imposed by subsection (a) and the amount with respect to such lien.

(5) ENFORCEMENT. —Any lien created under paragraph (1) may be perfected and enforced only by the Pension Benefit Guaranty Corporation, or at the direction of the Pension Benefit Guaranty Corporation, by the contributing sponsor (or any member of the controlled group of the contributing sponsor).

(6) DEFINITIONS. —For purposes of this subsection—

(A) CONTRIBUTION PAYMENT. —The term 'contribution payment' means, in connection with a plan, a contribution payment required to be made to the plan, including any required installment under paragraphs (3) and (4) of subsection (j).

(B) DUE DATE; REQUIRED INSTALLMENT. —The terms 'due date' and 'required installment' have the meanings given such terms by subsection (j).

(C) CONTROLLED GROUP. —The term 'controlled group' means any group treated as a single employer under subsections (b), (c), (m), and (o) of section 414 of the Internal Revenue Code of 1986.

Act Sec. 303. (l) QUALIFIED TRANSFERS TO HEALTH BENEFIT ACCOUNTS. —In the case of a qualified transfer (as defined in section 420 of the Internal Revenue Code of 1986), any assets so transferred shall not, for purposes of this section, be treated as assets in the plan.

Amendments

P.L. 114-74, §504(b)(1):

Amended the table in ERISA Sec. 303(h)(2)(C)(iv)(II) to read as above.

Prior to the amendment, ERISA Sec. 303(h)(2)(C)(iv)(II) read as follows:

(II) APPLICABLE MINIMUM PERCENTAGE; APPLICABLE MAXIMUM PERCENTAGE. For purposes of subclause (I), the applicable minimum percentage and the applicable maximum percentage for a plan year beginning in a calendar year shall be determined in accordance with the following table:

If the calendar year is:	The applicable minimum percentage is:	The applicable maximum percentage is:
2012, 2013, 2014, 2015, 2016, or 2017	90%	110%
2018	85%	115%
2019	80%	120%
2020	75%	125%
After 2020	70%	130%.

The above amendment shall apply to plan years beginning after December 31, 2015.

P.L. 114-74, §503 provides:

Sec. 503 MORTALITY TABLES.

(a) Credibility

For purposes of subclause (I) of section 430(h)(3)(C)(iii) of the Internal Revenue Code of 1986 and subclause (I) of section 303(h)(3)(C)(iii) of the Employee Retirement Income Security Act of 1974, the determination of whether plans have credible information shall be made in accordance with established actuarial credibility theory, which—

(1) is materially different from rules under such section of such Code, including Revenue Procedure 2007-37, that are in effect on the date of the enactment of this Act; and

(2) permits the use of tables that reflect adjustments to the tables described in subparagraphs (A) and (B) of section 430(h)(3) of such Code, and subparagraphs (A) and (B) of section 303(h)(3) of such Act, if such adjustments are based on the experience described in subclause (II) of section 430(h)(3)(C)(iii) of such Code and in subclause (II) of section 303(h)(3)(C)(iii) of such Act.

Act Sec. 503 shall apply to plan years beginning after December 31, 2015.

P.L. 113-295, §221(a)(57)(C)(ii), Div. A:

Amended ERISA Sec. 303(c)(5) by striking subparagraph (B) and by striking "(A) In general.—". Prior to being stricken, ERISA Sec. 303(c)(5)(B) read as follows:

(B) Transition rule.—

(i) In general.—Except as provided in clause (iii), in the case of plan years beginning after 2007 and before 2011, only the applicable percentage of the funding target shall be taken into account under paragraph (3)(A) in determining the funding shortfall for purposes of paragraph (3)(A) and subparagraph (A).

(ii) Applicable percentage.—For purposes of subparagraph (A), the applicable percentage shall be determined in accordance with the following table:

In the case of a plan year beginning in calendar year:	The applicable percentage is:
2008	92
2009	94
2010	96.

(iii) Transition relief not available for new or deficit reduction plans.—Clause (i) shall not apply to a plan—

(I) which was not in effect for a plan year beginning in 2007, or

(II) which was in effect for a plan year beginning in 2007 and which was subject to section 302(d) (as in effect for plan years beginning in 2007) for such year, determined after the application of paragraphs (6) and (9) thereof.

The above amendments shall take effect on the date of enactment of this Act [December 19, 2014.-CCH.]. For a special rule, see Act Sec. 221(b)(2), Div. A, below.

P. L. 113-295, §221(b)(2), Div. A, provides:

(2) Savings provision.—If—

(A) any provision amended or repealed by the amendments made by this section applied to—

(i) any transaction occurring before the date of the enactment of this Act,

(ii) any property acquired before such date of enactment, or

(iii) any item of income, loss, deduction, or credit taken into account before such date of enactment, and (B) the treatment of such transaction, property, or item under such provision would (without regard to the amendments or repeals made by this section) affect the liability for tax for periods ending after date of enactment, nothing in the amendments or repeals made by this section shall be construed to affect the treatment of such transaction, property, or item for purposes of determining liability for tax for periods ending after such date of enactment.

P.L. 113-295, §221(a)(57)(D)(ii), Div. A:

Amended ERISA Sec. 303(h)(2) by striking subparagraph (G). Prior to being stricken, ERISA Sec. 303(h)(2)(G) read as follows:

(G) Transition rule.—

(i) In general.—Notwithstanding the preceding provisions of this paragraph, for plan years beginning in 2008 or 2009, the first, second, or third segment rate for a plan with respect to any month shall be equal to the sum of—

(I) the product of such rate for such month determined without regard to this subparagraph, multiplied by the applicable percentage, and

(II) the product of the rate determined under the rules of section 302(b)(5)(B)(ii)(II) (as in effect for plan years beginning in 2007), multiplied by a percentage equal to 100 percent minus the applicable percentage.

(ii) Applicable percentage.—For purposes of clause (i), the applicable percentage is 33 1/3 percent for plan years beginning in 2008 and 66 2/3 percent for plan years beginning in 2009.

(iii) New plans ineligible.—

—Clause (i) shall not apply to any plan if the first plan year of the plan begins after December 31, 2007. (iv) Election.—The plan sponsor may elect not to have this subparagraph apply. Such election, once made, may be revoked only with the consent of the Secretary of the Treasury.

The above amendment shall take effect on the date of enactment of this Act [December 19, 2014.-CCH.]. For a special rule, see Act Sec. 221(b)(2), Div. A, below.

P.L. 113-295, §221(b)(2), Div. A, provides:

(2) Savings provision.—If—

(A) any provision amended or repealed by the amendments made by this section applied to—

(i) any transaction occurring before the date of the enactment of this Act,

(ii) any property acquired before such date of enactment, or

(iii) any item of income, loss, deduction, or credit taken into account before such date of enactment, and (B) the treatment of such transaction, property, or item under such provision would (without regard to the amendments or repeals made by this section) affect the liability for tax for periods ending after date of enactment, nothing in the amendments or repeals made by this section shall be construed to affect the treatment of such transaction, property, or item for purposes of determining liability for tax for periods ending after such date of enactment.

P.L. 113-159, §2003(b)(1):

Amended the table in ERISA Sec. 303(h)(2)(C)(iv)(II) to read as above.

The above amendment shall apply with respect to plan years beginning after December 31, 2012. For a special rule, see Act Sec. 2003(e)(2), below.

Prior to amendment, the table in ERISA Sec. 303(h)(2)(C)(iv)(II) read as follows:

If the calendar year is:	The applicable minimum percentage is:	The applicable maximum percentage is:
2012	90%	110%
2013	85%	115%
2014	80%	120%
2015	75%	125%
After 2015	70%	130%.

P.L. 113-159, §2003(d)(2):

Amended ERISA Sec. 303(h)(2)(B)(i) by striking "the first day of the plan year" and inserting "the valuation date for the plan year".

The above amendments shall apply with respect to plan years beginning after December 31, 2012. For a special rule, see Act Sec. 2003(e)(2), below

P.L. 113-159, §2003(e)(2) provides:

(2) ELECTIONS.—A plan sponsor may elect not to have the amendments made by subsections (a), (b), and (d) apply to any plan year beginning before January 1, 2014, either (as specified in the election)—

(A) for all purposes for which such amendments apply, or

(B) solely for purposes of determining the adjusted funding target attainment percentage under sections 436 of the Internal Revenue Code of 1986 and 206(g) of the Employee Retirement Income Security Act of 1974 (29 U.S.C. 1054(g)) for such plan year.

A plan shall not be treated as failing to meet the requirements of section 204(g) of such Act and section 411(d)(6) of such Code solely by reason of an election under this paragraph.

P.L. 112-141, §40211(b)(1):

Amended ERISA Sec. 303(h)(2)(C) by adding at the end new clause (iv) to read as above.

For effective date, see P.L. 112-141, §40211(c), below.

P.L. 112-141, §40211(b)(3)(A):

Amended ERISA Sec. 303(h)(2)(F) by inserting "and the averages determined under subparagraph (C)(iv)" after "subparagraph (C)".

For effective date, see P.L. 112-141, §40211(c), below.

P.L. 112-141, §40211(c):

(c) EFFECTIVE DATE.—

(1) IN GENERAL.—The amendments made by this section shall apply with respect to plan years beginning after December 31, 2011.

(2) RULES WITH RESPECT TO ELECTIONS.—

(A) ADJUSTED FUNDING TARGET ATTAINMENT PERCENTAGE.—A plan sponsor may elect not to have the amendments made by this section apply to any plan year beginning before January 1, 2013, either (as specified in the election)—

(i) for all purposes for which such amendments apply, or

(ii) solely for purposes of determining the adjusted funding target attainment percentage under sections 436 of the Internal Revenue Code of 1986 and 206(g) of the Employee Retirement Income Security Act of 1974 for such plan year.

A plan shall not be treated as failing to meet the requirements of sections 204(g) of such Act and 411(d)(6) of such Code solely by reason of an election under this paragraph.

(B) OPT OUT OF EXISTING ELECTIONS.—If, on the date of the enactment of this Act, an election is in effect with respect to any plan under sections 303(h)(2)(D)(ii) of the Employee Retirement Income Security Act of 1974 and 430(h)(2)(D)(ii) of the Internal Revenue Code of 1986, then, notwithstanding the last sentence of each such section, the plan sponsor may revoke such election without the consent of the Secretary of the Treasury. The plan sponsor may make such revocation at any time before the date which is 1 year after such date of enactment and such revocation shall be effective for the 1st plan year to which the amendments made by this section apply and all subsequent plan years. Nothing in this subparagraph shall preclude a plan sponsor from making a subsequent election in accordance with such sections.

P.L. 111-192, §201(a)(1):

Amended ERISA Sec. 303(c)(2) by adding new subparagraph (D) to read as above.

The above amendment applies to plan years beginning after December 31, 2007.

P.L. 111-192, §201(a)(2):

Amended ERISA Sec. 303(c) by adding new paragraph (7) to read as above.

The above amendment applies to plan years beginning after December 31, 2007.

P.L. 111-192, §201(a)(3)(A):

Amended ERISA Sec. 303(c)(1) by striking "the shortfall amortization bases for such plan year and each of the 6 preceding plan years" and inserting "any shortfall amortization base which has not been fully amortized under this subsection".

The above amendment applies to plan years beginning after December 31, 2007.

P.L. 111-192, §201(a)(3)(B):

Amended ERISA Sec. 303(j)(3) by adding new subparagraph (F) to read as above.

The above amendment applies to plan years beginning after December 31, 2007.

P.L. 111-192, §204(a):

Amended ERISA Sec. 303(f)(3) by adding new subparagraph (D) to read as above.

Except as provided below, the above amendment applies to plan years beginning after August 31, 2009. In the case of a plan for which the valuation date is not the first day of the plan year, the above amendment applies to plan years beginning after December 31, 2008.

P.L. 110-458, §101(b)(1)(A):

Amended ERISA Sec. 303(b) to read as above. Prior to amendment, ERISA Sec. 303(b) read as follows:

Act Sec. 303.

(b) TARGET NORMAL COST.—For purposes of this section, except as provided in subsection (i)(2) with respect to plans in at-risk status, the term 'target normal cost' means, for any plan year, the present value of all benefits which are expected to accrue or to be earned under the plan during the plan year. For purposes of this subsection, if any benefit attributable to services performed in a preceding plan year is increased by reason of any increase in compensation during the current plan year, the increase in such benefit shall be treated as having accrued during the current plan year.

The above amendment generally applies to plan years beginning after December 31, 2008. For special rule, see Act Sec. 101(b)(3) below.

P.L. 110-458, §101(b)(1)(B):

Amended ERISA Sec. 303(c)(5)(B)(iii) by inserting "beginning" before "after 2008". **Effective** as if included in the provision of the Pension Protection Act of 2006 (P.L. 109-280) to which the amendment relates [**effective** with respect to plan years beginning after 12-31-2007. —CCH].

P.L. 110-458, §101(b)(1)(C):

Amended ERISA Sec. 303(c)(5)(B)(iv)(II) by inserting "for such year" after "beginning in 2007". **Effective** as if included in the provision of the Pension Protection Act of 2006 to which the amendment relates [**effective** with respect to plan years beginning after 12-31-2007. —CCH].

P.L. 110-458, §101(b)(1)(D):

Amended ERISA Sec. 303(f)(4)(A) by striking "paragraph (2)" and inserting "paragraph (3)".

The above amendment is effective as if included in the provision of the Pension Protection Act of 2006 to which it relates [effective for plan years beginning after 2007—CCH].

P.L. 110-458, §101(b)(1)(E)(i):

Amended ERISA Sec. 303(h)(2)(F) by striking "section 205(g)(3)(B)(iii)(I)) for such month" and inserting "section 205(g)(3)(B)(iii)(I) for such month)".

The above amendment is effective as if included in the provision of the Pension Protection Act of 2006 to which it relates [effective for plan years beginning after 2007—CCH].

P.L. 110-458, §101(b)(1)(E)(ii):

Amended ERISA Sec. 303(h)(2)(F) by striking "subparagraph (B)" and inserting "subparagraph (C)".

The above amendment is effective as if included in the provision of the Pension Protection Act of 2006 to which it relates [effective for plan years beginning after 2007—CCH].

P.L. 110-458, §101(b)(1)(F)(i)(I):

Amended ERISA Sec. 303(i)(2) by striking subparagraph (A) and inserting a new subparagraph (A) to read as above. Prior to amendment, ERISA Sec. 303(i)(2)(A) read as follows:

(A) the present value of all benefits which are expected to accrue or be earned under the plan during the plan year, determined using the additional actuarial assumptions described in paragraph (1)(B), plus

The above amendment generally applies to plan years beginning after December 31, 2008. For special rule, see Act Sec. 101(b)(3) below.

P.L. 110-458, §101(b)(1)(F)(i)(II):

Amended ERISA Sec. 303(i)(2)(B) by striking "the target normal cost (determined without regard to this paragraph) of the plan for the plan year" and inserting "the amount determined under subsection (b)(1)(A)(i) with respect to the plan for the plan year".

The above amendment generally applies to plan years beginning after December 31, 2008. For special rule, see Act Sec. 101(b)(3) below.

P.L. 110-458, §101(b)(1)(F)(ii):

Amended ERISA Sec. 303(i)(4)(B) by striking "subparagraph (A)(ii)" in the last sentence of paragraph (4)(B) and inserting "subparagraph (A)".

The above amendment is effective as if included in the provision of the Pension Protection Act of 2006 to which it relates [effective for plan years beginning after 2007—CCH].

P.L. 110-458, §101(b)(1)(G)(i):

Amended ERISA Sec. 303(j)(3) by adding at the end of subparagraph (A) the following new sentence: "In the case of plan years beginning in 2008, the funding shortfall for the preceding plan year may be determined using such methods of estimation as the Secretary of the Treasury may provide."

The above amendment applies as if included in the provision of the Pension Protection Act of 2006 to which it relates [effective for plan years beginning after 2007—CCH].

P.L. 110-458, §101(b)(1)(G)(ii):

Amended ERISA Sec. 303(j)(3)(E) by adding at the end of subparagraph (E) a new clause (iii) to read as above.

The above amendment applies as if included in the provision of the Pension Protection Act of 2006 to which it relates [effective for plan years beginning after 2007—CCH].

P.L. 110-458, §101(b)(1)(G)(iii):

Amended ERISA Sec. 303(j)(3)(E) by striking "AND SHORT YEARS" in the heading of subparagraph (E) and inserting ", SHORT YEARS, AND YEARS WITH ALTERNATE VALUATION DATE".

The above amendment applies as if included in the provision of the Pension Protection Act of 2006 to which it relates [effective for plan years beginning after 2007—CCH].

P.L. 110-458, §101(b)(1)(H):

Amended ERISA Sec. 303(k)(6)(B) by striking ", except that in the case of a payment other than a required installment, the due date shall be the date such payment is required to be made under section 303." and inserting a period.

The above amendment applies as if included in the provision of the Pension Protection Act of 2006 to which it relates [effective for plan years beginning after 2007—CCH].

P.L. 110-458, §101(b)(3):

101(b)(3) EFFECTIVE DATES.—

101(b)(3)(A) IN GENERAL.—Except as provided in subparagraph (B), the amendments made by paragraphs (1)(A), (1)(F)(i), (2)(A), and (2)(F)(i) shall apply to plan years beginning after December 31, 2008.

101(b)(3)(B) ELECTION FOR EARLIER APPLICATION.—The amendments made by such paragraphs shall apply to a plan for the first plan year beginning after December 31, 2007, if the plan sponsor makes the election under this subparagraph. An election under this subparagraph shall be made at such time and in such manner as the Secretary of the Treasury or the Secretary's delegate may prescribe, and, once made, may be revoked only with the consent of the Secretary.

P.L. 110-458, §121(a):

Amended ERISA Sec. 303(g)(3)(B) by amending the last sentence to read as above. Prior to amendment, the last sentence read as follows: "Any such averaging shall be adjusted for contributions and distributions (as provided by the Secretary of the Treasury)."

The above amendment applies as if included in the provision of the Pension Protection Act of 2006 to which it relates [effective for plan years beginning after 2007—CCH].

P.L. 110-458, §202(a)(1)-(2):

Amended ERISA Sec. 303(c)(5)(B) by striking clause (iii) and redesignating clause (iv) as clause (iii); and by striking clause (i) and inserting a new clause (i). **Effective** as if included in Act Sec. 112 of the Pension Protection Act of 2006 (P.L. 109-280) [**effective** with respect to plan years beginning after 12-31-2007. —CCH]. Prior to being stricken, ERISA Sec. 303(c)(5)(B)(i) and (iii) read as follows:

303(c)(5)(B)(i) IN GENERAL.—Except as provided in clauses (iii) and (iv), in the case of plan years beginning after 2007 and before 2011, only the applicable percentage of the funding target shall be taken into account under paragraph (3)(A) in determining the funding shortfall for the plan year for purposes of subparagraph (A).

* * *

303(c)(5)(B)(iii) LIMITATION.—Clause (i) shall not apply with respect to any plan year beginning after 2008 unless the shortfall amortization base for each of the preceding years beginning after 2007 was zero (determined after application of this subparagraph).

P.L. 110-458, §202(a)(2):

Amended ERISA Sec. 303(c)(5)(B) by striking clause (i) and inserting a new clause (i) to read as above.

The above amendment applies as if included in the enactment of section 102 of the Pension Protection Act of 2006 [effective for plan years beginning after 2007—CCH].

P. L. 109-280, §101(a):

Repealed ERISA Sec. 303.

Prior to repeal, ERISA Sec. 303 read as follows:

(a) WAIVER OF REQUIREMENTS IN EVENT OF BUSINESS HARDSHIP.—If an employer, or in the case of a multiemployer plan, 10 percent or more of the number of employers contributing to or under the plan are unable to satisfy the minimum funding standard for a plan year without temporary substantial business hardship (substantial business hardship in the case of a multiemployer plan) and if application of the standard would be adverse to the interests of plan participants in the aggregate, the Secretary of the Treasury may waive the requirements of section 302(a) for such year with respect to all or any portion of the minimum funding standard other than the portion thereof determined under section 302(b)(2)(C). The Secretary of the Treasury shall not waive the minimum funding standard with respect to a plan for more than 3 of any 15 (5 of any 15 in the case of a multiemployer plan) consecutive plan years. The interest rate used for purposes of computing the amortization charge described in subsection (b)(2)(C) for any plan year shall be—

(a)(1) in the case of a plan other than a multiemployer plan, the greater of (A) 150 percent of the Federal mid-term rate (as in effect under section 1274 of the Internal Revenue Code of 1986 for the 1st month of such plan year), or (B) the rate of interest used under the plan in determining costs (including adjustments under section 302(b)(5)(B)), and

(a)(2) in the case of a multiemployer plan, the rate determined under section 6621(b) of such Code.

(b) MATTERS CONSIDERED IN DETERMINING BUSINESS HARDSHIP.—For purposes of this part, the factors taken into account in determining temporary substantial business hardship (substantial business hardship in the case of a multiemployer plan) shall include (but shall not be limited to) whether—

(b)(1) the employer is operating at an economic loss,

(b)(2) there is substantial unemployment or underemployment in the trade or business and in the industry concerned,

(b)(3) the sales and profits of the industry concerned are depressed or declining, and

(b)(4) it is reasonable to expect that the plan will be continued only if the waiver is granted.

(c) "WAIVED FUNDING DEFICIENCY" DEFINED.—For purposes of this part, the term "waived funding deficiency" means the portion of the minimum funding standard (determined without regard to subsection (b)(3)(C) of section 302) for a plan year waived by the Secretary of the Treasury and not satisfied by employer contributions.

(d) SPECIAL RULES.

(d)(1) APPLICATION MUST BE SUBMITTED BEFORE DATE 2 ½ MONTHS AFTER CLOSE OF YEAR. In the case of a plan other than a multiemployer plan, no waiver may be granted under this section with respect to any plan for any plan year unless an application therefor is submitted to the Secretary of the Treasury not later than the 15th day of the 3rd month beginning after the close of such plan year.

(d)(2) SPECIAL RULE IF EMPLOYER IS MEMBER OF CONTROLLED GROUP.

(d)(2)(A) IN GENERAL. In the case of a plan other than a multiemployer plan, if an employer is a member of a controlled group, the temporary substantial business hardship requirements of subsection (a) shall be treated as met only if such requirements are met—

(d)(2)(A)(i) with respect to such employer, and

(d)(2)(A)(ii) with respect to the controlled group of which such employer is a member (determined by treating all members of such group as a single employer).

The Secretary of the Treasury may provide that an analysis of trade or business or industry of a member need not be conducted if the Secretary of the Treasury determines such analysis is not necessary because the taking into account of such member would not significantly affect the determination under this subsection.

(d)(2)(B) CONTROLLED GROUP. For purposes of subparagraph (A), the term "controlled group" means any group treated as a single employer under subsection (b), (c), (m), or (o) of section 414 of the Internal Revenue Code of 1986.

(e)(1) NOTICE OF FILING OF APPLICATION FOR WAIVER.—The Secretary of the Treasury shall, before granting a waiver under this section, require each applicant to provide evidence satisfactory to such Secretary that the applicant has provided notice of the filing of the application for such waiver to each employee organization representing employees covered by the affected plan, and each affected party (as defined in section 4001(a)(21)) other than the Pension Benefit Guaranty Corporation. Such notice shall include a description of the extent to which the plan is funded for benefits which are guaranteed under title IV and for benefit liabilities.

(e)(2) The Secretary of the Treasury shall consider any relevant information provided by a person to whom notice was given under paragraph (1).

(f) CROSS REFERENCE. For corresponding duties of the Secretary of the Treasury with regard to implementation of the Internal Revenue Code of 1986, see section 412(d) of such Code.

The above amendment applies to plan years beginning after 2007.

P. L. 109-280, § 102(a):

Amended Part 3 of subtitle B of title I of the Employee Retirement Income Security Act of 1974 (as amended by section 101 of this Act) by inserting after section 302, the new section 303.

The above amendments apply to plan years beginning after 2007.

P.L. 101-239, § 7881(b)(6)(B)(ii):

Amended ERISA Sec. 303(a)(1)(B) by inserting "(including adjustments under section 302(b)(5)(B))" after "costs."

P.L. 101-239, § 7881(b)(7):

Amended ERISA Sec. 303(a) by redesignating subparagraphs (A) and (B) as paragraphs (1) and (2), respectively, and by adjusting the left-hand margination thereof 4 ems to the left; in paragraph (1) (as redesignated), by redesignating clauses (i) and (ii) as subparagraphs (A) and (B), respectively; and in paragraph (2) (as redesignated), by inserting "of such Code" after "section 6621(b)" effective for applications submitted after December 17, 1987 and waivers granted pursuant to such applications.

P.L. 101-239, § 7881(b)(8):

Amended ERISA Sec. 303(f) as redesignated by P.L. 100-203, § 9306(a)(2) by transferring it to immediately after subsection (e), effective for plan years beginning after December 31, 1987.

P.L. 101-239, § 7881(c)(2):

Amended ERISA Sec. 303(e)(1) by striking "the benefit liabilities" and inserting "for benefit liabilities" effective for applications submitted after March 21, 1987.

P.L. 101-239, § 7881(c)(3):

Amended P.L. 100-203, § 9306(f)(3) to read as below, effective December 22, 1987.

P.L. 100-203, § 9306(a)(2)(A):

Amended ERISA Sec. 303 by redesignating subsection (d) as (f) and inserting a new subsection (d)(1) to read as above, effective for plan years beginning after December 31, 1987.

P.L. 100-203, § 9306(a)(2)(B):

Amended ERISA Secs. 303(a) and (b) by striking out "substantial business hardship" and inserting in lieu thereof "temporary substantial business hardship (substantial business hardship in the case of a multiemployer plan)," effective for applications submitted after December 17, 1987 and waivers granted pursuant to such applications.

P.L. 100-203, § 9306(a)(2)(C):

Amended ERISA Sec. 303(d) by adding a new paragraph (2) to read as above, effective for applications submitted after December 17, 1987 and for waivers granted pursuant to such applications.

P.L. 100-203, § 9306(b)(2):

Amended ERISA Sec. 303(a) by striking out "more than 5 of any 15" and inserting "more than 3 of any 15 (5 of any 15 in the case of a multiemployer plan)," effective for applications submitted after December 17, 1987 and waivers granted pursuant to such applications.

P.L. 100-203, § 9306(c)(2)(A):

Amended ERISA Sec. 303(a) by striking out the last sentence and inserting the new last sentence to read as above, effective for applications submitted after December 17, 1987 and waivers granted pursuant to such applications. Prior to amendment, the last sentence read: "The interest rate used for purposes of computing the amortization charge described in section 302(b)(2)(C) for a variance granted under this subsection shall be the rate determined under section 6621(b) of the Internal Revenue Code of 1954.

P.L. 100-203, § 9306(d)(2):

Amended ERISA Sec. 303(e)(1) by striking out "plan," and adding the new material at the end of the sentence, effective for applications submitted after March 21, 1987.

P.L. 101-239, § 7891(a)(1):

Titles I, III, and IV of ERISA (other than sections 3(37)(E), 301(a)(7), and 308, the last sentence of section 408(d), and sections 414(c), 4001(a)(3)(ii), and 4303) are each amended by striking "Internal Revenue Code of 1954" each place it appears and inserting "Internal Revenue Code of 1986" effective October 22, 1986.

P.L. 100-203, § 9306(f)(3):

(3) SUBSECTION (b).—The amendments made by subsection (b) shall apply to waivers for plan years beginning after December 31, 1987. For purposes of applying such amendments, the number of waivers which may be granted for plan years after December 31, 1987, shall be determined without regard to any waivers granted for plan years beginning before January 1, 1988.

P.L. 99-272:

Act Sec. 11015(b)(1)(A) amended ERISA Sec. 303(a) by adding a new sentence at the end of the subsection, to read as above, effective with respect to terminations pursuant to notices of intent filed with the PBGC on or after January 1, 1986 or proceeding begun on or after that date.

Act Sec. 11016(c)(2) amended ERISA Sec. 303 by adding a new subsection (e) to read as above, effective on April 7, 1986.

[¶ 14,640]
MINIMUM FUNDING STANDARDS FOR MULTIEMPLOYER PLANS

Act Sec. 304.(a) IN GENERAL. —For purposes of section 302, the accumulated funding deficiency of a multiemployer plan for any plan year is the amount, determined as of the end of the plan year, equal to the excess (if any) of the total charges to the funding standard account of the plan for all plan years (beginning with the first plan year for which this part applies to the plan) over the total credits to such account for such years.

(b) FUNDING STANDARD ACCOUNT.—

(1) ACCOUNT REQUIRED. —Each multiemployer plan to which this part applies shall establish and maintain a funding standard account. Such account shall be credited and charged solely as provided in this section.

(2) CHARGES TO ACCOUNT. —For a plan year, the funding standard account shall be charged with the sum of—

(A) the normal cost of the plan for the plan year,

(B) the amounts necessary to amortize in equal annual installments (until fully amortized)—

(i) in the case of a plan which comes into existence on or after January 1, 2008, the unfunded past service liability under the plan on the first day of the first plan year to which this section applies, over a period of 15 plan years,

(ii) separately, with respect to each plan year, the net increase (if any) in unfunded past service liability under the plan arising from plan amendments adopted in such year, over a period of 15 plan years,

(iii) separately, with respect to each plan year, the net experience loss (if any) under the plan, over a period of 15 plan years, and

(iv) separately, with respect to each plan year, the net loss (if any) resulting from changes in actuarial assumptions used under the plan, over a period of 15 plan years,

(C) the amount necessary to amortize each waived funding deficiency (within the meaning of section 302(c)(3)) for each prior plan year in equal annual installments (until fully amortized) over a period of 15 plan years,

(D) the amount necessary to amortize in equal annual installments (until fully amortized) over a period of 5 plan years any amount credited to the funding standard account under section 302(b)(3)(D) (as in effect on the day before the date of the enactment of the Pension Protection Act of 2006), and

(E) the amount necessary to amortize in equal annual installments (until fully amortized) over a period of 20 years the contributions which would be required to be made under the plan but for the provisions of section 302(c)(7)(A)(i)(I) (as in effect on the day before the date of the enactment of the Pension Protection Act of 2006).

(3) CREDITS TO ACCOUNT. —For a plan year, the funding standard account shall be credited with the sum of —

(A) the amount considered contributed by the employer to or under the plan for the plan year,

(B) the amount necessary to amortize in equal annual installments (until fully amortized)—

(i) separately, with respect to each plan year, the net decrease (if any) in unfunded past service liability under the plan arising from plan amendments adopted in such year, over a period of 15 plan years,

(ii) separately, with respect to each plan year, the net experience gain (if any) under the plan, over a period of 15 plan years, and

(iii) separately, with respect to each plan year, the net gain (if any) resulting from changes in actuarial assumptions used under the plan, over a period of 15 plan years,

(C) the amount of the waived funding deficiency (within the meaning of section 302(c)(3)) for the plan year, and

(D) in the case of a plan year for which the accumulated funding deficiency is determined under the funding standard account if such plan year follows a plan year for which such deficiency was determined under the alternative minimum funding standard under section 305 (as in effect on the day before the date of the enactment of the Pension Protection Act of 2006), the excess (if any) of any debit balance in the funding standard account (determined without regard to this subparagraph) over any debit balance in the alternative minimum funding standard account.

(4) SPECIAL RULE FOR AMOUNTS FIRST AMORTIZED IN PLAN YEARS BEFORE 2008. —In the case of any amount amortized under section 302(b) (as in effect on the day before the date of the enactment of the Pension Protection Act of 2006) over any period beginning with a plan year beginning before 2008, in lieu of the amortization described in paragraphs (2)(B) and (3)(B), such amount shall continue to be amortized under such section as so in effect.

(5) COMBINING AND OFFSETTING AMOUNTS TO BE AMORTIZED. —Under regulations prescribed by the Secretary of the Treasury, amounts required to be amortized under paragraph (2) or paragraph (3), as the case may be—

(A) may be combined into one amount under such paragraph to be amortized over a period determined on the basis of the remaining amortization period for all items entering into such combined amount, and

(B) may be offset against amounts required to be amortized under the other such paragraph, with the resulting amount to be amortized over a period determined on the basis of the remaining amortization periods for all items entering into whichever of the two amounts being offset is the greater.

(6) INTEREST. —The funding standard account (and items therein) shall be charged or credited (as determined under regulations prescribed by the Secretary of the Treasury) with interest at the appropriate rate consistent with the rate or rates of interest used under the plan to determine costs.

(7) SPECIAL RULES RELATING TO CHARGES AND CREDITS TO FUNDING STANDARD ACCOUNT. —For purposes of this part—

(A) WITHDRAWAL LIABILITY. —Any amount received by a multiemployer plan in payment of all or part of an employer's withdrawal liability under part 1 of subtitle E of title IV shall be considered an amount contributed by the employer to or under the plan. The Secretary of the Treasury may prescribe by regulation additional charges and credits to a multiemployer plan's funding standard account to the extent necessary to prevent withdrawal liability payments from being unduly reflected as advance funding for plan liabilities.

(B) ADJUSTMENTS WHEN A MULTIEMPLOYER PLAN LEAVES REORGANIZATION. —If a multiemployer plan is not in reorganization in the plan year but was in reorganization in the immediately preceding plan year, any balance in the funding standard account at the close of such immediately preceding plan year—

(i) shall be eliminated by an offsetting credit or charge (as the case may be), but

(ii) shall be taken into account in subsequent plan years by being amortized in equal annual installments (until fully amortized) over 30 plan years.

The preceding sentence shall not apply to the extent of any accumulated funding deficiency under section 4243(a) as of the end of the last plan year that the plan was in reorganization.

(C) PLAN PAYMENTS TO SUPPLEMENTAL PROGRAM OR WITHDRAWAL LIABILITY PAYMENT FUND. —Any amount paid by a plan during a plan year to the Pension Benefit Guaranty Corporation pursuant to section 4222 of this Act or to a fund exempt under section 501(c)(22) of the Internal Revenue Code of 1986 pursuant to section 4223 of this Act shall reduce the amount of contributions considered received by the plan for the plan year.

(D) INTERIM WITHDRAWAL LIABILITY PAYMENTS. —Any amount paid by an employer pending a final determination of the employer's withdrawal liability under part 1 of subtitle E of title IV and subsequently refunded to the employer by the plan shall be charged to the funding standard account in accordance with regulations prescribed by the Secretary of the Treasury.

(E) ELECTION FOR DEFERRAL OF CHARGE FOR PORTION OF NET EXPERIENCE. —If an election is in effect under section 302(b)(7)(F) (as in effect on the day before the date of the enactment of the Pension Protection Act of 2006) for any plan year, the funding standard account shall be charged in the plan year to which the portion of the net experience loss deferred by such election was deferred with the amount so deferred (and paragraph (2)(B)(iii) shall not apply to the amount so charged).

(F) FINANCIAL ASSISTANCE. —Any amount of any financial assistance from the Pension Benefit Guaranty Corporation to any plan, and any repayment of such amount, shall be taken into account under this section and section 302 in such manner as is determined by the Secretary of the Treasury.

(G) SHORT-TERM BENEFITS. —To the extent that any plan amendment increases the unfunded past service liability under the plan by reason of an increase in benefits which are not payable as a life annuity but are payable under the terms of the plan for a period that does not exceed 14 years from the effective date of the amendment, paragraph (2)(B)(ii) shall be applied separately with respect to such increase in unfunded past service liability by substituting the number of years of the period during which such benefits are payable for '15'.

(8) SPECIAL RELIEF RULES. —Notwithstanding any other provision of this subsection—

(A) AMORTIZATION OF NET INVESTMENT LOSSES.—

(i) IN GENERAL. —A multiemployer plan with respect to which the solvency test under subparagraph (C) is met may treat the portion of any experience loss or gain attributable to net investment losses incurred in either or both of the first two plan years ending after August 31, 2008, as an item separate from other experience losses, to be amortized in equal annual installments (until fully amortized) over the period —

(I) beginning with the plan year in which such portion is first recognized in the actuarial value of assets, and

(II) ending with the last plan year in the 30-plan year period beginning with the plan year in which such net investment loss was incurred.

(ii) COORDINATION WITH EXTENSIONS. —If this subparagraph applies for any plan year—

(I) no extension of the amortization period under clause (i) shall be allowed under subsection (d), and

(II) if an extension was granted under subsection (d) for any plan year before the election to have this subparagraph apply to the plan year, such extension shall not result in such amortization period exceeding 30 years.

(iii) NET INVESTMENT LOSSES. —For purposes of this subparagraph—

(I) IN GENERAL. —Net investment losses shall be determined in the manner prescribed by the Secretary of the Treasury on the basis of the difference between actual and expected returns (including any difference attributable to any criminally fraudulent investment arrangement).

(II) CRIMINALLY FRAUDULENT INVESTMENT ARRANGEMENTS. —The determination as to whether an arrangement is a criminally fraudulent investment arrangement shall be made under rules substantially similar to the rules prescribed by the Secretary of the Treasury for purposes of section 165 of the Internal Revenue Code of 1986.

(B) EXPANDED SMOOTHING PERIOD.—

(i) IN GENERAL. —A multiemployer plan with respect to which the solvency test under subparagraph (C) is met may change its asset valuation method in a manner which—

(I) spreads the difference between expected and actual returns for either or both of the first 2 plan years ending after August 31, 2008, over a period of not more than 10 years,

(II) provides that for either or both of the first 2 plan years beginning after August 31, 2008, the value of plan assets at any time shall not be less than 80 percent or greater than 130 percent of the fair market value of such assets at such time, or

(III) makes both changes described in subclauses (I) and (II) to such method.

(ii) ASSET VALUATION METHODS. —If this subparagraph applies for any plan year—

(I) the Secretary of the Treasury shall not treat the asset valuation method of the plan as unreasonable solely because of the changes in such method described in clause (i), and

(II) such changes shall be deemed approved by such Secretary under section 302(d)(1) and section 412(d)(1) of such Code.

(iii) AMORTIZATION OF REDUCTION IN UNFUNDED ACCRUED LIABILITY. —If this subparagraph and subparagraph (A) both apply for any plan year, the plan shall treat any reduction in unfunded accrued liability resulting from the application of this subparagraph as a separate experience amortization base, to be amortized in equal annual installments (until fully amortized) over a period of 30 plan years rather than the period such liability would otherwise be amortized over.

(C) SOLVENCY TEST. —The solvency test under this paragraph is met only if the plan actuary certifies that the plan is projected to have sufficient assets to timely pay expected benefits and anticipated expenditures over the amortization period, taking into account the changes in the funding standard account under this paragraph.

(D) RESTRICTION ON BENEFIT INCREASES. —If subparagraph (A) or (B) apply to a multiemployer plan for any plan year, then, in addition to any other applicable restrictions on benefit increases, a plan amendment increasing benefits may not go into effect during either of the 2 plan years immediately following such plan year unless—

(i) the plan actuary certifies that—

(I) any such increase is paid for out of additional contributions not allocated to the plan immediately before the application of this paragraph to the plan, and

(II) the plan's funded percentage and projected credit balances for such 2 plan years are reasonably expected to be at least as high as such percentage and balances would have been if the benefit increase had not been adopted, or

(ii) the amendment is required as a condition of qualification under part I of subchapter D of chapter 1 of the Internal Revenue Code of 1986 or to comply with other applicable law.

(E) REPORTING. —A plan sponsor of a plan to which this paragraph applies shall—

(i) give notice of such application to participants and beneficiaries of the plan, and

(ii) inform the Pension Benefit Guaranty Corporation of such application in such form and manner as the Director of the Pension Benefit Guaranty Corporation may prescribe.

(c) ADDITIONAL RULES.—

(1) DETERMINATIONS TO BE MADE UNDER FUNDING METHOD. —For purposes of this part, normal costs, accrued liability, past service liabilities, and experience gains and losses shall be determined under the funding method used to determine costs under the plan.

(2) VALUATION OF ASSETS.—

(A) IN GENERAL. —For purposes of this part, the value of the plan's assets shall be determined on the basis of any reasonable actuarial method of valuation which takes into account fair market value and which is permitted under regulations prescribed by the Secretary of the Treasury.

(B) ELECTION WITH RESPECT TO BONDS. —The value of a bond or other evidence of indebtedness which is not in default as to principal or interest may, at the election of the plan administrator, be determined on an amortized basis running from initial cost at purchase to par value at maturity or earliest call date. Any election under this subparagraph shall be made at such time and in such manner as the Secretary of the Treasury shall by regulations provide, shall apply to all such evidences of indebtedness, and may be revoked only with the consent of such Secretary.

(3) ACTUARIAL ASSUMPTIONS MUST BE REASONABLE. —For purposes of this section, all costs, liabilities, rates of interest, and other factors under the plan shall be determined on the basis of actuarial assumptions and methods—

(A) each of which is reasonable (taking into account the experience of the plan and reasonable expectations), and

(B) which, in combination, offer the actuary's best estimate of anticipated experience under the plan.

(4) TREATMENT OF CERTAIN CHANGES AS EXPERIENCE GAIN OR LOSS. —For purposes of this section, if—

(A) a change in benefits under the Social Security Act or in other retirement benefits created under Federal or State law, or

(B) a change in the definition of the term 'wages' under section 3121 of the Internal Revenue Code of 1986, or a change in the amount of such wages taken into account under regulations prescribed for purposes of section 401(a)(5) of such Code,

results in an increase or decrease in accrued liability under a plan, such increase or decrease shall be treated as an experience loss or gain.

(5) FULL FUNDING. —If, as of the close of a plan year, a plan would (without regard to this paragraph) have an accumulated funding deficiency in excess of the full funding limitation—

(A) the funding standard account shall be credited with the amount of such excess, and

(B) all amounts described in subparagraphs (B), (C), and (D) of subsection (b)(2) and subparagraph (B) of subsection (b)(3) which are required to be amortized shall be considered fully amortized for purposes of such subparagraphs.

(6) FULL-FUNDING LIMITATION.—

(A) IN GENERAL. —For purposes of paragraph (5), the term 'full-funding limitation' means the excess (if any) of—

(i) the accrued liability (including normal cost) under the plan (determined under the entry age normal funding method if such accrued liability cannot be directly calculated under the funding method used for the plan), over

(ii) the lesser of—

(I) the fair market value of the plan's assets, or

(II) the value of such assets determined under paragraph (2).

(B) MINIMUM AMOUNT.—

(i) IN GENERAL. —In no event shall the full-funding limitation determined under subparagraph (A) be less than the excess (if any) of—

(I) 90 percent of the current liability of the plan (including the expected increase in current liability due to benefits accruing during the plan year), over

(II) the value of the plan's assets determined under paragraph (2).

(ii) Assets. —For purposes of clause (i), assets shall not be reduced by any credit balance in the funding standard account.

(C) Full funding limitation. —For purposes of this paragraph, unless otherwise provided by the plan, the accrued liability under a multiemployer plan shall not include benefits which are not nonforfeitable under the plan after the termination of the plan (taking into consideration section 411(d)(3) of the Internal Revenue Code of 1986).

(D) Current liability. —For purposes of this paragraph—

(i) In general. —The term 'current liability' means all liabilities to employees and their beneficiaries under the plan.

(ii) Treatment of unpredictable contingent event benefits. —For purposes of clause (i), any benefit contingent on an event other than —

(I) age, service, compensation, death, or disability, or

(II) an event which is reasonably and reliably predictable (as determined by the Secretary of the Treasury),

shall not be taken into account until the event on which the benefit is contingent occurs.

(iii) Interest rate used. —The rate of interest used to determine current liability under this paragraph shall be the rate of interest determined under subparagraph (E).

(iv) Mortality tables.—

(I) Commissioners' standard table. —In the case of plan years beginning before the first plan year to which the first tables prescribed under subclause (II) apply, the mortality table used in determining current liability under this paragraph shall be the table prescribed by the Secretary of the Treasury which is based on the prevailing commissioners' standard table (described in section 807(d)(5)(A) of the Internal Revenue Code of 1986) used to determine reserves for group annuity contracts issued on January 1, 1993.

(II) Secretarial authority. —The Secretary of the Treasury may by regulation prescribe for plan years beginning after December 31, 1999, mortality tables to be used in determining current liability under this subsection. Such tables shall be based upon the actual experience of pension plans and projected trends in such experience. In prescribing such tables, such Secretary shall take into account results of available independent studies of mortality of individuals covered by pension plans.

(v) Separate mortality tables for the disabled. —Notwithstanding clause (iv)—

(I) In general. —The Secretary of the Treasury shall establish mortality tables which may be used (in lieu of the tables under clause (iv)) to determine current liability under this subsection for individuals who are entitled to benefits under the plan on account of disability. Such Secretary shall establish separate tables for individuals whose disabilities occur in plan years beginning before January 1, 1995, and for individuals whose disabilities occur in plan years beginning on or after such date.

(II) Special rule for disabilities occurring after 1994. —In the case of disabilities occurring in plan years beginning after December 31, 1994, the tables under subclause (I) shall apply only with respect to individuals described in such subclause who are disabled within the meaning of title II of the Social Security Act and the regulations thereunder.

(vi) Periodic review. —The Secretary of the Treasury shall periodically (at least every 5 years) review any tables in effect under this subparagraph and shall, to the extent such Secretary determines necessary, by regulation update the tables to reflect the actual experience of pension plans and projected trends in such experience.

(E) Required change of interest rate. —For purposes of determining a plan's current liability for purposes of this paragraph—

(i) In general. —If any rate of interest used under the plan under subsection (b)(6) to determine cost is not within the permissible range, the plan shall establish a new rate of interest within the permissible range.

(ii) Permissible range. —For purposes of this subparagraph—

(I) In general. —Except as provided in subclause (II), the term 'permissible range' means a rate of interest which is not more than 5 percent above, and not more than 10 percent below, the weighted average of the rates of interest on 30-year Treasury securities during the 4-year period ending on the last day before the beginning of the plan year.

(II) Secretarial authority. —If the Secretary of the Treasury finds that the lowest rate of interest permissible under subclause (I) is unreasonably high, such Secretary may prescribe a lower rate of interest, except that such rate may not be less than 80 percent of the average rate determined under such subclause.

(iii) Assumptions. —Notwithstanding paragraph (3)(A), the interest rate used under the plan shall be—

(I) determined without taking into account the experience of the plan and reasonable expectations, but

(II) consistent with the assumptions which reflect the purchase rates which would be used by insurance companies to satisfy the liabilities under the plan.

(7) Annual valuation.—

(A) In general. —For purposes of this section, a determination of experience gains and losses and a valuation of the plan's liability shall be made not less frequently than once every year, except that such determination shall be made more frequently to the extent required in particular cases under regulations prescribed by the Secretary of the Treasury.

(B) Valuation date.—

(i) Current year. —Except as provided in clause (ii), the valuation referred to in subparagraph (A) shall be made as of a date within the plan year to which the valuation refers or within one month prior to the beginning of such year.

(ii) Use of prior year valuation. —The valuation referred to in subparagraph (A) may be made as of a date within the plan year prior to the year to which the valuation refers if, as of such date, the value of the assets of the plan are not less than 100 percent of the plan's current liability (as defined in paragraph (6)(D) without regard to clause (iv) thereof).

(iii) Adjustments. —Information under clause (ii) shall, in accordance with regulations, be actuarially adjusted to reflect significant differences in participants.

(iv) Limitation. —A change in funding method to use a prior year valuation, as provided in clause (ii), may not be made unless as of the valuation date within the prior plan year, the value of the assets of the plan are not less than 125 percent of the plan's current liability (as defined in paragraph (6)(D) without regard to clause (iv) thereof).

(8) TIME WHEN CERTAIN CONTRIBUTIONS DEEMED MADE. —For purposes of this section, any contributions for a plan year made by an employer after the last day of such plan year, but not later than two and one-half months after such day, shall be deemed to have been made on such last day. For purposes of this subparagraph, such two and one-half month period may be extended for not more than six months under regulations prescribed by the Secretary of the Treasury.

(d) EXTENSION OF AMORTIZATION PERIODS FOR MULTIEMPLOYER PLANS.—

(1) AUTOMATIC EXTENSION UPON APPLICATION BY CERTAIN PLANS.—

(A) IN GENERAL. —If the plan sponsor of a multiemployer plan—

(i) submits to the Secretary of the Treasury an application for an extension of the period of years required to amortize any unfunded liability described in any clause of subsection (b)(2)(B) or described in subsection (b)(4), and

(ii) includes with the application a certification by the plan's actuary described in subparagraph (B),

the Secretary of the Treasury shall extend the amortization period for the period of time (not in excess of 5 years) specified in the application. Such extension shall be in addition to any extension under paragraph (2).

(B) CRITERIA. —A certification with respect to a multiemployer plan is described in this subparagraph if the plan's actuary certifies that, based on reasonable assumptions—

(i) absent the extension under subparagraph (A), the plan would have an accumulated funding deficiency in the current plan year or any of the 9 succeeding plan years,

(ii) the plan sponsor has adopted a plan to improve the plan's funding status,

(iii) the plan is projected to have sufficient assets to timely pay expected benefits and anticipated expenditures over the amortization period as extended, and,

(iv) the notice required under paragraph (3)(A) has been provided.

(2) ALTERNATIVE EXTENSION.—

(A) IN GENERAL. —If the plan sponsor of a multiemployer plan submits to the Secretary of the Treasury an application for an extension of the period of years required to amortize any unfunded liability described in any clause of subsection (b)(2)(B) or described in subsection (b)(4), the Secretary of the Treasury may extend the amortization period for a period of time (not in excess of 10 years reduced by the number of years of any extension under paragraph (1) with respect to such unfunded liability) if the Secretary of the Treasury makes the determination described in subparagraph (B). Such extension shall be in addition to any extension under paragraph (1).

(B) DETERMINATION. —The Secretary of the Treasury may grant an extension under subparagraph (A) if such Secretary determines that—

(i) such extension would carry out the purposes of this Act and would provide adequate protection for participants under the plan and their beneficiaries, and

(ii) the failure to permit such extension would —

(I) result in a substantial risk to the voluntary continuation of the plan, or a substantial curtailment of pension benefit levels or employee compensation, and

(II) be adverse to the interests of plan participants in the aggregate.

(C) ACTION BY SECRETARY OF THE TREASURY. —The Secretary of the Treasury shall act upon any application for an extension under this paragraph within 180 days of the submission of such application. If such Secretary rejects the application for an extension under this paragraph, such Secretary shall provide notice to the plan detailing the specific reasons for the rejection, including references to the criteria set forth above.

(3) ADVANCE NOTICE.—

(A) IN GENERAL. —The Secretary of the Treasury shall, before granting an extension under this subsection, require each applicant to provide evidence satisfactory to such Secretary that the applicant has provided notice of the filing of the application for such extension to each affected party (as defined in section 4001(a)(21)) with respect to the affected plan. Such notice shall include a description of the extent to which the plan is funded for benefits which are guaranteed under title IV and for benefit liabilities.

(B) CONSIDERATION OF RELEVANT INFORMATION. —The Secretary of the Treasury shall consider any relevant information provided by a person to whom notice was given under paragraph (1).

Amendments

P.L. 113-235, § 108(a)(3)(B), Div. O:

Amended ERISA Sec. 304(a) to read as above. Prior to amendment, ERISA Sec. 304(a) read as follows:

(a) In General.—For purposes of section 302, the accumulated funding deficiency of a multiemployer plan for any plan year is—

(1) except as provided in paragraph (2), the amount, determined as of the end of the plan year, equal to the excess (if any) of the total charges to the funding standard account of the plan for all plan years (beginning with the first plan year for which this part applies to the plan) over the total credits to such account for such years, and

(2) if the multiemployer plan is in reorganization for any plan year, the accumulated funding deficiency of the plan determined under section 4243.

The above amendment shall apply with respect to plan years beginning after December 31, 2014.

P.L. 113-295, § 171(b), Div. A:

Amended ERISA Sec. 304(d)(1)(C) by striking "December 31, 2014" and inserting "December 31, 2015".

The above amendment shall apply to applications submitted under section 304(d)(1)(C) of the Employee Retirement Income Security Act of 1974 after December 31, 2014 [Note: P.L. 113-235, § 101(b)(1), struck ERISA Sec. 304(d)(1)(C). Therefore, this amendment cannot be made.—CCH.].

P.L. 113-235, § 101(b)(1), Div. O:

Amended ERISA Sec. 304(d)(1) by striking subparagraph (C). Prior to being stricken, ERISA Sec. 304(d)(1)(C) read as follows:

(C) Termination.—The preceding provisions of this paragraph shall not apply with respect to any application submitted after December 31, 2014.

The above amendment is effective on the date of enactment [December 16, 2014.-CCH.].

P.L. 111-192, § 211(a)(1):

Amended ERISA Sec. 304(b) by adding new paragraph (8) to read as above.

P.L. 111-192, § 211(b) provides:

211(b) EFFECTIVE DATES.—

(1) IN GENERAL.—The amendments made by this section shall take effect as of the first day of the first plan year ending after August 31, 2008, except that any election a plan makes pursuant to this section that affects the plan's funding standard account for the first plan year beginning after August 31, 2008, shall be disregarded for purposes of applying the provisions of section 305 of the Employee Retirement Income Security Act of 1974 and section 432 of the Internal Revenue Code of 1986 to such plan year.

(2) RESTRICTIONS ON BENEFIT INCREASES.—Notwithstanding paragraph (1), the restrictions on plan amendments increasing benefits in sections 304(b)(8)(D) of such Act and 431(b)(8)(D) of such Code, as added by this section, shall take effect on the date of enactment of this Act [i.e. June 25, 2010—CCH].

P. L. 109-280, § 101(a):

Repealed ERISA Sec. 304.

Prior to repeal, ERISA Sec. 304 read as follows:

(a) DETERMINATION BY SECRETARY IN GRANTING EXTENSION.—The period of years required to amortize any unfunded liability (described in any clause of subsection (b)(2)(B) of section 302) of any plan may be extended by the Secretary for a period of time (not in excess of 10 years) if he determines that such extension would carry out the purpose of this Act and would provide adequate protection for participants under the plan and their beneficiaries and if he determines that the failure to permit such extension would—

(a)(1) result in—

(a)(1)(A) a substantial risk to the voluntary continuation of the plan, or

(a)(1)(B) a substantial curtailment of pension benefit levels or employee compensation, and

(a)(2) be adverse to the interests of plan participants in the aggregate.

In the case of a plan other than a multiemployer plan, the interest rate applicable for any plan year under any arrangement entered into by the Secretary in connection with an extension granted under this subsection shall be the greater of (A) 150 percent of the Federal mid-term rate (as in effect under section 1274 of the Internal Revenue Code of 1986 for the 1st month of such plan year), or (B) the rate of interest used under the plan in determining costs. In the case of a multiemployer plan, such rate shall be the rate determined under section 6621(b) of such Code.

(b)(1) AMENDMENT OF PLAN.— No amendment of the plan which increases the liabilities of the plan by reason of any increase in benefits, any change in the accrual of benefits, or any change in the rate at which benefits become nonforfeitable under the plan shall be adopted if a waiver under section 303(a) or an extension of time under subsection (a) of this section is in effect with respect to the plan, or if a plan amendment described in section 302(c)(8) has been made at any time in the preceding 12 months (24 months in the case of a multiemployer plan). If a plan is amended in violation of the preceding sentence, any such waiver, or extension of time, shall not apply to any plan year ending on or after the date on which such amendment is adopted.

(b)(2) Paragraph (1) shall not apply to any plan amendment which—

(b)(2)(A) the Secretary determines to be reasonable and which provides for only de minimis increases in the liabilities of the plan,

(b)(2)(B) only repeals an amendment described in section 302(c)(8), or

(b)(2)(C) is required as a condition of qualification under part I of subchapter D, of chapter 1, of the Internal Revenue Code of 1986.

(c)(1) NOTICE OF FILING OF APPLICATION FOR EXTENSION.—The Secretary of the Treasury shall, before granting an extension under this section, require each applicant to provide evidence satisfactory to such Secretary that the applicant has provided notice of the filing of the application for such extension to each employee organization representing employees covered by the affected plan.

(c)(2) The Secretary of the Treasury shall consider any relevant information provided by a person to whom notice was given under paragraph (1).

The above amendment applies to plan years beginning after 2007.

P. L. 109-280, §201(a):

Amended Part 3 of subtitle B of title I of the Employee Retirement Income Security Act of 1974 (as amended by section 101 of this Act) by inserting after section 303 the new section 304.

The above amendment apply to plan years beginning after 2007.

P.L. 101-239, §7894(d)(3):

Amended ERISA Sec. 304(b)(2)(A), by striking the period and inserting a comma, effective September 2, 1974.

P.L. 101-239, §7894(a)(1):

Titles I, III, and IV of ERISA (other than sections 3(37)(E), 301(a)(7), and 308, the last sentence of section 408(d), and sections 414(c), 4001(a)(3)(ii), and 4303) are each amended by striking "Internal Revenue Code of 1954" each place it appears and inserting "Internal Revenue Code of 1986" effective October 22, 1986.

P.L. 100-203, §9306(c)(2)(B):

Amended ERISA Sec. 304(a) by striking out the last sentence and inserting a new last sentence to read as above, effective for applications for waivers submitted after December 17, 1987 and waivers granted pursuant to such waivers. Prior to amendment, the last sentence read as follows:

The interest rate applicable under any arrangement entered into by the Secretary in connection with an extension granted under this subsection shall be the rate determined under section 6621(b) of the Internal Revenue Code of 1954.

P.L. 99-272:

Act Sec. 11015(b)(1)(B) amended ERISA Sec. 304 by adding the new sentence following paragraph (2) to read as above, effective with respect to terminations pursuant to notices of intent filed with the PBGC on or after January 1, 1986 and proceedings begun on or after that date.

Act Sec. 11016(c)(3) amended ERISA Sec. 304 by adding a new subsection (c) to read as above, effective on April 7, 1986.

[¶ 14,650]
ADDITIONAL FUNDING RULES FOR MULTIEMPLOYER PLANS IN ENDANGERED STATUS OR CRITICAL STATUS

Act Sec. 305.(a) GENERAL RULE.—

—For purposes of this part, in the case of a multiemployer plan in effect on July 16, 2006—

(1) if the plan is in endangered status—

(A) the plan sponsor shall adopt and implement a funding improvement plan in accordance with the requirements of subsection (c), and

(B) the requirements of subsection (d) shall apply during the funding plan adoption period and the funding improvement period,

(2) if the plan is in critical status—

(A) the plan sponsor shall adopt and implement a rehabilitation plan in accordance with the requirements of subsection (e), and

(B) the requirements of subsection (f) shall apply during the rehabilitation plan adoption period and the rehabilitation period, and

(3) if the plan is in critical and declining status—

(A) the requirements of paragraph (2) shall apply to the plan; and

(B) the plan sponsor may, by plan amendment, suspend benefits in accordance with the requirements of subsection (e)(9).

Act Sec. 305. (b) DETERMINATION OF ENDANGERED AND CRITICAL STATUS.—For purposes of this section—

(1) ENDANGERED STATUS. —A multiemployer plan is in endangered status for a plan year if, as determined by the plan actuary under paragraph (3), the plan is not in critical status for the plan year and is not described in paragraph (5), and, as of the beginning of the plan year, either—

(A) the plan's funded percentage for such plan year is less than 80 percent, or

(B) the plan has an accumulated funding deficiency for such plan year, or is projected to have such an accumulated funding deficiency for any of the 6 succeeding plan years, taking into account any extension of amortization periods under section 304(d).

For purposes of this section, a plan shall be treated as in seriously endangered status for a plan year if the plan is described in both subparagraphs (A) and (B).

(2) CRITICAL STATUS. —A multiemployer plan is in critical status for a plan year if, as determined by the plan actuary under paragraph (3), the plan is described in 1 or more of the following subparagraphs as of the beginning of the plan year:

(A) A plan is described in this subparagraph if—

(i) the funded percentage of the plan is less than 65 percent, and

(ii) the sum of—

(I) the fair market value of plan assets, plus

(II) the present value of the reasonably anticipated employer contributions for the current plan year and each of the 6 succeeding plan years, assuming that the terms of all collective bargaining agreements pursuant to which the plan is maintained for the current plan year continue in effect for succeeding plan years,

is less than the present value of all nonforfeitable benefits projected to be payable under the plan during the current plan year and each of the 6 succeeding plan years (plus administrative expenses for such plan years).

(B) A plan is described in this subparagraph if—

(i) the plan has an accumulated funding deficiency for the current plan year, not taking into account any extension of amortization periods under section 304(d), or

(ii) the plan is projected to have an accumulated funding deficiency for any of the 3 succeeding plan years (4 succeeding plan years if the funded percentage of the plan is 65 percent or less), not taking into account any extension of amortization periods under section 304(d).

(C) A plan is described in this subparagraph if—

(i)(I) the plan's normal cost for the current plan year, plus interest (determined at the rate used for determining costs under the plan) for the current plan year on the amount of unfunded benefit liabilities under the plan as of the last date of the preceding plan year, exceeds

(II) the present value of the reasonably anticipated employer and employee contributions for the current plan year,

(ii) the present value, as of the beginning of the current plan year, of nonforfeitable benefits of inactive participants is greater than the present value of nonforfeitable benefits of active participants, and

(iii) the plan has an accumulated funding deficiency for the current plan year, or is projected to have such a deficiency for any of the 4 succeeding plan years, not taking into account any extension of amortization periods under section 304(d).

(D) A plan is described in this subparagraph if the sum of—

(i) the fair market value of plan assets, plus

(ii) the present value of the reasonably anticipated employer contributions for the current plan year and each of the 4 succeeding plan years, assuming that the terms of all collective bargaining agreements pursuant to which the plan is maintained for the current plan year continue in effect for succeeding plan years,

is less than the present value of all benefits projected to be payable under the plan during the current plan year and each of the 4 succeeding plan years (plus administrative expenses for such plan years).

(3) ANNUAL CERTIFICATION BY PLAN ACTUARY.—

(A) IN GENERAL.—Not later than the 90th day of each plan year of a multiemployer plan, the plan actuary shall certify to the Secretary of the Treasury and to the plan sponsor—

(i) whether or not the plan is in endangered status for such plan year, or would be in endangered status for such plan year but for paragraph (5), whether or not the plan is or will be in critical status for such plan year, and whether or not the plan is or will be in critical and declining status for such plan year, or for any of the succeeding 5 plan years, and

(ii) in the case of a plan which is in a funding improvement or rehabilitation period, whether or not the plan is making the scheduled progress in meeting the requirements of its funding improvement or rehabilitation plan.

(B) ACTUARIAL PROJECTIONS OF ASSETS AND LIABILITIES.—

(i) IN GENERAL.—Except as provided in clause (iv), in making the determinations and projections under this subsection, the plan actuary shall make projections required for the current and succeeding plan years of the current value of the assets of the plan and the present value of all liabilities to participants and beneficiaries under the plan for the current plan year as of the beginning of such year. The actuary's projections shall be based on reasonable actuarial estimates, assumptions, and methods that, except as provided in clause (iii), offer the actuary's best estimate of anticipated experience under the plan. The projected present value of liabilities as of the beginning of such year shall be determined based on the most recent of either—

(I) the actuarial statement required under section 103(d) with respect to the most recently filed annual report, or

(II) the actuarial valuation for the preceding plan year.

(ii) DETERMINATIONS OF FUTURE CONTRIBUTIONS.—Any actuarial projection of plan assets shall assume—

(I) reasonably anticipated employer contributions for the current and succeeding plan years, assuming that the terms of the one or more collective bargaining agreements pursuant to which the plan is maintained for the current plan year continue in effect for succeeding plan years, or

(II) that employer contributions for the most recent plan year will continue indefinitely, but only if the plan actuary determines there have been no significant demographic changes that would make such assumption unreasonable.

(iii) PROJECTED INDUSTRY ACTIVITY.—Any projection of activity in the industry or industries covered by the plan, including future covered employment and contribution levels, shall be based on information provided by the plan sponsor, which shall act reasonably and in good faith.

(iv) PROJECTIONS RELATING TO CRITICAL STATUS IN SUCCEEDING PLAN YEARS.—Clauses (i) and (ii) (other than the 2nd sentence of clause (i)) may be disregarded by a plan actuary in the case of any certification of whether a plan will be in critical status in a succeeding plan year, except that a plan sponsor may not elect to be in critical status for a plan year under paragraph (4) in any case in which the certification upon which such election would be based is made without regard to such clauses.

(iv)[(v)] PROJECTIONS OF CRITICAL AND DECLINING STATUS.—In determining whether a plan is in critical and declining status as described in subsection (e)(9), clauses (i), (ii), and (iii) shall apply, except that—

(I) if reasonable, the plan actuary shall assume that each contributing employer in compliance continues to comply through the end of the rehabilitation period or such later time as provided in subsection (e)(3)(A)(ii) with the terms of the rehabilitation plan that correspond to the schedule adopted or imposed under subsection (e), and

(II) the plan actuary shall take into account any suspensions of benefits described in subsection (e)(9) adopted in a prior plan year that are still in effect.

(C) PENALTY FOR FAILURE TO SECURE TIMELY ACTUARIAL CERTIFICATION.—Any failure of the plan's actuary to certify the plan's status under this subsection by the date specified in subparagraph (A) shall be treated for purposes of section 502(c)(2) as a failure or refusal by the plan administrator to file the annual report required to be filed with the Secretary under section 101(b)(1).

(D) NOTICE.—

(i) IN GENERAL.—In any case in which it is certified under subparagraph (A) that a multiemployer plan is or will be in endangered or critical status for a plan year or in which a plan sponsor elects to be in critical status for a plan year under paragraph (4), the plan sponsor shall, not later than 30 days after the date of the certification, provide notification of the endangered or critical status to the participants and beneficiaries, the bargaining parties, the Pension Benefit Guaranty Corporation, and the Secretary. In any case in which a plan sponsor elects to be in critical status for a plan year under paragraph (4), the plan sponsor shall notify the Secretary of the Treasury of such election not later than 30 days after the date of such certification or such other time as the Secretary of the Treasury may prescribe by regulations or other guidance.

(ii) PLANS IN CRITICAL STATUS.—If it is certified under subparagraph (A) that a multiemployer plan is or will be in critical status, the plan sponsor shall include in the notice under clause (i) an explanation of the possibility that—

(I) adjustable benefits (as defined in subsection (e)(8)) may be reduced, and

(II) such reductions may apply to participants and beneficiaries whose benefit commencement date is on or after the date such notice is provided for the first plan year in which the plan is in critical status.

(iii) In the case of a multiemployer plan that would be in endangered status but for paragraph (5), the plan sponsor shall provide notice to the bargaining parties and the Pension Benefit Guaranty Corporation that the plan would be in endangered status but for such paragraph..

(iv) MODEL NOTICE.—The Secretary of the Treasury, in consultation with the Secretary shall prescribe a model notice that a multiemployer plan may use to satisfy the requirements under clauses (ii) and (iii).

(v) NOTICE OF PROJECTION TO BE IN CRITICAL STATUS IN A FUTURE PLAN YEAR.—In any case in which it is certified under subparagraph (A)(i) that a multiemployer plan will be in critical status for any of 5 succeeding plan years (but not for the current plan year) and the plan sponsor of such plan has not made an election to be in critical status for the plan year under paragraph (4), the plan sponsor shall, not later than 30 days after the date of the certification, provide notification of the projected critical status to the Pension Benefit Guaranty Corporation.

(4) ELECTION TO BE IN CRITICAL STATUS. —Notwithstanding paragraph (2) and subject to paragraph (3)(B)(iv)—

(A) the plan sponsor of a multiemployer plan that is not in critical status for a plan year but that is projected by the plan actuary, pursuant to the determination under paragraph (3), to be in critical status in any of the succeeding 5 plan years may, not later than 30 days after the date of the certification under paragraph (3)(A), elect to be in critical status effective for the current plan year,

(B) the plan year in which the plan sponsor elects to be in critical status under subparagraph (A) shall be treated for purposes of this section as the first year in which the plan is in critical status, regardless of the date on which the plan first satisfies the criteria for critical status under paragraph (2), and

(C) a plan that is in critical status under this paragraph shall not emerge from critical status except in accordance with subsection (e)(4)(B).

(5) SPECIAL RULE. —A plan is described in this paragraph if—

(A) as part of the actuarial certification of endangered status under paragraph (3)(A) for the plan year, the plan actuary certifies that the plan is projected to no longer be described in either paragraph (1)(A) or paragraph (1)(B) as of the end of the tenth plan year ending after the plan year to which the certification relates, and

(B) the plan was not in critical or endangered status for the immediately preceding plan year.

(6) CRITICAL AND DECLINING STATUS. —For purposes of this section, a plan in critical status shall be treated as in critical and declining status if the plan is described in one or more of subparagraphs (A), (B), (C), and (D) of paragraph (2) and the plan is projected to become insolvent within the meaning of section 4245 during the current plan year or any of the 14 succeeding plan years (19 succeeding plan years if the plan has a ratio of inactive participants to active participants that exceeds 2 to 1 or if the funded percentage of the plan is less than 80 percent).

Act Sec. 305. (c) FUNDING IMPROVEMENT PLAN MUST BE ADOPTED FOR MULTIEMPLOYER PLANS IN ENDANGERED STATUS.—

(1) IN GENERAL. —In any case in which a multiemployer plan is in endangered status for a plan year, the plan sponsor, in accordance with this subsection—

(A) shall adopt a funding improvement plan not later than 240 days following the required date for the actuarial certification of endangered status under subsection (b)(3)(A), and

(B) within 30 days after the adoption of the funding improvement plan—

(i) shall provide to the bargaining parties 1 or more schedules showing revised benefit structures, revised contribution structures, or both, which, if adopted, may reasonably be expected to enable the multiemployer plan to meet the applicable benchmarks in accordance with the funding improvement plan, including—

(I) one proposal for reductions in the amount of future benefit accruals necessary to achieve the applicable benchmarks, assuming no amendments increasing contributions under the plan (other than amendments increasing contributions necessary to achieve the applicable benchmarks after amendments have reduced future benefit accruals to the maximum extent permitted by law), and

(II) one proposal for increases in contributions under the plan necessary to achieve the applicable benchmarks, assuming no amendments reducing future benefit accruals under the plan, and

(ii) may, if the plan sponsor deems appropriate, prepare and provide the bargaining parties with additional information relating to contribution rates or benefit reductions, alternative schedules, or other information relevant to achieving the applicable benchmarks in accordance with the funding improvement plan.

For purposes of this section, the term 'applicable benchmarks' means the requirements applicable to the multiemployer plan under paragraph (3) (as modified by paragraph (5)).

(2) EXCEPTION FOR YEARS AFTER PROCESS BEGINS. —Paragraph (1) shall not apply to a plan year if such year is in a funding plan adoption period or funding improvement period by reason of the plan being in endangered status for a preceding plan year. For purposes of this section, such preceding plan year shall be the initial determination year with respect to the funding improvement plan to which it relates.

(3) FUNDING IMPROVEMENT PLAN. —For purposes of this section—

(A) IN GENERAL. —A funding improvement plan is a plan which consists of the actions, including options or a range of options to be proposed to the bargaining parties, formulated to provide, based on reasonably anticipated experience and reasonable actuarial assumptions, for the attainment by the plan during the funding improvement period of the following requirements:

(i) INCREASE IN PLAN'S FUNDING PERCENTAGE. —The plan's funded percentage as of the close of the funding improvement period equals or exceeds a percentage equal to the sum of—

(I) such percentage as of the beginning of the first plan year for which the plan is certified to be in endangered status pursuant to paragraph (b)(3), plus

(II) 33 percent of the difference between 100 percent and the percentage under subclause (I).

(ii) AVOIDANCE OF ACCUMULATED FUNDING DEFICIENCIES. —No accumulated funding deficiency for the last plan year during the funding improvement period (taking into account any extension of amortization periods under section 304(d)).

(B) SERIOUSLY ENDANGERED PLANS. —In the case of a plan in seriously endangered status, except as provided in paragraph (5), subparagraph (A)(i)(II) shall be applied by substituting '20 percent' for '33 percent'.

(4) FUNDING IMPROVEMENT PERIOD. —For purposes of this section—

(A) IN GENERAL. —The funding improvement period for any funding improvement plan adopted pursuant to this subsection is the 10-year period beginning on the first day of the first plan year of the multiemployer plan beginning after the earlier of—

(i) the second anniversary of the date of the adoption of the funding improvement plan, or

(ii) the expiration of the collective bargaining agreements in effect on the due date for the actuarial certification of endangered status for the initial determination year under subsection (b)(3)(A) and covering, as of such due date, at least 75 percent of the active participants in such multiemployer plan.

(B) SERIOUSLY ENDANGERED PLANS. —In the case of a plan in seriously endangered status, except as provided in paragraph (5), subparagraph (A) shall be applied by substituting '15-year period' for '10-year period'.

(C) COORDINATION WITH CHANGES IN STATUS.—

(i) PLANS NO LONGER IN ENDANGERED STATUS. —If the plan's actuary certifies under subsection (b)(3)(A) for a plan year in any funding plan adoption period or funding improvement period that the plan is no longer in endangered status and is not in critical status, the funding plan adoption period or funding improvement period, whichever is applicable, shall end as of the close of the preceding plan year.

(ii) PLANS IN CRITICAL STATUS. —If the plan's actuary certifies under subsection (b)(3)(A) for a plan year in any funding plan adoption period or funding improvement period that the plan is in critical status, the funding plan adoption period or funding improvement period, whichever is applicable, shall end as of the close of the plan year preceding the first plan year in the rehabilitation period with respect to such status.

(D) PLANS IN ENDANGERED STATUS AT END OF PERIOD. —If the plan's actuary certifies under subsection (b)(3)(A) for the first plan year following the close of the period described in subparagraph (A) that the plan is in endangered status, the provisions of this subsection and subsection (d) shall be applied as if such first plan year were an initial determination year, except that the plan may not be amended in a manner inconsistent with the funding improvement plan in effect for the preceding plan year until a new funding improvement plan is adopted.

(5) SPECIAL RULES FOR SERIOUSLY ENDANGERED PLANS MORE THAN 70 PERCENT FUNDED.—

(A) IN GENERAL. —If the funded percentage of a plan in seriously endangered status was more than 70 percent as of the beginning of the initial determination year—

(i) paragraphs (3)(B) and (4)(B) shall apply only if the plan's actuary certifies, within 30 days after the certification under subsection (b)(3)(A) for the initial determination year, that, based on the terms of the plan and the collective bargaining agreements in effect at the time of such certification, the plan is not projected to meet the requirements of paragraph (3)(A) (without regard to paragraphs (3)(B) and (4)(B)), and

(ii) if there is a certification under clause (i), the plan may, in formulating its funding improvement plan, only take into account the rules of paragraph (3)(B) and (4)(B) for plan years in the funding improvement period beginning on or before the date on which the last of the collective bargaining agreements described in paragraph (4)(A)(ii) expires.

(B) SPECIAL RULE AFTER EXPIRATION OF AGREEMENTS. —Notwithstanding subparagraph (A)(ii), if, for any plan year ending after the date described in subparagraph (A)(ii), the plan actuary certifies (at the time of the annual certification under subsection (b)(3)(A) for such plan year) that, based on the terms of the plan and collective bargaining agreements in effect at the time of that annual certification, the plan is not projected to be able to meet the requirements of paragraph (3)(A) (without regard to paragraphs (3)(B) and (4)(B)), paragraphs (3)(B) and (4)(B) shall continue to apply for such year.

(6) UPDATES TO FUNDING IMPROVEMENT PLAN AND SCHEDULES.—

(A) FUNDING IMPROVEMENT PLAN. —The plan sponsor shall annually update the funding improvement plan and shall file the update with the plan's annual report under section 104.

(B) SCHEDULES. —The plan sponsor shall annually update any schedule of contribution rates provided under this subsection to reflect the experience of the plan.

(C) DURATION OF SCHEDULE. —A schedule of contribution rates provided by the plan sponsor and relied upon by bargaining parties in negotiating a collective bargaining agreement shall remain in effect for the duration of that collective bargaining agreement.

(7) IMPOSITION OF SCHEDULE WHERE FAILURE TO ADOPT FUNDING IMPROVEMENT PLAN.—

(A) INITIAL CONTRIBUTION SCHEDULE. —If—

(i) a collective bargaining agreement providing for contributions under a multiemployer plan that was in effect at the time the plan entered endangered status expires, and

(ii) after receiving one or more schedules from the plan sponsor under paragraph (1)(B), the bargaining parties with respect to such agreement fail to adopt a contribution schedule with terms consistent with the funding improvement plan and a schedule from the plan sponsor,

the plan sponsor shall implement the schedule described in paragraph (1)(B)(i)(I) beginning on the date specified in subparagraph (C).

(B) SUBSEQUENT CONTRIBUTION SCHEDULE. —If—

(i) a collective bargaining agreement providing for contributions under a multiemployer plan in accordance with a schedule provided by the plan sponsor pursuant to a funding improvement plan (or imposed under subparagraph (A)) expires while the plan is still in endangered status, and

(ii) after receiving one or more updated schedules from the plan sponsor under paragraph (6)(B), the bargaining parties with respect to such agreement fail to adopt a contribution schedule with terms consistent with the updated funding improvement plan and a schedule from the plan sponsor,

then the contribution schedule applicable under the expired collective bargaining agreement, as updated and in effect on the date the collective bargaining agreement expires, shall be implemented by the plan sponsor beginning on the date specified in subparagraph (C).

(C) DATE OF IMPLEMENTATION. —The date specified in this subparagraph is the date which is 180 days after the date on which the collective bargaining agreement described in subparagraph (A) or (B) expires.

(D) FAILURE TO MAKE SCHEDULED CONTRIBUTIONS. —Any failure to make a contribution under a schedule of contribution rates provided under this paragraph shall be treated as a delinquent contribution under section 515 and shall be enforceable as such.

(8) FUNDING PLAN ADOPTION PERIOD. —For purposes of this section, the term 'funding plan adoption period' means the period beginning on the date of the certification under subsection (b)(3)(A) for the initial determination year and ending on the day before the first day of the funding improvement period.

Act Sec. 305. (d) RULES FOR OPERATION OF PLAN DURING ADOPTION AND IMPROVEMENT PERIODS

(1) COMPLIANCE WITH FUNDING IMPROVEMENT PLAN.—

(A) IN GENERAL. —A plan may not be amended after the date of the adoption of a funding improvement plan under subsection (c) so as to be inconsistent with the funding improvement plan.

(B) SPECIAL RULES FOR BENEFIT INCREASES. —A plan may not be amended after the date of the adoption of a funding improvement plan under subsection (c) so as to increase benefits, including future benefit accruals, unless the plan actuary certifies that such increase is paid for out of additional contributions not contemplated by the funding improvement plan, and, after taking into account the benefit increase, the multiemployer plan still is reasonably expected to meet the applicable benchmark on the schedule contemplated in the funding improvement plan.

(2) SPECIAL RULES FOR PLAN ADOPTION PERIOD. —During the period beginning on the date of the certification under subsection (b)(3)(A) for the initial determination year and ending on the date of the adoption of a funding improvement plan—

(A) the plan sponsor may not accept a collective bargaining agreement or participation agreement with respect to the multiemployer plan that provides for—

(i) a reduction in the level of contributions for any participants,

(ii) a suspension of contributions with respect to any period of service, or

(iii) any new direct or indirect exclusion of younger or newly hired employees from plan participation, and

(B) no amendment of the plan which increases the liabilities of the plan by reason of any increase in benefits, any change in the accrual of benefits, or any change in the rate at which benefits become nonforfeitable under the plan may be adopted unless the amendment is required as a condition of qualification under part I of subchapter D of chapter 1 of the Internal Revenue Code of 1986 or to comply with other applicable law.

Act Sec. 305. (e) Rehabilitation plan must be adopted for multiemployer plans in critical status.—

(1) In general.—In any case in which a multiemployer plan is in critical status for a plan year, the plan sponsor, in accordance with this subsection—

(A) shall adopt a rehabilitation plan not later than 240 days following the required date for the actuarial certification of critical status under subsection (b)(3)(A), and

(B) within 30 days after the adoption of the rehabilitation plan—

(i) shall provide to the bargaining parties 1 or more schedules showing revised benefit structures, revised contribution structures, or both, which, if adopted, may reasonably be expected to enable the multiemployer plan to emerge from critical status in accordance with the rehabilitation plan, and

(ii) may, if the plan sponsor deems appropriate, prepare and provide the bargaining parties with additional information relating to contribution rates or benefit reductions, alternative schedules, or other information relevant to emerging from critical status in accordance with the rehabilitation plan.

The schedule or schedules described in subparagraph (B)(i) shall reflect reductions in future benefit accruals and adjustable benefits, and increases in contributions, that the plan sponsor determines are reasonably necessary to emerge from critical status. One schedule shall be designated as the default schedule and such schedule shall assume that there are no increases in contributions under the plan other than the increases necessary to emerge from critical status after future benefit accruals and other benefits (other than benefits the reduction or elimination of which are not permitted under section 204(g)) have been reduced to the maximum extent permitted by law.

(2) Exception for years after process begins.—Paragraph (1) shall not apply to a plan year if such year is in a rehabilitation plan adoption period or rehabilitation period by reason of the plan being in critical status for a preceding plan year. For purposes of this section, such preceding plan year shall be the initial critical year with respect to the rehabilitation plan to which it relates.

(3) Rehabilitation plan.—For purposes of this section—

(A) In general.—A rehabilitation plan is a plan which consists of—

(i) actions, including options or a range of options to be proposed to the bargaining parties, formulated, based on reasonably anticipated experience and reasonable actuarial assumptions, to enable the plan to cease to be in critical status by the end of the rehabilitation period and may include reductions in plan expenditures (including plan mergers and consolidations), reductions in future benefit accruals or increases in contributions, if agreed to by the bargaining parties, or any combination of such actions, or

(ii) if the plan sponsor determines that, based on reasonable actuarial assumptions and upon exhaustion of all reasonable measures, the plan can not reasonably be expected to emerge from critical status by the end of the rehabilitation period, reasonable measures to emerge from critical status at a later time or to forestall possible insolvency (within the meaning of section 4245).

A rehabilitation plan must provide annual standards for meeting the requirements of such rehabilitation plan. Such plan shall also include the schedules required to be provided under paragraph (1)(B)(i) and if clause (ii) applies, shall set forth the alternatives considered, explain why the plan is not reasonably expected to emerge from critical status by the end of the rehabilitation period, and specify when, if ever, the plan is expected to emerge from critical status in accordance with the rehabilitation plan.

(B) Updates to rehabilitation plan and schedules.—

(i) Rehabilitation plan.—The plan sponsor shall annually update the rehabilitation plan and shall file the update with the plan's annual report under section 104.

(ii) Schedules.—The plan sponsor shall annually update any schedule of contribution rates provided under this subsection to reflect the experience of the plan.

(iii) Duration of schedule.—A schedule of contribution rates provided by the plan sponsor and relied upon by bargaining parties in negotiating a collective bargaining agreement shall remain in effect for the duration of that collective bargaining agreement.

(C) Imposition of schedule where failure to adopt rehabilitation plan.—

(i) Initial contribution schedule.—If—

(I) a collective bargaining agreement providing for contributions under a multiemployer plan that was in effect at the time the plan entered critical status expires, and

(II) after receiving one or more schedules from the plan sponsor under paragraph (1)(B), the bargaining parties with respect to such agreement fail to adopt a contribution schedule with terms consistent with the rehabilitation plan and a schedule from the plan sponsor under paragraph (1)(B)(i),

the plan sponsor shall implement the schedule described in the last sentence of paragraph (1) beginning on the date specified in clause (iii).

(ii) Subsequent contribution schedule.—If—

(I) a collective bargaining agreement providing for contributions under a multiemployer plan in accordance with a schedule provided by the plan sponsor pursuant to a rehabilitation plan (or imposed under subparagraph (C)(i)) expires while the plan is still in critical status, and

(II) after receiving one or more updated schedules from the plan sponsor under subparagraph (B)(ii), the bargaining parties with respect to such agreement fail to adopt a contribution schedule with terms consistent with the updated rehabilitation plan and a schedule from the plan sponsor,

then the contribution schedule applicable under the expired collective bargaining agreement, as updated and in effect on the date the collective bargaining agreement expires, shall be implemented by the plan sponsor beginning on the date specified in clause (iii).

(iii) Date of implementation.—The date specified in this subparagraph is the date which is 180 days after the date on which the collective bargaining agreement described in clause (i) or (ii) expires.

(iv) Failure to make scheduled contributions.—Any failure to make a contribution under a schedule of contribution rates provided under this subsection shall be treated as a delinquent contribution under section 515 and shall be enforceable as such.

(4) Rehabilitation period.—For purposes of this section—

(A) In general.—The rehabilitation period for a plan in critical status is the 10-year period beginning on the first day of the first plan year of the multiemployer plan following the earlier of—

(i) the second anniversary of the date of the adoption of the rehabilitation plan, or

(ii) the expiration of the collective bargaining agreements in effect on the due date for the actuarial certification of critical status for the initial critical year under subsection (a)(1) and covering, as of such date at least 75 percent of the active participants in such multiemployer plan.

If a plan emerges from critical status as provided under subparagraph (B) before the end of such 10-year period, the rehabilitation period shall end with the plan year preceding the plan year for which the determination under subparagraph (B) is made.

(B) EMERGENCE.—

(i) IN GENERAL. —A plan in critical status shall remain in such status until a plan year for which the plan actuary certifies, in accordance with subsection (b)(3)(A), that—

(I) "the plan is not described in one or more of the subparagraphs in subsection (b)(2) as of the beginning of the plan year;

(II) the plan is not projected to have an accumulated funding deficiency for the plan year or any of the 9 succeeding plan years, without regard to the use of the shortfall method but taking into account any extension of amortization periods under section 304(d)(2) or section 304 (as in effect prior to the enactment of the Pension Protection Act of 2006); and

(III) the plan is not projected to become insolvent within the meaning of section 4245 for any of the 30 succeeding plan years.

(ii) PLANS WITH CERTAIN AMORTIZATION EXTENSIONS.—

(I) SPECIAL EMERGENCE RULE. —Notwithstanding clause (i), a plan in critical status that has an automatic extension of amortization periods under section 304(d)(1) shall no longer be in critical status if the plan actuary certifies for a plan year, in accordance with subsection (b)(3)(A), that—

(aa) the plan is not projected to have an accumulated funding deficiency for the plan year or any of the 9 succeeding plan years, without regard to the use of the shortfall method but taking into account any extension of amortization periods under section 304(d)(1); and

(bb) the plan is not projected to become insolvent within the meaning of section 4245 for any of the 30 succeeding plan years, regardless of whether the plan is described in one or more of the subparagraphs in subsection (b)(2) as of the beginning of the plan year.

(II) REENTRY INTO CRITICAL STATUS. —A plan that emerges from critical status under subclause (I) shall not reenter critical status for any subsequent plan year unless—

(aa) the plan is projected to have an accumulated funding deficiency for the plan year or any of the 9 succeeding plan years, without regard to the use of the shortfall method but taking into account any extension of amortization periods under section 304(d); or

(bb) the plan is projected to become insolvent within the meaning of section 4245 for any of the 30 succeeding plan years.

(5) REHABILITATION PLAN ADOPTION PERIOD. —For purposes of this section, the term 'rehabilitation plan adoption period' means the period beginning on the date of the certification under subsection (b)(3)(A) for the initial critical year and ending on the day before the first day of the rehabilitation period.

(6) LIMITATION ON REDUCTION IN RATES OF FUTURE ACCRUALS. —Any reduction in the rate of future accruals under the default schedule described in the last sentence of paragraph (1) shall not reduce the rate of future accruals below—

(A) a monthly benefit (payable as a single life annuity commencing at the participant's normal retirement age) equal to 1 percent of the contributions required to be made with respect to a participant, or the equivalent standard accrual rate for a participant or group of participants under the collective bargaining agreements in effect as of the first day of the initial critical year, or

(B) if lower, the accrual rate under the plan on such first day.

The equivalent standard accrual rate shall be determined by the plan sponsor based on the standard or average contribution base units which the plan sponsor determines to be representative for active participants and such other factors as the plan sponsor determines to be relevant. Nothing in this paragraph shall be construed as limiting the ability of the plan sponsor to prepare and provide the bargaining parties with alternative schedules to the default schedule that establish lower or higher accrual and contribution rates than the rates otherwise described in this paragraph.

(7) AUTOMATIC EMPLOYER SURCHARGE.—

(A) IMPOSITION OF SURCHARGE. —Each employer otherwise obligated to make contributions for the initial critical year shall be obligated to pay to the plan for such year a surcharge equal to 5 percent of the contributions otherwise required under the applicable collective bargaining agreement (or other agreement pursuant to which the employer contributes). For each succeeding plan year in which the plan is in critical status for a consecutive period of years beginning with the initial critical year, the surcharge shall be 10 percent of the contributions otherwise so required.

(B) ENFORCEMENT OF SURCHARGE. —The surcharges under subparagraph (A) shall be due and payable on the same schedule as the contributions on which the surcharges are based. Any failure to make a surcharge payment shall be treated as a delinquent contribution under section 515 and shall be enforceable as such.

(C) SURCHARGE TO TERMINATE UPON COLLECTIVE BARGAINING AGREEMENT RENEGOTIATION. —The surcharge under this paragraph shall cease to be effective with respect to employees covered by a collective bargaining agreement (or other agreement pursuant to which the employer contributes), beginning on the effective date of a collective bargaining agreement (or other such agreement) that includes terms consistent with a schedule presented by the plan sponsor under paragraph (1)(B)(i), as modified under subparagraph (B) of paragraph (3).

(D) SURCHARGE NOT TO APPLY UNTIL EMPLOYER RECEIVES NOTICE. —The surcharge under this paragraph shall not apply to an employer until 30 days after the employer has been notified by the plan sponsor that the plan is in critical status and that the surcharge is in effect.

(E) SURCHARGE NOT TO GENERATE INCREASED BENEFIT ACCRUALS. —Notwithstanding any provision of a plan to the contrary, the amount of any surcharge under this paragraph shall not be the basis for any benefit accrual under the plan.

(8) BENEFIT ADJUSTMENTS.—

(A) ADJUSTABLE BENEFITS.—

(i) IN GENERAL. —Notwithstanding section 204(g), the plan sponsor shall, subject to the notice requirements in subparagraph (C), make any reductions to adjustable benefits which the plan sponsor deems appropriate, based upon the outcome of collective bargaining over the schedule or schedules provided under paragraph (1)(B)(i).

(ii) EXCEPTION FOR RETIREES. —Except in the case of adjustable benefits described in clause (iv)(III), the plan sponsor of a plan in critical status shall not reduce adjustable benefits of any participant or beneficiary whose benefit commencement date is before the date on which the plan provides notice to the participant or beneficiary under subsection (b)(3)(D) for the initial critical year.

(iii) PLAN SPONSOR FLEXIBILITY. —The plan sponsor shall include in the schedules provided to the bargaining parties an allowance for funding the benefits of participants with respect to whom contributions are not currently required to be made, and shall reduce their benefits to the extent permitted under this title and considered appropriate by the plan sponsor based on the plan's then current overall funding status.

(iv) ADJUSTABLE BENEFIT DEFINED. —For purposes of this paragraph, the term 'adjustable benefit' means—

(I) benefits, rights, and features under the plan, including post-retirement death benefits, 60-month guarantees, disability benefits not yet in pay status, and similar benefits,

(II) any early retirement benefit or retirement-type subsidy (within the meaning of section 204(g)(2)(A)) and any benefit payment option (other than the qualified joint-and survivor annuity), and

(III) benefit increases that would not be eligible for a guarantee under section 4022A on the first day of initial critical year because the increases were adopted (or, if later, took effect) less than 60 months before such first day.

(B) NORMAL RETIREMENT BENEFITS PROTECTED. —Except as provided in subparagraph (A)(iv)(III), nothing in this paragraph shall be construed to permit a plan to reduce the level of a participant's accrued benefit payable at normal retirement age.

(C) NOTICE REQUIREMENTS.—

(i) IN GENERAL. —No reduction may be made to adjustable benefits under subparagraph (A) unless notice of such reduction has been given at least 30 days before the general effective date of such reduction for all participants and beneficiaries to—

(I) plan participants and beneficiaries,

(II) each employer who has an obligation to contribute (within the meaning of section 4212(a)) under the plan, and

(III) each employee organization which, for purposes of collective bargaining, represents plan participants employed by such an employer.

(ii) CONTENT OF NOTICE. —The notice under clause (i) shall contain—

(I) sufficient information to enable participants and beneficiaries to understand the effect of any reduction on their benefits, including an estimate (on an annual or monthly basis) of any affected adjustable benefit that a participant or beneficiary would otherwise have been eligible for as of the general effective date described in clause (i), and

(II) information as to the rights and remedies of plan participants and beneficiaries as well as how to contact the Department of Labor for further information and assistance where appropriate.

(iii) FORM AND MANNER. —Any notice under clause (i)—

(I) shall be provided in a form and manner prescribed in regulations of the Secretary of the Treasury, in consultation with the Secretary,

(II) shall be written in a manner so as to be understood by the average plan participant, and

(III) may be provided in written, electronic, or other appropriate form to the extent such form is reasonably accessible to persons to whom the notice is required to be provided.

The Secretary of the Treasury shall in the regulations prescribed under subclause (I) establish a model notice that a plan sponsor may use to meet the requirements of this subparagraph.

(9) BENEFIT SUSPENSIONS FOR MULTIEMPLOYER PLANS IN CRITICAL AND DECLINING STATUS.—

(A) IN GENERAL. —Notwithstanding section 204(g) and subject to subparagraphs (B) through (I), the plan sponsor of a plan in critical and declining status may, by plan amendment, suspend benefits which the sponsor deems appropriate.

(B) SUSPENSION OF BENEFITS.—

(i) SUSPENSION OF BENEFITS DEFINED. —For purposes of this subsection, the term 'suspension of benefits' means the temporary or permanent reduction of any current or future payment obligation of the plan to any participant or beneficiary under the plan, whether or not in pay status at the time of the suspension of benefits.

(ii) LENGTH OF SUSPENSIONS. —Any suspension of benefits made under subparagraph (A) shall remain in effect until the earlier of when the plan sponsor provides benefit improvements in accordance with subparagraph (E) or the suspension of benefits expires by its own terms.

(iii) NO LIABILITY. —The plan shall not be liable for any benefit payments not made as a result of a suspension of benefits under this paragraph.

(iv) APPLICABILITY. —For purposes of this paragraph, all references to suspensions of benefits, increases in benefits, or resumptions of suspended benefits with respect to participants shall also apply with respect to benefits of beneficiaries or alternative payees of participants.

(v) RETIREE REPRESENTATIVE.—

(I) IN GENERAL. —In the case of a plan with 10,000 or more participants, not later than 60 days prior to the plan sponsor submitting an application to suspend benefits, the plan sponsor shall select a participant of the plan in pay status to act as a retiree representative. The retiree representative shall advocate for the interests of the retired and deferred vested participants and beneficiaries of the plan throughout the suspension approval process.

(II) REASONABLE EXPENSES FROM PLAN. —The plan shall provide for reasonable expenses by the retiree representative, including reasonable legal and actuarial support, commensurate with the plan's size and funded status.

(III) SPECIAL RULE RELATING TO FIDUCIARY STATUS. —Duties performed pursuant to subclause (I) shall not be subject to section 404(a). The preceding sentence shall not apply to those duties associated with an application to suspend benefits pursuant to subparagraph (G) that are performed by the retiree representative who is also a plan trustee.

(C) CONDITIONS FOR SUSPENSIONS. —The plan sponsor of a plan in critical and declining status for a plan year may suspend benefits only if the following conditions are met:

(i) Taking into account the proposed suspensions of benefits (and, if applicable, a proposed partition of the plan under section 4233), the plan actuary certifies that the plan is projected to avoid insolvency within the meaning of section 4245, assuming the suspensions of benefits continue until the suspensions of benefits expire by their own terms or if no such expiration date is set, indefinitely.

(ii) The plan sponsor determines, in a written record to be maintained throughout the period of the benefit suspension, that the plan is still projected to become insolvent unless benefits are suspended under this paragraph, although all reasonable measures to avoid insolvency have been taken (and continue to be taken during the period of the benefit suspension). In its determination, the plan sponsor may take into account factors including the following:

(I) Current and past contribution levels.

(II) Levels of benefit accruals (including any prior reductions in the rate of benefit accruals).

(III) Prior reductions (if any) of adjustable benefits.

(IV) Prior suspensions (if any) of benefits under this subsection.

(V) The impact on plan solvency of the subsidies and ancillary benefits available to active participants.

(VI) Compensation levels of active participants relative to employees in the participants' industry generally.

(VII) Competitive and other economic factors facing contributing employers.

(VIII) The impact of benefit and contribution levels on retaining active participants and bargaining groups under the plan.

(IX) The impact of past and anticipated contribution increases under the plan on employer attrition and retention levels.

(X) Measures undertaken by the plan sponsor to retain or attract contributing employers.

(D) LIMITATIONS ON SUSPENSIONS. —Any suspensions of benefits made by a plan sponsor pursuant to this paragraph shall be subject to the following limitations:

(i) The monthly benefit of any participant or beneficiary may not be reduced below 110 percent of the monthly benefit which is guaranteed by the Pension Benefit Guaranty Corporation under section 4022A on the date of the suspension.

(ii)(I) In the case of a participant or beneficiary who has attained 75 years of age as of the effective date of the suspension, not more than the applicable percentage of the maximum suspendable benefits of such participant or beneficiary may be suspended under this paragraph.

(II) For purposes of subclause (I), the maximum suspendable benefits of a participant or beneficiary is the portion of the benefits of such participant or beneficiary that would be suspended pursuant to this paragraph without regard to this clause;

(III) For purposes of subclause (I), the applicable percentage is a percentage equal to the quotient obtained by dividing—

(aa) the number of months during the period beginning with the month after the month in which occurs the effective date of the suspension and ending with the month during which the participant or beneficiary attains the age of 80, by

(bb) 60 months.

(iii) No benefits based on disability (as defined under the plan) may be suspended under this paragraph.

(iv) Any suspensions of benefits, in the aggregate (and, if applicable, considered in combination with a partition of the plan under section 4233), shall be reasonably estimated to achieve, but not materially exceed, the level that is necessary to avoid insolvency.

(v) In any case in which a suspension of benefits with respect to a plan is made in combination with a partition of the plan under section 4233, the suspension of benefits may not take effect prior to the effective date of such partition.

(vi) Any suspensions of benefits shall be equitably distributed across the participant and beneficiary population, taking into account factors, with respect to participants and beneficiaries and their benefits, that may include one or more of the following:

(I) Age and life expectancy.

(II) Length of time in pay status.

(III) Amount of benefit.

(IV) Type of benefit: survivor, normal retirement, early retirement.

(V) Extent to which participant or beneficiary is receiving a subsidized benefit.

(VI) Extent to which participant or beneficiary has received post-retirement benefit increases.

(VII) History of benefit increases and reductions.

(VIII) Years to retirement for active employees.

(IX) Any discrepancies between active and retiree benefits.

(X) Extent to which active participants are reasonably likely to withdraw support for the plan, accelerating employer withdrawals from the plan and increasing the risk of additional benefit reductions for participants in and out of pay status.

(XI) Extent to which benefits are attributed to service with an employer that failed to pay its full withdrawal liability.

(vii) In the case of a plan that includes the benefits described in clause (III), benefits suspended under this paragraph shall—

(I) first, be applied to the maximum extent permissible to benefits attributable to a participant's service for an employer which withdrew from the plan and failed to pay (or is delinquent with respect to paying) the full amount of its withdrawal liability under section 4201(b)(1) or an agreement with the plan,

(II) second, except as provided by subclause (III), be applied to all other benefits that may be suspended under this paragraph, and

(III) third, be applied to benefits under a plan that are directly attributable to a participant's service with any employer which has, prior to the date of enactment of the Multiemployer Pension Reform Act of 2014—

(aa) withdrawn from the plan in a complete withdrawal under section 4203 and has paid the full amount of the employer's withdrawal liability under section 4201(b)(1) or an agreement with the plan, and

(bb) pursuant to a collective bargaining agreement, assumed liability for providing benefits to participants and beneficiaries of the plan under a separate, single-employer plan sponsored by the employer, in an amount equal to any amount of benefits for such participants and beneficiaries reduced as a result of the financial status of the plan.

(E) BENEFIT IMPROVEMENTS.—

(i) IN GENERAL. —The plan sponsor may, in its sole discretion, provide benefit improvements while any suspension of benefits under the plan remains in effect, except that the plan sponsor may not increase the liabilities of the plan by reason of any benefit improvement for any participant or beneficiary not in pay status by the first day of the plan year for which the benefit improvement takes effect, unless—

(I) such action is accompanied by equitable benefit improvements in accordance with clause (ii) for all participants and beneficiaries whose benefit commencement dates were before the first day of the plan year for which the benefit improvement for such participant or beneficiary not in pay status took effect; and

(II) the plan actuary certifies that after taking into account such benefits improvements the plan is projected to avoid insolvency indefinitely under section 4245.

(ii) EQUITABLE DISTRIBUTION OF BENEFIT IMPROVEMENTS.—

(I) LIMITATION. —The projected value of the total liabilities for benefit improvements for participants and beneficiaries not in pay status by the date of the first day of the plan year in which the benefit improvements are proposed to take effect, as determined as of such date, may not exceed the projected value of the liabilities arising from benefit improvements for participants and beneficiaries with benefit commencement dates prior to the first day of such plan year, as so determined.

(II) EQUITABLE DISTRIBUTION OF BENEFITS. —The plan sponsor shall equitably distribute any increase in total liabilities for benefit improvements in clause (i) to some or all of the participants and beneficiaries whose benefit commencement date is before the date of the first day of the plan year in which the benefit improvements are proposed to take effect, taking into account the relevant factors described in subparagraph (D)(vi) and the extent to which the benefits of the participants and beneficiaries were suspended.

(iii) SPECIAL RULE FOR RESUMPTIONS OF BENEFITS ONLY FOR PARTICIPANTS IN PAY STATUS. —The plan sponsor may increase liabilities of the plan through a resumption of benefits for participants and beneficiaries in pay status only if the plan sponsor equitably distributes the value of resumed benefits to some or all of the participants and beneficiaries in pay status, taking into account the relevant factors described in subparagraph (D)(vi).

(iv) SPECIAL RULE FOR CERTAIN BENEFIT INCREASES. —This subparagraph shall not apply to a resumption of suspended benefits or plan amendment which increases liabilities with respect to participants and beneficiaries not in pay status by the first day of the plan year in which the benefit improvements took effect which—

(I) the Secretary of the Treasury, in consultation with the Pension Benefit Guaranty Corporation and the Secretary of Labor, determines to be reasonable and which provides for only de minimis increases in the liabilities of the plan, or

(II) is required as a condition of qualification under part I of subchapter D of chapter 1 of subtitle A of the Internal Revenue Code of 1986 or to comply with other applicable law, as determined by the Secretary of the Treasury.

(v) ADDITIONAL LIMITATIONS. —Except for resumptions of suspended benefits described in clause (iii), the limitations on benefit improvements while a suspension of benefits is in effect under this paragraph shall be in addition to any other applicable limitations on increases in benefits imposed on a plan.

(vi) DEFINITION OF BENEFIT IMPROVEMENT. —For purposes of this subparagraph, the term 'benefit improvement' means, with respect to a plan, a resumption of suspended benefits, an increase in benefits, an increase in the rate at which benefits accrue, or an increase in the rate at which benefits become nonforfeitable under the plan.

(F) NOTICE REQUIREMENTS.—

(i) IN GENERAL. —No suspension of benefits may be made pursuant to this paragraph unless notice of such proposed suspension has been given by the plan sponsor concurrently with an application for approval of such suspension submitted under subparagraph (G) to the Secretary of the Treasury to—

(I) such plan participants and beneficiaries who may be contacted by reasonable efforts,

(II) each employer who has an obligation to contribute (within the meaning of section 4212(a)) under the plan, and

(III) each employee organization which, for purposes of collective bargaining, represents plan participants employed by such an employer.

(ii) CONTENT OF NOTICE. —The notice under clause (i) shall contain—

(I) sufficient information to enable participants and beneficiaries to understand the effect of any suspensions of benefits, including an individualized estimate (on an annual or monthly basis) of such effect on each participant or beneficiary,

(II) a description of the factors considered by the plan sponsor in designing the benefit suspensions,

(III) a statement that the application for approval of any suspension of benefits shall be available on the website of the Department of the Treasury and that comments on such application will be accepted,

(IV) information as to the rights and remedies of plan participants and beneficiaries,

(V) if applicable, a statement describing the appointment of a retiree representative, the date of appointment of such representative, identifying information about the retiree representative (including whether the representative is a plan trustee), and how to contact such representative, and

(VI) information on how to contact the Department of the Treasury for further information and assistance where appropriate.

(iii) FORM AND MANNER. —Any notice under clause (i)—

(I) shall be provided in a form and manner prescribed in guidance by the Secretary of the Treasury, in consultation with the Pension Benefit Guaranty Corporation and the Secretary of Labor, notwithstanding any other provision of law,

(II) shall be written in a manner so as to be understood by the average plan participant, and

(III) may be provided in written, electronic, or other appropriate form to the extent such form is reasonably accessible to persons to whom the notice is required to be provided.

(iv) OTHER NOTICE REQUIREMENT. —Any notice provided under clause (i) shall fulfill the requirement for notice of a significant reduction in benefits described in section 204(h).

(v) MODEL NOTICE. —The Secretary of the Treasury, in consultation with the Pension Benefit Guaranty Corporation and the Secretary of Labor, shall in the guidance prescribed under clause (iii)(I) establish a model notice that a plan sponsor may use to meet the requirements of this subparagraph.

(G) APPROVAL PROCESS BY THE SECRETARY OF THE TREASURY IN CONSULTATION WITH THE PENSION BENEFIT GUARANTY CORPORATION AND THE SECRETARY OF LABOR.—

(i) IN GENERAL. —The plan sponsor of a plan in critical and declining status for a plan year that seeks to suspend benefits must submit an application to the Secretary of the Treasury for approval of the suspensions of benefits. If the plan sponsor submits an application for approval of the suspensions, the Secretary of the Treasury, in consultation with the Pension Benefit Guaranty Corporation and the Secretary of Labor, shall approve the application upon finding that the plan is eligible for the suspensions and has satisfied the criteria of subparagraphs (C), (D), (E), and (F).

(ii) SOLICITATION OF COMMENTS. —Not later than 30 days after receipt of the application under clause (i), the Secretary of the Treasury, in consultation with the Pension Benefit Guaranty Corporation and the Secretary of Labor, shall publish a notice in the Federal Register soliciting comments from contributing employers, employee organizations, and participants and beneficiaries of the plan for which an application was made and other interested parties. The application for approval of the suspension of benefits shall be published on the website of the Secretary of the Treasury.

(iii) REQUIRED ACTION; DEEMED APPROVAL. —The Secretary of the Treasury, in consultation with the Pension Benefit Guaranty Corporation and the Secretary of Labor, shall approve or deny any application for suspensions of benefits under this paragraph within 225 days after the submission of such application. An application for suspension of benefits shall be deemed approved unless, within such 225 days, the Secretary of the Treasury notifies the plan sponsor that it has failed to satisfy one or more of the criteria described in this paragraph. If the Secretary of the Treasury, in consultation with the Pension Benefit Guaranty Corporation and the Secretary of Labor, rejects a plan sponsor's application, the Secretary of the Treasury shall provide notice to the plan sponsor detailing the specific reasons for the rejection, including reference to the specific requirement not satisfied. Approval or denial by the Secretary of the Treasury of an application shall be treated as a final agency action for purposes of section 704 of title 5, United States Code.

(iv) AGENCY REVIEW. —In evaluating whether the plan sponsor has met the criteria specified in clause (ii) of subparagraph (C), the Secretary of the Treasury, in consultation with the Pension Benefit Guaranty Corporation and the Secretary of Labor, shall review the plan sponsor's consideration of factors under such clause.

(v) STANDARD FOR ACCEPTING PLAN SPONSOR DETERMINATIONS. —In evaluating the plan sponsor's application, the Secretary of the Treasury shall accept the plan sponsor's determinations unless it concludes, in consultation with the Pension Benefit Guaranty Corporation and the Secretary of Labor, that the plan sponsor's determinations were clearly erroneous.

(H) PARTICIPANT RATIFICATION PROCESS.—

(i) IN GENERAL. —No suspension of benefits may take effect pursuant to this paragraph prior to a vote of the participants of the plan with respect to the suspension.

(ii) ADMINISTRATION OF VOTE. —Not later than 30 days after approval of the suspension by the Secretary of the Treasury, in consultation with the Pension Benefit Guaranty Corporation and the Secretary of Labor, under subparagraph (G), the Secretary of the Treasury, in consultation with the Pension Benefit Guaranty Corporation and the Secretary of Labor, shall administer a vote of participants and beneficiaries of the plan. Except as provided in clause (v), the suspension shall go into effect following the vote unless a majority of all participants and beneficiaries of the plan vote to reject the suspension. The plan sponsor may submit a new suspension application to the Secretary of the Treasury for approval in any case in which a suspension is prohibited from taking effect pursuant to a vote under this subparagraph.

(iii) BALLOTS. —The plan sponsor shall provide a ballot for the vote (subject to approval by the Secretary of the Treasury, in consultation with the Pension Benefit Guaranty Corporation and the Secretary of Labor) that includes the following:

(I) A statement from the plan sponsor in support of the suspension.

(II) A statement in opposition to the suspension compiled from comments received pursuant to subparagraph (G)(ii).

(III) A statement that the suspension has been approved by the Secretary of the Treasury, in consultation with the Pension Benefit Guaranty Corporation and the Secretary of Labor.

(IV) A statement that the plan sponsor has determined that the plan will become insolvent unless the suspension takes effect.

(V) A statement that insolvency of the plan could result in benefits lower than benefits paid under the suspension.

(VI) A statement that insolvency of the Pension Benefit Guaranty Corporation would result in benefits lower than benefits paid in the case of plan insolvency.

(iv) COMMUNICATION BY PLAN SPONSOR. —It is the sense of Congress that, depending on the size and resources of the plan and geographic distribution of the plan's participants, the plan sponsor should take such steps as may be necessary to inform participants about proposed benefit suspensions through in-person meetings, telephone or internet-based communications, mailed information, or by other means.

(v) SYSTEMICALLY IMPORTANT PLANS.—

(I) IN GENERAL. —Not later than 14 days after a vote under this subparagraph rejecting a suspension, the Secretary of the Treasury, in consultation with the Pension Benefit Guaranty Corporation and the Secretary of Labor, shall determine whether the plan is a systemically important plan. If the Secretary of the Treasury, in consultation with the Pension Benefit Guaranty Corporation and the Secretary of Labor, determines that the plan is a systemically important plan, not later than the end of the 90-day period beginning on the date the results of the vote are certified, the Secretary of the Treasury shall, notwithstanding such adverse vote—

(aa) permit the implementation of the suspension proposed by the plan sponsor; or

(bb) permit the implementation of a modification by the Secretary of the Treasury, in consultation with the Pension Benefit Guaranty Corporation and the Secretary of Labor, of such suspension (so long as the plan is projected to avoid insolvency within the meaning of section 4245 under such modification).

(II) RECOMMENDATIONS. —Not later than 30 days after a determination by the Secretary of the Treasury, in consultation with the Pension Benefit Guaranty Corporation and the Secretary of Labor, that the plan is systemically important, the Participant and Plan Sponsor Advocate selected under section 4004 may submit recommendations to the Secretary of the Treasury with respect to the suspension or any revisions to the suspension.

(III) SYSTEMICALLY IMPORTANT PLAN DEFINED.—

(aa) IN GENERAL. —For purposes of this subparagraph, a systemically important plan is a plan with respect to which the Pension Benefit Guaranty Corporation projects the present value of projected financial assistance payments exceeds $1,000,000,000 if suspensions are not implemented.

(bb) INDEXING. —For calendar years beginning after 2015, there shall be substituted for the dollar amount specified in item (aa) an amount equal to the product of such dollar amount and a fraction, the numerator of which is the contribution and benefit base (determined under section 230 of the Social Security Act) for the preceding calendar year and the denominator of which is such contribution and benefit base for calendar year 2014. If the amount otherwise determined under this item is not a multiple of $1,000,000, such amount shall be rounded to the next lowest multiple of $1,000,000.

(vi) FINAL AUTHORIZATION TO SUSPEND. —In any case in which a suspension goes into effect following a vote pursuant to clause (ii) (or following a determination under clause (v) that the plan is a systemically important plan), the Secretary of the Treasury, in consultation with the Pension Benefit Guaranty Corporation and the Secretary of Labor, shall issue a final authorization to suspend with respect to the suspension not later than 7 days after such vote (or, in the case of a suspension that goes into effect under clause (v), at a time sufficient to allow the implementation of the suspension prior to the end of the 90-day period described in clause (v)(I)).

(I) JUDICIAL REVIEW.—

(i) DENIAL OF APPLICATION. —An action by the plan sponsor challenging the denial of an application for suspension of benefits by the Secretary of the Treasury, in consultation with the Pension Benefit Guaranty Corporation and the Secretary of Labor, may only be brought following such denial.

(ii) APPROVAL OF SUSPENSION OF BENEFITS.—

(I) TIMING OF ACTION. —An action challenging a suspension of benefits under this paragraph may only be brought following a final authorization to suspend by the Secretary of the Treasury, in consultation with the Pension Benefit Guaranty Corporation and the Secretary of Labor, under subparagraph (H)(vi).

(II) STANDARDS OF REVIEW.—

(aa) IN GENERAL. —A court shall review an action challenging a suspension of benefits under this paragraph in accordance with section 706 of title 5, United States Code.

(bb) TEMPORARY INJUNCTION. —A court reviewing an action challenging a suspension of benefits under this paragraph may not grant a temporary injunction with respect to such suspension unless the court finds a clear and convincing likelihood that the plaintiff will prevail on the merits of the case.

(iii) RESTRICTED CAUSE OF ACTION. —A participant or beneficiary affected by a benefit suspension under this paragraph shall not have a cause of action under this title.

(iv) LIMITATION ON ACTION TO SUSPEND BENEFITS. —No action challenging a suspension of benefits following the final authorization to suspend or the denial of an application for suspension of benefits pursuant to this paragraph may be brought after one year after the earliest date on which the plaintiff acquired or should have acquired actual knowledge of the existence of such cause of action.

(J) SPECIAL RULE FOR EMERGENCE FROM CRITICAL STATUS. —A plan certified to be in critical and declining status pursuant to projections made under subsection (b)(3) for which a suspension of benefits has been made by the plan sponsor pursuant to this paragraph shall not emerge from critical status under paragraph (4)(B), until such time as—

(i) the plan is no longer certified to be in critical or endangered status under paragraphs (1) and (2) of subsection (b), and

(ii) the plan is projected to avoid insolvency under section 4245.

Act Sec. 305. (f) RULES FOR OPERATION OF PLAN DURING ADOPTION AND REHABILITATION PERIOD.—

(1) COMPLIANCE WITH REHABILITATION PLAN.—

(A) IN GENERAL. —A plan may not be amended after the date of the adoption of a rehabilitation plan under subsection (e) so as to be inconsistent with the rehabilitation plan.

(B) SPECIAL RULES FOR BENEFIT INCREASES. —A plan may not be amended after the date of the adoption of a rehabilitation plan under subsection (e) so as to increase benefits, including future benefit accruals, unless the plan actuary certifies that such increase is paid for out of additional contributions not contemplated by the rehabilitation plan, and, after taking into account the benefit increase, the multiemployer plan still is reasonably expected to emerge from critical status by the end of the rehabilitation period on the schedule contemplated in the rehabilitation plan.

(2) RESTRICTION ON LUMP SUMS AND SIMILAR BENEFITS.—

(A) IN GENERAL. —Effective on the date the notice of certification of the plan's critical status for the initial critical year under subsection (b)(3)(D) is sent, and notwithstanding section 204(g), the plan shall not pay—

(i) any payment, in excess of the monthly amount paid under a single life annuity (plus any social security supplements described in the last sentence of section 204(b)(1)(G)) to a participant or beneficiary whose annuity starting date (as defined in section 205(h)(2)) occurs after the date such notice is sent,

(ii) any payment for the purchase of an irrevocable commitment from an insurer to pay benefits, and

(iii) any other payment specified by the Secretary of the Treasury by regulations.

(B) EXCEPTION. —Subparagraph (A) shall not apply to a benefit which under section 203(e) may be immediately distributed without the consent of the participant or to any makeup payment in the case of a retroactive annuity starting date or any similar payment of benefits owed with respect to a prior period.

(3) SPECIAL RULES FOR PLAN ADOPTION PERIOD. —During the period beginning on the date of the certification under subsection (b)(3)(A) for the initial critical year and ending on the date of the adoption of a rehabilitation plan—

(A) the plan sponsor may not accept a collective bargaining agreement or participation agreement with respect to the multiemployer plan that provides for—

(i) a reduction in the level of contributions for any participants,

(ii) a suspension of contributions with respect to any period of service, or

(iii) any new direct or indirect exclusion of younger or newly hired employees from plan participation, and

(B) no amendment of the plan which increases the liabilities of the plan by reason of any increase in benefits, any change in the accrual of benefits, or any change in the rate at which benefits become nonforfeitable under the plan may be adopted unless the amendment is required as a condition of qualification under part I of subchapter D of chapter 1 of the Internal Revenue Code of 1986 or to comply with other applicable law.

Act Sec. 305 (g) ADJUSTMENTS DISREGARDED IN WITHDRAWAL LIABILITY DETERMINATION.—

(1) BENEFIT REDUCTION. —Any benefit reductions under subsection (e)(8) or (f) or benefit reductions or suspensions while in critical and declining status under subsection (e)(9)), unless the withdrawal occurs more than ten years after the effective date of a benefit suspension by a plan in critical and declining status, shall be disregarded in determining a plan's unfunded vested benefits for purposes of determining an employer's withdrawal liability under section 4201.

(2) SURCHARGES. —Any surcharges under subsection (e)(7) shall be disregarded in determining the allocation of unfunded vested benefits to an employer under section 4211 and in determining the highest contribution rate under section 4219(c), except for purposes of determining the unfunded vested benefits attributable to an employer under section 4211(c)(4) or a comparable method approved under section 4211(c)(5).

(3) CONTRIBUTION INCREASES REQUIRED BY FUNDING IMPROVEMENT OR REHABILITATION PLAN.—

(A) IN GENERAL. —Any increase in the contribution rate (or other increase in contribution requirements unless due to increased levels of work, employment, or periods for which compensation is provided) that is required or made in order to enable the plan to meet the requirement of the funding improvement plan or rehabilitation plan shall be disregarded in determining the allocation of unfunded vested benefits to an employer under section 4211 and in determining the highest contribution rate under section 4219(c), except for purposes of determining the unfunded vested benefits attributable to an employer under section 4211(c)(4) or a comparable method approved under section 4211(c)(5).

(B) SPECIAL RULES. —For purposes of this paragraph, any increase in the contribution rate (or other increase in contribution requirements) shall be deemed to be required or made in order to enable the plan to meet the requirement of the funding improvement plan or rehabilitation plan except for increases in contribution requirements due to increased levels of work, employment, or periods for which compensation is provided or additional contributions are used to provide an increase in benefits, including an increase in future benefit accruals, permitted by subsection (d)(1)(B) or (f)(1)(B).

(4) EMERGENCE FROM ENDANGERED OR CRITICAL STATUS. —In the case of increases in the contribution rate (or other increases in contribution requirements unless due to increased levels of work, employment, or periods for which compensation is provided) disregarded pursuant to paragraph (3), this subsection shall cease to apply as of the expiration date of the collective bargaining agreement in effect when the plan emerges from endangered or critical status. Notwithstanding the preceding sentence, once the plan emerges from critical or endangered status, increases in the contribution rate disregarded pursuant to paragraph (3) shall continue to be disregarded in determining the highest contribution rate under section 4219(c) for plan years during which the plan was in endangered or critical status.

(5) SIMPLIFIED CALCULATIONS. —The Pension Benefit Guaranty Corporation shall prescribe simplified methods for the application of this subsection in determining withdrawal liability and payment amounts under section 4219(c).

Act Sec. 305. (h) EXPEDITED RESOLUTION OF PLAN SPONSOR DECISIONS.—If, within 60 days of the due date for adoption of a funding improvement plan under subsection (c) or a rehabilitation plan under subsection (e), the plan sponsor of a plan in endangered status or a plan in critical status has not agreed on a funding improvement plan or rehabilitation plan, then any member of the board or group that constitutes the plan sponsor may require that the plan sponsor enter into an expedited dispute resolution procedure for the development and adoption of a funding improvement plan or rehabilitation plan.

Act Sec. 305. (i) NONBARGAINED PARTICIPATION.—

(1) BOTH BARGAINED AND NONBARGAINED EMPLOYEE-PARTICIPANTS. —In the case of an employer that contributes to a multiemployer plan with respect to both employees who are covered by one or more collective bargaining agreements and employees who are not so covered, if the plan is in endangered status or in critical status, benefits of and contributions for the nonbargained employees, including surcharges on those contributions, shall be determined as if those

nonbargained employees were covered under the first to expire of the employer's collective bargaining agreements in effect when the plan entered endangered or critical status.

(2) NONBARGAINED EMPLOYEES ONLY. —In the case of an employer that contributes to a multiemployer plan only with respect to employees who are not covered by a collective bargaining agreement, this section shall be applied as if the employer were the bargaining party, and its participation agreement with the plan were a collective bargaining agreement with a term ending on the first day of the plan year beginning after the employer is provided the schedule or schedules described in subsections (c) and (e).

Act Sec. 305. (j) DEFINITIONS; ACTUARIAL METHOD.—For purposes of this section—

(1) BARGAINING PARTY. The term 'bargaining party' means—

(A) (i) except as provided in clause (ii), an employer who has an obligation to contribute under the plan; or

(ii) in the case of a plan described under section 404(c) of the Internal Revenue Code of 1986, or a continuation of such a plan, the association of employers that is the employer settlor of the plan; and

(B) an employee organization which, for purposes of collective bargaining, represents plan participants employed by an employer who has an obligation to contribute under the plan.

(2) FUNDED PERCENTAGE. —The term 'funded percentage' means the percentage equal to a fraction—

(A) the numerator of which is the value of the plan's assets, as determined under section 304(c)(2), and

(B) the denominator of which is the accrued liability of the plan, determined using actuarial assumptions described in section 304(c)(3).

(3) ACCUMULATED FUNDING DEFICIENCY. —The term 'accumulated funding deficiency' has the meaning given such term in section 304(a).

(4) ACTIVE PARTICIPANT. —The term 'active participant' means, in connection with a multiemployer plan, a participant who is in covered service under the plan.

(5) INACTIVE PARTICIPANT. —The term 'inactive participant' means, in connection with a multiemployer plan, a participant, or the beneficiary or alternate payee of a participant, who—

(A) is not in covered service under the plan, and

(B) is in pay status under the plan or has a nonforfeitable right to benefits under the plan.

(6) PAY STATUS. —A person is in pay status under a multiemployer plan if—

(A) at any time during the current plan year, such person is a participant or beneficiary under the plan and is paid an early, late, normal, or disability retirement benefit under the plan (or a death benefit under the plan related to a retirement benefit), or

(B) to the extent provided in regulations of the Secretary of the Treasury, such person is entitled to such a benefit under the plan.

(7) OBLIGATION TO CONTRIBUTE. —The term 'obligation to contribute' has the meaning given such term under section 4212(a).

(8) ACTUARIAL METHOD. —Notwithstanding any other provision of this section, the actuary's determinations with respect to a plan's normal cost, actuarial accrued liability, and improvements in a plan's funded percentage under this section shall be based upon the unit credit funding method (whether or not that method is used for the plan's actuarial valuation).

(9) PLAN SPONSOR. —In the case of a plan described under section 404(c) of the Internal Revenue Code of 1986, or a continuation of such a plan, the term 'plan sponsor' means the bargaining parties described under paragraph (1).

(10) BENEFIT COMMENCEMENT DATE. —The term 'benefit commencement date' means the annuity starting date (or in the case of a retroactive annuity starting date, the date on which benefit payments begin).

Amendments

P.L. 113-235, § 201(a)(1)(A)-(C), Div. O:

Amended ERISA Sec. 305(a) by striking "and" in paragraph (1)(B) at the end; by striking the period at the end and inserting ", and" in paragraph 2(B); and by adding at the end a new paragraph (3).

The amendments take effect December 16, 2014.

P.L. 113-235, § 102(a)(1), Div. O:

Amended ERISA Sec. 305(b) by adding at the end a new paragraph (4).

Amendments are effective with respect to plan years beginning after December 31, 2014.

P.L. 113-235, § 102(a)(2)(A), Div. O:

Amended ERISA Sec. 305(b)(3)(A)(i) by striking ", and" and inserting "or for any of the succeeding 5 plan years, and".

Amendments are effective with respect to plan years beginning after December 31, 2014.

P.L. 113-235, § 102(a)(2)(B)(i)-(ii), Div. O:

Amended ERISA Sec. 305(b)(3)(B) by striking "In making the determinations" in clause (i) and inserting "Except as provided in clause (iv), in making the determinations"; and by adding at the end a new clause (iv).

Amendments are effective with respect to plan years beginning after December 31, 2014.

P.L. 113-235, § 102(a)(3)(A)(i)-(ii), Div. O:

Amended ERISA Sec. 305(b)(3)(D)(i) by inserting "or in which a plan sponsor elects to be in critical status for a plan year under paragraph (4)" after "for a plan year"; and by adding at the end a new sentence.

Amendments are effective with respect to plan years beginning after December 31, 2014.

P.L. 113-235, § 102(a)(3)(B), Div. O:

Amended ERISA Sec. 305(b)(3)(D) by adding at the end a new clause (iv).

Amendments are effective with respect to plan years beginning after December 31, 2014.

P.L. 113-235, § 104(a)(1)(A)-(B), Div. O:

Amended ERISA Sec. 305(b), as amended by Act Sec. 102, Div. O, by striking "the plan is not in critical status for the plan year" in paragraph (1) and inserting "the plan is

not in critical status for the plan year and is not described in paragraph (5),"; and by adding at the end a new paragraph (5).

Amendments are effective with respect to plan years beginning after December 31, 2014.

P.L. 113-235, § 104(a)(2)(A)-(B), Div. O:

Amended ERISA Sec. 305(b)(3)(D) by redesignating clause (iii) and clause (iv) (as added by Act Sec. 102(a)(3)(B)) as clauses (iv) and (v), respectively; and by inserting after clause (ii) a new clause (iii).

Amendments are effective with respect to plan years beginning after December 31, 2014.

P.L. 113-235, § 104(a)(2)(C), Div. O:

Amended ERISA Sec. 305(b)(3)(D)(iv) (as redesignated by Act Sec. 104(a)(2)(A)), by striking "clause (ii)" and inserting "clauses (ii) and (iii)."

Amendments are effective with respect to plan years beginning after December 31, 2014.

P.L. 113-235, § 104(a)(3), Div. O:

Amended ERISA Sec. 305(b)(3)(A)(i) by inserting ", or would be in endangered status for such plan year but for paragraph (5)," after "endangered status for a plan year". [Note: ERISA Sec. 305(b)(3)(A)(i) does not contain the text "endangered status for a plan year," therefore, this amendment cannot be made.—CCH].

Amendments are effective with respect to plan years beginning after December 31, 2014.

P.L. 113-235, § 201(a)(2), Div. O:

Amended ERISA Sec. 305(b), as amended by Act Secs. 102 and 104, by adding at the end a new paragraph (6).

The amendments take effect December 16, 2014.

P.L. 113-235, § 201(a)(3)(A)-(B), Div. O:

Amended ERISA Sec. 305(b)(3)(A)(i) by striking "and whether" and inserting ", whether", and by inserting ", and whether or not the plan is or will be in critical and declining status for such plan year" before ", and" at the end.

The amendments take effect December 16, 2014.

P.L. 113-235, § 201(a)(5), Div. O:

Amended ERISA Sec. 305(b)(3)(B) by adding at the end a new clause (iv)[(v)].

The amendments take effect December 16, 2014.

P.L. 113-235, § 105(a)(1)-(2), Div. O:

Amended ERISA Sec. 305(c)(3)(A) by striking "of such period" in clause (i)(I) and inserting "of the first plan year for which the plan is certified to be in endangered status pursuant to paragraph (b)(3)"; and by striking "any plan year" in clause (ii) and inserting "the last plan year".

Amendments are effective with respect to plan years beginning after December 31, 2014.

P.L. 113-235, § 107(a)(1), Div. O:

Amended ERISA Sec. 305(c)(7). Prior to amendment, ERISA Sec. 305(c)(7) read as follows:

(7)Imposition of default schedule where failure to adopt funding improvement plan.—

(A)In general.—

—If—

(i)a collective bargaining agreement providing for contributions under a multiemployer plan that was in effect at the time the plan entered endangered status expires, and

(ii) after receiving one or more schedules from the plan sponsor under paragraph (1)(B), the bargaining parties with respect to such agreement fail to adopt a contribution schedule with terms consistent with the funding improvement plan and a schedule from the plan sponsor,

the plan sponsor shall implement the schedule described in paragraph (1)(B)(i)(I) beginning on the date specified in subparagraph (B).

(B) Date of implementation.—

—The date specified in this subparagraph is the date which is 180 days after the date on which the collective bargaining agreement described in subparagraph (A) expires.

(C) Failure to make scheduled contributions.—

—Any failure to make a contribution under a schedule of contribution rates provided under this paragraph shall be treated as a delinquent contribution under section 515 and shall be enforceable as such.

—For purposes of this section, the term 'funding plan adoption period' means the period beginning on the date of the certification under subsection (b)(3)(A) for the initial determination year and ending on the day before the first day of the funding improvement period.

Amendments are effective with respect to plan years beginning after December 31, 2014.

P.L. 113-235, § 106(a), Div. O:

Amended ERISA Sec. 305(d). Prior to amendment, ERISA Sec. 305(d) read as follows:

(d) Rules for operation of plan during adoption and improvement periods.—

(1)Special rules for plan adoption period.—

—During the funding plan adoption period—

(A) the plan sponsor may not accept a collective bargaining agreement or participation agreement with respect to the multiemployer plan that provides for—

(i) a reduction in the level of contributions for any participants,

(ii) a suspension of contributions with respect to any period of service, or

(iii) any new direct or indirect exclusion of younger or newly hired employees from plan participation,

(B) no amendment of the plan which increases the liabilities of the plan by reason of any increase in benefits, any change in the accrual of benefits, or any change in the rate at which benefits become nonforfeitable under the plan may be adopted unless the amendment is required as a condition of qualification under part I of subchapter D of chapter 1 of the Internal Revenue Code of 1986 or to comply with other applicable law, and

(C) in the case of a plan in seriously endangered status, the plan sponsor shall take all reasonable actions which are consistent with the terms of the plan and applicable law and which are expected, based on reasonable assumptions, to achieve—

(i) an increase in the plan's funded percentage, and

(ii) postponement of an accumulated funding deficiency for at least 1 additional plan year.

Actions under subparagraph (C) include applications for extensions of amortization periods under section 304(d), use of the shortfall funding method in making funding standard account computations, amendments to the plan's benefit structure, reductions in future benefit accruals, and other reasonable actions consistent with the terms of the plan and applicable law.

(2) Compliance with funding improvement plan.—

(A) In general.—

—A plan may not be amended after the date of the adoption of a funding improvement plan so as to be inconsistent with the funding improvement plan.

(B) No reduction in contributions.—

—A plan sponsor may not during any funding improvement period accept a collective bargaining agreement or participation agreement with respect to the multiemployer plan that provides for—

(i) a reduction in the level of contributions for any participants,

(ii)

a suspension of contributions with respect to any period of service, or

(iii) any new direct or indirect exclusion of younger or newly hired employees from plan participation.

(C) Special rules for benefit increases.—

—A plan may not be amended after the date of the adoption of a funding improvement plan so as to increase benefits, including future benefit accruals, unless the plan actuary certifies that the benefit increase is consistent with the funding improvement

plan and is paid for out of contributions not required by the funding improvement plan to meet the applicable benchmark in accordance with the schedule contemplated in the funding improvement plan.

Amendments are effective with respect to plan years beginning after December 31, 2014.

P.L. 113-235, § 103(a), Div. O:

Amended ERISA Sec. 305(e)(4)(B). Prior to amendment, ERISA Sec. 305(e)(4)(B) read as follows:

(B)Emergence.—

—A plan in critical status shall remain in such status until a plan year for which the plan actuary certifies, in accordance with subsection (b)(3)(A), that the plan is not projected to have an accumulated funding deficiency for the plan year or any of the 9 succeeding plan years, without regard to the use of the shortfall method but taking into account any extension of amortization periods under section 304(d).

Amendments are effective with respect to plan years beginning after December 31, 2014.

P.L. 113-235, § 107(a)(2), Div. O:

Amended ERISA Sec. 305(e)(3)(C). Prior to amendment, ERISA Sec. 305(e)(3)(C) read as follows:

(C)Imposition of default schedule where failure to adopt rehabilitation plan.—

(i)In general.——If—

(I) a collective bargaining agreement providing for contributions under a multiemployer plan that was in effect at the time the plan entered critical status expires, and

(II) after receiving one or more schedules from the plan sponsor under paragraph (1)(B), the bargaining parties with respect to such agreement fail to adopt a contribution schedule with terms consistent with the rehabilitation plan and a schedule from the plan sponsor under paragraph (1)(B)(i),

the plan sponsor shall implement the default schedule described in the last sentence of paragraph (1) beginning on the date specified in clause (ii).

(ii)Date of implementation.—

—The date specified in this clause is the date which is 180 days after the date on which the collective bargaining agreement described in clause (i) expires.

(iii)Failure to make scheduled contributions.—

—Any failure to make a contribution under a schedule of contribution rates provided under this subsection shall be treated as a delinquent contribution under section 515 and shall be enforceable as such.

Amendments are effective with respect to plan years beginning after December 31, 2014.

P.L. 113-235, § 109(a)(1), Div. O:

Amended ERISA Sec. 305(e) by striking paragraph (9). Prior to being stricken, ERISA Sec. 305(e)(9) read as follows:

(9)Adjustments disregarded in withdrawal liability determination.—

(A)Benefit reductions.—

—Any benefit reductions under this subsection shall be disregarded in determining a plan's unfunded vested benefits for purposes of determining an employer's withdrawal liability under section 4201.

(B)Surcharges.—

—Any surcharges under paragraph (7) shall be disregarded in determining the allocation of unfunded vested benefits to an employer under section 4211, except for purposes of determining the unfunded vested benefits attributable to an employer under section 4211(c)(4) or a comparable method approved under section 4211(c)(5).

(C)Simplified calculations.—

—The Pension Benefit Guaranty Corporation shall prescribe simplified methods for the application of this paragraph in determining withdrawal liability.

Amendments are effective for benefit reductions and increases in the contribution rate or other required contribution increases that go into effect during plan years beginning after December 31, 2014 and to surcharges the obligation for which accrue on or after December 31, 2014.

P.L. 113-235, § 201(a)(6), Div. O:

Amended ERISA Sec. 305(e) (as amended by Act Sec. 109(a)(1), Division O) by inserting after paragraph (8) a new paragraph (9).

Amendments are effective December 16, 2014.

P.L. 113-235, § 109(a)(2)(A)-(B), Div. O:

Amended ERISA Sec. 305(f) by striking paragraph (3) and redesignating paragraph (4) as paragraph (3); and in paragraph (4) (as redesignated by Act Sec. 109(a)(2)(A)), striking "During the rehabilitation plan adoption period—" and inserting "During the period beginning on the date of the certification under subsection (b)(3)(A) for the initial critical year and ending on the date of the adoption of a rehabilitation plan—". Prior to being stricken, ERISA Sec. 305(f)(3) read as follows:

(3)Adjustments disregarded in withdrawal liability determination.—

—Any benefit reductions under this subsection shall be disregarded in determining a plan's unfunded vested benefits for purposes of determining an employer's withdrawal liability under section 4201.

Amendments are effective for benefit reductions and increases in the contribution rate or other required contribution increases that go into effect during plan years beginning after December 31, 2014 and to surcharges the obligation for which accrue on or after December 31, 2014.

P.L. 113-235, § 109(a)(3)-(4), Div. O:

Amended ERISA Sec. 305 by redesignating subsections (g), (h), and (i) as subsections (h), (i), and (j), respectively; and by inserting after subsection (f) a new subsection (g).

Amendments are effective for benefit reductions and increases in the contribution rate or other required contribution increases that go into effect during plan years beginning after December 31, 2014 and to surcharges the obligation for which accrue on or after December 31, 2014.

P.L. 113-235, § 201(a)(7), Div. O:

Amended ERISA Sec. 305(g)(1), as added by Act Sec. 109(a)(4), by inserting ", or benefit reductions or suspensions while in critical and declining status under subsection (e)(9)), unless the withdrawal occurs more than ten years after the effective date of a benefit suspension by a plan in critical and declining status," after "benefit reductions under subsection (e)(8) or (f)".

Amendments are effective December 16, 2014.

P.L. 110-458, § 102(b)(1)(B):

Amended ERISA Sec. 305(b)(3)(C) by striking "section 101(b)(4)" and inserting "section 101(b)(1)".

The above amendment is effective as if included in the provision of the Pension Protection Act of 2006 (P.L. 109-280) to which the amendment relates [effective with respect to plan years beginning after 2007.-CCH]

P.L. 110-458, § 102(b)(1)(C):

Amended ERISA Sec. 305(b)(3)(D) by striking "The Secretary" in clause (iii) and inserting "The Secretary of the Treasury, in consultation with the Secretary".

The above amendment is effective as if included in the provision of the Pension Protection Act of 2006 (P.L. 109-280) to which the amendment relates [effective with respect to plan years beginning after 2007.-CCH]

P.L. 110-458, § 102(b)(1)(D)(i):

Amended ERISA Sec. 305(c)(7)(A)(ii) by striking "to agree on" and all that follows in subparagraph (A)(ii) and inserting "to adopt a contribution schedule with terms consistent with the funding improvement plan and a schedule from the plan sponsor,".

The above amendment is effective as if included in the provision of the Pension Protection Act of 2006 (P.L. 109-280) to which the amendment relates [effective with respect to plan years beginning after 2007.-CCH]

P.L. 110-458, § 102(b)(1)(D)(ii):

Amended ERISA Sec. 305(c)(7)(B) by striking subparagraph (B) and inserting a new subparagraph (B) to read as above.

The above amendment is effective as if included in the provision of the Pension Protection Act of 2006 (P.L. 109-280) to which the amendment relates [effective with respect to plan years beginning after 2007.-CCH]

P.L. 110-458, § 102(b)(1)(D)(iii):

Amended ERISA Sec. 305(c)(7) by adding at the end a new subparagraph (C) to read as above.

The above amendment is effective as if included in the provision of the Pension Protection Act of 2006 (P.L. 109-280) to which the amendment relates [effective with respect to plan years beginning after 2007.-CCH] Prior to amendment, ERISA Sec. 305(c)(7) read as follows:

(7) IMPOSITION OF DEFAULT SCHEDULE WHERE FAILURE TO ADOPT FUNDING IMPROVEMENT PLAN.—

(A) IN GENERAL. —If—

(i) a collective bargaining agreement providing for contributions under a multiemployer plan that was in effect at the time the plan entered endangered status expires, and

(ii) after receiving one or more schedules from the plan sponsor under paragraph (1)(B), the bargaining parties with respect to such agreement fail to agree on changes to contribution or benefit schedules necessary to meet the applicable benchmarks in accordance with the funding improvement plan,

the plan sponsor shall implement the schedule described in paragraph (1)(B)(i)(I) beginning on the date specified in subparagraph (B).

(B) DATE OF IMPLEMENTATION. – The date specified in this subparagraph is the earlier of the date—

(i) on which the Secretary certifies that the parties are at an impasse, or

(ii) which is 180 days after the date on which the collective bargaining agreement described in subparagraph (A) expires.

P.L. 110-458, § 102(b)(1)(E)(i)(I):

Amended ERISA Sec. 305(e)(3)(C) by striking all that follows "to adopt a" in clause (i)(II) and inserting "to adopt a contribution schedule with terms consistent with the rehabilitation plan and a schedule from the plan sponsor under paragraph (1)(B)(i),".

The above amendment is effective as if included in the provision of the Pension Protection Act of 2006 (P.L. 109-280) to which the amendment relates [effective with respect to plan years beginning after 2007.-CCH]

P.L. 110-458, § 102(b)(1)(E)(i)(II):

Amended ERISA Sec. 305(e)(3)(C) by striking clause (ii) and inserting a new clause (ii) to read as above.

The above amendment is effective as if included in the provision of the Pension Protection Act of 2006 (P.L. 109-280) to which the amendment relates [effective with respect to plan years beginning after 2007.-CCH]

P.L. 110-458, § 102(b)(1)(E)(i)(III):

Amended ERISA Sec. 305(e)(3)(C) by adding at the end a new clause (iii) to read as above.

The above amendment is effective as if included in the provision of the Pension Protection Act of 2006 (P.L. 109-280) to which the amendment relates [effective with respect to plan years beginning after 2007.-CCH] Prior to amendment, ERISA Sec. 305(e)(3)(C) read as follows:

(C) IMPOSITION OF DEFAULT SCHEDULE WHERE FAILURE TO ADOPT REHABILITATION PLAN. —

(i) IN GENERAL. —If—

(I) a collective bargaining agreement providing for contributions under a multiemployer plan that was in effect at the time the plan entered critical status expires, and

(II) after receiving one or more schedules from the plan sponsor under paragraph (1)(B), the bargaining parties with respect to such agreement fail to adopt a contribution or benefit schedules with terms consistent with the rehabilitation plan and the schedule from the plan sponsor under paragraph (1)(B)(i),

the plan sponsor shall implement the default schedule described in the last sentence of paragraph (1) beginning on the date specified in clause (ii).

(ii) DATE OF IMPLEMENTATION. –The date specified in this clause is the earlier of the date—

(I) on which the Secretary certifies that the parties are at an impasse, or

(II) which is 180 days after the date on which the collective bargaining agreement described in clause (i) expires.

P.L. 110-458, § 102(b)(1)(E)(ii)(I):

Amended ERISA Sec. 305(e)(4)(A)(ii) by striking "the date of".

The above amendment is effective as if included in the provision of the Pension Protection Act of 2006 (P.L. 109-280) to which the amendment relates [effective with respect to plan years beginning after 2007.-CCH]

P.L. 110-458, § 102(b)(1)(E)(ii)(II):

Amended ERISA Sec. 305(e)(4)(B) by striking "and taking" and inserting "but taking".

The above amendment is effective as if included in the provision of the Pension Protection Act of 2006 (P.L. 109-280) to which the amendment relates [effective with respect to plan years beginning after 2007.-CCH]

P.L. 110-458, § 102(b)(1)(E)(iii)(I):

Amended ERISA Sec. 305(e)(6) by striking "paragraph (1)(B)(i)" and inserting "the last sentence of paragraph (1)".

The above amendment is effective as if included in the provision of the Pension Protection Act of 2006 (P.L. 109-280) to which the amendment relates [effective with respect to plan years beginning after 2007.-CCH]

P.L. 110-458, § 102(b)(1)(E)(iii)(II):

Amended ERISA Sec. 305(e)(6) by striking "established" and inserting "establish".

The above amendment is effective as if included in the provision of the Pension Protection Act of 2006 (P.L. 109-280) to which the amendment relates [effective with respect to plan years beginning after 2007.-CCH]

P.L. 110-458, § 102(b)(1)(E)(iv)(I):

Amended ERISA Sec. 305(e)(8)(C)(iii) by striking "the Secretary" in subclause (I) and inserting "the Secretary of the Treasury, in consultation with the Secretary".

The above amendment is effective as if included in the provision of the Pension Protection Act of 2006 (P.L. 109-280) to which the amendment relates [effective with respect to plan years beginning after 2007.-CCH]

P.L. 110-458, § 102(b)(1)(E)(iv)(II):

Amended ERISA Sec. 305(e)(8)(C)(iii) by striking "Secretary" in the last sentence and inserting "Secretary of the Treasury".

The above amendment is effective as if included in the provision of the Pension Protection Act of 2006 (P.L. 109-280) to which the amendment relates [effective with respect to plan years beginning after 2007.-CCH]

P.L. 110-458, § 102(b)(1)(E)(v):

Amended ERISA Sec. 305(e)(9)(B) by striking "an employer's withdrawal liability" and inserting "the allocation of unfunded vested benefits to an employer".

The above amendment is effective as if included in the provision of the Pension Protection Act of 2006 (P.L. 109-280) to which the amendment relates [effective with respect to plan years beginning after 2007.-CCH]

P.L. 110-458, § 102(b)(1)(F):

Amended ERISA Sec. 305(f)(2)(A)(i) by adding at the end the following: "to a participant or beneficiary whose annuity starting date (as defined in section 205(h)(2)) occurs after the date such notice is sent,".

The above amendment is effective as if included in the provision of the Pension Protection Act of 2006 (P.L. 109-280) to which the amendment relates [effective with respect to plan years beginning after 2007.-CCH]

P.L. 110-458, § 102(b)(1)(G):

Amended ERISA Sec. 305(g) by inserting "under subsection (c)" after "funding improvement plan" the first place it appears.

The above amendment is effective as if included in the provision of the Pension Protection Act of 2006 (P.L. 109-280) to which the amendment relates [effective with respect to plan years beginning after 2007.-CCH]

P. L. 109-280, § 101(a):

Repealed ERISA Sec. 305.

Prior to repeal, ERISA Sec. 305 read as follows:

(a) MAINTENANCE OF ACCOUNT.—A plan which uses a funding method that requires contributions in all years not less than those required under the entry age normal funding method may maintain an alternative minimum funding standard account for any plan year. Such account shall be credited and charged solely as provided in this section.

(b) OPERATION OF ACCOUNT.—For a plan year the alternative minimum funding standard accounts shall be—

(b)(1) charged with the sum of—

(b)(1)(A) the lesser of normal cost under the funding method used under the plan or normal cost determined under the unit credit method.

(b)(1)(B) the excess, if any, of the present value of accrued benefits under the plan over the fair market value of the assets, and

(b)(1)(C) an amount equal to the excess, if any, of credits to the alternative minimum funding standard account for all prior plan years over charges to such account for all such years, and

(b)(2) credited with the amount considered contributed by the employer to or under the plan (within the meaning of section 302(c)(10)) for the plan year.

(c) INTEREST.—The alternative minimum funding standard account (and items therein) shall be charged or credited with interest in the manner provided under section 302(b)(5) with respect to the funding standard account.

The above amendment applies to plan years beginning after 2007.

P. L. 109-280, § 202(a):

Amended Part 3 of subtitle B of title I of such Act (as amended by subsection (a)) by inserting after section 304 the new section 305.

The above amendment applies to plan years beginning after 2007.

[¶ 14,655]

SECURITY FOR WAIVERS OF MINIMUM FUNDING STANDARD AND EXTENSIONS OF AMORTIZATION PERIOD

[Act Sec. 306—Stricken]

Amendments

P. L. 109-280, § 101(a):

Repealed ERISA Sec. 306.

Prior to repeal, ERISA Sec. 306 read as follows:

(a) SECURITY MAY BE REQUIRED.

(a)(1) IN GENERAL. Except as provided in subsection (c), the Secretary of the Treasury may require an employer maintaining a defined benefit plan which is a single-employer plan (within the meaning of section 4001(a)(15)) to provide security to such plan as a condition for granting or modifying a waiver under section 303 or an extension under section 304.

(a)(2) SPECIAL RULES. Any security provided under paragraph (1) may be perfected and enforced only by the Pension Benefit Guaranty Corporation or, at the direction of the Corporation, by a contributing sponsor (within the meaning of section 4001(a)(13)) or a member of such sponsor's controlled group (within the meaning of section 4001(a)(14)).

(b) CONSULTATION WITH THE PENSION BENEFIT GUARANTY CORPORATION. Except as provided in subsection (c), the Secretary of the Treasury shall, before granting or modifying a waiver under section 303 or an extension under section 304 with respect to a plan described in subsection (a)(1)—

(b)(1) provide the Pension Benefit Guaranty Corporation with—

(b)(1)(A) notice of the compelled application for any waiver, extension, or modification, and

(b)(1)(B) an opportunity to comment on such application within 30 days after receipt of such notice, and

(b)(2) consider—

(b)(2)(A) any comments of the Corporation under paragraph (1)(B), and

(b)(2)(B) any views of any employee organization representing participants in the plan which are submitted in writing to the Secretary of the Treasury in connection with such application.

Information provided to the corporation under this subsection shall be considered tax return information and subject to the safeguarding and reporting requirements of section 6103(p) of the Internal Revenue Code of 1986.

(c) EXCEPTION FOR CERTAIN WAIVERS AND EXTENSIONS.

(c)(1) IN GENERAL. The preceding provisions of this section shall not apply to any plan with respect to which the sum of—

(c)(1)(A) the outstanding balance of the accumulated funding deficiencies (within the meaning of section 302(a)(2) of this Act and section 412(a) of the Internal Revenue Code of 1986) of the plan,

(c)(1)(B) the outstanding balance of the amount of waived funding deficiencies of the plan waived under section 303 of this Act or section 412(d) of such Code, and

(c)(1)(C) the outstanding balance of the amount of decreases in the minimum funding standard allowed under section 304 of this Act or section 412(e) of such Code,

(c)(2) ACCUMULATED FUNDING DEFICIENCIES. For purposes of paragraph (1)(A), accumulated funding deficiencies shall include any increase in such amount which would result if all applications for waivers of the minimum funding standard under section 303 of this Act or section 412(d) of the Internal Revenue Code of 1986 and for extensions of amortization period under section 304 of this Act or section 412(e) of such Code which are pending with respect to such plan were denied.

The above amendment applies to plan years beginning after 2007.

P.L. 101-239, § 7891(a)(1):

Titles I, III, and IV of ERISA (other than sections 3(37)(E), 301(a)(7), and 308, the last sentence of section 408(d), and sections 414(c), 4001(a)(3)(ii), and 4303) are each amended by striking "Internal Revenue Code of 1954" each place it appears and inserting "Internal Revenue Code of 1986" effective October 22, 1986.

P.L. 100-203, § 9306(e)(2):

Amended ERISA Sec. 306(c)(1) by striking out "$2,000,000" and inserting in lieu thereof "$1,000,000", effective for waiver applications submitted after December 17, 1987 and waivers granted pursuant to such applications.

P.L. § 99-272:

Act Sec. 11015(a)(1)(A) added new ERISA Sec. 306 to read as above, effective with respect to applications for waivers, extensions and modifications filed on or after April 7, 1986.

[¶ 14,656]

MINIMUM FUNDING STANDARDS

Act Sec. 306.(a) GENERAL RULE. For purposes of section 302, the term 'accumulated funding deficiency' for a CSEC plan means the excess of the total charges to the funding standard account for all plan years (beginning with the first plan year to which section 302 applies) over the total credits to such account for such years or, if less, the excess of the total charges to the alternative minimum funding standard account for such plan years over the total credits to such account for such years.

Act Sec. 306. (b) FUNDING STANDARD ACCOUNT—. (1) ACCOUNT REQUIRED. Each plan to which this section applies shall establish and maintain a funding standard account. Such account shall be credited and charged solely as provided in this section.

(2) CHARGES TO ACCOUNT. For a plan year, the funding standard account shall be charged with the sum of—

(A) the normal cost of the plan for the plan year,

(B) the amounts necessary to amortize in equal annual installments (until fully amortized)—

(i) in the case of a plan in existence on January 1, 1974, the unfunded past service liability under the plan on the first day of the first plan year to which section 302 applies, over a period of 40 plan years,

(ii) in the case of a plan which comes into existence after January 1, 1974, but before the first day of the first plan year beginning after December 31, 2013, the unfunded past service liability under the plan on the first day of the first plan year to which section 302 applies, over a period of 30 plan years,

(iii) separately, with respect to each plan year, the net increase (if any) in unfunded past service liability under the plan arising from plan amendments adopted in such year, over a period of 15 plan years,

(iv) separately, with respect to each plan year, the net experience loss (if any) under the plan, over a period of 5 plan years, and

(v) separately, with respect to each plan year, the net loss (if any) resulting from changes in actuarial assumptions used under the plan, over a period of 10 plan years,

(C) the amount necessary to amortize each waived funding deficiency (within the meaning of section 302(c)(3)) for each prior plan year in equal annual installments (until fully amortized) over a period of 5 plan years,

(D) the amount necessary to amortize in equal annual installments (until fully amortized) over a period of 5 plan years any amount credited to the funding standard account under paragraph (3)(D), and

(E) the amount necessary to amortize in equal annual installments (until fully amortized) over a period of 20 years the contributions which would be required to be made under the plan but for the provisions of section 302(c)(7)(A)(i)(I) (as in effect on the day before the enactment of the Pension Protection Act of 2006).

(3) CREDITS TO ACCOUNT. For a plan year, the funding standard account shall be credited with the sum of—

(A) the amount considered contributed by the employer to or under the plan for the plan year,

(B) the amount necessary to amortize in equal annual installments (until fully amortized)—

(i) separately, with respect to each plan year, the net decrease (if any) in unfunded past service liability under the plan arising from plan amendments adopted in such year, over a period of 15 plan years,

(ii) separately, with respect to each plan year, the net experience gain (if any) under the plan, over a period of 5 plan years, and

(iii) separately, with respect to each plan year, the net gain (if any) resulting from changes in actuarial assumptions used under the plan, over a period of 10 plan years,

(C) the amount of the waived funding deficiency (within the meaning of section 302(c)(3)) for the plan year, and

(D) in the case of a plan year for which the accumulated funding deficiency is determined under the funding standard account if such plan year follows a plan year for which such deficiency was determined under the alternative minimum funding standard, the excess (if any) of any debit balance in the funding standard account (determined without regard to this subparagraph) over any debit balance in the alternative minimum funding standard account.

(4) COMBINING AND OFFSETTING AMOUNTS TO BE AMORTIZED. Under regulations prescribed by the Secretary of the Treasury, amounts required to be amortized under paragraph (2) or paragraph (3), as the case may be—

(A) may be combined into one amount under such paragraph to be amortized over a period determined on the basis of the remaining amortization period for all items entering into such combined amount, and

(B) may be offset against amounts required to be amortized under the other such paragraph, with the resulting amount to be amortized over a period determined on the basis of the remaining amortization periods for all items entering into whichever of the two amounts being offset is the greater.

(5) INTEREST.—

(A) IN GENERAL. Except as provided in subparagraph (B), the funding standard account (and items therein) shall be charged or credited (as determined under regulations prescribed by the Secretary of the Treasury) with interest at the appropriate rate consistent with the rate or rates of interest used under the plan to determine costs.

(B) EXCEPTION. The interest rate used for purposes of computing the amortization charge described in subsection (b)(2)(C) or for purposes of any arrangement under subsection (d) for any plan year shall be the greater of—

(i) 150 percent of the Federal midterm rate (as in effect under section 1274 of the Internal Revenue Code of 1986 for the 1st month of such plan year), or

(ii) the rate of interest determined under subparagraph (A).

(6) AMORTIZATION SCHEDULES IN EFFECT. Amortization schedules for amounts described in paragraphs (2) and (3) that are in effect as of the last day of the last plan year beginning before January 1, 2014, by reason of section 104 of the Pension Protection Act of 2006 shall remain in effect pursuant to their terms and this section, except that such amounts shall not be amortized again under this section.

Act Sec. 306. (c) SPECIAL RULES.—

(1) DETERMINATIONS TO BE MADE UNDER FUNDING METHOD. For purposes of this section, normal costs, accrued liability, past service liabilities, and experience gains and losses shall be determined under the funding method used to determine costs under the plan.

(2) VALUATION OF ASSETS.—

(A) IN GENERAL. For purposes of this section, the value of the plan's assets shall be determined on the basis of any reasonable actuarial method of valuation which takes into account fair market value and which is permitted under regulations prescribed by the Secretary of the Treasury.

(B) DEDICATED BOND PORTFOLIO. The Secretary of the Treasury may by regulations provide that the value of any dedicated bond portfolio of a plan shall be determined by using the interest rate under section 302(b)(5) (as in effect on the day before the enactment of the Pension Protection Act of 2006).

(3) ACTUARIAL ASSUMPTIONS MUST BE REASONABLE. For purposes of this section, all costs, liabilities, rates of interest, and other factors under the plan shall be determined on the basis of actuarial assumptions and methods—

(A) each of which is reasonable (taking into account the experience of the plan and reasonable expectations), and

(B) which, in combination, offer the actuary's best estimate of anticipated experience under the plan.

(4) TREATMENT OF CERTAIN CHANGES AS EXPERIENCE GAIN OR LOSS. For purposes of this section, if—

(A) a change in benefits under the Social Security Act or in other retirement benefits created under Federal or State law, or

(B) a change in the definition of the term 'wages' under section 3121 of the Internal Revenue Code of 1986 or a change in the amount of such wages taken into account under regulations prescribed for purposes of section 401(a)(5) of such Code,

results in an increase or decrease in accrued liability under a plan, such increase or decrease shall be treated as an experience loss or gain.

(5) FUNDING METHOD AND PLAN YEAR.—

(A) FUNDING METHODS AVAILABLE. All funding methods available to CSEC plans under section 302 (as in effect on the day before the enactment of the Pension Protection Act of 2006) shall continue to be available under this section.

(B) CHANGES. If the funding method for a plan is changed, the new funding method shall become the funding method used to determine costs and liabilities under the plan only if the change is approved by the Secretary of the Treasury. If the plan year for a plan is changed, the new plan year shall become the plan year for the plan only if the change is approved by the Secretary of the Treasury.

(C) APPROVAL REQUIRED FOR CERTAIN CHANGES IN ASSUMPTIONS BY CERTAIN SINGLE-EMPLOYER PLANS SUBJECT TO ADDITIONAL FUNDING REQUIREMENT.—

(i) IN GENERAL. No actuarial assumption (other than the assumptions described in subsection (h)(3)) used to determine the current liability for a plan to which this subparagraph applies may be changed without the approval of the Secretary of the Treasury.

(ii) PLANS TO WHICH SUBPARAGRAPH APPLIES. This subparagraph shall apply to a plan only if—

(I) the plan is a CSEC plan,

(II) the aggregate unfunded vested benefits as of the close of the preceding plan year (as determined under section 4006(a)(3)(E)(iii)) of such plan and all other plans maintained by the contributing sponsors (as defined in section 4001(a)(13)) and members of such sponsors' controlled groups (as defined in section 4001(a)(14)) which are covered by title IV (disregarding plans with no unfunded vested benefits) exceed $50,000,000, and

(III) the change in assumptions (determined after taking into account any changes in interest rate and mortality table) results in a decrease in the funding shortfall of the plan for the current plan year that exceeds $50,000,000, or that exceeds $5,000,000 and that is 5 percent or more of the current liability of the plan before such change.

(6) FULL FUNDING. If, as of the close of a plan year, a plan would (without regard to this paragraph) have an accumulated funding deficiency (determined without regard to the alternative minimum funding standard account permitted under subsection (e)) in excess of the full funding limitation—

(A) the funding standard account shall be credited with the amount of such excess, and

(B) all amounts described in paragraphs (2)(B), (C), and (D) and (3)(B) of subsection (b) which are required to be amortized shall be considered fully amortized for purposes of such paragraphs.

(7) FULL-FUNDING LIMITATION. For purposes of paragraph (6), the term 'full-funding limitation' means the excess (if any) of—

(A) the accrued liability (including normal cost) under the plan (determined under the entry age normal funding method if such accrued liability cannot be directly calculated under the funding method used for the plan), over

(B) the lesser of—

(i) the fair market value of the plan's assets, or

(ii) the value of such assets determined under paragraph (2).

(C) MINIMUM AMOUNT.—

(i) IN GENERAL. In no event shall the full-funding limitation determined under subparagraph (A) be less than the excess (if any) of—

(I) 90 percent of the current liability (determined without regard to paragraph (4) of subsection (h)) of the plan (including the expected increase in such current liability due to benefits accruing during the plan year), over

(II) the value of the plan's assets determined under paragraph (2).

(ii) ASSETS. For purposes of clause (i), assets shall not be reduced by any credit balance in the funding standard account.

(8) ANNUAL VALUATION.—

(A) IN GENERAL. For purposes of this section, a determination of experience gains and losses and a valuation of the plan's liability shall be made not less frequently than once every year, except that such determination shall be made more frequently to the extent required in particular cases under regulations prescribed by the Secretary of the Treasury.

(B) VALUATION DATE.—

(i) CURRENT YEAR. Except as provided in clause (ii), the valuation referred to in subparagraph (A) shall be made as of a date within the plan year to which the valuation refers or within one month prior to the beginning of such year.

(ii) USE OF PRIOR YEAR VALUATION. The valuation referred to in subparagraph (A) may be made as of a date within the plan year prior to the year to which the valuation refers if, as of such date, the value of the assets of the plan are not less than 100 percent of the plan's current liability.

(iii) ADJUSTMENTS. Information under clause (ii) shall, in accordance with regulations, be actuarially adjusted to reflect significant differences in participants.

(iv) LIMITATION. A change in funding method to use a prior year valuation, as provided in clause (ii), may not be made unless as of the valuation date within the prior plan year, the value of the assets of the plan are not less than 125 percent of the plan's current liability.

(9) TIME WHEN CERTAIN CONTRIBUTIONS DEEMED MADE. For purposes of this section, any contributions for a plan year made by an employer during the period—

(A) beginning on the day after the last day of such plan year, and

(B) ending on the day which is 81.2 months after the close of the plan year,

shall be deemed to have been made on such last day.

(10) ANTICIPATION OF BENEFIT INCREASES EFFECTIVE IN THE FUTURE. In determining projected benefits, the funding method of a collectively bargained CSEC plan described in section 413(a) of the Internal Revenue Code of 1986 shall anticipate benefit increases scheduled to take effect during the term of the collective bargaining agreement applicable to the plan.

Act Sec. 306. (d) EXTENSION OF AMORTIZATION PERIODS. The period of years required to amortize any unfunded liability (described in any clause of subsection (b)(2)(B)) of any plan may be extended by the Secretary of the Treasury for a period of time (not in excess of 10 years) if such Secretary determines that such extension would carry out the purposes of this Act and provide adequate protection for participants under the plan and their beneficiaries, and if such Secretary determines that the failure to permit such extension would result in—

(1) a substantial risk to the voluntary continuation of the plan, or

(2) a substantial curtailment of pension benefit levels or employee compensation.

Act Sec. 306. (e) ALTERNATIVE MINIMUM FUNDING STANDARD.—

(1) IN GENERAL. A CSEC plan which uses a funding method that requires contributions in all years not less than those required under the entry age normal funding method may maintain an alternative minimum funding standard account for any plan year. Such account shall be credited and charged solely as provided in this subsection.

(2) CHARGES AND CREDITS TO ACCOUNT. For a plan year the alternative minimum funding standard account shall be—

(A) charged with the sum of—

(i) the lesser of normal cost under the funding method used under the plan or normal cost determined under the unit credit method,

(ii) the excess, if any, of the present value of accrued benefits under the plan over the fair market value of the assets, and

(iii) an amount equal to the excess (if any) of credits to the alternative minimum standard account for all prior plan years over charges to such account for all such years, and

(B) credited with the amount considered contributed by the employer to or under the plan for the plan year.

(3) INTEREST. The alternative minimum funding standard account (and items therein) shall be charged or credited with interest in the manner provided under subsection (b)(5) with respect to the funding standard account.

Act Sec. 306. (f) QUARTERLY CONTRIBUTIONS REQUIRED.—

(1) IN GENERAL. If a CSEC plan which has a funded current liability percentage for the preceding plan year of less than 100 percent fails to pay the full amount of a required installment for the plan year, then the rate of interest charged to the funding standard account under subsection (b)(5) with respect to the amount of the underpayment for the period of the underpayment shall be equal to the greater of—

(A) 175 percent of the Federal mid-term rate (as in effect under section 1274 of the Internal Revenue Code of 1986 for the 1st month of such plan year), or

(B) the rate of interest used under the plan in determining costs.

(2) AMOUNT OF UNDERPAYMENT, PERIOD OF UNDERPAYMENT. For purposes of paragraph (1)—

(A) AMOUNT. The amount of the underpayment shall be the excess of—

(i) the required installment, over

(ii) the amount (if any) of the installment contributed to or under the plan on or before the due date for the installment.

(B) PERIOD OF UNDERPAYMENT. The period for which interest is charged under this subsection with regard to any portion of the underpayment shall run from the due date for the installment to the date on which such portion is contributed to or under the plan (determined without regard to subsection (c)(9)).

(C) ORDER OF CREDITING CONTRIBUTIONS. For purposes of subparagraph (A)(ii), contributions shall be credited against unpaid required installments in the order in which such installments are required to be paid.

(3) NUMBER OF REQUIRED INSTALLMENTS; DUE DATES. For purposes of this subsection—

(A) PAYABLE IN 4 INSTALLMENTS. There shall be 4 required installments for each plan year.

(B) TIME FOR PAYMENT OF INSTALLMENTS.—

In the case of the following required installments:	The due date is:
1st	April 15
2nd	July 15
3rd	October 15
4th	January 15 of the following year.

(4) AMOUNT OF REQUIRED INSTALLMENT. For purposes of this subsection—

(A) IN GENERAL. The amount of any required installment shall be 25 percent of the required annual payment.

(B) REQUIRED ANNUAL PAYMENT. For purposes of subparagraph (A), the term 'required annual payment' means the lesser of—

(i) 90 percent of the amount required to be contributed to or under the plan by the employer for the plan year under section 302 (without regard to any waiver under subsection (c) thereof), or

(ii) 100 percent of the amount so required for the preceding plan year.

Clause (ii) shall not apply if the preceding plan year was not a year of 12 months.

(5) LIQUIDITY REQUIREMENT.—

(A) IN GENERAL. A plan to which this paragraph applies shall be treated as failing to pay the full amount of any required installment to the extent that the value of the liquid assets paid in such installment is less than the liquidity shortfall (whether or not such liquidity shortfall exceeds the amount of such installment required to be paid but for this paragraph).

(B) PLANS TO WHICH PARAGRAPH APPLIES. This paragraph shall apply to a CSEC plan other than a plan described in section 302(d)(6)(A) (as in effect on the day before the enactment of the Pension Protection Act of 2006) which—

(i) is required to pay installments under this subsection for a plan year, and

(ii) has a liquidity shortfall for any quarter during such plan year.

(C) PERIOD OF UNDERPAYMENT. For purposes of paragraph (1), any portion of an installment that is treated as not paid under subparagraph (A) shall continue to be treated as unpaid until the close of the quarter in which the due date for such installment occurs.

(D) LIMITATION ON INCREASE. If the amount of any required installment is increased by reason of subparagraph (A), in no event shall such increase exceed the amount which, when added to prior installments for the plan year, is necessary to increase the funded current liability percentage (taking into account the expected increase in current liability due to benefits accruing during the plan year) to 100 percent.

(E) DEFINITIONS. For purposes of this paragraph—

(i) LIQUIDITY SHORTFALL. The term 'liquidity shortfall' means, with respect to any required installment, an amount equal to the excess (as of the last day of the quarter for which such installment is made) of the base amount with respect to such quarter over the value (as of such last day) of the plan's liquid assets.

(ii) BASE AMOUNT.—

(I) IN GENERAL. The term 'base amount' means, with respect to any quarter, an amount equal to 3 times the sum of the adjusted disbursements from the plan for the 12 months ending on the last day of such quarter.

(II) SPECIAL RULE. If the amount determined under subclause (I) exceeds an amount equal to 2 times the sum of the adjusted disbursements from the plan for the 36 months ending on the last day of the quarter and an enrolled actuary certifies to the satisfaction of the Secretary of the Treasury that such excess is the result of nonrecurring circumstances, the base amount with respect to such quarter shall be determined without regard to amounts related to those nonrecurring circumstances.

(iii) DISBURSEMENTS FROM THE PLAN. The term 'disbursements from the plan' means all disbursements from the trust, including purchases of annuities, payments of single sums and other benefits, and administrative expenses.

(iv) ADJUSTED DISBURSEMENTS. The term 'adjusted disbursements' means disbursements from the plan reduced by the product of—

(I) the plan's funded current liability percentage for the plan year, and

(II) the sum of the purchases of annuities, payments of single sums, and such other disbursements as the Secretary of the Treasury shall provide in regulations.

(v) LIQUID ASSETS. The term 'liquid assets' means cash, marketable securities and such other assets as specified by the Secretary of the Treasury in regulations.

(vi) QUARTER. The term 'quarter' means, with respect to any required installment, the 3-month period preceding the month in which the due date for such installment occurs.

(F) REGULATIONS. The Secretary of the Treasury may prescribe such regulations as are necessary to carry out this paragraph.

(6) FISCAL YEARS AND SHORT YEARS.—

(A) FISCAL YEARS. In applying this subsection to a plan year beginning on any date other than January 1, there shall be substituted for the months specified in this subsection, the months which correspond thereto.

(B) SHORT PLAN YEAR. This subsection shall be applied to plan years of less than 12 months in accordance with regulations prescribed by the Secretary of the Treasury.

Act Sec. 306. (g) IMPOSITION OF LIEN WHERE FAILURE TO MAKE REQUIRED CONTRIBUTIONS.—

(1) IN GENERAL. In the case of a plan to which this section applies, if—

(A) any person fails to make a required installment under subsection (f) or any other payment required under this section before the due date for such installment or other payment, and

(B) the unpaid balance of such installment or other payment (including interest), when added to the aggregate unpaid balance of all preceding such installments or other payments for which payment was not made before the due date (including interest), exceeds $1,000,000,

then there shall be a lien in favor of the plan in the amount determined under paragraph (3) upon all property and rights to property, whether real or personal, belonging to such person and any other person who is a member of the same controlled group of which such person is a member.

(2) PLANS TO WHICH SUBSECTION APPLIES. This subsection shall apply to a CSEC plan for any plan year for which the funded current liability percentage of such plan is less than 100 percent. This subsection shall not apply to any plan to which section 4021 does not apply (as such section is in effect on the date of the enactment of the Retirement Protection Act of 1994).

(3) AMOUNT OF LIEN. For purposes of paragraph (1), the amount of the lien shall be equal to the aggregate unpaid balance of required installments and other payments required under this section (including interest)—

(A) for plan years beginning after 1987, and

(B) for which payment has not been made before the due date.

(4) NOTICE OF FAILURE; LIEN.—

(A) NOTICE OF FAILURE. A person committing a failure described in paragraph (1) shall notify the Pension Benefit Guaranty Corporation of such failure within 10 days of the due date for the required installment or other payment.

(B) PERIOD OF LIEN. The lien imposed by paragraph (1) shall arise on the due date for the required installment or other payment and shall continue until the last day of the first plan year in which the plan ceases to be described in paragraph (1)(B). Such lien shall continue to run without regard to whether such plan continues to be described in paragraph (2) during the period referred to in the preceding sentence.

(C) CERTAIN RULES TO APPLY. Any amount with respect to which a lien is imposed under paragraph (1) shall be treated as taxes due and owing the United States and rules similar to the rules of subsections (c), (d), and (e) of section 4068 shall apply with respect to a lien imposed by subsection (a) and the amount with respect to such lien.

(5) ENFORCEMENT. Any lien created under paragraph (1) may be perfected and enforced only by the Pension Benefit Guaranty Corporation, or at the direction of the Pension Benefit Guaranty Corporation, by any contributing employer (or any member of the controlled group of the contributing employer).

(6) DEFINITIONS. For purposes of this subsection—

(A) DUE DATE; REQUIRED INSTALLMENT. The terms 'due date' and 'required installment' have the meanings given such terms by subsection (f), except that in the case of a payment other than a required installment, the due date shall be the date such payment is required to be made under this section.

(B) CONTROLLED GROUP. The term 'controlled group' means any group treated as a single employer under subsections (b), (c), (m), and (o) of section 414 of the Internal Revenue Code of 1986.

Act Sec. 306. (h) CURRENT LIABILITY. For purposes of this section—

(1) IN GENERAL. The term 'current liability' means all liabilities to employees and their beneficiaries under the plan.

(2) TREATMENT OF UNPREDICTABLE CONTINGENT EVENT BENEFITS.—

(A) IN GENERAL. For purposes of paragraph (1), any unpredictable contingent event benefit shall not be taken into account until the event on which the benefit is contingent occurs.

(B) UNPREDICTABLE CONTINGENT EVENT BENEFIT. The term 'unpredictable contingent event benefit' means any benefit contingent on an event other than—

(i) age, service, compensation, death, or disability, or

(ii) an event which is reasonably and reliably predictable (as determined by the Secretary of the Treasury).

(3) INTEREST RATE AND MORTALITY ASSUMPTIONS USED.—

(A) INTEREST RATE. The rate of interest used to determine current liability under this section shall be the third segment rate determined under section 303(h)(2)(C).

(B) MORTALITY TABLES.—

(i) SECRETARIAL AUTHORITY. The Secretary of the Treasury may by regulation prescribe mortality tables to be used in determining current liability under this subsection. Such tables shall be based upon the actual experience of pension plans and projected trends in such experience. In prescribing such tables, the Secretary of the Treasury shall take into account results of available independent studies of mortality of individuals covered by pension plans.

(ii) PERIODIC REVIEW. The Secretary of the Treasury shall periodically (at least every 5 years) review any tables in effect under this subsection and shall, to the extent the Secretary of the Treasury determines necessary, by regulation update the tables to reflect the actual experience of pension plans and projected trends in such experience.

(C) SEPARATE MORTALITY TABLES FOR THE DISABLED. Notwithstanding subparagraph (B)—

(i) IN GENERAL. In the case of plan years beginning after December 31, 1995, the Secretary of the Treasury shall establish mortality tables which may be used (in lieu of the tables under subparagraph (B)) to determine current liability under this subsection for individuals who are entitled to benefits under the plan on account of disability. The Secretary of the Treasury shall establish separate tables for individuals whose disabilities occur in plan years beginning before January 1, 1995, and for individuals whose disabilities occur in plan years beginning on or after such date.

(ii) SPECIAL RULE FOR DISABILITIES OCCURRING AFTER 1994. In the case of disabilities occurring in plan years beginning after December 31, 1994, the tables under clause (i) shall apply only with respect to individuals described in such subclause who are disabled within the meaning of title II of the Social Security Act and the regulations thereunder.

(4) CERTAIN SERVICE DISREGARDED.—

(A) IN GENERAL. In the case of a participant to whom this paragraph applies, only the applicable percentage of the years of service before such individual became a participant shall be taken into account in computing the current liability of the plan.

(B) APPLICABLE PERCENTAGE. For purposes of this subparagraph, the applicable percentage shall be determined as follows:

If the years of participation are:	The applicable percentage is:
1	20
2	40
3	60
4	80
5 or more	100.

(C) PARTICIPANTS TO WHOM PARAGRAPH APPLIES. This subparagraph shall apply to any participant who, at the time of becoming a participant—

(i) has not accrued any other benefit under any defined benefit plan (whether or not terminated) maintained by the employer or a member of the same controlled group of which the employer is a member,

(ii) who first becomes a participant under the plan in a plan year beginning after December 31, 1987, and

(iii) has years of service greater than the minimum years of service necessary for eligibility to participate in the plan.

(D) ELECTION. An employer may elect not to have this subparagraph apply. Such an election, once made, may be revoked only with the consent of the Secretary of the Treasury.

Act Sec. 306. (i) FUNDED CURRENT LIABILITY PERCENTAGE. For purposes of this section, the term 'funded current liability percentage' means, with respect to any plan year, the percentage which—

(1) the value of the plan's assets determined under subsection (c)(2), is of

(2) the current liability under the plan.

Act Sec. 306. (j) FUNDING RESTORATION STATUS. Notwithstanding any other provisions of this section—

(1) NORMAL COST PAYMENT.—

(A) IN GENERAL. In the case of a CSEC plan that is in funding restoration status for a plan year, for purposes of section 302, the term 'accumulated funding deficiency' means, for such plan year, the greater of—

(i) the amount described in subsection (a), or

(ii) the excess of the normal cost of the plan for the plan year over the amount actually contributed to or under the plan for the plan year.

(B) NORMAL COST. In the case of a CSEC plan that uses a spread gain funding method, for purposes of this subsection, the term 'normal cost' means normal cost as determined under the entry age normal funding method.

(2) PLAN AMENDMENTS. In the case of a CSEC plan that is in funding restoration status for a plan year, no amendment to such plan may take effect during such plan year if such amendment has the effect of increasing liabilities of the plan by means of increases in benefits, establishment of new benefits, changing the rate of benefit accrual, or changing the rate at which benefits become non-forfeitable. This paragraph shall not apply to any plan amendment that is required to comply with any applicable law. This paragraph shall cease to apply with respect to any plan year, effective as of the first day of the plan year (or if later, the effective date of the amendment) upon payment by the plan sponsor of a contribution to the plan (in addition to any contribution required under this section without regard to this paragraph) in an amount equal to the increase in the funding liability of the plan attributable to the plan amendment.

(3) FUNDING RESTORATION PLAN. The sponsor of a CSEC plan shall establish a written funding restoration plan within 180 days of the receipt by the plan sponsor of a certification from the plan actuary that the plan is in funding restoration status for a plan year. Such funding restoration plan shall consist of actions that are calculated, based on reasonably anticipated experience and reasonable actuarial assumptions, to increase the plan's funded percentage to 100 percent over a period that is not longer than the greater of 7 years or the shortest amount of time practicable. Such funding restoration plan shall take into account contributions required under this section (without regard to this paragraph). If a plan remains in funding restoration status for 2 or more years, such funding restoration plan shall be updated each year after the 1st such year within 180 days of receipt by the plan sponsor of a certification from the plan actuary that the plan remains in funding restoration status for the plan year.

(4) ANNUAL CERTIFICATION BY PLAN ACTUARY. Not later than the 90th day of each plan year of a CSEC plan, the plan actuary shall certify to the plan sponsor whether or not the plan is in funding restoration status for the plan year, based on the plan's funded percentage as of the beginning of the plan year. For this purpose, the actuary may conclusively rely on an estimate of—

(A) the plan's funding liability, based on the funding liability of the plan for the preceding plan year and on reasonable actuarial estimates, assumptions, and methods, and

(B) the amount of any contributions reasonably anticipated to be made for the preceding plan year.

Contributions described in subparagraph (B) shall be taken into account in determining the plan's funded percentage as of the beginning of the plan year.

(5) DEFINITIONS. For purposes of this subsection—

(A) FUNDING RESTORATION STATUS. A CSEC plan shall be treated as in funding restoration status for a plan year if the plan's funded percentage as of the beginning of such plan year is less than 80 percent.

(B) FUNDED PERCENTAGE. The term 'funded percentage' means the ratio (expressed as a percentage) which—

(i) the value of plan assets (as determined under subsection (c)(2)), bears to

(ii) the plan's funding liability.

(C) FUNDING LIABILITY. The term 'funding liability' for a plan year means the present value of all benefits accrued or earned under the plan as of the beginning of the plan year, based on the assumptions used by the plan pursuant to this section, including the interest rate described in subsection (b)(5)(A) (without regard to subsection (b)(5)(B)).

(D) SPREAD GAIN FUNDING METHOD. The term 'spread gain funding method' has the meaning given such term under rules and forms issued by the Secretary of the Treasury.

Amendments

P.L. 113-97, §102(a):

Amended ERISA by adding new section 306 to read as above.

Effective for years beginning after 12-31-2013.

[¶ 14,657]
SECURITY REQUIRED UPON ADOPTION OF PLAN AMENDMENT RESULTING IN SIGNIFICANT UNDERFUNDING

[Act Sec. 307—Stricken]

Amendments

P. L. 109-280, §101(a):

Repealed ERISA Sec. 307.

Prior to repeal, ERISA Sec. 307 read as folows:

(a) IN GENERAL

(a)(1) a defined benefit plan (other than a multiemployer plan) to which the requirements of section 302 apply adopts an amendment an effect of which is to increase current liability under the plan for a plan year, and

(a)(2) the funded current liability percentage of the plan for the plan year in which the amendment takes effect is less than 60 percent, including the amount of the unfunded current liability under the plan attributable to the plan amendment.

the contributing sponsor (or any member of the controlled group of the contributing sponsor) shall provide security to the plan.

(b) FORM OF SECURITY. The security required under subsection (a) shall consist of—

(b)(1) a bond issued by a corporate surety company that is an acceptable surety for purposes of section 412,

(b)(2) cash, or United States obligations which mature in 3 years or less, held in escrow by a bank or similar financial institution, or

(b)(3) such other form of security as is satisfactory to the Secretary of the Treasury and the parties involved.

(c) AMOUNT OF SECURITY. The security shall be in an amount equal to the excess of—

(c)(1) the lesser of—

(c)(1)(A) the amount of additional plan assets which would be necessary to increase the funded current liability percentage under the plan to 60 percent, including the amount of the unfunded current liability under the plan attributable to the plan amendment, or

(c)(1)(B) the amount of the increase in current liability under the plan attributable to the plan amendment and any other plan amendments adopted after December 22, 1987, and before such plan amendment, over

(c)(2) $10,000,000.

(d) RELEASE OF SECURITY. The security shall be released (and any amounts thereunder shall be refunded together with any interest accrued thereon) at the end of the first plan year which ends after the provision of the security and for which the funded current liability percentage under the plan is not less than 60 percent. The Secretary of the Treasury may prescribe regulations for partial releases of the security by reason of increases in the funded current liability percentage.

(e) NOTICE. A contributing sponsor which is required to provide security under subsection (a) shall notify the Pension Benefit Guaranty Corporation within 30 days after the amendment requiring such security takes effect. Such notice shall contain such information as the Corporation may require.

(f) DEFINITIONS. For purposes of this section, the terms "current liability", "funded current liability percentage", and "unfunded current liability" shall have the meanings given such terms by section 302(d), except that in computing unfunded current liability there shall not be taken into account any unamortized portion of the unfunded old liability amount as of the close of the plan year.

The above amendment applies to plan years beginning after 2007.

P.L. 101-239, §7881(i)(1)(B):

Amended ERISA Sec. 307(c)(1)(B) by inserting "and any other plan amendments adopted after December 22, 1987, and before such plan amendment" after "amendment."

P.L. 101-239, §7881(i)(2):

Amended ERISA Sec. 307(d) by inserting "of the Treasury" after "Secretary."

P.L. 101-239, §7881(i)(3)(A):

Amended ERISA Sec. 307 by redesignating subsection (e) as subsection (f) and adding new subsection (e) to read as above.

P.L. 101-239, §7881(i)(4)(B):

Amended ERISA Sec. 307(a)(1) by inserting "to which the requirements of section 302 apply" after "multiemployer plan)."

The above amendments are effective as if included in P.L. 100-203, §9341(b).

P.L. 101-239, §7881(i)(5):

Amended P.L. 100-203, §9341(c) to read as below, effective December 22, 1987.

P.L. 100-203, §9341(b)(2):

Added ERISA Sec. 307, to read as above, effective for plan amendments made after December 22, 1987 except for plan amendments adopted by collective bargaining agreements ratified before December 22, 1987.

P.L. 100-203, §9341(c):

(c) EFFECTIVE DATE.—

(1) IN GENERAL.—Except as provided in this subsection, the amendments made by this section shall apply to plan amendments adopted after the date of the enactment of this Act.

(2) COLLECTIVE BARGAINING AGREEMENTS.—In the case of a plan maintained pursuant to 1 or more collective bargaining agreements between employee representatives and 1 or more employers ratified before the date of the enactment of this Act, the amendments made by this section shall not apply to plan amendments adopted pursuant to collective bargaining agreements ratified before the date of enactment (without regard to any extension, amendment, or modification of such agreements on or after such date of enactment).

[¶ 14,660]
EFFECTIVE DATES

[Act Sec. 308—Stricken]

Amendments

P. L. 109-280, §101(a):

Repealed ERISA Sec. 308.

Prior to repeal, ERISA Sec. 308 read as follows:

(a) Except as otherwise provided in this section, this part shall apply in the case of plan years beginning after the date of the enactment of this Act.

(b) Except as otherwise provided in subsections (c) and (d), in the case of a plan in existence on January 1, 1974, this part shall apply in the case of plan years beginning after December 31, 1975.

(c)(1) In the case of a plan maintained on January 1, 1974, pursuant to one or more agreements which the Secretary finds to be collective bargaining agreements between employee organizations and one or more employers, this part shall apply only with respect to plan years beginning after the earlier of the date specified in subparagraph (A) or (B) of section 211(c)(1).

(c)(2) This subsection shall apply with respect to a plan if (and only if) the application of this subsection results in a later effective date for this part than the effective date required by subsection (b).

(d) In the case of a plan the administrator of which elects under section 1017(d) of this Act to have the provisions of the Internal Revenue Code of 1954 relating to

participation, vesting, funding, and form of benefit to apply to a plan year and to all subsequent plan years, this part shall apply to plan years beginning on the earlier of the first plan year to which such election applies or the first plan year determined under subsections (a), (b), and (c) of this section.

(e) In the case of a plan maintained by a labor organization which is exempt from tax under section 501(c)(5) of the Internal Revenue Code of 1954 exclusively for the benefit of its employees and their beneficiaries, this part shall be applied by substituting for the term "December 31, 1975" in subsection (b), the earlier of—

(e)(1) the date on which the second convention of such labor organization held after the date of the enactment of this Act ends, or

(e)(2) December 31, 1980,

but in no event shall a date earlier than the later of December 31, 1975, or the date determined under subsection (c) be substituted.

(f) The preceding provisions of this section shall not apply with respect to amendments made to this part in provisions enacted after the date of the enactment of this Act.

The above amendment applies to plan years beginning after 2007.

P.L. 101-239, §7984(h)(3):

Amended ERISA by adding subsection (f).

P.L. 100-203, §9341(b):

Redesignated ERISA Sec. 307 as ERISA Sec. 308, to read as above, effective for plan amendments made after December 22, 1987 except for plan amendments adopted by collective bargaining agreements ratified before December 22, 1987.

P.L. 99-272, §11015(a)(1)(A):

Redesignated ERISA Sec. 306 as ERISA Sec. 307, effective with respect to applications for waivers, extensions and modifications filed on or after April 7, 1986.

Regulations

Interpretive Bulletin ERISA IB MS 75-1 has been redesignated as Reg. §2509.75-10 as section of "Part 2509—Interpretive Bulletins Relating to the Employee Retirement Income Security Act of 1974; Chapter XXV—Office of Employee Benefits Security—Title 29—Labor," filed with the Federal Register on January 21, 1976 (41 FR 3289).

»»→ *Caution: The Reliance Period and the deadline dates have expired.*

[¶ 14,671]

§2509.75-10 **Interpretive bulletin relating to the ERISA Guidelines and the Special Reliance Procedure.** On November 5, 1975, the Department of Labor (the "Department") and the Internal Revenue Service (the "Service") announced the publication of a compendium of authoritative rules (hereinafter referred to as the "ERISA Guidelines") relating to ERISA requirements. *See* T.I.R. No. 1415 (November 5, 1975) issued by the Service. These rules were published in recognition of the need to provide an immediate and complete set of interim guidelines to facilitate (1) adoption of new employee pension benefit plans (hereinafter referred to as "plans"), and (2) prompt amendment of existing plans, in conformance with the applicable requirements of the Employee Retirement Income Security Act of 1974 ("ERISA") pending the issuance of final regulations or other rules. These rules govern the application of (1) the qualification requirements of the Internal Revenue Code of 1954 (the "Code") added or amended by ERISA, and (2) the requirements of the provisions of parts 2 and 3 of Title I of ERISA paralleling such qualification requirements (both such sets of requirements hereinafter referred to collectively as the "new qualification requirements").

The ERISA Guidelines incorporate by reference the documents relating to the new qualification requirements heretofore published by the Department and by the Service as temporary or proposed regulations, revenue rulings, revenue procedures, questions and answers, technical information releases, and other issuances. The ERISA Guidelines also incorporate additional documents published on November 5, 1975, or to be published forthwith, which are necessary to complete the interim guidelines relating to the new qualification requirements. See the schedule set forth below for a complete list and brief description of the documents comprising the ERISA Guidelines.

The Department and the Service emphasized that the ERISA Guidelines constitute the entire set of interim rules of the Department and the Service for satisfying the new qualification requirements, and thus provide authoritative guidance in respect of the new statutory requirements bearing on qualification. These rules are applicable to individually designed plans and to multiemployer (or other multiple employer) plans, and may be relied upon until amended or supplemented by final regulations or other rules. Moreover, the Department and the Service announced that any provisions of final regulations or other rules which amend or supplement the rules contained in the ERISA Guidelines will generally be prospective only from the date of publication. Further, in the case of employee plan provisions adopted or amended before the date of such publication which satisfy the ERISA Guidelines, such final regulations or other rules will generally be made effective for plan years commencing after such date, except in unusual circumstances.

The Service further announced that the ERISA Guidelines incorporate the procedures that will enable employers to obtain determination letters as to the qualification of pension, annuity, profit sharing, stock bonus and bond purchase plans which satisfy the requirements of sections 401(a), 403(a) and 405(a) of the Code, as amended by ERISA.

The Service also pointed out that the ERISA Guidelines will enable sponsors of master and prototype plans (whether newly established or amended) to obtain opinion letters as to the acceptability of the form of such plans, and further, that employers who establish plans designed to meet the requirements of section 301(d) of the Tax Reduction Act of 1975 (relating to employee stock ownership plans) will be able to obtain determination letters as to the acceptability of such plans (whether or not such plans are intended to be qualified).

To facilitate further the adoption of new plans and the prompt amendment of existing plans in conformance with the new qualification requirements, the Service announced on November 5, 1975, the adoption of a special procedure (hereinafter referred to as the "Special Reliance Procedure") pursuant to which the adoption, on or before May 30, 1976, of new plans and amendments of existing plans may be effectuated with full reliance upon the rules which comprise the ERISA Guidelines and without regard to any amendment or supplementation of such rules before such date. Therefore, except in unusual circumstances (described in Technical Information Release No. 1416 (November 5, 1975)), plans which comply with the Special Reliance Procedure shall generally be considered by the Service as satisfying the qualification requirements of the Code added or amended by ERISA for plan years commencing on or before December 31, 1976, to which such requirements are applicable, notwithstanding the date when final regulations or other rules hereafter published which amend or supplement the rules comprising the ERISA Guidelines may otherwise be made effective. Reference is hereby made to Technical Information Release No. 1416 (November 5, 1975) for a description of the Special Reliance Procedure.

The Department announced that plans which comply with the Special Reliance Procedure will be considered by the Department as satisfying the requirements of the provisions of parts 2 and 3 of Title I of ERISA which parallel the qualification requirements of the Code added or amended by ERISA to the same extent as such plans are considered by the Service as satisfying, in accordance with the terms of the Special Reliance Procedure, such qualification requirements.

The availability of the Special Reliance Procedure will substantially diminish the occasions for plans to avail themselves of the right to satisfy, for tax purposes, the qualification requirements of the Code (added or amended by ERISA) by retroactive amendments adopted during or after the close of a plan year, in accordance with section 401(b) of the Code and the temporary regulations thereunder. The Department pointed out that no explicit parallel provision to section 401(b) of the Code is contained in Title I of ERISA. Nevertheless, to the extent retroactive amendments to a plan are made to satisfy the requirements of parts 2 and 3 of Title I of ERISA which parallel the qualification requirements of the Code added or amended by ERISA, the Department noted that such plan will be in compliance with such requirements if such an amendment designed to satisfy such requirements (1) is adopted by the end of the plan year to which such requirements are applicable, and (2) is made effective for all purposes for such entire plan year.

The schedule of documents comprising the ERISA Guidelines follows.

ERISA GUIDELINES
SCHEDULE OF DOCUMENTS

Publication Date [1]	Document [1]	Subject [1]	Code and ERISA Sections [1]
1/ 8/75	TIR 1334 [¶ 17,248]	Questions and answers relating to defined contribution plans subject to ERISA	410,411, *et al.*
4/21/75	40 F.R. 17576 [¶ 20,120]	Notice of Proposed Rule Making: Qualification (& other aspects) of HR-10 plans	401(c), 401(d), 401(e), 46, 50A, 72,404(e), 901 and 1379
6/ 4/75	T.D. 7358 [¶ 13,913—13,914]	Temporary Regulations: Notification of Interested Parties	7476
7/14/75	T.D. 7367 [¶ 13,915]	Temporary Regulations: Notice of determination of qualification	7476
9/ 8/75	40 F.R. 41654 [¶ 14,515]	Department of Labor — Minimum Standards for hours of service, years of service, and breaks in service relating to participation, vesting, and accrual of benefits[2]	401(a)(3)(B), 411(a)(5)(C), and ERISA sections 202, 203, and 204
9/17/75	TIR 1403 [¶ 17,443]	Questions and answers relating mainly to defined benefit plans subject to ERISA (addition to TIR 1334)	410, 411, *et al.*
9/18/75	40 F.R. 43034 [¶ 20,129]	Notice of Proposed Rule Making: Definitions of multiemployer plan and plan administrator	414(f) and (g)
9/29/75	T.D. 7377 [¶ 11,721]	Temporary Regulations: Certain retroactive amendments of employee plans[3]	401(b)
10/ 3/75	T.D. 7379 [¶ 11,719]	Temporary Regulations: Qualified joint and survivor annuities[4]	401(a)(11)
10/ 3/75	T.D. 7380 [¶ 12,155—12,171]	Temporary Regulations: Minimum Participation Standards[4a]	410
10/ 8/75	T.D. 7381 [¶ 11,720]	Temporary Regulations: Commencement of Benefits[5]	401(a)(14)
10/15/75	T.D. 7382 [¶ 11,720A]	Temporary Regulations: Requirement that benefits under a qualified plan are not decreased on account of certain Social Security increases[6]	401(a)(15)
10/16/75	T.D. 7383 [¶ 11,731]	Temporary Regulations: Nonbank trustees of pension and profit sharing trusts benefiting owner-employees	401(d)(1)
10/16/75	40 F.R. 48517 [¶ 20,136]	Notice of Proposed Rule Making: Certain Custodial Accounts	401(f)
10/30/75	TIR 1408 [¶ 17,445]	Questions & Answers relating to mergers, consolidations, etc.	401(a)(12) and 414(l)
11/ 3/75	Rev. Rul. 75-480,1975-44 IRB [¶ 19,394]	Updating of Rev. Rul. 71-446 to reflect changes mandated by ERISA	401(a)(5)
11/ 3/75	Rev. Rul. 75-481, 1975-44 IRB [¶ 19,395]	Guidelines for determining whether contributions or benefits under plan satisfy the limitations of section 415 of the Code[7]	401(a)(16) and 415
11/ 3/75	TIR 1411, Rev. Proc. 75-49, 1975-48 IRB [¶ 17,250]	Vesting and discrimination	401(a)(4) and 411(d)(1)
2/ 2/76	TIR 1441, Rev. Proc. 76-11, 1976-9 IRB [¶ 17,456]	[Vesting and discrimination]	[401(a)(4) and 411(d)(1)]

[1] [Bracketed material relates to additions made by CCH after ERISA IB-MS-75-1 was originally issued. Bracketed paragraph numbers refer to the paragraphs where the Documents are reported in the CCH PENSION PLAN GUIDE.—CCH.]

[2] [Final regulations on minimum standards for hours of service, years of service, and breaks in service relating to participation, vesting, and accrual of benefits have been adopted by the Department of Labor. They were published in the *Federal Register* (41 FR 56462) on December 28, 1976. The final regulations appear at ¶ 14,411—14,415, 14,421—14,422, 14,431—14,432, 14,441—14,444, and 14,501.—CCH.]

[3] [Final regulations on retroactive plan changes were adopted by T.D. 7437. The final regulations appear at ¶ 11,721.—CCH.]

[4] [Final regulations on joint and survivor annuities were adopted by T.D. 7458. The final regulations appear at ¶ 11,719.—CCH.]

[4a] [Final regulations on minimum participation standards were adopted by T.D. 7508. The final regulations appear at ¶ 12,156—12,163, 12,171, 12,311, and 12,312.—CCH.]

[5] [Final regulations on the commencement of benefits under qualified trusts were adopted by T.D. 7436. The final regulations appear at ¶ 11,720.—CCH.]

[6] [Final regulations under Code Sec. 401 on benefits under qualified plans not being decreased on account of certain social security increases were adopted by T.D. 7434. The final regulations appear at ¶ 11,720A.—CCH.]

[7] [Rev. Rul. 75-481: 1975-2 CB 188 has been modified by Rev. Rul. 76-318 at ¶ 19,415 and Rev. Rul. 77-24 at ¶ 19,424.—CCH.]

Publication Date[1]	Document [1]	Subject [1]	Code and ERISA Sections [1]
11/ 4/75	TIR 1413 [¶ 17,446]	Questions & Answers relating to Employee Stock Ownership Plans[8]	401, 4975, and section 301(d) of the Tax Reduction Act of 1975
11/ 5/75	T.D. 7387 [¶ 11,720D, 12,211—12,231]	Temporary Regulations on Minimum Vesting Standards[8a]	411
11/ 5/75	T.D. 7388 [¶ 12,365]	Controlled groups, businesses under common control, etc.	414(b) and (c)
4/ 6/76	IR-1589 [¶ 17,052]	Nonforfeiture of employee-derived accrued benefit upon death	411(a)(1)
1/21/76[9]	41 F.R. 3290	Department of Labor — Interpretive Bulletin; Definition of Seasonal Industries	410(a)(3)(B), 411(a)(5)(C), and ERISA sections 202(a)(3)(C), 203(b)(2)(C)
11/ 7/75	40 F.R. 52008 [¶ 14,139]	Department of Labor—additional requirements applicable to definition of multiemployer plan	404(f) and ERISA section 3(37)
		Department of Labor—suspension of benefits upon reemployment of retiree	411(a)(3)(B) and ERISA section 201(a)(3)(A)
12/ 3/75	TIR's 1422 and 1430 [¶ 17,450, 17,454]	Assignment or alienation of plan benefits[10]	401(a)(13)
12/ 3/75	TIR's 1422 and 1430 [¶ 17,450, 17,454]	Assignment or alienation of plan benefits[10]	401(a)(13)
1/28/76	TIR 1439; Rev. Rul. 76-47 [¶ 19,403]	Appropriate conversion factor	411(c)(2)(B)(ii)

Part 4—Fiduciary Responsibility

[¶ 14,710]
ERISA Sec. 401, COVERAGE

Act Sec. 401. (a) SCOPE OF COVERAGE.—This part shall apply to any employee benefit plan described in section 4(a) (and not exempted under section 4(b)), other than—

(1) a plan which is unfunded and is maintained by an employer primarily for the purpose of providing deferred compensation for a select group of management or highly compensated employees; or

(2) any agreement described in section 736 of the Internal Revenue Code of 1986, which provides payments to a retired partner or deceased partner or a deceased partner's successor in interest.

Act Sec. 401. (b) SECURITIES OR POLICIES DEEMED TO BE INCLUDED IN PLAN ASSETS.—For purposes of this part:

(1) In the case of a plan which invests in any security issued by an investment company registered under the Investment Company Act of 1940, the assets of such plan shall be deemed to include such security but shall not, solely by reason of such investment, be deemed to include any assets of such investment company.

(2) In the case of a plan to which a guaranteed benefit policy is issued by an insurer, the assets of such plan shall be deemed to include such policy, but shall not, solely by reason of the issuance of such policy, be deemed to include any assets of such insurer. For purposes of this paragraph:

(A) The term "insurer" means an insurance company, insurance service, or insurance organization, qualified to do business in a State.

(B) The term "guaranteed benefit policy" means an insurance policy or contract to the extent that such policy or contract provides for benefits the amount of which is guaranteed by the insurer. Such term includes any surplus in a separate account, but excludes any other portion of a separate account.

Act Sec. 401. (c)(1)(A) CLARIFICATION OF APPLICATION OF ERISA TO INSURANCE COMPANY GENERAL ACCOUNTS.—Not later than June 30, 1997, the Secretary shall issue proposed regulations to provide guidance for the purpose of determining, in cases where an insurer issues 1 or more policies to or for the benefit of an employee benefit plan (and such policies are supported by assets of such insurer's general account), which assets held by the insurer (other than plan assets held in its separate accounts) constitute assets of the plan for purposes of this part and section 4975 of the Internal Revenue Code of 1986 and to provide guidance with respect to the application of this title to the general account assets of insurers.

(B) The proposed regulations under subparagraph (A) shall be subject to public notice and comment until September 30, 1997.

(C) The Secretary shall issue final regulations providing the guidance described in subparagraph (A) not later than December 31, 1997.

(D) Such regulations shall only apply with respect to policies which are issued by an insurer on or before December 31, 1998, to or for the benefit of an employee benefit plan which is supported by assets of such insurer's general account. With respect to policies issued on or before December 31, 1998, such regulations shall take effect at the end of the 18-month period following the date on which such regulations become final.

(2) The Secretary shall ensure that the regulations issued under paragraph (1)—

(A) are administratively feasible, and

(B) protect the interests and rights of the plan and of its participants and beneficiaries (including meeting the requirements of paragraph (3)).

(3) The regulations prescribed by the Secretary pursuant to paragraph (1) shall require, in connection with any policy issued by an insurer to or for the benefit of an employee benefit plan to the extent that the policy is not a guaranteed benefit policy (as defined in subsection (b)(2)(B))—

---

[8] [Final regulations on excise taxes for employee stock ownership plans were adopted by T.D. 7506. The final regulations appear at ¶ 13,644, 13,647B, and 13,647C.]

[8a] [Final regulations on minimum vesting standards were adopted by T.D. 7501. The final regulations appear at ¶ 11,700A, 11,720D, 11,859, 12,211—12,231, 12,311, 12,312, and 13,302.]

[9] [The Interpretive Bulletin on Seasonal Industries, §2509.76-1, ¶ 14,520, was rescinded by ERISA IB 76-2 (§2509.76-2), reproduced at ¶14,521. It was officially withdrawn from the ERISA Guidelines by §2509.76-3 at ¶ 14,522.]

[10] [Final regulations on assignment or alienation of benefits were adopted by T.D. 7534 on February 5, 1978. The final regulations appear at ¶ 11,719B.]

[10] [Final regulations on assignment or alienation of benefits were adopted by T.D. 7534 on February 5, 1978. The final regulations appear at ¶ 11,719B.]

(A) that a plan fiduciary totally independent of the insurer authorize the purchase of such policy (unless such purchase is a transaction exempt under section 408(b)(5)),

(B) that the insurer describe (in such form and manner as shall be prescribed in such regulations), in annual reports and in policies issued to the policyholder after the date on which such regulations are issued in final form pursuant to paragraph (1)(C)—

(i) a description of the method by which any income and expenses of the insurer's general account are allocated to the policy during the term of the policy and upon the termination of the policy, and

(ii) for each report, the actual return to the plan under the policy and such other financial information as the Secretary may deem appropriate for the period covered by each such annual report,

(C) that the insurer disclose to the plan fiduciary the extent to which alternative arrangements supported by assets of separate accounts of the insurer (which generally hold plan assets) are available, whether there is a right under the policy to transfer funds to a separate account and the terms governing any such right, and the extent to which support by assets of the insurer's general account and support by assets of separate accounts of the insurer might pose differing risks to the plan, and

(D) that the insurer manage those assets of the insurer which are assets of such insurer's general account (irrespective of whether any such assets are plan assets) with the care, skill, prudence, and diligence under the circumstances then prevailing that a prudent man acting in a like capacity and familiar with such matters would use in the conduct of an enterprise of a like character and with like aims, taking into account all obligations supported by such enterprise.

(4) Compliance by the insurer with all requirements of the regulations issued by the Secretary pursuant to paragraph (1) shall be deemed compliance by such insurer with sections 404, 406, and 407 with respect to those assets of the insurer's general account which support a policy described in paragraph (3).

(5)(A) Subject to subparagraph (B), any regulations issued under paragraph (1) shall not take effect before the date on which such regulations become final.

(B) No person shall be subject to liability under this part or section 4975 of the Internal Revenue Code of 1986 for conduct which occurred before the date which is 18 months following the date described in subparagraph (A) on the basis of a claim that the assets of an insurer (other than plan assets held in a separate account) constitute assets of the plan, except—

(i) as otherwise provided by the Secretary in regulations intended to prevent avoidance of the regulations issued under paragraph (1), or

(ii) as provided in an action brought by the Secretary pursuant to paragraph (2) or (5) of section 502(a) for a breach of fiduciary responsibilities which would also constitute a violation of Federal or State criminal law.

The Secretary shall bring a cause of action described in clause (ii) if a participant, beneficiary, or fiduciary demonstrates to the satisfaction of the Secretary that a breach described in clause (ii) has occurred.

(6)»Nothing in this subsection shall preclude the application of any Federal criminal law.

(7) For purposes of this subsection, the term "policy" includes a contract.

Amendment

P.L. 104-188, § 1460(a):

Amended ERISA Act Sec. 401 by adding at the end a new subsection (c) to read as above.

The above amendment is effective January 1, 1975, except that it shall not apply to any civil action commenced before November 7, 1995.

P.L. 101-239, § 7891(a)(1):—

Titles I, III, and IV of ERISA (other than sections 3(37)(E), 301(a)(7), and 308, the last sentence of section 408(d), and sections 414(c), 4001(a)(3)(ii), and 4303) are each amended by striking "Internal Revenue Code of 1954" each place it appears and inserting "Internal Revenue Code of 1986" effective October 22, 1986.

Regulations

Reg. § 2550.401b-1 was adopted by FR Doc. 82-13400 and was filed with the Federal Register on May 13, 1982 (47 FR 21241). The regulation is effective June 17, 1982. **Note:** This regulation was removed from Part 2550 by 51 FR 41262 on Nov. 13, 1986, effective as of Mar. 13, 1987. Reg. § 2550.401c-1 was filed with the Federal Register January 5, 2000 (65 FR 613).

[¶ 14,713]

§ 2550.401b-1 **Definition of "plan assets"—Governmental mortgage pools.** (a) *In General.* (1) Where an employee benefit plan acquires a guaranteed governmental mortgage pool certificate, as defined in paragraph (b), then, for purposes of part 4 of Title I of the Act and section 4975 of the Internal Revenue Code, the plan's assets include the certificate and all of its rights with respect to such certificate under applicable law, but do not, solely by reason of the plan's holding of such certificate, include any of the mortgages underlying such certificate.

(b) A "guaranteed governmental mortgage pool certificate" is a certificate backed by, or evidencing an interest in, specified mortgages or participation interests therein and with respect to which interest and principal payable pursuant to the certificate is guaranteed by the United States or an agency or instrumentality thereof. The term "guaranteed governmental mortgage pool certificate" includes a mortgage pool certificate with respect to which interest and principal payable pursuant to the certificate is guaranteed by:

(1) The Government National Mortgage Association;

(2) The Federal Home Loan Mortgage Corporation; or

(3) The Federal National Mortgage Association.

[¶ 14,714]

§ 2550.401c-1 **Definition of "plan assets"—insurance company general accounts.** (a) *In General.* (1) This section describes, in the case where an insurer issues one or more policies to or for the benefit of an employee benefit plan (and such policies are supported by assets of an insurance company's general account), which assets held by the insurer (other than plan assets held in its separate accounts) constitute plan assets for purposes of Subtitle A, and Parts 1 and 4 of Subtitle B, of Title I of the Employee Retirement Income Security Act of 1974 (ERISA

or the Act) and section 4975 of the Internal Revenue Code (the Code), and provides guidance with respect to the application of Title I of the Act and section 4975 of the Code to the general account assets of insurers.

(2) Generally, when a plan has acquired a Transition Policy (as defined in paragraph (h)(6) of this section), the plan's assets include the Transition Policy, but do not include any of the underlying assets of the insurer's general account if the insurer satisfies the requirements of paragraphs (c) through (f) of this section or, if the requirements of paragraphs (c) through (f) were not satisfied, the insurer cures the non-compliance through satisfaction of the requirements in paragraph (i)(5) of this section.

(3) For purposes of paragraph (a)(2) of this section, a plan's assets will not include any of the underlying assets of the insurer's general account if the insurer fails to satisfy the requirements of paragraphs (c) through (f) of this section solely because of the takeover of the insurer's operations from management as a result of the granting of a petition filed in delinquency proceedings in the State court where the insurer is domiciled.

(b) *Approval by fiduciary independent of the issuer.*

(1) *In general.* An independent plan fiduciary who has the authority to manage and control the assets of the plan must expressly authorize the acquisition or purchase of the Transition Policy. For purposes of this paragraph, a fiduciary is not independent if the fiduciary is an affiliate of the insurer issuing the policy.

(2) Notwithstanding paragraph (b)(1) of this section, the authorization by an independent plan fiduciary is not required if:

(i) The insurer is the employer maintaining the plan, or a party in interest which is wholly owned by the employer maintaining the plan; and

(ii) The requirements of section 408(b)(5) of the Act are met.[1]

(c) *Duty of disclosure.*

(1) *In general.* An insurer shall furnish the information described in paragraphs (c)(3) and (c)(4) of this section to a plan fiduciary acting on behalf of a plan to which a Transition Policy has been issued. Paragraph (c)(2) of this section describes the style and format of such disclosure. Paragraph (c)(3) of this section describes the content of the initial disclosure. Paragraph (c)(4) of this section describes the information that must be disclosed by the insurer at least once per year for as long as the Transition Policy remains outstanding.

(2) *Style and format.* The disclosure required by this paragraph should be clear and concise and written in a manner calculated to be understood by a plan fiduciary, without relinquishing any of the substantive detail required by paragraphs (c)(3) and (c)(4) of this section. The information does not have to be organized in any particular order but should be presented in a manner which makes it easy to understand the operation of the Transition Policy.

(3) *Initial disclosure.* The insurer must provide to the plan, either as part of an amended policy, or as a separate written document, the disclosure information set forth in paragraphs (c)(3)(i) through (iv) of this section. The disclosure must include all of the following information which is applicable to the Transition Policy:

(i) A description of the method by which any income and any expense of the insurer's general account are allocated to the policy during the term of the policy and upon its termination, including:

(A) A description of the method used by the insurer to determine the fees, charges, expenses or other amounts that are, or may be, assessed against the policyholder or deducted by the insurer from any accumulation fund under the policy, including the extent and frequency with which such fees, charges, expenses or other amounts may be modified by the insurance company;

(B) A description of the method by which the insurer determines the return to be credited to any accumulation fund under the policy, including a description of the method used to allocate income and expenses to lines of business, business segments, and policies within such lines of business and business segments, and a description of how any withdrawals, transfers, or payments will affect the amount of the return credited;

(C) A description of the rights which the policyholder or plan participants have to withdraw or transfer all or a portion of any accumulation fund under the policy, or to apply the amount of a withdrawal to the purchase of guaranteed benefits or to the payment of benefits, and the terms on which such withdrawals or other applications of funds may be made, including a description of any charges, fees, credits, market value adjustments, or any other charges or adjustments, both positive and negative;

(D) A statement of the method used to calculate any charges, fees, credits or market value adjustments described in paragraph (c)(3)(i)(C) of this section, and, upon the request of a plan fiduciary, the insurer must provide within 30 days of the request:

(1) The formula actually used to calculate the market value adjustment, if any, to be applied to the unallocated amount in the accumulation fund upon distribution of a lump sum payment to the policyholder, and

(2) The actual calculation, as of a specified date that is no earlier than the last contract anniversary preceding the date of the request, of the applicable market value adjustment, including a description of the specific variables used in the calculation, the value of each of the variables, and a general description of how the value of each of those variables was determined.

(3) If the formula is based on interest rate guarantees applicable to new contracts of the same class or classes, and the duration of the assets underlying the accumulation fund, the contract must describe the process by which those components are ascertained or obtained. If the formula is based on an interest rate implicit in an index of publicly traded obligations, the identity of the index, the manner in which it is used, and identification of the source or publica-

tion where any data used in the formula can be found, must be disclosed;

(ii) A statement describing the expense, income and benefit guarantees under the policy, including a description of the length of such guarantees, and of the insurer's right, if any, to modify or eliminate such guarantees;

(iii) A description of the rights of the parties to make or discontinue contributions under the policy, and of any restrictions (such as timing, minimum or maximum amounts, and penalties and grace periods for late payments) on the making of contributions under the policy, and the consequences of the discontinuance of contributions under the policy; and

(iv) A statement of how any policyholder or participant-initiated withdrawals are to be made: first-in, first-out (FIFO) basis, last-in, first-out (LIFO) basis, pro rata or another basis.

(4) *Annual disclosure.* At least annually and not later than 90 days following the period to which it relates, an insurer shall provide the following information to each plan to which a Transition Policy has been issued:

(i) The balance of any accumulation fund on the first day and last day of the period covered by the annual report;

(ii) Any deposits made to the accumulation fund during such annual period;

(iii) An itemized statement of all income attributed to the policy or added to the accumulation fund during the period, and a description of the method used by the insurer to determine the precise amount of income;

(iv) The actual rate of return credited to the accumulation fund under the policy during such period, stating whether the rate of return was calculated before or after deduction of expenses charged to the accumulation fund;

(v) Any other additions to the accumulation fund during such period;

(vi) An itemized statement of all fees, charges, expenses or other amounts assessed against the policy or deducted from the accumulation fund during the reporting year, and a description of the method used by the insurer to determine the precise amount of the fees, charges and other expenses;

(vii) An itemized statement of all benefits paid, including annuity purchases, to participants and beneficiaries from the accumulation fund;

(viii) The dates on which the additions or subtractions were credited to, or deducted from, the accumulation fund during such period;

(ix) A description, if applicable, of all transactions with affiliates which exceed 1 percent of group annuity reserves of the general account for the prior reporting year;

(x) A statement describing any expense, income and benefit guarantees under the policy, including a description of the length of such guarantees, and of the insurer's right, if any, to modify or eliminate such guarantees. However, the information on guarantees does not have to be provided annually if it was previously disclosed in the insurance policy and has not been modified since that time;

(xi) A good faith estimate of the amount that would be payable in a lump sum at the end of such period pursuant to the request of a policyholder for payment or transfer of amounts in the accumulation fund under the policy after the insurer deducts any applicable charges and makes any appropriate market value adjustments, upward or downward, under the terms of the policy. However, upon the request of a plan fiduciary, the insurer must provide within 30 days of the request the information contained in paragraph (c)(3)(i)(D) as of a specified date that is no earlier than the last contract anniversary preceding the date of the request; and

(xii) An explanation that the insurer will make available promptly upon request of a plan, copies of the following publicly available financial data or other publicly available reports relating to the financial condition of the insurer:

[1] The Department notes that, because section 401(c)(1)(D) of the Act and the definition of Transition Policy preclude the issuance of any additional Transition Policies after December 31, 1998, the requirement for independent fiduciary authorization of the acquisition or purchase of the Transition Policy in paragraph (b) no longer has any application.

(A) National Association of Insurance Commissioners Statutory Annual Statement, with Exhibits, General Interrogatories, and Schedule D, Part 1A, Sections 1 and 2 and Schedule S—Part 3E;

(B) Rating agency reports on the financial strength and claims-paying ability of the insurer;

(C) Risk adjusted capital ratio, with a brief description of its derivation and significance, referring to the risk characteristics of both the assets and the liabilities of the insurer;

(D) Actuarial opinion of the insurer's Appointed Actuary certifying the adequacy of the insurer's reserves as required by New York State Insurance Department Regulation 126 and comparable regulations of other States; and

(E) The insurer's most recent SEC Form 10K and Form 10Q (stock companies only).

(d) *Alternative separate account arrangements.*

(1) In general. An insurer must provide the plan fiduciary with the following additional information at the same time as the initial disclosure required under paragraph (c)(3) of this section:

(i) A statement explaining the extent to which alternative contract arrangements supported by assets of separate accounts of insurers are available to plans;

(ii) A statement as to whether there is a right under the policy to transfer funds to a separate account and the terms governing any such right; and

(iii) A statement explaining the extent to which general account contracts and separate account contracts of the insurer may pose differing risks to the plan.

(2) An insurer will be deemed to comply with the requirements of paragraph (d)(1)(iii) of this section if the disclosure provided to the plan includes the following statement:

a. Contractual arrangements supported by assets of separate accounts may pose differing risks to plans from contractual arrangements supported by assets of general accounts. Under a general account contract, the plan's contributions or premiums are placed in the insurer's general account and commingled with the insurer's corporate funds and assets (excluding separate accounts and special deposit funds). The insurance company combines in its general account premiums received from all of its lines of business. These premiums are pooled and invested by the insurer. General account assets in the aggregate support the insurer's obligations under all of its insurance contracts, including (but not limited to) its individual and group life, health, disability, and annuity contracts. Experience rated general account policies may share in the experience of the general account through interest credits, dividends, or rate adjustments, but assets in the general account are not segregated for the exclusive benefit of any particular policy or obligation. General account assets are also available to the insurer for the conduct of its routine business activities, such as the payment of salaries, rent, other ordinary business expenses and dividends.

b. An insurance company separate account is a segregated fund which is not commingled with the insurer's general assets. Depending on the particular terms of the separate account contract, income, expenses, gains and losses associated with the assets allocated to a separate account may be credited to or charged against the separate account without regard to other income, expenses, gains, or losses of the insurance company, and the investment results passed through directly to the policyholders. While most, if not all, general account investments are maintained at book value, separate account investments are normally maintained at market value, which can fluctuate according to market conditions. In large measure, the risks associated with a separate account contract depend on the particular assets in the separate account.

c. The plan's legal rights vary under general and separate account contracts. In general, an insurer is subject to ERISA's fiduciary responsibility provisions with respect to the assets of a separate account (other than a separate account registered under the Investment Company Act of 1940) to the extent that the investment performance of such assets is passed directly through to the plan policyholders. ERISA requires insurers, in administering separate account assets, to act solely in the interest of the plan's participants and beneficiaries; prohibits self-dealing and conflicts of interest; and requires insurers to adhere

to a prudent standard of care. In contrast, ERISA generally imposes less stringent standards in the administration of general account contracts which were issued on or before December 31, 1998.

d. On the other hand, State insurance regulation is typically more restrictive with respect to general accounts than separate accounts. However, State insurance regulation may not provide the same level of protection to plan policyholders as ERISA regulation. In addition, insurance company general account policies often include various guarantees under which the insurer assumes risks relating to the funding and distribution of benefits. Insurers do not usually provide any guarantees with respect to the investment returns on assets held in separate accounts. Of course, the extent of any guarantees from any general account or separate account contract will depend upon the specific policy terms.

e. Finally, separate accounts and general accounts pose differing risks in the event of the insurer's insolvency. In the event of insolvency, funds in the general account are available to meet the claims of the insurer's general creditors, after payment of amounts due under certain priority claims, including amounts owed to its policyholders. Funds held in a separate account as reserves for its policy obligations, however, may be protected from the claims of creditors other than the policyholders participating in the separate account. Whether separate account funds will be granted this protection will depend upon the terms of the applicable policies and the provisions of any applicable laws in effect at the time of insolvency.

(e) *Termination procedures.* Within 90 days of written notice by a policyholder to an insurer, the insurer must permit the policyholder to exercise the right to terminate or discontinue the policy and to elect to receive without penalty either:

(1) A lump sum payment representing all unallocated amounts in the accumulation fund. For purposes of this paragraph (e)(1), the term penalty does not include a market value adjustment (as defined in paragraph (h)(7)of this section) or the recovery of costs actually incurred which would have been recovered by the insurer but for the termination or discontinuance of the policy, including any unliquidated acquisition expenses, to the extent not previously recovered by the insurer; or

(2) A book value payment of all unallocated amounts in the accumulation fund under the policy in approximately equal annual installments, over a period of no longer than 10 years, together with interest computed at an annual rate which is no less than the annual rate which was credited to the accumulation fund under the policy as of the date of the contract termination or discontinuance, minus 1 percentage point. Notwithstanding paragraphs (e)(1) and (e)(2) of this section, the insurer may defer, for a period not to exceed 180 days, amounts required to be paid to a policyholder under this paragraph for any period of time during which regular banking activities are suspended by State or federal authorities, a national securities exchange is closed for trading (except for normal holiday closings), or the Securities and Exchange Commission has determined that a state of emergency exists which may make such determination and payment impractical.

(f) *Insurer-initiated amendments.* In the event the insurer makes an insurer-initiated amendment (as defined in paragraph (h)(8) of this section), the insurer must provide written notice to the plan at least 60 days prior to the effective date of the insurer-initiated amendment. The notice must contain a complete description of the amendment and must inform the plan of its right to terminate or discontinue the policy and withdraw all unallocated funds without penalty by sending a written request within such 60 day period to the name and address contained in the notice. The plan must be offered the election to receive either a lump sum or an installment payment as described in paragraph (e)(1) and (e)(2) of this section. An insurer-initiated amendment shall not apply to a contract if the plan fiduciary exercises its right to terminate or discontinue the contract within such 60 day period and to receive a lump sum or installment payment.

(g) *Prudence.* An insurer shall manage those assets of the insurer which are assets of such insurer's general account (irrespective of whether any such assets are plan assets) with the care, skill, prudence and diligence under the circumstances then prevailing that a prudent man acting in a like capacity and familiar with such matters would use in the conduct of an enterprise of a like character and with like aims, taking into account all obligations supported by such enterprise. This prudence standard applies to the conduct of all insurers with respect to policies issued to plans on or before December 31, 1998, and differs from the prudence standard set forth in section 404(a)(1)(B) of the Act. Under the prudence standard provided in this paragraph, prudence must be determined by reference to all of the obligations supported by the general account, not just the obligations owed to plan policyholders. The more stringent standard of prudence set forth in section 404(a)(1)(B) of the Act continues to apply to any obligations which insurers may have as fiduciaries which do not arise from the management of general account assets, as well as to insurers' management of plan assets maintained in separate accounts. The terms of this section do not modify or reduce the fiduciary obligations applicable to insurers in connection with policies issued after December 31, 1998, which are supported by general account assets, including the standard of prudence under section 404(a)(1)(B) of the Act.

(h) *Definitions.* For purposes of this section:

(1) An affiliate of an insurer means:

(i) Any person, directly or indirectly, through one or more intermediaries, controlling, controlled by, or under common control with the insurer,

(ii) Any officer of, director of, 5 percent or more partner in, or highly compensated employee (earning 5 percent or more of the yearly wages of the insurer) of, such insurer or of any person described in paragraph (h)(1)(i) of this section including in the case of an insurer, an insurance agent or broker thereof (whether or not such person is a common law employee) if such agent or broker is an employee described in this paragraph or if the gross income received by such agent or broker from such insurer exceeds 5 percent of such agent's gross income from all sources for the year, and

(iii) Any corporation, partnership, or unincorporated enterprise of which a person described in paragraph (h)(1)(ii) of this section is an officer, director, or a 5 percent or more partner.

(2) The term control means the power to exercise a controlling influence over the management or policies of a person other than an individual.

(3) The term guaranteed benefit policy means a policy described in section 401(b)(2)(B) of the Act and any regulations promulgated thereunder.

(4) The term insurer means an insurer as described in section 401(b)(2)(A) of the Act.

(5) The term accumulation fund means the aggregate net considerations (i.e., gross considerations less all deductions from such considerations) credited to the Transition Policy plus all additional amounts, including interest and dividends, credited to such Transition Policy less partial withdrawals, benefit payments and less all charges and fees imposed against this accumulated amount under the Transition Policy other than surrender charges and market value adjustments.

(6) The term Transition Policy means:

(i) A policy or contract of insurance (other than a guaranteed benefit policy) that is issued by an insurer to, or on behalf of, an employee benefit plan on or before December 31, 1998, and which is supported by the assets of the insurer's general account.

(ii) A policy will not fail to be a Transition Policy merely because the policy is amended or modified:

(A) To comply with the requirements of section 401(c) of the Act and this section; or

(B) Pursuant to a merger, acquisition, demutualization, conversion, or reorganization authorized by applicable State law, provided that the premiums, policy guarantees, and the other terms and conditions of the policy remain the same, except that a membership interest in a mutual insurance company may be eliminated from the policy in exchange for separate consideration (e.g., shares of stock or policy credits).

(7) For purposes of this section, the term market value adjustment means an adjustment to the book value of the accumulation fund to accurately reflect the effect on the value of the accumulation fund of its liquidation in the prevailing market for fixed income obligations, taking into account the future cash flows that were anticipated under the policy. An adjustment is a market value adjustment within the meaning of this definition only if the insurer has determined the amount of the adjustment pursuant to a method which was previously disclosed to the policyholder in accordance with paragraph (c)(3)(i)(D) of this section, and the method permits both upward and downward adjustments to the book value of the accumulation fund.

(8) The term insurer-initiated amendment is defined in paragraphs (h)(8)(i), (ii) and (iii) of this section as:

(i) An amendment to a Transition Policy made by an insurer pursuant to a unilateral right to amend the policy terms that would have a material adverse effect on the policyholder; or

(ii) Any of the following unilateral changes in the insurer's conduct or practices with respect to the policyholder or the accumulation fund under the policy that result in a material reduction of existing or future benefits under the policy, a material reduction in the value of the policy or a material increase in the cost of financing the plan or plan benefits:

(A) A change in the methodology for assessing fees, expenses, or other charges against the accumulation fund or the policyholder;

(B) A change in the methodology used for allocating income between lines of business, or product classes within a line of business;

(C) A change in the methodology used for determining the rate of return to be credited to the accumulation fund under the policy;

(D) A change in the methodology used for determining the amount of any fees, charges, expenses, or market value adjustments applicable to the accumulation fund under the policy in connection with the termination of the contract or withdrawal from the accumulation fund;

(E) A change in the dividend class to which the policy or contract is assigned;

(F) A change in the policyholder's rights in connection with the termination of the policy, withdrawal of funds or the purchase of annuities for plan participants; and

(G) A change in the annuity purchase rates guaranteed under the terms of the contract or policy, unless the new rates are more favorable for the policyholder.

(iii) For purposes of this definition, an insurer-initiated amendment is material if a prudent fiduciary could reasonably conclude that the amendment should be considered in determining how or whether to exercise any rights with respect to the policy, including termination rights.

(iv) For purposes of this definition, the following amendments or changes are not insurer-initiated amendments:

(A) Any amendment or change which is made with the affirmative consent of the policyholder;

(B) Any amendment or change which is made in order to comply with the requirements of section 401(c) of the Act and this section; or

(C) Any amendment or change which is made pursuant to a merger, acquisition, demutualization, conversion, or reorganization authorized by applicable State law, provided that the premiums, policy guarantees, and the other terms and conditions of the policy remain the same, except that a membership interest in a mutual insurance company may be eliminated from the policy in exchange for separate consideration (e.g., shares of stock or policy credits).

(i) *Limitation on liability.*

(1) No person shall be subject to liability under Parts 1 and 4 of Title I of the Act or section 4975 of the Internal Revenue Code of 1986 for conduct which occurred prior to the applicability dates of the regulation on the basis of a claim that the assets of an insurer (other than plan assets held in a separate account) constitute plan assets. Notwithstanding the provisions of this paragraph (i)(1), this section shall not:

(i) Apply to an action brought by the Secretary of Labor pursuant to paragraphs (2) or (5) of section 502(a) of ERISA for a breach of fiduciary responsibility which would also constitute a violation of Federal or State criminal law;

(ii) Preclude the application of any Federal criminal law; or

(iii) Apply to any civil action commenced before November 7, 1995.

(2) Nothing in this section relieves any person from any State law regulating insurance which imposes additional obligations or duties upon insurers to the extent not inconsistent with the provisions of this section. Therefore, nothing in this section should be construed to preclude a State from requiring insurers to make additional disclosures to policyholders, including plans. Nor does this section prohibit a State from imposing additional substantive requirements with respect to the management of general accounts or from otherwise regulating the relationship between the policyholder and the insurer to the extent not inconsistent with the provisions of this section.

(3) Nothing in this section precludes any claim against an insurer or other person for violations of the Act which do not require a finding that the underlying assets of a general account constitute plan assets, regardless of whether the violation relates to a Transition Policy.

(4) If the requirements in paragraphs (c) through (f) of this section are not met with respect to a plan that has purchased or acquired a Transition Policy, and the insurer has not cured the non-compliance through satisfaction of the requirements in paragraph (i) (5) of this section, the plan's assets include an undivided interest in the underlying assets of the insurer's general account for that period of time for which the requirements are not met. However, an insurer's failure to comply with the requirements of this section with respect to any particular Transition Policy will not result in the underlying assets of the general account constituting plan assets with respect to other Transition Policies if the insurer is otherwise in compliance with the requirements contained in this section.

(5) Notwithstanding paragraphs (a) (2) and (i) (4) of this section, a plan's assets will not include an undivided interest in the underlying assets of the insurer's general account if the insurer made reasonable and good faith attempts at compliance with each of the requirements of paragraphs (c) through (f) of this section, and meets each of the following conditions:

(i) The insurer has in place written procedures that are reasonably designed to assure compliance with the requirements of paragraphs (c) through (f) of this section, including procedures reasonably designed to detect any instances of non-compliance.

(ii) No later than 60 days following the earlier of the insurer's detection of an instance of non-compliance or the receipt of written notice of non-compliance from the plan, the insurer complies with the requirements of paragraphs (c) through (f) of this section. If the insurer has failed to pay a plan the amounts required under paragraphs (e) or (f) of this section within 90 days of receiving written notice of termination or discontinuance of the policy, the insurer must make all corrections and adjustments necessary to restore to the plan the full amounts that the plan would have received but for the insurer's non-compliance within the applicable 60 day period; and

(iii) The insurer makes the plan whole for any losses resulting from the non-compliance as follows:

(A) If the insurer has failed to comply with the disclosure or notice requirements set forth in paragraphs (c), (d) and (f) of this section, then the insurer must make the plan whole for any losses resulting from its non-compliance within the earlier of 60 days of detection by the insurer or sixty days following the receipt of written notice from the plan; and

(B) If the insurer has failed to pay a plan any amounts required under paragraphs (e) or (f) of this section within 90 days of receiving written notice of termination or discontinuance of the policy, the insurer must pay to the plan interest on any amounts restored pursuant to paragraph (i) (5) (ii) of this section at the "underpayment rate" as set forth in 26 U.S.C. sections 6621 and 6622. Such interest must be paid within the earlier of 60 days of detection by the insurer or sixty days following receipt of written notice of non-compliance from the plan.

(j) *Applicability dates.*

(1) In general. Except as provided in paragraphs (j) (2) through (4) of this section, this section is applicable on July 5, 2001.

(2) Paragraph (c) relating to initial disclosures and paragraph (d) relating to separate account disclosures are applicable on July 5, 2000.

(3) The first annual disclosure required under paragraph (c) (4) of this section shall be provided to each plan not later than 18 months following January 5, 2000.

(4) Paragraph (f), relating to insurer-initiated amendments, is applicable on January 5, 2000.

(k) *Effective date.* This section is effective January 5, 2000.

[¶ 14,720]
ESTABLISHMENT OF PLAN

Act Sec. 402.(a)(1) NAMED FIDUCIARIES.—Every employee benefit plan shall be established and maintained pursuant to a written instrument. Such instrument shall provide for one or more named fiduciaries who jointly or severally shall have authority to control and manage the operation and administration of the plan.

(2) For purposes of this title, the term "named fiduciary" means a fiduciary who is named in the plan instrument, or who, pursuant to a procedure specified in the plan, is identified as a fiduciary (A) by a person who is an employer or employee organization with respect to the plan or (B) by such an employer and such an employee organization acting jointly.

Act Sec. 402. (b) REQUISITE FEATURES OF PLAN.—Every employee benefit plan shall—

(1) provide a procedure for establishing and carrying out a funding policy and method consistent with the objectives of the plan and the requirements of this title,

(2) describe any procedure under the plan for the allocation of responsibilities for the operation and administration of the plan (including any procedure described in section 405(c)(1)),

(3) provide a procedure for amending such plan, and for identifying the persons who have authority to amend the plan, and

(4) specify the basis on which payments are made to and from the plan.

Act Sec. 402. (c) OPTIONAL FEATURES OF PLAN.—Any employee benefit plan may provide—

(1) that any person or group of persons may serve in more than one fiduciary capacity with respect to the plan (including service both as trustee and administrator);

(2) that a named fiduciary, or a fiduciary designated by a named fiduciary pursuant to a plan procedure described in section 405(c)(1), may employ one or more persons to render advice with regard to any responsibility such fiduciary has under the plan; or

(3) that a person who is a named fiduciary with respect to control or management of the assets of the plan may appoint an investment manager or managers to manage (including the power to acquire and dispose of) any assets of a plan.

[¶ 14,730]
ESTABLISHMENT OF TRUST

Act Sec. 403.(a) BENEFIT PLAN ASSETS TO BE HELD IN TRUST; AUTHORITY OF TRUSTEES.—Except as provided in subsection (b), all assets of an employee benefit plan shall be held in trust by one or more trustees. Such trustee or trustees shall be either named in the trust instrument or in the plan instrument described in section 402(a) or appointed by a person who is a named fiduciary, and upon acceptance of being named or appointed, the trustee or trustees shall have exclusive authority and discretion to manage and control the assets of the plan, except to the extent that—

(1) the plan expressly provides that the trustee or trustees are subject to the direction of a named fiduciary who is not a trustee, in which case the trustees shall be subject to proper directions of such fiduciary which are made in accordance with the terms of the plan and which are not contrary to this Act, or

(2) authority to manage, acquire, or dispose of assets of the plan is delegated to one or more investment managers pursuant to section 402(c)(3).

Act Sec. 403. (b) EXCEPTIONS.—The requirements of subsection (a) of this section shall not apply—

(1) to any assets of a plan which consist of insurance contracts or policies issued by an insurance company qualified to do business in a State;

(2) to any assets of such an insurance company or any assets of a plan which are held by such an insurance company;

(3) to a plan—

(A) some or all of the participants of which are employees described in section 401(c)(1) of the Internal Revenue Code of 1986; or

(B) which consists of one or more individual retirement accounts described in section 408 of the Internal Revenue Code of 1986;

to the extent that such plan's assets are held in one or more custodial accounts which qualify under section 401(f) and 408(h) of such Code, whichever is applicable.

(4) to a plan which the Secretary exempts from the requirement of subsection (a) and which is not subject to any of the following provisions of this Act—

(A) part 2 of this subtitle,

(B) part 3 of this subtitle, or

(C) title IV of this Act;

(5) to a contract established and maintained under section 403(b) of the Internal Revenue Code of 1986 to the extent that the assets of the contract are held in one or more custodial accounts pursuant to section 403(b)(7) of such Code; or

(6) any plan, fund or program under which an employer, all of whose stock is directly or indirectly owned by employees, former employees or their beneficiaries, proposes through an unfunded arrangement to compensate retired employees for benefits which were forfeited by such employees under a pension plan maintained by a former employer prior to the date such pension plan became subject to this Act.

Act Sec. 403.(c)(1) ASSETS OF PLAN NOT TO INURE TO BENEFIT OF EMPLOYER; ALLOWABLE PURPOSES OF HOLDING PLAN ASSETS.—Except as provided in paragraph (2), (3) or (4) or subsection (d), or under section 4042 and 4044 (relating to termination of insured plans), or under section 420 of the Internal Revenue Code of 1986 (as in effect on the date of the enactment of the Surface Transportation and Veterans Health Care Choice Improvement Act of 2015), the assets of a plan shall never inure to the benefit of any employer and shall be held for the exclusive purposes of providing benefits to participants in the plan and their beneficiaries and defraying reasonable expenses of administering the plan.

(2)(A) In the case of a contribution, or a payment of withdrawal liability under part 1 of subtitle E of title IV—

(i) if such contribution or payment is made by an employer to a plan (other than a multiemployer plan) by a mistake of fact, paragraph (1) shall not prohibit the return of such contribution to the employer within one year after the payment of the contribution, and

(ii) if such contribution or payment is made by an employer to a multiemployer plan by a mistake of fact or law (other than a mistake relating to whether the plan is described in section 401(a) of the Internal Revenue Code of 1986 or the trust which is part of such plan is exempt from taxation under section 501(a) of such Code), paragraph (1) shall not prohibit the return of such contribution or payment to the employer within 6 months after the plan administrator determines that the contribution was made by such a mistake.

(B) If a contribution is conditioned on initial qualification of the plan under section 401 or 403(a) of the Internal Revenue Code of 1986, and if the plan receives an adverse determination with respect to its initial qualification, then paragraph (1) shall not prohibit the return of such contribution to the employer within one year after such determination, but only if the application for the determination is made by the time prescribed by law for filing the employer's return for the taxable year in which such plan was adopted, or such later date as the Secretary of the Treasury may prescribe.

(C) If a contribution is conditioned upon the deductibility of the contribution under section 404 of the Internal Revenue Code of 1986, then, to the extent the deduction is disallowed, paragraph (1) shall not prohibit the return to the employer of such contribution (to the extent disallowed) within one year after the disallowance of the deduction.

(3) In the case of a withdrawal liability payment which has been determined to be an overpayment, paragraph (1) shall not prohibit the return of such payment to the employer within 6 months after the date of such determination.

Act Sec. 403. (d) (1) TERMINATION OF PLAN.—Upon termination of a pension plan to which section 4021 does not apply at the time of termination and to which this part applies (other than a plan to which no employer contributions have been made) the assets of the plan shall be allocated in accordance with the provisions of section 4044 of this Act, except as otherwise provided in regulations of the Secretary.

(2) The assets of a welfare plan which terminates shall be distributed in accordance with the terms of the plan, except as otherwise provided in regulations of the Secretary.

Amendments

P.L. 114-41, § 2007(b)(1):

Amended ERISA Sec. 403(c)(1) by striking "MAP-21" and inserting "Surface Transportation and Veterans Health Care Choice Improvement Act of 2015".

The above amendments take effect on July 31, 2015.

P.L. 112-141, § 40241(b)(1):

Amended ERISA Sec. 403(c)(1) by striking "Pension Protection Act of 2006" and inserting "MAP-21".

For effective date, see P.L. 112-141, § 40241(c), below.

P.L. 112-141, § 40241(c), provides:

(c) EFFECTIVE DATE.—The amendments made by this Act [section]shall take effect on the date of the enactment of this Act [July 6, 2012].

P.L. 109-280, § 107(a)11):

Act Sec. 107(a)(11) amended ERISA Sec. 403(c)(1) by striking "American Jobs Creation Act of 2004" and inserting "Pension Protection Act of 2006."

The above amendment applies to plan years beginning after 2007.

P.L. 108-357, § 709(a)(2):

Act Sec. 709(a)(2) amended ERISA Sec. 403(c)(1) by striking "Pension Funding Equity Act of 2004" and inserting "American Jobs Creation Act of 2004."

P.L. 108-218, § 204(b):

Act Sec. 204(b)(2) amended ERISA Sec. 403(c)(1) by striking "Tax Relief Extension Act of 1999" and inserting "Pension Funding Equity Act of 2004."

P.L. 106-170, § 535(a)(2)(B):

Act Sec. 535(a)(2)(B) amended ERISA Sec. 403(c)(1) by striking "January 1, 1995" and inserting "the date of the enactment of the Tax Relief Extension Act of 1999".

The above amendment applies to qualified transfers occurring after December 17, 1999.

P.L. 101-508, Sec. 12012(a):

Amended ERISA Sec. 403(c)(1) by inserting ", or under section 420 of the Internal Revenue Code of 1986 (as in effect on January 1, 1991)" after "insured plans)" effective for qualified transfers under Code Sec. 420 made after November 5, 1990.

P.L. 101-239, § 7881(k):

Amended ERISA Sec. 403(c) by striking paragraph (3) and redesignating paragraph (4) as paragraph (3) effective December 22, 1987. Prior to being stricken, paragraph (3) read as follows:

(3) In the case of a contribution which would otherwise be an excess contribution (as defined in section 4979(c) of the Internal Revenue Code of 1986) paragraph (1) shall not prohibit a correcting distribution with respect to such contribution from the plan to the employer to the extent permitted in such section to avoid payment of an excise tax on excess contributions under such section.

P.L. 101-239, § 7891(a)(1):

Titles I, III, and IV of ERISA (other than sections 3(37)(E), 301(a)(7), and 308, the last sentence of section 408(d), and sections 414(c), 4001(a)(3)(ii), and 4303) are each amended by striking "Internal Revenue Code of 1954" each place it appears and inserting "Internal Revenue Code of 1986" effective October 22, 1986.

P.L. 101-239, § 7894(e)(3):

Amended ERISA Sec. 403(b)(3) by redesignating clauses (i) and (ii) as subparagraphs (A) and (B), respectively; by striking "to the extent" and all that followed through "applicable" in subparagraph (B) (as redesignated); and by adding the new material that follows subparagraph (B) effective September 2, 1974. Prior to amendment, ERISA Sec. 403(b)(3) read as follows:

(3) to a plan—

(i) some or all of the participants of which are employees described in section 401(c)(1) of the Internal Revenue Code of 1954; or

(ii) which consists of one or more individual retirement accounts described in section 408 of the Internal Revenue Code of 1954, to the extent that such plan's assets are held in one or more custodial accounts which qualify under section 401(f) or 408(h) of such Code, whichever is applicable;

P.L. 100-203, § 9343(c)(1):

Amended ERISA Sec. 403(c)(2)(B) to read as above, effective December 22, 1987. Prior to amendment, subparagraph (B) read as follows:

(B) If a contribution is conditioned on qualification of the plan under section 401, 403(a), or 405(a) of the Internal Revenue Code of 1954, and if the plan does not qualify, then paragraph (1) shall not prohibit the return of such contribution to the employer within one year after the date of denial of qualification of the plan.

P.L. 100-203, § 9343(c)(2):

Amended ERISA Sec. 403(c)(3) by striking out "4972(b) of the Internal Revenue Code of 1954" and inserting "4979(c) of the Internal Revenue Code of 1986" instead.

P.L. 96-364, §§ 310, 402(b)(2), 410(a) and 411(c):

Added new subsection 403(b)(6), amended section 403(c)(1) by substituting "(3) or (4)" for (3) and added new section 403(c)(4), effective September 26, 1980.

Sec. 403(c)(2)(A) was amended to read as above. Prior to its amendment, section 403(c)(2)(A) read:

"(2)(A) In the case of a contribution which is made by an employer by a mistake of fact, paragraph (1) shall not prohibit the return of such contribution to the employer within one year after the payment of the contribution."

Act Sec. 410(c) provides:

"(c) The amendment made by this section shall take effect on January 1, 1975, except that in the case of contributions received by a collectively bargained plan maintained by more than one employer before the date of enactment of this Act, any determination by the plan administrator that any such contribution was made by mistake of fact or law before such date shall be deemed to have been made on such date of enactment."

Regulations

Reg. §§ 2550.403a-1 and 2550.403b-1 were adopted by FR Doc. 82-13400 and were filed with the Federal Register on May 13, 1982 (47 FR 21241). The regulations are effective June 17, 1982.

Subchapter F—Fiduciary Responsibility Under the Employee Retirement Income Security Act of 1974

Part 2550—Rules and Regulations for Fiduciary Responsibility

[¶ 14,733]

§ 2550.403a-1 **Establishment of trust.** (a) *In General.* Except as otherwise provided in § 403b-1, all assets of an employee benefit plan shall be held in trust by one or more trustees pursuant to a written trust instrument.

(b) *Specific applications.* (1) The requirements of paragraph (a) of this section will not fail to be satisfied merely because securities of a plan are held in the name of a nominee or in street name, provided such securities are held on behalf of the plan by:

(i) A bank or trust company that is subject to supervision by the United States or a State, or a nominee of such bank or trust company;

(ii) A broker or dealer registered under the Securities Exchange Act of 1934, or a nominee of such broker or dealer; or

(iii) A "clearing agency," as defined in section 3(a)(23) of the Securities Exchange Act of 1934, or its nominee.

(2) Where a corporation described in section 501(c)(2) of the Internal Revenue Code holds property on behalf of a plan, the requirements of paragraph (a) of this section are satisfied with respect to such property if all the stock of such corporation is held in trust on behalf of the plan by one or more trustees.

(3) If the assets of an entity in which a plan invests include plan assets by reason of the plan's investment in the entity, the requirements of paragraph (a) of this section are satisfied with respect to such investment if the indicia of ownership of the plan's interest in the entity are held in trust on behalf of the plan by one or more trustees.

(c) *Requirements concerning trustees.* The trustee or trustees referred to in paragraphs (a) and (b) shall be either named in the trust instrument or in the plan instrument described in section 402(a) of the Act, or appointed by a person who is a named fiduciary (within the meaning of section 402(a)(2) of the Act). Upon acceptance of being named or appointed, the trustee or trustees shall have exclusive authority and discretion to manage and control the assets of the plan, except to the extent that:

(1) The plan instrument or the trust instrument expressly provides that the trustee or trustees are subject to the direction of a named fiduciary who is not a trustee, in which case the trustees shall be subject to the proper directions of such fiduciary which are made in accordance with the terms of the plan and which are not contrary to the provisions of Title I of the Act of Chapter XXV of this Title, or

(2) Authority to manage, acquire or dispose of assets of the plan is delegated to one or more investment managers (within the meaning of section 3(38) of the Act) pursuant to section 402(c)(3) of the Act.

[¶ 14,734]

§2550.403b-1 **Exemptions from trust requirement.** (a) *Statutory exemptions.* The requirements of section 403(a) of the Act and section 403a-1 shall not apply—

(1) To any assets of a plan which consist of insurance contracts or policies issued by an insurance company qualified to do business in a State;

(2) To any assets of such an insurance company or any assets of a plan which are held by such an insurance company.

(3) To plan—

(i) Some or all of the participants of which are employees described in section 401(c)(1) of the Internal Revenue Code of 1954; or

(ii) Which consists of one or more individual retirement accounts described in section 408 of the Internal Revenue Code of 1954 to the extent that such plan's assets are held in one or more custodial accounts which qualify under section 401(f) or 408(h) of such Code, whichever is applicable;

(4) To a contract established and maintained under section 403(b) of the Internal Revenue Code of 1954 to the extent that the assets of the contract are held in one or more custodial accounts pursuant to section 403(b)(7) of such Code.

(5) To any plan, fund or program under which as employer, all of whose stock is directly or indirectly owned by employees, former employees or their beneficiaries, proposes through an unfunded arrangement to compensate retired employees for benefits which were forfeited by such employees under a pension plan maintained by a former employer prior to the date such pension plan became subject to the Act.

(b) [Reserved]

[¶ 14,740]
FIDUCIARY DUTIES

Act Sec. 404. (a)(1) PRUDENT MAN STANDARD OF CARE.—Subject to sections 403(c) and (d), 4042, and 4044, a fiduciary shall discharge his duties with respect to a plan solely in the interest of the participants and beneficiaries and—

(A) for the exclusive purpose of:

(i) providing benefits to participants and their beneficiaries; and

(ii) defraying reasonable expenses of administering the plan;

(B) with the care, skill, prudence, and diligence under the circumstances then prevailing that a prudent man acting in a like capacity and familiar with such matters would use in the conduct of an enterprise of a like character and with like aims;

(C) by diversifying the investments of the plan so as to minimize the risk of large losses, unless under the circumstances it is clearly prudent not to do so; and

(D) in accordance with the documents and instruments governing the plan insofar as such documents and instruments are consistent with the provisions of this title and Title IV.

(2) In the case of an eligible individual account plan (as defined in section 407(d)(3)), the diversification requirement of paragraph (1)(C) and the prudence requirement (only to the extent that it requires diversification) of paragraph (1)(B) is not violated by acquisition or holding of qualifying employer real property or qualifying employer securities (as defined in section 407(d)(4) and (5)).

Act Sec. 404. (b) INDICIA OF OWNERSHIP OF ASSETS OUTSIDE JURISDICTION OF DISTRICT COURTS.—Except as authorized by the Secretary by regulation, no fiduciary may maintain the indicia of ownership of any assets of a plan outside the jurisdiction of the district courts of the United States.

Act Sec. 404. (c)(1)(A) CONTROL OVER ASSETS BY PARTICIPANT OR BENEFICIARY.—In the case of a pension plan which provides for individual accounts and permits a participant or beneficiary to exercise control over assets in his account, if a participant or beneficiary exercises control over the assets in his account (as determined under regulations of the Secretary)—

(i) such participant or beneficiary shall not be deemed to be a fiduciary by reason of such exercise, and

(ii) no person who is otherwise a fiduciary shall be liable under this part for any loss, or by reason of any breach, which results from such participant's or benficiary's exercise of control, except that this clause shall not apply in connection with such participant or beneficiary for any blackout period during which the ability of such participant or beneficiary to direct the investment of the assets in his or her account is suspended by a plan sponsor or fiduciary.

(B) If a person referred to in subparagraph (A)(ii) meets the requirements of this title in connection with authorizing and implementing the blackout period, any person who is otherwise a fiduciary shall not be liable under this title for any loss occurring during such period.

(C) For purposes of this paragraph, the term "blackout period" has the meaning given such term by section 101(i)(7).

(2) In the case of a simple retirement account established pursuant to a qualified salary reduction arrangement under section 408(p) of the Internal Revenue Code of 1986, a participant or beneficiary shall, for purposes of paragraph (1), be treated as exercising control over the assets in the account upon the earliest of—

(A) an affirmative election among investment options with respect to the initial investment of any contribution,

(B) a rollover to any other simple retirement account or individual retirement plan, or

(C) one year after the simple retirement account is established.

No reports, other than those required under section 101(g), shall be required with respect to a simple retirement account established pursuant to such a qualified salary reduction arrangement.

(3) In the case of a pension plan which makes a transfer to an individual retirement account or annuity of a designated trustee or issuer under section 401(a)(31)(B) of the Internal Revenue Code of 1986, the participant or beneficiary shall, for purposes of paragraph (1), be treated as exercising control over the assets in the account or annuity upon—

(A) the earlier of—

(i) a rollover of all or a portion of the amount to another individual retirement account or annuity; or

(ii) one year after the transfer is made; or

(B) a transfer that is made in a manner consistent with guidance provided by the Secretary.

(4)(A) In any case in which a qualified change in investment options occurs in connection with an individual account plan, a participant or beneficiary shall not be treated for purposes of paragraph (1) as not exercising control over the assets in his account in connection with such change if the requirements of subparagraph (C) are met in connection with such change.

(B) For purposes of subparagraph (A), the term "qualified change in investment options" means, in connection with an individual account plan, a change in the investment options offered to the participant or beneficiary under the terms of the plan, under which—

(i) the account of the participant or beneficiary is reallocated among one or more remaining or new investment options which are offered in lieu of one or more investment options offered immediately prior to the effective date of the change, and

(ii) the stated characteristics of the remaining or new investment options provided under clause (i), including characteristics relating to risk and rate of return, are, as of immediately after the change, reasonably similar to those of the existing investment options as of immediately before the change.

(C) The requirements of this subparagraph are met in connection with a qualified change in investment options if —

(i) at least 30 days and no more than 60 days prior to the effective date of the change, the plan administrator furnishes written notice of the change to the participants and beneficiaries, including information comparing the existing and new investment options and an explanation that, in the absence of affirmative investment instructions from the participant or beneficiary to the contrary, the account of the participant or beneficiary will be invested in the manner described in subparagraph (B),

(ii) the participant or beneficiary has not provided to the plan administrator, in advance of the effective date of the change, affirmative investment instructions contrary to the change, and

(iii) the investments under the plan of the participant or beneficiary as in effect immediately prior to the effective date of the change were the product of the exercise by such participant or beneficiary of control over the assets of the account within the meaning of paragraph (1).

(5) DEFAULT INVESTMENT ARRANGEMENTS.—

(A) IN GENERAL. —For purposes of paragraph (1), a participant or beneficiary in an individual account plan meeting the notice requirements of subparagraph (B) shall be treated as exercising control over the assets in the account with respect to the amount of contributions and earnings which, in the absence of an investment election by the participant or beneficiary, are invested by the plan in accordance with regulations prescribed by the Secretary. The regulations under this subparagraph shall provide guidance on the appropriateness of designating default investments that include a mix of asset classes consistent with capital preservation or long-term capital appreciation, or a blend of both.

(B) NOTICE REQUIREMENTS. —

(i) IN GENERAL. —The requirements of this subparagraph are met if each participant or beneficiary—

(I) receives, within a reasonable period of time before each plan year, a notice explaining the employee's right under the plan to designate how contributions and earnings will be invested and explaining how, in the absence of any investment election by the participant or beneficiary, such contributions and earnings will be invested, and

(II) has a reasonable period of time after receipt of such notice and before the beginning of the plan year to make such designation.

(ii) FORM OF NOTICE. —The requirements of clauses (i) and (ii) of section 401(k)(12)(D) of the Internal Revenue Code of 1986 shall apply with respect to the notices described in this subparagraph.

Act Sec. 404.(d)(1) PLAN TERMINATIONS.—If, in connection with the termination of a pension plan which is a single-employer plan, there is an election to establish or maintain a qualified replacement plan, or to increase benefits, as provided under section 4980(d) of the Internal Revenue Code of 1986, a fiduciary shall discharge the fiduciary's duties under this title and title IV in accordance with the following requirements:

(A) In the case of a fiduciary of the terminated plan, any requirement—

(i) under section 4980(d)(2)(B) of such Code with respect to the transfer of assets from the terminated plan to a qualified replacement plan, and

(ii) under section 4980(d)(2)(B)(ii) or 4980(d)(3) of such Code with respect to any increase in benefits under the terminated plan.

(B) In the case of a fiduciary of a qualified replacement plan, any requirement—

(i) under section 4980(d)(2)(A) of such Code with respect to participation in the qualified replacement plan of active participants in the terminated plan,

(ii) under section 4980(d)(2)(B) of such Code with respect to the receipt of assets from the terminated plan, and

(iii) under section 4980(d)(2)(C) of such Code with respect to the allocation of assets to participants of the qualified replacement plan.

(2) For purposes of this subsection—

(A) any term used in this subsection which is also used in section 4980(d) of the Internal Revenue Code of 1986 shall have the same meaning as when used in such section, and

(B) any reference in this subsection to the Internal Revenue Code of 1986 shall be a reference to such Code as in effect immediately after the enactment of the Omnibus Budget Reconciliation Act of 1990.

Amendments

P.L. 110-458, §106(d):

Amended ERISA 404(c)(5) by striking "participant" each place it appears and inserting "participant or beneficiary."

The above amendment applies to plan years beginning after December 31, 2006.

P.L. 109-280, §621(a)(1):

Amended ERISA Sec. 404(c) by redesignating subparagraphs (A) and (B) as clauses (i) and (ii), respectively, and by inserting "(A)" after "(c)(1)"; by inserting in subparagraph (A)(ii) (as redesignated) the following: ", except that this clause shall not apply in connection with such participant or beneficiary for any blackout period during which the ability of such participant or beneficiary to direct the investment of the assets in his or her account is suspended by a plan sponsor or fiduciary"; and by adding subparagraphs (B) and (C).

P.L. 109-280, §621(a)(2):

Amended ERISA Sec. 404(c) by adding at the end paragraph (4) to read as above.

P.L. 109-280, §621(b):

(b) EFFECTIVE DATE.—

(1) IN GENERAL. – The amendments made by this section shall apply to plan years beginning after December 31, 2007.

(2) SPECIAL RULE FOR COLLECTIVELY BARGAINED AGREEMENTS.—

In the case of a plan maintained pursuant to 1 or more collective bargaining agreements between employee representatives and 1 or more employers ratified on or before the date of the enactment of this Act, paragraph (1) shall be applied to benefits pursuant to, and individuals covered by, any such agreement by substituting for "December 31, 2007" the earlier of—

(A) the later of —

(i) December 31, 2008, or

(ii) the date on which the last of such collective bargaining agreements terminates (determined without regard to any extension thereof after such date of enactment), or

(B) December 31, 2009.

P.L. 109-280, §624(a):

Amended ERISA Sec. 404(c) by adding at the end paragraph (5) to read as above.

P.L. 109-280, §624(b):

(b) EFFECTIVE DATE.—

(1) IN GENERAL.—

The amendments made by this section shall apply to plan years beginning after December 31, 2006.

(2) REGULATIONS.—

Final regulations under section 404(c)(5)(A) of the Employee Retirement Income Security Act of 1974 (as added by this section) shall be issued no later than 6 months after the date of the enactment of this Act.

P.L. 109-280, §811, provides:

SEC. 811. PENSIONS AND INDIVIDUAL RETIREMENT ARRANGEMENT PROVISIONS OF ECONOMIC GROWTH AND TAX RELIEF RECONCILIATION ACT OF 2001 MADE PERMANENT.

Title IX of the Economic Growth and Tax Relief Reconciliation Act of 2001 [P.L. 107-16] shall not apply to the provisions of, and amendments made by, subtitles A through F of title VI [§§601-666]of such Act (relating to pension and individual retirement arrangement provisions).

P.L. 107-147, §411(t):

Amended ERISA Sec. 404(c)(3) by striking "the earlier of" the second place it appears in subparagraph (A) and by striking "if the transfer" and inserting "a transfer that."

The above amendments shall apply to distributions made after final regulations implementing Act Sec. 657(c)(2)(A) are amended, subject to sunset after 2010 under P.L. 107-16, Sec. 901.

P.L. 107-16, §657(c)(1):

Amended ERISA Sec. 404(c) by adding at the end a new paragraph (3) to read as above.

The above amendments shall apply to distributions made after final regulations implementing Act Sec. 657(c)(2)(A) are amended, subject to sunset after 2010 under P.L. 107-16, Sec. 901 [but see P.L. 109-280, §811, above].

P.L. 104-188, Sec. 1421(d)(2):

Amended ERISA Sec. 404(c) by inserting (1) after "(c)", by redesignating paragraphs (1) and (2) as subparagraphs (A) and (B), respectively, and by adding at the end a new paragraph (2) to read as above.

The above amendments apply to tax years beginning after December 31, 1996.

P.L. 101-508, Sec. 12001(b)(1):

Amended ERISA Sec. 404 by adding a new subsection (d) to read as above effective for reversions occurring after September 30, 1990 except for the provisions of Act Sec. 12003(b). See P.L. 101-508, Sec. 12001(b)(2)(A) below for exceptions to effective date.

P.L. 101-508, Sec. 12001(b)(2)(A):

Amended ERISA Sec. 404(a)(1)(D) by striking "or title IV" and inserting "and title IV" effective for reversions occurring after September 30, 1990 except for the provisions of Act Sec. 12003(b).

SEC. 12003. EFFECTIVE DATE.

* * *

(b) EXCEPTION.—The amendments made by this subtitle shall not apply to any reversion after September 30, 1990, if—

(1) in the case of plans subject to title IV of the Employee Retirement Income Security Act of 1974, a notice of intent to terminate under such title was provided to participants (or if no participants, to the Pension Benefit Guaranty Corporation) before October 1, 1990,

(2) in the case of plans subject to title I (and not to title IV) of such Act, a notice of intent to reduce future accruals under section 204(h) of such Act was provided to participants in connection with the termination before October 1, 1990,

(3) in the case of plans not subject to title I or IV of such Act, a request for a determination letter with respect to the termination was filed with the Secretary of the Treasury or the Secretary's delegate before October 1, 1990, or

(4) in the case of plans not subject to title I or IV of such Act and having only 1 participant, a resolution terminating the plan was adopted by the employer before October 1, 1990.

P.L. 96-364, §309:

Amended subsection 404(a)(1)(D) by adding "or Title IV" at the end of the subsection, effective September 26, 1980.

Regulations

Reg. §2550.404a-1 was filed with the Federal Register on June 25, 1979. Reg. §2550.404b-1 was adopted by FR Doc. 77-29187, filed with the Federal Register on September 30, 1977, and published in the Federal Register of October 4, 1977 (42 FR 54122). Reg. §2550.404c-1 was adopted by FR Doc. 92-24357, filed with the Federal Register on October 9, 1992 and published in the Federal Register of October 13, 1992 (57 FR 46906). Reg. §2550.404a-2 was adopted by FR Doc. 04-21591, filed with the Federal Register on September 27, 2004 and published in the Federal Register on September 28, 2004 (69 FR 58017). Reg. Sec. 2550.404a-3 was added on April 21, 2006 (71 FR 20820); effective May 22, 2006, amended on February 15, 2007 (72 FR 7516), effective March 19, 2007, and amended October 7, 2008 (73 FR 58459), effective November 6, 2008. Reg, Sec. 2550. 404a-4 was added October 7, 2008 (73 FR 58459), effective December 8, 2008. Reg. Sec. 2550.404c-5 was added on October 24, 2007 (72 FR 60452) and was effective December 24, 2007; it was amended on April 30, 2008 (73 FR 23349), with an effective date of April 30, 2008. Reg Sec. 2550.404a-5 was added October 20, 2010 (75 FR 64910), with an effective date of December 20, 2010. Reg Sec. 2550.404c-1 was amended October 20, 2010 (75 FR 64910), with an effective date of December 20, 2010. Reg Sec. 2550.404a-5(j)(3)(i) was amended July 19, 2011 (76 FR 42539). Reg Sec. 2550.404a-5(h)(1) was amended March 19, 2015 (80 FR 14301).

[¶ 14,742]

§2550.404a-1 **Investment duties.** (a) *In general.* Section 404(a)(1)(B) of the Employee Retirement Income Security Act of 1974 (the Act) provides, in part, that a fiduciary shall discharge his duties with respect to a plan with the care, skill, prudence, and diligence under the circumstances then prevailing that a prudent man acting in a like capacity and familiar with such matters would use in the conduct of an enterprise of a like character and with like aims.

(b) *Investment Duties.* (1) With regard to an investment or investment course of action taken by a fiduciary of an employee benefit plan pursuant to his investment duties, the requirements of section 404(a)(1)(B) of the Act set forth in subsection (a) of this section are satisfied if the fiduciary (A) has given appropriate consideration to those facts and circumstances that, given the scope of such fiduciary's investment duties, the fiduciary knows or should know are relevant to the particular investment or investment course of action involved, including the role the investment or investment course of action plays in that portion of the plan's investment portfolio with respect to which the fiduciary has investment duties; and (B) has acted accordingly.

(2) For purposes of paragraph (1) of this subsection, "appropriate consideration" shall include, but is not necessarily limited to, (A) a determination by the fiduciary that the particular investment or investment course of action is reasonably designed, as part of the portfolio (or, where applicable, that portion of the plan portfolio with respect to which the fiduciary has investment duties), to further the purposes of the plan, taking into consideration the risk of loss and the opportunity for gain (or other return) associated with the investment or investment course of action, and (B) consideration of the following factors as they relate to such portion of the portfolio:

(i) the composition of the portfolio with regard to diversification;

(ii) the liquidity and current return of the portfolio relative to the anticipated cash flow requirement of the plan, and

(iii) the projected return of the portfolio relative to the funding objectives of the plan.

(3) An investment manager appointed, pursuant to the provisions of section 402(c)(3) of the Act, to manage all or part of the assets of a plan, may, for purposes of compliance with the provisions of paragraphs (1) and (2) of this subsection, rely on, and act upon the basis of, information pertaining to the plan provided by or at the direction of the appointing fiduciary, if—

(A) such information is provided for the stated purpose of assisting the manager in the performance of his investment duties, and

(B) the manager does not know and has no reason to know that the information is incorrect.

(c) *Definitions.* For purposes of this section:

(1) The term "investment duties" means any duties imposed upon, or assumed or undertaken by, a person in connection with the investment of plan assets which make or will make such person a fiduciary of an employee benefit plan or which are performed by such person as a fiduciary of an employee benefit plan as defined in section 3(21)(A)(i) or (ii) of the Act.

(2) The term "investment course of action" means any series or program of investments or actions related to a fiduciary's performance of his investment duties.

(3) The term "plan" means an employee benefit plan to which Title I of the Act applies.

[¶ 14,742A]

§2550.404a-2 **Safe harbor for automatic rollovers to individual retirement plans.** (a) *In general.* (1) Pursuant to section 657(c) of the Economic Growth and Tax Relief Reconciliation Act of 2001, Public Law 107-16, June 7, 2001, 115 Stat. 38, this section provides a safe harbor under which a fiduciary of an employee pension benefit plan subject to Title I of the Employee Retirement Income Security Act of 1974, as amended (the Act), 29 USC 1001 et seq., will be deemed to have satisfied his or her fiduciary duties under section 404(a) of the Act in connection with an automatic rollover of a mandatory distribution described in section 401(a)(31)(B) of the Internal Revenue Code of 1986, as amended (the Code). This section also provides a safe harbor for certain other mandatory distributions not described in section 401(a)(31)(B) of the Code.

(2) The standards set forth in this section apply solely for purposes of determining whether a fiduciary meets the requirements of this safe harbor. Such standards are not intended to be the exclusive means by which a fiduciary might satisfy his or her responsibilities under the Act with respect to rollovers of mandatory distributions described in paragraphs (c) and (d) of this section.

(b) *Safe harbor.* A fiduciary that meets the conditions of paragraph (c) or paragraph (d) of this section is deemed to have satisfied his or her duties under section 404(a) of the Act with respect to both the selection of an individual retirement plan provider and the investment of funds in connection with the rollover of mandatory distributions described in those paragraphs to an individual retirement plan, within the meaning of section 7701(a)(37) of the Code.

(c) *Conditions.* With respect to an automatic rollover of a mandatory distribution described in section 401(a)(31)(B) of the Code, a fiduciary shall qualify for the safe harbor described in paragraph (b) of this section if:

(1) The present value of the nonforfeitable accrued benefit, as determined under section 411(a)(11) of the Code, does not exceed the maximum amount under section 401(a)(31)(B) of the Code;

(2) The mandatory distribution is to an individual retirement plan within the meaning of section 7701(a)(37) of the Code;

(3) In connection with the distribution of rolled-over funds to an individual retirement plan, the fiduciary enters into a written agreement with an individual retirement plan provider that provides:

(i) the rolled-over funds shall be invested in an investment product designed to preserve principal and provide a reasonable rate of return, whether or not such return is guaranteed, consistent with liquidity;

(ii) for purposes of paragraph (c)(3)(i) of this section, the investment product selected for the rolled-over funds shall seek to maintain, over the term of the investment, the dollar value that is equal to the amount invested in the product by the individual retirement plan;

(iii) the investment product selected for the rolled-over funds shall be offered by a state or federally regulated financial institution, which shall be: a bank or savings association, the deposits of which are insured by the Federal Deposit Insurance Corporation; a credit union, the member accounts of which are insured within the meaning of section 101(7) of the Federal Credit Union Act; an insurance company, the products of which are protected by state guaranty associations; or an investment company registered under the Investment Company Act of 1940;

(iv) all fees and expenses attendant to an individual retirement plan, including investments of such plan, (e.g., establishment charges, maintenance fees, investment expenses, termination costs and surrender charges) shall not exceed the fees and expenses charged by the individual retirement plan provider for comparable individual retirement plans established for reasons other than the receipt of a rollover distribution subject to the provisions of section 401(a)(31)(B) of the Code; and

(v) the participant on whose behalf the fiduciary makes an automatic rollover shall have the right to enforce the terms of the contractual agreement establishing the individual retirement plan, with regard to his or her rolled-over funds, against the individual retirement plan provider.

(4) Participants have been furnished a summary plan description, or a summary of material modifications, that describes the plan's automatic rollover provisions effectuating the requirements of section 401(a)(31)(B) of the Code, including an explanation that the mandatory distribution will be invested in an investment product designed to preserve principal and provide a reasonable rate of return and liquidity, a statement indicating how fees and expenses attendant to the individual retirement plan will be allocated (i.e., the extent to which expenses will be borne by the account holder alone or shared with the distributing plan or plan sponsor), and the name, address and phone number of a plan contact (to the extent not otherwise provided in the summary plan description or summary of material modifications) for further information concerning the plan's automatic rollover provisions, the individual retirement plan provider and the fees and expenses attendant to the individual retirement plan; and

(5) Both the fiduciary's selection of an individual retirement plan and the investment of funds would not result in a prohibited transaction under section 406 of the Act, unless such actions are exempted from the prohibited transaction provisions by a prohibited transaction exemption issued pursuant to section 408(a) of the Act.

(d) *Mandatory distributions of $1,000 or less.* A fiduciary shall qualify for the protection afforded by the safe harbor described in paragraph (b) of this section with respect to a mandatory distribution of one thousand dollars ($1,000) or less described in section 411(a)(11) of the Code, provided there is no affirmative distribution election by the participant and the fiduciary makes a rollover distribution of such amount into an individual retirement plan on behalf of such participant in accordance with the conditions described in paragraph (c) of this section, without regard to the fact that such rollover is not described in section 401(a)(31)(B) of the Code.

(e) *Effective date.* This section shall be effective and shall apply to any rollover of a mandatory distribution made on or after March 28, 2005.

[¶ 14,742B]

§ 2550.404a-3 **Safe Harbor for Distributions from Terminated Individual Account Plans.** (a) *General.* (1) This section provides a safe harbor under which a fiduciary (including a qualified termination administrator, within the meaning of § 2578.1(g) of this chapter) of a terminated individual account plan, as described in paragraph (a)(2) of this section, will be deemed to have satisfied its duties under section 404(a) of the Employee Retirement Income Security Act of 1974, as amended (the Act)), 29 U.S.C. 1001 *et seq.*, in connection with a distribution described in paragraph (b) of this section.

(2) This section shall apply to an individual account plan only if—

(i) In the case of an individual account plan that is an abandoned plan within the meaning of § 2578.1 of this chapter, such plan was intended to be maintained as a tax-qualified plan in accordance with the requirements of section 401(a), 403(a), or 403(b) of the Internal Revenue Code of 1986 (Code); or

(ii) In the case of any other individual account plan, such plan is maintained in accordance with the requirements of section 401(a), 403(a), or 403 (b) of the Code at the time of the distribution.

(3) The standards set forth in this section apply solely for purposes of determining whether a fiduciary meets the requirements of this safe harbor. Such standards are not intended to be the exclusive means by which a fiduciary might satisfy his or her responsibilities under the Act with respect to making distributions described in this section.

(b) *Distributions.* This section shall apply to a distribution from a terminated individual account plan if, in connection with such distribution:

(1) The participant or beneficiary, on whose behalf the distribution will be made, was furnished notice in accordance with paragraph (e) of this section or, in the case of an abandoned plan, § 2578.1(d)(2)(vi) of this chapter, and

(2) The participant or beneficiary failed to elect a form of distribution within 30 days of the furnishing of the notice described paragraph (b)(1) of this section.

(c) *Safe harbor.* A fiduciary that meets the conditions of paragraph (d) of this section shall, with respect to a distribution described in paragraph (b) of this section, be deemed to have satisfied its duties under section 404(a) of the Act with respect to the distribution of benefits, selection of a transferee entity described in paragraph (d)(1)(i) through (iii) of this section, and the investment of funds in connection with the distribution.

(d) *Conditions.* A fiduciary shall qualify for the safe harbor described in paragraph (c) of this section if:

(1) The distribution described in paragraph (b) of this section is made'

(i) To an individual retirement plan within the meaning of section 7701(a)(37) of the Code;

(ii) In the case of a distribution on behalf of a designated beneficiary (as defined by section 401(a)(9)(E) of the Code) who is not the surviving spouse of the deceased participant, to an inherited individual retirement plan (within the meaning of section 402(c)(11) of the Code) established to receive the distribution on behalf of the non-spouse beneficiary; or

(iii) In the case of a distribution by a qualified termination administrator with respect to which the amount to be distributed is $1000 or less and that amount is less than the minimum amount required to be invested in an individual retirement plan product offered by the qualified termination administrator to the public at the time of the distribution, to:

(A) An interest-bearing federally insured bank or savings association account in the name of the participant or beneficiary,

(B) The unclaimed property fund of the State in which the participant's or beneficiary's last known address is located, or

(C) An individual retirement plan (described in paragraph (d)(1)(i) or (d)(1)(ii) of this section) offered by a financial institution other than the qualified termination administrator to the public at the time of the distribution.

(2) Except with respect to distributions to State unclaimed property funds (described in paragraph (d)(1)(iii)(B) of this section), the fiduciary enters into a written agreement with the transferee entity which provides:

(i) The distributed funds shall be invested in an investment product designed to preserve principal and provide a reasonable rate of return, whether or not such return is guaranteed, consistent with liquidity (except that distributions under paragraph (d)(1)(iii)(A) of this section to a bank or savings account are not required to be invested in such a product);

(ii) For purposes of paragraph (d)(2)(i) of this section, the investment product shall—

(A) Seek to maintain, over the term of the investment, the dollar value that is equal to the amount invested in the product by the individual retirement plan (described in paragraph (d)(1)(i) or (d)(1)(ii) of this section), and

(B) Be offered by a State or federally regulated financial institution, which shall be: a bank or savings association, the deposits of which are insured by the Federal Deposit Insurance Corporation; a credit union, the member accounts of which are insured within the meaning of section 101(7) of the Federal Credit Union Act; an insurance company, the products of which are protected by State guaranty associations; or an investment company registered under the Investment Company Act of 1940;

(iii) All fees and expenses attendant to the transferee plan (described in paragraph (d)(1)(i) or (d)(1)(ii) of this section) or account (described in paragraph (d)(1)(iii)(A) of this section), including investments of such plan, (e.g., establishment charges, maintenance fees, investment expenses, termination costs and surrender charges), shall not exceed the fees and expenses charged by the provider of the plan or account for comparable plans or accounts established for reasons other than the receipt of a distribution under this section; and

(iv) The participant or beneficiary on whose behalf the fiduciary makes a distribution shall have the right to enforce the terms of the contractual agreement establishing the plan (described in paragraph (d)(1)(i) or (d)(1)(ii) of this section) or account (described in paragraph (d)(1)(iii)(A) of this section), with regard to his or her transferred account balance, against the plan or account provider.

(3) (3) Both the fiduciary's selection of a transferee plan (described in paragraph (d)(1)(i) or (d)(1)(ii) of this section) or account (described in paragraph (d)(1)(iii)(A) of this section) and the investment of funds would not result in a prohibited transaction under section 406 of the Act, unless such actions are exempted from the prohibited transaction provisions by a prohibited transaction exemption issued pursuant to section 408(a) of the Act.

(e) *Notice to participants and beneficiaries.* (1) *Content.* Each participant or beneficiary of the plan shall be furnished a notice written in a manner calculated to be understood by the average plan participant and containing the following:

(i) The name of the plan;

(ii) A statement of the account balance, the date on which the amount was calculated, and, if relevant, an indication that the amount to be distributed may be more or less than the amount stated in the notice, depending on investment gains or losses and the administrative cost of terminating the plan and distributing benefits;

(iii) A description of the distribution options available under the plan and a request that the participant or beneficiary elect a form of distribution and inform the plan administrator (or other fiduciary) identified in paragraph (e)(1)(vii) of this section of that election;

(iv) A statement explaining that, if a participant or beneficiary fails to make an election within 30 days from receipt of the notice, the plan will distribute the account balance of the participant or beneficiary to an individual retirement plan (i.e., individual retirement account or annuity described in paragraph (d)(1)(i) or (d)(1)(ii) of this section) and the account balance will be invested in an investment product designed to preserve principal and provide a reasonable rate of return and liquidity;

(v) A statement explaining what fees, if any, will be paid from the participant or beneficiary's individual retirement plan (described in paragraph (d)(1)(i) or (d)'(1)(ii) of this section), if such information is known at the time of the furnishing of this notice;

(vi) The name, address and phone number of the individual retirement plan (described in paragraph (d)(1)(i) or (d)(1)(ii) of this section) provider, if such information is known at the time of the furnishing of this notice; and

(vii) The name, address, and telephone number of the plan administrator (or other fiduciary) from whom a participant or beneficiary may obtain additional information concerning the termination.

(2) *Manner of furnishing notice.* (i) For purposes of paragraph (e)(1) of this section, a notice shall be furnished to each participant or beneficiary in accordance with the requirements of § 2520.104b-1(b)(1) of this chapter to the last known address of the participant or beneficiary; and

(ii) In the case of a notice that is returned to the plan as undeliverable, the plan fiduciary shall, consistent with its duties under section 404(a)(1) of ERISA, take steps to locate the participant or beneficiary and provide notice prior to making the distribution. If, after such steps, the fiduciary is unsuccessful in locating and furnishing notice to a participant or beneficiary, the participant or beneficiary shall be deemed to have been furnished the notice and to have failed to make an election within 30 days for purposes of paragraph (b)(2) of this section.

(f) *Model notice.* The appendix to this section contains a model notice that may be used to discharge the notification requirements under this section. Use of the model notice is not mandatory. However, use of an appropriately completed model notice will be deemed to satisfy the requirements of paragraph (e)(1) of this section.

[Added by 71 FR 20820, April 21, 2006; effective date May 22, 2006 and amended on February 15, 2007 (72 FR 7516), effective March 19, 2007 and on October 7, 2008 (73 FR 58459), effective November 6, 2008.]

APPENDIX TO § 2550.404a-3
NOTICE OF PLAN TERMINATION

[*Date of notice*]

[*Name and last known address of plan participant or beneficiary*]

Re: [*Name of plan*]

Dear [*Name of plan participant or beneficiary*]:

This notice is to inform you that [*name of the plan*](the Plan) has been terminated and we are in the process of winding it up.

We have determined that you have an interest in the Plan, either as a plan participant or beneficiary. Your account balance in the Plan on [*date*] is/was [*account balance*]. We will be distributing this money as permitted under the terms of the Plan and federal regulations. { *If applicable, insert the following sentence:* The actual amount of your distribution may be more or less than the amount stated in this notice depending on investment gains or losses and the administrative cost of terminating your plan and distributing your benefits.}

Your distribution options under the Plan are { *add a description of the Plan's distribution options* }. It is very important that you elect one of these forms of distribution and inform us of your election. The process for informing us of this election is { *enter a description of the Plan's election process* }.

If you do not make an election within 30 days from your receipt of this notice, your account balance will be transferred directly to an individual retirement plan (inherited individual retirement plan in the case of a nonspouse beneficiary). { *If the name of the provider of the individual retirement plan is known, include the following sentence:* The name of the provider of the individual retirement plan is [*name, address and phone number of the individual retirement plan provider*].} Pursuant to federal law, your money in the individual retirement plan would then be invested in an investment product designed to preserve principal and provide a reasonable rate of return and liquidity. { *If fee information is known, include the following sentence:* Should your money be transferred into an individual retirement plan, [*name of the financial institution*] charges the following fees for its services: { *add a statement of fees, if any, that will be paid from the participant or beneficiary's individual retirement plan* }.}

For more information about the termination, your account balance, or distribution options, please contact [*name, address, and telephone number of the plan administrator or other appropriate contact person*].

Sincerely,

[*Name of plan administrator or appropriate designee*]

[¶ 14,742C]

§ 2550.404a-4 **Selection of annuity providers—safe harbor for individual account plans.** (a) Scope.

(1) This section establishes a safe harbor for satisfying the fiduciary duties under section 404(a)(1)(B) of the Employee Retirement Income Security Act of 1974 (ERISA), 29 U.S.C. 1104-1114, in selecting an annuity provider and contract for benefit distributions from an individual account plan. For guidance concerning the selection of an annuity provider for defined benefit plans see 29 CFR 2509.95-1.

(2) This section sets forth an optional means for satisfying the fiduciary responsibilities under section 404(a)(1)(B) of ERISA with respect to the selection of an annuity provider or contract for benefit distributions. This section does not establish minimum requirements or the exclusive means for satisfying these responsibilities.

(b) Safe harbor. The selection of an annuity provider for benefit distributions from an individual account plan satisfies the requirements of section 404(a)(1)(B) of ERISA if the fiduciary:

(1) Engages in an objective, thorough and analytical search for the purpose of identifying and selecting providers from which to purchase annuities;

(2) Appropriately considers information sufficient to assess the ability of the annuity provider to make all future payments under the annuity contract;

(3) Appropriately considers the cost (including fees and commissions) of the annuity contract in relation to the benefits and administrative services to be provided under such contract;

(4) Appropriately concludes that, at the time of the selection, the annuity provider is financially able to make all future payments under the annuity contract and the cost of the annuity contract is reasonable in relation to the benefits and services to be provided under the contract; and

(5) If necessary, consults with an appropriate expert or experts for purposes of compliance with the provisions of this paragraph (b).

(c) Time of selection. For purposes of paragraph (b) of this section, the "time of selection" may be either:

(1) The time that the annuity provider and contract are selected for distribution of benefits to a specific participant or beneficiary; or

(2) The time that the annuity provider is selected to provide annuity contracts at future dates to participants or beneficiaries, provided that the selecting fiduciary periodically reviews the continuing appropriateness of the conclusion described in paragraph (b)(4) of this section, taking into account the factors described in paragraphs (b)(2), (3) and (5) of this section. For purposes of this paragraph (c)(2), a fiduciary is not required to review the appropriateness of this conclusion with respect to any annuity contract purchased for any specific participant or beneficiary.

[Added by 73 FR 58447, October 7, 2008, effective December 8, 2008.]

[¶ 14,742D]

§ 2550.404a-5 **Fiduciary requirements for disclosure in participant-directed individual account plans.** § 2550.404a-5(a) *General.* The investment of plan assets is a fiduciary act governed by the fiduciary standards of section 404(a)(1)(A) and (B) of the Employee Retirement Income Security Act of 1974, as amended (ERISA), 29 U.S.C. 1001 et seq. (all section references herein are references to ERISA unless otherwise indicated). Pursuant to section 404(a)(1)(A) and (B), fiduciaries must discharge their duties with respect to the plan prudently and solely in the interest of participants and beneficiaries. When the documents and instruments governing an individual account plan, described in paragraph (b)(2) of this section, provide for the allocation of investment responsibilities to participants or beneficiaries,

the plan administrator, as defined in section 3(16), must take steps to ensure, consistent with section 404(a)(1)(A) and (B), that such participants and beneficiaries, on a regular and periodic basis, are made aware of their rights and responsibilities with respect to the investment of assets held in, or contributed to, their accounts and are provided sufficient information regarding the plan, including fees and expenses, and regarding designated investment alternatives, including fees and expenses attendant thereto, to make informed decisions with regard to the management of their individual accounts.

(b) *Satisfaction of duty to disclose.* (1) In general. The plan administrator of a covered individual account plan must comply with the disclosure requirements set forth in paragraphs (c) and (d) of this section with respect to each participant or beneficiary that, pursuant to the terms of the plan, has the right to direct the investment of assets held in, or contributed to, his or her individual account. Compliance with paragraphs (c) and (d) of this section will satisfy the duty to make the regular and periodic disclosures described in paragraph (a) of this section, provided that the information contained in such disclosures is complete and accurate. A plan administrator will not be liable for the completeness and accuracy of information used to satisfy these disclosure requirements when the plan administrator reasonably and in good faith relies on information received from or provided by a plan service provider or the issuer of a designated investment alternative.

(2) *Covered individual account plan.* For purposes of paragraph (b)(1) of this section, a "covered individual account plan" is any participant-directed individual account plan as defined in section 3(34) of ERISA, except that such term shall not include plans involving individual retirement accounts or individual retirement annuities described in sections 408(k) ("simplified employee pension") or 408(p) ("simple retirement account") of the Internal Revenue Code of 1986.

(c) *Disclosure of plan-related information.* A plan administrator (or person designated by the plan administrator to act on its behalf) shall provide to each participant or beneficiary the plan-related information described in paragraphs (c)(1) through (4) of this section, based on the latest information available to the plan.

(1) *General.* (i) On or before the date on which a participant or beneficiary can first direct his or her investments and at least annually thereafter:

(A) An explanation of the circumstances under which participants and beneficiaries may give investment instructions;

(B) An explanation of any specified limitations on such instructions under the terms of the plan, including any restrictions on transfer to or from a designated investment alternative;

(C) A description of or reference to plan provisions relating to the exercise of voting, tender and similar rights appurtenant to an investment in a designated investment alternative as well as any restrictions on such rights;

(D) An identification of any designated investment alternatives offered under the plan;

(E) An identification of any designated investment managers; and

(F) A description of any "brokerage windows," "self-directed brokerage accounts," or similar plan arrangements that enable participants and beneficiaries to select investments beyond those designated by the plan.

(ii) If there is a change to the information described in paragraph (c)(1)(i)(A) through (F) of this section, each participant and beneficiary must be furnished a description of such change at least 30 days, but not more than 90 days, in advance of the effective date of such change, unless the inability to provide such advance notice is due to events that were unforeseeable or circumstances beyond the control of the plan administrator, in which case notice of such change must be furnished as soon as reasonably practicable.

(2) *Administrative expenses.* (i) (A) On or before the date on which a participant or beneficiary can first direct his or her investments and at least annually thereafter, an explanation of any fees and expenses for general plan administrative services (e.g., legal, accounting, recordkeeping), which may be charged against the individual accounts of participants and beneficiaries and are not reflected in the total annual operating expenses of any designated investment alternative, as well as the basis on which such charges will be allocated (e.g., pro rata, per capita) to, or affect the balance of, each individual account.

(B) If there is a change to the information described in paragraph (c) (2) (i) (A) of this section, each participant and beneficiary must be furnished a description of such change at least 30 days, but not more than 90 days, in advance of the effective date of such change, unless the inability to provide such advance notice is due to events that were unforeseeable or circumstances beyond the control of the plan administrator, in which case notice of such change must be furnished as soon as reasonably practicable.

(ii) At least quarterly, a statement that includes:

(A) The dollar amount of the fees and expenses described in paragraph (c) (2) (i) (A) of this section that are actually charged (whether by liquidating shares or deducting dollars) during the preceding quarter to the participant's or beneficiary's account for such services;

(B) A description of the services to which the charges relate (e.g., plan administration, including recordkeeping, legal, accounting services); and

(C) If applicable, an explanation that, in addition to the fees and expenses disclosed pursuant to paragraph (c) (2) (ii) of this section, some of the plan's administrative expenses for the preceding quarter were paid from the total annual operating expenses of one or more of the plan's designated investment alternatives (e.g., through revenue sharing arrangements, Rule 12b-1 fees, sub-transfer agent fees).

(3) *Individual expenses.* (i) (A) On or before the date on which a participant or beneficiary can first direct his or her investments and at least annually thereafter, an explanation of any fees and expenses that may be charged against the individual account of a participant or beneficiary on an individual, rather than on a plan-wide, basis (e.g., fees attendant to processing plan loans or qualified domestic relations orders, fees for investment advice, fees for brokerage windows, commissions, front or back-end loads or sales charges, redemption fees, transfer fees and similar expenses, and optional rider charges in annuity contracts) and which are not reflected in the total annual operating expenses of any designated investment alternative.

(B) If there is a change to the information described in paragraph (c) (3) (i) (A) of this section, each participant and beneficiary must be furnished a description of such change at least 30 days, but not more than 90 days, in advance of the effective date of such change, unless the inability to provide such advance notice is due to events that were unforeseeable or circumstances beyond the control of the plan administrator, in which case notice of such change must be furnished as soon as reasonably practicable.

(ii) At least quarterly, a statement that includes:

(A) The dollar amount of the fees and expenses described in paragraph (c) (3) (i) (A) of this section that are actually charged (whether by liquidating shares or deducting dollars) during the preceding quarter to the participant's or beneficiary's account for individual services; and

(B) A description of the services to which the charges relate (e.g., loan processing fee).

(4) *Disclosures on or before first investment.* The requirements of paragraphs (c) (1) (i), (c) (2) (i) (A), (c) (3) (i) (A) of this section to furnish information on or before the date on which a participant or beneficiary can first direct his or her investments may be satisfied by furnishing to the participant or beneficiary the most recent annual disclosure furnished to participants and beneficiaries pursuant those

paragraphs and any updates to the information furnished to participants and beneficiaries pursuant to paragraphs (c) (1) (ii), (c) (2) (i) (B) and (c) (3) (i) (B) of this section.

(d) *Disclosure of investment-related information.* The plan administrator (or person designated by the plan administrator to act on its behalf), based on the latest information available to the plan, shall:

(1) *Information to be provided automatically.* Except as provided in paragraph (i) of this section, furnish to each participant or beneficiary on or before the date on which he or she can first direct his or her investments and at least annually thereafter, the following information with respect to each designated investment alternative offered under the plan—

(i) *Identifying information.* Such information shall include:

(A) The name of each designated investment alternative; and

(B) The type or category of the investment (e.g., money market fund, balanced fund (stocks and bonds), large-cap stock fund, employer stock fund, employer securities).

(ii) *Performance data.* (A) For designated investment alternatives with respect to which the return is not fixed, the average annual total return of the investment for 1-, 5-, and 10-calendar year periods (or for the life of the alternative, if shorter) ending on the date of the most recently completed calendar year; as well as a statement indicating that an investment's past performance is not necessarily an indication of how the investment will perform in the future; and

(B) For designated investment alternatives with respect to which the return is fixed or stated for the term of the investment, both the fixed or stated annual rate of return and the term of the investment. If, with respect to such a designated investment alternative, the issuer reserves the right to adjust the fixed or stated rate of return prospectively during the term of the contract or agreement, the current rate of return, the minimum rate guaranteed under the contract, if any, and a statement advising participants and beneficiaries that the issuer may adjust the rate of return prospectively and how to obtain (e.g., telephone or Web site) the most recent rate of return required under this section.

(iii) *Benchmarks.* For designated investment alternatives with respect to which the return is not fixed, the name and returns of an appropriate broad-based securities market index over the 1-, 5-, and 10-calendar year periods (or for the life of the alternative, if shorter) comparable to the performance data periods provided under paragraph (d) (1) (ii) (A) of this section, and which is not administered by an affiliate of the investment issuer, its investment adviser, or a principal underwriter, unless the index is widely recognized and used.

(iv) *Fee and expense information.* (A) For designated investment alternatives with respect to which the return is not fixed:

(1) The amount and a description of each shareholder-type fee (fees charged directly against a participant's or beneficiary's investment, such as commissions, sales loads, sales charges, deferred sales charges, redemption fees, surrender charges, exchange fees, account fees, and purchase fees, which are not included in the total annual operating expenses of any designated investment alternative) and a description of any restriction or limitation that may be applicable to a purchase, transfer, or withdrawal of the investment in whole or in part (such as round trip, equity wash, or other restrictions);

(2) The total annual operating expenses of the investment expressed as a percentage (i.e., expense ratio), calculated in accordance with paragraph (h) (5) of this section;

(3) The total annual operating expenses of the investment for a one-year period expressed as a dollar amount for a $1,000 investment (assuming no returns and based on the percentage described in paragraph (d) (1) (iv) (A) (2) of this section);

(4) A statement indicating that fees and expenses are only one of several factors that participants and beneficiaries should consider when making investment decisions; and

(5) A statement that the cumulative effect of fees and expenses can substantially reduce the growth of a participant's or beneficiary's retirement account and that participants and beneficiaries

can visit the Employee Benefit Security Administration's Web site for an example demonstrating the long-term effect of fees and expenses.

(B) For designated investment alternatives with respect to which the return is fixed for the term of the investment, the amount and a description of any shareholder-type fees and a description of any restriction or limitation that may be applicable to a purchase, transfer or withdrawal of the investment in whole or in part.

(v) *Internet Web site address.* An Internet Web site address that is sufficiently specific to provide participants and beneficiaries access to the following information regarding the designated investment alternative:

(A) The name of the alternative's issuer;

(B) The alternative's objectives or goals in a manner consistent with Securities and Exchange Commission Form N-1A or N-3, as appropriate;

(C) The alternative's principal strategies (including a general description of the types of assets held by the investment) and principal risks in a manner consistent with Securities and Exchange Commission Form N-1A or N-3, as appropriate;

(D) The alternative's portfolio turnover rate in a manner consistent with Securities and Exchange Commission Form N-1A or N-3, as appropriate;

(E) The alternative's performance data described in paragraph (d)(1)(ii) of this section updated on at least a quarterly basis, or more frequently if required by other applicable law; and

(F) The alternative's fee and expense information described in paragraph (d)(1)(iv) of this section.

(vi) *Glossary.* A general glossary of terms to assist participants and beneficiaries in understanding the designated investment alternatives, or an Internet Web site address that is sufficiently specific to provide access to such a glossary along with a general explanation of the purpose of the address.

(vii) *Annuity options.* If a designated investment alternative is part of a contract, fund or product that permits participants or beneficiaries to allocate contributions toward the future purchase of a stream of retirement income payments guaranteed by an insurance company, the information set forth in paragraph (i)(2)(i) through (i)(2)(vii) of this section with respect to the annuity option, to the extent such information is not otherwise included in investment-related fees and expenses described in paragraph (d)(1)(iv).

(viii) *Disclosures on or before first investment.* The requirement in paragraph (d)(1) of this section to provide information to a participant or beneficiary on or before the date on which the participant or beneficiary can first direct his or her investments may be satisfied by furnishing to the participant or beneficiary the most recent annual disclosure furnished to participants and beneficiaries pursuant to paragraph (d)(1) of this section.

(2) *Comparative format.* (i) Furnish the information described in paragraph (d)(1) and, if applicable, paragraph (i) of this section in a chart or similar format that is designed to facilitate a comparison of such information for each designated investment alternative available under the plan and prominently displays the date, and that includes:

(A) A statement indicating the name, address, and telephone number of the plan administrator (or a person or persons designated by the plan administrator to act on its behalf) to contact for the provision of the information required by paragraph (d)(4) of this section;

(B) A statement that additional investment-related information (including more current performance information) is available at the listed Internet Web site addresses (see paragraph (d)(1)(v) of this section); and

(C) A statement explaining how to request and obtain, free of charge, paper copies of the information required to be made available on a Web site pursuant to paragraph (d)(1)(v), paragraph (i)(2)(vi), relating to annuity options, or paragraph (i)(3), relating to fixed-return investments, of this section.

(ii) Nothing in this section shall preclude a plan administrator from including additional information that the plan administrator determines appropriate for such comparisons, provided such information is not inaccurate or misleading.

(3) *Information to be provided subsequent to investment.* Furnish to each investing participant or beneficiary, subsequent to an investment in a designated investment alternative, any materials provided to the plan relating to the exercise of voting, tender and similar rights appurtenant to the investment, to the extent that such rights are passed through to such participant or beneficiary under the terms of the plan.

(4) *Information to be provided upon request.* Furnish to each participant or beneficiary, either at the times specified in paragraph (d)(1), or upon request, the following information relating to designated investment alternatives—

(i) Copies of prospectuses (or, alternatively, any short-form or summary prospectus, the form of which has been approved by the Securities and Exchange Commission) for the disclosure of information to investors by entities registered under either the Securities Act of 1933 or the Investment Company Act of 1940, or similar documents relating to designated investment alternatives that are provided by entities that are not registered under either of these Acts;

(ii) Copies of any financial statements or reports, such as statements of additional information and shareholder reports, and of any other similar materials relating to the plan's designated investment alternatives, to the extent such materials are provided to the plan;

(iii) A statement of the value of a share or unit of each designated investment alternative as well as the date of the valuation; and

(iv) A list of the assets comprising the portfolio of each designated investment alternative which constitute plan assets within the meaning of 29 CFR 2510.3-101 and the value of each such asset (or the proportion of the investment which it comprises).

(e) *Form of disclosure.* (1) The information required to be disclosed pursuant to paragraphs (c)(1)(i), (c)(2)(i)(A), and (c)(3)(i)(A) of this section may be provided as part of the plan's summary plan description furnished pursuant to ERISA section 102 or as part of a pension benefit statement furnished pursuant to ERISA section 105(a)(1)(A)(i), if such summary plan description or pension benefit statement is furnished at a frequency that comports with paragraph (c)(1)(i) of this section.

(2) The information required to be disclosed pursuant to paragraphs (c)(2)(ii) and (c)(3)(ii) of this section may be included as part of a pension benefit statement furnished pursuant to ERISA section 105(a)(1)(A)(i).

(3) A plan administrator that uses and accurately completes the model in the Appendix, taking into account each designated investment alternative offered under the plan, will be deemed to have satisfied the requirements of paragraph (d)(2) of this section.

(4) Except as otherwise explicitly required herein, fees and expenses may be expressed in terms of a monetary amount, formula, percentage of assets, or per capita charge.

(5) The information required to be prepared by the plan administrator for disclosure under this section shall be written in a manner calculated to be understood by the average plan participant.

(f) *Selection and monitoring.* Nothing herein is intended to relieve a fiduciary from its duty to prudently select and monitor providers of services to the plan or designated investment alternatives offered under the plan.

(g) *Manner of furnishing. Reserved.*

(h) *Definitions.* For purposes of this section, the term—

⋙→ *Caution: Reg. § 2550.404a-5(h)(1), below, as amended, is effective June 17, 2015, is applicable to disclosures made on or after June 17, 2015, and applies under a temporary enforcement policy prior to the effective date of the amendment.*

(1) *At least annually thereafter* means at least once in any 14-month period, without regard to whether the plan operates on a

calendar year or fiscal year basis. [Amended 3/19/2015 by 80 FR 14301.]

(2) *At least quarterly* means at least once in any 3-month period, without regard to whether the plan operates on a calendar or fiscal year basis.

(3) *Average annual total return* means the average annual compounded rate of return that would equate an initial investment in a designated investment alternative to the ending redeemable value of that investment calculated with the before tax methods of computation prescribed in Securities and Exchange Commission Form N-1A, N-3, or N-4, as appropriate, except that such method of computation may exclude any front-end, deferred or other sales loads that are waived for the participants and beneficiaries of the covered individual account plan.

(4) *Designated investment alternative* means any investment alternative designated by the plan into which participants and beneficiaries may direct the investment of assets held in, or contributed to, their individual accounts. The term "designated investment alternative" shall not include "brokerage windows," "self-directed brokerage accounts," or similar plan arrangements that enable participants and beneficiaries to select investments beyond those designated by the plan.

(5) *Total annual operating expenses* means:

(i) In the case of a designated investment alternative that is registered under the Investment Company Act of 1940, the annual operating expenses and other asset-based charges before waivers and reimbursements (e.g., investment management fees, distribution fees, service fees, administrative expenses, separate account expenses, mortality and expense risk fees) that reduce the alternative's rate of return, expressed as a percentage, calculated in accordance with the required Securities and Exchange Commission form, e.g., Form N-1A (open-end management investment companies) or Form N-3 or N-4 (separate accounts offering variable annuity contracts); or

(ii) In the case of a designated investment alternative that is not registered under the Investment Company Act of 1940, the sum of the fees and expenses described in paragraphs (h)(5)(ii)(A) through (C) of this section before waivers and reimbursements, for the alternative's most recently completed fiscal year, expressed as a percentage of the alternative's average net asset value for that year-

(A) Management fees as described in the Securities and Exchange Commission Form N-1A that reduce the alternative's rate of return,

(B) Distribution and/or servicing fees as described in the Securities and Exchange Commission Form N-1A that reduce the alternative's rate of return, and

(C) Any other fees or expenses not included in paragraphs (h)(5)(ii)(A) or (B) of this section that reduce the alternative's rate of return (e.g., externally negotiated fees, custodial expenses, legal expenses, accounting expenses, transfer agent expenses, recordkeeping fees, administrative fees, separate account expenses, mortality and expense risk fees), excluding brokerage costs described in Item 21 of Securities and Exchange Commission Form N-1A.

(i) *Special rules.* The rules set forth in this paragraph apply solely for purposes of paragraph (d)(1) of this section.

(1) *Qualifying employer securities.* In the case of designated investment alternatives designed to invest in, or primarily in, qualifying employer securities, within the meaning of section 407 of ERISA, the following rules shall apply -

(i) In lieu of the requirements of paragraph (d)(1)(v)(C) of this section (relating to principal strategies and principal risks), provide an explanation of the importance of a wellbalanced and diversified investment portfolio.

(ii) The requirements of paragraph (d)(1)(v)(D) of this section (relating to portfolio turnover rate) do not apply to such designated investment alternatives.

(iii) The requirements of paragraph (d)(1)(v)(F) of this section (relating to fee and expense information) do not apply to such designated investment alternatives, unless the designated investment

alternative is a fund with respect to which participants or beneficiaries acquire units of participation, rather than actual shares, in exchange for their investment.

(iv) The requirements of paragraph (d)(1)(iv)(A) *(2)* of this section (relating to total annual operating expenses expressed as a percentage) do not apply to such designated investment alternatives, unless the designated investment alternative is a fund with respect to which participants or beneficiaries acquire units of participation, rather than actual shares, in exchange for their investment.

(v) The requirements of paragraph (d)(1)(iv)(A) *(3)* of this section (relating to total annual operating expenses expressed as a dollar amount per $1,000 invested) do not apply to such designated investment alternatives, unless the designated investment alternative is a fund with respect to which participants or beneficiaries acquire units of participation, rather than actual shares, in exchange for their investment.

(vi)(A) With respect to the requirement in paragraph (d)(1)(ii)(A) of this section (relating to performance data for 1-, 5-, and 10-year periods), the definition of "average annual total return" as defined in paragraph (i)(1)(vi)(B) of this section shall apply to such designated investment alternatives in lieu of the definition in paragraph (h)(3) of this section if the qualifying employer securities are publicly traded on a national exchange or generally recognized market and the designated investment alternative is not a fund with respect to which participants or beneficiaries acquire units of participation, rather than actual shares, in exchange for their investment.

(B) The term "average annual total return" means the change in value of an investment in one share of stock on an annualized basis over a specified period, calculated by taking the sum of the dividends paid during the measurement period, assuming reinvestment, plus the difference between the stock price (consistent with ERISA section 3(18)) at the end and at the beginning of the measurement period, and dividing by the stock price at the beginning of the measurement period; reinvestment of dividends is assumed to be in stock at market prices at approximately the same time actual dividends are paid.

(C) The definition of "average annual total return" in paragraph (i)(1)(vi)(B) of this section shall apply to such designated investment alternatives consisting of employer securities that are not publicly traded on a national exchange or generally recognized market, unless the designated investment alternative is a fund with respect to which participants or beneficiaries acquire units of participation, rather than actual shares, in exchange for their investment. Changes in value shall be calculated using principles similar to those set forth in paragraph (i)(1)(vi)(B) of this section.

(2) *Annuity options.* In the case of a designated investment alternative that is a contract, fund or product that permits participants or beneficiaries to allocate contributions toward the current purchase of a stream of retirement income payments guaranteed by an insurance company, the plan administrator shall, in lieu of the information required by paragraphs (d)(1)(i) through (d)(1)(v), provide each participant or beneficiary the following information with respect to each such option:

(i) The name of the contract, fund or product;

(ii) The option's objectives or goals (e.g., to provide a stream of fixed retirement income payments for life);

(iii) The benefits and factors that determine the price (e.g., age, interest rates, form of distribution) of the guaranteed income payments;

(iv) Any limitations on the ability of a participant or beneficiary to withdraw or transfer amounts allocated to the option (e.g., lockups) and any fees or charges applicable to such withdrawals or transfers;

(v) Any fees that will reduce the value of amounts allocated by participants or beneficiaries to the option, such as surrender charges, market value adjustments, and administrative fees;

(vi) A statement that guarantees of an insurance company are subject to its long-term financial strength and claims-paying ability; and

(vii) An Internet Web site address that is sufficiently specific to provide participants and beneficiaries access to the following information -

(A) The name of the option's issuer and of the contract, fund or product;

(B) Description of the option's objectives or goals;

(C) Description of the option's distribution alternatives/ guaranteed income payments (e.g., payments for life, payments for a specified term, joint and survivor payments, optional rider payments), including any limitations on the right of a participant or beneficiary to receive such payments;

(D) Description of costs and/or factors taken into account in determining the price of benefits under an option's distribution alternatives/guaranteed income payments (e.g., age, interest rates, other annuitization assumptions);

(E) Description of any limitations on the right of a participant or beneficiary to withdraw or transfer amounts allocated to the option and any fees or charges applicable to a withdrawal or transfer; and

(F) Description of any fees that will reduce the value of amounts allocated by participants or beneficiaries to the option (e.g., surrender charges, market value adjustments, administrative fees).

(3) *Fixed-return investments*. In the case of a designated investment alternative with respect to which the return is fixed for the term of the investment, the plan administrator shall, in lieu of complying with the requirements of paragraph (d)(1)(v) of this section, provide an Internet Web site address that is sufficiently specific to provide participants and beneficiaries access to the following information -

(i) The name of the alternative's issuer;

(ii) The alternatives objectives or goals (e.g., to provide stability of principal and guarantee a minimum rate of return);

(iii) The alternative's performance data described in paragraph (d)(1)(ii)(B) of this section updated on at least a quarterly basis, or more frequently if required by other applicable law;

(iv) The alternative's fee and expense information described in paragraph (d)(1)(iv)(B) of this section.

(4) *Target date or similar funds. Reserved.*

(j) *Dates.* (1) *Effective Date.* This section shall be effective on December 20, 2010.

(2) *Applicability Date.* This section shall apply to covered individual account plans for plan years beginning on or after November 1, 2011.

(3) *Transitional rules.* (i)(A) Notwithstanding paragraphs (b), (c) and (d) of this section, the initial disclosures required on or before the date on which a participant or beneficiary can first direct his or her investments must be furnished no later than the later of 60 days after such applicability date or 60 days after the effective date of 29 CFR 2550.408b-2(c). [Amended July 19, 2011 by 76 FR 42539.]

(B) Notwithstanding paragraphs (b) and (c) of this section, the initial disclosures required under paragraphs (c)(2)(ii) and (c)(3)(ii) of this section must be furnished no later than 45 days after the end of the quarter in which the disclosure referred to in paragraph (j)(3)(i)(A) of this section was required to be furnished to participants and beneficiaries. [Added July 19, 2011 by 76 FR 42539.]

Notwithstanding paragraphs (b), (c) and (d) of this section, the initial disclosures required on or before the date on which a participant or beneficiary can first direct his or her investment must be furnished no later than 60 days after such applicability date to participants or beneficiaries who had the right to direct the investment of assets held in, or contributed to, their individual account on the applicability date.

(ii) For plan years beginning before October 1, 2021, if a plan administrator reasonably and in good faith determines that it does not have the information on expenses attributable to the plan that is necessary to calculate, in accordance with paragraph (h)(3) of this section, the 5-year and 10-year average annual total returns for a designated investment alternative that is not registered under the Investment Company Act of 1940, the plan administrator may use a reasonable estimate of such expenses or the plan administrator may use the most recently reported total annual operating expenses of the designated investment alternative as a substitute for such expenses. When a plan administrator uses a reasonable estimate or the most recently reported total annual operating expenses as a substitute for actual expenses pursuant to this paragraph, the administrator shall inform participants of the basis on which the returns were determined. Nothing in this section requires disclosure of returns for periods before the inception of a designated investment alternative. [Added by 75 FR 64910, October 20, 2010.]

APPENDIX to § 2550.404a-5 - Model Comparative Chart

ABC Corporation 401k Retirement Plan

Investment Options - January 1, 20XX

This document includes important information to help you compare the investment options under your retirement plan. If you want additional information about your investment options, you can go to the specific Internet Web site address shown below or you can contact [insert name of plan administrator or designee] at [insert telephone number and address]. A free paper copy of the information available on the Web site[s] can be obtained by contacting [insert name of plan administrator or designee] at [insert telephone number].

Document Summary

This document has 3 parts. Part I consists of performance information for plan investment options. This part shows you how well the investments have performed in the past. Part II shows you the fees and expenses you will pay if you invest in an option. Part III contains information about the annuity options under your retirement plan.

Part I. Performance Information

Table 1 focuses on the performance of investment options that do not have a fixed or stated rate of return. Table 1 shows how these options have performed over time and allows you to compare them with an appropriate benchmark for the same time periods. Past performance does not guarantee how the investment option will perform in the future. Your investment in these options could lose money. Information about an option's principal risks is available on the Web site[s].

Table 1—Variable Return Investments

Name/Type of Option	Average Annual Total Return as of 12/31/XX				Benchmark			
	1yr.	5yr.	10yr.	Since Inception	1yr.	5yr.	10yr.	Since Inception
Equity Funds								
A Index Fund/ S&P 500 www. website address	26.5%	.34%	-1.03%	9.25%	26.46%	.42%	-.95%	9.30% S&P 500

Table 1—Variable Return Investments

Name/Type of Option	Average Annual Total Return as of 12/31/XX				Benchmark			
	1yr.	5yr.	10yr.	Since Inception	1yr.	5yr.	10yr.	Since Inception
B Fund/Large Cap www. website address	27.6%	.99%	N/A	2.26%	27.80%	1.02%	N/A	2.77%
					US Prime Market 750 Index			
C Fund/Int'l Stock www. website address	36.73%	5.26%	2.29%	9.37%	40.40%	5.40%	2.40%	12.09%
					MSCI EAFE			
D Fund/Mid Cap www. website address	40.22%	2.28%	6.13%	3.29%	46.29%	2.40%	-.52%	4.16%
					Russell Midcap			
Bond Funds								
E Fund/Bond Index www. website address	6.45%	4.43%	6.08%	7.08%	5.93%	4.97%	6.33%	7.01%
					Barclays Cap. Aggr. Bd.			
Other								
F Fund/GICs www. website address	.72%	3.36%	3.11%	5.56%	1.8%	3.1%	3.3%	5.75%
					3-month US T-Bill Index			
G Fund/Stable Value www. website address	4.36%	4.64%	5.07%	3.75%	1.8%	3.1%	3.3%	4.99%
					3-month US T-Bill Index			
Generations 2020/ Lifecycle Fund www. website address	27.94%	N/A	N/A	2.45%	26.46%	N/A	N/A	3.09%
					S&P 500			
					23.95%	N/A	N/A	3.74%
					Generations 2020 Composite Index *			

*Generations 2020 composite index is a combination of a total market index and a US aggregate bond index proportional to the equity/bond allocation in the Generations 2020 Fund.

Table 2 focuses on the performance of investment options that have a fixed or stated rate of return. Table 2 shows the annual rate of return of each such option, the term or length of time that you will earn this rate of return, and other information relevant to performance.

Table 2—Fixed Return Investments

Name/Type of Option	Return	Term	Other
H 200X/GIC www. website address	4%	2 Yr.	The rate of return does not change during the stated term.
I LIBOR Plus/Fixed-Type Investment Account www. website address	LIBOR +2%	Quarterly	The rate of return on 12/31/xx was 2.45%. This rate is fixed quarterly, but will never fall below a guaranteed minimum rate of 2%. Current rate of return information is available on the option's Web site or at 1-800-yyyzzzz.
J Financial Services Co./ Fixed Account Investment www. website address	3.75%	6 Mos.	The rate of return on 12/31/xx was 3.75%. This rate of return is fixed for six months. Current rate of return information is available on the option's Web site or at 1- 800-yyy-zzzz.

Part II. Fee and Expense Information

Table 3 shows fee and expense information for the investment options listed in Table1 and Table 2. Table 3 shows the Total Annual Operating Expenses of the options in Table 1. Total Annual Operating Expenses are expenses that reduce the rate of return of the investment option. Table 3 also shows Shareholder-type Fees. These fees are in addition to Total Annual Operating Expenses.

Table 3—Fees and Expenses

Name / Type of Option	Total Annual Operating Expenses		Shareholder-Type Fees
	As a %	Per $1000	
Equity Funds			
A Index Fund/S&P 500	0.18%	$1.80	$20 annual service charge subtracted from investments held in this option if valued at less than $10,000.
B Fund/Large Cap	2.45%	$24.50	2.25% deferred sales charge subtracted from amounts withdrawn within 12 months of purchase.
C Fund/International Stock	0.79%	$7.90	5.75% sales charge subtracted from amounts invested.

Reg. §   ¶14,742D

Table 3—Fees and Expenses

Name / Type of Option	Total Annual Operating Expenses		Shareholder-Type Fees
	As a %	Per $1000	
D Fund/Mid Cap ETF	0.20%	$2.00	4.25% sales charge subtracted from amounts withdrawn.
Bond Funds			
E Fund/Bond Index	0.50%	$5.00	N/A
Other			
F Fund/GICs	0.46%	$4.60	10% charge subtracted from amounts withdrawn within 18 months of initial investment.
G Fund/Stable Value	0.65%	$6.50	Amounts withdrawn may not be transferred to a competing option for 90 days after withdrawal.
Generations 2020/Lifecycle Fund	1.50%	$15.00	Excessive trading restricts additional purchases (other than contributions and loan repayments) for 85 days.
Fixed Return Investments			
H 200X / GIC	N/A		12% charge subtracted from amounts withdrawn before maturity.
I LIBOR Plus/Fixed-Type Invest Account	N/A		5% contingent deferred sales charge subtracted from amounts withdrawn; charge reduced by 1% on 12-month anniversary of each investment.
J Financial Serv Co. / Fixed Account Investment	N/A		90 days of interest subtracted from amounts withdrawn before maturity.

The cumulative effect of fees and expenses can substantially reduce the growth of your retirement savings. Visit the Department of Labor's Web site for an example showing the long-term effect of fees and expenses at *http://www.dol.gov/ebsa/publications/401k employee.html*. Fees and expenses are only one of many factors to consider when you decide to invest in an option. You may also want to think about whether an investment in a particular option, along with your other investments, will help you achieve your financial goals.

Part III. Annuity Information

Table 4 focuses on the annuity options under the plan. Annuities are insurance contracts that allow you to receive a guaranteed stream of payments at regular intervals, usually beginning when you retire and lasting for your entire life. Annuities are issued by insurance companies. Guarantees of an insurance company are subject to its long-term financial strength and claims-paying ability.

Table 4—Annuity Options

Name	Objectives / Goals	Pricing Factors	Restrictions / Fees
Lifetime Income Option www. website address	To provide a guaranteed stream of income for your life, based on shares you acquire while you work. At age 65, you will receive monthly payments of $10 for each share you own, for your life. For example, if you own 30 shares at age 65, you will receive $300 per month over your life.	The cost of each share depends on your age and interest rates when you buy it. Ordinarily the closer you are to retirement, the more it will cost you to buy a share. The cost includes a guaranteed death benefit payable to a spouse or beneficiary if you die before payments begin. The death benefit is the total amount of your contributions, less any withdrawals.	Payment amounts are based on your life expectancy only and would be reduced if you choose a spousal joint and survivor benefit. You will pay a 25% surrender charge for any amount you withdraw before annuity payments begin. If your income payments are less than $50 per month, the option's issuer may combine payments and pay you less frequently, or return to you the larger of your net contributions or the cashout value of your income shares.
Generations 2020 Variable Annuity Option www. website address	To provide a guaranteed stream of income for your life, or some other period of time, based on your account balance in the Generations 2020 Lifecycle Fund. This option is available through a variable annuity contract that your plan has with ABC Insurance Company.	You have the right to elect fixed annuity payments in the form of a life annuity, a joint and survivor annuity, or a life annuity with a term certain, but the payment amounts will vary based on the benefit you choose. The cost of this right is included in the Total Annual Operating Expenses of the Generations 2020 Lifecycle Fund, listed in Table 3 above. The cost also includes a guaranteed death benefit payable to a spouse or beneficiary if you die before payments begin. The death benefit is the greater of your account balance or contributions, less any withdrawals.	Maximum surrender charge of 8% of account balance. Maximum transfer fee of $30 for each transfer over 12 in a year. Annual service charge of $50 for account balances below $100,000.

Please visit www.ABCPlanglossary.com for a glossary of investment terms relevant to the investment options under this plan. This glossary is intended to help you better understand your options.

[¶ 14,743]

§2550.404b-1 **Maintenance of the indicia of ownership of plan assets outside the jurisdiction of the district courts of the United States.** (a) No fiduciary may maintain the indicia of ownership of any assets of a plan outside the jurisdiction of the district courts of the United States, unless: [Amended by 64 FR 1266, originally scheduled to be effective February 6, 1981. However, the effective date was delayed under the President's regulation freeze until March 30, 1981 (46 FR 10465).]

(1) Such assets are (i) Securities issued by a person, as defined in section 3(9) of the Employee Retirement Income Security Act of 1974 (Act) (other than an individual), which is not organized under the laws of the United States or a State and does not have its principal place of business within the United States, (ii) securities issued by a government other than the government of the United States or of a State, or any political subdivision, agency or instrumentality of such a government, (iii) securities issued by a person, as defined in section 3(9) of the Act (other than an individual), the principal trading market for which securities is outside the jurisdiction of the district courts of the United States, or (iv) currency issued by a government other than the government of the United States if such currency is maintained outside the jurisdiction of the district courts of the United States solely as an incident to the purchase, sale or maintenance of securities described in paragraph (a)(1) of this section; and

(2)(i) Such assets are under the management and control of a fiduciary which is a corporation or partnership organized under the laws of the United States or a State, which fiduciary has its principal place of business within the United States and which is—

(A) A bank as defined in section 202(a)(2) of the Investment Advisers Act of 1940 that has, as of the last day of its most recent fiscal year, equity capital in excess of $1,000,000;

(B) An insurance company which is qualified under the laws of more than one State to manage, acquire, or dispose of any asset of a plan, which company has, as of the last day of its most recent fiscal year, net worth in excess of $1,000,000 and which is subject to supervision and examination by the State authority having supervision over insurance companies; or

(C) An investment adviser registered under the Investment Advisers Act of 1940 that has, as of the last day of its most recent fiscal year, total client assets under its management and control in excess [of] $50,000,000 and either *(1)* Shareholders' or partners' equity in excess of $750,000 or *(2)* all of its obligations and liabilities assumed or guaranteed by a person described in paragraph (a)(2)(i)(A), (B), or (C) *(1)* or (a)(2)(ii)(A) *(2)* of this section; or

(ii) Such indicia of ownership are either

(A) In the physical possession of, or, as a result of normal business operations, are in transit to the physical possession of, a person which is organized under the laws of the United States or a State, which person has its principal place of business in the United States and which is—

(1) A bank as defined in section 202(a)(2) of the Investment Advisers Act of 1940 that has, as of the last day of its most recent fiscal year, equity capital in excess of $1,000,000;

(2) A broker or dealer registered under the Securities Exchange Act of 1934 that has, as of the last day of its most recent fiscal year, net worth in excess of $750,000; or

(3) A broker or dealer registered under the Securities Exchange Act of 1934 that has all of its obligations and liabilities assumed or guaranteed by a person described in paragraph (a)(2)(i)(A), (B), or (C) *(1)* or (a)(2)(ii)(A) *(2)* of this section; or

(B) Maintained by a broker or dealer, described in paragraph (a)(2)(ii)(A) *(2)* or *(3)* of this section, in the custody of an entity designated by the Securities and Exchange Commission as a "satisfactory control location" with respect to such broker or dealer pursuant to Rule 15c3-3 under the Securities Exchange Act of 1934, provided that:

(1) Such entity holds the indicia of ownership as agent for the broker or dealer, and

(2) Such broker or dealer is liable to the plan to the same extent it would be if it retained the physical possession of the indicia of ownership pursuant to paragraph (a)(2)(ii)(A) of this section. [Amended by 46 FR 1266, originally scheduled to be effective February 6, 1981. However, the effective date was delayed under the President's regulation freeze until March 30, 1981 (46 FR 10465).]

(C) Maintained by a bank described in paragraph (a)(2)(ii)(A) *(1)*, in the custody of an entity that is a foreign securities depository, foreign clearing agency which acts as a securities depository, or foreign bank, which entity is supervised or regulated by a government agency or regulatory authority in the foreign jurisdiction having authority over such depositories, clearing agencies or banks, provided that:

(1) the foreign entity holds the indicia of ownership as agent for the bank;

(2) the bank is liable to the plan to the same extent it would be if it retained the physical possession of the indicia of ownership within the United States;

(3) the indicia of ownership are not subject to any right, charge, security interest, lien or claim of any kind in favor of the foreign entity except for their safe custody or administration;

(4) beneficial ownership of the assets represented by the indicia of ownership is freely transferable without the payment of money or value other than for safe custody or administration; and

(5) upon request by the plan fiduciary who is responsible for the selection and retention of the bank, the bank identifies to such fiduciary the name, address and principal place of business of the foreign entity which acts as custodian for the plan pursuant to this paragraph (a)(2)(ii)(C), and the name and address of the governmental agency or other regulatory authority that supervises or regulates that foreign entity. [Added by 46 FR 1266, originally scheduled to be effective February 6, 1981. However, the effective date was delayed under the President's regulation freeze until March 30, 1981 (46 FR 10465).]

(b) Notwithstanding any requirement of paragraph (a) of this section, a fiduciary with respect to a plan may maintain in Canada the indicia of ownership of plan assets which are attributable to a contribution made on behalf of a plan participant who is a citizen or resident of Canada, if such indicia of ownership must remain in Canada in order for the plan to qualify for and maintain tax exempt status under the laws of Canada or to comply with other applicable laws of Canada or any Province of Canada.

(c) For purposes of this regulation:

(1) the term "management and control" means the power to direct the acquisition or disposition through purchase, sale, pledging, or other means; and

(2) the term "depository" means any company, or agency or instrumentality of government, that acts as a custodian of securities in connection with a system for the central handling of securities whereby all securities of a particular class or series of any issuer deposited within the system are treated as fungible and may be transferred, loaned, or pledged by bookkeeping entry without physical delivery of securities certificates. [Amended by 46 FR 1266, originally scheduled to be effective February 6, 1981. However, the effective date was delayed under the President's regulation freeze until March 30, 1981 (46 FR 10465).]

[¶ 14,744]

§2550.404c-1 **ERISA section 404(c) plans.** (a) *In general.*

(1) Section 404(c) of the Employee Retirement Income Security Act of 1974 (ERISA or the Act) provides that if a pension plan that provides for individual accounts permits a participant or beneficiary to exercise control over assets in his account and that participant or beneficiary in fact exercises control over assets in his account, then the participant or beneficiary shall not be deemed to be a fiduciary by reason of his exercise of control and no person who is otherwise a fiduciary shall be liable for any loss, or by reason of any breach, which results from such exercise of control. This section describes the kinds of plans that are "ERISA section 404(c) plans," the circumstances in

which a participant or beneficiary is considered to have exercised independent control over the assets in his account as contemplated by section 404(c), and the consequences of a participant's or beneficiary's exercise of control.

(2) The standards set forth in this section are applicable solely for the purpose of determining whether a plan is an ERISA section 404(c) plan and whether a particular transaction engaged in by a participant or beneficiary of such plan is afforded relief by section 404(c). Such standards, therefore, are not intended to be applied in determining whether, or to what extent, a plan which does not meet the requirements for an ERISA section 404(c) plan or a fiduciary with respect to such a plan satisfies the fiduciary responsibility or other provisions of Title I of the Act.

(b) *ERISA section 404(c) plans.*

(1) *In general.* An "ERISA section 404(c) plan" is an individual account plan described in section 3(34) of the Act that:

(i) Provides an opportunity for a participant or beneficiary to exercise control over assets in his individual account (see paragraph (b)(2) of this section); and

(ii) Provides a participant or beneficiary an opportunity to choose, from a broad range of investment alternatives, the manner in which some or all of the assets in his account are invested (see paragraph (b)(3) of this section).

(2) *Opportunity to exercise control.* (i) A plan provides a participant or beneficiary an opportunity to exercise control over assets in his account only if:

(A) Under the terms of the plan, the participant or beneficiary has a reasonable opportunity to give investment instructions (in writing or otherwise, with an opportunity to obtain written confirmation of such instructions) to an identified plan fiduciary who is obligated to comply with such instructions except as otherwise provided in paragraphs (b)(2)(ii)(B) and (d)(2)(ii) of this section; and

(B) The participant or beneficiary is provided or has the opportunity to obtain sufficient information to make informed investment decisions with regard to investment alternatives available under the plan, and incidents of ownership appurtenant to such investments. For purposes of this paragraph, a participant or beneficiary will be considered to have sufficient information if the participant or beneficiary is provided by an identified plan fiduciary (or a person or persons designated by the plan fiduciary to act on his behalf):

(1) An explanation that the plan is intended to constitute a plan described in section 404(c) of the Employee Retirement Income Security Act, and 29 CFR 2550.404c-1, and that the fiduciaries of the plan may be relieved of liability for any losses which are the direct and necessary result of investment instructions given by such participant or beneficiary;

(2) The information required pursuant to 29 CFR 2550.404a-5; and

(3) In the case of plans which offer an investment alternative which is designed to permit a participant or beneficiary to directly or indirectly acquire or sell any employer security (employer security alternative), a description of the procedures established to provide for the confidentiality of information relating to the purchase, holding and sale of employer securities, and the exercise of voting, tender and similar rights, by participants and beneficiaries, and the name, address and phone number of the plan fiduciary responsible for monitoring compliance with the procedures (see paragraphs (d)(2)(ii)(E)(*4*)(*vii*), (*viii*) and (*ix*) of this section). [Amended October 20, 2010 (75 FR 64910.)]

(ii) A plan does not fail to provide an opportunity for a participant or beneficiary to exercise control over his individual account merely because it—

(A) *Imposes charges for reasonable expenses.* A plan may charge participants' and beneficiaries' accounts for the reasonable expenses of carrying out investment instructions, provided that procedures are established under the plan to periodically inform such participants and beneficiaries of actual expenses incurred with respect to their respective individual accounts;

(B) *Permits a fiduciary to decline to implement investment instructions by participants and beneficiaries.* A fiduciary may decline to implement participant and beneficiary instructions which are described at paragraph (d)(2)(ii) of this section, as well as instructions specified in the plan, including instructions—

(1) which would result in a prohibited transaction described in ERISA section 406 or section 4975 of the Internal Revenue Code, and

(2) which would generate income that would be taxable to the plan;

(C) *Imposes reasonable restrictions on frequency of investment instructions.* A plan may impose reasonable restrictions on the frequency with which participants and beneficiaries may give investment instructions. In no event, however, is such a restriction reasonable unless, with respect to each investment alternative made available by the plan, it permits participants and beneficiaries to give investment instructions with a frequency which is appropriate in light of the market volatility to which the investment alternative may reasonably be expected to be subject, provided that—

(1) At least three of the investment alternatives made available pursuant to the requirements of paragraph (b)(3)(i)(B) of this section, which constitute a broad range of investment alternatives, permit participants and beneficiaries to give investment instructions no less frequently than once within any three month period; and

(2)(i) At least one of the investment alternatives meeting the requirements of paragraph (b)(2)(ii)(C)(*1*) of this section permits participants and beneficiaries to give investment instructions with regard to transfers into the investment alternative as frequently as participants and beneficiaries are permitted to give investment instructions with respect to any investment alternative made available by the plan which permits participants and beneficiaries to give investment instructions more frequently than once within any three month period; or

(ii) With respect to each investment alternative which permits participants and beneficiaries to give investment instructions more frequently than once within any three month period, participants and beneficiaries are permitted to direct their investments from such alternative into an income producing, low risk, liquid fund, subfund, or account as frequently as they are permitted to give investment instructions with respect to each such alternative and, with respect to such fund, subfund or account, participants and beneficiaries are permitted to direct investments from the fund, subfund or account to an investment alternative meeting the requirements of paragraph (b)(2)(ii)(C)(*1*) as frequently as they are permitted to give investment instructions with respect to that investment alternative; and

(3) With respect to transfers from an investment alternative which is designed to permit a participant or beneficiary to directly or indirectly acquire or sell any employer security (employer security alternative) either:

(i) All of the investment alternatives meeting the requirements of paragraph (b)(2)(ii)(C)(*1*) of this section must permit participants and beneficiaries to give investment instructions with regard to transfers into each of the investment alternatives as frequently as participants and beneficiaries are permitted to give investment instructions with respect to the employer security alternative; or

(ii) Participants and beneficiaries are permitted to direct their investments from each employer security alternative into an income producing, low risk, liquid fund, subfund, or account as frequently as they are permitted to give investment instructions with respect to such employer security alternative and, with respect to such fund, subfund, or account, participants and beneficiaries are permitted to direct investments from the fund, subfund or account to each investment alternative meeting the requirements of paragraph (b)(2)(ii)(C)(*1*) as frequently as they are permitted to give investment instructions with respect to each such investment alternative.

(iii) Paragraph (c) of this section describes the circumstances under which a participant or beneficiary will be considered to have exercised independent control with respect to a particular transaction.

(3) *Broad range of investment alternatives.* (i) A plan offers a broad range of investment alternatives only if the available investment alternatives are sufficient to provide the participant or beneficiary with a reasonable opportunity to:

(A) Materially affect the potential return on amounts in his individual account with respect to which he is permitted to exercise control and the degree of risk to which such amounts are subject;

(B) Choose from at least three investment alternatives:

(1) each of which is diversified;

(2) each of which has materially different risk and return characteristics;

(3) which in the aggregate enable the participant or beneficiary by choosing among them to achieve a portfolio with aggregate risk and return characteristics at any point within the range normally appropriate for the participant or beneficiary; and

(4) each of which when combined with investments in the other alternatives tends to minimize through diversification the overall risk of a participant's or beneficiary's portfolio;

(C) Diversify the investment of that portion of his individual account with respect to which he is permitted to exercise control so as to minimize the risk of large losses, taking into account the nature of the plan and the size of participants' or beneficiaries' accounts. In determining whether a plan provides the participant or beneficiary with a reasonable opportunity to diversify his investments, the nature of the investment alternatives offered by the plan and the size of the portion of the individual's account over which he is permitted to exercise control must be considered. Where such portion of the account of any participant or beneficiary is so limited in size that the opportunity to invest in look-through investment vehicles is the only prudent means to assure an opportunity to achieve appropriate diversification, a plan may satisfy the requirements of this paragraph only by offering look-through investment vehicles.

(ii) *Diversification and look-through investment vehicles.* Where look-through investment vehicles are available as investment alternatives to participants and beneficiaries, the underlying investments of the look-through investment vehicles shall be considered in determining whether the plan satisfies the requirements of subparagraphs (b)(3)(i)(B) and (b)(3)(i)(C).

(c) *Exercise of control.* (1) *In general.* (i) Sections 404(c)(1) and 404(c)(2) of the Act and paragraphs (a) and (d) of this section apply only with respect to a transaction where a participant or beneficiary has exercised independent control in fact with respect to the investment of assets in his individual account under an ERISA section 404(c) plan.

(ii) For purposes of sections 404(c)(1) and 404(c)(2) of the Act and paragraphs (a) and (d) of this section, a participant or beneficiary will be deemed to have exercised control with respect to voting, tender or similar rights appurtenant to the participant's or beneficiary's ownership interest in an investment alternative, provided that the participant's or beneficiary's investment in the investment alternative was itself the result of an exercise of control; the participant or beneficiary was provided a reasonable opportunity to give instruction with respect to such incidents of ownership, including the provision of the information described in 29 CFR 2550.404a-5(d)(3); and the participant or beneficiary has not failed to exercise control by reason of the circumstances described in paragraph (c)(2) with respect to such incidents of ownership. [Amended October 20, 2010 (75 FR 64910).]

(2) *Independent control.* Whether a participant or beneficiary has exercised independent control in fact with respect to a transaction depends on the facts and circumstances of the particular case. However, a participant's or beneficiary's exercise of control is not independent in fact if:

(i) The participant or beneficiary is subjected to improper influence by a plan fiduciary or the plan sponsor with respect to the transaction;

(ii) A plan fiduciary has concealed material non-public facts regarding the investment from the participant or beneficiary, unless the disclosure of such information by the plan fiduciary to the participant or beneficiary would violate any provision of federal law or any provision of state law which is not preempted by the Act; or

(iii) The participant or beneficiary is legally incompetent and the responsible plan fiduciary accepts the instructions of the participant or beneficiary knowing him to be legally incompetent.

(3) *Transactions involving a fiduciary.* In the case of a sale, exchange or leasing of property (other than a transaction described in paragraph (d)(2)(ii)(E) of this section) between an ERISA section 404(c) plan and a plan fiduciary or an affiliate of such a fiduciary, or a loan to a plan fiduciary or an affiliate of such a fiduciary, the participant or beneficiary will not be deemed to have exercised independent control unless the transaction is fair and reasonable to him. For purposes of this paragraph (c)(3), a transaction will be deemed to be fair and reasonable to a participant or beneficiary if he pays no more than, or receives no less than, adequate consideration (as defined in section 3(18) of the Act) in connection with the transaction.

(4) *No obligation to advise.* A fiduciary has no obligation under part 4 of Title I of the Act to provide investment advice to a participant or beneficiary under an ERISA section 404(c) plan.

(d) *Effect of independent exercise of control.* (1) *Participant or beneficiary not a fiduciary.* If a participant or beneficiary of an ERISA section 404(c) plan exercises independent control over assets in his individual account in the manner described in paragraph (c), then such participant or beneficiary is not a fiduciary of the plan by reason of such exercise of control.

(2) *Limitation on liability of plan fiduciaries.* (i) If a participant or beneficiary of an ERISA section 404(c) plan exercises independent control over assets in his individual account in the manner described in paragraph (c), then no other person who is a fiduciary with respect to such plan shall be liable for any loss, or with respect to any breach of part 4 of Title I of the Act, that is the direct and necessary result of that participant's or beneficiary's exercise of control.

(ii) Paragraph (d)(2)(i) does not apply with respect to any instruction which, if implemented—

(A) Would not be in accordance with the documents and instruments governing the plan insofar as such documents and instruments are consistent with the provisions of Title I of ERISA;

(B) Would cause a fiduciary to maintain the indicia of ownership of any assets of the plan outside the jurisdiction of the district courts of the United States other than as permitted by section 404(b) of the Act and 29 C.F.R. § 2550.404b-1;

(C) Would jeopardize the plan's tax qualified status under the Internal Revenue Code;

(D) Could result in a loss in excess of a participant's or beneficiary's account balance; or

(E) Would result in a direct or indirect:

(1) Sale, exchange, or lease of property between a plan sponsor or any affiliate of the sponsor and the plan except for the acquisition or disposition of any interest in a fund, subfund or portfolio managed by a plan sponsor or an affiliate of the sponsor, or the purchase or sale of any qualifying employer security (as defined in section 407(d)(5) of the Act) which meets the conditions of section 408(e) of ERISA and section (d)(2)(ii)(E)(4) below;

(2) Loan to a plan sponsor or any affiliate of the sponsor;

(3) Acquisition or sale of any employer real property (as defined in section 407(d)(2) of the Act); or

(4) Acquisition or sale of any employer security except to the extent that:

(i) such securities are qualifying employer securities (as defined in section 407(d)(5) of the Act);

(ii) such securities are stock or an equity interest in a publicly traded partnership (as defined in section 7704(b) of the Internal Revenue Code of 1986), but only if such partnership is an existing partnership as defined in section 10211(c)(2)(A) of the Revenue Act of 1987 (Public Law 100-203);

(iii) such securities are publicly traded on a national exchange or other generally recognized market;

(iv) such securities are traded with sufficient frequency and in sufficient volume to assure that participant and beneficiary directions to buy or sell the security may be acted upon promptly and efficiently;

(v) information provided to shareholders of such securities is provided to participants and beneficiaries with accounts holding such securities;

(vi) voting, tender and similar rights with respect to such securities are passed through to participants and beneficiaries with accounts holding such securities;

(vii) information relating to the purchase, holding, and sale of securities, and the exercise of voting, tender and similar rights with respect to such securities by participants and beneficiaries, is maintained in accordance with procedures which are designed to safeguard the confidentiality of such information, except to the extent necessary to comply with Federal laws or state laws not preempted by the Act;

(viii) the plan designates a fiduciary who is responsible for ensuring that: the procedures required under subparagraph (d)(2)(ii)(E)(4)(vii) are sufficient to safeguard the confidentiality of the information described in that subparagraph, such procedures are being followed, and the independent fiduciary required by subparagraph (d)(2)(ii)(E)(4)(ix) is appointed; and

(ix) an independent fiduciary is appointed to carry out activities relating to any situations which the fiduciary designated by the plan for purposes of subparagraph (d)(2)(ii)(E)(4)(viii) determines involve a potential for undue employer influence upon participants and beneficiaries with regard to the direct or indirect exercise of shareholder rights. For purposes of this subparagraph, a fiduciary is not independent if the fiduciary is affiliated with any sponsor of the plan.

(iii) The individual investment decisions of an investment manager who is designated directly by a participant or beneficiary or who manages a look-through investment vehicle in which a participant or beneficiary has invested are not direct and necessary results of the designation of the investment manager or of investment in the look-through investment vehicle. However, this paragraph (d)(2)(iii) shall not be construed to result in liability under section 405 of ERISA with respect to a fiduciary (other than the investment manager) who would otherwise be relieved of liability by reason of section 404(c)(2) of the Act and paragraph (d) of this section.

(iv) Paragraph (d)(2)(i) does not serve to relieve a fiduciary from its duty to prudently select and monitor any service provider or designated investment alternative offered under the plan. [Added October 20, 2010 (75 FR 64910).]

(3) *Prohibited transactions.* The relief provided by section 404(c) of the Act and this section applies only to the provisions of part 4 of title I of the Act. Therefore, nothing in this section relieves a disqualified person from the taxes imposed by sections 4975(a) and (b) of the Internal Revenue Code with respect to the transactions prohibited by section 4975(c)(1) of the Code.

(e) *Definitions.* For purposes of this section:

(1) "Look-through investment vehicle" means:

(i) An investment company described in section 3(a) of the Investment Company Act of 1940, or a series investment company described in section 18(f) of the 1940 Act or any of the segregated portfolios of such company;

(ii) A common or collective trust fund or a pooled investment fund maintained by a bank or similar institution, a deposit in a bank or similar institution, or a fixed rate investment contract of a bank or similar institution;

(iii) A pooled separate account or a fixed rate investment contract of an insurance company qualified to do business in a State; or

(iv) Any entity whose assets include plan assets by reason of a plan's investment in the entity;

(2) "Adequate consideration" has the meaning given it in section 3(18) of the Act and in any regulations under this title;

(3) An "affiliate" of a person includes the following:

(i) Any person directly or indirectly controlling, controlled by, or under common control with the person;

(ii) Any officer, director, partner, employee, an employee of an affiliated employer, relative (as defined in section 3(15) of ERISA), brother, sister, or spouse of a brother or sister, of the person; and

(iii) Any corporation or partnership of which the person is an officer, director or partner.

For purposes of this paragraph (e)(3), the term "control" means, with respect to a person other than an individual, the power to exercise a controlling influence over the management or policies of such person.

(4) A "designated investment alternative" is a specific investment identified by a plan fiduciary as an available investment alternative under the plan.

(f) *Examples.* The provisions of this section are illustrated by the following examples. Examples (5) through (11) assume that the participant has exercised independent control with respect to his individual account under an ERISA section 404(c) plan described in paragraph (b) and has not directed a transaction described in paragraph (d)(2)(ii).

(1) Plan A is an individual account plan described in section 3(34) of the Act. The plan states that a plan participant or beneficiary may direct the plan administrator to invest any portion of his individual account in a particular diversified equity fund managed by an entity which is not affiliated with the plan sponsor, or any other asset administratively feasible for the plan to hold. However, the plan provides that the plan administrator will not implement certain listed instructions for which plan fiduciaries would not be relieved of liability under section 404(c) (see paragraph (d)(2)(ii) of this section). Plan participants and beneficiaries are permitted to give investment instructions during the first week of each month with respect to the equity fund and at any time with respect to other investments. The plan administrator of Plan A provides each participant and beneficiary with the information described in paragraph (b)(2)(i)(B) of this section, including the information that must be provided on or before the date on which a participant or beneficiary can first direct his or her investments and at least annually thereafter pursuant to 29 CFR 2550.404a-5, and provides updated information in the event of any change in the information provided. Subsequent to any investment by a participant or beneficiary, the plan administrator forwards to the investing participant or beneficiary any materials provided to the plan relating to the exercise of voting, tender or similar rights attendant to ownership of an interest in such investment (see paragraph (b)(2)(i)(B)(3) of this section and 29 CFR 2550.404a-5(d)(3)). Upon request, the plan administrator provides each participant or beneficiary with copies of any prospectuses (or similar documents relating to designated investment alternatives that are provided by entities that are not registered under the Securities Act of 1933 or the Investment Company Act of 1940), financial statements and reports, and any other materials relating to the designated investment alternatives available under the plan in accordance with 29 CFR 2550.404a-5(d)(4)(i) through (iv). Also upon request, the plan administrator provides each participant and beneficiary with other information required by 29 CFR 2550.404a-5(d)(4) with respect to the equity fund, which is a designated investment alternative, including a statement of the value of a share or unit of the participant's or beneficiary's interest in the equity fund and the date of the valuation. Plan A meets the requirements of paragraph (b)(2)(i)(B) of this section regarding the provision of investment information. [Amended October 20, 2010 (75 FR 64910).]

(2) Plan C is an individual account plan described in section 3(34) of the Act under which participants and beneficiaries may choose among three investment alternatives which otherwise meet the requirements of paragraph (b) of this section. The plan permits investment instruction with respect to each investment alternative only on the first 10 days of each calendar quarter, i.e. January 1-10, April 1-10, July 1-10 and October 1-10. Plan C satisfies the condition of paragraph (b)(2)(ii)(C)(1) that instruction be permitted not less frequently than once within any three month period, since there is not any three month period during which control could not be exercised.

(3) Assume the same facts as in paragraph (f)(2), except that investment instruction may only be given on January 1, April 4, July 1 and October 1. Plan C is not an ERISA section 404(c) plan because it does not satisfy the condition of paragraph (b)(2)(ii)(C)(1) that instruction be permitted not less frequently than once within any three month period. Under these facts, there is a three month period, e.g.,

January 2 through April 1, during which control could not be exercised by participants and beneficiaries.

(4) Plan D is an individual account plan described in section 3(34) of the Act under which participants and beneficiaries may choose among three diversified investment alternatives which constitute a broad range of investment alternatives. The plan also permits investment instruction with respect to an employer securities alternative but provides that a participant or beneficiary can invest no more than 25% of his account balance in this alternative. This restriction does not affect the availability of relief under section 404(c) inasmuch as it does not relate to the three diversified investment alternatives and, therefore, does not cause the plan to fail to provide an opportunity to choose from a broad range of investment alternatives.

(5) A participant, P, independently exercises control over assets in his individual account plan by directing a plan fiduciary, F, to invest 100% of his account balance in a single stock. P is not a fiduciary with respect to the plan by reason of his exercise of control and F will not be liable for any losses that necessarily result from P's investment instruction.

(6) Assume the same facts as in paragraph (f)(5), except that P directs F to purchase the stock from B, who is a party in interest with respect to the plan. Neither P nor F has engaged in a transaction prohibited under section 406 of the Act: P because he is not a fiduciary with respect to the plan by reason of his exercise of control and F because he is not liable for any breach of part 4 of Title I that is the direct and necessary consequence of P's exercise of control. However, a prohibited transaction under section 4975(c) of the Internal Revenue Code may have occurred, and, in the absence of an exemption, tax liability may be imposed pursuant to sections 4975(a) and (b) of the Code.

(7) Assume the same facts as in paragraph (f)(5), except that P does not specify that the stock be purchased from B, and F chooses to purchase the stock from B. In the absence of an exemption, F has engaged in a prohibited transaction described in 406(a) of ERISA because the decision to purchase the stock from B is not a direct or necessary result of P's exercise of control.

(8) Pursuant to the terms of the plan, plan fiduciary F designates three reputable investment managers whom participants may appoint to manage assets in their individual accounts. Participant P selects M, one of the designated managers, to manage the assets in his account. M prudently manages P's account for 6 months after which he incurs losses in managing the account through his imprudence. M has engaged in a breach of fiduciary duty because M's imprudent management of P's account is not a direct or necessary result of P's exercise of control (the choice of M as manager). F has no fiduciary liability for M's imprudence because he has no affirmative duty to advise P (see paragraph (c)(4)) and because F is relieved of co-fiduciary liability by reason of section 404(c)(2) (see paragraph (d)(2)(iii)). F does have a duty to monitor M's performance to determine the suitability of continuing M as an investment manager, however, and M's imprudence would be a factor which F must consider in periodically reevaluating its decision to designate M.

(9) Participant P instructs plan fiduciary F to appoint G as his investment manager pursuant to the terms of the plan which provide P total discretion in choosing an investment manager. Through G's imprudence, G incurs losses in managing P's account. G has engaged in a breach of fiduciary duty because G's imprudent management of P's account is not a direct or necessary result of P's exercise of control (the choice of G as manager). Plan fiduciary F has no fiduciary liability for G's imprudence because F has no obligation to advise P (see paragraph (c)(4)) and because F is relieved of co-fiduciary liability for G's actions by reason of section 404(c)(2) (see paragraph (d)(2)(iii)). In addition, F also has no duty to determine the suitability of G as an investment manager because the plan does not designate G as an investment manager.

(10) Participant P directs a plan fiduciary, F, a bank, to invest all of the assets in his individual account in a collective trust fund managed by F that is designed to be invested solely in a diversified portfolio of common stocks. Due to economic conditions, the value of the common stocks in the bank collective trust fund declines while the value of publicly-offered fixed income obligations remains relatively stable. F is not liable for any losses incurred by P solely because his individual account was not diversified to include fixed income obligations. Such losses are the direct result of P's exercise of control; moreover, under paragraph (c)(4) of this section F has no obligation to advise P regarding his investment decisions.

(11) Assume the same facts as in paragraph (f)(10) except that F, in managing the collective trust fund, invests the assets of the fund solely in a few highly speculative stocks. F is liable for losses resulting from its imprudent investment in the speculative stocks and for its failure to diversify the assets of the account. This conduct involves a separate breach of F's fiduciary duty that is not a direct or necessary result of P's exercise of control (see paragraph (d)(2)(iii)).

(g) *Effective date.* (1) *In general.* Except as provided in paragraph (g)(2), this section is effective with respect to transactions occurring on or after the first day of the second plan year beginning on or after October 13, 1992.

(2) This section is effective with respect to transactions occurring under a plan maintained pursuant to one or more collective bargaining agreements between employee representatives and one or more employers ratified before October 13, 1992 after the later of the date determined under paragraph (g)(1) or the date on which the last collective bargaining agreement terminates. For purposes of this paragraph (g)(2), any extension or renegotiation of a collective bargaining agreement which is ratified on or after October 13, 1992 is to be disregarded in determining the date on which the agreement terminates.

(3) Transactions occurring before the date determined under paragraph (g)(1) or (2) of this section, as applicable, are governed by section 404(c) of the Act without regard to the regulation.

[¶ 14,744D]

§ 2550.404c-5 Fiduciary relief for investments in qualified default investment alternatives.

(a) In general. (1) This section implements the fiduciary relief provided under section 404(c)(5) of the Employee Retirement Income Security Act of 1974, as amended (ERISA or the Act), 29 U.S.C. 1001 et seq., under which a participant or beneficiary in an individual account plan will be treated as exercising control over the assets in his or her account for purposes of ERISA section 404(c)(1) with respect to the amount of contributions and earnings that, in the absence of an investment election by the participant, are invested by the plan in accordance with this regulation. If a participant or beneficiary is treated as exercising control over the assets in his or her account in accordance with ERISA section 404(c)(1) no person who is otherwise a fiduciary shall be liable under part 4 of title I of ERISA for any loss or by reason of any breach which results from such participant's or beneficiary's exercise of control. Except as specifically provided in paragraph (c)(6) of this section, a plan need not meet the requirements for an ERISA section 404(c) plan under 29 CFR 2550.404c-1 in order for a plan fiduciary to obtain the relief under this section.

(2) The standards set forth in this section apply solely for purposes of determining whether a fiduciary meets the requirements of this regulation. Such standards are not intended to be the exclusive means by which a fiduciary might satisfy his or her responsibilities under the Act with respect to the investment of assets in the individual account of a participant or beneficiary.

(b) Fiduciary relief. (1) Except as provided in paragraphs (t)(2), (3), and (4) of this section, a fiduciary of an individual account plan that permits participants or beneficiaries to direct the investment of assets in their accounts and that meets the conditions of paragraph (c) of this section shall not be liable for any loss, or by reason of any breach under part 4 of title I of ERISA, that is the direct and necessary result of (i) investing all or part of a participant's or beneficiary's account in any qualified default investment alternative within the meaning of paragraph (e) of this section, or (ii) investment decisions made by the entity described in paragraph (e)(3) of this section in connection with the management of a qualified default investment alternative.

(2) Nothing in this section shall relieve a fiduciary from his or her duties under part 4 of title I of ERISA to prudently select and monitor any qualified default investment alternative under the plan or from any liability that results from a failure to satisfy these duties, including liability for any resulting losses.

(3) Nothing in this section shall relieve any fiduciary described in paragraph (e)(3)(i) of this section from its fiduciary duties under part 4 of title I of ERISA or from any liability that results from a failure to satisfy these duties, including liability for any resulting losses.

(4) Nothing in this section shall provide relief from the prohibited transaction provisions of section 406 of ERISA, or from any liability that results from a violation of those provisions, including liability for any resulting losses.

(c) Conditions. With respect to the investment of assets in the individual account of a participant or beneficiary, a fiduciary shall qualify for the relief described in paragraph (b)(1) of this section if:

(1) Assets are invested in a "qualified default investment alternative" within the meaning of paragraph (e) of this section;

(2) The participant or beneficiary on whose behalf the investment is made had the opportunity to direct the investment of the assets in his or her account but did not direct the investment of the assets;

(3) The participant or beneficiary on whose behalf an investment in a qualified default investment alternative may be made is furnished a notice that meets the requirements of paragraph (d) of this section:

(i)(A) At least 30 days in advance of the date of plan eligibility, or at least 30 days in advance of the date of any first investment in a qualified default investment alternative on behalf of a participant or beneficiary described in paragraph (c)(2) of this section, or

(B) On or before the date of plan eligibility provided the participant has the opportunity to make a permissible withdrawal (as determined under section 414(w) of the Internal Revenue Code of 1986, as amended (Code)); and

(ii) Within a reasonable period of time of at least 30 days in advance of each subsequent plan year;

(4) A fiduciary provides to a participant or beneficiary the material set forth in 29 CFR 2550.404c-1(b)(2)(i)(B)(1)(viii) and (ix) and 29 CFR 404c-1(b)(2)(i)(B)(2) relating to a participant's or beneficiary's investment in a qualified default investment alternative;

(5)(i) Any participant or beneficiary on whose behalf assets are invested in a qualified default investment alternative may transfer, in whole or in part, such assets to any other investment alternative available under the plan with a frequency consistent with that afforded to a participant or beneficiary who elected to invest in the qualified default investment alternative, but not less frequently than once within any three month period;

(ii)(A) Except as provided in paragraph (c)(5)(ii)(B) of this section, any transfer described in paragraph (c)(5)(i), or any permissible withdrawal as determined under section 414(w)(2) of the Code, by a participant or beneficiary of assets invested in a qualified default investment alternative, in whole or in part, resulting from the participant's or beneficiary's election to make such a transfer or withdrawal during the 90-day period beginning on the date of the participant's first elective contribution as determined under section 414(w)(2)(B) of the Code, or other first investment in a qualified default investment alternative on behalf of a participant or beneficiary described in paragraph (c)(2) of this section, shall not be subject to any restrictions, fees or expenses (including surrender charges, liquidation or exchange fees, redemption fees and similar expenses charged in connection with the liquidation of, or transfer from, the investment);

(B) Paragraph (c)(5)(ii)(A) of this section shall not apply to fees and expenses that are charged on an ongoing basis for the operation of the investment itself (such as investment management fees, distribution and/or service fees, "12b-1" fees, or legal, accounting, transfer agent and similar administrative expenses), and are not imposed, or do not vary, based on a participant's or beneficiary's decision to withdraw, sell or transfer assets out of the qualified default investment alternative; and

(iii) Following the end of the 90-day period described in paragraph (c)(5)(ii)(A) of this section, any transfer or permissible withdrawal described in this paragraph (c)(5) of this section shall not be subject to any restrictions, fees or expenses not otherwise applicable to a participant or beneficiary who elected to invest in that qualified default investment alternative; and

(6) The plan offers a "broad range of investment alternatives" within the meaning of 29 CFR 2550.404c-1(b)(3).

(d) Notice. The notice required by paragraph (c)(3) of this section shall be written in a manner calculated to be understood by the average plan participant and shall contain the following:

(1) A description of the circumstances under which assets in the individual account of a participant or beneficiary may be invested on behalf of the participant or beneficiary in a qualified default investment alternative; and, if applicable, an explanation of the circumstances under which elective contributions will be made on behalf of a participant, the percentage of such contributions, and the right of the participant to elect not to have such contributions made on the participant's behalf (or to elect to have such contributions made at a different percentage);

(2) An explanation of the right of participants and beneficiaries to direct the investment of assets in their individual accounts;

(3) A description of the qualified default investment alternative, including a description of the investment objectives, risk and return characteristics (if applicable), and fees and expenses attendant to the investment alternative;

(4) A description of the right of the participants and beneficiaries on whose behalf assets are invested in a qualified default investment alternative to direct the investment of those assets to any other investment alternative under the plan, including a description of any applicable restrictions, fees or expenses in connection with such transfer; and

(5) An explanation of where the participants and beneficiaries can obtain investment information concerning the other investment alternatives available under the plan.

(e) Qualified default investment alternative. For purposes of this section, a qualified default investment alternative means an investment alternative available to participants and beneficiaries that:

(1)(i) Does not hold or permit the acquisition of employer securities, except as provided in paragraph (ii).

(ii) Paragraph (e)(1)(i) of this section shall not apply to: (A) employer securities held or acquired by an investment company registered under the Investment Company Act of 1940 or a similar pooled investment vehicle regulated and subject to periodic examination by a State or Federal agency and with respect to which investment in such securities is made in accordance with the stated investment objectives of the investment vehicle and independent of the plan sponsor or an affiliate thereof; or (B) with respect to a qualified default investment alternative described in paragraph (e)(4)(iii) of this section, employer securities acquired as a matching contribution from the employer/plan sponsor, or employer securities acquired prior to management by the investment management service to the extent the investment management service has discretionary authority over the disposition of such employer securities;

(2) Satisfies the requirements of paragraph (c)(5) of this section regarding the ability of a participant or beneficiary to transfer, in whole or in part, his or her investment from the qualified default investment alternative to any other investment alternative available under the plan;

(3) Is:

(i) Managed by: (A) an investment manager, within the meaning of section 3(38) of the Act; (B) a trustee of the plan that meets the requirements of section 3(38)(A), (B) and (C) of the Act; or the plan sponsor, or a committee comprised primarily of employees of the plan sponsor, which is a named fiduciary within the meaning of section 402(a)(2) of the Act;

(ii) An investment company registered under the Investment Company Act of 1940; or

(iii) An investment product or fund described in paragraph (e)(4)(iv) or (v) of this section; and

(4) Constitutes one of the following:

(i) An investment fund product or model portfolio that applies generally accepted investment theories, is diversified so as to minimize the risk of large losses and that is designed to provide varying degrees of long-term appreciation and capital preservation through a mix of equity and fixed income exposures based on the participant's age, target retirement date (such as normal retirement age under the plan) or life expectancy. Such products and portfolios change their asset allocations and associated risk levels over time with the objective of becoming more conservative (i.e., decreasing risk of losses) with increasing age. For purposes of this paragraph (e)(4)(i), asset allocation decisions for such products and portfolios are not required to take into account risk tolerances, investments or other preferences of an individual participant. An example of such a fund or portfolio may be a "lifecycle" or "targeted-retirement-date" fund or account.

(ii) An investment fund product or model portfolio that applies generally accepted investment theories, is diversified so as to minimize the risk of large losses and that is designed to provide long-term appreciation and capital preservation through a mix of equity and fixed income exposures consistent with a target level of risk appropriate for participants of the plan as a whole. For purposes of this paragraph (e)(4)(ii), asset allocation decisions for such products and portfolios are not required to take into account the age, risk tolerances, investments or other preferences of an individual participant. An example of such a fund or portfolio may be a "balanced" fund.

(iii) An investment management service with respect to which a fiduciary, within the meaning of paragraph (e)(3)(i) of this section, applying generally accepted investment theories, allocates the assets of a participant's individual account to achieve varying degrees of long-term appreciation and capital preservation through a mix of equity and fixed income exposures, offered through investment alternatives available under the plan, based on the participant's age, target retirement date (such as normal retirement age under the plan) or life expectancy. Such portfolios are diversified so as to minimize the risk of large losses and change their asset allocations and associated risk levels for an individual account over time with the objective of becoming more conservative (i.e., decreasing risk of losses) with increasing age. For purposes of this paragraph (e)(4)(iii), asset allocation decisions are not required to take into account risk tolerances, investments or other preferences of an individual participant. An example of such a service may be a "managed account."

(iv)(A) Subject to paragraph (e)(4)(iv)(B) of this section, an investment product or fund designed to preserve principal and provide a reasonable rate of return, whether or not such return is guaranteed, consistent with liquidity. Such investment product shall for purposes of this paragraph (e)(4)(iv):

(1) Seek to maintain, over the term of the investment, the dollar value that is equal to the amount invested in the product; and

(2) Be offered by a State or federally regulated financial institution.

(B) An investment product described in this paragraph (e)(4)(iv) shall constitute a qualified default investment alternative for purposes of paragraph (e) of this section for not more than 120 days after the date of the participant's first elective contribution (as determined under section 414(w)(2)(B) of the Code).

(v)(A) Subject to paragraph (e)(4)(v)(B) of this section, an investment product or fund designed to preserve principal; provide a rate of return generally consistent with that earned on intermediate investment grade bonds; and provide liquidity for withdrawals by participants and beneficiaries, including transfers to other investment alternatives. Such investment product or fund shall, for purposes of this paragraph (e)(4)(v), meet the following requirements:

(1) There are no fees or surrender charges imposed in connection with withdrawals initiated by a participant or beneficiary; and

(2) Such investment product or fund invests primarily in investment products that are backed by State or federally regulated financial institutions.

(B) An investment product or fund described in this paragraph (e)(4)(v) shall constitute a qualified default investment alternative for purposes of paragraph (e) of this section solely for purposes of assets invested in such product or fund before December 24, 2007.

(vi) An investment fund product or model portfolio that otherwise meets the requirements of this section shall not fail to constitute a

product or portfolio for purposes of paragraph (e)(4)(i) or (ii) solely because the product or portfolio is offered through variable annuity or similar contracts or through common or collective trust funds or pooled investment funds and without regard to whether such contracts or funds provide annuity purchase rights, investment guarantees, death benefit guarantees or other features ancillary to the investment fund product or model portfolio.

(f) Preemption of State laws. (1) Section 514(e)(1) of the Act provides that title I of the Act supersedes any State law that would directly or indirectly prohibit or restrict the inclusion in any plan of an automatic contribution arrangement. For purposes of section 514(e) of the Act and this paragraph (f), an automatic contribution arrangement is an arrangement (or the provisions of a plan) under which:

(i) A participant may elect to have the plan sponsor make payments as contributions under the plan on his or her behalf or receive such payments directly in cash;

(ii) A participant is treated as having elected to have the plan sponsor make such contributions in an amount equal to a uniform percentage of compensation provided under the plan until the participant specifically elects not to have such contributions made (or specifically elects to have such contributions made at a different percentage); and

(iii) Contributions are invested in accordance with paragraphs (a) through (e) of this section.

(2) A State law that would directly or indirectly prohibit or restrict the inclusion in any pension plan of an automatic contribution arrangement is superseded as to any pension plan, regardless of whether such plan includes an automatic contribution arrangement as defined in paragraph (f)(1), of this section.

(3) The administrator of an automatic contribution arrangement within the meaning of paragraph (f)(1) of this section shall be considered to have satisfied the notice requirements of section 514(e)(3) of the Act if notices are furnished in accordance with paragraphs (c)(3) and (d) of this section.

(4) Nothing in this paragraph (f) precludes a pension plan from including an automatic contribution arrangement that does not meet the conditions of paragraphs (a) through (e) of this section. [Added October 24, 2007 (72 FR 60452); amended April 30, 2008 (73 FR 23349).]

[¶ 14,746]

§ 2509.94-1 **Interpretive Bulletin relating to the fiduciary standard under ERISA in considering economically targeted investments.** [Removed by EBSA on October 17, 2008. See § 2509.08-1 at ¶ 14,746D.]

[¶ 14,746A]

§ 2509.94-2 **Interpretive Bulletin relating to written statements of investment policy, including proxy voting policy or guidelines.** [Removed by EBSA on October 17, 2008. See § 2509.08-2 at ¶ 14,746E.]

[¶ 14,746AA]

§ 2509.94-3 **Interpretive Bulletin relating to in-kind contributions to employee benefit plans.** (a) *General.* This bulletin sets forth the views of the Department of Labor (the Department) concerning in-kind contributions (*i.e.*, contributions of property other than cash) in satisfaction of an obligation to contribute to an employee benefit plan to which part 4 of Title I of the Employee Retirement Income Security Act of 1974 (ERISA) or a plan to which section 4975 of the Internal Revenue Code (the Code) applies. (For purposes of this document the term "plan" shall refer to either or both types of such entities as appropriate). Section 406(a)(1)(A) of ERISA provides that a fiduciary with respect to a plan shall not cause the plan to engage in a transaction if the fiduciary knows or should know that the transaction constitutes a direct or indirect sale or exchange of any property between a plan and a "party in interest" as defined in section 3(14) of ERISA. The Code imposes a two-tier excise tax under section 4975(c)(1)(A) an any direct or indirect sale or exchange of any property between a plan and a "disqualified person" as defined in section 4975(e)(2) of the Code. An employer or employee organization that maintains a plan is included within the definitions of "party in interest" and "disqualified person."[1]

In *Commissioner of Internal Revenue v. Keystone Consolidated Industries, Inc.*,—U.S.—, 113 S. Ct. 2006 (1993), the Supreme Court held that an employer's contribution of unencumbered real property to a tax-qualified defined benefit pension plan was a sale or exchange prohibited under section 4975 of the Code where the stated fair market value of the property was credited against the employer's obligation to the defined benefit pension plan. The parties stipulated that the property was contributed to the plan free of encumbrances and the stated fair market value of the property was not challenged. 113 S. Ct. at 2009. In reaching its holding the Court construed section 4975(f)(3) of the Code (and therefore section 406(c) of ERISA), regarding transfers of encumbered property, not as a limitation but rather as extending the reach of section 4975(c)(1)(A) of the Code (and thus section 406(a)(1)(A) of ERISA) to include contributions of encumbered property that do not satisfy funding obligations. *Id.* at 2013. Accordingly, the Court concluded that the contribution of unencumbered property was prohibited under section 4975(c)(1)(A) of the Code (and thus section 406(a)(1)(A) of ERISA) as "at least both an indirect type of sale and a form of exchange, since the property is exchanged for diminution of the employer's funding obligation." 113 S. Ct. at 2012.

(b) *Defined benefit plans.* Consistent with the reasoning of the Supreme Court in *Keystone*, because an employer's or plan sponsor's in-kind contribution to a defined benefit pension plan is credited to the plan's funding standard account it would constitute a transfer to reduce an obligation of the sponsor or employer to the plan. Therefore, in the absence of an applicable exemption, such a contribution would be prohibited under section 406(a)(1)(A) of ERISA and section 4975(c)(1)(A) of the Code. Such an in-kind contribution would constitute a prohibited transaction even if the value of the contribution is in excess of the sponsor's or employer's funding obligation for the plan year in which the contribution is made and thus is not used to reduce the plan's accumulated funding deficiency for that plan year because the contribution would result in a credit against funding obligations which might arise in the future.

(c) *Defined contribution and welfare plans.* In the context of defined contribution pension plans and welfare plans, it is the view of the Department that an in-kind contribution to a plan that reduces an obligation of a plan sponsor or employer to make a contribution measured in terms of cash amounts would constitute a prohibited transaction under section 406(a)(1)(A) of ERISA (and section 4975(c)(1)(A) of the Code) unless a statutory or administrative exemption under section 408 of ERISA (or sections 4975(c)(2) or (d) of the Code) applies. For example, if a profit sharing plan required the employer to make annual contributions "in cash or in kind" equal to a given percentage of the employer's net profits for the year, an in-kind contribution used to reduce this obligation would constitute a prohibited transaction in the absence of an exemption because the amount of the contribution obligation is measured in terms of cash amounts (a percentage of profits) even though the terms of the plan purport to permit in-kind contributions.

Conversely, a transfer of unencumbered property to a welfare benefit plan that does not relieve the sponsor or employer of any present or future obligation to make a contribution that is measured in terms of cash amounts would not constitute a prohibited transaction under section 406(a)(1)(A) of ERISA or section 4975(c)(1)(A) of the Code. The same principles apply to defined contribution plans that are not subject to the minimum funding requirements of section 302 of ERISA or section 412 of the Code. For example, where a profit sharing or stock bonus plan, by its terms, is funded solely at the discretion of the sponsoring employer, and the employer is not otherwise obligated to make a contribution measured in terms of cash amounts, a contribution of unencumbered real property would not be a prohibited sale or exchange between the plan and the employer. If, however, the same employer had made an enforceable promise to make a contribution measured in terms of cash amounts to the plan, a subsequent contribution of unencumbered real property made to offset such an obligation would be a prohibited sale or exchange.

(d) *Fiduciary standards.* Independent of the application of the prohibited transaction provisions, fiduciaries of plans covered by part 4 of Title I of ERISA must determine that acceptance of an in-kind contribution is consistent with ERISA's general standards of fiduciary conduct. It is the view of the Department that acceptance of an in-kind contribution is a fiduciary act subject to section 404 of ERISA. In this regard, sections 406(a)(1)(A) and (B) of ERISA require that fiduciaries discharge their duties to a plan solely in the interests of the participants and beneficiaries, for the exclusive purpose of providing benefits and defraying reasonable administrative expenses, and with the care, skill, prudence, and diligence under the circumstances then prevailing that a prudent person acting in a like capacity and familiar with such matters would use in the conduct of an enterprise of a like character and with like aims. In addition, section 406(a)(1)(C) requires generally that fiduciaries diversify plan assets so as to minimize the risk of large losses. Accordingly, the fiduciaries of a plan must act "prudently," "solely in the interest" of the plan's participants and beneficiaries and with a view to the need to diversify plan assets when deciding whether to accept in-kind contributions. If accepting an in-kind contribution is not "prudent," not "solely in the interest" of the participants and beneficiaries of the plan, or would result in an improper lack of diversification of plan assets, the responsible fiduciaries of the plan would be liable for any losses resulting from such a breach of fiduciary responsibility, even if a contribution in kind does not constitute a prohibited transaction under section 406 of ERISA. In this regard, a fiduciary should consider any liabilities appurtenant to the in-kind contribution to which the plan would be exposed as a result of acceptance of the contribution.

[¶ 14,746B]

§ 2509.95-1 **Interpretive bulletin relating to the fiduciary standards under ERISA when selecting an annuity provider for a defined benefit pension plan..** (a) *Scope.* This Interpretive Bulletin provides guidance concerning certain fiduciary standards under part 4 of title I of the Employee Retirement Income Security Act of 1974 (ERISA), 29 U.S.C. 1104-1114, applicable to the selection of an annuity provider for the purpose of benefit distributions from a defined benefit pension plan (hereafter "pension plan") when the pension plan intends to transfer liability for benefits to an annuity provider. For guidance applicable to the selection of an annuity provider for benefit distributions from an individual account plan see 29 CFR 2550.404a-4.

(b) *In General.* Generally, when a pension plan purchases an annuity from an insurer as a distribution of benefits, it is intended that the plan's liability for such benefits is transferred to the annuity provider. The Department's regulation defining the term "participant covered under the plan" for certain purposes under title I of ERISA recognizes that such a transfer occurs [[Page 12330]] when the annuity is issued by an insurance company licensed to do business in a State. 29 CFR 2510.3-3(d)(2)(ii). Although the regulation does not define the term "participant" or "beneficiary" for purposes of standing to bring an action under ERISA Sec. 502(a), 29 U.S.C. 1132(a), it makes clear that the purpose of a benefit distribution annuity is to transfer the plan's liability with respect to the individual's benefits to the annuity provider.

Pursuant to ERISA section 404(a)(1), 29 U.S.C. 1104(a)(1), fiduciaries must discharge their duties with respect to the plan solely in the interest of the participants and beneficiaries. Section 404(a)(1)(A), 29 U.S.C. 1104(a)(1)(A), states that the fiduciary must act for the exclusive purpose of providing benefits to the participants and beneficiaries and defraying reasonable plan administration expenses. In addition, section 404(a)(1)(B), 29 U.S.C. 1104(a)(1)(B), requires a fiduciary to act with the care, skill, prudence and diligence under the prevailing circumstances that a prudent person acting in a like capacity and familiar with such matters would use.

(c) *Selection of Annuity Providers.* The selection of an annuity provider for purposes of a pension benefit distribution, whether upon separation or retirement of a participant or upon the termination of a

---

[1] Under Reorganization Plan No. 4 of 1978 (43 FR 47713, October 17, 1978), the authority of the Secretary of the Treasury to issue rulings under the prohibited transactions provisions of section 4975 of the Code has been transferred, with certain exceptions not here relevant, to the Secretary of Labor. Except with respect to the types of plans covered, the prohibited transaction provisions of section 406 of ERISA generally parallel the prohibited transaction of provisions of section 4975 of the Code.

plan, is a fiduciary decision governed by the provisions of part 4 of title I of ERISA. In discharging their obligations under section 404(a)(1), 29 U.S.C. 1104(a)(1), to act solely in the interest of participants and beneficiaries and for the exclusive purpose of providing benefits to the participants and beneficiaries as well as defraying reasonable expenses of administering the plan, fiduciaries choosing an annuity provider for the purpose of making a benefit distribution must take steps calculated to obtain the safest annuity available, unless under the circumstances it would be in the interests of participants and beneficiaries to do otherwise. In addition, the fiduciary obligation of prudence, described at section 404(a)(1)(B), 29 U.S.C. 1104(a)(1)(B), requires, at a minimum, that plan fiduciaries conduct an objective, thorough and analytical search for the purpose of identifying and selecting providers from which to purchase annuities. In conducting such a search, a fiduciary must evaluate a number of factors relating to a potential annuity provider's claims paying ability and creditworthiness. Reliance solely on ratings provided by insurance rating services would not be sufficient to meet this requirement. In this regard, the types of factors a fiduciary should consider would include, among other things:

(1) the quality and diversification of the annuity provider's investment portfolio;

(2) the size of the insurer relative to the proposed contract;

(3) the level of the insurer's capital and surplus;

(4) the lines of business of the annuity provider and other indications of an insurer's exposure to liability;

(5) the structure of the annuity contract and guarantees supporting the annuities, such as the use of separate accounts;

(6) the availability of additional protection through state guaranty associations and the extent of their guarantees. Unless they possess the necessary expertise to evaluate such factors, fiduciaries would need to obtain the advice of a qualified, independent expert. A fiduciary may conclude, after conducting an appropriate search, that more than one annuity provider is able to offer the safest annuity available.

(d) *Costs and Other Considerations.* The Department recognizes that there are situations where it may be in the interest of the participants and beneficiaries to purchase other than the safest available annuity. Such situations may occur where the safest available annuity is only marginally safer, but disproportionately more expensive than competing annuities, and the participants and beneficiaries are likely to bear a significant portion of that increased cost. For example, where the participants in a terminating pension plan are likely to receive, in the form of increased benefits, a substantial share of the cost savings that would result from choosing a competing annuity, it may be in the interest of the participants to choose the competing annuity. It may also be in the interest of the participants and beneficiaries to choose a competing annuity of the annuity provider offering the safest available annuity is unable to demonstrate the ability to administer the payment of benefits to the participants and beneficiaries. The Department notes, however, that increased cost or other considerations could never justify putting the benefits of annuitized participants and beneficiaries at risk by purchasing an unsafe annuity.

In contrast to the above, a fiduciary's decision to purchase more risky, lower-priced annuities in order to ensure or maximize a reversion of excess assets that will be paid solely to the employer-sponsor in connection with the termination of an over-funded pension plan would violate the fiduciary's duties under ERISA to act solely in the interest of the plan participants and beneficiaries. In such circumstances, the interests of those participants and beneficiaries who will receive annuities lies in receiving the safest annuity available and other participants and beneficiaries have no countervailing interests. The fiduciary in such circumstances must make diligent efforts to assure that the safest available annuity is purchased.

Similarly, a fiduciary may not purchase a riskier annuity solely because there are insufficient assets in a defined benefit plan to purchase a safer annuity. The fiduciary may have to condition the purchase of annuities on additional employer contributions sufficient to purchase the safest available annuity.

(e) *Conflicts of Interest.* Special care should be taken in reversion situations where fiduciaries selecting the annuity provider have an interest in the sponsoring employer which might affect their judgment and therefore create the potential for a violation of ERISA Sec. 406(b)(1). As a practical matter, many fiduciaries have this conflict of interest and therefore will need to obtain and follow independent expert advice calculated to identify those insurers with the highest claims-paying ability willing to write the business.

[Added by FR Doc. 95-5321, filed with the Federal Register on March 3, 1995, and published in the Federal Register on March 6, 1995 (60 FR 12328). Revised September 12, 2007 (72 FR 52004) and October 7, 2008 (73 FR 58445).]

»»→ Caution: *Reg. § 2509.96-1 was removed by the Department of Labor on April 8, 2016 (81 FR 20945). The removal is effective June 7, 2016 and applicable April 10, 2017.*

[¶ 14,746C]

§ 2509.96-1 **Interpretive Bulletin relating to participant investment education.** (a) *Scope.* This interpretive bulletin sets forth the Department of Labor's interpretation of section 3(21)(A)(ii) of the Employee Retirement Income Security Act of 1974, as amended (ERISA), and 29 CFR 2510.3-21(c) as applied to the provision of investment-related educational information to participants and beneficiaries in participant-directed individual account pension plans (*i.e.*, pension plans that permit participants and beneficiaries to direct the investment of assets in their individual accounts, including plans that meet the requirements of the Department's regulations at 29 CFR 2550.404c-1).

(b) *General.* Fiduciaries of an employee benefit plan are charged with carrying out their duties prudently and solely in the interest of participants and beneficiaries of the plan, and are subject to personal liability to, among other things, make good any losses to the plan resulting from a breach of their fiduciary duties. ERISA sections 403, 404 and 409, 29 U.S.C. 1103, 1104, and 1109. Section 404(c) of ERISA provides a limited exception to these rules for a pension plan that permits a participant or beneficiary to exercise control over the assets in his or her individual account. The Department of Labor's regulation, at 29 CFR 2550.404c-1, describes the kinds of plans to which section 404(c) applies, the circumstances under which a participant or beneficiary will be considered to have exercised independent control over the assets in his or her account, and the consequences of a participant's or beneficiary's exercise of such control.[1]

With both an increase in the number of participant-directed individual account plans and the number of investment options available to participants and beneficiaries under such plans, there has been an increasing recognition of the importance of providing participants and beneficiaries, whose investment decisions will directly affect their income at retirement, with information designed to assist them in making investment and retirement-related decisions appropriate to their particular situations. Concerns have been raised, however, that the provision of such information may in some situations be Viewed as rendering "investment advice for a fee or other compensation," within the meaning of ERISA section 3(21)(A)(ii), thereby giving rise to fiduciary status and potential liability under ERISA for investment decisions of plan participants and beneficiaries.

In response to these concerns, the Department of Labor is clarifying herein the applicability of ERISA section 3(21)(A)(ii) and 29 CFR 2510.3-21(c) to the provision of investment-related educational information to participants and beneficiaries in participant directed individual account plans.[2] In providing this clarification, the Department does not

---

[1] The section 404(c) regulation conditions relief from fiduciary liability on, among other things, the participant or beneficiary being provided or having the opportunity to obtain sufficient investment information regarding the investment alternatives available under the plan in order to make informed investment decisions. Compliance with this condition, however, does not require that participants and beneficiaries be offered or provided either investment advice or investment education, *e.g.* regarding general investment principles and strategies, to assist them in making investment decisions. 29 CFR 2550.404c-1(c)(4).

[2] Issues relating to the circumstances under which information provided to participants and beneficiaries may affect a participant's or beneficiary's ability to exercise independent control over the assets in his or her account for purposes of relief from fiduciary liability under ERISA section 404(c) are beyond the scope of this interpretive bulletin. Accordingly,

»»→ Caution: *Reg. § 2509.96-1 was removed by the Department of Labor on April 8, 2016 (81 FR 20945). The removal is effective June 7, 2016 and applicable April 10, 2017.*

address the "fee or other compensation, direct or indirect," which is a necessary element of fiduciary status under ERISA section 3(21)(A)(ii).[3]

(c) *Investment Advice.* Under ERISA section 3(21)(A)(ii), a person is considered a fiduciary with respect to an employee benefit plan to the extent that person "renders investment advice for a fee or other compensation, direct or indirect, with respect to any moneys or other property of such plan, or has any authority to do so . . . ." The Department issued a regulation, at 29 CFR 2510.3-21(c), describing the circumstances under which a person will be considered to be rendering "investment advice" within the meaning of section 3(21)(A)(ii). Because section 3(21)(A)(ii) applies to advice with respect to "any moneys or other property" of a plan and 29 CFR 2510.3-21(c) is intended to clarify the application of that section, it is the view of the Department of Labor that the criteria set forth in the regulation apply to determine whether a person renders "investment advice" to a pension plan participant or beneficiary who is permitted to direct the investment of assets in his or her individual account.

Applying 29 CFR 2510.3-21(c) in the context of providing investment-related information to participants and beneficiaries of participant-directed individual account pension plans, a person will be considered to be rendering "investment advice," within the meaning of ERISA section 3(21)(A)(ii), to a participant or beneficiary only if: (i) the person renders advice to the participant or beneficiary as to the value of securities or other property, or makes recommendations as to the advisability of investing in, purchasing, or selling securities or other property (2510.3-21(c)(1)(i)); and (ii) the person, either directly or indirectly, (A) has discretionary authority or control with respect to purchasing or selling securities or other property for the participant or beneficiary (2510.3-21(c)(1)(ii)(A)), or (B) renders the advice on a regular basis to the participant or beneficiary, pursuant to a mutual agreement, arrangement or understanding (written or otherwise) with the participant or beneficiary that the advice will serve as a primary basis for the participant's or beneficiary's investment decisions with respect to plan assets and that such person will render individualized advice based on the particular needs of the participant or beneficiary (2510.3-21(c)(1)(ii)(B)).[4]

Whether the provision of particular investment-related information or materials to a participant or beneficiary constitutes the rendering of "investment advice," within the meaning of 29 CFR 2510.3-21(c)(1), generally can be determined only by reference to the facts and circumstances of the particular case with respect to the individual plan participant or beneficiary. To facilitate such determinations, however, the Department of Labor has identified, in paragraph (d), below, examples of investment-related information and materials which if provided to plan participants and beneficiaries would not, in the view of the Department, result in the rendering of "investment advice" under ERISA section 3(21)(A)(ii) and 29 CFR 2510.3-21(c).

(d) *Investment Education.* For purposes of ERISA section 3(21)(A)(ii) and 29 CFR 2510.3-21(c), the Department of Labor has determined that the furnishing of the following categories of information and materials to a participant or beneficiary in a participant-directed individual account pension plan will not constitute the rendering of "investment advice," irrespective of who provides the information (*e.g.*, plan sponsor, fiduciary or service provider), the frequency with which the information is shared, the form in which the information and materials are provided (*e.g.*, on an individual or group basis, in writing or orally, or via video or computer software), or whether an identified category of information and materials is furnished alone or in combination with other identified categories of information and materials:

(1) *Plan Information.* (i) Information and materials that inform a participant or beneficiary about the benefits of plan participation, the benefits of increasing plan contributions, the impact of preretirement withdrawals on retirement income, the terms of the plan, or the operation of the plan; or

(ii) information such as that described in 29 CFR 2550.404c-1(b)(2)(i) on investment alternatives under the plan (*e.g.*, descriptions of investment objectives and philosophies, risk and return characteristics, historical return information, or related prospectuses).[5]

The information and materials described above relate to the plan and plan participation, without reference to the appropriateness of any individual investment option for a particular participant or beneficiary under the plan. The information, therefore, does not contain either "advice" or "recommendations" within the meaning of 29 CFR 2510.3-21(c)(1)(i). Accordingly, the furnishing of such information would not constitute the rendering of "investment advice" for purposes of section 3(21)(A)(ii) of ERISA.

(2) *General Financial and Investment Information.* Information and materials that inform a participant or beneficiary about: (i) general financial and investment concepts, such as risk and return, diversification, dollar cost averaging, compounded return, and tax deferred investment; (ii) historic differences in rates of return between different asset classes (*e.g.*, equities, bonds, or cash) based on standard market indices; (iii) effects of inflation; (iv) estimating future retirement income needs; (v) determining investment time horizons; and (vi) assessing risk tolerance.

The information and materials described above are general financial and investment information that have no direct relationship to investment alternatives available to participants and beneficiaries under a plan or to individual participants or beneficiaries. The furnishing of such information, therefore, would not constitute rendering "advice" or making "recommendations" to a participant or beneficiary within the meaning of 29 CFR 2510.3-21(c)(1)(i). Accordingly, the furnishing of such information would not constitute the rendering of "investment advice" for purposes of section 3(21)(A)(ii) of ERISA.

(3) *Asset Allocation Models.* Information and materials (*e.g.*, pie charts, graphs, or case studies) that provide a participant or beneficiary with models, available to all plan participants and beneficiaries, of asset allocation portfolios of hypothetical individuals with different time horizons and risk profiles, where: (i) such models are based on generally accepted investment theories that take into account the historic returns of different asset classes (*e.g.*, equities, bonds, or cash) over defined periods of time; (ii) all material facts and assumptions on which such models are based (*e.g.*, retirement ages, life expectancies, income levels, financial resources, replacement income ratios, inflation rates, and rates of return) accompany the models; (iii) to the extent that an asset allocation model identifies any specific investment alternative available under the plan, the model is accompanied by a statement indicating that other investment alternatives having similar risk and return characteristics may be available under the plan and identifying where information on those investment alternatives may be obtained; and (iv) the asset allocation models are accompanied by a statement indicating that, in applying particular asset allocation models to their individual situations, participants or beneficiaries should consider their other assets, income, and investments (*e.g.*, equity in a home, IRA investments, savings accounts, and interests in other qualified and non-qualified plans) in addition to their interests in the plan.

Because the information and materials described above would enable a participant or beneficiary to assess the relevance of an asset allocation model to his or her individual situation, the furnishing of

---

(Footnote Continued)

no inferences should be drawn regarding such issues. See 29 CFR 2550.404c-1(c)(2). It is the view of the Department, however, that the provision of investment-related information and material to participants and beneficiaries in accordance with paragraph (d) of this interpretive bulletin will not, in and of itself, affect the availability of relief under section 404(c).

[3] The Department has expressed the view that, for purposes of section 3(21)(A)(ii), such fees or other compensation need not come from the plan and should be deemed to include all fees or other compensation incident to the transaction in which the investment advice

has been or will be rendered. See A.O. 83-60A (Nov. 21, 1983); *Reich* v. *McManus*, 883 F. Supp. 1144 (N.D. *Ill.* 1995).

[4] This IB does not address the application of 29 CFR 2510.3-21(c) to communications with fiduciaries of participant-directed individual account pension plans.

[5] Descriptions of investment alternatives under the plan may include information relating to the generic asset class (*e.g.*, equities, bonds, or cash) of the investment alternatives. 29 CFR 2550.404c-1(b)(2)(i)(B)(*1*)(*ii*).

such information would not constitute a "recommendation" within the meaning of 29 CFR 2510.3-21(c)(1)(i) and, accordingly, would not constitute "investment advice" for purposes of section 3(21)(A)(ii) of ERISA. This result would not, in the view of the Department, be affected by the fact that a plan offers only one investment alternative in a particular asset class identified in an asset allocation model.

(4) *Interactive Investment Materials.* Questionnaires, worksheets, software, and similar materials which provide a participant or beneficiary the means to estimate future retirement income needs and assess the impact of different asset allocations on retirement income, where: (i) such materials are based on generally accepted investment theories that take into account the historic returns of different asset classes (*e.g.*, equities, bonds, or cash) over defined periods of time; (ii) there is an objective correlation between the asset allocations generated by the materials and the information and data supplied by the participant or beneficiary; (iii) all material facts and assumptions (*e.g.*, retirement ages, life expectancies, income levels, financial resources, replacement income ratios, inflation rates, and rates of return) which may affect a participant's or beneficiary's assessment of the different asset allocations accompany the materials or are specified by the participant or beneficiary; (iv) to the extent that an asset allocation generated by the materials identifies any specific investment alternative available under the plan, the asset allocation is accompanied by a statement indicating that other investment alternatives having similar risk and return characteristics may be available under the plan and identifying where information on those investment alternatives may be obtained; and (v) the materials either take into account or are accompanied by a statement indicating that, in applying particular asset allocations to their individual situations, participants or beneficiaries should consider their other assets, income, and investments (*e.g.*, equity in a home, IRA investments, savings accounts, and interests in other qualified and non-qualified plans) in addition to their interests in the plan.

The information provided through the use of the above-described materials enables participants and beneficiaries independently to design and assess multiple asset allocation models, but otherwise these materials do not differ from asset allocation models based on hypothetical assumptions. Such information would not constitute a "recommendation" within the meaning of 29 CFR 2510.3-21(c)(1)(i) and, accordingly, would not constitute "investment advice" for purposes of section 3(21)(A)(ii) of ERISA.

The Department notes that the information and materials described in subparagraphs (1)-(4) above merely represent examples of the type of information and materials which may be furnished to participants and beneficiaries without such information and materials constituting "investment advice." In this regard, the Department recognizes that there may be many other examples of information, materials, and educational services which, if furnished to participants and beneficiaries, would not constitute "investment advice." Accordingly, no inferences should be drawn from subparagraphs (1)-(4), above, with respect to whether the furnishing of any information, materials or educational services not described therein may constitute "investment advice." Determinations as to whether the provision of any information, materials or educational services not described herein constitutes the rendering of "investment advice" must be made by reference to the criteria set forth in 29 CFR 2510.3-21(c)(1).

(e) *Selection and Monitoring of Educators and Advisors.* As with any designation of a service provider to a plan, the designation of a person(s) to provide investment educational services or investment advice to plan participants and beneficiaries is an exercise of discretionary authority or control with respect to management of the plan; therefore, persons making the designation must act prudently and solely in the interest of the plan participants and beneficiaries, both in making the designation(s) and in continuing such designation(s). See ERISA sections 3(21)(A)(i) and 404(a), 29 U.S.C. 1002(21)(A)(i) and 1104(a). In addition, the designation of an investment advisor to serve as a fiduciary may give rise to co-fiduciary liability if the person making and continuing such designation in doing so fails to act prudently and solely in the interest of plan participants and beneficiaries; or knowingly participates in, conceals or fails to make reasonable efforts to

correct a known breach by the investment advisor. See ERISA section 405(a), 29 U.S.C. 1105(a). The Department notes, however, that, in the context of an ERISA section 404(c) plan, neither the designation of a person to provide education nor the designation of a fiduciary to provide investment advice to participants and beneficiaries would, in itself, give rise to fiduciary liability for loss, or with respect to any breach of part 4 of title I of ERISA, that is the direct and necessary result of a participant's or beneficiary's exercise of independent control. 29 CFR 2550.404c-1(d). The Department also notes that a plan sponsor or fiduciary would have no fiduciary responsibility or liability with respect to the actions of a third party selected by a participant or beneficiary to provide education or investment advice where the plan sponsor or fiduciary neither selects nor endorses the educator or advisor, nor otherwise makes arrangements with the educator or advisor to provide such services.

[Added by FR Doc. 96-14093, filed with the Federal Register on June 10, 1996, and published in the Federal Register on June 11, 1996 (61 FR 29586).]

[¶ 14,746D]
§ 2509.08-1 Supplemental guidance relating to fiduciary responsibility in considering economically targeted investments. [Removed by EBSA on October 26, 2015. See § 2509.2015-01 at ¶ 14,746F.]

[¶ 14,746E]
§ 2509.08-2 Interpretive bulletin relating to the exercise of shareholder rights and written statements of investment policy, including proxy voting policies or guidelines. [Removed by EBSA on December 29, 2016. See § 2509.2016-01 at ¶ 14,746G.]

[¶ 14,746F]
§ 2509.2015-01 Interpretive bulletin relating to the fiduciary standard under ERISA in considering economically targeted investments. This Interpretive Bulletin sets forth the Department of Labor's interpretation of sections 403 and 404 of the Employee Retirement Income Security Act of 1974 (ERISA), as applied to employee benefit plan investments in "economically targeted investments" (ETIs), that is, investments selected for the economic benefits they create apart from their investment return to the employee benefit plan. Sections 403 and 404, in part, require that a fiduciary of a plan act prudently, and to diversify plan investments so as to minimize the risk of large losses, unless under the circumstances it is clearly prudent not to do so. In addition, these sections require that a fiduciary act solely in the interest of the plan's participants and beneficiaries and for the exclusive purpose of providing benefits to their participants and beneficiaries. The Department has construed the requirements that a fiduciary act solely in the interest of, and for the exclusive purpose of providing benefits to, participants and beneficiaries as prohibiting a fiduciary from subordinating the interests of participants and beneficiaries in their retirement income to unrelated objectives.

With regard to investing plan assets, the Department has issued a regulation, at 29 CFR 2550.404a-1, interpreting the prudence requirements of ERISA as they apply to the investment duties of fiduciaries of employee benefit plans. The regulation provides that the prudence requirements of section 404(a)(1)(B) are satisfied if (1) the fiduciary making an investment or engaging in an investment course of action has given appropriate consideration to those facts and circumstances that, given the scope of the fiduciary's investment duties, the fiduciary knows or should know are relevant, and (2) the fiduciary acts accordingly. This includes giving appropriate consideration to the role that the investment or investment course of action plays (in terms of such factors as diversification, liquidity, and risk/return characteristics) with respect to that portion of the plan's investment portfolio within the scope of the fiduciary's responsibility.

Other facts and circumstances relevant to an investment or investment course of action would, in the view of the Department, include consideration of the expected return on alternative investments with similar risks available to the plan. It follows that, because every investment necessarily causes a plan to forgo other investment opportunities, an investment will not be prudent if it would be expected to provide a plan with a lower rate of return than available alternative investments with commensurate degrees of risk or is riskier than alternative available investments with commensurate rates of return.

The fiduciary standards applicable to ETIs are no different than the standards applicable to plan investments generally. Therefore, if the above requirements are met, the selection of an ETI, or the engaging in an investment course of action intended to result in the selection of ETIs, will not violate section 404(a)(1)(A) and (B) and the exclusive purpose requirements of section 403.

[¶ 14,746G]

§ 2509.2016-01 Interpretive Bulletin relating to the exercise of shareholder rights and written statements of investment policy, including proxy voting policies or guidelines. This interpretive bulletin sets forth the Department of Labor's (the Department) interpretation of sections 402, 403 and 404 of the Employee Retirement Income Security Act of 1974 (ERISA) as those sections apply to voting of proxies on securities held in employee benefit plan investment portfolios and the maintenance of and compliance with statements of investment policy, including proxy voting policy. In addition, this interpretive bulletin provides guidance on the appropriateness under ERISA of active engagement with corporate management by plan fiduciaries.

(1) Proxy Voting.

The fiduciary act of managing plan assets that are shares of corporate stock includes the voting of proxies appurtenant to those shares of stock. As a result, the responsibility for voting proxies lies exclusively with the plan trustee except to the extent that either (1) the trustee is subject to the directions of a named fiduciary pursuant to ERISA section 403(a)(1), or (2) the power to manage, acquire or dispose of the relevant assets has been delegated by a named fiduciary to one or more investment managers pursuant to ERISA section 403(a)(2). Where the authority to manage plan assets has been delegated to an investment manager pursuant to section 403(a)(2), no person other than the investment manager has authority to vote proxies appurtenant to such plan assets except to the extent that the named fiduciary has reserved to itself (or to another named fiduciary so authorized by the plan document) the right to direct a plan trustee regarding the voting of proxies. In this regard, a named fiduciary, in delegating investment management authority to an investment manager, could reserve to itself the right to direct a trustee with respect to the voting of all proxies or reserve to itself the right to direct a trustee as to the voting of only those proxies relating to specified assets or issues.

If the plan document or investment management agreement provides that the investment manager is not required to vote proxies, but does not expressly preclude the investment manager from voting proxies, the investment manager would have exclusive responsibility for voting proxies. Moreover, an investment manager would not be relieved of its own fiduciary responsibilities by following directions of some other person regarding the voting of proxies, or by delegating such responsibility to another person. If, however, the plan document or the investment management contract expressly precludes the investment manager from voting proxies, the responsibility for voting proxies would lie exclusively with the trustee. The trustee, however, consistent with the requirements of ERISA section 403(a)(1), may be subject to the directions of a named fiduciary if the plan so provides.

The fiduciary duties described at ERISA section 404(a)(1)(A) and (B), require that, in voting proxies, the responsible fiduciary consider those factors that may affect the value of the plan's investment and not subordinate the interests of the participants and beneficiaries in their retirement income to unrelated objectives. These duties also require that the named fiduciary appointing an investment manager periodically monitor the activities of the investment manager with respect to the management of plan assets, including decisions made and actions taken by the investment manager with regard to proxy voting decisions. The named fiduciary must carry out this responsibility solely in the interest of the participants and beneficiaries and without regard to its relationship to the plan sponsor.

It is the view of the Department that compliance with the duty to monitor necessitates proper documentation of the activities that are subject to monitoring. Thus, the investment manager or other responsible fiduciary would be required to maintain accurate records as to proxy voting. Moreover, if the named fiduciary is to be able to carry out its responsibilities under ERISA section 404(a) in determining whether the investment manager is fulfilling its fiduciary obligations in investing plans assets in a manner that justifies the continuation of the management appointment, the proxy voting records must enable the named fiduciary to review not only the investment manager's voting procedure with respect to plan-owned stock, but also to review the actions taken in individual proxy voting situations.

The fiduciary obligations of prudence and loyalty to plan participants and beneficiaries require the responsible fiduciary to vote proxies on issues that may affect the value of the plan's investment. This principle applies broadly. However, the Department recognizes that in some special cases voting proxies may involve out of the ordinary costs or unusual requirements, for example in the case of voting proxies on shares of certain foreign corporations. Thus, in such cases, a fiduciary should consider whether the plan's vote, either by itself or together with the votes of other shareholders, is expected to have an effect on the value of the plan's investment that warrants the additional cost of voting. Moreover, a fiduciary, in deciding whether to purchase shares for which this may be the case, should consider whether the difficulty and expense in voting the shares is reflected in their market price.

(2) Statements of Investment Policy.

The maintenance by an employee benefit plan of a statement of investment policy designed to further the purposes of the plan and its funding policy is consistent with the fiduciary obligations set forth in ERISA section 404(a)(1)(A) and (B). Since the fiduciary act of managing plan assets that are shares of corporate stock includes the voting of proxies appurtenant to those shares of stock, a statement of proxy voting policy would be an important part of any comprehensive statement of investment policy. For purposes of this document, the term "statement of investment policy" means a written statement that provides the fiduciaries who are responsible for plan investments with guidelines or general instructions concerning various types or categories of investment management decisions, which may include proxy voting decisions as well as policies concerning economically targeted investments or incorporating environmental, social or governance (ESG) factors in investment policy statements or integrating ESG-related tools, metrics and analyses to evaluate an investment's risk or return or choose among equivalent investments. A statement of investment policy is distinguished from directions as to the purchase or sale of a specific investment at a specific time or as to voting specific plan proxies.

In plans where investment management responsibility is delegated to one or more investment managers appointed by the named fiduciary pursuant to ERISA section 402(c)(3), the named fiduciary responsible for appointment of investment managers has the authority to condition the appointment on acceptance of a statement of investment policy. Thus, such a named fiduciary may expressly require, as a condition of the investment management agreement, that an investment manager comply with the terms of a statement of investment policy which sets forth guidelines concerning investments and investment courses of action which the investment manager is authorized or is not authorized to make. Such investment policy may include a policy or guidelines on the voting of proxies on shares of stock for which the investment manager is responsible. In the absence of such an express requirement to comply with an investment policy, the authority to manage the plan assets placed under the control of the investment manager would lie exclusively with the investment manager. Although a trustee may be subject to the directions of a named fiduciary pursuant to ERISA section 403(a)(1), an investment manager who has authority to make investment decisions, including proxy voting decisions, would never be relieved of its fiduciary responsibility if it followed directions as to specific investment decisions from the named fiduciary or any other person.

Statements of investment policy issued by a named fiduciary authorized to appoint investment managers would be part of the "documents and instruments governing the plan" within the meaning of ERISA section 404(a)(1)(D). An investment manager to whom such investment policy applies would be required to comply with such policy, pursuant to ERISA section 404(a)(1)(D) insofar as the policy directives or guidelines are consistent with titles I and IV of ERISA.

Therefore, if, for example, compliance with the guidelines in a given instance would be imprudent, then the investment manager's failure to follow the guidelines would not violate ERISA section 404(a)(1)(D). Moreover, ERISA section 404(a)(1)(D) does not shield the investment manager from liability for imprudent actions taken in compliance with a statement of investment policy.

The plan document or trust agreement may expressly provide a statement of investment policy to guide the trustee or may authorize a named fiduciary to issue a statement of investment policy applicable to a trustee. Where a plan trustee is subject to an investment policy, the trustee's duty to comply with such investment policy would also be analyzed under ERISA section 404(a)(1)(D). Thus, the trustee would be required to comply with the statement of investment policy unless, for example, it would be imprudent to do so in a given instance.

Maintenance of a statement of investment policy by a named fiduciary does not relieve the named fiduciary of its obligations under ERISA section 404(a) with respect to the appointment and monitoring of an investment manager or trustee. In this regard, the named fiduciary appointing an investment manager must periodically monitor the investment manager's activities with respect to management of the plan assets. Moreover, compliance with ERISA section 404(a)(1)(B) would require maintenance of proper documentation of the activities of the investment manager and of the named fiduciary of the plan in monitoring the activities of the investment manager. In addition, in the view of the Department, a named fiduciary's determination of the terms of a statement of investment policy is an exercise of fiduciary responsibility and, as such, statements may need to take into account factors such as the plan's funding policy and its liquidity needs as well as issues of prudence, diversification and other fiduciary requirements of ERISA.

An investment manager of a pooled investment vehicle that holds assets of more than one employee benefit plan may be subject to a proxy voting policy of one plan that conflicts with the proxy voting policy of another plan. Compliance with ERISA section 404(a)(1)(D) would require the investment manager to reconcile, insofar as possible, the conflicting policies (assuming compliance with each policy would be consistent with ERISA section 404(a)(1)(D)) and, if necessary and to the extent permitted by applicable law, vote the relevant proxies to reflect such policies in proportion to each plan's interest in the pooled investment vehicle. If, however, the investment manager determines that compliance with conflicting voting policies would violate ERISA section 404(a)(1)(D) in a particular instance, for example, by being imprudent or not solely in the interest of plan participants, the investment manager would be required to ignore the voting policy that would violate ERISA section 404(a)(1)(D) in that instance. Such an invest-

ment manager may, however, require participating investors to accept the investment manager's own investment policy statement, including any statement of proxy voting policy, before they are allowed to invest. As with investment policies originating from named fiduciaries, a policy initiated by an investment manager and adopted by the participating plans would be regarded as an instrument governing the participating plans, and the investment manager's compliance with such a policy would be governed by ERISA section 404(a)(1)(D).

(3) Shareholder Engagement.

An investment policy that contemplates activities intended to monitor or influence the management of corporations in which the plan owns stock is consistent with a fiduciary's obligations under ERISA where the responsible fiduciary concludes that there is a reasonable expectation that such monitoring or communication with management, by the plan alone or together with other shareholders, is likely to enhance the value of the plan's investment in the corporation, after taking into account the costs involved. Such a reasonable expectation may exist in various circumstances, for example, where plan investments in corporate stock are held as long-term investments, where a plan may not be able to easily dispose of such an investment, or where the same shareholder engagement issue is likely to exist in the case of available alternative investments. Active monitoring and communication activities would generally concern such issues as the independence and expertise of candidates for the corporation's board of directors and assuring that the board has sufficient information to carry out its responsibility to monitor management. Other issues may include such matters as governance structures and practices, particularly those involving board composition, executive compensation, transparency and accountability in corporate decision-making, responsiveness to shareholders, the corporation's policy regarding mergers and acquisitions, the extent of debt financing and capitalization, the nature of long-term business plans including plans on climate change preparedness and sustainability, governance and compliance policies and practices for avoiding criminal liability and ensuring employees comply with applicable laws and regulations, the corporation's workforce practices (e.g., investment in training to develop its work force, diversity, equal employment opportunity), policies and practices to address environmental or social factors that have an impact on shareholder value, and other financial and non-financial measures of corporate performance. Active monitoring and communication may be carried out through a variety of methods including by means of correspondence and meetings with corporate management as well as by exercising the legal rights of a shareholder.

[¶ 14,750]
LIABILITY FOR BREACH BY CO-FIDUCIARY

Act Sec. 405.(a) CIRCUMSTANCES GIVING RISE TO LIABILITY.—In addition to any liability which he may have under any other provision of this part, a fiduciary with respect to a plan shall be liable for a breach of fiduciary responsibility of another fiduciary with respect to the same plan in the following circumstances:

(1) if he participates knowingly in, or knowingly undertakes to conceal, an act or omission of such other fiduciary, knowing such act or omission is a breach;

(2) if, by his failure to comply with section 404(a)(1) in the administration of his specific responsibilities which give rise to his status as a fiduciary, he has enabled such other fiduciary to commit a breach; or

(3) if he has knowledge of a breach by such other fiduciary, unless he makes reasonable efforts under the circumstances to remedy the breach.

Act Sec. 405.(b)(1) ASSETS HELD BY TWO OR MORE TRUSTEES.—Except as otherwise provided in subsection (d) and in section 403(a)(1) and (2), if the assets of a plan are held by two or more trustees—

(A) each shall use reasonable care to prevent a co-trustee from committing a breach; and

(B) they shall jointly manage and control the assets of the plan, except that nothing in this subparagraph (B) shall preclude any agreement, authorized by the trust instrument, allocating specific responsibilities, obligations, or duties among trustees, in which event a trustee to whom certain responsibilities, obligations, or duties have not been allocated shall not be liable by reason of this subparagraph (B) either individually or as a trustee for any loss resulting to the plan arising from the acts or omissions on the part of another trustee to whom such responsibilities, obligations, or duties have been allocated.

(2) Nothing in this subsection shall limit any liability that a fiduciary may have under subsection (a) or any other provision of this part.

(3)(A) In the case of a plan the assets of which are held in more than one trust, a trustee shall not be liable under paragraph (1) except with respect to an act or omission of a trustee of a trust of which he is a trustee.

(B) No trustee shall be liable under this subsection for following instructions referred to in section 403(a)(1).

Act Sec. 405.(c)(1) ALLOCATION OF FIDUCIARY RESPONSIBILITY; DESIGNATED PERSONS TO CARRY OUT FIDUCIARY RESPONSIBILITIES.—The instrument under which a plan is maintained may expressly provide for procedures (A) for allocating fiduciary responsibilities (other than trustee responsibilities) among named fiduciaries, and (B) for named fiduciaries to designate persons other than named fiduciaries to carry out fiduciary responsibilities (other than trustee responsibilities) under the plan.

(2) If a plan expressly provides for a procedure described in paragraph (1), and pursuant to such procedure any fiduciary responsibility of a named fiduciary is allocated to any person, or a person is designated to carry out any such responsibility, then such named fiduciary shall not be liable for an act or omission of such person in carrying out such responsibility except to the extent that—

(A) the named fiduciary violated section 404(a)(1)—

    (i) with respect to such allocation or designation,

    (ii) with respect to the establishment or implementation of the procedure under paragraph (1), or

    (iii) in continuing the allocation or designation; or

(B) the named fiduciary would otherwise be liable in accordance with subsection (a).

(3) For purposes of this subsection, the term "trustee responsibility" means any responsibility provided in the plan's trust instrument (if any) to manage or control the assets of the plan, other than a power under the trust instrument of a named fiduciary to appoint an investment manager in accordance with section 402(c)(3).

Act Sec. 405.(d)(1) Investment managers.—If an investment manager or managers have been appointed under section 402(c)(3), then, notwithstanding subsections (a)(2) and (3) and subsection (b), no trustee shall be liable for the acts or omissions of such investment manager or managers, or be under an obligation to invest or otherwise manage any asset of the plan which is subject to the management of such investment manager.

(2) Nothing in this subsection shall relieve any trustee of any liability under this part for any act of such trustee.

[¶ 14,760]
PROHIBITED TRANSACTIONS

Act Sec. 406.(a) Transactions between plan and party in interest.—Except as provided in section 408:

(1) A fiduciary with respect to a plan shall not cause the plan to engage in a transaction, if he knows or should know that such transaction constitutes a direct or indirect—

(A) sale or exchange, or leasing, of any property between the plan and a party in interest;

(B) lending of money or other extension of credit between the plan and a party in interest;

(C) furnishing of goods, services, or facilities between the plan and a party in interest;

(D) transfer to, or use by or for the benefit of, a party in interest, of any assets of the plan; or

(E) acquisition, on behalf of the plan, of any employer security or employer real property in violation of section 407(a).

(2) No fiduciary who has authority or discretion to control or manage the assets of a plan shall permit the plan to hold any employer security or employer real property if he knows or should know that holding such security or real property violates section 407(a).

Act Sec. 406. (b) Transactions between plan and fiduciary.—A fiduciary with respect to a plan shall not—

(1) deal with the assets of the plan in his own interest or for his own account,

(2) in his individual or in any other capacity act in any transaction involving the plan on behalf of a party (or represent a party) whose interests are adverse to the interests of the plan or the interests of its participants or beneficiaries, or

(3) receive any consideration for his own personal account from any party dealing with such plan in connection with a transaction involving the assets of the plan.

Act Sec. 406. (c) Transfer of real or personal property to plan by party in interest.—A transfer of real or personal property by a party in interest to a plan shall be treated as a sale or exchange if the property is subject to a mortgage or similar lien which the plan assumes or if it is subject to a mortgage or similar lien which a party-in-interest placed on the property within the 10-year period ending on the date of the transfer.

[¶ 14,770]
10 PERCENT LIMITATION WITH RESPECT TO ACQUISITION AND HOLDING OF EMPLOYER SECURITIES AND EMPLOYER REAL PROPERTY BY CERTAIN PLANS

Act Sec. 407.(a) Percentage limitation.—Except as otherwise provided in this section and section 414:

(1) A plan may not acquire or hold—

(A) any employer security which is not a qualifying employer security, or

(B) any employer real property which is not qualifying employer real property.

(2) A plan may not acquire any qualifying employer security or qualifying employer real property, if immediately after such acquisition the aggregate fair market value of employer securities and employer real property held by the plan exceeds 10 percent of the fair market value of the assets of the plan.

(3)(A) After December 31, 1984, a plan may not hold any qualifying employer securities or qualifying employer real property (or both) to the extent that the aggregate fair market value of such securities and property determined on December 31, 1984, exceeds 10 percent of the greater of—

    (i) the fair market value of the assets of the plan, determined on December 31, 1984, or

    (ii) the fair market value of the assets of the plan determined on January 1, 1975.

(B) Subparagraph (A) of this paragraph shall not apply to any plan which on any date after December 31, 1974, and before January 1, 1985, did not hold employer securities or employer real property (or both) the aggregate fair market value of which determined on such date exceeded 10 percent of the greater of—

    (i) the fair market value of the assets of the plan, determined on such date, or

    (ii) the fair market value of the assets of the plan determined on January 1, 1975.

(4)(A) After December 31, 1979, a plan may not hold any employer securities or employer real property in excess of the amount specified in regulations under subparagraph (B). This subparagraph shall not apply to a plan after the earliest date after December 31, 1974, on which it complies with such regulations.

(B) Not later than December 31, 1976, the Secretary shall prescribe regulations which shall have the effect of requiring that a plan divest itself of 50 percent of the holdings of employer securities and employer real property which the plan would be required to divest before January 1, 1985, under paragraph (2) or subsection (c) (whichever is applicable).

Act Sec. 407.(b)(1) Exception.—Subsection (a) of this section shall not apply to any acquisition or holding of qualifying employer securities or qualifying employer real property by an eligible individual account plan.

(2)(A) If this paragraph applies to an eligible individual account plan, the portion of such plan which consists of applicable elective deferrals (and earnings allocable thereto) shall be treated as a separate plan—

    (i) which is not an eligible individual account plan, and

    (ii) to which the requirements of this section apply.

(B)(i) This paragraph shall apply to any eligible individual account plan if any portion of the plan's applicable elective deferrals (or earnings allocable thereto) are required to be invested in qualifying employer securities or qualifying employer real property or both—

    (I) pursuant to the terms of the plan, or

    (II) at the direction of a person other than the participant on whose behalf such elective deferrals are made to the plan (or a beneficiary).

(ii) This paragraph shall not apply to an individual account plan for a plan year if, on the last day of the preceding plan year, the fair market value of the assets of all individual account plans maintained by the employer equals not more than 10 percent of the fair market value of the assets of all pension plans (other than multiemployer plans) maintained by the employer.

(iii) This paragraph shall not apply to an individual account plan that is an employee stock ownership plan as defined in section 4975(e)(7) of the Internal Revenue Code of 1986.

(iv) This paragraph shall not apply to an individual account plan if, pursuant to the terms of the plan, the portion of any employee's applicable elective deferrals which is required to be invested in qualifying employer securities and qualifying employer real property for any year may not exceed 1 percent of the employee's compensation which is taken into account under the plan in determining the maximum amount of the employee's applicable elective deferrals for such year.

(C) For purposes of this paragraph, the term "applicable elective deferral" means any elective deferral (as defined in section 402(g)(3)(A) of the Internal Revenue Code of 1986) which is made pursuant to a qualified cash or deferred arrangement as defined in section 401(k) of the Internal Revenue Code of 1986.

(3) CROSS REFERENCES.—

(A) For exemption from diversification requirements for holding of qualifying employer securities and qualifying employer real property by eligible individual account plans, see section 404(a)(2).

(B) For exemption from prohibited transactions for certain acquisitions of qualifying employer securities and qualifying employer real property which are not in violation of 10 percent limitation, see section 408(e).

(C) For transitional rules respecting securities or real property subject to binding contracts in effect on June 30, 1974, see section 414(c).

(D) For diversification requirements for qualifying employer securities held in certain individual account plans, see section 204(j).

Act Sec. 407.(c)(1) ELECTION.—A plan which makes the election under paragraph (3) shall be treated as satisfying the requirement of subsection (a)(3) if and only if employer securities held on any date after December 31, 1974 and before January 1, 1985 have a fair market value, determined as of December 31, 1974, not in excess of 10 percent of the lesser of—

(A) the fair market value of the assets of the plan determined on such date (disregarding any portion of the fair market value of employer securities which is attributable to appreciation of such securities after December 31, 1974) but not less than the fair market value of plan assets on January 1, 1975, or

(B) an amount equal to the sum of (i) the total amount of the contributions to the plan received after December 31, 1974, and prior to such date, plus (ii) the fair market value of the assets of the plan, determined on January 1, 1975.

(2) For purposes of this subsection, in the case of an employer security held by a plan after January 1, 1975, the ownership of which is derived from ownership of employer securities held by the plan on January 1, 1975, or from the exercise of rights derived from such ownership, the value of such security held after January 1, 1975, shall be based on the value as of January 1, 1975, of the security from which ownership was derived. The Secretary shall prescribe regulations to carry out this paragraph.

(3) An election under this paragraph may not be made after December 31, 1975. Such an election shall be made in accordance with regulations prescribed by the Secretary, and shall be irrevocable. A plan may make an election under this paragraph only if on January 1, 1975, the plan holds no employer real property. After such election and before January 1, 1985 the plan may not acquire any employer real property.

Act Sec. 407. (d) DEFINITIONS.—For purposes of this section—

(1) The term "employer security" means a security issued by an employer of employees covered by the plan, or by an affiliate of such employer. A contract to which section 408(b)(5) applies shall not be treated as a security for purposes of this section.

(2) The term "employer real property" means real property (and related personal property) which is leased to an employer of employees covered by the plan, or to an affiliate of such employer. For purposes of determining the time at which a plan acquires employer real property for purposes of this section, such property shall be deemed to be acquired by the plan on the date on which the plan acquires the property or on the date on which the lease to the employer (or affiliate) is entered into, whichever is later.

(3)(A) The term "eligible individual account plan" means an individual account plan which is (i) a profit-sharing, stock bonus, thrift, or savings plan; (ii) an employee stock ownership plan; or (iii) a money purchase plan which was in existence on the date of enactment of this Act and which on such date invested primarily in qualifying employer securities. Such term excludes an individual retirement account or annuity described in section 408 of the Internal Revenue Code of 1986.

(B) Notwithstanding subparagraph (A), a plan shall be treated as an eligible individual account plan with respect to the acquisition or holding of qualifying employer real property or qualifying employer securities only if such plan explicitly provides for acquisition and holding of qualifying employer securities or qualifying employer real property (as the case may be). In the case of a plan in existence on the date of enactment of this Act, this subparagraph shall not take effect until January 1, 1976.

(C) The term "eligible individual account plan" does not include any individual account plan the benefits of which are taken into account in determining the benefits payable to a participant under any defined benefit plan.

(4) The term "qualifying employer real property" means parcels of employer real property—

(A) if a substantial number of the parcels are dispersed geographically;

(B) if each parcel of real property and the improvements thereon are suitable (or adaptable without excessive cost) for more than one use;

(C) even if all of such real property is leased to one lessee (which may be an employer, or an affiliate of an employer); and

(D) if the acquisition and retention of such property comply with the provisions of this part (other than section 404(a)(1)(B) to the extent it requires diversification, and sections 404(a)(1)(C), 406, and subsection (a) of this section).

(5) The term "qualifying employer security" means an employer security which is—

(A) stock,

(B) a marketable obligation (as defined in subsection (e)), or

(C) an interest in a publicly traded partnership (as defined in section 7704(b) of the Internal Revenue Code of 1986), but only if such partnership is an existing partnership as defined in section 10211(c)(2)(A) of the Revenue Act of 1987 (Public Law 100-203).

After December 17, 1987, in the case of a plan other than an eligible individual account plan, an employer security described in subparagraph (A) or (C) shall be considered a qualifying employer security only if such employer security satisfies the requirements of subsection (f)(1).

(6) The term "employee stock ownership plan" means an individual account plan—

(A) which is a stock bonus plan which is qualified, or a stock bonus plan and money purchase plan both of which are qualified, under section 401 of the Internal Revenue Code of 1954, and which is designed to invest primarily in qualifying employer securities, and

(B) which meets such other requirements as the Secretary of the Treasury may prescribe by regulation.

(7) A corporation is an affiliate of an employer if it is a member of any controlled group of corporations (as defined in section 1563(a) of the Internal Revenue Code of 1986, except that "applicable percentage" shall be substituted for "80 percent" wherever the latter percentage appears in such section) of which the employer who maintains the plan is a member. For purposes of the preceding sentence, the term "applicable percentage" means 50 percent, or such lower percentage as the Secretary may prescribe by regulation. A person other than a corporation shall be treated as an affiliate of an employer to the extent provided in regulations of the Secretary. An employer which is a person other than a corporation shall be treated as affiliated with another person to

the extent provided by regulations of the Secretary. Regulations under this paragraph shall be prescribed only after consultation and coordination with the Secretary of the Treasury.

(8) The Secretary may prescribe regulations specifying the extent to which conversion, splits, the exercise of rights, and similar transactions are not treated as acquisitions.

(9) For purposes of this section, an arrangement which consists of a defined benefit plan and an individual account plan shall be treated as 1 plan if the benefits of such individual account plan are taken into account in determining the benefits payable under such defined benefit plan.

Act Sec. 407. (e) MARKETABLE OBLIGATIONS.—For purposes of subsection (d)(5), the term "marketable obligation" means a bond, debenture, note, or certificate, or other evidence of indebtedness (hereinafter in this subsection referred to as "obligation") if—

(1) such obligation is acquired—

(A) on the market, either (i) at the price of the obligation prevailing on a national securities exchange which is registered with the Securities and Exchange Commission, or (ii) if the obligation is not traded on such a national securities exchange, at a price not less favorable to the plan than the offering price for the obligation as established by current bid and asked prices quoted by persons independent of the issuer;

(B) from an underwriter, at a price (i) not in excess of the public offering price for the obligation as set forth in a prospectus or offering circular filed with the Securities and Exchange Commission, and (ii) at which a substantial portion of the same issue is acquired by persons independent of the issuer; or

(C) directly from the issuer, at a price not less favorable to the plan than the price paid currently for a substantial portion of the same issue by persons independent of the issuer;

(2) immediately following acquisition of such obligation—

(A) not more than 25 percent of the aggregate amount of obligations issued in such issue and outstanding at the time of acquisition is held by the plan, and

(B) at least 50 percent of the aggregate amount referred to in subparagraph (A) is held by persons independent of the issuer; and

(3) immediately following acquisition of the obligation, not more than 25 percent of the assets of the plan is invested in obligations of the employer or an affiliate of the employer.

Act Sec. 407. (f)(1) MAXIMUM PERCENTAGE OF STOCK HELD BY PLAN; TIME OF HOLDING OR ACQUISITION; NECESSITY OF LEGALLY BINDING CONTRACT.—Stock satisfies the requirements of this paragraph if, immediately following the acquisition of such stock—

(A) no more than 25 percent of the aggregate amount of stock of the same class issued and outstanding at the time of acquisition is held by the plan, and

(B) at least 50 percent of the aggregate amount referred to in subparagraph (A) is held by persons independent of the issuer.

(2) Until January 1, 1993, a plan shall not be treated as violating subsection (a) solely by holding stock which fails to satisfy the requirements of paragraph (1) if such stock—

(A) has been so held since December 17, 1987, or

(B) was acquired after December 17, 1987, pursuant to a legally binding contract in effect on December 17, 1987, and has been so held at all times after the acquisition.

Amendments

P. L. 109-280, § 901(b)(2):

Amended ERISA Sec. 407(b)(3) by adding at the end subparagraph (D) to read as above.

For effective dates, see § 901(c) below.

P.L. 109-280, § 901(c):

901(c) EFFECTIVE DATES.—

901(c)(1) IN GENERAL.901(c)(2) SPECIAL RULE FOR COLLECTIVELY BARGAINED AGREEMENTS.—

Except as provided in paragraphs (2) and (3), the amendments made by this section shall apply to plan years beginning after December 31, 2006.

901(c)(2) SPECIAL RULE FOR COLLECTIVELY BARGAINED AGREE-MENTS.—

In the case of a plan maintained pursuant to 1 or more collective bargaining agreements between employee representatives and 1 or more employers ratified on or before the date of the enactment of this Act, paragraph (1) shall be applied to benefits pursuant to, and individuals covered by, any such agreement by substituting for "December 31, 2006" the earlier of—

901(c)(2)(A) the later of—

901(c)(2)(A)(i) December 31, 2007, or

901(c)(2)(A)(ii) the date on which the last of such collective bargaining agreements terminates (determined without regard to any extension thereof after such date of enactment), or

901(c)(2)(B) December 31, 2008.

901(c)(3) SPECIAL RULE FOR CERTAIN EMPLOYER SECURITIES HELD IN AN ESOP.—

901(c)(3)(A) IN GENERAL.—In the case of employer securities to which this paragraph applies, the amendments made by this section shall apply to plan years beginning after the earlier of—

901(c)(3)(A)(i) December 31, 2007, or

901(c)(3)(A)(ii) the first date on which the fair market value of such securities exceeds the guaranteed minimum value described in subparagraph (B)(ii).

901(c)(3)(B) APPLICABLE SECURITIES.—This paragraph shall apply to employer securities which are attributable to employer contributions other than elective deferrals, and which, on September 17, 2003—

901(c)(3)(B)(i) consist of preferred stock, and

901(c)(3)(B)(ii) are within an employee stock ownership plan (as defined in section 4975(e)(7) of the Internal Revenue Code of 1986), the terms of which provide that the value of the securities cannot be less than the guaranteed minimum value specified by the plan on such date.

901(c)(3)(C) COORDINATION WITH TRANSITION RULE.—In applying section 401(a)(35)(H) of the Internal Revenue Code of 1986 and section 204(j)(7) of the Employee Retirement Income Security Act of 1974 (as added by this section) to employer securities to which this paragraph applies, the applicable percentage shall be determined without regard to this paragraph.

P.L. 105-34, § 1524(a):

Amended ERISA Sec. 407(b) by redesignating paragraph (2) as paragraph (3) and by inserting after paragraph (1) new paragraph (2) to read as above.

The amendments made above apply to elective deferrals for plan years beginning after December 31, 1998.

P.L. 101-540, § 1:

Amended ERISA Sec. 407(d)(5) to read as above. Previously, Sec. 407(d)(5) read as follows:

(5) The term "qualifying employer security" means an employer security which is stock or a marketable obligation (as defined in subsection (e)). After December 17, 1987, in the case of a plan, other than an eligible individual account plan, stock shall be considered a qualifying employer security only if such stock satisfies the requirements of subsection (f)(1).

The above amendment is effective for interests in publicly traded partnerships acquired before, on, or after January 1, 1987.

P.L. 101-239, § 7881(1)(2):

Amended ERISA Sec. 407(d)(9) by striking "such arrangement" and inserting "such individual account plan."

The above amendment is effective for arrangements established after December 22, 1987.

P.L. 101-239, § 7881(1)(3):

Amended ERISA Sec. 407(f) in paragraph (1) by striking "this subsection" and inserting "this paragraph" and by striking paragraph (3). Prior to being stricken, paragraph (3) read as follows:

(3) After December 17, 1987, no plan may acquire stock which does not satisfy the requirements of paragraph (1) unless the acquisition is made pursuant to a legally binding contract in effect on such date.

The above changes are effective December 22, 1987.

P.L. 101-239, § 7881(1)(4):

Amended ERISA Sec. 407(f) in paragraph (1) by inserting ", immediately following the acquisition of such stock" after "if."

The above changes are effective December 22, 1987.

P.L. 101-239, § 7891(a)(1):

Titles I, III, and IV of ERISA (other than sections 3(37)(E), 301(a)(7), and 308, the last sentence of section 408(d), and sections 414(c), 4001(a)(3)(ii), and 4303) are each amended by striking "Internal Revenue Code of 1954" each place it appears and inserting "Internal Revenue Code of 1986."

The above changes are effective October 22, 1986.

P.L. 101-239, § 7894(e)(2):

Amended ERISA Sec. 407(d)(6)(A) by inserting "plan" after "money purchase" and by striking "employee securities" and inserting "employer securities." effective for arrangements established after December 17, 1987.

The above amendment is effective for arrangements established after December 22, 1987.

P.L. 100-203, §9345(a)(1):

Amended ERISA Sec. 407(d)(3) by adding subparagraph (c) to read as above.

The above amendment is effective for arrangements established after December 22, 1987.

P.L. 100-203, §9345(a)(2):

Amended ERISA Sec. 407(d) by adding paragraph (9) to read as above.

The above amendment is effective for arrangements established after December 22, 1987.

P.L. 100-203, §9345(b)(1):

Amended ERISA Sec. 407(d)(5) by adding the second sentence to read as above.

The above amendment is effective December 22, 1987.

P.L. 100-203, §9345(b)(2):

Amended ERISA Sec. 407 by adding subsection (f) to read as above.

The above amendment is effective December 22, 1987.

Regulations

The following regulations were adopted by FR Doc. 77-27315, filed with the Federal Register on September 19, 1977, and published in the Federal Register of September 20, 1977 (42 FR 47198).

[¶ 14,771]

§ 2550.407a-1 **General rule for the acquisition and holding of employer securities and employer real property.** (a) *In general.* Section 407(a)(1) of the Employee Retirement Income Security Act of 1974 (the act) states that except as otherwise provided in section 407 and section 414 of the Act, a plan may not acquire or hold any employer security which is not a qualifying employer security or any employer real property which is not qualifying employer real property. Section 406(a)(1)(E) prohibits a fiduciary from knowingly causing a plan to engage in a transaction which constitutes a direct or indirect acquisition, on behalf of a plan, of any employer security or employer real property in violation of section 407(a), and section 406(a)(2) prohibits a fiduciary who has authority or discretion to control or manage assets of a plan to permit the plan to hold any employer security or employer real property if he knows or should know that holding such security or real property violates section 407(a).

(b) *Requirements applicable to all plans.* A plan may hold or acquire only employer securities which are qualifying employer securities and employer real property which is qualifying employer real property. A plan may not hold employer securities and employer real property which are not qualifying employer securities and qualifying employer real property, except to the extent that:

(1) The employer security is held by a plan which has made an election under section 407(c)(3) of the Act; or

(2) The employer security is a loan or other extension of credit which satisfies the requirements of section 414(c)(1) of the Act or the employer real property is leased to the employer pursuant to a lease which satisfies the requirements of section 414(c)(2) of the Act.

[¶ 14,771A]

§ 2550.407a-2 **Limitation with respect to the acquisition of qualifying employer securities and qualifying employer real property.** (a) *In general.* Section 407(a)(2) of the Employee Retirement Income Security Act of 1974 (the Act) provides that a plan may not acquire any qualifying employer security or qualifying employer real property, if immediately after such acquisition the aggregate fair market value of qualifying employer securities and qualifying employer real property held by the plan exceeds 10 percent of the fair market value of the assets of the plan.

(b) *Acquisition.* For purposes of section 407(a) of the Act, an acquisition by a plan of qualifying employer securities or qualifying employer real property shall include, but not be limited to, an acquisition by purchase, by the exchange of plan assets, by the exercise of warrants or rights, by the conversion of a security (except any acquisition pursuant to a conversion exempt under section 408(b)(7) of the Act), by default of a loan where the qualifying employer security or qualifying employer real property was security for the loan, or by the contribution of such securities or real property to the plan. However, an acquisition of a security shall not be deemed to have occurred if a plan acquires the security as a result of a stock dividend or stock split.

(c) *Fair market value—Indebtedness incurred in connection with the acquisition of a plan asset.* In determining whether a plan is in compliance with the limitation on the acquisition of qualifying employer securities and qualifying employer real property in section 407(a)(2), the limitation on the holding of qualifying employer securities and qualifying employer real property in section 407(a)(3) and § 2550.407a-3 thereunder, and the requirement regarding the disposition of employer securities and employer real property in section 407(a)(4) and § 2550.407a-4 thereunder, the fair market value of total plan assets shall be the fair market value of such assets less the unpaid amount of:

(1) Any indebtedness incurred by the plan in acquiring such assets;

(2) Any indebtedness incurred before the acquisition of such assets if such indebtedness would not have been incurred but for such acquisition; and

(3) Any indebtedness incurred after the acquisition of such assets if such indebtedness would not have been incurred but for such acquisition and the incurrence of such indebtedness was reasonably foreseeable at the time of such acquisition. However, the fair market value of qualifying employer securities and qualifying employer real property shall be the fair market value of such assets without any reduction for the unpaid amount of any indebtedness incurred by the plan in connection with the acquisition of such employer securities and employer real property.

(d) *Examples.* (1) Plan assets have a fair market value of $100,000. The plan has no liabilities other than liabilities for vested benefits of participants and does not own any employer securities or employer real property. The plan proposes to acquire qualifying employer securities with a fair market value of $10,000 by paying $1,000 in cash and borrowing $9,000. The fair market value of plan assets would be $100,000 ($100,000 of plan assets less $1,000 cash payment plus $10,000 of employer securities less $9,000 indebtedness), the fair market value of the qualifying employer securities would be $10,000, which is 10 percent of the fair market value of plan assets. Accordingly, the acquisition would not contravene section 407(a).

(2) Plan assets have a fair market value of $100,000. The plan has liabilities of $20,000 which were incurred in connection with the acquisition of those assets, and does not own any employer securities or employer real property. The plan proposes to pay cash for qualifying employer securities with a fair market value of $10,000. The fair market value of plan assets would be $80,000 ($100,000 of plan assets less $10,000 cash payment plus $10,000 of employer securities less $20,000 indebtedness), the fair market value of the qualifying employer securities would be $10,000, which is 12.5 percent of the fair market value of plan assets. Accordingly, the acquisition would contravene section 407(a).

Regulations

The following regulations under Act Secs. 407 and 408 were adopted by FR Doc. 77-25695, filed with the Federal Register on August 30, 1977, and published in the Federal Register of September 2, 1977 (42 FR 44384).

[¶ 14,776E]

§ 2550.407d-5. **Definition of the term "qualifying employer security".** (a) *In general.* For purposes of this section and section 407(d)(5) of the Employee Retirement Income Security Act of 1974 (the Act), the term "qualifying employer security" means an employer security which is:

(1) Stock; or

(2) A marketable obligation, as defined in paragraph (b) of this section and section 407(e) of the Act.

Reg. §2550.407d-5(a)(2)   **¶14,776E**

(b) For purposes of paragraph (a)(2) of this section and section 407(d)(5) of the Act, the term "marketable obligation" means a bond, debenture, note, or certificate, or other evidence of indebtedness (hereinafter in this paragraph referred to as "obligation") if:

(1) Such obligation is acquired—

(i) On the market, either

(A) At the price of the obligation prevailing on a national securities exchange which is registered with the Securities and Exchange Commission, or

(B) If the obligation is not traded on such a national securities exchange, at a price not less favorable to the plan than the offering price for the obligation as established by current bid and asked prices quoted by persons independent of the issuer;

(ii) From an underwriter, at a price—

(A) Not in excess of the public offering price for the obligation as set forth in a prospectus or offering circular filed with the Securities and Exchange Commission, and

(B) At which a substantial portion of the same issue is acquired by persons independent of the issuer; or

(iii) Directly from the issuer at a price not less favorable to the plan than the price paid currently for a substantial portion of the same issue by persons independent of the issuer;

(2) Immediately following acquisition of such obligation,

(i) Not more than 25 percent of the aggregate amount of obligations issued in such issue and outstanding at the time of acquisition is held by the plan, and

(ii) At least 50 percent of the aggregate amount referred to in paragraph (A) is held by persons independent of the issuer; and

(3) Immediately following acquisition of the obligation, not more than 25 percent of the assets of the plan is invested in obligations of the employer or an affiliate of the employer.

[¶ 14,776F]

§ 2550.407d-6. **Definition of the term "employee stock ownership plan".** (a) *In general.* (1) *Type of plan.* To be an "ESOP" (employee stock ownership plan), a plan described in section 407(d)(6)(A) of the Employee Retirement Income Security Act of 1974 (the Act) must meet the requirements of this section. See section 407(d)(6)(B).

(2) *Designation as ESOP.* To be an ESOP, a plan must be formally designated as such in the plan document.

(3) *Retroactive amendment.* A plan meets the requirements of this section as of the date that it is designated as an ESOP if it is amended retroactively to meet, and in fact does meet, such requirements at any of the following times:

(i) 12 months after the date on which the plan is designated as an ESOP;

(ii) 90 days after a determination letter is issued with respect to the qualification of the plan as an ESOP under this section, but only if the determination is requested by the date in paragraph (a)(3)(i) of this section; or

(iii) A later date approved by the Internal Revenue Service district director.

(4) *Addition to other plan.* An ESOP may form a portion of a plan the balance of which includes a qualified pension, profit-sharing, or stock bonus plan which is not an ESOP. A reference to an ESOP includes an ESOP that forms a portion of another plan.

(5) *Conversion of existing plan to an ESOP.* If an existing pension, profit-sharing, or stock bonus plan is converted into an ESOP, the requirements of section 404 of the Act, relating to fiduciary duties, and section 401(a) of the Internal Revenue Code (the Code), relating to requirements for plans established for the exclusive benefit of employees, apply to such conversion. A conversion may constitute a termination of an existing plan. For definition of a termination, see the regulations under section 411(d)(3) of the Code and section 4041(f) of the Act.

(6) *Certain arrangements barred.* (i) *Buy-sell agreements.* An arrangement involving an ESOP that creates a put option must not provide for the issuance of put options other than as provided under § 2550.408b-3(j), (k) and (l). Also, an ESOP must not otherwise obligate itself to acquire securities from a particular security holder at an indefinite time determined upon the happening of an event such as the death of the holder.

(b) *Plan designed to invest primarily in qualifying employer securities.* A plan constitutes an ESOP only if the plan specifically states that it is designed to invest primarily in qualifying employer securities. Thus, a stock bonus plan or a money purchase pension plan constituting an ESOP may invest part of its assets in other than qualifying employer securities. Such plan will be treated the same as other stock bonus plans or money purchase pension plans qualified under section 401(a) of the Code with respect to those investments.

(c) *Regulations of the Secretary of the Treasury.* A plan constitutes an ESOP for a plan year only if it meets such other requirements as the Secretary of the Treasury may prescribe by regulation under section 4975(e)(7) of the Code. (See 26 CFR 54.4975-11.)

>»→ *Caution: Note: Various Prohibited Transaction Exemptions that have been granted are enumerated in the Finding Lists and the Current Finding Lists.—CCH.*

[¶ 14,780]
EXEMPTIONS FROM PROHIBITED TRANSACTIONS

Act Sec. 408. (a) Grant of exemptions.—

The Secretary shall establish an exemption procedure for purposes of this subsection. Pursuant to such procedure, he may grant a conditional or unconditional exemption of any fiduciary or transaction, or class of fiduciaries or transactions, from all or part of the restrictions imposed by sections 406 and 407(a). Action under this subsection may be taken only after consultation and coordination with the Secretary of the Treasury. An exemption granted under this section shall not relieve a fiduciary from any other applicable provision of this Act. The Secretary may not grant an exemption under this subsection unless he finds that such exemption is—

(1) administratively feasible,

(2) in the interests of the plan and of its participants and beneficiaries, and

(3) protective of the rights of participants and beneficiaries of such plan.

Before granting an exemption under this subsection from section 406(a) or 407(a), the Secretary shall publish notice in the Federal Register of the pendency of the exemption, shall require that adequate notice be given to interested persons, and shall afford interested persons opportunity to present views. The Secretary may not grant an exemption under this subsection from section 406(b) unless he affords an opportunity for a hearing and makes a determination on the record with respect to the findings required by paragraphs (1), (2), and (3) of this subsection.

Act Sec. 408. (b) Enumeration of transactions exempted from section 406 prohibitions.—

The prohibitions provided in section 406 shall not apply to any of the following transactions:

(1) Any loans made by the plan to parties in interest who are participants or beneficiaries of the plan if such loans (A) are available to all such participants and beneficiaries on a reasonably equivalent basis, (B) are not made available to highly compensated employees (within the meaning of section 414(g) of the Internal Revenue Code of 1986) in an amount greater than the amount made available to other employees, (C) are made in accordance with specific provisions regarding such loans set forth in the plan, (D) bear a reasonable rate of interest, and (E) are adequately secured. A loan made by a plan shall not fail to meet the requirements of the preceding sentence by reason of a loan repayment suspension described under section 414(u)(4) of the Internal Revenue Code of 1986.

(2) Contracting or making reasonable arrangements with a party in interest for office space, or legal, accounting, or other services necessary for the establishment or operation of the plan, if no more than reasonable compensation is paid therefor.

(3) A loan to an employee stock ownership plan (as defined in section 407(d)(6)), if—

(A) such loan is primarily for the benefit of participants and beneficiaries of the plan, and

(B) such loan is at an interest rate which is not in excess of a reasonable rate.

If the plan gives collateral to a party in interest for such loan, such collateral may consist only of qualifying employer securities (as defined in section 407(d)(5)).

(4) The investment of all or part of a plan's assets in deposits which bear a reasonable interest rate in a bank or similar financial institution supervised by the United States or a State, if such bank or other institution is a fiduciary of such plan and if—

(A) the plan covers only employees of such bank or other institution and employees of affiliates of such bank or other institution, or

(B) such investment is expressly authorized by a provision of the plan or by a fiduciary (other than such bank or institution or affiliate thereof) who is expressly empowered by the plan to so instruct the trustee with respect to such investment.

(5) Any contract for life insurance, health insurance, or annuities with one or more insurers which are qualified to do business in a State, if the plan pays no more than adequate consideration, and if each such insurer or insurers is—

(A) the employer maintaining the plan, or

(B) a party in interest which is wholly owned (directly or indirectly) by the employer maintaining the plan, or by any person which is a party in interest with respect to the plan, but only if the total premiums and annuity considerations written by such insurers for life insurance, health insurance, or annuities for all plans (and their employers) with respect to which such insurers are parties in interest (not including premiums or annuity considerations written by the employer maintaining the plan) do not exceed 5 percent of the total premiums and annuity considerations written for all lines of insurance in that year by such insurers (not including premiums or annuity considerations written by the employer maintaining the plan).

(6) The providing of any ancillary service by a bank or similar financial institution supervised by the United States or a State, if such bank or other institution is a fiduciary of such plan, and if—

(A) such bank or similar financial institution has adopted adequate internal safeguards which assure that the providing of such ancillary service is consistent with sound banking and financial practice, as determined by Federal or State supervisory authority, and

(B) the extent to which such ancillary service is provided is subject to specific guidelines issued by such bank or similar financial institution (as determined by the Secretary after consultation with Federal and State supervisory authority), and adherence to such guidelines would reasonably preclude such bank or similar financial institution from providing such ancillary service (i) in an excessive or unreasonable manner, and (ii) in a manner that would be inconsistent with the best interests of participants and beneficiaries of employee benefit plans.

Such ancillary services shall not be provided at more than reasonable compensation.

(7) The exercise of a privilege to convert securities, to the extent provided in regulations of the Secretary, but only if the plan receives no less than adequate consideration pursuant to such conversion.

(8) Any transaction between a plan and (i) a common or collective trust fund or pooled investment fund maintained by a party in interest which is a bank or trust company supervised by a State or Federal agency or (ii) a pooled investment fund of an insurance company qualified to do business in a State, if—

(A) the transaction is a sale or purchase of an interest in the fund,

(B) the bank, trust company, or insurance company receives not more than reasonable compensation, and

(C) such transaction is expressly permitted by the instrument under which the plan is maintained, or by a fiduciary (other than the bank, trust company, or insurance company, or an affiliate thereof) who has authority to manage and control the assets of the plan.

(9) The making by a fiduciary of a distribution of the assets of the plan in accordance with the terms of the plan if such assets are distributed in the same manner as provided under section 4044 of this Act (relating to allocation of assets).

(10) Any transaction required or permitted under part 1 of subtitle E of title IV.

(11) A merger of multiemployer plans, or the transfer of assets or liabilities between multiemployer plans, determined by the Pension Benefit Guaranty Corporation to meet the requirements of section 4231.

(12) The sale by a plan to a party in interest on or after December 18, 1987, of any stock, if—

(A) the requirements of paragraphs (1) and (2) of subsection (e) are met with respect to such stock,

(B) on the later of the date on which the stock was acquired by the plan, or January 1, 1975, such stock constituted a qualifying employer security (as defined in section 407(d)(5) as then in effect), and

(C) such stock does not constitute a qualifying employer security (as defined in section 407(d)(5) as in effect at the time of the sale).

(13) Any transfer made before January 1, 2026, of excess pension assets from a defined benefit plan to a retiree health account in a qualified transfer permitted under section 420 of the Internal Revenue Code of 1986 (as in effect on the date of the enactment of the Surface Transportation and Veterans Health Care Choice Improvement Act of 2015).

(14) Any transaction in connection with the provision of investment advice described in section 3(21)(A)(ii) to a participant or beneficiary of an individual account plan that permits such participant or beneficiary to direct the investment of assets in their individual account, if—

(A) the transaction is—

(i) the provision of the investment advice to the participant or beneficiary of the plan with respect to a security or other property available as an investment under the plan,

(ii) the acquisition, holding, or sale of a security or other property available as an investment under the plan pursuant to the investment advice, or

(iii) the direct or indirect receipt of fees or other compensation by the fiduciary adviser or an affiliate thereof (or any employee, agent, or registered representative of the fiduciary adviser or affiliate) in connection with the provision of the advice or in connection with an acquisition, holding, or sale of a security or other property available as an investment under the plan pursuant to the investment advice; and

(B) the requirements of subsection (g) are met.

(15)(A) Any transaction involving the purchase or sale of securities, or other property (as determined by the Secretary), between a plan and a party in interest (other than a fiduciary described in section 3(21)(A)) with respect to a plan if—

(i) the transaction involves a block trade,

(ii) at the time of the transaction, the interest of the plan (together with the interests of any other plans maintained by the same plan sponsor), does not exceed 10 percent of the aggregate size of the block trade,

(iii) the terms of the transaction, including the price, are at least as favorable to the plan as an arm's length transaction, and

(iv) the compensation associated with the purchase and sale is not greater than the compensation associated with an arm's length transaction with an unrelated party.

(B) For purposes of this paragraph, the term "block trade" means any trade of at least 10,000 shares or with a market value of at least $200,000 which will be allocated across two or more unrelated client accounts of a fiduciary.

(16) Any transaction involving the purchase or sale of securities, or other property (as determined by the Secretary), between a plan and a party in interest if—

(A) the transaction is executed through an electronic communication network, alternative trading system, or similar execution system or trading venue subject to regulation and oversight by—

    (i) the applicable Federal regulating entity, or

    (ii) such foreign regulatory entity as the Secretary may determine by regulation,

(B) either—

    (i) the transaction is effected pursuant to rules designed to match purchases and sales at the best price available through the execution system in accordance with applicable rules of the Securities and Exchange Commission or other relevant governmental authority, or

    (ii) neither the execution system nor the parties to the transaction take into account the identity of the parties in the execution of trades,

(C) the price and compensation associated with the purchase and sale are not greater than the price and compensation associated with an arm's length transaction with an unrelated party,

(D) if the party in interest has an ownership interest in the system or venue described in subparagraph (A), the system or venue has been authorized by the plan sponsor or other independent fiduciary for transactions described in this paragraph, and

(E) not less than 30 days prior to the initial transaction described in this paragraph executed through any system or venue described in subparagraph (A), a plan fiduciary is provided written or electronic notice of the execution of such transaction through such system or venue.

(17)(A) Transactions described in subparagraphs (A), (B), and (D) of section 406(a)(1) between a plan and a person that is a party in interest other than a fiduciary (or an affiliate) who has or exercises any discretionary authority or control with respect to the investment of the plan assets involved in the transaction or renders investment advice (within the meaning of section 3(21)(A)(ii)) with respect to those assets, solely by reason of providing services to the plan or solely by reason of a relationship to such a service provider described in subparagraph (F), (G), (H), or (I) of section 3(14), or both, but only if in connection with such transaction the plan receives no less, nor pays no more, than adequate consideration.

(B) For purposes of this paragraph, the term "adequate consideration" means—

    (i) in the case of a security for which there is a generally recognized market—

        (I) the price of the security prevailing on a national securities exchange which is registered under section 6 of the Securities Exchange Act of 1934, taking into account factors such as the size of the transaction and marketability of the security, or

        (II) if the security is not traded on such a national securities exchange, a price not less favorable to the plan than the offering price for the security as established by the current bid and asked prices quoted by persons independent of the issuer and of the party in interest, taking into account factors such as the size of the transaction and marketability of the security, and

    (ii) in the case of an asset other than a security for which there is a generally recognized market, the fair market value of the asset as determined in good faith by a fiduciary or fiduciaries in accordance with regulations prescribed by the Secretary.

(18) FOREIGN EXCHANGE TRANSACTIONS. —Any foreign exchange transactions, between a bank or broker-dealer (or any affiliate of either), and a plan (as defined in section 3(3)) with respect to which such bank or broker-dealer (or affiliate) is a trustee, custodian, fiduciary, or other party in interest, if—

(A) the transaction is in connection with the purchase, holding, or sale of securities or other investment assets (other than a foreign exchange transaction unrelated to any other investment in securities or other investment assets),

(B) at the time the foreign exchange transaction is entered into, the terms of the transaction are not less favorable to the plan than the terms generally available in comparable arm's length foreign exchange transactions between unrelated parties, or the terms afforded by the bank or broker-dealer (or any affiliate of either) in comparable arm's-length foreign exchange transactions involving unrelated parties,

(C) the exchange rate used by such bank or broker-dealer (or affiliate) for a particular foreign exchange transaction does not deviate by more than 3 percent from the interbank bid and asked rates for transactions of comparable size and maturity at the time of the transaction as displayed on an independent service that reports rates of exchange in the foreign currency market for such currency, and

(D) the bank or broker-dealer (or any affiliate of either) does not have investment discretion, or provide investment advice, with respect to the transaction.

(19) CROSS TRADING. —Any transaction described in sections 406(a)(1)(A) and 406(b)(2) involving the purchase and sale of a security between a plan and any other account managed by the same investment manager, if—

(A) the transaction is a purchase or sale, for no consideration other than cash payment against prompt delivery of a security for which market quotations are readily available,

(B) the transaction is effected at the independent current market price of the security (within the meaning of section 270.17a-7(b) of title 17, Code of Federal Regulations),

(C) no brokerage commission, fee (except for customary transfer fees, the fact of which is disclosed pursuant to subparagraph (D)), or other remuneration is paid in connection with the transaction,

(D) a fiduciary (other than the investment manager engaging in the cross-trades or any affiliate) for each plan participating in the transaction authorizes in advance of any crosstrades (in a document that is separate from any other written agreement of the parties) the investment manager to engage in cross trades at the investment manager's discretion, after such fiduciary has received disclosure regarding the conditions under which cross trades may take place (but only if such disclosure is separate from any other agreement or disclosure involving the asset management relationship), including the written policies and procedures of the investment manager described in subparagraph (H),

(E) each plan participating in the transaction has assets of at least $100,000,000, except that if the assets of a plan are invested in a master trust containing the assets of plans maintained by employers in the same controlled group (as defined in section 407(d)(7)), the master trust has assets of at least $100,000,000,

(F) the investment manager provides to the plan fiduciary who authorized cross trading under subparagraph (D) a quarterly report detailing all cross trades executed by the investment manager in which the plan participated during such quarter, including the following information, as applicable: (i) the identity of each security bought or sold; (ii) the number of shares or units traded, (iii) the parties involved in the cross-trade; and (iv) trade price and the method used to establish the trade price,

(G) the investment manager does not base its fee schedule on the plan's consent to cross trading, and no other service (other than the investment opportunities and cost savings available through a cross trade) is conditioned on the plan's consent to cross trading,

(H) the investment manager has adopted, and cross-trades are effected in accordance with, written cross-trading policies and procedures that are fair and equitable to all accounts participating in the cross-trading program, and that include a description of the manager's pricing policies and procedures, and the manager's policies and procedures for allocating cross trades in an objective manner among accounts participating in the cross-trading program, and

(I) the investment manager has designated an individual responsible for periodically reviewing such purchases and sales to ensure compliance with the written policies and procedures described in subparagraph (H), and following such review, the individual shall issue an annual written report no later than 90 days following the period to which it relates signed under penalty of perjury to the plan fiduciary who authorized cross trading under subparagraph (D) describing the steps performed during the course of the review, the level of compliance, and any specific instances of non-compliance.

The written report under subparagraph (I) shall also notify the plan fiduciary of the plan's right to terminate participation in the investment manager's cross-trading program at any time.

(20)(A) Except as provided in subparagraphs (B) and (C), a transaction described in section 406(a) in connection with the acquisition, holding, or disposition of any security or commodity, if the transaction is corrected before the end of the correction period.

(B) Subparagraph (A) does not apply to any transaction between a plan and a plan sponsor or its affiliates that involves the acquisition or sale of an employer security (as defined in section 407(d)(1)) or the acquisition, sale, or lease of employer real property (as defined in section 407(d)(2)).

(C) In the case of any fiduciary or other party in interest (or any other person knowingly participating in such transaction), subparagraph (A) does not apply to any transaction if, at the time the transaction occurs, such fiduciary or party in interest (or other person) knew (or reasonably should have known) that the transaction would (without regard to this paragraph) constitute a violation of section 406(a).

(D) For purposes of this paragraph, the term "correction period" means, in connection with a fiduciary or party in interest (or other person knowingly participating in the transaction), the 14-day period beginning on the date on which such fiduciary or party in interest (or other person) discovers, or reasonably should have discovered, that the transaction would (without regard to this paragraph) constitute a violation of section 406(a).

(E) For purposes of this paragraph—

(i) The term "security" has the meaning given such term by section 475(c)(2) of the Internal Revenue Code of 1986 (without regard to subparagraph (F)(iii) and the last sentence thereof).

(ii) The term "commodity" has the meaning given such term by section 475(e)(2) of such Code (without regard to subparagraph (D)(iii) thereof).

(iii) The term "correct" means, with respect to a transaction—

(I) to undo the transaction to the extent possible and in any case to make good to the plan or affected account any losses resulting from the transaction, and

(II) to restore to the plan or affected account any profits made through the use of assets of the plan.

Act Sec. 408. (c) FIDUCIARY BENEFITS AND COMPENSATION NOT PROHIBITED BY SECTION 406.—

Nothing in section 406 shall be construed to prohibit any fiduciary from—

(1) receiving any benefit to which he may be entitled as a participant or beneficiary in the plan, so long as the benefit is computed and paid on a basis which is consistent with the terms of the plan as applied to all other participants and beneficiaries;

(2) receiving any reasonable compensation for services rendered, or for the reimbursement of expenses properly and actually incurred, in the performance of his duties with the plan; except that no person so serving who already receives full-time pay from an employer or an association of employers, whose employees are participants in the plan, or from an employee organization whose members are participants in such plan shall receive compensation from such plan, except for reimbursement of expenses properly and actually incurred; or

(3) serving as a fiduciary in addition to being an officer, employee, agent, or other representative of a party in interest.

Act Sec. 408. (d) OWNER-EMPLOYEES; FAMILY MEMBERS; SHAREHOLDER EMPLOYEES.—

(1) Section 407(b) and subsections (b), (c), and (e) of this section shall not apply to a transaction in which a plan directly or indirectly—

(A) lends any part of the corpus or income of the plan to,

(B) pays any compensation for personal services rendered to the plan to, or

(C) acquires for the plan any property from, or sells any property to,

any person who is with respect to the plan an owner-employee (as defined in section 401(c)(3) of the Internal Revenue Code of 1986), a member of the family (as defined in section 267(c)(4) of such Code) of any such owner-employee, or any corporation in which any such owner-employee owns, directly or indirectly, 50 percent or more of the total combined voting power of all classes of stock entitled to vote or 50 percent or more of the total value of shares of all classes of stock of the corporation.

(2)(A) For purposes of paragraph (1), the following shall be treated as owner-employees:

(i) A shareholder-employee.

(ii) A participant or beneficiary of an individual retirement plan (as defined in section 7701(a)(37) of the Internal Revenue Code of 1986).

(iii) An employer or association of employees which establishes such an individual retirement plan under section 408(c) of such Code.

(B) Paragraph (1)(C) shall not apply to a transaction which consists of a sale of employer securities to an employee stock ownership plan (as defined in section 407(d)(6)) by a shareholder-employee, a member of the family (as defined in section 267(c)(4) of such Code) of any such owner-employee, or a corporation in which such a shareholder-employee owns stock representing a 50 percent or greater interest described in paragraph (1).

(C) For purposes of paragraph (1)(A), the term "owner-employee" shall only include a person described in clause (ii) or (iii) of subparagraph (A).

(3) For purposes of paragraph (2), the term "shareholder-employee" means an employee or officer of an S corporation (as defined in section 1361(a)(1) of such Code) who owns (or is considered as owning within the meaning of section 318(a)(1) of such Code) more than 5 percent of the outstanding stock of the corporation on any day during the taxable year of such corporation.

Act Sec. 408. (e) ACQUISITION OR SALE BY PLAN OF QUALIFYING EMPLOYER SECURITIES; ACQUISITION, SALE, OR LEASE BY PLAN OF QUALIFYING EMPLOYER REAL PROPERTY.—

Sections 406 and 407 shall not apply to the acquisition or sale by a plan of qualifying employer securities (as defined in section 407(d)(5)) or acquisition, sale or lease by a plan of qualifying employer real property (as defined in section 407(d)(4))—

(1) if such acquisition, sale, or lease is for adequate consideration (or in the case of a marketable obligation, at a price not less favorable to the plan than the price determined under section 407(e)(1)),

(2) if no commission is charged with respect thereto, and

(3) if—

(A) the plan is an eligible individual account plan (as defined in section 407(d)(3)), or

(B) in the case of an acquisition or lease of qualifying employer real property by a plan which is not an eligible individual account plan, or of an acquisition of qualifying employer securities by such a plan, the lease or acquisition is not prohibited by section 407(a).

Act Sec. 408. (f) APPLICABILITY STATUTORY PROHIBITIONS TO MERGERS OR TRANSFERS.—

Section 406(b)(2) shall not apply to any merger or transfer described in subsection (b)(11).

Act Sec. 408. (g) PROVISION OF INVESTMENT ADVICE TO PARTICIPANT AND BENEFICIARIES.—

(1) IN GENERAL. —The prohibitions provided in section 406 shall not apply to transactions described in subsection (b)(14) if the investment advice provided by a fiduciary adviser is provided under an eligible investment advice arrangement.

(2) ELIGIBLE INVESTMENT ADVICE ARRANGEMENT. —For purposes of this subsection, the term "eligible investment advice arrangement" means an arrangement—

(A) which either—

(i) provides that any fees (including any commission or other compensation) received by the fiduciary adviser for investment advice or with respect to the sale, holding, or acquisition of any security or other property for purposes of investment of plan assets do not vary depending on the basis of any investment option selected, or

(ii) uses a computer model under an investment advice program meeting the requirements of paragraph (3) in connection with the provision of investment advice by a fiduciary adviser to a participant or beneficiary, and

(B) with respect to which the requirements of paragraph (4), (5), (6), (7), (8), and (9) are met.

(3) INVESTMENT ADVICE PROGRAM USING COMPUTER MODEL.—

(A) IN GENERAL. —An investment advice program meets the requirements of this paragraph if the requirements of subparagraphs (B), (C), and (D) are met.

(B) COMPUTER MODEL. The requirements of this subparagraph are met if the investment advice provided under the investment advice program is provided pursuant to a computer model that—

(i) applies generally accepted investment theories that take into account the historic returns of different asset classes over defined periods of time,

(ii) utilizes relevant information about the participant, which may include age, life expectancy, retirement age, risk tolerance, other assets or sources of income, and preferences as to certain types of investments,

(iii) utilizes prescribed objective criteria to provide asset allocation portfolios comprised of investment options available under the plan,

(iv) operates in a manner that is not biased in favor of investments offered by the fiduciary adviser or a person with a material affiliation or contractual relationship with the fiduciary adviser, and

(v) takes into account all investment options under the plan in specifying how a participant's account balance should be invested and is not inappropriately weighted with respect to any investment option.

(C) CERTIFICATION.—

(i) IN GENERAL. —The requirements of this subparagraph are met with respect to any investment advice program if an eligible investment expert certifies, prior to the utilization of the computer model and in accordance with rules prescribed by the Secretary, that the computer model meets the requirements of subparagraph (B).

(ii) RENEWAL OF CERTIFICATIONS. —If, as determined under regulations prescribed by the Secretary, there are material modifications to a computer model, the requirements of this subparagraph are met only if a certification described in clause (i) is obtained with respect to the computer model as so modified.

(iii) ELIGIBLE INVESTMENT EXPERT. —The term "eligible investment expert" means any person—

(I) which meets such requirements as the Secretary may provide, and

(II) does not bear any material affiliation or contractual relationship with any investment adviser or a related person thereof (or any employee, agent, or registered representative of the investment adviser or related person).

(D) EXCLUSIVITY OF RECOMMENDATION. —The requirements of this subparagraph are met with respect to any investment advice program if—

(i) the only investment advice provided under the program is the advice generated by the computer model described in subparagraph (B), and

(ii) any transaction described in subsection (b)(14)(A)(ii) occurs solely at the direction of the participant or beneficiary.

Nothing in the preceding sentence shall preclude the participant or beneficiary from requesting investment advice other than that described in subparagraph (A), but only if such request has not been solicited by any person connected with carrying out the arrangement.

(4) EXPRESS AUTHORIZATION BY SEPARATE FIDUCIARY. —The requirements of this paragraph are met with respect to an arrangement if the arrangement is expressly authorized by a plan fiduciary other than the person offering the investment advice program, any person providing investment options under the plan, or any affiliate of either.

(5) ANNUAL AUDIT. —The requirements of this paragraph are met if an independent auditor, who has appropriate technical training or experience and proficiency and so represents in writing

(A) conducts an annual audit of the arrangement for compliance with the requirements of this subsection, and

(B) following completion of the annual audit, issues a written report to the fiduciary who authorized use of the arrangement which presents its specific findings regarding compliance of the arrangement with the requirements of this subsection.

For purposes of this paragraph, an auditor is considered independent if it is not related to the person offering the arrangement to the plan and is not related to any person providing investment options under the plan.

(6) DISCLOSURE. —The requirements of this paragraph are met if—

(A) the fiduciary adviser provides to a participant or a beneficiary before the initial provision of the investment advice with regard to any security or other property offered as an investment option, a written notification (which may consist of notification by means of electronic communication)—

(i) of the role of any party that has a material affiliation or contractual relationship with the fiduciary adviser in the development of the investment advice program and in the selection of investment options available under the plan,

(ii) of the past performance and historical rates of return of the investment options available under the plan,

(iii) of all fees or other compensation relating to the advice that the fiduciary adviser or any affiliate thereof is to receive (including compensation provided by any third party) in connection with the provision of the advice or in connection with the sale, acquisition, or holding of the security or other property,

(iv) of any material affiliation or contractual relationship of the fiduciary adviser or affiliates thereof in the security or other property,

(v) the manner, and under what circumstances, any participant or beneficiary information provided under the arrangement will be used or disclosed,

(vi) of the types of services provided by the fiduciary adviser in connection with the provision of investment advice by the fiduciary adviser,

(vii) that the adviser is acting as a fiduciary of the plan in connection with the provision of the advice, and

(viii) that a recipient of the advice may separately arrange for the provision of advice by another adviser, that could have no material affiliation with and receive no fees or other compensation in connection with the security or other property, and

(B) at all times during the provision of advisory services to the participant or beneficiary, the fiduciary adviser

(i) maintains the information described in subparagraph (A) in accurate form and in the manner described in paragraph (8),

(ii) provides, without charge, accurate information to the recipient of the advice no less frequently than annually,

(iii) provides, without charge, accurate information to the recipient of the advice upon request of the recipient, and

(iv) provides, without charge, accurate information to the recipient of the advice concerning any material change to the information required to be provided to the recipient of the advice at a time reasonably contemporaneous to the change in information.

(7) OTHER CONDITIONS. —The requirements of this paragraph are met if—

(A) the fiduciary adviser provides appropriate disclosure, in connection with the sale, acquisition, or holding of the security or other property, in accordance with all applicable securities laws,

(B) the sale, acquisition, or holding occurs solely at the direction of the recipient of the advice,

(C) the compensation received by the fiduciary adviser and affiliates thereof in connection with the sale, acquisition, or holding of the security or other property is reasonable, and

(D) the terms of the sale, acquisition, or holding of the security or other property are at least as favorable to the plan as an arm's length transaction would be.

(8) STANDARDS FOR PRESENTATION OF INFORMATION.—

(A) IN GENERAL. —The requirements of this paragraph are met if the notification required to be provided to participants and beneficiaries under paragraph (6)(A) is written in a clear and conspicuous manner and in a manner calculated to be understood by the average plan participant and is sufficiently accurate and comprehensive to reasonably apprise such participants and beneficiaries of the information required to be provided in the notification.

(B) MODEL FORM FOR DISCLOSURE OF FEES AND OTHER COMPENSATION. —The Secretary shall issue a model form for the disclosure of fees and other compensation required in paragraph (6)(A)(iii) which meets the requirements of subparagraph (A).

(9) MAINTENANCE FOR 6 YEARS OF EVIDENCE OF COMPLIANCE. —The requirements of this paragraph are met if a fiduciary adviser who has provided advice referred to in paragraph (1) maintains, for a period of not less than 6 years after the provision of the advice, any records necessary for determining whether the requirements of the preceding provisions of this subsection and of subsection (b)(14) have been met. A transaction prohibited under section 406 shall not be considered to have occurred solely because the records are lost or destroyed prior to the end of the 6-year period due to circumstances beyond the control of the fiduciary adviser.

(10) EXEMPTION FOR PLAN SPONSOR AND CERTAIN OTHER FIDUCIARIES.—

(A) IN GENERAL. —Subject to subparagraph (B), a plan sponsor or other person who is a fiduciary (other than a fiduciary adviser) shall not be treated as failing to meet the requirements of this part solely by reason of the provision of investment advice referred to in section 3(21)(A)(ii) (or solely by reason of contracting for or otherwise arranging for the provision of the advice), if—

(i) the advice is provided by a fiduciary adviser pursuant to an eligible investment advice arrangement between the plan sponsor or other fiduciary and the fiduciary adviser for the provision by the fiduciary adviser of investment advice referred to in such section,

(ii) the terms of the eligible investment advice arrangement require compliance by the fiduciary adviser with the requirements of this subsection, and

(iii) the terms of the eligible investment advice arrangement include a written acknowledgment by the fiduciary adviser that the fiduciary adviser is a fiduciary of the plan with respect to the provision of the advice.

(B) CONTINUED DUTY OF PRUDENT SELECTION OF ADVISOR AND PERIODIC REVIEW. —Nothing in subparagraph (A) shall be construed to exempt a plan sponsor or other person who is a fiduciary from any requirement of this part for the prudent selection and periodic review of a fiduciary adviser with whom the plan sponsor or other person enters into an eligible investment advice arrangement for the provision of investment advice referred to in section 3(21)(A)(ii). The plan sponsor or other person who is a fiduciary has no duty under this part to monitor the specific investment advice given by the fiduciary adviser to any particular recipient of the advice.

(C) AVAILABILITY OF PLAN ASSETS FOR PAYMENT FOR ADVICE. —Nothing in this part shall be construed to preclude the use of plan assets to pay for reasonable expenses in providing investment advice referred to in section 3(21)(A)(ii).

(11) DEFINITIONS. —For purposes of this subsection and subsection (b)(14)—

(A) FIDUCIARY ADVISER. —The term "fiduciary adviser" means, with respect to a plan, a person who is a fiduciary of the plan by reason of the provision of investment advice referred to in section 3(21)(A)(ii) by the person to a participant or beneficiary of the plan and who is—

(i) registered as an investment adviser under the Investment Advisers Act of 1940 (15 U.S.C. 80b-1 et seq.) or under the laws of the State in which the fiduciary maintains its principal office and place of business,

(ii) a bank or similar financial institution referred to in subsection (b)(4) or a savings association (as defined in section 3(b)(1) of the Federal Deposit Insurance Act (12 U.S.C. 1813(b)(1)), but only if the advice is provided through a trust department of the bank or similar financial institution or savings association which is subject to periodic examination and review by Federal or State banking authorities,

(iii) an insurance company qualified to do business under the laws of a State,

(iv) a person registered as a broker or dealer under the Securities Exchange Act of 1934 (15 U.S.C. 78a et seq.),

(v) an affiliate of a person described in any of clauses (i) through (iv), or

(vi) an employee, agent, or registered representative of a person described in clauses (i) through (v) who satisfies the requirements of applicable insurance, banking, and securities laws relating to the provision of the advice.

For purposes of this part, a person who develops the computer model described in paragraph (3)(B) or markets the investment advice program or computer model shall be treated as a person who is a fiduciary of the plan by reason of the provision of investment advice referred to in section 3(21)(A)(ii) to a participant or beneficiary and shall be treated as a fiduciary adviser for purposes of this subsection and subsection (b)(14), except that the Secretary may prescribe rules under which only 1 fiduciary adviser may elect to be treated as a fiduciary with respect to the plan.

(B) AFFILIATE. —The term "affiliate" of another entity means an affiliated person of the entity (as defined in section 2(a)(3) of the Investment Company Act of 1940 (15 U.S.C. 80a-2(a)(3))).

(C) REGISTERED REPRESENTATIVE. —The term "registered representative" of another entity means a person described in section 3(a)(18) of the Securities Exchange Act of 1934 (15 U.S.C. 78c(a)(18)) (substituting the entity for the broker or dealer referred to in such section) or a person described in section 202(a)(17) of the Investment Advisers Act of 1940 (15 U.S.C. 80b-2(a)(17)) (substituting the entity for the investment adviser referred to in such section).

Amendments

P.L. 114-41, §2007(b)(1):

Amended ERISA Sec. 408(b)(13) by striking "MAP-21" and inserting "Surface Transportation and Veterans Health Care Choice Improvement Act of 2015".

The above amendments take effect on July 31, 2015.

P.L. 114-41, §2007(b)(2):

Amended ERISA Sec. 408(b)(13) by striking "January 1, 2022" and inserting "January 1, 2026".

The above amendments take effect on July 31, 2015.

P.L. 112-141, §40241(b)(1) and (2):

Amended ERISA Sec. 408(b)(13) each by striking "Pension Protection Act of 2006" and inserting "MAP-21", and by striking "January 1, 2014" and inserting "January 1, 2022".

For effective date, see P.L. 112-141, §40241(c), below.

P.L. 112-141, §40241(c), provides:

(c) EFFECTIVE DATE.—The amendments made by this Act [section]shall take effect on the date of the enactment of this Act [July 6, 2012].

P.L. 110-458, §106(a)(1)(A):

Amended ERISA 408(g)(3)(D)(ii) by striking "subsection (b)(14)(B)(ii)" and inserting "subsection (b)(14)(A)(ii)".

The above amendment applies to advice referred to in ERISA Sec. 3(21)(A)(ii) provided after December 31, 2006.

P.L. 110-458, §106(a)(1)(B):

Amended ERISA 408(g)(6)(A)(i) by striking "financial adviser" and inserting "fiduciary adviser".

The above amendment applies to advice referred to in ERISA Sec. 3(21)(A)(ii) provided after December 31, 2006.

P.L. 110-458, §106(a)(1)(C)(i)-(ii):

Amended ERISA Sec. 408(g)(11)(A) by striking "the participant" each place it appears and inserting "a participant", and by striking "section 408(b)(4)" in clause (ii) and inserting "subsection (b)(4)".

The above amendment applies to advice referred to in ERISA Sec. 3(21)(A)(ii) provided after December 31, 2006.

P.L. 110-458, §106(b)(1):

Amended ERISA Sec. 408(b)(18)(C) by striking "or less".

The above amendment applies to transactions occurring after August 17, 2006.

P.L. 109-280, §601(a)(1):

Amended ERISA Sec. 408(b) by adding new paragraph (14) to read as above.

The above amendment applies to investment advice provided after December 31, 2006.

P.L. 109-280, §601(a)(2):

Amended ERISA Sec. 408 by adding new subsection (g) to read as above.

The above amendment applies to investment advice provided after December 31, 2006.

P.L. 109-280, §611(a)(1):

Amended ERISA Sec. 408(b) by adding new paragraph (15) to read as above.

The above amendment applies to transactions occurring after the date of the enactment (August 17, 2006).

P.L. 109-280, §611(c)(1):

Amended ERISA Sec. 408(b) by adding new paragraph (16) to read as above.

The above amendment applies to transactions occurring after the date of the enactment (August 17, 2006).

P.L. 109-280, §611(d)(1):

Amended ERISA Sec. 408(b) by adding new paragraph (17) to read as above.

The above amendment applies to transactions occurring after the date of the enactment (August 17, 2006).

P.L. 109-280, §611(e)(1):

Amended ERISA Sec. 408(b) by adding new paragraph (18) to read as above.

The above amendment applies to transactions occurring after the date of the enactment (August 17, 2006).

P.L. 109-280, §611(g)(1):

Amended ERISA Sec. 408(b) by adding new paragraph (19) to read as above.

The above amendment applies to transactions occurring after the date of the enactment (August 17, 2006).

P.L. 109-280, §612(a):

Amended ERISA Sec. 408(b) by adding new paragraph (20) to read as above.

The above amendment applies to any transaction which the fiduciary or disqualified person discovers, or reasonably should have discovered, after the date of the enactment (August 17, 2006) constitutes a prohibited transaction.

P.L. 109-280, §811, provides:

ACT SEC. 811. PENSIONS AND INDIVIDUAL RETIREMENT ARRANGEMENT PROVISIONS OF ECONOMIC GROWTH AND TAX RELIEF RECONCILIATION ACT OF 2001 MADE PERMANENT.

Title IX of the Economic Growth and Tax Relief Reconciliation Act of 2001 shall not apply to the provisions of, and amendments made by, subtitles A through F of title VI of such Act (relating to pension and individual retirement arrangement provisions).

P.L. 108-357, §709(a)(3):

Act Sec. 709(a)(3) amended ERISA Sec. 408(b)(13) by striking "Pension Funding Equity Act of 2004" and inserting "American Jobs Creation Act of 2004."

P.L. 108-218, §204(b):

Act Sec. 535(b)(3) amended ERISA Sec. 408(b)(13) by striking "January 1, 2006" and inserting "January 1, 2014" and by striking "Tax Relief Extension Act of 1999" and inserting "Pension Funding Equity Act of 2004".

P.L. 107-16, §612(b):

Act Sec. 612(b) amended ERISA Sec. 408(d)(2) by adding at the end new subparagraph (C) to read as above.

The above amendment applies to years beginning after December 31, 2001, subject to sunset after 2010 under P.L. 107-16, Sec. 901 [but see P.L. 109-280, §811, above].

P.L. 106-170, §535(b)(2)(C):

Act Sec. 535(b)(2)(C) amended ERISA Sec. 408(b)(13) by striking "in a taxable year beginning before January 1, 2001" and inserting "made before January 1, 2006" and by

striking "January 1, 1995" and inserting "the date of the enactment of the Tax Relief Extension Act of 1999".

The above amendment applies to qualified transfers occurring after December 17, 1999.

P.L. 105-34, Sec. 1506(b)(2):

Amended ERISA Sec. 408(d) to read as above. Prior to amendment, the subsection read as follows:

Act Sec. 408. (d) Section 407(b) and subsections (b), (c), and (e) of this section shall not apply to any transaction in which a plan, directly or indirectly—

(1) lends any part of the corpus or income of the plan to;

(2) pays any compensation for personal services rendered to the plan to; or

(3) acquires for the plan any property from or sells any property to;

any person who is with respect to the plan an owner-employee (as defined in section 401(c)(3) of the Internal Revenue Code of 1986), a member of the family (as defined in section 267(c)(4) of such Code) of any such owner-employee, or a corporation controlled by any such owner-employee through the ownership, directly or indirectly, of 50 percent or more of the total combined voting power of all classes of stock entitled to vote or 50 percent or more of the total value of shares of all classes of stock of the corporation. For purposes of this subsection a shareholder employee (as defined in section 1379 of the Internal Revenue Code of 1954 as in effect on the day before the date of the enactment of the Subchapter S Revision Act of 1982) and a participant or beneficiary of an individual retirement account or individual retirement annuity described in section 408 of the Internal Revenue Code of 1954 or a retirement bond described in section 409 of the Internal Revenue Code of 1954 (as effective for obligations issued before January 1, 1984) and an employer or association of employers which establishes such an account or annuity under section 408(c) of such Code shall be deemed to be an owner-employee.

The above amendment applies to taxable years beginning after December 31, 1997.

P.L. 104-188, Sec. 1704(n)(2):

Amended ERISA Sec. 408(b)(1) by adding a new sentence at the end to read as above.

The above amendment is effective as of December 12, 1994.

P.L. 101-508, Sec. 12012(b):

Amended ERISA Sec. 408(b) by adding new paragraph (13) effective for qualified transfers under Code Sec. 420 made after November 5, 1990.

P.L. 101-239, §7881(l)(5):

Amended ERISA Sec. 408(b) by adding a new paragraph (12) to read as above effective December 22, 1987.

P.L. 101-239, §7891(a)(2):

Amended ERISA Sec. 408(d), last sentence (as amended by section 7894(e)(4)(A)(i)), by striking "section 408 of the Internal Revenue Code of 1954" and inserting "section 408 of the Internal Revenue Code of 1986" and by striking "section 408(c) of such Code" and inserting "section 408(c) of the Internal Revenue Code of 1986" effective December 22, 1987.

P.L. 101-239, §7894(e)(4):

Amended ERISA Sec. 408(d), the last sentence, by striking "individual retirement account, individual retirement annuity, or an individual retirement bond (as defined in section 408 or 409 of the Internal Revenue Code of 1954)" and inserting "individual retirement account or individual retirement annuity described in section 408 of the Internal Revenue Code of 1954 or a retirement bond described in section 409 of the Internal Revenue Code of 1954 (as effective for obligations issued before January 1, 1984)"; and by striking "section 408(c) of such code" and inserting "section 408(c) of such Code" effective as if included in P.L. 98-369, §491(b).

P.L. 99-514, §1114(b)(15)(B):

Struck out "highly compensated employees, officers, or shareholders" and inserted "highly compensated employees (within the meaning of section 414(g) of the Internal Revenue Code of 1986)" in ERISA Sec. 408(b), effective for years beginning after December 31, 1988.

P.L. 99-514, §1898(i):

Amended ERISA Sec. 408(d) by striking out "(a)", effective for transactions after the date of enactment.

P.L. 97-354, §5(a)(43):

Added the words, "as in effect on the day before the date of the enactment of the Subchapter S Revision Act of 1982," after the words "section 1379 of the Internal Revenue Code of 1954" in subsection 408(d).

P.L. 96-364, §308:

Added new subsections 408(b)(10) and (11) and new section 408(f), effective September 26, 1980.

Regulations

The following regulations were adopted under "Title 29—Labor," "Chapter XXV—Pension and Welfare Benefit Programs," "Subchapter F—Employee Retirement Income Security Act of 1974," "Part 2550—Rules and Regulations for Fiduciary Responsibility." The regulations were filed with the Federal Register on June 21, 1977, and published in the Federal Register on June 24, 1977 (42 FR 32389). Reg. §2550.408b-1 was filed with the Federal Register on July 19, 1989, and published in the Federal Register on July 20, 1989 (54 FR 30520). Interim final regulations revising Reg. §2550.408b-2(c) were issued on July 16, 2010 (75 FR 41600), effective on July 16, 2011. Reg. §2550.408b-2(c) was amended on February 3, 2012 (77 FR 5632). Reg. §2550.408b-2(c) was amended on July 16, 2012 (77 FR 41678)).

[¶ 14,781]

§ 2550.408b-1 General statutory exemption for loans to plan participants and beneficiaries who are parties in interest with respect to the plan.

(a)(1) *In general.* Section 408(b)(1) of the Employee Retirement Income Security Act of 1974 (the Act or ERISA) exempts from the prohibitions of section 406(a), 406(b)(1) and 406(b)(2) loans by a plan to parties in interest who are participants or beneficiaries of the plan, provided that such loans:

(i) Are available to all such participants and beneficiaries on a reasonably equivalent basis;

(ii) Are not made available to highly compensated employees, officers or shareholders in an amount greater than the amount made available to other employees;

(iii) Are made in accordance with specific provisions regarding such loans set forth in the plan;

(iv) Bear a reasonable rate of interest; and

(v) Are adequately secured.

The Internal Revenue Code (the Code) contains parallel provisions to section 408(b)(1) of the Act. Effective, December 31, 1978, section 102 of Reorganization Plan No. 4 of 1987 (43 FR 47713, October 17, 1978) transferred the authority of the Secretary of the Treasury to promulgate regulations of the type published herein to the Secretary of Labor. Therefore, all references herein to section 408(b)(1) of the Act should be read to include reference to the parallel provisions of section 4975(d)(1) of the Code.

Section 1114(b)(15)(B) of the Tax Reform Act of 1986 amended section 408(b)(1)(B) of ERISA by deleting the phrase "highly compensated employees, officers or shareholders" and substituting the phrase "highly compensated employees (within the meaning of section 414(q) of the Internal Revenue Code of 1986)." Thus, for plans with participant loan programs which are subject to the amended section 408(b)(1)(B), the requirements of this regulation should be read to conform with the amendment.

(2) *Scope.* Section 408(b)(1) of the Act does not contain an exemption from acts described in section 406(b)(3) of the Act (prohibiting fiduciaries from receiving consideration for their own personal account from any party dealing with a plan in connection with a transaction involving plan assets). If a loan from a plan to a participant who is a party in interest with respect to that plan involves an act described in section 406(b)(3), such an act constitutes a separate transaction which is not exempt under section 408(b)(1) of the Act. The provisions of section 408(b)(1) are further limited by section 408(d) of the Act (relating to transactions with owner-employees and related persons).

(3) *Loans.* (i) Section 408(b)(1) of the Act provides relief from the prohibitions of section 406(a), 406(b)(1) and 406(b)(2) for the making of a participant loan. The term "participant loan" refers to a loan which is arranged and approved by the fiduciary administering the loan program primarily in the interest of the participant and which otherwise satisfies the criteria set forth in section 408(b)(1) of the Act. The existence of a participant loan or participant loan program will be determined upon consideration of all relevant facts and circumstances. Thus, for example, the mere presence of a loan document appearing to satisfy the requirements of section 408(b)(1) will not be dispositive of whether a participant loan exists where the subsequent administration of the loan indicates that the parties to the loan agreement did not intend the loan to be repaid. Moreover, a loan program containing a precondition designed to benefit a party in interest (other than the participant) is not afforded relief by section 408(b)(1) or this regulation. In this regard, section 408(b)(1) recognizes that a program of participant loans, like other plan investments, must be prudently established and administered for the exclusive purpose of providing benefits to participants and beneficiaries of the plan.

(ii) For the purpose of this regulation, the term "loan" will include any renewal or modification of an existing loan agreement, provided that, at the time of each such renewal or modification, the requirements of section 408(b)(1) and this regulation are met.

(4) *Examples.* The following examples illustrate the provisions of § 2550.408b-1(a).

Example (1): T, a trustee of plan P, has exclusive discretion over the management and disposition of plan assets. As a result, T is a fiduciary with respect to P under section 3(21)(A) of the Act and a party in interest with respect to P pursuant to section 3(14)(A) of the Act. T is also a participant in P. Among T's duties as fiduciary is the administration of a participant loan program which meets the requirements of section 408(b)(1) of the Act. Pursuant to strict objective criteria stated under the program, T, who participates in all loan decisions, receives a loan on the same terms as other participants. Although the exercise of T's discretion on behalf of himself may constitute an act of self-dealing described in section 406(b)(1), section 408(b)(1) provides an exemption from section 406(b)(1). As a result, the loan from P to T would be exempt under section 408(b)(1), provided the conditions of that section are otherwise satisfied.

Example (2): P is a plan covering all the employees of E, the employer who established and maintained P. F is a fiduciary with respect to P and an officer of E. The plan documents governing P give F the authority to establish a participant loan program in accordance with section 408(b)(1) of the Act. Pursuant to an arrangement with E, F establishes such a program but limits the use of loan funds to investments in a limited partnership which is established and maintained by E as general partner. Under these facts, the loan program and any loans made pursuant to this program are outside the scope of relief provided by section 408(b)(1) because the loan program is designed to operate for the benefit of E. Under the circumstances described, the diversion of plan assets for E's benefit would also violate sections 403(c)(1) and 404(a) of the Act.

Example (3): Assume the same facts as in Example 2, above, except that F does not limit the use of loan funds. However, E pressures his employees to borrow funds under P's participant loan program and then reloans the loan proceeds to E. F, unaware of E's activities, arranges and approves the loans. If the loans meet all the conditions of section 408(b)(1), such loans will be exempt under that section. However, E's activities would cause the entire transaction to be viewed as an indirect transfer of plan assets between P and E, who is a party in interest with respect to P, but not the participant borrowing from P. By coercing the employee to engage in loan transactions for its benefit, E has engaged in separate transactions that are not exempt under section 408(b)(1). Accordingly, E would be liable for the payment of excise taxes under section 4975 of the Code.

Example (4): Assume the same facts as in Example 2, above, except that, in return for structuring and administering the loan program as indicated, E agrees to pay F an amount equal to 10 percent of the funds loaned under the program. Such a payment would result in a separate transaction not covered by section 408(b)(1). This transaction would be prohibited under section 406(b)(3) since F would be receiving consideration from a party in connection with a transaction involving plan assets.

Example (5): F is a fiduciary with respect to plan P. D is a party in interest with respect to plan P. Section 406(a)(1)(B) of the Act would prohibit F from causing P to lend money to D. However, F enters into an agreement with Z, a plan participant, whereby F will cause P to make a participant loan to Z with the express understanding that Z will subsequently lend the loan proceeds to D. An examination of Z's credit standing indicates that he is not creditworthy and would not, under normal circumstances, receive a loan under the conditions established by the participant loan program. F's decision to approve the participant loan to Z on the basis of Z's prior agreement to lend the money to D violates the exclusive purpose requirements of sections 403(c) and 404(a). In effect, the entire transaction is viewed as an indirect transfer of plan assets between P and D, and not a loan to a participant exempt under section 408(b)(1). Z's lack of credit standing would also cause the transaction to fail under section 408(b)(1)(A) of the Act.

Example (6): F is a fiduciary with respect to Plan P. Z is a plan participant. Z and D are both parties in interest with respect to P. F approves a participant loan to Z in accordance with the conditions established under the participant loan program. Upon receipt of the loan, Z intends to lend the money to D. If F has approved this loan solely upon consideration of those factors which would be considered in a normal commercial setting by an entity in the business of making comparable loans, Z's subsequent use of the loan proceeds will not affect the determination of whether loans under P's program satisfy the conditions of section 408(b)(1).

Example (7): A is the trustee of a small individual account plan. D, the president of the plan sponsor, is also a participant in the plan. Pursuant to a participant loan program meeting the requirements of section 408(b)(1), D applies for a loan to be secured by a parcel of real property. D does not intend to repay the loan; rather, upon eventual default, he will permit the property to be foreclosed upon and transferred to the plan in discharge of his legal obligation to repay the loan. A, aware of D's intention, approves the loan. D fails to make two consecutive quarterly payments of principal and interest under the note evidencing the loan thereby placing the loan in default. The plan then acquires the real property upon foreclosure. Such facts and circumstances indicate that the payment of money from the plan to D was not a participant loan eligible for the relief afforded by section 408(b)(1). In effect, this transaction is a prohibited sale or exchange of property between a plan and a party in interest from the time D receives the money.

Example (8): Plan P establishes a participant loan program. All loans are subject to the condition that the borrowed funds must be used to finance home purchases. Interest rates on the loans are the same as those charged by a local savings and loan association under similar circumstances. A loan by P to a participant to finance a home purchase would be subject to the relief provided by section 408(b)(1) provided that the conditions of 408(b)(1) are met. A participant loan program which is established to make loans for certain stated purposes (e.g., hardship, college tuition, home purchases, etc.) but which is not otherwise designed to benefit parties in interest (other than plan participants) would not, in itself, cause such program to be ineligible for the relief provided by section 408(b)(1). However, fiduciaries are cautioned that operation of a loan program with limitations may result in loans not being made available to all participants and beneficiaries on a reasonably equivalent basis.

(b) *Reasonably Equivalent Basis.* (1) Loans will not be considered to have been made available to participants and beneficiaries on a reasonably equivalent basis unless:

(i) Such loans are available to all plan participants and beneficiaries without regard to any individual's race, color, religion, sex, age or national origin;

(ii) In making such loans, consideration has been given only to those factors which would be considered in a normal commercial setting by an entity in the business of making similar types of loans. Such factors may include the applicant's creditworthiness and financial need; and

(iii) An evaluation of all relevant facts and circumstances indicates that, in actual practice, loans are not unreasonably withheld from any applicant.

(2) A participant loan program will not fail the requirement of paragraph (b)(1) of this section or § 2550.408b-1(c) if the program establishes a minimum loan amount of up to $1,000, provided that the loans granted meet the requirements of § 2550.408b-1(f).

(3) *Examples.* The following examples illustrate the provisions of § 2550.408b-1(b)(1):

Example (1): T, a trustee of plan P, has exclusive discretion over the management and disposition of plan assets. T's duties include the administration of a participant loan program which meets the requirements of section 408(b)(1) of the Act. T receives a participant loan at a lower interest rate than the rate made available to other plan participants of similar financial condition or creditworthiness with similar security. The loan by P to T would not be covered by the relief provided by section 408(b)(1) because loans under P's program are not available to all plan participants on a reasonably equivalent basis.

Example (2): Same facts as in Example 1, except that T is a member of a committee of trustees responsible for approving participant loans. T pressures the committee to refuse loans to other qualified participants in order to assure that the assets allocated to the participant loan program would be available for a loan by P to T. The loan by P to T would not be covered by the relief provided by section 408(b)(1) since participant loans have not been made available to all participants and beneficiaries on a reasonably equivalent basis.

Example (3): T is the trustee of plan P, which covers the employees of E. A, B and C are employees of E, participants in P, and friends of T. The documents governing P provide that T, in his discretion, may establish a participant loan program meeting certain specified criteria. T institutes such a program and tells A, B and C of his decision. Before T is able to notify P's other participants and beneficiaries of the loan program, A, B, and C file loan applications which, if approved, will use up substantially all of the funds set aside for the loan program. Approval of these applications by T would represent facts and circumstances showing that loans under P's program are not available to all participants and beneficiaries on a reasonably equivalent basis.

(c) *Highly Compensated Employees.* (1) Loans will not be considered to be made available to highly compensated employees, officers or shareholders in an amount greater than the amount made available to other employees if, upon consideration of all relevant facts and circumstances, the program does not operate to exclude large numbers of plan participants from receiving loans under the program.

(2) A participant loan program will not fail to meet the requirement in paragraph (c)(1), of this section, merely because the plan documents specifically governing such loans set forth either (i) a maximum dollar limitation, or (ii) a maximum percentage of vested accrued benefit which no loan may exceed.

(3) If the second alternative in paragraph (c)(2) of this section (maximum percentage of vested accrued benefit) is chosen, a loan program will not fail to meet this requirement solely because maximum loan amounts will vary directly with the size of the participant's accrued benefit.

(4) *Examples.* The following examples illustrate the provisions of § 2550.408b-1(c).

Example (1): The documents governing plan P provide for the establishment of a participant loan program in which the amount of any loan under the program (when added to the outstanding balances of any other loans under the program to the same participant) does not exceed the lesser of (i) $50,000, or (ii) one-half of the present value of that participant's vested accrued benefit under the plan (but not less than $10,000). P's participant loan program does not fail to meet the requirement in section 408(b)(1)(B) of the Act, and would be covered by the relief provided by section 408(b)(1) if the other conditions of that section are met.

Example (2): The documents governing plan T provide for the establishment of a participant loan program in which the minimum loan amount would be $25,000. The documents also require that the only security acceptable under the program would be the participant's vested accrued benefit. A, the plan fiduciary administering the loan program, finds that because of the restrictions in the plan documents only 20 percent of the plan participants, all of whom earn in excess of $75,000 a year, would meet the threshold qualifications for a loan. Most of these participants are high-level supervisors or corporate officers. Based on these facts, it appears that loans under the program would be made available to highly compensated employees in an amount greater than the amount made available to other employees. As a result, the loan program would fail to meet the requirement in section 408(b)(1)(B) of the Act and would not be covered by the relief provided in section 408(b)(1).

(d) *Specific Plan Provisions.* For the purpose of section 408(b)(1) and this regulation, the Department will consider that participant loans granted or renewed at any time prior to the last day of the first plan year beginning on or after January 1, 1989, are made in accordance with specific provisions regarding such loans set forth in the plan if:

(1) The plan provisions regarding such loans contain (at a minimum) an explicit authorization for the plan fiduciary responsible for investing plan assets to establish a participant loan program; and

(2) For participant loans granted or renewed on or after the last day of the first plan year beginning on or after January 1, 1989, the participant loan program which is contained in the plan or in a written document forming part of the plan includes, but need not be limited to, the following:

(i) The identity of the person or positions authorized to administer the participant loan program;

(ii) A procedure for applying for loans;

(iii) The basis on which loans will be approved or denied;

(iv) Limitations (if any) on the types and amount of loans offered;

(v) The procedure under the program for determining a reasonable rate of interest;

(vi) The types of collateral which may secure a participant loan; and

(vii) The events constituting default and the steps that will be taken to preserve plan assets in the event of such default.

Example (1): Plan P authorizes the trustee to establish a participant loan program in accordance with section 408(b)(1) of the Act. Pursuant to this explicit authority, the trustee establishes a written program which contains all of the information required by § 2550.408b-1(d)(2). Loans made pursuant to this authorization and the written loan program will not fail under section 408(b)(1)(C) of the Act merely because the specific provisions regarding such loans are contained in a separate document forming part of the plan. The specific provisions describing the loan program, whether contained in the plan or in a written document forming part of a plan, do affect the rights and obligations of the participants and beneficiaries under the plan and, therefore, must in accordance with section 102(a)(1) of the Act, be disclosed in the plan's summary plan description.

(e) *Reasonable Rate of Interest*. A loan will be considered to bear a reasonable rate of interest if such loan provides the plan with a return commensurate with the interest rates charged by persons in the business of lending money for loans which would be made under similar circumstances.

Example (1): Plan P makes a participant loan to A at the fixed interest rate of 8% for 5 years. The trustees, prior to making the loan, contacted two local banks to determine under what terms the banks would make a similar loan taking into account A's creditworthiness and the collateral offered. One bank would charge a variable rate of 10% adjusted monthly for a similar loan. The other bank would charge a fixed rate of 12% under similar circumstances. Under these facts, the loan to A would not bear a reasonable rate of interest because the loan did not provide P with a return commensurate with interest rates charged by persons in the business of lending money for loans which would be made under similar circumstances. As a result, the loan would fail to meet the requirements of section 408(b)(1)(D) and would not be covered by the relief provided by section 408(b)(1) of the Act.

Example (2): Pursuant to the provisions of plan P's participant loan program, T, the trustee of P, approves a loan to M, a participant and party in interest with respect to P. At the time of execution, the loan meets all of the requirements of section 408(b)(1) of the Act. The loan agreement provides that at the end of two years M must pay the remaining balance in full or the parties may renew for an additional two-year period. At the end of the initial two-year period, the parties agree to renew the loan for an additional two years. At the time of renewal, however, A fails to adjust the interest rate charged on the loan in order to reflect current economic conditions. As a result, the interest rate on the renewal fails to provide a "reasonable rate of interest" as required by section 408(b)(1)(D) of the Act. Under such circumstances, the loan would not be exempt under section 408(b)(1) of the Act from the time of renewal.

Example (3): The documents governing plan P's participant loan program provide that loans must bear an interest rate no higher than the maximum interest rate permitted under State X's usury law. Pursuant to the loan program, P makes a participant loan to A, a plan participant, at a time when the interest rates charged by financial institutions in the community (not subject to the usury limit) for similar loans are higher than the usury limit. Under these circumstances, the loan would not bear a reasonable rate of interest because the loan does not provide P with a return commensurate with the interest rates charged by persons in the business of lending money under similar circumstances. In addition, participant loans that are artificially limited to the maximum usury ceiling then prevailing call into question the status of such loans under sections 403(c) and 404(a) where higher yielding comparable investment opportunities are available to the plan.

(f) *Adequate Security*. (1) A loan will be considered to be adequately secured if the security posted for such loan is something in addition to and supporting a promise to pay, which is so pledged to the plan that it may be sold, foreclosed upon, or otherwise disposed of upon default of repayment of the loan, the value and liquidity of which security is such that it may reasonably be anticipated that loss of principal or interest will not result from the loan. The adequacy of such security will be determined in light of the type and amount of security which would be required in the case of an otherwise identical transaction in a normal commercial setting between unrelated parties on arm's-length terms. A participant's vested accrued benefit under a plan may be used as security for a participant loan to the extent of the plan's ability to satisfy the participant's outstanding obligation in the event of default.

(2) For purposes of this paragraph, (i) no more than 50% of the present value of a participant's vested accrued benefit may be considered by a plan as security for the outstanding balance of all plan loans made to that participant; (ii) a plan will be in compliance with paragraph (f)(2)(i) of this section if, with respect to any participant, it meets the provisions of paragraph (f)(2)(i) of this section immediately after the origination of each participant loan secured in whole or in part by that participant's vested accrued benefit; and (iii) any loan secured in whole or in part by a portion of a participant's vested accrued benefit must also meet the requirements of paragraph (f)(1) of this section.

(g) *Effective Date*. This section is effective for all participant loans granted or renewed after October 18, 1989, except with respect to paragraph (d)(2) of this section relating to specific plan provisions. Paragraph (d)(2) of this section is effective for participant loans granted or renewed on or after the last day of the first plan year beginning on or after January 1, 1989.

[¶ 14,782]

§ 2550.408b-2 **General statutory exemption for services or office space.**

(a) *In general*. Section 408(b)(2) of the Employee Retirement Income Security Act of 1974 (the Act) exempts from the prohibitions of section 406(a) of the Act payment by a plan to a party in interest, including a fiduciary, for office space or any service (or a combination of services) if (1) such office space or service is necessary for the establishment or operation of the plan; (2) such office space or service is furnished under a contract or arrangement which is reasonable; and (3) no more than reasonable compensation is paid for such office space or service. However, section 408(b)((2) does not contain an exemption from acts described in section 406(b)(1) of the Act (relating to fiduciaries dealing with the assets of plans in their own interest or for their own account), section 406(b)(2) of the Act (relating to fiduciaries in their individual or in any other capacity acting in any transaction involving the plan on behalf of a party (or representing a party) whose interests are adverse to the interests of the plan or the interests of its participants or beneficiaries) or section 406(b)(3) of the Act (relating to fiduciaries receiving consideration for their own personal account from any party dealing with a plan in connection with a transaction involving the assets of the plan). Such acts are separate transactions not described in section 408(b)(2). See §§ 2550.408b-2(e) and (f) for guidance as to whether transactions relating to the furnishing of office space or services by fiduciaries to plans involve acts described in section 406(b)(1) of the Act. Section 408(b)(2) of the Act does not contain an exemption from other provisions of the Act, such as section 404, or other provisions of law which may impose requirements or restrictions relating to the transactions which are exempt under section 408(b)(2). See, for example, section 401 of the Internal Revenue Code of 1954. The provisions of section 408(b)(2) of the Act are further limited by section 408(d) of the Act (relating to transactions with owner-employees and related persons).

(b) *Necessary service*. A service is necessary for the establishment or operation of a plan within the meaning of section 408(b)(2) of the Act and § 2550.408b-2(a)(1) if the service is appropriate and helpful to the plan obtaining the service in carrying out the purposes for which the plan is established or maintained. A person providing such a service to a plan (or a person who is a party in interest solely by reason of a relationship to such a service provider described in section 3 (14) (F), (G), (H), or (I) of the Act) may furnish goods which are necessary for the establishment or operation of the plan in the course of, and incidental to, the furnishing of such service to the plan.

(c) *Reasonable contract or arrangement.* No contract or arrangement is reasonable within the meaning of section 408(b)(2) of the Act and § 2550.408b-2(a)(2) if it does not permit termination by the plan without penalty to the plan on reasonably short notice under the circumstances to prevent the plan from becoming locked into an arrangement that has become disadvantageous. A long-term lease which may be terminated prior to its expiration (without penalty to the plan) on reasonably short notice under the circumstances is not generally an unreasonable arrangement merely because of its long term. A provision in a contract or other arrangement which reasonably compensates the service provider or lessor for loss upon early termination of the contract, arrangement or lease is not a penalty. For example, a minimal fee in a service contract which is charged to allow recoupment of reasonable startup costs is not a penalty. Similarly, a provision in a lease for a termination fee that covers reasonably foreseeable expenses related to the vacancy and reletting of the office space upon early termination of the lease is not a penalty. Such a provision does not reasonably compensate for loss if it provides for payment in excess of actual loss or if it fails to require mitigation of damages.

(c) *Reasonable contract or arrangement—*

(1) *Pension plan disclosure.*

(i) *General.* No contract or arrangement for services between a covered plan and a covered service provider, nor any extension or renewal, is reasonable within the meaning of section 408(b)(2) of the Act and paragraph (a)(2) of this section unless the requirements of this paragraph (c)(1) are satisfied. The requirements of this paragraph (c)(1) are independent of fiduciary obligations under section 404 of the Act.

(ii) *Covered plan.* For purposes of this paragraph (c)(1), a "covered plan" is an "employee pension benefit plan" or a "pension plan" within the meaning of section 3(2)(A) (and not described in section 4(b)) of the Act, except that the term "covered plan" shall not include a "simplified employee pension" described in section 408(k) of the Internal Revenue Code of 1986 (the Code), a "simple retirement account" described in section 408(p) of the Code, an individual retirement account described in section 408(a) of the Code, or an individual retirement annuity described in section 408(b) of the Code.

(iii) *Covered service provider.* For purposes of this paragraph (c)(1), a "covered service provider" is a service provider that enters into a contract or arrangement with the covered plan and reasonably expects $1,000 or more in compensation, direct or indirect, to be received in connection with providing one or more of the services described in paragraphs (c)(1)(iii)(A), (B), or (C) of this section pursuant to the contract or arrangement, regardless of whether such services will be performed, or such compensation received, by the covered service provider, an affiliate, or a subcontractor.

(A) *Services as a fiduciary or registered investment adviser.*

(1) Services provided directly to the covered plan as a fiduciary (unless otherwise specified, a "fiduciary" in this paragraph (c)(1) is a fiduciary within the meaning of section 3(21) of the Act);

(2) Services provided as a fiduciary to an investment contract, product, or entity that holds plan assets (as determined pursuant to sections 3(42) and 401 of the Act and 29 CFR 2510.3-101) and in which the covered plan has a direct equity investment (a direct equity investment does not include investments made by the investment contract, product, or entity in which the covered plan invests); or

(3) Services provided directly to the covered plan as an investment adviser registered under either the Investment Advisers Act of 1940 or any State law.

(B) *Certain recordkeeping or brokerage services.* Recordkeeping services or brokerage services provided to a covered plan that is an individual account plan, as defined in section 3(34) of the Act, and that permits participants or beneficiaries to direct the investment of their accounts, if one or more designated investment alternatives will be made available (*e.g.,* through a platform or similar mechanism) in connection with such recordkeeping services or brokerage services.

(C) *Other services for indirect compensation..* Accounting, auditing, actuarial, appraisal, banking, consulting (i.e., consulting re-

lated to the development or implementation of investment policies or objectives, or the selection or monitoring of service providers or plan investments), custodial, insurance, investment advisory (for plan or participants), legal, recordkeeping, securities or other investment brokerage, third party administration, or valuation services provided to the covered plan, for which the covered service provider, an affiliate, or a subcontractor reasonably expects to receive indirect compensation (as defined in paragraph (c)(1)(viii)(B)(2) of this section) or compensation described in paragraph (c)(1)(iv)(C)(3) of this section).

(D) *Limitations.* Notwithstanding paragraphs (c)(1)(iii)(A), (B), or (C) of this section, no person or entity is a "covered service provider" solely by providing services -

(1) As an affiliate or a subcontractor that is performing one or more of the services described in paragraphs (c)(1)(iii)(A), (B), or (C) of this section under the contract or arrangement with the covered plan; or

(2) To an investment contract, product, or entity in which the covered plan invests, regardless of whether or not the investment contract, product, or entity holds assets of the covered plan, other than services as a fiduciary described in paragraph (c)(1)(iii)(A)(2) of this section.

(iv) *Initial disclosure requirements.* The covered service provider must disclose the following information to a responsible plan fiduciary, in writing -

(A) *Services.* A description of the services to be provided to the covered plan pursuant to the contract or arrangement (but not including non-fiduciary services described in paragraph (c)(1)(iii)(D)(2) of this section).

(B) *Status.* If applicable, a statement that the covered service provider, an affiliate, or a subcontractor will provide, or reasonably expects to provide, services pursuant to the contract or arrangement directly to the covered plan (or to an investment contract, product or entity that holds plan assets and in which the covered plan has a direct equity investment) as a fiduciary; and, if applicable, a statement that the covered service provider, an affiliate, or a subcontractor will provide, or reasonably expects to provide, services pursuant to the contract or arrangement directly to the covered plan as an investment adviser registered under either the Investment Advisers Act of 1940 or any State law.

(C) *Compensation.*

(1) *Direct compensation.* A description of all direct compensation (as defined in paragraph (c)(1)(viii)(B)(1) of this section), either in the aggregate or by service, that the covered service provider, an affiliate, or a subcontractor reasonably expects to receive in connection with the services described pursuant to paragraph (c)(1)(iv)(A) of this section.

(2) *Indirect compensation.* A description of all indirect compensation (as defined in paragraph (c)(1)(viii)(B)(2) of this section) that the covered service provider, an affiliate, or a subcontractor reasonably expects to receive in connection with the services described pursuant to paragraph (c)(1)(iv)(A) of this section; including identification of the services for which the indirect compensation will be received and identification of the payer of the indirect compensation.

(3) *Compensation paid among related parties.* A description of any compensation that will be paid among the covered service provider, an affiliate, or a subcontractor, in connection with the services described pursuant to paragraph (c)(1)(iv)(A) of this section if it is set on a transaction basis (e.g., commissions, soft dollars, finder's fees or other similar incentive compensation based on business placed or retained) or is charged directly against the covered plan's investment and reflected in the net value of the investment (e.g., Rule 12b-1 fees); including identification of the services for which such compensation will be paid and identification of the payers and recipients of such compensation (including the status of a payer or recipient as an affiliate or a subcontractor). Compensation must be disclosed pursuant to this paragraph (c)(1)(iv)(C)(3) regardless of whether such compensation also is disclosed pursuant to paragraph (c)(1)(iv)(C)(1) or (2), (F) or (G) of this section. This paragraph (c)(1)(iv)(C)(3) shall not apply to

compensation received by an employee from his or her employer on account of work performed by the employee.

(4) *Compensation for termination of contract or arrangement.* A description of any compensation that the covered service provider, an affiliate, or a subcontractor reasonably expects to receive in connection with termination of the contract or arrangement, and how any prepaid amounts will be calculated and refunded upon such termination.

(D) *Recordkeeping services.* Without regard to the disclosure of compensation pursuant to paragraph (c)(1)(iv)(C), (F), or (G) of this section, if recordkeeping services will be provided to the covered plan -

(1) A description of all direct and indirect compensation that the covered service provider, an affiliate, or a subcontractor reasonably expects to receive in connection with such recordkeeping services; and

(2) If the covered service provider reasonably expects recordkeeping services to be provided, in whole or in part, without explicit compensation for such recordkeeping services, or when compensation for recordkeeping services is offset or rebated based on other compensation received by the covered service provider, an affiliate, or a subcontractor, a reasonable and good faith estimate of the cost to the covered plan of such recordkeeping services, including an explanation of the methodology and assumptions used to prepare the estimate and a detailed explanation of the recordkeeping services that will be provided to the covered plan. The estimate shall take into account, as applicable, the rates that the covered service provider, an affiliate, or a subcontractor would charge to, or be paid by, third parties, or the prevailing market rates charged, for similar recordkeeping services for a similar plan with a similar number of covered participants and beneficiaries.

(E) *Manner of receipt.* A description of the manner in which the compensation described in paragraph (c)(1)(iv)(C) and (D) of this section will be received, such as whether the covered plan will be billed or the compensation will be deducted directly from the covered plan's account(s) or investments.

(F) *Investment disclosure - fiduciary services.* In the case of a covered service provider described in paragraph (c)(1)(iii)(A)(2) of this section, the following additional information with respect to each investment contract, product, or entity that holds plan assets and in which the covered plan has a direct equity investment, and for which fiduciary services will be provided pursuant to the contract or arrangement with the covered plan, unless such information is disclosed to the responsible plan fiduciary by a covered service provider providing recordkeeping services or brokerage services as described in paragraph (c)(1)(iii)(B) of this section -

(1) A description of any compensation that will be charged directly against the amount invested in connection with the acquisition, sale, transfer of, or withdrawal from the investment contract, product, or entity (e.g., sales loads, sales charges, deferred sales charges, redemption fees, surrender charges, exchange fees, account fees, and purchase fees);

(2) A description of the annual operating expenses (e.g., expense ratio) if the return is not fixed; and

(3) A description of any ongoing expenses in addition to annual operating expenses (e.g., wrap fees, mortality and expense fees).

(G) *Investment disclosure - recordkeeping and brokerage services.*

(1) In the case of a covered service provider described in paragraph (c)(1)(iii)(B) of this section, the additional information described in paragraph (c)(1)(iv)(F)(1) through (3) of this section with respect to each designated investment alternative for which recordkeeping services or brokerage services as described in paragraph (c)(1)(iii)(B) of this section will be provided pursuant to the contract or arrangement with the covered plan.

(2) A covered service provider may comply with this paragraph (c)(1)(iv)(G) by providing current disclosure materials of the issuer of the designated investment alternative that include the information described in such paragraph, provided that such issuer is not an affiliate, the disclosure materials are regulated by a State or federal agency, and the covered service provider does not know that the materials are incomplete or inaccurate.

(v) *Timing of initial disclosure requirements; changes.*

(A) A covered service provider must disclose the information required by paragraph (c)(1)(iv) of this section to the responsible plan fiduciary reasonably in advance of the date the contract or arrangement is entered into, and extended or renewed, except that -

(1) When an investment contract, product, or entity is determined not to hold plan assets upon the covered plan's direct equity investment, but subsequently is determined to hold plan assets while the covered plan's investment continues, the information required by paragraph (c)(1)(iv) of this section must be disclosed as soon as practicable, but not later than 30 days from the date on which the covered service provider knows that such investment contract, product, or entity holds plan assets; and

(2) The information described in paragraph (c)(1)(iv)(G) of this section relating to any investment alternative that is not designated at the time the contract or arrangement is entered into must be disclosed as soon as practicable, but not later than the date the investment alternative is designated by the responsible plan fiduciary.

(B) A covered service provider must disclose a change to the information required by paragraph (c)(1)(iv) of this section as soon as practicable, but not later than 60 days from the date on which the covered service provider is informed of such change, unless such disclosure is precluded due to extraordinary circumstances beyond the covered service provider's control, in which case the information must be disclosed as soon as practicable.

(vi) *Reporting and disclosure information; timing.*

(A) Upon request of the responsible plan fiduciary or covered plan administrator, the covered service provider must furnish any other information relating to the compensation received in connection with the contract or arrangement that is required for the covered plan to comply with the reporting and disclosure requirements of Title I of the Act and the regulations, forms and schedules issued thereunder.

(B) The covered service provider must disclose the information required by paragraph (c)(1)(vi)(A) of this section not later than 30 days following receipt of a written request from the responsible plan fiduciary or covered plan administrator, unless such disclosure is precluded due to extraordinary circumstances beyond the covered service provider's control, in which case the information must be disclosed as soon as practicable.

(vii) *Disclosure errors.* No contract or arrangement will fail to be reasonable under this paragraph (c)(1) solely because the covered service provider, acting in good faith and with reasonable diligence, makes an error or omission in disclosing the information required pursuant to paragraph (c)(1)(iv) or (vi) of this section, provided that the covered service provider discloses the correct information to the responsible plan fiduciary as soon as practicable, but not later than 30 days from the date on which the covered service provider knows of such error or omission.

(viii) *Definitions.* For purposes of paragraph (c)(1) of this section:

(A) *Affiliate.* A person's or entity's "affiliate" directly or indirectly (through one or more intermediaries) controls, is controlled by, or is under common control with such person or entity; or is an officer, director, or employee of, or partner in, such person or entity. Unless otherwise specified, an "affiliate" in this paragraph (c)(1) refers to an affiliate of the covered service provider.

(B) *Compensation.* Compensation is anything of monetary value (for example, money, gifts, awards, and trips), but does not include non-monetary compensation valued at $250 or less, in the aggregate, during the term of the contract or arrangement.

(1) *"Direct"* compensation is compensation received directly from the covered plan.

(2) "*Indirect*" compensation is compensation received from any source other than the covered plan, the plan sponsor, the covered service provider, an affiliate, or a subcontractor (if the subcontractor receives such compensation in connection with services performed under the subcontractor's contract or arrangement described in paragraph (c)(1)(viii)(F) of this section).

(3) A description or an estimate of compensation may be expressed as a monetary amount, formula, percentage of the covered plan's assets, or a per capita charge for each participant or beneficiary or, if the compensation cannot reasonably be expressed in such terms, by any other reasonable method. Any description or estimate must contain sufficient information to permit evaluation of the reasonableness of the compensation.

(C) *Designated investment alternative.* A "designated investment alternative" is any investment alternative designated by a fiduciary into which participants and beneficiaries may direct the investment of assets held in, or contributed to, their individual accounts. The term "designated investment alternative" shall not include brokerage windows, selfdirected brokerage accounts, or similar plan arrangements that enable participants and beneficiaries to select investments beyond those specifically designated.

(D) *Recordkeeping services.* "Recordkeeping services" include services related to plan administration and monitoring of plan and participant and beneficiary transactions (*e.g.*, enrollment, payroll deductions and contributions, offering designated investment alternatives and other covered plan investments, loans, withdrawals and distributions); and the maintenance of covered plan and participant and beneficiary accounts, records, and statements.

(E) *Responsible plan fiduciary.* A "responsible plan fiduciary" is a fiduciary with authority to cause the covered plan to enter into, or extend or renew, the contract or arrangement.

(F) *Subcontractor.* A "subcontractor" is any person or entity (or an affiliate of such person or entity) that is not an affiliate of the covered service provider and that, pursuant to a contract or arrangement with the covered service provider or an affiliate, reasonably expects to receive $1,000 or more in compensation for performing one or more services described pursuant to paragraph (c)(1)(iii)(A) through (C) of this section provided for by the contract or arrangement with the covered plan.

(ix) *Exemption for responsible plan fiduciary.* Pursuant to section 408(a) of the Act, the restrictions of section 406(a)(1)(C) and (D) of the Act shall not apply to a responsible plan fiduciary, notwithstanding any failure by a covered service provider to disclose information required by paragraph (c)(1)(iv) or (vi) of this section, if the following conditions are met:

(A) The responsible plan fiduciary did not know that the covered service provider failed or would fail to make required disclosures and reasonably believed that the covered service provider disclosed the information required by paragraph (c)(1)(iv) or (vi) of this section;

(B) The responsible plan fiduciary, upon discovering that the covered service provider failed to disclose the required information, requests in writing that the covered service provider furnish such information;

(C) If the covered service provider fails to comply with such written request within 90 days of the request, then the responsible plan fiduciary notifies the Department of Labor of the covered service provider's failure, in accordance with paragraph (c)(1)(ix)(E) of this section;

(D) The notice shall contain the following information -

(1) The name of the covered plan;

(2) The plan number used for the covered plan's Annual Report;

(3) The plan sponsor's name, address, and EIN;

(4) The name, address, and telephone number of the responsible plan fiduciary;

(5) The name, address, phone number, and, if known, EIN of the covered service provider;

(6) A description of the services provided to the covered plan;

(7) A description of the information that the covered service provider failed to disclose;

(8) The date on which such information was requested in writing from the covered service provider; and

(9) A statement as to whether the covered service provider continues to provide services to the plan;

(E) The notice shall be filed with the Department not later than 30 days following the earlier of -

(1) The covered service provider's refusal to furnish the information requested by the written request described in paragraph (c)(1)(ix)(B) of this section; or

(2) 90 days after the written request referred to in paragraph (c)(1)(ix)(B) of this section is made;

(F) The notice required by paragraph (c)(1)(ix)(C) of this section shall be sent to the following address: U.S. Department of Labor, Employee Benefits Security Administration, Office of Enforcement, 200 Constitution Ave., N.W., Suite 600, Washington, DC 20210; or may be sent electronically to *OEDelinquentSPnotice@dol.gov;* and

(G) The responsible plan fiduciary, following discovery of a failure to disclose required information, shall determine whether to terminate or continue the contract or arrangement. In making such a determination, the responsible plan fiduciary shall evaluate the nature of the failure, the availability, qualifications, and cost of replacement service providers, and the covered service provider's response to notification of the failure.

(x) *Preemption of State law.* Nothing in this section shall be construed to supersede any provision of State law that governs disclosures by parties that provide the services described in this section, except to the extent that such law prevents the application of a requirement of this section.

(xi) *Internal Revenue Code.* Section 4975(d)(2) of the Code contains provisions parallel to section 408(b)(2) of the Act. Effective December 31, 1978, section 102 of the Reorganization Plan No. 4 of 1978, 5 U.S.C. App. 214 (2000 ed.), transferred the authority of the Secretary of the Treasury to promulgate regulations of the type published herein to the Secretary of Labor. All references herein to section 408(b)(2) of the Act and the regulations thereunder should be read to include reference to the parallel provisions of section 4975(d)(2) of the Code and regulations thereunder at 26 CFR 54.4975-6.

(xii) *Effective date.* Paragraph (c) of this section shall be effective on April 1, 2012. Paragraph (c)(1) of this section shall apply to contracts or arrangements between covered plans and covered service providers as of the effective date, without regard to whether the contract or arrangement was entered into prior to such date; for contracts or arrangement entered into prior to the effective date, the information required to be disclosed pursuant to paragraph (c)(1)(iv) of this section must be furnished no later than the effective date. [Amended 7/19/2011 by 76 FR 42539.]

(2) *Welfare plan disclosure.* [Reserved]

(3) *Termination of contract or arrangement.* No contract or arrangement is reasonable within the meaning of section 408(b)(2) of the Act and paragraph (a)(2) of this section if it does not permit termination by the plan without penalty to the plan on reasonably short notice under the circumstances to prevent the plan from becoming locked into an arrangement that has become disadvantageous. A long-term lease which may be terminated prior to its expiration (without penalty to the plan) on reasonably short notice under the circumstances is not generally an unreasonable arrangement merely because of its long term. A provision in a contract or other arrangement which reasonably compensates the service provider or lessor for loss upon early termination of the contract, arrangement, or lease is not a penalty. For example, a minimal fee in a service contract which is charged to allow recoupment of reasonable start-up costs is not a penalty. Similarly, a provision in a lease for a termination fee that covers reasonably foreseeable expenses related to the vacancy and reletting of the office space upon early termination of the lease is not a penalty. Such a provision does not reasonably compensate for loss if it provides for payment in

excess of actual loss or if it fails to require mitigation of damages. [Added on July 16, 2010 by 75 FR 41600.]

(c) *Reasonable contract or arrangement—*

(1) *Pension plan disclosure.*

(i) *General.* No contract or arrangement for services between a covered plan and a covered service provider, nor any extension or renewal, is reasonable within the meaning of section 408(b)(2) of the Act and paragraph (a)(2) of this section unless the requirements of this paragraph (c)(1) are satisfied. The requirements of this paragraph (c)(1) are independent of fiduciary obligations under section 404 of the Act.

(ii) *Covered plan.* For purposes of this paragraph (c)(1), a "covered plan" is an "employee pension benefit plan" or a "pension plan" within the meaning of section 3(2)(A) (and not described in section 4(b)) of the Act, except that the term "covered plan" shall not include a "simplified employee pension" described in section 408(k) of the Internal Revenue Code of 1986 (the Code); a "simple retirement account" described in section 408(p) of the Code; an individual retirement account described in section 408(a) of the Code; an individual retirement annuity described in section 408(b) of the Code; or annuity contracts and custodial accounts described in section 403(b) of the Code issued to a current or former employee before January 1, 2009, for which the employer ceased to have any obligation to make contributions (including employee salary reduction contributions), and in fact ceased making contributions to the contract or account for periods before January 1, 2009, and for which all of the rights and benefits under the contract or account are legally enforceable against the insurer or custodian by the individual owner of the contract or account without any involvement by the employer, and for which such individual owner is fully vested in the contract or account.

(iii) *Covered service provider.* For purposes of this paragraph (c)(1), a "covered service provider" is a service provider that enters into a contract or arrangement with the covered plan and reasonably expects $1,000 or more in compensation, direct or indirect, to be received in connection with providing one or more of the services described in paragraphs (c)(1)(iii)(A), (B), or (C) of this section pursuant to the contract or arrangement, regardless of whether such services will be performed, or such compensation received, by the covered service provider, an affiliate, or a subcontractor.

(A) *Services as a fiduciary or registered investment adviser.*

(1) Services provided directly to the covered plan as a fiduciary (unless otherwise specified, a "fiduciary" in this paragraph (c)(1) is a fiduciary within the meaning of section 3(21) of the Act);

(2) Services provided as a fiduciary to an investment contract, product, or entity that holds plan assets (as determined pursuant to sections 3(42) and 401 of the Act and 29 CFR § 2510.3-101) and in which the covered plan has a direct equity investment (a direct equity investment does not include investments made by the investment contract, product, or entity in which the covered plan invests); or

(3) Services provided directly to the covered plan as an investment adviser registered under either the Investment Advisers Act of 1940 or any State law.

(B) *Certain recordkeeping or brokerage services.* Recordkeeping services or brokerage services provided to a covered plan that is an individual account plan, as defined in section 3(34) of the Act, and that permits participants or beneficiaries to direct the investment of their accounts, if one or more designated investment alternatives will be made available (*e.g.*, through a platform or similar mechanism) in connection with such recordkeeping services or brokerage services.

(C) *Other services for indirect compensation.* Accounting, auditing, actuarial, appraisal, banking, consulting (*i.e.*, consulting related to the development or implementation of investment policies or objectives, or the selection or monitoring of service providers or plan investments), custodial, insurance, investment advisory (for plan or participants), legal, recordkeeping, securities or other investment brokerage, third party administration, or valuation services provided to the covered plan, for which the covered service provider, an affiliate, or a subcontractor reasonably expects to receive indirect compensation (as

defined in paragraph (c)(1)(viii)(B)(*2*) of this section) or compensation described in paragraph (c)(1)(iv)(C)(*3*) of this section).

(D) *Limitations.* Notwithstanding paragraphs (c)(1)(iii)(A), (B), or (C) of this section, no person or entity is a "covered service provider" solely by providing services—

(1) As an affiliate or a subcontractor that is performing one or more of the services described in paragraphs (c)(1)(iii)(A), (B), or (C) of this section under the contract or arrangement with the covered plan; or

(2) To an investment contract, product, or entity in which the covered plan invests, regardless of whether or not the investment contract, product, or entity holds assets of the covered plan, other than services as a fiduciary described in paragraph (c)(1)(iii)(A)(*2*) of this section.

(iv) *Initial disclosure requirements.* The covered service provider must disclose the following information to a responsible plan fiduciary, in writing—

(A) *Services.* A description of the services to be provided to the covered plan pursuant to the contract or arrangement (but not including non-fiduciary services described in paragraph (c)(1)(iii)(D)(*2*) of this section).

(B) *Status.* If applicable, a statement that the covered service provider, an affiliate, or a subcontractor will provide, or reasonably expects to provide, services pursuant to the contract or arrangement directly to the covered plan (or to an investment contract, product or entity that holds plan assets and in which the covered plan has a direct equity investment) as a fiduciary (within the meaning of section 3(21) of the Act); and, if applicable, a statement that the covered service provider, an affiliate, or a subcontractor will provide, or reasonably expects to provide, services pursuant to the contract or arrangement directly to the covered plan as an investment adviser registered under either the Investment Advisers Act of 1940 or any State law.

(C) *Compensation.*

(1) *Direct compensation.* A description of all direct compensation (as defined in paragraph (c)(1)(viii)(B)(*1*) of this section), either in the aggregate or by service, that the covered service provider, an affiliate, or a subcontractor reasonably expects to receive in connection with the services described pursuant to paragraph (c)(1)(iv)(A) of this section.

(2) *Indirect compensation.* A description of all indirect compensation (as defined in paragraph (c)(1)(viii)(B)(*2*) of this section) that the covered service provider, an affiliate, or a subcontractor reasonably expects to receive in connection with the services described pursuant to paragraph (c)(1)(iv)(A) of this section; including identification of the services for which the indirect compensation will be received, identification of the payer of the indirect compensation, and a description of the arrangement between the payer and the covered service provider, an affiliate, or a subcontractor, as applicable, pursuant to which such indirect compensation is paid.

(3) *Compensation paid among related parties.* A description of any compensation that will be paid among the covered service provider, an affiliate, or a subcontractor, in connection with the services described pursuant to paragraph (c)(1)(iv)(A) of this section if it is set on a transaction basis (*e.g.*, commissions, soft dollars, finder's fees or other similar incentive compensation based on business placed or retained) or is charged directly against the covered plan's investment and reflected in the net value of the investment (*e.g.*, Rule 12b-1 fees); including identification of the services for which such compensation will be paid and identification of the payers and recipients of such compensation (including the status of a payer or recipient as an affiliate or a subcontractor). Compensation must be disclosed pursuant to this paragraph (c)(1)(iv)(C)(*3*) regardless of whether such compensation also is disclosed pursuant to paragraph (c)(1)(iv)(C)(*1*) or (*2*), (c)(1)(iv)(E), or (c)(1)(iv)(F) of this section. This paragraph (c)(1)(iv)(C)(*3*) shall not apply to compensation received by an employee from his or her employer on account of work performed by the employee.

(4) Compensation for termination of contract or arrangement. A description of any compensation that the covered service provider, an affiliate, or a subcontractor reasonably expects to receive in connection with termination of the contract or arrangement, and how any prepaid amounts will be calculated and refunded upon such termination.

(D) *Recordkeeping services.* Without regard to the disclosure of compensation pursuant to paragraph (c)(1)(iv)(C), (c)(1)(iv)(E), or (c)(1)(iv)(F) of this section, if recordkeeping services will be provided to the covered plan—

(1) A description of all direct and indirect compensation that the covered service provider, an affiliate, or a subcontractor reasonably expects to receive in connection with such recordkeeping services; and

(2) If the covered service provider reasonably expects recordkeeping services to be provided, in whole or in part, without explicit compensation for such recordkeeping services, or when compensation for recordkeeping services is offset or rebated based on other compensation received by the covered service provider, an affiliate, or a subcontractor, a reasonable and good faith estimate of the cost to the covered plan of such recordkeeping services, including an explanation of the methodology and assumptions used to prepare the estimate and a detailed explanation of the recordkeeping services that will be provided to the covered plan. The estimate shall take into account, as applicable, the rates that the covered service provider, an affiliate, or a subcontractor would charge to, or be paid by, third parties, or the prevailing market rates charged, for similar recordkeeping services for a similar plan with a similar number of covered participants and beneficiaries.

(E) *Investment disclosure—fiduciary services.* In the case of a covered service provider described in paragraph (c)(1)(iii)(A)(*2*) of this section, the following additional information with respect to each investment contract, product, or entity that holds plan assets and in which the covered plan has a direct equity investment, and for which fiduciary services will be provided pursuant to the contract or arrangement with the covered plan, unless such information is disclosed to the responsible plan fiduciary by a covered service provider providing recordkeeping services or brokerage services as described in paragraph (c)(1)(iii)(B) of this section—

(1) A description of any compensation that will be charged directly against an investment, such as commissions, sales loads, sales charges, deferred sales charges, redemption fees, surrender charges, exchange fees, account fees, and purchase fees; and that is not included in the annual operating expenses of the investment contract, product, or entity;

(2) A description of the annual operating expenses (*e.g.,* expense ratio) if the return is not fixed and any ongoing expenses in addition to annual operating expenses (*e.g.,* wrap fees, mortality and expense fees), or, for an investment contract, product, or entity that is a designated investment alternative, the total annual operating expenses expressed as a percentage and calculated in accordance with 29 CFR § 2550.404a-5(h)(5); and

(3) For an investment contract, product, or entity that is a designated investment alternative, any other information or data about the designated investment alternative that is within the control of, or reasonably available to, the covered service provider and that is required for the covered plan administrator to comply with the disclosure obligations described in 29 CFR § 2550.404a-5(d)(1).

(F) *Investment disclosure—recordkeeping and brokerage services.*

(1) In the case of a covered service provider described in paragraph (c)(1)(iii)(B) of this section, the additional information described in paragraph (c)(1)(iv)(E)(*1*) through (*3*) of this section with respect to each designated investment alternative for which recordkeeping services or brokerage services as described in paragraph (c)(1)(iii)(B) of this section will be provided pursuant to the contract or arrangement with the covered plan.

(2) A covered service provider may comply with this paragraph (c)(1)(iv)(F) by providing current disclosure materials of the issuer of the designated investment alternative, or information

replicated from such materials, that include the information described in such paragraph, provided that:

(i) The issuer is not an affiliate;

(ii) The issuer is a registered investment company, an insurance company qualified to do business in any State, an issuer of a publicly traded security, or a financial institution supervised by a State or federal agency; and

(iii) The covered service provider acts in good faith and does not know that the materials are incomplete or inaccurate, and furnishes the responsible plan fiduciary with a statement that the covered service provider is making no representations as to the completeness or accuracy of such materials.

(G) *Manner of receipt.* A description of the manner in which the compensation described in paragraph (c)(1)(iv)(C) through (F) of this section, as applicable, will be received, such as whether the covered plan will be billed or the compensation will be deducted directly from the covered plan's account(s) or investments.

(H) *Guide to initial disclosures.* [Reserved]

(v) *Timing of initial disclosure requirements; changes.*

(A) A covered service provider must disclose the information required by paragraph (c)(1)(iv) of this section to the responsible plan fiduciary reasonably in advance of the date the contract or arrangement is entered into, and extended or renewed, except that—

(1) When an investment contract, product, or entity is determined not to hold plan assets upon the covered plan's direct equity investment, but subsequently is determined to hold plan assets while the covered plan's investment continues, the information required by paragraph (c)(1)(iv) of this section must be disclosed as soon as practicable, but not later than 30 days from the date on which the covered service provider knows that such investment contract, product, or entity holds plan assets; and

(2) The information described in paragraph (c)(1)(iv)(F) of this section relating to any investment alternative that is not designated at the time the contract or arrangement is entered into must be disclosed as soon as practicable, but not later than the date the investment alternative is designated by the covered plan.

(B)*(1)* A covered service provider must disclose a change to the information required by paragraph (c)(1)(iv)(A) through (D), and (G) of this section as soon as practicable, but not later than 60 days from the date on which the covered service provider is informed of such change, unless such disclosure is precluded due to extraordinary circumstances beyond the covered service provider's control, in which case the information must be disclosed as soon as practicable.

(2) A covered service provider must, at least annually, disclose any changes to the information required by paragraph (c)(1)(iv)(E) and (F) of this section.

(vi) *Reporting and disclosure information; timing.*

(A) Upon the written request of the responsible plan fiduciary or covered plan administrator, the covered service provider must furnish any other information relating to the compensation received in connection with the contract or arrangement that is required for the covered plan to comply with the reporting and disclosure requirements of Title I of the Act and the regulations, forms and schedules issued thereunder.

(B) The covered service provider must disclose the information required by paragraph (c)(1)(vi)(A) of this section reasonably in advance of the date upon which such responsible plan fiduciary or covered plan administrator states that it must comply with the applicable reporting or disclosure requirement, unless such disclosure is precluded due to extraordinary circumstances beyond the covered service provider's control, in which case the information must be disclosed as soon as practicable.

(vii) *Disclosure errors.* No contract or arrangement will fail to be reasonable under this paragraph (c)(1) solely because the covered service provider, acting in good faith and with reasonable diligence, makes an error or omission in disclosing the information required pursuant to paragraph (c)(1)(iv) of this section (or a change to such information disclosed pursuant to paragraph (c)(1)(v)(B) of this section) or paragraph (c)(1)(vi) of this section, provided that the covered service provider discloses the correct information to the responsible plan fiduciary as soon as practicable, but not later than 30 days from the date on which the covered service provider knows of such error or omission.

(viii) *Definitions.* For purposes of paragraph (c)(1) of this section:

(A) *Affiliate.* A person's or entity's "affiliate" directly or indirectly (through one or more intermediaries) controls, is controlled by, or is under common control with such person or entity; or is an officer, director, or employee of, or partner in, such person or entity. Unless otherwise specified, an "affiliate" in this paragraph (c)(1) refers to an affiliate of the covered service provider.

(B) *Compensation.* Compensation is anything of monetary value (for example , money, gifts, awards, and trips), but does not include non-monetary compensation valued at $250 or less, in the aggregate, during the term of the contract or arrangement.

(1) "Direct" compensation is compensation received directly from the covered plan.

(2) "Indirect" compensation is compensation received from any source other than the covered plan, the plan sponsor, the covered service provider, or an affiliate. Compensation received from a subcontractor is indirect compensation, unless it is received in connection with services performed under the subcontractor's contract or arrangement described in paragraph (c)(1)(viii)(F) of this section.

(3) A description of compensation or cost may be expressed as a monetary amount, formula, percentage of the covered plan's assets, or a per capita charge for each participant or beneficiary or, if the compensation or cost cannot reasonably be expressed in such terms, by any other reasonable method. The description may include a reasonable and good faith estimate if the covered service provider cannot otherwise readily describe compensation or cost and the covered service provider explains the methodology and assumptions used to prepare such estimate. Any description, including any estimate of recordkeeping cost under paragraph (c)(1)(iv)(D), must contain sufficient information to permit evaluation of the reasonableness of the compensation or cost.

(C) *Designated investment alternative.* A "designated investment alternative" is any investment alternative designated by the covered plan into which participants and beneficiaries may direct the investment of assets held in, or contributed to, their individual accounts. The term "designated investment alternative" shall not include brokerage windows, self-directed brokerage accounts, or similar plan arrangements that enable participants and beneficiaries to select investments beyond those designated by the covered plan.

(D) *Recordkeeping services.* "Recordkeeping services" include services related to plan administration and monitoring of plan and participant and beneficiary transactions (*e.g.*, enrollment, payroll deductions and contributions, offering designated investment alternatives and other covered plan investments, loans, withdrawals and distributions); and the maintenance of covered plan and participant and beneficiary accounts, records, and statements.

(E) *Responsible plan fiduciary.* A "responsible plan fiduciary" is a fiduciary with authority to cause the covered plan to enter into, or extend or renew, the contract or arrangement.

(F) *Subcontractor.* A "subcontractor" is any person or entity (or an affiliate of such person or entity) that is not an affiliate of the covered service provider and that, pursuant to a contract or arrangement with the covered service provider or an affiliate, reasonably expects to receive $1,000 or more in compensation for performing one or more services described pursuant to paragraph (c)(1)(iii)(A) through (C) of this section provided for by the contract or arrangement with the covered plan.

(ix) *Exemption for responsible plan fiduciary.* Pursuant to section 408(a) of the Act, the restrictions of section 406(a)(1)(C) and (D) of the Act shall not apply to a responsible plan fiduciary, notwithstanding any failure by a covered service provider to disclose information required by paragraph (c)(1)(iv) or (vi) of this section, if the following conditions are met:

(A) The responsible plan fiduciary did not know that the covered service provider failed or would fail to make required disclosures and reasonably believed that the covered service provider disclosed the information required by paragraph (c)(1)(iv) or (vi) of this section;

(B) The responsible plan fiduciary, upon discovering that the covered service provider failed to disclose the required information, requests in writing that the covered service provider furnish such information;

(C) If the covered service provider fails to comply with such written request within 90 days of the request, then the responsible plan fiduciary notifies the Department of Labor of the covered service provider's failure, in accordance with paragraph (c)(1)(ix)(E) of this section;

(D) The notice shall contain the following information—

(1) The name of the covered plan;

(2) The plan number used for the covered plan's Annual Report;

(3) The plan sponsor's name, address, and EIN;

(4) The name, address, and telephone number of the responsible plan fiduciary;

(5) The name, address, phone number, and, if known, EIN of the covered service provider;

(6) A description of the services provided to the covered plan;

(7) A description of the information that the covered service provider failed to disclose;

(8) The date on which such information was requested in writing from the covered service provider; and

(9) A statement as to whether the covered service provider continues to provide services to the plan;

(E) The notice shall be filed with the Department not later than 30 days following the earlier of—

(1) The covered service provider's refusal to furnish the information requested by the written request described in paragraph (c)(1)(ix)(B) of this section; or

(2) 90 days after the written request referred to in paragraph (c)(1)(ix)(B) of this section is made;

(F) The notice required by paragraph (c)(1)(ix)(C) of this section shall be furnished to the U.S. Department of Labor electronically in accordance with instructions published by the Department; or may be sent to the following address: U.S. Department of Labor, Employee Benefits Security Administration, Office of Enforcement, P.O. Box 75296, Washington, DC 20013; and [Amended 7/16/2012 (77 FR 41678).]

(G) If the covered service provider fails to comply with the written request referred to in paragraph (c)(1)(ix)(C) of this section within 90 days of such request, the responsible plan fiduciary shall determine whether to terminate or continue the contract or arrangement consistent with its duty of prudence under section 404 of the Act. If the requested information relates to future services and is not disclosed promptly after the end of the 90-day period, then the responsible plan fiduciary shall terminate the contract or arrangement as expeditiously as possible, consistent with such duty of prudence.

(x) *Preemption of State law.* Nothing in this section shall be construed to supersede any provision of State law that governs disclosures by parties that provide the services described in this section, except to the extent that such law prevents the application of a requirement of this section.

(xi) *Internal Revenue Code.* Section 4975(d)(2) of the Code contains provisions parallel to section 408(b)(2) of the Act. Effective December 31, 1978, section 102 of the Reorganization Plan No. 4 of 1978, 5 U.S.C. App. 214 (2000 ed.), transferred the authority of the Secretary of the Treasury to promulgate regulations of the type published herein to the Secretary of Labor. All references herein to section 408(b)(2) of the Act and the regulations thereunder should be read to include reference to the parallel provisions of section 4975(d)(2) of the Code and regulations thereunder at 26 CFR 54.4975-6.

(xii) *Effective date.* Paragraph (c) of this section shall be effective on July 1, 2012. Paragraph (c)(1) of this section shall apply to contracts or arrangements between covered plans and covered service providers as of the effective date, without regard to whether the contract or arrangement was entered into prior to such date; for contracts or arrangement entered into prior to the effective date, the information required to be disclosed pursuant to paragraph (c)(1)(iv) of this section must be furnished no later than the effective date.

(2) *Welfare plan disclosure.* [Reserved]

(3) *Termination of contract or arrangement.* No contract or arrangement is reasonable within the meaning of section 408(b)(2) of the Act and paragraph (a)(2) of this section if it does not permit termination by the plan without penalty to the plan on reasonably short notice under the circumstances to prevent the plan from becoming locked into an arrangement that has become disadvantageous. A long-term lease which may be terminated prior to its expiration (without penalty to the plan) on reasonably short notice under the circumstances is not generally an unreasonable arrangement merely because of its long term. A provision in a contract or other arrangement which reasonably compensates the service provider or lessor for loss upon early termination of the contract, arrangement, or lease is not a penalty. For example, a minimal fee in a service contract which is charged to allow recoupment of reasonable start-up costs is not a penalty. Similarly, a provision in a lease for a termination fee that covers reasonably foreseeable expenses related to the vacancy and reletting of the office space upon early termination of the lease is not a penalty. Such a provision does not reasonably compensate for loss if it provides for payment in excess of actual loss or if it fails to require mitigation of damages. [Added on 2/3/2012 by 77 FR 5632.]

(d) *Reasonable compensation.* Section 408(b)(2) of the Act and § 2550.408b-2(a)(3) permit a plan to pay a party in interest reasonable compensation for the provision of office space or services described in section 408(b)(2). Section 2550.408c-2 of these regulations contains provisions relating to what constitutes reasonable compensation for the provision of services.

(e) *Transactions with fiduciaries.* (1) *In general.* If the furnishing of office space or a service involves an act described in section 406(b) of the Act (relating to acts involving conflicts of interest by fiduciaries), such an act constitutes a separate transaction which is not exempt under section 408(b)(2) of the Act. The prohibitions of section 406(b) supplement the other prohibitions of section 406(a) of the Act by imposing on parties in interest who are fiduciaries a duty of undivided loyalty to the plans for which they act. These prohibitions are imposed upon fiduciaries to deter them from exercising the authority, control, or responsibility which makes such persons fiduciaries when they have interests which may conflict with the interests of the plans for which they act. In such cases, the fiduciaries have interests in the transactions which may affect the exercise of their best judgment as fiduciaries. Thus, a fiduciary may not use the authority, control, or responsibility which makes such a person a fiduciary to cause a plan to pay an additional fee to such fiduciary (or to a person in which such fiduciary has an interest which may affect the exercise of such fiduciary's best judgment as a fiduciary) to provide a service. Nor may a fiduciary use such authority, control, or responsibility to cause a plan to enter into a transaction involving plan assets whereby such fiduciary (or a person in which such fiduciary has an interest which may affect the exercise of such fiduciary's best judgment as a fiduciary) will receive consideration from a third party in connection with such transaction. A person in which a fiduciary has an interest which may affect the exercise of such fiduciary's best judgment as a fiduciary includes, for example, a person who is a party in interest by reason of a relationship to such fiduciary described in section 3(14) (E), (F), (G), (H), or (I).

(2) *Transactions not described in section 406(b)(1).* A fiduciary does not engage in an act described in section 406(b)(1) of the Act if the fiduciary does not use any of the authority, control or responsibility which makes such person a fiduciary to cause a plan to pay additional fees for a service furnished by such fiduciary or to pay a fee for a service furnished by a person in which such fiduciary has an interest which may affect the exercise of such fiduciary's best judgment as a fiduciary. This may occur, for example, when one fiduciary is retained

on behalf of a plan by a second fiduciary to provide a service for an additional fee. However, because the authority, control or responsibility which makes a person a fiduciary may be exercised "in effect" as well as in form, mere approval of the transaction by a second fiduciary does not mean that the first fiduciary has not used any of the authority, control or responsibility which makes such person a fiduciary to cause the plan to pay the first fiduciary an additional fee for a service. See paragraph (f) below.

(3) *Services without compensation.* If a fiduciary provides services to a plan without the receipt of compensation or other consideration (other than reimbursement of direct expenses properly and actually incurred in the performance of such services within the meaning of § 2550.408c-2(b)(3)), the provision of such services does not, in and of itself, constitute an act described in section 406(b) of the Act. The allowance of a deduction to an employer under section 162 or 212 of the Code for the expense incurred in furnishing office space or services to a plan established or maintained by such employer does not constitute compensation or other consideration.

(f) *Examples.* The provisions of § 2550.408b-2(e) may be illustrated by the following examples.

Example (1). E, an employer whose employees are covered by plan P, is a fiduciary of P. I is a professional investment adviser in which E has no interest which may affect the exercise of E's best judgment as a fiduciary. E causes P to retain I to provide certain kinds of investment advisory services of a type which causes I to be a fiduciary of P under section 3(21)(A)(ii) of the Act. Thereafter, I proposes to perform for additional fees portfolio evaluation services in addition to the services currently provided. The provision of such services is arranged by I and approved on behalf of the plan by E. I has not engaged in an act described in section 406(b)(1) of the Act, because I did not use any of the authority, control or responsibility which makes I a fiduciary (the provision of investment advisory services) to cause the plan to pay I additional fees for the provision of the portfolio evaluation services. E has not engaged in an act which is described in section 406(b)(1). E, as the fiduciary who has the responsibility to be prudent in his selection and retention of I and the other investment advisers of the plan, has an interest in the purchase by the plan of portfolio evaluation services. However, such an interest is not an interest which may affect the exercise of E's best judgment as a fiduciary.

Example (2). D, a trustee of plan P with discretion over the management and disposition of plan assets, relies on the advice of C, a consultant to P, as to the investment of plan assets, thereby making C a fiduciary of the plan. On January 1, 1978, C recommends to D that the plan purchase an insurance policy from U, an insurance company which is not a party in interest with respect to P. C thoroughly explains the reasons for the recommendation and makes a full disclosure concerning the fact that C will receive a commission from U upon the purchase of the policy by P. D considers the recommendation and approves the purchase of the policy by P. C receives a commission. Under such circumstances, C has engaged in an act described in section 406(b)(1) of the Act (as well as sections 406(b)(2) and (3) of the Act) because C is in fact exercising the authority, control or responsibility which makes C a fiduciary to cause the plan to purchase the policy. However, the transaction is exempt from the prohibited transaction provisions of section 406 of the Act, if the requirements of Prohibited Transaction Exemption 77-9 are met.

Example (3). Assume the same facts as in Example (2) except that the nature of C's relationship with the plan is not such that C is a fiduciary of P. The purchase of the insurance policy does not involve an act described in section 406(b)(1) of the Act (or sections 406(b) (2) or (3) of the Act) because such sections only apply to acts by fiduciaries.

Example (4). E, an employer whose employees are covered by plan P, is a fiduciary with respect to P. A, who is not a party in interest with respect to P, persuades E that the plan needs the services of a professional investment adviser and that A should be hired to provide the investment advice. Accordingly, E causes P to hire A to provide investment advice of the type which makes A a fiduciary under § 2510.3-21(c)(1)(ii)(B). Prior to the expiration of A's first contract with P, A persuades E to cause P to renew A's contract with P to provide the same services for additional fees in view of the increased costs in providing such services. During the period of A's second contract, A provides additional investment advice services for which no additional charge is made. Prior to the expiration of A's second contract, A persuades E to cause P to renew his contract for additional fees in view of the additional services A is providing. A has not engaged in an act described in section 406(b)(1) of the Act, because A has not used any of the authority, control or responsibility which makes A a fiduciary (the provision of investment advice) to cause the plan to pay additional fees for A's services.

Example (5). F, a trustee of plan P with discretion over the management and disposition of plan assets, retains C to provide administrative services to P of the type which makes C a fiduciary under section 3(21)(A)(iii). Thereafter, C retains F to provide for additional fees actuarial and various kinds of administrative services in addition to the services F is currently providing to P. Both F and C have engaged in an act described in section 406(b)(1) of the Act. F, regardless of any intent which he may have had at the time he retained C, has engaged in such an act because F has, in effect, exercised the authority, control or responsibility which makes F a fiduciary to cause the plan to pay F additional fees for the services. C, whose continued employment by P depends on F, has also engaged in such an act, because C has an interest in the transaction which might affect the exercise of C's best judgment as a fiduciary. As a result, C has dealt with plan assets in his own interest under section 406(b)(1).

Example (6). F, a fiduciary of plan P with discretionary authority respecting the management of P, retains S, the son of F, to provide for a fee various kinds of administrative services necessary for the operation of the plan. F has engaged in an act described in section 406(b)(1) of the Act because S is a person in whom F has an interest which may affect the exercise of F's best judgment as a fiduciary. Such act is not exempt under section 408(b)(2) of the Act irrespective of whether the provision of the services by S is exempt.

Example (7). T, one of the trustees of plan P, is president of bank B. The bank proposes to provide administrative services to P for a fee. T physically absents himself from all consideration of B's proposal and does not otherwise exercise any of the authority, control or responsibility which makes T a fiduciary to cause the plan to retain B. The other trustees decide to retain B. T has not engaged in an act described in section 406(b)(1) of the Act. Further, the other trustees have not engaged in an act described in section 406(b)(1) merely because T is on the board of trustees of P. This fact alone would not make them have an interest in the transaction which might affect the exercise of their best judgment as fiduciaries.

[¶ 14,783]
§ 2550.408b-3 Loans to Employee Stock Ownership Plans.

(a) *Definitions*. When used in this section, the terms listed below have the following meanings:

(1) *ESOP*. The term "ESOP" refers to an employee stock ownership plan that meets the requirements of section 407(d)(6) of the Employee Retirement Income Security Act of 1974 (the Act) and 29 CFR 2550.407d-6. It is not synonymous with "stock bonus plan." A stock bonus plan must, however, be an ESOP to engage in an exempt loan. The qualification of an ESOP under section 401(a) of the Internal Revenue Code (the Code) and 26 CFR 54.4975-11 will not be adversely affected merely because it engages in a non-exempt loan.

(2) *Loan*. The term "loan" refers to a loan made to an ESOP by a party in interest or a loan to an ESOP which is guaranteed by a party in interest. It includes a direct loan of cash, a purchase-money transaction, and an assumption of the obligation of an ESOP. "Guarantee" includes an unsecured guarantee and the use of assets of a party in interest as collateral for a loan, even though the use of assets may not be a guarantee under applicable state law. An amendment of a loan in order to qualify as an exempt loan is not a refinancing of the loan or the making of another loan.

(3) *Exempt loan*. The term "exempt loan" refers to a loan that satisfies the provisions of this section. A "non-exempt loan" is one that fails to satisfy such provisions.

(4) *Publicly traded*. The term "publicly traded" refers to a security that is listed on a national securities exchange registered under section 6 of the Securities Exchange Act of 1934 (15 U.S.C. 78f) or that is quoted on a system sponsored by a national securities association registered under section 15 A(b) of the Securities Exchange Act (15 U.S.C. 78o).

(5) *Qualifying employer security*. The term "qualifying employer security" refers to a security described in 29 CFR 2550.407d-5.

(b) *Statutory exemption*. (1) *Scope*. Section 408(b)(3) of the Act provides an exemption from the prohibited transaction provisions of sections 406(a) and 406(b)(1) of the Act (relating to fiduciaries dealing with the assets of plans in their own interest or for their own account) and 406(b)(2) of the Act (relating to fiduciaries in their individual or in any other capacity acting in any transaction involving the plan on behalf of a party (or representing a party) whose interests are adverse to the interests of the plan or the interests of its participants or beneficiaries). Section 408(b)(3) does not provide an exemption from the prohibitions of section 406(b)(3) of the Act (relating to fiduciaries receiving consideration for their own personal account from any party dealing with a plan in connection with a transaction involving the income or assets of the plan).

(2) *Special scrutiny of transaction*. The exemption under section 408(b)(3) includes within its scope certain transactions in which the potential for self-dealing by fiduciaries exists and in which the interests of fiduciaries may conflict with the interests of participants. To guard against these potential abuses, the Department of Labor will subject these transactions to special scrutiny to ensure that they are primarily for the benefit of participants and their beneficiaries. Although the transactions need not be arranged and approved by an independent fiduciary, fiduciaries are cautioned to scrupulously exercise their discretion in approving them. For example, fiduciaries should be prepared to demonstrate compliance with the net effect test and the arm's-length standard under paragraphs (c)(2) and (3) of this section. Also, fiduciaries should determine that the transaction is truly arranged primarily in the interest of participants and their beneficiaries rather than, for example, in the interest of certain selling shareholders.

(c) *Primary benefit requirement*. (1) *In general*. An exempt loan must be primarily for the benefit of the ESOP participants and their beneficiaries. All the surrounding facts and circumstances, including those described in paragraphs (c)(2) and (3) of this section, will be considered in determining whether such loan satisfies this requirement. However, no loan will satisfy such requirement unless it satisfies the requirements of paragraphs (d), (e) and (f) of this section.

(2) *Net effect on plan assets*. At the time that a loan is made, the interest rate for the loan and the price of securities to be acquired with the loan proceeds should not be such that plan assets might be drained off.

(3) *Arm's-length standard*. The terms of a loan, whether or not between independent parties, must, at the time the loan is made, be at least as favorable to the ESOP as the terms of a comparable loan resulting from arm's-length negotiations between independent parties.

(d) *Use of loan proceeds*. The proceeds of an exempt loan must be used, within a reasonable time after their receipt, by the borrowing ESOP only for any or all of the following purposes:

(1) To acquire qualifying employer securities.

(2) To repay such loan.

(3) To repay a prior exempt loan. A new loan, the proceeds of which are so used, must satisfy the provisions of this section.

Except as provided in paragraphs (i) and (j) of this section or as otherwise required by applicable law, no security acquired with the proceeds of an exempt loan may be subject to a put, call, or other option, or buy-sell or similar arrangement while held by and when distributed from a plan, whether or not the plan is then an ESOP.

(e) *Liability and collateral of ESOP for loan*. An exempt loan must be without recourse against the ESOP. Furthermore, the only assets of the ESOP that may be given as collateral on an exempt loan are qualifying employer securities of two classes: those acquired with the proceeds of the exempt loan and those that were used as collateral on a prior exempt loan repaid with the proceeds of the current exempt loan.

No person entitled to payment under the exempt loan shall have any right to assets of the ESOP other than:

    (1) Collateral given for the loan,

    (2) Contributions (other than contributions of employer securities) that are made under an ESOP to meet its obligations under the loan, and

    (3) Earnings attributable to such collateral and the investment of such contributions.

The payments made with respect to an exempt loan by the ESOP during a plan year must not exceed an amount equal to the sum of such contributions and earnings received during or prior to the year less such payments in prior years. Such contributions and earnings must be accounted for separately in the books of account of the ESOP until the loan is repaid.

    (f) *Default.* In the event of default upon an exempt loan, the value of plan assets transferred in satisfaction of the loan must not exceed the amount of default. If the lender is a party in interest, a loan must provide for a transfer of plan assets upon default only upon and to the extent of the failure of the plan to meet the payment schedule of the loan. For purposes of this paragraph, the making of a guarantee does not make a person a lender.

    (g) *Reasonable rate of interest.* The interest rate of a loan must not be in excess of a reasonable rate of interest. All relevant factors will be considered in determining a reasonable rate of interest, including the amount and duration of the loan, the security and guarantee (if any) involved, the credit standing of the ESOP and the guarantor (if any), and the interest rate prevailing for comparable loans. When these factors are considered, a variable interest rate may be reasonable.

    (h) *Release from encumbrance.* (1) *General rule.* In general, an exempt loan must provide for the release from encumbrance of plan assets used as collateral for the loan under this paragraph. For each plan year during the duration of the loan, the number of securities released must equal the number of encumbered securities held immediately before release for the current plan year multiplied by a fraction. The numerator of the fraction is the amount of principal and interest paid for the year. The denominator of the fraction is the sum of the numerator plus the principal and interest to be paid for all future years. See § 2550.408b-3(h)(4). The number of future years under the loan must be definitely ascertainable and must be determined without taking into account any possible extensions or renewal periods. If the interest rate under the loan is variable, the interest to be paid in future years must be computed by using the interest rate applicable as of the end of the plan year. If collateral includes more than one class of securities, the number of securities of each class to be released for a plan year must be determined by applying the same fraction to each class.

    (2) *Special rule.* A loan will not fail to be exempt merely because the number of securities to be released from encumbrance is determined solely with reference to principal payments. However, if release is determined with reference to principal payments only, the following three additional rules apply. The first rule is that the loan must provide for annual payments of principal and interest at a cumulative rate that is not less rapid at any time than level annual payments of such amounts for 10 years. The second rule is that interest included in any payment is disregarded only to the extent that it would be determined to be interest under standard loan amortization tables. The third rule is that subdivision (2) is not applicable from the time that, by reason of a renewal, extension, or refinancing, the sum of the expired duration of the exempt loan, the renewal period, the extension period, and the duration of a new exempt loan exceeds 10 years.

    (3) *Caution against plan disqualification.* Under an exempt loan, the number of securities released from encumbrance may vary from year to year. The release of securities depends upon certain employer contributions and earnings under the ESOP. Under 26 CFR 54.4975-11(d)(2) actual allocations to participants' accounts are based upon assets withdrawn from the suspense account. Nevertheless, for purposes of applying the limitations under section 415 of the Code to these allocations, under 26 CFR 54.4975-11(a)(8)(ii) contributions used by the ESOP to pay the loan are treated as annual additions to participants' accounts. Therefore, particular caution must be exercised to

avoid exceeding the maximum annual additions under section 415 of the Code. At the same time, release from encumbrance in annually varying numbers may reflect a failure on the part of the employer to make substantial and recurring contributions to the ESOP which will lead to loss of qualification under section 401(a) of the Code. The Internal Revenue Service will observe closely the operation of ESOPs that release encumbered securities in varying annual amounts, particularly those that provide for the deferral of loan payments or for balloon payments. See 26 CFR 54.4975-7(b)(8)(iii).

    (4) *Illustration.* The general rule under paragraph (h)(1) of this section operates as illustrated in the following example:

    Example. Corporation X establishes an ESOP that borrows $750,000 from a bank. X guarantees the loan which is for 15 years at 5% interest and is payable in level annual amounts of $72,256.72. Total payments on the loan are $1,083,850.80. The ESOP uses the entire proceeds of the loan to acquire 15,000 shares of X stock which is used as collateral for the loan. The number of securities to be released for the first year is 1,000 shares, i.e., 15,000 shares × $72,256.72/$1,083,850.80 = 15,000 shares × $1/15$. The number of securities to be released for the second year is 1,000 shares, i.e., 14,000 shares × $72,256.72/$1,011,594.08 = 14,000 shares × $1/14$. If all loan payments are made as originally scheduled, the number of securities released in each succeeding year of the loan will also be 1,000.

    [Officially corrected by 42 FR 45907.]

    (i) *Right of first refusal.* Qualifying employer securities acquired with proceeds of an exempt loan may, but need not, be subject to a right of first refusal. However, any such right must meet the requirements of this paragraph. Securities subject to such right must be stock or an equity security, or a debt security convertible into stock or an equity security. Also, they must not be publicly traded at the time the right may be exercised. The right of first refusal must be in favor of the employer, the ESOP, or both in any order of priority. The selling price and other terms under the right must not be less favorable to the seller than the greater of the value of the security determined under 26 CFR 54.4975-11(d)(5), or the purchase price and other terms offered by a buyer, other than the employer or the ESOP, making a good faith offer to purchase the security. The right of first refusal must lapse no later than 14 days after the security holder gives written notice to the holder of the right that an offer by a third party to purchase the security has been received.

    (j) *Put option.* A qualifying employer security acquired with the proceeds of an exempt loan by an ESOP after September 30, 1976, must be subject to a put option if it is not publicly traded when distributed or if it is subject to a trading limitation when distributed. For purposes of this paragraph, a "trading limitation" on a security is a restriction under any Federal or State securities law or any regulation thereunder, or an agreement (not prohibited by this section) affecting the security which would make the security not as freely tradable as one not subject to such restriction. The put option must be exercisable only by a participant, by the participant's donees, or by a person (including an estate or its distributee) to whom the security passes by reason of a participant's death. (Under this paragraph "participant" means a participant and the beneficiaries of the participant under the ESOP.) The put option must permit a participant to put the security to the employer. Under no circumstances may the put option bind the ESOP. However, it may grant the ESOP an option to assume the rights and obligations of the employer at the time that the put option is exercised. If it is known at the time a loan is made that Federal or state law will be violated by the employer's honoring such put option, the put option must permit the security to be put, in a manner consistent with such law, to a third party (e.g., an affiliate of the employer or a shareholder other than the ESOP) that has substantial net worth at the time the loan is made and whose net worth is reasonably expected to remain substantial.

    [Officially corrected by 42 FR 45907.]

    (k) *Duration of put option.* (1) *General rule.* A put option must be exercisable at least during a 15-month period which begins the date the security subject to the put option is distributed by the ESOP.

    (2) *Special rule.* In the case of a security that is publicly traded without restriction when distributed but ceases to be so traded within 15 months after distribution, the employer must notify each security

holder in writing on or before the tenth day after the date the security ceases to be so traded that for the remainder of the 15-month period the security is subject to a put option. The number of days between the tenth day and the date on which notice is actually given, if later than the tenth day, must be added to the duration of the put option. The notice must inform distributees of the terms of the put options that they are to hold. The terms must satisfy the requirements of paragraphs (j) through (l) of this section.

(l) *Other put option provisions.* (1) *Manner of exercise.* A put option is exercised by the holder notifying the employer in writing that the put option is being exercised.

(2) *Time excluded from duration of put option.* The period during which a put option is exercisable does not include any time when a distributee is unable to exercise it because the party bound by the put option is prohibited from honoring it by applicable Federal or state law.

(3) *Price.* The price at which a put option must be exercisable is the value of the security, determined in accordance with paragraph (d)(5) of 26 CFR 54.4975-11.

(4) *Payment terms.* The provisions for payment under a put option must be reasonable. The deferral of payment is reasonable if adequate security and a reasonable interest rate are provided for any credit extended and if the cumulative payments at any time are no less than the aggregate of reasonable periodic payments as of such time. Periodic payments are reasonable if annual installments, beginning with 30 days after the date the put option is exercised, are substantially equal. Generally, the payment period may not end more than 5 years after the date the put option is exercised. However, it may be extended to a date no later than the earlier of 10 years from the date the put option is exercised or the date the proceeds of the loan used by the ESOP to acquire the security subject to such put option are entirely repaid.

(5) *Payment restrictions.* Payment under a put option may be restricted by the terms of a loan, including one used to acquire a security subject to a put option, made before November 1, 1977. Otherwise, payment under a put option must not be restricted by the provisions of a loan or any other arrangement, including the terms of the employer's articles of incorporation, unless so required by applicable state law.

(m) *Other terms of loan.* An exempt loan must be for a specific term. Such loan may not be payable at the demand of any person, except in the case of default.

(n) *Status of plan as ESOP.* To be exempt, a loan must be made to a plan that is an ESOP at the time of such loan. However, a loan to a plan formally designated as an ESOP at the time of the loan that fails to be an ESOP because it does not comply with section 401(a) of the Code or 26 CFR 54.4975-11 will be exempt as of the time of such loan if the plan is amended retroactively under section 401(b) of the Code or 26 CFR 54.4975-11(a)(4).

(o) *Special rules for certain loans.* (1) *Loans made before January 1, 1976.* A loan made before January 1, 1976, or made afterwards under a binding agreement in effect on January 1, 1976 (or under renewals permitted by the terms of such an agreement on that date) is exempt for the entire period of such loan if it otherwise satisfies the provisions of this section for such period, even though it does not satisfy the following provisions of this section:

(i) The last sentence of paragraph (d);

(ii) Paragraphs (e), (f), and (h) (1) and (2); and

(iii) Paragraphs (i) through (m), inclusive.

(2) *Loans made after December 31, 1975, but before (November 1, 1977).* A loan made after December 31, 1975, but before November 1, 1977, or made afterwards under a binding agreement in effect on November 1, 1977 (or under renewals permitted by the terms of such an agreement on that date) is exempt for the entire period of such loan if it otherwise satisfies the provisions of this section for such period even though it does not satisfy the following provisions of this section:

(i) Paragraph (f);

(ii) The three provisions of paragraph (h)(2); and (iii) paragraph (i).

(3) *Release rule.* Notwithstanding paragraphs (o) (1) and (2) of this section, if the proceeds of a loan are used to acquire securities after November 1, 1977, the loan must comply by such date with the provisions of paragraph (h) of this section.

(4) *Default rule.* Notwithstanding paragraphs (o) (1) and (2) of this section, a loan by a party in interest other than a guarantor must satisfy the requirements of paragraph (f) of this section. A loan will satisfy these requirements if it is retroactively amended before November 1, 1977, to satisfy these requirements.

(5) *Put option rule.* With respect to a security distributed before November 1, 1977, the put option provisions of paragraphs (j), (k), and (l) of this section will be deemed satisfied as of the date the security is distributed if by December 31, 1977, the security is subject to a put option satisfying such provisions. For purposes of satisfying such provisions, the security will be deemed distributed on the date the put option is issued. However, the put option provisions need not be satisfied with respect to a security that is not owned on November 1, 1977, by a person in whose hands a put option must be exercisable.

[Added August 30, 1977, by 42 FR 44384; officially corrected by 42 FR 45907.]

[¶ 14,784]

§ 2550.408b-4 Statutory exemption for investments in deposits of banks or similar financial institutions.

(a) *In general.* Section 408(b)(4) of the Employee Retirement Income Security Act of 1974 (the Act) exempts from the prohibitions of section 406 of the Act the investment of all or a part of a plan's assets in deposits bearing a reasonable rate of interest in a bank or similar financial institution supervised by the United States or a State, even though such bank or similar financial institution is a fiduciary or other party in interest with respect to the plan, if the conditions of either § 2550.408b-4(b)(1) or § 2550.408b-4(b)(2) are met. Section 408(b)(4) provides an exemption from sections 406(b)(1) of the Act (relating to fiduciaries dealing with the assets of plans in their own interest or for their own account) and 406(b)(2) of the Act (relating to fiduciaries in their individual or in any other capacity acting in any transaction involving the plan on behalf of a party (or representing a party) whose interests are adverse to the interests of the plan or the interests of its participants or beneficiaries), as well as section 406(a)(1), because section 408(b)(4) contemplates a bank or similar financial institution causing a plan for which it acts as a fiduciary to invest plan assets in its own deposits if the requirements of section 408(b)(4) are met. However, it does not provide an exemption from section 406(b)(3) of the Act (relating to fiduciaries receiving consideration for their own personal account from any party dealing with a plan in connection with a transaction involving the assets of the plan). The receipt of such consideration is a separate transaction not described in the statutory exemption. Section 408(b)(4) does not contain an exemption from other provisions of the Act, such as section 404, or other provisions of law which may impose requirements or restrictions relating to the transactions which are exempt under section 408(b)(4) of the Act. See, for example, section 401 of the Internal Revenue Code of 1954 (Code). The provisions of section 408(b)(4) of the Act are further limited by section 408(d) of the Act (relating to transactions with owner-employees and related persons).

[Officially corrected by 42 FR 36823.]

(b)(1) *Plan covering own employees.* Such investment may be made if the plan is one which covers only the employees of the bank or similar financial institution, the employees of any of its affiliates, or the employees of both.

(2) *Other plans.* Such investment may be made if the investment is expressly authorized by a provision of the plan or trust instrument or if the investment is expressly authorized (or made) by a fiduciary of the plan (other than the bank or similar financial institution or any of its affiliates) who has authority to make such investments, or to instruct the trustee or other fiduciary with respect to investments, and who has no interest in the transaction which may affect the exercise of such

authorizing fiduciary's best judgment as a fiduciary so as to cause such authorization to constitute an act described in section 406(b) of the Act. Any authorization to make investments contained in a plan or trust instrument will satisfy the requirement of express authorization for investments made prior to November 1, 1977. Effective November 1, 1977, in the case of a bank or similar financial institution that invests plan assets in deposits in itself or its affiliates under an authorization contained in a plan or trust instrument, such authorization must name such bank or similar financial institution and must state that such bank or similar financial institution may make investments in deposits which bear a reasonable rate of interest in itself (or in an affiliate).

(3) *Example.* B, a bank, is the trustee of plan P's assets. The trust instruments give the trustees the right to invest plan assets in its discretion. B invests in the certificates of deposit of bank C, which is a fiduciary of the plan by virtue of performing certain custodial and administrative services. The authorization is sufficient for the plan to make such investment under section 408(b)(4). Further, such authorization would suffice to allow B to make investments in deposits in itself prior to November 1, 1977. However, subsequent to October 31, 1977, B may not invest in deposits in itself, unless the plan or trust instrument specifically authorizes it to invest in deposits of B.

(c) *Definitions.* (1) The term "bank or similar financial institution" includes a bank (as defined in section 581 of the Code), a domestic building and loan association (as defined in section 7701(a)(19) of the Code), and a credit union (as defined in section 101(6) of the Federal Credit Union Act).

(2) A person is an affiliate of a bank or similar financial institution if such person and such bank or similar financial institution would be treated as members of the same controlled group of corporations or as members of two or more trades or businesses under common control within the meaning of section 414(b) or (c) of the Code and the regulations thereunder.

(3) The term "deposits" includes any account, temporary or otherwise, upon which a reasonable rate of interest is paid, including a certificate of deposit issued by a bank or similar financial institution.

[¶ 14,786]
§ 2550.408b-6 Statutory exemption for ancillary services by a bank or similar financial institution.

(a) *In general.* Section 408(b)(6) of the Employee Retirement Income Security Act of 1974 (the Act) exempts from the prohibitions of section 406 of the Act the provision of certain ancillary services by a bank or similar financial institution (as defined in §2550.408b-4(c)(1))

supervised by the United States or a State to a plan for which it acts as a fiduciary if the conditions of §2550.408b-6(b) are met. Such ancillary services include services which do not meet the requirements of section 408(b)(2) of the Act because the provision of such services involves an act described in section 406(b)(1) of the Act (relating to fiduciaries dealing with the assets of plans in their own interest or for their own account) by the fiduciary bank or similar financial institution or an act described in section 406(b)(2) of the Act (relating to fiduciaries in their individual or in any other capacity acting in any transaction involving the plan on behalf of a party (or representing a party) whose interests are adverse to the interests of the plan or the interests of its participants or beneficiaries). Section 408(b)(6) provides an exemption from sections 406(b)(1) and (2) because section 408(b)(6) contemplates the provision of such ancillary services without the approval of a second fiduciary (as described in §2550.408b-2(e)(2)) if the conditions of §2550.408b-6(b) are met. Thus, for example, plan assets held by a fiduciary bank which are reasonably expected to be needed to satisfy current plan expenses may be placed by the bank in a non-interest-bearing checking account in the bank if the conditions of §2550.408b-6(b) are met, notwithstanding the provisions of section 408(b)(4) of the Act (relating to investments in bank deposits). However, section 408(b)(6) does not provide an exemption for an act described in section 406(b)(3) of the Act (relating to fiduciaries receiving consideration for their own personal account from any party dealing with a plan in connection with a transaction involving the assets of the plan). The receipt of such consideration is a separate transaction not described in section 408(b)(6). Section 408(b)(6) does not contain an exemption from other provisions of the Act, such as section 404, or other provisions of law which may impose requirements or restrictions relating to the transactions which are exempt under section 408(b)(6) of the Act. See, for example, section 401 of the Internal Revenue Code of 1954. The provisions of section 408(b)(6) of the Act are further limited by section 408(d) of the Act (relating to transactions with owner-employees and related persons).

[Officially corrected by 42 FR 36823.]

(b) *Conditions.* Such service must be provided—

(1) At not more than reasonable compensation;

(2) Under adequate internal safeguards which assure that the provision of such service is consistent with sound banking and financial practice, as determined by Federal or State supervisory authority; and

(3) Only to the extent that such service is subject to specific guidelines issued by the bank or similar financial institution which meet the requirements of §2550.408b-6(c).

(c) *Specific guidelines.* [Reserved]

Regulations

The following regulations were adopted under "Title 29—Labor," "Chapter XXV—Pension and Welfare Benefit Programs," "Subchapter F—Employee Retirement Income Security Act of 1974," "Part 2550—Rules and Regulations for Fiduciary Responsibility." Reg. §2550.408b-19 was published in the Federal Register on February 12, 2007 (72 FR 6473) and amended on October 7, 2008 (73 FR 58450).

[¶ 14,786M]
§ 2550.408b-19 Statutory exemption for cross-trading of securities.

(a) In General.

(1) Section 408(b)(19) of the Employee Retirement Income Security Act of 1974 (the Act) exempts from the prohibitions of section 406(a)(1)(A) and 406(b)(2) of the Act any cross-trade of securities if certain conditions are satisfied. Among other conditions, the exemption requires that the investment manager adopt, and effect cross-trades in accordance with, written cross-trading policies and procedures that are fair and equitable to all accounts participating in the cross-trading program, and that include:

(i) A description of the investment manager's pricing policies and procedures; and

(ii) The investment manager's policies and procedures for allocating cross-trades in an objective manner among accounts participating in the cross-trading program.

(2) Section 4975(d)(22) of the Internal Revenue Code of 1986 (the Code) contains parallel provisions to section 408(b)(19) of the Act. Effective December 31, 1978, section 102 of Reorganization Plan No. 4

of 1978, 5 U.S.C. App. 214 (2000 ed.), transferred the authority of the Secretary of the Treasury to promulgate regulations of the type published herein to the Secretary of Labor. Therefore, all references herein to section 408(b)(19) of the Act should be read to include reference to the parallel provisions of section 4975(d)(22) of the Code.

(3) Section 408(b)(19)(D) of the Act requires that a plan fiduciary for each plan participating in the cross-trades receive in advance of any cross-trades disclosure regarding the conditions under which the cross-trades may take place, including the written policies and procedures described in section 408(b)(19)(H) of the Act. This disclosure must be in a document that is separate from any other agreement or disclosure involving the asset management relationship. For purposes of section 408(b)(19)(D) of the Act, the policies and procedures furnished to the authorizing fiduciary must conform with the requirements of this regulation.

(4) The standards set forth in this section apply solely for purposes of determining whether an investment manager's written policies and procedures satisfy the content requirements of section 408(b)(19)(H) of the Act. Accordingly, such standards do not determine whether the investment manager satisfies the other requirements for relief under section 408(b)(19) of the Act.

(b) Policies and Procedures.

(1) In General. This paragraph specifies the content of the written policies and procedures required to be adopted by an investment manager and disclosed to the plan fiduciary prior to authorizing cross-trading in order for transactions to qualify for relief under section 408(b)(19) of the Act.

(2) Style and Format. The content of the policies and procedures required by this paragraph must be clear and concise and written in a manner calculated to be understood by the plan fiduciary authorizing cross-trading. Although no specific format is required for the investment manager's written policies and procedures, the information contained in the policies and procedures must be sufficiently detailed to facilitate a periodic review by the compliance officer of the cross-trades and a determination by such compliance officer that the cross-trades comply with the investment manager's written cross-trading policies and procedures.

(3) Content. (i) An investment manager's policies and procedures must be fair and equitable to all accounts participating in its cross-trading program and reasonably designed to ensure compliance with the requirements of section 408(b)(19)(H) of the Act. Such policies and procedures must include:

(A) A statement of policy which describes the criteria that will be applied by the investment manager in determining that execution of a securities transaction as a cross-trade will be beneficial to both parties to the transaction;

(B) A description of how the investment manager will determine that cross-trades are effected at the independent "current market price" of the security (within the meaning of section 270.17a-7(b) of Title 17, Code of Federal Regulations and SEC no-action and interpretative letters thereunder) as required by section 408(b)(19)(B) of the Act, including the identity of sources used to establish such price;

(C) A description of the procedures for ensuring compliance with the $100,000,000 minimum asset size requirement of section 408(b)(19). A plan or master trust will satisfy the minimum asset size requirement as to a transaction if it satisfies the requirement upon its initial participation in the cross-trading program and on an annual basis thereafter;

(D) A statement that any investment manager participating in a cross-trading program will have conflicting loyalties and responsibilities to the parties involved in any cross-trade transaction and a description of how the investment manager will mitigate such conflicts;

(E) A requirement that the investment manager allocate cross-trades among accounts in an objective and equitable manner and a description of the allocation method(s) available to and used by the investment manager for assuring an objective allocation among accounts participating in the cross-trading program. If more than one allocation methodology may be used by the investment manager, a description of what circumstances will dictate the use of a particular methodology;

(F) Identification of the compliance officer responsible for periodically reviewing the investment manager's compliance with section 408(b)(19)(H) of the Act and a statement of the compliance officer's qualifications for this position;

(G) A statement that the cross-trading statutory exemption under section 408(b)(19) of the Act requires satisfaction of several objective conditions in addition to the requirements that the investment manager adopt and effect cross-trades in accordance with written cross-trading policies and procedures; and

(H) A statement which specifically describes the scope of the annual review conducted by the compliance officer.

(ii) Nothing herein is intended to preclude an investment manager from including such other policies and procedures not required by this regulation as the investment manager may determine appropriate to comply with the requirements of section 408(b)(19).

(c) Definitions. For purposes of this section:

(1) The term "account" includes any single customer or pooled fund or account.

(2) The term "compliance officer" means an individual designated by the investment manager who is responsible for periodically reviewing the cross-trades made for the plan to ensure compliance with the investment manager's written cross-trading policies and procedures and the requirements of section 408(b)(19)(H) of the Act.

(3) The term "plan fiduciary" means a person described in section 3(21)(A) of the Act with respect to a plan (other than the investment manager engaging in the cross-trades or an affiliate) who has the authority to authorize a plan's participation in an investment manager's cross-trading program.

(4) The term "investment manager" means a person described in section 3(38) of the Act.

(5) The term "plan" means any employee benefit plan as described in section 3(3) of the Act to which Title I of the Act applies or any plan defined in section 4975(e)(1) of the Code.

(6) The term "cross-trade" means the purchase and sale of a security between a plan and any other account managed by the same investment manager.

Regulation

The following regulation was adopted under "Title 29—Labor," "Chapter XXV—Pension and Welfare Benefit Programs," "Subchapter F—Employee Retirement Income Security Act of 1974," "Part 2550—Rules and Regulations for Fiduciary Responsibility." The regulations were filed with the Federal Register on June 21, 1977, and published in the Federal Register on June 24, 1977 (42 FR 32389).

[¶ 14,788]
§ 2550.408c-2 Compensation for services.

(a) *In general.* Section 408(b)(2) of the Employee Retirement Income Security Act of 1974 (the Act) refers to the payment of reasonable compensation by a plan to a party in interest for services rendered to the plan. Section 408(c)(2) of the Act and §§ 2550.408c-2(b)(1) through 2550.408c-2(b)(4) clarify what constitutes reasonable compensation for such services.

(b)(1) *General rule.* Generally, whether compensation is "reasonable" under sections 408(b)(2) and 408(c)(2) of the Act depends on the particular facts and circumstances of each case.

(2) *Payments to certain fiduciaries.* Under sections 408(b)(2) and 408(c)(2) of the Act, the term "reasonable compensation" does not include any compensation to a fiduciary who is already receiving full-time pay from an employer or association of employers (any of whose employees are participants in the plan) or from an employee organization (any of whose members are participants in the plan), except for the reimbursement of direct expenses properly and actually incurred and

not otherwise reimbursed. The restrictions of this paragraph (b)(2) do not apply to a party in interest who is not a fiduciary.

(3) *Certain expenses not direct expenses.* An expense is not a direct expense to the extent it would have been sustained had the service not been provided or if it represents an allocable portion of overhead costs.

(4) *Expense advances.* Under sections 408(b)(2) and 408(c)(2) of the Act, the term "reasonable compensation", as applied to a fiduciary or an employee of a plan, includes an advance to such a fiduciary or employee by the plan to cover direct expenses to be properly and actually incurred by such person in the performance of such person's duties with the plan if:

(i) The amount of such advance is reasonable with respect to the amount of the direct expense which is likely to be properly and actually incurred in the immediate future (such as during the next month); and

(ii) The fiduciary or employee accounts to the plan at the end of the period covered by the advance for the expenses properly and actually incurred.

(5) *Excessive compensation.* Under sections 408(b)(2) and 408(c)(2) of the Act, any compensation which would be considered excessive under 26 CFR 1.162-7 (Income Tax Regulations relating to compensation for personal services which constitutes an ordinary and necessary trade or business expense) will not be "reasonable compen-

sation". Depending upon the facts and circumstances of the particular situation, compensation which is not excessive under 26 CFR 1.162-7 may, nevertheless, not be "reasonable compensation" within the meaning of sections 408(b)(2) and 408(c)(2) of the Act.

Regulation

Reg. § 2550.408e was adopted on July 29, 1980, and published in the Federal Register on August 1, 1980 (45 FR 51194).

[¶ 14,789]

§ 2550.408e **Statutory exemption for acquisition or sale of qualifying employer securities and for acquisition, sale or lease of qualifying employer real property.**

(a) *General.* Section 408(e) of the Employee Retirement Income Security Act of 1974 (the Act) exempts from the prohibitions of section 406(a) and 406(b)(1) and (2) of the Act any acquisition or sale by a plan of qualifying employer securities (as defined in section 407(d)(5) of the Act), or any acquisition, sale or lease by a plan of qualifying employer real property (as defined in section 407(d)(4) of the Act) if certain conditions are met. The conditions are that

(1) The acquisition, sale or lease must be for adequate consideration (which is defined in paragraph (d) of this section);

(2) No commission may be charged directly or indirectly to the plan with respect to the transaction; and

(3) In the case of an acquisition or lease of qualifying employer real property, or an acquisition of qualifying employer securities, by a plan other than an eligible individual account plan (as defined in section 407(d)(3) of the Act), the acquisition or lease must comply with the requirements of section 407(a) of the Act.

(b) *Acquisition.* For purposes of section 408(e) and this section, an acquisition by a plan of qualifying employer securities or qualifying employer real property shall include, but not be limited to, an acquisition by purchase, by the exchange of plan assets, by the exercise of

warrants or rights, by the conversion of a security, by default of a loan where the qualifying employer security or qualifying employer real property was security for the loan, or in connection with the contribution of such securities or real property to the plan. However, an acquisition of a security shall not be deemed to have occurred if a plan acquires the security as a result of a stock dividend or stock split.

(c) *Sale.* For purposes of section 408(e) and this section, a sale of qualifying employer real property or qualifying employer securities shall include any disposition for value.

(d) *Adequate Consideration.* For purposes of section 408(e) and this section, adequate consideration means:

(1) In the case of a marketable obligation, a price not less favorable to the plan than the price determined under section 407(e)(1) of the Act; and

(2) In all other cases, a price not less favorable to the plan than the price determined under section 3(18) of the Act.

(e) *Commission.* For purposes of section 408(e) and this section, the term "commission" includes any fee, commission or similar charge paid in connection with a transaction, except that the term "commission" does not include a charge incurred for the purpose of enabling the appropriate plan fiduciaries to evaluate the desirability of entering into a transaction to which this section would apply, such as an appraisal or investment advisory fee.

Regulation

Reg. § 2550.408g-1, the Appendix to § 2550.408g-1 and § 2550.408g-2, was filed with Federal Register on January 16, 2009 and published in the Federal Register on January 21, 2009 (74 FR 3822). Reg. § 2550.408g-1 was amended March 20, 2009 by 74 FR 11847, further amended on May 22, 2009 (74 FR 23951), and further amended on November 17, 2009 (74 FR 59092). The regulations were withdrawn on November 20, 2009, effective January 19, 2010 (74 FR 60156). Reg. § 2550.408g-1, the Appendix to § 2550.408g-1 and § 2550.408g-2, was added on October 25, 2011 by 76 FR 66136.

[¶ 14,789B]

§ 2550.408g-1 Investment advice—participants and beneficiaries.

(a) *In general.* (1) This section provides relief from the prohibitions of section 406 of the Employee Retirement Income Security Act of 1974, as amended (ERISA or the Act), and section 4975 of the Internal Revenue Code of 1986, as amended (the Code), for certain transactions in connection with the provision of investment advice to participants and beneficiaries. This section, at paragraph (b), implements the statutory exemption set forth at sections 408(b)(14) and 408(g)(1) of ERISA and sections 4975(d)(17) and 4975(f)(8) of the Code. The requirements and conditions set forth in this section apply solely for the relief described in paragraph (b) of this section and, accordingly, no inferences should be drawn with respect to requirements applicable to the provision of investment advice not addressed by this section.

(2) Nothing contained in ERISA section 408(g)(1), Code section 4975(f)(8), or this regulation imposes an obligation on a plan fiduciary or any other party to offer, provide or otherwise make available any investment advice to a participant or beneficiary.

(3) Nothing contained in ERISA section 408(g)(1), Code section 4975(f)(8), or this regulation invalidates or otherwise affects prior regulations, exemptions, interpretive or other guidance issued by the Department of Labor pertaining to the provision of investment advice and the circumstances under which such advice may or may not constitute a prohibited transaction under section 406 of ERISA or section 4975 of the Code.

(b) *Statutory exemption.* (1) *General.* Sections 408(b)(14) and 408(g)(1) of ERISA provide an exemption from the prohibitions of section 406 of ERISA for transactions described in section 408(b)(14) of ERISA in connection with the provision of investment advice to a participant or a beneficiary if the investment advice is provided by a

fiduciary adviser under an "eligible investment advice arrangement." Sections 4975(d)(17) and (f)(8) of the Code contain parallel provisions to ERISA sections 408(b)(14) and (g)(1).

(2) *Eligible investment advice.* For purposes of section 408(g)(1) of ERISA and section 4975(f)(8) of the Code, an "eligible investment advice arrangement" means an arrangement that meets either the requirements of paragraph (b)(3) of this section or paragraph (b)(4) of this section, or both.

(3) *Arrangements that use fee leveling.* For purposes of this section, an arrangement is an eligible investment advice arrangement if—

(i)

(A) Any investment advice is based on generally accepted investment theories that take into account the historic risks and returns of different asset classes over defined periods of time, although nothing herein shall preclude any investment advice from being based on generally accepted investment theories that take into account additional considerations;

(B) Any investment advice takes into account investment management and other fees and expenses attendant to the recommended investments;

(C) Any investment advice takes into account, to the extent furnished by a plan, participant or beneficiary, information relating to age, time horizons (*e.g.,* life expectancy, retirement age), risk tolerance, current investments in designated investment options, other assets or sources of income, and investment preferences of the participant or beneficiary. A fiduciary adviser shall request such information, but nothing in this paragraph (b)(3)(i)(C) shall require that any investment advice take into account information requested, but not furnished by a participant or beneficiary, nor preclude requesting and taking into account additional information that a plan or participant or beneficiary may provide;

(D) No fiduciary adviser (including any employee, agent, or registered representative) that provides investment advice receives from any party (including an affiliate of the fiduciary adviser), directly or indirectly, any fee or other compensation (including commissions, salary, bonuses, awards, promotions, or other things of value) that varies depending on the basis of a participant's or beneficiary's selection of a particular investment option; and

(ii) The requirements of paragraphs (b)(5), (6), (7), (8) and (9) and paragraph (d) of this section are met.

(4) *Arrangements that use computer models.* For purposes of this section, an arrangement is an eligible investment advice arrangement if the only investment advice provided under the arrangement is advice that is generated by a computer model described in paragraphs (b)(4)(i) and (ii) of this section under an investment advice program and with respect to which the requirements of paragraphs (b)(5), (6), (7), (8) and (9) and paragraph (d) are met.

(i) A computer model shall be designed and operated to—

(A) Apply generally accepted investment theories that take into account the historic risks and returns of different asset classes over defined periods of time, although nothing herein shall preclude a computer model from applying generally accepted investment theories that take into account additional considerations;

(B) Take into account investment management and other fees and expenses attendant to the recommended investments;

(C) Appropriately weight the factors used in estimating future returns of investment options;

(D) Request from a participant or beneficiary and, to the extent furnished, utilize information relating to age, time horizons (*e.g.,* life expectancy, retirement age), risk tolerance, current investments in designated investment options, other assets or sources of income, and investment preferences; provided, however, that nothing herein shall preclude a computer model from requesting and taking into account additional information that a plan or a participant or beneficiary may provide;

(E) Utilize appropriate objective criteria to provide asset allocation portfolios comprised of investment options available under the plan;

(F) Avoid investment recommendations that:

(1) Inappropriately favor investment options offered by the fiduciary adviser or a person with a material affiliation or material contractual relationship with the fiduciary adviser over other investment options, if any, available under the plan; or

(2) Inappropriately favor investment options that may generate greater income for the fiduciary adviser or a person with a material affiliation or material contractual relationship with the fiduciary adviser; and

(G)

(1) Except as provided in paragraph (b)(4)(i)(G)(2) of this section, take into account all designated investment options, within the meaning of paragraph (c)(1) of this section, available under the plan without giving inappropriate weight to any investment option.

(2) A computer model shall not be treated as failing to meet the requirements of this paragraph merely because it does not make recommendations relating to the acquisition, holding or sale of an investment option that:

(i) Constitutes an annuity option with respect to which a participant or beneficiary may allocate assets toward the purchase of a stream of retirement income payments guaranteed by an insurance company, provided that, contemporaneous with the provision of investment advice generated by the computer model, the participant or beneficiary is also furnished a general description of such options and how they operate; or

(ii) The participant or beneficiary requests to be excluded from consideration in such recommendations.

(ii) Prior to utilization of the computer model, the fiduciary adviser shall obtain a written certification, meeting the requirements of paragraph (b)(4)(iv) of this section, from an eligible investment expert,

within the meaning of paragraph (b)(4)(iii) of this section, that the computer model meets the requirements of paragraph (b)(4)(i) of this section. If, following certification, a computer model is modified in a manner that may affect its ability to meet the requirements of paragraph (b)(4)(i), the fiduciary adviser shall, prior to utilization of the modified model, obtain a new certification from an eligible investment expert that the computer model, as modified, meets the requirements of paragraph (b)(4)(i).

(iii) The term "eligible investment expert" means a person that, through employees or otherwise, has the appropriate technical training or experience and proficiency to analyze, determine and certify, in a manner consistent with paragraph (b)(4)(iv) of this section, whether a computer model meets the requirements of paragraph (b)(4)(i) of this section; except that the term "eligible investment expert" does not include any person that: Has any material affiliation or material contractual relationship with the fiduciary adviser, with a person with a material affiliation or material contractual relationship with the fiduciary adviser, or with any employee, agent, or registered representative of the foregoing; or develops a computer model utilized by the fiduciary adviser to satisfy this paragraph (b)(4).

(iv) A certification by an eligible investment expert shall—

(A) Be in writing;

(B) Contain—

(1) An identification of the methodology or methodologies applied in determining whether the computer model meets the requirements of paragraph (b)(4)(i) of this section;

(2) An explanation of how the applied methodology or methodologies demonstrated that the computer model met the requirements of paragraph (b)(4)(i) of this section;

(3) A description of any limitations that were imposed by any person on the eligible investment expert's selection or application of methodologies for determining whether the computer model meets the requirements of paragraph (b)(4)(i) of this section;

(4) A representation that the methodology or methodologies were applied by a person or persons with the educational background, technical training or experience necessary to analyze and determine whether the computer model meets the requirements of paragraph (b)(4)(i); and

(5) A statement certifying that the eligible investment expert has determined that the computer model meets the requirements of paragraph (b)(4)(i) of this section; and

(C) Be signed by the eligible investment expert.

(v) The selection of an eligible investment expert as required by this section is a fiduciary act governed by section 404(a)(1) of ERISA.

(5) *Arrangement must be authorized by a plan fiduciary.* (i) Except as provided in paragraph (b)(5)(ii) of this section, the arrangement pursuant to which investment advice is provided to participants and beneficiaries pursuant to this section must be expressly authorized by a plan fiduciary (or, in the case of an Individual Retirement Account (IRA), the IRA beneficiary) other than: The person offering the arrangement; any person providing designated investment options under the plan; or any affiliate of either. Provided, however, that for purposes of the preceding, in the case of an IRA, an IRA beneficiary will not be treated as an affiliate of a person solely by reason of being an employee of such person.

(ii) In the case of an arrangement pursuant to which investment advice is provided to participants and beneficiaries of a plan sponsored by the person offering the arrangement or a plan sponsored by an affiliate of such person, the authorization described in paragraph (b)(5)(i) of this section may be provided by the plan sponsor of such plan, provided that the person or affiliate offers the same arrangement to participants and beneficiaries of unaffiliated plans in the ordinary course of its business.

(iii) For purposes of the authorization described in paragraph (b)(5)(i) of this section, a plan sponsor shall not be treated as a person providing a designated investment option under the plan merely because one of the designated investment options of the plan is an option that permits investment in securities of the plan sponsor or an affiliate.

(6) *Annual audit.* (i) The fiduciary adviser shall, at least annually, engage an independent auditor, who has appropriate technical training or experience and proficiency, and so represents in writing to the fiduciary adviser, to:

(A) Conduct an audit of the investment advice arrangements for compliance with the requirements of this section; and

(B) Within 60 days following completion of the audit, issue a written report to the fiduciary adviser and, except with respect to an arrangement with an IRA, to each fiduciary who authorized the use of the investment advice arrangement, in accordance with paragraph (b)(5) of this section, that—

(1) Identifies the fiduciary adviser,

(2) Indicates the type of arrangement (*i.e.,* fee leveling, computer models, or both),

(3) If the arrangement uses computer models, or both computer models and fee leveling, indicates the date of the most recent computer model certification, and identifies the eligible investment expert that provided the certification, and

(4) Sets forth the specific findings of the auditor regarding compliance of the arrangement with the requirements of this section.

(ii) With respect to an arrangement with an IRA, the fiduciary adviser:

(A) Within 30 days following receipt of the report from the auditor, as described in paragraph (b)(6)(i)(B) of this section, shall furnish a copy of the report to the IRA beneficiary or make such report available on its Web site, provided that such beneficiaries are provided information, with the information required to be disclosed pursuant to paragraph (b)(7) of this section, concerning the purpose of the report, and how and where to locate the report applicable to their account; and

(B) In the event that the report of the auditor identifies noncompliance with the requirements of this section, within 30 days following receipt of the report from the auditor, shall send a copy of the report to the Department of Labor at the following address: Investment Advice Exemption Notification, U.S. Department of Labor, Employee Benefits Security Administration, Room N-1513, 200 Constitution Ave., NW., Washington, DC 20210, or submit a copy electronically to *InvAdvNotification@dol.gov.*

(iii) For purposes of this paragraph (b)(6), an auditor is considered independent if it does not have a material affiliation or material contractual relationship with the person offering the investment advice arrangement to the plan or with any designated investment options under the plan, and does not have any role in the development of the investment advice arrangement, or certification of the computer model utilized under the arrangement.

(iv) For purposes of this paragraph (b)(6), the auditor shall review sufficient relevant information to formulate an opinion as to whether the investment advice arrangements, and the advice provided pursuant thereto, offered by the fiduciary adviser during the audit period were in compliance with this section. Nothing in this paragraph shall preclude an auditor from using information obtained by sampling, as reasonably determined appropriate by the auditor, investment advice arrangements, and the advice pursuant thereto, during the audit period.

(v) The selection of an auditor for purposes of this paragraph (b)(6) is a fiduciary act governed by section 404(a)(1) of ERISA.

(7) *Disclosure to participants.* (i) The fiduciary adviser must provide, without charge, to a participant or a beneficiary before the initial provision of investment advice with regard to any security or other property offered as an investment option, a written notification of:

(A) The role of any party that has a material affiliation or material contractual relationship with the fiduciary adviser in the development of the investment advice program, and in the selection of investment options available under the plan;

(B) The past performance and historical rates of return of the designated investment options available under the plan, to the extent that such information is not otherwise provided;

(C) All fees or other compensation that the fiduciary adviser or any affiliate thereof is to receive (including compensation provided by any third party) in connection with—

(1) The provision of the advice;

(2) The sale, acquisition, or holding of any security or other property pursuant to such advice; or

(3) Any rollover or other distribution of plan assets or the investment of distributed assets in any security or other property pursuant to such advice;

(D) Any material affiliation or material contractual relationship of the fiduciary adviser or affiliates thereof in the security or other property;

(E) The manner, and under what circumstances, any participant or beneficiary information provided under the arrangement will be used or disclosed;

(F) The types of services provided by the fiduciary adviser in connection with the provision of investment advice by the fiduciary adviser;

(G) The adviser is acting as a fiduciary of the plan in connection with the provision of the advice; and

(H) That a recipient of the advice may separately arrange for the provision of advice by another adviser that could have no material affiliation with and receive no fees or other compensation in connection with the security or other property.

(ii)

(A) The notification required under paragraph (b)(7)(i) of this section must be written in a clear and conspicuous manner and in a manner calculated to be understood by the average plan participant and must be sufficiently accurate and comprehensive to reasonably apprise such participants and beneficiaries of the information required to be provided in the notification.

(B) The appendix to this section contains a model disclosure form that may be used to provide notification of the information described in paragraph (b)(7)(i)(C) of this section. Use of the model form is not mandatory. However, use of an appropriately completed model disclosure form will be deemed to satisfy the requirements of paragraphs (b)(7)(i) and (ii) of this section with respect to such information.

(iii) The notification required under paragraph (b)(7)(i) of this section may, in accordance with 29 CFR 2520.104b-1, be provided in written or electronic form.

(iv) With respect to the information required to be disclosed pursuant to paragraph (b)(7)(i) of this section, the fiduciary adviser shall, at all times during the provision of advisory services to the participant or beneficiary pursuant to the arrangement—

(A) Maintain accurate, up-to-date information in a form that is consistent with paragraph (b)(7)(ii) of this section,

(B) Provide, without charge, accurate, up-to-date information to the recipient of the advice no less frequently than annually,

(C) Provide, without charge, accurate information to the recipient of the advice upon request of the recipient, and

(D) Provide, without charge, to the recipient of the advice any material change to the information described in paragraph (b)(7)(i) at a time reasonably contemporaneous to the change in information.

(8) *Disclosure to authorizing fiduciary.* The fiduciary adviser shall, in connection with any authorization described in paragraph (b)(5)(i) of this section, provide the authorizing fiduciary with a written notice informing the fiduciary that:

(i) The fiduciary adviser intends to comply with the conditions of the statutory exemption for investment advice under section 408(b)(14) and (g) of the Employee Retirement Income Security Act and this section;

(ii) The fiduciary adviser's arrangement will be audited annually by an independent auditor for compliance with the requirements of the statutory exemption and related regulations; and

(iii) The auditor will furnish the authorizing fiduciary a copy of that auditor's findings within 60 days of its completion of the audit.

(9) *Other conditions.* The requirements of this paragraph are met if—

(i) The fiduciary adviser provides appropriate disclosure, in connection with the sale, acquisition, or holding of the security or other property, in accordance with all applicable securities laws,

(ii) Any sale, acquisition, or holding of a security or other property occurs solely at the direction of the recipient of the advice,

(iii) The compensation received by the fiduciary adviser and affiliates thereof in connection with the sale, acquisition, or holding of the security or other property is reasonable, and

(iv) The terms of the sale, acquisition, or holding of the security or other property are at least as favorable to the plan as an arm's length transaction would be.

(c) *Definitions.* For purposes of this section:

(1) The term "*designated investment option*" means any investment option designated by the plan into which participants and beneficiaries may direct the investment of assets held in, or contributed to, their individual accounts. The term "*designated investment option*" shall not include "brokerage windows," "self-directed brokerage accounts," or similar plan arrangements that enable participants and beneficiaries to select investments beyond those designated by the plan. The term "*designated investment option*" has the same meaning as the term "*designated investment alternative*" as defined in 29 CFR 2550.404a-5(h).

(2)

(i) The term "*fiduciary adviser*" means, with respect to a plan, a person who is a fiduciary of the plan by reason of the provision of investment advice referred to in section 3(21)(A)(ii) of ERISA by the person to the participant or beneficiary of the plan and who is—

(A) Registered as an investment adviser under the Investment Advisers Act of 1940 (15 U.S.C. 80b-1 *et seq.*) or under the laws of the State in which the fiduciary maintains its principal office and place of business,

(B) A bank or similar financial institution referred to in section 408(b)(4) of ERISA or a savings association (as defined in section 3(b)(1) of the Federal Deposit Insurance Act (12 U.S.C. 1813(b)(1)), but only if the advice is provided through a trust department of the bank or similar financial institution or savings association which is subject to periodic examination and review by Federal or State banking authorities,

(C) An insurance company qualified to do business under the laws of a State,

(D) A person registered as a broker or dealer under the Securities Exchange Act of 1934 (15 U.S.C. 78a *et seq.*),

(E) An affiliate of a person described in paragraphs (c)(2)(i)(A) through (D), or

(F) An employee, agent, or registered representative of a person described in paragraphs (c)(2)(i)(A) through (E) of this section who satisfies the requirements of applicable insurance, banking, and securities laws relating to the provision of advice.

(ii) Except as provided under 29 CFR 2550.408g-2, a fiduciary adviser includes any person who develops the computer model, or markets the computer model or investment advice program, utilized in satisfaction of paragraph (b)(4) of this section.

(3) A "*registered representative*" of another entity means a person described in section 3(a)(18) of the Securities Exchange Act of 1934 (15 U.S.C. 78c(a)(18)) (substituting the entity for the broker or dealer referred to in such section) or a person described in section 202(a)(17) of the Investment Advisers Act of 1940 (15 U.S.C. 80b-2(a)(17)) (substituting the entity for the investment adviser referred to in such section).

(4) "*Individual Retirement Account*" or "*IRA*" means—

(i) An individual retirement account described in section 408(a) of the Code;

(ii) An individual retirement annuity described in section 408(b) of the Code;

(iii) An Archer MSA described in section 220(d) of the Code;

(iv) A health savings account described in section 223(d) of the Code;

(v) A Coverdell education savings account described in section 530 of the Code;

(vi) A trust, plan, account, or annuity which, at any time, has been determined by the Secretary of the Treasury to be described in any of paragraphs (c)(4)(i) through (v) of this section;

(vii) A "simplified employee pension" described in section 408(k) of the Code; or

(viii) A "simple retirement account" described in section 408(p) of the Code.

(5) An "*affiliate*" of another person means—

(i) Any person directly or indirectly owning, controlling, or holding with power to vote, 5 percent or more of the outstanding voting securities of such other person;

(ii) Any person 5 percent or more of whose outstanding voting securities are directly or indirectly owned, controlled, or held with power to vote, by such other person;

(iii) Any person directly or indirectly controlling, controlled by, or under common control with, such other person; and

(iv) Any officer, director, partner, copartner, or employee of such other person.

(6)

(i) A person with a "*material affiliation*" with another person means—

(A) Any affiliate of the other person;

(B) Any person directly or indirectly owning, controlling, or holding, 5 percent or more of the interests of such other person; and

(C) Any person 5 percent or more of whose interests are directly or indirectly owned, controlled, or held, by such other person.

(ii) For purposes of paragraph (c)(6)(i) of this section, "*interest*" means with respect to an entity—

(A) The combined voting power of all classes of stock entitled to vote or the total value of the shares of all classes of stock of the entity if the entity is a corporation;

(B) The capital interest or the profits interest of the entity if the entity is a partnership; or

(C) The beneficial interest of the entity if the entity is a trust or unincorporated enterprise.

(7) Persons have a "*material contractual relationship*" if payments made by one person to the other person pursuant to contracts or agreements between the persons exceed 10 percent of the gross revenue, on an annual basis, of such other person.

(8) "*Control*" means the power to exercise a controlling influence over the management or policies of a person other than an individual.

(d) *Retention of records.* The fiduciary adviser must maintain, for a period of not less than 6 years after the provision of investment advice under this section any records necessary for determining whether the applicable requirements of this section have been met. A transaction prohibited under section 406 of ERISA shall not be considered to have occurred solely because the records are lost or destroyed prior to the end of the 6-year period due to circumstances beyond the control of the fiduciary adviser.

(e) *Noncompliance.* (1) The relief from the prohibited transaction provisions of section 406 of ERISA and the sanctions resulting from the application of section 4975 of the Code described in paragraph (b) of this section shall not apply to any transaction described in such paragraphs in connection with the provision of investment advice to an individual participant or beneficiary with respect to which the applicable conditions of this section have not been satisfied.

(2) In the case of a pattern or practice of noncompliance with any of the applicable conditions of this section, the relief described in paragraph (b) of this section shall not apply to any transaction in connection with the provision of investment advice provided by the fiduciary adviser during the period over which the pattern or practice extended.

(f) *Effective date and applicability date.* This section shall be effective December 27, 2011. This section shall apply to transactions described in paragraph (b) of this section occurring on or after December 27, 2011.

[Added on October 25, 2011 by 76 FR 66136.]

[¶ 14,789B-1]
Appendix to § 2550.408g-1
Fiduciary Adviser Disclosure

This document contains important information about [*enter name of* Fiduciary Adviser] and how it is compensated for the investment advice provided to you. You should carefully consider this information in your evaluation of that advice.

[*enter name of* Fiduciary Adviser] has been selected to provide investment advisory services for the [*enter name of* Plan]. [*enter name of* Fiduciary Adviser] will be providing these services as a fiduciary under the Employee Retirement Income Security Act (ERISA). [*enter name of* Fiduciary Adviser], therefore, must act prudently and with only your interest in mind when providing you recommendations on how to invest your retirement assets.

Compensation of the Fiduciary Adviser and Related Parties

[*enter name of* Fiduciary Adviser] (is/is not) compensated by the plan for the advice it provides. *(if compensated by the plan, explain what and how compensation is charged (e.g., asset-based fee, flat fee, per advice)). (If applicable,* [*enter name of* Fiduciary Adviser] is not compensated on the basis of the investment(s) selected by you.)

Affiliates of [*enter name of* Fiduciary Adviser](*if applicable enter,* and other parties with whom [*enter name of* Fiduciary Adviser] is related or has a material financial relationship) also will be providing services for which they will be compensated. These services include: [*enter description of services, e.g., investment management, transfer agent, custodial, and shareholder services for some/all the investment funds available under the plan.*]

When [*enter name of* Fiduciary Adviser] recommends that you invest your assets in an investment fund of its own or one of its affiliates and you follow that advice, [*enter name* of Fiduciary Adviser] or that affiliate will receive compensation from the investment fund based on the amount you invest. The amounts that will be paid by you will vary depending on the particular fund in which you invest your assets and may range from 1% to 1%. Specific information concerning the fees and other charges of each investment fund is available from [*enter source, such as: your plan administrator, investment fund provider (possibly with Internet Web site address)*]. This information should be reviewed carefully before you make an investment decision.

(*if applicable enter,* [*enter name of* Fiduciary Adviser] or affiliates of [*enter name of* Fiduciary Adviser] also receive compensation from non-affiliated investment funds as a result of investments you make as a result of recommendations of [*enter name of* Fiduciary Adviser]. The amount of this compensation also may vary depending on the particular fund in which you invest. This compensation may range from 1% to 1%. Specific information concerning the fees and other charges of each investment fund is available from [*enter source, such as: your plan administrator, investment fund provider (possibly with Internet Web site address)*]. This information should be reviewed carefully before you make an investment decision.

(*if applicable enter,* In addition to the above, [*enter name of* Fiduciary Adviser] or affiliates of [*enter name of* Fiduciary Adviser] also receive other fees or compensation, such as commissions, in connection with the sale, acquisition or holding of investments selected by you as a result of recommendations of [*enter name of* Fiduciary Adviser]. These amounts are: [*enter description of all other fees or compensation to be received in connection with sale, acquisition or holding of investments*]. This information should be reviewed carefully before you make an investment decision.

(*if applicable enter,* When [*enter name of* Fiduciary Adviser] recommends that you take a rollover or other distribution of assets from the plan, or recommends how those assets should subsequently be invested, [*enter name of* Fiduciary Adviser] or affiliates of [*enter name of* Fiduciary Adviser] will receive additional fees or compensation. These amounts are: [*enter description of all other fees or compensation to be received in connection with any rollover or other distribution of plan assets or the investment of distributed assets*]. This information should be reviewed carefully before you make a decision to take a distribution.

Consider Impact of Compensation on Advice

The fees and other compensation that [*enter name of* Fiduciary Adviser] and its affiliates receive on account of assets in [*enter name of* Fiduciary Adviser](*enter if applicable,* and non-[*enter name of* Fiduciary Adviser]) investment funds are a significant source of revenue for the [*enter name of* Fiduciary Adviser] and its affiliates. You should carefully consider the impact of any such fees and compensation in your evaluation of the investment advice that [*enter name of* Fiduciary Adviser]provides to you. In this regard, you may arrange for the provision of advice by another adviser that may have no material affiliation with or receive no compensation in connection with the investment funds or products offered under the plan. This type of advice is/is not available through your plan.

Investment Returns

While understanding investment-related fees and expenses is important in making informed investment decisions, it is also important to consider additional information about your investment options, such as performance, investment strategies and risks. Specific information related to the past performance and historical rates of return of the investment options available under the plan (has/has not) been provided to you by [*enter source, such as: your plan administrator, investment fund provider*]. (*if applicable enter,* If not provided to you, the information is attached to this document.)

For options with returns that vary over time, past performance does not guarantee how your investment in the option will perform in the future; your investment in these options could lose money.

Parties Participating in Development of Advice Program or Selection of Investment Options

Name, and describe role of, affiliates or other parties with whom the fiduciary adviser has a material affiliation or contractual relationship that participated in the development of the investment advice program (if this is an arrangement that uses computer models) or the selection of investment options available under the plan.

Use of Personal Information

Include a brief explanation of the following— What personal information will be collected; How the information will be used; Parties with whom information will be shared; How the information will be protected; and When and how notice of the Fiduciary Adviser's privacy statement will be available to participants and beneficiaries.

Should you have any questions about [*enter name of* Fiduciary Adviser] or the information contained in this document, you may contact [*enter name of contact person for fiduciary adviser, telephone number, address*].

[Added on October 25, 2011 by 76 FR 66136.]

[¶ 14,789B-2]
§ 2550.408g-2 **Investment advice—fiduciary election.**

(a) *General.* Section 408(g)(11)(A) of the Employee Retirement Income Security Act, as amended (ERISA), provides that a person who develops a computer model or who markets a computer model or investment advice program used in an "eligible investment advice arrangement" shall be treated as a fiduciary of a plan by reason of the provision of investment advice referred to in ERISA section 3(21)(A)(ii) to the plan participant or beneficiary, and shall be treated as a "fiduciary adviser" for purposes of ERISA sections 408(b)(14) and 408(g), except that the Secretary of Labor may prescribe rules under which only one fiduciary adviser may elect to be treated as a fiduciary with respect to the plan. Section 4975(f)(8)(J)(i) of the Internal Revenue Code, as amended (the Code), contains a parallel provision to ERISA section 408(g)(11)(A) that applies for purposes of Code sections 4975(d)(17) and 4975(f)(8). This section sets forth requirements that must be satisfied in order for one such fiduciary adviser to elect to be treated as a fiduciary with respect to a plan under an eligible investment advice arrangement.

(b)(1) If an election meets the requirements in paragraph (b)(2) of this section, then the person identified in the election shall be the sole fiduciary adviser treated as a fiduciary by reason of developing or marketing the computer model, or marketing the investment advice program, used in an eligible investment advice arrangement.

(2) An election satisfies the requirements of this paragraph (b) with respect to an eligible investment advice arrangement if the election is in writing and such writing—

(i) Identifies the investment advice arrangement, and the person offering the arrangement, with respect to which the election is to be effective;

(ii) Identifies a person who—

(A) Is described in any of 29 CFR 2550.408g-1(c)(2)(i)(A) through (E),

(B) Develops the computer model, or markets the computer model or investment advice program, utilized in satisfaction of 29 CFR 2550.408g-1(b)(4) with respect to the arrangement, and

(C) Acknowledges that it elects to be treated as the only fiduciary, and fiduciary adviser, by reason of developing such computer model, or marketing such computer model or investment advice program;

(iii) Is signed by the person identified in paragraph (b)(2)(ii) of this section;

(iv) Is furnished to the person who authorized the arrangement, in accordance with 29 CFR 2550.408g-1(b)(5); and

(v) Is maintained in accordance with 29 CFR 2550.408g-1(d).

[Added on October 25, 2011 by 76 FR 66136.]

Regulations

The following regulations were adopted on October 27, 2011 by 76 FR 66637, effective on December 27, 2011.

Subpart B—Procedures Governing the Filing and Processing of Prohibited Transaction Exemption Applications

[¶ 14,789B-5]

§ 2570.30 **Scope of rules.**

(a) The rules of procedure set forth in this subpart apply to prohibited transaction exemptions issued by the Department under the authority of:

(1) Section 408(a) of the Employee Retirement Income Security Act of 1974 (ERISA);

(2) Section 4975(c)(2) of the Internal Revenue Code of 1986 (the Code)[1]; or

(3) The Federal Employees' Retirement System Act of 1986 (FERSA) (5 U.S.C. 8477(c)(3)).

(b) Under these rules of procedure, the Department may conditionally or unconditionally exempt any fiduciary or transaction, or class of fiduciaries or transactions, from all or part of the restrictions imposed by section 406 of ERISA and the corresponding restrictions of the Code and FERSA. While administrative exemptions granted under these rules are ordinarily prospective in nature, an applicant may also obtain retroactive relief for past prohibited transactions if certain safeguards described in this subpart were in place at the time the transaction was consummated.

(c) These rules govern the filing and processing of applications for both individual and class exemptions that the Department may propose and grant pursuant to the authorities cited in paragraph (a) of this section. The Department may also propose and grant exemptions on its own motion, in which case the procedures relating to publication of notices, hearings, evaluation and public inspection of the administrative record, and modification or revocation of previously granted exemptions will apply.

(d) The issuance of an administrative exemption by the Department under these procedural rules does not relieve a fiduciary or other party in interest or disqualified person with respect to a plan from the obligation to comply with certain other provisions of ERISA, the Code, or FERSA, including any prohibited transaction provisions to which the exemption does not apply, and the general fiduciary responsibility provisions of ERISA which require, among other things, that a fiduciary discharge his or her duties respecting the plan solely in the interests of the participants and beneficiaries of the plan and in a prudent fashion; nor does it affect the requirement of section 401(a) of the Code that the plan must operate for the exclusive benefit of the employees of the employer maintaining the plan and their beneficiaries.

(e) The Department will not propose or issue exemptions upon oral request alone, nor will the Department grant exemptions orally. An applicant for an administrative exemption may request and receive oral advice from Department employees in preparing an exemption application. However, such advice does not constitute part of the administrative record and is not binding on the Department in its processing of an exemption application or in its examination or audit of a plan.

(f) The Department will generally treat any exemption application that is filed solely under section 408(a) of ERISA or solely under section 4975(c)(2) of the Code as an exemption request filed under both section 408(a) and section 4975(c)(2) if it relates to a transaction that would be prohibited both by ERISA and the corresponding provisions of the Code.

[Amended on October 27, 2011 by 76 FR 66637.]

[¶ 14,789B-6]

§ 2570.31 **Definitions.**

For purposes of these procedures, the following definitions apply:

(a) An *affiliate* of a person means—

(1) Any person directly or indirectly through one or more intermediaries, controlling, controlled by, or under common control with the person. For purposes of this paragraph, the term "control" means the power to exercise a controlling influence over the management or policies of a person other than an individual;

(2) Any director of, relative of, or partner in, any such person;

(3) Any corporation, partnership, trust, or unincorporated enterprise of which such person is an officer, director, or a 5 percent or more partner or owner; or

(4) Any employee or officer of the person who—

(i) Is highly compensated (as defined in section 4975(e)(2)(H) of the Code), or

(ii) Has direct or indirect authority, responsibility, or control regarding the custody, management, or disposition of plan assets involved in the subject exemption transaction.

(b) A *class exemption* is an administrative exemption, granted under section 408(a) of ERISA, section 4975(c)(2) of the Code, and/or 5 U.S.C. 8477(c)(3), which applies to any transaction and party in interest within the class of transactions and parties in interest specified in the exemption when the conditions of the exemption are satisfied.

(c) *Department* means the U.S. Department of Labor and includes the Secretary of Labor or his or her delegate exercising authority with respect to prohibited transaction exemptions to which this subpart applies.

(d) *Exemption transaction* means the transaction or transactions for which an exemption is requested.

(e) An *individual exemption* is an administrative exemption, granted under section 408(a) of ERISA, section 4975(c)(2) of the Code, and/or 5 U.S.C. 8477(c)(3), which applies only to the specific parties in interest and transactions named or otherwise defined in the exemption.

(f) A *party in interest* means a person described in section 3(14) of ERISA or 5 U.S.C. 8477(a)(4) and includes a *disqualified person,* as defined in section 4975(e)(2) of the Code.

(g) *Pooled fund* means an account or fund for the collective investment of the assets of two or more unrelated plans, including (but not limited to) a pooled separate account maintained by an insurance company and a common or collective trust fund maintained by a bank or similar financial institution.

(h) A *qualified appraisal report* is any appraisal report that satisfies all of the requirements set forth in this subpart at § 2570.34(c)(4).

(i) A *qualified independent appraiser* is any individual or entity with appropriate training, experience, and facilities to provide a qualified appraisal report on behalf of the plan regarding the particular asset or property appraised in the report, that is independent of and unre-

---

[1] Section 102 of Presidential Reorganization Plan No. 4 of 1978 (3 CFR 332 (1978), *reprinted in* 5 U.S.C. app. at 672 (2006), *and in* 92 Stat. 3790 (1978)), effective December 31, 1978, generally transferred the authority of the Secretary of the Treasury to issue administrative exemptions under section 4975(c)(2) of the Code to the Department of Labor.

lated to any party in interest engaging in the exemption transaction and its affiliates; in general, the determination as to the independence of the appraiser is made by the Department on the basis of all relevant facts and circumstances. In making this determination, the Department generally will take into account the amount of both the appraiser's revenues and projected revenues for the current federal income tax year (including amounts received for preparing the appraisal report) that will be derived from the party in interest or its affiliates relative to the appraiser's revenues from all sources for the prior federal income tax year. Absent facts and circumstances demonstrating a lack of independence, the Department will operate according to the presumption that such appraiser will be independent if the revenues it receives or is projected to receive, within the current federal income tax year, from parties in interest (and their affiliates) to the transaction are not more than 2% of such appraiser's annual revenues based upon its prior income tax year. Although the presumption does not apply when the aforementioned percentage exceeds 2%, an appraiser nonetheless may be considered independent based upon other facts and circumstances provided that it receives or is projected to receive revenues that are not more than 5% within the current federal income tax year from parties in interest (and their affiliates) to the transaction based upon its prior income tax year.

(j) A *qualified independent fiduciary* is any individual or entity with appropriate training, experience, and facilities to act on behalf of the plan regarding the exemption transaction in accordance with the fiduciary duties and responsibilities prescribed by ERISA, that is independent of and unrelated to any party in interest engaging in the exemption transaction and its affiliates; in general, the determination as to the independence of a fiduciary is made by the Department on the basis of all relevant facts and circumstances. In making this determination, the Department generally will take into account the amount of both the fiduciary's revenues and projected revenues for the current federal income tax year (including amounts received for preparing fiduciary reports) that will be derived from the party in interest or its affiliates relative to the fiduciary's revenues from all sources for the prior federal income tax year. Absent facts and circumstances demonstrating a lack of independence, the Department will operate according to the presumption that such fiduciary will be independent if the revenues it receives or is projected to receive, within the current federal income tax year, from parties in interest (and their affiliates) to the transaction are not more than 2% of such fiduciary's annual revenues based upon its prior income tax year. Although the presumption does not apply when the aforementioned percentage exceeds 2%, a fiduciary nonetheless may be considered independent based upon other facts and circumstances provided that it receives or is projected to receive revenues that are not more than 5% within the current federal income tax year from parties in interest (and their affiliates) to the transaction based upon its prior income tax year.

[Amended on October 27, 2011 by 76 FR 66637.]

[¶ 14,789B-7]

§ 2570.32 **Persons who may apply for exemptions.**

(a) The Department will initiate exemption proceedings upon the application of:

(1) Any party in interest to a plan who is or may be a party to the exemption transaction;

(2) Any plan which is a party to the exemption transaction; or

(3) In the case of an application for an exemption covering a class of parties in interest or a class of transactions, in addition to any person described in paragraphs (a)(1) and (2) of this section, an association or organization representing parties in interest who may be parties to the exemption transaction.

(b) An application by or for a person described in paragraph (a) of this section, may be submitted by the applicant or by an authorized representative. An application submitted by a representative of the applicant must include proof of authority in the form of:

(1) A power of attorney; or

(2) A written certification from the applicant that the representative is authorized to file the application.

(c) If the authorized representative of an applicant submits an application for an exemption to the Department together with proof of

authority to file the application as required by paragraph (b) of this section, the Department will direct all correspondence and inquiries concerning the application to the representative unless requested to do otherwise by the applicant.

[Amended on October 27, 2011 by 76 FR 66637.]

[¶ 14,789B-8]

§ 2570.33 **Applications the Department will not ordinarily consider.**

(a) The Department ordinarily will not consider:

(1) An application that fails to include all the information required by §§ 2570.34 and 2570.35 of this subpart or otherwise fails to conform to the requirements of these procedures; or

(2) An application involving a transaction or transactions which are the subject of an investigation for possible violations of part 1 or 4 of subtitle B of Title I of ERISA or section 8477 or 8478 of FERSA or an application involving a party in interest who is the subject of such an investigation or who is a defendant in an action by the Department or the Internal Revenue Service to enforce the abovementioned provisions of ERISA or FERSA.

(b) An application for an individual exemption relating to a specific transaction or transactions ordinarily will not be considered if the Department has under consideration a class exemption relating to the same type of transaction or transactions. Notwithstanding the foregoing, the Department may consider such an application if the issuance of the final class exemption may not be imminent, and the Department determines that time constraints necessitate consideration of the transaction on an individual basis.

(c) The administrative record of an exemption application includes the initial exemption application and any supporting information provided by the applicant (as well as any comments and testimony received by the Department in connection with an application). If an applicant designates as confidential any information required by these regulations or requested by the Department, the Department will determine whether the information is material to the exemption determination. If it determines the information to be material, the Department will not process the application unless the applicant withdraws the claim of confidentiality.

(d) If for any reason the Department decides not to consider an exemption application, it will inform the applicant in writing of that decision and of the reasons therefore.

[Amended on October 27, 2011 by 76 FR 66637.]

[¶ 14,789B-9]

§ 2570.34 **Information to be included in every exemption application.**

(a) All applications for exemptions must contain the following information:

(1) The name(s) of the applicant(s);

(2) A detailed description of the exemption transaction including identification of all the parties in interest involved, a description of any larger integrated transaction of which the exemption transaction is a part, and a chronology of the events leading up to the transaction;

(3) The identity of any representatives for the affected plan(s) and parties in interest and what individuals or entities they represent;

(4) The reasons a plan would have for entering into the exemption transaction;

(5) The prohibited transaction provisions from which exemptive relief is requested and the reason why the transaction would violate each such provision;

(6) Whether the exemption transaction is customary for the industry or class involved;

(7) Whether the exemption transaction is or has been the subject of an investigation or enforcement action by the Department or by the Internal Revenue Service; and

(8) The hardship or economic loss, if any, which would result to the person or persons on behalf of whom the exemption is sought, to affected plans, and to their participants and beneficiaries from denial of the exemption.

(b) All applications for exemption must also contain the following:

(1) A statement explaining why the requested exemption would be—

(i) Administratively feasible;

(ii) In the interests of affected plans and their participants and beneficiaries; and

(iii) Protective of the rights of participants and beneficiaries of affected plans.

(2) With respect to the notification of interested persons required by § 2570.43:

(i) A description of the interested persons to whom the applicant intends to provide notice;

(ii) The manner in which the applicant will provide such notice; and

(iii) An estimate of the time the applicant will need to furnish notice to all interested persons following publication of a notice of the proposed exemption in the *Federal Register.*

(3) If an advisory opinion has been requested by any party to the exemption transaction from the Department with respect to any issue relating to the exemption transaction—

(i) A copy of the letter concluding the Department's action on the advisory opinion request; or

(ii) If the Department has not yet concluded its action on the request:

(A) A copy of the request or the date on which it was submitted together with the Department's correspondence control number as indicated in the acknowledgment letter; and

(B) An explanation of the effect of the issuance of an advisory opinion upon the exemption transaction.

(4) If the application is to be signed by anyone other than an individual party in interest seeking exemptive relief on his or her own behalf, a statement which—

(i) Identifies the individual signing the application and his or her position or title; and

(ii) Explains briefly the basis of his or her familiarity with the matters discussed in the application.

(5)(i) A declaration in the following form:

Under penalty of perjury, I declare that I am familiar with the matters discussed in this application and, to the best of my knowledge and belief, the representations made in this application are true and correct.

(ii) This declaration must be dated and signed by:

(A) The applicant, in its individual capacity, in the case of an individual party in interest seeking exemptive relief on his or her own behalf;

(B) A corporate officer or partner where the applicant is a corporation or partnership;

(C) A designated officer or official where the applicant is an association, organization or other unincorporated enterprise; or

(D) The plan fiduciary that has the authority, responsibility, and control with respect to the exemption transaction where the applicant is a plan.

(c) Specialized statements, as applicable, from a qualified independent appraiser acting solely on behalf of the plan, such as appraisal reports or analyses of market conditions, submitted to support an application for exemption must be accompanied by a statement of consent from such appraiser acknowledging that the statement is being submitted to the Department as part of an application for exemption. Such statements must also contain the following written information:

(1) A copy of the qualified independent appraiser's engagement letter with the plan describing the specific duties the appraiser shall undertake;

(2) A summary of the qualified independent appraiser's qualifications to serve in such capacity;

(3) A detailed description of any relationship that the qualified independent appraiser has had or may have with any party in interest engaging in the transaction with the plan, or its affiliates, that may influence the appraiser;

(4) A written appraisal report prepared by the qualified independent appraiser, acting solely on behalf of the plan, rather than, for example, on behalf of the plan sponsor, which satisfies the following requirements:

(i) The report must describe the method(s) used in determining the fair market value of the subject asset(s) and an explanation of why such method best reflects the fair market value of the asset(s);

(ii) The report must take into account any special benefit that the party in interest or its affiliate(s) may derive from control of the asset(s), such as from owning an adjacent parcel of real property or gaining voting control over a company; and

(iii) The report must be current and not more than one year old from the date of the transaction, and there must be a written update by the qualified independent appraiser affirming the accuracy of the appraisal as of the date of the transaction. If the appraisal report is a year old or more, a new appraisal shall be submitted to the Department by the applicant.

(5) If the subject of the appraisal report is real property, the qualified independent appraiser shall submit a written representation that he or she is a member of a professional organization of appraisers that can sanction its members for misconduct;

(6) If the subject of the appraisal report is an asset other than real property, the qualified independent appraiser shall submit a written representation describing the appraiser's prior experience in valuing assets of the same type; and

(7) The qualified independent appraiser shall submit a written representation disclosing the percentage of its current revenue that is derived from any party in interest involved in the transaction or its affiliates; in general, such percentage shall be computed by comparing, in fractional form:

(i) The amount of the appraiser's projected revenues from the current federal income tax year (including amounts received from preparing the appraisal report) that will be derived from the party in interest or its affiliates (expressed as a numerator); and

(ii) The appraiser's revenues from all sources for the prior federal income tax year (expressed as a denominator).

(d) For those exemption transactions requiring the retention of a qualified independent fiduciary to represent the interests of the plan, a statement must be submitted by such fiduciary that contains the following written information:

(1) A signed and dated declaration under penalty of perjury that, to the best of the qualified independent fiduciary's knowledge and belief, all of the representations made in such statement are true and correct;

(2) A copy of the qualified independent fiduciary's engagement letter with the plan describing the fiduciary's specific duties;

(3) An explanation for the conclusion that the fiduciary is a qualified independent fiduciary, which also must include a summary of that person's qualifications to serve in such capacity, as well as a description of any prior experience by that person or other demonstrated characteristics of the fiduciary (such as special areas of expertise) that render that person or entity suitable to perform its duties on behalf of the plan with respect to the exemption transaction;

(4) A detailed description of any relationship that the qualified independent fiduciary has had or may have with the party in interest engaging in the transaction with the plan or its affiliates;

(5) An acknowledgement by the qualified independent fiduciary that it understands its duties and responsibilities under ERISA in acting as a fiduciary on behalf of the plan rather than, for example, acting on behalf of the plan sponsor;

(6) The qualified independent fiduciary's opinion on whether the proposed transaction would be in the interests of the plan and of its participants and beneficiaries, and protective of the rights of participants and beneficiaries of such plan, along with a statement of the reasons on which the opinion is based;

(7) Where the proposed transaction is continuing in nature, a declaration by the qualified independent fiduciary that it is authorized to take all appropriate actions to safeguard the interests of the plan, and shall, during the pendency of the transaction:

(i) Monitor the transaction on behalf of the plan on a continuing basis;

(ii) Ensure that the transaction remains in the interests of the plan and, if not, take any appropriate actions available under the particular circumstances; and

(iii) Enforce compliance with all conditions and obligations imposed on any party dealing with the plan with respect to the transaction; and

(8) The qualified independent fiduciary shall submit a written representation disclosing the percentage of such fiduciary's current revenue that is derived from any party in interest involved in the transaction or its affiliates; in general, such percentage shall be computed by comparing, in fractional form:

(i) The amount of the fiduciary's projected revenues from the current federal income tax year that will be derived from the party in interest or its affiliates (expressed as a numerator); and

(ii) The fiduciary's revenues from all sources (excluding fixed, nondiscretionary retirement income) for the prior federal income tax year (expressed as a denominator).

(e) Specialized statements, as applicable, from other third-party experts, including but not limited to economists or market specialists, submitted on behalf of the plan to support an application for exemption must be accompanied by a statement of consent from such expert acknowledging that the statement prepared on behalf of the plan is being submitted to the Department as part of an application for exemption. Such statements must also contain the following written information:

(1) A copy of the expert's engagement letter with the plan describing the specific duties the expert will undertake;

(2) A summary of the expert's qualifications to serve in such capacity; and

(3) A detailed description of any relationship that the expert has had or may have with any party in interest engaging in the transaction with the plan, or its affiliates, that may influence the actions of the expert.

(f) An application for exemption may also include a draft of the requested exemption which describes the transaction and parties in interest for which exemptive relief is sought and the specific conditions under which the exemption would apply.

[Amended on October 27, 2011 by 76 FR 66637.]

[¶ 14,789B-10]

§ 2570.35 **Information to be included in applications for individual exemptions only.**

(a) Except as provided in paragraph (c) of this section, every application for an individual exemption must include, in addition to the information specified in § 2570.34 of this subpart, the following information:

(1) The name, address, telephone number, and type of plan or plans to which the requested exemption applies;

(2) The Employer Identification Number (EIN) and the plan number (PN) used by such plan or plans in all reporting and disclosure required by the Department;

(3) Whether any plan or trust affected by the requested exemption has ever been found by the Department, the Internal Revenue Service, or by a court to have violated the exclusive benefit rule of section 401(a) of the Code, section 4975(c)(1) of the Code, section 406 or 407(a) of ERISA, or 5 U.S.C. 8477(c)(3), including a description of the circumstances surrounding such violation;

(4) Whether any relief under section 408(a) of ERISA, section 4975(c)(2) of the Code, or 5 U.S.C. 8477(c)(3) has been requested by, or provided to, the applicant or any of the parties on behalf of whom the exemption is sought and, if so, the exemption application number or the prohibited transaction exemption number;

(5) Whether the applicant or any of the parties in interest involved in the exemption transaction is currently, or has been within the last five years, a defendant in any lawsuit or criminal action concerning such person's conduct as a fiduciary or party in interest with respect to any plan (other than a lawsuit with respect to a routine claim for benefits), and a description of the circumstances of such lawsuit or criminal action;

(6) Whether the applicant (including any person described in § 2570.34(b)(5)(ii)) or any of the parties in interest involved in the exemption transaction has, within the last 13 years, been either convicted or released from imprisonment, whichever is later, as a result of: any felony involving abuse or misuse of such person's position or employment with an employee benefit plan or a labor organization; any felony arising out of the conduct of the business of a broker, dealer, investment adviser, bank, insurance company or fiduciary; income tax evasion; any felony involving the larceny, theft, robbery, extortion, forgery, counterfeiting, fraudulent concealment, embezzlement, fraudulent conversion, or misappropriation of funds or securities; conspiracy or attempt to commit any such crimes or a crime of which any of the foregoing crimes is an element; or any other crime described in section 411 of ERISA, and a description of the circumstances of any such conviction. For purposes of this section, a person shall be deemed to have been "convicted" from the date of the judgment of the trial court, regardless of whether that judgment remains under appeal;

(7) Whether, within the last five years, any plan affected by the exemption transaction, or any party in interest involved in the exemption transaction, has been under investigation or examination by, or has been engaged in litigation or a continuing controversy with, the Department, the Internal Revenue Service, the Justice Department, the Pension Benefit Guaranty Corporation, or the Federal Retirement Thrift Investment Board involving compliance with provisions of ERISA, provisions of the Code relating to employee benefit plans, or provisions of FERSA relating to the Federal Thrift Savings Fund. If so, the applicant must provide a brief statement describing the investigation, examination, litigation or controversy. The Department reserves the right to require the production of additional information or documentation concerning any of the above matters. In this regard, a denial of the exemption application will result from a failure to provide additional information requested by the Department.

(8) Whether any plan affected by the requested exemption has experienced a reportable event under section 4043 of ERISA, and, if so, a description of the circumstances of any such reportable event;

(9) Whether a notice of intent to terminate has been filed under section 4041 of ERISA respecting any plan affected by the requested exemption, and, if so, a description of the circumstances for the issuance of such notice;

(10) Names, addresses, and taxpayer identifying numbers of all parties in interest involved in the subject transaction;

(11) The estimated number of participants and beneficiaries in each plan affected by the requested exemption as of the date of the application;

(12) The percentage of the fair market value of the total assets of each affected plan that is involved in the exemption transaction;

(13) Whether the exemption transaction has been consummated or will be consummated only if the exemption is granted;

(14) If the exemption transaction has already been consummated:

(i) The circumstances which resulted in plan fiduciaries causing the plan(s) to engage in the transaction before obtaining an exemption from the Department;

(ii) Whether the transaction has been terminated;

(iii) Whether the transaction has been corrected as defined in Code section 4975(f)(5);

(iv) Whether Form 5330, Return of Excise Taxes Related to Employee Benefit Plans, has been filed with the Internal Revenue Service with respect to the transaction; and

(v) Whether any excise taxes due under section 4975(a) and (b) of the Code, or any civil penalties due under section 502(i) or (l) of ERISA by reason of the transaction have been paid. If so, the applicant should submit documentation (e.g., a canceled check) demonstrating that the excise taxes or civil penalties were paid.

(15) The name of every person who has investment discretion over any plan assets involved in the exemption transaction and the relationship of each such person to the parties in interest involved in the exemption transaction and the affiliates of such parties in interest;

(16) Whether or not the assets of the affected plan(s) are invested in loans to any party in interest involved in the exemption transaction, in property leased to any such party in interest, or in securities issued by any such party in interest, and, if such investments exist, a statement for each of these three types of investments which indicates:

(i) The type of investment to which the statement pertains;

(ii) The aggregate fair market value of all investments of this type as reflected in the plan's most recent annual report;

(iii) The approximate percentage of the fair market value of the plan's total assets as shown in such annual report that is represented by all investments of this type; and

(iv) The statutory or administrative exemption covering these investments, if any.

(17) The approximate aggregate fair market value of the total assets of each affected plan;

(18) The person(s) who will bear the costs of the exemption application and of notifying interested persons; and

(19) Whether an independent fiduciary is or will be involved in the exemption transaction and, if so, the names of the persons who will bear the cost of the fee payable to such fiduciary.

(b) Each application for an individual exemption must also include:

(1) True copies of all contracts, deeds, agreements, and instruments, as well as relevant portions of plan documents, trust agreements, and any other documents bearing on the exemption transaction;

(2) A discussion of the facts relevant to the exemption transaction that are reflected in these documents and an analysis of their bearing on the requested exemption;

(3) A copy of the most recent financial statements of each plan affected by the requested exemption; and

(4) A net worth statement with respect to any party in interest that is providing a personal guarantee with respect to the exemption transaction.

(c) Special rule for applications for individual exemption involving pooled funds:

(1) The information required by paragraphs (a)(8) through (12) of this section is not required to be furnished in an application for individual exemption involving one or more pooled funds;

(2) The information required by paragraphs (a)(1) through (7) and (a)(13) through (19) of this section and by paragraphs (b)(1) through (3) of this section must be furnished in reference to the pooled fund, rather than to the plans participating therein. (For purposes of this paragraph, the information required by paragraph (a)(16) of this section relates solely to other pooled fund transactions with, and investments in, parties in interest involved in the exemption transaction which are also sponsors of plans which invest in the pooled fund.);

(3) The following information must also be furnished -

(i) The estimated number of plans that are participating (or will participate) in the pooled fund; and

(ii) The minimum and maximum limits imposed by the pooled fund (if any) on the portion of the total assets of each plan that may be invested in the pooled fund.

(4) Additional requirements for applications for individual exemption involving pooled funds in which certain plans participate.

(i) This paragraph applies to any application for an individual exemption involving one or more pooled funds in which any plan participating therein -

(A) Invests an amount which exceeds 20% of the total assets of the pooled fund, or

(B) Covers employees of:

(1) The party sponsoring or maintaining the pooled fund, or any affiliate of such party, or

(2) Any fiduciary with investment discretion over the pooled fund's assets, or any affiliate of such fiduciary.

(ii) The exemption application must include, with respect to each plan described in paragraph (c)(4)(i) of this section, the information required by paragraphs (a)(1) through (3), (a)(5) through (7),

(a)(10), (a)(12) through (16), and (a)(18) and (19), of this section. The information required by this paragraph must be furnished in reference to the plan's investment in the pooled fund (e.g., the names, addresses and taxpayer identifying numbers of all fiduciaries responsible for the plan's investment in the pooled fund (§ 2570.35(a) (10)), the percentage of the assets of the plan invested in the pooled fund (§ 2570.35(a)(12)), whether the plan's investment in the pooled fund has been consummated or will be consummated only if the exemption is granted (§ 2570.35(a)(13)), etc.).

(iii) The information required by paragraph (c)(4) of this section is in addition to the information required by paragraphs (c)(2) and (3) of this section relating to information furnished by reference to the pooled fund.

(5) The special rule and the additional requirements described in paragraphs (c)(1) through (4) of this section do not apply to an individual exemption request solely for the investment by a plan in a pooled fund. Such an application must provide the information required by paragraphs (a) and (b) of this section.

(d) Retroactive exemptions:

(1) Generally, the Department will favorably consider requests for retroactive relief, in all exemption applications, only where the safeguards necessary for the grant of a prospective exemption were in place at the time at which the parties entered into the transaction. An applicant for a retroactive exemption must have acted in good faith by taking reasonable and appropriate steps to protect the plan from abuse and unnecessary risk at the time of the transaction.

(2) Among the factors that the Department would take into account in making a finding that an applicant acted in good faith include the following:

(i) The participation of an independent fiduciary acting on behalf of the plan who is qualified to negotiate, approve and monitor the transaction;

(ii) The existence of a contemporaneous appraisal by a qualified independent appraiser or reference to an objective third party source, such as a stock or bond index;

(iii) The existence of a bidding process or evidence of comparable fair market transactions with unrelated third parties;

(iv) That the applicant has submitted an accurate and complete application for exemption containing documentation of all necessary and relevant facts and representations upon which the applicant relied. In this regard, additional weight will be given to facts and representations which are prepared and certified by a source independent of the applicant;

(v) That the applicant has submitted evidence that the plan fiduciary did not engage in an act or transaction knowing that such act or transaction was prohibited under section 406 of ERISA and/or section 4975 of the Code. In this regard, the Department will accord appropriate weight to the submission of a contemporaneous, reasoned legal opinion of counsel, upon which the plan fiduciary relied in good faith before entering the act or transaction;

(vi) That the applicant has submitted a statement of the circumstances which prompted the submission of the application for exemption and the steps taken by the applicant with regard to the transaction upon discovery of the violation;

(vii) That the applicant has submitted a statement, prepared and certified by an independent person familiar with the types of transactions for which relief is requested, demonstrating that the terms and conditions of the transaction (including, in the case of an investment, the return in fact realized by the plan) were at least as favorable to the plan as that obtainable in a similar transaction with an unrelated party; and

(viii) Such other undertakings and assurances with respect to the plan and its participants that may be offered by the applicant which are relevant to the criteria under section 408(a) of ERISA and section 4975(c)(2) of the Code.

(3) The Department, as a general matter, will not favorably consider requests for retroactive exemptions where transactions or conduct with respect to which an exemption is requested resulted in a loss to the plan. In addition, the Department will not favorably consider requests for exemptions where the transactions are inconsistent with the general fiduciary responsibility provisions of sections 403 or 404 of

ERISA or the exclusive benefit requirements of section 401(a) of the Code.

[Amended on October 27, 2011 by 76 FR 66637.]

[¶ 14,789B-11]
§ 2570.36 **Where to file an application.**

The Department's prohibited transaction exemption program is administered by the Employee Benefits Security Administration (EBSA). Any exemption application governed by these procedures may be mailed via first-class mail to: Employee Benefits Security Administration, Office of Exemption Determinations, U.S. Department of Labor, Room N-5700, 200 Constitution Avenue NW., Washington, DC 20210. Alternatively, applications may be e-mailed to the Department at *e-OED@dol.gov* or transmitted via facsimile at (202) 219-0204. Notwithstanding the foregoing methods of transmission, applicants are also required to submit one paper copy of the exemption application for the Department's file.

[Amended on October 27, 2011 by 76 FR 66637.]

[¶ 14,789B-12]
§ 2570.37 **Duty to amend and supplement exemption applications.**

(a) While an exemption application is pending final action with the Department, an applicant must promptly notify the Department in writing if he or she discovers that any material fact or representation contained in the application or in any documents or testimony provided in support of the application is inaccurate, if any such fact or representation changes during this period, or if, during the pendency of the application, anything occurs that may affect the continuing accuracy of any such fact or representation. In addition, an applicant must promptly notify the Department in writing if it learns that a material fact or representation has been omitted from the exemption application.

(b) If, at any time during the pendency of an exemption application, the applicant or any other party in interest who would participate in the exemption transaction becomes the subject of an investigation or enforcement action by the Department, the Internal Revenue Service, the Justice Department, the Pension Benefit Guaranty Corporation, or the Federal Retirement Thrift Investment Board involving compliance with provisions of ERISA, provisions of the Code relating to employee benefit plans, or provisions of FERSA relating to the Federal Thrift Savings Fund, the applicant must promptly notify the Department.

(c) The Department may require an applicant to provide documentation it considers necessary to verify any statements contained in the application or in supporting materials or documents.

[Amended on October 27, 2011 by 76 FR 66637.]

[¶ 14,789B-13]
§ 2570.38 **Tentative denial letters.**

(a) If, after reviewing an exemption file, the Department tentatively concludes that it will not propose or grant the exemption, it will notify the applicant in writing. At the same time, the Department will provide a brief statement of the reasons for its tentative denial.

(b) An applicant will have 20 days from the date of a tentative denial letter to request a conference under § 2570.40 of this subpart and/or to notify the Department of its intent to submit additional information under § 2570.39 of this subpart. If the Department does not receive a request for a conference or a notification of intent to submit additional information within that time, it will issue a final denial letter pursuant to § 2570.41.

(c) The Department need not issue a tentative denial letter to an applicant before issuing a final denial letter where the Department has conducted a hearing on the exemption pursuant to either § 2570.46 or § 2570.47.

[Amended on October 27, 2011 by 76 FR 66637.]

[¶ 14,789B-14]
§ 2570.39 **Opportunities to submit additional information.**

(a) An applicant may notify the Department of its intent to submit additional information supporting an exemption application either by telephone or by letter sent to the address furnished in the applicant's tentative denial letter, or electronically to the e-mail address provided in the tentative denial letter. At the same time, the applicant should indicate generally the type of information that will be submitted.

(b) The additional information an applicant intends to provide in support of the application must be in writing and be received by the Department within 40 days from the date of the tentative denial letter. All such information must be accompanied by a declaration under penalty of perjury attesting to the truth and correctness of the information provided, which is dated and signed by a person qualified under § 2570.34(b)(5) of this subpart to sign such a declaration.

(c) If, for reasons beyond its control, an applicant is unable to submit all the additional information he or she intends to provide in support of his application within the 40-day period described in paragraph (b) of this section, he or she may request an extension of time to furnish the information. Such requests must be made before the expiration of the 40-day period and will be granted only in unusual circumstances and for a limited period as determined, respectively, by the Department in its sole discretion.

(d) If an applicant is unable to submit all of the additional information he or she intends to provide within the 40-day period specified in paragraph (b) of this section, or within any additional period granted pursuant to paragraph (c) of this section, the applicant may withdraw the exemption application before expiration of the applicable time period and reinstate it later pursuant to § 2570.44.

(e) The Department will issue, without further notice, a final denial letter denying the requested exemption pursuant to § 2570.41 where—

(1) The Department has not received the additional information that the applicant stated his or her intention to submit within the 40-day period described in paragraph (b) of this section, or within any additional period granted pursuant to paragraph (c) of this section;

(2) The applicant did not request a conference pursuant to § 2570.38(b) of this subpart; and

(3) The applicant has not withdrawn the application as permitted by paragraph (d) of this section.

[Amended on October 27, 2011 by 76 FR 66637.]

[¶ 14,789B-15]
§ 2570.40 **Conferences.**

(a) Any conference between the Department and an applicant pertaining to a requested exemption will be held in Washington, DC, except that a telephone conference will be held at the applicant's request.

(b) An applicant is entitled to only one conference with respect to any exemption application. An applicant will not be entitled to a conference, however, where the Department has held a hearing on the exemption under either § 2570.46 or § 2570.47 of this subpart.

(c) Insofar as possible, conferences will be scheduled as joint conferences with all applicants present where:

(1) More than one applicant has requested an exemption with respect to the same or similar types of transactions;

(2) The Department is considering the applications together as a request for a class exemption;

(3) The Department contemplates not granting the exemption; and

(4) More than one applicant has requested a conference.

(d) In instances where the applicant has requested a conference pursuant to § 2570.38(b) and also has submitted additional information pursuant to § 2570.39, the Department will schedule a conference under this section for a date and time that occurs within 20 days after the date on which the Department has provided either oral or written notification to the applicant that, after reviewing the additional information, it is still not prepared to propose the requested exemption. If, for reasons beyond its control, the applicant cannot attend a conference within the 20-day limit described in this paragraph, the applicant may request an extension of time for the scheduling of a conference, provided that such request is made before the expiration of the 20-day limit. The Department will only grant such an extension in unusual circumstances and for a brief period as determined, respectively, by the Department in its sole discretion.

(e) In instances where the applicant has requested a conference pursuant to § 2570.38(b) but has not expressed an intent to submit additional information in support of the exemption application as provided in § 2570.39, the Department will schedule a conference under this section for a date and time that occurs within 40 days after the date of the issuance of the tentative denial letter described in § 2570.38(a). If, for reasons beyond its control, the applicant cannot attend a conference within the 40-day limit described in this paragraph, the applicant may request an extension of time for the scheduling of a conference, provided that such request is made before the expiration of the 40-day limit. The Department will only grant such an extension in unusual circumstances and for a brief period as determined, respectively, by the Department in its sole discretion.

(f) In instances where the applicant has requested a conference pursuant to § 2570.38(b) of this subpart, has notified the Department of its intent to submit additional information pursuant to § 2570.39, and has failed to furnish such information within 40 days from the date of the tentative denial letter, the Department will schedule a conference under this section for a date and time that occurs within 60 days after the date of the issuance of the tentative denial letter described in § 2570.38(a). If, for reasons beyond its control, the applicant cannot attend a conference within the 60-day limit described in this paragraph, the applicant may request an extension of time for the scheduling of a conference, provided that such request is made before the expiration of the 60-day limit. The Department will only grant such an extension in unusual circumstances and for a brief period as determined, respectively, by the Department in its sole discretion.

(g) If the applicant fails to either timely schedule or appear for a conference agreed to by the Department pursuant to this section, the applicant will be deemed to have waived its right to a conference.

(h) Within 20 days after the date of any conference held under this section, the applicant may submit to the Department (electronically or in paper form) any additional written data, arguments, or precedents discussed at the conference but not previously or adequately presented in writing. If, for reasons beyond its control, the applicant is unable to submit the additional information within this 20-day limit, the applicant may request an extension of time to furnish the information, provided that such request is made before the expiration of the 20-day limit described in this paragraph. The Department will only grant such an extension in unusual circumstances and for a brief period as determined, respectively, by the Department in its sole discretion.

[Amended on October 27, 2011 by 76 FR 66637.]

[¶ 14,789B-16]
§ 2570.41 **Final denial letters.**

The Department will issue a final denial letter denying a requested exemption where:

(a) The conditions for issuing a final denial letter specified in § 2570.38(b) or § 2570.39(e) of this subpart are satisfied;

(b) After issuing a tentative denial letter under § 2570.38 of this subpart and considering the entire record in the case, including all written information submitted pursuant to §§ 2570.39 and 2570.40 of this subpart, the Department decides not to propose an exemption or to withdraw an exemption already proposed; or

(c) After proposing an exemption and conducting a hearing on the exemption under either § 2570.46 or § 2570.47 of this subpart and after considering the entire record in the case, including the record of the hearing, the Department decides to withdraw the proposed exemption.

[Amended on October 27, 2011 by 76 FR 66637.]

[¶ 14,789B-17]
§ 2570.42 **Notice of proposed exemption.**

If the Department tentatively decides that an administrative exemption is warranted, it will publish a notice of a proposed exemption in the Federal Register. In addition to providing notice of the pendency of the exemption before the Department, the notice will:

(a) Explain the exemption transaction and summarize the information and reasons in support of proposing the exemption;

(b) Describe the scope of relief and any conditions of the proposed exemption;

(c) Inform interested persons of their right to submit comments to the Department (either electronically or in writing) relating to the proposed exemption and establish a deadline for receipt of such comments; and

(d) Where the proposed exemption includes relief from the prohibitions of section 406(b) of ERISA, section 4975(c)(1)(E) or (F) of the Code, or section 8477(c)(2) of FERSA, inform interested persons of their right to request a hearing under § 2570.46 of this subpart and establish a deadline for receipt of requests for such hearings.

[Amended on October 27, 2011 by 76 FR 66637.]

[¶ 14,789B-18]
§ 2570.43 **Notification of interested persons by applicant.**

(a) If a notice of proposed exemption is published in the *Federal Register* in accordance with § 2570.42 of this subpart, the applicant must notify interested persons of the pendency of the exemption in the manner and within the time period specified in the application. If the Department determines that this notification would be inadequate, the applicant must obtain the Department's consent as to the manner and time period of providing the notice to interested persons. Any such notification must include:

(1) A copy of the notice of proposed exemption as published in the *Federal Register*; and

(2) A supplemental statement in the following form:

You are hereby notified that the United States Department of Labor is considering granting an exemption from the prohibited transaction restrictions of the Employee Retirement Income Security Act of 1974, the Internal Revenue Code of 1986, or the Federal Employees' Retirement System Act of 1986. The exemption under consideration is summarized in the enclosed [Summary of Proposed Exemption, and described in greater detail in the accompanying][2] Notice of Proposed Exemption. As a person who may be affected by this exemption, you have the right to comment on the proposed exemption by [date].[3] [If you may be adversely affected by the grant of the exemption, you also have the right to request a hearing on the exemption by [date].][4]

All comments and/or requests for a hearing should be addressed to the Office of Exemption Determinations, Employee Benefits Security Administration, Room ___,[5] U.S. Department of Labor, 200 Constitution Avenue N.W., Washington, DC 20210, ATTENTION: Application No. ___.[6] Comments and hearing requests may also be transmitted to the Department electronically at *e-oed@dol.gov* or at *www.regulations.gov* (follow instructions for submission), and should prominently reference the application number listed above. In addition, comments and hearing requests may be transmitted to the Department via facsimile at (202) 219-0204. Individuals submitting comments or requests for a hearing on this matter are advised not to disclose sensitive personal data, such as social security numbers.

The Department will make no final decision on the proposed exemption until it reviews the comments received in response to the enclosed notice. If the Department decides to hold a hearing on the exemption request before making its final decision, you will be notified of the time and place of the hearing.

(b) The method used by an applicant to furnish notice to interested persons must be reasonably calculated to ensure that interested persons actually receive the notice. In all cases, personal delivery and delivery by first-class mail will be considered reasonable methods of furnishing notice. If the applicant elects to furnish notice electronically,

---

[2] To be added in instances where the Department requires the applicant to furnish a Summary of Proposed Exemption to interested persons as described in § 2570.43(d).

[3] The applicant will write in this space the date of the last day of the time period specified in the notice of proposed exemption.

[4] To be added in the case of an exemption that provides relief from section 406(b) of ERISA or corresponding sections of the Code or FERSA.

[5] The applicant will fill in the room number of the Office of Exemptions Determinations. As of the date of this final regulation, the room number of the Office of Exemption Determinations is N-5700.

[6] The applicant will fill in the exemption application number, which is stated in the notice of proposed exemption, as well as in all correspondence from the Department to the applicant regarding the application.

he or she must provide satisfactory proof of electronic delivery to the entire class of interested persons.

(c) After furnishing the notification described in paragraph (a) of this section, an applicant must provide the Department with a written statement confirming that notice was furnished in accordance with the foregoing requirements of this section. This statement must be accompanied by a declaration under penalty of perjury attesting to the truth of the information provided in the statement and signed by a person qualified under § 2570.34(b)(5) of this subpart to sign such a declaration. No exemption will be granted until such a statement and its accompanying declaration have been furnished to the Department.

(d) In addition to the provision of notification required by paragraph (a) of this section, the Department, in its discretion, may also require an applicant to furnish interested persons with a brief summary of the proposed exemption (Summary of Proposed Exemption), written in a manner calculated to be understood by the average recipient, which objectively describes:

(1) The exemption transaction and the parties in interest thereto;

(2) Why such transaction would violate the prohibited transaction provisions of ERISA, the Code, and/or FERSA from which relief is sought;

(3) The reasons why the plan seeks to engage in the transaction; and

(4) The conditions and safeguards proposed to protect the plan and its participants and beneficiaries from potential abuse or unnecessary risk of loss in the event the Department grants the exemption.

(e) Applicants who are required to provide interested persons with the Summary of Proposed Exemption described in paragraph (d) of this section shall furnish the Department with a copy of such summary for review and approval prior to its distribution to interested persons. Such applicants shall also provide confirmation to the Department that the Summary of Proposed Exemption was furnished to interested persons as part of the written statement and declaration required of exemption applicants by paragraph (c) of this section.

[Amended on October 27, 2011 by 76 FR 66637.]

[¶ 14,789B-19]
§ 2570.44 **Withdrawal of exemption applications.**

(a) An applicant may withdraw an application for an exemption at any time by oral or written (including electronic) notice to the Department. A withdrawn application generally shall not prejudice any subsequent applications for an exemption submitted by an applicant.

(b) Upon receiving an applicant's notice of withdrawal regarding an application for an individual exemption, the Department will confirm by letter the applicant's withdrawal of the application and will terminate all proceedings relating to the application. If a notice of proposed exemption has been published in the *Federal Register*, the Department will publish a notice withdrawing the proposed exemption.

(c) Upon receiving an applicant's notice of withdrawal regarding an application for a class exemption or for an individual exemption that is being considered with other applications as a request for a class exemption, the Department will inform any other applicants for the exemption of the withdrawal. The Department will continue to process other applications for the same exemption. If all applicants for a particular class exemption withdraw their applications, the Department may either terminate all proceedings relating to the exemption or propose the exemption on its own motion.

(d) If, following the withdrawal of an exemption application, an applicant decides to reapply for the same exemption, he or she may contact the Department in writing (including electronically) to request that the application be reinstated. The applicant should refer to the application number assigned to the original application. If, at the time the original application was withdrawn, any additional information to be submitted to the Department under § 2570.39 was outstanding, that information must accompany the request for reinstatement of the application. However, the applicant need not resubmit information previously furnished to the Department in connection with a withdrawn application unless reinstatement of the application is requested more than two years after the date of its withdrawal.

(e) Any request for reinstatement of a withdrawn application submitted, in accordance with paragraph (d) of this section, will be granted by the Department, and the Department will take whatever steps remained at the time the application was withdrawn to process the application.

[Amended on October 27, 2011 by 76 FR 66637.]

[¶ 14,789B-20]
§ 2570.45 **Requests for reconsideration.**

(a) The Department will entertain one request for reconsideration of an exemption application that has been finally denied pursuant to § 2570.41 if the applicant presents in support of the application significant new facts or arguments, which, for good reason, could not have been submitted for the Department's consideration during its initial review of the exemption application.

(b) A request for reconsideration of a previously denied application must be made within 180 days after the issuance of the final denial letter and must be accompanied by a copy of the Department's final letter denying the exemption and a statement setting forth the new information and/or arguments that provide the basis for reconsideration.

(c) A request for reconsideration must also be accompanied by a declaration under penalty of perjury attesting to the truth of the new information provided, which is signed by a person qualified under § 2570.34(b)(5) to sign such a declaration.

(d) If, after reviewing a request for reconsideration, the Department decides that the facts and arguments presented do not warrant reversal of its original decision to deny the exemption, it will send a letter to the applicant reaffirming that decision.

(e) If, after reviewing a request for reconsideration, the Department decides, based on the new facts and arguments submitted, to reconsider its final denial letter, it will notify the applicant of its intent to reconsider the application in light of the new information presented. The Department will then take whatever steps remained at the time it issued its final denial letter to process the exemption application.

(f) If, at any point during its subsequent processing of the application, the Department decides again that the exemption is unwarranted, it will issue a letter affirming its final denial.

[Amended on October 27, 2011 by 76 FR 66637.]

[¶ 14,789B-21]
§ 2570.46 **Hearings in opposition to exemptions from restrictions on fiduciary self-dealing.**

(a) Any interested person who may be adversely affected by an exemption which the Department proposes to grant from the restrictions of section 406(b) of ERISA, section 4975(c)(1)(E) or (F) of the Code, or section 8477(c)(2) of FERSA may request a hearing before the Department within the period of time specified in the *Federal Register* notice of the proposed exemption. Any such request must state:

(1) The name, address, telephone number, and e-mail address of the person making the request;

(2) The nature of the person's interest in the exemption and the manner in which the person would be adversely affected by the exemption; and

(3) A statement of the issues to be addressed and a general description of the evidence to be presented at the hearing.

(b) The Department will grant a request for a hearing made in accordance with paragraph (a) of this section where a hearing is necessary to fully explore material factual issues identified by the person requesting the hearing. A notice of such hearing shall be published by the Department in the *Federal Register*. The Department may decline to hold a hearing where:

(1) The request for the hearing does not meet the requirements of paragraph (a) of this section;

(2) The only issues identified for exploration at the hearing are matters of law; or

(3) The factual issues identified can be fully explored through the submission of evidence in written (including electronic) form.

(c) An applicant for an exemption must notify interested persons in the event that the Department schedules a hearing on the exemption. Such notification must be given in the form, time, and manner prescribed by the Department. Ordinarily, however, adequate notification can be given by providing to interested persons a copy of the notice of hearing published by the Department in the *Federal Register* within 10 days of its publication, using any of the methods approved in § 2570.43(b).

(d) After furnishing the notice required by paragraph (c) of this section, an applicant must submit a statement confirming that notice was given in the form, manner, and time prescribed. This statement must be accompanied by a declaration under penalty of perjury attesting to the truth of the information provided in the statement, which is signed by a person qualified under § 2570.34(b)(5) to sign such a declaration.

[Amended on October 27, 2011 by 76 FR 66637.]

[¶ 14,789B-22]
§ 2570.47 **Other hearings.**

(a) In its discretion, the Department may schedule a hearing on its own motion where it determines that issues relevant to the exemption can be most fully or expeditiously explored at a hearing. A notice of such hearing shall be published by the Department in the *Federal Register*.

(b) An applicant for an exemption must notify interested persons of any hearing on an exemption scheduled by the Department in the manner described in § 2570.46(c). In addition, the applicant must submit a statement subscribed as true under penalty of perjury like that required in § 2570.46(d).

[Amended on October 27, 2011 by 76 FR 66637.]

[¶ 14,789B-23]
§ 2570.48 **Decision to grant exemptions.**

(a) The Department may not grant an exemption under section 408(a) of ERISA, section 4975(c)(2) of the Code, or 5 U.S.C. 8477(c)(3) unless, following evaluation of the facts and representations comprising the administrative record of the proposed exemption (including any comments received in response to a notice of proposed exemption and the record of any hearing held in connection with the proposed exemption), it finds that the exemption is:

(1) Administratively feasible;

(2) In the interests of the plan (or the Thrift Savings Fund in the case of FERSA) and of its participants and beneficiaries; and

(3) Protective of the rights of participants and beneficiaries of such plan (or the Thrift Savings Fund in the case of FERSA).

(b) In each instance where the Department determines to grant an exemption, it shall publish a notice in the *Federal Register* which summarizes the transaction or transactions for which exemptive relief has been granted and specifies the conditions under which such exemptive relief is available.

[Amended on October 27, 2011 by 76 FR 66637.]

[¶ 14,789B-24]
§ 2570.49 **Limits on the effect of exemptions.**

(a) An exemption does not take effect with respect to the exemption transaction unless the material facts and representations contained in the application and in any materials and documents submitted in support of the application were true and complete.

(b) An exemption is effective only for the period of time specified and only under the conditions set forth in the exemption.

(c) Only the specific parties to whom an exemption grants relief may rely on the exemption. If the notice granting an exemption does not limit exemptive relief to specific parties, all parties to the exemption transaction may rely on the exemption.

(d) For transactions that are continuing in nature, an exemption ceases to be effective if, during the continuation of the transaction, there are material changes to the original facts and representations underlying such exemption or if one or more of the exemption's conditions cease to be met.

(e) The determination as to whether, under the totality of the facts and circumstances, a particular statement contained in (or omitted from) an exemption application constitutes a material fact or representation is made by the Department.

[Amended on October 27, 2011 by 76 FR 66637.]

[¶ 14,789B-25]
§ 2570.50 **Revocation or modification of exemptions.**

(a) If, after an exemption takes effect, changes in circumstances, including changes in law or policy, occur which call into question the continuing validity of the Department's original findings concerning the exemption, the Department may take steps to revoke or modify the exemption.

(b) Before revoking or modifying an exemption, the Department will publish a notice of its proposed action in the *Federal Register* and provide interested persons with an opportunity to comment on the proposed revocation or modification. Prior to the publication of such notice, the applicant will be notified of the Department's proposed action and the reasons therefore. Subsequent to the publication of the notice, the applicant will have the opportunity to comment on the proposed revocation or modification.

(c) Ordinarily the revocation or modification of an exemption will have prospective effect only.

[Amended on October 27, 2011 by 76 FR 66637.]

[¶ 14,789B-26]
§ 2570.51 **Public inspection and copies.**

(a) The administrative record of each exemption will be open to public inspection and copying at the EBSA Public Disclosure Room, U.S. Department of Labor, 200 Constitution Avenue, N.W., Washington, DC 20210.

(b) Upon request, the staff of the Public Disclosure Room will furnish photocopies of an administrative record, or any specified portion of that record, for a specified charge per page.

[Amended on October 27, 2011 by 76 FR 66637.]

[¶ 14,789B-27]
§ 2570.52 **Effective date.**

This subpart B is effective with respect to all exemptions filed with or initiated by the Department under section 408(a) of ERISA, section 4975(c)(2) of the Code, and/or 5 U.S.C. 8477(c)(3) at any time on or after December 27, 2011. Applications for exemptions under section 408(a) of ERISA, section 4975(c)(2) of the Code, and/or 5 U.S.C. 8477(c)(3) filed on or after September 10, 1990, but before December 27, 2011 are governed by part 2570 of chapter XXV of title 29 of the Code of Federal Regulations (title 29 CFR part 2570 as revised July 1, 1991).

[Amended on October 27, 2011 by 76 FR 66637.]

Regulations

[¶ 14,789C—14,789Y Reserved. Regulations adopted under "Title 29—Labor," "Chapter XXV—Pension and Welfare Benefit Programs," "Subchapter F—Employee Retirement Income Security Act of 1974," "Part 2570 Subpart B—Procedures for Filing and Processing Prohibited Transaction Exemption Applications" were formerly reproduced here. The regulations were filed with the Federal Register on August 9, 1990 and published in the Federal Register on August 10, 1990 (55 FR 32836). The regulations were amended on October 27, 2011 (76 FR 66637), effective for exemptions filed or initiated on or after December 27, 2011. See ¶ 14,789B-5 and following.]

Regulations

The following final regulations, published in the *Federal Register* on April 9, 2003 (68 FR 17484) set forth an administrative procedure for obtaining a determination by the Secretary of Labor as to whether a particular employee benefit plan is established or maintained under or pursuant to one or more agreements that are collective bargaining agreements for purposes of ERISA Sec. 3(40). They replace proposed regulations (CCH Pension Plan Guide ¶ 20,534F), published in the *Federal Register* on October 27, 2000 (65 FR 64498).

Subpart H—Procedures for Issuance of Findings Under ERISA Sec. 3(40)

[¶ 14,789Z-1]

§ 2570.150 **Scope of rules.**

The rules of practice set forth in this subpart H apply to "section 3(40) Finding Proceedings" (as defined in § 2570.152(g)), under section 3(40) of the Employee Retirement Income Security Act of 1974 (ERISA or the Act). Refer to 29 CFR 2510.3-40 for the definition of relevant terms of section 3(40) of ERISA, 29 U.S.C. 1002(40). To the extent that the regulations in this subpart differ from the regulations in subpart A of 29 CFR part 18, the regulations in this subpart apply to matters arising under section 3(40) of ERISA rather than the rules of procedure for administrative hearings published by the Department's Office of Administrative Law Judges in subpart A of 29 CFR part 18. These proceedings shall be conducted as expeditiously as possible, and the parties shall make every effort to avoid delay at each stage of the proceedings.

[¶ 14,789Z-2]

§ 2570.151 **In general.**

If there is an attempt to assert state jurisdiction or the application of state law, either by the issuance of a state administrative or court subpoena to, or the initiation of administrative or judicial proceedings against, a plan or other arrangement that alleges it is covered by title I of ERISA, 29 U.S.C. 1003, the plan or other arrangement may petition the Secretary to make a finding under section 3(40)(A)(i) of ERISA that it is a plan established or maintained under or pursuant to an agreement or agreements that the Secretary finds to be collective bargaining agreements for purposes of section 3(40) of ERISA.

[¶ 14,789Z-3]

§ 2570.152 **Definitions.**

For section 3(40) Finding Proceedings, this section shall apply instead of the definitions in 29 CFR 18.2.

(a) ERISA means the Employee Retirement Income Security Act of 1974, et seq., 29 U.S.C. 1001, et seq., as amended.

(b) Order means the whole or part of a final procedural or substantive disposition by the administrative law judge of a matter under section 3(40) of ERISA. No order will be appealable to the Secretary except as provided in this subpart.

(c) Petition means a written request under the procedures in this subpart for a finding by the Secretary under section 3(40) of ERISA that a plan is established or maintained under or pursuant to one or more collective bargaining agreements.

(d) Petitioner means the plan or arrangement filing a petition.

(e) Respondent means:

(1) A state government instrumentality charged with enforcing the law that is alleged to apply or which has been identified as asserting jurisdiction over a plan or other arrangement, including any agency, commission, board, or committee charged with investigating and enforcing state insurance laws, including parties joined under § 2570.153;

(2) The person or entity asserting that state law or state jurisdiction applies to the petitioner;

(3) The Secretary of Labor; and

(4) A state not named in the petition that has intervened under § 2570.153(b).

(f) Secretary means the Secretary of Labor, and includes, pursuant to any delegation or sub-delegation of authority, the Assistant Secretary for Employee Benefits Security or other employee of the Employee Benefits Security Administration.

(g) Section 3(40) Finding Proceeding means a proceeding before the Office of Administrative Law Judges (OALJ) relating to whether the Secretary finds an entity to be a plan to be established or maintained under or pursuant to one or more collective bargaining agreements within the meaning of section 3(40) of ERISA.

[¶ 14,789Z-4]

§ 2570.153 **Parties.**

For section 3(40) Finding Proceedings, this section shall apply instead of 29 CFR 18.10.

(a) The term "party" with respect to a Section 3(40) Finding Proceeding means the petitioner and the respondents.

(b) States not named in the petition may participate as parties in a Section 3(40) Finding Proceeding by notifying the OALJ and the other parties in writing prior to the date for filing a response to the petition. After the date for service of responses to the petition, a state not named in the petition may intervene as a party only with the consent of all parties or as otherwise ordered by the ALJ.

(c) The Secretary of Labor shall be named as a "respondent" to all actions.

(d) The failure of any party to comply with any order of the ALJ may, at the discretion of the ALJ, result in the denial of the opportunity to present evidence in the proceeding.

[¶ 14,789Z-5]

§ 2570.154 **Filing and contents of petition.**

(a) A person seeking a finding under section 3(40) of ERISA must file a written petition by delivering or mailing it to the Chief Docket Clerk, Office of Administrative Law Judges (OALJ), 800 K Street, NW., Suite 400, Washington, DC 20001-8002, or by making a filing by any electronic means permitted under procedures established by the OALJ.

(b) The petition shall—

(1) Provide the name and address of the entity for which the petition is filed;

(2) Provide the names and addresses of the plan administrator and plan sponsor(s) of the plan or other arrangement for which the finding is sought;

(3) Identify the state or states whose law or jurisdiction the petitioner claims has been asserted over the petitioner, and provide the addresses and names of responsible officials;

(4) Include affidavits or other written evidence showing that:

(i) State jurisdiction has been asserted over or legal process commenced against the petitioner pursuant to state law;

(ii) The petitioner is an employee welfare benefit plan as defined at section 3(1) of ERISA (29 U.S.C. 1002(1)) and 29 CFR 2510.3-1 and is covered by title I of ERISA (see 29 U.S.C. 1003);

(iii) The petitioner is established or maintained for the purpose of offering or providing benefits described in section 3(1) of ERISA (29 U.S.C. 1002(1)) to employees of two or more employers (including one or more self-employed individuals) or their beneficiaries;

(iv) The petitioner satisfies the criteria in 29 CFR 2510.3-40(b); and

(v) Service has been made as provided in § 2570.155.

(5) The affidavits shall set forth such facts as would be admissible in evidence in a proceeding under 29 CFR part 18 and shall show affirmatively that the affiant is competent to testify to the matters stated therein. The affidavit or other written evidence must set forth specific facts showing the factors required under paragraph (b)(4) of this section.

[¶ 14,789Z-6]

§ 2570.155 **Service.**

For section 3(40) proceedings, this section shall apply instead of 29 CFR 18.3.

(a) *In general.* Copies of all documents shall be served on all parties of record. All documents should clearly designate the docket number, if any, and short title of all matters. All documents to be filed shall be delivered or mailed to the Chief Docket Clerk, Office of Administrative Law Judges (OALJ), 800 K Street, NW., Suite 400, Washington, DC 20001-8002, or to the OALJ Regional Office to which the proceeding may have been transferred for hearing. Each document filed shall be clear and legible.

(b) *By parties.* All motions, petitions, pleadings, briefs, or other documents shall be filed with the Office of Administrative Law Judges with a copy, including any attachments, to all other parties of record. When a party is represented by an attorney, service shall be made upon the attorney. Service of any document upon any party may be made by personal delivery or by mailing by first class, prepaid U.S. mail, a copy to the last known address. The Secretary shall be served by delivery to the Associate Solicitor, Plan Benefits Security Division, ERISA Section 3(40) Proceeding, PO Box 1914, Washington, DC 20013. The person serving the document shall certify to the manner and date of service.

(c) *By the Office of Administrative Law Judges.* Service of orders, decisions and all other documents shall be made to all parties of record by regular mail to their last known address.

(d) *Form of pleadings.*

(1) Every pleading shall contain information indicating the name of the Employee Benefits Security Administration (EBSA) as the agency under which the proceeding is instituted, the title of the proceeding, the docket number (if any) assigned by the OALJ and a designation of the type of pleading or paper (e.g., notice, motion to dismiss, etc.). The pleading or paper shall be signed and shall contain the address and telephone number of the party or person representing the party. Although there are no formal specifications for documents, they should be typewritten when possible on standard size 8 1/2 × 11 inch paper.

(2) Illegible documents, whether handwritten, typewritten, photocopies, or otherwise, will not be accepted. Papers may be reproduced by any duplicating process provided all copies are clear and legible.

[¶ 14,789Z-7]

§ 2570.156 **Expedited proceedings.**

For section 3(40) Finding Proceedings, this section shall apply instead of 29 CFR 18.42.

(a) At any time after commencement of a proceeding, any party may move to advance the scheduling of a proceeding, including the time for conducting discovery.

(b) Except when such proceedings are directed by the Chief Administrative Law Judge or the administrative law judge assigned, any party filing a motion under this section shall:

(1) Make the motion in writing;

(2) Describe the circumstances justifying advancement;

(3) Describe the irreparable harm that would result if the motion is not granted; and

(4) Incorporate in the motion affidavits to support any representations of fact.

(c) Service of a motion under this section shall be accomplished by personal delivery, or by facsimile, followed by first class, prepaid, U.S. mail. Service is complete upon personal delivery or mailing.

(d) Except when such proceedings are required, or unless otherwise directed by the Chief Administrative Law Judge or the administrative law judge assigned, all parties to the proceeding in which the motion is filed shall have ten (10) days from the date of service of the motion to file an opposition in response to the motion.

(e) Following the timely receipt by the administrative law judge of statements in response to the motion, the administrative law judge may advance pleading schedules, discovery schedules, prehearing conferences, and the hearing, as deemed appropriate; provided, however, that a hearing on the merits shall not be scheduled with less than five (5) working days notice to the parties, unless all parties consent to an earlier hearing.

(f) When an expedited hearing is held, the decision of the administrative law judge shall be issued within twenty (20) days after receipt of the transcript of any oral hearing or within twenty (20) days after the filing of all documentary evidence if no oral hearing is conducted.

[¶ 14,789Z-8]

§ 2570.157 **Allocation of burden of proof.**

For purposes of a final decision under § 2570.158 (Decision of the Administrative Law Judge) or § 2570.159 (Review by the Secretary), the petitioner shall have the burden of proof as to whether it meets 29 CFR 2510.3-40.

[¶ 14,789Z-9]

§ 2570.158 **Decision of the Administrative Law Judge.**

For section 3(40) finding proceedings, this section shall apply instead of 29 CFR 18.57.

(a) *Proposed findings of fact, conclusions of law, and order.* Within twenty (20) days of filing the transcript of the testimony, or such additional time as the administrative law judge may allow, each party may file with the administrative law judge, subject to the judge's discretion under 29 CFR 18.55, proposed findings of fact, conclusions of law, and order together with the supporting brief expressing the reasons for such proposals. Such proposals and brief shall be served on all parties, and shall refer to all portions of the record and to all authorities relied upon in support of each proposal.

(b) *Decision based on oral argument in lieu of briefs.* In any case in which the administrative law judge believes that written briefs or proposed findings of fact and conclusions of law may not be necessary, the administrative law judge shall notify the parties at the opening of the hearing or as soon thereafter as is practicable that he or she may wish to hear oral argument in lieu of briefs. The administrative law judge shall issue his or her decision at the close of oral argument, or within 30 days thereafter.

(c) *Decision of the administrative law judge.* Within 30 days, or as soon as possible thereafter, after the time allowed for the filing of the proposed findings of fact, conclusions of law, and order, or within thirty (30) days after receipt of an agreement containing consent findings and order disposing of the disputed matter in whole, the administrative law judge shall make his or her decision. The decision of the administrative law judge shall include findings of fact and conclusions of law, with reasons therefore, upon each material issue of fact or law presented on the record. The decision of the administrative law judge shall be based upon the whole record. It shall be supported by reliable and probative evidence. Such decision shall be in accordance with the regulations found at 29 CFR 2510.3-40 and shall be limited to whether the petitioner, based on the facts presented at the time of the proceeding, is a plan established or maintained under or pursuant to collective bargaining for the purposes of section 3(40) of ERISA.

[¶ 14,789Z-10]

§ 2570.159 **Review by the Secretary.**

(a) A request for review by the Secretary of an appealable decision of the administrative law judge may be made by any party. Such a request must be filed within 20 days of the issuance of the final decision or the final decision of the administrative law judge will become the final agency order for purposes of 5 U.S.C. 701 et seq.

(b) A request for review by the Secretary shall state with specificity the issue(s) in the administrative law judge's final decision upon which review is sought. The request shall be served on all parties to the proceeding.

Reg. §2570.159(b) ¶14,789Z-10

(c) The review by the Secretary shall not be a de novo proceeding but rather a review of the record established by the administrative law judge.

(d) The Secretary may, in his or her discretion, allow the submission of supplemental briefs by the parties to the proceeding.

(e) The Secretary shall issue a decision as promptly as possible, affirming, modifying, or setting aside, in whole or in part, the decision under review, and shall set forth a brief statement of reasons therefor. Such decision by the Secretary shall be the final agency action within the meaning of 5 U.S.C. 704.

[¶ 14,790]
LIABILITY FOR BREACH OF FIDUCIARY DUTY

Act Sec. 409. (a) Any person who is a fiduciary with respect to a plan who breaches any of the responsibilities, obligations, or duties imposed upon fiduciaries by this title shall be personally liable to make good to such plan any losses to the plan resulting from each such breach, and to restore to such plan any profits of such fiduciary which have been made through use of assets of the plan by the fiduciary, and shall be subject to such other equitable or remedial relief as the court may deem appropriate, including removal of such fiduciary. A fiduciary may also be removed for a violation of section 411 of this Act.

Act Sec. 409. (b) No fiduciary shall be liable with respect to a breach of fiduciary duty under this title if such breach was committed before he became a fiduciary or after he ceased to be a fiduciary.

[¶ 14,800]
EXCULPATORY PROVISIONS; INSURANCE

Act Sec. 410. (a) Except as provided in section 405(b)(1) and 405(d), any provision in an agreement or instrument which purports to relieve a fiduciary from responsibility or liability for any responsibility, obligation, or duty under this part shall be void as against public policy.

Act Sec. 410. (b) Nothing in this subpart shall preclude—

(1) a plan from purchasing insurance for its fiduciaries or for itself to cover liability or losses occurring by reason of the act or omission of a fiduciary, if such insurance permits recourse by the insurer against the fiduciary in the case of a breach of a fiduciary obligation by such fiduciary;

(2) a fiduciary from purchasing insurance to cover liability under this part from and for his own account; or

(3) an employer or an employee organization from purchasing insurance to cover potential liability of one or more persons who serve in a fiduciary capacity with regard to an employee benefit plan.

[¶ 14,810]
PROHIBITION AGAINST CERTAIN PERSONS HOLDING CERTAIN POSITIONS

Act Sec. 411. (a) CONVICTION OR IMPRISONMENT.—No person who has been convicted of, or has been imprisoned as a result of his conviction of, robbery, bribery, extortion, embezzlement, fraud, grand larceny, burglary, arson, a felony violation of Federal or State law involving substances defined in section 102(6) of the Comprehensive Drug Abuse Prevention and Control Act of 1970, murder, rape, kidnaping, perjury, assault with intent to kill, any crime described in section 9(a)(1) of the Investment Company Act of 1940 (15 U.S.C. 80a-9(a)(1)), a violation of any provision of this Act, a violation of section 302 of the Labor-Management Relations Act, 1947 (29 U.S.C. 186), a violation of chapter 63 of title 18, United States Code, a violation of section 874, 1027, 1503, 1505, 1506, 1510, 1951, or 1954 of title 18, United States Code, a violation of the Labor-Management Reporting and Disclosure Act of 1959 (29 U.S.C. 401), any felony involving abuse or misuse of such person's position or employment in a labor organization or employee benefit plan to seek or obtain an illegal gain at the expense of the members of the labor organization or the beneficiaries of the employee benefit plan, or conspiracy to commit any such crimes or attempt to commit any such crimes, or a crime in which any of the foregoing crimes is an element, shall serve or be permitted to serve—

(1) as an administrator, fiduciary, officer, trustee, custodian, counsel, agent, employee, or representative in any capacity of any employee benefit plan,

(2) as a consultant or adviser to an employee benefit plan, including but not limited to any entity whose activities are in whole or substantial part devoted to providing goods or services to any employee benefit plan, or

(3) in any capacity that involves decisionmaking authority or custody or control of the moneys, funds, assets, or property of any employee benefit plan,

during or for the period of thirteen years after such conviction or after the end of such imprisonment, whichever is later, unless the sentencing court on the motion of the person convicted sets a lesser period of at least three years after such conviction or after the end of such imprisonment, whichever is later, or unless prior to the end of such period, in the case of a person so convicted or imprisoned (A) his citizenship rights, having been revoked as a result of such conviction, have been fully restored, or (B) if the offense is a Federal offense, the sentencing judge or, if the offense is a State or local offense, the United States district court for the district in which the offense was committed, pursuant to sentencing guidelines and policy statements under section 994(a) of title 28, United States Code, determines that such person's service in any capacity referred to in paragraphs (1) through (3) would not be contrary to the purposes of this title. Prior to making any such determination the court shall hold a hearing and shall give notice to such proceeding by certified mail to the Secretary of Labor and to State, county, and Federal prosecuting officials in the jurisdiction or jurisdictions in which such person was convicted. The court's determination in any such proceeding shall be final. No person shall knowingly hire, retain, employ, or otherwise place any other person to serve in any capacity in violation of this subsection. Notwithstanding the preceding provisions of this subsection, no corporation or partnership will be precluded from acting as an administrator, fiduciary, officer, trustee, custodian, counsel, agent, or employee of any employee benefit plan or as a consultant to any employee benefit plan without a notice, hearing, and determination by such court that such service would be inconsistent with the intention of this section.

Act Sec. 411. (b) PENALTY.—Any person who intentionally violates this section shall be fined not more than $10,000 or imprisoned for not more than five years, or both.

Act Sec. 411. (c) DEFINITIONS.—For the purposes of this section:

(1) A person shall be deemed to have been "convicted" and under the disability of "conviction" from the date of the judgment of the trial court, regardless of whether that judgment remains under appeal.

(2) The term "consultant" means any person who, for compensation, advises or represents an employee benefit plan or who provides other assistance to such plan, concerning the establishment or operation of such plan.

(3) A period of parole or supervised release shall not be considered as part of a period of imprisonment.

Act Sec. 411. (d) SALARY OF PERSON BARRED FROM EMPLOYEE BENEFIT PLAN OFFICE DURING APPEAL OF CONVICTION.—Whenever any person—

(1) by operation of this section, has been barred from office or other position in an employee benefit plan as a result of a conviction, and

(2) has filed an appeal of that conviction,

any salary which would be otherwise due such person by virtue of such office or position, shall be placed in escrow by the individual or organization responsible for payment of such salary. Payment of such salary into escrow shall continue for the duration of the appeal or for the period of time during which such salary would be otherwise due, whichever period is shorter. Upon the final reversal of such person's conviction on appeal, the amounts in escrow shall be paid to such person. Upon the final sustaining of that person's conviction on appeal, the amounts in escrow shall be returned to the individual or organization responsible for payments of those amounts. Upon final reversal of such person's conviction, such person shall no longer be barred by this statute from assuming any position from which such person was previously barred.

Amendments:

P.L. 100-182, § 15:

Amended Sec. 411(a), (1) by striking out "the United States Parole Commission" and inserting in lieu thereof "if the offense is a Federal offense, the sentencing judge or, if the offense is a State or local offense, the United States district court for the district in which the offense was committed, pursuant to sentencing guidelines and policy statements under section 994(a) of title 28, United States Code,";

(2) by striking out "Commission shall" and inserting in lieu thereof "court shall";

(3) by striking out "Commission's" and inserting in lieu thereof "court's";

(4) by striking out "such Parole Commission" and inserting in lieu thereof "such court"; and

(5) by striking out "and administrative hearing" and inserting in lieu thereof "a hearing".

P.L. 100-182, Sec. 26, provides that the amendments apply with respect to offenses committed after enactment (December 7, 1987).

P.L. 98-473, § 802:

Amended Sec. 411 to read as reflected above. Prior to the amendment, Sec. 411 read as follows:

" **Act Sec. 411.** (a) No person who has been convicted of, or has been imprisoned as a result of his conviction of, robbery, bribery, extortion, embezzlement, fraud, grand larceny, burglary, arson, a felony violation of Federal or State law involving substances defined in section 102(6) of the Comprehensive Drug Abuse Prevention and Control Act of 1970, murder, rape, kidnaping, perjury, assault with intent to kill, any crime described in section 9(a)(1) of the Investment Company Act of 1940 (15 U.S.C. 80a-9(a)(1)), a violation of any provision of this Act, a violation of section 302 of the Labor-Management Relations Act, 1947 (29 U.S.C. 186), a violation of chapter 63 of title 18, United States Code, a violation of section 874, 1027, 1503, 1505, 1506, 1510, 1951, or 1954 of title 18, United States Code, a violation of the Labor-Management Reporting and Disclosure Act of 1959 (29 U.S.C. 401), or conspiracy to commit any such crimes or attempt to commit any such crimes, or a crime in which any of the foregoing crimes is an element, shall serve or be permitted to serve—

"(1) as an administrator, fiduciary, officer, trustee, custodian, counsel, agent, or employee of any employee benefit plan, or

"(2) as a consultant to any employee benefit plan,

during or for five years after such conviction or after the end of such imprisonment, whichever is the later, unless prior to the end of such five-year period, in the case of a person so convicted or imprisoned, (A) his citizenship rights, having been revoked as a result of such conviction, have been fully restored, or (B) if the offense is a Federal offense, the sentencing judge or, if the offense is a State or local offense, on motion of the United States Department of Justice, the district court of the United States for the district in which the offense was committed, pursuant to sentencing guidelines and policy statements issued pursuant to 28 U.S.C. 994(a), determines that such person's service in any capacity referred to in paragraph (1) or (2) would not be contrary to the purposes of this title. Prior to making any such determination the court shall hold a hearing and shall give notice of such proceeding by certified mail to the State, county, and Federal prosecuting officials in the jurisdiction or jurisdictions in which such

person was convicted. The court's determination in any such proceeding shall be final. No person shall knowingly permit any other person to serve in any capacity referred to in paragraph (1) or (2) in violation of this subsection. Notwithstanding the preceding provisions of this subsection, no corporation or partnership will be precluded from acting as an administrator, fiduciary, officer, trustee, custodian, counsel, agent, or employee, of any employee benefit plan or as a consultant to any employee benefit plan without a notice, hearing, and determination by such court of parole that such service would be inconsistent with the intention of this section.

" **Act Sec. 411.** (b) Any person who intentionally violates this section shall be fined not more than $10,000 or imprisoned for not more than one year, or both.

" **Act Sec. 411.** (c) For the purposes of this section:

"(1) A person shall be deemed to have been 'convicted' and under the disability of 'conviction' from the date of the judgment of the trial court or the date of the final sustaining of such judgment on appeal, whichever is the later event.

"(2) The term 'consultant' means any person who, for compensation, advises or represents an employee benefit plan or who provides other assistance to such plan, concerning the establishment or operation of such plan.

"(3) A period of parole or supervised release shall not be considered as part of a period of imprisonment."

P.L. 98-473, Sec. 804, provides: "(a) The amendments made by section 802 and section 803 of this title shall take effect with respect to any judgment of conviction entered by the trial court after the date of enactment of this title (October 12, 1984), except that that portion of such amendments relating to the commencement of the period of disability shall apply to any judgment of conviction entered prior to the date of enactment of this title (October 12, 1984), if a right of appeal or an appeal from such judgment is pending on the date of enactment of this title.

"(b) Subject to subsection (a) the amendments made by sections 803 and 804 shall not affect any disability under section 411 of the Employee Retirement Income Security Act of 1974 or under section 504 of the Labor-Management Reporting and Disclosure Act of 1959 in effect on the date of enactment of this title (October 12, 1984)."

P.L. 98-473, §§ 229 and 230:

Amended Sec. 411(a) and 411(a)(3) to read as reflected in the amendment note immediately above as follows:

(1) in Sec. 411(a), by deleting "the Board of Parole of the United States Department of Justice" and substituting "if the offense is a Federal offense, the sentencing judge, or, if the offense is a State or local offense, on motion of the United States Department of Justice, the district court of the United States for the district in which the offense was committed, pursuant to sentencing guidelines and policy statements issued pursuant to 28 U.S.C. 994(a)",

(2) by deleting "Board" and "Board's" and substituting "court" and "court's" respectively, and

(3) by deleting "an administrative" and substituting "a."

In Sec. 411(c)(3) "or supervised release" was added after "parole."

Under Sec. 235 of P.L. 98-473, the above described amendments take effect on November 1, 1986.

Regulations

The following regulations were adopted effective March 5, 1979, under "Title 28—Judicial Administration; Chapter 1—Department of Justice; Part 4—Procedure Governing Applications for Certificates of Exemption under the Labor-Management Reporting and Disclosure Act of 1959, and the Employee Retirement Income Security Act of 1974." The regulations were published in the Federal Register of February 2, 1979 (44 FR 6890).

[¶ 14,811]

§ 4.1 **Definitions.** As used in this part:

(a) "Labor Act" means the Labor-Management Reporting and Disclosure Act of 1959 (73 Stat. 519).

(b) "Pension Act" means the Employee Retirement Income Security Act of 1974 (Pub. L. 93-406) (88 Stat. 829).

(c) "Acts" means both of the above statutes.

(d) "Commission" means the United States Parole Commission.

(e) "Secretary" means the Secretary of Labor or his designee.

(f) For proceedings under the "Labor Act"

(1) "Employer" means the labor organization, or person engaged in an industry or activity affecting commerce, or group or association of employers dealing with any labor organization, which an applicant under § 4.2 desires to serve in a capacity for which he is ineligible under section 504(a) of the "Labor Act".

(2) All other terms used in this part shall have the same meaning as identical or comparable terms when those terms are used in the "Labor Act".

(g) For proceedings under the "Pension Act"

(1) "Employer" means the employee benefit plan with which an applicant under § 4.2 desires to serve in a capacity for which he is ineligible under section 411(a) of the "Pension Act" (29 U.S.C. section 1111).

(2) All other terms used in this part shall have the same meaning as identical or comparable terms when those terms are used in the "Pension Act".

[¶ 14,811A]

§ 4.2 **Who may apply for Certificate of Exemption.** Any person who has been convicted of any of the crimes enumerated in section 504(a) of the "Labor Act" whose service, present or prospective, as described in that section is or would be prohibited by that section because of such a conviction or a prison term resulting therefrom; or any person who has been convicted of any of the crimes enumerated in section 411(a) of the "Pension Act" (29 U.S.C. section 1111) whose service, present or prospective, as described in that section is or would be prohibited by that section because of such a conviction or a prison term resulting therefrom, may apply to the Commission for a Certificate of Exemption from such a prohibition under the applicable Act.

[¶ 14,811B]

§ 4.3 **Contents of application.** A person applying for a Certificate of Exemption shall file with the Office of General Counsel, U.S. Parole Commission, 320 First St., NW., Washington, D.C. 20537, a signed application under oath, in seven copies, which shall set forth clearly and completely the following information:

(a) The name and address of the applicant and any other names used by the applicant and dates of such use.

(b) A statement of all convictions and imprisonments which prohibit the applicant's service under the provisions of the applicable Act.

(c) Whether any citizenship rights were revoked as a result of conviction or imprisonment and if so the name of the court and date of judgment thereof and the extent to which such rights have been restored.

(d) The name and location of the employer and a description of the office or paid position, including the duties thereof, for which a Certificate of Exemption is sought.

(e) A full explanation of the reasons or grounds relied upon to establish that the applicant's service in the office or employment for which a Certificate of Exemption is sought would not be contrary to the purposes of the applicable Act.

(f) A statement that the applicant does not, for the purpose of the proceeding, contest the validity of any conviction.

[¶ 14,811C]

§ 4.4 **Supporting affidavit; additional information.** (a) Each application filed with the Commission must be accompanied by a signed affidavit, in 7 copies, setting forth the following concerning the personal history of the applicant:

(1) Place and date of birth. If the applicant was not born in the United States, the time of first entry and port of entry, whether he is a citizen of the United States, and if naturalized, when, where and how he became naturalized and the number of his Certificate of Naturalization.

(2) Extent of education, including names of schools attended.

(3) History of marital and family status, including a statement as to whether any relatives by blood or marriage are currently serving in any capacity with any employee benefit plan, or labor organization, group or association of employers dealing with labor organizations or industrial labor relations group, or currently advising or representing any employer with respect to employee organizing, concerted activities, or collective bargaining activities.

(4) Present employment, including office or offices held, with a description of the duties thereof.

(5) History of employment, including military service, in chronological order.

(6) Licenses held, at the present time or at any time in the past five years, to possess or carry firearms.

(7) Veterans Administration claim number and regional office handling claim, if any.

(8) A listing (not including traffic offenses for which a fine of not more than $25 was imposed or collateral of not more than $25 was forfeited) by date and place of all arrests, convictions for felonies, misdemeanors, or offenses and all imprisonment or jail terms resulting therefrom, together with a statement of the circumstances of each violation which led to arrest or conviction.

(9) Whether applicant was ever on probation or parole, and if so the names of the courts by which convicted and the dates of conviction.

(10) Names and locations of all employee benefit plans, labor organizations or employer groups with which the applicant has ever been associated or employed, and all employers or employee benefit plans which he has advised or represented concerning employee organizing, concerted activities, or collective bargaining activities together with a description of the duties performed in each such employment or association.

(11) A statement of applicant's net worth, including all assets held by him or in the names of others for him, the amount of each liability owed by him or by him together with any other person and the amount and sources of all income during the immediately preceding five calendar years plus income to date of application.

(12) Any other information which the applicant feels will assist the Commission in making its determination.

(b) The Commission may require of the applicant such additional information as it deems appropriate for the proper consideration and disposition of his application.

[¶ 14,812]

§ 4.5 **Character endorsements.** Each application filed with the Commission must be accompanied by letters or other forms of statement (in three copies) from six persons addressed to the Chairman, U.S. Parole Commission, attesting to the character and reputation of the applicant. The statement as to character shall indicate the length of time the writer has known the applicant, and shall describe applicant's character traits as they relate to the position for which the exemption is sought and the duties and responsibilities thereof. The statement as to reputation shall attest to applicant's reputation in his community or in

his circle of business or social acquaintances. Each letter or other form of statement shall indicate that it has been submitted in compliance with procedures under the respective Act and that applicant has informed the writer of the factual basis of his application. The persons submitting letters or other forms of statement shall not include relatives by blood or marriage, prospective employers, or persons serving in any official capacity with an employee benefit plan, labor organization, group or association of employers dealing with labor organizations or industrial labor relations group.

[¶ 14,812A]

§ 4.6 **Institution of proceedings.** All applications and supporting documents received by the Commission shall be reviewed for completeness by the Office of General Counsel of the Parole Commission and if complete and fully in compliance with the regulations of this part the Office of General Counsel shall accept them for filing. Applicant and/or his representative will be notified by the Office of General Counsel of any deficiency in the application and supporting documents. The amount of time allowed for deficiencies to be remedied will be specified in said notice. In the event such deficiencies are not remedied within the specified period or any extension thereof, granted after application to the Commission in writing within the specified period, the application shall be deemed to have been withdrawn and notice thereof shall be given to applicant.

[¶ 14,812B]

§ 4.7 **Notice of hearing; postponements.** Upon the filing of an application, the Commission shall: (a) set the application for a hearing on a date within a reasonable time after its filing and notify the applicant of such date by certified mail; (b) give notice, as required by the respective Act, to the appropriate State, County, or Federal prosecuting officials in the jurisdiction or jurisdictions in which the applicant was convicted that an application for a Certificate of Exemption has been filed and the date for hearing thereon; and (c) notify the Secretary that an application has been filed and the date for hearing thereon and furnish him copies of the application and all supporting documents. Any party may request a postponement of a hearing date in writing from the Office of General Counsel at any time prior to ten (10) days before the scheduled hearing. No request for postponement other than the first for any party will be considered unless a showing is made of cause entirely beyond the control of the requester. The granting of such requests will be within the discretion of the Commission. In the event of a failure to appear on the hearing date as originally scheduled or extended, the absent party will be deemed to have waived his right to a hearing. The hearing will be conducted with the parties present participating and documentation, if any, of the absent party entered into the record.

[¶ 14,812C]

§ 4.8 **Hearing.** The hearing on the appplication shall be held at the offices of the Commission in Washington, D.C., or elsewhere as the Commission may direct. The hearing shall be held before the Commission, before one or more Commissioners or before one or more administrative law judges appointed as provided by section 11 of the Administrative Procedure Act (5 U.S.C. 3105) as the Commission by order shall determine. Hearings shall be conducted in accordance with sections 7 and 8 of the Administrative Procedure Act (5 U.S.C. 556, 557).

[¶ 14,813]

§ 4.9 **Representation.** The applicant may be represented before the Commission by any person who is a member in good standing of the bar of the Supreme Court of the United States or of the highest court of any State or territory of the United States, or the District of Columbia, and who is not under any order of any court suspending, enjoining, restraining, or disbarring him from, or otherwise restricting him in, the practice of law. Whenever a person acting in a representative capacity appears in person or signs a paper in practice before the Commission, his personal appearance or signature shall constitute a representation to the Commission that under the provisions of this part and applicable law he is authorized and qualified to represent the particular person in whose behalf he acts. Further proof of a person's authority to act in a representative capacity may be required. When any applicant is represented by an attorney at law, any notice or other written communication required or permitted to be given to or by such applicant shall be given to or by such attorney. If an applicant is represented by more than one attorney, service by or upon any one of such attorneys shall be sufficient.

[¶ 14,813A]

§ 4.10 **Waiver of oral hearing.** The Commission upon receipt of a statement from the Secretary that he does not object, and in the absence of any request for oral hearing from the others to whom notice has been sent pursuant to § 4.7 may grant an application without receiving oral testimony with respect to it.

[¶ 14,813B]

§ 4.11 **Appearance; testimony; cross-examination.** (a) The applicant shall appear and, except as otherwise provided in § 4.10, shall testify at the hearing and may cross-examine witnesses.

(b) The Secretary and others to whom notice has been sent pursuant to § 4.7 shall be afforded an opportunity to appear and present evidence and cross-examine witnesses, at any hearing.

(c) In the discretion of the Commission or presiding officer, other witnesses may testify at the hearing.

[¶ 14,813C]

§ 4.12 **Evidence which may be excluded.** The Commission or officer presiding at the hearing may exclude irrelevant, untimely, immaterial, or unduly repetitious evidence.

[¶ 14,814]

§ 4.13 **Record for decision; receipt of documents comprising record; timing and extension.** (a) The application and all supporting documents, the transcript of the testimony and oral argument at the hearing, together with any exhibits received and other documents filed pursuant to these procedures and/or the Administrative Procedures Act shall be made parts of the record for decision.

(b) At the conclusion of the hearing the presiding officer shall specify the time for submission of proposed findings of fact and conclusions of law (unless waived by the parties); transcript of the hearing, and supplemental exhibits, if any. He shall set a tentative date for the recommended decision based upon the timing of these preliminary steps. Extensions of time may be requested by any party, in writing, from the Parole Commission. Failure of any party to comply with the time frame as established or extended will be deemed to be a waiver on his part of his right to submit the document in question. The adjudication will proceed and the absence of said document and reasons therefor will be noted in the record.

[¶ 14,814A]

§ 4.14 **Administrative law judge's recommended decision; exceptions thereto; oral argument before Commission.** Whenever the hearing is conducted by an administrative law judge, at the conclusion of the hearing he shall submit a recommended decision to the Commission, which shall include a statement of findings and conclusions, as well as the reasons therefor. The applicant, the Secretary and others to whom notice has been sent pursuant to § 4.7 may file with the Commission, within 10 days after having been furnished a copy of the recommended decision, exceptions thereto and reasons in support thereof. The Commission may order the taking of additional evidence and may request the applicant and others to appear before it. The Commission may invite oral argument before it on such questions as it desires.

[¶ 14,814B]

§ 4.15 **Certificate of Exemption.** The applicant, the Secretary and others to whom notice has been sent pursuant to § 4.7 shall be served a copy of the Commission's decision and order with respect to each application. Whenever the Commission decision is that the application be granted, the Commission shall issue a Certificate of Exemption to the applicant. The Certificate of Exemption shall extend only to the stated employment with the prospective employer named in the application.

[¶ 14,814C]

§ 4.16 **Rejection of application.** No application for a Certificate of Exemption shall be accepted from any person whose application for a Certificate of Exemption has been withdrawn, deemed withdrawn due to failure to remedy deficiencies in a timely manner, or denied by the Commission within the preceding 12 months.

[¶ 14,815]

§ 4.17 **Availability of decisions.** The Commission's Decisions under both Acts are available for examination in the Office of the U.S. Parole Commission, 320 First Street, NW., Washington, D.C. 20537. Copies will be mailed upon written request to the Office of General Counsel, U.S. Parole Commission at the above address at a cost of ten cents per page.

Dated: January 26, 1979.

CECIL C. MCCALL,

Chairman,

United States Parole Commission.

[FR Doc. 79-3641, filed 2-1-79; 8:45 a.m.]

[¶ 14,820]
BONDING

Act Sec. 412. (a) REQUISITE BONDING OF PLAN OFFICIALS.—Every fiduciary of an employee benefit plan and every person who handles funds or other property of such a plan (hereafter in this section referred to as "plan official") shall be bonded as provided in this section; except that—

(1) where such plan is one under which the only assets from which benefits are paid are the general assets of a union or of an employer, the administrator, officers, and employees of such plan shall be exempt from the bonding requirements of this section,

(2) no bond shall be required of any entity which is registered as a broker or a dealer under section 15(b) of the Securities Exchange Act of 1934 (15 U.S.C. 78o(b)) if the broker or dealer is subject to the fidelity bond requirements of a self-regulatory organization (within the meaning of section 3(a)(26) of such Act (15 U.S.C. 78c(a)(26)).

(3) no bond shall be required of a fiduciary (or of any director, officer, or employee of such fiduciary) if such fiduciary—

(A) is a corporation organized and doing business under the laws of the United States or of any State;

(B) is authorized under such laws to exercise trust powers or to conduct an insurance business;

(C) is subject to supervision or examination by Federal or State authority; and

(D) has at all times a combined capital and surplus in excess of such a minimum amount as may be established by regulations issued by the Secretary, which amount shall be at least $1,000,000.

Paragraph (2) shall apply to a bank or other financial institution which is authorized to exercise trust powers and the deposits of which are not insured by the Federal Deposit Insurance Corporation, only if such bank or institution meets bonding or similar requirements under State law which the Secretary determines are at least equivalent to those imposed on banks by Federal law.

The amount of such bond shall be fixed at the beginning of each fiscal year of the plan. Such amount shall be not less than 10 per centum of the amount of funds handled. In no case shall such bond be less than $1,000 nor more than $500,000, except that the Secretary, after due notice and opportunity for hearing to all interested parties, and after consideration of the record, may prescribe an amount in excess of $500,000, subject to the 10 per centum limitation of the preceding sentence. For purposes of fixing the amount of such bond, the amount of funds handled shall be determined by the funds handled by the person, group, or class to be covered by such bond and by their predecessor or predecessors, if any, during the preceding reporting year, or if the plan has no preceding reporting year, the amount of funds to be handled during the current reporting year by such person, group, or class, estimated as provided in regulations of the Secretary. Such bond shall provide protection to the plan against loss by reason of acts of fraud or dishonesty on the part of the plan official, directly or through connivance with others. Any bond shall have as surety thereon a corporate surety company which is an acceptable surety on Federal bonds under authority granted by the Secretary of the Treasury pursuant to sections 9304-9308 of title 31. Any bond shall be in a form or of a type approved by the Secretary, including individual bonds or schedule or blanket forms of bonds which cover a group or class. In the case of a plan that holds employer securities (within the meaning of section 407(d)(1)), this subsection shall be applied by substituting "$1,000,000" for "$500,000'"each place it appears.

Act Sec. 412. (b) UNLAWFUL ACTS.—It shall be unlawful for any plan official to whom subsection (a) applies, to receive, handle, disburse, or otherwise exercise custody or control of any of the funds or other property of any employee benefit plan, without being bonded as required by subsection (a) and it shall be unlawful for any plan official of such plan, or any other person having authority to direct the performance of such functions, to permit such functions, or any of them, to be performed by any plan official, with respect to whom the requirements of subsection (a) have not been met.

Act Sec. 412. (c) CONFLICT OF INTEREST PROHIBITED IN PROCURING BONDS.—It shall be unlawful for any person to procure any bond required by subsection (a) from any surety or other company or through any agent or broker in whose business operations such plan or any party in interest in such plan has any control or significant financial interest, direct or indirect.

Act Sec. 412. (d) EXCLUSIVENESS OF STATUTORY BASIS FOR BONDING REQUIREMENT FOR PERSONS HANDLING FUNDS OR OTHER PROPERTY OF EMPLOYEE BENEFIT PLANS.— Nothing in any other provision of law shall require any person, required to be bonded as provided in subsection (a) because he handles funds or other property of an employee benefit plan, to be bonded insofar as the handling by such person of the funds or other property of such plan is concerned.

Act Sec. 412. (e) REGULATIONS.—The Secretary shall prescribe such regulations as may be necessarry to carry out the provisions of this section including exempting a plan from the requirements of this section where he finds that (1) other bonding arrangements or (2) the overall financial condition of the plan would be adequate to protect the interests of the beneficiaries and participants. When, in the opinion of the Secretary, the administrator of a plan offers adequate evidence of the financial responsibility of the plan, or that other bonding arrangements would provide adequate protection of the beneficiaries and participants, he may exempt such plan from the requirements of this section.

Amendment:

P.L. 109-280, §611(b)(1)-(3):

Amended ERISA Sec. 412(a) by striking "and" at the end of paragraph (1), redesignating paragraph (2) as paragraph (3), and inserting new paragraph (2) to read as above.

The above amendment applies to plan years beginning after August 17, 2006 (the date of enactment).

P.L. 109-208, §622(a):

Amended ERISA Sec. 412(a) by adding at the end a new sentence to read as above.

The above amendment applies to plan years beginning after December 31, 2007.

P.L. 97-258, §4(b):

In subsection (a), "sections 9304-9308 of Title 31" was substituted for "sections 6 through 13 of Title 6, United States Code" on authority of Pub. L. 97-258, §4(B), Sept. 13, 1982, 96 Stat. 1067, effective January 1, 1975.

ERISA Section 412, BONDING

The following temporary regulations were adopted effective January 10, 1975, under "Title 29—Labor; Chapter XXV—Office of Employee Benefits Security; Subchapter F—Fiduciary Responsibility; §2550.412-1 of Part 2550—Bonding Requirements." The temporary regulations were published in the Federal Register of January 10, 1975[1] and were amended on June 28, 1985 (50 FR 26705).

[¶ 14,821]

§2550.412-1 of Part 2550 **Temporary bonding requirements.** (a) Pending the issuance of permanent regulations with respect to the bonding provisions under section 412 of the Employee Retirement Income Security Act of 1974 (the Act), any plan official, as defined in section 412(a) of the Act, shall be deemed to be in compliance with the bonding requirements of the Act if he or she is bonded under a bond which would have been in compliance with section 13 of the Welfare and Pension Plans Disclosure Act, as amended (the WPPDA), and with the basic bonding requirements of Subparts A through E of Part 2580, Title 29, Code of Federal Regulations and with the prohibition against bonding by parties interested in the plan contained in Subpart G of Part 2580 of such Title, or would be exempt from such bonding requirements because bonding would not be required under the exemption provisions contained in Subpart F of Part 2580 of such Title. "Part 2580 of Title 29 of the *Code of Federal Regulations* incorporates material previously designated as Subparts A through E of Part 464, Subpart B of Part 465 and Part 485 of Title 29 of the *Code of Federal Regulations.*" The requirements which are set forth in the temporary regulations hereby adopted shall be applicable to all employee benefit plans covered by the Act, including those plans which were not covered by the WPPDA. Thus, for example, the regulations so adopted are applicable to plans containing fewer than 26 participants, although such plans were not covered by the WPPDA.

(b) For the purpose of this temporary regulation, any bond or rider thereto obtained by a plan official which contains a reference to the WPPDA will be construed by the Secretary to refer to the Act, provided that the surety company so agrees.

(c) For the purpose of this regulation, (1) any reference to section 13 of th WPPDA or any subsection thereof in the regulations issued under the WPPDA and which are incorporated by reference by this temporary regulation shall be deemed to refer to section 412 of the Act, or the corresponding subsection thereof, (2) where the particular phrases set forth in the Act are not identical to the phrases in the WPPDA and the regulations issued pursuant thereto, the phrases appearing in the Act shall be substituted by operation of law, and (3) where the phrases are identical but the meaning is different, the meaning given such phrases by the Act shall govern. For example, the phrase "administrators, officers, and employees of any employee welfare benefit plan or of any employee pension benefit plan subject to this Act who handle funds or other property of such plan" which appears in section 13 of the WPPDA and the regulations issued thereunder shall be construed to mean, for purposes of this regulation, "plan officials'", which is the term appearing in section 412 of the Act, and the terms "employee welfare benefit plan" and "employee pension benefit plan" shall be given the meaning assigned to them by the Act, and not the meaning set forth in the WPPDA.

(d) The requirements of this temporary regulation, as set forth in paragraphs (a) through (c), shall remain in effect pending the issuance of permanent regulations by the Secretary.

Temporary Regulations

The following temporary regulations were originally adopted on January 10, 1985 under Subchapter B of Chapter IV of Title 29 of the Code of Federal Regulations and were issued under the authority of the Office of Pension and Welfare Programs. As the result of a Department of Labor reorganization, the temporary regulations were transferred, effective June 28, 1985, to Chapter XXV (Office of Pension and Welfare Benefit Programs) of Title 29 (50 FR 26705).

---

[1] This was Part 2555 before redesignation by the Department of Labor. Part 2555 is reserved.

Subchapter I—Temporary Bonding Rules Under the Employee Retirement Income Security Act of 1974

Part 2580—Temporary Bonding Rules

Subpart A—Criteria for Determining Who Must Be Bonded

[¶ 14,822]

§ 2580.412-1. **Statutory Provisions.** Section 13(a) of the Welfare and Pension Plans Disclosure Act of 1958, as amended, states, in part, that—

Every administrator, officer and employee of any employee welfare benefit plan or of any employee pension benefit plan subject to this Act who handles funds or other property of such plan shall be bonded as herein provided; except that, where such plan is one under which the only assets from which benefits are paid are the general assets of a union or of an employer, the administrator, officers and employees of such plan shall be exempt from the bonding requirements of this section.

. . . Such bond shall provide protection to the plan against loss by reason of acts of fraud or dishonesty on the part of such administrator, officer, or employee, directly or through connivance with others.

[¶ 14,822A]

§ 2580.412-2. **Plans exempt from the coverage of section 13.** Only completely unfunded plans in which the plan benefits derive solely from the general assets of a union[1] or employer, and in which plan assets are not segregated in any way from the general assets of a union or employer and remain solely within the general assets until the time of distribution of benefits, shall be exempt from the bonding provisions. As such, the language "where such plan is one under which the only assets from which benefits are paid are the general assets of a union or of an employer" shall not be deemed to exempt a plan from the coverage of section 13 if the plan is one in which:

(a) Any benefits thereunder are provided or underwritten by an insurance carrier or service or other organization, or

(b) There is a trust or other separate entity to which contributions are made or out of which benefits are paid, or

(c) Contributions to the plan are made by the employees, either through withholding or otherwise, or from any source other than the employer or union involved, or

(d) There is a separately maintained bank account or separately maintained books and records for the plan or other evidence of the existence of a segregated or separately maintained or administered fund out of which plan benefits are to be provided.

As a general rule, the presence of special ledger accounts or accounting entries for plan funds as an integral part of the general books and records of an employer or union shall not, in and of itself, be deemed sufficient evidence of segregation of plan funds to take a plan out of the exempt category, but shall be considered along with the other factors and criteria discussed above in determining whether the exemption applies. Again, it should be noted, however, that the fact that a plan is not exempt from the coverage of section 13 does not necessarily mean that its administrators, officers or employees are required to be bonded. As stated previously, this will depend in each case on whether or not they "handle" funds or other property of the plan within the meaning of section 13 and under the standards set forth in section 2580.412-6.

[¶ 14,822B]

§ 2580.412-3. **Plan administrators, officers and employees for purposes of section 13.—**

(a) *Administrator.* (1) For purposes of the bonding provisions, the term "administrator" is defined in the same manner as under section 5 of the Act and refers to—

(i) The person or persons designated by the terms of the plan or the collective bargaining agreement with responsibility for the ulti-

mate control, disposition, or management of the money received or contributed; or

(ii) In the absence of such designation, the person or persons actually responsible for the control, disposition, or management of the money received or contributed, irrespective of whether such control, disposition, or management is exercised directly or through an agent or trustee designated by such person or persons.

(2) Where by virtue of this definition, or regulations, interpretations or opinions issued with respect thereto, the term embodies natural persons such as members of the board of trustees of a trust, the bonding requirements shall apply to such persons.

(3) However, when by virtue of this definition or regulations, interpretations, or opinions issued with respect thereto, the administrator in a given case is an entity such as a partnership, corporation, mutual company, joint stock company, trust, unincorporated organization, union or employees' beneficiary association, the term shall be deemed to apply, in meeting the bonding requirements, only to those natural persons who—

(i) Are vested under the authority of the entity-administrator with the responsibility for carrying out functions constituting control, disposition or management of the money received or contributed within the definition of administrator, or who, acting on behalf of or under the actual or apparent authority of the entity-administrator, actually perform such functions, and who

(ii) "Handle" funds or other property of the plan within the meaning of these regulations.

(b) *Officers.* For purposes of the bonding provisions, the term "officer" shall include any person designated by the terms of a plan or collective bargaining agreement as an officer, any person performing or authorized to perform executive functions of the plan or any member of a board of trustees or similar governing body of a plan. The term shall include such persons regardless of whether they are representatives of or selected by an employer, employees or an employee organization. In its most frequent application the term will encompass those natural persons appointed or elected as officers of the plan or as members of boards or committees performing executive or supervisory functions for the plan, but who do not fall within the definition of administrator.

(c) *Employees.* For purposes of the bonding provisions the term "employee" shall, to the extent a person performs functions not falling within the definition of officer or administrator, include any employee who performs work for or directly related to a covered plan, regardless of whether technically he is employed, directly or indirectly, by or for a plan, a plan administrator, a trust, or by an employee organization or employer within the meaning of section 3(3) or 3(4) of the Act.

(d) *Other persons covered.* For purposes of the bonding provisions, the terms "administrator, officer, or employee" shall include any persons performing functions for the plan normally performed by administrators, officers, or employees of a plan. As such, the terms shall include persons indirectly employed, or otherwise delegated, to perform such work for the plan, such as pension consultants and planners, and attorneys who perform "handling" functions within the meaning of § 2580.412-6. On the other hand, the terms would not include those brokers or independent contractors who have contracted for the performance of functions which are not ordinarily carried out by the administrators, officers, or employees of a plan, such as securities brokers who purchase and sell securities or armored motor vehicle companies. (Amended by F.R. Doc. 69-3030, published in Federal Register March 13, 1969.)

(e) [Deleted by F.R. Doc. 69-3030, published in Federal Register March 13, 1969.]

[¶ 14,822C]

§ 2580.412-4. **"Funds or other property" of a plan.** The affirmative requirement for bonding persons falling within the definition of administrator, officer or employee is applicable only if they handle "funds or other property" of the plan concerned. The term "funds or other property" is intended to encompass all property which is used or may

---

[1] For purposes of the exemption discussed in § 2580.412-2, the term "union" shall include "* * * any organization of any kind or any agency or employee representation committee, association, group, or plan, in which employees participate and which elects for

the purpose in whole or in part, of dealing with employers concerning an employee welfare or pension benefit plan, or other matters incidental to employment relationships * * *" (29 U.S.C. 302(a)(3)).

be used as a source for the payment of benefits to plan participants. It does not include permanent assets used in the operation of the plan such as land and buildings, furniture and fixtures or office and delivery equipment used in the operation of the plan. It does include all items in the nature of quick assets, such as cash, checks and other negotiable instruments, government obligations and marketable securities. It also includes all other property or items convertible into cash or having a cash value and held or acquired for the ultimate purpose of distribution to plan participants or beneficiaries. In the case of a plan which has investments, this would include all the investments of the plan even though not in the nature of quick assets, such as land and buildings, mortgages, and securities in closely held corporations. However, in a given case, the question of whether a person was "handling" such "funds or other property" so as to require bonding would depend on whether his relationship to this property was such that there was a risk that he, alone or in connivance with others, could cause a loss of such "funds or other property" through fraud or dishonesty.

[¶ 14,822D]

§ 2580.412-5. **Determining when "funds or other property" belong to a plan.** With respect to any contribution to a plan from any source, including employers, employees or employee organizations, the point at which any given item or amount becomes "funds or other property" of a plan for purposes of the bonding provisions shall be determined as described in this section.

(a) Where the plan administrator is a board of trustees, person or body other than the employer or employee organization establishing the plan, a contribution to the plan from any source shall become "funds or other property" of the plan at the time it is received by the plan administrator. Employee contributions collected by an employer and later turned over to the plan administrator would not become "funds or other property" of the plan until receipt by the plan administrator.

(b) Where the employer or employee organization establishing the plan is itself the plan administrator:

(1) Contributions from employees or other persons who are plan participants would normally become "funds or other property" of the plan at the time they are received by the employer or employee organization, except however that contributions made by withholding from employees' salaries shall not be considered "funds or other property" of the plan for purposes of the bonding provisions so long as they are retained in and not segregated in any way from the general assets of the withholding employer or employee organization.

(2) Contributions made to a plan by such employer or employee organization and contributions made by withholdings from employees' salaries would normally become "funds or other property" of the plan if and when they are taken out of the general assets of the employer or employee organization and placed in a special bank account or investment account; or identified on a separate set of books and records; or paid over to a corporate trustee or used to purchase benefits from an insurance carrier or service or other organization; or otherwise segregated, paid out or used for plan purposes, whichever shall occur first. Thus, if a plan is operated by a corporate trustee and no segregation from general assets is made of monies to be turned over to the corporate trustee prior to the actual transmittal of such monies, the contribution represented in the transmission becomes "funds or other property" of the plan at the time of receipt by the corporate trustee. On the other hand, if a special fund is first established from which monies are paid over to the corporate trustee, a given item would become "funds or other property" of the plan at the time it is placed in the special fund. Similarly, if plan benefits are provided through the medium of an insurance carrier or service or other organization and no segregation from general assets of monies used to purchase such benefits is made prior to turning such monies over to the organization contracting to provide benefits, plan funds or other property come into being at the time of receipt of payment for such benefits by the insurance carrier or service or other organization. In such a case, the "funds or other property" of the plan would be represented by the insurance contract or other obligations to pay benefits and would not be normally subject to "handling". Bonding would not be required for any person with respect to the purchase of such benefits directly from general assets nor with respect to the bare existence of the contract obligation to pay benefits. However, if the particular arrangement were such that monies

derived from, or by virtue of, the contract did subsequently flow back to the plan, bonding may be required if such monies returned to the plan are handled by plan administrators, officers or employees. (Further discussion on bonding of insured plans is contained in § 2580.412-6(b)(7).)

[¶ 14,822E]

§ 2580.412-6. **Determining when "funds or other property" are "handled" so as to require bonding.**—

(a) *General scope of term.* (1) A plan administrator, officer, or employee shall be deemed to be "handling" funds or other property of a plan, so as to require bonding under section 13, whenever his duties or activities with respect to given funds or other property are such that there is a risk that such funds or other property could be lost in the event of fraud or dishonesty on the part of such person, acting either alone or in collusion with others. While ordinarily, those plan administrators, officers and employees who "handle" within the meaning of section 13 will be those persons with duties related to the receipt, safekeeping and disbursement of funds, the scope of the term "handles" and the prohibitions of paragraph (b) of section 13 shall be deemed to encompass any relationship of an administrator, officer or employee with respect to funds or other property which can give rise to a risk of loss through fraud or dishonesty. This shall include relationships such as those which involve access to funds or other property or decision making powers with respect to funds or property which can give rise to such risk of loss.

(2) Section 13 contains no exemptions based on the amount or value of funds or other property "handled," nor is the determination of the existence of risk of loss based on the amount involved. However, regardless of the amount involved, a given duty or relationship to funds or other property shall not be considered "handling," and bonding is not required, where it occurs under conditions and circumstances in which the risk that a loss will occur through fraud or dishonesty is negligible. This may be the case where the risk of mishandling is precluded by the nature of the funds or other property (e.g., checks, securities or title papers which can not be negotiated by the persons performing duties with respect to them). It may also be the case where significant risk of mishandling in the performance of duties of an essentially clerical character is precluded by fiscal controls.

(b) *General criteria for determining "handling."*

Subject to the application of the basic standard of risk of loss to each situation, general criteria for determining whether there is "handling" so as to require bonding are:

(1) *Physial contact.* Physical contact with cash, checks or similar property generally constitutes "handling." However, persons who from time to time perform counting, packaging, tabulating, messenger or similar duties of an essentially clerical character involving physical contact with funds or other property would not be "handling" when they perform these duties under conditions and circumstances where risk of loss is negligible because of factors such as close supervision and control or the nature of the property.

(2) *Power to exercise physical contact or control.* Whether or not physical contact actually takes place, the power to secure physical possession of cash, checks or similar property through factors such as access to a safe deposit box or similar depository, access to cash or negotiable assets, powers of custody or safekeeping, power to withdraw funds from a bank or other account generally constitutes "handling," regardless of whether the person in question has specific duties in these matters regardless of whether the power or access is authorized.

(3) *Power to transfer to oneself or a third party or to negotiate for value.* With respect to property such as mortgages, title to land and buildings, or securities, while physical contact or the possibility of physical contact may not, of itself, give rise to risk of loss so as to constitute "handling," a person shall be regarded as "handling" such items where he, through actual or apparent authority, can cause those items to be transferred to himself or to a third party or to be negotiated for value.

(4) *Disbursement.* Persons who actually disburse funds or other property, such as officers or trustees authorized to sign checks or other

negotiable instruments, or persons who make cash disbursements, shall be considered to be "handling" such funds or property. Whether other persons who may influence, authorize or direct disbursements or the signing or endorsing of checks or similar instruments will be considered to be "handling" funds or other property shall be determined by reference to the particular duties or responsibilities of such persons as applied to the basic criteria of risk of loss.

(5) *Signing or endorsing checks or other negotiable instruments.* In connection with disbursements or otherwise, any persons with the power to sign or endorse checks or similar instruments or otherwise render them transferable, whether individually or as co-signers with one or more persons, shall each be considered to be "handling" such funds or other property.

(6) *Supervisory or decision making responsibility.* To the extent a person's supervisory or decision making responsibility involves factors in relationship to funds discussed in subparagraphs (1), (2), (3), (4), or (5) of this paragraph, such persons shall be considered to be "handling" in the same manner as any person to whom the criteria of those paragraphs apply. To the extent that only general responsibility for the conduct of the business affairs of the plan is involved, including such functions as approval of contracts, authorization of disbursements, auditing of accounts, investment decisions, determination of benefit claims and similar responsibilities, such persons shall be considered to be "handling" whenever the facts of the particular case raise the possibility that funds or other property of the plan are likely to be lost in the event of their fraud or dishonesty. The mere fact of general supervision would not necessarily, in and of itself, mean that such persons are "handling." Factors to be accorded weight are the system of fiscal controls, the closeness and continuity of supervision, who is in fact charged with, or actually exercising final responsibility for determining whether specific disbursements, investments, contracts, or benefit claims are bona fide, regular and made in accordance with the applicable trust instrument or other plan documents.

(i) For example, persons having supervisory or decision making responsibility would be "handling" to the extent they:

(a) Act in the capacity of plan "administrator" and have ultimate responsibility for the plan within the meaning of the definition of "administrator" (except to the extent that it can be shown that such persons could not, in fact, cause a loss to the plan to occur through fraud or dishonesty);

(b) Exercise close supervision over corporate trustees or other parties charged with dealing with plan funds or other property; exercise such close control over investment policy that they, in effect, determine all specific investments;

(c) Conduct, in effect, a continuing daily audit of the persons who "handle" funds;

(d) Regularly review and have veto power over the actions of a disbursing officer whose duties are essentially ministerial.

(ii) On the other hand, persons having supervisory or decision making responsibility would not be "handling" to the extent:

(a) They merely conduct a periodic or sporadic audit of the persons who "handle" funds;

(b) Their duties with repect to investment policy are essentially advisory;

(c) They make a broad general allocation of funds or general authorization of disbursements intended to permit expenditures by a disbursing officer who has final responsibility for determining the propriety of any specific expenditure and making the actual disbursement;

(d) A bank or corporate trustee has all the day to day functions of administering the plan;

(e) They are in the nature of a Board of Directors of a corporation or similar authority acting for the corporation rather than for the plan and do not perform specific functions with respect to the operations of the plan.

(7) *Insured plan arrangements.* In many cases, plan contributions made by employers or employee organizations or by withholding from employees' salaries are not segregated from the general assets of the employer or employee organization until payment for purchase of

benefits from an insurance carrier or service or other organization. No bonding is required with respect to the payment of premiums or other payments made to purchase such benefits directly from general assets, nor with respect to the bare existence of the contract obligation to pay benefits. Such arrangements would not normally be subject to bonding except to the extent that monies returned by way of benefit payments, cash surrender, dividends, credits or otherwise, and which by the terms of the plan belonged to the plan (rather than to the employer, employee organization, insurance carrier or service or other organization) were subject to "handling" by plan administrators, officers or employees.

Subpart B—Scope and Form of the Bond

[¶ 14,822F]

§ 2580.412-7. **Statutory provision—Scope of the bond.** The statute requires that the bond shall provide protection to the plan against loss by reason of acts of fraud or dishonesty on the part of a plan administrator, officer, or employee, directly or through connivance with others.

[¶ 14,822G]

§ 2580.412-8. **The nature of the duties or activities to which the bonding requirement relates.** The bond required under section 13 is limited to protection for those duties and activities from which loss can arise through fraud or dishonesty. It is not required to provide the same scope of coverage that is required in faithful discharge of duties bonds under the Labor-Management Reporting and Disclosure Act of 1959 or in the faithful performance bonds of public officials.

[¶ 14,822H]

§ 2580.412-9. **Meaning of fraud or dishonesty.** The term "fraud or dishonesty" shall be deemed to encompass all those risks of loss that might arise through dishonest or fraudulent acts in handling of funds as delineated in section 2580.412-6. As such, the bond must provide recovery for loss occasioned by such acts even though no personal gain accrues to the person committing the act and the act is not subject to punishment as a crime or misdemeanor, provided that within the law of the state in which the act is committed, a court would afford recovery under a bond providing protection against fraud or dishonesty. As usually applied under state laws, the term "fraud or dishonesty" encompasses such matters as larceny, theft, embezzlement, forgery, misappropriation, wrongful abstraction, wrongful conversion, willful misapplication or any other fraudulent or dishonest acts. For the purposes of section 13, other fraudulent or dishonest acts shall also be deemed to include acts where losses result through any act or arrangement prohibited by Title 18, Section 1954 of the United States Code.

[¶ 14,822I]

§ 2580.412-10. **Individual or schedule or blanket form of bonds.** Section 13 provides that "any bond shall be in a form or of a type approved by the Secretary, including individual bonds or schedule or blanket forms of bonds which cover a group or class". Any form of bond which may be described as individual, schedule or blanket in form or any combination of such forms of bonds shall be acceptable to meet the requirements of section 13, provided that in each case, the form of the bond, in its particular clauses and application, is not inconsistent with meeting the substantive requirements of the statute for the persons and plan involved and with meeting the specific requirements of the regulations in this part. Basic types of bonds in general usage are:

(a) *Individual Bond* covers a named individual in a stated penalty.

(b) *Name Schedule Bond* covers a number of named individuals in the respective amounts set opposite their names.

(c) *Position Schedule Bond* covers each of the occupants of positions listed in the schedule in the respective amounts set opposite such positions.

(d) *Blanket Bonds* cover all the insured's officers and employees with no schedule or list of those covered being necessary and with all new officers and employees bonded automatically, in a blanket penalty which takes two forms—an aggregate penalty bond and a multiple penalty bond—which are described below:

(1) The aggregate penalty blanket bond such as the Commercial Blanket Bond; the amount of the bond is available for dishonesty

losses caused by persons covered thereunder or losses in which such person is concerned or implicated. Payment of loss on account of any such person does not reduce the amount of coverage available for losses other than those caused by such person or in which he was concerned or implicated.

(2) The multiple penalty bond such as the Blanket Position Bond giving separate coverage on each person for a uniform amount—the net effect being the same as though a separate bond were issued on each person covered thereunder and all of such bonds being for a uniform amount.

> NOTE: For the purpose of section 13 blanket bonds which are either aggregate penalty or multiple penalty in form shall be permissible if they otherwise meet the requirements of the Act and the regulations in this part.

Bonding, to the extent required, of persons indirectly employed, or otherwise delegated, to perform functions for the plan which are normally performed by "administrators, officers, or employees" as described in section 2580.412-3 may be accomplished either by including them under individual or schedule bonds or other forms of bonds meeting the requirements of the Act, or naming them in what is known under general trade usage as an "Agents Rider" attached to a Blanket Bond.

Subpart C—Amount of the Bond

[¶ 14,822J]

§ 2580.412-11. **Statutory provision.** Section 13 requires that the amount of the bond be fixed at the beginning of each calendar, policy or other fiscal year, as the case may be, which constitutes the reporting year of the plan for purposes of the reporting provisions of the Act. The amount of the bond shall be not less than 10 per centum of the amount of funds handled, except that any such bond shall be in at least the amount of $1,000 and no such bond shall be required in an amount in excess of $500,000: *Provided,* That the Secretary, after due notice and opportunity for hearing to all interested parties, and after consideration of the record, may prescribe an amount in excess of $500,000, which in no event shall exceed 10 per centum of the funds handled. For purposes of fixing the amount of such bond, the amount of funds handled shall be determined by the funds handled by the person, group, or class to be covered by such bond and by their predecessor or predecessors, if any, during the preceding reporting year, or if the plan has no preceding reporting year, the amount of funds to be handled during the current reporting year by such person, group, or class, estimated as provided in the regulations in this part. With respect to persons required to be bonded, section 13 shall be deemed to require the bond to insure from the first dollar of loss up to the requisite bond amount and not to permit the use of deductible or similar features whereby a portion of the risk within such requisite bond amount is assumed by the insured. Any request for variance from these requirements shall be made pursuant to the provisions of section 13(e) of the Act.

[¶ 14,822K]

§ 2580.412-12. **Relationship of determining the amount of the bond to "handling."**. A determination of whether persons falling within the definition of administrator, officer or employee are required to be bonded depends on whether they "handle" funds or other property. Determining the amount of the bond is an aspect of the same process in that it requires a determination of what funds or other property are being handled or what amounts of funds of other property are subject to risk of loss with respect to the duties or powers of an administrator, officer or employee of a covered plan. Once this calculation is made, the required amount for which that person must be covered by a bond, either by himself or as a part of a group or class being bonded under a blanket or schedule bond, is not less than 10 percent of the amount "handled" or $1,000, whichever is the greater amount, except that no such bond shall be required in an amount greater than $500,000 by virtue of these regulations. (See § 2580.412-17).

[¶ 14,822L]

§ 2580.412-13. **The meaning of "funds" in determining the amount of the bond.** The amount of the bond depends on the amount of "funds" "handled," and shall be sufficient to provide bonding protection against risk of loss through fraud or dishonesty for all plan funds,

including other property similar to funds or in the nature of funds. As such, the term "funds" shall be deemed to include and be equivalent to "funds and other property" of the plan as described in ¶ 2580.412-4. With respect to any item of "funds or other property" which does not have a cash or readily ascertainable market value, the value of such property may be estimated on such basis as will reasonably reflect the loss the plan might suffer if it were mishandled.

[¶ 14,822M]

§ 2580.412-14. **Determining the amount of funds "handled" during the preceding reporting year.** (a) The amount of funds "handled" by each person falling within the definition of administrator, officer, or employee (or his predecessors) during the preceding reporting year shall be the total of funds subject to risk of loss, within the meaning of the definition of "handling" (see § 2580.412-6), through acts of fraud or dishonesty, directly or in connivance with others, by such person or his predecessors during the preceding reporting year. The relationship of the determination of the amount of funds "handled" to the determination of who is "handling" can best be illustrated by a situation that commonly arises with respect to executive personnel of a plan, where a bank or corporate trustee has the responsibility for the receipt, safekeeping, physical handling and investment of a plan's assets and the basic function of the executive personnel is to authorize payments to beneficiaries and payments for services to the corporate trustee, the actuary and the employees of the plan itself. Normally, in any given year, only a small portion of the plan's total assets is disbursed, and the question arises as to whether an administrator or executive personnel are "handling" only the amounts actually disbursed each year or whether they are "handling" the total amounts of the assets. The answer to this question depends on the same basic criterion that governs all questions of "handling", namely, the possibility of loss. If the authorized duties of the persons in question are strictly limited to disbursements of benefits and payments for services, and the fiscal controls and practical realities of the situation are such that these persons cannot gain access to funds which they are not legitimately allowed to disburse, the amount on which the bond is based may be limited to the amount actually disbursed in the reporting year. This would depend, in part, on the extent to which the bank or corporate trustee which has physical possession of the funds also has final responsibility for questioning and limiting disbursements from the plan, and on whether this responsibility is embodied in the original plan instruments. On the other hand, where insufficient fiscal controls exist so that the persons involved have free access to, or can obtain control of, the total amount of the fund, the bond shall reflect this fact and the amount "handled" shall be based on the total amount of the fund. This would generally occur with respect to persons such as the "administrator," regardless of what functions are performed by a bank or corporate trustee, since the "administrator" by definition retains ultimate power to revoke any arrangement with a bank or corporate trustee. In such case, the "administrator" would have the power to commit the total amount of funds involved to his control, unless the plan itself or other specific agreement (1) prevents the "administrator" from so doing or (2) requires that revocation cannot be had unless a new agreement providing for similar controls and limitations on the "handling" of funds is simultaneously entered into.

(b) Where the circumstances of "handling" are such that the total amount of a given account or fund is subject to "handling," the amount "handled" shall include the total of all such funds on hand at the beginning of the reporting year, plus any items received during the year for any reason, such as contributions or income, or items received as a result of sales, investments, reinvestments, interest or otherwise. It would not, however, be necessary to count the same item twice in arriving at the total funds "handled" by a given person during a reporting year. For example, a given person may have various duties or powers involving receipt, safekeeping or disbursement of funds which would place him in contact with the same funds at several times during the same year. Different duties, however, would not make it necessary to count the same item twice in arriving at the total "handled" by him. Similarly, where a person has several different positions with respect to a plan, it would not be necessary to count the same funds each time that they are "handled" by him in these different positions, so long as the amount of the bond is sufficient to meet the 10 percent requirement with respect to the total funds "handled" by him subject to risk of loss through fraud or dishonesty, whether acting alone or in a collusion with others. In general, once an item properly within the catergory of "funds" has been counted as "handled" by a given person, it need not be counted again even though it should subsequently be "handled" by the same person during the same year.

[¶ 14,822N]

§ 2580.412-15. **Procedures to be used for estimating the amount of funds to be "handled" during the current reporting year in those cases where there is no preceding reporting year**. If for any reason a plan does not have a complete preceding reporting year, the amount "handled" by persons required to be covered by a bond shall be estimated at the beginning of the calendar, policy or other fiscal year, as the case may be, which would constitute either the operating year or the reporting year of the plan, whichever shall occur first, as follows:

(a) In the case of a plan having a previous experience year, even though it has no preceding reporting year, the estimate of the amount to be "handled" for any person required to be covered shall be based on the experience in the previous year by applying the same standards and criteria as in a plan which has a preceding reporting year. Similarly, where a plan is recently established, but has had, at the time a bond is obtained, sufficient experience to reasonably estimate a complete year's experience for persons required to be bonded, the amount of funds to be "handled" shall be projected to the complete year on the basis of the period in which the plan has had experience, unless, to the knowledge of the plan administrator, the given period of experience is so seasonal or unrepresentative of the complete year's experience as not to provide a reasonable basis for projecting the estimate for the complete year.

(b) Where a plan does not have any prior experience sufficient to allow it to estimate the amount "handled" in the manner outlined in paragraph (a) of this section, the amount to be "handled" by the administrators, officers and employees of the plan during the current reporting year shall be that amount initially required to fund or set up the plan, plus the amount of contributions required to be made under the plan formula from any source during the current reporting year. In most cases, the amount of contributions will be calculated by multiplying the total yearly contribution per participant required by the plan formula from either employers, employees, employer organizations or any other source) by the number of participants in the plan at the beginning of such reporting year. In cases where the per capita contribution cannot readily be determined, such as in the case of certain insured plans covered by the Act, the amount of contributions shall be estimated on the amount of insurance premiums which are actuarially estimated as necessary to support the plan, or on such other actuarially estimated basis as may be applicable. In the case of a newly formed profit-sharing plan covered by the Act, if the employer establishing the plan has a previous year of experience, the amount of contributions required by the plan formula shall be estimated on the basis of the profits of the previous year. The amount of the bond shall then be fixed at 10 percent of this calculation, but not more than $500,000. A bond for such amount shall be obtained in any form the plan desires on all persons who are administrators, officers or employees of the plan and who "handle" funds or other property of the plan.

[¶ 14,822O]

§ 2580.412-16. **Amount of bond required in given types of bonds or where more than one plan is insured in the same bond**. (a) As indicated in § 464.11, the Act permits the use of blanket, schedule and individual forms of bonds so long as the amount of the bond penalty is sufficient to meet the requirements of the Act for any person who is an administrator, officer or employee of a plan handling funds or other property of the plan. Such person must be bonded for 10 percent of the amount he handles, and the amount of the bond must be sufficient to indemnify the plan for any losses in which such person is involved up to that amount.

(b) When individual or schedule bonds are written, the bond amount for each person must represent not less than 10 percent of the funds "handled" by the named individual or by the person in the position. When a blanket bond is written, the amount of the bond shall be at least 10% of the highest amount handled by any administrator, officer or employee to be covered under the bond. It should also be noted that if an individual or group or class covered under a blanket bond "handle" a large amount of funds or other property, while the remaining bondable persons "handle" only a smaller amount, it is permissible to obtain a blanket bond in an amount sufficient to meet the 10 percent requirements for all except the individual, group or class "handling" the larger amounts, with respect to whom excess indemnity shall be secured in an amount sufficient to meet the 10 percent requirement.

(c) The Act does not prohibit more than one plan from being named as insured under the same bond. However, any such bond must allow for recovery by each plan in an amount at least equal to that which would be required if bonded separately. This requirement has application where a person or persons sought to be bonded pursuant to the requirements of section 13 have "handling" functions in more than one plan covered under the bond. Where such is the case, the amount of the bond must be sufficient to cover any such persons having functions in more than one plan for at least 10 percent of the total amount "handled" by them in all the plans covered under the bond. For example, X is the administrator of two welfare plans run by the same employer and he "handled" $100,000 in the preceding reporting year for Plan A and $500,000 in the preceding reporting year for Plan B. If both plans are covered under the same bond, the amount of the bond with respect to X shall be at least $60,000 or ten percent of the total "handled" by X for both plans covered under the bond in which X has powers and duties of "handling" since Plan B is required to carry bond in at least the amount of $50,000 and Plan A, $10,000.

(d) Additionally, in order to meet the requirement that each plan be protected, it shall be necessary that arrangement be made either by the terms of the bond or rider to the bond or by separate agreement among the parties concerned, that payment of a loss sustained by one of such insureds shall not work to the detriment of any other plan covered under the bond with respect to the amount for which that plan is required to be covered. For example, if Plan A suffered a loss of $30,000 as described above and such loss was recompensed in its entirety by the surety company, it would receive $20,000 more than the $10,000 protection required under Section 13, and only $30,000 would be available for recovery with respect to further losses caused by X. In a subsequently discovered defalcation of $40,000 by X from Plan B, it would be necessary that the bond, rider, or separate agreement provide that such amount of recovery paid to Plan A, in excess of the $10,000 for which it is required to be covered, be made available by such insured to, or held for the use of, Plan B in such amount as Plan B would receive if bonded separately. Thus, in the instant case, Plan B would be able to recover the full $40,000 of its loss. Where the funds or other property of several plans are commingled (if permitted by law) with each other or with other funds, such arrangement shall allow recovery to be attributed proportionately to the amount for which each plan is required to be protectd. Thus, in the instant case, if funds or other property were commingled, and X caused a loss of these funds through fraud or dishonesty, one-sixth of the loss would be attributable to Plan A and five-sixths of the loss attributable to Plan B.

(e) The maximum amount of any bond with respect to any person in any one plan is $500,000, but bonds covering more than one plan may be required to be over $500,000 in order to meet the requirements of the Act, since persons covered by such a bond may have "handling" functions in more than one plan. The $500,000 limitations for such persons applies only with respect to each separate plan in which they have such functions. The minimum bond coverage for any administrator, officer, or employee "handling" funds or other property of a plan is $1,000 as respects each plan in which he has "handling" functions.

[¶ 14,822P]

§ 2580.412-17. **Bonds over $500,000.** The Labor-Management Services Administrator, after due notice and opportunity for hearing to all interested parties, and after consideration of the record, may prescribe an amount in excess of $500,000, which in no event shall exceed 10 per centum of the funds "handled." Any requirement for bonding in excess of $500,000 shall be according to such other regulations as the Secretary may prescribe.

Subpart D—General Bond Rules

[¶ 14,822Q]

§ 2580.412-18. **Naming of insureds.** Since section 13 is intended to protect funds or other property of all plans involved, bonds under this section shall allow for enforcement or recovery by those persons usually authorized to act for such plans in such matters. In most cases, the naming of the plan or plans as insured will provide for such recovery. Where it is not clear that such recovery will be provided, however, a rider shall be attached to the bond or separate agreement made among the parties concerned to make certain that any reimbursement collected under the bond will be for the benefit and use of the plan suffering a loss. Such rider or agreement shall always be required as respects any bond (a) where the employer or employee organization is first named joint insured with one or more plans, or (b) two or more plans are named joint insureds under a single bond with the first named acting for all insureds for the purpose of orderly servicing of the bond.

[¶ 14,822R]

§ 2580.412-19. **Term of the bond, discovery period, other bond clauses.**—

(a) *Term of the bond.* The amount of any required bond must in each instance be based on the amount of funds "handled" and must be fixed or estimated at the beginning of the plan's reporting year, that is, as soon after the date when such year begins as the necessary information from the preceding reporting year can practically be ascertained. This does not mean, however, that a new bond must be obtained each year. There is nothing in the Act that prohibits a bond for a term longer than one year, with whatever advantages such a bond might offer by way of a lower premium. However, at the beginning of each reporting year the bond shall be in at least the requisite amount. If, for any reason, the bond is below the required level at that time, the existing bond shall either be increased to the proper amount, or a supplemental bond shall be obtained.

(b) *Discovery period.* A discovery period of no less than one year after the termination or cancellation of the bond is required. Any standard form written on a "discovery" basis, i.e., providing that a loss must be discovered within the bond period as a prerequisite to recovery of such loss, however, will not be required to have a discovery period if it contains a provision giving the insured the right to purchase a discovery period of one year in the event of termination or cancellation and the insured has already given the surety notice that it desires such discovery period.

(c) *Other bond clauses.* A bond shall not be adequate to meet the requirements of section 13, if, with respect to bonding coverage required under section 13, it contains a clause, or is otherwise, in contravention of the law of the State in which it is executed.

[¶ 14,822S]

§ 2580.412-20. **Use of existing bonds, separate bonds and additional bonding.**—

(a) *Additional bonding.* Section 13 neither prevents additional bonding beyond that required by its terms, nor prescribes the form in which additional coverage may be taken. Thus, so long as a particular bond meets the requirements of the regulations in this part as to the persons required to be bonded and provides coverage for such persons in at least the minimum required amount, additional coverage as to persons or amount may be taken in any form, either on the same or separate bond.

(b) *Use of existing bonds.* Insofar as a bond currently in use is adequate to meet the requirements of the Act and the regulations in this part or may be made adequate to meet these requirements through rider, modification or separate agreement between the parties, no further bonding is required.

(c) *Use of separate bonds.* The choice of whether persons required to be bonded should be bonded separately or under the same bond, whether given plans should be bonded separately or under the same bond, whether existing bonds should be used or separate bonds for Welfare and Pension Plans Disclosure Act bonding should be obtained,

or whether the bond is underwritten by a single surety company or more than one surety company, either separately or on a cosurety basis, is left to the judgment of the parties concerned, so long as the bonding program adopted meets the requirements of the Act and the regulations in this part.

Subpart E—Qualified Agents, Brokers and Surety Companies for the Placing of Bonds

[¶ 14,822T]

§ 2580.412-21. **Corporate sureties holding, grants of authority from the Secretary of the Treasury.** (a) The provisions of section 13 require that any surety company with which a bond is placed pursuant to that section must be a corporate surety which holds a grant of authority from the Secretary of the Treasury under the Act of July 30, 1947 (6 U.S.C. 6-13), as an acceptable surety on Federal bonds. The Act provides, among other things, that in order for a surety company to be eligible for such grant of authority, it must be incorporated under the laws of the United States or of any State and the Secretary of the Treasury shall be satisfied of certain facts relating to its authority and capitalization. Such grants of authority are evidenced by Certificates of Authority which are issued by the Secretary of the Treasury and which expire on the April 30 following the date of their issuance. A list of the companies holding such Certificates of Authority is published annually in the Federal Register, usually in May or June. Changes in the list, occurring between May 1 and April 30, either by addition to or removal from the list of companies, are also published in the Federal Register following each such change.

(b) Where a surety becomes insolvent and is placed in receivership, or if for any other reason the Secretary of the Treasury determines that its financial condition is not satisfactory to him and he revokes the authority of such company to act as an acceptable surety under the Act of July 30, 1947, the "administrator" of the insured plan shall, upon knowledge of such facts, be responsible for securing a new bond with an acceptable surety.

(c) In obtaining or renewing a bond, the plan administrator shall assure that the surety is one which satisfies the requirements of this section. If the bond is for a term of more than one year, the plan administrator, at the beginning of each reporting year, shall assure that the surety continues to satisfy the requirements of this subpart.

[¶ 14,822U]

§ 2580.412-22. **Interests held in agents, brokers and surety companies.** Section 13(c) prohibits the placing of bonds, required to be obtained pursuant to section 13, with any surety or other company, or through any agent or broker in whose business operations a plan or any party in interest in a plan has significant control or financial interest, direct or indirect. An interpretation of this section has been issued (Part 485 of this chapter).

Subpart F—Exemptions

BONDS PLACED WITH CERTAIN REINSURING COMPANIES

[¶ 14,822V]

§ 2580.412-23. **Exemption.** An exemption from the bonding requirements of the Welfare and Pension Plans Disclosure Act is granted by this section whereby bonding arrangements (which otherwise comply with the requirements of section 13 of the Act and the regulations issued thereunder) with companies authorized by the Secretary of the Treasury as acceptable reinsurers on Federal bonds will satisfy the bonding requirements of the Act. (Amended by F.R. Doc. 63-11370, published in Federal Register October 29, 1963.)

[¶ 14,822W]

§ 2580.412-24. **Conditions of exemption.** (a) This exemption obtains only with respect to the requirement of section 13(a) of the Act that all bonds required thereunder shall have as surety thereon, a corporate surety company, which is an acceptable surety on Federal bonds under authority granted by the Secretary of the Treasury pursuant to the Act of July 30, 1947 (6 U.S.C. 6-13).

(b) The exemption is granted upon the condition that if for any reason the authority of any such company to act as an acceptable reinsuring company is terminated, the administrator of a plan insured with such company, shall, upon knowledge of such fact, be responsible for securing a new bond with a company acceptable under the Act and the exemptions issued thereunder.

(c) In obtaining or renewing a bond, the plan administrator shall ascertain that the surety is one which satisfies the requirements of the Act and the exemptions thereunder. If the bond is for a term of more than one year, the plan administrator, at the beginning of each reporting year, shall ascertain that the surety continues to do so. (Amended by F.R. Doc. 63-11370, published in Federal Register October 29, 1963.)

BONDS PLACED WITH UNDERWRITERS AT LLOYDS, LONDON

[¶ 14,822X]

§ 2580.412-25. **Exemption**. An exemption from the bonding requirements of subsection 13(a) of the Welfare and Pension Plans Disclosure Act is granted by this section whereby arrangements (which otherwise comply with the requirements of section 13 of the Act and the regulations issued thereunder), with the Underwriters at Lloyds, London will satisfy the bonding requirements of the Act.

[¶ 14,822Y]

§ 2580.412-26. **Conditions of exemption**. (a) This exemption obtains only with respect to the requirements of section 13(a) of the Act that all bonds required thereunder shall have assurety thereon, a corporate surety company, which is an acceptable surety on Federal bonds under authority granted by the Secretary of the Treasury, pursuant to the Act of July 30, 1947 (6 U.S.C. 6-13).

(b) This exemption is granted on the following conditions:

(1) Underwriters at Lloyds, London shall continue to be licensed in a state of the United States to enter into bonding arrangements of the type required by the Act.

(2) Underwriters at Lloyds, London shall file with the Office of Pension and Welfare Benefit Programs two (2) copies of each annual statement required to be made to the Commissioner of Insurance of those states in which Underwriters at Lloyds, London are licensed. Copies of annual statements shall be filed with the Office of Pension and Welfare Benefit Programs within the same period required by the respective states.

(3) All bonding arrangements entered into by Underwriters at Lloyds, London under section 13 of the Act shall contain a "Service of Suit Clause" in substantial conformity with that set forth in the petition for exemption.

BANKING INSTITUTIONS SUBJECT TO FEDERAL REGULATION

[¶ 14,822Z]

§ 2580.412-27. **Exemption**. An exemption from the bonding requirements of subsections 13(a) and (b) of the Welfare and Pension Plans Disclosure Act is granted whereby banking institutions and trust companies specified in § 2580.412-28 are not required to comply with subsections 13(a) and (b) of the Act, with respect to welfare and pension benefit plans covered by the Act. (Amended by F.R. Doc. 69-3030, published in Federal Register March 13, 1969.)

[¶ 14,823]

§ 2580.412-28. **Conditions of exemption**. This exemption applies only to those banking institutions and trust companies subject to regulation and examination by the Comptroller of the Currency or the Board of Governors of the Federal Reserve System, or the Federal Deposit Insurance Corporation.

[¶ 14,823A]

§ 2580.412-29. **Exemption**. An exemption from the bonding requirements of subsections 13(a) and (b) of the Welfare and Pension Plans Disclosure Act is granted whereby savings and loan associations (including building and loan associations, cooperative banks and homestead associations) specified in § 2580.412-30 are not required to comply with subsections 13(a) and (b) of the Act, with respect to welfare and pension benefit plans covered by the Act for the benefit of their own employees, where such a savings and loan association is the administrator of such plans. (Added by F.R. Doc. 67-4967, published in Federal Register May 4, 1967.)

[¶ 14,823B]

§ 2580.412-30. **Conditions of exemption**. This exemption applies only to those savings and loan associations (including building and loan associations, cooperative banks and homestead associations) subject to regulation and examination by the Federal Home Loan Bank Board. (Added by F.R. Doc. 67-4967, published in Federal Register May 4, 1967.)

INSURANCE CARRIERS, SERVICE AND OTHER SIMILAR ORGANIZATIONS

[¶ 14,823C]

§ 2580.412-31. **Exemption**. An exemption from the bonding requirements of subsections 13(a) and (b) of the Welfare and Pension Plans Disclosure Act is granted whereby any insurance carrier or service or other similar organization specified in § 2580.412-32 is not required to comply with subsections 13(a) and (b) of the Act with respect to any welfare or pension benefit plan covered by the Act which is established or maintained for the benefit of persons other than the employees of such insurance carrier or service or other similar organization. (Added by F.R. Doc. 69-3030, published in Federal Register March 13, 1969.)

[¶ 14,823D]

§ 2580.412-32. **Conditions of exemption**. This exemption applies only to those insurance carriers, service or other similar organizations providing or underwriting welfare or pension plan benefits in accordance with State law. (Added by F.R. Doc. 69-3030, published in Federal Register March 13, 1969.)

Subpart G—Prohibition Against Bonding by Parties Interested in the Plan

[¶ 14,823E]

§ 2580.412-33. **Introductory statement**. (a) This part discusses the meaning and scope of Section 13(c) of the Welfare and Pension Plans Disclosure Act of 1958 (76 Stat. 39, 29 U.S.C. 308d (c)) (hereinafter referred to as the Act). This provision makes it unlawful "for any person to procure any bond [required by the Act] from any surety or other company or through any agent or broker in whose business operations such plan or any party in interest in such plan has any significant control or financial interest, direct or indirect." Because the prohibition contained in this provision is broadly stated, it becomes a matter of importance to determine more specifically the types of arrangements intended to be prohibited.

(b) The provisions of Section 13 of the Act, including 13(c) are subject to the general investigatory authority of the Director, Office of Labor-Management and Welfare-Pension Reports, embodied in Section 9 of the Act. The correctness of an interpretation of these provisions can be determined finally and authoritatively only by the courts. It is necessary, however, for the Labor-Management Services Administrator (hereafter referred to as "the administrator") to reach informed conclusions as to the meaning of the law to enable him to carry out his statutory duties of administration and enforcement. The interpretations of the Administrator contained in this part, which are issued upon the advice of the Solicitor of Labor, indicate the construction of the law which will guide the Administrator in performing his duties unless and until he is directed otherwise by authoritative rulings of the courts or unless and until he subsequently decides that his prior interpretation is incorrect. Under Section 12 of the Act, the interpretations contained in this part, if relied upon in good faith, will constitute a defense in any action or proceeding based on any act or omission in alleged violation of Section 13(c) of the Act. The omission, however, to discuss a particular problem in this part, or in interpretations supplementing it, should not be taken to indicate the adoption of any position by the Administrator with respect to such problem or to constitute an administrative interpretation or practice. Interpretations of the Administrator with respect to 13(c) are set forth in this part to provide those affected by the provisions of the Act with "a practical guide * * * as to how the office representing the public interest in its enforcement will seek to apply it" (*Skidmore v. Swift & Co.*, 323 U.S. 134, 138).

(c) To the extent that prior opinions and interpretations relating to 13(c) are inconsistent with the principles stated in this part, they are hereby rescinded and withdrawn.

Reg. § 2580.412-33(c)   ¶ 14,823E

[¶ 14,823F]

§ 2580.412-34. **General**. The purpose of Section 13(c), as shown by its legislative history, is similar to a closely related provision contained in Section 502(a) of the Labor-Management Reporting and Disclosure Act of 1959 (73 Stat. 536; 29 U.S.C. 502(a)). The fundamental purpose of Congress under 13(c) is to insure against potential abuses arising from significant financial or other influential interests affecting the objectivity of the plan or parties in interest in the plan and agents, brokers, or surety or other companies, in securing and providing the bond specified in Section 13(a). As will be explained more fully below, this prohibition, however, was not intended to preclude the placing of bonds through or with certain parties in interest in plans which provide a variety of services to the plan, one of which is a bonding service.

[¶ 14,823G]

§ 2580.412-35. **Disqualification of agents, brokers and sureties**. Since 13(c) is to be construed as disqualifying any agent, broker, surety or other company from having a bond placed through or with it, if the plan or any party in interest in the plan has a significant financial interest or control in such agent, broker, surety or other company, a question of fact will necessarily arise in many cases as to whether the financial interest or control held is sufficiently significant to disqualify the agent, broker or surety. Although no rule of guidance can be established to govern each and every case in which this question arises, in general, the essential test is whether the existing financial interest or control held is incompatible with an unbiased exercise of judgment in regard to procuring the bond or bonding the plan's personnel. In regard to the foregoing, it is also to be pointed out that lack of knowledge or consent on the part of persons responsible for procuring bonds with respect to the existence of a significant financial interest or control rendering the bonding arrangement unlawful will not be deemed a mitigating factor where such persons have failed to make a reasonable examination into the pertinent circumstances affecting the procuring of the bond.

[¶ 14,823H]

§ 2580.412-36. **Application of 13(c) to "party in interest"**. (a) Under 13(c), an agent, broker or surety or other company is disqualified from having a bond placed through or with it if a "party in interest" in the plan has any significant control or financial interest in such agent, broker, surety or other company. Section 3(13) of the Act defines the term "party in interest" to mean "any administrator, officer, trustee, custodian, counsel, or employee of any employee welfare benefit plan or employee pension benefit plan, or a person providing benefit plan services to any such plan, or an employer any of whose employees are covered by such a plan or officer or employee or agent of such employer, or an officer or agent or employee of an employee organization having members covered by such plan."

(b) A basic question presented is whether the effect of 13(c) is to prohibit persons from placing a bond through or with any "party in interest" in the plan. The language used in 13(c) appears to indicate that in this connection the intent of Congress was to eliminate those instances where the existing financial interest or control held by the "party in interest" in the agent, broker, surety or other company is incompatible with an unbiased exercise of judgment in regard to procuring the bond or bonding the plan's personnel. Accordingly, not all parties in interest are disqualified from procuring or providing bonds for the plan. Thus where a "party in interest" or its affiliate provides multiple benefit plan services to plans, persons are not prohibited from availing themselves of the bonding services provided by the "party in interest" or its affiliate merely because the plan has already availed itself, or will avail itself, of other services provided by the "party in interest." In this case, it is inherent in the nature of the "party in interest" or its affiliate as an individual or organization providing multiple benefit plan services, one of which is a bonding service, that the existing financial interest or control held is not, in and of itself, incompatible with an unbiased exercise of judgment in regard to procuring the bond or bonding the plan's personnel. In short, there is no distinction between this type of relationship and the ordinary arm's length business relationship which may be established between a plan-customer and an agent, broker or surety company, a relationship which Congress could not have intended to disturb. On the other hand, where a "party in interest" in the plan or an affiliate does not provide a bonding service as part of its general business operations, 13(c) would prohibit any person from procuring the bond through or with any agent, broker, surety or other company, with respect to which the "party in interest" has any significant control or financial interest, direct or indirect. In this case, the failure of the "party in interest" or its affiliate to provide a bonding service as part of its general business operations misses the possibility of less than an arm's length business relationship between the plan and the agent, broker, surety or other company since the objectivity of either the plan or the agent, broker or surety may be influenced by the "party in interest".

(c) The application of the principles discussed in this section is illustrated by the following examples:

Example (1). B, a broker, renders actuarial and consultant services to plan P. B has also procured a group life insurance policy for plan P. B may also place a bond for P with surety company S, provided that neither B nor P has any significant control or financial interest, direct or indirect, in S and provided that neither P nor any other "party in interest" in P, e.g., an officer of the plan, has any significant control or financial interest, direct or indirect, in B or S.

Example (2). I, a life insurance company, has provided a group life insurance policy for plan P. I is affiliated with S, a surety company, and has a significant financial interest or control in S. P is not prohibited from obtaining a bond from S since I's affiliation with S does not ordinarily, in and of itself, affect the objectivity of P in procuring the bond or the objectivity of S in bonding P's personnel. However, if any other "party in interest" as defined in Section 3(13) of the Act, such as the employer whose employees are covered by P, should have a significant financial interest or control in S, S could not write the bond for P, since the employer's interest affects the objectivity of P and S.

[¶ 14,830]
LIMITATION ON ACTIONS

Act Sec. 413. No action may be commenced under this title with respect to a fiduciary's breach of any responsibility, duty, or obligation under this part, or with respect to a violation of this part, after the earlier of—

(1) six years after (A) the date of the last action which constituted a part of the breach or violation, or (B) in the case of an omission, the latest date on which the fiduciary could have cured the breach or violation, or

(2) three years after the earliest date on which the plaintiff had actual knowledge of the breach or violation

except that in the case of fraud or concealment, such action may be commenced not later than six years after the date of discovery of such breach or violation.

Amendments

P.L. 101-239, § 7881(j)(4):

Amended ERISA Sec. 413(2) by striking the comma effective December 17, for reports required to be filed after December 31, 1987.

P.L. 101-239, § 7894(e)(5):

Amended ERISA Sec. 413 by striking "(a)" effective September 2, 1974.

P.L. 100-203, § 9342(b):

Amended ERISA Sec. 413(a)(2) by striking "A" and "or B" and all that followed through "title", to read as above, effective December 17, 1987 for reports required to be filed after December 31, 1987. Prior to amendment, 413(a)(2) reads as follows:

(2) three years after the earliest date (A) on which the plaintiff had actual knowledge of the breach or violation, or (B) on which a report from which he could reasonably be expected to have obtained knowledge of such breach or violation was filed with the Secretary under this title;

[¶ 14,840]
EFFECTIVE DATE

Act Sec. 414. (a) Except as provided in subsections (b), (c), and (d), this part shall take effect on January 1, 1975.

Act Sec. 414. (b)(1) The provisions of this part authorizing the Secretary to promulgate regulations shall take effect on the date of enactment of this Act.

(2) Upon application of a plan, the Secretary may postpone until not later than January 1, 1976, the applicability of any provision of sections 402, 403 (other than 403(c)), 405 (other than 405(a) and (d)), and 410(a), as it applies to any plan in existence on the date of enactment of this Act if he determines such postponement is (A) necessary to amend the instrument establishing the plan under which the plan is maintained and (B) not adverse to the interest of participants and beneficiaries.

(3) This part shall take effect on the date of enactment of this Act with respect to a plan which terminates after June 30, 1974, and before January 1, 1975, and to which at the time of termination section 4021 applies.

Act Sec. 414. (c) Sections 406 and 407(a) (relating to prohibited transactions) shall not apply—

(1) until June 30, 1984, to a loan of money or other extension of credit between a plan and a party in interest under a binding contract in effect on July 1, 1974 (or pursuant to renewals of such a contract), if such loan or other extension of credit remains at least as favorable to the plan as an arm's-length transaction with an unrelated party would be, and if the execution of the contract, the making of the loan, or the extension of credit was not, at the time of such execution, making, or extension, a prohibited transaction (within the meaning of section 503(b) of the Internal Revenue Code of 1986 or the corresponding provisions of prior law);

(2) until June 30, 1984, to a lease or joint use of property involving the plan and a party in interest pursuant to a binding contract in effect on July 1, 1974 (or pursuant to renewals of such a contract), if such lease or joint use remains at least as favorable to the plan as an arm's-length transaction with an unrelated party would be and if the execution of the contract was not, at the time of such execution, a prohibited transaction (within the meaning of section 503(b) of the Internal Revenue Code of 1986 or the corresponding provisions of prior law);

(3) until June 30, 1984, to the sale, exchange, or other disposition of property described in paragraph (2) between a plan and a party in interest if—

(A) in the case of a sale, exchange, or other disposition of the property by the plan to the party in interest, the plan receives an amount which is not less than the fair market value of the property at the time of such disposition; and

(B) in the case of the acquisition of the property by the plan, the plan pays an amount which is not in excess of the fair market value of the property at the time of such acquisition;

(4) until June 30, 1977, to the provision of services, to which paragraphs (1), (2), and (3) do not apply between a plan and a party in interest—

(A) under a binding contract in effect on July 1, 1974 (or pursuant to renewals of such contract), or

(B) if the party in interest ordinarily and customarily furnished such services on June 30, 1974, if such provision of services remains at least as favorable to the plan as an arm's-length transaction with an unrelated party would be and if such provision of services was not, at the time of such provision, a prohibited transaction (within the meaning of section 503(b) of the Internal Revenue Code of 1954) or the corresponding provisions of prior law; or

(5) the sale, exchange, or other disposition of property which is owned by a plan on June 30, 1974, and all times thereafter, to a party in interest, if such plan is required to dispose of such property in order to comply with the provisions of section 407(a) (relating to the prohibition against holding excess employer securities and employer real property), and if the plan receives not less than adequate consideration.

Act Sec. 414. (d) Any election, or failure to elect, by a disqualified person under section 2003(c)(1)(B) of this Act shall be treated for purposes of this part (but not for purposes of section 514) as an act or omission occurring before the effective date of this part.

Act Sec. 414. (e) The preceding provisions of this section shall not apply with respect to amendments made to this part in provisions enacted after the date of the enactment of this Act.

Amendments

P.L. 101-239, §7891(a)(1):

Titles I, III, and IV of ERISA (other than sections 3(37)(E), 301(a)(7), and 308, the last sentence of section 408(d), and sections 414(c), 4001(a)(3)(ii), and 4303) are each amended by striking "Internal Revenue Code of 1954" each place it appears and inserting "Internal Revenue Code of 1986" effective October 22, 1986.

P.L. 101-239, §7894(e)(6):

Amended ERISA Sec. 414(c)(2) by striking "1954)" and inserting "1986" and by striking "prior law" and inserting "prior law)" effective September 2, 1974.

P.L. 101-239, §7894(h)(4):

Amended ERISA Sec. 414 by adding new subsection (e) to read as above.

Regulations

The following regulations were adopted under "Title 29—Labor; Chapter XXV—Office of Employee Benefits Security; Part 2555—Interpretive Bulletins Relating to Fiduciary Responsibility." The regulations were filed with the Federal Register on July 25, 1975, and published in the Federal Register of July 28, 1975. The regulations were renumbered under a new "Part 2509—Interpretive Bulletins Relating to the Employee Retirement Income Security Act of 1974" by FR Doc. 76-966, 41 FR 1906, filed with the Federal Register on January 12, 1976, and published in the Federal Register of January 13, 1976. Reg. Sec. 2509.75-1 was removed on July 1, 1996 by 61 FR 33847. Reg Sec. 2509.75-5 was amended on August 24, 2004 by 69 FR 52119.

[¶ 14,875]

§ 2509.75-1 **Interpretive bulletin relating to section 414(c)(4) of the Employee Retirement Income Security Act of 1974.** [Officially removed by 61 FR 33847 on 7/1/96.]

[¶ 14,876]

§ 2509.75-2 **Interpretive bulletin relating to prohibited transactions.** On February 6, 1975, the Department of Labor issued an an interpretive bulletin, ERISA IB 75-2, with respect to whether a party in interest has engaged in a prohibited transaction with an employee benefit plan where the party in interest has engaged in a transaction with a corporation or partnership (within the meaning of section 7701 of the Internal Revenue Code of 1954) in which the plan has invested.

On November 13, 1986 the Department published a final regulation dealing with the definition of "plan assets". See § 2510.3-101 of this title. Under that regulation, the assets of certain entities in which plans invest would include "plan assets" for purposes of the fiduciary responsibility provisions of the Act. Section 2510.3-101 applies only for purposes of identifying plan assets on or after the effective date of that section, however, and § 2510.3-101 does not apply to plan investments in certain entities that qualify for the transitional relief provided for in paragraph (k) of that section. The principles discussed in paragraph (a) of this Interpretive Bulletin continue to be applicable for purposes of identifying assets of a plan for periods prior to the effective date of § 2510.3-101 and for investments that are subject to the transitional rule

in § 2510.3-101(k). Paragraphs (b) and (c) of this Interpretive Bulletin, however, relate to matters outside the scope of § 2510.3-101, and nothing in that section affects the continuing application of the principles discussed in those parts.

(a) *Principles applicable to plan investments to which § 2510.3-101 does not apply.* Generally, investment by a plan in securities (within the meaning of section 3(20) of the Employee Retirement Income Security Act of 1974) of a corporation or partnership will not, solely by reason of such investment, be considered to be an investment in the underlying assets of such corporation or partnership so as to make such assets of the entity "plan assets" and thereby make a subsequent transaction between the party in interest and the corporation or partnership a prohibited transaction under section 406 of the Act.

For example, where a plan acquires a security of a corporation or a limited partnership interest in a partnership, a subsequent lease or sale of property between such corporation or partnership and a party in interest will not be a prohibited transaction solely by reason of the plan's investment in the corporation or partnership.

This general proposition, as applied to corporations and partnerships, is consistent with section 401(b)(1) of the Act, relating to plan investments in investment companies registered under the Investment Company Act of 1940. Under section 401(b)(1), an investment by a plan in securities of such an investment company may be made without causing, solely by reason of such investment, any of the assets of the investment company to be considered to be assets of the plan.

(b) *Contracts of policies of insurance.* [Removed and reserved by 61 FR 33847 on 7/1/96.]

(c) *Applications of the fiduciary responsibility rules.* The preceding paragraphs do not mean that an investment of plan assets in a security of a corporation or partnership may not be a prohibited transaction. For example, section 406(a)(1)(D) prohibits the direct or indirect transfer to, or use by or for the benefit of, a party in interest of any assets of the plan and section 406(b)(1) prohibits a fiduciary from dealing with the assets of the plan in his own interest or for his own account.

Thus, for example, if there is an arrangement under which a plan invests in, or retains its investment in, an investment company and as part of the arrangement it is expected that the investment company will purchase securities from a party in interest, such arrangement is a prohibited transaction.

Similarly, the purchase by a plan of an insurance policy pursuant to an arrangement under which it is expected that the insurance company will make a loan to a party in interest is a prohibited transaction.

Moreover, notwithstanding the foregoing, if a transaction between a party in interest and a plan would be a prohibited transaction, then such a transaction between a party in interest and such corporation or partnership will ordinarily be a prohibited transaction if the plan may, by itself, require the corporation or partnership to engage in such transaction.

Similarly, if a transaction between a party in interest and a plan would be a prohibited transaction, then such a transaction between a party in interest and such corporation or partnership will ordinarily be a prohibited transaction if such party in interest, together with one or more persons who are parties in interest by reason of such persons' relationship (within the meaning of section 3(14)(E) through (I)) to such party in interest may, with the aid of the plan but without the aid of any other persons, require the corporation or partnership to engage in such a transaction. However, the preceding sentence does not apply if the parties in interest engaging in the transaction, together with one or more persons who are parties in interest by reason of such persons' relationship (within the meaning of section 3(14)(E) through (I)) to such party in interest, may, by themselves, require the corporation or partnership to engage in the transaction.

Further, the Department of Labor emphasizes that it would consider a fiduciary who makes or retains an investment in a corporation or partnership for the purpose of avoiding the application of the fiduciary responsibility provisions of the Act to be in contravention of the provisions of section 404(a) of the Act. [Amended by 51 FR 41262 on November 13, 1986, effective Mar. 13, 1987.]

[¶ 14,877]

§ 2509.75-3 **Interpretive bulletin relating to investments by employee benefit plans in securities of registered investment companies.** On March 12, 1975, the Department of Labor issued an interpretive bulletin, ERISA IB 75-3, with regard to its interpretation of section 3(21)(B) of the Employee Retirement Income Security Act of 1974. That section provides that an investment by an employee benefit plan in securities issued by an investment company registered under the Investment Company Act of 1940 shall not by itself cause the investment company, its investment adviser or principal underwriter to be deemed to be a fiduciary or party in interest "except insofar as such investment company or its investment adviser or principal underwriter acts in connection with an employee benefit plan covering employees of the investment company, the investment adviser, or its principal underwriter."

The Department of Labor interprets this section as an elaboration of the principle set forth in section 401(b)(1) of the Act and ERISA IB 75-2 (issued February 6, 1975) that the assets of an investment company shall not be deemed to be assets of a plan solely by reason of an investment by such plan in the shares of such investment company. Consistent with this principle, the Department of Labor interprets this section to mean that a person who is connected with an investment company, such as the investment company itself, its investment adviser or its principal underwriter, is not to be deemed to be a fiduciary of or party in interest with respect to a plan solely because the plan has invested in the investment company's shares.

This principle applies, for example, to a plan covering employees of an investment adviser to an investment company where the plan invests in the securities of the investment company. In such a case the investment company or its principal underwriter is not be be deemed to be a fiduciary of or party in interest with respect to the plan solely because of such investment.

On the other hand, the exception clause in section 3(21) emphasizes that if an investment company, its investment adviser or its principal underwriter is a fiduciary or party in interest for a reason other than the investment in the securities of the investment company, such a person remains a party in interest or fiduciary. Thus, in the preceding example, since an employer is a party in interest, the investment adviser remains a party in interest with respect to a plan covering its employees.

The Department of Labor emphasized that an investment adviser, principal underwriter or investment company which is a fiduciary by virtue of section 3(21)(A) of the Act is subject to the fiduciary responsibility provisions of Part 4 of Title I of the Act, including those relating to fiduciary duties under section 404.

[¶ 14,878]

§ 2509.75-4 **Interpretive bulletin relating to indemnification of fiduciaries.** On June 4, 1975, the Department of Labor issued an interpretive bulletin, ERISA IB 75-4, announcing the Department's interpretation of section 410(a) of the Employee Retirement Income Security Act of 1974, insofar as that section relates to indemnification of fiduciaries. Section 410(a) states, in relevant part, that "any provision in an agreement or instrument which purports to relieve a fiduciary from responsibility or liability for any responsibilty, obligation, or duty under this part shall be void as against public policy."

The Department of Labor interprets this section to permit indemnification agreements which do not relieve a fiduciary of responsibility or liability under Part 4 of Title I. Indemnification provisions which leave the fiduciary fully responsible and liable, but merely permit another party to satisfy any liability incurred by the fiduciary in the same manner as insurance purchased under section 410(b)(3), are therefore not void under section 410(a).

Examples of such indemnification provisions are:

(1) Indemnification of a plan fiduciary by (a) an employer, any of whose employees are covered by the plan, or an affiliate (as defined in section 407(d)(7) of the Act) of such employer, or (b) an employee organization, any of whose members are covered by the plan; and

(2) Indemnification by a plan fiduciary of the fiduciary's employees who actually perform the fiduciary services.

The Department of Labor interprets section 410(a) as rendering void any arrangement for indemnification of a fiduciary of an employee benefit plan by the plan. Such an arrangement would have the same result as an exculpatory clause, in that it would, in effect, relieve the fiduciary of responsibility and liability to the plan by abrogating the plan's right to recovery from the fiduciary for breaches of fiduciary obligations.

While indemnification arrangements do not contravene the provisions of section 410(a), parties entering into an indemnification agreement should consider whether the agreement complies with the other provisions of Part 4 of Title I of the Act and with other applicable laws.

[¶ 14,879]

§ 2509.75-5 **Questions and answers relating to fiduciary responsibility.** On June 25, 1975, the Department of Labor issued an interpretive bulletin, ERISA IB 75-5, containing questions and answers relating to certain aspects of the recently enacted Employee Retirement Income Security Act of 1974 (the "Act").

Pending the issuance of regulations or other guidelines, persons may rely on the answers to these questions in order to resolve the issues that are specifically considered. No inferences should be drawn regarding issues not raised which may be suggested by a particular question and answer or as to why certain questions, and not others, are included. Furthermore, in applying the questions and answers, the effect of subsequent legislation, regulations, court decisions, and interpretive bulletins must be considered. To the extent that plans utilize or rely on these answers and the requirements of regulations subsequently adopted vary from the answers relied on, such plans may have to be amended.

An index of the questions and answers, relating them to the appropriate sections of the Act, is also provided.

INDEX KEY TO QUESTION PREFIXES

D—Refers to Definitions.
FR—Refers to Fiduciary Responsibility.

Section No.	Question No.
3(21)	D-1
3(38)	FR-6, FR-7
402(a)	FR-1, FR-2, FR-3
402(b)(1)	FR-4, FR-5
402(c)(3)	FR-6, FR-7
404(a)	FR-10
405(a)(3)	FR-10
405(b)(1)(A)	FR-10
406(a)	FR-9
409(a)	FR-10
412(a)	FR-8, FR-9

D-1 Q: Is an attorney, accountant, actuary or consultant who renders legal, accounting, actuarial or consulting services to an employee benefit plan (other than an investment adviser to the plan) a fiduciary to the plan solely by virtue of the rendering of such services, absent a showing that such consultant (a) exercises discretionary authority or discretionary control respecting the management of the plan, (b) exercises authority or control respecting management or disposition of the plan's assets, (c) renders investment advice for a fee, direct or indirect, with respect to the assets of the plan, or has any authority or responsibility to do so, or (d) has any discretionary authority or discretionary responsibility in the administration of the plan?

A: No. However, while attorneys, accountants, actuaries and consultants performing their usual professional functions will ordinarily not be considered fiduciaries, if the factual situation in a particular case falls within one of the categories described in clauses (a) through (d) of this question, such persons would be considered to be fiduciaries within the meaning of section 3(21) of the Act. The Internal Revenue Service notes that such persons would also be considered to be fiduciaries within the meaning of section 4975(e)(3) of the Internal Revenue Code of 1954.

FR-1 Q: If an instrument establishing an employee benefit plan provides that the plan committee shall control and manage the operation and administration of the plan and specifies who shall constitute the plan committee (either by position or by naming individuals to the committee), does such provision adequately satisfy the requirement in section 402(a) that a "named fiduciary" be provided for in a plan instrument?

A: Yes. While the better practice would be to state explicitly that the plan committee is the "named fiduciary" for purposes of the Act, clear identification of one or more persons, by name or title, combined with a statement that such person or persons have authority to control and manage the operation and administration of the plan, satisfies the "named fiduciary" requirement of section 402(a). The purpose of this requirement is to enable employees and other interested persons to ascertain who is responsible for operating the plan. The instrument in the above example, which provides that "the plan committee shall control and manage the operation and administration of the plan," and specifies, by name or position, who shall constitute the committee, fulfills this requirement.

FR-2 Q: In a union negotiated employee benefit plan, the instrument establishing the plan provides that a joint board on which employees and employers are equally represented shall control and manage the operation and administration of the plan. Does this provision adequately satisfy the requirement in section 402(a) that a "named fiduciary" be provided for in a plan instrument?

A: Yes, for the reasons stated in response to question FR-1. The joint board is clearly identified as the entity which has authority to control and manage the operation and administration of the plan, and the

persons designated to be members of such joint board would be named fiduciaries under section 402(a).

FR-3 Q: May an employee benefit plan covering employees of a corporation designate the corporation as the "named fiduciary" for purposes of section 402(a)(1) of the Act?

A: Yes, it may. Section 402(a)(2) of the Act states that a "named fiduciary" is a fiduciary either named in the plan instrument or designated according to a procedure set forth in the plan instrument. A fiduciary is a "person" falling within the definition of fiduciary set forth in section 3(21)(A) of the Act. A "person" may be a corporation under the definition of person contained in section 3(9) of the Act. While such designation satisfies the requirement of enabling employees and other interested persons to ascertain the person or persons responsible for operating the plan, a plan instrument which designates a corporation as "named fiduciary" should provide for designation by the corporation of specified individuals or other persons to carry out specified fiduciary responsibilities under the plan, in accordance with section 405(c)(1)(B) of the Act.

FR-4 Q: A defined benefit pension plan's procedure for establishing and carrying out a funding policy provides that the plan's trustees shall, at a meeting duly called for the purpose, establish a funding policy and method which satisfies the requirements of Part 3 of Title I of the Act, and shall meet annually at a stated time of the year to review such funding policy and method. It further provides that all actions taken with respect to such funding policy and method and the reasons therefor shall be recorded in the minutes of the trustees' meetings. Does this procedure comply with section 402(b)(1) of the Act?

A: Yes. The above procedure specifies who is to establish the funding policy and method for the plan, and provides for a written record of the actions taken with respect to such funding policy and method, including the reasons for such actions. The purpose of the funding policy requirement set forth in section 402(b)(1) is to enable plan participants and beneficiaries to ascertain that the plan has a funding policy that meets the requirements of Part 3 of Title I of the Act. The procedure set forth above meets that requirement.

FR-5 Q: Must a welfare plan in which the benefits are paid out of the general assets of the employer have a procedure for establishing and carrying out a funding policy set forth in the plan instrument?

A: No. Section 402(b)(1) requires that the plan provide for such a procedure "consistent with the objectives of the plan" and requirements of Title I of the Act. In stituations in which a plan is unfunded and Title I of the Act does not require the plan to be funded, there is no need to provide for such a procedure. If the welfare plan were funded, a procedure consistent with the objectives of the plan would have to be established.

FR-6 Q: May an investment adviser which is neither a bank nor an insurance company, and which is neither registered under the Investment Advisers Act of 1940 nor registered as an investment adviser in the State where it maintains its principal office and place of business, be appointed an investment manager under section 402(c)(3) of the Act?

A: No. The only persons who may be appointed an investment manager under section 402(c)(3) of the Act are persons who meet the requirements of section 3(38) of the Act—namely, banks (as defined in the Investment Advisers Act of 1940), insurance companies qualified under the laws of more than one state to manage, acquire and dispose of plan assets, persons registered as investment advisers under the Investment Advisers Act of 1940, or persons not registered under the Investment Advisers Act by reason of paragraph 1 of section 203A(a) of that Act who are registered as investment advisers in the State where they maintain their principal office and place of business in accordance with ERISA section 3(38) and who have met the filing requirements of 29 CFR 2510.3-38.

FR-7 Q: May an investment adviser that has a registration application pending for federal registration under the Investment Advisers Act of 1940, or pending with the appropriate state regulatory body under State investment adviser registration laws if relying on the provisions of 29 CFR 2510.3-38 to qualify as a state-registered investment manager, function as an investment manager under the Act prior to the effective date of their federal or state registration?

A: No, for the reasons stated in the answer to FR-6 above.

FR-8 Q: Under the temporary bonding regulation set forth in 29 CFR § 2550.412-1, must a person who renders investment advice to a plan for a fee or other compensation, direct or indirect, but who does not exercise or have the right to exercise discretionary authority with respect to the assets of the plan, be bonded solely by reason of the provision of such investment advice?

A: No. A person who renders investment advice, but who does not exercise or have the right to exercise discretionary authority with respect to plan assets, is not required to be bonded solely by reason of the provision of such investment advice. Such a person is not considered to be "handling" funds within the meaning of the temporary bonding regulation set forth in 29 CFR § 2550.412-1, which incorporates by reference 29 CFR § 464.7. For purposes of the temporary bonding regulation, only those fiduciaries who handle funds must be bonded. If, in addition to the rendering of investment advice, such person performs any additional function which constitutes the handling of plan funds under 29 CFR § 464.7, the person would have to be bonded.

FR-9 Q: May an employee benefit plan purchase a bond covering plan officials?

A: Yes. The bonding requirement, which applies, with certain exceptions, to every plan official under section 412(a) of the Act, is for the protection of the plan and does not benefit any plan official or relieve any plan official of any obligation to the plan. The purchase of such bond by a plan will not, therefore, be considered to be in contravention of sections 406(a) or (b) of the Act.

FR-10 Q: An employee benefit plan is considering the construction of a building to house the administration of the plan. One trustee has proposed that the building be constructed on a cost plus basis by a particular contractor without competitive bidding. When the trustee was questioned by another trustee as to the basis of choice of the contractor, the impact of the building on the plan's administrative costs, whether a cost plus contract would yield a better price to the plan than a fixed price basis, and why a negotiated contract would be better than letting the contract for competitive bidding, no satisfactory answers were provided. Several of the trustees have argued that letting such a contract would be a violation of their general fiduciary responsibilities. Despite their arguments, a majority of the trustees appear to be ready to vote to construct the building as proposed. What should the minority trustees do to protect themselves from liability under section 409(a) of the Act and section 405(b)(1)(A) of the Act?

A: Here, where a majority of trustees appear ready to take action which would clearly be contrary to the prudence requirement of section 404(a)(1)(B) of the Act, it is incumbent on the minority trustees to take all reasonable and legal steps to prevent the action. Such steps might include preparations to obtain an injunction from a Federal District court under section 502(a)(3) of the Act, to notify the Labor Department, or to publicize the vote if the decision is to proceed as proposed. If, having taken all reasonable and legal steps to prevent the imprudent action, the minority trustees have not succeeded, they will not incur liability for the action of the majority. Mere resignation, however, without taking steps to prevent the imprudent action, will not suffice to avoid liability for the minority trustees once they have knowledge that the imprudent action is under consideration.

More generally, trustees should take great care to document adequately all meetings where actions are taken with respect to management and control of plan assets. Written minutes of all actions taken should be kept describing the action taken, and stating how each trustee voted on each matter. If, as in the case above, trustees object to a proposed action on the grounds of possible violation of the fiduciary responsibility provisions of the Act, the trustees so objecting should insist that their objections and the responses to such objections be included in the record of the meeting. It should be noted that, where a trustee believes that a cotrustee has already committed a breach, resignation by the trustee as a protest against such breach will not generally be considered sufficient to discharge the trustee's positive duty under section 405(a)(3) to make reasonable efforts under the circumstances to remedy the breach. [Amended by 69 FR 52119 on August 24, 2004, effective October 25, 2004.]

[¶ 14,880]

§ 2509.75-6 **Interpretive bulletin relating to section 408(c)(2) of the Employee Retirement Income Security Act of 1974.** This

regulation, formerly reproduced at this point, was replaced by § 2550.408c-2 at ¶ 14,788 [FR Doc. 77-17895, filed with the Federal Register on June 21, 1977, and published in the Federal Register on June 24, 1977].

[¶ 14,881]

§ 2509.75-7 **Interpretive bulletin supplementing ERISA IB 75-1, relating to section 414(c)(4) of the Employee Retirement Income Security Act of 1974.** [Officially removed by 61 FR 33847 on 7/1/96.]

[¶ 14,882]

§ 2509.75-8 **Questions and answers relating to fiduciary responsibility under the Employee Retirement Income Security Act of 1974.** On October 3, 1975, the Department of Labor issued questions and answers relating to certain aspects of fiduciary responsibility under the Act, thereby supplementing ERISA IB 75-5 (29 CFR 2555.75-5) which was issued on June 24, 1975, and published in the FEDERAL REGISTER on July 28, 1975 (40 FR 31598).

Pending the issuance of regulations or other guidelines, persons may rely on the answers to these questions in order to resolve the issues that are specifically considered. No inferences should be drawn regarding issues not raised which may be suggested by a particular question and answer or as to why certain questions, and not others, are included. Furthermore, in applying the questions and answers, the effect of subsequent legislation, regulations, court decisions, and interpretive bulletins must be considered. To the extent that plans utilize or rely on these answers and the requirements of regulations subsequently adopted vary from the answers relied on, such plans may have to be amended.

An index of the questions and answers, relating them to the appropriate sections of the Act, is also provided.

INDEX KEY TO QUESTION PREFIXES

D—Refers to Definitions.

FR—Refers to Fiduciary Responsibility.

Sec. No.:	Question No.
3(21)(A)	D-2,D-3,D-4,D-5.
3(38)	FR-15.
402(c)(1)	FR-12.
402(c)(2)	FR-15.
402(c)(3)	FR-15.
403(a)(2)	FR-15.
404(a)(1)(B)	FR-11, FR-17.
405(a)	FR-13, FR-14, FR-16.
405(c)(1)	FR-12, FR-15.
405(c)(2)	D-4, FR-13, FR-14, FR-16.
412	D-2.

NOTE: Questions D-2, D-3, D-4, and D-5 relate to not only section 3(21)(A) of Title I of the Act, but also section 4975(c)(3) of the Internal Revenue Code (section 2003 of the Act). The Internal Revenue Service has indicated its concurrence with the answers to these questions.

D-2 Q: Are persons who have no power to make any decisions as to plan policy, interpretations, practices or procedures, but who perform the following administrative functions for an employee benefit plan, within a framework of policies, interpretations, rules, practices and procedures made by other persons, fiduciaries with respect to the plan:

(1) Application of rules determining eligibility for participation or benefits;
(2) Calculation of services and compensation credits for benefits;
(3) Preparation of employee communications material;
(4) Maintenance of participants' service and employment records;
(5) Preparation of reports required by government agencies;
(6) Calculation of benefits;
(7) Orientation of new participants and advising participants of their rights and options under the plan;
(8) Collection of contributions and application of contributions as provided in the plan;
(9) Preparation of reports concerning participants' benefits;

(10) Processing of claims; and

(11) Making recommendations to others for decisions with respect to plan administration?

A: No. Only persons who perform one or more of the functions described in section 3(21)(A) of the Act with respect to an employee benefit plan are fiduciaries. Therefore, a person who performs purely ministerial functions such as the types described above for an employee benefit plan within a framework of policies, interpretations, rules, practices and procedures made by other persons is not a fiduciary because such person does not have discretionary authority or discretionary control respecting management of the plan, does not exercise any authority or control respecting management or disposition of the assets of the plan, and does not render investment advice with respect to any money or other property of the plan and has no authority or responsibility to do so.

However, although such a person may not be a plan fiduciary, he may be subject to the bonding requirements contained in section 412 of the Act if he handles funds or other property of the plan within the meaning of applicable regulations.

The Internal Revenue Service notes that such persons would not be considered plan fiduciaries within the meaning of section 4975(e)(3) of the Internal Revenue Code of 1954.

D-3 Q: Does a person automatically become a fiduciary with respect to a plan by reason of holding certain positions in the administration of such plan?

A: Some offices or positions of an employee benefit plan by their very nature require persons who hold them to perform one or more of the functions described in section 3(21)(A) of the Act. For example, a plan administrator or a trustee of a plan must, by the very nature of his position, have "discretionary authority or discretionary responsibility in the administration" of the plan within the meaning of section 3(21)(A)(iii) of the Act. Persons who hold such positions will therefore be fiduciaries.

Other offices and positions should be examined to determine whether they involve the performance of any of the functions described in section 3(21)(A) of the Act. For example, a plan might designate as a "benefit supervisor" a plan employee whose sole function is to calculate the amount of benefits to which each plan participant is entitled in accordance with a mathematical formula contained in the written instrument pursuant to which the plan is maintained. The benefit supervisor, after calculating the benefits, would then inform the plan administrator of the results of his calculations, and the plan administrator would authorize the payment of benefits to a particular plan participant. The benefit supervisor does not perform any of the functions described in section 3(21)(A) of the Act and is not, therefore, a plan fiduciary. However, the plan might designate as a "benefit supervisor" a plan employee who has the final authority to authorize or disallow benefit payments in cases where a dispute exists as to the interpretation of plan provisions relating to eligibility for benefits. Under these circumstances, the benefit supervisor would be a fiduciary within the meaning of section 3(21)(A) of the Act.

The Internal Revenue Service notes that it would reach the same answer to this question under section 4975(e)(3) of the Internal Revenue Code of 1954.

D-4 Q: In the case of a plan established and maintained by an employer, are members of the board of directors of the employer fiduciaries with respect to the plan?

A: Members of the board of directors of an employer which maintains an employee benefit plan will be fiduciaries only to the extent that they have responsibility for the functions described in section 3(21)(A) of the Act. For example, the board of directors may be responsible for the selection and retention of plan fiduciaries. In such a case, members of the board of directors exercise "discretionary authority or discretionary control respecting management of such plan" and are, therefore, fiduciaries with respect to the plan. However, their responsibility, and, consequently, their liability, is limited to the selection and retention of fiduciaries (apart from co-fiduciary liability arising under circumstances described in section 405(a) of the Act). In addition, if the directors are made named fiduciaries of the plan, their liability may be limited pursuant to a procedure provided for in the plan instrument for the allocation of fiduciary responsibilities among named fiduciaries or for

the designation of persons other than named fiduciaries to carry out fiduciary responsibilities, as provided in section 405(c)(2).

The Internal Revenue Service notes that it would reach the same answer to this question under section 4975(e)(3) of the Internal Revenue Code of 1954.

D-5 Q: Is an officer or employee of an employer or employee organization which sponsors an employee benefit plan a fiduciary with respect to the plan solely by reason of holding such office or employment if he or she performs none of the functions described in section 3(21)(A) of the Act?

A: No, for the reasons stated in response to question D-2.

The Internal Revenue Service notes that it would reach the same answer to this question under section 4975(e)(3) of the Internal Revenue Code of 1954.

FR-11 Q: In discharging fiduciary responsibilities, may a fiduciary with respect to a plan rely on information, data, statistics or analyses provided by other persons who perform purely ministerial functions for such plan, such as those persons described in D-2 above?

A: A plan fiduciary may rely on information, data, statistics or analyses furnished by persons performing ministerial functions for the plan, provided that he has exercised prudence in the selection and retention of such persons. The plan fiduciary will be deemed to have acted prudently in such selection and retention if, in the exercise of ordinary care in such situation, he has no reason to doubt the competence, integrity or responsibility of such persons.

FR-12 Q: How many fiduciaries must an employee benefit plan have?

A: There is no required number of fiduciaries that a plan must have. Each plan must, of course, have at least one named fiduciary who serves as plan administrator and, if plan assets are held in trust, the plan must have at least one trustee. If these requirements are met, there is no limit on the number of fiduciaries a plan may have. A plan may have as few or as many fiduciaries as are necessary for its operation and administration. Under section 402(c)(1) of the Act, if the plan so provides, any person or group of persons may serve in more than one fiduciary capacity, including serving both as trustee and administrator. Conversely, fiduciary responsibilities not involving management and control of plan assets may, under section 405(c)(1) of the Act, be allocated among named fiduciaries and named fiduciaries may designate persons other than named fiduciaries to carry out such fiduciary responsibilities, if the plan instrument expressly provides procedures for such allocation or designation.

FR-13 Q: If the named fiduciaries of an employee benefit plan allocate their fiduciary responsibilities among themselves in accordance with a procedure set forth in the plan for the allocation of responsibilities for operation and administration of the plan, to what extent will a named fiduciary be relieved of liability for acts and omissions of other named fiduciaries in carrying out fiduciary responsibilities allocated to them?

A: If named fiduciaries of a plan allocate responsibilities in accordance with a procedure for such allocation set forth in the plan, a named fiduciary will not be liable for acts and omissions of other named fiduciaries in carrying out fiduciary responsibilities which have been allocated to them, except as provided in section 405(a) of the Act, relating to the general rules of co-fiduciary responsibility, and section 405(c)(2)(A) of the Act, relating in relevant part to standards for establishment and implementation of allocation procedures.

However, if the instrument under which the plan is maintained does not provide for a procedure for the allocation of fiduciary responsibilities among named fiduciaries, any allocation which the named fiduciaries may make among themselves will be ineffective to relieve a named fiduciary from responsibility or liability for the performance of fiduciary responsibilities allocated to other named fiduciaries.

FR-14 Q: If the named fiduciaries of an employee benefit plan designate a person who is not a named fiduciary to carry out fiduciary responsibilities, to what extent will the named fiduciaries be relieved of liability for the acts and omissions of such person in the performance of his duties?

A: If the instrument under which the plan is maintained provides for a procedure under which a named fiduciary may designate persons who are not named fiduciaries to carry out fiduciary responsibilities, named fiduciaries of the plan will not be liable for acts and omissions of a person who is not a named fiduciary in carrying out the fiduciary responsibilities which such person has been designated to carry out, except as provided in section 405(a) of the Act, relating to the general rules of co-fiduciary liability, and section 405(c)(2)(A) of the Act, relating in relevant part to the designation of persons to carry out fiduciary responsibilities.

However, if the instrument under which the plan is maintained does not provide for a procedure for the designation of persons who are not named fiduciaries to carry out fiduciary responsibilities, then any such designation which the named fiduciaries may make will not relieve the named fiduciaries from responsibility or liability for the acts and omissions of the persons so designated.

FR-15 Q: May a named fiduciary delegate responsibility for management and control of plan assets to anyone other than a person who is an investment manager as defined in section 3(38) of the Act so as to be relieved of liability for the acts and omissions of the person to whom such responsibility is delegated?

A: No. Section 405(c)(1) does not allow named fiduciaries to delegate to others authority or discretion to manage or control plan assets. However, under the terms of sections 403(a)(2) and 402(c)(3) of the Act, such authority and discretion may be delegated to persons who are investment managers as defined in section 3(38) of the Act. Further, under section 402(c)(2) of the Act, if the plan so provides, a named fiduciary may employ other persons to render advice to the named fiduciary to assist the named fiduciary in carrying out his investment responsibilities under the plan.

FR-16 Q: Is a fiduciary who is not a named fiduciary with respect to an employee benefit plan personally liable for all phases of the management and administration of the plan?

A: A fiduciary with respect to the plan who is not a named fiduciary is a fiduciary only to the extent that he or she performs one or more of the functions described in section 3(21)(A) of the Act. The personal liability of a fiduciary who is not a named fiduciary is generally limited to the fiduciary functions, which he or she performs with respect to the plan. With respect to the extent of liability of a named fiduciary of a plan where duties are properly allocated among named fiduciaries or where named fiduciaries properly designate other persons to carry out certain fiduciary duties, see question FR-13 and FR-14.

In addition, any fiduciary may become liable for breaches of fiduciary responsibility committed by another fiduciary of the same plan under circumstances giving rise to cofiduciary liability, as provided in section 405(a) of the Act.

FR-17 Q: What are the ongoing responsibilities of a fiduciary who has appointed trustees or other fiduciaries with respect to these appointments?

A: At reasonable intervals the performance of trustees and other fiduciaries should be reviewed by the appointing fiduciary in such manner as may be reasonably expected to ensure that their performance has been in compliance with the terms of the plan and statutory standards, and satisfies the needs of the plan. No single procedure will be appropriate in all cases; the procedure adopted may vary in accordance with the nature of the plan and other facts and circumstances relevant to the choice of the procedure.

Signed at Washington, D.C. this 3rd day of October 1975.

[§ 2555.75-8 filed with the Federal Register as FR Doc. 75-27156 on October 6, 1975, and published in the Federal Register of October 9, 1975 (40 FR 47491).]

[¶ 14,883]

§ 2509.78-1 **Interpretive Bulletin relating to payments by certain employee welfare benefit plans.** The Department of Labor today announced its interpretation of certain provisions of Part 4 of Title I of the Employee Retirement Income Security Act of 1974 (ERISA), as those sections apply to a payment by multiple employer vacation plans of a sum of money to which a participant or beneficiary of the plan is entitled to a party other than the participant or beneficiary.[1]

Section 402(b)(4) of ERISA requires every employee benefit plan to specify the basis on which payments are made to and from the plan.

Section 403(c)(1) of ERISA generally requires the assets of an employee benefit plan to be held for the exclusive purpose of providing benefits to participants in the plan and their beneficiaries[2] and defraying reasonable expenses of administering the plan. Similarly, section 404(a)(1)(A) requires a plan fiduciary to discharge his duties with respect to a plan solely in the interest of the participants and beneficiaries of the plan and for the exclusive purpose of providing benefits to participants and their beneficiaries and defraying reasonable expenses of administering the plan. Section 404(a)(1)(D) further requires the fiduciary to act in accordance with the documents and instruments governing the plan insofar as such documents and instruments are consistent with the provisions of Title I of ERISA.

In addition, section 406(a) of ERISA specifically prohibits a fiduciary with respect to a plan from causing the plan to engage in a transaction if he knows or should know that such transaction constitutes, *inter alia,* a direct or indirect: furnishing of goods, services or facilities between the plan and a party in interest (section 406(a)(1)(C)); or transfer to, or use by or for the benefit of, a party in interest of any assets of the plan (section 406(a)(1)(D)). Section 406(b)(2) of ERISA prohibits a plan fiduciary from acting in any transaction involving the plan on behalf of a party, or representing a party, whose interests are adverse to the interests of the plan or of its participants or beneficiaries.

In this regard, however, Prohibited Transaction Exemptions 76-1, Part C, (41 FR 12740, March 26, 1976) and 77-10 (42 FR 33918, July 1, 1977) exempt from the prohibitions of section 406(a) and 406(b)(2), respectively, the provision of administrative services by a multiple employer plan if specified conditions are met. These conditions are: (a) the plan receives reasonable compensation for the provision of the services (for purposes of the exemption, "reasonable compensation" need not include a profit which would ordinarily have been received in an arm's length transaction, but must be sufficient to reimburse the plan for its costs); (b) the arrangement allows any multiple employer plan which is a party to the transaction to terminate the relationship on a reasonably short notice under the circumstances; and (c) the plan complies with certain recordkeeping requirements. It should be noted that plans not subject to Prohibited Transaction Exemptions 76-1 and 77-10—i.e., plans that are not multiple employer plans—cannot rely upon these exemptions.

A payment by a vacation plan of all or any portion of benefits to which a plan participant or beneficiary is entitled to a party other than the participant or beneficiary will comply with the above-mentioned sections of ERISA if the arrangement pursuant to which payments are made does not constitute a prohibited transaction under ERISA and:

(1) The plan documents expressly state that benefits payable under the plan to a participant or beneficiary may, at the direction of the participant or beneficiary, be paid to a third party rather than to the participant or beneficiary;

(2) The participant or beneficiary directs in writing that the plan trustee(s) shall pay a named third party all or a specified portion of the sum of money which would otherwise be paid under the plan to him or her; and

(3) A payment is made to a third party only when or after the money would otherwise be payable to the plan participant or beneficiary.

In the case of a multiple employer plan (as defined in Prohibited Transaction Exemption 76-1, Part C, Section III), if the arrangement to make payments to a third party is a prohibited transaction under ERISA, the arrangement will comply with the above-mentioned sections of ERISA if the conditions of Prohibited Transaction Exemptions 76-1, Part C, and 77-10 and the above three paragraphs are met. In this regard, it is the view of the Department that the mere payment of money to which a participant or beneficiary is entitled, at the direction of the participant or beneficiary, to a third party who is a party in interest would not constitute a transfer of plan assets prohibited under section 406(a)(1)(D). It is also the view of the Department that if a trustee or other fiduciary of a plan, in addition to his duties with respect to the plan, serves in a decision making capacity with another party, the mere fact that the fiduciary effects payments to such party of money to

---

[1] Multiple employer vacation plans generally consist of trust funds to which employers are obligated to make contributions pursuant to collective bargaining agreements. Benefits are generally paid at specified intervals (usually annually or semi-annually) and such

benefits are neither contingent upon the occurrence of a specified event nor restricted to use for a specified purpose when paid to the participant.

[2] Section 403(c) and (d) provide certain exceptions to this requirement, not here relevant.

which a participant is entitled at the direction of the participant and in accordance with specific provisions of governing plan documents and instruments, does not amount to a prohibited transaction under section 406(b)(2).

It should be noted that the interpretation set forth herein deals solely with the application of the provisions of Title I of ERISA to the arrangements described herein. It does not deal with the application of any other statute to such arrangements. Specifically, no opinion is expressed herein as to the application of section 302 of the Labor Management Relations Act, 1947 or the Internal Revenue Code of 1954 (particularly the provisions of section 501(c)(9) of the Code). [Added by FR Doc. 78-34599, filed with the Federal Register on December 14, 1978, and published in the Federal Register of December 15, 1978 (43 FR 58565. The regulation is effective December 15, 1978.]

Part 5—Administration and Enforcement

[¶ 14,910]
CRIMINAL PENALTIES

Act Sec. 501. (a) Any person who willfully violates any provision of part 1 of this subtitle, or any regulation or order issued under any such provision, shall upon conviction be fined not more than $100,000 or imprisoned not more than 10 years, or both; except that in the case of such violation by a person not an individual, the fine imposed upon such person shall be a fine not exceeding $500,000.

(b) Any person that violates section 519 shall upon conviction be imprisoned not more than 10 years or fined under title 18, United States Code, or both.

<table>
<tr><td colspan="2" align="center">**Amendments**</td><td align="center">The above amendment is effective on the date of enactment (March 23, 2010).</td></tr>
<tr><td>**P.L. 111-148, §6601(b):**</td><td></td><td>**P.L. 107-204, §904**</td></tr>
<tr><td colspan="2">Amended ERISA Sec. 501 by inserting "(a)" before "Any person" and by adding at the end new subsection (b).</td><td>Act Sec. 904 amended ERISA Sec. 501 by striking "$5,000" and inserting "$100,000," by striking "one year" and inserting "10 years" and by striking "$100,000" and inserting "$500,000."</td></tr>
</table>

[¶ 14,920]
CIVIL ENFORCEMENT

Act Sec. 502. (a) PERSONS EMPOWERED TO BRING A CIVIL ACTION.—A civil action may be brought—

(1) by a participant or beneficiary—

(A) for the relief provided for in subsection (c) of this section, or

(B) to recover benefits due to him under the terms of his plan, to enforce his rights under the terms of the plan, or to clarify his rights to future benefits under the terms of the plan;

(2) by the Secretary, or by a participant, beneficiary or fiduciary for appropriate relief under section 409;

(3) by a participant, beneficiary, or fiduciary (A) to enjoin any act or practice which violates any provision of this title or the terms of the plan, or (B) to obtain other appropriate equitable relief (i) to redress such violations or (ii) to enforce any provisions of this title or the terms of the plan;

(4) by the Secretary, or by a participant, or beneficiary for appropriate relief in the case of a violation of [section] 105(c);

(5) except as otherwise provided in subsection (b), by the Secretary (A) to enjoin any act or practice which violates any provision of this title, or (B) to obtain other appropriate equitable relief (i) to redress such violation or (ii) to enforce any provision of this title;

(6) by the Secretary to collect any civil penalty under paragraph (2), (4), (5), (6), (7), (8), or (9) of subsection (c) or under subsection (i) or (l);

(7) by a State to enforce compliance with a qualified medical child support order (as defined in section 609(a)(2)(A));

(8) by the Secretary, or by an employer or other person referred to in section 101(f)(1), (A) to enjoin any act or practice which violates subsection (f) of section 101, or (B) to obtain appropriate equitable relief (i) to redress such violation or (ii) to enforce such subsection;

(9) in the event that the purchase of an insurance contract or insurance annuity in connection with termination of an individual's status as a participant covered under a pension plan with respect to all or any portion of the participant's pension benefit under such plan constitutes a violation of part 4 of this title or the terms of the plan, by the Secretary, by any individual who was a participant or beneficiary at the time of the alleged violation, or by a fiduciary, to obtain appropriate relief, including the posting of security if necessary, to assure receipt by the participant or beneficiary of the amounts provided or to be provided by such insurance contract or annuity, plus reasonable prejudgment interest on such amount;

(10) in the case of a multiemployer plan that has been certified by the actuary to be in endangered or critical status under section 305, if the plan sponsor—

(A) has not adopted a funding improvement or rehabilitation plan under that section by the deadline established in such section, or

(B) fails to update or comply with the terms of the funding improvement or rehabilitation plan in accordance with the requirements of such section,

by an employer that has an obligation to contribute with respect to the multiemployer plan or an employee organization that represents active participants in the multiemployer plan, for an order compelling the plan sponsor to adopt a funding improvement or rehabilitation plan or to update or comply with the terms of the funding improvement or rehabilitation plan in accordance with the requirements of such section and the funding improvement or rehabilitation plan; or

(11) in the case of a multiemployer plan, by an employee representative, or any employer that has an obligation to contribute to the plan, (A) to enjoin any act or practice which violates subsection (k) of section 101 (or, in the case of an employer, subsection (l) of such section), or (B) to obtain appropriate equitable relief (i) to redress such violation or (ii) to enforce such subsection.

Act Sec. 502. (b)(1) PLANS QUALIFIED UNDER INTERNAL REVENUE CODE; MAINTENANCE OF ACTIONS INVOLVING DELINQUENT CONTRIBUTIONS.—In the case of a plan which is qualified under section 401(a), 403(a), or 405(a) of the Internal Revenue Code of 1986 (or with respect to which an application to so qualify has been filed and has not been finally determined) the Secretary may exercise his authority under subsection (a)(5) with respect to a violation of or the enforcement of, parts 2 and 3 of this subtitle (relating to participation, vesting, and funding), only if—

(A) requested by the Secretary of the Treasury, or

(B) one or more participants, beneficiaries, or fiduciaries, of such plan request in writing (in such manner as the Secretary shall prescribe by regulation) that he exercise such authority on their behalf. In the case of such a request under this paragraph he may exercise such authority only if he determines that such violation affects, or such enforcement is necessary to protect, claims of participants or beneficiaries to benefits under the plan.

(2) The Secretary shall not initiate an action to enforce section 515.

(3) Except as provided in subsections (c)(9) and (a)(6) (with respect to collecting civil penalties under subsection (c)(9)), the Secretary is not authorized to enforce under this part any requirement of part 7 against a health insurance issuer offering health insurance coverage in connection with a group health plan (as defined in section 706(a)(1)). Nothing in this paragraph shall affect the authority of the Secretary to issue regulations to carry out such part.

Act Sec. 502. (c)(1) ADMINISTRATOR'S REFUSAL TO SUPPLY REQUESTED INFORMATION; PENALTY FOR FAILURE TO PROVIDE ANNUAL REPORT IN COMPLETE FORM.—Any administrator (A) who fails to meet the requirements of paragraph (1) or (4) of section 606, section 101(e)(1), section 101(f), or section 105(a) with respect to a participant or beneficiary, or (B) who fails or refuses to comply with a request for any information which such administrator is required by this title to furnish to a participant or beneficiary (unless such failure or refusal results from matters reasonably beyond the control of the administrator) by mailing the material requested to the last known address of the requesting participant or beneficiary within 30 days after such request may in the court's discretion be personally liable to such participant or beneficiary in the amount of up to $100 a day from the date of such failure or refusal, and the court may in its discretion order such other relief as it deems proper. For purposes of this paragraph, each violation described in subparagraph (A) with respect to any single participant, and each violation described in subparagraph (B) with respect to any single participant or beneficiary, shall be treated as a separate violation.

(2) The Secretary may assess a civil penalty against any plan administrator of up to $1,000 a day from the date of such plan administrator's failure or refusal to file the annual report required to be filed with the Secretary under section 101(b)(1). For purposes of this paragraph, an annual report, that has been rejected under section 104(a)(4) for failure to provide material information shall not be treated as having been filed with the Secretary.

(3) Any employer maintaining a plan who fails to meet the notice requirement of section 101(d) with respect to any participant or beneficiary or who fails to meet the requirements of section 101(e)(2) with respect to any person may in the court's discretion be liable to such participant or beneficiary or to such person in the amount of up to $100 a day from the date of such failure, and the court may in its discretion order such other relief as it deems proper.

(4) The Secretary may assess a civil penalty of not more than $1,000 a day for each violation by any person of subsection (j), (k), or (l) of section 101 or section 514(e)(3).

(5) The Secretary may asses a civil penalty against any person of up to $1,000 a day from the date of the persons' failure or refusal to file the information required to be filed by such person with the Secretary under regulations prescribed pursuant to section 101(g).

(6) If, within 30 days of a request by the Secretary to a plan administrator for documents under section 104(a)(6), the plan administrator fails to furnish the material requested to the Secretary, the Secretary may assess a civil penalty against the plan administrator of up to $100 a day from the date of such failure (but in no event in excess of $1,000 per request). No penalty shall be imposed under this paragraph for any failure resulting from matters reasonably beyond the control of the plan administrator.

(7) The Secretary may assess a civil penalty against a plan administrator of up to $100 a day from the date of the plan administrator's failure or refusal to provide notice to participants and beneficiaries in accordance with subsection (i) or (m) of section 101. For purposes of this paragraph, each violation with respect to any single participant or beneficiary shall be treated as a separate violation.

(8) The Secretary may assess against any plan sponsor of a multiemployer plan a civil penalty of not more than $1,100 per day—

(A) for each violation by such sponsor of the requirement under section 305 to adopt by the deadline established in that section a funding improvement plan or rehabilitation plan with respect to a multiemployer plan which is in endangered or critical status, or

(B) in the case of a plan in endangered status which is not in seriously endangered status, for failure by the plan to meet the applicable benchmarks under section 305 by the end of the funding improvement period with respect to the plan.

(9)(A) The Secretary may assess a civil penalty against any employer of up to $100 a day from the date of the employer's failure to meet the notice requirement of section 701(f)(3)(B)(i)(I). For purposes of this subparagraph, each violation with respect to any single employee shall be treated as a separate violation.

(B) The Secretary may assess a civil penalty against any plan administrator of up to $100 a day from the date of the plan administrator's failure to timely provide to any State the information required to be disclosed under section 701(f)(3)(B)(ii). For purposes of this subparagraph, each violation with respect to any single participant or beneficiary shall be treated as a separate violation.

(10) Secretarial enforcement authority relating to use of genetic information—

(A) General rule—The Secretary may impose a penalty against any plan sponsor of a group health plan, or any health insurance issuer offering health insurance coverage in connection with the plan, for any failure by such sponsor or issuer to meet the requirements of subsection (a)(1)(F), (b)(3), (c), or (d) of section 702 or section 701 or 702(b)(1) with respect to genetic information, in connection with the plan.

(B) Amount—

(i) In general—The amount of the penalty imposed by subparagraph (A) shall be $100 for each day in the noncompliance period with respect to each participant or beneficiary to whom such failure relates.

(ii) Noncompliance period—For purposes of this paragraph, the term "noncompliance period" means, with respect to any failure, the period—

(I) beginning on the date such failure first occurs; and

(II) ending on the date the failure is corrected.

(C) Minimum penalties where failure discovered—Notwithstanding clauses (i) and (ii) of subparagraph (D):

(i) In general—In the case of 1 or more failures with respect to a participant or beneficiary—

(I) which are not corrected before the date on which the plan receives a notice from the Secretary of such violation; and

(II) which occurred or continued during the period involved;

the amount of penalty imposed by subparagraph (A) by reason of such failures with respect to such participant or beneficiary shall not be less than $2,500.

(ii) Higher minimum penalty where violations are more than de minimis—To the extent violations for which any person is liable under this paragraph for any year are more than de minimis, clause (i) shall be applied by substituting "$15,000" for "$2,500" with respect to such person.

(D) Limitations—

(i) Penalty not to apply where failure not discovered exercising reasonable diligence—No penalty shall be imposed by subparagraph (A) on any failure during any period for which it is established to the satisfaction of the Secretary that the person otherwise liable for such penalty did not know, and exercising reasonable diligence would not have known, that such failure existed.

(ii) Penalty not to apply to failures corrected within certain periods—No penalty shall be imposed by subparagraph (A) on any failure if—

(I) such failure was due to reasonable cause and not to willful neglect; and

(II) such failure is corrected during the 30-day period beginning on the first date the person otherwise liable for such penalty knew, or exercising reasonable diligence would have known, that such failure existed.

(iii) Overall limitation for unintentional failures—In the case of failures which are due to reasonable cause and not to willful neglect, the penalty imposed by subparagraph (A) for failures shall not exceed the amount equal to the lesser of—

(I) 10 percent of the aggregate amount paid or incurred by the plan sponsor (or predecessor plan sponsor) during the preceding taxable year for group health plans; or

(II) $500,000.

(E) Waiver by secretary—In the case of a failure which is due to reasonable cause and not to willful neglect, the Secretary may waive part or all of the penalty imposed by subparagraph (A) to the extent that the payment of such penalty would be excessive relative to the failure involved.

(F) Definitions—Terms used in this paragraph which are defined in section 733 shall have the meanings provided such terms in such section.

(11) The Secretary and the Secretary of Health and Human Services shall maintain such ongoing consultation as may be necessary and appropriate to coordinate enforcement under this subsection with enforcement under section 1144(c)(8) of the Social Security Act.

(12) The Secretary may assess a civil penalty against any sponsor of a CSEC plan of up to $100 a day from the date of the plan sponsor's failure to comply with the requirements of section 306(j)(3) to establish or update a funding restoration plan..

Act Sec. 502.(d)(1) Status of employee benefit plan as entity.—An employee benefit plan may sue or be sued under this title as an entity. Service of summons, subpoena, or other legal process of a court upon a trustee or an administrator of an employee benefit plan in his capacity as such shall constitute service upon the employee benefit plan. In a case where a plan has not designated in the summary plan description of the plan an individual as agent for the service of legal process, service upon the Secretary shall constitute such service. The Secretary, not later than 15 days after receipt of service under the preceding sentence, shall notify the administrator or any trustee of the plan of receipt of such service.

(2) Any money judgment under this title against an employee benefit plan shall be enforceable only against the plan as an entity and shall not be enforceable against any other person unless liability against such person is established in his individual capacity under this title.

Act Sec. 502. (e)(1) JURISDICTION.—Except for actions under subsection (a)(1)(B) of this section, the district courts of the United States shall have exclusive jurisdiction of civil actions under this title brought by the Secretary or by a participant, beneficiary, fiduciary, or any person referred to in section 101(f)(1). State courts of competent jurisdiction and district courts of the United States shall have concurrent jurisdiction of actions under paragraphs (1)(B) and (7) of subsection (a) of this section.

(2) Where an action under this title is brought in a district court of the United States, it may be brought in the district where the plan is administered, where the breach took place, or where a defendant resides or may be found, and process may be served in any other district where a defendant resides or may be found.

Act Sec. 502. (f) AMOUNT IN CONTROVERSY; CITIZENSHIP OF PARTIES.—The district courts of the United States shall have jurisdiction, without respect to the amount in controversy or the citizenship of the parties, to grant the relief provided for in subsection (a) of this section in any action.

Act Sec. 502. (g)(1) ATTORNEY'S FEES AND COSTS; AWARDS IN ACTIONS INVOLVING DELINQUENT CONTRIBUTIONS.—In any action under this title (other than an action described in paragraph (2)) by a participant, beneficiary, or fiduciary, the court in its discretion may allow a reasonable attorney's fee and costs of action to either party.

(2) In any action under this title by a fiduciary for or on behalf of a plan to enforce section 515 in which a judgment in favor of the plan is awarded, the court shall award the plan—

(A) the unpaid contributions,

(B) interest on the unpaid contributions,

(C) an amount equal to the greater of—

(i) interest on the unpaid contributions, or

(ii) liquidated damages provided for under the plan in an amount not in excess of 20 percent (or such higher percentage as may be permitted under Federal or State law) of the amount determined by the court under subparagraph (A),

(D) reasonable attorney's fees and costs of the action, to be paid by the defendant, and

(E) such other legal or equitable relief as the court deems appropriate.

For purposes of this paragraph, interest on unpaid contributions shall be determined by using the rate provided under the plan, or, if none, the rate prescribed under section 6621 of the Internal Revenue Code of 1986.

Act Sec. 502. (h) SERVICE UPON SECRETARY OF LABOR AND SECRETARY OF THE TREASURY.—A copy of the complaint in any action under this title by a participant, beneficiary, or fiduciary (other than an action brought by one or more participants or beneficiaries under subsection (a)(1)(B) which is solely for the purpose of recovering benefits due such participants under the terms of the plan) shall be served upon the Secretary and the Secretary of the Treasury by certified mail. Either Secretary shall have the right in his discretion to intervene in any action, except that the Secretary of the Treasury may not intervene in any action under part 4 of this subtitle. If the Secretary brings an action under subsection (a) on behalf of a participant or beneficiary, he shall notify the Secretary of the Treasury.

Act Sec. 502. (i) ADMINISTRATIVE ASSESSMENT OF CIVIL PENALTY.—In the case of a transaction prohibited by section 406 by a party in interest with respect to a plan to which this part applies, the Secretary may assess a civil penalty against such party in interest. The amount of such penalty may not exceed 5 percent of the amount involved in each such transaction (as defined in section 4975(f)(4) of the Internal Revenue Code of 1986) for each year or part thereof during which the prohibited transaction continues, except that, if the transaction is not corrected (in such manner as the Secretary shall prescribe in regulations which shall be consistent with section 4975(f)(5) of such Code) within 90 days after notice from the Secretary (or such longer period as the Secretary may permit), such penalty may be in an amount not more than 100 percent of the amount involved. This subsection shall not apply to a transaction with respect to a plan described in section 4975(e)(1) of such Code.

Act Sec. 502. (j) DIRECTION AND CONTROL OF LITIGATION BY ATTORNEY GENERAL.—In all civil actions under this title, attorneys appointed by the Secretary may represent the Secretary (except as provided in section 518(a) of title 28, United States Code), but all such litigation shall be subject to the direction and control of the Attorney General.

Act Sec. 502. (k) JURISDICTION OF ACTION AGAINST SECRETARY OF LABOR.—Suits by an administrator, fiduciary, participant, or beneficiary of an employee benefit plan to review a final order of the Secretary, to restrain the Secretary from taking any action contrary to the provisions of this Act, or to compel him to take action required under this title, may be brought in the district court of the United States for the district where the plan has its principal office, or in the United States District Court for the District of Columbia.

Act Sec. 502. (l)(1) CIVIL PENALTIES ON VIOLATIONS BY FIDUCIARIES.—In the case of—

(A) any breach of fiduciary responsibility under (or other violation of) part 4 by a fiduciary, or

(B) any knowing participation in such a breach or violation by any other person,

the Secretary shall assess a civil penalty against such fiduciary or other person in an amount equal to 20 percent of the applicable recovery amount.

(2) For purposes of paragraph (1), the term "applicable recovery amount" means any amount which is recovered from a fiduciary or other person with respect to a breach or violation described in paragraph (1)—

(A) pursuant to any settlement agreement with the Secretary, or

(B) ordered by a court to be paid by such fiduciary or other person to a plan or its participants and beneficiaries in a judicial proceeding instituted by the Secretary under subsection (a)(2) or (a)(5).

(3) The Secretary may, in the Secretary's sole discretion, waive or reduce the penalty under paragraph (1) if the Secretary determines in writing that—

(A) the fiduciary or other person acted reasonably and in good faith, or

(B) it is reasonable to expect that the fiduciary or other person will not be able to restore all losses to the plan (or to provide the relief ordered pursuant to subsection (a)(9)) without severe financial hardship unless such waiver or reduction is granted.

(4) The penalty imposed on a fiduciary or other person under this subsection with respect to any transaction shall be reduced by the amount of any penalty or tax imposed on such fiduciary or other person with respect to such transaction under subsection (i) of this section and section 4975 of the Internal Revenue Code of 1986.

Act Sec. 502. (m) PENALTY FOR IMPROPER DISTRIBUTION.— In the case of a distribution to a pension plan participant or beneficiary in violation of section 206(e) by a plan fiduciary, the Secretary shall assess a penalty against such fiduciary in an amount equal to the value of the distribution. Such penalty shall not exceed $10,000 for each such distribution.

Amendments

P.L. 113-235, §111(d)(1)-(3), Div. O:

Amended ERISA Sec. 502(a) by (1) in paragraph (9), by striking "or" at the end; (2) in paragraph (10), by striking the period at the end and inserting "; or"; and by adding at the end a new paragraph (11) to read as above.

The above amendment shall apply with respect to plan years beginning after December 31, 2014.

P.L. 113-97, §102(b)(6):

Amended ERISA 502(c) by redesignating the last paragraph as paragraph (11) and inserting a new paragraph (12) to read as above.

Effective for years beginning after 12-31-2013.

P.L. 111-3, §311(b)(1)(E)(i):

Amended ERISA Sec. 502(a)(6) by striking "or 8" and inserting "(8), or (9)". For the **effective** date, see Act Sec. 3, below.

P.L. 111-3, §311(b)(1)(E)(ii):

Amended ERISA Sec. 502(c) by redesignating paragraph (9) as paragraph (10), and by inserting after paragraph (8) a new paragraph (9). For the **effective** date, see Act Sec. 3, below.

P.L. 111-3, §3, provides:

SEC. 3. GENERAL EFFECTIVE DATE; EXCEPTION FOR STATE LEGISLATION; CONTINGENT EFFECTIVE DATE; RELIANCE ON LAW.

(a) GENERAL EFFECTIVE DATE.—Unless otherwise provided in this Act, subject to subsections (b) through (d), this Act (and the amendments made by this Act) shall take effect on April 1, 2009, and shall apply to child health assistance and medical assistance provided on or after that date.

(b) EXCEPTION FOR STATE LEGISLATION.—In the case of a State plan under title XIX or State child health plan under XXI of the Social Security Act, which the Secretary of Health and Human Services determines requires State legislation in order for the respective plan to meet one or more additional requirements imposed by amendments made by this Act, the respective plan shall not be regarded as failing to comply with the requirements of such title solely on the basis of its failure to meet such an additional requirement before the first day of the first calendar quarter beginning after the close of the first regular session of the State legislature that begins after the date of enactment of this Act. For purposes of the previous sentence, in the case of a State that has a 2-year legislative session, each year of the session shall be considered to be a separate regular session of the State legislature.

(c) COORDINATION OF CHIP FUNDING FOR FISCAL YEAR 2009.—Notwithstanding any other provision of law, insofar as funds have been appropriated under section 2104(a)(11), 2104(k), or 2104(l) of the Social Security Act, as amended by section 201 of Public Law 110–173, to provide allotments to States under CHIP for fiscal year 2009—

(1) any amounts that are so appropriated that are not so allotted and obligated before April 1, 2009 are rescinded; and

(2) any amount provided for CHIP allotments to a State under this Act (and the amendments made by this Act) for such fiscal year shall be reduced by the amount of such appropriations so allotted and obligated before such date.

(d) RELIANCE ON LAW.—With respect to amendments made by this Act (other than title VII) that become effective as of a date—

(1) such amendments are effective as of such date whether or not regulations implementing such amendments have been issued; and

(2) Federal financial participation for medical assistance or child health assistance furnished under title XIX or XXI, respectively, of the Social Security Act on or after such date by a State in good faith reliance on such amendments before the date of promulgation of final regulations, if any, to carry out such amendments (or before the date of guidance, if any, regarding the implementation of such amendments) shall not be denied on the basis of the State's failure to comply with such regulations or guidance.

P.L. 110-458, §101(c)(1)(H):

Amended ERISA Sec. 502(c)(4) by striking "by any person" and all that follows through the period and inserting "by any person of subsection (j), (k), or (l) of section 101 or section 514(e)(3)."

The above amendment applies to plan years beginning after December 31, 2007.

P.L. 110-458, §102(b)(1)(H):

Amended ERISA Sec. 502(c)(2) by striking "101(b)(4)" and inserting "101(b)(1)".

For effective dates, see P.L. 110-458, §102(e), below.

P.L. 110-458, §102(b)(1)(I):

Amended ERISA 502(c)(8)(A) by inserting "plan" after "multiemployer".

For effective dates, see P.L. 110-458, §102(e), below.

P.L. 110-458, §102(e):

102(e) EFFECTIVE DATES.—

102(e)(1) IN GENERAL.—

The amendments made by this section shall apply with respect to plan years beginning after 2007, except that the amendments made by subsection (b) shall apply to taxable years beginning after 2007, but only with respect to plan years beginning after 2007 which end with or within any such taxable year.

102(e)(2) SPECIAL RULE FOR CERTAIN NOTICES.—

In any case in which a plan's actuary certifies that it is reasonably expected that a multiemployer plan will be in critical status under section 432(b)(3) of the Internal Revenue Code of 1986, as added by this section, with respect to the first plan year beginning after 2007, the notice required under subparagraph (D) of such section may be provided at any time after the date of enactment, so long as it is provided on or before the last date for providing the notice under such subparagraph.

P.L. 110-233, §101(e)(1):

Amended ERISA Sec. 502(a)(6) by striking "(7), or (8)" and inserting "(7), (8), or (9)".

P.L. 110-233, §101(e)(2):

Amended ERISA Sec. 502(b)(3) by striking "The Secretary" and inserting "Except as provided in subsections (c)(9) and (a)(6) (with respect to collecting civil penalties under subsection (c)(9)), the Secretary".

P.L. 110-233, §101(e)(3):

Amended ERISA Sec. 502(c) by redesignating paragraph (9) as paragraph (10) and inserting new paragraph (9) to read as above.

The above amendments apply with respect to group health plans for plan years beginning after the date that is 1 year after the date of enactment [May 21, 2009].

P.L. 109-280, §103(b)(2):

Amended ERISA Sec. 502(c)(4) by striking "section 302(b)(7)(F)(iv)" and inserting "section 101(j) or 302(b)(7)(F)(iv)".

For effective dates, see P.L. 109-280, §103(c) below.

P.L. 109-280, §103(c):

103(c) EFFECTIVE DATES.—

103(c)(1) IN GENERAL.—

The amendments made by this section shall apply to plan years beginning after December 31, 2007.

103(c)(2) COLLECTIVE BARGAINING EXCEPTION.—

In the case of a plan maintained pursuant to 1 or more collective bargaining agreements between employee representatives and 1 or more employers ratified before January 1, 2008, the amendments made by this section shall not apply to plan years beginning before the earlier of—

103(c)(2)(A) the later of—

103(c)(2)(A)(i) the date on which the last collective bargaining agreement relating to the plan terminates (determined without regard to any extension thereof agreed to after the date of the enactment of this Act), or

103(c)(2)(A)(ii) the first day of the first plan year to which the amendments made by this subsection would (but for this subparagraph) apply, or

103(c)(2)(B) January 1, 2010.

For purposes of subparagraph (A)(i), any plan amendment made pursuant to a collective bargaining agreement relating to the plan which amends the plan solely to conform to any requirement added by this section shall not be treated as a termination of such collective bargaining agreement.

P.L. 109-280, §202(b)(1):

Amended ERISA Sec. 502(a)(6) by striking "(6), or (7)" and inserting "(6), (7), or (8)".

For effective dates, see P.L. 109-280, §202(f) below.

P.L. 109-280, §202(b)(2)-(3):

Amended ERISA Sec. 502(c)(8)-(9) by redesignating subsection (c)(8) as subsection (c)(9) and by inserting after subsection (c)(7) a new subsection (c)(8) to read as above.

For effective dates, see P.L. 109-280, §202(f) below.

P.L. 109-280, §202(c):

Amended ERISA Sec. 502(a)(8)-(10) by striking "or" at the end of paragraph (8), by striking the period at the end of paragraph (9) and inserting "; or" and by adding at the end a new paragraph (10) to read as above.

For effective dates, see P.L. 109-280, §202(f) below.

P.L. 109-280, §202(f):

202(f) EFFECTIVE DATES.—

202(f)(1) IN GENERAL.—

The amendments made by this section shall apply with respect to plan years beginning after 2007.

202(f)(2) SPECIAL RULE FOR CERTAIN NOTICES.—

In any case in which a plan's actuary certifies that it is reasonably expected that a multiemployer plan will be in critical status under section 305(b)(3) of the Employee Retirement Income Security Act of 1974, as added by this section, with respect to the first plan year beginning after 2007, the notice required under subparagraph (D) of such section may be provided at any time after the date of enactment, so long as it is provided on or before the last date for providing the notice under such subparagraph.

202(f)(3) SPECIAL RULE FOR CERTAIN RESTORED BENEFITS.—

In the case of a multiemployer plan—

202(f)(3)(A) with respect to which benefits were reduced pursuant to a plan amendment adopted on or after January 1, 2002, and before June 30, 2005, and

202(f)(3)(B) which, pursuant to the plan document, the trust agreement, or a formal written communication from the plan sponsor to participants provided before June 30, 2005, provided for the restoration of such benefits,

the amendments made by this section shall not apply to such benefit restorations to the extent that any restriction on the providing or accrual of such benefits would otherwise apply by reason of such amendments.

P.L. 109-280, §502(a)(2):

Amended ERISA Sec. 502(c)(4), as amended by Act Sec. 103(b)(2) (see above), by striking "section 101(j)" and inserting "subsection (j) or (k) of section 101".

The above amendment applies to plan years beginning after December 31, 2007.

P.L. 109-280, §502(b)(2):

Amended ERISA Sec. 502(c)(4), as amended by Act Sec. 502(a)(2) (see above), by striking "section 101(j) or (k)" and inserting "subsection (j), (k), or (l) of section 101".

The above amendment applies to plan years beginning after December 31, 2007.

P.L. 109-280, §507(b):

Amended ERISA Sec. 502(c)(7) by striking "section 101(i)" and inserting "subsection (i) or (m) of section 101".

For effective dates, see P.L. 109-280, §507(d) below.

P.L. 109-280, §507(d):

507(d) EFFECTIVE DATES.—

507(d)(1) IN GENERAL.—

The amendments made by this section shall apply to plan years beginning after December 31, 2006.

507(d)(2) TRANSITION RULE.—

If notice under section 101(m) of the Employee Retirement Income Security Act of 1974 (as added by this section) would otherwise be required to be provided before the 90th day after the date of the enactment of this Act, such notice shall not be required to be provided until such 90th day.

P.L. 109-280, § 508(a)(2)(C):

Amended ERISA Sec. 502(c)(1) by striking "or section 101(f)" and inserting "section 101(f), or section 105(a)."

For effective dates, see P.L. 109-280 § 508(c) below.

P.L. 109-280, § 508(c):

508(c) EFFECTIVE DATE.—

508(c)(1) IN GENERAL.—

The amendments made by this section shall apply to plan years beginning after December 31, 2006.

508(c)(2) SPECIAL RULE FOR COLLECTIVELY BARGAINED AGREEMENTS.—

In the case of a plan maintained pursuant to 1 or more collective bargaining agreements between employee representatives and 1 or more employers ratified on or before the date of the enactment of this Act, paragraph (1) shall be applied to benefits pursuant to, and individuals covered by, any such agreement by substituting for "December 31, 2006" the earlier of—

508(c)(2)(A) the later of—

508(c)(2)(A)(i) December 31, 2007, or

508(c)(2)(A)(ii) the date on which the last of such collective bargaining agreements terminates (determined without regard to any extension thereof after such date of enactment), or

508(c)(2)(B) December 31, 2008.

P.L. 109-280, § 902(f)(2):

Amended ERISA Sec. 502(c)(4) by striking "or section 302(b)(7)(F)(vi)" and inserting ", section 302(b)(7)(F)(vi), or section 514(e)(3)". Prior to amendment, section 502(c)(4) read as follows:

(4) The Secretary may assess a civil penalty of not more than $1,000 a day for each violation by any person of section 302(b)(7)(F)(vi).

The above amendment applies on the date of enactment (August 17, 2006).

P.L. 108-218, § 104(a):

Act Sec. 103(a)(2) amended ERISA Sec. 502(c)(4) to read as above.

P.L. 108-218, § 103(b):

Act Sec. 103(b) amended ERISA Sec. 502(c)(1) by striking "or section 101(e)(1)" and inserting ", section 101(e)(1), or section 101(f)" The amendment shall apply to plan years beginning after December 31, 2004.

Act Sec. 103 provides:

(c) Regulations and Model Notice.—The Secretary of Labor shall, not later than 1 year after the date of the enactment of this Act, issue regulations (including a model notice) necessary to implement the amendments made by this section.

P.L. 107-204, § 306(b)(3)(A):

Act Sec. 306(b)(3)(A) amended ERISA Sec. 502(a)(6) by striking "(5), or (6)" and inserting "(5), (6), or (7)." See P.L. 107-204, § 306(c) below for effective date.

P.L. 107-204, § 306(b)(3)(B) and (C):

Act Sec. 306(b)(3)(B) amended ERISA Sec. 502(c) by redesignating paragraph (7) as paragraph (8) and inserting new paragraph (7) to read as above. See P.L. 107-204, § 306(c) for effective date.

P.L. 107-204, § 306(c):

(c) EFFECTIVE DATE—The provisions of this section (including the amendments made thereby) shall take effect 180 days after the date of the enactment of this Act. Good faith compliance with the requirements of such provisions in advance of the issuance of applicable regulations thereunder shall be treated as compliance with such provisions.

P.L. 105-34, § 1503(c)(2)(B):

Act Sec. 1503(c)(2)(B) amended ERISA Sec. 502(c) by redesignating paragraph (6) as paragraph (7) and by inserting after paragraph (5) a new paragraph (6) to read as above.

The above amendments are effective August 5, 1997.

P.L. 105-34, § 1503(d)(7):

Act Sec. 1503(d)(7) amended ERISA Sec. 502(a)(6) by striking "or (5)" and inserting "(5), or (6)"

The above amendment is effective August 5, 1997.

P.L. 104-191, § 101(b):

Act Sec. 101(b) amended ERISA Sec. 502(b) by adding at the end a new paragraph (3) to read as above.

P.L. 104-191, § 101(e)(2)(A):

Act Sec. 101(e)(2)(A) amended ERISA Sec. 502(a)(6) by striking "under subsection (c)(2) or (i) or (l)" and inserting "under paragraph (2), (4), or (5) of subsection (c) or under subsection (i) or (l)"; and ERISA Sec. 502(c), the last two sentences, by striking "For purposes of this paragraph" and all that follows through "The Secretary and" and inserting:

"(5) The Secretary may assess a civil penalty against any person of up to $1,000 a day from the date of the person's failure or refusal to file the information required to be filed by such person with the Secretary under regulations prescribed pursuant to section 101(g).

(6) The Secretary and"

P.L. 104-191, § 101(e)(2)(B):

Act Sec. 101(e)(2)(B) amended ERISA Sec. 502(c)(1) by adding at the end a new sentence to read as above.

The above amendments generally apply with respect to group health plans for plan years beginning after June 30, 1997. For special rules, see Act Sec. 101(g)(2)-(5), reproduced below.

Act Sec. 101(g)(2)-(5) reads as follows:

(g) EFFECTIVE DATES.—

(1) IN GENERAL.—Except as provided in this section, this section (and the amendments made by this section) shall apply with respect to group health plans for plan years beginning after June 30, 1997.

(2) DETERMINATION OF CREDITABLE COVERAGE.—

(A) PERIOD OF COVERAGE.—

(i) IN GENERAL.—Subject to clause (ii), no period before July 1, 1996, shall be taken into account under part 7 of subtitle B of title I of the Employee Retirement Income Security Act of 1974 (as added by this section) in determining creditable coverage.

(ii) SPECIAL RULE FOR CERTAIN PERIODS.—The Secretary of Labor, consistent with section 104, shall provide for a process whereby individuals who need to establish creditable coverage for periods before July 1, 1996, and who would have such coverage credited but for clause (i) may be given credit for creditable coverage for such periods through the presentation of documents or other means.

(B) CERTIFICATIONS, ETC.—

(i) IN GENERAL.—Subject to clauses (ii) and (iii), subsection (e) of section 701 of the Employee Retirement Income Security Act of 1974 (as added by this section) shall apply to events occurring after June 30, 1996.

(ii) NO CERTIFICATION REQUIRED TO BE PROVIDED BEFORE JUNE 1, 1997.—In no case is a certification required to be provided under such subsection before June 1, 1997.

(iii) CERTIFICATION ONLY ON WRITTEN REQUEST FOR EVENTS OCCURRING BEFORE OCTOBER 1, 1996.—In the case of an event occurring after June 30, 1996, and before October 1, 1996, a certification is not required to be provided under such subsection unless an individual (with respect to whom the certification is otherwise required to be made) requests such certification in writing.

(C) TRANSITIONAL RULE.—In the case of an individual who seeks to establish creditable coverage for any period for which certification is not required because it relates to an event occurring before June 30, 1996—

(i) the individual may present other credible evidence of such coverage in order to establish the period of creditable coverage; and

(ii) a group health plan and a health insurance issuer shall not be subject to any penalty or enforcement action with respect to the plan's or issuer's crediting (or not crediting) such coverage if the plan or issuer has sought to comply in good faith with the applicable requirements under the amendments made by this section.

(3) SPECIAL RULE FOR COLLECTIVE BARGAINING AGREEMENTS.—Except as provided in paragraph (2), in the case of a group health plan maintained pursuant to one or more collective bargaining agreements between employee representatives and one or more employers ratified before the date of the enactment of this Act, part 7 of subtitle B of title I of Employee Retirement Income Security Act of 1974 (other than section 701(e) thereof) shall not apply to plan years beginning before the later of—

(A) the date on which the last of the collective bargaining agreements relating to the plan terminates (determined without regard to any extension thereof agreed to after the date of the enactment of this Act), or

(B) July 1, 1997.

For purposes of subparagraph (A), any plan amendment made pursuant to a collective bargaining agreement relating to the plan which amends the plan solely to conform to any requirement of such part shall not be treated as a termination of such collective bargaining agreement.

(4) TIMELY REGULATIONS.—The Secretary of Labor, consistent with section 104, shall first issue by not later than April 1, 1997, such regulations as may be necessary to carry out the amendments made by this section.

(5) LIMITATION ON ACTIONS.—No enforcement action shall be taken, pursuant to the amendments made by this section, against a group health plan or health insurance issuer with respect to a violation of a requirement imposed by such amendments before January 1, 1998, or, if later, the date of issuance of regulations referred to in paragraph (4), if the plan or issuer has sought to comply in good faith with such requirements.

P.L. 103-465, § 761(a)(9)(B)(ii):

Act Sec. 761(a)(9)(B)(ii) amended ERISA Sec. 502 by adding subsection (m) to read as above.

The above amendment applies to plan years beginning after December 31, 1994.

P.L. 103-401:

Amended ERISA Sec. 502(a) by adding subparagraph (9). In addition, in ERISA Sec. 502(l)(3)(B), the words "(or to provide the relief ordered pursuant to subsection (a)(9))" were added after "to restore all losses to the plan".

Under Sec. 5 of P.L. 103-401, the above amendments apply to any legal proceeding pending, or brought, on or after May 31, 1993.

Sec. 4 of P.L. 103-401, entitled, "Effect on Other Provisions," provides, "Nothing in this Act shall be construed to limit the legal standing of individuals to bring a civil action as participants or beneficiaries under section 502(a) of the Employee Retirement Income Security Act of 1974 (29 U.S.C. § 1132(a)), and nothing in this Act shall affect the responsibilities, obligations, or duties imposed upon fiduciaries by title I of the Employee Retirement Income Security Act of 1974."

P.L. 103-66, § 4301(c)(1):

Amended ERISA Sec. 502(a) by striking "or" at the end of paragraph (5), by striking the period and inserting a semicolon in paragraph (6), and by adding new paragraphs (7) and (8) to read as above.

The above amendments are effective on August 10, 1993. Any plan amendment required to be made by Act. Sec. 4301 need not be made before the first plan year beginning on or after January 1, 1994 if: (1) the plan is operated in accordance with Act Sec. 4301 during the period after August 9, 1993 and before such first plan year; and (2) the amendment applies retroactively to this period. A plan will not be treated as failing to be operated in accordance with plan provisions merely because it operates in accordance with the effective date requirements.

P.L. 103-66, §4301(c)(2):

Amended ERISA Sec. 502(c) by adding at the end new paragraph (4) to read as above.

The above amendments are effective on August 10, 1993. Any plan amendment required to be made by Act. Sec. 4301 need not be made before the first plan year beginning on or after January 1, 1994 if: (1) the plan is operated in accordance with Act Sec. 4301 during the period after August 9, 1993 and before such first plan year; and (2) the amendment applies retroactively to this period. A plan will not be treated as failing to be operated in accordance with plan provisions merely because it operates in accordance with the effective date requirements.

P.L. 103-66, §4301(c)(3):

Amended ERISA Sec. 502(e)(1) by striking "or fiduciary" in the first sentence and inserting "fiduciary, or any person referred to in section 101(f)(1)"; and by striking "subsection (a)(1)(B)" in the second sentence and inserting "paragraphs (1)(B) and (7) of subsection (a)."

The above amendments are effective on August 10, 1993. Any plan amendment required to be made by Act. Sec. 4301 need not be made before the first plan year beginning on or after January 1, 1994 if: (1) the plan is operated in accordance with Act Sec. 4301 during the period after August 9, 1993 and before such first plan year; and (2) the amendment applies retroactively to this period. A plan will not be treated as failing to be operated in accordance with plan provisions merely because it operates in accordance with the effective date requirements.

P.L. 101-508, Sec. 12012(d)(2)(A):

Amended ERISA Sec. 502(c)(1) by inserting "or section 101(e)(1)" after "section 606" effective for qualified transfers under Code Sec. 420 made after November 5, 1990.

P.L. 101-508, Sec. 12012(d)(2)(B):

Amended ERISA Sec. 502(c)(3) by inserting "or who fails to meet the requirements of section 101(e)(2) with respect to any person" after "beneficiary" the first place it appears and by inserting "or to such person" after "beneficiary" the second place it appears effective for qualified transfers under Code Sec. 420 made after November 5, 1990.

P.L. 101-239, §2101(a):

Amended ERISA Sec. 502 by adding new subsection (l) to read as above, effective for any breach of fiduciary responsibility or other violation occurring on or after December 19, 1989.

P.L. 101-239, §2101(b):

Amended ERISA Sec. 502(a)(6) by inserting "or (l)" after "subsection (i)" effective for any breach of fiduciary responsibility or other violation occurring on or after December 19, 1989.

P.L. 101-239, §7881(b)(5)(B):

Amended ERISA Sec. 502(c) by adding a new paragraph (3) to read as above, effective for reports required to be filed after December 31, 1987.

P.L. 101-239, §7881(j)(2):

Amended ERISA Sec. 502(a)(6) by striking "subsection (i)" and inserting "subsection (c)(2) or (i)" effective December 22, 1987.

P.L. 101-239, §7881(j)(3):

Amended ERISA Sec. 502(c)(2) by inserting "against any plan administrator" after "civil penalty" and by striking "a plan administrator's" and inserting "such plan administrator's" effective for reports to be filed after December 31, 1987.

P.L. 101-239, §7894(f)(1):

Amended ERISA Sec. 502(b)(1) by striking "respct" and inserting "respect" effective September 2, 1974.

P.L. 101-239, §7891(a)(1):

Titles I, III, and IV of ERISA (other than sections 3(37)(E), 301(a)(7), and 308, the last sentence of section 408(d), and sections 414(c), 4001(a)(3)(ii), and 4303) are each amended by striking "Internal Revenue Code of 1954" each place it appears and inserting "Internal Revenue Code of 1986" effective October 22, 1986.

P.L. 100-203, §9342(c)(1):

Amended ERISA Sec. 502 by inserting (1) after (c) and by striking "(1) who" and "(2) who" and inserting "(A) who" and "(B) who", respectively, to read as above, effective for reports required to be filed after December 31, 1987.

P.L. 100-203, §9342(c)(2):

Amended ERISA Sec. 502(c) by adding paragraph (2) to read as above, effective for reports required to be filed after December 31, 1987.

P.L. 100-203, §9344:

Amended ERISA Sec. 502(i) by striking the second sentence and inserting a new sentence, to read as above, effective December 22, 1987. Prior to amendment, subsection (i) read as follows:

(i) In the case of a transaction prohibited by section 406 by a party in interest with respect to a plan to which this part applies, the Secretary may assess a civil penalty against such party in interest. The amount of such penalty may not exceed 5 percent of the amount involved (as defined in section 4975(f)(4) of the Internal Revenue Code of 1954); except that if the transaction is not corrected (in such manner as the Secretary shall prescribe by regulation, which regulations shall be consistent with section 4975(f)(5) of such Code) within 90 days after notice from the Secretary (or such longer period as the Secretary may permit), such penalty may be in an amount not more than 100 percent of the amount involved. This subsection shall not apply to a transaction with respect to a plan described in section 4975(e)(1) of such Code.

P.L. 99-272:

Act Sec. 10002(b) amended ERISA Sec. 502(c) by inserting after "any administrator (1) who fails to meet the requirements of paragraph (1) or (4) of section 606 with respect to a participant or beneficiary, or (2)," effective for plan years beginning on or after July 1, 1986, subject to the rules at ¶ 15,045.

P.L. 96-364, §306(b):

Act Sec. 306(b) renumbered subsections 502(b)(1)(A) and (B) and added new subsection 502(b)(2); renumbered section 502(g)(1) and inserted "(other than an action described in paragraph (2))" between "title" and "by" therein; and added new subsection 502(g)(2) effective September 26, 1980.

Regulations

The following regulations were adopted under "Title 29—Labor", "Chapter XXV—Pension and Welfare Benefit Programs, Department of Labor", "Subchapter G—Administration and Enforcement Under the Employee Retirement Income Security Act of 1974", "Part 2560—Rules and Regulations for Administration and Enforcement". The regulations were published in the *Federal Register* on October 27, 1978 (43 F.R. 50174), and filed October 20, 1978. The regulations are effective retroactively from January 1, 1975. ERISA Reg. Sec. 2560.502c-2 was amended effective March 8, 2002 and published in the *Federal Register* on January 7, 2002 (67 FR 771) and revised by the PWBA on January 24, 2003 (68 FR 3729).

Subchapter G—Administration and Enforcement Under the Employee Retirement Income Security Act of 1974

Part 2560—Rules and Regulations for Administration and Enforcement

[¶ 14,925]

§ 2560.502-1 **Requests for enforcement pursuant to section 502(b)(2).** (a) *Form, content, and filing.* All requests by participants, beneficiaries, and fiduciaries for the Secretary of Labor to exercise his enforcement authority pursuant to section 502(a)(5), 29 U.S.C. 1132(a)(5), with respect to a violation of, or the enforcement of, Parts 2 and 3 of Title I of the Employee Retirement Income Security Act of 1974 (Act) shall be in writing and shall contain information sufficient to form a basis for identifying the participant, beneficiary or fiduciary and the plan involved. All such requests shall be considered filed if they are directed to and received by any office or official of the Department of Labor or referred to and received by any such office or official by any party to whom such writing is directed.

(b) *Consideration.* The Secretary of Labor retains discretion to determine whether any enforcement proceeding should be commenced in the case of any request received pursuant to paragraph (a) of this section, and he may, but shall not be required to, exercise his authority pursuant to section 502(a)(5) of the Act only if he determines that such violation affects, or such enforcement is necessary to protect, claims of participants or beneficiaries to benefits under the plan.

Regulations

The following regulation was published in the *Federal Register* on June 23, 1989 (54 FR 26890). The regulation is effective with respect to annual reports required to be filed for plan years beginning on or after January 1, 1988. Regulation § 2560.502c-5 was added by 65 FR 7181 on February 11, 2000. Regulations § 2560.502c-2, § 2560.502c-5, § 2560.502c-6, and § 2560.502c-7 were revised by PWBA in 67 FR 64774 on October 21, 2002 and in 68 FR 3729 on January 24, 2003. Regulation § 2560.502c-5 was amended and revised by 68 FR 17503 on April 9, 2003. Regulation § 2560.502c-4 was added by 74

FR 17, on January 2, 2009. Regulations §§ 2560.502c-2, 2560.502c-4, 2560.502c-5, and 2560.502c-6 were amended by interim final regulations on July 1, 2016 (81 FR 43429).

[¶ 14,925A]
§ 2560.502c-2 Civil penalties under section 502(c)(2).

(a) *In general.* (1) Pursuant to the authority granted the Secretary under section 502(c)(2) of the Employee Retirement Income Security Act of 1974, as amended (the Act), the administrator (within the meaning of section 3(16)(A)) of an employee benefit plan (within the meaning of section 3(3) and § 2510.3-1, *et seq.*) for which an annual report is required to be filed under section 101(b)(1) shall be liable for civil penalties assessed by the Secretary under section 502(c)(2) of the Act in each case in which there is a failure or refusal to file the annual report required to be filed under section 101(b)(1).

(2) For purposes of this section, a failure or refusal to file the annual report required to be filed under section 101(b)(1) shall mean a failure or refusal to file, in whole or in part, that information described in section 103 and § 2520.103-1, et seq., on behalf of the plan at the time and in the manner prescribed therefor. [Revised by 67 FR 771, effective March 8, 2002.]

(b) *Amount assessed.*

»»→ Caution: *Reg. § 2560.502c-2(b)(1), as amended by interim final regulations to remove and replace the parenthetical material, is effective and generally applicable August 1, 2016.*

(1) The amount assessed under section 502(c)(2) shall be determined by the Department of Labor, taking into consideration the degree and/or willfulness of the failure or refusal to file the annual report. However, the amount assessed under section 502(c)(2) of the Act shall not exceed $1,000 a day (adjusted for inflation pursuant to the Federal Civil Penalties Inflation Adjustment Act of 1990, as amended), computed from the date of the administrator's failure or refusal to file the annual report and, except as provided in paragraph (b)(2) of this section, continuing up to the date on which an annual report satisfactory to the Secretary is filed. [Revised by PWBA in 68 FR 3729 on 1-24-03. Amended 7/1/16 (81 FR 43429) by interim final regulations that removed and replaced the parenthetical material in the second sentence.]

(2) If upon receipt of a notice of intent to assess a penalty (as described in paragraph (c) of this section) the administrator files a statement of reasonable cause for the failure to file, in accordance with paragraph (e) of this section, a penalty shall not be assessed for any day from the date the Department serves the administrator with a copy of such notice until the day after the Department serves notice on the administrator of its determination on reasonable cause and its intention to assess a penalty (as described in paragraph (g) of this section).

(3) For purposes of this paragraph, the date on which the administrator failed or refused to file the annual report shall be the date on which the annual report was due (determined without regard to any extension for filing). An annual report which is rejected under section 104(a)(4) for a failure to provide material information shall be treated as a failure to file an annual report when a revised report satisfactory to the Department is not filed within 45 days of the date of the Department's notice of rejection.

A penalty shall not be assessed under section 502(c)(2) for any day earlier than the day after the date of an administrator's failure or refusal to file the annual report if a revised filing satisfactory to the Department is not submitted within 45 days of the date of the notice of rejection by the Department.

(c) *Notice of intent to assess a penalty.* Prior to the assessment of any penalty under section 502(c)(2), the Department shall provide to the administrator of the plan a written notice indicating the Department's intent to assess a penalty under section 502(c)(2), the amount of such penalty, the period to which the penalty applies, and the reason(s) for the penalty.

(d) *Reconsideration or waiver of penalty to be assessed.* The Department may determine that all or part of the penalty amount in the notice of intent to assess a penalty shall not be assessed on a showing that the administrator complied with the requirements of section 101(b)(1) of the Act or on a showing by the administrator of mitigating circumstances regarding the degree or willfulness of the noncompliance.

[Revised by PWBA in 67 FR 64774 on 10-21-02 and in 68 FR 3729 on 1-24-03.]

(e) *Showing of reasonable cause.* Upon issuance by the Department of a notice of intent to assess a penalty, the administrator shall have thirty (30) days from the date of service of the notice, as described in paragraph (i) of this section, to file a statement of reasonable cause explaining why the penalty, as calculated, should be reduced, or not be assessed, for the reasons set forth in paragraph (d) of this section. Such statement must be made in writing and set forth all the facts alleged as reasonable cause for the reduction or nonassessment of the penalty. The statement must contain a declaration by the administrator that the statement is made under the penalties of perjury. [Revised by PWBA in 67 FR 64774 on 10-21-02 and in 68 FR 3729 on 1-24-03.]

(f) *Failure to file a statement of reasonable cause.* Failure of an administrator to file a statement of reasonable cause within the thirty (30) day period described in paragraph (e) of this section shall be deemed to constitute a waiver of the right to appear and contest the facts alleged in the notice of intent, and such failure shall be deemed an admission of the facts alleged in the notice for purposes of any proceeding involving the assessment of a civil penalty under section 502(c)(2) of the Act. Such notice shall then become a final order of the Secretary, within the meaning of section 2570.61(g) of this chapter, forty-five (45) days from the date of service of the notice. [Revised by PWBA in 67 FR 64774 on 10-21-02 and in 68 FR 3729 on 1-24-03.]

(g) *Notice of the determination on statement of reasonable cause.* (1) The Department, following a review of all the facts alleged in support of no assessment or a complete or partial waiver of the penalty, shall notify the administrator, in writing, of its determination to waive the penalty, in whole or in part, and/or assess a penalty. If it is the determination of the Department to assess a penalty, the notice shall indicate the amount of the penalty, not to exceed the amount described in paragraph (c) of this section. This notice is a "pleading" for purposes of Sec. 2570.61(m) of this chapter. [Revised by PWBA in 67 FR 64774 on 10-21-02 and in 58 FR 3729 on 1-24-03.]

(2) Except as provided in paragraph (h) of this section, a notice issued pursuant to paragraph (g)(1) of this section, indicating the Department's intention to assess a penalty shall become a final order, within the meaning of Sec. 2570.61(g), forty-five (45) days from the date of service of the notice. [Revised by PWBA in 67 FR 64774 on 10-21-02 and in 68 FR 3729 on 1-24-03.]

(h) *Administrative hearing.* A notice issued pursuant to paragraph (g) of this section will not become a final order, within the meaning of Sec. 2570.61(g) of this chapter, if, within 30 days from the date of the service of the notice, the administrator or a representative thereof files a request for a hearing under Sec. Sec. 2570.60 through 2570.71 of this chapter, and files an answer to the notice. The request for hearing and answer must be filed in accordance with Sec. 2570.62 of this chapter and Sec. 18.4 of this title. The answer opposing the proposed sanction shall be in writing, and supported by reference to specific circumstances or facts surrounding the notice of determination issued pursuant to paragraph (g) of this section. [Revised by PWBA in 67 FR 64774 on 10-21-02 and in 68 FR 3729 on 1-24-03.]

(i) *Service of notices and filing of statements.* (1) Service of a notice for purposes of paragraphs (c) and (g) of this section shall be made:[Revised by PWBA in 67 FR 64774 on 10-21-02 and in 68 FR 3729 on 1-24-03.]

(i) By delivering a copy to the administrator or representative thereof;

(ii) By leaving a copy at the principal office, place of business, or residence of the administrator or representative thereof; or

(iii) By mailing a copy to the last known address of the administrator or representative thereof.

(2) If service is accomplished by certified mail, service is complete upon mailing. If service is by regular mail, service is complete upon receipt by the addressee. When service of a notice under paragraph (c) or (g) of this section is by certified mail, five (5) days shall be added to the time allowed by these rules for the filing of a statement, or

a request for hearing and answer, as applicable. [Revised by PWBA in 67 FR 64774 on 10-21-02 and in 68 FR 3729 on 1-24-03.]

(3) For purposes of this section, a statement of reasonable cause shall be considered filed: [Added by PWBA in 67 FR 64774 on 10-21-02 and revised in 68 FR 3729 on 1-24-03.]

(i) Upon mailing, if accomplished using United States Postal Service certified mail or Express Mail; [Added by PWBA in 67 FR 64774 on 10-21-02 and revised in 68 FR 3729 on 1-24-03.]

(ii) Upon receipt by the delivery service, if accomplished using a "designated private delivery service" within the meaning of 26 U.S.C. 7502(f); [Added by PWBA in 67 FR 64774 on 10-21-02 and revised in 68 FR 3729 on 1-24-03.]

(iii) Upon transmittal, if transmitted in a manner specified in the notice of intent to assess a penalty as a method of transmittal to be accorded such special treatment; or [Added by PWBA in 67 FR 64774 on 10-21-02 and revised in 68 FR 3729 on 1-24-03.]

(iv) In the case of any other method of filing, upon receipt by the Department at the address provided in the notice of intent to assess a penalty. [Added by PWBA in 67 FR 64774 on 10-21-02 and revised in 68 FR 3729 on 1-24-03.]

(j) *Liability.* (1) If more than one person is responsible as administrator for the failure to file the annual report, all such persons shall be jointly and severally liable with respect to such failure.

(2) Any person against whom a civil penalty has been assessed under section 502(c)(2) pursuant to a final order, within the meaning of §2570.61(g), shall be personally liable for the payment of such penalty.

(k) *Cross-reference.* See §§2570.60 through 71 of this chapter for procedural rules relating to administrative hearings under section 502(c)(2) of the Act.

[¶ 14,925C]
§2560.502c-4 Civil penalties under section 502(c)(4).

Sec. 2560.502c-4(a) In general. (1) Pursuant to the authority granted the Secretary under section 502(c)(4) of the Employee Retirement Income Security Act of 1974, as amended (the Act), the administrator (within the meaning of section 3(16)(A) of the Act) shall be liable for civil penalties assessed by the Secretary under section 502(c)(4) of the Act, for failure or refusal to furnish:

(i) Notice of funding-based limits in accordance with section 101(j) of the Act;

(ii) Actuarial, financial or funding information in accordance with section 101(k) of the Act;

(iii) Notice of potential withdrawal liability in accordance with section 101(l) of the Act; or

(iv) Notice of rights and obligations under an automatic contribution arrangement in accordance with section 514(e)(3) of the Act.

(2) For purposes of this section, a failure or refusal to furnish the items referred to in paragraph (a)(1) above shall mean a failure or refusal to furnish, in whole or in part, the items required under section 101(j), (k), or (l), or section 514(e)(3) of the Act at the relevant times and manners prescribed in such sections.

(b) Amount assessed.

≫→ Caution: Reg. §2560.502c-4(b)(1), as amended by interim final regulations to remove and replace the parenthetical material, is effective and generally applicable August 1, 2016.

(1) The amount assessed under section 502(c)(4) of the Act for each separate violation shall be determined by the Department of Labor, taking into consideration the degree or willfulness of the failure or refusal to furnish the items referred to in paragraph (a) of this section. However, the amount assessed for each violation under section 502(c)(4) of the Act shall not exceed $1,000 a day (adjusted for inflation pursuant to the Federal Civil Penalties Inflation Adjustment Act of 1990, as amended), computed from the date of the administrator's failure or refusal to furnish the items referred to in paragraph (a) of this section. [Amended 7/1/16 (81 FR 43429) by interim final regulations that removed and replaced the parenthetical material in the second sentence.]

(2) For purposes of calculating the amount to be assessed under this section, a failure or refusal to furnish the item with respect to any person entitled to receive such item, shall be treated as a separate violation under section 101(j), (k), or (l), or section 514(e)(3) of the Act, as applicable.

(c) Notice of intent to assess a penalty. Prior to the assessment of any penalty under section 502(c)(4) of the Act, the Department shall provide to the administrator of the plan a written notice indicating the Department's intent to assess a penalty under section 502(c)(4) of the Act, the amount of such penalty, the number of individuals on which the penalty is based, the period to which the penalty applies, and the reason(s) for the penalty.

(d) Reconsideration or waiver of penalty to be assessed. The Department may determine that all or part of the penalty amount in the notice of intent to assess a penalty shall not be assessed on a showing that the administrator complied with the requirements of section 101(j), (k), or (l), or section 514(e)(3) of the Act, as applicable, or on a showing by such person of mitigating circumstances regarding the degree or willfulness of the noncompliance.

(e) Showing of reasonable cause. Upon issuance by the Department of a notice of intent to assess a penalty, the administrator shall have thirty (30) days from the date of service of the notice, as described in paragraph (i) of this section, to file a statement of reasonable cause explaining why the penalty, as calculated, should be reduced, or not be assessed, for the reasons set forth in paragraph (d) of this section. Such statement must be made in writing and set forth all the facts alleged as reasonable cause for the reduction or nonassessment of the penalty. The statement must contain a declaration by the administrator that the statement is made under the penalties of perjury.

(f) Failure to file a statement of reasonable cause. Failure to file a statement of reasonable cause within the thirty (30) day period described in paragraph (e) of this section shall be deemed to constitute a waiver of the right to appear and contest the facts alleged in the notice of intent, and such failure shall be deemed an admission of the facts alleged in the notice for purposes of any proceeding involving the assessment of a civil penalty under section 502(c)(4) of the Act. Such notice shall then become a final order of the Secretary, within the meaning of Sec. 2570.131(g) of this chapter, forty-five (45) days from the date of service of the notice.

(g) Notice of determination on statement of reasonable cause.. (1) The Department, following a review of all of the facts in a statement of reasonable cause alleged in support of nonassessment or a complete or partial waiver of the penalty, shall notify the administrator, in writing, of its determination on the statement of reasonable cause and its determination whether to waive the penalty in whole or in part, and/ or assess a penalty. If it is the determination of the Department to assess a penalty, the notice shall indicate the amount of the penalty assessment, not to exceed the amount described in paragraph (c) of this section. This notice is a "pleading" for purposes of Sec. 2570.131(m) of this chapter.

(2) Except as provided in paragraph (h) of this section, a notice issued pursuant to paragraph (g)(1) of this section, indicating the Department's determination to assess a penalty, shall become a final order, within the meaning of Sec. 2570.131(g) of this chapter, forty-five (45) days from the date of service of the notice.

(h) Administrative hearing. A notice issued pursuant to paragraph (g) of this section will not become a final order, within the meaning of Sec. 2570.131(g) of this chapter, if, within thirty (30) days from the date of the service of the notice, the administrator or a representative thereof files a request for a hearing under Sec. Sec. 2570.130 through 2570.141 of this chapter, and files an answer to the notice. The request for hearing and answer must be filed in accordance with Sec. 2570.132 of this chapter and Sec. 18.4 of this title. The answer opposing the proposed sanction shall be in writing, and supported by reference to specific circumstances or facts surrounding the notice of determination issued pursuant to paragraph (g) of this section.

(i) Service of notices and filing of statements.. (1) Service of a notice for purposes of paragraphs (c) and (g) of this section shall be made:

(i) By delivering a copy to the administrator or representative thereof;

(ii) By leaving a copy at the principal office, place of business, or residence of the administrator or representative thereof; or

(iii) By mailing a copy to the last known address of the administrator or representative thereof.

(2) If service is accomplished by certified mail, service is complete upon mailing. If service is by regular mail, service is complete upon receipt by the addressee. When service of a notice under paragraph (c) or (g) of this section is by certified mail, five days shall be added to the time allowed by these rules for the filing of a statement or a request for hearing and answer, as applicable.

(3) For purposes of this section, a statement of reasonable cause shall be considered filed:

(i) Upon mailing, if accomplished using United States Postal Service certified mail or express mail;

(ii) Upon receipt by the delivery service, if accomplished using a "designated private delivery service" within the meaning of 26 U.S.C. 7502(f);

(iii) Upon transmittal, if transmitted in a manner specified in the notice of intent to assess a penalty as a method of transmittal to be accorded such special treatment; or

(iv) In the case of any other method of filing, upon receipt by the Department at the address provided in the notice of intent to assess a penalty.

(j) *Liability.*. (1) If more than one person is responsible as administrator for the failure to furnish the items required under section 101(j), (k), or (l), or section 514(e)(3) of the Act, as applicable, all such persons shall be jointly and severally liable for such failure. For purposes of paragraph (a)(1)(iii) of this section, the term "administrator" shall include plan sponsor (within the meaning of section 3(16)(B) of the Act).

(2) Any person, or persons under paragraph (j)(1) of this section, against whom a civil penalty has been assessed under section 502(c)(4) of the Act, pursuant to a final order within the meaning of Sec. 2570.131(g) of this chapter shall be personally liable for the payment of such penalty.

(k) *Cross-references.*. (1) The procedural rules in Sec. Sec. 2570.130 through 2570.141 of this chapter apply to administrative hearings under section 502(c)(4) of the Act.

(2) When applying procedural rules in Sec. Sec. 2570.130 through 2570.140:

(i) Wherever the term "502(c)(7)" appears, such term shall mean "502(c)(4)"

(ii) Reference to Sec. 2560.502c-7(g) in 2570.131(c) shall be construed as reference to Sec. 2560.502c-4(g) of this chapter;

(iii) Reference to Sec. 2560.502c-7(e) in Sec. 2570.131(g) shall be construed as reference to Sec. 2560.502c-4(e) of this chapter;

(iv) Reference to Sec. 2560.502c-7(g) in Sec. 2570.131(m) shall be construed as reference to Sec. 2560.502c-4(g); and

(v) Reference to Sec. Sec. 2560.502c-7(g) and 2560.502c-7(h) in Sec. 2570.134 shall be construed as reference to Sec. Sec. 2560.502c-4(g) and 2560.502c-4(h), respectively.

[¶ 14,925D]

§ 2560.502c-5 **Civil penalties under section 502(c)(5).**

(a) *In general.* (1) Pursuant to the authority granted the Secretary under section 502(c)(5) of the Employee Retirement Income Security Act of 1974, as amended (the Act), the administrator of a multiple employer welfare arrangement (MEWA) (within the meaning of section 3(40)(A) of the Act) that is not a group health plan, and that provides benefits consisting of medical care (within the meaning of section 733(a)(2)), for which a report is required to be filed under section 101(g) of the Act and 29 CFR 2520.101-2, shall be liable for civil penalties assessed by the Secretary under section 502(c)(5) of the Act for each failure or refusal to file a completed report required to be filed under section 101(g) and 29 CFR 2520.101-2. The term "administrator" is defined in 29 CFR 2520.101-2(b).

(2) For purposes of this section, a failure or refusal to file the report required to be filed under section 101(g) shall mean a failure or refusal to file, in whole or in part, that information described in section 101(g) and 29 CFR 2520.101-2, on behalf of the MEWA, at the time and in the manner prescribed therefor.

(b) *Amount assessed.*

»»→ *Caution: Reg. § 2560.502c-5(b)(1), as amended by interim final regulations to revise the second sentence, is effective and generally applicable August 1, 2016.*

(1) The amount assessed under section 502(c)(5) shall be determined by the Department of Labor, taking into consideration the degree and/or willfulness of the failure to file the report. However, the amount assessed under section 502(c)(5) or the Act shall not exceed $1,000 a day (adjusted for inflation pursuant to the Federal Civil Penalties Inflation Adjustment Act of 1990, as amended), computed from the date of the administrator's failure or refusal to file the report and, except as provided in paragraph (b)(2) of this section, continuing up to the date on which a report meeting the requirements of section 101(g) of the Act and 29 CFR 2520.101-2, as determined by the Secretary, is filed. [Amended 7/1/16 (81 FR 43429) by interim final regulations that revised the second sentence.]

(2) If, upon receipt of a notice of intent to assess a penalty (as described in paragraph (c) of this section), the administrator files a statement of reasonable cause for the failure to file, in accordance with paragraph (e) of this section, a penalty shall not be assessed for any day from the date the Department serves the administrator with a copy of such notice until the day after the Department serves notice on the administrator of its determination on reasonable cause and its intention to assess a penalty (as described in paragraph (g) of this section).

(3) For purposes of this paragraph, the date on which the administrator failed or refused to file the report shall be the date on which the report was due (determined without regard to any extension of time for filing). A report which is rejected under 29 CFR 2520.101-2 shall be treated as a failure to file a report when a revised report meeting the requirements of this section is not filed within 45 days of the date of the Department's notice of rejection. If a revised report meeting the requirements of this section, as determined by the Secretary, is not submitted within 45 days of the date of the notice of rejection by the Department, a penalty shall be assessed under section 502(c)(5) beginning on the day after the date of the administrator's failure or refusal to file the report.

(c) *Notice of intent to assess a penalty.* Prior to the assessment of any penalty under section 502(c)(5), the Department shall provide to the administrator of the MEWA a written notice indicating the Department's intent to assess a penalty under section 502(c)(5), the amount of such penalty, the period to which the penalty applies, and a statement of the facts and the reason(s) for the penalty.

(d) *Reconsideration or waiver of penalty to be assessed.* The Department may determine that all or part of the penalty amount in the notice of intent to assess a penalty shall not be assessed on a showing that the administrator complied with the requirements of section 101(g) of the Act or on a showing by the administrator of mitigating circumstances regarding the degree or willfulness of the noncompliance.

(e) *Showing of reasonable cause.* Upon issuance by the Department of a notice of intent to assess a penalty, the administrator shall have thirty (30) days from the date of service of the notice, as described in paragraph (i) of this section, to file a statement of reasonable cause explaining why the penalty, as calculated, should be reduced, or not be assessed, for the reasons set forth in paragraph (d) of this section. Such statement must be made in writing and set forth all the facts alleged as reasonable cause for the reduction or nonassessment of the penalty. The statement must contain a declaration by the administrator that the statement is made under the penalties of perjury.

(f) *Failure to file a statement of reasonable cause.* Failure of an administrator to file a statement of reasonable cause within the thirty (30) day period described in paragraph (e) of this section shall be deemed to constitute a waiver of the right to appear and contest the facts alleged in the notice of intent, and such failure shall be deemed an admission of the facts alleged in the notice for purposes of any proceeding involving the assessment of a civil penalty under section 502(c)(5) of the Act. Such notice shall then become a final order of the Secretary, within the meaning of 29 CFR 2570.91(g), forty-five (45) days from the date of service of the notice.

(g) *Notice of the determination on statement of reasonable cause.* (1) The Department, following a review of all the facts alleged in support of no assessment or a complete or partial waiver of the penalty, shall notify the administrator, in writing, of its determination to waive the penalty, in whole or in part, and/or assess a penalty. If it is the determination of the Department to assess a penalty, the notice shall indicate the amount of the penalty, not to exceed the amount described in paragraph (c) of this section, and a brief statement of the reasons for assessing the penalty. This notice is a "pleading" for purposes of 29 CFR 2570.91(m).

(2) Except as provided in paragraph (h) of this section, a notice issued pursuant to paragraph (g)(1) of this section, indicating the Department's intention to assess a penalty, shall become a final order, within the meaning of 29 CFR 2570.91(g), forty-five (45) days from the date of service of the notice.

(h) *Administrative hearing.* A notice issued pursuant to paragraph (g) of this section will not become a final order, within the meaning of 29 CFR 2570.91(g), if, within thirty (30) days from the date of the service of the notice, the administrator or a representative thereof files a request for a hearing under 29 CFR 2570.90 through 2570.101, and files an answer to the notice. The request for hearing and answer must be filed in accordance with 29 CFR 2570.92 and 18.4. The answer opposing the proposed sanction shall be in writing, and supported by reference to specific circumstances or facts surrounding the notice of determination issued pursuant to paragraph (g) of this section.

(i) *Service of notices and filing of statements.* (1) Service of a notice for purposes of paragraphs (c) and (g) of this section shall be made:

(i) By delivering a copy to the administrator or representative thereof;

(ii) By leaving a copy at the principal office, place of business, or residence of the administrator or representative thereof; or

(iii) By mailing a copy to the last known address of the administrator or representative thereof.

(2) If service is accomplished by certified mail, service is complete upon mailing. If service is by regular mail, service is complete upon receipt by the addressee. When service of a notice under paragraph (c) or (g) of this section is by certified mail, five (5) days shall be added to the time allowed by these rules for the filing of a statement, or a request for hearing and answer, as applicable. ·

(3) For purposes of this section, a statement of reasonable cause shall be considered filed:

(i) Upon mailing, if accomplished using United States Postal Service certified mail or Express Mail;

(ii) Upon receipt by the delivery service, if accomplished using a "designated private delivery service" within the meaning of 26 U.S.C. 7502(f);

(iii) Upon transmittal, if transmitted in a manner specified in the notice of intent to assess a penalty as a method of transmittal to be accorded such special treatment; or

(iv) In the case of any other method of filing, upon receipt by the Department at the address provided in the notice of intent to assess a penalty.

(j) *Liability.* (1) If more than one person is responsible as administrator for the failure to file the report, all such persons shall be jointly and severally liable with respect to such failure.

(2) Any person against whom a civil penalty has been assessed under section 502(c)(5) pursuant to a final order, within the meaning of 29 CFR 2570.91(g), shall be personally liable for the payment of such penalty.

(k) *Cross-reference.* See 29 CFR 2570.90 through 2570.101 for procedural rules relating to administrative hearings under section 502(c)(5) of the Act.

[¶ 14,925E]

§2560.502c-6 Civil penalties under section 502(c)(6).

(a) *In general.* (1) Pursuant to the authority granted the Secretary under section 502(c)(6) of the Employee Retirement Income Security Act of 1974, as amended (the Act), the administrator (within the meaning of section 3(16)(A) of the Act) of an employee benefit plan (within the meaning of section 3(3) of the Act and §2510.3-1 of this chapter) shall be liable for civil penalties assessed by the Secretary under section 502(c)(6) of the Act in each case in which there is a failure or refusal to furnish to the Secretary documents requested under section 104(a)(6) of the Act and §2520.104a-8 of this chapter.

(2) For purposes of this section, a failure or refusal to furnish documents shall mean a failure or refusal to furnish, in whole or in part, the documents requested under section 104(a)(6) of the Act and §2520.104a-8 of this chapter at the time and in the manner prescribed in the request.

(b) *Amount assessed.*

⟫→ *Caution: Reg. §2560.502c-6(b)(1), as amended by interim final regulations to remove and replace the parenthetical material, is effective and generally applicable August 1, 2016.*

(1) The amount assessed under section 502(c)(6) of the Act shall be determined by the Department of Labor, taking into consideration the degree and/or willfulness of the failure or refusal to furnish any document or documents requested by the Department under section 104(a)(6) of the Act. However, the amount assessed under section 502(c)(6) of the Act shall not exceed $100 a day or $1,000 per request (such amounts to be adjusted for inflation pursuant to the Federal Civil Penalties Inflation Adjustment Act of 1990, as amended), computed from the date of the administrator's failure or refusal to furnish any document or documents requested by the Department. [Revised by PWBA in 68 FR 3729 on 1-24-03. Amended 7/1/16 (81 FR 43429) by interim final regulations that removed and replaced the parenthetical material in the second sentence.].

(2) For purposes of calculating the amount to be assessed under this section, the date of a failure or refusal to furnish documents shall not be earlier than the thirtieth day after service of the request under section 104(a)(6) of ERISA and §2520.104a-8 of this chapter.

(c) *Notice of intent to assess a penalty.* Prior to the assessment of any penalty under section 502(c)(6) of the Act, the Department shall provide to the administrator of the plan a written notice that indicates the Department's intent to assess a penalty under section 502(c)(6) of the Act, the amount of the penalty, the period to which the penalty applies, and the reason(s) for the penalty.

(d) *Reconsideration of waiver of penalty to be assessed.* The Department may determine that all or part of the penalty amount in the notice of intent to assess a penalty shall not be assessed on a showing that the administrator complied with the requirements of section 104(a)(6) of the Act or on a showing by the administrator of mitigating circumstances regarding the degree or willfulness of the noncompliance. [Revised by PWBA in 67 FR 64774 on 10-21-02 and in 68 FR 3729 on 1-24-03.]

(e) *Showing of reasonable cause.* Upon issuance by the Department of a notice of intent to assess a penalty, the administrator shall have thirty (30) days from the date of service of the notice, as described in paragraph (i) of this section, to file a statement of reasonable cause explaining why the penalty, as calculated, should be reduced, or not be assessed, for the reasons set forth in paragraph (d) of this section. Such statement must be in writing and set forth all the facts alleged as reasonable cause for the reduction or nonassessment of the penalty. The statement must contain a declaration by the administrator that the statement is made under the penalties of perjury. [Revised by PWBA in 67 FR 64774 on 10-21-02 and in 68 FR 3729 on 1-24-03.]

(f) *Failure to file a statement of reasonable cause.* Failure to file a statement of reasonable cause within the 30-day period described in paragraph (e) of this section shall be deemed to constitute a waiver of the right to appear and contest the facts alleged in the notice of intent, and such failure shall be deemed an admission of the facts alleged in the notice for purposes of any proceeding involving the assessment of a civil penalty under section 502(c)(6) of the Act. Such notice shall then become a final order of the Secretary, within the meaning of §2570.111(g) of this chapter, forty-five (45) days from the date of service of the notice. [Revised by PWBA in 67 FR 64774 on 10-21-02 and in 68 FR 3729 on 1-24-03.]

(g) *Notice of determination on statement of reasonable cause.* (1) The Department, following a review of all of the facts alleged in support of no assessment or a complete or partial waiver of the penalty, shall notify the administrator, in writing, of its determination not to assess or to waive the penalty, in whole or in part, and/or assess a penalty. If it is the determination of the Department to assess a penalty, the notice shall indicate the amount of the penalty, not to exceed the amount described in paragraph (c) of this section. This notice is a "pleading" for purposes of Sec. 2570.111(m) of this chapter. [Revised by PWBA in 67 FR 64774 on 10-21-02 and in 68 FR 3729 on 1-24-03.]

(2) Except as provided in paragraph (h) of this section, a notice issued pursuant to paragraph (g)(1) of this section, indicating the Department's intention to assess a penalty, shall become a final order, within the meaning of Sec. 2570.111(g) of this chapter, forty-five (45) days from the date of service of the notice. [Revised by PWBA in 67 FR 64774 on 10-21-02 and in 68 FR 3729 on 1-24-03.]

(h) *Administrative hearing.* A notice issued pursuant to paragraph (g) of this section will not become a final order, within the meaning of Sec. 2570.91(g) of this chapter, if, within thirty (30) days from the date of the service of the notice, the administrator or a representative thereof files a request for a hearing under Sec. Sec. 2570.110 through 2570.121 of this chapter, and files an answer to the notice. The request for hearing and answer must be filed in accordance with Sec. 2570.112 of this chapter and Sec. 18.4 of this title. The answer opposing the proposed sanction shall be in writing, and supported by reference to specific circumstances or facts surrounding the notice of determination issued pursuant to paragraph (g) of this section. [Revised by PWBA in 67 FR 64774 on 10-21-02 and in 68 FR 3729 on 1-24-03.]

(i) *Service of notices and filing of statements.* (1) Service of a notice for purposes of paragraphs (c) and (g) of this section shall be made:

(i) By delivering a copy to the administrator or representative thereof; [Revised by PWBA in 67 FR 64774 on 10-21-02 and in 68 FR 3729 on 1-24-03.]

(ii) By leaving a copy at the principal office, place of business, or residence of the administrator or representative thereof; or

(iii) By mailing a copy to the last known address of the administrator or representative thereof.

(2) If service is accomplished by certified mail, service is complete upon mailing. If service is by regular mail, service is complete upon receipt by the addressee. When service of a notice under paragraph (c) or (g) of this section is by certified mail, five (5) days shall be added to the time allowed by these rules for the filing of a statement, or a request for hearing and answer, as applicable. [Revised by PWBA in 67 FR 64774 on 10-21-02 and 68 FR 3729 on 1-24-03.]

(3) For purposes of this section, a statement of reasonable cause shall be considered filed: [Added by PWBA in 67 FR 64774 on 10-21-02.]

(i) Upon mailing, if accomplished using United States Postal Service certified mail or Express Mail; [Added by PWBA in 67 FR 64774 on 10-21-02.]

(ii) Upon receipt by delivery service, if accomplished using a "designated private delivery service" within the meaning of 26 U.S.C. 7502(f); [Added by PWBA in 67 FR 64774 on 10-21-02.]

(iii) Upon transmittal, if transmitted in a manner specified in the notice of intent to assess a penalty as a method of transmittal to be accorded such special treatment; or [Added by PWBA in 67 FR 64774 on 10-21-02.]

(iv) In the case of any other method of filing, upon receipt by the Department at the address provided in the notice of intent to assess a penalty. [Added by PWBA in 67 FR 64774 on 10-21-02.]

(j) *Liability.* (1) If more than one person is responsible as administrator for the failure to furnish the document or documents requested under section 104(a)(6) of the Act and its implementing regulations (§2520.104a-8 of this chapter), all such persons shall be jointly and severally liable with respect to such failure.

(2) Any person, or persons under paragraph (j)(1) of this section, against whom a civil penalty has been assessed under section 502(c)(6) of the Act pursuant to a final order, within the meaning of §2570.111(g) of this chapter, shall be personally liable for the payment of such penalty.

(k) *Cross-reference.* See §§2570.110 through 2570.121 of this chapter for procedural rules relating to administrative hearings under section 502(c)(6) of the Act.

Regulations

The following regulations regarding inflationary adjustments to ERISA civil monetary penalties were published in the *Federal Register* on October 21, 2002 (67 FR 64774) and revised by the PWBA on January 24, 2003 (68 FR 3729). The Employee Benefits Security Administration (EBSA) revised the regulations on August 10, 2007 (72 FR 44970). Reg. §2560.502c-8 was added February 26, 2010 by 75 FR 8796. Reg. §§ 2560.502c-7 and 2560.502c-8 were amended by interim final regulations on July 1, 2016 (81 FR 43429).

[¶ 14,925F]
§2560.502c-7 **Civil penalties under section 502(c)(7).**

(a) *In general.* (1) Pursuant to the authority granted the Secretary under section 502(c)(7) of the Employee Retirement Income Security Act of 1974, as amended (the Act), the administrator (within the meaning of section 3(16)(A) of the Act) of an individual account plan (within the meaning of section 101(i)(8) of the Act and Sec. 2520.101-3(d)(2) of this chapter), who fails or refuses to provide notice of a blackout period to affected participants and beneficiaries in accordance with section 101(i) of the Act and Sec. 2520.101-3 of this chapter, or the administrator (within the meaning of section 3(16)(A) of the Act) of an applicable individual account plan (within the meaning of section 101(m) of the Act), who fails or refuses to provide notice of diversification rights to applicable individuals in accordance with section 101(m) of the Act, shall be liable for civil penalties assessed by the Secretary under section 502(c)(7) of the Act.

(2) For purposes of this section, a failure or refusal to provide a notice of blackout period shall mean a failure or refusal, in whole or in part, to provide a notice of a blackout period to an affected plan participant or beneficiary at the time and in the manner prescribed by section 101(i) of the Act and Sec. 2520.101-3 of this chapter, and a failure or refusal to provide a notice of diversification rights shall mean a failure or refusal, in whole or in part, to provide notice of diversification rights

to an applicable individual at the time and in the manner prescribed by section 101(m) of the Act. [Revised by EBSA in 72 FR 44970 on 8-10-07.]

(b) *Amount assessed.*

≫→ *Caution: Reg. §2560.502c-7(b)(1), as amended by interim final regulations to remove and replace the parenthetical material, is effective and generally applicable August 1, 2016.*

(1) The amount assessed under section 502(c)(7) of the Act for each separate violation shall be determined by the Department of Labor, taking into consideration the degree and/or willfulness of the failure or refusal to provide a notice of blackout period or notice of diversification rights. However, the amount assessed for each violation under section 502(c)(7) of the Act shall not exceed $100 a day (adjusted for inflation pursuant to the Federal Civil Penalties Inflation Adjustment Act of 1990, as amended), computed from, in the case of a notice of blackout period under section 101(i) of the Act, the date of the administrator's failure or refusal to provide a notice of blackout period up to and including the date that is the final day of the blackout period for which the notice was required, or in the case of a notice of diversification rights under section 101(m) of the Act, computed from the date that is 30 days before the first date on which rights are exercisable under section 204(j) of the Act up to the date such a notice is furnished. [Amended 7/1/16 (81 FR 43429) by interim final regula-

tions that removed and replaced the parenthetical material in the second sentence.]

(2) For purposes of calculating the amount to be assessed under this section, a failure or refusal to provide a notice of blackout period or a notice of diversification rights with respect to any single participant or beneficiary shall be treated as a separate violation under section 101(i) of the Act and Sec. 2520.101-3 of this chapter or section 101(m) of the Act. [Revised by EBSA in 72 FR 44970 on 8-10-07.]

(c) *Notice of intent to assess a penalty.* Prior to the assessment of any penalty under section 502(c)(7) of the Act, the Department shall provide to the administrator of the plan a written notice indicating the Department's intent to assess a penalty under section 502(c)(7) of the Act, the amount of such penalty, the number of participants and beneficiaries on which the penalty is based, the period to which the penalty applies, and the reason(s) for the penalty. [Revised by PWBA in 68 FR 3729 on 1-24-03.]

(d) *Reconsideration or waiver of penalty to be assessed.* The Department may determine that all or part of the penalty amount in the notice of intent to assess a penalty shall not be assessed on a showing that the administrator complied with the applicable requirements of section 101(i) or section 101(m) of the Act or on a showing by the administrator of mitigating circumstances regarding the degree or willfulness of the noncompliance.[Revised by EBSA in 72 FR 44970 on 8-10-07.]

(e) *Showing of reasonable cause.* Upon issuance by the Department of a notice of intent to assess a penalty, the administrator shall have thirty (30) days from the date of service of the notice, as described in paragraph (i) of this section, to file a statement of reasonable cause explaining why the penalty, as calculated, should be reduced, or not be assessed, for the reasons set forth in paragraph (d) of this section. Such statement must be in writing and set forth all the facts alleged as reasonable cause for the reduction or nonassessment of the penalty. The statement must contain a declaration by the administrator that the statement is made under the penalties of perjury. [Revised by PWBA in 68 FR 3729 on 1-24-03.]

(f) *Failure to file a statement of reasonable cause.* Failure to file a statement of reasonable cause within the 30 day period described in paragraph (e) of this section shall be deemed to constitute a waiver of the right to appear and contest the facts alleged in the notice of intent, and such failure shall be deemed an admission of the facts alleged in the notice for purposes of any proceeding involving the assessment of a civil penalty under section 502(c)(7) of the Act. Such notice shall then become a final order of the Secretary, within the meaning of §2570.131(g) of this chapter, forty-five (45) days from the date of service of the notice. [Revised by PWBA in 68 FR 3729 on 1-24-03.]

(g) *Notice of determination on statement of reasonable cause.* (1) The Department, following a review of all of the facts in a statement of reasonable cause alleged in support of no assessment or a complete or partial waiver of the penalty, shall notify the administrator, in writing, of its determination on the statement of reasonable cause and its determination whether to waive the penalty, in whole or in part, and/or assess a penalty. If it is the determination of the Department to assess a penalty, the notice shall indicate the amount of the penalty assessment, not to exceed the amount described in paragraph (c) of this section. This notice is a "pleading" for purposes of Sec. 2570.131(m) of this chapter.

(2) Except as provided in paragraph (h) of this section, a notice issued pursuant to paragraph (g)(1) of this section, indicating the Department's determination to assess a penalty, shall become a final order, within the meaning of Sec. 2570.131(g) of this chapter, forty-five (45) days from the date of service of the notice. [Revised by PWBA in 68 FR 3729 on 1-24-03.]

(h) *Administrative hearing.* A notice issued pursuant to paragraph (g) of this section will not become a final order, within the meaning of Sec. 2570.131(g) of this chapter, if, within thirty (30) days from the date of the service of the notice, the administrator or a representative thereof files a request for a hearing under Sec. Sec. 2570.130 through 2570.141 of this chapter, and files an answer to the notice. The request for hearing and answer must be filed in accordance with Sec. 2570.132

of this chapter and Sec. 18.4 of this title. The answer opposing the proposed sanction shall be in writing, and supported by reference to specific circumstances or facts surrounding the notice of determination issued pursuant to paragraph (g) of this section. [Revised by PWBA in 68 FR 3729 on 1-24-03.]

(i) *Service of notices and filing of statements.* (1) Service of a notice for purposes of paragraphs (c) and (g) of this section shall be made:

(i) By delivering a copy to the administrator or representative thereof;

(ii) By leaving a copy at the principal office, place of business, or residence of the administrator or representative thereof; or

(iii) By mailing a copy to the last known address of the administrator or representative thereof.

(2) If service is accomplished by certified mail, service is complete upon mailing. If service is by regular mail, service is complete upon receipt by the addressee. When service of a notice under paragraph (c) or (g) of this section is by certified mail, five (5) days shall be added to the time allowed by these rules for the filing of a statement, or a request for hearing and answer, as applicable.

(3) For purposes of this section, a statement of reasonable cause shall be considered filed:

(i) Upon mailing, if accomplished using United States Postal Service certified mail or Express Mail;

(ii) Upon receipt by delivery service, if accomplished using a "designated private delivery service" within the meaning of 26 U.S.C. 7502(f);

(iii) Upon transmittal, if transmitted in a manner specified in the notice of intent to assess a penalty as a method of transmittal to be accorded such special treatment; or

(iv) In the case of any other method of filing, upon receipt by the Department at the address provided in the notice of intent to assess a penalty. [Revised by PWBA in 68 FR 3729 on 1-24-03.]

(j) *Liability.* (1) If more than one person is responsible as administrator for the failure to provide a notice of blackout period under section 101(i) of the Act and its implementing regulations (Sec. 2520.101-3 of this chapter), or the failure to provide a notice of diversification rights under section 101(m) of the Act, all such persons shall be jointly and severally liable for such failure. [Revised by EBSA in 72 FR 44970 on 8-10-07.]

(2) Any person, or persons under paragraph (j)(1) of this section, against whom a civil penalty has been assessed under section 502(c)(7) of the Act pursuant to a final order, within the meaning of §2570.131(g) of this chapter, shall be personally liable for the payment of such penalty. [Revised by PWBA in 68 FR 3729 on 1-24-03.]

(k) *Cross-reference.* See Sec. Sec. 2570.130 through 2570.141 of this chapter for procedural rules relating to administrative hearings under section 502(c)(7) of the Act. [Revised by PWBA in 68 FR 3729 on 1-24-03.]

[¶ 14,925G]
§ 2560.502c-8 Civil penalties under section 502(c)(8).

(a) *In general.* (1) Pursuant to the authority granted the Secretary under section 502(c)(8) of the Employee Retirement Income Security Act of 1974, as amended (the Act), the plan sponsor (within the meaning of section 3(16)(B)(iii) of the Act) shall be liable for civil penalties assessed by the Secretary under section 502(c)(8) of the Act, for:

(i) Each violation by such sponsor of the requirement under section 305 of the Act to adopt by the deadline established in that section a funding improvement plan or rehabilitation plan with respect to a multiemployer plan which is in endangered or critical status; or

(ii) In the case of a plan in endangered status which is not in seriously endangered status, a failure by the plan to meet the applicable benchmarks under section 305 by the end of the funding improvement period with respect to the plan.

(2) For purposes of this section, violations or failures referred to in paragraph (a)(1) of this section shall mean a failure or refusal, in whole or in part, to adopt a funding improvement or rehabilitation plan,

or to meet the applicable benchmarks, at the relevant times and manners prescribed in section 305 of the Act.

(b) *Amount assessed.*

»»→ Caution: Reg. § 2560.502c-8(b)(1), as amended by interim final regulations to remove and replace the parenthetical material, is effective and generally applicable August 1, 2016.

(1) The amount assessed under section 502(c)(8) of the Act for each separate violation shall be determined by the Department of Labor, taking into consideration the degree or willfulness of the failure or refusal to comply with the specific requirements referred to in paragraph (a) of this section. However, the amount assessed for each violation under section 502(c)(8) of the Act shall not exceed $1,100 a day (adjusted for inflation pursuant to the Federal Civil Penalties Inflation Adjustment Act of 1990, as amended), computed from the date of the plan sponsor's failure or refusal to comply with the specific requirements referred to in paragraph (a) of this section. [Amended 7/1/16 (81 FR 43429) by interim final regulations that removed and replaced the parenthetical material in the second sentence.]

(c) *Notice of intent to assess a penalty.* Prior to the assessment of any penalty under section 502(c)(8) of the Act, the Department shall provide to the plan sponsor of the plan a written notice indicating the Department's intent to assess a penalty under section 502(c)(8) of the Act, the amount of such penalty, the period to which the penalty applies, and the reason(s) for the penalty.

(d) *Reconsideration or waiver of penalty to be assessed.* The Department may determine that all or part of the penalty amount in the notice of intent to assess a penalty shall not be assessed on a showing that the plan sponsor complied with the requirements of section 305 of the Act, or on a showing by the plan sponsor of mitigating circumstances regarding the degree or willfulness of the noncompliance.

(e) *Showing of reasonable cause.* Upon issuance by the Department of a notice of intent to assess a penalty, the plan sponsor shall have thirty (30) days from the date of service of the notice, as described in paragraph (i) of this section, to file a statement of reasonable cause explaining why the penalty, as calculated, should be reduced, or not be assessed, for the reasons set forth in paragraph (d) of this section. Such statement must be made in writing and set forth all the facts alleged as reasonable cause for the reduction or nonassessment of the penalty. The statement must contain a declaration by the plan sponsor that the statement is made under the penalties of perjury.

(f) *Failure to file a statement of reasonable cause.* Failure to file a statement of reasonable cause within the thirty (30) day period described in paragraph (e) of this section shall be deemed to constitute a waiver of the right to appear and contest the facts alleged in the notice of intent, and such failure shall be deemed an admission of the facts alleged in the notice for purposes of any proceeding involving the assessment of a civil penalty under section 502(c)(8) of the Act. Such notice shall then become a final order of the Secretary, within the meaning of § 2570.161(g) of this chapter, forty-five (45) days from the date of service of the notice.

(g) *Notice of determination on statement of reasonable cause.* (1) The Department, following a review of all of the facts in a statement of reasonable cause alleged in support of nonassessment or a complete or partial waiver of the penalty, shall notify the plan sponsor, in writing, of its determination on the statement of reasonable cause and its determination whether to waive the penalty in whole or in part, and/or assess a penalty. If it is the determination of the Department to assess a penalty, the notice shall indicate the amount of the penalty assessment,

not to exceed the amount described in paragraph (c) of this section. This notice is a "pleading" for purposes of § 2570.161(m) of this chapter.

(2) Except as provided in paragraph (h) of this section, a notice issued pursuant to paragraph (g)(1) of this section, indicating the Department's determination to assess a penalty, shall become a final order, within the meaning of § 2570.161(g) of this chapter, forty-five (45) days from the date of service of the notice.

(h) *Administrative hearing.* A notice issued pursuant to paragraph (g) of this section will not become a final order, within the meaning of § 2570.161(g) of this chapter, if, within thirty (30) days from the date of the service of the notice, the plan sponsor or a representative thereof files a request for a hearing under §§ 2570.160 through 2570.171 of this chapter, and files an answer to the notice. The request for hearing and answer must be filed in accordance with § 2570.162 of this chapter and § 18.4 of this title. The answer opposing the proposed sanction shall be in writing, and supported by reference to specific circumstances or facts surrounding the notice of determination issued pursuant to paragraph (g) of this section.

(i) *Service of notices and filing of statements.* (1) Service of a notice for purposes of paragraphs (c) and (g) of this section shall be made:

(i) By delivering a copy to the plan sponsor or representative thereof;

(ii) By leaving a copy at the principal office, place of business, or residence of the plan sponsor or representative thereof; or

(iii) By mailing a copy to the last known address of the plan sponsor or representative thereof.

(2) If service is accomplished by certified mail, service is complete upon mailing. If service is by regular mail, service is complete upon receipt by the addressee. When service of a notice under paragraph (c) or (g) of this section is by certified mail, five days shall be added to the time allowed by these rules for the filing of a statement or a request for hearing and answer, as applicable.

(3) For purposes of this section, a statement of reasonable cause shall be considered filed:

(i) Upon mailing, if accomplished using United States Postal Service certified mail or express mail;

(ii) Upon receipt by the delivery service, if accomplished using a "designated private delivery service" within the meaning of 26 U.S.C. 7502(f);

(iii) Upon transmittal, if transmitted in a manner specified in the notice of intent to assess a penalty as a method of transmittal to be accorded such special treatment; or

(iv) In the case of any other method of filing, upon receipt by the Department at the address provided in the notice of intent to assess a penalty.

(j) *Liability.* (1) If more than one person is responsible as plan sponsor for violations referred to in paragraph (a) of this section, all such persons shall be jointly and severally liable for such violations.

(2) Any person, or persons under paragraph (j)(1) of this section, against whom a civil penalty has been assessed under section 502(c)(8) of the Act, pursuant to a final order within the meaning of § 2570.161(g) of this chapter, shall be personally liable for the payment of such penalty.

(k) *Cross-reference.* See §§ 2570.160 through 2570.171 of this chapter for procedural rules relating to administrative hearings under section 502(c)(8) of the Act.

Regulations

The following regulation was adopted under "Title 29—Labor, Chapter XXV—Pension and Welfare Benefit Administration, Department of Labor, Subchapter G—Administration and Enforcement under the Employee Retirement Income Security Act of 1974, Part 2560—Rules and Regulations for Administration and Enforcement." The regulation was filed with the Federal Register on September 23, 1988 and published in the Federal Register of September 26, 1988 (53 FR 37474). The regulation is effective October 26, 1988.

[¶ 14,926]

§ 2560.502i-1 **Civil Penalties Under Section 502(i).**

(a) *In general.* Section 502(i) of the Employee Retirement Income Security Act of 1974 (ERISA or the Act) permits the Secretary of Labor to assess a civil penalty against a party in interest who engages in a prohibited transaction with respect to an employee benefit plan other than a plan described in section 4975(e)(1) of the Internal Revenue Code (the Code). The initial penalty under section 502(i) is five percent of the total "amount involved" in the prohibited transaction (unless a lesser amount is otherwise agreed to by the parties). However, if the prohibited transaction is not corrected during the "correction period," the civil penalty shall be 100 percent of the "amount involved" (unless a lesser amount is otherwise agreed to by the parties). Paragraph (b) of this section defines the term "amount involved," paragraph (c) defines the term "correction," and paragraph (d) defines the term "correction period." Paragraph (e) illustrates the computation of the civil penalty under section 502(i). Paragraph (f) is a cross reference to the Department's procedural rules for section 502(i) proceedings.

(b) *Amount involved.* Section 502(i) of ERISA states that the term "amount involved" in that section shall be defined as it is defined under section 4975(f)(4) of the Code. As provided in 26 CFR 141.4975.13, 26 CFR 53.4941(e)-1(b) is controlling with respect to the interpretation of the term "amount involved" under section 4975 of the Code. Accordingly, the Department of Labor will apply the principles set out at 26 CFR 53.4941(e)-1(b) in determining the "amount involved" in a transaction subject to the civil penalty provided by section 502(i) of the Act and this section.

(c) *Correction.* Section 502(i) of ERISA states that the term "correction" shall be defined in a manner that is consistent with the definition of that term under section 4975(f)(5) of the Code. As provided in 26 CFR 141.4975-13, 26 CFR 53.4941(e)-1(c) is controlling with respect to the interpretation of the term "correction" for purposes of section 4975 of the Code. Accordingly, the Department of Labor will apply the principles set out in 26 CFR 53.4941(e)-(1)(c) in interpreting the term "correction" under section 502(i) of the Act and this section.

(d) *Correction Period.* (1) In general, the "correction period" begins on the date the prohibited transaction occurs and ends 90 days after a final agency order with respect to such transaction.

(2) When a party in interest seeks judicial review within 90 days of a final agency order in an ERISA section 502(i) proceeding, the correction period will end 90 days after the entry of a final order in the judicial action.

(3) The following examples illustrate the operation of this paragraph:

(i) A party in interest receives notice of the Department's intent to impose the section 502(i) penalty and does not invoke the ERISA section 502(i) prohibited transaction penalty proceedings described in § 2570.1 of this chapter within 30 days of such notice. As provided in § 2570.5 of this chapter, the notice of the intent to impose a penalty becomes a final order after 30 days. Thus, the "correction period" ends 90 days after the expiration of the 30-day period.

(ii) A party in interest contests a proposed section 502(i) penalty, but does not appeal an adverse decision of the administrative law judge in the proceeding. As provided in § 2570.10(a) of this chapter, the decision of the administrative law judge becomes a final order of the Department unless the decision is appealed within 20 days after the date of such order. Thus, the correction period ends 90 days after the expiration of such 20-day period.

(iii) The Secretary of Labor issues to a party in interest a decision upholding an administrative law judge's adverse decision. As provided in § 2570.12(b) of this chapter, the decision of the Secretary becomes a final order of the Department immediately. Thus, the correction period will end 90 days after the issuance of the Secretary's order unless the party in interest judicially contests the order within that 90-day period. If the party in interest so contests the order, the correction period will end 90 days after the entry of a final order in the judicial action.

(e) *Computation of the Section 502(i) penalty.* (1) In general, the civil penalty under section 502(i) is determined by applying the applicable percentage (five percent or one hundred percent) to the aggregate amount involved in the transaction. However, a continuing prohibited transaction, such as a lease or a loan, is treated as giving rise to a separate event subject to the sanction for each year (as measured from the anniversary date of the transaction) in which the transaction occurs.

(2) The following examples illustrate the computation of the section 502(i) penalty:

(i) An employee benefit plan purchases property from a party in interest at a price of $10,000. The fair market value of the property is $5,000. The "amount involved" in that transaction, as determined under 26 CFR 53.4941(e)-1(b), is $10,000 (the greater of the amount paid by the plan or the fair market value of the property). The initial five percent penalty under section 502(i) is $500 (five percent of $10,000).

(ii) An employee benefit plan executes a four-year lease with a party in interest at an annual rental of $10,000 (which is the fair rental value of the property). The amount involved in each year of that transaction, as determined under 26 CFR 53.4941(e)-1(b), is $10,000. The amount of the initial sanction under ERISA section 502(i) would be a total of $5,000: $2,000 ($10,000 × 5% × 4 with respect to the rentals paid in the first year of the lease); $1,500 ($10,000 × 5% × 3 with respect to the second year); $1,000 ($10,000 × 5% × 2 with respect to the third year); $500 ($10,000 × 5% × 1 with respect to the fourth year).

(f) *Cross Reference.* See §§ 2570.1-2570.12 of this chapter for procedural rules relating to section 502(i) penalty proceedings.

Regulations

The following regulations were adopted under "Title 29—Labor," "Chapter XXV—Pension and Welfare Benefits Administration, Department of Labor," "Subchapter G—Administration and Enforcement Under the Employee Retirement Income Security Act of 1974," "Part 2570—Procedural Regulations Under the Employee Retirement Income Security Act." The regulations were filed with the *Federal Register* on September 23, 1988 and published in the *Federal Register* of September 26, 1988 (53 FR 37474). The regulations are effective October 26, 1988. Subpart C (Reg. §§ 2570.60-2570.71) was published in the *Federal Register* on June 26, 1989 (54 FR 26895). It is effective on July 26, 1989. Regulations § 2570.61 and § 2570.64 were revised by PWBA in 67 FR 64774 on October 21, 2002 and in 68 FR 3729 on January 24, 2003. Regulation § 2570.3 was amended on April 9, 2003 (68 FR 17506).

Subpart A—Procedures for the Assessment of Civil Sanctions Under ERISA Section 502(i)

[¶ 14,928]

§ 2570.1 **Scope of rules.**

The rules of practice set forth in this part are applicable to "prohibited transaction penalty proceedings" (as defined in § 2570.2(o) of this part) under section 502(i) of the Employee Retirement Income Security Act of 1974. The rules of procedure for administrative hearings published by the department's Office of Administrative Law Judges at Part 18 of this Title will apply to matters arising under ERISA section 502(i) except as modified by this section. These proceedings shall be conducted as expeditiously as possible, and the parties shall make every effort to avoid delay at each stage of the proceedings.

[¶ 14,928A]

§ 2570.2 **Definitions.**

For prohibited transaction penalty proceedings, this section shall apply in lieu of the definitions in § 18.2 of this title:

(a) "Adjudicatory proceeding" means a judicial-type proceeding leading to the formulation of a final order;

(b) "Administrative law judge" means an administrative law judge appointed pursuant to the provisions of 5 U.S.C. 3105;

(c) "Answer" is defined for these proceedings as set forth in § 18.5(d)(2) of this title;

(d) "Commencement of proceeding" is the filing of an answer by the respondent;

(e) "Consent agreement" means any written document containing a specified proposed remedy or other relief acceptable to the Department and consenting parties;

(f) "ERISA" means the Employee Retirement Income Security Act of 1974, as amended;

(g) "Final order" means the final decision or action of the Department of Labor concerning the assessment of a civil sanction under ERISA section 502(i) against a particular party. Such final order may result from a decision of an administrative law judge or the Secretary, or the failure of a party to invoke the procedures for hearings or appeals under this title. Such a final order shall constitute final agency action within the meaning of 5 U.S.C. 704;

(h) "Hearing" means that part of a proceeding which involves the submission of evidence, either by oral presentation or written submission, to the administrative law judge;

(i) "Notice" means any document, however designated, issued by the Department of Labor which initiates an adjudicatory proceeding under ERISA section 502(i);

(j) "Order" means the whole or any part of a final procedural or substantive disposition of a matter under ERISA section 502(i);

(k) "Party" includes a person or agency named or admitted as a party to a proceeding;

(l) "Person" includes an individual, partnership, corporation, employee benefit plan, association, exchange or other entity or organization;

(m) "Petition" means a written request, made by a person or party, for some affirmative action;

(n) "Pleading" means the notice, the answer to the notice, any supplement or amendment thereto, and any reply that may be permitted to any answer, supplement or amendment;

(o) "Prohibited transaction penalty proceeding" means a proceeding relating to the assessment of the civil penalty provided for in section 502(i) of ERISA;

(p) "Respondent" means the party against whom the Department is seeking to assess a civil sanction under ERISA section 502(i);

(q) "Secretary" means the Secretary of Labor and includes, pursuant to any delegation of authority by the Secretary, any assistant secretary (including the Assistant Secretary for Employee Benefits Security), administrator, commissioner, appellate body, board, or other official; [EBSA technical correction, 68 FR 16399 (April 3, 2003).]

(r) "Solicitor" means the Solicitor of Labor or his or her delegate.

[¶ 14,928A-1]

§ 2570.3 **Service: copies of documents and pleadings**.

For prohibited transaction penalty proceedings, this section shall apply in lieu of § 18.3 of this title.

(a) *General.* Copies of all documents shall be served on all parties of record. All documents should clearly designate the docket number, if any, and short title of all matters. All documents shall be delivered or mailed to the Chief Docket Clerk, Office of Administrative Law Judges, 800 K Street, NW., Suite 400, Washington, DC 20001-8002, or to the OALJ Regional Office to which the proceeding may have been transferred for hearing. Each document filed shall be clear and legible.

(b) *By parties.* All motions, petitions, pleadings, briefs or other documents shall be filed with the Office of Administrative Law Judges with a copy including any attachments to all other parties of record. When a party is represented by an attorney, service shall be made upon the attorney. Service of any document upon any party may be made by personal delivery or by mailing a copy to the last known address. The Department shall be served by delivery to the Associate Solicitor, Plan Benefits Security Division, ERISA Section 502(i) Proceeding, P.O. Box 1914, Washington, DC 20013. The person serving the document shall certify to the manner and date of service.

(c) *By the Office of Administrative Law Judges.* Service of orders, decisions and all other documents, except notices, shall be made by regular mail to the last known address.

(d) *Service of notices.* (1) Service of notices shall be made either:

(i) By delivering a copy to the individual, any partner, any officer of a corporation, or any attorney of record;

(ii) By leaving a copy at the principal office, place of business, or residence of such individual, partner, officer or attorney; or

(iii) By mailing a copy to the last known address of such individual, partner, officer or attorney.

(2) If service is accomplished by certified mail, service is complete upon mailing. If done by regular mail, service is complete upon receipt by the addressee.

(e) *Form of pleadings.* (1) Every pleading shall contain information indicating the name of the Employee Benefits Security Administration (EBSA) as the agency under which the proceeding is instituted, the title of the proceeding, the docket number (if any) assigned by the Office of Administrative Law Judges and a designation of the type of pleading or paper (e.g., notice, motion to dismiss, etc.). The pleading or paper shall be signed and shall contain the address and telephone number of the party or person representing the party. Although there are no formal specifications for documents, they should be typewritten when possible on standard size 8 ½ × 11 inch paper. [EBSA technical correction, 68 FR 16399 (April 3, 2003).]

(2) Illegible documents, whether handwritten, typewritten, photocopied, or otherwise, will not be accepted. Papers may be reproduced by any duplicating process provided all copies are clear and legible.

[¶ 14,928A-2]

§ 2570.4 **Parties**.

For prohibited transaction penalty proceedings, this section shall apply in lieu of § 18.10 of this title.

(a) The term "party" wherever used in these rules shall include any natural person, corporation, employee benefit plan, association, firm, partnership, trustee, receiver, agency, public or private organization, or government agency. A party against whom a civil sanction is sought shall be designated as "respondent." The Department shall be designated as "complainant."

(b) Other persons organizations shall be permitted to participate as parties only if the administrative law judge finds that the final decision could directly and adversely affect them or the class they represent, that they may contribute materially to the disposition of the proceedings and their interest is not adequately represented by existing parties, and that in the discretion of the administrative law judge the participation of such persons or organizations would be appropriate.

(c) A person or organization not named as a respondent wishing to participate as a party under this section shall submit a petition to the administrative law judge within fifteen (15) days after the person or organization has knowledge of or should have known about the proceeding. The petition shall be filed with the administrative law judge and served on each person or organization who has been made a party at the time of filing. Such petition shall concisely state:

(1) Petitioner's interest in the proceeding;

(2) How his or her participation as a party will contribute materially to the disposition of the proceeding;

(3) Who will appear for petitioner;

(4) The issues on which petitioner wishes to participate; and

(5) Whether petitioner intends to present witnesses.

(d) Objections to the petition may be filed by a party within fifteen (15) days of the filing of the petition. If objections to the petition are filed, the administrative law judge shall then determine whether petitioners have the requisite interest to be a party in the proceedings, as defined in paragraph (b) of this section, and shall permit or deny participation accordingly. Where petitions to participate as parties are made by individuals or groups with common interests, the administrative law judge may request all such petitioners to designate a single representative, or he or she may recognize one or more of such petitioners. The administrative law judge shall give each such petitioner as well as the parties, written notice of the decision on his or her petition. For each petition granted, the administrative law judge shall provide a brief statement of the basis of the decision. If the petition is denied, he or she shall briefly state the grounds for denial and shall then treat the petition as a request for participation as amicus curiae.

[¶ 14,928A-3]
§ 2570.5 **Consequences of default**.

For prohibited transaction penalty proceedings, this section shall apply in lieu of § 18.5(b) of this title. Failure of the respondent to file an answer within the 30 day time period provided in § 18.5 of this title shall be deemed to constitute a waiver of his right to appear and contest the allegations of the notice, and such failure shall be deemed to be an admission of the facts as alleged in the notice for purposes of the prohibited transaction penalty proceeding. Such notice shall then become the final order of the Secretary, except that the administrative law judge may set aside a default entered under this provision where there is proof of defective notice.

[¶ 14,928A-4]
§ 2570.6 **Consent order or settlement**.

For prohibited transaction penalty proceedings, the following shall apply in lieu of § 18.9 of this title.

(a) *General*. At any time after the commencement of a proceeding, but at least five (5) days prior to the date set for hearing, the parties jointly may move to defer the hearing for a reasonable time to permit negotiation of a settlement or an agreement containing findings and an order disposing of the whole or any part of the proceeding. The allowance of such deferment and the duration thereof shall be in the discretion of the administrative law judge, after consideration of such factors as the nature of the proceeding, the requirements of the public interest, the representations of the parties and the probability of reaching an agreement which will result in a just disposition of the issues involved.

(b) *Content*. Any agreement containing consent findings and an order disposing of a proceeding or any part thereof shall also provide:

(1) That the order shall have the same force and effect as an order made after full hearing;

(2) That the entire record on which any order may be based shall consist solely of the notice and the agreement;

(3) A waiver of any further procedural steps before the administrative law judge;

(4) A waiver of any right to challenge or contest the validity of the order and decision entered into in accordance with the agreement; and

(5) That the order and decision of the administrative law judge shall be final agency action.

(c) *Submission*. On or before the expiration of the time granted for negotiations, but, in any case, at least five (5) days prior to the date set for hearing, the parties or their authorized representative or their counsel may:

(1) Submit the proposed agreement containing consent findings and an order to the administrative law judge; or

(2) Notify the administrative law judge that the parties have reached a full settlement and have agreed to dismissal of the action subject to compliance with the terms of the settlement; or

(3) Inform the administrative law judge that agreement cannot be reached.

(d) *Disposition*. In the event a settlement containing consent findings and an order is submitted within the time allowed therefor, the administrative law judge shall issue a decision incorporating such findings and agreement within thirty (30) days of his receipt of such document. The decision of the administrative law judge shall incorporate all of the findings, terms, and conditions of the settlement agreement and consent order of the parties. Such decision shall become final agency action within the meaning of 5 U.S.C. 704.

(e) *Settlement without consent of all parties*. In cases in which some, but not all, of the parties to a proceeding submit a consent agreement to the administrative law judge, the following procedure shall apply:

(1) If all of the parties have not consented to the proposed settlement submitted to the administrative law judge, then such non-consenting parties must receive notice, and a copy, of the proposed settlement at the time it is submitted to the administrative law judge;

(2) Any non-consenting party shall have fifteen (15) days to file any objections to the proposed settlement with the administrative law judge and all other parties;

(3) If any party submits an objection to the proposed settlement, the administrative law judge shall decide within thirty (30) days after receipt of such objections whether he shall sign or reject the proposed settlement. Where the record lacks substantial evidence upon which to base a decision or there is a genuine issue of material fact, then the administrative law judge may establish procedures for the purpose of receiving additional evidence upon which a decision on the contested issues may reasonably be based;

(4) If there are no objections to the proposed settlement, or if the administrative law judge decides to sign the proposed settlement after reviewing any such objections, the administrative law judge shall incorporate the consent agreement into a decision meeting the requirements of paragraph (d) of this section.

[¶ 14,928A-5]
§ 2570.7 **Scope of discovery**.

For prohibited transaction penalty proceedings, this section shall apply in lieu of § 18.14 of this title.

(a) A party may file a motion to conduct discovery with the administrative law judge. The motion for discovery shall be granted by the administrative law judge only upon a showing of good cause. In order to establish "good cause" for the purposes this section, a party must show that the discovery requested relates to a genuine issue as to a material fact that is relevant to the proceeding. The order of the administrative law judge shall expressly limit the scope and terms of discovery to that for which "good cause" has been shown, as provided in this paragraph.

(b) A party may obtain discovery of documents and tangible things otherwise discoverable under paragraph (a) of this section and prepared in anticipation of or for the hearing by or for another party's representative (including his or her attorney, consultant, surety, indemnitor, insurer, or agent) only upon a showing that the party seeking discovery has substantial need of the materials or information in the preparation of his or her case and that he or she is unable without undue hardship to obtain the substantial equivalent of the materials or information by other means. In ordering discovery of such materials when the required showing has been made, the administrative law judge shall protect against disclosure of the mental impressions, conclusions, opinions, or legal theories of an attorney or other representative of a party concerning the proceeding.

[¶ 14,928A-6]
§ 2570.8 **Summary decision**.

For prohibited transaction penalty proceedings, this section shall apply in lieu of § 18.41 of this title.

(a) *No genuine issue of material fact*. (1) Where no genuine issue of a material fact is found to have been raised, the administrative law judge may issue a decision which, in the absence of an appeal pursuant to §§ 2570.10-2570.12 of this part, shall become a final order.

(2) A decision made under this paragraph shall include a statement of:

(i) Findings of fact and conclusions of law, and the reasons therefor, on all issues presented; and

(ii) Any terms and conditions of the rule or order.

(3) A copy of any decision under this paragraph shall be served on each party.

(b) *Hearings on issue of fact*. Where a genuine question of material fact is raised, the administrative law judge shall, and in any other case may, set the case for an evidentiary hearing.

[¶ 14,928A-7]

§ 2570.9 **Decision of the administrative law judge.**

For prohibited transaction penalty proceedings, this section shall apply in lieu of § 18.57 of this title

(a) *Proposed findings of fact, conclusions, and order.* Within twenty (20) days of the filing of the transcript of the testimony or such additional time as the administrative law judge may allow, each party may file with the administrative law judge, subject to the judge's discretion, proposed findings of fact, conclusions of law, and order together with a supporting brief expressing the reasons for such proposals. Such proposals and brief shall be served on all parties, and shall refer to all portions of the record and to all authorities relied upon in support of each proposal.

(b) *Decision of the administrative law judge.* Within a reasonable time after the time allowed for the filing of the proposed findings of fact, conclusions of law, and order, or within thirty (30) days after receipt of an agreement containing consent findings and order disposing of the disputed matter in whole, the administrative law judge shall make his or her decision. The decision of the administrative law judge shall include findings of fact and conclusions of law with reasons therefor upon each material issue of fact of law presented on the record. The decision of the administrative law judge shall be based upon the whole record. In a contested case in which the Department and the Respondent have presented their positions to the administrative law judge pursuant to the procedures for prohibited transaction penalty proceedings as set forth in this part, the penalty (if any) which may be included in the decision of the administrative law judge shall be limited to the sanction expressly provided for in section 502(i) of ERISA. It shall be supported by reliable and probative evidence. The decision of the administrative law judge shall become final agency action within the meaning of 5 U.S.C. 704 unless an appeal is made pursuant to the procedures set forth in §§ 2570.10-2570.12.

[¶ 14,928A-8]

§ 2570.10 **Review by the Secretary.**

(a) The Secretary may review a decision of an administrative law judge. Such a review may occur only when a party files a notice of appeal from a decision of an administrative law judge within twenty (20) days of the issuance of such decision. In all other cases, the decision of the administrative law judge shall become final agency action within the meaning of 5 U.S.C. 704.

(b) A notice of appeal to the Secretary shall state with specificity the issue(s) in the decision of the administrative law judge on which the party is seeking review. Such notice of appeal must be served on all parties of record.

(c) Upon receipt of a notice of appeal, the Secretary shall request the Chief Administrative Law Judge to submit to him a copy of the entire record before the administrative law judge.

[¶ 14,928A-9]

§ 2570.11 **Scope of review.**

The review of the Secretary shall not be a *de novo* proceeding but rather a review of the record established before the administrative law judge. There shall be no opportunity for oral argument.

[¶ 14,928A-10]

§ 2570.12 **Procedures for review by the Secretary.**

(a) Upon receipt of a notice of appeal, the Secretary shall establish a briefing schedule which shall be served on all parties of record. Upon motion of one or more of the parties, the Secretary may, in his discretion, permit the submission of reply briefs.

(b) The Secretary shall issue a decision as promptly as possible after receipt of the briefs of the parties. The Secretary may affirm, modify, or set aside, in whole or in part, the decision on appeal and shall issue a statement of reasons and bases for the action(s) taken. Such decision by the Secretary shall be final agency action within the meaning of 5 U.S.C. 704.

Subpart C—Procedures for the Assessment of Civil Penalties Under ERISA Section 502(c)(2)

[¶ 14,928B]

§ 2570.60 **Scope of rules.**

The rules of practice set forth in this subpart are applicable to "502(c)(2) civil penalty proceedings" (as defined in § 2570.61(n) of this subpart) under section 502(c)(2) of the Employee Retirement Income Security Act of 1974. The rules of procedure for administrative hearings published by the Department's Office of Law Judges at Part 18 of this Title will apply to matters arising under ERISA section 502(c)(2) except as modified by this section. These proceedings shall be conducted as expeditiously as possible, and the parties shall make every effort to avoid delay at each stage of the proceedings.

[¶ 14,928B-1]

§ 2570.61 **Definitions.**

For 502(c)(2) civil penalty proceedings, this section shall apply in lieu of the definitions in § 18.2 of this title:

(a) "Adjudicatory proceeding" means a judicial-type proceeding before an administrative law judge leading to the formulation of a final order;

(b) "Administrative law judge" means an administrative law judge appointed pursuant to the provisions of 5 U.S.C. 3105;

(c) Answer means a written statement that is supported by reference to specific circumstances or facts surrounding the notice of determination issued pursuant to Sec. 2560.502c-2(g) of this chapter. [Revised by PWBA in 67 FR 64774 on 10-21-02 and in 68 FR 3729 on 1-24-03.]

(d) "Commencement of proceeding" is the filing of an answer by the respondent;

(e) "Consent agreement" means any written document containing a specified proposed remedy or other relief acceptable to the Department and consenting parties;

(f) "ERISA" means the Employee Retirement Income Security Act of 1974, as amended;

(g) "Final Order" means the final decision or action of the Department of Labor concerning the assessment of a civil penalty under ERISA section 502(c)(2) against a particular party. Such final order may result from a decision of an administrative law judge or the Secretary, the failure of a party to file a statement of reasonable cause described in § 2560.502c-2(e) within the prescribed time limits, or the failure of a party to invoke the procedures for hearings or appeals under this title within the prescribed time limits. Such a final order shall constitute final agency action within the meaning of 5 U.S.C. 704;

(h) "Hearing" means that part of a proceeding which involves the submission of evidence, either by oral presentation or written submission, to the administrative law judge;

(i) "Order" means the whole or any part of a final procedural or substantive disposition of a matter under ERISA section 502(c)(2);

(j) "Party" includes a person or agency named or admitted as a party to a proceeding;

(k) "Person" includes an individual, partnership, corporation, employee benefit plan, association, exchange or other entity or organization;

(l) "Petition" means a written request, made by a person or party, for some affirmative action;

(m) "Pleading" means the notice as defined in § 2560.502c-2(g), the answer to the notice, any supplement or amendment thereto, and any reply that may be permitted to any answer, supplement or amendment;

(n) "502(c)(2) civil penalty proceeding" means an adjudicatory proceeding relating to the assessment of a civil penalty provided for in section 502(c)(2) of ERISA;

(o) "Respondent" means the party against whom the Department is seeking to assess a civil sanction under ERISA section 502(c)(2);

(p) "Secretary" means the Secretary of Labor and includes, pursuant to any delegation of authority by the Secretary, any assistant secretary (including the Assistant Secretary for Employee Benefits

Security), administrator, commissioner, appellate body, board, or other official; and [EBSA technical correction, 68 FR 16399 (April 3, 2003).]

(q) "Solicitor" means the Solicitor of Labor or his or her delegate.

[¶ 14,928B-2]

§ 2570.62 **Service: Copies of documents and pleadings.**

For 502(c)(2) penalty proceedings, this section shall apply in lieu of § 18.3 of this title.

(a) *General.* Copies of all documents shall be served on all parties of record. All documents should clearly designate the docket number, if any, and short title of all matters. All documents to be filed shall be delivered or mailed to the Chief Docket Clerk, Office of Administrative Law Judges, 800 K Street, N.W., Suite 400, Washington, DC 20001-8002, or to the OALJ Regional Office to which the proceeding may have been transferred for hearing. Each document filed shall be clear and legible. [Address changed by 56 FR 54708 on October 22, 1991.]

(b) *By parties.* All motions, petitions, pleadings, briefs, or other documents shall be filed with the Office of Administrative Law Judges with a copy, including any attachments, to all other parties of record. When a party is represented by an attorney, service shall be made upon the attorney. Service of any document upon any party may be made by personal delivery or by mailing a copy to the last known address. The Department shall be served by delivery to the Associate Solicitor, Plan Benefits Security Division, ERISA section 502(c)(2) Proceeding, P.O. Box 1914, Washington, DC 20013. The person serving the document shall certify to the manner and date of service.

(c) *By the Office of Administrative Law Judges.* Service of orders, decisions and all other documents shall be made by regular mail to the last known address.

(d) *Form of pleadings.* (1) Every pleading shall contain information indicating the name of the Employee Benefits Security Administration (EBSA) as the agency under which the proceeding is instituted, the title of the proceeding, the docket number (if any) assigned by the Office of Administrative Law Judges and a designation of the type of pleading or paper (e.g., notice, motion to dismiss, etc.). The pleading or paper shall be signed and shall contain the address and telephone number of the party or person representing the party. Although there are no formal specifications for documents, they should be typewritten when possible on standard size 8 ½ × 11 inch paper. [EBSA technical correction, 68 FR 16399 (April 3, 2003).]

(2) Illegible documents, whether handwritten, typewritten, photocopies, or otherwise, will not be accepted. Papers may be reproduced by any duplicating process provided all copies are clear and legible.

[¶ 14,928B-3]

§ 2570.63 **Parties, how designated.**

For 502(c)(2) civil penalty proceedings, this section shall apply in lieu of § 18.10 of this title.

(a) The term "party" wherever used in these rules shall include any natural person, corporation, employee benefit plan, association, firm, partnership, trustee, receiver, agency, public or private organization, or government agency. A party against whom a civil penalty is sought shall be designated as "respondent." The Department shall be designated as the "complainant."

(b) Other persons or organizations shall be permitted to participate as parties only if the administrative law judge finds that the final decision could directly and adversely affect them or the class they represent, that they may contribute materially to the disposition of the proceedings and their interest is not adequately represented by existing parties, and that in the discretion of the administrative law judge the participation of such persons or organizations would be appropriate.

(c) A person or organization not named as a respondent wishing to participate as a party under this section shall submit a petition to the administrative law judge within fifteen (15) days after the person or organization has knowledge of or should have known about the proceeding. The petition shall be filed with the administrative law judge and served on each person or organization who has been made a party at the time of filing. Such petition shall concisely state:

(1) Petitioner's interest in the proceeding;

(2) How his or her participation as a party will contribute materially to the disposition of the proceeding;

(3) Who will appear for petitioner;

(4) The issues on which petitioner wishes to participate; and

(5) Whether petitioner intends to present witnesses.

(d) Objections to the petition may be filed by a party within fifteen (15) days of the filing of the petition. If objections to the petition are filed, the administrative law judge shall then determine whether petitioners have the requisite interest to be a party in the proceedings, as defined in paragraph (b) of this section, and shall permit or deny participation accordingly. Where petitions to participate as parties are made by individuals or groups with common interests, the administrative law judge may request all such petitioners to designate a single representative, or he or she may recognize one or more of such petitioners. The administrative law judge shall give each such petitioner as well as the parties, written notice of the decision on his or her petition. For each petition granted, the administrative law judge shall provide a brief statement of the basis of the decision. If the petition is denied, he or she shall briefly state the grounds for denial and shall then treat the petition as a request for participation as amicus curiae.

[¶ 14,928B-4]

§ 2570.64 **Consequences of default.**

For 502(c)(2) civil penalty proceedings, this section shall apply in lieu of Sec. 18.5(a) and (b) of this title. Failure of the respondent to file an answer to the notice of determination described in Sec. 2560.502c-2(g) of this chapter within the 30-day period provided by Sec. 2560.502c-2(h) of this chapter shall be deemed to constitute a waiver of his or her right to appear and contest the allegations of the notice of determination, and such failure shall be deemed to be an admission of the facts as alleged in the notice for purposes of any proceeding involving the assessment of a civil penalty under section 502(c)(2) of the Act. Such notice shall then become the final order of the Secretary, within the meaning of Sec. 2570.61(g) of this subpart, forty-five (45) days from the date of service of the notice. [Revised by PWBA in 67 FR 64774 on 10-21-02 and in 68 FR 3729 on 1-24-03.]

[¶ 14,928B-5]

§ 2570.65 **Consent order or settlement.**

For 502(c)(2) civil penalty proceedings, the following shall apply in lieu of § 18.9 of this title.

(a) *General.* At any time after the commencement of a proceeding, but at least five (5) days prior to the date set for hearing, the parties jointly may move to defer the hearing for a reasonable time to permit negotiation of a settlement or an agreement containing findings and an order disposing of the whole or any part of the proceeding. The allowance of such and the duration thereof shall be in the discretion of the administrative law judge, after consideration of such factors as the nature of the proceeding, the requirements of the public interest, the representations of the parties and the probability of reaching an agreement which will result in a just disposition of the issues involved.

(b) *Content.* Any agreement containing consent findings and an order disposing of a proceeding or any part thereof shall also provide:

(1) That the order shall have the same force and effect as an order made after full hearing;

(2) That the entire record on which any order may be based shall consist solely of the notice and the agreement;

(3) A waiver of any further procedural steps before the administrative law judge;

(4) A waiver of any right to challenge or contest the validity of the order and decision entered into in accordance with the agreement; and

(5) That the order and decision of the administrative law judge shall be final agency action.

(c) *Submission.* On or before the expiration of the time granted for negotiations, but, in any case, at least five (5) days prior to the date set for hearing, the parties or their authorized representative or their counsel may:

(1) Submit the proposed agreement containing consent findings and an order to the administrative law judge; or

(2) Notify the administrative law judge that the parties have reached a full settlement and have agreed to dismissal of the action subject to compliance with the terms of the settlement; or

(3) Inform the administrative law judge that agreement cannot be reached.

(d) *Disposition.* In the event a settlement agreement containing consent findings and an order is submitted within the time allowed therefore, the administrative law judge shall issue a decision incorporating such findings and agreement within thirty (30) days of his receipt of such document. The decision of the administrative law judge shall incorporate all of the findings, terms, and conditions of the settlement agreement and consent order of the parties. Such decision shall become final agency action within the meaning of 5 U.S.C. 704.

(e) *Settlement without consent of all parties.* In cases in which some, but not all, of the parties to a proceeding submit a consent agreement to the administrative law judge, the following procedure shall apply:

(1) If all of the parties have not consented to the proposed settlement submitted to the administrative law judge, then such non-consenting parties must receive notice, and a copy, of the proposed settlement at the time it is submitted to the administrative law judge;

(2) Any non-consenting party shall have fifteen (15) days to file any objections to the proposed settlement with the administrative law judge and all other parties;

(3) If any party submits an objection to the proposed settlement, the administrative law judge shall decide within thirty (30) days after receipt of such objections whether he shall sign or reject the proposed settlement. Where the record lacks substantial evidence upon which to base a decision or there is a genuine issue of material fact, then the administrative law judge may establish procedures for the purpose of receiving additional evidence upon which a decision on the contested issues may reasonably be based;

(4) If there are no objections to the proposed settlement, or if the administrative law judge decides to sign the proposed settlement after reviewing any such objections, the administrative law judge shall incorporate the consent agreement into a decision meeting the requirements of paragraph (d) of this section.

[¶ 14,928B-6]

§ 2570.66 **Scope of discovery**.

For 502(c)(2) civil penalty proceedings, this section shall apply in lieu of § 18.14 of this title.

(a) A party may file a motion to conduct discovery with the administrative law judge. The motion for discovery shall be granted by the administrative law judge only upon a showing of good cause. In order to establish "good cause" for the purposes of this section, a party must show that the discovery requested relates to a genuine issue as to a material fact that is relevant to the proceeding. The order of the administrative law judge shall expressly limit the scope and terms of discovery to that for which "good cause" has been shown, as provided in this paragraph.

(b) A party may obtain discovery of documents and tangible things otherwise discoverable under paragraph (a) of this section and prepared in anticipation of or for the hearing by or for another party's representative (including his or her attorney, consultant, surety, indemnitor, insurer, or agent) only upon showing that the party seeking discovery has substantial need of the materials or information in the preparation of his or her case and that he or she is unable without undue hardship to obtain the substantial equivalent of the materials or information by other means. In ordering discovery of such materials when the required showing has been made, the administrative law judge shall protect against disclosure of the mental impressions, conclusions, opinions, or legal theories of an attorney or other representatives of a party concerning the proceeding.

[¶ 14,928B-7]

§ 2570.67 **Summary decision**.

For 502(c)(2) civil penalty proceedings, this section shall apply in lieu of § 18.41 of this title.

(a) *No genuine issue of material of fact.* (1) Where no issue of a material of fact is found to have been raised, the administrative law judge may issue a decision which, in the absence of an appeal pursuant to §§ 2570.69 through 71 of this subpart, shall become a final order.

(2) A decision made under this paragraph shall include a statement of:

(i) Findings of fact and conclusions of law, and the reasons therefor, on all issues presented; and

(ii) Any terms and conditions of the rule or order.

(3) A copy of any decision under this paragraph shall be served on each party.

(b) *Hearings on issues of fact.* Where a genuine question of material of fact is raised, the administrative law judge shall, and in any other case may, set the case for an evidentiary hearing.

[¶ 14,928B-8]

§ 2570.68 **Decision of the administrative law judge**.

For 502(c)(2) civil penalty proceedings, this section shall apply in lieu of § 18.57 of this title.

(a) *Proposed findings of fact, conclusions, and order.* Within twenty (20) days of the filing of the transcript of the testimony of such additional time as the administrative law judge may allow, each party may file with the administrative law judge, subject to the judge's discretion, proposed findings of fact, conclusions of law, and order together with a supporting brief expressing the reasons for such proposals. Such proposals and briefs shall be served on all parties, and shall refer to all portions of the record and to all authorities relied upon in support of each proposal.

(b) *Decision of the administrative law judge.* Within a reasonable time after the time allowed for the filing of the proposed findings of fact, conclusions of law, and order, or within thirty (30) days after receipt of an agreement containing consent findings and order disposing of the disputed matter in whole, the administrative law judge shall make his or her decision. The decision of the administrative law judge shall include findings of fact and conclusions of law with reasons therefor upon each material issue of fact or law presented on the record. The decision of the administrative law judge shall be based upon the whole record. In a contested case in which the Department and the Respondent have presented their positions to the administrative law judge pursuant to the procedures for 502(c)(2) civil penalty proceedings as set forth in this subpart, the penalty (if any) which may be included in the decision of the administrative law judge shall be limited to the penalty expressly provided for in section 502(c)(2) of ERISA. It shall be supported by reliable and probative evidence. The decision of the administrative law judge shall become final agency action within the meaning of 5 U.S.C. 704 unless an appeal is made pursuant to the procedures set forth in §§ 2570.69 through 2570.71.

[¶ 14,928B-9]

§ 2570.69 **Review by the Secretary**.

(a) The Secretary may review a decision of an administrative law judge. Such a review may occur only when a party files a notice of appeal from a decision of an administrative law judge within twenty (20) days of the issuance of such decision. In all other cases, the decision of the administrative law judge shall become final agency action within the meaning of 5 U.S.C. 704.

(b) A notice of appeal to the Secretary shall state with specificity the issue(s) in the decision of the administrative law judge on which the party is seeking review. Such notice of appeal must be served on all parties of record.

(c) Upon receipt of a notice of appeal, the Secretary shall request the Chief Administrative Law Judge to submit to him or her a copy of the entire record before the administrative law judge.

[¶ 14,928B-10]

§ 2570.70 **Scope of review**.

The review of the Secretary shall not be *de novo* proceeding but rather a review of the record established before the administrative law judge. There shall be no opportunity for oral argument.

[¶ 14,928B-11]

§ 2570.71 **Procedures for review by the Secretary**.

(a) Upon receipt of the notice of appeal, the Secretary shall establish a briefing schedule which shall be served on all parties of record.

Upon motion of one or more of the parties, the Secretary may, in his or her discretion, permit the submission of reply briefs.

(b) The Secretary shall issue a decision as promptly as possible after receipt of the briefs of the parties. The Secretary may affirm, modify, or set aside, in whole or in part, the decision on appeal and shall issue a statement of reasons and bases for the action(s) taken. Such decision by the Secretary shall be final agency action within the meaning of 5 U.S.C. 704.

[Subpart C was added on June 26, 1989 (54 FR 26895).]

Interim Regulations

The following interim regulations were adopted under "Title 29—Labor," "Chapter XXV—Pension and Welfare Benefits Administration, Department of Labor," "Subchapter G—Administration and Enforcement Under the Employee Retirement Income Security Act of 1974," and "Part 2570—Procedural Regulations Under the Employee Retirement Income Security Act." The regulations were published in the *Federal Register* on June 20, 1990 (55 FR 25284). The regulations were effective June 20, 1990. Regulations § 2570.94 and § 2570.114 were revised by PWBA in 67 FR 64774 on October 21, 2002. Regulation 2570.82 was amended by EBSA in 68 FR 16399 on April 3, 2003.

Subpart D—Procedure for the Assessment of Civil Penalties Under ERISA Section 502(l)

[¶ 14,928C]

§ 2570.80 **Scope of rules**.

The rules of practice set forth in this subpart are applicable to "502(l) civil penalty proceedings" (as defined in § 2570.82 of this subpart) under section 502(l) of the Employee Retirement Income Security Act of 1974 (ERISA or the Act). Refer to 29 CFR 2560.5021 for the definition of the relevant terms of ERISA section 502(l).

[¶ 14,928D]

§ 2570.81 **In general**.

Section 502(l) of the Employee Retirement Income Security Act of 1974 (ERISA or the Act) requires the Secretary of Labor to assess a civil penalty against a fiduciary who breaches a fiduciary responsibility under, or commits any other violation of part 4 of Title I of ERISA or any other person who knowingly participates in such breach or violation. The penalty under section 502(l) is equal to 20 percent of the "applicable recovery amount" paid pursuant to any settlement agreement with the Secretary or ordered by a court to be paid in a judicial proceeding instituted by the Secretary under section 502(a)(2) or (a)(5). The Secretary may, in the Secretary's sole discretion, waive or reduce the penalty if the Secretary determines in writing that:

(a) The fiduciary or other person acted reasonably and in good faith, or

(b) It is reasonable to expect that the fiduciary or other person will not be able to restore all losses to the plan or any participant or beneficiary of such plan without severe financial hardship unless such waiver or reduction is granted.

The penalty imposed on a fiduciary or other person with respect to any transaction shall be reduced by the amount of any penalty or tax imposed on such fiduciary or other person with respect to such transaction under section 502(i) or section 4975 of the Internal Revenue Code of 1986 (the Code).

[¶ 14,928E]

§ 2570.82 **Definitions**.

For purposes of this section:

(a) *502(l) civil penalty proceedings* means an adjudicatory proceeding relating to the assessment of a civil penalty provided in section 502(l) of ERISA:

(b) *Notice of assessment* means any document, however designated, issued by the Secretary which contains a specified assessment, in monetary terms, of a civil penalty under ERISA section 502(l). A "notice of assessment" will contain a brief factual description of the violation for which the assessment is being made, the identity of the person being assessed, and the amount of the assessment and the basis for assessing that particular person that particular penalty amount;

(c) *Person* includes an individual, partnership, corporation, employee benefit plan, association, exchange or other entity or organization;

(d) *Petition* means a written request, made by a person, for a waiver or reduction of the civil penalty described herein; and

(e) *Secretary* means the Secretary of Labor and includes, pursuant to any delegation of authority by the Secretary, the Assistant Secretary for Pension and Welfare Benefits, Regional Directors for Employee Benefits Security, or Deputy Area Directors for Pension and Welfare Benefits. [Amended by EBSA, 68 FR 16399, April 3, 2003.]

[¶ 14,928F]

§ 2570.83 **Assessment of civil penalty**.

(a) Except as described in § § 2570.85 and 2570.86 below, subsequent to the payment of the applicable recovery amount pursuant to either a settlement agreement or a court order, the Secretary shall serve on the person liable for making such payment a notice of assessment of civil penalty equal to 20 percent of the applicable recovery amount.

(b) Service of such notice shall be made either:

(1) By delivering a copy to the person being assessed; if the person is an individual, to the individual; if the person is a partnership, to any partner; if the person is a corporation, association, exchange, or other entity or organization, to any officer of such entity; of the person is an employee benefit plan, to a trustee of such plan; or to any attorney representing any such person;

(2) By leaving a copy at the principal office, place of business, or residence of such individual, partner, officer, trustee, or attorney; or

(3) By mailing a copy to the last known address of such individual, partner, officer, trustee, or attorney.

If service is accomplished by certified mail, service is complete upon mailing. If done by regular mail, service is complete upon receipt by the addressee.

[¶ 14,928G]

§ 2570.84 **Payment of civil penalty**.

(a) The civil penalty must be paid within 60 days of service of the notice of assessment.

(b) At any time prior to the expiration of the payment period for the assessed penalty, any person who has committed, or knowingly participated in, a breach or violation, or has been alleged by the Secretary to have so committed or participated, may submit a written request for a conference with the Secretary to discuss the calculation of the assessed penalty. A person will be entitled under this section to one such conference per assessment. If such written request is submitted during the 60 day payment period described in subparagraph (a), such a request will not toll the running of that payment period.

(c) The notice of assessment will become a final order (within the meaning of 5 U.S.C. 704) on the first day following the 60 day payment period, subject to any tolling caused by a petition to waive or reduce described in paragraph 2570.85.

[¶ 14,928H]

§ 2570.85 **Waiver or reduction of civil penalty**.

(a) At any time prior to the expiration of the payment period for the assessed penalty, any person who has committed, or knowingly participated in, a breach or violation, or has been alleged by the Secretary to have so committed or participated, may petition the Secretary to waive or reduce the penalty under this section on the basis that:

(1) The person acted reasonably and in good faith in engaging in the breach or violation; or

(2) The person will not be able to restore all losses to the plan or participant or beneficiary of such plan without severe financial hardship unless such waiver or reduction is granted.

(b) All petitions for waiver or reduction shall be in writing and contain the following information:

(1) The name of the petitioner(s);

(2) A detailed description of the breach or violation which is the subject of the penalty;

(3) A detailed recitation of the facts which support one, or both, of the bases for waiver or reduction described in §2570.85(a) of this part, accompanied by underlying documentation supporting such factual allegations;

(4) A declaration, signed and dated by the petitioner(s), in the following form: Under penalty of perjury, I declare that, to the best of my knowledge and belief, the representations made in this petition are true and correct.

(c) If a petition for waiver or reduction is submitted during the 60 day payment period described in §2570.84(a) above, the payment period for the penalty in question will be tolled pending Departmental consideration of the petition. During such consideration, the applicant is entitled to one conference with the Secretary, but the Secretary, in his or her sole discretion, may schedule or hold additional conferences with the petitioner concerning the factual allegations contained in the petition.

(d) Based solely on his or her discretion, the Secretary will determine whether to grant such a waiver or reduction. Pursuant to the procedure described in §2570.83(b), the petitioner will be served with a written determination informing him or her of the Secretary's decision. Such written determination shall briefly state the grounds for the Secretary's decision, and shall be final and non-reviewable. In the case of a determination not to waive, the payment period for the penalty in question, if previously initiated, will resume as of the date of service of the Secretary's written determination.

[¶ 14,928I]

§2570.86 **Reduction of Penalty by Other Penalty Assessments**.

The penalty assessed on a person pursuant to this section with respect to any transaction shall be reduced by the amount of any penalty or tax imposed on such person with respect to such transaction under ERISA section 502(i) and section 4975 of the Code. Prior to a reduction of penalty under this paragraph, the person being assessed must provide proof to the Department of the payment of the penalty or tax and the amount of that payment.

Submissions of proof of other penalty or tax assessments will not toll the 60 day payment period, if previously initiated.

[¶ 14,928J]

§2570.87 **Revision of assessment**.

If, based on the procedures described in §§2570.84, 2570.85, or 2570.86, the assessed penalty amount is revised, the person being assessed will receive a revised notice of assessment and will be obligated to pay the revised assessed penalty within the relevant 60 day payment period (as determined by the applicable procedure in §§2570.84, 2570.85, or 2570.86), and, if necessary, any excess penalty payment will be refunded as soon as administratively feasible. The revised notice of assessment will revoke any previously issued notice of assessment with regard to the transaction in question and will become a final order (within the meaning of 5 U.S.C. 704) the later of the first day following the 60 day payment period or the date of its service on the person being assessed, pursuant to the service procedures described in §2570.83(b).

[¶ 14,928K]

§2570.88 **Effective Date**.

This section is effective June 20, 1990 and shall apply to assessments under section 502(l) made by the Secretary after June 20, 1990 based on any breach or violation occurring on or after December 19, 1989.

Regulations

The following regulations were adopted under "Title 29—Labor," "Chapter XXV—Pension and Welfare Benefits Administration, Department of Labor," "Subchapter G—Administration and Enforcement Under the Employee Retirement Income Security Act of 1974," "Part 2570—Procedural Regulations Under the Employee Retirement Income Security Act." The interim regulations were filed with the *Federal Register* on February 11, 2000 (65 FR 7185). The regulations are effective April 11, 2000. Regulation §2570.94 was revised by the PWBA on January 24, 2003 (68 FR 3729). They were amended and revised on April 9, 2003 (68 FR 17506).

Subpart E—Procedures for the Assessment of Civil Penalties Under ERISA Section 502(c)(5)

[¶ 14,928M]

§2570.90 **Scope of rules**.

The rules of practice set forth in this subpart are applicable to "502(c)(5) civil penalty proceedings" (as defined in 2570.91(n)) under section 502(c)(5) of the Employee Retirement Income Security Act of 1974. The rules of procedure for administrative hearings published by the Department's Office of Administrative Law Judges in subpart A of 29 CFR part 18 will apply to matters arising under ERISA section 502(c)(5) except as described by this section. These proceedings shall be conducted as expeditiously as possible, and the parties shall make every effort to avoid delay at each stage of the proceedings.

[¶ 14,928M-1]

§2570.91 **Definitions**.

For 502(c)(5) civil penalty proceedings, this section shall apply in lieu of the definitions in §18.2 of this title.

(a) *Adjudicatory proceeding* means a judicial-type proceeding before an administrative law judge leading to the formulation of a final order;

(b) *Administrative law judge* means an administrative law judge appointed pursuant to the provisions of 5 U.S.C. 3105;

(c) *Answer* means a written statement that is supported by reference to specific circumstances or facts surrounding the notice of determination issued pursuant to 29 CFR 2560.502c-5(g);

(d) *Commencement of proceeding* is the filing of an answer by the respondent;

(e) *Consent agreement* means any written document containing a specified proposed remedy or other relief acceptable to the Department and consenting parties;

(f) *ERISA* means the Employee Retirement Income Security Act of 1974, as amended;

(g) *Final order* means the final decision or action of the Department of Labor concerning the assessment of a civil penalty under ERISA section 502(c)(5) against a particular party. Such final order may result from a decision of an administrative law judge or the Secretary, the failure of a party to file a statement of reasonable cause described in 29 CFR 2560.502c-5(e) within the prescribed time limits, or the failure of a party to invoke the procedures for hearings or appeals under this title within the prescribed time limits. Such a final order shall constitute final agency action within the meaning of 5 U.S.C. 704;

(h) *Hearing* means that part of a proceeding which involves the submission of evidence, either by oral presentation or written submission, to the administrative law judge;

(i) *Order* means the whole or any part of a final procedural or substantive disposition of a matter under ERISA section 502(c)(5);

(j) *Party* includes a person or agency named or admitted as a party to a proceeding;

(k) *Person* includes an individual, partnership, corporation, employee benefit plan, association, exchange, or other entity or organization;

(l) *Petition* means a written request, made by a person or party, for some affirmative action;

(m) *Pleading* means the notice as defined in 29 CFR 2560.502c-5(g), the answer to the notice, any supplement or amendment thereto, and any reply that may be permitted to any answer, supplement or amendment;

(n) *502(c)(5) civil penalty proceeding* means an adjudicatory proceeding relating to the assessment of a civil penalty provided for in section 502(c)(5) of ERISA;

(o) *Respondent* means the party against whom the Department is seeking to assess a civil sanction under ERISA section 502(c)(5);

(p) *Secretary* means the Secretary of Labor and includes, pursuant to any delegation of authority by the Secretary, any assistant secretary (including the Assistant Secretary for Employee Benefits Security), administrator, commissioner, appellate body, board, or other official of the Department of Labor; and

(q) *Solicitor* means the Solicitor of Labor or his or her delegate.

[¶ 14,928M-2]

§2570.92 **Service: Copies of documents and pleadings**.

For 502(c)(5) penalty proceedings, this section shall apply in lieu of 29 CFR 18.3.

(a) *In general*. Copies of all documents shall be served on all parties of record. All documents should clearly designate the docket number, if any, and short title of all matters. All documents to be filed shall be delivered or mailed to the Chief Docket Clerk, Office of Administrative Law Judges (OALJ), 800 K Street, NW., Suite 400, Washington, DC 20001-8002, or to the OALJ Regional Office to which the proceeding may have been transferred for hearing. Each document filed shall be clear and legible.

(b) *By parties*. All motions, petitions, pleadings, briefs, or other documents shall be filed with the Office of Administrative Law Judges with a copy, including any attachments, to all other parties of record. When a party is represented by an attorney, service shall be made upon the attorney. Service of any document upon any party may be made by personal delivery or by mailing a copy to the last known address. The Department shall be served by delivery to the Associate Solicitor, Plan Benefits Security Division, ERISA Section 502(c)(5) Proceeding, P.O. Box 1914, Washington, DC 20013. The person serving the document shall certify to the manner and date of service.

(c) *By the Office of Administrative Law Judges*. Service of orders, decisions and all other documents shall be made by regular mail to the last known address.

(d) *Form of pleadings*—

(1) Every pleading shall contain information indicating the name of the Employee Benefits Security Administration (EBSA) as the agency under which the proceeding is instituted, the title of the proceeding, the docket number (if any) assigned by the Office of Administrative Law Judges and a designation of the type of pleading or paper (e.g., notice, motion to dismiss, etc.). The pleading or paper shall be signed and shall contain the address and telephone number of the party or person representing the party. Although there are no formal specifications for documents, they should be typewritten when possible on standard size 8 1/2 × 11 inch paper.

(2) Illegible documents, whether handwritten, typewritten, photocopies, or otherwise, will not be accepted. Papers may be reproduced by any duplicating process provided all copies are clear and legible.

[¶ 14,928M-3]

§2570.93 **Parties, how designated**.

For 502(c)(5) civil penalty proceedings, this section shall apply in lieu of 29 CFR 18.10.

(a) The term party wherever used in this subpart shall include any natural person, corporation, employee benefit plan, association, firm, partnership, trustee, receiver, agency, public or private organization, or government agency. A party against whom a civil penalty is sought shall be designated as "respondent." The Department shall be designated as the "complainant."

(b) Other persons or organizations shall be permitted to participate as parties only if the administrative law judge finds that the final decision could directly and adversely affect them or the class they represent, that they may contribute materially to the disposition of the proceedings and their interest is not adequately represented by existing parties, and that in the discretion of the administrative law judge the participation of such persons or organizations would be appropriate.

(c) A person or organization not named as a respondent wishing to participate as a party under this section shall submit a petition to the administrative law judge within fifteen (15) days after the person or organization has knowledge of or should have known about the proceeding. The petition shall be filed with the administrative law judge and served on each person or organization who has been made a party at the time of filing. Such petition shall concisely state:

(1) Petitioner's interest in the proceeding;

(2) How his or her participation as a party will contribute materially to the disposition of the proceeding;

(3) Who will appear for petitioner;

(4) The issues on which petitioner wishes to participate; and

(5) Whether petitioner intends to present witnesses.

(d) Objections to the petition may be filed by a party within fifteen (15) days of the filing of the petition. If objections to the petition are filed, the administrative law judge shall then determine whether petitioners have the requisite interest to be a party in the proceedings, as defined in paragraph (b) of this section, and shall permit or deny participation accordingly. Where petitions to participate as parties are made by individuals or groups with common interests, the administrative law judge may request all such petitioners to designate a single representative, or he or she may recognize one or more of such petitioners. The administrative law judge shall give each such petitioner as well as the parties, written notice of the decision on his or her petition. For each petition granted, the administrative law judge shall provide a brief statement of the basis of the decision. If the petition is denied, he or she shall briefly state the grounds for denial and shall then treat the petition as a request for participation as amicus curiae.

[¶ 14,928M-4]

§2570.94 **Consequences of default**.

For 502(c)(5) civil penalty proceedings, this section shall apply in lieu of 29 CFR 18.5(a) and (b). Failure of the respondent to file an answer to the notice of determination described in 29 CFR 2560.502c-5(g) within the 30 day period provided by 29 CFR 2560.502c-5(h) shall be deemed to constitute a waiver of his or her right to appear and contest the allegations of the notice of determination, and such failure shall be deemed to be an admission of the facts as alleged in the notice for purposes of any proceeding involving the assessment of a civil penalty under section 502(c)(5) of the Act. Such notice shall then become a final order of the Secretary, within the meaning of §2570.91(g), forty-five (45) days from the date of the service of the notice.

[¶ 14,928M-5]

§2570.95 **Consent order or settlement**.

For 502(c)(5) civil penalty proceedings, the following shall apply in lieu of 29 CFR 18.9.

(a) *In general*. At any time after the commencement of a proceeding, but at least five (5) days prior to the date set for hearing, the parties jointly may move to defer the hearing for a reasonable time to permit negotiation of a settlement or an agreement containing findings and an order disposing of the whole or any part of the proceeding. The allowance of such deferment and the duration thereof shall be in the discretion of the administrative law judge, after consideration of such factors as the nature of the proceeding, the requirements of the public interest, the representations of the parties and the probability of reaching an agreement which will result in a just disposition of the issues involved.

(b) *Content*. Any agreement containing consent findings and an order disposing of a proceeding or any part thereof shall also provide:

(1) That the order shall have the same force and effect as an order made after full hearing;

(2) That the entire record on which any order may be based shall consist solely of the notice and the agreement;

(3) A waiver of any further procedural steps before the administrative law judge;

(4) A waiver of any right to challenge or contest the validity of the order and decision entered into in accordance with the agreement; and

(5) That the order and decision of the administrative law judge shall be final agency action.

(c) *Submission.* On or before the expiration of the time granted for negotiations, but, in any case, at least five (5) days prior to the date set for hearing, the parties or their authorized representative or their counsel may:

(1) Submit the proposed agreement containing consent findings and an order to the administrative law judge;

(2) Notify the administrative law judge that the parties have reached a full settlement and have agreed to dismissal of the action subject to compliance with the terms of the settlement; or

(3) Inform the administrative law judge that agreement cannot be reached.

(d) *Disposition.* In the event that a settlement agreement containing consent findings and an order is submitted within the time allowed therefor, the administrative law judge shall issue a decision incorporating such findings and agreement within thirty (30) days of receipt of such document. The decision of the administrative law judge shall incorporate all of the findings, terms, and conditions of the settlement agreement and consent order of the parties. Such decision shall become a final agency action within the meaning of 5 U.S.C. 704.

(e) *Settlement without consent of all parties.* In cases in which some, but not all, of the parties to a proceeding submit a consent agreement to the administrative law judge, the following procedure shall apply:

(1) If all of the parties have not consented to the proposed settlement submitted to the administrative law judge, then such non-consenting parties must receive notice, and a copy, of the proposed settlement at the time it is submitted to the administrative law judge;

(2) Any non-consenting party shall have fifteen (15) days to file any objections to the proposed settlement with the administrative law judge and all other parties;

(3) If any party submits an objection to the proposed settlement, the administrative law judge shall decide within thirty (30) days after receipt of such objections whether to sign or reject the proposed settlement. Where the record lacks substantial evidence upon which to base a decision or there is a genuine issue of material fact, then the administrative law judge may establish procedures for the purpose of receiving additional evidence upon which a decision on the contested issues may reasonably be based;

(4) If there are no objections to the proposed settlement, or if the administrative law judge decides to sign the proposed settlement after reviewing any such objections, the administrative law judge shall incorporate the consent agreement into a decision meeting the requirements of paragraph (d) of this section.

[¶ 14,928M-6]

§ 2570.96 **Scope of discovery**.

For 502(c)(5) civil penalty proceedings, this section shall apply in lieu of 29 CFR 18.14.

(a) A party may file a motion to conduct discovery with the administrative law judge. The motion for discovery shall be granted by the administrative law judge only upon a showing of good cause. In order to establish "good cause" for the purposes of this section, a party must show that the discovery requested relates to a genuine issue as to a material fact that is relevant to the proceeding. The order of the administrative law judge shall expressly limit the scope and terms of discovery to that for which "good cause" has been shown, as provided in this paragraph.

(b) A party may obtain discovery of documents and tangible things otherwise discoverable under paragraph (a) of this section and prepared in anticipation of or for the hearing by or for another party's representative (including his or her attorney, consultant, surety, indemnitor, insurer, or agent) only upon showing that the party seeking discovery has substantial need of the materials or information in the preparation of his or her case and that he or she is unable without undue hardship to obtain the substantial equivalent of the materials or information by other means. In ordering discovery of such materials when the required showing has been made, the administrative law judge shall protect against disclosure of the mental impressions, conclusions, opinions, or legal theories of an attorney or other representative of a party concerning the proceeding.

[¶ 14,928M-7]

§ 2570.97 **Summary decision**.

For 502(c)(5) civil penalty proceedings, this section shall apply in lieu of 29 CFR 18.41.

(a) *No genuine issue of material fact.*

(1) Where no issue of material fact is found to have been raised, the administrative law judge may issue a decision which, in the absence of an appeal pursuant to §§ 2570.99 through 2570.101, shall become a final order.

(2) A decision made under this paragraph shall include a statement of:

(i) Findings of fact and conclusions of law, and the reasons therefore, on all issues presented; and

(ii) Any terms and conditions of the rule or order.

(3) A copy of any decision under this paragraph shall be served on each party.

(b) *Hearings on issues of fact.* Where a genuine question of material fact is raised, the administrative law judge shall, and in any other case may, set the case for an evidentiary hearing.

[¶ 14,928M-8]

§ 2570.98 **Decision of the administrative law judge**.

For 502(c)(5) civil penalty proceedings, this section shall apply in lieu of 29 CFR 18.57.

(a) *Proposed findings of fact, conclusions, and order.* Within twenty (20) days of the filing of the transcript of the testimony or such additional time as the administrative law judge may allow, each party may file with the administrative law judge, subject to the judge's discretion, proposed findings of fact, conclusions of law, and an order together with a supporting brief expressing the reasons for such proposals. Such proposals and briefs shall be served on all parties, and shall refer to all portions of the record and to all authorities relied upon in support of each proposal.

(b) *Decision of the administrative law judge.* Within a reasonable time after the time allowed for the filing of the proposed findings of fact, conclusions of law, and order, or within thirty (30) days after receipt of an agreement containing consent findings and an order disposing of the disputed matter in whole, the administrative law judge shall make his or her decision. The decision of the administrative law judge shall include findings of fact and conclusions of law with reasons therefor upon each material issue of fact or law presented on the record. The decision of the administrative law judge shall be based upon the whole record. In a contested case in which the Department and the Respondent have presented their positions to the administrative law judge pursuant to the procedures for 502(c)(5) civil penalty proceedings as set forth in this subpart, the penalty (if any) which may be included in the decision of the administrative law judge shall be limited to the penalty expressly provided for in section 502(c)(5) of ERISA. It shall be supported by reliable and probative evidence. The decision of the administrative law judge shall become a final agency action within the meaning of 5 U.S.C. 704 unless an appeal is made pursuant to the procedures set forth in §§ 2570.99 through 2570.101.

[¶ 14,928M-9]

§ 2570.99 **Review by the Secretary**.

(a) The Secretary may review a decision of an administrative law judge. Such a review may occur only when a party files a notice of appeal from a decision of an administrative law judge within twenty (20) days of the issuance of such decision. In all other cases, the decision of the administrative law judge shall become final agency action within the meaning of 5 U.S.C. 704.

(b) A notice of appeal to the Secretary shall state with specificity the issue(s) in the decision of the administrative law judge on which the party is seeking review. Such notice of appeal must be served on all parties of record.

(c) Upon receipt of a notice of appeal, the Secretary shall request the Chief Administrative Law Judge to submit to him or her a copy of the entire record before the administrative law judge.

[¶ 14,928M-10]

§ 2570.100 **Scope of review**.

The review of the Secretary shall not be a de novo proceeding but rather a review of the record established before the administrative law judge. There shall be no opportunity for oral argument.

[¶ 14,928M-11]

§ 2570.101 **Procedures for review by the Secretary**.

(a) Upon receipt of the notice of appeal, the Secretary shall establish a briefing schedule which shall be served on all parties of record. Upon motion of one or more of the parties, the Secretary may, in his or her discretion, permit the submission of reply briefs.

(b) The Secretary shall issue a decision as promptly as possible after receipt of the briefs of the parties. The Secretary may affirm, modify, or set aside, in whole or in part, the decision on appeal and shall issue a statement of reasons and bases for the action(s) taken. Such decision by the Secretary shall be final agency action within the meaning of 5 U.S.C. 704.

Regulations

The following regulations were adopted under "Title 29—Labor," "Chapter XXV—Pension and Welfare Benefits Administration, Department of Labor," "Subchapter—Administration and Enforcement Under the Employee Retirement Income Security Act of 1974," Part 2570—Procedural Regulations Under the Employee Retirement Income Security Act." The regulation was filed with the *Federal Register* on January 4, 2002 and published in the *Federal Register* on January 7, 2002 (67 FR 777). The regulation is effective March 8, 2002. Reg. § 2570.114 was revised by EBSA on January 24, 2003 (68 FR 3729).

Subpart F—Procedures for the Assessment of Civil Penalties Under ERISA Section 502(c)(6)

[¶ 14,928Q]

§ 2570.110 **Scope of rules**.

The rules of practice set forth in this subpart are applicable to "502(c)(6) civil penalty proceedings" (as defined in § 2570.111(n) of this subpart) under section 502(c)(6) of the Employee Retirement Income Security Act of 1974. The rules of procedure for administrative hearings published by the Department's Office of Law Judges at Part 18 of this title will apply to matters arising under ERISA section 502(c)(6) except as modified by this section. These proceedings shall be conducted as expeditiously as possible, and the parties shall make every effort to avoid delay at each stage of the proceedings.

[¶ 14,928R]

§ 2570.111 **Definitions**.

For section 502(c)(6) civil penalty proceedings, this section shall apply in lieu of the definitions in § 18.2 of this title:

(a) *Adjudicatory proceeding* means a judicial-type proceeding before an administrative law judge leading to the formulation of a final order;

(b) *Administrative law judge* means an administrative law judge appointed pursuant to the provisions of 5 U.S.C. 3105;

(c) *Answer* means a written statement that is supported by reference to specific circumstances or facts surrounding the notice of determination issued pursuant to § 2560.502c-6(g) of this chapter;

(d) *Commencement of proceeding* is the filing of an answer by the respondent;

(e) *Consent agreement* means any written document containing a specified proposed remedy or other relief acceptable to the Department and consenting parties;

(f) *ERISA* means the Employee Retirement Income Security Act of 1974, as amended;

(g) *Final order* means the final decision or action of the Department of Labor concerning the assessment of a civil penalty under ERISA section 502(c)(6) against a particular party. Such final order may result from a decision of an administrative law judge or the Secretary, the failure of a party to file a statement of matters reasonably beyond the control of the plan administrator described in § 2560.502c-6(e) of this chapter within the prescribed time limits, or the failure of a party to invoke the procedures for hearings or appeals under this title within the prescribed time limits. Such a final order shall constitute final agency action within the meaning of 5 U.S.C. 704;

(h) *Hearing* means that part of a proceeding which involves the submission of evidence, either by oral presentation or written submission, to the administrative law judge;

(i) *Order* means the whole or any part of a final procedural or substantive disposition of a matter under ERISA section 502(c)(6);

(j) *Party* includes a person or agency named or admitted as a party to a proceeding;

(k) *Person* includes an individual, partnership, corporation, employee benefit plan, association, exchange or other entity or organization;

(l) *Petition* means a written request, made by a person or party, for some affirmative action;

(m) *Pleading* means the notice as defined in § 2560.502c-6(g) of this chapter, the answer to the notice, any supplement or amendment thereto, and any reply that may be permitted to any answer, supplement or amendment;

(n) *502(c)(6) civil penalty proceeding* means an adjudicatory proceeding relating to the assessment of a civil penalty provided for in section 502(c)(6) of ERISA;

(o) *Respondent* means the party against whom the Department is seeking to assess a civil sanction under ERISA section 502(c)(6);

(p) *Secretary* means the Secretary of Labor and includes, pursuant to any delegation of authority by the Secretary, any assistant secretary (including the Assistant Secretary for Employee Benefits Security), administrator, commissioner, appellate body, board, or other official; and [EBSA technical correction, 68 FR 16399 (April 3, 2003).]

(q) *Solicitor* means the Solicitor of Labor or his or her delegate.

[¶ 14,928S]

§ 2570.112 **Service: Copies of documents and pleadings**.

For 502(c)(6) penalty proceedings, this section shall apply in lieu of § 18.3 of this title.

(a) *General*. Copies of all documents shall be served on all parties of record. All documents should clearly designate the docket number, if any, and short title of all matters. All documents to be filed shall be delivered or mailed to the Chief Docket Clerk, Office of Administrative Law Judges, 800 K Street, NW., Suite 400, Washington, DC 20001-8002, or to the OALJ Regional Office to which the proceeding may have been transferred for hearing. Each document filed shall be clear and legible.

(b) *By parties*. All motions, petitions, pleadings, briefs, or other documents shall be filed with the Office of Administrative Law Judges with a copy, including any attachments, to all other parties of record. When a party is represented by an attorney, service shall be made upon the attorney. Service of any document upon any party may be made by personal delivery or by mailing a copy to the last known address. The Department shall be served by delivery to the Associate Solicitor, Plan Benefits Security Division, ERISA section 502(c)(6) Proceeding, P.O. Box 1914, Washington, DC 20013. The person serving the document shall certify to the manner and date of service.

(c) *By the Office of Administrative Law Judges*. Service of orders, decisions and all other documents shall be made by regular mail to the last known address.

(d) *Form of pleadings*.

(1) Every pleading shall contain information indicating the name of the Employee Benefits Security Administration (EBSA) as the agency under which the proceeding is instituted, the title of the proceeding, the docket number (if any) assigned by the Office of Adminis-

trative Law Judges and a designation of the type of pleading or paper (e.g., notice, motion to dismiss, etc.). The pleading or paper shall be signed and shall contain the address and telephone number of the party or person representing the party. Although there are no formal specifications for documents, they should be typewritten when possible on standard size 8 1/2 x 11 inch paper. [EBSA technical correction, 68 FR 16399 (April 3, 2003).]

(2) Illegible documents, whether handwritten, typewritten, photocopied, or otherwise, will not be accepted. Papers may be reproduced by any duplicating process provided all copies are clear and legible.

[¶ 14,928T]
§ 2570.113 Parties, how designated.

For 502(c)(6) civil penalty proceedings, this section shall apply in lieu of § 18.10 of this title.

(a) The term "party" wherever used in this subpart shall include any natural person, corporation, employee benefit plan, association, firm, partnership, trustee, receiver, agency, public or private organization, or government agency. A party against whom a civil penalty is sought shall be designated as "respondent". The Department shall be designated as the "complainant".

(b) Other persons or organizations shall be permitted to participate as parties only if the administrative law judge finds that the final decision could directly and adversely affect them or the class they represent, that they may contribute materially to the disposition of the proceedings and their interest is not adequately represented by existing parties, and that in the discretion of the administrative law judge the participation of such persons or organizations would be appropriate.

(c) A person or organization not named as a respondent wishing to participate as a party under this section shall submit a petition to the administrative law judge within fifteen (15) days after the person or organization has knowledge of or should have known about the proceeding. The petition shall be filed with the administrative law judge and served on each person or organization who has been made a party at the time of filing. Such petition shall concisely state:

(1) Petitioner's interest in the proceeding;

(2) How his or her participation as a party will contribute materially to the disposition of the proceeding;

(3) Who will appear for petitioner;

(4) The issues on which petitioner wishes to participate; and

(5) Whether petitioner intends to present witnesses.

(d) Objections to the petition may be filed by a party within fifteen (15) days of the filing of the petition. If objections to the petition are filed, the administrative law judge shall then determine whether petitioner has the requisite interest to be a party in the proceedings, as defined in paragraph (b) of this section, and shall permit or deny participation accordingly. Where petitions to participate as parties are made by individuals or groups with common interests, the administrative law judge may request all such petitioners to designate a single representative, or he or she may recognize one or more of such petitioners. The administrative law judge shall give each such petitioner, as well as the parties, written notice of the decision on his or her petition. For each petition granted, the administrative law judge shall provide a brief statement of the basis of the decision. If the petition is denied, he or she shall briefly state the grounds for denial and shall then treat the petition as a request for participation as amicus curiae.

[¶ 14,928U]
§ 2570.114 Consequences of default.

For 502(c)(6) civil penalty proceedings, this section shall apply in lieu of § 18.5 (a) and (b) of this title. Failure of the respondent to file an answer to the notice of determination described in § 2560.502c-6(g) of this chapter within the 30-day period provided by § 2560.502c-6(h) of this chapter shall be deemed to constitute a waiver of his or her right to appear and contest the allegations of the notice of determination, and such failure shall be deemed to be an admission of the facts as alleged in the notice for purposes of any proceeding involving the assessment of a civil penalty under section 502(c)(6) of the Act. Such notice shall then become the final order of the Secretary, within the meaning of Sec. 2570.111(g) of this subpart, forty-five (45) days from the date of

service of the notice. [Revised by PWBA in 67 FR 64774 on 10-21-02 and in 68 FR 3729 on 1-24-03.]

[¶ 14,928V]
§ 2570.115 Consent order or settlement.

For 502(c)(6) civil penalty proceedings, the following shall apply in lieu of § 18.9 of this title.

(a) *General.* At any time after the commencement of a proceeding, but at least five (5) days prior to the date set for hearing, the parties jointly may move to defer the hearing for a reasonable time to permit negotiation of a settlement or an agreement containing findings and an order disposing of the whole or any part of the proceeding. The allowance of such a deferral and the duration thereof shall be in the discretion of the administrative law judge, after consideration of such factors as the nature of the proceeding, the requirements of the public interest, the representations of the parties, and the probability of reaching an agreement which will result in a just disposition of the issues involved.

(b) *Content.* Any agreement containing consent findings and an order disposing of a proceeding or any part thereof shall also provide:

(1) That the order shall have the same force and effect as an order made after full hearing;

(2) That the entire record on which any order may be based shall consist solely of the notice and the agreement;

(3) A waiver of any further procedural steps before the administrative law judge;

(4) A waiver of any right to challenge or contest the validity of the order and decision entered into in accordance with the agreement; and

(5) That the order and decision of the administrative law judge shall be final agency action.

(c) *Submission.* On or before the expiration of the time granted for negotiations, but, in any case, at least five (5) days prior to the date set for hearing, the parties or their authorized representative or their counsel may:

(1) Submit the proposed agreement containing consent findings and an order to the administrative law judge; or

(2) Notify the administrative law judge that the parties have reached a full settlement and have agreed to dismissal of the action subject to compliance with the terms of the settlement; or

(3) Inform the administrative law judge that agreement cannot be reached.

(d) *Disposition.* In the event a settlement agreement containing consent findings and an order is submitted within the time allowed therefor, the administrative law judge shall issue a decision incorporating such findings and agreement within 30 days of his receipt of such document. The decision of the administrative law judge shall incorporate all of the findings, terms, and conditions of the settlement agreement and consent order of the parties. Such decision shall become final agency action within the meaning of 5 U.S.C. 704.

(e) *Settlement without consent of all parties.* In cases in which some, but not all, of the parties to a proceeding submit a consent agreement to the administrative law judge, the following procedure shall apply:

(1) If all of the parties have not consented to the proposed settlement submitted to the administrative law judge, then such nonconsenting parties must receive notice, and a copy, of the proposed settlement at the time it is submitted to the administrative law judge;

(2) Any non-consenting party shall have fifteen (15) days to file any objections to the proposed settlement with the administrative law judge and all other parties;

(3) If any party submits an objection to the proposed settlement, the administrative law judge shall decide within 30 days after receipt of such objections whether he shall sign or reject the proposed settlement. Where the record lacks substantial evidence upon which to base a decision or there is a genuine issue of material fact, then the administrative law judge may establish procedures for the purpose of

receiving additional evidence upon which a decision on the contested issues may reasonably be based;

(4) If there are no objections to the proposed settlement, or if the administrative law judge decides to sign the proposed settlement after reviewing any such objections, the administrative law judge shall incorporate the consent agreement into a decision meeting the requirements of paragraph (d) of this section.

[¶ 14,928W]

§ 2570.116 **Scope of discovery**.

For 502(c)(6) civil penalty proceedings, this section shall apply in lieu of § 18.14 of this title.

(a) A party may file a motion to conduct discovery with the administrative law judge. The motion for discovery shall be granted by the administrative law judge only upon a showing of good cause. In order to establish "good cause" for the purposes of this section, a party must show that the discovery requested relates to a genuine issue as to a material fact that is relevant to the proceeding. The order of the administrative law judge shall expressly limit the scope and terms of discovery to that for which "good cause" has been shown, as provided in this paragraph.

(b) A party may obtain discovery of documents and tangible things otherwise discoverable under paragraph (a) of this section and prepared in anticipation of or for the hearing by or for another party's representative (including his or her attorney, consultant, surety, indemnitor, insurer, or agent) only upon showing that the party seeking discovery has substantial need of the materials or information in the preparation of his or her case and that he or she is unable without undue hardship to obtain the substantial equivalent of the materials or information by other means. In ordering discovery of such materials when the required showing has been made, the administrative law judge shall protect against disclosure of the mental impressions, conclusions, opinions, or legal theories of an attorney or other representatives of a party concerning the proceeding.

[¶ 14,928X]

§ 2570.117 **Summary decision**.

For 502(c)(6) civil penalty proceedings, this section shall apply in lieu of § 18.41 of this title.

(a) *No genuine issue of material fact*.

(1) Where no issue of a material fact is found to have been raised, the administrative law judge may issue a decision which, in the absence of an appeal pursuant to §§ 2570.119 through 2570.121 of this subpart, shall become a final order.

(2) A decision made under this paragraph (a) shall include a statement of:

(i) Findings of fact and conclusions of law, and the reasons therefor, on all issues presented; and

(ii) Any terms and conditions of the rule or order.

(3) A copy of any decision under this paragraph shall be served on each party.

(b) *Hearings on issues of fact*. Where a genuine question of a material fact is raised, the administrative law judge shall, and in any other case may, set the case for an evidentiary hearing.

[¶ 14,928Y]

§ 2570.118 **Decision of the administrative law judge**.

For 502(c)(6) civil penalty proceedings, this section shall apply in lieu of § 18.57 of this title.

(a) *Proposed findings of fact, conclusions, and order*. Within twenty (20) days of the filing of the transcript of the testimony, or such additional time as the administrative law judge may allow, each party may file with the administrative law judge, subject to the judge's discretion, proposed findings of fact, conclusions of law, and order together with a supporting brief expressing the reasons for such proposals. Such proposals and briefs shall be served on all parties, and shall refer to all portions of the record and to all authorities relied upon in support of each proposal.

(b) *Decision of the administrative law judge*. Within a reasonable time after the time allowed for the filing of the proposed findings of fact, conclusions of law, and order, or within 30 days after receipt of an agreement containing consent findings and order disposing of the disputed matter in whole, the administrative law judge shall make his or her decision. The decision of the administrative law judge shall include findings of fact and conclusions of law with reasons therefor upon each material issue of fact or law presented on the record. The decision of the administrative law judge shall be based upon the whole record. In a contested case in which the Department and the Respondent have presented their positions to the administrative law judge pursuant to the procedures for 502(c)(6) civil penalty proceedings as set forth in this subpart, the penalty (if any) which may be included in the decision of the administrative law judge shall be limited to the penalty expressly provided for in section 502(c)(6) of ERISA. It shall be supported by reliable and probative evidence. The decision of the administrative law judge shall become final agency action within the meaning of 5 U.S.C. 704 unless an appeal is made pursuant to the procedures set forth in §§ 2570.119 through 2570.121.

[¶ 14,928Z]

§ 2570.119 **Review by the Secretary**.

(a) The Secretary may review a decision of an administrative law judge. Such a review may occur only when a party files a notice of appeal from a decision of an administrative law judge within twenty (20) days of the issuance of such decision. In all other cases, the decision of the administrative law judge shall become final agency action within the meaning of 5 U.S.C. 704.

(b) A notice of appeal to the Secretary shall state with specificity the issue(s) in the decision of the administrative law judge on which the party is seeking review. Such notice of appeal must be served on all parties of record.

(c) Upon receipt of a notice of appeal, the Secretary shall request the Chief Administrative Law Judge to submit to him or her a copy of the entire record before the administrative law judge.

[¶ 14,928Z-1]

§ 2570.120 **Scope of review**.

The review of the Secretary shall not be a de novo proceeding but rather a review of the record established before the administrative law judge. There shall be no opportunity for oral argument.

[¶ 14,928Z-2]

§ 2570.121 **Procedures for review by the Secretary**.

(a) Upon receipt of the notice of appeal, the Secretary shall establish a briefing schedule which shall be served on all parties of record. Upon motion of one or more of the parties, the Secretary may, in his or her discretion, permit the submission of reply briefs.

(b) The Secretary shall issue a decision as promptly as possible after receipt of the briefs of the parties. The Secretary may affirm, modify, or set aside, in whole or in part, the decision on appeal and shall issue a statement of reasons and bases for the action(s) taken. Such decision by the Secretary shall be final agency action within the meaning of 5 U.S.C. 704.

Regulations

The following regulations regarding inflationary adjustments to ERISA civil monetary penalties were published in the *Federal Register* on October 21, 2002 (67 FR 64774) and revised by the PWBA on January 24, 2003 (68 FR 3729).

¶14,928W   Reg. § 2570.115(e)(4)

Subpart G—Procedures for the Assessment of Civil Penalties Under ERISA Section 502(c)(7)

[¶ 14,928MM]

§ 2570.130 **Scope of rules.** The rules of practice set forth in this subpart are applicable to "502(c)(7) civil penalty proceedings" (as defined in Sec. 2570.131(n) of this subpart) under section 502(c)(7) of the Employee Retirement Income Security Act of 1974, as amended (the Act). The rules of procedure for administrative hearings published by the Department's Office of Administrative Law Judges at Part 18 of this title will apply to matters arising under ERISA section 502(c)(7) except as modified by this subpart. These proceedings shall be conducted as expeditiously as possible, and the parties shall make every effort to avoid delay at each stage of the proceedings. [Revised by PWBA in 67 FR 64774 on 10-21-02 and in 68 FR 3729 on 1-24-03.]

[¶ 14,928NN]

§ 2570.131 **Definitions.** For 502(c)(7) civil penalty proceedings, this section shall apply in lieu of the definitions in Sec. 18.2 of this title:

(a) *Adjudicatory proceeding* means a judicial-type proceeding before an administrative law judge leading to the formulation of a final order;

(b) *Administrative law judge* means an administrative law judge appointed pursuant to the provisions of 5 U.S.C. 3105;

(c) *Answer* means a written statement that is supported by reference to specific circumstances or facts surrounding the notice of determination issued pursuant to Sec. 2560.502c-7(g) of this chapter;

(d) *Commencement of proceeding* is the filing of an answer by the respondent;

(e) *Consent agreement* means any written document containing a specified proposed remedy or other relief acceptable to the Department and consenting parties;

(f) *ERISA* means the Employee Retirement Income Security Act of 1974, as amended;

(g) *Final order* means the final decision or action of the Department of Labor concerning the assessment of a civil penalty under ERISA section 502(c)(7) against a particular party. Such final order may result from a decision of an administrative law judge or the Secretary, the failure of a party to file a statement of reasonable cause described in Sec. 2560.502c-7(e) of this chapter within the prescribed time limits, or the failure of a party to invoke the procedures for hearings or appeals under this title within the prescribed time limits. Such a final order shall constitute final agency action within the meaning of 5 U.S.C. 704;

(h) *Hearing* means that part of a proceeding which involves the submission of evidence, by either oral presentation or written submission, to the administrative law judge;

(i) *Order* means the whole or any part of a final procedural or substantive disposition of a matter under ERISA section 502(c)(7);

(j) *Party* includes a person or agency named or admitted as a party to a proceeding;

(k) *Person* includes an individual, partnership, corporation, employee benefit plan, association, exchange or other entity or organization;

(l) *Petition* means a written request, made by a person or party, for some affirmative action;

(m) *Pleading* means the notice as defined in Sec. 2560.502c-7(g) of this chapter, the answer to the notice, any supplement or amendment thereto, and any reply that may be permitted to any answer, supplement or amendment;

(n) *502(c)(7) civil penalty proceeding* means an adjudicatory proceeding relating to the assessment of a civil penalty provided for in section 502(c)(7) of ERISA;

(o) *Respondent* means the party against whom the Department is seeking to assess a civil sanction under ERISA section 502(c)(7);

(p) *Secretary* means the Secretary of Labor and includes, pursuant to any delegation of authority by the Secretary, any assistant secretary (including the Assistant Secretary for Employee Benefits Security), administrator, commissioner, appellate body, board, or other official; and [EBSA technical correction, 68 FR 16399 (April 3, 2003).]

(q) *Solicitor* means the Solicitor of Labor or his or her delegate. [Revised by PWBA in 67 FR 64774 on 10-21-02 and in 68 FR 3729 on 1-24-03.]

[¶ 14,928OO]

§ 2570.132 **Service: Copies of documents and pleadings.** For 502(c)(7) penalty proceedings, this section shall apply in lieu of Sec. 18.3 of this title.

(a) *General.* Copies of all documents shall be served on all parties of record. All documents should clearly designate the docket number, if any, and short title of all matters. All documents to be filed shall be delivered or mailed to the Chief Docket Clerk, Office of Administrative Law Judges, 800 K Street, NW, Suite 400, Washington, DC 20001-8002, or to the OALJ Regional Office to which the proceeding may have been transferred for hearing. Each document filed shall be clear and legible.

(b) *By parties.* All motions, petitions, pleadings, briefs, or other documents shall be filed with the Office of Administrative Law Judges with a copy, including any attachments, to all other parties of record. When a party is represented by an attorney, service shall be made upon the attorney. Service of any document upon any party may be made by personal delivery or by mailing a copy to the last known address. The Department shall be served by delivery to the Associate Solicitor, Plan Benefits Security Division, ERISA section 502(c)(7) Proceeding, P.O. Box 1914, Washington, DC 20013. The person serving the document shall certify to the manner and date of service.

(c) *By the Office of Administrative Law Judges.* Service of orders, decisions and all other documents shall be made by regular mail to the last known address.

(d) *Form of pleadings.* (1) Every pleading shall contain information indicating the name of the Employee Benefits Security Administration (EBSA) as the agency under which the proceeding is instituted, the title of the proceeding, the docket number (if any) assigned by the Office of Administrative Law Judges and a designation of the type of pleading or paper (e.g., notice, motion to dismiss, etc.). The pleading or paper shall be signed and shall contain the address and telephone number of the party or person representing the party. Although there are no formal specifications for documents, they should be typewritten when possible on standard size 8 1/2 x 11 inch paper. [EBSA technical correction, 68 FR 16399 (April 3, 2003).]

(2) Illegible documents, whether handwritten, typewritten, photocopied, or otherwise, will not be accepted. Papers may be reproduced by any duplicating process provided all copies are clear and legible. [Revised by PWBA in 67 FR 64774 on 10-21-02 and in 68 FR 3729 on 1-24-03.]

[¶ 14,928PP]

§ 2570.133 **Parties, how designated.** For 502(c)(7) civil penalty proceedings, this section shall apply in lieu of Sec. 18.10 of this title.

(a) The term "party" wherever used in this subpart shall include any natural person, corporation, employee benefit plan, association, firm, partnership, trustee, receiver, agency, public or private organization, or government agency. A party against whom a civil penalty is sought shall be designated as "respondent." The Department shall be designated as the "complainant."

(b) Other persons or organizations shall be permitted to participate as parties only if the administrative law judge finds that the final decision could directly and adversely affect them or the class they represent, that they may contribute materially to the disposition of the proceedings and their interest is not adequately represented by existing parties, and that in the discretion of the administrative law judge the participation of such persons or organizations would be appropriate.

(c) A person or organization not named as a respondent wishing to participate as a party under this section shall submit a petition to the administrative law judge within fifteen (15) days after the person or organization has knowledge of or should have known about the proceeding. The petition shall be filed with the administrative law judge and served on each person who or organization that has been made a party at the time of filing. Such petition shall concisely state:

(1) Petitioner's interest in the proceeding;

(2) How his or her participation as a party will contribute materially to the disposition of the proceeding;

(3) Who will appear for petitioner;

(4) The issues on which petitioner wishes to participate; and

(5) Whether petitioner intends to present witnesses.

(d) Objections to the petition may be filed by a party within fifteen (15) days of the filing of the petition. If objections to the petition are filed, the administrative law judge shall then determine whether petitioner has the requisite interest to be a party in the proceedings, as defined in paragraph (b) of this section, and shall permit or deny participation accordingly. Where petitions to participate as parties are made by individuals or groups with common interests, the administrative law judge may request all such petitioners to designate a single representative, or he or she may recognize one or more of such petitioners. The administrative law judge shall give each such petitioner, as well as the parties, written notice of the decision on his or her petition. For each petition granted, the administrative law judge shall provide a brief statement of the basis of the decision. If the petition is denied, he or she shall briefly state the grounds for denial and shall then treat the petition as a request for participation as amicus curiae. [Revised by PWBA in 67 FR 64774 on 10-21-02 and in 68 FR 3729 on 1-24-03.]

[¶ 14,928QQ]

§ 2570.134 **Consequences of default**. For 502(c)(7) civil penalty proceedings, this section shall apply in lieu of Sec. 18.5 (a) and (b) of this title. Failure of the respondent to file an answer to the notice of determination described in Sec. 2560.502c-7(g) of this chapter within the 30 day period provided by Sec. 2560.502c-7(h) of this chapter shall be deemed to constitute a waiver of his or her right to appear and contest the allegations of the notice of determination, and such failure shall be deemed to be an admission of the facts as alleged in the notice for purposes of any proceeding involving the assessment of a civil penalty under section 502(c)(7) of the Act. Such notice shall then become the final order of the Secretary, within the meaning of Sec. 2570.131(g) of this subpart, forty-five (45) days from the date of service of the notice. [Revised by PWBA in 67 FR 64774 on 10-21-02 and in 68 FR 3729 on 1-24-03.]

[¶ 14,928RR]

§ 2570.135 **Consent order or settlement**. For 502(c)(7) civil penalty proceedings, the following shall apply in lieu of Sec. 18.9 of this title.

(a) *General*. At any time after the commencement of a proceeding, but at least five (5) days prior to the date set for hearing, the parties jointly may move to defer the hearing for a reasonable time to permit negotiation of a settlement or an agreement containing findings and an order disposing of the whole or any part of the proceeding. The allowance of such a deferral and the duration thereof shall be in the discretion of the administrative law judge, after consideration of such factors as the nature of the proceeding, the requirements of the public interest, the representations of the parties, and the probability of reaching an agreement which will result in a just disposition of the issues involved.

(b) *Content*. Any agreement containing consent findings and an order disposing of a proceeding or any part thereof shall also provide:

(1) That the order shall have the same force and effect as an order made after full hearing;

(2) That the entire record on which any order may be based shall consist solely of the notice and the agreement;

(3) A waiver of any further procedural steps before the administrative law judge;

(4) A waiver of any right to challenge or contest the validity of the order and decision entered into in accordance with the agreement; and

(5) That the order and decision of the administrative law judge shall be final agency action.

(c) *Submission*. On or before the expiration of the time granted for negotiations, but, in any case, at least five (5) days prior to the date set

for hearing, the parties or their authorized representative or their counsel may:

(1) Submit the proposed agreement containing consent findings and an order to the administrative law judge; or

(2) Notify the administrative law judge that the parties have reached a full settlement and have agreed to dismissal of the action subject to compliance with the terms of the settlement; or

(3) Inform the administrative law judge that agreement cannot be reached.

(d) *Disposition*. In the event a settlement agreement containing consent findings and an order is submitted within the time allowed therefor, the administrative law judge shall issue a decision incorporating such findings and agreement within 30 days of his receipt of such document. The decision of the administrative law judge shall incorporate all of the findings, terms, and conditions of the settlement agreement and consent order of the parties. Such decision shall become final agency action within the meaning of 5 U.S.C. 704.

(e) *Settlement without consent of all parties*. In cases in which some, but not all, of the parties to a proceeding submit a consent agreement to the administrative law judge, the following procedure shall apply:

(1) If all of the parties have not consented to the proposed settlement submitted to the administrative law judge, then such nonconsenting parties must receive notice, and a copy, of the proposed settlement at the time it is submitted to the administrative law judge;

(2) Any non-consenting party shall have fifteen (15) days to file any objections to the proposed settlement with the administrative law judge and all other parties;

(3) If any party submits an objection to the proposed settlement, the administrative law judge shall decide within 30 days after receipt of such objections whether he shall sign or reject the proposed settlement. Where the record lacks substantial evidence upon which to base a decision or there is a genuine issue of material fact, then the administrative law judge may establish procedures for the purpose of receiving additional evidence upon which a decision on the contested issues may reasonably be based;

(4) If there are no objections to the proposed settlement, or if the administrative law judge decides to sign the proposed settlement after reviewing any such objections, the administrative law judge shall incorporate the consent agreement into a decision meeting the requirements of paragraph (d) of this section. [Revised by PWBA in 67 FR 64774 on 10-21-02 and in 68 FR 3729 on 1-24-03.]

[¶ 14,928SS]

§ 2570.136 **Scope of discovery**. For 502(c)(7) civil penalty proceedings, this section shall apply in lieu of Sec. 18.14 of this title.

(a) A party may file a motion to conduct discovery with the administrative law judge. The motion for discovery shall be granted by the administrative law judge only upon a showing of good cause. In order to establish "good cause" for the purposes of this section, a party must show that the discovery requested relates to a genuine issue as to a material fact that is relevant to the proceeding. The order of the administrative law judge shall expressly limit the scope and terms of discovery to that for which "good cause" has been shown, as provided in this paragraph.

(b) A party may obtain discovery of documents and tangible things otherwise discoverable under paragraph (a) of this section and prepared in anticipation of or for the hearing by or for another party's representative (including his or her attorney, consultant, surety, indemnitor, insurer, or agent) only upon showing that the party seeking discovery has substantial need of the materials or information in the preparation of his or her case and that he or she is unable without undue hardship to obtain the substantial equivalent of the materials or information by other means. In ordering discovery of such materials when the required showing has been made, the administrative law judge shall protect against disclosure of the mental impressions, conclusions, opinions, or legal theories of an attorney or other representatives of a party concerning the proceeding. [Revised by PWBA in 67 FR 64774 on 10-21-02 and in 68 FR 3729 on 1-24-03.]

[¶ 14,928TT]

§ 2570.137 **Summary decision**. For 502(c)(7) civil penalty proceedings, this section shall apply in lieu of Sec. 18.41 of this title.

(a) *No genuine issue of material fact.* (1) Where no issue of a material fact is found to have been raised, the administrative law judge may issue a decision which, in the absence of an appeal pursuant to Sec. Sec. 2570.139 through 2570.141 of this subpart, shall become a final order.

(2) A decision made under paragraph (a) of this section shall include a statement of:

(i) Findings of fact and conclusions of law, and the reasons therefor, on all issues presented; and

(ii) Any terms and conditions of the rule or order.

(3) A copy of any decision under this paragraph shall be served on each party.

(b) *Hearings on issues of fact.* Where a genuine question of a material fact is raised, the administrative law judge shall, and in any other case may, set the case for an evidentiary hearing. [Revised by PWBA in 67 FR 64774 on 10-21-02 and in 68 FR 3729 on 1-24-03.]

[¶ 14,928UU]

§ 2570.138 **Decision of the administrative law judge**. For 502(c)(7) civil penalty proceedings, this section shall apply in lieu of Sec. 18.57 of this title.

(a) *Proposed findings of fact, conclusions, and order.* Within twenty (20) days of the filing of the transcript of the testimony, or such additional time as the administrative law judge may allow, each party may file with the administrative law judge, subject to the judge's discretion, proposed findings of fact, conclusions of law, and order together with a supporting brief expressing the reasons for such proposals. Such proposals and briefs shall be served on all parties, and shall refer to all portions of the record and to all authorities relied upon in support of each proposal.

(b) *Decision of the administrative law judge.* Within a reasonable time after the time allowed for the filing of the proposed findings of fact, conclusions of law, and order, or within thirty (30) days after receipt of an agreement containing consent findings and order disposing of the disputed matter in whole, the administrative law judge shall make his or her decision. The decision of the administrative law judge shall include findings of fact and conclusions of law with reasons therefor upon each material issue of fact or law presented on the record. The decision of the administrative law judge shall be based upon the whole record. In a contested case in which the Department and the Respondent have presented their positions to the administrative law judge pursuant to the procedures for 502(c)(7) civil penalty

proceedings as set forth in this subpart, the penalty (if any) which may be included in the decision of the administrative law judge shall be limited to the penalty expressly provided for in section 502(c)(7) of ERISA. It shall be supported by reliable and probative evidence. The decision of the administrative law judge shall become final agency action within the meaning of 5 U.S.C. 704 unless an appeal is made pursuant to the procedures set forth in Sec. Sec. 2570.139 through 2570.141 of this subpart. [Revised by PWBA in 67 FR 64774 on 10-21-02 and in 68 FR 3729 on 1-24-03.]

[¶ 14,928VV]

§ 2570.139 **Review by the Secretary**.

(a) The Secretary may review a decision of an administrative law judge. Such a review may occur only when a party files a notice of appeal from a decision of an administrative law judge within twenty (20) days of the issuance of such decision. In all other cases, the decision of the administrative law judge shall become final agency action within the meaning of 5 U.S.C. 704.

(b) A notice of appeal to the Secretary shall state with specificity the issue(s) in the decision of the administrative law judge on which the party is seeking review. Such notice of appeal must be served on all parties of record.

(c) Upon receipt of a notice of appeal, the Secretary shall request the Chief Administrative Law Judge to submit to him or her a copy of the entire record before the administrative law judge. [Revised by PWBA in 67 FR 64774 on 10-21-02 and in 68 FR 3729 on 1-24-03.]

[¶ 14,928WW]

§ 2570.140 **Scope of review**. The review of the Secretary shall not be a de novo proceeding but rather a review of the record established before the administrative law judge. There shall be no opportunity for oral argument. [Revised by PWBA in 67 FR 64774 on 10-21-02 and in 68 FR 3729 on 1-24-03.]

[¶ 14,928XX]

§ 2570.141 **Procedures for review by the Secretary**.

(a) Upon receipt of the notice of appeal, the Secretary shall establish a briefing schedule which shall be served on all parties of record. Upon motion of one or more of the parties, the Secretary may, in his or her discretion, permit the submission of reply briefs.

(b) The Secretary shall issue a decision as promptly as possible after receipt of the briefs of the parties. The Secretary may affirm, modify, or set aside, in whole or in part, the decision on appeal and shall issue a statement of reasons and bases for the action(s) taken. Such decision by the Secretary shall be final agency action within the meaning of 5 U.S.C. 704. [Revised by PWBA in 67 FR 64774 on 10-21-02 and in 68 FR 3729 on 1-24-03.]

Regulations

The following subpart and regulations concerning procedures for assessment of civil penalties under ERISA § 502(c)(8) were published in the Federal Register on February 26, 2010 (75 FR 8796).

Subpart I—Procedures for the Assessment of Civil Penalties Under ERISA Section 502(c)(8)

[¶ 14,928YY-1]

§ 2570.160 **Scope of rules.**

The rules of practice set forth in this subpart are applicable to "502(c)(8) civil penalty proceedings" (as defined in § 2570.161(n) of this subpart) under section 502(c)(8) of the Employee Retirement Income Security Act of 1974, as amended (the Act). The rules of procedure for administrative hearings published by the Department's Office of Administrative Law Judges at Part 18 of this title will apply to matters arising under ERISA section 502(c)(8) except as modified by this subpart. These proceedings shall be conducted as expeditiously as possible, and the parties shall make every effort to avoid delay at each stage of the proceedings.

[¶ 14,928YY-2]

§ 2570.161 **Definitions.**

For 502(c)(8) civil penalty proceedings, this section shall apply in lieu of the definitions in § 18.2 of this title:

(a) *Adjudicatory proceeding* means a judicial-type proceeding before an administrative law judge leading to the formulation of a final order;

(b) *Administrative law judge* means an administrative law judge appointed pursuant to the provisions of 5 U.S.C. 3105;

(c) *Answer* means a written statement that is supported by reference to specific circumstances or facts surrounding the notice of determination issued pursuant to § 2560.502c-8(g) of this chapter;

(d) *Commencement of proceeding* is the filing of an answer by the respondent;

(e) *Consent agreement* means any written document containing a specified proposed remedy or other relief acceptable to the Department and consenting parties;

(f) *ERISA* means the Employee Retirement Income Security Act of 1974, as amended;

(g) *Final order* means the final decision or action of the Department of Labor concerning the assessment of a civil penalty under ERISA section 502(c)(8) against a particular party. Such final order may result from a decision of an administrative law judge or the Secretary, the failure of a party to file a statement of reasonable cause described in § 2560.502c-8(e) of this chapter within the prescribed time limits, or the failure of a party to invoke the procedures for hearings or appeals under this title within the prescribed time limits. Such a final order shall constitute final agency action within the meaning of 5 U.S.C. 704;

(h) *Hearing* means that part of a proceeding which involves the submission of evidence, by either oral presentation or written submission, to the administrative law judge;

(i) *Order* means the whole or any part of a final procedural or substantive disposition of a matter under ERISA section 502(c)(8);

(j) *Party* includes a person or agency named or admitted as a party to a proceeding;

(k) *Person* includes an individual, partnership, corporation, employee benefit plan, association, exchange or other entity or organization;

(l) *Petition* means a written request, made by a person or party, for some affirmative action;

(m) *Pleading* means the notice as defined in § 2560.502c-8(g) of this chapter, the answer to the notice, any supplement or amendment thereto, and any reply that may be permitted to any answer, supplement or amendment;

(n) *502(c)(8) civil penalty proceeding* means an adjudicatory proceeding relating to the assessment of a civil penalty provided for in section 502(c)(8) of ERISA;

(o) *Respondent* means the party against whom the Department is seeking to assess a civil sanction under ERISA section 502(c)(8);

(p) *Secretary* means the Secretary of Labor and includes, pursuant to any delegation of authority by the Secretary, any assistant secretary (including the Assistant Secretary for Employee Benefits Security), administrator, commissioner, appellate body, board, or other official; and

(q) *Solicitor* means the Solicitor of Labor or his or her delegate.

[¶ 14,928YY-3]
§ 2570.162 Service: Copies of documents and pleadings.

For 502(c)(8) penalty proceedings, this section shall apply in lieu of § 18.3 of this title.

(a) *General.* Copies of all documents shall be served on all parties of record. All documents should clearly designate the docket number, if any, and short title of all matters. All documents to be filed shall be delivered or mailed to the Chief Docket Clerk, Office of Administrative Law Judges, 800 K Street, NW., Suite 400, Washington, DC 20001-8002, or to the OALJ Regional Office to which the proceeding may have been transferred for hearing. Each document filed shall be clear and legible.

(b) *By parties.* All motions, petitions, pleadings, briefs, or other documents shall be filed with the Office of Administrative Law Judges with a copy, including any attachments, to all other parties of record. When a party is represented by an attorney, service shall be made upon the attorney. Service of any document upon any party may be made by personal delivery or by mailing a copy to the last known address. The Department shall be served by delivery to the Associate Solicitor, Plan Benefits Security Division, ERISA section 502(c)(8) Proceeding, P.O. Box 1914, Washington, DC 20013. The person serving the document shall certify to the manner and date of service.

(c) *By the Office of Administrative Law Judges.* Service of orders, decisions and all other documents shall be made by regular mail to the last known address.

(d) *Form of pleadings.* (1) Every pleading shall contain information indicating the name of the Employee Benefits Security Administration (EBSA) as the agency under which the proceeding is instituted, the title of the proceeding, the docket number (if any) assigned by the Office of Administrative Law Judges and a designation of the type of pleading or paper (*e.g.,* notice, motion to dismiss, *etc.*). The pleading or paper shall be signed and shall contain the address and telephone number of the party or person representing the party. Although there are no formal specifications for documents, they should be typewritten when possible on standard size 8 ½ × 11-inch paper.

(2) Illegible documents, whether handwritten, typewritten, photocopied, or otherwise, will not be accepted. Papers may be reproduced by any duplicating process provided all copies are clear and legible.

[¶ 14,928YY-4]
§ 2570.163 Parties, how designated.

For 502(c)(8) civil penalty proceedings, this section shall apply in lieu of § 18.10 of this title.

(a) The term "party" wherever used in this subpart shall include any natural person, corporation, employee benefit plan, association, firm, partnership, trustee, receiver, agency, public or private organization, or government agency. A party against whom a civil penalty is sought shall be designated as "respondent." The Department shall be designated as the "complainant."

(b) Other persons or organizations shall be permitted to participate as parties only if the administrative law judge finds that the final decision could directly and adversely affect them or the class they represent, that they may contribute materially to the disposition of the proceedings and their interest is not adequately represented by existing parties, and that in the discretion of the administrative law judge the participation of such persons or organizations would be appropriate.

(c) A person or organization not named as a respondent wishing to participate as a party under this section shall submit a petition to the administrative law judge within fifteen (15) days after the person or organization has knowledge of or should have known about the proceeding. The petition shall be filed with the administrative law judge and served on each person who or organization that has been made a party at the time of filing. Such petition shall concisely state:

(1) Petitioner's interest in the proceeding;

(2) How his or her participation as a party will contribute materially to the disposition of the proceeding;

(3) Who will appear for petitioner;

(4) The issues on which petitioner wishes to participate; and

(5) Whether petitioner intends to present witnesses.

(d) Objections to the petition may be filed by a party within fifteen (15) days of the filing of the petition. If objections to the petition are filed, the administrative law judge shall then determine whether petitioner has the requisite interest to be a party in the proceedings, as defined in paragraph (b) of this section, and shall permit or deny participation accordingly. Where petitions to participate as parties are made by individuals or groups with common interests, the administrative law judge may request all such petitioners to designate a single representative, or he or she may recognize one or more of such petitioners. The administrative law judge shall give each such petitioner, as well as the parties, written notice of the decision on his or her petition. For each petition granted, the administrative law judge shall provide a brief statement of the basis of the decision. If the petition is denied, he or she shall briefly state the grounds for denial and shall then treat the petition as a request for participation as *amicus curiae.*

[¶ 14,928YY-5]
§ 2570.164 Consequences of default.

For 502(c)(8) civil penalty proceedings, this section shall apply in lieu of § 18.5(a) and (b) of this title. Failure of the respondent to file an answer to the notice of determination described in § 2560.502c-8(g) of this chapter within the 30 day period provided by § 2560.502c-8(h) of this chapter shall be deemed to constitute a waiver of his or her right to appear and contest the allegations of the notice of determination, and such failure shall be deemed to be an admission of the facts as alleged in the notice for purposes of any proceeding involving the assessment of a civil penalty under section 502(c)(8) of the Act. Such notice shall then become the final order of the Secretary, within the meaning of § 2570.161(g) of this subpart, forty-five (45) days from the date of service of the notice.

[¶ 14,928YY-6]
§ 2570.165 Consent order or settlement.

For 502(c)(8) civil penalty proceedings, the following shall apply in lieu of § 18.9 of this title.

(a) *General.* At any time after the commencement of a proceeding, but at least five (5) days prior to the date set for hearing, the parties jointly may move to defer the hearing for a reasonable time to permit negotiation of a settlement or an agreement containing findings and an order disposing of the whole or any part of the proceeding. The allowance of such a deferral and the duration thereof shall be in the discretion of the administrative law judge, after consideration of such factors as the nature of the proceeding, the requirements of the public interest, the representations of the parties, and the probability of reaching an agreement which will result in a just disposition of the issues involved.

(b) *Content.* Any agreement containing consent findings and an order disposing of a proceeding or any part thereof shall also provide:

(1) That the order shall have the same force and effect as an order made after full hearing;

(2) That the entire record on which any order may be based shall consist solely of the notice and the agreement;

(3) A waiver of any further procedural steps before the administrative law judge;

(4) A waiver of any right to challenge or contest the validity of the order and decision entered into in accordance with the agreement; and

(5) That the order and decision of the administrative law judge shall be final agency action.

(c) *Submission.* On or before the expiration of the time granted for negotiations, but, in any case, at least five (5) days prior to the date set for hearing, the parties or their authorized representative or their counsel may:

(1) Submit the proposed agreement containing consent findings and an order to the administrative law judge; or

(2) Notify the administrative law judge that the parties have reached a full settlement and have agreed to dismissal of the action subject to compliance with the terms of the settlement; or

(3) Inform the administrative law judge that agreement cannot be reached.

(d) *Disposition.* In the event a settlement agreement containing consent findings and an order is submitted within the time allowed therefor, the administrative law judge shall issue a decision incorporating such findings and agreement within 30 days of his receipt of such document. The decision of the administrative law judge shall incorporate all of the findings, terms, and conditions of the settlement agreement and consent order of the parties. Such decision shall become final agency action within the meaning of 5 U.S.C. 704.

(e) *Settlement without consent of all parties.* In cases in which some, but not all, of the parties to a proceeding submit a consent agreement to the administrative law judge, the following procedure shall apply:

(1) If all of the parties have not consented to the proposed settlement submitted to the administrative law judge, then such non-consenting parties must receive notice, and a copy, of the proposed settlement at the time it is submitted to the administrative law judge;

(2) Any non-consenting party shall have fifteen (15) days to file any objections to the proposed settlement with the administrative law judge and all other parties;

(3) If any party submits an objection to the proposed settlement, the administrative law judge shall decide within 30 days after receipt of such objections whether he shall sign or reject the proposed settlement. Where the record lacks substantial evidence upon which to base a decision or there is a genuine issue of material fact, then the administrative law judge may establish procedures for the purpose of receiving additional evidence upon which a decision on the contested issues may reasonably be based;

(4) If there are no objections to the proposed settlement, or if the administrative law judge decides to sign the proposed settlement after reviewing any such objections, the administrative law judge shall incorporate the consent agreement into a decision meeting the requirements of paragraph (d) of this section.

[¶ 14,928YY-7]

§ 2570.166 Scope of discovery.

For 502(c)(8) civil penalty proceedings, this section shall apply in lieu of § 18.14 of this title.

(a) A party may file a motion to conduct discovery with the administrative law judge. The motion for discovery shall be granted by the administrative law judge only upon a showing of good cause. In order to establish "good cause" for the purposes of this section, a party must show that the discovery requested relates to a genuine issue as to a material fact that is relevant to the proceeding. The order of the administrative law judge shall expressly limit the scope and terms of discovery to that for which "good cause" has been shown, as provided in this paragraph.

(b) A party may obtain discovery of documents and tangible things otherwise discoverable under paragraph (a) of this section and prepared in anticipation of or for the hearing by or for another party's representative (including his or her attorney, consultant, surety, indemnitor, insurer, or agent) only upon showing that the party seeking discovery has substantial need of the materials or information in the preparation of his or her case and that he or she is unable without undue hardship to obtain the substantial equivalent of the materials or information by other means. In ordering discovery of such materials when the required showing has been made, the administrative law judge shall protect against disclosure of the mental impressions, conclusions, opinions, or legal theories of an attorney or other representatives of a party concerning the proceeding.

[¶ 14,928YY-8]

§ 2570.167 Summary decision.

For 502(c)(8) civil penalty proceedings, this section shall apply in lieu of § 18.41 of this title.

(a) *No genuine issue of material fact.*

(1) Where no issue of a material fact is found to have been raised, the administrative law judge may issue a decision which, in the absence of an appeal pursuant to §§ 2570.169 through 2570.171 of this subpart, shall become a final order.

(2) A decision made under paragraph (a) of this section shall include a statement of:

(i) Findings of fact and conclusions of law, and the reasons therefor, on all issues presented; and

(ii) Any terms and conditions of the rule or order.

(3) A copy of any decision under this paragraph shall be served on each party.

(b) *Hearings on issues of fact.* Where a genuine question of a material fact is raised, the administrative law judge shall, and in any other case may, set the case for an evidentiary hearing.

[¶ 14,928YY-9]

§ 2570.168 Decision of the administrative law judge.

For 502(c)(8) civil penalty proceedings, this section shall apply in lieu of § 18.57 of this title.

(a) *Proposed findings of fact, conclusions, and order.* Within twenty (20) days of the filing of the transcript of the testimony, or such additional time as the administrative law judge may allow, each party may file with the administrative law judge, subject to the judge's discretion, proposed findings of fact, conclusions of law, and order together with a supporting brief expressing the reasons for such proposals. Such proposals and briefs shall be served on all parties, and shall refer to all portions of the record and to all authorities relied upon in support of each proposal.

(b) *Decision of the administrative law judge.* Within a reasonable time after the time allowed for the filing of the proposed findings of fact, conclusions of law, and order, or within thirty (30) days after receipt of an agreement containing consent findings and order disposing of the disputed matter in whole, the administrative law judge shall make his or her decision. The decision of the administrative law judge shall include findings of fact and conclusions of law with reasons therefor upon each material issue of fact or law presented on the record. The decision of the administrative law judge shall be based upon the whole record. In a contested case in which the Department and the Respondent have presented their positions to the administrative law judge pursuant to the procedures for 502(c)(8) civil penalty proceedings as set forth in this subpart, the penalty (if any) which may be included in the decision of the administrative law judge shall be limited to the penalty expressly provided for in section 502(c)(8) of ERISA. It shall be supported by reliable and probative evidence. The decision of the administrative law judge shall become final agency action within the meaning of 5 U.S.C. 704 unless an appeal is made pursuant to the procedures set forth in §§ 2570.169 through 2570.171 of this subpart.

[¶ 14,928YY-10]

§ 2570.169 **Review by the Secretary.**

(a) The Secretary may review a decision of an administrative law judge. Such a review may occur only when a party files a notice of appeal from a decision of an administrative law judge within twenty (20) days of the issuance of such decision. In all other cases, the decision of the administrative law judge shall become final agency action within the meaning of 5 U.S.C. 704.

(b) A notice of appeal to the Secretary shall state with specificity the issue(s) in the decision of the administrative law judge on which the party is seeking review. Such notice of appeal must be served on all parties of record.

(c) Upon receipt of a notice of appeal, the Secretary shall request the Chief Administrative Law Judge to submit to him or her a copy of the entire record before the administrative law judge.

[¶ 14,928YY-11]

§ 2570.170 **Scope of review.**

The review of the Secretary shall not be a de novo proceeding but rather a review of the record established before the administrative law judge. There shall be no opportunity for oral argument.

[¶ 14,928YY-12]

§ 2570.171 **Procedures for review by the Secretary.**

(a) Upon receipt of the notice of appeal, the Secretary shall establish a briefing schedule which shall be served on all parties of record. Upon motion of one or more of the parties, the Secretary may, in his or her discretion, permit the submission of reply briefs.

(b) The Secretary shall issue a decision as promptly as possible after receipt of the briefs of the parties. The Secretary may affirm, modify, or set aside, in whole or in part, the decision on appeal and shall issue a statement of reasons and bases for the action(s) taken. Such decision by the Secretary shall be final agency action within the meaning of 5 U.S.C. 704.

Interim Final Regulations

Reg. §§ 2575.1, 2575.2, and 2575.3 were adopted by interim final regulations published in the Federal Register on July 1, 2016 (81 FR 43429). The new regulations are effective August 1, 2016 and are applicable only to civil penalties assessed after August 1, 2016, whose associated violations occurred after November 2, 2015. Reg. § 2575.3 was revised and finalized on January 18, 2017 (82 FR 5373). In the same final regulations document, the DOL set forth the 2017 annual adjustments for inflation to the civil monetary penalties in Reg. § 2575.2 in an Appendix (see the Appendix in ¶ 24,810Q for the 2017 adjusted civil monetary penalties). The adjusted penalty amounts apply to any violation occurring after November 2, 2015 for a penalty assessed after January 13, 2017. The DOL has set forth the 2018 annual adjustments for inflation to the civil monetary penalties in Reg. § 2575.2 in an Appendix (see the Appendix in ¶ 24,811).

Part 2575, Subpart A—Adjustment of Civil Penalties Under ERISA Title I

[¶ 14,928ZZ]

§ 2575.1 **In general.**

In accordance with the requirements of the Federal Civil Penalties Inflation Adjustment Act of 1990, Pub. L. 104-410, 104 Stat. 890, as amended by the section 31001(s) of the Debt Collection Improvement Act of 1996, Pub. L. 104-34, 110 Stat. 1321-373, and section 701 of the Federal Civil Penalties Inflation Adjustment Act Improvements Act of 2015, Pub. L. 114-74, 129 Stat. 584, (collectively the Inflation Adjustment Act), the applicable civil monetary penalties of title I of the Employee Retirement Income Security Act of 1974, as amended (ERISA), under the jurisdiction of the U.S. Department of Labor (Department) and listed in 29 CFR 2575.2 are adjusted as set forth in this subpart, effective as of the relevant dates specified in § 2575.2.

[¶ 14,928ZZ-1]

§ 2575.2 **Catch-up adjustments to civil monetary penalties.**

The civil monetary penalties set forth in paragraphs (a) through (m) of this section are adjusted for inflation as required by section 4(b)(1) of the Inflation Adjustment Act and 29 CFR 2575.1 as follows:

(a) The civil monetary penalty of $10 for each employee established by section 209(b) of ERISA, is adjusted to $11 for violations occurring after July 29, 1997, for which a penalty is assessed before August 1, 2016 and to $28 for penalties assessed after August 1, 2016, and before the effective date of the next adjustment for inflation made by the Secretary in accordance with the Inflation Adjustment Act and § 2575.3.

(b) The civil monetary penalty of up to $1,000 established by Section 502(c)(2) of ERISA is adjusted to $1,100 for violations occurring after July 29, 1997, for which a penalty is assessed before August 1, 2016, and to $2,063 for penalties assessed after August 1, 2016, and before the effective date of the next adjustment for inflation made by the Secretary in accordance with the Inflation Adjustment Act and § 2575.3.

(c) The civil monetary penalty of up to $1,000 established by section 502(c)(4) of ERISA is adjusted to $1,632 for penalties assessed

after August 1, 2016, and before the effective date of the next adjustment for inflation made by the Secretary in accordance with the Inflation Adjustment Act and § 2575.3.

(d) The civil monetary penalty of up to $1,000 established by Section 502(c)(5) of ERISA is adjusted to $1,100 for violations occurring after March 24, 2003, for which a penalty is assessed before August 1, 2016, and to $1,502 for penalties assessed after August 1, 2016, and before the effective date of the next adjustment for inflation made by the Secretary in accordance with the Inflation Adjustment Act and § 2575.3.

(e) The civil monetary penalty of up to $100 not to exceed $1,000 per request, established by section 502(c)(6) of ERISA, is adjusted to $110 not to exceed $1,100 per request for violations occurring after March 24, 2003, for which a penalty is assessed before August 1, 2016, and to $147 not to exceed $1,472 per request for penalties assessed after August 1, 2016, and before the effective date of the next adjustment for inflation made by the Secretary in accordance with the Inflation Adjustment Act and § 2575.3.

(f) The civil monetary penalty of up to $100 established by section 502(c)(7) of ERISA is adjusted to $131 for penalties assessed after August 1, 2016, and before the effective date of the next adjustment for inflation made by the Secretary in accordance with the Inflation Adjustment Act and § 2575.3.

(g) The civil monetary penalty of up to $1,100 established by section 502(c)(8) of ERISA is adjusted to $1,296 for penalties assessed after August 1, 2016, and before the effective date of the next adjustment for inflation made by the Secretary in accordance with the Inflation Adjustment Act and § 2575.3.

(h) The civil monetary penalty of up to $100 established by section 502(c)(9)(A) of ERISA is adjusted to $110 for penalties assessed after August 1, 2016, and before the effective date of the next adjustment for inflation made by the Secretary in accordance with the Inflation Adjustment Act and § 2575.3.

(i) The civil monetary penalty of up to $100 established by section 502(c)(9)(B) of ERISA is adjusted to $110 for penalties assessed after August 1, 2016, and before the effective date of the next adjustment for inflation made by the Secretary in accordance with the Inflation Adjustment Act and § 2575.3.

(j) The civil monetary penalties established by section 502(c)(10) of ERISA are adjusted in accordance with paragraphs (j)(1) through (4) of this section:

(1) The $100 civil monetary penalty of section 502(c)(10)(B)(i) of ERISA is adjusted to $110 to for penalties assessed after August 1, 2016, and before the effective date of the next adjustment for inflation made by the Secretary in accordance with the Inflation Adjustment Act and § 2575.3;

(2) The $2,500 minimum civil monetary penalty of section 502(c)(10)(C)(i) of ERISA for de minimis uncorrected violations is adjusted to $2,745 for penalties assessed after August 1, 2016, and before the effective date of the next adjustment for inflation made by the Secretary in accordance with the Inflation Adjustment Act and § 2575.3;

(3) The $15,000 minimum civil monetary penalty of section 502(c)(10)(C)(ii) of ERISA for uncorrected violations that are not de minimis is adjusted to $16,473 for penalties assessed after August 1, 2016, and before the effective date of the next adjustment for inflation made by the Secretary in accordance with the Inflation Adjustment Act and § 2575.3; and

(4) The $500,000 maximum civil monetary penalty for unintentional failures set in Section 502 (c)(10)(D)(iii)(II) of ERISA is adjusted to $549,095, for penalties assessed after August 1, 2016, and before the effective date of the next adjustment for inflation made by the Secretary in accordance with the Inflation Adjustment Act and § 2575.3.

(k) The civil monetary penalty of up to $100 established by section 502(c)(12) of ERISA remains at $100 for penalties assessed after August 1, 2016, and before the effective date of the next adjustment for inflation made by the Secretary in accordance with the Inflation Adjustment Act and § 2575.3.

(l) The maximum civil monetary penalty of $10,000 established by section 502(m) of ERISA is adjusted to $15,909 for penalties assessed after August 1, 2016, and before the effective date of the next adjustment for inflation made by the Secretary in accordance with the Inflation Adjustment Act and § 2575.3.

(m) The civil monetary penalty of not more than $1,000, established by Public Health Services Act section 2715(f) and incorporated into ERISA by section 715 of ERISA, is adjusted to $1,087 for penalties assessed after August 1, 2016, and before the effective date of the next adjustment for inflation made by the Secretary in accordance with the Inflation Adjustment Act and § 2575.3.

Regulations

Reg. § 2575.3 was adopted by interim final regulations published in the Federal Register on July 1, 2016 (81 FR 43429). The new regulations were effective August 1, 2016 and were applicable only to civil penalties assess after August 1, 2016 but on or before January 13, 2017, whose associated violations occurred after November 2, 2015. Reg. § 2575.3 was revised and finalized on January 18, 2017 (82 FR 5373).

[¶ 14,928ZZ-2]
§ 2575.3 Subsequent adjustments to civil monetary penalties.

No later than January 15, starting in 2017, and each subsequent year, the Secretary shall adjust for inflation, as required by the Inflation Adjustment Act, the civil monetary penalties described in § 2575.2 for violations occurring on or after November 2, 2015, and any future civil monetary penalties enforceable by the Secretary under title I of ERISA.

The Secretary shall publish such annual adjustments in the **Federal Register** notwithstanding section 553 of the Administrative Procedure Act. Future penalties or adjustments to the amount of the penalty that are enacted by statute or regulation (other than an adjustment for inflation under the Inflation Adjustment Act) will not be adjusted for inflation in the first year those penalty levels take effect. Annual inflation adjustments shall apply to penalties assessed after the date notice of the annual inflation adjustment is published in the **Federal Register**.

Regulations

The following regulations regarding inflationary adjustments to ERISA civil monetary penalties were published in the *Federal Register* on July 29, 1997 (62 FR 40696). The regulations are to be applied to violations occurring after the effective date. On August 3, 1999 (64 FR 42246), the regulations contained herein were transferred from Subpart E of part 2570 to Subpart A of a new part 2575 of Chapter XXV of title 29 of the Code of Federal Regulation (CFR) and were redesignated accordingly. The transfer was performed to simplify the organization and numbering of procedure regulations in part 2570 of the CFR. The contents of the regulations was not altered during the redesign. The regulations were amended and revised at § 2575.100, § 2575.502c-5, and § 2575.502c-6 by PWBA final regulations published in the *Federal Register* on January 22, 2003 (68 FR 2875). Reg. §§ 2575.100, 2575.209b-1, 2575.502c-2, 2575.502c-5, and 2575.502c-6 were removed by interim final regulations on July 1, 2016 (81 FR 43429). The interim final regulations are effective August 1, 2016. The civil penalties in the removed regulations are applicable to violations occurring on or before November 2, 2015, as well as assessments made prior to August 1, 2016 whose associated violations occurred after November 2, 2015. See new interim final Reg. § 2575.1 at ¶ 14,928ZZ, Reg. § 2575.2 at ¶ 14,928ZZ-1, and Reg. § 2575.3 at ¶ 14,928ZZ-2 for inflation-adjusted civil penalties.

[¶ 14,929A]
§ 2575.100 In general.

[Redesignated as ERISA Reg. Sec. 2575.100, 64 FR 42245, August 3, 1999. Amended and revised by PWBA on January 22, 2003 (68 FR 1875). Removed 7/1/16 (81 FR 43429) by interim final regulations.].

[¶ 14,929B]
§ 2575.209b-1 Adjusted civil penalty under section 209(b).

[Redesignated as ERISA Reg. Sec. 2575.209b-1, 64 FR 42245, August 3, 1999. Removed 7/1/16 (81 FR 43429) by interim final regulations.].

[¶ 14,929C]
§ 2575.502c-1 Adjusted civil penalty under section 502(c)(1).

In accordance with the requirements of the 1990 Act, as amended, the maximum amount of the civil monetary penalty established by section 502(c)(1) of the Employee Retirement Income Security Act of 1974, as amended (ERISA), is hereby increased from $100 a day to $110 a day. This adjusted penalty applies only to violations occurring after July 29, 1997 [Redesignated as ERISA Reg. Sec. 2575.502c-1, 64 FR 42245, August 3, 1999].

[¶ 14,929D]
§ 2575.502c-2 Adjusted civil penalty under section 502(c)(2).

[Redesignated as ERISA Reg. Sec. 2575.502c-2, 64 FR 42245, August 3, 1999. Removed 7/1/16 (81 FR 43429) by interim final regulations.].

[¶ 14,929E]
§ 2575.502c-3 Adjusted civil penalty under section 502(c)(3).

In accordance with the requirements of the 1990 Act, as amended, the maximum amount of the civil monetary penalty established by section 502(c)(3) of the Employee Retirement Income Security Act of 1974, as amended (ERISA), is hereby increased from $100 a day to $110 a day. This adjusted penalty applies only to violations occurring after July 29, 1997 [Redesignated as ERISA Reg. Sec. 2575.502c-3, 64 FR 42245, August 3, 1999].

[¶ 14,929G]
§ 2575.502c-5 Adjusted civil penalty under section 502(c)(5).

[Redesignated as ERISA Reg. Sec. 2575.502c-3, 64 FR 42245, August 3, 1999. Amended and revised by PWBA on January 22, 2003 (68 FR 2875). Removed 7/1/16 (81 FR 43429) by interim final regulations.].

[¶ 14,929H]
§ 2575.502c-6 Adjusted civil penalty under section 502(c)(6).

[Redesignated as ERISA Reg. Sec. 2575.502c-3, 64 FR 42245, August 3, 1999. Amended and revised by PWBA on January 22, 2003 (68 FR 2875). Removed 7/1/16 (81 FR 43429) by interim final regulations.].

[¶ 14,929L]
Part 2575, Subpart B. Reserved [Added and Reserved, 64 FR 42245, August 3, 1999].

Regulations

The following regulation was adopted on April 21, 2006 (71 FR 20820) under 29 Code of Federal Regulations, Chapter XXV, Title 29-Labor, Subchapter G-Administration and Enforcement Under the Employee Retirement Income Security Act of 1974, Part 2578-Rules and Regulations for Abandoned Plans. It is effective May 22, 2006. Reg. Sec. 2578.1 was amended on February 15, 2007 (72 FR 7516) and on October 7, 2008 (73 FR 58459).

[¶ 14,929S]

§ 2578.1 Termination of Abandoned Individual Account Plans.

(a) *General.* The purpose of this part is to establish standards for the termination and winding up of an individual account plan (as defined in section 3(34) of the Employee Retirement Income Security Act of 1974 (ERISA or the Act)) with respect to which a qualified termination administrator (as defined in paragraph (g) of this section) has determined there is no responsible plan sponsor or plan administrator within the meaning of section 3(16)(B) and (A) of the Act, respectively, to perform such acts.

(b) *Finding of abandonment.* (1) A qualified termination administrator may find an individual account plan to be abandoned when:

(i) Either:. (A) No contributions to, or distributions from, the plan have been made for a period of at least 12 consecutive months immediately preceding the date on which the determination is being made; or

(B) Other facts and circumstances (such as a filing by or against the plan sponsor for liquidation under title 11 of the United States Code, or communications from participants and beneficiaries regarding distributions) known to the qualified termination administrator suggest that the plan is or may become abandoned by the plan sponsor; and

(ii) Following reasonable efforts to locate or communicate with the plan sponsor, the qualified termination administrator determines that the plan sponsor:

(A) No longer exists;

(B) Cannot be located; or

(C) Is unable to maintain the plan.

(2) Notwithstanding paragraph (b)(1) of this section, a qualified termination administrator may not find a plan to be abandoned if, at any time before the plan is deemed terminated pursuant to paragraph (c) of this section, the qualified termination administrator receives an objection from the plan sponsor regarding the finding of abandonment and proposed termination.

(3) A qualified termination administrator shall, for purposes of paragraph (b)(1)(ii) of this section, be deemed to have made a reasonable effort to locate or communicate with the plan sponsor if the qualified termination administrator sends to the last known address of the plan sponsor, and, in the case of a plan sponsor that is a corporation, to the address of the person designated as the corporation's agent for service of legal process, by a method of delivery requiring acknowledgement of receipt, the notice described in paragraph (b)(5) of this section.

(4) If receipt of the notice described in paragraph (b)(5) of this section is not acknowledged pursuant to paragraph (b)(3) of this section, the qualified termination administrator shall be deemed to have made a reasonable effort to locate or communicate with the plan sponsor if the qualified termination administrator contacts known service providers (other than itself) of the plan and requests the current address of the plan sponsor from such service providers and, if such information is provided, the qualified termination administrator sends to each such address, by a method of delivery requiring acknowledgement of receipt, the notice described in paragraph (b)(5) of this section.

(5) The notice referred to in paragraph (b)(3) of this section shall contain the following information:

(i) The name and address of the qualified termination administrator;

(ii) The name of the plan;

(iii) The account number or other identifying information relating to the plan;

(iv) A statement that the plan may be terminated and benefits distributed pursuant to 29 CFR 2578.1 if the plan sponsor fails to contact the qualified termination administrator within 30 days;

(v) The name, address, and telephone number of the person, office, or department that the plan sponsor must contact regarding the plan;

(vi) A statement that if the plan is terminated pursuant to 29 CFR 2578.1, notice of such termination will be furnished to the U.S. Department of Labor's Employee Benefits Security Administration;

(vii) The following statement: "The U.S. Department of Labor requires that you be informed that, as a fiduciary or plan administrator or both, you may be personally liable for costs, civil penalties, excise taxes, etc. as a result of your acts or omissions with respect to this plan. The termination of this plan will not relieve you of your liability for any such costs, penalties, taxes, etc."; and

(viii) A statement that the plan sponsor may contact the U.S Department of Labor for more information about the federal law governing the termination and winding-up process for abandoned plans and the telephone number of the appropriate Employee Benefit Security Administration contact person.

(c) *Deemed termination.* (1) Except as provided in paragraph (c)(2) of this section, if a qualified termination administrator finds, pursuant to paragraph (b)(1) of this section, that an individual account plan has been abandoned, the plan shall be deemed to be terminated on the ninetieth (90th) day following the date of the letter from EBSA's Office of Enforcement acknowledging receipt of the notice of plan abandonment, described in paragraph (c)(3) of this section.

(2) If, prior to the end of the 90-day period described in paragraph (c)(1) of this section, the Department notifies the qualified termination administrator that it—

(i) Objects to the termination of the plan, the plan shall not be deemed terminated under paragraph (c)(1) of this section until the qualified termination administrator is notified that the Department has withdrawn its objection; or

(ii) Waives the 90-day period described in paragraph (c)(1), the plan shall be deemed terminated upon the qualified termination administrator's receipt of such notification.

(3) Following a qualified termination administrator's finding, pursuant to paragraph (b)(1) of this section, that an individual account plan has been abandoned, the qualified termination administrator shall furnish to the U.S. Department of Labor a notice of plan abandonment that is signed and dated by the qualified termination administrator and that includes the following information:

(i) *Qualified termination administrator information.* (A) The name, EIN, address, and telephone number of the person electing to be the qualified termination administrator, including the address, e-mail address, and telephone number of the person signing the notice (or other contact person, if different from the person signing the notice);

(B) A statement that the person (identified in paragraph (c)(3)(i)(A) of this section) is a qualified termination administrator within the meaning of paragraph (g) of this section and elects to terminate and wind up the plan (identified in paragraph (c)(3)(ii)(A) of this section) in accordance with the provisions of this section; and

(C) An identification whether the person electing to be the qualified termination administrator or its affiliate is, or within the past 24 months has been, the subject of an investigation, examination, or enforcement action by the Department, Internal Revenue Service, or Securities and Exchange Commission concerning such entity's conduct as a fiduciary or party in interest with respect to any plan covered by the Act.

(ii) *Plan information.* (A) The name, address, telephone number, account number, EIN, and plan number of the plan with respect to which the person is electing to serve as the qualified termination administrator;

(B) The name and last known address and telephone number of the plan sponsor; and

(C) The estimated number of participants in the plan;

(iii) *Findings.* A statement that the person electing to be the qualified termination administrator finds that the plan (identified in paragraph (c)(3)(ii)(A) of this section) is abandoned pursuant to paragraph (b) of this section. This statement shall include an explanation of the basis for such a finding, specifically referring to the provisions in paragraph (b)(1) of this section, a description of the specific steps (set forth in paragraphs (b)(3) and (b)(4) of this section) taken to locate or communicate with the known plan sponsor, and a statement that no objection has been received from the plan sponsor;

(iv) *Plan asset information.* (A) The estimated value of the plan's assets held by the person electing to be the qualified termination administrator;

(B) The length of time plan assets have been held by the person electing to be the qualified termination administrator, if such period of time is less than 12 months;

(C) An identification of any assets with respect to which there is no readily ascertainable fair market value, as well as information, if any, concerning the value of such assets; and

(D) An identification of known delinquent contributions pursuant to paragraph (d)(2)(iii) of this section;

(v) *Service provider information.* (A) The name, address, and telephone number of known service providers (*e.g.*, record keeper, accountant, lawyer, other asset custodian(s)) to the plan; and

(B) An identification of any services considered necessary to wind up the plan in accordance with this section, the name of the service provider(s) that is expected to provide such services, and an itemized estimate of expenses attendant thereto expected to be paid out of plan assets by the qualified termination administrator; and

(vi) *Perjury statement.* A statement that the information being provided in the notice is true and complete based on the knowledge of the person electing to be the qualified termination administrator, and that the information is being provided by the qualified termination administrator under penalty of perjury.

(d) *Winding up the affairs of the plan.* (1) In any case where an individual account plan is deemed to be terminated pursuant to paragraph (c) of this section, the qualified termination administrator shall take steps as may be necessary or appropriate to wind up the affairs of the plan and distribute benefits to the plan's participants and beneficiaries.

(2) For purposes of paragraph (d)(1) of this section, the qualified termination administrator shall:

(i) *Update plan records.* (A) Undertake reasonable and diligent efforts to locate and update plan records necessary to determine the benefits payable under the terms of the plan to each participant and beneficiary.

(B) For purposes of paragraph (d)(2)(i)(A) of this section, a qualified termination administrator shall not have failed to make reasonable and diligent efforts to update plan records merely because the administrator determines in good faith that updating the records is either impossible or involves significant cost to the plan in relation to the total assets of the plan.

(ii) *Calculate benefits.* Use reasonable care in calculating the benefits payable to each participant or beneficiary based on plan records described in paragraph (d)(2)(i) of this section. A qualified termination administrator shall not have failed to use reasonable care in calculating benefits payable solely because the qualified termination administrator—

(A) Treats as forfeited an account balance that, taking into account estimated forfeitures and other assets allocable to the account, is less than the estimated share of plan expenses allocable to that account, and reallocates that account balance to defray plan expenses or to other plan accounts in accordance with (d)(2)(ii)(B) of this section;

(B) Allocates expenses and unallocated assets in accordance with the plan documents, or, if the plan document is not available, is ambiguous, or if compliance with the plan is unfeasible,

(1) Allocates unallocated assets (including forfeitures and assets in a suspense account) to participant accounts on a per capita basis (allocated equally to all accounts); and

(2) Allocates expenses on a pro rata basis (proportionately in the ratio that each individual account balance bears to the total of all individual account balances) or on a per capita basis (allocated equally to all accounts).

(iii) *Report delinquent contributions.* (A) Notify the Department of any known contributions (either employer or employee) owed to the plan in conjunction with the filing of either the notification required in paragraph (c)(3) or (d)(2)(ix) of this section.

(B) Nothing in paragraph (d)(2)(iii)(A) of this section or any other provision of the Act shall be construed to impose an obligation on the qualified termination administrator to collect delinquent contributions on behalf of the plan, provided that the qualified termination administrator satisfies the requirements of paragraph (d)(2)(iii)(A) of this section.

(iv) *Engage service providers.* Engage, on behalf of the plan, such service providers as are necessary for the qualified termination administrator to wind up the affairs of the plan and distribute benefits to the plan's participants and beneficiaries in accordance with paragraph (d)(1) of this section.

(v) *Pay reasonable expenses.* (A) Pay, from plan assets, the reasonable expenses of carrying out the qualified termination administrator's authority and responsibility under this section.

(B) Expenses of plan administration shall be considered reasonable solely for purposes of paragraph (d)(2)(v)(A) of this section if:

(1) Such expenses are for services necessary to wind up the affairs of the plan and distribute benefits to the plan's participants and beneficiaries,

(2) Such expenses:. (i) Are consistent with industry rates for such or similar services, based on the experience of the qualified termination administrator; and

(ii) Are not in excess of rates ordinarily charged by the qualified termination administrator (or affiliate) for same or similar services provided to customers that are not plans terminated pursuant to this section, if the qualified termination administrator (or affiliate) provides same or similar services to such other customers, and

(3) The payment of such expenses would not constitute a prohibited transaction under the Act or is exempted from such prohibited transaction provisions pursuant to section 408(a) of the Act.

(vi) *Notify participants.* (A) Furnish to each participant or beneficiary of the plan a notice written in a manner calculated to be understood by the average plan participant and containing the following:

(1) The name of the plan;

(2) A statement that the plan has been determined to be abandoned by the plan sponsor and, therefore, has been terminated pursuant to regulations issued by the U.S. Department of Labor;

(3)(i) A statement of the account balance and the date on which it was calculated by the qualified termination administrator, and

(ii) The following statement: "The actual amount of your distribution may be more or less than the amount stated in this letter depending on investment gains or losses and the administrative cost of terminating your plan and distributing your benefits.";

(4) A description of the distribution options available under the plan and a request that the participant or beneficiary elect a form of distribution and inform the qualified termination administrator (or designee) of that election;

(5) A statement explaining that, if a participant or beneficiary fails to make an election within 30 days from receipt of the notice, the qualified termination administrator (or designee) will distribute the account balance of the participant or beneficiary directly:

(i) To an individual retirement plan (*i.e.*, individual retirement account or annuity),

(ii) To an inherited individual retirement plan described in Sec. 2550.404a-3(d)(1)(ii) of this chapter (in the case of a distribution on behalf of a distributee other than a participant or spouse),

(iii) In any case where the amount to be distributed meets the conditions in Sec. 2550.404a-3 (d)(1)(iii), to an interest-bearing federally insured bank account, the unclaimed property fund of the State of the last known address of the participant or beneficiary, or an individual retirement plan (described in Sec. 2550.404a-3(d)(1)(i) or (d)(1)(ii) of this chapter) or

(iv) To an annuity provider in any case where the qualified termination administrator determines that the survivor annuity requirements in sections 401(a)(11) and 417 of the Internal Revenue Code (or section 205 of ERISA) prevent a distribution under paragraph (d)(2)(vii)(B)(*1*) of this section;

(6) In the case of a distribution to an individual retirement plan (described in Sec. 2550.404a-3(d)(1)(i) or (d)(1)(ii) of this chapter) a statement explaining that the account balance will be invested in an investment product designed to preserve principal and provide a reasonable rate of return and liquidity;

(7) A statement of the fees, if any, that will be paid from the participant or beneficiary's individual retirement plan (described in Sec. 2550.404a-3(d)(1)(i) or (d)(1)(ii) of this chapter) or other account (described in Sec. 2550.404a-3(d)(1)(iii)(A) of this chapter), if such information is known at the time of the furnishing of this notice;

(8) The name, address and phone number of the provider of the individual retirement plan (described in Sec. 2550.404a-3(d)(1)(i) or (d)(1)(ii) of this chapter), qualified survivor annuity, or other account (described in Sec. 2550.404a-3(d)(1)(iii)(A) of this chapter), if such information is known at the time of the furnishing of this notice; and

(9) The name, address, and telephone number of the qualified termination administrator and, if different, the name, address and phone number of a contact person (or entity) for additional information concerning the termination and distribution of benefits under this section.

(B) *(1)* For purposes of paragraph (d)(2)(vi)(A) of this section, a notice shall be furnished to each participant or beneficiary in accordance with the requirements of § 2520.104b-1(b)(1) of this chapter to the last known address of the participant or beneficiary; and

(2) In the case of a notice that is returned to the plan as undeliverable, the qualified termination administrator shall, consistent with the duties of a fiduciary under section 404(a)(1) of ERISA, take steps to locate and provide notice to the participant or beneficiary prior to making a distribution pursuant to paragraph (d)(2)(vii) of this section. If, after such steps, the qualified termination administrator is unsuccessful in locating and furnishing notice to a participant or beneficiary, the participant or beneficiary shall be deemed to have been furnished the notice and to have failed to make an election within the 30-day period described in paragraph (d)(2)(vii) of this section.

(vii) *Distribute benefits.* (A) Distribute benefits in accordance with the form of distribution elected by each participant or beneficiary with spousal consent, if required.

(B) If the participant or beneficiary fails to make an election within 30 days from the date the notice described in paragraph (d)(2)(vi) of this section is furnished, distribute benefits—

(1) In accordance with § 2550.404a-3 of this chapter; or

(2) If a qualified termination administrator determines that the survivor annuity requirements in sections 401(a)(11) and 417 of the Internal Revenue Code (or section 205 of ERISA) prevent a distribution under paragraph (d)(2)(vii)(B)(*1*) of this section, in any manner reasonably determined to achieve compliance with those requirements.

(C) For purposes of distributions pursuant to paragraph (d)(2)(vii)(B) of this section, the qualified termination administrator may designate itself (or an affiliate) as the transferee of such proceeds, and invest such proceeds in a product in which it (or an affiliate) has an interest, only if such designation and investment is exempted from the prohibited transaction provisions under the Act pursuant to section 408(a) of the Act.

(viii) *Special Terminal Report for Abandoned Plans.* File the Special Terminal Report for Abandoned Plans in accordance with § 2520.103-13 of this chapter.

(ix) *Final Notice.* No later than two months after the end of the month in which the qualified termination administrator satisfies the requirements in paragraph (d)(2)(i) through (d)(2)(vii) of this section, furnish to the Office of Enforcement, Employee Benefits Security Administration, U.S. Department of Labor, 200 Constitution Avenue, NW., Washington, DC 20210, a notice, signed and dated by the qualified termination administrator, containing the following information:

(A) The name, EIN, address, e-mail address, and telephone number of the qualified termination administrator, including the address and telephone number of the person signing the notice (or other contact person, if different from the person signing the notice);

(B) The name, account number, EIN, and plan number of the plan with respect to which the person served as the qualified termination administrator;

(C) A statement that the plan has been terminated and all the plan's assets have been distributed to the plan's participants and beneficiaries on the basis of the best available information;

(D) A statement that plan expenses were paid out of plan assets by the qualified termination administrator in accordance with the requirements of paragraph (d)(2)(v) of this section;

(E) If fees and expenses paid to the qualified termination administrator (or its affiliate) exceed by 20 percent or more the estimate required by paragraph (c)(3)(v)(B) of this section, a statement that actual fees and expenses exceeded estimated fees and expenses and the reasons for such additional costs;

(F) An identification of known delinquent contributions pursuant to paragraph (d)(2)(iii) of this section (if not already reported under paragraph (c)(3)(iv)(D)); and

(G) A statement that the information being provided in the notice is true and complete based on the knowledge of the qualified termination administrator, and that the information is being provided by the qualified termination administrator under penalty of perjury.

(3) The terms of the plan shall, for purposes of title I of ERISA, be deemed amended to the extent necessary to allow the qualified termination administrator to wind up the plan in accordance with this section.

(e) *Limited liability.* (1)(i) Except as otherwise provided in paragraph (e)(1)(ii) and (iii) of this section, to the extent that the activities enumerated in paragraph (d)(2) of this section involve the exercise of discretionary authority or control that would make the qualified termination administrator a fiduciary within the meaning of section 3(21) of the Act, the qualified termination administrator shall be deemed to satisfy its responsibilities under section 404(a) of the Act with respect to such activities, provided that the qualified termination administrator complies with the requirements of paragraph (d)(2) of this section.

(ii) A qualified termination administrator shall be responsible for the selection and monitoring of any service provider (other than monitoring a provider selected pursuant to paragraph (d)(2)(vii)(B) of this section) determined by the qualified termination administrator to be necessary to the winding up of the affairs of the plan, as well as ensuring the reasonableness of the compensation paid for such services. If a qualified termination administrator selects and monitors a service provider in accordance with the requirements of section 404(a)(1) of the Act, the qualified termination administrator shall not be liable for the acts or omissions of the service provider with respect to which the qualified termination administrator does not have knowledge.

(iii) For purposes of a distribution pursuant to paragraph (d)(2)(vii)(B)(*2*) of this section, a qualified termination administrator shall be responsible for the selection of an annuity provider in accordance with section 404 of the Act.

(2) Nothing herein shall be construed to impose an obligation on the qualified termination administrator to conduct an inquiry or review to determine whether or what breaches of fiduciary responsibility may have occurred with respect to a plan prior to becoming the qualified termination administrator for such plan.

(3) If assets of an abandoned plan are held by a person other than the qualified termination administrator, such person shall not be treated as in violation of section 404 (a) the Act solely on the basis that the person cooperated with and followed the directions of the qualified termination administrator in carrying out its responsibilities under this section with respect to such plan, provided that, in advance of any transfer or disposition of any assets at the direction of the qualified termination administrator, such person confirms with the Department of Labor that the person representing to be the qualified termination administrator with respect to the plan is the qualified termination administrator recognized by the Department of Labor.

(f) *Continued liability of plan sponsor.* Nothing in this section shall serve to relieve or limit the liability of any person other than the qualified termination administrator due to a violation of ERISA.

(g) *Qualified termination administrator.* A termination administrator is qualified under this section only if:

(1) It is eligible to serve as a trustee or issuer of an individual retirement plan, within the meaning of section 7701(a)(37) of the Internal Revenue Code, and

(2) It holds assets of the plan that is considered abandoned pursuant to paragraph (b) of this section.

(h) *Affiliate.* (1) Except as provided in paragraph (h)(2) of this section, the term affiliate means any person directly or indirectly controlling, controlled by, or under common control with, the person; or any officer, director, partner or employee of the person.

(2) For purposes of paragraph (c)(3)(i)(C) of this section, the term affiliate means a 50 percent or more owner of a qualified termination administrator, or any person described in paragraph (h)(1) of this section that provides services to the plan.

(3) For purposes of paragraph (h)(1) of this section, the term control means the power to exercise a controlling influence over the management or policies of a person other than an individual.

(i) *Model notices.* Appendices to this section contain model notices that are intended to assist qualified termination administrators in discharging the notification requirements under this section. Their use is not mandatory. However, the use of appropriately completed model notices will be deemed to satisfy the requirements of paragraphs (b)(5), (c)(3), (d)(2)(vi), and (d)(2)(ix) of this section.

[Added by 71 FR 20820, April 21, 2006, amended by 72 FR 7516, February 15, 2007].

APPENDIX A TO § 2578.1
NOTICE OF INTENT TO TERMINATE PLAN

[*Date of notice*]

[*Name of plan sponsor*]

[*Last known address of plan sponsor*]

Re: [*Name of plan and account number or other identifying information*]

Dear [*Name of plan sponsor*]:

We are writing to advise you of our concern about the status of the subject plan. Our intention is to terminate the plan and distribute benefits in accordance with federal law if you do not contact us within 30 days of your receipt of this notice. See 29 CFR 2578.1.

Our basis for taking this action is that our records reflect that there have been no contributions to, or distributions from, the plan within the past 12 months. *[If the basis for sending this notice is under § 29 CFR 2578.1(b)(1)(i)(B), complete and include the sentence below rather than the sentence above.]* Our basis for taking this action is *[provide a description of the facts and circumstances indicating plan abandonment]*.

We are sending this notice to you because our records show that you are the sponsor of the subject plan. The U.S. Department of Labor requires that you be informed that, as a fiduciary or plan administrator or both, you may be personally liable for all costs, civil penalties, excise taxes, etc. as a result of your acts or omissions with respect to this plan. The termination of this plan by us will not relieve you of your liability for any such costs, penalties, taxes, etc. Federal law also requires us to notify the U.S. Department of Labor, Employee Benefits Security Administration, of the termination of any abandoned plan. For information about the federal law governing the termination of abandoned plans, you may contact the U.S. Department of Labor at [*telephone number of appropriate EBSA contact person*].

Please contact [*name, address, and telephone number of the person, office, or department that the sponsor must contact regarding the plan*] within 30 days in order to prevent this action.

Sincerely,

[*Name and address of qualified termination administrator or appropriate designee*]

APPENDIX B TO § 2578.1
NOTIFICATION OF PLAN ABANDONMENT AND INTENT TO SERVE AS QUALIFIED TERMINATION ADMINISTRATOR

[*Date of notice*]

Abandoned Plan Coordinator, Office of Enforcement
Employee Benefits Security Administration
U.S. Department of Labor
200 Constitution Ave., NW
Suite 600
Washington, DC, 20210

Re:	*Plan Identification*	*Qualified Termination Administrator*
	[*Plan name and plan number*]	[*Name*]
	[*EIN*]	[*Address*]
	[*Plan account number*]	[*E-mail address*]
	[*Address*]	[*Telephone number*]
	[*Telephone number*]	[*EIN*]

Abandoned Plan Coordinator:

Pursuant to 29 CFR 2578.1(b), we have determined that the subject plan is or may become abandoned by its sponsor. We are eligible to serve as a Qualified Termination Administrator for purposes of terminating and winding up the plan in accordance with 29 CFR 2578.1, and hereby elect to do so.

We find that the { *check the appropriate box below and provide additional information as necessary* }:

☐ There have been no contributions to, or distributions from, the plan for a period of at least 12 consecutive months immediately preceding the date of this letter. Our records indicate that the date of the last contribution or distribution was { *enter appropriate date* }.

☐ The following facts and circumstances suggest that the plan is or may become abandoned by the plan sponsor { *add description below* }:

_____

_____

_____

We have also determined that the plan sponsor { *check appropriate box below* }:

☐ No longer exists

☐ Cannot be located

☐ Is unable to maintain the plan

We have taken the following steps to locate or communicate with the known plan sponsor and have received no objection { *provide an explanation below* }:

_____

_____

_____

Part I *Plan Information*

1. Estimated number of individuals (participants and beneficiaries) with accounts under the plan: [*number*]

2. Plan assets held by Qualified Termination Administrator:

   A. Estimated value of assets: [*value*]

   B. Months we have held plan assets, if less than 12: [*number*]

   C. Hard to value assets { *select "yes" or "no" to identify any assets with no readily ascertainable fair market value, and include for those identified assets the best known estimate of their value* }:

		Yes	No	
(a)	Partnership/joint venture interests	☐	☐	[*value*]
(b)	Employer real property	☐	☐	[*value*]
(c)	Real estate (other than (b))	☐	☐	[*value*]
(d)	Employer securities	☐	☐	[*value*]
(e)	Participant loans	☐	☐	[*value*]
(f)	Loans (other than (e))	☐	☐	[*value*]
(g)	Tangible personal property	☐	☐	[*value*]

3. Name and last known address and telephone number of plan sponsor:

   _____

   _____

   _____

4. Other:

   _____

   _____

   _____

Part II *Known Service Providers of the Plan*

	Name	Address	Telephone
1.			
2.			
3.			

Part III *Services and Related Expenses to be Paid*

	Services	Service Provider	Estimated Cost
1.			
2.			
3.			

Part IV *Investigation*

In the past 24 months { *check one box* }:

☐ Neither we nor our affiliates are or have been the subject of an investigation, examination, or enforcement action by the Department, Internal Revenue Service, or Securities and Exchange Commission concerning such entity's conduct as a fiduciary or party in interest with respect to any plan covered by the Act.

☐ We or our affiliates are or have been the subject of an investigation, examination, or enforcement action by the Department, Internal Revenue Service, or Securities and Exchange Commission concerning such entity's conduct as a fiduciary or party in interest with respect to any plan covered by the Act.

Part V   *Contact Person { enter information only if different from signatory }*:

[*Name*]

[*Address*]

[*E-mail address*]

[*Telephone number*]

Under penalties of perjury, I declare that I have examined this notice and to the best of my knowledge and belief, it is true, correct and complete.

[*Signature*]

[*Title of person signing on behalf the Qualified Termination Administrator*]

[*Address, e-mail address, and telephone number*]

APPENDIX C TO § 2578.1
NOTICE OF PLAN TERMINATION

[*Date of notice*]

[*Name and last known address of plan participant or beneficiary*]

Re: [*Name of plan*]

Dear [*Name of plan participant or beneficiary*]:

We are writing to inform you that the [*name of plan*](Plan) has been terminated pursuant to regulations issued by the U.S. Department of Labor. The Plan was terminated because it was abandoned by [*name of the plan sponsor*].

We have determined that you have an interest in the Plan, either as a plan participant or beneficiary. Your account balance on [*date*]is/was [*account balance*]. We will be distributing this money as permitted under the terms of the Plan and federal regulations. The actual amount of your distribution may be more or less than the amount stated in this letter depending on investment gains or losses and the administrative cost of terminating the Plan and distributing your benefits.

Your distribution options under the Plan are { *add a description of the Plan's distribution options* }. It is very important that you elect one of these forms of distribution and inform us of your election. The process for informing us of this election is { *enter a description of the election process established by the qualified termination administrator* }.

{ *Select the next paragraph from options I through 3, as appropriate.* }

{*Option 1: If this notice is for a participant or beneficiary, complete and include the following paragraph provided the account balance does not meet the conditions of § 2550.404a-3(d)(1)(iii).*}

If you do not make an election within 30 days from your receipt of this notice, your account balance will be transferred directly to an individual retirement plan (inherited individual retirement plan in the case of a nonspouse beneficiary) maintained by {*insert the name, address, and phone number of the provider if known, other wise insert the following language}* a bank or insurance company or other similar financial institution]}. Pursuant to federal law, your money in the individual retirement plan would then be invested in an investment product designed to preserve principal and provide a reasonable rate of return and liquidity. {If fee information is known, include the following sentence: Should your money be transferred into an individual retirement plan, [*name of the financial institution*] charges the following fees for its services: *{add a statement of fees, if any, that will be paid from the participant or beneficiary's individual retirement plan}.}*

{ *Option 2: If this notice is for a participant or beneficiary whose account balance meets the conditions of § 2550.404a-3(d)(1)(iii), complete and include the following paragraph.* }

If you do not make an election within 30 days from your receipt of this notice, and your account balance is $1,000 or less, federal law permits us to transfer your balance to an interest-bearing federally insured bank account, to the unclaimed property fund of the State of your last known address, or to an individual retirement plan (inherited individual retirement plan in the case of a nonspouse beneficiary). Pursuant to federal law, your money, if transferred to an individual retirement plan would then be invested in an investment product designed to preserve principal and provide a reasonable rate of return and liquidity. { *If known, include the name, address, and telephone number of the financial institution or State fund into which the individual's account balance will be transferred or deposited. If the individual's account balance is to be transferred to a financial institution and fee information is known, include the following sentence:* } Should your money be transferred into a plan or account, [*name of the financial institution*] charges the following fees for its services: { *add a statement of fees, if any, that will be paid from the individual's account* }.}

{ *Option 3: If this notice is for a participant or participant's spouse whose distribution is subject to the survivor annuity requirements in sections 401(a)(11) and 417 of the Internal Revenue Code (or section 205 of ERISA), complete and include the following paragraph.* }

If you do not make an election within 30 days from your receipt of this notice, your account balance will be distributed in the form of a qualified joint and survivor annuity or qualified preretirement annuity as required by the Internal Revenue Code. { *If the name of the annuity provider is known, include the following sentence:* The name of the annuity provider is [*name, address and phone number of the provider*].}

For more information about the termination, your account balance, or distribution options, please contact [*name, address, and telephone number of the qualified termination administrator and, if different, the name, address, and telephone number of the appropriate contact person*].

Sincerely,

[*Name of qualified termination administrator or appropriate designee*]

APPENDIX D TO § 2578.1
FINAL NOTICE

[*Date of notice*]

Abandoned Plan Coordinator, Office of Enforcement
Employee Benefits Security Administration
U.S. Department of Labor

Reg. §2578.1   ¶14,929S

200 Constitution Ave., NW
Suite 600
Washington, DC, 20210

Re: *Plan Identification*   *Qualified Termination Administrator*

          [*Plan name and plan number*]   [*Name*]

          [*Plan acount number*]   [*Address and e-mail address*]

          [*EIN*]   [*Telephone number*]

                                                        [*EIN*]

Abandoned Plan Coordinator:

General Information

The termination and winding-up process of the subject plan has been completed pursuant to 29 CFR 2578.1. Benefits were distributed to participants and beneficiaries on the basis of the best available information pursuant to 29 CFR 2578.1(d)(2)(i). Plan expenses were paid out of plan assets pursuant to 29 CFR 2578.1(d)(2)(v).

{ *Include and complete the next section, entitled "Contact Person," only if the contact person is different from the signatory of this notice.* }

Contact Person

[*Name*]

[*Address and e-mail address*]

[*Telephone number*]

{ *Include and complete the next section, entitled "Expenses Paid to Qualified Termination Administrator," only if fees and expenses paid to the QTA (or its affiliate) exceeded by 20 percent or more the estimate required by 29 CFR 2578.1(c)(3)(v)(B).* }

Expenses Paid to Qualified Termination Administrator

The actual fees and/or expenses we received in connection with winding up the Plan exceeded by { *insert either*: [20 percent or more] *or* [*enter the actual percentage*]} the estimate required by 29 CFR 2578.1(c)(3)(v)(B). The reason or reasons for such additional costs are { *provide an explanation of the additional costs* }.

Other

_____

_____

_____

_____

Under penalties of perjury, I declare that I have examined this notice and to the best of my knowledge and belief, it is true, correct and complete.

[*Signature*]

[*Title of person signing on behalf the Qualified Termination Administrator*]

[*Address, e-mail address, and telephone number*]

Attachment

[¶ 14,930]
CLAIMS PROCEDURE

Act Sec. 503. In accordance with regulations of the Secretary, every employee benefit plan shall—

(1) provide adequate notice in writing to any participant or beneficiary whose claim for benefits under the plan has been denied, setting forth the specific reasons for such denial, written in a manner calculated to be understood by the participant, and

(2) afford a reasonable opportunity to any participant whose claim for benefits has been denied for a full and fair review by the appropriate named fiduciary of the decision denying the claim.

Regulations

The following regulations were adopted under "Title 29—Labor," "Chapter XXV—Pension and Welfare Benefit Programs," "Subchapter G—Administration and Enforcement Under the Employee Retirement Income Security Act of 1974," "Part 2560—Rules and Regulations for Administration and Enforcement." The regulations were filed with the Federal Register on May 25, 1977, and published in the *Federal Register* of May 27, 1977 (42 FR 27426). The regulations are effective for claims filed on or after October 1, 1977. Regulation § 2560.503-1 was amended by revising paragraph (b)(1)(i) and adding a new paragraph (j) by 46 FR 5882 and published in the *Federal Register* on January 21, 1981. The regulations were amended by 65 FR 70264 and published in the *Federal Register* on November 21, 2000. Regulation Sec. 2560.503-1 was amended by revising paragraph (o) by 66 FR 35885 and published in the *Federal Register* on July 9, 2001. Reg. § 2560.503-1 was amended on December 19, 2016 (81 FR 92316). Reg. § 2560.503-1 was amended on November 29, 2017 (82 FR 56560) to delay the applicability date of certain amendments made on December 19, 2016 from January 1, 2018 to after April 1, 2018.

[¶ 14,931]

§ 2560.503-1 **Claims procedure.**

(a) *Scope and purpose.* In accordance with the authority of sections 503 and 505 of the Employee Retirement Income Security Act of 1974 (ERISA or the Act), 29 U.S.C. 1133, 1135, this section sets forth minimum requirements for employee benefit plan procedures pertaining to claims for benefits by participants and beneficiaries (hereinafter referred to as claimants). Except as otherwise specifically provided in this section, these requirements apply to every employee benefit plan described in section 4(a) and not exempted under section 4(b) of the Act.

(b) *Obligation to establish and maintain reasonable claims procedures.* Every employee benefit plan shall establish and maintain reasonable procedures governing the filing of benefit claims, notification of benefit determinations, and appeal of adverse benefit determinations (hereinafter collectively referred to as claims procedures). The claims procedures for a plan will be deemed to be reasonable only if—

(1) The claims procedures comply with the requirements of paragraphs (c), (d), (e), (f), (g), (h), (i), and (j) of this section, as appropriate, except to the extent that the claims procedures are deemed to comply with some or all of such provisions pursuant to paragraph (b)(6) of this section;

(2) A description of all claims procedures (including, in the case of a group health plan within the meaning of paragraph (m)(6) of this section, any procedures for obtaining prior approval as a prerequisite for obtaining a benefit, such as preauthorization procedures or utilization review procedures) and the applicable time frames is included as part of a summary plan description meeting the requirements of 29 CFR 2520.102-3;

(3) The claims procedures do not contain any provision, and are not administered in a way, that unduly inhibits or hampers the initiation or processing of claims for benefits. For example, a provision or practice that requires payment of a fee or costs as a condition to making a claim or to appealing an adverse benefit determination would be considered to unduly inhibit the initiation and processing of claims for benefits. Also, the denial of a claim for failure to obtain a prior approval under circumstances that would make obtaining such prior approval impossible or where application of the prior approval process could seriously jeopardize the life or health of the claimant (e.g., in the case of a group health plan, the claimant is unconscious and in need of immediate care at the time medical treatment is required) would constitute a practice that unduly inhibits the initiation and processing of a claim;

(4) The claims procedures do not preclude an authorized representative of a claimant from acting on behalf of such claimant in pursuing a benefit claim or appeal of an adverse benefit determination. Nevertheless, a plan may establish reasonable procedures for determining whether an individual has been authorized to act on behalf of a claimant, provided that, in the case of a claim involving urgent care, within the meaning of paragraph (m)(1) of this section, a health care professional, within the meaning of paragraph (m)(7) of this section, with knowledge of a claimant's medical condition shall be permitted to act as the authorized representative of the claimant; and

(5) The claims procedures contain administrative processes and safeguards designed to ensure and to verify that benefit claim determinations are made in accordance with governing plan documents and that, where appropriate, the plan provisions have been applied consistently with respect to similarly situated claimants.

(6) In the case of a plan established and maintained pursuant to a collective bargaining agreement (other than a plan subject to the provisions of section 302(c)(5) of the Labor Management Relations Act, 1947 concerning joint representation on the board of trustees)—

(i) Such plan will be deemed to comply with the provisions of paragraphs (c) through (j) of this section if the collective bargaining agreement pursuant to which the plan is established or maintained sets forth or incorporates by specific reference—

(A) Provisions concerning the filing of benefit claims and the initial disposition of benefit claims, and

(B) A grievance and arbitration procedure to which adverse benefit determinations are subject.

(ii) Such plan will be deemed to comply with the provisions of paragraphs (h), (i), and (j) of this section (but will not be deemed to comply with paragraphs (c) through (g) of this section) if the collective bargaining agreement pursuant to which the plan is established or maintained sets forth or incorporates by specific reference a grievance and arbitration procedure to which adverse benefit determinations are subject (but not provisions concerning the filing and initial disposition of benefit claims).

»»→ Caution: Reg. Sec. 2560.503-1(b)(7), as amended, is effective January 18, 2017 and applicable for claims for disability benefits filed under a plan after April 1, 2018.

(7) In the case of a plan providing disability benefits, the plan must ensure that all claims and appeals for disability benefits are adjudicated in a manner designed to ensure the independence and impartiality of the persons involved in making the decision. Accordingly, decisions regarding hiring, compensation, termination, promotion, or other similar matters with respect to any individual (such as a claims adjudicator or medical or vocational expert) must not be made based upon the likelihood that the individual will support the denial of benefits. [Added 12/19/16 (81 FR 92316).]

(c) *Group health plans.* The claims procedures of a group health plan will be deemed to be reasonable only if, in addition to complying with the requirements of paragraph (b) of this section—

(1)(i) The claims procedures provide that, in the case of a failure by a claimant or an authorized representative of a claimant to follow the plan's procedures for filing a pre-service claim, within the meaning of paragraph (m)(2) of this section, the claimant or representative shall be notified of the failure and the proper procedures to be followed in filing a claim for benefits. This notification shall be provided to the claimant or authorized representative, as appropriate, as soon as possible, but not later than 5 days (24 hours in the case of a failure to file a claim involving urgent care) following the failure. Notification may be oral, unless written notification is requested by the claimant or authorized representative.

(ii) Paragraph (c)(1)(i) of this section shall apply only in the case of a failure that—

(A) Is a communication by a claimant or an authorized representative of a claimant that is received by a person or organizational unit customarily responsible for handling benefit matters; and

(B) Is a communication that names a specific claimant; a specific medical condition or symptom; and a specific treatment, service, or product for which approval is requested.

(2) The claims procedures do not contain any provision, and are not administered in a way, that requires a claimant to file more than two appeals of an adverse benefit determination prior to bringing a civil action under section 502(a) of the Act;

(3) To the extent that a plan offers voluntary levels of appeal (except to the extent that the plan is required to do so by State law), including voluntary arbitration or any other form of dispute resolution, in addition to those permitted by paragraph (c)(2) of this section, the claims procedures provide that:

(i) The plan waives any right to assert that a claimant has failed to exhaust administrative remedies because the claimant did not elect to submit a benefit dispute to any such voluntary level of appeal provided by the plan;

(ii) The plan agrees that any statute of limitations or other defense based on timeliness is tolled during the time that any such voluntary appeal is pending;

(iii) The claims procedures provide that a claimant may elect to submit a benefit dispute to such voluntary level of appeal only after exhaustion of the appeals permitted by paragraph (c)(2) of this section;

(iv) The plan provides to any claimant, upon request, sufficient information relating to the voluntary level of appeal to enable the claimant to make an informed judgment about whether to submit a benefit dispute to the voluntary level of appeal, including a statement that the decision of a claimant as to whether or not to submit a benefit dispute to the voluntary level of appeal will have no effect on the claimant's rights to any other benefits under the plan and information about the applicable rules, the claimant's right to representation, the process for selecting the decisionmaker, and the circumstances, if any, that may affect the impartiality of the decisionmaker, such as any financial or personal interests in the result or any past or present relationship with any party to the review process; and

(v) No fees or costs are imposed on the claimant as part of the voluntary level of appeal.

(4) The claims procedures do not contain any provision for the mandatory arbitration of adverse benefit determinations, except to the extent that the plan or procedures provide that:

(i) The arbitration is conducted as one of the two appeals described in paragraph (c)(2) of this section and in accordance with the requirements applicable to such appeals; and

(ii) The claimant is not precluded from challenging the decision under section 502(a) of the Act or other applicable law.

(d) *Plans providing disability benefits.* The claims procedures of a plan that provides disability benefits will be deemed to be reasonable only if the claims procedures comply, with respect to claims for disability benefits, with the requirements of paragraphs (b), (c)(2), (c)(3), and (c)(4) of this section.

(e) *Claim for benefits.* For purposes of this section, a claim for benefits is a request for a plan benefit or benefits made by a claimant in accordance with a plan's reasonable procedure for filing benefit claims. In the case of a group health plan, a claim for benefits includes any pre-service claims within the meaning of paragraph (m)(2) of this section and any post-service claims within the meaning of paragraph (m)(3) of this section.

(f) *Timing of notification of benefit determination.* (1) *In general.* Except as provided in paragraphs (f)(2) and (f)(3) of this section, if a claim is wholly or partially denied, the plan administrator shall notify the claimant, in accordance with paragraph (g) of this section, of the plan's adverse benefit determination within a reasonable period of time, but not later than 90 days after receipt of the claim by the plan, unless the plan administrator determines that special circumstances require an extension of time for processing the claim. If the plan administrator determines that an extension of time for processing is required, written notice of the extension shall be furnished to the claimant prior to the termination of the initial 90day period. In no event shall such extension exceed a period of 90 days from the end of such initial period. The extension notice shall indicate the special circumstances requiring an extension of time and the date by which the plan expects to render the benefit determination.

(2) *Group health plans.* In the case of a group health plan, the plan administrator shall notify a claimant of the plan's benefit determination in accordance with paragraph (f)(2)(i), (f)(2)(ii), or (f)(2)(iii) of this section, as appropriate.

(i) *Urgent care claims.* In the case of a claim involving urgent care, the plan administrator shall notify the claimant of the plan's benefit determination (whether adverse or not) as soon as possible, taking into account the medical exigencies, but not later than 72 hours after receipt of the claim by the plan, unless the claimant fails to provide sufficient information to determine whether, or to what extent, benefits are covered or payable under the plan. In the case of such a failure, the plan administrator shall notify the claimant as soon as possible, but not later than 24 hours after receipt of the claim by the plan, of the specific information necessary to complete the claim. The claimant shall be afforded a reasonable amount of time, taking into account the circumstances, but not less than 48 hours, to provide the specified information. Notification of any adverse benefit determination pursuant to this paragraph (f)(2)(i) shall be made in accordance with paragraph (g) of this section. The plan administrator shall notify the claimant of the plan's benefit determination as soon as possible, but in no case later than 48 hours after the earlier of—

(A) The plan's receipt of the specified information, or

(B) The end of the period afforded the claimant to provide the specified additional information.

(ii) *Concurrent care decisions.* If a group health plan has approved an ongoing course of treatment to be provided over a period of time or number of treatments—

(A) Any reduction or termination by the plan of such course of treatment (other than by plan amendment or termination) before the end of such period of time or number of treatments shall constitute an adverse benefit determination. The plan administrator shall notify the claimant, in accordance with paragraph (g) of this section, of the adverse benefit determination at a time sufficiently in advance of the reduction or termination to allow the claimant to appeal and obtain a determination on review of that adverse benefit determination before the benefit is reduced or terminated.

(B) Any request by a claimant to extend the course of treatment beyond the period of time or number of treatments that is a claim involving urgent care shall be decided as soon as possible, taking into account the medical exigencies, and the plan administrator shall notify the claimant of the benefit determination, whether adverse or not, within 24 hours after receipt of the claim by the plan, provided that any such claim is made to the plan at least 24 hours prior to the expiration of the prescribed period of time or number of treatments. Notification of any adverse benefit determination concerning a request to extend the course of treatment, whether involving urgent care or not, shall be made in accordance with paragraph (g) of this section, and

appeal shall be governed by paragraph (i)(2)(i), (i)(2)(ii), or (i)(2)(iii), as appropriate.

(iii) *Other claims.* In the case of a claim not described in paragraphs (f)(2)(i) or (f)(2)(ii) of this section, the plan administrator shall notify the claimant of the plan's benefit determination in accordance with either paragraph (f)(2)(iii)(A) or (f)(2)(iii)(B) of this section, as appropriate.

(A) *Pre-service claims.* In the case of a pre-service claim, the plan administrator shall notify the claimant of the plan's benefit determination (whether adverse or not) within a reasonable period of time appropriate to the medical circumstances, but not later than 15 days after receipt of the claim by the plan. This period may be extended one time by the plan for up to 15 days, provided that the plan administrator both determines that such an extension is necessary due to matters beyond the control of the plan and notifies the claimant, prior to the expiration of the initial 15-day period, of the circumstances requiring the extension of time and the date by which the plan expects to render a decision. If such an extension is necessary due to a failure of the claimant to submit the information necessary to decide the claim, the notice of extension shall specifically describe the required information, and the claimant shall be afforded at least 45 days from receipt of the notice within which to provide the specified information. Notification of any adverse benefit determination pursuant to this paragraph (f)(2)(iii)(A) shall be made in accordance with paragraph (g) of this section.

(B) *Post-service claims.* In the case of a post-service claim, the plan administrator shall notify the claimant, in accordance with paragraph (g) of this section, of the plan's adverse benefit determination within a reasonable period of time, but not later than 30 days after receipt of the claim. This period may be extended one time by the plan for up to 15 days, provided that the plan administrator both determines that such an extension is necessary due to matters beyond the control of the plan and notifies the claimant, prior to the expiration of the initial 30-day period, of the circumstances requiring the extension of time and the date by which the plan expects to render a decision. If such an extension is necessary due to a failure of the claimant to submit the information necessary to decide the claim, the notice of extension shall specifically describe the required information, and the claimant shall be afforded at least 45 days from receipt of the notice within which to provide the specified information.

(3) *Disability claims.* In the case of a claim for disability benefits, the plan administrator shall notify the claimant, in accordance with paragraph (g) of this section, of the plan's adverse benefit determination within a reasonable period of time, but not later than 45 days after receipt of the claim by the plan. This period may be extended by the plan for up to 30 days, provided that the plan administrator both determines that such an extension is necessary due to matters beyond the control of the plan and notifies the claimant, prior to the expiration of the initial 45-day period, of the circumstances requiring the extension of time and the date by which the plan expects to render a decision. If, prior to the end of the first 30-day extension period, the administrator determines that, due to matters beyond the control of the plan, a decision cannot be rendered within that extension period, the period for making the determination may be extended for up to an additional 30 days, provided that the plan administrator notifies the claimant, prior to the expiration of the first 30-day extension period, of the circumstances requiring the extension and the date as of which the plan expects to render a decision. In the case of any extension under this paragraph (f)(3), the notice of extension shall specifically explain the standards on which entitlement to a benefit is based, the unresolved issues that prevent a decision on the claim, and the additional information needed to resolve those issues, and the claimant shall be afforded at least 45 days within which to provide the specified information.

(4) *Calculating time periods.* For purposes of paragraph (f) of this section, the period of time within which a benefit determination is required to be made shall begin at the time a claim is filed in accordance with the reasonable procedures of a plan, without regard to whether all the information necessary to make a benefit determination accompanies the filing. In the event that a period of time is extended as

permitted pursuant to paragraph (f)(2)(iii) or (f)(3) of this section due to a claimant's failure to submit information necessary to decide a claim, the period for making the benefit determination shall be tolled from the date on which the notification of the extension is sent to the claimant until the date on which the claimant responds to the request for additional information.

(g) *Manner and content of notification of benefit determination.* (1) Except as provided in paragraph (g)(2) of this section, the plan administrator shall provide a claimant with written or electronic notification of any adverse benefit determination. Any electronic notification shall comply with the standards imposed by 29 CFR 2520.104b-1(c)(1)(i), (iii), and (iv). The notification shall set forth, in a manner calculated to be understood by the claimant—

(i) The specific reason or reasons for the adverse determination;

(ii) Reference to the specific plan provisions on which the determination is based;

(iii) A description of any additional material or information necessary for the claimant to perfect the claim and an explanation of why such material or information is necessary;

(iv) A description of the plan's review procedures and the time limits applicable to such procedures, including a statement of the claimant's right to bring a civil action under section 502(a) of the Act following an adverse benefit determination on review;

(v) In the case of an adverse benefit determination by a group health plan—[Revised 12/19/16 (81 FR 92316).]

(vi) In the case of an adverse benefit determination by a group health plan concerning a claim involving urgent care, a description of the expedited review process applicable to such claims.

⟫→ Caution: Reg. Sec. 2560.503-1(g)(1)(vii), as added, is effective January 18, 2017 and applicable for claims for disability benefits filed under a plan after April 1, 2018.

(vii) In the case of an adverse benefit determination with respect to disability benefits—

(A) A discussion of the decision, including an explanation of the basis for disagreeing with or not following:

(i) The views presented by the claimant to the plan of health care professionals treating the claimant and vocational professionals who evaluated the claimant;

(ii) The views of medical or vocational experts whose advice was obtained on behalf of the plan in connection with a claimant's adverse benefit determination, without regard to whether the advice was relied upon in making the benefit determination; and

(iii) A disability determination regarding the claimant presented by the claimant to the plan made by the Social Security Administration;

(B) If the adverse benefit determination is based on a medical necessity or experimental treatment or similar exclusion or limit, either an explanation of the scientific or clinical judgment for the determination, applying the terms of the plan to the claimant's medical circumstances, or a statement that such explanation will be provided free of charge upon request;

(C) Either the specific internal rules, guidelines, protocols, standards or other similar criteria of the plan relied upon in making the adverse determination or, alternatively, a statement that such rules, guidelines, protocols, standards or other similar criteria of the plan do not exist; and

(D) A statement that the claimant is entitled to receive, upon request and free of charge, reasonable access to, and copies of, all documents, records, and other information relevant to the claimant's claim for benefits. Whether a document, record, or other information is relevant to a claim for benefits shall be determined by reference to paragraph (m)(8) of this section. [Added 12/19/16 (81 FR 92316).]

⟫→ Caution: Reg. Sec. 2560.503-1(g)(1)(viii), as added, is effective January 18, 2017 and applicable for claims for disability benefits filed under a plan after April 1, 2018.

(viii) In the case of an adverse benefit determination with respect to disability benefits, the notification shall be provided in a culturally and linguistically appropriate manner (as described in paragraph (o) of this section). [Added 12/19/16 (81 FR 92316).]

(2) In the case of an adverse benefit determination by a group health plan concerning a claim involving urgent care, the information described in paragraph (g)(1) of this section may be provided to the claimant orally within the time frame prescribed in paragraph (f)(2)(i) of this section, provided that a written or electronic notification in accordance with paragraph (g)(1) of this section is furnished to the claimant not later than 3 days after the oral notification.

(h) *Appeal of adverse benefit determinations.* (1) In general. Every employee benefit plan shall establish and maintain a procedure by which a claimant shall have a reasonable opportunity to appeal an adverse benefit determination to an appropriate named fiduciary of the plan, and under which there will be a full and fair review of the claim and the adverse benefit determination.

(2) *Full and fair review.* Except as provided in paragraphs (h)(3) and (h)(4) of this section, the claims procedures of a plan will not be deemed to provide a claimant with a reasonable opportunity for a full and fair review of a claim and adverse benefit determination unless the claims procedures—

(i) Provide claimants at least 60 days following receipt of a notification of an adverse benefit determination within which to appeal the determination;

(ii) Provide claimants the opportunity to submit written comments, documents, records, and other information relating to the claim for benefits;

(iii) Provide that a claimant shall be provided, upon request and free of charge, reasonable access to, and copies of, all documents, records, and other information relevant to the claimant's claim for benefits. Whether a document, record, or other information is relevant to a claim for benefits shall be determined by reference to paragraph (m)(8) of this section;

(iv) Provide for a review that takes into account all comments, documents, records, and other information submitted by the claimant relating to the claim, without regard to whether such information was submitted or considered in the initial benefit determination.

(3) *Group health plans.* The claims procedures of a group health plan will not be deemed to provide a claimant with a reasonable opportunity for a full and fair review of a claim and adverse benefit determination unless, in addition to complying with the requirements of paragraphs (h)(2)(ii) through (iv) of this section, the claims procedures—

(i) Provide claimants at least 180 days following receipt of a notification of an adverse benefit determination within which to appeal the determination;

(ii) Provide for a review that does not afford deference to the initial adverse benefit determination and that is conducted by an appropriate named fiduciary of the plan who is neither the individual who made the adverse benefit determination that is the subject of the appeal, nor the subordinate of such individual;

(iii) Provide that, in deciding an appeal of any adverse benefit determination that is based in whole or in part on a medical judgment, including determinations with regard to whether a particular treatment, drug, or other item is experimental, investigational, or not medically necessary or appropriate, the appropriate named fiduciary shall consult with a health care professional who has appropriate training and experience in the field of medicine involved in the medical judgment;

(iv) Provide for the identification of medical or vocational experts whose advice was obtained on behalf of the plan in connection with a claimant's adverse benefit determination, without regard to whether the advice was relied upon in making the benefit determination;

(v) Provide that the health care professional engaged for purposes of a consultation under paragraph (h)(3)(iii) of this section shall be an individual who is neither an individual who was consulted in connection with the adverse benefit determination that is the subject of the appeal, nor the subordinate of any such individual; and

(vi) Provide, in the case of a claim involving urgent care, for an expedited review process pursuant to which—

(A) A request for an expedited appeal of an adverse benefit determination may be submitted orally or in writing by the claimant; and

(B) All necessary information, including the plan's benefit determination on review, shall be transmitted between the plan and the claimant by telephone, facsimile, or other available similarly expeditious method.

(4) *Plans providing disability benefits.* The claims procedures of a plan providing disability benefits will not, with respect to claims for such benefits, be deemed to provide a claimant with a reasonable opportunity for a full and fair review of a claim and adverse benefit determination unless, in addition to complying with the requirements of paragraphs (h)(2)(ii) through (iv) and (h)(3)(i) through (v) of this section, the claims procedures—

(i) Provide that before the plan can issue an adverse benefit determination on review on a disability benefit claim, the plan administrator shall provide the claimant, free of charge, with any new or additional evidence considered, relied upon, or generated by the plan, insurer, or other person making the benefit determination (or at the direction of the plan, insurer or such other person) in connection with the claim; such evidence must be provided as soon as possible and sufficiently in advance of the date on which the notice of adverse benefit determination on review is required to be provided under paragraph (i) of this section to give the claimant a reasonable opportunity to respond prior to that date; and

(ii) Provide that, before the plan can issue an adverse benefit determination on review on a disability benefit claim based on a new or additional rationale, the plan administrator shall provide the claimant, free of charge, with the rationale; the rationale must be provided as soon as possible and sufficiently in advance of the date on which the notice of adverse benefit determination on review is required to be provided under paragraph (i) of this section to give the claimant a reasonable opportunity to respond prior to that date. [Revised 12/19/16 (81 FR 92316).]

(i) *Timing of notification of benefit determination on review.* (1) *In general.* (i) Except as provided in paragraphs (i)(1)(ii), (i)(2), and (i)(3) of this section, the plan administrator shall notify a claimant in accordance with paragraph (j) of this section of the plan's benefit determination on review within a reasonable period of time, but not later than 60 days after receipt of the claimant's request for review by the plan, unless the plan administrator determines that special circumstances (such as the need to hold a hearing, if the plan's procedures provide for a hearing) require an extension of time for processing the claim. If the plan administrator determines that an extension of time for processing is required, written notice of the extension shall be furnished to the claimant prior to the termination of the initial 60-day period. In no event shall such extension exceed a period of 60 days from the end of the initial period. The extension notice shall indicate the special circumstances requiring an extension of time and the date by which the plan expects to render the determination on review.

(ii) In the case of a plan with a committee or board of trustees designated as the appropriate named fiduciary that holds regularly scheduled meetings at least quarterly, paragraph (i)(1)(i) of this section shall not apply, and, except as provided in paragraphs (i)(2) and (i)(3) of this section, the appropriate named fiduciary shall instead make a benefit determination no later than the date of the meeting of the committee or board that immediately follows the plan's receipt of a request for review, unless the request for review is filed within 30 days preceding the date of such meeting. In such case, a benefit determination may be made by no later than the date of the second meeting following the plan's receipt of the request for review. If special circumstances (such as the need to hold a hearing, if the plan's procedures provide for a hearing) require a further extension of time for processing, a benefit determination shall be rendered not later than the third meeting of the committee or board following the plan's receipt of the request for review. If such an extension of time for review is required because of special circumstances, the plan administrator shall provide the claimant with written notice of the extension, describing the special circumstances and the date as of which the benefit determination will be made, prior to the commencement of the extension. The plan administrator shall notify the claimant, in accordance with paragraph

(j) of this section, of the benefit determination as soon as possible, but not later than 5 days after the benefit determination is made.

(2) *Group health plans.* In the case of a group health plan, the plan administrator shall notify a claimant of the plan's benefit determination on review in accordance with paragraphs (i)(2)(i) through (iii), as appropriate.

(i) *Urgent care claims.* In the case of a claim involving urgent care, the plan administrator shall notify the claimant, in accordance with paragraph (j) of this section, of the plan's benefit determination on review as soon as possible, taking into account the medical exigencies, but not later than 72 hours after receipt of the claimant's request for review of an adverse benefit determination by the plan.

(ii) *Pre-service claims.* In the case of a pre-service claim, the plan administrator shall notify the claimant, in accordance with paragraph (j) of this section, of the plan's benefit determination on review within a reasonable period of time appropriate to the medical circumstances. In the case of a group health plan that provides for one appeal of an adverse benefit determination, such notification shall be provided not later than 30 days after receipt by the plan of the claimant's request for review of an adverse benefit determination. In the case of a group health plan that provides for two appeals of an adverse determination, such notification shall be provided, with respect to any one of such two appeals, not later than 15 days after receipt by the plan of the claimant's request for review of the adverse determination.

(iii) *Post-service claims.* (A) In the case of a post-service claim, except as provided in paragraph (i)(2)(iii)(B) of this section, the plan administrator shall notify the claimant, in accordance with paragraph (j) of this section, of the plan's benefit determination on review within a reasonable period of time. In the case of a group health plan that provides for one appeal of an adverse benefit determination, such notification shall be provided not later than 60 days after receipt by the plan of the claimant's request for review of an adverse benefit determination. In the case of a group health plan that provides for two appeals of an adverse determination, such notification shall be provided, with respect to any one of such two appeals, not later than 30 days after receipt by the plan of the claimant's request for review of the adverse determination.

(B) In the case of a multiemployer plan with a committee or board of trustees designated as the appropriate named fiduciary that holds regularly scheduled meetings at least quarterly, paragraph (i)(2)(iii)(A) of this section shall not apply, and the appropriate named fiduciary shall instead make a benefit determination no later than the date of the meeting of the committee or board that immediately follows the plan's receipt of a request for review, unless the request for review is filed within 30 days preceding the date of such meeting. In such case, a benefit determination may be made by no later than the date of the second meeting following the plan's receipt of the request for review. If special circumstances (such as the need to hold a hearing, if the plan's procedures provide for a hearing) require a further extension of time for processing, a benefit determination shall be rendered not later than the third meeting of the committee or board following the plan's receipt of the request for review. If such an extension of time for review is required because of special circumstances, the plan administrator shall notify the claimant in writing of the extension, describing the special circumstances and the date as of which the benefit determination will be made, prior to the commencement of the extension. The plan administrator shall notify the claimant, in accordance with paragraph (j) of this section, of the benefit determination as soon as possible, but not later than 5 days after the benefit determination is made.

(3) *Disability claims.* (i) Except as provided in paragraph (i)(3)(ii) of this section, claims involving disability benefits (whether the plan provides for one or two appeals) shall be governed by paragraph (i)(1)(i) of this section, except that a period of 45 days shall apply instead of 60 days for purposes of that paragraph. [Revised 12/19/16 (81 FR 92316).]

(ii) In the case of a multiemployer plan with a committee or board of trustees designated as the appropriate named fiduciary that holds regularly scheduled meetings at least quarterly, paragraph (i)(3)(i) of this section shall not apply, and the appropriate named fiduciary shall instead make a benefit determination no later than the date of the meeting of the committee or board that immediately follows the plan's receipt of a request for review, unless the request for review is filed within 30 days preceding the date of such meeting. In such case, a benefit determination may be made by no later than the date of the second meeting following the plan's receipt of the request for review. If special circumstances (such as the need to hold a hearing, if the plan's procedures provide for a hearing) require a further extension of time for processing, a benefit determination shall be rendered not later than the third meeting of the committee or board following the plan's receipt of the request for review. If such an extension of time for review is required because of special circumstances, the plan administrator shall notify the claimant in writing of the extension, describing the special circumstances and the date as of which the benefit determination will be made, prior to the commencement of the extension. The plan administrator shall notify the claimant, in accordance with paragraph (j) of this section, of the benefit determination as soon as possible, but not later than 5 days after the benefit determination is made.

(4) *Calculating time periods.* For purposes of paragraph (i) of this section, the period of time within which a benefit determination on review is required to be made shall begin at the time an appeal is filed in accordance with the reasonable procedures of a plan, without regard to whether all the information necessary to make a benefit determination on review accompanies the filing. In the event that a period of time is extended as permitted pursuant to paragraph (i)(1), (i)(2)(iii)(B), or (i)(3) of this section due to a claimant's failure to submit information necessary to decide a claim, the period for making the benefit determination on review shall be tolled from the date on which the notification of the extension is sent to the claimant until the date on which the claimant responds to the request for additional information.

(5) *Furnishing documents.* In the case of an adverse benefit determination on review, the plan administrator shall provide such access to, and copies of, documents, records, and other information described in paragraphs (j)(3), (j)(4), and (j)(5) of this section as is appropriate.

(j) *Manner and content of notification of benefit determination on review.* The plan administrator shall provide a claimant with written or electronic notification of a plan's benefit determination on review. Any electronic notification shall comply with the standards imposed by 29 CFR 2520.104b-1(c)(1)(i), (iii), and (iv). In the case of an adverse benefit determination, the notification shall set forth, in a manner calculated to be understood by the claimant—

(1) The specific reason or reasons for the adverse determination;

(2) Reference to the specific plan provisions on which the benefit determination is based;

(3) A statement that the claimant is entitled to receive, upon request and free of charge, reasonable access to, and copies of, all documents, records, and other information relevant to the claimant's claim for benefits. Whether a document, record, or other information is relevant to a claim for benefits shall be determined by reference to paragraph (m)(8) of this section;

(4)(i) A statement describing any voluntary appeal procedures offered by the plan and the claimant's right to obtain the information about such procedures described in paragraph (c)(3)(iv) of this section, and a statement of the claimant's right to bring an action under section 502(a) of the Act; and,

>>>→ *Caution: Reg. Sec. 2560.503-1(j)(4)(ii), as amended, is effective January 18, 2017 and applicable for claims for disability benefits filed under a plan after April 1, 2018.*

(ii) In the case of a plan providing disability benefits, in addition to the information described in paragraph (j)(4)(i) of this section, the statement of the claimant's right to bring an action under section 502(a) of the Act shall also describe any applicable contractual limitations period that applies to the claimant's right to bring such an action, including the calendar date on which the contractual limitations period expires for the claim. [Revised 12/19/16 (81 FR 92316).]

(5) In the case of a group health plan—[Revised 12/19/16 (81 FR 92316).]

(i) If an internal rule, guideline, protocol, or other similar criterion was relied upon in making the adverse determination, either the specific rule, guideline, protocol, or other similar criterion; or a statement that such rule, guideline, protocol, or other similar criterion was relied upon in making the adverse determination and that a copy of the rule, guideline, protocol, or other similar criterion will be provided free of charge to the claimant upon request;

(ii) If the adverse benefit determination is based on a medical necessity or experimental treatment or similar exclusion or limit, either an explanation of the scientific or clinical judgment for the determination, applying the terms of the plan to the claimant's medical circumstances, or a statement that such explanation will be provided free of charge upon request; and

(iii) The following statement: "You and your plan may have other voluntary alternative dispute resolution options, such as mediation. One way to find out what may be available is to contact your local U.S. Department of Labor Office and your State insurance regulatory agency."

>>>→ *Caution: Reg. Sec. 2560.503-1(j)(6) and (7), as amended, is effective January 18, 2017 and applicable for claims for disability benefits filed under a plan after April 1, 2018.*

(6) In the case of an adverse benefit decision with respect to disability benefits—

(i) A discussion of the decision, including an explanation of the basis for disagreeing with or not following:

(A) The views presented by the claimant to the plan of health care professionals treating the claimant and vocational professionals who evaluated the claimant;

(B) The views of medical or vocational experts whose advice was obtained on behalf of the plan in connection with a claimant's adverse benefit determination, without regard to whether the advice was relied upon in making the benefit determination; and

(C) A disability determination regarding the claimant presented by the claimant to the plan made by the Social Security Administration;

(ii) If the adverse benefit determination is based on a medical necessity or experimental treatment or similar exclusion or limit, either an explanation of the scientific or clinical judgment for the determination, applying the terms of the plan to the claimant's medical circumstances, or a statement that such explanation will be provided free of change upon request; and

(iii) Either the specific internal rules, guidelines, protocols, standards or other similar criteria of the plan relied upon in making the adverse determination or, alternatively, a statement that such rules, guidelines, protocols, standards or other similar criteria of the plan do not exist. [Added 12/19/16 (81 FR 92316).]

(7) In the case of an adverse benefit determination on review with respect to a claim for disability benefits, the notification shall be provided in a culturally and linguistically appropriate manner (as described in paragraph (o) of this section). [Added 12/19/16 (81 FR 92316).]

(k) *Preemption of State law.* (1) Nothing in this section shall be construed to supersede any provision of State law that regulates insurance, except to the extent that such law prevents the application of a requirement of this section.

(2)(i) For purposes of paragraph (k)(1) of this section, a State law ~~regulating insurance~~ shall not be considered to prevent the application ~~of a requirement~~ of this section merely because such State law ~~establishes a pr~~ocedure to evaluate and resolve disputes involv~~ing benefit dete~~rminations under group health plans so long as ~~the procedure i~~s conducted by a person or entity other than the ~~plan, the plan~~ fiduciaries, the employer, or any employee or ~~agent of the fore~~going.

~~(ii) Stat~~e law procedures described in paragraph ~~(k)(2)(i)~~ are not part of the full and fair review required ~~by this Ac~~t. Claimants therefore need not exhaust such ~~procedures pr~~ior to bringing suit under section 502(a) of the

(l) *Failure to establish and follow reasonable claims procedures.* (1) *In general.* Except as provided in paragraph (l)(2) of this section, in the case of the failure of a plan to establish or follow claims procedures consistent with the requirements of this section, a claimant shall be deemed to have exhausted the administrative remedies available under the plan and shall be entitled to pursue any available remedies under section 502(a) of the Act on the basis that the plan has failed to provide a reasonable claims procedure that would yield a decision on the merits of the claim.

>>> *Caution: Reg. Sec. 2560.503-1(l)(2), as amended, is effective January 18, 2017 and applicable for claims for disability benefits filed under a plan after April 1, 2018.*

(2) *Plans providing disability benefits.* (i) In the case of a claim for disability benefits, if the plan fails to strictly adhere to all the requirements of this section with respect to a claim, the claimant is deemed to have exhausted the administrative remedies available under the plan, except as provided in paragraph (l)(2)(ii) of this section. Accordingly, the claimant is entitled to pursue any available remedies under section 502(a) of the Act on the basis that the plan has failed to provide a reasonable claims procedure that would yield a decision on the merits of the claim. If a claimant chooses to pursue remedies under section 502(a) of the Act under such circumstances, the claim or appeal is deemed denied on review without the exercise of discretion by an appropriate fiduciary.

(ii) Notwithstanding paragraph (l)(2)(i) of this section, the administrative remedies available under a plan with respect to claims for disability benefits will not be deemed exhausted based on *de minimis* violations that do not cause, and are not likely to cause, prejudice or harm to the claimant so long as the plan demonstrates that the violation was for good cause or due to matters beyond the control of the plan and that the violation occurred in the context of an ongoing, good faith exchange of information between the plan and the claimant. This exception is not available if the violation is part of a pattern or practice of violations by the plan. The claimant may request a written explanation of the violation from the plan, and the plan must provide such explanation within 10 days, including a specific description of its bases, if any, for asserting that the violation should not cause the administrative remedies available under the plan to be deemed exhausted. If a court rejects the claimant's request for immediate review under paragraph (l)(2)(i) of this section on the basis that the plan met the standards for the exception under this paragraph (l)(2)(ii), the claim shall be considered as re-filed on appeal upon the plan's receipt of the decision of the court. Within a reasonable time after the receipt of the decision, the plan shall provide the claimant with notice of the resubmission. [Revised 12/19/16 (81 FR 92316).]

(m) *Definitions.* The following terms shall have the meaning ascribed to such terms in this paragraph (m) whenever such term is used in this section:

(1)(i) A "claim involving urgent care" is any claim for medical care or treatment with respect to which the application of the time periods for making non-urgent care determinations—

(A) Could seriously jeopardize the life or health of the claimant or the ability of the claimant to regain maximum function, or,

(B) In the opinion of a physician with knowledge of the claimant's medical condition, would subject the claimant to severe pain that cannot be adequately managed without the care or treatment that is the subject of the claim.

(ii) Except as provided in paragraph (m)(1)(iii) of this section, whether a claim is a "claim involving urgent care" within the meaning of paragraph (m)(1)(i)(A) of this section is to be determined by an individual acting on behalf of the plan applying the judgment of a prudent layperson who possesses an average knowledge of health and medicine.

(iii) Any claim that a physician with knowledge of the claimant's medical condition determines is a "claim involving urgent care" within the meaning of paragraph (m)(1)(i) of this section shall be treated as a "claim involving urgent care" for purposes of this section.

(2) The term "pre-service claim" means any claim for a benefit under a group health plan with respect to which the terms of the plan condition receipt of the benefit, in whole or in part, on approval of the benefit in advance of obtaining medical care.

(3) The term "post-service claim" means any claim for a benefit under a group health plan that is not a pre-service claim within the meaning of paragraph (m)(2) of this section.

(4) The term "adverse benefit determination" means:

(i) Any of the following: A denial, reduction, or termination of, or a failure to provide or make payment (in whole or in part) for, a benefit, including any such denial, reduction, termination, or failure to provide or make payment that is based on a determination of a participant's or beneficiary's eligibility to participate in a plan, and including, with respect to group health plans, a denial, reduction, or termination of, or a failure to provide or make payment (in whole or in part) for, a benefit resulting from the application of any utilization review, as well as a failure to cover an item or service for which benefits are otherwise provided because it is determined to be experimental or investigational or not medically necessary or appropriate; and

>>> *Caution: Reg. Sec. 2560.503-1(m)(4)(ii), as amended, is effective January 18, 2017 and applicable for claims for disability benefits filed under a plan after April 1, 2018.*

(ii) In the case of a plan providing disability benefits, the term "adverse benefit determination" also means any rescission of disability coverage with respect to a participant or beneficiary (whether or not, in connection with the rescission, there is an adverse effect on any particular benefit at that time). For this purpose, the term "rescission" means a cancellation or discontinuance of coverage that has retroactive effect, except to the extent it is attributable to a failure to timely pay required premiums or contributions towards the cost of coverage. [Revised 12/19/16 (81 FR 92316).]

(5) The term "notice" or "notification" means the delivery or furnishing of information to an individual in a manner that satisfies the standards of 29 CFR 2520.104b-1(b) as appropriate with respect to material required to be furnished or made available to an individual.

(6) The term "group health plan" means an employee welfare benefit plan within the meaning of section 3(1) of the Act to the extent that such plan provides "medical care" within the meaning of section 733(a) of the Act.

(7) The term "health care professional" means a physician or other health care professional licensed, accredited, or certified to perform specified health services consistent with State law.

(8) A document, record, or other information shall be considered "relevant" to a claimant's claim if such document, record, or other information

(i) Was relied upon in making the benefit determination;

(ii) Was submitted, considered, or generated in the course of making the benefit determination, without regard to whether such document, record, or other information was relied upon in making the benefit determination;

(iii) Demonstrates compliance with the administrative processes and safeguards required pursuant to paragraph (b)(5) of this section in making the benefit determination; or

(iv) In the case of a group health plan or a plan providing disability benefits, constitutes a statement of policy or guidance with respect to the plan concerning the denied treatment option or benefit for the claimant's diagnosis, without regard to whether such advice or statement was relied upon in making the benefit determination.

(n) *Apprenticeship plans.* This section does not apply to employee benefit plans that solely provide apprenticeship training benefits.

>>> *Caution: Reg. Sec. 2560.503-1(o), as amended, is effective January 18, 2017 and applicable for claims for disability benefits filed under a plan after April 1, 2018.*

(o) *Standards for culturally and linguistically appropriate notices.* A plan is considered to provide relevant notices in a "culturally and linguistically appropriate manner" if the plan meets all the requirements of paragraph (o)(1) of this section with respect to the applicable non-English languages described in paragraph (o)(2) of this section.

(1) *Requirements.* (i) The plan must provide oral language services (such as a telephone customer assistance hotline) that include

answering questions in any applicable non-English language and providing assistance with filing claims and appeals in any applicable non-English language;

(ii) The plan must provide, upon request, a notice in any applicable non-English language; and

(iii) The plan must include in the English versions of all notices, a statement prominently displayed in any applicable non-English language clearly indicating how to access the language services provided by the plan.

(2) *Applicable non-English language.* With respect to an address in any United States county to which a notice is sent, a non-English language is an applicable non-English language if ten percent or more of the population residing in the county is literate only in the same non-English language, as determined in guidance published by the Secretary. [Revised 12/19/16 (81 FR 92316).]

(p) *Applicability dates and temporarily applicable provisions.* (1) Except as provided in paragraphs (p)(2), (p)(3) and (p)(4) of this section, this section shall apply to claims filed under a plan on or after January 1, 2002.

(2) This section shall apply to claims filed under a group health plan on or after the first day of the first plan year beginning on or after July 1, 2002, but in no event later than January 1, 2003.

(3) Paragraphs (b)(7), (g)(1)(vii) and (viii), (j)(4)(ii), (j)(6) and (7), (l)(2), (m)(4)(ii), and (o) of this section shall apply to claims for disability benefits filed under a plan after April 1, 2018, in addition to the other paragraphs in this rule applicable to such claims. [Amended 11/29/17 (82 FR 56560).]

(4) With respect to claims for disability benefits filed under a plan from January 18, 2017 through April 1, 2018, this paragraph (p)(4) shall apply instead of paragraphs (g)(1)(vii), (g)(1)(viii), (h)(4), (j)(6) and (j)(7). [Amended 11/29/17 (82 FR 56560).]

(i) In the case of a notification of benefit determination and a notification of benefit determination on review by a plan providing disability benefits, the notification shall set forth, in a manner calculated to be understood by the claimant—

(A) If an internal rule, guideline, protocol, or other similar criterion was relied upon in making the adverse determination, either the specific rule, guideline, protocol, or other similar criterion; or a statement that such a rule, guideline, protocol, or other similar criterion was relied upon in making the adverse determination and that a copy of such rule, guideline, protocol, or other criterion will be provided free of charge to the claimant upon request; and

(B) If the adverse benefit determination is based on a medical necessity or experimental treatment or similar exclusion or limit, either an explanation of the scientific or clinical judgment for the determination, applying the terms of the plan to the claimant's medical circumstances, or a statement that such explanation will be provided free of charge upon request.

(ii) The claims procedures of a plan providing disability benefits will not, with respect to claims for such benefits, be deemed to provide a claimant with a reasonable opportunity for a full and fair review of a claim and adverse benefit determination unless the claims procedures comply with the requirements of paragraphs (h)(2)(ii) through (iv) and (h)(3)(i) through (v) of this section. [Redesignated and revised 12/19/16 (81 FR 92316).]

[¶ 14,940]
INVESTIGATIVE AUTHORITY

Act Sec. 504. (a) INVESTIGATION AND SUBMISSION OF REPORTS, BOOKS, ETC.—The Secretary shall have the power, in order to determine whether any person has violated or is about to violate any provision of this title or any regulation or order thereunder—

(1) to make an investigation, and in connection therewith to require the submission of reports, books, and records, and the filing of data in support of any information required to be filed with the Secretary under this title, and

(2) to enter such places, inspect such books and records and question such persons as he may deem necessary to enable him to determine the facts relative to such investigation, if he has reasonable cause to believe there may exist a violation of this title or any rule or regulation issued thereunder or if the entry is pursuant to an agreement with the plan.

The Secretary may make available to any person actually affected by any matter which is the subject of an investigation under this section, and to any department or agency of the United States, information concerning any matter which may be the subject of such investigation; except that any information obtained by the Secretary pursuant to section 6103(g) of the Internal Revenue Code of 1986 shall be made available only in accordance with regulations prescribed by the Secretary of the Treasury.

Act Sec. 504. (b) FREQUENCY OF SUBMISSION OF BOOKS AND RECORDS.—The Secretary may not under the authority of this section require any plan to submit to the Secretary any books or records of the plan more than once in any 12 month period, unless the Secretary has reasonable cause to believe there may exist a violation of this title or any regulation or order thereunder.

Act Sec. 504. (c) OTHER PROVISIONS APPLICABLE RELATING TO ATTENDANCE OF WITNESS AND PRODUCTION OF BOOKS, RECORDS, ETC.—For the purposes of any investigation provided for in this title, the provisions of section 9 and 10 (relating to the attendance of witnesses and the production of books, records, and documents) of the Federal Trade Commission Act (15 U.S.C. 49, 50) are hereby made applicable (without regard to any limitation in such sections respecting persons, partnerships, banks, or common carriers) to the jurisdiction, powers, and duties of the Secretary or any officers designated by him. To the extent he considers appropriate, the Secretary may delegate his investigative functions under this section with respect to insured banks acting as fiduciaries of employee benefit plans to the appropriate Federal banking agency (as defined in section 3(q) of the Federal Deposit Insurance Act (12 U.S.C. 1813(q))).

Act Sec. 504. (d) The Secretary may promulgate a regulation that provides an evidentiary privilege for, and provides for the confidentiality of communications between or among, any of the following entities or their agents, consultants, or employees:

(1) A State insurance department.

(2) A State attorney general.

(3) The National Association of Insurance Commissioners.

(4) The Department of Labor.

(5) The Department of the Treasury.

(6) The Department of Justice.

(7) The Department of Health and Human Services.

(8) Any other Federal or State authority that the Secretary determines is appropriate for the purposes of enforcing the provisions of this title.

Act Sec. 504. (e) The privilege established under subsection (d) shall apply to communications related to any investigation, audit, examination, or inquiry conducted or coordinated by any of the agencies. A communication that is privileged under subsection (d) shall not waive any privilege otherwise available to the communicating agency or to any person who provided the information that is communicated.

Amendments

P.L. 111-148, §6607:

Amended ERISA Sec. 504 by inserting at the end new subsections (d) and (e).

The above amendment is effective on the date of enactment (March 23, 2010).

P.L. 101-239, §3111:

Amended ERISA Sec. 504(a) by striking "Internal Revenue Code of 1954" and inserting "Internal Revenue Code of 1986".

The above amendment is effective as if originally included in the provision of the Tax Reform Act of 1986 to which it relates.

[¶ 14,950]
REGULATIONS

Act Sec. 505. Subject to title III and section 109, the Secretary may prescribe such regulations as he finds necessary or appropriate to carry out the provisions of this title. Among other things, such regulations may define accounting, technical and trade terms used in such provisions; may prescribe forms; and may provide for the keeping of books and records, and for the inspection of such books and records (subject to section 504(a) and (b)).

[¶ 14,960]
COORDINATION AND RESPONSIBILITY OF AGENCIES ENFORCING EMPLOYEE RETIREMENT INCOME SECURITY ACT AND RELATED FEDERAL LAWS

Act Sec. 506.(a) Coordination With Other Agencies and Departments. In order to avoid unnecessary expense and duplication of functions among Government agencies, the Secretary may make such arrangements or agreements for cooperation or mutual assistance in the performance of his functions under this title and the functions of any such agency as he may find to be practicable and consistent with law. The Secretary may utilize, on a reimbursable or other basis, the facilities or services of any department, agency, or establishment of the United States or of any State or political subdivision of a State, including the services of any of its employees, with the lawful consent of such department, agency, or establishment; and each department, agency, or establishment of the United States is authorized and directed to cooperate with the Secretary and, to the extent permitted by law, to provide such information and facilities as he may request for his assistance in the performance of his functions under this title. The Attorney General or his representative shall receive from the Secretary for appropriate action such evidence developed in the performance of his functions under this title as may be found to warrant consideration for criminal prosecution under the provisions of this title or other Federal law.

(b) Responsibility for Detecting and Investigating Civil and Criminal Violations of Employee Retirement Income Security Act and Related Federal Laws. The Secretary shall have the responsibility and authority to detect and investigate and refer, where appropriate, civil and criminal violations related to the provisions of this title and other related Federal laws, including the detection, investigation, and appropriate referrals of related violations of title 18 of the United States Code. Nothing in this subsection shall be construed to preclude other appropriate Federal agencies from detecting and investigating civil and criminal violations of this title and other related Federal laws.

(c) Coordination of Enforcement with States with Respect to Certain Arrangements. A State may enter into an agreement with the Secretary for delegation to the State of some or all of the Secretary's authority under sections 502 and 504 to enforce the requirements under part 7 in connection with multiple employer welfare arrangements, providing medical care (within the meaning of section 733(a)(2)), which are not group health plans.

Amendment

P.L. 104-204, § 603(b)(3)(F):

Amended Sec. 506(c) by striking "section 706(a)(2)" and inserting "section 733(a)(2)".

The above amendment is effective for group health plans for plan years beginning on or after January 1, 1998.

P.L. 104-191, § 101(e)(3):

Added Sec. 506(c) to read as above.

The above amendment generally applies with respect to group health plans for plan years beginning after June 30, 1997. For special rules, see Act Sec. 101(g)(2)-(5), reproduced after ERISA Act Sec. 502.

P.L. 98-473, § 805:

Added Sec. 506(b) and the section heading to Sec. 506(a) and amended the title of the section. Prior to amendment, the section heading was as follows: "OTHER AGENCIES AND DEPARTMENTS."

[¶ 14,970]
ADMINISTRATION

Act Sec. 507.(a) Subchapter II of chapter 5, and chapter 7, of title 5, United States Code (relating to administrative procedure), shall be applicable to this title.

Act Sec. 507. (b) Section 5108 of title 5, United States Code, is amended by adding at the end thereof the following new subsection:

"(f) In addition to the number of positions authorized by subsection (a), the Secretary of Labor is authorized, without regard to any other provision of this section, to place 1 position in the Department of Labor in grade GS-18, and a total of 20 positions in the Department of Labor in grades GS-16 and 17."

Act Sec. 507. (c) No employee of the Department of Labor or the Department of the Treasury shall administer or enforce this title or the Internal Revenue Code of 1986 with respect to any employee benefit plan under which he is a participant or beneficiary, any employee organization of which he is a member, or any employer organization in which he has an interest. This subsection does not apply to an employee benefit plan which covers only employees of the United States.

Amendments

P.L. 101-239, § 3111:

Amended ERISA Sec. 507(c) by striking "Internal Revenue Code of 1954" and inserting "Internal Revenue Code of 1986".

The above amendment is effective as if originally included in the provision of the Tax Reform Act of 1986 to which it relates.

[¶ 14,980]
APPROPRIATIONS

Act Sec. 508. There are hereby authorized to be appropriated such sums as may be necessary to enable the Secretary to carry out his functions and duties under this Act.

[¶ 14,990]
SEPARABILITY PROVISIONS

Act Sec. 509. If any provision of this Act, or the application of such provision to any person or circumstances, shall be held invalid, the remainder of this Act, or the application of such provision to persons or circumstances other than those as to which it is held invalid, shall not be affected thereby.

[¶ 15,000]
INTERFERENCE WITH RIGHTS PROTECTED UNDER ACT

Act Sec. 510. It shall be unlawful for any person to discharge, fine, suspend, expel, discipline, or discriminate against a participant or beneficiary for exercising any right to which he is entitled under the provisions of an employee benefit plan, this title, section 3001, or the Welfare and Pension Plans Disclosure Act, or for the purpose of interfering with the attainment of any right to which such participant may become entitled under the plan, this title, or the Welfare and Pension Plans Disclosure Act. It shall be unlawful for any person to discharge, fine, suspend, expel, or discriminate against any person because he has given information or has testified or is about to testify in any inquiry or proceeding relating to this Act or the Welfare and Pension Plans Disclosure Act. In the case of a multiemployer plan, it shall be unlawful for the plan sponsor or any other person to discriminate against any contributing employer for exercising rights under this Act or for giving information or testifying in any inquiry or proceeding relating to this Act before Congress. The provisions of section 502 shall be applicable in the enforcement of this section.

Amendments

P.L. 109-280, §205:

Added the second to the last sentence to read as above.

The above amendment is effective the date of enactment (August 17, 2006).

[¶ 15,010]
COERCIVE INTERFERENCE

Act Sec. 511. It shall be unlawful for any person through the use of fraud, force, violence, or threat of the use of force or violence, to restrain, coerce, intimidate, or attempt to restrain, coerce, or intimidate any participant or beneficiary for the purpose of interfering with or preventing the exercise of any right to which he is or may become entitled under the plan, this title, section 3001, or the Welfare and Pension Plans Disclosure Act. Any person who willfully violates this section shall be fined $100,000 or imprisoned for not more than ten years, or both.

Amendments

P.L. 109-280, §623(a)(1):

Amended the above by striking "$10,000" and inserting "$100,000".

The above amendment applies to violations occurring on and after the date of enactment (August 17, 2006).

P.L. 109-280, §623(a)(2):

Amended the above by striking "one year" and inserting "10 years".

The above amendment applies to violations occurring on and after the date of enactment (August 17, 2006).

[¶ 15,020]
ADVISORY COUNCIL

Act Sec. 512. (a)(1) ESTABLISHMENT; MEMBERSHIP; TERMS; APPOINTMENT AND REAPPOINTMENT; VACANCIES; QUORUM.—There is hereby established an Advisory Council on Employee Welfare and Pension Benefit Plans (hereinafter in this section referred to as the "Council") consisting of fifteen members appointed by the Secretary. Not more than eight members of the Council shall be members of the same political party.

(2) Members shall be persons qualified to appraise the programs instituted under this Act.

(3) Of the members appointed, three shall be representatives of employee organizations (at least one of whom shall be representative of any organization members of which are participants in a multiemployer plan); three shall be representatives of employers (at least one of whom shall be representative of employers maintaining or contributing to multiemployer plans); three representatives shall be appointed from the general public, one of whom shall be a person representing those receiving benefits from a pension plan; and there shall be one representative each from the fields of insurance, corporate trust, actuarial counseling, investment counseling, investment management, and the accounting field.

(4) Members shall serve for terms of three years except that of those first appointed, five shall be appointed for terms of one year, five shall be appointed for terms of two years, and five shall be appointed for terms of three years. A member may be reappointed. A member appointed to fill a vacancy shall be appointed only for the remainder of such term. A majority of members shall constitute a quorum and action shall be taken only by a majority vote of those present and voting.

Act Sec. 512. (b) DUTIES AND FUNCTIONS.—It shall be the duty of the Council to advise the Secretary with respect to the carrying out of his functions under this Act and to submit to the Secretary recommendations with respect thereto. The Council shall meet at least four times each year and at such other times as the Secretary requests. In his annual report submitted pursuant to section 513(b), the Secretary shall include each recommendation which he has received from the Council during the preceding calendar year.

Act Sec. 512. (c) EXECUTIVE SECRETARY; SECRETARIAL AND CLERICAL SERVICES.—The Secretary shall furnish to the Council an executive secretary and such secretarial, clerical, and other services as are deemed necessary to conduct its business. The Secretary may call upon other agencies of the Government for statistical data, reports, and other information which will assist the Council in the performance of its duties.

Act Sec. 512. (d)(1) COMPENSATION.—Members of the Council shall each be entitled to receive the daily equivalent of the annual rate of basic pay in effect for grade GS-18 of the General Schedule for each day (including travel time) during which they are engaged in the actual performance of duties vested in the Council.

(2) While away from their homes or regular places of business in the performance of services for Council, members of the Council shall be allowed travel expenses, including per diem in lieu of subsistence, in the same manner as persons employed intermittently in the Government service are allowed expenses under section 5703(b) of title 5 of the United States Code.

Act Sec. 512. (e) TERMINATION.—Section 14(a) of the Federal Advisory Committee Act (relating to termination) shall not apply to the Council.

[¶ 15,030]
RESEARCH, STUDIES, AND ANNUAL REPORT

Act Sec. 513. (a)(1) AUTHORIZATION TO UNDERTAKE RESEARCH AND SURVEYS.—The Secretary is authorized to undertake research and surveys and in connection therewith to collect, compile, analyze and publish data, information, and statistics relating to employee benefit plans, including retirement, deferred compensation, and welfare plans, and types of plans not subject to this Act.

(2) The Secretary is authorized and directed to undertake research studies relating to pension plans, including but not limited to (A) the effects of this title upon the provisions and costs of pension plans, (B) the role of private pensions in meeting the economic security needs of the Nation, and (C) the operation of private pension plans including types and levels of benefits, degree of reciprocity of portability, and financial and actuarial characteristics and practice, and methods of encouraging the growth of the private pension system.

(3) The Secretary may, as he deems appropriate or necessary, undertake other studies relating to employee benefit plans, the matters regulated by this title, and the enforcement procedures provided for under this title.

(4) The research, surveys, studies, and publications referred to in this subsection may be conducted directly, or indirectly through grant or contract agreements.

Act Sec. 513. (b) SUBMISSION OF ANNUAL REPORT TO CONGRESS; CONTENTS.—The Secretary shall submit annually a report to the Congress covering his administration of this title for the preceding year, and including (1) an explanation of any variances or extensions granted under section 110, 207, 303, or 304 and the projected date for terminating the variance; (2) the status of cases in enforcement status; (3) recommendations received from the Advisory Council during the preceding year; and (4) such information, data, research findings, studies, and recommendations for further legislation in connection with the matters covered by this title as he may find advisable.

Act Sec. 513. (c) COOPERATION WITH CONGRESS.—The Secretary is authorized and directed to cooperate with the Congress and its appropriate committees, subcommittees, and staff in supplying data and any other information, and personnel and services, required by the Congress in any study, examination, or report by the Congress relating to pension benefit plans established or maintained by States or their political subdivisions.

[¶ 15,040]
OTHER LAWS

Act Sec. 514. (a) SUPERSEDURE; EFFECTIVE DATE.—Except as provided in subsection (b) of this section, the provisions of this title and title IV shall supersede any and all State laws insofar as they may now or hereafter relate to any employee benefit plan described in section 4(a) and not exempt under section 4(b). This section shall take effect on January 1, 1975.

Act Sec. 514.(b)(1) CONSTRUCTION AND APPLICATION.—This section shall not apply with respect to any cause of action which arose, or any act or omission which occurred, before January 1, 1975.

(2)(A) Except as provided in subparagraph (B), nothing in this title shall be construed to exempt or relieve any person from any law of any State which regulates insurance, banking, or securities.

(B) Neither an employee benefit plan described in section 4(a), which is not exempt under section 4(b) (other than a plan established primarily for the purpose of providing death benefits), nor any trust established under such a plan, shall be deemed to be an insurance company or other insurer, bank, trust company, or investment company or to be engaged in the business of insurance or banking for purposes of any law of any State purporting to regulate insurance companies, insurance contracts, banks, trust companies, or investment companies.

(3) Nothing in this section shall be construed to prohibit use by the Secretary of services or facilities of a State agency as permitted under section 506 of this Act.

(4) Subsection (a) shall not apply to any generally applicable criminal law of a state.

(5)(A) Except as provided in subparagraph (B), subsection (a) shall not apply to tthe Hawaii Prepaid Health Care Act (Haw.Rev.Stat. §§ 393-1 through 393-51).

(B) Nothing in subparagraph (A) shall be construed to exempt from subsection (a)—

(i) any State tax law relating to employee benefit plans, or

(ii) any amendment of the Hawaii Prepaid Health Care Act enacted after September 2, 1974, to the extent it provides for more than the effective administration of such Act as in effect on such date.

(C) Notwithstanding subparagraph (A), parts 1 and 4 of this subtitle, and the preceding sections of this part to the extent they govern matters which are governed by the provisions of such parts 1 and 4 and the preceding sections of this part, shall supersede the Hawaii Prepaid Health Care Act (as in effect on or after the date of the enactment of this paragraph), but the Secretary may enter into cooperative arrangements under paragraph and section 506 with officials of the State of Hawaii to assist them in effectuating the policies of provisions of such Act which are superseded by such parts 1 and 4 and the preceding sections of this part.

(6)(A) Notwithstanding any other provision of this section—

(i) in the case of an employee welfare benefit plan which is a multiple employer welfare arrangement and is fully insured (or which is a multiple employer welfare arrangement subject to an exemption under subparagraph (B)), any law of any State which regulates insurance may apply to such arrangement to the extent that such law provides—

(I) standards, requiring the maintenance of specified levels of reserves and specified levels of contributions, which any such plan, or any trust established under such a plan, must meet in order to be considered under such law able to pay benefits in full when due, and

(II) provisions to enforce such standards, and

(ii) in the case of any other employee welfare benefit plan which is a multiple employer welfare arrangement, in addition to this title, any law of any State which regulates insurance may apply to the extent not inconsistent with the preceding sections of this title.

(B) The Secretary may, under regulations which may be prescribed by the Secretary, exempt from subparagraph (A)(ii), individually or by class, multiple employer welfare arrangements which are not fully insured. Any such exemption may be granted with respect to any arrangement or class of arrangements only if such arrangement or each arrangement which is a member of such class meets the requirements of section 3(1) and section 4 necessary to be considered an employee welfare benefit plan to which this title applies.

(C) Nothing in subparagraph (A) shall affect the manner or extent to which the provisions of this title apply to an employee welfare benefit plan which is not a multiple employer welfare arrangement and which is a plan, fund, or program participating in, subscribing to, or otherwise using a multiple employer welfare arrangement to fund or administer benefits to such plan's participants and beneficiaries.

(D) For purposes of this paragraph, a multiple employer welfare arrangement shall be considered fully insured only if the terms of the arrangement provide for benefits the amount of all of which the Secretary determines are guaranteed under a contract, or policy of insurance, issued by an insurance company, insurance service, or insurance organization, qualified to conduct business in a State.

(7) Subsection (a) shall not apply to qualified domestic relations orders (within the meaning of section 206(d)(3)(B)(i)), qualified medical child support orders (within the meaning of section 609(a)(2)(A)), and the provisions of law referred to in section 609(a)(2)(B)(ii) to the extent they apply to qualified medical child support orders.

(8) Subsection (a) of this section shall not be construed to preclude any State cause of action—

(A) with respect to which the State exercises its acquired rights under section 609(b)(3) with respect to a group health plan (as defined in section 607(1)), or

(B) for recoupment of payment with respect to items or services pursuant to a State plan for medical assistance approved under title XIX of the Social Security Act which would not have been payable if such acquired rights had been executed before payment with respect to such items or services by the group health plan.

(9) For additional provisions relating to group health plans, see section 731.

Act Sec. 514. (c) DEFINITIONS.—For purposes of this section:

(1) The term "State law" includes all laws, decisions, rules, regulations, or other State action having the effect of law, of any State. A law of the United States applicable only to the District of Columbia shall be treated as a State law rather than a law of the United States.

(2) The term "State" includes a State, any political subdivisions thereof, or any agency or intrumentality of either, which purports to regulate, directly or indirectly, the terms and conditions of employee benefit plans covered by this title.

Act Sec. 514. (d) ALTERATION, AMENDMENT, MODIFICATION, INVALIDATION, IMPAIRMENT OR SUPERSEDURE OF ANY LAW OF THE UNITED STATES PROHIBITED.—Nothing in this title shall be construed to alter, amend, modify, invalidate, impair, or supersede any law of the United States (except as provided in sections 111 and 507(b)) or any rule or regulation issued under any such law.

Act Sec. 514.(e)(1) Notwithstanding any other provision of this section, this title shall supersede any law of a State which would directly or indirectly prohibit or restrict the inclusion in any plan of an automatic contribution arrangement. The Secretary may prescribe regulations which would establish minimum standards that such an arrangement would be required to satisfy in order for this subsection to apply in the case of such arrangement.

(2) For purposes of this subsection, the term "automatic contribution arrangement" means an arrangement—

(A) under which a participant may elect to have the plan sponsor make payments as contributions under the plan on behalf of the participant, or to the participant directly in cash,

(B) under which a participant is treated as having elected to have the plan sponsor make such contributions in an amount equal to a uniform percentage of compensation provided under the plan until the participant specifically elects not to have such contributions made (or specifically elects to have such contributions made at a different percentage), and

(C) under which such contributions are invested in accordance with regulations prescribed by the Secretary under section 404(c)(5).

(3)(A) The plan administrator of an automatic contribution arrangement shall, within a reasonable period before such plan year, provide to each participant to whom the arrangement applies for such plan year notice of the participant's rights and obligations under the arrangement which—

(i) is sufficiently accurate and comprehensive to apprise the participant of such rights and obligations, and

(ii) is written in a manner calculated to be understood by the average participant to whom the arrangement applies.

(B) A notice shall not be treated as meeting the requirements of subparagraph (A) with respect to a participant unless—

(i) the notice includes an explanation of the participant's right under the arrangement not to have elective contributions made on the participant's behalf (or to elect to have such contributions made at a different percentage),

(ii) the participant has a reasonable period of time, after receipt of the notice described in clause (i) and before the first elective contribution is made, to make such election, and

(iii) the notice explains how contributions made under the arrangement will be invested in the absence of any investment election by the participant.

Amendments

P.L. 109-280, §902(f)(1):

Amended ERISA Sec. 514 by adding new subsection (e).

The above amendment is effective on the date of enactment (August 17, 2006).

P.L. 105-200, §402(h)(2)(A)(ii):

Amended ERISA Sec. 514(b)(7) by striking "enforced by" and inserting "they apply to" to read as above.

The above amendment is effective August 10, 1993, as if included in ther enactment of P.L. 103-66, Sec. 4301(c)(4)(A).

P.L. 104-191, §101(f)(1):

Amended ERISA Sec. 514(b) by adding at the end a new paragraph (9) to read as above.

The above amendment generally applies with respect to group health plans for plan years beginning after June 30, 1997. For special rules, see Act Sec. 101(g)(2)-(5), reproduced after ERISA Act Sec. 701.

P.L. 103-66, §4301(c)(4)(A):

Amended ERISA Sec. 514 by inserting in subsection (b)(7) ", qualified medical child support orders (within the meaning of section 609(a)(2)(A)), and the provisions of law referred to in section 609(a)(2)(B)(ii) to the extent enforced by qualified medical child support orders" before the period.

The above amendment is effective on August 10, 1993. Any plan amendment required to be made by Act Sec. 4301 need not be made before the first plan year beginning on or after January 1, 1994 if: (1) the plan is operated in accordance with Act Sec. 4301 during the period after August 9, 1993 and before such first plan year; and (2) the amendment applies retroactively to this period. A plan will not be treated as failing to be operated in accordance with plan provisions merely because it operates in accordance with the effective date requirements.

P.L. 103-66, Sec. 4301(c)(4)(A) was amended by Sec. 402(h)(1)(i) of P.L. 105-200 by striking "subsection (b)(7)(D)" and inserting "subsection (b)(7)" effective August 10, 1993.

P.L. 103-66, §4301(c)(4)(B):

Amended ERISA Sec. 514 by striking subsection (b)(8) and inserting new subsection (b)(8) to read as above.

The above amendment is effective on August 10, 1993. Any plan amendment required to be made by Act Sec. 4301 need not be made before the first plan year beginning on or after January 1, 1994 if: (1) the plan is operated in accordance with Act Sec. 4301 during the period after August 9, 1993 and

before such first plan year; and (2) the amendment applies retroactively to this period. A plan will not be treated as failing to be operated in accordance with plan provisions merely because it operates in accordance with the effective date requirements.

P.L. 101-239, §7894(f)(2):

Amended ERISA Sec. 514(b)(5)(C) by striking "such parts" the second place it appeared and inserting "such parts 1 and 4 and the preceding sections of this part" effective as if included in P.L. 97-473, §301.

P.L. 101-239, §7894(f)(3):

Amended ERISA Sec. 514(b)(6)(B) by striking section 3(l) and inserting "section 3(1)" effective as if included in P.L. 97-473, §302.

P.L. 99-272, §9503(d)(1):

Amended ERISA Sec. 514 by adding new paragraph (8), to take effect pursuant to §9503(d)(2), which provided:

(2)(A) Except as provided in subparagraph (B), the amendment made by paragraph (1) shall become effective on October 1, 1986.

(B) In the case of a plan maintained pursuant to one or more collective bargaining agreements between employee representatives and one or more employers ratified on or before the date of the enactment of this Act, the amendment made by paragraph (1) shall become effective on the later of—

(i) October 1, 1986; or

(ii) the earlier of—

(I) the date on which the last of the collective bargaining agreements under which the plan is maintained, which were in effect on the date of the enactment of this Act, terminates (determined without regard to any extension thereof agreed to after the date of the enactment of this Act); or

(II) three years after the date of the enactment of this Act.

P.L. 98-397, §104:

Act Sec. 104(b) amended ERISA Sec. 514(b) by adding new paragraph (7).

For the effective date of the above amendment, see Act Sec. 303(d), which appears in the amendment note for ERISA Sec. 206 at ¶ 14,460.

P.L. 97-473, §301:

Amended Sec. 514(b) by adding new paragraph (5), effective January 14, 1983. Sec. 301(b) of the Act provided: "The amendment made by this section shall not be considered a precedent with respect to extending such amendment to any other State law."

P.L. 97-473, §302:

Amended Sec. 514(b) by adding new paragraph (6), effective January 14, 1983.

Regulations

Reg. § 2509.2015-02 was published in the Federal Register on November 18, 2015 (80 FR 71936).

[¶ 15,041]

§ 2509.2015-02 **Interpretive bulletin relating to state savings programs that sponsor or facilitate plans covered by the Employee Retirement Income Security Act of 1974.**

(a) *Scope.* This document sets forth the views of the Department of Labor (Department) concerning the application of the Employee Retirement Income Security Act of 1974 (ERISA) to certain state laws designed to expand the retirement savings options available to private sector workers through ERISA-covered retirement plans. Concern over adverse social and economic consequences of inadequate retirement savings levels has prompted several states to adopt or consider legislation to address this problem.[1] An impediment to state adoption of such measures is uncertainty about the effect of ERISA's broad preemption of state laws that "relate to" private sector employee benefit plans. In the Department's view, ERISA preemption principles leave room for states to sponsor or facilitate ERISA-based retirement savings options for private sector employees, provided employers participate volunta-

rily and ERISA's requirements, liability provisions, and remedies fully apply to the state programs.

(b) *In General.* There are advantages to utilizing an ERISA plan approach. Employers as well as employees can make contributions to ERISA plans, contribution limits are higher than for other state approaches that involve individual retirement plans (IRAs) that are not intended to be ERISA-covered plans,[2] and ERISA plan accounts have stronger protection from creditors. Tax credits may also allow small employers to offset part of the costs of starting certain types of retirement plans.[3] Utilizing ERISA plans also provides a well-established uniform regulatory structure with important consumer protections, including fiduciary obligations, automatic enrollment rules, recordkeeping and disclosure requirements, legal accountability provisions, and spousal protections.

The Department is not aware of judicial decisions or other ERISA guidance directly addressing the application of ERISA to state programs that facilitate or sponsor ERISA plans, and, therefore, believes

---

[1] For information on the problem of inadequate retirement savings, *see* the May 2015 Report of the United States Government Accountability Office (GAO), RETIREMENT SECURITY—Most Households Approaching Retirement Have Low Savings (GAO Report-15-419) (available at *www.gao.gov/assets/680/670153.pdf*). *Also see* GAO's September 2015 Report-15-566, RETIREMENT SECURITY—Federal Action Could Help State Efforts to Expand Private Sector Coverage (available at *www.gao.gov/assets/680/672419.pdf*).

[2] Some states are developing programs to encourage employees to establish tax-favored IRAs funded by payroll deductions rather than encouraging employers to adopt ERISA plans. Oregon, Illinois, and California, for example, have adopted laws along these lines. Oregon 2015 Session Laws, Ch. 557 (H.B. 2960) (June 2015); Illinois Secure Choice Savings Program Act, 2014 Ill. Legis. Serv. P.A. 98-1150 (S.B. 2758) (West); California

Secure Choice Retirement Savings Act, 2012 Cal. Legis. Serv. Ch. 734 (S.B. 1234) (West). These IRA-based initiatives generally require specified employers to deduct amounts from their employees' paychecks, unless the employee affirmatively elects not to participate, in order that those amounts may be remitted to state-administered IRAs for the employees. The Department is addressing these state "payroll deduction IRA" initiatives separately through a proposed regulation that describes safe-harbor conditions for employers to avoid creation of ERISA-covered plans when they comply with state laws that require payroll deduction IRA programs. This Interpretive Bulletin does not address those laws.

[3] For more information, *see Choosing a Retirement Solution for Your Small Business*, a joint project of the U.S. Department of Labor's Employee Benefits Security Administration (EBSA) and the Internal Revenue Service. Available at *www.irs.gov/pub/irs-pdf/p3998.pdf*.

that the states, employers, other plan sponsors, workers, and other stakeholders would benefit from guidance setting forth the general views of the Department on the application of ERISA to these state initiatives. The application of ERISA in an individual case would present novel preemption questions and, if decided by a court, would turn on the particular features of the state-sponsored program at issue, but, as discussed below, the Department believes that neither ERISA section 514 specifically, nor federal preemption generally, are insurmountable obstacles to all state programs that promote retirement saving among private sector workers through the use of ERISA-covered plans.

Marketplace Approach

One state approach is reflected in the 2015 Washington State Small Business Retirement Savings Marketplace Act.[4] This law requires the state to contract with a private sector entity to establish a program that connects eligible employers with qualifying savings plans available in the private sector market. Only products that the state determines are suited to small employers, provide good quality, and charge low fees would be included in the state's "marketplace." Washington State employers would be free to use the marketplace or not and would not be required to establish any savings plans for their employees. Washington would merely set standards for arrangements marketed through the marketplace. The marketplace arrangement would not itself be an ERISA-covered plan, and the arrangements available to employers through the marketplace could include ERISA-covered plans and other non-ERISA savings arrangements. The state would not itself establish or sponsor any savings arrangement. Rather, the employer using the state marketplace would establish the savings arrangement, whether it is an ERISA-covered employee pension benefit plan or a non-ERISA savings program. ERISA's reporting and disclosure requirements, protective standards and remedies would apply to the ERISA plans established by employers using the marketplace. On the other hand, if the plan or arrangement is of a type that would otherwise be exempt from ERISA (such as a payroll deduction IRA arrangement that satisfies the conditions of the existing safe harbor at 29 CFR 2510.3-2(d)), the state's involvement as organizer or facilitator of the marketplace would not by itself cause that arrangement to be covered by ERISA. Similarly, if, as in Washington State, a marketplace includes a type of plan that is subject to special rules under ERISA, such as the SIMPLE-IRA under section 101(h) of ERISA, the state's involvement as organizer or facilitator of the marketplace would not by itself affect the application of the special rules.

Prototype Plan Approach

Another potential approach is a state sponsored "prototype plan." At least one state, Massachusetts, has enacted a law to allow nonprofit organizations with fewer than 20 employees to adopt a contributory retirement plan developed and administered by the state.[5] Banks, insurance companies and other regulated financial institutions commonly market prototype plans to employers as simple means for them to establish and administer employee pension benefit plans.[6] The financial institutions develop standard form 401(k) or other tax-favored retirement plans (such as SIMPLE-IRA plans) and secure IRS approval. Typically, employers may choose features such as contribution rates to meet their specific needs. Each employer that adopts the prototype sponsors an ERISA plan for its employees. The individual employers would assume the same fiduciary obligations associated with sponsorship of any ERISA-covered plans. For example, the prototype plan documents often specify that the employer is the plan's "named fiduci-

ary" and "plan administrator" responsible for complying with ERISA, but they may allow the employer to delegate these responsibilities to others. The plan documents for a state-administered prototype plan could designate the state or a state designee to perform these functions. Thus, the state or a designated third-party could assume responsibility for most administrative and asset management functions of an employer's prototype plan. The state could also designate low-cost investment options and a third-party administrative service provider for its prototype plans.

Multiple Employer Plan (MEP) Approach

A third approach, (referenced, for example, in the "Report of the Governor's Task Force to Ensure Retirement Security for All Marylanders"),[7] involves a state establishing and obtaining IRS tax qualification for a "multiple employer" 401(k)-type plan, defined benefit plan, or other tax-favored retirement savings program. The Department anticipates that such an approach would generally involve permitting employers that meet specified eligibility criteria to join the state multiple employer plan. The plan documents would provide that the plan is subject to Title I of ERISA and is intended to comply with Internal Revenue Code tax qualification requirements. The plan would have a separate trust holding contributions made by the participating employers, the employer's employees, or both. The state, or a designated governmental agency or instrumentality, would be the plan sponsor under ERISA section 3(16)(B) and the named fiduciary and plan administrator responsible (either directly or through one or more contract agents, which could be private-sector providers) for administering the plan, selecting service providers, communicating with employees, paying benefits, and providing other plan services. A state could take advantage of economies of scale to lower administrative and other costs.

As a state-sponsored multiple employer plan ("state MEP"), this type of arrangement could also reduce overall administrative costs for participating employers in large part because the Department would consider this arrangement as a single ERISA plan. Consequently, only a single Form 5500 Annual Return/Report would be filed for the whole arrangement. In order to participate in the plan, employers simply would be required to execute a participation agreement. Under a state MEP, each employer that chose to participate would not be considered to have established its own ERISA plan, and the state could design its defined contribution MEP so that the participating employers could have limited fiduciary responsibilities (the duty to prudently select the arrangement and to monitor its operation would continue to apply). The continuing involvement by participating employers in the ongoing operation and administration of a 401(k)-type individual account MEP, however, generally could be limited to enrolling employees in the state plan and forwarding voluntary employee and employer contributions to the plan. When an employer joins a carefully structured MEP, the employer is not the "sponsor" of the plan under ERISA, and also would not act as a plan administrator or named fiduciary. Those fiduciary roles, and attendant fiduciary responsibilities, would be assigned to other parties responsible for administration and management of the state MEP.[8] Adoption of a defined benefit plan structure would involve additional funding and other employer obligations.[9]

For a person (other than an employee organization) to sponsor an employee benefit plan under Title I of ERISA, such person must either act directly as the employer of the covered employees or "indirectly in

---

[4] 2015 Wash. Sess. Laws chap. 296 (SB 5826) (available at *http://app.leg.wa.gov/billinfo/summary.aspx?bill=5826&year=2015*).

[5] The retirement plan will be overseen by the Massachusetts State Treasurer's Office. Mass. Gen. Laws ch.29, §64E (2012). In June 2014, the Massachusetts Treasurer's Office announced that the IRS had issued a favorable ruling on the proposal, but noted that additional approval from the IRS is still needed (*see www.massnonprofitnet.org/blog/nonprofitretirement/*). *See also* GAO's Report 2015 Report-15-566, RETIREMENT SECURITY—Federal Action Could Help State Efforts to Expand Private Sector Coverage, which included the following statement at footnote 93 regarding the Massachusetts program: "The Massachusetts official told us that each participating employer would be considered to have created its own plan, characterizing the state's effort as development of a volume submitter 401(k) plan, which is a type of employee benefit plan that is typically pre-approved by the Internal Revenue Service." (GAO report is available at *www.gao.gov/assets/680/672419.pdf*).

[6] *See* IRS Online Publication, *Types of Pre-Approved Retirement Plans* at *www.irs.gov/Retirement-Plans/Types-of-Pre-Approved-Retirement-Plans*.

[7] Governor's Task Force to Ensure Retirement Security for All Marylanders, *1,000,000 of Our Neighbors at Risk: Improving Retirement Security for Marylanders* (February 2015) (available at *www.dllr.state.md.us/retsecurity/*).

[8] A state developing a state sponsored MEP could submit an advisory opinion request to the Department under ERISA Procedure 76-1 to confirm that the MEP at least in form has assigned those fiduciary functions to persons other than the participating employers. ERISA Procedure 76-1 is available at *www.dol.gov/ebsa/regs/aos/aorequests.html*.

[9] State laws authorizing defined benefit plans for private sector employers (as prototypes or as multiple employer plans) might create plans covered by Title IV of ERISA and subject to the jurisdiction of the Pension Benefit Guaranty Corporation (PBGC). Subject to some exceptions, the PBGC protects the retirement incomes of workers in private-sector defined benefit pension plans. A defined benefit plan provides a specified monthly benefit at retirement, often based on a combination of salary and years of service. PBGC was created by ERISA to encourage the continuation and maintenance of private-sector defined benefit pension plans, provide timely and uninterrupted payment of pension benefits, and keep pension insurance premiums at a minimum. More information is available on the PBGC's Web site at *www.pbgc.gov*.

the interest of an employer" in relation to a plan.[10] ERISA sections 3(2), 3(5). A person will be considered to act "indirectly in the interest of an employer, in relation to a plan," if such person is tied to the contributing employers or their employees by genuine economic or representational interests unrelated to the provision of benefits.[11] In the Department's view, a state has a unique representational interest in the health and welfare of its citizens that connects it to the in-state employers that choose to participate in the state MEP and their employees, such that the state should be considered to act indirectly in the interest of the participating employers.[12] Having this unique nexus distinguishes the state MEP from other business enterprises that underwrite benefits or provide administrative services to several unrelated employers.[13]

(c) *ERISA Preemption*. The Department is aware that a concern for states adopting an ERISA plan approach is whether or not those state laws will be held preempted. ERISA preemption analysis begins with the "presumption that Congress does not intend to supplant state law." *New York State Conference of Blue Cross & Blue Shield Plans* v. *Travelers Ins. Co.*, 514 U.S. 645, 654 (1995). The question turns on Congress's intent "to avoid a multiplicity of regulation in order to permit nationally uniform administration of employee benefit plans." *Id.* at 654, 657. *See also Fort Halifax Packing Co.* v. *Coyne*, 482 U.S. 1, 11 (1987) (goal of ERISA preemption is to "ensure . . . that the administrative practices of a benefit plan will be governed by only a single set of regulations.").

Section 514 of ERISA provides that Title I "shall supersede any and all State laws insofar as they . . . relate to any employee benefit plan" covered by the statute. The U.S. Supreme Court has held that "[a] law 'relates to' an employee benefit plan, in the normal sense of the phrase, if it has a connection with or reference to such a plan." *Shaw* v. *Delta Air Lines, Inc.*, 463 U.S. 85, 96-97 (1983) (footnote omitted); *see, e.g., Travelers*, 514 U.S. at 656. A law has a "reference to" ERISA plans if the law "acts immediately and exclusively upon ERISA plans" or "the existence of ERISA plans is essential to the law's operation." *California Div. of Labor Standards Enforcement* v. *Dillingham Constr., N.A.*, 519 U.S. 316, 325-326 (1997). In determining whether a state law has a "connection with ERISA plans," the U.S. Supreme Court "look[s] both to 'the objectives of the ERISA statute as a guide to the scope of the state laws that Congress understood would survive,' as well as to the nature of the effect of the state law on ERISA plans," to "determine whether [the] state law has the forbidden connection" with ERISA plans. *Egelhoff* v. *Egelhoff*, 532 U.S. 141, 147 (2001) (quoting *Dillingham*, 519 U.S. at 325). In various decisions, the Court has concluded that ERISA preempts state laws that: (1) Mandate employee benefit structures or their administration; (2) provide alternative enforcement mechanisms; or (3) bind employers or plan fiduciaries to particular choices or preclude uniform administrative practice, thereby functioning as a regulation of an ERISA plan itself.[14]

In the Department's view, state laws of the sort outlined above interact with ERISA in such a way that section 514 preemption principles and purposes would not appear to come into play in the way they have in past preemption cases. Although the approaches described above involve ERISA plans, they do not appear to undermine ERISA's exclusive regulation of ERISA-covered plans. The approaches do not mandate employee benefit structures or their administration, provide alternative regulatory or enforcement mechanisms, bind employers or plan fiduciaries to particular choices, or preclude uniform administrative practice in any way that would regulate ERISA plans.

Moreover, the approaches appear to contemplate a state acting as a participant in a market rather than as a regulator. The U.S. Supreme Court has found that, when a state or municipality acts as a participant in the market and does so in a narrow and focused manner consistent with the behavior of other market participants, such action does not constitute state regulation. *Compare Building and Construction Trades Council* v. *Associated Builders and Contractors of Massachusetts/Rhode Island, Inc.*, 507 U.S. 218 (1993); *Wisconsin Department of Industry, Labor and Human Relations* v. *Gould*, 475 U.S. 282 (1986); *see also American Trucking Associations, Inc.* v. *City of Los Angeles*, 133 S. Ct. 2096, 2102 (2013) (Section 14501(c)(1) of the Federal Aviation Administration Authorization Act, which preempts a state "law, regulation, or other provision having the force and effect of law related to a price, route, or service of any motor carrier," 49 U.S.C. 14501(c)(1), "draws a rough line between a government's exercise of regulatory authority and its own contract-based participation in a market"); *Associated General Contractors of America* v. *Metropolitan Water District of Southern California*, 159 F.3d 1178, 1182-84 (9th Cir. 1998) (recognizing a similar distinction between state regulation and state market participation). By merely offering employers particular ERISA-covered plan options[15] (or non-ERISA plan options), these approaches (whether used separately or together as part of a multi-faceted state initiative) do not dictate how an employer's plan is designed or operated or make offering a plan more costly for employers or employees. Nor do they make it impossible for employers operating across state lines to offer uniform benefits to their employees.[16] Rather than impair federal regulation of employee benefit plans, the state laws would leave the plans wholly subject to ERISA's regulatory requirements and protections.

Of course, a state must implement these approaches without establishing standards inconsistent with ERISA or providing its own regulatory or judicial remedies for conduct governed exclusively by ERISA. ERISA's system of rules and remedies would apply to these arrangements. A contractor retained by a state using the marketplace approach would be subject to the same ERISA standards and remedies that apply to any company offering the same services to employers. Similarly, a prototype plan or multiple employer plan program that a state offers to employers would have to comply with the same ERISA requirements and would have to be subject to the same remedies as any private party offering such products and services.[17]

Even if the state laws enacted to establish programs of the sort described above "reference" employee benefit plans in a literal sense, they should not be seen as laws that "relate to" ERISA plans in the sense ERISA section 514(a) uses that statutory term because they are completely voluntary from the employer's perspective, the state program would be entirely subject to ERISA, and state law would not impose any outside regulatory requirements beyond ERISA. They do not require employers to establish ERISA-covered plans, forbid any type of plan or restrict employers' choices with respect to benefit structures or their administration. These laws would merely offer a program that employers could accept or reject. *See Dillingham*, 519 U.S. at 325-28.

---

[10] Different rules may apply under the Internal Revenue Code for purposes of determining the plan sponsor of a tax-qualified retirement plan.

[11] *See, e.g.,* Advisory Opinion 2012-04A. *See also MDPhysicians & Associates, Inc.* v. *State Bd. Ins.*, 957 F.2d 178,185 (5th Cir.), *cert. denied*, 506 U.S. 861 (1992) ("the entity that maintains the plan and the individuals that benefit from the plan [must be] tied by a common economic or representation interest, unrelated to the provision of benefits." (quoting *Wisconsin Educ. Assoc. Ins. Trust* v. *Iowa State Bd.*, 804 F.2d 1059, 1063 (8th Cir. 1986)).

[12] The Department has also recognized other circumstances when a person sponsoring a plan is acting as an "employer" indirectly rather than as an entity that underwrites benefits or provides administrative services. *See* Advisory Opinion 89-06A (Department would consider a member of a controlled group which establishes a benefit plan for its employees and/or the employees of other members of the controlled group to be an employer within the meaning of section 3(5) of ERISA); Advisory Opinion 95-29A (employee leasing company may act either directly or indirectly in the interest of an employer in establishing and maintaining employee benefit plan).

[13] *See* Advisory Opinion 2012-04A (holding that a group of employers can collectively act as the "employer" in sponsoring a multiple employer plan only if the employers group was formed for purposes other than the provision of benefits, the employers have a basic level of commonality (such as the participating employers all being in the same industry), and the employers participating in the plan in fact act as the "employer" by controlling the plan).

[14] *Travelers*, 514 U.S. at 658 (1995); *Ingersoll-Rand Co.* v. *McClendon*, 498 U.S. 133, 142 (1990); *Egelhoff* v. *Egelhoff*, 532 U.S. 141, 148 (2001); *Fort Halifax Packing Co.* v. *Coyne*, 482 U.S. 1, 14 (1987).

[15] In the Department's view, a state law that required employers to participate in a state prototype plan or state sponsored multiple employer plan unless they affirmatively opted out would effectively compel the employer to decide whether to sponsor an ERISA plan in a way that would be preempted by ERISA.

[16] The Court in *Travelers* approved a New York statute that gave employers a strong incentive to provide health care benefits through Blue Cross and Blue Shield as opposed to other providers. The Court noted that the law did not "mandate" employee benefit plans or their administration, or produce such acute economic effects, either directly or indirectly, by intent or otherwise "as to force an ERISA plan to adopt a certain scheme of substantive coverage or effectively restrict its choice of insurers." *Travelers*, 514 U.S. at 668. *See also De Buono* v. *NYSA-ILA Medical and Clinical Services Fund*, 520 U.S. 806, 816 (1997).

[17] State laws relating to sovereign immunity for state governments and their employees would have to be evaluated carefully to ensure they do not conflict with ERISA's remedial provisions.

In addition, none of the state approaches described above resemble the state laws that the Court held preempted in its pre- *Travelers* "reference to" cases. Those laws targeted ERISA plans as a class with affirmative requirements or special exemptions. *See, e.g., District of Columbia* v. *Greater Wash. Bd. of Trade*, 506 U.S. 125, 128, 129-133 (1992) (workers' compensation law that required employee benefits "set by reference to [ERISA] plans") (citation omitted); *Ingersoll-Rand Co.* v. *McClendon*, 498 U.S. 133, 135-136, 140 (1990) (common law claim for wrongful discharge to prevent attainment of ERISA benefits); *Mackey* v. *Lanier Collection Agency & Serv., Inc.*, 486 U.S. 825, 828 & n.2, 829-830 (1988) (exemption from garnishment statute for ERISA plans). In the case of the state actions outlined above, any restriction on private economic activity arises, not from state regulatory actions, but from the application of ERISA requirements to the plans, service providers, and investment products, that the state, as any other private sector participant in the market, selects in deciding what it is willing to offer.

Finally, it is worth noting that even if the state laws implementing these approaches "relate to" ERISA plans in some sense of that term, it is only because they create or authorize arrangements that are fully governed by ERISA's requirements. By embracing ERISA in this way, the state would not on that basis be running afoul of section 514(a) because ERISA fully applies to the arrangement and there is nothing in the state law for ERISA to "supersede." In this regard, section 514(a) of ERISA, in relevant part, provides that Title I of ERISA "shall supersede any and all state laws insofar as they may now or hereafter relate to any employee benefit plan . . . ." To the extent that the state makes plan design decisions in fashioning its prototype plan or state sponsored plan, or otherwise adopts rules necessary to run the plan, those actions would be the same as any other prototype plan provider or employer sponsor of any ERISA-covered plan, and the arrangement would be fully and equally subject to ERISA.

This conclusion is supported by the Department's position regarding state governmental participation in ERISA plans in another context. Pursuant to section 4(b)(1) of ERISA, the provisions of Title I of ERISA do not apply to a plan that a state government establishes for its own employees, which ERISA section 3(32) defines as a "governmental plan." The Department has long held the view, however, that if a plan covering governmental employees fails to qualify as a governmental plan, it would still be subject to Title I of ERISA.[18] In these circumstances, the failure to qualify as a governmental plan does not prohibit a governmental employer from providing benefits through, and making contributions to, an ERISA-covered employee benefit plan.[19] Thus, the effect of ERISA is not to prohibit the state from offering benefits, but rather to make those benefits subject to ERISA. Here too, ERISA does not supersede state law to the extent it merely creates an arrangement that is fully governed by ERISA.

[¶ 15,043]
DELINQUENT CONTRIBUTIONS

Act Sec. 515. Every employer who is obligated to make contributions to a multi-employer plan under the terms of the plan or under the terms of a collectively bargained agreement shall to the extent not inconsistent with law, make such contributions in accordance with the terms and conditions of such plan or such agreement.

Amendment

P.L. 96-364, §306:

Added new section 515, effective September 26, 1980.

[¶ 15,043C]
OUTREACH TO PROMOTE RETIREMENT INCOME SAVINGS

Act Sec. 516.(a) IN GENERAL. The Secretary shall maintain an ongoing program of outreach to the public designed to effectively promote retirement income savings by the public.

(b) METHODS. The Secretary shall carry out the requirements of subsection (a) by means which shall ensure effective communication to the public, including publication of public service announcements, public meetings, creation of educational materials, and establishment of a site on the Internet.

(c) INFORMATION TO BE MADE AVAILABLE. The information to be made available by the Secretary as part of the program of outreach required under subsection (a) shall include the following:

(1) a description of the vehicles currently available to individuals and employers for creating and maintaining retirement income savings, specifically including information explaining to employers, in simple terms, the characteristics and operation of the different retirement savings vehicles, including the steps to establish each such vehicle; and

(2) information regarding matters relevant to establishing retirement income savings, such as—

    (A) the forms of retirement income savings;

    (B) the concept of compound interest;

    (C) the importance of commencing savings early in life;

    (D) savings principles;

    (E) the importance of prudence and diversification in investing;

    (F) the importance of the timing of investments; and

    (G) the impact on retirement savings of life's uncertainties, such as living beyond one's life expectancy.

(d) ESTABLISHMENT OF SITE ON THE INTERNET. The Secretary shall establish a permanent site on the Internet concerning retirement income savings. The site shall contain at least the following information:

(1) a means for individuals to calculate their estimated retirement savings needs, based on their retirement income goal as a percentage of their preretirement income;

(2) a description in simple terms of the common types of retirement income savings arrangements available to both individuals and employers (specifically including small employers), including information on the amount of money that can be placed into a given vehicle, the tax treatment of the money, the amount of accumulation possible through different typical investment options and interest rate projections, and a directory of resources of more descriptive information;

(3) materials explaining to employers in simple terms, the characteristics and operation of the different retirement savings arrangements for their workers and what the basic legal requirements are under this Act and the Internal Revenue Code of 1986, including the steps to establish each such arrangement;

(4) copies of all educational materials developed by the Department of Labor, and by other Federal agencies in consultation with such Department, to promote retirement income savings by workers and employers; and

---

[18] *See, e.g.*, Advisory Opinion 2004-04A.

[19] *See* Information Letter to Michael T. Scaraggi and James M. Steinberg from John J. Canary (April 12, 2004).

(5) links to other sites maintained on the Internet by governmental agencies and nonprofit organizations that provide additional detail on retirement income savings arrangements and related topics on savings or investing.

(e) COORDINATION. The Secretary shall coordinate the outreach program under this section with similar efforts undertaken by other public and private entities.

Amendment

P.L. 105-92, §3(a):

Added new section 516, to read as above.

[¶ 15,043F]
NATIONAL SUMMIT ON RETIREMENT SAVINGS

Act Sec. 517.(a) AUTHORITY TO CALL SUMMIT. Not later than July 15, 1998, the President shall convene a National Summit on Retirement Income Savings at the White House, to be co-hosted by the President and the Speaker and the Minority Leader of the House of Representatives and the Majority Leader and Minority Leader of the Senate. Such a National Summit shall be convened thereafter in 2001 and 2005 on or after September 1 of each year involved. Such a National Summit shall—

(1) advance the public's knowledge and understanding of retirement savings and its critical importance to the future well-being of American workers and their families;

(2) facilitate the development of a broad-based, public education program to encourage and enhance individual commitment to a personal retirement savings strategy;

(3) develop recommendations for additional research, reforms, and actions in the field of private pensions and individual retirement savings; and

(4) disseminate the report of, and information obtained by, the National Summit and exhibit materials and works of the National Summit.

(b) PLANNING AND DIRECTION. The National Summit shall be planned and conducted under the direction of the Secretary, in consultation with, and with the assistance of, the heads of such other Federal departments and agencies as the President may designate. Such assistance may include the assignment of personnel. The Secretary shall, in planning and conducting the National Summit, consult with the congressional leaders specified in subsection (e)(2). The Secretary shall also, in carrying out the Secretary's duties under this subsection, consult and coordinate with at least one organization made up of private sector businesses and associations partnered with Government entities to promote long-term financial security in retirement through savings.

(c) PURPOSE OF NATIONAL SUMMIT. The purpose of the National Summit shall be—

(1) to increase the public awareness of the value of personal savings for retirement;

(2) to advance the public's knowledge and understanding of retirement savings and its critical importance to the future well-being of American workers and their families;

(3) to facilitate the development of a broad-based, public education program to encourage and enhance individual commitment to a personal retirement savings strategy;

(4) to identify the problems workers have in setting aside adequate savings for retirement;

(5) to identify the barriers which employers, especially small employers, face in assisting their workers in accumulating retirement savings;

(6) to examine the impact and effectiveness of individual employers to promote personal savings for retirement among their workers and to promote participation in company savings options;

(7) to examine the impact and effectiveness of government programs at the Federal, State, and local levels to educate the public about, and to encourage, retirement income savings;

(8) to develop such specific and comprehensive recommendations for the legislative and executive branches of the Government and for private sector action as may be appropriate for promoting private pensions and individual retirement savings; and

(9) to develop recommendations for the coordination of Federal, State, and local retirement income savings initiatives among the Federal, State, and local levels of government and for the coordination of such initiatives.

(d) SCOPE OF NATIONAL SUMMIT. The scope of the National Summit shall consist of issues relating to individual and employer-based retirement savings and shall not include issues relating to the old-age, survivors, and disability insurance program under title II of the Social Security Act.

(e) NATIONAL SUMMIT PARTICIPANTS.—

(1) IN GENERAL. To carry out the purposes of the National Summit, the National Summit shall bring together—

(A) professionals and other individuals working in the fields of employee benefits and retirement savings;

(B) Members of Congress and officials in the executive branch;

(C) representatives of State and local governments;

(D) representatives of private sector institutions, including individual employers, concerned about promoting the issue of retirement savings and facilitating savings among American workers; and

(E) representatives of the general public.

(2) STATUTORILY REQUIRED PARTICIPATION. The participants in the National Summit shall include the following individuals or their designees:

(A) the Speaker and the Minority Leader of the House of representatives;

(B) the Majority Leader and the Minority Leader of the Senate;

(C) the Chairman and ranking Member of the Committee on Education and the Workforce of the House of Representatives;

(D) the Chairman and ranking Member of the Committee on Labor and Human Resources of the Senate;

(E) the Chairman and ranking Member of the Special Committee on Aging of the Senate;

(F) the Chairman and ranking Member of the Subcommittees on Labor, Health and Human Services, and Education of the Senate and House of Representatives; and

(G) the parties referred to in subsection (b).

(3) ADDITIONAL PARTICIPANTS.—

(A) IN GENERAL. There shall be not more than 200 additional participants. Of such additional participants—

(i) one-half shall be appointed by the President, in consultation with the elected leaders of the President's party in Congress (either the Speaker of the House of Representatives or the Minority Leader of the House of Representatives, and either the Majority Leader or the Minority Leader of the Senate; and

(ii) one-half shall be appointed by the elected leaders of Congress of the party to which the President does not belong (one-half of that allotment to be appointed by either the Speaker of the House of Representatives or the Minority Leader of the House of Representatives, and one-half of that allotment to be appointed by either the Majority Leader or the Minority Leader of the Senate).

(B) APPOINTMENT REQUIREMENTS. The additional participants described in subparagraph (A) shall be—

(i) appointed not later than January 31, 1998;

(ii) selected without regard to political affiliation or past partisan activity; and

(iii) representative of the diversity of thought in the fields of employee benefits and retirement income savings.

(4) PRESIDING OFFICERS. The National Summit shall be presided over equally by representatives of the executive and legislative branches.

(f) NATIONAL SUMMIT ADMINISTRATION—

(1) ADMINISTRATION. In administering this section, the Secretary shall—

(A) request the cooperation and assistance of such other Federal departments and agencies and other parties referred to in subsection (b) as may be appropriate in the carrying out of this section;

(B) furnish all reasonable assistance to State agencies, area agencies, and other appropriate organizations to enable them to organize and conduct conferences in conjunction with the National Summit;

(C) make available for public comment a proposed agenda for the National Summit that reflects to the greatest extent possible the purposes for the National Summit set out in this section;

(D) prepare and make available background materials for the use of participants in the National Summit that the Secretary considers necessary; and

(E) appoint and fix the pay of such additional personnel as may be necessary to carry out the provisions of this section without regard to provisions of title 5, United States Code, governing appointments in the competitive service, and without regard to chapter 51 and subchapter III of chapter 53 of such title relating to classification and General Schedule pay rates.

(2) DUTIES. The Secretary shall, in carrying out the responsibilities and functions of the Secretary under this section, and as part of the National Summit, ensure that—

(A) the National Summit shall be conducted in a manner that ensures broad participation of Federal, State, and local agencies and private organizations, professionals, and others involved in retirement income savings and provides a strong basis for assistance to be provided under paragraph (1)(B);

(B) the agenda prepared under paragraph (1)(C) for the National Summit is published in the Federal Register; and

(C) the personnel appointed under paragraph (1)(E) shall be fairly balanced in terms of points of views represented and shall be appointed without regard to political affiliation or previous partisan activities.

(3) NONAPPLICATION OF FACA. The provisions of the Federal Advisory Committee Act (5 U.S.C. App.) shall not apply to the National Summit.

(g) REPORT. The Secretary shall prepare a report describing the activities of the National Summit and shall submit the report to the President, the Speaker and Minority Leader of the House of Representatives, the Majority and Minority Leaders of the Senate, and the chief executive officers of the States not later than 90 days after the date on which the National Summit is adjourned.

(h) DEFINITION. For purposes of this section, the term 'State' means a State, the District of Columbia, the Commonwealth of Puerto Rico, the Commonwealth of the Northern Mariana Islands, Guam, the Virgin Islands, American Samoa, and any other territory or possession of the United States.

(i) AUTHORIZATION OF APPROPRIATIONS.—

(1) IN GENERAL. There is authorized to be appropriated for fiscal years beginning on or after October 1, 1997, such sums as are necessary to carry out this section.

(2) AUTHORIZATION TO ACCEPT PRIVATE CONTRIBUTIONS. In order to facilitate the National Summit as a public-private partnership, the Secretary may accept private contributions, in the form of money, supplies, or services, to defray the costs of the National Summit.

(j) FINANCIAL OBLIGATION FOR FISCAL YEAR 1998. The financial obligation for the Department of Labor for fiscal year 1998 shall not exceed the lesser of—

(1) one-half of the costs of the National Summit; or

(2) $250,000.

The private sector organization described in subsection (b) and contracted with by the Secretary shall be obligated for the balance of the cost of the National Summit.

(k) CONTRACTS. The Secretary may enter into contracts to carry out the Secretary's responsibilities under this section. The Secretary shall enter into a contract on a sole-source basis to ensure the timely completion of the National Summit in fiscal year 1998.

Amendment

P.L. 105-92, §4(a):

Added new section 517, to read as above.

[¶ 15,043H]

AUTHORITY TO POSTPONE CERTAIN DEADLINES BY REASON OF A PRESIDENTIALLY DECLARED DISASTER OR TERRORISTIC OR MILITARY ACTIONS

Act Sec. 518. In the case of a pension or other employee benefit plan, or any sponsor, administrator, participant, beneficiary, or other person with respect to such plan, affected by a Presidentially declared disaster (as defined in section 1033 (h) (3) of the Internal Revenue Code of 1986) or a terroristic or military action (as defined in section 692 (c) (2) of such Code), the Secretary may, notwithstanding any other provision of law prescribe, by notice or otherwise, a period of up to 1 year which may be disregarded in determining the date by which any action is required or permitted to be completed underthis Act. No plan shall be treated as failing to be operated in accordance with the terms of the plan solely as the result of disregarding any period by reason of the preceding sentence.

Amendment

P.L. 107-134, §112(c)(1):

Added new section 518, to read as above. This section applies to disasters and terroristic or military actions occurring on or after September 11, 2001, with respect to

any action of the Secretary of the Treasury, Secretary of Labor, or the PBGC occurring on or after January 23, 2002.

[¶ 15,043K]
PROHIBITION ON FALSE STATEMENTS AND REPRESENTATIONS

Act Sec. 519. No person, in connection with a plan or other arrangement that is multiple employer welfare arrangement described in section 3(40), shall make a false statement or false representation of fact, knowing it to be false, in connection with the marketing or sale of such plan or arrangement, to any employee, any member of an employee organization, any beneficiary, any employer, any employee organization, the Secretary, or any State, or the representative or agent of any such person, State, or the Secretary, concerning—

(1) the financial condition or solvency of such plan or arrangement;

(2) the benefits provided by such plan or arrangement;

(3) the regulatory status of such plan or other arrangement under any Federal or State law governing collective bargaining, labor management relations, or intern union affairs; or

(4) the regulatory status of such plan or other arrangement regarding exemption from state regulatory authority under this Act.

This section shall not apply to any plan or arrangement that does not fall within the meaning of the term 'multiple employer welfare arrangement' under section 3(40)(A).

Amendments	The above amendment is effective on the date of enactment (March 23, 2010).

P.L. 111-148, § 6601(a):

Added ERISA Sec. 519 to read as above.

[¶ 15,043N]
APPLICABILITY OF STATE LAW TO COMBAT FRAUD AND ABUSE

Act Sec. 520. The Secretary may, for the purpose of identifying, preventing, or prosecuting fraud and abuse, adopt regulatory standards establishing, or issue an order relating to a specific person establishing, that a person engaged in the business of providing insurance through a multiple employer welfare arrangement described in section 3(40) is subject to the laws of the States in which such person operates which regulate insurance in such State, notwithstanding section 514(b)(6) of this Act or the Liability Risk Retention Act of 1986, and regardless of whether the law of the State is otherwise preempted under any of such provisions. This section shall not apply to any plan or arrangement that does not fall within the meaning of the term 'multiple employer welfare arrangement' under section 3(40)(A).

Amendments	The above amendment is effective on the date of enactment (March 23, 2010).

P.L. 111-148, § 6604(a):

Added ERISA Sec. 520 to read as above.

[¶ 15,043Q]
ADMINISTRATIVE SUMMARY CEASE AND DESIST ORDERS AND SUMMARY SEIZURE ORDERS AGAINST MULTIPLE EMPLOYER WELFARE ARRANGEMENTS IN FINANCIALLY HAZARDOUS CONDITION

Act Sec. 521.(a) IN GENERAL. The Secretary may issue a cease and desist (ex parte) order under this title if it appears to the Secretary that the alleged conduct of a multiple employer welfare arrangement described in section 3(40), other than a plan or arrangement described in subsection (g), is fraudulent, or creates an immediate danger to the public safety or welfare, or is causing or can be reasonably expected to cause significant, imminent, and irreparable public injury.

(b) HEARING. A person that is adversely affected by the issuance of a cease and desist order under subsection (a) may request a hearing by the Secretary regarding such order. The Secretary may require that a proceeding under this section, including all related information and evidence, be conducted in a confidential manner.

(c) BURDEN OF PROOF. The burden of proof in any hearing conducted under subsection (b) shall be on the party requesting the hearing to show cause why the cease and desist order should be set aside.

(d) DETERMINATION. Based upon the evidence presented at a hearing under subsection (b), the cease and desist order involved may be affirmed, modified, or set aside by the Secretary in whole or in part.

(e) SEIZURE. The Secretary may issue a summary seizure order under this title if it appears that a multiple employer welfare arrangement is in a financially hazardous condition.

(f) REGULATIONS. The Secretary may promulgate such regulations or other guidance as may be necessary or appropriate to carry out this section.

(g) EXCEPTION. This section shall not apply to any plan or arrangement that does not fall within the meaning of the term 'multiple employer welfare arrangement' under section 3(40)(A).

Amendments	The above amendment is effective on the date of enactment (March 23, 2010).

P.L. 111-148, § 6605(a):

Added ERISA Sec. 521 to read as above.

Regulations

The following regulations were adopted on March 1, 2013 by 78 FR 13797, effective on April 1, 2013.

[¶ 15,043Q-1]

§ 2560.521-1 Cease and desist and seizure orders under section 521.

(a) *Purpose.* Section 521(a) of the Employee Retirement Income Security Act of 1974 (ERISA), 29 U.S.C. 1151(a), authorizes the Secretary of Labor to issue an ex parte cease and desist order if it appears to the Secretary that the alleged conduct of a multiple employer welfare arrangement (MEWA) under section 3(40) of ERISA is fraudulent, or creates an immediate danger to the public safety or welfare, or is causing or can be reasonably expected to cause significant, imminent, and irreparable public injury. Section 521(e) of ERISA authorizes the Secretary to issue a summary seizure order if it appears that a MEWA is in a financially hazardous condition. An order may apply to a MEWA or to persons having custody or control of assets of the subject MEWA, any authority over management of the subject MEWA, or any role in the transaction of the subject MEWA's business. This section sets forth standards and procedures for the Secretary to issue ex parte cease and desist and summary seizure orders and for administrative review of the issuance of such cease and desist orders.

(b) *Definitions.* When used in this section, the following terms shall have the meanings ascribed in this paragraph (b).

(1) *Multiple employer welfare arrangement* (MEWA) is an arrangement as defined in section 3(40) of ERISA that either is an employee welfare benefit plan subject to Title I of ERISA or offers benefits in connection with one or more employee welfare benefit plans subject to Title I of ERISA. For purposes of section 521 of ERISA, a

MEWA does not include a health insurance issuer (including a health maintenance organization) that is licensed to offer or provide health insurance coverage to the public and employers at large in each State in which it offers or provides health insurance coverage, and that, in each such State, is subject to comprehensive licensure, solvency, and examination requirements that the State customarily requires for issuing health insurance policies to the public and employers at large. The term health insurance issuer does not include group health plans. For purposes of this section, the term "health insurance coverage" has the same meaning as in ERISA section 733(b)(1).

(2) *The conduct of a MEWA is fraudulent:*

(i) When the MEWA or any person acting as an agent or employee of the MEWA commits an act or omission knowingly and with an intent to deceive or defraud plan participants, plan beneficiaries, employers or employee organizations, or other members of the public, the Secretary, or a State regarding:

(A) The financial condition of the MEWA (including the MEWA's solvency and the management of plan assets);

(B) The benefits provided by or in connection with the MEWA;

(C) The management, control, or administration of the MEWA;

(D) The existing or lawful regulatory status of the MEWA under Federal or State law; or,

(E) Any other material fact, as determined by the Secretary, relating to the MEWA or its operation.

(ii) Fraudulent conduct includes any false statement regarding any of paragraphs (b)(2)(i)(A) through (b)(2)(i)(E) of this section that is made with knowledge of its falsity or that is made with reckless indifference to the statement's truth or falsity, and the knowing concealment of material information regarding any of paragraphs (b)(2)(i)(A) through (b)(2)(i)(E) of this section. Examples of fraudulent conduct include, but are not limited to, misrepresenting the terms of the benefits offered by or in connection with the MEWA or the financial condition of the MEWA or engaging in deceptive acts or omissions in connection with marketing or sales or fees charged to employers or employee organizations.

(3) *The conduct of a MEWA creates an immediate danger to the public safety or welfare* if the conduct of a MEWA or any person acting as an agent or employee of the MEWA impairs, or threatens to impair, a MEWA's ability to pay claims or otherwise unreasonably increases the risk of nonpayment of benefits. Intent to create an immediate danger is not required for this criterion. Examples of such conduct include, but are not limited to, a systematic failure to properly process or pay benefit claims, including failure to establish and maintain a claims procedure that complies with the Secretary's claims procedure regulations (29 CFR 2560.503-1 and 29 CFR 2590.715-2719), failure to establish or maintain a recordkeeping system that tracks the claims made, paid, or processed or the MEWA's financial condition, a substantial failure to meet applicable disclosure, reporting, and other filing requirements, including the annual reporting and registration requirements under sections 101(g) and 104 of ERISA, failure to establish and implement a policy or method to determine that the MEWA is actuarially sound with appropriate reserves and adequate underwriting, failure to comply with a cease and desist order issued by a government agency or court, and failure to hold plan assets in trust.

(4) *The conduct of a MEWA is causing or can be reasonably expected to cause significant, imminent, and irreparable public injury:*

(i) If the conduct of a MEWA, or of a person acting as an agent or employee of the MEWA, is having, or is reasonably expected to have, a significant and imminent negative effect on one or more of the following:

(A) An employee welfare benefit plan that is, or offers benefits in connection with, a MEWA;

(B) The sponsor of such plan or the employer or employee organization that makes payments for benefits provided by or in connection with a MEWA; or

(C) Plan participants and plan beneficiaries; and

(ii) If it is not reasonable to expect that such effect will be fully repaired or rectified.

Intent to cause injury is not required for this criterion. Examples of such conduct include, but are not limited to, conversion or concealment of property of the MEWA; improper disposal, transfer, or removal of funds or other property of the MEWA, including unreasonable compensation or payments to MEWA operators and service providers (e.g. brokers, marketers, and third party administrators); employment by the MEWA of a person prohibited from such employment pursuant to section 411 of ERISA, and embezzlement from the MEWA. For purposes of section 521 of ERISA, compensation that would be excessive under 26 CFR 1.162-7 will be considered unreasonable compensation or payments for purposes of this regulation. Depending upon the facts and circumstances, compensation may be unreasonable under this regulation even it is not excessive under 26 CFR 1.162-7.

(5) *A MEWA is in a financially hazardous condition if:*

(i) The Secretary has probable cause to believe that a MEWA:

(A) Is, or is in imminent danger of becoming, unable to pay benefit claims as they come due, or

(B) Has sustained, or is in imminent danger of sustaining, a significant loss of assets; or

(ii) A person responsible for management, control, or administration of the MEWA's assets is the subject of a cease and desist order issued by the Secretary.

(6) A *person,* for purposes of this section, is an individual, partnership, corporation, employee welfare benefit plan, association, or other entity or organization.

(c) *Temporary cease and desist order.* (1)(i) The Secretary may issue a temporary cease and desist order when the Secretary finds there is reasonable cause to believe that the conduct of a MEWA, or any person acting as an agent or employee of the MEWA, is -

(A) Fraudulent;

(B) Creates an immediate danger to the public safety or welfare; or

(C) Is causing or can be reasonably expected to cause significant, imminent, and irreparable public injury.

(ii) A single act or omission may be the basis for a temporary cease and desist order.

(2) A temporary cease and desist order, as the Secretary determines is necessary and appropriate to stop the conduct on which the order is based, and to protect the interests of plan participants, plan beneficiaries, employers or employee organizations, or other members of the public, may—

(i) Prohibit specific conduct or prohibit the transaction of any business of the MEWA;

(ii) Prohibit any person from taking specified actions, or exercising authority or control, concerning funds or property of a MEWA or of any employee benefit plan, regardless of whether such funds or property have been commingled with other funds or property; and,

(iii) Bar any person either directly or indirectly, from providing management, administrative, or other services to any MEWA or to an employee benefit plan or trust.

(3) The Secretary may require documentation from the subject of the order verifying compliance.

(d) *Effect of order on other remedies.* The issuance of a temporary or final cease and desist order shall not foreclose the Secretary from seeking additional remedies under ERISA.

(e) *Administrative hearing.* (1) A temporary cease and desist order shall become a final order as to any MEWA or other person named in the order 30 days after such person receives notice of the order unless, within this period, such person requests a hearing in accordance with the requirements of this paragraph (e).

(2) A person requesting a hearing must file a written request and an answer to the order showing cause why the order should be modified or set aside. The request and the answer must be filed in accordance with 29 CFR part 2571 and § 18.4 of this title.

(3) A hearing shall be held expeditiously following the receipt of the request for a hearing by the Office of the Administrative Law Judges, unless the parties mutually consent, in writing, to a later date.

(4) The decision of the administrative law judge shall be issued expeditiously after the conclusion of the hearing.

(5) The Secretary must offer evidence supporting the findings made in issuing the order that there is reasonable cause to believe that the MEWA (or a person acting as an employee or agent of the MEWA) engaged in conduct specified in paragraph (c)(1) of this section.

(6) The person requesting the hearing has the burden to show that the order should be modified or set aside. To meet this burden such person must show by a preponderance of the evidence that the MEWA (or a person acting as an employee or agent of the MEWA) did not engage in conduct specified in paragraph (c)(1) of this section or must show that the requirements imposed by the order, are, in whole or part, arbitrary and capricious.

(7) Any temporary cease and desist order for which a hearing has been requested shall remain in effect and enforceable, pending completion of the administrative proceedings, unless stayed by the Secretary, an administrative law judge, or by a court.

(8) The Secretary may require that the hearing and all evidence be treated as confidential.

(f) *Summary seizure order.* (1) Subject to paragraphs (f)(2) and (3) of this section, the Secretary may issue a summary seizure order when the Secretary finds there is probable cause to believe that a MEWA is in a financially hazardous condition.

(2) Except as provided in paragraph (f)(3) of this section, the Secretary, before issuing a summary seizure order to remove assets and records from the control and management of the MEWA or any persons having custody or control of such assets or records, shall obtain judicial authorization from a federal court in the form of a warrant or other appropriate form of authorization and may at that time pursue other actions such as those set forth in paragraph (f)(5) of this section.

(3) If the Secretary reasonably believes that any delay in issuing the order is likely to result in the removal, dissipation, or concealment of plan assets or records, the Secretary may issue and serve a summary seizure order before seeking court authorization. Promptly following service of the order, the Secretary shall seek authorization from a federal court and may at that time pursue other actions such as those set forth in paragraph (f)(5) of this section.

(4) A summary seizure order may authorize the Secretary to take possession or control of all or part of the books, records, accounts, and property of the MEWA (including the premises in which the MEWA transacts its business) to protect the benefits of plan participants, plan beneficiaries, employers or employee organizations, or other members of the public, and to safeguard the assets of employee welfare benefit plans. The order may also direct any person having control and custody of the assets that are the subject of the order not to allow any transfer or disposition of such assets except upon the written direction of the Secretary, or of a receiver or independent fiduciary appointed by a court.

(5) In connection with or following the execution of a summary seizure order, the Secretary may—

(i) Secure court appointment of a receiver or independent fiduciary to perform any necessary functions of the MEWA;

(ii) Obtain court authorization for the Secretary, the receiver or independent fiduciary to take any other action to seize, secure, maintain, or preserve the availability of the MEWA's assets; and

(iii) Obtain such other appropriate relief available under ERISA to protect the interest of employee welfare benefit plan participants, plan beneficiaries, employers or employee organizations or other members of the public. Other appropriate equitable relief may include the liquidation and winding up of the MEWA's affairs and, where applicable, the affairs of any person sponsoring the MEWA.

(g) *Effective date of orders.* Cease and desist and summary seizure orders are effective immediately upon issuance by the Secretary and shall remain effective, except to the extent and until any provision is modified or the order is set aside by the Secretary, an administrative law judge, or a court.

(h) *Service of orders.* (1) As soon as practicable after the issuance of a temporary or final cease and desist order and no later than five business days after issuance of a summary seizure order, the Secretary shall serve the order either:

(i) By delivering a copy to the person who is the subject of the order. If the person is a partnership, service may be made to any partner. If the person is a corporation, association, or other entity or organization, service may be made to any officer of such entity or any person designated for service of process under State law or the applicable plan document. If the person is an employee welfare benefit plan, service may be made to a trustee or administrator. A person's attorney may accept service on behalf of such person;

(ii) By leaving a copy at the principal office, place of business, or residence of such person or attorney; or

(iii) By mailing a copy to the last known address of such person or attorney.

(2) If service is accomplished by certified mail, service is complete upon mailing. If service is done by regular mail, service is complete upon receipt by the addressee.

(3) Service of a temporary or final cease and desist order and of a summary seizure order shall include a statement of the Secretary's findings giving rise to the order, and, where applicable, a copy of any warrant or other authorization by a court.

[¶ 15,043Q-2]

§ 2560.521-2 Disclosure of order and proceedings.

(a) Notwithstanding § 2560.521-1(e)(8), the Secretary shall make available to the public final cease and desist and summary seizure orders or modifications and terminations of such final orders.

(b) Except as prohibited by applicable law, and at his or her discretion, the Secretary may disclose the issuance of a temporary cease and desist order or summary seizure order and information and evidence of any proceedings and hearings related to an order, to any Federal, State, or foreign authorities responsible for enforcing laws that apply to MEWAs and parties associated with, or providing services to, MEWAs.

(c) The sharing of such documents, material, or other information and evidence under this section does not constitute a waiver of any applicable privilege or claim of confidentiality.

[¶ 15,043Q-3]

§ 2560.521-3 Effect on other enforcement authority.

The Secretary's authority under section 521 shall not be construed to limit the Secretary's ability to exercise his or her enforcement or investigatory authority under any other provision of title I of ERISA. 29 U.S.C. 1001 *et seq.* The Secretary may, in his or her sole discretion, initiate court proceedings without using the procedures in this section.

[¶ 15,043Q-4]

§ 2560.521-4 Cross-reference.

See 29 CFR 2571.1 through 2571.13 for procedural rules relating to administrative hearings under section 521 of ERISA.

Regulations

The following regulations were adopted on March 1, 2013 by 78 FR 13797, effective on April 1, 2013.

Subpart A—Procedures for Administrative Hearings on the Issuance of Cease and Desist Orders Under ERISA Section 521—Multiple Employer Welfare Arrangements

2571.1 Scope of rules.

2571.2 Definitions.

2571.3 Service: copies of documents and pleadings.

Subpart B—[Reserved]

Part 2571—Procedural Regulations for Administration and Enforcement under the Employee Retirement Income Security Act

Subpart A—Procedures for Administrative Hearings on the Issuance of Cease and Desist Orders Under ERISA Section 521—Multiple Employer Welfare Arrangements

[¶ 15,043Q-50]

§ 2571.1 Scope of rules.

The rules of practice set forth in this part apply to ex parte cease and desist order proceedings under section 521 of the Employee Retirement Income Security Act of 1974, as amended (ERISA). The rules of procedure for administrative hearings published by the Department's Office of Administrative Law Judges at Part 18 of this Title will apply to matters arising under ERISA section 521 except as modified by this section. These proceedings shall be conducted as expeditiously as possible, and the parties and the Office of the Administrative Law Judges shall make every effort to avoid delay at each stage of the proceedings.

[¶ 15,043Q-51]

§ 2571.2 Definitions.

For section 521 proceedings, this section shall apply in lieu of the definitions in § 18.2 of this title:

(a) *Adjudicatory proceeding* means a judicial-type proceeding before an administrative law judge leading to an order;

(b) *Administrative law judge* means an administrative law judge appointed pursuant to the provisions of 5 U.S.C. 3105;

(c) *Answer* means a written statement that is supported by reference to specific circumstances or facts surrounding the temporary order issued pursuant to 29 CFR 2560.521-1(c);

(d) *Commencement of proceeding* is the filing of an answer by the respondent;

(e) *Consent agreement* means a proposed written agreement and order containing a specified proposed remedy or other relief acceptable to the Secretary and consenting parties;

(f) *Final order* means a cease and desist order that is a final order of the Secretary of Labor under ERISA section 521. Such final order may result from a decision of an administrative law judge or of the Secretary on review of a decision of an administrative law judge, or from the failure of a party to invoke the procedures for a hearing under 29 CFR 2560.521-1 within the prescribed time limit. A final order shall constitute a final agency action within the meaning of 5 U.S.C. 704;

(g) *Hearing* means that part of a section 521 proceeding which involves the submission of evidence, either by oral presentation or written submission, to the administrative law judge;

(h) *Order* means the whole or any part of a final procedural or substantive disposition of a section 521 proceeding;

(i) *Party* includes a person or agency named or admitted as a party to a section 521 proceeding;

(j) *Person* includes an individual, partnership, corporation, employee welfare benefit plan, association, or other entity or organization;

(k) *Petition* means a written request, made by a person or party, for some affirmative action;

(l) *Respondent* means the party against whom the Secretary is seeking to impose a cease and desist order under ERISA section 521;

(m) *Secretary* means the Secretary of Labor or his or her delegate;

(n) *Section 521 proceeding* means an adjudicatory proceeding relating to the issuance of a temporary order under 29 CFR 2560.521-1 and section 521 of ERISA;

(o) *Solicitor* means the Solicitor of Labor or his or her delegate; and

(p) *Temporary order* means the temporary cease and desist order issued by the Secretary under 29 CFR 2560.521-1(c) and section 521 of ERISA.

[¶ 15,043Q-52]

§ 2571.3 Service: copies of documents and pleadings.

For section 521 proceedings, this section shall apply in lieu of § 18.3 of this title:

(a) *In general.* Copies of all documents shall be served on all parties of record. All documents should clearly designate the docket number, if any, and short title of all matters. All documents to be filed shall be delivered or mailed to the Chief Docket Clerk, Office of Administrative Law Judges, 800 K Street NW., Suite 400, Washington, DC 20001-8002, or to the OALJ Regional Office to which the section 521 proceeding may have been transferred for hearing. Each document filed shall be clear and legible.

(b) *By parties.* All motions, petitions, pleadings, briefs, or other documents shall be filed with the Office of Administrative Law Judges with a copy, including any attachments, to all other parties of record. When a party is represented by an attorney, service shall be made upon the attorney. Service of any document upon any party may be made by personal delivery or by mailing a copy to the last known address. The Secretary shall be served by delivery to the Associate Solicitor, Plan Benefits Security Division, ERISA Section 521 Proceeding, P.O. Box 1914, Washington, DC 20013 and any attorney named for service of process as set forth in the temporary order. The person serving the document shall certify to the manner of date and service.

(c) *By the Office of Administrative Law Judges.* Service of orders, decisions, and all other documents shall be made in such manner as the Office of Administrative Law Judges determines to the last known address.

(d) *Form of pleadings.*

(1) Every pleading or other paper filed in a section 521 proceeding shall designate the Employee Benefits Security Administration (EBSA) as the agency under which the proceeding is instituted, the title of the proceeding, the docket number (if any) assigned by the Office of Administrative Law Judges and a designation of the type of pleading or paper (e.g., notice, motion to dismiss, etc.). The pleading or paper shall be signed and shall contain the address and telephone number of the party or person representing the party. Although there are no formal specifications for documents, they should be printed when possible on standard size 8 ½ × 11 inch paper.

(2) Illegible documents, whether handwritten, printed, photocopies, or otherwise, will not be accepted. Papers may be reproduced by any duplicating process provided all copies are clear and legible.

[¶ 15,043Q-53]

§ 2571.4 Parties.

For section 521 proceedings, this section shall apply in lieu of § 18.10 of this title:

(a) The term "party" wherever used in these rules shall include any person that is a subject of the temporary order and is challenging the temporary order under these section 521 proceedings, and the Secretary. A party challenging a temporary order shall be designated as the "respondent." The Secretary shall be designated as the "complainant."

(b) Other persons shall be permitted to participate as parties only if the administrative law judge finds that the final decision could directly and adversely affect them or the class they represent, that they may contribute materially to the disposition of the section 521 proceeding and their interest is not adequately represented by the existing parties, and that in the discretion of the administrative law judge the participation of such persons would be appropriate.

(c) A person not named in a temporary order, but wishing to participate as a respondent under this section shall submit a petition to the administrative law judge within fifteen (15) days after the person has knowledge of, or should have known about, the section 521 proceeding. The petition shall be filed with the administrative law judge and served on each person who has been made a party at the time of filing. Such petition shall concisely state:

(1) Petitioner's interest in the section 521 proceeding (including how the section 521 proceedings will directly and adversely affect them or the class they represent and why their interest is not adequately represented by the existing parties);

(2) How his or her participation as a party will contribute materially to the disposition of the section 521 proceeding;

(3) Who will appear for the petitioner;

(4) The issues on which petitioner wishes to participate; and

(5) Whether petitioner intends to present witnesses.

(d) Objections to the petition may be filed by a party within fifteen (15) days of the filing of the petition. If objections to the petition are filed, the administrative law judge shall then determine whether petitioners have the requisite interest to be a party in the section 521 proceeding, as defined in paragraph (b) of this section, and shall permit or deny participation accordingly. Where persons with common interest file petitions to participate as parties in a section 521 proceeding, the administrative law judge may request all such petitioners to designate a single representative, or the administrative law judge may designate one or more of the petitioners to represent the others. The administrative law judge shall give each such petitioner, as well as the parties, written notice of the decision on his or her petition. For each petition granted, the administrative law judge shall provide a brief statement of the basis of the decision. If the petition is denied, he or she shall briefly state the grounds for denial and may consider whether to treat the petition as a request for participation as amicus curiae.

[¶ 15,043Q-54]
§ 2571.5 **Consequences of default.**

For section 521 proceedings, this section shall apply in lieu of § 18.5(b) of this title. Failure of the respondent to file an answer to the temporary order within the 30-day period provided by 29 CFR 2560.521-1(e) shall constitute a waiver of the respondent's right to appear and contest the temporary order. Such failure shall also be deemed to be an admission of the facts as alleged in the temporary order for purposes of any proceeding involving the order issued under section 521 of ERISA. The temporary order shall then become the final order of the Secretary, within the meaning of 29 CFR 2571.2(f), 30 days from the date of the service of the temporary order.

[¶ 15,043Q-55]
§ 2571.6 **Consent order or settlement.**

For section 521 proceedings, this section shall apply in lieu of § 18.9 of this title:

(a) *In general.* At any time after the commencement of a section 521 proceeding, the parties jointly may move to defer the hearing for a reasonable time in order to negotiate a settlement or an agreement containing findings and a consent order disposing of the whole or any part of the section 521 proceeding. The administrative law judge shall have discretion to allow or deny such a postponement and to determine its duration. In exercising this discretion, the administrative law judge shall consider the nature of the section 521 proceeding, the requirements of the public interest, the representations of the parties and the probability of reaching an agreement that will result in a just disposition of the issues involved.

(b) *Content.* Any agreement containing consent findings and an order disposing of the section 521 proceeding or any part thereof shall also provide:

(1) That the consent order shall have the same force and effect as an order made after full hearing;

(2) That the entire record on which the consent order is based shall consist solely of the notice and the agreement;

(3) A waiver of any further procedural steps before the administrative law judge;

(4) A waiver of any right to challenge or contest the validity of the consent order and decision entered into in accordance with the agreement; and

(5) That the consent order and decision of the administrative law judge shall be final agency action within the meaning of 5 U.S.C. 704.

(c) *Submission.* On or before the expiration of the time granted for negotiations, the parties or their authorized representatives or their counsel may:

(1) Submit the proposed agreement containing consent findings and an order to the administrative law judge;

(2) Notify the administrative law judge that the parties have reached a full settlement and have agreed to dismissal of the action subject to compliance with the terms of the settlement; or

(3) Inform the administrative law judge that agreement cannot be reached.

(d) *Disposition.* If a settlement agreement containing consent findings and an order, agreed to by all the parties to a section 521 proceeding, is submitted within the time allowed therefor, the administrative law judge shall incorporate all of the findings, terms, and conditions of the settlement agreement and consent order of the parties. Such decision shall become a final agency action within the meaning of 5 U.S.C. 704.

(e) *Settlement without consent of all respondents.* In cases in which some, but not all, of the respondents to a section 521 proceeding submit an agreement and consent order to the administrative law judge, the following procedure shall apply:

(1) If all of the respondents have not consented to the proposed settlement submitted to the administrative law judge, then such non-consenting parties must receive notice and a copy of the proposed settlement at the time it is submitted to the administrative law judge;

(2) Any non-consenting respondent shall have fifteen (15) days to file any objections to the proposed settlement with the administrative law judge and all other parties;

(3) If any respondent submits an objection to the proposed settlement, the administrative law judge shall decide within thirty (30) days after receipt of such objections whether to sign or reject the proposed settlement. Where the record lacks substantial evidence upon which to base a decision or there is a genuine issue of material fact, then the administrative law judge may establish procedures for the purpose of receiving additional evidence upon which a decision on the contested issue may be reasonably based;

(4) If there are no objections to the proposed settlement, or if the administrative law judge decides to sign the proposed settlement after reviewing any such objections, the administrative law judge shall incorporate the consent agreement into a decision meeting the requirements of paragraph (d) of this section; and

(5) If the consent agreement is incorporated into a decision meeting the requirements of paragraph (d) of this section, the administrative law judge shall continue the section 521 proceeding with respect to any non-consenting respondents.

[¶ 15,043Q-56]
§ 2571.7 **Scope of discovery.**

For section 521 proceedings, this section shall apply in lieu of § 18.14 of this title:

(a) A party may file a motion to conduct discovery with the administrative law judge. The administrative law judge may grant a motion for discovery only upon a showing of good cause. In order to establish "good cause" for the purposes of this section, the moving party must show that the requested discovery relates to a genuine issue as to a fact that is material to the section 521 proceeding. The order of the administrative law judge shall expressly limit the scope and terms of the discovery to that for which "good cause" has been shown, as provided in this paragraph.

(b) Any evidentiary privileges apply as they would apply in a civil proceeding in federal district court. For example, legal advice provided by an attorney to a client is generally protected from disclosure. Mental impressions, conclusions, opinions, or legal theories of a party's attorney or other representative developed in anticipation of litigation are also generally protected from disclosure. The administrative law judge may not, however, protect from discovery or use, relevant communications between an attorney and a plan administrator or other plan fiduciary, or work product, that fall under the fiduciary exception to the attorney-client or work product privileges. The fiduciary exception to these privileges exists when an attorney advises the plan administrator or other plan fiduciary on matters concerning plan administration or other fiduciary activities. Consequently, the administrative law judge may not protect such communications from discovery or from use by the Secretary in the proceedings. The administrative law judge also may also not protect attorney work product prepared to assist the fiduciary in its fiduciary capacity from discovery or from use by the Secretary in the proceedings. The fiduciary exception does not apply, however, to the extent that communications were made or documents were prepared exclusively to aid the fiduciary personally or for non-fiduciary matters (*e.g.* settlor acts), provided that the plan did not pay for the legal services. The Secretary need not make a special showing, such as good cause, merely to obtain information or documents covered by the fiduciary exception. Other relevant exceptions to the attorney-client or work product privileges shall also apply.

[¶ 15,043Q-57]

§ 2571.8 **Summary decision.**

For section 521 proceedings, this section shall apply in lieu of § 18.41 of this title:

(a) *No genuine issue of material fact.* Where the administrative law judge finds that no issue of a material fact has been raised, he or she may issue a decision which, in the absence of an appeal, pursuant to § § 2571.10 through 2571.12, shall become a final agency action within the meaning of 5 U.S.C. 704.

(b) A decision made under this section, shall include a statement of:

(1) Findings of fact and conclusions of law, and the reasons thereof, on all issues presented; and

(2) Any terms and conditions of the ruling.

(c) A copy of any decision under this section shall be served on each party.

[¶ 15,043Q-58]

§ 2571.9 **Decision of the administrative law judge.**

For section 521 proceedings, this section shall apply in lieu of § 18.57 of this title:

(a) *Proposed findings of fact, conclusions, and order.* Within twenty (20) days of the filing of the transcript of the testimony, or such additional time as the administrative law judge may allow, each party may file with the administrative law judge, subject to the judge's discretion, proposed findings of fact, conclusions of law, and order together with a supporting brief expressing the reasons for such proposals. Such proposals and briefs shall be served on all parties, and shall refer to all portions of the record and to all authorities relied upon in support of each proposal.

(b) *Decision of the administrative law judge.* The administrative law judge shall make his or her decision expeditiously after the conclusion of the section 521 proceeding. The decision of the administrative law judge shall include findings of fact and conclusions of law with reasons therefore upon each material issue of fact or law presented on the record. The decision of the administrative law judge shall be based upon the whole record and shall be supported by reliable and probative evidence. The decision of the administrative law judge shall become final agency action within the meaning of 5 U.S.C. 704 unless an appeal is made pursuant to the procedures set forth in § § 2571.10 through 2571.12.

[¶ 15,043Q-59]

§ 2571.10 **Review by the Secretary.**

(a) The Secretary may review the decision of an administrative law judge. Such review may occur only when a party files a notice of appeal from a decision of an administrative law judge within twenty (20) days of the issuance of such a decision. In all other cases, the decision of the administrative law judge shall become the final agency action within the meaning of 5 U.S.C. 704.

(b) A notice of appeal to the Secretary shall state with specificity the issue(s) in the decision of the administrative law judge on which the party is seeking review. Such notice of appeal must be served on all parties of record.

(c) Upon receipt of an appeal, the Secretary shall request the Chief Administrative Law Judge to submit to the Secretary a copy of the entire record before the administrative law judge.

[¶ 15,043Q-60]

§ 2571.11 **Scope of review by the Secretary.**

The review of the Secretary shall be based on the record established before the administrative law judge. There shall be no opportunity for oral argument.

[¶ 15,043Q-61]

§ 2571.12 **Procedures for review by the Secretary.**

(a) Upon receipt of a notice of appeal, the Secretary shall establish a briefing schedule which shall be served on all parties of record. Upon motion of one or more of the parties, the Secretary may, in her discretion, permit the submission of reply briefs.

(b) The Secretary shall issue a decision as promptly as possible after receipt of the briefs of the parties. The Secretary may affirm, modify, or set aside, in whole or in part, the decision on appeal and shall issue a statement of reasons and bases for the action(s) taken. Such decision by the Secretary shall be the final agency action with the meaning of 5 U.S.C. 704.

[¶ 15,043Q-62]

§ 2571.13 **Effective date.**

This regulation is effective with respect to all cease and desist orders issued by the Secretary under section 521 of ERISA at any time after April 1, 2013.

Subpart B—[Reserved]

Part 6—Group Health Plans

[¶ 15,045]
PLANS MUST PROVIDE CONTINUATION COVERAGE TO CERTAIN INDIVIDUALS

Act Sec. 601.(a) In General. The plan sponsor of each group health plan shall provide, in accordance with this part, that each qualified beneficiary who would lose coverage under the plan as a result of a qualifying event is entitled, under the plan, to elect, within the election period, continuation coverage under the plan.

Act Sec. 601. (b) Exception for Certain Plans. Subsection (a) shall not apply to any group health plan for any calendar year if all employers maintaining such plan normally employed fewer than 20 employees on a typical business day during the preceding calendar year.

Amendments

P.L. 101-239, § 7862(c)(1)(B):

Amended ERISA Sec. 601(b) by striking the last sentence, effective for years beginning after December 31, 1986. Prior to being stricken, the last sentence read:

Under regulations, rules similar to the rules of subsections (a) and (b) of section 52 of the Internal Revenue Code of 1954 (relating to employers under common control) shall apply for purposes of this subsection.

P.L. 99-272:

Act Sec. 10002(a) added new ERISA Sec. 601 to read as above, effective for plan years beginning after July 1, 1986 except for the special rule which applies to collective bargaining agreements. When the amendments become effective the plan is subject to certain notification requirements. Act Secs. 10002(d) and (e) provide as follows:

(d) Effective Dates.—

(1) General rule.—The amendments made by this section shall apply to plan years beginning on or after July 1, 1986.

(2) Special rule for collective bargaining agreements.—In the case of a group health plan maintained pursuant to one or more collective bargaining agreements.—In the case of a group health plan maintained pursuant to one or more collective bargaining agreements between employee representatives and one or more employers ratified before the date of the enactment of this Act, the amendments made by this section shall not apply to plan years beginning before the later of—

(A) the date on which the last of the collective bargaining agreements relating to the plan terminates (determined without regard to any extension thereof agreed to after the date of the enactment of this Act), or

(B) January 1, 1987.

For purposes of subparagraph (A), any plan amendment made pursuant to a collective bargaining agreement relating to the plan which amends the plan solely to conform to any requirement added by this section shall not be treated as a termination of such collective bargaining agreement.

(e) Notification to Covered Employees.—At the time that the amendments made by this section apply to a group health plan (within the meaning of section 607(1) of the Employee Retirement Income Security Act of 1974), the plan shall notify each covered employee, and spouse of the employee (if any), who is covered under the plan at that time of the continuation coverage required under part 6 of subtitle B of title I of such Act. The notice furnished under this subsection is in lieu of notice that may otherwise be required under section 601(1) of such Act with respect to such individuals.

[¶ 15,045F]
CONTINUATION COVERAGE

Act Sec. 602. For purposes of section 601, the term "continuation coverage" means coverage under the plan which meets the following requirements:

(1) TYPE OF BENEFIT COVERAGE. The coverage must consist of coverage which, as of the time the coverage is being provided, is identical to the coverage provided under the plan to similarly situated beneficiaries under the plan with respect to whom a qualifying event has not occurred. If coverage is modified under the plan for any group of similarly situated beneficiaries, such coverage shall also be modified in the same manner for all individuals who are qualified beneficiaries under the plan pursuant to this part in connection with such group.

(2) PERIOD OF COVERAGE. The coverage must extend for at least the period beginning on the date of the qualifying event and ending not earlier than the earliest of the following:

(A) MAXIMUM REQUIRED PERIOD.—

(i) GENERAL RULE FOR TERMINATIONS AND REDUCED HOURS. In the case of a qualifying event described in section 603(2), except as provided in clause (ii), the date which is 18 months after the date of the qualifying event.

(ii) SPECIAL RULE FOR MULTIPLE QUALIFYING EVENTS. If a qualifying event (other than a qualifying event described in section 603(6)) occurs during the 18 months after the date of a qualifying event described in section 603(2), the date which is 36 months after the date of the qualifying event described in section 603(2).

(iii) SPECIAL RULE FOR CERTAIN BANKRUPTCY PROCEEDINGS. In the case of a qualifying event described in section 603(6) (relating to bankruptcy proceedings), the date of the death of the covered employee or qualified beneficiary (described in section 607(3)(C)(iii)), or in the case of the surviving spouse or dependent children of the covered employee, 36 months after the date of the death of the covered employee.

(iv) GENERAL RULE FOR OTHER QUALIFYING EVENTS. In the case of a qualifying event not described in section 603(2) or 603(6), the date which is 36 months after the date of the qualifying event.

(v) SPECIAL RULE FOR PBGC RECIPIENTS. In the case of a qualifying event described in section 603(2) with respect to a covered employee who (as of such qualifying event) has a nonforfeitable right to a benefit any portion of which is to be paid by the Pension Benefit Guaranty Corporation under title IV, notwithstanding clause (i) or (ii), the date of the death of the covered employee, or in the case of the surviving spouse or dependent children of the covered employee, 24 months after the date of the death of the covered employee. The preceding sentence shall not require any period of coverage to extend beyond January 1, 2014.

(vi) SPECIAL RULE FOR TAA-ELIGIBLE INDIVIDUALS. In the case of a qualifying event described in section 603(2) with respect to a covered employee who is (as of the date that the period of coverage would, but for this clause or clause (vii), otherwise terminate under clause (i) or (ii)) a TAA-eligible individual (as defined in section 605(b)(4)(B)), the period of coverage shall not terminate by reason of clause (i) or (ii), as the case may be, before the later of the date specified in such clause or the date on which such individual ceases to be such a TAA-eligible individual. The preceding sentence shall not require any period of coverage to extend beyond January 1, 2014.

(vii) MEDICARE ENTITLEMENT FOLLOWED BY QUALIFYING EVENT. In the case of a qualifying event described in section 603(2) that occurs less than 18 months after the date the covered employee became entitled to benefits under title XVIII of the Social Security Act, the period of coverage for qualified beneficiaries other than the covered employee shall not terminate under this subparagraph before the close of the 36-month period beginning on the date the covered employee became so entitled.

(viii) SPECIAL RULE FOR DISABILITY. In the case of a qualified beneficiary who is determined, under title II or XVI of the Social Security Act, to have been disabled at any time during the first 60 days of continuation coverage under this part, any reference in clause (i) or (ii) to 18 months is deemed a reference to 29 months (with respect to all qualified beneficiaries), but only if the qualified beneficiary has provided notice of such determination under section 606(3) before the end of such 18 months.

(B) END OF PLAN. The date on which the employer ceases to provide any group health plan to any employee.

(C) FAILURE TO PAY PREMIUM. The date on which coverage ceases under the plan by reason of a failure to make timely payment of any premium required under the plan with respect to the qualified beneficiary. The payment of any premium (other than any payment referred to in the last sentence of paragraph (3)) shall be considered to be timely if made within 30 days after the date due or within such longer period as applies to or under the plan.

(D) GROUP HEALTH PLAN COVERAGE OR MEDICARE ENTITLEMENT. The date on which the qualified beneficiary first becomes, after the date of the election—

(i) covered under any other group health plan (as an employee or otherwise which does not contain any exclusion or limitation with respect to any preexisting condition of such beneficiary) (other than such an exclusion or limitation which does not apply to (or is satisfied by) such beneficiary by reason of chapter 100 of the Internal Revenue Code of 1986, part 7 of this subtitle, or title XXVII of the Public Health Service Act), or

(ii) in the case of a qualified beneficiary other than a qualified beneficiary described in section 607(3)(C) entitled to benefits under title XVIII of the Social Security Act.

(E) TERMINATION OF EXTENDED COVERAGE FOR DISABILITY. In the case of a qualified beneficiary who is disabled at any time during the first 60 days of continuation coverage under this part, the month that begins more than 30 days after the date of the final determination under title II or XVI of the Social Security Act that the qualified beneficiary is no longer disabled.

(3) PREMIUM REQUIREMENTS. The plan may require payment of a premium for any period of continuation coverage, except that such premium—

(A) shall not exceed 102 percent of the applicable premium for such period, and

(B) may, at the election of the payor, be made in monthly installments.

In no event may the plan require the payment of any premium before the day which is 45 days after the day on which the qualified beneficiary made the initial election for continuation coverage. In the case of an individual described in the last sentence of paragraph (2)(A), any reference in subparagraph (A) of this paragraph to "102 percent" is deemed a reference to "150 percent" for any month after the 18th month of continuation coverage described in clause (i) or (ii) of paragraph (2)(A).

(4) NO REQUIREMENT OF INSURABILITY. The coverage may not be conditioned upon, or discriminate on the basis of lack of, evidence of insurability.

(5) CONVERSION OPTION. In the case of a qualified beneficiary whose period of continuation coverage expires under paragraph (2)(A), the plan must, during the 180-day period ending on such expiration date, provide to the qualified beneficiary the option of enrollment under a conversion health plan otherwise generally available under the plan.

Amendments

P.L. 112-040, §242(a)(1):

Amended ERISA Sec. 602(2)(A)(v) by striking "February 12, 2011" and inserting "January 1, 2014".

The above amendment applies to periods of coverage which would (without regard to the amendments made by this section) end on or after the date which is 30 days after the date of the enactment of this Act.

P.L. 112-040, §242(a)(2):

Amended ERISA Sec. 602(2)(A)(vi) by striking "February 12, 2011" and inserting "January 1, 2014".

The above amendment applies to periods of coverage which would (without regard to the amendments made by this section) end on or after the date which is 30 days after the date of the enactment of this Act.

P.L. 111-344, §116(a)(1):

Amended ERISA Sec. 602(2)(A)(v) by striking "December 31 2010" and inserting "February 12, 2011".

The above amendment applies to periods of coverage which would (without regard to the amendments made by this section) end on or after December 31, 2010.

P.L. 111-344, §116(a)(2):

Amended ERISA Sec. 602(2)(A)(vi) by striking "December 31 2010" and inserting "February 12, 2011".

The above amendment applies to periods of coverage which would (without regard to the amendments made by this section) end on or after December 31, 2010.

P.L. 111-5, §1899F(a):

Act Sec. 1899F(a) amended ERISA Sec. 602(2)(A) by moving clause (v) to after clause (iv) and before the flush left sentence beginning with "In the case of a qualified beneficiary"; by striking "In the case of a qualified beneficiary" and inserting "(vi) SPECIAL RULE FOR DISABILITY.—In the case of a qualified beneficiary"; and by redesignating clauses (v) and (vi), as amended, as clauses (vii) and (viii), respectively, and by inserting after clause (iv) new clauses (v) and (vi) to read as above.

The above amendments apply to periods of coverage which would (without regard to the amendments made by this section) end on or after the date of the enactment [February 17, 2009].

P.L. 104-191, §421(b)(1)(A):

Act Sec. 421(b)(1)(A) amended ERISA Sec. 602(2)(A), the last sentence thereof, by striking "an individual" and inserting "a qualified beneficiary"; by striking "at the time of a qualifying event described in section 603(2)" and inserting "at any time during the first 60 days of continuation coverage under this part"; by striking "with respect to such event"; and by inserting "(with respect to all qualified beneficiaries)" after "29 months". Prior to amendment, the last sentence of ERISA Sec. 602(2)(A) read as follows:

In the case of an individual who is determined, under title II or XVI of the Social Security Act, to have been disabled at the time of a qualifying event described in section 603(2), any reference in clause (i) or (ii) to 18 months with respect to such event is deemed a reference to 29 months, but only if the qualified beneficiary has provided notice of such determination under section 606(3) before the end of such 18 months.

P.L. 104-191, §421(b)(2):

Act Sec. 421(b)(2) amended ERISA Sec. 602(2)(D)(i) by inserting before ", or" the following: "(other than such an exclusion or limitation which does not apply to (or is satisfied by) such beneficiary by reason of chapter 100 of the Internal Revenue Code of 1986, part 7 of this subtitle, or title XXVII of the Public Health Service Act)".

P.L. 104-191, §421(b)(3):

Act Sec. 421(b)(3) amended ERISA Sec. 602(2)(E) by striking "at the time of a qualifying event described in section 603(2)" and inserting "at any time during the first 60 days of continuation coverage under this part".

The above amendments are effective on January 1, 1997, regardless of whether the qualifying event occurred before, on, or after such date. For a special rule, see Act Sec. 421(e), reproduced below.

Act Sec. 421(e) provides:

(e) NOTIFICATION OF CHANGES.—Not later than November 1, 1996, each group health plan (covered under title XXII of the Public Health Service Act, part 6 of subtitle B of title I of the Employee Retirement Income Security Act of 1974, and section 4980B(f) of the Internal Revenue Code of 1986) shall notify each qualified beneficiary who has elected continuation coverage under such title, part or section of the amendments made by this section.

P.L. 104-188, §1704(g)(1)(B):

Act Sec. 1704(g)(1)(B) amended ERISA Sec. 602(2)(A) by striking clause (v) and adding a new clause (v) to read as above. Prior to amendment, clause (v) read as follows:

(v) QUALIFYING EVENT INVOLVING MEDICARE ENTITLEMENT.—In the case of an event described in section 603(4) (without regard to whether such event is a qualifying event), the period of coverage for qualified beneficiaries other than the covered employee for such event or any subsequent qualifying event shall not terminate before the close of the 36-month period beginning on the date the covered employee becomes entitled to benefits under title XVIII of the Social Security Act.

The above amendment is effective as of December 12, 1994.

P.L. 101-239, §6703(a):

Act Sec. 6703(a)(1) amended ERISA Sec. 602(2)(A) by adding a new sentence after and below clause (iv) to read as above.

Act Sec. 6703(a)(2) amended ERISA Sec. 602(2) by adding a new subparagraph (E) to read as above.

P.L. 101-239, §6703(b):

Act Sec. 6703(b) amended ERISA Sec. 602(3) by adding in the matter after and below subparagraph (B) a new sentence to read as above.

The above amendments apply to plan years beginning on or after December 19, 1989, regardless of whether the qualifying event occurred before, on, or after that date.

P.L. 101-239, §7862(c)(2)(A):

Amended ERISA Sec. 602(2)(D) by striking "ELIGIBILITY" in the heading and inserting "ENTITLEMENT" and by inserting "which does not contain any exclusion or limitation with respect to any preexisting condition of such beneficiary" after "or otherwise)" in subclause (i), applicable to qualifying events occurring after December 31, 1989.

P.L. 101-239, §7862(c)(4)(A):

Amended the last sentence of ERISA Sec. 602(3) to read as above effective October 22, 1986.

P.L. 101-239, §7862(c)(5)(B):

Amended ERISA Sec. 602(2)(A) by adding a new clause at the end effective October 22, 1986.

P.L. 101-239, §7871(c):

Amended ERISA Sec. 602(2)(A)(iii) by inserting "section" before "603(6)" effective as if included in P.L. 99-509, §9501(b)(1)(B).

P.L. 99-514, §1895(d)(1)(B), (d)(2)(B), (d)(3)(B), and (d)(4)(B):

Amended Sec. 602(1) by adding the sentence at the end to read as above.

Amended Sec. 602(2)(A) to read as above. Prior to amendment, the section read as follows:

(A) MAXIMUM PERIOD.—In the case of—

(i) a qualifying event described in section 603(2) (relating to terminations and reduced hours), the date which is 18 months after the date of the qualifying event, and

(ii) any qualifying event not described in clause (i), the date which is 36 months after the date of the qualifying event.

Amended Sec. 602(2)(C) by adding the last sentence to read as above.

Amended Sec. 602(2) by striking out subparagraph (E), by amending clause (i) of subparagraph (D) to read as above and by amending the heading to read as above. Prior to amendment, the heading and Secs. 602(2)(D)(i) and (E) read as follows:

(2) PERIOD OF COVERAGE.—

(D) REEMPLOYMENT OR MEDICARE ELIGIBILITY.—The date on which the qualified beneficiary first becomes, after the date of the election—

(i) a covered employee under any other group health plan, or

(ii) entitled to benefits under title XVIII of the Social Security Act.

(E) REMARRIAGE OF SPOUSE.—In the case of an individual who is a qualified beneficiary by reason of being the spouse of a covered employee, the date on which the beneficiary remarries and becomes covered under a group health plan.

The above amendments are effective for plan years beginning after July 1, 1986 except for plans maintained under collective bargaining agreements in which case the amendments do not apply to plan years beginning before the later of (1) the date the last of the collective bargaining agreements terminate, or (2) January 1, 1987.

P.L. 99-509, §9501(b)(1)(B):

Amended ERISA Sec. 602(2)(A)

(i) in clause (ii), by inserting "(other than a qualifying event described in section 603(6))" after "qualifying event" the first place it appears,

(ii) in clause (iii), by inserting "or 603(6)" after "603(2)",

(iii) by redesignating clause (iii) as clause (iv),

and by adding a new subclause (iii) to read as above, effective for plan years beginning after July 1, 1986 except for plans maintained under collective bargaining agreements in which case the amendments do not apply to plan years beginning before the later of (1) the date the last of the collective bargaining agreements terminate, or (2) January 1, 1987.

P.L. 99-509, §9501(b)(2)(B):

Amended ERISA Sec. 602(2)(D) by inserting "in the case of a qualified beneficiary other than a qualified beneficiary described in section 607(3)(C)" before "entitled", effective for plan years beginning after July 1, 1986 except for plans maintained under collective bargaining agreements in which case the amendments do not apply to plan years beginning before the later of (1) the date the last of the collective bargaining agreements terminate, or (2) January 1, 1987.

P.L. 99-272:

Act Sec. 10002(a) added ERISA Sec. 602 to read as above, effective for plan years beginning after July 1, 1986, subject to the special rules discussed at ¶ 15,045.

[¶ 15,045L]
QUALIFYING EVENT

Act Sec. 603. For purposes of this part, the term "qualifying event" means, with respect to any covered employee, any of the following events which, but for the continuation coverage required under this part, would result in the loss of coverage of a qualified beneficiary:

(1) The death of the covered employee.

(2) The termination (other than by reason of such employee's gross misconduct), reduction of hours, of the covered employee's employment.

(3) The divorce or legal separation of the covered employee from the employee's spouse.

(4) The covered employee becoming entitled to benefits under title XVIII of the Social Security Act.

(5) A dependent child ceasing to be a dependent child under the generally applicable requirements of the plan.

(6) A proceeding in a case under title 11, United States Code, commencing on or after July 1, 1986, with respect to the employer from whose employment the covered employee retired at any time.

In the case of an event described in paragraph (6), a loss of coverage includes a substantial elimination of coverage with respect to a qualified beneficiary described in section 607(3)(C) within one year before or after the date of commencement of the proceeding.

Amendment

P.L. 99-509, §9501(a)(2):

Amended ERISA Sec. 603 by adding a new subsection (6) to read as above, effective for plan years beginning after July 1, 1986 except for plans maintained under collective bargaining agreements in which case the amendments do not apply to plan years

beginning before the later of (1) the date the last of the collective bargaining agreements terminate, or (2) January 1, 1987.

P.L. 99-272:

Act Sec. 10002(a) added ERISA Sec. 603 to read as above, effective for plan years beginning after July 1, 1986, subject to the special rules discussed at ¶ 15,045.

[¶ 15,045P]
APPLICABLE PREMIUM

Act Sec. 604. For purposes of this part—

(1) IN GENERAL. The term "applicable premium" means, with respect to any period of continuation coverage of qualified beneficiaries, the cost to the plan for such period of the coverage for similarly situated beneficiaries with respect to whom a qualifying event has not occurred (without regard to whether such cost is paid by the employer or employee).

(2) SPECIAL RULE FOR SELF-INSURED PLANS. To the extent that a plan is a self-insured plan—

(A) IN GENERAL. Except as provided in subparagraph (B), the applicable premium for any period of continuation coverage of qualified beneficiaries shall be equal to a reasonable estimate of the cost of providing coverage for such period for similarly situated beneficiaries which—

(i) is determined on an actuarial basis, and

(ii) takes into account such factors as the Secretary may prescribe in regulations.

(B) DETERMINATION ON BASIS OF PAST COST. If an administrator elects to have this subparagraph apply, the applicable premium for any period of continuation coverage of qualified beneficiaries shall be equal to—

(i) the cost to the plan for similarly situated beneficiaries for same period occurring during the preceding determination period under paragraph (3), adjusted by

(ii) the percentage increase or decrease in the implicit price deflator of the gross national product (calculated by the Department of Commerce and published in the Survey of Current Business) for the 12-month period ending on the last day of the sixth month of such preceding determination period.

(C) SUBPARAGRAPH (B) NOT TO APPLY WHERE SIGNIFICANT CHANGE. An administrator may not elect to have subparagraph (B) apply in any case in which there is any significant difference, between the determination period and the preceding determination period, in coverage under, or in employees covered by, the plan. The determination under the preceding sentence for any determination period shall be made at the same time as the determination under paragraph (3).

(3) DETERMINATION PERIOD. The determination of any applicable premium shall be made for a period of 12 months and shall be made before the beginning of such period.

Amendment:

P.L. 99-272:

Act Sec. 10002(a) added ERISA Sec. 604 to read as above, effective for plan years beginning after July 1, 1986, subject to the special rules discussed at ¶ 15,045.

[¶ 15,045T]
ELECTION

Act Sec. 605.(a) IN GENERAL. For purposes of this part—

(1) ELECTION PERIOD. The term "election period" means the period which—

(A) begins not later than the date on which coverage terminates under the plan by reason of a qualifying event,

(B) is of at least 60 days' duration, and

(C) ends not earlier than 60 days after the later of—

(i) the date described in subparagraph (A), or

(ii) in the case of any qualified beneficiary who receives notice under section 606(4), the date of such notice.

(2) EFFECT OF ELECTION ON OTHER BENEFICIARIES. Except as otherwise specified in an election, any election of continuation coverage by a qualified beneficiary described in subparagraph (A)(i) or (B) of section 607(3) shall be deemed to include an election of continuation coverage on behalf of any other qualified beneficiary who would lose coverage under the plan by reason of the qualifying event. If there is a choice among types of coverage under the plan, each qualified beneficiary is entitled to make a separate election among such types of coverage.

(b) TEMPORARY EXTENSION OF COBRA ELECTION PERIOD FOR CERTAIN INDIVIDUALS—

(b)(1) IN GENERAL. In the case of a nonelecting TAA-eligible individual and notwithstanding subsection (a), such individual may elect continuation coverage under this part during the 60-day period that begins on the first day of the month in which the individual becomes a TAA-eligible individual, but only if such election is made not later than 6 months after the date of the TAA-related loss of coverage.

(2) COMMENCEMENT OF COVERAGE; NO REACH-BACK. Any continuation coverage elected by a TAA-eligible individual under paragraph (1) shall commence at the beginning of the 60-day election period described in such paragraph and shall not include any period prior to such 60-day election period.

(3) PREEXISTING CONDITIONS. With respect to an individual who elects continuation coverage pursuant to paragraph (1), the period—

(A) beginning on the date of the TAA-related loss of coverage, and

(B) ending on the first day of the 60-day election period described in paragraph (1), shall be disregarded for purposes of determining the 63-day periods referred to in section 701(c)(2), section 2701(c)(2) of the Public Health Service Act, and section 9801(c)(2) of the Internal Revenue Code of 1986.

(4) DEFINITIONS. For purposes of this subsection:

(A) NONELECTING TAA-ELIGIBLE INDIVIDUAL. The term 'nonelecting TAA-eligible individual' means a TAA-eligible individual who—

(i) has a TAA-related loss of coverage; and

(ii) did not elect continuation coverage under this part during the TAA-related election period.

(B) TAA- ELIGIBLE INDIVIDUAL. The term 'TAA-eligible individual' means—

(i) an eligible TAA recipient (as defined in paragraph (2) of section 35(c) of the Internal Revenue Code of 1986), and

(ii) an eligible alternative TAA recipient (as defined in paragraph (3) of such section).

(C) TAA- RELATED ELECTION PERIOD. The term 'TAA-related election period' means, with respect to a TAA-related loss of coverage, the 60-day election period under this part which is a direct consequence of such loss.

(D) TAA- RELATED LOSS OF COVERAGE. The term 'TAA-related loss of coverage' means, with respect to an individual whose separation from employment gives rise to being an TAA-eligible individual, the loss of health benefits coverage associated with such separation.

P.L. 107-210, § 203(e)(1):

Act Sec. 203(e)(1) amended ERISA Sec. 605 by inserting "(a) IN GENERAL—" before "For purposes of this part"; and by adding paragraph (b) to read as above.

P.L. 99-514, § 1895(d)(5)(B):

Amended Sec. 605(2) by inserting "of continuation coverage" after "any election" and by adding the sentence at the end of the section, effective for plan years beginning after July 1, 1986, subject to the special rules at ¶ 15,045.

P.L. 99-272:

Act Sec. 10002(a) added ERISA Sec. 605 to read as above, effective for plan years beginning after July 1, 1986, subject to the special rules discussed at ¶ 15,045.

[¶ 15,046]
NOTICE REQUIREMENTS

Act Sec. 606.(a) IN GENERAL. In accordance with regulations prescribed by the Secretary—

(1) the group health plan shall provide, at the time of commencement of coverage under the plan, written notice to each covered employee and spouse of the employee (if any) of the rights provided under this subsection,

(2) the employer of an employee under a plan must notify the administrator of a qualifying event described in paragraph (1), (2), (4), or (6) of section 603 within 30 days (or, in the case of a group health plan which is a multiemployer plan, such longer period of time as may be provided in the terms of the plan) of the date of the qualifying event,

(3) each covered employee or qualified beneficiary is responsible for notifying the administrator of the occurrence of any qualifying event described in paragraph (3) or (5) of section 603 within 60 days after the date of the qualifying event and each qualified beneficiary who is determined, under title II or XVI of the Social Security Act, to have been disabled at any time during the first 60 days of continuation coverage under this part is responsible for notifying the plan administrator of such determination within 60 days after the date of the determination and for notifying the plan administrator within 30 days after the date of any final determination under such title or titles that the qualified beneficiary is no longer disabled, and

(4) the administrator shall notify—

(A) in the case of a qualifying event described in paragraph (1), (2), (4) or (6) of section 603, any qualified beneficiary with respect to such event, and

(B) in the case of a qualifying event described in paragraph (3) or (5) of section 603 where the covered employee notifies the administrator under paragraph (3), any qualified beneficiary with respect to such event, of such beneficiary's rights under this subsection.

Act Sec. 606(b). ALTERNATIVE MEANS OF COMPLIANCE WITH REQUIREMENT FOR NOTIFICATION OF MULTIEMPLOYER PLANS BY EMPLOYERS. The requirements of subsection (a)(2) shall be considered satisfied in the case of a multiemployer plan in connection with a qualifying event described in paragraph (2) of section 603 if the plan provides that the determination of the occurrence of such qualifying event will be made by the plan administrator.

Act Sec. 606(c). RULES RELATING TO NOTIFICATION OF QUALIFIED BENEFICIARIES BY PLAN ADMINISTRATOR. For purposes of subsection (a)(4), any notification shall be made within 14 days (or, in the case of a group health plan which is a multiemployer plan, such longer period of time as may be provided in the terms of the plan) of the date on which the administrator is notified under paragraph (2) or (3), whichever is applicable, and any such notification to an individual who is a qualified beneficiary as the spouse of the covered employee shall be treated as notification to all other qualified beneficiaries residing with such spouse at the time such notification is made.

P.L. 104-191, § 421(b)(2):

Act Sec. 421(b)(2) amended ERISA Sec. 606(a)(3) by striking "at the time of a qualifying event described in section 603(2)" and inserting "at any time during the first 60 days of continuation coverage under this part".

The above amendment is effective on January 1, 1997, regardless of whether the qualifying event occurred before, on, or after such date. For a special rule, see Act Sec. 421(e), reproduced below.

Act Sec. 421(e) provides:

(e) NOTIFICATION OF CHANGES.—Not later than November 1, 1996, each group health plan (covered under title XXII of the Public Health Service Act, part 6 of subtitle B of title I of the Employee Retirement Income Security Act of 1974, and section 4980B(f) of the Internal Revenue Code of 1986) shall notify each qualified beneficiary who has elected continuation coverage under such title, part or section of the amendments made by this section.

P.L. 101-239, § 6703(c):

Act Sec. 6703(c) amended ERISA Sec. 606(a)(3) by inserting before the comma the following:

"and each qualified beneficiary who is determined, under title II or XVI of the Social Security Act, to have been disabled at the time of a qualifying event described in section 603(2) is responsible for notifying the plan administrator of such determination within 60 days after the date of the determination and for notifying the plan administrator within 30 days after the date of any final determination under such title or titles that the qualified beneficiary is no longer disabled".

The above amendment applies to plan years beginning on or after December 19, 1989, regardless of whether the qualifying event occurred before, on, or after that date.

P.L. 101-239, § 7891(d)(1)(A)(i)(I):

Amended ERISA Sec. 606(2) by inserting after "30 days" new material to read as above, effective for plan years beginning on or after January 1, 1990.

P.L. 101-239, § 7891(d)(1)(A)(i)(II):

Amended ERISA Sec. 606(c) (as redesignated) by inserting after "14 days" new material to read as above, effective for plan years beginning on or after January 1, 1990.

P.L. 101-239, § 7891(d)(1)(A)(ii):

Amended ERISA Sec. 606 by inserting "(a) IN GENERAL.—" before "In accordance", by striking "for purposes of paragraph (4)," and inserting "(c) RULES RELATING TO NOTIFICATION OF QUALIFIED BENEFICIARIES BY PLAN ADMINISTRATOR.—For purposes of subsection (a)(4)," and by inserting after subsection (a)(4) (as designated by this amendment) new subsection (b) to read as above, effective for plan years beginning on or after January 1, 1990.

P.L. 99-514, § 1895(d)(6)(B):

Amended Sec. 606(3) by inserting "within 60 days after the date of the qualifying event" after "section 603" effective with respect to qualifying events occurring after the date of enactment.

P.L. 99-272:

Act Sec. 10002(a) added ERISA Sec. 606 to read as above, effective for plan years beginning after July 1, 1986, subject to the special rules discussed at ¶ 15,045.

Regulations

The following regulations were adopted and published in the *Federal Register* on May 26, 2004 (69 FR 30084), amending Part 2590, Subpart A under "Chapter XXV of Title 29 of the Code of Federal Regulations; Subchapter L—Group Health Plans; Part 2590—Rules and Regulations for Group Health Plans."

Subchapter L—Group Health Plans

Part 2590—Rules and Regulations for Group Health Plans

Subpart A—Requirements Relating to Access and Renewability of Coverage, and Limitations on Preexisting Condition Exclusion Periods

[¶ 15,046B-1]

§ 2590.606-1. **General Notice of Continuation Coverage.**

(a) *General.* Pursuant to section 606(a)(1) of the Employee Retirement Income Security Act of 1974, as amended (the Act), the adminis-

trator of a group health plan subject to the continuation coverage requirements of Part 6 of title I of the Act shall provide, in accordance with this section, written notice to each covered employee and spouse of the covered employee (if any) of the right to continuation coverage provided under the plan.

(b) *Timing of notice.* (1) The notice required by paragraph (a) of this section shall be furnished to each employee and each employee's spouse, not later than the earlier of:

(i) The date that is 90 days after the date on which such individual's coverage under the plan commences, or, if later, the date that is 90 days after the date on which the plan first becomes subject to the continuation coverage requirements; or

(ii) The first date on which the administrator is required, pursuant to § 2590.606-4(b), to furnish the covered employee, spouse, or dependent child of such employee notice of a qualified beneficiary's right to elect continuation coverage.

(2) A notice that is furnished in accordance with paragraph (b)(1) of this section shall, for purposes of section 606(a)(1) of the Act, be deemed to be provided at the time of commencement of coverage under the plan.

(3) In any case in which an administrator is required to furnish a notice to a covered employee or spouse pursuant to paragraph (b)(1)(ii) of this section, the furnishing of a notice to such individual in accordance with § 2590.606-4(b) shall be deemed to satisfy the requirements of this section.

(c) *Content of notice*. The notice required by paragraph (a) of this section shall be written in a manner calculated to be understood by the average plan participant and shall contain the following information:

(1) The name of the plan under which continuation coverage is available, and the name, address and telephone number of a party or parties from whom additional information about the plan and continuation coverage can be obtained;

(2) A general description of the continuation coverage under the plan, including identification of the classes of individuals who may become qualified beneficiaries, the types of qualifying events that may give rise to the right to continuation coverage, the obligation of the employer to notify the plan administrator of the occurrence of certain qualifying events, the maximum period for which continuation coverage may be available, when and under what circumstances continuation coverage may be extended beyond the applicable maximum period, and the plan's requirements applicable to the payment of premiums for continuation coverage;

(3) An explanation of the plan's requirements regarding the responsibility of a qualified beneficiary to notify the administrator of a qualifying event that is a divorce, legal separation, or a child's ceasing to be a dependent under the terms of the plan, and a description of the plan's procedures for providing such notice;

(4) An explanation of the plan's requirements regarding the responsibility of qualified beneficiaries who are receiving continuation coverage to provide notice to the administrator of a determination by the Social Security Administration, under title II or XVI of the Social Security Act (42 U.S.C. 401 *et seq.* or 1381 *et seq.*), that a qualified beneficiary is disabled, and a description of the plan's procedures for providing such notice;

(5) An explanation of the importance of keeping the administrator informed of the current addresses of all participants or beneficiaries under the plan who are or may become qualified beneficiaries; and

(6) A statement that the notice does not fully describe continuation coverage or other rights under the plan and that more complete information regarding such rights is available from the plan administrator and in the plan's SPD.

(d) *Single notice rule*. A plan administrator may satisfy the requirement to provide notice in accordance with this section to a covered employee and the covered employee's spouse by furnishing a single notice addressed to both the covered employee and the covered employee's spouse, if, on the basis of the most recent information available to the plan, the covered employee's spouse resides at the same location as the covered employee, and the spouse's coverage under the plan commences on or after the date on which the covered employee's coverage commences, but not later than the date on which the notice required by this section is required to be provided to the covered employee. Nothing in this section shall be construed to create a requirement to provide a separate notice to dependent children who share a residence with a covered employee or a covered employee's spouse to whom notice is provided in accordance with this section. [Technical correction made June 23, 2004 (69 FR 34920)]

(e) *Notice in summary plan description*. A plan administrator may satisfy the requirement to provide notice in accordance with this section by including the information described in paragraphs (c)(1), (2), (3), (4), and (5) of this section in a summary plan description

meeting the requirements of § 2520.102-3 of this Chapter furnished in accordance with paragraph (b) of this section.

(f) *Delivery of notice*. The notice required by this section shall be furnished in a manner consistent with the requirements of § 2520.104b-1 of this Chapter, including paragraph (c) of that section relating to the use of electronic media.

(g) *Model notice*. The appendix to this section contains a model notice that is intended to assist administrators in discharging the notice obligations of this section. Use of the model notice is not mandatory. The model notice reflects the requirements of this section as they would apply to single-employer group health plans and must be modified if used to provide notice with respect to other types of group health plans, such as multiemployer plans or plans established and maintained by employee organizations for their members. In order to use the model notice, administrators must appropriately add relevant information where indicated in the model notice, select among alternative language, and supplement the model notice to reflect applicable plan provisions. Items of information that are not applicable to a particular plan may be deleted. Use of the model notice, appropriately modified and supplemented, will be deemed to satisfy the notice content requirements of paragraph (c) of this section.

(h) *Applicability*. This section shall apply to any notice obligation described in this section that arises on or after the first day of the first plan year beginning on or after November 26, 2004.

[¶ 15,046B-2]

§ 2590.606-1. **Appendix to § 2590.606-1.**

MODEL GENERAL NOTICE OF COBRA CONTINUATION COVERAGE RIGHTS

(For use by single-employer group health plans)

** CONTINUATION COVERAGE RIGHTS UNDER COBRA **

Introduction

You are receiving this notice because you have recently become covered under a group health plan (the Plan). This notice contains important information about your right to COBRA continuation coverage, which is a temporary extension of coverage under the Plan. **This notice generally explains COBRA continuation coverage, when it may become available to you and your family, and what you need to do to protect the right to receive it.**

The right to COBRA continuation coverage was created by a federal law, the Consolidated Omnibus Budget Reconciliation Act of 1985 (COBRA). COBRA continuation coverage can become available to you when you would otherwise lose your group health coverage. It can also become available to other members of your family who are covered under the Plan when they would otherwise lose their group health coverage. For additional information about your rights and obligations under the Plan and under federal law, you should review the Plan's Summary Plan Description or contact the Plan Administrator.

What is COBRA Continuation Coverage?

COBRA continuation coverage is a continuation of Plan coverage when coverage would otherwise end because of a life event known as a "qualifying event." Specific qualifying events are listed later in this notice. After a qualifying event, COBRA continuation coverage must be offered to each person who is a "qualified beneficiary." You, your spouse, and your dependent children could become qualified beneficiaries if coverage under the Plan is lost because of the qualifying event. Under the Plan, qualified beneficiaries who elect COBRA continuation coverage [*choose and enter appropriate information:* must pay *or* are not required to pay] for COBRA continuation coverage.

If you are an employee, you will become a qualified beneficiary if you lose your coverage under the Plan because either one of the following qualifying events happens:

• Your hours of employment are reduced, or

• Your employment ends for any reason other than your gross misconduct.

If you are the spouse of an employee, you will become a qualified beneficiary if you lose your coverage under the Plan because any of the following qualifying events happens:

• Your spouse dies;

- Your spouse's hours of employment are reduced;

- Your spouse's employment ends for any reason other than his or her gross misconduct;

- Your spouse becomes entitled to Medicare benefits (under Part A, Part B, or both); or

- You become divorced or legally separated from your spouse.

Your dependent children will become qualified beneficiaries if they lose coverage under the Plan because any of the following qualifying events happens:

- The parent-employee dies;

- The parent-employee's hours of employment are reduced;

- The parent-employee's employment ends for any reason other than his or her gross misconduct;

- The parent-employee becomes entitled to Medicare benefits (Part A, Part B, or both);

- The parents become divorced or legally separated; or

- The child stops being eligible for coverage under the plan as a "dependent child."

[*If the Plan provides retiree health coverage, add the following paragraph:*]

Sometimes, filing a proceeding in bankruptcy under title 11 of the United States Code can be a qualifying event. If a proceeding in bankruptcy is filed with respect to [*enter name of employer sponsoring the plan*], and that bankruptcy results in the loss of coverage of any retired employee covered under the Plan, the retired employee will become a qualified beneficiary with respect to the bankruptcy. The retired employee's spouse, surviving spouse, and dependent children will also become qualified beneficiaries if bankruptcy results in the loss of their coverage under the Plan.

When is COBRA Coverage Available?

The Plan will offer COBRA continuation coverage to qualified beneficiaries only after the Plan Administrator has been notified that a qualifying event has occurred. When the qualifying event is the end of employment or reduction of hours of employment, death of the employee, [*add if Plan provides retiree health coverage:* commencement of a proceeding in bankruptcy with respect to the employer,] or the employee's becoming entitled to Medicare benefits (under Part A, Part B, or both), the employer must notify the Plan Administrator of the qualifying event.

You Must Give Notice of Some Qualifying Events

For the other qualifying events (*divorce* or *legal separation* **of the employee and spouse or a** *dependent child's losing eligibility for coverage* **as a dependent child), you must notify the Plan Administrator within 60 days [** *or enter longer period permitted under the terms of the Plan***] after the qualifying event occurs. You must provide this notice to: [** *Enter name of appropriate party*]**. [** *Add description of any additional Plan procedures for this notice, including a description of any required information or documentation.*]

How is COBRA Coverage Provided?

Once the Plan Administrator receives notice that a qualifying event has occurred, COBRA continuation coverage will be offered to each of the qualified beneficiaries. Each qualified beneficiary will have an independent right to elect COBRA continuation coverage. Covered employees may elect COBRA continuation coverage on behalf of their spouses, and parents may elect COBRA continuation coverage on behalf of their children.

COBRA continuation coverage is a temporary continuation of coverage. When the qualifying event is the death of the employee, the employee's becoming entitled to Medicare benefits (under Part A, Part B, or both), your divorce or legal separation, or a dependent child's losing eligibility as a dependent child, COBRA continuation coverage lasts for up to a total of 36 months. When the qualifying event is the end of employment or reduction of the employee's hours of employment, and the employee became entitled to Medicare benefits less than 18 months before the qualifying event, COBRA continuation coverage for qualified beneficiaries other than the employee lasts until 36 months after the date of Medicare entitlement. For example, if a covered employee becomes entitled to Medicare 8 months before the date on which his employment terminates, COBRA continuation coverage for his spouse and children can last up to 36 months after the date of Medicare entitlement, which is equal to 28 months after the date of the qualifying event (36 months minus 8 months). Otherwise, when the qualifying event is the end of employment or reduction of the employee's hours of employment, COBRA continuation coverage generally lasts for only up to a total of 18 months. There are two ways in which this 18-month period of COBRA continuation coverage can be extended.

Disability extension of 18-month period of continuation coverage

If you or anyone in your family covered under the Plan is determined by the Social Security Administration to be disabled and you notify the Plan Administrator in a timely fashion, you and your entire family may be entitled to receive up to an additional 11 months of COBRA continuation coverage, for a total maximum of 29 months. The disability would have to have started at some time before the 60th day of COBRA continuation coverage and must last at least until the end of the 18-month period of continuation coverage. [*Add description of any additional Plan procedures for this notice, including a description of any required information or documentation, the name of the appropriate party to whom notice must be sent, and the time period for giving notice*].

Second qualifying event extension of 18-month period of continuation coverage

If your family experiences another qualifying event while receiving 18 months of COBRA continuation coverage, the spouse and dependent children in your family can get up to 18 additional months of COBRA continuation coverage, for a maximum of 36 months, if notice of the second qualifying event is properly given to the Plan. This extension may be available to the spouse and any dependent children receiving continuation coverage if the employee or former employee dies, becomes entitled to Medicare benefits (under Part A, Part B, or both), or gets divorced or legally separated, or if the dependent child stops being eligible under the Plan as a dependent child, but only if the event would have caused the spouse or dependent child to lose coverage under the Plan had the first qualifying event not occurred.

If You Have Questions

Questions concerning your Plan or your COBRA continuation coverage rights should be addressed to the contact or contacts identified below. For more information about your rights under ERISA, including COBRA, the Health Insurance Portability and Accountability Act (HIPAA), and other laws affecting group health plans, contact the nearest Regional or District Office of the U.S. Department of Labor's Employee Benefits Security Administration (EBSA) in your area or visit the EBSA website at www.dol.gov/ebsa. (Addresses and phone numbers of Regional and District EBSA Offices are available through EBSA's website.)

Keep Your Plan Informed of Address Changes

In order to protect your family's rights, you should keep the Plan Administrator informed of any changes in the addresses of family members. You should also keep a copy, for your records, of any notices you send to the Plan Administrator.

Plan Contact Information

[*Enter name of group health plan and name (or position), address and phone number of party or parties from whom information about the plan and COBRA continuation coverage can be obtained on request.*]

[¶ 15,046B-3]
§ 2590.606-2. **Notice Requirement for Employers.**

(a) *General.* Pursuant to section 606(a)(2) of the Employee Retirement Income Security Act of 1974, as amended (the Act), except as otherwise provided herein, the employer of a covered employee under a group health plan subject to the continuation coverage requirements of Part 6 of title I of the Act shall provide, in accordance with this section, notice to the administrator of the plan of the occurrence of a qualifying event that is the covered employee's death, termination of employment (other than by reason of gross misconduct), reduction in hours of employment, Medicare entitlement, or a proceeding in a case under title 11, United States Code, with respect to the employer from whose employment the covered employee retired at any time.

(b) *Timing of notice.* The notice required by this section shall be furnished to the administrator of the plan —

(1) In the case of a plan that provides, with respect to a qualifying event, pursuant to section 607(5) of the Act, that continuation coverage and the applicable period for providing notice under section 606(a)(2) of the Act shall commence on the date of loss of coverage, not later than 30 days after the date on which a qualified beneficiary loses coverage under the plan due to the qualifying event;

(2) In the case of a multiemployer plan that provides, pursuant to section 606(a)(2) of the Act, for a longer period of time within which employers may provide notice of a qualifying event, not later than the end of the period provided pursuant to the plan's terms for such notice; and

(3) In all other cases, not later than 30 days after the date on which the qualifying event occurred.

(c) *Content of notice.* The notice required by this section shall include sufficient information to enable the administrator to determine the plan, the covered employee, the qualifying event, and the date of the qualifying event.

(d) *Multiemployer plan special rules.* This section shall not apply to any employer that maintains a multiemployer plan, with respect to qualifying events affecting coverage under such plan, if the plan provides, pursuant to section 606(b) of the Act, that the administrator shall determine whether such a qualifying event has occurred.

(e) *Applicability.* This section shall apply to any notice obligation described in this section that arises on or after the first day of the first plan year beginning on or after November 26, 2004.

[¶ 15,046B-4]

§ 2590.606-3. **Notice Requirements for Covered Employees and Qualified Beneficiaries.**

(a) *General.* In accordance with the authority of sections 505 and 606(a)(3) of the Employee Retirement Income Security Act of 1974, as amended (the Act), this section sets forth requirements for group health plans subject to the continuation coverage requirements of Part 6 of title I of the Act with respect to the responsibility of covered employees and qualified beneficiaries to provide the following notices to administrators:

(1) Notice of the occurrence of a qualifying event that is a divorce or legal separation of a covered employee from his or her spouse;

(2) Notice of the occurrence of a qualifying event that is a beneficiary's ceasing to be covered under a plan as a dependent child of a participant;

(3) Notice of the occurrence of a second qualifying event after a qualified beneficiary has become entitled to continuation coverage with a maximum duration of 18 (or 29) months;

(4) Notice that a qualified beneficiary entitled to receive continuation coverage with a maximum duration of 18 months has been determined by the Social Security Administration, under title II or XVI of the Social Security Act (42 U.S.C. 401 *et seq.* or 1381 *et seq.*) (SSA), to be disabled at any time during the first 60 days of continuation coverage; and

(5) Notice that a qualified beneficiary, with respect to whom a notice described in paragraph (a)(4) of this section has been provided, has subsequently been determined by the Social Security Administration, under title II or XVI of the SSA to no longer be disabled.

(b) *Reasonable procedures.* (1) A plan subject to the continuation coverage requirements shall establish reasonable procedures for the furnishing of the notices described in paragraph (a) of this section.

(2) For purposes of this section, a plan's notice procedures shall be deemed reasonable only if such procedures:

(i) Are described in the plan's summary plan description required by § 2520.102-3 of this Chapter;

(ii) Specify the individual or entity designated to receive such notices;

(iii) Specify the means by which notice may be given;

(iv) Describe the information concerning the qualifying event or determination of disability that the plan deems necessary in order to provide continuation coverage rights consistent with the requirements of the Act; and

(v) Comply with the requirements of paragraphs (c), (d), and (e) of this section.

(3) A plan's procedures will not fail to be reasonable, pursuant to this section, solely because the procedures require a covered employee or qualified beneficiary to utilize a specific form to provide notice to the administrator, provided that any such form is easily available, without cost, to covered employees and qualified beneficiaries.

(4) If a plan has not established reasonable procedures for providing a notice required by this section, such notice shall be deemed to have been provided when a written or oral communication identifying a specific event is made in a manner reasonably calculated to bring the information to the attention of any of the following:

(i) In the case of a single-employer plan, the person or organizational unit that customarily handles employee benefits matters of the employer;

(ii) In the case of a plan to which more than one unaffiliated employer contributes, or which is established or maintained by an employee organization, either the joint board, association, committee, or other similar group (or any member of any such group) administering the plan, or the person or organizational unit to which claims for benefits under the plan customarily are referred; or

(iii) In the case of a plan the benefits of which are provided or administered by an insurance company, insurance service, or other similar organization subject to regulation under the insurance laws of one or more States, the person or organizational unit that customarily handles claims for benefits under the plan or any officer of the insurance company, insurance service, or other similar organization.

(c) *Periods of time for providing notice.* A plan may establish a reasonable period of time for furnishing any of the notices described in paragraph (a) of this section, provided that any time limit imposed by the plan with respect to a particular notice may not be shorter than the time limit described in this paragraph (c) with respect to that notice.

(1) *Time limits for notices of qualifying events.* The period of time for furnishing a notice described in paragraph (a)(1), (2), or (3) of this section may not end before the date that is 60 days after the latest of:

(i) The date on which the relevant qualifying event occurs;

(ii) The date on which the qualified beneficiary loses (or would lose) coverage under the plan as a result of the qualifying event; or

(iii) The date on which the qualified beneficiary is informed, through the furnishing of the plan's summary plan description or the notice described in § 2590.606-1, of both the responsibility to provide the notice and the plan's procedures for providing such notice to the administrator.

(2) *Time limits for notice of disability determination.* (i) Subject to paragraph (c)(2)(ii) of this section, the period of time for furnishing the notice described in paragraph (a)(4) of this section may not end before the date that is 60 days after the latest of:

(A) The date of the disability determination by the Social Security Administration;

(B) The date on which a qualifying event occurs;

(C) The date on which the qualified beneficiary loses (or would lose) coverage under the plan as a result of the qualifying event; or

(D) The date on which the qualified beneficiary is informed, through the furnishing of the summary plan description or the notice described in § 2590.606-1, of both the responsibility to provide the notice and the plan's procedures for providing such notice to the administrator.

(ii) Notwithstanding paragraph (c)(2)(i) of this section, a plan may require the notice described in paragraph (a)(4) of this section to be furnished before the end of the first 18 months of continuation coverage.

(3) *Time limits for notice of change in disability status.* The period of time for furnishing the notice described in paragraph (a)(5) of this section may not end before the date that is 30 days after the later of:

(i) The date of the final determination by the Social Security Administration, under title II or XVI of the SSA, that the qualified beneficiary is no longer disabled; or

(ii) The date on which the qualified beneficiary is informed, through the furnishing of the plan's summary plan description or the notice described in § 2590.606-1, of both the responsibility to provide the notice and the plan's procedures for providing such notice to the administrator.

(d) *Required contents of notice.* (1) A plan may establish reasonable requirements for the content of any notice described in this section, provided that a plan may not deem a notice to have been provided untimely if such notice, although not containing all of the information required by the plan, is provided within the time limit established under the plan in conformity with paragraph (c) of this section, and the administrator is able to determine from such notice the plan, the covered employee and qualified beneficiary(ies), the qualifying event or disability, and the date on which the qualifying event (if any) occurred.

(2) An administrator may require a notice that does not contain all of the information required by the plan to be supplemented with the additional information necessary to meet the plan's reasonable content requirements for such notice in order for the notice to be deemed to have been provided in accordance with this section.

(e) *Who may provide notice.* With respect to each of the notice requirements of this section, any individual who is either the covered employee, a qualified beneficiary with respect to the qualifying event, or any representative acting on behalf of the covered employee or qualified beneficiary may provide the notice, and the provision of notice by one individual shall satisfy any responsibility to provide notice on behalf of all related qualified beneficiaries with respect to the qualifying event.

(f) *Plan provisions.* To the extent that a plan provides a covered employee or qualified beneficiary a period of time longer than that specified in this section to provide notice to the administrator, the terms of the plan shall govern the time frame for such notice.

(g) *Additional rights to continuation coverage.* Nothing in this section shall be construed to preclude a plan from providing, in accordance with its terms, continuation coverage to a qualified beneficiary although a notice requirement of this section was not satisfied.

(h) *Applicability.* This section shall apply to any notice obligation described in this section that arises on or after the first day of the first plan year beginning on or after November 26, 2004.

[¶ 15,046B-5]
§ 2590.606-4. **Notice Requirements for Plan Administrators.**

(a) *General.* Pursuant to section 606(a)(4) of the Employee Retirement Income Security Act of 1974, as amended (the Act), the administrator of a group health plan subject to the continuation coverage requirements of Part 6 of title I of the Act shall provide, in accordance with this section, notice to each qualified beneficiary of the qualified beneficiary's rights to continuation coverage under the plan.

(b) *Notice of right to elect continuation coverage.* (1) Except as provided in paragraph (b)(2) or (3) of this section, upon receipt of a notice of qualifying event furnished in accordance with § 2590.606-2 or § 2590.606-3, the administrator shall furnish to each qualified beneficiary, not later than 14 days after receipt of the notice of qualifying event, a notice meeting the requirements of paragraph (b)(4) of this section.

(2) In the case of a plan with respect to which an employer of a covered employee is also the administrator of the plan, except as provided in paragraph (b)(3) of this section, if the employer is otherwise required to furnish a notice of a qualifying event to an administrator pursuant to § 2590.606-2, the administrator shall furnish to each qualified beneficiary a notice meeting the requirements of paragraph (b)(4) of this section not later than 44 days after:

(i) In the case of a plan that provides, with respect to the qualifying event, that continuation coverage and the applicable period for providing notice under section 606(a)(2) of the Act shall commence with the date of loss of coverage, the date on which a qualified beneficiary loses coverage under the plan due to the qualifying event; or

(ii) In all other cases, the date on which the qualifying event occurred.

(3) In the case of a plan that is a multiemployer plan, a notice meeting the requirements of paragraph (b)(4) of this section shall be furnished not later than the later of:

(i) The end of the time period provided in paragraph (b)(1) of this section; or

(ii) The end of the time period provided in the terms of the plan for such purpose.

(4) The notice required by this paragraph (b) shall be written in a manner calculated to be understood by the average plan participant and shall contain the following information:

(i) The name of the plan under which continuation coverage is available; and the name, address and telephone number of the party responsible under the plan for the administration of continuation coverage benefits;

(ii) Identification of the qualifying event;

(iii) Identification, by status or name, of the qualified beneficiaries who are recognized by the plan as being entitled to elect continuation coverage with respect to the qualifying event, and the date on which coverage under the plan will terminate (or has terminated) unless continuation coverage is elected;

(iv) A statement that each individual who is a qualified beneficiary with respect to the qualifying event has an independent right to elect continuation coverage, that a covered employee or a qualified beneficiary who is the spouse of the covered employee (or was the spouse of the covered employee on the day before the qualifying event occurred) may elect continuation coverage on behalf of all other qualified beneficiaries with respect to the qualifying event, and that a parent or legal guardian may elect continuation coverage on behalf of a minor child;

(v) An explanation of the plan's procedures for electing continuation coverage, including an explanation of the time period during which the election must be made, and the date by which the election must be made;

(vi) An explanation of the consequences of failing to elect or waiving continuation coverage, including an explanation that a qualified beneficiary's decision whether to elect continuation coverage will affect the future rights of qualified beneficiaries to portability of group health coverage, guaranteed access to individual health coverage, and special enrollment under Part 7 of title I of the Act, with a reference to where a qualified beneficiary may obtain additional information about such rights; and a description of the plan's procedures for revoking a waiver of the right to continuation coverage before the date by which the election must be made;

(vii) A description of the continuation coverage that will be made available under the plan, if elected, including the date on which such coverage will commence, either by providing a description of the coverage or by reference to the plan's summary plan description;

(viii) An explanation of the maximum period for which continuation coverage will be available under the plan, if elected; an explanation of the continuation coverage termination date; and an explanation of any events that might cause continuation coverage to be terminated earlier than the end of the maximum period;

(ix) A description of the circumstances (if any) under which the maximum period of continuation coverage may be extended due either to the occurrence of a second qualifying event or a determination by the Social Security Administration, under title II or XVI of the Social Security Act (42 U.S.C. 401 *et seq.* or 1381 *et seq.*) (SSA), that the qualified beneficiary is disabled, and the length of any such extension;

(x) In the case of a notice that offers continuation coverage with a maximum duration of less than 36 months, a description of the plan's requirements regarding the responsibility of qualified beneficiaries to provide notice of a second qualifying event and notice of a disability determination under the SSA, along with a description of the plan's procedures for providing such notices, including the times within which such notices must be provided and the consequences of failing to provide such notices. The notice shall also explain the responsibility of qualified beneficiaries to provide notice that a disabled qualified beneficiary has subsequently been determined to no longer be disabled;

(xi) A description of the amount, if any, that each qualified beneficiary will be required to pay for continuation coverage;

(xii) A description of the due dates for payments, the qualified beneficiaries' right to pay on a monthly basis, the grace periods for payment, the address to which payments should be sent, and the consequences of delayed payment and non-payment;

(xiii) An explanation of the importance of keeping the administrator informed of the current addresses of all participants or beneficiaries under the plan who are or may become qualified beneficiaries; and

(xiv) A statement that the notice does not fully describe continuation coverage or other rights under the plan, and that more complete information regarding such rights is available in the plan's summary plan description or from the plan administrator.

(c) *Notice of unavailability of continuation coverage.* (1) In the event that an administrator receives a notice furnished in accordance with § 2590.606-3 relating to a qualifying event, second qualifying event, or determination of disability by the Social Security Administration regarding a covered employee, qualified beneficiary, or other individual and determines that the individual is not entitled to continuation coverage under Part 6 of title I of the Act, the administrator shall provide to such individual an explanation as to why the individual is not entitled to continuation coverage.

(2) The notice required by this paragraph (c) shall be written in a manner calculated to be understood by the average plan participant and shall be furnished by the administrator in accordance with the time frame set out in paragraph (b) of this section that would apply if the administrator received a notice of qualifying event and determined that the individual was entitled to continuation coverage.

(d) *Notice of termination of continuation coverage.* (1) The administrator of a plan that is providing continuation coverage to one or more qualified beneficiaries with respect to a qualifying event shall provide, in accordance with this paragraph (d), notice to each such qualified beneficiary of any termination of continuation coverage that takes effect earlier than the end of the maximum period of continuation coverage applicable to such qualifying event.

(2) The notice required by this paragraph (d) shall be written in a manner calculated to be understood by the average plan participant and shall contain the following information:

(i) The reason that continuation coverage has terminated earlier than the end of the maximum period of continuation coverage applicable to such qualifying event;

(ii) The date of termination of continuation coverage; and

(iii) Any rights the qualified beneficiary may have under the plan or under applicable law to elect an alternative group or individual coverage, such as a conversion right.

(3) The notice required by this paragraph (d) shall be furnished by the administrator as soon as practicable following the administrator's determination that continuation coverage shall terminate.

☐ End of employment

☐ Death of employee

☐ Entitlement to Medicare

Each person ("qualified beneficiary") in the category(ies) checked below is entitled to elect COBRA continuation coverage, which will continue group health care coverage under the Plan for up to ___ months [*enter 18 or 36, as appropriate and check appropriate box or boxes; names may be added*]:

☐ Employee or former employee

☐ Spouse or former spouse

☐ Dependent child(ren) covered under the Plan on the day before the event that caused the loss of coverage

(e) *Special notice rules.* The notices required by paragraphs (b), (c), and (d) of this section shall be furnished to each qualified beneficiary or individual, except that:

(1) An administrator may provide notice to a covered employee and the covered employee's spouse by furnishing a single notice addressed to both the covered employee and the covered employee's spouse, if, on the basis of the most recent information available to the plan, the covered employee's spouse resides at the same location as the covered employee; and

(2) An administrator may provide notice to each qualified beneficiary who is the dependent child of a covered employee by furnishing a single notice to the covered employee or the covered employee's spouse, if, on the basis of the most recent information available to the plan, the dependent child resides at the same location as the individual to whom such notice is provided.

(f) *Delivery of notice.* The notices required by this section shall be furnished in any manner consistent with the requirements of § 2520.104b-1 of this Chapter, including paragraph (c) of that section relating to the use of electronic media.

(g) *Model notice.* The appendix to this section contains a model notice that is intended to assist administrators in discharging the notice obligations of paragraph (b) of this section. Use of the model notice is not mandatory. The model notice reflects the requirements of this section as they would apply to single-employer group health plans and must be modified if used to provide notice with respect to other types of group health plans, such as multiemployer plans or plans established and maintained by employee organizations for their members. In order to use the model notice, administrators must appropriately add relevant information where indicated in the model notice, select among alternative language and supplement the model notice to reflect applicable plan provisions. Items of information that are not applicable to a particular plan may be deleted. Use of the model notice, appropriately modified and supplemented, will be deemed to satisfy the notice content requirements of paragraph (b)(4) of this section.

(h) *Applicability.* This section shall apply to any notice obligation described in this section that arises on or after the first day of the first plan year beginning on or after November 26, 2004.

[¶ 15,046B-6]

§ 2590.606-4. **Appendix to § 2590.606-4.**

MODEL COBRA CONTINUATION COVERAGE ELECTION NOTICE

(For use by single-employer group health plans)

[*Enter date of notice*]

Dear: [*Identify the qualified beneficiary(ies), by name or status*]

This notice contains important information about your right to continue your health care coverage in the [*enter name of group health plan*] (the Plan). Please read the information contained in this notice very carefully.

To elect COBRA continuation coverage, follow the instructions on the next page to complete the enclosed Election Form and submit it to us.

If you do not elect COBRA continuation coverage, your coverage under the Plan will end on [*enter date*] due to [*check appropriate box*]:

☐ Reduction in hours of employment

☐ Divorce or legal separation

☐ Loss of dependent child status

☐ Child who is losing coverage under the Plan because he or she is no longer a dependent under the Plan

If elected, COBRA continuation coverage will begin on [*enter date*] and can last until [*enter date*]. [*Add, if appropriate:* You may elect any of the following options for COBRA continuation coverage: [*list available coverage options*].

COBRA continuation coverage will cost: [*enter amount each qualified beneficiary will be required to pay for each option per month of coverage and any other permitted coverage periods.*]You do not have to send any payment with the Election Form. Important additional information about payment for COBRA continuation coverage is included in the pages following the Election Form.

If you have any questions about this notice or your rights to COBRA continuation coverage, you should contact [*enter name of party responsible for COBRA administration for the Plan, with telephone number and address*].

COBRA CONTINUATION COVERAGE ELECTION FORM

INSTRUCTIONS: To elect COBRA continuation coverage, complete this Election Form and return it to us. Under federal law, you must have 60 days after the date of this notice to decide whether you want to elect COBRA continuation coverage under the Plan.

Send completed Election Form to: [*Enter Name and Address*]

Name	Date of Birth	Relationship to Employee

a. _____

[*Add if appropriate:* Coverage option elected:]

_____

c. _____

[*Add if appropriate:* Coverage option elected:]

_____

_____

Signature

_____

Print Name

_____

_____

Print Address

IMPORTANT INFORMATION ABOUT YOUR COBRA CONTINUATION COVERAGE RIGHTS

What is continuation coverage?

Federal law requires that most group health plans (including this Plan) give employees and their families the opportunity to continue their health care coverage when there is a "qualifying event" that would result in a loss of coverage under an employer's plan. Depending on the type of qualifying event, "qualified beneficiaries" can include the employee (or retired employee) covered under the group health plan, the covered employee's spouse, and the dependent children of the covered employee.

Continuation coverage is the same coverage that the Plan gives to other participants or beneficiaries under the Plan who are not receiving continuation coverage. Each qualified beneficiary who elects continuation coverage will have the same rights under the Plan as other participants or beneficiaries covered under the Plan, including [*add if applicable:* open enrollment and] special enrollment rights.

How long will continuation coverage last?

In the case of a loss of coverage due to end of employment or reduction in hours of employment, coverage generally may be continued only for up to a total of 18 months. In the case of losses of coverage due to an employee's death, divorce or legal separation, the employee's becoming entitled to Medicare benefits or a dependent child ceasing to be a dependent under the terms of the plan, coverage may be continued for up to a total of 36 months. When the qualifying event is the end of employment or reduction of the employee's hours of employment, and the employee became entitled to Medicare benefits less than 18 months before the qualifying event, COBRA continuation coverage for qualified beneficiaries other than the employee lasts until 36 months after the date of Medicare entitlement. This notice shows the maxi-

This Election Form must be completed and returned by mail [*or describe other means of submission and due date*]. If mailed, it must be post-marked no later than [*enter date*].

If you do not submit a completed Election Form by the due date shown above, you will lose your right to elect COBRA continuation coverage. If you reject COBRA continuation coverage before the due date, you may change your mind as long as you furnish a completed Election Form before the due date. However, if you change your mind after first rejecting COBRA continuation coverage, your COBRA continuation coverage will begin on the date you furnish the completed Election Form.

Read the important information about your rights included in the pages after the Election Form.

I (We) elect COBRA continuation coverage in the [*enter name of plan*] (the Plan) as indicated below:

	SSN (or other identifier)

b. _____

[*Add if appropriate:* Coverage option elected:]

_____

_____

Date

_____

Relationship to individual(s) listed above

_____

_____

Telephone number

mum period of continuation coverage available to the qualified beneficiaries.

Continuation coverage will be terminated before the end of the maximum period if:

- any required premium is not paid in full on time,

- a qualified beneficiary becomes covered, after electing continuation coverage, under another group health plan that does not impose any pre-existing condition exclusion for a pre-existing condition of the qualified beneficiary,

- a qualified beneficiary becomes entitled to Medicare benefits (under Part A, Part B, or both) after electing continuation coverage, [Technical correction made June 23, 2004 (69 FR 34920)] or

- the employer ceases to provide any group health plan for its employees.

Continuation coverage may also be terminated for any reason the Plan would terminate coverage of a participant or beneficiary not receiving continuation coverage (such as fraud).

[*If the maximum period shown on page 1 of this notice is less than 36 months, add the following three paragraphs:*]

How can you extend the length of COBRA continuation coverage?

If you elect continuation coverage, an extension of the maximum period of coverage may be available if a qualified beneficiary is disabled or a second qualifying event occurs. You must notify [*enter name of party responsible for COBRA administration*] of a disability or a second qualifying event in order to extend the period of continuation coverage. Failure to provide notice of a disability or second qualifying event may affect the right to extend the period of continuation coverage.

Disability

An 11-month extension of coverage may be available if any of the qualified beneficiaries is determined by the Social Security Administration (SSA) to be disabled. The disability has to have started at some time before the 60th day of COBRA continuation coverage and must last at least until the end of the 18-month period of continuation coverage. [*Describe Plan provisions for requiring notice of disability determination, including time frames and procedures.*] Each qualified beneficiary who has elected continuation coverage will be entitled to the 11-month disability extension if one of them qualifies. If the qualified beneficiary is determined by SSA to no longer be disabled, you must notify the Plan of that fact within 30 days after SSA's determination.

Second Qualifying Event

An 18-month extension of coverage will be available to spouses and dependent children who elect continuation coverage if a second qualifying event occurs during the first 18 months of continuation coverage. The maximum amount of continuation coverage available when a second qualifying event occurs is 36 months. Such second qualifying events may include the death of a covered employee, divorce or separation from the covered employee, the covered employee's becoming entitled to Medicare benefits (under Part A, Part B, or both), or a dependent child's ceasing to be eligible for coverage as a dependent under the Plan. These events can be a second qualifying event only if they would have caused the qualified beneficiary to lose coverage under the Plan if the first qualifying event had not occurred. You must notify the Plan within 60 days after a second qualifying event occurs if you want to extend your continuation coverage.

How can you elect COBRA continuation coverage?

To elect continuation coverage, you must complete the Election Form and furnish it according to the directions on the form. Each qualified beneficiary has a separate right to elect continuation coverage. For example, the employee's spouse may elect continuation coverage even if the employee does not. Continuation coverage may be elected for only one, several, or for all dependent children who are qualified beneficiaries. A parent may elect to continue coverage on behalf of any dependent children. The employee or the employee's spouse can elect continuation coverage on behalf of all of the qualified beneficiaries.

In considering whether to elect continuation coverage, you should take into account that a failure to continue your group health coverage will affect your future rights under federal law. First, you can lose the right to avoid having pre-existing condition exclusions applied to you by other group health plans if you have more than a 63-day gap in health coverage, and election of continuation coverage may help you not have such a gap. Second, you will lose the guaranteed right to purchase individual health insurance policies that do not impose such pre-existing condition exclusions if you do not get continuation coverage for the maximum time available to you. Finally, you should take into account that you have special enrollment rights under federal law. You have the right to request special enrollment in another group health plan for which you are otherwise eligible (such as a plan sponsored by your spouse's employer) within 30 days after your group health coverage ends because of the qualifying event listed above. You will also have the same special enrollment right at the end of continuation coverage if you get continuation coverage for the maximum time available to you.

How much does COBRA continuation coverage cost?

Generally, each qualified beneficiary may be required to pay the entire cost of continuation coverage. The amount a qualified beneficiary may be required to pay may not exceed 102 percent (or, in the case of an extension of continuation coverage due to a disability, 150 percent) of the cost to the group health plan (including both employer and employee contributions) for coverage of a similarly situated plan participant or beneficiary who is not receiving continuation coverage. The required payment for each continuation coverage period for each option is described in this notice.

[*If employees might be eligible for trade adjustment assistance, the following information may be added*: The Trade Act of 2002 created a new tax credit for certain individuals who become eligible for trade adjustment assistance and for certain retired employees who are receiving pension payments from the Pension Benefit Guaranty Corporation (PBGC) (eligible individuals). Under the new tax provisions, eligible individuals can either take a tax credit or get advance payment of 65% of premiums paid for qualified health insurance, including continuation coverage. If you have questions about these new tax provisions, you may call the Health Coverage Tax Credit Customer Contact Center toll-free at 1-866-628-4282. TTD/TTY callers may call toll-free at 1-866-626-4282. More information about the Trade Act is also available at *www.doleta.gov/tradeact/2002act_index.asp*.

When and how must payment for COBRA continuation coverage be made?

First payment for continuation coverage

If you elect continuation coverage, you do not have to send any payment with the Election Form. However, you must make your first payment for continuation coverage not later than 45 days after the date of your election. (This is the date the Election Notice is post-marked, if mailed.) If you do not make your first payment for continuation coverage in full not later than 45 days after the date of your election, you will lose all continuation coverage rights under the Plan. You are responsible for making sure that the amount of your first payment is correct. You may contact [*enter appropriate contact information, e.g., the Plan Administrator or other party responsible for COBRA administration under the Plan*] to confirm the correct amount of your first payment.

Periodic payments for continuation coverage

After you make your first payment for continuation coverage, you will be required to make periodic payments for each subsequent coverage period. The amount due for each coverage period for each qualified beneficiary is shown in this notice. The periodic payments can be made on a monthly basis. Under the Plan, each of these periodic payments for continuation coverage is due on the [*enter due day for each monthly payment*] for that coverage period. [*If Plan offers other payment schedules, enter with appropriate dates:* You may instead make payments for continuation coverage for the following coverage periods, due on the following dates:]. If you make a periodic payment on or before the first day of the coverage period to which it applies, your coverage under the Plan will continue for that coverage period without any break. The Plan [*select one:* will *or* will not] send periodic notices of payments due for these coverage periods.

Grace periods for periodic payments

Although periodic payments are due on the dates shown above, you will be given a grace period of 30 days after the first day of the coverage period [*or enter longer period permitted by Plan*] to make each periodic payment. Your continuation coverage will be provided for each coverage period as long as payment for that coverage period is made before the end of the grace period for that payment. [*If Plan suspends coverage during grace period for nonpayment, enter and modify as necessary:* However, if you pay a periodic payment later than the first day of the coverage period to which it applies, but before the end of the grace period for the coverage period, your coverage under the Plan will be suspended as of the first day of the coverage period and then retroactively reinstated (going back to the first day of the coverage period) when the periodic payment is received. This means that any claim you submit for benefits while your coverage is suspended may be denied and may have to be resubmitted once your coverage is reinstated.]

If you fail to make a periodic payment before the end of the grace period for that coverage period, you will lose all rights to continuation coverage under the Plan.

Your first payment and all periodic payments for continuation coverage should be sent to:

[*enter appropriate payment address*]

For more information

This notice does not fully describe continuation coverage or other rights under the Plan. More information about continuation coverage and your rights under the Plan is available in your summary plan description or from the Plan Administrator.

If you have any questions concerning the information in this notice, your rights to coverage, or if you want a copy of your summary plan description, you should contact [*enter name of party responsible for COBRA administration for the Plan, with telephone number and address*].

For more information about your rights under ERISA, including COBRA, the Health Insurance Portability and Accountability Act (HIPAA), and other laws affecting group health plans, contact the U.S.

Department of Labor's Employee Benefits Security Administration (EBSA) in your area or visit the EBSA website at *www.dol.gov/ebsa*. (Addresses and phone numbers of Regional and District EBSA Offices are available through EBSA's website.)

Keep Your Plan Informed of Address Changes

In order to protect your and your family's rights, you should keep the Plan Administrator informed of any changes in your address and the addresses of family members. You should also keep a copy, for your records, of any notices you send to the Plan Administrator.

[¶ 15,046F]
DEFINITIONS AND SPECIAL RULES

Act Sec. 607. For purposes of this part—

»»→ Caution: *ERISA Sec. 607(1), below, prior to amendment by P.L. 114-255, applies to plan years beginning on or before December 31, 2016.*

(1) GROUP HEALTH PLAN. The term "group health plan" means an employee welfare benefit plan providing medical care (as defined in section 213(d) of the Internal Revenue Code of 1986) to participants or beneficiaries directly or through insurance, reimbursement, or otherwise. Such term shall not include any plan substantially all of the coverage under which is for qualified long-term care services (as defined in section 7702B(c) of such Code).

»»→ Caution: *ERISA Sec. 607(1), below, as amended by P.L. 114-255, applies to plan years beginning after December 31, 2016.*

(1) GROUP HEALTH PLAN. The term "group health plan" means an employee welfare benefit plan providing medical care (as defined in section 213(d) of the Internal Revenue Code of 1986) to participants or beneficiaries directly or through insurance, reimbursement, or otherwise. Such term shall not include any plan substantially all of the coverage under which is for qualified long-term care services (as defined in section 7702B(c) of such Code). Such term shall not include any qualified small employer health reimbursement arrangement (as defined in section 9831(d)(2) of the Internal Revenue Code of 1986).

(2) COVERED EMPLOYEE. The term "covered employee" means an individual who is (or was) provided coverage under a group health plan by virtue of the performance of services by the individual for 1 or more persons maintaining the plan (including as an employee defined in section 401(c)(1) of the Internal Revenue Code of 1986).

(3) QUALIFIED BENEFICIARY—

(A) IN GENERAL. The term "qualified beneficiary" means, with respect to a covered employee under a group health plan, any other individual who, on the day before the qualifying event for that employee, is a beneficiary under the plan—

    (i) as the spouse of the covered employee, or

    (ii) as the dependent child of the employee.

Such term shall also include a child who is born to or placed for adoption with the covered employee during the period of continuation coverage under this part.

(B) SPECIAL RULE FOR TERMINATIONS AND REDUCED EMPLOYMENT. In the case of a qualifying event described in section 603(2), the term "qualified beneficiary" includes the covered employee.

(C) SPECIAL RULE FOR RETIREES AND WIDOWS. In the case of a qualifying event described in section 603(6), the term qualified beneficiary includes a covered employee who had retired on or before the date of substantial elimination of coverage and any other individual who, on the day before such qualifying event, is a beneficiary under the plan—

    (i) as the spouse of the covered employee,

    (ii) as the dependent child of the employee, or

    (iii) as the surviving spouse of the covered employee.

(4) EMPLOYER. Subsection (n) (relating to leased employees) and subsection (t) (relating to application of controlled group rules to certain employee benefits) of section 414 of the Internal Revenue Code of 1986 shall apply for purposes of this part in the same manner and to the same extent as such subsections apply for purposes of section 106 of such Code. Any regulations prescribed by the Secretary pursuant to the preceding sentence shall be consistent and coextensive with any regulations prescribed for similar purposes by the Secretary of the Treasury (or such Secretary's delegate) under such subsections.

(5) OPTIONAL EXTENSION OF REQUIRED PERIODS. A group health plan shall not be treated as failing to meet the requirements of this part solely because the plan provides both—

    (A) that the period of extended coverage referred to in section 602(2) commences with the date of the loss of coverage, and

    (B) that the applicable notice period provided under section 606(a)(2) commences with the date of the loss of coverage.

Amendments

P.L. 114-255, §18001(b)(2):

Amended ERISA Sec. 607(1) by adding at the end the following: "Such term shall not include any qualified small employer health reimbursement arrangement (as defined in section 9831(d)(2) of the Internal Revenue Code of 1986)."

The above amendment applies to plan years beginning after December 31, 2016.

P.L. 104-191, §321(d)(2):

Amended ERISA Sec. 607(1) by adding a new sentence at the end to read as above.

The above amendment applies to contracts issued after December 31, 1996. For special rules, see Act Sec. 321(f)(2)-(5), reproduced below:

(2) CONTINUATION OF EXISTING POLICIES.—In the case of any contract issued before January 1, 1997, which met the long-term care insurance requirements of the State in which the contract was sitused at the time the contract was issued—

(A) such contract shall be treated for purposes of the Internal Revenue Code of 1986 as a qualified long-term care insurance contract (as defined in section 7702B(b) of such Code), and

(B) services provided under, or reimbursed by, such contract shall be treated for such purposes as qualified long-term care services (as defined in section 7702B(c) of such Code).

In the case of an individual who is covered on December 31, 1996, under a State long-term care plan (as defined in section 7702B(f)(2) of such Code), the terms of such plan on such date shall be treated for purposes of the preceding sentence as a contract issued on such date which met the long-term care insurance requirements of such State.

(3) EXCHANGES OF EXISTING POLICIES.—If, after the date of enactment of this Act and before January 1, 1998, a contract providing for long-term care insurance coverage is exchanged solely for a qualified long-term care insurance contract (as defined in section 7702B(b) of such Code), no gain or loss shall be recognized on the exchange. If, in addition to a qualified long-term care insurance contract, money or other property is received in the exchange, then any gain shall be recognized to the extent of the sum of the money and the fair market value of the other property received. For purposes of this paragraph, the cancellation of a contract providing for long-term care insurance coverage and reinvestment of the cancellation proceeds in a qualified long-term care insurance contract within 60 days thereafter shall be treated as an exchange.

(4) ISSUANCE OF CERTAIN RIDERS PERMITTED.—For purposes of applying sections 101(f), 7702, and 7702A of the Internal Revenue Code of 1986 to any contract—

(A) the issuance of a rider which is treated as a qualified long-term care insurance contract under section 7702B, and

(B) the addition of any provision required to conform any other long-term care rider to be so treated,

shall not be treated as a modification or material change of such contract.

(5) APPLICATION OF PER DIEM LIMITATION TO EXISTING CONTRACTS.—The amount of per diem payments made under a contract issued on or before July 31, 1996, with respect to an insured which are excludable from gross income by reason of section 7702B of the Internal Revenue Code of 1986 (as added by this section) shall not be reduced under subsection (d)(2)(B) thereof by reason of reimbursements received under a contract issued on or before such date. The preceding sentence shall cease to apply as of the date (after July 31, 1996) such contract is exchanged or there is any contract modification which results in an increase in the amount of such per diem payments or the amount of such reimbursements.

P.L. 104-191, § 421(b)(3):

Amended ERISA Sec. 607(3)(A) by adding a new flush sentence at the end to read as above.

The above amendment is effective on January 1, 1997, regardless of whether the qualifying event occurred before, on, or after such date. For a special rule, see Act Sec. 421(e), reproduced below.

Act Sec. 421(e) provides:

(e) NOTIFICATION OF CHANGES.—Not later than November 1, 1996, each group health plan (covered under title XXII of the Public Health Service Act, part 6 of subtitle B of title I of the Employee Retirement Income Security Act of 1974, and section 4980B(f) of the Internal Revenue Code of 1986) shall notify each qualified beneficiary who has elected continuation coverage under such title, part or section of the amendments made by this section.

P.L. 101-239, § 7862(c)(2)(A):

Amended ERISA Sec. 607(2) by striking "the individual's employment or previous employment with an employer" and inserting "the performance of services by the individual for 1 or more persons maintaining the plan (including as an employee defined in section 401(c)(1) of the Internal Revenue Code of 1986)," effective for plan years beginning after December 31, 1989.

P.L. 101-239, § 7891(a)(1):

Titles I, III, and IV of ERISA (other than sections 3(37)(E), 301(a)(7), and 308, the last sentence of section 408(d), and sections 414(c), 4001(a)(3)(ii), and 4303) are each amended by striking "Internal Revenue Code of 1954" each place it appears and inserting "Internal Revenue Code of 1986" effective October 22, 1986.

P.L. 101-239, § 7891(d)(2)(B)(i):

Amended ERISA Sec. 607 by inserting "AND SPECIAL RULES" after "DEFINITIONS" in the heading and by adding new paragraph (5) to read as above, effective for plan years beginning on or after January 1, 1990.

P.L. 101-239, § 7862(c)(6):

Repealed Sec. 3011(b)(6) of the Technical and Miscellaneous Revenue Act of 1988 (P.L. 100-647), effective as if included in Sec. 3011(b).

P.L. 100-647, § 3011(b)(6):

Amended ERISA Sec. 607(1) by striking out "section 162(i)(3) of the Internal Revenue Code of 1954" and inserting in lieu thereof "section 162(i)(2) of the Internal Revenue Code of 1986".

The above amendment shall apply to tax years beginning after December 31, 1988, but shall not apply to any plan for any plan year to which section 162(k) of the Internal Revenue Code of 1986 (as in effect on the date before the date of enactment of this Act) did not apply by reason of section 10001(e)(2) of the Consolidated Budget Reconciliation Act of 1985.

P.L. 99-514, § 1895(d)(8):

Added Sec. 607(1) to read as above, effective for plan years beginning after July 1, 1986, subject to the special rules discussed at ¶ 15,045. Prior to amendment, Sec. 607(1) read as follows:

(1) GROUP HEALTH PLAN.—The term "group health plan" means an employee welfare benefit plan that is a group health plan (within the meaning of section 162(i)(3) of the Internal Revenue Code of 1954).

P.L. 99-514 § 1895(d)(9):

Added Sec. 607(4) to read as above, effective subject to the rules under Act Sec. 1151(k), which provides as follows:

(k) EFFECTIVE DATES.—

(l) IN GENERAL.—The amendments made by this section shall apply to years beginning after the later of—

(A) December 31, 1987, or

(B) the earlier of—

(i) the date which is 3 months after the date on which the Secretary of the Treasury or his delegate issues such regulations as are necessary to carry out the provisions of section 89 of the Internal Revenue Code of 1986 (as added by this section), or

(ii) December 31, 1988.

(2) SPECIAL RULE FOR COLLECTIVE BARGAINING PLAN.—In the case of a plan maintained pursuant to 1 or more collective bargaining agreements between employee representatives and 1 or more employers ratified before March 1, 1986, the amendments made by this section shall not apply to employees covered by such an agreement in years beginning before the earlier of—

(A) the date on which the last of such collective bargaining agreements terminates (determined without regard to any extension thereof after February 28, 1986), or

(B) January 1, 1991.

A plan shall not be required to take into account employees to which the preceding sentence applies for purposes of applying section 89 of the Internal Revenue Code of 1986 (as added by this section) to employees to which the preceding sentence does not apply for any year preceding the year described in the preceding sentence.

* * *

P.L. 99-509, § 9501(c)(2):

Amended ERISA Sec. 607(3) by adding a new paragraph (C) to read as above effective for plan years beginning after July 1, 1986 except for plans maintained under collective bargaining agreements in which case the amendments do not apply to plan years beginning before the later of (1) the date the last of the collective bargaining agreements terminates, or (2) January 1, 1987.

P.L. 99-272:

Act Sec. 10002(a) added ERISA Sec. 607 to read as above, effective for plan years beginning after July 1, 1986, subject to the special rules discussed at ¶ 15,045.

[¶ 15,046L]
REGULATIONS

Act Sec. 608. The Secretary may prescribe regulations to carry out the provisions of this part.

Amendment

P.L. 99-272:

Act Sec. 10002(a) added ERISA Sec. 608 to read as above, effective for plan years beginning after July 1, 1986, subject to the special rules discussed at ¶ 15,045.

[¶ 15,046M]
ADDITIONAL STANDARDS FOR GROUP HEALTH PLANS

Act Sec. 609.(a) GROUP HEALTH PLAN COVERAGE PURSUANT TO MEDICAL CHILD SUPPORT ORDERS.—

(1) IN GENERAL. Each group health plan shall provide benefits in accordance with the applicable requirements of any qualified medical child support order. A qualified medical child support order with respect to any participant or beneficiary shall be deemed to apply to each group health plan which has received such order, from which the participant or beneficiary is eligible to receive benefits, and with respect to which the requirements of paragraph (4) are met.

(2) DEFINITIONS. For purposes of this subsection—

(A) QUALIFIED MEDICAL CHILD SUPPORT ORDER. The term "qualified medical child support order" means a medical child support order—

(i) which creates or recognizes the existence of an alternate recipient's right to, or assigns to an alternate recipient the right to, receive benefits for which a participant or beneficiary is eligible under a group health plan, and

(ii) with respect to which the requirements of paragraphs (3) and (4) are met.

(B) MEDICAL CHILD SUPPORT ORDER. The term "medical child support order" means any judgment, decree, or order (including approval of a settlement agreement) which—

(i) provides for child support with respect to a child of a participant under a group health plan or provides for health benefit coverage to such a child, is made pursuant to a State domestic relations law (including a community property law), and relates to benefits under such plan, or

(ii) is made pursuant to a law relating to medical child support described in section 1908 of the Social Security Act (as added by section 13822 of the Omnibus Budget Reconciliation Act of 1993) with respect to a group health plan,

if such judgment, decree, or order (I) is issued by a court of competent jurisdiction or (II) is issued through an administrative process established under State law and has the force and effect of law under applicable State law.

For purposes of this subparagraph, an administrative notice which is issued pursuant to an administrative process referred to in subclause (II) of the preceding sentence and which has the effect of an order described in clause (i) or (ii) of the preceding sentence shall be treated as such an order.

(C) ALTERNATE RECIPIENT. The term "alternate recipient" means any child of a participant who is recognized under a medical child support order as having a right to enrollment under a group health plan with respect to such participant.

(D) CHILD. The term "child" includes any child adopted by, or placed for adoption with, a participant of a group health plan.

(3) INFORMATION TO BE INCLUDED IN QUALIFIED ORDER. A medical child support order meets the requirements of this paragraph only if such order clearly specifies—

(A) the name and the last known mailing address (if any) of the participant and the name and address of each alternate recipient covered by the order, except that, to the extent provided in the order, the name and mailing address of an official of a State or a political subdivision thereof may be substituted for the mailing address of any such alternate recipient,

(B) a reasonable description of the type of coverage to be provided to each such alternate recipient, or the manner in which such type of coverage is to be determined, and

(C) the period to which such order applies.

(4) RESTRICTIONS ON NEW TYPES OR FORMS OF BENEFITS. A medical child support order meets the requirements of this paragraph only if such order does not require a plan to provide any type or form of benefit, or any option, not otherwise provided under the plan, except to the extent necessary to meet the requirements of a law relating to medical child support described in section 1908 of the Social Security Act (as added by section 13822 of the Omnibus Budget Reconciliation Act of 1993).

(5) PROCEDURAL REQUIREMENTS.—

(A) TIMELY NOTIFICATIONS AND DETERMINATIONS. In the case of any medical child support order received by a group health plan—

(i) the plan administrator shall promptly notify the participant and each alternate recipient of the receipt of such order and the plan's procedures for determining whether medical child support orders are qualified medical child support orders, and

(ii) within a reasonable period after receipt of such order, the plan administrator shall determine whether such order is a qualified medical child support order and notify the participant and each alternate recipient of such determination.

(B) ESTABLISHMENT OF PROCEDURES FOR DETERMINING QUALIFIED STATUS OF ORDERS. Each group health plan shall establish reasonable procedures to determine whether medical child support orders are qualified medical child support orders and to administer the provision of benefits under such qualified orders. Such procedures—

(i) shall be in writing,

(ii) shall provide for the notification of each person specified in a medical child support order as eligible to receive benefits under the plan (at the address included in the medical child support order) of such procedures promptly upon receipt by the plan of the medical child support order, and

(iii) shall permit an alternate recipient to designate a representative for receipt of copies of notices that are sent to the alternate recipient with respect to a medical child support order.

(C) NATIONAL MEDICAL SUPPORT NOTICE DEEMED TO BE A QUALIFIED MEDICAL CHILD SUPPORT ORDER.—

(i) IN GENERAL. If the plan administrator of a group health plan which is maintained by the employer of a noncustodial parent of a child or to which such an employer contributes receives an appropriately completed National Medical Support Notice promulgated pursuant to section 401(b) of the Child Support Performance and Incentive Act of 1998 in the case of such child, and the Notice meets the requirements of paragraphs (3) and (4), the Notice shall be deemed to be a qualified medical child support order in the case of such child.

(ii) ENROLLMENT OF CHILD IN PLAN. In any case in which an appropriately completed National Medical Support Notice is issued in the case of a child of a participant under a group health plan who is a noncustodial parent of the child, and the Notice is deemed under clause (i) to be a qualified medical child support order, the plan administrator, within 40 business days after the date of the Notice, shall—

(I) notify the State agency issuing the Notice with respect to such child whether coverage of the child is available under the terms of the plan and, if so, whether such child is covered under the plan and either the effective date of the coverage or, if necessary, any steps to be taken by the custodial parent (or by the official of a State or political subdivision thereof substituted for the name of such child pursuant to paragraph (3)(A)) to effectuate the coverage; and

(II) provide to the custodial parent (or such substituted official) a description of the coverage available and any forms or documents necessary to effectuate such coverage.

(iii) RULE OF CONSTRUCTION. Nothing in this subparagraph shall be construed as requiring a group health plan, upon receipt of a National Medical Support Notice, to provide benefits under the plan (or eligibility for such benefits) in addition to benefits (or eligibility for benefits) provided under the terms of the plan as of immediately before receipt of such Notice.

(6) ACTIONS TAKEN BY FIDUCIARIES. If a plan fiduciary acts in accordance with part 4 of this subtitle in treating a medical child support order as being (or not being) a qualified medical child support order, then the plan's obligation to the participant and each alternate recipient shall be discharged to the extent of any payment made pursuant to such act of the fiduciary.

(7) TREATMENT OF ALTERNATE RECIPIENTS.—

(A) TREATMENT AS BENEFICIARY GENERALLY. A person who is an alternate recipient under a qualified medical child support order shall be considered a beneficiary under the plan for purposes of any provision of this Act.

(B) TREATMENT AS PARTICIPANT FOR PURPOSES OF REPORTING AND DISCLOSURE REQUIREMENTS. A person who is an alternate recipient under any medical child support order shall be considered a participant under the plan for purposes of the reporting and disclosure requirements of part 1.

(8) DIRECT PROVISION OF BENEFITS PROVIDED TO ALTERNATE RECIPIENTS. Any payment for benefits made by a group health plan pursuant to a medical child support order in reimbursement for expenses paid by an alternate recipient or an alternate recipient's custodial parent or legal guardian shall be made to the alternate recipient or the alternate recipient's custodial parent or legal guardian.

(9) PAYMENT TO STATE OFFICIAL TREATED AS SATISFACTION OF PLAN'S OBLIGATION TO MAKE PAYMENT TO ALTERNATE RECIPIENT. Payment of benefits by a group health plan to an official of a State or a political subdivision thereof whose name and address have been substituted for the address of an alternate recipient in a qualified medical child support order, pursuant to paragraph (3)(A), shall be treated, for purposes of this title, as payment of benefits to the alternate recipient.

(b) RIGHTS OF STATES WITH RESPECT TO GROUP HEALTH PLANS WHERE PARTICIPANTS OR BENEFICIARIES THEREUNDER ARE ELIGIBLE FOR MEDICAID BENEFITS.—

(b)(1) COMPLIANCE BY PLANS WITH ASSIGNMENT OF RIGHTS. A group health plan shall provide that payment for benefits with respect to a participant under the plan will be made in accordance with any assignment of rights made by or on behalf of such participant or a beneficiary of the participant as required by a

State plan for medical assistance approved under title XIX of the Social Security Act pursuant to section 1912(a)(1)(A) of such Act (as in effect on the date of the enactment of the Omnibus Budget Reconciliation Act of 1993).

(2) ENROLLMENT AND PROVISION OF BENEFITS WITHOUT REGARD TO MEDICAID ELIGIBILITY. A group health plan shall provide that, in enrolling an individual as a participant or beneficiary or in determining or making any payments for benefits of an individual as a participant or beneficiary, the fact that the individual is eligible for or is provided medical assistance under a State plan for medical assistance approved under title XIX of the Social Security Act will not be taken into account.

(3) ACQUISITION BY STATES OF RIGHTS OF THIRD PARTIES. A group health plan shall provide that, to the extent that payment has been made under a State plan for medical assistance approved under title XIX of the Social Security Act in any case in which a group health plan has a legal liability to make payment for items or services constituting such assistance, payment for benefits under the plan will be made in accordance with any State law which provides that the State has acquired the rights with respect to a participant to such payment for such items or services.

(c) GROUP HEALTH PLAN COVERAGE OF DEPENDENT CHILDREN IN CASES OF ADOPTION.—

(c)(1) COVERAGE EFFECTIVE UPON PLACEMENT FOR ADOPTION. In any case in which a group health plan provides coverage for dependent children of participants or beneficiaries, such plan shall provide benefits to dependent children placed with participants or beneficiaries for adoption under the same terms and conditions as apply in the case of dependent children who are natural children of participants or beneficiaries under the plan, irrespective of whether the adoption has become final.

(2) RESTRICTIONS BASED ON PREEXISTING CONDITIONS AT TIME OF PLACEMENT FOR ADOPTION PROHIBITED. A group health plan may not restrict coverage under the plan of any dependent child adopted by a participant or beneficiary, or placed with a participant or beneficiary for adoption, solely on the basis of a preexisting condition of such child at the time that such child would otherwise become eligible for coverage under the plan, if the adoption or placement for adoption occurs while the participant or beneficiary is eligible for coverage under the plan.

(3) DEFINITIONS. For purposes of this subsection—

(A) CHILD. The term "child" means, in connection with any adoption, or placement for adoption, of the child, an individual who has not attained age 18 as of the date of such adoption or placement for adoption.

(B) PLACEMENT FOR ADOPTION. The term "placement," or being "placed," for adoption, in connection with any placement for adoption of a child with any person, means the assumption and retention by such person of a legal obligation for total or partial support of such child in anticipation of adoption of such child. The child's placement with such person terminates upon the termination of such legal obligation.

(d) CONTINUED COVERAGE OF COSTS OF A PEDIATRIC VACCINE UNDER GROUP HEALTH PLANS. (d) A group health plan may not reduce its coverage of the costs of pediatric vaccines (as defined under section 1928(h)(6) of the Social Security Act as amended by section 13830 of the Omnibus Budget Reconciliation Act of 1993) below the coverage it provided as of May 1, 1993.

(e) REGULATIONS. (e) Any regulations prescribed under this section shall be prescribed by the Secretary of Labor, in consultation with the Secretary of Health and Human Services.

Amendments

P.L. 105-200, §401(d):

Amended ERISA Sec. 609(a)(5) by adding subparagraph (C) to read as above.

The above amendment is effective July 16, 1998.

P.L. 105-200, §402(h)(2)(A)(iii):

Amended ERISA Sec. 609(a)(2)(B)(ii) by striking "enforced by" and inserting "is made pursuant to" to read as above.

The above amendment is effective August 10, 1993.

P.L. 105-200, §402(h)(2)(B):

Amended ERISA Sec. 609(a)(2) by adding subparagraph (D) to read as above.

The above amendment is effective July 16, 1998.

P.L. 105-200, §402(h)(3)(A):

Amended ERISA Sec. 609(a)(9) by striking "the name and address" and inserting "the address" to read as above.

The above amendment is effective with respect to medical child support orders issued on or after August 5, 1997.

P.L. 105-33, §5611(a):

Amended ERISA Sec. 609(a)(3)(A) by adding at the end new material to read as above.

The above amendment is effective with respect to medical child support orders issued on or after August 5, 1997.

P.L. 105-33, §5611(b):

Amended ERISA Sec. 609(a) by adding a new paragraph (9) to read as above.

The above amendment is effective with respect to medical child support orders issued on or after August 5, 1997.

P.L. 105-33, §5612(a):

Amended ERISA Sec. 609(a)(2)(B) by adding at the end a new sentence to read as above.

The above amendment is effective on August 22, 1996. For a special rule, see Act Sec. 381(b)(2), reproduced below.

P.L. 105-33, §5613(a):

Amended ERISA Sec. 609(a)(3) in subparagraph (B), by striking "by the plan;" by adding "and" at the end of subparagraph (B); in subparagraph (C), by striking ", and"

and inserting a period; and by striking subparagraph (D). Prior to being striken, subparagraph (D) read as follows:

(D) each plan to which such order applies.

The above amendments are effective with respect to medical child support orders issued on or after August 5, 1997.

P.L. 104-193, §381(a):

Amended ERISA Sec. 609(a)(2)(B) by striking "issued by a court of competent jurisdiction"; by striking the period at the end of clause (ii) and inserting a comma; and by adding, after and below clause (ii), the following: "if such judgment, decree, or order (I) is issued by a court of competent jurisdiction or (II) is issued through an administrative process established under State law and has the force and effect of law under applicable State law."

The above amendments are effective on August 22, 1996. For a special rule, see Act Sec. 381(b)(2), reproduced below.

Act Sec. 381(b)(2) provides:

(2) PLAN AMENDMENTS NOT REQUIRED UNTIL JANUARY 1, 1997.—Any amendment to a plan required to be made by an amendment made by this section shall not be required to be made before the 1st plan year beginning on or after January 1, 1997, if—

(A) during the period after the date before the date of the enactment of this Act and before such 1st plan year, the paln is operated in accordance with the requirements of the amendments made by this section; and

(B) such plan amendment applies retroactively to the period after the date before the date of the enactment of this Act and before such 1st plan year.

A plan shall not be treated as failing to be operated in accordance with the provisions of the plan merely because it operates in accordance with this paragraph.

P.L. 103-66, §4301(a):

Added ERISA Sec. 609 to read as above.

The above amendments are effective on August 10, 1993. Any plan amendment required to be made by Act Sec. 4301 need not be made before the first plan year beginning on or after January 1, 1994 if: (1) the plan is operated in accordance with Act Sec. 4301 during the period after August 9, 1993 and before such first plan year; and (2) the amendment applies retroactively to this period. A plan will not be treated as failing to be operated in accordance with plan provisions merely because it operates in accordance with the effective date requirements.

Regulations

The following regulations regarding a National Medical Support Notice were adopted by the Pension and Welfare Benefits Administration. The regulations were published in the *Federal Register* on December 27, 2000 (65 FR 82127) and became effective January 26, 2001. Reg. §2590.609-1 was reserved and §2590.609-2 was added on December 27, 2000 (65 FR 82127).

§ 2590.609-1 **[Reserved on 12/27/00 by 65 FR 82129].**

[¶ 15,047I]

§ 2590.609-2 **National Medical Support Notice.** (a) This section promulgates the National Medical Support Notice (the Notice), as mandated by section 401(b) of the Child Support Performance and Incentive Act of 1998 (Pub. L. 105-200). If the Notice is appropriately completed and satisfies paragraphs (3) and (4) of section 609(a) of the Employee Retirement Income Security Act (ERISA), the Notice is deemed to be a qualified medical child support order (QMCSO) pursuant to ERISA section 609(a)(5)(C). Section 609(a) of ERISA delineates the rights and obligations of the alternate recipient (child), the participant, and the group health plan under a QMCSO. A copy of the Notice is available on the Internet at http://www.dol.gov/dol/ebsa. [EBSA technical correction, 68 FR 16399 (April 3, 2003).]

(b) For purposes of this section, a plan administrator shall find that a Notice is appropriately completed if it contains the name of an Issuing Agency, the name and mailing address (if any) of an employee who is a participant under the plan, the name and mailing address of one or more alternate recipient(s) (child(ren) of the participant) (or the name and address of a substituted official or agency which has been substituted for the mailing address of the alternate recipient(s)), and identifies an underlying child support order.

(c)(1) Under section 609(a)(3)(A) of ERISA, in order to be qualified, a medical child support order must clearly specify the name and the last known mailing address (if any) of the participant and the name and mailing address of each alternate recipient covered by the order, except that, to the extent provided in the order, the name and mailing address of an official of a State or a political subdivision thereof may be substituted for the mailing address of any such alternate recipient. Section 609(a)(3)(B) of ERISA requires a reasonable description of the type of coverage to be provided to each such alternate recipient, or the manner in which such type of coverage is to be determined. Section 609(a)(3)(C) of ERISA requires that the order specify the period to which such order applies.

(2) The Notice satisfies ERISA section 609(a)(3)(A) by including the necessary identifying information described in § 2590.609-2(b).

(3) The Notice satisfies ERISA section 609(a)(3)(B) by having the Issuing Agency identify either the specific type of coverage or all available group health coverage. If an employer receives a Notice that does not designate either specific type(s) of coverage or all available coverage, the employer and plan administrator should assume that all are designated. The Notice further satisfies ERISA section 609(a)(3)(B) by instructing the plan administrator that if a group health plan has multiple options and the participant is not enrolled, the Issuing Agency will make a selection after the Notice is qualified, and, if the Issuing Agency does not respond within 20 days, the child will be enrolled under the plan's default option (if any).

(4) Section 609(a)(3)(C) of ERISA is satisfied because the Notice specifies that the period of coverage may only end for the alternate recipient(s) when similarly situated dependents are no longer eligible for coverage under the terms of the plan, or upon the occurrence of certain specified events.

(d)(1) Under ERISA section 609(a)(4), a qualified medical child support order may not require a plan to provide any type or form of benefit, or any option, not otherwise provided under the plan, except to the extent necessary to meet the requirements of a law relating to medical child support described in section 1908 of the Social Security Act, 42 U.S.C. 1396g-1.

(2) The Notice satisfies the conditions of ERISA section 609(a)(4) because it requires the plan to provide to an alternate recipient only those benefits that the plan provides to any dependent of a participant who is enrolled in the plan, and any other benefits that are necessary to meet the requirements of a State law described in such section 1908.

(e) For the purposes of this section, an "Issuing Agency" is a State agency that administers the child support enforcement program under Part D of Title IV of the Social Security Act. [Added on 12/27/00 by 65 FR 82127.]

Appendix: National Medical Support Notice.

CCH Note: The following Appendix, which follows Reg. § 2590.609-2 in the Federal Register dated December 27, 2000, does not appear in the Code of Federal Regulations.

APPENDIX
NATIONAL MEDICAL SUPPORT NOTICE
PART A
NOTICE TO WITHHOLD FOR HEALTH CARE COVERAGE

This Notice is issued under section 466(a)(19) of the Social Security Act, section 609(a)(5)(C) of the Employee Retirement Income Security Act of 1974 (ERISA), and for State and local government and church plans, sections 401(e) and (f) of the Child Support Performance and Incentive Act of 1998.

Issuing Agency: _____	Court or Administrative Authority: _____
Issuing Agency Address: _____	Date of Support Order: _____
_____	Support Order Number: _____
Date of Notice: _____	
Case Number: _____	
Telephone Number: _____	
FAX Number: _____	

RE*

_____)   _____
Employer/Withholder's Federal EIN Number   Employee's Name (Last, First, MI)

_____)   _____
Employer/Withholder's Name   Employee's Social Security Number

_____)   _____
Employer/Withholder's Address   Employee's Mailing Address

_____)
Custodial Parent's Name (Last, First, MI)

_____)   _____
Custodial Parent's Mailing Address   Substituted Official/Agency Name and Address

_____)
Child(ren)'s Mailing Address (if different from Custodial
Parent's)

_____)
_____)
_____)
Name, Mailing Address, and Telephone
Number of a Representative of the Child(ren)

Child(ren)'s Name(s)	DOB	SSN	Child(ren)'s Name(s)	DOB	SSN
_____	_____	_____	_____	_____	_____
_____	_____	_____	_____	_____	_____
_____	_____	_____	_____	_____	_____

The order requires the child(ren) to be enrolled in [ ] any health coverages available; or [] only the following coverage(s): __Medical; __Dental; __Vision; __Prescription drug; __Mental health; __Other (specify): _____

THE PAPERWORK REDUCTION ACT OF 1995 (P.L. 104-13) Public reporting burden for this collection of information is estimated to average 10 minutes per response, including the time reviewing instructions, gathering and maintaining the data needed, and reviewing the collection of information. An agency may not conduct or sponsor, and a person is not required to respond to, a collection of information unless it displays a currently valid OMB control number. OMB control number: 0970-0222 Expiration Date: 12/31/2003.

EMPLOYER RESPONSE

If either 1, 2, or 3 below applies, check the appropriate box and return this Part A to the Issuing Agency within 20 business days after the date of the Notice, or sooner if reasonable. NO OTHER ACTION IS NECESSARY. If neither 1, 2, nor 3 applies, forward Part B to the appropriate plan administrator(s) within 20 business days after the date of the Notice, or sooner if reasonable. Check number 4 and return this Part A to the Issuing Agency if the Plan Administrator informs you that the child(ren) is/are enrolled in an option under the plan for which you have determined that the employee contribution exceeds the amount that may be withheld from the employee's income due to State or Federal withholding limitations and/or prioritization.

☐ 1. Employer does not maintain or contribute to plans providing dependent or family health care coverage.

☐ 2. The employee is among a class of employees (for example, part-time or non-union) that are not eligible for family health coverage under any group health plan maintained by the employer or to which the employer contributes.

☐ 3. Health care coverage is not available because employee is no longer employed by the employer:

> Date of termination: _____
>
> Last known address: _____
>
> Last known telephone number: _____
>
> New employer (if known): _____
>
> New employer address: _____
>
> New employer telephone number: _____

☐ 4. State or Federal withholding limitations and/or prioritization prevent the withholding from the employee's income of the amount required to obtain coverage under the terms of the plan.

Employer Representative:

Name: _____   Telephone Number: _____

Title: _____   Date: _____

EIN (if not provided by Issuing Agency on Notice to Withhold for Health Care Coverage):_____

INSTRUCTIONS TO EMPLOYER

This document serves as notice that the employee identified on this National Medical Support Notice is obligated by a court or administrative child support order to provide health care coverage for the child(ren) identified on this Notice. This National Medical Support Notice replaces any Medical Support Notice that the Issuing Agency has previously served on you with respect to the employee and the children listed on this Notice.

The document consists of **Part A - Notice to Withhold for Health Care Coverage** for the employer to withhold any employee contributions required by the group health plan(s) in which the child(ren) is/are enrolled; and **Part B - Medical Support Notice to the Plan Administrator**, which must be forwarded to the administrator of each group health plan identified by the employer to enroll the eligible child(ren).

EMPLOYER RESPONSIBILITIES

1.   If the individual named above is not your employee, or if family health care coverage is not available, please complete item 1, 2, or 3 of the Employer Response as appropriate, and return it to the Issuing Agency. NO FURTHER ACTION IS NECESSARY.

2.   If family health care coverage is available for which the child(ren) identified above may be eligible, you are required to:

   a.   Transfer, not later than 20 business days after the date of this Notice, a copy of **Part B - Medical Support Notice to the Plan Administrator** to the administrator of each appropriate group health plan for which the child(ren) may be eligible, and

   b.   Upon notification from the plan administrator(s) that the child(ren) is/are enrolled, either

   1) withhold from the employee's income any employee contributions required under each group health plan, in accordance with the applicable law of the employee's principal place of employment and transfer employee contributions to the appropriate plan(s), or

   2) complete item 4 of the Employer Response to notify the Issuing Agency that enrollment cannot be completed because of prioritization or limitations on withholding.

   c.   If the plan administrator notifies you that the employee is subject to a waiting period that expires more than 90 days from the date of its receipt of **Part B of** this Notice, or whose duration is determined by a measure other than the passage of time (for example, the completion of a certain number of hours worked), notify

¶15,047I   Reg. §2590.609-2(e)

the plan administrator when the employee is eligible to enroll in the plan and that this Notice requires the enrollment of the child(ren) named in the Notice in the plan.

LIMITATIONS ON WITHHOLDING

The total amount withheld for both cash and medical support cannot exceed ___% of the employee's aggregate disposable weekly earnings. The employer may not withhold more under this National Medical Support Notice than the lesser of:

    1.   The amounts allowed by the Federal Consumer Credit Protection Act (15 U.S.C., section 1673(b));

    2.   The amounts allowed by the State of the employee's principal place of employment; or

    3.   The amounts allowed for health insurance premiums by the child support order, as indicated here:_____.

The Federal limit applies to the aggregate disposable weekly earnings (ADWE). ADWE is the net income left after making mandatory deductions such as State, Federal, local taxes; Social Security taxes; and Medicare taxes.

PRIORITY OF WITHHOLDING

If withholding is required for employee contributions to one or more plans under this notice and for a support obligation under a separate notice and available funds are insufficient for withholding for both cash and medical support contributions, the employer must withhold amounts for purposes of cash support and medical support contributions in accordance with the law, if any, of the State of the employee's principal place of employment requiring prioritization between cash and medical support, as described here:_____
_____.

DURATION OF WITHHOLDING

The child(ren) shall be treated as dependents under the terms of the plan. Coverage of a child as a dependent will end when similarly situated dependents are no longer eligible for coverage under the terms of the plan. However, the continuation coverage provisions of ERISA may entitle the child to continuation coverage under the plan. The employer must continue to withhold employee contributions and may not disenroll (or eliminate coverage for) the child(ren) unless:

    1.   The employer is provided satisfactory written evidence that:

a.   The court or administrative child support order referred to above is no longer in effect; or

b.   The child(ren) is or will be enrolled in comparable coverage which will take effect no later than the effective date of disenrollment from the plan; or

2.   The employer eliminates family health coverage for all of its employees.

POSSIBLE SANCTIONS

An employer may be subject to sanctions or penalties imposed under State law and/or ERISA for discharging an employee from employment, refusing to employ, or taking disciplinary action against any employee because of medical child support withholding, or for failing to withhold income, or transmit such withheld amounts to the applicable plan(s) as the Notice directs.

NOTICE OF TERMINATION OF EMPLOYMENT

In any case in which the above employee's employment terminates, the employer must promptly notify the Issuing Agency listed above of such termination. This requirement may be satisfied by sending to the Issuing Agency a copy of any notice the employer is required to provide under the continuation coverage provisions of ERISA or the Health Insurance Portability and Accountability Act.

EMPLOYEE LIABILITY FOR CONTRIBUTION TO PLAN

The employee is liable for any employee contributions that are required under the plan(s) for enrollment of the child(ren) and is subject to appropriate enforcement. The employee may contest the withholding under this Notice based on a mistake of fact (such as the identity of the obligor). Should an employee contest the withholding under this Notice, the employer must proceed to comply with the employer responsibilities in this Notice until notified by the Issuing Agency to discontinue withholding. To contest the withholding under this Notice, the employee should contact the Issuing Agency at the address and telephone number listed on the Notice. With respect to plans subject to ERISA, it is the view of the Department of Labor that Federal Courts have jurisdiction if the employee challenges a determination that the Notice constitutes a Qualified Medical Child Support Order.

CONTACT FOR QUESTIONS

If you have any questions regarding this Notice, you may contact the Issuing Agency at the address and telephone number listed above.

NATIONAL MEDICAL SUPPORT NOTICE   OMB NO. 1210-0113
PART B
MEDICAL SUPPORT NOTICE TO PLAN ADMINISTRATOR

This Notice is issued under section 466(a)(19) of the Social Security Act, section 609(a)(5)(C) of the Employee Retirement Income Security Act of 1974, and for State and local government and church plans, sections 401(e) and (f) of the Child Support Performance and Incentive Act of 1998. Receipt of this Notice from the Issuing Agency constitutes receipt of a Medical Child Support Order under applicable law. The rights of the parties and the duties of the plan administrator under this Notice are in addition to the existing rights and duties established under such law.

Issuing Agency: _____   Court or Administrative Authority: _____
Issuing Agency Address: _____   Date of Support Order: _____
_____   Support Order Number: _____
Date of Notice: _____
Case Number: _____
Telephone Number: _____
FAX Number: _____

_____)   RE* _____
Employer/Withholder's Federal EIN Number   Employee's Name (Last, First, MI)

_____)   _____
Employer/Withholder's Name   Employee's Social Security Number

_____)   _____
Employer/Withholder's Address   Employee's Address

_____)   _____
Custodial Parent's Name (Last, First, MI)

_____)   _____
Custodial Parent's Mailing Address   Substituted Official/Agency Name and Address

_____)
Child(ren)'s Mailing Address (if Different from Custodial
Parent's)
_____)
_____)
_____)
Name(s), Mailing Address, and Telephone
Number of a Representative of the Child(ren)

Child(ren)'s Name(s)   DOB   SSN   Child(ren)'s Name(s)   DOB   SSN
_____   _____ _____ _____   _____ _____
_____   _____ _____ _____   _____ _____
_____   _____ _____ _____   _____ _____

The order requires the child(ren) to be enrolled in [] any health coverages available; or [] only the following coverage(s): __medical; __dental; __vision; __prescription drug; __mental health; __other (specify):_____

Reg. §2590.609-2(e)   ¶15,047I

PLAN ADMINISTRATOR RESPONSE
(To be completed and returned to the Issuing Agency within 40 business days after the date of
the Notice, or sooner if reasonable)

This Notice was received by the plan administrator on _____.

☐ 1. This Notice was determined to be a "qualified medical child support order," on _____.
Complete **Response 2 or 3, and 4**, if applicable.

2. The participant (employee) and alternate recipient(s) (child(ren)) are to be enrolled in the
following family coverage.
    ☐ a. The child(ren) is/are currently enrolled in the plan as a dependent of the participant.
    ☐ b. There is only one type of coverage provided under the plan. The child(ren) is/are
included as dependents of the participant under the plan.
    ☐ c. The participant is enrolled in an option that is providing dependent coverage and the
child(ren) will be enrolled in the same option.
    ☐ d. The participant is enrolled in an option that permits dependent coverage that has not
been elected; dependent coverage will be provided.

Coverage is effective as of __/__/____ (includes waiting period of less than 90 days from date of
receipt of this Notice). The child(ren) has/have been enrolled in the following option:
_____. Any necessary withholding should commence if the employer
determines that it is permitted under State and Federal withholding and/or prioritization
limitations.

☐ 3. There is more than one option available under the plan and the participant is not enrolled.
The Issuing Agency must select from the available options. Each child is to be included as a
dependent under one of the available options that provide family coverage. If the Issuing
Agency does not reply within 20 business days of the date this Response is returned, the
child(ren), and the participant if necessary, will be enrolled in the plan's default option, if any:
_____.

☐ 4. The participant is subject to a waiting period that expires __/__/____ (more than 90 days
from the date of receipt of this Notice), or has not completed a waiting period which is
determined by some measure other than the passage of time, such as the completion of a certain
number of hours worked (describe here: _____). At the completion of
the waiting period, the plan administrator will process the enrollment.

☐ 5. This Notice does not constitute a "qualified medical child support order" because:
    ☐ The name of the ☐ child(ren) or ☐ participant is unavailable.
    ☐ The mailing address of the ☐ child(ren) (or a substituted official) or ☐ participant is
unavailable.
    ☐ The following child(ren) is/are at or above the age at which dependents are no longer
eligible for coverage under the plan _____ (insert
name(s) of child(ren)).

Plan Administrator or Representative:

Name: _____ Telephone Number: _____

Title: _____ Date: _____

Address: _____

INSTRUCTIONS TO PLAN ADMINISTRATOR

This Notice has been forwarded from the employer identified above to you as the plan administrator of a group health plan maintained by the employer (or a group health plan to which the employer contributes) and in which the noncustodial parent/participant identified above is enrolled or is eligible for enrollment.

This Notice serves to inform you that the noncustodial parent/participant is obligated by an order issued by the court or agency identified above to provide health care coverage for the child(ren) under the group health plan(s) as described on **Part B**.

(A) If the participant and child(ren) and their mailing addresses (or that of a Substituted Official or Agency) are identified above, and if coverage for the child(ren) is or will become available, this Notice constitutes a "qualified medical child support order"(QMCSO) under ERISA or CSPIA, as applicable. (If any mailing address is not present, but it is reasonably accessible, this Notice will not fail to be a QMCSO on that basis.) You must, within 40 business days of the date of this Notice, or sooner if reasonable:

   (1) Complete Part B - Plan Administrator Response - and send it to the Issuing Agency:

   (a) if you checked Response 2:

        (i) notify the noncustodial parent/participant named above, each named child, and the custodial parent that coverage of the child(ren) is or will become available (notification of the custodial parent will be deemed notification of the child(ren) if they reside at the same address);

        (ii) furnish the custodial parent a description of the coverage available and the effective date of the coverage, including, if not already provided, a summary plan description and any forms, documents, or information necessary to effectuate such coverage, as well as information necessary to submit claims for benefits;

   (b) if you checked Response 3:

        (i) if you have not already done so, provide to the Issuing Agency copies of applicable summary plan descriptions or other documents that describe available coverage including the additional participant contribution necessary to obtain coverage for the child(ren) under each option and whether there is a limited service area for any option;

        (ii) if the plan has a default option, you are to enroll the child(ren) in the default option if you have not received an election from the Issuing Agency within 20 business days of the date you returned the Response. If the plan does not have a default option, you are to enroll the child(ren) in the option selected by the Issuing Agency.

(c) if the participant is subject to a waiting period that expires more than 90 days from the date of receipt of this Notice, or has not completed a waiting period whose duration is determined by a measure other than the passage of time (for example, the completion of a certain number of hours worked), complete Response 4 on the Plan Administrator Response and return to the employer and the Issuing Agency, and notify the participant and the custodial parent; and upon satisfaction of the period or requirement, complete enrollment under Response 2 or 3, and

(d) upon completion of the enrollment, transfer the applicable information on Part B - Plan Administrator Response to the employer for a determination that the necessary employee contributions are available. Inform the employer that the enrollment is pursuant to a National Medical Support Notice.

(B) If within 40 business days of the date of this Notice, or sooner if reasonable, you determine that this Notice does not constitute a QMCSO, you must complete Response 5 of Part B - Plan Administrator Response and send it to the Issuing Agency, and inform the noncustodial parent/participant, custodial parent, and child(ren) of the specific reasons for your determination.

(C) Any required notification of the custodial parent, child(ren) and/or participant that is required may be satisfied by sending the party a copy of the Plan Administrator Response, if appropriate.

UNLAWFUL REFUSAL TO ENROLL

Enrollment of a child may not be denied on the ground that: (1) the child was born out of wedlock; (2) the child is not claimed as a dependent on the participant's Federal income tax return; (3) the child does not reside with the participant or in the plan's service area; or (4) because the child is receiving benefits or is eligible to receive benefits under the State Medicaid plan. If the plan requires that the participant be enrolled in order for the child(ren) to be enrolled, and the participant is not currently enrolled, you must enroll both the participant and the child(ren). All enrollments are to be made without regard to open season restrictions.

PAYMENT OF CLAIMS

A child covered by a QMCSO, or the child's custodial parent, legal guardian, or the provider of services to the child, or a State agency to the extent assigned the child's rights, may file claims and the plan shall make payment for covered benefits or reimbursement directly to such party.

PERIOD OF COVERAGE

The alternate recipient(s) shall be treated as dependents under the terms of the plan. Coverage of an alternate recipient as a dependent will end when similarly situated dependents are no longer eligible for coverage under the terms of the plan. However, the continuation coverage provisions of ERISA or other applicable law may entitle the alternate recipient to continue coverage under the plan. Once a child is enrolled in the plan as directed above, the alternate recipient may not be disenrolled unless:

(1) The plan administrator is provided satisfactory written evidence that either:
(a) the court or administrative child support order referred to above is no longer in effect, or
(b) the alternate recipient is or will be enrolled in comparable coverage which will take effect no later than the effective date of disenrollment from the plan;

(2) The employer eliminates family health coverage for all of its employees; or

(3) Any available continuation coverage is not elected, or the period of such coverage expires.

CONTACT FOR QUESTIONS

If you have any questions regarding this Notice, you may contact the Issuing Agency at the address and telephone number listed above.

Paperwork Reduction Act Notice

The Issuing Agency asks for the information on this form to carry out the law as specified in the Employee Retirement Income Security Act or the Child Support Performance and Incentive Act, as applicable. You are required to give the Issuing Agency the information. You are not required to respond to this collection of information unless it displays a currently valid OMB control number. The Issuing Agency needs the information to determine whether health care coverage is provided in accordance with the underlying child support order. The Average time needed to complete and file the form is estimated below. These times will vary depending on the individual circumstances.

__Learning about the law or the form__	__Preparing the form__
First Notice 1 hr.__	1 hr., 45 min.
Subsequent ----- Notices	35 min.

Part 7 Group Health Plan Portability, Access, and Renewability Requirements

[¶ 15,049H]
INCREASED PORTABILITY THROUGH LIMITATION ON PREEXISTING CONDITION EXCLUSIONS

Act Sec. 701.(a) LIMITATIONS ON PREEXISTING CONDITION EXCLUSION PERIOD; CREDITING FOR PERIODS OF PREVIOUS COVERAGE. Subject to subsection (d), a group health plan, and a health insurance issuer offering group health insurance coverage, may, with respect to a participant or beneficiary, impose a preexisting condition exclusion only if—

(1) such exclusion relates to a condition (whether physical or mental), regardless of the cause of the condition, for which medical advice, diagnosis, care, or treatment was recommended or received within the 6-month period ending on the enrollment date;

(2) such exclusion extends for a period of not more than 12 months (or 18 months in the case of a late enrollee) after the enrollment date; and

(3) the period of any such preexisting condition exclusion is reduced by the aggregate of the periods of creditable coverage (if any, as defined in subsection (c)(1)) applicable to the participant or beneficiary as of the enrollment date.

(b) DEFINITIONS. (b) For purposes of this part—

(1) PREEXISTING CONDITION EXCLUSION.—

(A) IN GENERAL. The term "preexisting condition exclusion" means, with respect to coverage, a limitation or exclusion of benefits relating to a condition based on the fact that the condition was present before the date of enrollment for such coverage, whether or not any medical advice, diagnosis, care, or treatment was recommended or received before such date.

Act Sec. 701(b)(1)(A)   ¶ 15,049H

(B) TREATMENT OF GENETIC INFORMATION. Genetic information shall not be treated as a condition described in subsection (a)(1) in the absence of a diagnosis of the condition related to such information.

(2) ENROLLMENT DATE. The term "enrollment date" means, with respect to an individual covered under a group health plan or health insurance coverage, the date of enrollment of the individual in the plan or coverage or, if earlier, the first day of the waiting period for such enrollment.

(3) LATE ENROLLEE. The term "late enrollee" means, with respect to coverage under a group health plan, a participant or beneficiary who enrolls under the plan other than during—

(A) the first period in which the individual is eligible to enroll under the plan, or

(B) a special enrollment period under subsection (f).

(4) WAITING PERIOD. The term "waiting period" means, with respect to a group health plan and an individual who is a potential participant or beneficiary in the plan, the period that must pass with respect to the individual before the individual is eligible to be covered for benefits under the terms of the plan.

(c) RULES RELATING TO CREDITING PREVIOUS COVERAGE.—

(c)(1) CREDITABLE COVERAGE DEFINED. For purposes of this part, the term "creditable coverage" means, with respect to an individual, coverage of the individual under any of the following:

(A) A group health plan.

(B) Health insurance coverage.

(C) Part A or part B of title XVIII of the Social Security Act.

(D) Title XIX of the Social Security Act, other than coverage consisting solely of benefits under section 1928.

(E) Chapter 55 of title 10, United States Code.

(F) A medical care program of the Indian Health Service or of a tribal organization.

(G) A State health benefits risk pool.

(H) A health plan offered under chapter 89 of title 5, United States Code.

(I) A public health plan (as defined in regulations).

(J) A health benefit plan under section 5(e) of the Peace Corps Act (22 U.S.C. 2504(e)).

Such term does not include coverage consisting solely of coverage of excepted benefits (as defined in section 733(c)).

(2) NOT COUNTING PERIODS BEFORE SIGNIFICANT BREAKS IN COVERAGE.—

(A) IN GENERAL. A period of creditable coverage shall not be counted, with respect to enrollment of an individual under a group health plan, if, after such period and before the enrollment date, there was a 63-day period during all of which the individual was not covered under any creditable coverage.

(B) WAITING PERIOD NOT TREATED AS A BREAK IN COVERAGE. For purposes of subparagraph (A) and subsection (d)(4), any period that an individual is in a waiting period for any coverage under a group health plan (or for group health insurance coverage) or is in an affiliation period (as defined in subsection (g)(2)) shall not be taken into account in determining the continuous period under subparagraph (A).

(C) TAA-ELIGIBLE INDIVIDUALS. In the case of plan years beginning before January 1, 2014—

(i) TAA PRE-CERTIFICATION PERIOD RULE. In the case of a TAA-eligible individual, the period beginning on the date the individual has a TAA-related loss of coverage and ending on the date that is 7 days after the date of the issuance by the Secretary (or by any person or entity designated by the Secretary) of a qualified health insurance costs credit eligibility certificate for such individual for purposes of section 7527 of the Internal Revenue Code of 1986 shall not be taken into account in determining the continuous period under subparagraph (A).

(ii) DEFINITIONS. The terms "TAA-eligible individual" and "TAA-related loss of coverage" have the meanings given such terms in section 605(b)(4).

(3) METHOD OF CREDITING COVERAGE.—

(A) STANDARD METHOD. Except as otherwise provided under subparagraph (B), for purposes of applying subsection (a)(3), a group health plan, and a health insurance issuer offering group health insurance coverage, shall count a period of creditable coverage without regard to the specific benefits covered during the period.

(B) ELECTION OF ALTERNATIVE METHOD. A group health plan, or a health insurance issuer offering group health insurance coverage, may elect to apply subsection (a)(3) based on coverage of benefits within each of several classes or categories of benefits specified in regulations rather than as provided under subparagraph (A). Such election shall be made on a uniform basis for all participants and beneficiaries. Under such election a group health plan or issuer shall count a period of creditable coverage with respect to any class or category of benefits if any level of benefits is covered within such class or category.

(C) PLAN NOTICE. In the case of an election with respect to a group health plan under subparagraph (B) (whether or not health insurance coverage is provided in connection with such plan), the plan shall—

(i) prominently state in any disclosure statements concerning the plan, and state to each enrollee at the time of enrollment under the plan, that the plan has made such election, and

(ii) include in such statements a description of the effect of this election.

(4) ESTABLISHMENT OF PERIOD. Periods of creditable coverage with respect to an individual shall be established through presentation of certifications described in subsection (e) or in such other manner as may be specified in regulations.

(d) EXCEPTIONS.—

(d)(1) EXCLUSION NOT APPLICABLE TO CERTAIN NEWBORNS. Subject to paragraph (4), a group health plan, and a health insurance issuer offering group health insurance coverage, may not impose any preexisting condition exclusion in the case of an individual who, as of the last day of the 30-day period beginning with the date of birth, is covered under creditable coverage.

(2) EXCLUSION NOT APPLICABLE TO CERTAIN ADOPTED CHILDREN. Subject to paragraph (4), a group health plan, and a health insurance issuer offering group health insurance coverage, may not impose any preexisting condition exclusion in the case of a child who is adopted or placed for adoption before attaining 18 years of age and who, as of the last day of the 30-day period beginning on the date of the adoption or placement for adoption, is covered under creditable coverage. The previous sentence shall not apply to coverage before the date of such adoption or placement for adoption.

(3) EXCLUSION NOT APPLICABLE TO PREGNANCY. A group health plan, and health insurance issuer offering group health insurance coverage, may not impose any preexisting condition exclusion relating to pregnancy as a preexisting condition.

(4) LOSS IF BREAK IN COVERAGE. Paragraphs (1) and (2) shall no longer apply to an individual after the end of the first 63-day period during all of which the individual was not covered under any creditable coverage.

(e) CERTIFICATIONS AND DISCLOSURE OF COVERAGE.—

(e)(1) REQUIREMENT FOR CERTIFICATION OF PERIOD OF CREDITABLE COVERAGE.—

(A) IN GENERAL. A group health plan, and a health insurance issuer offering group health insurance coverage, shall provide the certification described in subparagraph (B)—

(i) at the time an individual ceases to be covered under the plan or otherwise becomes covered under a COBRA continuation provision,

(ii) in the case of an individual becoming covered under such a provision, at the time the individual ceases to be covered under such provision, and

(iii) on the request on behalf of an individual made not later than 24 months after the date of cessation of the coverage described in clause (i) or (ii), whichever is later.

The certification under clause (i) may be provided, to the extent practicable, at a time consistent with notices required under any applicable COBRA continuation provision.

(B) CERTIFICATION. The certification described in this subparagraph is a written certification of—

(i) the period of creditable coverage of the individual under such plan and the coverage (if any) under such COBRA continuation provision, and

(ii) the waiting period (if any) (and affiliation period, if applicable) imposed with respect to the individual for any coverage under such plan.

(C) ISSUER COMPLIANCE. To the extent that medical care under a group health plan consists of group health insurance coverage, the plan is deemed to have satisfied the certification requirement under this paragraph if the health insurance issuer offering the coverage provides for such certification in accordance with this paragraph.

(2) DISCLOSURE OF INFORMATION ON PREVIOUS BENEFITS. In the case of an election described in subsection (c)(3)(B) by a group health plan or health insurance issuer, if the plan or issuer enrolls an individual for coverage under the plan and the individual provides a certification of coverage of the individual under paragraph (1)—

(A) upon request of such plan or issuer, the entity which issued the certification provided by the individual shall promptly disclose to such requesting plan or issuer information on coverage of classes and categories of health benefits available under such entity's plan or coverage, and

(B) such entity may charge the requesting plan or issuer for the reasonable cost of disclosing such information.

(3) REGULATIONS. The Secretary shall establish rules to prevent an entity's failure to provide information under paragraph (1) or (2) with respect to previous coverage of an individual from adversely affecting any subsequent coverage of the individual under another group health plan or health insurance coverage.

(f) SPECIAL ENROLLMENT PERIODS.—

(f)(1) INDIVIDUALS LOSING OTHER COVERAGE. A group health plan, and a health insurance issuer offering group health insurance coverage in connection with a group health plan, shall permit an employee who is eligible, but not enrolled, for coverage under the terms of the plan (or a dependent of such an employee if the dependent is eligible, but not enrolled, for coverage under such terms) to enroll for coverage under the terms of the plan if each of the following conditions is met:

(A) The employee or dependent was covered under a group health plan or had health insurance coverage at the time coverage was previously offered to the employee or dependent.

(B) The employee stated in writing at such time that coverage under a group health plan or health insurance coverage was the reason for declining enrollment, but only if the plan sponsor or issuer (if applicable) required such a statement at such time and provided the employee with notice of such requirement (and the consequences of such requirement) at such time.

(C) The employee's or dependent's coverage described in subparagraph (A)—

(i) was under a COBRA continuation provision and the coverage under such provision was exhausted; or

(ii) was not under such a provision and either the coverage was terminated as a result of loss of eligibility for the coverage (including as a result of legal separation, divorce, death, termination of employment, or reduction in the number of hours of employment) or employer contributions toward such coverage were terminated.

(D) Under the terms of the plan, the employee requests such enrollment not later than 30 days after the date of exhaustion of coverage described in subparagraph (C)(i) or termination of coverage or employer contribution described in subparagraph (C)(ii).

(2) FOR DEPENDENT BENEFICIARIES—

(A) IN GENERAL. If—

(i) a group health plan makes coverage available with respect to a dependent of an individual,

(ii) the individual is a participant under the plan (or has met any waiting period applicable to becoming a participant under the plan and is eligible to be enrolled under the plan but for a failure to enroll during a previous enrollment period), and

(iii) a person becomes such a dependent of the individual through marriage, birth, or adoption or placement for adoption,

the group health plan shall provide for a dependent special enrollment period described in subparagraph (B) during which the person (or, if not otherwise enrolled, the individual) may be enrolled under the plan as a dependent of the individual, and in the case of the birth or adoption of a child, the spouse of the individual may be enrolled as a dependent of the individual if such spouse is otherwise eligible for coverage.

(B) DEPENDENT SPECIAL ENROLLMENT PERIOD. A dependent special enrollment period under this subparagraph shall be a period of not less than 30 days and shall begin on the later of—

(i) the date dependent coverage is made available, or

(ii) the date of the marriage, birth, or adoption or placement for adoption (as the case may be) described in subparagraph (A)(iii).

(C) NO WAITING PERIOD. If an individual seeks to enroll a dependent during the first 30 days of such a dependent special enrollment period, the coverage of the dependent shall become effective—

(i) in the case of marriage, not later than the first day of the first month beginning after the date the completed request for enrollment is received;

(ii) in the case of a dependent's birth, as of the date of such birth; or

(iii) in the case of a dependent's adoption or placement for adoption, the date of such adoption or placement for adoption.

(3) SPECIAL RULES FOR APPLICATION IN CASE OF MEDICAID AND CHIP.—

(A) IN GENERAL. —A group health plan, and a health insurance issuer offering group health insurance coverage in connection with a group health plan, shall permit an employee who is eligible, but not enrolled, for coverage under the terms of the plan (or a dependent of such an employee if the dependent is eligible, but not enrolled, for coverage under such terms) to enroll for coverage under the terms of the plan if either of the following conditions is met:

(i) TERMINATION OF MEDICAID OR CHIP COVERAGE. —The employee or dependent is covered under a Medicaid plan under title XIX of the Social Security Act or under a State child health plan under title XXI of such Act and coverage of the employee or dependent under such a plan is terminated as a result of loss of eligibility for such coverage and the employee requests coverage under the group health plan (or health insurance coverage) not later than 60 days after the date of termination of such coverage.

(ii) ELIGIBILITY FOR EMPLOYMENT ASSISTANCE UNDER MEDICAID OR CHIP. —The employee or dependent becomes eligible for assistance, with respect to coverage under the group health plan or health insurance coverage, under such Medicaid plan or State child health plan (including under any waiver or demonstration project conducted under or in relation to such a plan), if the employee requests coverage under the group health plan or health insurance coverage not later than 60 days after the date the employee or dependent is determined to be eligible for such assistance.

(B) COORDINATION WITH MEDICAID AND CHIP.—

(i) OUTREACH TO EMPLOYEES REGARDING AVAILABILITY OF MEDICAID AND CHIP COVERAGE.—

(I) IN GENERAL. —Each employer that maintains a group health plan in a State that provides medical assistance under a State Medicaid plan under title XIX of the Social Security Act, or child health assistance under a State child health plan under title XXI of such Act, in the form of premium assistance for the purchase of coverage under a group health plan, shall provide to each employee a written notice informing the employee of potential opportunities then currently available in the State in which the employee resides for premium assistance under such plans for health coverage of the employee or the employee's dependents.

(II) MODEL NOTICE. —Not later than 1 year after the date of enactment of the Children's Health Insurance Program Reauthorization Act of 2009, the Secretary and the Secretary of Health and Human Services, in consultation with Directors of State Medicaid agencies under title XIX of the Social Security Act and Directors of State CHIP agencies under title XXI of such Act, shall jointly develop national and State-specific model notices for purposes of subparagraph (A). The Secretary shall also provide employers with such model notices so as to enable employers to timely comply with the requirements of subparagraph (A). Such model notices shall include information regarding how an employee may contact the State in which the employee resides for additional information regarding potential opportunities for such premium assistance, including how to apply for such assistance.

(III) OPTION TO PROVIDE CONCURRENT WITH PROVISION OF PLAN MATERIALS TO EMPLOYEE. —An employer may provide the model notice applicable to the State in which an employee resides concurrent with the furnishing of materials notifying the employee of health plan eligibility, concurrent with materials provided to the employee in connection with an open season or election process conducted under the plan, or concurrent with the furnishing of the summary plan description as provided in section 104(b).

(ii) DISCLOSURE ABOUT GROUP HEALTH PLAN BENEFITS TO STATES FOR MEDICAID AND CHIP ELIGIBLE INDIVIDUALS. —In the case of a participant or beneficiary of a group health plan who is covered under a Medicaid plan of a State under title XIX of the Social Security Act or under a State child health plan under title XXI of such Act, the plan administrator of the group health plan shall disclose to the State, upon request, information about the benefits available under the group health plan in sufficient specificity, as determined under regulations of the Secretary of Health and Human Services in consultation with the Secretary that require use of the model coverage coordination disclosure form developed under section 311(b)(1)(C) of the Children's Health Insurance Program Reauthorization Act of 2009, so as to permit the State to make a determination (under paragraph (2)(B), (3), or (10) of section 2105(c) of the Social Security Act or otherwise) concerning the cost-effectiveness of the State providing medical or child health assistance through premium assistance for the purchase of coverage under such group health plan and in order for the State to provide supplemental benefits required under paragraph (10)(E) of such section or other authority.

(g) USE OF AFFILIATION PERIOD BY HMOs AS ALTERNATIVE TO PREEXISTING CONDITION EXCLUSION.—

(g)(1) IN GENERAL. In the case of a group health plan that offers medical care through health insurance coverage offered by a health maintenance organization, the plan may provide for an affiliation period with respect to coverage through the organization only if—

(A) no preexisting condition exclusion is imposed with respect to coverage through the organization,

(B) the period is applied uniformly without regard to any health status-related factors, and

(C) such period does not exceed 2 months (or 3 months in the case of a late enrollee).

(2) AFFILIATION PERIOD.—

(A) DEFINED. For purposes of this part, the term "affiliation period" means a period which, under the terms of the health insurance coverage offered by the health maintenance organization, must expire before the health insurance coverage becomes effective. The organization is not required to provide health care services or benefits during such period and no premium shall be charged to the participant or beneficiary for any coverage during the period.

(B) BEGINNING. Such period shall begin on the enrollment date.

(C) RUNS CONCURRENTLY WITH WAITING PERIODS. An affiliation period under a plan shall run concurrently with any waiting period under the plan.

(3) ALTERNATIVE METHODS. A health maintenance organization described in paragraph (1) may use alternative methods, from those described in such paragraph, to address adverse selection as approved by the State insurance commissioner or official or officials designated by the State to enforce the requirements of part A of title XXVII of the Public Health Service Act for the State involved with respect to such issuer.

Amendments

P.L. 112-040, §242(a)(2)(a):

Amended ERISA Sec. 701(c)(2)(C) by striking "February 13, 2011" and inserting "January 1, 2014".

The above amendment is effective for plan years beginning after February 12, 2011.

P.L. 112-040, §242(b)(2) provides:

(2) TRANSITIONAL RULES-

(A) BENEFIT DETERMINATIONS- Notwithstanding the amendments made by this section (and the provisions of law amended thereby), a plan shall not be required to modify benefit determinations for the period beginning on February 13, 2011, and ending 30 days after the date of the enactment of this Act, but a plan shall not fail to be qualified health insurance within the meaning of section 35(e) of the Internal Revenue Code of 1986 during this period merely due to such failure to modify benefit determinations.

(B) GUIDANCE CONCERNING PERIODS BEFORE 30 DAYS AFTER ENACTMENT- Except as provided in subparagraph (A), the Secretary of the Treasury (or his designee), in consultation with the Secretary of Health and Human Services and the Secretary of Labor, may issue regulations or other guidance regarding the scope of the application of the amendments made by this section to periods before the date which is 30 days after the date of the enactment of this Act.

(C) SPECIAL RULE RELATING TO CERTAIN LOSS OF COVERAGE-In the case of a TAA-related loss of coverage (as defined in section 4980B(f)(5)(C)(iv) of the Internal Revenue Code of 1986) that occurs during the period beginning on February 13, 2011, and ending 30 days after the date of the enactment of this Act, the 7-day period described in section 9801(c)(2)(D) of the Internal Revenue Code of 1986, section 701(c)(2)(C) of the Employee Retirement Income Security Act of 1974, and section 2701(c)(2)(C) of the Public Health Service Act shall be extended until 30 days after such date of enactment.

P.L. 111-344, §114(b):

Amended ERISA Sec. 701(c)(2)(C) by striking "January 1, 2011" and inserting "February 13, 2011".

The above amendment applies to plan years beginning after December 31, 2010.

P.L. 111-5, §1899D(b):

Amended ERISA Sec. 701(c)(2) by adding subparagraph (C) to read as above.

The above amendment applies to plan years beginning after the date of enactment [February 17, 2009].

P.L. 111-3, §311(b)(1)(A):

Amended ERISA Sec. 701(f) by adding at the end a new paragraph (3). For the **effective** date, see Act Sec. 3, below.

P.L. 111-3, §3, provides:

SEC. 3. GENERAL EFFECTIVE DATE; EXCEPTION FOR STATE LEGISLATION; CONTINGENT EFFECTIVE DATE; RELIANCE ON LAW.

(a) GENERAL EFFECTIVE DATE.—Unless otherwise provided in this Act, subject to subsections (b) through (d), this Act (and the amendments made by this Act) shall take effect on April 1, 2009, and shall apply to child health assistance and medical assistance provided on or after that date.

(b) EXCEPTION FOR STATE LEGISLATION.—In the case of a State plan under title XIX or State child health plan under XXI of the Social Security Act, which the Secretary of Health and Human Services determines requires State legislation in order for the respective plan to meet one or more additional requirements imposed by amendments made by this Act, the respective plan shall not be regarded as failing to comply with the requirements of such title solely on the basis of its failure to meet such an additional requirement before the first day of the first calendar quarter beginning after the close of the first regular session of the State legislature that begins after the date of enactment of this Act. For purposes of the previous sentence, in the case of a State that has a 2-year legislative session, each year of the session shall be considered to be a separate regular session of the State legislature.

(c) COORDINATION OF CHIP FUNDING FOR FISCAL YEAR 2009.—Notwithstanding any other provision of law, insofar as funds have been appropriated under section 2104(a)(11), 2104(k), or 2104(l) of the Social Security Act, as amended by section 201 of Public Law 110–173, to provide allotments to States under CHIP for fiscal year 2009—

(1) amounts that are so appropriated that are not so allotted and obligated before April 1, 2009 are rescinded; and

(2) any amount provided for CHIP allotments to a State under this Act (and the amendments made by this Act) for such fiscal year shall be reduced by the amount of such appropriations so allotted and obligated before such date.

(d) RELIANCE ON LAW.—With respect to amendments made by this Act (other than title VII) that become effective as of a date—

(1) such amendments are effective as of such date whether or not regulations implementing such amendments have been issued; and

(2) Federal financial participation for medical assistance or child health assistance furnished under title XIX or XXI, respectively, of the Social Security Act on or after such date by a State in good faith reliance on such amendments before the date of promulgation of final regulations, if any, to carry out such amendments (or before the date of guidance, if any, regarding the implementation of such amendments) shall not be denied on the basis of the State's failure to comply with such regulations or guidance.

P.L. 104-204, §603(b)(3)(H):

Amended ERISA Sec. 701(c)(1) by striking "section 706(c)" and inserting "section 733(c)".

The above amendment is effective for group health plans for plan years beginning on or after January 1, 1998.

P.L. 104-191, §101(a):

Added ERISA Sec. 701 to read as above.

The above amendments generally apply with respect to group health plans for plan years beginning after June 30, 1997. For special rules, see Act Sec. 101(g)(2)-(5), reproduced below.

Act Sec. 101(g)(2)-(5) reads as follows:

(g) EFFECTIVE DATES.—

(1) IN GENERAL.—Except as provided in this section, this section (and the amendments made by this section) shall apply with respect to group health plans for plan years beginning after June 30, 1997.

(2) DETERMINATION OF CREDITABLE COVERAGE.—

(A) PERIOD OF COVERAGE.—

(i) IN GENERAL.—Subject to clause (ii), no period before July 1, 1996, shall be taken into account under part 7 of subtitle B of title I of the Employee Retirement Income Security Act of 1974 (as added by this section) in determining creditable coverage.

(ii) SPECIAL RULE FOR CERTAIN PERIODS.—The Secretary of Labor, consistent with section 104, shall provide for a process whereby individuals who need to establish creditable coverage for periods before July 1, 1996, and who would have such coverage credited but for clause (i) may be given credit for creditable coverage for such periods through the presentation of documents or other means.

(B) CERTIFICATIONS, ETC.—

(i) IN GENERAL.—Subject to clauses (ii) and (iii), subsection (e) of section 701 of the Employee Retirement Income Security Act of 1974 (as added by this section) shall apply to events occurring after June 30, 1996.

(ii) NO CERTIFICATION REQUIRED TO BE PROVIDED BEFORE JUNE 1, 1997.—In no case is a certification required to be provided under such subsection before June 1, 1997.

(iii) CERTIFICATION ONLY ON WRITTEN REQUEST FOR EVENTS OCCURRING BEFORE OCTOBER 1, 1996.—In the case of an event occurring after June 30, 1996, and before October 1, 1996, a certification is not required to be provided under such subsection unless an individual (with respect to whom the certification is otherwise required to be made) requests such certification in writing.

(C) TRANSITIONAL RULE.—In the case of an individual who seeks to establish creditable coverage for any period for which certification is not required because it relates to an event occurring before June 30, 1996—

(i) the individual may present other credible evidence of such coverage in order to establish the period of creditable coverage; and

(ii) a group health plan and a health insurance issuer shall not be subject to any penalty or enforcement action with respect to the plan's or issuer's crediting (or not crediting) such coverage if the plan or issuer has sought to comply in good faith with the applicable requirements under the amendments made by this section.

(3) SPECIAL RULE FOR COLLECTIVE BARGAINING AGREEMENTS.—Except as provided in paragraph (2), in the case of a group health plan maintained pursuant to one or more collective bargaining agreements between employee representatives and one or more employers ratified before the date of the enactment of this Act, part 7 of subtitle B of title I of Employee Retirement Income Security Act of 1974 (other than section 701(e) thereof) shall not apply to plan years beginning before the later of—

(A) the date on which the last of the collective bargaining agreements relating to the plan terminates (determined without regard to any extension thereof agreed to after the date of the enactment of this Act), or

(B) July 1, 1997.

For purposes of subparagraph (A), any plan amendment made pursuant to a collective bargaining agreement relating to the plan which amends the plan solely to conform to any requirement of such part shall not be treated as a termination of such collective bargaining agreement.

(4) TIMELY REGULATIONS.—The Secretary of Labor, consistent with section 104, shall first issue by not later than April 1, 1997, such regulations as may be necessary to carry out the amendments made by this section.

(5) LIMITATION ON ACTIONS.—No enforcement action shall be taken, pursuant to the amendments made by this section, against a group health plan or health insurance issuer with respect to a violation of a requirement imposed by such amendments before January 1, 1998, or, if later, the date of issuance of regulations referred to in paragraph (4), if the plan or issuer has sought to comply in good faith with such requirements.

Regulations

The following regulations were adopted by 62 FR 16894 and published in the Federal Register on April 8, 1997, under "Chapter XXV of Title 29 of the Code of Federal Regulations; Subchapter L—Health Insurance Portability and Renewability for Group Health Plans; Part 2590—Rules and Regulations for Health Insurance Portability and Renewability for Group Health Plans." Reg. §§2590.701-2—2590.701-6 were officially corrected on June 10, 1997, by 62 FR 31690. Reg. §§2590.701-3—2590.701-6 were amended by 62 FR 35904 and published in the *Federal Register* on July 2, 1997. Reg. §§2590.701-1, 2590.701-2, 2590.701-3, 2590.701-4, 2590.701-5, 2590.701-6, and 2590.701-7 were revised by T.D. 9166 on December 30, 2004 (69 FR 78720). Reg. §§2590.701-1 and 2590.701-2 were amended October 7, 2009 (74 FR 51663). Reg. §§2590.701-2 and 2590.701-3 were amended June 28, 2010 (75 FR 37187). Reg. §§2590.701-1—2590.701-7 were amended February 24, 2014 (79 FR 10295). Reg. §§2590.701-2 and 2590.701-3 were amended November 18, 2015 (80 FR 72191). Reg. §2590.701-2 was amended October 31, 2016 (81 FR 75316).

[¶ 15,049I]

§2590.701-1 **Basis and scope.** (a) *Statutory basis.* This Subpart B implements Part 7 of Subtitle B of Title I of the Employee Retirement Income Security Act of 1974, as amended (hereinafter ERISA or the Act).

(b) *Scope.* A group health plan or health insurance issuer offering group health insurance coverage may provide greater rights to participants and beneficiaries than those set forth in this Subpart B. This Subpart B sets forth minimum requirements for group health plans and group health insurance issuers offering group health insurance coverage concerning certain consumer protections of the Health Insurance Portability and Accountability Act (HIPAA), including special enrollment periods and the prohibition against discrimination based on a health factor, as amended by the Patient Protection and Affordable Care Act (Affordable Care Act). Other consumer protection provisions, including other protections provided by the Affordable Care Act and the Mental Health Parity and Addiction Equity Act, are set forth in Subpart C of this part. [Amended 2/24/14 by 79 FR 10295.]

[¶ 15,049J]

§ 2590.701-2 **Definitions.** Unless otherwise provided, the definitions in this section govern in applying the provisions of §§ 2590.701 through 2590.734.

Affiliation period means a period of time that must expire before health insurance coverage provided by an HMO becomes effective, and during which the HMO is not required to provide benefits.

COBRA definitions:

(1) *COBRA* means Title X of the Consolidated Omnibus Budget Reconciliation Act of 1985, as amended.

(2) *COBRA continuation coverage* means coverage, under a group health plan, that satisfies an applicable COBRA continuation provision.

(3) *COBRA continuation provision* means sections 601-608 of the Act, section 4980B of the Internal Revenue Code (other than paragraph (f)(1) of such section 4980B insofar as it relates to pediatric vaccines), or Title XXII of the PHS Act.

(4) *Exhaustion of COBRA continuation coverage* means that an individual's COBRA continuation coverage ceases for any reason other than either failure of the individual to pay premiums on a timely basis, or for cause (such as making a fraudulent claim or an intentional misrepresentation of a material fact in connection with the plan). An individual is considered to have exhausted COBRA continuation coverage if such coverage ceases—

(i) Due to the failure of the employer or other responsible entity to remit premiums on a timely basis;

(ii) When the individual no longer resides, lives, or works in the service area of an HMO or similar program (whether or not within the choice of the individual) and there is no other COBRA continuation coverage available to the individual; or

(iii) When the individual incurs a claim that would meet or exceed a lifetime limit on all benefits and there is no other COBRA continuation coverage available to the individual.

Condition means a *medical condition.*

Creditable coverage means *creditable coverage* within the meaning of § 2590.701-4(a).

Dependent means any individual who is or may become eligible for coverage under the terms of a group health plan because of a relationship to a participant.

Enroll means to become covered for benefits under a group health plan (that is, when coverage becomes effective), without regard to when the individual may have completed or filed any forms that are required in order to become covered under the plan. For this purpose, an individual who has health coverage under a group health plan is enrolled in the plan regardless of whether the individual elects coverage, the individual is a dependent who becomes covered as a result of an election by a participant, or the individual becomes covered without an election.

Enrollment date means the first day of coverage or, if there is a waiting period, the first day of the waiting period. If an individual receiving benefits under a group health plan changes benefit packages, or if the plan changes group health insurance issuers, the individual's enrollment date does not change. [Amended 2/24/14 by 79 FR 10295.]

Excepted benefits means the benefits described as excepted in § 2590.732(c).

First day of coverage means, in the case of an individual covered for benefits under a group health plan, the first day of coverage under the plan and, in the case of an individual covered by health insurance coverage in the individual market, the first day of coverage under the policy or contract. [Added 2/24/14 by 79 FR 10295.]

Genetic information has the meaning given the term in § 2590.702-1(a)(3) of this Part [Amended 10/7/09 by 74 FR 51663.]

Group health insurance coverage means health insurance coverage offered in connection with a group health plan.

Group health plan or *plan* means a *group health plan* within the meaning of § 2590.732(a).

Group market means the market for health insurance coverage offered in connection with a group health plan. (However, certain very small plans may be treated as being in the individual market, rather than the group market; see the definition of *individual market* in this section.)

Health insurance coverage means benefits consisting of medical care (provided directly, through insurance or reimbursement, or otherwise) under any hospital or medical service policy or certificate, hospital or medical service plan contract, or HMO contract offered by a health insurance issuer. Health insurance coverage includes group health insurance coverage, individual health insurance coverage, and short-term, limited-duration insurance.

Health insurance issuer or *issuer* means an insurance company, insurance service, or insurance organization (including an HMO) that is required to be licensed to engage in the business of insurance in a State and that is subject to State law that regulates insurance (within the meaning of section 514(b)(2) of the Act). Such term does not include a group health plan.

Health maintenance organization or *HMO* means—

(1) A federally qualified health maintenance organization (as defined in section 1301(a) of the PHS Act);

(2) An organization recognized under State law as a health maintenance organization; or

(3) A similar organization regulated under State law for solvency in the same manner and to the same extent as such a health maintenance organization.

Individual health insurance coverage means health insurance coverage offered to individuals in the individual market, but does not include short-term, limited-duration insurance. Individual health insurance coverage can include dependent coverage.

Individual market means the market for health insurance coverage offered to individuals other than in connection with a group health plan. Unless a State elects otherwise in accordance with section 2791(e)(1)(B)(ii) of the PHS Act, such term also includes coverage offered in connection with a group health plan that has fewer than two participants who are current employees on the first day of the plan year.

Internal Revenue Code means the Internal Revenue Code of 1986, as amended (Title 26, United States Code).

Issuer means a *health insurance issuer.*

Late enrollee means an individual whose enrollment in a plan is a late enrollment. [Added 2/24/14 by 79 FR 10295.]

Late enrollment means enrollment of an individual under a group health plan other than on the earliest date on which coverage can become effective for the individual under the terms of the plan; or through special enrollment. (For rules relating to special enrollment, see § 2590.701-6.) If an individual ceases to be eligible for coverage under a plan, and then subsequently becomes eligible for coverage under the plan, only the individual's most recent period of eligibility is taken into account in determining whether the individual is a late enrollee under the plan with respect to the most recent period of coverage. Similar rules apply if an individual again becomes eligible for coverage following a suspension of coverage that applied generally under the plan. [Amended 2/24/14 by 79 FR 10295.]

Medical care means amounts paid for—

(1) The diagnosis, cure, mitigation, treatment, or prevention of disease, or amounts paid for the purpose of affecting any structure or function of the body;

(2) Transportation primarily for and essential to medical care referred to in paragraph (1) of this definition; and

(3) Insurance covering medical care referred to in paragraphs (1) and (2) of this definition.

Medical condition or *condition* means any condition, whether physical or mental, including, but not limited to, any condition resulting from illness, injury (whether or not the injury is accidental), pregnancy, or congenital malformation. However, genetic information is not a condition.

Participant means *participant* within the meaning of section 3(7) of the Act.

Placement, or being placed, for adoption means the assumption and retention of a legal obligation for total or partial support of a child by a person with whom the child has been placed in anticipation of the child's adoption. The child's placement for adoption with such person ends upon the termination of such legal obligation.

Plan year means the year that is designated as the plan year in the plan document of a group health plan, except that if the plan document does not designate a plan year or if there is no plan document, the plan year is—

(1) The deductible or limit year used under the plan;

(2) If the plan does not impose deductibles or limits on a yearly basis, then the plan year is the policy year;

(3) If the plan does not impose deductibles or limits on a yearly basis, and either the plan is not insured or the insurance policy is not renewed on an annual basis, then the plan year is the employer's taxable year; or

(4) In any other case, the plan year is the calendar year.

Preexisting condition exclusion means a limitation or exclusion of benefits (including a denial of coverage) based on the fact that the condition was present before the effective date of coverage (or if coverage is denied, the date of the denial) under a group health plan or group or individual health insurance coverage (or other coverage provided to Federally eligible individuals pursuant to 45 CFR part 148), whether or not any medical advice, diagnosis, care, or treatment was recommended or received before that day. A preexisting condition exclusion includes any limitation or exclusion of benefits (including a denial of coverage) applicable to an individual as a result of information relating to an individual's health status before the individual's effective date of coverage (or if coverage is denied, the date of the denial) under a group health plan, or group or individual health insurance coverage (or other coverage provided to Federally eligible individuals pursuant to 45 CFR part 148), such as a condition identified as a result of a pre-enrollment questionnaire or physical examination given to the individual, or review of medical records relating to the pre- enrollment period. [Amended 6/28/10 by 75 FR 37187. Amended 11/18/15 by 80 FR 72191.]

Public health plan means *public health plan* within the meaning of § 2590.701-4(a)(1)(ix).

Public Health Service Act (PHS Act) means the Public Health Service Act (42 U.S.C. 201, *et seq.*).

Short-term, limited-duration insurance means health insurance coverage provided pursuant to a contract with an issuer that:

(1) Has an expiration date specified in the contract (taking into account any extensions that may be elected by the policyholder with or without the issuer's consent) that is less than 3 months after the original effective date of the contract; and

(2) Displays prominently in the contract and in any application materials provided in connection with enrollment in such coverage in at least 14 point type the following: "THIS IS NOT QUALIFYING HEALTH COVERAGE ("MINIMUM ESSENTIAL COVERAGE") THAT SATISFIES THE HEALTH COVERAGE REQUIREMENT OF THE AFFORDABLE CARE ACT. IF YOU DON'T HAVE MINIMUM ESSENTIAL COVERAGE, YOU MAY OWE AN ADDITIONAL PAYMENT WITH YOUR TAXES." [Revised 10/31/16 by 81 FR 75316.]

Significant break in coverage means a *significant break in coverage* within the meaning of § 2590.701-4(b)(2)(iii).

Special enrollment means enrollment in a group health plan or group health insurance coverage under the rights described in § 2590.701-6.

State means each of the several States, the District of Columbia, Puerto Rico, the Virgin Islands, Guam, American Samoa, and the Northern Mariana Islands.

State health benefits risk pool means a *State health benefits risk pool* within the meaning of § 2590.701-4(a)(1)(vii).

Travel insurance means insurance coverage for personal risks incident to planned travel, which may include, but is not limited to, interruption or cancellation of trip or event, loss of baggage or personal effects, damages to accommodations or rental vehicles, and sickness, accident, disability, or death occurring during travel, provided that the health benefits are not offered on a stand-alone basis and are incidental to other coverage. For this purpose, the term travel insurance does not include major medical plans that provide comprehensive medical protection for travelers with trips lasting 6 months or longer, including, for

example, those working overseas as an expatriate or military personnel being deployed. [Added 10/31/16 by 81 FR 75316.]

Waiting period means *waiting period* within the meaning of § 2590.715-2708(b). [Amended 2/24/14 by 79 FR 10295.]

[¶ 15,049K]

§ 2590.701-3 **Limitations on preexisting condition exclusion period. [Amended 2/24/14 by 79 FR 10295. Amended 11/18/15 by 80 FR 72191.].** (a) *Preexisting condition exclusion defined*— [Amended 2/24/14 by 79 FR 10295.]. (1) A *preexisting condition exclusion* means a *preexisting condition exclusion* within the meaning of § 2590.701–2. [Redesignated 2/24/14 by 79 FR 10295). Amended 11/18/15 by 80 FR 72191.]

(2) *Examples.* The rules of this paragraph (a)(1) are illustrated by the following examples:

Example 1. (i) *Facts.* A group health plan provides benefits solely through an insurance policy offered by Issuer *S.* At the expiration of the policy, the plan switches coverage to a policy offered by Issuer *T.* Issuer *T*'s policy excludes benefits for any prosthesis if the body part was lost before the effective date of coverage under the policy.

(ii) *Conclusion.* In this *Example 1,* the exclusion of benefits for any prosthesis if the body part was lost before the effective date of coverage is a preexisting condition exclusion because it operates to exclude benefits for a condition based on the fact that the condition was present before the effective date of coverage under the policy. The exclusion of benefits, therefore, is prohibited. [Amended 2/24/14 by 79 FR 10295.]

Example 2. (i) *Facts.* A group health plan provides coverage for cosmetic surgery in cases of accidental injury, but only if the injury occurred while the individual was covered under the plan.

(ii) *Conclusion.* In this *Example 2,* the plan provision excluding cosmetic surgery benefits for individuals injured before enrolling in the plan is a preexisting condition exclusion because it operates to exclude benefits relating to a condition based on the fact that the condition was present before the effective date of coverage. The plan provision, therefore, is prohibited. [Amended 2/24/14 by 79 FR 10295.]

Example 3. (i) *Facts.* A group health plan provides coverage for the treatment of diabetes, generally not subject to any requirement to obtain an approval for a treatment plan. However, if an individual was diagnosed with diabetes before the effective date of coverage under the plan, diabetes coverage is subject to a requirement to obtain approval of a treatment plan in advance.

(ii) *Conclusion.* In this *Example 3,* the requirement to obtain advance approval of a treatment plan is a preexisting condition exclusion because it limits benefits for a condition based on the fact that the condition was present before the effective date of coverage. The plan provision, therefore, is prohibited. [Amended 2/24/14 by 79 FR 10295.]

Example 4. (i) *Facts.* A group health plan provides coverage for three infertility treatments. The plan counts against the three-treatment limit benefits provided under prior health coverage.

(ii) *Conclusion.* In this *Example 4,* counting benefits for a specific condition provided under prior health coverage against a treatment limit for that condition is a preexisting condition exclusion because it operates to limit benefits for a condition based on the fact that the condition was present before the effective date of coverage. The plan provision, therefore, is prohibited. [Amended 2/24/14 by 79 FR 10295.]

Example 5. (i) *Facts.* When an individual's coverage begins under a group health plan, the individual generally becomes eligible for all benefits. However, benefits for pregnancy are not available until the individual has been covered under the plan for 12 months.

(ii) *Conclusion.* In this *Example 5,* the requirement to be covered under the plan for 12 months to be eligible for pregnancy benefits is a subterfuge for a preexisting condition exclusion because it is designed to exclude benefits for a condition (pregnancy) that arose before the effective date of coverage. The plan provision, therefore, is prohibited. [Amended 2/24/14 by 79 FR 10295.]

Example 6. (i) *Facts.* A group health plan provides coverage for medically necessary items and services, generally including treatment of heart conditions. However, the plan does not cover those same items and services when used for treatment of congenital heart conditions.

(ii) *Conclusion.* In this *Example 6,* the exclusion of coverage for treatment of congenital heart conditions is a preexisting condition exclusion because it operates to exclude benefits relating to a condition based on the fact that the condition was present before the effective date of coverage. The plan provision, therefore, is prohibited. [Amended 2/24/14 by 79 FR 10295.]

Example 7. (i) *Facts.* A group health plan generally provides coverage for medically necessary items and services. However, the plan excludes coverage for the treatment of cleft palate.

(ii) *Conclusion.* In this *Example 7,* the exclusion of coverage for treatment of cleft palate is not a preexisting condition exclusion because the exclusion applies regardless of when the condition arose relative to the effective date of coverage. The plan provision, therefore, is not prohibited. (But see 45 CFR 147.150, which may require coverage of cleft palate as an essential health benefit for health insurance coverage in the individual or small group market, depending on the essential health benefits benchmark plan as defined in 45 CFR 156.20). [Amended 2/24/14 by 79 FR 10295.]

Example 8. (i) *Facts.* A group health plan provides coverage for treatment of cleft palate, but only if the individual being treated has been continuously covered under the plan from the date of birth.

(ii) *Conclusion.* In this *Example 8,* the exclusion of coverage for treatment of cleft palate for individuals who have not been covered under the plan from the date of birth operates to exclude benefits in relation to a condition based on the fact that the condition was present before the effective date of coverage. The plan provision, therefore, is prohibited. [Redesignated and amended 2/24/14 by 79 FR 10295.]

(3) *Enrollment definitions.* [Removed 2/24/14 by 79 FR 10295.]

(b) *General rules. See* § 2590.715-2704 for rules prohibiting the imposition of a preexisting condition exclusion. [Amended 2/24/14 by 79 FR 10295.]

(c) *General notice of preexisting condition exclusion.* [Removed 2/24/14 by 79 FR 10295.]

(d) *Determination of creditable coverage.* [Removed 2/24/14 79 FR 10295.]

(e) *Individual notice of period of preexisting condition exclusion.* [Removed 2/24/14 by 79 FR 10295.]

(f) *Reconsideration.* [Removed 2/24/14 by 79 FR 10295.]

[¶ 15,049L]

§ 2590.701-4 **Rules relating to creditable coverage.** (a) *General rules.* (1) *Creditable coverage.* For purposes of this section, except as provided in paragraph (a)(2) of this section, the term *creditable coverage* means coverage of an individual under any of the following:

(i) A group health plan as defined in § 2590.732(a).

(ii) Health insurance coverage as defined in § 2590.701-2 (whether or not the entity offering the coverage is subject to Part 7 of Subtitle B of Title I of the Act, and without regard to whether the coverage is offered in the group market, the individual market, or otherwise).

(iii) Part A or B of Title XVIII of the Social Security Act (Medicare).

(iv) Title XIX of the Social Security Act (Medicaid), other than coverage consisting solely of benefits under section 1928 of the Social Security Act (the program for distribution of pediatric vaccines).

(v) Title 10 U.S.C. Chapter 55 (medical and dental care for members and certain former members of the uniformed services, and for their dependents; for purposes of Title 10 U.S.C. Chapter 55, *uniformed services* means the armed forces and the Commissioned Corps of the National Oceanic and Atmospheric Administration and of the Public Health Service).

(vi) A medical care program of the Indian Health Service or of a tribal organization.

(vii) A State health benefits risk pool. For purposes of this section, a *State health benefits risk pool* means—

(A) An organization qualifying under section 501(c)(26) of the Internal Revenue Code;

(B) A qualified high risk pool described in section 2744(c)(2) of the PHS Act; or

(C) Any other arrangement sponsored by a State, the membership composition of which is specified by the State and which is established and maintained primarily to provide health coverage for individuals who are residents of such State and who, by reason of the existence or history of a medical condition—

(1) Are unable to acquire medical care coverage for such condition through insurance or from an HMO, or

(2) Are able to acquire such coverage only at a rate which is substantially in excess of the rate for such coverage through the membership organization.

(viii) A health plan offered under Title 5 U.S.C. Chapter 89 (the Federal Employees Health Benefits Program).

(ix) A public health plan. For purposes of this section, a *public health plan* means any plan established or maintained by a State, the U.S. government, a foreign country, or any political subdivision of a State, the U.S. government, or a foreign country that provides health coverage to individuals who are enrolled in the plan.

(x) A health benefit plan under section 5(e) of the Peace Corps Act (22 U.S.C. 2504(e)).

(xi) Title XXI of the Social Security Act (State Children's Health Insurance Program).

(2) *Excluded coverage.* Creditable coverage does not include coverage of solely excepted benefits (described in § 2590.732).

(3) *Methods of counting creditable coverage.* [Removed 2/24/14 by 79 FR 10295.]

(b) *Counting creditable coverage rules superseded by prohibition on preexisting condition exclusion. See* § 2590.715-2704 for rules prohibiting the imposition of a preexisting condition exclusion. [Amended 2/24/14 by 79 FR 10295.]

(c) *Alternative method.* [Removed 2/24/14 by 79 FR 10295.]

[¶ 15,049M]

§ 2590.701-5 **Evidence of creditable coverage.** (a) *In general.* The rules for providing certificates of creditable coverage and demonstrating creditable coverage have been superseded by the prohibition on preexisting condition exclusions. *See* section 2704 of the Public Health Service Act, incorporated into section 9815 of the Code, and its implementing regulations for rules prohibiting the imposition of a preexisting condition exclusion.

(b) *Applicability.* The provisions of this section apply beginning December 31, 2014. [Amended 2/24/14 by 79 FR 10295.]

[¶ 15,049N]

§ 2590.701-6 **Special enrollment periods.** (a) *Special enrollment for certain individuals who lose coverage.* (1) *In general.* A group health plan, and a health insurance issuer offering health insurance coverage in connection with a group health plan, is required to permit current employees and dependents (as defined in § 2590.701-2) who are described in paragraph (a)(2) of this section to enroll for coverage under the terms of the plan if the conditions in paragraph (a)(3) of this section are satisfied. The special enrollment rights under this paragraph (a) apply without regard to the dates on which an individual would otherwise be able to enroll under the plan.

(2) *Individuals eligible for special enrollment.* (i) *When employee loses coverage.* A current employee and any dependents (including the employee's spouse) each are eligible for special enrollment in any benefit package under the plan (subject to plan eligibility rules conditioning dependent enrollment on enrollment of the employee) if—

(A) The employee and the dependents are otherwise eligible to enroll in the benefit package;

(B) When coverage under the plan was previously offered, the employee had coverage under any group health plan or health insurance coverage; and

(C) The employee satisfies the conditions of paragraph (a)(3)(i), (ii), or (iii) of this section and, if applicable, paragraph (a)(3)(iv) of this section.

(ii) *When dependent loses coverage.* (A) A dependent of a current employee (including the employee's spouse) and the employee each are eligible for special enrollment in any benefit package under the plan (subject to plan eligibility rules conditioning dependent enrollment on enrollment of the employee) if—

(1) The dependent and the employee are otherwise eligible to enroll in the benefit package;

(2) When coverage under the plan was previously offered, the dependent had coverage under any group health plan or health insurance coverage; and

(3) The dependent satisfies the conditions of paragraph (a)(3)(i), (ii), or (iii) of this section and, if applicable, paragraph (a)(3)(iv) of this section.

(B) However, the plan or issuer is not required to enroll any other dependent unless that dependent satisfies the criteria of this paragraph (a)(2)(ii), or the employee satisfies the criteria of paragraph (a)(2)(i) of this section.

(iii) *Examples.* The rules of this paragraph (a)(2) are illustrated by the following examples:

Example 1. (i) *Facts.* Individual *A* works for Employer *X*. *A*, *A*'s spouse, and *A*'s dependent children are eligible but not enrolled for coverage under *X*'s group health plan. *A*'s spouse works for Employer *Y* and at the time coverage was offered under *X*'s plan, *A* was enrolled in coverage under *Y*'s plan. Then, *A* loses eligibility for coverage under *Y*'s plan.

(ii) *Conclusion.* In this *Example 1*, because *A* satisfies the conditions for special enrollment under paragraph (a)(2)(i) of this section, *A*, *A*'s spouse, and *A*'s dependent children are eligible for special enrollment under *X*'s plan.

Example 2. (i) *Facts.* Individual *A* and *A*'s spouse are eligible but not enrolled for coverage under Group Health Plan *P* maintained by *A*'s employer. When *A* was first presented with an opportunity to enroll *A* and *A*'s spouse, they did not have other coverage. Later, *A* and *A*'s spouse enroll in Group Health Plan *Q* maintained by the employer of *A*'s spouse. During a subsequent open enrollment period in *P*, *A* and *A*'s spouse did not enroll because of their coverage under *Q*. They then lose eligibility for coverage under *Q*.

(ii) *Conclusion.* In this *Example 2*, because *A* and *A*'s spouse were covered under *Q* when they did not enroll in *P* during open enrollment, they satisfy the conditions for special enrollment under paragraphs (a)(2)(i) and (ii) of this section. Consequently, *A* and *A*'s spouse are eligible for special enrollment under *P*.

Example 3. (i) *Facts.* Individual *B* works for Employer *X*. *B* and *B*'s spouse are eligible but not enrolled for coverage under *X*'s group health plan. *B*'s spouse works for Employer *Y* and at the time coverage was offered under *X*'s plan, *B*'s spouse was enrolled in self-only coverage under *Y*'s group health plan. Then, *B*'s spouse loses eligibility for coverage under *Y*'s plan.

(ii) *Conclusion.* In this *Example 3*, because *B*'s spouse satisfies the conditions for special enrollment under paragraph (a)(2)(ii) of this section, both *B* and *B*'s spouse are eligible for special enrollment under *X*'s plan.

Example 4. (i) *Facts.* Individual *A* works for Employer *X*. *X* maintains a group health plan with two benefit packages—an HMO option and an indemnity option. Self-only and family coverage are available under both options. *A* enrolls for self-only coverage in the HMO option. *A*'s spouse works for Employer *Y* and was enrolled for self-only coverage under *Y*'s plan at the time coverage was offered under *X*'s plan. Then, *A*'s spouse loses coverage under *Y*'s plan. *A* requests special enrollment for *A* and *A*'s spouse under the plan's indemnity option.

(ii) *Conclusion.* In this *Example 4*, because *A*'s spouse satisfies the conditions for special enrollment under paragraph (a)(2)(ii) of this section, both *B* and *A*'s spouse can enroll in either benefit package under *X*'s plan. Therefore, if *A* requests enrollment in accordance with the requirements of this section, the plan must allow *A* and *A*'s spouse to enroll in the indemnity option.

(3) *Conditions for special enrollment.* (i) *Loss of eligibility for coverage.* In the case of an employee or dependent who has coverage that is not COBRA continuation coverage, the conditions of this paragraph (a)(3)(i) are satisfied at the time the coverage is terminated as a result of loss of eligibility (regardless of whether the individual is eligible for or elects COBRA continuation coverage). Loss of eligibility under this paragraph (a)(3)(i) does not include a loss due to the failure of the employee or dependent to pay premiums on a timely basis or termination of coverage for cause (such as making a fraudulent claim or an intentional misrepresentation of a material fact in connection with the plan). Loss of eligibility for coverage under this paragraph (a)(3)(i) includes (but is not limited to)—

(A) Loss of eligibility for coverage as a result of legal separation, divorce, cessation of dependent status (such as attaining the maximum age to be eligible as a dependent child under the plan), death of an employee, termination of employment, reduction in the number of hours of employment, and any loss of eligibility for coverage after a period that is measured by reference to any of the foregoing;

(B) In the case of coverage offered through an HMO, or other arrangement, in the individual market that does not provide benefits to individuals who no longer reside, live, or work in a service area, loss of coverage because an individual no longer resides, lives, or works in the service area (whether or not within the choice of the individual);

(C) In the case of coverage offered through an HMO, or other arrangement, in the group market that does not provide benefits to individuals who no longer reside, live, or work in a service area, loss of coverage because an individual no longer resides, lives, or works in the service area (whether or not within the choice of the individual), and no other benefit package is available to the individual; and [Amended 2/24/14 by 79 FR 10295.]

(D) A situation in which a plan no longer offers any benefits to the class of similarly situated individuals (as described in § 2590.702(d)) that includes the individual. [Amended 2/24/14 by 79 FR 10295.]

(E) [Removed 2/24/14 by 79 FR 10295.]

(ii) *Termination of employer contributions.* In the case of an employee or dependent who has coverage that is not COBRA continuation coverage, the conditions of this paragraph (a)(3)(ii) are satisfied at the time employer contributions towards the employee's or dependent's coverage terminate. Employer contributions include contributions by any current or former employer that was contributing to coverage for the employee or dependent.

(iii) *Exhaustion of COBRA continuation coverage.* In the case of an employee or dependent who has coverage that is COBRA continuation coverage, the conditions of this paragraph (a)(3)(iii) are satisfied at the time the COBRA continuation coverage is exhausted. For purposes of this paragraph (a)(3)(iii), an individual who satisfies the conditions for special enrollment of paragraph (a)(3)(i) of this section, does not enroll, and instead elects and exhausts COBRA continuation coverage satisfies the conditions of this paragraph (a)(3)(iii). (*Exhaustion of COBRA continuation coverage* is defined in § 2590.701-2.)

(iv) *Written statement.* A plan may require an employee declining coverage (for the employee or any dependent of the employee) to State in writing whether the coverage is being declined due to other health coverage only if, at or before the time the employee declines coverage, the employee is provided with notice of the requirement to provide the statement (and the consequences of the employee's failure to provide the statement). If a plan requires such a statement, and an employee does not provide it, the plan is not required to provide special enrollment to the employee or any dependent of the employee under this paragraph (a)(3). A plan must treat an employee as having satisfied the plan requirement permitted under this paragraph (a)(3)(iv) if the employee provides a written statement that coverage was being declined because the employee or dependent had other coverage; a plan cannot require anything more for the employee to satisfy the plan's requirement to provide a written statement. (For example, the plan cannot require that the statement be notarized.)

(v) The rules of this paragraph (a)(3) are illustrated by the following examples:

Example 1. (i) *Facts.* Individual *D* enrolls in a group health plan maintained by Employer *Y.* At the time *D* enrolls, *Y* pays 70 percent of the cost of employee coverage and *D* pays the rest. *Y* announces that beginning January 1, *Y* will no longer make employer contributions towards the coverage. Employees may maintain coverage, however, if they pay the total cost of the coverage.

(ii) *Conclusion.* In this *Example 1,* employer contributions towards *D*'s coverage ceased on January 1 and the conditions of paragraph (a)(3)(ii) of this section are satisfied on this date (regardless of whether *D* elects to pay the total cost and continue coverage under *Y*'s plan).

Example 2. (i) *Facts.* A group health plan provides coverage through two options—Option 1 and Option 2. Employees can enroll in either option only within 30 days of hire or on January 1 of each year. Employee *A* is eligible for both options and enrolls in Option 1. Effective July 1 the plan terminates coverage under Option 1 and the plan does not create an immediate open enrollment opportunity into Option 2.

(ii) *Conclusion.* In this *Example 2,* A has experienced a loss of eligibility for coverage that satisfies paragraph (a)(3)(i) of this section, and has satisfied the other conditions for special enrollment under paragraph (a)(2)(i) of this section. Therefore, if *A* satisfies the other conditions of this paragraph (a), the plan must permit *A* to enroll in Option 2 as a special enrollee. (*A* may also be eligible to enroll in another group health plan, such as a plan maintained by the employer of *A*'s spouse, as a special enrollee.) The outcome would be the same if Option 1 was terminated by an issuer and the plan made no other coverage available to *A.*

Example 3. (i) *Facts.* Individual *C* is covered under a group health plan maintained by Employer *X.* While covered under *X*'s plan, *C* was eligible for but did not enroll in a plan maintained by Employer *Z,* the employer of *C*'s spouse. *C* terminates employment with *X* and loses eligibility for coverage under *X*'s plan. *C* has a special enrollment right to enroll in *Z*'s plan, but *C* instead elects COBRA continuation coverage under *X*'s plan. *C* exhausts COBRA continuation coverage under *X*'s plan and requests special enrollment in *Z*'s plan.

(ii) *Conclusion.* In this *Example 3, C* has satisfied the conditions for special enrollment under paragraph (a)(3)(iii) of this section, and has satisfied the other conditions for special enrollment under paragraph (a)(2)(i) of this section. The special enrollment right that *C* had into *Z*'s plan immediately after the loss of eligibility for coverage under *X*'s plan was an offer of coverage under *Z*'s plan. When *C* later exhausts COBRA coverage under *X*'s plan, *C* has a second special enrollment right in *Z*'s plan.

(4) *Applying for special enrollment and effective date of coverage.* (i) A plan or issuer must allow an employee a period of at least 30 days after an event described in paragraph (a)(3) of this section to request enrollment (for the employee or the employee's dependent). [Amended 2/24/14 by 79 FR 10295.]

(ii) Coverage must begin no later than the first day of the first calendar month beginning after the date the plan or issuer receives the request for special enrollment.

(b) *Special enrollment with respect to certain dependent beneficiaries.* (1) *In general.* A group health plan, and a health insurance issuer offering health insurance coverage in connection with a group health plan, that makes coverage available with respect to dependents is required to permit individuals described in paragraph (b)(2) of this section to be enrolled for coverage in a benefit package under the terms of the plan. Paragraph (b)(3) of this section describes the required special enrollment period and the date by which coverage must begin. The special enrollment rights under this paragraph (b) apply without regard to the dates on which an individual would otherwise be able to enroll under the plan.

(2) *Individuals eligible for special enrollment.* An individual is described in this paragraph (b)(2) if the individual is otherwise eligible for coverage in a benefit package under the plan and if the individual is described in paragraph (b)(2)(i), (ii), (iii), (iv), (v), or (vi) of this section.

(i) *Current employee only.* A current employee is described in this paragraph (b)(2)(i) if a person becomes a dependent of the individual through marriage, birth, adoption, or placement for adoption.

(ii) *Spouse of a participant only.* An individual is described in this paragraph (b)(2)(ii) if either —

(A) The individual becomes the spouse of a participant; or

(B) The individual is a spouse of a participant and a child becomes a dependent of the participant through birth, adoption, or placement for adoption.

(iii) *Current employee and spouse.* A current employee and an individual who is or becomes a spouse of such an employee, are described in this paragraph (b)(2)(iii) if either—

(A) The employee and the spouse become married; or

(B) The employee and spouse are married and a child becomes a dependent of the employee through birth, adoption, or placement for adoption.

(iv) *Dependent of a participant only.* An individual is described in this paragraph (b)(2)(iv) if the individual is a dependent (as defined in § 2590.701- 2) of a participant and the individual has become a dependent of the participant through marriage, birth, adoption, or placement for adoption.

(v) *Current employee and a new dependent.* A current employee and an individual who is a dependent of the employee, are described in this paragraph (b)(2)(v) if the individual becomes a dependent of the employee through marriage, birth, adoption, or placement for adoption.

(vi) *Current employee, spouse, and a new dependent.* A current employee, the employee's spouse, and the employee's dependent are described in this paragraph (b)(2)(vi) if the dependent becomes a dependent of the employee through marriage, birth, adoption, or placement for adoption.

(3) *Applying for special enrollment and effective date of coverage.* (i) *Request.* A plan or issuer must allow an individual a period of at least 30 days after the date of the marriage, birth, adoption, or placement for adoption (or, if dependent coverage is not generally made available at the time of the marriage, birth, adoption, or placement for adoption, a period of at least 30 days after the date the plan makes dependent coverage generally available) to request enrollment (for the individual or the individual's dependent).

(ii) *Reasonable procedures for special enrollment.* [Reserved]

(iii) *Date coverage must begin.* (A) *Marriage.* In the case of marriage, coverage must begin no later than the first day of the first calendar month beginning after the date the plan or issuer receives the request for special enrollment.

(B) *Birth, adoption, or placement for adoption.* Coverage must begin in the case of a dependent's birth on the date of birth and in the case of a dependent's adoption or placement for adoption no later than the date of such adoption or placement for adoption (or, if dependent coverage is not made generally available at the time of the birth, adoption, or placement for adoption, the date the plan makes dependent coverage available).

(4) *Examples.* The rules of this paragraph (b) are illustrated by the following examples:

Example 1. (i) *Facts.* An employer maintains a group health plan that offers all employees employee-only coverage, employee-plus-spouse coverage, or family coverage. Under the terms of the plan, any employee may elect to enroll when first hired (with coverage beginning on the date of hire) or during an annual open enrollment period held each December (with coverage beginning the following January 1). Employee *A* is hired on September 3. *A* is married to *B,* and they have no children. On March 15 in the following year a child *C* is born to *A* and *B.* Before that date, *A* and *B* have not been enrolled in the plan.

(ii) *Conclusion.* In this *Example 1,* the conditions for special enrollment of an employee with a spouse and new dependent under paragraph (b)(2)(vi) of this section are satisfied. If *A* satisfies the conditions of paragraph (b)(3) of this section for requesting enrollment timely, the plan will satisfy this paragraph (b) if it allows *A* to enroll either with employee-only coverage, with employee-plus-spouse coverage (for *A* and *B*), or with family coverage (for *A, B,* and *C*). The plan must allow whatever coverage is chosen to begin on March 15, the date of *C*'s birth.

Example 2. (i) *Facts.* Individual *D* works for Employer X. *X* maintains a group health plan with two benefit packages—an HMO option and an indemnity option. Self-only and family coverage are available under both options. *D* enrolls for self-only coverage in the HMO option. Then, a child, E, is placed for adoption with *D*. Within 30 days of the placement of *E* for adoption, *D* requests enrollment for *D* and *E* under the plan's indemnity option.

(ii) *Conclusion.* In this *Example 2, D* and *E* satisfy the conditions for special enrollment under paragraphs (b)(2)(v) and (b)(3) of this section. Therefore, the plan must allow *D* and *E* to enroll in the indemnity coverage, effective as of the date of the placement for adoption.

(c) *Notice of special enrollment.* At or before the time an employee is initially offered the opportunity to enroll in a group health plan, the plan must furnish the employee with a notice of special enrollment that complies with the requirements of this paragraph (c).

(1) *Description of special enrollment rights.* The notice of special enrollment must include a description of special enrollment rights. The following model language may be used to satisfy this requirement:

If you are declining enrollment for yourself or your dependents (including your spouse) because of other health insurance or group health plan coverage, you may be able to enroll yourself and your dependents in this plan if you or your dependents lose eligibility for that other coverage (or if the employer stops contributing towards your or your dependents' other coverage). However, you must request enrollment within [insert "30 days" or any longer period that applies under the plan] after your or your dependents' other coverage ends (or after the employer stops contributing toward the other coverage).

In addition, if you have a new dependent as a result of marriage, birth, adoption, or placement for adoption, you may be able to enroll yourself and your dependents. However, you must request enrollment within [insert "30 days" or any longer period that applies under the plan] after the marriage, birth, adoption, or placement for adoption.

To request special enrollment or obtain more information, contact [insert the name, title, telephone number, and any additional contact information of the appropriate plan representative].

(2) *Additional information that may be required.* The notice of special enrollment must also include, if applicable, the notice described in paragraph (a)(3)(iv) of this section (the notice required to be furnished to an individual declining coverage if the plan requires the reason for declining coverage to be in writing).

(d) *Treatment of special enrollees.* (1) If an individual requests enrollment while the individual is entitled to special enrollment under either paragraph (a) or (b) of this section, the individual is a special enrollee, even if the request for enrollment coincides with a late enrollment opportunity under the plan. Therefore, the individual cannot be treated as a late enrollee.

(2) Special enrollees must be offered all the benefit packages available to similarly situated individuals who enroll when first eligible. For this purpose, any difference in benefits or cost-sharing requirements for different individuals constitutes a different benefit package. In addition, a special enrollee cannot be required to pay more for coverage than a similarly situated individual who enrolls in the same coverage when first eligible. [Amended 2/24/14 by 79 FR 10295.]

(3) The rules of this section are illustrated by the following example:

Example. (i) *Facts.* Employer *Y* maintains a group health plan that has an enrollment period for late enrollees every November 1 through November 30 with coverage effective the following January 1. On October 18, Individual *B* loses coverage under another group health plan and satisfies the requirements of paragraphs (a)(2), (3), and (4) of this section. *B* submits a completed application for coverage on November 2.

(ii) *Conclusion.* In this *Example, B* is a special enrollee. Therefore, even though *B*'s request for enrollment coincides with an open enrollment period, *B*'s coverage is required to be made effective no later than December 1 (rather than the plan's January 1 effective date for late enrollees).

[¶ 15,049O]

§ 2590.701-7 **HMO affiliation period as an alternative to a preexisting condition exclusion.** The rules for HMO affiliation periods have been superseded by the prohibition on preexisting condition exclusions. *See* § 2590.715-2704 for rules prohibiting the imposition of a preexisting condition exclusion. [Amended 2/24/14 by 79 FR 10295.]

[¶ 15,049P]

§ 2590.701-8 **Interaction with the Family and Medical Leave Act.** [Reserved].

[¶ 15,050A]
PROHIBITING DISCRIMINATION AGAINST INDIVIDUAL PARTICIPANTS AND BENEFICIARIES BASED ON HEALTH STATUS

Act Sec. 702.(a) In Eligibility to Enroll.—

(1) In GENERAL. Subject to paragraph (2), a group health plan, and a health insurance issuer offering group health insurance coverage in connection with a group health plan, may not establish rules for eligibility (including continued eligibility) of any individual to enroll under the terms of the plan based on any of the following health status-related factors in relation to the individual or a dependent of the individual:

(A) Health status.

(B) Medical condition (including both physical and mental illnesses).

(C) Claims experience.

(D) Receipt of health care.

(E) Medical history.

(F) Genetic information.

(G) Evidence of insurability (including conditions arising out of acts of domestic violence).

(H) Disability.

(2) No APPLICATION TO BENEFITS OR EXCLUSIONS. To the extent consistent with section 701, paragraph (1) shall not be construed—

(A) to require a group health plan, or group health insurance coverage, to provide particular benefits other than those provided under the terms of such plan or coverage, or

(B) to prevent such a plan or coverage from establishing limitations or restrictions on the amount, level, extent, or nature of the benefits or coverage for similarly situated individuals enrolled in the plan or coverage.

(3) CONSTRUCTION. For purposes of paragraph (1), rules for eligibility to enroll under a plan include rules defining any applicable waiting periods for such enrollment.

Act Sec. 702(b). In Premium Contributions.—

(1) In GENERAL.—A group health plan, and a health insurance issuer offering health insurance coverage in connection with a group health plan, may not require any individual (as a condition of enrollment or continued enrollment under the plan) to pay a premium or contribution which is greater than such

premium or contribution for a similarly situated individual enrolled in the plan on the basis of any health status-related factor in relation to the individual or to an individual enrolled under the plan as a dependent of the individual.

(2) CONSTRUCTION.—Nothing in paragraph (1) shall be construed—

(A) to restrict the amount that an employer may be charged for coverage under a group health plan except as provided in paragraph (3); or

(B) to prevent a group health plan, and a health insurance issuer offering group health insurance coverage, from establishing premium discounts or rebates or modifying otherwise applicable copayments or deductibles in return for adherence to programs of health promotion and disease prevention.

(3) NO GROUP-BASED DISCRIMINATION ON BASIS OF GENETIC INFORMATION—

(A) IN GENERAL—For purposes of this section, a group health plan, and a health insurance issuer offering group health insurance coverage in connection with a group health plan, may not adjust premium or contribution amounts for the group covered under such plan on the basis of genetic information.

(B) RULE OF CONSTRUCTION—Nothing in subparagraph (A) or in paragraphs (1) and (2) of subsection (d) shall be construed to limit the ability of a health insurance issuer offering health insurance coverage in connection with a group health plan to increase the premium for an employer based on the manifestation of a disease or disorder of an individual who is enrolled in the plan. In such case, the manifestation of a disease or disorder in one individual cannot also be used as genetic information about other group members and to further increase the premium for the employer.

Act Sec. 702(c). LIMITATION ON REQUESTING OR REQUIRING GENETIC TESTING—

(1) —A group health plan, and a health insurance issuer offering health insurance coverage in connection with a group health plan, shall not request or require an individual or a family member of such individual to undergo a genetic test.

(2) RULE OF CONSTRUCTION—Paragraph (1) shall not be construed to limit the authority of a health care professional who is providing health care services to an individual to request that such individual undergo a genetic test.

(3) RULE OF CONSTRUCTION REGARDING PAYMENT—

(A) IN GENERAL—Nothing in paragraph (1) shall be construed to preclude a group health plan, or a health insurance issuer offering health insurance coverage in connection with a group health plan, from obtaining and using the results of a genetic test in making a determination regarding payment (as such term is defined for the purposes of applying the regulations promulgated by the Secretary of Health and Human Services under part C of title XI of the Social Security Act and section 264 of the Health Insurance Portability and Accountability Act of 1996, as may be revised from time to time) consistent with subsection (a).

(B) LIMITATION—For purposes of subparagraph (A), a group health plan, or a health insurance issuer offering health insurance coverage in connection with a group health plan, may request only the minimum amount of information necessary to accomplish the intended purpose.

(4) RESEARCH EXCEPTION—Notwithstanding paragraph (1), a group health plan, or a health insurance issuer offering health insurance coverage in connection with a group health plan, may request, but not require, that a participant or beneficiary undergo a genetic test if each of the following conditions is met:

(A) The request is made, in writing, pursuant to research that complies with part 46 of title 45, Code of Federal Regulations, or equivalent Federal regulations, and any applicable State or local law or regulations for the protection of human subjects in research.

(B) The plan or issuer clearly indicates to each participant or beneficiary, or in the case of a minor child, to the legal guardian of such beneficiary, to whom the request is made that—

(i) compliance with the request is voluntary; and

(ii) non-compliance will have no effect on enrollment status or premium or contribution amounts.

(C) No genetic information collected or acquired under this paragraph shall be used for underwriting purposes.

(D) The plan or issuer notifies the Secretary in writing that the plan or issuer is conducting activities pursuant to the exception provided for under this paragraph, including a description of the activities conducted.

(E) The plan or issuer complies with such other conditions as the Secretary may by regulation require for activities conducted under this paragraph.

Act Sec. 702(d). PROHIBITION ON COLLECTION OF GENETIC INFORMATION—

(1) IN GENERAL—A group health plan, and a health insurance issuer offering health insurance coverage in connection with a group health plan, shall not request, require, or purchase genetic information for underwriting purposes (as defined in section 733).

(2) PROHIBITION ON COLLECTION OF GENETIC INFORMATION PRIOR TO ENROLLMENT—A group health plan, and a health insurance issuer offering health insurance coverage in connection with a group health plan, shall not request, require, or purchase genetic information with respect to any individual prior to such individual's enrollment under the plan or coverage in connection with such enrollment.

(3) INCIDENTAL COLLECTION—If a group health plan, or a health insurance issuer offering health insurance coverage in connection with a group health plan, obtains genetic information incidental to the requesting, requiring, or purchasing of other information concerning any individual, such request, requirement, or purchase shall not be considered a violation of paragraph (2) if such request, requirement, or purchase is not in violation of paragraph (1).

Act Sec. 702(e) APPLICATION TO ALL PLANS—The provisions of subsections (a)(1)(F), (b)(3), (c), and (d), and subsection (b)(1) and section 701 with respect to genetic information, shall apply to group health plans and health insurance issuers without regard to section 732(a).

Act Sec. 702(f) GENETIC INFORMATION OF A FETUS OR EMBRYO—Any reference in this part to genetic information concerning an individual or family member of an individual shall—

(1) with respect to such an individual or family member of an individual who is a pregnant woman, include genetic information of any fetus carried by such pregnant woman; and

(2) with respect to an individual or family member utilizing an assisted reproductive technology, include genetic information of any embryo legally held by the individual or family member.

Amendments

P.L. 110-233, § 101(a):

Amended ERISA Sec. 702(b)(2)(A) by inserting before the semicolon the following: "except as provided in paragraph (3)" and by adding (c)(3) to read as above.

P.L. 110-233, § 101(b):

Amended ERISA Sec. 702 by adding subsections (c), (d), and (e) to read as above.

P.L. 110-233, § 101(c):

Amended ERISA Sec. 702 by adding subsection (f) to read as above.

The above amendments apply with respect to group health plans for plan years beginning after the date that is 1 year after the date of enactment [May 21, 2009].

P.L. 104-191, § 101(a):

Added ERISA Act Sec. 702 to read as above.

The above amendments generally apply with respect to group health plans for plan years beginning after June 30, 1997. For special rules, see Act Sec. 101(g)(2)-(5), reproduced after ERISA Act Sec. 701 above.

Regulations

The following regulations were adopted by 62 FR 16894 and published in the Federal Register on April 8, 1997, under "Chapter XXV of Title 29 of the Code of Federal Regulations; Subchapter L—Health Insurance Portability and Renewability for Group Health Plans; Part 2590—Rules and Regulations for Health Insurance Portability and Renewability for Group Health Plans." They were revised January 8, 2001 by 66 FR 1377 and amended March 9, 2001 by 66 FR 14,076. Reg. § 2590.702 was revised in its entirety on December 13, 2006 by 71 FR 75014. Reg. § 2590.702 was amended and

Reg. §2590.702-1 was added October 7, 2009 by 74 FR 51663. Reg. §2590.702(f) was amended June 3, 2013 by 78 FR 33157. Reg. §2590.702 was amended February 24, 2014 (79 FR 10295).

[¶ 15,050A-1]

§2590.702 Prohibiting discrimination against participants and beneficiaries based on a health factor.

(a) *Health factors.* (1) The term *health factor* means, in relation to an individual, any of the following health status-related factors:

(i) Health status;

(ii) Medical condition (including both physical and mental illnesses), as defined in §2590.701-2;

(iii) Claims experience;

(iv) Receipt of health care;

(v) Medical history;

(vi) Genetic information, as defined in §2590.702-1(a)(3) of this Part; [Amended 10/7/09 by 74 FR 51663.]

(vii) Evidence of insurability; or

(viii) Disability.

(2) Evidence of insurability includes. (i) Conditions arising out of acts of domestic violence; and

(ii) Participation in activities such as motorcycling, snowmobiling, all-terrain vehicle riding, horseback riding, skiing, and other similar activities.

(3) The decision whether health coverage is elected for an individual (including the time chosen to enroll, such as under special enrollment or late enrollment) is not, itself, within the scope of any health factor. (However, under §2590.701-6, a plan or issuer must treat special enrollees the same as similarly situated individuals who are enrolled when first eligible.)

(b) *Prohibited discrimination in rules for eligibility.* (1) *In general.* (i) A group health plan, and a health insurance issuer offering health insurance coverage in connection with a group health plan, may not establish any rule for eligibility (including continued eligibility) of any individual to enroll for benefits under the terms of the plan or group health insurance coverage that discriminates based on any health factor that relates to that individual or a dependent of that individual. This rule is subject to the provisions of paragraph (b)(2) of this section (explaining how this rule applies to benefits), paragraph (d) of this section (containing rules for establishing groups of similarly situated individuals), paragraph (e) of this section (relating to nonconfinement, actively-at-work, and other service requirements), paragraph (f) of this section (relating to wellness programs), and paragraph (g) of this section (permitting favorable treatment of individuals with adverse health factors). [Amended 2/24/14 by 79 FR 10295.]

(ii) For purposes of this section, rules for eligibility include, but are not limited to, rules relating to —

(A) Enrollment;

(B) The effective date of coverage;

(C) Waiting (or affiliation) periods;

(D) Late and special enrollment;

(E) Eligibility for benefit packages (including rules for individuals to change their selection among benefit packages);

(F) Benefits (including rules relating to covered benefits, benefit restrictions, and cost-sharing mechanisms such as coinsurance, copayments, and deductibles), as described in paragraphs (b)(2) and (3) of this section;

(G) Continued eligibility; and

(H) Terminating coverage (including disenrollment) of any individual under the plan.

(iii) The rules of this paragraph (b)(1) are illustrated by the following examples:

Example 1. (i) *Facts.* An employer sponsors a group health plan that is available to all employees who enroll within the first 30 days of their employment. However, employees who do not enroll within the first 30 days cannot enroll later unless they pass a physical examination.

(ii) *Conclusion.* In this *Example 1*, the requirement to pass a physical examination in order to enroll in the plan is a rule for eligibility that discriminates based on one or more health factors and thus violates this paragraph (b)(1).

Example 2. (i) *Facts.* Under an employer's group health plan, employees who enroll during the first 30 days of employment (and during special enrollment periods) may choose between two benefit packages: an indemnity option and an HMO option. However, employees who enroll during late enrollment are permitted to enroll only in the HMO option and only if they provide evidence of good health.

(ii) *Conclusion.* In this *Example 2*, the requirement to provide evidence of good health in order to be eligible for late enrollment in the HMO option is a rule for eligibility that discriminates based on one or more health factors and thus violates this paragraph (b)(1). However, if the plan did not require evidence of good health but limited late enrollees to the HMO option, the plan's rules for eligibility would not discriminate based on any health factor, and thus would not violate this paragraph (b)(1), because the time an individual chooses to enroll is not, itself, within the scope of any health factor.

Example 3. (i) *Facts.* Under an employer's group health plan, all employees generally may enroll within the first 30 days of employment. However, individuals who participate in certain recreational activities, including motorcycling, are excluded from coverage.

(ii) *Conclusion.* In this *Example 3*, excluding from the plan individuals who participate in recreational activities, such as motorcycling, is a rule for eligibility that discriminates based on one more health factors and thus violates this paragraph (b)(1).

Example 4. (i) *Facts.* A group health plan applies for a group health policy offered by an issuer. As part of the application, the issuer receives health information about individuals to be covered under the plan. Individual *A* is an employee of the employer maintaining the plan. *A* and *A*'s dependents have a history of high health claims. Based on the information about *A* and *A*'s dependents, the issuer excludes *A* and *A*'s dependents from the group policy it offers to the employer.

(ii) *Conclusion.* In this *Example 4*, the issuer's exclusion of *A* and *A*'s dependents from coverage is a rule for eligibility that discriminates based on one or more health factors, and thus violates this paragraph (b)(1). (If the employer is a small employer under 45 CFR 144.103 (generally, an employer with 50 or fewer employees), the issuer also may violate 45 CFR 146.150, which requires issuers to offer all the policies they sell in the small group market on a guaranteed available basis to all small employers and to accept every eligible individual in every small employer group.) If the plan provides coverage through this policy and does not provide equivalent coverage for *A* and *A*'s dependents through other means, the plan will also violate this paragraph (b)(1).

(2) *Application to benefits.* (i) *General rule.* (A) Under this section, a group health plan or group health insurance issuer is not required to provide coverage for any particular benefit to any group of similarly situated individuals.

(B) However, benefits provided under a plan must be uniformly available to all similarly situated individuals (as described in paragraph (d) of this section). Likewise, any restriction on a benefit or benefits must apply uniformly to all similarly situated individuals and must not be directed at individual participants or beneficiaries based on any health factor of the participants or beneficiaries (determined based on all the relevant facts and circumstances). Thus, for example, a plan may limit or exclude benefits in relation to a specific disease or condition, limit or exclude benefits for certain types of treatments or drugs, or limit or exclude benefits based on a determination of whether the benefits are experimental or not medically necessary, but only if the benefit limitation or exclusion applies uniformly to all similarly situated individuals and is not directed at individual participants or beneficiaries based on any health factor of the participants or beneficiaries. In addition, a plan or issuer may require the satisfaction of a deductible, copayment, coinsurance, or other cost-sharing requirement in order to obtain a benefit if the limit or cost-sharing requirement applies uniformly to all similarly situated individuals and is not directed at individual participants or beneficiaries based on any health factor of the participants or beneficiaries. In the case of a cost-sharing requirement, see also paragraph (b)(2)(ii) of this section, which permits variances in the application of a cost-sharing mechanism made available under a wellness program. (Whether any plan provision or practice with respect to benefits complies with this paragraph (b)(2)(i) does not affect whether the provision or practice is permitted under ERISA, the Affordable Care Act (including the requirements related to essential health benefits), the Americans with Disabilities Act, or any other law, whether State or Federal.) [Amended 2/24/14 by 79 FR 10295.]

(C) For purposes of this paragraph (b)(2)(i), a plan amendment applicable to all individuals in one or more groups of similarly situated individuals under the plan and made effective no earlier than the first day of the first plan year after the amendment is adopted is not considered to be directed at any individual participants or beneficiaries.

(D) The rules of this paragraph (b)(2)(i) are illustrated by the following examples:

Example 1. (i) *Facts.* A group health plan applies a $10,000 annual limit on a specific covered benefit that is not an essential health benefit to each participant or beneficiary covered under the plan. The limit is not directed at individual participants or beneficiaries. [Amended 2/24/14 by 79 FR 10295.]

(ii) *Conclusion.* In this *Example 1,* the limit does not violate this paragraph (b)(2)(i) because coverage of the specific, non-essential health benefit up to $10,000 is available uniformly to each participant and beneficiary under the plan and because the limit is applied uniformly to all participants and beneficiaries and is not directed at individual participants or beneficiaries. [Amended 2/24/14 by 79 FR 10295.]

Example 2. (i) *Facts.* A group health plan has a $500 deductible on all benefits for participants covered under the plan. Participant *B* files a claim for the treatment of AIDS. At the next corporate board meeting of the plan sponsor, the claim is discussed. Shortly thereafter, the plan is modified to impose a $2,000 deductible on benefits for the treatment of AIDS, effective before the beginning of the next plan year. [Amended 2/24/14 by 79 FR 10295.]

(ii) *Conclusion.* The facts of this *Example 2* strongly suggest that the plan modification is directed at *B* based on *B*'s claim. Absent outweighing evidence to the contrary, the plan violates this paragraph (b)(2)(i).

Example 3. (i) A group health plan applies for a group health policy offered by an issuer. Individual *C* is covered under the plan and has an adverse health condition. As part of the application, the issuer receives health information about the individuals to be covered, including information about *C*'s adverse health condition. The policy form offered by the issuer generally provides benefits for the adverse health condition that *C* has, but in this case the issuer offers the plan a policy modified by a rider that excludes benefits for *C* for that condition. The exclusionary rider is made effective the first day of the next plan year.

(ii) *Conclusion.* In this *Example 3,* the issuer violates this paragraph (b)(2)(i) because benefits for *C*'s condition are available to other individuals in the group of similarly situated individuals that includes *C* but are not available to *C*. Thus, the benefits are not uniformly available to all similarly situated individuals. Even though the exclusionary rider is made effective the first day of the next plan year, because the rider does not apply to all similarly situated individuals, the issuer violates this paragraph (b)(2)(i).

Example 4. (i) *Facts.* A group health plan has a $2,000 lifetime limit for the treatment of temporomandibular joint syndrome (TMJ). The limit is applied uniformly to all similarly situated individuals and is not directed at individual participants or beneficiaries.

(ii) *Conclusion.* In this *Example 4,* the limit does not violate this paragraph (b)(2)(i) because $2,000 of benefits for the treatment of TMJ are available uniformly to all similarly situated individuals and a plan may limit benefits covered in relation to a specific disease or condition if the limit applies uniformly to all similarly situated individuals and is not directed at individual participants or beneficiaries. (However, applying a lifetime limit on TMJ may violate §2590.715-2711, if TMJ coverage is an essential health benefit, depending on the essential health benefits benchmark plan as defined in 45 CFR 156.20. This example does not address whether the plan provision is permissible

under any other applicable law, including PHS Act section 2711 or the Americans with Disabilities Act.) [Amended 2/24/14 by 79 FR 10295.]

Example 5. (i) *Facts.* A group health plan applies a $2 million lifetime limit on all benefits. However, the $2 million lifetime limit is reduced to $10,000 for any participant or beneficiary covered under the plan who has a congenital heart defect.

(ii) *Conclusion.* In this *Example 5,* the lower lifetime limit for participants and beneficiaries with a congenital heart defect violates this paragraph (b)(2)(i) because benefits under the plan are not uniformly available to all similarly situated individuals and the plan's lifetime limit on benefits does not apply uniformly to all similarly situated individuals. Additionally, this plan provision is prohibited under §2590.715-2711 because it imposes a lifetime limit on essential health benefits. [Amended 2/24/14 by 79 FR 10295.]

Example 6. (i) *Facts.* A group health plan limits benefits for prescription drugs to those listed on a drug formulary. The limit is applied uniformly to all similarly situated individuals and is not directed at individual participants or beneficiaries.

(ii) *Conclusion.* In this *Example 6,* the exclusion from coverage of drugs not listed on the drug formulary does not violate this paragraph (b)(2)(i) because benefits for prescription drugs listed on the formulary are uniformly available to all similarly situated individuals and because the exclusion of drugs not listed on the formulary applies uniformly to all similarly situated individuals and is not directed at individual participants or beneficiaries.

Example 7. (i) *Facts.* Under a group health plan, doctor visits are generally subject to a $250 annual deductible and 20 percent coinsurance requirement. However, prenatal doctor visits are not subject to any deductible or coinsurance requirement. These rules are applied uniformly to all similarly situated individuals and are not directed at individual participants or beneficiaries.

(ii) *Conclusion.* In this *Example 7,* imposing different deductible and coinsurance requirements for prenatal doctor visits and other visits does not violate this paragraph (b)(2)(i) because a plan may establish different deductibles or coinsurance requirements for different services if the deductible or coinsurance requirement is applied uniformly to all similarly situated individuals and is not directed at individual participants or beneficiaries.

Example 8. [Removed 2/24/14 by 79 FR 10295.]

(ii) *Exception for wellness programs.* A group health plan or group health insurance issuer may vary benefits, including cost-sharing mechanisms (such as a deductible, copayment, or coinsurance), based on whether an individual has met the standards of a wellness program that satisfies the requirements of paragraph (f) of this section.

(iii) *Specific rule relating to source-of-injury exclusions.* (A) If a group health plan or group health insurance coverage generally provides benefits for a type of injury, the plan or issuer may not deny benefits otherwise provided for treatment of the injury if the injury results from an act of domestic violence or a medical condition (including both physical and mental health conditions). This rule applies in the case of an injury resulting from a medical condition even if the condition is not diagnosed before the injury.

(B) The rules of this paragraph (b)(2)(iii) are illustrated by the following examples:

Example 1. (i) *Facts.* A group health plan generally provides medical/surgical benefits, including benefits for hospital stays, that are medically necessary. However, the plan excludes benefits for self-inflicted injuries or injuries sustained in connection with attempted suicide. Because of depression, Individual *D* attempts suicide. As a result, *D* sustains injuries and is hospitalized for treatment of the injuries. Under the exclusion, the plan denies *D* benefits for treatment of the injuries.

(ii) *Conclusion.* In this *Example 1,* the suicide attempt is the result of a medical condition (depression). Accordingly, the denial of benefits for the treatments of *D*'s injuries violates the requirements of this paragraph (b)(2)(iii) because the plan provision excludes benefits for treatment of an injury resulting from a medical condition.

Example 2. (i) *Facts.* A group health plan provides benefits for head injuries generally. The plan also has a general exclusion for any injury sustained while participating in any of a number of recreational activities, including bungee jumping. However, this exclusion does not apply to any injury that results from a medical condition (nor from domestic violence). Participant *E* sustains a head injury while bungee jumping. The injury did not result from a medical condition (nor from domestic violence). Accordingly, the plan denies benefits for *E*'s head injury.

(ii) *Conclusion*. In this *Example 2*, the plan provision that denies benefits based on the source of an injury does not restrict benefits based on an act of domestic violence or any medical condition. Therefore, the provision is permissible under this paragraph (b)(2)(iii) and does not violate this section. (However, if the plan did not allow *E* to enroll in the plan (or applied different rules for eligibility to *E*) because *E* frequently participates in bungee jumping, the plan would violate paragraph (b)(1) of this section.)

(3) *Relationship to § 2590.701-3*. [Removed 2/24/14 by 79 FR 10295.]

(c) *Prohibited discrimination in premiums or contributions*. (1) *In general*. (i) A group health plan, and a health insurance issuer offering health insurance coverage in connection with a group health plan, may not require an individual, as a condition of enrollment or continued enrollment under the plan or group health insurance coverage, to pay a premium or contribution that is greater than the premium or contribution for a similarly situated individual (described in paragraph (d) of this section) enrolled in the plan or group health insurance coverage based on any health factor that relates to the individual or a dependent of the individual.

(ii) Discounts, rebates, payments in kind, and any other premium differential mechanisms are taken into account in determining an individual's premium or contribution rate. (For rules relating to cost-sharing mechanisms, see paragraph (b)(2) of this section (addressing benefits).)

(2) *Rules relating to premium rates*. (i) *Group rating based on health factors not restricted under this section*. Nothing in this section restricts the aggregate amount that an employer may be charged for coverage under a group health plan. But see § 2590.702-1(b) of this Part, which prohibits adjustments in group premium or contribution rates based on genetic information. [Amended 10/7/09 by 74 FR 51663.]

(ii) *List billing based on a health factor prohibited*. However, a group health insurance issuer, or a group health plan, may not quote or charge an employer (or an individual) a different premium for an individual in a group of similarly situated individuals based on a health factor. (But see paragraph (g) of this section permitting favorable treatment of individuals with adverse health factors.)

(iii) *Examples*. The rules of this paragraph (c)(2) are illustrated by the following examples:

Example 1. (i) *Facts*. An employer sponsors a group health plan and purchases coverage from a health insurance issuer. In order to determine the premium rate for the upcoming plan year, the issuer reviews the claims experience of individuals covered under the plan. The issuer finds that Individual *F* had significantly higher claims experience than similarly situated individuals in the plan. The issuer quotes the plan a higher per-participant rate because of *F*'s claims experience.

(ii) *Conclusion*. In this *Example 1*, the issuer does not violate the provisions of this paragraph (c)(2) because the issuer blends the rate so that the employer is not quoted a higher rate for *F* than for a similarly situated individual based on *F*'s claims experience. (However, if the issuer used genetic information in computing the group rate, it would violate § 2590.702-1(b) of this Part.) [Amended 10/7/09 by 74 FR 51663.]

Example 2. (i) *Facts*. Same facts as *Example 1*, except that the issuer quotes the employer a higher premium rate for *F*, because of *F*'s claims experience, than for a similarly situated individual.

(ii) *Conclusion*. In this *Example 2*, the issuer violates this paragraph (c)(2). Moreover, even if the plan purchased the policy based on the quote but did not require a higher participant contribution for *F* than for a similarly situated individual, the issuer would still

violate this paragraph (c)(2) (but in such a case the plan would not violate this paragraph (c)(2)).

(3) *Exception for wellness programs*. Notwithstanding paragraphs (c)(1) and (2) of this section, a plan or issuer may vary the amount of premium or contribution it requires similarly situated individuals to pay based on whether an individual has met the standards of a wellness program that satisfies the requirements of paragraph (f) of this section.

(d) *Similarly situated individuals*. The requirements of this section apply only within a group of individuals who are treated as similarly situated individuals. A plan or issuer may treat participants as a group of similarly situated individuals separate from beneficiaries. In addition, participants may be treated as two or more distinct groups of similarly situated individuals and beneficiaries may be treated as two or more distinct groups of similarly situated individuals in accordance with the rules of this paragraph (d). Moreover, if individuals have a choice of two or more benefit packages, individuals choosing one benefit package may be treated as one or more groups of similarly situated individuals distinct from individuals choosing another benefit package.

(1) *Participants*. Subject to paragraph (d)(3) of this section, a plan or issuer may treat participants as two or more distinct groups of similarly situated individuals if the distinction between or among the groups of participants is based on a bona fide employment-based classification consistent with the employer's usual business practice. Whether an employment-based classification is bona fide is determined on the basis of all the relevant facts and circumstances. Relevant facts and circumstances include whether the employer uses the classification for purposes independent of qualification for health coverage (for example, determining eligibility for other employee benefits or determining other terms of employment). Subject to paragraph (d)(3) of this section, examples of classifications that, based on all the relevant facts and circumstances, may be bona fide include full-time versus part-time status, different geographic location, membership in a collective bargaining unit, date of hire, length of service, current employee versus former employee status, and different occupations. However, a classification based on any health factor is not a bona fide employment-based classification, unless the requirements of paragraph (g) of this section are satisfied (permitting favorable treatment of individuals with adverse health factors).

(2) *Beneficiaries*. (i) Subject to paragraph (d)(3) of this section, a plan or issuer may treat beneficiaries as two or more distinct groups of similarly situated individuals if the distinction between or among the groups of beneficiaries is based on any of the following factors:

(A) A bona fide employment-based classification of the participant through whom the beneficiary is receiving coverage;

(B) Relationship to the participant (for example, as a spouse or as a dependent child);

(C) Marital status;

(D) With respect to children of a participant, age or student status; or

(E) Any other factor if the factor is not a health factor.

(ii) Paragraph (d)(2)(i) of this section does not prevent more favorable treatment of individuals with adverse health factors in accordance with paragraph (g) of this section.

(3) *Discrimination directed at individuals*. Notwithstanding paragraphs (d)(1) and (2) of this section, if the creation or modification of an employment or coverage classification is directed at individual participants or beneficiaries based on any health factor of the participants or beneficiaries, the classification is not permitted under this paragraph (d), unless it is permitted under paragraph (g) of this section (permitting favorable treatment of individuals with adverse health factors). Thus, if an employer modified an employment-based classification to single out, based on a health factor, individual participants and beneficiaries and deny them health coverage, the new classification would not be permitted under this section.

(4) *Examples*. The rules of this paragraph (d) are illustrated by the following examples:

Example 1. (i) *Facts.* An employer sponsors a group health plan for full-time employees only. Under the plan (consistent with the employer's usual business practice), employees who normally work at least 30 hours per week are considered to be working full-time. Other employees are considered to be working part-time. There is no evidence to suggest that the classification is directed at individual participants or beneficiaries.

(ii) *Conclusion.* In this *Example 1*, treating the full-time and part-time employees as two separate groups of similarly situated individuals is permitted under this paragraph (d) because the classification is bona fide and is not directed at individual participants or beneficiaries.

Example 2. (i) *Facts.* Under a group health plan, coverage is made available to employees, their spouses, and their children. However, coverage is made available to a child only if the child is under age 26 (or under age 29 if the child is continuously enrolled full-time in an institution of higher learning (full-time students)). There is no evidence to suggest that these classifications are directed at individual participants or beneficiaries.

(ii) *Conclusion.* In this Example 2, treating spouses and children differently by imposing an age limitation on children, but not on spouses, is permitted under this paragraph (d). Specifically, the distinction between spouses and children is permitted under paragraph (d)(2) of this section and is not prohibited under paragraph (d)(3) of this section because it is not directed at individual participants or beneficiaries. It is also permissible to treat children who are under age 26 (or full-time students under age 29) as a group of similarly situated individuals separate from those who are age 26 or older (or age 29 or older if they are not full-time students) because the classification is permitted under paragraph (d)(2) of this section and is not directed at individual participants or beneficiaries. [Amended 2/24/14 by 79 FR 10295.]

Example 3. (i) *Facts.* A university sponsors a group health plan that provides one health benefit package to faculty and another health benefit package to other staff. Faculty and staff are treated differently with respect to other employee benefits such as retirement benefits and leaves of absence. There is no evidence to suggest that the distinction is directed at individual participants or beneficiaries.

(ii) *Conclusion.* In this *Example 3*, the classification is permitted under this paragraph (d) because there is a distinction based on a bona fide employment-based classification consistent with the employer's usual business practice and the distinction is not directed at individual participants and beneficiaries.

Example 4. (i) *Facts.* An employer sponsors a group health plan that is available to all current employees. Former employees may also be eligible, but only if they complete a specified number of years of service, are enrolled under the plan at the time of termination of employment, and are continuously enrolled from that date. There is no evidence to suggest that these distinctions are directed at individual participants or beneficiaries.

(ii) *Conclusion.* In this *Example 4*, imposing additional eligibility requirements on former employees is permitted because a classification that distinguishes between current and former employees is a bona fide employment-based classification that is permitted under this paragraph (d), provided that it is not directed at individual participants or beneficiaries. In addition, it is permissible to distinguish between former employees who satisfy the service requirement and those who do not, provided that the distinction is not directed at individual participants or beneficiaries. (However, former employees who do not satisfy the eligibility criteria may, nonetheless, be eligible for continued coverage pursuant to a COBRA continuation provision or similar State law.)

Example 5. (i) *Facts.* An employer sponsors a group health plan that provides the same benefit package to all seven employees of the employer. Six of the seven employees have the same job title and responsibilities, but Employee *G* has a different job title and different responsibilities. After *G* files an expensive claim for benefits under the plan, coverage under the plan is modified so that employees with *G*'s job title receive a different benefit package that includes a higher deductible than in the benefit package made available to the other six employees. [Amended 2/24/14 by 79 FR 10295.]

(ii) *Conclusion.* Under the facts of this *Example 5*, changing the coverage classification for *G* based on the existing employment classifi-

cation for *G* is not permitted under this paragraph (d) because the creation of the new coverage classification for *G* is directed at *G* based on one or more health factors.

(e) *Nonconfinement and actively-at-work provisions.* (1) *Nonconfinement provisions.* (i) *General rule.* Under the rules of paragraphs (b) and (c) of this section, a plan or issuer may not establish a rule for eligibility (as described in paragraph (b)(1)(ii) of this section) or set any individual's premium or contribution rate based on whether an individual is confined to a hospital or other health care institution. In addition, under the rules of paragraphs (b) and (c) of this section, a plan or issuer may not establish a rule for eligibility or set any individual's premium or contribution rate based on an individual's ability to engage in normal life activities, except to the extent permitted under paragraphs (e)(2)(ii) and (3) of this section (permitting plans and issuers, under certain circumstances, to distinguish among employees based on the performance of services).

(ii) *Examples.* The rules of this paragraph (e)(1) are illustrated by the following examples:

Example 1. (i) *Facts.* Under a group health plan, coverage for employees and their dependents generally becomes effective on the first day of employment. However, coverage for a dependent who is confined to a hospital or other health care institution does not become effective until the confinement ends.

(ii) *Conclusion.* In this *Example 1*, the plan violates this paragraph (e)(1) because the plan delays the effective date of coverage for dependents based on confinement to a hospital or other health care institution.

Example 2. (i) *Facts.* In previous years, a group health plan has provided coverage through a group health insurance policy offered by Issuer *M*. However, for the current year, the plan provides coverage through a group health insurance policy offered by Issuer *N*. Under Issuer *N*'s policy, items and services provided in connection with the confinement of a dependent to a hospital or other health care institution are not covered if the confinement is covered under an extension of benefits clause from a previous health insurance issuer.

(ii) *Conclusion.* In this *Example 2*, Issuer *N* violates this paragraph (e)(1) because the group health insurance coverage restricts benefits (a rule for eligibility under paragraph (b)(1)) based on whether a dependent is confined to a hospital or other health care institution that is covered under an extension of benefits clause from a previous issuer. State law cannot change the obligation of Issuer *N* under this section. However, under State law Issuer *M* may also be responsible for providing benefits to such a dependent. In a case in which Issuer *N* has an obligation under this section to provide benefits and Issuer *M* has an obligation under State law to provide benefits, any State laws designed to prevent more than 100% reimbursement, such as State coordination-of-benefits laws, continue to apply.

(2) *Actively-at-work and continuous service provisions.* (i) *General rule.* (A) Under the rules of paragraphs (b) and (c) of this section and subject to the exception for the first day of work described in paragraph (e)(2)(ii) of this section, a plan or issuer may not establish a rule for eligibility (as described in paragraph (b)(1)(ii) of this section) or set any individual's premium or contribution rate based on whether an individual is actively at work (including whether an individual is continuously employed), unless absence from work due to any health factor (such as being absent from work on sick leave) is treated, for purposes of the plan or health insurance coverage, as being actively at work.

(B) The rules of this paragraph (e)(2)(i) are illustrated by the following examples:

Example 1. (i) *Facts.* Under a group health plan, an employee generally becomes eligible to enroll 30 days after the first day of employment. However, if the employee is not actively at work on the first day after the end of the 30-day period, then eligibility for enrollment is delayed until the first day the employee is actively at work.

(ii) *Conclusion.* In this *Example 1*, the plan violates this paragraph (e)(2) (and thus also violates paragraph (b) of this section). However, the plan would not violate paragraph (e)(2) or (b) of this section if, under the plan, an absence due to any health factor is considered being actively at work.

Example 2. (i) *Facts.* Under a group health plan, coverage for an employee becomes effective after 90 days of continuous service; that is, if an employee is absent from work (for any reason) before completing 90 days of service, the beginning of the 90-day period is measured from the day the employee returns to work (without any credit for service before the absence).

(ii) *Conclusion.* In this Example 2, the plan violates this paragraph (e)(2) (and thus also paragraph (b) of this section) because the 90-day continuous service requirement is a rule for eligibility based on whether an individual is actively at work. However, the plan would not violate this paragraph (e)(2) or paragraph (b) of this section if, under the plan, an absence due to any health factor is not considered an absence for purposes of measuring 90 days of continuous service. (In addition, any eligibility provision that is time-based must comply with the requirements of PHS Act section 2708 and its implementing regulations.) [Amended 2/24/14 by 79 FR 10295.]

(ii) *Exception for the first day of work.* (A) Notwithstanding the general rule in paragraph (e)(2)(i) of this section, a plan or issuer may establish a rule for eligibility that requires an individual to begin work for the employer sponsoring the plan (or, in the case of a multiemployer plan, to begin a job in covered employment) before coverage becomes effective, provided that such a rule for eligibility applies regardless of the reason for the absence.

(B) The rules of this paragraph (e)(2)(ii) are illustrated by the following examples:

Example 1. (i) *Facts.* Under the eligibility provision of a group health plan, coverage for new employees becomes effective on the first day that the employee reports to work. Individual *H* is scheduled to begin work on August 3. However, *H* is unable to begin work on that day because of illness. *H* begins working on August 4, and *H*'s coverage is effective on August 4.

(ii) *Conclusion.* In this *Example 1*, the plan provision does not violate this section. However, if coverage for individuals who do not report to work on the first day they were scheduled to work for a reason unrelated to a health factor (such as vacation or bereavement) becomes effective on the first day they were scheduled to work, then the plan would violate this section.

Example 2. (i) *Facts.* Under a group health plan, coverage for new employees becomes effective on the first day of the month following the employee's first day of work, regardless of whether the employee is actively at work on the first day of the month. Individual *J* is scheduled to begin work on March 24. However, *J* is unable to begin work on March 24 because of illness. *J* begins working on April 7 and *J*'s coverage is effective May 1.

(ii) *Conclusion.* In this *Example 2*, the plan provision does not violate this section. However, as in *Example 1*, if coverage for individuals absent from work for reasons unrelated to a health factor became effective despite their absence, then the plan would violate this section.

(3) *Relationship to plan provisions defining similarly situated individuals.* (i) Notwithstanding the rules of paragraphs (e)(1) and (2) of this section, a plan or issuer may establish rules for eligibility or set any individual's premium or contribution rate in accordance with the rules relating to similarly situated individuals in paragraph (d) of this section. Accordingly, a plan or issuer may distinguish in rules for eligibility under the plan between full-time and part-time employees, between permanent and temporary or seasonal employees, between current and former employees, and between employees currently performing services and employees no longer performing services for the employer, subject to paragraph (d) of this section. However, other Federal or State laws (including the COBRA continuation provisions and the Family and Medical Leave Act of 1993) may require an employee or the employee's dependents to be offered coverage and set limits on the premium or contribution rate even though the employee is not performing services.

(ii) The rules of this paragraph (e)(3) are illustrated by the following examples:

Example 1. (i) *Facts.* Under a group health plan, employees are eligible for coverage if they perform services for the employer for 30 or more hours per week or if they are on paid leave (such as vacation, sick, or bereavement leave). Employees on unpaid leave are treated as a separate group of similarly situated individuals in accordance with the rules of paragraph (d) of this section.

(ii) *Conclusion.* In this *Example 1*, the plan provisions do not violate this section. However, if the plan treated individuals performing services for the employer for 30 or more hours per week, individuals on vacation leave, and individuals on bereavement leave as a group of similarly situated individuals separate from individuals on sick leave, the plan would violate this paragraph (e) (and thus also would violate paragraph (b) of this section) because groups of similarly situated individuals cannot be established based on a health factor (including the taking of sick leave) under paragraph (d) of this section.

Example 2. (i) *Facts.* To be eligible for coverage under a bona fide collectively bargained group health plan in the current calendar quarter, the plan requires an individual to have worked 250 hours in covered employment during the three-month period that ends one month before the beginning of the current calendar quarter. The distinction between employees working at least 250 hours and those working less than 250 hours in the earlier three-month period is not directed at individual participants or beneficiaries based on any health factor of the participants or beneficiaries.

(ii) *Conclusion.* In this *Example 2*, the plan provision does not violate this section because, under the rules for similarly situated individuals allowing full-time employees to be treated differently than part-time employees, employees who work at least 250 hours in a three-month period can be treated differently than employees who fail to work 250 hours in that period. The result would be the same if the plan permitted individuals to apply excess hours from previous periods to satisfy the requirement for the current quarter.

Example 3. (i) *Facts.* Under a group health plan, coverage of an employee is terminated when the individual's employment is terminated, in accordance with the rules of paragraph (d) of this section. Employee *B* has been covered under the plan. *B* experiences a disabling illness that prevents *B* from working. *B* takes a leave of absence under the Family and Medical Leave Act of 1993. At the end of such leave, *B* terminates employment and consequently loses coverage under the plan. (This termination of coverage is without regard to whatever rights the employee (or members of the employee's family) may have for COBRA continuation coverage.)

(ii) *Conclusion.* In this *Example 3*, the plan provision terminating *B*'s coverage upon *B*'s termination of employment does not violate this section.

Example 4. (i) *Facts.* Under a group health plan, coverage of an employee is terminated when the employee ceases to perform services for the employer sponsoring the plan, in accordance with the rules of paragraph (d) of this section. Employee *C* is laid off for three months. When the layoff begins, *C*'s coverage under the plan is terminated. (This termination of coverage is without regard to whatever rights the employee (or members of the employee's family) may have for COBRA continuation coverage.)

(ii) *Conclusion.* In this *Example 4*, the plan provision terminating *C*'s coverage upon the cessation of *C*'s performance of services does not violate this section.

(f) *Nondiscriminatory wellness programs—in general.* A wellness program is a program of health promotion or disease prevention. Paragraphs (b)(2)(ii) and (c)(3) of this section provide exceptions to the general prohibitions against discrimination based on a health factor for plan provisions that vary benefits (including cost-sharing mechanisms) or the premium or contribution for similarly situated individuals in connection with a wellness program that satisfies the requirements of this paragraph (f).

(1) *Definitions.* The definitions in this paragraph (f)(1) govern in applying the provisions of this paragraph (f).

(i) *Reward.* Except where expressly provided otherwise, references in this section to an individual obtaining a reward include both obtaining a reward (such as a discount or rebate of a premium or contribution, a waiver of all or part of a cost-sharing mechanism, an additional benefit, or any financial or other incentive) and avoiding a penalty (such as the absence of a premium surcharge or other financial or nonfinancial disincentive). References in this section to a plan providing a reward include both providing a reward (such as a discount or rebate of a premium or contribution, a waiver of all or part of a cost-sharing mechanism, an additional benefit, or any financial or other incentive) and imposing a penalty (such as a surcharge or other financial or nonfinancial disincentive).

(ii) *Participatory wellness programs.* If none of the conditions for obtaining a reward under a wellness program is based on an individual satisfying a standard that is related to a health factor (or if a wellness program does not provide a reward), the wellness program is a participatory wellness program. Examples of participatory wellness programs are:

(A) A program that reimburses employees for all or part of the cost for membership in a fitness center.

(B) A diagnostic testing program that provides a reward for participation in that program and does not base any part of the reward on outcomes.

(C) A program that encourages preventive care through the waiver of the copayment or deductible requirement under a group health plan for the costs of, for example, prenatal care or well-baby visits. (Note that, with respect to non-grandfathered plans, § 2590.715-2713 of this part requires benefits for certain preventive health services without the imposition of cost sharing.)

(D) A program that reimburses employees for the costs of participating, or that otherwise provides a reward for participating, in a smoking cessation program without regard to whether the employee quits smoking.

(E) A program that provides a reward to employees for attending a monthly, no-cost health education seminar.

(F) A program that provides a reward to employees who complete a health risk assessment regarding current health status, without any further action (educational or otherwise) required by the employee with regard to the health issues identified as part of the assessment. (*See also* § 2590.702-1 for rules prohibiting collection of genetic information.)

(iii) *Health-contingent wellness programs.* A health-contingent wellness program is a program that requires an individual to satisfy a standard related to a health factor to obtain a reward (or requires an individual to undertake more than a similarly situated individual based on a health factor in order to obtain the same reward). A health-contingent wellness program may be an activity-only wellness program or an outcome-based wellness program.

(iv) *Activity-only wellness programs.* An activity-only wellness program is a type of health-contingent wellness program that requires an individual to perform or complete an activity related to a health factor in order to obtain a reward but does not require the individual to attain or maintain a specific health outcome. Examples include walking, diet, or exercise programs, which some individuals may be unable to participate in or complete (or have difficulty participating in or completing) due to a health factor, such as severe asthma, pregnancy, or a recent surgery. *See* paragraph (f)(3) of this section for requirements applicable to activity-only wellness programs.

(v) *Outcome-based wellness programs.* An outcome-based wellness program is a type of health-contingent wellness program that requires an individual to attain or maintain a specific health outcome (such as not smoking or attaining certain results on biometric screenings) in order to obtain a reward. To comply with the rules of this paragraph (f), an outcome-based wellness program typically has two tiers. That is, for individuals who do not attain or maintain the specific health outcome, compliance with an educational program or an activity may be offered as an alternative to achieve the same reward. This alternative pathway, however, does not mean that the overall program, which has an outcome-based component, is not an outcome-based wellness program. That is, if a measurement, test, or screening is used as part of an initial standard and individuals who meet the standard are granted the reward, the program is considered an outcome-based wellness program. For example, if a wellness program tests individuals for specified medical conditions or risk factors (including biometric screening such as testing for high cholesterol, high blood pressure, abnormal body mass index, or high glucose level) and provides a reward to individuals identified as within a normal or healthy range for these medical conditions or risk factors, while requiring individuals

who are identified as outside the normal or healthy range (or at risk) to take additional steps (such as meeting with a health coach, taking a health or fitness course, adhering to a health improvement action plan, complying with a walking or exercise program, or complying with a health care provider's plan of care) to obtain the same reward, the program is an outcome-based wellness program. *See* paragraph (f)(4) of this section for requirements applicable to outcome-based wellness programs.

(2) *Requirement for participatory wellness programs.* A participatory wellness program, as described in paragraph (f)(1)(ii) of this section, does not violate the provisions of this section only if participation in the program is made available to all similarly situated individuals, regardless of health status.

(3) *Requirements for activity-only wellness programs.* A health-contingent wellness program that is an activity-only wellness program, as described in paragraph (f)(1)(iv) of this section, does not violate the provisions of this section only if all of the following requirements are satisfied:

(i) *Frequency of opportunity to qualify.* The program must give individuals eligible for the program the opportunity to qualify for the reward under the program at least once per year.

(ii) *Size of reward.* The reward for the activity-only wellness program, together with the reward for other health-contingent wellness programs with respect to the plan, must not exceed the applicable percentage (as defined in paragraph (f)(5) of this section) of the total cost of employee-only coverage under the plan. However, if, in addition to employees, any class of dependents (such as spouses, or spouses and dependent children) may participate in the wellness program, the reward must not exceed the applicable percentage of the total cost of the coverage in which an employee and any dependents are enrolled. For purposes of this paragraph (f)(3)(ii), the cost of coverage is determined based on the total amount of employer and employee contributions towards the cost of coverage for the benefit package under which the employee is (or the employee and any dependents are) receiving coverage.

(iii) *Reasonable design.* The program must be reasonably designed to promote health or prevent disease. A program satisfies this standard if it has a reasonable chance of improving the health of, or preventing disease in, participating individuals, and it is not overly burdensome, is not a subterfuge for discriminating based on a health factor, and is not highly suspect in the method chosen to promote health or prevent disease. This determination is based on all the relevant facts and circumstances.

(iv) *Uniform availability and reasonable alternative standards.* The full reward under the activity-only wellness program must be available to all similarly situated individuals.

(A) Under this paragraph (f)(3)(iv), a reward under an activity-only wellness program is not available to all similarly situated individuals for a period unless the program meets both of the following requirements:

(1) The program allows a reasonable alternative standard (or waiver of the otherwise applicable standard) for obtaining the reward for any individual for whom, for that period, it is unreasonably difficult due to a medical condition to satisfy the otherwise applicable standard; and

(2) The program allows a reasonable alternative standard (or waiver of the otherwise applicable standard) for obtaining the reward for any individual for whom, for that period, it is medically inadvisable to attempt to satisfy the otherwise applicable standard.

(B) While plans and issuers are not required to determine a particular reasonable alternative standard in advance of an individual's request for one, if an individual is described in either paragraph (f)(3)(iv)(A)(*1*) or (*2*) of this section, a reasonable alternative standard must be furnished by the plan or issuer upon the individual's request or the condition for obtaining the reward must be waived.

(C) All the facts and circumstances are taken into account in determining whether a plan or issuer has furnished a reasonable alternative standard, including but not limited to the following:

(1) If the reasonable alternative standard is completion of an educational program, the plan or issuer must make the educational program available or assist the employee in finding such a program (instead of requiring an individual to find such a program unassisted), and may not require an individual to pay for the cost of the program.

(2) The time commitment required must be reasonable (for example, requiring attendance nightly at a one-hour class would be unreasonable).

(3) If the reasonable alternative standard is a diet program, the plan or issuer is not required to pay for the cost of food but must pay any membership or participation fee.

(4) If an individual's personal physician states that a plan standard (including, if applicable, the recommendations of the plan's medical professional) is not medically appropriate for that individual, the plan or issuer must provide a reasonable alternative standard that accommodates the recommendations of the individual's personal physician with regard to medical appropriateness. Plans and issuers may impose standard cost sharing under the plan or coverage for medical items and services furnished pursuant to the physician's recommendations.

(D) To the extent that a reasonable alternative standard under an activity-only wellness program is, itself, an activity-only wellness program, it must comply with the requirements of this paragraph (f)(3) in the same manner as if it were an initial program standard. (Thus, for example, if a plan or issuer provides a walking program as a reasonable alternative standard to a running program, individuals for whom it is unreasonably difficult due to a medical condition to complete the walking program (or for whom it is medically inadvisable to attempt to complete the walking program) must be provided a reasonable alternative standard to the walking program.) To the extent that a reasonable alternative standard under an activity-only wellness program is, itself, an outcome-based wellness program, it must comply with the requirements of paragraph (f)(4) of this section, including paragraph (f)(4)(iv)(D).

(E) If reasonable under the circumstances, a plan or issuer may seek verification, such as a statement from an individual's personal physician, that a health factor makes it unreasonably difficult for the individual to satisfy, or medically inadvisable for the individual to attempt to satisfy, the otherwise applicable standard of an activity-only wellness program. Plans and issuers may seek verification with respect to requests for a reasonable alternative standard for which it is reasonable to determine that medical judgment is required to evaluate the validity of the request.

(v) *Notice of availability of reasonable alternative standard.* The plan or issuer must disclose in all plan materials describing the terms of an activity-only wellness program the availability of a reasonable alternative standard to qualify for the reward (and, if applicable, the possibility of waiver of the otherwise applicable standard), including contact information for obtaining a reasonable alternative standard and a statement that recommendations of an individual's personal physician will be accommodated. If plan materials merely mention that such a program is available, without describing its terms, this disclosure is not required. Sample language is provided in paragraph (f)(6) of this section, as well as in certain examples of this section.

(vi) *Example.* The provisions of this paragraph (f)(3) are illustrated by the following example:

Example. (i) *Facts.* A group health plan provides a reward to individuals who participate in a reasonable specified walking program. If it is unreasonably difficult due to a medical condition for an individual to participate (or if it is medically inadvisable for an individual to attempt to participate), the plan will waive the walking program requirement and provide the reward. All materials describing the terms of the walking program disclose the availability of the waiver.

(ii) *Conclusion.* In this *Example,* the program satisfies the requirements of paragraph (f)(3)(iii) of this section because the walking program is reasonably designed to promote health and prevent disease. The program satisfies the requirements of paragraph (f)(3)(iv) of this section because the reward under the program is available to all similarly situated individuals. It accommodates individuals for whom it

is unreasonably difficult to participate in the walking program due to a medical condition (or for whom it would be medically inadvisable to attempt to participate) by providing them with the reward even if they do not participate in the walking program (that is, by waiving the condition). The plan also complies with the disclosure requirement of paragraph (f)(3)(v) of this section. Thus, the plan satisfies paragraphs (f)(3)(iii), (iv), and (v) of this section.

(4) *Requirements for outcome-based wellness programs.* A health-contingent wellness program that is an outcome-based wellness program, as described in paragraph (f)(1)(v) of this section, does not violate the provisions of this section only if all of the following requirements are satisfied:

(i) *Frequency of opportunity to qualify.* The program must give individuals eligible for the program the opportunity to qualify for the reward under the program at least once per year.

(ii) *Size of reward.* The reward for the outcome-based wellness program, together with the reward for other health-contingent wellness programs with respect to the plan, must not exceed the applicable percentage (as defined in paragraph (f)(5) of this section) of the total cost of employee-only coverage under the plan. However, if, in addition to employees, any class of dependents (such as spouses, or spouses and dependent children) may participate in the wellness program, the reward must not exceed the applicable percentage of the total cost of the coverage in which an employee and any dependents are enrolled. For purposes of this paragraph (f)(4)(ii), the cost of coverage is determined based on the total amount of employer and employee contributions towards the cost of coverage for the benefit package under which the employee is (or the employee and any dependents are) receiving coverage.

(iii) *Reasonable design.* The program must be reasonably designed to promote health or prevent disease. A program satisfies this standard if it has a reasonable chance of improving the health of, or preventing disease in, participating individuals, and it is not overly burdensome, is not a subterfuge for discriminating based on a health factor, and is not highly suspect in the method chosen to promote health or prevent disease. This determination is based on all the relevant facts and circumstances. To ensure that an outcome-based wellness program is reasonably designed to improve health and does not act as a subterfuge for underwriting or reducing benefits based on a health factor, a reasonable alternative standard to qualify for the reward must be provided to any individual who does not meet the initial standard based on a measurement, test, or screening that is related to a health factor, as explained in paragraph (f)(4)(iv) of this section.

(iv) *Uniform availability and reasonable alternative standards.* The full reward under the outcome-based wellness program must be available to all similarly situated individuals.

(A) Under this paragraph (f)(4)(iv), a reward under an outcome-based wellness program is not available to all similarly situated individuals for a period unless the program allows a reasonable alternative standard (or waiver of the otherwise applicable standard) for obtaining the reward for any individual who does not meet the initial standard based on the measurement, test, or screening, as described in this paragraph (f)(4)(iv).

(B) While plans and issuers are not required to determine a particular reasonable alternative standard in advance of an individual's request for one, if an individual is described in paragraph (f)(4)(iv)(A) of this section, a reasonable alternative standard must be furnished by the plan or issuer upon the individual's request or the condition for obtaining the reward must be waived.

(C) All the facts and circumstances are taken into account in determining whether a plan or issuer has furnished a reasonable alternative standard, including but not limited to the following:

(1) If the reasonable alternative standard is completion of an educational program, the plan or issuer must make the educational program available or assist the employee in finding such a program (instead of requiring an individual to find such a program unassisted), and may not require an individual to pay for the cost of the program.

Reg. §2590.702(f)(4)(iv)(C)(1)   ¶ 15,050A-1

(2) The time commitment required must be reasonable (for example, requiring attendance nightly at a one-hour class would be unreasonable).

(3) If the reasonable alternative standard is a diet program, the plan or issuer is not required to pay for the cost of food but must pay any membership or participation fee.

(4) If an individual's personal physician states that a plan standard (including, if applicable, the recommendations of the plan's medical professional) is not medically appropriate for that individual, the plan or issuer must provide a reasonable alternative standard that accommodates the recommendations of the individual's personal physician with regard to medical appropriateness. Plans and issuers may impose standard cost sharing under the plan or coverage for medical items and services furnished pursuant to the physician's recommendations.

(D) To the extent that a reasonable alternative standard under an outcome-based wellness program is, itself, an activity-only wellness program, it must comply with the requirements of paragraph (f)(3) of this section in the same manner as if it were an initial program standard. To the extent that a reasonable alternative standard under an outcome-based wellness program is, itself, another outcome-based wellness program, it must comply with the requirements of this paragraph (f)(4), subject to the following special provisions:

(1) The reasonable alternative standard cannot be a requirement to meet a different level of the same standard without additional time to comply that takes into account the individual's circumstances. For example, if the initial standard is to achieve a BMI less than 30, the reasonable alternative standard cannot be to achieve a BMI less than 31 on that same date. However, if the initial standard is to achieve a BMI less than 30, a reasonable alternative standard for the individual could be to reduce the individual's BMI by a small amount or small percentage, over a realistic period of time, such as within a year.

(2) An individual must be given the opportunity to comply with the recommendations of the individual's personal physician as a second reasonable alternative standard to meeting the reasonable alternative standard defined by the plan or issuer, but only if the physician joins in the request. The individual can make a request to involve a personal physician's recommendations at any time and the personal physician can adjust the physician's recommendations at any time, consistent with medical appropriateness.

(E) It is not reasonable to seek verification, such as a statement from an individual's personal physician, under an outcome-based wellness program that a health factor makes it unreasonably difficult for the individual to satisfy, or medically inadvisable for the individual to attempt to satisfy, the otherwise applicable standard as a condition of providing a reasonable alternative to the initial standard. However, if a plan or issuer provides an alternative standard to the otherwise applicable measurement, test, or screening that involves an activity that is related to a health factor, then the rules of paragraph (f)(3) of this section for activity-only wellness programs apply to that component of the wellness program and the plan or issuer may, if reasonable under the circumstances, seek verification that it is unreasonably difficult due to a medical condition for an individual to perform or complete the activity (or it is medically inadvisable to attempt to perform or complete the activity). (For example, if an outcome-based wellness program requires participants to maintain a certain healthy weight and provides a diet and exercise program for individuals who do not meet the targeted weight, a plan or issuer may seek verification, as described in paragraph (f)(3)(iv)(D) of this section, if reasonable under the circumstances, that a second reasonable alternative standard is needed for certain individuals because, for those individuals, it would be unreasonably difficult due to a medical condition to comply, or medically inadvisable to attempt to comply, with the diet and exercise program, due to a medical condition.)

(v) *Notice of availability of reasonable alternative standard.* The plan or issuer must disclose in all plan materials describing the terms of an outcome-based wellness program, and in any disclosure that an individual did not satisfy an initial outcome-based standard, the availability of a reasonable alternative standard to qualify for the reward (and, if applicable, the possibility of waiver of the otherwise applicable standard), including contact information for obtaining a reasonable alternative standard and a statement that recommendations of an indi-

vidual's personal physician will be accommodated. If plan materials merely mention that such a program is available, without describing its terms, this disclosure is not required. Sample language is provided in paragraph (f)(6) of this section, as well as in certain examples of this section.

(vi) *Examples.* The provisions of this paragraph (f)(4) are illustrated by the following examples:

Example 1—Cholesterol screening with reasonable alternative standard to work with personal physician. (i) *Facts.* A group health plan offers a reward to participants who achieve a count under 200 on a total cholesterol test. If a participant does not achieve the targeted cholesterol count, the plan allows the participant to develop an alternative cholesterol action plan in conjunction with the participant's personal physician that may include recommendations for medication and additional screening. The plan allows the physician to modify the standards, as medically necessary, over the year. (For example, if a participant develops asthma or depression, requires surgery and convalescence, or some other medical condition or consideration makes completion of the original action plan inadvisable or unreasonably difficult, the physician may modify the original action plan.) All plan materials describing the terms of the program include the following statement: "Your health plan wants to help you take charge of your health. Rewards are available to all employees who participate in our Cholesterol Awareness Wellness Program. If your total cholesterol count is under 200, you will receive the reward. If not, you will still have an opportunity to qualify for the reward. We will work with you and your doctor to find a Health Smart program that is right for you." In addition, when any individual participant receives notification that his or her cholesterol count is 200 or higher, the notification includes the following statement: "Your plan offers a Health Smart program under which we will work with you and your doctor to try to lower your cholesterol. If you complete this program, you will qualify for a reward. Please contact us at [contact information] to get started."

(ii) *Conclusion.* In this *Example 1,* the program is an outcome-based wellness program because the initial standard requires an individual to attain or maintain a specific health outcome (a certain cholesterol level) to obtain a reward. The program satisfies the requirements of paragraph (f)(4)(iii) of this section because the cholesterol program is reasonably designed to promote health and prevent disease. The program satisfies the requirements of paragraph (f)(4)(iv) of this section because it makes available to all participants who do not meet the cholesterol standard a reasonable alternative standard to qualify for the reward. Lastly, the plan also discloses in all materials describing the terms of the program and in any disclosure that an individual did not satisfy the initial outcome-based standard the availability of a reasonable alternative standard (including contact information and the individual's ability to involve his or her personal physician), as required by paragraph (f)(4)(v) of this section. Thus, the program satisfies the requirements of paragraphs (f)(4)(iii), (iv), and (v) of this section.

Example 2—Cholesterol screening with plan alternative and no opportunity for personal physician involvement. (i) *Facts.* Same facts as *Example 1,* except that the wellness program's physician or nurse practitioner (rather than the individual's personal physician) determines the alternative cholesterol action plan. The plan does not provide an opportunity for a participant's personal physician to modify the action plan if it is not medically appropriate for that individual.

(ii) *Conclusion.* In this *Example 2,* the wellness program does not satisfy the requirements of paragraph (f)(4)(iii) of this section because the program does not accommodate the recommendations of the participant's personal physician with regard to medical appropriateness, as required under paragraph (f)(4)(iv)(C)(*3*) of this section. Thus, the program is not reasonably designed under paragraph (f)(4)(iii) of this section and is not available to all similarly situated individuals under paragraph (f)(4)(iv) of this section. The notice also does not provide all the content required under paragraph (f)(4)(v) of this section.

Example 3—Cholesterol screening with plan alternative that can be modified by personal physician. (i) *Facts.* Same facts as *Example 2,* except that if a participant's personal physician disagrees with any part of the action plan, the personal physician may modify the action plan at any time, and the plan discloses this to participants.

(ii) *Conclusion.* In this *Example 3,* the wellness program satisfies the requirements of paragraph (f)(4)(iii) of this section because the participant's personal physician may modify the action plan determined by the wellness program's physician or nurse practitioner at any time if the physician states that the recommendations are not medically appropriate, as required under paragraph (f)(4)(iv)(C)(*3*) of this section. Thus, the program is reasonably designed under paragraph (f)(4)(iii) of this section and is available to all similarly situated individuals under paragraph (f)(4)(iv) of this section. The notice, which includes a statement that recommendations of an individual's personal physician will be accommodated, also complies with paragraph (f)(4)(v) of this section.

Example 4—BMI screening with walking program alternative. *(i) Facts.* A group health plan will provide a reward to participants who have a body mass index (BMI) that is 26 or lower, determined shortly before the beginning of the year. Any participant who does not meet the target BMI is given the same discount if the participant complies with an exercise program that consists of walking 150 minutes a week. Any participant for whom it is unreasonably difficult due to a medical condition to comply with this walking program (and any participant for whom it is medically inadvisable to attempt to comply with the walking program) during the year is given the same discount if the participant satisfies an alternative standard that is reasonable taking into consideration the participant's medical situation, is not unreasonably burdensome or impractical to comply with, and is otherwise reasonably designed based on all the relevant facts and circumstances. All plan materials describing the terms of the wellness program include the following statement: "Fitness is Easy! Start Walking! Your health plan cares about your health. If you are considered overweight because you have a BMI of over 26, our Start Walking program will help you lose weight and feel better. We will help you enroll. (**If your doctor says that walking isn't right for you, that's okay too. We will work with you (and, if you wish, your own doctor) to develop a wellness program that is.)" Participant *E* is unable to achieve a BMI that is 26 or lower within the plan's timeframe and receives notification that complies with paragraph (f)(4)(v) of this section. Nevertheless, it is unreasonably difficult due to a medical condition for *E* to comply with the walking program. *E* proposes a program based on the recommendations of *E*'s physician. The plan agrees to make the same discount available to *E* that is available to other participants in the BMI program or the alternative walking program, but only if *E* actually follows the physician's recommendations.

(ii) *Conclusion.* In this *Example 4,* the program is an outcome-based wellness program because the initial standard requires an individual to attain or maintain a specific health outcome (a certain BMI level) to obtain a reward. The program satisfies the requirements of paragraph (f)(4)(iii) of this section because it is reasonably designed to promote health and prevent disease. The program also satisfies the requirements of paragraph (f)(4)(iv) of this section because it makes available to all individuals who do not satisfy the BMI standard a reasonable alternative standard to qualify for the reward (in this case, a walking program that is not unreasonably burdensome or impractical for individuals to comply with and that is otherwise reasonably designed based on all the relevant facts and circumstances). In addition, the walking program is, itself, an activity-only standard and the plan complies with the requirements of paragraph (f)(3) of this section (including the requirement of paragraph (f)(3)(iv) that, if there are individuals for whom it is unreasonably difficult due to a medical condition to comply, or for whom it is medically inadvisable to attempt to comply, with the walking program, the plan provide a reasonable alternative to those individuals). Moreover, the plan satisfies the requirements of paragraph (f)(4)(v) of this section because it discloses, in all materials describing the terms of the program and in any disclosure that an individual did not satisfy the initial outcome-based standard, the availability of a reasonable alternative standard (including contact information and the individual's option to involve his or her personal physician) to qualify for the reward or the possibility of waiver of the otherwise applicable standard. Thus, the program satisfies the requirements of paragraphs (f)(4)(iii), (iv), and (v) of this section.

Example 5—BMI screening with alternatives available to either lower BMI or meet personal physician's recommendations. (i) Facts. Same facts as *Example 4* except that, with respect to any participant who does not meet the target BMI, instead of a walking program, the participant is expected to reduce BMI by one point. At any point during the year upon request, any individual can obtain a second reasonable alternative standard, which is compliance with the recommendations of the participant's personal physician regarding weight, diet, and exercise as set forth in a treatment plan that the physician recommends or to which the physician agrees. The participant's personal physician is permitted to change or adjust the treatment plan at any time and the option of following the participant's personal physician's recommendations is clearly disclosed.

(ii) *Conclusion.* In this *Example 5,* the reasonable alternative standard to qualify for the reward (the alternative BMI standard requiring a one-point reduction) does not make the program unreasonable under paragraph (f)(4)(iii) or (iv) of this section because the program complies with paragraph (f)(4)(iv)(C)(*4*) of this section by allowing a second reasonable alternative standard to qualify for the reward (compliance with the recommendations of the participant's personal physician, which can be changed or adjusted at any time). Accordingly, the program continues to satisfy the applicable requirements of paragraph (f) of this section.

Example 6—Tobacco use surcharge with smoking cessation program alternative. (i) *Facts.* In conjunction with an annual open enrollment period, a group health plan provides a premium differential based on tobacco use, determined using a health risk assessment. The following statement is included in all plan materials describing the tobacco premium differential: "Stop smoking today! We can help! If you are a smoker, we offer a smoking cessation program. If you complete the program, you can avoid this surcharge." The plan accommodates participants who smoke by facilitating their enrollment in a smoking cessation program that requires participation at a time and place that are not unreasonably burdensome or impractical for participants, and that is otherwise reasonably designed based on all the relevant facts and circumstances, and discloses contact information and the individual's option to involve his or her personal physician. The plan pays for the cost of participation in the smoking cessation program. Any participant can avoid the surcharge for the plan year by participating in the program, regardless of whether the participant stops smoking, but the plan can require a participant who wants to avoid the surcharge in a subsequent year to complete the smoking cessation program again.

(ii) *Conclusion.* In this *Example 6,* the premium differential satisfies the requirements of paragraphs (f)(4)(iii), (iv), and (v). The program is an outcome-based wellness program because the initial standard for obtaining a reward is dependent on the results of a health risk assessment (a measurement, test, or screening). The program is reasonably designed under paragraph (f)(4)(iii) because the plan provides a reasonable alternative standard (as required under paragraph (f)(4)(iv) of this section) to qualify for the reward to all tobacco users (a smoking cessation program). The plan discloses, in all materials describing the terms of the program, the availability of the reasonable alternative standard (including contact information and the individual's option to involve his or her personal physician). Thus, the program satisfies the requirements of paragraphs (f)(4)(iii), (iv), and (v) of this section.

Example 7—Tobacco use surcharge with alternative program requiring actual cessation. (i) *Facts.* Same facts as *Example 6,* except the plan does not provide participant *F* with the reward in subsequent years unless *F* actually stops smoking after participating in the tobacco cessation program.

(ii) *Conclusion.* In this *Example 7,* the program is not reasonably designed under paragraph (f)(4)(iii) of this section and does not provide a reasonable alternative standard as required under paragraph (f)(4)(iv) of this section. The plan cannot cease to provide a reasonable alternative standard merely because the participant did not stop smoking after participating in a smoking cessation program. The plan must continue to offer a reasonable alternative standard whether it is the same or different (such as a new recommendation from *F*'s personal physician or a new nicotine replacement therapy).

Example 8—Tobacco use surcharge with smoking cessation program alternative that is not reasonable. (i) *Facts.* Same facts as *Example 6,* except the plan does not facilitate participant *F*'s enrollment in a smoking cessation program. Instead the plan advises *F* to find a program, pay for it, and provide a certificate of completion to the plan.

(ii) *Conclusion.* In this *Example 8,* the requirement for *F* to find and pay for *F*'s own smoking cessation program means that the alternative program is not reasonable. Accordingly, the plan has not offered a reasonable alternative standard that complies with paragraphs (f)(4)(iii) and (iv) of this section and the program fails to satisfy the requirements of paragraph (f) of this section.

(5) *Applicable percentage.* (i) For purposes of this paragraph (f), the applicable percentage is 30 percent, except that the applicable percentage is increased by an additional 20 percentage points (to 50 percent) to the extent that the additional percentage is in connection with a program designed to prevent or reduce tobacco use.

(ii) The rules of this paragraph (f)(5) are illustrated by the following examples:

Example 1. (i) *Facts.* An employer sponsors a group health plan. The annual premium for employee-only coverage is $6,000 (of which the employer pays $4,500 per year and the employee pays $1,500 per year). The plan offers employees a health-contingent wellness program with several components, focused on exercise, blood sugar, weight, cholesterol, and blood pressure. The reward for compliance is an annual premium rebate of $600.

(ii) *Conclusion.* In this *Example 1,* the reward for the wellness program, $600, does not exceed the applicable percentage of 30 percent of the total annual cost of employee-only coverage, $1,800. ($6,000 × 30% = $1,800.)

Example 2. (i) *Facts.* Same facts as *Example 1,* except the wellness program is exclusively a tobacco prevention program. Employees who have used tobacco in the last 12 months and who are not enrolled in the plan's tobacco cessation program are charged a $1,000 premium surcharge (in addition to their employee contribution towards the coverage). (Those who participate in the plan's tobacco cessation program are not assessed the $1,000 surcharge.)

(ii) *Conclusion.* In this *Example 2,* the reward for the wellness program (absence of a $1,000 surcharge), does not exceed the applicable percentage of 50 percent of the total annual cost of employee-only coverage, $3,000. ($6,000 × 50% = $3,000.)

Example 3. (i) *Facts.* Same facts as *Example 1,* except that, in addition to the $600 reward for compliance with the health-contingent wellness program, the plan also imposes an additional $2,000 tobacco premium surcharge on employees who have used tobacco in the last 12 months and who are not enrolled in the plan's tobacco cessation program. (Those who participate in the plan's tobacco cessation program are not assessed the $2,000 surcharge.)

(ii) *Conclusion.* In this *Example 3,* the total of all rewards (including absence of a surcharge for participating in the tobacco program) is $2,600 ($600 + $2,000 = $2,600), which does not exceed the applicable percentage of 50 percent of the total annual cost of employee-only coverage ($3,000); and, tested separately, the $600 reward for the wellness program unrelated to tobacco use does not exceed the applicable percentage of 30 percent of the total annual cost of employee-only coverage ($1,800).

Example 4. (i) *Facts.* An employer sponsors a group health plan. The total annual premium for employee-only coverage (including both employer and employee contributions towards the coverage) is $5,000. The plan provides a $250 reward to employees who complete a health risk assessment, without regard to the health issues identified as part of the assessment. The plan also offers a Healthy Heart program, which is a health-contingent wellness program, with an opportunity to earn a $1,500 reward.

(ii) *Conclusion.* In this *Example 4,* even though the total reward for all wellness programs under the plan is $1,750 ($250 + $1,500 = $1,750, which exceeds the applicable percentage of 30 percent of the cost of the annual premium for employee-only coverage ($5,000 × 30% = $1,500)), only the reward offered for compliance with the health-contingent wellness program ($1,500) is taken into account in determining whether the rules of this paragraph (f)(5) are met. (The $250 reward is offered in connection with a participatory wellness program and therefore is not taken into account.) Accordingly, the health-contingent wellness program offers a reward that does not exceed the applicable percentage of 30 percent of the total annual cost of employee-only coverage.

(6) *Sample language.* The following language, or substantially similar language, can be used to satisfy the notice requirement of paragraphs (f)(3)(v) or (f)(4)(v) of this section: "Your health plan is committed to helping you achieve your best health. Rewards for participating in a wellness program are available to all employees. If you think you might be unable to meet a standard for a reward under this wellness program, you might qualify for an opportunity to earn the same reward by different means. Contact us at [insert contact information] and we will work with you (and, if you wish, with your doctor) to find a wellness program with the same reward that is right for you in light of your health status."

[Amended by 6/3/13 by 78 FR 33157.]

(g) *More favorable treatment of individuals with adverse health factors permitted.* (1) *In rules for eligibility.* (i) Nothing in this section prevents a group health plan or group health insurance issuer from establishing more favorable rules for eligibility (described in paragraph (b)(1) of this section) for individuals with an adverse health factor, such as disability, than for individuals without the adverse health factor. Moreover, nothing in this section prevents a plan or issuer from charging a higher premium or contribution with respect to individuals with an adverse health factor if they would not be eligible for the coverage were it not for the adverse health factor. (However, other laws, including State insurance laws, may set or limit premium rates; these laws are not affected by this section.)

(ii) The rules of this paragraph (g)(1) are illustrated by the following examples:

Example 1. (i) *Facts.* An employer sponsors a group health plan that generally is available to employees, spouses of employees, and dependent children until age 26. However, dependent children who are disabled are eligible for coverage beyond age 26.

(ii) *Conclusion.* In this Example 1, the plan provision allowing coverage for disabled dependent children beyond age 26 satisfies this paragraph (g)(1) (and thus does not violate this section). [Amended 2/24/14 by 79 FR 10295.]

Example 2. (i) *Facts.* An employer sponsors a group health plan, which is generally available to employees (and members of the employee's family) until the last day of the month in which the employee ceases to perform services for the employer. The plan generally charges employees $50 per month for employee-only coverage and $125 per month for family coverage. However, an employee who ceases to perform services for the employer by reason of disability may remain covered under the plan until the last day of the month that is 12 months after the month in which the employee ceased to perform services for the employer. During this extended period of coverage, the plan charges the employee $100 per month for employee-only coverage and $250 per month for family coverage. (This extended period of coverage is without regard to whatever rights the employee (or members of the employee's family) may have for COBRA continuation coverage.)

(ii) *Conclusion.* In this *Example 2,* the plan provision allowing extended coverage for disabled employees and their families satisfies this paragraph (g)(1) (and thus does not violate this section). In addition, the plan is permitted, under this paragraph (g)(1), to charge the disabled employees a higher premium during the extended period of coverage.

Example 3. (i) *Facts.* To comply with the requirements of a COBRA continuation provision, a group health plan generally makes COBRA continuation coverage available for a maximum period of 18 months in connection with a termination of employment but makes the coverage available for a maximum period of 29 months to certain disabled individuals and certain members of the disabled individual's family. Although the plan generally requires payment of 102 percent of the applicable premium for the first 18 months of COBRA continuation coverage, the plan requires payment of 150 percent of the applicable premium for the disabled individual's COBRA continuation coverage during the disability extension if the disabled individual would not be entitled to COBRA continuation coverage but for the disability.

(ii) *Conclusion.* In this *Example 3,* the plan provision allowing extended COBRA continuation coverage for disabled individuals satisfies this paragraph (g)(1) (and thus does not violate this section). In addition, the plan is permitted, under this paragraph (g)(1), to charge the disabled individuals a higher premium for the extended coverage if the individuals would not be eligible for COBRA continuation coverage were it not for the disability. (Similarly, if the plan provided an extended period of coverage for disabled individuals pursuant to State law or plan provision rather than pursuant to a COBRA continuation coverage provision, the plan could likewise charge the disabled individuals a higher premium for the extended coverage.)

(2) *In premiums or contributions.* (i) Nothing in this section prevents a group health plan or group health insurance issuer from charging individuals a premium or contribution that is less than the premium (or contribution) for similarly situated individuals if the lower charge is based on an adverse health factor, such as disability.

(ii) The rules of this paragraph (g)(2) are illustrated by the following example:

Example. (i) *Facts.* Under a group health plan, employees are generally required to pay $50 per month for employee-only coverage and $125 per month for family coverage under the plan. However, employees who are disabled receive coverage (whether employee-only or family coverage) under the plan free of charge.

(ii) *Conclusion.* In this *Example*, the plan provision waiving premium payment for disabled employees is permitted under this paragraph (g)(2) (and thus does not violate this section).

(h) *No effect on other laws.* Compliance with this section is not determinative of compliance with any other provision of the Act (including the COBRA continuation provisions) or any other State or Federal law, such as the Americans with Disabilities Act. Therefore, although the rules of this section would not prohibit a plan or issuer from treating one group of similarly situated individuals differently from another (such as providing different benefit packages to current and former employees), other Federal or State laws may require that two separate groups of similarly situated individuals be treated the same for certain purposes (such as making the same benefit package available to COBRA qualified beneficiaries as is made available to active employees). In addition, although this section generally does not impose new disclosure obligations on plans and issuers, this section does not affect any other laws, including those that require accurate disclosures and prohibit intentional misrepresentation.

(i) *Applicability dates.* This section applies for plan years beginning on or after July 1, 2007.

[Revised 12/13/06 by 71 FR 75014.]

Historical Comment: Amended 3/9/01 by 66 FR 14,076. Revised 12/13/06 by 71 FR 75014. Amended 10/7/09 by 74 FR 51663. Amended by 6/3/13 by 78 FR 33157. Amended 2/24/2014 by 79 FR 10295.

[¶ 15,050A-2]

§ 2590.702-1 Additional requirements prohibiting discrimination based on genetic information.

§ 2590.702-1(a) *Definitions.*. Unless otherwise provided, the definitions in this paragraph (a) govern in applying the provisions of this section.

(1) *Collect* means, with respect to information, to request, require, or purchase such information.

(2) *Family member* means, with respect to an individual -

(i) A dependent (as defined for purposes of § 2590.701-2 of this Part) of the individual; or

(ii) Any other person who is a first-degree, second-degree, third-degree, or fourthdegree relative of the individual or of a dependent of the individual. Relatives by affinity (such as by marriage or adoption) are treated the same as relatives by consanguinity (that is, relatives who share a common biological ancestor). In determining the degree of the relationship, relatives by less than full consanguinity (such as half-siblings, who share only one parent) are treated the same as relatives by full consanguinity (such as siblings who share both parents).

(A) First-degree relatives include parents, spouses, siblings, and children.

(B) Second-degree relatives include grandparents, grandchildren, aunts, uncles, nephews, and nieces.

(C) Third-degree relatives include great-grandparents, great-grandchildren, great aunts, great uncles, and first cousins.

(D) Fourth-degree relatives include great-great grandparents, great-great grandchildren, and children of first cousins.

(3) *Genetic information* means. (i) Subject to paragraphs (a)(3)(ii) and (a)(3)(iii) of this section, with respect to an individual, information about -

(A) The individual's genetic tests (as defined in paragraph (a)(5) of this section);

(B) The genetic tests of family members of the individual;

(C) The manifestation (as defined in paragraph (a)(6) of this section) of a disease or disorder in family members of the individual; or

(D) Any request for, or receipt of, genetic services (as defined in paragraph (a)(4) of this section), or participation in clinical research which includes genetic services, by the individual or any family member of the individual.

(ii) The term *genetic information* does not include information about the sex or age of any individual.

(iii) The term *genetic information* includes -

(A) With respect to a pregnant woman (or a family member of the pregnant woman), genetic information of any fetus carried by the pregnant woman; and

(B) With respect to an individual (or a family member of the individual) who is utilizing an assisted reproductive technology, genetic information of any embryo legally held by the individual or family member.

(4) *Genetic services* means -

(i) A genetic test, as defined in paragraph (a)(5) of this section;

(ii) Genetic counseling (including obtaining, interpreting, or assessing genetic information); or

(iii) Genetic education.

(5)(i) *Genetic test* means an analysis of human DNA, RNA, chromosomes, proteins, or metabolites, if the analysis detects genotypes, mutations, or chromosomal changes. However, a genetic test does not include an analysis of proteins or metabolites that is directly related to a manifested disease, disorder, or pathological condition. Accordingly, a test to determine whether an individual has a BRCA1 or BRCA2 variant is a genetic test. Similarly, a test to determine whether an individual has a genetic variant associated with hereditary nonpolyposis colorectal cancer is a genetic test. However, an HIV test, complete blood count, cholesterol test, liver function test, or test for the presence of alcohol or drugs is not a genetic test.

(ii) The rules of this paragraph (a)(5) are illustrated by the following example:

Example. (i) *Facts.* Individual *A* is a newborn covered under a group health plan. *A* undergoes a phenylketonuria (PKU) screening, which measures the concentration of a metabolite, phenylalanine, in *A*'s blood. In PKU, a mutation occurs in the phenylalanine hydroxylase (PAH) gene which contains instructions for making the enzyme needed to break down the amino acid phenylalanine. Individuals with the mutation, who have a deficiency in the enzyme to break down phenylalanine, have high concentrations of phenylalanine.

(ii) *Conclusion.* In this *Example*, the PKU screening is a genetic test with respect to *A* because the screening is an analysis of metabolites that detects a genetic mutation.

(6)(i) *Manifestation* or *manifested* means, with respect to a disease, disorder, or pathological condition, that an individual has been or could reasonably be diagnosed with the disease, disorder, or pathological condition by a health care professional with appropriate training and expertise in the field of medicine involved. For purposes of this section, a disease, disorder, or pathological condition is not manifested if a diagnosis is based principally on genetic information.

(ii) The rules of this paragraph (a)(6) are illustrated by the following examples:

Example 1. (i) *Facts.* Individual *A* has a family medical history of diabetes. *A* begins to experience excessive sweating, thirst, and fatigue. *A*'s physician examines *A* and orders blood glucose testing (which is not a genetic test). Based on the physician's examination, *A*'s symptoms, and test results that show elevated levels of blood glucose, *A*'s physician diagnoses *A* as having adult onset diabetes mellitus (Type 2 diabetes).

(ii) *Conclusion.* In this *Example 1*, *A* has been diagnosed by a health care professional with appropriate training and expertise in the field of medicine involved. The diagnosis is not based principally on genetic information. Thus, Type 2 diabetes is manifested with respect to *A*.

Example 2. (i) *Facts.* Individual *B* has several family members with colon cancer. One of them underwent genetic testing which detected a mutation in the MSH2 gene associated with hereditary nonpolyposis colorectal cancer (HNPCC). *B*'s physician, a health care professional with appropriate training and expertise in the field of medicine involved, recommends that *B* undergo a targeted genetic test to look for the specific mutation found in *B*'s relative to determine if *B* has an elevated risk for cancer. The genetic test with respect to *B* showed that *B* also carries the mutation and is at increased risk to develop colorectal and other cancers associated with HNPCC. *B* has a colonoscopy which indicates no signs of disease, and *B* has no symptoms.

(ii) *Conclusion.* In this *Example 2*, because *B* has no signs or symptoms of colorectal cancer, *B* has not been and could not reasonably be diagnosed with HNPCC. Thus, HNPCC is not manifested with respect to *B*.

Example 3. (i) *Facts.* Same facts as *Example 2*, except that *B*'s colonoscopy and subsequent tests indicate the presence of HNPCC. Based on the colonoscopy and subsequent test results, *B*'s physician makes a diagnosis of HNPCC.

(ii) *Conclusion.* In this *Example 3*, HNPCC is manifested with respect to *B* because a health care professional with appropriate training and expertise in the field of medicine involved has made a diagnosis that is not based principally on genetic information.

Example 4. (i) *Facts.* Individual *C* has a family member that has been diagnosed with Huntington's Disease. A genetic test indicates that *C* has the Huntington's Disease gene variant. At age 42, *C* begins suffering from occasional moodiness and disorientation, symptoms which are associated with Huntington's Disease. *C* is examined by a neurologist (a physician with appropriate training and expertise for diagnosing Huntington's Disease). The examination includes a clinical neurological exam. The results of the examination do not support a diagnosis of Huntington's Disease.

(ii) *Conclusion.* In this *Example 4*, *C* is not and could not reasonably be diagnosed with Huntington's Disease by a health care professional with appropriate training and expertise. Therefore, Huntington's Disease is not manifested with respect to *C*.

Example 5. (i) *Facts.* Same facts as *Example 4*, except that *C* exhibits additional neurological and behavioral symptoms, and the results of the examination support a diagnosis of Huntington's Disease with respect to *C*.

(ii) *Conclusion.* In this *Example 5*, *C* could reasonably be diagnosed with Huntington's Disease by a health care professional with appropriate training and expertise. Therefore, Huntington's Disease is manifested with respect to *C*.

(7) *Underwriting purposes* has the meaning given in paragraph (d)(1) of this section.

(b) *No group-based discrimination based on genetic information.* (1) *In general..* For purposes of this section, a group health plan, and a health insurance issuer offering health insurance coverage in connection with a group health plan, must not adjust premium or contribution amounts for the plan, or any group of similarly situated individuals under the plan, on the basis of genetic information. For this purpose, "similarly situated individuals" are those described in § 2590.702(d) of this Part.

(2) *Rule of construction..* Nothing in paragraph (b)(1) of this section (or in paragraph (d)(1) or (d)(2) of this section) limits the ability of a health insurance issuer offering health insurance coverage in connection with a group health plan to increase the premium for a group health plan or a group of similarly situated individuals under the

plan based on the manifestation of a disease or disorder of an individual who is enrolled in the plan. In such a case, however, the manifestation of a disease or disorder in one individual cannot also be used as genetic information about other group members to further increase the premium for a group health plan or a group of similarly situated individuals under the plan.

(3) *Examples..* The rules of this paragraph (b) are illustrated by the following examples:

Example 1. (i) *Facts.* An employer sponsors a group health plan that provides coverage through a health insurance issuer. In order to determine the premium rate for the upcoming plan year, the issuer reviews the claims experience of individuals covered under the plan and other health status information of the individuals, including genetic information. The issuer finds that three individuals covered under the plan had unusually high claims experience. In addition, the issuer finds that the genetic information of two other individuals indicates the individuals have a higher probability of developing certain illnesses although the illnesses are not manifested at this time. The issuer quotes the plan a higher per-participant rate because of both the genetic information and the higher claims experience.

(ii) *Conclusion.* In this *Example 1*, the issuer violates the provisions of this paragraph (b) because the issuer adjusts the premium based on genetic information. However, if the adjustment related solely to claims experience, the adjustment would not violate the requirements of this section (nor would it violate the requirements of paragraph (c) of § 2590.702 of this Part, which prohibits discrimination in individual premiums or contributions based on a health factor but permits increases in the group rate based on a health factor).

Example 2. (i) *Facts.* An employer sponsors a group health plan that provides coverage through a health insurance issuer. In order to determine the premium rate for the upcoming plan year, the issuer reviews the claims experience of individuals covered under the plan and other health status information of the individuals, including genetic information. The issuer finds that Employee *A* has made claims for treatment of polycystic kidney disease. *A* also has two dependent children covered under the plan. The issuer quotes the plan a higher per-participant rate because of both *A*'s claims experience and the family medical history of *A*'s children (that is, the fact that *A* has the disease).

(ii) *Conclusion.* In this *Example 2*, the issuer violates the provisions of this paragraph (b) because, by taking the likelihood that *A*'s children may develop polycystic kidney disease into account in computing the rate for the plan, the issuer adjusts the premium based on genetic information relating to a condition that has not been manifested in *A*'s children. However, it is permissible for the issuer to increase the premium based on *A*'s claims experience.

(c) *Limitation on requesting or requiring genetic testing.* (1) *General rule..* Except as otherwise provided in this paragraph (c), a group health plan, and a health insurance issuer offering health insurance coverage in connection with a group health plan, must not request or require an individual or a family member of the individual to undergo a genetic test.

(2) *Health care professional may recommend a genetic test..* Nothing in paragraph (c)(1) of this section limits the authority of a health care professional who is providing health care services to an individual to request that the individual undergo a genetic test.

(3) *Examples..* The rules of paragraphs (c)(1) and (2) of this section are illustrated by the following examples:

Example 1. (i) *Facts.* Individual *A* goes to a physician for a routine physical examination. The physician reviews *A*'s family medical history and *A* informs the physician that *A*'s mother has been diagnosed with Huntington's Disease. The physician advises *A* that Huntington's Disease is hereditary and recommends that *A* undergo a genetic test.

(ii) *Conclusion.* In this *Example 1*, the physician is a health care professional who is providing health care services to *A*. Therefore, the physician's recommendation that *A* undergo the genetic test does not violate this paragraph (c).

Example 2. (i) *Facts.* Individual *B* is covered by a health maintenance organization (HMO). *B* is a child being treated for leukemia. *B*'s physician, who is employed by the HMO, is considering a treatment plan that includes six-mercaptopurine, a drug for treating leukemia in most children. However, the drug could be fatal if taken by a small percentage of children with a particular gene variant. *B*'s physician recommends that *B* undergo a genetic test to detect this variant before proceeding with this course of treatment.

(ii) *Conclusion.* In this *Example 2*, even though the physician is employed by the HMO, the physician is nonetheless a health care professional who is providing health care services to *B*. Therefore, the physician's recommendation that *B* undergo the genetic test does not violate this paragraph (c).

(4) *Determination regarding payment..* (i) *In general..* As provided in this paragraph (c)(4), nothing in paragraph (c)(1) of this section precludes a plan or issuer from obtaining and using the results of a genetic test in making a determination regarding payment. For this purpose, "payment" has the meaning given such term in 45 CFR 164.501 of the privacy regulations issued under the Health Insurance Portability and Accountability Act. Thus, if a plan or issuer conditions payment for an item or service based on its medical appropriateness and the medical appropriateness of the item or service depends on the genetic makeup of a patient, then the plan or issuer is permitted to condition payment for the item or service on the outcome of a genetic test. The plan or issuer may also refuse payment if the patient does not undergo the genetic test.

(ii) *Limitation..* A plan or issuer is permitted to request only the minimum amount of information necessary to make a determination regarding payment. The minimum amount of information necessary is determined in accordance with the minimum necessary standard in 45 CFR 164.502(b) of the privacy regulations issued under the Health Insurance Portability and Accountability Act.

(iii) *Examples..* See paragraph (e) of this section for examples illustrating the rules of this paragraph (c)(4), as well as other provisions of this section.

(5) *Research exception..* Notwithstanding paragraph (c)(1) of this section, a plan or issuer may request, but not require, that a participant or beneficiary undergo a genetic test if all of the conditions of this paragraph (c)(5) are met:

(i) *Research in accordance with Federal regulations and applicable State or local law or regulations..* The plan or issuer makes the request pursuant to research, as defined in 45 CFR 46.102(d), that complies with 45 CFR Part 46 or equivalent Federal regulations, and any applicable State or local law or regulations for the protection of human subjects in research.

(ii) *Written request for participation in research..* The plan or issuer makes the request in writing, and the request clearly indicates to each participant or beneficiary (or, in the case of a minor child, to the legal guardian of the beneficiary) that -

(A) Compliance with the request is voluntary; and

(B) Noncompliance will have no effect on eligibility for benefits (as described in § 2590.702(b)(1) of this Part) or premium or contribution amounts.

(iii) *Prohibition on underwriting..* No genetic information collected or acquired under this paragraph (c)(5) can be used for underwriting purposes (as described in paragraph (d)(1) of this section).

(iv) *Notice to Federal agencies..* The plan or issuer completes a copy of the "Notice of Research Exception under the Genetic Information Nondiscrimination Act" authorized by the Secretary and provides the notice to the address specified in the instructions thereto.

(d) *Prohibitions on collection of genetic information.* (1) *For underwriting purposes.* (i) *General rule..* A group health plan, and a health insurance issuer offering health insurance coverage in connection with a group health plan, must not collect (as defined in paragraph (a)(1) of this section) genetic information for underwriting purposes. See paragraph (e) of this section for examples illustrating the rules of this paragraph (d)(1), as well as other provisions of this section.

(ii) *Underwriting purposes defined..* Subject to paragraph (d)(1)(iii) of this section, *underwriting purposes* means, with respect to any group health plan, or health insurance coverage offered in connection with a group health plan -

(A) Rules for, or determination of, eligibility (including enrollment and continued eligibility) for benefits under the plan or coverage as described in § 2590.702(b)(1)(ii) of this Part (including changes in deductibles or other cost-sharing mechanisms in return for activities such as completing a health risk assessment or participating in a wellness program);

(B) The computation of premium or contribution amounts under the plan or coverage (including discounts, rebates, payments in kind, or other premium differential mechanisms in return for activities such as completing a health risk assessment or participating in a wellness program);

(C) The application of any preexisting condition exclusion under the plan or coverage; and

(D) Other activities related to the creation, renewal, or replacement of a contract of health insurance or health benefits.

(iii) *Medical appropriateness..* If an individual seeks a benefit under a group health plan or health insurance coverage, the plan or coverage may limit or exclude the benefit based on whether the benefit is medically appropriate, and the determination of whether the benefit is medically appropriate is not within the meaning of underwriting purposes. Accordingly, if an individual seeks a benefit under the plan and the plan or issuer conditions the benefit based on its medical appropriateness and the medical appropriateness of the benefit depends on genetic information of the individual, then the plan or issuer is permitted to condition the benefit on the genetic information. A plan or issuer is permitted to request only the minimum amount of genetic information necessary to determine medical appropriateness. The plan or issuer may deny the benefit if the patient does not provide the genetic information required to determine medical appropriateness. If an individual is not seeking a benefit, the medical appropriateness exception of this paragraph (d)(1)(iii) to the definition of underwriting purposes does not apply. See paragraph (e) of this section for examples illustrating the medical appropriateness provisions of this paragraph (d)(1)(iii), as well as other provisions of this section.

(2) *Prior to or in connection with enrollment..* (i) *In general..* A group health plan, and a health insurance issuer offering health insurance coverage in connection with a group health plan, must not collect genetic information with respect to any individual prior to that individual's effective date of coverage under that plan or coverage, nor in connection with the rules for eligibility (as defined in § 2590.702(b)(1)(ii) of this Part) that apply to that individual. Whether or not an individual's information is collected prior to that individual's effective date of coverage is determined at the time of collection.

(ii) *Incidental collection exception..* (A) *In general..* If a group health plan, or a health insurance issuer offering health insurance coverage in connection with a group health plan, obtains genetic information incidental to the collection of other information concerning any individual, the collection is not a violation of this paragraph (d)(2), as long as the collection is not for underwriting purposes in violation of paragraph (d)(1) of this section.

(B) *Limitation..* The incidental collection exception of this paragraph (d)(2)(ii) does not apply in connection with any collection where it is reasonable to anticipate that health information will be received, unless the collection explicitly states that genetic information should not be provided.

(3) *Examples..* The rules of this paragraph (d) are illustrated by the following examples:

Example 1. (i) *Facts.* A group health plan provides a premium reduction to enrollees who complete a health risk assessment. The health risk assessment is requested to be completed after enrollment. Whether or not it is completed or what responses are given on it has no effect on an individual's enrollment status, or on the enrollment status of members of the individual's family. The health risk assessment includes questions about the individual's family medical history.

(ii) *Conclusion.* In this *Example 1*, the health risk assessment includes a request for genetic information (that is, the individual's family medical history). Because completing the health risk assessment results in a premium reduction, the request for genetic information is for underwriting purposes. Consequently, the request violates the prohibition on the collection of genetic information in paragraph (d)(1) of this section.

Example 2. (i) *Facts.* The same facts as *Example 1*, except there is no premium reduction or any other reward for completing the health risk assessment.

(ii) *Conclusion.* In this *Example 2*, the request is not for underwriting purposes, nor is it prior to or in connection with enrollment. Therefore, it does not violate the prohibition on the collection of genetic information in this paragraph (d).

Example 3. (i) *Facts.* A group health plan requests that enrollees complete a health risk assessment prior to enrollment, and includes questions about the individual's family medical history. There is no reward or penalty for completing the health risk assessment.

(ii) *Conclusion.* In this *Example 3*, because the health risk assessment includes a request for genetic information (that is, the individual's family medical history), and requests the information prior to enrollment, the request violates the prohibition on the collection of genetic information in paragraph (d)(2) of this section. Moreover, because it is a request for genetic information, it is not an incidental collection under paragraph (d)(2)(ii) of this section.

Example 4. (i) *Facts.* The facts are the same as in *Example 1*, except there is no premium reduction or any other reward given for completion of the health risk assessment. However, certain people completing the health risk assessment may become eligible for additional benefits under the plan by being enrolled in a disease management program based on their answers to questions about family medical history. Other people may become eligible for the disease management program based solely on their answers to questions about their individual medical history.

(ii) *Conclusion.* In this *Example 4*, the request for information about an individual's family medical history could result in the individual being eligible for benefits for which the individual would not otherwise be eligible. Therefore, the questions about family medical history on the health risk assessment are a request for genetic information for underwriting purposes and are prohibited under this paragraph (d). Although the plan conditions eligibility for the disease management program based on determinations of medical appropriateness, the exception for determinations of medical appropriateness does not apply because the individual is not seeking benefits.

Example 5. (i) *Facts.* A group health plan requests enrollees to complete two distinct health risk assessments (HRAs) after and unrelated to enrollment. The first HRA instructs the individual to answer only for the individual and not for the individual's family. The first HRA does not ask about any genetic tests the individual has undergone or any genetic services the individual has received. The plan offers a reward for completing the first HRA. The second HRA asks about family medical history and the results of genetic tests the individual has undergone. The plan offers no reward for completing the second HRA and the instructions make clear that completion of the second HRA is wholly voluntary and will not affect the reward given for completion of the first HRA.

(ii) *Conclusion.* In this *Example 5*, no genetic information is collected in connection with the first HRA, which offers a reward, and no benefits or other rewards are conditioned on the request for genetic information in the second HRA. Consequently, the request for genetic information in the second HRA is not for underwriting purposes, and the two HRAs do not violate the prohibition on the collection of genetic information in this paragraph (d).

Example 6. (i) *Facts.* A group health plan waives its annual deductible for enrollees who complete an HRA. The HRA is requested to be completed after enrollment. Whether or not the HRA is completed or what responses are given on it has no effect on an individual's enrollment status, or on the enrollment status of members of the individual's family. The HRA does not include any direct questions about the individual's genetic information (including family medical history). However, the last question reads, "Is there anything else

relevant to your health that you would like us to know or discuss with you?"

(ii) *Conclusion.* In this *Example 6*, the plan's request for medical information does not explicitly state that genetic information should not be provided. Therefore, any genetic information collected in response to the question is not within the incidental collection exception and is prohibited under this paragraph (d).

Example 7. (i) *Facts.* Same facts as *Example 6*, except that the last question goes on to state, "In answering this question, you should not include any genetic information. That is, please do not include any family medical history or any information related to genetic testing, genetic services, genetic counseling, or genetic diseases for which you believe you may be at risk."

(ii) *Conclusion.* In this *Example 7*, the plan's request for medical information explicitly states that genetic information should not be provided. Therefore, any genetic information collected in response to the question is within the incidental collection exception. However, the plan may not use any genetic information it obtains incidentally for underwriting purposes.

Example 8. (i) *Facts.* Issuer *M* acquires Issuer *N*. *M* requests *N*'s records, stating that *N* should not provide genetic information and should review the records to excise any genetic information. *N* assembles the data requested by *M* and, although *N* reviews it to delete genetic information, the data from a specific region included some individuals' family medical history. Consequently, *M* receives genetic information about some of *N*'s covered individuals.

(ii) *Conclusion.* In this *Example 8*, *M*'s request for health information explicitly stated that genetic information should not be provided. Therefore, the collection of genetic information was within the incidental collection exception. However, *M* may not use the genetic information it obtained incidentally for underwriting purposes.

(e) *Examples regarding determinations of medical appropriateness..* The application of the rules of paragraphs (c) and (d) of this section to plan or issuer determinations of medical appropriateness is illustrated by the following examples:

Example 1. (i) *Facts.* Individual *A*'s group health plan covers genetic testing for celiac disease for individuals who have family members with this condition. After *A*'s son is diagnosed with celiac disease, *A* undergoes a genetic test and promptly submits a claim for the test to *A*'s issuer for reimbursement. The issuer asks *A* to provide the results of the genetic test before the claim is paid.

(ii) *Conclusion.* In this *Example 1*, under the rules of paragraph (c)(4) of this section the issuer is permitted to request only the minimum amount of information necessary to make a decision regarding payment. Because the results of the test are not necessary for the issuer to make a decision regarding the payment of *A*'s claim, the issuer's request for the results of the genetic test violates paragraph (c) of this section.

Example 2. (i) *Facts.* Individual *B*'s group health plan covers a yearly mammogram for participants and beneficiaries starting at age 40, or at age 30 for those with increased risk for breast cancer, including individuals with BRCA1 or BRCA2 gene mutations. *B* is 33 years old and has the BRCA2 mutation. *B* undergoes a mammogram and promptly submits a claim to *B*'s plan for reimbursement. Following an established policy, the plan asks *B* for evidence of increased risk of breast cancer, such as the results of a genetic test or a family history of breast cancer, before the claim for the mammogram is paid. This policy is applied uniformly to all similarly situated individuals and is not directed at individuals based on any genetic information.

(ii) *Conclusion.* In this *Example 2*, the plan does not violate paragraphs (c) or (d) of this section. Under paragraph (c), the plan is permitted to request and use the results of a genetic test to make a determination regarding payment, provided the plan requests only the minimum amount of information necessary. Because the medical appropriateness of the mammogram depends on the genetic makeup of the patient, the minimum amount of information necessary includes the results of the genetic test. Similarly, the plan does not violate paragraph (d) of this section because the plan is permitted to request genetic information in making a determination regarding the medical appropriateness of a claim if the genetic information is necessary to make the determination (and if the genetic information is not used for underwriting purposes).

Example 3. (i) *Facts.* Individual *C* was previously diagnosed with and treated for breast cancer, which is currently in remission. In accordance with the recommendation of *C*'s physician, *C* has been taking a regular dose of tamoxifen to help prevent a recurrence. *C*'s group health plan adopts a new policy requiring patients taking tamoxifen to undergo a genetic test to ensure that tamoxifen is medically appropriate for their genetic makeup. In accordance with, at the time, the latest scientific research, tamoxifen is not helpful in up to 7 percent of breast cancer patients, those with certain variations of the gene for making the CYP $_2$D6 enzyme. If a patient has a gene variant making tamoxifen not medically appropriate, the plan does not pay for the tamoxifen prescription.

(ii) *Conclusion.* In this *Example 3*, the plan does not violate paragraph (c) of this section if it conditions future payments for the tamoxifen prescription on *C*'s undergoing a genetic test to determine what genetic markers *C* has for making the CYP $_2$D6 enzyme. Nor does the plan violate paragraph (c) of this section if the plan refuses future payment if the results of the genetic test indicate that tamoxifen is not medically appropriate for *C*.

Example 4. (i) *Facts.* A group health plan offers a diabetes disease management program to all similarly situated individuals for whom it is medically appropriate based on whether the individuals have or are at risk for diabetes. The program provides enhanced benefits related only to diabetes for individuals who qualify for the program. The plan sends out a notice to all participants that describes the diabetes disease management program and explains the terms for eligibility. Individuals interested in enrolling in the program are advised to contact the plan to demonstrate that they have diabetes or that they are at risk for diabetes. For individuals who do not currently have diabetes, genetic information may be used to demonstrate that an individual is at risk.

(ii) *Conclusion.* In this *Example 4*, the plan may condition benefits under the disease management program upon a showing by an individual that the individual is at risk for diabetes, even if such showing may involve genetic information, provided that the plan requests genetic information only when necessary to make a determination regarding whether the disease management program is medically appropriate for the individual and only requests the minimum amount of information necessary to make that determination.

Example 5. (i) *Facts.* Same facts as *Example 4*, except that the plan includes a questionnaire that asks about the occurrence of diabetes in members of the individual's family as part of the notice describing the disease management program.

(ii) *Conclusion.* In this *Example 5*, the plan violates the requirements of paragraph (d)(1) of this section because the requests for genetic information are not limited to those situations in which it is necessary to make a determination regarding whether the disease management program is medically appropriate for the individuals.

Example 6. (i) *Facts.* Same facts as *Example 4*, except the disease management program provides an enhanced benefit in the form of a lower annual deductible to individuals under the program; the lower deductible applies with respect to all medical expenses incurred by the individual. Thus, whether or not a claim relates to diabetes, the individual is provided with a lower deductible based on the individual providing the plan with genetic information.

(ii) *Conclusion.* In this *Example 6*, because the enhanced benefits include benefits not related to the determination of medical appropriateness, making available the enhanced benefits is within the meaning of underwriting purposes. Accordingly, the plan may not request or require genetic information (including family history information) in determining eligibility for enhanced benefits under the program because such a request would be for underwriting purposes and would violate paragraph (d)(1) of this section.

(f) *Applicability date.*. This section applies for plan years beginning on or after December 7, 2009.

Historical Comment: Added 10/7/09 by 74 FR 51663.

[¶ 15,050B]
GUARANTEED RENEWABILITY IN MULTIEMPLOYER PLANS AND MULTIPLE EMPLOYER WELFARE ARRANGEMENTS

Act Sec. 703. A group health plan which is a multiemployer plan or which is a multiple employer welfare arrangement may not deny an employer whose employees are covered under such a plan continued access to the same or different coverage under the terms of such a plan, other than—

(1) for nonpayment of contributions;

(2) for fraud or other intentional misrepresentation of material fact by the employer;

(3) for noncompliance with material plan provisions;

(4) because the plan is ceasing to offer any coverage in a geographic area;

(5) in the case of a plan that offers benefits through a network plan, there is no longer any individual enrolled through the employer who lives, resides, or works in the service area of the network plan and the plan applies this paragraph uniformly without regard to the claims experience of employers or any health status-related factor in relation to such individuals or their dependents; and

(6) for failure to meet the terms of an applicable collective bargaining agreement, to renew a collective bargaining or other agreement requiring or authorizing contributions to the plan, or to employ employees covered by such an agreement.

Amendments

P.L. 104-191, § 101(a):

Added ERISA Act Sec. 703 to read as above.

The above amendments generally apply with respect to group health plans for plan years beginning after June 30, 1997. For special rules, see Act Sec. 101(g)(2)- (5), reproduced after ERISA Act Sec. 701 above.

Regulations

The following regulations were adopted by 62 FR 16894 and published in the Federal Register on April 8, 1997, under "Chapter XXV of Title 29 of the Code of Federal Regulations; Subchapter L—Health Insurance Portability and Renewability for Group Health Plans; Part 2590—Rules and Regulations for Health Insurance Portability and Renewability for Group Health Plans."

[¶ 15,050B-1]
§ 2590.703 **Guaranteed renewability in multiemployer plans and multiple employer welfare arrangements. [Reserved]**

[¶ 15,050C] Act Sec. 704. [Reserved]

[¶ 15,050D] Act Sec. 705 [Reserved]

[¶ 15,050E] Act Sec. 706. [Reserved]

[¶ 15,050F] Act Sec. 707. [Reserved]

[¶ 15,050J]
STANDARDS RELATING TO BENEFITS FOR MOTHERS AND NEWBORNS

Act Sec. 711.(a) REQUIREMENTS FOR MINIMUM HOSPITAL STAY FOLLOWING BIRTH. (1) IN GENERAL. A group health plan, and a health insurance issuer offering group health insurance coverage, may not—

(A) except as provided in paragraph (2)—

(i) restrict benefits for any hospital length of stay in connection with childbirth for the mother or newborn child, following a normal vaginal delivery, to less than 48 hours, or

(ii) restrict benefits for any hospital length of stay in connection with childbirth for the mother or newborn child, following a cesarean section, to less than 96 hours; or

(B) require that a provider obtain authorization from the plan or the issuer for prescribing any length of stay required under subparagraph (A) (without regard to paragraph (2)).

(2) EXCEPTION. Paragraph (1)(A) shall not apply in connection with any group health plan or health insurance issuer in any case in which the decision to discharge the mother or her newborn child prior to the expiration of the minimum length of stay otherwise required under paragraph (1)(A) is made by an attending provider in consultation with the mother.

(b) PROHIBITIONS. (b) A group health plan, and a health insurance issuer offering group health insurance coverage in connection with a group health plan, may not—

(1) deny to the mother or her newborn child eligibility, or continued eligibility, to enroll or to renew coverage under the terms of the plan, solely for the purpose of avoiding the requirements of this section;

(2) provide monetary payments or rebates to mothers to encourage such mothers to accept less than the minimum protections available under this section;

(3) penalize or otherwise reduce or limit the reimbursement of an attending provider because such provider provided care to an individual participant or beneficiary in accordance with this section;

(4) provide incentives (monetary or otherwise) to an attending provider to induce such provider to provide care to an individual participant or beneficiary in a manner inconsistent with this section; or

(5) subject to subsection (c)(3), restrict benefits for any portion of a period within a hospital length of stay required under subsection (a) in a manner which is less favorable than the benefits provided for any preceding portion of such stay.

(c) RULES OF CONSTRUCTION.—

(c)(1) Nothing in this section shall be construed to require a mother who is a participant or beneficiary—

(A) to give birth in a hospital; or

(B) to stay in the hospital for a fixed period of time following the birth of her child.

(2) This section shall not apply with respect to any group health plan, or any group health insurance coverage offered by a health insurance issuer, which does not provide benefits for hospital lengths of stay in connection with childbirth for a mother or her newborn child.

(3) Nothing in this section shall be construed as preventing a group health plan or issuer from imposing deductibles, coinsurance, or other cost-sharing in relation to benefits for hospital lengths of stay in connection with childbirth for a mother or newborn child under the plan (or under health insurance coverage offered in connection with a group health plan), except that such coinsurance or other cost-sharing for any portion of a period within a hospital length of stay required under subsection (a) may not be greater than such coinsurance or cost-sharing for any preceding portion of such stay.

(d) Notice under Group Health Plan. The imposition of the requirements of this section shall be treated as a material modification in the terms of the plan described in section 102(a)(1), for purposes of assuring notice of such requirements under the plan; except that the summary description required to be provided under the last sentence of section 104(b)(1) with respect to such modification shall be provided by not later than 60 days after the first day of the first plan year in which such requirements apply.

(e) Level and Type of Reimbursements. Nothing in this section shall be construed to prevent a group health plan or a health insurance issuer offering group health insurance coverage from negotiating the level and type of reimbursement with a provider for care provided in accordance with this section.

(f) Preemption; Exception for Health Insurance Coverage in Certain States.—

(f)(1) In general. The requirements of this section shall not apply with respect to health insurance coverage if there is a State law (as defined in section 731(d)(1)) for a State that regulates such coverage that is described in any of the following subparagraphs:

(A) Such State law requires such coverage to provide for at least a 48-hour hospital length of stay following a normal vaginal delivery and at least a 96-hour hospital length of stay following a cesarean section.

(B) Such State law requires such coverage to provide for maternity and pediatric care in accordance with guidelines established by the American College of Obstetricians and Gynecologists, the American Academy of Pediatrics, or other established professional medical associations.

(C) Such State law requires, in connection with such coverage for maternity care, that the hospital length of stay for such care is left to the decision of (or required to be made by) the attending provider in consultation with the mother.

(2) Construction. Section 731(a)(1) shall not be construed as superseding a State law described in paragraph (1).

Amendments

P.L. 104-204, §603(a)(5):

Added ERISA Sec. 711 to read as above.

The above amendment shall apply with respect to group health plans for plan years beginning on or after January 1, 1998.

Regulations

The following regulations were adopted by 62 FR 16894 and published in the Federal Register on April 8, 1997, under "Chapter XXV of Title 29 of the Code of Federal Regulations; Subchapter L—Health Insurance Portability and Renewability for Group Health Plans; Part 2590—Rules and Regulations for Health Insurance Portability and Renewability for Group Health Plans." The regulations were amended by 63 FR 5745 and published in the Federal Register on October 27, 1998. The heading was revised by T.D. 9166 (69 FR 78720) on December 30, 2004. Reg. §2590.711 was revised in its entirety on October 20, 2008 (73 FR 62410).

Subpart B—Health Coverage Portability, Nondiscrimination, and Renewability

[¶ 15,050J-1]

§2590.711 Standards relating to benefits for mothers and newborns.

(a) *Hospital length of stay*—. (1) *General rule.* Except as provided in paragraph (a)(5) of this section, a group health plan, or a health insurance issuer offering group health insurance coverage, that provides benefits for a hospital length of stay in connection with childbirth for a mother or her newborn may not restrict benefits for the stay to less than—

(i) 48 hours following a vaginal delivery; or

(ii) 96 hours following a delivery by cesarean section.

(2) *When stay begins.* (i) *Delivery in a hospital.* If delivery occurs in a hospital, the hospital length of stay for the mother or newborn child begins at the time of delivery (or in the case of multiple births, at the time of the last delivery).

(ii) *Delivery outside a hospital.* If delivery occurs outside a hospital, the hospital length of stay begins at the time the mother or newborn is admitted as a hospital inpatient in connection with childbirth. The determination of whether an admission is in connection with childbirth is a medical decision to be made by the attending provider.

(3) *Examples.* The rules of paragraphs (a)(1) and (2) of this section are illustrated by the following examples. In each example, the group health plan provides benefits for hospital lengths of stay in connection with childbirth and is subject to the requirements of this section, as follows:

(i) *Example 1.* (i) *Facts.* A pregnant woman covered under a group health plan goes into labor and is admitted to the hospital at 10 p.m. on June 11. She gives birth by vaginal delivery at 6 a.m. on June 12.

(ii) *Conclusion.* In this Example 1, the 48-hour period described in paragraph (a)(1)(i) of this section ends at 6 a.m. on June 14.

(i) *Example 2.* (i) *Facts.* A woman covered under a group health plan gives birth at home by vaginal delivery. After the delivery,

the woman begins bleeding excessively in connection with the childbirth and is admitted to the hospital for treatment of the excessive bleeding at 7 p.m. on October 1.

(ii) *Conclusion.* In this Example 2, the 48-hour period described in paragraph (a)(1)(i) of this section ends at 7 p.m. on October 3.

(i) *Example 3.* (i) *Facts.* A woman covered under a group health plan gives birth by vaginal delivery at home. The child later develops pneumonia and is admitted to the hospital. The attending provider determines that the admission is not in connection with childbirth.

(ii) *Conclusion.* In this Example 3, the hospital length-of-stay requirements of this section do not apply to the child's admission to the hospital because the admission is not in connection with childbirth.

(4) *Authorization not required*— (i) *In general.* A plan or issuer is prohibited from requiring that a physician or other health care provider obtain authorization from the plan or issuer for prescribing the hospital length of stay specified in paragraph (a)(1) of this section. (See also paragraphs (b)(2) and (c)(3) of this section for rules and examples regarding other authorization and certain notice requirements.)

(ii) *Example.* The rule of this paragraph (a)(4) is illustrated by the following example:

(i) *Example.* (i) *Facts.* In the case of a delivery by cesarean section, a group health plan subject to the requirements of this section automatically provides benefits for any hospital length of stay of up to 72 hours. For any longer stay, the plan requires an attending provider to complete a certificate of medical necessity. The plan then makes a determination, based on the certificate of medical necessity, whether a longer stay is medically necessary.

(ii) *Conclusion.* In this Example, the requirement that an attending provider complete a certificate of medical necessity to obtain authorization for the period between 72 hours and 96 hours following a delivery by cesarean section is prohibited by this paragraph (a)(4).

(5) *Exceptions.* (i) *Discharge of mother*—. If a decision to discharge a mother earlier than the period specified in paragraph (a)(1) of

this section is made by an attending provider, in consultation with the mother, the requirements of paragraph (a)(1) of this section do not apply for any period after the discharge.

(ii) *Discharge of newborn.* If a decision to discharge a newborn child earlier than the period specified in paragraph (a)(1) of this section is made by an attending provider, in consultation with the mother (or the newborn's authorized representative), the requirements of paragraph (a)(1) of this section do not apply for any period after the discharge.

(iii) *Attending provider defined.* For purposes of this section, attending provider means an individual who is licensed under applicable state law to provide maternity or pediatric care and who is directly responsible for providing maternity or pediatric care to a mother or newborn child. Therefore, a plan, hospital, managed care organization, or other issuer is not an attending provider.

(iv) *Example.* The rules of this paragraph (a)(5) are illustrated by the following example:

(i) *Example.* (i) *Facts.* A pregnant woman covered under a group health plan subject to the requirements of this section goes into labor and is admitted to a hospital. She gives birth by cesarean section. On the third day after the delivery, the attending provider for the mother consults with the mother, and the attending provider for the newborn consults with the mother regarding the newborn. The attending providers authorize the early discharge of both the mother and the newborn. Both are discharged approximately 72 hours after the delivery. The plan pays for the 72-hour hospital stays.

(ii) *Conclusion.* In this Example, the requirements of this paragraph (a) have been satisfied with respect to the mother and the newborn. If either is readmitted, the hospital stay for the readmission is not subject to this section.

(b) *Prohibitions—.* (1) *With respect to mothers.* (i) *In general.* A group health plan, and a health insurance issuer offering group health insurance coverage, may not—

(A) Deny a mother or her newborn child eligibility or continued eligibility to enroll or renew coverage under the terms of the plan solely to avoid the requirements of this section; or

(B) Provide payments (including payments-in-kind) or rebates to a mother to encourage her to accept less than the minimum protections available under this section.

(ii) *Examples.* The rules of this paragraph (b)(1) are illustrated by the following examples. In each example, the group health plan is subject to the requirements of this section, as follows:

(i) *Example 1.* (i) *Facts.* A group health plan provides benefits for at least a 48-hour hospital length of stay following a vaginal delivery. If a mother and newborn covered under the plan are discharged within 24 hours after the delivery, the plan will waive the copayment and deductible.

(ii) *Conclusion.* In this Example 1, because waiver of the copayment and deductible is in the nature of a rebate that the mother would not receive if she and her newborn remained in the hospital, it is prohibited by this paragraph (b)(1). (In addition, the plan violates paragraph (b)(2) of this section because, in effect, no copayment or deductible is required for the first portion of the stay and a double copayment and a deductible are required for the second portion of the stay.)

(i) *Example 2.* (i) *Facts.* A group health plan provides benefits for at least a 48-hour hospital length of stay following a vaginal delivery. In the event that a mother and her newborn are discharged earlier than 48 hours and the discharges occur after consultation with the mother in accordance with the requirements of paragraph (a)(5) of this section, the plan provides for a follow-up visit by a nurse within 48 hours after the discharges to provide certain services that the mother and her newborn would otherwise receive in the hospital.

(ii) *Conclusion.* In this Example 2, because the follow-up visit does not provide any services beyond what the mother and her

newborn would receive in the hospital, coverage for the follow-up visit is not prohibited by this paragraph (b)(1).

(2) *With respect to benefit restrictions.* (i) *In general.* Subject to paragraph (c)(3) of this section, a group health plan, and a health insurance issuer offering group health insurance coverage, may not restrict the benefits for any portion of a hospital length of stay specified in paragraph (a) of this section in a manner that is less favorable than the benefits provided for any preceding portion of the stay.

(ii) *Example.* The rules of this paragraph (b)(2) are illustrated by the following example:

(i) *Example.* (i) *Facts.* A group health plan subject to the requirements of this section provides benefits for hospital lengths of stay in connection with childbirth. In the case of a delivery by cesarean section, the plan automatically pays for the first 48 hours. With respect to each succeeding 24-hour period, the participant or beneficiary must call the plan to obtain precertification from a utilization reviewer, who determines if an additional 24-hour period is medically necessary. If this approval is not obtained, the plan will not provide benefits for any succeeding 24-hour period.

(ii) *Conclusion.* In this Example, the requirement to obtain precertification for the two 24-hour periods immediately following the initial 48-hour stay is prohibited by this paragraph (b)(2) because benefits for the latter part of the stay are restricted in a manner that is less favorable than benefits for a preceding portion of the stay. (However, this section does not prohibit a plan from requiring precertification for any period after the first 96 hours.) In addition, the requirement to obtain precertification from the plan based on medical necessity for a hospital length of stay within the 96-hour period would also violate paragraph (a) of this section.

(3) *With respect to attending providers.* A group health plan, and a health insurance issuer offering group health insurance coverage, may not directly or indirectly—

(i) Penalize (for example, take disciplinary action against or retaliate against), or otherwise reduce or limit the compensation of, an attending provider because the provider furnished care to a participant or beneficiary in accordance with this section; or

(ii) Provide monetary or other incentives to an attending provider to induce the provider to furnish care to a participant or beneficiary in a manner inconsistent with this section, including providing any incentive that could induce an attending provider to discharge a mother or newborn earlier than 48 hours (or 96 hours) after delivery.

(c) *Construction.* With respect to this section, the following rules of construction apply:

(1) *Hospital stays not mandatory.* This section does not require a mother to—

(i) Give birth in a hospital; or

(ii) Stay in the hospital for a fixed period of time following the birth of her child.

(2) *Hospital stay benefits not mandated.* This section does not apply to any group health plan, or any group health insurance coverage, that does not provide benefits for hospital lengths of stay in connection with childbirth for a mother or her newborn child.

(3) *Cost-sharing rules—*(i) *In general.* This section does not prevent a group health plan or a health insurance issuer offering group health insurance coverage from imposing deductibles, coinsurance, or other cost-sharing in relation to benefits for hospital lengths of stay in connection with childbirth for a mother or a newborn under the plan or coverage, except that the coinsurance or other cost-sharing for any portion of the hospital length of stay specified in paragraph (a) of this section may not be greater than that for any preceding portion of the stay.

(ii) *Examples.* The rules of this paragraph (c)(3) are illustrated by the following examples. In each example, the group health plan is subject to the requirements of this section, as follows:

(i) *Example 1.* (i) *Facts.* A group health plan provides benefits for at least a 48-hour hospital length of stay in connection with vaginal deliveries. The plan covers 80 percent of the cost of the stay for the first 24-hour period and 50 percent of the cost of the stay for the second 24-hour period. Thus, the coinsurance paid by the patient increases from 20 percent to 50 percent after 24 hours.

(ii) *Conclusion.* In this Example 1, the plan violates the rules of this paragraph (c)(3) because coinsurance for the second 24-hour period of the 48-hour stay is greater than that for the preceding portion of the stay. (In addition, the plan also violates the similar rule in paragraph (b)(2) of this section.)

(i) *Example 2.* (i) *Facts.* A group health plan generally covers 70 percent of the cost of a hospital length of stay in connection with childbirth. However, the plan will cover 80 percent of the cost of the stay if the participant or beneficiary notifies the plan of the pregnancy in advance of admission and uses whatever hospital the plan may designate.

(ii) *Conclusion.* In this Example 2, the plan does not violate the rules of this paragraph (c)(3) because the level of benefits provided (70 percent or 80 percent) is consistent throughout the 48-hour (or 96-hour) hospital length of stay required under paragraph (a) of this section. (In addition, the plan does not violate the rules in paragraph (a)(4) or (b)(2) of this section.)

(4) *Compensation of attending provider.* This section does not prevent a group health plan or a health insurance issuer offering group health insurance coverage from negotiating with an attending provider the level and type of compensation for care furnished in accordance with this section (including paragraph (b) of this section).

(d) *Notice requirement.* See 29 CFR 2520.102-3(u) (relating to the disclosure requirement under section 711(d) of the Act).

(e) *Applicability in certain States*—(1) *Health insurance coverage.* The requirements of section 711 of the Act and this section do not apply with respect to health insurance coverage offered in connection with a group health plan if there is a state law regulating the coverage that meets any of the following criteria:

(i) The state law requires the coverage to provide for at least a 48-hour hospital length of stay following a vaginal delivery and at least a 96-hour hospital length of stay following a delivery by cesarean section.

(ii) The state law requires the coverage to provide for maternity and pediatric care in accordance with guidelines that relate to care following childbirth established by the American College of Obstetricians and Gynecologists, the American Academy of Pediatrics, or any other established professional medical association.

(iii) The state law requires, in connection with the coverage for maternity care, that the hospital length of stay for such care is left to the decision of (or is required to be made by) the attending provider in consultation with the mother. State laws that require the decision to be made by the attending provider with the consent of the mother satisfy the criterion of this paragraph (e)(1)(iii).

(2) *Group health plans*—(i) *Fully-insured plans.* Fully-insured plans. For a group health plan that provides benefits solely through health insurance coverage, if the state law regulating the health insurance coverage meets any of the criteria in paragraph (e)(1) of this section, then the requirements of section 711 of the Act and this section do not apply.

(ii) *Self-insured plans.* For a group health plan that provides all benefits for hospital lengths of stay in connection with childbirth other than through health insurance coverage, the requirements of section 711 of the Act and this section apply.

(iii) *Partially-insured plans.* For a group health plan that provides some benefits through health insurance coverage, if the state law regulating the health insurance coverage meets any of the criteria in paragraph (e)(1) of this section, then the requirements of section 711 of the Act and this section apply only to the extent the plan provides benefits for hospital lengths of stay in connection with childbirth other than through health insurance coverage.

(3) *Relation to section 731(a) of the Act.* The preemption provisions contained in section 731(a)(1) of the Act and § 2590.731(a) do not supersede a state law described in paragraph (e)(1) of this section.

(4) *Examples.* The rules of this paragraph (e) are illustrated by the following examples:

(i) *Example 1.* (i) *Facts.* A group health plan buys group health insurance coverage in a state that requires that the coverage provide for at least a 48-hour hospital length of stay following a vaginal delivery and at least a 96-hour hospital length of stay following a delivery by cesarean section.

(ii) *Conclusion.* In this Example 1, the coverage is subject to state law, and the requirements of section 711 of the Act and this section do not apply.

(i) *Example 2.* (i) *Facts.* A self-insured group health plan covers hospital lengths of stay in connection with childbirth in a state that requires health insurance coverage to provide for maternity and pediatric care in accordance with guidelines that relate to care following childbirth established by the American College of Obstetricians and Gynecologists and the American Academy of Pediatrics.

(ii) *Conclusion.* In this Example 2, even though the state law satisfies the criterion of paragraph (e)(1)(ii) of this section, because the plan provides benefits for hospital lengths of stay in connection with childbirth other than through health insurance coverage, the plan is subject to the requirements of section 711 of the Act and this section.

(f) *Applicability date..* This section applies to group health plans, and health insurance issuers offering group health insurance coverage, for plan years beginning on or after January 1, 2009.

[¶ 15,050K]
PARITY IN MENTAL HEALTH AND SUBSTANCE USE DISORDER BENEFITS

Act Sec. 712.(a) IN GENERAL. (a) IN GENERAL. (1) Aggregate lifetime limits. In the case of a group health plan (or health insurance coverage offered in connection with such a plan) that provides both medical and surgical benefits and mental health or substance use disorder benefits—

(A) NO LIFETIME LIMIT. If the plan or coverage does not include an aggregate lifetime limit on substantially all medical and surgical benefits, the plan or coverage may not impose any aggregate lifetime limit on mental health or substance use disorder benefits.

(B) LIFETIME LIMIT. If the plan or coverage includes an aggregate lifetime limit on substantially all medical and surgical benefits (in this paragraph referred to as the "applicable lifetime limit"), the plan or coverage shall either—

(i) apply the applicable lifetime limit both to the medical and surgical benefits to which it otherwise would apply and to mental health and substance use disorder benefits and not distinguish in the application of such limit between such medical and surgical benefits and mental health and substance use disorder benefits; or

(ii) not include any aggregate lifetime limit on mental health or substance use disorder benefits that is less than the applicable lifetime limit.

(C) RULE IN CASE OF DIFFERENT LIMITS. In the case of a plan or coverage that is not described in subparagraph (A) or (B) and that includes no or different aggregate lifetime limits on different categories of medical and surgical benefits, the Secretary shall establish rules under which subparagraph (B) is applied to such plan or coverage with respect to mental health and substance use disorder benefits by substituting for the applicable lifetime limit an average aggregate lifetime limit that is computed taking into account the weighted average of the aggregate lifetime limits applicable to such categories.

(2) ANNUAL LIMITS. In the case of a group health plan (or health insurance coverage offered in connection with such a plan) that provides both medical and surgical benefits and mental health or substance use disorder benefits—

(A) NO ANNUAL LIMIT. If the plan or coverage does not include an annual limit on substantially all medical and surgical benefits, the plan or coverage may not impose any annual limit on mental health or substance use disorder benefits.

(B) ANNUAL LIMIT. If the plan or coverage includes an annual limit on substantially all medical and surgical benefits (in this paragraph referred to as the "applicable annual limit"), the plan or coverage shall either—

(i) apply the applicable annual limit both to medical and surgical benefits to which it otherwise would apply and to mental health and substance use disorder benefits and not distinguish in the application of such limit between such medical and surgical benefits and mental health and substance use disorder benefits; or

(ii) not include any annual limit on mental health or substance use disorder benefits that is less than the applicable annual limit.

(C) RULE IN CASE OF DIFFERENT LIMITS. In the case of a plan or coverage that is not described in subparagraph (A) or (B) and that includes no or different annual limits on different categories of medical and surgical benefits, the Secretary shall establish rules under which subparagraph (B) is applied to such plan or coverage with respect to mental health and substance use disorder benefits by substituting for the applicable annual limit an average annual limit that is computed taking into account the weighted average of the annual limits applicable to such categories.

(3) FINANCIAL REQUIREMENTS AND TREATMENT LIMITATIONS. (A) IN GENERAL. In the case of a group health plan (or health insurance coverage offered in connection with such a plan) that provides both medical and surgical benefits and mental health or substance use disorder benefits, such plan or coverage shall ensure that—

(i) the financial requirements applicable to such mental health or substance use disorder benefits are no more restrictive than the predominant financial requirements applied to substantially all medical and surgical benefits covered by the plan (or coverage), and there are no separate cost sharing requirements that are applicable only with respect to mental health or substance use disorder benefits; and

(ii) the treatment limitations applicable to such mental health or substance use disorder benefits are no more restrictive than the predominant treatment limitations applied to substantially all medical and surgical benefits covered by the plan (or coverage) and there are no separate treatment limitations that are applicable only with respect to mental health or substance use disorder benefits.

(B) DEFINITIONS—. In this paragraph:

(i) FINANCIAL REQUIREMENT—. The term `financial requirement' includes deductibles, copayments, coinsurance, and out-of-pocket expenses, but excludes an aggregate lifetime limit and an annual limit subject to paragraphs (1) and (2),

(ii) PREDOMINANT—. A financial requirement or treatment limit is considered to be predominant if it is the most common or frequent of such type of limit or requirement.

(iii) TREATMENT LIMITATION—. The term `treatment limitation' includes limits on the frequency of treatment, number of visits, days of coverage, or other similar limits on the scope or duration of treatment.

(4) AVAILABILITY OF PLAN INFORMATION—. The criteria for medical necessity determinations made under the plan with respect to mental health or substance use disorder benefits (or the health insurance coverage offered in connection with the plan with respect to such benefits) shall be made available by the plan administrator (or the health insurance issuer offering such coverage) in accordance with regulations to any current or potential participant, beneficiary, or contracting provider upon request. The reason for any denial under the plan (or coverage) of reimbursement or payment for services with respect to mental health or substance use disorder benefits in the case of any participant or beneficiary shall, on request or as otherwise required, be made available by the plan administrator (or the health insurance issuer offering such coverage) to the participant or beneficiary in accordance with regulations.

(5) OUT-OF-NETWORK PROVIDERS—. In the case of a plan or coverage that provides both medical and surgical benefits and mental health or substance use disorder benefits, if the plan or coverage provides coverage for medical or surgical benefits provided by out-of-network providers, the plan or coverage shall provide coverage for mental health or substance use disorder benefits provided by out-of-network providers in a manner that is consistent with the requirements of this section.

(b) CONSTRUCTION. (b) Nothing in section shall be construed—

(1) as requiring a group health plan (or health insurance coverage offered in connection with such a plan) to provide any mental health or substance use disorder benefits; or

(2) in the case of a group health plan (or health insurance coverage offered in connection with such a plan) that provides mental health or substance use disorder benefits, as affecting the terms and conditions of the plan or coverage relating to such benefits under the plan or coverage, except as provided in subsection (a).

(c) EXEMPTIONS.—

(c)(1) SMALL EMPLOYER EXEMPTION.—

(A) IN GENERAL. This section shall not apply to any group health plan (and group health insurance coverage offered in connection with a group health plan) for any plan year of a small employer.

(B) SMALL EMPLOYER. For purposes of subparagraph (A), the term "small employer" means, in connection with a group health plan with respect to a calendar year and a plan year, an employer who employed an average of at least 2 (or 1 in the case of an employer residing in a state that permits small groups to include a single individual) but not more than 50 employees on business days during the preceding calendar year.

(C) APPLICATION OF CERTAIN RULES IN DETERMINATION OF EMPLOYER SIZE. For purposes of this paragraph—

(i) APPLICATION OF AGGREGATION RULE FOR EMPOYERS. Rules similar to the rules under subsections (b), (c), (m), and (o) of section 414 of the Internal Revenue Code of 1986 shall apply for purposes of treating persons as a single employer.

(ii) EMPLOYERS NOT IN EXISTENCE IN PRECEDING YEAR. In the case of an employer which was not in existence throughout the preceding calendar year, the determination of whether such employer is a small employer shall be based on the average number of employees that it is reasonably expected such employer will employ on business days in the current calendar year.

(iii) PREDECESSORS. Any reference in this paragraph to an employer shall include a reference to any predecessor of such employer.

(2) COST EXEMPTION. (A) IN GENERAL. With respect to a group health plan (or health insurance coverage offered in connection with such a plan), if the application of this section to such plan (or coverage) results in an increase for the plan year involved of the actual total costs of coverage with respect to medical and surgical benefits and mental health and substance use disorder benefits under the plan (as determined and certified under subparagraph by an amount that exceeds the applicable percentage described in subparagraph (B) of the actual Total Plan costs, the provisions of this section shall not apply to such plan (or coverage) during the following plan year, and such exemption shall apply to the plan (or coverage) for 1 plan year. An employer may elect to

continue to apply mental health and substance use disorder parity pursuant to this section with respect to the group health plan (or coverage) involved regardless of any increase in total costs.

(B) APPLICABLE PERCENTAGE. With respect to a plan (or coverage), the applicable percentage described in this subparagraph shall be—

(i) 2 percent in the case of the first plan year in which this section is applied; and

(ii) 1 percent in the case of each subsequent plan year.

(C) DETERMINATIONS BY ACTUARIES. Determinations as to increases in actual costs under a plan (or coverage) for purposes of this section shall be made and certified by a qualified and licensed actuary who is a member in good standing of the American Academy of Actuaries. All such determinations shall be in a written report prepared by the actuary. The report, and all underlying documentation relied upon by the actuary, shall be maintained by the group health plan or health insurance issuer for a period of 6 years following the notification made under subparagraph (E).

(D) 6-MONTH DETERMINATIONS. If a group health plan (or a health insurance issuer offering coverage in connection with a group health plan) seeks an exemption under this paragraph, determinations under subparagraph (A) shall be made after such plan (or coverage) has complied with this section for the first 6 months of the plan year involved.

(E) NOTIFICATION—. (i) IN GENERAL. A group health plan (or a health insurance issuer offering coverage in connection with a group health plan) that, based upon a certification described under subparagraph (C), qualifies for an exemption under this paragraph, and elects to implement the exemption, shall promptly notify the Secretary, the appropriate State agencies, and participants and beneficiaries in the plan of such election.

(ii) REQUIREMENT. A notification to the Secretary under clause (i) shall include—

(I) a description of the number of covered lives under the plan (or coverage) involved at the time of the notification, and as applicable, at the time of any prior election of the cost-exemption under this paragraph by such plan (or coverage);

(II) for both the plan year upon which a cost exemption is sought and the year prior, a description of the actual total costs of coverage with respect to medical and surgical benefits and mental health and substance use disorder benefits under the plan; and

(III) for both the plan year upon which a cost exemption is sought and the year prior, the actual total costs of coverage with respect to mental health and substance use disorder benefits under the plan.

(iii) CONFIDENTIALITY. A notification to the Secretary under clause (i) shall be confidential. The Secretary shall make available, upon request and on not more than an annual basis, an anonymous itemization of such notifications, that includes—

(I) a breakdown of States by the size and type of employers submitting such notification; and

(II) a summary of the data received under clause (ii).

(F) AUDITS BY APPROPRIATE AGENCIES. To determine compliance with this paragraph, the Secretary may audit the books and records of a group health plan or health insurance issuer relating to an exemption, including any actuarial reports prepared pursuant to subparagraph (C), during the 6 year period following the notification of such exemption under subparagraph (E). A State agency receiving a notification under subparagraph (E) may also conduct such an audit with respect to an exemption covered by such notification.

(d) SEPARATE APPLICATION TO EACH OPTION OFFERED. In the case of a group health plan that offers a participant or beneficiary two or more benefit package options under the plan, the requirements of this section shall be applied separately with respect to each such option.

(e) DEFINITIONS. For purposes of this section—

(1) AGGREGATE LIFETIME LIMIT. The term "aggregate lifetime limit" means, with respect to benefits under a group health plan or health insurance coverage, a dollar limitation on the total amount that may be paid with respect to such benefits under the plan or health insurance coverage with respect to an individual or other coverage unit.

(2) ANNUAL LIMIT. The term "annual limit" means, with respect to benefits under a group health plan or health insurance coverage, a dollar limitation on the total amount of benefits that may be paid with respect to such benefits in a 12-month period under the plan or health insurance coverage with respect to an individual or other coverage unit.

(3) MEDICAL OR SURGICAL BENEFITS. The term "medical or surgical benefits" means benefits with respect to medical or surgical services, as defined under the terms of the plan or coverage (as the case may be), but does not include mental health or substance use disorder benefits.

(4) MENTAL HEALTH BENEFITS. The term "mental health benefits" means benefits with respect to services for mental health conditions, as defined under the terms of the plan and in accordance with applicable Federal and State law.

(5) SUBSTANCE USE DISORDER BENEFITS. The term `substance use disorder benefits' means benefits with respect to services for substance use disorders, as defined under the terms of the plan and in accordance with applicable Federal and State law.

(f) SECRETARY REPORT. The Secretary shall, by January 1, 2012, and every two years thereafter, submit to the appropriate committees of Congress a report on compliance of group health plans (and health insurance coverage offered in connection with such plans) with the requirements of this section. Such report shall include the results of any surveys or audits on compliance of group health plans (and health insurance coverage offered in connection with such plans) with such requirements and an analysis of the reasons for any failures to comply.

(g) NOTICE AND ASSISTANCE. The Secretary, in cooperation with the Secretaries of Health and Human Services and Treasury, as appropriate, shall publish and widely disseminate guidance and information for group health plans, participants and beneficiaries, applicable State and local regulatory bodies, and the National Association of Insurance Commissioners concerning the requirements of this section and shall provide assistance concerning such requirements and the continued operation of applicable State law. Such guidance and information shall inform participants and beneficiaries of how they may obtain assistance under this section, including, where appropriate, assistance from State consumer and insurance agencies.

Amendments

P.L. 110-343, Division C, §512(a)(1):

Amended ERISA Sec. 712(a) by adding subsections (3)-(5) to read as above.

For the effective date and special rules, see Act Sec. 512(d)-(f), below.

P.L. 110-343, Division C, §512(a)(2):

Amended ERISA Sec. 712(b)(2) to read as above. Prior to amendment, ERISA Sec. 712(b)(2) read as follows: "(2) in the case of a group health plan (or health insurance coverage offered in connection with such a plan) that provides mental health benefits, as affecting the terms and conditions (including cost sharing, limits on numbers of visits or days of coverage, and requirements relating to medical necessity) relating to the amount, duration, or scope of mental health benefits under the plan or coverage, except as specifically provided in subsection (a) (in regard to parity in the imposition of aggregate lifetime limits and annual limits for mental health benefits).

For the effective date and special rules, see Act Sec. 512(d)-(f), below.

P.L. 110-343, Division C, §512(a)(3):

Amended ERISA Sec. 712(c)(1)(B) by inserting "(or 1 in the case of an employer residing in a State that permits small groups to include a single individual)" after "at least 2" the first place that such appears; and by striking "and who employs at least 2 employees on the first day of the plan year".

Amended ERISA Sec. 712(c)(2) to read as above. Prior to amendment, ERISA Sec. 712(c)(2) read as follows: "(2) INCREASED COST EXEMPTION.—This section shall not apply with respect to a group health plan (or health insurance coverage offered in connection with a group health plan) if the application of this section to such plan (or to such coverage) results in an increase in the cost under the plan (or for such coverage) of at least 1 percent."

For the effective date and special rules, see Act Sec. 512(d)-(f), below.

P.L. 110-343, Division C, §512(a)(4):

Amended ERISA Sec. 712(e) by striking paragraph (4) and inserting paragraph (4) and (5) to read as above. Prior to amendment, ERISA Sec. 712(e)(4) read as follows:

"(4) MENTAL HEALTH BENEFITS. – The term "mental health benefits" means benefits with respect to mental health services, as defined under the terms of the plan or coverage (as the case may be), but does not include benefits with respect to treatment of substance abuse or chemical dependency."

For the effective date and special rules, see Act Sec. 512(d)-(f), below.

P.L. 110-343, Division C, §512(a)(5):

Amended ERISA Sec. 712 by striking subsection (f). Prior to amendment, ERISA Sec. 712(f) read as follows: "(f) SUNSET.— This section shall not apply to benefits for services furnished – (1) on or after January 1, 2008, and before the date of the enactment of the Heroes Earnings Assistance and Relief Tax Act of 2008, and (2) after December 31, 2008.

The amendment takes effect on January 1, 2009.

P.L. 110-343, Division C, §512(a)(6):

Amended ERISA Sec. 712 by added subsection (f) and (g) to read as above.

For the effective date and special rules, see Act Sec. 512(d)-(f), below.

P.L. 110-343, Division C, §512(a)(7) and (a)(8):

Amended ERISA Sec. 712 by striking "mental health benefits" and inserting "mental health and substance use disorder benefits" each place it appears in subsections (a)(1)(B)(i), (a)(1)(C), (a)(2)(B)(i), and (a)(2)(C) and by striking "mental health benefits" and inserting "mental health or substance use disorder benefits" each place it appears (other than in any provision amended by the previous paragraph) including subsection (e)(3).

For the effective date and special rules, see Act Sec. 512(d)-(f), below.

P.L. 110-343, Division C, §512(g):

Provided a conforming clerical amendment to the heading of ERISA Sec. 712 to read as above. Prior to the clerical amendment, the heading read as follows: "SEC. 712 PARITY IN THE APPLICATION OF CERTAIN LIMITS TO MENTAL HEALTH BENEFITS."

For the effective date and special rules, see Act Sec. 512(d)-(f), below.

P.L. 110-343, Division C, §512(d)-(f) [as amended by P.L.110-460], provides:

(d) REGULATIONS. —Not later than 1 year after the date of enactment of this Act, the Secretaries of Labor, Health and Human Services, and the Treasury shall issue regulations to carry out the amendments made by subsections (a), (b), and (c), respectively.

(e) EFFECTIVE DATE.—

(1) IN GENERAL. —The amendments made by this section shall apply with respect to group health plans for plan years beginning after the date that is 1 year after the date of enactment of this Act, regardless of whether regulations have been issued to carry out such amendments by such effective date, except that the amendments made by subsections (a)(5), (b)(5), and (c)(5), relating to striking of certain sunset provisions, shall take effect on January 1, 2009.

(2) SPECIAL RULE FOR COLLECTIVE BARGAINING AGREEMENTS. –In the case of a group health plan maintained pursuant to one or more collective bargaining agreements between employee representatives and one or more employers ratified before the date of the enactment of this Act, the amendments made by this section shall not apply to plan years beginning before the later of –

(A) the date on which the last of the collective bargaining agreements relating to the plan terminates (determined without regard to any extension thereof agreed to after the date of the enactment of this Act), or

(B) January 1, 2010.

For purposes of subparagraph (A), any plan amendment made pursuant to a collective bargaining agreement relating to the plan which amends the plan solely to conform to any requirement added by this section shall not be treated as a termination of such collective bargaining agreement.

(f) ASSURING COORDINATION. —The Secretary of Health and Human Services, the Secretary of Labor, and the Secretary of the Treasury may ensure, through the execution or revision of an interagency memorandum of understanding among such Secretaries, that—

(1) regulations, rulings, and interpretations issued by such Secretaries relating to the same matter over which two or more such Secretaries have responsibility under this section (and the amendments made by this section) are administered so as to have the same effect at all times; and

(2) coordination of policies relating to enforcing the same requirements through such Secretaries in order to have a coordinated enforcement strategy that avoids duplication of enforcement efforts and assigns priorities in enforcement.

P.L. 110-245, §401(b):

Amended ERISA §712(f) by striking "services furnished after December 31, 2007" and inserting "services furnished—

"(1) on or after January 1, 2008, and before the date of the enactment of the Heroes Earnings Assistance and Relief Tax Act of 2008, and

"(2) after December 31, 2008.".

The above amendment is effective on the date of enactment of this Act (June 17, 2008).

P.L. 109-432, §115(b):

Act Sec. 115(b) amended ERISA §712(f) by striking "2006" and inserting "2007".

The above amendment is effective on the date of enactment of this Act (December 20, 2006).

P.L. 109-151, §1(a):

Act Sec. 1(a) amended ERISA §712(f) by striking "December 31, 2005" and inserting "December 31, 2006".

The above amendment is effective on the date of enactment of this Act (December 30, 2005).

P.L. 108-311, §302(b):

Amended ERISA §712(f) by striking "on or after December 31, 2004" and inserting "after December 31, 2005".

The above amendment is effective on October 4, 2004 (the date of enactment of P.L. 108-311).

P.L. 108-197, §2:

Amended ERISA Sec. 712 (f) by striking "December 31, 2003," and inserting "December 31, 2004."

P.L. 107-313, §2:

Amended ERISA Sec. 712 (f) by striking "December 31, 2002," and inserting "December 31, 2003."

P.L. 107-116, §701(a):

Amended ERISA Sec. 712(f) by striking "September 30, 2001," and inserting "December 31, 2002."

P.L. 104-204, §702(a):

Added ERISA Sec. 712 to read as above.

The above amendment shall apply with respect to group health plans for plan years beginning on or after January 1, 1998.

Interim Final Regulations

The following regulations were adopted by 62 FR 16894 and published in the *Federal Register* on April 8, 1997, under "Chapter XXV of Title 29 of the Code of Federal Regulations; Subchapter LHealth Insurance Portability and Renewability for Group Health Plans; Part 2590Rules and Regulations for Health Insurance Portability and Renewability for Group Health Plans." Reg. 2590.712 was amended by T.D. 8741, which was published in the *Federal Register* on Dec. 22, 1997 (62 FR 66932) and was amended on Sept. 27, 2002 (67 FR 60859), on April 14, 2003 (68 FR 18048), on January 26, 2004 (69 FR 3815), on December 17, 2004 (69 FR 75797), on March 20, 2006 (71 FR 13937) and on February 27, 2007 (72 FR 8628). Reg. §2590.712 was revised and replaced on February 2, 2010 (75 FR 5409). Reg. §2590.712 was revised and published in the Federal Register on November 13, 2013 (78 FR 68239). See ¶ 15,050K-3.

[¶ 15,050K-1]

§2590.712 Parity in the application of certain limits to mental health benefits.

[Amended December 19, 1997 by T.D. 8741 and by EBSA on 9/27/02 (67 FR 60859), on 4/14/03 (68 FR 18048), on 1/26/2004 (69 FR 3815), on 12/17/2004 (69 FR 75797), on 3/20/2006 (71 FR 13937), and on 2/27/2007 (72 FR 8628). Revised and replaced 2/2/2010 (75 FR 5409). See ¶ 15,050K-2.]

[¶ 15,050K-2]

§ 2590.712 Parity in mental health and substance use disorder benefits.

(a) *Meaning of terms.* For purposes of this section, except where the context clearly indicates otherwise, the following terms have the meanings indicated:

Aggregate lifetime dollar limit means a dollar limitation on the total amount of specified benefits that may be paid under a group health plan (or health insurance coverage offered in connection with such a plan) for any coverage unit.

Annual dollar limit means a dollar limitation on the total amount of specified benefits that may be paid in a 12-month period under a group health plan (or health insurance coverage offered in connection with such a plan) for any coverage unit.

Coverage unit means coverage unit as described in paragraph (c)(1)(iv) of this section.

Cumulative financial requirements are financial requirements that determine whether or to what extent benefits are provided based on accumulated amounts and include deductibles and out-of-pocket maximums. (However, cumulative financial requirements do not include aggregate lifetime or annual dollar limits because these two terms are excluded from the meaning of financial requirements.)

Cumulative quantitative treatment limitations are treatment limitations that determine whether or to what extent benefits are provided based on accumulated amounts, such as annual or lifetime day or visit limits.

Financial requirements include deductibles, copayments, coinsurance, or out-of-pocket maximums. Financial requirements do not include aggregate lifetime or annual dollar limits.

Medical/surgical benefits means benefits for medical or surgical services, as defined under the terms of the plan or health insurance coverage, but does not include mental health or substance use disorder benefits. Any condition defined by the plan as being or as not being a medical/surgical condition must be defined to be consistent with generally recognized independent standards of current medical practice (for example, the most current version of the International Classification of Diseases (ICD) or State guidelines).

Mental health benefits means benefits with respect to services for mental health conditions, as defined under the terms of the plan and in accordance with applicable Federal and State law. Any condition defined by the plan as being or as not being a mental health condition must be defined to be consistent with generally recognized independent standards of current medical practice (for example, the most current version of the Diagnostic and Statistical Manual of Mental Disorders (DSM), the most current version of the ICD, or State guidelines).

Substance use disorder benefits means benefits with respect to services for substance use disorders, as defined under the terms of the plan and in accordance with applicable Federal and State law. Any disorder defined by the plan as being or as not being a substance use disorder must be defined to be consistent with generally recognized independent standards of current medical practice (for example, the most current version of the DSM, the most current version of the ICD, or State guidelines).

Treatment limitations include limits on benefits based on the frequency of treatment, number of visits, days of coverage, days in a waiting period, or other similar limits on the scope or duration of treatment. Treatment limitations include both quantitative treatment limitations, which are expressed numerically (such as 50 outpatient visits per year), and nonquantitative treatment limitations, which otherwise limit the scope or duration of benefits for treatment under a plan. (See paragraph (c)(4)(ii) of this section for an illustrative list of nonquantitative treatment limitations.) A permanent exclusion of all benefits for a particular condition or disorder, however, is not a treatment limitation.

(b) *Parity requirements with respect to aggregate lifetime and annual dollar limits.* (1) *General.* (i) *General parity requirement.* A group health plan (or health insurance coverage offered by an issuer in connection with a group health plan) that provides both medical/surgical benefits and mental health or substance use disorder benefits must comply with paragraph (b)(2), (b)(3), or (b)(6) of this section.

(ii) *Exception.* The rule in paragraph (b)(1)(i) of this section does not apply if a plan (or health insurance coverage) satisfies the requirements of paragraph (f) or (g) of this section (relating to exemptions for small employers and for increased cost).

(2) *Plan with no limit or limits on less than one-third of all medical/surgical benefits.* If a plan (or health insurance coverage) does not include an aggregate lifetime or annual dollar limit on any medical/surgical benefits or includes an aggregate lifetime or annual dollar limit that applies to less than one-third of all medical/surgical benefits, it may not impose an aggregate lifetime or annual dollar limit, respectively, on mental health or substance use disorder benefits.

(3) *Plan with a limit on at least two-thirds of all medical/surgical benefits.* If a plan (or health insurance coverage) includes an aggregate lifetime or annual dollar limit on at least two-thirds of all medical/surgical benefits, it must either—

(i) Apply the aggregate lifetime or annual dollar limit both to the medical/surgical benefits to which the limit would otherwise apply and to mental health or substance use disorder benefits in a manner that does not distinguish between the medical/surgical benefits and mental health or substance use disorder benefits; or

(ii) Not include an aggregate lifetime or annual dollar limit on mental health or substance use disorder benefits that is less than the aggregate lifetime or annual dollar limit, respectively, on medical/

surgical benefits. (For cumulative limits other than aggregate lifetime or annual dollar limits, see paragraph (c)(3)(v) of this section prohibiting separately accumulating cumulative financial requirements or cumulative quantitative treatment limitations.)

(4) *Examples.* The rules of paragraphs (b)(2) and (b)(3) of this section are illustrated by the following examples:

Example 1. (i) *Facts.* A group health plan has no annual limit on medical/surgical benefits and a $10,000 annual limit on mental health and substance use disorder benefits. To comply with the requirements of this paragraph (b), the plan sponsor is considering each of the following options -

(A) Eliminating the plan's annual dollar limit on mental health and substance use disorder benefits;

(B) Replacing the plan's annual dollar limit on mental health and substance use disorder benefits with a $500,000 annual limit on all benefits (including medical/surgical and mental health and substance use disorder benefits); and

(C) Replacing the plan's annual dollar limit on mental health and substance use disorder benefits with a $250,000 annual limit on medical/surgical benefits and a $250,000 annual limit on mental health and substance use disorder benefits.

(ii) *Conclusion.* In this *Example 1*, each of the three options being considered by the plan sponsor would comply with the requirements of this paragraph (b).

Example 2. (i) *Facts.* A plan has a $100,000 annual limit on medical/surgical inpatient benefits and a $50,000 annual limit on medical/surgical outpatient benefits. To comply with the parity requirements of this paragraph (b), the plan sponsor is considering each of the following options -

(A) Imposing a $150,000 annual limit on mental health and substance use disorder benefits; and

(B) Imposing a $100,000 annual limit on mental health and substance use disorder inpatient benefits and a $50,000 annual limit on mental health and substance use disorder outpatient benefits.

(ii) *Conclusion.* In this *Example 2*, each option under consideration by the plan sponsor would comply with the requirements of this section.

(5) *Determining one-third and two-thirds of all medical/surgical benefits.* For purposes of this paragraph (b), the determination of whether the portion of medical/surgical benefits subject to an aggregate lifetime or annual dollar limit represents one-third or two-thirds of all medical/surgical benefits is based on the dollar amount of all plan payments for medical/surgical benefits expected to be paid under the plan for the plan year (or for the portion of the plan year after a change in plan benefits that affects the applicability of the aggregate lifetime or annual dollar limits). Any reasonable method may be used to determine whether the dollar amount expected to be paid under the plan will constitute one-third or two-thirds of the dollar amount of all plan payments for medical/surgical benefits.

(6) *Plan not described in paragraph (b)(2) or (b)(3) of this section.* (i) *In general.* A group health plan (or health insurance coverage) that is not described in paragraph (b)(2) or (b)(3) of this section with respect to aggregate lifetime or annual dollar limits on medical/surgical benefits, must either—

(A) Impose no aggregate lifetime or annual dollar limit, as appropriate, on mental health or substance use disorder benefits; or

(B) Impose an aggregate lifetime or annual dollar limit on mental health or substance use disorder benefits that is no less than an average limit calculated for medical/surgical benefits in the following manner. The average limit is calculated by taking into account the weighted average of the aggregate lifetime or annual dollar limits, as appropriate, that are applicable to the categories of medical/surgical benefits. Limits based on delivery systems, such as inpatient/outpatient treatment or normal treatment of common, low-cost conditions (such as treatment of normal births), do not constitute categories for purposes of this paragraph (b)(6)(i)(B). In addition, for purposes of determining weighted averages, any benefits that are not within a category that is subject to a separately-designated dollar limit under the plan are taken into account as a single separate category by using an estimate of the upper limit on the dollar amount that a plan may reasonably be expected to incur with respect to such benefits, taking into account any other applicable restrictions under the plan.

(ii) *Weighting*. For purposes of this paragraph (b)(6), the weighting applicable to any category of medical/surgical benefits is determined in the manner set forth in paragraph (b)(5) of this section for determining one-third or two-thirds of all medical/surgical benefits.

(iii) *Example*. The rules of this paragraph (b)(6) are illustrated by the following example:

Example. (i) *Facts*. A group health plan that is subject to the requirements of this section includes a $100,000 annual limit on medical/surgical benefits related to cardio-pulmonary diseases. The plan does not include an annual dollar limit on any other category of medical/surgical benefits. The plan determines that 40% of the dollar amount of plan payments for medical/surgical benefits are related to cardio-pulmonary diseases. The plan determines that $1,000,000 is a reasonable estimate of the upper limit on the dollar amount that the plan may incur with respect to the other 60% of payments for medical/surgical benefits.

(ii) *Conclusion*. In this *Example*, the plan is not described in paragraph (b)(3) of this section because there is not one annual dollar limit that applies to at least two-thirds of all medical/surgical benefits. Further, the plan is not described in paragraph (b)(2) of this section because more than one-third of all medical/surgical benefits are subject to an annual dollar limit. Under this paragraph (b)(6), the plan sponsor can choose either to include no annual dollar limit on mental health or substance use disorder benefits, or to include an annual dollar limit on mental health or substance use disorder benefits that is not less than the weighted average of the annual dollar limits applicable to each category of medical/surgical benefits. In this example, the minimum weighted average annual dollar limit that can be applied to mental health or substance use disorder benefits is $640,000 (40% × $100,000 + 60% × $1,000,000 = $640,000).

(c) *Parity requirements with respect to financial requirements and treatment limitations*. (1) *Clarification of terms*. (i) *Classification of benefits*. When reference is made in this paragraph (c) to a classification of benefits, the term "classification" means a classification as described in paragraph (c)(2)(ii) of this section.

(ii) *Type of financial requirement or treatment limitation*. When reference is made in this paragraph (c) to a type of financial requirement or treatment limitation, the reference to type means its nature. Different types of financial requirements include deductibles, copayments, coinsurance, and out-of-pocket maximums. Different types of quantitative treatment limitations include annual, episode, and lifetime day and visit limits. See paragraph (c)(4)(ii) of this section for an illustrative list of nonquantitative treatment limitations.

(iii) *Level of a type of financial requirement or treatment limitation*. When reference is made in this paragraph (c) to a level of a type of financial requirement or treatment limitation, level refers to the magnitude of the type of financial requirement or treatment limitation. For example, different levels of coinsurance include 20 percent and 30 percent; different levels of a copayment include $15 and $20; different levels of a deductible include $250 and $500; and different levels of an episode limit include 21 inpatient days per episode and 30 inpatient days per episode.

(iv) *Coverage unit*. When reference is made in this paragraph (c) to a coverage unit, coverage unit refers to the way in which a plan (or health insurance coverage) groups individuals for purposes of determining benefits, or premiums or contributions. For example, different coverage units include self-only, family, and employee-plus-spouse.

(2) *General parity requirement*. (i) *General rule*. A group health plan (or health insurance coverage offered by an issuer in connection with a group health plan) that provides both medical/surgical benefits and mental health or substance use disorder benefits may not apply any financial requirement or treatment limitation to mental health or substance use disorder benefits in any classification that is more restrictive than the predominant financial requirement or treatment limitation of that type applied to substantially all medical/surgical

benefits in the same classification. Whether a financial requirement or treatment limitation is a predominant financial requirement or treatment limitation that applies to substantially all medical/surgical benefits in a classification is determined separately for each type of financial requirement or treatment limitation. The application of the rules of this paragraph (c)(2) to financial requirements and quantitative treatment limitations is addressed in paragraph (c)(3) of this section; the application of the rules of this paragraph (c)(2) to nonquantitative treatment limitations is addressed in paragraph (c)(4) of this section.

(ii) *Classifications of benefits used for applying rules*. (A) *In general*. If a plan (or health insurance coverage) provides mental health or substance use disorder benefits in any classification of benefits described in this paragraph (c)(2)(ii), mental health or substance use disorder benefits must be provided in every classification in which medical/surgical benefits are provided. In determining the classification in which a particular benefit belongs, a plan (or health insurance issuer) must apply the same standards to medical/surgical benefits and to mental health or substance use disorder benefits. To the extent that a plan (or health insurance coverage) provides benefits in a classification and imposes any separate financial requirement or treatment limitation (or separate level of a financial requirement or treatment limitation) for benefits in the classification, the rules of this paragraph (c) apply separately with respect to that classification for all financial requirements or treatment limitations. The following classifications of benefits are the only classifications used in applying the rules of this paragraph (c):

(1) *Inpatient, in-network*. Benefits furnished on an inpatient basis and within a network of providers established or recognized under a plan or health insurance coverage.

(2) *Inpatient, out-of-network*. Benefits furnished on an inpatient basis and outside any network of providers established or recognized under a plan or health insurance coverage. This classification includes inpatient benefits under a plan (or health insurance coverage) that has no network of providers.

(3) *Outpatient, in-network*. Benefits furnished on an outpatient basis and within a network of providers established or recognized under a plan or health insurance coverage.

(4) *Outpatient, out-of-network*. Benefits furnished on an outpatient basis and outside any network of providers established or recognized under a plan or health insurance coverage. This classification includes outpatient benefits under a plan (or health insurance coverage) that has no network of providers.

(5) *Emergency care*. Benefits for emergency care.

(6) *Prescription drugs*. Benefits for prescription drugs. See special rules for multi-tiered prescription drug benefits in paragraph (c)(3)(iii) of this section.

(B) *Application to out-of-network providers*. See paragraph (c)(2)(ii)(A) of this section, under which a plan (or health insurance coverage) that provides mental health or substance use disorder benefits in any classification of benefits must provide mental health or substance use disorder benefits in every classification in which medical/surgical benefits are provided, including out-of-network classifications.

(C) *Examples*. The rules of this paragraph (c)(2)(ii) are illustrated by the following examples. In each example, the group health plan is subject to the requirements of this section and provides both medical/surgical benefits and mental health and substance use disorder benefits.

Example 1. (i) *Facts*. A group health plan offers inpatient and outpatient benefits and does not contract with a network of providers. The plan imposes a $500 deductible on all benefits. For inpatient medical/surgical benefits, the plan imposes a coinsurance requirement. For outpatient medical/surgical benefits, the plan imposes copayments. The plan imposes no other financial requirements or treatment limitations.

(ii) *Conclusion*. In this *Example 1*, because the plan has no network of providers, all benefits provided are out-of-network. Because inpatient, out-of-network medical/surgical benefits are subject to separate financial requirements from outpatient, out-of-network medical/surgical benefits, the rules of this paragraph (c) apply separately with respect to any financial requirements and treatment limitations, including the deductible, in each classification.

Example 2. (i) *Facts.* A plan imposes a $500 deductible on all benefits. The plan has no network of providers. The plan generally imposes a 20 percent coinsurance requirement with respect to all benefits, without distinguishing among inpatient, outpatient, emergency, or prescription drug benefits. The plan imposes no other financial requirements or treatment limitations.

(ii) *Conclusion.* In this *Example 2*, because the plan does not impose separate financial requirements (or treatment limitations) based on classification, the rules of this paragraph (c) apply with respect to the deductible and the coinsurance across all benefits.

Example 3. (i) *Facts.* Same facts as *Example 2*, except the plan exempts emergency care benefits from the 20 percent coinsurance requirement. The plan imposes no other financial requirements or treatment limitations.

(ii) *Conclusion.* In this *Example 3*, because the plan imposes separate financial requirements based on classifications, the rules of this paragraph (c) apply with respect to the deductible and the coinsurance separately for -

(A) Benefits in the emergency classification; and

(B) All other benefits.

Example 4. (i) *Facts.* Same facts as *Example 2*, except the plan also imposes a preauthorization requirement for all inpatient treatment in order for benefits to be paid. No such requirement applies to outpatient treatment.

(ii) *Conclusion.* In this *Example 4*, because the plan has no network of providers, all benefits provided are out-of-network. Because the plan imposes a separate treatment limitation based on classifications, the rules of this paragraph (c) apply with respect to the deductible and coinsurance separately for -

(A) Inpatient, out-of-network benefits; and

(B) All other benefits.

(3) *Financial requirements and quantitative treatment limitations.* (i) *Determining "substantially all" and "predominant".* (A) *Substantially all.* For purposes of this paragraph (c), a type of financial requirement or quantitative treatment limitation is considered to apply to substantially all medical/surgical benefits in a classification of benefits if it applies to at least two-thirds of all medical/surgical benefits in that classification. (For this purpose, benefits expressed as subject to a zero level of a type of financial requirement are treated as benefits not subject to that type of financial requirement, and benefits expressed as subject to a quantitative treatment limitation that is unlimited are treated as benefits not subject to that type of quantitative treatment limitation.) If a type of financial requirement or quantitative treatment limitation does not apply to at least two-thirds of all medical/surgical benefits in a classification, then that type cannot be applied to mental health or substance use disorder benefits in that classification.

(B) *Predominant. (1)* If a type of financial requirement or quantitative treatment limitation applies to at least two-thirds of all medical/surgical benefits in a classification as determined under paragraph (c)(3)(i)(A) of this section, the level of the financial requirement or quantitative treatment limitation that is considered the predominant level of that type in a classification of benefits is the level that applies to more than one-half of medical/surgical benefits in that classification subject to the financial requirement or quantitative treatment limitation.

(2) If, with respect to a type of financial requirement or quantitative treatment limitation that applies to at least two-thirds of all medical/surgical benefits in a classification, there is no single level that applies to more than one-half of medical/surgical benefits in the classi-

fication subject to the financial requirement or quantitative treatment limitation, the plan (or health insurance issuer) may combine levels until the combination of levels applies to more than onehalf of medical/surgical benefits subject to the financial requirement or quantitative treatment limitation in the classification. The least restrictive level within the combination is considered the predominant level of that type in the classification. (For this purpose, a plan may combine the most restrictive levels first, with each less restrictive level added to the combination until the combination applies to more than one-half of the benefits subject to the financial requirement or treatment limitation.)

(C) *Portion based on plan payments.* For purposes of this paragraph (c), the determination of the portion of medical/surgical benefits in a classification of benefits subject to a financial requirement or quantitative treatment limitation (or subject to any level of a financial requirement or quantitative treatment limitation) is based on the dollar amount of all plan payments for medical/surgical benefits in the classification expected to be paid under the plan for the plan year (or for the portion of the plan year after a change in plan benefits that affects the applicability of the financial requirement or quantitative treatment limitation).

(D) *Clarifications for certain threshold requirements.* For any deductible, the dollar amount of plan payments includes all plan payments with respect to claims that would be subject to the deductible if it had not been satisfied. For any out-of-pocket maximum, the dollar amount of plan payments includes all plan payments associated with out-of-pocket payments that are taken into account towards the out-of-pocket maximum as well as all plan payments associated with out-of-pocket payments that would have been made towards the out-of-pocket maximum if it had not been satisfied. Similar rules apply for any other thresholds at which the rate of plan payment changes.

(E) *Determining the dollar amount of plan payments.* Subject to paragraph (c)(3)(i)(D) of this section, any reasonable method may be used to determine the dollar amount expected to be paid under a plan for medical/surgical benefits subject to a financial requirement or quantitative treatment limitation (or subject to any level of a financial requirement or quantitative treatment limitation).

(ii) *Application to different coverage units.* If a plan (or health insurance coverage) applies different levels of a financial requirement or quantitative treatment limitation to different coverage units in a classification of medical/surgical benefits, the predominant level that applies to substantially all medical/surgical benefits in the classification is determined separately for each coverage unit.

(iii) *Special rule for multi-tiered prescription drug benefits.* If a plan (or health insurance coverage) applies different levels of financial requirements to different tiers of prescription drug benefits based on reasonable factors determined in accordance with the rules in paragraph (c)(4)(i) of this section (relating to requirements for nonquantitative treatment limitations) and without regard to whether a drug is generally prescribed with respect to medical/surgical benefits or with respect to mental health or substance use disorder benefits, the plan (or health insurance coverage) satisfies the parity requirements of this paragraph (c) with respect to prescription drug benefits. Reasonable factors include cost, efficacy, generic versus brand name, and mail order versus pharmacy pick-up.

(iv) *Examples.* The rules of paragraphs (c)(3)(i), (c)(3)(ii), and (c)(3)(iii) of this section are illustrated by the following examples. In each example, the group health plan is subject to the requirements of this section and provides both medical/surgical benefits and mental health and substance use disorder benefits.

Example 1. (i) *Facts.* For inpatient, out-of-network medical/surgical benefits, a group health plan imposes five levels of coinsurance. Using a reasonable method, the plan projects its payments for the upcoming year as follows:

Coinsurance rate	0 %	10%	15%	20%	30%	Total
Projected payments	$200x	$100x	$450x	$100x	$150x	$1,000x
Percent of total plan costs	20%	10%	45%	10%	15%	

Percent subject to coinsurance level	N/A	12.5% (100x/800x)	56.25% (450x/800x)	12.5% (100x/800x)	18.75% (150x/800x)

The plan projects plan costs of $800x to be subject to coinsurance ($100x + $450x + $100x + $150x = $800x). Thus, 80 percent ($800x/$1,000x) of the benefits are projected to be subject to coinsurance, and 56.25 percent of the benefits subject to coinsurance are projected to be subject to the 15 percent coinsurance level.

(ii) *Conclusion.* In this *Example 1*, the two-thirds threshold of the substantially all standard is met for coinsurance because 80 percent of all inpatient, out-of-network medical/surgical benefits are subject to coinsurance. Moreover, the 15 percent coinsurance is the predominant level because it is applicable to more than one-half of inpatient, out-of-network medical/surgical benefits subject to the coinsurance requirement. The plan may not impose any level of coinsurance with respect to inpatient, out-of-network mental health or substance use disorder benefits that is more restrictive than the 15 percent level of coinsurance.

Example 2. (i) *Facts.* For outpatient, in-network medical/surgical benefits, a plan imposes five different copayment levels. Using a reasonable method, the plan projects payments for the upcoming year as follows:

Copayment amount	$0	$10	$15	$20	$50	Total
Projected payments	$200x	$200x	$200x	$300x	$100x	$1,000x
Percent of total plan costs	20%	20%	20%	30%	10%	
Percent subject to copayments	N/A	25% (200x/800x)	25% (200x/800x)	37.5% (300x/800x)	12.5% (100x/800x)	

The plan projects plan costs of $800x to be subject to copayments ($200x + $200x +$300x + $100x = $800x). Thus, 80 percent ($800x/$1,000x) of the benefits are projected to be subject to a copayment.

(ii) *Conclusion.* In this *Example 2*, the two-thirds threshold of the substantially all standard is met for copayments because 80 percent of all outpatient, in-network medical/surgical benefits are subject to a copayment. Moreover, there is no single level that applies to more than one-half of medical/surgical benefits in the classification subject to a copayment (for the $10 copayment, 25%; for the $15 copayment, 25%; for the $20 copayment, 37.5%; and for the $50 copayment, 12.5%). The plan can combine any levels of copayment, including the highest levels, to determine the predominant level that can be applied to mental health or substance use disorder benefits. If the plan combines the highest levels of copayment, the combined projected payments for the two highest copayment levels, the $50 copayment and the $20 copayment, are not more than one-half of the outpatient, in-network medical/surgical benefits subject to a copayment because they are exactly one-half ($300x + $100x = $400x; $400x/$800x = 50%). The combined projected payments for the three highest copayment levels - the $50 copayment, the $20 copayment, and the $15 copayment - are more than one-half of the outpatient, innetwork medical/surgical benefits subject to the copayments ($100x + $300x + $200x = $600x; $600x/$800x = 75%). Thus, the plan may not impose any copayment on outpatient, innetwork mental health or substance use disorder benefits that is more restrictive than the least restrictive copayment in the combination, the $15 copayment.

Example 3. (i) *Facts.* A plan imposes a $250 deductible on all medical/surgical benefits for self-only coverage and a $500 deductible on all medical/surgical benefits for family coverage. The plan has no network of providers. For all medical/surgical benefits, the plan imposes a coinsurance requirement. The plan imposes no other financial requirements or treatment limitations.

(ii) *Conclusion.* In this *Example 3*, because the plan has no network of providers, all benefits are provided out-of-network. Because self-only and family coverage are subject to different deductibles, whether the deductible applies to substantially all medical/surgical benefits is determined separately for self-only medical/surgical benefits and family medical/surgical benefits. Because the coinsurance is applied without regard to coverage units, the predominant coinsurance that applies to substantially all medical/surgical benefits is determined without regard to coverage units.

Example 4. (i) *Facts.* A plan applies the following financial requirements for prescription drug benefits. The requirements are applied without regard to whether a drug is generally prescribed with respect to medical/surgical benefits or with respect to mental health or substance use disorder benefits. Moreover, the process for certifying a particular drug as "generic", "preferred brand name", "non-preferred brand name", or "specialty" complies with the rules of paragraph (c)(4)(i) of this section (relating to requirements for nonquantitative treatment limitations).

	Tier 1	Tier 2	Tier 3	Tier 4
Tier description	Generic drugs	Preferred brand name drugs	Non-preferred brand name drugs (which may have Tier 1 or Tier 2 alternatives)	Specialty drugs
Percent paid by plan	90%	80%	60%	50%

(ii) *Conclusion.* In this *Example 4*, the financial requirements that apply to prescription drug benefits are applied without regard to whether a drug is generally prescribed with respect to medical/surgical benefits or with respect to mental health or substance use disorder benefits; the process for certifying drugs in different tiers complies with paragraph (c)(4) of this section; and the bases for establishing different levels or types of financial requirements are reasonable. The financial requirements applied to prescription drug benefits do not violate the parity requirements of this paragraph (c)(3).

(v) *No separate cumulative financial requirements or cumulative quantitative treatment limitations.* (A) A group health plan (or health insurance coverage offered in connection with a group health plan) may not apply any cumulative financial requirement or cumulative quantitative treatment limitation for mental health or substance use disorder benefits in a classification that accumulates separately from any established for medical/surgical benefits in the same classification.

(B) The rules of this paragraph (c)(3)(v) are illustrated by the following examples:

Example 1. (i) *Facts.* A group health plan imposes a combined annual $500 deductible on all medical/surgical, mental health, and substance use disorder benefits.

(ii) *Conclusion.* In this *Example 1*, the combined annual deductible complies with the requirements of this paragraph (c)(3)(v).

Example 2. (i) *Facts.* A plan imposes an annual $250 deductible on all medical/surgical benefits and a separate annual $250 deductible on all mental health and substance use disorder benefits.

(ii) *Conclusion.* In this *Example 2*, the separate annual deductible on mental health and substance use disorder benefits violates the requirements of this paragraph (c)(3)(v).

Example 3. (i) *Facts.* A plan imposes an annual $300 deductible on all medical/surgical benefits and a separate annual $100 deductible on all mental health or substance use disorder benefits.

(ii) *Conclusion.* In this *Example 3*, the separate annual deductible on mental health and substance use disorder benefits violates the requirements of this paragraph (c)(3)(v).

Example 4. (i) *Facts.* A plan generally imposes a combined annual $500 deductible on all benefits (both medical/surgical benefits and mental health and substance use disorder benefits) except prescription drugs. Certain benefits, such as preventive care, are provided without regard to the deductible. The imposition of other types of financial requirements or treatment limitations varies with each classification. Using reasonable methods, the plan projects its payments for medical/surgical benefits in each classification for the upcoming year as follows:

Classification	Benefits Subject to Deductible	Total Benefits	Percent Subject to Deductible
Inpatient, in-network	$1,800x	$2,000x	90%
Inpatient, out-of-network	$1,000x	$1,000x	100%
Outpatient, in-network	$1,400x	$2,000x	70%
Outpatient, out-of-network	$1,880x	$2,000x	94%
Emergency care	$300x	$500x	60%

(ii) *Conclusion.* In this *Example 4*, the two-thirds threshold of the substantially all standard is met with respect to each classification except emergency care because in each of those other classifications at least two-thirds of medical/surgical benefits are subject to the $500 deductible. Moreover, the $500 deductible is the predominant level in each of those other classifications because it is the only level. However, emergency care mental health and substance use disorder benefits cannot be subject to the $500 deductible because it does not apply to substantially all emergency care medical/surgical benefits.

(4) *Nonquantitative treatment limitations.* (i) *General rule.* A group health plan (or health insurance coverage) may not impose a nonquantitative treatment limitation with respect to mental health or substance use disorder benefits in any classification unless, under the terms of the plan (or health insurance coverage) as written and in operation, any processes, strategies, evidentiary standards, or other factors used in applying the nonquantitative treatment limitation to mental health or substance use disorder benefits in the classification are comparable to, and are applied no more stringently than, the processes, strategies, evidentiary standards, or other factors used in applying the limitation with respect to medical surgical/benefits in the classification, except to the extent that recognized clinically appropriate standards of care may permit a difference.

(ii) *Illustrative list of nonquantitative treatment limitations.* Nonquantitative treatment limitations include -

(A) Medical management standards limiting or excluding benefits based on medical necessity or medical appropriateness, or based on whether the treatment is experimental or investigative;

(B) Formulary design for prescription drugs;

(C) Standards for provider admission to participate in a network, including reimbursement rates;

(D) Plan methods for determining usual, customary, and reasonable charges;

(E) Refusal to pay for higher-cost therapies until it can be shown that a lower-cost therapy is not effective (also known as fail-first policies or step therapy protocols); and

(F) Exclusions based on failure to complete a course of treatment.

(iii) *Examples.* The rules of this paragraph (c)(4) are illustrated by the following examples. In each example, the group health plan is subject to the requirements of this section and provides both medical/surgical benefits and mental health and substance use disorder benefits.

Example 1. (i) *Facts.* A group health plan limits benefits to treatment that is medically necessary. The plan requires concurrent review for inpatient, in-network mental health and substance use disorder benefits but does not require it for any inpatient, in-network medical/surgical benefits. The plan conducts retrospective review for inpatient, in-network medical/surgical benefits.

(ii) *Conclusion.* In this *Example 1*, the plan violates the rules of this paragraph (c)(4). Although the same nonquantitative treatment limitation - medical necessity - applies to both mental health and substance use disorder benefits and to medical/surgical benefits for inpatient, in-network services, the concurrent review process does not apply to medical/surgical benefits. The concurrent review process is not comparable to the retrospective review process. While such a difference might be permissible in certain individual cases based on recognized clinically appropriate standards of care, it is not permissible for distinguishing between all medical/surgical benefits and all mental health or substance use disorder benefits.

Example 2. (i) *Facts.* A plan requires prior approval that a course of treatment is medically necessary for outpatient, in-network medical/surgical, mental health, and substance use disorder benefits. For mental health and substance use disorder treatments that do not have prior approval, no benefits will be paid; for medical/surgical treatments that do not have prior approval, there will only be a 25 percent reduction in the benefits the plan would otherwise pay.

(ii) *Conclusion.* In this *Example 2*, the plan violates the rules of this paragraph (c)(4). Although the same nonquantitative treatment limitation - medical necessity - is applied both to mental health and substance use disorder benefits and to medical/surgical benefits for outpatient, in-network services, the penalty for failure to obtain prior approval for mental health and substance use disorder benefits is not comparable to the penalty for failure to obtain prior approval for medical/surgical benefits.

Example 3. (i) *Facts.* A plan generally covers medically appropriate treatments. For both medical/surgical benefits and mental health and substance use disorder benefits, evidentiary standards used in determining whether a treatment is medically appropriate (such as the number of visits or days of coverage) are based on recommendations made by panels of experts with appropriate training and experience in the fields of medicine involved. The evidentiary standards are applied in a manner that may differ based on clinically appropriate standards of care for a condition.

(ii) *Conclusion.* In this *Example 3*, the plan complies with the rules of this paragraph (c)(4) because the nonquantitative treatment limitation - medical appropriateness - is the same for both medical/surgical benefits and mental health and substance use disorder benefits, and the processes for developing the evidentiary standards and the application of them to mental health and substance use disorder benefits are comparable to and are applied no more stringently than for medical/surgical benefits. This is the result even if, based on clinically appropriate standards of care, the application of the evidentiary standards does not result in similar numbers of visits, days of coverage, or other benefits utilized for mental health conditions or substance use disorders as it does for any particular medical/surgical condition.

Example 4. (i) *Facts.* A plan generally covers medically appropriate treatments. In determining whether prescription drugs are medically appropriate, the plan automatically excludes coverage for antidepressant drugs that are given a black box warning label by the

Food and Drug Administration (indicating the drug carries a significant risk of serious adverse effects). For other drugs with a black box warning (including those prescribed for other mental health conditions and substance use disorders, as well as for medical/surgical conditions), the plan will provide coverage if the prescribing physician obtains authorization from the plan that the drug is medically appropriate for the individual, based on clinically appropriate standards of care.

(ii) *Conclusion*. In this *Example 4*, the plan violates the rules of this paragraph (c)(4). Although the same nonquantitative treatment limitation - medical appropriateness - is applied to both mental health and substance use disorder benefits and medical/surgical benefits, the plan's unconditional exclusion of antidepressant drugs given a black box warning is not comparable to the conditional exclusion for other drugs with a black box warning.

Example 5. (i) *Facts*. An employer maintains both a major medical program and an employee assistance program (EAP). The EAP provides, among other benefits, a limited number of mental health or substance use disorder counseling sessions. Participants are eligible for mental health or substance use disorder benefits under the major medical program only after exhausting the counseling sessions provided by the EAP. No similar exhaustion requirement applies with respect to medical/surgical benefits provided under the major medical program.

(ii) *Conclusion*. In this *Example 5*, limiting eligibility for mental health and substance use disorder benefits only after EAP benefits are exhausted is a nonquantitative treatment limitation subject to the parity requirements of this paragraph (c). Because no comparable requirement applies to medical/surgical benefits, the requirement may not be applied to mental health or substance use disorder benefits.

(5) *Exemptions*. The rules of this paragraph (c) do not apply if a group health plan (or health insurance coverage) satisfies the requirements of paragraph (f) or (g) of this section (relating to exemptions for small employers and for increased cost).

(d) *Availability of plan information*. (1) *Criteria for medical necessity determinations*. The criteria for medical necessity determinations made under a group health plan with respect to mental health or substance use disorder benefits (or health insurance coverage offered in connection with the plan with respect to such benefits) must be made available by the plan administrator (or the health insurance issuer offering such coverage) to any current or potential participant, beneficiary, or contracting provider upon request.

(2) *Reason for any denial*. The reason for any denial under a group health plan (or health insurance coverage) of reimbursement or payment for services with respect to mental health or substance use disorder benefits in the case of any participant or beneficiary must be made available by the plan administrator (or the health insurance issuer offering such coverage) to the participant or beneficiary in a form and manner consistent with the rules in § 2560.503-1 of this Part for group health plans.

(e) *Applicability*. (1) *Group health plans*. The requirements of this section apply to a group health plan offering medical/surgical benefits and mental health or substance use disorder benefits. If, under an arrangement or arrangements to provide medical care benefits by an employer or employee organization (including for this purpose a joint board of trustees of a multiemployer trust affiliated with one or more multiemployer plans), any participant (or beneficiary) can simultaneously receive coverage for medical/surgical benefits and coverage for mental health or substance use disorder benefits, then the requirements of this section (including the exemption provisions in paragraph (g) of this section) apply separately with respect to each combination of medical/surgical benefits and of mental health or substance use disorder benefits that any participant (or beneficiary) can simultaneously receive from that employer's or employee organization's arrangement or arrangements to provide medical care benefits, and all such combinations are considered for purposes of this section to be a single group health plan.

(2) *Health insurance issuers*. The requirements of this section apply to a health insurance issuer offering health insurance coverage for mental health or substance use disorder benefits in connection with a group health plan subject to paragraph (e)(1) of this section.

(3) *Scope*. This section does not -

(i) Require a group health plan (or health insurance issuer offering coverage in connection with a group health plan) to provide any mental health benefits or substance use disorder benefits, and the provision of benefits by a plan (or health insurance coverage) for one or more mental health conditions or substance use disorders does not require the plan or health insurance coverage under this section to provide benefits for any other mental health condition or substance use disorder; or

(ii) Affect the terms and conditions relating to the amount, duration, or scope of mental health or substance use disorder benefits under the plan (or health insurance coverage) except as specifically provided in paragraphs (b) and (c) of this section.

(f) *Small employer exemption*. (1) *In general*. The requirements of this section do not apply to a group health plan (or health insurance issuer offering coverage in connection with a group health plan) for a plan year of a small employer. For purposes of this paragraph (f), the term *small employer* means, in connection with a group health plan with respect to a calendar year and a plan year, an employer who employed an average of at least two (or one in the case of an employer residing in a state that permits small groups to include a single individual) but not more than 50 employees on business days during the preceding calendar year. See section 732(a) of ERISA and § 2590.732(b) of this Part, which provide that this section (and certain other sections) does not apply to any group health plan (and health insurance issuer offering coverage in connection with a group health plan) for any plan year if, on the first day of the plan year, the plan has fewer than two participants who are current employees.

(2) *Rules in determining employer size*. For purposes of paragraph (f)(1) of this section—

(i) All persons treated as a single employer under subsections (b), (c), (m), and (o) of section 414 of the Code are treated as one employer;

(ii) If an employer was not in existence throughout the preceding calendar year, whether it is a small employer is determined based on the average number of employees the employer reasonably expects to employ on business days during the current calendar year; and

(iii) Any reference to an employer for purposes of the small employer exemption includes a reference to a predecessor of the employer.

(g) *Increased cost exemption*. [Reserved]

(h) *Sale of nonparity health insurance coverage*. A health insurance issuer may not sell a policy, certificate, or contract of insurance that fails to comply with paragraph (b) or (c) of this section, except to a plan for a year for which the plan is exempt from the requirements of this section because the plan meets the requirements of paragraph (f) or (g) of this section.

(i) *Applicability dates*. (1) *In general*. Except as provided in paragraph (i)(2) of this section, the requirements of this section are applicable for plan years beginning on or after July 1, 2010.

(2) *Special effective date for certain collectively-bargained plans*. For a group health plan maintained pursuant to one or more collective bargaining agreements ratified before October 3, 2008, the requirements of this section do not apply to the plan (or health insurance coverage offered in connection with the plan) for plan years beginning before the later of either -

(i) The date on which the last of the collective bargaining agreements relating to the plan terminates (determined without regard to any extension agreed to after October 3, 2008); or

(ii) July 1, 2010.

[Revised on 2/2/2010 (75 FR 5409).]

Regulations

Reg. § 2590.712 was adopted and published in the Federal Register on November 13, 2013 (78 FR 68239).

»»→ *Caution: EBSA Reg. § 2590.712 is effective on January 13, 2014, and generally applicable to group health plans and health insurance issuers offering group health insurance coverage for plan years beginning on or after July 1, 2014. Until the final regulations become applicable, plans and issuers must continue to comply with the mental health parity provisions of the interim final regulations at ¶ 15,050K-2.*

[¶ 15,050K-3]

§ 2590.712 Parity in mental health and substance use disorder benefits.

(a) *Meaning of terms*. For purposes of this section, except where the context clearly indicates otherwise, the following terms have the meanings indicated:

Aggregate lifetime dollar limit means a dollar limitation on the total amount of specified benefits that may be paid under a group health plan (or health insurance coverage offered in connection with such a plan) for any coverage unit.

Annual dollar limit means a dollar limitation on the total amount of specified benefits that may be paid in a 12-month period under a group health plan (or health insurance coverage offered in connection with such a plan) for any coverage unit.

Coverage unit means coverage unit as described in paragraph (c)(1)(iv) of this section.

Cumulative financial requirements are financial requirements that determine whether or to what extent benefits are provided based on accumulated amounts and include deductibles and out-of-pocket maximums. (However, cumulative financial requirements do not include aggregate lifetime or annual dollar limits because these two terms are excluded from the meaning of financial requirements.)

Cumulative quantitative treatment limitations are treatment limitations that determine whether or to what extent benefits are provided based on accumulated amounts, such as annual or lifetime day or visit limits.

Financial requirements include deductibles, copayments, coinsurance, or out-of-pocket maximums. Financial requirements do not include aggregate lifetime or annual dollar limits.

Medical/surgical benefits means benefits with respect to items or services for medical conditions or surgical procedures, as defined under the terms of the plan or health insurance coverage and in accordance with applicable Federal and State law, but does not include mental health or substance use disorder benefits. Any condition defined by the plan or coverage as being or as not being a medical/surgical condition must be defined to be consistent with generally recognized independent standards of current medical practice (for example, the most current version of the International Classification of Diseases (ICD) or State guidelines).

Mental health benefits means benefits with respect to items or services for mental health conditions, as defined under the terms of the plan or health insurance coverage and in accordance with applicable Federal and State law. Any condition defined by the plan or coverage as being or as not being a mental health condition must be defined to be consistent with generally recognized independent standards of current medical practice (for example, the most current version of the Diagnostic and Statistical Manual of Mental Disorders (DSM), the most current version of the ICD, or State guidelines).

Substance use disorder benefits means benefits with respect to items or services for substance use disorders, as defined under the terms of the plan or health insurance coverage and in accordance with applicable Federal and State law. Any disorder defined by the plan as being or as not being a substance use disorder must be defined to be consistent with generally recognized independent standards of current medical practice (for example, the most current version of the DSM, the most current version of the ICD, or State guidelines).

Treatment limitations include limits on benefits based on the frequency of treatment, number of visits, days of coverage, days in a waiting period, or other similar limits on the scope or duration of treatment. Treatment limitations include both quantitative treatment limitations, which are expressed numerically (such as 50 outpatient visits per year), and nonquantitative treatment limitations, which otherwise limit the scope or duration of benefits for treatment under a plan

or coverage. (See paragraph (c)(4)(ii) of this section for an illustrative list of nonquantitative treatment limitations.) A permanent exclusion of all benefits for a particular condition or disorder, however, is not a treatment limitation for purposes of this definition.

(b) *Parity requirements with respect to aggregate lifetime and annual dollar limits*. This paragraph (b) details the application of the parity requirements with respect to aggregate lifetime and annual dollar limits. This paragraph (b) does not address the provisions of PHS Act section 2711, as incorporated in ERISA section 715 and Code section 9815, which prohibit imposing lifetime and annual limits on the dollar value of essential health benefits. For more information, see 29 CFR 2590.715-2711.

(1) *General*. (i) *General parity requirement*. A group health plan (or health insurance coverage offered by an issuer in connection with a group health plan) that provides both medical/surgical benefits and mental health or substance use disorder benefits must comply with paragraph (b)(2), (b)(3), or (b)(5) of this section.

(ii) *Exception*. The rule in paragraph (b)(1)(i) of this section does not apply if a plan (or health insurance coverage) satisfies the requirements of paragraph (f) or (g) of this section (relating to exemptions for small employers and for increased cost).

(2) *Plan with no limit or limits on less than one-third of all medical/surgical benefits*. If a plan (or health insurance coverage) does not include an aggregate lifetime or annual dollar limit on any medical/surgical benefits or includes an aggregate lifetime or annual dollar limit that applies to less than one-third of all medical/surgical benefits, it may not impose an aggregate lifetime or annual dollar limit, respectively, on mental health or substance use disorder benefits.

(3) *Plan with a limit on at least two-thirds of all medical/surgical benefits*. If a plan (or health insurance coverage) includes an aggregate lifetime or annual dollar limit on at least two-thirds of all medical/surgical benefits, it must either—

(i) Apply the aggregate lifetime or annual dollar limit both to the medical/surgical benefits to which the limit would otherwise apply and to mental health or substance use disorder benefits in a manner that does not distinguish between the medical/surgical benefits and mental health or substance use disorder benefits; or

(ii) Not include an aggregate lifetime or annual dollar limit on mental health or substance use disorder benefits that is less than the aggregate lifetime or annual dollar limit, respectively, on medical/surgical benefits. (For cumulative limits other than aggregate lifetime or annual dollar limits, see paragraph (c)(3)(v) of this section prohibiting separately accumulating cumulative financial requirements or cumulative quantitative treatment limitations.)

(4) *Determining one-third and two-thirds of all medical/surgical benefits*. For purposes of this paragraph (b), the determination of whether the portion of medical/surgical benefits subject to an aggregate lifetime or annual dollar limit represents one-third or two-thirds of all medical/surgical benefits is based on the dollar amount of all plan payments for medical/surgical benefits expected to be paid under the plan for the plan year (or for the portion of the plan year after a change in plan benefits that affects the applicability of the aggregate lifetime or annual dollar limits). Any reasonable method may be used to determine whether the dollar amount expected to be paid under the plan will constitute one-third or two-thirds of the dollar amount of all plan payments for medical/surgical benefits.

(5) *Plan not described in paragraph (b)(2) or (b)(3) of this section*. (i) *In general*. A group health plan (or health insurance coverage) that is not described in paragraph (b)(2) or (b)(3) of this section with respect to aggregate lifetime or annual dollar limits on medical/surgical benefits, must either—

(A) Impose no aggregate lifetime or annual dollar limit, as appropriate, on mental health or substance use disorder benefits; or

(B) Impose an aggregate lifetime or annual dollar limit on mental health or substance use disorder benefits that is no less than an average limit calculated for medical/surgical benefits in the following manner. The average limit is calculated by taking into account the weighted average of the aggregate lifetime or annual dollar limits, as appropriate, that are applicable to the categories of medical/surgical benefits. Limits based on delivery systems, such as inpatient/outpatient treatment or normal treatment of common, low-cost conditions (such as treatment of normal births), do not constitute categories for purposes of this paragraph (b)(5)(i)(B). In addition, for purposes of determining weighted averages, any benefits that are not within a category that is subject to a separately-designated dollar limit under the plan are taken into account as a single separate category by using an estimate of the upper limit on the dollar amount that a plan may reasonably be expected to incur with respect to such benefits, taking into account any other applicable restrictions under the plan.

(ii) *Weighting.* For purposes of this paragraph (b)(5), the weighting applicable to any category of medical/surgical benefits is determined in the manner set forth in paragraph (b)(4) of this section for determining one-third or two-thirds of all medical/surgical benefits.

(c) *Parity requirements with respect to financial requirements and treatment limitations.* (1) *Clarification of terms.* (i) *Classification of benefits.* When reference is made in this paragraph (c) to a classification of benefits, the term "classification" means a classification as described in paragraph (c)(2)(ii) of this section.

(ii) *Type of financial requirement or treatment limitation.* When reference is made in this paragraph (c) to a type of financial requirement or treatment limitation, the reference to type means its nature. Different types of financial requirements include deductibles, copayments, coinsurance, and out-of-pocket maximums. Different types of quantitative treatment limitations include annual, episode, and lifetime day and visit limits. See paragraph (c)(4)(ii) of this section for an illustrative list of nonquantitative treatment limitations.

(iii) *Level of a type of financial requirement or treatment limitation.* When reference is made in this paragraph (c) to a level of a type of financial requirement or treatment limitation, level refers to the magnitude of the type of financial requirement or treatment limitation. For example, different levels of coinsurance include 20 percent and 30 percent; different levels of a copayment include $15 and $20; different levels of a deductible include $250 and $500; and different levels of an episode limit include 21 inpatient days per episode and 30 inpatient days per episode.

(iv) *Coverage unit.* When reference is made in this paragraph (c) to a coverage unit, coverage unit refers to the way in which a plan (or health insurance coverage) groups individuals for purposes of determining benefits, or premiums or contributions. For example, different coverage units include self-only, family, and employee-plus-spouse.

(2) *General parity requirement.* (i) *General rule.* A group health plan (or health insurance coverage offered by an issuer in connection with a group health plan) that provides both medical/surgical benefits and mental health or substance use disorder benefits may not apply any financial requirement or treatment limitation to mental health or substance use disorder benefits in any classification that is more restrictive than the predominant financial requirement or treatment limitation of that type applied to substantially all medical/surgical benefits in the same classification. Whether a financial requirement or treatment limitation is a predominant financial requirement or treatment limitation that applies to substantially all medical/surgical benefits in a classification is determined separately for each type of financial requirement or treatment limitation. The application of the rules of this paragraph (c)(2) to financial requirements and quantitative treatment limitations is addressed in paragraph (c)(3) of this section; the application of the rules of this paragraph (c)(2) to nonquantitative treatment limitations is addressed in paragraph (c)(4) of this section.

(ii) *Classifications of benefits used for applying rules.* (A) *In general.* If a plan (or health insurance coverage) provides mental health

or substance use disorder benefits in any classification of benefits described in this paragraph (c)(2)(ii), mental health or substance use disorder benefits must be provided in every classification in which medical/surgical benefits are provided. In determining the classification in which a particular benefit belongs, a plan (or health insurance issuer) must apply the same standards to medical/surgical benefits and to mental health or substance use disorder benefits. To the extent that a plan (or health insurance coverage) provides benefits in a classification and imposes any separate financial requirement or treatment limitation (or separate level of a financial requirement or treatment limitation) for benefits in the classification, the rules of this paragraph (c) apply separately with respect to that classification for all financial requirements or treatment limitations (illustrated in examples in paragraph (c)(2)(ii)(C) of this section). The following classifications of benefits are the only classifications used in applying the rules of this paragraph (c):

(1) *Inpatient, in-network.* Benefits furnished on an inpatient basis and within a network of providers established or recognized under a plan or health insurance coverage. See special rules for plans with multiple network tiers in paragraph (c)(3)(iii) of this section.

(2) *Inpatient, out-of-network.* Benefits furnished on an inpatient basis and outside any network of providers established or recognized under a plan or health insurance coverage. This classification includes inpatient benefits under a plan (or health insurance coverage) that has no network of providers.

(3) *Outpatient, in-network.* Benefits furnished on an outpatient basis and within a network of providers established or recognized under a plan or health insurance coverage. See special rules for office visits and plans with multiple network tiers in paragraph (c)(3)(iii) of this section.

(4) *Outpatient, out-of-network.* Benefits furnished on an outpatient basis and outside any network of providers established or recognized under a plan or health insurance coverage. This classification includes outpatient benefits under a plan (or health insurance coverage) that has no network of providers. See special rules for office visits in paragraph (c)(3)(iii) of this section.

(5) *Emergency care.* Benefits for emergency care.

(6) *Prescription drugs.* Benefits for prescription drugs. See special rules for multi-tiered prescription drug benefits in paragraph (c)(3)(iii) of this section.

(B) *Application to out-of-network providers.* See paragraph (c)(2)(ii)(A) of this section, under which a plan (or health insurance coverage) that provides mental health or substance use disorder benefits in any classification of benefits must provide mental health or substance use disorder benefits in every classification in which medical/surgical benefits are provided, including out-of-network classifications.

(C) *Examples.* The rules of this paragraph (c)(2)(ii) are illustrated by the following examples. In each example, the group health plan is subject to the requirements of this section and provides both medical/surgical benefits and mental health and substance use disorder benefits.

Example 1. (i) *Facts.* A group health plan offers inpatient and outpatient benefits and does not contract with a network of providers. The plan imposes a $500 deductible on all benefits. For inpatient medical/surgical benefits, the plan imposes a coinsurance requirement. For outpatient medical/surgical benefits, the plan imposes copayments. The plan imposes no other financial requirements or treatment limitations.

(ii) *Conclusion.* In this *Example 1,* because the plan has no network of providers, all benefits provided are out-of-network. Because inpatient, out-of-network medical/surgical benefits are subject to separate financial requirements from outpatient, out-of-network medical/surgical benefits, the rules of this paragraph (c) apply separately with respect to any financial requirements and treatment limitations, including the deductible, in each classification.

Example 2. (i) *Facts.* A plan imposes a $500 deductible on all benefits. The plan has no network of providers. The plan generally imposes a 20 percent coinsurance requirement with respect to all benefits, without distinguishing among inpatient, outpatient, emergency care, or prescription drug benefits. The plan imposes no other financial requirements or treatment limitations.

(ii) *Conclusion.* In this *Example 2,* because the plan does not impose separate financial requirements (or treatment limitations) based on classification, the rules of this paragraph (c) apply with respect to the deductible and the coinsurance across all benefits.

Example 3. (i) *Facts.* Same facts as *Example 2,* except the plan exempts emergency care benefits from the 20 percent coinsurance requirement. The plan imposes no other financial requirements or treatment limitations.

(ii) *Conclusion.* In this *Example 3,* because the plan imposes separate financial requirements based on classifications, the rules of this paragraph (c) apply with respect to the deductible and the coinsurance separately for—

(A) Benefits in the emergency care classification; and

(B) All other benefits.

Example 4. (i) *Facts.* Same facts as *Example 2,* except the plan also imposes a preauthorization requirement for all inpatient treatment in order for benefits to be paid. No such requirement applies to outpatient treatment.

(ii) *Conclusion.* In this *Example 4,* because the plan has no network of providers, all benefits provided are out-of-network. Because the plan imposes a separate treatment limitation based on classifications, the rules of this paragraph (c) apply with respect to the deductible and coinsurance separately for—

(A) Inpatient, out-of-network benefits; and

(B) All other benefits.

(3) *Financial requirements and quantitative treatment limitations.* (i) *Determining "substantially all" and "predominant".* (A) *Substantially all.* For purposes of this paragraph (c), a type of financial requirement or quantitative treatment limitation is considered to apply to substantially all medical/surgical benefits in a classification of benefits if it applies to at least two-thirds of all medical/surgical benefits in that classification. (For this purpose, benefits expressed as subject to a zero level of a type of financial requirement are treated as benefits not subject to that type of financial requirement, and benefits expressed as subject to a quantitative treatment limitation that is unlimited are treated as benefits not subject to that type of quantitative treatment limitation.) If a type of financial requirement or quantitative treatment limitation does not apply to at least two-thirds of all medical/surgical benefits in a classification, then that type cannot be applied to mental health or substance use disorder benefits in that classification.

(B) *Predominant.* (1) If a type of financial requirement or quantitative treatment limitation applies to at least two-thirds of all medical/surgical benefits in a classification as determined under paragraph (c)(3)(i)(A) of this section, the level of the financial requirement or quantitative treatment limitation that is considered the predominant level of that type in a classification of benefits is the level that applies to more than one-half of medical/surgical benefits in that classification subject to the financial requirement or quantitative treatment limitation.

(2) If, with respect to a type of financial requirement or quantitative treatment limitation that applies to at least two-thirds of all medical/surgical benefits in a classification, there is no single level that applies to more than one-half of medical/surgical benefits in the classification subject to the financial requirement or quantitative treatment limitation, the plan (or health insurance issuer) may combine levels until the combination of levels applies to more than one-half of medical/surgical benefits subject to the financial requirement or quantitative treatment limitation in the classification. The least restrictive level within the combination is considered the predominant level of that type in the classification. (For this purpose, a plan may combine the most restrictive levels first, with each less restrictive level added to the combination until the combination applies to more than one-half of the benefits subject to the financial requirement or treatment limitation.)

(C) *Portion based on plan payments.* For purposes of this paragraph (c), the determination of the portion of medical/surgical benefits in a classification of benefits subject to a financial requirement or quantitative treatment limitation (or subject to any level of a financial requirement or quantitative treatment limitation) is based on the dollar amount of all plan payments for medical/surgical benefits in the classification expected to be paid under the plan for the plan year (or for the portion of the plan year after a change in plan benefits that affects the applicability of the financial requirement or quantitative treatment limitation).

(D) *Clarifications for certain threshold requirements.* For any deductible, the dollar amount of plan payments includes all plan payments with respect to claims that would be subject to the deductible if it had not been satisfied. For any out-of-pocket maximum, the dollar amount of plan payments includes all plan payments associated with out-of-pocket payments that are taken into account towards the out-of-pocket maximum as well as all plan payments associated with out-of-pocket payments that would have been made towards the out-of-pocket maximum if it had not been satisfied. Similar rules apply for any other thresholds at which the rate of plan payment changes. (See also PHS Act section 2707(b) and Affordable Care Act section 1302(c), which establish limitations on annual deductibles for non-grandfathered health plans in the small group market and annual limitations on out-of-pocket maximums for all non-grandfathered health plans.)

(E) *Determining the dollar amount of plan payments.* Subject to paragraph (c)(3)(i)(D) of this section, any reasonable method may be used to determine the dollar amount expected to be paid under a plan for medical/surgical benefits subject to a financial requirement or quantitative treatment limitation (or subject to any level of a financial requirement or quantitative treatment limitation).

(ii) *Application to different coverage units.* If a plan (or health insurance coverage) applies different levels of a financial requirement or quantitative treatment limitation to different coverage units in a classification of medical/surgical benefits, the predominant level that applies to substantially all medical/surgical benefits in the classification is determined separately for each coverage unit.

(iii) *Special rules.* (A) *Multi-tiered prescription drug benefits.* If a plan (or health insurance coverage) applies different levels of financial requirements to different tiers of prescription drug benefits based on reasonable factors determined in accordance with the rules in paragraph (c)(4)(i) of this section (relating to requirements for nonquantitative treatment limitations) and without regard to whether a drug is generally prescribed with respect to medical/surgical benefits or with respect to mental health or substance use disorder benefits, the plan (or health insurance coverage) satisfies the parity requirements of this paragraph (c) with respect to prescription drug benefits. Reasonable factors include cost, efficacy, generic versus brand name, and mail order versus pharmacy pick-up.

(B) *Multiple network tiers.* If a plan (or health insurance coverage) provides benefits through multiple tiers of in-network providers (such as an in-network tier of preferred providers with more generous cost-sharing to participants than a separate in-network tier of participating providers), the plan may divide its benefits furnished on an in-network basis into sub-classifications that reflect network tiers, if the tiering is based on reasonable factors determined in accordance with the rules in paragraph (c)(4)(i) of this section (such as quality, performance, and market standards) and without regard to whether a provider provides services with respect to medical/surgical benefits or mental health or substance use disorder benefits. After the sub-classifications are established, the plan or issuer may not impose any financial requirement or treatment limitation on mental health or substance use disorder benefits in any sub-classification that is more restrictive than the predominant financial requirement or treatment limitation that applies to substantially all medical/surgical benefits in the sub-classification using the methodology set forth in paragraph (c)(3)(i) of this section.

(C) *Sub-classifications permitted for office visits, separate from other outpatient services.* For purposes of applying the financial requirement and treatment limitation rules of this paragraph (c), a plan or issuer may divide its benefits furnished on an outpatient basis into the two sub-classifications described in this paragraph (c)(3)(iii)(C). After the sub-classifications are established, the plan or issuer may not impose any financial requirement or quantitative treatment limitation on mental health or substance use disorder benefits in any sub-classification that is more restrictive than the predominant financial requirement or quantitative treatment limitation that applies to substantially all medical/surgical benefits in the sub-classification using the methodology set forth in paragraph (c)(3)(i) of this section. Sub-classifications other than these special rules, such as separate sub-classifications for generalists and specialists, are not permitted. The two sub-classifications permitted under this paragraph (c)(3)(iii)(C) are:

(1) Office visits (such as physician visits), and

(2) All other outpatient items and services (such as outpatient surgery, facility charges for day treatment centers, laboratory charges, or other medical items).

Coinsurance rate	0%	10%	15%	20%	30% Total.
Projected payments	$200x	$100x	$450x	$100x	$150x $1,000x.
Percent of total plan costs . . .	20%	10%	45%	10%	15%
Percent subject to coinsurance level	N/A	12.5%	56.25%	12.5%	18.75%
		(100x/800x)	(450x/800x)	(100x/800x)	(150x/800x)

The plan projects plan costs of $800x to be subject to coinsurance ($100x + $450x + $100x + $150x = $800x). Thus, 80 percent ($800x/$1,000x) of the benefits are projected to be subject to coinsurance, and 56.25 percent of the benefits subject to coinsurance are projected to be subject to the 15 percent coinsurance level.

(ii) *Conclusion.* In this *Example 1,* the two-thirds threshold of the substantially all standard is met for coinsurance because 80 percent of all inpatient, out-of-network medical/surgical benefits are subject to coinsurance. Moreover, the 15 percent coinsurance is the predominant

Copayment amount	$0	$10	$15	$20	$50 Total.
Projected payments	$200x	$200x	$200x	$300x	$100x $1,000x.
Percent of total plan costs . . .	20%	20%	20%	30%	10%
Percent subject to copayments	N/A	25%	25%	37.5%	12.5%
		(200x/800x)	(200x/800x)	(300x/800x)	(100x/800x)

The plan projects plan costs of $800x to be subject to copayments ($200x + $200x +$300x + $100x = $800x). Thus, 80 percent ($800x/$1,000x) of the benefits are projected to be subject to a copayment.

(ii) *Conclusion.* In this *Example 2,* the two-thirds threshold of the substantially all standard is met for copayments because 80 percent of all outpatient, in-network medical/surgical benefits are subject to a copayment. Moreover, there is no single level that applies to more than one-half of medical/surgical benefits in the classification subject to a copayment (for the $10 copayment, 25%; for the $15 copayment, 25%; for the $20 copayment, 37.5%; and for the $50 copayment, 12.5%). The plan can combine any levels of copayment, including the highest levels, to determine the predominant level that can be applied to mental health or substance use disorder benefits. If the plan combines the highest levels of copayment, the combined projected payments for the two highest copayment levels, the $50 copayment and the $20 copayment, are not more than one-half of the outpatient, in-network medical/surgical benefits subject to a copayment because they are exactly one-half ($300x + $100x = $400x; $400x/$800x = 50%). The combined projected payments for the three highest copayment levels—the $50 copayment, the $20 copayment, and the $15 copayment—are more than one-half of the outpatient, in-network medical/surgical benefits subject to the copayments ($100x + $300x + $200x = $600x; $600x/$800x = 75%). Thus, the plan may not impose any copayment on outpatient, in-network mental health or substance use disorder benefits

(iv) *Examples.* The rules of paragraphs (c)(3)(i), (c)(3)(ii), and (c)(3)(iii) of this section are illustrated by the following examples. In each example, the group health plan is subject to the requirements of this section and provides both medical/surgical benefits and mental health and substance use disorder benefits.

Example 1. (i) *Facts.* For inpatient, out-of-network medical/surgical benefits, a group health plan imposes five levels of coinsurance. Using a reasonable method, the plan projects its payments for the upcoming year as follows:

level because it is applicable to more than one-half of inpatient, out-of-network medical/surgical benefits subject to the coinsurance requirement. The plan may not impose any level of coinsurance with respect to inpatient, out-of-network mental health or substance use disorder benefits that is more restrictive than the 15 percent level of coinsurance.

Example 2. (i) *Facts.* For outpatient, in-network medical/surgical benefits, a plan imposes five different copayment levels. Using a reasonable method, the plan projects payments for the upcoming year as follows:

that is more restrictive than the least restrictive copayment in the combination, the $15 copayment.

Example 3. (i) *Facts.* A plan imposes a $250 deductible on all medical/surgical benefits for self-only coverage and a $500 deductible on all medical/surgical benefits for family coverage. The plan has no network of providers. For all medical/surgical benefits, the plan imposes a coinsurance requirement. The plan imposes no other financial requirements or treatment limitations.

(ii) *Conclusion.* In this *Example 3,* because the plan has no network of providers, all benefits are provided out-of-network. Because self-only and family coverage are subject to different deductibles, whether the deductible applies to substantially all medical/surgical benefits is determined separately for self-only medical/surgical benefits and family medical/surgical benefits. Because the coinsurance is applied without regard to coverage units, the predominant coinsurance that applies to substantially all medical/surgical benefits is determined without regard to coverage units.

Example 4. (i) *Facts.* A plan applies the following financial requirements for prescription drug benefits. The requirements are applied without regard to whether a drug is generally prescribed with respect to medical/surgical benefits or with respect to mental health or substance use disorder benefits. Moreover, the process for certifying a particular drug as "generic", "preferred brand name", "non-preferred brand name", or "specialty" complies with the rules of paragraph (c)(4)(i) of this section (relating to requirements for nonquantitative treatment limitations).

Tier description	Tier 1 Generic drugs	Tier 2 Preferred brand name drugs	Tier 3 Non-preferred brand name drugs (which may have Tier 1 or Tier 2 alternatives)	Tier 4 Specialty drugs
Percent paid by plan	90%	80%	60%	50%

(ii) *Conclusion.* In this *Example 4,* the financial requirements that apply to prescription drug benefits are applied without regard to whether a drug is generally prescribed with respect to medical/surgical benefits or with respect to mental health or substance use disorder benefits; the process for certifying drugs in different tiers complies with paragraph (c)(4) of this section; and the bases for establishing different levels or types of financial requirements are reasonable. The financial requirements applied to prescription drug benefits do not violate the parity requirements of this paragraph (c)(3).

Example 5. (i) *Facts.* A plan has two-tiers of network of providers: a preferred provider tier and a participating provider tier. Providers are placed in either the preferred tier or participating tier based on reasonable factors determined in accordance with the rules in paragraph (c)(4)(i) of this section, such as accreditation, quality and performance measures (including customer feedback), and relative reimbursement rates. Furthermore, provider tier placement is determined without regard to whether a provider specializes in the treatment of mental health conditions or substance use disorders, or medical/surgical conditions. The plan divides the in-network classifications into two sub-classifications (in-network/preferred and in-network/participating). The plan does not impose any financial requirement or treatment limitation on mental health or substance use disorder benefits in either of these sub-classifications that is more restrictive than the predominant financial requirement or treatment limitation that applies to substantially all medical/surgical benefits in each sub-classification.

(ii) *Conclusion.* In this *Example 5,* the division of in-network benefits into sub-classifications that reflect the preferred and participating provider tiers does not violate the parity requirements of this paragraph (c)(3).

Example 6. (i) *Facts.* With respect to outpatient, in-network benefits, a plan imposes a $25 copayment for office visits and a 20 percent coinsurance requirement for outpatient surgery. The plan divides the outpatient, in-network classification into two sub-classifications (in-network office visits and all other outpatient, in-network items and services). The plan or issuer does not impose any financial requirement or quantitative treatment limitation on mental health or substance use disorder benefits in either of these sub-classifications that is more restrictive than the predominant financial requirement or quantitative treatment limitation that applies to substantially all medical/surgical benefits in each sub-classification.

(ii) *Conclusion.* In this *Example 6,* the division of outpatient, in-network benefits into sub-classifications for office visits and all other outpatient, in-network items and services does not violate the parity requirements of this paragraph (c)(3).

Example 7. (i) *Facts.* Same facts as *Example 6,* but for purposes of determining parity, the plan divides the outpatient, in-network classification into outpatient, in-network generalists and outpatient, in-network specialists.

(ii) *Conclusion.* In this *Example 7,* the division of outpatient, in-network benefits into any sub-classifications other than office visits and all other outpatient items and services violates the requirements of paragraph (c)(3)(iii)(C) of this section.

(v) *No separate cumulative financial requirements or cumulative quantitative treatment limitations.* (A) A group health plan (or health insurance coverage offered in connection with a group health plan) may not apply any cumulative financial requirement or cumulative quantitative treatment limitation for mental health or substance use disorder benefits in a classification that accumulates separately from any established for medical/surgical benefits in the same classification.

(B) The rules of this paragraph (c)(3)(v) are illustrated by the following examples:

Example 1. (i) *Facts.* A group health plan imposes a combined annual $500 deductible on all medical/surgical, mental health, and substance use disorder benefits.

(ii) *Conclusion.* In this *Example 1,* the combined annual deductible complies with the requirements of this paragraph (c)(3)(v).

Example 2. (i) *Facts.* A plan imposes an annual $250 deductible on all medical/surgical benefits and a separate annual $250 deductible on all mental health and substance use disorder benefits.

(ii) *Conclusion.* In this *Example 2,* the separate annual deductible on mental health and substance use disorder benefits violates the requirements of this paragraph (c)(3)(v).

Example 3. (i) *Facts.* A plan imposes an annual $300 deductible on all medical/surgical benefits and a separate annual $100 deductible on all mental health or substance use disorder benefits.

(ii) *Conclusion.* In this *Example 3,* the separate annual deductible on mental health and substance use disorder benefits violates the requirements of this paragraph (c)(3)(v).

Example 4. (i) *Facts.* A plan generally imposes a combined annual $500 deductible on all benefits (both medical/surgical benefits and mental health and substance use disorder benefits) except prescription drugs. Certain benefits, such as preventive care, are provided without regard to the deductible. The imposition of other types of financial requirements or treatment limitations varies with each classification. Using reasonable methods, the plan projects its payments for medical/surgical benefits in each classification for the upcoming year as follows:

Classification	Benefits subject to deductible	Total benefits	Percent subject to deductible
Inpatient, in-network	$1,800x	$2,000x	90
Inpatient, out-of-network	1,000x	1,000x	100
Outpatient, in-network	1,400x	2,000x	70
Outpatient, out-of-network	1,880x	2,000x	94
Emergency care	300x	500x	60

(ii) *Conclusion.* In this *Example 4,* the two-thirds threshold of the substantially all standard is met with respect to each classification except emergency care because in each of those other classifications at least two-thirds of medical/surgical benefits are subject to the $500 deductible. Moreover, the $500 deductible is the predominant level in each of those other classifications because it is the only level. However, emergency care mental health and substance use disorder benefits cannot be subject to the $500 deductible because it does not apply to substantially all emergency care medical/surgical benefits.

(4) *Nonquantitative treatment limitations.* (i) *General rule.* A group health plan (or health insurance coverage) may not impose a nonquantitative treatment limitation with respect to mental health or substance use disorder benefits in any classification unless, under the terms of the plan (or health insurance coverage) as written and in operation, any processes, strategies, evidentiary standards, or other factors used in applying the nonquantitative treatment limitation to mental health or substance use disorder benefits in the classification

are comparable to, and are applied no more stringently than, the processes, strategies, evidentiary standards, or other factors used in applying the limitation with respect to medical/surgical benefits in the classification.

(ii) *Illustrative list of nonquantitative treatment limitations.* Nonquantitative treatment limitations include—

(A) Medical management standards limiting or excluding benefits based on medical necessity or medical appropriateness, or based on whether the treatment is experimental or investigative;

(B) Formulary design for prescription drugs;

(C) For plans with multiple network tiers (such as preferred providers and participating providers), network tier design;

(D) Standards for provider admission to participate in a network, including reimbursement rates;

(E) Plan methods for determining usual, customary, and reasonable charges;

(F) Refusal to pay for higher-cost therapies until it can be shown that a lower-cost therapy is not effective (also known as fail-first policies or step therapy protocols);

(G) Exclusions based on failure to complete a course of treatment; and

(H) Restrictions based on geographic location, facility type, provider specialty, and other criteria that limit the scope or duration of benefits for services provided under the plan or coverage.

(iii) *Examples*. The rules of this paragraph (c)(4) are illustrated by the following examples. In each example, the group health plan is subject to the requirements of this section and provides both medical/surgical benefits and mental health and substance use disorder benefits.

Example 1. (i) *Facts*. A plan requires prior authorization from the plan's utilization reviewer that a treatment is medically necessary for all inpatient medical/surgical benefits and for all inpatient mental health and substance use disorder benefits. In practice, inpatient benefits for medical/surgical conditions are routinely approved for seven days, after which a treatment plan must be submitted by the patient's attending provider and approved by the plan. On the other hand, for inpatient mental health and substance use disorder benefits, routine approval is given only for one day, after which a treatment plan must be submitted by the patient's attending provider and approved by the plan.

(ii) *Conclusion*. In this Example 1, the plan violates the rules of this paragraph (c)(4) because it is applying a stricter nonquantitative treatment limitation in practice to mental health and substance use disorder benefits than is applied to medical/surgical benefits.

Example 2. (i) *Facts*. A plan applies concurrent review to inpatient care where there are high levels of variation in length of stay (as measured by a coefficient of variation exceeding 0.8). In practice, the application of this standard affects 60 percent of mental health conditions and substance use disorders, but only 30 percent of medical/surgical conditions.

(ii) *Conclusion*. In this *Example 2,* the plan complies with the rules of this paragraph (c)(4) because the evidentiary standard used by the plan is applied no more stringently for mental health and substance use disorder benefits than for medical/surgical benefits, even though it results in an overall difference in the application of concurrent review for mental health conditions or substance use disorders than for medical/surgical conditions.

Example 3. (i) *Facts*. A plan requires prior approval that a course of treatment is medically necessary for outpatient, in-network medical/surgical, mental health, and substance use disorder benefits and uses comparable criteria in determining whether a course of treatment is medically necessary. For mental health and substance use disorder treatments that do not have prior approval, no benefits will be paid; for medical/surgical treatments that do not have prior approval, there will only be a 25 percent reduction in the benefits the plan would otherwise pay.

(ii) *Conclusion*. In this *Example 3,* the plan violates the rules of this paragraph (c)(4). Although the same nonquantitative treatment limitation—medical necessity—is applied both to mental health and substance use disorder benefits and to medical/surgical benefits for outpatient, in-network services, it is not applied in a comparable way. The penalty for failure to obtain prior approval for mental health and substance use disorder benefits is not comparable to the penalty for failure to obtain prior approval for medical/surgical benefits.

Example 4. (i) *Facts*. A plan generally covers medically appropriate treatments. For both medical/surgical benefits and mental health and substance use disorder benefits, evidentiary standards used in determining whether a treatment is medically appropriate (such as the number of visits or days of coverage) are based on recommendations made by panels of experts with appropriate training and experience in the fields of medicine involved. The evidentiary standards are applied in a manner that is based on clinically appropriate standards of care for a condition.

(ii) *Conclusion*. In this *Example 4,* the plan complies with the rules of this paragraph (c)(4) because the processes for developing the evidentiary standards used to determine medical appropriateness and the application of these standards to mental health and substance use disorder benefits are comparable to and are applied no more strin-

gently than for medical/surgical benefits. This is the result even if the application of the evidentiary standards does not result in similar numbers of visits, days of coverage, or other benefits utilized for mental health conditions or substance use disorders as it does for any particular medical/surgical condition.

Example 5. (i) *Facts*. A plan generally covers medically appropriate treatments. In determining whether prescription drugs are medically appropriate, the plan automatically excludes coverage for antidepressant drugs that are given a black box warning label by the Food and Drug Administration (indicating the drug carries a significant risk of serious adverse effects). For other drugs with a black box warning (including those prescribed for other mental health conditions and substance use disorders, as well as for medical/surgical conditions), the plan will provide coverage if the prescribing physician obtains authorization from the plan that the drug is medically appropriate for the individual, based on clinically appropriate standards of care.

(ii) *Conclusion*. In this *Example 5,* the plan violates the rules of this paragraph (c)(4). Although the standard for applying a nonquantitative treatment limitation is the same for both mental health and substance use disorder benefits and medical/surgical benefits—whether a drug has a black box warning—it is not applied in a comparable manner. The plan's unconditional exclusion of antidepressant drugs given a black box warning is not comparable to the conditional exclusion for other drugs with a black box warning.

Example 6. (i) *Facts*. An employer maintains both a major medical plan and an employee assistance program (EAP). The EAP provides, among other benefits, a limited number of mental health or substance use disorder counseling sessions. Participants are eligible for mental health or substance use disorder benefits under the major medical plan only after exhausting the counseling sessions provided by the EAP. No similar exhaustion requirement applies with respect to medical/surgical benefits provided under the major medical plan.

(ii) *Conclusion*. In this *Example 6,* limiting eligibility for mental health and substance use disorder benefits only after EAP benefits are exhausted is a nonquantitative treatment limitation subject to the parity requirements of this paragraph (c). Because no comparable requirement applies to medical/surgical benefits, the requirement may not be applied to mental health or substance use disorder benefits.

Example 7. (i) *Facts*. Training and State licensing requirements often vary among types of providers. A plan applies a general standard that any provider must meet the highest licensing requirement related to supervised clinical experience under applicable State law in order to participate in the plan's provider network. Therefore, the plan requires master's-level mental health therapists to have post-degree, supervised clinical experience but does not impose this requirement on master's-level general medical providers because the scope of their licensure under applicable State law does require clinical experience. In addition, the plan does not require post-degree, supervised clinical experience for psychiatrists or Ph.D. level psychologists since their licensing already requires supervised training.

(ii) *Conclusion*. In this *Example 7,* the plan complies with the rules of this paragraph (c)(4). The requirement that master's-level mental health therapists must have supervised clinical experience to join the network is permissible, as long as the plan consistently applies the same standard to all providers even though it may have a disparate impact on certain mental health providers.

Example 8. (i) *Facts*. A plan considers a wide array of factors in designing medical management techniques for both mental health and substance use disorder benefits and medical/surgical benefits, such as cost of treatment; high cost growth; variability in cost and quality; elasticity of demand; provider discretion in determining diagnosis, or type or length of treatment; clinical efficacy of any proposed treatment or service; licensing and accreditation of providers; and claim types with a high percentage of fraud. Based on application of these factors in a comparable fashion, prior authorization is required for some (but not all) mental health and substance use disorder benefits, as well as for some medical/surgical benefits, but not for others. For example, the plan requires prior authorization for: outpatient surgery; speech, occupational, physical, cognitive and behavioral therapy extending for more than six months; durable medical equipment; diagnostic imaging; skilled nursing visits; home infusion therapy; coordinated home care; pain management; high-risk prenatal care;

delivery by cesarean section; mastectomy; prostate cancer treatment; narcotics prescribed for more than seven days; and all inpatient services beyond 30 days. The evidence considered in developing its medical management techniques includes consideration of a wide array of recognized medical literature and professional standards and protocols (including comparative effectiveness studies and clinical trials). This evidence and how it was used to develop these medical management techniques is also well documented by the plan.

(ii) *Conclusion.* In this *Example 8,* the plan complies with the rules of this paragraph (c)(4). Under the terms of the plan as written and in operation, the processes, strategies, evidentiary standards, and other factors considered by the plan in implementing its prior authorization requirement with respect to mental health and substance use disorder benefits are comparable to, and applied no more stringently than, those applied with respect to medical/surgical benefits.

Example 9. (i) *Facts.* A plan generally covers medically appropriate treatments. The plan automatically excludes coverage for inpatient substance use disorder treatment in any setting outside of a hospital (such as a freestanding or residential treatment center). For inpatient treatment outside of a hospital for other conditions (including freestanding or residential treatment centers prescribed for mental health conditions, as well as for medical/surgical conditions), the plan will provide coverage if the prescribing physician obtains authorization from the plan that the inpatient treatment is medically appropriate for the individual, based on clinically appropriate standards of care.

(ii) *Conclusion.* In this *Example 9,* the plan violates the rules of this paragraph (c)(4). Although the same nonquantitative treatment limitation—medical appropriateness—is applied to both mental health and substance use disorder benefits and medical/surgical benefits, the plan's unconditional exclusion of substance use disorder treatment in any setting outside of a hospital is not comparable to the conditional exclusion of inpatient treatment outside of a hospital for other conditions.

Example 10. (i) *Facts.* A plan generally provides coverage for medically appropriate medical/surgical benefits as well as mental health and substance use disorder benefits. The plan excludes coverage for inpatient, out-of-network treatment of chemical dependency when obtained outside of the State where the policy is written. There is no similar exclusion for medical/surgical benefits within the same classification.

(ii) *Conclusion.* In this Example 10, the plan violates the rules of this paragraph (c)(4). The plan is imposing a nonquantitative treatment limitation that restricts benefits based on geographic location. Because there is no comparable exclusion that applies to medical/surgical benefits, this exclusion may not be applied to mental health or substance use disorder benefits.

Example 11. (i) *Facts.* A plan requires prior authorization for all outpatient mental health and substance use disorder services after the ninth visit and will only approve up to five additional visits per authorization. With respect to outpatient medical/surgical benefits, the plan allows an initial visit without prior authorization. After the initial visit, the plan pre-approves benefits based on the individual treatment plan recommended by the attending provider based on that individual's specific medical condition. There is no explicit, predetermined cap on the amount of additional visits approved per authorization.

(ii) *Conclusion.* In this *Example 11,* the plan violates the rules of this paragraph (c)(4). Although the same nonquantitative treatment limitation—prior authorization to determine medical appropriateness—is applied to both mental health and substance use disorder benefits and medical/surgical benefits for outpatient services, it is not applied in a comparable way. While the plan is more generous with respect to the number of visits initially provided without pre-authorization for mental health benefits, treating all mental health conditions and substance use disorders in the same manner, while providing for individualized treatment of medical conditions, is not a comparable application of this nonquantitative treatment limitation.

(5) *Exemptions.* The rules of this paragraph (c) do not apply if a group health plan (or health insurance coverage) satisfies the requirements of paragraph (f) or (g) of this section (relating to exemptions for small employers and for increased cost).

(d) *Availability of plan information.* (1) *Criteria for medical necessity determinations.* The criteria for medical necessity determinations made under a group health plan with respect to mental health or substance use disorder benefits (or health insurance coverage offered in connection with the plan with respect to such benefits) must be made available by the plan administrator (or the health insurance issuer offering such coverage) to any current or potential participant, beneficiary, or contracting provider upon request.

(2) *Reason for any denial.* The reason for any denial under a group health plan (or health insurance coverage offered in connection with such plan) of reimbursement or payment for services with respect to mental health or substance use disorder benefits in the case of any participant or beneficiary must be made available by the plan administrator (or the health insurance issuer offering such coverage) to the participant or beneficiary in a form and manner consistent with the requirements of § 2560.503-1 of this chapter for group health plans.

(3) *Provisions of other law.* Compliance with the disclosure requirements in paragraphs (d)(1) and (d)(2) of this section is not determinative of compliance with any other provision of applicable Federal or State law. In particular, in addition to those disclosure requirements, provisions of other applicable law require disclosure of information relevant to medical/surgical, mental health, and substance use disorder benefits. For example, ERISA section 104 and § 2520.104b-1 of this chapter provide that, for plans subject to ERISA, instruments under which the plan is established or operated must generally be furnished to plan participants within 30 days of request. Instruments under which the plan is established or operated include documents with information on medical necessity criteria for both medical/surgical benefits and mental health and substance use disorder benefits, as well as the processes, strategies, evidentiary standards, and other factors used to apply a nonquantitative treatment limitation with respect to medical/surgical benefits and mental health or substance use disorder benefits under the plan. In addition, §§ 2560.503-1 and 2590.715-2719 of this chapter set forth rules regarding claims and appeals, including the right of claimants (or their authorized representative) upon appeal of an adverse benefit determination (or a final internal adverse benefit determination) to be provided upon request and free of charge, reasonable access to and copies of all documents, records, and other information relevant to the claimant's claim for benefits. This includes documents with information on medical necessity criteria for both medical/surgical benefits and mental health and substance use disorder benefits, as well as the processes, strategies, evidentiary standards, and other factors used to apply a nonquantitative treatment limitation with respect to medical/surgical benefits and mental health or substance use disorder benefits under the plan.

(e) *Applicability.* (1) *Group health plans.* The requirements of this section apply to a group health plan offering medical/surgical benefits and mental health or substance use disorder benefits. If, under an arrangement or arrangements to provide medical care benefits by an employer or employee organization (including for this purpose a joint board of trustees of a multiemployer trust affiliated with one or more multiemployer plans), any participant (or beneficiary) can simultaneously receive coverage for medical/surgical benefits and coverage for mental health or substance use disorder benefits, then the requirements of this section (including the exemption provisions in paragraph (g) of this section) apply separately with respect to each combination of medical/surgical benefits and of mental health or substance use disorder benefits that any participant (or beneficiary) can simultaneously receive from that employer's or employee organization's arrangement or arrangements to provide medical care benefits, and all such combinations are considered for purposes of this section to be a single group health plan.

(2) *Health insurance issuers.* The requirements of this section apply to a health insurance issuer offering health insurance coverage for mental health or substance use disorder benefits in connection with a group health plan subject to paragraph (e)(1) of this section.

(3) *Scope.* This section does not—

(i) Require a group health plan (or health insurance issuer offering coverage in connection with a group health plan) to provide any mental health benefits or substance use disorder benefits, and the provision of benefits by a plan (or health insurance coverage) for one or more mental health conditions or substance use disorders does not require the plan or health insurance coverage under this section to provide benefits for any other mental health condition or substance use disorder;

(ii) Require a group health plan (or health insurance issuer offering coverage in connection with a group health plan) that provides coverage for mental health or substance use disorder benefits only to the extent required under PHS Act section 2713 to provide additional mental health or substance use disorder benefits in any classification in accordance with this section; or

(iii) Affect the terms and conditions relating to the amount, duration, or scope of mental health or substance use disorder benefits under the plan (or health insurance coverage) except as specifically provided in paragraphs (b) and (c) of this section.

(4) *Coordination with EHB requirements.* Nothing in paragraph (f) or (g) of this section changes the requirements of 45 CFR 147.150 and 45 CFR 156.115, providing that a health insurance issuer offering non-grandfathered health insurance coverage in the individual or small group market providing mental health and substance use disorder services, including behavioral health treatment services, as part of essential health benefits required under 45 CFR 156.110(a)(5) and 156.115(a), must comply with the provisions of 45 CFR 146.136 to satisfy the requirement to provide essential health benefits.

(f) *Small employer exemption.* (1) *In general.* The requirements of this section do not apply to a group health plan (or health insurance issuer offering coverage in connection with a group health plan) for a plan year of a small employer. For purposes of this paragraph (f), the term *small employer* means, in connection with a group health plan with respect to a calendar year and a plan year, an employer who employed an average of at least two (or one in the case of an employer residing in a State that permits small groups to include a single individual) but not more than 50 employees on business days during the preceding calendar year. See section 732(a) of ERISA and § 2590.732(b), which provide that this section (and certain other sections) does not apply to any group health plan (and health insurance issuer offering coverage in connection with a group health plan) for any plan year if, on the first day of the plan year, the plan has fewer than two participants who are current employees.

(2) *Rules in determining employer size.* For purposes of paragraph (f)(1) of this section—

(i) All persons treated as a single employer under subsections (b), (c), (m), and (o) of section 414 of the Code are treated as one employer;

(ii) If an employer was not in existence throughout the preceding calendar year, whether it is a small employer is determined based on the average number of employees the employer reasonably expects to employ on business days during the current calendar year; and

(iii) Any reference to an employer for purposes of the small employer exemption includes a reference to a predecessor of the employer.

(g) *Increased cost exemption.* (1) *In general.* If the application of this section to a group health plan (or health insurance coverage offered in connection with such plans) results in an increase for the plan year involved of the actual total cost of coverage with respect to medical/surgical benefits and mental health and substance use disorder benefits as determined and certified under paragraph (g)(3) of this section by an amount that exceeds the applicable percentage described in paragraph (g)(2) of this section of the actual total plan costs, the provisions of this section shall not apply to such plan (or coverage) during the following plan year, and such exemption shall apply to the plan (or coverage) for one plan year. An employer or issuer may elect to continue to provide mental health and substance use disorder benefits in compliance with this section with respect to the plan or coverage involved regardless of any increase in total costs.

(2) *Applicable percentage.* With respect to a plan or coverage, the applicable percentage described in this paragraph (g) is—

(i) 2 percent in the case of the first plan year in which this section is applied to the plan or coverage; and

(ii) 1 percent in the case of each subsequent plan year.

(3) *Determinations by actuaries.* (i) Determinations as to increases in actual costs under a plan or coverage that are attributable to implementation of the requirements of this section shall be made and certified by a qualified and licensed actuary who is a member in good standing of the American Academy of Actuaries. All such determinations must be based on the formula specified in paragraph (g)(4) of this section and shall be in a written report prepared by the actuary.

(ii) The written report described in paragraph (g)(3)(i) of this section shall be maintained by the group health plan or health insurance issuer, along with all supporting documentation relied upon by the actuary, for a period of six years following the notification made under paragraph (g)(6) of this section.

(4) *Formula.* The formula to be used to make the determination under paragraph (g)(3)(i) of this section is expressed mathematically as follows: $[(E_1 - E_0)/T_0] - D > k$

(i) E_1 is the actual total cost of coverage with respect to mental health and substance use disorder benefits for the base period, including claims paid by the plan or issuer with respect to mental health and substance use disorder benefits and administrative costs (amortized over time) attributable to providing these benefits consistent with the requirements of this section.

(ii) E_0 is the actual total cost of coverage with respect to mental health and substance use disorder benefits for the length of time immediately before the base period (and that is equal in length to the base period), including claims paid by the plan or issuer with respect to mental health and substance use disorder benefits and administrative costs (amortized over time) attributable to providing these benefits.

(iii) T_0 is the actual total cost of coverage with respect to all benefits during the base period.

(iv) k is the applicable percentage of increased cost specified in paragraph (g)(2) of this section that will be expressed as a fraction for purposes of this formula.

(v) D is the average change in spending that is calculated by applying the formula $(E_1 - E_0)/T_0$ to mental health and substance use disorder spending in each of the five prior years and then calculating the average change in spending.

(5) *Six month determination.* If a group health plan or health insurance issuer seeks an exemption under this paragraph (g), determinations under paragraph (g)(3) of this section shall be made after such plan or coverage has complied with this section for at least the first 6 months of the plan year involved.

(6) *Notification.* A group health plan or health insurance issuer that, based on the certification described under paragraph (g)(3) of this section, qualifies for an exemption under this paragraph (g), and elects to implement the exemption, must notify participants and beneficiaries covered under the plan, the Secretary, and the appropriate State agencies of such election.

(i) *Participants and beneficiaries.* (A) *Content of notice.* The notice to participants and beneficiaries must include the following information:

(1) A statement that the plan or issuer is exempt from the requirements of this section and a description of the basis for the exemption.

(2) The name and telephone number of the individual to contact for further information.

(3) The plan or issuer name and plan number (PN).

(4) The plan administrator's name, address, and telephone number.

(5) For single-employer plans, the plan sponsor's name, address, and telephone number (if different from paragraph (g)(6)(i)(A)(3) of this section) and the plan sponsor's employer identification number (EIN).

(6) The effective date of such exemption.

(7) A statement regarding the ability of participants and beneficiaries to contact the plan administrator or health insurance issuer to see how benefits may be affected as a result of the plan's or issuer's election of the exemption.

(8) A statement regarding the availability, upon request and free of charge, of a summary of the information on which the exemption is based (as required under paragraph (g)(6)(i)(D) of this section).

(B) Use of summary of material reductions in covered services or benefits. A plan or issuer may satisfy the requirements of paragraph (g)(6)(i)(A) of this section by providing participants and beneficiaries (in accordance with paragraph (g)(6)(i)(C) of this section) with a summary of material reductions in covered services or benefits consistent with § 2520.104b-3(d) of this chapter that also includes the information specified in paragraph (g)(6)(i)(A) of this section. However, in all cases, the exemption is not effective until 30 days after notice has been sent.

(C) Delivery. The notice described in this paragraph (g)(6)(i) is required to be provided to all participants and beneficiaries. The notice may be furnished by any method of delivery that satisfies the requirements of section 104(b)(1) of ERISA (29 U.S.C. 1024(b)(1)) and its implementing regulations (for example, first-class mail). If the notice is provided to the participant and any beneficiaries at the participant's last known address, then the requirements of this paragraph (g)(6)(i) are satisfied with respect to the participant and all beneficiaries residing at that address. If a beneficiary's last known address is different from the participant's last known address, a separate notice is required to be provided to the beneficiary at the beneficiary's last known address.

(D) Availability of documentation. The plan or issuer must make available to participants and beneficiaries (or their representatives), on request and at no charge, a summary of the information on which the exemption was based. (For purposes of this paragraph (g), an individual who is not a participant or beneficiary and who presents a notice described in paragraph (g)(6)(i) of this section is considered to be a representative. A representative may request the summary of information by providing the plan a copy of the notice provided to the participant under paragraph (g)(6)(i) of this section with any personally identifiable information redacted.) The summary of information must include the incurred expenditures, the base period, the dollar amount of claims incurred during the base period that would have been denied under the terms of the plan or coverage absent amendments required to comply with paragraphs (b) and (c) of this section, the administrative costs related to those claims, and other administrative costs attributable to complying with the requirements of this section. In no event should the summary of information include any personally identifiable information.

(ii) Federal agencies. (A) *Content of notice.* The notice to the Secretary must include the following information:

(1) A description of the number of covered lives under the plan (or coverage) involved at the time of the notification, and as applicable, at the time of any prior election of the cost exemption under this paragraph (g) by such plan (or coverage);

(2) For both the plan year upon which a cost exemption is sought and the year prior, a description of the actual total costs of coverage with respect to medical/surgical benefits and mental health and substance use disorder benefits; and

(3) For both the plan year upon which a cost exemption is sought and the year prior, the actual total costs of coverage with respect to mental health and substance use disorder benefits under the plan.

(B) Reporting. A group health plan, and any health insurance coverage offered in connection with a group health plan, must provide notice to the Department of Labor. This requirement is satisfied if the plan sends a copy, to the address designated by the Secretary in generally applicable guidance, of the notice described in paragraph (g)(6)(ii)(A) of this section identifying the benefit package to which the exemption applies.

(iii) Confidentiality. A notification to the Secretary under this paragraph (g)(6) shall be confidential. The Secretary shall make available, upon request and not more than on an annual basis, an anonymous itemization of each notification that includes—

(A) A breakdown of States by the size and type of employers submitting such notification; and

(B) A summary of the data received under paragraph (g)(6)(ii) of this section.

(iv) Audits. The Secretary may audit the books and records of a group health plan or a health insurance issuer relating to an exemption, including any actuarial reports, during the 6 year period following notification of such exemption under paragraph (g)(6) of this section. A State agency receiving a notification under paragraph (g)(6) of this section may also conduct such an audit with respect to an exemption covered by such notification.

(h) Sale of nonparity health insurance coverage. A health insurance issuer may not sell a policy, certificate, or contract of insurance that fails to comply with paragraph (b) or (c) of this section, except to a plan for a year for which the plan is exempt from the requirements of this section because the plan meets the requirements of paragraph (f) or (g) of this section.

(i) Applicability dates. (1) *In general.* Except as provided in paragraph (i)(2) of this section, this section applies to group health plans and health insurance issuers offering group health insurance coverage on the first day of the first plan year beginning on or after July 1, 2014. Until the applicability date, plans and issuers are required to continue to comply with the corresponding sections of 29 CFR 2590.712 contained in the 29 CFR, parts 1927 to end, edition revised as of July 1, 2013.

(2) Special effective date for certain collectively-bargained plans. For a group health plan maintained pursuant to one or more collective bargaining agreements ratified before October 3, 2008, the requirements of this section do not apply to the plan (or health insurance coverage offered in connection with the plan) for plan years beginning before the date on which the last of the collective bargaining agreements terminates (determined without regard to any extension agreed to after October 3, 2008).

[¶ 15,050P]
MANDATED COVERAGE OF POST-MASTECTOMY RECONSTRUCTIVE SURGERY

Act Sec. 713 REQUIRED COVERAGE FOR RECONSTRUCTIVE SURGERY FOLLOWING MASTECTOMIES—

(a) IN GENERAL. A group health plan, and a health insurance issuer providing health insurance coverage in connection with a group health plan, that provides medical and surgical benefits with respect to a mastectomy shall provide, in a case of a participant or beneficiary who is receiving benefits in connection with a mastectomy and who elects breast reconstruction in connection with such mastectomy, coverage for—

(1) all stages of reconstruction of the breast on which the mastectomy has been performed;

(2) surgery and reconstruction of the other breast to produce a symmetrical appearance; and

(3) prostheses and physical complications all stages of mastectomy, including lymphedemas; in a manner determined in consultation with the attending physician and the patient. Such coverage may be subject to annual deductibles and coinsurance provisions as may be deemed appropriate and as are consistent with those established for other benefits under the plan or coverage. Written notice of the availability of such coverage shall be delivered to the participant upon enrollment and annually thereafter.

(b) NOTICE. A group health plan, and a health insurance issuer providing health insurance coverage in connection with a group health plan shall provide notice to each participant and beneficiary under such plan regarding the coverage required by this section in accordance with regulations promulgated by the

Secretary. Such notice shall be in writing and prominently positioned in any literature or correspondence made available or distributed by the plan or issuer and shall be transmitted—

(1) in the next mailing made by the plan or issuer to the participant or beneficiary;

(2) as part of any yearly informational packet sent to the participant or beneficiary; or

(3) not later than January 1, 1999; whichever is earlier.

(c) PROHIBITIONS. A group health plan, and a health insurance issuer offering group health insurance coverage in connection with a group health plan, may not—

(1) deny to a patient eligibility, or continued eligibility, to enroll or to renew coverage under the terms of the plan, solely for the purpose of avoiding the requirements of this section; and

(2) penalize or otherwise reduce or limit the reimbursement of an attending provider, or provide incentives (monetary or otherwise) to an attending provider, to induce such provider to provide care to an individual participant or beneficiary in a manner inconsistent with this section.

(d) RULE OF CONSTRUCTION. Nothing in this section shall be construed to prevent a group health plan or a health insurance issuer offering group health insurance coverage from negotiating the level and type of reimbursement with a provider for care provided in accordance with this section.

(e) PREEMPTION, RELATION TO STATE LAWS.—

(1) IN GENERAL. Nothing in this section shall be construed to preempt any State law in effect on October 21, 1998, with respect to health insurance coverage that requires coverage of at least the coverage of reconstructive breast surgery otherwise required under this section.

(2) ERISA. Nothing in this section shall be construed to affect or modify the provisions of section 514 with respect to group health plans.

Amendments

P.L. 105-277, §902(a):

Subpart B of part 7 of subtitle B of title I of the Employee Retirement Income Security Act of 1974 (29 U.S.C. 1185 et seq.) is amended by adding at the end the above new section:

(b) Clerical Amendment. The table of contents in section 1 of the Employee Retirement Income Security Act of 1974 (29 U.S.C. 1001 note) is amended by inserting after the item relating to section 712 the following new item:

Sec. 713. Required coverage reconstructive surgery following mastectomies.".

(c) Effective Dates.

(1) In General. The amendments made by this section shall apply with respect to plan years beginning on or after the date of enactment of this Act.

(2) Special Rule for Collective Bargaining Agreements. In the case of a group health plan maintained pursuant to 1 or more collective bargaining agreements between employee representatives and 1 or more employers, any plan amendment made pursuant to a collective bargaining agreement relating to the plan which amends the plan solely to conform to any requirement added by this section shall not be treated as a termination of such collective bargaining agreement.

[¶ 15,050R]
COVERAGE OF DEPENDENT STUDENTS ON MEDICALLY NECESSARY LEAVE OF ABSENCE

Act Sec. 714.(a) MEDICALLY NECESSARY LEAVE OF ABSENCE.. In this section, the term "medically necessary leave of absence" means, with respect to a dependent child described in subsection (b)(2) in connection with a group health plan or health insurance coverage offered in connection with such plan, a leave of absence of such child from a postsecondary educational institution (including an institution of higher education as defined in section 102 of the Higher Education Act of 1965), or any other change in enrollment of such child at such an institution, that—

(1) commences while such child is suffering from a serious illness or injury;

(2) is medically necessary; and

(3) causes such child to lose student status for purposes of coverage under the terms of the plan or coverage.

(b) REQUIREMENT TO CONTINUE COVERAGE—

(1) IN GENERAL. In the case of a dependent child described in paragraph (2), a group health plan, or a health insurance issuer that provides health insurance coverage in connection with a group health plan, shall not terminate coverage of such child under such plan or health insurance coverage due to a medically necessary leave of absence before the date that is the earlier of

(A) the date that is 1 year after the first day of the medically necessary leave of absence; or

(B) the date on which such coverage would otherwise terminate under the terms of the plan or health insurance coverage.

(2) DEPENDENT CHILD DESCRIBED. A dependent child described in this paragraph is, with respect to a group health plan or health insurance coverage offered in connection with the plan, a beneficiary under the plan who—

(A) is a dependent child, under the terms of the plan or coverage, of a participant or beneficiary under the plan or coverage; and

(B) was enrolled in the plan or coverage, on the basis of being a student at a postsecondary educational institution (as described in subsection (a)), immediately before the first day of the medically necessary leave of absence involved.

(3) CERTIFICATION BY PHYSICIAN. Paragraph (1) shall apply to a group health plan or health insurance coverage offered by an issuer in connection with such plan only if the plan or issuer of the coverage has received written certification by a treating physician of the dependent child which states that the child is suffering from a serious illness or injury and that the leave of absence (or other change of enrollment) described in subsection (a) is medically necessary.

(c) NOTICE. A group health plan, and a health insurance issuer providing health insurance coverage in connection with a group health plan, shall include, with any notice regarding a requirement for certification of student status for coverage under the plan or coverage, a description of the terms of this section for continued coverage during medically necessary leaves of absence. Such description shall be in language which is understandable to the typical plan participant.

(d) NO CHANGE IN BENEFITS. A dependent child whose benefits are continued under this section shall be entitled to the same benefits as if (during the medically necessary leave of absence) the child continued to be a covered student at the institution of higher education and was not on a medically necessary leave of absence.

(e) CONTINUED APPLICATION IN CASE OF CHANGED COVERAGE. If—

(1) a dependent child of a participant or beneficiary is in a period of coverage under a group health plan or health insurance coverage offered in connection with such a plan, pursuant to a medically necessary leave of absence of the child described in subsection (b);

(2) the manner in which the participant or beneficiary is covered under the plan changes, whether through a change in health insurance coverage or health insurance issuer, a change between health insurance coverage and self-insured coverage, or otherwise; and

(3) the coverage as so changed continues to provide coverage of beneficiaries as dependent children, this section shall apply to coverage of the child under the changed coverage for the remainder of the period of the medically necessary leave of absence of the dependent child under the plan in the same manner as it would have applied if the changed coverage had been the previous coverage.

Amendments

P.L. 110-381, §2(a)(1):

Act Sec. 2(a)(1) added ERISA Sec. 714 to read as above, effective with respect to plan years beginning on or after the date that is one year after the date of the enactment

[October 9, 2008] and to medically necessary leaves of absence beginning during such plan years.

[¶ 15,050R-50]
ADDITIONAL MARKET REFORMS

Act Sec. 715.(a) GENERAL RULE. Except as provided in subsection (b)—

(1) the provisions of part A of title XXVII of the Public Health Service Act (as amended by the Patient Protection and Affordable Care Act) shall apply to group health plans, and health insurance issuers providing health insurance coverage in connection with group health plans, as if included in this subpart; and

(2) to the extent that any provision of this part conflicts with a provision of such part A with respect to group health plans, or health insurance issuers providing health insurance coverage in connection with group health plans, the provisions of such part A shall apply.

(b) EXCEPTION. Notwithstanding subsection (a), the provisions of sections 2716 and 2718 of title XXVII of the Public Health Service Act (as amended by the Patient Protection and Affordable Care Act) shall not apply with respect to self-insured group health plans, and the provisions of this part shall continue to apply to such plans as if such sections of the Public Health Service Act (as so amended) had not been enacted.

Amendments

The above amendment is effective on the date of enactment (March 23, 2010).

P.L. 111-148, §1563(e) [as redesignated by Act Sec. 101 7(b):

Added ERISA Sec. 715 to read as above.

Interim Final Regulations

Reg. §2590.715-1251 was adopted and published in the *Federal Register* on June 17, 2010 (75 FR 34537). Reg. §§2590.715-2704 was amended on June 28, 2010 (75 FR 37187). Reg. §2590.715-1251 was amended on November 17, 2010 (75 FR 70114). Reg. §2590.715-2704 was adopted and published in the Federal Register on June 28, 2010 (75 FR 37187).

⟫⟶ Caution: Until final Reg. § 2590.715-1251 at ¶ 15,050R-50BA is applicable on the first day of the plan year beginning on or after January 1, 2017, plans and issuers must continue to comply with the below interim final regulation.

[¶ 15,050R-50B]

§ 2590.715-1251 **Preservation of right to maintain existing coverage.**

(a) *Definition of grandfathered health plan coverage.* (1) *In general.* (i) *Grandfathered health plan coverage. Grandfathered health plan coverage* means coverage provided by a group health plan, or a health insurance issuer, in which an individual was enrolled on March 23, 2010 (for as long as it maintains that status under the rules of this section). A group health plan or group health insurance coverage does not cease to be grandfathered health plan coverage merely because one or more (or even all) individuals enrolled on March 23, 2010 cease to be covered, provided that the plan has continuously covered someone since March 23, 2010 (not necessarily the same person, but at all times at least one person). In addition, subject to the limitation set forth in paragraph (a)(1)(ii) of this section, a group health plan (and any health insurance coverage offered in connection with the group health plan) does not cease to be a grandfathered health plan merely because the plan (or its sponsor) enters into a new policy, certificate, or contract of insurance after March 23, 2010 (for example, a plan enters into a contract with a new issuer or a new policy is issued with an existing issuer). For purposes of this section, a plan or health insurance coverage that provides grandfathered health plan coverage is referred to as a grandfathered health plan. The rules of this section apply separately to each benefit package made available under a group health plan or health insurance coverage. [Amended 11/17/2010 (75 FR 70114.]

(ii) *Changes in group health insurance coverage.* Subject to paragraphs (f) and (g)(2) of this section, if a group health plan (including a group health plan that was self-insured on March 23, 2010) or its sponsor enters into a new policy, certificate, or contract of insurance after March 23, 2010 that is effective before November 15, 2010, then the plan ceases to be a grandfathered health plan. [Amended 11/17/2010 (75 FR 70114.]

(2) *Disclosure of grandfather status.* (i) To maintain status as a grandfathered health plan, a plan or health insurance coverage must include a statement, in any plan materials provided to a participant or beneficiary describing the benefits provided under the plan or health insurance coverage, that the plan or coverage believes it is a grandfathered health plan within the meaning of section 1251 of the Patient Protection and Affordable Care Act and must provide contact information for questions and complaints.

(ii) The following model language can be used to satisfy this disclosure requirement:

This [group health plan or health insurance issuer] believes this [plan or coverage] is a "grandfathered health plan" under the Patient Protection and Affordable Care Act (the Affordable Care Act). As permitted by the Affordable Care Act, a grandfathered health plan can preserve certain basic health coverage that was already in effect when that law was enacted. Being a grandfathered health plan means that your [plan or policy] may not include certain consumer protections of the Affordable Care Act that apply to other plans, for example, the requirement for the provision of preventive health services without any cost sharing. However, grandfathered health plans must comply with certain other consumer protections in the Affordable Care Act, for example, the elimination of lifetime limits on benefits.

Questions regarding which protections apply and which protections do not apply to a grandfathered health plan and what might cause a plan to change from grandfathered health plan status can be directed to the plan administrator at [insert contact information]. [For ERISA plans, insert: You may also contact the Employee Benefits Security Administration, U.S. Department of Labor at 1-866-444-3272 or *www.dol.gov/ebsa/healthreform*. This website has a table summarizing which protections do and do not apply to grandfathered health plans.] [For individual market policies and nonfederal governmental plans, insert: You may also contact the U.S. Department of Health and Human Services at *www.healthreform.gov*.]

(3) *Documentation of plan or policy terms on March 23, 2010..* (i) To maintain status as a grandfathered health plan, a group health plan, or group health insurance coverage, must, for as long as the plan or health insurance coverage takes the position that it is a grandfathered health plan - [Redesignated 11/17/2010 (75 FR 70114.]

(A) Maintain records documenting the terms of the plan or health insurance coverage in connection with the coverage in effect on March 23, 2010, and any other documents necessary to verify, explain, or clarify its status as a grandfathered health plan; and [Redesignated 11/17/2010 (75 FR 70114.]

(B) Make such records available for examination upon request. [Redesignated 11/17/2010 (75 FR 70114.]

(ii) *Change in group health insurance coverage.* To maintain status as a grandfathered health plan, a group health plan that enters into a new policy, certificate, or contract of insurance must provide to the new health insurance issuer (and the new health insurance issuer must require) documentation of plan terms (including benefits, cost sharing, employer contributions, and annual limits) under the prior health coverage sufficient to determine whether a change causing a cessation of grandfathered health plan status under paragraph (g)(1) of this section has occurred. [Added 11/17/2010 (75 FR 70114.]

(4) *Family members enrolling after March 23, 2010..* With respect to an individual who is enrolled in a group health plan or health insurance coverage on March 23, 2010, grandfathered health plan coverage includes coverage of family members of the individual who enroll after March 23, 2010 in the grandfathered health plan coverage of the individual.

(b) *Allowance for new employees to join current plan.* (1) *In general..* Subject to paragraph (b)(2) of this section, a group health plan (including health insurance coverage provided in connection with the group health plan) that provided coverage on March 23, 2010 and has retained its status as a grandfathered health plan (consistent with the rules of this section, including paragraph (g) of this section) is grandfathered health plan coverage for new employees (whether newly hired or newly enrolled) and their families enrolling in the plan after March 23, 2010.

(2) *Anti-abuse rules*. (i) *Mergers and acquisitions*.. If the principal purpose of a merger, acquisition, or similar business restructuring is to cover new individuals under a grandfathered health plan, the plan ceases to be a grandfathered health plan.

(ii) *Change in plan eligibility*.. A group health plan or health insurance coverage (including a benefit package under a group health plan) ceases to be a grandfathered health plan if -

(A) Employees are transferred into the plan or health insurance coverage (the transferee plan) from a plan or health insurance coverage under which the employees were covered on March 23, 2010 (the transferor plan);

(B) Comparing the terms of the transferee plan with those of the transferor plan (as in effect on March 23, 2010) and treating the transferee plan as if it were an amendment of the transferor plan would cause a loss of grandfather status under the provisions of paragraph (g)(1) of this section; and

(C) There was no bona fide employment-based reason to transfer the employees into the transferee plan. For this purpose, changing the terms or cost of coverage is not a bona fide employment-based reason.

(3) *Examples*.. The rules of this paragraph (b) are illustrated by the following examples:

Example 1. (i) *Facts*. A group health plan offers two benefit packages on March 23, 2010, Options *F* and *G*. During a subsequent open enrollment period, some of the employees enrolled in Option *F* on March 23, 2010 switch to Option *G*.

(ii) *Conclusion*. In this *Example 1*, the group health coverage provided under Option *G* remains a grandfathered health plan under the rules of paragraph (b)(1) of this section because employees previously enrolled in Option *F* are allowed to enroll in Option *G* as new employees.

Example 2. (i) *Facts*. Same facts as *Example 1*, except that the plan sponsor eliminates Option *F* because of its high cost and transfers employees covered under Option *F* to Option *G*. If instead of transferring employees from Option *F* to Option *G*, Option *F* was amended to match the terms of Option *G*, then Option *F* would cease to be a grandfathered health plan.

(ii) *Conclusion*. In this *Example 2*, the plan did not have a bona fide employment-based reason to transfer employees from Option *F* to Option *G*. Therefore, Option *G* ceases to be a grandfathered health plan with respect to all employees. (However, any other benefit package maintained by the plan sponsor is analyzed separately under the rules of this section.)

Example 3. (i) *Facts*. A group health plan offers two benefit packages on March 23, 2010, Options *H* and *I*. On March 23, 2010, Option *H* provides coverage only for employees in one manufacturing plant. Subsequently, the plant is closed, and some employees in the closed plant are moved to another plant. The employer eliminates Option *H* and the employees that are moved are transferred to Option *I*. If instead of transferring employees from Option *H* to Option *I*, Option *H* was amended to match the terms of Option *I*, then Option *H* would cease to be a grandfathered health plan.

(ii) *Conclusion*. In this *Example 3*, the plan has a bona fide employment-based reason to transfer employees from Option *H* to Option *I*. Therefore, Option *I* does not cease to be a grandfathered health plan.

(c) *General grandfathering rule*. (1) Except as provided in paragraphs (d) and (e) of this section, subtitles A and C of title I of the Patient Protection and Affordable Care Act (and the amendments made

by those subtitles, and the incorporation of those amendments into ERISA section 715 and Internal Revenue Code section 9815) do not apply to grandfathered health plan coverage. Accordingly, the provisions of PHS Act sections 2701, 2702, 2703, 2705, 2706, 2707, 2709 (relating to coverage for individuals participating in approved clinical trials, as added by section 10103 of the Patient Protection and Affordable Care Act), 2713, 2715A, 2716, 2717, 2719, and 2719A, as added or amended by the Patient Protection and Affordable Care Act, do not apply to grandfathered health plans. (In addition, *see* 45 CFR 147.140(c), which provides that the provisions of PHS Act section 2704, and PHS Act section 2711 insofar as it relates to annual limits, do not apply to grandfathered health plans that are individual health insurance coverage.)

(2) To the extent not inconsistent with the rules applicable to a grandfathered health plan, a grandfathered health plan must comply with the requirements of the PHS Act, ERISA, and the Internal Revenue Code applicable prior to the changes enacted by the Patient Protection and Affordable Care Act.

(d) *Provisions applicable to all grandfathered health plans*.. The provisions of PHS Act section 2711 insofar as it relates to lifetime limits, and the provisions of PHS Act sections 2712, 2714, 2715, and 2718, apply to grandfathered health plans for plan years beginning on or after September 23, 2010. The provisions of PHS Act section 2708 apply to grandfathered health plans for plan years beginning on or after January 1, 2014.

(e) *Applicability of PHS Act sections 2704, 2711, and 2714 to grandfathered group health plans and group health insurance coverage.* (1) The provisions of PHS Act section 2704 as it applies with respect to enrollees who are under 19 years of age, and the provisions of PHS Act section 2711 insofar as it relates to annual limits, apply to grandfathered health plans that are group health plans (including group health insurance coverage) for plan years beginning on or after September 23, 2010. The provisions of PHS Act section 2704 apply generally to grandfathered health plans that are group health plans (including group health insurance coverage) for plan years beginning on or after January 1, 2014.

(2) For plan years beginning before January 1, 2014, the provisions of PHS Act section 2714 apply in the case of an adult child with respect to a grandfathered health plan that is a group health plan only if the adult child is not eligible to enroll in an eligible employer-sponsored health plan (as defined in section 5000A(f)(2) of the Internal Revenue Code) other than a grandfathered health plan of a parent. For plan years beginning on or after January 1, 2014, the provisions of PHS Act section 2714 apply with respect to a grandfathered health plan that is a group health plan without regard to whether an adult child is eligible to enroll in any other coverage.

(f) *Effect on collectively bargained plans*. In the case of health insurance coverage maintained pursuant to one or more collective bargaining agreements between employee representatives and one or more employers that was ratified before March 23, 2010, the coverage is grandfathered health plan coverage at least until the date on which the last of the collective bargaining agreements relating to the coverage that was in effect on March 23, 2010 terminates. Any coverage amendment made pursuant to a collective bargaining agreement relating to the coverage that amends the coverage solely to conform to any requirement added by subtitles A and C of title I of the Patient Protection and Affordable Care Act (and the amendments made by those subtitles, and the incorporation of those amendments into ERISA section 715 and Internal Revenue Code section 9815) is not treated as a termination of the collective bargaining agreement. After the date on which the last of the collective bargaining agreements relating to the coverage that was in effect on March 23, 2010 terminates, the determination of whether health insurance coverage maintained pursuant to a collective bargaining agreement is grandfathered health plan coverage is made under the rules of this section other than this paragraph (f) (comparing the terms of the health insurance coverage after the date the last collective bargaining agreement terminates with the terms of the health insurance coverage that were in effect on March 23, 2010). [Redesignated and amended 11/17/2010 (75 FR 70114.]

>>>→ *Caution: Until final Reg. § 2590.715-1251 at ¶ 15,050R-50BA is applicable on the first day of the plan year beginning on or after January 1, 2017, plans and issuers must continue to comply with the below interim final regulation.*

(g) *Maintenance of grandfather status.* (1) *Changes causing cessation of grandfather status..* Subject to paragraph (g)(2) of this section, the rules of this paragraph (g)(1) describe situations in which a group health plan or health insurance coverage ceases to be a grandfathered health plan.

(i) *Elimination of benefits..* The elimination of all or substantially all benefits to diagnose or treat a particular condition causes a group health plan or health insurance coverage to cease to be a grandfathered health plan. For this purpose, the elimination of benefits for any necessary element to diagnose or treat a condition is considered the elimination of all or substantially all benefits to diagnose or treat a particular condition.

(ii) *Increase in percentage cost-sharing requirement..* Any increase, measured from March 23, 2010, in a percentage cost-sharing requirement (such as an individual's coinsurance requirement) causes a group health plan or health insurance coverage to cease to be a grandfathered health plan.

(iii) *Increase in a fixed-amount cost-sharing requirement other than a copayment..* Any increase in a fixed-amount cost-sharing requirement other than a copayment (for example, deductible or out-of-pocket limit), determined as of the effective date of the increase, causes a group health plan or health insurance coverage to cease to be a grandfathered health plan, if the total percentage increase in the cost-sharing requirement measured from March 23, 2010 exceeds the maximum percentage increase (as defined in paragraph (g)(3)(ii) of this section).

(iv) *Increase in a fixed-amount copayment..* Any increase in a fixed-amount copayment, determined as of the effective date of the increase, causes a group health plan or health insurance coverage to cease to be a grandfathered health plan, if the total increase in the copayment measured from March 23, 2010 exceeds the greater of:

(A) An amount equal to $5 increased by medical inflation, as defined in paragraph (g)(3)(i) of this section (that is, $5 times medical inflation, plus $5), or

(B) The maximum percentage increase (as defined in paragraph (g)(3)(ii) of this section), determined by expressing the total increase in the copayment as a percentage.

(v) *Decrease in contribution rate by employers and employee organizations.* (A) *Contribution rate based on cost of coverage..* A group health plan or group health insurance coverage ceases to be a grandfathered health plan if the employer or employee organization decreases its contribution rate based on cost of coverage (as defined in paragraph (g)(3)(iii)(A) of this section) towards the cost of any tier of coverage for any class of similarly situated individuals (as described in § 2590.702(d) of this part) by more than 5 percentage points below the contribution rate for the coverage period that includes March 23, 2010.

(B) *Contribution rate based on a formula..* A group health plan or group health insurance coverage ceases to be a grandfathered health plan if the employer or employee organization decreases its contribution rate based on a formula (as defined in paragraph (g)(3)(iii)(B) of this section) towards the cost of any tier of coverage for any class of similarly situated individuals (as described in section 2590.702(d) of this part) by more than 5 percent below the contribution rate for the coverage period that includes March 23, 2010.

(vi) *Changes in annual limits.* (A) *Addition of an annual limit..* A group health plan, or group health insurance coverage, that, on March 23, 2010, did not impose an overall annual or lifetime limit on the dollar value of all benefits ceases to be a grandfathered health plan if the plan or health insurance coverage imposes an overall annual limit on the dollar value of benefits.

(B) *Decrease in limit for a plan or coverage with only a lifetime limit..* A group health plan, or group health insurance coverage, that, on March 23, 2010, imposed an overall lifetime limit on the dollar value of all benefits but no overall annual limit on the dollar value of all benefits ceases to be a grandfathered health plan if the plan or health insurance coverage adopts an overall annual limit at a dollar value that is lower than the dollar value of the lifetime limit on March 23, 2010.

(C) *Decrease in limit for a plan or coverage with an annual limit..* A group health plan, or group health insurance coverage, that, on March 23, 2010, imposed an overall annual limit on the dollar value of all benefits ceases to be a grandfathered health plan if the plan or health insurance coverage decreases the dollar value of the annual limit (regardless of whether the plan or health insurance coverage also imposed an overall lifetime limit on March 23, 2010 on the dollar value of all benefits).

(2) *Transitional rules.* (i) *Changes made prior to March 23, 2010..* If a group health plan or health insurance issuer makes the following changes to the terms of the plan or health insurance coverage, the changes are considered part of the terms of the plan or health insurance coverage on March 23, 2010 even though they were not effective at that time and such changes do not cause a plan or health insurance coverage to cease to be a grandfathered health plan:

(A) Changes effective after March 23, 2010 pursuant to a legally binding contract entered into on or before March 23, 2010;

(B) Changes effective after March 23, 2010 pursuant to a filing on or before March 23, 2010 with a State insurance department; or

(C) Changes effective after March 23, 2010 pursuant to written amendments to a plan that were adopted on or before March 23, 2010.

(ii) *Changes made after March 23, 2010 and adopted prior to issuance of regulations..* If, after March 23, 2010, a group health plan or health insurance issuer makes changes to the terms of the plan or health insurance coverage and the changes are adopted prior to June 14, 2010, the changes will not cause the plan or health insurance coverage to cease to be a grandfathered health plan if the changes are revoked or modified effective as of the first day of the first plan year (in the individual market, policy year) beginning on or after September 23, 2010, and the terms of the plan or health insurance coverage on that date, as modified, would not cause the plan or coverage to cease to be a grandfathered health plan under the rules of this section, including paragraph (g)(1) of this section. For this purpose, changes will be considered to have been adopted prior to June 14, 2010 if:

(A) The changes are effective before that date;

(B) The changes are effective on or after that date pursuant to a legally binding contract entered into before that date;

(C) The changes are effective on or after that date pursuant to a filing before that date with a State insurance department; or

(D) The changes are effective on or after that date pursuant to written amendments to a plan that were adopted before that date.

(3) *Definitions.* (i) *Medical inflation defined..* For purposes of this paragraph (g), the term *medical inflation* means the increase since March 2010 in the overall medical care component of the Consumer Price Index for All Urban Consumers (CPI-U) (unadjusted) published by the Department of Labor using the 1982 - 1984 base of 100. For this purpose, the increase in the overall medical care component is computed by subtracting 387.142 (the overall medical care component of the CPI-U (unadjusted) published by the Department of Labor for March 2010, using the 1982 - 1984 base of 100) from the index amount for any month in the 12 months before the new change is to take effect and then dividing that amount by 387.142.

(ii) *Maximum percentage increase defined..* For purposes of this paragraph (g), the term *maximum percentage increase* means medical inflation (as defined in paragraph (g)(3)(i) of this section), expressed as a percentage, plus 15 percentage points.

(iii) *Contribution rate defined..* For purposes of paragraph (g)(1)(v) of this section:

(A) *Contribution rate based on cost of coverage..* The term *contribution rate based on cost of coverage* means the amount of contributions made by an employer or employee organization compared to the total cost of coverage, expressed as a percentage. The total cost of coverage is determined in the same manner as the applicable premium is calculated under the COBRA continuation provisions of section 604 of ERISA, section 4980B(f)(4) of the Internal Revenue Code, and section 2204 of the PHS Act. In the case of a self-insured plan, contributions by an employer or employee organization are equal to the total cost of coverage minus the employee contributions towards the total cost of coverage.

(B) *Contribution rate based on a formula.*. The term *contribution rate based on a formula* means, for plans that, on March 23, 2010, made contributions based on a formula (such as hours worked or tons of coal mined), the formula.

(4) *Examples.*. The rules of this paragraph (g) are illustrated by the following examples:

Example 1. (i) *Facts.* On March 23, 2010, a grandfathered health plan has a coinsurance requirement of 20% for inpatient surgery. The plan is subsequently amended to increase the coinsurance requirement to 25%.

(ii) *Conclusion.* In this *Example 1*, the increase in the coinsurance requirement from 20% to 25% causes the plan to cease to be a grandfathered health plan.

Example 2. (i) *Facts.* Before March 23, 2010, the terms of a group health plan provide benefits for a particular mental health condition, the treatment for which is a combination of counseling and prescription drugs. Subsequently, the plan eliminates benefits for counseling.

(ii) *Conclusion.* In this *Example 2*, the plan ceases to be a grandfathered health plan because counseling is an element that is necessary to treat the condition. Thus the plan is considered to have eliminated substantially all benefits for the treatment of the condition.

Example 3. (i) *Facts.* On March 23, 2010, a grandfathered health plan has a copayment requirement of $30 per office visit for specialists. The plan is subsequently amended to increase the copayment requirement to $40. Within the 12-month period before the $40 copayment takes effect, the greatest value of the overall medical care component of the CPI-U (unadjusted) is 475.

(ii) *Conclusion.* In this *Example 3*, the increase in the copayment from $30 to $40, expressed as a percentage, is 33.33% (40 − 30 = 10; 10 ÷ 30 = 0.3333; 0.3333 = 33.33%). Medical inflation (as defined in paragraph (g)(3)(i) of this section) from March 2010 is 0.2269 (475 − 387.142 = 87.858; 87.858 ÷ 387.142 = 0.2269). The maximum percentage increase permitted is 37.69% (0.2269 = 22.69%; 22.69% + 15% = 37.69%). Because 33.33% does not exceed 37.69%, the change in the copayment requirement at that time does not cause the plan to cease to be a grandfathered health plan.

Example 4. (i) *Facts.* Same facts as *Example 3*, except the grandfathered health plan subsequently increases the $40 copayment requirement to $45 for a later plan year. Within the 12-month period before the $45 copayment takes effect, the greatest value of the overall medical care component of the CPI-U (unadjusted) is 485.

(ii) *Conclusion.* In this *Example 4*, the increase in the copayment from $30 (the copayment that was in effect on March 23, 2010) to $45, expressed as a percentage, is 50% (45 − 30 = 15; 15 ÷ 30 = 0.5; 0.5 = 50%). Medical inflation (as defined in paragraph (g)(3)(i) of this section) from March 2010 is 0.2527 (485 − 387.142 = 97.858; 97.858 ÷ 387.142 = 0.2527). The increase that would cause a plan to cease to be a grandfathered health plan under paragraph (g)(1)(iv) of this section is the greater of the maximum percentage increase of 40.27% (0.2527 = 25.27%; 25.27% + 15% = 40.27%), or $6.26 ($5 × 0.2527 = $1.26; $1.26 + $5 = $6.26). Because 50% exceeds 40.27% and $15 exceeds $6.26, the change in the copayment requirement at that time causes the plan to cease to be a grandfathered health plan.

Example 5. (i) *Facts.* On March 23, 2010, a grandfathered health plan has a copayment of $10 per office visit for primary care providers. The plan is subsequently amended to increase the copayment requirement to $15. Within the 12-month period before the $15 copayment

takes effect, the greatest value of the overall medical care component of the CPI-U (unadjusted) is 415.

(ii) *Conclusion.* In this *Example 5*, the increase in the copayment, expressed as a percentage, is 50% (15 − 10 = 5; 5 ÷ 10 = 0.5; 0.5 = 50%). Medical inflation (as defined in paragraph (g)(3) of this section) from March 2010 is 0.0720 (415.0 − 387.142 = 27.858; 27.858 ÷ 387.142 = 0.0720). The increase that would cause a plan to cease to be a grandfathered health plan under paragraph (g)(1)(iv) of this section is the greater of the maximum percentage increase of 22.20% (0.0720 = 7.20%; 7.20% + 15% = 22.20), or $5.36 ($5 × 0.0720 = $0.36; $0.36 + $5 = $5.36). The $5 increase in copayment in this *Example 5* would not cause the plan to cease to be a grandfathered health plan pursuant to paragraph (g)(1)(iv)this section, which would permit an increase in the copayment of up to $5.36.

Example 6. (i) *Facts.* The same facts as *Example 5*, except on March 23, 2010, the grandfathered health plan has no copayment ($0) for office visits for primary care providers. The plan is subsequently amended to increase the copayment requirement to $5.

(ii) *Conclusion.* In this *Example 6*, medical inflation (as defined in paragraph (g)(3)(i) of this section) from March 2010 is 0.0720 (415.0 − 387.142 = 27.858; 27.858 ÷ 387.142 = 0.0720). The increase that would cause a plan to cease to be a grandfathered health plan under paragraph (g)(1)(iv)(A) of this section is $5.36 ($5 × 0.0720 = $0.36; $0.36 + $5 = $5.36). The $5 increase in copayment in this *Example 6* is less than the amount calculated pursuant to paragraph (g)(1)(iv)(A) of this section of $5.36. Thus, the $5 increase in copayment does not cause the plan to cease to be a grandfathered health plan.

Example 7. (i) *Facts.* On March 23, 2010, a self-insured group health plan provides two tiers of coverage — self-only and family. The employer contributes 80% of the total cost of coverage for self-only and 60% of the total cost of coverage for family. Subsequently, the employer reduces the contribution to 50% for family coverage, but keeps the same contribution rate for self-only coverage.

(ii) *Conclusion.* In this *Example 7*, the decrease of 10 percentage points for family coverage in the contribution rate based on cost of coverage causes the plan to cease to be a grandfathered health plan. The fact that the contribution rate for self-only coverage remains the same does not change the result.

Example 8. (i) *Facts.* On March 23, 2010, a self-insured grandfathered health plan has a COBRA premium for the 2010 plan year of $5000 for self-only coverage and $12,000 for family coverage. The required employee contribution for the coverage is $1000 for self-only coverage and $4000 for family coverage. Thus, the contribution rate based on cost of coverage for 2010 is 80% ((5000 − 1000)/5000) for self-only coverage and 67% ((12,000 − 4000)/12,000) for family coverage. For a subsequent plan year, the COBRA premium is $6000 for self-only coverage and $15,000 for family coverage. The employee contributions for that plan year are $1200 for selfonly coverage and $5000 for family coverage. Thus, the contribution rate based on cost of coverage is 80% ((6000 − 1200)/6000) for self-only coverage and 67% ((15,000 − 5000)/15,000) for family coverage.

(ii) *Conclusion.* In this *Example 8*, because there is no change in the contribution rate based on cost of coverage, the plan retains its status as a grandfathered health plan. The result would be the same if all or part of the employee contribution was made pre-tax through a cafeteria plan under section 125 of the Internal Revenue Code.

Example 9. (i) *Facts.* A group health plan not maintained pursuant to a collective bargaining agreement offers three benefit packages on March 23, 2010. Option *F* is a self-insured option. Options *G* and *H* are insured options. Beginning July 1, 2013, the plan increases coinsurance under Option *H* from 10% to 15%. [Amended 11/17/2010 (75 FR 70114.]

(ii) *Conclusion.* In this *Example 9*, the coverage under Option *H* is not grandfathered health plan coverage as of July 1, 2013, consistent with the rule in paragraph (g)(1)(ii) of this section. Whether the coverage under Options *F* and *G* is grandfathered health plan coverage is determined separately under the rules of this paragraph (g). [Amended 11/17/2010 (75 FR 70114.]

Regulations

Reg. § 2590.715-1251 was revised and finalized on November 18, 2015 (80 FR 72191). See the caution line for applicability information.

>>>→ *Caution: Reg. § 2590.715-1251 is effective January 19, 2016, and applies to group health plans beginning on the first day of the first plan year beginning on or after January 1, 2017. Until the final regulations become applicable, plans and issuers are required to continue to comply with the corresponding EBSA interim final regulations, which apply for purposes of ERISA and the Code.*

[¶ 15,050R-50BA]

§ 2590.715-1251 Preservation of right to maintain existing coverage.

(a) *Definition of grandfathered health plan coverage—*

(1) *In general—*

(i) *Grandfathered health plan coverage.* means coverage provided by a group health plan, or a health insurance issuer, in which an individual was enrolled on March 23, 2010 (for as long as it maintains that status under the rules of this section). A group health plan or group health insurance coverage does not cease to be grandfathered health plan coverage merely because one or more (or even all) individuals enrolled on March 23, 2010 cease to be covered, provided that the plan or group health insurance coverage has continuously covered someone since March 23, 2010 (not necessarily the same person, but at all times at least one person). In addition, subject to the limitation set forth in paragraph (a)(1)(ii) of this section, a group health plan (and any health insurance coverage offered in connection with the group health plan) does not cease to be a grandfathered health plan merely because the plan (or its sponsor) enters into a new policy, certificate, or contract of insurance after March 23, 2010 (for example, a plan enters into a contract with a new issuer or a new policy is issued with an existing issuer). For purposes of this section, a plan or health insurance coverage that provides grandfathered health plan coverage is referred to as a grandfathered health plan. The rules of this section apply separately to each benefit package made available under a group health plan or health insurance coverage. Accordingly, if any benefit package relinquishes grandfather status, it will not affect the grandfather status of the other benefit packages.

(ii) *Changes in group health insurance coverage.* Subject to paragraphs (f) and (g)(2) of this section, if a group health plan (including a group health plan that was self-insured on March 23, 2010) or its sponsor enters into a new policy, certificate, or contract of insurance after March 23, 2010 that is effective before November 15, 2010, then the plan ceases to be a grandfathered health plan.

(2) *Disclosure of grandfather status—*

(i) To maintain status as a grandfathered health plan, a plan or health insurance coverage must include a statement that the plan or coverage believes it is a grandfathered health plan within the meaning of section 1251 of the Patient Protection and Affordable Care Act, and must provide contact information for questions and complaints, in any summary of benefits provided under the plan.

(ii) The following model language can be used to satisfy this disclosure requirement:

This [group health plan or health insurance issuer] believes this [plan or coverage] is a "grandfathered health plan" under the Patient Protection and Affordable Care Act (the Affordable Care Act). As permitted by the Affordable Care Act, a grandfathered health plan can preserve certain basic health coverage that was already in effect when that law was enacted. Being a grandfathered health plan means that your [plan or policy] may not include certain consumer protections of the Affordable Care Act that apply to other plans, for example, the requirement for the provision of preventive health services without any cost sharing. However, grandfathered health plans must comply with certain other consumer protections in the Affordable Care Act, for example, the elimination of lifetime dollar limits on benefits.

Questions regarding which protections apply and which protections do not apply to a grandfathered health plan and what might cause a plan to change from grandfathered health plan status can be directed to the plan administrator at [insert contact information]. [For ERISA plans, insert: You may also contact the Employee Benefits Security Administration, U.S. Department of Labor at 1-866-444-3272 or *www.dol.gov/ebsa/healthreform*. This Web site has a table summarizing which protections do and do not apply to grandfathered health plans.] [For individual market policies and nonfederal governmental plans, insert: You may also contact the U.S. Department of Health and Human Services at *www.healthcare.gov*.]

(3)(i) *Documentation of plan or policy terms on March 23, 2010.* To maintain status as a grandfathered health plan, a group health plan, or group health insurance coverage, must, for as long as the plan or health insurance coverage takes the position that it is a grandfathered health plan—

(A) Maintain records documenting the terms of the plan or health insurance coverage in connection with the coverage in effect on March 23, 2010, and any other documents necessary to verify, explain, or clarify its status as a grandfathered health plan; and

(B) Make such records available for examination upon request.

(ii) *Change in group health insurance coverage.* To maintain status as a grandfathered health plan, a group health plan that enters into a new policy, certificate, or contract of insurance must provide to the new health insurance issuer (and the new health insurance issuer must require) documentation of plan terms (including benefits, cost sharing, employer contributions, and annual dollar limits) under the prior health coverage sufficient to determine whether a change causing a cessation of grandfathered health plan status under paragraph (g)(1) of this section has occurred.

(4) *Family members enrolling after March 23, 2010.* With respect to an individual who is enrolled in a group health plan or health insurance coverage on March 23, 2010, grandfathered health plan coverage includes coverage of family members of the individual who enroll after March 23, 2010 in the grandfathered health plan coverage of the individual.

(b) *Allowance for new employees to join current plan—*

(1) *In general.* Subject to paragraph (b)(2) of this section, a group health plan (including health insurance coverage provided in connection with the group health plan) that provided coverage on March 23, 2010 and has retained its status as a grandfathered health plan (consistent with the rules of this section, including paragraph (g) of this section) is grandfathered health plan coverage for new employees (whether newly hired or newly enrolled) and their families enrolling in the plan after March 23, 2010. Further, the addition of a new contributing employer or new group of employees of an existing contributing employer to a grandfathered multiemployer health plan will not affect the plan's grandfather status.

(2) *Anti-abuse rules—*

(i) *Mergers and acquisitions.* If the principal purpose of a merger, acquisition, or similar business restructuring is to cover new individuals under a grandfathered health plan, the plan ceases to be a grandfathered health plan.

(ii) *Change in plan eligibility.* A group health plan or health insurance coverage (including a benefit package under a group health plan) ceases to be a grandfathered health plan if—

(A) Employees are transferred into the plan or health insurance coverage (the transferee plan) from a plan or health insurance coverage under which the employees were covered on March 23, 2010 (the transferor plan);

(B) Comparing the terms of the transferee plan with those of the transferor plan (as in effect on March 23, 2010) and treating the transferee plan as if it were an amendment of the transferor plan would cause a loss of grandfather status under the provisions of paragraph (g)(1) of this section; and

(C) There was no bona fide employment-based reason to transfer the employees into the transferee plan. For this purpose, changing the terms or cost of coverage is not a bona fide employment-based reason.

(iii) *Illustrative list of bona fide employment-based reasons.* For purposes of this paragraph (b)(2)(ii)(C), bona fide employment-based reasons include—

(A) When a benefit package is being eliminated because the issuer is exiting the market;

(B) When a benefit package is being eliminated because the issuer no longer offers the product to the employer;

(C) When low or declining participation by plan participants in the benefit package makes it impractical for the plan sponsor to continue to offer the benefit package;

(D) When a benefit package is eliminated from a multiemployer plan as agreed upon as part of the collective bargaining process; or

(E) When a benefit package is eliminated for any reason and multiple benefit packages covering a significant portion of other employees remain available to the employees being transferred.

(3) *Examples.* The rules of this paragraph (b) are illustrated by the following examples:

Example 1. (i) *Facts.* A group health plan offers two benefit packages on March 23, 2010, Options *F* and *G*. During a subsequent open enrollment period, some of the employees enrolled in Option *F* on March 23, 2010 switch to Option *G*.

(ii) *Conclusion.* In this *Example 1*, the group health coverage provided under Option *G* remains a grandfathered health plan under the rules of paragraph (b)(1) of this section because employees previously enrolled in Option *F* are allowed to enroll in Option *G* as new employees.

Example 2. (i) *Facts.* A group health plan offers two benefit packages on March 23, 2010, Options *H* and *I*. On March 23, 2010, Option *H* provides coverage only for employees in one manufacturing plant. Subsequently, the plant is closed, and some employees in the closed plant are moved to another plant. The employer eliminates Option *H* and the employees that are moved are transferred to Option *I*. If instead of transferring employees from Option *H* to Option *I*, Option *H* was amended to match the terms of Option *I*, then Option *H* would cease to be a grandfathered health plan.

(ii) *Conclusion.* In this *Example 2*, the plan has a bona fide employment-based reason to transfer employees from Option *H* to Option *I*. Therefore, Option *I* does not cease to be a grandfathered health plan.

(c) *General grandfathering rule*—

(1) Except as provided in paragraphs (d) and (e) of this section, subtitles A and C of title I of the Patient Protection and Affordable Care Act (and the amendments made by those subtitles, and the incorporation of those amendments into ERISA section 715 and Internal Revenue Code section 9815) do not apply to grandfathered health plan coverage. Accordingly, the provisions of PHS Act sections 2701, 2702, 2703, 2705, 2706, 2707, 2709 (relating to coverage for individuals participating in approved clinical trials, as added by section 10103 of the Patient Protection and Affordable Care Act), 2713, 2715A, 2716, 2717, 2719, and 2719A, as added or amended by the Patient Protection and Affordable Care Act, do not apply to grandfathered health plans. (In addition, *see* 45 CFR 147.140(c), which provides that the provisions of PHS Act section 2704, and PHS Act section 2711 insofar as it relates to annual dollar limits, do not apply to grandfathered health plans that are individual health insurance coverage.)

(2) To the extent not inconsistent with the rules applicable to a grandfathered health plan, a grandfathered health plan must comply with the requirements of the PHS Act, ERISA, and the Internal Revenue Code applicable prior to the changes enacted by the Patient Protection and Affordable Care Act.

(d) *Provisions applicable to all grandfathered health plans.* The provisions of PHS Act section 2711 insofar as it relates to lifetime dollar limits, and the provisions of PHS Act sections 2712, 2714, 2715, and 2718, apply to grandfathered health plans for plan years beginning on or after September 23, 2010. The provisions of PHS Act section 2708 apply to grandfathered health plans for plan years beginning on or after January 1, 2014.

(e) *Applicability of PHS Act sections 2704, 2711, and 2714 to grandfathered group health plans and group health insurance coverage*—

(1) The provisions of PHS Act section 2704 as it applies with respect to enrollees who are under 19 years of age, and the provisions of PHS Act section 2711 insofar as it relates to annual dollar limits, apply to grandfathered health plans that are group health plans (including group health insurance coverage) for plan years beginning on or after September 23, 2010. The provisions of PHS Act section 2704 apply generally to grandfathered health plans that are group health plans (including group health insurance coverage) for plan years beginning on or after January 1, 2014.

(2) For plan years beginning before January 1, 2014, the provisions of PHS Act section 2714 apply in the case of an adult child with respect to a grandfathered health plan that is a group health plan only if the adult child is not eligible to enroll in an eligible employer-sponsored health plan (as defined in section 5000A(f)(2) of the Internal Revenue Code) other than a grandfathered health plan of a parent. For plan years beginning on or after January 1, 2014, the provisions of PHS Act section 2714 apply with respect to a grandfathered health plan that is a group health plan without regard to whether an adult child is eligible to enroll in any other coverage.

(f) *Effect on collectively bargained plans*—

In general. In the case of health insurance coverage maintained pursuant to one or more collective bargaining agreements between employee representatives and one or more employers that was ratified before March 23, 2010, the coverage is grandfathered health plan coverage at least until the date on which the last of the collective bargaining agreements relating to the coverage that was in effect on March 23, 2010 terminates. Any coverage amendment made pursuant to a collective bargaining agreement relating to the coverage that amends the coverage solely to conform to any requirement added by subtitles A and C of title I of the Patient Protection and Affordable Care Act (and the amendments made by those subtitles, and the incorporation of those amendments into ERISA section 715 and Internal Revenue Code section 9815) is not treated as a termination of the collective bargaining agreement. After the date on which the last of the collective bargaining agreements relating to the coverage that was in effect on March 23, 2010 terminates, the determination of whether health insurance coverage maintained pursuant to a collective bargaining agreement is grandfathered health plan coverage is made under the rules of this section other than this paragraph (f) (comparing the terms of the health insurance coverage after the date the last collective bargaining agreement terminates with the terms of the health insurance coverage that were in effect on March 23, 2010).

(g) *Maintenance of grandfather status*—

(1) *Changes causing cessation of grandfather status.* Subject to paragraph (g)(2) of this section, the rules of this paragraph (g)(1) describe situations in which a group health plan or health insurance coverage ceases to be a grandfathered health plan. A plan or coverage will cease to be a grandfathered health plan when an amendment to plan terms that results in a change described in this paragraph (g)(1) becomes effective, regardless of when the amendment was adopted. Once grandfather status is lost, it cannot be regained.

(i) *Elimination of benefits.* The elimination of all or substantially all benefits to diagnose or treat a particular condition causes a group health plan or health insurance coverage to cease to be a grandfathered health plan. For this purpose, the elimination of benefits for any necessary element to diagnose or treat a condition is considered the elimination of all or substantially all benefits to diagnose or treat a particular condition. Whether or not a plan or coverage has eliminated substantially all benefits to diagnose or treat a particular condition must be determined based on all the facts and circumstances, taking into account the items and services provided for a particular condition under the plan on March 23, 2010, as compared to the benefits offered at the time the plan or coverage makes the benefit change effective.

(ii) *Increase in percentage cost-sharing requirement.* Any increase, measured from March 23, 2010, in a percentage cost-sharing requirement (such as an individual's coinsurance requirement) causes a group health plan or health insurance coverage to cease to be a grandfathered health plan.

(iii) *Increase in a fixed-amount cost-sharing requirement other than a copayment.* Any increase in a fixed-amount cost-sharing requirement other than a copayment (for example, deductible or out-of-pocket limit), determined as of the effective date of the increase, causes a group health plan or health insurance coverage to cease to be a grandfathered health plan, if the total percentage increase in the cost-sharing requirement measured from March 23, 2010 exceeds the maximum percentage increase (as defined in paragraph (g)(3)(ii) of this section).

(iv) *Increase in a fixed-amount copayment.* Any increase in a fixed-amount copayment, determined as of the effective date of the increase, and determined for each copayment level if a plan has different copayment levels for different categories of services, causes a group health plan or health insurance coverage to cease to be a grandfathered health plan, if the total increase in the copayment measured from March 23, 2010 exceeds the greater of:

(A) An amount equal to $5 increased by medical inflation, as defined in paragraph (g)(3)(i) of this section (that is, $5 times medical inflation, plus $5), or

(B) The maximum percentage increase (as defined in paragraph (g)(3)(ii) of this section), determined by expressing the total increase in the copayment as a percentage.

(v) *Decrease in contribution rate by employers and employee organizations—*

(A) *Contribution rate based on cost of coverage.* A group health plan or group health insurance coverage ceases to be a grandfathered health plan if the employer or employee organization decreases its contribution rate based on cost of coverage (as defined in paragraph (g)(3)(iii)(A) of this section) towards the cost of any tier of coverage for any class of similarly situated individuals (as described in § 2590.702(d)) by more than 5 percentage points below the contribution rate for the coverage period that includes March 23, 2010.

(B) *Contribution rate based on a formula.* A group health plan or group health insurance coverage ceases to be a grandfathered health plan if the employer or employee organization decreases its contribution rate based on a formula (as defined in paragraph (g)(3)(iii)(B) of this section) towards the cost of any tier of coverage for any class of similarly situated individuals (as described in § 2590.702(d)) by more than 5 percent below the contribution rate for the coverage period that includes March 23, 2010.

(C) *Special rules regarding decreases in contribution rates.* An insured group health plan (or a multiemployer plan) that is a grandfathered health plan will not cease to be a grandfathered health plan based on a change in the employer contribution rate unless the issuer (or multiemployer plan) knows, or should know, of the change, provided:

(1) Upon renewal (or, in the case of a multiemployer plan, before the start of a new plan year), the issuer (or multiemployer plan) requires relevant employers, employee organizations, or plan sponsors, as applicable, to make a representation regarding its contribution rate for the plan year covered by the renewal, as well as its contribution rate on March 23, 2010 (if the issuer, or multiemployer plan, does not already have it); and

(2) The relevant policies, certificates, contracts of insurance, or plan documents disclose in a prominent and effective manner that employers, employee organizations, or plan sponsors, as applicable, are required to notify the issuer (or multiemployer plan) if the contribution rate changes at any point during the plan year.

(D) *Application to plans with multi-tiered coverage structures.* The standards for employer contributions in this paragraph (g)(1)(v) apply on a tier-by-tier basis. Therefore, if a group health plan modifies the tiers of coverage it had on March 23, 2010 (for example, from self-only and family to a multi-tiered structure of self-only, self-plus-one, self-plus-two, and self-plus-three-or-more), the employer contribution for any new tier would be tested by comparison to the contribution rate for the corresponding tier on March 23, 2010. For example, if the employer contribution rate for family coverage was 50 percent on March 23, 2010, the employer contribution rate for any new tier of coverage other than self-only (*i.e.*, self-plus-one, self-plus-two, self-plus-three or more) must be within 5 percentage points of 50 percent (*i.e.*, at least 45 percent). If, however, the plan adds one or more new coverage tiers without eliminating or modifying any previous tiers and those new coverage tiers cover classes of individuals that were not covered previously under the plan, the new tiers would not be analyzed under the standards for changes in employer contributions. For example, if a plan with self-only as the sole coverage tier added a family coverage tier, the level of employer contributions toward the family coverage would not cause the plan to lose grandfather status.

(E) *Group health plans with fixed-dollar employee contributions or no employee contributions.* A group health plan that requires either fixed-dollar employee contributions or no employee contributions will not cease to be a grandfathered health plan solely because the employer contribution rate changes so long as there continues to be no employee contributions or no increase in the fixed-dollar employee contributions towards the cost of coverage.

(vi) *Changes in annual limits—*

(A) *Addition of an annual limit.* A group health plan, or group health insurance coverage, that, on March 23, 2010, did not impose an overall annual or lifetime limit on the dollar value of all benefits ceases to be a grandfathered health plan if the plan or health insurance coverage imposes an overall annual limit on the dollar value of benefits. (But see § 2590.715-2711, which prohibits all annual dollar limits on essential health benefits for plan years beginning on or after January 1, 2014).

(B) *Decrease in limit for a plan or coverage with only a lifetime limit.* A group health plan, or group health insurance coverage, that, on March 23, 2010, imposed an overall lifetime limit on the dollar value of all benefits but no overall annual limit on the dollar value of all benefits ceases to be a grandfathered health plan if the plan or health insurance coverage adopts an overall annual limit at a dollar value that is lower than the dollar value of the lifetime limit on March 23, 2010. (But see § 2590.715-2711, which prohibits all annual dollar limits on essential health benefits for plan years beginning on or after January 1, 2014).

(C) *Decrease in limit for a plan or coverage with an annual limit.* A group health plan, or group health insurance coverage, that, on March 23, 2010, imposed an overall annual limit on the dollar value of all benefits ceases to be a grandfathered health plan if the plan or health insurance coverage decreases the dollar value of the annual limit (regardless of whether the plan or health insurance coverage also imposed an overall lifetime limit on March 23, 2010 on the dollar value of all benefits). (But see § 2590.715-2711, which prohibits all annual dollar limits on essential health benefits for plan years beginning on or after January 1, 2014).

(2) *Transitional rules—*

(i) *Changes made prior to March 23, 2010.* If a group health plan or health insurance issuer makes the following changes to the terms of the plan or health insurance coverage, the changes are considered part of the terms of the plan or health insurance coverage on March 23, 2010 even though they were not effective at that time and such changes do not cause a plan or health insurance coverage to cease to be a grandfathered health plan:

Reg. § 2590.715-1251(g)(2)(i)   ¶ 15,050R-50BA

>>>→ *Caution: Reg. § 2590.715-1251 is effective January 19, 2016, and applies to group health plans beginning on the first day of the first plan year beginning on or after January 1, 2017. Until the final regulations become applicable, plans and issuers are required to continue to comply with the corresponding EBSA interim final regulations, which apply for purposes of ERISA and the Code.*

(A) Changes effective after March 23, 2010 pursuant to a legally binding contract entered into on or before March 23, 2010;

(B) Changes effective after March 23, 2010 pursuant to a filing on or before March 23, 2010 with a State insurance department; or

(C) Changes effective after March 23, 2010 pursuant to written amendments to a plan that were adopted on or before March 23, 2010.

(ii) *Changes made after March 23, 2010 and adopted prior to issuance of regulations.* If, after March 23, 2010, a group health plan or health insurance issuer makes changes to the terms of the plan or health insurance coverage and the changes are adopted prior to June 14, 2010, the changes will not cause the plan or health insurance coverage to cease to be a grandfathered health plan if the changes are revoked or modified effective as of the first day of the first plan year (in the individual market, policy year) beginning on or after September 23, 2010, and the terms of the plan or health insurance coverage on that date, as modified, would not cause the plan or coverage to cease to be a grandfathered health plan under the rules of this section, including paragraph (g)(1) of this section. For this purpose, changes will be considered to have been adopted prior to June 14, 2010 if:

(A) The changes are effective before that date;

(B) The changes are effective on or after that date pursuant to a legally binding contract entered into before that date;

(C) The changes are effective on or after that date pursuant to a filing before that date with a State insurance department; or

(D) The changes are effective on or after that date pursuant to written amendments to a plan that were adopted before that date.

(3) *Definitions—*

(i) *Medical inflation defined.* For purposes of this paragraph (g), the term *medical inflation* means the increase since March 2010 in the overall medical care component of the Consumer Price Index for All Urban Consumers (CPI-U) (unadjusted) published by the Department of Labor using the 1982-1984 base of 100. For this purpose, the increase in the overall medical care component is computed by subtracting 387.142 (the overall medical care component of the CPI-U (unadjusted) published by the Department of Labor for March 2010, using the 1982-1984 base of 100) from the index amount for any month in the 12 months before the new change is to take effect and then dividing that amount by 387.142.

(ii) *Maximum percentage increase defined.* For purposes of this paragraph (g), the term *maximum percentage increase* means medical inflation (as defined in paragraph (g)(3)(i) of this section), expressed as a percentage, plus 15 percentage points.

(iii) *Contribution rate defined.* For purposes of paragraph (g)(1)(v) of this section:

(A) *Contribution rate based on cost of coverage.* The term *contribution rate based on cost of coverage* means the amount of contributions made by an employer or employee organization compared to the total cost of coverage, expressed as a percentage. The total cost of coverage is determined in the same manner as the applicable premium is calculated under the COBRA continuation provisions of section 604 of ERISA, section 4980B(f)(4) of the Internal Revenue Code, and section 2204 of the PHS Act. In the case of a self-insured plan, contributions by an employer or employee organization are equal to the total cost of coverage minus the employee contributions towards the total cost of coverage.

(B) *Contribution rate based on a formula.* The term *contribution rate based on a formula* means, for plans that, on March 23, 2010, made contributions based on a formula (such as hours worked or tons of coal mined), the formula.

(4) *Examples.* The rules of this paragraph (g) are illustrated by the following examples:

Example 1. (i) *Facts.* On March 23, 2010, a grandfathered health plan has a coinsurance requirement of 20% for inpatient surgery. The plan is subsequently amended to increase the coinsurance requirement to 25%.

(ii) *Conclusion.* In this *Example 1*, the increase in the coinsurance requirement from 20% to 25% causes the plan to cease to be a grandfathered health plan.

Example 2. (i) *Facts.* Before March 23, 2010, the terms of a group health plan provide benefits for a particular mental health condition, the treatment for which is a combination of counseling and prescription drugs. Subsequently, the plan eliminates benefits for counseling.

(ii) *Conclusion.* In this *Example 2*, the plan ceases to be a grandfathered health plan because counseling is an element that is necessary to treat the condition. Thus the plan is considered to have eliminated substantially all benefits for the treatment of the condition.

Example 3. (i) *Facts.* On March 23, 2010, a grandfathered health plan has a copayment requirement of $30 per office visit for specialists. The plan is subsequently amended to increase the copayment requirement to $40. Within the 12-month period before the $40 copayment takes effect, the greatest value of the overall medical care component of the CPI-U (unadjusted) is 475.

(ii) *Conclusion.* In this *Example 3*, the increase in the copayment from $30 to $40, expressed as a percentage, is 33.33% (40-30 = 10; 10 ÷ 30 = 0.3333; 0.3333 = 33.33%). Medical inflation (as defined in paragraph (g)(3)(i) of this section) from March 2010 is 0.2269 (475-387.142 = 87.858; 87.858 ÷ 387.142 = 0.2269). The maximum percentage increase permitted is 37.69% (0.2269 = 22.69%; 22.69% + 15% = 37.69%). Because 33.33% does not exceed 37.69%, the change in the copayment requirement at that time does not cause the plan to cease to be a grandfathered health plan.

Example 4. (i) *Facts.* Same facts as *Example 3*, except the grandfathered health plan subsequently increases the $40 copayment requirement to $45 for a later plan year. Within the 12-month period before the $45 copayment takes effect, the greatest value of the overall medical care component of the CPI-U (unadjusted) is 485.

(ii) *Conclusion.* In this *Example 4*, the increase in the copayment from $30 (the copayment that was in effect on March 23, 2010) to $45, expressed as a percentage, is 50% (45-30 = 15; 15 ÷ 30 = 0.5; 0.5 = 50%). Medical inflation (as defined in paragraph (g)(3)(i) of this section) from March 2010 is 0.2527 (485-387.142 = 97.858; 97.858 ÷ 387.142 = 0.2527). The increase that would cause a plan to cease to be a grandfathered health plan under paragraph (g)(1)(iv) of this section is the greater of the maximum percentage increase of 40.27% (0.2527 = 25.27%; 25.27% + 15% = 40.27%), or $6.26 ($5 × 0.2527 = $1.26; $1.26 + $5 = $6.26). Because 50% exceeds 40.27% and $15 exceeds $6.26, the change in the copayment requirement at that time causes the plan to cease to be a grandfathered health plan.

Example 5. (i) *Facts.* On March 23, 2010, a grandfathered health plan has a copayment of $10 per office visit for primary care providers. The plan is subsequently amended to increase the copayment requirement to $15. Within the 12-month period before the $15 copayment takes effect, the greatest value of the overall medical care component of the CPI-U (unadjusted) is 415.

(ii) *Conclusion.* In this *Example 5*, the increase in the copayment, expressed as a percentage, is 50% (15-10 = 5; 5 ÷ 10 = 0.5; 0.5 = 50%). Medical inflation (as defined in paragraph (g)(3) of this section) from March 2010 is 0.0720 (415.0-387.142 = 27.858; 27.858 ÷ 387.142 = 0.0720). The increase that would cause a plan to cease to be a grandfathered health plan under paragraph (g)(1)(iv) of this section is the greater of the maximum percentage increase of 22.20% (0.0720 = 7.20%; 7.20% + 15% = 22.20), or $5.36 ($5 × 0.0720 = $0.36; $0.36 + $5 = $5.36). The $5 increase in copayment in this *Example 5* would not cause the plan to cease to be a grandfathered health plan pursuant to paragraph (g)(1)(iv) this section, which would permit an increase in the copayment of up to $5.36.

Example 6. (i) *Facts.* The same facts as *Example 5*, except on March 23, 2010, the grandfathered health plan has no copayment ($0)

»»→ *Caution: Reg. § 2590.715-1251 is effective January 19, 2016, and applies to group health plans beginning on the first day of the first plan year beginning on or after January 1, 2017. Until the final regulations become applicable, plans and issuers are required to continue to comply with the corresponding EBSA interim final regulations, which apply for purposes of ERISA and the Code.*

for office visits for primary care providers. The plan is subsequently amended to increase the copayment requirement to $5.

(ii) *Conclusion.* In this *Example 6*, medical inflation (as defined in paragraph (g)(3)(i) of this section) from March 2010 is 0.0720 (415.0-387.142 = 27.858; 27.858 ÷ 387.142 = 0.0720). The increase that would cause a plan to cease to be a grandfathered health plan under paragraph (g)(1)(iv)(A) of this section is $5.36 ($5 × 0.0720 = $0.36; $0.36 + $5 = $5.36). The $5 increase in copayment in this *Example 6* is less than the amount calculated pursuant to paragraph (g)(1)(iv)(A) of this section of $5.36. Thus, the $5 increase in copayment does not cause the plan to cease to be a grandfathered health plan.

Example 7. (i) *Facts.* On March 23, 2010, a self-insured group health plan provides two tiers of coverage—self-only and family. The employer contributes 80% of the total cost of coverage for self-only and 60% of the total cost of coverage for family. Subsequently, the employer reduces the contribution to 50% for family coverage, but keeps the same contribution rate for self-only coverage.

(ii) *Conclusion.* In this *Example 7*, the decrease of 10 percentage points for family coverage in the contribution rate based on cost of coverage causes the plan to cease to be a grandfathered health plan. The fact that the contribution rate for self-only coverage remains the same does not change the result.

Example 8. (i) *Facts.* On March 23, 2010, a self-insured grandfathered health plan has a COBRA premium for the 2010 plan year of $5,000 for self-only coverage and $12,000 for family coverage.

The required employee contribution for the coverage is $1,000 for self-only coverage and $4,000 for family coverage. Thus, the contribution rate based on cost of coverage for 2010 is 80% ((5,000-1,000)/5,000) for self-only coverage and 67% ((12,000-4,000)/12,000) for family coverage. For a subsequent plan year, the COBRA premium is $6,000 for self-only coverage and $15,000 for family coverage. The employee contributions for that plan year are $1,200 for self-only coverage and $5,000 for family coverage. Thus, the contribution rate based on cost of coverage is 80% ((6,000-1,200)/6,000) for self-only coverage and 67% ((15,000-5,000)/15,000) for family coverage.

(ii) *Conclusion.* In this *Example 8*, because there is no change in the contribution rate based on cost of coverage, the plan retains its status as a grandfathered health plan. The result would be the same if all or part of the employee contribution was made pre-tax through a cafeteria plan under section 125 of the Internal Revenue Code.

Example 9. (i) *Facts.* A group health plan not maintained pursuant to a collective bargaining agreement offers three benefit packages on March 23, 2010. Option *F* is a self-insured option. Options *G* and *H* are insured options. Beginning July 1, 2013, the plan increases coinsurance under Option *H* from 10% to 15%.

(ii) *Conclusion.* In this *Example 9*, the coverage under Option *H* is not grandfathered health plan coverage as of July 1, 2013, consistent with the (rule in paragraph (g)(1)(ii) of this section. Whether the coverage under Options *F* and *G* is grandfathered health plan coverage is determined separately under the rules of this paragraph (g).

Interim Final Regulations

Reg. § 2590.715-2704 was adopted and published in the Federal Register on June 28, 2010 (75 FR 37187).

»»»→ *Caution: Until final Reg. § 2590.715-2704 at ¶ 15,050R-50GA is applicable on the first day of the plan year beginning on or after January 1, 2017, plans and issuers must continue to comply with the below interim final regulation.*

[¶ 15,050R-50G]

§ 2590.715-2704 Prohibition of preexisting condition exclusions.

(a) *No preexisting condition exclusions.* (1) *In general..* A group health plan, or a health insurance issuer offering group health insurance coverage, may not impose any preexisting condition exclusion (as defined in § 2590.701-2 of this part).

(2) *Examples..* The rules of this paragraph (a) are illustrated by the following examples (for additional examples illustrating the definition of a preexisting condition exclusion, *see* § 2590.701-3(a)(1)(ii) of this part):

Example 1. (i) *Facts.* A group health plan provides benefits solely through an insurance policy offered by Issuer *P*. At the expiration of the policy, the plan switches coverage to a policy offered by Issuer *N*. *N*'s policy excludes benefits for oral surgery required as a result of a traumatic injury if the injury occurred before the effective date of coverage under the policy.

(ii) *Conclusion.* In this *Example 1*, the exclusion of benefits for oral surgery required as a result of a traumatic injury if the injury occurred before the effective date of coverage is a preexisting condition exclusion because it operates to exclude benefits for a condition based on the fact that the condition was present before the effective date of coverage under the policy.

Example 2. (i) *Facts.* Individual *C* applies for individual health insurance coverage with Issuer *M*. *M* denies *C*'s application for coverage because a pre-enrollment physical revealed that *C* has type 2 diabetes.

(ii) *Conclusion. See Example 2* in 45 CFR 147.108(a)(2) for a conclusion that *M*'s denial of *C*'s application for coverage is a preexisting condition exclusion because a denial of an application for coverage based on the fact that a condition was present before the date of denial is an exclusion of benefits based on a preexisting condition.

(b) *Applicability.* (1) *General applicability date..* Except as provided in paragraph (b)(2) of this section, the rules of this section apply for plan years beginning on or after January 1, 2014.

(2) *Early applicability date for children..* The rules of this section apply with respect to enrollees, including applicants for enrollment, who are under 19 years of age for plan years beginning on or after September 23, 2010.

(3) *Applicability to grandfathered health plans..* See § 2590.715-1251 of this part for determining the application of this section to grandfathered health plans (providing that a grandfathered health plan that is a group health plan or group health insurance coverage must comply with the prohibition against preexisting condition exclusions).

(4) *Example..* The rules of this paragraph (b) are illustrated by the following example:

Example. (i) *Facts.* Individual *F* commences employment and enrolls *F* and *F*'s 16-year-old child in the group health plan maintained by *F*'s employer, with a first day of coverage of October 15, 2010. *F*'s child had a significant break in coverage because of a lapse of more than 63 days without creditable coverage immediately prior to enrolling in the plan. *F*'s child was treated for asthma within the six-month period prior to the enrollment date and the plan imposes a 12-month preexisting condition exclusion for coverage of asthma. The next plan year begins on January 1, 2011.

(ii) *Conclusion.* In this *Example,* the plan year beginning January 1, 2011 is the first plan year of the group health plan beginning on or after September 23, 2010. Thus, beginning on January 1, 2011, because the child is under 19 years of age, the plan cannot impose a preexisting condition exclusion with respect to the child's asthma regardless of the fact that the preexisting condition exclusion was imposed by the plan before the applicability date of this provision.

Final Regulations

Reg. § 2590.715-2705 was adopted and published in the *Federal Register* on June 3, 2013 by 78 FR 33157. Reg. § 2590.715-2708 was adopted and published in the Federal Register on February 24, 2014 by 79 FR 10295. Reg. § 2590.715-2708 was amended on June 25, 2014 (79 FR 35942). Reg. § 2590.715-2704 was revised and finalized on November 18, 2015 (80 FR 72191). See the caution line for applicability information.

⫸→ *Caution: Reg. § 2590.715-2704 is effective January 19, 2016, and applies to group health plans beginning on the first day of the first plan year beginning on or after January 1, 2017. Until the final regulations become applicable, plans and issuers are required to continue to comply with the corresponding EBSA interim final regulations, which apply for purposes of ERISA and the Code.*

[¶ 15,050R-50GA]

§ 2590.715-2704 Prohibition of preexisting condition exclusions.

(a) *No preexisting condition exclusions.* A group health plan, or a health insurance issuer offering group health insurance coverage, may not impose any preexisting condition exclusion (as defined in § 2590.701-2).

(b) *Examples.* The rules of paragraph (a) of this section are illustrated by the following examples (for additional examples illustrating the definition of a preexisting condition exclusion, *see* § 2590.701-3(a)(2)):

Example 1. (i) *Facts.* A group health plan provides benefits solely through an insurance policy offered by Issuer *P*. At the expiration of the policy, the plan switches coverage to a policy offered by Issuer *N*. *N*'s policy excludes benefits for oral surgery required as a result of a traumatic injury if the injury occurred before the effective date of coverage under the policy.

(ii) *Conclusion.* In this *Example 1*, the exclusion of benefits for oral surgery required as a result of a traumatic injury if the injury occurred before the effective date of coverage is a preexisting condition exclusion because it operates to exclude benefits for a condition based on the fact that the condition was present before the effective date of coverage under the policy. Therefore, such an exclusion is prohibited.

Example 2. (i) *Facts.* Individual *C* applies for individual health insurance coverage with Issuer *M*. *M* denies *C*'s application for coverage because a pre-enrollment physical revealed that *C* has type 2 diabetes.

(ii) *Conclusion. See Example 2* in 45 CFR 147.108(a)(2) for a conclusion that *M*'s denial of *C*'s application for coverage is a preexisting condition exclusion because a denial of an application for coverage based on the fact that a condition was present before the date of denial is an exclusion of benefits based on a preexisting condition. Therefore, such an exclusion is prohibited.

(c) *Applicability date.* The provisions of this section are applicable to group health plans and health insurance issuers for plan years beginning on or after January 1, 2017. Until the applicability date for this regulation, plans and issuers are required to continue to comply with the corresponding sections of 29 CFR part 2590, contained in the 29 CFR, parts 1927 to end, edition revised as of July 1, 2015.

[¶ 15,050R-50H]

§ 2590.715-2705 Prohibiting discrimination against participants and beneficiaries based on a health factor.

(a) *In general.* A group health plan and a health insurance issuer offering group health insurance coverage must comply with the requirements of § 2590.702 of this part.

(b) *Applicability date.* This section is applicable to group health plans and health insurance issuers offering group health insurance coverage for plan years beginning on or after January 1, 2014.

[¶ 15,050R-50K]

§ 2590.715-2708 Prohibition on waiting periods that exceed 90 days.

(a) *General rule.* A group health plan, and a health insurance issuer offering group health insurance coverage, must not apply any waiting period that exceeds 90 days, in accordance with the rules of this section. If, under the terms of a plan, an individual can elect coverage that would begin on a date that is not later than the end of the 90-day waiting period, this paragraph (a) is considered satisfied. Accordingly, in that case, a plan or issuer will not be considered to have violated this paragraph (a) solely because individuals take, or are permitted to take, additional time (beyond the end of the 90-day waiting period) to elect coverage.

(b) *Waiting period defined.* For purposes of this part, a waiting period is the period that must pass before coverage for an individual who is otherwise eligible to enroll under the terms of a group health plan can become effective. If an individual enrolls as a late enrollee (as

defined under § 2590.701-2) or special enrollee (as described in § 2590.701-6), any period before such late or special enrollment is not a waiting period.

(c) *Relation to a plan's eligibility criteria.* (1) *In general.* Except as provided in paragraphs (c)(2) and (c)(3) of this section, being otherwise eligible to enroll under the terms of a group health plan means having met the plan's substantive eligibility conditions (such as, for example, being in an eligible job classification, achieving job-related licensure requirements specified in the plan's terms, or satisfying a reasonable and bona fide employment-based orientation period). Moreover, except as provided in paragraphs (c)(2) and (c)(3) of this section, nothing in this section requires a plan sponsor to offer coverage to any particular individual or class of individuals (including, for example, part-time employees). Instead, this section prohibits requiring otherwise eligible individuals to wait more than 90 days before coverage is effective. *See also* section 4980H of the Code and its implementing regulations for an applicable large employer's shared responsibility to provide health coverage to full-time employees.

(2) *Eligibility conditions based solely on the lapse of time.* Eligibility conditions that are based solely on the lapse of a time period are permissible for no more than 90 days.

(3) *Other conditions for eligibility.* Other conditions for eligibility under the terms of a group health plan are generally permissible under PHS Act section 2708, unless the condition is designed to avoid compliance with the 90-day waiting period limitation, determined in accordance with the rules of this paragraph (c)(3).

(i) *Application to variable-hour employees in cases in which a specified number of hours of service per period is a plan eligibility condition.* If a group health plan conditions eligibility on an employee regularly having a specified number of hours of service per period (or working full-time), and it cannot be determined that a newly-hired employee is reasonably expected to regularly work that number of hours per period (or work full-time), the plan may take a reasonable period of time, not to exceed 12 months and beginning on any date between the employee's start date and the first day of the first calendar month following the employee's start date, to determine whether the employee meets the plan's eligibility condition. Except in cases in which a waiting period that exceeds 90 days is imposed in addition to a measurement period, the time period for determining whether such an employee meets the plan's eligibility condition will not be considered to be designed to avoid compliance with the 90-day waiting period limitation if coverage is made effective no later than 13 months from the employee's start date plus, if the employee's start date is not the first day of a calendar month, the time remaining until the first day of the next calendar month.

(ii) *Cumulative service requirements.* If a group health plan or health insurance issuer conditions eligibility on an employee's having completed a number of cumulative hours of service, the eligibility condition is not considered to be designed to avoid compliance with the 90-day waiting period limitation if the cumulative hours-of-service requirement does not exceed 1,200 hours.

(iii) *Limitation on orientation periods.* To ensure that an orientation period is not used as a subterfuge for the passage of time, or designed to avoid compliance with the 90-day waiting period limitation, an orientation period is permitted only if it does not exceed one month. For this purpose, one month is determined by adding one calendar month and subtracting one calendar day, measured from an employee's start date in a position that is otherwise eligible for coverage. For example, if an employee's start date in an otherwise eligible position is May 3, the last permitted day of the orientation period is June 2. Similarly, if an employee's start date in an otherwise eligible position is October 1, the last permitted day of the orientation period is October 31. If there is not a corresponding date in the next calendar month upon adding a calendar month, the last permitted day of the orientation period is the last day of the next calendar month. For example, if the employee's start date is January 30, the last permitted day of the orientation period is February 28 (or February 29 in a leap year). Similarly, if the employee's start date is August 31, the last permitted day of the orientation period is September 30. [Added 6/25/2014 (79 FR 35942).]

(d) *Application to rehires.* A plan or issuer may treat an employee whose employment has terminated and who then is rehired as newly eligible upon rehire and, therefore, required to meet the plan's eligibility criteria and waiting period anew, if reasonable under the circumstances (for example, the termination and rehire cannot be a subterfuge to avoid compliance with the 90-day waiting period limitation).

(e) *Counting days.* Under this section, all calendar days are counted beginning on the enrollment date (as defined in §2590.701-2), including weekends and holidays. A plan or issuer that imposes a 90-day waiting period may, for administrative convenience, choose to permit coverage to become effective earlier than the 91st day if the 91st day is a weekend or holiday.

(f) *Examples.* The rules of this section are illustrated by the following examples:

Example 1. (i) *Facts.* A group health plan provides that full-time employees are eligible for coverage under the plan. Employee *A* begins employment as a full-time employee on January 19.

(ii) *Conclusion.* In this *Example 1,* any waiting period for *A* would begin on January 19 and may not exceed 90 days. Coverage under the plan must become effective no later than April 19 (assuming February lasts 28 days).

Example 2. (i) *Facts.* A group health plan provides that only employees with job title *M* are eligible for coverage under the plan. Employee *B* begins employment with job title *L* on January 30.

(ii) *Conclusion.* In this *Example 2,* B is not eligible for coverage under the plan, and the period while *B* is working with job title *L* and therefore not in an eligible class of employees, is not part of a waiting period under this section.

Example 3. (i) *Facts.* Same facts as in *Example 2,* except that *B* transfers to a new position with job title *M* on April 11.

(ii) *Conclusion.* In this *Example 3,* B becomes eligible for coverage on April 11, but for the waiting period. Any waiting period for *B* begins on April 11 and may not exceed 90 days; therefore, coverage under the plan must become effective no later than July 10.

Example 4. (i) *Facts.* A group health plan provides that only employees who have completed specified training and achieved specified certifications are eligible for coverage under the plan. Employee *C* is hired on May 3 and meets the plan's eligibility criteria on September 22.

(ii) *Conclusion.* In this *Example 4,* C becomes eligible for coverage on September 22, but for the waiting period. Any waiting period for *C* would begin on September 22 and may not exceed 90 days; therefore, coverage under the plan must become effective no later than December 21.

Example 5. (i) *Facts.* A group health plan provides that employees are eligible for coverage after one year of service.

(ii) *Conclusion.* In this *Example 5,* the plan's eligibility condition is based solely on the lapse of time and, therefore, is impermissible under paragraph (c)(2) of this section because it exceeds 90 days.

Example 6. (i) *Facts.* Employer *V*'s group health plan provides for coverage to begin on the first day of the first payroll period on or after the date an employee is hired and completes the applicable enrollment forms. Enrollment forms are distributed on an employee's start date and may be completed within 90 days. Employee *D* is hired and starts on October 31, which is the first day of a pay period. *D* completes the enrollment forms and submits them on the 90th day after *D*'s start date, which is January 28. Coverage is made effective 7 days later, February 4, which is the first day of the next pay period.

(ii) *Conclusion.* In this *Example 6,* under the terms of *V*'s plan, coverage may become effective as early as October 31, depending on when *D* completes the applicable enrollment forms. Under the terms of the plan, when coverage becomes effective depends solely on the length of time taken by *D* to complete the enrollment materials. Therefore, under the terms of the plan, *D* may elect coverage that would begin on a date that does not exceed the 90-day waiting period limitation, and the plan complies with this section.

Example 7. (i) *Facts.* Under Employer *W*'s group health plan, only employees who are full-time (defined under the plan as regularly averaging 30 hours of service per week) are eligible for coverage. Employee *E* begins employment for Employer *W* on November 26 of Year 1. *E*'s hours are reasonably expected to vary, with an opportunity to work between 20 and 45 hours per week, depending on shift availability and *E*'s availability. Therefore, it cannot be determined at *E*'s start date that *E* is reasonably expected to work full-time. Under the terms of the plan, variable-hour employees, such as *E*, are eligible to enroll in the plan if they are determined to be a full-time employee after a measurement period of 12 months that begins on the employee's start date. Coverage is made effective no later than the first day of the first calendar month after the applicable enrollment forms are received. *E*'s 12-month measurement period ends November 25 of Year 2. *E* is determined to be a full-time employee and is notified of *E*'s plan eligibility. If *E* then elects coverage, *E*'s first day of coverage will be January 1 of Year 3.

(ii) *Conclusion.* In this *Example 7,* the measurement period is permissible because it is not considered to be designed to avoid compliance with the 90-day waiting period limitation. The plan may use a reasonable period of time to determine whether a variable-hour employee is a full-time employee, provided that (a) the period of time is no longer than 12 months; (b) the period of time begins on a date between the employee's start date and the first day of the next calendar month (inclusive); (c) coverage is made effective no later than 13 months from *E*'s start date plus, if the employee's start date is not the first day of a calendar month, the time remaining until the first day of the next calendar month; and (d) in addition to the measurement period, no more than 90 days elapse prior to the employee's eligibility for coverage.

Example 8. (i) *Facts.* Employee *F* begins working 25 hours per week for Employer *X* on January 6 and is considered a part-time employee for purposes of *X*'s group health plan. *X* sponsors a group health plan that provides coverage to part-time employees after they have completed a cumulative 1,200 hours of service. *F* satisfies the plan's cumulative hours of service condition on December 15.

(ii) *Conclusion.* In this *Example 8,* the cumulative hours of service condition with respect to part-time employees is not considered to be designed to avoid compliance with the 90-day waiting period limitation. Accordingly, coverage for *F* under the plan must begin no later than the 91st day after *F* completes 1,200 hours. (If the plan's cumulative hours-of-service requirement was more than 1,200 hours, the requirement would be considered to be designed to avoid compliance with the 90-day waiting period limitation.)

Example 9. (i) *Facts.* A multiemployer plan operating pursuant to an arms-length collective bargaining agreement has an eligibility provision that allows employees to become eligible for coverage by working a specified number of hours of covered employment for multiple contributing employers. The plan aggregates hours in a calendar quarter and then, if enough hours are earned, coverage begins the first day of the next calendar quarter. The plan also permits coverage to extend for the next full calendar quarter, regardless of whether an employee's employment has terminated.

(ii) *Conclusion.* In this *Example 9,* these eligibility provisions are designed to accommodate a unique operating structure, and, therefore, are not considered to be designed to avoid compliance with the 90-day waiting period limitation, and the plan complies with this section.

Example 10. (i) *Facts.* Employee *G* retires at age 55 after 30 years of employment with Employer *Y* with no expectation of providing further services to Employer *Y*. Three months later, *Y* recruits *G* to return to work as an employee providing advice and transition assistance for *G*'s replacement under a one-year employment contract. *Y*'s plan imposes a 90-day waiting period from an employee's start date before coverage becomes effective.

(ii) *Conclusion.* In this *Example 10,* Y's plan may treat *G* as newly eligible for coverage under the plan upon rehire and therefore may impose the 90-day waiting period with respect to *G* for coverage offered in connection with *G*'s rehire.

Example 11. (i) *Facts.* Employee *H* begins working full time for Employer *Z* on October 16. *Z* sponsors a group health plan, under which full time employees are eligible for coverage after they have successfully completed a bona fide one-month orientation period. *H* completes the orientation period on November 15.

(ii) *Conclusion.* In this *Example 11*, the orientation period is not considered a subterfuge for the passage of time and is not considered to be designed to avoid compliance with the 90-day waiting period limitation. Accordingly, plan coverage for *H* must begin no later than February 14, which is the 91st day after *H* completes the orientation period. (If the orientation period was longer than one month, it would be considered to be a subterfuge for the passage of time and designed to avoid compliance with the 90-day waiting period limitation. Accordingly it would violate the rules of this section.) [Added 6/25/2014 (79 FR 35942).]

(g) *Special rule for health insurance issuers.* To the extent coverage under a group health plan is insured by a health insurance issuer, the issuer is permitted to rely on the eligibility information reported to it by the employer (or other plan sponsor) and will not be considered to violate the requirements of this section with respect to its administration of any waiting period, if both of the following conditions are satisfied:

(1) The issuer requires the plan sponsor to make a representation regarding the terms of any eligibility conditions or waiting periods imposed by the plan sponsor before an individual is eligible to become covered under the terms of the plan (and requires the plan sponsor to update this representation with any changes), and

(2) The issuer has no specific knowledge of the imposition of a waiting period that would exceed the permitted 90-day period.

(h) *No effect on other laws.* Compliance with this section is not determinative of compliance with any other provision of State or Federal law (including ERISA, the Code, or other provisions of the Patient Protection and Affordable Care Act). *See e.g.,* § 2590.702, which prohibits discrimination in eligibility for coverage based on a health factor and Code section 4980H, which generally requires applicable large employers to offer coverage to full-time employees and their dependents or make an assessable payment.

(i) *Applicability date.* The provisions of this section apply for plan years beginning on or after January 1, 2015. *See* § 2590.715-1251 providing that the prohibition on waiting periods exceeding 90 days applies to all group health plans and group health insurance issuers, including grandfathered health plans.

Interim Final Regulations

Reg. §§ 2590.715-2711 and 2590.715-2712 were adopted and published in the *Federal Register* on June 28, 2010 (75 FR 37187). Reg. § 2590.715-2713 was adopted and published in the *Federal Register* on July 19, 2010 (75 FR 41726). Reg. § 2590.715-2713 was amended on August 3, 2011 (76 FR 46621). Reg. § 2590.715-2713 was finalized on July 14, 2015 (80 FR 41317). See ¶ 15,050R-50PA for the final version of the regulations.

>>>→ *Caution: Until final Reg. § 2590.715-2711 at ¶ 15,050R-50NA is applicable on the first day of the plan year beginning on or after January 1, 2017, plans and issuers must continue to comply with the below interim final regulation.*

[¶ 15,050R-50N]

§ 2590.715-2711 No lifetime or annual limits.

(a) *Prohibition.* (1) *Lifetime limits..* Except as provided in paragraph (b) of this section, a group health plan, or a health insurance issuer offering group health insurance coverage, may not establish any lifetime limit on the dollar amount of benefits for any individual.

(2) *Annual limits.* (i) *General rule..* Except as provided in paragraphs (a)(2)(ii), (b), and (d) of this section, a group health plan, or a health insurance issuer offering group health insurance coverage, may not establish any annual limit on the dollar amount of benefits for any individual.

(ii) *Exception for health flexible spending arrangements..* A health flexible spending arrangement (as defined in section 106(c)(2) of the Internal Revenue Code) is not subject to the requirement in paragraph (a)(2)(i) of this section.

(b) *Construction.* (1) *Permissible limits on specific covered benefits..* The rules of this section do not prevent a group health plan, or a health insurance issuer offering group health insurance coverage, from placing annual or lifetime dollar limits with respect to any individual on specific covered benefits that are not essential health benefits to the extent that such limits are otherwise permitted under applicable Federal or State law. (The scope of essential health benefits is addressed in paragraph (c) of this section).

(2) *Condition-based exclusions..* The rules of this section do not prevent a group health plan, or a health insurance issuer offering group health insurance coverage, from excluding all benefits for a condition. However, if any benefits are provided for a condition, then the requirements of this section apply. Other requirements of Federal or State law may require coverage of certain benefits.

(c) *Definition of essential health benefits..* The term "essential health benefits" means essential health benefits under section 1302(b) of the Patient Protection and Affordable Care Act and applicable regulations.

(d) *Restricted annual limits permissible prior to 2014.* (1) *In general..* With respect to plan years beginning prior to January 1, 2014, a group health plan, or a health insurance issuer offering group health insurance coverage, may establish, for any individual, an annual limit on the dollar amount of benefits that are essential health benefits, provided the limit is no less than the amounts in the following schedule:

(i) For a plan year beginning on or after September 23, 2010, but before September 23, 2011, $750,000.

(ii) For a plan year beginning on or after September 23, 2011, but before September 23, 2012, $1,250,000.

(iii) For plan years beginning on or after September 23, 2012, but before January 1, 2014, $2,000,000.

(2) *Only essential health benefits taken into account..* In determining whether an individual has received benefits that meet or exceed the applicable amount described in paragraph (d)(1) of this section, a plan or issuer must take into account only essential health benefits.

(3) *Waiver authority of the Secretary of Health and Human Services..* For plan years beginning before January 1, 2014, the Secretary of Health and Human Services may establish a program under which the requirements of paragraph (d)(1) of this section relating to annual limits may be waived (for such period as is specified by the Secretary of Health and Human Services) for a group health plan or health insurance coverage that has an annual dollar limit on benefits below the restricted annual limits provided under paragraph (d)(1) of this section if compliance with paragraph (d)(1) of this section would result in a significant decrease in access to benefits under the plan or health insurance coverage or would significantly increase premiums for the plan or health insurance coverage.

(e) *Transitional rules for individuals whose coverage or benefits ended by reason of reaching a lifetime limit.* (1) *In general..* The relief provided in the transitional rules of this paragraph (e) applies with respect to any individual—

(i) Whose coverage or benefits under a group health plan or group health insurance coverage ended by reason of reaching a lifetime limit on the dollar value of all benefits for any individual (which, under this section, is no longer permissible); and

(ii) Who becomes eligible (or is required to become eligible) for benefits not subject to a lifetime limit on the dollar value of all benefits under the group health plan or group health insurance coverage on the first day of the first plan year beginning on or after September 23, 2010, by reason of the application of this section.

(2) *Notice and enrollment opportunity requirements.* (i) If an individual described in paragraph (e)(1) of this section is eligible for benefits (or is required to become eligible for benefits) under the group health plan—or group health insurance coverage—described in paragraph (e)(1) of this section, the plan and the issuer are required to give the individual written notice that the lifetime limit on the dollar

value of all benefits no longer applies and that the individual, if covered, is once again eligible for benefits under the plan. Additionally, if the individual is not enrolled in the plan or health insurance coverage, or if an enrolled individual is eligible for but not enrolled in any benefit package under the plan or health insurance coverage, then the plan and issuer must also give such an individual an opportunity to enroll that continues for at least 30 days (including written notice of the opportunity to enroll). The notices and enrollment opportunity required under this paragraph (e)(2)(i) must be provided beginning not later than the first day of the first plan year beginning on or after September 23, 2010.

(ii) The notices required under paragraph (e)(2)(i) of this section may be provided to an employee on behalf of the employee's dependent. In addition, the notices may be included with other enrollment materials that a plan distributes to employees, provided the statement is prominent. For either notice, if a notice satisfying the requirements of this paragraph (e)(2) is provided to an individual, the obligation to provide the notice with respect to that individual is satisfied for both the plan and the issuer.

(3) *Effective date of coverage..* In the case of an individual who enrolls under paragraph (e)(2) of this section, coverage must take effect not later than the first day of the first plan year beginning on or after September 23, 2010.

(4) *Treatment of enrollees in a group health plan..* Any individual enrolling in a group health plan pursuant to paragraph (e)(2) of this section must be treated as if the individual were a special enrollee, as provided under the rules of § 2590.701-6(d) of this part. Accordingly, the individual (and, if the individual would not be a participant once enrolled in the plan, the participant through whom the individual is otherwise eligible for coverage under the plan) must be offered all the benefit packages available to similarly situated individuals who did not lose coverage by reason of reaching a lifetime limit on the dollar value of all benefits. For this purpose, any difference in benefits or cost-sharing requirements constitutes a different benefit package. The individual also cannot be required to pay more for coverage than similarly situated individuals who did not lose coverage by reason of reaching a lifetime limit on the dollar value of all benefits.

(5) *Examples..* The rules of this paragraph (e) are illustrated by the following examples:

Example 1. (i) *Facts.* Employer *Y* maintains a group health plan with a calendar year plan year. The plan has a single benefit package. For plan years beginning before September 23, 2010, the plan has a lifetime limit on the dollar value of all benefits. Individual *B*, an employee of *Y*, was enrolled in *Y*'s group health plan at the beginning of the 2008 plan year. On June 10, 2008, *B* incurred a claim for benefits that exceeded the lifetime limit under *Y*'s plan and ceased to be enrolled in the plan. *B* is still eligible for coverage under *Y*'s group health plan. On or before January 1, 2011, *Y*'s group health plan gives *B* written notice informing *B* that the lifetime limit on the dollar value of all benefits no longer applies, that individuals whose coverage ended by reason of reaching a lifetime limit under the plan are eligible to enroll in the plan, and that individuals can request such enrollment through February 1, 2011 with enrollment effective retroactively to January 1, 2011.

(ii) *Conclusion.* In this *Example 1,* the plan has complied with the requirements of this paragraph (e) by providing a timely written notice and enrollment opportunity to *B* that lasts at least 30 days.

Example 2. (i) *Facts.* Employer *Z* maintains a group health plan with a plan year beginning October 1 and ending September 30. Prior to October 1, 2010, the group health plan has a lifetime limit on the dollar value of all benefits. Individual *D*, an employee of *Z*, and Individual *E*, *D*'s child, were enrolled in family coverage under *Z*'s group health plan for the plan year beginning on October 1, 2008. On May 1, 2009, *E* incurred a claim for benefits that exceeded the lifetime limit under *Z*'s plan. *D* dropped family coverage but remains an employee of *Z* and is still eligible for coverage under *Z*'s group health plan.

(ii) *Conclusion.* In this *Example 2,* not later than October 1, 2010, the plan must provide *D* and *E* an opportunity to enroll (including written notice of an opportunity to enroll) that continues for at least 30 days, with enrollment effective not later than October 1, 2010.

Example 3. (i) *Facts.* Same facts as *Example 2,* except that *Z*'s plan had two benefit packages (a low-cost and a high-cost option). Instead of dropping coverage, *D* switched to the low-cost benefit package option.

(ii) *Conclusion.* In this *Example 3,* not later than October 1, 2010, the plan must provide *D* and *E* an opportunity to enroll in any benefit package available to similarly situated individuals who enroll when first eligible. The plan would have to provide *D* and *E* the opportunity to enroll in any benefit package available to similarly situated individuals who enroll when first eligible, even if *D* had not switched to the low-cost benefit package option.

Example 4. (i) *Facts.* Employer *Q* maintains a group health plan with a plan year beginning October 1 and ending September 30. For the plan year beginning on October 1, 2009, *Q* has an annual limit on the dollar value of all benefits of $500,000.

(ii) *Conclusion.* In this *Example 4,* Q must raise the annual limit on the dollar value of essential health benefits to at least $750,000 for the plan year beginning October 1, 2010. For the plan year beginning October 1, 2011, *Q* must raise the annual limit to at least $1.25 million. For the plan year beginning October 1, 2012, *Q* must raise the annual limit to at least $2 million. *Q* may also impose a restricted annual limit of $2 million for the plan year beginning October 1, 2013. After the conclusion of that plan year, *Q* cannot impose an overall annual limit.

Example 5. (i) *Facts.* Same facts as *Example 4,* except that the annual limit for the plan year beginning on October 1, 2009 is $1 million and *Q* lowers the annual limit for the plan year beginning October 1, 2010 to $750,000.

(ii) *Conclusion.* In this *Example 5,* Q complies with the requirements of this paragraph (e). However, *Q*'s choice to lower its annual limit means that under § 2590.715-1251(g)(1)(vi)(C), the group health plan will cease to be a grandfathered health plan and will be generally subject to all of the provisions of PHS Act sections 2701 through 2719A.

(f) *Applicability date..* The provisions of this section apply for plan years beginning on or after September 23, 2010. *See* § 2590.715-1251 of this Part for determining the application of this section to grandfathered health plans (providing that the prohibitions on lifetime and annual limits apply to all grandfathered health plans that are group health plans and group health insurance coverage, including the special rules regarding restricted annual limits).

Regulations

Reg. § 2590.715-2711 was revised and finalized on November 18, 2015 (80 FR 72191). Reg. § 2590.715-2711 was amended on October 31, 2016 (81 FR 75316).

[¶ 15,050R-50NA]

§ 2590.715-2711 No lifetime or annual limits.

(a) *Prohibition—*

(1) *Lifetime limits.* Except as provided in paragraph (b) of this section, a group health plan, or a health insurance issuer offering group health insurance coverage, may not establish any lifetime limit on the dollar amount of essential health benefits for any individual, whether provided in-network or out-of-network.

>→ *Caution: Reg. §2590.715-2711 is effective January 19, 2016, and applies to group health plans beginning on the first day of the first plan year beginning on or after January 1, 2017. Until the final regulations become applicable, plans and issuers are required to continue to comply with the corresponding EBSA interim final regulations, which apply for purposes of ERISA and the Code.*

(2) *Annual limits*—

(i) *General rule.* Except as provided in paragraphs (a)(2)(ii) and (b) of this section, a group health plan, or a health insurance issuer offering group health insurance coverage, may not establish any annual limit on the dollar amount of essential health benefits for any individual, whether provided in-network or out-of-network.

(ii) *Exception for health flexible spending arrangements.* A health flexible spending arrangement (as defined in section 106(c)(2) of the Internal Revenue Code) offered through a cafeteria plan pursuant to section 125 of the Internal Revenue Code is not subject to the requirement in paragraph (a)(2)(i) of this section.

(b) *Construction*—

(1) *Permissible limits on specific covered benefits.* The rules of this section do not prevent a group health plan, or a health insurance issuer offering group health insurance coverage, from placing annual or lifetime dollar limits with respect to any individual on specific covered benefits that are not essential health benefits to the extent that such limits are otherwise permitted under applicable Federal or State law. (The scope of essential health benefits is addressed in paragraph (c) of this section).

(2) *Condition-based exclusions.* The rules of this section do not prevent a group health plan, or a health insurance issuer offering group health insurance coverage, from excluding all benefits for a condition. However, if any benefits are provided for a condition, then the requirements of this section apply. Other requirements of Federal or State law may require coverage of certain benefits.

(c) *Definition of essential health benefits.* The term "essential health benefits" means essential health benefits under section 1302(b) of the Patient Protection and Affordable Care Act and applicable regulations. For this purpose, a group health plan or a health insurance issuer that is not required to provide essential health benefits under section 1302(b) must define "essential health benefits" in a manner that is consistent with—

(1) One of the EHB-benchmark plans applicable in a State under 45 CFR 156.110, and includes coverage of any additional required benefits that are considered essential health benefits consistent with 45 CFR 155.170(a)(2); or

(2) One of the three Federal Employees Health Benefits Program (FEHBP) plan options as defined by 45 CFR 156.100(a)(3), supplemented, as necessary, to meet the standards in 45 CFR 156.110. [Revised 10/31/16 by 81 FR 75316.]

(d) *Special rule for health reimbursement arrangements (HRAs) and other account-based plans*—

(1) *In general.* If an HRA or other account-based plan is integrated with other coverage under a group health plan and the other group health plan coverage alone satisfies the requirements in paragraph (a)(2) of this section, the fact that the benefits under the HRA or other account-based plan are limited does not mean that the HRA or other account-based plan fails to meet the requirements of paragraph (a)(2) of this section. Similarly, if an HRA or other account-based plan is integrated with other coverage under a group health plan and the other group health plan coverage alone satisfies the requirements in PHS Act section 2713 and §2590.715-2713(a)(1), the HRA or other account-based plan will not fail to meet the requirements of PHS Act section 2713 and §2590.715-2713(a)(1).

(2) *Integration requirements.* An HRA or other account-based plan is integrated with a group health plan for purposes of paragraph (a)(2) of this section if it meets the requirements under either the integration method set forth in paragraph (d)(2)(i) of this section or the integration method set forth in paragraph (d)(2)(ii) of this section. Integration does not require that the HRA (or other account-based plan) and the group health plan with which it is integrated share the same plan sponsor, the same plan document, or governing instru-

ments, or file a single Form 5500, if applicable. The term "excepted benefits" is used throughout the integration methods; for a definition of the term "excepted benefits" see Internal Revenue Code section 9832(c), ERISA section 733(c), and PHS Act section 2791(c).

(i) *Integration Method: Minimum value not required.* An HRA or other account-based plan is integrated with another group health plan for purposes of this paragraph if:

(A) The plan sponsor offers a group health plan (other than the HRA or other account-based plan) to the employee that does not consist solely of excepted benefits;

(B) The employee receiving the HRA or other account-based plan is actually enrolled in a group health plan (other than the HRA or other account-based plan) that does not consist solely of excepted benefits, regardless of whether the plan is offered by the same plan sponsor (referred to as non-HRA group coverage);

(C) The HRA or other account-based plan is available only to employees who are enrolled in non-HRA group coverage, regardless of whether the non-HRA group coverage is offered by the plan sponsor of the HRA or other account-based plan (for example, the HRA may be offered only to employees who do not enroll in an employer's group health plan but are enrolled in other non-HRA group coverage, such as a group health plan maintained by the employer of the employee's spouse);

(D) The benefits under the HRA or other account-based plan are limited to reimbursement of one or more of the following—co-payments, co-insurance, deductibles, and premiums under the non-HRA group coverage, as well as medical care (as defined under section 213(d) of the Internal Revenue Code) that does not constitute essential health benefits as defined in paragraph (c) of this section; and

(E) Under the terms of the HRA or other account-based plan, an employee (or former employee) is permitted to permanently opt out of and waive future reimbursements from the HRA or other account-based plan at least annually and, upon termination of employment, either the remaining amounts in the HRA or other account-based plan are forfeited or the employee is permitted to permanently opt out of and waive future reimbursements from the HRA or other account-based plan.

(ii) *Integration Method: Minimum value required.* An HRA or other account-based plan is integrated with another group health plan for purposes of this paragraph if:

(A) The plan sponsor offers a group health plan (other than the HRA or other account-based plan) to the employee that provides minimum value pursuant to Code section 36B(c)(2)(C)(ii) (and its implementing regulations and applicable guidance);

(B) The employee receiving the HRA or other account-based plan is actually enrolled in a group health plan that provides minimum value pursuant to section 36B(c)(2)(C)(ii) of the Internal Revenue Code (and applicable guidance), regardless of whether the plan is offered by the plan sponsor of the HRA or other account-based plan (referred to as non-HRA MV group coverage);

(C) The HRA or other account-based plan is available only to employees who are actually enrolled in non-HRA MV group coverage, regardless of whether the non-HRA MV group coverage is offered by the plan sponsor of the HRA or other account-based plan (for example, the HRA may be offered only to employees who do not enroll in an employer's group health plan but are enrolled in other non-HRA MV group coverage, such as a group health plan maintained by an employer of the employee's spouse); and

(D) Under the terms of the HRA or other account-based plan, an employee (or former employee) is permitted to permanently opt out of and waive future reimbursements from the HRA or other account-based plan at least annually, and, upon termination of employment, either the remaining amounts in the HRA or other account-based plan are forfeited or the employee is permitted to permanently opt out of and waive future reimbursements from the HRA or other account-based plan.

(3) *Forfeiture.* For purpose of integration under paragraphs (d)(2)(i)(E) and (d)(2)(ii)(D) of this section, forfeiture or waiver occurs even if the forfeited or waived amounts may be reinstated upon a fixed date, a participant's death, or the earlier of the two events (the reinstatement event). For this purpose coverage under an HRA or other account-based plan is considered forfeited or waived prior to a reinstatement event only if the participant's election to forfeit or waive is irrevocable, meaning that, beginning on the effective date of the election and through the date of the reinstatement event, the participant and the participant's beneficiaries have no access to amounts credited to the HRA or other account-based plan. This means that upon and after reinstatement, the reinstated amounts under the HRA or other account-based plan may not be used to reimburse or pay medical expenses incurred during the period after forfeiture and prior to reinstatement.

(4) *No integration with individual market coverage.* A group health plan, including an HRA or other account-based plan, used to purchase coverage on the individual market is not integrated with that individual market coverage for purposes of paragraph (a)(2) of this section (or for purposes of the requirements of PHS Act section 2713).

(5) *Integration with Medicare parts B and D.* For employers that are not required to offer their non-HRA group health plan coverage to employees who are Medicare beneficiaries, an HRA or other account-based plan that may be used to reimburse premiums under Medicare part B or D may be integrated with Medicare (and deemed to comply with PHS Act sections 2711 and 2713) if the following requirements are satisfied with respect to employees who would be eligible for the employer's non-HRA group health plan but for their eligibility for Medicare (and the integration rules under paragraphs (d)(2)(i) and (d)(2)(ii) of this section continue to apply to employees who are not eligible for Medicare):

(i) The plan sponsor offers a group health plan (other than the HRA or other account-based plan and that does not consist solely of excepted benefits) to employees who are not eligible for Medicare;

(ii) The employee receiving the HRA or other account-based plan is actually enrolled Medicare part B or D;

(iii) The HRA or other account-based plan is available only to employees who are enrolled in Medicare part B or D; and

(iv) The HRA or other account-based plan complies with paragraphs (d)(2)(i)(E) and (d)(2)(ii)(D) of this section.

(6) *Account-based plan.* An account-based plan for purposes of this section is an employer-provided group health plan that provides reimbursements of medical expenses other than individual market policy premiums with the reimbursement subject to a maximum fixed dollar amount for a period. An HRA is a type of account-based plan.

(e) *Applicability date.* The provisions of this section are applicable to group health plans and health insurance issuers for plan years beginning on or after January 1, 2017. Until the applicability date for this regulation, plans and issuers are required to continue to comply with the corresponding sections of 29 CFR part 2590, contained in the 29 CFR, parts 1927 to end, edition revised as of July 1, 2015.

Interim Final Regulations

Reg. § 2590.715-2712 was adopted and published in the Federal Register on June 28, 2010 (75 FR 37187).

[¶ 15,050R-50O]

§ 2590.715-2712 Rules regarding rescissions.

(a) *Prohibition on rescissions.* (1) A group health plan, or a health insurance issuer offering group health insurance coverage, must not rescind coverage under the plan, or under the policy, certificate, or contract of insurance, with respect to an individual (including a group to which the individual belongs or family coverage in which the individual is included) once the individual is covered under the plan or coverage, unless the individual (or a person seeking coverage on behalf of the individual) performs an act, practice, or omission that constitutes fraud, or unless the individual makes an intentional misrepresentation of material fact, as prohibited by the terms of the plan or coverage. A group health plan, or a health insurance issuer offering group health insurance coverage, must provide at least 30 days advance written notice to each participant who would be affected before coverage may be rescinded under this paragraph (a)(1), regardless of whether the coverage is insured or self-insured, or whether the rescission applies to an entire group or only to an individual within the group. (The rules of this paragraph (a)(1) apply regardless of any contestability period that may otherwise apply.)

(2) For purposes of this section, a rescission is a cancellation or discontinuance of coverage that has retroactive effect. For example, a cancellation that treats a policy as void from the time of the individual's or group's enrollment is a rescission. As another example, a cancellation that voids benefits paid up to a year before the cancellation is also a rescission for this purpose. A cancellation or discontinuance of coverage is not a rescission if -

(i) The cancellation or discontinuance of coverage has only a prospective effect; or

(ii) The cancellation or discontinuance of coverage is effective retroactively to the extent it is attributable to a failure to timely pay required premiums or contributions towards the cost of coverage.

(3) The rules of this paragraph (a) are illustrated by the following examples:

Example 1. (i) *Facts.* Individual *A* seeks enrollment in an insured group health plan. The plan terms permit rescission of coverage with respect to an individual if the individual engages in fraud or makes an intentional misrepresentation of a material fact. The plan requires *A* to complete a questionnaire regarding *A's* prior medical history, which affects setting the group rate by the health insurance issuer. The questionnaire complies with the other requirements of this part. The questionnaire includes the following question: "Is there anything else relevant to your health that we should know?" *A* inadvertently fails to list that *A* visited a psychologist on two occasions, six years previously. *A* is later diagnosed with breast cancer and seeks benefits under the plan. On or around the same time, the issuer receives information about *A's* visits to the psychologist, which was not disclosed in the questionnaire.

(ii) *Conclusion.* In this *Example 1,* the plan cannot rescind *A's* coverage because *A's* failure to disclose the visits to the psychologist was inadvertent. Therefore, it was not fraudulent or an intentional misrepresentation of material fact.

Example 2. (i) *Facts.* An employer sponsors a group health plan that provides coverage for employees who work at least 30 hours per week. Individual *B* has coverage under the plan as a full-time employee. The employer reassigns *B* to a part-time position. Under the terms of the plan, *B* is no longer eligible for coverage. The plan mistakenly continues to provide health coverage, collecting premiums from *B* and paying claims submitted by *B*. After a routine audit, the plan discovers that *B* no longer works at least 30 hours per week. The plan rescinds *B's* coverage effective as of the date that *B* changed from a full-time employee to a part-time employee.

(ii) *Conclusion.* In this *Example 2,* the plan cannot rescind *B's* coverage because there was no fraud or an intentional misrepresentation of material fact. The plan may cancel coverage for *B* prospectively, subject to other applicable Federal and State laws.

(b) *Compliance with other requirements..* Other requirements of Federal or State law may apply in connection with a rescission of coverage.

>>>→ *Caution: Until final Reg. § 2590.715-2712 at ¶ 15,050R-50OA is applicable on the first day of the plan year beginning on or after January 1, 2017, plans and issuers must continue to comply with the below interim final regulation.*

(c) *Applicability date.*. The provisions of this section apply for plan years beginning on or after September 23, 2010. *See* § 2590.715-1251 of this part for determining the application of this section to grandfathered health plans (providing that the rules regarding rescissions and advance notice apply to all grandfathered health plans).

Regulations

Reg. § 2590.715-2712 was revised and finalized on November 18, 2015 (80 FR 72191).

>>>→ *Caution: Reg. § 2590.715-2712 is effective January 19, 2016, and applies to group health plans beginning on the first day of the first plan year beginning on or after January 1, 2017. Until the final regulations become applicable, plans and issuers are required to continue to comply with the corresponding EBSA interim final regulations, which apply for purposes of ERISA and the Code.*

[¶ 15,050R-50OA]

§ 2590.715-2712 Rules regarding rescissions.

(a) *Prohibition on rescissions—*

(1) A group health plan, or a health insurance issuer offering group health insurance coverage, must not rescind coverage under the plan, or under the policy, certificate, or contract of insurance, with respect to an individual (including a group to which the individual belongs or family coverage in which the individual is included) once the individual is covered under the plan or coverage, unless the individual (or a person seeking coverage on behalf of the individual) performs an act, practice, or omission that constitutes fraud, or makes an intentional misrepresentation of material fact, as prohibited by the terms of the plan or coverage. A group health plan, or a health insurance issuer offering group health insurance coverage, must provide at least 30 days advance written notice to each participant who would be affected before coverage may be rescinded under this paragraph (a)(1), regardless of whether the coverage is insured or self-insured, or whether the rescission applies to an entire group or only to an individual within the group. (The rules of this paragraph (a)(1) apply regardless of any contestability period that may otherwise apply.)

(2) For purposes of this section, a rescission is a cancellation or discontinuance of coverage that has retroactive effect. For example, a cancellation that treats a policy as void from the time of the individual's or group's enrollment is a rescission. As another example, a cancellation that voids benefits paid up to a year before the cancellation is also a rescission for this purpose. A cancellation or discontinuance of coverage is not a rescission if—

(i) The cancellation or discontinuance of coverage has only a prospective effect;

(ii) The cancellation or discontinuance of coverage is effective retroactively to the extent it is attributable to a failure to timely pay required premiums or contributions (including COBRA premiums) towards the cost of coverage;

(iii) The cancellation or discontinuance of coverage is initiated by the individual (or by the individual's authorized representative) and the sponsor, employer, plan, or issuer does not, directly or indirectly, take action to influence the individual's decision to cancel or discontinue coverage retroactively or otherwise take any adverse action or retaliate against, interfere with, coerce, intimidate, or threaten the individual; or

(iv) The cancellation or discontinuance of coverage is initiated by the Exchange pursuant to 45 CFR 155.430 (other than under paragraph (b)(2)(iii)).

(3) The rules of this paragraph (a) are illustrated by the following examples:

Example 1. (i) *Facts.* Individual *A* seeks enrollment in an insured group health plan. The plan terms permit rescission of coverage with respect to an individual if the individual engages in fraud or makes an intentional misrepresentation of a material fact. The plan requires *A* to complete a questionnaire regarding *A*'s prior medical history, which affects setting the group rate by the health insurance issuer. The questionnaire complies with the other requirements of this part. The questionnaire includes the following question: "Is there anything else relevant to your health that we should know?" *A* inadvertently fails to list that *A* visited a psychologist on two occasions, six years previously. *A* is later diagnosed with breast cancer and seeks benefits under the plan. On or around the same time, the issuer receives information about *A*'s visits to the psychologist, which was not disclosed in the questionnaire.

(ii) *Conclusion.* In this *Example 1*, the plan cannot rescind *A*'s coverage because *A*'s failure to disclose the visits to the psychologist was inadvertent. Therefore, it was not fraudulent or an intentional misrepresentation of material fact.

Example 2. (i) *Facts.* An employer sponsors a group health plan that provides coverage for employees who work at least 30 hours per week. Individual *B* has coverage under the plan as a full-time employee. The employer reassigns *B* to a part-time position. Under the terms of the plan, *B* is no longer eligible for coverage. The plan mistakenly continues to provide health coverage, collecting premiums from *B* and paying claims submitted by *B*. After a routine audit, the plan discovers that *B* no longer works at least 30 hours per week. The plan rescinds *B*'s coverage effective as of the date that *B* changed from a full-time employee to a part-time employee.

(ii) *Conclusion.* In this *Example 2*, the plan cannot rescind *B*'s coverage because there was no fraud or an intentional misrepresentation of material fact. The plan may cancel coverage for *B* prospectively, subject to other applicable Federal and State laws.

(b) *Compliance with other requirements.* Other requirements of Federal or State law may apply in connection with a rescission of coverage.

(c) *Applicability date.* The provisions of this section are applicable to group health plans and health insurance issuers for plan years beginning on or after January 1, 2017. Until the applicability date for this regulation, plans and issuers are required to continue to comply with the corresponding sections of 29 CFR part 2590, contained in the 29 CFR, parts 1927 to end, edition revised as of July 1, 2015.

Interim Final Regulations

Reg. § 2590.715-2713 was adopted and published in the Federal Register on July 19, 2010 (75 FR 41726). Reg. § 2590.715-2713 was amended on August 3, 2011 (76 FR 46621). Reg. § 2590.715-2713 was finalized on July 14, 2015 (80 FR 41317). See ¶ 15,050R-50PA for the final version of the regulations. Reg. § 2590.715-2713 was amended October 13, 2017 (82 FR 47792). Reg. § 2590.715-2713 was amended October 13, 2017 (82 FR 47838).

[¶ 15,050R-50P]

§ 2590.715-2713 Coverage of preventive health services.

(a) *Services—*

(1) *In general.* Beginning at the time described in paragraph (b) of this section and subject to § 2590.715-2713A, a group health plan, or a health insurance issuer offering group health insurance coverage, must provide coverage for and must not impose any cost-sharing requirements (such as a copayment, coinsurance, or a deductible) for—

* * * * *

(iv) With respect to women, such additional preventive care and screenings not described in paragraph (a)(1)(i) of this section as provided for in comprehensive guidelines supported by the Health Resources and Services Administration for purposes of section 2713(a)(4) of the Public Health Service Act, subject to 45 CFR 147.131, 147.132, and 147.133. [Amended 10/13/2017 by 82 FR 47838.]

[Amended 10/13/2017 by 82 FR 47792. Amended 10/13/2017 by 82 FR 47838.]

Final Regulations

Reg. §2590.715-2713(a)(1)(iv) was finalized on February 15, 2012 (77 FR 8725). Reg. §2590.715-2713(a)(1) was finalized and Reg. §2590.715-2713(a)(1)(iv) was amended on July 2, 2013 by 78 FR 39869. Reg. §2590.715-2713A was added on July 2, 2013 by 78 FR 39869. Reg. §2590.715-2713 was amended on July 14, 2015 (80 FR 41317). Reg. §2590.715-2713A was amended on July 14, 2015 (80 FR 41317).

[¶ 15,050R-50PA]

§ 2590.715-2713 Coverage of preventive health services.

(a) *Services.* (1) *In general.* Beginning at the time described in paragraph (b) of this section and subject to §2590.715–2713A, a group health plan, or a health insurance issuer offering group health insurance coverage, must provide coverage for all of the following items and services, and may not impose any cost-sharing requirements (such as a copayment, coinsurance, or a deductible) with respect to those items and services:

(i) Evidence-based items or services that have in effect a rating of A or B in the current recommendations of the United States Preventive Services Task Force with respect to the individual involved (except as otherwise provided in paragraph (c) of this section); [Amended 7/14/15 by 80 FR 41317.]

(ii) Immunizations for routine use in children, adolescents, and adults that have in effect a recommendation from the Advisory Committee on Immunization Practices of the Centers for Disease Control and Prevention with respect to the individual involved (for this purpose, a recommendation from the Advisory Committee on Immunization Practices of the Centers for Disease Control and Prevention is considered in effect after it has been adopted by the Director of the Centers for Disease Control and Prevention, and a recommendation is considered to be for routine use if it is listed on the Immunization Schedules of the Centers for Disease Control and Prevention); [Amended 7/14/15 by 80 FR 41317.]

(iii) With respect to infants, children, and adolescents, evidence-informed preventive care and screenings provided for in comprehensive guidelines supported by the Health Resources and Services Administration; and [Amended 7/14/15 by 80 FR 41317.]

(iv) With respect to women, to the extent not described in paragraph (a)(1)(i) of this section, evidence-informed preventive care and screenings provided for in binding comprehensive health plan coverage guidelines supported by the Health Resources and Services Administration, in accordance with 45 CFR 147.131(a). [Amended 7/2/13 by 78 FR 39869.]

(2) *Office visits.* (i) If an item or service described in paragraph (a)(1) of this section is billed separately (or is tracked as individual encounter data separately) from an office visit, then a plan or issuer may impose cost-sharing requirements with respect to the office visit.

(ii) If an item or service described in paragraph (a)(1) of this section is not billed separately (or is not tracked as individual encounter data separately) from an office visit and the primary purpose of the office visit is the delivery of such an item or service, then a plan or issuer may not impose cost-sharing requirements with respect to the office visit.

(iii) If an item or service described in paragraph (a)(1) of this section is not billed separately (or is not tracked as individual encounter data separately) from an office visit and the primary purpose of the office visit is not the delivery of such an item or service, then a plan or issuer may impose cost-sharing requirements with respect to the office visit.

(iv) The rules of this paragraph (a)(2) are illustrated by the following examples:

Example 1. (i) *Facts.* An individual covered by a group health plan visits an in-network health care provider. While visiting the provider, the individual is screened for cholesterol abnormalities, which has in effect a rating of A or B in the current recommendations of the United States Preventive Services Task Force with respect to the individual. The provider bills the plan for an office visit and for the laboratory work of the cholesterol screening test.

(ii) *Conclusion.* In this *Example 1,* the plan may not impose any cost-sharing requirements with respect to the separately-billed laboratory work of the cholesterol screening test. Because the office visit is billed separately from the cholesterol screening test, the plan may impose cost-sharing requirements for the office visit.

Example 2. (i) *Facts.* Same facts as *Example 1.* As the result of the screening, the individual is diagnosed with hyperlipidemia and is prescribed a course of treatment that is not included in the recommendations under paragraph (a)(1) of this section.

(ii) *Conclusion.* In this *Example 2,* because the treatment is not included in the recommendations under paragraph (a)(1) of this section, the plan is not prohibited from imposing cost-sharing requirements with respect to the treatment.

Example 3. (i) *Facts.* An individual covered by a group health plan visits an in-network health care provider to discuss recurring abdominal pain. During the visit, the individual has a blood pressure screening, which has in effect a rating of A or B in the current recommendations of the United States Preventive Services Task Force with respect to the individual. The provider bills the plan for an office visit.

(ii) *Conclusion.* In this *Example 3,* the blood pressure screening is provided as part of an office visit for which the primary purpose was not to deliver items or services described in paragraph (a)(1) of this section. Therefore, the plan may impose a cost-sharing requirement for the office visit charge.

Example 4. (i) *Facts.* A child covered by a group health plan visits an in-network pediatrician to receive an annual physical exam described as part of the comprehensive guidelines supported by the Health Resources and Services Administration. During the office visit, the child receives additional items and services that are not described in the comprehensive guidelines supported by the Health Resources and Services Administration, nor otherwise described in paragraph (a)(1) of this section. The provider bills the plan for an office visit.

(ii) *Conclusion.* In this *Example 4,* the service was not billed as a separate charge and was billed as part of an office visit. Moreover, the primary purpose for the visit was to deliver items and services described as part of the comprehensive guidelines supported by the Health Resources and Services Administration. Therefore, the plan may not impose a cost-sharing requirement with respect to the office visit. [Amended 7/14/15 by 80 FR 41317.]

(3) *Out-of-network providers.*

(i) Subject to paragraph (a)(3)(ii) of this section, nothing in this section requires a plan or issuer that has a network of providers to provide benefits for items or services described in paragraph (a)(1) of this section that are delivered by an out-of-network provider. Moreover, nothing in this section precludes a plan or issuer that has a network of providers from imposing cost-sharing requirements for items or services described in paragraph (a)(1) of this section that are delivered by an out-of-network provider.

(ii) If a plan or issuer does not have in its network a provider who can provide an item or service described in paragraph (a)(1) of this section, the plan or issuer must cover the item or service when performed by an out-of-network provider, and may not impose cost sharing with respect to the item or service. [Amended 7/14/15 by 80 FR 41317.]

(4) *Reasonable medical management.* Nothing prevents a plan or issuer from using reasonable medical management techniques to determine the frequency, method, treatment, or setting for an item or service described in paragraph (a)(1) of this section to the extent not specified in the relevant recommendation or guideline. To the extent not specified in a recommendation or guideline, a plan or issuer may rely on the relevant clinical evidence base and established reasonable medical management techniques to determine the frequency, method, treatment, or setting for coverage of a recommended preventive health service. [Amended 7/14/15 by 80 FR 41317.]

(5) *Services not described.* Nothing in this section prohibits a plan or issuer from providing coverage for items and services in addition to those recommended by the United States Preventive Services Task Force or the Advisory Committee on Immunization Practices of the Centers for Disease Control and Prevention, or provided for

by guidelines supported by the Health Resources and Services Administration, or from denying coverage for items and services that are not recommended by that task force or that advisory committee, or under those guidelines. A plan or issuer may impose cost-sharing requirements for a treatment not described in paragraph (a)(1) of this section, even if the treatment results from an item or service described in paragraph (a)(1) of this section. [Amended 7/14/15 by 80 FR 41317.]

(b) *Timing.* (1) *In general.* A plan or issuer must provide coverage pursuant to paragraph (a)(1) of this section for plan years that begin on or after September 23, 2010, or, if later, for plan years that begin on or after the date that is one year after the date the recommendation or guideline is issued. [Amended 7/14/15 by 80 FR 41317.]

(2) *Changes in recommendations or guidelines.* (i) A plan or issuer that is required to provide coverage for any items and services specified in any recommendation or guideline described in paragraph (a)(1) of this section on the first day of a plan year must provide coverage through the last day of the plan year, even if the recommendation or guideline changes or is no longer described in paragraph (a)(1) of this section, during the plan year.

(ii) Notwithstanding paragraph (b)(2)(i) of this section, to the extent a recommendation or guideline described in paragraph (a)(1)(i) of this section that was in effect on the first day of a plan year is downgraded to a "D" rating, or any item or service associated with any recommendation or guideline specified in paragraph (a)(1) of this section is subject to a safety recall or is otherwise determined to pose a significant safety concern by a federal agency authorized to regulate the item or service during a plan year, there is no requirement under this section to cover these items and services through the last day of the plan year. [Amended 7/14/15 by 80 FR 41317.]

(c) *Recommendations not current.* For purposes of paragraph (a)(1)(i) of this section, and for purposes of any other provision of law, recommendations of the United States Preventive Services Task Force regarding breast cancer screening, mammography, and prevention issued in or around November 2009 are not considered to be current. [Amended 7/14/15 by 80 FR 41317.]

(d) *Applicability date.* The provisions of this section apply for plan years beginning on or after September 23, 2010. *See* § 2590.715-1251 of this Part for determining the application of this section to grandfathered health plans (providing that these rules regarding coverage of preventive health services do not apply to grandfathered health plans). [Amended 7/14/15 by 80 FR 41317.]

[¶ 15,050R-50PB]

§ 2590.715-2713A Accommodations in connection with coverage of preventive health services.

(a) *Eligible organizations.* An eligible organization is an organization that meets the criteria of paragraphs (a)(1) through (3) of this section.

(1) The organization opposes providing coverage for some or all of any contraceptive items or services required to be covered under § 2590.715-2713(a)(1)(iv) on account of religious objections.

(2)(i) The organization is organized and operates as a nonprofit entity and holds itself out as a religious organization; or

(ii) The organization is organized and operates as a closely held for-profit entity, as defined in paragraph (a)(4) of this section, and the organization's highest governing body (such as its board of directors, board of trustees, or owners, if managed directly by its owners) has adopted a resolution or similar action, under the organization's applicable rules of governance and consistent with state law, establishing that it objects to covering some or all of the contraceptive services on account of the owners' sincerely held religious beliefs.

(3) The organization must self-certify in the form and manner specified by the Secretary or provide notice to the Secretary of Health and Human Services as described in paragraph (b) or (c) of this section. The organization must make such self-certification or notice available for examination upon request by the first day of the first plan year to which the accommodation in paragraph (b) or (c) of this section applies. The self-certification or notice must be executed by a person authorized to make the certification or notice on behalf of the

organization, and must be maintained in a manner consistent with the record retention requirements under section 107 of ERISA.

(4) A closely held for-profit entity is an entity that—

(i) Is not a nonprofit entity;

(ii) Has no publicly traded ownership interests (for this purpose, a publicly traded ownership interest is any class of common equity securities required to be registered under section 12 of the Securities Exchange Act of 1934); and

(iii) Has more than 50 percent of the value of its ownership interest owned directly or indirectly by five or fewer individuals, or has an ownership structure that is substantially similar thereto, as of the date of the entity's self-certification or notice described in paragraph (b) or (c) of this section.

(iv) For the purpose of the calculation in paragraph (a)(4)(iii) of this section, the following rules apply:

(A) Ownership interests owned by a corporation, partnership, estate, or trust are considered owned proportionately by such entity's shareholders, partners, or beneficiaries. Ownership interests owned by a nonprofit entity are considered owned by a single owner.

(B) An individual is considered to own the ownership interests owned, directly or indirectly, by or for his or her family. Family includes only brothers and sisters (including half-brothers and half-sisters), a spouse, ancestors, and lineal descendants.

(C) If a person holds an option to purchase ownership interests, he or she is considered to be the owner of those ownership interests.

(v) A for-profit entity that seeks further information regarding whether it qualifies for the accommodation described in this section may send a letter describing its ownership structure to the Department of Health and Human Services. An entity must submit the letter in the manner described by the Department of Health and Human Services. If the entity does not receive a response from the Department of Health and Human Services to a properly submitted letter describing the entity's current ownership structure within 60 calendar days, as long as the entity maintains that structure it will be considered to meet the requirement set forth in paragraph (a)(4)(iii) of this section. [Amended 7/14/15 by 80 FR 41317.]

(b) *Contraceptive coverage—self-insured group health plans—*

(1) A group health plan established or maintained by an eligible organization that provides benefits on a self-insured basis complies for one or more plan years with any requirement under § 2590.715-2713(a)(1)(iv) to provide contraceptive coverage if all of the requirements of this paragraph (b)(1) are satisfied:

(i) The eligible organization or its plan contracts with one or more third party administrators.

(ii) The eligible organization provides either a copy of the self-certification to each third party administrator or a notice to the Secretary of Health and Human Services that it is an eligible organization and of its religious objection to coverage of all or a subset of contraceptive services.

(A) When a copy of the self-certification is provided directly to a third party administrator, such self-certification must include notice that obligations of the third party administrator are set forth in § 2510.3-16 of this chapter and this section.

(B) When a notice is provided to the Secretary of Health and Human Services, the notice must include the name of the eligible organization and the basis on which it qualifies for an accommodation; its objection based on sincerely held religious beliefs to coverage of some or all contraceptive services (including an identification of the subset of contraceptive services to which coverage the eligible organization objects, if applicable); the plan name and type (*i.e.,* whether it is a student health insurance plan within the meaning of 45 CFR 147.145(a) or a church plan within the meaning of ERISA section 3(33)); and the name and contact information for any of the plan's third party administrators and health insurance issuers. If there is a change in any of the information required to be included in the notice, the organization must provide updated information to the Secretary of Health and Human Services. The Department of Labor (working with the Department of Health and Human Services), shall send a separate notification to each of the plan's third party administrators informing the third party administrator that the Secretary of Health and Human Services has received a notice under paragraph (b)(1)(ii) of this section and describing the obligations of the third party administrator under § 2510.3–16 of this chapter and this section.

(2) If a third party administrator receives a copy of the self-certification from an eligible organization or a notification from the Department of Labor, as described in paragraph (b)(1)(ii) of this section, and agrees to enter into or remain in a contractual relationship with the eligible organization or its plan to provide administrative services for the plan, the third party administrator shall provide or arrange payments for contraceptive services using one of the following methods—

(i) Provide payments for contraceptive services for plan participants and beneficiaries without imposing any cost-sharing requirements (such as a copayment, coinsurance, or a deductible), or imposing a premium, fee, or other charge, or any portion thereof, directly or indirectly, on the eligible organization, the group health plan, or plan participants or beneficiaries; or

(ii) Arrange for an issuer or other entity to provide payments for contraceptive services for plan participants and beneficiaries without imposing any cost-sharing requirements (such as a copayment, coinsurance, or a deductible), or imposing a premium, fee, or other charge, or any portion thereof, directly or indirectly, on the eligible organization, the group health plan, or plan participants or beneficiaries.

(3) If a third party administrator provides or arranges payments for contraceptive services in accordance with either paragraph (b)(2)(i) or (ii) of this section, the costs of providing or arranging such payments may be reimbursed through an adjustment to the Federally-facilitated Exchange user fee for a participating issuer pursuant to 45 CFR 156.50(d).

(4) A third party administrator may not require any documentation other than a copy of the self-certification from the eligible organization or notification from the Department of Labor described in paragraph (b)(1)(ii) of this section. [Amended 7/14/15 by 80 FR 41317.]

(c) *Contraceptive coverage—insured group health plans.* (1) *General rule.* A group health plan established or maintained by an eligible organization that provides benefits through one or more group health insurance issuers complies for one or more plan years with any requirement under § 2590.715-2713(a)(1)(iv) to provide contraceptive coverage if the eligible organization or group health plan provides either a copy of the self-certification to each issuer providing coverage in connection with the plan or a notice to the Secretary of Health and Human Services that it is an eligible organization and of its religious objection to coverage for all or a subset of contraceptive services.

(i) When a copy of the self-certification is provided directly to an issuer, the issuer has sole responsibility for providing such coverage in accordance with § 2590.715–2713. An issuer may not require any further documentation from the eligible organization regarding its status as such.

(ii) When a notice is provided to the Secretary of Health and Human Services, the notice must include the name of the eligible organization and the basis on which it qualifies for an accommodation; its objection based on its sincerely held religious beliefs to coverage of some or all contraceptive services, as applicable (including an identification of the subset of contraceptive services to which coverage the eligible organization objects, if applicable); the plan name and type (*i.e.,* whether it is a student health insurance plan within the meaning of 45 CFR 147.145(a) or a church plan within the meaning of ERISA section 3(33)); and the name and contact information for any of the plan's third party administrators and health insurance issuers. If there is a change in any of the information required to be included in the notice, the organization must provide updated information to the Secretary of Health and Human Services. The Department of Health and Human Services will send a separate notification to each of the plan's health insurance issuers informing the issuer that the Secretary of Health and Human Services has received a notice under paragraph (c)(1) of this section and describing the obligations of the issuer under this section. [Amended 7/14/15 by 80 FR 41317.]

(2) *Payments for contraceptive services.* (i) A group health insurance issuer that receives a copy of the self-certification or notification described in paragraph (c)(1)(ii) of this section with respect to a group health plan established or maintained by an eligible organization in connection with which the issuer would otherwise provide contraceptive coverage under § 2590.715-2713(a)(1)(iv) must—[Amended 7/14/15 by 80 FR 41317.]

(A) Expressly exclude contraceptive coverage from the group health insurance coverage provided in connection with the group health plan; and

(B) Provide separate payments for any contraceptive services required to be covered under § 2590.715-2713(a)(1)(iv) for plan participants and beneficiaries for so long as they remain enrolled in the plan.

(ii) With respect to payments for contraceptive services, the issuer may not impose any cost-sharing requirements (such as a copayment, coinsurance, or a deductible), or impose any premium, fee, or other charge, or any portion thereof, directly or indirectly, on the eligible organization, the group health plan, or plan participants or beneficiaries. The issuer must segregate premium revenue collected from the eligible organization from the monies used to provide payments for contraceptive services. The issuer must provide payments for contraceptive services in a manner that is consistent with the requirements under sections 2706, 2709, 2711, 2713, 2719, and 2719A of the PHS Act, as incorporated into section 9815. If the group health plan of the eligible organization provides coverage for some but not all of any contraceptive services required to be covered under § 2590.715-2713(a)(1)(iv), the issuer is required to provide payments only for those contraceptive services for which the group health plan does not provide coverage. However, the issuer may provide payments for all contraceptive services, at the issuer's option.

(d) *Notice of availability of separate payments for contraceptive services—self-insured and insured group health plans.* For each plan year to which the accommodation in paragraph (b) or (c) of this section is to apply, a third party administrator required to provide or arrange payments for contraceptive services pursuant to paragraph (b) of this section, and an issuer required to provide payments for contraceptive services pursuant to paragraph (c) of this section, must provide to plan participants and beneficiaries written notice of the availability of separate payments for contraceptive services contemporaneous with (to the extent possible), but separate from, any application materials distributed in connection with enrollment (or re-enrollment) in group health coverage that is effective beginning on the first day of each applicable plan year. The notice must specify that the eligible organization does not administer or fund contraceptive benefits, but that the third party administrator or issuer, as applicable, provides separate payments for contraceptive services, and must provide contact information for questions and complaints. The following model language, or substantially similar language, may be used to satisfy the notice requirement of this paragraph (d): "Your employer has certified that your group health plan qualifies for an accommodation with respect to the federal requirement to cover all Food and Drug Administration-approved contraceptive services for women, as prescribed by a health care provider, without cost sharing. This means that your employer will not contract, arrange, pay, or refer for contraceptive coverage. Instead, [name of third party administrator/health insurance issuer] will provide or arrange separate payments for contraceptive services that you use, without cost sharing and at no other cost, for so long as you are enrolled in your group health plan. Your employer will not administer or fund these payments. If you have any questions about this notice, contact [contact information for third party administrator/health insurance issuer]."

(e) *Reliance—insured group health plans.* (1) If an issuer relies reasonably and in good faith on a representation by the eligible organization as to its eligibility for the accommodation in paragraph (c) of this section, and the representation is later determined to be incorrect, the issuer is considered to comply with any requirement under § 2590.715-2713(a)(1)(iv) to provide contraceptive coverage if the issuer complies with the obligations under this section applicable to such issuer.

(2) A group health plan is considered to comply with any requirement under § 2590.715-2713(a)(1)(iv) to provide contraceptive

coverage if the plan complies with its obligations under paragraph (c) of this section, without regard to whether the issuer complies with the obligations under this section applicable to such issuer.

Interim Final Regulations

Reg. § 2590.715-2714 was adopted and published in the *Federal Register* on May 13, 2010 by 75 FR 27121. Reg. § 2590.715-2714(h) was amended on June 17, 2010 (75 FR 34537). Reg. 2590.715-2713A was adopted and published in the *Federal Register* on August 27, 2014 (79 FR 51092). Reg. § 2590.715-2713A was finalized on July 14, 2015 (80 FR 41317). See ¶ 15,050R-50PB for the final version of the regulations. Reg. § 2590.715-2713A was revised October 13, 2017 (82 FR 47792). Reg. § 2590.715-2713A was amended October 13, 2017 (82 FR 47838).

[¶ 15,050R-50PC]

§ 2590.715-2713A **Accommodations in connection with coverage of preventive health services.**

(a) *Eligible organizations for optional accommodation.* An eligible organization is an organization that meets the criteria of paragraphs (a)(1) through (4) of this section.

(1) The organization is an objecting entity described in 45 CFR 147.132(a)(1)(i) or (ii), or 45 CFR 147.133(a)(1)(i) or (ii); [Amended 10/13/2017 by 82 FR 47838.]

(2) Notwithstanding its exempt status under 45 CFR 147.132(a) or 147.133(a), the organization voluntarily seeks to be considered an eligible organization to invoke the optional accommodation under paragraph (b) or (c) of this section as applicable; and [Amended 10/13/2017 by 82 FR 47838.]

(3) [Reserved]

(4) The organization self-certifies in the form and manner specified by the Secretary or provides notice to the Secretary of the Department of Health and Human Services as described in paragraph (b) or (c) of this section. To qualify as an eligible organization, the organization must make such self-certification or notice available for examination upon request by the first day of the first plan year to which the accommodation in paragraph (b) or (c) of this section applies. The self-certification or notice must be executed by a person authorized to make the certification or provide the notice on behalf of the organization, and must be maintained in a manner consistent with the record retention requirements under section 107 of ERISA.

(5) An eligible organization may revoke its use of the accommodation process, and its issuer or third party administrator must provide participants and beneficiaries written notice of such revocation as specified in guidance issued by the Secretary of the Department of Health and Human Services. If contraceptive coverage is currently being offered by an issuer or third party administrator through the accommodation process, the revocation will be effective on the first day of the first plan year that begins on or after 30 days after the date of the revocation (to allow for the provision of notice to plan participants in cases where contraceptive benefits will no longer be provided). Alternatively, an eligible organization may give 60-days notice pursuant to PHS Act section 2715(d)(4) and § 2590.715-2715(b), if applicable, to revoke its use of the accommodation process.

(b) *Optional accommodation-self-insured group health plans.*

(1) A group health plan established or maintained by an eligible organization that provides benefits on a self-insured basis may voluntarily elect an optional accommodation under which its third party administrator(s) will provide or arrange payments for all or a subset of contraceptive services for one or more plan years. To invoke the optional accommodation process:

(i) The eligible organization or its plan must contract with one or more third party administrators.

(ii) The eligible organization must provide either a copy of the self-certification to each third party administrator or a notice to the Secretary of the Department of Health and Human Services that it is an eligible organization and of its objection as described in 45 CFR 147.132 or 147.133 to coverage of all or a subset of contraceptive services. [Amended 10/13/2017 by 82 FR 47838.]

(A) When a copy of the self-certification is provided directly to a third party administrator, such self-certification must include notice that obligations of the third party administrator are set forth in § 2510.3-16 of this chapter and this section.

(B) When a notice is provided to the Secretary of Health and Human Services, the notice must include the name of the eligible organization; a statement that it objects as described in 45 CFR 147.132

or 147.133 to coverage of some or all contraceptive services (including an identification of the subset of contraceptive services to which coverage the eligible organization objects, if applicable), but that it would like to elect the optional accommodation process; the plan name and type (that is, whether it is a student health insurance plan within the meaning of 45 CFR 147.145(a) or a church plan within the meaning of section 3(33) of ERISA); and the name and contact information for any of the plan's third party administrators. If there is a change in any of the information required to be included in the notice, the eligible organization must provide updated information to the Secretary of the Department of Health and Human Services for the optional accommodation process to remain in effect. The Department of Labor (working with the Department of Health and Human Services), will send a separate notification to each of the plan's third party administrators informing the third party administrator that the Secretary of the Department of Health and Human Services has received a notice under paragraph (b)(1)(ii) of this section and describing the obligations of the third party administrator under § 2510.3-16 of this chapter and this section. [Amended 10/13/2017 by 82 FR 47838.]

(2) If a third party administrator receives a copy of the self-certification from an eligible organization or a notification from the Department of Labor, as described in paragraph (b)(1)(ii) of this section, and is willing to enter into or remain in a contractual relationship with the eligible organization or its plan to provide administrative services for the plan, then the third party administrator will provide or arrange payments for contraceptive services, using one of the following methods—

(i) Provide payments for the contraceptive services for plan participants and beneficiaries without imposing any cost-sharing requirements (such as a copayment, coinsurance, or a deductible), premium, fee, or other charge, or any portion thereof, directly or indirectly, on the eligible organization, the group health plan, or plan participants or beneficiaries; or

(ii) Arrange for an issuer or other entity to provide payments for contraceptive services for plan participants and beneficiaries without imposing any cost-sharing requirements (such as a copayment, coinsurance, or a deductible), premium, fee, or other charge, or any portion thereof, directly or indirectly, on the eligible organization, the group health plan, or plan participants or beneficiaries.

(3) If a third party administrator provides or arranges payments for contraceptive services in accordance with either paragraph (b)(2)(i) or (ii) of this section, the costs of providing or arranging such payments may be reimbursed through an adjustment to the Federally facilitated Exchange user fee for a participating issuer pursuant to 45 CFR 156.50(d).

(4) A third party administrator may not require any documentation other than a copy of the self-certification from the eligible organization or notification from the Department of Labor described in paragraph (b)(1)(ii) of this section.

(5) Where an otherwise eligible organization does not contract with a third party administrator and it files a self-certification or notice under paragraph (b)(1)(ii) of this section, the obligations under paragraph (b)(2) of this section do not apply, and the otherwise eligible organization is under no requirement to provide coverage or payments for contraceptive services to which it objects. The plan administrator for that otherwise eligible organization may, if it and the otherwise eligible organization choose, arrange for payments for contraceptive services from an issuer or other entity in accordance with paragraph (b)(2)(ii) of this section, and such issuer or other entity may receive reimbursements in accordance with paragraph (b)(3) of this section.

(c) *Optional accommodation—insured group health plans—*

(1) *General rule.* A group health plan established or maintained by an eligible organization that provides benefits through one or more

group health insurance issuers may voluntarily elect an optional accommodation under which its health insurance issuer(s) will provide payments for all or a subset of contraceptive services for one or more plan years. To invoke the optional accommodation process:

(i) The eligible organization or its plan must contract with one or more health insurance issuers.

(ii) The eligible organization must provide either a copy of the self-certification to each issuer providing coverage in connection with the plan or a notice to the Secretary of the Department of Health and Human Services that it is an eligible organization and of its objection as described in 45 CFR 147.132 or 147.133 to coverage for all or a subset of contraceptive services. [Amended 10/13/2017 by 82 FR 47838.]

(A) When a self-certification is provided directly to an issuer, the issuer has sole responsibility for providing such coverage in accordance with § 2590.715-2713.

(B) When a notice is provided to the Secretary of the Department of Health and Human Services, the notice must include the name of the eligible organization; a statement that it objects as described in 45 CFR 147.132 or 147.133 to coverage of some or all contraceptive services (including an identification of the subset of contraceptive services to which coverage the eligible organization objects, if applicable) but that it would like to elect the optional accommodation process; the plan name and type (that is, whether it is a student health insurance plan within the meaning of 45 CFR 147.145(a) or a church plan within the meaning of section 3(33) of ERISA); and the name and contact information for any of the plan's health insurance issuers. If there is a change in any of the information required to be included in the notice, the eligible organization must provide updated information to the Secretary of Department Health and Human Services for the optional accommodation process to remain in effect. The Department of Health and Human Services will send a separate notification to each of the plan's health insurance issuers informing the issuer that the Secretary of Health and Human Services has received a notice under paragraph (c)(2)(ii) of this section and describing the obligations of the issuer under this section. [Amended 10/13/2017 by 82 FR 47838.]

(2) If an issuer receives a copy of the self-certification from an eligible organization or the notification from the Department of Health and Human Services as described in paragraph (c)(2)(ii) of this section and does not have its own objection as described in 45 CFR 147.132 or 147.133 to providing the contraceptive services to which the eligible organization objects, then the issuer will provide payments for contraceptive services as follows—[Amended 10/13/2017 by 82 FR 47838.]

(i) The issuer must expressly exclude contraceptive coverage from the group health insurance coverage provided in connection with the group health plan and provide separate payments for any contraceptive services required to be covered under § 2590.715-2713(a)(1)(iv) for plan participants and beneficiaries for so long as they remain enrolled in the plan.

(ii) With respect to payments for contraceptive services, the issuer may not impose any cost-sharing requirements (such as a copayment, coinsurance, or a deductible), or impose any premium, fee, or other charge, or any portion thereof, directly or indirectly, on the eligible organization, the group health plan, or plan participants or beneficiaries. The issuer must segregate premium revenue collected from the eligible organization from the monies used to provide payments for contraceptive services. The issuer must provide payments for contraceptive services in a manner that is consistent with the require-

ments under sections 2706, 2709, 2711, 2713, 2719, and 2719A of the PHS Act, as incorporated into section 715 of ERISA. If the group health plan of the eligible organization provides coverage for some but not all of any contraceptive services required to be covered under § 2590.715-2713(a)(1)(iv), the issuer is required to provide payments only for those contraceptive services for which the group health plan does not provide coverage. However, the issuer may provide payments for all contraceptive services, at the issuer's option.

(3) A health insurance issuer may not require any documentation other than a copy of the self-certification from the eligible organization or the notification from the Department of Health and Human Services described in paragraph (c)(1)(ii) of this section.

(d) *Notice of availability of separate payments for contraceptive services—self-insured and insured group health plans.* For each plan year to which the optional accommodation in paragraph (b) or (c) of this section is to apply, a third party administrator required to provide or arrange payments for contraceptive services pursuant to paragraph (b) of this section, and an issuer required to provide payments for contraceptive services pursuant to paragraph (c) of this section, must provide to plan participants and beneficiaries written notice of the availability of separate payments for contraceptive services contemporaneous with (to the extent possible), but separate from, any application materials distributed in connection with enrollment (or re-enrollment) in group health coverage that is effective beginning on the first day of each applicable plan year. The notice must specify that the eligible organization does not administer or fund contraceptive benefits, but that the third party administrator or issuer, as applicable, provides or arranges separate payments for contraceptive services, and must provide contact information for questions and complaints. The following model language, or substantially similar language, may be used to satisfy the notice requirement of this paragraph (d): "Your employer has certified that your group health plan qualifies for an accommodation with respect to the Federal requirement to cover all Food and Drug Administration-approved contraceptive services for women, as prescribed by a health care provider, without cost sharing. This means that your employer will not contract, arrange, pay, or refer for contraceptive coverage. Instead, [name of third party administrator/health insurance issuer] will provide or arrange separate payments for contraceptive services that you use, without cost sharing and at no other cost, for so long as you are enrolled in your group health plan. Your employer will not administer or fund these payments. If you have any questions about this notice, contact [contact information for third party administrator/health insurance issuer]."

(e) *Definition.* For the purposes of this section, reference to "contraceptive" services, benefits, or coverage includes contraceptive or sterilization items, procedures, or services, or related patient education or counseling, to the extent specified for purposes of § 2590.715-2713(a)(1)(iv).

(f) *Severability.* Any provision of this section held to be invalid or unenforceable by its terms, or as applied to any person or circumstance, shall be construed so as to continue to give maximum effect to the provision permitted by law, unless such holding shall be one of utter invalidity or unenforceability, in which event the provision shall be severable from this section and shall not affect the remainder thereof or the application of the provision to persons not similarly situated or to dissimilar circumstances.

[Added 8/27/2014 by 79 FR 51092. Finalized on 7/14/2015 by 80 FR 41317. Revised 10/13/2017 by 82 FR 47792. Amended 10/13/2017 by 82 FR 47838.]

»»→ Caution: Until final Reg. § 2590.715-2714 at ¶ 15,050R-50QA is applicable on the first day of the plan year beginning on or after January 1, 2017, plans and issuers must continue to comply with the below interim final regulation.

[¶ 15,050R-50Q]
§ 2590.715-2714 **Eligibility of children until at least age 26.**

(a) *In general.* (1) A group health plan, or a health insurance issuer offering group health insurance coverage, that makes available dependent coverage of children must make such coverage available for children until attainment of 26 years of age.

(2) The rule of this paragraph (a) is illustrated by the following example:

Example. (i) *Facts.* For the plan year beginning January 1, 2011, a group health plan provides health coverage for employees, employees' spouses, and employees' children until the child turns 26. On the birthday of a child of an employee, July 17, 2011, the child turns 26. The last day the plan covers the child is July 16, 2011.

(ii) *Conclusion.* In this *Example*, the plan satisfies the requirement of this paragraph (a) with respect to the child.

(b) *Restrictions on plan definition of dependent.* With respect to a child who has not attained age 26, a plan or issuer may not define dependent for purposes of eligibility for dependent coverage of children other than in terms of a relationship between a child and the participant. Thus, for example, a plan or issuer may not deny or restrict coverage for a child who has not attained age 26 based on the presence or absence of the child's financial dependency (upon the participant or any other person), residency with the participant or with any other person, student status, employment, or any combination of those factors. In addition, a plan or issuer may not deny or restrict coverage of a child based on eligibility for other coverage, except that paragraph (g) of this section provides a special rule for plan years beginning before January 1, 2014 for grandfathered health plans that are group health plans. (Other requirements of Federal or State law, including section 609 of ERISA or section 1908 of the Social Security Act, may mandate coverage of certain children.)

(c) *Coverage of grandchildren not required.* Nothing in this section requires a plan or issuer to make coverage available for the child of a child receiving dependent coverage.

(d) *Uniformity irrespective of age.* The terms of the plan or health insurance coverage providing dependent coverage of children cannot vary based on age (except for children who are age 26 or older).

(e) *Examples.* The rules of paragraph (d) of this section are illustrated by the following examples:

Example 1. (i) *Facts.* A group health plan offers a choice of self-only or family health coverage. Dependent coverage is provided under family health coverage for children of participants who have not attained age 26. The plan imposes an additional premium surcharge for children who are older than age 18.

(ii) *Conclusion.* In this *Example 1*, the plan violates the requirement of paragraph (d) of this section because the plan varies the terms for dependent coverage of children based on age.

Example 2. (i) *Facts.* A group health plan offers a choice among the following tiers of health coverage: self-only, self-plus-one, self-plus-two, and self-plus-three-or-more. The cost of coverage increases based on the number of covered individuals. The plan provides dependent coverage of children who have not attained age 26.

(ii) *Conclusion.* In this *Example 2*, the plan does not violate the requirement of paragraph (d) of this section that the terms of dependent coverage for children not vary based on age. Although the cost of coverage increases for tiers with more covered individuals, the increase applies without regard to the age of any child.

Example 3. (i) *Facts.* A group health plan offers two benefit packages — an HMO option and an indemnity option. Dependent coverage is provided for children of participants who have not attained age 26. The plan limits children who are older than age 18 to the HMO option.

(ii) *Conclusion.* In this *Example 3*, the plan violates the requirement of paragraph (d) of this section because the plan, by limiting children who are older than age 18 to the HMO option, varies the terms for dependent coverage of children based on age.

(f) *Transitional rules for individuals whose coverage ended by reason of reaching a dependent eligibility threshold.* (1) *In general.* The relief provided in the transitional rules of this paragraph (f) applies with respect to any child—

(i) Whose coverage ended, or who was denied coverage (or was not eligible for coverage) under a group health plan or group health insurance coverage because, under the terms of the plan or coverage, the availability of dependent coverage of children ended before the attainment of age 26 (which, under this section, is no longer permissible); and

(ii) Who becomes eligible (or is required to become eligible) for coverage under a group health plan or group health insurance coverage on the first day of the first plan year beginning on or after September 23, 2010 by reason of the application of this section.

(2) *Opportunity to enroll required.* (i) If a group health plan, or group health insurance coverage, in which a child described in paragraph (f)(1) of this section is eligible to enroll (or is required to become eligible to enroll) is the plan or coverage in which the child's coverage ended (or did not begin) for the reasons described in paragraph (f)(1)(i) of this section, and if the plan, or the issuer of such coverage, is subject to the requirements of this section, the plan and the issuer are required to give the child an opportunity to enroll that continues for at least 30 days (including written notice of the opportunity to enroll). This opportunity (including the written notice) must be provided beginning not later than the first day of the first plan year beginning on or after September 23, 2010.

(ii) The written notice must include a statement that children whose coverage ended, or who were denied coverage (or were not eligible for coverage), because the availability of dependent coverage of children ended before attainment of age 26 are eligible to enroll in the plan or coverage. The notice may be provided to an employee on behalf of the employee's child. In addition, the notice may be included with other enrollment materials that a plan distributes to employees, provided the statement is prominent. If a notice satisfying the requirements of this paragraph (f)(2) is provided to an employee whose child is entitled to an enrollment opportunity under this paragraph (f), the obligation to provide the notice of enrollment opportunity under this paragraph (f)(2) with respect to that child is satisfied for both the plan and the issuer.

(3) *Effective date of coverage.* In the case of an individual who enrolls under paragraph (f)(2) of this section, coverage must take effect not later than the first day of the first plan year beginning on or after September 23, 2010.

(4) *Treatment of enrollees in a group health plan.* Any child enrolling in a group health plan pursuant to paragraph (f)(2) of this section must be treated as if the child were a special enrollee, as provided under the rules of § 2590.701-6(d) of this Part. Accordingly, the child (and, if the child would not be a participant once enrolled in the plan, the participant through whom the child is otherwise eligible for coverage under the plan) must be offered all the benefit packages available to similarly situated individuals who did not lose coverage by reason of cessation of dependent status. For this purpose, any difference in benefits or cost-sharing requirements constitutes a different benefit package. The child also cannot be required to pay more for coverage than similarly situated individuals who did not lose coverage by reason of cessation of dependent status.

(5) *Examples.* The rules of this paragraph (f) are illustrated by the following examples:

Example 1. (i) *Facts.* Employer *Y* maintains a group health plan with a calendar year plan year. The plan has a single benefit package. For the 2010 plan year, the plan allows children of employees to be covered under the plan until age 19, or until age 23 for children who are full-time students. Individual *B*, an employee of *Y*, and Individual *C*, *B*'s child and a fulltime student, were enrolled in *Y*'s group health plan at the beginning of the 2010 plan year. On June 10, 2010, *C* turns 23 years old and loses dependent coverage under *Y*'s plan. On or before January 1, 2011, *Y*'s group health plan gives *B* written notice that individuals who lost coverage by reason of ceasing to be a dependent before attainment of age 26 are eligible to enroll in the plan, and that individuals may request enrollment for such children through February 14, 2011 with enrollment effective retroactively to January 1, 2011.

(ii) *Conclusion.* In this *Example 1*, the plan has complied with the requirements of this paragraph (f) by providing an enrollment opportunity to *C* that lasts at least 30 days.

Example 2. (i) *Facts.* Employer *Z* maintains a group health plan with a plan year beginning October 1 and ending September 30. Prior to October 1, 2010, the group health plan allows children of employees to be covered under the plan until age 22. Individual *D*, an employee of *Z*, and Individual *E*, *D*'s child, are enrolled in family coverage under *Z*'s group health plan for the plan year beginning on October 1, 2008. On May 1, 2009, *E* turns 22 years old and ceases to be eligible as a dependent under *Z*'s plan and loses coverage. *D* drops coverage but remains an employee of *Z*.

(ii) *Conclusion.* In this *Example 2*, not later than October 1, 2010, the plan must provide D and E an opportunity to enroll (including

>>>→ *Caution: Until final Reg. § 2590.715-2714 at ¶ 15,050R-50QA is applicable on the first day of the plan year beginning on or after January 1, 2017, plans and issuers must continue to comply with the below interim final regulation.*

written notice of an opportunity to enroll) that continues for at least 30 days, with enrollment effective not later than October 1, 2010.

Example 3. (i) *Facts.* Same facts as *Example 2*, except that *D* did not drop coverage. Instead, *D* switched to a lower-cost benefit package option.

(ii) *Conclusion.* In this *Example 3*, not later than October 1, 2010, the plan must provide *D* and *E* an opportunity to enroll in any benefit package available to similarly situated individuals who enroll when first eligible.

Example 4. (i) *Facts.* Same facts as *Example 2*, except that *E* elected COBRA continuation coverage.

(ii) *Conclusion.* In this *Example 4*, not later than October 1, 2010, the plan must provide *D* and *E* an opportunity to enroll other than as a COBRA qualified beneficiary (and must provide, by that date, written notice of the opportunity to enroll) that continues for at least 30 days, with enrollment effective not later than October 1, 2010.

Example 5. (i) *Facts.* Employer *X* maintains a group health plan with a calendar year plan year. Prior to 2011, the plan allows children of employees to be covered under the plan until the child attains age 22. During the 2009 plan year, an individual with a 22-year old child joins the plan; the child is denied coverage because the child is 22.

(ii) *Conclusion.* In this *Example 5*, notwithstanding that the child was not previously covered under the plan, the plan must provide the

child, not later than January 1, 2011, an opportunity to enroll (including written notice to the employee of an opportunity to enroll the child) that continues for at least 30 days, with enrollment effective not later than January 1, 2011.

(g) *Special rule for grandfathered group health plans.* (1) For plan years beginning before January 1, 2014, a group health plan that qualifies as a grandfathered health plan under section 1251 of the Patient Protection and Affordable Care Act and that makes available dependent coverage of children may exclude an adult child who has not attained age 26 from coverage only if the adult child is eligible to enroll in an eligible employer-sponsored health plan (as defined in section 5000A(f)(2) of the Internal Revenue Code) other than a group health plan of a parent.

(2) For plan years beginning on or after January 1, 2014, a group health plan that qualifies as a grandfathered health plan under section 1251 of the Patient Protection and Affordable Care Act must comply with the requirements of paragraphs (a) through (f) of this section.

(h) *Applicability date.* The provisions of this section apply for plan years beginning on or after September 23, 2010. *See* § 2590.715-1251 of this Part for determining the application of this section to grandfathered health plans. [Amended 6/17/10 (75 FR 34537).]

Final Regulations

Reg. § 2590.715-2715 was adopted and published in the *Federal Register* on February 14, 2012 by 77 FR 8668. Reg. § 2590.715-2715 was revised by 80 FR 34292 on June 16, 2015. Reg. § 2590.715-2714 was revised and finalized on November 18, 2015 (80 FR 72191). Reg. § 2590.715-2715 was amended by interim final regulations on July 1, 2016 (81 FR 43429).

>>>→ *Caution: Reg. § 2590.715-2714 is effective January 19, 2016, and applies to group health plans beginning on the first day of the first plan year beginning on or after January 1, 2017. Until the final regulations become applicable, plans and issuers are required to continue to comply with the corresponding EBSA interim final regulations, which apply for purposes of ERISA and the Code.*

[¶ 15,050R-50QA]

§ 2590.715-2714 Eligibility of children until at least age 26.

(a) *In general—*

(1) A group health plan, or a health insurance issuer offering group health insurance coverage, that makes available dependent coverage of children must make such coverage available for children until attainment of 26 years of age.

(2) The rule of this paragraph (a) is illustrated by the following example:

Example. (i) *Facts.* For the plan year beginning January 1, 2011, a group health plan provides health coverage for employees, employees' spouses, and employees' children until the child turns 26. On the birthday of a child of an employee, July 17, 2011, the child turns 26. The last day the plan covers the child is July 16, 2011.

(ii) *Conclusion.* In this *Example*, the plan satisfies the requirement of this paragraph (a) with respect to the child.

(b) *Restrictions on plan definition of dependent—*

(1) *In general.* With respect to a child who has not attained age 26, a plan or issuer may not define dependent for purposes of eligibility for dependent coverage of children other than in terms of a relationship between a child and the participant. Thus, for example, a plan or issuer may not deny or restrict dependent coverage for a child who has not attained age 26 based on the presence or absence of the child's financial dependency (upon the participant or any other person); residency with the participant or with any other person; whether the child lives, works, or resides in an HMO's service area or other network service area; marital status; student status; employment; eligibility for other coverage; or any combination of those factors. (Other requirements of Federal or State law, including section 609 of ERISA or section 1908 of the Social Security Act, may require coverage of certain children.)

(2) *Construction.* A plan or issuer will not fail to satisfy the requirements of this section if the plan or issuer limits dependent child coverage to children under age 26 who are described in section 152(f)(1) of the Code. For an individual not described in Code section

152(f)(1), such as a grandchild or niece, a plan may impose additional conditions on eligibility for dependent child health coverage, such as a condition that the individual be a dependent for income tax purposes.

(c) *Coverage of grandchildren not required.* Nothing in this section requires a plan or issuer to make coverage available for the child of a child receiving dependent coverage.

(d) *Uniformity irrespective of age.* The terms of the plan or health insurance coverage providing dependent coverage of children cannot vary based on age (except for children who are age 26 or older).

(e) *Examples.* The rules of paragraph (d) of this section are illustrated by the following examples:

Example 1. (i) *Facts.* A group health plan offers a choice of self-only or family health coverage. Dependent coverage is provided under family health coverage for children of participants who have not attained age 26. The plan imposes an additional premium surcharge for children who are older than age 18.

(ii) *Conclusion.* In this *Example 1*, the plan violates the requirement of paragraph (d) of this section because the plan varies the terms for dependent coverage of children based on age.

Example 2. (i) *Facts.* A group health plan offers a choice among the following tiers of health coverage: Self-only, self-plus-one, self-plus-two, and self-plus-three-or-more. The cost of coverage increases based on the number of covered individuals. The plan provides dependent coverage of children who have not attained age 26.

(ii) *Conclusion.* In this *Example 2*, the plan does not violate the requirement of paragraph (d) of this section that the terms of dependent coverage for children not vary based on age. Although the cost of coverage increases for tiers with more covered individuals, the increase applies without regard to the age of any child.

Example 3. (i) *Facts.* A group health plan offers two benefit packages—an HMO option and an indemnity option. Dependent coverage is provided for children of participants who have not attained age 26. The plan limits children who are older than age 18 to the HMO option.

(ii) *Conclusion.* In this *Example 3*, the plan violates the requirement of paragraph (d) of this section because the plan, by limiting

***→** *Caution: Reg. § 2590.715-2714 is effective January 19, 2016, and applies to group health plans beginning on the first day of the first plan year beginning on or after January 1, 2017. Until the final regulations become applicable, plans and issuers are required to continue to comply with the corresponding EBSA interim final regulations, which apply for purposes of ERISA and the Code.*

children who are older than age 18 to the HMO option, varies the terms for dependent coverage of children based on age.

Example 4. (i) *Facts.* A group health plan sponsored by a large employer normally charges a copayment for physician visits that do not constitute preventive services. The plan charges this copayment to individuals age 19 and over, including employees, spouses, and dependent children, but waives it for those under age 19.

(ii) *Conclusion.* In this *Example 4*, the plan does not violate the requirement of paragraph (d) of this section that the terms of dependent coverage for children not vary based on age. While the requirement of paragraph (d) of this section generally prohibits distinctions based upon age in dependent coverage of children, it does not prohibit distinctions based upon age that apply to all coverage under the plan, including coverage for employees and spouses as well as dependent children. In this *Example 4*, the copayments charged to dependent children are the same as those charged to employees and spouses. Accordingly, the arrangement described in this *Example 4* (including waiver, for individuals under age 19, of the generally applicable copayment) does not violate the requirement of paragraph (d) of this section.

(f) *Applicability date.* The provisions of this section are applicable to group health plans and health insurance issuers for plan years beginning on or after January 1, 2017. Until the applicability date for this regulation, plans and issuers are required to continue to comply with the corresponding sections of 29 CFR part 2590, contained in the 29 CFR, parts 1927 to end, edition revised as of July 1, 2015.

***→** *Caution: Reg. § 2590.715-2715 is effective on August 17, 2015, and is applicable for disclosures for relevant participants and beneficiaries beginning on the first day of the first open enrollment period that begins on or after September 1, 2015 or beginning on the first day of the first plan year that begins on or after September 1, 2015.*

[¶ 15,050R-50RR]

§ 2590.715-2715 Summary of benefits and coverage and uniform glossary.

(a) *Summary of benefits and coverage—*

(1) *In general.* A group health plan (and its administrator as defined in section 3(16)(A) of ERISA)), and a health insurance issuer offering group health insurance coverage, is required to provide a written summary of benefits and coverage (SBC) for each benefit package without charge to entities and individuals described in this paragraph (a)(1) in accordance with the rules of this section.

(i) *SBC provided by a group health insurance issuer to a group health plan—*

(A) *Upon application.* A health insurance issuer offering group health insurance coverage must provide the SBC to a group health plan (or its sponsor) upon application for health coverage, as soon as practicable following receipt of the application, but in no event later than seven business days following receipt of the application. If an SBC was provided before application pursuant to paragraph (a)(1)(i)(D) of this section (relating to SBCs upon request), this paragraph (a)(1)(i)(A) is deemed satisfied, provided there is no change to the information required to be in the SBC. However, if there has been a change in the information required, a new SBC that includes the changed information must be provided upon application pursuant to this paragraph (a)(1)(i)(A).

(B) *By first day of coverage (if there are changes).* If there is any change in the information required to be in the SBC that was provided upon application and before the first day of coverage, the issuer must update and provide a current SBC to the plan (or its sponsor) no later than the first day of coverage.

(C) *Upon renewal, reissuance, or reenrollment.* If the issuer renews or reissues a policy, certificate, or contract of insurance for a succeeding policy year, or automatically re-enrolls the policyholder or its participants and beneficiaries in coverage, the issuer must provide a new SBC as follows:

(1) If written application is required (in either paper or electronic form) for renewal or reissuance, the SBC must be provided no later than the date the written application materials are distributed.

(2) If renewal, reissuance, or reenrollment is automatic, the SBC must be provided no later than 30 days prior to the first day of the new plan or policy year; however, with respect to an insured plan, if the policy, certificate, or contract of insurance has not been issued or renewed before such 30-day period, the SBC must be provided as soon as practicable but in no event later than seven business days after issuance of the new policy, certificate, or contract of insurance, or the receipt of written confirmation of intent to renew, whichever is earlier.

(D) *Upon request.* If a group health plan (or its sponsor) requests an SBC or summary information about a health insurance product from a health insurance issuer offering group health insurance coverage, an SBC must be provided as soon as practicable, but in no event later than seven business days following receipt of the request.

(ii) *SBC provided by a group health insurance issuer and a group health plan to participants and beneficiaries—*

(A) *In general.* A group health plan (including its administrator, as defined under section 3(16) of ERISA), and a health insurance issuer offering group health insurance coverage, must provide an SBC to a participant or beneficiary (as defined under sections 3(7) and 3(8) of ERISA), and consistent with the rules of paragraph (a)(1)(iii) of this section, with respect to each benefit package offered by the plan or issuer for which the participant or beneficiary is eligible.

(B) *Upon application.* The SBC must be provided as part of any written application materials that are distributed by the plan or issuer for enrollment. If the plan or issuer does not distribute written application materials for enrollment, the SBC must be provided no later than the first date on which the participant is eligible to enroll in coverage for the participant or any beneficiaries. If an SBC was provided before application pursuant to paragraph (a)(1)(ii)(F) of this section (relating to SBCs upon request), this paragraph (a)(1)(ii)(B) is deemed satisfied, provided there is no change to the information required to be in the SBC. However, if there has been a change in the information that is required to be in the SBC, a new SBC that includes the changed information must be provided upon application pursuant to this paragraph (a)(1)(ii)(B).

(C) *By first day of coverage (if there are changes).* (1) If there is any change to the information required to be in the SBC that was provided upon application and before the first day of coverage, the plan or issuer must update and provide a current SBC to a participant or beneficiary no later than the first day of coverage.

(2) If the plan sponsor is negotiating coverage terms after an application has been filed and the information required to be in the SBC changes, the plan or issuer is not required to provide an updated SBC (unless an updated SBC is requested) until the first day of coverage.

(D) *Special enrollees.* The plan or issuer must provide the SBC to special enrollees (as described in § 2590.701-6) no later than the date by which a summary plan description is required to be provided under the timeframe set forth in ERISA section 104(b)(1)(A) and its implementing regulations, which is 90 days from enrollment.

(E) *Upon renewal, reissuance, or reenrollment.* If the plan or issuer requires participants or beneficiaries to renew in order to maintain coverage (for example, for a succeeding plan year), or automatically re-enrolls participants and beneficiaries in coverage, the plan or issuer must provide a new SBC, as follows:

(1) If written application is required for renewal, reissuance, or reenrollment (in either paper or electronic form), the SBC must be provided no later than the date on which the written application materials are distributed.

>»→ *Caution: Reg. §2590.715-2715 is effective on August 17, 2015, and is applicable for disclosures for relevant participants and beneficiaries beginning on the first day of the first open enrollment period that begins on or after September 1, 2015 or beginning on the first day of the first plan year that begins on or after September 1, 2015.*

(2) If renewal, reissuance, or reenrollment is automatic, the SBC must be provided no later than 30 days prior to the first day of the new plan or policy year; however, with respect to an insured plan, if the policy, certificate, or contract of insurance has not been issued or renewed before such 30-day period, the SBC must be provided as soon as practicable but in no event later than seven business days after issuance of the new policy, certificate, or contract of insurance, or the receipt of written confirmation of intent to renew, whichever is earlier.

(F) *Upon request.* A plan or issuer must provide the SBC to participants or beneficiaries upon request for an SBC or summary information about the health coverage, as soon as practicable, but in no event later than seven business days following receipt of the request.

(iii) *Special rules to prevent unnecessary duplication with respect to group health coverage—*

(A) An entity required to provide an SBC under this paragraph (a)(1) with respect to an individual satisfies that requirement if another party provides the SBC, but only to the extent that the SBC is timely and complete in accordance with the other rules of this section. Therefore, for example, in the case of a group health plan funded through an insurance policy, the plan satisfies the requirement to provide an SBC with respect to an individual if the issuer provides a timely and complete SBC to the individual. An entity required to provide an SBC under this paragraph (a)(1) with respect to an individual that contracts with another party to provide such SBC is considered to satisfy the requirement to provide such SBC if:

(1) The entity monitors performance under the contract;

(2) If the entity has knowledge that the SBC is not being provided in a manner that satisfies the requirements of this section and the entity has all information necessary to correct the noncompliance, the entity corrects the noncompliance as soon as practicable; and

(3) If the entity has knowledge the SBC is not being provided in a manner that satisfies the requirements of this section and the entity does not have all information necessary to correct the noncompliance, the entity communicates with participants and beneficiaries who are affected by the noncompliance regarding the noncompliance, and begins taking significant steps as soon as practicable to avoid future violations.

(B) If a single SBC is provided to a participant and any beneficiaries at the participant's last known address, then the requirement to provide the SBC to the participant and any beneficiaries is generally satisfied. However, if a beneficiary's last known address is different than the participant's last known address, a separate SBC is required to be provided to the beneficiary at the beneficiary's last known address.

(C) With respect to a group health plan that offers multiple benefit packages, the plan or issuer is required to provide a new SBC automatically to participants and beneficiaries upon renewal or reenrollment only with respect to the benefit package in which a participant or beneficiary is enrolled (or will be automatically re-enrolled under the plan); SBCs are not required to be provided automatically upon renewal or reenrollment with respect to benefit packages in which the participant or beneficiary is not enrolled (or will not automatically be enrolled). However, if a participant or beneficiary requests an SBC with respect to another benefit package (or more than one other benefit package) for which the participant or beneficiary is eligible, the SBC (or SBCs, in the case of a request for SBCs relating to more than one benefit package) must be provided upon request as soon as practicable, but in no event later than seven business days following receipt of the request.

(D) Subject to paragraph (a)(2)(ii) of this section, a plan administrator of a group health plan that uses two or more insurance products provided by separate health insurance issuers with respect to a single group health plan may synthesize the information into a single SBC or provide multiple partial SBCs provided that all the SBC include the content in paragraph (a)(2)(iii) of this section.

(2) Content—

(i) *In general.* Subject to paragraph (a)(2)(iii) of this section, the SBC must include the following:

(A) Uniform definitions of standard insurance terms and medical terms so that consumers may compare health coverage and understand the terms of (or exceptions to) their coverage, in accordance with guidance as specified by the Secretary;

(B) A description of the coverage, including cost sharing, for each category of benefits identified by the Secretary in guidance;

(C) The exceptions, reductions, and limitations of the coverage;

(D) The cost-sharing provisions of the coverage, including deductible, coinsurance, and copayment obligations;

(E) The renewability and continuation of coverage provisions;

(F) Coverage examples, in accordance with the rules of paragraph (a)(2)(ii) of this section;

(G) With respect to coverage beginning on or after January 1, 2014, a statement about whether the plan or coverage provides minimum essential coverage as defined under section 5000A(f) and whether the plan's or coverage's share of the total allowed costs of benefits provided under the plan or coverage meets applicable requirements;

(H) A statement that the SBC is only a summary and that the plan document, policy, certificate, or contract of insurance should be consulted to determine the governing contractual provisions of the coverage;

(I) Contact information for questions;

(J) For issuers, an Internet web address where a copy of the actual individual coverage policy or group certificate of coverage can be reviewed and obtained;

(K) For plans and issuers that maintain one or more networks of providers, an Internet address (or similar contact information) for obtaining a list of network providers;

(L) For plans and issuers that use a formulary in providing prescription drug coverage, an Internet address (or similar contact information) for obtaining information on prescription drug coverage; and

(M) An Internet address for obtaining the uniform glossary, as described in paragraph (c) of this section, as well as a contact phone number to obtain a paper copy of the uniform glossary, and a disclosure that paper copies are available.

(ii) *Coverage examples.* The SBC must include coverage examples specified by the Secretary in guidance that illustrate benefits provided under the plan or coverage for common benefits scenarios (including pregnancy and serious or chronic medical conditions) in accordance with this paragraph (a)(2)(ii).

(A) *Number of examples.* The Secretary may identify up to six coverage examples that may be required in an SBC.

(B) *Benefits scenarios.* For purposes of this paragraph (a)(2)(ii), a benefits scenario is a hypothetical situation, consisting of a sample treatment plan for a specified medical condition during a specific period of time, based on recognized clinical practice guidelines as defined by the National Guideline Clearinghouse, Agency for Healthcare Research and Quality. The Secretary will specify, in guidance, the assumptions, including the relevant items and services and reimbursement information, for each claim in the benefits scenario.

(C) *Illustration of benefit provided.* For purposes of this paragraph (a)(2)(ii), to illustrate benefits provided under the plan or coverage for a particular benefits scenario, a plan or issuer simulates claims processing in accordance with guidance issued by the Secretary to generate an estimate of what an individual might expect to pay under the plan, policy, or benefit package. The illustration of benefits provided will take into account any cost sharing, excluded benefits, and

Reg. §2590.715-2715(a)(2)(ii)(C)   ¶15,050R-50RR

⫸ *Caution: Reg. § 2590.715-2715 is effective on August 17, 2015, and is applicable for disclosures for relevant participants and beneficiaries beginning on the first day of the first open enrollment period that begins on or after September 1, 2015 or beginning on the first day of the first plan year that begins on or after September 1, 2015.*

other limitations on coverage, as specified by the Secretary in guidance.

(iii) *Coverage provided outside the United States.* In lieu of summarizing coverage for items and services provided outside the United States, a plan or issuer may provide an Internet address (or similar contact information) for obtaining information about benefits and coverage provided outside the United States. In any case, the plan or issuer must provide an SBC in accordance with this section that accurately summarizes benefits and coverage available under the plan or coverage within the United States.

(3) *Appearance.* (i) A group health plan and a health insurance issuer must provide an SBC in the form, and in accordance with the instructions for completing the SBC, that are specified by the Secretary in guidance. The SBC must be presented in a uniform format, use terminology understandable by the average plan enrollee, not exceed four double-sided pages in length, and not include print smaller than 12-point font.

(ii) A group health plan that utilizes two or more benefit packages (such as major medical coverage and a health flexible spending arrangement) may synthesize the information into a single SBC, or provide multiple SBCs.

(4) *Form.* (i) An SBC provided by an issuer offering group health insurance coverage to a plan (or its sponsor), may be provided in paper form. Alternatively, the SBC may be provided electronically (such as by email or an Internet posting) if the following three conditions are satisfied—

(A) The format is readily accessible by the plan (or its sponsor);

(B) The SBC is provided in paper form free of charge upon request; and

(C) If the electronic form is an Internet posting, the issuer timely advises the plan (or its sponsor) in paper form or email that the documents are available on the Internet and provides the Internet address.

(ii) An SBC provided by a group health plan or health insurance issuer to a participant or beneficiary may be provided in paper form. Alternatively, the SBC may be provided electronically (such as by email or an Internet posting) if the requirements of this paragraph (a)(4)(ii) are met.

(A) With respect to participants and beneficiaries covered under the plan or coverage, the SBC may be provided electronically as described in this paragraph (a)(4)(ii)(A). However, in all cases, the plan or issuer must provide the SBC in paper form if paper form is requested.

(1) In accordance with the Department of Labor's disclosure regulations at 29 CFR 2520.104b-1;

(2) In connection with online enrollment or online renewal of coverage under the plan; or

(3) In response to an online request made by a participant or beneficiary for the SBC.

(B) With respect to participants and beneficiaries who are eligible but not enrolled for coverage, the SBC may be provided electronically if:

(1) The format is readily accessible;

(2) The SBC is provided in paper form free of charge upon request; and

(3) In a case in which the electronic form is an Internet posting, the plan or issuer timely notifies the individual in paper form (such as a postcard) or email that the documents are available on the Internet, provides the Internet address, and notifies the individual that the documents are available in paper form upon request.

(5) *Language.* A group health plan or health insurance issuer must provide the SBC in a culturally and linguistically appropriate manner. For purposes of this paragraph (a)(5), a plan or issuer is considered to provide the SBC in a culturally and linguistically appro-

priate manner if the thresholds and standards of § 2590.715-2719(e) are met as applied to the SBC.

(b) *Notice of modification.* If a group health plan, or health insurance issuer offering group health insurance coverage, makes any material modification (as defined under section 102 of ERISA) in any of the terms of the plan or coverage that would affect the content of the SBC, that is not reflected in the most recently provided SBC, and that occurs other than in connection with a renewal or reissuance of coverage, the plan or issuer must provide notice of the modification to enrollees not later than 60 days prior to the date on which the modification will become effective. The notice of modification must be provided in a form that is consistent with the rules of paragraph (a)(4) of this section.

(c) *Uniform glossary*—

(1) *In general.* A group health plan, and a health insurance issuer offering group health insurance coverage, must make available to participants and beneficiaries the uniform glossary described in paragraph (c)(2) of this section in accordance with the appearance and form and manner requirements of paragraphs (c)(3) and (4) of this section.

(2) *Health-coverage-related terms and medical terms.* The uniform glossary must provide uniform definitions, specified by the Secretary in guidance, of the following health-coverage-related terms and medical terms:

(i) Allowed amount, appeal, balance billing, co-insurance, complications of pregnancy, co-payment, deductible, durable medical equipment, emergency medical condition, emergency medical transportation, emergency room care, emergency services, excluded services, grievance, habilitation services, health insurance, home health care, hospice services, hospitalization, hospital outpatient care, in-network coinsurance, in-network co-payment, medically necessary, network, non-preferred provider, out-of-network coinsurance, out-of-network co-payment, out-of-pocket limit, physician services, plan, preauthorization, preferred provider, premium, prescription drug coverage, prescription drugs, primary care physician, primary care provider, provider, reconstructive surgery, rehabilitation services, skilled nursing care, specialist, usual customary and reasonable (UCR), and urgent care; and

(ii) Such other terms as the Secretary determines are important to define so that individuals and employers may compare and understand the terms of coverage and medical benefits (including any exceptions to those benefits), as specified in guidance.

(3) *Appearance.* A group health plan, and a health insurance issuer, must provide the uniform glossary with the appearance specified by the Secretary in guidance to ensure the uniform glossary is presented in a uniform format and uses terminology understandable by the average plan enrollee.

(4) *Form and manner.* A plan or issuer must make the uniform glossary described in this paragraph (c) available upon request, in either paper or electronic form (as requested), within seven business days after receipt of the request.

(d) *Preemption.* See § 2590.731. State laws that conflict with this section (including a state law that requires a health insurance issuer to provide an SBC that supplies less information than required under paragraph (a) of this section) are preempted.

⫸ *Reg. Sec. 2590.715-2715(e), as amended by interim final regulations to revise the first sentence, is effective and generally applicable August 1, 2016.*

(e) *Failure to provide.* A group health plan that willfully fails to provide information under this section to a participant or beneficiary is subject to a fine of not more than $1,000 (adjusted for inflation pursuant to the Federal Civil Penalties Inflation Adjustment Act of 1990, as amended) for each such failure. A failure with respect to each participant or beneficiary constitutes a separate offense for purposes of this paragraph (e). The Department will enforce this section using a pro-

⫸→ *Caution: Reg. § 2590.715-2715 is effective on August 17, 2015, and is applicable for disclosures for relevant participants and beneficiaries beginning on the first day of the first open enrollment period that begins on or after September 1, 2015 or beginning on the first day of the first plan year that begins on or after September 1, 2015.*

cess and procedure consistent with § 2560.502c-2 of this chapter and 29 CFR part 2570, subpart C. [Amended 7/1/16 (81 FR 43429) by interim final regulations that revised the first sentence.]

(f) *Applicability to Medicare Advantage benefits.* The requirements of this section do not apply to a group health plan benefit package that provides Medicare Advantage benefits pursuant to or 42 U.S.C. Chapter 7, Subchapter XVIII, Part C.

(g) *Applicability date.* (1) This section is applicable to group health plans and group health insurance issuers in accordance with this paragraph (g). (See § 2590.715-1251(d), providing that this section applies to grandfathered health plans.)

(i) For disclosures with respect to participants and beneficiaries who enroll or re-enroll through an open enrollment period (including re-enrollees and late enrollees), this section applies beginning on the first day of the first open enrollment period that begins on or after September 1, 2015; and

(ii) For disclosures with respect to participants and beneficiaries who enroll in coverage other than through an open enrollment period (including individuals who are newly eligible for coverage and special enrollees), this section applies beginning on the first day of the first plan year that begins on or after September 1, 2015.

(2) For disclosures with respect to plans, this section is applicable to health insurance issuers beginning September 1, 2015. [Revised 6/16/15 by 80 FR 34292.]

Interim Final Regulations

Reg. § 2590.715-2719 was adopted and published in the *Federal Register* on July 23, 2010 by 75 FR 43329. Reg § 2590.715-2719 was amended on June 24, 2011 (76 FR 37208). Reg § 2590.715-2719(d)(1)(ii) was corrected on July 26, 2011 (76 FR 44491). Reg. § § 2590.715-2719(d) and (d)(1)(i) were amended and finalized on November 13, 2013 (78 FR 68239). See ¶ 15,050R-50VV.

⫸→ *Caution: Until final Reg. § 2590.715-2719 at ¶ 15,050R-50VV is applicable on the first day of the plan year beginning on or after January 1, 2017, plans and issuers must continue to comply with the below interim final regulation.*

[¶ 15,050R-50V]

§ 2590.715-2719 **Internal claims and appeals and external review processes.**

§ 2590.715-2719(a) *Scope and definitions—*

(1) *Scope.* This section sets forth requirements with respect to internal claims and appeals and external review processes for group health plans and health insurance issuers that are not grandfathered health plans under § 2590.715-1251 of this part. Paragraph (b) of this section provides requirements for internal claims and appeals processes. Paragraph (c) of this section sets forth rules governing the applicability of State external review processes. Paragraph (d) of this section sets forth a Federal external review process for plans and issuers not subject to an applicable State external review process. Paragraph (e) of this section prescribes requirements for ensuring that notices required to be provided under this section are provided in a culturally and linguistically appropriate manner. Paragraph (f) of this section describes the authority of the Secretary to deem certain external review processes in existence on March 23, 2010 as in compliance with paragraph (c) or (d) of this section. Paragraph (g) of this section sets forth the applicability date for this section.

(2) *Definitions.* For purposes of this section, the following definitions apply—

(i) *Adverse benefit determination.* An *adverse benefit determination* means an adverse benefit determination as defined in 29 CFR 2560.503-1, as well as any rescission of coverage, as described in § 2590.715-2712(a)(2) of this part (whether or not, in connection with the rescission, there is an adverse effect on any particular benefit at that time).

(ii) *Appeal (or internal appeal).* An *appeal* or *internal appeal* means review by a plan or issuer of an adverse benefit determination, as required in paragraph (b) of this section.

(iii) *Claimant. Claimant* means an individual who makes a claim under this section. For purposes of this section, references to claimant include a claimant's authorized representative.

(iv) *External review. External review* means a review of an adverse benefit determination (including a final internal adverse benefit determination) conducted pursuant to an applicable State external review process described in paragraph (c) of this section or the Federal external review process of paragraph (d) of this section.

(v) *Final internal adverse benefit determination.* A *final internal adverse benefit determination* means an adverse benefit determination that has been upheld by a plan or issuer at the completion of the internal appeals process applicable under paragraph (b) of this section (or an adverse benefit determination with respect to which the internal appeals process has been exhausted under the deemed exhaustion rules of paragraph (b)(2)(ii)(F) of this section).

(vi) *Final external review decision.* A *final external review decision,* as used in paragraph (d) of this section, means a determination by an independent review organization at the conclusion of an external review.

(vii) *Independent review organization (or IRO).* An independent review organization (or *IRO*) means an entity that conducts independent external reviews of adverse benefit determinations and final internal adverse benefit determinations pursuant to paragraph (c) or (d) of this section.

(viii) *NAIC Uniform Model Act.* The *NAIC Uniform Model Act* means the Uniform Health Carrier External Review Model Act promulgated by the National Association of Insurance Commissioners in place on July 23, 2010.

(b) *Internal claims and appeals process—*

(1) *In general.* A group health plan and a health insurance issuer offering group health insurance coverage must implement an effective internal claims and appeals process, as described in this paragraph (b).

(2) *Requirements for group health plans and group health insurance issuers.* A group health plan and a health insurance issuer offering group health insurance coverage must comply with all the requirements of this paragraph (b)(2). In the case of health insurance coverage offered in connection with a group health plan, if either the plan or the issuer complies with the internal claims and appeals process of this paragraph (b)(2), then the obligation to comply with this paragraph (b)(2) is satisfied for both the plan and the issuer with respect to the health insurance coverage.

(i) *Minimum internal claims and appeals standards.* A group health plan and a health insurance issuer offering group health insurance coverage must comply with all the requirements applicable to group health plans under 29 CFR 2560.503-1, except to the extent those requirements are modified by paragraph (b)(2)(ii) of this section. Accordingly, under this paragraph (b), with respect to health insurance coverage offered in connection with a group health plan, the group health insurance issuer is subject to the requirements in 29 CFR 2560.503-1 to the same extent as the group health plan.

(ii) *Additional standards.* In addition to the requirements in paragraph (b)(2)(i) of this section, the internal claims and appeals processes of a group health plan and a health insurance issuer offering group health insurance coverage must meet the requirements of this paragraph (b)(2)(ii).

(A) *Clarification of meaning of adverse benefit determination.* For purposes of this paragraph (b)(2), an "adverse benefit determination" includes an adverse benefit determination as defined in paragraph (a)(2)(i) of this section. Accordingly, in complying with 29 CFR 2560.503-1, as well as the other provisions of this paragraph (b)(2), a plan or issuer must treat a rescission of coverage (whether or not the rescission has an adverse effect on any particular benefit at that time) as an adverse benefit determination. (Rescissions of coverage are subject to the requirements of § 2590.715-2712 of this part.)

(B) *Expedited notification of benefit determinations involving urgent care.* The requirements of 29 CFR 2560.503-1(f)(2)(i) (which generally provide, among other things, in the case of urgent care claims for notification of the plan's benefit determination (whether adverse or not) as soon as possible, taking into account the medical exigencies, but not later than 72 hours after receipt of the claim) continue to apply to the plan and issuer. For purposes of this paragraph (b)(2)(ii)(B), a claim involving urgent care has the meaning given in 29 CFR 2560.503-1(m)(1), as determined by the attending provider, and the plan or issuer shall defer to such determination of the attending provider. [Amended by 76 FR 37208 on 6/24/2011.]

(C) *Full and fair review.* A plan and issuer must allow a claimant to review the claim file and to present evidence and testimony as part of the internal claims and appeals process. Specifically, in addition to complying with the requirements of 29 CFR 2560.503-1(h)(2)—

(1) The plan or issuer must provide the claimant, free of charge, with any new or additional evidence considered, relied upon, or generated by the plan or issuer (or at the direction of the plan or issuer) in connection with the claim; such evidence must be provided as soon as possible and sufficiently in advance of the date on which the notice of final internal adverse benefit determination is required to be provided under 29 CFR 2560.503-1(i) to give the claimant a reasonable opportunity to respond prior to that date; and

(2) Before the plan or issuer can issue a final internal adverse benefit determination based on a new or additional rationale, the claimant must be provided, free of charge, with the rationale; the rationale must be provided as soon as possible and sufficiently in advance of the date on which the notice of final internal adverse benefit determination is required to be provided under 29 CFR 2560.503-1(i) to give the claimant a reasonable opportunity to respond prior to that date.

(D) *Avoiding conflicts of interest.* In addition to the requirements of 29 CFR 2560.503-1(b) and (h) regarding full and fair review, the plan and issuer must ensure that all claims and appeals are adjudicated in a manner designed to ensure the independence and impartiality of the persons involved in making the decision. Accordingly, decisions regarding hiring, compensation, termination, promotion, or other similar matters with respect to any individual (such as a claims adjudicator or medical expert) must not be made based upon the likelihood that the individual will support the denial of benefits.

(E) *Notice.* A plan and issuer must provide notice to individuals, in a culturally and linguistically appropriate manner (as described in paragraph (e) of this section) that complies with the requirements of 29 CFR 2560.503-1(g) and (j). The plan and issuer must also comply with the additional requirements of this paragraph (b)(2)(ii)(E).

(1) The plan and issuer must ensure that any notice of adverse benefit determination or final internal adverse benefit determination includes information sufficient to identify the claim involved (including the date of service, the health care provider, the claim amount (if applicable), and a statement describing the availability, upon request, of the diagnosis code and its corresponding meaning, and the treatment code and its corresponding meaning). [Amended by 76 FR 37208 on 6/24/2011.]

(2) The plan and issuer must provide to participants and beneficiaries, as soon as practicable, upon request, the diagnosis code and its corresponding meaning, and the treatment code and its corresponding meaning, associated with any adverse benefit determination or final internal adverse benefit determination. The plan or issuer must not consider a request for such diagnosis and treatment information, in itself, to be a request for an internal appeal under this paragraph (b) or an external review under paragraphs (c) and (d) of this section. [Amended by 76 FR 37208 on 6/24/2011.]

(3) The plan and issuer must ensure that the reason or reasons for the adverse benefit determination or final internal adverse benefit determination includes the denial code and its corresponding meaning, as well as a description of the plan's or issuer's standard, if any, that was used in denying the claim. In the case of a notice of final internal adverse benefit determination, this description must include a discussion of the decision. [Redesignated by 76 FR 37208 on 6/24/2011.]

(4) The plan and issuer must provide a description of available internal appeals and external review processes, including information regarding how to initiate an appeal. [Redesignated by 76 FR 37208 on 6/24/2011.]

(5) The plan and issuer must disclose the availability of, and contact information for, any applicable office of health insurance consumer assistance or ombudsman established under PHS Act section 2793 to assist individuals with the internal claims and appeals and external review processes. [Redesignated by 76 FR 37208 on 6/24/2011.]

(F) *Deemed exhaustion of internal claims and appeals processes.*

(1) In the case of a plan or issuer that fails to adhere to all the requirements of this paragraph (b)(2) with respect to a claim, the claimant is deemed to have exhausted the internal claims and appeals process of this paragraph (b), except as provided in paragraph (b)(2)(ii)(F)(2) of this section. Accordingly, the claimant may initiate an external review under paragraph (c) or (d) of this section, as applicable. The claimant is also entitled to pursue any available remedies under section 502(a) of ERISA or under State law, as applicable, on the basis that the plan or issuer has failed to provide a reasonable internal claims and appeals process that would yield a decision on the merits of the claim. If a claimant chooses to pursue remedies under section 502(a) of ERISA under such circumstances, the claim or appeal is deemed denied on review without the exercise of discretion by an appropriate fiduciary.

(2) Notwithstanding paragraph (b)(2)(ii)(F)(1) of this section, the internal claims and appeals process of this paragraph (b) will not be deemed exhausted based on *de minimis* violations that do not cause, and are not likely to cause, prejudice or harm to the claimant so long as the plan or issuer demonstrates that the violation was for good cause or due to matters beyond the control of the plan or issuer and that the violation occurred in the context of an ongoing, good faith exchange of information between the plan and the claimant. This exception is not available if the violation is part of a pattern or practice of violations by the plan or issuer. The claimant may request a written explanation of the violation from the plan or issuer, and the plan or issuer must provide such explanation within 10 days, including a specific description of its bases, if any, for asserting that the violation should not cause the internal claims and appeals process of this paragraph (b) to be deemed exhausted. If an external reviewer or a court rejects the claimant's request for immediate review under paragraph (b)(2)(ii)(F)(1) of this section on the basis that the plan met the standards for the exception under this paragraph (b)(2)(ii)(F)(2), the claimant has the right to resubmit and pursue the internal appeal of the claim. In such a case, within a reasonable time after the external reviewer or court rejects the claim for immediate review (not to exceed 10 days), the plan shall provide the claimant with notice of the opportunity to resubmit and pursue the internal appeal of the claim. Time periods for re-filing the claim shall begin to run upon claimant's receipt of such notice. [Amended by 76 FR 37208 on 6/24/2011.]

(iii) *Requirement to provide continued coverage pending the outcome of an appeal.* A plan and issuer subject to the requirements of this paragraph (b)(2) are required to provide continued coverage pending the outcome of an appeal. For this purpose, the plan and issuer must comply with the requirements of 29 CFR 2560.503-1(f)(2)(ii), which generally provides that benefits for an ongoing course of treatment cannot be reduced or terminated without providing advance notice and an opportunity for advance review.

(c) *State standards for external review*—

(1) *In general.*

(i) If a State external review process that applies to and is binding on a health insurance issuer offering group health insurance coverage includes at a minimum the consumer protections in the NAIC Uniform Model Act, then the issuer must comply with the applicable State external review process and is not required to comply with the Federal external review process of paragraph (d) of this section. In such a case, to the extent that benefits under a group health plan are provided through health insurance coverage, the group health plan is not required to comply with either this paragraph (c) or the Federal external review process of paragraph (d) of this section.

(ii) To the extent that a group health plan provides benefits other than through health insurance coverage (that is, the plan is self-insured) and is subject to a State external review process that applies to and is binding on the plan (for example, is not preempted by ERISA) and the State external review process includes at a minimum the consumer protections in the NAIC Uniform Model Act, then the plan must comply with the applicable State external review process and is not required to comply with the Federal external review process of paragraph (d) of this section.

(iii) If a plan or issuer is not required under paragraph (c)(1)(i) or (c)(1)(ii) of this section to comply with the requirements of this paragraph (c), then the plan or issuer must comply with the Federal external review process of paragraph (d) of this section, except to the extent, in the case of a plan, the plan is not required under paragraph (c)(1)(i) of this section to comply with paragraph (d) of this section.

(2) *Minimum standards for State external review processes.* An applicable State external review process must meet all the minimum consumer protections in this paragraph (c)(2). The Department of Health and Human Services will determine whether State external review processes meet these requirements.

(i) The State process must provide for the external review of adverse benefit determinations (including final internal adverse benefit determinations) by issuers (or, if applicable, plans) that are based on the issuer's (or plan's) requirements for medical necessity, appropriateness, health care setting, level of care, or effectiveness of a covered benefit.

(ii) The State process must require issuers (or, if applicable, plans) to provide effective written notice to claimants of their rights in connection with an external review for an adverse benefit determination.

(iii) To the extent the State process requires exhaustion of an internal claims and appeals process, exhaustion must be unnecessary where the issuer (or, if applicable, the plan) has waived the requirement, the issuer (or the plan) is considered to have exhausted the internal claims and appeals process under applicable law (including by failing to comply with any of the requirements for the internal appeal process, as outlined in paragraph (b)(2) of this section), or the claimant has applied for expedited external review at the same time as applying for an expedited internal appeal.

(iv) The State process provides that the issuer (or, if applicable, the plan) against which a request for external review is filed must pay the cost of the IRO for conducting the external review. Notwithstanding this requirement, the State external review process may require a nominal filing fee from the claimant requesting an external review. For this purpose, to be considered nominal, a filing fee must not exceed $25, it must be refunded to the claimant if the adverse benefit determination (or final internal adverse benefit determination) is reversed through external review, it must be waived if payment of the fee would impose an undue financial hardship, and the annual limit on filing fees for any claimant within a single plan year must not exceed $75.

(v) The State process may not impose a restriction on the minimum dollar amount of a claim for it to be eligible for external review. Thus, the process may not impose, for example, a $500 minimum claims threshold.

(vi) The State process must allow at least four months after the receipt of a notice of an adverse benefit determination or final internal adverse benefit determination for a request for an external review to be filed.

(vii) The State process must provide that IROs will be assigned on a random basis or another method of assignment that assures the independence and impartiality of the assignment process (such as rotational assignment) by a State or independent entity, and in no event selected by the issuer, plan, or the individual.

(viii) The State process must provide for maintenance of a list of approved IRO qualified to conduct the external review based on the nature of the health care service that is the subject of the review. The State process must provide for approval only of IROs that are accredited by a nationally recognized private accrediting organization.

(ix) The State process must provide that any approved IRO has no conflicts of interest that will influence its independence. Thus, the IRO may not own or control, or be owned or controlled by a health insurance issuer, a group health plan, the sponsor of a group health plan, a trade association of plans or issuers, or a trade association of health care providers. The State process must further provide that the IRO and the clinical reviewer assigned to conduct an external review may not have a material professional, familial, or financial conflict of interest with the issuer or plan that is the subject of the external review; the claimant (and any related parties to the claimant) whose treatment is the subject of the external review; any officer, director, or management employee of the issuer; the plan administrator, plan fiduciaries, or plan employees; the health care provider, the health care provider's group, or practice association recommending the treatment that is subject to the external review; the facility at which the recommended treatment would be provided; or the developer or manufacturer of the principal drug, device, procedure, or other therapy being recommended.

(x) The State process allows the claimant at least five business days to submit to the IRO in writing additional information that the IRO must consider when conducting the external review and it requires that the claimant is notified of the right to do so. The process must also require that any additional information submitted by the claimant to the IRO must be forwarded to the issuer (or, if applicable, the plan) within one business day of receipt by the IRO.

(xi) The State process must provide that the decision is binding on the plan or issuer, as well as the claimant, except to the extent other remedies are available under State or Federal law, and except that the requirement that the decision be binding shall not preclude the plan or issuer from making payment on the claim or otherwise providing benefits at any time, including after a final external review decision that denies the claim or otherwise fails to require such payment or benefits. For this purpose, the plan or issuer must provide benefits (including by making payment on the claim) pursuant to the final external review decision without delay, regardless of whether the plan or issuer intends to seek judicial review of the external review decision and unless or until there is a judicial decision otherwise. [Amended by 76 FR 37208 on 6/24/2011.]

(xii) The State process must require, for standard external review, that the IRO provide written notice to the issuer (or, if applicable, the plan) and the claimant of its decision to uphold or reverse the adverse benefit determination (or final internal adverse benefit determination) within no more than 45 days after the receipt of the request for external review by the IRO.

(xiii) The State process must provide for an expedited external review if the adverse benefit determination (or final internal adverse benefit determination) concerns an admission, availability of care, continued stay, or health care service for which the claimant received emergency services, but has not been discharged from a facility; or involves a medical condition for which the standard external review timeframe would seriously jeopardize the life or health of the claimant or jeopardize the claimant's ability to regain maximum function. As expeditiously as possible but within no more than 72 hours after the receipt of the request for expedited external review by the IRO, the IRO must make its decision to uphold or reverse the adverse benefit determination (or final internal adverse benefit determination) and notify the claimant and the issuer (or, if applicable, the plan) of the determination. If the notice is not in writing, the IRO must provide written confirmation of the decision within 48 hours after the date of the notice of the decision.

⟫⟫→ Caution: Until final Reg. § 2590.715-2719 at ¶ 15,050R-50VV is applicable on the first day of the plan year beginning on or after January 1, 2017, plans and issuers must continue to comply with the below interim final regulation.

(xiv) The State process must require that issuers (or, if applicable, plans) include a description of the external review process in or attached to the summary plan description, policy, certificate, membership booklet, outline of coverage, or other evidence of coverage it provides to participants, beneficiaries, or enrollees, substantially similar to what is set forth in section 17 of the NAIC Uniform Model Act.

(xv) The State process must require that IROs maintain written records and make them available upon request to the State, substantially similar to what is set forth in section 15 of the NAIC Uniform Model Act.

(xvi) The State process follows procedures for external review of adverse benefit determinations (or final internal adverse benefit determinations) involving experimental or investigational treatment, substantially similar to what is set forth in section 10 of the NAIC Uniform Model Act.

(3) *Transition period for external review processes*—

(i) Through December 31, 2011, an applicable State external review process applicable to a health insurance issuer or group health plan is considered to meet the requirements of PHS Act section 2719(b). Accordingly, through December 31, 2011, an applicable State external review process will be considered binding on the issuer or plan (in lieu of the requirements of the Federal external review process). If there is no applicable State external review process, the issuer or plan is required to comply with the requirements of the Federal external review process in paragraph (d) of this section. [Amended by 76 FR 37208 on 6/24/2011.]

(ii) For final internal adverse benefit determinations (or, in the case of simultaneous internal appeal and external review, adverse benefit determinations) provided on or after January 1, 2012, the Federal external review process will apply unless the Department of Health and Human Services determines that a State law meets all the minimum standards of paragraph (c)(2) of this section. [Amended by 76 FR 37208 on 6/24/2011.]

(d) *Federal external review process.* A plan or issuer not subject to an applicable State external review process under paragraph (c) of this section must provide an effective Federal external review process in accordance with this paragraph (d) (except to the extent, in the case of a plan, the plan is described in paragraph (c)(1)(i) of this section as not having to comply with this paragraph (d)). In the case of health insurance coverage offered in connection with a group health plan, if either the plan or the issuer complies with the Federal external review process of this paragraph (d), then the obligation to comply with this paragraph (d) is satisfied for both the plan and the issuer with respect to the health insurance coverage. [Amended and finalized by 78 FR 68239 on November 13, 2013—¶ 15,050R-50VV.]

(1) *Scope.* (i) *In general.* Subject to the suspension provision in paragraph (d)(1)(ii) of this section and except to the extent provided otherwise by the Secretary in guidance, the Federal external review process established pursuant to this paragraph (d) applies to any adverse benefit determination or final internal adverse benefit determination (as defined in paragraphs (a)(2)(i) and (a)(2)(v) of this section), except that a denial, reduction, termination, or a failure to provide payment for a benefit based on a determination that a participant or beneficiary fails to meet the requirements for eligibility under the terms of a group health plan is not eligible for the Federal external review process under this paragraph (d). [Amended and finalized by 78 FR 68239 on November 13, 2013— ¶ 15,050R-50VV.]

(ii) *Suspension of general rule.* Unless or until this suspension is revoked in guidance by the Secretary, with respect to claims for which external review has not been initiated before September 20, 2011, the Federal external review process established pursuant to this paragraph (d) applies only to: [Corrected July 26, 2011 (76 FR 44491).]

(A) An adverse benefit determination (including a final internal adverse benefit determination) by a plan or issuer that involves medical judgment (including, but not limited to, those based on the plan's or issuer's requirements for medical necessity, appropriateness, health care setting, level of care, or effectiveness of a covered benefit;

or its determination that a treatment is experimental or investigational), as determined by the external reviewer; and

(B) A rescission of coverage (whether or not the rescission has any effect on any particular benefit at that time).

(iii) *Examples.* This rules of paragraph (d)(1)(ii) of this section are illustrated by the following examples:

Example 1. (i) *Facts.* A group health plan provides coverage for 30 physical therapy visits generally. After the 30th visit, coverage is provided only if the service is preauthorized pursuant to an approved treatment plan that takes into account medical necessity using the plan's definition of the term. Individual *A* seeks coverage for a 31st physical therapy visit. *A*'s health care provider submits a treatment plan for approval, but it is not approved by the plan, so coverage for the 31st visit is not preauthorized. With respect to the 31st visit, *A* receives a notice of final internal adverse benefit determination stating that the maximum visit limit is exceeded.

(ii) *Conclusion.* In this *Example 1,* the plan's denial of benefits is based on medical necessity and involves medical judgment. Accordingly, the claim is eligible for external review during the suspension period under paragraph (d)(1)(ii) of this section. Moreover, the plan's notification of final internal adverse benefit determination is inadequate under paragraphs (b)(2)(i) and (b)(2)(ii)(E)(3) of this section because it fails to make clear that the plan will pay for more than 30 visits if the service is preauthorized pursuant to an approved treatment plan that takes into account medical necessity using the plan's definition of the term. Accordingly, the notice of final internal adverse benefit determination should refer to the plan provision governing the 31st visit and should describe the plan's standard for medical necessity, as well as how the treatment fails to meet the plan's standard.

Example 2. (i) *Facts.* A group health plan does not provide coverage for services provided out of network, unless the service cannot effectively be provided in network. Individual *B* seeks coverage for a specialized medical procedure from an out-of-network provider because *B* believes that the procedure cannot be effectively provided in network. *B* receives a notice of final internal adverse benefit determination stating that the claim is denied because the provider is out-of-network.

(ii) *Conclusion.* In this *Example 2,* the plan's denial of benefits is based on whether a service can effectively be provided in network and, therefore, involves medical judgment. Accordingly, the claim is eligible for external review during the suspension period under paragraph (d)(1)(ii) of this section. Moreover, the plan's notice of final internal adverse benefit determination is inadequate under paragraphs (b)(2)(i) and (b)(2)(ii)(E)(3) of this section because the plan does provide benefits for services on an out-of-network basis if the services cannot effectively be provided in network. Accordingly, the notice of final internal adverse benefit determination is required to refer to the exception to the out-of-network exclusion and should describe the plan's standards for determining effectiveness of services, as well as how services available to the claimant within the plan's network meet the plan's standard for effectiveness of services. [Amended by 76 FR 37208 on 6/24/2011.]

(2) *External review process standards.* The Federal external review process established pursuant to this paragraph (d) will be similar to the process set forth in the NAIC Uniform Model Act and will meet standards issued by the Secretary. These standards will comply with all of the requirements described in this paragraph (d)(2).

(i) These standards will describe how a claimant initiates an external review, procedures for preliminary reviews to determine whether a claim is eligible for external review, minimum qualifications for IROs, a process for approving IROs eligible to be assigned to conduct external reviews, a process for random assignment of external reviews to approved IROs, standards for IRO decisionmaking, and rules for providing notice of a final external review decision.

(ii) These standards will provide an expedited external review process for—

(A) An adverse benefit determination, if the adverse benefit determination involves a medical condition of the claimant for which the timeframe for completion of an expedited internal appeal under paragraph (b) of this section would seriously jeopardize the life or health of the claimant, or would jeopardize the claimant's ability to regain maximum function and the claimant has filed a request for an expedited internal appeal under paragraph (b) of this section; or

(B) A final internal adverse benefit determination, if the claimant has a medical condition where the timeframe for completion of a standard external review pursuant to paragraph (d)(3) of this section would seriously jeopardize the life or health of the claimant or would jeopardize the claimant's ability to regain maximum function, or if the final internal adverse benefit determination concerns an admission, availability of care, continued stay or health care service for which the claimant received emergency services, but has not been discharged from a facility.

(iii) With respect to claims involving experimental or investigational treatments, these standards will also provide additional consumer protections to ensure that adequate clinical and scientific experience and protocols are taken into account as part of the external review process.

(iv) These standards will provide that an external review decision is binding on the plan or issuer, as well as the claimant, except to the extent other remedies are available under State or Federal law, and except that the requirement that the decision be binding shall not preclude the plan or issuer from making payment on the claim or otherwise providing benefits at any time, including after a final external review decision that denies the claim or otherwise fails to require such payment or benefits. For this purpose, the plan or issuer must provide any benefits (including by making payment on the claim) pursuant to the final external review decision without delay, regardless of whether the plan or issuer intends to seek judicial review of the external review decision and unless or until there is a judicial decision otherwise. [Amended by 76 FR 37208 on 6/24/2011.]

(v) These standards may establish external review reporting requirements for IROs.

(vi) These standards will establish additional notice requirements for plans and issuers regarding disclosures to participants and beneficiaries describing the Federal external review procedures (including the right to file a request for an external review of an adverse benefit determination or a final internal adverse benefit determination in the summary plan description, policy, certificate, membership booklet, outline of coverage, or other evidence of coverage it provides to participants or beneficiaries.

(vii) These standards will require plans and issuers to provide information relevant to the processing of the external review, including, but not limited to, the information considered and relied on in making the adverse benefit determination or final internal adverse benefit determination.

(e) *Form and manner of notice.* (1) *In general.* For purposes of this section, a group health plan and a health insurance issuer offering group health insurance coverage are considered to provide relevant notices in a culturally and linguistically appropriate manner if the plan or issuer meets all the requirements of paragraph (e)(2) of this section with respect to the applicable non-English languages described in paragraph (e)(3) of this section.

(2) *Requirements.* (i) The plan or issuer must provide oral language services (such as a telephone customer assistance hotline) that include answering questions in any applicable non-English language and providing assistance with filing claims and appeals (including external review) in any applicable non-English language;

(ii) The plan or issuer must provide, upon request, a notice in any applicable non-English language; and

(iii) The plan or issuer must include in the English versions of all notices, a statement prominently displayed in any applicable non-English language clearly indicating how to access the language services provided by the plan or issuer.

(3) *Applicable non-English language.* With respect to an address in any United States county to which a notice is sent, a non-English language is an applicable non-English language if ten percent or more of the population residing in the county is literate only in the same non-English language, as determined in guidance published by the Secretary. [Amended by 76 FR 37208 on 6/24/2011.]

(f) *Secretarial authority.* The Secretary may determine that the external review process of a group health plan or health insurance issuer, in operation as of March 23, 2010, is considered in compliance with the applicable process established under paragraph (c) or (d) of this section if it substantially meets the requirements of paragraph (c) or (d) of this section, as applicable.

(g) *Applicability date.* The provisions of this section apply for plan years beginning on or after September 23, 2010. See § 2590.715-1251 of this part for determining the application of this section to grandfathered health plans (providing that these rules regarding internal claims and appeals and external review processes do not apply to grandfathered health plans).

Final Regulations

Reg. §§2590.715-2719(d) and (d)(1)(i) were amended and finalized on November 13, 2013 (78 FR 68239). EBSA Reg. §§2590.715-2719(d) and (d)(1)(i) are effective on December 13, 2013. Reg. § 2590.715-2719 was revised and finalized on November 18, 2015 (80 FR 72191).

[¶ 15,050R-50VV]

§ 2590.715-2719 Internal claims and appeals and external review processes.

(a) *Scope and definitions-*

(1) *Scope.* This section sets forth requirements with respect to internal claims and appeals and external review processes for group health plans and health insurance issuers that are not grandfathered health plans under §2590.715-1251. Paragraph (b) of this section provides requirements for internal claims and appeals processes. Paragraph (c) of this section sets forth rules governing the applicability of State external review processes. Paragraph (d) of this section sets forth a Federal external review process for plans and issuers not subject to an applicable State external review process. Paragraph (e) of this section prescribes requirements for ensuring that notices required to be provided under this section are provided in a culturally and linguistically appropriate manner. Paragraph (f) of this section describes the authority of the Secretary to deem certain external review processes in

existence on March 23, 2010 as in compliance with paragraph (c) or (d) of this section.

(2) *Definitions.* For purposes of this section, the following definitions apply—

(i) *Adverse benefit determination.* An *adverse benefit determination* means an adverse benefit determination as defined in 29 CFR 2560.503-1, as well as any rescission of coverage, as described in §2590.715-2712(a)(2) (whether or not, in connection with the rescission, there is an adverse effect on any particular benefit at that time).

(ii) *Appeal (or internal appeal).* An *appeal* or *internal appeal* means review by a plan or issuer of an adverse benefit determination, as required in paragraph (b) of this section.

(iii) *Claimant. Claimant* means an individual who makes a claim under this section. For purposes of this section, references to claimant include a claimant's authorized representative.

»»→ *Caution: Reg. § 2590.715-2719 is effective January 19, 2016, and applies to group health plans beginning on the first day of the first plan year beginning on or after January 1, 2017. Until the final regulations become applicable, plans and issuers are required to continue to comply with the corresponding EBSA interim final regulations, which apply for purposes of ERISA and the Code.*

(iv) *External review. External review* means a review of an adverse benefit determination (including a final internal adverse benefit determination) conducted pursuant to an applicable State external review process described in paragraph (c) of this section or the Federal external review process of paragraph (d) of this section.

(v) *Final internal adverse benefit determination.* A *final internal adverse benefit determination* means an adverse benefit determination that has been upheld by a plan or issuer at the completion of the internal appeals process applicable under paragraph (b) of this section (or an adverse benefit determination with respect to which the internal appeals process has been exhausted under the deemed exhaustion rules of paragraph (b)(2)(ii)(F) of this section).

(vi) *Final external review decision.* A *final external review decision* means a determination by an independent review organization at the conclusion of an external review.

(vii) *Independent review organization (or IRO).* An *independent review organization* (or *IRO*) means an entity that conducts independent external reviews of adverse benefit determinations and final internal adverse benefit determinations pursuant to paragraph (c) or (d) of this section.

(viii) *NAIC Uniform Model Act.* The *NAIC Uniform Model Act* means the Uniform Health Carrier External Review Model Act promulgated by the National Association of Insurance Commissioners in place on July 23, 2010.

(b) *Internal claims and appeals process—*

(1) *In general.* A group health plan and a health insurance issuer offering group health insurance coverage must implement an effective internal claims and appeals process, as described in this paragraph (b).

(2) *Requirements for group health plans and group health insurance issuers.* A group health plan and a health insurance issuer offering group health insurance coverage must comply with all the requirements of this paragraph (b)(2). In the case of health insurance coverage offered in connection with a group health plan, if either the plan or the issuer complies with the internal claims and appeals process of this paragraph (b)(2), then the obligation to comply with this paragraph (b)(2) is satisfied for both the plan and the issuer with respect to the health insurance coverage.

(i) *Minimum internal claims and appeals standards.* A group health plan and a health insurance issuer offering group health insurance coverage must comply with all the requirements applicable to group health plans under 29 CFR 2560.503-1, except to the extent those requirements are modified by paragraph (b)(2)(ii) of this section. Accordingly, under this paragraph (b), with respect to health insurance coverage offered in connection with a group health plan, the group health insurance issuer is subject to the requirements in 29 CFR 2560.503-1 to the same extent as the group health plan.

(ii) *Additional standards.* In addition to the requirements in paragraph (b)(2)(i) of this section, the internal claims and appeals processes of a group health plan and a health insurance issuer offering group health insurance coverage must meet the requirements of this paragraph (b)(2)(ii).

(A) *Clarification of meaning of adverse benefit determination.* For purposes of this paragraph (b)(2), an "adverse benefit determination" includes an adverse benefit determination as defined in paragraph (a)(2)(i) of this section. Accordingly, in complying with 29 CFR 2560.503-1, as well as the other provisions of this paragraph (b)(2), a plan or issuer must treat a rescission of coverage (whether or not the rescission has an adverse effect on any particular benefit at that time) as an adverse benefit determination. (Rescissions of coverage are subject to the requirements of § 2590.715-2712.)

(B) *Expedited notification of benefit determinations involving urgent care.* The requirements of 29 CFR 2560.503-1(f)(2)(i) (which

generally provide, among other things, in the case of urgent care claims for notification of the plan's benefit determination (whether adverse or not) as soon as possible, taking into account the medical exigencies, but not later than 72 hours after the receipt of the claim) continue to apply to the plan and issuer. For purposes of this paragraph (b)(2)(ii)(B), a claim involving urgent care has the meaning given in 29 CFR 2560.503-1(m)(1), as determined by the attending provider, and the plan or issuer shall defer to such determination of the attending provider.

(C) *Full and fair review.* A plan and issuer must allow a claimant to review the claim file and to present evidence and testimony as part of the internal claims and appeals process. Specifically, in addition to complying with the requirements of 29 CFR 2560.503-1(h)(2)—

(1) The plan or issuer must provide the claimant, free of charge, with any new or additional evidence considered, relied upon, or generated by the plan or issuer (or at the direction of the plan or issuer) in connection with the claim; such evidence must be provided as soon as possible and sufficiently in advance of the date on which the notice of final internal adverse benefit determination is required to be provided under 29 CFR 2560.503-1(i) to give the claimant a reasonable opportunity to respond prior to that date; and

(2) Before the plan or issuer can issue a final internal adverse benefit determination based on a new or additional rationale, the claimant must be provided, free of charge, with the rationale; the rationale must be provided as soon as possible and sufficiently in advance of the date on which the notice of final internal adverse benefit determination is required to be provided under 29 CFR 2560.503-1(i) to give the claimant a reasonable opportunity to respond prior to that date. Notwithstanding the rules of 29 CFR 2560.503-1(i), if the new or additional evidence is received so late that it would be impossible to provide it to the claimant in time for the claimant to have a reasonable opportunity to respond, the period for providing a notice of final internal adverse benefit determination is tolled until such time as the claimant has a reasonable opportunity to respond. After the claimant responds, or has a reasonable opportunity to respond but fails to do so, the plan administrator shall notify the claimant of the plan's benefit determination as soon as a plan acting in a reasonable and prompt fashion can provide the notice, taking into account the medical exigencies.

(D) *Avoiding conflicts of interest.* In addition to the requirements of 29 CFR 2560.503-1(b) and (h) regarding full and fair review, the plan and issuer must ensure that all claims and appeals are adjudicated in a manner designed to ensure the independence and impartiality of the persons involved in making the decision. Accordingly, decisions regarding hiring, compensation, termination, promotion, or other similar matters with respect to any individual (such as a claims adjudicator or medical expert) must not be made based upon the likelihood that the individual will support the denial of benefits.

(E) *Notice.* A plan and issuer must provide notice to individuals, in a culturally and linguistically appropriate manner (as described in paragraph (e) of this section) that complies with the requirements of 29 CFR 2560.503-1(g) and (j). The plan and issuer must also comply with the additional requirements of this paragraph (b)(2)(ii)(E).

(1) The plan and issuer must ensure that any notice of adverse benefit determination or final internal adverse benefit determination includes information sufficient to identify the claim involved (including the date of service, the health care provider, the claim amount (if applicable), and a statement describing the availability, upon request, of the diagnosis code and its corresponding meaning, and the treatment code and its corresponding meaning).

(2) The plan and issuer must provide to participants and beneficiaries, as soon as practicable, upon request, the diagnosis code and its corresponding meaning, and the treatment code and its corresponding meaning, associated with any adverse benefit determination or final internal adverse benefit determination. The plan or issuer must

not consider a request for such diagnosis and treatment information, in itself, to be a request for an internal appeal under this paragraph (b) or an external review under paragraphs (c) and (d) of this section.

(3) The plan and issuer must ensure that the reason or reasons for the adverse benefit determination or final internal adverse benefit determination includes the denial code and its corresponding meaning, as well as a description of the plan's or issuer's standard, if any, that was used in denying the claim. In the case of a notice of final internal adverse benefit determination, this description must include a discussion of the decision.

(4) The plan and issuer must provide a description of available internal appeals and external review processes, including information regarding how to initiate an appeal.

(5) The plan and issuer must disclose the availability of, and contact information for, any applicable office of health insurance consumer assistance or ombudsman established under PHS Act section 2793 to assist individuals with the internal claims and appeals and external review processes.

(F) Deemed exhaustion of internal claims and appeals processes—

(1) In the case of a plan or issuer that fails to strictly adhere to all the requirements of this paragraph (b)(2) with respect to a claim, the claimant is deemed to have exhausted the internal claims and appeals process of this paragraph (b), except as provided in paragraph (b)(2)(ii)(F)(*2*) of this section. Accordingly the claimant may initiate an external review under paragraph (c) or (d) of this section, as applicable. The claimant is also entitled to pursue any available remedies under section 502(a) of ERISA or under State law, as applicable, on the basis that the plan or issuer has failed to provide a reasonable internal claims and appeals process that would yield a decision on the merits of the claim. If a claimant chooses to pursue remedies under section 502(a) of ERISA under such circumstances, the claim or appeal is deemed denied on review without the exercise of discretion by an appropriate fiduciary.

(2) Notwithstanding paragraph (b)(2)(ii)(F)(*1*) of this section, the internal claims and appeals process of this paragraph (b) will not be deemed exhausted based on *de minimis* violations that do not cause, and are not likely to cause, prejudice or harm to the claimant so long as the plan or issuer demonstrates that the violation was for good cause or due to matters beyond the control of the plan or issuer and that the violation occurred in the context of an ongoing, good faith exchange of information between the plan and the claimant. This exception is not available if the violation is part of a pattern or practice of violations by the plan or issuer. The claimant may request a written explanation of the violation from the plan or issuer, and the plan or issuer must provide such explanation within 10 days, including a specific description of its bases, if any, for asserting that the violation should not cause the internal claims and appeals process of this paragraph (b) to be deemed exhausted. If an external reviewer or a court rejects the claimant's request for immediate review under paragraph (b)(2)(ii)(F)(*1*) of this section on the basis that the plan met the standards for the exception under this paragraph (b)(2)(ii)(F)(*2*), the claimant has the right to resubmit and pursue the internal appeal of the claim. In such a case, within a reasonable time after the external reviewer or court rejects the claim for immediate review (not to exceed 10 days), the plan shall provide the claimant with notice of the opportunity to resubmit and pursue the internal appeal of the claim. Time periods for re-filing the claim shall begin to run upon claimant's receipt of such notice.

(iii) Requirement to provide continued coverage pending the outcome of an appeal. A plan and issuer subject to the requirements of this paragraph (b)(2) are required to provide continued coverage pending the outcome of an appeal. For this purpose, the plan and issuer must comply with the requirements of 29 CFR 2560.503-1(f)(2)(ii), which generally provides that benefits for an ongoing course of treatment cannot be reduced or terminated without providing advance notice and an opportunity for advance review.

(c) State standards for external review—

(1) In general.

(i) If a State external review process that applies to and is binding on a health insurance issuer offering group health insurance coverage includes at a minimum the consumer protections in the NAIC Uniform Model Act, then the issuer must comply with the applicable State external review process and is not required to comply with the Federal external review process of paragraph (d) of this section. In such a case, to the extent that benefits under a group health plan are provided through health insurance coverage, the group health plan is not required to comply with either this paragraph (c) or the Federal external review process of paragraph (d) of this section.

(ii) To the extent that a group health plan provides benefits other than through health insurance coverage (that is, the plan is self-insured) and is subject to a State external review process that applies to and is binding on the plan (for example, is not preempted by ERISA) and the State external review process includes at a minimum the consumer protections in the NAIC Uniform Model Act, then the plan must comply with the applicable State external review process and is not required to comply with the Federal external review process of paragraph (d) of this section. Where a self-insured plan is not subject to an applicable State external review process, but the State has chosen to expand access to its process for plans that are not subject to the applicable State laws, the plan may choose to comply with either the applicable State external review process or the Federal external review process of paragraph (d) of this section.

(iii) If a plan or issuer is not required under paragraph (c)(1)(i) or (c)(1)(ii) of this section to comply with the requirements of this paragraph (c), then the plan or issuer must comply with the Federal external review process of paragraph (d) of this section, except to the extent, in the case of a plan, the plan is not required under paragraph (c)(1)(i) of this section to comply with paragraph (d) of this section.

(2) Minimum standards for State external review processes. An applicable State external review process must meet all the minimum consumer protections in this paragraph (c)(2). The Department of Health and Human Services will determine whether State external review processes meet these requirements.

(i) The State process must provide for the external review of adverse benefit determinations (including final internal adverse benefit determinations) by issuers (or, if applicable, plans) that are based on the issuer's (or plan's) requirements for medical necessity, appropriateness, health care setting, level of care, or effectiveness of a covered benefit.

(ii) The State process must require issuers (or, if applicable, plans) to provide effective written notice to claimants of their rights in connection with an external review for an adverse benefit determination.

(iii) To the extent the State process requires exhaustion of an internal claims and appeals process, exhaustion must be unnecessary where the issuer (or, if applicable, the plan) has waived the requirement; the issuer (or the plan) is considered to have exhausted the internal claims and appeals process under applicable law (including by failing to comply with any of the requirements for the internal appeal process, as outlined in paragraph (b)(2) of this section), or the claimant has applied for expedited external review at the same time as applying for an expedited internal appeal.

(iv) The State process provides that the issuer (or, if applicable, the plan) against which a request for external review is filed must pay the cost of the IRO for conducting the external review. Notwithstanding this requirement, a State external review process that expressly authorizes, as of November 18, 2015, a nominal filing fee may continue to permit such fees. For this purpose, to be considered nominal, a filing fee must not exceed $25; it must be refunded to the claimant if the adverse benefit determination (or final internal adverse benefit determination) is reversed through external review; it must be waived if payment of the fee would impose an undue financial hardship;

»»→ Caution: Reg. §2590.715-2719 is effective January 19, 2016, and applies to group health plans beginning on the first day of the first plan year beginning on or after January 1, 2017. Until the final regulations become applicable, plans and issuers are required to continue to comply with the corresponding EBSA interim final regulations, which apply for purposes of ERISA and the Code.

and the annual limit on filing fees for any claimant within a single plan year must not exceed $75.

(v) The State process may not impose a restriction on the minimum dollar amount of a claim for it to be eligible for external review. Thus, the process may not impose, for example, a $500 minimum claims threshold.

(vi) The State process must allow at least four months after the receipt of a notice of an adverse benefit determination or final internal adverse benefit determination for a request for an external review to be filed.

(vii) The State process must provide that IROs will be assigned on a random basis or another method of assignment that assures the independence and impartiality of the assignment process (such as rotational assignment) by a State or independent entity, and in no event selected by the issuer, plan, or the individual.

(viii) The State process must provide for maintenance of a list of approved IROs qualified to conduct the external review based on the nature of the health care service that is the subject of the review. The State process must provide for approval only of IROs that are accredited by a nationally recognized private accrediting organization.

(ix) The State process must provide that any approved IRO has no conflicts of interest that will influence its independence. Thus, the IRO may not own or control, or be owned or controlled by a health insurance issuer, a group health plan, the sponsor of a group health plan, a trade association of plans or issuers, or a trade association of health care providers. The State process must further provide that the IRO and the clinical reviewer assigned to conduct an external review may not have a material professional, familial, or financial conflict of interest with the issuer or plan that is the subject of the external review; the claimant (and any related parties to the claimant) whose treatment is the subject of the external review; any officer, director, or management employee of the issuer; the plan administrator, plan fiduciaries, or plan employees; the health care provider, the health care provider's group, or practice association recommending the treatment that is subject to the external review; the facility at which the recommended treatment would be provided; or the developer or manufacturer of the principal drug, device, procedure, or other therapy being recommended.

(x) The State process allows the claimant at least five business days to submit to the IRO in writing additional information that the IRO must consider when conducting the external review, and it requires that the claimant is notified of the right to do so. The process must also require that any additional information submitted by the claimant to the IRO must be forwarded to the issuer (or, if applicable, the plan) within one business day of receipt by the IRO.

(xi) The State process must provide that the decision is binding on the plan or issuer, as well as the claimant except to the extent the other remedies are available under State or Federal law, and except that the requirement that the decision be binding shall not preclude the plan or issuer from making payment on the claim or otherwise providing benefits at any time, including after a final external review decision that denies the claim or otherwise fails to require such payment or benefits. For this purpose, the plan or issuer must provide benefits (including by making payment on the claim) pursuant to the final external review decision without delay, regardless of whether the plan or issuer intends to seek judicial review of the external review decision and unless or until there is a judicial decision otherwise.

(xii) The State process must require, for standard external review, that the IRO provide written notice to the issuer (or, if applicable, the plan) and the claimant of its decision to uphold or reverse the adverse benefit determination (or final internal adverse benefit determination) within no more than 45 days after the receipt of the request for external review by the IRO.

(xiii) The State process must provide for an expedited external review if the adverse benefit determination (or final internal adverse benefit determination) concerns an admission, availability of care, continued stay, or health care service for which the claimant received emergency services, but has not been discharged from a facility; or involves a medical condition for which the standard external review time frame would seriously jeopardize the life or health of the claimant or jeopardize the claimant's ability to regain maximum function. As expeditiously as possible but within no more than 72 hours after the receipt of the request for expedited external review by the IRO, the IRO must make its decision to uphold or reverse the adverse benefit determination (or final internal adverse benefit determination) and notify the claimant and the issuer (or, if applicable, the plan) of the determination. If the notice is not in writing, the IRO must provide written confirmation of the decision within 48 hours after the date of the notice of the decision.

(xiv) The State process must require that issuers (or, if applicable, plans) include a description of the external review process in or attached to the summary plan description, policy, certificate, membership booklet, outline of coverage, or other evidence of coverage it provides to participants, beneficiaries, or enrollees, substantially similar to what is set forth in section 17 of the NAIC Uniform Model Act.

(xv) The State process must require that IROs maintain written records and make them available upon request to the State, substantially similar to what is set forth in section 15 of the NAIC Uniform Model Act.

(xvi) The State process follows procedures for external review of adverse benefit determinations (or final internal adverse benefit determinations) involving experimental or investigational treatment, substantially similar to what is set forth in section 10 of the NAIC Uniform Model Act.

(3) *Transition period for external review processes—*

(i) Through December 31, 2017, an applicable State external review process applicable to a health insurance issuer or group health plan is considered to meet the requirements of PHS Act section 2719(b). Accordingly, through December 31, 2017, an applicable State external review process will be considered binding on the issuer or plan (in lieu of the requirements of the Federal external review process). If there is no applicable State external review process, the issuer or plan is required to comply with the requirements of the Federal external review process in paragraph (d) of this section.

(ii) An applicable State external review process must apply for final internal adverse benefit determinations (or, in the case of simultaneous internal appeal and external review, adverse benefit determinations) provided on or after January 1, 2018. The Federal external review process will apply to such internal adverse benefit determinations unless the Department of Health and Human Services determines that a State law meets all the minimum standards of paragraph (c)(2) of this section. Through December 31, 2017, a State external review process applicable to a health insurance issuer or group health plan may be considered to meet the minimum standards of paragraph (c)(2) of this section, if it meets the temporary standards established by the Secretary in guidance for a process similar to the NAIC Uniform Model Act.

(d) *Federal external review process.* A plan or issuer not subject to an applicable State external review process under paragraph (c) of this section must provide an effective Federal external review process in accordance with this paragraph (d) (except to the extent, in the case of a plan, the plan is described in paragraph (c)(1)(i) of this section as not having to comply with this paragraph (d)). In the case of health insurance coverage offered in connection with a group health plan, if either the plan or the issuer complies with the Federal external review process of this paragraph (d), then the obligation to comply with this paragraph (d) is satisfied for both the plan and the issuer with respect to the health insurance coverage. A Multi State Plan or MSP, as defined by 45 CFR 800.20, must provide an effective Federal external review process in accordance with this paragraph (d). In such circumstances, the requirement to provide external review under this paragraph (d) is satisfied when a Multi State Plan or MSP complies with standards established by the Office of Personnel Management.

>>> *Caution: Reg. § 2590.715-2719 is effective January 19, 2016, and applies to group health plans beginning on the first day of the first plan year beginning on or after January 1, 2017. Until the final regulations become applicable, plans and issuers are required to continue to comply with the corresponding EBSA interim final regulations, which apply for purposes of ERISA and the Code.*

(1) *Scope*—

(i) *In general.* The Federal external review process established pursuant to this paragraph (d) applies to the following:

(A) An adverse benefit determination (including a final internal adverse benefit determination) by a plan or issuer that involves medical judgment (including, but not limited to, those based on the plan's or issuer's requirements for medical necessity, appropriateness, health care setting, level of care, or effectiveness of a covered benefit; its determination that a treatment is experimental or investigational; its determination whether a participant or beneficiary is entitled to a reasonable alternative standard for a reward under a wellness program; or its determination whether a plan or issuer is complying with the nonquantitative treatment limitation provisions of Code section 9812 and § 54.9812, which generally require, among other things, parity in the application of medical management techniques), as determined by the external reviewer. (A denial, reduction, termination, or a failure to provide payment for a benefit based on a determination that a participant or beneficiary fails to meet the requirements for eligibility under the terms of a group health plan or health insurance coverage is not eligible for the Federal external review process under this paragraph (d)); and

(B) A rescission of coverage (whether or not the rescission has any effect on any particular benefit at that time).

(ii) *Examples.* The rules of paragraph (d)(1)(i) of this section are illustrated by the following examples:

Example 1. (i) *Facts.* A group health plan provides coverage for 30 physical therapy visits generally. After the 30th visit, coverage is provided only if the service is preauthorized pursuant to an approved treatment plan that takes into account medical necessity using the plan's definition of the term. Individual *A* seeks coverage for a 31st physical therapy visit. *A*'s health care provider submits a treatment plan for approval, but it is not approved by the plan, so coverage for the 31st visit is not preauthorized. With respect to the 31st visit, *A* receives a notice of final internal adverse benefit determination stating that the maximum visit limit is exceeded.

(ii) *Conclusion.* In this *Example 1*, the plan's denial of benefits is based on medical necessity and involves medical judgment. Accordingly, the claim is eligible for external review under paragraph (d)(1)(i) of this section. Moreover, the plan's notification of final internal adverse benefit determination is inadequate under paragraphs (b)(2)(i) and (b)(2)(ii)(E)(*3*) of this section because it fails to make clear that the plan will pay for more than 30 visits if the service is preauthorized pursuant to an approved treatment plan that takes into account medical necessity using the plan's definition of the term. Accordingly, the notice of final internal adverse benefit determination should refer to the plan provision governing the 31st visit and should describe the plan's standard for medical necessity, as well as how the treatment fails to meet the plan's standard.

Example 2. (i) *Facts.* A group health plan does not provide coverage for services provided out of network, unless the service cannot effectively be provided in network. Individual *B* seeks coverage for a specialized medical procedure from an out-of-network provider because *B* believes that the procedure cannot be effectively provided in network. *B* receives a notice of final internal adverse benefit determination stating that the claim is denied because the provider is out-of-network.

(ii) *Conclusion.* In this *Example 2*, the plan's denial of benefits is based on whether a service can effectively be provided in network and, therefore, involves medical judgment. Accordingly, the claim is eligible for external review under paragraph (d)(1)(i) of this section. Moreover, the plan's notice of final internal adverse benefit determination is inadequate under paragraphs (b)(2)(i) and (b)(2)(ii)(E)(*3*) of this section because the plan does provide benefits for services on an out-of-network basis if the services cannot effectively be provided in network. Accordingly, the notice of final internal adverse benefit determination is required to refer to the exception to the out-of-network exclusion and should describe the plan's standards for determining effectiveness of services, as well as how services available to the claimant within the plan's network meet the plan's standard for effectiveness of services.

(2) *External review process standards.* The Federal external review process established pursuant to this paragraph (d) is considered similar to the process set forth in the NAIC Uniform Model Act and, therefore satisfies the requirements of paragraph (d)(2)) if such process provides the following.

(i) *Request for external review.* A group health plan or health insurance issuer must allow a claimant to file a request for an external review with the plan or issuer if the request is filed within four months after the date of receipt of a notice of an adverse benefit determination or final internal adverse benefit determination. If there is no corresponding date four months after the date of receipt of such a notice, then the request must be filed by the first day of the fifth month following the receipt of the notice. For example, if the date of receipt of the notice is October 30, because there is no February 30, the request must be filed by March 1. If the last filing date would fall on a Saturday, Sunday, or Federal holiday, the last filing date is extended to the next day that is not a Saturday, Sunday, or Federal holiday.

(ii) *Preliminary review*—

(A) *In general.* Within five business days following the date of receipt of the external review request, the group health plan or health insurance issuer must complete a preliminary review of the request to determine whether:

(1) The claimant is or was covered under the plan or coverage at the time the health care item or service was requested or, in the case of a retrospective review, was covered under the plan or coverage at the time the health care item or service was provided;

(2) The adverse benefit determination or the final adverse benefit determination does not relate to the claimant's failure to meet the requirements for eligibility under the terms of the group health plan or health insurance coverage (*e.g.*, worker classification or similar determination);

(3) The claimant has exhausted the plan's or issuer's internal appeal process unless the claimant is not required to exhaust the internal appeals process under paragraph (b)(1) of this section; and

(4) The claimant has provided all the information and forms required to process an external review.

(B) Within one business day after completion of the preliminary review, the plan or issuer must issue a notification in writing to the claimant. If the request is complete but not eligible for external review, such notification must include the reasons for its ineligibility and current contact information, including the phone number, for the Employee Benefits Security Administration. If the request is not complete, such notification must describe the information or materials needed to make the request complete, and the plan or issuer must allow a claimant to perfect the request for external review within the four-month filing period or within the 48 hour period following the receipt of the notification, whichever is later.

(iii) *Referral to Independent Review Organization.*

(A) *In general.* The group health plan or health insurance issuer must assign an IRO that is accredited by URAC or by similar nationally-recognized accrediting organization to conduct the external review. The IRO referral process must provide for the following:

(1) The plan or issuer must ensure that the IRO process is not biased and ensures independence;

(2) The plan or issuer must contract with at least three (3) IROs for assignments under the plan or coverage and rotate claims assignments among them (or incorporate other independent, unbiased methods for selection of IROs, such as random selection); and

(3) The IRO may not be eligible for any financial incentives based on the likelihood that the IRO will support the denial of benefits.

⋙→ *Caution: Reg. §2590.715-2719 is effective January 19, 2016, and applies to group health plans beginning on the first day of the first plan year beginning on or after January 1, 2017. Until the final regulations become applicable, plans and issuers are required to continue to comply with the corresponding EBSA interim final regulations, which apply for purposes of ERISA and the Code.*

(4) The IRO process may not impose any costs, including filing fees, on the claimant requesting the external review.

(B) IRO contracts. A group health plan or health insurance issuer must include the following standards in the contract between the plan or issuer and the IRO:

(1) The assigned IRO will utilize legal experts where appropriate to make coverage determinations under the plan or coverage.

(2) The assigned IRO will timely notify a claimant in writing whether the request is eligible for external review. This notice will include a statement that the claimant may submit in writing to the assigned IRO, within ten business days following the date of receipt of the notice, additional information. This additional information must be considered by the IRO when conducting the external review. The IRO is not required to, but may, accept and consider additional information submitted after ten business days.

(3) Within five business days after the date of assignment of the IRO, the plan or issuer must provide to the assigned IRO the documents and any information considered in making the adverse benefit determination or final internal adverse benefit determination. Failure by the plan or issuer to timely provide the documents and information must not delay the conduct of the external review. If the plan or issuer fails to timely provide the documents and information, the assigned IRO may terminate the external review and make a decision to reverse the adverse benefit determination or final internal adverse benefit determination. Within one business day after making the decision, the IRO must notify the claimant and the plan.

(4) Upon receipt of any information submitted by the claimant, the assigned IRO must within one business day forward the information to the plan or issuer. Upon receipt of any such information, the plan or issuer may reconsider its adverse benefit determination or final internal adverse benefit determination that is the subject of the external review. Reconsideration by the plan or issuer must not delay the external review. The external review may be terminated as a result of the reconsideration only if the plan decides, upon completion of its reconsideration, to reverse its adverse benefit determination or final internal adverse benefit determination and provide coverage or payment. Within one business day after making such a decision, the plan must provide written notice of its decision to the claimant and the assigned IRO. The assigned IRO must terminate the external review upon receipt of the notice from the plan or issuer.

(5) The IRO will review all of the information and documents timely received. In reaching a decision, the assigned IRO will review the claim de novo and not be bound by any decisions or conclusions reached during the plan's or issuer's internal claims and appeals process applicable under paragraph (b). In addition to the documents and information provided, the assigned IRO, to the extent the information or documents are available and the IRO considers them appropriate, will consider the following in reaching a decision:

(i) The claimant's medical records;

(ii) The attending health care professional's recommendation;

(iii) Reports from appropriate health care professionals and other documents submitted by the plan or issuer, claimant, or the claimant's treating provider;

(iv) The terms of the claimant's plan or coverage to ensure that the IRO's decision is not contrary to the terms of the plan or coverage, unless the terms are inconsistent with applicable law;

(v) Appropriate practice guidelines, which must include applicable evidence-based standards and may include any other practice guidelines developed by the Federal government, national or professional medical societies, boards, and associations;

(vi) Any applicable clinical review criteria developed and used by the plan or issuer, unless the criteria are inconsistent with the terms of the plan or coverage or with applicable law; and

(vii) To the extent the final IRO decision maker is different from the IRO's clinical reviewer, the opinion of such clinical reviewer, after considering information described in this notice, to the extent the information or documents are available and the clinical reviewer or reviewers consider such information or documents appropriate.

(6) The assigned IRO must provide written notice of the final external review decision within 45 days after the IRO receives the request for the external review. The IRO must deliver the notice of the final external review decision to the claimant and the plan or issuer.

(7) The assigned IRO's written notice of the final external review decision must contain the following:

(i) A general description of the reason for the request for external review, including information sufficient to identify the claim (including the date or dates of service, the health care provider, the claim amount (if applicable), and a statement describing the availability, upon request, of the diagnosis code and its corresponding meaning, the treatment code and its corresponding meaning, and the reason for the plan's or issuer's denial);

(ii) The date the IRO received the assignment to conduct the external review and the date of the IRO decision;

(iii) References to the evidence or documentation, including the specific coverage provisions and evidence-based standards, considered in reaching its decision;

(iv) A discussion of the principal reason or reasons for its decision, including the rationale for its decision and any evidence-based standards that were relied on in making its decision;

(v) A statement that the IRO's determination is binding except to the extent that other remedies may be available under State or Federal law to either the group health plan or health insurance issuer or to the claimant, or to the extent the health plan or health insurance issuer voluntarily makes payment on the claim or otherwise provides benefits at any time, including after a final external review decision that denies the claim or otherwise fails to require such payment or benefits;

(vi) A statement that judicial review may be available to the claimant; and

(vii) Current contact information, including phone number, for any applicable office of health insurance consumer assistance or ombudsman established under PHS Act section 2793.

(viii) After a final external review decision, the IRO must maintain records of all claims and notices associated with the external review process for six years. An IRO must make such records available for examination by the claimant, plan, issuer, or State or Federal oversight agency upon request, except where such disclosure would violate State or Federal privacy laws.

(iv) Reversal of plan's or issuer's decision. Upon receipt of a notice of a final external review decision reversing the adverse benefit determination or final adverse benefit determination, the plan or issuer immediately must provide coverage or payment (including immediately authorizing care or immediately paying benefits) for the claim.

(3) Expedited external review. A group health plan or health insurance issuer must comply with the following standards with respect to an expedited external review:

(i) Request for external review. A group health plan or health insurance issuer must allow a claimant to make a request for an expedited external review with the plan or issuer at the time the claimant receives:

(A) An adverse benefit determination if the adverse benefit determination involves a medical condition of the claimant for which the timeframe for completion of an expedited internal appeal under paragraph (b) of this section would seriously jeopardize the life or health of the claimant or would jeopardize the claimant's ability to regain maximum function and the claimant has filed a request for an expedited internal appeal; or

(B) A final internal adverse benefit determination, if the claimant has a medical condition where the timeframe for completion of a standard external review would seriously jeopardize the life or

>>→ *Caution: Reg. § 2590.715-2719 is effective January 19, 2016, and applies to group health plans beginning on the first day of the first plan year beginning on or after January 1, 2017. Until the final regulations become applicable, plans and issuers are required to continue to comply with the corresponding EBSA interim final regulations, which apply for purposes of ERISA and the Code.*

health of the claimant or would jeopardize the claimant's ability to regain maximum function, or if the final internal adverse benefit determination concerns an admission, availability of care, continued stay, or health care item or service for which the claimant received emergency services, but has not been discharged from the facility.

(ii) *Preliminary review.* Immediately upon receipt of the request for expedited external review, the plan or issuer must determine whether the request meets the reviewability requirements set forth in paragraph (d)(2)(ii) of this section for standard external review. The plan or issuer must immediately send a notice that meets the requirements set forth in paragraph (d)(2)(ii)(B) for standard review to the claimant of its eligibility determination.

(iii) *Referral to independent review organization.*

(A) Upon a determination that a request is eligible for expedited external review following the preliminary review, the plan or issuer will assign an IRO pursuant to the requirements set forth in paragraph (d)(2)(iii) of this section for standard review. The plan or issuer must provide or transmit all necessary documents and information considered in making the adverse benefit determination or final internal adverse benefit determination to the assigned IRO electronically or by telephone or facsimile or any other available expeditious method.

(B) The assigned IRO, to the extent the information or documents are available and the IRO considers them appropriate, must consider the information or documents described above under the procedures for standard review. In reaching a decision, the assigned IRO must review the claim de novo and is not bound by any decisions or conclusions reached during the plan's or issuer's internal claims and appeals process.

(iv) *Notice of final external review decision.* The plan's or issuer's contract with the assigned IRO must require the IRO to provide notice of the final external review decision, in accordance with the requirements set forth in paragraph (d)(2)(iii)(B) of this section, as expeditiously as the claimant's medical condition or circumstances require, but in no event more than 72 hours after the IRO receives the request for an expedited external review. If the notice is not in writing, within 48 hours after the date of providing that notice, the assigned IRO must provide written confirmation of the decision to the claimant and the plan or issuer.

(4) *Alternative, Federally-administered external review process.* Insured coverage not subject to an applicable State external review process under paragraph (c) of this section may elect to use either the Federal external review process, as set forth under paragraph (d) of this section or the Federally-administered external review process, as set forth by HHS in guidance. In such circumstances, the requirement to provide external review under this paragraph (d) is satisfied.

(e) *Form and manner of notice—*

(1) *In general.* For purposes of this section, a group health plan and a health insurance issuer offering group health insurance coverage are considered to provide relevant notices in a culturally and linguistically appropriate manner if the plan or issuer meets all the requirements of paragraph (e)(2) of this section with respect to the applicable non-English languages described in paragraph (e)(3) of this section.

(2) *Requirements—*

(i) The plan or issuer must provide oral language services (such as a telephone customer assistance hotline) that includes answering questions in any applicable non-English language and providing assistance with filing claims and appeals (including external review) in any applicable non-English language;

(ii) The plan or issuer must provide, upon request, a notice in any applicable non-English language; and

(iii) The plan or issuer must include in the English versions of all notices, a statement prominently displayed in any applicable non-English language clearly indicating how to access the language services provided by the plan or issuer.

(3) *Applicable non-English language.* With respect to an address in any United States county to which a notice is sent, a non-English language is an applicable non-English language if ten percent or more of the population residing in the county is literate only in the same non-English language, as determined in guidance published by the Secretary.

(f) *Secretarial authority.* The Secretary may determine that the external review process of a group health plan or health insurance issuer, in operation as of March 23, 2010, is considered in compliance with the applicable process established under paragraph (c) or (d) of this section if it substantially meets the requirements of paragraph (c) or (d) of this section, as applicable.

(g) *Applicability date.* The provisions of this section are applicable to group health plans and health insurance issuers for plan years beginning on or after January 1, 2017. Until the applicability date for this regulation, plans and issuers are required to continue to comply with the corresponding sections of 29 CFR part 2590, contained in the 29 CFR, parts 1927 to end, edition revised as of July 1, 2015.

Interim Final Regulations

Reg. § 2590.715-2719A was adopted and published in the *Federal Register* on June 28, 2010 by 75 FR 37187).

>>→ *Caution: Until final Reg. § 2590.715-2719A at ¶ 15,050R-50WA is applicable on the first day of the plan year beginning on or after January 1, 2017, plans and issuers must continue to comply with the below interim final regulation.*

[¶ 15,050R-50W]

§ 2590.715-2719A Patient protections.

(a) *Choice of health care professional.* (1) *Designation of primary care provider.* (i) *In general..* If a group health plan, or a health insurance issuer offering group health insurance coverage, requires or provides for designation by a participant or beneficiary of a participating primary care provider, then the plan or issuer must permit each participant or beneficiary to designate any participating primary care provider who is available to accept the participant or beneficiary. In such a case, the plan or issuer must comply with the rules of paragraph (a)(4) of this section by informing each participant of the terms of the plan or health insurance coverage regarding designation of a primary care provider.

(ii) *Example..* The rules of this paragraph (a)(1) are illustrated by the following example:

Example. (i) *Facts.* A group health plan requires individuals covered under the plan to designate a primary care provider. The plan permits each individual to designate any primary care provider participating in the plan's network who is available to accept the individual as the individual's primary care provider. If an individual has not designated a primary care provider, the plan designates one until one has been designated by the individual. The plan provides a notice that satisfies the requirements of paragraph (a)(4) of this section regarding the ability to designate a primary care provider.

(ii) *Conclusion.* In this *Example,* the plan has satisfied the requirements of paragraph (a) of this section.

(2) *Designation of pediatrician as primary care provider.* (i) *In general..* If a group health plan, or a health insurance issuer offering group health insurance coverage, requires or provides for the designation of a participating primary care provider for a child by a participant or beneficiary, the plan or issuer must permit the participant or beneficiary to designate a physician (allopathic or osteopathic) who specializes in pediatrics as the child's primary care provider if the provider participates in the network of the plan or issuer and is available to accept the child. In such a case, the plan or issuer must comply with

the rules of paragraph (a)(4) of this section by informing each participant of the terms of the plan or health insurance coverage regarding designation of a pediatrician as the child's primary care provider.

(ii) *Construction.*. Nothing in paragraph (a)(2)(i) of this section is to be construed to waive any exclusions of coverage under the terms and conditions of the plan or health insurance coverage with respect to coverage of pediatric care.

(iii) *Examples.*. The rules of this paragraph (a)(2) are illustrated by the following examples:

Example 1. (i) *Facts.* A group health plan's HMO designates for each participant a physician who specializes in internal medicine to serve as the primary care provider for the participant and any beneficiaries. Participant *A* requests that Pediatrician *B* be designated as the primary care provider for *A*'s child. *B* is a participating provider in the HMO's network.

(ii) *Conclusion.* In this *Example 1,* the HMO must permit *A*'s designation of *B* as the primary care provider for *A*'s child in order to comply with the requirements of this paragraph (a)(2).

Example 2. (i) *Facts.* Same facts as *Example 1,* except that *A* takes *A*'s child to *B* for treatment of the child's severe shellfish allergies. *B* wishes to refer *A*'s child to an allergist for treatment. The HMO, however, does not provide coverage for treatment of food allergies, nor does it have an allergist participating in its network, and it therefore refuses to authorize the referral.

(ii) *Conclusion.* In this *Example 2,* the HMO has not violated the requirements of this paragraph (a)(2) because the exclusion of treatment for food allergies is in accordance with the terms of *A*'s coverage.

(3) *Patient access to obstetrical and gynecological care.* (i) *General rights.* (A) *Direct access.*. A group health plan, or a health insurance issuer offering group health insurance coverage, described in paragraph (a)(3)(ii) of this section may not require authorization or referral by the plan, issuer, or any person (including a primary care provider) in the case of a female participant or beneficiary who seeks coverage for obstetrical or gynecological care provided by a participating health care professional who specializes in obstetrics or gynecology. In such a case, the plan or issuer must comply with the rules of paragraph (a)(4) of this section by informing each participant that the plan may not require authorization or referral for obstetrical or gynecological care by a participating health care professional who specializes in obstetrics or gynecology. The plan or issuer may require such a professional to agree to otherwise adhere to the plan's or issuer's policies and procedures, including procedures regarding referrals and obtaining prior authorization and providing services pursuant to a treatment plan (if any) approved by the plan or issuer. For purposes of this paragraph (a)(3), a health care professional who specializes in obstetrics or gynecology is any individual (including a person other than a physician) who is authorized under applicable State law to provide obstetrical or gynecological care.

(B) *Obstetrical and gynecological care.*. A group health plan or health insurance issuer described in paragraph (a)(3)(ii) of this section must treat the provision of obstetrical and gynecological care, and the ordering of related obstetrical and gynecological items and services, pursuant to the direct access described under paragraph (a)(3)(i)(A) of this section, by a participating health care professional who specializes in obstetrics or gynecology as the authorization of the primary care provider.

(ii) *Application of paragraph.*. A group health plan, or a health insurance issuer offering group health insurance coverage, is described in this paragraph (a)(3) if the plan or issuer—

(A) Provides coverage for obstetrical or gynecological care; and

(B) Requires the designation by a participant or beneficiary of a participating primary care provider.

(iii) *Construction.*. Nothing in paragraph (a)(3)(i) of this section is to be construed to—

(A) Waive any exclusions of coverage under the terms and conditions of the plan or health insurance coverage with respect to coverage of obstetrical or gynecological care; or

(B) Preclude the group health plan or health insurance issuer involved from requiring that the obstetrical or gynecological provider notify the primary care health care professional or the plan or issuer of treatment decisions.

(iv) *Examples.*. The rules of this paragraph (a)(3) are illustrated by the following examples:

Example 1. (i) *Facts.* A group health plan requires each participant to designate a physician to serve as the primary care provider for the participant and the participant's family. Participant *A*, a female, requests a gynecological exam with Physician *B,* an in-network physician specializing in gynecological care. The group health plan requires prior authorization from *A*'s designated primary care provider for the gynecological exam.

(ii) *Conclusion.* In this *Example 1,* the group health plan has violated the requirements of this paragraph (a)(3) because the plan requires prior authorization from *A*'s primary care provider prior to obtaining gynecological services.

Example 2. (i) *Facts.* Same facts as *Example 1* except that *A* seeks gynecological services from *C,* an out-of-network provider.

(ii) *Conclusion.* In this *Example 2,* the group health plan has not violated the requirements of this paragraph (a)(3) by requiring prior authorization because *C* is not a participating health care provider.

Example 3. (i) *Facts.* Same facts as *Example 1* except that the group health plan only requires *B* to inform *A*'s designated primary care physician of treatment decisions.

(ii) *Conclusion.* In this *Example 3,* the group health plan has not violated the requirements of this paragraph (a)(3) because *A* has direct access to *B* without prior authorization. The fact that the group health plan requires notification of treatment decisions to the designated primary care physician does not violate this paragraph (a)(3).

Example 4. (i) *Facts.* A group health plan requires each participant to designate a physician to serve as the primary care provider for the participant and the participant's family. The group health plan requires prior authorization before providing benefits for uterine fibroid embolization.

(ii) *Conclusion.* In this *Example 4,* the plan requirement for prior authorization before providing benefits for uterine fibroid embolization does not violate the requirements of this paragraph (a)(3) because, though the prior authorization requirement applies to obstetrical services, it does not restrict access to any providers specializing in obstetrics or gynecology.

(4) *Notice of right to designate a primary care provider.* (i) *In general.*. If a group health plan or health insurance issuer requires the designation by a participant or beneficiary of a primary care provider, the plan or issuer must provide a notice informing each participant of the terms of the plan or health insurance coverage regarding designation of a primary care provider and of the rights—

(A) Under paragraph (a)(1)(i) of this section, that any participating primary care provider who is available to accept the participant or beneficiary can be designated;

(B) Under paragraph (a)(2)(i) of this section, with respect to a child, that any participating physician who specializes in pediatrics can be designated as the primary care provider; and

(C) Under paragraph (a)(3)(i) of this section, that the plan may not require authorization or referral for obstetrical or gynecological care by a participating health care professional who specializes in obstetrics or gynecology.

(ii) *Timing.*. The notice described in paragraph (a)(4)(i) of this section must be included whenever the plan or issuer provides a participant with a summary plan description or other similar description of benefits under the plan or health insurance coverage.

(iii) *Model language.*. The following model language can be used to satisfy the notice requirement described in paragraph (a)(4)(i) of this section:

(A) For plans and issuers that require or allow for the designation of primary care providers by participants or beneficiaries, insert:

[Name of group health plan or health insurance issuer] generally [requires/allows] the designation of a primary care provider. You have the right to designate any primary care provider who participates in our network and who is available to accept you or your family members. [If the plan or health insurance coverage designates a primary care provider automatically, insert: Until you make this designation, [name of group health plan or health insurance issuer] designates one for you.] For information on how to select a primary care provider, and for a list of the participating primary care providers, contact the [plan administrator or issuer] at [insert contact information].

(B) For plans and issuers that require or allow for the designation of a primary care provider for a child, add:

For children, you may designate a pediatrician as the primary care provider.

(C) For plans and issuers that provide coverage for obstetric or gynecological care and require the designation by a participant or beneficiary of a primary care provider, add:

You do not need prior authorization from [name of group health plan or issuer] or from any other person (including a primary care provider) in order to obtain access to obstetrical or gynecological care from a health care professional in our network who specializes in obstetrics or gynecology. The health care professional, however, may be required to comply with certain procedures, including obtaining prior authorization for certain services, following a pre-approved treatment plan, or procedures for making referrals. For a list of participating health care professionals who specialize in obstetrics or gynecology, contact the [plan administrator or issuer] at [insert contact information].

(b) *Coverage of emergency services.* (1) *Scope.*. If a group health plan, or a health insurance issuer offering group health insurance coverage, provides any benefits with respect to services in an emergency department of a hospital, the plan or issuer must cover emergency services (as defined in paragraph (b)(4)(ii) of this section) consistent with the rules of this paragraph (b).

(2) *General rules.*. A plan or issuer subject to the requirements of this paragraph (b) must provide coverage for emergency services in the following manner—

(i) Without the need for any prior authorization determination, even if the emergency services are provided on an out-of-network basis;

(ii) Without regard to whether the health care provider furnishing the emergency services is a participating network provider with respect to the services;

(iii) If the emergency services are provided out of network, without imposing any administrative requirement or limitation on coverage that is more restrictive than the requirements or limitations that apply to emergency services received from in-network providers;

(iv) If the emergency services are provided out of network, by complying with the cost-sharing requirements of paragraph (b)(3) of this section; and

(v) Without regard to any other term or condition of the coverage, other than—

(A) The exclusion of or coordination of benefits;

(B) An affiliation or waiting period permitted under part 7 of ERISA, part A of title XXVII of the PHS Act, or chapter 100 of the Internal Revenue Code; or

(C) Applicable cost sharing.

(3) *Cost-sharing requirements.* (i) *Copayments and coinsurance.*. Any cost-sharing requirement expressed as a copayment amount or coinsurance rate imposed with respect to a participant or beneficiary for out-of-network emergency services cannot exceed the cost-sharing requirement imposed with respect to a participant or beneficiary if the services were provided in-network. However, a participant or beneficiary may be required to pay, in addition to the in-network cost sharing, the excess of the amount the out-of-network provider charges over the amount the plan or issuer is required to pay under this paragraph (b)(3)(i). A group health plan or health insurance issuer complies with the requirements of this paragraph (b)(3) if it provides benefits with respect to an emergency service in an amount equal to the greatest of the three amounts specified in paragraphs (b)(3)(i)(A), (b)(3)(i)(B), and (b)(3)(i)(C) of this section (which are adjusted for in-network cost-sharing requirements).

(A) The amount negotiated with in-network providers for the emergency service furnished, excluding any in-network copayment or coinsurance imposed with respect to the participant or beneficiary. If there is more than one amount negotiated with in-network providers for the emergency service, the amount described under this paragraph (b)(3)(i)(A) is the median of these amounts, excluding any in-network copayment or coinsurance imposed with respect to the participant or beneficiary. In determining the median described in the preceding sentence, the amount negotiated with each in-network provider is treated as a separate amount (even if the same amount is paid to more than one provider). If there is no per-service amount negotiated with in-network providers (such as under a capitation or other similar payment arrangement), the amount under this paragraph (b)(3)(i)(A) is disregarded.

(B) The amount for the emergency service calculated using the same method the plan generally uses to determine payments for out-of-network services (such as the usual, customary, and reasonable amount), excluding any in-network copayment or coinsurance imposed with respect to the participant or beneficiary. The amount in this paragraph (b)(3)(i)(B) is determined without reduction for out-of-network cost sharing that generally applies under the plan or health insurance coverage with respect to out-of-network services. Thus, for example, if a plan generally pays 70 percent of the usual, customary, and reasonable amount for out-of-network services, the amount in this paragraph (b)(3)(i)(B) for an emergency service is the total (that is, 100 percent) of the usual, customary, and reasonable amount for the service, not reduced by the 30 percent coinsurance that would generally apply to out-of-network services (but reduced by the in-network copayment or coinsurance that the individual would be responsible for if the emergency service had been provided in-network).

(C) The amount that would be paid under Medicare (part A or part B of title XVIII of the Social Security Act, 42 U.S.C. 1395 *et seq.*) for the emergency service, excluding any in-network copayment or coinsurance imposed with respect to the participant or beneficiary.

(ii) *Other cost sharing.*. Any cost-sharing requirement other than a copayment or coinsurance requirement (such as a deductible or out-of-pocket maximum) may be imposed with respect to emergency services provided out of network if the cost-sharing requirement generally applies to out-of-network benefits. A deductible may be imposed with respect to out-of-network emergency services only as part of a deductible that generally applies to out-of-network benefits. If an out-of-pocket maximum generally applies to out-of-network benefits, that out-of-pocket maximum must apply to out-of-network emergency services.

(iii) *Examples.*. The rules of this paragraph (b)(3) are illustrated by the following examples. In all of these examples, the group health plan covers benefits with respect to emergency services.

Example 1. (i) *Facts.* A group health plan imposes a 25% coinsurance responsibility on individuals who are furnished emergency services, whether provided in network or out of network. If a covered individual notifies the plan within two business days after the day an individual receives treatment in an emergency department, the plan reduces the coinsurance rate to 15%.

(ii) *Conclusion.* In this *Example 1,* the requirement to notify the plan in order to receive a reduction in the coinsurance rate does not violate the requirement that the plan cover emergency services without the need for any prior authorization determination. This is the result

>>→ *Caution: Until final Reg. § 2590.715-2719A at ¶ 15,050R-50WA is applicable on the first day of the plan year beginning on or after January 1, 2017, plans and issuers must continue to comply with the below interim final regulation.*

even if the plan required that it be notified before or at the time of receiving services at the emergency department in order to receive a reduction in the coinsurance rate.

Example 2. (i) *Facts.* A group health plan imposes a $60 copayment on emergency services without preauthorization, whether provided in network or out of network. If emergency services are preauthorized, the plan waives the copayment, even if it later determines the medical condition was not an emergency medical condition.

(ii) *Conclusion.* In this *Example 2,* by requiring an individual to pay more for emergency services if the individual does not obtain prior authorization, the plan violates the requirement that the plan cover emergency services without the need for any prior authorization determination. (By contrast, if, to have the copayment waived, the plan merely required that it be notified rather than a prior authorization, then the plan would not violate the requirement that the plan cover emergency services without the need for any prior authorization determination.)

Example 3. (i) *Facts.* A group health plan covers individuals who receive emergency services with respect to an emergency medical condition from an out-of-network provider. The plan has agreements with in-network providers with respect to a certain emergency service. Each provider has agreed to provide the service for a certain amount. Among all the providers for the service: one has agreed to accept $85, two have agreed to accept $100, two have agreed to accept $110, three have agreed to accept $120, and one has agreed to accept $150. Under the agreement, the plan agrees to pay the providers 80% of the agreed amount, with the individual receiving the service responsible for the remaining 20%.

(ii) *Conclusion.* In this *Example 3,* the values taken into account in determining the median are $85, $100, $100, $110, $110, $120, $120, $120, and $150. Therefore, the median amount among those agreed to for the emergency service is $110, and the amount under paragraph (b)(3)(i)(A) of this section is 80% of $110 ($88).

Example 4. (i) *Facts.* Same facts as *Example 3.* Subsequently, the plan adds another provider to its network, who has agreed to accept $150 for the emergency service.

(ii) *Conclusion.* In this *Example 4,* the median amount among those agreed to for the emergency service is $115. (Because there is no one middle amount, the median is the average of the two middle amounts, $110 and $120.) Accordingly, the amount under paragraph (b)(3)(i)(A) of this section is 80% of $115 ($92).

Example 5. (i) *Facts.* Same facts as *Example 4.* An individual covered by the plan receives the emergency service from an out-of-network provider, who charges $125 for the service. With respect to services provided by out-of-network providers generally, the plan reimburses covered individuals 50% of the reasonable amount charged by the provider for medical services. For this purpose, the reasonable amount for any service is based on information on charges by all providers collected by a third party, on a zip code by zip code basis, with the plan treating charges at a specified percentile as reasonable. For the emergency service received by the individual, the reasonable amount calculated using this method is $116. The amount that would be paid under Medicare for the emergency service, excluding any copayment or coinsurance for the service, is $80.

(ii) *Conclusion.* In this *Example 5,* the plan is responsible for paying $92.80, 80% of $116. The median amount among those agreed to for the emergency service is $115 and the amount the plan would pay is

$92 (80% of $115); the amount calculated using the same method the plan uses to determine payments for out-of-network services—$116—excluding the in-network 20% coinsurance, is $92.80; and the Medicare payment is $80. Thus, the greatest amount is $92.80. The individual is responsible for the remaining $32.20 charged by the out-of-network provider.

Example 6. (i) *Facts.* Same facts as *Example 5.* The group health plan generally imposes a $250 deductible for in-network health care. With respect to all health care provided by out-of-network providers, the plan imposes a $500 deductible. (Covered in-network claims are credited against the deductible.) The individual has incurred and submitted $260 of covered claims prior to receiving the emergency service out of network.

(ii) *Conclusion.* In this *Example 6,* the plan is not responsible for paying anything with respect to the emergency service furnished by the out-of-network provider because the covered individual has not satisfied the higher deductible that applies generally to all health care provided out of network. However, the amount the individual is required to pay is credited against the deductible.

(4) *Definitions..* The definitions in this paragraph (b)(4) govern in applying the provisions of this paragraph (b).

(i) *Emergency medical condition..* The term *emergency medical condition* means a medical condition manifesting itself by acute symptoms of sufficient severity (including severe pain) so that a prudent layperson, who possesses an average knowledge of health and medicine, could reasonably expect the absence of immediate medical attention to result in a condition described in clause (i), (ii), or (iii) of section 1867(e)(1)(A) of the Social Security Act (42 U.S.C. 1395dd(e)(1)(A)). (In that provision of the Social Security Act, clause (i) refers to placing the health of the individual (or, with respect to a pregnant woman, the health of the woman or her unborn child) in serious jeopardy; clause (ii) refers to serious impairment to bodily functions; and clause (iii) refers to serious dysfunction of any bodily organ or part.)

(ii) *Emergency services..* The term *emergency services* means, with respect to an emergency medical condition—

(A) A medical screening examination (as required under section 1867 of the Social Security Act, 42 U.S.C. 1395dd) that is within the capability of the emergency department of a hospital, including ancillary services routinely available to the emergency department to evaluate such emergency medical condition, and

(B) Such further medical examination and treatment, to the extent they are within the capabilities of the staff and facilities available at the hospital, as are required under section 1867 of the Social Security Act (42 U.S.C. 1395dd) to stabilize the patient.

(iii) *Stabilize..* The term *to stabilize,* with respect to an emergency medical condition (as defined in paragraph (b)(4)(i) of this section) has the meaning given in section 1867(e)(3) of the Social Security Act (42 U.S.C. 1395dd(e)(3)).

(c) *Applicability date..* The provisions of this section apply for plan years beginning on or after September 23, 2010. *See* § 2590.715-1251 of this part for determining the application of this section to grandfathered health plans (providing that these rules regarding patient protections do not apply to grandfathered health plans).

Regulations

Reg. § 2590.715-2719A was revised and finalized on November 18, 2015 (80 FR 72191).

[¶ 15,050R-50WA]

§ 2590.715-2719A Patient protections.

(a) *Choice of health care professional*—

(1) *Designation of primary care provider*—

(i) *In general*. If a group health plan, or a health insurance issuer offering group health insurance coverage, requires or provides for designation by a participant or beneficiary of a participating primary care provider, then the plan or issuer must permit each participant or beneficiary to designate any participating primary care provider who is available to accept the participant or beneficiary. In such a case, the plan or issuer must comply with the rules of paragraph (a)(4) of this section by informing each participant of the terms of the plan or health insurance coverage regarding designation of a primary care provider.

(ii) *Construction*. Nothing in paragraph (a)(1)(i) of this section is to be construed to prohibit the application of reasonable and appropriate geographic limitations with respect to the selection of primary care providers, in accordance with the terms of the plan or coverage, the underlying provider contracts, and applicable State law.

(iii) *Example*. The rules of this paragraph (a)(1) are illustrated by the following example:

Example. (i) *Facts*. A group health plan requires individuals covered under the plan to designate a primary care provider. The plan permits each individual to designate any primary care provider participating in the plan's network who is available to accept the individual as the individual's primary care provider. If an individual has not designated a primary care provider, the plan designates one until one has been designated by the individual. The plan provides a notice that satisfies the requirements of paragraph (a)(4) of this section regarding the ability to designate a primary care provider.

(ii) *Conclusion*. In this *Example*, the plan has satisfied the requirements of paragraph (a) of this section.

(2) *Designation of pediatrician as primary care provider*—

(i) *In general*. If a group health plan, or a health insurance issuer offering group health insurance coverage, requires or provides for the designation of a participating primary care provider for a child by a participant or beneficiary, the plan or issuer must permit the participant or beneficiary to designate a physician (allopathic or osteopathic) who specializes in pediatrics (including pediatric subspecialties, based on the scope of that provider's license under applicable State law) as the child's primary care provider if the provider participates in the network of the plan or issuer and is available to accept the child. In such a case, the plan or issuer must comply with the rules of paragraph (a)(4) of this section by informing each participant of the terms of the plan or health insurance coverage regarding designation of a pediatrician as the child's primary care provider.

(ii) *Construction*. Nothing in paragraph (a)(2)(i) of this section is to be construed to waive any exclusions of coverage under the terms and conditions of the plan or health insurance coverage with respect to coverage of pediatric care.

(iii) *Examples*. The rules of this paragraph (a)(2) are illustrated by the following examples:

Example 1. (i) *Facts*. A group health plan's HMO designates for each participant a physician who specializes in internal medicine to serve as the primary care provider for the participant and any beneficiaries. Participant *A* requests that Pediatrician *B* be designated as the primary care provider for *A*'s child. *B* is a participating provider in the HMO's network and is available to accept the child.

(ii) *Conclusion*. In this *Example 1*, the HMO must permit *A*'s designation of *B* as the primary care provider for *A*'s child in order to comply with the requirements of this paragraph (a)(2).

Example 2. (i) *Facts*. Same facts as *Example 1*, except that *A* takes *A*'s child to *B* for treatment of the child's severe shellfish allergies. *B* wishes to refer *A*'s child to an allergist for treatment. The HMO, however, does not provide coverage for treatment of food allergies, nor does it have an allergist participating in its network, and it therefore refuses to authorize the referral.

(ii) *Conclusion*. In this *Example 2*, the HMO has not violated the requirements of this paragraph (a)(2) because the exclusion of treatment for food allergies is in accordance with the terms of *A*'s coverage.

(3) *Patient access to obstetrical and gynecological care*—

(i) *General rights*—

(A) *Direct access*. A group health plan, or a health insurance issuer offering group health insurance coverage, described in paragraph (a)(3)(ii) of this section may not require authorization or referral by the plan, issuer, or any person (including a primary care provider) in the case of a female participant or beneficiary who seeks coverage for obstetrical or gynecological care provided by a participating health care professional who specializes in obstetrics or gynecology. In such a case, the plan or issuer must comply with the rules of paragraph (a)(4) of this section by informing each participant that the plan may not require authorization or referral for obstetrical or gynecological care by a participating health care professional who specializes in obstetrics or gynecology. The plan or issuer may require such a professional to agree to otherwise adhere to the plan's or issuer's policies and procedures, including procedures regarding referrals and obtaining prior authorization and providing services pursuant to a treatment plan (if any) approved by the plan or issuer. For purposes of this paragraph (a)(3), a health care professional who specializes in obstetrics or gynecology is any individual (including a person other than a physician) who is authorized under applicable State law to provide obstetrical or gynecological care.

(B) *Obstetrical and gynecological care*. A group health plan or health insurance issuer described in paragraph (a)(3)(ii) of this section must treat the provision of obstetrical and gynecological care, and the ordering of related obstetrical and gynecological items and services, pursuant to the direct access described under paragraph (a)(3)(i)(A) of this section, by a participating health care professional who specializes in obstetrics or gynecology as the authorization of the primary care provider.

(ii) *Application of paragraph*. A group health plan, or a health insurance issuer offering group health insurance coverage, is described in this paragraph (a)(3) if the plan or issuer—

(A) Provides coverage for obstetrical or gynecological care; and

(B) Requires the designation by a participant or beneficiary of a participating primary care provider.

(iii) *Construction*. Nothing in paragraph (a)(3)(i) of this section is to be construed to—

(A) Waive any exclusions of coverage under the terms and conditions of the plan or health insurance coverage with respect to coverage of obstetrical or gynecological care; or

(B) Preclude the group health plan or health insurance issuer involved from requiring that the obstetrical or gynecological provider notify the primary care health care professional or the plan or issuer of treatment decisions.

(iv) *Examples*. The rules of this paragraph (a)(3) are illustrated by the following examples:

Example 1. (i) *Facts*. A group health plan requires each participant to designate a physician to serve as the primary care provider for the participant and the participant's family. Participant *A*, a female, requests a gynecological exam with Physician *B*, an in-network physician specializing in gynecological care. The group health plan requires prior authorization from *A*'s designated primary care provider for the gynecological exam.

(ii) *Conclusion*. In this *Example 1*, the group health plan has violated the requirements of this paragraph (a)(3) because the plan requires prior authorization from *A*'s primary care provider prior to obtaining gynecological services.

Example 2. (i) *Facts.* Same facts as *Example 1* except that *A* seeks gynecological services from *C*, an out-of-network provider.

(ii) *Conclusion.* In this *Example 2*, the group health plan has not violated the requirements of this paragraph (a)(3) by requiring prior authorization because *C* is not a participating health care provider.

Example 3. (i) *Facts.* Same facts as *Example 1* except that the group health plan only requires *B* to inform *A*'s designated primary care physician of treatment decisions.

(ii) *Conclusion.* In this *Example 3*, the group health plan has not violated the requirements of this paragraph (a)(3) because *A* has direct access to *B* without prior authorization. The fact that the group health plan requires notification of treatment decisions to the designated primary care physician does not violate this paragraph (a)(3).

Example 4. (i) *Facts.* A group health plan requires each participant to designate a physician to serve as the primary care provider for the participant and the participant's family. The group health plan requires prior authorization before providing benefits for uterine fibroid embolization.

(ii) *Conclusion.* In this *Example 4*, the plan requirement for prior authorization before providing benefits for uterine fibroid embolization does not violate the requirements of this paragraph (a)(3) because, though the prior authorization requirement applies to obstetrical services, it does not restrict access to any providers specializing in obstetrics or gynecology.

(4) *Notice of right to designate a primary care provider—*

(i) *In general.* If a group health plan or health insurance issuer requires the designation by a participant or beneficiary of a primary care provider, the plan or issuer must provide a notice informing each participant of the terms of the plan or health insurance coverage regarding designation of a primary care provider and of the rights—

(A) Under paragraph (a)(1)(i) of this section, that any participating primary care provider who is available to accept the participant or beneficiary can be designated;

(B) Under paragraph (a)(2)(i) of this section, with respect to a child, that any participating physician who specializes in pediatrics can be designated as the primary care provider; and

(C) Under paragraph (a)(3)(i) of this section, that the plan may not require authorization or referral for obstetrical or gynecological care by a participating health care professional who specializes in obstetrics or gynecology.

(ii) *Timing.* The notice described in paragraph (a)(4)(i) of this section must be included whenever the plan or issuer provides a participant with a summary plan description or other similar description of benefits under the plan or health insurance coverage.

(iii) *Model language.* The following model language can be used to satisfy the notice requirement described in paragraph (a)(4)(i) of this section:

(A) For plans and issuers that require or allow for the designation of primary care providers by participants or beneficiaries, insert:

[Name of group health plan or health insurance issuer] generally [requires/allows] the designation of a primary care provider. You have the right to designate any primary care provider who participates in our network and who is available to accept you or your family members. [If the plan or health insurance coverage designates a primary care provider automatically, insert: Until you make this designation, [name of group health plan or health insurance issuer] designates one for you.] For information on how to select a primary care provider, and for a list of the participating primary care providers, contact the [plan administrator or issuer] at [insert contact information].

(B) For plans and issuers that require or allow for the designation of a primary care provider for a child, add:

For children, you may designate a pediatrician as the primary care provider.

(C) For plans and issuers that provide coverage for obstetric or gynecological care and require the designation by a participant or beneficiary of a primary care provider, add:

You do not need prior authorization from [name of group health plan or issuer] or from any other person (including a primary care provider) in order to obtain access to obstetrical or gynecological care from a health care professional in our network who specializes in obstetrics or gynecology. The health care professional, however, may be required to comply with certain procedures, including obtaining prior authorization for certain services, following a pre-approved treatment plan, or procedures for making referrals. For a list of participating health care professionals who specialize in obstetrics or gynecology, contact the [plan administrator or issuer] at [insert contact information].

(b) *Coverage of emergency services—*

(1) *Scope.* If a group health plan, or a health insurance issuer offering group health insurance coverage, provides any benefits with respect to services in an emergency department of a hospital, the plan or issuer must cover emergency services (as defined in paragraph (b)(4)(ii) of this section) consistent with the rules of this paragraph (b).

(2) *General rules.* A plan or issuer subject to the requirements of this paragraph (b) must provide coverage for emergency services in the following manner—

(i) Without the need for any prior authorization determination, even if the emergency services are provided on an out-of-network basis;

(ii) Without regard to whether the health care provider furnishing the emergency services is a participating network provider with respect to the services;

(iii) If the emergency services are provided out of network, without imposing any administrative requirement or limitation on coverage that is more restrictive than the requirements or limitations that apply to emergency services received from in-network providers;

(iv) If the emergency services are provided out of network, by complying with the cost-sharing requirements of paragraph (b)(3) of this section; and

(v) Without regard to any other term or condition of the coverage, other than—

(A) The exclusion of or coordination of benefits;

(B) An affiliation or waiting period permitted under part 7 of ERISA, part A of title XXVII of the PHS Act, or chapter 100 of the Internal Revenue Code; or

(C) Applicable cost sharing.

(3) *Cost-sharing requirements—*

(i) *Copayments and coinsurance.* Any cost-sharing requirement expressed as a copayment amount or coinsurance rate imposed with respect to a participant or beneficiary for out-of-network emergency services cannot exceed the cost-sharing requirement imposed with respect to a participant or beneficiary if the services were provided in-network. However, a participant or beneficiary may be required to pay, in addition to the in-network cost sharing, the excess of the amount the out-of-network provider charges over the amount the plan or issuer is required to pay under this paragraph (b)(3)(i). A group health plan or health insurance issuer complies with the requirements of this paragraph (b)(3) if it provides benefits with respect to an emergency service in an amount at least equal to the greatest of the three amounts specified in paragraphs (b)(3)(i)(A), (B), and (C) of this section (which are adjusted for in-network cost-sharing requirements).

»»→ *Caution: Reg. § 2590.715-2719A is effective January 19, 2016, and applies to group health plans beginning on the first day of the first plan year beginning on or after January 1, 2017. Until the final regulations become applicable, plans and issuers are required to continue to comply with the corresponding EBSA interim final regulations, which apply for purposes of ERISA and the Code.*

(A) The amount negotiated with in-network providers for the emergency service furnished, excluding any in-network copayment or coinsurance imposed with respect to the participant or beneficiary. If there is more than one amount negotiated with in-network providers for the emergency service, the amount described under this paragraph (b)(3)(i)(A) is the median of these amounts, excluding any in-network copayment or coinsurance imposed with respect to the participant or beneficiary. In determining the median described in the preceding sentence, the amount negotiated with each in-network provider is treated as a separate amount (even if the same amount is paid to more than one provider). If there is no per-service amount negotiated with in-network providers (such as under a capitation or other similar payment arrangement), the amount under this paragraph (b)(3)(i)(A) is disregarded.

(B) The amount for the emergency service calculated using the same method the plan generally uses to determine payments for out-of-network services (such as the usual, customary, and reasonable amount), excluding any in-network copayment or coinsurance imposed with respect to the participant or beneficiary. The amount in this paragraph (b)(3)(i)(B) is determined without reduction for out-of-network cost sharing that generally applies under the plan or health insurance coverage with respect to out-of-network services. Thus, for example, if a plan generally pays 70 percent of the usual, customary, and reasonable amount for out-of-network services, the amount in this paragraph (b)(3)(i)(B) for an emergency service is the total (that is, 100 percent) of the usual, customary, and reasonable amount for the service, not reduced by the 30 percent coinsurance that would generally apply to out-of-network services (but reduced by the in-network copayment or coinsurance that the individual would be responsible for if the emergency service had been provided in-network).

(C) The amount that would be paid under Medicare (part A or part B of title XVIII of the Social Security Act, 42 U.S.C. 1395 *et seq.*) for the emergency service, excluding any in-network copayment or coinsurance imposed with respect to the participant or beneficiary.

(ii) *Other cost sharing.* Any cost-sharing requirement other than a copayment or coinsurance requirement (such as a deductible or out-of-pocket maximum) may be imposed with respect to emergency services provided out of network if the cost-sharing requirement generally applies to out-of-network benefits. A deductible may be imposed with respect to out-of-network emergency services only as part of a deductible that generally applies to out-of-network benefits. If an out-of-pocket maximum generally applies to out-of-network benefits, that out-of-pocket maximum must apply to out-of-network emergency services.

(iii) *Special rules regarding out-of-network minimum payment standards—*

(A) The minimum payment standards set forth under paragraph (b)(3) of this section do not apply in cases where State law prohibits a participant or beneficiary from being required to pay, in addition to the in-network cost sharing, the excess of the amount the out-of-network provider charges over the amount the plan or issuer provides in benefits, or where a group health plan or health insurance issuer is contractually responsible for such amounts. Nonetheless, in such cases, a plan or issuer may not impose any copayment or coinsurance requirement for out-of-network emergency services that is higher than the copayment or coinsurance requirement that would apply if the services were provided in network.

(B) A group health plan and health insurance issuer must provide a participant or beneficiary adequate and prominent notice of their lack of financial responsibility with respect to the amounts described under this paragraph (b)(3)(iii), to prevent inadvertent payment by the participant or beneficiary.

(iv) *Examples.* The rules of this paragraph (b)(3) are illustrated by the following examples. In all of these examples, the group health plan covers benefits with respect to emergency services.

Example 1. (i) *Facts.* A group health plan imposes a 25% coinsurance responsibility on individuals who are furnished emergency services, whether provided in network or out of network. If a covered individual notifies the plan within two business days after the day an individual receives treatment in an emergency department, the plan reduces the coinsurance rate to 15%.

(ii) *Conclusion.* In this *Example 1*, the requirement to notify the plan in order to receive a reduction in the coinsurance rate does not violate the requirement that the plan cover emergency services without the need for any prior authorization determination. This is the result even if the plan required that it be notified before or at the time of receiving services at the emergency department in order to receive a reduction in the coinsurance rate.

Example 2. (i) *Facts.* A group health plan imposes a $60 copayment on emergency services without preauthorization, whether provided in network or out of network. If emergency services are preauthorized, the plan waives the copayment, even if it later determines the medical condition was not an emergency medical condition.

(ii) *Conclusion.* In this *Example 2*, by requiring an individual to pay more for emergency services if the individual does not obtain prior authorization, the plan violates the requirement that the plan cover emergency services without the need for any prior authorization determination. (By contrast, if, to have the copayment waived, the plan merely required that it be notified rather than a prior authorization, then the plan would not violate the requirement that the plan cover emergency services without the need for any prior authorization determination.)

Example 3. (i) *Facts.* A group health plan covers individuals who receive emergency services with respect to an emergency medical condition from an out-of-network provider. The plan has agreements with in-network providers with respect to a certain emergency service. Each provider has agreed to provide the service for a certain amount. Among all the providers for the service: One has agreed to accept $85, two have agreed to accept $100, two have agreed to accept $110, three have agreed to accept $120, and one has agreed to accept $150. Under the agreement, the plan agrees to pay the providers 80% of the agreed amount, with the individual receiving the service responsible for the remaining 20%.

(ii) *Conclusion.* In this *Example 3*, the values taken into account in determining the median are $85, $100, $100, $110, $110, $120, $120, $120, and $150. Therefore, the median amount among those agreed to for the emergency service is $110, and the amount under paragraph (b)(3)(i)(A) of this section is 80% of $110 ($88).

Example 4. (i) *Facts.* Same facts as *Example 3*. Subsequently, the plan adds another provider to its network, who has agreed to accept $150 for the emergency service.

(ii) *Conclusion.* In this *Example 4*, the median amount among those agreed to for the emergency service is $115. (Because there is no one middle amount, the median is the average of the two middle amounts, $110 and $120.) Accordingly, the amount under paragraph (b)(3)(i)(A) of this section is 80% of $115 ($92).

Example 5. (i) *Facts.* Same facts as *Example 4*. An individual covered by the plan receives the emergency service from an out-of-network provider, who charges $125 for the service. With respect to services provided by out-of-network providers generally, the plan reimburses covered individuals 50% of the reasonable amount charged by the provider for medical services. For this purpose, the reasonable amount for any service is based on information on charges by all providers collected by a third party, on a zip code by zip code basis, with the plan treating charges at a specified percentile as reasonable. For the emergency service received by the individual, the reasonable amount calculated using this method is $116. The amount that would be paid under Medicare for the emergency service, excluding any copayment or coinsurance for the service, is $80.

(ii) *Conclusion.* In this *Example 5*, the plan is responsible for paying $92.80, 80% of $116. The median amount among those agreed to for the emergency service is $115 and the amount the plan would pay is $92 (80% of $115); the amount calculated using the same method the plan uses to determine payments for out-of-network services—$116— excluding the in-network 20% coinsurance, is $92.80; and the Medicare payment is $80. Thus, the greatest amount is $92.80. The individual is

>>> *Caution: Reg. § 2590.715-2719A is effective January 19, 2016, and applies to group health plans beginning on the first day of the first plan year beginning on or after January 1, 2017. Until the final regulations become applicable, plans and issuers are required to continue to comply with the corresponding EBSA interim final regulations, which apply for purposes of ERISA and the Code.*

responsible for the remaining $32.20 charged by the out-of-network provider.

Example 6. (i) *Facts.* Same facts as *Example 5.* The group health plan generally imposes a $250 deductible for in-network health care. With respect to all health care provided by out-of-network providers, the plan imposes a $500 deductible. (Covered in-network claims are credited against the deductible.) The individual has incurred and submitted $260 of covered claims prior to receiving the emergency service out of network.

(ii) *Conclusion.* In this *Example 6,* the plan is not responsible for paying anything with respect to the emergency service furnished by the out-of-network provider because the covered individual has not satisfied the higher deductible that applies generally to all health care provided out of network. However, the amount the individual is required to pay is credited against the deductible.

(4) *Definitions.* The definitions in this paragraph (b)(4) govern in applying the provisions of this paragraph (b).

(i) *Emergency medical condition.* The term *emergency medical condition* means a medical condition manifesting itself by acute symptoms of sufficient severity (including severe pain) so that a prudent layperson, who possesses an average knowledge of health and medicine, could reasonably expect the absence of immediate medical attention to result in a condition described in clause (i), (ii), or (iii) of section 1867(e)(1)(A) of the Social Security Act (42 U.S.C. 1395dd(e)(1)(A)). (In that provision of the Social Security Act, clause (i) refers to placing the health of the individual (or, with respect to a pregnant woman, the health of the woman or her unborn child) in serious jeopardy; clause (ii) refers to serious impairment to bodily functions; and clause (iii) refers to serious dysfunction of any bodily organ or part.)

(ii) *Emergency services.* The term *emergency services* means, with respect to an emergency medical condition—

(A) A medical screening examination (as required under section 1867 of the Social Security Act, 42 U.S.C. 1395dd) that is within the capability of the emergency department of a hospital, including ancillary services routinely available to the emergency department to evaluate such emergency medical condition, and

(B) Such further medical examination and treatment, to the extent they are within the capabilities of the staff and facilities available at the hospital, as are required under section 1867 of the Social Security Act (42 U.S.C. 1395dd) to stabilize the patient.

(iii) *Stabilize.* The term *to stabilize,* with respect to an emergency medical condition (as defined in paragraph (b)(4)(i) of this section) has the meaning given in section 1867(e)(3) of the Social Security Act (42 U.S.C. 1395dd(e)(3)).

(c) *Applicability date.* The provisions of this section are applicable to group health plans and health insurance issuers for plan years beginning on or after January 1, 2017. Until the applicability date for this regulation, plans and issuers are required to continue to comply with the corresponding sections of 29 CFR part 2590, contained in the 29 CFR, parts 1927 to end, edition revised as of July 1, 2015.

[¶ 15,051A]
PREEMPTION; STATE FLEXIBILITY; CONSTRUCTION

Act Sec. 731.(a) CONTINUED APPLICABILITY OF STATE LAW WITH RESPECT TO HEALTH INSURANCE ISSUERS.—

(1) IN GENERAL. Subject to paragraph (2) and except as provided in subsection (b), this part shall not be construed to supersede any provision of State law which establishes, implements, or continues in effect any standard or requirement solely relating to health insurance issuers in connection with group health insurance coverage except to the extent that such standard or requirement prevents the application of a requirement of this part.

(2) CONTINUED PREEMPTION WITH RESPECT TO GROUP HEALTH PLANS. Nothing in this part shall be construed to affect or modify the provisions of section 514 with respect to group health plans.

(b) SPECIAL RULES IN CASE OF PORTABILITY REQUIREMENTS.—

(b)(1) IN GENERAL. Subject to paragraph (2), the provisions of this part relating to health insurance coverage offered by a health insurance issuer supersede any provision of State law which establishes, implements, or continues in effect a standard or requirement applicable to imposition of a preexisting condition exclusion specifically governed by section 701 which differs from the standards or requirements specified in such section.

(2) EXCEPTIONS. Only in relation to health insurance coverage offered by a health insurance issuer, the provisions of this part do not supersede any provision of State law to the extent that such provision—

(A) substitutes for the reference to "6-month period" in section 701(a)(1) a reference to any shorter period of time;

(B) substitutes for the reference to "12 months" and "18 months" in section 701(a)(2) a reference to any shorter period of time;

(C) substitutes for the references to "63 days" in sections 701(c)(2)(A) and (d)(4)(A) a reference to any greater number of days;

(D) substitutes for the reference to "30-day period" in sections 701(b)(2) and (d)(1) a reference to any greater period;

(E) prohibits the imposition of any preexisting condition exclusion in cases not described in section 701(d) or expands the exceptions described in such section;

(F) requires special enrollment periods in addition to those required under section 701(f); or

(G) reduces the maximum period permitted in an affiliation period under section 701(g)(1)(B).

(c) RULES OF CONSTRUCTION. Except as provided in section 711, nothing in this part shall be construed as requiring a group health plan or health insurance coverage to provide specific benefits under the terms of such plan or coverage.

(d) DEFINITIONS. For purposes of this section—

(1) STATE LAW. The term "State law" includes all laws, decisions, rules, regulations, or other State action having the effect of law, of any State. A law of the United States applicable only to the District of Columbia shall be treated as a State law rather than a law of the United States.

(2) STATE. The term "State" includes a State, the Northern Mariana Islands, any political subdivisions of a State or such Islands, or any agency or instrumentality of either.

Amendments

P.L. 104-204, § 603(a)(3):

Redesignated ERISA Act Sec. 704 as ERISA Act Sec. 731.

P.L. 104-204, § 603(b)(1):

Amended ERISA Act Sec. 731 by striking "Nothing" and inserting "Except as provided in section 711, nothing".

The above amendments shall apply with respect to group health plans for plan years beginning on or after January 1, 1998.

P.L. 104-191, § 101(a):

Added ERISA Act Sec. 704 to read as above.

The above amendments generally apply with respect to group health plans for plan years beginning after June 30, 1997. For special rules, see Act Sec. 101(g)(2)-(5), reproduced after ERISA Act Sec. 701 above.

Regulations

The following regulations were adopted by 62 FR 16894 and published in the Federal Register on April 8, 1997, under "Chapter XXV of Title 29 of the Code of Federal Regulations; Subchapter L—Health Insurance Portability and Renewability for Group Health Plans; Part 2590—Rules and Regulations for Health Insurance Portability and Renewability for Group Health Plans." They were officially corrected on June 10, 1997, by 62 FR 31690. Reg. §2590.731 was revised by T.D. 9166 on December 30, 2004 (69 FR 78720) and corrected on April 25, 2005 (70 FR 21146). Reg. §2590.731 was amended February 24, 2014 (79 FR 10295).

Subpart C—General Provisions

[¶ 15,051A-1]

§2590.731. **Preemption; State flexibility; construction**. (a) *Continued applicability of State law with respect to health insurance issuers.* Subject to paragraph (b) of this section and except as provided in paragraph (c) of this section, part 7 of subtitle B of Title I of the Act is not to be construed to supersede any provision of State law which establishes, implements, or continues in effect any standard or requirement solely relating to health insurance issuers in connection with group health insurance coverage except to the extent that such standard or requirement prevents the application of a requirement of this part.

(b) *Continued preemption with respect to group health plans.* Nothing in part 7 of subtitle B of Title I of the Act affects or modifies the provisions of section 514 of the Act with respect to group health plans.

(c) *Special rules.* (1) *In general.* Subject to paragraph (c)(2) of this section, the provisions of part 7 of subtitle B of Title I of the Act relating to health insurance coverage offered by a health insurance issuer supersede any provision of State law which establishes, implements, or continues in effect a standard or requirement applicable to imposition of a preexisting condition exclusion specifically governed by section 701 which differs from the standards or requirements specified in such section.

(2) *Exceptions.* Only in relation to health insurance coverage offered by a health insurance issuer, the provisions of this part do not supersede any provision of State law to the extent that such provision requires special enrollment periods in addition to those required under section 701(f) of the Act. [Amended 2/24/14 by 79 FR 10295.]

(d) *Definitions.* (1) *State law.* For purposes of this section the term *State law* includes all laws, decisions, rules, regulations, or other State action having the effect of law, of any State. A law of the United States applicable only to the District of Columbia is treated as a State law rather than as a law of the United States.

(2) *State.* For purposes of this section the term *State* includes a State (as defined in §2590.701-2), any political subdivisions of a State, or any agency or instrumentality of either.

[¶ 15,051B]
SPECIAL RULES RELATING TO GROUP HEALTH PLANS

Act Sec. 732.(a) GENERAL EXCEPTION FOR CERTAIN SMALL GROUP HEALTH PLANS. The requirements of this part (other than section 711) shall not apply to any group health plan (and group health insurance coverage offered in connection with a group health plan) for any plan year if, on the first day of such plan year, such plan has less than 2 participants who are current employees.

(b) EXCEPTION FOR CERTAIN BENEFITS. The requirements of this part shall not apply to any group health plan (and group health insurance coverage) in relation to its provision of excepted benefits described in section 733(c)(1).

(c) EXCEPTION FOR CERTAIN BENEFITS OF CERTAIN CONDITIONS MET.—

(c)(1) LIMITED, EXCEPTED BENEFITS. The requirements of this part shall not apply to any group health plan (and group health insurance coverage offered in connection with a group health plan) in relation to its provision of excepted benefits described in section 733(c)(2) if the benefits—

(A) are provided under a separate policy, certificate, or contract of insurance; or

(B) are otherwise not an integral part of the plan.

(2) NONCOORDINATED, EXCEPTED BENEFITS. The requirements of this part shall not apply to any group health plan (and group health insurance coverage offered in connection with a group health plan) in relation to its provision of excepted benefits described in section 733(c)(3) if all of the following conditions are met:

(A) The benefits are provided under a separate policy, certificate, or contract of insurance.

(B) There is no coordination between the provision of such benefits and any exclusion of benefits under any group health plan maintained by the same plan sponsor.

(C) Such benefits are paid with respect to an event without regard to whether benefits are provided with respect to such an event under any group health plan maintained by the same plan sponsor.

(3) SUPPLEMENTAL EXCEPTED BENEFITS. The requirements of this part shall not apply to any group health plan (and group health insurance coverage) in relation to its provision of excepted benefits described in section 733(c)(4) if the benefits are provided under a separate policy, certificate, or contract of insurance.

(d) TREATMENT OF PARTNERSHIPS. For purposes of this part—

(1) TREATMENT AS A GROUP HEALTH PLAN. Any plan, fund, or program which would not be (but for this subsection) an employee welfare benefit plan and which is established or maintained by a partnership, to the extent that such plan, fund, or program provides medical care (including items and services paid for as medical care) to present or former partners in the partnership or to their dependents (as defined under the terms of the plan, fund, or program), directly or through insurance, reimbursement, or otherwise, shall be treated (subject to paragraph (2)) as an employee welfare benefit plan which is a group health plan.

(2) EMPLOYER. In the case of a group health plan, the term "employer" also includes the partnership in relation to any partner.

(3) PARTICIPANTS OF GROUP HEALTH PLANS. In the case of a group health plan, the term "participant" also includes—

(A) in connection with a group health plan maintained by a partnership, an individual who is a partner in relation to the partnership, or

(B) in connection with a group health plan maintained by a self-employed individual (under which one or more employees are participants), the self-employed individual,

if such individual is, or may become, eligible to receive a benefit under the plan or such individual's beneficiaries may be eligible to receive any such benefit.

Amendments

P.L. 104-204, §603(a)(3):

Redesignated ERISA Act Sec. 705 as ERISA Act Sec. 732.

P.L. 104-204, §603(b)(2):

Amended ERISA Act Sec. 732(a) by inserting "(other than section 711)" after "part".

P.L. 104-204, §603(b)(3)(I):

Amended ERISA Act Sec. 732(b) by striking "section 706(c)(1)" and inserting "section 733(c)(1)".

P.L. 104-204, § 603(b)(3)(J):

Amended ERISA Act Sec. 732(c)(1) by striking "section 706(c)(2)" and inserting "section 733(c)(2)".

P.L. 104-204, § 603(a)(3)(K):

Amended ERISA Act Sec. 732(c)(2) by striking "section 706(c)(3)" and inserting "section 733(c)(3)".

P.L. 104-204, § 603(a)(3)(L):

Amended ERISA Act Sec. 732(c)(3) by striking "section 706(c)(4)" and inserting "section 733(c)(4)".

The above amendments shall apply with respect to group health plans for plan years beginning on or after January 1, 1998.

P.L. 104-191, § 101(a):

Added ERISA Act Sec. 705 to read as above.

The above amendments generally apply with respect to group health plans for plan years beginning after June 30, 1997. For special rules, see Act Sec. 101(g)(2)-(5), reproduced after ERISA Act Sec. 701 above.

Regulations

The following regulations were adopted by 62 FR 16894 and published in the Federal Register on April 8, 1997, under "Chapter XXV of Title 29 of the Code of Federal Regulations; Subchapter L—Health Insurance Portability and Renewability for Group Health Plans; Part 2590—Rules and Regulations for Health Insurance Portability and Renewability for Group Health Plans." Reg. § 2590.732 was revised by T.D. 9166 on December 30, 2004 (69 FR 78720) and was amended October 7, 2009 by 74 FR 51663. Reg. § 2590.732 was amended February 24, 2014 (79 FR 10295). Reg. § 2590.732 was amended by T.D. 9697 on October 1, 2014 (79 FR 59130). Reg. 2590.732 was amended by 80 FR 13995 on March 18, 2015 and by 81 FR 75316 on October 31, 2016.

[¶ 15,051B-1]

§ 2590.732. **Special rules relating to group health plans.**
(a) *Group health plan.* (1) *Defined.* A group health plan means an employee welfare benefit plan to the extent that the plan provides medical care (including items and services paid for as medical care) to employees (including both current and former employees) or their dependents (as defined under the terms of the plan) directly or through insurance, reimbursement, or otherwise.

(2) *Determination of number of plans.* [Reserved]

(b) *General exception for certain small group health plans.* (1) Subject to paragraph (b)(2) of this section, the requirements of this part do not apply to any group health plan (and group health insurance coverage) for any plan year, if on the first day of the plan year, the plan has fewer than two participants who are current employees.

(2) The following requirements apply without regard to paragraph (b)(1) of this section:

(i) Section 2590.702(b) of this Part, as such section applies with respect to genetic information as a health factor. [Redesignated 2/24/14 by 79 FR 10295.]

(ii) Section 2590.702(c) of this Part, as such section applies with respect to genetic information as a health factor. [Redesignated 2/24/14 by 79 FR 10295.]

(iii) Section 2590.702(e) of this Part, as such section applies with respect to genetic information as a health factor. [Redesignated 2/24/14 by 79 FR 10295.]

(iv) Section 2590.702-1(b) of this Part. [Redesignated 2/24/14 by 79 FR 10295.]

(v) Section 2590.702-1(c) of this Part. [Redesignated 2/24/14 by 79 FR 10295.]

(vi) Section 2590.702-1(d) of this Part. [Redesignated 2/24/14 by 79 FR 10295.]

(vii) Section 2590.702-1(e) of this Part. [Redesignated 2/24/14 by 79 FR 10295.]

(viii) Section 2590.711 of this Part. [Redesignated 2/24/14 by 79 FR 10295.]

[Amended 10-7-09 by 74 FR 51663 and 2/24/14 by 79 FR 10295.]

(c) *Excepted benefits.* (1) *In general.* The requirements of this Part do not apply to any group health plan (or any group health insurance coverage) in relation to its provision of the benefits described in paragraph (c)(2), (3), (4), or (5) of this section (or any combination of these benefits).

(2) *Benefits excepted in all circumstances.* The following benefits are excepted in all circumstances—

(i) Coverage only for accident (including accidental death and dismemberment);

(ii) Disability income coverage;

(iii) Liability insurance, including general liability insurance and automobile liability insurance;

(iv) Coverage issued as a supplement to liability insurance;

(v) Workers' compensation or similar coverage;

(vi) Automobile medical payment insurance;

(vii) Credit-only insurance (for example, mortgage insurance); and

(viii) Coverage for on-site medical clinics.

(ix) Travel insurance, within the meaning of § 2590.701–2. [Added 10/31/16 by 81 FR 75316.]

(3) *Limited excepted benefits.* (i) *In general.* Limited-scope dental benefits, limited-scope vision benefits, or long-term care benefits are excepted if they are provided under a separate policy, certificate, or contract of insurance, or are otherwise not an integral part of a group health plan as described in paragraph (c)(3)(ii) of this section. In addition, benefits provided under a health flexible spending arrangement are excepted benefits if they satisfy the requirements of paragraph (c)(3)(v) of this section. Furthermore, benefits provided under an employee assistance program are excepted benefits if they satisfy the requirements of paragraph (c)(3)(vi) of this section. [Revised 10/1/14 by T.D. 9697 (79 FR 59130).]

⟫⟫→ Caution: Reg. § 2590.732(c)(3)(ii), below, prior to amendment by T.D. 9697, is generally applicable for plan years beginning before January 1, 2015.

(ii) *Not an integral part of a group health plan.* For purposes of this paragraph (c)(3), benefits are not an integral part of a group health plan (whether the benefits are provided through the same plan or a separate plan) only if the following two requirements are satisfied—

⟫⟫→ Caution: Reg. § 2590.732(c)(3)(ii), below, as amended by T.D. 9697, is generally applicable for plan years beginning on or after January 1, 2015, but may be relied upon prior to that date.

(ii) *Not an integral part of a group health plan.* For purposes of this paragraph (c)(3), benefits are not an integral part of a group health plan (whether the benefits are provided through the same plan, a separate plan, or as the only plan offered to participants) if either paragraph (c)(3)(ii)(A) or (B) are satisfied.

(A) Participants may decline coverage. For example, a participant may decline coverage if the participant can opt out of the

(A) Participants must have the right to elect not to receive coverage for the benefits; and

(B) If a participant elects to receive coverage for the benefits, the participant must pay an additional premium or contribution for that coverage.

coverage upon request, whether or not there is a participant contribution required for the coverage.

(B) Claims for the benefits are administered under a contract separate from claims administration for any other benefits under the plan. [Revised 10/1/14 by T.D. 9697 (79 FR 59130).]

(iii) *Limited scope.* (A) *Dental benefits.* Limited scope dental benefits are benefits substantially all of which are for treatment of the mouth (including any organ or structure within the mouth).

(B) *Vision benefits.* Limited scope vision benefits are benefits substantially all of which are for treatment of the eye.

(iv) *Long-term care.* Long-term care benefits are benefits that are either—

(A) Subject to State long-term care insurance laws;

(B) For qualified long-term care services, as defined in section 7702B(c)(1) of the Internal Revenue Code, or provided under a qualified long-term care insurance contract, as defined in section 7702B(b) of the Internal Revenue Code; or

(C) Based on cognitive impairment or a loss of functional capacity that is expected to be chronic.

»»→ Caution: *Reg. § 2590.732(c)(3)(vi), below, as added by T.D. 9697, is generally applicable for plan years beginning on or after January 1, 2015, but may be relied upon prior to that date.*

(vi) *Employee assistance programs.* Benefits provided under employee assistance programs are excepted if they satisfy all of the requirements of this paragraph (c)(3)(vi).

(A) The program does not provide significant benefits in the nature of medical care. For this purpose, the amount, scope and duration of covered services are taken into account.

(B) The benefits under the employee assistance program are not coordinated with benefits under another group health plan, as follows:

(1) Participants in the other group health plan must not be required to use and exhaust benefits under the employee assistance

(v) *Health flexible spending arrangements.* Benefits provided under a health flexible spending arrangement (as defined in section 106(c)(2) of the Internal Revenue Code) are excepted for a class of participants only if they satisfy the following two requirements—

(A) Other group health plan coverage, not limited to excepted benefits, is made available for the year to the class of participants by reason of their employment; and

(B) The arrangement is structured so that the maximum benefit payable to any participant in the class for a year cannot exceed two times the participant's salary reduction election under the arrangement for the year (or, if greater, cannot exceed $500 plus the amount of the participant's salary reduction election). For this purpose, any amount that an employee can elect to receive as taxable income but elects to apply to the health flexible spending arrangement is considered a salary reduction election (regardless of whether the amount is characterized as salary or as a credit under the arrangement).

program (making the employee assistance program a gatekeeper) before an individual is eligible for benefits under the other group health plan; and

(2) Participant eligibility for benefits under the employee assistance program must not be dependent on participation in another group health plan.

(C) No employee premiums or contributions are required as a condition of participation in the employee assistance program.

(D) There is no cost sharing under the employee assistance program. [Added 10/1/14 by T.D. 9697 (79 FR 59130).]

»»→ Caution: *Reg. § 2590.732(c)(3)(vii) is effective on May 18, 2015, and applies to limited wraparound coverage that is first offered no earlier than January 1, 2016 and no later than December 31, 2018.*

(vii) *Limited wraparound coverage.* Limited benefits provided through a group health plan that wrap around eligible individual health insurance (or Basic Health Plan coverage described in section 1331 of the Patient Protection and Affordable Care Act); or that wrap around coverage under a Multi-State Plan described in section 1334 of the Patient Protection and Affordable Care Act, collectively referred to as "limited wraparound coverage," are excepted benefits if all of the following conditions are satisfied. For this purpose, eligible individual health insurance is individual health insurance coverage that is not a grandfathered health plan (as described in section 1251 of the Patient Protection and Affordable Care Act and § 2590.715-1251), not a transitional individual health insurance plan (as described in the March 5, 2014 Insurance Standards Bulletin Series—Extension of Transitional Policy through October 1, 2016), and does not consist solely of excepted benefits (as defined in paragraph (c) of this section).

(A) *Covers additional benefits.* The limited wraparound coverage provides meaningful benefits beyond coverage of cost sharing under either the eligible individual health insurance, Basic Health Program coverage, or Multi-State Plan coverage. The limited wraparound coverage must not provide benefits only under a coordination-of-benefits provision and must not consist of an account-based reimbursement arrangement.

(B) *Limited in amount.* The annual cost of coverage per employee (and any covered dependents, as defined in § 2590.701-2) under the limited wraparound coverage does not exceed the greater of the amount determined under either paragraph (c)(3)(vii)(B)(*1*) or (*2*) of this section. Making a determination regarding the annual cost of coverage per employee must occur on an aggregate basis relying on sound actuarial principles.

(1) The maximum permitted annual salary reduction contribution toward health flexible spending arrangements, indexed in the manner prescribed under section 125(i)(2) of the Code. For this purpose, the cost of coverage under the limited wraparound includes both employer and employee contributions towards coverage and is determined in the same manner as the applicable premium is calculated under a COBRA continuation provision.

(2) Fifteen percent of the cost of coverage under the primary plan. For this purpose, the cost of coverage under the primary

plan and under the limited wraparound coverage includes both employer and employee contributions towards the coverage and each is determined in the same manner as the applicable premium is calculated under a COBRA continuation provision.

(C) *Nondiscrimination.* All of the conditions of this paragraph (c)(3)(vii)(C) are satisfied.

(1) *No preexisting condition exclusion.* The limited wraparound coverage does not impose any preexisting condition exclusion, consistent with the requirements of section 2704 of the PHS Act (incorporated by reference into section 715 of ERISA) and § 2590.715-2704.

(2) *No discrimination based on health status.* The limited wraparound coverage does not discriminate against individuals in eligibility, benefits, or premiums based on any health factor of an individual (or any dependent of the individual, as defined in § 2590.701-2), consistent with the requirements of section 702 of ERISA and section 2705 of the PHS Act (incorporated by reference into section 715 of ERISA).

(3) *No discrimination in favor of highly compensated individuals.* Neither the limited wraparound coverage, nor any other group health plan coverage offered by the plan sponsor, fails to comply with section 2716 of the PHS Act (incorporated by reference into section 715 of ERISA) or fails to be excludible from income for any individual due to the application of section 105(h) of the Code (as applicable).

(D) *Plan eligibility requirements.* Individuals eligible for the wraparound coverage are not enrolled in excepted benefit coverage under paragraph (c)(3)(v) of this section (relating to health FSAs). In addition, the conditions set forth in either paragraph (c)(3)(vii)(D)(*1*) or (*2*) of this section are met.

(1) *Limited wraparound coverage that wraps around eligible individual insurance for persons who are not full-time employees.* Coverage that wraps around eligible individual health insurance (or that wraps around Basic Health Plan coverage) must satisfy all of the conditions of this paragraph (c)(3)(vii)(D)(*1*).

(i) For each year for which limited wraparound coverage is offered, the employer that is the sponsor of the plan offering limited wraparound coverage, or the employer participating in a plan

»»→ *Caution: Reg. §2590.732(c)(3)(vii) is effective on May 18, 2015, and applies to limited wraparound coverage that is first offered no earlier than January 1, 2016 and no later than December 31, 2018.*

offering limited wraparound coverage, offers to its full-time employees coverage that is substantially similar to coverage that the employer would need to offer to its full-time employees in order not to be subject to a potential assessable payment under the employer shared responsibility provisions of section 4980H(a) of the Code, if such provisions were applicable; provides minimum value (as defined in section 36B(c)(2)(C)(ii) of the Code); and is reasonably expected to be affordable (applying the safe harbor rules for determining affordability set forth in 26 CFR 54.4980H-5(e)(2)). If a plan or issuer providing limited wraparound coverage takes reasonable steps to ensure that employers disclose to the plan or issuer necessary information regarding their coverage offered and affordability information, the plan or issuer is permitted to rely on reasonable representations by employers regarding this information, unless the plan or issuer has specific knowledge to the contrary. In the event that the employer that is the sponsor of the plan offering wraparound coverage, or the employer participating in a plan offering wraparound coverage, has no full-time employees for any plan year limited wraparound coverage is offered, the requirement of this paragraph (c)(3)(vii)(D)(*1*)(*i*) is considered satisfied.

(ii) Eligibility for the limited wraparound coverage is limited to employees who are reasonably determined at the time of enrollment to not be full-time employees (and their dependents, as defined in §2590.701-2), or who are retirees (and their dependents, as defined in §2590.701-2). For this purpose, full-time employees are employees who are reasonably expected to work at least an average of 30 hours per week.

(iii) Other group health plan coverage, not limited to excepted benefits, is offered to the individuals eligible for the limited wraparound coverage. Only individuals eligible for the other group health plan coverage are eligible for the limited wraparound coverage.

(2) Limited coverage that wraps around Multi-State Plan coverage. Coverage that wraps around Multi-State Plan coverage must satisfy all of the conditions of this paragraph (c)(3)(vii)(D)(*2*). For this purpose, the term "full-time employee" means a "full-time employee" as defined in 26 CFR 54.4980H-1(a)(21) who is not in a limited non-assessment period for certain employees (as defined in 26 CFR 54.4980H-1(a)(26)). Moreover, if a plan or issuer providing limited wraparound coverage takes reasonable steps to ensure that employers disclose to the plan or issuer necessary information regarding their coverage offered and contribution levels for 2013 or 2014 (as applicable), and for any year in which limited wraparound coverage is offered, the plan or issuer is permitted to rely on reasonable representations by employers regarding this information, unless the plan or issuer has specific knowledge to the contrary. Consistent with the reporting and evaluation criteria of paragraph (c)(3)(vii)(E) of this section, the Office of Personnel Management may verify that plans and issuers have reasonable mechanisms in place to ensure that contributing employers meet these standards.

(i) The limited wraparound coverage is reviewed and approved by the Office of Personnel Management, consistent with the reporting and evaluation criteria of paragraph (c)(3)(vii)(E) of this section, to provide benefits in conjunction with coverage under a Multi-State Plan authorized under section 1334 of the Patient Protection and Affordable Care Act. The Office of Personnel Management may revoke approval if it determines that continued approval is inconsistent with the reporting and evaluation criteria of paragraph (c)(3)(vii)(E) of this section.

(ii) The employer offered coverage in the plan year that began in either 2013 or 2014 that is substantially similar to coverage that the employer would need to have offered to its full-time employees in order to not be subject to an assessable payment under the employer shared responsibility provisions of section 4980H(a) of the Code, if such provisions had been applicable. In the event that a plan that offered coverage in 2013 or 2014 has no full-time employees for any plan year limited wraparound coverage is offered, the requirement of this paragraph (c)(3)(vii)(D)(*2*)(*ii*) is considered satisfied.

(iii) In the plan year that began in either 2013 or 2014, the employer offered coverage to a substantial portion of full-time employees that provided minimum value (as defined in section

36B(c)(2)(C)(ii) of the Code) and was affordable (applying the safe harbor rules for determining affordability set forth in 26 CFR 54.4980H-5(e)(2)). In the event that the plan that offered coverage in 2013 or 2014 has no full-time employees for any plan year limited wraparound coverage is offered, the requirement of this paragraph (c)(3)(vii)(D)(*2*)(*iii*) is considered satisfied.

(iv) For the duration of the pilot program, as described in paragraph (c)(3)(vii)(F) of this section, the employer's annual aggregate contributions for both primary and limited wraparound coverage are substantially the same as the employer's total contributions for coverage offered to full-time employees in 2013 or 2014.

(E) *Reporting*

(1) Reporting by group health plans and group health insurance issuers. A self-insured group health plan, or a health insurance issuer, offering or proposing to offer limited wraparound coverage in connection with Multi-State Plan coverage pursuant to paragraph (c)(3)(vii)(D)(*2*) of this section reports to the Office of Personnel Management (OPM), in a form and manner specified in guidance, information OPM reasonably requires to determine whether the plan or issuer qualifies to offer such coverage or complies with the applicable requirements of this section.

(2) Reporting by group health plan sponsors. The plan sponsor of a group health plan offering limited wraparound coverage under paragraph (c)(3)(vii) of this section, must report to the Department of Health and Human Services (HHS), in a form and manner specified in guidance, information HHS reasonably requires.

(F) Pilot program with sunset. The provisions of paragraph (c)(3)(vii) of this section apply to limited wraparound coverage that is first offered no earlier than January 1, 2016 and no later than December 31, 2018 and that ends no later than on the later of:

(1) The date that is three years after the date limited wraparound coverage is first offered; or

(2) The date on which the last collective bargaining agreement relating to the plan terminates after the date limited wraparound coverage is first offered (determined without regard to any extension agreed to after the date limited wraparound coverage is first offered). [Added 3/18/15 by 80 FR 13995.]

(4) *Noncoordinated benefits.* (i) *Excepted benefits that are not coordinated.* Coverage for only a specified disease or illness (for example, cancer-only policies) or hospital indemnity or other fixed indemnity insurance is excepted only if it meets each of the conditions specified in paragraph (c)(4)(ii) of this section. To be hospital indemnity or other fixed indemnity insurance, the insurance must pay a fixed dollar amount per day (or per other period) of hospitalization or illness (for example, $100/day) regardless of the amount of expenses incurred.

(ii) *Conditions.* Benefits are described in paragraph (c)(4)(i) of this section only if—

(A) The benefits are provided under a separate policy, certificate, or contract of insurance;

(B) There is no coordination between the provision of the benefits and an exclusion of benefits under any group health plan maintained by the same plan sponsor; and

(C) The benefits are paid with respect to an event without regard to whether benefits are provided with respect to the event under any group health plan maintained by the same plan sponsor.

(iii) *Example.* The rules of this paragraph (c)(4) are illustrated by the following example:

Example. (i) *Facts.* An employer sponsors a group health plan that provides coverage through an insurance policy. The policy provides benefits only for hospital stays at a fixed percentage of hospital expenses up to a maximum of $100 a day.

(ii) *Conclusion.* In this *Example,* even though the benefits under the policy satisfy the conditions in paragraph (c)(4)(ii) of this section, because the policy pays a percentage of expenses incurred rather than a fixed dollar amount, the benefits under the policy are not excepted benefits under this paragraph (c)(4). This is the result even if, in practice, the policy pays the maximum of $100 for every day of hospitalization.

(5) *Supplemental benefits.* (i) The following benefits are excepted only if they are provided under a separate policy, certificate, or contract of insurance—

(A) Medicare supplemental health insurance (as defined under section 1882(g)(1) of the Social Security Act; also known as Medigap or MedSupp insurance);

(B) Coverage supplemental to the coverage provided under Chapter 55, Title 10 of the United States Code (also known as TRICARE supplemental programs); and

(C) *Similar supplemental coverage provided to coverage under a group health plan.* To be similar supplemental coverage, the coverage must be specifically designed to fill gaps in the primary coverage. The preceding sentence is satisfied if the coverage is designed to fill gaps in cost sharing in the primary coverage, such as coinsurance or deductibles, or the coverage is designed to provide benefits for items and services not covered by the primary coverage and that are not essential health benefits (as defined under section 1302(b) of the Patient Protection and Affordable Care Act) in the State where the coverage is issued, or the coverage is designed to both fill such gaps in cost sharing under, and cover such benefits not covered by, the primary coverage. Similar supplemental coverage does not include coverage that becomes secondary or supplemental only under a coordination-of-benefits provision. [Revised 10/31/16 by 81 FR 75316.]

(ii) The rules of this paragraph (c)(5) are illustrated by the following example:

Example. (i) *Facts.* An employer sponsors a group health plan that provides coverage for both active employees and retirees. The coverage for retirees supplements benefits provided by Medicare, but does not meet the requirements for a supplemental policy under section 1882(g)(1) of the Social Security Act.

(ii) *Conclusion.* In this *Example,* the coverage provided to retirees does not meet the definition of supplemental excepted benefits under this paragraph (c)(5) because the coverage is not Medicare supplemental insurance as defined under section 1882(g)(1) of the Social Security Act, is not a TRICARE supplemental program, and is not supplemental to coverage provided under a group health plan.

(d) *Treatment of partnerships.* For purposes of this part:

(1) *Treatment as a group health plan.* Any plan, fund, or program that would not be (but for this paragraph (d)) an employee welfare benefit plan and that is established or maintained by a partnership, to the extent that the plan, fund, or program provides medical care (including items and services paid for as medical care) to present or former partners in the partnership or to their dependents (as defined under the terms of the plan, fund, or program), directly or through insurance, reimbursement, or otherwise, is treated (subject to paragraph (d)(2)) as an employee welfare benefit plan that is a group health plan.

(2) *Employment relationship.* In the case of a group health plan, the term *employer* also includes the partnership in relation to any bona fide partner. In addition, the term *employee* also includes any bona fide partner. Whether or not an individual is a bona fide partner is determined based on all the relevant facts and circumstances, including whether the individual performs services on behalf of the partnership.

(3) *Participants of group health plans.* In the case of a group health plan, the term participant also includes any individual described in paragraph (d)(3)(i) or (ii) of this section if the individual is, or may become, eligible to receive a benefit under the plan or the individual's beneficiaries may be eligible to receive any such benefit.

(i) In connection with a group health plan maintained by a partnership, the individual is a partner in relation to the partnership.

(ii) In connection with a group health plan maintained by a self-employed individual (under which one or more employees are participants), the individual is the self-employed individual.

(e) *Determining the average number of employees.* [Reserved]

[¶ 15,051C]
DEFINITIONS

Act Sec. 733.(a) Group Health Plan. For purposes of this part—

⫸→ Caution: ERISA Sec. 733(a)(1), below, prior to amendment by P.L. 114-255, applies to plan years beginning on or before December 31, 2016.

(a)(1) In general. The term "group health plan" means an employee welfare benefit plan to the extent that the plan provides medical care (as defined in paragraph (2) and including items and services paid for as medical care) to employees or their dependents (as defined under the terms of the plan) directly or through insurance, reimbursement or otherwise.

⫸→ Caution: ERISA Sec. 733(a)(1), below, as amended by P.L. 114-255, applies to plan years beginning after December 31, 2016.

(a)(1) In general. The term "group health plan" means an employee welfare benefit plan to the extent that the plan provides medical care (as defined in paragraph (2) and including items and services paid for as medical care) to employees or their dependents (as defined under the terms of the plan) directly or through insurance, reimbursement, or otherwise. Such term shall not include any qualified small employer health reimbursement arrangement (as defined in section 9831(d)(2) of the Internal Revenue Code of 1986).

(2) Medical care. The term "medical care" means amounts paid for—

(A) the diagnosis, cure, mitigation, treatment, or prevention of disease, or amounts paid for the purpose of affecting any structure or function of the body,

(B) amounts paid for transportation primarily for and essential to medical care referred to in subparagraph (A), and

(C) amounts paid for insurance covering medical care referred to in subparagraphs (A) and (B).

(b) Definitions Relating to Health Insurance. For purposes of this part—

(b)(1) Health insurance coverage. The term "health insurance coverage" means benefits consisting of medical care (provided directly, through insurance or reimbursement, or otherwise and including items and services paid for as medical care) under any hospital or medical service policy or certificate, hospital or medical service plan contract, or health maintenance organization contract offered by a health insurance issuer.

(2) Health insurance issuer. The term "health insurance issuer" means an insurance company, insurance service, or insurance organization (including a health maintenance organization, as defined in paragraph (3)) which is licensed to engage in the business of insurance in a State and which is subject to State law which regulates insurance (within the meaning of section 514(b)(2)). Such term does not include a group health plan.

(3) Health maintenance organization. The term "health maintenance organization" means—

(A) a federally qualified health maintenance organization (as defined in section 1301(a) of the Public Health Service Act (42 U.S.C. 300e(a))),

(B) an organization recognized under State law as a health maintenance organization, or

(C) a similar organization regulated under State law for solvency in the same manner and to the same extent as such a health maintenance organization.

(4) GROUP HEALTH INSURANCE COVERAGE. The term "group health insurance coverage" means, in connection with a group health plan, health insurance coverage offered in connection with such plan.

(c) EXCEPTED BENEFITS. For purposes of this part, the term "excepted benefits" means benefits under one or more (or any combination thereof) of the following:

(1) BENEFITS NOT SUBJECT TO REQUIREMENTS.—

(A) Coverage only for accident, or disability income insurance, or any combination thereof.

(B) Coverage issued as a supplement to liability insurance.

(C) Liability insurance, including general liability insurance and automobile liability insurance.

(D) Workers' compensation or similar insurance.

(E) Automobile medical payment insurance.

(F) Credit-only insurance.

(G) Coverage for on-site medical clinics.

(H) Other similar insurance coverage, specified in regulations, under which benefits for medical care are secondary or incidental to other insurance benefits.

(2) BENEFITS NOT SUBJECT TO REQUIREMENTS IF OFFERED SEPARATELY.—

(A) Limited scope dental or vision benefits.

(B) Benefits for long-term care, nursing home care, home health care, community-based care, or any combination thereof.

(C) Such other similar, limited benefits as are specified in regulations.

(3) BENEFITS NOT SUBJECT TO REQUIREMENTS IF OFFERED AS INDEPENDENT, NONCOORDINATED BENEFITS.—

(A) Coverage only for a specified disease or illness.

(B) Hospital indemnity or other fixed indemnity insurance.

(4) BENEFITS NOT SUBJECT TO REQUIREMENTS IF OFFERED AS SEPARATE INSURANCE POLICY. Medicare supplemental health insurance (as defined under section 1882(g)(1) of the Social Security Act), coverage supplemental to the coverage provided under chapter 55 of title 10, United States Code, and similar supplemental coverage provided to coverage under a group health plan.

(d) OTHER DEFINITIONS. For purposes of this part—

(1) COBRA CONTINUATION PROVISION. The term "COBRA continuation provision" means any of the following:

(A) Part 6 of this subtitle.

(B) Section 4980B of the Internal Revenue Code of 1986, other than subsection (f)(1) of such section insofar as it relates to pediatric vaccines.

(C) Title XXII of the Public Health Service Act.

(2) HEALTH STATUS-RELATED FACTOR. The term "health status-related factor" means any of the factors described in section 702(a)(1).

(3) NETWORK PLAN. The term "network plan" means health insurance coverage offered by a health insurance issuer under which the financing and delivery of medical care (including items and services paid for as medical care) are provided, in whole or in part, through a defined set of providers under contract with the issuer.

(4) PLACED FOR ADOPTION. The term "placement", or being "placed", for adoption, has the meaning given such term in section 609(c)(3)(B).

(5) FAMILY MEMBER. The term "family member" means, with respect to an individual—

(A) a dependent (as such term is used for purposes of section 701(f)(2)) of such individual, and

(B) any other individual who is a first-degree, second-degree, third-degree, or fourth-degree relative of such individual or of an individual described in subparagraph (A).

(6) GENETIC INFORMATION—

(A) IN GENERAL—The term "genetic information" means, with respect to any individual, information about—

(i) such individual's genetic tests,

(ii) the genetic tests of family members of such individual, and

(iii) the manifestation of a disease or disorder in family members of such individual.

(B) INCLUSION OF GENETIC SERVICES AND PARTICIPATION IN GENETIC RESEARCH—Such term includes, with respect to any individual, any request for, or receipt of, genetic services, or participation in clinical research which includes genetic services, by such individual or any family member of such individual.

(C) EXCLUSIONS—The term "genetic information" shall not include information about the sex or age of any individual.

(7) GENETIC TEST—

(A) IN GENERAL—The term "genetic test" means an analysis of human DNA, RNA, chromosomes, proteins, or metabolites, that detects genotypes, mutations, or chromosomal changes.

(B) EXCEPTIONS—The term "genetic test" does not mean—

(i) an analysis of proteins or metabolites that does not detect genotypes, mutations, or chromosomal changes; or

(ii) an analysis of proteins or metabolites that is directly related to a manifested disease, disorder, or pathological condition that could reasonably be detected by a health care professional with appropriate training and expertise in the field of medicine involved.

(8) GENETIC SERVICES—

The term "genetic services" means—

(A) a genetic test;

(B) genetic counseling (including obtaining, interpreting, or assessing genetic information); or

(C) genetic education.

(9) UNDERWRITING PURPOSES—

The term "underwriting purposes" means, with respect to any group health plan, or health insurance coverage offered in connection with a group health plan—

(A) rules for, or determination of, eligibility (including enrollment and continued eligibility) for benefits under the plan or coverage;

(B) the computation of premium or contribution amounts under the plan or coverage;

(C) the application of any pre-existing condition exclusion under the plan or coverage; and

(D) other activities related to the creation, renewal, or replacement of a contract of health insurance or health benefits.

Amendments

P.L. 114-255, §18001(b)(1):

Amended ERISA Sec. 733(a)(1) by adding at the end the following: "Such term shall not include any qualified small employer health reimbursement arrangement (as defined in section 9831(d)(2) of the Internal Revenue Code of 1986)."

The above amendment applies to plan years beginning after December 31, 2016.

P.L. 110-233, §101(c):

Amended ERISA Sec. 733(d) by adding subsections (5) to (9) to read as above.

The above amendment applies with respect to group health plans for plan years beginning after the date that is 1 year after the date of enactment [May 21, 2009].

P.L. 104-204, §603(a)(3):

Redesignated ERISA Act Sec. 706 as ERISA Act Sec. 733.

The above amendment shall apply with respect to group health plans for plan years beginning on or after January 1, 1998.

P.L. 104-191, §101(a):

Added ERISA Act Sec. 706 to read as above.

The above amendments generally apply with respect to group health plans for plan years beginning after June 30, 1997. For special rules, see Act Sec. 101(g)(2)-(5), reproduced after ERISA Act Sec. 701 above.

[¶ 15,051D]
REGULATIONS

Act Sec. 734. The Secretary, consistent with section 104 of the Health Care Portability and Accountability Act of 1996, may promulgate such regulations as may be necessary or appropriate to carry out the provisions of this part. The Secretary may promulgate any interim final rules as the Secretary determines are appropriate to carry out this part.

Amendments

P.L. 104-204, §603(a)(3):

Redesignated ERISA Act Sec. 707 as ERISA Act Sec. 734.

The above amendment shall apply with respect to group health plans for plan years beginning on or after January 1, 1998.

P.L. 104-191, §101(a):

Added ERISA Act Sec. 707 to read as above.

The above amendments generally apply with respect to group health plans for plan years beginning after June 30, 1997. For special rules, see Act Sec. 101(g)(2)-(5), reproduced after ERISA Act Sec. 701 above.

Regulations

The following regulations were adopted by 62 FR 16894 and published in the Federal Register on April 8, 1997, under "Chapter XXV of Title 29 of the Code of Federal Regulations; Subchapter L—Health Insurance Portability and Renewability for Group Health Plans; Part 2590—Rules and Regulations for Health Insurance Portability and Renewability for Group Health Plans."

[¶ 15,051D-1]
§ 2590.734. **Enforcement.** [Reserved.]

Regulations

The following regulations were adopted by 62 FR 16894 and published in the Federal Register on April 8, 1997, under "Chapter XXV of Title 29 of the Code of Federal Regulations; Subchapter L—Health Insurance Portability and Renewability for Group Health Plans; Part 2590—Rules and Regulations for Health Insurance Portability and Renewability for Group Health Plans." They were officially corrected on June 10, 1997, by 62 FR 31690. Revised January 8, 2001 by 66 FR 1377. Reg. § 2590.736 was revised December 30, 2004 by 69 FR 78720. Reg. § 2590.736 was amended October 31, 2016 by 81 FR 75316.

[¶ 15,051E-1]
§ 2590.736. **Applicability dates.** Sections 2590.701-1 through 2590.701-8 and 2590.731 through 2590.736 are applicable for plan years beginning on or after July 1, 2005. Until the applicability date for this regulation, plans and issuers are required to continue to comply with the corresponding sections of 29 CFR part 2590, contained in the 29 CFR, parts 1927 to end, edition revised as of July 1, 2004. Notwithstanding the previous sentence, the definition of "short-term, limited-duration insurance" in § 2590.701–2 and paragraph (c)(5)(i)(C) of § 2590.732 apply for plan years beginning on or after January 1, 2017. [Amended 10/31/16 by 81 FR 75316.]

TITLE II—AMENDMENTS TO THE INTERNAL REVENUE CODE RELATING TO RETIREMENT PLANS

Subtitle A—Participation, Vesting, Funding Administration, Etc.

Part 1—Participation, Vesting, and Funding

[¶ 15,052]
AMENDMENT OF INTERNAL REVENUE CODE OF 1954

Act Sec. 1001. Except as otherwise expressly provided, whenever in this title an amendment or repeal is expressed in terms of an amendment to, or repeal of, a section or other provision, the reference shall be considered to be made to a section or other provision of the Internal Revenue Code of 1954.

CCH Note: New and Amended Code Provisions

Title II amendments to the Internal Revenue Code of 1954, encompassing Act Secs. 1011-2008, are incorporated in place in the "Internal Revenue Code—Regulations.". The division contains the new and amended code provisions with controlling committee reports and applicable regulations.

Excerpts from Title II that do not amend the Internal Revenue Code are reproduced below.

[¶ 15,060]
MINIMUM VESTING STANDARDS

Act Sec. 1012.

* * *

(c) VARIATIONS FROM CERTAIN VESTING AND ACCRUED BENEFITS REQUIREMENTS. In the case of any plan maintained on January 1, 1974, if, not later than 2 years after the date of the enactment of this Act, the plan administrator petitions the Secretary of Labor, the Secretary of Labor may prescribe an alternate method which shall be treated as satisfying the requirements of subsection (a)(2) of section 411 of the Internal Revenue Code of 1954, or of subsection (b)(1) (other than subparagraph (D) thereof) of such section 411, or of both such provisions for a period of not more than 4 years. The Secretary may prescribe such alternate method only when he finds that—

(1) the application of such requirements would increase the costs of the plan to such an extent that there would result a substantial risk to the voluntary continuation of the plan or a substantial curtailment of benefit levels or the levels of employees' compensation,

(2) the application of such requirements or discontinuance of the plan would be adverse to the interests of plan participants in the aggregate, and

(3) a waiver or extension of time granted under section 412(d) or (e) would be inadequate.

In the case of any plan withh respect to which an alternate method has been prescribed under the preceding provisions of this subsection for a period of not more than 4 years, if, not later than 1 year before the expiration of such period, the plan administrator petitions the Secretary of Labor for an extension of such alternate method, and the Secretary makes the findings required by the preceding sentence, such alternate method may be extended for not more than 3 years.

[¶ 15,061]
MINIMUM FUNDING STANDARDS

Act Sec. 1013.

* * *

(d) ALTERNATIVE AMORTIZATION METHOD FOR CERTAIN MULTIEMPLOYER PLANS. —

(1) GENERAL RULE. In the case of any multiemployer plan (as defined in section 414(f) of the Internal Revenue Code of 1954) to which section 412 of such Code applies, if—

(A) on January 1, 1974, the contributions under the plan were based on a percentage of pay,

(B) the actuarial assumptions with respect to pay are reasonably related to past and projected experience, and

(C) the rates of interest under the plan are determined on the basis of reasonable actuarial assumptions,

the plan may elect (in such manner and at such time as may be provided under regulations prescribed by the Secretary of the Treasury or his delegate) to fund the unfunded past service liability under the plan existing as of the date 12 months following the first date on which such section 412 first applies to the plan by charging the funding standard account with an equal annual percentage of the aggregate pay of all participants in the plan in lieu of the level dollar charges to such account required under clauses (i), (ii), and (iii) of section 412(b)(2)(B) of such Code and section 302(b)(2)(B)(i), (ii), and (iii) of this Act.

(2) LIMITATION. In the case of a plan which makes an election under paragraph (1), the aggregate of the charges required under such paragraph for a plan year shall not be less than the interest on the unfunded past service liabilities described in clauses (i), (ii), and (iii) of section 412(b)(2)(B) of the Internal Revenue Code of 1954.

[¶ 15,062]
CERTAIN PUERTO RICAN PENSION PLANS

Act Sec. 1022.

* * *

(i) CERTAIN PUERTO RICAN PENSION, ETC., PLANS TO BE EXEMPT FROM TAX UNDER SECTION 501(A).—

(1) GENERAL RULE. Effective for taxable years beginning after December 31, 1973, for purposes of section 501(a) of the Internal Revenue Code of 1954 (relating to exemption from tax), any trust forming part of a pension, profitsharing, or stock bonus plan all of the participants of which are residents of the Commonwealth of Puerto Rico shall be treated as an organization described in section 401(a) of such Code if such trust—

(A) forms part of a pension, profitsharing, or stock bonus plan, and

(B) is exempt from income tax under the laws of the Commonwealth of Puerto Rico.

(2) Election to have provisions of, and amendments made by, title II of this act apply.—

(A) If the administrator of a pension, profitsharing, or stock bonus plan which is created or organized in Puerto Rico elects, at such time and in such manner as the Secretary of the Treasury may require, to have the provisions of this paragraph apply, for plan years beginning after the date of election, any trust forming a part of such plan shall be treated as a trust created or organized in the United States for purposes of section 401(a) of the Internal Revenue Code of 1954.

(B) An election under subparagraph (A), once made, is irrevocable.

(C) This paragraph applies to plan years beginning after the date of enactment of this Act.

(D) The source of any distributions made under a plan which makes an election under this paragraph to participants and beneficiaries residing outside of the United States shall be determined, for purposes of subchapter N of chapter 1 of the Internal Revenue Code of 1954, by the Secretary of the Treasury in accordance with regulations prescribed by him. For purposes of this subparagraph the United States means the United States as defined in section 7701(a)(9) of the Internal Revenue Code of 1954.

[¶ 15,065]
EFFECTIVE DATES

Act Sec. 1024. Except as otherwise provided in section 1021, the amendments made by section 1021 shall apply to plan years to which part I applies. Except as otherwise provided in section 1022, the amendments made by section 1022 shall apply to plan years in which part I applies. Section 1023 shall take effect on the date of the enactment of this Act.

[¶ 15,070]
DUTIES OF SECRETARY OF HEALTH, EDUCATION, AND WELFARE

Act Sec. 1032. Title XI of the Social Security Act (relating to general provisions) is amended by adding at the end of part A thereof the following new section:

"NOTIFICATION OF SOCIAL SECURITY CLAIMANT WITH RESPECT TO DEFERRED VESTED BENEFITS

"Sec. 1131. (a) Whenever—

"(1) the Secretary makes a finding of fact and a decision as to—

"(A) the entitlement of any individual to monthly benefits under section 202, 223, or 228,

"(B) the entitlement of any individual to a lump-sum death payment payable under section 202(i) on account of the death of any person to whom such individual is related by blood, marriage, or adoption, or

"(C) the entitlement under section 226 of any individual to hospital insurance benefits under part A of title XVIII, or

"(2) the Secretary is requested to do so—

"(A) by any individual with respect to whom the Secretary holds information obtained under section 6057 of the Internal Revenue Code of 1954, or

"(B) in the case of the death of the individual referred to in subparagraph (A), by the individual who would be entitled to payment under section 204(d) of this Act,

he shall transmit to the individual referred to in paragraph (1) or the individual making the request under paragraph (2) any information, as reported by the employer, regarding any deferred vested benefit transmitted to the Secretary pursuant to such section 6057 with respect to the individual referred to in paragraph (1) or (2)(A) or the person on whose wages and self-employment income entitlement (or claim of entitlement) is based.

"(b)(1) For purposes of section 201(g)(1), expenses incurred in the administration of subsection (a) shall be deemed to be expenses incurred for the administration of title II.

"(2) There are hereby authorized to be appropriated to the Federal Old-Age and Survivors Insurance Trust Fund for each fiscal year (commencing with the fiscal year ending June 30, 1974) such sums as the Secretary deems necessary on account of additional administrative expenses resulting from the enactment of the provisions of subsection (a)."

[¶ 15,075]
EFFECTIVE DATES

Act Sec. 1034. This part shall take effect upon the date of the enactment of this Act; except that—

(1) the requirements of section 6059 of the Internal Revenue Code of 1954 shall apply only with respect to plan years to which part I of this title applies,

(2) the requirements of section 6057 of such Code shall apply only with respect to plan years beginning after December 31, 1975,

(3) the requirements of section 6058(a) of such Code shall apply only with respect to plan years beginning after the date of the enactment of this Act, and

(4) the amendments made by section 1032 shall take effect on January 1, 1978.

[¶ 15,080]
TAX COURT PROCEDURE

Act Sec. 1041.

* * *

(d) EFFECTIVE DATE. The amendments made by this section shall apply to pleadings filed more than 1 year after the date of the enactment of this Act.

Part 5—Internal Revenue Service

[¶ 15,081]
ESTABLISHMENT OF OFFICE

Act Sec. 1051.

* * *

(b) SALARIES.—

(1) ASSISTANT COMMISSIONER. Section 5109 of title 5, United States Code, is amended by adding at the end thereof the following new subsection:

"(c) The position held by the employee appointed under section 7802(b) of the Internal Revenue Code of 1954 is classified at GS-18, and is in addition to the number of positions authorized by section 5108(a) of this title."

(2) CLASSIFICATION OF POSITIONS AT GS-16 AND 17. Section 5108 of title 5, United States Code, is amended by adding at the end thereof the following new subsection:

"(e) In addition to the number of positions authorized by subsection (a), the Commissioner of Internal Revenue is authorized, without regard to any other provision of this section, to place a total of 20 positions in the Internal Revenue Service in GS-16 and 17."

* * *

(d) EFFECTIVE DATE. The amendments made by this section shall take effect on the 90th day after the date of the enactment of this Act.

[¶ 15,082]
AUTHORIZATION OF APPROPRIATIONS

Act Sec. 1052. There is authorized to be appropriated to the Department of the Treasury for the purpose of carrying out all functions of the Office of Employee Plans and Exempt Organizations for each fiscal year beginning after June 30, 1974, an amount equal to the sum of—

(1) so much of the collections from the taxes imposed under section 4940 of such Code (relating to excise tax based on investment income) as would have been collected if the rate of tax under such section was 2 percent during the second preceding fiscal year, and

(2) the greater of—

(A) an amount equal to the amount described in paragraph (1), or

(B) $30,000,000.

Subtitle B—Other Amendments to the Internal Revenue Code Relating to Retirement Plans

[¶ 15,090]
CONTRIBUTIONS ON BEHALF OF SELF-EMPLOYED INDIVIDUALS AND SHAREHOLDER-EMPLOYEES

Act Sec. 2001.(i) EFFECTIVE DATES.—

(1) The amendments made by subsections (a) and (b) apply to taxable years beginning after December 31, 1973.

(2) The amendments made by subsection (c) apply to—

(A) taxable years beginning after December 31, 1975, and

(B) any other taxable years beginning after December 31, 1973, for which contributions were made under the plan in excess of the amounts permitted to be made under sections 404(e) and 1379(b) as in effect on the day before the date of the enactment of this Act.

(3) The amendments made by subsection (d) apply to taxable years beginning after December 31, 1975.

(4) The amendments made by subsections (e) and (f) apply to contributions made in taxable years beginning after December 31, 1975.

(5) The amendments made by subsection (g) apply to distributions made in taxable years beginning after December 31, 1975.

(6) The amendments made by subsection (h) apply to taxable years ending after the date of enactment of this Act.

[¶ 15,091]
LIMITATIONS ON BENEFITS AND CONTRIBUTIONS

Act Sec. 2004.(a) PLAN REQUIREMENTS.—

* * *

(3) SPECIAL RULE FOR CERTAIN PLANS IN EFFECT ON DATE OF ENACTMENT [September 2, 1974]. In any case in which, on the date of enactment [September 2, 1974] of this Act, an individual is a participant in both a defined benefit plan and a definedcontribution plan maintained by the same employer, and the sum of the defined benefit plan fraction and the defined contribution plan fraction for the year during which such date occurs exceeds 1.4, the sum of such fractions may continue to exceed 1.4 if—

(A) the defined benefit plan fraction is not increased, by amendment of the plan or otherwise, after the date of enactment [September 2, 1974] of this Act, and

(B) no contributions are made under the defined contribution plan after such date.

A trust which is part of a pension, profit-sharing, or stock bonus plan described in the preceding sentence shall not be treated as not constituting a qualified trust under section 401(a) of the Internal Revenue Code of 1954 on account of the provisions of section 415(e) of such Code, as long as it is described in the preceding sentence of this subsection.

* * *

(d) EFFECTIVE DATE.—

(d)(1) GENERAL RULE. The amendments made by this section shall apply to years beginning after December 31, 1975. The Secretary of the Treasury shall prescribe such regulations as may be necessary to carry out the provisions of this paragraph.

(2) TRANSITION RULE FOR DEFINED BENEFIT PLANS. In the case of an individual who was an active participant in a defined benefit plan before October 3, 1973, if—

(A) the annual benefit (within the meaning of section 415(b)(2) of the Internal Revenue Code of 1954) payable to such participant on retirement does not exceed 100 percent of his annual rate of compensation on the earlier of (i) October 2, 1973, or (ii) the date on which he separated from the service of the employer,

(B) such annual benefit is no greater than the annual benefit which would have been payable to such participant on retirement if (i) all the terms and conditions of such plan in existence on such date had remained in existence until such retirement, and (ii) his compensation taken into account for any period after October 2, 1973, had not exceeded his annual rate of compensation on such date, and

(C) in the case of a participant who separated from the service of the employer prior to October 2, 1973, such annual benefit is no greater than his vested accrued benefit as of the date he separated from the service,

then such annual benefit shall be treated as not exceeding the limitation of subsection (b) of section 415 of the Internal Revenue Code of 1954.

[¶ 15,093]
TAXATION OF CERTAIN LUMP SUM DISTRIBUTIONS

Act Sec. 2005.

* * *

(d) EFFECTIVE DATE. The amendments made by this section shall apply only with respect to distributions or payments made after December 31, 1973, in taxable years beginning after such date.

[¶ 15,095]
RULES FOR CERTAIN NEGOTIATED PLANS

Act Sec. 2007.

* * *

(c) EFFECTIVE DATE. The amendments made by this section shall apply to taxable years ending on or after June 30, 1972.

[¶ 15,096]
CERTAIN ARMED FORCES SURVIVOR ANNUITIES

Act Sec. 2008.

* * *

(c) EFFECTIVE DATES. The amendments made by this section apply to taxable years ending on or after September 21, 1972. The amendments made by paragraphs (3) and (4) of subsection (b) apply with respect to individuals dying on or after such date.

TITLE III—JURISDICTION, ADMINISTRATION, ENFORCEMENT; JOINT PENSION TASK FORCE, ETC.

Subtitle A—Jurisdiction, Administration, and Enforcement

[¶ 15,110]

PROCEDURES IN CONNECTION WITH THE ISSUANCE OF CERTAIN DETERMINATION LETTERS BY THE SECRETARY OF THE TREASURY

Act Sec. 3001.(a) ADDITIONAL MATERIAL REQUIRED OF APPLICANTS—.Before issuing an advance determination of whether a pension, profit-sharing, or stock bonus plan, a trust which is a part of such a plan, or an annuity or bond purchase plan meets the requirements of part I of subchapter D of chapter 1 of the Internal Revenue Code of 1986, the Secretary of the Treasury shall require the person applying for the determination to provide, in addition to any material and information necessary for such determination, such other material and information as may reasonably be made available at the time such application is made as the Secretary of Labor may require under title I of this Act for the administration of that title. The Secretary of the Treasury shall also require that the applicant provide evidence satisfactory to the Secretary that the applicant has notified each employee who qualifies as an interested party (within the meaning of regulations prescribed under section 7476(b)(1) of such Code (relating to declaratory judgments in connection with the qualification of certain retirement plans)) of the application for a determination.

Act Sec. 3001.(b)(1) OPPORTUNITY TO COMMENT ON APPLICATION.—Whenever an application is made to the Secretary of the Treasury for a determination of whether a pension, profit-sharing, or stock bonus plan, a trust which is a part of such a plan, or an annuity or bond purchase plan meets the requirements of part I of subchapter D of chapter 1 of the Internal Revenue Code of 1986, the Secretary shall upon request afford an opportunity to comment on the application at any time within 45 days after receipt thereof to—

(A) any employee or class of employee qualifying as an interested party within the meaning of the regulations referred to in subsection (a),

(B) the Secretary of Labor, and

(C) the Pension Benefit Guaranty Corporation.

(2) The Secretary of Labor may not request an opportunity to comment upon such an application unless he has been requested in writing to do so by the Pension Benefit Guaranty Corporation or by the lesser of—

(A) 10 employees, or

(B) 10 percent of the employees

who qualify as interested parties within the meaning of the regulations referred to in subsection (a). Upon receiving such a request, the Secretary of Labor shall furnish a copy of the request to the Secretary of the Treasury within 5 days (excluding Saturdays, Sundays, and legal public holidays (as set forth in section 6103 of title 5, United States Code).

(3) Upon receiving such a request from the Secretary of Labor, the Secretary of the Treasury shall furnish to the Secretary of Labor such information held by the Secretary of the Treasury relating to the application as the Secretary of Labor may request.

(4) The Secretary of Labor shall, within 30 days after receiving a request from the Pension Benefit Guaranty Corporation or from the necessary number of employees who qualify as interested parties, notify the Secretary of the Treasury, the Pension Benefit Guaranty Corporation, and such employees with respect to whether he is going to comment on the application to which the request relates and with respect to any matters raised in such request on which he is not going to comment. If the Secretary of Labor indicates in the notice required under the preceding sentence that he is not going to comment on all or part of the matters raised in such request, the Secretary of the Treasury shall afford the corporation, and such employees, an opportunity to comment on the application with respect to any matter on which the Secretary of Labor has declined to comment.

Act Sec. 3001. (c) INTERVENTION BY PENSION BENEFIT GUARANTY CORPORATION OR SECRETARY OF LABOR INTO DECLARATORY JUDGEMENT ACTION UNDER SECTION 7476 OF TITLE 26; ACTION BY CORPORATION AUTHORIZED.—The Pension Benefit Guaranty Corporation and, upon petition of a group of employees referred to in subsection (b)(2), the Secretary of Labor, may intervene in any action brought for declaratory judgment under section 7476 of the Internal Revenue Code of 1986 in accordance with the provisions of such section. The Pension Benefit Guaranty Corporation is permitted to bring an action under such section 7476 under such rules as may be prescribed by the United States Tax Court.

Act Sec. 3001. (d) NOTIFICATION AND INFORMATION BY SECRETARY OF THE TREASURY TO SECRETARY OF LABOR UPON ISSUANCE BY SECRETARY OF THE TREASURY OF A DETERMINATION LETTER TO APPLICANT.—If the Secretary of the Treasury determines that a plan or trust to which this section applies meets the applicable requirements of part I of subchapter D of chapter 1 of the Internal Revenue Code of 1986 and issues a determination letter to the applicant, the Secretary shall notify the Secretary of Labor of his determination and furnish such information and material relating to the application and determination held by the Secretary of the Treasury as the Secretary of Labor may request for the proper administration of title I of this Act. The Secretary of Labor shall accept the determination of the Secretary of the Treasury as prima facie evidence of initial compliance by the plan with the standards of parts 2, 3, and 4 of subtitle B of title I of this Act. The determination of the Secretary of the Treasury shall not be prima facie evidence on issues relating solely to part 4 of subtitle B of title I. If an application for such a determination is withdrawn, or if the Secretary of the Treasury issues a determination that the plan or trust does not meet the requirements of such part I, the Secretary shall notify the Secretary of Labor of the withdrawal or determination.

Act Sec. 3001. (e) EFFECTIVE DATE.—This section does not apply with respect to an application for any plan received by the Secretary of the Treasury before the date on which section 410 of the Internal Revenue Code of 1986 applies to the plan, or on which such section will apply if the plan is determined by the Secretary to be a qualified plan.

Amendments

P.L. 101-239, § 7891(a)(1):

Titles I, III, and IV of ERISA (other than sections 3(37)(E), 301(a)(7), and 308, the last sentence of section 408(d), and sections 414(c), 4001(a)(3)(ii), and 4303) are each amended by striking "Internal Revenue Code of 1954" each place it appears and inserting "Internal Revenue Code of 1986" effective October 22, 1986.

P.L. 100-203, § 9343(b):

Amended ERISA Sec. 3001(d) by adding a new sentence after the second sentence, to read as above, effective December 22, 1987.

[¶ 15,120]

PROCEDURES WITH RESPECT TO CONTINUED COMPLIANCE WITH REQUIREMENTS RELATING TO PARTICIPATION, VESTING, AND FUNDING STANDARDS

Act Sec. 3002.(a) NOTIFICATION BY SECRETARY OF THE TREASURY TO SECRETARY OF LABOR OF ISSUANCE OF A PRELIMINARY NOTICE OF INTENT TO DISQUALIFY OR OF COMMENCEMENT OF PROCEEDINGS TO DETERMINE SATISFACTION OF REQUIREMENTS.—In carrying out the provisions of part I of subchapter D of chapter 1 of the Internal Revenue Code of 1986 with respect to whether a plan or a trust meets the requirements of section 410(a) or 411 of such Code (relating to minimum participation standards and minimum vesting standards, respectively), the Secretary of the Treasury shall notify the Secretary of Labor when the Secretary of the Treasury issues a preliminary notice of intent to disqualify related to the plan or trust or, if earlier, at the time of commencing any proceeding to determine whether the plan or trust satisfies such requirements. Unless the Secretary of the Treasury finds that the collection of a tax imposed under the Internal Revenue Code of 1986 is in jeopardy, the Secretary of the Treasury shall not issue a determination that the plan or trust does not satisfy the requirements of such section until the expiration of a period of 60 days after the date on which he notifies the Secretary of Labor of such review. The Secretary of the Treasury, in his discretion, may extend the 60-day period referred to in the preceding sentence if he determines that such an extension would enable the Secretary of Labor to obtain compliance with such requirements by the plan within the extension period. Except as otherwise provided in this Act, the Secretary of Labor shall not generally apply part 2 of title I of this Act to any plan or trust subject to sections 410(a) and 411 of such Code, but shall refer alleged general violations of the vesting or participation standards to the Secretary of the Treasury. (The preceding sentence shall not apply to matters relating to individual benefits.)

Act Sec. 3002 (b) Notification to Secretary of Labor before Secretary of the Treasury sends notice of deficiency under section 4971 of title 26; waiver of imposition of tax; requests for investigation; consultation—.Unless the Secretary of the Treasury finds that the collection of a tax is in jeopardy, in carrying out the provisions of section 4971 of the Internal Revenue Code of 1986 (relating to taxes on the failure to meet minimum funding standards), the Secretary of the Treasury shall notify the Secretary of Labor before sending a notice of deficiency with respect to any tax imposed under that section on an employer, and, in accordance with the provisions of subsection (d) of that section, afford the Secretary of Labor an opportunity to comment on the imposition of the tax in the case. The Secretary of the Treasury may waive the imposition of the tax imposed under section 4971(b) of such Code in appropriate cases. Upon receiving a written request from the Secretary of Labor or from the Pension Benefit Guaranty Corporation, the Secretary of the Treasury shall cause an investigation to be commenced expeditiously with respect to whether the tax imposed under section 4971 of such Code should be applied with respect to any employer to which the request relates. The Secretary of the Treasury and the Secretary of Labor shall consult with each other from time to time with respect to the provisions of section 412 of the Internal Revenue Code of 1986 (relating to minimum funding standards) and with respect to the funding standards applicable under title I of this Act in order to coordinate the rules applicable under such standards.

Act Sec. 3002 (c) Extended application of regulations prescribed by Secretary of the Treasury relating to minimum participation standards, minimum vesting standards, and minimum funding standards.—Regulations prescribed by the Secretary of the Treasury under sections 410(a), 411, and 412 of the Internal Revenue Code of 1986 (relating to minimum participation standards, minimum vesting standards, and minimum funding standards, respectively) shall also apply to the minimum participation, vesting, and funding standards set forth in parts 2 and 3 of subtitle B of title I of this Act. Except as otherwise expressly provided in this Act, the Secretary of Labor shall not prescribe other regulations under such parts, or apply the regulations prescribed by the Secretary of the Treasury under sections 410(a), 411, 412 of the Internal Revenue Code of 1986 and applicable to the minimum participation, vesting, and funding standards under such parts in a manner inconsistent with the way such regulations apply under sections 410(a), 411, and 412 of such Code.

Act Sec. 3002 (d) Opportunity afforded Secretary of the Treasury to intervene in cases involving construction or application of minimum standards; review of briefs filed by Pension Benefit Guaranty Corporation of Secretary of Labor.—The Secretary of Labor and the Pension Benefit Guaranty Corporation, before filing briefs in any case involving the construction or application of minimum participation standards, minimum vesting standards, or minimum funding standards under title I of this Act, shall afford the Secretary of the Treasury a reasonable opportunity to review any such brief. The Secretary of the Treasury shall have the right to intervene in any such case.

Act Sec. 3002 (e) Consultative requirements respecting promulgation of proposed or final regulations.—The Secretary of the Treasury shall consult with the Pension Benefit Guaranty Corporation with respect to any proposed or final regulation authorized by subpart C of part I of subchapter D of chapter 1 of the Internal Revenue Code of 1986, or by sections 4241 through 4245 of this Act, before publishing any such proposed or final regulation.

Amendments

P.L. 101-239, § 7891(a)(1):

Titles I, III, and IV of ERISA (other than sections 3(37)(E), 301(a)(7), and 308, the last sentence of section 408(d), and sections 414(c), 4001(a)(3)(ii), and 4303) are each

amended by striking "Internal Revenue Code of 1954" each place it appears and inserting "Internal Revenue Code of 1986".

P.L. 96-364, § 402(b)(3):

Amended Sec. 3002 effective September 26, 1980 by adding at the end thereof the new subsection (e).

[¶ 15,130]
PROCEDURES IN CONNECTION WITH PROHIBITED TRANSACTIONS

Act Sec. 3003. (a) Notification to Secretary of Labor; opportunity to comment on imposition of tax under section 4975 of title 26; waiver; requests for investigation.—Unless the Secretary of the Treasury finds that the collection of a tax is in jeopardy, in carrying out the provisions of section 4975 of the Internal Revenue Code of 1986 (relating to tax on prohibited transactions) the Secretary of the Treasury shall, in accordance with the provisions of subsection (h) of such section, notify the Secretary of Labor before sending a notice of deficiency with respect to the tax imposed by subsection (a) or (b) of such section, and, in accordance with the provisions of subsection (h) of such section, afford the Secretary an opportunity to comment on the imposition of the tax in any case. The Secretary of the Treasury shall have authority to waive the imposition of the tax imposed under section 4975(b) in appropriate cases. Upon receiving a written request from the Secretary of Labor or from the Pension Benefit Guaranty Corporation, the Secretary of the Treasury shall cause an investigation to be carried out with respect to whether the tax imposed by section 4975 of such Code should be applied to any person referred to in the request.

Act Sec. 3003 (b) Consultation.—The Secretary of the Treasury and the Secretary of Labor shall consult with each other from time to time with respect to the provisions of section 4975 of the Internal Revenue Code of 1986 (relating to tax on prohibited transactions) and with respect to the provisions of title I of this Act relating to prohibited transactions and exemptions therefrom in order to coordinate the rules applicable under such standards.

Act Sec. 3003 (c) Transmission of information to Secretary of the Treasury Whenever the Secretary of Labor obtains information indicating that a party-in-interest or disqualified person is violating section 406 of this Act, he shall transmit such information to the Secretary of the Treasury.

Amendment

P.L. 101-239, § 7891(a)(1):

Titles I, III, and IV of ERISA (other than sections 3(37)(E), 301(a)(7), and 308, the last sentence of section 408(d), and sections 414(c), 4001(a)(3)(ii), and 4303) are each

amended by striking "Internal Revenue Code of 1954" each place it appears and inserting "Internal Revenue Code of 1986".

[¶ 15,140]
COORDINATION BETWEEN THE DEPARTMENT OF THE TREASURY AND THE DEPARTMENT OF LABOR

Act Sec. 3004. (a) Whenever in this Act or in any provision of law amended by this Act the Secretary of the Treasury and the Secretary of Labor are required to carry out provisions relating to the same subject matter (as determined by them) they shall consult with each other and shall develop rules, regulations, practices, and forms which, to the extent appropriate for the efficient administration of such provisions are designed to reduce duplication of effort, duplication of reporting, conflicting or overlapping requirements, and the burden of compliance with such provisions by plan administrators, employers, and participants and beneficiaries.

Act Sec. 3004. (b) In order to avoid unnecessary expense and duplication of functions among Government agencies, the Secretary of the Treasury and the Secretary of Labor may make such arrangements or agreements for cooperation or mutual assistance in the performance of their functions under this Act, and the functions of any such agency as they find to be practicable and consistent with law. The Secretary of the Treasury and the Secretary of Labor may utilize, on a reimbursable or other basis, the facilities or services, of any department, agency, or establishment of the United States or of any State or political subdivision of a State, including the services of any of its employees, with the lawful consent of such department, agency, or establishment; and each department, agency, or establishment of the United States is authorized and directed to cooperate with the Secretary of the Treasury and the Secretary of Labor and, to the extent permitted by law, to provide such information and facilities as they may request for their assistance in the performance of their functions under this Act. The Attorney General or his representative shall receive from the Secretary of the Treasury and the Secretary of Labor for appropriate action such evidence developed in the performance of their functions under this Act as may be found to warrant consideration for criminal prosecution under the provisions of this title or other Federal law.

Subtitle B—Joint Pension, Profit-Sharing, and Employee Stock Ownership Plan Task Force; Studies

Part 1—Joint Pension, Profit-Sharing, and Employee Stock Ownership Plan Task Force

[¶ 15,150]
ESTABLISHMENT

Act Sec. 3021. The staffs of the Committee on Ways and Means and the Committee on Education and Labor of the House of Representatives, the Joint Committee on Internal Revenue Taxation, and the Committee on Finance and the Committee on Labor and Public Welfare of the Senate shall carry out the duties assigned under this title to the Joint Pension, Profit-Sharing, and Employee Stock Ownership Plan Task Force. By agreement among the chairmen of such Committees, the Joint Pension, Profit-Sharing, and Employee Stock Ownership Plan Task Force shall be furnished with office space, clerical personnel, and such supplies and equipment as may be necessary for the Joint Pension, Profit-Sharing, and Employee Stock Ownership Plan Task Force to carry out its duties under this title.

Amendment

P.L. 94-455, §803(i):

Amended Sec. 3021 by striking out "Joint Pension" each place it appeared and substituting in its place "Joint Pension, Profit-Sharing, and Employee Stock Ownership

Plan." The amendment is applicable to taxable years beginning after December 31, 1974.

[¶ 15,160]
DUTIES

Act Sec. 3022.(a) The Joint Pension, Profit-Sharing, and Employee Stock Ownership Plan Task Force shall, within 24 months after the date of enactment of this Act, make a full study and review of—

(1) the effect of the requirements of section 411 of the Internal Revenue Code of 1986 and of section 203 of this Act to determine the extent of discrimination, if any, among employees in various age groups resulting from the application of such requirements;

(2) means of providing for the portability of pension rights among different pension plans;

(3) the appropriate treatment under title IV of this Act (relating to termination insurance) of plans established and maintained by small employers;

(4) the broadening of stock ownership, particularly with regard to employee stock ownership plans (as defined in section 4975(e)(7) of the Internal Revenue Code of 1986 and section 407(d)(6) of this Act) and all other alternative methods for broadening stock ownership to the American labor force and others;

(5) the effects and desirability of the Federal preemption of State and local law with respect to matters relating to pension and similar plans; and

(6) such other matter as any of the committees referred to in section 3021 may refer to it.

Act Sec. 3022. (b) The Joint Pension, Profit-Sharing, and Employee Stock Ownership Plan Task Force shall report the results of its study and review to each of the committees referred to in section 3021.

Amendments

P.L. 101-239, §7891(a)(1):

Title I, III, and IV of ERISA (other than sections 3(37)(E), 301(a)(7), and 308, the last sentence of section 408(d), and sections 414(c), 4001(a)(3)(ii), and 4303) are each amended by striking "Internal Revenue Code of 1954" each place it appears and inserting "Internal Revenue Code of 1986".

P.L. 94-455, §803(i):

Amended Sec. 3022 by striking out "Joint Pension" each place it appeared and substituting in its place "Joint Pension, Profit-Sharing, and Employee Stock Ownership Plan." In addition, subsection (a)(4) was added. The amendments are applicable to taxable years beginning after December 31, 1974.

Part 2—Other Studies

[¶ 15,170]
CONGRESSIONAL STUDY

Act Sec. 3031.(a) The Committee on Education and Labor and the Committee on Ways and Means of the House of Representatives and the Committee on Finance and the Committee on Labor and Public Welfare of the Senate shall study retirement plans established and maintained or financed (directly or indirectly) by the Government of the United States, by any State (including the District of Columbia) or political subdivision thereof, or by any agency or instrumentality of any of the foregoing. Such study shall include analysis of—

(1) the adequacy of existing levels of participation, vesting, and financing arrangements,

(2) existing fiduciary standards, and

(3) the necessity for Federal legislation and standards with respect to such plans.

In determining whether any such plan is adequately financed, each committee shall consider the necessity for minimum funding standards, as well as the taxing power of the government maintaining the plan.

Act Sec. 3031. (b) Not later than December 31, 1976, the Committee on Education and Labor and the Committee on Ways and Means shall each submit to the House of Representatives the results of the studies conducted under this section, together with such recommendations as they deem appropriate. The Committee on Finance and the Committee on Labor and Public Welfare shall each submit to the Senate the results of the studies conducted under this section together with such recommendations as they deem appropriate not later than such date.

[¶ 15,180]
PROTECTION FOR EMPLOYEES UNDER FEDERAL PROCUREMENT, CONSTRUCTION, AND RESEARCH CONTRACTS AND GRANTS

Act Sec. 3032.(a) Study and investigation by Secretary of Labor.—The Secretary of Labor shall, during the 2-year period beginning on the date of the enactment of this Act, conduct a full and complete study and investigation of the steps necessary to be taken to insure that professional, scientific, and technical personnel and others working in associated occupations employed under Federal procurement, construction, or research contracts or grants will, to the extent feasible, be protected against forfeitures of pension or retirement rights or benefits, otherwise provided, as a consequence of job transfers or loss of employment resulting from terminations or modifications of Federal contracts, grants, or procurement policies. The Secretary of Labor shall report the results of his study and investigation to the Congress within 2 years after the date of the enactment of this Act. The Secretary of Labor is authorized, to the extent provided by law, to obtain the services of private research institutions and such other persons by contract or other arrangement as he determines necessary in carrying out the provisions of this section.

Act Sec. 3032. (b) Consultation.—In the course of conducting the study and investigation described in subsection (a), and in developing the regulations referred to in subsection (c), the Secretary of Labor shall consult—

(1) with appropriate professional societies, business organizations, and labor organizations, and

(2) with the heads of interested Federal departments and agencies.

Act Sec. 3032. (c) REGULATIONS.—Within 1 year after the date on which he submits his report to the Congress under subsection (a), the Secretary of Labor shall, if he determines it to be feasible, develop regulations which will provide the protection of pension and retirement rights and benefits referred to in subsection (a).

Act Sec. 3032. (d) (1) CONGRESSIONAL REVIEW OF REGULATIONS; RESOLUTION OF DISAPPROVAL. Any regulations developed pursuant to subsection (c) shall take effect if, and only if—

(A) the Secretary of Labor, not later than the day which is 3 years after the date of the enactment of this Act, delivers a copy of such regulations to the House of Representatives and a copy to the Senate, and

(B) before the close of the 120-day period which begins on the day on which the copies of such regulations are delivered to the House of Representatives and to the Senate, neither the House of Representatives nor the Senate adopts, by an affirmative vote of a majority of those present and voting in that House, a resolution of disapproval.

(2) For purposes of this subsection, the term "resolution of disapproval" means only a resolution of either House of Congress, the matter after the resolving clause of which is as follows: "That the . . . does not favor the taking effect of the regulations transmitted to the Congress by the Secretary of Labor on . . .", the first blank space therein being filled with the name of the resolving House and the second blank space therein being filled with the day and year.

(3) A resolution of disapproval in the House of Representatives shall be referred to the Committee on Education and Labor. A resolution of disapproval in the Senate shall be referred to the Committee on Labor and Public Welfare.

(4) (A) If the committee to which a resolution of disapproval has been referred has not reported it at the end of 7 calendar days after its introduction, it is in order to move either to discharge the committee from further consideration of the resolution or to discharge the committee from further consideration of any other resolution of disapproval which has been referred to the committee.

(B) A motion to discharge may be made only by an individual favoring the resolution, is highly privileged (except that it may not be made after the committee has reported a resolution of disapproval), and debate thereon shall be limited to not more than 1 hour, to be divided equally between those favoring and those opposing the resolution. An amendment to the motion is not in order, and it is not in order to move to reconsider the vote by which the motion is agreed to or disagreed to.

(C) If the motion to discharge is agreed to or disagreed to, the motion may not be renewed, nor may another motion to discharge the committee be made with respect to any other resolution of disapproval.

(5) (A) When the committee has reported, or has been discharged from further consideration of, a resolution of disapproval, it is at any time thereafter in order (even though a previous motion to the same effect has been disagreed to) to move to proceed to the consideration of the resolution. The motion is highly privileged and is not debatable. An amendment to the motion is not in order, and it is not in order to move to reconsider the vote by which the motion is agreed to or disagreed to.

(B) Debate on the resolution of disapproval shall be limited to not more than 10 hours, which shall be divided equally between those favoring and those opposing the resolution. A motion further to limit debate is not debatable. An amendment to, or motion to recommit, the resolution is not in order, and it is not in order to move to reconsider the vote by which the resolution is agreed to or disagreed to.

(6) (A) Motions to postpone, made with respect to the discharge from committee or the consideration of a resolution of disapproval, and motions to proceed to the consideration of other business, shall be decided without debate.

(B) Appeals from the decisions of the Chair relating to the application of the rules of the House of Representatives or the Senate, as the case may be, to the procedure relating to any resolution of disapproval shall be decided without debate.

(7) Whenever the Secretary of Labor transmits copies of the regulations to the Congress, a copy of such regulations shall be delivered to each House of Congress on the same day and shall be delivered to the Clerk of the House of Representatives if the House is not in session and to the Secretary of the Senate if the Senate is not in session.

(8) The 120 day period referred to in paragraph (1) shall be computed by excluding—

(A) the days on which either House is not in session because of an adjournment of more than 3 days to a day certain or an adjournment of the Congress sine die, and

(B) any Saturday and Sunday, not excluded under subparagraph (A), when either House is not in session.

(9) This subsection is enacted by the Congress—

(A) as an exercise of the rulemaking power of the House of Representatives and the Senate, respectively, and as such they are deemed a part of the rules of each House, respectively, but applicable only with respect to the procedure to be followed in that House in the case of resolutions of disapproval described in paragraph (2); and they supersede other rules only to the extent that they are inconsistent therewith; and

(B) with full recognition of the constitutional right of either House to change the rules (so far as relating to the procedures of that House) at any time, in the same manner and to the same extent as in the case of any other rule of that House.

Subtitle C—Enrollment of Actuaries

[¶ 15,210]
ESTABLISHMENT OF JOINT BOARD FOR THE ENROLLMENT OF ACTUARIES

Act Sec. 3041. The Secretary of Labor and the Secretary of the Treasury shall, not later than the last day of the first calendar month beginning after the date of the enactment of this Act, establish a Joint Board for the Enrollment of Actuaries (hereinafter in this part referred to as the "Joint Board").

Regulations

The following regulations were adopted by 40 FR 18776, filed with the Federal Register on April 25, 1975, and published in the Federal Register on April 30, 1975, under "Title 20—Employees' Benefits;" "Chapter VIII—Joint Board for the Enrollment of Actuaries;" "Part 900—Statement of Organization." The Bylaws of the Joint Board for the Enrollment of Actuaries are reproduced following the regulations. Reg. §900.3 was revised on February 23, 2016 by 81 FR 8832.

[¶ 15,211]

§900.1 **Basis.** This Statement is issued by the Joint Board for the Enrollment of Actuaries (the Joint Board) pursuant to the requirement of section 552 of Title 5 of the United States Code that every agency shall publish in the FEDERAL REGISTER a description of its central and field organization.

[¶ 15,212]

§900.2 **Establishment.** The Joint Board has been established by the Secretary of Labor and the Secretary of the Treasury pursuant to section 3041 of the Employee Retirement Income Security Act of 1974 (29 U.S.C. 1241). Bylaws of the Board have been issued by the two Secretaries.[1]

---

[1] Copy filed with the Office of the Federal Register. Copies may also be obtained from the Executive Director of the Board.

BYLAWS OF THE JOINT BOARD FOR THE ENROLLMENT OF ACTUARIES

⋙→ CCH Note:: The Bylaws signed on April 27, 1981, appear below

Pursuant to the Provisions of the Employee Retirement Income Security Act of 1974

(Public Law No. 93-406)

SECTION 1. *Name.*

The name of the organization is the Joint Board for the Enrollment of Actuaries, hereinafter referred to as the Joint Board.

SECTION 2. *Offices.*

The principal office of the Joint Board shall be in the City of Washington, District of Columbia. The Joint Board may have additional offices at such other places as it may deem necessary or desirable for the conduct of its business.

SECTION 3. *Membership.*

(a)(i) The Joint Board shall be composed of five members, three to be appointed by and to serve at the pleasure of the Secretary of the Treasury for three-year terms and two to be appointed by and to serve at the pleasure of the Secretary of Labor for three-year terms. Members of the Joint Board may be appointed for successive three-year terms. To the extent feasible, two of the members appointed by the Secretary of the Treasury and one of the members appointed by the Secretary of Labor shall be actuaries.

(ii) Any Joint Board member who has served three years or more on the date the Bylaws are adopted shall be considered to have served a three-year term and will be subject to reappointment within 30 days from the date of such adoption. The terms of all Joint Board members shall run from the dates of appointment.

(b) A Chairman shall be elected for a one-year term by the Board from among its members. No Chairman shall serve in that capacity for two consecutive terms. The Chairman may designate an Acting Chairman from among the Joint Board members.

(c) A Secretary of the Joint Board shall be elected for a one-year term by the Board from among its members. No Secretary shall serve in that capacity for two consecutive terms. The Secretary of the Joint Board may designate an Acting Secretary from among the Joint Board members.

(d) The Pension Benefit Guaranty Corporation may designate a representative to sit with, and participate in, the discussions of the Joint Board.

(e) The Secretary of the Treasury may appoint one alternate member of the Joint Board. The alternate member shall serve at the pleasure of the Secretary of the Treasury for a three-year term. An alternate member may be appointed for successive three-year terms. The alternate member shall serve on the Joint Board only at such time that one of the Joint Board members appointed by the Secretary of the Treasury (i) has left service on the Joint Board, (ii) is incapacitated for health reasons, or (iii) is unable to participate at meetings of the Joint Board because of a detail or assignment away from his/her regular employment. An alternate member serving on the Joint Board pursuant to this subsection shall be considered a Joint Board member for quorum and voting purposes.

(f) The Secretary of Labor may appoint one alternate member of the Joint Board. The alternate member shall serve at the pleasure of the Secretary of Labor for a three-year term. An alternate member may be appointed for successive three-year terms. The alternate member shall serve on the Joint Board only at such time that one of the Joint Board members appointed by the Secretary of Labor (i) has left service on the Joint Board, (ii) is incapacitated for health reasons, or (iii) is unable to participate at meetings of the Joint Board because of a detail or assignment away from his/her regular employment. An alternate member serving on the Joint Board pursuant to this subsection shall be considered a Joint Board member for quorum and voting purposes.

(g) Members of the Joint Board, who shall be Federal employees, shall serve without compensation from the Board.

SECTION 4. *Powers of the Joint Board.*

(a) The Joint Board shall issue, after approval by the Secretaries of Labor and Treasury, or their delegates, regulations establishing standards and qualifications for the enrollment of persons performing actuarial services with respect to certain employee-benefit plans covered by the Employee Retirement Income Security Act of 1974.

(b) If the Joint Board finds that any person applying for enrollment satisfies the standards and qualifications referred to in Section 4(a) above, the Joint Board shall enroll such individual.

(c) The Joint Board may after an opportunity for a hearing suspend or terminate the enrollment of an individual if the Board finds that such individual has failed to discharge his duties under the Act or does not satisfy the requirement for enrollment in effect at the time of his enrollment.

(d) The Joint Board shall have all such powers, and shall establish and administer necessary policies and procedures, for the performance of the functions assigned to it under Title III, Subtitle C, of the Employee Retirement Income Security Act of 1974.

SECTION 5. *Administration.*

(a) There is established in the Joint Board, an Executive Director. The Executive Director shall be appointed by the Secretary of the Treasury. Authority for administration of the Joint Board, including the hiring of appropriate staff, supervision of personnel, organization, and budget practices, shall be delegated to the Executive Director. In addition, the Executive Director shall provide for the conduct of disciplinary proceedings relating to enrolled actuaries; shall make inquiries with respect to matters under his/her jurisdiction; and shall perform such other duties as are necessary or appropriate to carry out his/her functions under these Bylaws or as are prescribed by the Joint Board.

(b) The Departments of Treasury and Labor shall provide the Joint Board with sufficient support services to perform its functions.

(c) Administrative expenses incurred by the Joint Board in the performance of its duties shall be paid by the Departments of Treasury and Labor.

SECTION 6. *Meetings.*

Regular meetings of the Joint Board shall be held at such times as the Chairman shall select. Special meetings of the Joint Board shall be called by the Chairman on the request of any other member. Reasonable notice of any meetings shall be given to each member. The Secretary of the Joint Board shall keep its minutes, and as soon as practicable after each meeting a draft of the minutes of such meeting shall be distributed to each member of the Board for correction or approval.

SECTION 7. *Quorum.*

(a) A majority of the members, including at least one member appointed by each Department, shall constitute a quorum for the transaction of business. Any act of a majority of the members present at any meeting at which there is a quorum shall be the act of the Board.

(b) A resolution of the Joint Board signed by all of its members shall have the same force and effect as if agreed to at a duly called meeting and shall be recorded in the minutes of the Joint Board.

SECTION 8. *Place of Meetings: Use of Conference Call Communications Equipment.*

Meetings of the Joint Board shall be held in the offices of the Department of the Treasury unless otherwise determined by the Joint Board or the Chairman. Any member may participate in a meeting of the Board through the use of conference call telephone or similar communications equipment, by means of which all persons participating in the meeting can simultaneously speak to and hear each other. Any member so participating in a meeting shall be deemed present for all purposes. Actions taken by the Joint Board at meetings conducted through the use of such equipment, including the votes of each member, shall be recorded in the usual manner in the minutes of the meetings of the Joint Board.

SECTION 9. *Amendments.*

These bylaws may be amended or new bylaws adopted by the Secretaries of Treasury and Labor acting jointly. The Joint Board may recommend such amendment or revision, provided a copy of any proposed amendments has been delivered to each member at least seven days prior to the adoption of such recommendation.

Pursuant to Paragraph 4 of the Order dated October 31, 1974, establishing the Joint Board for the Enrollment of Actuaries, we hereby approve these Bylaws as the Bylaws of the Joint Board, thereby revoking all other Bylaws previously approved.

Raymond J. Donovan

Secretary of Labor

Date: April 10, 1981

Donald T. Regan

Secretary of the Treasury

Date: April 27, 1981

[¶ 15,213]

§ 900.3 **Composition.** Pursuant to the Bylaws, the Joint Board consists of three members appointed by the Secretary of the Treasury and two members appointed by the Secretary of Labor. The Board elects a Chairman and a Secretary from among the Department of the Treasury and the Department of Labor members. The Pension Benefit Guaranty Corporation may designate a non-voting representative to sit with, and participate in, the discussions of the Board. All decisions of the Board are made by simple majority vote. [Revised 2/23/2016 by 81 FR 8832.]

[¶ 15,214]

§ 900.4 **Meetings.** The Joint Board meets on the call of the Chairman at such times as are necessary in order to consider matters requiring action. Minutes are kept of each meeting by the Secretary.

[¶ 15,215]

§ 900.5 **Staff.** (a) The Executive Director advises and assists the Joint Board directly in carrying out its responsibilities under the Act and performs such other functions as the Board may delegate to him.

(b) Members of the staffs of the Departments of the Treasury and of Labor, by arrangement with the Joint Board, perform such services as may be appropriate in assisting the Board in the discharge of its responsibilities.

[¶ 15,216]

§ 900.6 **Offices.** The Joint Board does not maintain offices separate from those of the Departments of the Treasury and Labor. Its post office address is Joint Board for the Enrollment of Actuaries, c/o Department of the Treasury, Washington, D.C. 20220.

[¶ 15,217]

§ 900.7 **Delegations of authority.** As occasion warrants, the Joint Board may delegate functions to the Chairman or the Executive Director, including the authority to receive applications and to give notice of actions. Any such delegation of authority is conferred by resolution of the Board.

[¶ 15,220]

ENROLLMENT BY BOARD; STANDARDS AND QUALIFICATIONS; SUSPENSION OR TERMINATION OF ENROLLMENT

Act Sec. 3042. (a) The Joint Board shall, by regulations, establish reasonable standards and qualifications for persons performing actuarial services with respect to plans to which this Act applies and, upon application by any individual, shall enroll such individual if the Joint Board finds that such individual satisfies such standards and qualifications. With respect to individuals applying for enrollment before January 1, 1976, such standards and qualifications shall include a requirement for an appropriate period of responsible actuarial experience relating to pension plans. With respect to individuals applying for enrollment on or after January 1, 1976, such standards and qualifications shall include—

    (1) education and training in actuarial mathematics and methodology, as evidenced by—

        (A) a degree in actuarial mathematics or its equivalent from an accredited college or university,

        (B) successful completion of an examination in actuarial mathematics and methodology to be given by the Joint Board, or

        (C) successful completion of other actuarial examinations deemed adequate by the Joint Board, and

    (2) an appropriate period of responsible actuarial experience.

Notwithstanding the preceding provisions of this subsection, the Joint Board may provide for the temporary enrollment for the period ending on January 1, 1976, of actuaries under such interim standards as it deems adequate.

Act Sec. 3042. (b) The Joint Board may, after notice and an opportunity for a hearing, suspend or terminate the enrollment of an individual under this section if the Joint Board finds that such individual—

    (1) has failed to discharge his duties under this Act, or

    (2) does not satisfy the requirements for enrollment as in effect at the time of his enrollment.

The Joint Board may also, after notice and opportunity for hearing, suspend or terminate the temporary enrollment of an individual who fails to discharge his duties under this Act or who does not satisfy the interim enrollment standards.

Regulations

The following regulations were adopted by FR Doc. 76-1156 (41 FR 2080) under "Title 20—Employees' Benefits"; "Chapter VIII—Joint Board for the Enrollment of Actuaries"; "Part 901—Regulations Governing the Performance of Actuarial Services Under the Employee Retirement Income Security Act of 1974" and "Part 902—Rules Regarding Availability of Information." The temporary regulations which were filed with the Federal Register on August 26, 1975, published in the Federal Register of August 27, 1975, have been superseded. Identical proposed regulations that were also published in the Federal Register of August 27, 1975, have been adopted with certain changes (41 FR 2080). In the case of *Sol Tabor v. Joint Board for the Enrollment of Actuaries* the regulations were vacated for failure to comply with the Administrative Procedure Act. The regulations have been reissued (42 FR 39200). They were filed with the Federal Register on July 29, 1977, and published in the Federal Register on August 3, 1977.

Regulations under Title 20—"Employee Benefits," Chapter VIII, Part 901, "Regulations Governing the Performance of Actuarial Services Under the Employee Retirement Income Security Act of 1974" were amended in Subpart B, § 901.11 and Subpart C, § 901.20 and Subparts D and E were adopted by FR Doc. 78-25172 (43 FR 39756) which was filed with the Federal Register on September 6, 1978 and published in the Register on September 7, 1978.

Reg. Secs. 901.0, 901.1, 901.11, 901.12, 901.20, 901.31, 901.32, and 901.47 were amended and Reg. Sec. 901.72 was added on March 31, 2011 (76 FR 17762). Reg. Sec. 901.11 was corrected on December 28, 2011 (76 FR 81362).

[¶ 15,221]
§ 901.0 Performance of Actuarial Services Under ERISA

Scope. This part contains rules governing the performance of actuarial services under the Employee Retirement Income Security Act of 1974, hereinafter also referred to as ERISA. Subpart A of this part sets forth definitions and eligibility to perform actuarial services; Subpart B of this part sets forth rules governing the enrollment of actuaries; Subpart C of this part sets forth standards of performance to which enrolled actuaries must adhere; Subpart D sets forth rules applicable to suspension and termination of enrollment; and Subpart E of this part sets forth general provisions. [Amended 3/31/2011 by 76 FR 17762.]

Subpart A—Definitions and Eligibility to Perform Actuarial Services

[¶ 15,222]
§ 901.1 **Definitions.** As used in this part, the term:

(a) "*Actuarial experience*" means the performance of or the direct supervision of, services involving the application of principles of probability and compound interest to determine the present value of payments to be made upon the fulfillment of certain specified conditions or the occurrence of certain specified events.

(b) "*Responsible actuarial experience*" means actuarial experience:

(1) involving participation in making determinations that the methods and assumptions adopted in the procedures followed in actuarial services are appropriate in the light of all pertinent circumstances, and

(2) Demonstrating a thorough understanding of the principles and alternatives involved in such actuarial services.

(c) "*Month of responsible actuarial experience*" means a month during which the actuary spent a substantial amount of time in responsible actuarial experience.

(d) "*Responsible pension actuarial experience*" means responsible actuarial experience involving valuations of the liabilities of pension plans, wherein the performance of such valuations requires the application of principles of life contingencies and compound interest in the determination, under one or more standard actuarial cost methods, of such of the following as may be appropriate in the particular case:

(1) Normal cost.

(2) Accrued liability.

(3) Payment required to amortize a liability or other amount over a period of time.

(4) Actuarial gain or loss.

(e) "*Month of responsible pension actuarial experience*" means a month during which the actuary spent a substantial amount of time in responsible pension actuarial experience.

(f) "*Applicant*" means an individual who has filed an application to become an enrolled actuary.

(g) "*Enrolled actuary*" means an individual who has satisfied the standards and qualifications as set forth in this part and who has been approved by the Joint Board (the Joint Board), or its designee, to perform actuarial services required under ERISA or regulations thereunder. [Amended 3/31/2011 by 76 FR 17762.]

(h) "*Actuarial services*" means performance of actuarial valuations and preparation of any actuarial reports.

(i) *Certified responsible actuarial experience* means responsible actuarial experience of an individual that has been certified in writing by the individual's supervisor. [Added 3/31/2011 by FR 17762.]

(j) *Certified responsible pension actuarial experience* means responsible pension actuarial experience of an individual that has been certified in writing by the individual's supervisor if the supervisor is an enrolled actuary. If the individual's supervisor is not an enrolled actuary, the pension actuarial experience must be certified in writing by both the supervisor and an enrolled actuary with knowledge of the individual's pension actuarial experience. [Added 3/31/2011 by FR 17762.]

(k) *Enrollment cycle* means the three-year period from January 1, 2011, to December 31, 2013, and every three-year period thereafter. [Added 3/31/2011 by FR 17762.]

[¶ 15,222A]
§ 901.2 **Eligibility to perform actuarial services.** (a) *Enrolled actuary.* Subject to the standards of performance set forth in Subpart C of this part, any individual who is an enrolled actuary as defined in § 901.1(g) may perform actuarial services required under ERISA or regulations thereunder. Where a corporation, partnership, or other entity is engaged to provide actuarial services, such services may be provided on its behalf only by an enrolled actuary who is an employee, partner or consultant.

(b) *Government officers and employees.* No officer or employee of the United States in the executive, legislative, or judicial branch of the Government, or in any agency of the United States, including the District of Columbia, may perform actuarial services required under ERISA or regulations thereunder if such services would be in violation of 18 U.S.C. 205. No Member of Congress or Resident Commissioner (elect or serving) may perform such actuarial services if such services would be in violation of 18 U.S.C. 203 or 205.

(c) *Former government officers and employees.* (1) *Personal and substantial participation in the performance of actuarial services.* No former officer or employee of the executive branch of the United States Government, of any independent agency of the United States, or of the District of Columbia, shall perform actuarial services required under ERISA or regulations thereunder or aid or assist in the performance of such actuarial services, in regard to particular matters, involving a specific party or parties, in which the individual participated personally and substantially as such officer or employee.

(2) *Official responsibility.* No former officer or employee of the executive branch of the United States Government, of any independent agency of the United States, or of the District of Columbia, shall, within 1 year after his employment has ceased, perform actuarial services required under ERISA or regulations thereunder in regard to any particular matter involving a specific party or parties which was under the individual's official responsibility as an officer or employee of the Government at any time within a period of 1 year prior to the termination of such responsibility.

Subpart B—Enrollment of Actuaries

[¶ 15,223]
§ 901.10 **Application for enrollment.** (a) *Form.* As a requirement for enrollment, an applicant shall file with the Executive Director of the Joint Board a properly executed application on a form or forms specified by the Joint Board, and shall agree to comply with these regulations and any other guidance as required by the Joint Board. A reasonable nonrefundable fee may be charged for each application for enrollment filed. [Amended 3/31/2011 by 76 FR 17762.]

(b) *Additional information.* The Joint Board or Executive Director, as a condition to consideration of an application for enrollment, may require the applicant to file additional information and to submit to written or oral examination under oath or otherwise.

(c) *Denial of application.* If the Joint Board proposes to deny an application for enrollment, the Executive Director shall notify the applicant in writing of the proposed denial and the reasons therefor, of his rights to request reconsideration, of the address to which such request should be made and the date by which such request must be made. The applicant may, within 30 days from the date of the written proposed denial, file a written request for reconsideration therefrom, together with his reasons in support thereof, to the Joint Board. The Joint Board may afford an applicant the opportunity to make a personal appearance before the Joint Board. A decision on the request for reconsideration shall be rendered by the Joint Board as soon as practicable. In the absence of a request for reconsideration within the aforesaid 30 days, the proposed denial shall, without further proceeding, constitute a final decision of denial by the Joint Board.

[¶ 15,223A]
§ 901.11 **Enrollment procedures.** (a) *Enrollment.* The Joint Board shall enroll each applicant it determines has met the requirements of these regulations and any other guidance as required by the Joint Board, and shall so notify the applicant. Subject to the provisions of Subpart D of this part, an individual must renew his or her enrollment

in the manner described in paragraph (d) of this section. [Amended by 9/7/98 by 53 FR 34484 and 3/31/2011 by 76 FR 17762].

(b) *Enrollment certificate*. The Joint Board (or its designee) shall issue a certificate of enrollment to each actuary who is duly enrolled under this part.

(c) *Rosters*. (1) *Maintenance of rosters.*

The Executive Director shall maintain rosters of—

(i) All actuaries who are duly enrolled under this part;

(ii) All individuals whose enrollment has been suspended or terminated; and

(iii) All individuals who are in inactive status.

(2) *Publication of Rosters..* The Executive Director may publish any or all of the rosters, including display on the Joint Board's Web site, to the extent permitted by law. [Amended 3/31/2011 by 76 FR 17762].

(d) *Renewal of enrollment*. To maintain active enrollment to perform actuarial services under ERISA, each enrolled actuary is required to have his/her enrollment renewed as set forth herein.

(1) Each enrolled actuary must file an application for renewal of enrollment on the prescribed form no earlier than October 1, 2010, and no later than March 1, 2011, and no earlier than October 1 and no later than March 1 of every third year thereafter. If March 1 is a Saturday, Sunday, or holiday, the due date shall be the next day that is not a Saturday, Sunday, or holiday.

(2) The effective date of renewal of enrollment for an individual who files a complete renewal application within the time period described in paragraph (d)(1) of this section is the April 1 immediately following the date of application. The effective date of renewal of enrollment for an individual who files a complete renewal application after the due date described in paragraph (d)(1) of this section is the later of the April 1 immediately following the due date of application and the date of the notice of renewal.

(3) Forms required for renewal may be obtained from the Executive Director.

(4) A reasonable non-refundable fee may be charged for each application for renewal of enrollment filed. [Amended 3/31/2011 by 76 FR 17762].

(e) *Condition for renewal: continuing professional education*. To qualify for renewal of enrollment, an enrolled actuary must certify, on the form prescribed by the Executive Director, that he/she has completed the applicable minimum number of hours of continuing professional education credit required by this paragraph (e) and satisfied the recordkeeping requirements of paragraph (j) of this section.

(1) *Transition rule for renewal of enrollment effective April 1, 2011.*

(i) A minimum of 36 hours of continuing professional education credit must be completed between January 1, 2008 and December 31, 2010. Of the 36 hours, at least 18 must consist of core subject matter; the remainder may be non-core subject matter.

(ii) An individual who received initial enrollment in 2008 must complete 24 hours of continuing professional education by December 31, 2010. An individual who received initial enrollment in 2009 must complete 12 hours of continuing professional education by December 31, 2010. In either case, at least one-half of the applicable hours must consist of core subject matter; the remainder may consist of non-core subject matter. For purposes of this paragraph (e)(1)(ii), credit will be awarded for continuing professional education completed after January 1 of the year in which initial enrollment was received.

(iii) An individual who receives initial enrollment during 2010 is exempt from the continuing professional education requirements during 2010, but must file a timely application for renewal during the time period described in paragraph (d)(1) of this section. [Amended 3/31/2011 by 76 FR 17762].

(2) *For renewal of enrollment effective April 1, 2014, and every third year thereafter.*

(i) A minimum of 36 hours of continuing professional education credit must be completed between January 1, 2011 and December 31, 2013, and between January 1 and December 31 for each three-year period subsequent thereto. [Amended 3/31/2011 by 76 FR 17762].

(ii) An individual who receives initial enrollment during the first or second year of an enrollment cycle must satisfy the following requirements by the end of the enrollment cycle: Those enrolled during the first year of an enrollment cycle must complete 24 hours of continuing education; those enrolled during the second year of an enrollment cycle must complete 12 hours of continuing education. At least one half of the applicable hours must be comprised of core subject matter; the remainder may be comprised of non-core subject matter. For purposes of this paragraph (e)(2)(ii), credit will be awarded for continuing professional education completed after January 1 of the year in which initial enrollment was received. [Amended 3/31/2011 by 76 FR 17762].

(iii) An individual who receives initial enrollment during the third year of an enrollment cycle is exempt from the continuing education requirements until the next enrollment cycle, but must file a timely application for renewal.

(iv) For an individual who was initially enrolled before January 1, 2008 (and who has therefore completed at least one full enrollment cycle as of January 1, 2011), at least 12 hours of the 36 hours of continuing professional education required for each enrollment cycle must consist of core subject matter; the remainder may consist of non-core subject matter. [Amended 3/31/2011 by 76 FR 17762].

(v) For an individual who was initially enrolled on or after January 1, 2008, at least 18 hours of his or her 36 hours of continuing professional education required for the first full enrollment cycle must consist of core subject matter. Thereafter, for such individuals, for each subsequent enrollment cycle at least 12 hours of the 36 hours must consist of core subject matter. In each instance, the remainder may consist of non-core subject matter. [Amended 3/31/2011 by 76 FR 17762].

(vi) When core subject matter hours are required (including when an individual seeks to return to active status from inactive status), an individual must complete a minimum of two hours of continuing professional education credit relating to ethical standards, regardless of the total number of core hours required. [Amended 3/31/2011 by 76 FR 17762].

(f) *Qualifying continuing professional education*. (1) *In general*. To qualify for continuing professional education credit an enrolled actuary must complete his/her hours of continuing professional education credit under a qualifying program, within the meaning of paragraph (f)(2) of this section, consisting of core and/or non-core subject matter. In addition, a portion of the continuing professional education credit may be earned under the provisions of paragraph (g) of this section. In any event, no less than 1.3 of the total hours of continuing professional education credit required for an enrollment cycle must be obtained by participation in a formal program or programs, within the meaning of paragraph (f)(2)(ii)(A) of this section.

(i) Core subject matter is program content and knowledge that is integral and necessary to the satisfactory performance of pension actuarial services and actuarial certifications under ERISA and the Internal Revenue Code. Such core subject matter includes the characteristics of actuarial cost methods under ERISA, actuarial assumptions, minimum funding standards, titles I, II, and IV of ERISA, requirements with respect to the valuation of plan assets, requirements for qualification of pension plans, maximum deductible contributions, tax treatment of distributions from qualified pension plans, excise taxes related to the funding of qualified pension plans and standards of performance (including ethical standards) for actuarial services. Core subject matter includes all materials included on the syllabi of any of the pension actuarial examinations offered by the Joint Board during the current enrollment cycle and the enrollment cycle immediately preceding the current enrollment cycle. [Amended 3/31/2011 by 76 FR 17762 and corrected 12/28/11 by 76 FR 81362].

(ii) Non-core subject matter is program content designed to enhance knowledge of an enrolled actuary in matters related to the performance of pension actuarial services. Examples include economics, computer programs, pension accounting, investment and finance, risk theory, communication and business and general tax law. [Amended 3/31/2011 by 76 FR 17762].

(iii) The Joint Board my publish other topics or approve other topics which may be included in a qualifying program as core or non-core subject matter.

(iv) The same course of study cannot be used more than once within a given 36-month period to satisfy the continuing professional education requirements of these regulations. A program or session bearing the same or a similar title to a previous one may be used to satisfy the requirements of these regulations if the major content of the program or session differs substantively from the previous one. [Amended 3/31/2011 by 76 FR 17762].

(2) *Qualifying Program.* (i) *In general.* A qualifying program is a course of learning that—

(A) Is conducted by a qualifying sponsor, within the meaning of paragraph (f)(3) of this section, who identifies the program as a qualifying program;

(B) Is developed by individual(s) qualified in the subject matter;

(C) Covers current subject matter;

(D) Includes written outlines or textbooks;

(E) Is taught by instructors, discussion leaders, and speakers qualified with respect to the course content;

(F) Includes means for evaluation by the Joint Board of technical content and presentation;

(G) Provides a certificate of completion, within the meaning of paragraph (f)(3)(iv) of this section, to each person who successfully completed the program; and

(H) Provides a certificate of instruction, within the meaning of paragraph (f)(3)(v) of this section, to each person who served an instructor, discussion leader, or speaker.

(ii) *Formal programs.* (A) *Participants.* Formal programs are programs that meet all of the requirements of this paragraph (f)(2)(ii) and paragraph (f)(2)(i) of this section. Whether a program qualifies as a formal program is determined on a participant-by-participant basis. A qualifying program qualifies as a formal program with respect to a participant if the participant simultaneously participates in the program in the same physical location with at least two other participants engaged in substantive pension service, and the participants have the opportunity to interact with another individual qualified with respect to the course content who serves as an instructor, whether or not the instructor is in the same physical location. Groups of three or more participants who are in the same physical location may participate in a formal program in person or via the internet, videoconferencing, or teleconferencing. If the qualifying program is prerecorded, to qualify as a formal program, there must be a qualified individual who serves as the instructor and is available to answer questions immediately following the pre-recorded program.

(B) *Instructor.* A qualifying program is a formal program with respect to the instructor only if the program is a formal program under paragraph (f)(2)(ii)(A) of this section with respect to at least three participants and the instructor is in the physical presence of at least three other individuals engaged in substantive pension service. [Amended 3/31/2011 by 76 FR 17762].

(3) *Qualifying sponsor.* (i) *In general.* Qualifying sponsors are organizations recognized by the Executive Director whose programs offer opportunities for continuing professional education in subject matter within the scope of this section.

(ii) *Recognition by the Executive Director.* An organization requesting qualifying sponsor status shall file a sponsor agreement request with the Executive Director and furnish information in support of such request as deemed necessary for approval by the Executive Director. Such information shall include sufficient information to establish that all programs designated as qualifying programs offered by the qualifying sponsor will satisfy the requirements of paragraph (f)(2) of this section. Recognition as a qualifying sponsor by the Executive Director shall be effective when approved, unless the Executive Director provides that it shall be effective on a different date, and shall terminate at the end of the sponsor enrollment cycle. The Executive Director may publish the names of such sponsors on a periodic basis.

(iii) *Sponsor enrollment cycle.* (A) *Transition sponsor enrollment cycle.* The transition sponsor enrollment cycle is the period beginning on January 1, 2008 and ending December 31, 2011.

(B) *Subsequent sponsor enrollment cycles.* After the transition sponsor enrollment cycle, the sponsor enrollment cycle means the three-year period from January 1, 2012, to December 31, 2014, and every three-year period thereafter.

(iv) *Certificates of completion.* Upon verification of successful completion of a qualifying program, the program's qualifying sponsor shall furnish each individual who successfully completed the qualifying program with a certificate listing the following information:

(A) The name of the participant.

(B) The name of the qualifying sponsor.

(C) The title, location, and speaker(s) of each session attended.

(D) The dates of the program.

(E) The total credit hours earned, the total core and non-core credit hours earned, and how many of those hours relate to ethics.

(F) Whether or not the program is a formal program with respect to the participant.

(v) *Certificates of instruction.* The program's qualifying sponsor shall furnish to each instructor, discussion leader, or speaker, a certificate listing the following information:

(A) The name of the instructor, discussion leader, or speaker.

(B) The name of the qualifying sponsor.

(C) The title and location of the program.

(D) The dates of the program.

(E) The total credit hours earned and the total core and non-core credit hours earned for the program, and how many of those hours relate to ethics.

(F) Whether or not the program is a formal program with respect to the instructor. [Amended 3/31/2011 by 76 FR 17762].

(g) *Alternative means for completion of credit hours.* (1) *In general.* In addition to credit hours completed under paragraph (f) of this section, an enrolled actuary may be awarded continuing professional education credit under the provisions of this paragraph (g).

(2) *Serving as an instructor, discussion leader or speaker.* (i) Four credit hours (that is, 200 minutes) of continuing professional education credit will be awarded for each 50 minutes completed as an instructor, discussion leader, or speaker at a qualifying program which meets the continuing professional education requirements of paragraph (f) of this section. If the qualifying program is a formal program with respect to the instructor, only the time spent during the actual program is counted toward satisfaction of the formal program requirement.

(ii) The credit for instruction and preparation may not exceed 50 percent of the continuing professional education requirement for an enrollment cycle.

(iii) Presentation of the same material as an instructor, discussion leader, or speaker more than one time in any 36-month period will not qualify for continuing professional education credit. A program will not be considered to consist of the same material if a substantial portion of the content has been revised to reflect changes in the law or practices relative to the performance of pension actuarial service.

(iv) Credit as an instructor, discussion leader, or speaker will not be awarded to panelists, moderators, or others who are not required to prepare substantive subject matter for their portion of the program. However, such individuals may be awarded credit for attendance, provided the other provisions of this section are met.

(v) The nature of the subject matter will determine if credit will be of a core or non-core nature.

(3) *Credit for publications.* (i) Continuing professional education credit will be awarded for the creation of peer-reviewed materials for publication or distribution with respect to matters directly related to the continuing professional education requirements of this section.

Reg. §901.11(g)(3)(i)   ¶15,223A

Credit will be awarded to the author, coauthor, or a person listed as a major contributor.

(ii) One hour of credit will be allowed for each hour of preparation time of the material. It will be the responsibility of the person claiming the credit to maintain records to verify preparation time.

(iii) Publication or distribution may utilize any available technology for the dissemination of written, visual or auditory materials.

(iv) The materials must be available on reasonable terms for acquisition and use by all enrolled actuaries.

(v) The credit for the creation of materials may not exceed 25 percent of the continuing professional education requirement of any enrollment cycle.

(vi) The nature of the subject matter will determine if credit will be of a core or non-core nature.

(vii) Publication of the same material more than one time will not qualify for continuing professional education credit. A publication will not be considered to consist of the same material if a substantial portion has been revised to reflect changes in the law or practices relative to the performance of pension actuarial service.

(4) *Service on Joint Board advisory committee(s)*. Continuing professional education credit may be awarded by the Joint Board for service on (any of) its advisory committee(s), to the extent that the Joint Board considers warranted by the service rendered.

(5) *Preparation of Joint Board examinations*. Continuing professional education credit may be awarded by the Joint Board for participation in drafting questions for use on Joint Board examinations or in pretesting its examinations, to the extent the Joint Board determines suitable. Such credit may not exceed 50 percent of the continuing professional education requirement for the applicable enrollment cycle.

(6) *Examinations sponsored by professional organizations or societies*. Individuals may earn continuing professional education credit for achieving a passing grade on proctored examinations sponsored by a professional organization or society recognized by the Joint Board. Such credit is limited to the number of hours scheduled for each examination and may be applied only as non-core credit provided the content of the examination is core or non-core. No credit may be earned for hours attributable to any content that is neither core nor non-core.

(7) *Joint Board pension examination*. Individuals may establish eligibility for renewal of enrollment for any enrollment cycle by—

(i) Achieving a passing score on the Joint Board pension examination, as described in §901.12(d)(1)(i), administered under this part during the applicable enrollment cycle; and

(ii) Completing a minimum of 12 hours of qualifying continuing professional education by attending formal program(s) during the same applicable enrollment cycle. This option of satisfying the continuing professional education requirements is not available to those who receive initial enrollment during the enrollment cycle. [Amended 3/31/2011 by 76 FR 17762].

(h) *Measurement of continuing education course work*. (1) All continuing education programs will be measured in terms of credit hours. The shortest recognized program will be one credit hour.

(2) A credit hour is 50 minutes of continuous participation in a program. Each session in a program must be at least one full credit hour, i.e., 50 minutes. For example, a single-session program lasting 100 minutes will count as two credit hours, and a program comprised of three 75 minute sessions (225 minutes) constitutes four credit hours. However, at the end of an enrollment cycle, an individual may total the number of minutes of sessions of at least one credit hour in duration attended during the cycle and divided by fifty. For example, attending three 75 minutes segments at two separate programs will accord an individual nine credit hours (450 minutes divided by 50) toward fulfilling the minimum number of continuing professional education hours. It will not be permissible to merge non-core hours with core hours. [Amended 3/31/2011 by 76 FR 17762].

(i) [Reserved].

(j) *Recordkeeping requirements*. (1) *Qualifying sponsors*. A qualifying sponsor must maintain records to verify that each program it sponsors is a qualifying program within the meaning of paragraph (f)(2) of this section, including the certificates of completion, certificates of instruction, and outlines and course material. In the case of programs of more than one session, records must be maintained to verify each session of the program that is completed by each participant. Records required to be maintained under this paragraph must be retained by the qualifying sponsor for a period of six years following the end of the sponsor enrollment cycle in which the program is held.

(2) *Enrolled actuaries*—. (i) *Qualifying program credits as a participant*. To receive continuing professional education credit for completion of hours of continuing professional education under paragraph (f) of this section, an enrolled actuary must retain all certificates of completion evidencing completion of such hours for the three-year period following the end of the enrollment cycle in which the credits are earned.

(ii) *Qualifying program credits as an instructor, discussion leader, or speaker*. To receive continuing professional education credit for completion of hours earned under paragraph (g)(2) of this section, an enrolled actuary must retain all certificates of instruction evidencing completion of such hours for the three-year period following the end of the enrollment cycle in which the credits are earned.

(iii) *Credit for publications*. To receive continuing professional education credit for a publication under paragraph (g)(3) of this section, the following information must be maintained by the enrolled actuary for the three-year period following the end of the enrollment cycle in which the credits are earned:

(A) The name of the publisher.

(B) The title and author of the publication.

(C) A copy of the publication.

(D) The date of the publication.

(E) The total credit hours earned, and the total core and non-core credit hours earned, and how many of those hours relate to ethics.

(iv) *Other credits*. To receive continuing professional education credit for hours earned under paragraphs (g)(4) through (g)(7) of this section, an enrolled actuary must retain sufficient documentation to establish completion of such hours for the three-year period following the end of the enrollment cycle in which the credits are earned. [amended 3/31/2011 by 76 FR 17762].

(k) *Waivers*. (1) Waiver from the continuing professional education requirements for a given period may be granted by the Executive Director only under extraordinary circumstances, and upon submission of sufficient evidence that every effort was made throughout the enrollment cycle to participate in one or more qualifying programs that would have satisfied the continuing professional education requirements.

(2) A request for waiver must be accompanied by appropriate documentation. The individual will be required to furnish any additional documentation or explanation deemed necessary by the Executive Director.

(3) The individual will be notified by the Executive Director of the disposition of the request for waiver. If the waiver is not approved, and the individual does not otherwise satisfy the continuing professional education requirements within the allotted time, the individual will be placed on the roster of inactive enrolled individuals.

(4) Individuals seeking to rely on a waiver of the continuing professional education requirements must receive the waiver from the Executive Director before filing an application for renewal of enrollment. [Amended 3/31/2011 by 76 FR 17762].

(l) *Failure to comply*. (1) Compliance by an individual with the requirements of this part shall be determined by the Executive Director. An individual who applies for renewal of enrollment but who fails to meet the requirements of eligibility for renewal will be notified by the Executive Director at his/her last known address by first class mail. The notice will state the basis for the non-compliance and will provide the individual an opportunity to furnish in writing, within 60 days of the date of the notice, information relating to the matter. Such information will be considered by the Executive Director in making a final determination as to eligibility for renewal of enrollment. [Amended 3/31/2011 by 76 FR 17762].

(2) The Executive Director may require any individual, by first class mail sent to his/her mailing address of record with the Joint Board, to provide copies of any records required to be maintained under this section. The Executive Director may disallow any continuing professional education hours claimed if the individual concerned fails to comply with such requirements. [Amended 3/31/2011 by 76 FR 17762].

(3) An individual whose application for renewal is not approved may seek review of the matter by the Joint Board. A request for review and the reasons in support of the request must be filed with the Joint Board within 30 days of the date of the notice of failure to comply. [Amended 3/31/2011 by 76 FR 17762].

(4) *Inactive status.* (i) *Automatic placement on the inactive roster.* To remain on the roster of active enrolled actuaries, an enrolled actuary must submit a timely application for renewal showing satisfaction of the requirements for reenrollment, including completion of the required continuing professional education hours, within the appropriate time frame. The Executive Director will move an enrolled actuary who does not submit such an application for reenrollment from the roster of enrolled actuaries to the roster of inactive enrolled actuaries as of April 1 following the March 1 due date for the application. However, if an enrolled actuary completes the required number of continuing professional education hours after the close of the enrollment cycle, submits an application for reenrollment, and is informed by the Executive Director before April 1st that the enrollment has been renewed, then the Executive Director will not move such individual to the roster of inactive enrolled actuaries at that time.

(ii) *Placement on the inactive roster after notice and right to respond.* The Executive Director will move an enrolled actuary who does not submit a timely application of renewal that shows timely completion of the required continuing professional education to the inactive roster only after giving the enrolled actuary 60 days to respond as described in paragraph (l)(1) of this section. [Corrected on 12/28/11 by 76 FR 81362].

(iii) *Length on time on inactive roster.* An individual may remain on the roster of inactive enrolled actuaries for a period up to three enrollment cycles from the date renewal would have been effective.

(iv) *Consequence of being on the inactive roster.* An individual in inactive status will be ineligible to perform pension actuarial services as an enrolled actuary under ERISA and the Internal Revenue Code. During such time in inactive status or at any other time an individual is ineligible to perform pension actuarial services as an enrolled actuary, the individual shall not in any manner, directly or indirectly, indicate he or she is so enrolled, or use the term "enrolled actuary," the designation "E.A.," or other form of reference to eligibility to perform pension actuarial services as an enrolled actuary.

(v) *Returning to active status.* An individual placed in inactive status may return to active status by filing an application for renewal of enrollment (with the appropriate fee) and providing evidence of the completion of all required continuing professional education hours and of satisfaction of any applicable requirements for qualifying experience under paragraph (l)(7) of this section. If an application for return to active status is approved, the individual will be eligible to perform services as an enrolled actuary effective with the date the notice of approval is mailed to that individual by the Executive Director. [Amended 3/31/2011 by 76 FR 17762].

(5) *Time for return to active enrollment.* (i) An individual placed in inactive status must file an application for return to active enrollment, and satisfy the requirements for return to active enrollment as set forth in this section, within three enrollment cycles of being placed in inactive status. Otherwise, the name of such individual will be removed from the inactive enrollment roster and his/her enrollment will terminate.

(ii) For purposes of paragraph (l)(5)(i) of this section, an individual who is in inactive or retired status as of April 1, 2010, will be deemed to have been placed in inactive status on April 1, 2010. [Amended 3/31/2011 by 76 FR 17762].

(6) An individual in inactive status may satisfy the requirements for return to active enrollment at any time during his/her period of inactive enrollment. If only completion of the continuing professional education requirement is necessary, the application for return to active enrollment may be filed immediately upon such completion. If qualifying experience is also required, the application for return to active enrollment may not be filed until the completion of both the continuing professional education and qualifying experience requirements set forth in this subsection. Continuing professional education credits applied to meet the requirements for reenrollment under this paragraph (l)(6) may not be used to satisfy the requirements of the enrollment cycle in which the individual has been placed back on the active roster. [Amended 3/31/2011 by 76 FR 17762].

(7) *Continuing professional education requirements for return to active enrollment from inactive status.* (i) During the first inactive enrollment cycle; 36 hours of qualifying continuing professional education as set forth in paragraph (e)(2) of this section, without regard to paragraph (e)(2)(ii) or (e)(2)(iii) of this section, must be completed. Any hours of continuing professional education credit earned during the immediately prior enrollment cycle may be applied in satisfying this requirement.

(ii) During the second inactive enrollment cycle; four-thirds of the qualifying continuing professional education requirements as set forth in paragraph (e)(2) of this section (that is, 48 hours), without regard to paragraph (e)(2)(ii) or (e)(2)(iii) of this section, plus eighteen months of certified responsible pension actuarial experience, must be completed since the start of the first inactive enrollment cycle. Any hours of continuing professional education credit earned during the first inactive enrollment cycle may be applied in satisfying this requirement.

(iii) During the third inactive enrollment cycle: five-thirds of the qualifying continuing professional education requirements as set forth in paragraph (e)(2) of this section, (that is, 60 hours), without regard to paragraph (e)(2)(ii) or (e)(2)(iii) of this section plus eighteen months of certified responsible pension actuarial experience, must be completed since the start of the second inactive enrollment cycle. Any hours of continuing professional education credit earned during the second inactive enrollment cycle may be applied in satisfying this requirement. No hours earned during the first inactive enrollment cycle may be applied in satisfying this requirement. [Amended 3/31/2011 by 76 FR 17762].

(8) An individual in inactive status remains subject to the jurisdiction of the Joint Board and/or the Department of the Treasury with respect to disciplinary matters.

(9) An individual who has certified in good faith that he/she has satisfied the continuing professional education requirements of this section will not be considered to be in non-compliance with such requirements on the basis of a program he/she has attended later being found inadequate or not in compliance with the requirements for continuing professional education. Such individual will be granted renewal, but the Executive Director may require such individual to remedy the resulting shortfall by earning replacement credit during the cycle in which renewal was granted or within a reasonable time period as determined by the Executive Director. For example, if six of the credit hours claimed were disallowed, the individual may be required to present 42 credit hours instead of the minimum 36 credit hours to qualify for renewal related to the next cycle. [Amended 3/31/2011 by 76 FR 17762].

(m) *Renewal while under suspension or disbarment.* An individual who is ineligible to perform actuarial services and/or to practice before the Internal Revenue Service by virtue of disciplinary action is required to meet the requirements for renewal of enrollment during the period of such ineligibility.

(n) *Verification.* The Executive Director or his/her designee may request and review the continuing professional education records of an enrolled actuary, including programs attended, in a manner deemed appropriate to determine compliance with the requirements and standards for the renewal of enrollment as provided in this section. The Executive Director may also request and review the records of any qualifying sponsor in a manner deemed appropriate to determine compliance with the requirements of paragraphs (f)(3) and (j)(1) of this section. [Added 3/31/2011 by 76 FR 17762].

(o) *Examples*. The following examples illustrate the application of the rules of paragraph (l)(7) of this section and the effective date of an enrolled actuary's renewal:

Example 1. Individual E, who was initially enrolled before January 1, 2008, completes 12 hours of core continuing professional education credit and 24 hours of non-core continuing professional education credit between January 1, 2011, and December 31, 2013. E files a complete application for reenrollment on February 28, 2014. E's reenrollment is effective as of April 1, 2014.

Example 2. Individual F, who was initially enrolled before January 1, 2008, also completes 12 hours of core continuing professional education credit and 24 hours of non-core continuing professional education credit between January 1, 2011, and December 31, 2013. However, F does not file an application for reenrollment until March 20, 2014. The Joint Board notifies F that it has granted F's application on June 25, 2014. Accordingly, effective April 1, 2014, F is placed on the roster of inactive enrolled actuaries. F returns to active status as of June 25, 2014. F is ineligible to perform pension actuarial services as an enrolled actuary under ERISA and the Internal Revenue Code from April 1 through June 24, 2014.

Example 3. Individual G, who was initially enrolled before January 1, 2008, completes only 8 hours of core continuing professional education credit and 24 hours of non-core continuing professional education credit between January 1, 2011, and December 31, 2013. G completes another 6 hours of core continuing professional education on January 15, 2014, and files an application for return to active status on January 20, 2014. G's application shows the timely completion of 32 hours of continuing professional education plus the additional 4 hours of continuing professional education earned after the end of the enrollment cycle. The Joint Board notifies G that it has granted the application on April 20, 2014. Accordingly, effective April 1, 2014, G is placed on the roster of inactive enrolled actuaries. G returns to active status as of April 20, 2014. G is ineligible to perform pension actuarial services as an enrolled actuary under ERISA and the Internal Revenue Code from April 1 through April 19, 2014. Of the 6 hours of continuing professional education earned by G on January 15, 2014, only 2 hours may be applied to the enrollment cycle that ends December 31, 2016.

Example 4. (i) Individual H, who was initially enrolled before January 1, 2008, completes 5 hours of core continuing professional education credit and 10 hours of non-core continuing professional education credit between January 1, 2011, and December 31, 2013. Accordingly, effective April 1, 2014, H is placed on the roster of inactive enrolled actuaries and is ineligible to perform pension actuarial services as an enrolled actuary under ERISA and the Internal Revenue Code. [Corrected 12/28/11 by 76 FR 81362].

(ii) H completes 7 hours of core continuing professional education credit and 14 hours of noncore continuing professional education credit between January 1, 2014, and May 24, 2016. Because H has completed 12 hours of core continuing professional education and 24 hours of non-core continuing professional education during the last active enrollment period and the initial period when on inactive status, H has satisfied the requirements for reenrollment during the first inactive cycle. Accordingly, H may file an application for return to active enrollment on May 24, 2016. If this application is approved, H will be eligible to perform pension actuarial services as an enrolled actuary under ERISA and the Internal Revenue Code, effective with the date of such approval.

(iii) Because H used the 21 hours of continuing professional education credit earned after January 1, 2014, for return from inactive status, H may not apply any of these 21 hours of core and non-core continuing professional education credits towards the requirements for renewed enrollment effective April 1, 2017. Accordingly, H must complete an additional 36 hours of continuing professional education (12 core and 24 non-core) prior to December 31, 2016, to be eligible for renewed enrollment effective April 1, 2017.

Example 5. (i) The facts are the same as in *Example 4* except H completes 2 hours of core continuing professional education credit and 8 hours of non-core continuing professional education credit between January 1, 2014, and December 31, 2016. Thus, because H did not fulfill the requirements for return to active status during his first inactive cycle, H must satisfy the requirements of paragraph (l)(7)(ii) of this section in order to return to active status.

(ii) Accordingly, in order to be eligible to file an application for return to active status on or before December 31, 2019, H must complete an additional 38 hours of continuing professional education credit (of which at least 14 hours must consist of core subject matter) between January 1, 2017, and December 31, 2019, and have 18 months of certified responsible pension actuarial experience during the period beginning on January 1, 2014.

(iii) Note that the 5 hours of core continuing professional education credit and the 10 hours of non-core continuing professional education credit that H completes between January 1, 2011, and December 31, 2013, are not counted toward H's return to active status and are also not taken into account toward the additional hours of continuing professional education credit that H must complete between January 1, 2017, and December 31, 2019, in order to apply for renewal of enrollment effective April 1, 2020.

Example 6. (i) The facts are the same as in *Example 4* except H completes 2 hours of core continuing professional education credit and 8 hours of non-core continuing professional education credit between January 1, 2014, and December 31, 2016, and 12 hours of core continuing professional education credit and 24 hours of non-core continuing professional education credit between January 1, 2017, and December 31, 2019. Thus, because H did not fulfill the requirements for return to active status during his first or second inactive cycles, H must satisfy the requirements of paragraph (l)(7)(iii) of this section in order to return to active status.

(ii) Accordingly, in order to be eligible to file an application for return to active status on or before December 31, 2022, H must complete an additional 24 hours of continuing professional education credit (of which, at least 8 hours must consist of core subject matter) between January 1, 2020 and December 31, 2022, and have at least 18 months of certified responsible pension actuarial experience during the period beginning on January 1, 2017.

(iii) Note that the total of 15 hours of continuing professional education credit that H completes between January 1, 2011, and December 31, 2013, as well as the 10 hours of continuing professional education credit between January 1, 2014, and December 31, 2016, are not counted toward H's return to active status and are not taken into account toward the additional hours of continuing professional education credit that H must complete between January 1, 2020, and December 31, 2022, in order to be eligible to file an application for renewal of enrollment active status effective April 1, 2023. [Corrected 12/28/11 by 76 FR 81362].

Example 7. (i) Individual J, who was initially enrolled July 1, 2012, completes 1 hour of core continuing professional education credit and 2 hours of non-core continuing professional education credit between January 1, 2012, and December 31, 2013. Accordingly, effective April 1, 2014, J is placed on the roster of inactive enrolled actuaries and is ineligible to perform pension actuarial services as an enrolled actuary under ERISA and the Internal Revenue Code.

(ii) J completes 5 hours of core continuing professional education credit and 4 hours of non-core continuing professional education credit between January 1, 2014, and October 6, 2014. Because J did not complete the required 12 hours of continuing professional education (of which at least 6 hours must consist of core subject matter) during J's initial enrollment cycle, J is not eligible to file an application for a return to active enrollment on October 6, 2014, notwithstanding the fact that had J completed such hours between January 1, 2012, and December 31, 2013, J would have satisfied the requirements for renewed enrollment effective April 1, 2014. [Corrected 12/28/11 by 76 FR 81362].

(iii) Accordingly, J must complete an additional 24 hours of continuing professional education (of which at least 12 hours must consist of core subject matter) during his/her first inactive enrollment cycle before applying for renewal of enrollment.

Example 8. The facts are the same as in *Example 7* except that J completes 17 hours of core continuing professional education credit and 16 hours of non-core continuing professional education credit between January 1, 2014, and February 12, 2015. Accordingly, because as of February 12, 2015, J satisfied the continuing professional education requirements as set forth in paragraph (e)(2) of this section without regard to paragraph (e)(2)(ii) thereof, J may file an application for return to active enrollment status on February 12, 2015. [Added 3/31/2011 by 76 FR 17762].

(p) With the exception of paragraphs (e)(1) and (f)(3)(iii) of this section, this section applies to the enrollment cycle beginning January 1, 2011, and all subsequent enrollment cycles. [Added 3/31/2011 by 76 FR 17762].

[¶ 15,223C]

§ 901.12 *Eligibility for enrollment.* (a) *In general.* An individual applying to be an enrolled actuary must fulfill the experience requirement of paragraph (b) of this section, the basic actuarial knowledge requirement of paragraph (c) of this section, and the pension actuarial knowledge requirement of paragraph (d) of this section.

(b) *Qualifying experience.* Within the 10-year period immediately preceding the date of application, the applicant shall have completed either—

(1) A minimum of 36 months of certified responsible pension actuarial experience; or [Added 3/31/2011 by 76 FR 17762].

(2) A minimum of 60 months of certified responsible actuarial experience, including at least 18 months of certified responsible pension actuarial experience. [Added 3/31/2011 by 76 FR 17762].

(c) *Basic actuarial knowledge.* The applicant shall demonstrate knowledge of basic actuarial mathematics and methodology by one of the following:

(1) *Joint Board basic examination.* Successful completion, to a score satisfactory to the Joint Board, of an examination, prescribed by the Joint Board, in basic actuarial mathematics and methodology including compound interest, principles of life contingencies, commutation functions, multiple-decrement functions, and joint life annuities.

(2) *Organization basic examinations.* Successful completion, to a score satisfactory to the Joint Board, of one or more proctored examinations which are given by an actuarial organization and which the Joint Board has determined cover substantially the same subject areas, have at least a comparable level of difficulty, and require at least the same competence as the Joint Board basic examination referred to in paragraph (c)(1) of this section.

(3) *Qualifying formal education.* Receipt of a bachelor's or higher degree from an accredited college or university after the satisfactory completion of a course of study:

(i) In which the major area of concentration was actuarial mathematics, or

(ii) Which included at least as many semester hours or quarter hours each in mathematics, statistics, actuarial mathematics and other subjects as the Board determines represent equivalence to paragraph (c)(3)(i) of this section.

(d) *Pension actuarial knowledge.* (1) The applicant shall demonstrate pension actuarial knowledge by one of the following:

(i) *Joint Board pension examination.* Successful completion, within the 10-year period immediately preceding the date of the application, to a score satisfactory to the Joint Board, of an examination prescribed by the Joint Board in actuarial mathematics and methodology relating to pension plans, including the provisions of ERISA relating to the minimum funding requirements and allocation of assets on plan termination.

(ii) *Organization pension examinations.* Successful completion, within the 10-year period immediately preceding the date of the application, to a score satisfactory to the Joint Board, of one or more proctored examinations which are given by an actuarial organization and which the Joint Board has determined cover substantially the same subject areas, have at least a comparable level of difficulty, and require

at least the same competence as the Joint Board pension examination referred to in paragraph (d)(1)(i) of this section.

(2) For purposes of this section, the date of successful completion of an examination is generally the date a candidate sits for the examination, provided that the candidate receives a passing grade on that examination. However, an applicant who sat for an examination prior to the effective date of these regulations will be deemed to have sat for such examination on the effective date. [Amended 3/31/2011 by 76 FR 17762].

(e) *Form; fee.* An applicant who wishes to take an examination administered by the Joint Board under paragraph (c)(1) or (d)(1) of this section shall file an application on a form prescribed by the Joint Board. Such application shall be accompanied by payment in the amount set forth on the application form. The amount represents a fee charged to each applicant for examination and is designed to cover the costs for the administration of the examination. The fee shall be retained whether or not the applicant successfully completes the examination or is enrolled. [Added by 44 FR 68457, effective November 13, 1979 and amended 3/31/2011 by 76 FR 17762].

(f) *Denial of enrollment.* An applicant may be denied enrollment if:

(1) The Joint Board finds that the applicant, during the 15-year period immediately preceding the date of application and on or after the applicant's eighteenth birthday has engaged in disreputable conduct. The term disreputable conduct includes, but is not limited to:

(i) An adjudication, decision, or determination by a court of law, a duly constituted licensing or accreditation authority (other than the Joint Board), or by any federal or state agency, board, commission, hearing examiner, administrative law judge, or other official administrative authority, that the applicant has engaged in conduct evidencing fraud, dishonesty or breach of trust.

(ii) Giving false or misleading information, or participating in any way in the giving of false or misleading information, to the Department of the Treasury or the Department of Labor or the Pension Benefit Guaranty Corporation or any officer or employee thereof in connection with any matter pending or likely to be pending before them, knowing such information to be false or misleading.

(iii) Willfully failing to make a federal tax return in violation of the revenue laws of the United States, or evading, attempting to evade, or participating in any way in evading or attempting to evade any federal tax or payment thereof, knowingly counseling or suggesting to a client or prospective client an illegal plan to evade federal taxes or payment thereof, or concealing assets of himself or another to evade federal taxes or payment thereof.

(iv) Directly or indirectly attempting to influence, or offering or agreeing to attempt to influence, the official action of any officer or employee of the Department of the Treasury or the Department of Labor or the Pension Benefit Guaranty Corporation by the use of threats, false accusations, duress or coercion, by the offer of any special inducement or promise of advantage or by the bestowing of any gift, favor, or thing of value.

(v) Disbarment or suspension from practice as an actuary, attorney, certified public accountant, public accountant, or an enrolled agent by any duly constituted authority of any state, possession, territory, commonwealth, the District of Columbia, by any Federal Court of record, or by the Department of the Treasury.

(vi) Contemptuous conduct in connection with matters before the Department of Labor or the Pension Benefit Guaranty Corporation, including the use of abusive language, making false accusations and statements knowing them to be false, or circulating or publishing malicious or libelous matter.

(2) The applicant has been convicted of any of the offenses referred to in section 411 of ERISA.

(3) The applicant has submitted false or misleading information on an application for enrollment to perform actuarial services or in any oral or written information submitted in connection therewith or in any report presenting actuarial information to any person, knowing the same to be false or misleading. [Added November 12, 1976, by 41 FR 49970. Amended by 43 FR 39756, filed with the Federal Register September 6, 1978, and published in the Federal Register on September 6, 1978.]

Subpart C—Standards of Performance for Enrolled Actuaries

[¶ 15,224]

§ 901.20 **Standards of performance of actuarial services.** In the discharge of duties required by ERISA of enrolled actuaries with respect to any plan to which the Act applies:

(a) *In general.* An enrolled actuary shall undertake an actuarial assignment only when qualified to do so.

(b) *Professional duty.* (1) An enrolled actuary shall perform actuarial services only in a manner that is fully in accordance with all of the duties and requirements for such persons under applicable law and consistent with relevant generally accepted standards for professional responsibility and ethics.

(2) An enrolled actuary shall not perform actuarial services for any person or organization which he/she believes, or has reasonable grounds to believe, may utilize his/her services in a fraudulent manner or in a manner inconsistent with law. [Amended 3/31/2011 by 76 FR 17762].

(c) *Advice or explanations.* An enrolled actuary shall provide to the plan administrator upon appropriate request, supplemental advice or explanation relative to any report signed or certified by such enrolled actuary.

(d) *Conflicts of interest.* (1) Except as provided in paragraph (d)(2) of this section, an enrolled actuary shall not perform actuarial services for a client if the representation involves a conflict of interest. A conflict of interest exists if—

(i) The representation of one client will be directly adverse to another client; or

(ii) There is a significant risk that the representation of one or more clients will be materially limited by the enrolled actuary's responsibilities to another client, a former client, or by a personal interest of the enrolled actuary.

(2) Notwithstanding the existence of a conflict of interest under paragraph (d)(1) of this section, the enrolled actuary may represent a client if—

(i) The enrolled actuary reasonably believes that he or she will be able to provide competent and diligent representation to each affected client;

(ii) The representation is not prohibited by law; and

(iii) Each affected client waives the conflict of interest and gives informed consent at the time the existence of the conflict of interest is known by the enrolled actuary. [Amended 3/31/2011 by 76 FR 17762].

(e) *Assumptions, calculations and recommendations.* (1) The enrolled actuary shall exercise due care, skill, prudence and diligence when performing actuarial services under ERISA and the Internal Revenue Code. In particular, in the course of preparing a report or certificate stating actuarial costs or liabilities, the enrolled actuary shall ensure that—

(i) Except as mandated by law, the actuarial assumptions are reasonable individually and in combination, and the actuarial cost method and the actuarial method of valuation of assets are appropriate;

(ii) The calculations are accurately carried out and properly documented; and

(iii) The report, any recommendations, and any supplemental advice or explanation relative to the report reflect the results of the calculations.

(2) An enrolled actuary shall include in any report or certificate stating actuarial costs or liabilities, a statement or reference describing or clearly identifying the data, any material inadequacies therein and the implications thereof, and the actuarial methods and assumptions employed. [Amended 3/31/2011 by 76 FR 17762].

(f) *Due diligence.* (1) An enrolled actuary must exercise due diligence—

(i) In preparing or assisting in the preparation of, approving, and filing tax returns, documents, affidavits, and other papers relating to the Department of the Treasury, the Department of Labor, the

Pension Benefit Guaranty Corporation, or any other applicable Federal or State entity;

(ii) In determining the correctness of oral or written representations made by the enrolled actuary to the Department of the Treasury, the Department of Labor, the Pension Benefit Guaranty Corporation, or any other applicable Federal or State entity; and

(iii) In determining the correctness of oral or written representations made by the enrolled actuary to clients.

(2) An enrolled actuary advising a client to take a position on any document to be filed with the Department of the Treasury, the Department of Labor, the Pension Benefit Guaranty Corporation, or any other applicable Federal or State entity (or preparing or signing such a return or document) generally may rely in good faith without verification upon information furnished by the client. The enrolled actuary may not, however, ignore the implications of information furnished to, or actually known by, the enrolled actuary, and must make reasonable inquiries if the information as furnished appears to be incorrect, inconsistent with an important fact or another factual assumption, or incomplete. [Amended 3/31/2011 by 76 FR 17762].

(g) *Solicitations regarding actuarial services.* An enrolled actuary may not in any way use or participate in the use of any form of public communication or private solicitation related to the performance of actuarial services containing a false, fraudulent, or coercive statement or claim, or a misleading or deceptive statement or claim. An enrolled actuary may not make, directly or indirectly, an uninvited written or oral solicitation of employment related to actuarial services if the solicitation violates Federal or State law, nor may such person employ, accept employment in partnership form, corporate form, or any other form, or share fees with, any individual or entity who so solicits. Any lawful solicitation related to the performance of actuarial services made by or on behalf of an enrolled actuary must clearly identify the solicitation as such and, if applicable, identify the source of the information used in choosing the recipient. [Amended 3/31/2011 by 76 FR 17762].

(h) *Prompt disposition of pending matters.* An enrolled actuary may not unreasonably delay the prompt disposition of any matter before the Internal Revenue Service, the Department of Labor, the Pension Benefit Guaranty Corporation, or any other applicable Federal or State entity. [Amended 3/31/2011 by 76 FR 17762].

(i) *[Reserved].*

(j) *Return of client's records.* (1) In general, an enrolled actuary must, at the request of a client, promptly return any and all records of the client that are necessary for the client to comply with his or her legal obligations. The enrolled actuary may retain copies of the records returned to a client. The existence of a dispute over fees generally does not relieve the enrolled actuary of his or her responsibility under this section. Nevertheless, if applicable state law allows or permits the retention of a client's records by an enrolled actuary in the case of a dispute over fees for services rendered, the enrolled actuary need only return those records that must be attached to the client's required forms under ERISA and the Internal Revenue Code. The enrolled actuary, however, must provide the client with reasonable access to review and copy any additional records of the client retained by the enrolled actuary under state law that are necessary for the client to comply with his or her obligations under ERISA and the Internal Revenue Code. [Amended 3/31/2011 by 76 FR 17762].

(2) For purposes of this section, records of the client include all documents or written or electronic materials provided to the enrolled actuary, or obtained by the enrolled actuary in the course of the enrolled actuary's representation of the client, that preexisted the retention of the enrolled actuary by the client. The term "records of the client" also includes materials that were prepared by the client or a third party (not including an employee or agent of the enrolled actuary) at any time and provided to the enrolled actuary with respect to the subject matter of the representation. The term "records of the client" also includes any return, claim for refund, schedule, affidavit, appraisal or any other document prepared by the enrolled actuary, or his or her employee or agent, that was presented to the client with respect to a prior representation if such document is necessary for the taxpayer to comply with his or her current obligations under ERISA and the Internal Revenue Code. The term "records of the client" does not include any return, claim for refund, schedule, affidavit, appraisal or

any other document prepared by the enrolled actuary or the enrolled actuary's firm, employees or agents if the enrolled actuary is withholding such document pending the client's performance of its contractual obligation to pay fees with respect to such document. [Amended 3/31/2011 by 76 FR 17762].

(k) *Notification.* An enrolled actuary shall provide written notification of the nonfiling of any actuarial document he/she has signed upon discovery of the non-filing. Such notification shall be made to the office of the Internal Revenue Service, the Department of Labor, or the Pension Benefit Guaranty Corporation where such document should have been filed. [Amended by 43 FR 39756, filed with the Federal Register September 6, 1978, and published in the Federal Register on September 6, 1978. amended 3/31/2011 by 76 FR 17762].

(l) The rules of this section apply to all actuarial services and related acts performed on or after May 2, 2011. [Added 3/31/2011 by 76 FR 17762].

Subpart D—Suspension and Termination of Enrollment

[¶ 15,224A]

§ 901.30 *Authority to suspend or terminate enrollment.* Under Section 3042(b) of ERISA the Joint Board may, after notice and opportunity for a hearing, suspend or terminate the enrollment of an enrolled actuary if the Joint Board finds that such enrolled actuary

(a) has failed to discharge his/her duties under ERISA, or

(b) does not satisfy the requirements for enrollment in effect at the time of his/her enrollment.

[¶ 15,224B]

§ 901.31 *Grounds for suspension or termination of enrollment.* (a) *Failure to satisfy requirements for enrollment.* The enrollment of an actuary may be terminated if it is found that the actuary did not satisfy the eligibility requirements set forth in § 901.11 or § 901.12. [Amended 3/31/2011 by 76 FR 17762].

(b) *Failure to discharge duties.* The enrollment of an actuary may be suspended or terminated if it is found that the actuary, following enrollment, failed to discharge his/her duties under ERISA. Such duties include those set forth in § 901.20.

(c) *Disreputable conduct.* The enrollment of an actuary may be suspended or terminated if it is found that the actuary has, at any time after he/she applied for enrollment, engaged in any conduct set forth in § 901.12(f) or other conduct evidencing fraud, dishonesty, or breach of trust. Such other conduct includes, but is not limited to, the following:

(1) Conviction of any criminal offense under the laws of the United States (including Section 411 of ERISA, 29 U.S.C. 1111), any State thereof, the District of Columbia, or any territory or possession of the United States, which evidences fraud, dishonesty, or breach of trust.

(2) Knowingly filing false or altered documents, affidavits, financial statements or other papers on matters relating to employee benefit plans or actuarial services.

(3) Knowingly making false or misleading representations, either orally or in writing, on matters relating to employee benefit plans or actuarial services, or knowingly failing to disclose information relative to such matters.

(4) The use of false or misleading representations with intent to deceive a client or prospective client, or of intimations that the actuary is able to obtain special consideration or action from an officer or employee of any agency or court authorized to determine the validity of pension plans under ERISA.

(5) Willful violation of any of the regulations contained in this part. [Amended 3/31/2011 by 76 FR 17762].

[¶ 15,224C]

§ 901.32 *Receipt of information concerning enrolled actuaries.* If an officer or employee of the Department of the Treasury, the Department of Labor, the Pension Benefit Guaranty Corporation, or a member of the Joint Board has reason to believe that an enrolled actuary has violated any provision of this part, or if any such officer, employee or member receives information to that effect, he/she may make a written report thereof, which report or a copy thereof shall be forwarded to the Executive Director. If any other person has information of any such violation, he/she may make a report thereof to the Executive Director. [Amended 3/31/2011 by 76 FR 17762].

[¶ 15,224D]

§ 901.33 *Initiation of proceeding.* Whenever the Executive Director has reason to believe that an enrolled actuary has violated any provision of the laws or regulations governing enrollment, such individual may be reprimanded or a proceeding may be initiated for the suspension or termination of such individual's enrollment. A reprimand as used in this paragraph is a statement informing the enrolled actuary that, in the opinion of the Executive Director, his/her conduct is in violation of the regulations and admonishing the enrolled actuary that repetition of the conduct occasioning the reprimand may result in the institution of a proceeding for the suspension or termination of the actuary's enrollment. A proceeding for suspension or termination of enrollment shall be initiated by a complaint naming the respondent actuary, signed by the Executive Director and filed in the Executive Director's office. Except in cases where the nature of the proceeding or the public interest does not permit, a proceeding will not be initiated under this section until the facts which may warrant such a proceeding have been called to the attention of the actuary in writing and he/she has been given an opportunity to respond to the allegations of misconduct.

[¶ 15,224E]

§ 901.34 *Conferences.* (a) *In general.* The Executive Director may confer with an enrolled actuary concerning allegations of his/her misconduct whether or not a proceeding for suspension or termination has been initiated against him/her. If the conference results in agreement as to certain facts or other matters in connection with such a proceeding, such agreement may be entered in the record at the request of the actuary or the Executive Director.

(b) *Voluntary suspension or termination of enrollment.* An enrolled actuary, in order to avoid the initiation or conclusion of a suspension or termination proceeding, may offer his/her consent to suspension or termination of enrollment or may offer his/her resignation. The Executive Director may accept the offered resignation or may suspend or terminate enrollment in accordance with the consent offered.

[¶ 15,224F]

§ 901.35 *Contents of complaint.* (a) *Charges.* A complaint initiating a suspension or termination proceeding shall describe the allegations which are the basis for the proceeding, and fairly inform the respondent of the charges against him/her.

(b) *Answer.* In the complaint, or in a separate paper attached to the complaint, notice shall be given of the place at, and time within which the respondent shall file an answer, which time shall not be less than 15 days from the date of service of the complaint. Notice shall be given that a decision by default may be rendered against the respondent if an answer is not filed as required.

[¶ 15,224G]

§ 901.36 *Service of complaint and other papers.* (a) *Complaint.* The complaint or a copy thereof may be served upon the respondent by certified mail, or first-class mail as hereinafter provided, by delivering it to the respondent, or the respondent's attorney or agent of record either in person or by leaving it at the office or place of business of the respondent, the attorney or agent, or in any other manner which may have been agreed to in writing by the respondent. Where the service is by certified mail, the return post office receipt signed by or on behalf of the respondent shall be proof of service. If the certified matter is not claimed or accepted by the respondent and is returned undelivered, complete service may be made upon the respondent by mailing the complaint to him/her by first-class mail, addressed to the respondent at the last address known to the Executive Director. If service is made upon the respondent or his/her attorney or agent in person or by leaving the complaint at the office or place of business of the respondent, attorney, or agent, the verified return by the person making service, setting forth the manner of service, shall be proof of such service.

(b) *Service of papers other than complaint.* Any paper other than the complaint may be served upon the respondent as provided in paragraph (a) of this section or by mailing the paper by first-class mail to the respondent at the last address known to the Executive Director or by mailing the paper by first-class mail to the respondent's attorney or agent. Such mailing shall constitute complete service. Notices may also be served upon the respondent or his/her attorney or agent by telegraph.

(c) *Filing of papers.* Whenever the filing of a paper is required or permitted in connection with a suspension or termination proceeding, and the place of filing is not specified by this subpart or by rule or order of the Administrative Law Judge, the paper shall be filed with the Executive Director of the Joint Board for the Enrollment of Actuaries, Treasury Department, Washington, D.C. 20220. All papers shall be filed in duplicate.

[¶ 15,224H]

§ 901.37 **Answer.** (a) *Filing.* The respondent's answer shall be filed in writing within the time specified in the complaint or notice of initiation of the proceeding, unless, on application, the time is extended by the Executive Director or the Administrative Law Judge. The answer shall be filed in duplicate with the Executive Director.

(b) *Contents.* The answer shall contain a statement of facts which constitute the grounds of defense and it shall specifically admit or deny each allegation set forth in the complaint, except that the respondent shall not deny a material allegation in the complaint which he/she knows to be true, or state that he/she is without sufficient information to form a belief when in fact the respondent possesses such information. The respondent may also state affirmatively special matters of defense.

(c) *Failure to deny or answer allegations in the complaint.* Every allegation in the complaint which is not denied in the answer shall be deemed to be admitted and may be considered as proven, and no further evidence in respect of such allegation need be adduced at a hearing. Failure to file an answer within the time prescribed in the notice to the respondent, except as the time for answer is extended by the Executive Director or the Administrative Law Judge, shall constitute an admission of the allegations of the complaint and a waiver of hearing, and the Administrative Law Judge may make a decision by default, without a hearing or further procedure.

[¶ 15,224I]

§ 901.38 **Supplemental charges.** If it appears to the Executive Director that the respondent in his/her answer falsely and in bad faith denies a material allegation of fact in the complaint or states that the respondent has no knowledge sufficient to form a belief when he/she in fact possesses such knowledge, or if it appears that the respondent has knowingly introduced false testimony during proceedings for suspension or termination of his/her enrollment, the Executive Director may file supplemental charges against the respondent. Such supplemental charges may be tried with other charges in the case, provided the respondent is given due notice thereof and is afforded an opportunity to prepare a defense thereto.

[¶ 15,224J]

§ 901.39 **Reply to answer.** No reply to the respondent's answer shall be required, but the Executive Director may file a reply at his/her discretion or at the request of the Administrative Law Judge.

[¶ 15,224K]

§ 901.40 **Proof; variance; amendment of pleadings.** In the case of a variance between the allegations in a pleading and the evidence adduced in support of the pleading, the Administrative Law Judge may order or authorize amendment of the pleading to conform to the evidence, provided that the party who would otherwise be prejudiced by the amendment is given reasonable opportunity to meet the allegations of the pleading as amended. The Administrative Law Judge shall make findings on any issue presented by the pleadings as so amended.

[¶ 15,224L]

§ 901.41 **Motions and requests.** Motions and requests may be filed with the Executive Director or with the Administrative Law Judge.

[¶ 15,224M]

§ 901.42 **Representation.** A respondent or proposed respondent may appear at conference or hearing in person or may be represented by counsel or other representative. The Executive Director may be represented by an attorney or other employee of the Treasury Department.

[¶ 15,224N]

§ 901.43 **Administrative Law Judge.** (a) *Appointment.* An Administrative Law Judge, appointed as provided by section 11 of the Administrative Procedure Act, 60 Stat. 244 (5 U.S.C. 3105), shall conduct proceedings upon complaints for the suspension or termination of enrolled actuaries.

(b) *Power of Administrative Law Judge.* Among other powers, the Administrative Law Judge shall have authority, in connection with any suspension or termination proceeding of an enrolled actuary, to do the following:

(1) Administer oaths and affirmations;

(2) Make rulings upon motions and requests, which may not be appealed before the close of a hearing except at the discretion of the Administrative Law Judge;

(3) Determine the time and place of hearing and regulate its course of conduct;

(4) Adopt rules of procedure and modify the same as required for the orderly disposition of proceedings;

(5) Rule upon offers of proof, receive relevant evidence, and examine witnesses;

(6) Take or authorize the taking of depositions;

(7) Receive and consider oral or written argument on facts or law;

(8) Hold or provide for the holding of conferences for the settlement or simplification of the issues by consent of the parties;

(9) Perform such acts and take such measures as are necessary or appropriate to the efficient conduct of any proceeding; and

(10) Make initial decisions.

[¶ 15,224O]

§ 901.44 **Hearings.** (a) *In general.* The Administrative Law Judge shall preside at the hearing on a complaint for the suspension or termination of an enrolled actuary. Hearing shall be stenographically recorded and transcribed and the testimony of witnesses shall be taken under oath or affirmation. Hearings will be conducted pursuant to Section 7 of the Administrative Procedure Act, 60 Stat. 241 (5 U.S.C. 556).

(b) *Failure to appear.* If either party to the proceeding fails to appear at the hearing, after due notice thereof has been sent to the parties, the Administrative Law Judge may make a decision against the absent party by default.

[¶ 15,224P]

§ 901.45 **Evidence.** (a) *In general.* The rules of evidence prevailing in courts of law and equity are not controlling in hearings on complaints for the suspension or the termination of the enrollment of enrolled actuaries. However, the Administrative Law Judge shall exclude evidence which is irrelevant, immaterial, or unduly repetitious.

(b) *Depositions.* The deposition of any witness taken pursuant to § 901.46 may be admitted.

(c) *Proof of documents.* Official documents, records, and papers of the Department of the Treasury, the Department of Labor, the Pension Benefit Guaranty Corporation, the Joint Board for the Enrollment of Actuaries or the Office of the Executive Director of the Joint Board for the Enrollment of Actuaries shall be admissible into evidence without the production of an officer or employee to authenticate them. Any such documents, records, and papers may be evidenced by a copy attested to or identified by an officer or employee of the Department of the Treasury, the Department of Labor, the Pension Benefit Guaranty Corporation, the Joint Board for the Enrollment of Actuaries, or the Office of the Executive Director of the Joint Board for the Enrollment of Actuaries, as the case may be.

(d) *Exhibits*. If any document, record, or other paper is introduced into evidence as an exhibit, the Administrative Law Judge may authorize the withdrawal of the exhibit subject to any conditions which he/she deems proper.

(e) *Objections*. Objections to evidence shall state the grounds relied upon, and the record shall not include argument thereon, except as ordered by the Administrative Law Judge. Rulings on such objections shall be part of the record. No exception to the ruling is necessary to preserve the rights of the parties.

[¶ 15,224Q]

§ 901.46 *Depositions*. Depositions for use at a hearing may, with the written approval of the Administrative Law Judge, be taken by either the Executive Director or the respondent or their duly authorized representatives. Depositions may be taken upon oral or written interrogatories, upon not less than 10 days written notice to the other party, before any officer duly authorized to administer an oath for general purposes or before an officer or employee of the Department of the Treasury, the Department of Labor, the Pension Benefit Guaranty Corporation, or the Joint Board who is authorized to administer an oath. Such notice shall state the names of the witnesses and the time and place where the depositions are to be taken. The requirement of 10 days notice may be waived by the parties in writing, and depositions may then be taken from the persons and at the times and places mutually agreed upon by the parties. When a deposition is taken upon written interrogatories, any cross-examination shall be upon written interrogatories. Copies of such written interrogatories shall be served upon the other party with the notice, and the copies of any written cross-interrogatories shall be mailed or delivered to the opposing party at least five days before the date of taking the depositions, unless the parties mutually agree otherwise. A party upon whose behalf a deposition is taken must file it with the Administrative Law Judge and serve one copy upon the opposing party. Expenses in the reporting of depositions shall be borne by the party at whose instance the deposition is taken.

[¶ 15,224R]

§ 901.47 *Transcript*. In cases where the hearing is stenographically reported by a Government contract reporter, copies of the transcript may be obtained from the reporter at rates not to exceed the minimum rates fixed by contract between the Government and the reporter. Where the hearing is stenographically reported by a regular employee of the Department of the Treasury, the Department of Labor, the Pension Benefit Guaranty Corporation, or the Joint Board, a copy thereof will be supplied to the respondent either without charge or upon the payment of a reasonable fee. Copies of exhibits introduced at the hearing or at the taking of depositions will be supplied to parties upon the payment of a reasonable fee (31 U.S.C. 9701). [Amended 3/31/2011 by 76 FR 17762].

[¶ 15,224S]

§ 901.48 *Proposed findings and conclusions*. Except in cases where the respondent has failed to answer the complaint or where a party has failed to appear at the hearing, the Administrative Law Judge, before making his/her decision, shall give the parties a reasonable opportunity to submit proposed findings and conclusions and supporting reasons therefor.

[¶ 15,224T]

§ 901.49 *Decision of the Administrative Law Judge*. As soon as practicable after the conclusion of a hearing and the receipt of any proposed findings and conclusions timely submitted by the parties, the Administrative Law Judge shall make the initial decision in the case. The decision should be based solely upon the pleading, the testimony and exhibits received in evidence at the hearing or specifically authorized to be subsequently submitted under the applicable laws and regulations. The decision shall include (a) a statement of findings and conclusions, as well as the reasons or basis therefor, upon all the material issues of fact or law presented on the record, and (b) an order of suspension, termination or reprimand or an order of dismissal of the complaint. The Administrative Law Judge shall file the decision with the Executive Director and shall transmit a copy thereof to the respondent or his/her attorney or agent of record. In the absence of an appeal to the Joint Board or review of the decision upon motion of the Joint Board, the decision of the Administrative Law Judge shall without further proceedings become the decision of the Joint Board 30 days from the date of the Administrative Law Judge's decision.

[¶ 15,224U]

§ 901.50 *Appeal to the Joint Board*. Within 30 days from the date of the Administrative Law Judge's decision, either party may appeal to the Joint Board for the Enrollment of Actuaries. The appeal shall be filed with the Executive Director in duplicate and shall include exceptions to the decision of the Administrative Law Judge and supporting reasons for such exceptions. If an appeal is filed by the Executive Director, a copy of it shall be transmitted to the respondent. Within 30 days after receipt of an appeal or copy thereof, the other party may file a reply brief in duplicate with the Executive Director. If the reply brief is filed by the Executive Director, a copy thereof shall be transmitted to the respondent. Upon the filing of an appeal and a reply brief, if any, the Executive Director shall transmit the entire record to the joint board.

[¶ 15,224V]

§ 901.51 *Decision of the Joint Board*. On appeal from or review of the initial decision of the Administrative Law Judge, the Joint Board for the Enrollment of Actuaries will make the final decision. In making its decision the Joint Board will review the record of such portions thereof as may be cited by the parties to permit limiting of the issues. A copy of the Joint Board's decision shall be transmitted to the respondent by the Executive Director.

[¶ 15,224W]

§ 901.52 *Effect of suspension, termination or resignation of enrollment; surrender of enrollment certificate*. If the respondent's enrollment is suspended, the respondent shall not thereafter be permitted to perform actuarial services under ERISA during the period of suspension. If the respondent's enrollment is terminated, the respondent shall not thereafter be permitted to perform actuarial services under ERISA unless and until authorized to do so by the Executive Director pursuant to § 901.54. The respondent shall surrender his/her enrollment certificate to the Executive Director for cancellation in the case of a termination or resignation of enrollment or for retention during a period of suspension.

[¶ 15,224X]

§ 901.53 *Notice of suspension, termination or resignation of enrollment*. Upon the resignation or the issuance of a final order suspending or terminating the enrollment of an actuary, the Executive Director shall give notice thereof to appropriate officers and employees of the Department of the Treasury, the Department of Labor, the Pension Benefit Guaranty Corporation, and to other interested departments and agencies of the Federal Government.

[¶ 15,224Y]

§ 901.54 *Petition for reinstatement*. Any individual whose enrollment has been terminated may petition the Executive Director for reinstatement after the expiration of five years following such termination. Reinstatement may not be granted unless the Executive Director, with the approval of the Joint Board, is satisfied that the petitioner is not likely to conduct himself/herself thereafter contrary to the regulations in this part, and that granting such reinstatement would not be contrary to the public interest.

Subpart E—General Provisions

[¶ 15,225]

§ 901.70 *Records*. (a) *Availability*. There are made available for public inspection at the Office of the Executive Director of the Joint Board for the Enrollment of Actuaries a roster of all persons enrolled to perform actuarial services under ERISA and a roster of all persons whose enrollments to perform such services have been suspended or terminated. Other records may be disclosed upon specific request, in accordance with the applicable disclosure and privacy statutes.

(b) *Disciplinary procedures*. A request by an enrolled actuary that a hearing in a disciplinary proceeding concerning him/her be public, and that the record thereof be made available for inspection by interested persons may be granted if written agreement is reached in advance to protect from disclosure tax information which is confidential, in accordance with applicable statutes and regulations.

[¶ 15,225A]

§ 901.71 *Special orders*. The Joint Board reserves the power to issue such special orders as it may deem proper in any case within the purview of this part.

[¶ 15,225B]

§ 901.72 *Additional rules*. The Joint Board may, in notice or other guidance of general applicability, provide additional rules regarding the enrollment of actuaries. [Added 3/31/2011 by 76 FR 17762].

[¶ 15,226]
Availability of Information

§ 902.1 *Scope*. This part is issued by the Joint Board for the Enrollment of Actuaries (the "Joint Board") pursuant to the requirements of section 552 of Title 5 of the United States Code, including the requirements that every Federal agency shall publish in the FEDERAL REGISTER, for the guidance of the public, descriptions of the established places at which, the officers from whom, and the methods whereby, the public may obtain information, make submittals or requests, or obtain decisions.

[¶ 15,226A]

§ 902.2 *Definitions*. (a) *"Records of the Joint Board"*. For purposes of this Part, the term "records of the Joint Board" means rules, statements, opinions, orders, memoranda, letters, reports, accounts and other papers containing information in the possession of the Joint Board that constitute part of the Joint Board's official files.

(b) *"Unusual Circumstances"*. For purposes of this part, "unusual circumstances" means, but only to the extent reasonably necessary for the proper processing of the particular request:

(1) The need to search for and collect the requested records from other establishments that are separate from the Joint Board's office processing the request;

(2) The need to search for, collect, and appropriately examine a voluminous amount of separate and distinct records which are demanded in a single request; or

(3) The need for consultation, which shall be conducted with all practicable speed, with another agency having a substantial interest in the determination of the request.

[¶ 15,226B]

§ 902.3 *Published information*. (a) *Federal Register*. Pursuant to sections 552 and 553 of Title 5 of the United States Code, and subject to the provisions of § 902.5, the Joint Board publishes in the FEDERAL REGISTER for the guidance of the public, in addition to this part, descriptions of its organization and procedures, substantive rules of general applicability, and, as may from time to time be appropriate, statements of general policy, and interpretations of general applicability.

(b) *Other published information*. From time to time, the Joint Board issues statements to the press relating to its operations.

(c) *Obtaining printed information*. If not available through the Government Printing Office, printed information released by the Joint Board may be obtained without cost from the Executive Director of the Joint Board ("Executive Director").

[¶ 15,226C]

§ 902.4 *Access to records*. (a) *General rule*. All records of the Joint Board, including information set forth in section 552(a)(2) of Title 5 of the United States Code, are made available to any person, upon request, for inspection and copying in accordance with the provisions of this section and subject to the limitations stated in section 552(b) of Title 5 of the United States Code. Records falling within such limitations may nevertheless be made available in accordance with this section to the extent consistent, in the judgment of the Chairman of the Joint Board ("Chairman"), with the effective performance of the Joint Board's statutory responsibilities and with the avoidance of injury to a public or private interest intended to be protected by such limitations.

(b) *Obtaining access to records*. Records of the Joint Board subject to this section are available by appointment for public inspection or copying during regular business hours on regular business days at the office of the Executive Director. Every request for access to such records, other than published records described in § 902.3, shall be signed and submitted in writing to the Executive Director, Joint Board for the Enrollment of Actuaries, c/o Department of the Treasury, Washington, D.C. 20220, shall state the name and address of the person requesting such access, and shall describe such records in a manner reasonably sufficient to permit their identification without undue difficulty.

(c) *Fees*. A fee at the rate of $5.00 per hour or fraction thereof or the time required to locate such records, plus ten cents per standard page for any copying thereof, shall be paid by any person requesting records other than published records described in § 902.3. In addition, the cost of postage and any packaging and special handling shall be paid by the requester. Documents shall be provided without charge or at a reduced charge where the Chairman determines that waiver or reduction of the fee is in the public interest because furnishing the information can be considered as primarily benefitting the general public.

(d) *Actions on request*. The Executive Director shall within ten days (excepting Saturdays, Sundays and legal public holidays) from receipt of request, determine whether to comply with such requests for records and shall immediately notify in writing the person making such request of such determination and the reason therefor, and of the right of such person to appeal any adverse determination, as provided in § 902.5. In unusual circumstances, the time limit for the determination may be extended by written notice to the person making such request, setting forth the reasons for such extension and the date on which the determination is expected to be dispatched. No such notice shall specify a date that will result in an extension of more than ten working days.

[¶ 15,226D]

§ 902.5 *Appeal*. (a) Any person denied access to records requested under § 902.4, may within thirty days after notification of such denial, file a signed written appeal to the Joint Board. The appeal shall provide the name and address of the appellant, the identification of the records denied, and the dates of the original request and its denial.

(b) The Joint Board shall act upon any such appeal within twenty days (excepting Saturdays, Sundays and legal public holidays) of its receipt unless for unusual circumstances the time for such action is deferred, subject to § 902.4(b), for not more than ten days. If action upon any such appeal is so deferred, the Joint Board shall notify the requester of the reasons for such deferral and the date on which the final reply is expected to be dispatched. If it is determined that the appeal from the initial denial shall be denied (in whole or in part), the requester shall be notified in writing of the denial, of the reasons therefor, of the fact the Joint Board is responsible for the denial, and of the provisions of section 552(a)(4) of Title 5 of the United States Code for judicial review of the determination.

(c) Any extension or extensions of time under §§ 902.4(d) and 902.5(b) shall not cumulatively total more than ten days (excepting Saturdays, Sundays and legal public holidays). If an extension is invoked in connection with an initial determination under § 902.4(d), any unused days of such extension may be invoked in connection with the determination on appeal under § 902.5(a), by written notice from the Joint Board.

[¶ 15,230]
AMENDMENT OF INTERNAL REVENUE CODE

Act Sec. 3043. Section 7701(a) of the Internal Revenue Code of 1986 (relating to definitions) is amended by adding at the end thereof the following new paragraph:

[Code Sec. 7701(a)(35)]

(35) **ENROLLED ACTUARY.** The term 'enrolled actuary' means a person who is enrolled by the Joint Board for the Enrollment of Actuaries established under subtitle C of the title III of the Employee Retirement Income Security Act of 1974."

[The above amendment to the Internal Revenue Code of 1954 is incorporated in place in the "Internal Revenue Code—Regulations."]

Amendment

P.L. 101-239, §7891(a)(1):

Titles I, III, and IV of ERISA (other than sections 3(37)(E), 301(a)(7), and 308, the last sentence of section 408(d), and sections 414(c), 4001(a)(3)(ii) and 4303) are each amended by striking "Internal Revenue Code of 1954" each place it appears and inserting "Internal Revenue Code of 1986" effective October 22, 1986.

TITLE IV—PLAN TERMINATION INSURANCE

Subtitle A—Pension Benefit Guaranty Corporation (Part 4000)

[¶ 15,300]
Part 4000—Filing, Issuance, Computation of Time, and Record Retention

Regulations

The following regulations were adopted by the Pension Benefit Guaranty Corporation on July 1, 1996 (61 FR 34002), and officially corrected on December 26, 1996 (61 FR 67942). Prior to July 1, 1996, PBGC regulations were under Chapter XXVI of Title 29 of the Code of Federal Regulations. Effective July 1, 1996, PBGC regulations were moved to Chapter XL, and were renumbered and reorganized. Reg. §4000.2 was amended effective August 11, 1997 (62 FR 36993). Reg. §4000.1—4000.54 were revised on October 28, 2003 (68 FR 61344). Reg. §§ 4000.3, 4000.4, 4000.23, and 4000.29 were revised on March 9, 2005 (70 FR 11540). Reg. § 4000.3 was revised on June 1, 2006 (71 FR 31077), effective July 1, 2006. Reg. §4000.3 was amended on March 11, 2014 (79 FR 13547). Reg. §§4000.3 and 4000.53 were amended on September 11, 2015 (80 FR 54979). Reg. §4000.3 was amended on September 17, 2015 (80 FR 55742). Amendatory instructions from September 17, 2015 and Reg. §4000.3 were corrected to add (b)(4) on September 25, 2015 (80 FR 57717). Reg. §4000.41 was amended on December 22, 2017 (82 FR 60800).

Subpart A—Filing Rules

[¶ 15,301]
§4000.1 What are these filing rules about?

Where a particular regulation calls for their application, the rules in this subpart A of part 4000 tell you what filing methods you may use for any submission (including a payment) to us. They do not cover an issuance from you to anyone other than the PBGC, such as a notice to participants. Also, they do not cover filings with us that are not made under our regulations, such as procurement filings, litigation filings, and applications for employment with us. (Subpart B tells you what methods you may use to issue a notice or otherwise provide information to any person other than us. Subpart C tells you how we determine your filing or issuance date. Subpart D tells you how to compute various periods of time. Subpart E tells you how to maintain required records in electronic form.)

[¶ 15,302]
§4000.2 What definitions do I need to know for these rules?

You need to know two definitions from Sec. 4001.2 of this chapter: PBGC and person. You also need to know the following definitions:

Filing means any notice, information, or payment that you submit to us under our regulations.

Issuance means any notice or other information you provide to any person other than us under our regulations.

We means the PBGC.

You means the person filing with us.

⋙→ *Caution: Reg. §4000.3(b)(4), as added, applies to filings made on or after January 1, 2016.*

(4) When making filings to PBGC under parts 4041A, 4245, and 4281 of this chapter (except for notices of benefit reductions and notices of restoration of benefits under part 4281), you must submit the information required under these parts electronically in accordance with the instructions on the PBGC's Web site, except as otherwise provided by the PBGC. [Added 9/25/2015 by 80 FR 57717.]

(c) *Information on how to file.* Current information on how to file, including permitted filing methods, fax numbers, and mail and e-mail addresses, is—

(1) On our Web site, *http://www.pbgc.gov;*

(2) In our various printed forms and instructions packages; and

[¶ 15,302A]
§4000.3 What methods of filing may I use?

(a) *Paper filings.* Except for the filings listed in paragraph (b) of this section, you may file any submission with us by hand, mail, or commercial delivery service.

(b) *Electronic filings.* (1) You must file premium declarations under part 4007 of this chapter electronically in accordance with the instructions on the PBGC's Web site subject to the following provisions:

(i) This electronic filing requirement does not apply to premium information to the extent that the PBGC grants an exemption for good cause in appropriate circumstances. [Redesignated 3/11/14 by 79 FR 13547.]

(ii) This electronic filing requirement does not apply to premium payments except to the extent that the PBGC so provides in the instructions on the PBGC's Web site. [Redesignated 3/11/14 by 79 FR 13547.]

(iii) This electronic filing reqtirement does not apply to information you file to comply with a request we make under § 4007.10(c) of this chapter (dealing with providing record information in connection with a premium compliance review). [Redesignated 3/11/14 by 79 FR 13547.]

(2) You must submit the information required under part 4010 of this chapter electronically in accordance with the instructions on the PBGC's Web site, except as otherwise provided by the PBGC. [Revised 6/1/2006 by 71 FR 31077.]

(3) You must file notices under part 4043 of this chapter electronically in accordance with the instructions on PBGC's Web site, http://www.pbgc.gov, except as otherwise provided by PBGC. [Added 9/11/15 by 80 FR 54979.]

(3) Available by contacting our Customer Service Center at 1200 K Street, NW., Washington, DC, 20005- 4026; telephone 1-800-400-7242 (for participants), or 1-800-736-2444 (for practitioners). (TTY/TDD users may call the Federal relay service toll-free at 1-800-877-8339 and ask to be connected to the appropriate number.)

[Revised 6/1/2006 by 71 FR 31077.]

[¶ 15,302B]
§4000.4 Where do I file my submission?

To find out where to send your submission, visit our Web site at http://www.pbgc.gov, see the instructions to our forms, or call our Customer Service Center (1-800-400-7242 for participants, or

1-800-736-2444 for practitioners; TTY/TDD users may call the Federal relay service toll-free at 1-800-877-8339 and ask to be connected to the appropriate number.) Because we have different addresses for different types of filings, you should make sure to use the appropriate address for your type of filing. For example, some filings (such as premium payments) must be sent to a specified bank, while other filings (such as the Standard Termination Notice (Form 500)) must be sent to the appropriate department at our offices in Washington, DC. You do not have to address electronic submissions made through our Web site. We are responsible for ensuring that such submissions go to the proper place.

[¶ 15,302C]

§ 4000.5   Does the PBGC have discretion to waive these filing requirements?

We retain the discretion to waive any requirement under this part, at any time, if warranted by the facts and circumstances.

Subpart B—Issuance Rules

[¶ 15,302I]

§ 4000.11   What are these issuance rules about?

Where a particular regulation calls for their application, the rules in this subpart B of part 4000 tell you what methods you may use to issue a notice or otherwise provide information to any person other than us (e.g., a participant or beneficiary). They do not cover payments to third parties. In some cases, the PBGC regulations tell you to comply with requirements that are found somewhere other than in the PBGC's own regulations (e.g., requirements under the Internal Revenue Code). If so, you must comply with any applicable issuance rules under those other requirements. (Subpart A tells you what filing methods you may use for filings with us. Subpart C tells you how we determine your filing or issuance date. Subpart D tells you how to compute various periods of time. Subpart E tells you how to maintain required records in electronic form.)

[¶ 15,302J]

§ 4000.12   What definitions do I need to know for these rules?

You need to know two definitions from Sec. 4001.2 of this chapter: PBGC and person. You also need to know the following definitions:

Filing means any notice, information, or payment that you submit to us under our regulations.

Issuance means any notice or other information you provide to any person other than us under our regulations.

We means the PBGC.

You means the person providing the issuance to a third party.

[¶ 15,302K]

§ 4000.13   What methods of issuance may I use?

(a) *In general.* You may use any method of issuance, provided you use measures reasonably calculated to ensure actual receipt of the material by the intended recipient. Posting is not a permissible method of issuance under the rules of this part.

(b) *Electronic safe-harbor method.* Section 4000.14 provides a safe-harbor method for meeting the requirements of paragraph (a) of this section when providing an issuance using electronic media.

[¶ 15,302L]

§ 4000.14   What is the safe-harbor method for providing an issuance by electronic media?

(a) *In general.* Except as otherwise provided by applicable law, rule or regulation, you satisfy the requirements of Sec. 4000.13 if you follow the methods described at paragraph (b) of this section when providing an issuance by electronic media to any person described in paragraph (c) or (d) of this section.

(b) *Issuance requirements.* (1) You must take appropriate and necessary measures reasonably calculated to ensure that the system for furnishing documents—

(i) Results in actual receipt of transmitted information (e.g., using return-receipt or notice of undelivered electronic mail features,

conducting periodic reviews or surveys to confirm receipt of the transmitted information); and

(ii) Protects confidential information relating to the intended recipient (e.g., incorporating into the system measures designed to preclude unauthorized receipt of or access to such information by anyone other than the intended recipient);

(2) You prepare and furnish electronically delivered documents in a manner that is consistent with the style, format and content requirements applicable to the particular document;

(3) You provide each intended recipient with a notice, in electronic or non-electronic form, at the time a document is furnished electronically, that apprises the intended recipient of—

(i) The significance of the document when it is not otherwise reasonably evident as transmitted (e.g., "The attached participant notice contains information on the funding level of your defined benefit pension plan and the benefits guaranteed by the Pension Benefit Guaranty Corporation."); and

(ii) The intended recipient's right to request and obtain a paper version of such document; and

(4) You give the intended recipient, upon request, a paper version of the electronically furnished documents.

(c) *Employees with electronic access.* This section applies to a participant who—

(1) Has the ability to effectively access the document furnished in electronic form at any location where the participant is reasonably expected to perform duties as an employee; and

(2) With respect to whom access to the employer's electronic information system is an integral part of those duties.

(d) *Any person.* This section applies to any person who—

(1) Except as provided in paragraph (d)(2) of this section, has affirmatively consented, in electronic or non-electronic form, to receiving documents through electronic media and has not withdrawn such consent;

(2) In the case of documents to be furnished through the Internet or other electronic communication network, has affirmatively consented or confirmed consent electronically, in a manner that reasonably demonstrates the person's ability to access information in the electronic form that will be used to provide the information that is the subject of the consent, and has provided an address for the receipt of electronically furnished documents;

(3) Prior to consenting, is provided, in electronic or non-electronic form, a clear and conspicuous statement indicating:

(i) The types of documents to which the consent would apply;

(ii) That consent can be withdrawn at any time without charge;

(iii) The procedures for withdrawing consent and for updating the participant's, beneficiary's or other person's address for receipt of electronically furnished documents or other information;

(iv) The right to request and obtain a paper version of an electronically furnished document, including whether the paper version will be provided free of charge;

(v) Any hardware and software requirements for accessing and retaining the documents; and

(4) Following consent, if a change in hardware or software requirements needed to access or retain electronic documents creates a material risk that the person will be unable to access or retain electronically furnished documents,

(i) Is provided with a statement of the revised hardware or software requirements for access to and retention of electronically furnished documents;

(ii) Is given the right to withdraw consent without charge and without the imposition of any condition or consequence that was not disclosed at the time of the initial consent; and

(iii) Again consents, in accordance with the requirements of paragraph (d)(1) or paragraph (d)(2) of this section, as applicable, to the receipt of documents through electronic media.

[¶ 15,302M]

§ 4000.15 Does the PBGC have discretion to waive these issuance requirements?

We retain the discretion to waive any requirement under this part, at any time, if warranted by the facts and circumstances.

Subpart C—Determining Filing and Issuance Dates

[¶ 15,302S]

§ 4000.21 What are these rules for determining the filing or issuance date about?

Where the particular regulation calls for their application, the rules in this subpart C of part 4000 tell you how we will determine the date you send us a filing and the date you provide an issuance to someone other than us (such as a participant). These rules do not cover payments to third parties. In addition, they do not cover filings with us that are not made under our regulations, such as procurement filings, litigation filings, and applications for employment with us. In some cases, the PBGC regulations tell you to comply with requirements that are found somewhere other than in the PBGC's own regulations (e.g., requirements under the Internal Revenue Code (Title 26, USC)). In meeting those requirements, you should follow any applicable rules under those requirements for determining the filing and issuance date. (Subpart A tells you what filing methods you may use for filings with us. Subpart B tells you what methods you may use to issue a notice or otherwise provide information to any person other than us. Subpart D tells you how to compute various periods of time. Subpart E tells you how to maintain required records in electronic form.)

[¶ 15,302T]

§ 4000.22 What definitions do I need to know for these rules?

You need to know two definitions from Sec. 4001.2 of this chapter: PBGC and person. You also need to know the following definitions:

Business day means a day other than a Saturday, Sunday, or Federal holiday. We means the PBGC.

You means the person filing with us or the person providing the issuance to a third party.

[¶ 15,302U]

§ 4000.23 When is my submission or issuance treated as filed or issued?

(a) *Filed or issued when sent.* Generally, we treat your submission as filed, or your issuance as provided, on the date you send it, if you meet certain requirements. The requirements depend upon the method you use to send your submission or issuance (see Sec. Sec. 4000.24 through 4000.29). (Certain filings are always treated as filed when received, as explained in paragraph (b)(2) of this section.) A submission made through our Web site is considered to have been sent when you perform the last act necessary to indicate that your submission is filed and cannot be further edited or withdrawn.

(b) *Filed or issued when received.* (1) *In genera* l. If you do not meet the requirements for your submission or issuance to be treated as filed or issued when sent (see Sec. Sec. 4000.24 through 4000.32), we treat it as filed or issued on the date received in a permitted format at the proper address.

(2) *Certain filings always treated as filed when received.* We treat the following submissions as filed on the date we receive your submission, no matter what method you use:

(i) *Applications for benefits.* An application for benefits or related submission (unless the instructions for the applicable forms provide for an earlier date);

(ii) *Advance notice of reportable events.* Information required under subpart C of part 4043 of this chapter, dealing with advance notice of reportable events;

(iii) *Form 200 filings.* Information required under subpart D of part 4043 of this chapter, dealing with notice of certain missed minimum funding contributions; and

(iv) *Requests for approval of multiemployer plan amendments.* A request for approval of an amendment filed with the PBGC pursuant to part 4220 of this chapter.

(3) *Determining our receipt date for your filing.* If we receive your submission at the correct address by 5 p.m. (our time) on a business day, we treat it as received on that date. If we receive your submission at the correct address after 5 p.m. on a business day, or anytime on a weekend or Federal holiday, we treat it as received on the next business day. For example, if you send your fax or e-mail of a Form 200 filing to us in Washington, DC, on Friday, March 15, from California at 3 p.m. (Pacific standard time), and we receive it immediately at 6 p.m. (our time), we treat it as received on Monday, March 18. A submission made through our Web site is considered to have been received when we receive an electronic signal that you have performed the last act necessary to indicate that your submission is filed and cannot be further edited or withdrawn.

[¶ 15,302V]

§ 4000.24 What if I mail my submission or issuance using the U.S. Postal Service?

(a) *In general.* Your filing or issuance date is the date you mail your submission or issuance using the U.S. Postal Service if you meet the requirements of paragraph (b) of this section, and you mail it by the last scheduled collection of the day. If you mail it later than that, or if there is no scheduled collection that day, your filing or issuance date is the date of the next scheduled collection. If you do not meet the requirements of paragraph (b), your filing or issuance date is the date of receipt at the proper address.

(b) *Requirements for "send date".* Your submission or issuance must meet the applicable postal requirements, be properly addressed, and you must use First-Class Mail (or a U.S. Postal Service mail class that is at least the equivalent of First-Class Mail, such as Priority Mail or Express Mail). However, if you are filing an advance notice of reportable event or a Form 200 (notice of certain missed contributions), see Sec. 4000.23(b); these filings are always treated as filed when received.

(c) *Presumptions.* We make the following presumptions—

(1) *U.S. Postal Service postmark.* If you meet the requirements of paragraph (b) of this section and your submission or issuance has a legible U.S. Postal Service postmark, we presume that the postmark date is the filing or issuance date. However, you may prove an earlier date under paragraph (a) of this section.

(2) *Private meter postmark.* If you meet the requirements of paragraph (b) of this section and your submission or issuance has a legible postmark made by a private postage meter (but no legible U.S. Postal Service postmark) and arrives at the proper address by the time reasonably expected, we presume that the metered postmark date is your filing or issuance date. However, you may prove an earlier date under paragraph (a) of this section.

(d) *Examples.* (1) You mail your issuance using the U.S. Postal Service and meet the requirements of paragraph (b) of this section. You deposit your issuance in a mailbox at 4 p.m. on Friday, March 15 and the next scheduled collection at that mailbox is 5 p.m. that day. Your issuance date is March 15. If on the other hand you deposit it at 6 p.m. and the next collection at that mailbox is not until Monday, March 18, your issuance date is March 18.

(2) You mail your submission using the U.S. Postal Service and meet the requirements of paragraph (b) of this section. You deposit your submission in the mailbox at 4 p.m. on Friday, March 15, and the next scheduled collection at that mailbox is 5 p.m. that day. If your submission does not show a March 15 postmark, then you may prove to us that you mailed your submission by the last scheduled collection on March 15.

[¶ 15,302W]

§ 4000.25 What if I use the postal service of a foreign country?

If you send your submission or issuance using the postal service of a foreign country, your filing or issuance date is the date of receipt at the proper address.

Reg. §4000.25   ¶15,302W

[¶ 15,302X]
§ 4000.26 What if I use a commercial delivery service?

(a) *In general.* Your filing or issuance date is the date you deposit your submission or issuance with the commercial delivery service if you meet the requirements of paragraph (b) of this section, and you deposit it by the last scheduled collection of the day for the type of delivery you use (such as two-day delivery or overnight delivery). If you deposit it later than that, or if there is no scheduled collection that day, your filing or issuance date is the date of the next scheduled collection. If you do not meet the requirements of paragraph (b), your filing or issuance date is the date of receipt at the proper address. However, if you are filing an advance notice of reportable event or a Form 200 (notice of certain missed contributions), see Sec. 4000.23(b); these filings are always treated as filed when received.

(b) *Requirements for "send date".* Your submission or issuance must meet the applicable requirements of the commercial delivery service, be properly addressed, and—

(1) *Delivery within two days.* It must be reasonable to expect your submission or issuance will arrive at the proper address by 5 p.m. on the second business day after the next scheduled collection; or

(2) *Designated delivery service.* You must use a "designated delivery service" under section 7502(f) of the Internal Revenue Code (Title 26, USC). Our Web site, http://www.pbgc.gov, lists those designated delivery services. You should make sure that both the provider and the particular type of delivery (such as two-day delivery) are designated.

(c) *Example.* You send your submission by commercial delivery service using two-day delivery. In addition, you meet the requirements of paragraph (b) of this section. Suppose that the deadline for two-day delivery at the place you make your deposit is 8 p.m. on Friday, March 15. If you deposit your submission by that the deadline, your filing date is March 15. If, instead, you deposit it after the 8 p.m. deadline and the next collection at that site for two-day delivery is on Monday, March 18, your filing date is March 18.

[¶ 15,302Y]
§ 4000.27 What if I hand deliver my submission or issuance?

Your filing or issuance date is the date of receipt of your hand-delivered submission or issuance at the proper address. A hand-delivered issuance need not be delivered while the intended recipient is physically present. For example, unless you have reason to believe that the intended recipient will not receive the notice within a reasonable amount of time, a notice is deemed to be received when you place it in the intended recipient's office mailbox. Our Web site, http://www.pbgc.gov, and the instructions to our forms, identify the proper addresses for filings with us.

[¶ 15,302Z]
§ 4000.28 What if I send a computer disk?

(a) *In general.* We determine your filing or issuance date for a computer disk as if you had sent a paper version of your submission or issuances if you meet the requirements of paragraph (b) of this section.

(1) *Filings.* For computer-disk filings, we may treat your submission as invalid if you fail to meet the requirements of paragraph (b)(1) or (b)(3) of this section.

(2) *Issuances.* For computer-disk issuances, we may treat your issuance as invalid if—

(i) You fail to meet the requirements ("using measures reasonably calculated to ensure actual receipt") of Sec. 4000.13(a), or

(ii) You fail to meet the contact information requirements of paragraph (b)(3) of this section.

(b) *Requirements.* To get the filing date under paragraph (a) of this section, you must meet the requirements of paragraphs (b)(1) and (b)(3). To get the issuance date under paragraph (a), you must meet the requirements of paragraphs (b)(2) and (b)(3).

(1) *Technical requirements for filing* s. For filings, your electronic disk must comply with any technical requirements for that type of submission (our Web site, http://www.pbgc.gov, identifies the technical requirements for each type of filing).

(2) *Technical requirements for issuance* s. For issuances, you must comply with the safe-harbor method under Sec. 4000.14.

(3) *Identify contact person.* For filings and issuances, you must include, in a paper cover letter or on the disk's label, the name and telephone number of the person to contact if we or the intended recipient is unable to read the disk.

[¶ 15,302AA]
§ 4000.29 What if I use electronic delivery?

(a) *In general.* Your filing or issuance date is the date you electronically transmit your submission or issuance to the proper address if you meet the requirements of paragraph (b) of this section. Note that we always treat an advance notice of reportable event and a Form 200 (notice of certain missed contributions) as filed when received. A submission made through our Web site is considered to have been transmitted when you perform the last act necessary to indicate that your submission is filed and cannot be further edited or withdrawn. You do not have to address electronic submissions made through our Web site. We are responsible for ensuring that such submissions go to the proper place.

(1) *Filings.* For electronic filings, if you fail to meet the requirements of paragraph (b)(1) or (b)(3) of this section, we may treat your submission as invalid.

(2) *Issuances.* For electronic issuances, we may treat your issuance as invalid if—

(i) You fail to meet the requirements ("using measures reasonably calculated to ensure actual receipt") of Sec. 4000.13(a), or

(ii) You fail to meet the contact information requirements of paragraph (b)(3) of this section.

(b) *Requirements.* To get the filing date under paragraph (a) of this section, you must meet the requirements of paragraphs (b)(1) and (b)(3). To get the issuance date under paragraph (a), you must meet the requirement of paragraphs (b)(2) and (b)(3).

(1) *Technical requirements for filings.* For filings, your electronic submission must comply with any technical requirements for that type of submission (our Web site, http://www.pbgc.gov, identifies the technical requirements for each type of filing).

(2) T *echnical requirements for issuances.* For issuances, you must comply with the safe-harbor method under Sec. 4000.14.

(3) *Identify contact person.* For an e-mail submission or issuance with an attachment, you must include, in the body of your e-mail, the name and telephone number of the person to contact if we or the intended recipient needs you to resubmit your filing or issuance.

(c) *Failure to meet address requirement.* If you send your electronic submission or issuance to the wrong address (but you meet the requirements of paragraph (b) of this section), your filing or issuance date is the date of receipt at the proper address.

[¶ 15,302BB]
§ 4000.30 What if I need to resend my filing or issuance for technical reasons?

(a) *Request to resubmit.* (1) *Filing.* We may ask you to resubmit all or a portion of your filing for technical reasons (for example, because we are unable to open an attachment to your e-mail). In that case, your submission (or portion) is invalid. However, if you comply with the request or otherwise resolve the problem (e.g., by providing advice that allows us to open the attachment to your e-mail) by the date we specify, your filing date for the submission (or portion) that we asked you to resubmit is the date you filed your original submission. If you comply with our request late, your submission (or portion) will be treated as filed on the date of your resubmission.

(2) *Issuance.* The intended recipient may, for good reason (of a technical nature), ask you to resend all or a portion of your issuance (for example, because of a technical problem in opening an attachment

to your e-mail). In that case, your issuance (or portion) is invalid. However, if you comply with the request or otherwise resolve the problem (e.g., by providing advice that the recipient uses to open the attachment to your e-mail), within a reasonable time, your issuance date for the issuance (or portion) that the intended recipient asked you to resend is the date you provided your original issuance. If you comply with the request late, your issuance (or portion) will be treated as provided on the date of your reissuance.

(b) *Reason to believe submission or issuance not received or defective.* If you have reason to believe that we have not received your submission (or have received it in a form that is not useable), or that the intended recipient has not received your issuance (or has received it in a form that is not useable), you must promptly resend your submission or issuance to get your original filing or issuance date. However, we may require evidence to support your original filing or issuance date. If you are not prompt, or you do not provide us with any evidence we may require to support your original filing or issuance date, your filing or issuance date is the filing or issuance date of your resubmission or reissuance.

[¶ 15,302CC]

§ 4000.31 **Is my issuance untimely if I miss a few participants or beneficiaries?**

The PBGC will not treat your issuance as untimely based on your failure to provide the issuance to a participant or beneficiary in a timely manner if—

(a) The failure resulted from administrative error;

(b) The failure involved only a de minimis percentage of intended recipients; and

(c) You resend the issuance to the intended recipient promptly after discovering the error.

[¶ 15,302DD]

§ 4000.32 **Does the PBGC have discretion to waive any requirements under this part?**

We retain the discretion to waive any requirement under this part, at any time, if warranted by the facts and circumstances.

Subpart D—Computation of Time

[¶ 15,302MM]

§ 4000.41 **What are these computation-of-time rules about?**

The rules in this subpart D of part 4000 tell you how to compute time periods under our regulations (e.g., for filings with us and issuances to third parties) where the particular regulation calls for their application. (There are specific exceptions or modifications to these rules in Sec. 4007.6 of this chapter (premium payments), and Sec. 4062.10 of this chapter (employer liability payments). In some cases, the PBGC regulations tell you to comply with requirements that are found somewhere other than in the PBGC's own regulations (e.g., requirements under the Internal Revenue Code (Title 26, USC)). In meeting those requirements, you should follow any applicable computation-of-time rules under those other requirements. (Subpart A tells you what filing methods you may use for filings with us. Subpart B tells you what methods you may use to issue a notice or otherwise provide information to any person other than us. Subpart C tells you how we determine your filing or issuance date. Subpart E tells you how to maintain required records in electronic form.) [Amended 12/22/2017 by 82 FR 60800.]

[¶ 15,302NN]

§ 4000.42 **What definitions do I need to know for these rules?**

You need to know two definitions from Sec. 4001.2 of this chapter: PBGC and person. You also need to know the following definitions:

Business day means a day other than a Saturday, Sunday, or Federal holiday.

We means the PBGC.

You means the person responsible, under our regulations, for the filing or issuance to which these rules apply.

[¶ 15,302OO]

§ 4000.43 **How do I compute a time period?**

(a) *In general.* If you are computing a time period to which this part applies, whether you are counting forwards or backwards, the day after (or before) the act, event, or default that begins the period is day one, the next day is day two, and so on. Count all days, including weekends and Federal holidays. However, if the last day you count is a weekend or Federal holiday, extend or shorten the period (whichever benefits you in complying with the time requirement) to the next regular business day. The examples in paragraph (d) of this section illustrate these rules.

(b) *When date is designated.* In some cases, our regulations designate a specific day as the end of a time period, such as "the last day" of a plan year or "the fifteenth day" of a calendar month. In these cases, you simply use the designated day, together with the weekend and holiday rule of paragraph (a) of this section.

(c) *When counting months.* If a time period is measured in months, first identify the date (day, month, and year) of the act, event, or default that begins the period. The corresponding day of the following (or preceding) month is one month later (or earlier), and so on. For example, two months after July 15 is September 15. If the period ends on a weekend or Federal holiday, follow the weekend and holiday rule of paragraph (a) of this section. There are two special rules for determining what the corresponding day is when you start counting on a day that is at or near the end of a calendar month:

(1) *Special "last-day" rule.* If you start counting on the last day of a calendar month, the corresponding day of any calendar month is the last day of that calendar month. For example, a three-month period measured from November 30 ends (if counting forward) on the last day of February (the 28th or 29th) or (if counting backward) on the last day of August (the 31st).

(2) *Special February rule.* If you start counting on the 29th or 30th of a calendar month, the corresponding day of February is the last day of February. For example, a one-month period measured from January 29 ends on the last day of February (the 28th or 29th).

(d) *Examples.* (1) *Counting backwards.* Suppose you are required to file an advance notice of reportable event for a transaction that is effective December 31. Under our regulations, the notice is due at least 30 days before the effective date of the event. To determine your deadline, count December 30 as day 1, December 29 as day 2, December 28 as day 3, and so on. Therefore, December 1 is day 30. Assuming that day is not a weekend or holiday, your notice is timely if you file it on or before December 1.

(2) *Weekend or holiday rule.* Suppose you are filing a notice of intent to terminate. The notice must be issued at least 60 days and no more than 90 days before the proposed termination date. Suppose the 60th day before the proposed termination date is a Saturday. Your notice is timely if you issue it on the following Monday even though that is only 58 days before the proposed termination date. Similarly, if the 90th day before the proposed termination date is Wednesday, July 4 (a Federal holiday), your notice is timely if you issue it on Tuesday, July 3, even though that is 91 days before the proposed termination date.

(3) *Counting months.* Suppose you are required to issue a Participant Notice two months after December 31. The deadline for the Participant Notice is the last day of February (the 28th or 29th). If the last day of February is a weekend or Federal holiday, your deadline is extended until the next day that is not a weekend or Federal holiday.

Subpart E—Electronic Means of Record Retention

[¶ 15,302WW]

§ 4000.51 **What are these record retention rules about?**

The rules in this subpart E of part 4000 tell you what methods you may use to meet any record retention requirement under our regulations if you choose to use electronic means. The rules for who must retain the records, how long the records must be maintained, and how records must be made available to us are contained in the specific part where the record retention requirement is found. (Subpart A tells you what filing methods you may use for filings with us and how we determine your filing date. Subpart B tells you what methods you may use to issue a notice or otherwise provide information to any person other than us. Subpart C tells you how we determine your filing or issuance date. Subpart D tells you how to compute various periods of time.)

[¶ 15,302XX]

§ 4000.52 **What definitions do I need to know for these rules?**

You need to know two definitions from Sec. 4001.2 of this chapter: PBGC and person. You also need to know the following definitions:

We means the PBGC.

You means the person subject to the record retention requirement.

[¶ 15,302YY]

§ 4000.53 **May I use electronic media to satisfy PBGC's record retention requirements?**

General requirements. You may use electronic media to satisfy the record maintenance and retention requirements of this chapter if:

(a) The electronic recordkeeping system has reasonable controls to ensure the integrity, accuracy, authenticity and reliability of the records kept in electronic form;

(b) The electronic records are maintained in reasonable order and in a safe and accessible place, and in such manner as they may be readily inspected or examined (for example, the recordkeeping system should be capable of indexing, retaining, preserving, retrieving and reproducing the electronic records);

(c) The electronic records are readily convertible into legible and readable paper copy as may be needed to satisfy reporting and disclosure requirements or any other obligation under section 101(f), section 303(k)(4), or Title IV of ERISA; [Amended 9/11/15 by 80 FR 54979.]

(d) The electronic recordkeeping system is not subject, in whole or in part, to any agreement or restriction that would, directly or indirectly, compromise or limit a person's ability to comply with any reporting and disclosure requirement or any other obligation under section 101(f), section 303(k)(4), or Title IV of ERISA; [Amended 9/11/15 by 80 FR 54979.]

(e) Adequate records management practices are established and implemented (for example, following procedures for labeling of electronically maintained or retained records, providing a secure storage environment, creating back-up electronic copies and selecting an off-site storage location, observing a quality assurance program evidenced by regular evaluations of the electronic recordkeeping system including periodic checks of electronically maintained or retained records; and retaining paper copies of records that cannot be clearly, accurately or completely transferred to an electronic recordkeeping system); and

(f) All electronic records exhibit a high degree of legibility and readability when displayed on a video display terminal or other method of electronic transmission and when reproduced in paper form. The term "legibility" means the observer must be able to identify all letters and numerals positively and quickly to the exclusion of all other letters or numerals. The term "readability" means that the observer must be able to recognize a group of letters or numerals as words or complete numbers.

[¶ 15,302ZZ]

§ 4000.54 **May I dispose of original paper records if I keep electronic copies?**

You may dispose of original paper records any time after they are transferred to an electronic recordkeeping system that complies with the requirements of this subpart, except such original records may not be discarded if the electronic record would not constitute a duplicate or substitute record under the terms of the plan and applicable federal or state law.

[¶ 15,310]
DEFINITIONS

Act Sec. 4001. (a) For purposes of this title, the term—

(1) "administrator" means the person or persons described in paragraph (16) of section 3 of this Act;

(2) "substantial employer", for any plan year of a single-employer plan, means one or more persons—

    (A) who are contributing sponsors of the plan in such plan year,

    (B) who, at any time during such plan year, are members of the same control group, and

    (C) whose required contributions to the plan for each plan year constituting one of—

        (i) the two immediately preceding plan years, or

        (ii) the first two of the three immediately preceding plan years,

total an amount greater than or equal to 10 percent of all contributions required to be paid to or under the plan for such plan year;

(3) "multiemployer plan" means a plan—

    (A) to which more than one employer is required to contribute,

    (B) which is maintained pursuant to one or more collective bargaining agreements between one or more employee organizations and more than one employer, and

    (C) which satisfies such other requirements as the Secretary of Labor may prescribe by regulation,

    except that, in applying this paragraph—

        (i) a plan shall be considered a multiemployer plan on and after its termination date if the plan was a multiemployer plan under this paragraph for the plan year preceding such termination, and

        (ii) for any plan year which began before the date of the enactment of the Multiemployer Pension Plan Amendments Act of 1980, the term "multiemployer plan" means a plan described in section 414(f) of the Internal Revenue Code of 1954 as in effect immediately before such date;

(4) "corporation", except where the context clearly requires otherwise, means the Pension Benefit Guaranty Corporation established under section 4002;

(5) "fund" means the appropriate fund established under section 4005;

(6) "basic benefits" means benefits guaranteed under section 4022 (other than under section 4022(c)), or under section 4022A (other than under section 4022A(g));

(7) "non-basic benefits" means benefits guaranteed under section 4022(c) or 4022A(g);

(8) "nonforfeitable benefit" means, with respect to a plan, a benefit for which a participant has satisfied the conditions for entitlement under the plan or the requirements of this Act (other than submission of a formal application, retirement, completion of a required waiting period, or death in the case of a benefit which returns all or a portion of a participant's accumulated mandatory employee contributions upon the participant's death), whether or not the benefit may subsequently be reduced or suspended by a plan amendment, an occurrence of any condition, or operation of this Act or the Internal Revenue Code of 1986;

(9) [Stricken]

(10) "plan sponsor" means, with respect to a multiemployer plan—

    (A) the plan's joint board of trustees, or

    (B) if the plan has no joint board of trustees, the plan administrator;

(11) "contribution base unit" means a unit with respect to which an employer has an obligation to contribute under a multiemployer plan, as defined in regulations prescribed by the Secretary of the Treasury;

(12) "outstanding claim for withdrawal liability" means a plan's claim for the unpaid balance of the liability determined under part 1 of subtitle E for which demand has been made, valued in accordance with regulations prescribed by the corporation;

(13) "contributing sponsor", of a single-employer plan, means a person described in section 302(b)(1) of this Act (without regard to section 302(b)(2) of this Act) or section 412(b)(1) of the Internal Revenue Code of 1986 (without regard to section 412(b)(2) of such Code).

(14) in the case of a single-employer plan—

(A) "controlled group" means, in connection with any person, a group consisting of such person and all other persons under common control with such person;

(B) the determination of whether two or more persons are under "common control" shall be made under regulations of the corporation which are consistent and coextensive with regulations prescribed for similar purposes by the Secretary of the Treasury under subsections (b) and (c) of section 414 of the Internal Revenue Code of 1986; and

(C)(i) notwithstanding any other provision of this title, during any period in which an individual possesses, directly or indirectly, the power to direct or cause the direction of the management and policies of an affected air carrier of which he was an accountable owner, whether through the ownership of voting securities, by contract, or otherwise, the affected air carrier shall be considered to be under common control not only with those persons described in subparagraph (B), but also with all related persons; and

(ii) for purposes of this subparagraph, the term—

(I) "affected air carrier" means an air carrier, as defined in section 101(3) of the Federal Aviation Act of 1958, that holds a certificate of public convenience and necessity under section 401 of such Act for route number 147, as of November 12, 1991;

(II) "related person" means any person which was under common control (as determined under subparagraph (B)) with an affected air carrier on October 10, 1991, or any successor to such related person;

(III) "accountable owner" means any individual who on October 10, 1991, owned directly or indirectly through the application of section 318 of the Internal Revenue Code of 1986 more than 50 percent of the total voting power of the stock of an affected air carrier;

(IV) "successor" means any person that acquires, directly or indirectly through the application of section 318 of the Internal Revenue Code of 1986, more than 50 percent of the total voting power of the stock of a related person, more than 50 percent of the total value of the securities (as defined in section 3(20) of this Act) of the related person, more than 50 percent of the total value of the assets of the related person, or any person into which such related person shall be merged or consolidated; and

(V) "individual" means a living human being;

(15) "single-employer plan" means any defined benefit plan (as defined in section 3(35)) which is not a multiemployer plan;

(16) "benefit liabilities" means the benefits of their employees and their beneficiaries under the plan (within the meaning of section 401(a)(2) of the Internal Revenue Code of 1986);

(17) "amount of unfunded guaranteed benefits", of a participant or beneficiary as of any date under a single-employer plan, means an amount equal to the excess of—

(A) the actuarial present value (determined as of such date on the basis of assumptions prescribed by the corporation for purposes of section 4044) of the benefits of the participant or beneficiary under the plan which are guaranteed under section 4022, over

(B) the current value (as of such date) of the assets of the plan which are required to be allocated to those benefits under section 4044;

(18) "amount of unfunded benefit liabilities" means, as of any date, the excess (if any) of—

(A) the value of the benefit liabilities under the plan (determined as of such date on the basis of assumptions prescribed by the corporation for purposes of section 4044), over

(B) the current value (as of such date) of the assets of the plan;

(19) "outstanding amount of benefit liabilities" means, with respect to any plan, the excess (if any) of—

◆ (A) the value of the benefit liabilities under the plan (determined as of the termination date on the basis of assumptions prescribed by the corporation for purposes of section 4044), over

(B) the value of the benefit liabilities which would be so determined by only taking into account benefits which are guaranteed under section 4022 or to which assets of the plan are allocated under section 4044;

(20) "person" has the meaning set forth in section 3(9);

(21) "affected party" means, with respect to a plan—

(A) each participant in the plan,

(B) each beneficiary under the plan who is a beneficiary of a deceased participant or who is an alternate payee (within the meaning of section 206(d)(3)(K)) under an applicable qualified domestic relations order (within the meaning of section 206(d)(3)(B)(i)),

(C) each employee organization representing participants in the plan, and

(D) the corporation,

except that, in connection with any notice required to be provided to the affected party, if an affected party has designated, in writing, a person to receive such notice on behalf of the affected party, any reference to the affected party shall be construed to refer to such person.

Act Sec. 4001. (b)(1) An individual who owns the entire interest in an unincorporated trade or business is treated as his own employer, and a partnership is treated as the employer of each partner who is an employee within the meaning of section 401(c)(1) of the Internal Revenue Code of 1986. For purposes of this title, under regulations prescribed by the corporation, all employees of trades or businesses (whether or not incorporated) which are under common control shall be treated as employed by a single employer and all such trades and businesses as a single employer. The regulations prescribed under the preceding sentence shall be consistent and coextensive with regulations prescribed for similar purposes by the Secretary of the Treasury under section 414(c) of the Internal Revenue Code of 1986.

(2) For purposes of subtitle E—

(A) except as otherwise provided in subtitle E, contributions or other payments shall be considered under a plan for a plan year if they are made within the period prescribed under section 412(c)(10) of the Internal Revenue Code of 1986 (determined, in the case of a terminated plan, as if the plan had continued beyond the termination date), and

(B) the term "Secretary of the Treasury" means the Secretary of the Treasury or such Secretary's delegate.

Amendments

P.L. 113-235, § 108(a)(3)(A), Div. O:

Amended ERISA Sec. 4001(a) by striking paragraph (a).

Prior to amendment, ERISA Sec. 4001(a)(9) read as follows:

"reorganization index" means the amount determined under section 4241(b);

The amendment applies with respect to plan years beginning after December 31, 2014.

P.L. 109-280, § 107(b)(1):

Amended ERISA Sec. 4001(a)(13), by striking "302(c)(11)(A)" and inserting "302(b)(1)", by striking "412(c)(11)(A)" and inserting "412(b)(1)", by striking "302(c)(11)(B)" and inserting "302(b)(2)", and by striking "412(c)(11)(B)" and inserting "412(b)(2)".

The above amendment applies to plan years beginning after 2007.

P.L. 103-465, § 761(a)(11):

Act Sec. 761(a)(11) amended ERISA Sec. 4001(a)(13) by striking "means a person—" and all that follows and inserting "means a person described in section 302(c)(11)(A) of this Act (without regard to section 302(c)(11)(B) of this Act) or section 412(c)(11)(A) of the Internal Revenue Code of 1986 (without regard to section 412(c)(11)(B) of such Code)." Prior to amendment, ERISA Sec. 4001(a)(13) read as follows:

(13) "contributing sponsor", of a single-employer plan, means a person—

(A) who is responsible, in connection with such plan, for meeting the funding requirements under section 302 of this Act or section 412 of the Internal Revenue Code of 1986, or

(B) who is a member of the controlled group of a person described in subparagraph (A), has been responsible for meeting such funding requirements, and has employed a significant number (as may be defined in regulations of the corporation) of participants under such plan while such person was so responsible;

The above amendment is effective as if included in the Pension Protection Act.

P.L. 102-229, §214:

Amended ERISA Sec. 4001(a)(14) by striking "and" at the end of subparagraph (A), adding "and" at the end of subparagraph (B) and by adding a new subparagraph (C) to read as above, effective December 13, 1991.

P.L. 101-239, §7891(a)(1):

Titles I, III, and IV of ERISA (other than sections 3(37)(E), 301(a)(7), and 308, the last sentence of section 408(d), and sections 414(c), 4001(a)(3)(ii), and 4303) are each amended by striking "Internal Revenue Code of 1954" each place it appears and inserting "Internal Revenue Code of 1986" effective October 22, 1986.

P.L. 100-203, §9312(b)(4):

Amended ERISA Sec. 4001(a)(16) to read as above, effective for (A) plan terminations under section 4041(c) of ERISA with respect to which notices of intent to terminate are provided under section 4041(a)(2) of ERISA after December 17, 1987, and (B) plan terminations with respect to which proceedings are instituted by the Pension Benefit Guaranty Corporation under section 4042 of ERISA after December 17, 1987.

Prior to amendment ERISA Sec. 4001(a)(16) read as follows:

(16) "benefit commitments", to a participant or beneficiary as of any date under a single-employer plan, means all benefits provided by the plan with respect to the participant or beneficiary which—

(A) are guaranteed under section 4022,

(B) would be guaranteed under section 4022, but for the operation of subsection 4022(b), or

(C) constitute—

(i) early retirement supplements or subsidies, or

(ii) plant closing benefits,

irrespective of whether any such supplements, subsidies, or benefits are benefits guaranteed under section 4022, if the participant or beneficiary has satisfied, as of such date, all of the conditions required of him or her under the provisions of the plan to establish entitlement to the benefits, except for the submission of a formal application, retirement, completion of a required waiting period subsequent to application for benefits, or designation of a beneficiary;

P.L. 100-203, §9312(b)(5):

Amended ERISA Sec. 4001(a)(19) to read as above. For the effective date, see Act Sec. 9312(b)(4), above.

Prior to amendment, ERISA Sec. 4001(a)(19) read as follows:

(19) "outstanding amount of benefit commitments", of a participant or beneficiary under a terminated single-employer plan, means the excess of—

(A) the actuarial present value (determined as of the termination date on the basis of assumptions prescribed by the corporation for purposes of section 4044) of the benefit commitments to such participant or beneficiary under the plan, over

(B) the actuarial present value (determined as of such date on the basis of assumptions prescribed by the corporation for purposes of section 4044) of the benefits of such participants or beneficiary which are guaranteed under section 4022 or to which assets of the plan are required to be allocated under section 4044;

P.L. 100-203, §9313(a)(3)(F):

Amended ERISA Sec. 4001(a)(18) to read as above, effective for plan termination under section 4041 of ERISA for which notices of intent to terminate are provided under section 4041(a)(2) of ERISA after December 17, 1987.

Prior to amendment, ERISA Sec. 4001(a)(18) read as follows:

(18) "amounts of unfunded benefit commitments", of a participant or beneficiary as of any date under a single-employer plan, means an amount equal to the excess of—

(A) the actuarial present value (determined as of such date on the basis of assumptions prescribed by the corporation for purposes of section 4044) of the benefit commitments to the patricipant or beneficiary under the plan, over

(B) the current value (as of such date) of the assets of the plan which are required to be allocated to those benefit commitments under section 4044;

P.L. 99-272:

Act Sec. 11004(a) amended ERISA Sec. 4001(a) by striking paragraph (2) and inserting a new paragraph (2) to read as above.

Prior to amendment, ERISA Sec. 4001(a)(2) read as follows:

(2) "substantial employer" means for any plan year an employer (treating employers who are members of the same affiliated group, within the meaning of section 1563(a) of the Internal Revenue Code of 1954, determined without regard to section 1563(a)(4) and (e)(3)(C) of such Code, as one employer) who has made contributions to or under a plan under which more than one employer (other than a multiemployer plan) makes contributions for each of—

(A) the two immediately preceding plan years, or

(B) the second and third preceding plan years,

equaling or exceeding 10 percent of all employer contributions paid to or under that plan for each such year;

Act Sec. 11004(a) also amended ERISA Sec. 4001(a) by striking "and" which followed paragraph (11), struck the period following "corporation" at the end of paragraph (12) and inserted a semicolon and added new paragraphs (13)—(21) to read as above.

Act Sec. 11004(b) amended ERISA Sec. 4001(b) by inserting (1) and (b) and by adding new paragraph (2) to read as above.

Act Sec. 11004(b) also struck out amendments made by section 402(a)(1)(F) of the Multiemployer Pension Plan Amendments Act of 1980 which added new paragraphs to ERISA Sec. 4001(c)(1) which read:

(2) For purposes of this title, "single-employer plan" means, except as otherwise specifically provided in this title, any plan which is not a multiemployer plan.

(3) For purposes of this title, except as otherwise provided in this title, contributions or other payments shall be considered made under a plan for a plan year if they are made within the period prescribed under section 412(c)(10) of the Internal Revenue Code of 1954.

(4) For purposes of subtitle E, "Secretary of the Treasury" means the Secretary of the Treasury or such Secretary's delegate.

These amendments apply with respect to terminations pursuant to notices of intent filed with the PBGC on or after January 1, 1986 and proceedings begun after that date.

P.L. 96-364, §402(a)(1):

Amended Sec. 4001, effective September 26, 1980 by: inserting in subsection (a)(2) "(other than a multiemployer plan)"; inserting subsection (a)(3), prior to the amendment subsection (a)(3) read "'multiemployer plan' means a multi-employer plan as defined in section 414(f) of the Internal Revenue Code of 1954 (as added by this Act but without regard to whether such section is in effect on the date of enactment of this Act)"; inserting subsection (a)(6), prior to the amendment subsection (A)(6) read "'basic benefits' means benefits guaranteed under section 4022 other than under section 4022(c)"; inserting "or 4022(A)g;" at the end of subsection (a)(7); inserting new subsections (a)(8) through (a)(12). Act Sec. 402(a)(1) added new paragraphs (2), (3), (4) to subsection (c)(1) (as redesignated); however, no redesignation was made in the law. Therefore, the provisions of subsection (b) have been designated as paragraph (b)(1) to which paragraphs (2) through (4) have been added.

Regulations

The following regulations were adopted by the Pension Benefit Guaranty Corporation on July 1, 1996 (61 FR 34002). Prior to July 1, 1996, PBGC regulations were under Chapter XXVI of Title 29 of the Code of Federal Regulations. Effective July 1, 1996, PBGC regulations were moved to Chapter XL, and were renumbered and reorganized. Reg. §4001.2 was amended December 2, 1996 (61 FR 63988), effective January 1, 1997 and was corrected July 1, 1997 (62 FR 35342), effective July 1, 1996. Reg. §4001.2 was amended November 7, 1997 (62 FR 60424), effective January 1, 1998. Reg. §4001.2 was officially corrected on December 30, 1997 (62 FR 67728). Reg. §4001.2 was amended on December 30, 2008 (73 FR 79628) and on March 16, 2009 (74 FR 11022). Reg. §4001.2 was amended on June 8, 2009 (74 FR 27080), effective July 8, 2009. Reg. §4001.2 was amended on November 17, 2009 (74 FR 59093), effective December 17, 2009. Reg. §4001.2 was amended on June 14, 2011 (76 FR 34590), effective July 14, 2011. Reg. §4001.2 was amended on November 25, 2014 (79 FR 70090). Reg. §4001.2 was amended on September 11, 2015 (80 FR 54979). Reg. §§4001.1 and 4001.2 were amended on December 22, 2017 (82 FR 60800).

[¶ 15,315]

§4001.1 **Purpose and scope.** (a) *In general.* This part contains definitions of certain terms used in this chapter and the regulations under which the PBGC makes various controlled group determinations. [Amended 12/22/2017 by 82 FR 60800.]

(b) *Title IV coverage.* Coverage by section 4050 of ERISA is not and does not result in or confer coverage by title IV of ERISA. [Added 12/22/2017 by 82 FR 60800.]

[¶ 15,315A]

§4001.2 **Definitions.** For purposes of this chapter (unless otherwise indicated or required by the context):

Affected party means, with respect to a plan—

(1) Each participant in the plan;

(2) Each beneficiary of a deceased participant;

(3) Each alternate payee under an applicable qualified domestic relations order, as defined in section 206(d)(3) of ERISA;

(4) Each employee organization that currently represents any group of participants;

(5) For any group of participants not currently represented by an employee organization, the employee organization, if any, that last represented such group of participants within the 5-year period preceding issuance of the notice of intent to terminate; and

(6) the PBGC. If an affected party has designated, in writing, a person to receive a notice on behalf of the affected party, any reference to the affected party (in connection with the notice) shall be construed to refer to such person.

Annuity means a series of periodic payments to a participant or surviving beneficiary for a fixed or contingent period.

Bankruptcy filing date means, with respect to a plan, the date on which a petition commencing a case under the United States Bankruptcy Code is filed, or the date on which any similar filing is made commencing a case under any similar Federal law or law of a State or political subdivision, with respect to the contributing sponsor of the plan, if such case has not been dismissed as of the termination date of the plan. If a bankruptcy petition is filed under one chapter of the United States Bankruptcy Code, or under one chapter or provision of any such similar law, and the case is converted to a case under a different chapter or provision of such Code or similar law (for example, a Chapter 11 reorganization case is converted to a Chapter 7 liquidation case), the date of the original petition is the bankruptcy filing date. If such a plan has more than one contributing sponsor:

(1) If all contributing sponsors entered bankruptcy on the same date, that date is the bankruptcy filing date;

(2) If all contributing sponsors did not enter bankruptcy on the same date (or if not all contributing sponsors are in bankruptcy), PBGC will determine the date that will be treated as the bankruptcy filing date based on the facts and circumstances, which may include such things as the relative sizes of the contributing sponsors, the relative amounts of their minimum required contributions to the plan, the timing of the different bankruptcies, and the expectations of participants. [Added 6/14/11 by 76 FR 34590.]

Basic-type benefit means a benefit that is guaranteed under the provisions of part 4022 of this chapter or would be guaranteed if the guarantee limits in §§ 4022.22 through 4022.27 of this chapter did not apply. In a PPA 2006 bankruptcy termination, it also includes a benefit accrued by a participant, or to which a participant otherwise became entitled, on or before the plan's termination date but that is not guaranteed solely because of the provisions of §§ 4022.3(b) or 4022.4(c). [Corrected 12/30/97 by 62 FR 67728. Amended 6/14/11 by 76 FR 34590.]

Benefit liabilities means the benefits of participants and their beneficiaries under the plan (within the meaning of section 401(a)(2) of the Code).

Code means the Internal Revenue Code of 1986, as amended.

Complete withdrawal means a complete withdrawal as described in section 4203 of ERISA.

Contributing sponsor means a person who is a contributing sponsor as defined in section 4001(a)(13) of ERISA.

Controlled group means, in connection with any person, a group consisting of such person and all other persons under common control with such person, determined under section 4001.3 of this part. For purposes of determining the persons liable for contributions under section 412(b)(2) of the Code or section 302(b)(2) of ERISA, or for premiums under section 4007(e)(2) of ERISA, a controlled group also includes any group treated as a single employer under section 414(m) or (o) of the Code. Any reference to a plan's controlled group means all contributing sponsors of the plan and all members of each contributing sponsor's controlled group. [Amended 12/2/96 by 61 FR 63989; 9/11/15 by 80 FR 54979.]

Corporation means the Pension Benefit Guaranty Corporation, except where the context demonstrates that a different meaning is intended.

Defined benefit plan means a plan described in section 3(35) of ERISA.

Disclosure officer means the official designated as disclosure officer in the Office of the General Counsel, PBGC. [Added 6/8/2009 by 74 FR 27080.]

Distress termination means the voluntary termination of a single-employer plan in accordance with section 4041(c) of ERISA and part 4041, subpart C, of this chapter.

Distribution date means:

(1) For benefits provided through the purchase of irrevocable commitments, the date on which the obligation to provide the benefits passes from the plan to the insurer; and [Redesignated 12/22/2017 by 82 FR 60800.]

(2) For benefits provided other than through the purchase of irrevocable commitments, the date on which the benefits are delivered to the participant or beneficiary (or to another plan or benefit arrangement or other recipient authorized by the participant or beneficiary in accordance with applicable law and regulations) personally or by deposit with a mail or courier service (as evidenced by a postmark or written receipt); or [Redesignated 12/22/2017 by 82 FR 60800.]

Earliest retirement age at valuation date means the later of: a participant's age on his or her birthday nearest to the valuation date, or the participant's attained age as of his or her Earliest PBGC Retirement Date (as determined under § 4022.10 of this chapter). [Added 3/16/2009 by 74 FR 11022.]

EIN means the nine-digit employer identification number assigned by the Internal Revenue Service to a person. [Amended 12/2/96 by 61 FR 63988.]

Employer means all trades or businesses (whether or not incorporated) that are under common control, within the meaning of § 4001.3 of this chapter.

ERISA means the Employee Retirement Income Security Act of 1974, as amended.

Expected retirement age (XRA) means the age, determined in accordance with §§ 4044.55 through 4044.57 of this chapter, at which a participant is expected to begin receiving benefits when the participant has not elected, before the allocation date, an annuity starting date. This is the age to which a participant's benefit payment is assumed to be deferred for valuation purposes. An XRA is equal to or greater than the participant's earliest retirement age at valuation date but less than his or her normal retirement age. [Added 3/16/2009 by 74 FR 11022.]

Fair market value means the price at which property would change hands between a willing buyer and a willing seller, neither being under any compulsion to buy or sell and both having reasonable knowledge of relevant facts.

FOIA means the Freedom of Information Act, as amended (5 U.S.C. 552).

Funding standard account means an account established and maintained under section 304(b) of ERISA or section 431(b) of the Code. [Amended 9/11/15 by 80 FR 54979.]

Guaranteed benefit means a benefit under a single-employer plan that is guaranteed by the PBGC under section 4022(a) of ERISA and part 4022 of this chapter, or a benefit under a multiemployer plan that is guaranteed by the PBGC under section 4022A of ERISA.

Insurer means a company authorized to do business as an insurance carrier under the laws of a State or the District of Columbia.

Irrevocable commitment means an obligation by an insurer to pay benefits to a named participant or surviving beneficiary, if the obligation cannot be cancelled under the terms of the insurance contract (except for fraud or mistake) without the consent of the participant or beneficiary and is legally enforceable by the participant or beneficiary.

IRS means the Internal Revenue Service.

Mandatory employee contributions means amounts contributed to the plan by a participant that are required as a condition of employment, as a condition of participation in such plan, or as a condition of obtaining benefits under the plan attributable to employer contributions.

Mass withdrawal means:

(1) The withdrawal of every employer from the plan (2) The cessation of the obligation of all employers to contribute under the plan, or (3) The withdrawal of substantially all employers pursuant to an agreement or arrangement to withdraw. [Corrected 7/1/97 by 62 FR 35342.]

Multiemployer Act means the Multiemployer Pension Plan Amendments Act of 1980.

Multiemployer plan means a plan that is described in section 4001(a)(3) of ERISA and that is covered by title IV of ERISA. Multiemployer plan also means a plan that elects to be a multiemployer plan under ERISA section 3(37)(G) and Code section 414(f)(6), pursuant to procedures prescribed by PBGC. [Amended 12/30/2008 by 73 FR 79628.]

Multiple employer plan means a single-employer plan maintained by two or more contributing sponsors that are not members of the same controlled group, under which all plan assets are available to pay benefits to all plan participants and beneficiaries.

Nonbasic-type benefit means any benefit provided by a plan other than a basic-type benefit.

Nonforfeitable benefit means a benefit described in section 4001(a)(8) of ERISA. Benefits that become nonforfeitable solely as a result of the termination of a plan will be considered forfeitable.

Non-PPA 2006 bankruptcy termination means a plan termination that is not a PPA 2006 bankruptcy termination. [Added 6/14/11 by 76 FR 34590.]

Normal retirement age means the age specified in the plan as the normal retirement age. This age shall not exceed the later of age 65 or the age attained after 5 years of participation in the plan. If no normal retirement age is specified in the plan, it is age 65.

Notice of intent to terminate means the notice of a proposed termination of a single-employer plan, as required by section 4041(a)(2) of ERISA and §4041.21 (in a standard termination) or §4041.41 (in a distress termination) of this chapter.

PBGC means the Pension Benefit Guaranty Corporation.

Person means a person defined in section 3(9) of ERISA.

Plan means a defined benefit plan within the meaning of section 3(35) of ERISA that is covered by title IV of ERISA.

Plan administrator means an administrator, as defined in section 3(16)(A) of ERISA.

Plan sponsor means, with respect to a multiemployer plan, the person described in section 4001(a)(10) of ERISA.

Plan year means the calendar, policy, or fiscal year on which the records of the plan are kept.

PN means the three-digit plan number assigned to a plan. [Amended 12/2/96 by 61 FR 63988.]

PPA 2006 bankruptcy termination means a plan termination to which section 404 of the Pension Protection Act of 2006 applies. Section 404 of the Pension Protection Act of 2006 applies to any plan termination in which the termination date occurs while bankruptcy proceedings are pending with respect to the contributing sponsor of the plan, if the bankruptcy proceedings were initiated on or after September 16, 2006. Bankruptcy proceedings are pending, for this purpose, if a contributing sponsor has filed or has had filed against it a petition seeking liquidation or reorganization in a case under title 11, United States Code, or under any similar Federal law or law of a State or political subdivision, and the case has not been dismissed as of the termination date of the plan.

[Added 11/17/09 by 74 FR 59093.]

Proposed termination date means the date specified as such by the plan administrator of a single-employer plan in a notice of intent to terminate or, if later, in the standard or distress termination notice, in accordance with section 4041 of ERISA and part 4041 of this chapter.

Rollover amounts means the dollar amount of all or any part of a distribution that is rolled over from a defined contribution plan into a defined benefit plan in accordance with section 401(a)(31) or 402(c) or similar provisions under the Internal Revenue Code. Rollover amounts include salary deferral contributions made by the participant, any additional employer contributions provided for under the defined con-

tribution plan, and earnings on both. [Added 11/25/14 by 79 FR 70090.]

Single-employer plan means any defined benefit plan (as defined in section 3(35) of ERISA) that is not a multiemployer plan (as defined in section 4001(a)(3) of ERISA) and that is covered by title IV of ERISA.

Standard termination means the voluntary termination, in accordance with section 4041(b) of ERISA and part 4041, subpart B, of this chapter, of a single-employer plan that is able to provide for all of its benefit liabilities when plan assets are distributed.

Substantial owner means a substantial owner as defined in section 4021(d) of ERISA. [Amended 9/11/15 by 80 FR 54979.]

Sufficient for benefit liabilities means that there is no amount of unfunded benefit liabilities, as defined in section 4001(a)(18) of ERISA.

Sufficient for guaranteed benefits means that there is no amount of unfunded guaranteed benefits, as defined in section 4001(a)(17) of ERISA. In a PPA 2006 bankruptcy termination, the determination whether a plan is sufficient for guaranteed benefits is made taking into account the limitations in sections 4022(g) and 4044(e) of ERISA (and corresponding provisions of these regulations). The determinations of which benefits are guaranteed and which benefits are in priority category 3 under section 4044(a)(3) of ERISA are made by reference to the bankruptcy filing date, but the present values of those benefits are determined as of the proposed termination date and the date of distribution. [Amended 6/14/11 by 76 FR 34590.]

Termination date means the date established pursuant to section 4048(a) of ERISA.

Title IV benefit means the guaranteed benefit plus any additional benefits to which plan assets are allocated pursuant to section 4044 of ERISA and part 4044 of this chapter.

Unreduced retirement age (URA) means the earlier of the normal retirement age specified in the plan or the age at which an unreduced benefit is first payable. [Added 3/16/2009 by 74 FR 11022.]

Voluntary employee contributions means amounts contributed by an employee to a plan, pursuant to the provisions of the plan, that are not mandatory employee contributions. [Amended 12/2/96 by 61 FR 63988; corrected 7/1/97 by 62 FR 35342.]

[¶ 15,315B]

§4001.3 **Trades or businesses under common control; controlled groups.** For purposes of title IV of ERISA:

(a)(1) The PBGC will determine that trades and businesses (whether or not incorporated) are under common control if they are "two or more trades or businesses under common control", as defined in regulations prescribed under section 414(c) of the Code.

(2) The PBGC will determine that all employees of trades or businesses (whether or not incorporated) which are under common control shall be treated as employed by a single employer, and all such trades and businesses shall be treated as a single employer.

(3) An individual who owns the entire interest in an unincorporated trade or business is treated as his own employer, and a partnership is treated as the employer of each partner who is an employee within the meaning of section 401(c)(1) of the Code.

(b) In the case of a single-employer plan:

(1) In connection with any person, a controlled group consists of that person and all other persons under common control with such person.

(2) Persons are under common control if they are members of a "controlled group of corporations", as defined in regulations prescribed under section 414(b) of the Code, or if they are "two or more trades or businesses under common control", as defined in regulations prescribed under section 414(c) of the Code.

[¶ 15,320]

PENSION BENEFIT GUARANTY CORPORATION

Act Sec. 4002. (a) ESTABLISHMENT WITHIN DEPARTMENT OF LABOR.—There is established within the Department of Labor a body corporate to be known as the Pension Benefit Guaranty Corporation. In carrying out its functions under this title, the corporation shall be administered by a Director, who shall be appointed by the President, by and with the advice and consent of the Senate, and who shall act in accordance with the policies established by the board. The purposes of this title, which are to be carried out by the corporation, are—

(1) to encourage the continuation and maintenance of voluntary private pension plans for the benefit of their participants,

(2) to provide for the timely and uninterrupted payment of pension benefits to participants and beneficiaries under plans to which this title applies, and

(3) to maintain premiums established by the corporation under section 4006 at the lowest level consistent with carrying out its obligations under this title.

(b) POWERS OF CORPORATION.—To carry out the purposes of this title, the corporation has the powers conferred on a nonprofit corporation under the District of Columbia Nonprofit Corporation Act and, in addition to any specific power granted to the corporation elsewhere in this title or under that Act, the corporation has the power—

(1) to sue and be sued, complain and defend, in its corporate name and through its own counsel, in any court, State or Federal;

(2) to adopt, alter, and use a corporate seal, which shall be judicially noticed;

(3) to adopt, amend, and repeal, by the board of directors, bylaws, rules, and regulations relating to the conduct of its business and the exercise of all other rights and powers granted to it by this Act and such other bylaws, rules, and regulations as may be necessary to carry out the purposes of this title;

(4) to conduct its business (including the carrying on of operations and the maintenance of offices) and to exercise all other rights and powers granted to it by this Act in any State or other jurisdiction without regard to qualification, licensing, or other requirements imposed by law in such State or other jurisdiction;

(5) to lease, purchase, accept gifts or donations of, or otherwise to acquire, to own, hold, improve, use, or otherwise deal in or with, and to sell, convey, mortgage, pledge, lease, exchange, or otherwise dispose of, any property, real, personal or mixed, or any interest therein wherever situated;

(6) to appoint and fix the compensation of such officers, attorneys, employees, and agents as may be required, to determine their qualifications, to define their duties, and, to the extent desired by the corporation, require bonds for them and fix the penalty thereof, and to appoint and fix the compensation of experts and consultants in accordance with the provisions of section 3109 of title 5, United States Code;

(7) to utilize the personnel and facilities of any other agency or department of the United States Government, with or without reimbursement, with the consent of the head of such agency or department; and

(8) to enter into contracts, to execute instruments, to incur liabilities, and to do any and all other acts and things as may be necessary or incidental to the conduct of its business and the exercise of all other rights and powers granted to the corporation by this Act.

(c) The Director shall be accountable to the board of directors. The Director shall serve for a term of 5 years unless removed by the President or the board of directors before the expiration of such 5year term.

(d) BOARD OF DIRECTORS; COMPENSATION; REIMBURSEMENT FOR EXPENSES.—

(1) The board of directors of the corporation consists of the Secretary of the Treasury, the Secretary of Labor, and the Secretary of Commerce. Members of the board shall serve without compensation, but shall be reimbursed for travel, subsistence, and other necessary expenses incurred in the performance of their duties as members of the board. The Secretary of Labor is the chairman of the board of directors.

(2) A majority of the members of the board of directors in office shall constitute a quorum for the transaction of business. The vote of the majority of the members present and voting at a meeting at which a quorum is present shall be the act of the board of directors.

(3) Each member of the board of directors shall designate in writing an official, not below the level of Assistant Secretary, to serve as the voting representative of such member on the board. Such designation shall be effective until revoked or until a date or event specified therein. Any such representative may refer for board action any matter under consideration by the designating board member, but such representative shall not count toward establishment of a quorum as described under paragraph (2).

(4) The Inspector General of the corporation shall report to the board of directors, and not less than twice a year, shall attend a meeting of the board of directors to provide a report on the activities and findings of the Inspector General, including with respect to monitoring and review of the operations of the corporation.

(5) The General Counsel of the corporation shall—

(A) serve as the secretary to the board of directors, and advise such board as needed; and

(B) have overall responsibility for all legal matters affecting the corporation and provide the corporation with legal advice and opinions on all matters of law affecting the corporation, except that the authority of the General Counsel shall not extend to the Office of Inspector General and the independent legal counsel of such Office.

(6) Notwithstanding any other provision of this Act, the Office of Inspector General and the legal counsel of such Office are independent of the management of the corporation and the General Counsel of the corporation.

(7) The board of directors may appoint and fix the compensation of employees as may be required to enable the board of directors to perform its duties. The board of directors shall determine the qualifications and duties of such employees and may appoint and fix the compensation of experts and consultants in accordance with the provisions of section 3109 of title 5, United States Code.

(e) MEETINGS.—

(1) The board of directors shall meet at the call of its chairman, or as otherwise provided by the bylaws of the corporation, but in no case less than 4 times a year with not fewer than 2 members present. Not less than 1 meeting of the board of directors during each year shall be a joint meeting with the advisory committee under subsection (h).

(2)(A) Except as provided in subparagraph (B), the chairman of the board of directors shall make available to the public the minutes from each meeting of the board of directors.

(B) The minutes of a meeting of the board of directors, or a portion thereof, shall not be subject to disclosure under subparagraph (A) if the chairman reasonably determines that such minutes, or portion thereof, contain confidential employer information including information obtained under section 4010, information about the investment activities of the corporation, or information regarding personnel decisions of the corporation,

(c) The minutes of a meeting, or portion of thereof exempt from disclosure pursuant to subparagraph (B) shall be exempt from disclosure under section 552(b) of title 5, United States Code. For purposes of such section 552, this subparagraph shall be considered a statute described in subsection (b)(3) of such section 552.

(f) ADOPTION OF BYLAWS; AMENDMENT; ALTERATION; PUBLICATION IN THE FEDERAL REGISTER.—As soon as practicable, but not later than 180 days after the date of enactment of this Act, the board of directors shall adopt initial bylaws and rules relating to the conduct of the business of the corporation. Thereafter, the board of directors may alter, supplement, or repeal any existing bylaw or rule, and may adopt additional bylaws and rules from time to time as may be necessary. The chairman of the board shall cause a copy of the bylaws of the corporation to be published in the Federal Register not less often than once each year.

(g)(1) EXEMPTION FROM TAXATION.—The corporation, its property, its franchise, capital, reserves, surplus, and its income (including, but not limited to, any income of any fund established under section 4005), shall be exempt from all taxation now or hereafter imposed by the United States (other than taxes imposed under chapter 21 of the Internal Revenue Code of 1986, relating to Federal Insurance Contributions Act, and chapter 23 of such Code, relating to Federal Unemployment Tax Act), or by any State or local taxing authority, except that any real property and any tangible personal property (other than cash and securities) of the corporation shall be subject to State and local taxation to the same extent according to its value as other real and tangible personal property is taxed.

(2) The receipts and disbursements of the corporation in the discharge of its functions shall be included in the totals of the budget of the United States Government. The United States is not liable for any obligation or liability incurred by the corporation.

(3) Section 101 of the Government Corporation Control Act (31 U.S.C. 846) is amended by inserting before the period a semicolon and the following: "and Pension Benefit Guaranty Corporation".

(h)(1) ADVISORY COMMITTEE TO CORPORATION.—There is established an advisory committee to the corporation, for the purpose of advising the corporation as to its policies and procedures relating to (A) the appointment of trustees in termination proceedings, (B) investment of moneys, (C) whether plans being terminated should be liquidated immediately or continued in operation under a trustee, (D) such other issues as the corporation may request from time to time, and (E) other issues as determined appropriate by the advisory committee. The advisory committee may also recommend persons for appointment as trustees in termination proceedings, make recommendations with respect to the investment of moneys in the funds, and advise the corporation as to whether a plan subject to being terminated should be liquidated immediately or continued in operation under a trustee. In the event of a vacancy or impending vacancy in the office of the Participant and Plan Sponsor Advocate established under section 4004, the Advisory Committee shall, in consultation with the Director of the corporation and participant and plan sponsor advocacy groups, nominate at least two but no more than three individuals to serve as the Participant and Plan Sponsor Advocate.

(2) The advisory committee consists of seven members appointed, from among individuals recommended by the board of directors, by the President. Of the seven members, two shall represent the interests of employee organizations, two shall represent the interests of employers who maintain pension plans, and three shall represent the interests of the general public. The President shall designate one member as chairman at the time of the appointment of that member.

(3) Members shall serve for terms of 3 years each, except that, of the members first appointed, one of the members representing the interests of employee organizations, one of the members representing the interests of employers, and one of the members representing the interests of the general public shall be appointed for terms of 2 years each, one of the members representing the interests of the general public shall be appointed for a term of 1 year, and the other members shall be appointed to full 3-year terms. The advisory committee shall meet at least six times each year and at such other times as may be determined by the chairman or requested by any three members of the advisory committee. Not less than 1 meeting of the advisory committee during each year shall be a joint meeting with the board of directors under subsection (e).

(4) Members shall be chosen on the basis of their experience with employee organizations, with employers who maintain pension plans, with the administration of pension plans, or otherwise on account of outstanding demonstrated ability in related fields. Of the members serving on the advisory committee at any time, no more than four shall be affiliated with the same political party.

(5) An individual appointed to fill a vacancy occurring other than by the expiration of a term of office shall be appointed only for the unexpired term of the member he succeeds. Any vacancy occurring in the office of a member of the advisory committee shall be filled in the manner in which that office was originally filled.

(6) The advisory committee shall appoint and fix the compensation of such employees as it determines necessary to discharge its duties, including experts and consultants in accordance with the provisions of section 3109 of title 5, United States Code. The corporation shall furnish to the advisory committee such professional, secretarial, and other services as the committee may request.

(7) Members of the advisory committee shall, for each day (including travel time) during which they are attending meetings or conferences of the committee or otherwise engaged in the business of the committee, be compensated at a rate fixed by the corporation which is not in excess of the daily equivalent of the annual rate of basic pay in effect for grade GS-18 of the General Schedule, and while away from their homes or regular places of business they may be allowed travel expenses, including per diem in lieu of subsistence, as authorized by section 5703 of title 5, United States Code.

(8) The Federal Advisory Committee Act does not apply to the advisory committee established by this subsection.

(i) SPECIAL RULES REGARDING DISASTERS, ETC.—In the case of a pension or other employee benefit plan, or any sponsor, administrator, participant, beneficiary, or other person with respect to such plan, affected by a Presidentially declared disaster (as defined in section 1033 (h)(3) of the Internal Revenue Code of 1986) or a terroristic or military action (as defined in section 692 (c)(2) of such Code), the corporation may, notwithstanding any other provision of law, prescribe, by notice or otherwise, a period of up to 1 year which may be disregarded in determining the date by which any action is required or permitted to be completed under this Act. No plan shall be treated as failing to be operated in accordance with the terms of the plan solely as the result of disregarding any period by reason of the preceding sentence.

(j) CONFLICTS OF INTEREST.—

(1) IN GENERAL. The Director of the corporation and each member of the board of directors shall not participate in a decision of the corporation in which the Director or such member has a direct financial interest. The Director of the corporation shall not participate in any activities that would present a potential conflict of interest or appearance of a conflict of interest without approval of the board of directors.

(2) ESTABLISHMENT OF POLICY. The board of directors shall establish a policy that will inform the identification of potential conflicts of interests of the members of the board of directors and mitigate perceived conflicts of interest of such members and the Director of the corporation.

(k) RISK MANAGEMENT OFFICER.—The corporation shall have a risk management officer whose duties include evaluating and mitigating the risk that the corporation might experience. The individual in such position shall coordinate the risk management efforts of the corporation, explain risks and controls to senior management and the board of directors of the corporation, and make recommendations.

Amendments:

P.L. 112-141, §40231(a)(1)(A) and (B):

Amended ERISA Sec. 4002(d) by striking "(d) The board of directors" and inserting "(d)(1) The board of directors"; and by adding at the end adding new paragraphs (2)-(7) to read as above.

The above amendment is effective on the date of enactment (July 6, 2012).

P.L. 112-141, §40231(a)(2)(A), (B), and (C):

Amended ERISA Sec. 4002(e) by striking "The board" and inserting "(1) The board", by striking "the corporation." and inserting "the corporation, but in no case less than 4 times a year with not fewer than 2 members present. Not less than 1 meeting of the board of directors during each year shall be a joint meeting with the advisory committee under subsection (h).", and by adding at the end new paragraph (2) to read as above.

The above amendment is effective on the date of enactment (July 6, 2012).

P.L. 112-141, §40231(a)(3)(A)(i) and (ii):

Amended ERISA Sec. 4002(h)(1) by striking ", and (D)" and inserting ", (D)"; and by striking "time to time." and inserting "time to time, and (E) other issues as determined appropriate by the advisory committee.".

The above amendment is effective on the date of enactment (July 6, 2012).

P.L. 112-141, §40231(a)(3)(B):

Amended ERISA Sec. 4002(h)(3) by adding at the end the following: "Not less than 1 meeting of the advisory committee during each year shall be a joint meeting with the board of directors under subsection (e).".

The above amendment is effective on the date of enactment (July 6, 2012).

P.L. 112-141, §40231(b):

Amended ERISA Sec. 4002 by adding at the end new subsection (j) to read as above.

The above amendment is effective on the date of enactment (July 6, 2012).

P.L. 112-141, §40231(c):

Amended ERISA Sec. 4002 by adding at the end new subsection (k) to read as above.

The above amendment is effective on the date of enactment (July 6, 2012).

P.L. 112-141, §40231(d):

Amended ERISA Sec. 4002(c) to read as above. Prior to amendment, ERISA Sec. 4002(c) read as follows:

(c) Section 5108 of title 5, United States Code, is amended by adding at the end thereof the following new subsection:

"(g) In addition to the number of positions authorized by subsection (a), the Pension Benefit Guaranty Corporation is authorized, without regard to any other provision of this section, to place one position in the corporation at GS-18 and a total of 10 positions in the corporation at GS-16 and 17.".

The above amendment is effective on the date of enactment (July 6, 2012).

P.L. 112-141, §40232(b):

Amended ERISA Sec. 4002(h)(1) by adding at the end the following new sentence: "In the event of a vacancy or impending vacancy in the office of the Participant and Plan Sponsor Advocate established under section 4004, the Advisory Committee shall, in consultation with the Director of the corporation and participant and plan sponsor advocacy groups, nominate at least two but no more than three individuals to serve as the Participant and Plan Sponsor Advocate.".

The above amendment is effective on the date of enactment (July 6, 2012).

P.L. 109-280, §411(a)(1):

Amended ERISA Sec. 4002(a) by striking the second sentence and inserting a new second sentence to read as above. Prior to being stricken, the second sentence read as follows: "In carrying out its functions under this title, the corporation shall be administered by the chairman of the board of directors in accordance with policies established by the board."

The above amendment is effective on the date of enactment (August 17, 2006).

P.L. 107-134, §112(c)(2):

Amended Sec. 4002 by adding subsection (i). The amendment applies to disasters and terroristic or military actions occurring on or after September 11, 2001, with respect to any action of the Secretary of the Treasury, Secretary of Labor, or the PBGC occurring on or after January 23, 2002.

Regulations

Prior to July 1, 1996, the following PBGC bylaws regulations were under Chapter XXVI of Title 29 of the Code of Federal Regulations. Effective July 1, 1996, the PBGC regulations were moved to Chapter XL, and were renumbered and reorganized. The bylaws were amended and replaced May 23, 2008 (73 FR 29985), effective June 23, 2008. The bylaws were revised and replaced September 12, 2017 (82 FR 42733), effective September 12, 2017.

[¶ 15,321]

§ 4002.1 **Board of Directors, Chair, and Representatives of Board Members.** (a) *Composition and responsibilities of the Board of Directors.* (1) *Board.* Section 4002(d)(1) of ERISA establishes the Board membership as the Secretaries of Labor (Chair), the Treasury, and Commerce. A person who, at the time of a meeting of the Board of Directors, is serving in an acting capacity as, or performing the duties of, a Member of the Board of Directors will serve as a Member of the Board of Directors with the same authority and effect as the designated Secretary.

(2) *Chair of the Board.* As Chair of the Board, the Secretary of Labor will preside over all Board meetings. As a direct report to the Board under section 4002(d)(4) of ERISA, the Inspector General of the Corporation reports to the Board through the Chair. The Participant and Plan Sponsor Advocate also reports to the Board through the Chair.

(3) *Board responsibilities.* Except as provided in paragraph (b) of this section, the Board may not delegate any of the following responsibilities—

(i) Voting on an amendment to these bylaws.

(ii) Approval of the Annual Report, which includes the Annual Management Report (AMR) (and its components the financial statements, management's discussion and analysis, annual performance report and independent auditor's report), the Chair's message, and other documentation in conformance with guidance issued by the Office of Management and Budget (OMB).

(iii) Approval of the Corporation's Investment Policy Statement.

(iv) Approval of all reports or recommendations to the Congress required by Title IV of ERISA.

(v) Approval of any policy matter (other than administrative policies) that would have a significant impact on the pension insurance program.

(vi) Review of reports from the Corporation's Inspector General that the Inspector General deems appropriate to deliver to the Board.

(4) *Investment Policy Statement review.* The Board must review the Corporation's Investment Policy Statement at least every two years and approve the Investment Policy Statement at least every four years.

(b) *Designation of and responsibilities of Board Representatives and Alternate Representatives.* (1) *Board Representatives.* A Board Representative, as designated under section 4002(d)(3) of ERISA, may act for all purposes under these bylaws, except that an action of a Board Representative on a Board Member's behalf with respect to the powers described in paragraphs (a)(3)(i) through (iii) of this section, will be valid only upon ratification in writing by the Board Member. Any Board Representative may refer for Board action any matter under consideration by the Board Representatives.

(2) *Alternate Representatives.* A Board Member may designate in writing an official, not below the level of Assistant Secretary, to serve as the Board Member's Alternate Representative at a meeting. An Alternate Representative may act for all purposes at that meeting, except that the Alternate Representative's actions will be valid only upon ratification in writing by either the Board Member or the Board Representative. Any action of the Alternate Representative involving the powers described in paragraphs (a)(3)(i) through (iii) of this section or any matter that has been referred to the Board under paragraph (b)(1) of this section must be ratified in writing by the Board Member.

(3) *Ratification.* For purposes of this section, ratification of a Board Representative or Alternative Representative action includes approval of the minutes of the meeting of the Board of Directors by voice vote or otherwise.

(c) *Review and approval of regulations.* Regulations may be issued by the Director of the Corporation, subject to the following conditions—

(1) Regulations must first be reviewed for comment by each Board Representative except for routine updates of PBGC valuation factors and actuarial assumptions.

(2) A Board Representative may, within 21 days of receiving a regulation for review, request that it be referred to the Board Representatives for approval.

(3) Nonsignificant regulations and significant proposed regulations within the meaning of Executive Order 12866 and subject to review under paragraph (c)(1) of this section may be issued by the Director upon either the expiration of the time specified in paragraph (c)(2) of this section, or, if the approval option is exercised, upon Board Representative approval.

(4) Significant final regulations must be approved by the Board Representatives or the Board.

(5) The Director may submit regulations subject to approval by the Board Representatives or the Board to OMB for concurrent review after they have been pending without comment before the Board Representatives or the Board for more than 60 days.

[¶ 15,321A]

§ 4002.2 **Quorum.** Section 4002(d)(2) of ERISA establishes that a majority of the Board Members will constitute a quorum for the transaction of business. Any act of a majority of the Members present at any meeting at which there is a quorum will be the act of the Board.

[¶ 15,321B]

§ 4002.3 **Meetings.** (a) *General.* Meetings of the Board of Directors are called by the Chair in accordance with section 4002(e)(1) of ERISA and on the request of any Board Member. The Chair must provide reasonable notice of any meetings to each Board Member.

(b) *Minutes.* The General Counsel of the Corporation serves as Secretary to the Board of Directors pursuant to section 4002(d)(5) of ERISA. The General Counsel must keep Board minutes. As soon as practicable after each meeting, the General Counsel must distribute a draft of the minutes of such meeting to each Member of the Board for approval. The Board of Directors may approve minutes by resolution or by voice vote at a subsequent meeting. Subject to appropriate redactions authorized by section 4002(e)(2)(C) of ERISA, approved minutes will be posted on PBGC's Web site.

[¶ 15,321C]

§ 4002.4 **Place of meetings; use of conference call communications equipment.** (a) *Place of meetings.* Meetings of the Board of Directors will be held at the principal office of the Corporation or the Department of Labor unless otherwise determined by the Board of Directors or the Chair.

Reg. § 4002.4(a)   ¶ 15,321C

(b) *Teleconference.* Any Member may participate in a meeting of the Board of Directors through the use of conference call telephone or similar communications equipment, by means of which all persons participating in the meeting can speak to and hear each other. Any Board Member so participating in a meeting will be deemed present for all purposes. Actions taken by the Board of Directors at meetings conducted through the use of such equipment, including the votes of each Member, must be recorded in the minutes of the meetings of the Board of Directors.

[¶ 15,321D]

§ 4002.5 **Voting without a meeting.** A resolution of the Board of Directors signed by all of the Board Members or all of the Board Representatives will have the same effect as if agreed to at a meeting and must be kept in the Corporate Minutes Book. A resolution for an action taken on any matter for which a Board Member has been disqualified under § 4002.6 may be signed by the Board Representative of the disqualified Board Member to the extent the matter is delegable under these bylaws.

[¶ 15,321E]

§ 4002.6 **Conflict of interest.** (a) *Board Members and Director.* The Board Members and the Director must work with their respective ethics office to identify actual or potential conflicts of interest under 18 U.S.C. 208 or section 4002(j) of ERISA or the appearance of the loss of impartiality under 5 CFR 2635.502.

(b) *Disqualification.* A Board Member and the Director must notify the Board Members of disqualification in any decision or activity based on a conflict of interest under paragraph (a) of this section. To the extent a matter is delegable under these bylaws, the disqualified Board Member's Board Representative, acting independently of that Member, may vote on the matter in the Member's place. The disqualified Board Member may not ratify any action taken on the matter giving rise to his or her disqualification.

[¶ 15,321F]

§ 4002.7 **Director of the Corporation and senior officers.** (a) *Director of the Corporation.* Section 4002(a) and (c) of ERISA establish that the Corporation is administered by a Director. Subject to policies established by the Board, the Director is responsible for the Corporation's management, including its personnel, organization and budget practices, and for carrying out the Corporation's functions under Title IV of ERISA. The Director will timely provide the Board any information necessary to assist the Board in exercising its statutory responsibilities. The Director must submit the Corporation's budget to the Chair of the Board for review and approval before formally submitting the budget to OMB.

(b) *Senior officers.* The senior officers of the Corporation report directly to the Director. The Director must consult with the Board before eliminating or creating a senior officer position or making an appointment to a senior officer position.

[¶ 15,321G]

§ 4002.8 **Emergency procedures.** (a) An emergency exists if a quorum of the Corporation's Board cannot readily be assembled or act through written contact because of the declaration of a government-wide emergency. These emergency procedures must remain in effect during the emergency and upon the termination of the emergency will cease to be operative unless and until another emergency occurs. The emergency procedures operate in conjunction with the PBGC Continuity of Operations Plan ("COOP Plan") of the current year, and any government-wide COOP protocols in effect.

(b) During an emergency, the business of the PBGC must continue to be managed in accordance with its COOP Plan. The functions of the Board of Directors must be carried out by those Members of the Board of Directors in office at the time the emergency arises, or by persons designated by the agencies' COOP plans to act in place of the Board Members, who are available to act during the emergency. If no such persons are available, then the authority of the Board must be transferred to the Board Representatives who are available. If no Board Representatives are available, then the Director of the Corporation must perform essential Board functions.

(c) During an emergency, meetings of the Board may be called by any available Member of the Board. The notice thereof must specify the time and place of the meeting. To the extent possible, notice must be given in accordance with these bylaws. Notice must be given to those Board Members whom it is feasible to reach at the time of the emergency, and notice may be given at a time less than 24 hours before the meeting if deemed necessary by the person giving notice.

[¶ 15,321H]

§ 4002.9 **Seal.** The seal of the Corporation must be in such form as may be approved from time to time by the Board.

[¶ 15,321I]

§ 4002.10 **Authority and amendments.** (a) Section 4002 of ERISA and the bylaws establish the authority and responsibilities of the Board, the Board Representatives, and the Director.

(b) These bylaws may be amended or new bylaws adopted by unanimous vote of the Board.

[¶ 15,330]
OPERATION OF CORPORATION

Act Sec. 4003. (a) INVESTIGATING AUTHORITY; AUDIT OF STATISTICALLY SIGNIFICANT NUMBER OF TERMINATING PLANS.—The corporation may make such investigations as it deems necessary to enforce any provision of this title or any rule or regulation thereunder, and may require or permit any person to file with it a statement in writing, under oath or otherwise as the corporation shall determine, as to all the facts and circumstances concerning the matter to be investigated. The corporation shall annually audit a statistically significant number of plans terminating under section 4041(b) to determine whether participants and beneficiaries have received their benefit commitments and whether section 4050(a) has been satisfied. Each audit shall include a statistically significant number of participants and beneficiaries.

Act Sec. 4003. (b) DISCOVERY POWERS VESTED IN BOARD MEMBERS OR OFFICERS DESIGNATED BY THE CHAIRMAN.—For the purpose of any such investigation, or any other proceeding under this title, the Director, any member of the board of directors of the corporation, or any officer designated by the Director or chairman, may administer oaths and affirmations, subpoena witnesses, compel their attendance, take evidence, and require the production of any books, papers, correspondence, memoranda, or other records which the corporation deems relevant or material to the inquiry.

Act Sec. 4003. (c) CONTEMPT.—In case of contumacy by, or refusal to obey a subpena issued to, any person, the corporation may invoke the aid of any court of the United States within the jurisdiction of which such investigation or proceeding is carried on, or where such person resides or carries on business, in requiring the attendance and testimony of witnesses and the production of books, papers, correspondence, memoranda, and other records. The court may issue an order requiring such person to appear before the corporation, or member or officer designated by the corporation, and to produce records or to give testimony related to the matter under investigation or in question. Any failure to obey such order of the court may be punished by the court as a contempt thereof. All process in any such case may be served in the judicial district in which such person is an inhabitant or may be found.

Act Sec. 4003. (d) COOPERATION WITH OTHER GOVERNMENTAL AGENCIES.—In order to avoid unnecessary expense and duplication of functions among government agencies, the corporation may make such arrangements or agreements for cooperation or mutual assistance in the performance of its functions under this title as is practicable and consistent with law. The corporation may utilize the facilities or services of any department, agency, or establishment of the United States or of any State or political subdivision of a State, including the services of any of its employees, with the lawful consent of such department, agency, or establishment. The head of each department, agency, or establishment of the United States shall cooperate with the corporation and, to the extent permitted by law, provide such information and facilities as it may request for its assistance in the performance of its functions under this title. The Attorney General or his representative shall receive from the corporation for appropriate action such evidence developed in the performance of its functions under this title as may be found to warrant consideration for criminal prosecution under the provisions of this or any other Federal law.

Act Sec. 4003. (e)(1) CIVIL ACTIONS BY CORPORATION; JURISDICTION; PROCESS; EXPEDITIOUS HANDLING OF CASE; COSTS; LIMITATIONS ON ACTIONS.—Civil actions may be brought by the corporation for appropriate relief, legal or equitable or both, to enforce

(A) the provisions of this title, and

(B) In the case of a plan which is covered under this title (other than a multiemployer plan) and for which the conditions for imposition for a lien described in section 303(k)(1)(A) and (B) or 306(g)(1)(A) and (B) of this Act or section 430(k)(1)(A) and (B) or 433(g)(1)(A) and (B) of the Internal Revenue Code of 1986 have been met, section 302 of this Act and section 412 of such Code.

(2) Except as otherwise provided in this title, where such an action is brought in a district court of the United States, it may be brought in the district where the plan is administered, where the violation took place, or where a defendant resides or may be found, and process may be served in any other district where a defendant resides or may be found.

(3) The district courts of the United States shall have jurisdiction of actions brought by the corporation under this title without regard to the amount in controversy in any such action.

(4) [Repealed]

(5) In any action brought under this title, whether to collect premiums, penalties, and interest under section 4007 or for any other purpose, the court may award to the corporation all or a portion of the costs of litigation incurred by the corporation in connection with such action.

(6)(A) Except as provided in subparagraph (C), an action under this subsection may not be brought after the later of—

(i) 6 years after the date on which the cause of action arose, or

(ii) 3 years after the applicable date specified in subparagraph (B).

(B)(i) Except as provided in clause (ii), the applicable date specified in this subparagraph is the earliest date on which the corporation acquired or should have acquired actual knowledge of the existence of such cause of action.

(ii) If the corporation brings the action as a trustee, the applicable date specified in this subparagraph is the date on which the corporation became a trustee with respect to the plan if such date is later than the date described in clause (i).

(C) In the case of fraud or concealment, the period described in subparagraph (A)(ii) shall be extended to 6 years after the applicable date specified in subparagraph (B).

Act Sec. 4003.(f)(1) CIVIL ACTIONS AGAINST THE CORPORATION; APPROPRIATE COURT; AWARD OF COSTS AND EXPENSES; LIMITATION ON ACTIONS; JURISDICTION; REMOVAL OF ACTIONS.—Except with respect to withdrawal liability disputes under part 1 of subtitle E, any person who is a plan sponsor, fiduciary, employer, contributing sponsor, member of a contributing sponsor's controlled group, participant, or beneficiary, and is adversely affected by any action of the corporation with respect to a plan in which such person has an interest, or who is an employee organization representing such a participant or beneficiary so adversely affected for purposes of collective bargaining with respect to such plan, may bring an action against the corporation for appropriate equitable relief in the appropriate court.

(2) For purposes of this subsection, the term "appropriate court" means—

(A) the United States district court before which proceedings under section 4041 or 4042 are being conducted,

(B) if no such proceedings are being conducted, the United States district court for the judicial district in which the plan has its principal office, or

(C) the United States District Court for the District of Columbia.

(3) In any action brought under this subsection, the court may award all or a portion of the costs and expenses incurred in connection with such action to any party who prevails or substantially prevails in such action.

(4) This subsection shall be the exclusive means for bringing actions against the corporation under this title, including actions against the corporation in its capacity as a trustee under section 4042 or 4049.

(5)(A) Except as provided in subparagraph (C), an action under this subsection may not be brought after the later of—

(i) 6 years after the date on which the cause of action arose, or

(ii) 3 years after the applicable date specified in subparagraph (B).

(B)(i) Except as provided in clause (ii), the applicable date specified in this subparagraph is the earliest date on which the plaintiff acquired or should have acquired actual knowledge of the existence of such cause of action.

(ii) In the case of a plaintiff who is a fiduciary bringing the action in the exercise of fiduciary duties, the applicable date specified in this subparagraph is the date on which the plaintiff became a fiduciary with respect to the plan if such date is later than the date specified in clause (i).

(C) In the case of fraud or concealment, the period described in subparagraph (A)(ii) shall be extended to 6 years after the applicable date specified in subparagraph (B).

(6) The district courts of the United States have jurisdiction of actions brought under this subsection without regard to the amount in controversy.

(7) In any suit, action, or proceeding in which the corporation is a party, or intervenes under section 4301, in any State court, the corporation may, without bond or security, remove such suit, action, or proceeding from the state court to the United States district court for the district or division in which such suit, action, or proceeding is pending by following any procedure for removal now or hereafter in effect.

Amendments:

P.L. 113-235, §201(a)(7)(C), Div. O:

Amended ERISA Sec. 4003(f)(1) by inserting "plan sponsor," before "fiduciary".

The amendment is effective as of the date of enactment (December 16, 2014).

P.L. 113-97, §102(b)(7):

Amended ERISA 4003(e)(1)(B) by striking "303(k)(1)(A) and (B) of this Act or section 430(k)(1)(A) and (B) of the Internal Revenue Code of 1986" and inserting "303(k)(1)(A) and (B) or 306(g)(1)(A) and (B) of this Act or section 430(k)(1)(A) and (B) or 433(g)(1)(A) and (B) of the Internal Revenue Code of 1986".

Effective for years beginning after 12-31-2013.

P.L. 109-280, Sec. 107(b)(2):

Amended ERISA Sec. 4003(e)(1)(B) by striking "302(f)(1)(A) and (B)" and inserting "303(k)(1)(A) and (B)", and by striking "412(n)(1)(A) and (B) and inserting "430(k)(1)(A) and (B)".

The above amendment applies to plan years beginning after 2007.

P.L. 109-280, Sec. 411(a)(2)(A)-(B):

Amended ERISA Sec. 4003(b) by striking "under the title, any member" and inserting "under this title, the Director, any member", and by striking "designated by the chairman" and inserting "designated by the Director or chairman"

The above amendment is effective as of the date of enactment (August 17, 2006).

P.L. 103-465, §773(a):

Act Sec. 773(a) amended ERISA Sec. 4003(e)(1) to read as above. Prior to amendment, ERISA Sec. 4003(e)(1) read as follows:

(e)(1) Civil actions may be brought by the corporation for appropriate relief, legal or equitable or both, to enforce the provisions of this title.

The above amendment is effective for installments and other payments required under ERISA Sec. 302 or Code Sec. 412 that become due on or after December 8, 1994.

P.L. 103-465, §776(b)(1):

Act Sec. 776(b)(1) amended ERISA Sec. 4003(a) in the second sentence by inserting before the period the following: "and whether section 4050(a) has been satisfied".

The above amendment is effective with respect to distributions that occur in plan years commencing after final regulations implementing the amendment are prescribed by the Pension Benefit Guaranty Corporation.

P.L. 99-272:

Act Sec. 11014(b)(2) amended ERISA Sec. 4003(e) by adding a new paragraph (6) to read as above, effective with respect to actions filed after April 7, 1986.

Act Sec. 11014(b)(1) amended ERISA Sec. 4003(f) to read as above, effective with respect to actions filed after April 7, 1986. Prior to amendment, Sec. 4003(f) read as follows:

Act Sec. 4003. (f) Except as provided in section 4301(a)(2), any participant beneficiary plan administrator, or employer adversely affected by any action of the corporation, or by a receiver or trustee appointed by the corporation, with respect to a plan in which such participant, beneficiary, plan administrator or employer has an interest, may bring an action against the corporation, receiver or trustee in the appropriate court. For purposes of this subsection the term "appropriate court" means the United States district court before which proceedings under section 4041 or 4042 of this title are being conducted, or if no such proceedings are being conducted the United States district court for the district in which the plan has its principal office, or the United States district court for the District of Columbia. The district courts of the United States have jurisdiction of actions brought under this subsection without regard to the amount in controversy. In any suit, action, or proceeding in which the corporation is a party, or intervenes under section 4301, an [sic] any State court, the corporation may, without bond or security, remove such suit, action, or proceeding from the State court to the

Act Sec. 4003(f)(7) ¶15,330

United States District Court for the district or division embracing the place where the same is pending by following any procedure for removal now or hereafter in effect.

Act Sec. 11016(c)(5) amended ERISA Sec. 4003(a) by adding a new sentence at the end of the subsection, effective on April 7, 1986.

P.L. 98-620, §402(33):

Repealed ERISA Sec. 4003(e)(4) effective November 8, 1984, but the repeal does not apply to cases pending on that date. Prior to repeal, ERISA Sec. 4003(e)(4) read:

"(4) Upon application by the corporation to a court of the United States for expedited handling of any case in which the corporation is a party, it is the duty of that court to assign such case for hearing at the earliest practical date and to cause such case to be in every way expedited."

P.L. 96-364, §§402(a)(2) and 403(k):

Amended Sec. 4003 effective September 26, 1980 by: striking out in subsection (a) "determine whether any person has violated or is about to violate" and inserting "enforce"; striking out in subsection (e)(1) "redress violations of" and inserting "enforce"; and inserting at the end of subsection (f) the new sentence.

Regulations

The following regulations were adopted by the Pension Benefit Guaranty Corporation on July 1, 1996 (61 FR 34002). Prior to July 1, 1996, PBGC regulations were under Chapter XXVI of Title 29 of the Code of Federal Regulations. Effective July 1, 1996, PBGC regulations were moved to Chapter XL, and were renumbered and reorganized. On October 28, 2003, §4003.9 and §4003.10 were revised and §4003.33 and §4003.53 were amended (68 FR 61344). On July 3, 2008, §4003.1, §4003.2, §4003.4, §4003.33, §4003.35, §4003.53, and §4003.60 were amended; §4003.54 was revised; and the existing text in §4003.58 was redesignated as (a) and paragraph (b) was added (73 FR 38117). Reg. §§4003.32 and 4003.52 were amended on November 5, 2010 (75 FR 68203). Reg. §4003.1 was amended on April 16, 2012 (77 FR 22488). Reg. §4003.1 was amended on December 22, 2017 (82 FR 60800).

Subpart A—General Provisions

[¶ 15,331]

§4003.1 **Purpose and scope.** (a) *Purpose.* This part sets forth the rules governing the issuance of all initial determinations by the PBGC on cases pending before it involving the matters set forth in paragraph (b) of this section and the procedures for requesting and obtaining administrative review by the PBGC of those determinations. Subpart A contains general provisions. Subpart B sets forth rules governing the issuance of all initial determinations of the PBGC on matters covered by this part. Subpart C establishes procedures governing the reconsideration by the PBGC of initial determinations relating to the matters set forth in paragraphs (b)(1) through (b)(5). Subpart D establishes procedures governing administrative appeals from initial determinations relating to the matters set forth in paragraphs (b)(6) through (b)(11). [Amended 4/16/12 by 77 FR 22488.]

(b) *Scope.* This part applies to the following determinations made by the PBGC in cases pending before it and to the review of those determinations:

(1) Determinations that a plan is covered under section 4021 of ERISA;

(2) Determinations with respect to premiums, interest and late payment penalties pursuant to section 4007 of ERISA;

(3) Determinations with respect to voluntary terminations under section 4041 of ERISA, including—

(i) A determination that a notice requirement or a certification requirement under section 4041 of ERISA has not been met,

(ii) A determination that the requirements for demonstrating distress under section 4041(c)(2)(B) of ERISA have not been met, and

(iii) A determination with respect to the sufficiency of plan assets for benefit liabilities or for guaranteed benefits;

(4) Determinations with respect to allocation of assets under section 4044 of ERISA, including distribution of excess assets under section 4044(d);

(5) Determinations with respect to penalties under section 4071 of ERISA; [Added 4/16/12 by 77 FR 22488.]

(6) Determinations that a plan is not covered under section 4021 of ERISA; [Redesignated 4/16/12 by 77 FR 22488.]

(7) Determinations under section 4022(a) or (c) of ERISA with respect to benefit entitlement of participants and beneficiaries under covered plans and determinations that a domestic relations order is or is not a qualified domestic relations order under section 206(d)(3) of ERISA and section 414(p) of the Code; [Amended 7/3/08 by 73 FR 38117 and redesignated 4/16/12 by 77 FR 22488.]

(8) Determinations under section 4022(b) or (c) or section 4022B of ERISA of the amount of benefits payable to participants and beneficiaries under covered plans; [Amended 7/3/08 by 73 FR 38117 and redesignated 4/16/12 by 77 FR 22488.]

(9) Determinations of the amount of money subject to recapture pursuant to section 4045 of ERISA; [Redesignated 4/16/12 by 77 FR 22488.]

(10) Determinations of the amount of liability under section 4062(b)(1), section 4063, or section 4064 of ERISA; [Redesignated 4/16/12 by 77 FR 22488.]

(11) Determinations with respect to benefits payable by PBGC under section 4050 of ERISA and part 4050 of this chapter. [Redesignated 4/16/12 by 77 FR 22488. Revised 12/22/2017 by 82 FR 60800.]

(c) *Matters not covered by this part. Nothing in this part limits—*

(1) The authority of the PBGC to review, either upon request or on its own initiative, a determination to which this part does not apply when, in its discretion, the PBGC determines that it would be appropriate to do so, or

(2) The procedure that the PBGC may utilize in reviewing any determination to which this part does not apply.

[¶ 15,331A]

§4003.2 **Definitions.** The following terms are defined in §4001.2 of this chapter: Code, contributing sponsor, controlled group, ERISA, multiemployer plan, PBGC, person, plan administrator, and single-employer plan.

In addition, for purposes of this part:

Aggrieved person means any participant, beneficiary, plan administrator, contributing sponsor of a single-employer plan or member of such a contributing sponsor's controlled group, plan sponsor of a multiemployer plan, or employer that is adversely affected by an initial determination of the PBGC with respect to a pension plan in which such person has an interest. The term "beneficiary" includes an alternate payee (within the meaning of section 206(d)(3)(K) of ERISA) under a qualified domestic relations order (within the meaning of section 206(d)(3)(B) of ERISA).

Appeals Board means a board consisting of three PBGC officials. The Director shall appoint a senior PBGC official to serve as Chairperson and three or more other PBGC officials to serve as regular Appeals Board members. The Chairperson shall designate the three officials who will constitute the Appeals Board with respect to a case, provided that a person may not serve on the Appeals Board with respect to a case in which he or she made a decision regarding the merits of the determination being appealed. The Chairperson need not serve on the Appeals Board with respect to all cases. [Amended 7/3/08 by 73 FR 38117.]

Appellant means any person filing an appeal under subpart D of this part.

Director means the Director of any department of the PBGC and includes the Director of the PBGC, Deputy Directors, and the General Counsel. [Amended 7/3/08 by 73 FR 38117.]

[¶ 15,331B]

§4003.3 **PBGC assistance in obtaining information.** A person who lacks information or documents necessary to file a request for review pursuant to subpart C or D of this part, or necessary to a decision whether to seek review, or necessary to participate in an appeal pursuant to §4003.57 of this part or necessary to a decision whether to participate, may request the PBGC's assistance in obtaining information or documents in the possession of a party other than the PBGC. The request shall state or describe the missing information or documents, the reason why the person needs the information or documents, and the reason why the person needs the assistance of the PBGC in obtaining the information or documents. The request may also include a request for an extension of time to file pursuant to §4003.4 of this part.

[¶ 15,331C]

§4003.4 **Extension of time**. (a) *General rule*. When a document is required under this part to be filed within a prescribed period of time, an extension of time to file will be granted only upon good cause shown and only when the request for an extension is made before the expiration of the time prescribed. The request for an extension shall be in writing and state why additional time is needed and the amount of additional time requested. The filing of a request for an extension shall stop the running of the prescribed period of time. When a request for an extension is granted, the PBGC shall notify the person requesting the extension, in writing, of the amount of additional time granted. When a request for an extension is denied, the PBGC shall so notify the requestor in writing, and the prescribed period of time shall resume running from the date of denial.

(b) *Disaster relief*. When the President of the United States declares that, under the Disaster Relief Act of 1974, as amended (42 U.S.C. 5121, 5122(2), 5141(b)), a major disaster exists, the Director of the PBGC (or his or her designee) may, by issuing one or more notices of disaster relief, extend the due date for filing a request for reconsideration under §4003.32 or an appeal under §4003.52 by up to 180 days. [Amended 7/3/08 by 73 FR 38117.]

(1) The due date extension or extensions shall be available only to an aggrieved person who is residing in, or whose principal place of business is within, a designated disaster area, or with respect to whom the office of the service provider, bank, insurance company, or other person maintaining the information necessary to file the request for reconsideration or appeal is within a designated disaster area; and

(2) The request for reconsideration or appeal shall identify the filing as one for which the due date extension is available.

[¶ 15,331D]

§4003.5 **Non-timely request for review**. The PBGC will process a request for review of an initial determination that was not filed within the prescribed period of time for requesting review (see §§4003.32 and 4003.52) if—

(a) The person requesting review demonstrates in his or her request that he or she did not file a timely request for review because he or she neither knew nor, with due diligence, could have known of the initial determination; and

(b) The request for review is filed within 30 days after the date the aggrieved person, exercising due diligence at all relevant times, first learned of the initial determination where the requested review is reconsideration, or within 45 days after the date the aggrieved person, exercising due diligence at all relevant times, first learned of the initial determination where the request for review is an appeal.

[¶ 15,331E]

§4003.6 **Representation**. A person may file any document or make any appearance that is required or permitted by this part on his or her own behalf or he or she may designate a representative. When the representative is not an attorney-at-law, a notarized power of attorney, signed by the person making the designation, which authorizes the representation and specifies the scope of representation shall be filed with the PBGC in accordance with §4003.9(b) of this part.

[¶ 15,331F]

§4003.7 **Exhaustion of administrative remedies**. Except as provided in §4003.22(b), a person aggrieved by an initial determination of the PBGC covered by this part, other than a determination subject to reconsideration that is issued by a Department Director, has not exhausted his or her administrative remedies until he or she has filed a request for reconsideration under subpart C of this part or an appeal under subpart D of this part, whichever is applicable, and a decision granting or denying the relief requested has been issued.

[¶ 15,331G]

§4003.8 **Request for confidential treatment**. If any person filing a document with the PBGC believes that some or all of the information contained in the document is exempt from the mandatory public disclosure requirements of the Freedom of Information Act, 5 U.S.C. 552, he

or she shall specify the information with respect to which confidentiality is claimed and the grounds therefor.

[¶ 15,331H]

§4003.9 **Method and date of filing**. (a) *Method of filing*. The PBGC applies the rules in subpart A of part 4000 of this chapter to determine permissible methods of filing with the PBGC under this part.

(b) *Date of filing*. The PBGC applies the rules in subpart C of part 4000 of this chapter to determine the date that a submission under this part was filed with the PBGC.

[¶ 15,331I]

§4003.10 **Computation of time**. The PBGC applies the rules in subpart D of part 4000 of this chapter to compute any time period under this part.

Subpart B—Initial Determinations

[¶ 15,332]

§4003.21 **Form and contents of initial determinations**. All determinations to which this subpart applies shall be in writing, shall state the reason for the determination, and, except when effective on the date of issuance as provided in §4003.22(b), shall contain notice of the right to request review of the determination pursuant to subpart C or subpart D of this part, as applicable, and a brief description of the procedures for requesting review.

[¶ 15,332A]

§4003.22 **Effective date of determinations**. (a) *General Rule*. Except as provided in paragraph (b) of this section, an initial determination covered by this subpart will not become effective until the prescribed period of time for filing a request for reconsideration under subpart C of this part or an appeal under subpart D of this part, whichever is applicable, has elapsed. The filing of a request for review under subpart C or D of this part shall automatically stay the effectiveness of a determination until a decision on the request for review has been issued by the PBGC.

(b) *Exception*. The PBGC may, in its discretion, order that the initial determination in a case is effective on the date it is issued. When the PBGC makes such an order, the initial determination shall state that the determination is effective on the date of issuance and that there is no obligation to exhaust administrative remedies with respect to that determination by seeking review of it by the PBGC.

Subpart C—Reconsideration of Initial Determinations

[¶ 15,333]

§4003.31 **Who may request reconsideration**. Any person aggrieved by an initial determination of the PBGC to which this subpart applies may request reconsideration of the determination.

[¶ 15,333A]

§4003.32 **When to request reconsideration**. Except as provided in §§4003.4 and 4003.5, a request for reconsideration must be filed within 30 days after the date of the initial determination of which reconsideration is sought or, when administrative review includes a procedure in part 4903 of this chapter, by the date that is specified in the PBGC's notice of the right to request review. [Amended 11/5/2010 (75 FR 68203).]

[¶ 15,333B]

§4003.33 **Where to submit request for reconsideration**. A request for reconsideration shall be submitted to the Director of the department within the PBGC that issued the initial determination, except that a request for reconsideration of a determination described in §4003.1(b)(3)(ii) shall be submitted to the Director. See Sec. 4000.4 of this chapter for information on where to file. [Amended 7/3/08 by 73 FR 38117.]

[¶ 15,333C]

§4003.34 **Form and contents of request for reconsideration**. A request for reconsideration shall—

(a) Be in writing;

(b) Be clearly designated as a request for reconsideration;

(c) Contain a statement of the grounds for reconsideration and the relief sought; and

(d) Reference all pertinent information already in the possession of the PBGC and include any additional information believed to be relevant.

[¶ 15,333D]

§ 4003.35 **Final decision on request for reconsideration**. (a) Except as provided in paragraphs (a)(1) or (a)(2), final decisions on requests for reconsideration will be issued by the same department of the PBGC that issued the initial determination, by an official whose level of authority in that department is higher than that of the person who issued the initial determination.

(1) When an initial determination is issued by a Department Director, the Department Director (or an official designated by the Department Director) will issue the final decision on request for reconsideration of a determination other than one described in § 4003.1(b)(3)(ii).

(2) The Director (or an official designated by the Director) will issue the final decision on a request for reconsideration of a determination described in § 4003.1(b)(3)(ii). [Amended 7/3/08 by 73 FR 38117.]

(b) The final decision on a request for reconsideration shall be in writing, specify the relief granted, if any, state the reason(s) for the decision, and state that the person has exhausted his or her administrative remedies.

Subpart D—Administrative Appeals

[¶ 15,334]

§ 4003.51 **Who may appeal or participate in appeals**. Any person aggrieved by an initial determination to which this subpart applies may file an appeal. Any person who may be aggrieved by a decision under this subpart granting the relief requested in whole or in part may participate in the appeal in the manner provided in § 4003.57.

[¶ 15,334A]

§ 4003.52 **When to file**. Except as provided in §§ 4003.4 and 4003.5, an appeal under this subpart must be filed within 45 days after the date of the initial determination being appealed or, when administrative review includes a procedure in part 4903 of this chapter, by the date that is specified in the PBGC's notice of the right to request review. [Amended 11/5/2010 (75 FR 68203).]

[¶ 15,334B]

§ 4003.53 **Where to file**. An appeal or a request for an extension of time to appeal shall be submitted to the Appeals Board. See Sec. 4000.4 of this chapter for additional information on where to file. [Amended 7/3/08 by 73 FR 38117.]

[¶ 15,334C]

§ 4003.54 **Contents of appeal**. (a) An appeal shall—

(1) Be in writing;

(2) Be clearly designated as an appeal;

(3) Specifically explain why PBGC's determination is wrong and the result the appellant is seeking; [Revised 7/3/08 by 73 FR 38117.]

(4) Describe the relevant information the appellant believes is known by PBGC, and summarize any other information the appellant believes is relevant. It is important to include copies of any documentation that support the appellant's claim or the appellant's assertions about this information; [Revised 7/3/08 by 73 FR 38117.]

(5) State whether the appellant desires to appear in person or through a representative before the Appeals Board; and

(6) State whether the appellant desires to present witnesses to testify before the Appeals Board, and if so, state why the presence of witnesses will further the decision-making process.

(b) In any case where the appellant believes that another person may be aggrieved if the PBGC grants the relief sought, the appeal shall also include the name(s) and address(es) (if known) of such other person(s).

[¶ 15,334D]

§ 4003.55 **Opportunity to appear and to present witnesses**. (a) At the discretion of the Appeals Board, any appearance permitted under this subpart may be before a hearing officer designated by the Appeals Board.

(b) An opportunity to appear before the Appeals Board (or a hearing officer) and an opportunity to present witnesses will be permitted at the discretion of the Appeals Board. In general, an opportunity to appear will be permitted if the Appeals Board determines that there is a dispute as to a material fact; an opportunity to present witnesses will be permitted when the Appeals Board determines that witnesses will contribute to the resolution of a factual dispute.

(c) Appearances permitted under this section will take place at the main offices of the PBGC, 1200 K Street NW., Washington, DC 20005-4026, unless the Appeals Board, in its discretion, designates a different location, either on its own initiative or at the request of the appellant or a third party participating in the appeal.

[¶ 15,334E]

§ 4003.56 **Consolidation of appeals**. (a) *When consolidation may be required*. Whenever multiple appeals are filed that arise out of the same or similar facts and seek the same or similar relief, the Appeals Board may, in its discretion, order the consolidation of all or some of the appeals.

(b) *Representation of parties*. Whenever the Appeals Board orders the consolidation of appeals, the appellants may designate one (or more) of their number to represent all of them for all purposes relating to their appeals.

(c) *Decision by Appeals Board*. The decision of the Appeals Board in a consolidated appeal shall be binding on all appellants whose appeals were subject to the consolidation.

[¶ 15,334F]

§ 4003.57 **Appeals affecting third parties**. (a) Before the Appeals Board issues a decision granting, in whole or in part, the relief requested in an appeal, it shall make a reasonable effort to notify third persons who will be aggrieved by the decision of the following:

(1) The pendency of the appeal;

(2) The grounds upon which the appeal is based;

(3) The grounds upon which the Appeals Board is considering reversing the initial determination;

(4) The right to submit written comments on the appeal;

(5) The right to request an opportunity to appear in person or through a representative before the Appeals Board and to present witnesses; and

(6) That no further opportunity to present information to the PBGC with respect to the determination under appeal will be provided.

(b) Written comments and a request to appear before the Appeals Board must be filed within 45 days after the date of the notice from the Appeals Board.

(c) If more than one third party is involved, their participation in the appeal may be consolidated pursuant to the provisions of § 4003.56.

[¶ 15,334G]

§ 4003.58 **Powers of the Appeals Board**. (a) In addition to the powers specifically described in this part, the Appeals Board may request the submission of any information or the appearance of any person it considers necessary to resolve a matter before it and to enter any order it considers necessary for or appropriate to the disposition of any matter before it. [Redesignated as paragraph (a) 7/3/08 by 73 FR 38117.]

(b) The Appeals Board may refer certain appeals to another PBGC department or to Appeals Board staff to provide a response to the appellant. The response from another PBGC department or Board staff shall be in writing and address the matters raised in the appeal. The response may be in the form of an explanation or corrected benefit determination. In either case, the appellant will have 45 calendar-days from the date of the response to file a written request for review by the Appeals Board. If a written request for review is not filed with the Appeals Board within the 45-calendar-day period the determination shall become effective pursuant to § 4003.22(a).

(1) Appeals that may be referred to another PBGC department or to the Board staff include those that—

(i) Request an explanation of the initial determination being appealed;

(ii) Dispute specific data used in the determination, such as date of hire, date of retirement, date of termination of employment, length of service, compensation, marital status and form of benefit elected; or

(iii) Request an explanation of the limits on benefits payable by PBGC under Part 4022, Subpart B, such as the maximum guarantee-able benefit and phase-in of the PBGC guarantee.

(2) An explanation or corrected benefit determination issued under this subsection is not considered a decision of the Appeals Board. If an appellant aggrieved by PBGC's initial determination is issued an explanation or corrected benefit determination under this section, the appellant has not exhausted his or her administrative remedies until the appellant has filed a timely request with the Appeals Board for review and the Appeals Board has issued a decision granting or denying the relief requested. See § 4003.7 of this part. [Added 7/3/08 by 73 FR 38117.]

[¶ 15,334H]

§ 4003.59 **Decision by the Appeals Board**. (a) In reaching its decision, the Appeals Board shall consider those portions of the file relating to the initial determination, all material submitted by the appellant and any third parties in connection with the appeal, and any additional information submitted by PBGC staff.

(b) The decision of the Appeals Board constitutes the final agency action by the PBGC with respect to the determination which was the subject of the appeal and is binding on all parties who participated in the appeal and who were notified pursuant to § 4003.57 of their right to participate in the appeal.

(c) The decision of the Appeals Board shall be in writing, specify the relief granted, if any, state the bases for the decision, including a brief statement of the facts or legal conclusions supporting the decision, and state that the appellant has exhausted his or her administrative remedies.

[¶ 15,334I]

§ 4003.60 **Referral of appeal to the Director**. The Appeals Board may, in its discretion, refer any appeal to the Director of the PBGC for decision. In such a case, the Director shall have all the powers vested in the Appeals Board by this subpart and the decision of the Director shall meet the requirements of and have the effect of a decision issued under § 4003.59 of this part. [Amended 7/3/08 by 73 FR 38117.]

[¶ 15,334J]

§ 4003.61 **Action by a single Appeals Board member**. (a) *Authority to act.* Notwithstanding any other provision of this part, any member of the Appeals Board has the authority to take any action that the Appeals Board could take with respect to a routine appeal as defined in paragraph (b) of this section.

(b) *Routine appeal defined.* For purposes of this section, a routine appeal is any appeal that does not raise a significant issue of law or a precedent-setting issue. This would generally include any appeal that—

(1) Is outside the jurisdiction of the Appeals Board (for example, an appeal challenging the plan's termination date);

(2) Is filed by a person other than an aggrieved person or an aggrieved person's authorized representative;

(3) Is untimely and presents no grounds for waiver or extension of the time limit for filing the appeal, or only grounds that are clearly without merit;

(4) Presents grounds that clearly warrant or clearly do not warrant the relief requested;

(5) Presents only factual issues that are not reasonably expected to affect other appeals (for example, the participant's date of birth or date of hire); or

(6) Presents only issues that are controlled by settled principles of existing law, including Appeals Board precedent (for example, an issue of plan interpretation that has been resolved by the Appeals Board in a decision on an appeal by another participant in the same plan).

[¶ 15,339]
PARTICIPANT AND PLAN SPONSOR ADVOCATE

Act Sec. 4004.(a) IN GENERAL. The board of directors of the corporation shall select a Participant and Plan Sponsor Advocate from the candidates nominated by the advisory committee to the corporation under section 4002(h)(1) and without regard to the provisions of title 5, United States Code, relating to appointments in the competitive service or Senior Executive Service.

(b) DUTIES. The Participant and Plan Sponsor Advocate shall—

(1) act as a liaison between the corporation, sponsors of defined benefit pension plans insured by the corporation, and participants in pension plans trusteed by the corporation;

(2) advocate for the full attainment of the rights of participants in plans trusteed by the corporation;

(3) assist pension plan sponsors and participants in resolving disputes with the corporation;

(4) identify areas in which participants and plan sponsors have persistent problems in dealings with the corporation;

(5) to the extent possible, propose changes in the administrative practices of the corporation to mitigate problems;

(6) identify potential legislative changes which may be appropriate to mitigate problems; and

(7) refer instances of fraud, waste, and abuse, and violations of law to the Office of the Inspector General of the corporation.

(c) REMOVAL. If the Participant and Plan Sponsor Advocate is removed from office or is transferred to another position or location within the corporation or the Department of Labor, the board of the directors of the corporation shall communicate in writing the reasons for any such removal or transfer to Congress not less than 30 days before the removal or transfer. Nothing in this subsection shall prohibit a personnel action otherwise authorized by law, other than transfer or removal.

(d) COMPENSATION. The annual rate of basic pay for the Participant and Plan Sponsor Advocate shall be the same rate as the highest rate of basic pay established for the Senior Executive Service under section 5382 of title 5, United States Code, or, if the board of directors of the corporation so determines, at a rate fixed under section 9503 of such title.

(e) ANNUAL REPORT.—

(1) IN GENERAL. Not later than December 31 of each calendar year, the Participant and Plan Sponsor Advocate shall report to the Health, Education, Labor, and Pensions Committee of the Senate, the Committee on Finance of the Senate, the Committee on Education and the Workforce of the House of Representatives, and the Committee on Ways and Means of the House of Representatives on the activities of the Office of the Participant and Plan Sponsor Advocate during the fiscal year ending during such calendar year.

(2) CONTENT. Each report submitted under paragraph (1) shall—

(A) summarize the assistance requests received from participants and plan sponsors and describe the activities, and evaluate the effectiveness, of the Participant and Plan Sponsor Advocate during the preceding year;

(B) identify significant problems the Participant and Plan Sponsor Advocate has identified;

(C) include specific legislative and regulatory changes to address the problems; and

(D) identify any actions taken to correct problems identified in any previous report.

(3) CONCURRENT SUBMISSION. The Participant and Plan Sponsor Advocate shall submit a copy of each report to the Secretary of Labor, the Director of the corporation, and any other appropriate official at the same time such report is submitted to the committees of Congress under paragraph (1).

Amendments

The above amendment is effective on the date of enactment (July 6, 2012).

P.L. 112-141, §40232(a):

Added new ERISA Sec. 4004 to read as above.

[¶ 15,340]
[SEC. 4004 REPEALED]

Act Sec. 4004 Repealed.

Amendment:

P.L. 99-272:

Act Sec. 11016(c)(6) repealed ERISA Sec. 4004, effective on April 7, 1986.

Prior to repeal, ERISA Sec. 4004 read as follows:

TEMPORARY AUTHORITY FOR INITIAL PERIOD

Act Sec. 4004. (a) Notwithstanding anything to the contrary in this title, the corporation may, upon receipt of notice that a plan is to be terminated or upon making a determination described in section 4042, appoint a receiver whose powers shall take effect immediately. The receiver shall assume control of such plan and its assets, protecting the interests of all interested persons during subsequent proceedings.

(b)(1) Within a reasonable time, not exceeding 20 days, after the appointment of a receiver under subsection (a), the corporation shall apply to an appropriate United States district court for a decree approving such appointment. The court to which application is made shall issue a decree approving such appointment unless it determines that such approval would not be in the best interests of the participants and beneficiaries of the plan.

(2) If the court to which application is made under paragraph (1) dismisses the application with prejudice, or if the corporation fails to apply for a degree under paragraph (1) within 20 days after the appointment of the receiver, the receiver shall transfer all assets and records of the plan held by him to the plan administrator within 3 business days after such dismissal or the expiration of the 20 day period. The receiver shall not be liable to the plan or to any other person for his acts as receiver other than for willful misconduct, or for conduct in violation of the provisions of part 4 of subpart B of title I of this Act (except to the extent that the provisions of section 4042(d)(1)(A) provide otherwise).

(c) The corporation is authorized, as an alternative to appointing a receiver under subsection (a), to direct a plan administrator to apply to a district court of the United States for the appointment of a receiver to assume control of the plan and its assets for the purpose of protecting the interests of all interested persons until the plan can be terminated under the provisions of this title.

(d) A receiver appointed under this section has the powers of a trustee under section 4042(d)(1)(A) and (B), and shall report to the corporation and the court on the plan from time to time as required by either the corporation or the court. As soon as practicable after his appointment, a receiver appointed under this section shall determine whether the assets of the plan are sufficient to discharge when due all obligations of the plan with respect to benefits guaranteed under this title in accordance with the requirements of section 4044. If the determination of the receiver is approved by the corporation and the court, the receiver shall proceed as if he were a trustee appointed under section 4042.

(e) A receiver may not be appointed under this section more than 270 days after the date of enactment of this Act.

(f) In addition to its other powers under this title, for only the first 270 days after the date of enactment of this Act the corporation may—

(1) contract for printing without regard to the provisions of chapter 5 of this title 44, United States Code,

(2) waive any notice required under this title if the corporation finds that a waiver is necessary or appropriate.

(3) extend the 90-day period referred to in section 4041(a) for an additional 90 days without the agreement of the plan administrator and without application to a court as required under section 4041(d), and

(4) Waive the application of the provisions of sections 4062, 4063, and 4064 to, or reduce the liability imposed under such sections on, any employer with respect to a plan terminating during that 270 day period if the corporation determines that such waiver or reduction is necessary to avoid unreasonable hardship in any case in which the employer was not able, as a practical matter, to continue the plan.

[¶ 15,350]
PENSION BENEFIT GUARANTY FUNDS

Act Sec. 4005.(a) ESTABLISHMENT OF FOUR REVOLVING FUNDS ON BOOKS OF TREASURY OF THE UNITED STATES.—There are established on the books of the Treasury of the United States four revolving funds to be used by the corporation in carrying out its duties under this title. One of the funds shall be used with respect to basic benefits guaranteed under section 4022, one of the funds shall be used with respect to basic benefits guaranteed under section 4022A, one of the funds shall be used with respect to nonbasic benefits guaranteed under section 4022 (if any), and the remaining fund shall be used with respect to nonbasic benefits guaranteed under section 4022A (if any), other than subsection (g)(2) thereof (if any). Whenever in this title reference is made to the term "fund" the reference shall be considered to refer to the appropriate fund established under this subsection.

Act Sec. 4005.(b)(1) CREDITS TO FUNDS; AVAILABILITY OF FUNDS; INVESTMENT OF MONEYS IN EXCESS OF CURRENT NEEDS.—Each fund established under this section shall be credited with the appropriate portion of—

(A) premiums, penalties, interest, and charges collected under this title,

(B) the value of the assets of a plan administered under section 4042 by a trustee to the extent that they exceed the liabilities of such plan,

(C) the amount of any employer liability payments under subtitle D, to the extent that such payments exceed liabilities of the plan (taking into account all other plan assets),

(D) earnings on investments of the fund or on assets credited to the fund under this subsection,

(E) attorney's fees awarded to the corporation, and

(F) receipts from any other operations under this title.

(2) Subject to the provisions of subsection (a), each fund shall be available—

(A) for making such payments as the corporation determines are necessary to pay benefits guaranteed under section 4022 or 4022A or benefits payable under section 4050,

(B) to purchase assets from a plan being terminated by the corporation when the corporation determines such purchase will best protect the interests of the corporation, participants in the plan being terminated, and other insured plans,

(C) to pay the operational and administrative expenses of the corporation, including reimbursement of the expenses incurred by the Department of the Treasury in maintaining the funds, and the Comptroller General in auditing the corporation and,

(D) to pay to participants and beneficiaries the estimated amount of benefits which are guaranteed by the corporation under this title and the estimated amount of other benefits to which plan assets are allocated under section 4044, under single-employer plans which are unable to pay benefits when due or which are abandoned.

(3)(A) Whenever the corporation determines that the moneys of any fund are in excess of current needs, it may request the investment of such amounts as it determines advisable by the Secretary of the Treasury in obligations issued or guaranteed by the United States.

(B) Notwithstanding subparagraph (A)—

(i) the amounts of premiums received under section 4006 with respect to the fund to be used for basic benefits under section 4022A in a fiscal year in the period beginning with fiscal year 2016 and ending with fiscal year 2020 shall be placed in a noninterest-bearing account within such fund in the following amounts:

(I) for fiscal year 2016, $108,000,000;

(II) for fiscal year 2017, $111,000,000;

(III) for fiscal year 2018, $113,000,000;

(IV) for fiscal year 2019, $149,000,000; and

(V) for fiscal year 2020, $296,000,000;

(ii) premiums received in fiscal years specified in subclauses (I) through (V) of clause (i) shall be allocated in order first to the noninterest-bearing account in the amount specified and second to any other accounts within such fund; and

(iii) financial assistance, as provided under section 4261, shall be withdrawn proportionately from the noninterest-bearing and other accounts within the fund.

Act Sec. 4005. (c) [Repealed]

Act Sec. 4005. (d)(1) ESTABLISHMENT OF FIFTH FUND; PURPOSE; AVAILABILITY; ETC.—A fifth fund shall be established for the reimbursement of uncollectible withdrawal liability under section 4222, and shall be credited with the appropriate—

(A) premiums, penalties, and interest charges collected under this title, and

(B) earnings on investments of the fund or on assets credited to the fund.

The fund shall be available to make payments pursuant to the supplemental program established under section 4222, including those expenses and other charges determined to be appropriate by the corporation.

(2) The corporation may invest amounts of the fund in such obligations as the corporation considers appropriate.

Act Sec. 4005. (e)(1) ESTABLISHMENT OF SIXTH FUND; PURPOSE; AVAILABILITY; ETC.—A sixth fund shall be established for the supplemental benefit guarantee program provided under section 4022A(g)(2).

(2) Such fund shall be credited with the appropriate—

(A) premiums, penalties, and interest charges collected under section 4022A(g)(2), and

(B) earnings on investments of the fund or on assets credited to the fund.

The fund shall be available for making payments pursuant to the supplemental benefit guarantee program established under section 4022A(g)(2), including those expenses and other charges determined to be appropriate by the corporation.

(3) The corporation may invest amounts of the fund in such obligations as the corporation considers appropriate.

Act Sec. 4005. (f)(1) DEPOSIT OF PREMIUMS INTO A SEPARATE REVOLVING FUND.—A seventh fund shall be established and credited with—

(A) premiums, penalties, and interest charges collected under section 4006(a)(3)(A)(i) (not described in subparagraph (B)) to the extent attributable to the amount of the premium in excess of $8.50,

(B) premiums, penalties, and interest charges collected under section 4006(a)(3)(E), and

(C) earnings on investments of the fund or on assets credited to the fund.

(2) Amounts in the fund shall be available for transfer to other funds established under this section with respect to a single-employer plan but shall not be available to pay—

(A) administrative costs of the corporation, or

(B) benefits under any plan which was terminated before October 1, 1988, unless no other amounts are available for such payment.

The corporation may invest amounts of the fund in such obligations as the corporation considers appropriate.

Act Sec. 4005. (g)(1) OTHER USE OF FUNDS; DEPOSITS OF REPAYMENTS.—Amounts in any fund established under this section may be used only for the purposes for which such fund was established and may not be used to make loans to (or on behalf of) any other fund or to finance any other activity of the corporation.

(2) Any repayment to the corporation of any amount paid out of any fund in connection with a multiemployer plan shall be deposited in such fund.

Act Sec. 4005. (h) VOTING BY CORPORATION OF STOCK PAID AS LIABILITY.—Any stock in a person liable to the corporation under this title which is paid to the corporation by such person or a member of such person's controlled group in satisfaction of such person's liability under this title may be voted only by the custodial trustees or outside money managers of the corporation.

Amendment:

P.L. 113-235, §131(b)(1), Div. O:

Amended ERISA Sec. 4005(b)(3) by striking "Whenever" and inserting "(A) Whenever" to read as above.

The above amendment is effective on the date of enactment (December 16, 2014).

P.L. 113-235, §131(b)(2), Div. O:

Amended ERISA Sec. 4005(b)(3) by inserting at the end a new subparagraph (B) to read as above.

The above amendment is effective on the date of enactment (December 16, 2014).

P.L. 112-141, §40234(a):

Amended ERISA Sec. 4005 by repealing subsection (c). Prior to amendment, ERISA Sec. 4005(c) read as follows:

"(c) AUTHORITY TO ISSUE NOTES OR OTHER OBLIGATIONS; PURCHASE BY SECRETARY OF THE TREASURY AS PUBLIC DEBT TRANSACTIONS.—The corporation is authorized to issue to the Secretary of the Treasury notes or other obligations in an aggregate amount of not to exceed $100,000,000, in such forms and denominations, bearing such maturities, and subject to such terms and conditions as may be prescribed by the Secretary of the Treasury. Such notes or other obligations shall bear interest at a rate determined by the Secretary of the Treasury, taking into consideration the current average market yield on outstanding marketable obligations of the United States of comparable maturities during the month preceding the issuance of such notes or other obligations of the corporation. The Secretary of the Treasury is authorized and directed to purchase any notes or other obligations issued by the corporation under this subsection, and for that purpose he is authorized to use as a public debt transaction the proceeds from the sale of any securities issued under the Second Liberty Bond Act, as amended, and the purposes for which securities may be issued under that Act, as amended, are extended to include any purchase of such notes and obligations. The Secretary of the Treasury may at any time sell any of the notes or other obligations acquired by him under this subsection. All redemptions, purchases, and sales by the Secretary of the Treasury of such notes or other obligations shall be treated as public debt transactions of the United States."

The above amendment is effective on the date of enactment (July 6, 2012).

P.L. 112-141, §40234(b)(1)(A)(i)(I) and (II):

Amended ERISA Sec. 4005(b)(1)(A)-(G) by striking subparagraph (A); and by redesignating subparagraphs (B) through (G) as subparagraphs (A) through (F), respectively. Prior to amendment, subparagraph (A) read as follows:

"(A) funds borrowed under subsection (c),"

The above amendment is effective on the date of enactment (July 6, 2012).

P.L. 112-141, §40234(b)(1)(A)(ii)(I) and (II):

Amended ERISA Sec. 4005(b)(2)(C)-(E) by striking subparagraph (C); and by redesignating subparagraphs (D) and (E) as subparagraphs (C) and (D), respectively. Prior to amendment, subparagraph (C) read as follows:

"(C) to repay to the Secretary of the Treasury such sums as may be borrowed (together with interest thereon) under subsection (c),"

The above amendment is effective on the date of enactment (July 6, 2012).

P.L. 112-141, §40234(b)(1)(A)(iii):

Amended ERISA Sec. 4005(b)(3) by striking "but," and all that follows through the end and inserting a period. Prior to amendment, paragraph (3) read as follows:

"(3) Whenever the corporation determines that the moneys of any fund are in excess of current needs, it may request the investment of such amounts as it determines advisable by the Secretary of the Treasury in obligations issued or guaranteed by the United States but, until all borrowings under subsection (c) have been repaid, the obligations in which such excess moneys are invested may not yield a rate of return in excess of the rate of interest payable on such borrowings."

The above amendment is effective on the date of enactment (July 6, 2012).

P.L. 112-141, §40234(b)(1)(B)(i) and (ii):

Amended ERISA Sec. 4005(g)(2) and (3) by striking paragraph (2); and by redesignating paragraph (3) as paragraph (2). Prior to amendment, paragraph (2) read as follows:

"(2) None of the funds borrowed under subsection (c) may be used to make loans to (or on behalf of) any fund other than a fund described in the second sentence of subsection (a)."

The above amendment is effective on the date of enactment (July 6, 2012).

P.L. 103-465, §776(b)(2):

Act Sec. 776(b)(2) amended ERISA Sec. 4005(b)(2)(A) by inserting "or benefits payable under section 4050" after "section 4022A".

The above amendment is effective with respect to distributions that occur in plan years commencing after final regulations implementing the amendment are prescribed by the Pension Benefit Guaranty Corporation.

P.L. 100-203, §9312(c)(4):

Amended ERISA Sec. 4005(g) by striking out "or fiduciaries with respect to trusts to which the requirements of section 4049 apply", effective for (A) plan terminations under section 4041(c) of ERISA with respect to which notices of intent to terminate are provided under section 4041(a)(2) of ERISA after December 17, 1987, and (B) plan terminations with respect to which proceedings are instituted by the Pension Benefit Guaranty Corporation under section 4042 of ERISA after December 17, 1987.

P.L. 100-203, §9331(d):

Amending ERISA Sec. 4005 by redesignating subsections (f) and (g) as subsections (g) and (h) and by adding subsection (f), to read as above, effective for fiscal years beginning after September 30, 1988.

P.L. 99-272:

Act Sec. 11016(a)(1) amended ERISA Sec. 4005(b)(2) by striking out "and" at the end of subparagraph (C), striking out the period at the end of subparagraph (D) and by adding a new subparagraph (E) to read as above.

Act Sec. 11016(a)(2) amended ERISA Sec. 4005(b)(1) by striking out "and" at the end of subparagraph (E), by redesignating subparagraph (F) as (G) and by adding a new subparagraph (F) to read as above.

Act Sec. 11016(c)(7) amended ERISA Sec. 4005 by adding a new subsection (g) to read as above.

These amendments take effect on the date of enactment.

P.L. 96-364, §403(a):

Amended Sec. 4005(a) to read as above and added new subsections (d), (e), and (f), effective September 26, 1980. Prior to amendment, Sec. 4005(a) read as follows:

"(a) There are established on the books of the Treasury of the United States four revolving funds to be used by the corporation in carrying out its duties under this title. One of the funds shall be used in connection with benefits guaranteed under sections 4022 and 4023 (but not non-basic benefits) with respect to plans other than multiemployer plans, one of the funds shall be used with respect to such benefits guaranteed under such sections (other than non-basic benefits) for multiemployer plans, one of the funds shall be used with respect to non-basic benefits, if any are guaranteed by the corporation under section 4022, for plans which are not multiemployer plans, and the remaining fund shall be used with respect to non-basic benefits, if any are guaranteed by the corporation under section 4022, for multiemployer plans. Whenever in this title reference is made to the term 'fund' the reference shall be considered to refer to the appropriate fund established under this subsection."

[¶ 15,360]
PREMIUM RATES

Act Sec. 4006. (a)(1) SCHEDULES FOR PREMIUM RATES AND BASES FOR APPLICATION; ESTABLISHMENT, COVERAGE, ETC.—The corporation shall prescribe such schedules of premium rates and bases for the application of those rates as may be necessary to provide sufficient revenue to the fund for the corporation to carry out its functions under this title. The premium rates charged by the corporation for any period shall be uniform for all plans, other than multiemployer plans, insured by the corporation with respect to basic benefits guaranteed by it under section 4022, and shall be uniform for all multiemployer plans with respect to basic benefits guaranteed by it under section 4022A.

(2) The corporation shall maintain separate schedules of premium rates, and bases for the application of those rates, for—

(A) basic benefits guaranteed by it under section 4022 for single-employer plans,

(B) basic benefits guaranteed by it under section 4022A for multiemployer plans,

(C) nonbasic benefits guaranteed by it under section 4022 for single-employer plans,

(D) nonbasic benefits guaranteed by it under section 4022A for multiemployer plans, and

(E) reimbursements of uncollectible withdrawal liability under section 4222.

The corporation may revise such schedules whenever it determines that revised schedules are necessary. Except as provided in section 4022A(f), in order to place a revised schedule described in subparagraph (A) and (B) in effect, the corporation shall proceed in accordance with subsection (b)(1), and such schedule shall apply only to plan years beginning more than 30 days after the date on which a joint resolution approving such revised schedule is enacted.

⟫⟫→ *Caution: ERISA Sec. 4006(a)(3)(A), below, prior to amendment by P.L. 114-74, applies to plan years beginning on or before December 31, 2016.*

(3)(A) Except as provided in subparagraph (C), the annual premium rate payable to the corporation by all plans for basic benefits guaranteed under this title is—

(i) in the case of a single-employer plan, an amount for each individual who is a participant in such plan during the plan year equal to the sum of the additional premium (if any) determined under subparagraph (E) and—

(I) for plan years beginning after December 31, 2005, and before January 1, 2013, $30;

(II) for plan years beginning after December 31, 2012, and before January 1, 2014, $42;

(III) for plan years beginning after December 31, 2013, and before January 1, 2015, $49;

(IV) for plan years beginning after December 31, 2014, and before January 1, 2016, $57; and

(V) for plan years beginning after December 31, 2015, and before January 1, 2017, $64.

(ii) in the case of a multiemployer plan, for the plan year within which the date of enactment of the Multiemployer Pension Plan Amendments Act of 1980 falls, an amount for each individual who is a participant in such plan for such plan year equal to the sum of—

(I) 50 cents, multiplied by a fraction the numerator of which is the number of months in such year ending on or before such date and the denominator of which is 12, and

(II) $1.00, multiplied by a fraction equal to 1 minus the fraction determined under clause (i),

(iii) in the case of a multiemployer plan, for plan years beginning after the date of enactment of the Multiemployer Pension Plan Amendments Act of 1980 and before January 1, 2006, an amount equal to—

(I) $1.40 for each participant, for the first, second, third, and fourth plan years,

(II) $1.80 for each participant, for the fifth and sixth plan years,

(III) $2.20 for each participant, for the seventh and eighth plan years, and

(IV) $2.60 for each participant, for the ninth plan year, and for each succeeding plan year,

(iv) in the case of a multiemployer plan, for plan years beginning after December 31, 2005, and before January 1, 2013, $8.00 for each individual who is a participant in such plan during the applicable plan year,

(v) in the case of a multiemployer plan, for plan years beginning after December 31, 2012, and before January 1, 2015, $12.00 for each individual who is a participant in such plan during the applicable plan year, or

(vi) in the case of a multiemployer plan, for plan years beginning after December 31, 2014, $26 for each individual who is a participant in such plan during the applicable plan year.

(B) the corporation may prescribe by regulation the extent to which the rate described in subparagraph (A)(i) applies more than once for any plan year to an individual participating in more than one plan maintained by the same employer and the corporation may prescribe regulations under which the rate described in clause (iii) or (iv) of subparagraph (A) will not apply to the same participant in any multiemployer plan more than once for any plan year.

(C)(i) If the sum of—

(I) the amounts in any fund for basic benefits guaranteed for multiemployer plans, and

(II) the value of any assets held by the corporation for payment of basic benefits guaranteed for multiemployer plans,

is for any calendar year less than 2 times the amount of basic benefits guaranteed by the corporation under this title for multiemployer plans which were paid out of any such fund or assets during the preceding calendar year, the annual premium rates under subparagraph (A) shall be increased to the next highest premium level necessary to insure that such sum will be at least 2 times greater than such amount during the following calendar year.

(ii) If the board of directors of the corporation determines that an increase in the premium rates under subparagraph (A) is necessary to provide assistance to plans which are receiving assistance under section 4261 and to plans the board finds are reasonably likely to require such assistance, the board may order such increase in the premium rates.

(iii) The maximum annual premium rate which may be established under this subparagraph is $2.60 for each participant.

(iv) The provisions of this subparagraph shall not apply if the annual premium rate is increased to a level in excess of $2.60 per participant under any other provisions of this title.

(D)(i) Not later than 120 days before the date on which an increase under subparagraph (C)(ii) is to become effective, the corporation shall publish in the Federal Register a notice of the determination described in subparagraph (C)(ii), the basis for the determination, the amount of the increase in the premium, and the anticipated increase in premium income that would result from the increase in the premium rate. The notice shall invite public comment, and shall provide for a public hearing if one is requested. Any such hearing shall be commenced not later than 60 days before the date on which the increase is to become effective.

(ii) The board of directors shall review the hearing record established under clause (i) and shall, not later than 30 days before the date on which the increase is to become effective, determine (after the consideration of the comments received) whether the amount of the increase should be changed and shall publish its determination in the Federal Register.

(E)(i) Except as provided in subparagraph (H), the additional premium determined under this subparagraph with respect to any plan for any plan year—

(I) shall be an amount equal to the amount determined under clause (ii) divided by the number of participants in such plan as of the close of the preceding plan year;

(II) in the case of plan years beginning in a calendar year after 2012 and before 2016, shall not exceed $400; and

(III) in the case of plan years beginning in a calendar year after 2015, shall not exceed $500.

(ii) The amount determined under this clause for any plan year shall be an amount equal to the applicable dollar amount under paragraph (8) for each $1,000 (or fraction thereof) of unfunded vested benefits under the plan as of the close of the preceding plan year.

(iii) For purposes of clause (ii), the term "unfunded vested benefits" means, for a plan year, the excess (if any) of—

(I) the funding target of the plan as determined under section 303(d) for the plan year by only taking into account vested benefits and by using the interest rate described in clause (iv), over

(II) the fair market value of plan assets for the plan year which are held by the plan on the valuation date.

(iv) The interest rate used in valuing benefits for purposes of subclause (I) of clause (iii) shall be equal to the first, second, or third segment rate for the month preceding the month in which the plan year begins, which would be determined under section 303(h)(2)(C) (notwithstanding any regulations issued by the corporation, determined by not taking into account any adjustment under clause (iv) thereof) if section 303(h)(2)(D) were applied by using the monthly yields for the month preceding the month in which the plan year begins on investment grade corporate bonds with varying maturities and in the top 3 quality levels rather than the average of such yields for a 24-month period.

(F) For each plan year beginning in a calendar year after 2006 and before 2013, there shall be substituted for the premium rate specified in clause (i) of subparagraph (A) an amount equal to the greater of—

(i) the product derived by multiplying the premium rate specified in clause (i) of subparagraph (A) by the ratio of—

(I) the national average wage index (as defined in section 209(k)(1) of the Social Security Act) for the first of the 2 calendar years preceding the calendar year in which such plan year begins, to

(II) the national average wage index (as so defined) for 2004 (2012 in the case of plan years beginning after calendar year 2014); and

(ii) the premium rate in effect under clause (i) of subparagraph (A) for plan years beginning in the preceding calendar year.

If the amount determined under this subparagraph is not a multiple of $1, such product shall be rounded to the nearest multiple of $1.

(G) For each plan year beginning in a calendar year after 2016, there shall be substituted for the premium rate specified in clause (i) of subparagraph (A) an amount equal to the greater of—

(i) the product derived by multiplying the premium rate specified in clause (i) of subparagraph (A) by the ratio of—

(I) the national average wage index (as defined in section 209(k)(1) of the Social Security Act) for the first of the 2 calendar years preceding the calendar year in which such plan year begins, to

(II) the national average wage index (as so defined) for 2014; and

(ii) the premium rate in effect under clause (i) of subparagraph (A) for plan years beginning in the preceding calendar year.

If the amount determined under this subparagraph is not a multiple of $1, such product shall be rounded to the nearest multiple of $1.

(H) For each plan year beginning in a calendar year after 2006, there shall be substituted for the premium rate specified in clause (iv) of subparagraph (A) an amount equal to the greater of—

(i) the product derived by multiplying the premium rate specified in clause (iv) of subparagraph (A) by the ratio of—

(I) the national average wage index (as defined in section 209(k)(1) of the Social Security Act) for the first of the 2 calendar years preceding the calendar year in which such plan year begins, to

(II) the national average wage index (as so defined) for 2004; and

(ii) the premium rate in effect under clause (iv) of subparagraph (A) for plan years beginning in the preceding calendar year.

If the amount determined under this subparagraph is not a multiple of $1, such product shall be rounded to the nearest multiple of $1.

(I)(i) In the case of an employer who has 25 or fewer employees on the first day of the plan year, the additional premium determined under subparagraph (E) for each participant shall not exceed $5 multiplied by the number of participants in the plan as of the close of the preceding plan year.

(ii) For purposes of clause (i), whether an employer has 25 or fewer employees on the first day of the plan year is determined by taking into consideration all of the employees of all members of the contributing sponsor's controlled group. In the case of a plan maintained by two or more contributing sponsors, the employees of all contributing sponsors and their controlled groups shall be aggregated for purposes of determining whether the 25-or-fewer-employees limitation has been satisfied.

(J) For each plan year beginning in a calendar year after 2013, there shall be substituted for the premium rate specified in clause (v) of subparagraph (A) an amount equal to the greater of—

(i) the product derived by multiplying the premium rate specified in clause (v) of subparagraph (A) by the ratio of—

(I) the national average wage index (as defined in section 209(k)(1) of the Social Security Act) for the first of the 2 calendar years preceding the calendar year in which such plan year begins, to

(II) the national average wage index (as so defined) for 2011; and

(ii) the premium rate in effect under clause (v) of subparagraph (A) for plan years beginning in the preceding calendar year.

If the amount determined under this subparagraph is not a multiple of $1, such product shall be rounded to the nearest multiple of $1.

(K) For each plan year beginning in a calendar year after 2013 and before 2016, there shall be substituted for the dollar amount specified in subclause (II) of subparagraph (E)(i) an amount equal to the greater of—

(i) the product derived by multiplying such dollar amount by the ratio of—

(I) the national average wage index (as defined in section 209(k)(1) of the Social Security Act) for the first of the 2 calendar years preceding the calendar year in which such plan year begins, to

(II) the national average wage index (as so defined) for 2011; and

(ii) such dollar amount for plan years beginning in the preceding calendar year.

If the amount determined under this subparagraph is not a multiple of $1, such product shall be rounded to the nearest multiple of $1.

(L) For each plan year beginning in a calendar year after 2016, there shall be substituted for the dollar amount specified in subclause (III) of subparagraph (E)(i) an amount equal to the greater of—

(i) the product derived by multiplying such dollar amount by the ratio of—

(I) the national average wage index (as defined in section 209(k)(1) of the Social Security Act) for the first of the 2 calendar years preceding the calendar year in which such plan year begins, to

(II) the national average wage index (as so defined) for 2014; and

(ii) such dollar amount for plan years beginning in the preceding calendar year.

If the amount determined under this subparagraph is not a multiple of $1, such product shall be rounded to the nearest multiple of $1.

(M) For each plan year beginning in a calendar year after 2015, there shall be substituted for the dollar amount specified in clause (vi) of subparagraph (A) an amount equal to the greater of—

(i) the product derived by multiplying such dollar amount by the ratio of—

(I) the national average wage index (as defined in section 209(k)(1) of the Social Security Act) for the first of the 2 calendar years preceding the calendar year in which such plan year begins, to

(II) the national average wage index (as so defined) for 2013; and

(ii) such dollar amount for plan years beginning in the preceding calendar year.

If the amount determined under this subparagraph is not a multiple of $1, such product shall be rounded to the nearest multiple of $1.

⯈⯈→ *Caution: ERISA Sec. 4006(a)(3)(A), below, as amended by P.L. 114-74, applies to plan years beginning after December 31, 2016.*

(3)(A) Except as provided in subparagraph (C), the annual premium rate payable to the corporation by all plans for basic benefits guaranteed under this title is—

(i) in the case of a single-employer plan, an amount for each individual who is a participant in such plan during the plan year equal to the sum of the additional premium (if any) determined under subparagraph (E) and—

(I) for plan years beginning after December 31, 2005, and before January 1, 2013, $30;

(II) for plan years beginning after December 31, 2012, and before January 1, 2014, $42;

(III) for plan years beginning after December 31, 2013, and before January 1, 2015, $49;

(IV) for plan years beginning after December 31, 2014, and before January 1, 2016, $57; and

(V) for plan years beginning after December 31, 2015, and before January 1, 2017, $64;

(VI) for plan years beginning after December 31, 2016, and before January 1, 2018, $69;

(VII) for plan years beginning after December 31, 2017, and before January 1, 2019, $74; and

(VIII) for plan years beginning after December 31, 2018, $80.

(ii) in the case of a multiemployer plan, for the plan year within which the date of enactment of the Multiemployer Pension Plan Amendments Act of 1980 falls, an amount for each individual who is a participant in such plan for such plan year equal to the sum of—

(I) 50 cents, multiplied by a fraction the numerator of which is the number of months in such year ending on or before such date and the denominator of which is 12, and

(II) $1.00, multiplied by a fraction equal to 1 minus the fraction determined under clause (i),

(iii) in the case of a multiemployer plan, for plan years beginning after the date of enactment of the Multiemployer Pension Plan Amendments Act of 1980 and before January 1, 2006, an amount equal to—

(I) $1.40 for each participant, for the first, second, third, and fourth plan years,

(II) $1.80 for each participant, for the fifth and sixth plan years,

(III) $2.20 for each participant, for the seventh and eighth plan years, and

(IV) $2.60 for each participant, for the ninth plan year, and for each succeeding plan year,

(iv) in the case of a multiemployer plan, for plan years beginning after December 31, 2005, and before January 1, 2013, $8.00 for each individual who is a participant in such plan during the applicable plan year,

(v) in the case of a multiemployer plan, for plan years beginning after December 31, 2012, and before January 1, 2015, $12.00 for each individual who is a participant in such plan during the applicable plan year, or

(vi) in the case of a multiemployer plan, for plan years beginning after December 31, 2014, $26 for each individual who is a participant in such plan during the applicable plan year.

(B) the corporation may prescribe by regulation the extent to which the rate described in subparagraph (A)(i) applies more than once for any plan year to an individual participating in more than one plan maintained by the same employer and the corporation may prescribe regulations under which the rate described in clause (iii) or (iv) of subparagraph (A) will not apply to the same participant in any multiemployer plan more than once for any plan year.

(C)(i) If the sum of—

(I) the amounts in any fund for basic benefits guaranteed for multiemployer plans, and

(II) the value of any assets held by the corporation for payment of basic benefits guaranteed for multiemployer plans,

is for any calendar year less than 2 times the amount of basic benefits guaranteed by the corporation under this title for multiemployer plans which were paid out of any such fund or assets during the preceding calendar year, the annual premium rates under subparagraph (A) shall be increased to the next highest premium level necessary to insure that such sum will be at least 2 times greater than such amount during the following calendar year.

(ii) If the board of directors of the corporation determines that an increase in the premium rates under subparagraph (A) is necessary to provide assistance to plans which are receiving assistance under section 4261 and to plans the board finds are reasonably likely to require such assistance, the board may order such increase in the premium rates.

(iii) The maximum annual premium rate which may be established under this subparagraph is $2.60 for each participant.

(iv) The provisions of this subparagraph shall not apply if the annual premium rate is increased to a level in excess of $2.60 per participant under any other provisions of this title.

(D)(i) Not later than 120 days before the date on which an increase under subparagraph (C)(ii) is to become effective, the corporation shall publish in the Federal Register a notice of the determination described in subparagraph (C)(ii), the basis for the determination, the amount of the increase in the premium, and the anticipated increase in premium income that would result from the increase in the premium rate. The notice shall invite public comment, and shall provide for a public hearing if one is requested. Any such hearing shall be commenced not later than 60 days before the date on which the increase is to become effective.

(ii) The board of directors shall review the hearing record established under clause (i) and shall, not later than 30 days before the date on which the increase is to become effective, determine (after the consideration of the comments received) whether the amount of the increase should be changed and shall publish its determination in the Federal Register.

(E)(i) Except as provided in subparagraph (H), the additional premium determined under this subparagraph with respect to any plan for any plan year—

(I) shall be an amount equal to the amount determined under clause (ii) divided by the number of participants in such plan as of the close of the preceding plan year;

(II) in the case of plan years beginning in a calendar year after 2012 and before 2016, shall not exceed $400; and

(III) in the case of plan years beginning in a calendar year after 2015, shall not exceed $500.

(ii) The amount determined under this clause for any plan year shall be an amount equal to the applicable dollar amount under paragraph (8) for each $1,000 (or fraction thereof) of unfunded vested benefits under the plan as of the close of the preceding plan year.

(iii) For purposes of clause (ii), the term "unfunded vested benefits" means, for a plan year, the excess (if any) of—

(I) the funding target of the plan as determined under section 303(d) for the plan year by only taking into account vested benefits and by using the interest rate described in clause (iv), over

(II) the fair market value of plan assets for the plan year which are held by the plan on the valuation date.

(iv) The interest rate used in valuing benefits for purposes of subclause (I) of clause (iii) shall be equal to the first, second, or third segment rate for the month preceding the month in which the plan year begins, which would be determined under section 303(h)(2)(C) (notwithstanding any regulations issued by the corporation, determined by not taking into account any adjustment under clause (iv) thereof) if section 303(h)(2)(D) were applied by using the monthly yields for the month preceding the month in which the plan year begins on investment grade corporate bonds with varying maturities and in the top 3 quality levels rather than the average of such yields for a 24-month period.

(F) For each plan year beginning in a calendar year after 2006 and before 2013, there shall be substituted for the premium rate specified in clause (i) of subparagraph (A) an amount equal to the greater of—

(i) the product derived by multiplying the premium rate specified in clause (i) of subparagraph (A) by the ratio of—

(I) the national average wage index (as defined in section 209(k)(1) of the Social Security Act) for the first of the 2 calendar years preceding the calendar year in which such plan year begins, to

(II) the national average wage index (as so defined) for 2004 (2012 in the case of plan years beginning after calendar year 2014); and

(ii) the premium rate in effect under clause (i) of subparagraph (A) for plan years beginning in the preceding calendar year.

If the amount determined under this subparagraph is not a multiple of $1, such product shall be rounded to the nearest multiple of $1.

⫸→ Caution: ERISA Sec. 4006(a)(3)(G), below, prior to amendment by P.L. 114-74, applies to plan years beginning on or before December 31, 2016.

(G) For each plan year beginning in a calendar year after 2016, there shall be substituted for the premium rate specified in clause (i) of subparagraph (A) an amount equal to the greater of—

(i) the product derived by multiplying the premium rate specified in clause (i) of subparagraph (A) by the ratio of—

(I) the national average wage index (as defined in section 209(k)(1) of the Social Security Act) for the first of the 2 calendar years preceding the calendar year in which such plan year begins, to

(II) the national average wage index (as so defined) for 2014; and

(ii) the premium rate in effect under clause (i) of subparagraph (A) for plan years beginning in the preceding calendar year.

If the amount determined under this subparagraph is not a multiple of $1, such product shall be rounded to the nearest multiple of $1.

⫸→ Caution: ERISA Sec. 4006(a)(3)(G), below, as amended by P.L. 114-74, applies to plan years beginning after December 31, 2016.

(G) For each plan year beginning in a calendar year after 2019, there shall be substituted for the premium rate specified in clause (i) of subparagraph (A) an amount equal to the greater of—

(i) the product derived by multiplying the premium rate specified in clause (i) of subparagraph (A) by the ratio of—

(I) the national average wage index (as defined in section 209(k)(1) of the Social Security Act) for the first of the 2 calendar years preceding the calendar year in which such plan year begins, to

(II) the national average wage index (as so defined) for 2017; and

(ii) the premium rate in effect under clause (i) of subparagraph (A) for plan years beginning in the preceding calendar year.

If the amount determined under this subparagraph is not a multiple of $1, such product shall be rounded to the nearest multiple of $1.

(H) For each plan year beginning in a calendar year after 2006, there shall be substituted for the premium rate specified in clause (iv) of subparagraph (A) an amount equal to the greater of—

(i) the product derived by multiplying the premium rate specified in clause (iv) of subparagraph (A) by the ratio of—

(I) the national average wage index (as defined in section 209(k)(1) of the Social Security Act) for the first of the 2 calendar years preceding the calendar year in which such plan year begins, to

(II) the national average wage index (as so defined) for 2004; and

(ii) the premium rate in effect under clause (iv) of subparagraph (A) for plan years beginning in the preceding calendar year.

If the amount determined under this subparagraph is not a multiple of $1, such product shall be rounded to the nearest multiple of $1.

(I)(i) In the case of an employer who has 25 or fewer employees on the first day of the plan year, the additional premium determined under subparagraph (E) for each participant shall not exceed $5 multiplied by the number of participants in the plan as of the close of the preceding plan year.

(ii) For purposes of clause (i), whether an employer has 25 or fewer employees on the first day of the plan year is determined by taking into consideration all of the employees of all members of the contributing sponsor's controlled group. In the case of a plan maintained by two or more contributing sponsors, the employees of all contributing sponsors and their controlled groups shall be aggregated for purposes of determining whether the 25-or-fewer-employees limitation has been satisfied.

(J) For each plan year beginning in a calendar year after 2013, there shall be substituted for the premium rate specified in clause (v) of subparagraph (A) an amount equal to the greater of—

(i) the product derived by multiplying the premium rate specified in clause (v) of subparagraph (A) by the ratio of—

(I) the national average wage index (as defined in section 209(k)(1) of the Social Security Act) for the first of the 2 calendar years preceding the calendar year in which such plan year begins, to

(II) the national average wage index (as so defined) for 2011; and

(ii) the premium rate in effect under clause (v) of subparagraph (A) for plan years beginning in the preceding calendar year.

If the amount determined under this subparagraph is not a multiple of $1, such product shall be rounded to the nearest multiple of $1.

(K) For each plan year beginning in a calendar year after 2013 and before 2016, there shall be substituted for the dollar amount specified in subclause (II) of subparagraph (E)(i) an amount equal to the greater of—

    (i) the product derived by multiplying such dollar amount by the ratio of—

       (I) the national average wage index (as defined in section 209(k)(1) of the Social Security Act) for the first of the 2 calendar years preceding the calendar year in which such plan year begins, to

       (II) the national average wage index (as so defined) for 2011; and

    (ii) such dollar amount for plan years beginning in the preceding calendar year.

If the amount determined under this subparagraph is not a multiple of $1, such product shall be rounded to the nearest multiple of $1.

    (L) For each plan year beginning in a calendar year after 2016, there shall be substituted for the dollar amount specified in subclause (III) of subparagraph (E)(i) an amount equal to the greater of—

    (i) the product derived by multiplying such dollar amount by the ratio of—

       (I) the national average wage index (as defined in section 209(k)(1) of the Social Security Act) for the first of the 2 calendar years preceding the calendar year in which such plan year begins, to

       (II) the national average wage index (as so defined) for 2014; and

    (ii) such dollar amount for plan years beginning in the preceding calendar year.

If the amount determined under this subparagraph is not a multiple of $1, such product shall be rounded to the nearest multiple of $1.

    (M) For each plan year beginning in a calendar year after 2015, there shall be substituted for the dollar amount specified in clause (vi) of subparagraph (A) an amount equal to the greater of—

    (i) the product derived by multiplying such dollar amount by the ratio of—

       (I) the national average wage index (as defined in section 209(k)(1) of the Social Security Act) for the first of the 2 calendar years preceding the calendar year in which such plan year begins, to

       (II) the national average wage index (as so defined) for 2013; and

    (ii) such dollar amount for plan years beginning in the preceding calendar year.

If the amount determined under this subparagraph is not a multiple of $1, such product shall be rounded to the nearest multiple of $1.

    (4) The corporation may prescribe, subject to the enactment of a joint resolution in accordance with this section or section 4022A(f), alternative schedules of premium rates, and bases for the application of those rates, for basic benefits guaranteed by it under sections 4022 and 4022A based, in whole or in part, on the risks insured by the corporation in each plan.

    (5)(A) In carrying out its authority under paragraph (1) to establish schedules of premium rates, and bases for the application of those rates, for nonbasic benefits guaranteed under sections 4022 and 4022A, the premium rates charged by the corporation for any period for nonbasic benefits guaranteed shall—

    (i) be uniform by category of nonbasic benefits guaranteed,

    (ii) be based on the risks insured in each category, and

    (iii) reflect the experience of the corporation (including experience which may be reasonably anticipated) in guaranteeing such benefits.

    (B) Notwithstanding subparagraph (A), premium rates charged to any multiemployer plan by the corporation for any period for supplemental guarantees under section 4022A(g)(2) may reflect any reasonable considerations which the corporation determines to be appropriate.

    (6)(A) In carrying out its authority under paragraph (1) to establish premium rates and bases for basic benefits guaranteed under section 4022 with respect to single-employer plans, the corporation shall establish such rates and bases in coverage schedules is accordance with the provisions of this paragraph.

    (B) The corporation may establish annual premiums for single-employer plans composed of the sum of—

    (i) a charge based on a rate applicable to the excess, if any, of the present value of the basic benefits of the plan which are guaranteed over the value of the assets of the plan, not in excess of 0.1 percent, and

    (ii) an additional charge based on a rate applicable to the present value of the basic benefits of the plan which are guaranteed.

The rate for the additional charge referred to in clause (ii) shall be set by the corporation for every year at a level which the corporation estimates will yield total revenue approximately equal to the total revenue to be derived by the corporation from the charges referred to in clause (i) of this subparagraph.

    (C) The corporation may establish annual premiums for single-employer plans based on—

    (i) the number of participants in a plan, but such premium rates shall not exceed the rates described in paragraph (3),

    (ii) unfunded basic benefits guaranteed under this title, but such premium rates shall not exceed the limitations applicable to charges referred to in subparagraph (B)(i), or

    (iii) total guaranteed basic benefits, but such premium rates shall not exceed the rates for additional charges referred to in subparagraph (B)(ii).

If the corporation uses two or more of the rate bases described in this subparagraph, the premium rates shall be designed to produce approximately equal amounts of aggregate premium revenue from each of the rate bases used.

    (D) For purposes of this paragraph, the corporation shall by regulation define the terms "value of assets" and "present value of the benefits of the plan which are guaranteed" in a manner consistent with the purposes of this title and the provisions of this section.

    (7) PREMIUM RATE FOR CERTAIN TERMINATED SINGLE-EMPLOYER PLANS.—

    (A) IN GENERAL. —If there is a termination of a single-employer plan under clause (ii) or (iii) of section 4041(c)(2)(B) or section 4042, there shall be payable to the corporation, with respect to each applicable 12-month period, a premium at a rate equal to $1,250 multiplied by the number of individuals who were participants in the plan immediately before the termination date. Such premium shall be in addition to any other premium under this section.

    (B) SPECIAL RULE FOR PLANS TERMINATED IN BANKRUPTCY REORGANIZATION. —In the case of a single-employer plan terminated under section 4041(c)(2)(B)(ii) or under section 4042 during pendency of any bankruptcy reorganization proceeding under chapter 11 of title 11, United States Code, or under any similar law of a State or a political subdivision of a State (or a case described in section 4041(c)(2)(B)(i) filed by or against such person has been converted, as of such date, to such a case in which reorganization is sought), subparagraph (A) shall not apply to such plan until the date of the discharge or dismissal of such person in such case.

    (C) APPLICABLE 12-MONTH PERIOD. —For purposes of subparagraph (A)—

    (i) IN GENERAL. The term "applicable 12-month period" means—

       (I) the 12-month period beginning with the first month following the month in which the termination date occurs, and

       (II) each of the first two 12-month periods immediately following the period described in subclause (I).

    (ii) PLANS TERMINATED IN BANKRUPTCY REORGANIZATION. —In any case in which the requirements of subparagraph (B) are met in connection with the termination of the plan with respect to 1 or more persons described in such subparagraph, the 12-month period described in clause (i)(I) shall be the 12-month period beginning with the first month following the month which includes the earliest date as of which each such person is discharged or dismissed in the case described in such clause in connection with such person.

(D) COORDINATION WITH SECTION 4007.—

(i) Notwithstanding section 4007—

(I) premiums under this paragraph shall be due within 30 days after the beginning of any applicable 12-month period, and

(II) the designated payor shall be the person who is the contributing sponsor as of immediately before the termination date.

(ii) The fifth sentence of section 4007(a) shall not apply in connection with premiums determined under this paragraph.

⋙→ *Caution: ERISA Sec. 4006(a)(8), below, prior to amendment by P.L. 114-74, applies to plan years beginning on or before December 31, 2016.*

(8) APPLICABLE DOLLAR AMOUNT FOR VARIABLE RATE PREMIUM. For purposes of paragraph (3)(E)(ii)—

(A) IN GENERAL. Except as provided in subparagraphs (B) and (C), the applicable dollar amount shall be—

(i) $9 for plan years beginning in a calendar year before 2015;

(ii) for plan years beginning in calendar year 2015, the amount in effect for plan years beginning in 2014 (determined after application of subparagraph (C));

(iii) for plan years beginning after calendar year 2015, the amount in effect for plan years beginning in 2015 (determined after application of subparagraph (C)); and

(iv) for plan years beginning after calendar year 2016, the amount in effect for plan years beginning in 2016 (determined after application of subparagraph (C)).

(B) ADJUSTMENT FOR INFLATION. For each plan year beginning in a calendar year after 2012, there shall be substituted for the applicable dollar amount specified under subparagraph (A) an amount equal to the greater of—

(i) the product derived by multiplying such applicable dollar amount for plan years beginning in that calendar year by the ratio of—

(I) the national average wage index (as defined in section 209(k)(1) of the Social Security Act) for the first of the 2 calendar years preceding the calendar year in which such plan year begins, to

(II) the national average wage index (as so defined) for the base year; and

(ii) such applicable dollar amount in effect for plan years beginning in the preceding calendar year.

If the amount determined under this subparagraph is not a multiple of $1, such product shall be rounded to the nearest multiple of $1.

(C) ADDITIONAL INCREASE IN 2014 AND 2015. The applicable dollar amount determined under subparagraph (A) (after the application of subparagraph (B)) shall be increased—

(i) in the case of plan years beginning in calendar year 2014, by $4;

(ii) in the case of plan years beginning in calendar year 2015, by $10; and

(iii) in the case of plan years beginning in calendar year 2016, by $5.

(D) BASE YEAR. For purposes of subparagraph (B), the base year is—

(i) 2010, in the case of plan years beginning in calendar year 2013 or 2014;

(ii) 2012, in the case of plan years beginning in calendar year 2015;

(iii) 2013, in the case of plan years beginning after calendar year 2015; and

(iv) 2014, in the case of plan years beginning after calendar year 2016.

⋙→ *Caution: ERISA Sec. 4006(a)(8), below, as amended by P.L. 114-74, applies to plan years beginning after December 31, 2016.*

(8) APPLICABLE DOLLAR AMOUNT FOR VARIABLE RATE PREMIUM. For purposes of paragraph (3)(E)(ii)—

(A) IN GENERAL. Except as provided in subparagraphs (B) and (C), the applicable dollar amount shall be—

(i) $9 for plan years beginning in a calendar year before 2015;

(ii) for plan years beginning in calendar year 2015, the amount in effect for plan years beginning in 2014 (determined after application of subparagraph (C));

(iii) for plan years beginning after calendar year 2015, the amount in effect for plan years beginning in 2015 (determined after application of subparagraph (C));

(iv) for plan years beginning after calendar year 2016, the amount in effect for plan years beginning in 2016 (determined after application of subparagraph (C));

(v) for plan years beginning after calendar year 2017, the amount in effect for plan years beginning in 2017 (determined after application of subparagraph (C));

(vi) for plan years beginning after calendar year 2018, the amount in effect for plan years beginning in 2018 (determined after application of subparagraph (C)); and

(vii) for plan years beginning after calendar year 2019, the amount in effect for plan years beginning in 2019 (determined after application of subparagraph (C)).

(B) ADJUSTMENT FOR INFLATION. For each plan year beginning in a calendar year after 2012, there shall be substituted for the applicable dollar amount specified under subparagraph (A) an amount equal to the greater of—

(i) the product derived by multiplying such applicable dollar amount for plan years beginning in that calendar year by the ratio of—

(I) the national average wage index (as defined in section 209(k)(1) of the Social Security Act) for the first of the 2 calendar years preceding the calendar year in which such plan year begins, to

(II) the national average wage index (as so defined) for the base year; and

(ii) such applicable dollar amount in effect for plan years beginning in the preceding calendar year.

If the amount determined under this subparagraph is not a multiple of $1, such product shall be rounded to the nearest multiple of $1.

(C) ADDITIONAL INCREASES. The applicable dollar amount determined under subparagraph (A) (after the application of subparagraph (B)) shall be increased—

(i) in the case of plan years beginning in calendar year 2014, by $4;

(ii) in the case of plan years beginning in calendar year 2015, by $10;

(iii) in the case of plan years beginning in calendar year 2016, by $5;

(iv) in the case of plan years beginning in calendar year 2017, by $3;

(v) in the case of plan years beginning in calendar year 2018, by $4; and

⟫→ *Caution: ERISA Sec. 4006(a)(8), below, as amended by P.L. 114-74, applies to plan years beginning after December 31, 2016.*

     (vi) in the case of plan years beginning in calendar year 2019, by $4.

    (D) BASE YEAR. For purposes of subparagraph (B), the base year is—

     (i) 2010, in the case of plan years beginning in calendar year 2013 or 2014;

     (ii) 2012, in the case of plan years beginning in calendar year 2015;

     (iii) 2013, in the case of plan years beginning after calendar year 2015;

     (iv) 2014, in the case of plan years beginning after calendar year 2016;

     (v) 2015, in the case of plan years beginning after calendar year 2017;

     (vi) 2016, in the case of plan years beginning after calendar year 2018; and

     (vii) 2017, in the case of plan years beginning after calendar year 2019.

Act Sec. 4006.(b)(1) REVISED SCHEDULE; CONGRESSIONAL PROCEDURES APPLICABLE.—In order to place a revised schedule (other than a schedule described in subsection (a)(2)(C), (D), or (E)) in effect, the corporation shall transmit the proposed schedule, its proposed effective date, and the reasons for its proposal to the Committee on Ways and Means and the Committee on Education and Labor of the House of Representatives, and to the Committee on Finance and the Committee on Labor and Human Resources of the Senate.

    (2) The succeeding paragraphs of this subsection are enacted by Congress as an exercise of the rulemaking power of the Senate and the House of Representatives, respectively, and as such they shall be deemed a part of the rules of each House, respectively, but applicable only with respect to the procedure to be followed in that House in the case of resolutions described in paragraph (3). They shall supersede other rules only to the extent that they are inconsistent therewith. They are enacted with full recognition of the constitutional right of either House to change the rules (so far as relating to the procedure of that House) at any time, in the same manner and to the same extent as in the case of any rule of that House.

    (3) For the purpose of the succeeding paragraphs of this subsection, "resolution" means only a joint resolution, the matter after the resolving clause of which is as follows: "The proposed revised schedule transmitted to Congress by the Pension Benefit Guaranty Corporation on . . . is hereby approved.", the blank space therein being filled with the date on which the corporation's message proposing the rate was delivered.

    (4) A resolution shall be referred to the Committee on Ways and Means and the Committee on Education and Labor of the House of Representatives and to the Committee on Finance and the Committee on Labor and Human Resources of the Senate.

    (5) If a committee to which has been referred a resolution has not reported it before the expiration of 10 calendar days after its introduction, it shall then (but not before) be in order to move to discharge the committee from further consideration of that resolution, or to discharge the committee from further consideration of any other resolution with respect to the proposed adjustment which has been referred to the committee. The motion to discharge may be made only by a person favoring the resolution, shall be highly privileged (except that it may not be made after the committee has reported a resolution with respect to the same proposed rate), and debate thereon shall be limited to not more than 1 hour, to be divided equally between those favoring and those opposing the resolution. An amendment to the motion is not in order, and it is not in order to move to reconsider the vote by which the motion is agreed to or disagreed to. If the motion to discharge is agreed to or disagreed to, the motion may not be renewed, nor may another motion to discharge the committee be made with respect to any other resolution with respect to the same proposed rate.

    (6) When a committee has reported, or has been discharged from further consideration of a resolution, it is at any time thereafter in order (even though a previous motion to the same effect has been disagreed to) to move to proceed to the consideration of the resolution. The motion is highly privileged and is not debatable. An amendment to the motion is not in order, and it is not in order to move to reconsider the vote by which the motion is agreed to or disagreed to. Debate on the resolution shall be limited to not more than 10 hours, which shall be divided equally between those favoring and those opposing the resolution. A motion further to limit debate is not debatable. An amendment to, or motion to recommit, the resolution is not in order, and it is not in order to move to reconsider the vote by which the resolution is agreed to or disagreed to.

    (7) Motions to postpone, made with respect to the discharge from committee, or the consideration of, a resolution and motions to proceed to the consideration of other business shall be decided without debate. Appeals from the decisions of the Chair relating to the application of the rules of the Senate or the House of Representatives, as the case may be, to the procedure relating to a resolution shall be decided without debate.

Act Sec. 4006.(c)(1) RATES FOR PLANS FOR BASIC BENEFITS.—Except as provided in subsection (a)(3), and subject to paragraph (2), the rate for all plans for basic benefits guaranteed under this title with respect to plan years ending after September 2, 1974, is—

    (A) in the case of each plan which was not a multiemployer plan in a plan year—

     (i) with respect to each plan year beginning before January 1, 1978, an amount equal to $1 for each individual who was a participant in such plan during the plan year, and

     (ii) with respect to each plan year beginning after December 31, 1977, and before January 1, 1986, an amount equal to $2.60 for each individual who was a participant in such plan during the plan year, and

     (iii) with respect to each plan year beginning after December 31, 1985, and before January 1, 1988, an amount equal to $8.50 for each individual who was a participant in such plan during the plan year, and

     (iv) with respect to each plan year beginning after December 31, 1987, and before January 1, 1991, an amount equal to $16 for each individual who was a participant in such plan during the plan year, and

    (B) in the case of each plan which was a multiemployer plan in a plan year, an amount equal to 50 cents for each individual who was a participant in such plan during the plan year.

    (2) The rate applicable under this subsection for the plan year preceding September 1, 1975, is the product of—

    (A) the rate described in the preceding sentence; and

    (B) a fraction—

     (i) the numerator of which is the number of calendar months in the plan year which ends after September 2, 1974, and before the date on which the new plan year commences, and

     (ii) the denominator of which is 12.

Amendments

P.L. 114-74, §501(a)(1):

Amended ERISA Sec. 4006(a)(3)(A)(i) by striking "and" at the end of subclause (IV), by striking the period at the end of subclause (V) and inserting a semicolon, and by inserting subclause (VI) to read as above.

The above amendment shall apply to plan years beginning after December 31, 2016.

P.L. 114-74, §501(a)(2):

Amended ERISA Sec. 4006(a)(3)(G) by, in the matter preceding clause (i), striking "2016" and inserting "2019"; and, in clause (i)(II) by striking "2014" and inserting "2017".

The above amendment shall apply to plan years beginning after December 31, 2016.

P.L. 114-74, §501(b)(1):

Amended ERISA Sec. 4006(a)(8)(C) by (A) in the subparagraph heading, by striking "increase in 2014 and 2015" and inserting "increases"; (B) in clause (ii), by striking "and" at the end; (C) in clause (iii), by striking the period at the end and inserting a semicolon; and (D) by adding at the end clauses (iv), (v) and (vi), to read as above.

The above amendment shall apply to plan years beginning after December 31, 2016.

P.L. 114-74, §501(b)(2)(A):

Amended ERISA Sec. 4006(a)(8)(A) by (i) in clause (iii), striking "and" at the end; (ii) in clause (iv), striking the period at the end and inserting a semicolon; and (iii) adding at the end clauses (v), (vi), and (vii) to read as above.

The above amendment shall apply to plan years beginning after December 31, 2016.

P.L. 114-74, §501(b)(2)(B):

Amended ERISA Sec. 4006(a)(8)(D) by (i) in clause (iii), striking "and" at the end; (ii) in clause (iv), striking the period at the end and inserting a semicolon; and (iii) by adding at the end clauses (v), (vi), and (vii) to read as above.

The above amendment shall apply to plan years beginning after December 31, 2016.

P.L. 113-235, §131(a)(1), Div. O:

Amended ERISA Sec. 4006(a)(3)(A) by striking "or" at the end of clause (iv), by inserting "and before January 1, 2015," after "December 31, 2012," in clause (v), by striking the period at the end and inserting ", or" in clause (v), and by adding at the end a new clause (vi) to read as above.

The above amendment shall apply with respect to plan years beginning after December 31, 2014.

P.L. 113-235, §131(a)(2), Div. O:

Amended ERISA Sec. 4006(a)(3) by inserting at the end a new subparagraph (M) to read as above.

The above amendment shall apply with respect to plan years beginning after December 31, 2014.

P.L. 113-67, Act Sec. 703(a):

Amended ERISA Sec. 4006(a)(3)(A)(i) in subclause (II) by striking "and" at the end, in subclause (III) by inserting "and before January 1, 2015," after "December 31, 2013", and by inserting after subclause (III), subclauses (IV) and (V) to read as above.

P.L. 113-67, Act Sec. 703(b)(1):

Amended ERISA Sec. 4006(a)(3) by redesignating subparagraphs (G) through (J) as subparagraphs (H) through (K), respectively and by inserting after subparagraph (F) subparagraph (G) to read as above.

P.L. 113-67, Act Sec. 703(b)(2):

Amended ERISA Sec. 4006(a)(3)(F) by inserting "and before 2013" after "after 2006" preceding clause (i) and by striking the second sentence in the flush text following clause (ii).

Prior to being stricken, the second sentence read as follows: "This subparagraph shall not apply to plan years beginning in 2013 or 2014."

P.L. 113-67, Act Sec. 703(c)(1):

Amended ERISA Sec. 4006(a)(8)(C) in clause (i) by striking "and" at the end, in clause (ii) by striking "$5." and inserting "$10; and", and by adding clause (iii) to read as above.

P.L. 113-67, Act Sec. 703(c)(2):

Amended ERISA Sec. 4006(a)(8)(A) by striking "and" at the end of clause (ii), by striking the period at the end of clause (iii) and inserting "; and", and by adding clause (iv) to read as above.

Amended ERISA Sec. 4006(a)(8)(D) by striking "and" at the end of clause (ii), by striking the period at the end of clause (iii) and inserting "; and", and by adding clause (iv) to read as above.

P.L. 113-67, Act Sec. 703(d)(1):

Amended ERISA Sec. 4006(a)(3)(E)(i) by striking "and" at the end of subclause (I), by inserting "and before 2016" after "2012" in subclause (II), by striking the period at the end and inserting "and", and by adding at the end subclause (III) to read as above.

P.L. 113-67, Act Sec. 703(d)(2):

Amended ERISA Sec. 4006(a)(3)(K), as redesignated, by inserting "and before 2016" after "2013" and by inserting at the end subparagraph (L) to read as above.

The above amendments apply to plan years beginning after December 31, 2013.

P.L. 112-141, §40211(b)(3)(C):

Amended ERISA Sec. 4006(a)(3)(E)(iv) by striking "section 303(h)(2)(C)" and inserting "section 303(h)(2)(C) (notwithstanding any regulations issued by the corporation, determined by not taking into account any adjustment under clause (iv) thereof)".

For effective date, see P.L. 112-141, §40211(c), below.

P.L. 112-141, §40211(c):

(c) EFFECTIVE DATE.—

(1) IN GENERAL.—The amendments made by this section shall apply with respect to plan years beginning after December 31, 2011.

(2) RULES WITH RESPECT TO ELECTIONS.—

(A) ADJUSTED FUNDING TARGET ATTAINMENT PERCENTAGE.—A plan sponsor may elect not to have the amendments made by this section apply to any plan year beginning before January 1, 2013, either (as specified in the election)—

(i) for all purposes for which such amendments apply, or

(ii) solely for purposes of determining the adjusted funding target attainment percentage under sections 436 of the Internal Revenue Code of 1986 and 206(g) of the Employee Retirement Income Security Act of 1974 for such plan year.

A plan shall not be treated as failing to meet the requirements of sections 204(g) of such Act and 411(d)(6) of such Code solely by reason of an election under this paragraph.

(B) OPT OUT OF EXISTING ELECTIONS.—If, on the date of the enactment of this Act, an election is in effect with respect to any plan under sections 303(h)(2)(D)(ii) of the Employee Retirement Income Security Act of 1974 and 430(h)(2)(D)(ii) of the Internal Revenue Code of 1986, then, notwithstanding the last sentence of each such section, the plan sponsor may revoke such election without the consent of the Secretary of the Treasury. The plan sponsor may make such revocation at any time before the date which is 1 year after such date of enactment and such revocation shall be effective for the 1st plan year to which the amendments made by this section apply and all

subsequent plan years. Nothing in this subparagraph shall preclude a plan sponsor from making a subsequent election in accordance with such sections.

P.L. 112-141, §40221(a):

Amended ERISA Sec. 4006(a)(3)(A) by inserting clause (i) to read as above. Prior to the amendment, ERISA Sec. 4006(a)(3)(A)(i) read as follows:

"(i) in the case of a single-employer plan, for plan years beginning after December 31, 2005, an amount equal to the sum of $30 plus the additional premium (if any) determined under subparagraph (E) for each individual who is a participant in such plan during the plan year;"

The above amendment is effective on the date of enactment (July 6, 2012).

P.L. 112-141, §40221(a)(2)(A) and (B):

Amended ERISA Sec. 4006(a)(3)(F)(i)(II) by inserting "(2012 in the case of plan years beginning after calendar year 2014)" after "2004", and by adding at the end of ERISA Sec. 4006(a)(3)(F) the following new sentence: "This subparagraph shall not apply to plan years beginning in 2013 or 2014.".

The above amendment is effective on the date of enactment (July 6, 2012).

P.L. 112-141, §40221(b)(1):

Amended ERISA Sec. 4006(a)(3)(E)(ii) by striking "$9.00" and inserting "the applicable dollar amount under paragraph (8)".

The above amendment is effective on the date of enactment (July 6, 2012).

P.L. 112-141, §40221(b)(2):

Amended ERISA Sec. 4006(a) by adding at the end new paragraph (8) to read as above.

The above amendment is effective on the date of enactment (July 6, 2012).

P.L. 112-141, §40221(b)(3)(A):

Amended ERISA Sec. 4006(a)(3)(E)(i) by striking "for any plan year shall be" and all that follows through the end and inserting the following "for any plan year—"

"(I) shall be an amount equal to the amount determined under clause (ii) divided by the number of participants in such plan as of the close of the preceding plan year; and"

"(II) in the case of plan years beginning in a calendar year after 2012, shall not exceed $400.".

The above amendment is effective on the date of enactment (July 6, 2012).

P.L. 112-141, §40221(b)(3)(B):

Amended ERISA Sec. 4006(a)(3) by adding at the end new subparagraph (J) to read as above.

The above amendment is effective on the date of enactment (July 6, 2012).

P.L. 112-141, §40222(a)(1):

Amended ERISA Sec. 4006(a)(3)(A)(iv) by inserting "and before January 1, 2013," after "December 31, 2005,".

The above amendment is effective on the date of enactment (July 6, 2012).

P.L. 112-141, §40222(a)(2), (3), and (4):

Amended ERISA Sec. 4006(a)(3)(A)(iii), and (iv) by striking "or" at the end of clause (iii), striking the period at the end of clause (iv) and inserting ", or", and by adding at the end the following new clause (v) to read as above.

The above amendment is effective on the date of enactment (July 6, 2012).

P.L. 112-141, §40222(b):

Amended ERISA Sec. 4006(a)(3) by adding at the end new subparagraph (I) to read as above.

The above amendment is effective on the date of enactment (July 6, 2012).

P.L. 110-458, §104(a):

Amended ERISA Sec. 4006(a)(3)(A)(i) by striking "1990" and inserting "2005".

The above amendment applies to plan years beginning after December 31, 2007.

P.L. 109-280, Sec. 301(a)(3):

Amended ERISA Sec. 4006(a)(3)(E)(iii)(V) by striking "2006" and inserting "2008."

The above amendment is effective as of the date of enactment (August 17, 2006).

P.L. 109-280, Sec. 401(a)(1):

Amended ERISA Sec. 4006(a)(3)(E) by striking clauses (iii) and (iv) and new clauses (iii) and (iv) to read as above.

Prior to being stricken, clauses (iii) and (iv) read as follows:

(iii) For purposes of clause (ii)—

(I) Except as provided in subclause (II) or (III) the term "unfunded vested benefits" means the amount which would be the unfunded current liability (within the meaning of section 302(d)(8)(A)) if only vested benefits were taken in account.

(II) The interest rate used in valuing vested benefits for purposes of subclause (I) shall be equal to the applicable percentage of the annual yield on 30-year Treasury securities for the month preceding the month in which the plan years begins. For purposes of this subclause, the applicable percentage is 80 percent for plan years beginning before July 1, 1997, 85 percent for plan years beginning after June 30, 1997, and before the 1st plan year to which the first tables prescribed under section 302(d)(7)(C)(ii)(II) apply, and 100 percent for such 1st plan year and subsequent plan years.

(III) In the case of any plan year for which the applicable percentage under subclause (II) is 100 percent, the value of the plan's assets used in determining unfunded current liability under subclause (I) shall be their fair market value.

(IV) In the case of plan years beginning after December 31, 2001, and before January 1, 2004, subclause (II) shall be applied to substituting '100 percent' for '85 percent'.

Subclause (III) shall be applied for such years without regard to the preceding sentence. Any reference to this clause or this subparagraph by any other sections or subsections (other than sections 4005, 4010, 4011, and 4043) shall be treated as a reference to this clause or this subparagraph without regard to this subclause.

(V) In the case of plan years beginning after December 31, 2003, and before January 1, 2008, the annual yield taken into account under subclause (II) shall be the annual rate of interest determined by the Secretary of the Treasury on amounts invested conservatively in long-term investment grade corporate bonds for the month preceding the month in which the plan year begins. For purposes of the preceding sentence, the Secretary of the Treasury shall determine such rate of interest on the basis of 2 or more indices that are selected periodically by the Secretary of the Treasury and that are in the top 3 quality levels available. The Secretary of the Treasury shall make the permissible range, and the indices and methodology used to determine the rate, publicly available.

(iv) No premium shall be determined under this subparagraph for any plan year if, as of the close of the preceding plan year, contributions to the plan for the preceding plan year were not less than the full funding limitation for the preceding year under section 412(c)(7) of the Internal Revenue Code of 1986.

The above amendment applies with respect to plan years beginning after 2007.

P.L. 109-280, Sec. 401(b)(1):

Amended ERISA Sec. 4006(a)(7) by repealing subparagraph (E). Prior to repeal, subparagraph (E) read as follows:

TERMINATION. Subparagraph (A) shall not apply with respect to any plan terminated after December 31, 2010.

The above amendment shall take effect as if included in the provision of the Deficit Reduction Act of 2005 to which it relates.

P.L. 109-280, Sec. 401(b)(2)(A):

Amended ERISA Sec. 4006(a)(7)(C)(ii) by striking "subparagraph (B)(i)(I)" and inserting "subparagraph (B)."

The above amendment shall take effect as if included in the provision of the Deficit Reduction Act of 2005 to which it relates.

P.L. 109-280, Sec. 405(a)(1):

Amended ERISA Sec. 4006(a)(3) by striking "The additional" in subparagraph (E)(i) and inserting "Except as provided in subparagraph (H), the additional."

The above amendment is effective for plan years beginning after December 31, 2006.

P.L. 109-280, Sec. 405(a)(2):

Amended ERISA Sec. 4006(a)(3) by inserting after subparagraph (G) a new subparagraph (H) to read as above:

The above amendment is effective for plan years beginning after December 31, 2006.

P.L. 109-171, §8101(a)(1)(A):

Amended ERISA § 4006(a)(3)(A)(i) by striking "$19" and inserting "$30".

P.L. 109-171, §8101(a)(1)(B):

Amended ERISA § 4006(a)(3) by adding subparagraph (F) to read as above.

P.L. 109-171, §8101(a)(2)(A):

Amended ERISA § 4006(a)(3)(A)(iii) by inserting "and before January 1, 2006," after "Act of 1980," ; by striking the period at the end and inserting ", or" ; and by adding at the end subclause (iv) to read as above.

P.L. 109-171, §8101(a)(2)(B):

Amended ERISA § 4006(a)(3) by adding subparagraph (G) to read as above.

The above amendments are effective for plan years beginning after December 31, 2005.

P.L. 109-171, §8101(b):

Amended ERISA § 4006(a) by adding subsection (7) to read as above.

The above amendment is generally effective for plans terminated after December 31, 2005. However, see the special rules in Act Sec. 8101(d)(2)(B) below.

(2) PREMIUM RATE FOR CERTAIN TERMINATED SINGLE-EMPLOYER PLANS—

(A) IN GENERAL—Except as provided in subparagraph (B), the amendment made by subsection (b) shall apply to plans terminated after December 31, 2005.

(B) SPECIAL RULE FOR PLANS TERMINATED IN BANKRUPTCY—The amendment made by subsection (b) shall not apply to a termination of a single-employer plan that is terminated during the pendency of any bankruptcy reorganization proceeding under chapter 11 of title 11, United States Code (or under any similar law of a State or political subdivision of a State), if the proceeding is pursuant to a bankruptcy filing occurring before October 18, 2005.

P.L. 109-171, §8101(c):

Amended ERISA § 4006(a)(3)(B) by striking "subparagraph (A)(iii)" and inserting "clause (iii) or (iv) of subparagraph (A).".

The above amendment is effective for plan years beginning after December 31, 2005.

P.L. 108-311, §403(d):

Amended ERISA § 4006(a)(3)(E)(iii)(IV) by inserting "or this subparagraph" after "this clause" both places it appears and by inserting "(other than sections 4005, 4010, 4011, and 4043" after "subsections".

The above amendment is effective as if included in the provisions of the Job Creation and Worker Assistance Act of 2002 to which they relate.

P.L. 108-218, §101(a):

Act Sec. 101(a) amended ERISA Sec. 4006(a)(3)(E) by adding subclause V to read as above.

Act Sec. 101 provides:

(c) Provisions Relating to Plan Amendments.—

(1) In general.

If this subsection applies to any plan or annuity contract amendment—

(A) such plan or contract shall be treated as being operated in accordance with the terms of the plan or contract during the period described in paragraph (2)(B)(i), and

(B) except as provided by the Secretary of the Treasury, such plan shall not fail to meet the requirements of section 411(d)(6) of the Internal Revenue Code of 1986 and section 204(g) of the Employee Retirement Income Security Act of 1974 by reason of such amendment.

(2) Amendments to which section applies.—

(A) In general.—

This subsection shall apply to any amendment to any plan or annuity contract which is made—

(i) pursuant to any amendment made by this section, and

(ii) on or before the last day of the first plan year beginning on or after January 1, 2006.

(B) Conditions.—

This subsection shall not apply to any plan or annuity contract amendment unless—

(i) during the period beginning on the date the amendment described in subparagraph (A)(i) takes effect and ending on the date described in subparagraph (A)(ii) (or, if earlier, the date the plan or contract amendment is adopted), the plan or contract is operated as if such plan or contract amendment were in effect; and

(ii) such plan or contract amendment applies retroactively for such period.

(d) Effective Dates.—

(1) In general.—Except as provided in paragraphs (2) and (3), the amendments made by this section shall apply to plan years beginning after December 31, 2003.

(2) Lookback rules.—For purposes of applying subsections (d)(9)(B)(ii) and (e)(1) of section 302 of the Employee Retirement Income Security Act of 1974 and subsections (l)(9)(B)(ii) and (m)(1) of section 412 of the Internal Revenue Code of 1986 to plan years beginning after December 31, 2003, the amendments made by this section may be applied as if such amendments had been in effect for all prior plan years. The Secretary of the Treasury may prescribe simplified assumptions which may be used in applying the amendments made by this section to such prior plan years.

(3) Transition rule for section 415 limitation.—In the case of any participant or beneficiary receiving a distribution after December 31, 2003 and before January 1, 2005, the amount payable under any form of benefit subject to section 417(e)(3) of the Internal Revenue Code of 1986 and subject to adjustment under section 415(b)(2)(B) of such Code shall not, solely by reason of the amendment made by subsection (b)(4), be less than the amount that would have been so payable had the amount payable been determined using the applicable interest rate in effect as of the last day of the last plan year beginning before January 1, 2004.

P.L. 107-147, §405(c):

Act Sec. 405(c) amended ERISA Sec. 4006(a)(3)(E)(iii) to add subclause III to read as above.

P.L. 103-465, §774(b)(1):

Act Sec. 774(b)(1) amended ERISA Sec. 4006(a)(3)(E)(iii)(II) by striking "80 percent" and inserting "the applicable percentage", and by adding at the end a new sentence to read as above.

P.L. 103-465, §774(b)(2):

Act Sec. 774(b)(2) amended ERISA Sec. 4006(a)(3)(E)(iii) by inserting "or (III)" after "subclause (II)" in subclause (I), and by adding new subclause (III) to read as above.

The above amendments apply to plan years beginning after December 8, 1994. For special rules, see Act Sec. 774(c) below.

P.L. 103-465, §774(a)(1):

Act Sec. 774(a)(1) amended ERISA Sec. 4006(a)(3)(E) by striking clause (iv), and by redesignating clause (v) as clause (iv) to read as above. Prior to amendment, ERISA Sec. 4006(a)(3)(E)(iv) read as follows:

(iv)(I) Except as provided in this clause, the aggregate increase in the premium payable with respect to any participant by reason of this subparagraph shall not exceed $53.

(II) If an employer made contributions to a plan during 1 or more of the 5 plan years preceding the 1st plan year to which this subparagraph applies in an amount not less than the maximum amount allowable as a deduction with respect to such contributions under section 404 of such Code, the dollar amount in effect under subclause (I) for the 1st 5 plan years to which this subparagraph applies shall be reduced by $3 for each plan year for which such contributions were made in such amount.

The above amendment is effective for plan years beginning on or after July 1, 1994. For special rules, see Act Secs. 774(a)(2)(B) and 774(c), below.

Act Sec. 774(a)(2)(B) provides:

(B) TRANSITION RULE.—In the case of plan years beginning on or after July 1, 1994, and before July 1, 1996, the additional premium payable with respect to any participant by reason of the amendments made by this section shall not exceed the sum of—

(i) $53, and

(ii) the product derived by multiplying—

(I) the excess (if any) of the amount determined under clause (i) of section 4006(a)(3)(E) of the Employee Retirement Income Security Act of 1974, over $53, by

(II) the applicable percentage.

For purposes of this subparagraph, the applicable percentage shall be the percentage specified in the following table:

For the plan year beginning:		The applicable percentage
on or after	but before	is:
July 1, 1994	July 1, 1995	20 percent
July 1, 1995	July 1, 1996	60 percent

Act Sec. 774(c) provides:

(e) TRANSITION RULE FOR CERTAIN REGULATED PUBLIC UTILITIES.—In the case of a regulated public utility described in section 7701(a)(33)(A)(i) of the Internal Revenue Code of 1986, the amendments made by this section shall not apply to plan years beginning before the earlier of—

(1) January 1, 1998, or

(2) the date the regulated public utility begins to collect from utility customers rates that reflect the costs incurred or projected to be incurred for additional premiums under section 4006(a)(3)(E) of the Employee Retirement Income Security Act of 1974 pursuant to final and nonappealable determinations by all public utility commissions (or other authorities having jurisdiction over the rates and terms of service by the regulated public utility) that the costs are just and reasonable and recoverable from customers of the regulated public utility.

P.L. 101-508, Sec. 12021(a)(1):

Amended ERISA Sec. 4006(a)(3)(A)(i) by striking "for plan years beginning after December 31, 1987, an amount equal to the sum of $16" and inserting "for plan years beginning after December 31, 1990, an amount equal to the sum of $19" effective for plan years beginning after December 31, 1990.

P.L. 101-508, Sec. 12021(a)(2):

Amended ERISA Sec. 4006(c)(1)(A) by adding a new clause (iv) to read as above effective for plan years beginning after December 31, 1990.

P.L. 101-508, Sec. 12021(b):

Amended ERISA Sec. 4006(a)(3)(E) by striking "$6.00" in clause (ii) and inserting "$9.00" and by striking "$34" in clause (iv)(I) and inserting "$53" effective for plan years beginning after December 31, 1990.

P.L. 101-239, § 7881(h)(1):

Amended ERISA Sec. 4006(a)(3)(E) by adding a new clause (v) at the end.

P.L. 100-203, § 9331(a):

Amended ERISA Sec. 4006(a)(3)(A)(i) by striking out "for plan years beginning after December 31, 1985, an amount equal to $8.50" and inserting "for plan years beginning after December 31, 1987, an amount equal to the sum of $16 plus the additional premium (if any) determined under subparagraph (E), to read as above, effective December 22, 1987.

P.L. 100-203, § 9331(b):

Amended ERISA Sec. 4006(a)(3) by adding subparagraph (E), to read as above, effective December 22, 1987.

P.L. 100-203, § 9331(e):

Amended ERISA Sec. 4006(c)(1)(A) by striking out "and" at the end of clause (i), by inserting "and before January 1, 1986," after "after December 31, 1977," and by adding subparagraph (iii), to read as above, effective for plan years beginning after December 31, 1987.

P.L. 99-272:

Act Sec. 11005(a)(1) amended ERISA Sec. 4006(a)(3)(A)(i) by striking out "for plan years beginning after December 31, 1977, an amount equal to $2.60" and inserting "for plan years beginning after December 31, 1985, an amount equal to $8.50."

Act Sec. 11005(a)(2) amended ERISA Sec. 4006(c)(1) by striking out subparagraph (A) and inserting a new subparagraph (A) to read as above. Prior to the amendment, ERISA Sec. 4006(c)(1)(A) read as follows:

(A) in the case of each plan which was not a multiemployer plan in a plan year, an amount equal to $1 for each individual who was a participant in such plan during the plan year, and

Act Sec. 11005(b) amended ERISA Sec. 4006(a) by striking out the last sentence in paragraph (1) and by adding a new paragraph (6) to read as above. Prior to amendment, the last sentence of ERISA Sec. 4006(a)(1) read as follows:

In establishing annual premiums with respect to plans, other than multiemployer plans, paragraphs (5) and (6) of this subsection (as in effect before the enactment of the Multiemployer Pension Plan Amendments Act of 1980) shall continue to apply.

Act Sec. 11005(c)(1) amended ERISA Sec. 4006(a)(2) by striking out "the Congress approves such revised schedule by a concurrent resolution" and inserting "a joint resolution approving such revised schedule is enacted."

Act Sec. 11005(c)(2) amended ERISA Sec. 4006(a)(4) by striking out "approval by the Congress" and inserting "the enactment of a joint resolution."

Act Sec. 11005(c)(3) amended ERISA Sec. 4006(b)(3) by striking out "concurrent" and inserting "joint," by striking out "That the Congress favors the" and inserting "The," and by inserting "is hereby approved." before the period preceding the quotation marks,

The above amendments are effective for plan years beginning after December 31, 1985 except for the amendment made by Act Sec. 11005(b) which is effective as of September 26, 1980.

P.L. 96-364, § 105:

Amended section 4006(a) to read as above; amended section 4006(b) by substituting "Committee on Labor and Human Resources" for "Committee on Labor and Public

Welfare," striking out "coverage" and by substituting "(C), (D), or (E)" for "(B) or (C)"; and by adding new section 4006(c), effective September 26, 1980.

Section 4006(a) prior to amendment read:

"(a)(1) The corporation shall prescribe such insurance premium rates and such coverage schedules for the application of those rates as may be necessary to provide sufficient revenue to the fund for the corporation to carry out its functions under this title. The premium rates charged by the corporation for any period shall be uniform for all plans, other than miltiemployer plans insured by the corporation, with respect to basic benefits guaranteed by it under section 4022, and shall be uniform for all multiemployer plans with respect to basic benefits guaranteed by it under such section. The premium rates charged by the corporation for any period for non-basic benefits guaranteed by it shall be uniform by category of non-basic benefit guaranteed, shall be based on the risk insured in each category, and shall reflect the experience of the corporation (including reasonably anticipated experience) in guaranteeing such benefits.

(2) The corporation shall maintain separate coverage schedules for—

(A) basic benefits guaranteed by it under section 4022 for—

(i) plans which are multiemployer plans, and

(ii) plans which are not multiemployer plans,

(B) employers insured under section 4023 against liability under subtitle D of this title, and

(C) non-basic benefits.

Except as provided in paragraph (3), the corporation may revise such schedules whenever it determines that revised rates are necessary, but a revised schedule described in subparagraph (A) shall apply only to plan years beginning more than 30 days after the date on which the Congress approves such revised schedule by a concurrent resolution.

(3) Except as provided in paragraph (4), the rate for all plans for benefits guaranteed under section 4022 (other than non-basic benefits) with respect to plan years ending no more than 35 months after the effective date of this title is—

(A) in the case of each plan which is not a multiemployer plan, an amount equal to one dollar for each individual who is a participant in such plan at any time during the plan year; and

(B) in the case of a multiemployer plan, an amount equal to fifty cents for each individual who is a participant in such plan at any time during the plan year.

The rate applicable under this paragraph to any plan the plan year of which does not begin on the date of enactment of this Act is a fraction of the rate described in the preceding sentence, the numerator of which is the number of months which end before the date on which the new plan year commences and the denominator of which is 12. The corporation is authorized to prescribe regulations under which the rate described in subparagraph (B) will not apply to the same participant in any multiemployer plan more than once for any plan year.

(4) Upon notification filed with the corporation not less than 60 days after the date on which the corporation publishes the rates applicable under paragraph (5), at the election of a plan the rate applicable to that plan with respect to the second full plan year to which this section applies beginning after the date of enactment of this Act shall be the greater of—

(A) an alternative rate determined under paragraph (5), or

(B) one-half of the rate applicable to the plan under paragraph (3).

In the case of a multiemployer plan, the rate prescribed by this paragraph (at the election of a plan) for the second full plan year is also the applicable rate for plan years succeeding the second full plan year and ending before the full plan year first commencing after December 31, 1977.

(5) In carrying out its authority under paragraph (1) to establish premium rates and bases for basic benefits guaranteed under section 4022 the corporation shall establish such rates and bases in coverage schedules for plan years beginning 24 months or more after the date of enactment of this Act in accordance with the provisions of the paragraph. The corporation shall publish the rate schedules first applicable under this paragraph in the Federal Register not later than 270 days after the date of enactment of this Act.

(A) The corporation may establish annual premiums composed of—

(i) a rate applicable to the excess, if any, of the present value of the basic benefits of the plan which are guaranteed over the value of the assets of the plan, not in excess of 0.1 percent for plans which are not multiemployer plans and not in excess of 0.025 percent for multiemployer plans, and

(ii) an additional charge base on the rate applicable to the present value of the basic benefits of the plan which are guaranteed, determined separately for multiemployer plans and for plans which are not multiemployer plans.

The rate for the additional charge referred to in clause (ii) shall be set by the corporation for every year at a level (determined separately for multiemployer plans and for plans which are not multiemployer plans) which the corporation estimates will yield total revenue approximately equal to the total revenue to be derived by the corporation from the premiums referred to in clause (i) of this subparagraph.

(B) The corporation may establish annual premiums based on—

(i) the number of participants in a plan, but such premium rates shall not exceed the rates described in paragraph (3),

(ii) unfunded basic benefits guaranteed under this title, but such premium rates shall not exceed the limitations applicable under subparagraph (A)(i), or

(iii) total guaranteed basic benefits, but such premium rates may not exceed the rates determined under subparagraph (A)(ii).

If the corporation uses 2 or more of the rate bases described in this subparagraph, the premium rates shall be designed to produce approximately equal amounts of aggregate premium revenue from each of the rate bases used.

(6) The corporation shall by regulation define the terms 'value or the assets' and 'present value of the benefits of the plan which are guaranteed' in a manner consistent with the purposes of this title and the provisions of this section."

Regulations

The following regulations were adopted by the Pension Benefit Guaranty Corporation on July 1, 1996 (61 FR 34002). Prior to July 1, 1996, PBGC regulations were under Chapter XXVI of Title 29 of the Code of Federal Regulations. Effective July 1, 1996, PBGC regulations were moved to Chapter XL, and were renumbered and reorganized. Reg. § 4006.5 was amended November 7, 1997 (62 FR 60424), effective January 1, 1998. Regs. § 4006.2, § 4006.5, and § 4006.6 were amended December 1, 2000 (65 FR 75160), effective January 1, 2001. Reg. § 4006.4 and § 4006.5 were revised on June 1, 2006 (71 FR 31077), effective July 1, 2006. Reg. § 4006.3 was amended, and Reg. § 4006.7 was added, on December 17, 2007 by 72 FR 71222. Reg. § 4006.2— § 4006.6 were amended on March 21, 2008 (73 FR 15065). Reg. §§ 4006.2, 4006.3, 4006.4, 4006.5, and 4006.7 were amended on March 11, 2014 (79 FR 13547).

[¶ 15,361]

§ 4006.1 **Purpose and scope.** This part, which applies to all plans covered by title IV of ERISA, provides rules for computing the premiums imposed by sections 4006 and 4007 of ERISA. (See part 4007 of this chapter for rules for the payment of premiums, including due dates and late payment charges.)

[¶ 15,361A]

§ 4006.2 **Definitions.** The following terms are defined in § 4001.2 of this chapter: benefit liabilities, Code, contributing sponsor, ERISA, fair market value, insurer, irrevocable commitment, mandatory employee contributions, multiemployer plan, notice of intent to terminate, PBGC, plan administrator, plan, plan year, single-employer plan, and termination date. [Amended 3/11/14 by 79 FR 13547.]

In addition, for purposes of this part:

Continuation plan means a new plan resulting from a consolidation or spinoff that is not *de minimis* pursuant to the regulations under section 414(*l*) of the Code. [Added 3/11/14 by 79 FR 13547.]

New plan means a plan that did not exist before the premium payment year and includes a plan resulting from a consolidation or spinoff. A plan that meets this definition is considered to be a new plan even if the plan constitutes a successor plan within the meaning of section 4021(a) of ERISA.

Newly covered plan means a plan that becomes covered by title IV of ERISA during the premium payment year and that existed as an uncovered plan immediately before the first date in the premium payment year on which it was a covered plan. [Amended 3/11/14 by 79 FR 13547.]

Participant has the meaning described in Sec. 4006.6. [Amended 12/1/00 by 65 FR 75160.]

Participant count of a plan means the number of participants in the plan on the participant count date of the plan. [Amended 3/11/14 by 79 FR 13547.]

Participant count date of a plan means the date provided for in § 4006.5(c), (d), or (e) as applicable. [Amended 3/11/14 by 79 FR 13547.]

Premium funding target has the meaning described in § 4006.4(b)(1).

Premium payment year means the plan year for which the premium is being paid.

Short plan year means a plan year of coverage that is shorter than a normal plan year.

Small plan means a plan—

(1) Whose participant count is not more than 100, or

(2) Whose funding valuation date for the premium payment year, determined in accordance with ERISA section 303(g)(2), is not the first day of the premium payment year. [Added 3/11/14 by 79 FR 13547.]

UVB valuation date of a plan means the plan's funding valuation date for the UVB valuation year, determined in accordance with ERISA section 303(g)(2). [Amended 3/11/14 by 79 FR 13547.]

UVB valuation year of a plan means—

(1) In general,—

(i) The plan year preceding the premium payment year, if the plan is a small plan other than a continuation plan, or

(ii) The premium payment year, in any other case; or

(2) For a small plan that so opts subject to PBGC premium instructions, the premium payment year. [Added 3/11/14 by 79 FR 13547.]

[Revised 3/21/2008 by 73 FR 15065.]

[¶ 15,361B]

§ 4006.3 **Premium rate.** Subject to the provisions of § 4006.5 (dealing with exemptions and special rules) and § 4006.7 (dealing with premiums for certain terminated single-employer plans), the premium paid for basic benefits guaranteed under section 4022(a) or section 4022A(a) of ERISA shall equal the flat-rate premium under paragraph (a) of this section plus, in the case of a single-employer plan, the variable-rate premium under paragraph (b) of this section. Premium rates (and the MAP–21 cap rate referred to in paragraph (b)(2) of this section) are subject to change each year under inflation indexing provisions in section 4006 of ERISA. [Amended 3/11/14 by 79 FR 13547.]

(a) *Flat-rate premium.* The flat-rate premium for a plan is equal to the applicable flat premium rate multiplied by the plan's participant count. The applicable flat premium rate is the amount prescribed for the calendar year in which the premium payment year begins by the applicable provisions of—[Revised 3/21/2008 by 73 FR 15065.]

(1) ERISA section 4006(a)(3)(A), (F), and (G) for a single-employer plan, or

(2) ERISA section 4006(a)(3)(A), (H), and (J) for a multiemployer plan.

[Amended 3/11/14 by 79 FR 13547.]

(b) *Variable-rate premium.*

(1) *In general.* Subject to the cap provisions in paragraphs (b)(2) and (b)(3) of this section, the variable-rate premium for a single-employer plan is equal to a specified dollar amount for each $1,000 (or fraction thereof) of the plan's unfunded vested benefits as determined under § 4006.4 for the UVB valuation year. The specified dollar amount is the applicable variable premium rate prescribed by the applicable provisions of ERISA section 4006(a)(8) for the calendar year in which the premium payment year begins. [Revised 3/21/2008 by 73 FR 15065.]

(2) *MAP–21 cap.* The variable-rate premium for a plan is not more than the applicable MAP–21 cap rate multiplied by the plan's participant count. The applicable MAP–21 cap rate is the amount prescribed by the applicable provisions of ERISA section 4006(a)(3)(E)(i)(II), (E)(i)(III), (K), and (L) for the calendar year in which the premium payment year begins.

(3) *Small-employer cap.*

(i) *In general.* If a plan is described in paragraph (b)(3)(ii) of this section for the premium payment year, the variable-rate premium is not more than $5 multiplied by the square of the participant count. For example, if the participant count is 20, the variable-rate premium is not more than $2,000 ($5 × 20^2 = $5 × 400 = $2,000).

(ii) *Plans eligible for cap.* A plan is described in paragraph (b)(3)(ii) of this section for the premium payment year if the aggregate number of employees of all employers in the plan's controlled group on the first day of the premium payment year is 25 or fewer.

(iii) *Meaning of "employee."* For purposes of paragraph (b)(3)(ii) of this section, the aggregate number of employees is determined in the same manner as under section 410(b)(1) of the Code, taking into account the provisions of section 414(m) and (n) of the Code, but without regard to section 410(b)(3), (4), and (5) of the Code.

[Amended 3/11/14 by 79 FR 13547.]

(c) *Applicable flat premium rate.* [Removed 3/11/14 by 79 FR 13547.]

(d) *Adjusted flat rate.* [Removed 3/11/14 by 79 FR 13547.]

[¶ 15,361C]

§ 4006.4 Determination of unfunded vested benefits.

(a) *In general.* Except as provided in the exemptions and special rules under § 4006.5, the amount of a plan's unfunded vested benefits for the UVB valuation year is the excess (if any) of the plan's premium funding target for the UVB valuation year (determined under paragraph (b) of this section) over the fair market value of the plan's assets for the UVB valuation year (determined under paragraph (c) of this section). Unfunded vested benefits for the UVB valuation year must be determined as of the plan's UVB valuation date, based on the plan provisions and the plan's population as of that date. The determination must be made in a manner consistent with generally accepted actuarial principles and practices. [Amended 3/11/14 by 79 FR 13547.]

(b) *Premium funding target.* (1) *In general.* A plan's premium funding target is its standard premium funding target under paragraph (b)(2) of this section or, if an election to use the alternative premium funding target under § 4006.5(g) is in effect, its alternative premium funding target under § 4006.5(g).

(2) *Standard premium funding target.* A plan's standard premium funding target under this section is the plan's funding target as determined under ERISA section 303(d) (or 303(i), if applicable) for the UVB valuation year using the same assumptions that are used for funding purposes, except that— [Amended 3/11/14 by 79 FR 13547.]

(i) Only vested benefits are taken into account, and

(ii) The interest rates to be used are the segment rates for the month preceding the month in which the UVB valuation year begins that are determined in accordance with ERISA section 4006(a)(3)(E)(iv). These are the rates that would be determined under ERISA section 303(h)(2)(C) if ERISA section 303(h)(2)(D) were applied by using the monthly yields for the month preceding the month in which the UVB valuation year begins on investment grade corporate bonds with varying maturities and in the top 3 quality levels rather than the average of such yields for a 24-month period. For this purpose, the transition rule in ERISA section 303(h)(2)(G) is inapplicable. [Amended 3/11/14 by 79 FR 13547.]

(3) *"At-risk" plans; transition rules; loading factor.* . The transition rules in ERISA section 303(i)(5) apply to the determination of the premium funding target of a plan in at-risk status for funding purposes. If a plan in at-risk status is also described in ERISA section 303(i)(1)(A)(ii) for the UVB valuation year, its premium funding target reflects a loading factor pursuant to ERISA section 303(i)(1)(C) equal to the sum of—

(i) *Per-participant portion of loading factor.* The amount determined for funding purposes under ERISA section 303(i)(1)(C)(i) for the UVB valuation year, and

(ii) *Four percent portion of loading factor.* Four percent of the premium funding target determined as if the plan were not in at-risk status.

[Added 3/11/14 by 79 FR 13547.]

(c) *Value of assets.* The fair market value of a plan's assets under this section is determined in the same manner as for funding purposes under ERISA section 303(g)(3) and (4), except that averaging as described in ERISA section 303(g)(3)(B) must not be used and prior year contributions are included only to the extent received by the plan by the date the premium is filed. Contribution receipts must be accounted for as described in ERISA section 303(g)(4), using effective interest rates determined under ERISA section 303(h)(2)(A) (not rates that could be determined based on the segment rates described in paragraph (b)(2) of this section).

(d) *"Vested".* For purposes of ERISA section 4006(a)(3)(E), this part, and part 4007 of this chapter:

(1) A participant's benefit that is otherwise vested does not fail to be vested merely because of the circumstance that the participant is living, in the case of the following death benefits:

(i) A qualified pre-retirement survivor annuity (as described in ERISA section 205(e)), (ii) A post-retirement survivor annuity that pays some or all of the participant's benefit amount for a fixed or contingent period (such as a joint and survivor annuity or a certain and continuous annuity), and

(iii) A benefit that returns the participant's accumulated mandatory employee contributions (as described in ERISA section 204(c)(2)(C)).

(2) A benefit otherwise vested does not fail to be vested merely because of the circumstance that the benefit may be eliminated or reduced by the adoption of a plan amendment or by the occurrence of a condition or event (such as a change in marital status).

(3) A participant's pre-retirement lump-sum death benefit (other than a benefit described in paragraph (d)(1)(iii) of this section) is not vested if the participant is living.

(4) A participant's disability benefit is not vested if the participant is not disabled.

(e) *Illustration of vesting principle.* The vesting principles set forth in paragraph (d) of this section are illustrated by the following examples:

(1) *Example 1.* Under Plan A, if a participant retires at or after age 55 but before age 62, the participant receives a temporary supplement from retirement until age 62. The supplement is not a QSUPP (qualified social security supplement), as defined in Treasury Reg. § 1.401(a)(4)-12, and is not protected under Code section 411(d)(6). The temporary supplement is considered vested, and its value is included in the premium funding target, for each participant who, on the UVB valuation date, is at least 55 but less than 62, and thus eligible for the supplement. The calculation is unaffected by the fact that the plan could be amended to remove the supplement after the UVB valuation date.

(2) *Example 2.* Plan B provides a qualified pre-retirement survivor annuity (QPSA) upon the death of a participant who has five years of service, at no charge to the participant. The QPSA is considered vested, and its value is included in the premium funding target, for each participant who, on the UVB valuation date, has five years of service and is thus eligible for the QPSA. The calculation is unaffected by the fact that the participant is alive on that date.

(f) *Plans to which special funding rules apply.* Unfunded vested benefits must be determined (whether the standard premium funding target or the alternative premium funding target is used) without regard to the following provisions of the Pension Protection Act of 2006 (Pub. L. 109-280):

(1) Section 104, dealing generally with plans of cooperatives.

(2) Section 105, dealing generally with plans affected by settlement agreements with PBGC.

(3) Section 106, dealing generally with plans of government contractors.

(4) Section 402, dealing generally with plans of commercial passenger airlines and airline caterers.

[Revised 3/21/2008 by 73 FR 15065.]

[¶ 15,361D]

§ 4006.5 Exemptions and special rules.

(a) *Variable-rate premium exemptions.* A plan described in any of paragraphs (a)(1)-(a)(4) of this section is not required to determine or report its unfunded vested benefits under § 4006.4 and does not owe a variable-rate premium under § 4006.3(b). [Revised 3/21/2008 by 73 FR 15065. Amended 3/11/14 by 79 FR 13547.]

(1) *Plans without vested participants.* A plan is described in this paragraph if it does not have any participants with vested benefits as of the UVB valuation date. [Revised 3/21/2008 by 73 FR 15065.]

(2) *Section 412(e)(3) plans.* A plan is described in this paragraph if the plan is a plan described in section 412(e)(3) of the Code and the regulations thereunder on the UVB valuation date.

[Revised 3/21/2008 by 73 FR 15065.]

(3) *Plans terminating in standard terminations.* The exemption for a plan described in this paragraph is conditioned upon the plan's making a final distribution of assets in a standard termination. If a plan is ultimately unable to do so, the exemption is revoked and all variable-rate amounts not paid pursuant to this exemption are due retroactive to

the applicable due date(s). A plan is described in this paragraph if it makes a final distribution of assets in a standard termination during the premium payment year or if—[Amended 3/11/14 by 79 FR 13547.]

(i) The plan administrator has issued notices of intent to terminate the plan in a standard termination in accordance with section 4041(a)(2) of ERISA; and

(ii) The proposed termination date set forth in the notice of intent to terminate is before the beginning of the premium payment year. [Amended 3/11/14 by 79 FR 13547.]

[Revised 3/21/2008 by 73 FR 15065.]

(4) *Certain small new and newly covered plans.* A plan is described in this paragraph if—

(i) It is a small plan other than a continuation plan, and

(ii) It is a new plan or a newly covered plan

[Added 3/11/14 by 79 FR 13547.]

(b) *Reporting exemption for plans paying capped variable-rate premium.* A plan that qualifies for the variable-rate premium cap described in ERISA section 4006(a)(3)(H) is not required to determine or report its unfunded vested benefits under § 4006.4 if it reports that it qualifies for the cap and pays a variable-rate premium equal to the amount of the cap.

[Revised 3/21/2008 by 73 FR 15065.]

(c) *Participant count date; in general.* Except as provided in paragraphs (d) and (e) of this section, the participant count date of a plan is the last day of the plan year preceding the premium payment year.

[Revised 3/21/2008 by 73 FR 15065 and 3/11/14 by 79 FR 13547.]

(d) *Participant count date; new and newly covered plans.* The participant count date of a new plan or a newly covered plan is the first day of the premium payment year. For this purpose, a new plan's premium payment year begins on the plan's effective date.

[Revised 3/21/2008 by 73 FR 15065 and 3/11/14 by 79 FR 13547.]

(e) *Participant count date; certain mergers and spinoffs.*

(1) The participant count date of a plan described in paragraph (e)(2) of this section is the first day of the premium payment year.

[Revised 3/11/14 by 79 FR 13547.]

(2) A plan is described in this paragraph (e)(2) for a plan year if—

(i) The plan engages in a merger or spinoff that is not de minimis pursuant to the regulations under section 414(l) of the Code (in the case of single-employer plans) or pursuant to part 4231 of this chapter (in the case of multiemployer plans), as applicable;

(ii) The merger or spinoff is effective at the beginning of the premium payment year; and

[Revised 3/21/2008 by 73 FR 15065. Amended 3/11/14 by 79 FR 13547.]

(iii) The plan is the transferee plan in the case of a merger or the transferor plan in the case of a spinoff.

(f) *Proration for certain short plan years.* The premium for a plan that has a short plan year described in this paragraph (f) is prorated by the number of months in the short plan year (treating a part of a month as a month). The proration applies whether or not the short plan year ends by the premium due date for the short plan year. For purposes of this paragraph (f), there is a short plan year in the following circumstances: [Revised 3/21/2008 by 73 FR 15065]

(1) *New or newly covered plan.* A new plan becomes effective less than one full year before the beginning of its second plan year, or a newly covered plan becomes covered on a date other than the first day of its plan year. (Cessation of coverage before the end of a plan year does not give rise to proration under this section.)

[Revised 3/21/2008 by 73 FR 15065. Amended 3/11/14 by 79 FR 13547.]

(2) *Change in plan year.* A plan amendment changes the plan year, but only if the plan does not merge into or consolidate with another plan or otherwise cease its independent existence either during the short plan year or at the beginning of the full plan year following the short plan year.

(3) *Distribution of assets.* The plan's assets (other than any excess assets) are distributed pursuant to the plan's termination.

(4) *Appointment of trustee.* The plan is a single-employer plan, and a plan trustee is appointed pursuant to section 4042 of ERISA. [Amended 12/1/00 by 65 FR 75160.]

(g) *Alternative premium funding target.* A plan's alternative premium funding target is determined in the same way as its standard premium funding target except that the discount rates described in ERISA section 4006(a)(3)(E)(iv) are not used. Instead, the alternative premium funding target is determined using the discount rates that would have been used to determine the funding target for the plan under ERISA section 303 for the purpose of determining the plan's minimum contribution under ERISA section 303 for the UVB valuation year if the segment rate stabilization provisions of ERISA section 303(h)(2)(iv) were disregarded. A plan may elect to compute unfunded vested benefits using the alternative premium funding target instead of the standard premium funding target described in §4006.4(b)(2), and may revoke such an election, in accordance with the provisions of this paragraph (g). A plan must compute its unfunded vested benefits using the alternative premium funding target instead of the standard premium funding target described in §4006.4(b)(2) if an election under this paragraph (g) to use the alternative premium funding target is in effect for the premium payment year.

(1) An election under this paragraph (g) to use the alternative premium funding target for a plan must specify the premium payment year to which it first applies and must be filed by the plan's variable-rate premium due date for that premium payment year. The premium payment year to which the election first applies must begin at least five years after the beginning of the premium payment year to which a revocation of a prior election first applied. The election will be effective—

(i) For the premium payment year for which made and for all plan years that begin less than five years thereafter, and

(ii) For all succeeding plan years until the premium payment year to which a revocation of the election first applies.

(2) A revocation of an election under this paragraph (g) to use the alternative premium funding target for a plan must specify the premium payment year to which it first applies and must be filed by the plan's variable-rate premium due date for that premium payment year. The premium payment year to which the revocation first applies must begin at least five years after the beginning of the premium payment year to which the election first applied.

[Added 3/21/2008 by 73 FR 15065. Revised 3/11/14 by 79 FR 13547.]

[¶ 15,361E]

§4006.6 **Definition of "participant".** (a) *General rule.* For purposes of this part and part 4007 of this chapter, an individual is considered to be a participant in a plan on any date if the plan has benefit liabilities with respect to the individual on that date.

(b) *Loss or distribution of benefit.* For purposes of this section, an individual is treated as no longer being a participant—

(1) In the case of an individual with no vested accrued benefit, after—

(i) The individual incurs a one-year break in service under the terms of the plan,

(ii) The individual's entire "zero-dollar" vested accrued benefit is deemed distributed under the terms of the plan, or

(iii) The individual dies; and

(2) In the case of a living individual whose accrued benefit is fully or partially vested, or a deceased individual whose accrued benefit was fully or partially vested at the time of death, after—

(i) An insurer makes an irrevocable commitment to pay all benefit liabilities with respect to the individual, or

(ii) All benefit liabilities with respect to the individual are otherwise distributed.

(c) *Examples.* The operation of this section is illustrated by the following examples:

Example 1. Participation under a calendar-year plan begins upon commencement of employment, and the only benefit provided by the plan is an accrued benefit (expressed as a life annuity beginning at age 65) of $30 per month times full years of service. The plan credits a ratable portion of a full year of service for service of at least 1,000 hours but less than 2,000 hours in a service computation period that begins on the date when the participant commences employment and each anniversary of that date. John and Mary both commence employment on July 1, 2008. On December 31, 2008 (the participant count date for the plan's 2009 premium), John has credit for 988 hours of service and Mary has credit for 1,006 hours of service. For purposes of this section, Mary is considered to have an accrued benefit, and John is considered not to have an accrued benefit. Thus, the plan is considered to have benefit liabilities with respect to Mary, but not John, on December 31, 2008; and Mary, but not John, must be counted as a participant for purposes of computing the plan's 2009 premium.

Example 2. The plan also provides that a participant becomes vested five years after commencing employment and defines a one-year break in service as a service computation period in which less than 500 hours of service is performed. On February 1, 2010, John has an accrued benefit of $18 per month beginning at age 65 based on credit for 1,200 hours of service in the service computation period that began July 1, 2008. However, John has credit for only 492 hours of service in the service computation period that began July 1, 2009. On February 1, 2010, John terminates his employment. On December 31, 2010 (the participant count date for the 2011 premium), John has incurred a one-year break in service, and thus is not counted as a participant for purposes of computing the plan's 2011 premium.

Example 3. On January 1, 2012, the plan is amended to provide that if a vested participant whose accrued benefit has a present value of $5,000 or less leaves employment, the benefit will be immediately cashed out. On December 30, 2013, Jane, who has a vested benefit with a present value of less than $5,000, leaves employment. Because of reasonable administrative delay in determining the amount of the benefit to be paid, the plan does not pay Jane the value of her benefit until January 9, 2014. Under the provisions of this section, Jane is treated as not having an accrued benefit on December 31, 2013 (the

participant count date for the 2014 premium), because Jane's benefit is treated as having been paid on December 30, 2013. Thus, Jane is not counted as a participant for purposes of computing the plan's 2014 premium.

Example 4. If the plan amendment had instead provided for cashouts as of the first of the month following termination of employment, and the plan paid Jane the value of her benefit on January 1, 2014, Jane would be treated under the provisions of this section as having an accrued benefit on December 31, 2013, and would thus be counted as a participant for purposes of computing the plan's 2014 premium. [Added 12/1/00 by 65 FR 75160; revised 3/21/08 by 73 FR 15065.]

[¶ 15,361F]

§ 4006.7 **Premium rate for certain terminated single-employer plans.** (a) The premium under this section ("termination premium") applies to a DRA 2005 termination described in § 4007.13 of this chapter.

(b) The amount of the premium under this section that is payable with respect to each applicable 12-month period (as described in § 4007.13 of this chapter) is the number of participants in the plan, determined as of the day before the termination date, multiplied by the termination premium rate. In general, the termination premium rate is $1,250. However, the termination premium rate is $2,500 for an "eligible plan" under section 402(c)(1) of the Pension Protection Act of 2006 (dealing with certain plans of commercial passenger airlines and airline catering services) while an election under section 402(a)(1) of the Pension Protection Act of 2006 (dealing with alternative funding schedules) is in effect for the plan if the plan terminates during the five-year period beginning on the first day of the first applicable plan year (as defined in section 402(c)(2) of that Act) with respect to the plan, unless the Secretary of Labor determines that the plan terminated as a result of extraordinary circumstances such as a terrorist attack or other similar event. [Amended 3/11/14 by 79 FR 13547.]

(c) The premium under this section is in addition to any other premium under this part.

(d) See § 4007.13 of this chapter for further rules about termination premiums.

[Adopted 12/17/2007 by 72 FR 71222.]

[¶ 15,370]
PAYMENT OF PREMIUMS

Act Sec. 4007.(a) PREMIUMS PAYABLE WHEN DUE; ACCRUAL; WAIVER OR REDUCTION.—The designated payor of each plan shall pay the premiums imposed by the corporation under this title with respect to that plan when they are due. Premiums under this title are payable at the time, and on an estimated, advance, or other basis, as determined by the corporation. Premiums imposed by this title on the date of enactment (applicable to that portion of any plan year during which such date occurs) are due within 30 days after such date. Premiums imposed by this title on the first plan year commencing after the date of enactment of this Act are due within 30 days after such plan year commences. Premiums shall continue to accrue until a plan's assets are distributed pursuant to a termination procedure, or until a trustee is appointed pursuant to section 4042, whichever is earlier. The corporation may waive or reduce premiums for a multiemployer plan for any plan year during which such plan receives financial assistance from the corporation under section 4261, except that any amount so waived or reduced shall be treated as financial assistance under such section.

Act Sec. 4007. (b)(1) LATE PAYMENT CHARGE; WAIVER.—If any basic benefit premium is not paid when it is due the corporation is authorized to assess a late payment charge of not more than 100 percent of the premium payment which was not timely paid. The preceding sentence shall not apply to any payment of premium made within 60 days after the date on which payment is due, if before such date, the designated payor obtains a waiver from the corporation based upon a showing of substantial hardship arising from the timely payment of the premium. The corporation is authorized to grant a waiver under this subsection upon application made by the designated payor, but the corporation may not grant a waiver if it appears that the designated payor will be unable to pay the premium within 60 days after the date on which it is due. If any premium is not paid by the last date prescribed for a payment, interest on the amount of such premium at the rate imposed under section 6601(a) of the Internal Revenue Code of 1986 (relating to interest on underpayment, nonpayment, or extensions of time for payment of tax) shall be paid for the period from such last date to the date paid.

(2) The corporation is authorized to pay, subject to regulations prescribed by the corporation, interest on the amount of any overpayment of premium refunded to a designated payor. Interest under this paragraph shall be calculated at the same rate and in the same manner as interest is calculated for underpayments under paragraph (1).

Act Sec. 4007. (c) CIVIL ACTION TO RECOVER PREMIUM PENALTY AND INTEREST.—If any designated payor fails to pay a premium when due, the corporation is authorized to bring a civil action in any district court of the United States within the jurisdiction of which the plan assets are located, the plan is administered, or in which a defendant resides or is found for the recovery of the amount of the premium, penalty, and interest, and process may be served in any other district. The district courts of the United States shall have jurisdiction over actions brought under this subsection by the corporation without regard to the amount in controversy.

Act. Sec. 4007. (d) BASIC BENEFIT GUARANTEE NOT STOPPED BY DESIGNATED PAYOR'S FAILURE TO PAY PREMIUMS WHEN DUE.—The corporation shall not cease to guarantee basic benefits on account of the failure of a designated payor to pay any premium when due.

Act Sec. 4007.(e)(1) DESIGNATED PAYOR.—For purposes of this section, the term "designated payor" means—

    (A) the contributing sponsor or plan administrator in the case of a single-employer plan, and

    (B) the plan administrator in the case of a multiemployer plan.

(2) If the contributing sponsor of any single-employer plan is a member of a controlled group, each member of such group shall be jointly and severally liable for any premiums required to be paid by such contributing sponsor. For purposes of the preceding sentence, the term "controlled group" means any group treated as a single employer under subsection (b), (c), (m), or (o) of section 414 of the Internal Revenue Code of 1986.

Amendments

P.L. 114-74, § 502, provides:

Sec. 502 PENSION PAYMENT ACCELERATION.

Notwithstanding section 4007(a) of the Employee Retirement Income Security Act of 1974 (29 U.S.C. 1307(a)) and section 4007.11 of title 29, Code of Federal Regulations, for plan years commencing after December 31, 2024, and before January 1, 2026, the premium due date for such plan years shall be the fifteenth day of the ninth calendar month that begins on or after the first day of the premium payment year.

P.L. 109-280, § 406(a):

Amended ERISA Sec. 4007(b) by striking "(b)" and replacing it with "(b)(1)" and by adding a new subparagraph (b)(2) to read as above.

The above amendment applies to interest accruing for periods beginning not earlier than the date of the enactment (August 17, 2006).

P.L. 101-239, § 7891(a)(1):

Titles I, III, and IV of ERISA (other than sections 3(37)(E), 301(a)(7), and 308, the last sentence of section 408(d), and sections 414(c), 4001(a)(3)(ii), and 4303) are each amended by striking "Internal Revenue Code of 1954" each place it appears and inserting "Internal Revenue Code of 1986" effective October 22, 1986.

P.L. 100-203, § 9331(c)(1):

Amended ERISA Sec. 4007 by striking out "plan administrator" and replacing it with "designated payor", to read as above, effective for plan years beginning after December 31, 1987.

P.L. 100-203, § 9331(c)(2):

Amended ERISA Sec. 4007 by adding subsection (e), to read as above, effective from plan years beginning after December 31, 1987.

P.L. 96-364, §§ 402(a)(3) and 403(b):

Amended Sec. 4007(a), effective September 26, 1980 by striking out the second sentence and by inserting a new sentence at the end thereof.

Regulations

The following regulations were adopted by the Pension Benefit Guaranty Corporation on July 1, 1996 (61 FR 34002). Prior to July 1, 1996, PBGC regulations were under Chapter XXVI of Title 29 of the Code of Federal Regulations. Effective July 1, 1996, PBGC regulations were moved to Chapter XL, and were renumbered and reorganized. Reg. § 4007.10 was amended July 9, 1997 (62 FR 36663), effective August 8, 1997. Reg. § 4007.8 was revised November 26, 1999 (64 FR 66383), effective December 27, 1999. Reg § 4007.8 was amended December 1, 2000 (65 FR 75160), effective January 1, 2001. Reg. § 4007.3, Reg. § 4007.5, Reg. § 4007.6, and Reg. § 4007.10 were amended October 28, 2003 (68 FR 61344). Reg. § 4007.3, § 4007.4. and § 4007.11 were revised June 1, 2006 (71 FR 31077), effective July 1, 2006. Reg. § 4007.8 was amended and revised and an Appendix was added November 17, 2006 (71 FR 66867). Reg. § 4007.3, § 4007.7, § 4007.8, § 4007.9, § 4007.10, § 4007.11, § 4007.12 were amended, and Reg. § 4007.13 was added, on December 17, 2007 by 72 FR 71222. Reg. § 4007.2, § 4007.3, § 4007.7, § 4007.8, § 4007.10 and § 4007.11 were amended on March 21, 2008 (73 FR 15065). Reg. § 4007.8(f), (g), (h), and (i) were amended on January 3, 2014 (78 FR 347). Reg. § 4007.11(a) was amended on January 3, 2014 (79 FR 347). Reg. §§ 4007.2, 4007.3, 4007.8, 4007.11, 4007.12, 4007.13, and the Appendix to Part 4007 were amended on March 11, 2014 (79 FR 13547). Reg. § 4007.8 was amended on September 23, 2016 (81 FR 65542).

[¶ 15,371]

§ 4007.1 **Purpose and scope.** This part, which applies to all plans that are covered by title IV of ERISA, provides procedures for paying the premiums imposed by sections 4006 and 4007 of ERISA. (See part 4006 of this chapter for premium rates and computational rules.)

[¶ 15,371A]

§ 4007.2 **Definitions.** (a) The following terms are defined in § 4001.2 of this chapter: Code, contributing sponsor, ERISA, multiemployer plan, IRS, multiemployer plan, notice of intent to terminate, PBGC, plan, plan administrator, plan year, single-employer plan, and termination date. [Amended 3/11/14 by 79 FR 13547.]

(b) For purposes of this part, the following terms are defined in § 4006.2 of this chapter: continuation plan, new plan, newly covered plan, participant, participant count, premium, funding target, premium payment year, short plan year, small plan, and UVB valuation date. [Amended 3/11/14 by 79 FR 13547.]

[¶ 15,371B]

§ 4007.3 **Filing requirements; method of filing.** (a) *In general.* The estimation, determination, declaration, and payment of premiums must be made in accordance with the premium instructions on PBGC's Web site (*www.pbgc.gov*). Subject to the provisions of § 4007.13, the plan administrator of each covered plan is responsible for filing prescribed premium information and payments. Each required premium payment and related information, certified as provided in the premium instructions, must be filed by the applicable due date specified in this part in the manner and format prescribed in the instructions. [Revised 3/11/14 by 79 FR 13547.]

(b) *Electronic filing.* Information must be filed electronically except to the extent that PBGC grants an exemption for good cause in appropriate circumstances. (The requirement to file electronically applies to all estimated and final flat-rate and variable-rate premium filings (including amended filings) but does not apply to information filed to comply with a PBGC request under (4007.10(c) (dealing with providing record information in connection with a premium compliance review).) Unless an exemption applies, filing on paper or in any other manner other than by a prescribed electronic filing method does not satisfy the requirement to file. Failure to file electronically as required is subject to penalty under ERISA section 4071. [Amended 3/11/14 by 79 FR 13547.]

[Amended 6/1/2006 by 71 FR 31077 and 12/17/07 by 72 FR 71222; Revised 3/21/2008 by 73 FR 15065.]

[¶ 15,371C]

§ 4007.4 **Where to file.** See ERISA Reg. § 4000.4 of this chapter for information on where to file.

[Revised 6/1/2006 by 71 FR 31077.]

[¶ 15,371D]

§ 4007.5 **Date of filing.** The PBGC applies the rules in subpart C of part 4000 of this chapter to determine the date that a submission under this part was filed with the PBGC.

[Amended 10/28/2003 by 68 FR 61344]

[¶ 15,371E]

§ 4007.6 **Computation of time.** The PBGC applies the rules in subpart D of part 4000 of this chapter to compute any time period under this part. However, for purposes of determining the amount of a late payment interest charge under Sec. 4007.7 or of a late payment penalty charge under Sec. 4007.8, the rule in Sec. 4000.43(a) of this chapter governing periods ending on weekends or Federal holidays does not apply.

[Amended 10/28/2003 by 68 FR 61344]

[¶ 15,371F]

§ 4007.7 **Late payment interest charges.** (a) If any premium payment due under this part is not paid by the due date prescribed for such payment by this part, an interest charge will accrue on the unpaid amount at the rate imposed under section 6601(a) of the Code for the period from the date payment is due to the date payment is made. Late payment interest charges are compounded daily.

(b) With respect to any PBGC bill for a premium underpayment and/or interest thereon, interest will accrue only until the date of the bill if the premium underpayment and interest billed are paid within 30 days after the date of the bill.

[Amended 12/17/07 by 72 FR 71222; revised 3/21/2008 by 73 FR 15065.]

[¶ 15,371G]

§ 4007.8 **Late payment penalty charges.** (a) *Penalty charge.* Subject to the provisions of § 4007.13, if any premium payment due under this part is not paid by the due date under this part, PBGC will assess a late payment penalty charge as determined under this paragraph (a), except to the extent the charge is waived under paragraphs (b) through (h) of this section. The amount determined under this paragraph (a) will be based on the number of months (counting any portion of a month as a whole month) from the due date to the date of payment. The penalty rate is — [Amended 11/17/06 by 71 FR 66867 12/17/07 by

72 FR 71222, and revised 3/21/2008 by 73 FR 15065. Amended 3/11/14 by 79 FR 13547 and 9/23/16 by 81 FR 65542.]

(1) For any amount of unpaid premium that is paid on or before the date PBGC issues the first written notice to any person liable for the premium that there is or may be a premium delinquency (for example, a premium bill, a letter initiating a premium compliance review, a notice of filing error in premium determination, or a letter questioning a failure to make a premium filing), 1/2 percent per month, to a maximum penalty charge of 25 percent of the unpaid premium; or [Amended 3/11/14 by 79 FR 13547 and 9/23/16 by 81 FR 65542.]

(2) For any amount of unpaid premium that is paid after that date, 2 1/2 percent per month, to a maximum penalty charge of 50 percent of the unpaid premium. [Amended 12/17/07 by 72 FR 71222 and revised 3/21/2008 by 73 FR 15065. Amended 3/11/14 by 79 FR 13547 and 9/23/16 by 81 FR 65542.]

(b) *Hardship waiver.* The PBGC may grant a waiver based upon a showing of substantial hardship as provided in section 4007(b) of ERISA.

(c) *Reasonable cause waivers.* PBGC will waive all or part of a late payment penalty charge if PBGC determines that there is reasonable cause for the late payment. Policy guidelines for applying the "reasonable cause" standard are in §§ 22 through 25 of the Appendix to this part. [Revised 11/17/06 by 71 FR 66867.]

(d) *Other waivers.* PBGC may waive all or part of a late payment penalty charge in other circumstances without regard to whether there is reasonable cause. Policy guidelines for waivers without reasonable cause are in § 21(b)(1), (b)(3), (b)(4), and (b)(5) of the Appendix to this part. [Revised 11/17/06 by 71 FR 66867.]

(e) *Grace period.* With respect to any PBGC bill for a premium underpayment, the PBGC will waive any late payment penalty charge accruing after the date of the bill, provided the premium underpayment is paid within 30 days after the date of the bill.

(f) *Filings not more than 7 days late.* PBGC will waive premium payment penalties that arise solely because premium payments are late by not more than seven calendar days, as described in this paragraph (f). In applying this waiver, PBGC will assume that each premium payment with respect to a plan year was made seven calendar days before it was actually made. All other rules will then be applied as usual. If the result of this procedure is that no penalty would arise for that plan year, then any penalty that would apply on the basis of the actual payment date(s) will be waived. [Added 3/11/14 by 79 FR 13547.]

(g) *Variable-rate premium penalty relief.* PBGC will waive the penalty on any underpayment of the variable-rate premium for the period that ends on the earlier of the date the reconciliation filing is due or the date the reconciliation filing is made if, by the date the variable-rate premium for the premium payment year is due under § 4007.11(a)(1),—[Amended 3/11/14 by 79 FR 13547.]

(1) The plan administrator reports—

(i) The fair market value of the plan's assets for the premium payment year, and

(ii) An estimate of the plan's premium funding target for the premium payment year that is certified by an enrolled actuary to be a reasonable estimate that takes into account the most current data available to the enrolled actuary and that has been determined in accordance with generally accepted actuarial principles and practices; and

(2) The plan administrator pays at least the amount of variable-rate premium determined from the value of assets and estimated premium funding target so reported. [Added 3/21/2008 by 73 FR 15065. Redesignated 3/11/14 by 79 FR 13547.]

(h) *Demonstrated compliance.* PBGC will waive 80 percent of the premium payment penalty assessed under paragraph (a)(2) of this section if the criteria in paragraphs (h)(1) and (2) of this section are met.

(1) For each plan year within the last five plan years of coverage preceding the plan year for which the penalty rate is being determined,—

(i) Any required premium filing for the plan has been made; and

(ii) PBGC has not required payment of a penalty for the plan under this section.

(2) For the plan year for which the penalty rate is being determined, the total amount of premium is paid no later than 30 days after PBGC issues the first written notice as described in paragraph (a)(1) of this section. [Added 9/23/2016 by 81 FR 65542.]

[¶ 15,371H]

§ 4007.9 **Coverage for guaranteed basic benefits.** (a) The failure to pay the premiums due under this part will not result in a plan's loss of coverage for basic benefits guaranteed under sections 4022(a) or 4022A(a) of ERISA.

(b) The payment of the premiums imposed by this part will not result in coverage for basic benefits guaranteed under sections 4022(a) or 4022A(a) of ERISA for plans not covered under title IV of ERISA.

[Amended 12/17/07 by 72 FR 71222.]

[¶ 15,371I]

§ 4007.10 **Recordkeeping; audits; disclosure of information.** (a) *Retention of records to support premium payments.* (1) *In general.* The designated recordkeeper under paragraph (a)(3) of this section must retain, for a period of six years after the premium due date, all plan records that are necessary to establish, support, and validate the amount of any premium required to be paid and any information required to be reported ("premium-related information") under this part and part 4006 of this chapter and under PBGC's premium filing instructions. Records that must be retained pursuant to this paragraph include, but are not limited to, records that establish the number of plan participants and that support and demonstrate the calculation of unfunded vested benefits.

[Revised 3/21/08 by 73 FR 15065.]

(2) *Electronic recordkeeping.* A designated record keeper may use electronic media for maintenance and retention of records required by this part in accordance with the requirements of subpart E of part 4000 of this chapter.

[Amended 10/28/2003 by 68 FR 61344 and 12/17/07 by 72 FR 71222.]

(3) *Designated recordkeepers..* (i) With respect to the flat-rate and variable-rate premiums described in § 4006.3 of this chapter, the plan administrator is the designated recordkeeper.

(ii) With respect to the premium for certain terminated single-employer plans described in § 4006.7 of this chapter, each person who was a contributing sponsor of such a plan, or was a member of a contributing sponsor's controlled group, as of the day before the plan's termination date is a designated recordkeeper.

[Added 12/17/07 by 72 FR 71222.]

(4) *Records.* (i) Records that must be retained pursuant to paragraph (a)(1) of this section include, but are not limited to, records prepared by the plan administrator, a plan sponsor, an employer required to contribute to the plan with respect to its employees, an enrolled actuary performing services for the plan, or an insurance carrier issuing any contract to pay benefits under the plan.

(ii) For purposes of this section, "records" include, but are not limited to, plan documents; participant data records; personnel and payroll records; actuarial tables, worksheets, and reports; records of computations, projections, and estimates; benefit statements, disclosures, and applications; financial and tax records; insurance contracts; records of plan procedures and practices; and any other records, whether in written, electronic, or other format, that are relevant to the determination of the amount of any premium required to be paid or any premium-related information required to be reported.

(iii) When a record to be produced for PBGC inspection and copying exists in more than one format, it must be produced in the format specified by PBGC.

[Added 3/21/2008 by 73 FR 15065.]

(b) *PBGC audit.* (1) *In general.* In order to determine the correctness of any premium paid or premium-related information reported or to determine the amount of any premium required to be paid or any premium-related information required to be reported, PBGC may—

(i) Audit any premium filing,

(ii) Inspect and copy any records that are relevant to the determination of the amount of any premium required to be paid and any premium-related information required to be reported, including (without limitation) the records described in paragraph (a) of this section, and

(iii) Require disclosure of any manual or automated system or process used to determine any premium paid or premium-related information reported, and demonstration of its operation in order to permit PBGC to determine the effectiveness of the system or process and the reliability of information produced by the system or process.

(2) *Deficiencies found on audit.* If, upon audit, PBGC determines that a premium due under this part was underpaid, late payment interest and penalty charges will apply as provided for in this part. If, upon audit, PBGC determines that required information was not timely and accurately reported, a penalty may be assessed under ERISA section 4071.

(3) *Insufficient records*

In determining the premium due, if, in the judgment of PBGC, a plan's records fail to establish the participant count or (for a single-employer plan) the plan's unfunded vested benefits for any premium payment year, PBGC may rely on data it obtains from other sources (including the IRS and the Department of Labor) for presumptively establishing the participant count and/or unfunded vested benefits for premium computation purposes.

[Revised 3/21/2008 by 73 FR 15065.]

(c) *Providing record information.* (1) *In general.* A designated recordkeeper must make the records retained pursuant to paragraph (a) of this section available to PBGC promptly upon request for inspection and photocopying (or, for electronic records, inspection, electronic copying, and printout) at the location where they are kept (or another, mutually agreeable, location). If PBGC requests in writing that records retained pursuant to paragraph (a) of this section, or information in such records, be submitted to PBGC, the designated recordkeeper must submit the requested materials to PBGC either electronically or by hand, mail, or commercial delivery service within 45 days of the date of PBGC's request therefor, or by a different time specified in the request.

[Revised 3/21/2008 by 73 FR 15065.]

(2) *Extension.* Except as provided in paragraph (c)(3) of this section, a designated record keeper may automatically extend the period described in paragraph (c)(1) by submitting a certification to the PBGC prior to the expiration of that time period. The certification shall—

(i) Specify a date to which the time period described in paragraph (c)(1) is extended that is no more than 90 days from the date of the PBGC's written request for information; and

(ii) Contain a statement, certified to by the designated record keeper under penalty of perjury (18 U.S.C. § 1001), that, despite reasonable efforts, the additional time is necessary to comply with the PBGC's request.

[Amended 12/17/07 by 72 FR 71222.]

(3) *Shortening of time period.* The PBGC may in its discretion shorten the time period described in paragraph (c)(1) or (c)(2) of this section where it determines that the interests of PBGC may be prejudiced by a delay in the receipt of the information (e.g., where collection of unpaid premiums (or any associated interest or penalties) would otherwise be jeopardized) If the PBGC shortens the time period described in paragraph (c)(1), no extension is available under paragraph (c)(2).

[Revised 3/21/08 by 73 FR 15065.]

(d) *Address and timeliness.* Information required to be submitted under paragraph (c) of this section shall be submitted to the address specified in the PBGC's request. The timeliness of a submission shall be determined in accordance with §§ 4007.5 and 4007.6. [Amended 7/9/97 by 62 FR 36663.]

[¶ 15,371J]

§ 4007.11 **Due dates.** (a) *In general.* In general:

(1) The flat-rate and variable-rate premium filing due date is the fifteenth day of the tenth calendar month that begins on or after the first day of the premium payment year.

(2) If the variable-rate premium paid by the premium filing due date is estimated as described in § 4007.8(g)(1)(ii), a reconciliation filing and any required variable-rate premium payment must be made by the end of the sixth calendar month that begins on or after the premium filing due date.

(3) *Small plan transition rule.* Notwithstanding paragraph (a)(1) of this section, if a plan had fewer than 100 participants for whom flat-rate premiums were payable for the plan year preceding the last plan year that began before 2014, then the plan's due date for the first plan year beginning after 2013 is the fifteenth day of the fourteenth calendar month that begins on or after the first day of that plan year.

(b) *Plans that change plan years.* For a plan that changes its plan year, the flat-rate and variable-rate premium filing due date for the short plan year is as specified in paragraph (a) of this section. For the plan year that follows a short plan year, the due date is the later of—

(1) The due date specified in paragraph (a) of this section, or

(2) 30 days after the date on which the amendment changing the plan year was adopted.

(c) *New and newly covered plans.* For a new plan or newly covered plan, the flat-rate and variable-rate premium filing due date for the first plan year of coverage is the latest of—

(1) The due date specified in paragraph (a) of this section, or

(2) 90 days after the date of the plan's adoption, or

(3) 90 days after the date on which the plan became covered by title IV of ERISA, or

(4) In the case of a small plan that is a continuation plan, 90 days after the plan's UVB valuation date.

(d) *Terminating plans.* For a plan that terminates in a standard termination, the flat-rate and variable-rate premium filing due date for the plan year in which all plan assets are distributed pursuant to the plan's termination is the earlier of—

(1) The due date specified in paragraph (a) of this section, or

(2) The date when the post-distribution certification under § 4041.29 of this chapter is filed.

(e) *Continuing obligation to file.* The obligation to make flat-rate and variable-rate premium filings and payments under this part continues through the plan year in which all plan assets are distributed pursuant to a plan's termination or in which a trustee is appointed under section 4042 of ERISA, whichever occurs earlier.

[Revised 3/11/14 by 79 FR 13547.]

[¶ 15,371K]

§ 4007.12 **Liability for single-employer premiums.** (a) The designation under this part of the plan administrator as the person required to make flat-rate and variable-rate premium filings and payments under this part for a single-employer plan is a procedural requirement only and does not alter the liability for premium payments imposed by section 4007 of ERISA. Pursuant to section 4007(e) of ERISA, both the plan administrator and the contributing sponsor of a single-employer plan are liable for flat-rate and variable-rate premium payments, and, if the contributing sponsor is a member of a controlled group, each member of the controlled group is jointly and severally liable for the required premiums. Any entity that is liable for required premiums is also liable for any interest and penalties assessed with respect to such premiums.

[Amended 12/17/07 by 72 FR 71222.]

(b) After a plan administrator issues (pursuant to section 4041(a)(2) of ERISA) the first notice of intent to terminate in a distress termination under section 4041(c) of ERISA or PBGC issues a notice of determination under section 4042(a) of ERISA, the obligation to pay the premiums (and any interest or penalties thereon) imposed by ERISA and this part for a single-employer plan shall be an obligation solely of the contributing sponsor and the members of its controlled group, if any.

Sec.

General Provisions

Premium Penalty Assessment

[Reserved.]

Waiver Standards

Procedures

[Reserved.]

General Provisions

§ 1 What is the purpose of this Appendix?

This appendix sets forth principles and guidelines that we intend to follow in assessing, reviewing, and waiving premium penalties. However, this is only general policy guidance. Our action in each case is guided by the facts and circumstances of the case.

§ 2 What defined terms are used in this Appendix?

The following terms are defined in part 4001 of this chapter: contributing sponsor, ERISA, PBGC, person, plan, and plan administrator. In addition, in this appendix:

(a) *Premium penalty* means a penalty under ERISA section 4007 and under this part for failing to pay a premium in full and on time.

(b) *Waiver* means reduction or elimination of a premium penalty that is being or has been assessed.

(c) *We* means PBGC.

(d) *You* means, according to the context,—

(1) A plan administrator, contributing sponsor, or other person, if—

(i) The person's action or inaction may be the basis for a premium penalty assessment,

(ii) The person may be required to pay the premium penalty, or

(iii) The person is requesting review of the premium penalty; or

(2) An employee or agent of, or advisor to, any of these persons.

§ 3 What is the purpose of a premium penalty?

The basic purpose of a premium penalty is to encourage you to pay premiums in full and on time and to voluntarily self-correct any failure to do so.

§ 4 What information is in this Appendix and how is it organized?

This Appendix has four divisions:

(a) *General provisions.* The General Provisions division (§§ 1-4) tells you the purpose and organization of the Appendix, the purpose of a premium penalty, and the definitions of terms used in the Appendix.

(b) *Premium penalty assessment.* The Premium Penalty Assessment division is reserved.

(c) *Waiver standards.* The Waiver Standards division (§§ 21-25) explains the principles that PBGC follows in waiving premium penalties.

(Approved by the Office of Management and Budget under control number 1212-0009)

[Amended 7/9/97 by 62 FR 36663 and 3/11/14 by 79 FR 13547.]

[¶ 15,373]

§ 4007.12a **Appendix to Part 4007. Policy Guidelines on Premium Penalties.**

(1) *Reasonable cause.* We waive premium penalties for reasonable cause, as explained in §§ 22-25.

(2) *Other waivers.* We also waive premium penalties in some other circumstances, such as mistake of law, as explained in § 21.

(d) *Procedures.* The Procedures division is reserved.

Premium Penalty Assessment

[Reserved.]

Waiver Standards

§ 21 What are the standards for waiving a premium penalty?

(a) *Facts and circumstances.* In deciding whether to waive a premium penalty in whole or in part under paragraph (b), we consider the facts and circumstances of each case.

(b) *Waivers.*

(1) *Provisions of law.* We waive all or part of a premium penalty if a statute or regulation requires that we do so. For example, ERISA section 4007(b) and § 4007.8 of this part provide for a waiver in certain circumstances involving business hardship, and § 4007.8 of this part also provides for a waiver of a premium penalty that accrues after the date of a bill for a premium underpayment if you pay the premium owed within 30 days after the date of the bill, and for waivers in certain cases where you pay not more than a week late or where you estimate the variable-rate premium and then timely correct any underpayment. [Amended 3/11/14 by 79 FR 13547.]

(2) *Reasonable cause.* We waive a premium penalty if you show reasonable cause for a failure to pay a premium in full and on time. See §§ 22 through 25 for guidelines on "reasonable cause" waivers. If there is reasonable cause for only part of a failure to pay a premium, we waive the premium penalty only for that part.

(3) *Legal errors.* We may waive all or part of a premium penalty if the failure to pay a premium in full and on time that gives rise to the premium penalty results from certain kinds of legal errors.

(i) *Erroneous legal interpretation—disclosed.* If a failure to pay a premium in full and on time results from your reliance on an erroneous interpretation of the law, we waive a premium penalty that arises from the failure if you promptly and adequately call our attention to the interpretation and the relevant facts, and the erroneous interpretation is not frivolous. If the interpretation affects a filing that you make with us, you should call our attention to the interpretation in writing with the filing. If you rely on the interpretation to justify not making a filing with us, you should call our attention to the interpretation in writing by the time prescribed for the filing not made.

(ii) *Erroneous legal interpretation—undisclosed.* If a failure to pay a premium in full and on time results from your reliance on an erroneous interpretation of the law, and you do not promptly and adequately call our attention to the interpretation and the relevant facts, we may nevertheless waive a premium penalty if the weight of authority supporting the interpretation is substantial in relation to the weight of opposing authority and it is reasonable for you to rely on the interpretation.

(iii) *Recent change in the law.* We may waive all or part of a premium penalty if the law changes shortly before the date a premium payment is due and the premium payment that you make by the due date would have been correct under the law as in effect before the change. In determining whether and to what extent to grant a waiver in a case of this kind, we consider such factors as the length of time between the change in the law and the premium due date, the nature and timing of any publicity given to the change in the law, the complexity of the legal issues, and your general familiarity with those issues.

(4) *Pendency of PBGC procedures.* We may waive all or a part of a premium penalty that is attributable to the pendency of PBGC review or other procedures. For example:

(i) If you request review of a premium penalty, and you make a non-frivolous argument in your request for review that you were not required to pay the premium or that you were, and still are, unable to obtain the information needed to determine the premium, we may waive the portion of the premium penalty that accrues during the review process. If you make such a non-frivolous argument with respect to a portion of the premium, we may apply this principle to that portion.

(ii) We may waive all or a part of a premium penalty if we believe that the pendency of PBGC procedures for identifying a premium delinquency and notifying you of the delinquency contributed to your failure to correct the delinquency more promptly.

(5) *Other circumstances.* We may waive all or part of a premium penalty in other circumstances if we determine that it is appropriate to do so. [Amended 3/11/14 by 79 FR 13547.]

(c) *Action or inaction of outside parties.* In some cases an accountant, actuary, lawyer, pension consultant, or other individual or firm that is not part of your organization may assist you in complying with PBGC requirements. If the outside individual's or firm's action, inaction, or advice causes or contributes to a failure to pay a premium in full and on time, we apply our waiver authority as if the outside individual or firm were part of your organization. In the case of an outside individual who is part of a firm, we generally consider both the individual and the firm to be part of your organization.

§ 22 What is "reasonable cause"?

(a) *General rule.* In general, there is "reasonable cause" for a failure to pay a premium in full and on time to the extent that—

(1) The failure arises from circumstances beyond your control, and

(2) You could not avoid the failure by the exercise of ordinary business care and prudence.

(b) *Overlooking legal requirements.* Overlooking legal requirements does not constitute reasonable cause.

(c) *Action or inaction of outside parties.* If an accountant, actuary, lawyer, pension consultant, or other individual or firm that is not part of your organization assists you in complying with PBGC requirements, there is generally no reasonable cause for a failure to pay a premium in full and on time that arises from circumstances within the control of the outside individual or firm, or could be avoided by the exercise of ordinary business care and prudence by the outside individual or firm. The fact that you exercised care and prudence in selecting and monitoring the outside individual or firm is not a basis for a reasonable cause waiver.

(d) *Size of organization.* If an organization or one or more of its employees is responsible for taking action, the size of the organization may affect what ordinary business care and prudence would require. For example, ordinary business care and prudence would typically require a larger organization to establish more comprehensive backup procedures than a smaller organization for dealing with situations such as computer failure, the loss of important records, and the inability of

an individual to carry out assigned responsibilities. Thus, there may be reasonable cause for a small organization's failure to pay a premium in full and on time even though, if the organization were larger, the exercise of ordinary business care and prudence would have avoided the failure.

(e) *Size of premium underpayment.* In general, the larger a premium, the more care and prudence you should use to make sure that you pay it in full and on time. Thus, there may be reasonable cause for a small underpayment even though, under the same circumstances, we would conclude that a larger underpayment could have been avoided by the exercise of ordinary business care and prudence.

(f) *Collection and enforcement.* In determining whether reasonable cause exists, we do not consider either—

(i) The likelihood or cost of collecting the premium penalty, or

(ii) The costs and risks of enforcing the premium penalty by litigation.

§ 23 What kinds of facts does PBGC consider in determining whether there is reasonable cause for a failure to pay a premium?

In determining the extent to which a failure to pay a premium in full and on time arose from circumstances beyond your control and the extent to which you could have avoided the failure by the exercise of ordinary business care and prudence—and thus the extent to which waiver of a premium penalty for reasonable cause is appropriate—we consider facts such as the following:

(a) What event or circumstance caused the underpayment and when the event happened or the circumstance arose. The dates you give should clearly correspond with the underpayment upon which the premium penalty is based.

(b) How that event or circumstance kept you from paying the premium in full and on time. The explanation you give should relate directly to the failure to pay a premium that is the subject of the premium penalty.

(c) Whether you could have anticipated the event or circumstance.

(d) How you responded to the event or circumstance, including what steps you took, and how quickly you took them, to pay the premium and how you conducted other business affairs. Knowing how you responded to the event or circumstance may help us determine what degree of business care and prudence you were capable of exercising during that period and thus whether the failure to pay the premium could or could not have been avoided by the exercise of ordinary business care and prudence.

§ 24 What are some situations that might justify a "reasonable cause" waiver?

The following examples illustrate some of the reasons often given for failures to pay premiums for which we may assess penalties. The situation described in each example may constitute reasonable cause, and each example lists factors we consider in determining whether to grant a premium penalty waiver for reasonable cause in a case of that kind.

(a) *An individual with responsibility for taking action was suddenly and unexpectedly absent or unable to act.* We consider such factors as the following: The nature of the event that caused the individual's absence or inability to act, for example, the resignation of the individual or the death or serious illness of the individual or a member of the individual's immediate family; the size of the organization and what kind of backup procedures it had to cope with such events; how close the event was to the deadline that was missed; how abrupt and unanticipated the event was; how the individual's absence or inability to act prevented compliance; how expensive it would have been to comply without the absent individual; whether and how other business operations and obligations were affected; how quickly and prudently a replacement for the absent individual was selected or other arrangements for compliance were made; and how quickly a replacement for the absent individual took appropriate action.

(b) *A fire or other casualty or natural disaster destroyed relevant records or prevented compliance in some other way.* We consider such factors as the following: The nature of the event; how close the event was to the deadline that was missed; how the event caused the failure to pay the premium; whether other efforts were made to get needed information; how expensive it would have been to comply; and how you responded to the event.

(c) *You reasonably relied on erroneous oral or written advice given by a PBGC employee.* We consider such factors as the following: Whether there was a clear relationship between your situation and the advice sought; whether you provided the PBGC employee with adequate and accurate information; and whether the surrounding circumstances should have led you to question the correctness of the advice or information provided.

(d) *You were unable to obtain information, including records and calculations, needed to comply.* We consider such factors as the following: What information was needed; why the information was unavailable; when and how you discovered that the information was not available; what attempts you made to get the information or reconstruct it through other means; and how much it would have cost to comply.

§ 25 What are some situations that might justify a partial "reasonable cause" waiver?

(a) Assume that a fire destroyed the records needed to compute a premium payment. If in the exercise of ordinary business care and prudence it should take you one month to reconstruct the records and pay the premium, but the payment was made two months late, it might be appropriate to waive that part of the premium penalty attributable to the first month the payment was late, but not the part attributable to the second month.

(b) Assume that a plan administrator underpaid the plan's flat-rate premium because of reasonable reliance on erroneous advice from a PBGC employee, and also underpaid the plan's variable-rate premium because the plan actuary used the wrong interest rate. A PBGC audit revealed both errors. PBGC billed the plan for a premium penalty of $5,000—$1,000 for underpayment of the flat-rate premium and $4,000 for underpayment of the variable-rate premium. The plan administrator requested a waiver of the premium penalty. While the erroneous PBGC advice constituted reasonable cause for underpaying the flat-rate premium, there was no showing of reasonable cause for the error in the variable-rate premium. Therefore, we would waive only the part of the premium penalty based on underpayment of the flat-rate portion of the premium ($1,000).

Procedures

[Reserved.]

[Added 11/17/06 by 71 FR 66867.]

[¶ 15,374]

§4007.13 **Premiums for certain terminated single-employer plans.** (a) *Applicability*—(1) *In general.* This section applies where there is a "DRA 2005 termination" of a plan. Subject to paragraph (a)(2) of this section, there is a DRA 2005 termination where a single-employer plan's termination date is after 2005 and either—[Amended 3/11/14 by 79 FR 13547.]

(i) The plan terminates under section 4042 of ERISA, or

(ii) The plan terminates under section 4041(c) of ERISA and at least one contributing sponsor or member of a contributing sponsor's controlled group meets the requirements of section 4041(c)(2)(B)(ii) or (iii) of ERISA.

(2) *Plans terminated during reorganization proceedings.* Except as provided in paragraph (a)(3) of this section, a DRA 2005 termination of a plan does not occur where as of the plan's termination date—[Amended 3/11/14 by 79 FR 13547.]

(i) A bankruptcy proceeding has been filed by or against any person that was a contributing sponsor of the plan on the day before the plan's termination date or that was on that day a member of any controlled group of which any such contributing sponsor was a member,

(ii) The proceeding is pending as a reorganization proceeding under chapter 11 of title 11, United States Code (or under any similar law of a State or political subdivision of a State),

(iii) The person has not been discharged from the proceeding, and

(iv) The proceeding was filed before October 18, 2005.

(3) *Special rule for certain airline-related plans.* Paragraph (a)(2) of this section does not apply to an "eligible plan" under section 402(c)(1) of the Pension Protection Act of 2006 (dealing with certain plans of commercial passenger airlines and airline catering services) while an election under section 402(a)(1) of the Pension Protection Act of 2006 (dealing with alternative funding schedules) is in effect for the plan.

(4) *Termination premium.* A premium as described in § 4006.7 of this chapter is payable to PBGC with respect to a DRA 2005 termination each year for three years after the termination (the "termination premium").

(b) *Filing requirements; method of filing.* Notwithstanding § 4007.3, in the case of a DRA 2005 termination of a plan, each person that was a contributing sponsor of the plan on the day before the plan's termination date or that was on that day a member of any controlled group of which any such contributing sponsor was a member is responsible for filing prescribed termination premium information and payments. Any such person may file on behalf of all such persons.

(c) *Late payment penalty charges.* Notwithstanding § 4007.8(a), if any required termination premium payment is not filed by the due date under paragraph (d) of this section, PBGC may assess a late payment penalty charge based on the facts and circumstances, subject to waiver under § 4007.8(b), (c), (d), or (e). The charge will not exceed the amount of termination premium not timely filed.

(d) *Due dates.* Notwithstanding § 4007.11, the due date for the termination premium is the 30th day of each of three applicable 12-month periods. The three applicable 12-month periods with respect to a DRA 2005 termination of a plan are—

(1) *First applicable 12-month period.* Except as provided in paragraph (e) or (f) of this section, the period of 12 calendar months beginning with the first calendar month following the calendar month in which occurs the plan's termination date, and [Amended 3/11/14 by 79 FR 13547.]

(2) *Subsequent applicable 12-month periods.* Each of the first two periods of 12 calendar months that immediately follow the first applicable 12-month period.

(e) *Certain reorganization cases.* (1) This paragraph (e) applies with respect to a DRA 2005 termination of a plan if the conditions in both paragraph (e)(2) and paragraph (e)(3) of this section are satisfied.

(2) The condition of this paragraph (e)(2) is that either—

(i) The plan terminates under section 4042 of ERISA, or

(ii) The plan terminates under section 4041(c) of ERISA and at least one contributing sponsor or member of a contributing sponsor's controlled group meets the requirements of section 4041(c)(2)(B)(ii) of ERISA.

(3) The condition of this paragraph (e)(3) is that as of the plan's termination date—[Amended 3/11/14 by 79 FR 13547.]

(i) A bankruptcy proceeding has been filed by or against any person that was a contributing sponsor of the plan on the day before the plan's termination date or that was on that day a member of any controlled group of which any such contributing sponsor was a member,

(ii) The proceeding is pending as a reorganization proceeding under chapter 11 of title 11, United States Code (or under any similar law of a State or political subdivision of a State), and

(iii) The person has not been discharged from the proceeding.

(4) If this paragraph (e) applies with respect to a DRA 2005 termination of a plan, then except as provided in paragraph (f) of this section, the first applicable 12-month period with respect to the plan is the period of 12 calendar months beginning with the first calendar month following the calendar month in which occurs the earliest date when, for every person that was a contributing sponsor of the plan on the day before the plan's termination date, or that was on that day a member of any controlled group of which any such contributing sponsor was a member, either—[Amended 3/11/14 by 79 FR 13547.]

(i) There is not pending any bankruptcy proceeding that was filed by or against such person and that was, as of the plan's termination date, a reorganization proceeding under chapter 11 of title 11,

United States Code (or under any similar law of a State or political subdivision of a State), or [Amended 3/11/14 by 79 FR 13547.]

(ii) The person has been discharged in any such proceeding, or

(iii) The person no longer exists.

(f) *Plan termination date in past when set.* If a plan's termination date is in the past when it is established by agreement or court action as described in section 4048 of ERISA, then the first applicable 12-month period for determining the due dates of the termination premium begins with the later of—[Amended 3/11/14 by 79 FR 13547.]

(1) The first calendar month following the calendar month in which the termination date is established by agreement or court action as described in section 4048 of ERISA, or

(2) The first calendar month specified in paragraph (d)(1) of this section or (if paragraph (e) of this section applies) paragraph (e)(4) of this section.

(g) *Liability for termination premiums.* In the case of a DRA 2005 termination of a plan, each person that was a contributing sponsor of the plan on the day before the plan's termination date, or that was on that day a member of any controlled group of which any such contributing sponsor was a member, is jointly and severally liable for termination premiums with respect to the plan.

[Adopted 12/17/07 by 72 FR 71222.]

[¶ 15,380]
REPORT BY THE CORPORATION

Act Sec. 4008. (a) As soon as practicable after the close of each fiscal year the corporation shall transmit to the President and the Congress a report relative to the conduct of its business under this title for that fiscal year. The report shall include financial statements setting forth the finances of the corporation at the end of such fiscal year and the result of its operations (including the source and application of its funds) for the fiscal year and shall include an actuarial evaluation of the expected operations and status of the funds established under section 4005 for the next five years (including a detailed statement of the actuarial assumptions and methods used in making such evaluation).

(b) The report under subsection (a) shall include—

(1) a summary of the Pension Insurance Modeling System microsimulation model, including the specific simulation parameters, specific initial values, temporal parameters, and policy parameters used to calculate the financial statements for the corporation;

(2) a comparison of —

(A) the average return on investments earned with respect to assets invested by the corporation for the year to which the report relates; and

(B) an amount equal to 60 percent of the average return on investment for such year in the Standard & Poor's 500 Index, plus 40 percent of the average return on investment for such year in the Lehman Aggregate Bond Index (or in a similar fixed income index); and

(3) a statement regarding the deficit or surplus for such year that the corporation would have had if the corporation had earned the return described in paragraph (2)(B) with respect to assets invested by the corporation.

Amendments

P.L. 109-280, § 412(1):

Amended ERISA Sec. 4008 by adding by striking "As soon as practicable" and inserting "(a) As soon as practicable" and by adding a new subparagraph (b).

The amendments are effective on the date of enactment (August 17, 2006).

[¶ 15,390]
PORTABILITY ASSISTANCE

Act Sec. 4009. The corporation shall provide advice and assistance to individuals with respect to evaluating the economic desirability of establishing individual retirement accounts or other forms of individual retirement savings for which a deduction is allowable under section 219 of the Internal Revenue Code of 1986 and with respect to evaluating the desirability, in particular cases, of transferring amounts representing an employee's interest in a qualified plan to such an account upon the employee's separation from service with an employer.

Amendment

P.L. 101-239, § 7891(a)(1):

Titles I, III, and IV of ERISA (other than sections 3(37)(E), 301(a)(7), and 308, the last sentence of section 408(d), and sections 414(c), 4001(a)(3)(ii), and 4303) are each

amended by striking "Internal Revenue Code of 1954" each place it appears and inserting "Internal Revenue Code of 1986" effective October 22, 1986.

[¶ 15,395]
AUTHORITY TO REQUIRE CERTAIN INFORMATION

Act Sec. 4010.(a) INFORMATION REQUIRED. Each person described in subsection (b) shall provide the corporation annually, on or before a date specified by the corporation in regulations, with—

(1) such records, documents, or other information that the corporation specifies in regulations as necessary to determine the liabilities and assets of plans covered by this title; and

(2) copies of such person's audited (or, if unavailable, unaudited) financial statements, and such other financial information as the corporation may prescribe in regulations.

(b) PERSONS REQUIRED TO PROVIDE INFORMATION. The persons covered by subsection (a) are each contributing sponsor, and each member of a contributing sponsor's controlled group, of a single-employer plan covered by this title, if—

(1) the funding target attainment percentage (as defined in subsection (d)) at the end of the preceding plan year of a plan maintained by the contributing sponsor or any member of its controlled group is less than 80 percent;

(2) the conditions for imposition of a lien described in section 303(k)(1)(A) and (B) or 306(g)(1)(A) and (B) of this Act or section 430(k)(1)(A) and (B) or 433 (g)(1)(A) and (B) of the Internal Revenue Code of 1986 have been met with respect to any plan maintained by the contributing sponsor or any member of its controlled group; or

(3) minimum funding waivers in excess of $1,000,000 have been granted with respect to any plan maintained by the contributing sponsor or any member of its controlled group, and any portion thereof is still outstanding.

(c) INFORMATION EXEMPT FROM DISCLOSURE REQUIREMENTS. —Any information or documentary material submitted to the corporation pursuant to this section shall be exempt from disclosure under section 552 of title 5, United States Code, and no such information or documentary material may be made public, except as may be relevant to any administrative or judicial action or proceeding. Nothing in this section is intended to prevent disclosure to either body of Congress or to any duly authorized committee or subcommittee of the Congress.

(d) ADDITIONAL INFORMATION REQUIRED.—

(1) IN GENERAL. —The information submitted to the corporation under subsection (a) shall include—

(A) the amount of benefit liabilities under the plan determined using the assumptions used by the corporation in determining liabilities;

(B) the funding target of the plan determined as if the plan has been in at-risk status for at least 5 plan years; and

(C) the funding target attainment percentage of the plan.

(2) DEFINITIONS. —For purposes of this subsection:

(A) FUNDING TARGET. —The term "funding target" has the meaning provided under section 303(d)(1).

(B) FUNDING TARGET ATTAINMENT PERCENTAGE. —The term "funding target attainment percentage" has the meaning provided under section 303(d)(2).

(C) AT-RISK STATUS. —The term "at-risk status" has the meaning provided in section 303(i)(4).

(3) PENSION STABILIZATION DISREGARDED. For purposes of this section, the segment rates used in determining the funding target and funding target attainment percentage shall be determined by not taking into account any adjustment under section 302(h)((2)(C)(iv).

(e) NOTICE TO CONGRESS. —The corporation shall, on an annual basis, submit to the Committee on Health, Education, Labor, and Pensions and the Committee on Finance of the Senate and the Committee on Education and the Workforce and the Committee on Ways and Means of the House of Representatives, a summary report in the aggregate of the information submitted to the corporation under this section.

Amendments

P.L. 113-97, §102(b)(8):

Amended ERISA 4010(b)(2) by striking "303(k)(1)(A) and (B) of this Act or section 430(k)(1)(A) and (B) of the Internal Revenue Code of 1986" and inserting "303(k)(1)(A) and (B) or 306(g)(1)(A) and (B) of this Act or section 430(k)(1)(A) and (B) or 433(g)(1)(A) and (B) of the Internal Revenue Code of 1986".

Effective for years beginning after 12-31-2013.

P.L. 112-141, §40211(b)(3)(D):

Amended ERISA Sec. 4010(d) by adding at the end new paragraph (3) to read as above.

For effective date, see P.L. 112-141, §40211(c), below.

P.L. 112-141, §40211(c):

(c) EFFECTIVE DATE.—

(1) IN GENERAL.—The amendments made by this section shall apply with respect to plan years beginning after December 31, 2011.

(2) RULES WITH RESPECT TO ELECTIONS.—

(A) ADJUSTED FUNDING TARGET ATTAINMENT PERCENTAGE.—A plan sponsor may elect not to have the amendments made by this section apply to any plan year beginning before January 1, 2013, either (as specified in the election)—

(i) for all purposes for which such amendments apply, or

(ii) solely for purposes of determining the adjusted funding target attainment percentage under sections 436 of the Internal Revenue Code of 1986 and 206(g) of the Employee Retirement Income Security Act of 1974 for such plan year.

A plan shall not be treated as failing to meet the requirements of sections 204(g) of such Act and 411(d)(6) of such Code solely by reason of an election under this paragraph.

(B) OPT OUT OF EXISTING ELECTIONS.—If, on the date of the enactment of this Act, an election is in effect with respect to any plan under sections 303(h)((2)(D)(ii) of the Employee Retirement Income Security Act of 1974 and 430(h)((2)(D)(ii) of the Internal Revenue Code of 1986, then, notwithstanding the last sentence of each such section, the plan sponsor may revoke such election without the consent of the Secretary of the Treasury. The plan sponsor may make such revocation at any time before the date which is 1 year after such date of enactment and such revocation shall be effective for the 1st plan year to which the amendments made by this section apply and all subsequent plan years. Nothing in this subparagraph shall preclude a plan sponsor from making a subsequent election in accordance with such sections.

P.L. 110-458, §105(d):

Amended ERISA Sec. 4010(d)(2)(B) by striking "section 302(d)(2)" and inserting "section 303(d)(2)".

The above amendment applies to years beginning after December 31, 2007.

P.L. 109-280, §107(b)(3):

Amended ERISA Sec. 4010(b)(2) by striking "302(f)(1)(A) and (B)" and inserting "303(k)(1)(A) and (B)", and by striking "412(n)(1)(A) and (B)" and inserting "430(k)(1)(A) and (B)".

The above amendment applies to plan years beginning after 2007.

P.L. 109-280, §505(a):

Amended ERISA Sec. 4010(b)(1) to read as above.

Prior to amendment, paragraph (1) read as follows:

(1) the aggregate unfunded vested benefits at the end of the preceding plan year (as determined under section 4006(a)(3)(E)(iii)) of plans maintained by the contributing sponsor and the members of its controlled group exceed $50,000,000 (disregarding plans with no unfunded vested benefits);

The above amendment applies to years beginning after 2007.

P.L. 109-280, §505(b):

Amended ERISA Sec. 4010 by adding new subsections (d) and (e) to read as above.

The above amendment applies to years beginning after 2007.

P.L. 103-465, §772(a):

Act Sec. 772(a) amended subtitle A of title IV of ERISA by adding new section 4010 to read as above.

The above amendment is effective on December 8, 1994.

Regulations

The following regulations were adopted by the Pension Benefit Guaranty Corporation on July 1, 1996 (61 FR 34002). Prior to July 1, 1996, PBGC regulations were under Chapter XXVI of Title 29 of the Code of Federal Regulations. Effective July 1, 1996, PBGC regulations were moved to Chapter XL, and were renumbered and reorganized. Reg. 4010.13 was amended effective August 11, 1997 (62 FR 36993). Reg. §4010.10 was amended on October 28, 2003 (68 FR 61344). Reg. Secs. 4010.3—4010.9 were revised on March 9, 2005 (70 FR 11540). Reg. Secs. 4010.0—4010.11 were amended, Reg. Secs. 4010.12—4010.14 were redesignated as Reg. Secs. 4010.13—4010.15, and Reg. Sec. 4010.12 was added on March 16, 2009 (74 FR 11022). Reg. §§4010.2, 4010.4, 4010.8, and 4010.11 were amended on March 23, 2016 (81 FR 15432). Effective and applicable August 1, 2016, Reg. Sec. 4010.14 was amended in interim final regulations on May 13, 2016 (81 FR 29765), removing the words "of up to $1,100 a day for each day that the failure continues". Reg. Sec. 4010.14 was finalized on January 31, 2017 (82 FR 8813).

[¶ 15,396]

§4010.1 **Purpose and scope.** This part prescribes the requirements for annual filings with PBGC under ERISA section 4010. [Amended 3/16/2009 by 74 FR 11022.]

[¶ 15,396A]

§4010.2 **Definitions.** The following terms are defined in §4001.2 of this chapter: benefit liabilities, Code, contributing sponsor, controlled group, earliest retirement age at valuation date, ERISA, expected retirement age, fair market value, IRS, PBGC, person, plan, plan year, and unreduced retirement age (URA). [Amended 3/16/2009 by 74 FR 11022.]

In addition, for purposes of this part:

4010 funding target attainment percentage means, with respect to a plan for a plan year, the percentage as determined under § 4010.4(b) for the plan year. [Added 3/23/2016 by 81 FR 15432.]

At-risk status means, with respect to a plan for a plan year, at-risk status as defined in ERISA section 303(i)(4) and Code section 430(i)(4). [Added 3/16/2009 by 74 FR 11022.]

Exempt entity means a person that does not have to file information and about which information does not have to be filed, as described in §4010.4(c). [Amended 3/16/2009 by 74 FR 11022.]

Exempt plan means a plan about which actuarial information does not have to be filed, as described in §4010.8(c). [Amended 3/16/2009 by 74 FR 11022.]

Fair market value of the plan's assets means the fair market value of the plan's assets at the end of the plan year ending within the filer's information year (determined without regard to any contributions receivable).

Filer means a person who is required to file reports, as described in §4010.4. [Amended 3/16/2009 by 74 FR 11022.]

Fiscal year means, with respect to a person, the person's annual accounting period or, if the person has not adopted a closing date, the calendar year.

Funding target means, with respect to a plan for a plan year, the funding target as provided under ERISA section 303(d)(1) and Code section 430(d)(1) determined as of the valuation date for the plan year. [Added 3/16/2009 by 74 FR 11022.]

Information year means the information year determined under § 4010.5. [Amended 3/16/2009 by 74 FR 11022.]

Valuation date means, with respect to a plan for a plan year, the valuation date as determined under ERISA section 303(g)(2) and Code section 430(g)(2). [Added 3/16/2009 by 74 FR 11022.]

[¶ 15,396B]

§ 4010.3 **Filing requirement.** (a) *General.* Except as provided in § 4010.8(c) (relating to exempt plans) and except where one or more waivers under § 4010.11 apply, each filer must submit to PBGC annually, on or before the due date specified in § 4010.10, all information specified in § 4010.6(a) with respect to all members of a controlled group and all plans maintained by members of the filer's controlled group. Under § 4000.3(b) of this chapter, except as otherwise provided by PBGC, the information must be submitted electronically in accordance with the instructions on PBGC's Web site, *http://www.pbgc.gov.* [Amended 3/16/2009 by 74 FR 11022.]

(b) *Single controlled group submission.* Any filer or other person may submit the information specified in § 4010.6(a) on behalf of one or more members of a filer's controlled group.

[¶ 15,396C]

§ 4010.4 **Filers.** (a) *General.* Unless a waiver in § 4010.11 of this part applies, a contributing sponsor of a plan and each member of the contributing sponsor's controlled group on the last day of the information year is a filer with respect to an information year (unless exempted under paragraph (c) of this section) if—[Amended 3/23/2016 by 81 FR 15432.]

(1) For any plan (including an exempt plan) maintained by the members of the contributing sponsor's controlled group on the last day of the information year, the 4010 funding target attainment percentage for the plan year ending within the information year is less than 80 percent; [Amended 3/23/2016 by 81 FR 15432.]

(2) Any member of the controlled group fails to make a required installment or other required payment to a plan and, as a result, the conditions for imposition of a lien described in ERISA section 303(k) or 306(g) and Code section 430(k) or 433(g) have been met during the information year, and the required installment or other required payment is not made within ten days after its due date; or [Amended 3/23/2016 by 81 FR 15432.]

(3) Any plan maintained by a member of the controlled group has been granted one or more minimum funding waivers under ERISA section 302(c) and Code section 412(c) totaling in excess of $1 million, and as of the end of the plan year ending within the information year, any portion thereof is still outstanding.

(b) *4010 Funding target attainment percentage—*

(1) *General.* The 4010 funding target attainment percentage for a plan for a plan year equals the funding target attainment percentage as provided under ERISA section 303(d)(2) and Code section 430(d)(2) determined without regard to the interest rate stabilization provisions of ERISA section 303(h)(2)(C)(iv) and Code section 430(h)(2)(C)(iv).

(2) *Assets used to determine 4010 funding target attainment percentage.* For purposes of determining the 4010 funding target attainment percentage for a plan for the plan year, the value of plan assets determined under ERISA section 303(g)(3) and Code section 430(g)(3) may (but need not) be substituted for the asset value determined without regard to the interest rate stabilization provisions of ERISA section 303(h)(2)(C)(iv) and Code section 430(h)(2)(C)(iv).

(3) *Prefunding balance and funding standard carryover balance elections.* For purposes of determining the 4010 funding target attainment percentage for a plan for the plan year, prefunding balances and funding standard carryover balances must reflect any elections (or deemed elections) under ERISA section 303(f) and Code section 430(f) that affect the value of such balances as of the beginning of the plan year, regardless of when the elections (or deemed elections) are made. [Revised 3/23/2016 by 81 FR 15432.]

(c) *Exempt entities.* A person is an exempt entity for an information year if the conditions of paragraphs (c)(1) through (4) of this section are satisfied.

(1) The person is not a contributing sponsor of a plan (other than an exempt plan) as of the last day of the information year.

(2) The person has revenue for its fiscal year ending within the controlled group's information year that is five percent or less of the revenue of the person's controlled group for the fiscal year(s) ending within the information year.

(3) The person has annual operating income for the fiscal year ending within the controlled group's information year that is no more than the greater of—

(i) Five percent of the controlled group's annual operating income for the fiscal year(s) ending within the information year, or

(ii) $5 million.

(4) The person has net assets at the end of the fiscal year ending within the controlled group's information year that is no more than the greater of—

(i) Five percent of the controlled group's annual operating income for the fiscal year(s) ending within the information year, or

(ii) $5 million.

(d) *Minimum funding waiver.* (1) *General.* For purposes of § 4010.4(a)(3), a portion of the minimum funding waiver for a plan is considered outstanding unless prior to the plan year ending within the information year the statutory amortization period has ended, or, as of the valuation date for the plan year ending within the information year, the amortization bases are deemed to be reduced to zero pursuant to ERISA section 303(e)(5) and Code section 430(e)(5).

(2) *Example.* Company A sponsors Plan X, which received a minimum funding waiver of $700,000 for the plan year ending December 31, 2004, and another waiver of $500,000 for the plan year ending December 31, 2008. Assume that the amortization bases of the waivers are not reduced to zero pursuant to ERISA section 303(e)(5) and Code section 430(e)(5), and the waivers are therefore outstanding for the full five-year statutory amortization period. Also, assume Company A has a calendar information year. For the 2009 information year, Company A must report under ERISA section 4010. However, for the 2010 information year, Company A, assuming no other obligation to report under ERISA section 4010, is not required to report. [Redesignated 3/23/2016 by 81 FR 15432.]

(e) *Certain plans to which special funding rules apply.* Except for purposes of determining the information to be submitted under § 4010.8(h) (in connection with the actuarial valuation report), the following statutory provisions are disregarded for purposes of this part:

(1) Section of 402(b) of the Pension Protection Act of 2006, Public Law 109-280, dealing with certain frozen plans of commercial passenger airlines and airline caterers.

(2) Section 104 of the Pension Protection Act of 2006 as amended by the Preservation of Access to Care for Medicare Beneficiaries and Pension Relief Act of 2010, Public Law 111-192, dealing with eligible charity plans and plans of certain rural cooperatives.

(3) The Cooperative and Small Employer Charity Pension Flexibility Act, Public Law 113-97, dealing with certain defined benefit pension plans maintained by certain cooperatives and charities. [Redesignated and revised 3/23/2016 by 81 FR 15432.]

[¶ 15,396D]

§ 4010.5 **Information year.** (a) *Determinations based on information year.* An information year is used under this part to determine which persons are filers (§ 4010.4), what information a filer must submit (§§ 4010.6-4010.9), whether a plan is an exempt plan (§ 4010.8(c)), and the due date for submitting the information (§ 4010.10(a)).

(b) *General.* Except as provided in paragraph (c) of this section, a person's information year is the fiscal year of the person. A filer is not required to change its fiscal year or the plan year of a plan, to report financial information for any accounting period other than an existing fiscal year, or to report actuarial information for any plan year other than an existing plan year. [Amended 3/16/2009 by 74 FR 11022.]

(c) *Controlled group members with different fiscal years.* If members of a controlled group (disregarding any exempt entity) report financial information on the basis of different fiscal years, the information year is the calendar year. (If any two members of the controlled group report financial information on the basis of different fiscal years, the determination of whether an entity is an exempt entity is based on a calendar year information year for purposes of this paragraph (c) and § 4010.4(c).) [Amended 3/16/2009 by 74 FR 11022.]

(d) *Examples.* The following examples illustrate the rule in paragraph (c) of this section.

(1) *Example 1.* Companies A and B are the only members of the same controlled group, and both are contributing sponsors to nonexempt plans. Company A has a July 1 fiscal year, and Company B has an October 1 fiscal year. The information year is the calendar year. Company A's financial information with respect to its fiscal year ending June 30, 2009, and Company B's financial information with respect to its fiscal year ending September 30, 2009, must be submitted to the PBGC following the end of the 2009 calendar year information year.

(2) *Example 2.* The facts are the same as in Example 1 except that Company B is not a contributing sponsor of a plan and would be an exempt entity using the calendar year as the information year. Because Company B is an exempt entity based on a calendar year information year, it is excluded when determining the information year. Thus, the information year is the July 1 fiscal year. Note that Company B is an exempt entity even if it would not be exempt based on the July information year.

(3) *Example 3.* The facts are the same as in Example 2 except that Company B would not be an exempt entity using the calendar year information year but would be exempt based on an information year that is the July 1 fiscal year. Since Company B is not exempt based on a calendar year information year, it may not be excluded when determining the information year. Therefore, the information year is the calendar year and Company B is not an exempt entity. [Added 3/16/2009 by 74 FR 11022.]

(e) *Special rules for certain plan years.* If a plan maintained by the members of the contributing sponsor's controlled group has two plan years that end in the information year or has no plan year that ends in the information year, the last plan year ending on or immediately before the end of information year is deemed to be the plan year ending within the information year. [Added 3/16/2009 by 74 FR 11022.]

[¶ 15,396E]

§ 4010.6 **Information to be filed.** (a) *General.* (1) *Current filers.* A filer must submit the information specified in § 4010.7 (identifying information), § 4010.8 (plan actuarial information) and § 4010.9 (financial information) with respect to each member of the filer's controlled group and each plan maintained by any member of the filer's controlled group, and any other information relating to the information specified in §§ 4010.7 through 4010.9, as specified in the instructions on PBGC's Web site, http://www.pbgc.gov. [Amended 3/16/2009 by 74 FR 11022.]

(2) *Previous filers.* If a filer for the immediately preceding information year is not required to file for the current information year, the filer must submit information, in accordance with the instructions on PBGC's Web site, http://www.pbgc.gov, demonstrating why a filing is not required for the current information year. [Amended 3/16/2009 by 74 FR 11022.]

(b) *Additional information.* By written notification, PBGC may require any filer to submit additional actuarial or financial information that is necessary to determine plan assets and liabilities for any period through the end of the filer's information year, or the financial status of a filer for any period through the end of the filer's information year (including information on exempt entities and exempt plans). The information must be submitted within ten days after the date of the written notification or by a different time specified therein. [Amended 3/16/2009 by 74 FR 11022.]

(c) *Previous submissions.* If any required information has been previously submitted to PBGC, a filer may incorporate this information into the required submission by referring to the previous submission. [Amended 3/16/2009 by 74 FR 11022.]

[¶ 15,396F]

§ 4010.7 **Identifying information.** (a) *Filers.* Each filer is required to provide, in accordance with the instructions on PBGC's Web site, http://www.pbgc.gov, the following identifying information with respect to each member of the filer's controlled group (excluding exempt entities)—

(1) *Current members.* For an entity that is a member of the controlled group as of the end of the filer's information year—

(i) The name, address, and telephone number of the entity and the legal relationships with other members of the controlled group (for example, parent, subsidiary);

(ii) The nine-digit Employer Identification Number (EIN) assigned by the IRS to the entity (or if there is no EIN for the entity, an explanation); and

(iii) If the entity became a member of the controlled group during the information year, the date the entity became a member of the controlled group; and [Amended 3/16/2009 by 74 FR 11022.]

(2) *Former members.* For any entity that ceased to be a member of the controlled group during the filer's information year, the date the entity ceased to be a member of the controlled group and the identifying information required by paragraph (a)(1) of this section as of the day before the entity left the controlled group. [Amended 3/16/2009 by 74 FR 11022.]

(b) *Plans.* Each filer is required to provide, in accordance with the instructions on PBGC's Web site, http://www.pbgc.gov, the following identifying information with respect to each plan (including exempt plans) maintained by any member of the filer's controlled group (including exempt entities)—

(1) *Current plans..* For a plan that is maintained by the controlled group as of the last day of the filer's information year—

(i) The name of the plan;

(ii) The EIN and the three-digit Plan Number (PN) assigned by the contributing sponsor to the plan (or if there is no EIN or PN for the plan, an explanation);

(iii) If the EIN or PN of the plan has changed during the filer's information year, the previous EIN or PN and an explanation;

(iv) If the plan was not maintained by the controlled group immediately before the filer's information year, the date the plan was first maintained by the controlled group during the information year;

(v) If, as of any day during the information year, the plan was frozen (for eligibility or benefit accrual purposes), a description of the date and the nature of the freeze (*e.g.*, service is frozen but pay is not); and

(vi) In the case of a multiple employer plan, a list of the contributing sponsors as of the end of the plan year ending within the filer's information year, including the name, employer identification number, contact information, fiscal year, and a statement as to whether each contributing sponsor is a publicly-traded company; and [Amended 3/16/2009 by 74 FR 11022.]

(2) *Former plans.* For a plan that ceased to be maintained by the controlled group during the filer's information year, the date the plan ceased to be so maintained, identification of the controlled group currently maintaining the plan, and the identifying information required by paragraph (b)(1) of this section as of the day before that date. [Amended 3/16/2009 by 74 FR 11022.]

[¶ 15,396G]

§ 4010.8 **Plan actuarial information.** (a) *Required information.* Except as provided elsewhere in this part, for each plan (other than an exempt plan) maintained by any member of the filer's controlled group, each filer is required to provide, in accordance with the instructions on PBGC's Web site, *http://www.pbgc.gov,* the following actuarial information determined (except as specified below) as of the end of plan year ending within the filer's information year—

(1) The number of—

(i) Retired participants and beneficiaries receiving payments,

(ii) Terminated vested participants, and

(iii) Active participants;

(2) The fair market value of the plan's assets (excluding any contributions received after year-end);

(3) The amount of benefit liabilities under the plan, setting forth separately the amount of the liabilities attributable to retired participants and beneficiaries receiving payments, terminated vested participants, and active participants, determined, for this purpose in accordance with paragraph (d) of this section;

(4) A description of the actuarial assumptions used to determine the benefit liabilities in paragraph (a)(3) of this section;

(5) The at-risk funding target for the plan year ending within the information year determined under ERISA section 303(i) and Code section 430(i)—

(i) As if the plan has been in at-risk status for a consecutive period of at least five years, and

(ii) Without regard to the interest rate stabilization provisions of ERISA section 303(h)(2)(C)(iv) and Code section 430(h)(2)(C)(iv); [Revised 3/23/2016 by 81 FR 15432.]

(6) The 4010 funding target attainment percentage (as of the valuation date) for the plan year ending within the information year; [Amended 3/23/2016 by 81 FR 15432.]

(7) The adjusted funding target attainment percentage as defined in ERISA section 206(g)(9)(B) and Code section 436(j)(2) for the plan year ending within the information year;

(8) Whether the plan, at any time during the plan year, was subject to any of the limitations described in ERISA section 206(g) and Code section 436, and, if so, which limitations applied, when such limitations applied, and when (if applicable) they were lifted;

(9) Whether a required installment or other required payment to the plan was not made, and, as a result, a lien described in ERISA section 303(k) or 306(g) and Code section 430(k) or 433(g) was triggered during the information year, and the required installment or other required payment was not made within ten days after its due date; [Amended 3/23/2016 by 81 FR 15432.]

(10) Whether any portion of the total minimum funding waiver(s) in excess of $1 million granted with respect to such plan is outstanding;

(11) A copy of the actuarial valuation report for the plan year ending within the filer's information year that contains or is supplemented by the following information for that plan year—

(i) The funding target calculated pursuant to ERISA section 303 without regard to subsection 303(i)(1) (and Code section 430 without regard to subsection 430(i)(1)), setting forth separately the value of the liabilities attributable to retirees and beneficiaries receiving payment, terminated vested participants, and active participants (showing vested and nonvested benefits separately);

(ii) A summary of the actuarial assumptions and methods used for purposes of ERISA section 303 and Code section 430, including the form of payment and benefit commencement date assumptions for all active and deferred vested participants not yet receiving benefits, information on how lump sums are valued (for plans that provide lump sums other than *de minimis* lump sums), and any changes in those assumptions and methods since the previous valuation and the justifications for such changes;

(iii) The effective interest rate (as defined in ERISA section 303(h)(2)(A) and Code section 430(h)(2)(A));

(iv) The target normal cost calculated pursuant to ERISA section 303 without regard to subsection 303(i)(2) (and Code section 430 without regard to subsection 430(i)(2));

(v) For the plan year and each of the four preceding plan years, a statement as to whether the plan was in at-risk status for that plan year;

(vi) In the case of a plan that is in at-risk status, the target normal cost and funding target calculated pursuant to ERISA section 303 and Code section 430 as if the plan has been in at-risk status for five consecutive years; [Amended 3/23/2016 by 81 FR 15432.]

(vii) The value of the plan's assets (reflecting any averaging method) as of the valuation date and the fair market value of the plan's assets as of the valuation date;

(viii) The funding standard carryover balance and the prefunding balance (maintained pursuant to ERISA section 303(f)(1)

and Code section 430(f)(1)) as of the beginning of the plan year and a summary of any changes in such balances in the past year (e.g., amounts used to offset the minimum funding requirement, amounts reduced in accordance with any elections under ERISA section 303(f)(5) and Code section 430(f)(5), interest credited to such balances, and excess contributions used to increase such balances);

(ix) A list of amortization bases (shortfall and waiver) under ERISA section 303 and Code section 430, including the year each base was established, the original amount, the installment amount, and the remaining balance at the beginning of the plan year;

(x) An age/service scatter for active participants including average compensation information for pay-related plans and average account balance information for hybrid plans presented in a format similar to that described in the instructions to Schedule SB of the Form 5500;

(xi) Expected disbursements (benefit payments and expenses) during the plan year;

(xii) A summary of the principal eligibility and benefit provisions on which the valuation of the plan was based (and any changes to those provisions since the previous valuation), along with descriptions of any benefits not included in the valuation, any significant events that occurred during the plan year, and the plan's early retirement factors; in the case of a plan that provides lump sums, other than de minimis lump sums, the summary must include information on how annuity benefits are converted to lump sum amounts (e.g., whether early retirement subsidies are reflected); and

(xiii) Any other similar information as specified in instructions on PBGC's Web site, *http://www.pbgc.gov;* and

(12) A written certification by an enrolled actuary that, to the best of his or her knowledge and belief, the actuarial information submitted is true, correct, and complete and conforms to all applicable laws and regulations, provided that this certification may be qualified in writing, but only to the extent the qualification(s) are permitted under 26 CFR 301.6059-1(d).

(b) *Alternative methods of compliance—*

(1) *At-risk funding target.* Notwithstanding any other provision of this section, a filer is not required to provide the information specified in paragraph (a)(5) of this section for the plan year for which actuarial information is being reported unless PBGC requests in writing that the information be provided, in which case the filer must provide the information within 30 days of such request or such later date as PBGC specifies in the request.

(2) *Actuarial valuation report.* If any of the information specified in paragraph (a)(11) of this section is not available by the date specified in §4010.10(a), a filer may satisfy the requirement to provide such information by—

(i) Including a statement, with the material that is submitted to PBGC, that the filer will file the unavailable information by the alternative due date specified in §4010.10(b), and

(ii) Filing such information (along with a certification by an enrolled actuary under paragraph (a)(12) of this section) with PBGC by that alternative due date. [Revised 3/23/2016 by 81 FR 15432.]

(c) *Exempt plan.* The actuarial information specified in this section is not required with respect to a plan if the plan satisfies the conditions in paragraph (c)(1) through (3).

(1) The plan—

(i) Has fewer than 500 participants as of the end of the plan year ending within the information year or as of the valuation date for that plan year and has a 4010 funding shortfall (as defined in §4010.11(a)(1)) for the plan year ending within the information year that is not in excess of $15 million, or [Amended 3/23/2016 by 81 FR 15432.]

(ii) Has benefit liabilities as of the end of the plan year ending within the filer's information year, (determined in accordance with paragraph (d) of this section) equal to or less than the fair market value of the plan's assets.

(2) The plan has received, by or within ten days after the due dates, all required installments or other payments required to be made

during the information year under ERISA sections 302 and 303 and Code sections 412 and 430.

(3) The plan has no outstanding minimum funding waivers (as described in § 4010.4(a)(3)) as of the end of the plan year ending within the information year.

(d) *Value of benefit liabilities.* The value of a plan's benefit liabilities at the end of a plan year must be determined using the plan census data described in paragraph (d)(1) of this section and the actuarial assumptions and methods described in paragraph (d)(2) or, where applicable, (d)(3) of this section.

(1) *Census data.* (i) *Census data period.* Plan census data must be determined (for all plans for any information year) either as of the end of the plan year or as of the beginning of the next plan year.

(ii) *Projected census data.* If actual plan census data are not available, a plan may use a projection of plan census data from a date within the plan year. The projection must be consistent with projections used to measure pension obligations of the plan for financial statement purposes and must give a result appropriate for the end of the plan year for these obligations. For example, adjustments to the projection process are required where there has been a significant event (such as a plan amendment or a plant shutdown) that has not been reflected in the projection data.

(2) *Actuarial assumptions and methods.* The value of benefit liabilities must be determined using the following rules in paragraphs (d)(2)(i) through (iv) of this section:

(i) *Assumptions included in §§ 4044.51 through 4044.57.* Interest, form of payment, expenses, mortality and retirement assumptions must be as prescribed in §§ 4044.51 through 4044.57 of this chapter. [Amended 3/23/2016 by 81 FR 15432.]

(ii) *Assumptions not included in §§ 4044.51 through 4044.57.* Assumptions for decrements other than mortality and retirement (such as turnover or disability) used to determine the minimum required contribution under ERISA section 303 and Code section 430 for the plan year ending within the filer's information year may be used, but only if all such assumptions are used. For plans where there is no distinction between termination and retirement assumptions, any termination/retirement rates at ages after the Earliest PBGC Retirement Date (as defined in § 4022.10 of this chapter) must be treated as retirement rates and replaced by expected retirement ages; termination/retirement rates at ages below the Earliest PBGC Retirement Date must be treated as pre-retirement decrements. Assumptions used to determine the minimum required contribution for the plan year ending within the filer's information year, other than assumptions for decrements, interest, form of payment, and expenses (*e.g.*, cost-of-living increases, marital status), must be used. [Amended 3/23/2016 by 81 FR 15432.]

(iii) *Benefits to be valued.* Benefits to be valued include all benefits earned or accrued under the plan as of the end of the plan year ending within the information year and other benefits payable from the plan including, but not limited to, ancillary benefits and retirement supplements, regardless of whether such benefits are protected by the anti-cutback provisions of Code section 411(d)(6).

(iv) *Future service.* Future service expected to be accrued by an active participant in an ongoing plan during future employment (based on the assumptions used to determine benefit liabilities) must be included in determining the earliest and unreduced retirement ages used to determine the expected retirement age and in determining an active participant's entitlement to early retirement subsidies and supplements at the expected retirement age. See the examples in paragraph (e) of this section.

(3) *Special actuarial assumptions for exempt plan determination.* Solely for purposes of determining whether a plan is an exempt plan for an information year, the value of benefit liabilities may be determined by substituting for the retirement age assumptions in paragraph (d)(2) of this section the retirement age assumptions used by the plan for the plan year ending within the information year for purposes of section 303 of ERISA without regard to the at-risk assumption of subsection

303(i) of ERISA and Code section 430 without regard to the at-risk assumption of subsection 430(i).

(e) *Examples.* The following examples demonstrate how XRA is determined and applied for purposes of determining benefit liabilities under paragraph (d) of this section:

(1) *Example 1.* (i) *Facts.* Plan X has a normal retirement age of 65, but allows benefits to commence as early as age 55 for participants who complete at least 10 years of service before termination. Early retirement benefits are reduced for participants with fewer than 25 years of service. Employee A is an active participant who is age 40 and has completed 5 years of service. Assume the "medium" XRA look-up table applies, and that for purposes of § 4010.8(d), the filer has decided not to take pre-retirement decrements other than mortality table into account as permitted under § 4010.8(d)(2)(i).

(ii) *Determination of XRA.* The benefit liability is the present value of A's benefit accrued as of the measurement date assuming A retires at age 58 and elects to have benefits commence immediately. Since A will not be eligible to receive unreduced benefits at that time, the accrued benefit is reduced in accordance with the plan's early retirement reduction provisions, including any subsidies to which A will be entitled under the assumption that A works until age 58.

(iii) *Determination of Benefit Liabilities.* The benefit liability is the present value of A's benefit accrued as of the measurement date assuming A retires at age 58 and elects to have benefits commence immediately. Since A will not be eligible to receive unreduced benefits at that time, the accrued benefit is reduced in accordance with the plan's early retirement reduction provisions, including any subsidies to which A will be entitled under the assumption that A works until age 58.

(2) *Example 2.* Employee B is also an active participant in plan X and is age 40 with 15 years of service. B will complete 25 years of service at age 50. However, because the plan does not allow for benefit commencement before age 55, B's ERA, URA and thus, XRA are all age 55. The benefit liability is the present value of B's benefit accrued as of the measurement date assuming B retires at age 55 and elects to commence benefits immediately. Since B will be eligible to receive an unreduced benefit at that time, the full unreduced benefit amount is valued.

(3) *Example 3.* (i) *Facts.* Assume the same facts as in Example 1, except that for purposes of § 4010.8(d), the filer has decided to take pre-retirement decrements other than mortality into account as permitted under § 4010.8(d)(2)(i). Assume the only pre-retirement decrement other than mortality is turnover. The plan's turnover rates go from age 21 to age 54, and the retirement rates go from age 55 to age 65.

(ii) *Determination of XRA.* If A terminates employment at or before age 45, A will not be eligible to receive benefits until age 65. Therefore, the portion of Employee A that is assumed to terminate before age 45 has an ERA, URA, and XRA of age 65. The portion of A that remains in service to age 45, after the application of the applicable turnover decrements, and then terminates at or after age 45, but before age 55, will be entitled to receive a reduced benefit as early as 55. Therefore, the portion of A that is assumed to terminate during this period has an ERA of 55, a URA of 65 and an XRA of 60. Since the turnover rates stop at age 55, the portion of A that remains in service to age 55 is assumed to remain in service until the XRA for that portion of A. For that portion of A, the ERA is 55, the URA is 60 and the XRA is 58. (For purposes of § 4010.8(d), the plan's assumed retirement rates are replaced by XRAs.)

(iii) *Determination of benefit liabilities.* The benefit liability of A is the sum of the present value of A's full accrued benefit at age 65 for the portion of A that terminates between age 40 and age 45, the present value of A's accrued benefit reduced for commencement at age 60 for the portion of A that terminates between age 45 and age 54, and the present value of A's accrued benefit reduced for commencement at age 58 for the portion of A that remains employed until age 55.

(4) *Example 4.* Assume the same facts as in Example 3, except that Employee B, the sole active participant, is age 40 with 15 years of

service. The portion of B that is assumed to terminate before age 50 would be entitled to receive a reduced benefit as early as age 55 or an unreduced benefit at age 65. That portion of B has an ERA of 55, a URA of 65, and an XRA of 60. The benefit liability for that portion of B is the present value of B's benefit accrued as of the measurement date assuming B commences a reduced benefit at age 60. The portion of B that survives to age 50 would be entitled to receive an unreduced benefit as early as age 55. That portion of B has an ERA, URA and XRA of 55. The benefit liability for this portion of B is the present value of B's benefit accrued as of the measurement date assuming B retires and commences unreduced payments at age 55.

(f) *Multiple employer plans.* If, with respect to a multiple employer plan, the actuarial information required under this section 4010 for the plan year ending within the filer's information year has been filed under part 4010 by another filer, the filer may include this actuarial information by reference. The filer must report the name, EIN and plan number of the multiple employer plan and the name of the other filer that submitted this information.

(g) *Previous filing for plan year.* If the actuarial information for the plan year as required under this § 4010.8 has been submitted by the filer in a previous 4010 submission, the filing may include that actuarial information by reference to the previous submission.

(h) *Plans subject to special funding rules.* Instead of the requirements of paragraph (a)(11) of this section:

(1) In the case of a plan year for which a plan is subject to section 402(b) of the Pension Protection Act of 2006, Public Law 109-280, dealing with certain frozen plans of commercial passenger airlines and airline caterers, the plan must meet the requirements in connection with the actuarial valuation report in accordance with instructions on PBGC's Web site, *http://www.pbgc.gov.*

(2) In the case of a plan year for which the application of new funding rules is deferred for a plan under section 104 of the Pension Protection Act of 2006, Public Law 109-280, as amended by the Preservation of Access to Care for Medicare Beneficiaries and Pension Relief Act of 2010, Public Law 111-192, dealing with eligible charity plans and plans of certain rural cooperatives, the plan must meet the requirements in paragraph (a)(5) of this section (in connection with the actuarial valuation report) in effect as of December 31, 2007.

(3) In the case of a plan year for which a plan is subject to the Cooperative and Small Employer Charity Pension Flexibility Act, Public Law 113-97, dealing with certain defined benefit pension plans maintained by more than one employer, the plan must meet the requirements in connection with the actuarial valuation report in accordance with instructions on PBGC's Web site, *http://www.pbgc.gov.* [Redesignated and revised 3/23/2016 by 81 FR 15432.]

[¶ 15,396H]

§4010.9 **Financial information.** (a) *General.* Except as provided in this section, each filer is required to provide, in accordance with the instructions on PBGC's Web site, http://www.pbgc.gov, the following financial information for each member of the filer's controlled group (other than an exempt entity)—[Amended 3/16/2009 by 74 FR 11022.]

(1) audited financial statements for the fiscal year ending within the information year (including balance sheets, income statements, cash flow statements, and notes to the financial statements);

(2) if audited financial statements are not available by the date specified in §4010.10(a), unaudited financial statements for the fiscal year ending within the information year; or

(3) if neither audited nor unaudited financial statements are available by the date specified in §4010.10(a), copies of federal tax returns for the tax year ending within the information year.

(b) *Consolidated financial statements.* If the financial information of a controlled group member is combined with the information of other group members in consolidated financial statements, a filer may provide the following financial information in lieu of the information required in paragraph (a) of this section—

(1) the audited consolidated financial statements for the filer's information year or, if the audited consolidated financial statements are not available by the date specified in §4010.10(a), unaudited consoli-

dated financial statements for the fiscal year ending within the information year; and

(2) for each controlled group member included in the consolidated financial statements (other than an exempt entity), the member's revenues and operating income for the information year, and net assets at the end of the information year.

(c) *Subsequent submissions.* If unaudited financial statements are submitted as provided in paragraph (a)(2) or (b)(1) of this section, audited financial statements must thereafter be filed within 15 days after they are prepared, if they are prepared. If federal tax returns are submitted as provided in paragraph (a)(3) of this section, audited and unaudited financial statements, if prepared, must thereafter be filed within 15 days after they are prepared. [Amended 3/16/2009 by 74 FR 11022.]

(d) *Submission of public information.* If any of the financial information required by paragraphs (a) through (c) of this section is publicly available, the filer, in lieu of submitting such information to PBGC, may include a statement with the other information that is submitted to PBGC indicating when such financial information was made available to the public and where PBGC may obtain it. For example, if the controlled group member has filed audited financial statements with the Securities and Exchange Commission, it need not file the financial statements with PBGC but instead can identify the SEC filing as part of its submission under this part. [Amended 3/16/2009 by 74 FR 11022.]

(e) *Inclusion of information about non-filers and exempt entities.* Consolidated financial statements provided pursuant to paragraph (b)(1) of this section may include financial information of persons who are not controlled group members (e.g., joint ventures) or are exempt entities.

[¶ 15,396I]

§4010.10 **Due date and filing with the PBGC.** (a) *Due date.* Except as permitted under paragraph (b) of this section, a filer must file the information required under this part with PBGC on or before the 105th day after the close of the filer's information year. The filing deadline is extended to the 106th date after the close of the filer's information year if the 105-day reporting period includes February 29. [Amended 3/16/2009 by 74 FR 11022.]

(b) *Alternative due date.* A filer that includes the statement specified in §4010.8(b)(1) with its submission to PBGC by the date specified in paragraph (a) of this section must submit the actuarial information specified in §4010.8(b)(2) within 15 days after the deadline for filing the plan's annual report (Form 5500 series) for the plan year ending within the filer's information year (see §2520.104a-5(a)(2) of this title). [Amended 3/16/2009 by 74 FR 11022.]

(c) *How and where to file.* PBGC applies the rules in subpart A of part 4000 of this chapter to determine permissible methods of filing with PBGC under this part. See Sec. 4000.4 of this chapter for information on where to file [Amended 10/28/2003 by 68 FR 61344 and 3/16/2009 by 74 FR 11022].

(d) *Date of filing.* PBGC applies the rules in subpart C of part 4000 of this chapter to determine the date that a submission under this part was filed with PBGC. [Amended 10/28/2003 by 68 FR 61344 and 3/16/2009 by 74 FR 11022.]

(e) *Computation of time.* PBGC applies the rules in subpart D of part 4000 of this chapter to compute any time period under this part. [Amended 10/28/2003 by 68 FR 61344 and 3/16/2009 by 74 FR 11022.]

[¶ 15,396J]

§4010.11 **Waivers.**

(a) *Aggregate funding shortfall not in excess of $15 million waiver.* Unless reporting is required by §4010.4(a)(2) or (3), reporting is waived for a person (that would be a filer if not for the waiver) for an information year if, for the plan year ending within the information year, the aggregate 4010 funding shortfall for all plans (including any exempt plans) maintained by the person's controlled group (disregarding those plans with no 4010 funding shortfall) does not exceed $15 million, as determined under paragraphs (a)(1) and (2) of this section.

(1) *4010 funding shortfall; in general.* A plan's 4010 funding shortfall for a plan year equals the funding shortfall for the plan year as provided under ERISA section 303(c)(4) and Code section 430(c)(4), with the following exceptions:

(i) The funding target used to calculate the 4010 funding shortfall is determined without regard to the interest rate stabilization provisions of ERISA section 303(h)(2)(C)(iv) and Code section 430(h)(2)(C)(iv).

(ii) The value of plan assets used to calculate the 4010 funding shortfall is determined without regard to the reduction under ERISA section 303(f)(4)(B) and Code section 430(f)(4)(B) (dealing with reduction of assets by the amount of prefunding and funding standard carryover balances).

(2) *Multiple employer plans.* For purposes of § 4010.8(c) and paragraph (a) of this section, the entire 4010 funding shortfall of any multiple employer plan of which the filer or any member of the filer's controlled group is a contributing sponsor is included.

(b) *Smaller plans waiver—*

(1) *General.* Unless reporting is required by § 4010.4(a)(2) or (a)(3), reporting is waived for a person (that would be a filer if not for the waiver) for an information year if, for the plan year ending within the information year, the aggregate number of participants in all plans (including any exempt plans) maintained by the person's controlled group is fewer than 500. For this purpose, the number of participants in any plan may be determined either as of the end of the plan year ending within the information year or as of the valuation date for that plan year.

(2) *Multiple employer plans.* For purposes of this paragraph (b), the aggregate number of participants in all plans maintained by a person's controlled group includes any participants covered by a multiple employer plan in which the person participates (including participants covered by the multiple employer plan who are not or were not employed by the person).

(c) *Missed contributions resulting in a lien or outstanding minimum funding waivers.* Reporting is waived for a person (that would be a filer if not for the waiver) for an information year if, for the plan year ending within the information year, reporting would have been required solely under § 4010.4(a)(2) or (3), provided that the missed contributions or applications for minimum funding waivers (as applicable) were reported to PBGC under part 4043 of this chapter by the due date for the 4010 filing.

(d) *Other waiver authority.* PBGC may waive the requirement to submit information with respect to one or more filers or plans or may extend the applicable due date or dates specified in § 4010.10. PBGC will exercise this discretion in appropriate cases where it finds convincing evidence supporting a waiver or extension; any waiver or extension may be subject to conditions. A request for a waiver or extension must be filed in writing with PBGC at the address provided in § 4010.10(c) no later than 15 days before the applicable due date specified in

§ 4010.10, and must state the facts and circumstances on which the request is based. [Revised 3/23/2016 by 81 FR 15432.]

[¶ 15,396J-50]

§ 4010.12 **Alternative method of compliance for certain sponsors of multiple employer plans.** (a) *In general.* Subject to paragraph (b) of this section, an eligible contributing sponsor (as defined in paragraph (c) of this section) of a multiple employer plan satisfies the requirements of this part for an information year if any contributing sponsor of the multiple employer plan provides a timely filing under this part for an information year that coincides with or overlaps with the eligible contributing sponsor's information year.

(b) *PBGC request for additional information.* PBGC may request some or all of the information that would otherwise be required under this part from an eligible contributing sponsor that uses the alternative method of compliance in this section. PBGC will make such a request no earlier than the date the information would otherwise have been due. The eligible contributing sponsor must provide the requested information no later than 30 days after PBGC makes the request. The requested information need not be submitted electronically.

(c) *Eligible contributing sponsor.* For purposes of this section, an eligible contributing sponsor of a multiple employer plan is a contributing sponsor that would not be subject to reporting if the plan were disregarded in applying the gateway tests in § 4010.4(a). [Added 3/16/2009 by 74 FR 11022.]

[¶ 15,396K]

§ 4010.13 **Confidentiality of information submitted.** In accordance with § 4901.21(a)(3) of this chapter and ERISA section 4010(c) any information or documentary material that is not publicly available and is submitted to PBGC pursuant to this part will not be made public, except as may be relevant to any administrative or judicial action or proceeding or for disclosures to either body of Congress or to any duly authorized committee or subcommittee of the Congress. [Redesignated and amended 3/16/2009 by 74 FR 11022.]

[¶ 15,396L]

§ 4010.14 **Penalties.** If all of the information required under this part is not provided within the specified time limit, PBGC may assess a separate penalty under ERISA section 4071 against the filer and each member of the filer's controlled group (other than an exempt entity). PBGC may also pursue other equitable or legal remedies available to it under the law. [Amended by 62 FR 36993, effective August 11, 1997. Redesignated and amended 3/16/2009 by 74 FR 11022. Interim final regulations removed the words "of up to $1,100 a day for each day that the failure continues" on 5/13/2016 by 81 FR 29765. Finalized 1/31/17 by 82 FR 8813]

[¶ 15,396M]

§ 4010.15 **OMB control number.** The collection of information requirements contained in this part have been approved by the Office of Management and Budget under OMB Control Number 1212-0049. [Redesignated 3/16/2009 by 74 FR 11022.]

[¶ 15,400]
SEC. 4011 STRICKEN

Act Sec. 4011 Stricken.

Amendment

P.L. 109-280, § 501(b)(1):

Amended ERISA Sec. 4011 by striking the section.

Prior to being stricken, ERISA Sec. 4011 read as follows:

Act Sec. 4011. (a) IN GENERAL.—The plan administrator of a plan subject to the additional premium under section 4006(a)(3)(E) shall provide, in a form and manner and at such time as prescribed in regulations of the corporation, notice to plan participants and beneficiaries of the plan's funding status and the limits on the corporation's guaranty should the plan terminate while underfunded.

Such notice shall be written in a manner as to be understood by the average plan participant.

(b) EXCEPTION.—Subsection (a) shall not apply to any plan to which section 302(d) does not apply for the plan year by reason of paragraph (9) thereof.

The above amendment applies to plan years beginning after December 31, 2006.

P.L. 103-465, § 775(a):

Act Sec. 775(a) amended subtitle A of title IV of ERISA by adding new section 4011 to read as above.

The above amendment is effective for plan years beginning after December 8, 1994.

Subtitle B—Coverage

[¶ 15,410]
COVERAGE

Act Sec. 4021.(a) PLANS COVERED.—Except as provided in subsection (b), this title applies to any plan (including a successor plan) which, for a plan year—

(1) is an employee pension benefit plan (as defined in paragraph (2) of section 3 of this Act) established or maintained—

(A) by an employer engaged in commerce or in any industry or activity affecting commerce, or

(B) by any employee organization, or organization representing employees, engaged in commerce or in any industry or activity affecting commerce, or

(C) by both, which has, in practice, met the requirements of part I of subchapter D of chapter 1 of the Internal Revenue Code of 1986 (as in effect for the preceding 5 plan years of the plan) applicable to plans described in paragraph (2) for the preceding 5 plan years; or

(2) is, or has been determined by the Secretary of the Treasury to be, a plan described in section 401(a) of the Internal Revenue Code of 1986, or which meets, or has been determined by the Secretary of the Treasury to meet, the requirements of section 404(a)(2) of such Code.

For purposes of this title, a successor plan is considered to be a continuation of a predecessor plan. For this purpose, unless otherwise specifically indicated in this title, a successor plan is a plan which covers a group of employees which includes substantially the same employees as a previously established plan, and provides substantially the same benefits as that plan provided.

Act Sec. 4021.(b) PLANS NOT COVERED.—This section does not apply to any plan—

(1) which is an individual account plan, as defined in paragraph (34) of section 3 of this Act,

(2) established and maintained for its employees by the Government of the United States, by the government of any State or political subdivision thereof, or by any agency or instrumentality of any of the foregoing, or to which the Railroad Retirement Act of 1935 or 1937 applies and which is financed by contributions required under that Act or which is described in the last sentence of section 3(32),

(3) which is a church plan as defined in section 414(e) of the Internal Revenue Code of 1986, unless that plan has made an election under section 410(d) of such Code, and has notified the corporation in accordance with procedures prescribed by the corporation, that it wishes to have the provisions of this part apply to it,

(4)(A) established and maintained by a society, order, or association described in section 501(c)(8) or (9) of the Internal Revenue Code of 1986, if no part of the contributions to or under the plan is made by employers of participants in the plan, or

(B) of which a trust described in section 501(c)(18) of such Code is a part;

(5) which has not at any time after the date of enactment of this Act provided for employer contributions;

(6) which is unfunded and which is maintained by an employer primarily for the purpose of providing deferred compensation for a select group of management or highly compensated employees;

(7) which is established and maintained outside of the United States primarily for the benefit of individuals substantially all of whom are nonresident aliens;

(8) which is maintained by an employer solely for the purpose of providing benefits for certain employees in excess of the limitations on contributions and benefits imposed by section 415 of the Internal Revenue Code of 1986 on plans to which that section applies, without regard to whether the plan is funded, and, to the extent that a separable part of a plan (as determined by the corporation) maintained by an employer is maintained for such purpose, that part shall be treated for purposes of this title, as a separate plan which is an excess benefit plan;

(9) which is established and maintained exclusively for substantial owners;

(10) of an international organization which is exempt from taxation under the International Organizations Immunities Act;

(11) maintained solely for the purpose of complying with applicable workmen's compensation laws or unemployment compensation or disability insurance laws;

(12) which is a defined benefit plan, to the extent that it is treated as an individual account plan under paragraph (35)(B) of section 3 of this Act or;

(13) established and maintained by a professional service employer which does not at any time after the date of enactment of this Act have more than 25 active participants in the plan.

Act Sec. 4021.(c)(1) DEFINITIONS.—For purposes of subsection (b)(1), the term "individual account plan" does not include a plan under which a fixed benefit is promised if the employer or his representative participated in the determination of that benefit.

(2) For purposes of this paragraph and for purposes of subsection (b)(13)—

(A) the term "professional service employer" means any proprietorship, partnership, corporation, or other association or organization (i) owned or controlled by professional individuals or by executors or administrators of professional individuals, (ii) the principal business of which is the performance of professional services, and

(B) the term "professional individuals" includes[,] but is not limited to, physicians, dentists, chiropractors, osteopaths, optometrists, other licensed practitioners of the healing arts, attorneys at law, public accountants, public engineers, architects, draftsmen, actuaries, psychologists, social or physical scientists, and performing artists.

(3) In the case of a plan established and maintained by more than one professional service employer, the plan shall not be treated as a plan described in subsection (b)(13) if, at any time after the date of enactment of this Act the plan has more than 25 active participants.

Act Sec. 4021.(d) For purposes of subsection (b)(9), the term "substantial owner" means an individual who, at any time during the 60-month period ending on the date the determination is being made—

(1) owns the entire interest in an unincorporated trade or business,

(2) in the case of a partnership, is a partner who owns, directly or indirectly, more than 10 percent of either the capital interest or the profits interest in such partnership, or

(3) in the case of a corporation, owns, directly or indirectly, more than 10 percent in value of either the voting stock of that corporation or all the stock of that corporation.

For purposes of paragraph (3), the constructive ownership rules of section 1563(e) of the Internal Revenue Code of 1986 (other than paragraph (3)(C) thereof) shall apply, including the application of such rules under section 414(c) of such Code.

Amendments

P.L. 110-458, § 109(d)(2):

Amended ERISA Sec. 4021(b) by inserting "or" at the end of paragraph (12), by striking "; or" at the end of paragraph (13) and inserting a period, and by striking paragraph (14).

Prior to being stricken, ERISA Sec. 4021(b)(14) read as follows:

ERISA Sec. 4021(b)(14)—

established and maintained by an Indian tribal government (as defined in section 7701(a)(40) of the Internal Revenue Code of 1986), a subdivision of an Indian tribal government (determined in accordance with section 7871(d) of such Code), or an agency or instrumentality of either, and all of the participants of which are employees of such entity substantially all of whose services as such employee are in the performance of essential governmental functions but not in the performance of commercial activities (whether or not an essential government function).

The above amendment applies to any year beginning on or after August 17, 2006.

P.L. 109-280, § 407(c)(1)(A):

Amended ERISA Sec. 4021(b)(9) by striking "as defined in section 4022(b)(6)."

The above amendment is effective on January 1, 2006.

P.L. 109-280, §407(c)(1)(B):

Amended ERISA Sec. 4021 by adding subsection (d).

The above amendment is effective on January 1, 2006.

P.L. 109-280, §906(a)(2)(B):

Amended ERISA Sec. 4021(b)(2) by adding "or which is described in the last sentence of section 3(32)."

The above amendment applies to any year beginning on or after the date of the enactment of the Act (August 17, 2006).

P.L. 109-280, §906(b)(2)(A)-(C):

Amended ERISA Sec. 4021(b) by striking, in paragraph (12) "or" at the end, by striking, in paragraph (13) "plan." and adding "plan; or" and by adding new paragraph (14).

The above amendment applies to any year beginning on or after the date of the enactment of the Act (August 17, 2006).

P.L. 101-239, §7891(a)(1):

Titles I, III, and IV of ERISA (other than sections 3(37)(E), 301(a)(7), and 308, the last sentence of section 408(d), and sections 414(c), 4001(a)(3)(ii), and 4303) are each amended by striking "Internal Revenue Code of 1954" each place it appears and inserting "Internal Revenue Code of 1986" effective October 22, 1986.

P.L. 101-239, §7894(g)(3)(A):

Amended ERISA Sec. 4021(a) by striking "this section" and inserting "this title" effective September 2, 1974.

P.L. 96-364, §402(a)(4):

Amended Sec. 4021(a) effective September 26, 1980 by inserting in the last sentence "unless otherwise specifically indicated in this title," before "a successor plan".

[¶ 15,420]
SINGLE-EMPLOYER PLAN BENEFITS GUARANTEED

Act Sec. 4022.(a) NONFORFEITABLE BENEFITS.—Subject to the limitations contained in subsection (b), the corporation shall guarantee, in accordance with this section, the payment of all nonforfeitable benefits (other than benefits becoming nonforfeitable solely on account of the termination of a plan) under a single-employer plan which terminates at a time when this title applies to it.

Act Sec. 4022.(b)(1) EXCEPTIONS.—Except to the extent provided in paragraph (7)—

(A) no benefits provided by a plan which has been in effect for less than 60 months at the time the plan terminates shall be guaranteed under this section, and

(B) any increase in the amount of benefits under a plan resulting from a plan amendment which was made, or became effective, whichever is later, within 60 months before the date on which the plan terminates shall be disregarded.

(2) For purposes of this subsection, the time a successor plan (within the meaning of section 4021(a)) has been in effect includes the time a previously established plan (within the meaning of section 4021(a)) was in effect. For purposes of determining what benefits are guaranteed under this section in the case of a plan to which section 4021 does not apply on the day after the date of enactment of this Act, the 60-month period referred to in paragraph (1) shall be computed beginning on the first date on which such section does apply to the plan.

(3) The amount of monthly benefits described in subsection (a) provided by a plan, which are guaranteed under this section with respect to a participant, shall not have an actuarial value which exceeds the actuarial value of a monthly benefit in the form of a life annuity commencing at age 65 equal to the lesser of—

(A) his average monthly gross income from his employer during the 5 consecutive calendar year period (or, if less, during the number of calendar years in such period in which he actively participates in the plan) during which his gross income from that employer was greater than during any other such period with that employer determined by dividing ¹⁄₁₂ of the sum of all such gross income by the number of such calendar years in which he had such gross income, or

(B) $750 multiplied by a fraction, the numerator of which is the contribution and benefit base (determined under section 230 of the Social Security Act) in effect at the time the plan terminates and the denominator of which is such contribution and benefit base in effect in calendar year 1974.

The provisions of this paragraph do not apply to non-basic benefits.

The maximum guaranteed monthly benefit shall not be reduced solely on account of the age of a participant in the case of a benefit payable by reason of disability that occurred on or before the termination date, if the participant demonstrates to the satisfaction of the corporation that the Social Security Administration has determined that the participant satisfies the definition of disability under title II or XVI of the Social Security Act, and the regulations thereunder. If a benefit payable by reason of disability is converted to an early or normal retirement benefit for reasons other than a change in the health of the participant, such early or normal retirement benefit shall be treated as a continuation of the benefit payable by reason of disability and this subparagraph shall continue to apply.

(4)(A) The actuarial value of a benefit, for purposes of this subsection, shall be determined in accordance with regulations prescribed by the corporation.

(B) For purposes of paragraph (3)—

(i) the term "gross income" means "earned income" within the meaning of section 911(b) of the Internal Revenue Code of 1986 (determined without regard to any community property laws),

(ii) in the case of a participant in a plan under which contributions are made by more than one employer, amounts received as gross income from any employer under that plan shall be aggregated with amounts received from any other employer under that plan during the same period, and

(iii) any non-basic benefit shall be disregarded.

(5)(A) For purposes of this paragraph, the term "majority owner" means an individual who, at any time during the 60-month period ending on the date the determination is being made—

(i) owns the entire interest in an unincorporated trade or business,

(ii) in the case of a partnership, is a partner who owns, directly or indirectly, 50 percent or more of either the capital interest or the profits interest in such partnership, or

(iii) in the case of a corporation, owns, directly or indirectly, 50 percent or more in value of either the voting stock of that corporation or all the stock of that corporation.

For purposes of clause (iii), the constructive ownership rules of section 1563(e) of the Internal Revenue Code of 1986 (other than paragraph (3)(C) thereof) shall apply, including the application of such rules under section 414(c) of such Code.

(B) In the case of a participant who is a majority owner, the amount of benefits guaranteed under this section shall equal the product of—

(i) a fraction (not to exceed 1) the numerator of which is the number of years from the later of the effective date or the adoption date of the plan to the termination date, and the denominator of which is 10, and

(ii) the amount of benefits that would be guaranteed under this section if the participant were not a majority owner.

(C) In the case of a participant in a plan, other than a plan described in subparagraph (B), who is covered by the plan as a substantial owner, the amount of the benefit guaranteed under this section shall, under regulations prescribed by the corporation, treat each benefit increase attributable to a plan amendment as if it were provided under a new plan. The benefits guaranteed under this section with respect to all such amendments shall not exceed the amount which would be determined under subparagraph (B) if subparagraph (B) applied.

(6)(A) No benefits accrued under a plan after the date on which the Secretary of the Treasury issues notice that he has determined that any trust which is a part of a plan does not meet the requirements of section 401(a) of the Internal Revenue Code of 1986, or that the plan does not meet the requirements of section 404(a)(2) of such Code, are guaranteed under this section unless such determination is erroneous. This subparagraph does not apply if the Secretary subsequently issues a notice that such trust meets the requirements of section 401(a) of such Code or that the plan meets the requirements of section

404(a)(2) of such Code and if the Secretary determines that the trust or plan has taken action necessary to meet such requirements during the period between the issuance of the notice referred to in the preceding sentence and the issuance of the notice referred to in this sentence.

(B) No benefits accrued under a plan after the date on which an amendment of the plan is adopted which causes the Secretary of the Treasury to determine that any trust under the plan has ceased to meet the requirements of section 401(a) of the Internal Revenue Code of 1986 or that the plan has ceased to meet the requirements of section 404(a)(2) of such Code, are guaranteed under this section unless such determination is erroneous. This subparagraph shall not apply if the amendment is revoked as of the date it was first effective or amended to comply with such requirements.

(7) Benefits described in paragraph (1) are guaranteed only to the extent of the greater of—

(A) 20 percent of the amount which, but for the fact that the plan or amendment has not been in effect for 60 months or more, would be guaranteed under this section, or

(B) $20 per month,

multiplied by the number of years (but not more than 5) the plan or amendment, as the case may be, has been in effect. In determining how many years a plan or amendment has been in effect for purposes of this paragraph, the first 12 months beginning with the date on which the plan or amendment is made or first becomes effective (whichever is later) constitutes one year, and each consecutive period of 12 months thereafter constitutes an additional year. This paragraph does not apply to benefits payable under a plan unless the corporation finds substantial evidence that the plan was terminated for a reasonable business purpose and not for the purpose of obtaining the payment of benefits by the corporation under this title.

(8) If an unpredictable contingent event benefit (as defined in section 206(g)(1)) is payable by reason of the occurrence of any event, this section shall be applied as if a plan amendment had been adopted on the date such event occurred.

Act Sec. 4022.(c)(1) PAYMENT BY CORPORATION TO PARTICIPANTS AND BENEFICIARIES OF RECOVERY PERCENTAGE OF OUTSTANDING AMOUNT OF BENEFIT LIABILITIES.—In addition to benefits paid under the preceding provision of this section with respect to a terminated plan, the corporation shall pay the portion of the amount determined under paragraph (2) which is allocated with respect to each participant under section 4044(a). Such payment shall be made to such participant or to such participant's beneficiaries (including alternate payees, within the meaning of section 206(d)(3)(K)).

(2) The amount determined under this paragraph is an amount equal to the product derived by multiplying—

(A) the outstanding amount of benefit liabilities under the plan (including interest calculated from the termination date), by

(B) the applicable recovery ratio.

(3)(A) IN GENERAL. —Except as provided in subparagraph (C), the term "recovery ratio" means the ratio which—

(i) the sum of the values of all recoveries under section 4062, 4063, or 4064, determined by the corporation in connection with plan terminations described under subparagraph (B), bears to

(ii) the sum of all unfunded benefit liabilities under such plans as of the termination date in connection with any such prior termination.

(B) A plan termination described in this subparagraph is a termination with respect to which—

(i) the corporation has determined the value of recoveries under section 4062, 4063, or 4064, and

(ii) notices of intent to terminate were provided (or in the case of a termination by the corporation, a notice of determination under section 4042 was issued) during the 5-Federal fiscal year period ending with the third fiscal year preceding the fiscal year in which occurs the date of the notice of intent to terminate (or the notice of determination under section 4042) with respect to the plan termination for which the recovery ratio is being determined.

(C) In the case of a terminated plan with respect to which the outstanding amount of benefit liabilities exceeds $20,000,000, for purposes of this section, the term "recovery ratio" means, with respect to the termination of such plan, the ratio of—

(i) the value of the recoveries of the corporation under section 4062, 4063, or 4064 in connection with such plan, to

(ii) the amount of unfunded benefit liabilities under such plan as of the termination date.

(4) Determinations under this subsection shall be made by the corporation. Such determinations shall be binding unless shown by clear and convincing evidence to be unreasonable.

Act Sec. 4022. (d) AUTHORIZATION TO GUARANTEE OTHER CLASSES OF BENEFITS.—The corporation is authorized to guarantee the payment of such other classes of benefits and to establish the terms and conditions under which such other classes of benefits are guaranteed as it determines to be appropriate.

Act Sec. 4022. (e) NONFORFEITABLILITY OF PRERETIREMENT SURVIVOR ANNUITY.—For purposes of subsection (a), a qualified preretirement survivor annuity (as defined in section 205(e)(1)) with respect to a participant under a terminated single-employer plan shall not be treated as forfeitable solely because the participant has not died as of the termination date.

Act Sec. 4022. (f) EFFECTIVE DATE OF PLAN AMENDMENT.—For purposes of this section, the effective date of a plan amendment described in section 204(i)(1) shall be the effective date of the plan of reorganization of the employer described in section 204(i)(1) or, if later, the effective date stated in such amendment.

Act Sec. 4022. (g) BANKRUPTCY FILING SUBSTITUTED FOR TERMINATION DATE.—If a contributing sponsor of a plan has filed or has had filed against such person a petition seeking liquidation or reorganization in a case under title 11, United States Code, or under any similar Federal law or law of a State or political subdivision, and the case has not been dismissed as of the termination date of the plan, then this section shall be applied by treating the date such petition was filed as the termination date of the plan.

Act Sec. 4022. (h) SPECIAL RULE FOR PLANS ELECTING CERTAIN FUNDING REQUIREMENTS.—If any plan makes an election under section 402(a)(1) of the Pension Protection Act of 2006 and is terminated effective before the end of the 10-year period beginning on the first day of the first applicable plan year—

(1) this section shall be applied—

(A) by treating the first day of the first applicable plan year as the termination date of the plan, and

(B) by determining the amount of guaranteed benefits on the basis of plan assets and liabilities as of such assumed termination date, and

(2) notwithstanding section 4044(a), plan assets shall first be allocated to pay the amount, if any, by which—

(A) the amount of guaranteed benefits under this section (determined without regard to paragraph (1) and on the basis of plan assets and liabilities as of the actual date of plan termination), exceeds

(B) the amount determined under paragraph (1).

Amendments

P.L. 109-280, §402(g)(2)(A):

Amended ERISA Sec. 4022 by adding new subsection (h) to read as above.

The above amendment applies to plan years ending after the date of the enactment of this Act [August 17, 2006].

P.L. 109-280, §403(a):

Amended ERISA Sec. 4022(b) by adding a new paragraph (8) to read as above.

The above amendment applies to benefits that become payable as a result of an event which occurs after July 26, 2005.

P.L. 109-280, 404(a):

Amended ERISA Sec. 4022 by adding new subsection (g) to read as above.

The above amendment applies with respect to proceedings initiated under title 11, United States Code, or under any similar Federal law or law of a State or

political subdivision, on or after the date that is 30 days after the date of enactment of this Act [August 17, 2006].

P.L. 109-280, §407(a):

Amended ERISA Sec. 4022(b)(5) to read as above. Prior to amendment, paragraph (5) read as follows:

(5)(A) For purposes of this title, the term "substantial owner" means an individual who—

(i) owns the entire interest in an unincorporated trade or business,

(ii) in the case of a partnership, is a partner who owns, directly or indirectly, more than 10 percent of either the capital interest or the profits interest in such partnership, or

(iii) in the case of a corporation, owns, directly or indirectly, more than 10 percent in value of either the voting stock of that corporation or all the stock of that corporation.

For purposes of clause (iii) the constructive ownership rules of section 1563(e) of the Internal Revenue Code of 1986 shall apply (determined without regard to section 1563(e)(3)(C)). For purposes of this title an individual is also treated as a substantial owner with respect to a plan if, at any time within the 60 months preceding the date on which the determination is made, he was a substantial owner under the plan.

(B) In the case of a participant in a plan under which benefits have not been increased by reason of any plan amendments and who is covered by the plan as a substantial owner, the amount of benefits guaranteed under this section shall not exceed the product of—

(i) a fraction (not to exceed 1) the numerator of which is the number of years the substantial owner was an active participant in the plan, and the denominator of which is 30, and

(ii) the amount of the substantial owner's monthly benefits guaranteed under subsection (a) (as limited under paragraph (3) of this subsection).

(C) In the case of a participant in a plan, other than a plan described in subparagraph (B), who is covered by the plan as a substantial owner, the amount of the benefit guaranteed under this section shall, under regulations prescribed by the corporation, treat each benefit increase attributable to a plan amendment as if it were provided under a new plan. The benefits guaranteed under this section with respect to all such amendments shall not exceed the amount which would be determined under subparagraph (B) if subparagraph (B) applied.

For effective date, see §407(d) below.

P.L. 109-280, §407(d):

(d) EFFECTIVE DATES.—(1) IN GENERAL.—* * * The amendments made by this section shall apply to plan terminations—

(A) under section 4041(c) of the Employee Retirement Income Security Act of 1974 (29 U.S.C. 1341(c)) with respect to which notices of intent to terminate are provided under section 4041(a)(2) of such Act (29 U.S.C. 1341(a)(2)) after December 31, 2005, and

(B) under section 4042 of such Act (29 U.S.C. 1342) with respect to which notices of determination are provided under such section after such date.

* * *

P.L. 109-280, §408(a):

Amended ERISA Sec. 4022(c)(3)(B)(ii) to read as above. Prior to amendment, subparagraph (ii) read as follows:

(ii) notices of intent to terminate were provided after December 17, 1987, and during the 5-Federal fiscal year period ending with the fiscal year preceding the fiscal year in which occurs the date of the notice of intent to terminate with respect to the plan termination for which the recovery ratio is being determined.

For effective date, see §408(c) below.

P.L. 109-280, §408(b)(1):

Amended ERISA Sec. 4022(c)(3)(A) to read as above. Prior to amendment, subparagraph (A) read as follows:

(A) Except as provided in subparagraph (C), for purposes of this subsection, the term "recovery ratio" means the average ratio, with respect to prior plan terminations described in subparagraph (B), of—

(i) the value of the recovery of the corporation under section 4062, 4063, or 4064 in connection with such prior terminations, to

(ii) the amount of unfunded benefit liabilities under such plans as of the termination date in connection with such prior terminations.

For effective date, see §408(c) below.

P.L. 109-280, §408(c):

EFFECTIVE DATE. – The amendments made by this section shall apply for any termination for which notices of intent to terminate are provided (or in the case of a termination by the corporation, a notice of determination under section 4042 under the Employee Retirement Income Security Act of 1974 is issued) on or after the date which is 30 days after the date of enactment of this section [August 17, 2006].

The above amendment is effective for plan terminations under ERISA Sec. 4041(c) with respect to which notices of intent to terminate are provided under ERISA Sec. 4041(a)(2), or under ERISA Sec. 4042 with respect to which proceedings are instituted by the corporation, on or after December 8, 1994.

P.L. 103-465, §777(a):

Act Sec. 777(a) amended ERISA Sec. 4022(b)(3) by adding at the end new sentences to read as above.

The above amendment is effective for plan terminations under ERISA Sec. 4041(c) with respect to which notices of intent to terminate are provided under ERISA Sec. 4041(a)(2), or under ERISA Sec. 4042 with respect to which proceedings are instituted by the corporation, on or after December 8, 1994.

P.L. 103-465, §766(c):

Act Sec. 766(c) amended ERISA Sec. 4022 by inserting new subsection (f) to read as above.

The above amendment applies to plan amendments adopted on or after December 8, 1994.

P.L. 101-239, §7881(f)(1):

Amended P.L. 100-203, §9312(b)(3)(B)(i) by striking "section 4022(c)(1)" in subclause (I) and inserting "section 4022(c)(3)", and by striking "subparagraph (B) of section 4022(c)(1)" and inserting "subparagraph (C) of section 4022(c)(3)."

P.L. 101-239, §7881(f)(4):

Amended ERISA Sec. 4022(c)(1) by striking "(in the case of a deceased participant)."

P.L. 101-239, §7881(f)(5):

Amended ERISA Sec. 4022(c)(3)(B)(ii) by inserting new material after "1987."

P.L. 101-239, §7881(f)(6):

Amended P.L. 100-203, §9312(b)(3)(B) by striking clause (ii).

P.L. 101-239, §7881(f)(11):

Amended ERISA Sec. 4022(c)(1) by striking "section 4044(a), to such participant" and inserting "section 4044(a). Such payment shall be made to such participant".

The above amendments are effective as if included in P.L. 100-203, §9312(b)(3)(A).

P.L. 101-239, §7891(a)(1):

Titles I, III, and IV of ERISA (other than sections 3(37)(E), 301(a)(7), and 308, the last sentence of section 408(d), and sections 414(c), 4001(a)(3)(ii), and 4303) are each amended by striking "Internal Revenue Code of 1954" each place it appears and inserting "Internal Revenue Code of 1986" effective October 22, 1986.

P.L. 101-239, §7894(g)(1):

Amended ERISA Sec. 4022(b)(2) by striking "60 month" and inserting "60-month."

P.L. 101-239, §7894(g)(3)(B):

Amended ERISA Sec. 4022(a) by striking "section 4021" and inserting "this title."

The above amendments are effective September 2, 1974.

P.L. 100-203, §9312(b)(3)(A):

Amended ERISA Sec. 4022 by redesignating subsections (c) and (d) as (d) and (e) and adding new subsection (c) to read as above, effective for (A) plan terminations under section 4041(c) of ERISA with respect to which notices of intent to terminate are provided under section 4041(a)(2) of ERISA after December 17, 1987, and (B) plan terminations with respect to which proceedings are instituted by the Pension Benefit Guaranty Corporation under section 4042 of ERISA after December 17, 1987.

P.L. 100-203, §9312(b)(3)(B):

(B) TRANSITIONAL RULE.—

(i) IN GENERAL.—In the case of any plan termination to which the amendments made by this section apply and with respect to which notices of intent to terminate were provided on or before December 17, 1990—

(I) subparagraph (A) of section 4022(c)(3) of ERISA (as amended by this paragraph) shall not apply, and

(II) subparagraph (C) of section 4022(c)(3) of ERISA (as so amended) shall apply irrespective of the outstanding amount of benefit liabilities under the plan.

P.L. 99-272:

Act Sec. 11016(c)(8) amended ERISA Sec. 4022(b)(7) by striking "following" and inserting "beginning with" in its place. Act Sec. 11016(c)(9) added a new subsection (d) to read as above. These amendments apply on April 7, 1986.

P.L. 99-364, §403(c):

Amended Sec. 4022, effective September 26, 1980 by changing the title to read as above (previously it read "Benefits Guaranteed"), amended subsection (a) to read as above, substituted "(7)" for "(8)" in subparagraph (b)(1), and struck subparagraph (b)(5) and renumbered subparagraphs (b)(6)-(8) as (b)(5), (b)(6) and (b)(7). Prior to amendment, subsection (a) read:

"Subject to the limitations contained in subsection (b), the corporation shall guarantee the payment of all nonforfeitable benefits (other than benefits becoming nonforfeitable solely on account of the termination of a plan) under the terms of a plan which terminates at a time when section 4021 applies to it."

Prior to amendment, subparagraph (b)(5) read:

"Notwithstanding paragraph (3), no person shall receive from the corporation for basic benefits with respect to a participant an amount, or amounts, with an actuarial value which exceeds a monthly benefit in the form of a life annuity commencing at age 65 equal to the amount determined under paragraph (3)(B) at the time of the last plan termination."

Regulations

The following regulations were adopted by the Pension Benefit Guaranty Corporation on July 1, 1996 (61 FR 34002). Prior to July 1, 1996, PBGC regulations were under Chapter XXVI of Title 29 of the Code of Federal Regulations. Effective July 1, 1996, PBGC regulations were moved to Chapter XL, and were renumbered and reorganized. Reg. §4022.61 was amended November 7, 1997 (62 FR 60424), effective January 1, 1998. Reg. §§4022.1, 4022.24 and 4022.26 were officially corrected December 30, 1997 (62 FR 67728). Reg. §§4022.81, 4022.82, and 4022.83 were amended May 28, 1998 (63 FR 29353), effective May 29, 1998. Reg. §4022.7 was amended July 15, 1998 (63 FR 38305), effective July 16, 1998 and on March 17, 2000 (65 FR 14751), effective May 1, 2000. The Appendix to Part 4022 was amended and added to on March 17, 2000 (65 FR 14751 and 14753), effective May 1, 2000. Reg. §§4022.4, 4022.6, 4022.7, 4022.21, 4022.25, 4022.81 were amended April 8, 2002 (67 FR 16949), effective June 1, 2002. Reg §§4022.8, 4022.9, 4022.10, 4022.91, 4022.92, 4022.93, 4022.94, 4022.95, 4022.101, 4022.102, 4022.103, and 4022.104 were added April 8, 2002 (67 FR 16949), effective June 1, 2002. Reg. §4022.9 was amended on October 28, 2003 (68 FR 61344). Reg. §4022.11 was added on November 17, 2009 (74 FR 59093), effective December 17, 2009. Reg. §§4022.2, 4022.3, 4022.4, 4022.6, 4022.21, 4022.22, 4022.23, 4022.24, 4022.25, 4022.61, 4022.62, 4022.63, 4022.81, and 4022.82 were amended on June 14, 2011 (76 FR 34590). Reg. § 4022.51 was added on June 14, 2011 (76 FR 34590). Reg. §§ 4022.2, 4022.24, and 4022.62 were amended, Reg. § 4022.27 was redesignated as Reg. § 4022.28, and Reg. § 4022.27 was added May 6, 2014 (79 FR 25667), effective June 5, 2014. Reg. §§ 4022.2, 4022.7, 4022.8, 4022.22, and 4022.24 were amended on November 25, 2014 (79 FR 70090).

Subpart A—General Provisions; Guaranteed Benefits

[¶ 15,421]

§ 4022.1 **Purpose and scope.** The purpose of this part is to prescribe rules governing the calculation and payment of benefits payable in terminated single-employer plans under section 4022 of ERISA. Subpart A, which applies to each plan providing benefits guaranteed under title IV of ERISA, contains definitions applicable to all subparts, and describes benefits that are guaranteed by the PBGC subject to the limitations set forth in Subpart B. Subpart C is reserved for rules relating to the calculation and payment of unfunded nonguaranteed benefits under section 4022(c) of ERISA. Subpart D prescribes procedures that minimize the overpayment of benefits by plan administrators after initiating distress terminations of single-employer plans that are not expected to be sufficient for guaranteed benefits. Subpart E sets forth the method of recoupment of benefit payments in excess of the amounts permitted under sections 4022, 4022B, and 4044 of ERISA from participants and beneficiaries in PBGC-trusteed plans, and provides for reimbursement of benefit underpayments. (The provisions of this part have not been amended to take account of changes made in section 4022 of ERISA by sections 766 and 777 of the Retirement Protection Act of 1994.) [Corrected 12/30/97 by 62 FR 67728.]

[¶ 15,421A]

§ 4022.2 **Definitions.** The following terms are defined in § 4001.2 of this chapter: annuity, bankruptcy filing date, Code, employer, ERISA, guaranteed benefit, non-PPA 2006 bankruptcy termination, mandatory employee contributions, nonforfeitable benefit, non-PPA 2006 bankruptcy termination, normal retirement age, notice of intent to terminate, PBGC, person, plan, plan administrator, plan year, proposed termination date, substantial owner, and title IV benefit. [Amended 6/14/11 by 76 FR 34590.]

In addition, for purposes of this part (unless otherwise required by the context):

Accumulated mandatory employee contributions means mandatory employee contributions plus interest credited on those contributions under the plan, or, if greater, interest required by section 204(c) of ERISA.

Benefit in pay status means that one or more benefit payments have been made or would have been made except for administrative delay.

Benefit increase means any benefit arising from the adoption of a new plan or an increase in the value of benefits payable arising from an amendment to an existing plan. Such increases include, but are not limited to, a scheduled increase in benefits under a plan or plan amendment, such as a cost-of-living increase, and any change in plan provisions which advances a participant's or beneficiary's entitlement to a benefit, such as liberalized participation requirements or vesting schedules, reductions in the normal or early retirement age under a plan, an unpredictable contingent event benefit, and changes in the form of benefit payments. In the case of a plan under which the amount of benefits depends on the participant's salary and the participant receives a salary increase the resulting increase in benefits to which the participant becomes entitled will not, for the purpose of this part, be treated as a benefit increase. Similarly, in the case of a plan under which the amount of benefits depends on the participant's age or service, and the participant becomes entitled to increased benefits solely because of advancement in age or service, the increased benefits to which the participant becomes entitled will not, for the purpose of this part, be treated as a benefit increase. [Amended 5/6/2014 (79 FR 25667).]

Covered employment means employment with respect to which benefits accrue under a plan.

Pension benefit means a benefit payable as an annuity, or one or more payments related thereto, to a participant who permanently leaves or has permanently left covered employment, or to a surviving beneficiary, which payments by themselves or in combination with Social Security, Railroad Retirement, or workmen's compensation benefits provide a substantially level income to the recipient. An annuity benefit

resulting from a rollover amount is a pension benefit. [Amended 11/25/14 by 79 FR 70090.]

Straight life annuity means a series of level periodic payments payable for the life of the recipient, but does not include any combined annuity form, including an annuity payable for a term certain and life.

Unpredictable contingent event (UCE) has the same meaning as unpredictable contingent event in section 206(g)(1)(C) of ERISA and Treas. Reg. § 1.436–1(j)(9) (26 CFR 1.436–1(j)(9)). It includes a plant shutdown (full or partial) or a similar event (such as a full or partial closing of another type of facility, or a layoff or other workforce reduction), or any event other than the attainment of any age, performance of any service, receipt or derivation of any compensation, or occurrence of death or disability. [Added 5/6/2014 (79 FR 25667).]

Unpredictable contingent event benefit (UCEB) has the same meaning as unpredictable contingent event benefit in section 206(g)(1)(C) of ERISA and Treas. Reg. § 1.436–1(j)(9) (26 CFR 1.436–1(j)(9)). Thus, a UCEB is any benefit or benefit increase to the extent that it would not be payable but for the occurrence of a UCE. A benefit or benefit increase that is conditioned upon the occurrence of a UCE does not cease to be a UCEB as a result of the contingent event having occurred or its occurrence having become reasonably predictable. [Added 5/6/2014 (79 FR 25667).]

[¶ 15,421B]

§ 4022.3 **Guaranteed benefits.** (a) *General.* Except as otherwise provided in this part, the PBGC will guarantee the amount, as of the termination date, of a benefit provided under a plan to the extent that the benefit does not exceed the limitations in ERISA and in subpart B, if—

(1) The benefit is a nonforfeitable benefit;

(2) The benefit qualifies as a pension benefit as defined in § 4022.2; and

(3) The participant is entitled to the benefit under § 4022.4. [Amended 6/14/11 by 76 FR 34590.]

(b) *PPA 2006 bankruptcy termination.*

(1) *Substitution of bankruptcy filing date.* In a PPA 2006 bankruptcy termination, "bankruptcy filing date" is substituted for "termination date" each place that "termination date" appears in paragraph (a) of this section.

(2) *Condition for entitlement satisfied between bankruptcy filing date and termination date.* If a participant becomes entitled to a subsidized early retirement or other benefit before the termination date (or on or before the termination date, in the case of a requirement that a participant attain a particular age, earn a particular amount of service, become disabled, or die) but on or after the bankruptcy filing date (or after the bankruptcy filing date, in the case of a requirement that a participant attain a particular age, earn a particular amount of service, become disabled, or die), the subsidy or other benefit is not guaranteed because the participant had not satisfied the conditions for entitlement by the bankruptcy filing date. In such a case, the participant may have been put into pay status with the subsidized early retirement or other benefit by the plan administrator, because the plan was ongoing at the time. Even though the subsidy or other benefit is not guaranteed, the participant may be entitled to another benefit from PBGC (at that time or in the future). If so, PBGC will continue paying the participant a benefit, but in an amount reduced to reflect that the subsidy or other benefit is not guaranteed. PBGC will also allow a similarly situated participant who had not started receiving a subsidized early retirement or other benefit before PBGC became trustee of the plan to begin receiving a benefit (if the participant would have been allowed under the plan to begin receiving benefits and has reached his Earliest PBGC Retirement Date, as defined in § 4022.10), but in an amount that does not include the subsidy or other benefit.

(3) *Examples.* (i) *Vesting.* A plan provides for 5-year "cliff" vesting—*i.e.,* benefits become 100% vested when the participant completes five years of service; before the five-year mark, benefits are 0% vested. The contributing sponsor of the plan files a bankruptcy petition on November 15, 2006. The plan terminates with a termination date of

December 4, 2007, and PBGC becomes statutory trustee of the plan. A participant had four years and six months of service at the bankruptcy filing date and became vested in May 2007. None of the participant's benefit is guaranteed because none of the benefit was nonforfeitable as of the bankruptcy filing date.

(ii) *Subsidized early retirement benefit.* The facts regarding the plan are the same as in Example (i) (paragraph (b)(3)(i) of this section), but the plan also provides that a participant may retire from active employment at any age with a fully subsidized (*i.e.,* not actuarially reduced) early retirement benefit if he has completed 30 years of service. The plan also provides that a participant who is age 60 and has completed 20 years of service may retire from active employment with an early retirement benefit, reduced by three percent for each year by which the participant's age at benefit commencement is less than 65. A participant was age 61 and had 29 years and 6 months of service at the bankruptcy filing date. The participant continued working for another six months, then retired as of June 1, 2007, and immediately began receiving from the plan the fully subsidized "30-and-out" early retirement benefit. PBGC will continue paying the participant a benefit, but PBGC's guarantee does not include the full subsidy for the "30-and-out" benefit, because the participant satisfied the conditions for that benefit after the bankruptcy filing date. The guarantee does include, however, the partial subsidy associated with the "60/20" early retirement benefit, because the participant satisfied the conditions for that benefit before the bankruptcy filing date.

(iii) *Accruals after bankruptcy filing date.* The facts regarding the plan are the same as in Example (i) (paragraph (b)(3)(i) of this section). A participant has a vested, accrued benefit of $500 per month as of the bankruptcy filing date. At the plan's termination date, the participant has a vested, accrued benefit of $512 per month. His guaranteed benefit is limited to $500 per month—the accrued, nonforfeitable benefit as of the bankruptcy filing date. [Add 6/14/11 by 76 FR 34590.]

[¶ 15,421C]

§ 4022.4 **Entitlement to a benefit.** (a) A participant or his surviving beneficiary is entitled to a benefit if under the provisions of a plan:

(1) The benefit was in pay status on the termination date of the plan. [Amended 6/14/11 by 76 FR 34590.]

(2) The benefit is payable in an optional life-annuity form of benefit that the participant or beneficiary elected on or before the termination date of the plan or, if later, the date on which PBGC became statutory trustee of the plan.

(3) Except for a benefit described in paragraph (a)(2) of this section, before the termination date or on or before the termination date, in the case of a requirement that a participant attain a particular age, earn a particular amount of service, become disabled, or die the participant had satisfied the conditions of the plan necessary to establish the right to receive the benefit prior to such date prior to or on such date, in the case of a requirement that a participant attain a particular age, earn a particular amount of service, become disabled, or die other than application for the benefit, satisfaction of a waiting period described in the plan, or retirement; or [Amended by 67 FR 16949, April 8, 2002.]

(4) Absent an election by the participant, the benefit would be payable upon retirement.

(5) In the case of a benefit that returns all or a portion of a participant's accumulated mandatory employee contributions upon death, the participant (or beneficiary) had satisfied the conditions of the plan necessary to establish the right to the benefit other than death or designation of a beneficiary.

(b) If none of the conditions set forth in paragraph (a) of this section is met, the PBGC will determine whether the participant is entitled to a benefit on the basis of the provisions of the plan and the circumstances of the case.

(c) In a PPA 2006 bankruptcy termination, "bankruptcy filing date" is substituted for "termination date" each place that "termination date" appears in paragraphs (a)(1) and (3) of this section. In making this substitution for purposes of paragraph (a)(3) of this section, the rule in § 4022.3(b)(2) (dealing with the situation where the condition for entitlement was satisfied between the bankruptcy filing date and the termination date) shall apply. [Added 6/14/11 by 76 FR 34590.]

[¶ 15,421D]

§ 4022.5 **Determination of nonforfeitable benefits.** (a) A guaranteed benefit payable to a surviving beneficiary is not considered to be forfeitable solely because the plan provides that the benefit will cease upon the remarriage of such beneficiary or his attaining a specified age. However, the PBGC will observe the provisions of the plan relating to the effect of such remarriage or attainment of such specified age on the surviving beneficiary's eligibility to continue to receive benefit payments.

(b) Any other provision in a plan that the right to a benefit in pay status will cease or be suspended upon the occurrence of any specified condition does not automatically make that benefit forfeitable. In each such case the PBGC will determine whether the benefit is forfeitable.

(c) A benefit guaranteed under § 4022.6 shall not be considered forfeitable solely because the plan provides that upon recovery of the participant the benefit will cease.

[¶ 15,421E]

§ 4022.6 **Annuity payable for total disability.** (a) Except as otherwise provided in this section, an annuity which is payable (or would be payable after a waiting period described in the plan, whether or not the participant is in receipt of other benefits during such waiting period), under the terms of a plan on account of the total and permanent disability of a participant which is expected to last for the life of the participant and which began on or before the termination date is considered to be a pension benefit. [Amended by 67 FR 16949, April 8, 2002 and by 76 FR 34590, June 14, 2011.]

(b) In any case in which the PBGC determines that the standards for determining such total and permanent disability under a plan were unreasonable, or were modified in anticipation of termination of the plan, the disability benefits payable to a participant under such standard shall not be guaranteed unless the participant meets the standards of the Social Security Act and the regulations promulgated thereunder for determining total disability.

(c) For the purpose of this section, a participant may be required, upon the request of the PBGC, to submit to an examination or to submit proof of continued total and permanent disability. If the PBGC finds that a participant is no longer so disabled, it may suspend, modify, or discontinue the payment of the disability benefit.

(d) *PPA 2006 bankruptcy termination.* In a PPA 2006 bankruptcy termination, "bankruptcy filing date" is substituted for "termination date" in paragraph (a) of this section. [Added 6/14/11 by 76 FR 34590.]

[¶ 15,421F]

§ 4022.7 **Benefits payable in a single installment.** (a) *Alternative benefit.* If a benefit that is guaranteed under this part is payable in a single installment or substantially so under the terms of the plan, or an option elected under the plan by the participant, the benefit will not be guaranteed or paid as such, but the PBGC will guarantee the alternative benefit, if any, in the plan which provides for the payment of equal periodic installments for the life of the recipient. If the plan provides more than one such annuity, the recipient may within 30 days after notification of the proposed termination of the plan elect to receive one of those annuities. If the plan does not provide such an annuity, the PBGC will guarantee an actuarially equivalent life annuity.

(b)(1) *Payment in lump sum.* Notwithstanding paragraph (a) of this section:

(i) *In general.* If the lump sum value of a benefit (or of an estimated benefit) payable by the PBGC is $5,000 or less and the benefit is not yet in pay status, the benefit (or estimated benefit) may be paid in a lump sum.

(ii) *Annuity option.* If the PBGC would otherwise make a lump sum payment in accordance with paragraph (b)(1)(i) of this section and the monthly benefit (or the estimated monthly benefit) is equal to or greater than $25 (at normal retirement age and in the normal form for an unmarried participant), the PBGC will provide the option to receive the benefit in the form of an annuity.

(iii) *Election of QPSA lump sum.* If the lump sum value of annuity payments under a qualified preretirement survivor annuity (or under an estimated qualified preretirement survivor annuity) is $5,000 or less, the benefit is not yet in pay status, and the participant dies after the termination date, the benefit (or estimated benefit) may be paid in a lump sum if so elected by the surviving spouse.

(iv) *Payments to estates.* The PBGC may pay any annuity payments payable to an estate in a single installment without regard to the threshold in paragraph (b)(1)(i) of this section if so elected by the estate. The PBGC will discount the annuity payments using the federal mid-term rate (as determined by the Secretary of the Treasury pursuant to section 1274(d)(1)(C)(ii) of the Code) applicable for the month the participant died based on monthly compounding. [Amended by 67 FR 16949, April 8, 2002.]

(2) *Return of employee contributions—*

(i) *General.* Notwithstanding any other provision of this part, except as provided in paragraph (b)(2)(iii) of this section, the PBGC may pay in a single installment (or a series of installments) instead of as an annuity, the value of the portion of an individual's basic-type benefit derived from mandatory employee contributions, if: [Amended 11/25/14 by 79 FR 70090.]

(A) The individual elects payment in a single installment (or a series of installments) before the sixty-first (61st) day after the date he or she receives notice that such an election is available; and

(B) Payment in a single installment (or a series of installments) is consistent with the plan's provisions. For purposes of this part, the portion of an individual's basic-type benefit derived from mandatory employee contributions is determined under § 4044.12 (priority category 2 benefits) of this chapter, and the value of that portion is computed under the applicable rules contained in part 4044, subpart B, of this chapter.

(ii) *Set-off for distributions after termination.* The amount to be returned under paragraph (b)(2)(i) of this section is reduced by the set-off amount. The set-off amount is the amount by which distributions made to the individual after the termination date exceed the amount that would have been distributed, exclusive of mandatory employee contributions, if the individual had withdrawn the mandatory employee contributions on the termination date.

Example: Participant A is receiving a benefit of $600 per month when the plan terminates, $200 of which is derived from mandatory employee contributions. If the participant had withdrawn his contributions on the termination date, his benefit would have been reduced to $400 per month. The participant receives two monthly payments after the termination date. The set-off amount is $400. (The $600 actual payment minus the $400 the participant would have received if he had withdrawn his contributions multiplied by the two months for which he received the extra payment.)

(iii) *Rollover amounts.* The rule in paragraph (b)(2) of this section (dealing with return of employee contributions) does not apply to a participant's accumulated mandatory employee contributions resulting from rollover amounts (as determined under § 4044.12(c)(4)(i) of this chapter) or the benefit derived from such mandatory employee contributions. [Added 11/25/14 by 79 FR 70090.]

(c) *Death benefits—*

(1) *General.* Notwithstanding paragraph (a) of this section, a benefit that would otherwise be guaranteed under the provisions of this subpart, except for the fact that it is payable solely in a single installment (or substantially so) upon the death of a participant, shall be paid by the PBGC as an annuity that has the same value as the single installment. The PBGC will in each case determine the amount and duration of the annuity based on all the facts and circumstances.

(2) *Exception.* Except in the case of accumulated mandatory employee contributions resulting from rollover amounts (as determined under § 4044.12(c)(4)(i) of this chapter), upon the death of a participant the PBGC may pay in a single installment (or a series of installments) that portion of the participant's accumulated mandatory employee contributions that is payable under the plan in a single installment (or a series of installments) upon the participant's death. [Revised 11/25/14 by 79 FR 70090.]

(d) *Determination of lump sum amount.* For purposes of paragraph (b)(1) of this section—

(1) *Benefits disregarded.* In determining whether the lump-sum value of a benefit is $5,000 or less, the PBGC may disregard the value of any benefits the plan or the PBGC previously paid in lump-sum form or the plan paid by purchasing an annuity contract, the value of any benefits returned under paragraph (b)(2) of this section, and the value of any benefits the PBGC has not yet determined under section 4022(c) of ERISA.

(2) *Actuarial assumptions.* The PBGC will calculate the lump sum value of a benefit by valuing the monthly annuity benefits payable in the form determined under § 4044.51(a) of this chapter and commencing at the time determined under § 4044.51(b) of this chapter. The actuarial assumptions used will be those described in § 4044.52, except that—

(i) *Loading for expenses.* There will be no adjustment to reflect the loading for expenses;

(ii) *Mortality rates and interest assumptions.* The mortality rates in appendix A to this part and the interest assumptions in appendix B to this part will apply; and

(iii) *Date for determining lump sum value.* The date as of which a lump sum value is calculated is the termination date, except that in the case of a subsequent insufficiency it is the date described in section 4062(b)(1)(B) of ERISA. [Amended by 67 FR 16949, April 8, 2002.]

(3) *Date for determining lump sum value.* The date as of which a lump sum value is calculated is the termination date, except that in the case of a subsequent insufficiency it is the date described in section 4062(b)(1)(B) of ERISA. [Amended on 3/17/00 by 65 FR 14751.]

(e) *Publication of lump sum rates.* The PBGC will provide two sets of lump sum interest rates as follows—

(1) In appendix B to this part, the lump sum interest rates for PBGC payments, as provided under paragraph (d)(2) of this section; and

(2) In appendix C to this part, the lump sum interest rates for private-sector payments. [Added on 3/17/00 by 65 FR 14753.]

[¶ 15,421G]

§ 4022.8 Form of payment.

(a) *In general.* This section applies where benefits are not already in pay status. Except as provided in § 4022.7 (relating to the payment of lump sums), the PBGC will pay benefits—

(1) In the automatic PBGC form described in paragraph (b) of this section; or

(2) If an optional PBGC form described in paragraph (c) of this section is elected, in that optional form.

(b) *Automatic PBGC form.*

(1) *Participants.*

(i) *Married participants.* The automatic PBGC form with respect to a participant who is married at the time the benefit enters pay status is the form a married participant would be entitled to receive from the plan in the absence of an election.

(ii) *Unmarried participants.* The automatic PBGC form with respect to a participant who is unmarried at the time the benefit enters pay status is the form an unmarried person would be entitled to receive from the plan in the absence of an election.

(2) *Beneficiaries.*

(i) *QPSA beneficiaries.* The automatic PBGC form with respect to the spouse of a married participant in a plan with a termination date on or after August 23, 1984, who dies before his or her benefit enters pay status is the qualified preretirement survivor annuity such a spouse would be entitled to receive from the plan in the absence of an election. The PBGC will not charge the participant or beneficiary for this survivor benefit coverage for the time period beginning on the plan's termination date (regardless of whether the plan would have charged).

(ii) *Alternate payees*. The automatic PBGC form with respect to an alternate payee with a separate interest under a qualified domestic relations order is the form an unmarried participant would be entitled to receive from the plan in the absence of an election.

(c) *Optional PBGC forms.*

(1) *Participant and beneficiary elections.* A participant may elect any optional form described in paragraphs (c)(4) or (c)(5) of this section. A beneficiary described in paragraph (b)(2) of this section (a QPSA beneficiary or an alternate payee) may elect any optional form described in paragraphs (c)(4)(i) through (c)(4)(iv) of this section.

(2) *Permitted designees.* A participant or beneficiary, whether married or unmarried, who elects an optional form with a survivor feature (e.g., a 5-year certain-and-continuous annuity or, in the case of a participant, a joint-and-50%-survivor annuity) may designate either a spouse or a non-spouse beneficiary to receive survivor benefits. An optional joint-life form must be payable to a natural person or (with the consent of the PBGC) to a trust for the benefit of one or more natural persons.

(3) *Spousal consent.* In the case of a participant who is married at the time the benefit enters pay status, the election of an optional form or the designation of a non-spouse beneficiary is valid only if the participant's spouse consents.

(4) *Permitted optional single-life forms.* The PBGC may offer benefits in the following single-life forms:

(i) A straight-life annuity;

(ii) A 5-year certain-and-continuous annuity;

(iii) A 10-year certain-and-continuous annuity;

(iv) A 15-year certain-and-continuous annuity; and

(v) The form an unmarried person would be entitled to receive from the plan in the absence of an election.

(5) *Permitted optional joint-life forms.* The PBGC may offer benefits in the following joint-life forms:

(i) A joint-and-50%-survivor annuity;

(ii) A joint-and-50%-survivor- "pop-up" annuity (i.e., where the participant's benefit "pops up" to the unreduced level if the beneficiary dies first);

(iii) A joint-and-75%-survivor annuity; and

(iv) A joint-and-100%-survivor annuity.

(6) *Determination of benefit amount; starting benefit.* To determine the amount of the benefit in an optional PBGC form—

(i) *Single-life forms.* In the case of an optional PBGC form under paragraph (c)(4) of this section, the PBGC will first determine the amount of the benefit in the form the plan would pay to an unmarried participant in the absence of an election.

(ii) *Joint-life forms.* In the case of an optional PBGC form under paragraph (c)(5) of this section, the PBGC will first determine the amount of the benefit in the form the plan would pay to a married participant in the absence of an election. For this purpose, the PBGC will treat a participant who designates a non-spouse beneficiary as being married to a person who is the same age as that non-spouse beneficiary.

(7) *Determination of benefit amount; conversion factors.* The PBGC will convert the benefit amount determined under paragraph (c)(6) of this section to the optional form elected, using PBGC factors based on—

(i) *Mortality.* Unisex mortality rates that are a fixed blend of 50 percent of the male mortality rates and 50 percent of the female mortality rates from the 1983 Group Annuity Mortality Table as prescribed in Rev. Rul. 95-6, 1995-1 C.B. 80 (Internal Revenue Service Cumulative Bulletins are available from the Superintendent of Documents, Government Printing Office, Washington, DC 20402); and

(ii) *Interest.* An interest rate of six percent.

(8) *Determination of benefit amount; limitation.* The PBGC will limit the benefit amount determined under paragraph (c)(7) of this section to the amount of the benefit it would pay in the form of a straight life annuity under paragraph (c)(4)(i) of this section.

(9) *Incidental benefits.* The PBGC will not pay an optional PBGC form with a death benefit (e.g., a joint-and-50%-survivor annuity) unless the death benefit would be an "incidental death benefit" under 26 CFR 1.401-1(b)(1)(i). If the death benefit would not be an "incidental death benefit," the PBGC may instead offer a modified version of the optional form under which the death benefit would be an "incidental death benefit."

(d) *Change in benefit form.* Once payment of a benefit starts, the benefit form cannot be changed.

(e) *PBGC discretion.* The PBGC may make other optional annuity forms available subject to the rules in paragraph (c) of this section.

(f) *Rollover amounts.* The annuity benefit resulting from rollover amounts (as determined under § 4044.12(c)(4) of this chapter) is combined with any other benefit under the plan and paid in the same form and at the same time as the other benefit. [Added 11/25/14 by 79 FR 70090.]

[¶ 15,421H]
§ 4022.9 **Time of payment; benefit applications**.

(a) *Time of payment.* A participant may start receiving an annuity benefit from —the PBGC (subject to the PBGC's rules for starting benefit payments) on his or her Earliest PBGC Retirement Date as determined under § 4022.10 of this subchapter or, if later, the plan's termination date.

(b) *Elections and consents.* The PBGC may prescribe the time and manner for benefit elections to be made and spousal consents to be provided.

(c) *Benefit applications.* The PBGC is not required to accept any application for benefits not made in accordance with its forms and instructions.

(d) *Filing with the PBGC—.* (1) *Method and date of filing.* The PBGC applies the rules in subpart A of part 4000 of this chapter to determine permissible methods of filing with the PBGC under this part. Benefit applications and related submissions are treated as filed on the date received by the PBGC unless the instructions for the applicable form provide for an earlier date. Subpart C of part 4000 of this chapter provides rules for determining when the PBGC receives a submission.

(2) *Where to file.* See Sec. 4000.4 of this chapter for information on where to file.

(3) *Computation of time.* The PBGC applies the rules in subpart D of part 4000 of this chapter to compute any time period for filing under this part.

[Amended 10/28/2003 by 68 FR 61344]

[¶ 15,421I]
§ 4022.10 **Earliest PBGC Retirement Date.**
The Earliest PBGC Retirement Date for a participant is the earliest date on which the participant could retire under plan provisions for purposes of section 4044(a)(3)(B) of ERISA. The Earliest PBGC Retirement Date is determined in accordance with this § 4022.10. For purposes of this § 4022.10, "age" means the participant's age as of his or her last birthday (unless otherwise required by the context).

(a) *Immediate annuity at or after age 55.* If the earliest date on which a participant could separate from service with the right to receive an immediate annuity is on or after the date the participant reaches age 55, the Earliest PBGC Retirement Date for the participant is the earliest date on which the participant could separate from service with the right to receive an immediate annuity.

(b) *Immediate annuity before age 55.* If the earliest date on which a participant could separate from service with the right to receive an immediate annuity is before the date the participant reaches age 55, the Earliest PBGC Retirement Date for the participant is the date the participant reaches age 55 (except as provided in paragraph (c) of this section).

(c) *Facts and circumstances.* If a participant could separate from service with the right to receive an immediate annuity before the date the participant reaches age 55, the PBGC will make a determination, under the facts and circumstances, as to whether the participant could retire under plan provisions for purposes of section 4044(a)(3)(B) of ERISA on an earlier date. If the PBGC determines, under the facts and circumstances, that the participant could retire under plan provisions for those purposes on an earlier date, that earlier date is the Earliest PBGC Retirement Date for the participant. In making this determination, the PBGC will take into account plan provisions (e.g., the general structure of the provisions, the extent to which the benefit is subsidized, and whether eligibility for the benefit is based on a substantial service or age-and-service requirement), the age at which employees customarily retire (under the particular plan or in the particular company or industry, as appropriate), and all other relevant considerations. Neither a plan's reference to a separation from service at a particular age as a "retirement" nor the ability of a participant to receive an immediate annuity at a particular age necessarily makes the date the participant reaches that age the Earliest PBGC Retirement Date for the participant. The Earliest PBGC Retirement Date determined by the PBGC under this paragraph (c) will never be earlier than the earliest date the participant could separate from service with the right to receive an immediate annuity.

(d) *Examples.* The following examples illustrate the operation of the rules in paragraphs (a) through (c) of this section.

(1) *Normal retirement age.* A plan's normal retirement age is age 65. The plan does not offer a consensual lump sum or an immediate annuity upon separation before normal retirement age. The Earliest PBGC Retirement Date for a participant who, as of the plan's termination date, is age 50 is the date the participant reaches age 65.

(2) *Early retirement age.* A plan's normal retirement age is age 65. The plan specifies an early retirement age of 60 with 10 years of service. The plan does not offer a consensual lump sum or an immediate annuity upon separation before early retirement age. The Earliest PBGC Retirement Date for a participant who, as of the plan's termination date, is age 55 and has completed 10 years of service is the date the participant reaches age 60.

(3) *Separation at any age.* A plan's normal retirement age is age 65. The plan specifies an early retirement age of 60 but offers an immediate annuity upon separation regardless of age. The Earliest PBGC Retirement Date for a participant who, as of the plan's termination date, is age 35 is the date the participant reaches age 55, unless the PBGC determines under the facts and circumstances that the participant could "retire" for purposes of ERISA section 4044(a)(3)(B) on an earlier date, in which case the participant's Earliest PBGC Retirement Date would be that earlier date.

(4) *Age 50 retirement common.* A plan's normal retirement age is age 60. The plan specifies an early retirement age of 50 but offers an immediate annuity upon separation regardless of age. The Earliest PBGC Retirement Date for a participant who, as of the plan's termination date, is age 35 is the date the participant reaches age 55, unless the PBGC determines under the facts and circumstances that the participant could retire for purposes of ERISA section 4044(a)(3)(B) on an earlier date, in which case the Earliest PBGC Retirement Date would be that earlier date. For example, if it were common for participants to retire at age 50, the PBGC could determine that the participant's Earliest PBGC Retirement Date would be the date the participant reached age 50.

(5) *"30-and-out" benefit.* A plan's normal retirement age is age 65. The plan offers an immediate annuity upon separation regardless of age and a fully-subsidized annuity upon separation with 30 years of service. The Earliest PBGC Retirement Date for a participant who, as of the plan's termination date, is age 48 and has completed 30 years of service is the date the participant reaches age 55, unless the PBGC

determines under the facts and circumstances that the participant could retire for purposes of ERISA section 4044(a)(3)(B) on an earlier date, in which case the participant's Earliest PBGC Retirement Date would be that earlier date. In this example, the PBGC generally would determine under the facts and circumstances that the participant's Earliest PBGC Retirement Date is the date the participant completed 30 years of service.

(6) *Typical airline pilots' plan.* An airline pilots' plan has a normal retirement age of 60. The plan specifies an early retirement age of 50 (with 5 years of service). The Earliest PBGC Retirement Date for a participant who, as of the plan's termination date, is age 48 and has completed five years of service would be the date the participant reaches age 55, unless the PBGC determines under the facts and circumstances that the participant could retire for purposes of ERISA section 4044(a)(3)(B) on an earlier date, in which case the participant's Earliest PBGC Retirement Date would be that earlier date. In this example, the PBGC generally would determine under the facts and circumstances that the participant's Earliest PBGC Retirement Date is the date the participant reaches age 50. If the plan instead had provided for early retirement before age 50, the PBGC would consider all the facts and circumstances (including the plan's normal retirement age and the age at which employees customarily retire in the airline industry) in determining whether to treat the date the participant reaches the plan's early retirement age as the participant's Earliest PBGC Retirement Date.

(e) *Special rule for "window" provisions.* For purposes of paragraphs (a), (b), and (c) of this section, the PBGC will treat a participant as being able, under plan provisions, to separate from service with the right to receive an immediate annuity on a date before the plan's termination date only if—

(1) Eligibility for that immediate annuity continues through the earlier of—

(i) The plan's termination date; or

(ii) The date the participant actually separates from service with the right to receive an immediate annuity; and

(2) The participant satisfies the conditions for eligibility for that immediate annuity on or before the plan's termination date.

[¶ 15,421J]

§ 4022.11 **Guarantee of benefits relating to uniformed service.**

This section applies to a benefit of a participant who becomes reemployed after service in the uniformed services that is covered by the Uniformed Services Employment and Reemployment Rights Act of 1994 (USERRA).

(a) A benefit described in paragraph (b) of this section that would satisfy the requirements of § 4022.3(a) and (c) (together with any benefit earned for the period preceding military service) except for the fact that the participant was not reemployed on or before the termination date will be deemed to satisfy those requirements if PBGC determines, based upon a demonstration by the participant or otherwise, that he or she became reemployed after the termination date and entitled to the benefit under USERRA.

(b) A benefit described in this paragraph (b) is a benefit attributable to a period of service commencing before the termination date and ending on the termination date during which the participant was serving in the uniformed services as defined in 38 U.S.C. 4303(13) (or was in a subsequent reemployment eligibility period) and to which the participant is entitled under USERRA.

(c) Example: A plan's vesting requirement is 5 years of service with the employer. A participant has completed 4 years of service when he leaves employment for uniformed service. The plan terminates while the participant is in military service. As of the termination date, the participant would have had 5 years of service and 5 years of benefit accruals if he had remained continuously employed. Upon reemployment after the termination date but within the time limits set by USERRA, the participant would have had 6 years of service under the plan for vesting and benefit accrual purposes, if the plan had not terminated. PBGC would treat the participant as having a vested, nonforfeitable plan benefit with 5 years of vesting service and benefit accruals as of the termination date.

(d) In the case of a PPA 2006 bankruptcy termination, "bankruptcy filing date" is substituted for "termination date" each place that "termination date" appears in this section.

[Added on 11/17/2009 by 74 FR 59093.]

Subpart B—Limitations on Guaranteed Benefits

[¶ 15,422]

§ 4022.21 **Limitations; in general**. (a)(1) Subject to paragraphs (b), (c), (d), and (e) of this section, the PBGC will not guarantee that part of an installment payment that exceeds the dollar amount payable as a straight life annuity commencing at normal retirement age, or thereafter, to which a participant would have been entitled under the provisions of the plan in effect on the termination date, on the basis of his credited service to such date. If the plan does not provide a straight life annuity either as its normal form of retirement benefit or as an option to the normal form, the PBGC will for purposes of this paragraph convert the plan's normal form benefit to a straight life annuity of equal actuarial value as determined by the PBGC. [Amended 6/14/11 by 76 FR 34590.]

(2) The limitation of paragraph (a)(1) of this section shall not apply to:

(i) A survivor's benefit payable as an annuity on account of the death of a participant that occurred on or before the plan's termination date and before the participant retired; [Amended by 67 FR 16949, April 8, 2002.]

(ii) A disability pension described in section 4022.6 of this part; or

(iii) A benefit payable in non-level installments that in combination with Social Security, Railroad Retirement, or workman's compensation benefits yields a substantially level income if the projected income from the plan benefit over the expected life of the recipient does not exceed the value of the straight life annuity described in paragraph (a)(1) of this section.

(b) The PBGC will not guarantee the payment of that part of any benefit that exceeds the limitations in section 4022(b) of ERISA and this subpart B.

(c)(1) Except as provided in paragraph (c)(2) of this section, the PBGC does not guarantee a benefit payable in a single installment (or substantially so) upon the death of a participant or his surviving beneficiary unless that benefit is substantially derived from a reduction in the pension benefit payable to the participant or surviving beneficiary.

(2) Paragraphs (a) and (c)(1) of this section do not apply to that portion of accumulated mandatory employee contributions payable under a plan upon the death of a participant, and such a benefit is a pension benefit for purposes of this part.

(d) The PBGC will not guarantee a joint-life annuity benefit payable to other than—

(1) Natural persons; or

(2) A trust or estate for the benefit of one or more natural persons. [Amended by 67 FR 16949, April 8, 2002.]

(e) *PPA 2006 bankruptcy termination.*

(1) *Substitution of bankruptcy filing date.* In a PPA 2006 bankruptcy termination, "bankruptcy filing date" is substituted for "termination date" each place that "termination date" appears in paragraph (a)(1) of this section.

(2) *Examples.*

(i) *Straight-life annuity.* A plan provides for normal retirement at age 65. If a participant terminates employment at or after age 55 with 25 years of service, the plan will pay an unreduced early retirement benefit, plus a temporary supplement of $400 per month until the participant reaches age 62. When the plan's contributing sponsor files a bankruptcy petition in 2008, a participant who is still working has a vested, accrued benefit of $1,500 per month (as a straight-life annuity) and has satisfied the age and service requirements for the unreduced early retirement benefit. The participant retires eight months later, when his vested, accrued benefit is $1,530 per month (as a straight-life annuity). He elects to receive his benefit as a straight-life annuity, and begins receiving a total benefit of $1,930: His $1,530 accrued benefit plus the $400 temporary supplement. The plan terminates six months later, during the sponsor's bankruptcy. No Title IV limitations apply to the participant's benefit, other than the limitation in paragraph (a)(1) of this section. PBGC will guarantee $1,500, the amount of the participant's accrued benefit (as a straight-life annuity) as of the bankruptcy filing date.

(ii) *Joint-and-survivor annuity.* The facts are the same as Example (i) (paragraph (e)(2)(i) of this section), except that the participant elects to receive his benefit as a 50% joint-and-survivor annuity. Before plan termination, the participant was receiving a total benefit of $1,777: His $1,530 accrued benefit, reduced by 10% for the survivor benefit, plus the $400 temporary supplement. From the termination date until the participant reaches age 62, PBGC will guarantee $1,500: The $1,500 accrued benefit (as a straight-life annuity) as of the bankruptcy filing date, reduced to $1,350 to reflect the 10% reduction for the survivor benefit, plus $150 of the temporary supplement that, in combination with the $1,350, does not exceed the $1,500 accrued-at-normal limit. When the participant reaches age 62, his guaranteed benefit is reduced to $1,350, because under plan provisions the temporary supplement ceases at that time. [Added 6/14/11 by 76 FR 34590.]

[¶ 15,422A]

§ 4022.22 **Maximum guaranteeable benefit**. (a) *In general.* Subject to section 4022B of ERISA and part 4022B of this chapter, and except as provided in paragraph (b) of this section, benefits payable with respect to a participant under a plan shall be guaranteed only to the extent that such benefits do not exceed the actuarial value of a benefit in the form of a life annuity payable in monthly installments, commencing at age 65, equal to the lesser of—

(1) One-twelfth of the participant's average annual gross income from his employer during either his highest-paid five consecutive calendar years in which he was an active participant under the plan, or if he was not an active participant throughout the entire such period, the lesser number of calendar years within that period in which he was an active participant under the plan; or

(2) $750 multiplied by the fraction x/$13,200 where "x" is the Social Security contribution and benefit base determined under section 230 of the Social Security Act in effect at the termination date of the plan.

(b) *PPA 2006 bankruptcy termination.* In a PPA 2006 bankruptcy termination—

(1) The five-year period described in paragraph (a)(1) of this section shall not include any calendar years that end after the bankruptcy filing date.

(2) "Bankruptcy filing date" is substituted for "termination date of the plan" in paragraph (a)(2) of this section. Example: A contributing sponsor files a bankruptcy petition in 2007. The sponsor's plan terminates in a distress termination with a termination date in 2008. PBGC will compute participants' maximum guaranteeable benefits based on the amount determined under paragraph (a)(2) for 2007 ($4,125.00 as a straight-life annuity starting at age 65).

(c) *Gross income.* For purposes of paragraph (a)(1) of this section—

(1) Gross income means "earned income" as defined in section 911(d)(2) of the Code, determined without regard to any community property laws.

(2) If the plan is one to which more than one employer contributes, and during any calendar year the participant received gross income from more than one such contributing employer, then the amounts so received shall be aggregated in determining the participant's gross income for the calendar year. [Amended 6/14/11 by 76 FR 34590.]

(d) *Rollover amounts.* Any portion of a benefit derived from mandatory employee contributions resulting from rollover amounts (as determined under § 4044.12(c)(4)(i) of this chapter) is disregarded in applying the provisions of §§ 4022.22 and 4022.23. However, any portion of a benefit derived from employer contributions resulting from rollover amounts (as determined under § 4044.12(c)(4)(ii) of this chapter) is combined with any other benefit under the plan for purposes of determining the maximum guaranteeable benefit under §§ 4022.22 and 4022.23. For example, assume that a participant has an $80,000 total annual plan benefit at age 65, of which $15,000 is derived from mandatory employee contributions resulting from rollover amounts and $5,000 is derived from employer contributions resulting from rollover amounts. The $15,000 benefit derived from employee contributions resulting from rollover amounts would be excluded in the determination of the participant's maximum guaranteeable amount. The participant's remaining $65,000 benefit (including the $5,000 benefit derived from employer contributions resulting from rollover amounts) would be subject to the maximum guaranteeable benefit limitation. Assuming the plan terminated in 2014, the participant's maximum guaranteeable benefit of approximately $59,000 for a straight life annuity at age 65 would effectively be increased by the $15,000 benefit derived from employee contributions resulting from rollover amounts, resulting in total guaranteeable benefits of approximately $74,000. (The maximum guaranteeable benefit limitation would apply to the participant's benefit derived from employer contributions; as a result, $6,000 of the participant's benefit derived from employer contributions would not be guaranteeable by PBGC.) [Added 11/25/14 by 79 FR 70090.]

[¶ 15,422B]

§ 4022.23 **Computation of maximum guaranteeable benefits**. (a) *General*. Where a benefit is payable in any manner other than as a monthly benefit payable for life commencing at age 65, the maximum guaranteeable monthly amount of such benefit shall be computed by applying the applicable factor or factors set forth in paragraphs (c)-(e) of this section to the monthly amount computed under § 4022.22. In the case of a step-down life annuity, the maximum guaranteeable monthly amount of such benefit shall be computed in accordance with paragraph (f) of this section.

(b) *Application of adjustment factors to monthly amount computed under § 4022.22*. (1) Each percentage increase or decrease computed under paragraphs (c), (d), and (e) of this section shall be added to or subtracted from a base of 1.00, and the resulting amounts shall be multiplied.

(2) The monthly amount computed under § 4022.22 shall be multiplied by the product computed pursuant to paragraph (b)(1) of this section in order to determine the participant's and/or beneficiary's maximum benefit guaranteeable.

(c) *Annuitant's age factor*. If a participant or the beneficiary of a deceased participant is entitled to and chooses to receive his benefit at an age younger than 65, the monthly amount computed under § 4022.22 shall be reduced by the following amounts for each month up to the number of whole months below age 65 that corresponds to the later of the participant's age at the termination date or his age at the time he begins to receive the benefit: For each of the 60 months immediately preceding the 65th birthday, the reduction shall be 7/12 of 1%; For each of the 60 months immediately preceding the 60th birthday, the reduction shall be 4/12 of 1%; For each of the 120 months immediately preceding the 55th birthday, the reduction shall be 2/12 of 1%; and For each succeeding 120 months period, the monthly percentage reduction shall be 1/2 of that used for the preceding 120 month period.

(d) *Factor for benefit payable in a form other than as a life annuity*. When a benefit is in a form other than a life annuity payable in monthly installments, the monthly amount computed under § 4022.22 shall be adjusted by the appropriate factors on a case-by-case basis by PBGC. This paragraph sets forth the adjustment factors to be used for several common benefit forms payable in monthly installments.

(1) *Period certain and continuous annuity*. A period certain and continuous annuity means an annuity which is payable in periodic installments for the participant's life, but for not less than a specified period of time whether or not the participant dies during that period. The monthly amount of a period certain and continuous annuity computed under § 4022.22 shall be reduced by the following amounts for each month of the period certain subsequent to the termination date:

For each month up to 60 months deduct 1/24 of 1%;

For each month beyond 60 months deduct 1/12 of 1%.

(i) A cash refund annuity means an annuity under which if the participant dies prior to the time when he has received pension payments equal to a fixed sum specified in the plan, then the balance is paid as a lump-sum death benefit. A cash refund annuity shall be treated as a benefit payable for a period certain and continuous. The period of certainty shall be computed by dividing the amount of the lump-sum refund by the monthly amount to which the participant is entitled under the terms of the plan.

(ii) An installment refund annuity means an annuity under which if the participant dies prior to the time he has received pension payments equal to a fixed sum specified in the plan, then the balance is paid as a death benefit in periodic installments equal in amount to the participant's periodic benefit. An installment refund annuity shall be treated as a benefit payable for a period certain and continuous. The period of certainty shall be computed by dividing the amount of the remaining refund by the monthly amount to which the participant is entitled under the terms of the plan.

(2) *Joint and survivor annuity (contingent basis)*. A joint and survivor annuity (contingent basis) means an annuity which is payable in periodic installments to a participant for his life and upon his death is payable to his beneficiary for the beneficiary's life in the same or in a reduced amount. The monthly amount of a joint and survivor annuity (contingent basis) computed under § 4022.22 shall be reduced by an amount equal to 10% plus 2/10 of 1% for each percentage point in excess of 50% of the participant's benefit that will continue to be paid to the beneficiary. If the benefit payable to the beneficiary is less than 50 percent of the participant's benefit, PBGC shall provide the adjustment factors to be used.

(3) *Joint and survivor annuity (joint basis)*. A joint and survivor annuity (joint basis) means an annuity which is payable in periodic installments to a participant and upon his death or the death of his beneficiary is payable to the survivor for the survivor's life in the same or in a reduced amount. The monthly amount of a joint and survivor annuity (joint basis) computed under § 4022.22 shall be reduced by an amount equal to 4/10 of 1% for each percentage point in excess of 50% of the participant's original benefit that will continue to be paid to the survivor. If the benefit payable to the survivor is less than 50 percent of the participant's original benefit, PBGC shall provide the adjustment factors to be used.

(e) When a benefit is payable in a form described in paragraph (d) (2) or (3) of this section, and the beneficiary's age is different from the participant's age, by 15 years or less, the monthly amount computed under § 4022.22 shall be adjusted by the following amounts: If the beneficiary is younger than the participant, deduct 1% for each year of the age difference; If the beneficiary is older than the participant, add 1/2 of 1% for each year of the age difference. In computing the difference in ages, years over 65 years of age shall not be counted. If the difference in age between the beneficiary and the participant is greater than 15 years, PBGC shall provide the adjustment factors to be used.

(f) *Step-down life annuity*. A step-down life annuity means an annuity payable in a certain amount for the life of the participant plus a temporary additional amount payable until the participant attains an age specified in the plan.

(1) The temporary additional amount payable under a step-down life annuity shall be converted to a life annuity payable in monthly installments by multiplying the appropriate factor based on the participant's age and the number of remaining years of the temporary additional benefit by the amount of the temporary additional benefit. The factors to be used are set forth in the table below. The amount of the monthly benefit so calculated shall be added to the level amount of the monthly benefit payable for life to determine the level-life annuity that is equivalent to the step-down life annuity.

Factors for Converting Temporary Additional Benefit Under Step-Down Life Annuity

Age of participant[1] at the later of the date the temporary additional benefit commences or the date of plan termination	Number of years temporary additional benefit is payable under the plan as of the date of plan termination[2]									
	1	2	3	4	5	6	7	8	9	10
45	0.060	0.117	0.170	0.220	0.268	0.315	0.355	0.395	0.435	0.475
46	.061	.119	.173	.224	.273	.321	.362	.403	.444	.485
47	.062	.121	.176	.228	.278	.327	.369	.411	.453	.495
48	.063	.123	.179	.232	.283	.333	.376	.419	.462	.505
49	.064	.125	.182	.236	.288	.339	.383	.427	.471	.515
50	.065	.127	.185	.240	.293	.345	.390	.435	.480	.525
51	.066	.129	.188	.244	.298	.351	.397	.443	.489	.535
52	.067	.131	.191	.248	.303	.357	.404	.451	.498	.545
53	.068	.133	.194	.252	.308	.363	.411	.459	.507	.555
54	.069	.135	.197	.256	.313	.369	.418	.467	.516	.565
55	.070	.137	.200	.260	.318	.375	.425	.475	.525	.575
56	.072	.141	.206	.268	.328	.387	.439	.491	.543	. . .
57	.074	.145	.212	.276	.338	.399	.453	.507	. . .	. . .
58	.076	.149	.218	.284	.348	.411	.467	. . .		. . .
59	.078	153	.224	.292	.358	.423	. . .			
60	.080	.157	.230	.300	.368	. . .				
61	.082	.161	.236	.308	. . .					
62	.084	.165	.242	. . .	. . .					
63	.086	.169	. . .	. . .	. . .					
64	.088	. . .	. . .	. . .	. . .					

[1] Age of participant is his age at his last birthday.

[2] If the benefit is payable for less than 1 yr, the appropriate factor is obtained by multiplying the factor for 1 yr by a fraction, the numerator of which is the number of months the benefit is payable, and the denominator of which is 12. If the benefit is payable for 1 or more whole years, plus an additional number of months less than 12, the appropriate factor is obtained by linear interpolation between the factor for the number of whole years the benefit is payable and the factor for the next year.

(2) If a participant is entitled to and chooses to receive a step-down life annuity at an age younger than 65, the monthly amount computed under § 4022.22 shall be adjusted by applying the factors set forth in paragraph (c) of this section in the manner described in paragraph (b) of this section.

(3) If the level-life monthly benefit calculated pursuant to paragraph (f)(1) of this section exceeds the monthly amount calculated pursuant to paragraph (f)(2) of this section, then the monthly maximum benefit guaranteeable shall be a step-down life annuity under which the monthly amount of the temporary additional benefit and the amount of the monthly benefit payable for life, respectively, shall bear the same ratio to the monthly amount of the temporary additional benefit and the monthly benefit payable for life provided under the plan, respectively, as the monthly benefit calculated pursuant to paragraph (f)(2) of this section bears to the monthly benefit calculated pursuant to paragraph (f)(1) of this section.

(g) *PPA 2006 bankruptcy termination.*

(1) In a PPA 2006 bankruptcy termination, except as provided in the next sentence, "bankruptcy filing date" is substituted for "termination date" and "date of plan termination" each place that "termination date" or "date of plan termination" appears in paragraphs (c), (d), and (f) of this section. In any case in which an event (such as the death of a participant or beneficiary who was alive on the bankruptcy filing date) that affects who is receiving or will receive a benefit from PBGC has occurred on or before the termination date, PBGC will determine the factors in paragraphs (d), (e), and (f) based on the form of benefit that was being paid (or was payable) and the person who was receiving or was entitled to receive the benefit from PBGC as of the termination date. (The case of Participant C in the example below illustrates this exception.)

(2) *Example.* (i) *Facts.* The contributing sponsor of a plan files a bankruptcy petition in July 2007, and the sponsor's plan terminates in a PBGC-initiated termination with a termination date in July 2008. At the bankruptcy filing date:

(A) Participant A was age 64 and receiving a benefit from the plan in the form of a 10-year certain-and-continuous annuity, with 4 years remaining in the certain period.

(B) Participant B was age 60 and 6 months and was still working. She began receiving a benefit from the plan in the form of a 50% joint-and-survivor annuity when she turned 61 in January 2008. Her spouse was the same age as she.

(C) Participant C was age 60 and was receiving a $3,000/month benefit from the plan in the form of a 50% joint-and-survivor annuity, with his spouse, age 58, as his beneficiary. Participant C he died in February 2008 and in March 2008 his spouse began receiving a 50% survivor annuity of $1,500/month.

(D) Participant D was age 59 and was still working; he began receiving a straight-life annuity from the PBGC in July 2010 when he was 62 years old.

(ii) *Conclusions.* In accordance with § 4022.22(b)(2), PBGC computes the maximum guaranteeable monthly benefit for Participants A, B, and D and for the spouse of Participant C based on the $4,125.00 amount determined under § 4022.22(a)(2) for 2007. (The gross-income-based limitation in § 4022.22(a)(1) does not apply to any of these participants.)

(A) Participant A's maximum guaranteeable monthly benefit is $3,759.53 [$4,125.00 × .93 (7% reduction for a benefit starting at age 64) × .98 (2% reduction for a certain-and-continuous annuity with 4 years remaining in the certain period)].

(B) Participant B's maximum guaranteeable monthly benefit is $2,673.00 [$4,125.00 × .72 (28% reduction for a benefit starting at age 61) × .90 (10% reduction due to the 50% joint-and-survivor feature)].

(C) Participant C's spouse's maximum guaranteeable monthly benefit is $2,351.25 [$4,125.00 × .57 (43% reduction for a benefit starting at age 58; no reduction for the form of benefit because the spouse's survivor benefit is a straight-life annuity)]. Because that amount exceeds the spouse's $1,500 monthly survivor benefit, the spouse's benefit is not reduced by the maximum guaranteeable benefit limitation.

(D) Participant D's maximum guaranteeable monthly benefit is $3,258.75 [$4,125.00 × .79 (21% reduction for a benefit starting at age 62)]. [Added 6/14/11 by 76 FR 34590.]

[¶ 15,422C]

§ 4022.24 **Benefit increases.** (a) *Scope.* This section applies:

(1) To all benefit increases, as defined in § 4022.2, payable with respect to a participant other than a substantial owner, which have been in effect for less than five years preceding the termination date; and

(2) To all benefit increases payable with respect to a substantial owner, which have been in effect for less than 30 years preceding the termination date.

(b) *General rule.* Benefit increases described in paragraph (a) of this section shall be guaranteed only to the extent provided in § 4022.25 with respect to a participant other than a substantial owner and in § 4022.26 with respect to a participant who is a substantial owner.

(c) *Computation of guaranteeable benefit increases.* Except as provided in paragraph (d) of this section pertaining to multiple benefit increases, the amount of a guaranteeable benefit increase shall be the amount, if any, by which the monthly benefit calculated pursuant to paragraph (c)(1) of this section (the monthly benefit provided under the terms of the plan as of the termination date, as limited by § 4022.22) exceeds the monthly benefit calculated pursuant to paragraph (c)(4) of this section (the monthly benefit which would have been payable on the termination date if the benefit provided subsequent to the increase were equivalent, as of the date of the increase, to the benefit provided prior to the increase).

(1) Determine the amount of the monthly benefit payable on the termination date (or, in the case of a deferred benefit, the monthly benefit which will become payable thereafter) under the terms of the plan subsequent to the increase, using service credited to the participant as of the termination date, that is guaranteeable pursuant to § 4022.22;

(2) Determine, as of the date of the benefit increase, in accordance with the provisions of § 4022.23, the factors which would be used to calculate the monthly maximum benefit guaranteeable (i) under the terms of the plan prior to the increase and (ii) under the terms of the plan subsequent to the increase. However, when the benefit referred to in paragraph (c)(2)(ii) of this section is a joint and survivor benefit deferred as of the termination date and there is no beneficiary on that date, the factors computed in paragraph (c)(2)(ii) of this section shall be determined as if the benefit were payable only to the participant. Each set of factors determined under this paragraph shall be stated in the manner set forth in § 4022.23(b)(1);

(3) Multiply the monthly benefit which would have been payable (or, in the case of a deferred benefit, would have become payable) under the terms of the plan prior to the increase based on service credited to the participant as of the termination date by a fraction, the numerator of which is the product of the factors computed pursuant to paragraph (c)(2)(ii) of this section and the denominator of which is the product of the factors computed pursuant to paragraph (c)(2)(i) of this section.

(4) Calculate the amount of the monthly benefit which would be payable on the termination date if the monthly benefit computed in paragraph (c)(3) of this section had been payable commencing on the date of the benefit increase (or, in the case of a deferred benefit, would have become payable thereafter.) In the case of a benefit which does not become payable until subsequent to the termination date, the amount of the monthly benefit determined pursuant to this paragraph is the same as the amount of the monthly benefit calculated pursuant to paragraph (c)(3) of this section.

(d) *Multiple benefit increases.* (1) Where there has been more than one benefit increase described in paragraph (a) of this section, the amounts of guaranteeable benefit increases shall be calculated begin-

ning with the earliest increase, and each such amount (except for the amount resulting from the final benefit increase) shall be multiplied by a fraction, the numerator of which is the product of the factors, stated in the manner set forth in § 4022.23(b)(1), used to calculate the monthly maximum guaranteeable benefit under § 4022.22 and the denominator of which is the product of the factors used in the calculation under paragraph (c)(2)(i) of this section.

(2) Each benefit increase shall be treated separately for the purposes of § 4022.25, except as otherwise provided in paragraph (d) of that section, and for the purposes of § 4022.26, as appropriate.

(e) Except as provided in § 4022.27(c), for the purposes of §§ 4022.22 through 4022.28, a benefit increase is deemed to be in effect commencing on the later of its adoption date or its effective date. [Corrected 12/30/97 by 62 FR 67728. Amended 5/6/2014 (79 FR 25667).]

(f) *PPA 2006 bankruptcy termination.* In a PPA 2006 bankruptcy termination, except as provided in the next sentence, "bankruptcy filing date" is substituted for "termination date" each place that "termination date" appears in paragraphs (a) and (c) of this section. In any case in which an event (such as the death of a participant or beneficiary who was alive on the bankruptcy filing date) that affects who is receiving or will receive a benefit from PBGC has occurred on or before the termination date, PBGC will compute the benefit based on the form of benefit that was being paid (or was payable) and the person who was receiving or was entitled to receive the benefit from PBGC as of the termination date, consistent with § 4022.23(g). [Added 6/14/11 by 76 FR 34590.]

(g) *Rollover amounts.* Any portion of a benefit derived from mandatory employee contributions resulting from rollover amounts (as determined under § 4044.12(c)(4)(i) of this chapter) is disregarded in applying the provisions of §§ 4022.24 through 4022.26. However, any portion of a benefit derived from employer contributions resulting from rollover amounts (as determined under § 4044.12(c)(4)(ii) of this chapter) is combined with any other benefit under the plan in applying the provisions of §§ 4022.24 through 4022.26. In such case, the benefit increase is deemed to be in effect on the date the rollover amounts are received by the plan. [Added 11/25/14 by 79 FR 70090.]

[¶ 15,422D]

§ 4022.25 **Five-year phase-in of benefit guarantee for participants other than substantial owners.** (a) *Scope.* This section applies to the guarantee of benefit increases which have been in effect for less than five years with respect to participants other than substantial owners.

(b) *Phase-in formula.* The amount of a benefit increase computed pursuant to § 4022.24 shall be guaranteed to the extent provided in the following formula: the number of years the benefit increase has been in effect, not to exceed five, multiplied by the greater of (1) 20 percent of the amount computed pursuant to § 4022.24; or (2) $20 per month.

(c) *Computation of years.* In computing the number of years a benefit increase has been in effect, each complete 12-month period ending on or before the termination date during which such benefit increase was in effect constitutes one year. [Amended by 67 FR 16949, April 8, 2002.]

(d) *Multiple benefit increases.* In applying the formula contained in paragraph (b) of this section, multiple benefit increases within any 12-month period ending on or before the termination date and calculated from that date are aggregated and treated as one benefit increase. [Amended by 67 FR 16949, April 8, 2002.]

(e) Notwithstanding the provisions of paragraph (b) of this section, a benefit increase described in paragraph (a) of this section shall be guaranteed only if PBGC determines that the plan was terminated for a reasonable business purpose and not for the purpose of obtaining the payment of benefits by PBGC.

(f) *PPA 2006 bankruptcy termination.* In a PPA 2006 bankruptcy termination, "bankruptcy filing date" is substituted for "termination date" each place that "termination date" appears in paragraphs (c) and (d) of this section. Example: A plan amendment that was adopted and effective in February 2007 increased a participant's benefit by $300 per month (as computed under § 4022.24). The contributing sponsor of the plan filed a bankruptcy petition in March 2009 and the plan has a termination date in April 2010. PBGC's guarantee of the participant's benefit increase is limited to $120 ($300 × 40%), because the increase was made more than 2 years but less than 3 years before the bankruptcy filing date. [Added 6/14/11 by 76 FR 34590.]

[¶ 15,422E]

§ 4022.26 **Phase-in of benefit guarantee for participants who are substantial owners**. (a) *Scope.* This section shall apply to the guarantee of all benefits described in subpart A (subject to the limitations in § 4022.21) with respect to participants who are substantial owners at the termination date or who were substantial owners at any time within the 5-year period preceding that date. [Corrected 12/30/97 by 62 FR 67728.]

(b) *Phase-in formula when there have been no benefit increases.* Benefits provided by a plan under which there has been no benefit increase, other than the adoption of the plan, shall be guaranteed to the extent provided in the following formula: The monthly amount computed under § 4022.22 multiplied by a fraction not to exceed 1, the numerator of which is the number of full years prior to the termination date that the substantial owner was an active participant under the plan, and the denominator of which is 30. Active participation under a plan commences at the later of the date on which the plan is adopted or becomes effective.

(c) *Phase-in formula when there have been benefit increases.* If there has been a benefit increase under the plan, other than the adoption of the plan, benefits provided by each such increase shall be guaranteed to the extent provided in the following formula: The amount of the guaranteeable benefit increase computed under § 4022.24 multiplied by a fraction not to exceed 1, the numerator of which is the number of full years prior to the termination date that the benefit increase was in effect and during which the substantial owner was an active participant under the plan, and the denominator of which is 30. However, in no event shall the total benefits guaranteed under all such benefit increases exceed the benefits which are guaranteed under paragraph (b) of this section with respect to a plan described therein.

(d) For the purpose of computing the benefits guaranteed under this section, in the case of a substantial owner who becomes an active participant under a plan after a benefit increase (other than the adoption of the plan) has been put into effect, the plan as it exists at the time he commences his participation shall be deemed to be the original plan with respect to him.

[¶ 15,422F]

§ 4022.27 **Phase-in of guarantee of unpredictable contingent event benefits**. (a) *Scope.* This section applies to a benefit increase, as defined in § 4022.2, that is an unpredictable contingent event benefit (UCEB) and that is payable with respect to an unpredictable contingent event (UCE) that occurs after July 26, 2005.

(1) Examples of benefit increases within the scope of this section include unreduced early retirement benefits or other early retirement subsidies, or other benefits to the extent that such benefits would not be payable but for the occurrence of one or more UCEs.

(2) Examples of UCEs within the scope of this section include full and partial closings of plants or other facilities, and permanent workforce reductions, such as permanent layoffs. Permanent layoffs include layoffs during which an idled employee continues to earn credited service (creep-type layoff) for a period of time at the end of which the layoff is deemed to be permanent. Permanent layoffs also include layoffs that become permanent upon the occurrence of an additional event such as a declaration by the employer that the participant's return to work is unlikely or a failure by the employer to offer the employee suitable work in a specified area.

(3) The examples in this section are not an exclusive list of UCEs or UCEBs and are not intended to narrow the statutory definitions, as further delineated in Treasury Regulations.

(b) *Facts and circumstances.* If PBGC determines that a benefit is a shutdown benefit or other type of UCEB, the benefit will be treated as a UCEB for purposes of this subpart. PBGC will make such determinations based on the facts and circumstances, consistent with these regulations; how a benefit is characterized by the employer or other parties may be relevant but is not determinative.

(c) *Date phase-in begins.* (1) The date the phase-in of PBGC's guarantee of a UCEB begins is determined in accordance with subpart B of this part. For purposes of this subpart, a UCEB is deemed to be in effect as of the latest of-

(i) The adoption date of the plan provision that provides for the UCEB,

(ii) The effective date of the UCEB, or

(iii) The date the UCE occurs.

(2) The date the phase-in of PBGC's guarantee of a UCEB begins is not affected by any delay that may occur in placing participants in pay status due to removal of a restriction under section 436(b) of the Code. See the example in paragraph (e)(8) of this section.

(d) *Date UCE occurs.* For purposes of this section, PBGC will determine the date the UCE occurs based on plan provisions and other facts and circumstances, including the nature and level of activity at a facility that is closing and the permanence of the event. PBGC will also consider, to the extent relevant, statements or determinations by the employer, the plan administrator, a union, an arbitrator under a collective bargaining agreement, or a court, but will not treat such statements or determinations as controlling.

(1) The date a UCE occurs is determined on a participant-by-participant basis, or on a different basis, such as a facility-wide or company-wide basis, depending upon plan provisions and the facts and circumstances. For example, a benefit triggered by a permanent layoff of a participant would be determined with respect to each participant, and thus layoffs that occur on different dates would generally be distinct UCEs. In contrast, a benefit payable only upon a complete plant shutdown would apply facility-wide, and generally the shutdown date would be the date of the UCE for all participants who work at that plant. Similarly, a benefit payable only upon the complete shutdown of the employer's entire operations would apply plan-wide, and thus the shutdown date of company operations generally would be the date of the UCE for all participants.

(2) For purposes of paragraph (c)(1)(iii) of this section, if a benefit is contingent upon more than one UCE, PBGC will apply the rule under Treas. Reg. § 1.436-1(b)(3)(ii) (26 CFR 1.436-1(b)(3)(ii)) (i.e., the date the UCE occurs is the date of the latest UCE).

(e) *Examples.* The following examples illustrate the operation of the rules in this section. Except as provided in Example 8, no benefit limitation under Code section 436 applies in any of these examples. Unless otherwise stated, the termination is not a PPA 2006 bankruptcy termination.

Example 1. Date of UCE. (i) Facts: On January 1, 2006, a Company adopts a plan that provides an unreduced early retirement benefit for participants with specified age and service whose continuous service is broken by a permanent plant closing or permanent layoff that occurs on or after January 1, 2007. On January 1, 2013, the Company informally and without announcement decides to close Facility A within a two-year period. On January 1, 2014, the Company's Board of Directors passes a resolution directing the Company's officers to close Facility A on or before September 1, 2014. On June 1, 2014, the Company issues a notice pursuant to the Worker Adjustment and Retraining Notification (WARN) Act, 29 U.S.C. 2101, et seq., that Facility A will close, and all employees will be permanently laid off, on or about August 1, 2014. The Company and the Union representing the employees enter into collective bargaining concerning the closing of Facility A and on July 1, 2014, they jointly agree and announce that Facility A will close and employees who work there will be permanently laid off as of November 1, 2014. However, due to unanticipated business conditions, Facility A continues to operate until December 31, 2014, when operations cease and all employees are permanently laid off. The plan terminates as of December 1, 2015.

(ii) *Conclusion:* PBGC would determine that the UCE is the facility closing and permanent layoff that occurred on December 31, 2014. Because the date that the UCE occurred (December 31, 2014) is later than both the date the plan provision that established the UCEB was adopted (January 1, 2006) and the date the UCEB became effective (January 1, 2007), December 31, 2014, would be the date the phase-in period under ERISA section 4022 begins. In light of the plan termination date of December 1, 2015, the guarantee of the UCEBs of participants laid off on December 31, 2014, would be 0 percent phased in.

Reg. § 4022.27(e)   **¶ 15,422F**

Example 2. Sequential layoffs. (i) *Facts*: The same facts as Example 1, with these exceptions: Not all employees are laid off on December 31, 2014. The Company and Union agree to and subsequently implement a shutdown in which employees are permanently laid off in stages-one third of the employees are laid off on October 31, 2014, another third are laid off on November 30, 2014, and the remaining one-third are laid off on December 31, 2014.

(ii) *Conclusion*: Because the plan provides that a UCEB is payable in the event of either a permanent layoff or a plant shutdown, PBGC would determine that phase-in begins on the date of the UCE applicable to each of the three groups of employees. Because the first two groups of employees were permanently laid off before the plant closed, October 31, 2014, and November 30, 2014, are the dates that the phase-in period under ERISA section 4022 begins for those groups. Because the third group was permanently laid off on December 31, 2014, the same date the plant closed, the phase-in period would begin on that date for that group. Based on the plan termination date of December 1, 2015, participants laid off on October 31, 2014, and November 30, 2014, would have 20 percent of the UCEBs (or $20 per month, if greater) guaranteed under the phase-in rule. The guarantee of the UCEBs of participants laid off on December 31, 2014, would be 0 percent phased in.

Example 3. Skeleton shutdown crews. (i) *Facts*: The same facts as Example 1, with these exceptions: The plan provides for an unreduced early retirement benefit for age/ service-qualified participants only in the event of a break in continuous service due to a permanent and complete plant closing. A minimal skeleton crew remains to perform primarily security and basic maintenance functions until March 31, 2015, when skeleton crew members are permanently laid off and the facility is sold to an unrelated investment group that does not assume the plan or resume business operations at the facility. The plan has no specific provision or past practice governing benefits of skeleton shutdown crews. The plan terminates as of January 1, 2015.

(ii) *Conclusion*: Because the continued employment of the skeleton crew does not effectively continue operations of the facility, PBGC would determine that there is a permanent and complete plant closing (for purposes of the plan's plant closing provision) as of December 31, 2014, which is the date the phase-in period under ERISA section 4022 begins with respect to employees who incurred a break in continuous service at that time. The UCEB of those participants would be a nonforfeitable benefit as of the plan termination date, but PBGC's guarantee of the UCEB would be 0 percent phased in. In the case of the skeleton crew members, such participants would not be eligible for the UCEB because they did not incur a break in continuous service until after the plan termination date. (If the plan had a provision that there is no shutdown until all employees, including any skeleton crew are terminated, or if the plan were reasonably interpreted to so provide in light of past practice, PBGC would determine that the date that the UCE occurred was after the plan termination date. Thus the UCEB would not be a nonforfeitable benefit as of the plan termination date and therefore would not be guaranteeable.)

Example 4. Creep-type layoff benefit/ bankruptcy of contributing sponsor. (i) *Facts*: A plan provides that participants who are at least age 55 and whose age plus years of continuous service equal at least 80 are entitled to an unreduced early retirement benefit if their continuous service is broken due to a permanent layoff. The plan further provides that a participant's continuous service is broken due to a permanent layoff when the participant is terminated due to the permanent shutdown of a facility, or the participant has been on layoff status for two years. These provisions were adopted and effective in 1990. Participant A is 56 years old and has 25 years of continuous service when he is laid off in a reduction-in-force on May 15, 2014. He is not recalled to employment, and on May 15, 2016, under the terms of the plan, his continuous service is broken due to the layoff. He goes into pay status on June 1, 2016, with an unreduced early retirement benefit. The contributing sponsor of Participant A's plan files a bankruptcy petition under Chapter 11 of the U.S. Bankruptcy Code on September 1, 2017, and the plan terminates during the bankruptcy proceedings with a termination date of October 1, 2018. Under section 4022(g) of ERISA, because the plan terminated while the contributing sponsor was in bankruptcy, the five-year phase-in period ended on the bankruptcy filing date.

(ii) *Conclusion*: PBGC would determine that the guarantee of the UCEB is phased in beginning on May 15, 2016, the date of the later of the two UCEs necessary to make this benefit payable (i.e., the first UCE is the initial layoff and the second UCE is the expiration of the two-year period without rehire). Since that date is more than one year (but less than two years) before the September 1, 2017, bankruptcy filing date, 20 percent of Participant A's UCEB (or $20 per month, if greater) would be guaranteed under the phase-in rule.

Example 5. Creep-type layoff benefit with provision for declaration that return to work unlikely. (i) *Facts*: A plan provides that participants who are at least age 60 and have at least 20 years of continuous service are entitled to an unreduced early retirement benefit if their continuous service is broken by a permanent layoff. The plan further provides that a participant's continuous service is broken by a permanent layoff if the participant is laid off and the employer declares that the participant's return to work is unlikely. Participants may earn up to 2 years of credited service while on layoff. The plan was adopted and effective in 1990. On March 1, 2014, Participant B, who is age 60 and has 20 years of service, is laid off. On June 15, 2014, the employer declares that Participant B's return to work is unlikely. Participant B retires and goes into pay status as of July 1, 2014. The employer files for bankruptcy on September 1, 2016, and the plan terminates during the bankruptcy.

(ii) *Conclusion*: PBGC would determine that the phase-in period of the guarantee of the UCEB would begin on June 15, 2014-the later of the two UCEs necessary to make the benefit payable (i.e., the first UCE is the initial layoff and the second UCE is the employer's declaration that it is unlikely that Participant B will return to work). The phase-in period would end on September 1, 2016, the date of the bankruptcy filing. Thus 40 percent of Participant B's UCEB (or $40 per month, if greater) would be guaranteed under the phase-in rule.

Example 6. Shutdown benefit with special post-employment eligibility provision. (i) *Facts*: A plan provides that, in the event of a permanent shutdown of a plant, a participant age 60 or older who terminates employment due to the shutdown and who has at least 20 years of service is entitled to an unreduced early retirement benefit. The plan also provides that a participant with at least 20 years of service who terminates employment due to a plant shutdown at a time when the participant is under age 60 also will be entitled to an unreduced early retirement benefit, provided the participant's commencement of benefits is on or after attainment of age 60 and the time required to attain age 60 does not exceed the participant's years of service with the plan sponsor. The plan imposes no other conditions on receipt of the benefit. Plan provisions were adopted and effective in 1990. On January 1, 2014, Participant C's plant is permanently shut down. At the time of the shutdown, Participant C had 20 years of service and was age 58. On June 1, 2015, Participant C reaches age 60 and retires. The plan terminates as of September 1, 2015.

(ii) *Conclusion*: PBGC would determine that the guarantee of the shutdown benefit is phased in from January 1, 2014, which is the date of the only UCE (the permanent shutdown of the plant) necessary to make the benefit payable. Thus 20 percent of Participant C's UCEB (or $20 per month, if greater) would be guaranteed under the phase-in rule.

Example 7. Phase-in of retroactive UCEB. (i) *Facts*: As the result of a settlement in a class-action lawsuit, a plan provision is adopted on September 1, 2014, to provide that age/service-qualified participants are entitled to an unreduced early retirement benefit if permanently laid off due to a plant shutdown occurring on or after January 1, 2014. Benefits under the provision are payable prospectively only, beginning March 1, 2015. Participant A, who was age/service-qualified, was permanently laid off due to a plant shutdown occurring on January 1, 2014, and therefore he is scheduled to be placed in pay status as of March 1, 2015. The unreduced early retirement benefit is paid to Participant A beginning on March 1, 2015. The plan terminates as of February 1, 2017.

(ii) *Conclusion*: PBGC would determine that the guarantee of the UCEB is phased in beginning on March 1, 2015. This is the date the benefit was effective (since it was the first date on which the new benefit was payable), and it is later than the adoption date of the plan provision (September 1, 2014) and the date of the UCE (January 1, 2014). Thus 20 percent of Participant A's UCEB (or $20 per month, if greater) would be guaranteed under the phase-in rule.

Example 8. Removal of IRC section 436 restriction. (i)(A) *Facts*: A plan provision was adopted on September 1, 1989, to provide that age/service-qualified participants are entitled to an unreduced early retirement benefit if permanently laid off due to a plant shutdown occurring after January 1, 1990. Participant A, who was age/service-qualified, was permanently laid off due to a plant shutdown occurring on April 15, 2014. The plan is a calendar year plan.

(B) Under the rules of Code section 436 (ERISA section 206(g)) and Treasury regulations thereunder, a plan cannot provide a UCEB payable with respect to an unpredictable contingent event, if the event occurs during a plan year in which the plan's adjusted funding target attainment percentage is less than 60%. On March 17, 2014, the plan's enrolled actuary issued a certification stating that the plan's adjusted funding target attainment percentage for 2014 is 58%. Therefore, the plan restricts payment of the unreduced early retirement benefit payable with respect to the shutdown on April 15, 2014.

(C) On August 15, 2014, the plan sponsor makes an additional contribution to the plan that is designated as a contribution under Code section 436(b)(2) to eliminate the restriction on payment of the shutdown benefits. On September 15, 2014, the plan's enrolled actuary issues a certification stating that, due to the additional section 436(b)(2) contribution, the plan's adjusted funding target attainment percentage for 2014 is 60%. On October 1, 2014, Participant A is placed in pay status for the unreduced early retirement benefit and, as required under Code section 436 and Treasury regulations thereunder, is in addition paid retroactively the unreduced benefit for the period May 1, 2014 (the date the unreduced early retirements would have become payable) through September 1, 2014. The plan terminates as of September 1, 2016.

(ii) *Conclusion*: PBGC would determine that the guarantee of the UCEB is phased in beginning on April 15, 2014, the date the UCE occurred. Because April 15, 2014, is later than both the date the UCEB was adopted (September 1, 1989) and the date the UCEB became effective (January 1, 1990), it would be the date the phase-in period under ERISA section 4022 begins. Commencement of the phase-in period is not affected by the delay in providing the unreduced early retirement benefit to Participant A due to the operation of the rules of Code section 436 and the Treasury regulations thereunder. Thus 40 percent of Participant A's UCEB (or $40 per month, if greater) would be guaranteed under the phase-in rule.

[Added 5/6/14 (79 FR 25667).]

[¶ 15,422G]

§ 4022.28 **Effect of tax disqualification**. (a) *General rule*. Except as provided in paragraph (b) of this section, benefits accrued under a plan after the date on which the Secretary of the Treasury or his delegate issues a notice that any trust which is part of the plan no longer meets the requirements of section 401(a) of the Code or that the plan no longer meets the requirements of section 404(a) of the Code or after the date of adoption of a plan amendment that causes the issuance of such a notice shall not be guaranteed under this part.

(b) *Exceptions*. The restriction on the guarantee of benefits set forth in paragraph (a) of this section shall not apply if:

(1) The Secretary of the Treasury or his delegate issues a notice stating that the original notice referred to in paragraph (a) of this section was erroneous;

(2) The Secretary of the Treasury or his delegate finds that, subsequent to the issuance of the notice referred to in paragraph (a) of this section, appropriate action has been taken with respect to the trust or plan to cause it to meet the requirements of sections 401(a) or 404(a)(2) of the Code, respectively, and issues a subsequent notice stating that the trust or plan meets such requirements; or

(3) The plan amendment is revoked retroactively to its original effective date. [Redesignated 5/6/14 (79 FR 25667).]

Subpart C—Section 4022(c) Benefits

[¶ 15,422DD]

§ 4022.51 **Determination of section 4022(c) benefits in a PPA 2006 bankruptcy termination.**

(a) *Amount of unfunded nonguaranteed benefits*. For purposes of this section, and subject to paragraph (b) of this section, a plan's amount of unfunded nonguaranteed benefits means the plan's outstanding amount of benefit liabilities, as defined in section 4001(a)(19) of ERISA, determined as of the plan's termination date. A plan's amount of unfunded nonguaranteed benefits is multiplied by the applicable recovery ratio to determine the aggregate amount to be allocated with respect to participants of the plan under section 4022(c)(1) of ERISA.

(b) *Benefits included in unfunded nonguaranteed benefits*. For purposes of computing benefits under section 4022(c) of ERISA in a PPA 2006 bankruptcy termination, unfunded nonguaranteed benefits are benefits under a plan as of the plan's termination date that are neither guaranteed by PBGC (taking into account section 4022(g) of ERISA) nor funded by the plan's assets (taking into account section 4044(e) of ERISA).

(c) *Determination of recovery ratio*. In a PPA 2006 bankruptcy termination, the recovery ratio under section 4022(c)(3) of ERISA is determined as follows. The numerator is based on PBGC's recoveries under section 4062, 4063, or 4064, valued as of the plan's (or plans') termination date (or dates). The denominator of the recovery ratio is based on the amount of unfunded benefit liabilities, as defined in section 4001(a)(18) of ERISA, as of the plan's (or plans') termination date (or dates). [Added 6/14/11 by 76 FR 34590.]

Subpart D—Benefit Reductions in Terminating Plans

[¶ 15,423]

§ 4022.61 **Limitations on benefit payments by plan administrator.** (a) *General*. When section 4041.42 of this chapter requires a plan administrator to reduce benefits, the plan administrator shall limit benefit payments in accordance with this section. [Amended 11/7/97 by 62 FR 60424. Generally, for fully-funded, single-employer pension plans which issued their first notice of intent to terminate before January 1, 1998, an unamended regulation applies. The paragraph previously read: (a) General. When section 4041.4 of this chapter requires a plan administrator to reduce benefits, the plan administrator shall limit benefit payments in accordance with this section.]

(b) *Accrued benefit at normal retirement*. Except to the extent permitted by paragraph (d) of this section, a plan administrator may not pay that portion of a monthly benefit payable with respect to any participant that exceeds the participant's accrued benefit payable at normal retirement age under the plan. For the purpose of applying this limitation, post-retirement benefit increases, such as cost-of-living adjustments, are not considered to increase a participant's benefit beyond his or her accrued benefit payable at normal retirement age.

(c) *Maximum guaranteeable benefit*. Except to the extent permitted by paragraph (d) of this section, a plan administrator may not pay that portion of a monthly benefit payable with respect to any participant, as limited by paragraph (b) of this section, that exceeds the maximum guaranteeable benefit under section 4022(b)(3)(B) of ERISA and § 4022.22(a)(2) of this part, adjusted for age and benefit form, for the year of the proposed termination date. In a PPA 2006 bankruptcy termination, the maximum guaranteeable benefit is determined as of the bankruptcy filing date, in accordance with §§ 4022.22(b) and 4022.23(g). [Amended 6/14/11 by 76 FR 34950.]

(d) *Estimated benefit payments*. A plan administrator shall pay the monthly benefit payable with respect to each participant as determined under § 4022.62 or § 4022.63, whichever produces the higher benefit.

(e) *PBGC authority to modify procedures*. In order to avoid abuse of the plan termination insurance system, inequitable treatment of participants and beneficiaries, or the imposition of unreasonable burdens on terminating plans, the PBGC may authorize or direct the use of alternative procedures for determining benefit reductions.

(f) *Examples*. This section is illustrated by the following examples. (For examples addressing issues specific to a PPA 2006 bankruptcy termination, see §§ 4022.21(e), 4022.22(b), and 4022.23(g).) [Amended 6/14/11 by 76 FR 34950.]

Example 1— Facts. On October 10, 1992, a plan administrator files with the PBGC a notice of intent to terminate in a distress termination that includes December 31, 1992, as the proposed termination date. A participant who is in pay status on December 31, 1992, has been receiving his accrued benefit of $2,500 per month under the plan. The benefit is in the form of a joint and survivor annuity (contingent basis) that will pay 50 percent of the participant's benefit amount (i.e., $1,250 per month) to his surviving spouse following the death of the participant. On December 31, 1992, the participant is age 66, and his wife is age 56.

Benefit reductions. Paragraph (b) of this section requires the plan administrator to cease paying benefits in excess of the accrued benefit payable at normal retirement age. Because the participant is receiving only his accrued benefit, no reduction is required under paragraph (b).

Paragraph (c) of this section requires the plan administrator to cease paying benefits in excess of the maximum guaranteeable benefit, adjusted for age and benefit form in accordance with the provisions of subpart B. The maximum guaranteeable benefit for plans terminating in 1992, the year of the proposed termination date, is $2,352.27 per month, payable in the form of a single life annuity at age 65. Because the participant is older than age 65, no adjustment is required under § 4022.23(c) based on the annuitant's age factor. The benefit form is a joint and survivor annuity (contingent basis), as defined in § 4022.23(d)(2). The required benefit reduction for this benefit form under § 4022.23(d) is 10 percent. The corresponding adjustment factor is 0.90 (1.00 − 0.10). The benefit reduction factor to adjust for the age difference between the participant and the beneficiary is computed under § 4022.23(e). In computing the difference in ages, years over 65 years of age are not taken into account. Therefore, the age difference is 9 years (65 − 56). The required percentage reduction when the beneficiary is 9 years younger than the participant is 9 percent. The corresponding adjustment factor is 0.91 (1.00 − 0.09).

The maximum guaranteeable benefit adjusted for age and benefit form is $1,926.51 ($2,352.27 × 0.90 × 0.91) per month. Therefore, the plan administrator must reduce the participant's benefit payment from $2,500 to $1,926.51. If the participant dies after December 31, 1992, the plan administrator will pay his spouse $963.26 (0.50 × $1,926.51) per month.

Example 2— Facts. The benefit of a participant who retired under a plan at age 60 is a reduced single life annuity of $400 per month plus a temporary supplement of $400 per month payable until age 62 (i.e., a step-down benefit). The participant's accrued benefit under the plan is $450 per month, payable from the plan's normal retirement age. On the proposed termination date, June 30, 1992, the participant is 61 years old.

The maximum guaranteeable benefit adjusted for age under § 4022.23(c) of this chapter is $1,693.63 ($2,352.27 × 0.72) per month. Since the benefit is payable as a single life annuity, no adjustment is required under § 4022.23(d) for benefit form.

Benefit reductions. The plan benefit of $800 per month payable until age 62 exceeds the participant's accrued benefit at normal requirement age of $450 per month. Paragraph (b) of this section requires that, except to the extent permitted by paragraph (d), the plan benefit must be reduced to $450 per month. Since the levelized benefit of $404.10 ((0.082 × 50) + $400) per month, determined under § 4022.23(f), is less than the adjusted maximum guaranteeable benefit of $1,693.63 per month, no further reduction in the $450 per month benefit payment is required under paragraph (c) of this section. The plan administrator next would determine the amount of the participant's estimated benefit under paragraph (d).

Example 3— Facts. A retired participant is receiving a reduced early retirement benefit of $1,100 per month plus a temporary supplement of $700 per month payable until age 62. The benefit is in the form of a single life annuity. On the proposed termination date, November 30, 1992, the participant is 56 years old.

The participant's accrued benefit at normal retirement age under the plan is $1,200 per month. The maximum guaranteeable benefit adjusted for age is $1,152.61 ($2,352.27 × 0.49) per month. A form adjustment is not required.

Benefit reductions. The plan benefit of $1,800 per month payable from age 56 to age 62 exceeds the participant's accrued benefit at normal retirement age of $1,200 per month. Therefore, under paragraph (b) of this section, the plan administrator must reduce the temporary supplement to $100 per month.

For the purpose of determining whether the reduced benefit, i.e., a level-life annuity of $1,100 per month and a temporary annuity supple-

ment of $100 per month to age 62, exceeds the maximum guaranteeable benefit adjusted for age, the temporary annuity supplement of $100 per month is converted to a level-life annuity equivalent in accordance with § 4022.23(f) of this chapter. The level-life annuity equivalent is $38.70 ($100 × 0.387). This, added to the life annuity of $1,100 per month, equals $1,138.70. Since the maximum guaranteeable benefit of $1,152.61 per month exceeds $1,138.70 per month, no further reduction is required under paragraph (c) of this section.

The plan administrator next would determine the participant's estimated benefit under paragraph (d). Assume that the estimated benefit under paragraph (d) is $780 per month until age 62 and $715 per month thereafter. The plan administrator would pay the participant $780 per month, reduced to $715 per month at age 62, subject to the final benefit determination made under title IV.

Example 4— Facts. A retired participant is receiving a reduced early retirement benefit of $2,650 per month plus a temporary supplement of $800 per month payable until age 62. The benefit is in the form of a joint and survivor annuity (contingent basis) that will pay 50 percent of the participant's benefit amount to his surviving spouse following the death of the participant. On the proposed termination date, December 20, 1992, the participant and his spouse are each 56 years old.

The participant's accrued benefit at normal retirement age under the plan is $3,000 per month. The maximum guaranteeable benefit adjusted for age and the joint and survivor annuity (contingent basis) annuity form is $1,037.35 per month. An adjustment for age difference is not required because the participant and his spouse are the same age.

Benefit reductions. The plan benefit of $3,450 per month payable from age 56 to age 62 exceeds the participant's accrued benefit at normal retirement age, which is $3,000 per month. Therefore, under paragraph (b) of this section, the plan administrator must reduce the participant's benefit so that it does not exceed $3,000 per month.

The level-life equivalent of the participant's reduced benefit, determined using the § 4022.23(f) adjustment factor, is $2,785.45 (($350 × 0.387) + $2,650) per month. Since this benefit exceeds the participant's maximum guaranteeable benefit of $1,037.35 per month, the plan administrator must reduce the participant's benefit payment so that it does not exceed the maximum guaranteeable benefit.

The ratio of (i) the participant's maximum guaranteeable benefit to (ii) the level-life equivalent of the participant's reduced benefit (computed under the "accrued for normal retirement age" limitation) is used in converting the level-life maximum guaranteeable benefit to the step-down benefit form. The level-life equivalent of the reduced benefit computed under the "accrued for normal retirement age" limitation is 37.24 percent ($1,037.35/$2,785.45). Thus, the plan administrator must reduce the participant's level-life benefit of $2,650 per month to $986.86 ($2,650 x 0.3724) and must further reduce the reduced temporary benefit of $350 per month to $130.34 ($350 × 0.3724). Under paragraph (c) of this section, therefore, the participant's maximum guaranteeable benefit is $1,117.20 ($986.86 + $130.34) per month to age 62 and $986.86 per month thereafter, subject to any adjustment under paragraph (d) of this section.

Assume that the estimated benefit under paragraph (d) is $1,005.48 per month to age 62 and $888.17 per month thereafter. The plan administrator would reduce the participant's benefit from $3,450 per month to $1,005.48 per month and pay this amount until age 62, at which time the benefit payment would be reduced to $888.17 per month, subject to the final benefit determination made under title IV.

[¶ 15,423A]

§ 4022.62 **Estimated guaranteed benefit.** (a) *General.* The estimated guaranteed benefit payable with respect to each participant who is not a substantial owner is computed under paragraph (c) of this section. The estimated guaranteed benefit payable with respect to each participant who is a substantial owner is computed under paragraph (d) of this section.

(b) *Rules for determining benefits.* For the purposes of determining entitlement to a benefit and the amount of the estimated benefit under this section, the following rules apply:

(1) *Non-PPA 2006 bankruptcy termination.* In a non-PPA 2006 bankruptcy termination:

(i) For benefits payable with respect to a participant who is in pay status on or before the proposed termination date, the plan administrator shall use the participant's age and benefit payable under the plan as of the proposed termination date.

(ii) For benefits payable with respect to a participant who enters pay status after the proposed termination date, the plan administrator shall use the participant's age as of the benefit commencement date and his service and compensation as of the proposed termination date.

(2) *PPA 2006 bankruptcy termination.* In a PPA 2006 bankruptcy termination:

(i) For benefits payable with respect to a participant who is in pay status on or before the bankruptcy filing date, the plan administrator shall use the participant's age and benefit payable under the plan as of the bankruptcy filing date.

(ii) For benefits payable with respect to a participant who enters pay status after the bankruptcy filing date, the plan administrator shall use the participant's age as of the benefit commencement date and his service and compensation as of the bankruptcy filing date. [Amended 6/14/11 by 76 FR 34590.]

(3) *Participants with new benefits or benefit improvements.* For the purpose of determining the estimated guaranteed benefit under paragraph (c) of this section, only new benefits and benefit improvements that affect the benefit of the participant or beneficiary for whom the determination is made are taken into account.

(4) *Limitations on estimated guaranteed benefits.* For the purpose of determining the estimated guaranteed benefit under paragraph (c) or (d) of this section, the benefit determined under paragraph (b)(1) or (b)(2) of this section is subject to the limitations set forth in § 4022.61(b) and (c).

(5) Nothing in this paragraph (b) overrides the provisions of subparts A and B of part 4022 with respect to the requirements necessary for a benefit to be guaranteed by PBGC. [Added 6/14/11 by 76 FR 34590.]

(c) *Estimated guaranteed benefit payable with respect to a participant who is not a substantial owner.* For benefits payable with respect to a participant who is not a substantial owner, the estimated guaranteed benefit is determined under paragraph (c)(1) of this section, if no portion of the benefit is subject to the phase-in of plan termination insurance guarantees set forth in section 4022(b)(1) of ERISA. In any other case, the estimated guaranteed benefit is determined under paragraph (c)(2). "Benefit subject to phase-in" means a benefit that is subject to the phase-in of plan termination insurance guarantees set forth in section 4022(b)(1) of ERISA, determined without regard to section 4022(b)(7) of ERISA.

(1) *Participants with no benefits subject to phase-in.* In the case of a participant or beneficiary with no benefit improvement (as defined in paragraph (c)(2)(ii)) or new benefit (as defined in paragraph (c)(2)(i)) in the five years preceding the proposed termination date, the estimated guaranteed benefit is the benefit to which he or she is entitled under the rules in paragraph (b) of this section.

(2) *Participants with benefits subject to phase-in.* In the case of a participant or beneficiary with a benefit improvement or new benefit in the five years preceding the proposed termination date, the estimated guaranteed benefit is the benefit to which he or she is entitled under the rules in paragraph (b) of this section, multiplied by the multiplier determined according to paragraphs (i), (ii), and (iii), but not less than the benefit to which he or she would have been entitled if the benefit improvement or new benefit had not been adopted.

(i) From column (a) of Table I, select the line that applies according to the number of full years before the proposed termination date since the plan was last amended to provide for a new benefit (or the number of full years since the plan was established, if it has never been amended to provide for a new benefit). "New benefit" means a change in the terms of the plan that results in (a) a participant's or a beneficiary's eligibility for a benefit that was not previously available or to which he or she was not entitled (excluding a benefit that is

actuarially equivalent to the normal retirement benefit to which the participant was previously entitled) or (b) an increase of more than twenty percent in the benefit to which a participant is entitled upon entering pay status before his or her normal retirement age under the plan. "New benefits" result from liberalized participation or vesting requirements, reductions in the age or service requirements for receiving unreduced benefits, additions of actuarially subsidized benefits, and increases in actuarial subsidies. "New benefits" also result from increases that become payable by reason of the occurrence of an unpredictable contingent event (provided the event occurred after July 26, 2005), to the extent the increase would not be payable but for the occurrence of the event; in the case of such new benefits, the date of the occurrence of the unpredictable contingent event is treated as the amendment date for purposes of Table I. The establishment of a plan creates a new benefit as of the effective date of the plan. A change in the amount of a benefit is not deemed to be a "new benefit" if it results solely from a benefit improvement. "New benefit" and "benefit improvement" are mutually exclusive terms. [Amended 5/6/2014 (79 FR 25667).]

(ii) If there was no benefit improvement under the plan during the one-year period ending on the proposed termination date, use the multiplier set forth in column (b) of Table I on the line selected from column (a). "Benefit improvement" means a change in the terms of the plan that results in (a) an increase in the benefit to which a participant is entitled at his or her normal retirement age under the plan or (b) an increase in the benefit to which a participant or beneficiary in pay status is entitled.

(iii) If there was any benefit improvement during the one-year period ending on the proposed termination date, use the multiplier set forth in column (c) of Table I on the line selected from column (a).

TABLE I.—APPLICABLE MULTIPLIER IF—

Full years since last new benefit (a)	No benefit improvement during last year (b)	Benefit improvement during last year (c)
Five or more	.90	.80
Four	.80	.70
Three	.65	.55
Two	.50	.45
Fewer than two	.35	.30

Note: The foregoing method of estimating guaranteed benefits is based upon the PBGC's experience with a wide range of plans and may not provide accurate estimates in certain circumstances. In accordance with § 4022.61(e), a plan administrator may use a different method of estimation if he or she demonstrates to the PBGC that his proposed method will be more equitable to participants and beneficiaries. The PBGC may require the use of a different method in certain cases.

(d) *Estimated guaranteed benefit payable with respect to a substantial owner.* For benefits payable with respect to each participant who is a substantial owner and who commenced participation under the plan fewer than five full years before the proposed termination date, the estimated guaranteed benefit is determined under paragraph (d)(1). With respect to any other substantial owner, the estimated guaranteed benefit is determined under paragraph (d)(2).

(1) *Fewer than five years of participation.* The estimated guaranteed benefit under this paragraph is the benefit to which the substantial owner is entitled, as determined under paragraph (b) of this section, multiplied by a fraction, not to exceed one, the numerator of which is the number of full years prior to the proposed termination date that the substantial owner was an active participant under the plan and the denominator of which is thirty.

(2) *Five or more years of participation.* The estimated guaranteed benefit under this paragraph is the lesser of—

(i) the estimated guaranteed benefit calculated under paragraph (d)(1) of this section; or

(ii) the benefit to which the substantial owner would have been entitled as of the proposed termination date (or benefit commencement date in the case of a substantial owner whose benefit commences after the proposed termination date) under the terms of the plan in effect when he or she first began participation, as limited by § 4022.61 (b) and (c), multiplied by a fraction, not to exceed one, the numerator of which is two times the number of full years of his or her active participation under the plan prior to the proposed termination date and the denominator of which is thirty.

(e) *PPA 2006 bankruptcy termination.* In a PPA 2006 bankruptcy termination, "bankruptcy filing date" is substituted for "proposed termination date" each place that "proposed termination date" appears in paragraph (c) of this section. [Added 6/14/11 by 76 FR 34590.]

(f) *Examples.* This section is illustrated by the following examples. (For an example addressing issues specific to a PPA 2006 bankruptcy termination, see § 4022.25(f).). [Redesignated and amended 6/14/11 by 76 FR 34590.]

Example 1— Facts. A participant who is not a substantial owner retired on December 31, 1991, at age 60 and began receiving a benefit of $600 per month. On January 1, 1989, the plan had been amended to allow participants to retire with unreduced benefits at age 60. Previously, a participant who retired before age 65 was subject to a reduction of 1/15 for each year by which his or her actual retirement age preceded age 65. On January 1, 1992, the plan's benefit formula was amended to increase benefits for participants who retired before January 1, 1992. As a result, the participant's benefit was increased to $750 per month. There have been no other pertinent amendments. The proposed termination date is December 15, 1992.

Estimated guaranteed benefit. No reduction is required under § 4022.61(b) or (c) because the participant's benefit does not exceed either the participant's accrued benefit at normal retirement age or the maximum guaranteeable benefit. (Post-retirement benefit increases are not considered as increasing accrued benefits payable at normal retirement age.)

The amendment as of January 1, 1989, resulted in a "new benefit" because the reduction in the age at which the participant could receive unreduced benefits increased the participant's benefit entitlement at actual retirement age by 5/15, which is more than a 20 percent increase. The amendment of January 1, 1992, which increased the participant's benefit to $750 per month, is a "benefit improvement" because it is an increase in the amount of benefit for persons in pay status. (No percentage test applies in determining whether such an increase is a benefit improvement.)

The multiplier for computing the amount of the estimated guaranteed benefit is taken from the third row of Table I (because the last new benefit had been in effect for 3 full years as of the proposed termination date) and column (c) (because there was a benefit improvement within the 1-year period preceding the proposed termination date). This multiplier is 0.55. Therefore, the amount of the participant's estimated guaranteed benefit is $412.50 (0.55 × $750) per month.

Example 2— Facts. A participant who is not a substantial owner terminated employment on December 31, 1990. On January 1, 1992, she reached age 65 and began receiving a benefit or $250 per month. She had completed 3 years of service at her termination of employment and was fully vested in her accrued benefit. The plan's vesting schedule had been amended on July 1, 1988. Under the schedule in effect before the amendment, a participant with 5 years of service was 100 percent vested. There have been no other pertinent amendments. The proposed termination date is December 31, 1992.

Estimated guaranteed benefit. No reduction is required under § 4022.61(b) or (c) because the participant's benefit does not exceed either her accrued benefit at normal retirement age or the maximum guaranteeable benefit. The plan's change of vesting schedule created a new benefit for the participant. Because the amendment was in effect for 4 full years before the proposed termination date, the second row of Table I is used to determine the applicable multiplier for estimating the amount of the participant's guaranteed benefit. Because the participant did not receive any benefit improvement during the 12-month period ending on the proposed termination date, column (b) of the table is used. Therefore, the multiplier is 0.80, and the amount of the participant's estimated guaranteed benefit is $200 (0.80 × $250) per month.

Example 3— Facts. A participant who is a substantial owner retired prior to the proposed termination date after 5 1/2 years of active

participation in the plan. The benefit under the terms of the plan when he first began active participation was $800 per month. On the proposed termination date of April 30, 1992, he was entitled to receive a benefit of $2000 per month. No reduction of this benefit is required under § 4022.61(b) or (c).

Estimated guaranteed benefit. Paragraph (d)(2) of this section is used to compute the amount of the estimated guaranteed benefit of substantial owners with 5 or more years of active participation prior to the proposed termination date. Consequently, the amount of this participant's estimated guaranteed benefit is the lesser of—

(i) the amount calculated as if he had been an active participant in the plan for fewer than 5 full years on the proposed termination date, or $333.33 ($2000 × 5/30) per month, or

(ii) the amount to which he would have been entitled as of the proposed termination date under the terms of the plan when he first began participation, as limited by § 4022.61(b) and (c), multiplied by 2 times the number of years of active participation and divided by 30, or $266.67 ($800 × 2 × 5/30) per month. Therefore, the amount of the participant's estimated guaranteed benefit is $266.67 per month.

[¶ 15,423B]

§ 4022.63 **Estimated title IV benefit.** (a) *General.* If the conditions specified in paragraph (b) exist, the plan administrator shall determine each participant's estimated title IV benefit. The estimated title IV benefit payable with respect to each participant who is not a substantial owner is computed under paragraph (c) of this section. The estimated title IV benefit payable with respect to each participant who is a substantial owner is computed under paragraph (d) of this section.

(b) *Conditions for use of this section.* The conditions set forth in this paragraph must be satisfied in order to make use of the procedures set forth in this section. If the specified conditions exist, estimated title IV benefits must be determined in accordance with these procedures (or in accordance with alternative procedures authorized by the PBGC under § 4022.61(f)) for each participant and beneficiary whose benefit under the plan exceeds the limitations contained in § 4022.61(b) or (c) or who is a substantial owner or the beneficiary of a substantial owner. If the specified conditions do not exist, title IV benefits may be estimated by the plan administrator in accordance with procedures authorized by the PBGC, but no such estimate is required. The conditions are as follows:

(1) An actuarial valuation of the plan has been performed for a plan year beginning not more than eighteen months before the proposed termination date. If the interest rate used to value plan liabilities in this valuation exceeded the applicable valuation interest rates and factors under appendix B to part 4044 of this chapter in effect on the proposed termination date, the value of benefits in pay status and the value of vested benefits not in pay status on the valuation date must be converted to the PBGC's valuation rates and factors.

(2) The plan has been in effect for at least five full years before the proposed termination date, and the most recent actuarial valuation demonstrates that the value of plan assets, reduced by employee contributions remaining in the plan and interest credited thereon under the terms of the plan, exceeds the present value, adjusted as required under paragraph (b)(1), of all plan benefits in pay status on the valuation date.

(3) *PPA 2006 bankruptcy termination.* In a PPA 2006 bankruptcy termination, "bankruptcy filing date" is substituted for "proposed termination date" in the first sentence of paragraph (b)(2) of this section. [Added 6/14/11 by 76 FR 34590.]

(c)(1) *In general.* For benefits payable with respect to a participant who is not a substantial owner, the estimated title IV benefit is the estimated priority category 3 benefit computed under this paragraph. Priority category 3 benefits are payable with respect to participants who were, or could have been, in pay status three full years prior to the proposed termination date. The estimated priority category 3 benefit is computed by multiplying the benefit payable with respect to the participant under § 4022.62(b)(1) and (b)(2) by a fraction, not to exceed one—[Redesignated 6/14/11 by 76 FR 34590.]

(i) The numerator of which is the benefit that would be payable with respect to the participant at normal retirement age under the provisions of the plan in effect on the date five full years before the proposed termination date, based on the participant's age, service, and compensation as of the earlier of the participant's benefit commencement date or the proposed termination date, and [Redesignated 6/14/11 by 76 FR 34590.]

(ii) The denominator of which is the benefit that would be payable with respect to the participant at normal retirement age under the provisions of the plan in effect on the proposed termination date, based on the participant's age, service, and compensation as of the earlier of the participant's benefit commencement date or the proposed termination date. [Redesignated 6/14/11 by 76 FR 34590.]

(2) *PPA 2006 bankruptcy termination.* In a PPA 2006 bankruptcy termination, "bankruptcy filing date" is substituted for "proposed termination date" each place that "proposed termination date" appears in paragraph (c)(1) of this section. [Added 6/14/11 by 76 FR 34590.]

(d) *Estimated title IV benefit payable with respect to a substantial owner.* For benefits payable with respect to a participant who is a substantial owner, the estimated title IV benefit is the higher of the benefit computed under paragraph (c) of this section or the benefit computed under this paragraph.

(1) The plan administrator shall first calculate the estimated guaranteed benefit payable with respect to the substantial owner as if he or she were not a substantial owner, using the method set forth in § 4022.62(c).

(2) The benefit computed under paragraph (d)(1) shall be multiplied by the priority category 4 funding ratio. The category 4 funding ratio is the ratio of x to y, not to exceed one, where—

(i) in a plan with priority category 3 benefits, x equals plan assets minus employee contributions remaining in the plan on the valuation date, with interest credited thereon under the terms of the plan, and the present value of benefits in pay status, and y equals the present value of all vested benefits not in pay status minus such employee contributions and interest; or

(ii) in a plan with no priority category 3 benefits, x equals plan assets minus employee contributions remaining in the plan on the valuation date, with interest credited thereon under the terms of the plan, and y equals the present value of all vested benefits minus such employee contributions and interest.

(e) *Examples.* This section is illustrated by the following examples:

Example 1— Facts. A participant who is not a substantial owner was eligible to retire 3 1/2 years before the proposed termination date. The participant retired 2 years before the proposed termination date with 20 years of service. Her final 5 years' average salary was $45,000, and she was entitled to an unreduced early retirement benefit of $1,500 per month payable as a single life annuity. This retirement benefit does not exceed the limitation in § 4022.61(b) or (c).

On the participant's benefit commencement date, the plan provided for a normal retirement benefit of 2 percent of the final 5 years' salary times the number of years of service. Five years before the proposed termination date, the percentage was 1 1/2 percent. The amendments improving benefits were put into effect 3 1/2 years prior to the proposed termination date. There were no other amendments during the 5-year period.

The participant's estimated guaranteed benefit computed under § 4022.62(c) is $1,500 per month times 0.90 (the factor from column (b) of Table I in § 4022.62(c)(2)), or $1,350 per month. It is assumed that the plan meets the conditions set forth in paragraph (b) of this section, and the plan administrator is therefore required to estimate the title IV benefit.

Estimated title IV benefit. For a participant who is not a substantial owner, the amount of the estimated title IV benefit is the estimated priority category 3 benefit computed under paragraph (c) of this section. This amount is computed by multiplying the participant's benefit under the plan as of the later of the proposed termination date or the benefit commencement date by the ratio of (i) the normal retirement benefit under the provisions of the plan in effect 5 years before the proposed termination date and (ii) the normal retirement benefit under the plan provisions in effect on the proposed termination date.

Thus, the numerator of the ratio is the benefit that would be payable to the participant under the normal retirement provisions of

the plan 5 years before the proposed termination date, based on her age, service, and compensation on her benefit commencement date. The denominator of the ratio is the benefit that would be payable to the participant under the normal retirement provisions of the plan in effect on the proposed termination date, based on her age, service, and compensation as of the earlier of her benefit commencement date or the proposed termination date. Since the only different factor in the numerator and denominator is the salary percentage, the amount of the estimated title IV benefit is $1,125 (0.015/0.020 × $1,500) per month. This amount is less than the estimated guaranteed benefit of $1,350 per month. Therefore, in accordance with § 4022.61(d), the benefit payable to the participant is $1,350 per month.

PPA 2006 bankruptcy termination. In a PPA 2006 bankruptcy termination, the methodology would be the same, but "bankruptcy filing date" would be substituted for "proposed termination date" each place that "proposed termination date" appears in the example, and the numbers would change accordingly. [Added 6/14/11 by 76 FR 34590.]

Example 2— Facts. A participant who is a substantial owner retires at the plan's normal retirement age, having completed 5 years of active participation in the plan, on October 31, 1992, which is the proposed termination date. Under provisions of the plan in effect 5 years prior to the proposed termination date, the participant is entitled to a single life annuity of $500 per month. Under the most recent plan amendments, which were put into effect 1 1/2 years prior to the proposed termination date, the participant is entitled to a single life annuity of $1,000 per month. The participant's estimated guaranteed benefit computed under § 4022.62(d)(2) is $166.67 per month.

It is assumed that all of the conditions in paragraph (b) of this section have been met. Plan assets equal $2 million. The present value of all benefits in pay status is $1.5 million based on applicable PBGC interest rates. There are no employee contributions and the present value of all vested benefits that are not in pay status is $0.75 million based on applicable PBGC interest rates.

Estimated title IV benefit. Paragraph (d) of this section provides that the amount of the estimated title IV benefit payable with respect to a participant who is a substantial owner is the higher of the estimated priority category 3 benefit computed under paragraph (c) of this section or the estimated priority category 4 benefit computed under paragraph (d) of this section.

Under paragraph (c), the participant's estimated priority category 3 benefit is $500 ($1,000 × $500/$1000) per month.

Under paragraph (d), the participant's estimated priority category 4 benefit is the estimated guaranteed benefit computed under § 4022.62(c) (i.e., as if the participant were not a substantial owner) multiplied by the priority category 4 funding ratio. Since the plan has priority category 3 benefits, the ratio is determined under paragraph (d)(2)(i). The numerator of the ratio is plan assets minus the present value of benefits in pay status. The denominator of the ratio is the present value of all vested benefits that are not in pay status. The participant's estimated guaranteed benefit under § 4022.62(c) is $1,000 per month times 0.90 (the factor from column (b) of Table I in § 4022.62(c)(2)), or $900 per month. Multiplying $900 by the category 4 funding ratio of 2/3 (($2 million—$1.5 million)/$0.75 million) produces an estimated category 4 benefit of $600 per month.

Because the estimated category 4 benefit so computed is greater than the estimated category 3 benefit so computed, the estimated category 4 benefit is the estimated title IV benefit. Because the estimated category 4 benefit so computed is greater than the estimated guaranteed benefit of $166.67 per month, in accordance with § 4022.61(d), the benefit payable to the participant is the estimated category 4 benefit of $600 per month.

Subpart E—PBGC Recoupment and Reimbursement of Benefit Overpayments and Underpayments

[¶ 15,424]

§ 4022.81 **General rules.** (a) *Recoupment of benefit overpayments.* If at any time the PBGC determines that net benefits paid with respect to any participant in a PBGC-trusteed plan exceed the total amount to which the participant (and any beneficiary) is entitled up to that time under title IV of ERISA, and the participant (or beneficiary) is, as of the termination date, entitled to receive future benefit payments, the PBGC will recoup the net overpayment in accordance with paragraph (c) of this section and § 4022.82. Notwithstanding the previous sentence, the PBGC may, in its discretion, recover overpayments by methods other than recouping in accordance with the rules in this subpart. The PBGC will not normally do so unless net benefits paid after the termination date exceed those to which a participant (and any beneficiary) is entitled under the terms of the plan before any reductions under subpart D.

(b) *Reimbursement of benefit underpayments.* If at any time the PBGC determines that net benefits paid with respect to a participant in a PBGC-trusteed plan are less than the amount to which the participant (and any beneficiary) is entitled up to that time under title IV of ERISA, the PBGC will reimburse the participant or beneficiary for the net underpayment in accordance with paragraphs (c) and (d) of this section and § 4022.83.

(c) *Amount to be recouped or reimbursed.* In order to determine the amount to be recouped from, or reimbursed to, a participant (or beneficiary), the PBGC will calculate a monthly account balance for each month ending after the termination date. The PBGC will start with a balance of zero as of the end of the calendar month ending immediately prior to the termination date and determine the account balance as of the end of each month thereafter as follows:

(1) *Debit for overpayments.* the PBGC will subtract from the account balance the amount of overpayments made in that month. Only overpayments made on or after the latest of the proposed termination date, the termination date, or, if no notice of intent to terminate was issued, the date on which proceedings to terminate the plan are instituted pursuant to section 4042 of ERISA will be included.

(2) *Credit for underpayments.* The PBGC will add to the account balance the amount of underpayments made in that month. Only underpayments made on or after the termination date will be included.

(3) *PPA 2006 bankruptcy termination.* The provisions of paragraphs (c)(1) and (2) of this section regarding the overpayments and underpayments that will be included in the account balance apply regardless of whether the termination is a PPA 2006 bankruptcy termination. [Added 6/14/11 by 76 FR 34590.]

(4) *Credit for interest on net underpayments.* If at the end of a month there is a positive account balance (a net underpayment), the PBGC will add to the account balance interest thereon for that month using—

(i) For months after May 1998, the applicable federal midterm rate (as determined by the Secretary of the Treasury pursuant to section 1274(d)(1)(c)(ii) of the Code) for that month (or, where the rate for a month is not available at the time the PBGC calculates the amount to be recouped or reimbursed, the most recent month for which the rate is available) based on monthly compounding; and

(ii) For May 1998 and earlier months, the immediate annuity rate established for lump sum valuations as set forth in Table II of Appendix B of part 4044 of this chapter. [Redesignated 6/14/11 by 76 FR 34590.]

(5) *No interest on net overpayments.* If at the end of the month, there is a negative account balance (a net overpayment), there will be no interest adjustment for that month. [Redesignated 6/14/11 by 76 FR 34590.]

(d) *Death of participant.* (1) *Benefit overpayments.* If the PBGC determines that, at the time of a participant's death, there was a net overpayment to the participant—

(i) *Future annuity payments.* If the participant was entitled to future annuity payments as of the plan's termination date, the PBGC will (except as provided in paragraph (a) of this section) recoup the overpayment from the person (if any) who is receiving survivor benefits under the annuity.

(ii) *No future annuity payments.* If the participant was not entitled to future annuity benefits as of the plan's termination date, the PBGC may seek repayment of the overpayment from the participant's estate.

(2) *Benefit underpayments.* If the PBGC determines that, at the time of a participant's death, there was a net underpayment to the participant—

(i) *Future annuity payments.* If the benefit is in the form of a joint-and-survivor or other annuity under which payments may continue after the participant's death, the PBGC will pay the underpayment to the person who is receiving survivor benefits; for this purpose, if the person receiving survivor benefits is an alternate payee under a qualified domestic relations order, the PBGC will treat the benefit as if payments do not continue after the participant's death (see paragraph (d)(2)(ii) of this section).

(ii) *No future annuity payments.* If the benefit is not in the form of a joint-and-survivor or other annuity (e.g., a certain-and-continuous annuity) under which payments may continue after the participant's death or although the benefit is in such a form payments do not continue after the participant's death (i.e., in the case of a joint-and-survivor annuity, the person designated to receive survivor benefits predeceased the participant or, in the case of another annuity under which payments may continue after the participant's death the participant died with no payments owed for future periods), the PBGC will pay the underpayment to the person determined under the rules in §§ 4022.91 through 4022.95. [Added by 67 FR 16949, April 8, 2002.]

[¶ 15,424A]

§ 4022.82 **Method of recoupment.** (a) *Future benefit reductions.* The PBGC will recoup net overpayments of benefits by reducing the amount of each future benefit payment to which the participant or any beneficiary is entitled by the fraction determined under paragraphs (a)(1) and (a)(2) of this section, except that benefit reduction will cease when the amount (without interest) of the net overpayment is recouped. Notwithstanding the preceding sentence, the PBGC may accept repayment ahead of the recoupment schedule.

(1) *Computation..* The PBGC will determine the fractional multiplier by dividing the amount of the net overpayment by the present value of the benefit payable with respect to the participant under title IV of ERISA.

(i) *Non-PPA 2006 bankruptcy termination.* In a non-PPA bankruptcy termination, the PBGC will determine the present value of the benefit to which a participant or beneficiary is entitled under title IV of ERISA as of the termination date, using the PBGC interest rates and factors in effect on that date.

(ii) *PPA 2006 bankruptcy termination.* In a PPA 2006 bankruptcy termination, PBGC will determine the amount of benefit payable with respect to the participant under title IV of ERISA taking into account the limitations in sections 4022(g) and 4044(e) (and corresponding provisions of these regulations), and will determine the present value of that amount as of the termination date, using PBGC interest rates and factors in effect on the termination date.

(iii) *Facts and circumstances.* The PBGC may, however, utilize a different date of determination if warranted by the facts and circumstances of a particular case. [Amended 6/14/11 by 76 FR 34590.]

(2) *Limitation on benefit reduction.* Except as provided in paragraph (a)(1) of this section, the PBGC will reduce benefits with respect to a participant or beneficiary by no more than the greater of—

(i) ten percent per month; or

(ii) the amount of benefit per month in excess of the maximum guaranteeable benefit payable under section 4022(b)(3)(B) of ERISA, determined without adjustment for age and benefit form.

(3) *PBGC notice to participant or beneficiary.* Before effecting a benefit reduction pursuant to this paragraph, the PBGC will notify the participant or beneficiary in writing of the amount of the net overpayment and of the amount of the reduced benefit computed under this section.

(4) *Waiver of de minimis amounts.* The PBGC may, in its discretion, decide not to recoup net overpayments that it determines to be de minimis.

(5) *Final installment.* The PBGC will cease recoupment one month early if the amount remaining to be recouped in the final month is less than the amount of the monthly reduction.

(b) *Full repayment through repayment.* Recoupment under this section constitutes full repayment of the net overpayment.

[¶ 15,424B]

§ 4022.83 **PBGC reimbursement of benefit underpayments.** When the PBGC determines that there has been a net benefit underpayment made with respect to a participant, it shall pay the participant or beneficiary the amount of the net underpayment, determined in accordance with § 4022.81(c), in a single payment.

[¶ 15,424C]

§ 4022.83 **Appendix A to Part 4022: Lump Sum Mortality Rates.**

Age x	q_x	Age x	q_x	Age x	q_x	Age x	q_x
12	0.000000	37	0.001643	62	0.017010	87	0.143179
13	0.000000	38	0.001792	63	0.018685	88	0.155147
14	0.000000	39	0.001948	64	0.020517	89	0.168208
15	0.000000	40	0.002125	65	0.022562	90	0.182461
16	0.001437	41	0.002327	66	0.024847	91	0.198030
17	0.001414	42	0.002556	67	0.027232	92	0.215035
18	0.001385	43	0.002818	68	0.029634	93	0.232983
19	0.001351	44	0.003095	69	0.032073	94	0.252545
20	0.001311	45	0.003410	70	0.034743	95	0.273878
21	0.001267	46	0.003769	71	0.037667	96	0.297152
22	0.001219	47	0.004180	72	0.040871	97	0.322553
23	0.001167	48	0.004635	73	0.044504	98	0.349505
24	0.001149	49	0.005103	74	0.048504	99	0.378865
25	0.001129	50	0.005616	75	0.052913	100	0.410875
26	0.001107	51	0.006196	76	0.057775	101	0.445768
27	0.001083	52	0.006853	77	0.063142	102	0.483830
28	0.001058	53	0.007543	78	0.068628	103	0.524301
29	0.001083	54	0.008278	79	0.074648	104	0.568365
30	0.001111	55	0.009033	80	0.081256	105	0.616382
31	0.001141	56	0.009875	81	0.088518	106	0.668696
32	0.001173	57	0.010814	82	0.096218	107	0.725745
33	0.001208	58	0.011863	83	0.104310	108	0.786495
34	0.001297	59	0.012952	84	0.112816	109	0.852659
35	0.001398	60	0.014162	85	0.122079	110	0.924666
36	0.001513	61	0.015509	86	0.132174	111	1.000000

[Amended 3/17/2000 by 65 FR 14753.]

[¶ 15,424D]

§ 4022.83 **Appendix B to Part 4022: Lump Sum Interest Rates for PBGC Payments.**

[In using this table: (1) For benefits for which the participant or beneficiary is entitled to be in pay status on the valuation date, the immediate annuity rate shall apply; (2) For benefits for which the deferral period is y years (where y is an integer and $0 < y$ [is less than or equal to] n_1), interest rate i_1 shall apply from the valuation date for a period of y years; thereafter the immediate annuity rate shall apply; (3) For benefits for which the deferral period is y years (where y is an integer and $n_1 < y$ [is less than or equal to] $n_1 + n_2$); interest rate i_2 shall apply from the valuation date for a period of y n_1 years, interest rate i_1 shall apply for the following n_1 years; thereafter the immediate annuity rate shall apply; (4) For benefits for which the deferral period is y years (where y is an integer and $y < n_1 + n_2$), interest rate i_3 shall apply from the valuation date for a period of y n_1 n_2 years; interest rate i_2 shall apply for the following n_2 years; interest rate i_1 shall apply for the following n_1 years; thereafter the immediate annuity rate shall apply.][Amended 31700 by 65 FR 14751, 14753.]

Rate set	For plans with a valuation date		Immediate annuity rate (percent)	Deferred annuities (percent)				
	On or After	Before		i_1	i_2	i_3	n_1	n_2
1	11-1-93	12-1-93	4.25	4.00	4.00	4.00	7	8
2	12-1-93	1-1-94	4.25	4.00	4.00	4.00	7	8
3	1-1-94	2-1-94	4.50	4.00	4.00	4.00	7	8
4	2-1-94	3-1-94	4.50	4.00	4.00	4.00	7	8
5	3-1-94	4-1-94	4.50	4.00	4.00	4.00	7	8
6	4-1-94	5-1-94	4.75	4.00	4.00	4.00	7	8
7	5-1-94	6-1-94	5.25	4.50	4.00	4.00	7	8
8	6-1-94	7-1-94	5.25	4.50	4.00	4.00	7	8
9	7-1-94	8-1-94	5.50	4.75	4.00	4.00	7	8
10	8-1-94	9-1-94	5.75	5.00	4.00	4.00	7	8

Rate set	For plans with a valuation date		Immediate annuity rate (percent)	Deferred annuities (percent)				
	On or After	Before		i_1	i_2	i_3	n_1	n_2
11	9-1-94	10-1-94	5.50	4.75	4.00	4.00	7	8
12	10-1-94	11-1-94	5.50	4.75	4.00	4.00	7	8
13	11-1-94	12-1-94	6.00	5.25	4.00	4.00	7	8
14	12-1-94	1-1-95	6.25	5.50	4.25	4.00	7	8
15	1-1-95	2-1-95	6.00	5.25	4.00	4.00	7	8
16	2-1-95	3-1-95	6.00	5.25	4.00	4.00	7	8
17	3-1-95	4-1-95	6.00	5.25	4.00	4.00	7	8
18	4-1-95	5-1-95	5.75	5.00	4.00	4.00	7	8
19	5-1-95	6-1-95	5.50	4.75	4.00	4.00	7	8
20	6-1-95	7-1-95	5.50	4.75	4.00	4.00	7	8

Rate set	For plans with a valuation date		Immediate annuity rate (percent)	Deferred annuities (percent)				
	On or After	Before		i_1	i_2	i_3	n_1	n_2
21	7-1-95	8-1-95	4.75	4.00	4.00	4.00	7	8
22	8-1-95	9-1-95	4.75	4.00	4.00	4.00	7	8
23	9-1-95	10-1-95	5.00	4.25	4.00	4.00	7	8
24	10-1-95	11-1-95	4.75	4.00	4.00	4.00	7	8
25	11-1-95	12-1-95	4.75	4.00	4.00	4.00	7	8
26	12-1-95	1-1-96	4.50	4.00	4.00	4.00	7	8
27	1-1-96	2-1-96	4.50	4.00	4.00	4.00	7	8
28	2-1-96	3-1-96	4.25	4.00	4.00	4.00	7	8
29	3-1-96	4-1-96	4.25	4.00	4.00	4.00	7	8
30	4-1-96	5-1-96	4.75	4.00	4.00	4.00	7	8

Rate set	For plans with a valuation date		Immediate annuity rate (percent)	Deferred annuities (percent)				
	On or After	Before		i_1	i_2	i_3	n_1	n_2
31	5-1-96	6-1-96	5.00	4.25	4.00	4.00	7	8
32	6-1-96	7-1-96	5.00	4.25	4.00	4.00	7	8
33	7-1-96	8-1-96	5.00	4.25	4.00	4.00	7	8
34	8-1-96	9-1-96	5.25	4.50	4.00	4.00	7	8
35	9-1-96	10-1-96	5.25	4.50	4.00	4.00	7	8
36	10-1-96	11-1-96	5.25	4.50	4.00	4.00	7	8
37	11-1-96	12-1-96	5.00	4.25	4.00	4.00	7	8
38	12-1-96	1-1-97	4.75	4.00	4.00	4.00	7	8
39	1-1-97	2-1-97	4.50	4.00	4.00	4.00	7	8
40	2-1-97	3-1-97	4.75	4.00	4.00	4.00	7	8

Rate set	For plans with a valuation date		Immediate annuity rate (percent)	Deferred annuities (percent)				
	On or After	Before		i_1	i_2	i_3	n_1	n_2
41	3-1-97	4-1-97	5.00	4.25	4.00	4.00	7	8
42	4-1-97	5-1-97	4.75	4.00	4.00	4.00	7	8
43	5-1-97	6-1-97	5.00	4.25	4.00	4.00	7	8
44	6-1-97	7-1-97	5.25	4.50	4.00	4.00	7	8
45	7-1-97	8-1-97	5.25	4.50	4.00	4.00	7	8
46	8-1-97	9-1-97	4.75	4.00	4.00	4.00	7	8
47	9-1-97	10-1-97	4.50	4.00	4.00	4.00	7	8
48	10-1-97	11-1-97	4.75	4.00	4.00	4.00	7	8
49	11-1-97	12-1-97	4.50	4.00	4.00	4.00	7	8
50	12-1-97	1-1-98	4.50	4.00	4.00	4.00	7	8

Rate set	For plans with a valuation date		Immediate annuity rate (percent)	Deferred annuities (percent)				
	On or After	Before		i_1	i_2	i_3	n_1	n_2
51	1-1-98	2-1-98	4.25	4.00	4.00	4.00	7	8
52	2-1-98	3-1-98	4.25	4.00	4.00	4.00	7	8
53	3-1-98	4-1-98	4.25	4.00	4.00	4.00	7	8
54	4-1-98	5-1-98	4.25	4.00	4.00	4.00	7	8
55	5-1-98	6-1-98	4.25	4.00	4.00	4.00	7	8
56	6-1-98	7-1-98	4.25	4.00	4.00	4.00	7	8
57	7-1-98	8-1-98	4.00	4.00	4.00	4.00	7	8
58	8-1-98	9-1-98	4.00	4.00	4.00	4.00	7	8
59	9-1-98	10-1-98	4.00	4.00	4.00	4.00	7	8
60	10-1-98	11-1-98	4.00	4.00	4.00	4.00	7	8

Rate set	For plans with a valuation date		Immediate annuity rate (percent)	Deferred annuities (percent)				
	On or After	Before		i_1	i_2	i_3	n_1	n_2
61	11-1-98	12-1-98	3.75	4.00	4.00	4.00	7	8
62	12-1-98	1-1-99	4.00	4.00	4.00	4.00	7	8
63	1-1-99	2-1-99	4.00	4.00	4.00	4.00	7	8
64	2-1-99	3-1-99	4.00	4.00	4.00	4.00	7	8
65	3-1-99	4-1-99	4.00	4.00	4.00	4.00	7	8
66	4-1-99	5-1-99	4.25	4.00	4.00	4.00	7	8
67	5-1-99	6-1-99	4.25	4.00	4.00	4.00	7	8
68	6-1-99	7-1-99	4.25	4.00	4.00	4.00	7	8
69	7-1-99	8-1-99	4.50	4.00	4.00	4.00	7	8
70	8-1-99	9-1-99	5.00	4.25	4.00	4.00	7	8

Rate set	For plans with a valuation date		Immediate annuity rate (percent)	Deferred annuities (percent)				
	On or After	Before		i_1	i_2	i_3	n_1	n_2
71	9-1-99	10-1-99	5.00	4.25	4.00	4.00	7	8
72	10-1-99	11-1-99	5.00	4.25	4.00	4.00	7	8
73	11-1-99	12-1-99	5.00	4.25	4.00	4.00	7	8
74	12-1-99	1-1-00	5.25	4.50	4.00	4.00	7	8
75	1-1-00	2-1-00	5.00	4.25	4.00	4.00	7	8
76	2-1-00	3-1-00	5.25	4.50	4.00	4.00	7	8
77	3-1-00	4-1-00	5.25	4.50	4.00	4.00	7	8
78	4-1-00	5-1-00	5.25	4.50	4.00	4.00	7	8
79	5-1-00	6-1-00	5.25	4.50	4.00	4.00	7	8
80	6-1-00	7-1-00	5.25	4.50	4.00	4.00	7	8

Rate set	For plans with a valuation date		Immediate annuity rate (percent)	Deferred annuities (percent)				
	On or After	Before		i_1	i_2	i_3	n_1	n_2
81	7-1-00	8-1-00	5.50	4.75	4.00	4.00	7	8
82[1]	8-1-00	9-1-00	5.25	4.50	4.00	4.00	7	8
83[2]	9-1-00	10-1-00	5.25	4.50	4.00	4.00	7	8
84[3]	10-1-00	11-1-00	5.00	4.25	4.00	4.00	7	8
85[4]	11-1-00	12-1-00	5.25	4.50	4.00	4.00	7	8
86[5]	12-1-00	1-1-01	5.25	4.50	4.00	4.00	7	8
87[6]	1-1-01	2-1-01	5.00	4.25	4.00	4.00	7	8
88[7]	2-1-01	3-1-01	4.75	4.00	4.00	4.00	7	8
89[8]	3-1-01	4-1-01	4.75	4.00	4.00	4.00	7	8
90[9]	4-1-01	5-1-01	4.75	4.00	4.00	4.00	7	8

Rate set	For plans with a valuation date		Immediate annuity rate (percent)	Deferred annuities (percent)				
	On or After	Before		i_1	i_2	i_3	n_1	n_2
91[10]	5-1-01	6-1-01	4.75	4.00	4.00	4.00	7	8
92[11]	6-1-01	7-1-01	5.00	4.25	4.00	4.00	7	8
93[12]	7-1-01	8-1-01	5.00	4.25	4.00	4.00	7	8
94[13]	8-1-01	9-1-01	4.75	4.00	4.00	4.00	7	8
95[14]	9-1-01	10-1-01	4.50	4.00	4.00	4.00	7	8
96[15]	10-1-01	11-1-01	4.50	4.00	4.00	4.00	7	8
97[16]	11-1-01	12-1-01	4.75	4.00	4.00	4.00	7	8
98[17]	12-1-01	1-1-02	4.50	4.00	4.00	4.00	7	8
100[19]	2-1-02	3-1-02	4.75	4.00	4.00	4.00	7	8

Rate set	For plans with a valuation date		Immediate annuity rate (percent)	Deferred annuities (percent)				
	On or After	Before		i_1	i_2	i_3	n_1	n_2
101[20]	3-1-02	4-1-02	4.50	4.00	4.00	4.00	7	8
102[21]	4-1-02	5-1-02	4.25	4.00	4.00	4.00	7	8
103[22]	5-1-02	6-1-02	4.75	4.00	4.00	4.00	7	8
104[23]	6-1-02	7-1-02	4.50	4.00	4.00	4.00	7	8
105[24]	7-1-02	8-1-02	4.50	4.00	4.00	4.00	7	8
106[25]	8-1-02	9-1-02	4.25	4.00	4.00	4.00	7	8
107[26]	9-1-02	10-1-02	4.25	4.00	4.00	4.00	7	8
108[27]	10-1-02	11-1-02	4.00	4.00	4.00	4.00	7	8
109[28]	11-1-02	12-1-02	3.75	4.00	4.00	4.00	7	8
110[29]	12-1-02	1-1-03	4.00	4.00	4.00	4.00	7	8

Rate set	For plans with a valuation date		Immediate annuity rate (percent)	Deferred annuities (percent)				
	On or After	Before		i_1	i_2	i_3	n_1	n_2
111[30]	1-1-03	2-1-03	4.00	4.00	4.00	4.00	7	8
112[31]	2-1-03	3-1-03	3.75	4.00	4.00	4.00	7	8
113[32]	3-1-03	4-1-03	3.75	4.00	4.00	4.00	7	8
114[33]	4-1-03	5-1-03	3.50	4.00	4.00	4.00	7	8
115[34]	5-1-03	6-1-03	3.50	4.00	4.00	4.00	7	8
116[35]	6-1-03	7-1-03	3.50	4.00	4.00	4.00	7	8
117[36]	7-1-03	8-1-03	3.00	4.00	4.00	4.00	7	8
118[37]	8-1-03	9-1-03	3.00	4.00	4.00	4.00	7	8
119[38]	9-1-03	10-1-03	3.50	4.00	4.00	4.00	7	8
120[39]	10-1-03	11-1-03	3.50	4.00	4.00	4.00	7	8
121[40]	11-1-03	12-1-03	3.25	4.00	4.00	4.00	7	8
122[41]	12-1-03	1-1-04	3.25	4.00	4.00	4.00	7	8

Rate set	For plans with a valuation date		Immediate annuity rate (percent)	Deferred annuities (percent)				
	On or After	Before		i_1	i_2	i_3	n_1	n_2
123[42]	1-1-04	2-1-04	3.25	4.00	4.00	4.00	7	8
124[43]	2-1-04	3-1-04	3.25	4.00	4.00	4.00	7	8
125[44]	3-1-04	4-1-04	3.00	4.00	4.00	4.00	7	8
126[45]	4-1-04	5-1-04	3.00	4.00	4.00	4.00	7	8
127[46]	5-1-04	6-1-04	3.00	4.00	4.00	4.00	7	8
128[47]	6-1-04	7-1-04	3.50	4.00	4.00	4.00	7	8
129[48]	7-1-04	8-1-04	3.50	4.00	4.00	4.00	7	8
130[49]	8-1-04	9-1-04	3.50	4.00	4.00	4.00	7	8
131[50]	9-1-04	10-1-04	3.25	4.00	4.00	4.00	7	8
132[51]	10-1-04	11-1-04	3.00	4.00	4.00	4.00	7	8
133[52]	11-1-04	12-1-04	2.75	4.00	4.00	4.00	7	8
134[53]	12-1-04	1-1-05	2.75	4.00	4.00	4.00	7	8

Rate set	For plans with a valuation date		Immediate annuity rate (percent)	Deferred annuities (percent)				
	On or After	Before		i_1	i_2	i_3	n_1	n_2
135[54]	1-1-05	2-1-05	3.00	4.00	4.00	4.00	7	8
136[55]	2-1-05	3-1-05	3.00	4.00	4.00	4.00	7	8
137[56]	3-1-05	4-1-05	2.75	4.00	4.00	4.00	7	8
138[57]	4-1-05	5-1-05	2.75	4.00	4.00	4.00	7	8
139[58]	5-1-05	6-1-05	2.75	4.00	4.00	4.00	7	8
140[59]	6-1-05	7-1-05	2.50	4.00	4.00	4.00	7	8
141[60]	7-1-05	8-1-05	2.50	4.00	4.00	4.00	7	8
142[61]	8-1-05	9-1-05	2.25	4.00	4.00	4.00	7	8
143[62]	9-1-05	10-1-05	2.50	4.00	4.00	4.00	7	8
144[63]	10-1-05	11-1-05	2.25	4.00	4.00	4.00	7	8
145[64]	11-1-05	12-1-05	2.50	4.00	4.00	4.00	7	8
146[65]	12-1-05	1-1-06	2.75	4.00	4.00	4.00	7	8

Rate set	For plans with a valuation date		Immediate annuity rate (percent)	Deferred annuities (percent)				
	On or After	Before		i_1	i_2	i_3	n_1	n_2
147[66]	1-1-06	2-1-06	2.75	4.00	4.00	4.00	7	8
148[67]	2-1-06	3-1-06	2.75	4.00	4.00	4.00	7	8
149[68]	3-1-06	4-1-06	2.75	4.00	4.00	4.00	7	8
150[69]	4-1-06	5-1-06	2.75	4.00	4.00	4.00	7	8
151[70]	5-1-06	6-1-06	3.00	4.00	4.00	4.00	7	8
152[71]	6-1-06	7-1-06	3.25	4.00	4.00	4.00	7	8
153[72]	7-1-06	8-1-06	3.50	4.00	4.00	4.00	7	8
154[73]	8-1-06	9-1-06	3.50	4.00	4.00	4.00	7	8
155[74]	9-1-06	10-1-06	3.25	4.00	4.00	4.00	7	8
156[75]	10-1-06	11-1-06	3.00	4.00	4.00	4.00	7	8
158[77]	12-1-06	1-1-07	3.00	4.00	4.00	4.00	7	8

Rate set	For plans with a valuation date		Immediate annuity rate (percent)	Deferred annuities (percent)				
	On or After	Before		i_1	i_2	i_3	n_1	n_2
159[78]	1-1-07	2-1-07	2.75	4.00	4.00	4.00	7	8
160[79]	2-1-07	3-1-07	3.00	4.00	4.00	4.00	7	8
161[80]	3-1-07	4-1-07	3.00	4.00	4.00	4.00	7	8
162[81]	4-1-07	5-1-07	2.75	4.00	4.00	4.00	7	8
163[82]	5-1-07	6-1-07	3.00	4.00	4.00	4.00	7	8
164[83]	6-1-07	7-1-07	3.00	4.00	4.00	4.00	7	8
165[84]	7-1-07	8-1-07	3.25	4.00	4.00	4.00	7	8
166[85]	8-1-07	9-1-07	3.50	4.00	4.00	4.00	7	8
167[86]	9-1-07	10-1-07	3.25	4.00	4.00	4.00	7	8
168[87]	10-1-07	11-1-07	3.25	4.00	4.00	4.00	7	8
169[88]	11-1-07	12-1-07	3.25	4.00	4.00	4.00	7	8
170[89]	12-1-07	1-1-08	3.00	4.00	4.00	4.00	7	8

Rate set	For plans with a valuation date		Immediate annuity rate (percent)	Deferred annuities (percent)				
	On or After	Before		i_1	i_2	i_3	n_1	n_2
171[90]	1-1-08	2-1-08	3.00	4.00	4.00	4.00	7	8
172[91]	2-1-08	3-1-08	3.25	4.00	4.00	4.00	7	8
173[92]	3-1-08	4-1-08	3.00	4.00	4.00	4.00	7	8
174[93]	4-1-08	5-1-08	3.25	4.00	4.00	4.00	7	8
175[94]	5-1-08	6-1-08	3.25	4.00	4.00	4.00	7	8
176[95]	6-1-08	7-1-08	3.25	4.00	4.00	4.00	7	8
177[96]	7-1-08	8-1-08	3.50	4.00	4.00	4.00	7	8
178[97]	8-1-08	9-1-08	3.25	4.00	4.00	4.00	7	8
179[98]	9-1-08	10-1-08	3.50	4.00	4.00	4.00	7	8
180[99]	10-1-08	11-1-08	3.25	4.00	4.00	4.00	7	8
181[100]	11-1-08	12-1-08	3.75	4.00	4.00	4.00	7	8

Rate set	For plans with a valuation date		Immediate annuity rate (percent)	Deferred annuities (percent)				
	On or After	Before		i_1	i_2	i_3	n_1	n_2
182[101]	12-1-08	1-1-09	4.75	4.00	4.00	4.00	7	8
183[102]	1-1-09	2-1-09	4.00	4.00	4.00	4.00	7	8
184[103]	2-1-09	3-1-09	3.00	4.00	4.00	4.00	7	8
185[104]	3-1-09	4-1-09	3.50	4.00	4.00	4.00	7	8
186[105]	4-1-09	5-1-09	3.25	4.00	4.00	4.00	7	8
187[106]	5-1-09	6-1-09	3.50	4.00	4.00	4.00	7	8
188[107]	6-1-09	7-1-09	3.75	4.00	4.00	4.00	7	8
189[108]	7-1-09	8-1-09	3.75	4.00	4.00	4.00	7	8
190[109]	8-1-09	9-1-09	3.00	4.00	4.00	4.00	7	8
191[110]	9-1-09	10-1-09	3.00	4.00	4.00	4.00	7	8
192[111]	10-1-09	11-1-09	2.50	4.00	4.00	4.00	7	8
193[112]	11-1-09	12-1-09	2.25	4.00	4.00	4.00	7	8
194[113]	12-1-09	1-1-10	2.50	4.00	4.00	4.00	7	8
195[114]	1-1-10	2-1-10	2.50	4.00	4.00	4.00	7	8
196[115]	2-1-10	3-1-10	2.75	4.00	4.00	4.00	7	8
197[116]	3-1-10	4-1-10	2.75	4.00	4.00	4.00	7	8
198[117]	4-1-10	5-1-10	2.75	4.00	4.00	4.00	7	8
199[118]	5-1-10	6-1-10	3.00	4.00	4.00	4.00	7	8
200[119]	6-1-10	7-1-10	2.75	4.00	4.00	4.00	7	8
201[120]	7-1-10	8-1-10	2.50	4.00	4.00	4.00	7	8
202[121]	8-1-10	9-1-10	2.25	4.00	4.00	4.00	7	8
203[122]	9-1-10	10-1-10	2.25	4.00	4.00	4.00	7	8
204[123]	10-1-10	11-1-10	1.75	4.00	4.00	4.00	7	8
205[124]	11-1-10	12-1-10	1.75	4.00	4.00	4.00	7	8
206[125]	12-1-10	1-1-11	2.25	4.00	4.00	4.00	7	8
207[126]	1-1-11	2-1-11	2.25	4.00	4.00	4.00	7	8
208[127]	2-1-11	3-1-11	2.50	4.00	4.00	4.00	7	8
209[128]	3-1-11	4-1-11	2.50	4.00	4.00	4.00	7	8
210[129]	4-1-11	5-1-11	2.50	4.00	4.00	4.00	7	8
211[130]	5-1-11	6-1-11	2.50	4.00	4.00	4.00	7	8
212[131]	6-1-11	7-1-11	2.50	4.00	4.00	4.00	7	8
213[132]	7-1-11	8-1-11	2.25	4.00	4.00	4.00	7	8
214[133]	8-1-11	9-1-11	2.25	4.00	4.00	4.00	7	8
215[134]	9-1-11	10-1-11	2.25	4.00	4.00	4.00	7	8
216[135]	10-1-11	11-1-11	1.75	4.00	4.00	4.00	7	8
217[136]	11-1-11	12-1-11	1.50	4.00	4.00	4.00	7	8
218[137]	12-1-11	1-1-12	1.50	4.00	4.00	4.00	7	8
219[138]	1-1-12	2-1-12	1.25	4.00	4.00	4.00	7	8
220[139]	2-1-12	3-1-12	1.25	4.00	4.00	4.00	7	8
221[140]	3-1-12	4-1-12	1.25	4.00	4.00	4.00	7	8
222[141]	4-1-12	5-1-12	1.25	4.00	4.00	4.00	7	8
223[142]	5-1-12	6-1-12	1.50	4.00	4.00	4.00	7	8
224[143]	6-1-12	7-1-12	1.25	4.00	4.00	4.00	7	8
225[144]	7-1-12	8-1-12	1.00	4.00	4.00	4.00	7	8
226[145]	8-1-12	9-1-12	1.00	4.00	4.00	4.00	7	8
227[146]	9-1-12	10-1-12	0.75	4.00	4.00	4.00	7	8
228[147]	10-1-12	11-1-12	0.75	4.00	4.00	4.00	7	8
229[148]	11-1-12	12-1-12	0.75	4.00	4.00	4.00	7	8
230[149]	12-1-12	1-1-13	0.75	4.00	4.00	4.00	7	8
231[150]	1-1-13	2-1-13	0.75	4.00	4.00	4.00	7	8
232[151]	2-1-13	3-1-13	0.75	4.00	4.00	4.00	7	8
233[152]	3-1-13	4-1-13	1.00	4.00	4.00	4.00	7	8
234[153]	4-1-13	5-1-13	1.00	4.00	4.00	4.00	7	8
235[154]	5-1-13	6-1-13	1.00	4.00	4.00	4.00	7	8
236[155]	6-1-13	7-1-13	0.75	4.00	4.00	4.00	7	8

¶ 15,424D   Reg. § 4022.83

Rate set	For plans with a valuation date		Immediate annuity rate (percent)	Deferred annuities (percent)				
	On or After	Before		i_1	i_2	i_3	n_1	n_2
237[156]	7-1-13	8-1-13	1.25	4.00	4.00	4.00	7	8
238[157]	8-1-13	9-1-13	1.75	4.00	4.00	4.00	7	8
239[158]	9-1-13	10-1-13	1.50	4.00	4.00	4.00	7	8
240[159]	10-1-13	11-1-13	1.75	4.00	4.00	4.00	7	8
241[160]	11-1-13	12-1-13	1.75	4.00	4.00	4.00	7	8
242[161]	12-1-13	1-1-14	1.75	4.00	4.00	4.00	7	8
243[162]	1-1-14	2-1-14	1.75	4.00	4.00	4.00	7	8
244[163]	2-1-14	3-1-14	1.75	4.00	4.00	4.00	7	8
245[164]	3-1-14	4-1-14	1.50	4.00	4.00	4.00	7	8
246[165]	4-1-14	5-1-14	1.50	4.00	4.00	4.00	7	8
247[166]	5-1-14	6-1-14	1.50	4.00	4.00	4.00	7	8
248[167]	6-1-14	7-1-14	1.25	4.00	4.00	4.00	7	8
249[168]	7-1-14	8-1-14	1.25	4.00	4.00	4.00	7	8
250[169]	8-1-14	9-1-14	1.25	4.00	4.00	4.00	7	8
251[170]	9-1-14	10-1-14	1.25	4.00	4.00	4.00	7	8
252[171]	10-1-14	11-1-14	1.00	4.00	4.00	4.00	7	8
253[172]	11-1-14	12-1-14	1.25	4.00	4.00	4.00	7	8
254[173]	12-1-14	1-1-15	1.00	4.00	4.00	4.00	7	8
255[174]	1-1-15	2-1-15	1.00	4.00	4.00	4.00	7	8
256[175]	2-1-15	3-1-15	1.00	4.00	4.00	4.00	7	8
257[176]	3-1-15	4-1-15	0.50	4.00	4.00	4.00	7	8
258[177]	4-1-15	5-1-15	0.75	4.00	4.00	4.00	7	8
259[178]	5-1-15	6-1-15	0.75	4.00	4.00	4.00	7	8
260[179]	6-1-15	7-1-15	0.75	4.00	4.00	4.00	7	8
261[180]	7-1-15	8-1-15	1.25	4.00	4.00	4.00	7	8
262[181]	8-1-15	9-1-15	1.50	4.00	4.00	4.00	7	8
263[182]	9-1-15	10-1-15	1.25	4.00	4.00	4.00	7	8
264[183]	10-1-15	11-1-15	1.25	4.00	4.00	4.00	7	8
265[184]	11-1-15	12-1-15	1.25	4.00	4.00	4.00	7	8
266[185]	12-1-15	1-1-16	1.25	4.00	4.00	4.00	7	8
267[186]	1-1-16	2-1-16	1.25	4.00	4.00	4.00	7	8
268[187]	2-1-16	3-1-16	1.25	4.00	4.00	4.00	7	8
269[188]	3-1-16	4-1-16	1.25	4.00	4.00	4.00	7	8
270[189]	4-1-16	5-1-16	1.00	4.00	4.00	4.00	7	8
271[190]	5-1-16	6-1-16	1.00	4.00	4.00	4.00	7	8
272[191]	6-1-16	7-1-16	0.75	4.00	4.00	4.00	7	8
273[192]	7-1-16	8-1-16	0.75	4.00	4.00	4.00	7	8
274[193]	8-1-16	9-1-16	0.50	4.00	4.00	4.00	7	8
275[194]	9-1-16	10-1-16	0.50	4.00	4.00	4.00	7	8
276[195]	10-1-16	11-1-16	0.50	4.00	4.00	4.00	7	8
277[196]	11-1-16	12-1-16	0.50	4.00	4.00	4.00	7	8
278[197]	12-1-16	1-1-17	0.75	4.00	4.00	4.00	7	8
279[198]	1-1-17	2-1-17	1.25	4.00	4.00	4.00	7	8
280[199]	2-1-17	3-1-17	1.25	4.00	4.00	4.00	7	8
281[200]	3-1-17	4-1-17	1.25	4.00	4.00	4.00	7	8
282[201]	4-1-17	5-1-17	1.00	4.00	4.00	4.00	7	8
283[202]	5-1-17	6-1-17	1.00	4.00	4.00	4.00	7	8
284[203]	6-1-17	7-1-17	1.00	4.00	4.00	4.00	7	8
285[204]	7-1-17	8-1-17	1.00	4.00	4.00	4.00	7	8
286[205]	8-1-17	9-1-17	0.75	4.00	4.00	4.00	7	8
287[206]	9-1-17	10-1-17	1.00	4.00	4.00	4.00	7	8
288[207]	10-1-17	11-1-17	0.75	4.00	4.00	4.00	7	8
289[208]	11-1-17	12-1-17	0.75	4.00	4.00	4.00	7	8
290[209]	12-1-17	1-1-18	0.75	4.00	4.00	4.00	7	8
291[210]	1-1-18	2-1-18	0.75	4.00	4.00	4.00	7	8

[1] 65 FR 4369471400.

[2] 65 FR 497378 1500.

[3] 65 FR 5598691500.

[4] 65 FR 60859101300.

[5] 65 FR 68892111500.

[6] 65 FR 78414121500.

[7] 66 FR 282211201.

[8] 66 FR 1036521501.

[9] 66 FR 1503131501.

[10] 66 FR 1908941301.

[11] 66 FR 2679151501.

[12] 66 FR 3254361501.

[13] 66 FR 3670271301.

[14] 66 FR 4273781501.

[15] 66 FR 4788591401.

[16] 66 FR 52315101501.

[17] 66 FR 57369111501.

[18] 66 FR 64744121401.

[19] 67 FR 186111502.

[20] 67 FR 707621502.

[21] 67 FR 1157231502.

[22] 67 FR 1811241502.

[23] 67 FR 3461051502.

[24] 67 FR 4085061402.

[25] 67 FR 4637671502.

[26] 67 FR 5330781502.

[27] 67 FR 5794991302.

[28] 67 FR 63544101502.

[29] 67 FR 69121111502.

[30] 67 FR 76682121302.

[31] 68 FR 196511503.

[32] 68 FR 741921403.

[33] 68 FR 1230331403.

[34] 68 FR 1812241503.

[35] 68 FR 2620651503.

[36] 68 FR 3529461303.

[37] 68 FR 4171471503.

[38] 68 FR 4878781503.

[39] 68 FR 5388091503.

[40] 68 FR 59315101503.

[41] 68 FR 64525111403.

[42] 68 FR 69606121503.

[43] 69 FR 229911504.

[44] 69 FR 711921304.

[45] 69 FR 1207231504.

[46] 69 FR 1992541504.

[47] 69 FR 2676951404.

[48] 69 FR 3330261504.

[49] 69 FR 4233371504.

[50] 69 FR 5007081304.

[51] 69 FR 5550091504.

[52] 69 FR 61150101504.

[53] 69 FR 65543111504.

[54] 69 FR 74973121504.

[55] 70 FR 256811405.

[56] 70 FR 765121505.

[57] 70 FR 1258531505.

[58] 70 FR 1989041505.

[59] 70 FR 2547051305.

[60] 70 FR 34655—6\15\05.

[61] 70 FR 40882—7/15/05.

[62] 70 FR 47725—8/15/05.

[63] 70 FR 54477—9/15/05.

[64] 70 FR 60002—10/14/05.

[65] 70 FR 69277—11/15/\05.

[66] 70 FR 74200—12/15/05.

[67] 71 FR 2147—1/13/06.

[68] 71 FR 7871—2/15/06.

[69] 71 FR 13258—3/15/06.

[70] 71 FR 19429—4/14/06.

[71] 71 FR 27959—5/15/06.

[72] 71 FR 34532—6/15/06.

[73] 71 FR 40011—7/14/06.

¶15,424D   Reg. §4022.83

[74] 71 FR 47090—8/16/06.
[75] 71 FR 54415—9/15/06.
[76] 71 FR 60428—10/13/06.
[77] 71 FR 66455—11/15/06.
[78] 71 FR 75420—12/15/06.
[79] 72 FR 1460—1/12/07.
[80] 72 FR 7349—2/15/07.
[81] 72 FR 12087—3/15/07.
[82] 72 FR 18576—4/13/07.
[83] 72 FR 27243—5/15/07.
[84] 72 FR 33152—6/15/07.
[85] 72 FR 38484—7/13/07.
[86] 72 FR 45637—8/15/07.
[87] 72 FR 52471 9/14/07.
[88] 72 FR 58249—10/15/07.
[89] 72 FR 64150—11/15/07.
[90] 72 FR 71071—12/14/07.
[91] 73 FR 2420—1/15/08.
[92] 73 FR 8816—2/15/08.
[93] 73 FR 13754—3/14/08.
[94] 73 FR 20164—4/15/08.
[95] 73 FR 28037—5/15/08.
[96] 73 FR 33695—6/13/08.
[97] 73 FR 40464—7/15/08.
[98] 73 FR 47831—8/15/08.
[99] 73 FR 53115—9/15/08.
[100] 73 FR 61352—10/16/08.
[101] 73 FR 67389—11/14/08.
[102] 73 FR 78621—12/23/08.
[103] 74 FR 2864—1/16/09.
[104] 74 FR 7180—2/13/09.
[105] 74 FR 11035—3/16/09.
[106] 74 FR 17395—4/15/09 corrected by 74 FR 18290, 4/22/09.
[107] 74 FR 22827—5/15/09.
[108] 74 FR 28163—6/15/09.
[109] 74 FR 34238—7/15/09.
[110] 74 FR 41039—8/14/09.
[111] 74 FR 47098—9/15/09.
[112] 74 FR 52886—10/15/09.
[113] 74 FR 58544—11/13/09.
[114] 74 FR 66234—12/15/09.
[115] 75 FR 2437—1/15/10.
[116] 75 FR 6857—2/12/10.
[117] 75 FR 12122—3/15/10.
[118] 75 FR 19542—4/15/10.
[119] 75 FR 27189—5/14/10.
[120] 75 FR 33689—6/15/10.
[121] 75 FR 41091—7/15/10.
[122] 75 FR 49408—8/13/10.
[123] 75 FR 55966—9/15/10.
[124] 75 FR 63380—10/15/10.
[125] 75 FR 69588—11/15/10.
[126] 75 FR 78161—12/15/10.
[127] 76 FR 2578—1/14/11.
[128] 76 FR 8649—2/15/11.
[129] 76 FR 13883—3/15/11.
[130] 76 FR 21252—4/15/11.
[131] 76 FR 27889—5/13/11.
[132] 76 FR 34847—6/15/11.
[133] 76 FR 41689—7/15/11.
[134] 76 FR 50413—8/15/11.
[135] 76 FR 56974—9/15/11.
[136] 76 FR 63836—10/14/11.
[137] 76 FR 70639—11/15/11.
[138] 76 FR 77900—12/15/11.
[139] 77 FR 2015—1/13/12.
[140] 77 FR 8730—2/15/12.
[141] 77 FR 15256—3/15/12.
[142] 77 FR 22215—4/13/12.
[143] 77 FR 28477—5/15/12.
[144] 77 FR 35838—6/15/12.
[145] 77 FR 41270—7/13/12.
[146] 77 FR 48855—8/15/12.

[147] 77 FR 56770—9/14/12.
[148] 77 FR 62434—10/15/12.
[149] 77 FR 68685—11/16/12.
[150] 77 FR 74353—12/14/12.
[151] 78 FR 2881—1/15/13.
[152] 78 FR 11093—2/15/13.
[153] 78 FR 16401—3/15/13.
[154] 78 FR 22192—4/15/13.
[155] 78 FR 28490—5/15/13.
[156] 78 FR 35754—6/14/13.
[157] 78 FR 42009—7/15/13.
[158] 78 FR 49682—8/15/13.
[159] 78 FR 56603—9/13/13.
[160] 78 FR 62426—10/22/13.
[161] 78 FR 68739—11/15/13.
[162] 78 FR 75897—12/13/13.
[163] 79 FR 2591—1/15/14.
[164] 79 FR 8857—2/14/14.
[165] 79 FR 15009—3/18/14.
[166] 79 FR 21127—4/15/14.
[167] 79 FR 27731—5/15/14.
[168] 79 FR 33860—6/13/14.
[169] 79 FR 41133—7/15/14.
[170] 79 FR 48038—8/15/14.
[171] 79 FR 54904—9/15/14.
[172] 79 FR 61761—10/15/14.
[173] 79 FR 68116—11/14/14.
[174] 79 FR 74021—12/15/14.
[175] 80 FR 2010—1/15/15.
[176] 80 FR 7967—2/13/15.
[177] 80 FR 13239—3/13/15.
[178] 80 FR 20158—4/15/15.
[179] 80 FR 27857—5/15/15.
[180] 80 FR 34052—6/15/15.
[181] 80 FR 41436—7/15/15.
[182] 80 FR 48688—8/14/15.
[183] 80 FR 55249—9/15/15.
[183] 80 FR 55249—9/15/15.
[184] 80 FR 61981—10/15/15.
[185] 80 FR 70170—11/13/15.
[186] 80 FR 77569—12/15/15.
[187] 81 FR 2088—1/15/16.
[188] 81 FR 7454—2/12/16.
[189] 81 FR 13742—3/15/16.
[190] 81 FR 22184—4/15/16.
[191] 81 FR 29767—5/13/16.
[192] 81 FR 38948—6/15/16.
[193] 81 FR 45969—7/15/16.
[194] 81 FR 53921—8/15/16.
[195] 81 FR 63414—9/15/16.
[196] 81 FR 70940—10/14/16.
[197] 81 FR 80002—11/15/16.
[198] 81 FR 91032—12/16/16.
[199] 82 FR 6243—1/19/17.
[200] 82 FR 10707—2/15/17.
[201] 82 FR 13755—3/15/17.
[202] 82 FR 17938—4/14/17.
[203] 82 FR 22279—5/15/17.
[204] 82 FR 27422—6/15/17.
[205] 82 FR 32463—7/14/17.
[206] 82 FR 38597—8/15/17.
[207] 82 FR 43299—9/15/17.
[208] 82 FR 47613—10/13/17.
[209] 82 FR 52848—11/15/17.
[210] 82 FR 59515—12/15/17.

[¶ 15,424E]

§ 4022.83 Appendix C to Part 4022: Lump Sum Interest Rates for Private-Sector payments.

[In using this table: (1) For benefits for which the participant or beneficiary is entitled to be in pay status on the valuation date, the immediate annuity rate shall apply; (2) For benefits for which the deferral period is y years (where y is an integer and $0 \leq y \leq n_1$), interest rate i_1 shall apply from the valuation date for a period of y years, and thereafter the immediate annuity rate shall apply; (3) For benefits for which the deferral period is y years (where y is an integer and $n_1 \leq y \leq n_1 + n_2$), interest rate i_2 shall apply from the valuation date for a period of $y - n_1$ years, interest rate i_1 shall apply for the following n_1 years, and thereafter the immediate annuity rate shall apply; (4) For benefits for which the deferral period is y years (where y is an integer and $y > n_1 + n_2$), interest rate i_3 shall apply from the valuation date for a period of $y - n_1 - n_2$ years, interest rate i_2 shall apply for the following n_2 years, interest rate i_1 shall apply for the following n_1 years, and thereafter the immediate annuity rate shall apply.][Amended 3/17/00 by 65 FR 14751, 14753.]

Rate set	For plans with a valuation date		Immediate annuity rate (percent)	Deferred annuities (percent)				
	On or After	Before		i_1	i_2	i_3	n_1	n_2
1	11-1-93	12-1-93	4.25	4.00	4.00	4.00	7	8
2	12-1-93	1-1-94	4.25	4.00	4.00	4.00	7	8
3	1-1-94	2-1-94	4.50	4.00	4.00	4.00	7	8
4	2-1-94	3-1-94	4.50	4.00	4.00	4.00	7	8
5	3-1-94	4-1-94	4.50	4.00	4.00	4.00	7	8
6	4-1-94	5-1-94	4.75	4.00	4.00	4.00	7	8
7	5-1-94	6-1-94	5.25	4.50	4.00	4.00	7	8
8	6-1-94	7-1-94	5.25	4.50	4.00	4.00	7	8
9	7-1-94	8-1-94	5.50	4.75	4.00	4.00	7	8
10	8-1-94	9-1-94	5.75	5.00	4.00	4.00	7	8

Rate set	For plans with a valuation date		Immediate annuity rate (percent)	Deferred annuities (percent)				
	On or After	Before		i_1	i_2	i_3	n_1	n_2
11	9-1-94	10-1-94	5.50	4.75	4.00	4.00	7	8
12	10-1-94	11-1-94	5.50	4.75	4.00	4.00	7	8
13	11-1-94	12-1-94	6.00	5.25	4.00	4.00	7	8
14	12-1-94	1-1-95	6.25	5.50	4.25	4.00	7	8
15	1-1-95	2-1-95	6.00	5.25	4.00	4.00	7	8
16	2-1-95	3-1-95	6.00	5.25	4.00	4.00	7	8
17	3-1-95	4-1-95	6.00	5.25	4.00	4.00	7	8
18	4-1-95	5-1-95	5.75	5.00	4.00	4.00	7	8
19	5-1-95	6-1-95	5.50	4.75	4.00	4.00	7	8
20	6-1-95	7-1-95	5.50	4.75	4.00	4.00	7	8

Rate set	For plans with a valuation date		Immediate annuity rate (percent)	Deferred annuities (percent)				
	On or After	Before		i_1	i_2	i_3	n_1	n_2
21	7-1-95	8-1-95	4.75	4.00	4.00	4.00	7	8
22	8-1-95	9-1-95	4.75	4.00	4.00	4.00	7	8
23	9-1-95	10-1-95	5.00	4.25	4.00	4.00	7	8
24	10-1-95	11-1-95	4.75	4.00	4.00	4.00	7	8
25	11-1-95	12-1-95	4.75	4.00	4.00	4.00	7	8
26	12-1-95	1-1-96	4.50	4.00	4.00	4.00	7	8
27	1-1-96	2-1-96	4.50	4.00	4.00	4.00	7	8
28	2-1-96	3-1-96	4.25	4.00	4.00	4.00	7	8
29	3-1-96	4-1-96	4.25	4.00	4.00	4.00	7	8
30	4-1-96	5-1-96	4.75	4.00	4.00	4.00	7	8

Rate set	For plans with a valuation date		Immediate annuity rate (percent)	Deferred annuities (percent)				
	On or After	Before		i_1	i_2	i_3	n_1	n_2
31	5-1-96	6-1-96	5.00	4.25	4.00	4.00	7	8
32	6-1-96	7-1-96	5.00	4.25	4.00	4.00	7	8
33	7-1-96	8-1-96	5.00	4.25	4.00	4.00	7	8
34	8-1-96	9-1-96	5.25	4.50	4.00	4.00	7	8
35	9-1-96	10-1-96	5.25	4.50	4.00	4.00	7	8
36	10-1-96	11-1-96	5.25	4.50	4.00	4.00	7	8

Rate set	For plans with a valuation date		Immediate annuity rate (percent)	Deferred annuities (percent)				
	On or After	Before		i_1	i_2	i_3	n_1	n_2
37	11-1-96	12-1-96	5.00	4.25	4.00	4.00	7	8
38	12-1-96	1-1-97	4.75	4.00	4.00	4.00	7	8
39	1-1-97	2-1-97	4.50	4.00	4.00	4.00	7	8

Rate set	For plans with a valuation date		Immediate annuity rate (percent)	Deferred annuities (percent)				
	On or After	Before		i_1	i_2	i_3	n_1	n_2
40	2-1-97	3-1-97	4.75	4.00	4.00	4.00	7	8
41	3-1-97	4-1-97	5.00	4.25	4.00	4.00	7	8
42	4-1-97	5-1-97	4.75	4.00	4.00	4.00	7	8
43	5-1-97	6-1-97	5.00	4.25	4.00	4.00	7	8
44	6-1-97	7-1-97	5.25	4.50	4.00	4.00	7	8
45	7-1-97	8-1-97	5.25	4.50	4.00	4.00	7	8
46	8-1-97	9-1-97	4.75	4.00	4.00	4.00	7	8
47	9-1-97	10-1-97	4.50	4.00	4.00	4.00	7	8
48	10-1-97	11-1-97	4.75	4.00	4.00	4.00	7	8
49	11-1-97	12-1-97	4.50	4.00	4.00	4.00	7	8

Rate set	For plans with a valuation date		Immediate annuity rate (percent)	Deferred annuities (percent)				
	On or After	Before		i_1	i_2	i_3	n_1	n_2
50	12-1-97	1-1-98	4.50	4.00	4.00	4.00	7	8
51	1-1-98	2-1-98	4.25	4.00	4.00	4.00	7	8
52	2-1-98	3-1-98	4.25	4.00	4.00	4.00	7	8
53	3-1-98	4-1-98	4.25	4.00	4.00	4.00	7	8
54	4-1-98	5-1-98	4.25	4.00	4.00	4.00	7	8
55	5-1-98	6-1-98	4.25	4.00	4.00	4.00	7	8
56	6-1-98	7-1-98	4.25	4.00	4.00	4.00	7	8
57	7-1-98	8-1-98	4.00	4.00	4.00	4.00	7	8
58	8-1-98	9-1-98	4.00	4.00	4.00	4.00	7	8
59	9-1-98	10-1-98	4.00	4.00	4.00	4.00	7	8

Rate set	For plans with a valuation date		Immediate annuity rate (percent)	Deferred annuities (percent)				
	On or After	Before		i_1	i_2	i_3	n_1	n_2
60	10-1-98	11-1-98	4.00	4.00	4.00	4.00	7	8
61	11-1-98	12-1-98	3.75	4.00	4.00	4.00	7	8
62	12-1-98	1-1-99	4.00	4.00	4.00	4.00	7	8
63	1-1-99	2-1-99	4.00	4.00	4.00	4.00	7	8
64	2-1-99	3-1-99	4.00	4.00	4.00	4.00	7	8
65	3-1-99	4-1-99	4.00	4.00	4.00	4.00	7	8
66	4-1-99	5-1-99	4.25	4.00	4.00	4.00	7	8
67	5-1-99	6-1-99	4.25	4.00	4.00	4.00	7	8
68	6-1-99	7-1-99	4.25	4.00	4.00	4.00	7	8
69	7-1-99	8-1-99	4.50	4.00	4.00	4.00	7	8

Rate set	For plans with a valuation date		Immediate annuity rate (percent)	Deferred annuities (percent)				
	On or After	Before		i_1	i_2	i_3	n_1	n_2
70	8-1-99	9-1-99	5.00	4.25	4.00	4.00	7	8
71	9-1-99	10-1-99	5.00	4.25	4.00	4.00	7	8
72	10-1-99	11-1-99	5.00	4.25	4.00	4.00	7	8
73	11-1-99	12-1-99	5.00	4.25	4.00	4.00	7	8
74	12-1-99	1-1-00	5.25	4.50	4.00	4.00	7	8
75	1-1-00	2-1-00	5.00	4.25	4.00	4.00	7	8
76	2-1-00	3-1-00	5.25	4.50	4.00	4.00	7	8
77	3-1-00	4-1-00	5.25	4.50	4.00	4.00	7	8

¶15,424E   Reg. §4022.83

Rate set	For plans with a valuation date		Immediate annuity rate (percent)	Deferred annuities (percent)				
	On or After	Before		i_1	i_2	i_3	n_1	n_2
78	4-1-00	5-1-00	5.25	4.50	4.00	4.00	7	8
79	5-1-00	6-1-00	5.25	4.50	4.00	4.00	7	8

Rate set	For plans with a valuation date		Immediate annuity rate (percent)	Deferred annuities (percent)				
	On or After	Before		i_1	i_2	i_3	n_1	n_2
80	6-1-00	7-1-00	5.25	4.50	4.00	4.00	7	8
81	7-1-00	8-1-00	5.50	4.75	4.00	4.00	7	8
82 [1]	8-1-00	9-1-00	5.25	4.50	4.00	4.00	7	8
83 [2]	9-1-00	10-1-00	5.25	4.50	4.00	4.00	7	8
84 [3]	10-1-00	11-1-00	5.00	4.25	4.00	4.00	7	8
85 [4]	11-1-00	12-1-00	5.25	4.50	4.00	4.00	7	8
86 [5]	12-1-00	1-1-01	5.25	4.50	4.00	4.00	7	8
87 [6]	1-1-01	2-1-01	5.00	4.25	4.00	4.00	7	8
88 [7]	2-1-01	3-1-01	4.75	4.00	4.00	4.00	7	8
89 [8]	3-1-01	4-1-01	4.75	4.00	4.00	4.00	7	8
90 [9]	4-1-01	5-1-01	4.75	4.00	4.00	4.00	7	8

Rate set	For plans with a valuation date		Immediate annuity rate (percent)	Deferred annuities (percent)				
	On or After	Before		i_1	i_2	i_3	n_1	n_2
91 [10]	5-1-01	6-1-01	4.75	4.00	4.00	4.00	7	8
92 [11]	6-1-01	7-1-01	5.00	4.25	4.00	4.00	7	8
93 [12]	7-1-01	8-1-01	5.00	4.25	4.00	4.00	7	8
94 [13]	8-1-01	9-1-01	4.75	4.00	4.00	4.00	7	8
95 [14]	9-1-01	10-1-01	4.50	4.00	4.00	4.00	7	8
96 [15]	10-1-01	11-1-01	4.50	4.00	4.00	4.00	7	8
97 [16]	11-1-01	12-1-01	4.75	4.00	4.00	4.00	7	8
98 [17]	12-1-01	1-1-02	4.50	4.00	4.00	4.00	7	8
99 [18]	1-1-02	2-1-02	4.50	4.00	4.00	4.00	7	8
100 [19]	2-1-02	3-1-02	4.75	4.00	4.00	4.00	7	8

Rate set	For plans with a valuation date		Immediate annuity rate (percent)	Deferred annuities (percent)				
	On or After	Before		i_1	i_2	i_3	n_1	n_2
101 [20]	3-1-02	4-1-02	4.50	4.00	4.00	4.00	7	8
102 [21]	4-1-02	5-1-02	4.25	4.00	4.00	4.00	7	8
103 [22]	5-1-02	6-1-02	4.75	4.00	4.00	4.00	7	8
104 [23]	6-1-02	7-1-02	4.50	4.00	4.00	4.00	7	8
105 [24]	7-1-02	8-1-02	4.50	4.00	4.00	4.00	7	8
106 [25]	8-1-02	9-1-02	4.25	4.00	4.00	4.00	7	8
107 [26]	9-1-02	10-1-02	4.25	4.00	4.00	4.00	7	8
108 [27]	10-1-02	11-1-02	4.00	4.00	4.00	4.00	7	8
109 [28]	11-1-02	12-1-02	3.75	4.00	4.00	4.00	7	8
110 [29]	12-1-02	1-1-03	4.00	4.00	4.00	4.00	7	8

Rate set	For plans with a valuation date		Immediate annuity rate (percent)	Deferred annuities (percent)				
	On or After	Before		i_1	i_2	i_3	n_1	n_2
111 [30]	1-1-03	2-1-03	4.00	4.00	4.00	4.00	7	8
112 [31]	2-1-03	3-1-03	3.75	4.00	4.00	4.00	7	8
113 [32]	3-1-03	4-1-03	3.75	4.00	4.00	4.00	7	8
114 [33]	4-1-03	5-1-03	3.50	4.00	4.00	4.00	7	8
115 [34]	5-1-03	6-1-03	3.50	4.00	4.00	4.00	7	8
116 [35]	6-1-03	7-1-03	3.50	4.00	4.00	4.00	7	8
117 [36]	7-1-03	8-1-03	3.00	4.00	4.00	4.00	7	8
118 [37]	8-1-03	9-1-03	3.00	4.00	4.00	4.00	7	8
119 [38]	9-1-03	10-1-03	3.50	4.00	4.00	4.00	7	8

Rate set	For plans with a valuation date		Immediate annuity rate (percent)	Deferred annuities (percent)				
	On or After	Before		i_1	i_2	i_3	n_1	n_2
120[39]	10-1-03	11-1-03	3.50	4.00	4.00	4.00	7	8
121[40]	11-1-03	12-1-03	3.25	4.00	4.00	4.00	7	8
122[41]	12-1-03	1-1-04	3.25	4.00	4.00	4.00	7	8

Rate set	For plans with a valuation date		Immediate annuity rate (percent)	Deferred annuities (percent)				
	On or After	Before		i_1	i_2	i_3	n_1	n_2
123[42]	1-1-04	2-1-04	3.25	4.00	4.00	4.00	7	8
124[43]	2-1-04	3-1-04	3.25	4.00	4.00	4.00	7	8
125[44]	3-1-04	4-1-04	3.00	4.00	4.00	4.00	7	8
126[45]	4-1-04	5-1-04	3.00	4.00	4.00	4.00	7	8
127[46]	5-1-04	6-1-04	3.00	4.00	4.00	4.00	7	8
128[47]	6-1-04	7-1-04	3.50	4.00	4.00	4.00	7	8
129[48]	7-1-04	8-1-04	3.50	4.00	4.00	4.00	7	8
130[49]	8-1-04	9-1-04	3.50	4.00	4.00	4.00	7	8
131[50]	9-1-04	10-1-04	3.25	4.00	4.00	4.00	7	8
132[51]	10-1-04	11-1-04	3.00	4.00	4.00	4.00	7	8
133[52]	11-1-04	12-1-04	2.75	4.00	4.00	4.00	7	8
134[53]	12-1-04	1-1-05	2.75	4.00	4.00	4.00	7	8

Rate set	For plans with a valuation date		Immediate annuity rate (percent)	Deferred annuities (percent)				
	On or After	Before		i_1	i_2	i_3	n_1	n_2
135[54]	1-1-05	2-1-05	3.00	4.00	4.00	4.00	7	8
136[55]	2-1-05	3-1-05	3.00	4.00	4.00	4.00	7	8
137[56]	3-1-05	4-1-05	2.75	4.00	4.00	4.00	7	8
138[57]	4-1-05	5-1-05	2.75	4.00	4.00	4.00	7	8
139[58]	5-1-05	6-1-05	2.75	4.00	4.00	4.00	7	8
140[59]	6-1-05	7-1-05	2.50	4.00	4.00	4.00	7	8
141[60]	7-1-05	8-1-05	2.50	4.00	4.00	4.00	7	8
142[61]	8-1-05	9-1-05	2.25	4.00	4.00	4.00	7	8
143[62]	9-1-05	10-1-05	2.50	4.00	4.00	4.00	7	8
144[63]	10-1-05	11-1-05	2.25	4.00	4.00	4.00	7	8
145[64]	11-1-05	12-1-05	2.50	4.00	4.00	4.00	7	8
146[65]	12-1-05	1-1-06	2.75	4.00	4.00	4.00	7	8

Rate set	For plans with a valuation date		Immediate annuity rate (percent)	Deferred annuities (percent)				
	On or After	Before		i_1	i_2	i_3	n_1	n_2
147[66]	1-1-06	2-1-06	2.75	4.00	4.00	4.00	7	8
148[67]	2-1-06	3-1-06	2.75	4.00	4.00	4.00	7	8
149[68]	3-1-06	4-1-06	2.75	4.00	4.00	4.00	7	8
150[69]	4-1-06	5-1-06	2.75	4.00	4.00	4.00	7	8
151[70]	5-1-06	6-1-06	3.00	4.00	4.00	4.00	7	8
152[71]	6-1-06	7-1-06	3.25	4.00	4.00	4.00	7	8
153[72]	7-1-06	8-1-06	3.50	4.00	4.00	4.00	7	8
154[73]	8-1-06	9-1-06	3.50	4.00	4.00	4.00	7	8
155[74]	9-1-06	10-1-06	3.25	4.00	4.00	4.00	7	8
156[75]	10-1-06	11-1-06	3.00	4.00	4.00	4.00	7	8
157[76]	11-1-06	12-1-06	2.75	4.00	4.00	4.00	7	8
158[77]	12-1-06	1-1-07	3.00	4.00	4.00	4.00	7	8

Rate set	For plans with a valuation date		Immediate annuity rate (percent)	Deferred annuities (percent)				
	On or After	Before		i_1	i_2	i_3	n_1	n_2
159[78]	1-1-07	2-1-07	2.75	4.00	4.00	4.00	7	8
160[79]	2-1-07	3-1-07	3.00	4.00	4.00	4.00	7	8
161[80]	3-1-07	4-1-07	3.00	4.00	4.00	4.00	7	8

¶ 15,424E   Reg. § 4022.83

Rate set	For plans with a valuation date		Immediate annuity rate (percent)	Deferred annuities (percent)				
	On or After	Before		i_1	i_2	i_3	n_1	n_2
162[81]	4-1-07	5-1-07	2.75	4.00	4.00	4.00	7	8
163[82]	5-1-07	6-1-07	3.00	4.00	4.00	4.00	7	8
164[83]	6-1-07	7-1-07	3.00	4.00	4.00	4.00	7	8
165[84]	7-1-07	8-1-07	3.25	4.00	4.00	4.00	7	8
166[85]	8-1-07	9-1-07	3.50	4.00	4.00	4.00	7	8
168[87]	10-1-07	11-1-07	3.25	4.00	4.00	4.00	7	8
169[88]	11-1-07	12-1-07	3.25	4.00	4.00	4.00	7	8
170[89]	12-1-07	1-1-08	3.00	4.00	4.00	4.00	7	8

Rate set	For plans with a valuation date		Immediate annuity rate (percent)	Deferred annuities (percent)				
	On or After	Before		i_1	i_2	i_3	n_1	n_2
171[90]	1-1-08	2-1-08	3.00	4.00	4.00	4.00	7	8
172[91]	2-1-08	3-1-08	3.25	4.00	4.00	4.00	7	8
173[92]	3-1-08	4-1-08	3.00	4.00	4.00	4.00	7	8
174[93]	4-1-08	5-1-08	3.25	4.00	4.00	4.00	7	8
175[94]	5-1-08	6-1-08	3.25	4.00	4.00	4.00	7	8
176[95]	6-1-08	7-1-08	3.25	4.00	4.00	4.00	7	8
177[96]	7-1-08	8-1-08	3.50	4.00	4.00	4.00	7	8
178[97]	8-1-08	9-1-08	3.25	4.00	4.00	4.00	7	8
179[98]	9-1-08	10-1-08	3.50	4.00	4.00	4.00	7	8
180[99]	10-1-08	11-1-08	3.25	4.00	4.00	4.00	7	8
181[100]	11-1-08	12-1-08	3.75	4.00	4.00	4.00	7	8
182[101]	12-1-08	1-1-09	4.75	4.00	4.00	4.00	7	8
183[102]	1-1-09	2-1-09	4.00	4.00	4.00	4.00	7	8
184[103]	2-1-09	3-1-09	3.00	4.00	4.00	4.00	7	8
185[104]	3-1-09	4-1-09	3.50	4.00	4.00	4.00	7	8
186[105]	4-1-09	5-1-09	3.25	4.00	4.00	4.00	7	8
187[106]	5-1-09	6-1-09	3.50	4.00	4.00	4.00	7	8
187[106]	5-1-09	6-1-09	3.50	4.00	4.00	4.00	7	8
188[107]	6-1-09	7-1-09	3.75	4.00	4.00	4.00	7	8
189[108]	7-1-09	8-1-09	3.75	4.00	4.00	4.00	7	8
190[109]	8-1-09	9-1-09	3.00	4.00	4.00	4.00	7	8
191[110]	9-1-09	10-1-09	3.00	4.00	4.00	4.00	7	8
192[111]	10-1-09	11-1-09	2.50	4.00	4.00	4.00	7	8
193[112]	11-1-09	12-1-09	2.25	4.00	4.00	4.00	7	8
194[113]	12-1-09	1-1-10	2.50	4.00	4.00	4.00	7	8
195[114]	1-1-10	2-1-10	2.50	4.00	4.00	4.00	7	8
196[115]	2-1-10	3-1-10	2.75	4.00	4.00	4.00	7	8
197[116]	3-1-10	4-1-10	2.75	4.00	4.00	4.00	7	8
198[117]	4-1-10	5-1-10	2.75	4.00	4.00	4.00	7	8
199[118]	5-1-10	6-1-10	3.00	4.00	4.00	4.00	7	8
200[119]	6-1-10	7-1-10	2.75	4.00	4.00	4.00	7	8
201[120]	7-1-10	8-1-10	2.50	4.00	4.00	4.00	7	8
202[121]	8-1-10	9-1-10	2.25	4.00	4.00	4.00	7	8
203[122]	9-1-10	10-1-10	2.25	4.00	4.00	4.00	7	8
204[123]	10-1-10	11-1-10	1.75	4.00	4.00	4.00	7	8
205[124]	11-1-10	12-1-10	1.75	4.00	4.00	4.00	7	8
206[125]	12-1-10	1-1-11	2.25	4.00	4.00	4.00	7	8
207[126]	1-1-11	2-1-11	2.25	4.00	4.00	4.00	7	8
208[127]	2-1-11	3-1-11	2.50	4.00	4.00	4.00	7	8
209[128]	3-1-11	4-1-11	2.50	4.00	4.00	4.00	7	8
210[129]	4-1-11	5-1-11	2.50	4.00	4.00	4.00	7	8
211[130]	5-1-11	6-1-11	2.50	4.00	4.00	4.00	7	8
212[131]	6-1-11	7-1-11	2.50	4.00	4.00	4.00	7	8
213[132]	7-1-11	8-1-11	2.25	4.00	4.00	4.00	7	8

Rate set	For plans with a valuation date		Immediate annuity rate (percent)	Deferred annuities (percent)				
	On or After	Before		i_1	i_2	i_3	n_1	n_2
214[133]	8-1-11	9-1-11	2.25	4.00	4.00	4.00	7	8
215[134]	9-1-11	10-1-11	2.25	4.00	4.00	4.00	7	8
216[135]	10-1-11	11-1-11	1.75	4.00	4.00	4.00	7	8
217[136]	11-1-11	12-1-11	1.50	4.00	4.00	4.00	7	8
218[137]	12-1-11	1-1-12	1.50	4.00	4.00	4.00	7	8
219[138]	1-1-12	2-1-12	1.25	4.00	4.00	4.00	7	8
220[139]	2-1-12	3-1-12	1.25	4.00	4.00	4.00	7	8
221[140]	3-1-12	4-1-12	1.25	4.00	4.00	4.00	7	8
222[141]	4-1-12	5-1-12	1.25	4.00	4.00	4.00	7	8
223[142]	5-1-12	6-1-12	1.50	4.00	4.00	4.00	7	8
224[143]	6-1-12	7-1-12	1.25	4.00	4.00	4.00	7	8
225[144]	7-1-12	8-1-12	1.00	4.00	4.00	4.00	7	8
226[145]	8-1-12	9-1-12	1.00	4.00	4.00	4.00	7	8
227[146]	9-1-12	10-1-12	0.75	4.00	4.00	4.00	7	8
228[147]	10-1-12	11-1-12	0.75	4.00	4.00	4.00	7	8
229[148]	11-1-12	12-1-12	0.75	4.00	4.00	4.00	7	8
230[149]	12-1-12	1-1-13	0.75	4.00	4.00	4.00	7	8
231[150]	1-1-13	2-1-13	0.75	4.00	4.00	4.00	7	8
232[151]	2-1-13	3-1-13	0.75	4.00	4.00	4.00	7	8
233[152]	3-1-13	4-1-13	1.00	4.00	4.00	4.00	7	8
234[153]	4-1-13	5-1-13	1.00	4.00	4.00	4.00	7	8
235[154]	5-1-13	6-1-13	1.00	4.00	4.00	4.00	7	8
236[155]	6-1-13	7-1-13	0.75	4.00	4.00	4.00	7	8
237[156]	7-1-13	8-1-13	1.25	4.00	4.00	4.00	7	8
238[157]	8-1-13	9-1-13	1.75	4.00	4.00	4.00	7	8
239[158]	9-1-13	10-1-13	1.50	4.00	4.00	4.00	7	8
240[159]	10-1-13	11-1-13	1.75	4.00	4.00	4.00	7	8
241[160]	11-1-13	12-1-13	1.75	4.00	4.00	4.00	7	8
242[161]	12-1-13	1-1-14	1.75	4.00	4.00	4.00	7	8
243[162]	1-1-14	2-1-14	1.75	4.00	4.00	4.00	7	8
244[163]	2-1-14	3-1-14	1.75	4.00	4.00	4.00	7	8
245[164]	3-1-14	4-1-14	1.50	4.00	4.00	4.00	7	8
246[165]	4-1-14	5-1-14	1.50	4.00	4.00	4.00	7	8
247[166]	5-1-14	6-1-14	1.50	4.00	4.00	4.00	7	8
248[167]	6-1-14	7-1-14	1.25	4.00	4.00	4.00	7	8
249[168]	7-1-14	8-1-14	1.25	4.00	4.00	4.00	7	8
250[169]	8-1-14	9-1-14	1.25	4.00	4.00	4.00	7	8
251[170]	9-1-14	10-1-14	1.25	4.00	4.00	4.00	7	8
252[171]	10-1-14	11-1-14	1.00	4.00	4.00	4.00	7	8
253[172]	11-1-14	12-1-14	1.25	4.00	4.00	4.00	7	8
254[173]	12-1-14	1-1-15	1.00	4.00	4.00	4.00	7	8
255[174]	1-1-15	2-1-15	1.00	4.00	4.00	4.00	7	8
256[175]	2-1-15	3-1-15	1.00	4.00	4.00	4.00	7	8
257[176]	3-1-15	4-1-15	0.50	4.00	4.00	4.00	7	8
258[177]	4-1-15	5-1-15	0.75	4.00	4.00	4.00	7	8
259[178]	5-1-15	6-1-15	0.75	4.00	4.00	4.00	7	8
260[179]	6-1-15	7-1-15	0.75	4.00	4.00	4.00	7	8
261[180]	7-1-15	8-1-15	1.25	4.00	4.00	4.00	7	8
262[181]	8-1-15	9-1-15	1.50	4.00	4.00	4.00	7	8
263[182]	9-1-15	10-1-15	1.25	4.00	4.00	4.00	7	8
264[183]	10-1-15	11-1-15	1.25	4.00	4.00	4.00	7	8
265[184]	11-1-15	12-1-15	1.25	4.00	4.00	4.00	7	8
266[185]	12-1-15	1-1-16	1.25	4.00	4.00	4.00	7	8
267[186]	1-1-16	2-1-16	1.25	4.00	4.00	4.00	7	8
268[187]	2-1-16	3-1-16	1.25	4.00	4.00	4.00	7	8

¶15,424E   Reg. §4022.83

Rate set	For plans with a valuation date		Immediate annuity rate (percent)	Deferred annuities (percent)				
	On or After	Before		i_1	i_2	i_3	n_1	n_2
269[188]	3-1-16	4-1-16	1.25	4.00	4.00	4.00	7	8
270[189]	4-1-16	5-1-16	1.00	4.00	4.00	4.00	7	8
271[190]	5-1-16	6-1-16	1.00	4.00	4.00	4.00	7	8
272[191]	6-1-16	7-1-16	0.75	4.00	4.00	4.00	7	8
273[192]	7-1-16	8-1-16	0.75	4.00	4.00	4.00	7	8
274[193]	8-1-16	9-1-16	0.50	4.00	4.00	4.00	7	8
275[194]	9-1-16	10-1-16	0.50	4.00	4.00	4.00	7	8
276[195]	10-1-16	11-1-16	0.50	4.00	4.00	4.00	7	8
277[196]	11-1-16	12-1-16	0.50	4.00	4.00	4.00	7	8
278[197]	12-1-16	1-1-17	0.75	4.00	4.00	4.00	7	8
279[198]	1-1-17	2-1-17	1.25	4.00	4.00	4.00	7	8
280[199]	2-1-17	3-1-17	1.25	4.00	4.00	4.00	7	8
281[200]	3-1-17	4-1-17	1.25	4.00	4.00	4.00	7	8
282[201]	4-1-17	5-1-17	1.00	4.00	4.00	4.00	7	8
283[202]	5-1-17	6-1-17	1.00	4.00	4.00	4.00	7	8
284[203]	6-1-17	7-1-17	1.00	4.00	4.00	4.00	7	8
285[204]	7-1-17	8-1-17	1.00	4.00	4.00	4.00	7	8
286[205]	8-1-17	9-1-17	0.75	4.00	4.00	4.00	7	8
287[206]	9-1-17	10-1-17	1.00	4.00	4.00	4.00	7	8
288[207]	10-1-17	11-1-17	0.75	4.00	4.00	4.00	7	8
289[208]	11-1-17	12-1-17	0.75	4.00	4.00	4.00	7	8
290[209]	12-1-17	1-1-18	0.75	4.00	4.00	4.00	7	8
291[210]	1-1-18	2-1-18	0.75	4.00	4.00	4.00	7	8

[1] 65 FR 43694—7/14/00.
[2] 65 FR 49737—8/15/00.
[3] 65 FR 55896—9/15/00.
[4] 65 FR 60859—10/13/00.
[5] 65 FR 68892—11/15/00.
[6] 65 FR 78414—12/15/00.
[7] 66 FR 2822—1/12/01.
[8] 66 FR 10365—2/15/01.
[9] 66 FR 15031—3/15/01.
[10] 66 FR 19089—4/13/01.
[11] 66 FR 26791—5/15/01.
[12] 66 FR 32543—6/15/01.
[13] 66 FR 36702—7/13/01.
[14] 66 FR 42737—8/15/01.
[15] 66 FR 47885—9/14/01.
[16] 66 FR 52315—10/15/01.
[17] 66 FR 57369—11/15/01.
[18] 66 FR 64744—12/14/01.
[19] 67 FR 1861—1/15/02.
[20] 67 FR 7076—2/15/02.
[21] 67 FR 11572—3/15/02.
[22] 67 FR 18112—4/15/02.
[23] 67 FR 34610—5/15/02.
[24] 67 FR 40850—6/14/02.
[25] 67 FR 46376—7/15/02.
[26] 67 FR 53307—8/15/02.
[27] 67 FR 57949—9/13/02.
[28] 67 FR 63544—10/15/02.
[29] 67 FR 69121—11/15/02.
[30] 67 FR 76682—12/13/02.
[31] 68 FR 1965—1/15/03.
[32] 68 FR 7419—2/14/03.
[33] 68 FR 12303—3/14/03.
[34] 68 FR 18122—4/15/03.
[35] 68 FR 26206—5/15/03.
[36] 68 FR 35294—6/13/03.
[37] 68 FR 41714—7/15/03.
[38] 68 FR 48787—8/15/03.
[39] 68 FR 53880—9/15/03.

[40] 68 FR 59315—10/15/03.
[41] 68 FR 64525—11/14/03.
[42] 68 FR 69606—12/15/03.
[43] 69 FR 2299—1/15/04.
[44] 69 FR 7119—2/13/04.
[45] 69 FR 12072—3/15/04.
[46] 69 FR 19925—4/15/04.
[47] 69 FR 26769—5/14/04.
[48] 69 FR 33302—6/15/04.
[49] 69 FR 42333—7/15/04.
[50] 69 FR 50070—8/13/04.
[51] 69 FR 55500—9/15/04.
[52] 69 FR 61150—10/15/04.
[53] 69 FR 65543—11/15/04.
[54] 69 FR 74973—12/15/04.
[55] 70 FR 2568—1/14/05.
[56] 70 FR 7651—2/15/05.
[57] 70 FR 12585—3/15/05.
[58] 70 FR 19890—4/15/05.
[59] 70 FR 25470—5/13/05.
[60] 70 FR 34655—6/15/05.
[61] 70 FR 40882—7/15/05.
[62] 70 FR 47725—8/15/05.
[63] 70 FR 54477—9/15/05.
[64] 70 FR 60002—10/14/05.
[65] 70 FR 69277—11/15/05.
[66] 70 FR 74200—12/15/05.
[67] 71 FR 2147—1/13/06.
[68] 71 FR 7871—2/15/06.
[69] 71 FR 13258—3/15/06.
[70] 71 FR 19429—4/14/06.
[71] 71 FR 27959—5/15/06.
[72] 71 FR 34532—6/15/06.
[73] 71 FR 40011—7/14/06.
[74] 71 FR 47090—8/16/06.
[75] 71 FR 54415—9/15/06.
[76] 71 FR 60428—10/13/06.
[77] 71 FR 66455—11/15/06.
[78] 71 FR 75420—12/15/06.
[79] 72 FR 1460—1/12/07.
[80] 72 FR 7349—2/15/07.
[81] 72 FR 12087—3/15/07.
[82] 72 FR 18576—4/13/07.
[83] 72 FR 27243—5/15/07.
[84] 72 FR 33152—6/15/07.
[85] 72 FR 38484—7/13/07.
[86] 72 FR 45637—8/15/07.
[87] 72 FR 52471—9/14/07.
[88] 72 FR 58249—10/15/07.
[89] 72 FR 64150—11/15/07.
[90] 72 FR 71071—12/14/07.
[91] 73 FR 2420—1/15/08.
[92] 73 FR 8816—2/15/08.
[93] 73 FR 13754—3/14/08.
[94] 73 FR 20164—4/15/08.
[95] 73 FR 28037—5/15/08.
[96] 73 FR 33695—6/13/08.
[97] 73 FR 40464—7/15/08.
[98] 73 FR 47831—8/15/08.
[99] 73 FR 53115—9/15/08.
[100] 73 FR 61352—10/16/08.
[101] 73 FR 67389—11/14/08.
[102] 73 FR 78621—12/23/08.
[103] 74 FR 2864—1/16/09.
[104] 74 FR 7180—2/13/09.
[105] 74 FR 11035—3/16/09.
[106] 74 FR 17395—4/15/09 [corrected by 74 FR 18290, 4/22/09].
[107] 74 FR 22828—5/15/09.
[108] 74 FR 28163—6/15/09.
[109] 74 FR 34238—7/15/09.
[110] 74 FR 41039—8/14/09.
[111] 74 FR 47098—9/15/09.
[112] 74 FR 52886—10/15/09.

¶15,424E   Reg. §4022.83

[113] 74 FR 58544—11/13/09.
[114] 74 FR 66234—12/15/09.
[115] 75 FR 2437—1/15/10.
[116] 75 FR 6858—2/12/10.
[117] 75 FR 12122—3/15/10.
[118] 75 FR 19542—4/15/10.
[119] 75 FR 27190—5/14/10.
[120] 75 FR 33689—6/15/10.
[121] 75 FR 41092—7/15/10.
[122] 75 FR 49408—8/13/10.
[123] 75 FR 55966—9/15/10.
[124] 75 FR 63380—10/15/10.
[125] 75 FR 69588—11/15/10.
[126] 75 FR 78161—12/15/10.
[127] 76 FR 2578—1/14/11.
[128] 76 FR 8649—2/15/11.
[129] 76 FR 13883—3/15/11.
[130] 76 FR 21252—4/15/11.
[131] 76 FR 27889—5/13/11.
[132] 76 FR 34847—6/15/11.
[133] 76 FR 41689—7/15/11.
[134] 76 FR 50413—8/15/11.
[135] 76 FR 56974—9/15/11.
[136] 76 FR 63836—10/14/11.
[137] 76 FR 70639—11/15/11.
[138] 76 FR 77900—12/15/11.
[139] 77 FR 2015—1/13/12.
[140] 77 FR 8730—2/15/12.
[141] 77 FR 15256—3/15/12.
[142] 77 FR 22215—4/13/12.
[143] 77 FR 28477—5/15/12.
[144] 77 FR 35838—6/15/12.
[145] 77 FR 41270—7/13/12.
[146] 77 FR 48855—8/15/12.
[147] 77 FR 56770—9/14/12.
[148] 77 FR 62434—10/15/12.
[149] 77 FR 68685—11/16/12.
[150] 77 FR 74353—12/14/12.
[151] 78 FR 2881—1/15/13.
[152] 78 FR 11093—2/15/13.
[153] 78 FR 16401—3/15/13.
[154] 78 FR 22192—4/15/13.
[155] 78 FR 28490—5/15/13.
[156] 78 FR 35754—6/14/13.
[157] 78 FR 42009—7/15/13.
[158] 78 FR 49682—8/15/13.
[159] 78 FR 56603—9/13/13.
[160] 78 FR 62426—10/22/13.
[161] 78 FR 68739—11/15/13.
[162] 78 FR 75897—12/13/13.
[163] 79 FR 2591—1/15/14.
[164] 79 FR 8857—2/14/14.
[165] 79 FR 15009—3/18/14.
[166] 79 FR 21127—4/15/14.
[167] 79 FR 27731—5/15/14.
[168] 79 FR 33860—6/13/14.
[169] 79 FR 41133—7/15/14.
[170] 79 FR 48038—8/15/14.
[171] 79 FR 54904—9/15/14.
[172] 79 FR 61761—10/15/14.
[173] 79 FR 68116—11/14/14.
[174] 79 FR 74021—12/15/14.
[175] 80 FR 2010—1/15/15.
[176] 80 FR 7967—2/13/15.
[177] 80 FR 13239—3/13/15.
[178] 80 FR 20158—4/15/15.
[179] 80 FR 27857—5/15/15.
[180] 80 FR 34052—6/15/15.
[181] 80 FR 41436—7/15/15.
[182] 80 FR 48688—8/14/15.
[183] 80 FR 55249—9/15/15.
[184] 80 FR 61981—10/15/15.
[185] 80 FR 70170—11/13/15.

[186] 80 FR 77569—12/15/15.
[187] 81 FR 2088—1/15/16.
[188] 81 FR 7454—2/12/16.
[189] 81 FR 13742—3/15/16.
[190] 81 FR 22184—4/15/16.
[191] 81 FR 29767—5/13/16.
[192] 81 FR 38948—6/15/16.
[193] 81 FR 45969—7/15/16.
[194] 81 FR 53921—8/15/16.
[195] 81 FR 63414—9/15/16.
[196] 81 FR 70940—10/14/16.
[197] 81 FR 80002—11/15/16.
[198] 81 FR 91032—12/16/16.
[199] 82 FR 6243—1/19/17.
[200] 82 FR 10707—2/15/17.
[201] 82 FR 13755—3/15/17.
[202] 82 FR 17938—4/14/17.
[203] 82 FR 22279—5/15/17.
[204] 82 FR 27422—6/15/17.
[205] 82 FR 32463—7/14/17.
[206] 82 FR 38597—8/15/17.
[207] 82 FR 43299—9/15/17.
[208] 82 FR 47613—10/13/17.
[209] 82 FR 52848—11/15/17.
[210] 82 FR 59515—12/15/17.

[¶ 15,424F]

§ 4022.83 **Appendix D to Part 4022: Maximum Guaranteeable Monthly Benefit.**

[Appendix D was removed by the PBGC on December 1, 2009 (74 FR 62697). For a historical list of the maximum guaranteed benefits for participants retiring at age 65, see CCH PENSION PLAN GUIDE ¶ 49. In addition, the PBGC maintains a list of maximum monthly guaranteed benefits at www.pbgc.gov—click on "Workers & Retirees", then on "Maximum monthly guarantee tables" under the heading "Benefits Information" in the center column.]

Subpart F—Certain Payments Owed Upon Death

[¶ 15,425]

§ 4022.91 **When do these rules apply?**

(a) *Types of benefits.* Provided the conditions in paragraphs (b) and (c) of this section are satisfied, these rules (§§ 4022.91 through 4022.95) apply to any benefits we may owe you (including benefits we owe you because your plan owed them) at the time of your death, such as a payment of a lump-sum benefit that we calculated as of your plan's termination date but have not yet paid you or a back payment to reimburse you for monthly underpayments. We may owe you benefits at the time of your death if—

(1) You are a participant in a terminated plan;

(2) You are a beneficiary (including an alternate payee) of a participant; or

(3) You are a designee or other payee (e.g., a participant's next of kin) under these rules, as explained in § 4022.93.

(b) *Payments do not continue after death.* These rules apply only if payments do not continue after your death. (If payments continue after your death, we will make up any underpayment to you at the time of your death under the rule in § 4022.81(d)(2)(i) by paying it to the person who is entitled to receive those continuing payments.) Payments do not continue after your death if—

(1) Your benefit is not in the form of a joint-and-survivor or other annuity under which payments may continue after your death (e.g., a certain-and-continuous annuity);

(2) Your benefit is in the form of a joint-and-survivor annuity and the person designated to receive survivor benefits died before you; or

(3) Your benefit is in the form of another type of annuity under which payments may continue after your death (e.g., a certain-and-continuous annuity) but you die with no payments owed for future periods.

(c) *Time of death.* These rules apply only if you die—

(1) On or after the date we take over your plan (as trustee); or

(2) Before the date we take over your plan, to the extent that, by that date, the plan administrator has not paid all benefits owed to you at the time of your death.

(d) *Effect of plan or will.* These rules apply even if there is a contrary provision in a plan or will.

[¶ 15,425A]

§ 4022.92 **What definitions do I need to know for these rules?**

You need to know three definitions from § 4001.2 of this chapter (PBGC, person, and plan) and the following definitions:

"We" means the PBGC.

"You" means the person to whom we may owe benefits at the time of death.

[¶ 15,425B]

§ 4022.93 **Who will get benefits the PBGC may owe me at the time of my death?**

(a) *In general.* Except as provided in paragraphs (b) and (c) of this section (which explain what happens if you die before the date we take over your plan or within 180 days after the date we take over your plan), we will pay any benefits we owe you at the time of your death to the person(s) surviving you in the following order—

(1) *Designee with the PBGC.* The person(s) you designated with us to get any benefits we may owe you at the time of your death. See § 4022.94 for information on designating with us.

(2) *Spouse. Your spouse.* We will consider a person to whom you are married to be your spouse even if you and that person are separated, unless a decree of divorce or annulment has been entered in a court.

(3) *Children.* Your children and descendants of your deceased children.

(i) *Adopted children.* In determining who is a child or descendant, an adopted child is treated the same way as a natural child.

(ii) *Child dies before parent.* If one of your children dies before you, any of your grandchildren through that deceased child will equally divide that deceased child's share; if one of your grandchildren through that deceased child dies before that deceased child, any of your great-grandchildren through that deceased grandchild will equally divide that deceased grandchild's share; and so on.

(4) *Parents. Your parents.* A parent includes an adoptive parent.

(5) *Estate.* Your estate, provided your estate is open.

(6) *Next of kin.* Your next of kin in accordance with applicable state law.

(b) *Pre-trusteeship deaths.* If you die before the date we take over your plan and, by that date, the plan administrator has not paid all benefits owed to you at the time of your death, we will pay any benefits we owe you at the time of your death to the person(s) designated by or under the plan to get those benefits (provided the designation clearly applies to those benefits). If there is no such designation, we will pay those benefits to your spouse, children, parents, estate, or next of kin under the rules in paragraphs (a) (2) through (a)(6) of this section.

(c) *Deaths shortly after trusteeship.* If you die within 180 days after the date we take over your plan and you have not designated anyone with the PBGC under paragraph (a)(1) of this section, we will pay any benefits we owe you at the time of your death to the person(s) designated by or under the plan to get those benefits (provided the designation clearly applies to those benefits) before paying those benefits to your spouse, children, parents, estate, or next of kin under the rules in paragraphs (a) (2) through (a)(6) of this section.

[¶ 15,425C]

§ 4022.94 **What are the PBGC's rules on designating a person to get benefits the PBGC may owe me at the time of my death?**

(a) *When you may designate.* At any time on or after the date we take over your plan, you may designate with us who will get any benefits we owe you at the time of your death.

(b) *Change of designee.* If you want to change the person(s) you designate with us, you must submit another designation to us.

(c) *If your designee dies before you.*

(1) *In general.* If the person(s) you designate with us dies before you or at the same time as you, we will treat you as not having designated anyone with us (unless you named an alternate designee who survives you). Therefore, you should keep your designation with us current.

(2) *Simultaneous deaths.* If you and a person you designated die as a result of the same event, we will treat you and that person as having died at the same time, provided you and that person die within 30 days of each other.

[¶ 15,425D]

§ 4022.95 **Examples.**

The following examples show how the rules in § § 4022.91 through 4022.94 apply. For examples on how these rules apply in the case of a certain-and-continuous annuity, see § 4022.104.

At the time of his death, Charlie was receiving payments under a joint-and-survivor annuity. Charlie designated Ellen to receive survivor benefits under his joint-and-survivor annuity. We underpaid Charlie for periods before his death. At the time of his death, we owed Charlie a back payment to reimburse him for those underpayments.

(a) *Example 1:* where surviving beneficiary is alive at participant's death. Ellen survived Charlie. As explained in § 4022.91(b), because Ellen is entitled to survivor benefits under the joint-and-survivor annuity, we would pay Ellen the back payment.

(b) *Example 2:* where surviving beneficiary predeceases participant. Ellen died before Charlie. As explained in § § 4022.91(b) and 4022.93, because benefits do not continue after Charlie's death under the joint-and-survivor annuity, we would pay the back payment to the person(s) Charlie designated to receive any payments we might owe him at the time of his death. If Charlie did not designate anyone to receive those payments or his designee died before him, we would pay the back payment to the person(s) surviving Charlie in the following order: spouse, children, parents, estate and next of kin.

Subpart G—Certain-and-Continuous and Similar Annuity Payments Owed for Future Periods After Death

[¶ 15,426]

§ 4022.101 **When do these rules apply?**

(a) *In general.* These rules (§ § 4022.101 through 4022.104) apply only if you die—

(1) *Required payments for future periods.* Without having received all required payments for future periods under a form of annuity promising that, regardless of a participant's death, there will be annuity payments for a certain period of time (e.g., a certain-and-continuous annuity) or until a certain amount is paid (e.g., a cash-refund annuity or installment-refund annuity);

(2) *No surviving beneficiary.* Without a surviving beneficiary designated to receive the payments described in paragraph (a)(1) of this section; and

(3) *Time of death.*

(i) On or after the date we take over your plan (as trustee); or

(ii) Before the date we take over your plan, to the extent that, by that date, the plan administrator has not paid any required payments for future periods.

(b) *Effect of plan or will.* These rules apply even if there is a contrary provision in a plan or will.

(c) *Payments owed at time of death.* See § § 4022.91 through 4022.95 for rules that apply to benefits we may owe you at the time of your death, such as a correction for monthly underpayments.

[¶ 15,426A]

§ 4022.102 **What definitions do I need to know for these rules?**

You need to know three definitions from § 4001.2 of this chapter (PBGC, person, and plan) and the following definitions:

"We" means the PBGC.

"You" means the person who might die—

(1) Without having received all required payments for future periods under a form of annuity promising that, regardless of a participant's death, there will be annuity payments for a certain period of time (e.g., a certain-and-continuous annuity) or until a certain amount is paid (e.g., a cash-refund annuity or installment-refund annuity); and

(2) Without a surviving beneficiary designated to receive the payments described in paragraph (1) of this definition.

[¶ 15,426B]

§ 4022.103 **Who will get benefits if I die when payments for future periods under a certain-and-continuous or similar annuity are owed upon my death?**

If you die at a time when payments are owed for future periods under a form of annuity promising that, regardless of a participant's death, there will be annuity payments for a certain period of time (e.g., a certain-and-continuous annuity) or until a certain amount is paid (e.g., a cash-refund annuity or installment-refund annuity), and there is no surviving beneficiary designated to receive such payments, we will pay the remaining payments to the person determined under the rules in § 4022.93.

[¶ 15,426C]

§ 4022.104 **Examples.**

The following examples show how the rules in § § 4022.101 through 4022.103 and 4022.91 through 4022.94 apply in the case of a certain-and-continuous annuity.

(a) *C&C annuity with no underpayment.* At the time of his death, Charlie was receiving payments (in the correct amount) under a 5-year certain-and-continuous annuity. Charlie designated Ellen to receive any payments we might owe for periods after his death (but did not designate an alternate beneficiary to receive those payments in case Ellen died before him). Charlie died with three years of payments remaining.

(1) *Example 1:* where surviving beneficiary predeceases participant. Ellen died before Charlie. As explained in § § 4022.103 and 4022.93, we would pay the remaining three years of payments to the person(s) surviving Charlie in the following order: spouse, children, parents, estate and next of kin.

(2) *Example 2:* where surviving beneficiary dies during certain period. Ellen survived Charlie and lived another year. We pay Ellen one year of payments. As explained in § § 4022.103 and 4022.93, we would pay the remaining two years of payments to the person Ellen designated to receive any payments we might owe for periods after Ellen's death. If Ellen did not designate anyone to receive those payments or her designee died before her, we would pay the remaining year of payments to the person(s) surviving Ellen in the following order: spouse, children, parents, estate, next of kin.

(b) *C&C annuity with underpayment.* At the time of his death, Charlie was receiving payments under a 5-year certain-and-continuous annuity. Charlie designated Ellen to receive any payments we might owe for periods after his death. We underpaid Charlie for periods before his death. At the time of his death, we owed Charlie a back payment to reimburse him for those underpayments.

(1) *Example 3:* where participant dies during certain period. Charlie died with three years of payments remaining. Ellen survived Charlie and lived at least another three years. We pay Ellen the remaining three years of payments. As explained in § 4022.91(b), because Ellen is entitled to survivor benefits under the certain-and-continuous annuity, we would pay Ellen the back payment for the underpayments to Charlie (and for any underpayments to Ellen).

(2) *Example 4:* where participant and surviving beneficiary die during certain period. Charlie died with three years of payments remaining. Ellen survived Charlie and lived another year. We paid Ellen one year of payments. Ellen designated Jean to receive any payments we might owe for periods after Ellen's death. Jean survived Ellen and lives at least another two years. We pay Jean the remaining two years of payments. As explained in § 4022.91(b), because Jean is entitled to survivor benefits under the certain-and-continuous annuity, we would pay Jean the back payment for the underpayments to Charlie (and for any underpayments to Ellen).

(3) *Example 5:* where participant dies after certain period. Charlie died after receiving seven years of payments. As explained in §§ 4022.91(b) and 4022.93, because benefits do not continue after Charlie's death under the certain-and-continuous annuity, we would pay the back payment to the person(s) Charlie designated to receive any payments we might owe him at the time of his death in case he died after the end of certain period. If Charlie did not designate anyone to receive those payments or his designee died before him, we would pay the back payment to the person(s) surviving Charlie in the following order: spouse, children, parents, estate and next of kin.

[¶ 15,429H]
MULTIEMPLOYER PLAN BENEFITS GUARANTEED

Act Sec. 4022A. (a) BENEFITS OF COVERED PLANS SUBJECT TO GUARANTEE.—The corporation shall guarantee, in accordance with this section, the payment of all nonforfeitable benefits (other than benefits becoming nonforfeitable solely on account of the termination of a plan) under a multiemployer plan—

(1) to which this title applies, and

(2) which is insolvent under section 4245(b) or 4281(d)(2).

Act Sec. 4022A. (b)(1)(A) BENEFITS OR BENEFIT INCREASES NOT ELIGIBLE FOR GUARANTEE.—For purposes of this section, a benefit or benefit increase which has been in effect under a plan for less than 60 months is not eligible for the corporation's guarantee. For purposes of this paragraph, any month of any plan year during which the plan was insolvent or terminated (within the meaning of section 4041A(a)(2)) shall not be taken into account.

(B) For purposes of this section, a benefit or benefit increase which has been in effect under a plan for less than 60 months before the first day of the plan year for which an amendment reducing the benefit or the benefit increase is taken into account under section 4244A(a)(2) in determining the minimum contribution requirement for the plan year under section 4243(b) is not eligible for the corporation's guarantee.

(2) For purposes of this section—

(A) the date on which a benefit or a benefit increase under a plan is first in effect is the later of—

(i) the date on which the documents establishing or increasing the benefit were executed, or

(ii) the effective date of the benefit or benefit increase;

(B) the period of time for which a benefit or a benefit increase has been in effect under a successor plan includes the period of time for which the benefit or benefit increase was in effect under a previous established plan; and

(C) in the case of a plan to which section 4021 did not apply on September 3, 1974, the time periods referred to in this section are computed beginning on the date on which section 4021 first applies to the plan.

Act Sec. 4022A. (c)(1) DETERMINATIONS RESPECTING AMOUNT OF GUARANTEE.—Except as provided in subsection (g), the monthly benefit of a participant or a beneficiary which is guaranteed under this section by the corporation with respect to a plan is the product of—

(A) 100 percent of the accrual rate up to $11, plus 75 percent of the lesser of—

(i) $33, or

(ii) the accrual rate, if any, in excess of $11, and

(B) the number of the participant's years of credited service.

(2) For purposes of this section, the accrual rate is—

(A) the monthly benefit of the participant or beneficiary which is described in subsection (a) and which is eligible for the corporation's guarantee under subsection (b), except that such benefit shall be—

(i) no greater than the monthly benefit which would be payable under the plan at normal retirement age in the form of a single life annuity, and

(ii) determined without regard to any reduction under section 411(a)(3)(E) of the Internal Revenue Code of 1986; divided by

(B) the participant's years of credited service.

(3) For purposes of this subsection—

(A) a year of credited service is a year in which the participant completed—

(i) a full year of participation in the plan, or

(ii) any period of service before participation which is credited for purposes of benefit accrual as the equivalent of a full year of participation;

(B) any year for which the participant is credited for purposes of benefit accrual with a fraction of the equivalent of a full year of participation shall be counted as such a fraction of a year of credited service; and

(C) years of credited service shall be determined by including service which may otherwise be disregarded by the plan under section 411(a)(3)(E) of the Internal Revenue Code of 1986.

(4) For purposes of subsection (a), in the case of a qualified preretirement survivor annuity (as defined in section 205(e)(1)) payable to the surviving spouse of a participant under a multiemployer plan which becomes insolvent under section 4245(b) or 4281(d)(2) or is terminated, such annuity shall not be treated as forfeitable solely because the participant has not died as of the date on which the plan became so insolvent or the termination date.

Act Sec. 4022A. (d) AMOUNT OF GUARANTEE OF REDUCED BENEFIT.—In the case of a benefit which has been reduced under section 411(a)(3)(E) of the Internal Revenue Code of 1954, the corporation shall guarantee the lesser of—

(1) the reduced benefit, or

(2) the amount determined under subsection (c).

Act Sec. 4022A. (e) INELIGIBILITY OF BENEFITS FOR GUARANTEE.—The corporation shall not guarantee benefits under a multiemployer plan which, under section 4022(b)(6), would not be guaranteed under a single-employer plan.

Act Sec. 4022A. (f)(1) STUDY, REPORT, ETC. RESPECTING PREMIUM INCREASE IN EXISTING BASIC-BENEFIT GUARANTEE LEVELS; CONGRESSIONAL PROCEDURES APPLICABLE FOR REVISION OF SCHEDULES.—No later than 5 years after the date of the enactment of the Multiemployer Pension Plan Amendments Act of 1980, and at least every fifth year thereafter, the corporation shall—

(A) conduct a study to determine—

(i) the premiums needed to maintain the basic-benefit guarantee levels for multiemployer plans described in subsection (c), and

(ii) whether the basic-benefit guarantee levels for multiemployer plans may be increased without increasing the basic-benefit premiums for multiemployer plans under this title; and

(B) report such determinations to the Committee on Ways and Means and the Committee on Education and Labor of the House of Representatives and to the Committee on Finance and the Committee on Labor and Human Resources of the Senate.

(2)(A) If the last report described in paragraph (1) indicates that a premium increase is necessary to support the existing basic-benefit guarantee levels for multiemployer plans, the corporation shall transmit to the Committee on Ways and Means and the Committee on Education and Labor of the House of Representatives and to the Committee on Finance and the Committee on Labor and Human Resources of the Senate by March 31 of any calendar year in which congressional action under this subsection is requested—

(i) a revised schedule of basic-benefit guarantees for multiemployer plans which would be necessary in the absence of an increase in premiums approved in accordance with section 4006(b),

(ii) a revised schedule of basic-benefit premiums for multiemployer plans which is necessary to support the existing basic-benefit guarantees for such plans, and

(iii) a revised schedule of basic-benefit guarantees for multiemployer plans for which the schedule of premiums necessary is higher than the existing premium schedule for such plans but lower than the revised schedule of premiums for such plans specified in clause (ii), together with such schedule of premiums.

(B) The revised schedule of increased premiums referred to in subparagraph (A)(ii) or (A)(iii) shall go into effect as approved by the enactment of a joint resolution.

(C) If an increase in premiums is not so enacted, the revised guarantee schedule described in subparagraph (A)(i) shall go into effect on the first day of the second calendar year following the year in which such revised guarantee schedule was submitted to the Congress.

(3)(A) If the last report described in paragraph (1) indicates that basic-benefit guarantees for multiemployer plans can be increased without increasing the basic-benefit premiums for multiemployer plans under this title, the corporation shall submit to the Committee on Ways and Means and the Committee on Education and Labor of the House of Representatives and to the Committee on Finance and the Committee on Labor and Human Resources of the Senate by March 31 of the calendar year in which congressional action under this paragraph is requested—

(i) a revised schedule of increases in the basic-benefit guarantees which can be supported by the existing schedule of basic-benefit premiums for multiemployer plans, and

(ii) a revised schedule of basic-benefit premiums sufficient to support the existing basic-benefit guarantees.

(B) The revised schedules referred to in subparagraph (A)(i) or subparagraph (A)(ii) shall go into effect as approved by the enactment of a joint resolution.

(4)(A) The succeeding subparagraphs of this paragraph are enacted by the Congress as an exercise of the rulemaking power of the Senate and the House of Representatives, respectively, and as such they shall be deemed a part of the rules of each House, respectively, but applicable only with respect to the procedure to be followed in that House in the case of joint resolutions (as defined in subparagraph (B)). Such subparagraphs shall supersede other rules only to the extent that they are inconsistent therewith. They are enacted with full recognition of the constitutional right of either House to change the rules (so far as relating to the procedure of that House) at any time, in the same manner, and to the same extent as in the case of any rule of that House.

(B) For purposes of this subsection, "joint resolution" means only a joint resolution, the matter after the resolving clause of which is as follows: "The proposed schedule described in   transmitted to the Congress by the Pension Benefit Guaranty Corporation on   is hereby approved.", the first blank space therein being filled with "section 4022A(f)(2)(A)(ii) of the Employee Retirement Income Security Act of 1974", "section 4022A(f)(2)(A)(iii) of the Employee Retirement Income Security Act of 1974", "section 4022A(f)(3)(A)(i) of the Employee Retirement Income Security Act of 1974", or "section 4022A(f)(3)(A)(ii) of the Employee Retirement Income Security Act of 1974" (whichever is applicable), and the second blank space therein being filled with the date on which the corporation's message proposing the revision was submitted.

(C) The procedure for disposition of a joint resolution shall be the procedure described in section 4006(b)(4) through (7).

Act Sec. 4022A. (g)(1) GUARANTEE OF PAYMENT OF OTHER CLASSES OF BENEFITS AND ESTABLISHMENT OF TERMS AND CONDITIONS OF GUARANTEE; PROMULGATION OF REGULATIONS FOR ESTABLISHMENT OF SUPPLEMENTAL PROGRAM TO GUARANTEE BENEFITS OTHERWISE INELIGIBLE; STATUS OF BENEFITS; APPLICABILITY OF REVISED SCHEDULE OF PREMIUMS.—The corporation may guarantee the payment of such other classes of benefits under multiemployer plans, and establish the terms and conditions under which those other classes of benefits are guaranteed, as it determines to be appropriate.

(2)(A) The corporation shall prescribe regulations to establish a supplemental program to guarantee benefits under multiemployer plans which would be guaranteed under this section but for the limitations in subsection (c). Such regulations shall be proposed by the corporation no later than the end of the 18th calendar month following the date of the enactment of the Multiemployer Pension Plan Amendment Act of 1980. The regulations shall make coverage under the supplemental program available no later than January 1, 1983. Any election to participate in the supplemental program shall be on a voluntary basis and a plan electing such coverage shall continue to pay the premiums required under section 4006(a)(2)(B) to the revolving fund used pursuant to section 4005 in connection with benefits otherwise guaranteed under this section. Any such election shall be irrevocable, except to the extent otherwise provided by regulations prescribed by the corporation.

(B) The regulations prescribed under this paragraph shall provide—

(i) that a plan must elect coverage under the supplemental program within the time permitted by the regulations;

(ii) unless the corporation determines otherwise, that a plan may not elect supplemental coverage unless the value of the assets of the plan as of the end of the plan year preceding the plan year in which the election must be made is an amount equal to 15 times the total amount of the benefit payments made under the plan for that year; and

(iii) such other reasonable terms and conditions for supplemental coverage, including funding standards and any other reasonable limitations with respect to plans or benefits covered or to means of program financing, as the corporation determines are necessary and appropriate for a feasible supplemental program consistent with the purposes of this title.

(3) Any benefits guaranteed under this subsection shall be considered nonbasic benefits for purposes of this title.

(4)(A) No revised schedule of premiums under this subsection, after the initial schedule, shall go into effect unless—

(i) the revised schedule is submitted to the Congress, and

(ii) a joint resolution described in subparagraph (B) is not enacted before the close of the 60th legislative day after such schedule is submitted to the Congress.

(B) For purposes of subparagraph (A), a joint resolution described in this subparagraph is a joint resolution the matter after the resolving clause of which is as follows: "The revised premium schedule transmitted to the Congress by the Pension Benefit Guaranty Corporation under section 4022A(g)(4) of the Employee Retirement Income Security Act of 1974 on   is hereby disapproved.", the blank space therein being filed with the date on which the revised schedule was submitted.

(C) For purposes of subparagraph (A), the term "legislative day" means any calendar day other than a day on which either House is not in session because of a sine die adjournment or an adjournment of more than 3 days to a day certain.

(D) The procedure for disposition of a joint resolution described in subparagraph (B) shall be the procedure described in paragraphs (4) through (7) of section 4006(b).

(5) Regulations prescribed by the corporation to carry out the provisions of this subsection, may, to the extent provided therein, supersede the requirements of sections 4245, 4261, and 4281, and the requirements of section 418E of the Internal Revenue Code of 1986, but only with respect to benefits guaranteed under this subsection.

Act Sec. 4022A. (h)(1) APPLICABILITY TO NONFORFEITABLE BENEFITS ACCRUED AS OF JULY 30, 1980; MANNER AND EXTENT OF GUARANTEE.—Except as provided in paragraph (3), subsections (b) and (c) shall not apply with respect to the nonforfeitable benefits accrued as of July 29, 1980, with respect to a participant or beneficiary under a multiemployer plan—

(1) who is in pay status on July 29, 1980, or

(2) who is within 36 months of the normal retirement age and has a nonforfeitable right to a pension as of that date.

(2) The benefits described in paragraph (1) shall be guaranteed by the corporation in the same manner and to the same extent as benefits are guaranteed by the corporation under section 4022 (without regard to this section).

(3) This subsection does not apply with respect to a plan for plan years following a plan year—

(A) in which the plan has terminated within the meaning of section 4041A(a)(2), or

(B) in which it is determined by the corporation that substantially all the employers have withdrawn from the plan pursuant to an agreement or arrangement to withdraw.

Amendments

P.L. 113-235, § 110(a), Div. O:

Amended ERISA Sec. 4022A(c) by inserting at the end a new paragraph (4) to read as above.

The above amendment shall apply with respect to multiemployer plan benefit payments becoming payable on or after January 1, 1985, except that the amendment shall not apply in any case where the surviving spouse has died before the date of enactment of this Act (December 16, 2014).

P.L. 106-554, § 951:

Act Sec. 951(a)(1) amended ERISA Sec. 4022A(c)(1) by striking "$5" each place it appears and inserting "$11".

Act Sec. 951(a)(2) amended ERISA Sec. 4022A(c)(1)(A)(i) by striking "$15" and inserting "$33".

Act Sec. 951(a)(3) amended ERISA Sec. 4022A(c) by striking paragraphs (2), (5), and (6) and by redesignating paragraphs (3) and (4) as paragraphs (2) and (3).

Prior to amendment, ERISA Sec. 4022A(c)(2) read as follows:

"(2) Except as provided in paragraph (6) of this subsection and in subsection (g), in applying paragraph (1) with respect to a plan described in paragraph (5)(A), the term '65 percent' shall be substituted in paragraph (1)(A) for the term '75 percent'."

Prior to amendment, ERISA Sec. 4022A(c)(5) read as follows:

"(5)(A) A plan is described in this subparagraph if—

(i) the first plan year—

(I) in which the plan is insolvent under section 4245(b) or 4281(d)(2), and

(II) for which benefits are required to be suspended under section 4245, or reduced or suspended under section 4281, until they do not exceed the levels provided in this subsection,

begins before the year 2000; and

(ii) the plan sponsor has not established to the satisfaction of the corporation that, during the period of 10 consecutive plan years (or of such lesser number of plan years for which the plan was maintained) immediately preceding the first plan year to which the minimum funding standards of section 412 of the Internal Revenue Code of 1986 apply, the total amount of the contributions required under the plan for each plan year was at least equal to the sum of—

(I) the normal cost for that plan year, and

(II) the interest for the plan year (determined under the plan) on the unfunded past service liability for that plan year, determined as of the beginning of that plan year.

(B) A plan shall not be considered to be described in subparagraph (A) if—

(i) it is established to the satisfaction of the corporation that—

(I) the total amount of the contributions received under the plan for the plan years for which the actuarial valuations (performed during the period described in subparagraph (A)(ii)) were performed was at least equal to the sum described in subparagraph (A)(ii); or

(II) the rates of contribution to the plan under the collective bargaining agreements negotiated when the findings of such valuations were available were reasonably expected to provide such contributions;

(ii) the number of actuarial valuations performed during the period described in subparagraph (A)(ii) is—

(I) at least 2, in any case in which such period consists of more than 6 plan years, and

(II) at least 1, in any case in which such period consists of 6 or fewer plan years; and

(iii) if the proposition described in clause (i)(I) is to be established, the plan sponsor certifies that to the best of the plan sponsor's knowledge there is no information available which establishes that the total amount of the contributions received under the plan for any plan year during the period described in subparagraph (A)(ii) for which no valuation was performed is less than the sum described in subparagraph (A)(ii)."

Prior to amendment, ERISA Sec. 4022A(c)(6) read as follows:

"(6) Notwithstanding paragraph (2), in the case of a plan described in paragraph (5)(A), if for any period of 3 consecutive plan years beginning with the first plan year to which the minimum funding standards of section 412 of the Internal Revenue Code of 1986 apply, the value of the assets of the plan for each such plan year is an amount equal to at least 8 times the benefit payments for such plan year—

(A) paragraph (2) shall not apply to such plan; and

(B) the benefit of a participant or beneficiary guaranteed by the corporation with respect to the plan shall be an amount determined under paragraph (1)."

The above amendements shall apply to any multiemployer plan that has not received financial assistance (within the meaning of section 4261 of the Employee Retirement Income Security Act of 1974) within the 1-year period ending on the date of the enactment of this Act.

Amendments

P.L. 101-239, § 7891(a)(1):

Titles I, III, and IV of ERISA (other than sections 3(37)(E), 301(a)(7), and 308, the last sentence of section 408(d), and sections 414(c), 4001(a)(3)(ii), and 4303) are each amended by striking "Internal Revenue Code of 1954" each place it appears and inserting "Internal Revenue Code of 1986" effective October 22, 1986.

P.L. 101-239, § 7893(b):

Amended ERISA Sec. 4022A(f)(2)(B) by striking "the the enactment" and inserting "the enactment" effective for plan years beginning after December 31, 1985.

P.L. 101-239, § 7894(g)(3)(C):

Amended ERISA Sec. 4022A(a)(1) by striking "section 4021" and inserting "this title" effective as if included in P.L. 96-364, § 102.

P.L. 99-272:

Act Sec. 11005(c)(4) amended ERISA Sec. 4022A(f)(2)(B) by striking out "Congress by concurrrent resolution" and inserting "the enactment of a joint resolution."

Act Sec. 11005(c)(5) amended ERISA Sec. 4022A(f)(2)(C) by striking out "approved" and inserting "so enacted."

Act Sec. 11005(c)(6) amended ERISA Sec. 4022A(f)(3)(B) by striking out "Congress by a concurrent resolution" and inserting "enactment of a joint resolution."

Act Sec. 11005(c)(7) amended ERISA Sec. 4022A(f)(4)(A) by striking out "concurrent" and inserting "joint."

Act Sec. 11005(c)(8) amended ERISA Sec. 4022A(f)(4)(B) by striking out "concurrent" each place it appeared and inserting "joint" instead; by striking out "That the Congress favors the" and inserting "The;" and, by inserting "is hereby approved" immediately before the period preceding the quotation marks.

Act Sec. 11005(c)(9) amended ERISA Sec. 4022A(f)(4)(C) by striking out "concurrent" and inserting "joint."

Act Sec. 11005(c)(10) amended ERISA Sec. 4022A(g)(4)(A)(ii) by striking out "concurrent" and inserting "joint" and by striking out "adopted" and inserting "enacted."

Act Sec. 11005(c)(11) amended ERISA Sec. 4022A(g)(4)(B) by striking out "concurrent" each place it appeared and inserting "joint" instead; by striking out "That the Congress disapproves the" and inserting "The;" and by inserting "is hereby disapproved" immediately before the period preceding the quotation marks.

Act Sec. 11005(c)(12) amended ERISA Sec. 4022A(g)(4)(D) by striking out "concurrent" and inserting "joint."

These amendments are effective for plan years beginning after December 31, 1985.

P.L. 96-364, § 102:

Added new section 4022A, effective September 26, 1980.

[¶ 15,429L]
AGGREGATE LIMIT ON BENEFITS GUARANTEED

Act Sec. 4022B. (a) Notwithstanding sections 4022 and 4022A, no person shall receive from the corporation pursuant to a guarantee by the corporation of basic benefits with respect to a participant under all multiemployer and single employer plans an amount, or amounts, with an actuarial value which exceeds the actuarial value of a monthly benefit in the form of a life annuity commencing at age 65 equal to the amount determined under section 4022(b)(3)(B) as of the date of the last plan termination.

Act Sec. 4022B. (b) For purposes of this section—

(1) the receipt of benefits under a multiemployer plan receiving financial assistance from the corporation shall be considered the receipt of amounts from the corporation pursuant to a guarantee by the corporation of basic benefits except to the extent provided in regulations prescribed by the corporation, and

(2) the date on which a multiemployer plan, whether or not terminated, begins receiving financial assistance from the corporation shall be considered a date of plan termination.

Amendment:

P.L. 96-364, §102:

Added new ERISA section 4022B, effective September 26, 1980.

Regulations

The following regulations were adopted by the Pension Benefit Guaranty Corporation on July 1, 1996 (61 FR 34002). Prior to July 1, 1996, PBGC regulations were under Chapter XXVI of Title 29 of the Code of Federal Regulations. Effective July 1, 1996, PBGC regulations were moved to Chapter XL, and were renumbered and reorganized. Reg. §4022B.1 was revised April 8, 2002 (67 FR 16949), effective June 1, 2002.

[¶ 15,429M]

§4022B.1 **Aggregate payments limitation.** (a) *Benefits with respect to two or more plans.* If a person (or persons) is entitled to benefits payable with respect to one participant in two or more plans, the aggregate benefits payable by PBGC from its funds is limited by §4022.22 of this chapter (without regard to §4022.22(a)). The PBGC will determine the limitation as of the date of the last plan termination.

(b) *Benefits with respect to two or more participants.* The PBGC will not aggregate the benefits payable with respect to one participant with the benefits payable with respect to any other participant (e.g., if an individual is entitled to benefits both as a participant and as the spouse of a deceased participant). [Revised by 67 FR 16949, April 8, 2002.]

[¶ 15,430]
PLAN FIDUCIARIES

Act Sec. 4023. Notwithstanding any other provision of this Act, a fiduciary of a plan to which section 4021 applies is not in violation of the fiduciary's duties as a result of any act or of any withholding of action required by this title.

Amendments:

P.L. 96-364, §402(a)(5):

Added new ERISA section 4023 to read as above, effective September 26, 1980.

P.L. 96-364, §107:

Repealed ERISA section 4023 (as in effect immediately before the date of enactment of this Act [September 26, 1980]). Prior to its repeal, section 4023 read:

" **CONTINGENT LIABILITY COVERAGE**

"(a) The corporation shall insure any employer who maintains or contributes to or under a plan to which section 4021 applies against the payment of any liability imposed on him under subtitle D of this title in the event of a termination of that plan. The corporation may develop arrangements with persons engaged in the business of providing insurance under which the insurance coverage described in the preceding sentence could be provided in whole or in part by such private insurers. In developing such arrangements the corporation shall devise a system under which risks are equitably distributed between the corporation and private insurers with respect to the classes of employers insured by each.

(b) The corporation is authorized to prescribe and collect in such manner as it determines to be appropriate premiums for insurance offered under subsection (a). If the corporation requires all employers to which this title applies to purchase coverage under this section, the provisions of section 4007(b) and (c) apply to the collection of premiums under this section. The premiums shall be determined by the corporation and revised by it from time to time as may be necessary, and shall be chargeable at a rate sufficient to fund any payment by the corporation becoming necessary under such coverage.

(c) If the corporation is, in its determination, able to develop a satisfactory arrangement with private insurers, within 36 months after the date of enactment of this Act, to carry out the program of insurance authorized by this section in whole or in part, the corporation is authorized to require employers to elect coverage by such private insurance or by the corporation at such times and in such manner as the corporation determines necessary.

(d) No payment may be made by the corporation under any insurance provided by it under this section unless the premiums on such insurance have been paid by the employer and the insurance has been in effect (with respect to any benefit) for more than 60 months. The corporation is authorized to prescribe conditions under which no payment will be made by it under any insurance offered under this section without regard to whether premiums for such insurance have been paid.

(e) Nothing in this section precludes the purchase by the employer of insurance from any other person, or limits the circumstances under which that insurance is payable, or in any way limits the terms and conditions of such insurance, except that the corporation may prescribe as a condition precedent to the purchase of such insurance the payment of a reinsurance premium or other reasonable fee under this section determined by the corporation to be necessary to assure the liquidity and adequacy of any fund or funds established to carry out the provisions of this section.

(f) In carrying out its duties under subsection (a) to develop arrangements with private insurers the corporation shall consider as an alternative or as a supplement to private insurance the feasibility of using private industry guarantees, indemnities, or letters of credit."

Subtitle C—Terminations

[¶ 15,440]
TERMINATION OF SINGLE-EMPLOYER PLANS

Act Sec. 4041.(a) GENERAL RULES GOVERNING SINGLE-EMPLOYER PLAN TERMINATIONS.—

(1) EXCLUSIVE MEANS OF PLAN TERMINATION. Except in the case of a termination for which proceedings are otherwise instituted by the corporation as provided in section 4042, a single-employer plan may be terminated only in a standard termination under subsection (b) or a distress termination under subsection (c).

(2) 60-DAY NOTICE OF INTENT TO TERMINATE. Not less than 60 days before the proposed termination date of a standard termination under subsection (b) or a distress termination under subsection (c), the plan administrator shall provide to each affected party (other than the corporation in the case of a standard termination) a written notice of intent to terminate stating that such termination is intended and the proposed termination date. The written notice shall include any related additional information required in regulations of the corporation.

(3) ADHERENCE TO COLLECTIVE BARGAINING AGREEMENTS. The corporation shall not proceed with a termination of a plan under this section if the termination would violate the terms and conditions of an existing collective bargaining agreement. Nothing in the preceding sentence shall be construed as limiting the authority of the corporation to institute proceedings to involuntarily terminate a plan under section 4042.

(b) STANDARD TERMINATION OF SINGLE-EMPLOYER PLANS.—

(b)(1) GENERAL REQUIREMENTS. A single-employer plan may terminate under a standard termination only if—

(A) the plan administrator provides the 60-day advance notice of intent to terminate to affected parties required under subsection (a)(2),

(B) the requirements of subparagraphs (A) and (B) of paragraph (2) are met,

(C) the corporation does not issue a notice of noncompliance under subparagraph (C) of paragraph (2), and

(D) when the final distribution of assets occurs, the plan is sufficient for benefit liabilities (determined as of the termination date).

(2) TERMINATION PROCEDURE.—

(A) NOTICE TO THE CORPORATION. As soon as practicable after the date on which the notice of intent to terminate is provided pursuant to subsection (a)(2), the plan administrator shall send a notice to the corporation setting forth—

(i) certification by an enrolled actuary—

(I) of the projected amount of the assets of the plan (as of a proposed date of final distribution of assets),

(II) of the actuarial present value (as of such date) of the benefit liabilities (determined as of the proposed termination date) under the plan, and

(III) that the plan is projected to be sufficient (as of such proposed date of final distribution) for such benefit liabilities,

(ii) such information as the corporation may prescribe in regulations as necessary to enable the corporation to make determinations under subparagraph (C), and

(iii) certification by the plan administrator that—

(I) the information on which the enrolled actuary based the certification under clause (i) is accurate and complete, and

(II) the information provided to the corporation under clause (ii) is accurate and complete.

Clause (i) and clause (iii)(I) shall not apply to a plan described in section 412(i) of the Internal Revenue Code of 1986.

(B) NOTICE TO PARTICIPANTS AND BENEFICIARIES OF BENEFIT COMMITMENTS [LIABILITIES]. No later than the date on which a notice is sent by the plan administrator under subparagraph (A), the plan administrator shall send a notice to each person who is a participant or beneficiary under the plan—

(i) specifying the amount of the benefit liabilities (if any) attributable to such person as of the proposed termination date and the benefit form on the basis of which such amount is determined and

(ii) including the following information used in determining such benefit liabilities:

(I) the length of service,

(II) the age of the participant or beneficiary,

(III) wages,

(IV) the assumptions, including the interest rate, and

(V) such other information as the corporation may require.

Such notice shall be written in such manner as is likely to be understood by the participant or beneficiary and as may be prescribed in regulations of the corporation.

(C) NOTICE FROM THE CORPORATION OF NONCOMPLIANCE.—

(i) IN GENERAL. Within 60 days after receipt of the notice under subparagraph (A), the corporation shall issue a notice of noncompliance to the plan administrator if—

(I) it determines, based on the notice sent under paragraph (2)(A) of subsection (b), that there is reason to believe that the plan is not sufficient for benefit liabilities,

(II) it otherwise determines, on the basis of information provided by affected parties or otherwise obtained by the corporation, that there is reason to believe that the plan is not sufficient for benefit liabilities, or

(III) it determines that any other requirement of subparagraph (A) or (B) of this paragraph or of subsection (a)(2) has not been met, unless it further determines that the issuance of such notice would be inconsistent with the interests of participants and beneficiaries.

(ii) EXTENSION. The corporation and the plan administrator may agree to extend the 60-day period referred to in clause (i) by a written agreement signed by the corporation and the plan administrator before the expiration of the 60-day period. The 60-day period shall be extended as provided in the agreement and may be further extended by subsequent written agreements signed by the corporation and the plan administrator made before the expiration of a previously agreed upon extension of the 60-day period. Any extension may be made upon such terms and conditions (including the payment of benefits) as are agreed upon by the corporation and the plan administrator.

(D) FINAL DISTRIBUTION OF ASSETS IN ABSENCE OF NOTICE OF NONCOMPLIANCE. The plan administrator shall commence the final distribution of assets pursuant to the standard termination of the plan as soon as practicable after the expiration of the 60-day (or extended) period referred to in subparagraph (C), but such final distribution may occur only if—

(i) the plan administrator has not received during such period a notice of noncompliance from the corporation under subparagraph (C), and

(ii) when such final distribution occurs, the plan is sufficient for benefit liabilities (determined as of the termination date).

(3) METHODS OF FINAL DISTRIBUTION OF ASSETS.—

(A) IN GENERAL. In connection with any final distribution of assets pursuant to the standard termination of the plan under this subsection, the plan administrator shall distribute the assets in accordance with section 4044. In distributing such assets, the plan administrator shall—

(i) purchase irrevocable commitments from an insurer to provide all benefit liabilities under the plan, or

(ii) in accordance with the provisions of the plan and any applicable regulations, otherwise fully provide all benefit liabilities under the plan. A transfer of assets to the corporation in accordance with section 4050 on behalf of a missing participant shall satisfy this subparagraph with respect to such participant.

(B) CERTIFICATION TO THE CORPORATION OF FINAL DISTRIBUTION OF ASSETS. Within 30 days after the final distribution of assets is completed pursuant to the standard termination of the plan under this subsection, the plan administrator shall send a notice to the corporation certifying that the assets of the plan have been distributed in accordance with the provisions of subparagraph (A) so as to pay all benefit liablities under the plan.

(4) CONTINUING AUTHORITY. Nothing in this section shall be construed to preclude the continued exercise by the corporation, after the termination date of a plan terminated in a standard termination under this subsection, of its authority under section 4003 with respect to matters relating to the termination. A certification under paragraph (3)(B) shall not affect the corporation's obligations under section 4022.

(5) SPECIAL RULE FOR CERTAIN PLANS WHERE CESSATION OR CHANGE IN MEMBERSHIP OF A CONTROLLED GROUP.—

(A) IN GENERAL. —Except as provided in subparagraphs (B) and (D), if —

(i) there is transaction or series of transactions which result in a person ceasing to be a member of a controlled group, and

(ii) such person immediately before the transaction or series of transactions maintained a single-employer plan which is a defined benefit plan which is fully funded,

then the interest rate used in determining whether the plan is sufficient for benefit liabilities or to otherwise assess plan liabilities for purposes of this subsection or section 4042(a)(4) shall be not less than the interest rate used in determining whether the plan is fully funded.

(B) LIMITATIONS. —Subparagraph (A) shall not apply to any transaction or series of transactions unless —

(i) any employer maintaining the plan immediately before or after such transaction or series of transactions —

(I) has an outstanding senior unsecured debt instrument which is rated investment grade by each of the nationally recognized statistical rating organizations for corporate bonds that has issued a credit rating for such instrument, or

(II) if no such debt instrument of such employer has been rated by such an organization but 1 or more of such organizations has made an issuer credit rating for such employer, all such organizations which have so rated the employer have rated such employer investment grade, and

(ii) the employer maintaining the plan after the transaction or series of transactions employs at least 20 percent of the employees located in the United States who were employed by such employer immediately before the transaction or series of transactions.

(C) FULLY FUNDED. —For purposes of subparagraph (A), a plan shall be treated as fully funded with respect to any transaction or series of transactions if—

(i) in the case of a transaction or series of transactions which occur in a plan year beginning before January 1, 2008, the funded current liability percentage determined under section 302(d) for the plan year is at least 100 percent, and

(ii) in the case of a transaction or series of transactions which occur in a plan year beginning on or after such date, the funding target attainment percentage determined under section 303 is, as of the valuation date for such plan year, at least 100 percent.

(D) 2 YEAR LIMITATION. —Subparagraph (A) shall not apply to any transaction or series of transaction if the plan referred to in subparagraph (A)(ii) is terminated under section 4041(c) or 4042 after the close of the 2-year period beginning on the date on which the first such transaction occurs.

(c) DISTRESS TERMINATION OF SINGLE-EMPLOYER PLANS.—

(c)(1) IN GENERAL. A single-employer plan may terminate under a distress termination only if—

(A) the plan administrator provides the 60-day advance notice of intent to terminate to affected parties required under subsection (a)(2),

(B) the requirements of subparagraph (A) of paragraph (2) are met, and

(C) the corporation determines that the requirements of subparagraphs (B) and (D) of paragraph (2) are met.

(2) TERMINATION REQUIREMENTS.—

(A) INFORMATION SUBMITTED TO THE CORPORATION. As soon as practicable after the date on which the notice of intent to terminate is provided pursuant to subsection (a)(2), the plan administrator shall provide the corporation, in such form as may be prescribed by the corporation in regulations, the following information:

(i) such information as the corporation may prescribe by regulation as necessary to make determinations under subparagraph (B) and paragraph (3);

(ii) unless the corporation determines the information is not necessary for purposes of paragraph (3)(A) or section 4062, certification by an enrolled actuary of—

(I) the amount (as of the proposed termination date and, if applicable, the proposed distribution date) of the current value of the assets of the plan,

(II) the actuarial present value (as of such dates) of the benefit liabilities under the plan,

(III) whether the plan is sufficient for benefit liabilities as of such dates,

(IV) the actuarial present value (as of such dates) of benefits under the plan guaranteed under section 4022, and

(V) whether the plan is sufficient for guaranteed benefits as of such dates;

(iii) in any case in which the plan is not sufficient for benefit liabilities as of such date—

(I) the name and address of each participant and beneficiary under the plan as of such date, and

(II) such other information as shall be prescribed by the corporation by regulation as necessary to enable the corporation to be able to make payments to participants and beneficiaries as required under section 4022(c); and

(iv) certification by the plan administrator that—

(I) the information on which the enrolled actuary based the certifications under clause (ii) as accurate and complete, and

(II) the information provided to the corporation under clauses (i) and (iii) is accurate and complete.

Clause (ii) and clause (iv)(I) shall not apply to a plan described in section 412(i) of the Internal Revenue Code of 1986.

(B) DETERMINATION BY THE CORPORATION OF NECESSARY DISTRESS CRITERIA. Upon receipt of the notice of intent to terminate required under subsection (a)(2) and the information required under subparagraph (A), the corporation shall determine whether the requirements of this subparagraph are met as provided in clause (i), (ii), or (iii). The requirements of this subparagraph are met if each person who is (as of the proposed termination date) a contributing sponsor of such plan or a member of such sponsor's controlled group meets the requirements of any of the following clauses:

(i) LIQUIDATION IN BANKRUPTCY OR INSOLVENCY PROCEEDINGS. The requirements of this clause are met by a person if—

(I) such person has filed or has had filed against such person, as of the proposed termination date, a petition seeking liquidation in a case under title 11, United States Code, or under any similar Federal law or law of a State or political subdivision of a State (or a case described in clause (ii) filed by or against such person has been converted, as of such date, to a case in which liquidation is sought), and

(II) such case has not, as of the proposed termination date, been dismissed.

(ii) REORGANIZATION IN BANKRUPTCY OR INSOLVENCY PROCEEDINGS. The requirements of this clause are met by a person if—

(I) such person has filed, or has had filed against such person, as of the proposed termination date, a petition seeking reorganization in a case under title 11, United States Code, or under any similar law of a State or political subdivision of a State (or a case described in clause (i) filed by or against such person has been converted, as of such date, to such a case in which reorganization is sought),

(II) such case has not, as of the proposed termination date, been dismissed,

(III) such person timely submits to the corporation any request for the approval of the bankruptcy court (or other appropriate court in a case under such similar law of a State or political subdivision) of the plan termination, and

(IV) the bankruptcy court (or such other appropriate court) determines that, unless the plan is terminated, such person will be unable to pay all its debts pursuant to a plan of reorganization and wil be unable to continue in business outside a Chapter 11 reorganization process and approves the termination.

(iii) TERMINATION REQUIRED TO ENABLE PAYMENT OF DEBTS WHILE STAYING IN BUSINESS OR TO AVOID UNREASONABLY BURDENSOME PENSION COSTS CAUSED BY DECLINING WORKFORCE. The requirements of this clause are met by a person if such person demonstrates to the satisfaction of the corporation that—

(I) unless a distress termination occurs, such person will be unable to pay such person's debts when due and will be unable to continue in business, or

(II) the costs of providing pension coverage have become unreasonably burdensome to such person, solely as a result of a decline of such person's workforce covered by participants under all single-employer plans of which such person is a contributing sponsor.

(C) NOTIFICATION OF DETERMINATIONS BY THE CORPORATION. The corporation shall notify the plan administrator as soon as practicable of its determinations made pursuant to subparagraph (B).

(D) DISCLOSURE OF TERMINATION INFORMATION.—

(i) IN GENERAL. —A plan administrator that has filed a notice of intent to terminate under subsection (a)(2) shall provide to an affected party any information provided to the corporation under subparagraph (A) or the regulations under subsection (a)(2) not later than 15 days after—

(I) receipt of a request from the affected party for the information; or

(II) the provision of new information to the corporation relating to a previous request.

(ii) CONFIDENTIALITY.—

(I) IN GENERAL. —The plan administrator shall not provide information under clause (i) in a form that includes any information that may directly or indirectly be associated with, or otherwise identify, an individual participant or beneficiary.

(II) LIMITATION. —A court may limit disclosure under this subparagraph of confidential information described in section 552(b) of title 5, United States Code, to any authorized representative of the participants or beneficiaries that agrees to ensure the confidentiality of such information.

(iii) FORM AND MANNER OF INFORMATION; CHARGES.—

(I) FORM AND MANNER. —The corporation may prescribe the form and manner of the provision of information under this subparagraph, which shall include delivery in written, electronic, or other appropriate form to the extent that such form is reasonably accessible to individuals to whom the information is required to be provided.

(II) REASONABLE CHARGES. —A plan administrator may charge a reasonable fee for any information provided under this subparagraph in other than electronic form.

(iv) AUTHORIZED REPRESENTATIVE. —For purposes of this subparagraph, the term "authorized representative" means any employee organization representing participants in the pension plan.

(3) TERMINATION PROCEDURE.—

(A) DETERMINATIONS BY THE CORPORATION RELATING TO PLAN SUFFICIENCY FOR GUARANTEED BENEFITS AND FOR BENEFIT LIABILITIES. If the corporation determines that the requirements for a distress termination set forth in paragraphs (1) and (2) are met, the corporation shall—

(i) determine that the plan is sufficient for guaranteed benefits (as of the termination date) or that the corporation is unable to make such determination on the basis of information made available to the corporation,

(ii) determine that the plan is sufficient for benefit liabilities (as of the termination date) or that the corporation is unable to make such determination on the basis of information made available to the corporation, and

(iii) notify the plan administrator of the determinations made pursuant to this subparagraph as soon as practicable.

(B) IMPLEMENTATION OF TERMINATION. After the corporation notifies the plan administrator of its determinations under subparagraph (A), the termination of the plan shall be carried out as soon as practicable, as provided in clause (i), (ii), or (iii).

(i) CASES OF SUFFICIENCY FOR BENEFIT LIABILITIES. In any case in which the corporation determines that the plan is sufficient for benefit liabilities, the plan administrator shall proceed to distribute the plan's assets, and make certification to the corporation with respect to such distribution, in the manner described in subsection (b)(3), and shall take such other actions as may be appropriate to carry out the termination of the plan.

(ii) CASES OF SUFFICIENCY FOR GUARANTEED BENEFITS WITHOUT A FINDING OF SUFFICIENCY FOR BENEFIT LIABILITIES. In any case in which the corporation determines that the plan is sufficient for guaranteed benefits, but further determines that it is unable to determine that the plan is sufficient for benefit liabilities on the basis of the information made available to it, the plan administrator shall proceed to distribute the plan's assets in the manner described in subsection (b)(3), make certification to the corporation that the distribution has occurred, and take such actions as may be appropriate to carry out the termination of the plan.

(iii) CASES WITHOUT ANY FINDING OF SUFFICIENCY. In any case in which the corporation determines that it is unable to determine that the plan is sufficient for guaranteed benefits on the basis of the information made available to it, the corporation shall commence proceedings in accordance with section 4042.

(C) FINDINGS AFTER AUTHORIZED COMMENCEMENT OF TERMINATION THAT PLAN IS UNABLE TO PAY BENEFITS. (i) FINDING WITH RESPECT TO BENEFIT LIABILITIES WHICH ARE NOT GUARANTEED BENEFITS. If, after the plan administrator has begun to terminate the plan as authorized under subparagraph (B)(i), the plan administrator finds that the plan is unable, or will be unable, to pay benefit liabilities which are not benefits guaranteed by the corporation under section 4022, the plan administrator shall notify the corporation of such findings as soon as practicable thereafter.

(ii) FINDING WITH RESPECT TO GUARANTEED BENEFITS. If, after the plan administrator has begun to terminate the plan as authorized by subparagraph (B)(i) or (ii), the plan administrator finds that the plan is unable, or will be unable, to pay all benefits under the plan which are guaranteed by the corporation under section 4022, the plan administrator shall notify the corporation of such finding as soon as practicable thereafter. If the corporation concurs in the finding of the plan administrator (or the corporation itself makes such a finding), the corporation shall institute appropriate proceedings under section 4042.

(D) ADMINISTRATION OF THE PLAN DURING INTERIM PERIOD. (i) IN GENERAL. The plan administrator shall—

(I) meet the requirements of clause (ii) for the period commencing on the date on which the plan administrator provides a notice of distress termination to the corporation under subsection (a)(2) and ending on the date on which the plan administrator receives notification from the corporation of its determinations under subparagraph (A), and

(II) meet the requirements of clause (ii) commencing on the date on which the plan administrator or the corporation makes a finding under subparagraph (C)(ii).

(ii) REQUIREMENTS. The requirements of this clause are met by the plan administrator if the plan administrator—

(I) refrains from distributing assets or taking any other actions to carry out the proposed termination under this subsection,

(II) pays benefits attributable to employer contributions, other than death benefits, only in the form of an annuity,

(III) does not use plan assets to purchase irrevocable commitments to provide benefits from an insurer, and

(IV) continues to pay all benefit liabilities under the plan, but, commencing on the proposed termination date, limits the payment of benefits under the plan to those benefits which are guaranteed by the corporation under section 4022 or to which assets are required to be allocated under section 4044.

In the event the plan administrator is later determined not to have met the requirements for distress termination, any benefits which are not paid solely by reason of compliance with subclause (IV) shall be due and payable immediately (together with interest, at a reasonable rate, in accordance with regulations of the corporation).

(d) SUFFICIENCY. For purposes of this section—

(1) SUFFICIENCY FOR BENEFIT LIABILITIES. A single-employer plan is sufficient for benefit liabilities if there is no amount of unfunded benefit liabilities under the plan.

(2) SUFFICIENCY FOR GUARANTEED BENEFITS. A single-employer plan is sufficient for guaranteed benefits if there is no amount of unfunded guaranteed benefits under the plan.

(e) LIMITATION ON THE CONVERSION OF A DEFINED BENEFIT PLAN TO A DEFINED CONTRIBUTION PLAN. The adoption of an amendment to a plan which causes the plan to become a plan described in section 4021(b)(1) constitutes a termination of the plan. Such an amendment may take effect only after the plan satisfies the requirements for standard termination under subsection (b) or distress termination under subsection (c).

Amendments

P.L. 110-458, § 104(d):

Amended ERISA Sec. 4041(b)(5)(A) by striking "subparagraph (B)" and inserting "subparagraphs (B) and (D)".

The above amendment applies to any transaction or series of transactions occurring on and after August 17, 2006.

P.L. 110-458, § 105(e)(1):

Amended ERISA Sec. 4041(c)(2)(D)(i) by striking "subsection (a)(2)" the second place it appears and inserting "subparagraph (A) or the regulations under subsection (a)(2)".

The above amendment applies to any plan termination under Title IV of ERISA with respect to which the notice of intent to terminate (or in the case of a termination by the PBGC, a notice of determination under ERISA Sec. 4042 occurs after August 17, 2006 generally.

P.L. 109-280, § 409(a):

Amended ERISA Sec. 4041(b) by adding new paragraph (5) to read as above.

The above amendment applies to any transaction or series of transactions occurring on and after the date of the enactment of this Act [August 17, 2006].

P.L. 109-280, § 506(a)(1):

Amended ERISA Sec. 4041(c)(2) by adding new subparagraph (D) to read as above.

P.L. 109-280, § 506(a)(2):

Amended ERISA Sec. 4041(c)(1)(C) by striking "subparagraph (B)" and inserting "subparagraphs (B) and (D)".

P.L. 109-280, § 506(c):

(c) EFFECTIVE DATE.—

(1) IN GENERAL.—

The amendments made by this section shall apply to any plan termination under title IV of the Employee Retirement Income Security Act of 1974 (29 U.S.C. 1301 et seq.) with respect to which the notice of intent to terminate (or in the case of a termination by the Pension Benefit Guaranty Corporation, a notice of determination under section 4042 of such Act (29 U.S.C. 1342)) occurs after the date of enactment of this Act.

(2) TRANSITION RULE.—

If notice under section 4041(c)(2)(D) or 4042(c)(3) of the Employee Retirement Income Security Act of 1974 (as added by this section) would otherwise be required to be provided before the 90th day after the date of the enactment of this Act, such notice shall not be required to be provided until such 90th day.

P.L. 103-465, § 776(b)(3):

Act Sec. 776(b)(3) amended ERISA Sec. 4041(b)(3)(A)(ii) by adding at the end a new sentence to read as above.

The above amendment is effective with respect to distributions that occur in plan years commencing after final regulations implementing the amendment are prescribed by the Pension Benefit Guaranty Corporation.

P.L. 103-465, § 778(a):

Act Sec. 778(a) amended ERISA Sec. 4041(b)(2)(C)(i) by striking subclause (I) and inserting new subclause (I) to read as above. Prior to amendment, ERISA Sec. 4041(b)(2)(C)(i)(I) read as follows:

(I) it has reason to believe that any requirement of subsection (a)(2) and subparagraph (A) or (B) has not been met, or

Act Sec. 778(a) also amended ERISA Sec. 4041(b)(2)(C)(i) by striking the period at the end of subclause (II) and inserting ", or"; and by adding a new subclause (III) to read as above.

The above amendments apply to any plan termination under ERISA Sec. 4041(b) with respect to which the Pension Benefit Guaranty Corporation has not, as of the date of enactment, issued a notice of noncompliance that has become final, or otherwise issued a final determination that the plan termination is nullified.

P.L. 103-465, § 778(b):

Act Sec. 778(b) amended ERISA Sec. 4041(c)(2)(B)(i)(I) by inserting after "under any similar" the following: "Federal law or".

The above amendment is effective as if included in the Single-Employer Pension Plan Amendments Act of 1986.

P.L. 101-239, § 7881(f)(7):

Amended ERISA Sec. 4041(c) by striking "(or its designee under section 4049(b))" in paragraph (2)(A)(iii)(II), by striking "section 4049" in paragraph (2)(A)(iii)(II) and inserting "section 4022(c)", and by striking the last sentence of paragraph (3)(C)(i) effective as if included in P.L. 100-203, § 9312(c).

Prior to being stricken, the last sentence of clause (i) read as follows:

If the corporation concurs in the findings of the plan administrator (or the corporation itself makes such a finding) the corporation shall take the actions set forth in subparagraph (B)(ii)(II) relating to the trust established for purposes of section 4049.

P.L. 101-239, § 7881(g)(1):

Amended ERISA Sec. 4041(d)(1) by striking "sufficient for benefit commitments" and inserting "sufficient for benefit liabilities," effective as if included in P.L. 100-203, § 9313.

P.L. 101-239, § 7881(g)(2):

Amended ERISA Sec. 4041(c)(2)(B) by inserting "proposed" before "termination" in the parenthetical material in the second sentence, effective as if included in P.L. 100-203, § 9313.

P.L. 101-239, § 7881(g)(3):

Amended ERISA Sec. 4041(c)(2)(A)(ii) by inserting new material before "certification," by inserting new material after "termination date" in subclause (I) and by striking "date" and inserting "dates" in subclauses (II) through (V), effective as if included in P.L. 100-203, § 9313(a)(2)(D).

P.L. 101-239, § 7881(g)(4):

Amended ERISA Sec. 4041(b)(3)(B) by adding a period at the end, effective December 22, 1987.

P.L. 101-239, § 7881(g)(5):

Amended P.L. 100-203, § 9313(b)(3) by inserting "each place it appears" before the period, effective December 22, 1987.

P.L. 101-239, § 7893(d)(2):

Amended ERISA Sec. 4041(c)(3)(D)(ii)(I) by striking "of" and inserting "under," effective as if included in P.L. 99-272, § 11009(a).

P.L. 100-203, § 9312(c)(1):

Amended ERISA Sec. 4041(c)(3)(B)(ii) by striking subclause (II); by striking "plan, and" at the end of subclause (I) and inserting "plan."; and by striking "available to it—"and all that follows through "the plan administrator" and inserting "available to it, the plan administrator" effective for

(A) plan terminations under section 4041(c) of ERISA with respect to which notices of intent to terminate are provided under section 4041(a)(2) of ERISA after December 17, 1987, and

(B) plan terminations with respect to which proceedings are instituted by the Pension Benefit Guaranty Corporation under section 4042 of ERISA after December 17, 1987.

Prior to amendment ERISA Sec. 4041(c)(3)(B)(ii)(II) read as follows:

(II) the corporation shall establish a separate trust in connection with the plan for purposes of section 4049.

P.L. 100-203, ERISA § 9312(c)(2):

Amended ERISA Sec. 4041(c)(3)(B)(iii) by striking subclause (II); by striking "section 4042, and" at the end of subclause (I) and inserting "section 4042."; and by striking "available to it—"and all that follows through "the corporation" in subclause (I) and inserting "available to it, the corporation".

For the effective date, see Act Sec. 9312(c)(1), above. Prior to amendment, ERISA Sec. 4041(c)(3)(B)(iii)(II) read as follows:

(II) the corporation shall establish a separate trust in connection with the plan for purposes of section 4049 unless the corporation determines that all benefit commitments under the plan are benefits guaranteed by the corporation under section 4022.

P.L. 100-203, § 9313(a)(1):

Amended ERISA Sec. 4041(b)(1)(D) by striking out "commitments" and inserting "liabilities" instead, to read as above.

P.L. 100-203, § 9313(a)(2)(A):

Amended ERISA Sec. 4041(b)(2)(A), (2)(C), (2)(D), (3) by striking out "benefit commitments" and inserting "benefit liabilities" instead each place it appeared, to read as above.

P.L. 100-203, § 9313(a)(2)(B):

Amended ERISA Sec. 4041(b)(2)(B)

(i) by striking out "the amount of such person's benefit commitments (if any)" and inserting in lieu thereof "the amount of the benefit liabilities (if any) attributable to such person"; and

(ii) by striking out "such benefit commitments" and inserting in lieu thereof "such benefit liabilities".

Prior to amendment, ERISA Sec. 4041(b)(2)(B) read as follows:

(B) Notice to Participants and Beneficiaries of Benefit Commitments.—No later than the date on which a notice is sent by the plan administrator under subparagraph (A), the plan administrator shall send a notice to each person who is a participant or beneficiary under the plan—

(i) specifying the amount of such person's benefit commitments (if any) as of the proposed termination date and the benefit form on the basis of which such amount is determined and

(ii) including the following information used in determining such benefit commitments:

(I) the length of service,

(II) the age of the participant or beneficiary,

(III) wages,

(IV) the assumptions, including the interest rate, and

(V) such other information as the corporation may require.

Such notice shall be written in such manner as is likely to be understood by the participant or beneficiary and as may be prescribed in regulations of the corporation.

P.L. 100-203, §9313(a)(2)(C)(i):

Amended ERISA Sec. 4041(b)(3)(A) by striking out clauses (i) and (ii) and inserting

"(i) purchase irrevocable commitments from an insurer to provide all benefit liabilities under the plan, or

"(ii) in accordance with the provisions of the plan and any applicable regulations, otherwise fully provide all benefit liabilities under the plan." instead, to read as above.

Prior to amendment, ERISA Sec. 4041(b)(3)(A) read as follows:

(3) Methods of Final Distribution of Assets.—

(A) In General.—In connection with any final distribution of assets pursuant to the standard termination of the plan under this subsection, the plan administrator shall distribute the assets in accordance with section 4044. In distributing such assets, the plan administrator shall—

(i) purchase irrevocable commitments from an insurer to provide the benefit commitments under the plan and all other benefits (if any) under the plan to which assets are required to be allocated under section 4044, or

(ii) in accordance with the provisions of the plan and any applicable regulations of the corporation, otherwise fully provide the benefit commitments under the plan and all other benefits (if any) under the plan to which assets are required to be allocated under section 4044.

P.L. 100-203, §9313(a)(2)(C)(ii):

Amended ERISA Sec. 4041(b)(3)(B) by striking out "so as to pay" and all that followed and inserting "so as to pay all benefit liabilities under the plan" instead, to read as above.

Prior to amendment, ERISA sec. 4041(b)(3)(B) read as follows:

(B) Certification to the Corporation of Final Distribution of Assets.—Within 30 days after the final distribution of assets is completed pursuant to the standard termination of the plan under this subsection, the plan administrator shall send a notice to the corporation certifying that the assets of the plan have been distributed in accordance with the provisions of subparagraph (A) so as to pay the benefit commitments under the plan and all other benefits under the plan to which assets are required to be allocated under section 4044.

P.L. 100-203, §9313(a)(2)(D):

Amended ERISA Secs. 4041(c)(2) and (3) by striking out "benefit commitment" each place it appears (including in any heading) and inserting in lieu thereof "benefit liabilities."

Prior to amendment, ERISA Secs. 4041(c)(2) and (3) read as follows:

(2) Termination Requirements.—

(A) Information Submitted to the Corporation.—As soon as practicable after the date on which the notice of intent to terminate is provided pursuant to subsection (a)(2), the plan administrator shall provide the corporation, in such form as may be prescribed by the corporation in regulations, the following information:

(i) such information as the corporation may prescribe by regulation as necessary to make determinations under subparagraph (B) and paragraph (3);

(ii) certification by an enrolled actuary of—

(I) the amount (as of the proposed termination date) of the current value of the assets of the plan,

(II) the actuarial present value (as of such date) of the benefit commitments under the plan,

(III) whether the plan is sufficient for benefit commitments as of such date,

(IV) the actuarial present value (as of such date) of benefits under the plan guaranteed under section 4022, and

(V) whether the plan is sufficient for guaranteed benefits as of such date;

(iii) in any case in which the plan is not sufficient for benefit commitments as of such date—

(I) the name and address of each participant and beneficiary under the plan as of such date, and

(II) such other information as shall be prescribed by the corporation by regulation as necessary to enable the corporation (or its designee under section 4049(b)) to be able to make payments to participants and beneficiaries required under section 4049, and

(iv) certification by the plan administrator that the information on which the enrolled actuary based the certifications under clause (ii) and the information provided to the corporation and under clauses (i) and (iii) are accurate and complete.

(B) Determination By the Corporation of Necessary Distress Criteria.—Upon receipt of the notice of intent to terminate required under subsection (a)(2) and the information required under subparagraph (A), the corporation shall determine whether the requirements of this subparagraph are met as provided in clause (i), (ii), or (iii). The requirements of this subparagraph are met if each person who is (as of the termination date) a contributing sponsor of such plan or a substantial member of such sponsor's controlled group meets the requirements of any of the following clauses:

(i) Liquidation in Bankruptcy or Insolvency Proceedings.—The requirements of this clause are met by a person if—

(I) such person has filed or has had filed against such person, as of the termination date, a petition seeking liquidation in a case under title 11, United States Code, or under any similar law of a State or political subdivision of a State, and

(II) such case has not, as of the termination date, been dismissed.

(ii) Reorganization in Bankruptcy or Insolvency Proceedings.—The requirements of this clause are met by a person if—

(I) such person has filed, or has had filed against such person, as of the termination date, a petition seeking reorganization in a case under title 11, United States Code, or under any similar law of a State or political subdivision of a State (or a case described in clause (i) filed by or against such person has been converted, as of such date, to such a case in which reorganization is sought),

(II) such case has not, as of the termination date, been dismissed, and

(III) the bankruptcy court (or other appropriate court in a case under such similar law of a State or political subdivision) approves the termination.

(iii) Termination Required to Enable Payment of Debts While Staying in Business or to Avoid Unreasonably Burdensome Pension Costs Caused by Declining Workforce.— The requirements of this clause are met by a person if such person demonstrates to the satisfaction of the corporation that—

(I) unless a distress termination occurs, such person will be unable to pay such person's debts when due and will be unable to continue in business, or

(II) the costs of providing pension coverage have become unreasonably burdensome to such person, solely as a result of a decline of such person's workforce covered as participants under all single-employer plans of which such person is a contributing sponsor.

(C) Substantial Member.—For purposes of subparagraph (B), the term "substantial member" of a controlled group means a person whose assets comprise 5 percent or more of the total assets of the controlled group as a whole.

(D) Notification of Determinations by the Corporation.— The corporation shall notify the plan administrator as soon as practicable of its determinations made pursuant to subparagraph (B).

(3) Termination Procedure.—

(A) Determinations by the Corporation Relating to Plan Sufficiency for Guaranteed Benefits and for Benefit Commitments.—If the corporation determines that the requirements for a distress termination set forth in paragraphs (1) and (2) are met, the corporation shall—

(i) determine that the plan is sufficient for guaranteed benefits (as of the termination date) or that the corporation is unable to make such determinations on the basis of information made available to the corporation,

(ii) determine that the plan is sufficient for benefit commitments (as of the termination date) or that the corporation is unable to make such determination on the basis of information made available to the corporation, and

(iii) notify the plan administrator of the determinations made pursuant to this subparagraph as soon as practicable.

(B) Implementation of Termination.—After the corporation notifies the plan administrator of its determinations under subparagraph (A), the termination of the plan shall be carried out as soon as practicable, as provided in clause (i), (ii), or (iii).

(i) Cases of Sufficiency for Benefit Commitments.—In any case in which the corporation determines that the plan is sufficient for benefit commitments, the plan administrator shall proceed to distribute the plan's assets, and make certification to the corporation with respect to such distribution, in the manner described in subsection (b)(3), and shall take such other actions as may be appropriate to carry out the termination of the plan.

(ii) Cases of Sufficiency for Guaranteed Benefits Without a Finding of Sufficiency for Benefit Commitments.—In any case in which the corporation determines that the plan is sufficient for guaranteed benefits, but further determines that it is unable to determine that the plan is sufficient for benefit commitments on the basis of the information made available to it—

(I) the plan administrator shall proceed to distribute the plan's assets in the manner described in subsection (b)(3), make certification to the corporation that the distribution has occurred, and take such actions as may be appropriate to carry out the termination of the plan, and

(II) the corporation shall establish a separate trust in connection with the plan for purposes of section 4049.

(iii) Cases Without Any Finding of Sufficiency.—In any case in which the corporation determines that it is unable to determine that the plan is sufficient for guaranteed benefits on the basis of the information made available to it—

(I) the corporation shall commence proceedings in accordance with section 4042, and

(II) the corporation shall establish a separate trust in connection with the plan for purposes of section 4049 unless the corporation determines that all benefit commitments under the plan are benefits guaranteed by the corporation under section 4022.

P.L. 100-203, §9313(a)(2)(E):

Amended ERISA Sec. 4041(d)(1) by striking out "no amount of unfunded benefit commitments" and inserting in lieu thereof "no amount of unfunded benefit liabilities", and by striking out "Benefit Commitments" in the paragraph heading and inserting in lieu thereof "Benefit Liabilities," to read as above.

Prior to amendment, ERISA Sec. 4041(d)(1) read as follows:

Act Sec. 4041. (d) Sufficiency.—For purposes of this section—

(1) Sufficiency for Benefit Commitments.—A single-employer plan is sufficient for benefit commitments if there is no amount of unfunded benefit commitments under the plan.

P.L. 100-203, §9313(b)(1):

Amended ERISA Sec. 4041(c)(2)(B) of ERISA by striking "a substantial member" in the matter preceding clause (i) and inserting "a member"; and by striking subparagraph (C) and by redesignating subparagraph (D) as subparagraph (C), to read as above.

P.L. 100-203, §9313(b)(2):

Amended ERISA Sec. 4041(c)(2)(B)(ii)(III) by striking "approves the termination" and inserting "determines that, unless the plan is terminated, such person will be unable to pay all its debts pursuant to a plan of reorganization and will be unable to continue in business outside the chapter 11 reorganization process and approves the termination."

P.L. 100-203, §9313(b)(3):

Amended ERISA Sec. 4041(c)(2)(B) by inserting "proposed" before "termination date", each place it appeared.

P.L. 100-203, §9313(b)(4):

Amended ERISA Sec. 4041(c)(2)(B)(i)(I) by inserting before the comma at the end the following: "(or a case described in clause (ii) filed by or against such person has been converted, as of such date, to a case in which liquidation is sought), to read as above.

P.L. 100-203, §9313(b)(5):

Amended ERISA Sec. 4041(c)(2)(B)(ii) by striking "and" at the end;

by redesignating subclause (III) as subclause (IV);

by inserting after subclause (II) the following new subclause:

"(III) such person timely submits to the corporation any request for the approval of the bankruptcy court (or other appropriate court in a case under such similar law of a State or political subdivision) of the plan termination, and";

and

in subclause (IV) (as redesignated), by striking "(or other" and all that follows through "subdivision)" and inserting "(or such other appropriate court)," to read as above.

The above amendments apply to plan terminations under ERISA Sec. 4041 with respect to which notices of intent to terminate are provided under ERISA Sec. 4041(a)(2) after December 17, 1987.

P.L. 100-203, §9314(a)(1):

Amended ERISA Sec. 4041(b)(2)(A)(iii) to read as above, effective December 22, 1987. Prior to amendment, subparagraph (iii) read as follows:

(iii) certification by the plan administrator that the information on which the enrolled actuary based the certification under clause (i) and the information provided to the corporation under clause (ii) are accurate and complete.

P.L. 100-203, §9314(a)(2):

Amended ERISA Sec. 4041(c)(2)(A)(iv) to read as above, effective December 22, 1987. Prior to amendment, Subparagraph (iv) read as follows:

(iv) certification by the plan administrator that the information on which the enrolled actuary based the certifications under clause (ii) and the information provided to the corporation under clauses (i) and (iii) are accurate and complete.

P.L. 99-272:

Act Sec. 11007(a) amended ERISA Sec. 4041 by striking out subsections (a) through (c) and inserting a new subsection (a) to read as above.

Act Sec. 11008(a) added a new subsection (b) to read as above.

Act Sec. 11009(a) added a new subsection (c) to read as above.

Act Sec. 11007(b) amended subsection (d) to read as above.

Act Sec. 11008(b) amended subsection (f) to read as above.

Act Sec. 11009(b) struck out subsection (e) and renumbered subsection (f) as subsection (e).

These amendments apply with respect to terminations pursuant to notices of intent filed with the PBGC on or after January 1, 1986 or proceedings begun on or after that date.

Prior to the above amendments, ERISA Secs. 4041(a) through (e) read as follows:

Sec. 4041. (a) Before the effective date of the termination of a single-employer plan, the plan administrator shall file a notice with the corporation that the plan is to be terminated on a proposed date (which may not be earlier than 10 days after the filing of the notice), and for a period of 90 days after the proposed termination date the plan administrator shall pay no amount pursuant to the termination procedure of the plan unless, before the expiration of such period, he receives a notice of sufficiency under subsection (b). Upon receiving such a notice, the plan administrator may proceed with the termination of the plan in a manner consistent with this subtitle.

Sec. 4041. (b) If the corporation determines that, after application of section 4044, the assets held under the plan are sufficient to discharge when due all obligations of the plan with respect to basic benefits, it shall notify the plan administrator of such determination as soon as practicable.

Sec. 4041. (c) If, within such 90-day period, the corporation finds that it is unable to determine that, if the assets of the plan are allocated in accordance with the provisions of section 4044, the assets held under the plan are sufficient to discharge when due all obligations of the plan with respect to basic benefits, it shall notify the plan administrator within such 90-day period of that finding. When the corporation issues a notice under this subsection, it shall commence proceedings in accordance with the provisions of section 4042. Upon receiving a notice under this subsection, the plan administrator shall refrain from taking any action under the proposed termination.

Sec. 4041. (d) The corporation and the plan administrator may agree to extend the 90-day period provided by this section by a written agreement signed by the corporation and the plan administrator before the expiration of the 90-day period, or the corporation may apply to an appropriate court (as defined in section 4042(g)) for an order extending the 90-day period provided by this section. The 90-day period shall be extended as provided in the agreement or in any court order obtained by the corporation. The 90-day period may be further extended by subsequent written agreements signed by the corporation and the plan administrator made before the expiration of a previously agreed upon extension of the 90-day period, or by subsequent order of the court. Any extension may be made upon such terms and conditions (including the payment of benefits) as are agreed upon by the corporation and the plan administrator or as specified in the court order.

Sec. 4041. (e) If, after the plan administrator has begun to terminate the plan as authorized by this section, the corporation or the plan administrator finds that the plan is unable, or will be unable, to pay basic benefits when due, the plan administrator shall notify the corporation of such finding as soon as practicable thereafter. If the corporation makes such a finding or concurs with the finding of the plan administrator, it shall institute appropriate proceedings under section 4042. The plan administrator terminating a plan shall furnish such reports to the corporation as it may require for purposes of its duties under this section.

P.L. 96-364, §403(g):

Amended ERISA Sec. 4041 by changing the title of the section to read as above (previously it read: "Termination by Plan Administrator"), amended subsection (a) by inserting "single-employer" after "termination of a" and by striking out subsection (g), effective September 26, 1980. Prior to its being stricken, subsection (g) read as follows:

"Notwithstanding any other provision of this title, a plan administrator or the corporation may petition the appropriate court for the appointment of a trustee in accordance with the provisions of section 4042 if the interests of the participants and beneficiaries would be better served by the appointment of the trustee."

Regulations

The following regulations were adopted by the Pension Benefit Guaranty Corporation on July 1, 1996 (61 FR 34002). Prior to July 1, 1996, PBGC regulations were under Chapter XXVI of Title 29 of the Code of Federal Regulations. Effective July 1, 1996, PBGC regulations were moved to Chapter XL, and were renumbered and reorganized. Reg. §4041 was amended November 7, 1997 (62 FR 60424), effective January 1, 1998. Reg. §4041.42 was amended May 28, 1998 (63 FR 29353), effective May 29, 1998. Reg §§4041.3 and 4041.5 were amended October 28, 2003 (68 FR 61344). Reg. §4041.51, added on November 18, 2008 (73 FR 68333), is applicable to terminations initiated on or after August 17, 2006, but only to requests for information made on or after December 18, 2008. Effective and applicable August 1, 2016, Reg. Sec. 4041.6 was amended in interim final regulations on May 13, 2016 (81 FR 29765), removing the words "of up to $1,100 a day for each day that the failure continues". Reg. Sec. 4041.6 was finalized on January 31, 2017 (82 FR 8813). Reg. §4041.28 was amended on December 22, 2017 (82 FR 60800).

Subpart A—General Provisions

[¶ 15,440A]

§4041.1 **Purpose and scope.** This part sets forth the rules and procedures for terminating a single-employer plan in a standard or distress termination under section 4041 of ERISA, the exclusive means of voluntarily terminating a plan. [Amended 11/7/97 by 62 FR 60424.]

[¶ 15,440A-1]

§4041.2 **Definitions.** The following terms are defined in §4001.2 of this chapter: affected party, annuity, benefit liabilities, Code, contributing sponsor, controlled group, distress termination, distribution date, EIN, employer, ERISA, guaranteed benefit, insurer, irrevocable commitment, IRS, mandatory employee contributions, normal retirement age, notice of intent to terminate, PBGC, person, plan administrator, plan year, PN, single-employer plan, standard termination, termination date, and title IV benefit. In addition, for purposes of this part:

Distress termination notice means the notice filed with the PBGC pursuant to §4041.45.

Distribution notice means the notice issued to the plan administrator by the PBGC pursuant to §4041.47(c) upon the PBGC's determination that the plan has sufficient assets to pay at least guaranteed benefits.

Majority owner means, with respect to a contributing sponsor of a single-employer plan, an individual who owns, directly or indirectly, 50 percent or more (taking into account the constructive ownership rules of section 414(b) and (c) of the Code) of—

(1) An unincorporated trade or business;

(2) The capital interest or the profits interest in a partnership; or

(3) Either the voting stock of a corporation or the value of all of the stock of a corporation.

Notice of noncompliance means a notice issued to a plan administrator by the PBGC pursuant to §4041.31 advising the plan administrator that the requirements for a standard termination have not been satisfied and that the plan is an ongoing plan.

Notice of plan benefits means the notice to each participant and beneficiary required by §4041.24.

Participant means—

(1) Any individual who is currently in employment covered by the plan and who is earning or retaining credited service under the plan, including any individual who is considered covered under the plan for purposes of meeting the minimum participation requirements but who, because of offset or similar provisions, does not have any accrued benefits;

(2) Any nonvested individual who is not currently in employment covered by the plan but who is earning or retaining credited service under the plan; and

(3) Any individual who is retired or separated from employment covered by the plan and who is receiving benefits under the plan or is entitled to begin receiving benefits under the plan in the future, excluding any such individual to whom an insurer has made an irrevocable commitment to pay all the benefits to which the individual is entitled under the plan.

Plan benefits means benefit liabilities determined as of the termination date (taking into account the rules in § 4041.8(a)).

Proposed termination date means the date specified as such by the plan administrator in the notice of intent to terminate or, if later, in the standard or distress termination notice.

Residual assets means the plan assets remaining after all plan benefits and other liabilities (e.g., PBGC premiums) of the plan have been satisfied (taking into account the rules in § 4041.8(b)).

Standard termination notice means the notice filed with the PBGC pursuant to § 4041.25.

State guaranty association means an association of insurers created by a State, the District of Columbia, or the Commonwealth of Puerto Rico to pay benefits and to continue coverage, within statutory limits, under life and health insurance policies and annuity contracts when an insurer fails. [Amended 11/7/97 by 62 FR 60424.]

[¶ 15,440A-2]

§ 4041.3 **Computation of time; filing and issuance rules**. (a) *Computation of time*. The PBGC applies the rules in subpart D of part 4000 of this chapter to compute any time period under this part. A proposed termination date may be any day, including a weekend or Federal holiday.

(b) *Filing with the PBGC*.

(1) *Method and date of filing*. The PBGC applies the rules in subpart A of part 4000 of this chapter to determine permissible methods of filing with the PBGC under this part. The PBGC applies the rules in subpart C of part 4000 of this chapter to determine the date that a submission under this part was filed with the PBGC.

(2) *Where to file*. See Sec. 4000.4 of this chapter for information on where to file.

(c) *Issuance to third parties*. The following rules apply to affected parties (other than the PBGC). For purposes of this paragraph (c), a person entitled to notice under the spin-off/termination transaction rules of Sec. 4041.23(c) or Sec. 4041.24(f) is treated as an affected party.

(1) *Method and date of issuance*. The PBGC applies the rules in subpart B of part 4000 of this chapter to determine permissible methods of issuance under this part. The PBGC applies the rules in subpart C of part 4000 of this chapter to determine the date that an issuance under this part was provided.

(2) *Omission of affected parties*. The failure to issue any notice to an affected party (other than any employee organization) within the specified time period will not cause the notice to be untimely if—

(i) *After-discovered affected parties*. The plan administrator could not reasonably have been expected to know of the affected party, and issues the notice promptly after discovering the affected party; or

(ii) *Unlocated participants*. The plan administrator could not locate the affected party after making reasonable efforts, and issues the notice promptly in the event the affected party is located.

(3) *Deceased participants*. In the case of a deceased participant, the plan administrator need not issue a notice to the participant's estate if the estate is not entitled to a distribution.

(4) *Form of notices to affected parties*. All notices to affected parties must be readable and written in a manner calculated to be understood by the average plan participant. The plan administrator

may provide additional information with a notice only if the information is not misleading.

(5) *Foreign language* s. The plan administrator of a plan that (as of the proposed termination date) covers the numbers or percentages in § 2520.104b-10(e) of this title of participants literate only in the same non-English language must, for any notice to affected parties—

(i) Include a prominent legend in that common non-English language advising them how to obtain assistance in understanding the notice; or

(ii) Provide the notice in that common non-English language to those affected parties literate only in that language.

[Amended 11/7/97 by 62 FR 60424 and 10/28/2003 by 68 FR 61344.]

[¶ 15,440A-3]

§ 4041.4 **Disaster relief**. When the President of the United States declares that, under the Disaster Relief Act (42 U.S.C. 5121, 5122(2), 5141(b)), a major disaster exists, the Executive Director of the PBGC (or his or her designee) may, by issuing one or more notices of disaster relief, extend by up to 180 days any due date under this part. [Amended 11/7/97 by 62 FR 60424.]

[¶ 15,440A-4]

§ 4041.5 **Record retention and availability**. (a) *Retention requirement*. (1) *Persons subject to requirement; records to be retained*. Each contributing sponsor and the plan administrator of a plan terminating in a standard termination, or in a distress termination that closes out in accordance with Sec. 4041.50, must maintain all records necessary to demonstrate compliance with section 4041 of ERISA and this part. If a contributing sponsor or the plan administrator maintains information in accordance with this section, the other(s) need not maintain that information.

(2) *Retention period*. The records described in paragraph (a)(1) of this section must be preserved for six years after the date when the post-distribution certification under this part is filed with the PBGC.

(3) *Electronic recordkeeping*. The contributing sponsor or plan administrator may use electronic media for maintenance and retention of records required by this part in accordance with the requirements of subpart E of part 4000 of this chapter.

(b) *Availability of records*. The contributing sponsor or plan administrator must make all records needed to determine compliance with section 4041 of ERISA and this part available to the PBGC upon request for inspection and photocopying (or, for electronic records, inspection, electronic copying, and printout) at the location where they are kept (or another, mutually agreeable, location) and must submit such records to the PBGC within 30 days after the date of a written request by the PBGC or by a later date specified therein.

[Amended 11/7/97 by 62 FR 60424 and 10/28/2003 by 68 FR 61344]

[¶ 15,440A-5]

§ 4041.6 **Effect of failure to provide required information**. If a plan administrator fails to provide any information required under this part within the specified time limit, the PBGC may assess a penalty under section 4071 of ERISA. The PBGC may also pursue any other equitable or legal remedies available to it under the law, including, if appropriate, the issuance of a notice of noncompliance under § 4041.31. [Amended 11/7/97 by 62 FR 60424. Interim final regulations removed the words "of up to $1,100 a day for each day that the failure continues" on 5/13/2016 by 81 FR 29765. Finalized 1/31/17 by 82 FR 8813.]

[¶ 15,440A-6]

§ 4041.7 **Challenges to plan termination under collective bargaining agreement**. (a) *Suspension upon formal challenge to termination*. (1) Notice of formal challenge. (i) If the PBGC is advised, before its review period under § 4041.26(a) ends, or before issuance of a notice of inability to determine sufficiency or a distribution notice under § 4041.47(b) or (c), that a formal challenge to the termination has been initiated as described in paragraph (c) of this section, the PBGC will suspend the termination proceeding and so advise the plan administrator in writing.

(ii) If the PBGC is advised of a challenge described in paragraph (a)(1)(i) of this section after the time specified therein, the

PBGC may suspend the termination proceeding and will so advise the plan administrator in writing.

(2) *Standard terminations.* During any period of suspension in a standard termination—

(i) The running of all time periods specified in ERISA or this part relevant to the termination will be suspended; and

(ii) The plan administrator must comply with the prohibitions in § 4041.22.

(3) *Distress terminations.* During any period of suspension in a distress termination—

(i) The issuance by the PBGC of any notice of inability to determine sufficiency or distribution notice will be stayed or, if any such notice was previously issued, its effectiveness will be stayed;

(ii) The plan administrator must comply with the prohibitions in § 4041.42; and

(iii) The plan administrator must file a distress termination notice with the PBGC pursuant to § 4041.45.

(b) *Existing collective bargaining agreement.* For purposes of this section, an existing collective bargaining agreement means a collective bargaining agreement that has not been made inoperative by a judicial ruling and, by its terms, either has not expired or is extended beyond its stated expiration date because neither of the collective bargaining parties took the required action to terminate it. When a collective bargaining agreement no longer meets these conditions, it ceases to be an "existing collective bargaining agreement," whether or not any or all of its terms may continue to apply by operation of law.

(c) *Formal challenge to termination.* A formal challenge to a plan termination asserting that the termination would violate the terms and conditions of an existing collective bargaining agreement is initiated when—

(1) Any procedure specified in the collective bargaining agreement for resolving disputes under the agreement commences; or

(2) Any action before an arbitrator, administrative agency or board, or court under applicable labor-management relations law commences.

(d) *Resolution of challenge.* Immediately upon the final resolution of the challenge, the plan administrator must notify the PBGC in writing of the outcome of the challenge, provide the PBGC with a copy of any award or order, and, if the validity of the proposed termination has been upheld, advise the PBGC whether the proposed termination is to proceed. The final resolution ends the suspension period under paragraph (a) of this section.

(1) *Challenge sustained.* If the final resolution is that the proposed termination violates an existing collective bargaining agreement, the PBGC will dismiss the termination proceeding, all actions taken to effect the plan termination will be null and void, and the plan will be an ongoing plan. In this event, in a distress termination, § 4041.42(d) will apply as of the date of the dismissal by the PBGC.

(2) *Termination sustained.* If the final resolution is that the proposed termination does not violate an existing collective bargaining agreement and the plan administrator has notified the PBGC that the termination is to proceed, the PBGC will reactivate the termination proceeding by sending a written notice thereof to the plan administrator, and—

(i) The termination proceeding will continue from the point where it was suspended;

(ii) All actions taken to effect the termination before the suspension will be effective;

(iii) Any time periods that were suspended will resume running from the date of the PBGC's notice of the reactivation of the proceeding;

(iv) Any time periods that had fewer than 15 days remaining will be extended to the 15th day after the date of the PBGC's notice, or such later date as the PBGC may specify; and

(v) In a distress termination, the PBGC will proceed to issue a notice of inability to determine sufficiency or a distribution notice (or reactivate any such notice stayed under paragraph (a)(3) of this section), either with or without first requesting updated information from the plan administrator pursuant to § 4041.45(c).

(e) *Final resolution of challenge.* A formal challenge to a proposed termination is finally resolved when—

(1) The parties involved in the challenge enter into a settlement that resolves the challenge;

(2) A final award, administrative decision, or court order is issued that is not subject to review or appeal; or

(3) A final award, administrative decision, or court order is issued that is not appealed, or review or enforcement of which is not sought, within the time for filing an appeal or requesting review or enforcement.

(f) *Involuntary termination by the PBGC.* Notwithstanding any other provision of this section, the PBGC retains the authority in any case to initiate a plan termination in accordance with the provisions of section 4042 of ERISA. [Amended 11/7/97 by 62 FR 60424.]

[¶ 15,440A-7]

§ 4041.8 **Post-termination amendments.** (a) *Plan benefits.* A participant's or beneficiary's plan benefits are determined under the plan's provisions in effect on the plan's termination date. Notwithstanding the preceding sentence, an amendment that is adopted after the plan's termination date is taken into account with respect to a participant's or beneficiary's plan benefits to the extent the amendment—

(1) Does not decrease the value of the participant's or beneficiary's plan benefits under the plan's provisions in effect on the termination date; and

(2) Does not eliminate or restrict any form of benefit available to the participant or beneficiary on the plan's termination date.

(b) *Residual assets.* In a plan in which participants or beneficiaries will receive some or all of the plan's residual assets based on an allocation formula, the amount of the plan's residual assets and each participant's or beneficiary's share thereof is determined under the plan's provisions in effect on the plan's termination date. Notwithstanding the preceding sentence, an amendment adopted after the plan's termination date is taken into account with respect to a participant's or beneficiary's allocation of residual assets to the extent the amendment does not decrease the value of the participant's or beneficiary's allocation of residual assets under the plan's provisions in effect on the termination date.

(c) *Permitted decreases.* For purposes of this section, an amendment shall not be treated as decreasing the value of a participant's or beneficiary's plan benefits or allocation of residual assets to the extent—

(1) The decrease is necessary to meet a qualification requirement under section 401 of the Code;

(2) The participant's or beneficiary's allocation of residual assets is paid in the form of an increase in the participant's or beneficiary's plan benefits; or

(3) The decrease is offset by assets that would otherwise revert to the contributing sponsor or by additional contributions.

(d) *Distress terminations.* In the case of a distress termination, a participant's or beneficiary's benefit liabilities are determined as of the termination date in the same manner as plan benefits under this section. [Amended 11/7/97 by 62 FR 60424.]

Subpart B—Standard Termination Process

[¶ 15,440F]

§ 4041.21 **Requirements for a standard termination.** (a) *Notice and distribution requirements.* A standard termination is valid if the plan administrator—

(1) Issues a notice of intent to terminate to all affected parties (other than the PBGC) in accordance with § 4041.23;

(2) Issues notices of plan benefits to all affected parties entitled to plan benefits in accordance with § 4041.24;

(3) Files a standard termination notice with the PBGC in accordance with § 4041.25;

(4) Distributes the plan's assets in satisfaction of plan benefits in accordance with § 4041.28(a) and (c); and

(5) In the case of a spin-off/termination transaction (as defined in § 4041.23(c)), issues the notices required by § 4041.23(c), § 4041.24(f), and § 4041.27(a)(2) in accordance with such sections.

(b) *Plan sufficiency.* (1) *Commitment to make plan sufficient.* A contributing sponsor of a plan or any other member of the plan's controlled group may make a commitment to contribute any additional sums necessary to enable the plan to satisfy plan benefits in accordance with § 4041.28. A commitment will be valid only if—

(i) It is made to the plan;

(ii) It is in writing, signed by the contributing sponsor or controlled group member(s); and

(iii) In any case in which the person making the commitment is the subject of a bankruptcy liquidation or reorganization proceeding, as described in § 4041.41(c)(1) or (c)(2), the commitment is approved by the court before which the liquidation or reorganization proceeding is pending or a person not in bankruptcy unconditionally guarantees to meet the commitment at or before the time distribution of assets is required.

(2) *Alternative treatment of majority owner's benefit.* A majority owner may elect to forgo receipt of his or her plan benefits to the extent necessary to enable the plan to satisfy all other plan benefits in accordance with § 4041.28. Any such alternative treatment of the majority owner's plan benefits is valid only if—

(i) The majority owner's election is in writing;

(ii) In any case in which the plan would require the spouse of the majority owner to consent to distribution of the majority owner's receipt of his or her plan benefits in a form other than a qualified joint and survivor annuity, the spouse consents in writing to the election;

(iii) The majority owner makes the election and the spouse consents during the time period beginning with the date of issuance of the first notice of intent to terminate and ending with the date of the last distribution; and

(iv) Neither the majority owner's election nor the spouse's consent is inconsistent with a qualified domestic relations order (as defined in section 206(d)(3) of ERISA). [Amended 11/7/97 by 62 FR 60424.]

[¶ 15,440F-1]

§ 4041.22 **Administration of plan during pendency of termination process.** (a) *In general.* A plan administrator may distribute plan assets in connection with the termination of the plan only in accordance with the provisions of this part. From the first day the plan administrator issues a notice of intent to terminate to the last day of the PBGC's review period under § 4041.26(a), the plan administrator must continue to carry out the normal operations of the plan. During that time period, except as provided in paragraph (b) of this section, the plan administrator may not—

(1) Purchase irrevocable commitments to provide any plan benefits; or

(2) Pay benefits attributable to employer contributions, other than death benefits, in any form other than an annuity.

(b) *Exception.* The plan administrator may pay benefits attributable to employer contributions either through the purchase of irrevocable commitments or in a form other than an annuity if—

(1) The participant has separated from active employment or is otherwise permitted under the Code to receive the distribution;

(2) The distribution is consistent with prior plan practice; and

(3) The distribution is not reasonably expected to jeopardize the plan's sufficiency for plan benefits. [Amended 11/7/97 by 62 FR 60424.]

[¶ 15,440F-2]

§ 4041.23 **Notice of intent to terminate.** (a) *Notice requirement.* (1) *In general.* At least 60 days and no more than 90 days before the proposed termination date, the plan administrator must issue a notice of intent to terminate to each person (other than the PBGC) that is an affected party as of the proposed termination date. In the case of a beneficiary of a deceased participant or an alternate payee, the plan administrator must issue a notice of intent to terminate promptly to any person that becomes an affected party after the proposed termination date and on or before the distribution date.

(2) *Early issuance of NOIT.* The PBGC may consider a notice of intent to terminate to be timely under paragraph (a)(1) of this section if

the notice was early by a de minimis number of days and the PBGC finds that the early issuance was the result of administrative error.

(b) *Contents of notice.* The PBGC's standard termination forms and instructions package includes a model notice of intent to terminate. The notice of intent to terminate must include—

(1) *Identifying information.* The name and PN of the plan, the name and EIN of each contributing sponsor, and the name, address, and telephone number of the person who may be contacted by an affected party with questions concerning the plan's termination;

(2) *Intent to terminate plan.* A statement that the plan administrator intends to terminate the plan in a standard termination as of a specified proposed termination date and will notify the affected party if the proposed termination date is changed to a later date or if the termination does not occur;

(3) *Sufficiency requirement.* A statement that, in order to terminate in a standard termination, plan assets must be sufficient to provide all plan benefits under the plan;

(4) *Cessation of accruals.* A statement (as applicable) that—

(i) Benefit accruals will cease as of the termination date, but will continue if the plan does not terminate;

(ii) A plan amendment has been adopted under which benefit accruals will cease, in accordance with section 204(h) of ERISA, as of the proposed termination date or a specified date before the proposed termination date, whether or not the plan is terminated; or

(iii) Benefit accruals ceased, in accordance with section 204(h) of ERISA, as of a specified date before the notice of intent to terminate was issued;

(5) *Annuity information.* If required under § 4041.27, the annuity information described therein;

(6) *Benefit information.* A statement that each affected party entitled to plan benefits will receive a written notification regarding his or her plan benefits;

(7) *Summary plan description.* A statement as to how an affected party entitled to receive the latest updated summary plan description under section 104(b) of ERISA can obtain it.

(8) *Continuation of monthly benefits.* For persons who are, as of the proposed termination date, in pay status, a statement (as applicable)—

(i) That their monthly (or other periodic) benefit amounts will not be affected by the plan's termination; or

(ii) Explaining how their monthly (or other periodic) benefit amounts will be affected under plan provisions); and

(9) *Extinguishment of guarantee.* A statement that after plan assets have been distributed in full satisfaction of all plan benefits under the plan with respect to a participant or a beneficiary of a deceased participant, either by the purchase of irrevocable commitments (annuity contracts) or by an alternative form of distribution provided for under the plan, the PBGC no longer guarantees that participant's or beneficiary's plan benefits.

(c) *Spin-off/termination transactions.* In the case of a transaction in which a single defined benefit plan is split into two or more plans and there is a reversion of residual assets to an employer upon the termination of one or more but fewer than all of the resulting plans (a "spin-off/termination transaction"), the plan administrator must, within the time period specified in paragraph (a) of this section, provide a notice describing the transaction to all participants, beneficiaries of deceased participants, and alternate payees in the original plan who are, as of the proposed termination date, covered by an ongoing plan. [Amended 11/7/97 by 62 FR 60424.]

[¶ 15,440F-3]

§ 4041.24 **Notices of plan benefits.** (a) *Notice requirement.* The plan administrator must, no later than the time the plan administrator files the standard termination notice with the PBGC, issue a notice of plan benefits to each person (other than the PBGC and any employee organization) who is an affected party as of the proposed termination date. In the case of a beneficiary of a deceased participant or an alternate payee, the plan administrator must issue a notice of plan benefits promptly to any person that becomes an affected party after the proposed termination date and on or before the distribution date.

(b) *Contents of notice.* The plan administrator must include in each notice of plan benefits—

(1) The name and PN of the plan, the name and EIN of each contributing sponsor, and the name, address, and telephone number of an individual who may be contacted to answer questions concerning plan benefits;

(2) The proposed termination date given in the notice of intent to terminate and any extended proposed termination date under § 4041.25(b);

(3) If the amount of plan benefits set forth in the notice is an estimate, a statement that the amount is an estimate and that plan benefits paid may be greater than or less than the estimate;

(4) Except in the case of an affected party in pay status for more than one year as of the proposed termination date—

(i) The personal data (if available) needed to calculate the affected party's plan benefits, along with a statement requesting that the affected party promptly correct any information he or she believes to be incorrect; and

(ii) If any of the personal data needed to calculate the affected party's plan benefits is not available, the best available data, along with a statement informing the affected party of the data not available and affording him or her the opportunity to provide it; and

(5) The information in paragraphs (c) through (e) of this section, as applicable.

(c) *Benefits of persons in pay status.* For an affected party in pay status as of the proposed termination date, the plan administrator must include in the notice of plan benefits—

(1) The amount and form of the participant's or beneficiary's plan benefits payable as of the proposed termination date;

(2) The amount and form of plan benefits, if any, payable to a beneficiary upon the participant's death and the name of the beneficiary; and

(3) The amount and date of any increase or decrease in the benefit scheduled to occur (or that has already occurred) after the proposed termination date and an explanation of the increase or decrease, including, where applicable, a reference to the pertinent plan provision.

(d) *Benefits of persons with valid elections or de minimis benefits.* For an affected party who, as of the proposed termination date, has validly elected a form and starting date with respect to plan benefits not yet in pay status, or with respect to whom the plan administrator has determined that a nonconsensual lump sum distribution will be made, the plan administrator must include in the notice of plan benefits—

(1) The amount and form of the person's plan benefits payable as of the projected benefit starting date, and what that date is;

(2) The information in paragraphs (c)(2) and (c)(3) of this section;

(3) If the plan benefits will be paid in any form other than a lump sum and the age at which, or form in which, the plan benefits will be paid differs from the normal retirement benefit—

(i) The age or form stated in the plan; and

(ii) The age or form adjustment factors; and

(4) If the plan benefits will be paid in a lump sum—

(i) An explanation of when a lump sum may be paid without the consent of the participant or the participant's spouse;

(ii) A description of the mortality table used to convert to the lump sum benefit (e.g., the mortality table published by the IRS in Revenue Ruling 95-6, 1995-1 C.B. 80) and a reference to the pertinent plan provisions;

(iii) A description of the interest rate to be used to convert to the lump sum benefit (e.g., the 30-year Treasury rate for the third month before the month in which the lump sum is distributed), a reference to the pertinent plan provision, and (if known) the applicable interest rate;

(iv) An explanation of how interest rates are used to calculate lump sums;

(v) A statement that the use of a higher interest rate results in a smaller lump sum amount; and

(vi) A statement that the applicable interest rate may change before the distribution date.

(e) *Benefits of all other persons not in pay status.* For any other affected party not described in paragraph (c) or (d) of this section (or described therein only with respect to a portion of the affected party's plan benefits), the plan administrator must include in the notice of plan benefits—

(1) The amount and form of the person's plan benefits payable at normal retirement age in any one form permitted under the plan;

(2) Any alternative benefit forms, including those payable to a beneficiary upon the person's death either before or after benefits commence;

(3) If the person is or may become entitled to a benefit that would be payable before normal retirement age, the amount and form of benefit that would be payable at the earliest benefit commencement date (or, if more than one such form is payable at the earliest benefit commencement date, any one of those forms) and whether the benefit commencing on such date would be subject to future reduction; and

(4) If the plan benefits may be paid in a lump sum, the information in paragraph (d)(4) of this section.

(f) *Spin-off/termination transactions.* In the case of a spin-off/termination transaction (as defined in § 4041.23(c)), the plan administrator must, no later than the time the plan administrator files the standard termination notice for any terminating plan, provide all participants, beneficiaries of deceased participants, and alternate payees in the original plan who are (as of the proposed termination date) covered by an ongoing plan with a notice of plan benefits containing the information in paragraphs (b) through (e) of this section. [Amended 11/6/97 by 62 FR 60424.]

[¶ 15,440F-4]

§ 4041.25 **Standard termination notice.** (a) *Notice requirement.* The plan administrator must file with the PBGC a standard termination notice, consisting of the PBGC Form 500, completed in accordance with the instructions thereto, on or before the 180th day after the proposed termination date.

(b) *Change of proposed termination date.* The plan administrator may, in the standard termination notice, select a proposed termination date that is later than the date specified in the notice of intent to terminate, provided it is not later than 90 days after the earliest date on which a notice of intent to terminate was issued to any affected party.

(c) *Request for IRS determination letter.* To qualify for the distribution deadline in § 4041.28(a)(1)(ii), the plan administrator must submit to the IRS a valid request for a determination of the plan's qualification status upon termination ("determination letter") by the time the standard termination notice is filed. [Amended 11/7/97 by 62 FR 60424.]

[¶ 15,440F-5]

§ 4041.26 **PBGC review of standard termination notice.** (a) *Review period.* (1) *In general.* The PBGC will notify the plan administrator in writing of the date on which it received a complete standard termination notice at the address provided in the PBGC's standard termination forms and instructions package. If the PBGC does not issue a notice of noncompliance under § 4041.31 during its 60-day review period following such date, the plan administrator must proceed to close out the plan in accordance with § 4041.28.

(2) *Extension of review period.* The PBGC and the plan administrator may, before the expiration of the PBGC review period in paragraph (a)(1) of this section, agree in writing to extend that period.

(b) *If standard termination notice is incomplete.* (1) For purposes of timely filing. If the standard termination notice is incomplete, the PBGC may, based on the nature and extent of the omission, provide the plan administrator an opportunity to complete the notice. In such a case, the standard termination notice will be deemed to have been complete as of the date when originally filed for purposes of

§ 4041.25(a), provided the plan administrator provides the missing information by the later of—

   (i) The 180th day after the proposed termination date; or

   (ii) The 30th day after the date of the PBGC notice that the filing was incomplete.

   (2) *For purposes of PBGC review period.* If the standard termination notice is completed under paragraph (b)(1) of this section, the PBGC will determine whether the notice will be deemed to have been complete as of the date when originally filed for purposes of determining when the PBGC's review period begins under § 4041.26(a)(1).

   (c) *Additional information.* (1) *Deadline for providing additional information.* The PBGC may in any case require the submission of additional information relevant to the termination proceeding. Any such additional information becomes part of the standard termination notice and must be submitted within 30 days after the date of a written request by the PBGC, or within a different time period specified therein. The PBGC may in its discretion shorten the time period where it determines that the interests of the PBGC or participants may be prejudiced by a delay in receipt of the information.

   (2) *Effect on termination proceeding.* A request for additional information will suspend the running of the PBGC's 60-day review period. The review period will begin running again on the day the required information is received and continue for the greater of—

   (i) The number of days remaining in the review period; or

   (ii) Five regular business days. [Amended 11/7/97 by 62 FR 60424.]

[¶ 15,440F-6]

§ 4041.27 **Notice of annuity information.** (a) *Notice requirement.* (1) *In general.* The plan administrator must provide notices in accordance with this section to each affected party entitled to plan benefits other than an affected party whose plan benefits will be distributed in the form of a nonconsensual lump sum.

   (2) *Spin-off/termination transactions.* The plan administrator must provide the information in paragraph (d) of this section to a person entitled to notice under §§ 4041.23(c) or 4041.24(f), at the same time and in the same manner as required for an affected party.

   (b) *Content of notice.* The plan administrator must include, as part of the notice of intent to terminate—

   (1) *Identity of insurers.* The name and address of the insurer or insurers from whom (if known), or (if not) from among whom, the plan administrator intends to purchase irrevocable commitments (annuity contracts);

   (2) *Change in identity of insurers.* A statement that if the plan administrator later decides to select a different insurer, affected parties will receive a supplemental notice no later than 45 days before the distribution date; and

   (3) *State guaranty association coverage information.* A statement informing the affected party—

   (i) That once the plan distributes a benefit in the form of an annuity purchased from an insurance company, the insurance company takes over the responsibility for paying that benefit;

   (ii) That all states, the District of Columbia, and the Commonwealth of Puerto Rico have established "guaranty associations" to protect policy holders in the event of an insurance company's financial failure;

   (iii) That a guaranty association is responsible for all, part, or none of the annuity if the insurance company cannot pay;

   (iv) That each guaranty association has dollar limits on the extent of its guaranty coverage, along with a general description of the applicable dollar coverage limits;

   (v) That in most cases the policy holder is covered by the guaranty association for the state where he or she lives at the time the insurance company fails to pay; and

   (vi) How to obtain the addresses and telephone numbers of guaranty association offices from the PBGC (as described in the applicable forms and instructions package).

   (c) *Where insurer(s) not known.* (1) *Extension of deadline for notice.* If the identity-of-insurer information in paragraph (b)(1) of this section is not known at the time the plan administrator is required to provide it to an affected party as part of a notice of intent to terminate, the plan administrator must instead provide it in a supplemental notice under paragraph (d) of this section.

   (2) *Alternative NOIT information.* A plan administrator that qualifies for the extension in paragraph (c)(1) of this section with respect to a notice of intent to terminate must include therein (in lieu of the information in paragraph (b) of this section) a statement that—

   (i) Irrevocable commitments (annuity contracts) may be purchased from an insurer to provide some or all of the benefits under the plan;

   (ii) The insurer or insurers have not yet been identified; and

   (iii) Affected parties will be notified at a later date (but no later than 45 days before the distribution date) of the name and address of the insurer or insurers from whom (if known), or (if not) from among whom, the plan administrator intends to purchase irrevocable commitments (annuity contracts).

   (d) *Supplemental notice.* The plan administrator must provide a supplemental notice to an affected party in accordance with this paragraph (d) if the plan administrator did not previously notify the affected party of the identity of insurer(s) or, after having previously notified the affected party of the identity of insurer(s), decides to select a different insurer. A failure to provide a required supplemental notice to an affected party will be deemed to be a failure to comply with the notice of intent to terminate requirements.

   (1) *Deadline for supplemental notice.* The deadline for issuing the supplemental notice is 45 days before the affected party's distribution date (or, in the case of an employee organization, 45 days before the earliest distribution date for any affected party that it represents).

   (2) *Content of supplemental notice.* The supplemental notice must include—

   (i) The identity-of-insurer information in paragraph (b)(1) of this section;

   (ii) The information regarding change of identity of insurer(s) in paragraph (b)(2) of this section; and

   (iii) Unless the state guaranty association coverage information in paragraph (b)(3) of this section was previously provided to the affected party, such information and the extinguishment-of-guarantee information in § 4041.23(b)(9). [Amended 11/7/97 by 62 FR 60424.]

[¶ 15,440F-7]

§ 4041.28 **Closeout of plan.** (a) *Distribution deadline.* (1) *In general.* Unless a notice of noncompliance is issued under § 4041.31(a), the plan administrator must complete the distribution of plan assets in satisfaction of plan benefits (through priority category 6 under section 4044 of ERISA and part 4044 of this chapter) by the later of—

   (i) 180 days after the expiration of the PBGC's 60-day (or extended) review period under § 4041.26(a); or

   (ii) If the plan administrator meets the requirements of § 4041.25(c), 120 days after receipt of a favorable determination from the IRS.

   (2) *Revocation of notice of noncompliance.* If the PBGC revokes a notice of noncompliance issued under § 4041.31(a), the distribution deadline is extended until the 180th day after the date of the revocation.

   (3) *Missing participants and beneficiaries.* The distribution deadline is considered met with respect to a missing distributee to whom subpart A of part 4050 of this chapter applies if the benefit transfer amount for the missing distributee is considered timely transferred to PBGC under subpart A of part 4050 of this chapter. [Added 12/22/2017 by 82 FR 60800.]

   (b) *Assets insufficient to satisfy plan benefits.* If, at the time of any distribution, the plan administrator determines that plan assets are not sufficient to satisfy all plan benefits (with assets determined net of other liabilities, including PBGC premiums), the plan administrator may not make any further distribution of assets to effect the plan's termination and must promptly notify the PBGC.

(c) *Method of distribution.* (1) *In general.* The plan administrator must, in accordance with all applicable requirements under the Code and ERISA, distribute plan assets in satisfaction of all plan benefits by purchase of an irrevocable commitment from an insurer or in another permitted form.

(2) *Lump sum calculations.* In the absence of evidence establishing that another date is the "annuity starting date" under the Code, the distribution date is the "annuity starting date" for purposes of—

(i) Calculating the present value of plan benefits that may be provided in a form other than by purchase of an irrevocable commitment from an insurer (e.g., in selecting the interest rate(s) to be used to value a lump sum distribution); and

(ii) Determining whether plan benefits will be paid in such other form.

(3) *Selection of insurer.* In the case of plan benefits that will be provided by purchase of an irrevocable commitment from an insurer, the plan administrator must select the insurer in accordance with the fiduciary standards of Title I of ERISA.

(4) *Participating annuity contracts.* In the case of a plan in which any residual assets will be distributed to participants, a participating annuity contract may be purchased to satisfy the requirement that annuities be provided by the purchase of irrevocable commitments only if the portion of the price of the contract that is attributable to the participation feature—

(i) Is not taken into account in determining the amount of residual assets; and

(ii) Is not paid from residual assets allocable to participants.

(5) *Missing participants.* The plan administrator must distribute plan benefits to missing participants in accordance with subpart A of part 4050 of this chapter. [Amended 12/22/2017 by 82 FR 60800.]

(d) *Provision of annuity contract.* If plan benefits are provided through the purchase of irrevocable commitments—

(1) Either the plan administrator or the insurer must, within 30 days after it is available, provide each participant and beneficiary with a copy of the annuity contract or certificate showing the insurer's name and address and clearly reflecting the insurer's obligation to provide the participant's or beneficiary's plan benefits; and

(2) If such a contract or certificate is not provided to the participant or beneficiary by the date on which the post-distribution certification is required to be filed in order to avoid the assessment of penalties under § 4041.29(b), the plan administrator must, no later than that date, provide the participant and beneficiary with a notice that includes—

(i) A statement that the obligation for providing the participant's or beneficiary's plan benefits has transferred to the insurer;

(ii) The name and address of the insurer;

(iii) The name, address, and telephone number of the person designated by the insurer to answer questions concerning the annuity; and

(iv) A statement that the participant or beneficiary will receive from the plan administrator or insurer a copy of the annuity contract or a certificate showing the insurer's name and address and clearly reflecting the insurer's obligation to provide the participant's or beneficiary's plan benefits. [Amended 11/7/97 by 62 FR 60424.]

[¶ 15,440F-8]

§ 4041.29 **Post-distribution certification.** (a) *Deadline.* Within 30 days after the last distribution date for any affected party, the plan administrator must file with the PBGC a post-distribution certification consisting of the PBGC Form 501, completed in accordance with the instructions thereto.

(b) *Assessment of penalties.* The PBGC will assess a penalty for late filing of a post-distribution certification only to the extent the certification is filed more than 90 days after the distribution deadline (including extensions) under § 4041.28(a). [Amended 11/7/97 by 62 FR 60424.]

[¶ 15,440F-9]

§ 4041.30 **Requests for deadline extensions.** (a) *In general.* The PBGC may in its discretion extend a deadline for taking action under this subpart to a later date. The PBGC will grant such an extension where it finds compelling reasons why it is not administratively feasible for the plan administrator (or other persons acting on behalf of the plan administrator) to take the action until the later date and the delay is brief. The PBGC will consider—

(1) The length of the delay; and

(2) Whether ordinary business care and prudence in attempting to meet the deadline is exercised.

(b) *Time of extension request.* Any request for an extension under paragraph (a) of this section that is filed later than the 15th day before the applicable deadline must include a justification for not filing the request earlier.

(c) *IRS determination letter requests.* Any request for an extension under paragraph (a) of this section of the deadline in § 4041.25(c) for submitting a determination letter request to the IRS (in order to qualify for the distribution deadline in § 4041.28(a)(1)(ii)) will be deemed to be granted unless the PBGC notifies the plan administrator otherwise within 60 days after receipt of the request (or, if later, by the end of the PBGC's review period under § 4041.26(a)). The PBGC will notify the plan administrator in writing of the date on which it receives such request.

(d) *Statutory deadlines not extendable.* The PBGC will not—

(1) *Pre-distribution deadlines.* (i) Extend the 60-day time limit under § 4041.23(a) for issuing the notice of intent to terminate; or

(ii) Waive the requirement in § 4041.24(a) that the notice of plan benefits be issued by the time the plan administrator files the standard termination notice with the PBGC; or

(2) *Post-distribution deadlines.* Extend the deadline under § 4041.29(a) for filing the post-distribution certification. However, the PBGC will assess a penalty for late filing of a post-distribution certification only under the circumstances described in § 4041.29(b). [Amended 11/7/97 by 62 FR 60424.]

[¶ 15,440F-10]

§ 4041.31 **Notice of noncompliance.** (a) *Failure to meet pre-distribution requirements.* (1) *In general.* Except as provided in paragraphs (a)(2) and (c) of this section, the PBGC will issue a notice of noncompliance within the 60-day (or extended) time period prescribed by § 4041.26(a) whenever it determines that—

(i) The plan administrator failed to issue the notice of intent to terminate to all affected parties (other than the PBGC) in accordance with § 4041.23;

(ii) The plan administrator failed to issue notices of plan benefits to all affected parties entitled to plan benefits in accordance with § 4041.24;

(iii) The plan administrator failed to file the standard termination notice in accordance with § 4041.25;

(iv) As of the distribution date proposed in the standard termination notice, plan assets will not be sufficient to satisfy all plan benefits under the plan; or

(v) In the case of a spin-off/termination transaction (as described in § 4041.23(c)), the plan administrator failed to issue any notice required by § 4041.23(c), § 4041.24(f), or § 4041.27(a)(2) in accordance with such section.

(2) *Interests of participants.* The PBGC may decide not to issue a notice of noncompliance based on a failure to meet a requirement under paragraphs (a)(1)(i) through (a)(1)(iii) or (a)(1)(v) of this section if it determines that issuance of the notice would be inconsistent with the interests of participants and beneficiaries.

(3) *Continuing authority.* The PBGC may issue a notice of noncompliance or suspend the termination proceeding based on a failure to meet a requirement under paragraphs (a)(1)(i) through (a)(1)(v) of this section after expiration of the 60-day (or extended) time period

prescribed by §4041.26(a) (including upon audit) if the PBGC determines such action is necessary to carry out the purposes of Title IV.

(b) *Failure to meet distribution requirements*. (1) *In general*. If the PBGC determines, as part of an audit or otherwise, that the plan administrator has not satisfied any distribution requirement of §4041.28(a) or (c), it may issue a notice of noncompliance.

(2) *Criteria*. In deciding whether to issue a notice of noncompliance under paragraph (b)(1) of this section, the PBGC may consider—

(i) The nature and extent of the failure to satisfy a requirement of §4041.28(a) or (c);

(ii) Any corrective action taken by the plan administrator; and

(iii) The interests of participants and beneficiaries.

(3) *Late distributions*. The PBGC will not issue a notice of noncompliance for failure to distribute timely based on any facts disclosed in the post-distribution certification if 60 or more days have passed from the PBGC's receipt of the post-distribution certification. The 60-day period may be extended by agreement between the plan administrator and the PBGC.

(c) *Correction of errors*. The PBGC will not issue a notice of noncompliance based solely on the plan administrator's inclusion of erroneous information (or omission of correct information) in a notice required to be provided to any person under this part if—

(1) The PBGC determines that the plan administrator acted in good faith in connection with the error;

(2) The plan administrator corrects the error no later than—

(i) In the case of an error in the notice of plan benefits under §4041.24, the latest date an election notice may be provided to the person; or

(ii) In any other case, as soon as practicable after the plan administrator knows or should know of the error, or by any later date specified by the PBGC; and

(3) The PBGC determines that the delay in providing the correct information will not substantially harm any person.

(d) *Reconsideration*. A plan administrator may request reconsideration of a notice of noncompliance in accordance with the rules prescribed in part 4003, subpart C.

(e) *Consequences of notice of noncompliance*. (1) *Effect on termination*. A notice of noncompliance ends the standard termination proceeding, nullifies all actions taken to terminate the plan, and renders the plan an ongoing plan. A notice of noncompliance is effective upon the expiration of the period within which the plan administrator may request reconsideration under paragraph (d) of this section or, if reconsideration is requested, a decision by the PBGC upholding the notice. However, once a notice is issued, the running of all time periods specified in ERISA or this part relevant to the termination will be suspended, and the plan administrator may take no further action to terminate the plan (except by initiation of a new termination) unless and until the notice is revoked. A plan administrator that still desires to terminate a plan must initiate the termination process again, starting with the issuance of a new notice of intent to terminate.

(2) *Effect on plan administration*. If the PBGC issues a notice of noncompliance, the prohibitions in §4041.22(a)(1) and (a)(2) will cease to apply—

(i) Upon expiration of the period during which reconsideration may be requested or, if earlier, at the time the plan administrator decides not to request reconsideration; or

(ii) If reconsideration is requested, upon PBGC issuance of a decision on reconsideration upholding the notice of noncompliance.

(3) *Revocation of notice of noncompliance*. If a notice of noncompliance is revoked, unless the PBGC provides otherwise, any time period suspended by the issuance of the notice will resume running from the date of the revocation. In no case will the review period under §4041.26(a) end less than 60 days from the date the PBGC received the standard termination notice.

(f) *If no notice of noncompliance is issued*. A standard termination is deemed to be valid if—

(1) The plan administrator files a standard termination notice under §4041.25 and the PBGC does not issue a notice of noncompliance pursuant to §4041.31(a); and

(2) The plan administrator files a post-distribution certification under §4041.29 and the PBGC does not issue a notice of noncompliance pursuant to §4041.31(b).

(g) *Notice to affected parties*. Upon a decision by the PBGC on reconsideration affirming the issuance of a notice of noncompliance or, if earlier, upon the plan administrator's decision not to request reconsideration, the plan administrator must notify the affected parties (other than the PBGC), and any persons who were provided notice under §4041.23(c), in writing that the plan is not going to terminate or, if applicable, that the termination was invalid but that a new notice of intent to terminate is being issued. [Amended 11/7/97 by 62 FR 60424.]

Subpart C—Distress Termination Process

[¶ 15,440J]

§4041.41 **Requirements for a distress termination**. (a) *Distress requirements*. A plan may be terminated in a distress termination only if—

(1) The plan administrator issues a notice of intent to terminate to each affected party in accordance with §4041.43 at least 60 days and (except with PBGC approval) not more than 90 days before the proposed termination date;

(2) The plan administrator files a distress termination notice with the PBGC in accordance with §4041.45 no later than 120 days after the proposed termination date; and

(3) The PBGC determines that each contributing sponsor and each member of its controlled group satisfy one of the distress criteria set forth in paragraph (c) of this section.

(b) *Effect of failure to satisfy requirements*. (1) Except as provided in paragraph (b)(2)(i) of this section, if the plan administrator does not satisfy all of the requirements for a distress termination, any action taken to effect the plan termination is null and void, and the plan is an ongoing plan. A plan administrator who still desires to terminate the plan must initiate the termination process again, starting with the issuance of a new notice of intent to terminate.

(2)(i) The PBGC may, upon its own motion, waive any requirement with respect to notices to be filed with the PBGC under paragraph (a)(1) or (a)(2) of this section if the PBGC believes that it will be less costly or administratively burdensome to the PBGC to do so. The PBGC will not entertain requests for waivers under this paragraph.

(ii) Notwithstanding any other provision of this part, the PBGC retains the authority in any case to initiate a plan termination in accordance with the provisions of section 4042 of ERISA.

(c) *Distress criteria*. In a distress termination, each contributing sponsor and each member of its controlled group must satisfy at least one (but not necessarily the same one) of the following criteria in order for a distress termination to occur:

(1) *Liquidation*. This criterion is met if, as of the proposed termination date—

(i) A person has filed or had filed against it a petition seeking liquidation in a case under title 11, United States Code, or under a similar federal law or law of a State or political subdivision of a State, or a case described in paragraph (e)(2) of this section has been converted to such a case; and

(ii) The case has not been dismissed.

(2) *Reorganization*. This criterion is met if—

(i) As of the proposed termination date, a person has filed or had filed against it a petition seeking reorganization in a case under title 11, United States Code, or under a similar law of a state or a political subdivision of a state, or a case described in paragraph (e)(1) of this section has been converted to such a case;

(ii) As of the proposed termination date, the case has not been dismissed;

(iii) The person notifies the PBGC of any request to the bankruptcy court (or other appropriate court in a case under such similar law of a state or a political subdivision of a state) for approval of the plan termination by concurrently filing with the PBGC a copy of the motion requesting court approval, including any documents submitted in support of the request; and

(iv) The bankruptcy court or other appropriate court determines that, unless the plan is terminated, such person will be unable to pay all its debts pursuant to a plan of reorganization and will be unable to continue in business outside the reorganization process and approves the plan termination.

(3) *Inability to continue in business.* This criterion is met if a person demonstrates to the satisfaction of the PBGC that, unless a distress termination occurs, the person will be unable to pay its debts when due and to continue in business.

(4) *Unreasonably burdensome pension costs.* This criterion is met if a person demonstrates to the satisfaction of the PBGC that the person's costs of providing pension coverage have become unreasonably burdensome solely as a result of declining covered employment under all single-employer plans for which that person is a contributing sponsor.

(d) *Non-duplicative efforts.* (1) If a person requests approval of the plan termination by a court, as described in paragraph (c)(2) of this section, the PBGC—

(i) Will normally enter an appearance to request that the court make specific findings as to whether the contributing sponsor or controlled group member meets the distress test in paragraph (c)(3) of this section, or state that it is unable to make such findings;

(ii) Will provide the court with any information it has that may be germane to the court's ruling;

(iii) Will, if the person has requested, or later requests, a determination by the PBGC under paragraph (c)(3) of this section, defer action on the request until the court makes its determination; and

(iv) Will be bound by a final and non-appealable order of the court.

(2) If a person requests a determination by the PBGC under paragraph (c)(3) of this section, the PBGC determines that the distress criterion is not met, and the person thereafter requests approval of the plan termination by a court, as described in paragraph (c)(2) of this section, the PBGC will advise the court of its determination and make its administrative record available to the court.

(e) *Non-recognition of certain actions.* If the PBGC finds that a person undertook any action or failed to act for the principal purpose of satisfying any of the distress criteria contained in paragraph (c) of this section, rather than for a reasonable business purpose, the PBGC will disregard such act or failure to act in determining whether the person has satisfied any of those criteria.

(f) *Requests for deadline extensions.* The PBGC may extend any deadline under this subpart in accordance with the rules described in section §4041.30, except that the PBGC will not extend—

(1) *Pre-distribution deadlines.* The 60-day time limit under §4041.43(a) for issuing the notice of intent to terminate; or

(2) *Post-distribution deadlines.* The deadline under §4041.50 for filing the post-distribution certification. [Amended 11/7/97 by 62 FR 60424.]

[¶ 15,440J-1]

§4041.42 **Administration of plan during termination process**. (a) *General rule.* Except to the extent specifically prohibited by this section, during the pendency of termination proceedings the plan administrator must continue to carry out the normal operations of the plan, such as putting participants into pay status, collecting contributions due the plan, and investing plan assets.

(b) *Prohibitions after issuing notice of intent to terminate.* The plan administrator may not make loans to plan participants beginning on the first day he or she issues a notice of intent to terminate, and from that date until a distribution is permitted pursuant to §4041.50, the plan administrator may not—

(1) Distribute plan assets pursuant to, or (except as required by this part) take any other actions to implement, the termination of the plan;

(2) Pay benefits attributable to employer contributions, other than death benefits, in any form other than as an annuity; or

(3) Purchase irrevocable commitments to provide benefits from an insurer.

(c) *Limitation on benefit payments on or after proposed termination date.* Beginning on the proposed termination date, the plan administrator must reduce benefits to the level determined under part 4022, subpart D, of this chapter.

(d) *Failure to qualify for distress termination.* In any case where the PBGC determines, pursuant to §4041.44(c) or §4041.46(c)(1), that the requirements for a distress termination are not satisfied—

(1) The prohibitions in paragraph (b) of this section, other than those in paragraph (b)(1), will cease to apply—

(i) Upon expiration of the period during which reconsideration may be requested under §§4041.44(e) and 4041.46(e) or, if earlier, at the time the plan administrator decides not to request reconsideration; or

(ii) If reconsideration is requested, upon PBGC issuance of its decision on reconsideration.

(2) Any benefits that were not paid pursuant to paragraph (c) of this section will be due and payable as of the effective date of the PBGC's determination, together with interest from the date (or dates) on which the unpaid amounts were originally due until the date on which they are paid in full at the rate or rates prescribed under §4022.81(c)(3) of this chapter.

(e) *Effect of subsequent insufficiency.* If the plan administrator makes a finding of subsequent insufficiency for guaranteed benefits pursuant to §4041.49(b), or the PBGC notifies the plan administrator that it has made a finding of subsequent insufficiency for guaranteed benefits pursuant to §4041.40(d), the prohibitions in paragraph (b) of this section will apply in accordance with §4041.49(e). [Amended 11/7/97 by 62 FR 60424.]

[¶ 15,440J-2]

§4041.43 **Notice of intent to terminate**. (a) *General rules.* (1) At least 60 days and (except with PBGC approval) no more than 90 days before the proposed termination date, the plan administrator must issue a written notice of intent to terminate to each person who is an affected party as of the proposed termination date.

(2) The plan administrator must issue the notice of intent to terminate to all affected parties other than the PBGC at or before the time he or she files the notice with the PBGC.

(3) The notice to affected parties other than the PBGC must contain all of the information specified in paragraph (b) of this section.

(4) The notice to the PBGC must be filed on PBGC Form 600, Distress Termination, Notice of Intent to Terminate, completed in accordance with the instructions thereto.

(5) In the case of a beneficiary of a deceased participant or an alternate payee, the plan administrator must issue a notice of intent to terminate promptly to any person that becomes an affected party after the proposed termination date and on or before the date a trustee is appointed for the plan pursuant to section 4042(c) of ERISA (or, in the case of a plan that distributes assets pursuant to §4041.50, the distribution date).

(b) *Contents of notice to affected parties other than the PBGC.* The plan administrator must include in the notice of intent to terminate to each affected party other than the PBGC all of the following information:

(1) The name of the plan and of the contributing sponsor;

(2) The EIN of the contributing sponsor and the PN; if there is no EIN or PN, the notice must so state;

(3) The name, address, and telephone number of the person who may be contacted by an affected party with questions concerning the plan's termination;

(4) A statement that the plan administrator expects to terminate the plan in a distress termination on a specified proposed termination date;

(5) The cessation of accruals information in §4041.23(b)(4);

(6) A statement as to how an affected party entitled to receive the latest updated summary plan description under section 104(b) of ERISA can obtain it;

(7) A statement of whether plan assets are sufficient to pay all guaranteed benefits or all benefit liabilities;

(8) A brief description of what benefits are guaranteed by the PBGC (e.g., if only a portion of the benefits are guaranteed because of the phase-in rule, this should be explained), and a statement that participants and beneficiaries also may receive a portion of the benefits to which each is entitled under the terms of the plan in excess of guaranteed benefits; and

(9) A statement, if applicable, that benefits may be subject to reduction because of the limitations on the amounts guaranteed by the PBGC or because plan assets are insufficient to pay for full benefits (pursuant to part 4022, subparts B and D, of this chapter) and that payments in excess of the amount guaranteed by the PBGC may be recouped by the PBGC (pursuant to part 4022, subpart E, of this chapter).

(c) *Spin-off/termination transactions.* In the case of a spin-off/termination transaction (as described in §4041.23(c)), the plan administrator must provide all participants and beneficiaries in the original plan who are also participants or beneficiaries in the ongoing plan (as of the proposed termination date) with a notice describing the transaction no later than the date on which the plan administrator completes the issuance of notices of intent to terminate under this section. [Amended 11/7/97 by 62 FR 60424.]

[¶ 15,440J-3]

§4041.44 **PBGC review of notice of intent to terminate.** (a) *General.* When a notice of intent to terminate is filed with it, the PBGC—

(1) Will determine whether the notice was issued in compliance with §4041.43; and

(2) Will advise the plan administrator of its determination, in accordance with paragraph (b) or (c) of this section, no later than the proposed termination date specified in the notice.

(b) *Tentative finding of compliance.* If the PBGC determines that the issuance of the notice of intent to terminate appears to be in compliance with §4041.43, it will notify the plan administrator in writing that—

(1) The PBGC has made a tentative determination of compliance;

(2) The distress termination proceeding may continue; and

(3) After reviewing the distress termination notice filed pursuant to §4041.45, the PBGC will make final, or reverse, this tentative determination.

(c) *Finding of noncompliance.* If the PBGC determines that the issuance of the notice of intent to terminate was not in compliance with §4041.43 (except for requirements that the PBGC elects to waive under §4041.41(b)(2)(i) with respect to the notice filed with the PBGC), the PBGC will notify the plan administrator in writing—

(1) That the PBGC has determined that the notice of intent to terminate was not properly issued; and

(2) That the proposed distress termination is null and void and the plan is an ongoing plan.

(d) *Information on need to institute section 4042 proceedings.* The PBGC may require the plan administrator to submit, within 20 days after the plan administrator's receipt of the PBGC's written request (or such other period as may be specified in such written request), any information that the PBGC determines it needs in order to decide whether to institute termination or trusteeship proceedings pursuant to section 4042 of ERISA, whenever—

(1) A notice of intent to terminate indicates that benefits currently in pay status (or that should be in pay status) are not being paid

or that this is likely to occur within the 180-day period following the issuance of the notice of intent to terminate;

(2) The PBGC issues a determination under paragraph (c) of this section; or

(3) The PBGC has any reason to believe that it may be necessary or appropriate to institute proceedings under section 4042 of ERISA.

(e) *Reconsideration of finding of noncompliance.* A plan administrator may request reconsideration of the PBGC's determination of noncompliance under paragraph (c) of this section in accordance with the rules prescribed in part 4003, subpart C, of this chapter. Any request for reconsideration automatically stays the effectiveness of the determination until the PBGC issues its decision on reconsideration, but does not stay the time period within which information must be submitted to the PBGC in response to a request under paragraph (d) of this section.

(f) *Notice to affected parties.* Upon a decision by the PBGC affirming a finding of noncompliance or upon the expiration of the period within which the plan administrator may request reconsideration of a finding of noncompliance (or, if earlier, upon the plan administrator's decision not to request reconsideration), the plan administrator must notify the affected parties (and any persons who were provided notice under §4041.43(e)) in writing that the plan is not going to terminate or, if applicable, that the termination is invalid but that a new notice of intent to terminate is being issued. [Amended 11/7/97 by 62 FR 60424.]

[¶ 15,440J-4]

§4041.45 **Distress termination notice.** (a) *General rule.* The plan administrator must file with the PBGC a PBGC Form 601, Distress Termination Notice, Single-Employer Plan Termination, with Schedule EA-D, Distress Termination Enrolled Actuary Certification, that has been completed in accordance with the instructions thereto, on or before the 120th day after the proposed termination date.

(b) *Participant and benefit information.* (1) *Plan insufficient for guaranteed benefits.* Unless the enrolled actuary certifies, in the Schedule EA-D filed in accordance with paragraph (a) of this section, that the plan is sufficient either for guaranteed benefits or for benefit liabilities, the plan administrator must file with the PBGC the participant and benefit information described in PBGC Form 601 and the instructions thereto by the later of—

(i) 120 days after the proposed termination date, or

(ii) 30 days after receipt of the PBGC's determination, pursuant to §4041.46(b), that the requirements for a distress termination have been satisfied.

(2) *Plan sufficient for guaranteed benefits or benefit liabilities.* If the enrolled actuary certifies that the plan is sufficient either for guaranteed benefits or for benefit liabilities, the plan administrator need not submit the participant and benefit information described in PBGC Form 601 and the instructions thereto unless requested to do so pursuant to paragraph (c) of this section.

(3) *Effect of failure to provide information.* The PBGC may void the distress termination if the plan administrator fails to provide complete participant and benefit information in accordance with this section.

(c) *Additional information.* The PBGC may in any case require the submission of any additional information that it needs to make the determinations that it is required to make under this part or to pay benefits pursuant to section 4061 or 4022(c) of ERISA. The plan administrator must submit any information requested under this paragraph within 30 days after receiving the PBGC's written request (or such other period as may be specified in such written request). [Amended 11/7/97 by 62 FR 60424.]

[¶ 15,440J-5]

§4041.46 **PBGC determination of compliance with requirements for distress termination.** (a) *General.* Based on the information contained and submitted with the PBGC Form 600 and the PBGC Form 601, with Schedule EA-D, and on any information submitted by an affected party or otherwise obtained by the PBGC, the PBGC will determine whether the requirements for a distress termination set forth in § 4041.41(c) have been met and will notify the plan administrator in writing of its determination, in accordance with paragraph (b) or (c) of this section.

(b) *Qualifying termination.* If the PBGC determines that all of the requirements of § 4041.41(c) have been satisfied, it will so advise the plan administrator and will also advise the plan administrator of whether participant and benefit information must be submitted in accordance with § 4041.45(b).

(c) *Non-qualifying termination.* (1) Except as provided in paragraph (c)(2) of this section, if the PBGC determines that any of the requirements of § 4041.41 have not been met, it will notify the plan administrator of its determination, the basis therefor, and the effect thereof (as provided in § 4041.41(b)).

(2) If the only basis for the PBGC's determination described in paragraph (c)(1) of this section is that the distress termination notice is incomplete, the PBGC will advise the plan administrator of the missing item(s) of information and that the information must be filed with the PBGC no later than the 120th day after the proposed termination date or the 30th day after the date of the PBGC's notice of its determination, whichever is later.

(d) *Reconsideration of determination of non-qualification.* A plan administrator may request reconsideration of the PBGC's determination under paragraph (c)(1) of this section in accordance with the rules prescribed in part 4003, subpart C, of this chapter. The filing of a request for reconsideration automatically stays the effectiveness of the determination until the PBGC issues its decision on reconsideration.

(e) *Notice to affected parties.* Upon a decision by the PBGC affirming a determination of non-qualification or upon the expiration of the period within which the plan administrator may request reconsideration of a determination of non-qualification (or, if earlier, upon the plan administrator's decision not to request reconsideration), the plan administrator must notify the affected parties (and any persons who were provided notice under § 4041.43(e)) in writing that the plan is not going to terminate or, if applicable, that the termination is invalid but that a new notice of intent to terminate is being issued. [Amended 11/7/97 by 62 FR 60424.]

[¶ 15,440J-6]

§ 4041.47 **PBGC determination of plan sufficiency/insufficiency.** (a) *General.* Upon receipt of participant and benefit information filed pursuant to § 4041.45(b)(1) or (c), the PBGC will determine the degree to which the plan is sufficient and notify the plan administrator in writing of its determination in accordance with paragraph (b) or (c) of this section.

(b) *Insufficiency for guaranteed benefits.* If the PBGC finds that it is unable to determine that a plan is sufficient for guaranteed benefits, it will issue a "notice of inability to determine sufficiency" notifying the plan administrator of this finding and advising the plan administrator that—

(1) The plan administrator must continue to administer the plan under the restrictions imposed by § 4041.42; and

(2) The termination will be completed under section 4042 of ERISA.

(c) *Sufficiency for guaranteed benefits or benefit liabilities.* If the PBGC determines that a plan is sufficient for guaranteed benefits but not for benefit liabilities or is sufficient for benefit liabilities, the PBGC will issue to the plan administrator a distribution notice advising the plan administrator—

(1) To issue notices of benefit distribution in accordance with § 4041.48;

(2) To close out the plan in accordance with § 4041.50;

(3) To file a timely post-distribution certification with the PBGC in accordance with § 4041.50(b); and

(4) That either the plan administrator or the contributing sponsor must preserve and maintain plan records in accordance with § 4041.5.

(d) *Alternative treatment of majority owner's benefit.* A majority owner may elect to forgo receipt of all or part of his or her plan benefits in connection with a distress termination. Any such alternative treatment—

(1) Is valid only if the conditions in § 4041.21(b)(2)(i) through (iv) are met (except that, in the case of a plan that does not distribute assets pursuant to § 4041.50, the majority owner may make the election and the spouse may consent any time on or after the date of issuance of the first notice of intent to terminate); and—

(2) Is subject to the PBGC's approval if the election—

(i) Is made after the termination date; and

(ii) Would result in the PBGC determining that the plan is sufficient for guaranteed benefits under paragraph (c). [Amended 11/7/97 by 62 FR 60424.]

[¶ 15,440J-7]

§ 4041.48 **Sufficient plans; notice requirements.** (a) *Notices of benefit distribution.* When a distribution notice is issued by the PBGC pursuant to § 4041.47, the plan administrator must issue notices of benefit distribution in accordance with the rules regarding notices of plan benefits in § 4041.24, except that—

(1) The deadline for issuing the notices of benefit distribution is the 60th day after receipt of the distribution notice; and

(2) With respect to the information described in § 4041.24(b) through (e), the term "plan benefits" is replaced with "title IV benefits" and the term "proposed termination date" is replaced with "termination date".

(b) *Certification to PBGC.* No later than 15 days after the date on which the plan administrator completes the issuance of the notices of benefit distribution, the plan administrator must file with the PBGC a certification that the notices were so issued in accordance with the requirements of this section.

(c) *Notice of annuity information.* (1) *In general.* Unless all title IV benefits will be distributed in the form of nonconsensual lump sums, the plan administrator must provide a notice of annuity information to each affected party other than—

(i) An affected party whose title IV benefits will be distributed in the form of a nonconsensual lump sum; and

(ii) The PBGC.

(2) *Spin-off/termination transactions.* The plan administrator must provide the information in paragraph (c)(4) of this section to a person entitled to notice under § 4041.43(c), at the same time and in the same manner as required for an affected party described in paragraph (c)(1) of this section.

(3) *Selection of different insurer.* A plan administrator that decides to select a different insurer after having previously notified the affected party of the identity of insurer(s) under this paragraph must provide another notice of annuity information.

(4) *Content of notice.* The notice must include—

(i) The identity-of-insurer information in § 4041.27(b)(1);

(ii) The information regarding change in identity of insurer(s) in § 4041.27(b)(2); and

(iii) Unless the state guaranty coverage information in § 4041.27(b)(3) was previously provided to the affected party, such information and the extinguishment-of-guaranty information in § 4041.23(b)(9) (replacing the term "plan benefits" with "title IV benefits").

(5) *Deadline for notice.* The plan administrator must issue the notice of annuity information to each affected party by the deadline in § 4041.27(d)(1).

(d) *Request for IRS determination letter.* To qualify for the distribution deadline in § 4041.28(a)(1)(ii) (as modified and made applicable by § 4041.50(c)), the plan administrator must submit to the IRS a valid request for a determination of the plan's qualification status upon termination ("determination letter") by the day on which the plan administrator completes the issuance of the notices of benefit distribution. [Amended 11/7/97 by 62 FR 60424.]

§ 4041.49 **Verification of plan sufficiency prior to closeout**. (a) *General rule*. Before distributing plan assets pursuant to a closeout under § 4041.50, the plan administrator must verify whether the plan's assets are still sufficient to provide for benefits at the level determined by the PBGC, i.e., guaranteed benefits or benefit liabilities. If the plan administrator finds that the plan is no longer able to provide for benefits at the level determined by the PBGC, then paragraph (b) or (c) of this section, as appropriate, will apply.

(b) *Subsequent insufficiency for guaranteed benefits*. When a plan administrator finds that a plan is no longer sufficient for guaranteed benefits, the plan administrator must promptly notify the PBGC in writing of that fact and may take no further action to implement the plan termination, pending the PBGC's determination and notice pursuant to paragraph (b)(1) or (b)(2) of this section.

(1) *PBGC concurrence with finding*. If the PBGC concurs with the plan administrator's finding, the distribution notice will be void, and the PBGC will—

(i) Issue the plan administrator a notice of inability to determine sufficiency in accordance with § 4041.47(b); and

(ii) Require the plan administrator to submit a new valuation, certified to by an enrolled actuary, of the benefit liabilities and guaranteed benefits under the plan, valued in accordance with § § 4044.41 through 4044.57 of this chapter as of the date of the plan administrator's notice to the PBGC.

(2) *PBGC non-concurrence with finding*. If the PBGC does not concur with the plan administrator's finding, it will so notify the plan administrator in writing, and the distribution notice will remain in effect.

(c) *Subsequent insufficiency for benefit liabilities*. When a plan administrator finds that a plan is sufficient for guaranteed benefits but is no longer sufficient for benefit liabilities, the plan administrator must immediately notify the PBGC in writing of this fact, but must continue with the distribution of assets in accordance with § 4041.50.

(d) *Finding by PBGC of subsequent insufficiency*. In any case in which the PBGC finds on its own initiative that a subsequent insufficiency for guaranteed benefits has occurred, paragraph (b)(1) of this section will apply, except that the guaranteed benefits must be revalued as of the date of the PBGC's finding.

(e) *Restrictions upon finding of subsequent insufficiency*. When the plan administrator makes the finding described in paragraph (b) of this section or receives notice that the PBGC has made the finding described in paragraph (d) of this section, the plan administrator is (except to the extent the PBGC otherwise directs) subject to the prohibitions in § 4041.42. [Amended 11/7/97 by 62 FR 60424.]

§ 4041.50 **Closeout of plan**. If a plan administrator receives a distribution notice from the PBGC pursuant to § 4041.47 and neither the plan administrator nor the PBGC makes the finding described in § 4041.49(b) or (d), the plan administrator must distribute plan assets in accordance with § 4041.28 and file a post-distribution certification in accordance with § 4041.29, except that—

(a) The term "plan benefits" is replaced with "title IV benefits";

(b) For purposes of applying the distribution deadline in § 4041.28(a)(1)(i), the phrase "after the expiration of the PBGC's 60-day (or extended) review period under § 4041.26(a)" is replaced with "the day on which the plan administrator completes the issuance of the notices of benefit distribution pursuant to § 4041.48(a)"; and

(c) For purposes of applying the distribution deadline in § 4041.28(a)(1)(ii), the phrase "the requirements of § 4041.25(c)" is replaced with "the requirements of § 4041.48(d)". [Amended 11/7/97 by 62 FR 60424.]

§ 4041.51 **Disclosure of information by plan administrator in distress termination**.

(a) *Request for Information*. (1) *In general*. If a notice of intent to terminate under § 4041.43 is issued with respect to a plan, an affected party may make a request to the plan administrator for information submitted to PBGC under sections 4041(a)(2) and 4041(c)(2) of ERISA and § § 4041.43 and 4041.45.

(2) *Requirements*. A request under paragraph (a) of this section must:

(i) Be in writing to the plan administrator;

(ii) State the name of the plan and that the request is for information submitted to PBGC with respect to the application for a distress termination of the plan;

(iii) State the name of the person making the request for information and such person's relationship to the plan (e.g., plan participant), and that such relationship meets the definition of affected party under § 4001.2 of this chapter; and

(iv) Be signed by the person making the request.

(b) *Response by Plan Administrator*. (1) *Information*. The information that a plan administrator must provide in response to a request under paragraph (a) of this section includes PBGC Form 600, and any information submitted to PBGC pursuant to section 4041(c)(2) of ERISA and § 4041.45.

(2) *Timing of response*. A plan administrator that receives a request under paragraph (a) of this section must provide the information requested not later than the 15th business day (as defined in § 4000.22 of this chapter) after receipt of the request.

(3) *Deferral of due date*. If, at the time the plan administrator receives a request under paragraph (a) of this section, the plan administrator has not filed a PBGC Form 600, the plan administrator must provide the information requested under paragraph (a) not later than the 15th business day (as defined in § 4000.22 of this chapter) after a PBGC Form 600 is filed with PBGC.

(4) *Supplemental responses*. If, at any time after the later of the receipt of a request under paragraph (a) of this section, or the filing of PBGC Form 600, the plan administrator submits additional information to PBGC with respect to the plan termination under section 4041(c)(2) of ERISA and § 4041.45, the plan administrator must, not later than the 15th business day (as defined in § 4000.22 of this chapter) after each additional submission, provide the additional information to any affected party that has made a request under paragraph (a) of this section.

(5) *Confidential information*. (i) In responding to a request under paragraph (a) of this section, the plan administrator shall not provide information that may, directly or indirectly, identify an individual participant or beneficiary of the plan.

(ii) A plan administrator that has received a request under paragraph (a) of this section may seek a court order under which confidential information described in section 552(b) of title 5, United States Code—

(A) Will be disclosed only to authorized representatives (within the meaning of section 4041(c)(2)(D)(iv) of ERISA) that agree to ensure the confidentiality of such information, and,

(B) Will not be disclosed to other affected parties.

(6) *Reasonable fees*. Under section 4041(c)(2)(D)(iii)(II) of ERISA, a plan administrator may charge a reasonable fee for any information provided under this section in other than electronic form.

[Added 11/18/2008 by 73 FR 68333.]

TERMINATION OF MULTIEMPLOYER PLANS

Act Sec. 4041A. (a) DETERMINATION FACTORS.—Termination of a multiemployer plan under this section occurs as a result of—

(1) the adoption after the date of enactment of the Multiemployer Pension Plan Amendments Act of 1980 of a plan amendment which provides that participants will receive no credit for any purpose under the plan for service with any employer after the date specified by such amendment;

(2) the withdrawal of every employer from the plan, within the meaning of section 4203, or the cessation of the obligation of all employers to contribute under the plan; or

(3) the adoption of an amendment to the plan which causes the plan to become a plan described in section 4021(b)(1).

Act Sec. 4041A. (b)(1) DATE OF TERMINATION.—The date on which a plan terminates under paragraph (1) or (3) of subsection (a) is the later of—

(A) the date on which the amendment is adopted, or

(B) the date on which the amendment takes effect.

(2) The date on which a plan terminates under paragraph (2) of subsection (a) is the earlier of—

(A) the date on which the last employer withdraws, or

(B) the first day of the first plan year for which no employer contributions were required under the plan.

Act Sec. 4041A. (c) DUTIES OF PLAN SPONSOR OF AMENDED PLAN.—Except as provided in subsection (f)(1), the plan sponsor of a plan which terminates under paragraph (2) of subsection (a) shall—

(1) limit the payment of benefits to benefits which are nonforfeitable under the plan as of the date of the termination, and

(2) pay benefits attributable to employer contributions, other than death benefits, only in the form of an annuity, unless the plan assets are distributed in full satisfaction of all nonforfeitable benefits under the plan.

Act Sec. 4041A. (d) DUTIES OF PLAN SPONSOR OF NONOPERATIVE PLAN.—The plan sponsor of a plan which terminates under paragraph (2) of subsection (a) shall reduce benefits and suspend benefit payments in accordance with section 4281.

Act Sec. 4041A. (e) AMOUNT OF CONTRIBUTION OF EMPLOYER UNDER AMENDED PLAN FOR EACH PLAN YEAR SUBSEQUENT TO PLAN TERMINATION DATE.—In the case of a plan which terminates under paragraph (1) or (3) of subsection (a), the rate of an employer's contributions under the plan for each plan year beginning on or after the plan termination date shall equal or exceed the highest rate of employer contributions at which the employer had an obligation to contribute under the plan in the 5 preceding plan years ending on or before the plan termination date, unless the corporation approves a reduction in the rate based on a finding that the plan is or soon will be fully funded.

Act Sec. 4041A. (f)(1) PAYMENT OF BENEFITS; REPORTING REQUIREMENTS FOR TERMINATED PLANS AND RULES AND STANDARDS FOR ADMINISTRATION OF SUCH PLANS.— The plan sponsor of a terminated plan may authorize the payment other than in the form of an annuity of a participant's entire nonforfeitable benefit attributable to employer contributions, other than a death benefit, if the value of the entire nonforfeitable benefit does not exceed $1,750. The corporation may authorize the payment of benefits under the terms of a terminated plan other than nonforfeitable benefits, or the payment other than in the form of an annuity of benefits having a value greater than $1,750, if the corporation determines that such payment is not adverse to the interest of the plan's participants and beneficiaries generally and does not unreasonably increase the corporation's risk of loss with respect to the plan.

(2) The corporation may prescribe reporting requirements for terminated plans, and rules and standards for the administration of such plans, which the corporation considers appropriate to protect the interests of plan participants and beneficiaries or to prevent unreasonable loss to the corporation.

Amendment:

P.L. 96-364, §103

Added new section 4041A, effective September 26, 1980.

Regulations

The following regulations were adopted by the Pension Benefit Guaranty Corporation on July 1, 1996 (61 FR 34002). Prior to July 1, 1996, PBGC regulations were under Chapter XXVI of Title 29 of the Code of Federal Regulations. Effective July 1, 1996, PBGC regulations were moved to Chapter XL, and were renumbered and reorganized. Reg. §4041A.43 was amended July 15, 1998 (63 FR38305), effective July 16, 1998. Reg. §4041A.3 was amended October 28, 2003 (68 FR 61344). Reg. §4041A.24 was amended May 28, 2014 (79 FR 30459). Reg. §§4041A.11 and 4041A.25 were amended on September 17, 2015 (80 FR 55742). Reg. §4041A.42 was amended on December 22, 2017 (82 FR 60800).

Subpart A—General Provisions

[¶ 15,449G]

§4041A.1 **Purpose and scope.** The purpose of this part is to establish rules for notifying the PBGC of the termination of a multiemployer plan and rules for the administration of multiemployer plans that have terminated by mass withdrawal. Subpart B prescribes the contents of and procedures for filing a Notice of Termination for a multiemployer plan. Subpart C prescribes basic duties of plan sponsors of mass-withdrawal-terminated plans. (Other duties are prescribed in part 4281 of this chapter.) Subpart D contains procedures for closing out sufficient plans. This part applies to terminated multiemployer plans covered by title IV of ERISA but, in the case of subparts C and D, only to plans terminated by mass withdrawal under section 4041A(a)(2) of ERISA (including plans created by partition pursuant to section 4233 of ERISA).

[¶ 15,449H]

§4041A.2 **Definitions.** The following terms are defined in §4001.1 of this chapter: annuity, ERISA, insurer, IRS, mass withdrawal, multiemployer plan, nonforfeitable benefit, PBGC, plan, and plan year.

In addition, for purposes of this part:

Available resources means, for a plan year, available resources as described in section 4245(b)(3) of ERISA.

Benefits subject to reduction means those benefits accrued under plan amendments (or plans) adopted after March 26, 1980, or under collective bargaining agreements entered into after March 26, 1980, that are not eligible for the PBGC's guarantee under section 4022A(b) of ERISA.

Financial assistance means financial assistance from the PBGC under section 4261 of ERISA.

Insolvency benefit level means the greater of the resource benefit level or the benefit level guaranteed by the PBGC for each participant and beneficiary in pay status.

Insolvency year means insolvency year as described in section 4245(b)(4) of ERISA.

Insolvent means that a plan is unable to pay benefits when due during the plan year. A plan terminated by mass withdrawal is not insolvent unless it has been amended to eliminate all benefits that are subject to reduction under section 4281(c) of ERISA, or, in the absence of an amendment, no benefits under the plan are subject to reduction under section 4281(c) of ERISA.

Nonguaranteed benefits means those benefits that are eligible for the PBGC's guarantee under section 4022A(b) of ERISA, but exceed the guarantee limits under section 4022A(c).

Resource benefit level means resource benefit level as described in section 4245(b)(2) of ERISA.

[¶ 15,449I]

§4041A.3 **Method and date of filing; where to file; computation of time; issuances to third parties.** (a) *Method and date of filing.* The PBGC applies the rules in subpart A of part 4000 of this chapter to determine permissible methods of filing with the PBGC under this part. The PBGC applies the rules in subpart C of part 4000 of this chapter to determine the date that a submission under this part was filed with the PBGC.

(b) *Where to file.* See Sec. 4000.4 of this chapter for information on where to file.

(c) *Computation of time.* The PBGC applies the rules in subpart D of part 4000 of this chapter to compute any time period for filing or issuance under this part.

(d) *Method and date of issuance*. The PBGC applies the rules in subpart B of part 4000 of this chapter to determine permissible methods of issuance under this part. The PBGC applies the rules in subpart C of part 4000 of this chapter to determine the date that an issuance under this part was provided. [Amended 10/28/2003 by 68 FR 61344.]

Subpart B—Notice of Termination

[¶ 15,449J]

§ 4041A.11 **Requirement of notice**. (a) *General*. A Notice of Termination shall be filed with the PBGC by a multiemployer plan when the plan has terminated as described in section 4041A(a) of ERISA.

⟫→ *Caution: Reg. § 4041A.11(d) applies to filings made on or after January 1, 2016.*

(d) *How and where to file*. Filings to PBGC under this subpart must be submitted in accordance with the rules in subpart A of part 4000 of this chapter. See § 4000.4 of this chapter for information on where to file. [Added 9/17/15 by 80 FR 55742.]

[¶ 15,449K]

§ 4041A.12 **Contents of notice**. (a) *Information to be contained in notice*. Except to the extent provided in paragraph (d), each Notice shall contain:

(1) The name of the plan;

(2) The name, address and telephone number of the plan sponsor and of the plan sponsor's duly authorized representative, if any;

(3) The name, address, and telephone number of the person that will administer the plan after the date of termination, if other than the plan sponsor;

(4) A copy of the plan's most recent Form 5500 (Annual Report Form), including schedules; and

(5) The date of termination of the plan.

(b) *Information to be contained in a notice involving a mass withdrawal*. In addition to the information contained in paragraph (a) and except as provided in paragraph (d), the following information shall be contained in a Notice filed by a plan that has terminated by mass withdrawal:

(1) A copy of the plan document in effect 5 years prior to the date of termination and copies of any amendments adopted after that date.

(2) A copy (or copies) of the trust agreement (or agreements), if any, authorizing the plan sponsor to control and manage the operation and administration of the plan.

(3) A copy of the most recent actuarial statement and opinion (if any) relating to the plan.

(4) A statement of any material change in the assets or liabilities of the plan occurring after either the date of the actuarial statement referred to in item (5) or the date of the plan's Form 5500 submitted as part of the Notice.

(5) Complete copies of any letters of determination issued by the IRS relating to the establishment of the plan, any letters of determination relating to the disqualification of the plan and any subsequent requalification, and any letters of determination relating to the termination of the plan.

(6) A statement whether the plan assets will be sufficient to pay all benefits in pay status during the 12-month period following the date of termination.

(7) If plan assets on hand are sufficient to satisfy all nonforfeitable benefits under the plan, and if the plan sponsor intends to distribute such assets, a brief description of the proposed method of distributing the plan assets.

(8) If plan assets on hand are not sufficient to satisfy all nonforfeitable benefits under the plan, the name and address of any employer who contributed to the plan within 3 plan years prior to the date of termination.

(c) *Certification*. As part of the Notice, the plan sponsor or duly authorized representatives shall certify that all information and documents submitted pursuant to this section are true and correct to the best of the plan sponsor's or representative's knowledge and belief.

(b) *Who shall file*. The plan sponsor or a duly authorized representative acting on behalf of the plan sponsor shall sign and file the Notice.

(c) *When to file*. (1) For a termination pursuant to a plan amendment, the Notice shall be filed with the PBGC within thirty days after the amendment is adopted or effective, whichever is later.

(2) For a termination that results from a mass withdrawal, the Notice shall be filed with the PBGC within thirty days after the last employer withdrew from the plan or thirty days after the first day of the first plan year for which no employer contributions were required under the plan, whichever is earlier.

(Approved by the Office of Management and Budget under control number 1212-0020)

(d) *Avoiding duplication*. Information described in paragraphs (a) and (b) of this section need not be supplied if it duplicates information contained in Form 5500, or a schedule thereof, that a plan submits as part of the Notice.

(e) *Additional information*. In addition to the information described in paragraphs (a) and (b) of this section, the PBGC may require the submission of any other information which the PBGC determines is necessary for review of a Notice of Termination.

Subpart C—Plan Sponsor Duties

[¶ 15,449L]

§ 4041A.21 **General rule**. The plan sponsor of a multiemployer plan that terminates by mass withdrawal shall continue to administer the plan in accordance with applicable statutory provisions, regulations, and plan provisions until a trustee is appointed under section 4042 of ERISA or until plan assets are distributed in accordance with subpart D of this part. In addition, the plan sponsor shall be responsible for the specific duties described in this subpart.

[¶ 15,449M]

§ 4041A.22 **Payment of benefits**. (a) Except as provided in paragraph (b), the plan sponsor shall pay any benefit attributable to employer contributions, other than a death benefit, only in the form of an annuity.

(b) The plan sponsor may pay a benefit in a form other than an annuity if—

(1) The plan distributes plan assets in accordance with subpart D of this part;

(2) The PBGC approves the payment of the benefit in an alternative form pursuant to § 4041A.27; or

(3) The value of the entire nonforfeitable benefit does not exceed $1,750.

(c) Except to the extent provided in the next sentence, the plan sponsor shall not pay benefits in excess of the amount that is nonforfeitable under the plan as of the date of termination, unless authorized to do so by the PBGC pursuant to § 4041A.27. Subject to the restriction stated in paragraph (d) of this section, however, the plan sponsor may pay a qualified preretirement survivor annuity with respect to a participant who died after the date of termination.

(d) The payment of benefits subject to reduction shall be discontinued to the extent provided in § 4281.31 if the plan sponsor determines, in accordance with § 4041A.24, that the plan's assets are insufficient to provide all nonforfeitable benefits.

(e) The plan sponsor shall, to the extent provided in § 4281.41, suspend the payment of nonguaranteed benefits if the plan sponsor determines, in accordance with § 4041A.25, that the plan is insolvent.

(f) The plan sponsor shall, to the extent required by § 4281.42, make retroactive payments of suspended benefits if it determines under that section that the level of the plan's available resources requires such payments.

[¶ 15,449N]

§ 4041A.23 **Imposition and collection of withdrawal liability**. Until plan assets are distributed in accordance with subpart D of this part, or until the end of the plan year as of which the PBGC determines that plan assets (exclusive of claims for withdrawal liability) are sufficient to satisfy all nonforfeitable benefits under the plan, the plan sponsor shall be responsible for determining, imposing and collecting withdrawal liability (including the liability arising as a result of the mass withdrawal), in accordance with part 4219, subpart C, of this chapter and sections 4201 through 4225 of ERISA.

[¶ 15,449O]

§ 4041A.24 **Plan valuations and monitoring**. [Revised 5/28/14 by 79 FR 30459.]

(a) *Annual valuation.* The plan sponsor shall determine or cause to be determined in writing the value of nonforfeitable benefits under the plan and the value of the plan's assets, in accordance with part 4281, subpart B. This valuation shall be done not later than 150 days after the end of the plan year in which the plan terminates and each plan year thereafter except as provided in this paragraph. A plan year for which a valuation is performed is called a valuation year.

(1) If the value of nonforfeitable benefits for the plan is $25 million or less as determined for a valuation year, the plan sponsor may use the valuation for the next two plan years and, subject to paragraphs (a)(2) and (3) of this section, perform a new valuation pursuant to this paragraph for the third plan year after the previous valuation year.

(2) No valuation is required for a plan year for which the plan receives financial assistance from PBGC under section 4261 of ERISA.

(3) No valuation is required for the plan year in which the plan is closed out in accordance with subpart D of this part. [Revised 5/28/14 by 79 FR 30459.]

(b) *Plan monitoring.* Upon receipt of the valuation described in paragraph (a) of this section, the plan sponsor shall determine whether the value of nonforfeitable benefits exceeds the value of the plan's assets, including claims for withdrawal liability owed to the plan. When benefits do exceed assets, the plan sponsor shall—[Amended 5/28/14 by 79 FR 30459.]

(1) If the plan provides benefits subject to reduction, amend the plan to reduce those benefits in accordance with the procedures in part 4281, subpart C, of this chapter to the extent necessary to ensure that the plan's assets are sufficient to discharge when due all of the plan's obligations with respect to nonforfeitable benefits; or

⯈⯈⯈→ *Caution: Reg. § § 4041A.25(d) applies to filings made on or after January 1, 2016.*

(d) *Insolvency notices.* If the plan sponsor determines that the plan is, or is expected to be, insolvent for a plan year, it shall issue notices of insolvency or annual updates and notices of insolvency benefit level to the PBGC and to plan participants and beneficiaries in accordance with part 4281, subpart D. [Amended 9/17/15 by 80 FR 55742.]

[¶ 15,449Q]

§ 4041A.26 **Financial assistance**. A plan sponsor that determines a resource benefit level under section 4245(b)(2) of ERISA that is below the level of guaranteed benefits or that determines that the plan will be unable to pay guaranteed benefits for any month during an insolvency year shall apply for financial assistance from the PBGC in accordance with § 4281.47.

[¶ 15,449R]

§ 4041A.27 **PBGC approval to pay benefits not otherwise permitted.** Upon written application by the plan sponsor, the PBGC may authorize the plan to pay benefits other than nonforfeitable benefits or to pay benefits valued at more than $1,750 in a form other than an annuity. The PBGC will approve such payments if it determines that the plan sponsor has demonstrated that the payments are not adverse to the interests of the plan's participants and beneficiaries generally and do not unreasonably increase the PBGC's risk of loss with respect to the plan.

Subpart D—Closeout of Sufficient Plans

[¶ 15,449S]

§ 4041A.41 **General rule**. If a plan's assets, excluding any claim of the plan for unpaid withdrawal liability, are sufficient to satisfy all obligations for nonforfeitable benefits provided under the plan, the plan

(2) If the plan provides no benefits subject to reduction, make periodic determinations of plan solvency in accordance with § 4041A.25.

(c) *Notices of benefit reductions.* The plan sponsor of a plan that has been amended to reduce benefits shall provide participants and beneficiaries and the PBGC notice of the benefit reduction in accordance with § 4281.32.

[¶ 15,449P]

§ 4041A.25 **Periodic determinations of plan solvency**. (a) *Annual insolvency determination.* The plan sponsor of a plan that has been amended to eliminate all benefits that are subject to reduction under section 4281(c) of ERISA shall determine in writing whether the plan is expected to be insolvent for the first plan year beginning after the effective date of the amendment and for each plan year thereafter. In the event that a plan adopts more than one amendment reducing benefits under section 4281(c) of ERISA, the initial determination shall be made for the first plan year beginning after the effective date of the amendment that effects the elimination of all such benefits, and a determination shall be made for each plan year thereafter. The plan sponsor of a plan under which no benefits are subject to reduction under section 4281(c) of ERISA as of the date the plan terminated shall determine in writing whether the plan is expected to be insolvent. The initial determination shall be made for the second plan year beginning after the first plan year for which it is determined under section 4281(b) of ERISA that the value of nonforfeitable benefits under the plan exceeds the value of the plan's assets. The plan sponsor shall also make a solvency determination for each plan year thereafter. A determination required under this paragraph shall be made no later than six months before the beginning of the plan year to which it applies.

(b) *Other determination of insolvency.* Whether or not a prior determination of plan solvency has been made under paragraph (a) of this section (or under section 4245 of ERISA), a plan sponsor that has reason to believe, taking into account the plan's recent and anticipated financial experience, that the plan is or may be insolvent for the current or next plan year shall determine in writing whether the plan is expected to be insolvent for that plan year.

(c) *Benefit suspensions.* If the plan sponsor determines that the plan is, or is expected to be, insolvent for a plan year, it shall suspend benefits in accordance with § 4281.41.

sponsor may close out the plan in accordance with this subpart by distributing plan assets in full satisfaction of all nonforfeitable benefits under the plan.

[¶ 15,449T]

§ 4041A.42 **Method of distribution**. (a) *In general.* The plan sponsor shall distribute plan assets by purchasing from an insurer contracts to provide all benefits required by § 4041A.43 to be provided in annuity form and by paying in a lump sum (or other alternative elected by the participant) all other benefits. [Redesignated 12/22/2017 by 82 FR 60800.]

(b) *Missing participants and beneficiaries.* The plan sponsor must distribute plan benefits of missing distributees in accordance with subpart D of part 4050 of this chapter. [Added 12/22/2017 by 82 FR 60800.]

[¶ 15,449U]

§ 4041A.43 **Benefit forms**. (a) *General rule.* Except as provided in paragraph (b) of this section, the sponsor of a plan that is closed out shall provide for the payment of any benefit attributable to employer contributions only in the form of an annuity.

(b) *Exceptions.* The plan sponsor may pay a benefit attributable to employer contributions in a form other than an annuity if:

(1) The present value of the participant's entire nonforfeitable benefit, determined using the interest assumption under § § 4044.41 through 4044.57, does not exceed $5,000.

(2) The payment is for death benefits provided under the plan.

(3) The participant elects an alternative form of distribution under paragraph (c) of this section.

Reg. § 4041A.43(b)(3)   ¶ 15,449U

(c) *Alternative forms of distribution.* The plan sponsor may allow participants to elect alternative forms of distribution in accordance with this paragraph. When a form of distribution is offered as an alternative to the normal form, the plan sponsor shall notify each participant, in writing, of the form and estimated amount of the participant's normal form of distribution. The notification shall also describe any risks attendant to the alternative form. Participants' elections of alternative forms shall be in writing.

§ 4041A.44 **Cessation of withdrawal liability**. The obligation of an employer to make payments of initial withdrawal liability and mass withdrawal liability shall cease on the date on which the plan's assets are distributed in full satisfaction of all nonforfeitable benefits provided by the plan.

[¶ 15,450]
INSTITUTION OF TERMINATION PROCEEDINGS BY THE CORPORATION

Act Sec. 4042.(a) Authority to institute proceedings to terminate a plan.—The corporation may institute proceedings under this section to terminate a plan whenever it determines that—

(1) the plan has not met the minimum funding standard required under section 412 of the Internal Revenue Code of 1986, or has been notified by the Secretary of the Treasury that a notice of deficiency under section 6212 of such Code has been mailed with respect to the tax imposed under section 4971(a) of such Code,

(2) the plan will be unable to pay benefits when due,

(3) the reportable event described in section 4043(c)(7) has occurred, or

(4) the possible long-run loss of the corporation with respect to the plan may reasonably be expected to increase unreasonably if the plan is not terminated.

The corporation shall as soon as practicable institute proceedings under this section to terminate a single-employer plan whenever the corporation determines that the plan does not have assets available to pay benefits which are currently due under the terms of the plan. The corporation may prescribe a simplified procedure to follow in terminating small plans as long as that procedure includes substantial safeguards for the rights of the participants and beneficiaries under the plans, and for the employers who maintain such plans (including the requirement for a court decree under subsection (c)). Notwithstanding any other provision of this title, the corporation is authorized to pool assets of terminated plans for purposes of administration, investment, payment of liabilities of all such terminated plans, and such other purposes as it determines to be appropriate in the administration of this title.

Act Sec. 4042.(b)(1) Appointment of trustee.—Whenever the corporation makes a determination under subsection (a) with respect to a plan or is required under subsection (a) to institute proceedings under this section, it may, upon notice to the plan, apply to the appropriate United States district court for the appointment of a trustee to administer the plan with respect to which the determination is made pending the issuance of a decree under subsection (c) ordering the termination of the plan. If within 3 business days after the filing of an application under this subsection, or such other period as the court may order, the administrator of the plan consents to the appointment of a trustee, or fails to show why a trustee should not be appointed, the court may grant the application and appoint a trustee to administer the plan in accordance with its terms until the corporation determines that the plan should be terminated or that termination is unnecessary. The corporation may request that it be appointed as trustee of a plan in any case.

(2) Notwithstanding any other provision of this title—

(A) upon the petition of a plan administrator or the corporation, the appropriate United States district court may appoint a trustee in accordance with the provisions of this section if the interests of the plan participants would be better served by the appointment of the trustee, and

(B) upon the petition of the corporation, the appropriate United States district court shall appoint a trustee proposed by the corporation for a multiemployer plan which is in reorganization or to which section 4041A(d) applies, unless such appointment would be adverse to the interests of the plan participants and beneficiaries in the aggregate.

(3) The corporation and plan administrator may agree to the appointment of a trustee without proceeding in accordance with the requirements of paragraphs (1) and (2).

Act Sec. 4042. (c)(1) Adjudication that plan must be terminated.—If the corporation is required under subsection (a) of this section to commence proceedings under this section with respect to a plan or, after issuing a notice under this section to a plan administrator, has determined that the plan should be terminated, it may, upon notice to the plan administrator, apply to the appropriate United States district court for a decree adjudicating that the plan must be terminated in order to protect the interests of the participants *or* to avoid any unreasonable deterioration of the financial condition of the plan or any unreasonable increase in the liability of the fund. If the trustee appointed under subsection (b) disagrees with the determination of the corporation under the preceding sentence he may intervene in the proceeding relating to the application for the decree, or make application for such decree himself. Upon granting a decree for which the corporation or trustee has applied under this subsection the court shall authorize the trustee appointed under subsection (b) (or appoint a trustee if one has not been appointed under such subsection and authorize him) to terminate the plan in accordance with the provisions of this subtitle. If the corporation and the plan administrator agree that a plan should be terminated and agree to the appointment of a trustee without proceeding in accordance with the requirements of this subsection (other than this sentence) the trustee shall have the power described in subsection (d)(1) and, in addition to any other duties imposed on the trustee under law or by agreement between the corporation and the plan administrator, the trustee is subject to the duties described in subsection (d)(3). Whenever a trustee appointed under this title is operating a plan with discretion as to the date upon which final distribution of the assets is to be commenced, the trustee shall notify the corporation at least 10 days before the date on which he proposes to commence such distribution.

(2) In the case of a proceeding initiated under this section, the plan administrator shall provide the corporation, upon the request of the corporation, the information described in clauses (ii), (iii), and (iv) of section 4041(c)(2)(A).

(3) Disclosure of termination information.—

(A) In general.—

(i) Information from plan sponsor or administrator. —A plan sponsor or plan administrator of a single-employer plan that has received a notice from the corporation of a determination that the plan should be terminated under this section shall provide to an affected party any information provided to the corporation in connection with the plan termination.

(ii) Information from corporation. —The corporation shall provide a copy of the administrative record, including the trusteeship decision record of a termination of a plan described under clause (i).

(B) Timing of disclosure. —The plan sponsor, plan administrator, or the corporation, as applicable, shall provide the information described in subparagraph (A) not later than 15 days after—

(i) receipt of a request from an affected party for such information; or

(ii) in the case of information described under subparagraph (A)(i), the provision of any new information to the corporation relating to a previous request by an affected party.

(C) Confidentiality.—

(i) In general. —The plan administrator, the plan sponsor, or the corporation shall not provide information under subparagraph (A) in a form which includes any information that may directly or indirectly be associated with, or otherwise identify, an individual participant or beneficiary.

(ii) LIMITATION. —A court may limit disclosure under this paragraph of confidential information described in section 552(b) of title 5, United States Code, to authorized representatives (within the meaning of section 4041(c)(2)(D)(iv)) of the participants or beneficiaries that agree to ensure the confidentiality of such information.

(D) FORM AND MANNER OF INFORMATION; CHARGES.—

(i) FORM AND MANNER. —The corporation may prescribe the form and manner of the provision of information under this paragraph, which shall include delivery in written, electronic, or other appropriate form to the extent that such form is reasonably accessible to individuals to whom the information is required to be provided.

(ii) REASONABLE CHARGES. —A plan sponsor may charge a reasonable fee for any information provided under this paragraph in other than electronic form.

Act Sec. 4042. (d)(1)(A) POWERS OF TRUSTEE.—A trustee appointed under subsection (b) shall have the power—

(i) to do any act authorized by the plan or this title to be done by the plan administrator or any trustee of the plan;

(ii) to require the transfer of all (or any part) of the assets and records of the plan to himself as trustee;

(iii) to invest any assets of the plan which he holds in accordance with the provisions of the plan, regulations of the corporation, and applicable rules of law;

(iv) to limit payment of benefits under the plan to basic benefits or to continue payment of some or all of the benefits which were being paid prior to his appointment;

(v) in the case of a multiemployer plan, to reduce benefits or suspend benefit payments under the plan, give appropriate notices, amend the plan, and perform other acts required or authorized by subtitle (E) to be performed by the plan sponsor or administrator;

(vi) to do such other acts as he deems necessary to continue operation of the plan without increasing the potential liability of the corporation if such acts may be done under the provisions of the plan; and

(vii) to require the plan sponsor, the plan administrator, any contributing or withdrawn employer, and any employee organization representing plan participants to furnish any information with respect to the plan which the trustee may reasonably need in order to administer the plan.

If the court to which application is made under subsection (c) dismisses the application with prejudice, or if the corporation fails to apply for a decree under subsection (c) within 30 days after the date on which the trustee is appointed under subsection (b), the trustee shall transfer all assets and records of the plan held by him to the plan administrator within 3 business days after such dismissal or the expiration of such 30-day period, and shall not be liable to the plan or any other person for his acts as trustee except for willful misconduct, or for conduct in violation of the provisions of part 4 of subtitle B of title I of this Act (except as provided in subsection (d)(1)(A)(v)). The 30-day period referred to in this subparagraph may be extended as provided by agreement between the plan administrator and the corporation or by court order obtained by the corporation.

(B) If the court to which an application is made under subsection (c) issues the decree requested in such application, in addition to the powers described in subparagraph (A), the trustee shall have the power—

(i) to pay benefits under the plan in accordance with the requirements of this title;

(ii) to collect for the plan any amounts due the plan, including but not limited to the power to collect from the persons obligated to meet the requirements of section 302 or the terms of the plan;

(iii) to receive any payment made by the corporation to the plan under this title;

(iv) to commence, prosecute, or defend on behalf of the plan any suit or proceeding involving the plan;

(v) to issue, publish, or file such notices, statements, and reports as may be required by the corporation or any order of the court;

(vi) to liquidate the plan assets;

(vii) to recover payments under section 4045(a); and

(viii) to do such other acts as may be necessary to comply with this title or any order of the court and to protect the interests of plan participants and beneficiaries.

(2) As soon as practicable after his appointment, the trustee shall give notice to interested parties of the institution of proceedings under this title to determine whether the plan should be terminated or to terminate the plan, whichever is applicable. For purposes of this paragraph, the term "interested party" means—

(A) the plan administrator,

(B) each participant in the plan and each beneficiary of a deceased participant,

(C) each employer who may be subject to liability under section 4062, 4063, or 4064,

(D) each employer who is or may be liable to the plan under section part 1 of subtitle E,

(E) each employer who has an obligation to contribute, within the meaning of section 4212(a), under a multiemployer plan, and

(F) each employee organization which, for purposes of collective bargaining, represents plan participants employed by an employer described in subparagraph (C), (D), or (E).

(3) Except to the extent inconsistent with the provisions of this Act, or as may be otherwise ordered by the court, a trustee appointed under this section shall be subject to the same duties as those of a trustee under section 704, title 11, United States Code, and shall be, with respect to the plan, a fiduciary within the meaning of paragraph (21) of section 3 of this Act and under section 4975(e) of the Internal Revenue Code of 1986 (except to the extent that the provisions of this title are inconsistent with the requirements applicable under part 4 of subtitle B of title I of this Act and of such section 4975).

Act Sec. 4042. (e) FILING OF APPLICATION NOTWITHSTANDING PENDENCY OF OTHER PROCEEDINGS.—An application by the corporation under this section may be filed notwithstanding the pendency in the same or any other court of any bankruptcy, mortgage foreclosure, or equity receivership proceeding, or any proceeding to reorganize, conserve, or liquidate such plan or its property, or any proceeding to enforce a lien against property of the plan.

Act Sec. 4042. (f) EXCLUSIVE JURISDICTION; STAY OF OTHER PROCEEDINGS.—Upon the filing of an application for the appointment of a trustee or the issuance of a decree under this section, the court to which an application is made shall have exclusive jurisdiction of the plan involved and its property wherever located with the powers, to the extent consistent with the purposes of this section, of a court of the United States having jurisdiction over cases under chapter 11 of title 11 of the United States Code. Pending an adjudication under subsection (c) such court shall stay, and upon appointment by it of a trustee, as provided in this section such court shall continue the stay of, any pending mortgage foreclosure, equity receivership, or other proceeding to reorganize, conserve, or liquidate the plan or its property and any other suit against any receiver, conservator, or trustee of the plan or its property. Pending such adjudication and upon the appointment by it of such trustee, the court may stay any proceeding to enforce a lien against property of the plan or any other suit against the plan.

Act Sec. 4042. (g) VENUE.—An action under this subsection may be brought in the judicial district where the plan administrator resides or does business or where any asset of the plan is situated. A district court in which such action is brought may issue process with respect to such action in any other judicial district.

Act Sec. 4042. (h)(1) COMPENSATION OF TRUSTEE AND PROFESSIONAL SERVICE PERSONNEL APPOINTED OR RETAINED BY TRUSTEE.—The amount of compensation paid to each trustee appointed under the provisions of this title shall require the prior approval of the corporation, and, in the case of a trustee appointed by a court, the consent of that court.

(2) Trustees shall appoint, retain, and compensate accountants, actuaries, and other professional service personnel in accordance with regulations prescribed by the corporation.

Act Sec. 4042. (i) [Repealed]

Amendments:

P.L. 110-458, § 105(e)(2)(A)-(B):

Amended ERISA Sec. 4042(c)(3)(C)(i) by striking "and plan sponsor" and inserting ", the plan sponsor, or the corporation", and by striking "subparagraph (A)(i)" and inserting "subparagraph (A)".

The above amendment applies to any plan termination under Title IV of ERISA with respect to which the notice of intent to terminate (or in the case of a termination by the PBGC, a notice of determination under ERISA Sec. 4042 occurs after August 17, 2006 generally.

P.L. 109-280, § 506(b)(1)(A):

Amended ERISA Sec. 4042(c) by adding striking "(c) If the" and inserting "(c)(1) If the".

P.L. 109-280, § 506(b)(1)(B):

Amended ERISA Sec. 4042(c) by redesignating paragraph (3) as paragraph (2).

P.L. 109-280, § 506(b)(1)(C):

Amended ERISA Sec. 4042(c) by adding new paragraph (3) to read as above.

P.L. 109-280, § 506(c):

(c) EFFECTIVE DATE.—

(1) IN GENERAL.—

The amendments made by this section shall apply to any plan termination under title IV of the Employee Retirement Income Security Act of 1974 (29 U.S.C. 1301 et seq.) with respect to which the notice of intent to terminate (or in the case of a termination by the Pension Benefit Guaranty Corporation, a notice of determination under section 4042 of such Act (29 U.S.C. 1342)) occurs after the date of enactment of this Act [August 17, 2006].

(2) TRANSITION RULE.—

If notice under section 4041(c)(2)(D) or 4042(c)(3) of the Employee Retirement Income Security Act of 1974 (as added by this section) would otherwise be required to be provided before the 90th day after the date of the enactment of this Act, such notice shall not be required to be provided until such 90th day.

P.L. 103-465, § 771(e)(2):

Act Sec. 771(e)(2) amended ERISA Sec. 4042(a)(3) by striking "4043(b)(7)" and inserting "4043(c)(7)".

The above amendment is effective for events occurring 60 days or more after December 8, 1994.

P.L. 101-239, § 7881(g)(7):

Amended P.L. 100-203, § 9314(b) by striking "section 4042" and inserting "section 4042(a)" and by striking "third sentence" and inserting "last sentence," effective December 22, 1987.

P.L. 101-239, § 7891(a)(1):

Titles I, III, and IV of ERISA (other than sections 3(37)(E), 301(a)(7), and 308, the last sentence of section 408(d), and sections 414(c), 4001(a)(3)(ii), and 4303) are each amended by striking "Internal Revenue Code of 1954" each place it appears and inserting "Internal Revenue Code of 1986" effective October 22, 1986.

P.L. 101-239, § 7893(e):

Amended ERISA Sec. 4042(a) by inserting a period after "terms of the plan" in the matter following paragraph (4), effective as if included in P.L. 99-272, § 11010(a)(1).

P.L. 100-203, § 9312(c)(3):

Repealed ERISA Sec. 4042(i) effective for (A) plan terminations under section 4041(c) of ERISA with respect to which notices of intent to terminate are provided under section 4041(a)(2) of ERISA after December 17, 1987, and (B) plan termination with respect to which proceedings are instituted by the Pension Benefit Guaranty Corporation under section 4042 of ERISA after December 17, 1987.

Prior to repeal, ERISA Sec. 4042(i) read as follows:

(i) In any case in which a plan is terminated under this section in a termination proceeding initiated by the corporation pursuant to subsection (a), the corporation shall establish a separate trust in connection with the plan for purposes of section 4049, unless the corporation determines that all benefit commitments under the plan are benefits guaranteed by the corporation under section 4022 or that there is no amount of unfunded benefit commitments under the plan.

P.L. 100-203, § 9314(b):

Amended ERISA Sec. 4042(a) by striking the last sentence and inserting a new last sentence, to read as above, effective December 22, 1987. Prior to amendment, ERISA Sec. 4042(a), last sentence, read as follows:

The corporation is authorized to pool the assets of terminated plans for purposes of administration and such other purposes, not inconsistent with its duties to the plan participants and the employer maintaining the plan under this title, as it determines to be required for the efficient administration of this title.

Amended ERISA Sec. 4042(c) by adding paragraph (3), to read as above, effective December 22, 1987.

P.L. 96-364, § 402(a)(6):

Amended Sec. 4042 effective September 26, 1980 by: striking out "such small" in subsection (a) and inserting "terminated"; redesignating subsection (b) as subsection (b)(1) and inserting at the end thereof ERISA Secs. 4042(b)(2) and (3); striking out "and" after "interests of the participants" in subsection (c) and inserting "or"; striking out "further" each place it appears in subsection (c) and inserting "unreasonable"; in subsection (d)(1)(A), striking out "and" in clause (iv), redesignating clause (v) as clause (vi) and inserting new ERISA Sec. 4042(d)(1)(A)(v) and (vii); by striking out "allocation requirements of section 4044" in subsection (d)(1)(B)(i) and inserting "requirements of this title"; striking out ", except to the extent that the corporation is an adverse party in a suit or proceeding" in subsection (d)(1)(B)(iv); by striking out "and" in subsection (d)(2)(B); and striking out the period in subsection (d)(2)(C), inserting a comma, and inserting new ERISA Sec. 4042(d)(2)(D) through (F).

P.L. 95-598, § 321(a):

Amended Sec. 4042, effective October 1, 1979, by striking out the word "bankruptcy" after the word "pending" in subsection (f) and by substituting the words "the United States having jurisdiction over cases under chapter 11 of title 11 of the United States Code" for the words "bankruptcy and of a court in a proceeding under chapter X of the Bankruptcy Act" in subsection (f).

P.L. 92-272, § 11010(a)(1):

Amended ERISA Sec. 4042(a) by striking "is" in paragraph (2) and inserting "will be" and amended the matter following paragraph (4) by adding a new sentence at the beginning of the matter to read as above.

Act Sec. 11010(a)(2) amended ERISA Sec. 4042(b)(1) by inserting "or is required under subsection (a) to institute court proceedings under this section," after "to a plan" and amended ERISA Sec. 4042(c) by striking out "If the corporation has issued a notice under this section to a plan administrator and (whether or not a trustee has been appointed under subsection (b)) has determined" and inserted "If the corporation is required under subsection (a) of this section to commence court proceedings under this section with respect to a plan or, after issuing a notice under this section to a plan administrator, has determined in its place."

Act Sec. 11010(b) added ERISA Sec. 4042(i) to read as above.

Act Sec. 11010(c) amended the heading of ERISA Sec. 4042 to read as above.

The above amendments are effective with respect to notices of intent to terminate filed with the PBGC or with proceedings begun on or after January 1, 1986.

Act Sec. 11016(c)(10) amended ERISA Sec. 4042(d)(1)(B)(ii) by inserting after "amounts due the plan ", including but not limited to the power to collect from the persons obligated to meet the requirements of section 302 or the terms of the plan." Act Sec. 11016(c)(11) added ERISA Sec. 4042(d)(3) to read as above, effective on April 7, 1986.

Regulations

The following regulations were adopted by the Pension Benefit Guaranty Corporation on November 18, 2008 (73 FR 68333). They are applicable to terminations initiated on or after August 17, 2006, but only to requests for information made on or after December 18, 2008.

Subpart A—General Provisions

[¶ 15,451]

§ 4042.1 **Purpose and scope.** This part sets forth rules and procedures relating to single-employer plan terminations initiated by PBGC under section 4042 of ERISA.

[¶ 15,451A]

§ 4042.2 **Definitions**. The following terms used in this part are defined in § 4001.2 of this chapter: *Affected party, ERISA, PBGC,* and *plan administrator.*

[¶ 15,451B]

§ 4042.3 **Issuance rules**. PBGC applies the rules in subpart B of part 4000 of this chapter to determine permissible methods of issuance under this part. PBGC applies the rules in subpart C of part 4000 of this chapter to determine the date that an issuance under this part was provided.

Subpart B—Reserved

Subpart C—Disclosure

[¶ 15,451C]

§ 4042.4 **Disclosure of information by plan administrator or plan sponsor.**

(a) *Request for Information.* (1) *In general.* Beginning on the third business day (as defined in § 4000.22 of this chapter) after PBGC has issued a notice under section 4042 of ERISA that a plan should be terminated, an affected party may make a request to the plan sponsor or the plan administrator (or both) for any information that such plan administrator or plan sponsor has submitted to PBGC in connection with the plan termination.

(2) *Requirements.* A request under paragraph (a) of this section must:

(i) Be in writing to the plan administrator or plan sponsor;

(ii) State the name of the plan and that the request is for information submitted to PBGC in connection with the plan termination;

(iii) State the name of the person making the request for information and such person's relationship to the plan (e.g., plan participant), and that such relationship meets the definition of affected party under § 4001.2 of this chapter; and

(iv) Be signed by the person making the request.

(b) *Response by Plan Administrator or Plan Sponsor.* (1) *Timing of response.* A plan administrator or plan sponsor that receives a request under paragraph (a) of this section must provide the information requested not later than the 15th business day (as defined in § 4000.22 of this chapter) after receipt of the request.

(2) *Supplemental responses.* If, at any time after receipt of a request under paragraph (a), the plan administrator or plan sponsor submits additional information to PBGC in connection with the plan termination, the plan administrator or plan sponsor must provide such additional information to any affected party that has made a request under paragraph (a), not later than the 15th business day (as defined in § 4000.22 of this chapter) after the information is submitted to PBGC.

(3) *Confidential information.* (i) In responding to a request under paragraph (a) of this section, the plan administrator or plan sponsor shall not provide information that may, directly or indirectly, identify an individual participant or beneficiary.

(ii) A plan administrator or plan sponsor that has received a request under paragraph (a) of this section may seek a court order under which confidential information described in section 552(b) of title 5, United States Code—

(A) Will be disclosed only to authorized representatives (within the meaning of section 4041(c)(2)(D)(iv) of ERISA) that agree, to ensure the confidentiality of such information, and

(B) Will not be disclosed to other affected parties.

(4) *Reasonable fees.* Under section 4042(c)(3)(D)(ii) of ERISA, a plan administrator or plan sponsor may charge a reasonable fee for any information provided under this section in other than electronic form.

[¶ 15,451D]
§ 4042.5 **Disclosure of administrative record by PBGC.**

(a) *Request for Administrative Record.* (1) *In general.* Beginning on the third business day (as defined in § 4000.22 of this chapter) after PBGC has issued a notice under section 4042 of ERISA that a plan should be terminated, an affected party with respect to the plan may make a request to PBGC for the administrative record of PBGC's determination that the plan should be terminated.

(2) *Requirements.* A request under paragraph (a) of this section must:

(i) Be in writing;

(ii) State the name of the plan and that the request is for the administrative record with respect to a notice issued by PBGC under section 4042 of ERISA that a plan should be terminated;

(iii) State the name of the person making the request, the person's relationship to the plan (e.g., plan participant), and that such relationship meets the definition of affected party under § 4001.2 of this chapter; and

(iv) Be signed by the person making the request.

(3) A request under paragraph (a) of this section must be sent to PBGC's Disclosure Officer at the address provided on PBGC's Web site. To expedite processing, the request should be prominently identified as an "Administrative Record Request."

(b) *PBGC Response to Request for Administrative Record.* (1) *Notification of plan administrator and plan sponsor.* Upon receipt of a request under paragraph (a) of this section, PBGC will promptly notify the plan administrator and plan sponsor that it has received a request for the administrative record, and the date by which PBGC will provide the information to the affected party that made the request.

(2) *Confidential information.* (i) In responding to a request under paragraph (a) of this section, PBGC will not disclose any portions of the administrative record that are prohibited from disclosure under the Privacy Act, 5 U.S.C. 552a.

(ii) A plan administrator or plan sponsor that has received notification pursuant to paragraph (b)(1) of this section may seek a court order under which those portions of the administrative record that contain confidential information described in section 552(b) of title 5, United States Code—

(A) Will be disclosed only to authorized representatives (within the meaning of section 4041(c)(2)(D)(iv)) of ERISA) that agree to ensure the confidentiality of such information, and

(B) Will not be disclosed to other affected parties.

(iii) If, before the 15th business day (as defined in § 4000.22 of this chapter) after PBGC has received a request under paragraph (a), PBGC receives a court order as described in paragraph (b)(2)(ii) of this section, PBGC will disclose those portions of the administrative record that contain confidential information described in section 552(b) of title 5, United States Code, only as provided in the order.

(3) *Timing of response.* PBGC will send the administrative record to the affected party that made the request not later than the 15th business day (as defined in § 4000.22 of this chapter) after it receives the request.

(4) *Form and manner.* PBGC will provide the administrative record using measures (including electronic measures) reasonably calculated to ensure actual receipt of the material by the intended recipient.

[¶ 15,460]
REPORTABLE EVENTS

Act Sec. 4043. (a) NOTIFICATION THAT EVENT HAS OCCURRED.—Within 30 days after the plan administrator or the contributing sponsor knows or has reason to know that a reportable event described in subsection (c) has occurred, he shall notify the corporation that such event has occurred, unless a notice otherwise required under this subsection has already been provided with respect to such event. The corporation is authorized to waive the requirement of the preceding sentence with respect to any or all reportable events with respect to any plan, and to require the notification to be made by including the event in the annual report made by the plan.

Act Sec. 4043. (b)(1) NOTIFICATION THAT EVENT IS ABOUT TO OCCUR.—The requirements of this subsection shall be applicable to a contributing sponsor if, as of the close of the preceding plan year—

(A) the aggregate unfunded vested benefits (as determined under section 4006(a)(3)(E)(iii)) of plans subject to this title which are maintained by such sponsor and members of such sponsor's controlled groups (disregarding plans with no unfunded vested benefits) exceed $50,000,000, and

(B) the funded vested benefit percentage for such plans is less than 90 percent.

For purposes of subparaprah (B), the funded vested benefit percentage means the percentage which the aggregate value of the assets of such plans bears to the aggregate vested benefits of such plans (determined in accordance with section 4006(a)(3)(E)(iii)).

(2) This subsection shall not apply to an event if the contributing sponser, or the member of the contributing sponser's controlled group to which the event relates, is—

(A) a person subject to the reporting requirements of section 13 or 15(d) of the Securities Exchange Act of 1934, or

(B) a subsidiary (as defined for purposes of such Act) of a person subject to such reporting requirements.

(3) No later than 30 days prior to the effective date of an event described in paragraph (9), (10), (11), (12), or (13) of subsection (c), a contributing sponsor to which the requirements of this subsection apply shall notify the corporation that the event is about to occur.

(4) The corporation may waive the requirement of this subsection with respect to any or all reportable events with respect to any contributing sponsor.

Act Sec. 4043. (c) ENUMERATION OF REPORTABLE EVENTS.—For purposes of this section a reportable event occurs—

(1) when the Secretary of the Treasury issues notice that a plan has ceased to be a plan described in section 4021(a)(2), or when the Secretary of Labor determines the plan is not in compliance with title I of this Act;

(2) when an amendment of the plan is adopted if, under the amendment, the benefit payable with respect to any participant may be decreased;

(3) when the number of active participants is less than 80 percent of the number of such participants at the beginning of the plan year, or is less than 75 percent of the number of such participants at the beginning of the previous plan year;

(4) when the Secretary of the Treasury determines that there has been a termination or partial termination of the plan within the meaning of section 411(d)(3) of the Internal Revenue Code of 1986, but the occurrence of such a termination or partial termination does not, by itself, constitute or require a termination of a plan under this title;

(5) when the plan fails to meet the minimum funding standards under section 412 of such Code (without regard to whether the plan is a plan described in section 4021(a)(2) of this Act) or under section 302 of this Act;

(6) when the plan is unable to pay benefits thereunder when due;

(7) when there is a distribution under the plan to a participant who is a substantial owner as defined in section 4021(d) if—

(A) such distribution has a value of $10,000 or more;

(B) such distribution is not made by reason of the death of the participant; and

(C) immediately after the distribution, the plan has nonforfeitable benefits which are not funded;

(8) when a plan merges, consolidates, or transfers its assets under section 208 of this Act, or when an alternative method of compliance is prescribed by the Secretary of Labor under section 110 of this Act;

(9) when, as a result of an event, a person ceases to be a member of the controlled group;

(10) when a contributing sponsor or a member of a contributing sponsor's controlled group liquidates in a case under title 11, United States Code, or under any similar Federal law or law of a State or political subdivision of a State;

(11) when a contributing sponsor or a member of a contributing sponsor's controlled group declares an extraordinary dividend (as defined in section 1059(c) of the Internal Revenue Code of 1986) or redeems, in any 12-month period, an aggregate of 10 percent or more of the total combined voting power of, all classes of stock entitled to vote, or an aggregate of 10 percent of [or] more of the total value of shares of all classes of stock, of a contributing sponsor and all members of its controlled group;

(12) when, in any 12-month period, an aggregate of 3 percent or more of the benefit liabilities of a plan covered by this title and maintained by a contributing sponsor or a member of its controlled group are transferred to a person that is not a member of the controlled group or to a plan or plans maintained by a person or persons that are not such a contributing sponsor or a member of its controlled group; or

(13) when any other event occurs that may be indicative of a need to terminate the plan and that is prescribed by the corporation in regulations.

For purposes of paragraph (7), all distributions to a participant within any 24-month period are treated as a single distribution.

Act Sec. 4043. (d) NOTIFICATION TO CORPORATION BY SECRETARY OF THE TREASURY.—The Secretary of the Treasury shall notify the corporation—

(1) whenever a reportable event described in paragraph (1), (4), or (5) of subsection (c) occurs, or

(2) whenever any other event occurs which the Secretary of the Treasury believes indicates that the plan may not be sound.

Act Sec. 4043. (e) NOTIFICATION TO CORPORATION BY SECRETARY OF LABOR.—The Secretary of Labor shall notify the corporation—

(1) whenever a reportable event described in paragraph (1), (5), or (8) of subsection (c) occurs, or

(2) whenever any other event occurs which the Secretary of Labor believes indicates that the plan may not be sound.

Act Sec. 4043. (f) DISCLOSURE EXEMPTION.—Any information or documentary material submitted to the corporation pursuant to this section shall be exempt from disclosure under section 552 of title 5, United States Code, and no such information or documentary material may be made public, except as may be relevant to any administrative or judicial action or proceeding. Nothing in this section is intended to prevent disclosure to either body of Congress or to any duly authorized committee or subcommittee of the Congress.

Amendments

P.L. 109-280, §407(c)(2):

Amended ERISA Sec. 4043(c)(7) by striking "section 4022(b)(6)" and inserting "section 4021(d)" to read as above.

This amendment is effective on January 1, 2006.

P.L. 103-465, §771(a):

Act Sec. 771(a) amended ERISA Sec. 4043(a) by inserting in the first sentence "or the contributing sponsor" before "knows or has reason to know"; by inserting in the first sentence ", unless a notice otherwise required under this subsection has already been provided with respect to such event" before the period at the end; and by striking the last sentence. Prior to amendment, the last sentence of ERISA Sec. 4043(a) read as follows:

Whenever an employer making contributions under a plan to which section 4021 applies knows or has reason to know that a reportable event has occurred he shall notify the plan administrator immediately.

P.L. 103-465, §771(b):

Act Sec. 771(b) amended ERISA Sec. 4043 by redesignating subsection (b) as subsection (c) and by inserting after subsection (a) a new subsection (b) to read as above.

Act Sec. 771(b) amended ERISA Sec. 4043 by redesignating subsection (c) as subsection (d).

Act Sec. 771(b) amended ERISA Sec. 4043 by redesignating subsection (d) as subsection (e).

P.L. 103-465, §771(c):

Act Sec. 771(c) amended ERISA Sec. 4043(c) (as redesignated by Act Sec. 771(b)) by striking the "or" at the end of paragraph (8); by striking paragraph (9); and by inserting after paragraph (8) new paragraphs (9)-(13) to read as above. Prior to amendment, ERISA Sec. 4043(b)(9) read as follows:

(9) when any other event occurs which the corporation determines may be indicative of a need to terminate the plan.

P.L. 103-465, §771(d):

Act Sec. 771(d) amended ERISA Sec. 4043 by adding at the end a new subsection (f) to read as above.

P.L. 103-465, §771(e)(1):

Act Sec. 771(e)(1) amended ERISA Sec. 4043(a) by striking "subsection (b)" and inserting "subsection (c)".

Act Sec. 771(e)(1) amended ERISA Sec. 4043(d) (as redesignated by Act Sec. 771(b)) by striking "subsection (b)" and inserting "subsection (c)".

The above amendments are effective for events occurring 60 days or more after December 8, 1994.

P.L. 101-239, §7891(a)(1):

Titles I, III, and IV of ERISA (other than sections 3(37)(E), 301(a)(7), and 308, the last sentence of section 408(d), and sections 414(c), 4001(a)(3)(ii), and 4303) are each amended by striking "Internal Revenue Code of 1954" each place it appears and inserting "Internal Revenue Code of 1986" effective October 22, 1986.

Regulations

The following regulations were adopted by the Pension Benefit Guaranty Corporation on December 2, 1996 (61 FR 63988), effective January 1, 1997. Reg. 4043.3 was amended effective August 11, 1997 (62 FR 36993). Reg. §§4043.5, 4043.6 and 4043.7 were amended October 28, 2003 (68 FR 61344). Reg. §§4043.1—4043.8, §§4043.20—4043.35, §§4043.61—4043.68, and §4043.81 were revised and Reg. §§4043.9—4043.10 were added on September 11, 2015 (80 FR 54979).

»»→ *Caution: Part 4043, as revised, applies to post-event reports for reportable events occurring on or after January 1, 2016, and to advance reports due on or after that date.*

Subpart A—General Provisions

[¶ 15,461]

§ 4043.1 **Purpose and scope.** This part prescribes the requirements for notifying PBGC of a reportable event under section 4043 of ERISA or of a failure to make certain required contributions under section 303(k)(4) of ERISA or section 430(k)(4) of the Code. Subpart A contains definitions and general rules. Subpart B contains rules for post-event notice of a reportable event. Subpart C contains rules for advance notice of a reportable event. Subpart D contains rules for notifying PBGC of a failure to make certain required contributions. [Revised 9/11/15 by 80 FR 54979.]

[¶ 15,461A]

§ 4043.2 **Definitions.** The following terms are defined in § 4001.2 of this chapter: benefit liabilities, Code, contributing sponsor, controlled group, ERISA, fair market value, irrevocable commitment, multiemployer plan, PBGC, person, plan, plan administrator, plan year, single-employer plan, and substantial owner.

In addition, for purposes of this part:

De minimis 10-percent segment means, in connection with a plan's controlled group, one or more entities that in the aggregate have for a fiscal year—

(1) Revenue not exceeding 10 percent of the controlled group's revenue;

(2) Annual operating income not exceeding the greater of—

(i) 10 percent of the controlled group's annual operating income; or

(ii) $5 million; and

(3) Net tangible assets at the end of the fiscal year(s) not exceeding the greater of—

(i) 10 percent of the controlled group's net tangible assets at the end of the fiscal year(s); or

(ii) $5 million.

De minimis 5-percent segment has the same meaning as *de minimis* 10-percent segment, except that "5 percent" is substituted for "10 percent" each time it appears.

Event year means the plan year in which a reportable event occurs.

Foreign entity means a member of a controlled group that—

(1) Is not a contributing sponsor of a plan;

(2) Is not organized under the laws of (or, if an individual, is not a domiciliary of) any state (as defined in section 3(10) of ERISA); and

(3) For the fiscal year that includes the date the reportable event occurs, meets one of the following tests—

(i) Is not required to file any United States federal income tax form;

(ii) Has no income reportable on any United States federal income tax form other than passive income not exceeding $1,000; or

(iii) Does not own substantial assets in the United States (disregarding stock of a member of the plan's controlled group) and is not required to file any quarterly United States tax returns for employee withholding.

Foreign parent means a foreign entity that is a direct or indirect parent of a person that is a contributing sponsor of a plan.

Low-default-risk has the meaning described in § 4043.9.

Notice due date means the deadline (including extensions) for filing notice of a reportable event with PBGC.

Participant means a participant as defined in § 4006.2 of this chapter.

Public company means a person subject to the reporting requirements of section 13 or 15(d) of the Securities Exchange Act of 1934 or a subsidiary (as defined for purposes of the Securities Exchange Act of 1934) of a person subject to such reporting requirements.

U.S. entity means an entity subject to the personal jurisdiction of the U.S. district court.

Well-funded plan safe harbor has the meaning described in § 4043.10. [Revised 9/11/15 by 80 FR 54979.]

[¶ 15,461B]

§ 4043.3 **Requirement of notice.** (a) *Obligation to file—.* (1) *In general.* Each person that is required to file a notice under this part, or a duly authorized representative, must submit the information required under this part by the time specified in § 4043.20 (for post-event notices), § 4043.61 (for advance notices), or § 4043.81 (for Form 200 filings). Any information filed with PBGC in connection with another matter may be incorporated by reference. If an event is subject to both post-event and advance notice requirements, the notice filed first satisfies both filing requirements.

(2) *Multiple plans.* If a reportable event occurs for more than one plan, the filing obligation with respect to each plan is independent of the filing obligation with respect to any other plan.

(3) *Optional consolidated filing.* A filing of a notice with respect to a reportable event by any person required to file will be deemed to be a filing by all persons required to give PBGC notice of the event under this part. If notices are required for two or more events, the notices may be combined in one filing.

(b) *Contents of reportable event notice.* A person required to file a reportable event notice under subpart B or C of this part must file, by the notice date, the form specified by PBGC for that purpose, with the information specified in PBGC's reportable events instructions.

(c) *Reportable event forms and instructions.* PBGC will issue reportable events forms and instructions and make them available on its Web site (*http://www.pbgc.gov*).

(d) *Requests for additional information.* PBGC may, in any case, require the submission of additional relevant information not specified in its forms and instructions. Any such information must be submitted for subpart B of this part within 30 days, and for subpart C or D of this part within 7 days, after the date of a written request by PBGC, or within a different time period specified therein. PBGC may in its discretion shorten the time period where it determines that the interests of PBGC or participants may be prejudiced by a delay in receipt of the information.

(e) *Effect of failure to file.* If a notice (or any other information required under this part) is not provided within the specified time limit, PBGC may pursue any equitable or legal remedies available to it under the law, including assessing against each person required to provide the notice a separate penalty under section 4071 of ERISA. [Revised 9/11/15 by 80 FR 54979.]

[¶ 15,461C]

§ 4043.4 **Waivers and extensions.** (a) *Waivers and extensions—in general.* PBGC may extend any deadline or waive any other requirement under this part where it finds convincing evidence that the waiver or extension is appropriate under the circumstances. Any waiver or extension may be subject to conditions. A request for a waiver or extension must be filed with PBGC in writing (which may be in electronic form) and must state the facts and circumstances on which the request is based.

(b) *Waivers and extensions—specific events.* For some reportable events, automatic waivers from reporting and extensions of time are provided in subparts B and C of this part. If an occurrence constitutes two or more reportable events, reporting requirements for each event are determined independently. For example, reporting is automatically waived for an occurrence that constitutes a reportable event under more than one section only if the requirements for an automatic waiver under each section are satisfied.

(c) *Multiemployer plans.* The requirements of section 4043 of ERISA are waived with respect to multiemployer plans.

(d) *Terminating plans.* No notice is required from the plan administrator or contributing sponsor of a plan if the notice date is on or after the date on which—

(1) All of the plan's assets (other than any excess assets) are distributed pursuant to a termination under part 4041 of this chapter; or

›››→ *Caution: Part 4043, as revised, applies to post-event reports for reportable events occurring on or after January 1, 2016, and to advance reports due on or after that date.*

(2) A trustee is appointed for the plan under section 4042 of ERISA.

(e) *Events not described in this part.* Notice of a reportable event described in section 4043(c) of ERISA is waived except to the extent that reporting is required under this part. [Revised 9/11/15 by 80 FR 54979.]

[¶ 15,461D]

§ 4043.5 **How and where to file.** Reportable event notices required under this part must be filed electronically in accordance with the instructions posted on PBGC's Web site, *http://www.pbgc.gov.* Filing guidance is provided by the instructions and by subpart A of part 4000 of this chapter. [Revised 9/11/15 by 80 FR 54979.]

[¶ 15,461E]

§ 4043.6 **Date of filing.** (a) *Post-event notice filings.* PBGC applies the rules in subpart C of part 4000 of this chapter to determine the date that a submission under subpart B of this part was filed with PBGC.

(b) *Advance notice and Form 200 filings.* Information filed under subpart C or D of this part is treated as filed on the date it is received by PBGC. Subpart C of part 4000 of this chapter provides rules for determining when PBGC receives a submission. [Revised 9/11/15 by 80 FR 54979.]

[¶ 15,461F]

§ 4043.7 **Computation of time.** PBGC applies the rules in subpart D of part 4000 of this chapter to compute any time period under this part. [Revised 9/11/15 by 80 FR 54979.]

[¶ 15,461G]

§ 4043.8 **Confidentiality.** In accordance with section 4043(f) of ERISA and § 4901.21(a)(3) of this chapter, any information or documentary material that is not publicly available and is submitted to PBGC pursuant to subpart B or C of this part will not be made public, except as may be relevant to any administrative or judicial action or proceeding or for disclosures to either body of Congress or to any duly authorized committee or subcommittee of the Congress. This provision does not apply to information or material submitted to PBGC pursuant to subpart D of this part, even where the submission serves as an alternative method of compliance with § 4043.25. [Revised 9/11/15 by 80 FR 54979.]

[¶ 15,461H]

§ 4043.9 **Company low-default-risk safe harbor.** (a) *Low-default-risk.* An entity (a "company") that is a contributing sponsor of a plan or the highest level U.S. parent of a contributing sponsor is "low-default-risk" on the date of an event if that date falls within a safe harbor period of the company as described in paragraph (b) of this section.

(b) *Safe harbor period.* A safe harbor period for a company means a period that—

(1) Begins on a financial information date (as described in paragraph (c) of this section) on which the company satisfies the low-default-risk standard in paragraph (e) of this section, and

(2) Ends 13 months later or (if earlier) on the company's next financial information date.

(c) *Financial information date.* A financial information date for a company means—

(1) A date on which the company files on Form 10-K with the Securities and Exchange Commission ("SEC") audited annual financial statements (including balance sheets, income statements, cash flow statements, and notes to the financial statements) for the company's most recent completed fiscal year preceding the date of such filing;

(2) The date (the "closing date") on which the company closes the annual accounting period that results in the production of audited or unaudited annual financial statements for the company's most recent completed fiscal year preceding the closing date, if audited annual financial statements are not required to be filed with the SEC; or

(3) A date on which the company files with IRS an annual federal income tax return or IRS Form 990 (in either case, a "return") for the company's most recent completed fiscal year preceding the date of such filing, if at the time the return is filed there are no annual financial statements for the year of the return.

(d) *Supporting financial information.* For purposes of this section, the "supporting financial information" is the annual financial statements or return associated with the establishment of the financial information date.

(e) *Low-default-risk standard—.* (1) *Adequate capacity.* For purposes of this part, except as provided in paragraph (e)(4) of this section, a company meets the low-default-risk standard as of a financial information date (the "qualifying date") if the company has adequate capacity to meet its obligations in full and on time on the qualifying date as evidenced by satisfying either:

(i) Both of the criteria described in paragraphs (e)(2)(i) and (ii) of this section, or

(ii) Any four of the seven criteria described in paragraphs (e)(2)(i) through (vii) of this section.

(2) *Criteria evidencing adequate capacity.* The criteria referred to in paragraph (e)(1) of this section are:

(i) The probability that the company will default on its financial obligations is not more than four percent over the next five years or not more than 0.4 percent over the next year, in either case determined on the basis of widely available financial information on the company's credit quality.

(ii) The company's secured debt (disregarding leases and debt incurred to acquire or improve property and secured only by that property) does not exceed 10 percent of the company's total assets.

(iii) The company has a ratio of retained-earnings-to-total-assets of 0.25 or more.

(iv) The company has a ratio of total-debt-to-EBITDA (earnings before interest, taxes, depreciation, and amortization) of 3.0 or less.

(v) The company has positive net income for the two most recently completed fiscal years preceding the qualifying date.

(vi) During the two-year period ending on the qualifying date, the company has not experienced an event described in § 4043.34(a)(1) or (2) (dealing with a default on a loan with an outstanding balance of $10 million or more) with respect to any loan with an outstanding balance of $10 million or more to the company regardless of whether reporting was waived under § 4043.34(b).

(vii) During the two-year period ending on the qualifying date, there has not been any failure to make when due any contribution described in § 4043.25(a)(1) or (2) (dealing with failure to make required minimum funding payments), unless reporting was waived under § 4043.25(c).

(3) *Using financial information to evaluate criteria—.* (i) Subject to paragraph (e)(3)(ii) of this section with respect to evaluating the criterion described in paragraph (e)(2)(v) of this section, to evaluate whether criteria described in paragraphs (e)(2)(ii) through (v) of this section are met, a company must use the supporting financial information described in paragraph (d) of this section associated with the qualifying date.

(ii) In addition to the use of the supporting financial information to evaluate criteria as described in paragraph (e)(3)(i) of this section, to evaluate whether the criterion described in paragraph (e)(2)(v) of this section is met, the company must also use the supporting financial information as described in paragraph (d) of this section associated with the financial information date for the fiscal year preceding the fiscal year covered by the supporting financial information associated with the qualifying date.

(iii) For purposes of paragraph (e)(2)(v) of this section, the excess of total revenue over total expenses as reported on the IRS Form 990 is considered to be net income.

»»→ *Caution: Part 4043, as revised, applies to post-event reports for reportable events occurring on or after January 1, 2016, and to advance reports due on or after that date.*

(4) *Exception.* If a company receives an audit or review report for supporting financial information described in paragraph (d) of this section associated with the qualifying date that expresses a material adverse view or qualification, the company does not satisfy the low-default-risk standard. [Added 9/11/15 by 80 FR 54979.]

»»→ *Caution: Part 4043, as revised, applies to post-event reports for reportable events occurring on or after January 1, 2016, and to advance reports due on or after that date.*

Subpart B—Post-Event Notice of Reportable Events

[¶ 15,462]

§ 4043.20 **Post-event filing obligation**. The plan administrator and each contributing sponsor of a plan for which a reportable event under this subpart has occurred are required to notify PBGC within 30 days after that person knows or has reason to know that the reportable event has occurred, unless a waiver or extension applies. If there is a change in plan administrator or contributing sponsor, the responsibility for any failure to file or defective filing lies with the person who is the plan administrator or contributing sponsor of the plan on the 30th day after the reportable event occurs. [Revised 9/11/15 by 80 FR 54979.]

[¶ 15,462A]

§ 4043.21 **Tax disqualification and Title I noncompliance.** (a) *Reportable event.* A reportable event occurs when the Secretary of the Treasury issues notice that a plan has ceased to be a plan described in section 4021(a)(2) of ERISA, or when the Secretary of Labor determines that a plan is not in compliance with title I of ERISA.

(b) *Waiver.* Notice is waived for this event. [Revised 9/11/15 by 80 FR 54979.]

[¶ 15,462B]

§ 4043.22 **Amendment decreasing benefits payable.** (a) *Reportable event.* A reportable event occurs when an amendment to a plan is adopted under which the retirement benefit payable from employer contributions with respect to any participant may be decreased.

(b) *Waiver.* Notice is waived for this event. [Revised 9/11/15 by 80 FR 54979.]

[¶ 15,462C]

§ 4043.23 **Active participant reduction.** (a) *Reportable event.* A reportable event occurs for a plan:

(1) *Single-cause event.* On the date in a plan year when, as a result of a single cause—such as a reorganization, the discontinuance of an operation, a natural disaster, a mass layoff, or an early retirement incentive program—the number of active participants is reduced to less than 80 percent of the number of active participants at the beginning of such plan year or less than 75 percent of the number of active participants at the beginning of the plan year preceding such plan year.

(2) *Attrition event.* At the end of a plan year if the number of active participants covered by the plan at the end of such plan year is less than 80 percent of the number of active participants at the beginning of such plan year, or less than 75 percent of the number of active participants at the beginning of the plan year preceding such plan year.

(b) *Determination rules—.* (1) *Determination dates.* The number of active participants at the beginning of a plan year may be determined by using the number of active participants at the end of the previous plan year, and the number of active participants at the end of a plan year may be determined by using the number of active participants at the beginning of the next plan year.

(2) *Active participant.* "Active participant" means a participant who—

(i) Is receiving compensation for work performed;

(ii) Is on paid or unpaid leave granted for a reason other than a layoff;

[¶ 15,461I]

§ 4043.10 **Well-funded plan safe harbor.** For purposes of this part, a plan is in the well-funded plan safe harbor for an event year if no variable-rate premium was required to be paid for the plan under parts 4006 and 4007 of this chapter for the plan year preceding the event year. [Added 9/11/15 by 80 FR 54979.]

(iii) Is laid off from work for a period of time that has lasted less than 30 days; or

(iv) Is absent from work due to a recurring reduction in employment that occurs at least annually.

(3) *Employment relationship.* The employment relationship referred to in this paragraph (b) is between the participant and all members of the plan's controlled group.

(c) *Reductions due to cessations and withdrawals.* For purposes of paragraph (a)(1) of this section, a reduction in the number of active participants is to be disregarded to the extent that it—

(1) Is attributable to an event described in ERISA section 4062(e) or 4063(a), and

(2) Is timely reported to PBGC under ERISA section 4063(a).

(d) *Waivers—.* (1) *Small plan.* Notice under this section is waived if the plan had 100 or fewer participants for whom flat-rate premiums were payable for the plan year preceding the event year.

(2) *Low-default-risk.* Notice under this section is waived if each contributing sponsor of the plan and the highest level U.S. parent of each contributing sponsor are low-default-risk on the date of the event.

(3) *Well-funded plan.* Notice under this section is waived if the plan is in the well-funded plan safe harbor for the event year.

(4) *Public company.* Notice under this section is waived if any contributing sponsor of the plan before the transaction is a public company and the contributing sponsor timely files a SEC Form 8-K disclosing the event under an item of the Form 8-K other than under Item 2.02 (Results of Operations and Financial Condition) or in financial statements under Item 9.01 (Financial Statements and Exhibits).

(e) *Extension—attrition event.* For an event described in paragraph (a)(2) of this section, the notice date is extended until the premium due date for the plan year following the event year. [Revised 9/11/15 by 80 FR 54979.]

[¶ 15,462D]

§ 4043.24 **Termination or partial termination.** (a) *Reportable event.* A reportable event occurs when the Secretary of the Treasury determines that there has been a termination or partial termination of a plan within the meaning of section 411(d)(3) of the Code.

(b) *Waiver.* Notice is waived for this event. [Revised 9/11/15 by 80 FR 54979.]

[¶ 15,462E]

§ 4043.25 **Failure to make required minimum funding payment.** (a) *Reportable event.* A reportable event occurs when—

(1) A contribution required under sections 302 and 303 of ERISA or sections 412 and 430 of the Code is not made by the due date for the payment under ERISA section 303(j) or Code section 430(j), or

(2) Any other contribution required as a condition of a funding waiver is not made when due.

(b) *Alternative method of compliance—Form 200 filed.* If, with respect to the same failure, a filing is made in accordance with § 4043.81, that filing (while not considered to be submitted to PBGC pursuant to section 4043 of ERISA for purposes of section 4043(f) of ERISA) satisfies the requirements of this section.

(c) *Waivers—.* (1) *Small plan.* Notice under this section is waived with respect to a failure to make a required quarterly contribution

⟫⟶ Caution: Part 4043, as revised, applies to post-event reports for reportable events occurring on or after January 1, 2016, and to advance reports due on or after that date.

under section 303(j)(3) of ERISA or section 430(j)(3) of the Code if the plan had 100 or fewer participants for whom flat-rate premiums were payable for the plan year preceding the event year.

(2) *30-day grace period.* Notice under this section is waived if the missed contribution is made by the 30th day after its due date.

(3) *Late funding balance election.* Notice under this section is waived if the failure to make a timely required contribution is solely because of the plan sponsor's failure to timely make a funding balance election. [Revised 9/11/15 by 80 FR 54979.]

[¶ 15,462F]

§ 4043.26 **Inability to pay benefits when due.** (a) *Reportable event.* A reportable event occurs when a plan is currently unable or projected to be unable to pay benefits.

(1) *Current inability.* A plan is currently unable to pay benefits if it fails to provide any participant or beneficiary the full benefits to which the person is entitled under the terms of the plan, at the time the benefit is due and in the form in which it is due. A plan is not treated as being currently unable to pay benefits if its failure to pay is caused solely by—

(i) A limitation under section 436 of the Code and section 206(g) of ERISA (dealing with funding-based limits on benefits and benefit accruals under single-employer plans),

(ii) The inability to locate a person, or

(iii) Any other administrative delay, including the need to verify a person's eligibility for benefits, to the extent that the delay is for less than the shorter of two months or two full benefit payment periods.

(2) *Projected inability.* A plan is projected to be unable to pay benefits when, as of the last day of any quarter of a plan year, the plan's "liquid assets" are less than two times the amount of the "disbursements from the plan" for such quarter. "Liquid assets" and "disbursements from the plan" have the same meaning as under section 303(j)(4)(E) of ERISA and section 430(j)(4)(E) of the Code.

(b) *Waiver—plans subject to liquidity shortfall rules.* Notice under this section is waived unless the reportable event occurs during a plan year for which the plan is exempt from the liquidity shortfall rules in section 303(j)(4) of ERISA and section 430(j)(4) of the Code because it is described in section 303(g)(2)(B) of ERISA and section 430(g)(2)(B) of the Code. [Revised 9/11/15 by 80 FR 54979.]

[¶ 15,462G]

§ 4043.27 **Distribution to a substantial owner.** (a) *Reportable event.* A reportable event occurs for a plan when—

(1) There is a distribution to a substantial owner of a contributing sponsor of the plan;

(2) The total of all distributions made to the substantial owner within the one-year period ending with the date of such distribution exceeds $10,000;

(3) The distribution is not made by reason of the substantial owner's death;

(4) Immediately after the distribution, the plan has nonforfeitable benefits (as provided in § 4022.5 of this chapter) that are not funded; and

(5) Either—

(i) The sum of the values of all distributions to any one substantial owner within the one-year period ending with the date of the distribution is more than one percent of the end-of-year total amount of the plan's assets (as required to be reported on Schedule H or Schedule I to Form 5500) for each of the two plan years immediately preceding the event year, or

(ii) The sum of the values of all distributions to all substantial owners within the one-year period ending with the date of the distribution is more than five percent of the end-of-year total amount of the plan's assets (as required to be reported on Schedule H or Schedule I

to Form 5500) for each of the two plan years immediately preceding the event year.

(b) *Determination rules—.* (1) *Valuation of distribution.* The value of a distribution under this section is the sum of—

(i) The cash amounts actually received by the substantial owner;

(ii) The purchase price of any irrevocable commitment; and

(iii) The fair market value of any other assets distributed, determined as of the date of distribution to the substantial owner.

(2) *Date of substantial owner distribution.* The date of distribution to a substantial owner of a cash distribution is the date it is received by the substantial owner. The date of distribution to a substantial owner of an irrevocable commitment is the date on which the obligation to provide benefits passes from the plan to the insurer. The date of any other distribution to a substantial owner is the date when the plan relinquishes control over the assets transferred directly or indirectly to the substantial owner.

(3) *Determination date.* The determination of whether a participant is (or has been in the preceding 60 months) a substantial owner is made on the date when there has been a distribution that would be reportable under this section if made to a substantial owner.

(c) *Alternative method of compliance—annuity.* In the case of an annuity for a substantial owner, a filing that satisfies the requirements of this section with respect to any payment under the annuity and that discloses the period, the amount of the payment, and the duration of the annuity satisfies the requirements of this section with respect to all subsequent payments under the annuity.

(d) *Waivers—.* (1) *Low-default-risk.* Notice under this section is waived if each contributing sponsor of the plan and the highest level U.S. parent of each contributing sponsor are low-default-risk on the date of the event.

(2) *Well-funded plan.* Notice under this section is waived if the plan is in the well-funded plan safe harbor for the event year.

(3) *Public company.* Notice under this section is waived if any contributing sponsor of the plan before the transaction is a public company and the contributing sponsor timely files a SEC Form 8-K disclosing the event under an item of the Form 8-K other than under Item 2.02 (Results of Operations and Financial Condition) or in financial statements under Item 9.01 (Financial Statements and Exhibits). [Revised 9/11/15 by 80 FR 54979.]

[¶ 15,462H]

§ 4043.28 **Plan merger, consolidation or transfer.** (a) *Reportable event.* A reportable event occurs when a plan merges, consolidates, or transfers its assets or liabilities under section 208 of ERISA or section 414(*l*) of the Code.

(b) *Waiver.* Notice under this section is waived for this event. However, notice may be required under § 4043.29 (for a controlled group change) or § 4043.32 (for a transfer of benefit liabilities). [Revised 9/11/15 by 80 FR 54979.]

[¶ 15,462I]

§ 4043.29 **Change in contributing sponsor or controlled group.** (a) *Reportable event.* A reportable event occurs for a plan when there is a transaction that results, or will result, in one or more persons' ceasing to be members of the plan's controlled group (other than by merger involving members of the same controlled group). For purposes of this section, the term "transaction" includes, but is not limited to, a legally binding agreement, whether or not written, to transfer ownership, an actual transfer of ownership, and an actual change in ownership that occurs as a matter of law or through the exercise or lapse of preexisting rights. Whether an agreement is legally binding is to be determined without regard to any conditions in the agreement. A transaction is not reportable if it will result solely in a reorganization involving a mere change in identity, form, or place of organization, however effected.

>>→ *Caution: Part 4043, as revised, applies to post-event reports for reportable events occurring on or after January 1, 2016, and to advance reports due on or after that date.*

(b) *Waivers.* (1) De minimis *10-percent segment.* Notice under this section is waived if the person or persons that will cease to be members of the plan's controlled group represent a *de minimis* 10-percent segment of the plan's old controlled group for the most recent fiscal year(s) ending on or before the date the reportable event occurs.

(2) *Foreign entity.* Notice under this section is waived if each person that will cease to be a member of the plan's controlled group is a foreign entity other than a foreign parent.

(3) *Small plan.* Notice under this section is waived if the plan had 100 or fewer participants for whom flat-rate premiums were payable for the plan year preceding the event year.

(4) *Low-default-risk.* Notice under this section is waived if each post-event contributing sponsor of the plan and the highest level U.S. parent of each post-event contributing sponsor are low-default-risk on the date of the event.

(5) *Well-funded plan.* Notice under this section is waived if the plan is in the well-funded plan safe harbor for the event year.

(6) *Public company.* Notice under this section is waived if any contributing sponsor of the plan before the transaction is a public company and the contributing sponsor timely files a SEC Form 8-K disclosing the event under an item of the Form 8-K other than under Item 2.02 (Results of Operations and Financial Condition) or in financial statements under Item 9.01 (Financial Statements and Exhibits).

(c) *Examples.* The following examples assume that no waiver applies.

(1) *Controlled group breakup.* Plan A's controlled group consists of Company A (its contributing sponsor), Company B (which maintains Plan B), and Company C. As a result of a transaction, the controlled group will break into two separate controlled groups — one segment consisting of Company A and the other segment consisting of Companies B and C. Both Company A (Plan A's contributing sponsor) and the plan administrator of Plan A are required to report that Companies B and C will leave Plan A's controlled group. Company B (Plan B's contributing sponsor) and the plan administrator of Plan B are required to report that Company A will leave Plan B's controlled group. Company C is not required to report because it is not a contributing sponsor or a plan administrator.

(2) *Change in contributing sponsor.* Plan Q is maintained by Company Q. Company Q enters into a binding contract to sell a portion of its assets and to transfer employees participating in Plan Q, along with Plan Q, to Company R, which is not a member of Company Q's controlled group. There will be no change in the structure of Company Q's controlled group. On the effective date of the sale, Company R will become the contributing sponsor of Plan Q. A reportable event occurs on the date of the transaction (*i.e.*, the date the binding contract was executed), because as a result of the transaction, Company Q (and any other member of its controlled group) will cease to be a member of Plan Q's controlled group. The event is not reported before the notice date. If on the notice date the change in the contributing sponsor has not yet become effective, Company Q has the reporting obligation. If the change in the contributing sponsor has become effective by the notice date, Company R has the reporting obligation. [Revised 9/11/15 by 80 FR 54979.]

[¶ 15,462J]

§ 4043.30 **Liquidation.** (a) *Reportable event.* A reportable event occurs for a plan when a member of the plan's controlled group—

(1) Is involved in any transaction to implement its complete liquidation (including liquidation into another controlled group member);

(2) Institutes or has instituted against it a proceeding to be dissolved or is dissolved, whichever occurs first; or

(3) Liquidates in a case under the Bankruptcy Code, or under any similar law.

(b) *Waivers—.* (1) *De minimis 10-percent segment.* Notice under this section is waived if the person or persons that liquidate do not include any contributing sponsor of the plan and represent a *de minimis* 10-percent segment of the plan's controlled group for the most recent fiscal year(s) ending on or before the date the reportable event occurs.

(2) *Foreign entity.* Notice under this section is waived if each person that liquidates is a foreign entity other than a foreign parent. [Revised 9/11/15 by 80 FR 54979.]

[¶ 15,462K]

§ 4043.31 **Extraordinary dividend or stock redemption.** (a) *Reportable event.* A reportable event occurs for a plan when any member of the plan's controlled group declares a dividend or redeems its own stock and the amount or net value of the distribution, when combined with other such distributions during the same fiscal year of the person, exceeds the person's net income before after-tax gain or loss on any sale of assets, as determined in accordance with generally accepted accounting principles, for the prior fiscal year. A distribution by a person to a member of its controlled group is disregarded.

(b) *Determination rules.* For purposes of paragraph (a) of this section, the net value of a non-cash distribution is the fair market value of assets transferred by the person making the distribution, reduced by the fair market value of any liabilities assumed or consideration given by the recipient in connection with the distribution. Net value determinations should be based on readily available fair market value(s) or independent appraisal(s) performed within one year before the distribution is made. To the extent that fair market values are not readily available and no such appraisals exist, the fair market value of an asset transferred in connection with a distribution or a liability assumed by a recipient of a distribution is deemed to be equal to 200 percent of the book value of the asset or liability on the books of the person making the distribution. Stock redeemed is deemed to have no value.

(c) *Waivers—.* (1) *De minimis 10-percent segment.* Notice under this section is waived if the person making the distribution is a *de minimis* 10-percent segment of the plan's controlled group for the most recent fiscal year(s) ending on or before the date the reportable event occurs.

(2) *Foreign entity.* Notice under this section is waived if the person making the distribution is a foreign entity other than a foreign parent.

(3) *Small plan.* Notice under this section is waived if the plan had 100 or fewer participants for whom flat-rate premiums were payable for the plan year preceding the event year.

(4) *Low-default-risk.* Notice under this section is waived if each contributing sponsor of the plan and the highest level U.S. parent of each contributing sponsor are low-default-risk on the date of the event.

(5) *Well-funded plan.* Notice under this section is waived if the plan is in the well-funded plan safe harbor for the event year.

(6) *Public company.* Notice under this section is waived if any contributing sponsor of the plan before the transaction is a public company and the contributing sponsor timely files a SEC Form 8-K disclosing the event under an item of the Form 8-K other than under Item 2.02 (Results of Operations and Financial Condition) or in financial statements under Item 9.01 (Financial Statements and Exhibits). [Revised 9/11/15 by 80 FR 54979.]

[¶ 15,462L]

§ 4043.32 **Transfer of benefit liabilities.** (a) *Reportable event.* A reportable event occurs for a plan when—

(1) The plan makes a transfer of benefit liabilities to a person, or to a plan or plans maintained by a person or persons, that are not members of the transferor plan's controlled group; and

(2) The amount of benefit liabilities transferred, in conjunction with other benefit liabilities transferred during the 12-month period ending on the date of the transfer, is 3 percent or more of the plan's

total benefit liabilities. Both the benefit liabilities transferred and the plan's total benefit liabilities are to be valued as of any one date in the plan year in which the transfer occurs, using actuarial assumptions that comply with section 414(*l*) of the Code.

(b) *Determination rules—*. (1) *Date of transfer.* The date of transfer is to be determined on the basis of the facts and circumstances of the particular situation. For transfers subject to the requirements of section 414(*l*) of the Code, the date determined in accordance with 26 CFR 1.414(*l*)-1(b)(11) will be considered the date of transfer.

(2) *Distributions of lump sums and annuities.* For purposes of paragraph (a) of this section, the payment of a lump sum, or purchase of an irrevocable commitment to provide an annuity, in satisfaction of benefit liabilities is not a transfer of benefit liabilities.

(c) *Waivers—*. (1) *Small plan.* Notice under this section is waived if the plan had 100 or fewer participants for whom flat-rate premiums were payable for the plan year preceding the event year.

(2) *Low-default-risk.* Notice under this section is waived if each contributing sponsor of the plan and the highest level U.S. parent of each contributing sponsor are low-default-risk on the date of the event.

(3) *Well-funded plan.* Notice under this section is waived if the plan is in the well-funded plan safe harbor for the event year.

(4) *Public company.* Notice under this section is waived if any contributing sponsor of the plan before the transaction is a public company and the contributing sponsor timely files a SEC Form 8-K disclosing the event under an item of the Form 8-K other than under Item 2.02 (Results of Operations and Financial Condition) or in financial statements under Item 9.01 (Financial Statements and Exhibits). [Revised 9/11/15 by 80 FR 54979.]

[¶ 15,462M]

§ 4043.33 **Application for minimum funding waiver.** A reportable event for a plan occurs when an application for a minimum funding waiver for the plan is submitted under section 302(c) of ERISA or section 412(c) of the Code. [Revised 9/11/15 by 80 FR 54979.]

[¶ 15,462N]

§ 4043.34 **Loan default.** (a) *Reportable event.* A reportable event occurs for a plan when, with respect to a loan with an outstanding balance of $10 million or more to a member of the plan's controlled group—

(1) There is an acceleration of payment or a default under the loan agreement, or

(2) The lender waives or agrees to an amendment of any covenant in the loan agreement the effect of which is to cure or avoid a breach that would trigger a default.

(b) *Waivers—*. (1) *De minimis 10-percent segment.* Notice under this section is waived if the debtor is not a contributing sponsor of the plan and represents a *de minimis* 10-percent segment of the plan's controlled group for the most recent fiscal year(s) ending on or before the date the reportable event occurs.

(2) *Foreign entity.* Notice under this section is waived if the debtor is a foreign entity other than a foreign parent. [Revised 9/11/15 by 80 FR 54979.]

[¶ 15,462O]

§ 4043.35 **Insolvency or similar settlement.** (a) *Reportable event.* A reportable event occurs for a plan when any member of the plan's controlled group—

(1) Commences or has commenced against it any insolvency proceeding (including, but not limited to, the appointment of a receiver) other than a bankruptcy case under the Bankruptcy Code;

(2) Commences, or has commenced against it, a proceeding to effect a composition, extension, or settlement with creditors;

(3) Executes a general assignment for the benefit of creditors; or

(4) Undertakes to effect any other nonjudicial composition, extension, or settlement with substantially all its creditors.

(b) *Waivers—*. (1) *De minimis 10-percent segment.* Notice under this section is waived if the person described in paragraph (a) of this section is not a contributing sponsor of the plan and represents a *de minimis* 10-percent segment of the plan's controlled group for the most recent fiscal year(s) ending on or before the date the reportable event occurs.

(2) *Foreign entity.* Notice under this section is waived if the person described in paragraph (a) of this section is a foreign entity other than a foreign parent. [Revised 9/11/15 by 80 FR 54979.]

Subpart C—Advance Notice of Reportable Events

[¶ 15,463]

§ 4043.61 **Advance reporting filing obligation.** (a) *In general.* Unless a waiver or extension applies with respect to the plan, each contributing sponsor of a plan is required to notify PBGC no later than 30 days before the effective date of a reportable event described in this subpart C if the contributing sponsor is subject to advance reporting for the reportable event. If there is a change in contributing sponsor, the responsibility for any failure to file or defective filing lies with the person who is the contributing sponsor of the plan on the notice date.

(b) *Persons subject to advance reporting.* A contributing sponsor of a plan is subject to the advance reporting requirement under paragraph (a) of this section for a reportable event if —

(1) On the notice date, neither the contributing sponsor nor any member of the plan's controlled group to which the event relates is a public company; and

(2) The aggregate unfunded vested benefits, determined in accordance with paragraph (c) of this section, are more than $50 million; and

(3) The aggregate value of plan assets, determined in accordance with paragraph (c) of this section, is less than 90 percent of the aggregate premium funding target, determined in accordance with paragraph (c) of this section.

(c) *Funding determinations.* For purposes of paragraph (b) of this section, the aggregate unfunded vested benefits, aggregate value of plan assets, and aggregate premium funding target are determined by aggregating the unfunded vested benefits, values of plan assets, and premium funding targets (respectively), as determined in accordance with part 4006 of this chapter for purposes of the variable-rate premium for the plan year preceding the effective date of the event, of plans maintained (on the notice date) by the contributing sponsor and any members of the contributing sponsor's controlled group, disregarding plans with no unfunded vested benefits (as so determined).

(d) *Shortening of 30-day period.* Pursuant to § 4043.3(d), PBGC may, upon review of an advance notice, shorten the notice period to allow for an earlier effective date. [Revised 9/11/15 by 80 FR 54979.]

[¶ 15,463A]

§ 4043.62 **Change in contributing sponsor or controlled group.** (a) *Reportable event.* Advance notice is required for a change in a plan's contributing sponsor or controlled group, as described in § 4043.29(a).

(b) *Waivers—*. (1) *Small and mid-size plans.* Notice under this section is waived with respect to a change of contributing sponsor if the transferred plan has fewer than 500 participants.

(2) *De minimis 5-percent segment.* Notice under this section is waived if the person or persons that will cease to be members of the plan's controlled group represent a *de minimis* 5-percent segment of the plan's old controlled group for the most recent fiscal year(s) ending

»»→ *Caution: Part 4043, as revised, applies to post-event reports for reportable events occurring on or after January 1, 2016, and to advance reports due on or after that date.*

on or before the effective date of the reportable event. [Revised 9/11/15 by 80 FR 54979.]

[¶ 15,463B]

§ 4043.63 **Liquidation**. (a) *Reportable event*. Advance notice is required for a liquidation of a member of a plan's controlled group, as described in § 4043.30.

(b) *Waiver—de minimis 5-percent segment and ongoing plans*. Notice under this section is waived if the person that liquidates is a *de minimis* 5-percent segment of the plan's controlled group for the most recent fiscal year(s) ending on or before the effective date of the reportable event, and each plan that was maintained by the liquidating member is maintained by another member of the plan's controlled group. [Revised 9/11/15 by 80 FR 54979.]

[¶ 15,463C]

§ 4043.64 **Extraordinary dividend or stock redemption**. (a) *Reportable event*. Advance notice is required for a distribution by a member of a plan's controlled group, as described in § 4043.31(a).

(b) *Waiver—de minimis 5-percent segment*. Notice under this section is waived if the person making the distribution is a *de minimis* 5-percent segment of the plan's controlled group for the most recent fiscal year(s) ending on or before the effective date of the reportable event. [Revised 9/11/15 by 80 FR 54979.]

[¶ 15,463D]

§ 4043.65 **Transfer of benefit liabilities**. (a) *Reportable event*. Advance notice is required for a transfer of benefit liabilities, as described in § 4043.32(a).

(b) *Waivers—*. (1) *Complete plan transfer*. Notice under this section is waived if the transfer is a transfer of all of the transferor plan's benefit liabilities and assets to one other plan.

(2) *Transfer of less than 3 percent of assets*. Notice under this section is waived if the value of the assets being transferred—

(i) Equals the present value of the accrued benefits (whether or not vested) being transferred, using actuarial assumptions that comply with section 414(*l*) of the Code; and

(ii) In conjunction with other assets transferred during the same plan year, is less than 3 percent of the assets of the transferor plan as of at least one day in that year.

(3) *Section 414(l) safe harbor*. Notice under this section is waived if the benefit liabilities of 500 or fewer participants are transferred and the transfer complies with section 414(*l*) of the Code using the actuarial assumptions prescribed for valuing benefits in trusteed plans under § § 4044.51 through 4044.57 of this chapter.

(4) *Fully funded plans*. Notice under this section is waived if the transfer complies with section 414(*l*) of the Code using reasonable actuarial assumptions and, after the transfer, the transferor and transferee plans are fully funded as determined in accordance with § § 4044.51 through 4044.57 of this chapter and § 4010.8(d)(1)(ii) of this chapter. [Revised 9/11/15 by 80 FR 54979.]

[¶ 15,463E]

§ 4043.66 **Application for minimum funding waiver**. (a) *Reportable event*. Advance notice is required for an application for a minimum funding waiver, as described in § 4043.33.

(b) *Extension*. The notice date is extended until 10 days after the reportable event has occurred. [Revised 9/11/15 by 80 FR 54979.]

[¶ 15,463F]

§ 4043.67 **Loan default**. Advance notice is required for an acceleration of payment, a default, a waiver, or an agreement to an amendment with respect to a loan agreement described in § 4043.34(a). [Revised 9/11/15 by 80 FR 54979.]

[¶ 15,463G]

§ 4043.68 **Insolvency or similar settlement**. (a) *Reportable event*. Advance notice is required for an insolvency or similar settlement, as described in § 4043.35.

(b) *Extension*. For a case or proceeding under § 4043.35(a)(1) or (2) that is not commenced by a member of the plan's controlled group, the notice date is extended to 10 days after the commencement of the case or proceeding. [Revised 9/11/15 by 80 FR 54979.]

»»→ *Caution: Part 4043, as revised, applies to post-event reports for reportable events occurring on or after January 1, 2016, and to advance reports due on or after that date.*

Subpart D—Notice of Failure To Make Required Contributions

[¶ 15,464]

§ 4043.81 **PBGC Form 200, notice of failure to make required contributions; supplementary information**. (a) *General rules*. To comply with the notification requirement in section 303(k)(4) of ERISA and section 430(k)(4) of the Code, a contributing sponsor of a single-employer plan that is covered under section 4021 of ERISA and (if that contributing sponsor is a member of a parent-subsidiary controlled group) the ultimate parent must complete and submit in accordance with this section a properly certified Form 200 that includes all required documentation and other information, as described in the related filing instructions. Notice is required whenever the unpaid balance of a contribution payment required under sections 302 and 303 of ERISA and sections 412 and 430 of the Code (including interest), when added to the aggregate unpaid balance of all preceding such payments for which payment was not made when due (including interest), exceeds $1 million.

(1) Form 200 must be filed with PBGC no later than 10 days after the due date for any required payment for which payment was not made when due.

(2) If a contributing sponsor or the ultimate parent completes and submits Form 200 in accordance with this section, PBGC will consider the notification requirement in section 303(k)(4) of ERISA and section 430(k)(4) of the Code to be satisfied by all members of a controlled group of which the person who has filed Form 200 is a member.

(b) *Supplementary information*. If, upon review of a Form 200, PBGC concludes that it needs additional information in order to make decisions regarding enforcement of a lien imposed by section 303(k) of ERISA and section 430(k) of the Code, PBGC may require any member of the contributing sponsor's controlled group to supplement the Form 200 in accordance with § 4043.3(d).

(c) *Ultimate parent*. For purposes of this section, the term "ultimate parent" means the parent at the highest level in the chain of corporations and/or other organizations constituting a parent-subsidiary controlled group. [Revised 9/11/15 by 80 FR 54979.]

[¶ 15,470]
ALLOCATION OF ASSETS

Act Sec. 4044. (a) ORDER OF PRIORITY OF PARTICIPANTS AND BENEFICIARIES.—In the case of the termination of a single-employer plan, the plan administrator shall allocate the assets of the plan (available to provide benefits) among the participants and beneficiaries of the plan in the following order:

(1) First, to that portion of each individual's accrued benefit which is derived from the participant's contributions to the plan which were not mandatory contributions.

(2) Second, to that portion of each individual's accrued benefit which is derived from the participant's mandatory contributions.

(3) Third, in the case of benefits payable as an annuity—

(A) in the case of the benefit of a participant or beneficiary which was in pay status as of the beginning of the 3-year period ending on the termination date of the plan, to each such benefit, based on the provisions of the plan (as in effect during the 5-year period ending on such date) under which such benefit would be the least.

(B) in the case of a participant's or beneficiary's benefit (other than a benefit described in subparagraph (A)) which would have been in pay status as of the beginning of such 3-year period if the participant had retired prior to the beginning of the 3-year period and if his benefits had commenced (in the normal form of annuity under the plan) as of the beginning of such period, to each such benefit based on the provisions of the plan (as in effect during the 5-year period ending on such date) under which such benefit would be the least.

For purposes of subparagraph (A), the lowest benefit in pay status during a 3-year period shall be considered the benefit in pay status for such period.

(4) Fourth—

(A) to all other benefits (if any) of individuals under the plan guaranteed under this title (determined without regard to section 4022B(a)), and

(B) to the additional benefits (if any) which would be determined under subparagraph (A) if section 4022(b)(5)(B) did not apply.

For purposes of this paragraph, section 4021 shall be applied without regard to subsection (c) thereof.

(5) Fifth, to all other nonforfeitable benefits under the plan.

(6) Sixth, to all other benefits under the plan.

Act Sec. 4044. (b) ADJUSTMENT OF ALLOCATIONS; REALLOCATIONS; MANDATORY CONTRIBUTIONS; ESTABLISHMENT OF SUBCLASSES AND CATEGORIES.—For purposes of subsection (a)—

(1) The amount allocated under any paragraph of subsection (a) with respect to any benefit shall be properly adjusted for any allocation of assets with respect to that benefit under a prior paragraph of subsection (a).

(2) If the assets available for allocation under any paragraph of subsection (a) (other than paragraphs (4), (5), and (6)) are insufficient to satisfy in full the benefits of all individuals which are described in that paragraph, the assets shall be allocated pro rata among such individuals on the basis of the present value (as of the termination date) of their respective benefits described in that paragraph.

(3) If assets available for allocation under paragraph (4) of subsection (a) are insufficient to satisfy in full the benefits of all individuals who are described in that paragraph, the assets shall be allocated first to benefits described in subparagraph (A) of that paragraph. Any remaining assets shall then be allocated to benefits described in subparagraph (B) of that paragraph. If assets allocated to such subparagraph (B) are insufficient to satisfy in full the benefits described in that subparagraph, the assets shall be allocated pro rata among individuals on the basis of the present value (as of the termination date) of their respective benefits described in that subparagraph.

(4) This paragraph applies if the assets available for allocation under paragraph (5) of subsection (a) are not sufficient to satisfy in full the benefits of individuals described in that paragraph.

(A) If this paragraph applies, except as provided in subparagraph (B), the assets shall be allocated to the benefits of individuals described in such paragraph (5) on the basis of the benefits of individuals which would have been described in such paragraph (5) under the plan as in effect at the beginning of the 5-year ending on the date of plan termination.

(B) If the assets available for allocation under subparagraph (A) are sufficient to satisfy in full the benefits described in such subparagraph (without regard to this subparagraph), then for purposes of subparagraph (A), benefits of individuals described in such subparagraph shall be determined on the basis of the plan as amended by the most recent plan amendment effective during such 5-year period under which the assets available for allocation are sufficient to satisfy in full the benefits of individuals described in subparagraph (A) and any assets remaining to be allocated under such subparagraph shall be allocated under subparagraph (A) on the basis of the plan as amended by the next succeeding plan amendment effective during such period.

(5) If the Secretary of the Treasury determines that the allocation made pursuant to this section (without regard to this paragraph) results in discrimination prohibited by section 401(a)(4) of the Internal Revenue Code of 1986 then, if required to prevent the disqualification of the plan (or any trust under the plan) under section 401(a) or 403(a) of such Code, the assets allocated under subsection (a)(4)(B), (a)(5), and (a)(6) shall be reallocated to the extent necessary to avoid such discrimination.

(6) The term "mandatory contributions" means amounts contributed to the plan by a participant which are required as a condition of employment, as a condition of participation in such plan, or as a condition of obtaining benefits under the plan attributable to employer contributions. For this purpose, the total amount of mandatory contributions of a participant is the amount of such contributions reduced (but not below zero) by the sum of the amounts paid or distributed to him under the plan before its termination.

(7) A plan may establish subclasses and categories within the classes described in paragraphs (1) through (6) of subsection (a) in accordance with regulations prescribed by the corporation.

Act Sec. 4044. (c) INCREASE OR DECREASE IN VALUE OF ASSETS.—Any increase or decrease in the value of the assets of a single-employer plan occurring during the period beginning on the later of (1) the date a trustee is appointed under section 4042(b) or (2) the date on which the plan is terminated is to be allocated between the plan and the corporation in the manner determined by the court (in the case of a court-appointed trustee) or as agreed upon by the corporation and the plan administrator in any other case. Any increase or decrease in the value of the assets of a single-employer plan occurring after the date on which the plan is terminated shall be credited to, or suffered by, the corporation.

Act Sec. 4044.(d)(1) DISTRIBUTION OF RESIDUAL ASSETS; RESTRICTION ON REVERSIONS PURSUANT TO RECENTLY AMENDED PLANS; ASSETS ATTRIBUTABLE TO EMPLOYEE CONTRIBUTIONS; CALCULATION OR REMAINING ASSETS.—Subject to paragraph (3), any residual assets of a single-employer plan may be distributed to the employer if,—

(A) all liabilities of the plan to participants and their beneficiaries have been satisfied,

(B) the distribution does not contravene any provision of law, and

(C) the plan provides for such a distribution in these circumstances.

(2)(A) In determining the extent to which a plan provides for the distribution of plan assets to the employer for purposes of paragraph (1)(C), any such provision, and any amendment increasing the amount which may be distributed to the employer, shall not be treated as effective before the end of the fifth calendar year following the date of the adoption of such provision or amendment.

(B) A distribution to the employer from a plan shall not be treated as failing to satisfy the requirements of this paragraph if the plan has been in effect for fewer than 5 years and the plan has provided for such a distribution since the effective date of the plan.

(C) Except as otherwise provided in regulations of the Secretary of the Treasury, in any case in which a transaction described in section 208 occurs, subparagraph (A) shall continue to apply separately with respect to the amounts of any assets transferred in such transaction.

(D) For purposes of this subsection, the term "employer" includes any member of the controlled group of which the employer is a member. For purposes of the preceding sentence, the term "controlled group" means any group treated as a single employer under subsection (b), (c), (m) or (o) of section 414 of the Internal Revenue Code of 1986.

(3)(A) Before any distribution from a plan pursuant to paragraph (1), if any assets of the plan attributable to employee contributions remain after satisfaction of all liabilities described in subsection (a), such remaining assets shall be equitably distributed to the participants who made such contributions or their beneficiaries (including alternate payees, within the meaning of section 206(d)(3)(K)).

(B) For purposes of subparagraph (A), the portion of the remaining assets which are attributable to employee contributions shall be an amount equal to the product derived by multiplying—

(i) the market value of the total remaining assets, by

(ii) a fraction—

(I) the numerator of which is the present value of all portions of the accrued benefits with respect to participants which are derived from participants' mandatory contributions (referred to in subsection (a)(2)), and

(II) the denominator of which is present value of all benefits with respect to which assets are allocated under paragraph (2) through (6) of subsection (a).

(C) For purposes of this paragraph, each person who is, as of the termination date—

(i) a participant under the plan, or

(ii) an individual who has received, during the 3-year period ending with the termination date, a distribution from the plan of such individual's entire nonforfeitable benefit in the form of a single sum distribution in accordance with section 203(e) or in the form of irrevocable commitments purchased by the plan from an insurer to provide such nonforfeitable benefit,

shall be treated as a participant with respect to the termination, if all or part of the nonforfeitable benefit with respect to such person is or was attributable to participants' mandatory contributions (referred to in subsection (a)(2)).

(4) Nothing in this subsection shall be construed to limit the requirements of section 4980(d) of the Internal Revenue Code of 1986 (as in effect immediately after the enactment of the Omnibus Budget Reconciliation Act of 1990) or section 404(d) of this Act with respect to any distribution of residual assets of a single-employer plan to the employer.

Act Sec. 4044. (e) BANKRUPTCY FILING SUBSTITUTED FOR TERMINATION DATE.—If a contributing sponsor of a plan has filed or has had filed against such person a petition seeking liquidation or reorganization in a case under title 11, United States Code, or under any similar Federal law or law of a State or political subdivision, and the case has not been dismissed as of the termination date of the plan, then subsection (a)(3) shall be applied by treating the date such petition was filed as the termination date of the plan.

Act Sec. 4044. (f) VALUATION OF SECTION 4062(C) LIABILITY FOR DETERMINING AMOUNTS PAYABLE BY CORPORATION TO PARTICIPANTS AND BENEFICIARIES.—

(1) IN GENERAL.—In the case of a terminated plan, the value of the recovery of liability under section 4062(c) allocable as a plan asset under this section for purposes of determining the amount of benefits payable by the corporation shall be determined by multiplying—

(A) the amount of liability under section 4062(c) as of the termination date of the plan, by

(B) the applicable section 4062(c) recovery ratio.

(2) SECTION 4062(C) RECOVERY RATIO.—For purposes of this subsection—

(A) IN GENERAL.—Except as provided in subparagraph (C), the term "section 4062(c) recovery ratio" means the ratio which—

(i) the sum of the values of all recoveries under section 4062(c) determined by the corporation in connection with plan terminations described under subparagraph (B), bears to

(ii) the sum of all the amounts of liability under section 4062(c) with respect to such plans as of the termination date in connection with any such prior termination.

(B) PRIOR TERMINATIONS.—A plan termination described in this subparagraph is a termination with respect to which—

(i) the value of recoveries under section 4062(c) have been determined by the corporation, and

(ii) notices of intent to terminate were provided (or in the case of a termination by the corporation, a notice of determination under section 4042 was issued) during the 5-Federal fiscal year period ending with the third fiscal year preceding the fiscal year in which occurs the date of the notice of intent to terminate (or the notice of determination under section 4042) with respect to the plan termination for which the recovery ratio is being determined.

(C) EXCEPTION.—In the case of a terminated plan with respect to which the outstanding amount of benefit liabilities exceeds $20,000,000, the term "section 4062(c) recovery ratio" means, with respect to the termination of such plan, the ratio of—

(i) the value of the recoveries on behalf of the plan under section 4062(c), to

(ii) the amount of the liability owed under section 4062(c) as of the date of plan termination to the trustee appointed under section 4042 (b) or (c).

(3) SUBSECTION NOT TO APPLY.—This subsection shall not apply with respect to the determination of—

(A) whether the amount of outstanding benefit liabilities exceeds $20,000,000, or

(B) the amount of any liability under section 4062 to the corporation or the trustee appointed under section 4042 (b) or (c).

(4) DETERMINATIONS.—Determinations under this subsection shall be made by the corporation. Such determinations shall be binding unless shown by clear and convincing evidence to be unreasonable.

Amendments

P.L. 110-458, §104(c):

Amended ERISA Sec. 4044(e), as added by P.L. 109-280, by redesignating it as subsection (f).

The above amendment applies to any termination for which notices of intent to terminate are provided (or in the case of a termination by the corporation, a notice of determination under ERISA Sec. 4042 is issued) on or after September 17, 2006.

P.L. 109-280, §404(b):

Amended ERISA Sec. 4044 by adding a new paragraph (e) to read as above.

The above amendment applies with respect to proceeding initiated under title 11, United States Code, or under any similar Federal law or law of a State or political subdivision, on or after the date that is 30 days after the date of enactment of this Act (September 16, 2006).

P.L. 109-280, §407(b)(1):

Amended ERISA Sec. 4044(a)(4)(B) by striking "section 4022(b)(5)" and inserting "section 4022(b)(5)(B)".

The above amendment applies to plan terminations (1) under ERISA Sec. 4041(c) with respect to which notices of intent to terminate are provided under ERISA Sec. 4041(a)(2) after December 31, 2005, and (2) under ERISA Sec. 4042 with respect to which notices of determination are provided under such section after such date.

P.L. 109-280, §407(b)(2):

Amended ERISA Sec. 4044(b) by striking "(5)" in paragraph (2) and inserting "(4), (5),", and by redesignating paragraphs (3) through (6) as paragraphs (4) through (7), respectively, and inserting after paragraph (2) a new paragraph (3) to read as above.

The above amendment applies to plan terminations (1) under ERISA Sec. 4041(c) with respect to which notices of intent to terminate are provided under ERISA Sec. 4041(a)(2) after December 31, 2005, and (2) under ERISA Sec. 4042 with respect to which notices of determination are provided under such section after such date.

P.L. 109-280, §408(b)(2):

Amended ERISA Sec. 4044 by adding a new paragraph (e) [f] to read as above.

The above amendment applies to any termination for which notices of intent to terminate are provided (or in the case of a termination by the corporation, a notice of determination under ERISA Sec. 4042 is issued) on or after the date that is 30 days after the date of enactment of this Act (September 16, 2006).

P.L. 101-508, Sec. 12001(b)(2)(B):

Amended ERISA Sec. 4044(d) by adding a new paragraph (4) to read as above effective for reversions occurring after September 30, 1990 except for the provisions of Act Sec. 12003(b).

SEC. 12003. EFFECTIVE DATE.

* * *

(b) EXCEPTION.—The amendments made by this subtitle shall not apply to any reversion after September 30, 1990, if—

(1) in the case of plans subject to title IV of the Employee Retirement Income Security Act of 1974, a notice of intent to terminate under such title was provided to participants (or if no participants, to the Pension Benefit Guaranty Corporation) before October 1, 1990,

(2) in the case of plans subject to title I (and not to title IV) of such Act, a notice of intent to reduce future accruals under section 204(h) of such Act was provided to participants in connection with the termination before October 1, 1990,

(3) in the case of plans not subject to title I or IV of such Act, a request for a determination letter with respect to the termination was filed with the Secretary of the Treasury or the Secretary's delegate before October 1, 1990, or

(4) in the case of plans not subject to title I or IV of such Act and having only 1 participant, a resolution terminating the plan was adopted by the employer before October 1, 1990.

P.L. 101-239, §§7881(e)(1) and (4):

Amended P.L. 100-203, §9311(a)(2) to read as below effective December 22, 1987.

P.L. 101-239, §7881(e)(2):

Amended P.L. 100-203, §9311(d) to read as below effective December 22, 1987.

P.L. 101-239, §7894(g)(2):

Amended ERISA Sec. 4044(a)(1) by striking "accured" and inserting "accrued" effective September 2, 1974.

P.L. 101-239, §7891(a)(1):

Titles I, III, and IV of ERISA (other than sections 3(37)(E), 301(a)(7), and 308, the last sentence of section 408(d), and sections 414(c), 4001(a)(3)(ii), and 4303) are each amended by striking "Internal Revenue Code of 1954" each place it appears and inserting "Internal Revenue Code of 1986" effective October 22, 1986.

P.L. 100-203, §9311(a)(1):

Amended ERISA Sec. 4044(d) by redesignating paragraph (2) as (3) and adding a new paragraph (2) to read as above.

P.L. 100-203, §9311(a)(2):

(2) TRANSITIONAL RULE.—The amendments made by paragraph (1) shall apply, in the case of plans which, as of December 17, 1987, have no provision relating to the distribution of residual plan assets upon termination only with respect to plan amendments providing for the distribution of plan assets to the employer which are adopted after December 17, 1988.

P.L. 100-203, §9311(b)(1):

Amended ERISA Sec. 4044(d)(1) by striking "Any" and inserting "Subject to paragraph (3), any."

P.L. 100-203, §9311(b)(2):

Amended ERISA Sec. 4044(d) by striking paragraph (3) (as redesignated) and adding a new paragraph (3) to read as above. Prior to being stricken paragraph (3) read as follows:

(3) Notwithstanding the provisions of paragraph (1), if any assets of the plan attributable to employee contributions remain after all liabilities of the plan to participants and their beneficiaries have been satisfied, such assets shall be equitably distributed to the employees who made such contributions (or their beneficaries) in accordance with their rate of contributions.

P.L. 100-203, §9311(c):

Amended ERISA Sec. 4044(b)(4) by striking "section 401(a), 403(a), or 405(a)" and inserting "section 401(a) or 403(a)".

The above amendments are effective for: (1) plan terminations under section 4041(c) of ERISA for which notices of intent to terminate are provided under section 4041(a)(2) of ERISA after December 17, 1987, and (2) plan terminations for which proceedings are instituted by the Pension Benefit Guaranty Corporation under section 4042 of ERISA after December 17, 1987.

P.L. 100-203, §9311(d):

(d) EFFECTIVE DATE.—The amendments made by this section shall apply with respect to—

(1) plan terminations under section 4041 of ERISA with respect to which notices of intent to terminate are provided under section 4041(a)(2) of ERISA after December 17, 1987, and

(2) plan terminations with respect to which proceedings are instituted by the Pension Benefit Guaranty Corporation under section 4042 of ERISA after December 17, 1987.

Except as provided in subsection (a)(2), the amendments made by subsection (a) shall apply to any provision of the plan or plan amendment adopted after December 17, 1987.

P.L. 99-2762, §11016(c)(12):

Amended ERISA Sec. 4044(a), first sentence, by deleting "defined benefit."

Act Sec. 11016(c)(13) amended ERISA Sec. 4044(a)(4)(A) by striking out "section 4022(b)(5)" and inserting "section 4022B(a)" and amended ERISA Sec. 4044(a)(4)(B) by striking out "section 4022(b)(6)" and inserting "section 4022(b)(5)," effective on April 7, 1986.

P.L. 96-364, §402(a)(7):

Amended Sec. 4044 effective September 26, 1980 by: inserting "single-employer" before "defined benefit plan" in subsection (a); inserting "single-employer" before "plan occurring during" and before "plan occurring after" in subsection (c); and inserting "single-employer" before "plan may be distributed" in subsection (d)(1).

Regulations

The following regulations were adopted by the Pension Benefit Guaranty Corporation on July 1, 1996 (61 FR 34002). Prior to July 1, 1996, PBGC regulations were under Chapter XXVI of Title 29 of the Code of Federal Regulations. Effective July 1, 1996, PBGC regulations were moved to Chapter XL, and were renumbered and reorganized. Reg. §4044.13 was officially corrected December 30, 1997 (62 FR 67728). Reg. §§4044.52 and 4044.54 were amended July 15, 1998 (63 FR 38305), effective July 16, 1998 and March 17, 2000 (65 FR 14751), effective May 1, 2000. Reg. §4044.53 was amended March 17, 2000 (65 FR 14751), effective May 1, 2000. The Appendices to Part 4044 were amended on March 17, 2000 (65 FR 14751), effective May 1, 2000. Reg. §4044.2 was amended and Reg. §4044.13 was revised April 8, 2002 (67 FR 16949), effective June 1, 2002. Reg. §4044.2 was amended March 16, 2009 (74 FR 11022). Reg. §§4044.1, 4044.2, 4044.3, 4044.10, 4044.13, 4044.14, 4044.41, 4044.71, 4044.72, 4044.73, and 4044.75 were amended on June 14, 2011 (76 FR 34590). Reg. §4044.12 was amended on November 25, 2014 (79 FR 70090).

Note: Certain provisions of part 4044 have been superseded by legislative changes. For example, there are references to provisions formerly codified in 29 CFR part 2617, subpart C (and to the Notice of Sufficiency provided for thereunder) that no longer exist because of changes in the PBGC's plan termination regulations in response to the Single-Employer Pension Plan Amendments Act of 1986 and the Pension Protection Act of 1987. The PBGC intends to amend part 4044 at a later date to conform it to current statutory provisions.

Subpart A—Allocation of Assets

General Provisions

[¶ 15,471]

§4044.1 **Purpose and scope.** This part implements section 4044 of ERISA, which contains rules for allocating a plan's assets when the plan terminates. These rules have been in effect since September 2, 1974, the date of enactment of ERISA. This part applies to any single-employer plan covered by title IV of ERISA that submits a notice of intent to terminate, or for which PBGC commences an action to terminate the plan under section 4042 of ERISA.

(a) *Subpart A.* Sections 4044.1 through 4044.4 set forth general rules for applying §§4044.10 through 4044.17. Sections 4044.10 through 4044.17 interpret the rules and describe procedures for allocating plan assets to priority categories 1 through 6.

(b) *Subpart B.* The purpose of subpart B is to establish the method of determining the value of benefits and assets under terminating single-employer pension plans covered by title IV of ERISA. This valuation is needed for both plans trusteed under title IV and plans which are not trusteed. For the former, the valuation is needed to allocate plan assets in accordance with subpart A of this part and to determine the amount of any plan asset insufficiency. For the latter, the valuation is needed to allocate assets in accordance with subpart A and to distribute the assets in accordance with subpart B of part 4041 of this chapter.

(1) Section 4044.41 sets forth the general provisions of subpart B and applies to all terminating single-employer plans. Sections 4044.51 through 4044.57 prescribe the benefit valuation rules for plans that are placed into trusteeship by PBGC, including (in §§4044.55 through 4044.57) the rules and procedures a plan administrator shall follow to determine the expected retirement age (XRA) for a plan participant entitled to early retirement benefits for whom the annuity starting date is not known as of the valuation date. This applies to all trusteed plans which have such early retirement benefits. The plan administrator shall determine an XRA under §4044.55, §4044.56 or §4044.57, as appropriate, for each active participant or participant with a deferred vested benefit who is entitled to an early retirement benefit and who as of the valuation date has not selected an annuity starting date. [Amended 6/14/11 by 76 FR 34590.]

(2) Sections 4044.71 through 4044.75 prescribe the benefit valuation rules for calculating the value of a benefit to be paid a participant or beneficiary under a terminating pension plan that is distributing assets where the plan has not been placed into trusteeship by PBGC. [Amended 6/14/11 by 76 FR 34590.]

[¶ 15,471A]

§4044.2 **Definitions.** (a) The following terms are defined in §4001.2 of this chapter: annuity, bankruptcy filing date, basic-type benefit, Code, distribution date, earliest retirement age at valuation date, ERISA, expected retirement age (XRA), fair market value, guaranteed benefit, insurer, IRS, irrevocable commitment, mandatory employee contributions, nonbasic-type benefit, nonforfeitable benefit, non-PPA 2006 bankruptcy termination, normal retirement age, notice of intent to terminate, PBGC, person, plan, plan administrator, single-employer plan, substantial owner, termination date, unreduced retirement age (URA), and voluntary employee contributions. [Amended 3/16/2009 by 74 FR 11022 and 6/14/11 by 76 FR 34590.]

(b) For purposes of this part:

Deferred annuity means an annuity under which the specified date or age at which payments are to begin occurs after the valuation date.

Early retirement benefit means an annuity benefit payable under the terms of the plan, under which the participant is entitled to begin receiving payments before his or her normal retirement age and which is not payable on account of the disability of the participant. It may be reduced according to the terms of the plan.

Non-trusteed plan means a single-employer plan which is able to close out by purchasing annuities in the private sector. [Amended 6/14/11 by 76 FR 34590.]

Priority category means one of the categories contained in sections 4044(a)(1) through (a)(6) of ERISA that establish the order in which plan assets are to be allocated.

Trusteed plan means a single-employer plan which has been placed into trusteeship by PBGC.

Valuation date means (1) for non-trusteed plans, the date of distribution and (2) for trusteed plans, the termination date. [Amended 6/14/11 by 76 FR 34590.]

(c) For purposes of subpart B of this part (unless otherwise required by the context):

Age means the participant's age at his or her nearest birthday and is determined by rounding the individual's exact age to the nearest whole year. Half years are rounded to the next highest year. This is also known as the "insurance age."

(d) For purposes of §§ 4044.55 through 4044.57:

Monthly benefit means the guaranteed benefit payable by PBGC.

(e) For purposes of §§ 4044.71 through 4044.75:

Lump sum payable in lieu of an annuity means a benefit that is payable in a single installment and is derived from an annuity payable under the plan.

Other lump sum benefit means a benefit in priority category 5 or 6, determined under subpart A of this part, that is payable in a single installment (or substantially so) under the terms of the plan, and that is not derived from an annuity payable under the plan. The benefit may be a severance pay benefit, a death benefit or other single installment benefit.

[¶ 15,471B]

§ 4044.3 **General rule**. (a) *Asset allocation*. Upon the termination of a single-employer plan, the plan administrator shall allocate the plan assets available to pay for benefits under the plan in the manner prescribed by this subpart. Plan assets available to pay for benefits include all plan assets (valued according to § 4044.41(b)) remaining after the subtraction of all liabilities, other than liabilities for future benefit payments, paid or payable from plan assets under the provisions of the plan. Liabilities include expenses, fees and other administrative costs, and benefit payments due before the allocation date. Except as provided in § 4044.4(b), an irrevocable commitment by an insurer to pay a benefit, which commitment is in effect on the date of the asset allocation, is not considered a plan asset, and a benefit payable under such a commitment is excluded from the allocation process.

(b) *Allocation date*. For plans that close out under § 4041.28 or § 4041.50, assets shall be allocated as of the date plan assets are to be distributed. For other plans, assets shall be allocated as of the termination date. [Amended 6/14/11 by 76 FR 34590.]

[¶ 15,471C]

§ 4044.4 **Violations**. (a) *General*. A plan administrator violates ERISA if plan assets are allocated or distributed upon plan termination in a manner other than that prescribed in section 4044 of ERISA and this subpart, except as may be required to prevent disqualification of the plan under the Code and regulations thereunder.

(b) *Distributions in anticipation of termination*. A distribution, transfer, or allocation of assets to a participant or to an insurance company for the benefit of a participant, made in anticipation of plan termination, is considered to be an allocation of plan assets upon termination, and is covered by paragraph (a) of this section. In determining whether a distribution, transfer, or allocation of assets has been made in anticipation of plan termination PBGC will consider all of the facts and circumstances including—

(1) Any change in funding or operation procedures;

(2) Past practice with regard to employee requests for forms of distribution;

(3) Whether the distribution is consistent with plan provisions; and

(4) Whether an annuity contract that provides for a cutback based on the guarantee limits in subpart B of part 4022 of this chapter could have been purchased from an insurance company.

Allocation of Assets to Benefit Categories

[¶ 15,472]

§ 4044.10 **Manner of allocation**. (a) *General*. The plan administrator shall allocate plan assets available to pay for benefits under the plan using the rules and procedures set forth in paragraphs (b) through (f) of this section, or any other procedure that results in each participant (or beneficiary) receiving the same benefits he or she would receive if the procedures in paragraphs (b) through (f) were followed.

(b) *Assigning benefits*. The basic-type and nonbasic-type benefits payable with respect to each participant in a terminated plan shall be assigned to one or more priority categories in accordance with §§ 4044.11 through 4044.16. Benefits derived from voluntary employee contributions, which are assigned only to priority category 1, are treated, under section 204(c)(4) of ERISA and section 411(d)(5) of the Code, as benefits under a separate plan. The amount of a benefit payable with respect to each participant shall be determined as of the termination date, but, in a PPA 2006 bankruptcy termination, subject to the limitations in sections 4022(g) and 4044(e) of ERISA (and corresponding provisions of these regulations). [Amended 6/14/11 by 76 FR 34590.]

(c) *Valuing benefits*. The value of a participant's benefit or benefits assigned to each priority category shall be determined, as of the allocation date, in accordance with the provisions of subpart B of this part. The value of each participant's basic-type benefit or benefits in a priority category shall be reduced by the value of the participant's benefit of the same type that is assigned to a higher priority category. Except as provided in the next two sentences, the same procedure shall be followed for nonbasic-type benefits. The value of a participant's nonbasic-type benefits in priority categories 3, 5, and 6 shall not be reduced by the value of the participant's nonbasic-type benefit assigned to priority category 2. Benefits in priority category 1 shall neither be included in nor subtracted from lower priority categories. In no event shall a benefit assigned to a priority category be valued at less than zero.

(d) *Allocating assets to priority categories*. Plan assets available to pay for benefits under the plan shall be allocated to each priority category in succession, beginning with priority category 1. If the plan has sufficient assets to pay for all benefits in a priority category, the remaining assets shall then be allocated to the next lower priority category. This process shall be repeated until all benefits in priority categories 1 through 6 have been provided or until all available plan assets have been allocated.

(e) *Allocating assets within priority categories*. Except for priority category 5, if the plan assets available for allocation to any priority category are insufficient to pay for all benefits in that priority category, those assets shall be distributed among the participants according to the ratio that the value of each participant's benefit or benefits in that priority category bears to the total value of all benefits in that priority category. If the plan assets available for allocation to priority category 5 are insufficient to pay for all benefits in that category, the assets shall be allocated, first, to the value of each participant's nonforfeitable benefits that would be assigned to priority category 5 under § 4044.15 after reduction for the value of benefits assigned to higher priority categories, based only on the provisions of the plan in effect at the beginning of the 5-year period immediately preceding the termination date. If assets available for allocation to priority category 5 are sufficient to fully satisfy the value of those benefits, assets shall then be allocated to the value of the benefit increase under the oldest amendment during the 5-year period immediately preceding the termination date, reduced by the value of benefits assigned to higher priority categories (including higher subcategories in priority category 5). This allocation procedure shall be repeated for each succeeding plan amendment within the 5-year period until all plan assets available for allocation have been exhausted. If an amendment decreased benefits, amounts previously allocated with respect to each participant in excess of the value of the reduced benefit shall be reduced accordingly. In the subcategory in which assets are exhausted, the assets shall be distributed among the participants according to the ratio that the value of each participant's benefit or benefits in that subcategory bears to the total value of all benefits in that subcategory.

(f) *Applying assets to basic-type or nonbasic-type benefits within priority categories.* The assets allocated to a participant's benefit or benefits within each priority category shall first be applied to pay for the participant's basic-type benefit or benefits assigned to that priority category. Any assets allocated on behalf of that participant remaining after satisfying the participant's basic-type benefit or benefits in that priority category shall then be applied to pay for the participant's nonbasic-type benefit or benefits assigned to that priority category. If the assets allocable to a participant's basic-type benefit or benefits in all priority categories are insufficient to pay for all of the participant's guaranteed benefits, the assets allocated to that participant's benefit in priority category 4 shall be applied, first, to the guaranteed portion of the participant's benefit in priority category 4. The remaining assets allocated to that participant's benefit in priority category 4, if any, shall be applied to the nonguaranteed portion of the participant's benefit.

(g) *Allocation to established subclasses.* Notwithstanding paragraphs (e) and (f) of this section, the assets of a plan that has established subclasses within any priority category may be allocated to the plan's subclasses in accordance with the rules set forth in § 4044.17.

[¶ 15,472A]

§ 4044.11 **Priority category 1 benefits**. (a) *Definition.* The benefits in priority category 1 are participants' accrued benefits derived from voluntary employee contributions.

(b) *Assigning benefits.* Absent an election described in the next sentence, the benefit assigned to priority category 1 with respect to each participant is the balance of the separate account maintained for the participant's voluntary contributions. If a participant has elected to receive an annuity in lieu of his or her account balance, the benefit assigned to priority category 1 with respect to that participant is the present value of that annuity.

[¶ 15,472B]

§ 4044.12 **Priority category 2 benefits**. (a) *Definition.* The benefits in priority category 2 are participants' accrued benefits derived from mandatory employee contributions, whether to be paid as an annuity benefit with a pre-retirement death benefit that returns mandatory employee contributions or, if a participant so elects under the terms of the plan and subpart A of part 4022 of this chapter, as a lump sum benefit. Benefits are primarily basic-type benefits although nonbasic-type benefits may also be included as follows:

(1) *Basic-type benefits.* The basic-type benefit in priority category 2 with respect to each participant is the sum of the values of the annuity benefit and the pre-retirement death benefit determined under the provisions of paragraph (c)(1) of this section.

(2) *Nonbasic-type benefits.* If a participant elects to receive a lump sum benefit and if the value of the lump sum benefit exceeds the value of the basic-type benefit in priority category 2 determined with respect to the participant, the excess is a nonbasic-type benefit. There is no nonbasic-type benefit in priority category 2 for a participant who does not elect to receive a lump sum benefit.

(b) *Conversion of mandatory employee contributions to an annuity benefit.* Subject to the limitation set forth in paragraph (b)(3) of this

section, a participant's accumulated mandatory employee contributions shall be converted to an annuity form of benefit payable at the normal retirement age or, if the plan provides for early retirement, at the expected retirement age. The conversion shall be made using the interest rates and factors specified in paragraph (b)(2) of this section. The form of the annuity benefit (e.g., straight life annuity, joint and survivor annuity, cash refund annuity, etc.) is the form that the participant or beneficiary is entitled to on the termination date. If the participant does not have a nonforfeitable right to a benefit, other than the return of his or her mandatory contributions in a lump sum, the annuity form of benefit is the form the participant would be entitled to if the participant had a nonforfeitable right to an annuity benefit under the plan on the termination date.

(1) *Accumulated mandatory employee contributions.* Subject to any addition for the cost of ancillary benefits plus interest, as provided in the following sentence, the amount of the accumulated mandatory employee contributions for each participant is the participant's total nonforfeitable mandatory employee contributions remaining in the plan on the termination date plus interest, if any, under the plan provisions. Mandatory employee contributions, if any, used after the effective date of the minimum vesting standards in section 203 of ERISA and section 411 of the Code for costs or to provide ancillary benefits such as life insurance or health insurance, plus interest under the plan provisions, shall be added to the contributions that remain in the plan to determine the accumulated mandatory employee contributions.

(2) *Interest rates and conversion factors.* The interest rates and conversion factors used in the administration of the plan shall be used to convert a participant's accumulated mandatory contributions to the annuity form of benefit. In the absence of plan rules and factors, the interest rates and conversion factors established by the IRS for allocation of accrued benefits between employer and employee contributions under the provisions of section 204(c) of ERISA and section 411(c) of the Code shall be used.

(3) *Minimum accrued benefit.* The annuity benefit derived from mandatory employee contributions may not be less than the minimum accrued benefit under the provisions of section 204(c) of ERISA and section 411(c) of the Code.

(4) *Rollover amounts.* In the case of a benefit resulting from rollover amounts, notwithstanding the provisions of paragraph (b)(2) of this section, the interest rates and conversion factors in paragraph (c)(4) of this section are used to determine the portion of the accrued benefit derived from the employee's contributions and, if any, the portion of the accrued benefit derived from employer contributions. [Added 11/25/14 by 79 FR 70090.]

(c) *Assigning benefits.* If a participant or beneficiary elects to receive a lump sum benefit, his or her benefit shall be determined under paragraph (c)(2) of this section. Otherwise, the benefits with respect to a participant shall be determined under paragraph (c)(1) of this section.

(1) *Annuity benefit and pre-retirement death benefit.* The annuity benefit and the pre-retirement death benefit assigned to priority category 2 with respect to a participant are determined as follows:

(i) The annuity benefit is the benefit computed under paragraph (b) of this section.

(ii) Except for adjustments necessary to meet the minimum lump sum requirements as hereafter provided, the pre-retirement death benefit is the benefit under the plan that returns all or a portion of the participant's mandatory employee contributions upon the death of the participant before retirement. A benefit that became payable in a single installment (or substantially so) because the participant died before the termination date is a liability of the plan within the meaning of § 4044.3(a) and should not be assigned to priority category 2. A benefit payable upon a participant's death that is included in the annuity form of the benefit derived from mandatory employee contributions (e.g., the survivor's portion of a joint and survivor annuity or the cash refund portion of a cash refund annuity) is assigned to priority category 2 as part of the annuity benefit under paragraph (c)(1)(i) of this section and is not assigned as a death benefit. The pre-retirement death benefit may not be less than the minimum lump sum required upon withdrawal of mandatory employee contributions by the IRS under section 204(c) of ERISA and section 411(c) of the Code.

(2) *Lump sum benefit.* Except for adjustments necessary to meet the minimum lump sum requirements as hereafter provided, if a participant elects to receive a lump sum benefit under the provisions of the plan, the amount of the benefit that is assigned to priority category 2 with respect to the participant is—

(i) The combined value of the annuity benefit and the pre-retirement death benefit determined according to paragraph (c)(1) (which constitutes the basic-type benefit) plus

(ii) The amount, if any, of the participant's accumulated mandatory employee contributions that exceeds the combined value of the annuity benefit and the pre-retirement death benefit (which constitutes the nonbasic-type benefit), but not more than

(iii) The amount of the participant's accumulated mandatory contributions.

(3) For purposes of paragraph (c)(2) of this section, accumulated mandatory contributions means the contributions with interest, if any, payable under plan provisions to the participant or beneficiary on termination of the plan or, in the absence of such provisions, the amount that is payable if the participant withdrew his or her contributions on the termination date. The lump sum benefit may not be less than the minimum lump required by the IRS under section 204(c) of ERISA and section 411(c) of the Code upon withdrawal of mandatory employee contributions.

(4) *Special rules for benefit resulting from rollover amounts.* (i) *Mandatory employee contributions.* Notwithstanding paragraphs (c)(1) through (3) of this section, in the case of a benefit resulting from rollover amounts, the accrued benefit derived from mandatory employee contributions is determined using the interest rates and conversion factors under section 411(c)(2)(B) and (C) of the Code for purposes of computing an employee's accrued benefit derived from the employee's contributions. The annuity benefit and the pre-retirement death benefit, as determined on this basis, is the benefit resulting from rollover amounts in priority category 2.

(ii) *Employer contributions.* Any portion of a participant's accrued benefit resulting from rollover amounts that is in excess of the accrued benefit derived from mandatory employee contributions determined in accordance with paragraph (c)(4)(i) of this section (*i.e.*, the accrued benefit derived from employer contributions) is a guaranteeable benefit in priority category 3, priority category 4, or priority category 5, as applicable under this part. [Added 11/25/14 by 79 FR 70090.]

[¶ 15,472C]

§ 4044.13 **Priority category 3 benefits.** (a) *Definition.* The benefits in priority category 3 are those annuity benefits that were in pay status before the beginning of the 3-year period ending on the termination date, and those annuity benefits that could have been in pay status (then or as of the next payment date under the plan's rules for starting benefit payments) for participants who, before the beginning of the 3-year period ending on the termination date, had reached their Earliest PBGC Retirement Date (as determined under § 4022.10 of this chapter) based on plan provisions in effect on the day before the beginning of the 3-year period ending on the termination date. For example, in a plan with a termination date of September 1, 2012, the benefits in priority category 3 are those annuity benefits that were in pay status on or before September 1, 2009, and those annuity benefits that could have been in pay status for participants who, on or before September 1, 2009, had reached their Earliest PBGC Retirement Date based on plan provisions in effect on September 1, 2009. Benefit increases, as defined in § 4022.2, that were in effect throughout the 5-year period ending on the termination date, including automatic benefit increases during that period to the extent provided in paragraph (b)(5) of this section, shall be included in determining the priority category 3 benefit. For example, in a plan with a termination date of September 1, 2012, a benefit increase that was in effect throughout the 5-year period from September 2, 2007, to September 1, 2012, is included in priority category 3. Benefits are primarily basic-type benefits, although nonbasic-type benefits will be included if any portion of a

participant's priority category 3 benefit is not guaranteeable under the provisions of subpart A of part 4022 and § 4022.21 of this chapter. [Amended 6/14/11 by 76 FR 34590.]

(b) *Assigning benefits.* The annuity benefit that is assigned to priority category 3 with respect to each participant is the lowest annuity that was paid or payable under the rules in paragraphs (b)(2) through (b)(6) of this section.

(1) *Eligibility of participants and beneficiaries.* A participant or beneficiary is eligible for a priority category 3 benefit if either of the following applies [Revised by 67 FR 16959, April 8, 2002]:

(i) The participant's (or beneficiary's) benefit was in pay status before the beginning of the 3-year period ending on the termination date.

(ii) Before the beginning of the 3-year period ending on the termination date, the participant was eligible for an annuity benefit that could have been in pay status and had reached his or her Earliest PBGC Retirement Date (as determined in § 4022.10 of this chapter, based on plan provisions in effect on the day before the beginning of the 3-year period ending on the termination date). Whether a participant was eligible to receive an annuity before the beginning of the 3-year period shall be determined using the plan provisions in effect on the day before the beginning of the 3-year period.

(iii) If a participant described in either of the preceding two paragraphs died during the 3-year period ending on the date of the plan termination and his or her beneficiary is entitled to an annuity, the beneficiary is eligible for a priority category 3 benefit. [Revised by 67 FR 16949, April 8, 2002.]

(2) *Plan provisions governing determination of benefit.* In determining the amount of the priority category 3 annuity with respect to a participant, the plan administrator shall use the participant's age, service, actual or expected retirement age, and other relevant facts as of the following dates:

(i) Except as provided in paragraph (b)(3), for a participant or beneficiary whose benefit was in pay status before the beginning of the 3-year period ending on the termination date, the priority category 3 benefit shall be determined according to plan provisions in effect on the date the benefit commenced. The form of annuity elected by a retiree is considered the normal form of annuity for that participant [Corrected by 67 FR 38003, May 31, 2002. Amended 6/14/11 by 76 FR 34590.]

(ii) Except as provided in paragraph (b)(3), for a participant who was eligible to receive an annuity before the beginning of the 3-year period ending on the termination date but whose benefit was not in pay status, the priority category 3 benefit and the normal form of annuity shall be determined according to plan provisions in effect on the day before the beginning of the 3-year period ending on the termination date as if the benefit had commenced at that time. [Amended 6/14/11 by 76 FR 34590.]

(3) *General benefit limitations.* The general benefit limitation is determined as follows:

(i) If a participant's benefit was in pay status before the beginning of the 3-year period, the benefit assigned to priority category 3 with respect to that participant is limited to the lesser of the lowest annuity benefit in pay status during the 3-year period ending on the termination date and the lowest annuity benefit payable under the plan provisions at any time during the 5-year period ending on the termination date.

(ii) Unless a benefit was in pay status before the beginning of the 3-year period ending on the termination date, the benefit assigned to priority category 3 with respect to a participant is limited to the lowest annuity benefit payable under the plan provisions, including any reduction for early retirement, at any time during the 5-year period ending on the termination date. If the annuity form of benefit under a formula that appears to produce the lowest benefit differs from the normal annuity form for the participant under paragraph (b)(2)(ii) of this section, the benefits shall be compared after the differing form is converted to the normal annuity form, using plan factors. In the absence of plan factors, the factors in subpart B of part 4022 of this chapter shall be used.

(iii) For purposes of this paragraph, if a terminating plan has been in effect less than five years on the termination date, computed in accordance with paragraph (b)(6) of this section, the lowest annuity benefit under the plan during the 5-year period ending on the termination date is zero. If the plan is a successor to a previously established defined benefit plan within the meaning of section 4021(a) of ERISA, the time it has been in effect will include the time the predecessor plan was in effect.

(4) *Determination of beneficiary's benefit.* If a beneficiary is eligible for a priority category 3 benefit because of the death of a participant during the 3-year period ending on the termination date, the benefit assigned to priority category 3 for the beneficiary shall be determined as if the participant had died the day before the 3-year period began.

(5) *Automatic benefit increases.* If plan provisions adopted and effective on or before the first day of the 5-year period ending on the termination date provided for automatic increases in the benefit formula for both active participants and those in pay status or for participants in pay status only, the lowest annuity benefit payable during the 5-year period ending on the termination date determined under paragraph (b)(3) of this section includes the automatic increases scheduled during the fourth and fifth years preceding termination, subject to the restriction that benefit increases for active participants in excess of the increases for retirees shall not be taken into account [Corrected by 67 FR 38003, May 31, 2002].

(6) *Computation of time periods.* For purposes of this section, a plan or amendment is "in effect" on the later of the date on which it is adopted or the date it becomes effective.

(c) *PPA 2006 bankruptcy termination.* In a PPA 2006 bankruptcy termination:

(1) For purposes of this paragraph (c), "applicable pre-termination period" means the period—

(i) Beginning on the first day of the 5-year period ending on the bankruptcy filing date; and

(ii) Ending on the termination date. For example, if the bankruptcy filing date is January 15, 2008, and the termination date is March 22, 2009, the applicable pre-termination period is the period beginning on January 16, 2003, and ending on March 22, 2009.

(2) "Applicable pre-termination period" is substituted for "5-year period ending on the termination date" each place that "5-year period ending on the termination date" appears in paragraphs (a) and (b) of this section.

(3) Except as provided in paragraph (a)(2) of this section, "bankruptcy filing date" is substituted for "termination date" and "date of the plan termination" each place that "termination date" and "date of the plan termination" appear in paragraphs (a) and (b) of this section. In paragraph (b)(5) of this section, "the bankruptcy filing date" is substituted for "termination" in the phrase "during the fourth and fifth years preceding termination."

(4) Example: A plan provides for normal retirement at age 65 and has only one early retirement benefit: a subsidized early retirement benefit for participants who terminate employment on or after age 60 with 20 years of service. These plan provisions have been unchanged since 1990. The contributing sponsor of the plan files a bankruptcy petition in June 2008, and the plan terminates during the bankruptcy with a termination date in September 2010. A participant retired in July 2007, at which time he was age 60 and had 20 years of service, and began receiving the subsidized early retirement benefit. The participant has no benefit in priority category 3, because he was not eligible to retire three or more years before the June 2008 bankruptcy filing date. [Added by 6/14/11 by 76 FR 34590.]

[¶ 15,472D]

§ 4044.14 **Priority category 4 benefits.** The benefits assigned to priority category 4 with respect to each participant are the participant's guaranteed benefits, except as provided in the next sentence. The benefit assigned to priority category 4 with respect to a participant is not limited by the aggregate benefits limitations set forth in § 4022B.1 of this chapter for individuals who are participants in more than one

plan or by the phase-in limitation applicable to substantial owners set forth in § 4022.26. [Amended by 6/14/11 by 76 FR 34590.]

[¶ 15,472E]

§ 4044.15 **Priority category 5 benefits.** The benefits assigned to priority category 5 with respect to each participant are all of the participant's nonforfeitable benefits under the plan.

[¶ 15,472F]

§ 4044.16 **Priority category 6 benefits.** The benefits assigned to priority category 6 with respect to each participant are all of the participant's benefits under the plan, whether forfeitable or nonforfeitable.

[¶ 15,472G]

§ 4044.17 **Subclasses.** (a) *General rule.* A plan may establish one or more subclasses within any priority category, other than priority categories 1 and 2, which subclasses will govern the allocation of assets within that priority category. The subclasses may be based only on a participant's longer service, older age, or disability, or any combination thereof.

(b) *Limitation.* Except as provided in paragraph (c) of this section, whenever the allocation within a priority category on the basis of the subclasses established by the plan increases or decreases the cumulative amount of assets that otherwise would be allocated to guaranteed benefits, the assets so shifted shall be reallocated to other participants' benefits within the priority category in accordance with the subclasses.

(c) *Exception for subclasses in effect on September 2, 1974.* A plan administrator may allocate assets to subclasses within any priority category, other than priority categories 1 and 2, without regard to the limitation in paragraph (b) of this section if, on September 2, 1974, the plan provided for allocation of plan assets upon termination of the plan based on a participant's longer service, older age, or disability, or any combination thereof, and—

(1) Such provisions are still in effect; or

(2) The plan, if subsequently amended to modify or remove those subclasses, is re-amended to re-establish the same subclasses on or before July 28, 1981.

(d) *Discrimination under Code.* Notwithstanding the provisions of paragraphs (a) through (c) of this section, allocation of assets to subclasses established under this section is permitted only to the extent that the allocation does not result in discrimination prohibited under the Code and regulations thereunder.

Allocation of Residual Assets

[¶ 15,473]

§ 4044.30 **[Reserved].**

Subpart B—Valuation of Benefits and Assets

General Provisions

[¶ 15,474]

§ 4044.41 **General valuation rules.** (a) *Valuation of benefits—*

(1) *Trusteed plans.* The plan administrator of a plan that has been or will be placed into trusteeship by the PBGC shall value plan benefits in accordance with §§ 4044.51 through 4044.57.

(2) *Non-trusteed plans.* The plan administrator of a non-trusteed plan shall value plan benefits in accordance with § 4044.71 through 4044.75. If a plan is unable to satisfy all benefits assigned to priority categories 1 through 4 on the distribution date, the PBGC will place it into trusteeship and the plan administrator shall re-value the benefits in accordance with §§ 4044.51 through 4044.57. [Amended 6/14/11 by 76 FR 34590.]]

(b) *Valuation of assets.* Plan assets shall be valued at their fair market value, based on the method of valuation that most accurately reflects such fair market value.

Trusteed Plans

[¶ 15,475]

§ 4044.51 **Benefits to be valued**. (a) *Form of benefit*. The plan administrator shall determine the form of each benefit to be valued in accordance with the following rules:

(1) If a benefit is in pay status as of the valuation date, the plan administrator shall value the form of the benefit being paid.

(2) If a benefit is not in pay status as of the valuation date but a valid election with respect to the form of benefit has been made on or before the valuation date, the plan administrator shall value the form of benefit so elected.

(3) If a benefit is not in pay status as of the valuation date and no valid election with respect to the form of benefit has been made on or before the valuation date, the plan administrator shall value the form of benefit that, under the terms of the plan, is payable in the absence of a valid election.

(b) *Timing of benefit*. The plan administrator shall value benefits whose starting date is subject to election using the assumption specified in paragraph (b)(1) or (b)(2) of this section.

(1) *Where election made*. If a valid election of the starting date of a benefit has been made on or before the valuation date, the plan administrator shall assume that the starting date of the benefit is the starting date so elected.

(2) *Where no election made*. If no valid election of the starting date of a benefit has been made on or before the valuation date, the plan administrator shall assume that the starting date of the benefit is the later of—

(i) The expected retirement age, as determined under §§ 4044.55 through 4044.57, of the participant with respect to whom the benefit is payable, or

(ii) The valuation date.

[¶ 15,475A]

§ 4044.52 **Valuation of benefits**. The plan administrator shall value all benefits as of the valuation date by—

(a) Using the mortality assumptions prescribed by Sec. 4044.53 and the interest assumptions prescribed in appendix B to this part;

(b) Using interpolation methods, where necessary, at least as accurate as linear interpolation;

(c) Using valuation formulas that accord with generally accepted actuarial principles and practices; and

(d) Adjusting the values to reflect loading expenses in accordance with appendix C to this part.

[Amended 3/17/00 by 65 FR 14751; 12/2/2005 by 70 FR 72207.]

[¶ 15,475B]

§ 4044.53 **Mortality assumptions**. (a) *General rule*. Subject to paragraph (b) of this section (regarding certain death benefits), the plan administrator shall use the mortality factors prescribed in paragraphs (c), (d), (e), (f), and (g) of this section to value benefits under § 4044.52.

(b) *Certain death benefits*. If an annuity for one person is in pay status on the valuation date, and if the payment of a death benefit after the valuation date to another person, who need not be identifiable on the valuation date, depends in whole or in part on the death of the pay status annuitant, then the plan administrator shall value the death benefit using—

(1) The mortality rates that are applicable to the annuity in pay status under this section to represent the mortality of the pay status annuitant; and

(2) The mortality rates under paragraph (c) of this section to represent the mortality of the death beneficiary.

(c) *Healthy lives*. If the individual is not disabled under paragraph (f) of this section, the plan administrator will value the benefit using—

(1) For male participants, the rates in Table 1 of Appendix A to this part projected from 1994 to the calendar year in which the valua-

tion date occurs plus 10 years using Scale AA from Table 2 of Appendix A to this part; and

(2) For female participants, the rates in Table 3 of Appendix A to this part projected from 1994 to the calendar year in which the valuation date occurs plus 10 years using Scale AA from Table 4 of Appendix A to this part.

(d) *Social Security disabled lives*. If the individual is Social Security disabled under paragraph (f)(1) of this section, the plan administrator will value the benefit using—

(1) For male participants, the rates in Table 5 of Appendix A to this part; and

(2) For female participants, the rates in Table 6 of Appendix A to this part.

(e) *Non-Social Security disabled lives*. If the individual is non-Social Security disabled under paragraph (f)(2) of this section, the plan administrator will value the benefit at each age using—

(1) For male participants, the lesser of—

(i) The rate determined from Table 1 of Appendix A to this part projected from 1994 to the calendar year in which the valuation date occurs plus 10 years using Scale AA from Table 2 of Appendix A to this part and setting the resulting table forward three years, or

(ii) The rate in Table 5 of Appendix A to this part.

(2) For female participants, the lesser of—

(i) The rate determined from Table 3 of Appendix A to this part projected from 1994 to the calendar year in which the valuation date occurs plus 10 years using Scale AA from Table 4 of Appendix A to this part and setting the resulting table forward three years, or

(ii) The rate in Table 6 of Appendix A to this part.

(f) *Definitions of disability*. (1) *Social Security disabled*. A participant is Social Security disabled if, on the valuation date, the participant is less than age 65 and has a benefit in pay status that—

(i) Is being received as a disability benefit under a plan provision requiring either receipt of or eligibility for Social Security disability benefits, or

(ii) Was converted under the plan's terms from a disability benefit under a plan provision requiring either receipt of or eligibility for Social Security disability benefits to an early or normal retirement benefit for any reason other than a change in the participant's health status.

(2) *Non-Social Security disabled*. A participant is non-Social Security disabled if, on the valuation date, the participant is less than age 65, is not Social Security disabled, and has a benefit in pay status that—

(i) Is being received as a disability benefit under the plan, or

(ii) Was converted under the plan's terms from a disability benefit to an early or normal retirement benefit for any reason other than a change in the participant's health status.

(g) *Contingent annuitant mortality during deferral period*. If a participant's joint and survivor benefit is valued as a deferred annuity, the mortality of the contingent annuitant during the deferral period will be disregarded.

[Revised 12/2/2005 by 70 FR 72207.]

[¶ 15,475C]

§ 4044.54 **Removed and Reserved**. [Removed and Reserved 3/17/00 by 65 FR 14751.]

[¶ 15,475D]

§ 4044.55 **Expected Retirement Age**. XRA when a participant must retire to receive a benefit.—

(a) *Applicability*. Except as provided in § 4044.57, the plan administrator shall determine the XRA under this section when plan provisions or established plan practice require a participant to retire from his or her job to begin receiving an early retirement benefit.

(b) *Data needed*. The plan administrator shall determine for each participant who is entitled to an early retirement benefit—

(1) The amount of the participant's monthly benefit payable at unreduced retirement age in the normal form payable under the terms of the plan or in the form validly elected by the participant before the termination date;

(2) The calendar year in which the participant reaches unreduced retirement age ("URA");

(3) The participant's URA; and

(4) The participant's earliest retirement age at the valuation date.

(c) *Procedure.* (1) The plan administrator shall determine whether a participant is in the high, medium or low retirement rate category using the applicable Selection of Retirement Rate Category Table in appendix D, based on the participant's benefit determined under paragraph (b)(1) of this section and the year in which the participant reaches URA.

(2) Based on the retirement rate category determined under paragraph (c)(1), the plan administrator shall determine the XRA from Table II-A, II-B or II-C, as appropriate, by using the participant's URA and earliest retirement age at valuation date.

[¶ 15,475E]

§ 4044.56 **XRA when a participant need not retire to receive a benefit**. (a) *Applicability.* Except as provided in § 4044.57, the plan administrator shall determine the XRA under this section when plan provisions or established plan practice do not require a participant to retire from his or her job to begin receiving his or her early retirement benefit.

(b) *Data needed.* The plan administrator shall determine for each participant—

(1) The participant's URA; and

(2) The participant's earliest retirement age at valuation date.

(c) *Procedure.* Participants in this case are always assigned to the high retirement rate category and therefore the plan administrator shall use Table II-C of appendix D to determine the XRA. The plan administrator shall determine the XRA from Table II-C by using the participant's URA and earliest retirement age at termination date.

[¶ 15,475F]

§ 4044.57 **Special rule for facility closing**. (a) *Applicability.* The plan administrator shall determine the XRA under this section, rather than § 4044.55 or § 4044.56, when both the conditions set forth in paragraphs (a)(1) and (a)(2) of this section exist.

(1) The facility at which the participant is or was employed permanently closed within one year before the valuation date, or is in the process of being permanently closed on the valuation date.

(2) The participant left employment at the facility less than one year before the valuation date or was still employed at the facility on the valuation date.

(b) *XRA.* The XRA is equal to the earliest retirement age at valuation date.

Non-Trusteed Plans

[¶ 15,476]

§ 4044.71 **Valuation of annuity benefits**. The value of a benefit which is to be paid as an annuity is the cost of purchasing the annuity on the date of distribution from an insurer. [Amended 6/14/11 by 76 FR 34590.]

[¶ 15,476A]

§ 4044.72 **Form of annuity to be valued**. (a) When both the participant and beneficiary are alive on the date of distribution, the form of annuity to be valued is—

(1) For a participant or beneficiary already receiving a monthly benefit, that form which is being received, or

(2) For a participant or beneficiary not receiving a monthly benefit, the normal annuity form payable under the plan or the optional form for which the participant has made a valid election. [Amended by 6/14/11 by 76 FR 34590.]

(b) When the participant dies after the date of plan termination but before the date of distribution, the form of annuity to be valued is determined under paragraph (b)(1) or (b)(2) of this section:

(1) For a participant who was entitled to a deferred annuity—

(i) If the form was a single or joint life annuity, no benefit shall be valued; or

(ii) If the participant had made a valid election of a lump sum benefit before he or she died, the form to be valued is the lump sum.

(2) For a participant who was eligible for immediate retirement, and for a participant who was in pay status at the date of termination—

(i) If the form was a single life annuity, no benefit shall be valued;

(ii) If the form was an annuity for a period certain and life thereafter, the form to be valued is an annuity for the certain period;

(iii) If the form was a joint and survivor annuity, the form to be valued is a single life annuity payable to the beneficiary, unless the beneficiary has also died, in which case no benefit shall be valued;

(iv) If the form was an annuity for a period certain and joint and survivor thereafter, the form to be valued is an annuity for the certain period and the life of the beneficiary thereafter, unless the beneficiary has also died, in which case the form to be valued is an annuity for the certain period;

(v) If the form was a cash refund annuity, the form to be valued is the remaining lump sum death benefit; or

(vi) If the participant had elected a lump sum benefit before he or she died, the form to be valued is the lump sum.

(c) When the participant is still living and the named beneficiary or spouse dies after the date of termination but before the date of distribution, the form of annuity to be valued is determined under paragraph (c)(1) or (c)(2) of this section:

(1) For a participant entitled to a deferred annuity—

(i) If the form was a joint and survivor annuity, the form to be valued is a single life annuity payable to the participant; or

(ii) If the form was an annuity for a period certain and joint and survivor thereafter, the form to be valued is an annuity for the certain period and the life of the participant thereafter.

(2) For a participant eligible for immediate retirement and for a participant in pay status at the date of termination—

(i) If the form was a joint and survivor annuity, the form to be valued is a single life annuity payable to the participant; or

(ii) If the form was an annuity for a period certain and joint survivor thereafter annuity, the form to be valued is an annuity for the certain period and for the life of the participant thereafter.

[¶ 15,476B]

§ 4044.73 **Lump sums and other alternative forms of distribution in lieu of annuities**. (a) *Valuation.* (1) The value of the lump sum or other alternative form of distribution is the present value of the normal form of benefit provided by the plan payable at normal retirement age, determined as of the date of distribution using reasonable actuarial assumptions as to interest and mortality.

(2) If the participant dies before the date of distribution, but had elected a lump sum benefit, the present value shall be determined as if the participant were alive on the date of distribution.

(b) *Actuarial assumptions.* The plan administrator shall specify the actuarial assumptions used to determine the value calculated under paragraph (a) of this section when the plan administrator submits the benefit valuation data to the PBGC. The same actuarial assumptions shall be used for all such calculations. The PBGC reserves the right to review the actuarial assumptions used and to re-value the benefits determined by the plan administrator if the actuarial assumptions are found to be unreasonable. [Amended 6/14/11 by 76 FR 34590.]

[¶ 15,476C]

§ 4044.74 **Withdrawal of employee contributions**. (a) If a participant has not started to receive monthly benefit payments on the date of distribution, the value of the lump sum which returns mandatory employee contributions is equal to the total amount of contributions made by the participant, plus interest that is payable to the participant under the terms of the plan, plus interest on that total amount from the date of termination to the date of distribution. The rate of interest credited on employee contributions up to the date of termination shall be the greater of the interest rate provided under the terms of the plan or the interest rate required under section 204(c) of ERISA or section 411(c) of the IRC.

(b) If a participant has started to receive monthly benefit payments on the date of distribution, part of which are attributable to his or her contributions, the value of the lump sum which returns employee contributions is equal to the excess of the amount described in paragraph (b)(1) of this section over the amount computed in paragraph (b)(2) of this section.

(1) The amount of accumulated mandatory employee contributions remaining in the plan as of the date of termination plus interest from the date of termination to the date of distribution.

(2) The excess of benefit payments made from the plan between date of plan termination and the date of distribution, over the amount of payments that would have been made if the employee contributions had been paid as a lump sum on the date of plan termination, with interest accumulated on the excess from the date of payment to the date of distribution.

(c) *Interest assumptions.* The interest rate used under this section to credit interest between the date of termination to the date of distribution shall be a reasonable rate and shall be the same for both paragraphs (a) and (b).

[¶ 15,476D]

§ 4044.75 **Other lump sum benefits**. The value of a lump sum benefit which is not covered under § 4044.73 or § 4044.74 is equal to—

(a) The value under the irrevocable comment, if an insurer provides the benefit; or [Amended 6/14/11 by 76 FR 34590.]

(b) The present value of the benefit as of the date of distribution, determined using reasonable actuarial assumptions, if the benefit is to be distributed other than by the purchase of the benefit from an insurer. The PBGC reserves the right to review the actuarial assumptions as to reasonableness and re-value the benefit if the actuarial assumptions are unreasonable.

[¶ 15,476E]

§ 4044.75 **Appendix A to Part 4044—Mortality Rate Tables**

The mortality tables in this appendix set forth for each age x the probability qX that an individual aged x (in 1994, when using Table 1 or Table 3) will not survive to attain age x + 1. The projection scales in this appendix set forth for each age x the annual reduction AAX in the mortality rate at age x.

TABLE 1.—MORTALITY TABLE FOR HEALTHY MALE PARTICIPANTS
[94 GAM basic]

Age x	q_x
15	0.000371
16	0.000421
17	0.000463
18	0.000495
19	0.000521
20	0.000545
21	0.000570
22	0.000598
23	0.000633
24	0.000671
25	0.000711
26	0.000749
27	0.000782
28	0.000811
29	0.000838
30	0.000862
31	0.000883
32	0.000902
33	0.000912
34	0.000913
35	0.000915
36	0.000927
37	0.000958
38	0.001010
39	0.001075
40	0.001153
41	0.001243
42	0.001346
43	0.001454
44	0.001568
45	0.001697
46	0.001852
47	0.002042
48	0.002260
49	0.002501
50	0.002773
51	0.003088
52	0.003455
53	0.003854
54	0.004278
55	0.004758
56	0.005322
57	0.006001
58	0.006774
59	0.007623
60	0.008576
61	0.009663
62	0.010911
63	0.012335
64	0.013914
65	0.015629
66	0.017462
67	0.019391
68	0.021354
69	0.023364
70	0.025516
71	0.027905
72	0.030625
73	0.033549
74	0.036614
75	0.040012
76	0.043933
77	0.048570
78	0.053991
79	0.060066
80	0.066696
81	0.073780
82	0.081217
83	0.088721
84	0.096358
85	0.104559
86	0.113755
87	0.124377

Age x	q_x
88	0.136537
89	0.149949
90	0.164442
91	0.179849
92	0.196001
93	0.213325
94	0.231936
95	0.251189
96	0.270441
97	0.289048
98	0.306750
99	0.323976
100	0.341116
101	0.358560
102	0.376699
103	0.396884
104	0.418855
105	0.440585
106	0.460043
107	0.475200
108	0.485670
109	0.492807
110	0.497189
111	0.499394
112	0.500000
113	0.500000
114	0.500000
115	0.500000
116	0.500000
117	0.500000
118	0.500000
119	0.500000
120	1.000000

TABLE 2.—PROJECTION SCALE AA FOR HEALTHY MALE PARTICIPANTS

Age x	AA_x
15	0.019
16	0.019
17	0.019
18	0.019
19	0.019
20	0.019
21	0.018
22	0.017
23	0.015
24	0.013
25	0.010
26	0.006
27	0.005
28	0.005
29	0.005
30	0.005
31	0.005
32	0.005
33	0.005

Age x	AA_x
34	0.005
35	0.005
36	0.005
37	0.005
38	0.006
39	0.007
40	0.008
41	0.009
42	0.010
43	0.011
44	0.012
45	0.013
46	0.014
47	0.015
48	0.016
49	0.017
50	0.018
51	0.019
52	0.020
53	0.020
54	0.020
55	0.019
56	0.018
57	0.017
58	0.016
59	0.016
60	0.016
61	0.015
62	0.015
63	0.014
64	0.014
65	0.014
66	0.013
67	0.013
68	0.014
69	0.014
70	0.015
71	0.015
72	0.015
73	0.015
74	0.015
75	0.014
76	0.014
77	0.013
78	0.012
79	0.011
80	0.010
81	0.009
82	0.008
83	0.008
84	0.007
85	0.007
86	0.007
87	0.006
88	0.005
89	0.005

Age x	AA$_x$
90	0.004
91	0.004
92	0.003
93	0.003
94	0.003
95	0.002
96	0.002
97	0.002
98	0.001
99	0.001
100	0.001
101	0.000
102	0.000
103	0.000
104	0.000
105	0.000
106	0.000
107	0.000
108	0.000
109	0.000
110	0.000
111	0.000
112	0.000
113	0.000
114	0.000
115	0.000
116	0.000
117	0.000
118	0.000
119	0.000
120	0.000

TABLE 3.—MORTALITY TABLE FOR HEALTHY FEMALE PARTICIPANTS
[94 GAM Basic]

Age x	q$_x$
15	0.000233
16	0.000261
17	0.000281
18	0.000293
19	0.000301
20	0.000305
21	0.000308
22	0.000311
23	0.000313
24	0.000313
25	0.000313
26	0.000316
27	0.000324
28	0.000338
29	0.000356
30	0.000377
31	0.000401
32	0.000427
33	0.000454
34	0.000482

Age x	q$_x$
35	0.000514
36	0.000550
37	0.000593
38	0.000643
39	0.000701
40	0.000763
41	0.000826
42	0.000888
43	0.000943
44	0.000992
45	0.001046
46	0.001111
47	0.001196
48	0.001297
49	0.001408
50	0.001536
51	0.001686
52	0.001864
53	0.002051
54	0.002241
55	0.002466
56	0.002755
57	0.003139
58	0.003612
59	0.004154
60	0.004773
61	0.005476
62	0.006271
63	0.007179
64	0.008194
65	0.009286
66	0.010423
67	0.011574
68	0.012648
69	0.013665
70	0.014763
71	0.016079
72	0.017748
73	0.019724
74	0.021915
75	0.024393
76	0.027231
77	0.030501
78	0.034115
79	0.038024
80	0.042361
81	0.047260
82	0.052853
83	0.058986
84	0.065569
85	0.072836
86	0.081018
87	0.090348
88	0.100882
89	0.112467
90	0.125016

Age x	q_x
91	0.138442
92	0.152660
93	0.167668
94	0.183524
95	0.200229
96	0.217783
97	0.236188
98	0.255605
99	0.276035
100	0.297233
101	0.318956
102	0.340960
103	0.364586
104	0.389996
105	0.415180
106	0.438126
107	0.456824
108	0.471493
109	0.483473
110	0.492436
111	0.498054
112	0.500000
113	0.500000
114	0.500000
115	0.500000
116	0.500000
117	0.500000
118	0.500000
119	0.500000
120	1.000000

TABLE 4.—PROJECTION SCALE AA FOR HEALTHY FEMALE PARTICIPANTS

Age x	AA_x
15	0.016
16	0.015
17	0.014
18	0.014
19	0.015
20	0.016
21	0.017
22	0.017
23	0.016
24	0.015
25	0.014
26	0.012
27	0.012
28	0.012
29	0.012
30	0.010
31	0.008
32	0.008
33	0.009
34	0.010
35	0.011
36	0.012

Age x	AA_x
37	0.013
38	0.014
39	0.015
40	0.015
41	0.015
42	0.015
43	0.015
44	0.015
45	0.016
46	0.017
47	0.018
48	0.018
49	0.018
50	0.017
51	0.016
52	0.014
53	0.012
54	0.010
55	0.008
56	0.006
57	0.005
58	0.005
59	0.005
60	0.005
61	0.005
62	0.005
63	0.005
64	0.005
65	0.005
66	0.005
67	0.005
68	0.005
69	0.005
70	0.005
71	0.006
72	0.006
73	0.007
74	0.007
75	0.008
76	0.008
77	0.007
78	0.007
79	0.007
80	0.007
81	0.007
82	0.007
83	0.007
84	0.007
85	0.006
86	0.005
87	0.004
88	0.004
89	0.003
90	0.003
91	0.003
92	0.003

Age x	AA$_x$
93	0.002
94	0.002
95	0.002
96	0.002
97	0.001
98	0.001
99	0.001
100	0.001
101	0.000
102	0.000
103	0.000
104	0.000
105	0.000
106	0.000
107	0.000
108	0.000
109	0.000
110	0.000
111	0.000
112	0.000
113	0.000
114	0.000
115	0.000
116	0.000
117	0.000
118	0.000
119	0.000
120	0.000

TABLE 5.—MORTALITY TABLE FOR SOCIAL SECURITY DISABLED MALE
PARTICIPANTS

Age x	q$_x$
15	0.022010
16	0.022502
17	0.023001
18	0.023519
19	0.024045
20	0.024583
21	0.025133
22	0.025697
23	0.026269
24	0.026857
25	0.027457
26	0.028071
27	0.028704
28	0.029345
29	0.029999
30	0.030661
31	0.031331
32	0.032006
33	0.032689
34	0.033405
35	0.034184
36	0.034981
37	0.035796

Age x	q$_x$
38	0.036634
39	0.037493
40	0.038373
41	0.039272
42	0.040189
43	0.041122
44	0.042071
45	0.043033
46	0.044007
47	0.044993
48	0.045989
49	0.046993
50	0.048004
51	0.049021
52	0.050042
53	0.051067
54	0.052093
55	0.053120
56	0.054144
57	0.055089
58	0.056068
59	0.057080
60	0.058118
61	0.059172
62	0.060232
63	0.061303
64	0.062429
65	0.063669
66	0.065082
67	0.066724
68	0.068642
69	0.070834
70	0.073284
71	0.075979
72	0.078903
73	0.082070
74	0.085606
75	0.088918
76	0.092208
77	0.095625
78	0.099216
79	0.103030
80	0.107113
81	0.111515
82	0.116283
83	0.121464
84	0.127108
85	0.133262
86	0.139974
87	0.147292
88	0.155265
89	0.163939
90	0.173363
91	0.183585
92	0.194653
93	0.206615

Age x	q_x
94	0.219519
95	0.234086
96	0.248436
97	0.263954
98	0.280803
99	0.299154
100	0.319185
101	0.341086
102	0.365052
103	0.393102
104	0.427255
105	0.469531
106	0.521945
107	0.586518
108	0.665268
109	0.760215
110	1.000000

TABLE 6.—MORTALITY TABLE FOR SOCIAL SECURITY DISABLED FEMALE PARTICIPANTS

Age x	q_x
15	0.007777
16	0.008120
17	0.008476
18	0.008852
19	0.009243
20	0.009650
21	0.010076
22	0.010521
23	0.010984
24	0.011468
25	0.011974
26	0.012502
27	0.013057
28	0.013632
29	0.014229
30	0.014843
31	0.015473
32	0.016103
33	0.016604
34	0.017121
35	0.017654
36	0.018204
37	0.018770
38	0.019355
39	0.019957
40	0.020579
41	0.021219
42	0.021880
43	0.022561
44	0.023263
45	0.023988
46	0.024734
47	0.025504
48	0.026298

Age x	q_x
49	0.027117
50	0.027961
51	0.028832
52	0.029730
53	0.030655
54	0.031609
55	0.032594
56	0.033608
57	0.034655
58	0.035733
59	0.036846
60	0.037993
61	0.039176
62	0.040395
63	0.041653
64	0.042950
65	0.044287
66	0.045666
67	0.046828
68	0.048070
69	0.049584
70	0.051331
71	0.053268
72	0.055356
73	0.057573
74	0.059979
75	0.062574
76	0.065480
77	0.068690
78	0.072237
79	0.076156
80	0.080480
81	0.085243
82	0.090480
83	0.096224
84	0.102508
85	0.109368
86	0.116837
87	0.124948
88	0.133736
89	0.143234
90	0.153477
91	0.164498
92	0.176332
93	0.189011
94	0.202571
95	0.217045
96	0.232467
97	0.248870
98	0.266289
99	0.284758
100	0.303433
101	0.327385
102	0.359020
103	0.395842
104	0.438360

Age x	q_x
105	0.487816
106	0.545886
107	0.614309
108	0.694884
109	0.789474

Age x	q_x
110	1.000000

[Revised 12/2/2005 by 70 FR 72208.]

[¶ 15,476F]

§ 4044.75 Appendix B to Part 4044: Interest Rates Used To Value Benefits.

[This table sets forth, for each indicated calendar month, the interest rates (denoted by i_1, i_2, ..., and referred to generally as i_t) assumed to be in effect between specified anniversaries of a valuation date thatoccurs within that calendar month; those anniversaries are specified in the columns adjacent to the rates. The last listed rate is assumed to be in effect after the last listed anniversary date.] [Amended 3/17/00 by 65 FR 14751]

The values of i_t are:

For valuation dates occurring in the month —	i_t for $t =$		i_t for $t =$		i_t for $t =$	
Nov. 1993	.0560	1-25	.0525	> 25	N/A	N/A
Dec. 1993	.0560	1-25	.0525	> 25	N/A	N/A
Jan. 1994	.0590	1-25	.0525	> 25	N/A	N/A
Feb. 1994	.0590	1-25	.0525	> 25	N/A	N/A
March 1994	.0580	1-25	.0525	> 25	N/A	N/A
April 1994	.0620	1-25	.0525	> 25	N/A	N/A
May 1994	.0650	1-25	.0525	> 25	N/A	N/A
June 1994	.0670	1-25	.0525	> 25	N/A	N/A
July 1994	.0690	1-25	.0525	> 25	N/A	N/A
Aug. 1994	.0700	1-25	.0525	> 25	N/A	N/A
Sep. 1994	.0690	1-25	.0525	> 25	N/A	N/A
Oct. 1994	.0700	1-25	.0525	> 25	N/A	N/A
Nov. 1994	.0730	1-25	.0525	> 25	N/A	N/A
Dec. 1994	.0750	1-25	.0525	> 25	N/A	N/A

The values of i_t are:

For valuation dates occurring in the month —	i_t for $t =$		i_t for $t =$		i_t for $t =$	
Jan. 1995	.0750	1-20	.0575	> 20	N/A	N/A
Feb. 1995	.0730	1-20	.0575	> 20	N/A	N/A
March 1995	.0730	1-20	.0575	> 20	N/A	N/A
April 1995	.0710	1-20	.0575	> 20	N/A	N/A
May 1995	.0690	1-20	.0575	> 20	N/A	N/A
June 1995	.0680	1-20	.0575	> 20	N/A	N/A
July 1995	.0630	1-20	.0575	> 20	N/A	N/A
Aug. 1995	.0620	1-20	.0575	> 20	N/A	N/A
Sep. 1995	.0640	1-20	.0575	> 20	N/A	N/A
Oct. 1995	.0630	1-20	.0575	> 20	N/A	N/A
Nov. 1995	.0620	1-20	.0575	> 20	N/A	N/A
Dec. 1995	.0600	1-20	.0575	> 20	N/A	N/A

The values of i_t are:

For valuation dates occurring in the month —	i_t for $t =$		i_t for $t =$		i_t for $t =$	
Jan. 1996	.0560	1-20	.0475	> 20	N/A	N/A
Feb. 1996	.0540	1-20	.0475	> 20	N/A	N/A
March 1996	.0550	1-20	.0475	> 20	N/A	N/A
April 1996	.0580	1-20	.0475	> 20	N/A	N/A
May 1996	.0600	1-20	.0475	> 20	N/A	N/A
June 1996	.0620	1-20	.0475	> 20	N/A	N/A
July 1996	.0620	1-20	.0475	> 20	N/A	N/A
Aug. 1996	.0630	1-20	.0475	> 20	N/A	N/A
Sep. 1996	.0630	1-20	.0475	> 20	N/A	N/A
Oct. 1996	.0630	1-20	.0475	> 20	N/A	N/A

	The values of i_t are:					
For valuation dates occurring in the month —	i_t for $t =$		i_t for $t =$		i_t for $t =$	
Nov. 1996	.0620	1-20	.0475	> 20	N/A	N/A
Dec. 1996	.0600	1-20	.0475	> 20	N/A	N/A

	The values of i_t are:					
For valuation dates occurring in the month —	i_t for $t =$		i_t for $t =$		i_t for $t =$	
Jan. 1997	.0580	1-25	.0500	> 25	N/A	N/A
Feb. 1997	.0590	1-25	.0500	> 25	N/A	N/A
March 1997	.0620	1-25	.0500	> 25	N/A	N/A
April 1997	.0610	1-25	.0500	> 25	N/A	N/A
May 1997	.0630	1-25	.0500	> 25	N/A	N/A
June 1997	.0640	1-25	.0500	> 25	N/A	N/A
July 1997	.0630	1-25	.0500	> 25	N/A	N/A
Aug. 1997	.0610	1-25	.0500	> 25	N/A	N/A
Sep. 1997	.0570	1-25	.0500	> 25	N/A	N/A
Oct. 1997	.0590	1-25	.0500	> 25	N/A	N/A
Nov. 1997	.0570	1-25	.0500	> 25	N/A	N/A
Dec. 1997	.0560	1-25	.0500	> 25	N/A	N/A

	The values of i_t are:					
For valuation dates occurring in the month —	i_t for $t =$		i_t for $t =$		i_t for $t =$	
Jan. 1998	.0560	1-25	.0525	> 25	N/A	N/A
Feb. 1998	.0550	1-25	.0525	> 25	N/A	N/A
March 1998	.0550	1-25	.0525	> 25	N/A	N/A
April 1998	.0550	1-25	.0525	> 25	N/A	N/A
May 1998	.0560	1-25	.0525	> 25	N/A	N/A
June 1998	.0560	1-25	.0525	> 25	N/A	N/A
July 1998	.0550	1-25	.0525	> 25	N/A	N/A
Aug. 1998	.0540	1-25	.0525	> 25	N/A	N/A
Sep. 1998	.0540	1-25	.0525	> 25	N/A	N/A
Oct. 1998	.0540	1-25	.0525	> 25	N/A	N/A
Nov. 1998	.0530	1-25	.0525	> 25	N/A	N/A
Dec. 1998	.0540	1-25	.0525	> 25	N/A	N/A

	The values of i_t are:					
For valuation dates occurring in the month —	i_t for $t =$		i_t for $t =$		i_t for $t =$	
Jan. 1999	.0530	1-20	.0525	> 20	N/A	N/A
Feb. 1999	.0540	1-20	.0525	> 20	N/A	N/A
March 1999	.0530	1-20	.0525	> 20	N/A	N/A
April 1999	.0560	1-20	.0525	> 20	N/A	N/A
May 1999	.0570	1-20	.0525	> 20	N/A	N/A
June 1999	.0570	1-20	.0525	> 20	N/A	N/A
July 1999	.0600	1-20	.0525	> 20	N/A	N/A
Aug. 1999	.0630	1-20	.0525	> 20	N/A	N/A
Sep. 1999	.0630	1-20	.0525	> 20	N/A	N/A
Oct. 1999	.0630	1-20	.0525	> 20	N/A	N/A
Nov. 1999	.0630	1-20	.0525	> 20	N/A	N/A
Dec. 1999	.0650	1-20	.0525	> 20	N/A	N/A
Jan. 2000	.0690	1-25	.0625	> 25	N/A	N/A
Feb. 2000	.0710	1-25	.0625	> 25	N/A	N/A
March 2000	.0710	1-25	.0625	> 25	N/A	N/A
April 2000	.0710	1-25	.0625	> 25	N/A	N/A

The values of i_t are:

For valuation dates occurring in the month —	i_t for $t =$		i_t for $t =$		i_t for $t =$	
May 2000	.0700	1-25	.0625	> 25	N/A	N/A
June 2000	.0710	1-25	.0625	> 25	N/A	N/A
July 2000	.0740	1-25	.0625	> 25	N/A	N/A
Aug. 2000[1]	.0710	1-25	.0625	> 25	N/A	N/A
Sep. 2000[2]	.0700	1-25	.0625	> 25	N/A	N/A
Oct. 2000[3]	.0700	1-25	.0625	> 25	N/A	N/A
Nov. 2000[4]	.0710	1-25	.0625	> 25	N/A	N/A
Dec. 2000[5]	.0700	1-25	.0625	> 25	N/A	N/A

The values of i_t are:

For valuation dates occurring in the month —	i_t for $t =$		i_t for $t =$		i_t for $t =$	
Jan. 2001[6]	.0670	1-20	.0625	> 20	N/A	N/A
Feb. 2001[7]	.0650	1-20	.0625	> 20	N/A	N/A
Mar. 2001[8]	.0640	1-20	.0625	> 20	N/A	N/A
Apr. 2001[9]	.0640	1-20	.0625	> 20	N/A	N/A
May 2001[10]	.0640	1-20	.0625	> 20	N/A	N/A
June 2001[11]	.0660	1-20	.0625	> 20	N/A	N/A
July 2001[12]	.0660	1-20	.0625	> 20	N/A	
Aug. 2001[13]	.0640	1-20	.0625	> 20	N/A	N/A
Sep. 2001[14]	.0630	1-20	.0625	> 20	N/A	N/A
Oct. 2001[15]	.0610	1-20	.0625	> 20	N/A	N/A
Nov. 2001[16]	.0650	1-20	.0625	> 20	N/A	N/A
Dec. 2001[17]	.0610	1-20	.0625	> 20	N/A	N/A

The values of i_t are:

For valuation dates occurring in the month —	i_t for $t =$		i_t for $t =$		i_t for $t =$	
Jan. 2002[18]	.0580	1-25	.0425	> 25	N/A	N/A
Feb. 2002[19]	.0580	1-25	.0425	> 25	N/A	N/A
Mar. 2002[20]	.0560	1-25	.0425	> 25	N/A	N/A
Apr. 2002[21]	.0550	1-25	.0425	> 25	N/A	N/A
May 2002[22]	.0590	1-25	.0425	> 25	N/A	N/A
June 2002[23]	.0570	1-25	.0425	> 25	N/A	N/A
July 2002[24]	.0570	1-25	.0425	> 25	N/A	N/A
Aug. 2002[25]	.0550	1-25	.0425	> 25	N/A	N/A
Sep. 2002[26]	.0540	1-25	.0425	> 25	N/A	N/A
Oct. 2002[27]	.0530	1-25	.0425	> 25	N/A	N/A
Nov. 2002[28]	.0500	1-25	.0425	> 25	N/A	N/A
Dec. 2002[29]	.0530	1-25	.0425	> 25	N/A	N/A

The values of i_t are:

For valuation dates occurring in the month —	i_t for $t =$		i_t for $t =$		i_t for $t =$	
Jan. 2003[30]	.0530	1-20	.0525	> 20	N/A	N/A
Feb. 2003[31]	.0510	1-20	.0525	> 20	N/A	N/A
Mar. 2003[32]	.0510	1-20	.0525	> 20	N/A	N/A
Apr. 2003[33]	.0490	1-20	.0525	> 20	N/A	N/A
May 2003[34]	.0490	1-20	.0525	> 20	N/A	N/A
June 2003[35]	.0470	1-20	.0525	> 20	N/A	N/A
July 2003[36]	.0430	1-20	.0525	> 20	N/A	N/A
Aug. 2003[37]	.0440	1-20	.0525	> 20	N/A	N/A
Sep. 2003[38]	.0490	1-20	.0525	> 20	N/A	N/A
Oct. 2003[39]	.0490	1-20	.0525	> 20	N/A	N/A

The values of i_t are:

For valuation dates occurring in the month —	i_t for $t =$		i_t for $t =$		i_t for $t =$	
Nov. 2003[40]	.04960	1-20	.0525	> 20	N/A	N/A
Dec. 2003[41]	.0470	1-20	.0525	> 20	N/A	N/A

The values of i_t are:

For valuation dates occurring in the month —	i_t for $t =$		i_t for $t =$		i_t for $t =$	
Jan. 2004[42]	.0420	1-20	.0500	> 20	N/A	N/A
Feb. 2004[43]	.0410	1-20	.0500	> 20	N/A	N/A
Mar. 2004[44]	.0410	1-20	.0500	> 20	N/A	N/A
Apr. 2004[45]	.0400	1-20	.0500	> 20	N/A	N/A
May 2004[46]	.0390	1-20	.0500	> 20	N/A	N/A
June 2004[47]	.0430	1-20	.0500	> 20	N/A	N/A
July 2004[48]	.0450	1-20	.0500	> 20	N/A	N/A
Aug. 2004[49]	.0430	1-20	.0500	> 20	N/A	N/A
Sep. 2004[50]	.0420	1-20	.0500	> 20	N/A	N/A
Oct. 2004[51]	.0400	1-20	.0500	> 20	N/A	N/A
Nov. 2004[52]	.0380	1-20	.0500	> 20	N/A	N/A
Dec. 2004[53]	.0380	1-20	.0500	> 20	N/A	N/A

The values of i_t are:

For valuation dates occurring in the month —	i_t for $t =$		i_t for $t =$		i_t for $t =$	
Jan. 2005[54]	.0410	1-20	.0475	> 20	N/A	N/A
Feb. 2005[55]	.0400	1-20	.0475	> 20	N/A	N/A
Mar. 2005[56]	.0380	1-20	.0475	> 20	N/A	N/A
Apr. 2005[57]	.0380	1-20	.0475	> 20	N/A	N/A
May 2005[58]	.0390	1-20	.0475	> 20	N/A	N/A
June 2005[59]	.0370	1-20	.0475	> 20	N/A	N/A
July 2005[60]	.0360	1-20	.0475	> 20	N/A	N/A
Aug. 2005[61]	.0340	1-20	.0475	> 20	N/A	N/A
Sep. 2005[62]	.0360	1-20	.0475	> 20	N/A	N/A
Oct. 2005[63]	.0350	1-20	.0475	> 20	N/A	N/A
Nov. 2005[64]	.0370	1-20	.0475	> 20	N/A	N/A
Dec. 2005[65]	.0400	1-20	.0475	> 20	N/A	N/A

The values of i_t are:

For valuation dates occurring in the month —	i_t for $t =$		i_t for $t =$		i_t for $t =$	
Jan. 2006[66]	.0570	1-20	.0475	> 20	N/A	N/A
Feb. 2006[67]	.0560	1-20	.0475	> 20	N/A	N/A
Mar. 2006[68]	.0570	1-20	.0475	> 20	N/A	N/A
Apr. 2006[69]	.0560	1-20	.0475	> 20	N/A	N/A
May 2006[70]	.0590	1-20	.0475	> 20	N/A	N/A
June 2006[71]	.0620	1-20	.0475	> 20	N/A	N/A
July 2006[72]	.0630	1-20	.0475	> 20	N/A	N/A
Aug. 2006[73]	.0640	1-20	.0475	> 20	N/A	N/A
Sep. 2006[74]	.0620	1-20	.0475	> 20	N/A	N/A
Oct. 2006[75]	.0600	1-20	.0475	> 20	N/A	N/A
Nov. 2006[76]	.0570	1-20	.0475	> 20	N/A	N/A
Dec. 2006[77]	.0580	1-20	.0475	> 20	N/A	N/A

For valuation dates occurring in the month —	The values of i_t are:					
	i_t for $t =$		i_t for $t =$		i_t for $t =$	
Jan. 2007[78]	.0488	1-20	.0455	> 20	N/A	N/A
Feb. 2007[79]	.0513	1-20	.0480	> 20	N/A	N/A
March 2007[80]	.0522	1-20	.0489	> 20	N/A	N/A
April 2007[81]	.0499	1-20	.0466	> 20	N/A	N/A
May 2007[82]	.0520	1-20	.0487	> 20	N/A	N/A
June 2007[83]	.0514	1-20	.0481	> 20	N/A	N/A
July 2007[84]	.0533	1-20	.0500	> 20	N/A	N/A
Aug. 2007[85]	.0549	1-20	.0516	> 20	N/A	N/A
Sept. 2007[86]	.0553	1-20	.0520	> 20	N/A	N/A
Oct. 2007[87]	.0551	1-20	.0518	> 20	N/A	N/A
Nov. 2007[88]	.0546	1-20	.0513	> 20	N/A	N/A
Dec. 2007[89]	.0537	1-20	.0504	> 20	N/A	N/A

For valuation dates occurring in the month —	The values of i_t are:					
	i_t for $t =$		i_t for $t =$		i_t for $t =$	
Jan. 2008[90]	.0542	1-20	.0449	> 20	N/A	N/A
Feb. 2008[91]	.0550	1-20	.0457	> 20	N/A	N/A
Mar. 2008[92]	.0554	1-20	.0461	> 20	N/A	N/A
Apr. 2008[93]	.0564	1-20	.0471	> 20	N/A	N/A
May 2008[94]	.0581	1-20	.0488	> 20	N/A	N/A
June 2008[95]	.0568	1-20	.0475	> 20	N/A	N/A
July 2008[96]	.0595	1-20	.0502	> 20	N/A	N/A
August 2008[97]	.0605	1-20	.0512	> 20	N/A	N/A
September 2008[98]	.0624	1-20	.0531	> 20	N/A	N/A
October 2008[99]	.0618	1-20	.0525	> 20	N/A	N/A
November 2008[100]	.0709	1-20	.0616	> 20	N/A	N/A
December 2008[101]	.0792	1-20	.0699	> 20	N/A	N/A
January 2009[102]	.0602	1-20	.0548	> 20	N/A	N/A
February 2009[102]	.0602	1-20	.0548	> 20	N/A	N/A
March 2009[102]	.0602	1-20	.0548	> 20	N/A	N/A
April 2009[103]	.0550	1-20	.0502	> 20	N/A	N/A
May 2009[103]	.0550	1-20	.0502	> 20	N/A	N/A
June 2009[103]	.0550	1-20	.0502	> 20	N/A	N/A
July 2009[104]	.0531	1-20	.0504	> 20	N/A	N/A
August 2009[104]	.0531	1-20	.0504	> 20	N/A	N/A
September 2009[104]	.0531	1-20	.0504	> 20	N/A	N/A
October 2009[105]	.0530	1-20	.0501	> 20	N/A	N/A
November 2009[105]	.0530	1-20	.0501	> 20	N/A	N/A
December 2009[105]	.0530	1-20	.0501	> 20	N/A	N/A
January 2010[106]	.0489	1-20	.0463	> 20	N/A	N/A
February 2010[106]	.0489	1-20	.0463	> 20	N/A	N/A
March 2010[106]	.0489	1-20	.0463	> 20	N/A	N/A
April 2010[107]	.0463	1-20	.0451	> 20	N/A	N/A
May 2010[107]	.0463	1-20	.0451	> 20	N/A	N/A
June 2010[107]	.0463	1-20	.0451	> 20	N/A	N/A
July 2010[108]	.0493	1-20	.0466	> 20	N/A	N/A
August 2010[108]	.0493	1-20	.0466	> 20	N/A	N/A
September 2010[108]	.0493	1-20	.0466	> 20	N/A	N/A
October 2010[109]	.0448	1-25	.0451	> 25	N/A	N/A
November 2010[109]	.0448	1-25	.0451	> 25	N/A	N/A
December 2010[109]	.0448	1-25	.0451	> 25	N/A	N/A
January 2011[110]	.0407	1-25	.0393	> 25	N/A	N/A
February 2011[110]	.0407	1-25	.0393	> 25	N/A	N/A

The values of i_t are:

For valuation dates occurring in the month —	i_t for $t =$		i_t for $t =$		i_t for $t =$	
March 2011[110]	.0407	1-25	.0393	> 25	N/A	N/A
April 2011[111]	.0396	1-20	.0432	> 20	N/A	N/A
May 2011[111]	.0396	1-20	.0432	> 20	N/A	N/A
June 2011[111]	.0396	1-20	.0432	> 20	N/A	N/A
July 2011[112]	.0422	1-20	.0434	> 20	N/A	N/A
August 2011[112]	.0422	1-20	.0434	> 20	N/A	N/A
September 2011[112]	.0422	1-20	.0434	> 20	N/A	N/A
October 2011[113]	.0409	1-20	.0430	> 20	N/A	N/A
November 2011[113]	.0409	1-20	.0430	> 20	N/A	N/A
December 2011[113]	.0409	1-20	.0430	> 20	N/A	N/A
January 2012[114]	.0374	1-20	.0370	> 20	N/A	N/A
February 2012[114]	.0374	1-20	.0370	> 20	N/A	N/A
March 2012[114]	.0374	1-20	.0370	> 20	N/A	N/A
April 2012[115]	.0311	1-20	.0336	> 20	N/A	N/A
May 2012[115]	.0311	1-20	.0336	> 20	N/A	N/A
June 2012[115]	.0311	1-20	.0336	> 20	N/A	N/A
July 2012[116]	.0295	1-20	.0366	> 20	N/A	N/A
August 2012[116]	.0295	1-20	.0366	> 20	N/A	N/A
September 2012[116]	.0295	1-20	.0366	> 20	N/A	N/A
October 2012[117]	.0307	1-20	.0300	> 20	N/A	N/A
November 2012[117]	.0307	1-20	.0300	> 20	N/A	N/A
December 2012[117]	.0307	1-20	.0300	> 20	N/A	N/A
January 2013[118]	.0267	1-20	.0301	> 20	N/A	N/A
February 2013[118]	.0267	1-20	.0301	> 20	N/A	N/A
March 2013[118]	.0267	1-20	.0301	> 20	N/A	N/A
April 2013[119]	.0250	1-20	.0320	> 20	N/A	N/A
May 2013[119]	.0250	1-20	.0320	> 20	N/A	N/A
June 2013[119]	.0250	1-20	.0320	> 20	N/A	N/A
July 2013[120]	.0260	1-20	.0343	> 20	N/A	N/A
August 2013[120]	.0260	1-20	.0343	> 20	N/A	N/A
September 2013[120]	.0260	1-20	.0343	> 20	N/A	N/A
October 2013[121]	.0300	1-20	.0331	> 20	N/A	N/A
November 2013[121]	.0300	1-20	.0331	> 20	N/A	N/A
December 2013[121]	.0300	1-20	.0331	> 20	N/A	N/A
January 2014[122]	.0335	1-20	.0350	> 20	N/A	N/A
February 2014[122]	.0335	1-20	.0350	> 20	N/A	N/A
March 2014[122]	.0335	1-20	.0350	> 20	N/A	N/A
April 2014[123]	.0347	1-20	.0364	> 20	N/A	N/A
May 2014[123]	.0347	1-20	.0364	> 20	N/A	N/A
June 2014[123]	.0347	1-20	.0364	> 20	N/A	N/A
July 2014[124]	.0343	1-20	.0366	> 20	N/A	N/A
August 2014[124]	.0343	1-20	.0366	> 20	N/A	N/A
September 2014[124]	.0343	1-20	.0366	> 20	N/A	N/A
October 2014[125]	.0310	1-20	.0329	> 20	N/A	N/A
November 2014[125]	.0310	1-20	.0329	> 20	N/A	N/A
December 2014[125]	.0310	1-20	.0329	> 20	N/A	N/A
January 2015[126]	.0289	1-20	.0312	> 20	N/A	N/A
February 2015[126]	.0289	1-20	.0312	> 20	N/A	N/A
March 2015[126]	.0289	1-20	.0312	> 20	N/A	N/A
April 2015[127]	.0271	1-20	.0278	> 20	N/A	N/A
May 2015[127]	.0271	1-20	.0278	> 20	N/A	N/A
June 2015[127]	.0271	1-20	.0278	> 20	N/A	N/A
July 2015[128]	.0232	1-20	.0237	> 20	N/A	N/A
August 2015[128]	.0232	1-20	.0237	> 20	N/A	N/A

For valuation dates occurring in the month —	The values of i_t are:					
	i_t for $t =$		i_t for $t =$		i_t for $t =$	
September 2015[128]	.0232	1-20	.0237	> 20	N/A	N/A
October 2015[129]	.0246	1-20	.0298	> 20	N/A	N/A
November 2015[129]	.0246	1-20	.0298	> 20	N/A	N/A
December 2015[129]	.0246	1-20	.0298	> 20	N/A	N/A
January 2016[130]	.0282	1-20	.0295	> 20	N/A	N/A
February 2016[130]	.0282	1-20	.0295	> 20	N/A	N/A
March 2016[130]	.0282	1-20	.0295	> 20	N/A	N/A
April 2016[131]	.0277	1-20	.0286	> 20	N/A	N/A
May 2016[131]	.0277	1-20	.0286	> 20	N/A	N/A
June 2016[131]	.0277	1-20	.0286	> 20	N/A	N/A
July 2016[132]	.0250	1-20	.0285	> 20	N/A	N/A
August 2016[132]	.0250	1-20	.0285	> 20	N/A	N/A
September 2016[132]	.0250	1-20	.0285	> 20	N/A	N/A
October 2016[133]	.0198	1-20	.0267	> 20	N/A	N/A
November 2016[133]	.0198	1-20	.0267	> 20	N/A	N/A
December 2016[133]	.0198	1-20	.0267	> 20	N/A	N/A
January 2017[134]	.0187	1-20	.0237	> 20	N/A	N/A
February 2017[134]	.0187	1-20	.0237	> 20	N/A	N/A
March 2017[134]	.0187	1-20	.0237	> 20	N/A	N/A
April 2017[135]	.0215	1-20	.0260	> 20	N/A	N/A
May 2017[135]	.0215	1-20	.0260	> 20	N/A	N/A
June 2017[135]	.0215	1-20	.0260	> 20	N/A	N/A
July 2017[136]	.0244	1-20	.0274	> 20	N/A	N/A
August 2017[136]	.0244	1-20	.0274	> 20	N/A	N/A
September 2017[136]	.0244	1-20	.0274	> 20	N/A	N/A
October 2017[137]	.0234	1-20	.0263	> 20	N/A	N/A
November 2017[137]	.0234	1-20	.0263	> 20	N/A	N/A
December 2017[137]	.0234	1-20	.0263	> 20	N/A	N/A
January 2018[138]	.0239	1-20	.0260	> 20	N/A	N/A
February 2018[138]	.0239	1-20	.0260	> 20	N/A	N/A
March 2018[138]	.0239	1-20	.0260	> 20	N/A	N/A

[1] 65 FR 43694, 7/14/2000.
[2] 65 FR 49737, 8/15/2000.
[3] 65 FR 55896, 9/15/2000.
[4] 65 FR 60859, 10/13/2000.
[5] 65 FR 68892, 11/15/2000.
[6] 65 FR 78415, 12/15/2000.
[7] 66 FR 2822, 1/12/2001.
[8] 66 FR 10365, 2/15/2001.
[9] 66 FR 15031, 3/15/2001.
[10] 66 FR 19089, 4/13/2001.
[11] 66 FR 26791, 5/15/2001.
[12] 66 FR 32543, 6/15/2001.
[13] 66 FR 36702, 7/13/2001.
[14] 66 FR 42737, 8/15/2001.
[15] 66 FR 47885, 9/14/2001.
[16] 66 FR 52315, 10/15/2001.
[17] 66 FR 57369, 11/15/2001.
[18] 66 FR 64744, 12/14/2001.
[19] 67 FR 1861, 1/15/2002.
[20] 67 FR 7076, 2/15/2002.
[21] 67 FR 11572, 3/15/2002.
[22] 67 FR 18112, 4/15/2002.
[23] 67 FR 34610, 5/15/2002.
[24] 67 FR 40850, 6/14/2002.
[25] 67 FR 46376, 7/15/2002.
[26] 67 FR 53307, 8/15/2002.
[27] 67 FR 57949, 9/13/2002.

[28] 67 FR 63544, 10/15/2002.
[29] 67 FR 69121, 11/15/2002.
[30] 67 FR 76682, 12/13/2002.
[31] 68 FR 1965, 1/15/2003.
[32] 68 FR 7419, 2/14/2003.
[33] 68 FR 12303, 3/14/2003.
[34] 68 FR 18122, 4/15/2003.
[35] 68 FR 26206, 5/15/2003.
[36] 68 FR 35294, 6/13/2003.
[37] 68 FR 41714, 7/15/2003.
[38] 68 FR 48787, 8/15/2003.
[39] 68 FR 53880, 9/15/2003.
[40] 68 FR 59315, 10/15/2003.
[41] 68 FR 64525, 11/14/2003.
[42] 68 FR 69606, 12/15/2003.
[43] 69 FR 2299, 1/15/2004.
[44] 69 FR 7119, 2/13/2004.
[45] 69 FR 12072, 3/15/2004.
[46] 69 FR 20079, 4/15/2004.
[47] 69 FR 26769, 5/14/2004.
[48] 69 FR 33302, 6/15/2004.
[49] 69 FR 42333, 7/15/2004.
[50] 69 FR 50070, 8/13/2004.
[50] 69 FR 50070, 8/13/2004.
[51] 69 FR 55500, 9/15/2004.
[52] 69 FR 61150, 10/15/2004.
[53] 69 FR 65543, 11/15/2004.
[54] 69 FR 74973, 12/15/2004.
[55] 70 FR 2568, 1/14/2005.
[56] 70 FR 7651, 2/15/2005.
[57] 70 FR 12585, 3/15/2005.
[58] 70 FR 19890, 4/15/2005.
[59] 70 FR 25470, 5/13/2005.
[60] 70 FR 34655, 6/15/2005.
[61] 70 FR 40882, 7/15/2005.
[62] 70 FR 47725, 8/15/2005.
[63] 70 FR 54477, 9/15/2005.
[64] 70 FR 60002, 10/14/2005.
[65] 70 FR 69277, 11/15/2005.
[66] 70 FR 74200, 12/15/2005.
[67] 71 FR 2147, 1/13/2006.
[68] 71 FR 7871, 2/15/2006.
[69] 71 FR 13258, 3/15/2006.
[70] 71 FR 19429, 4/14/2006.
[71] 71 FR 27959, 5/15/2006.
[72] 71 FR 34532, 6/15/2006.
[73] 71 FR 40011, 7/14/2006.
[74] 71 FR 47090, 8/16/2006.
[75] 71 FR 54415, 9/15/2006.
[76] 71 FR 60428, 10/13/2006.
[77] 71 FR 66455, 11/15/2006.
[78] 71 FR 75420, 12/15/2006.
[79] 72 FR 1460, 1/12/2007.
[80] 72 FR 7349, 2/15/2007.
[81] 72 FR 12087, 3/15/2007.
[82] 72 FR 18576, 4/13/2007.
[83] 72 FR 27243, 5/15/2007.
[84] 72 FR 33152, 6/15/2007.
[85] 72 FR 38484, 7/13/2007.
[86] 72 FR 45637, 8/15/2007.
[87] 72 FR 52471, 9/14/2007.
[88] 72 FR 58249, 10/15/2007.
[89] 72 FR 64150, 11/15/2007.
[90] 72 FR 71071, 12/14/2007.
[91] 73 FR 2420, 1/15/2008.
[92] 73 FR 8816, 2/15/2008.
[93] 73 FR 13754, 3/14/2008.
[94] 73 FR 20164, 4/15/2008.
[95] 73 FR 28037, 5/15/2008.
[96] 73 FR 33695, 6/13/2008.
[97] 73 FR 40464, 7/15/2008.
[98] 73 FR 47831, 8/15/2008.
[99] 73 FR 53115, 9/15/2008.

¶15,476F   Reg. §4044.75

[100] 73 FR 61352, 10/16/2008.
[101] 73 FR 67389, 11/14/2008.
[102] 73 FR 79362, 12/29/2008 [corrected by 74 FR 772, 1/8/09].
[103] 74 FR 11035, 3/16/2009.
[104] 74 FR 28163, 6/15/2009.
[105] 74 FR 47099, 9/15/2009.
[106] 74 FR 66234, 12/15/2009.
[107] 75 FR 12123, 3/15/2010.
[108] 75 FR 33689, 6/15/2010.
[109] 75 FR 55966, 9/15/2010.
[110] 75 FR 78161, 12/15/2010.
[111] 76 FR 13884, 3/15/2011.
[112] 76 FR 34847, 6/15/2011 [corrected by 77 FR 14276, 3/9/2012].
[113] 76 FR 56975, 9/15/2011 [corrected by 77 FR 14275, 3/9/2012].
[114] 76 FR 77901, 12/15/2011.
[115] 77 FR 15256, 3/15/2012.
[116] 77 FR 35838, 6/15/2012.
[117] 77 FR 56770, 9/14/2012.
[118] 77 FR 75549, 12/21/2012.
[119] 78 FR 16401, 3/15/2013.
[120] 78 FR 35754, 6/14/2013.
[121] 78 FR 56603, 9/13/2013.
[122] 78 FR 75897, 12/13/2013.
[123] 79 FR 15009, 3/18/2014.
[124] 79 FR 33860, 6/13/2014.
[125] 79 FR 54904, 9/15/2014.
[126] 79 FR 74023, 12/15/2014.
[127] 80 FR 13239, 3/13/2015.
[128] 80 FR 34052, 6/15/2015.
[129] 80 FR 55249, 9/15/2015.
[130] 80 FR 79476, 12/22/2015.
[131] 81 FR 13742, 3/15/2016.
[132] 81 FR 38948, 6/15/2016.
[133] 81 FR 63414, 9/15/2016.
[134] 81 FR 93599, 12/21/2016.
[135] 82 FR 13755, 3/15/2017.
[136] 82 FR 27422, 6/15/2017.
[137] 82 FR 43299, 9/15/2017.
[138] 82 FR 59515, 12/15/2017.

[¶ 15,476G]

§ 4044.75 Appendix C to Part 4044: Loading Assumptions.

If the total value of the plan's benefit liabilities (as defined in 29 U.S.C. Sec. 1301(a)(16)), exclusive of the loading charge, is—		The loading charge equals—
greater than	but less than or equal to	
$0	$200,000	5% of the total value of the plan's benefits, plus $200 for each plan participant.
$200,000	_____	$10,000, plus a percentage of the excess of the total value over $200,000, plus $200 for each plan participant; the percentage is equal to $1\% + [(P\%-7.50\%)/10]$, where P% is the initial rate, expressed as a percentage, set forth in appendix B of this part for the valuation of benefits. [Amended 3/17/00 by 65 FR 14751.]

[¶ 15,476H]

§ 4044.75 Appendix D to Part 4044: Tables Used to Determine Expected Retirement Age

[(For Plans with valuation dates after December 31, 2017, and before January 1, 2019)]

TABLE I-18—SELECTION OF RETIREMENT RATE CATEGORY [For plans with valuation dates after December 31, 2017, and before January 1, 2019]

If participant reaches URA in year—	Participant's retirement rate category is—			
	Low[1] if monthly benefit at URA is less than—	Medium[2] if monthly benefit at URA is		High[3] if monthly benefit at URA is greater than—
		From—	To—	
2019	647	647	2,734	2,734
2020	662	662	2,797	2,797
2021	678	678	2,862	2,862
2022	693	693	2,927	2,927

If participant reaches URA in year—	Participant's retirement rate category is—			
	Low[1] if monthly benefit at URA is less than—	Medium[2] if monthly benefit at URA is—		High[3] if monthly benefit at URA is greater than—
		From—	To—	
2023	709	709	2,995	2,995
2024	725	725	3,064	3,064
2025	742	742	3,134	3,134
2026	759	759	3,206	3,206
2027	777	777	3,280	3,280
2028 or later	794	794	3,355	3,355

[1] Table II-A.
[2] Table II-B.
[3] Table II-C.

Table II-A.—Expected Retirement Ages for Individuals in the Low Category

Participant's earliest retirement age at valuation date.	Unreduced retirement age										
	60	61	62	63	64	65	66	67	68	69	70
42	53	53	53	54	54	54	54	54	54	54	54
43	53	54	54	54	55	55	55	55	55	55	55
44	54	54	55	55	55	55	55	56	56	56	56
45	54	55	55	56	56	56	56	56	56	56	56
46	55	55	56	56	56	57	57	57	57	57	57
47	56	56	56	57	57	57	57	57	57	57	57
48	56	57	57	57	58	58	58	58	58	58	58
49	56	57	58	58	58	58	59	59	59	59	59
50	57	57	58	58	59	59	59	59	59	59	59
51	57	58	58	59	59	60	60	60	60	60	60
52	58	58	59	59	60	60	60	60	60	60	60
53	58	59	59	60	60	61	61	61	61	61	61
54	58	59	60	60	61	61	61	61	61	61	61
55	59	59	60	61	61	61	62	62	62	62	62
56	59	60	60	61	61	62	62	62	62	62	62
57	59	60	61	61	62	62	62	62	62	62	62
58	59	60	61	61	62	62	63	63	63	63	63
59	59	60	61	62	62	63	63	63	63	63	63
60	60	60	61	62	62	63	63	63	63	63	63
61		61	61	62	63	63	63	63	64	64	64
62			62	62	63	63	63	64	64	64	64
63				63	63	64	64	65	65	65	65
64					64	64	65	65	65	65	65
65						65	65	65	65	65	65
66							66	66	66	66	66
67								67	67	67	67
68									68	68	68
69										69	69
70											70

Table II-B.—Expected Retirement Ages for Individuals in the Medium Category

Participant's earliest retirement age at valuation date.	Unreduced retirement age										
	60	61	62	63	64	65	66	67	68	69	70
42	49	49	49	49	49	49	49	49	49	49	49
43	50	50	50	50	50	50	50	50	50	50	50
44	50	51	51	51	51	51	51	51	51	51	51
45	51	51	52	52	52	52	52	52	52	52	52
46	52	52	52	53	53	53	53	53	53	53	53

Unreduced retirement age

Participant's earliest retirement age at valuation date.	60	61	62	63	64	65	66	67	68	69	70
47	53	53	53	53	53	54	54	54	54	54	54
48	54	54	54	54	54	54	54	54	54	54	54
49	54	55	55	55	55	55	55	55	55	55	55
50	55	55	56	56	56	56	56	56	56	56	56
51	56	56	56	57	57	57	57	57	57	57	57
52	56	57	57	57	57	58	58	58	58	58	58
53	57	57	58	58	58	58	58	58	58	58	58
54	57	58	58	59	59	59	59	59	59	59	59
55	58	58	59	59	59	60	60	60	60	60	60
56	58	59	59	60	60	60	60	60	60	60	60
57	59	59	60	60	61	61	61	61	61	61	61
58	59	60	60	61	61	61	61	61	61	61	61
59	59	60	61	61	62	62	62	62	62	62	62
60	60	60	61	62	62	62	62	62	62	62	62
61	..	61	61	62	62	63	63	63	63	63	63
62	..	..	62	62	62	63	63	63	63	63	63
63	..	..	..	63	63	64	64	64	64	64	64
64	..	..	..	..	64	64	64	64	64	64	64
65	..	..	..	..	..	65	65	65	65	65	65
66	..	..	..	..	..	..	66	66	66	66	66
67	..	..	..	..	..	..	..	67	67	67	67
68	..	..	..	..	..	..	..	..	68	68	68
69	..	..	..	..	..	..	..	..	..	69	69
70	..	..	..	..	..	..	..	..	..	..	70

Table II-C.—Expected Retirement Ages for Individuals in the High Category

Unreduced retirement age

Participant's earliest retirement age at valuation date.	60	61	62	63	64	65	66	67	68	69	70
42	46	46	46	46	46	47	47	47	47	47	47
43	47	47	47	47	47	47	47	47	47	47	47
44	48	48	48	48	48	48	48	48	48	48	48
45	49	49	49	49	49	49	49	49	49	49	49
46	50	50	50	50	50	50	50	50	50	50	50
47	51	51	51	51	51	51	51	51	51	51	51
48	52	52	52	52	52	52	52	52	52	52	52
49	53	53	53	53	53	53	53	53	53	53	53
50	54	54	54	54	54	54	54	54	54	54	54
51	54	55	55	55	55	55	55	55	55	55	55
52	55	55	56	56	56	56	56	56	56	56	56
53	56	56	56	57	57	57	57	57	57	57	57
54	57	57	57	57	57	58	58	58	58	58	58
55	57	58	58	58	58	58	58	58	58	58	58
56	58	58	59	59	59	59	59	59	59	59	59
57	58	59	59	60	60	60	60	60	60	60	60
58	59	59	60	60	60	60	61	61	61	61	61
59	59	60	60	61	61	61	61	61	61	61	61
60	60	60	61	61	61	62	62	62	62	62	62
61	..	61	61	62	62	62	62	62	62	62	62
62	..	..	62	62	62	62	62	62	62	62	62
63	..	..	..	63	63	63	64	64	64	64	64
64	..	..	..	..	64	64	64	64	64	64	64
65	..	..	..	..	..	65	65	65	65	65	65
66	..	..	..	..	..	..	66	66	66	66	66
67	..	..	..	..	..	..	..	67	67	67	67
68	..	..	..	..	..	..	..	..	68	68	68

Participant's earliest retirement age at valuation date.	60	61	62	63	64	65	66	67	68	69	70
							Unreduced retirement age				
69	..	..	..	..	..	..	..	..	..	69	69
70	..	..	..	..	..	..	..	..	..	..	70

[¶ 15,480]
RECAPTURE OF CERTAIN PAYMENTS

Act Sec. 4045. (a) AUTHORIZATION TO RECOVER BENEFITS.—Except as provided in subsection (c), the trustee is authorized to recover for the benefit of a plan from a participant the recoverable amount (as defined in subsection (b)) of all payments from the plan to him which commenced within the 3-year period immediately preceding the time the plan is terminated.

Act Sec. 4045. (b) RECOVERABLE AMOUNT.—For purposes of subsection (a) the recoverable amount is the excess of the amount determined under paragraph (1) over the amount determined under paragraph (2).

(1) The amount determined under this paragraph is the sum of the amount of the actual payments received by the participant within the 3-year period.

(2) The amount determined under this paragraph is the sum of—

(A) the sum of the amount such participant would have received during each consecutive 12-month period within the 3 years if the participant received the benefit in the form described in paragraph (3),

(B) the sum for each of the consecutive 12-month periods of the lesser of—

(i) the excess, if any, of $10,000 over the benefit in the form described in paragraph (3), or

(ii) the excess of the actual payment, if any, over the benefit in the form described in paragraph (3), and

(C) the present value at the time of termination of the participant's future benefits guaranteed under this title as if the benefits commenced in the form described in paragraph (3).

(3) The form of benefit for purposes of this subsection shall be the monthly benefit the participant would have received during the consecutive 12-month period, if he had elected at the time of the first payment made during the 3-year period, to receive his interest in the plan as a monthly benefit in the form of a life annuity commencing at the time of such first payment.

Act Sec. 4045. (c) (1) PAYMENTS MADE ON OR AFTER DEATH OR DISABILITY OF PARTICIPANT; WAIVER OF RECOVERY IN CASE OF HARDSHIP.—In the event of a distribution described in section 4043(b)(7) the 3-year period referred to in subsection (b) shall not end sooner than the date on which the corporation is notified of the distribution.

(2) The trustee shall not recover any payment made from a plan after or on account of the death of a participant, or to a participant who is disabled (within the meaning of section 72(m)(7) of the Internal Revenue Code of 1986).

(3) The corporation is authorized to waive, in whole or in part, the recovery of any amount which the trustee is authorized to recover for the benefit of a plan under this section in any case in which it determines that substantial economic hardship would result to the participant or his beneficiaries from whom such amount is recoverable.

Amendment

P.L. 101-239, § 7891(a)(1):

Titles I, III, and IV of ERISA (other than sections 3(37)(E), 301(a)(7), and 308, the last sentence of section 408(d), and sections 414(c), 4001(a)(3)(ii), and 4303) are each amended by striking "Internal Revenue Code of 1954" each place it appears and inserting "Internal Revenue Code of 1986" effective October 22, 1986.

[¶ 15,490]
REPORTS TO TRUSTEE

Act Sec. 4046. The corporation and the plan administrator of any plan to be terminated under this subtitle shall furnish to the trustee such information as the corporation or the plan administrator has and, to the extent practicable, can obtain regarding—

(1) the amount of benefits payable with respect to each participant under a plan to be terminated,

(2) the amount of basic benefits guaranteed under section 4022 or 4022A which are payable with respect to each participant in the plan,

(3) the present value, as of the time of termination, of the aggregate amount of basic benefits payable under section 4022 or 4022A (determined without regard to section 4022B),

(4) the fair market value of the assets of the plan at the time of termination,

(5) the computations under section 4044, and all actuarial assumptions under which the items described in paragraphs (1) through (4) were computed, and

(6) any other information with respect to the plan the trustee may require in order to terminate the plan.

Amendment

P.L. 96-364, § 403(e):

Amended Sec. 4046 by inserting "or 4022A" after "4022" in paragraphs (2) and (3) and by inserting "basic" after "benefits" in paragraphs (2) and (3) and by inserting "4022B" in place of "4022(b)(5)" in paragraph (3), effective September 26, 1980.

[¶ 15,500]
RESTORATION OF PLANS

Act Sec. 4047. Whenever the corporation determines that a plan which is to be terminated under section 4041 or 4042, or which is in the process of being terminated under section 4041 or 4042, should not be terminated under section 4041 or 4042 as a result of such circumstances as the corporation determines to be relevant, the corporation is authorized to cease any activities undertaken to terminate the plan, and to take whatever action is necessary and within its power to restore the plan to its status prior to the determination that the plan was to be terminated under section 4041 or 4042. In the case of a plan which has been terminated under section 4041 or 4042 the corporation is authorized in any such case in which the corporation determines such action to be appropriate and consistent with its duties under this title, to take such action as may be necessary to restore the plan to its pretermination status, including, but not limited to, the transfer to the employer or a plan administrator of control of part or all of the remaining assets and liabilities of the plan.

Amendments

P.L. 101-239, § 7893(g)(1):

Amended ERISA Sec. 4047 in the first sentence by striking "under this subtitle" effective April 7, 1986.

P.L. 99-272:

Act Sec. 11016(a)(3) amended ERISA Sec. 4047 by inserting "under section 4041 or 4042" after "terminated" each place it appears in the first sentence and by striking out "section 4042" and inserting "section 4041 or 4042" in the second sentence.

These changes take effect on April 7, 1986.

Regulations

The following regulations were adopted by the Pension Benefit Guaranty Corporation on July 1, 1996 (61 FR 34002). Prior to July 1, 1996, PBGC regulations were under Chapter XXVI of Title 29 of the Code of Federal Regulations. Effective July 1, 1996, PBGC regulations were moved to Chapter XL, and were renumbered and reorganized. Reg. §4047.4 was amended on March 11, 2014 (79 FR 13547).

[¶ 15,501]

§4047.1 **Purpose and scope.** Section 4047 of ERISA gives the PBGC broad authority to take any necessary actions in furtherance of a plan restoration order issued pursuant to section 4047. This part (along with Treasury regulation 26 CFR 1.412(c)(1)-3) describes certain legal obligations that arise incidental to a plan restoration under section 4047. This part also establishes procedures with respect to these obligations that are intended to facilitate the orderly transition of a restored plan from terminated (or terminating) status to ongoing status, and to help ensure that the restored plan will continue to be ongoing consistent with the best interests of the plan's participants and beneficiaries and the single-employer insurance program. This part applies to terminated and terminating single-employer plans (except for plans terminated and terminating under ERISA section 4041(b)) with respect to which the PBGC has issued or is issuing a plan restoration order pursuant to ERISA section 4047.

[¶ 15,501A]

§4047.2 **Definitions.** The following terms are defined in §4001.2 of this chapter: *controlled group, ERISA, IRS, PBGC, plan, plan administrator, plan year,* and *single-employer plan.*

[¶ 15,501B]

§4047.3 **Funding of restored plan.** (a) *General.* Whenever the PBGC issues or has issued a plan restoration order under ERISA section 4047, it shall issue to the plan sponsor a restoration payment schedule order in accordance with the rules of this section. PBGC, through its Executive Director, shall also issue a certification to its Board of Directors and the IRS, as described in paragraph (c) of this section. If more than one plan is or has been restored, the PBGC shall issue a separate restoration payment schedule order and separate certification with respect to each restored plan.

(b) *Restoration payment schedule order.* A restoration payment schedule order shall set forth a schedule of payments sufficient to amortize the initial restoration amortization base described in paragraph (b) of 26 CFR 1.412(c)(1)-3 over a period extending no more than 30 years after the initial post-restoration valuation date, as defined in paragraph (a)(1) of 26 CFR 1.412(c)(1)-3. The restoration payment schedule shall be consistent with the requirements of 26 CFR 1.412(c)(1)-3 and may require payments at intervals of less than one year, as determined by the PBGC. The PBGC may, in its discretion, amend the restoration payment schedule at any time, consistent with the requirements of 26 CFR 1.412(c)(1)-3.

(c) *Certification.* The Executive Director's certification to the Board of Directors and the IRS pursuant to paragraph (a) of this section shall state that the PBGC has reviewed the funding of the plan, the financial condition of the plan sponsor and its controlled group members, the payments required under the restoration payment schedule (taking into account the availability of deferrals as permitted under paragraph (c)(4) of 26 CFR 1.412(c)(1)-3) and any other factor that the PBGC deems relevant, and, based on that review, determines that it is in the best interests of the plan's participants and beneficiaries and the single-employer insurance program that the restored plan not be reterminated.

(d) *Periodic PBGC review.* As long as a restoration payment schedule order issued under this section is in effect, the PBGC shall review annually the funding status of the plan with respect to which the order

applies. As part of this review, the PBGC, through its Executive Director, shall issue a certification in the form described in paragraph (c) of this section. As a result of its funding review, PBGC may amend the restoration payment schedule, consistent with the requirements of paragraph (c)(2) of 26 CFR 1.412(c)(1)-3.

[¶ 15,501C]

§4047.4 **Payment of premiums.** (a) *General.* Upon restoration of a plan pursuant to ERISA section 4047, the obligation to pay PBGC premiums pursuant to ERISA section 4007 is reinstated as of the date on which the plan was trusteed under section 4042 of ERISA. Except as otherwise specifically provided in paragraphs (b) and (c) of this section, the amount of the outstanding premiums owed shall be computed and paid by the plan administrator in accordance with part 4006 of this chapter (Premium Rates) and the forms and instructions issued pursuant thereto, as in effect for the plan years for which premiums are owed.

(b) *Notification of premiums owed.* Whenever the PBGC issues or has issued a plan restoration order, it shall send a written notice to the plan administrator of the restored plan advising the plan administrator of the plan year(s) for which premiums are owed. PBGC will include with the notice the necessary premium payment forms and instructions. The notice shall prescribe the payment due dates for the outstanding premiums.

(c) *Methods for determining variable rate portion of the premium.* In general, the variable rate portion of the outstanding premiums shall be determined in accordance with the premium regulation and forms, as provided in paragraph (a) of this section, except that for any plan year following a plan year for which Form 5500, Schedule B was not filed because the plan was terminated, the alternative calculation method may not be used. [Amended 3/11/14 by 79 FR 13547.]

[¶ 15,501D]

§4047.5 **Repayment of PBGC payments of guaranteed benefits.** (a) *General.* Upon restoration of a plan pursuant to ERISA section 4047, amounts paid by the PBGC from its single-employer insurance fund (the fund established pursuant to ERISA section 4005(a)) to pay guaranteed benefits and related expenses under the plan while it was terminated are a debt of the restored plan. The terms and conditions for payment of this debt shall be determined by the PBGC.

(b) *Repayment terms.* The PBGC shall prescribe reasonable terms and conditions for payment of the debt described in paragraph (a) of this section, including the number, amount and commencement date of the payments. In establishing the terms, PBGC will consider the cash needs of the plan, the timing and amount of contributions owed to the plan, the liquidity of plan assets, the interests of the single-employer insurance program, and any other factors PBGC deems relevant. PBGC may, in its discretion, revise any of the payment terms and conditions, upon written notice to the plan administrator in accordance with paragraph (c) of this section.

(c) *Notification to plan administrator.* Whenever the PBGC issues or has issued a plan restoration order, it shall send a written notice to the plan administrator of the restored plan advising the plan administrator of the amount owed the PBGC pursuant to paragraph (a) of this section. The notice shall also include the terms and conditions for payment of this debt, as established under paragraph (b) of this section.

[¶ 15,510]
TERMINATION DATE

Act Sec. 4048. (a) For purposes of this title, the termination date of a single-employer plan is—

(1) in the case of a plan terminated in a standard termination in accordance with the provisions of section 4041(b), the termination date proposed in the notice provided under section 4041(a)(2),

(2) in the case of a plan terminated in a distress termination in accordance with the provisions of section 4041(c), the date established by the plan administrator and agreed to by the corporation,

(3) in the case of a plan terminated in accordance with the provisions of section 4042, the date established by the corporation and agreed to by the plan administrator, or

(4) In the case of a plan terminated under section 4041(c) or 4042 in any case in which no agreement is reached between the plan administrator and the corporation (or the trustee), the date established by the court.

Act Sec. 4048. (b) For purposes of this title, the date of termination of a multiemployer plan is—

(1) in the case of a plan terminated in accordance with the provisions of section 4041A, the date determined under subsection (b) of that section; or

(2) in the case of a plan terminated in accordance with the provisions of section 4042, the date agreed to between the plan administrator and the corporation (or the trustee appointed under section 4042(b)(2), if any), or, if no agreement is reached, the date established by the court.

Amendments

P.L. 99-272:

Act Sec. 11016(a)(4) amended ERISA Sec. 4048(a) by redesignating paragraphs (1) through (3) as paragraphs (2) through (4) and adding new paragraph (1) to read as above; by striking out "date of termination" and inserting "termination date;" by inserting "in a distress termination" after "terminated" and by striking out "section 4041" and inserting "section 4041(c)" in paragraph (2); and by striking out "in accor-

dance with the provisions of either section" and inserting "under section 4041(c) or 4042" in paragraph (4).

These amendments take effect on April 7, 1986.

P.L. 96-364, §402(a)(8):

Amended Sec. 4048, effective September 26, 1980 by: inserting "(a)" before "For"; inserting "of a single-employer plan" after "date of termination"; and added new subsection (b).

[¶ 15,520]

DISTRIBUTION TO PARTICIPANTS AND BENEFICIARIES OF LIABILITY PAYMENTS TO SECTION 4049 TRUST

Act Sec. 4049. [Repealed]

Amendments

P.L. 100-203, §9312(a):

Repealed ERISA Sec. 4049 effective for (A) plan termination under section 4041(c) of ERISA for which notices of intent to terminate are provided under section 4041(a)(2) of ERISA after December 17, 1987, and (B) plan terminations for which proceedings are instituted by the Pension Benefit Guaranty Corporation under section 4042 of ERISA after December 17, 1987.

Prior to repeal, ERISA Sec. 4049 read as follows:

(a) Trust Requirements.—The requirements of this section apply to a trust established by the corporation in connection with a terminated plan pursuant to section 4041(c)(3)(B)(ii) or (iii) or 4042(i), the trust shall be used exclusively for—

(1) receiving liability payments under section 4062(c) from the persons who were (as of the termination date) contributing sponsors of the terminated plan and members of their controlled groups,

(2) making distributions as provided in this section to the persons who were (as of the termination date) participants and beneficiaries under the terminated plan, and

(3) defraying the reasonable administrative expenses incurred in carrying out responsibilities under this section.

The trust shall be maintained for such period of time as is necessary to receive all liability payments required to be made to the trust under section 4062(c) with respect to the terminated plan and to make all distributions required to be made to participants and beneficiaries under this section with respect to the terminated plan.

Reasonable administrative expenses incurred in carrying out the responsibilities under this section prior to the receipt of any liability payments under section 4062(c) shall be paid by the persons described in section 4062(a) in accordance with procedures which shall be prescribed by the corporation by regulation, and the amount of the liability determined under section 4062(c) shall be reduced by the amount of such expenses so paid.

(b) Designation of Fiduciary by the Corporation.—

(1) Purposes for Designation of Fiduciary.—

(A) Collection of Liability.—The corporation shall designate a fiduciary (within the meaning of section 3(21)) to serve as trustee of the trust for purposes of conducting negotiations and assessing and collecting liability pursuant to section 4062(c).

(B) Administration of Trust.—

(i) Corporation's Functions.—Except as provided in clause (ii), the corporation shall serve as trustee of the trust for purposes of administering the trust, including making distributions from the trust to participants and beneficiaries.

(ii) Designation of Fiduciary If Cost-Effective.—If the corporation determines that it would be cost-effective to do so, it may designate a fiduciary (within the meaning of section 3(21)), including the fiduciary designated under subparagraph (A), to perform the functions described in clause (i).

(2) Fiduciary Requirements.—A fiduciary designated under paragraph (1) shall be—

(A) independent of each contributing sponsor of the plan and the members of such sponsor's controlled group, and

(B) subject to the requirements of part 4 of subtitle B of title I (other than section 406(a)) as if such trust were a plan subject to such part.

(c) Distribution From Trust.—

(1) In General.—Not later than 30 days after the end of each liability payment year (described in section 4062(e)(3)) with respect to a terminated single-employer plan, the corporation, or its designee under subsection (b), shall distribute from the trust maintained pursuant to subsection (a) to each person who was (as of the termination date) a participant or beneficiary under the plan—

(A) in any case not described in subparagraph (B), an amount equal to the outstanding amount of benefit commitments to such person under the plan (including interest calculated from the termination date), to the extent not previously paid under this paragraph, or

(B) in any case in which the balance in the trust at the end of such year which is in cash or may be prudently converted to cash (after taking into account liability payments received under subsection (a)(1) and administrative expenses paid under subsection (a)(3)) is less than the total of all amounts described in subparagraph (A) in connection with all persons who were (as of the termination date) participants and beneficiaries under the terminated plan, the product derived by multiplying—

(i) the amount described in subparagraph (A) in connection with each such person, by

(ii) a fraction—

(I) the numerator of which is such balance in the trust, and

(II) the denominator of which is equal to the total of all amounts described in subparagraph (A) in connection with all persons who were (as of the termination date) participants and beneficiaries under the terminated plan.

(2) Carry-Over of Minimal Payment Amounts.—The corporation, or its designee under subsection (b), may withhold a payment to any person under this subsection in connection with any liability payment year (other than the last liability payment year with respect to which payments under paragraph (1) are payable) if such payment does not exceed $100. In any case in which such a payment is so withheld, the payment to such person in connection with the next following liability payment year shall be increased by the amount of such withheld payment.

Act Sec. 4049. (d) Regulations.—The corporation may issue such regulations as it considers necessary to carry out the purposes of this section.

P.L. 100-203, §9312(d)(2):

Amended ERISA Sec. 4049(a), as in effect prior to its repeal, by adding a new sentence at the end of the subsection, to read as above.

P.L. 99-514, §1879(u)(2):

Amended Sec. 4049(a) by inserting "or 4042(i)" after "section 4041(c)(3)(B)(ii) or (iii)", effective on date of enactment.

P.L. 99-272:

Act Sec. 11012(a) added new ERISA Sec. 4049 to read as above, effective with respect to terminations pursuant to notices of intent filed with the PBGC on or after January 1, 1986 or proceedings begun on or after that date.

[¶ 15,530]

MISSING PARTICIPANTS

Act Sec. 4050.(a) General rule.—

(1) Payment to the Corporation. A plan administrator satisfies section 4041(b)(3)(A) in the case of a missing participant only if the plan administrator—

(A) transfers the participant's designated benefit to the corporation or purchases an irrevocable commitment from an insurer in accordance with clause (i) of section 4041(b)(3)(A), and

(B) provides the corporation such information and certifications with respect to such designated benefits or irrevocable commitments as the corporation shall specify.

(2) Treatment Of Transferred Assets. A transfer to the corporation under this section shall be treated as a transfer of assets from a terminated plan to the corporation as trustee, and shall be held with assets of terminated plans for which the corporation is trustee under section 4042, subject to the rules set forth in that section.

(3) PAYMENT BY THE CORPORATION. After a missing participant whose designated benefit was transferred to the corporation is located—

(A) in any case in which the plan could have distributed the benefit of the missing participant in a single sum without participant or spousal consent under section 205(g), the corporation shall pay the participant or beneficiary a single sum benefit equal to the designated benefit paid the corporation plus interest as specified by the corporation, and

(B) in any other case, the corporation shall pay a benefit based on the designated benefit and the assumptions prescribed by the corporation at the time that the corporation received the designated benefit.

The corporation shall make payments under subparagraph (B) available in the same forms and at the same times as a guaranteed benefit under section 4022 would be available to be paid, except that the corporation may make a benefit available in the form of a single sum if the plan provided a single sum benefit (other than a single sum described in subsection (b)(2)(A)).

(b) DEFINITIONS. For purposes of this section—

(1) MISSING PARTICIPANT. The term "missing participant" means a participant or beneficiary under a terminating plan whom the plan administrator cannot locate after a diligent search.

(2) DESIGNATED BENEFIT. The term "designated benefit" means the single sum benefit the participant would receive—

(A) under the plan's assumptions, in the case of a distribution that can be made without participant or spousal consent under section 205(g);

(B) under the assumptions of the corporation in effect on the date that the designated benefit is transferred to the corporation, in the case of a plan that does not pay any single sums other than those described in subparagraph (A); or

(C) under the assumptions of the corporation or of the plan, whichever provides the higher single sum, in the case of a plan that pays a single sum other than those described in subparagraph (A).

(c) MULTIEMPLOYER PLANS. —The corporation shall prescribe rules similar to the rules in subsection (a) for multiemployer plans covered by this title that terminate under section 4041A.

(d) PLANS NOT OTHERWISE SUBJECT TO TITLE.—

(1) TRANSFER TO CORPORATION. —The plan administrator of a plan described in paragraph (4) may elect to transfer a missing participant's benefits to the corporation upon termination of the plan.

(2) INFORMATION TO THE CORPORATION. —To the extent provided in regulations, the plan administrator of a plan described in paragraph (4), shall, upon termination of the plan, provide the corporation information with respect to benefits of a missing participant if the plan transfers such benefits—

(A) to the corporation, or

(B) to an entity other than the corporation or a plan described in paragraph (4)(B)(ii).

(3) PAYMENT BY THE CORPORATION. —If benefits of a missing participant were transferred to the corporation under paragraph (1), the corporation shall, upon location of the participant or beneficiary, pay to the participant or beneficiary the amount transferred (or the appropriate survivor benefit) either—

(A) in a single sum (plus interest), or

(B) in such other form as is specified in regulations of the corporation.

(4) PLANS DESCRIBED. —A plan is described in this paragraph if—

(A) the plan is a pension plan (within the meaning of section 3(2))

(i) to which the provisions of this section do not apply (without regard to the subsection),

(ii) which is not a plan described in paragraph (2), (3), (4), (6), (7), (8), (9), (10), or (11) of section 4021(b), and

(iii) which, was a plan described in section 401(a) of the Internal Revenue Code of 1986 which includes a trust exempt from tax under section 501(a) of such Code, and

(B) at the time the assets are to be distributed upon termination, the plan—

(i) has missing participants, and

(ii) has not provided for the transfer of assets to pay the benefits of all missing participants to another pension plan (within the meaning of section 3(2)).

(5) CERTAIN PROVISIONS NOT TO APPLY. —Subsections (a)(1) and (a)(3) shall not apply to a plan described in paragraph (4).

(e) REGULATORY AUTHORITY. —The corporation shall prescribe such regulations as are necessary to carry out the purposes of this section, including rules relating to what will be considered a diligent search, the amount payable to the corporation, and the amount to be paid by the corporation.

Amendment

P.L. 110-458, §104(e)(1):

Amended ERISA Sec. 4050(d)(4)(A) by striking "and" at the end of clause (i).

The above amendment applies to distributions made after final regulations implementing subsections (c) and (d) of section 4050 of the Employee Retirement Income Security Act of 1974 are prescribed.

P.L. 110-458, §104(e)(2):

Amended ERISA Sec. 4050(d)(4)(A) by striking clause (ii) and inserting the following new clauses:

"(ii) which is not a plan described in paragraph (2), (3), (4), (6), (7), (8), (9), (10), or (11) of section 4021(b), and

"(iii) which, was a plan described in section 401(a) of the Internal Revenue Code of 1986 which includes a trust exempt from tax under section 501(a) of such Code, and".

The above amendment applies to distributions made after final regulations implementing subsections (c) and (d) of section 4050 of the Employee Retirement Income Security Act of 1974 are prescribed.

Prior to amendment, ERISA 4050(d)(4)(A)(ii) read as follows:

ERISA 4050(d)(4)(A)(ii)

which is not a plan described in paragraphs (2) through (11) of section 4021(b), and

P.L. 109-280, Sec. 410(a):

Amended ERISA Sec. 4050 by redesignating subsection (c) as subsection (e) and by inserting after subsection (b) new subsections (c)—(e) to read as above.

The above amendment shall apply to distributions made after final regulations implementing subsections (c) and (d) of ERISA Sec. 4050 (as added by subsection (a)), respectively, are prescribed.

P.L. 103-465, §776(a):

Act Sec. 776(a) amended subtitle C of title IV of ERISA by adding a new section 4050 to read as above.

The above amendment is effective with respect to distributions that occur in plan years commencing after final regulations implementing the provision are prescribed by the Pension Benefit Guaranty Corporation.

Regulations

The following regulations were adopted by the Pension Benefit Guaranty Corporation on July 1, 1996 (61 FR 34002). Prior to July 1, 1996, PBGC regulations were under Chapter XXVI of Title 29 of the Code of Federal Regulations. Effective July 1, 1996, PBGC regulations were moved to Chapter XL, and were renumbered and reorganized. Reg. §4051 was amended November 7, 1997 (62 FR 60424), effective January 1, 1998. Reg. §4050.2 was amended May 28, 1998 (63 FR 29353), effective May 29, 1998. Reg. §§4050.2 and 4050.5 were amended July 15, 1998 (63 FR 38305), effective August 17, 1998. Appendix A to Part 4050 was amended July 15, 1998 (63 FR 38305), effective August 17, 1998. Reg. §4050.2 was amended March 17, 2000 (65 FR 14751), effective May 1, 2000 and December 14, 2006 (71 FR 75117), effective February 27, 2007. Reg. §4050.6 was amended October 28, 2003 (68

FR 61344). Part 4050 was revised December 22, 2017 (82 FR 60800), effective January 22, 2018 and generally applicable to plans that terminated on or after January 1, 2018.

>>>→ *Caution: Reg. Secs. 4050.1—4050.12 as in effect before January 22, 2018, apply to the PBGC's payment of missing participant benefits attributable to prior plan terminations (i.e., terminations prior to calendar year 2018).*

[¶ 15,530A]

§4050.1 **Purpose and scope.** This part prescribes rules for distributing benefits under a terminating single-employer plan for any individual whom the plan administrator has not located when distributing

>>>→ *Caution: Reg. Secs. 4050.1—4050.12 as in effect before January 22, 2018, apply to the PBGC's payment of missing participant benefits attributable to prior plan terminations (i.e., terminations prior to calendar year 2018).*

[¶ 15,530B]

§4050.2 **Definitions.** The following terms are defined in §4001.2 of this chapter: *annuity, Code, ERISA, insurer, irrevocable commitment, mandatory employee contributions, normal retirement age, PBGC, person, plan, plan administrator, plan year,* and *title IV benefit.*

In addition, for purposes of this part:

Deemed distribution date means—

(1) The last day of the period in which distribution may be made under part 4041 of this chapter; or

(2) If the plan administrator selects an earlier date that is no earlier than the date when all benefit distributions have been made under the plan except for distributions to missing participants whose designated benefits are paid to the PBGC, such earlier date.

Designated benefit means the amount payable to the PBGC for a missing participant pursuant to §4050.5.

Designated benefit interest rate means the rate of interest applicable to underpayments of guaranteed benefits by the PBGC under §4022.81(c) of this chapter.

Guaranteed benefit form means, with respect to a benefit, the form in which the PBGC would pay a guaranteed benefit to a participant or beneficiary in the PBGC's program for trusteed plans under subparts A and B of part 4022 of this chapter (treating the deemed distribution date as the termination date for this purpose).

Missing participant means a participant or beneficiary entitled to a distribution under a terminating plan whom the plan administrator has not located as of the date when the plan administrator pays the individual's designated benefit to the PBGC (or distributes the individual's benefit by purchasing an irrevocable commitment from an insurer). In the absence of proof of death, individuals not located are presumed living.

Missing participant annuity assumptions means the interest rate assumptions and actuarial methods for valuing benefits under Sec. 4044.52 of this chapter, applied—

(1) As if the deemed distribution date were the termination date;

(2) Using mortality rates that are a fixed blend of 50 percent of the healthy male mortality rates in Sec. 4044.53(c)(1) of this chapter and 50

percent of the healthy female mortality rates in Sec. 4044.53(c)(2) of this chapter;

[Amended 12/14/2006 (71 FR 75117).]

(3) Without using the expected retirement age assumptions in Secs. 4044.55 through 4044.57 of this chapter;

(4) Without making the adjustment for expenses provided for in Sec. 4044.52(d) of this chapter; and

[Amended 12/14/2006 (71 FR 75117).]

(5) By adding $300, as an adjustment (loading) for expenses, for each missing participant whose designated benefit without such adjustment would be greater than $5,000. [Amended 3/17/00 by 65 FR 14751.]

Missing participant forms and instructions means PBGC Forms 501 and 602, Schedule MP thereto, and related forms, and their instructions.

Missing participant lump sum assumptions means the interest rate and mortality assumptions and actuarial methods for determining the lump sum value of a benefit under Sec. 4022.7(d) of this chapter applied—

(1) As if the deemed distribution date were the termination date; and

(2) Without using the expected retirement age assumptions in Secs. 4044.55 through 4044.57 of this chapter. [Amended 3/17/00 by 65 FR 14751.]

Pay status means, with respect to a benefit under a plan, that the plan administrator has made or (except for administrative delay or a waiting period) would have made one or more benefit payments.

Post-distribution certification means the post-distribution certification required by §4041.29 or §4041.50 of this chapter.

Unloaded designated benefit means the designated benefit reduced by $300; except that the reduction does not apply in the case of a designated benefit determined using the missing participant annuity assumptions without adding the $300 load described in paragraph (5) of the definition of "missing participant annuity assumptions." [Amended 11/7/97 by 62 FR 60424.]

benefits under §4041.28 of this chapter. This part applies to a plan if the plan's deemed distribution date (or the date of a payment made in accordance with §4050.12) is in a plan year beginning on or after January 1, 1996. [Amended 11/7/97 by 62 FR 60424.]

>>>→ *Caution: Reg. Secs. 4050.1—4050.12 as in effect before January 22, 2018, apply to the PBGC's payment of missing participant benefits attributable to prior plan terminations (i.e., terminations prior to calendar year 2018).*

[¶ 15,530C]

§4050.3 **Method of distribution for missing participants.** The plan administrator of a terminating plan must distribute benefits for each missing participant by—

(a) Purchasing from an insurer an irrevocable commitment that satisfies the requirements of §4041.28(c) or §4041.50 of this chapter (whichever is applicable); or

(b) Paying the PBGC a designated benefit in accordance with §§4050.4 through 4050.6 (subject to the special rules in §4050.12). [Amended 11/7/97 by 62 FR 60424.]

>>>→ *Caution: Reg. Secs. 4050.1—4050.12 as in effect before January 22, 2018, apply to the PBGC's payment of missing participant benefits attributable to prior plan terminations (i.e., terminations prior to calendar year 2018).*

[¶ 15,530D]

§4050.4 **Diligent search.** (a) *Search required.* A diligent search must be made for each missing participant before information about the missing participant or payment is submitted to the PBGC pursuant to §4050.6.

(b) *Diligence.* A search is a diligent search only if the search—

(1) Begins not more than 6 months before notices of intent to terminate are issued and is carried on in such a manner that if the

individual is found, distribution to the individual can reasonably be expected to be made on or before the deemed distribution date;

(2) Includes inquiry of any plan beneficiaries (including alternate payees) of the missing participant whose names and addresses are known to the plan administrator; and

(3) Includes use of a commercial locator service to search for the missing participant (without charge to the missing participant or reduction of the missing participant's plan benefit). [Amended 11/7/97 by 62 FR 60424.]

>>>→ *Caution: Reg. Secs. 4050.1—4050.12 as in effect before January 22, 2018, apply to the PBGC's payment of missing participant benefits attributable to prior plan terminations (i.e., terminations prior to calendar year 2018).*

[¶ 15,530E]

§ 4050.5 **Designated benefit.** (a) *Amount of designated benefit.* The amount of the designated benefit is the amount determined under paragraph (a)(1), (a)(2), (a)(3), or (a)(4) of this section (whichever is applicable) or, if less, the maximum amount that could be provided under the plan to the missing participant in the form of a single sum in accordance with section 415 of the Code.

(1) *Mandatory lump sum.* The designated benefit of a missing participant required under a plan to receive a mandatory lump sum as of the deemed distribution date is the lump sum payment that the plan administrator would have distributed to the missing participant as of the deemed distribution date.

(2) *De minimis lump sum.* The designated benefit of a missing participant not described in paragraph (a)(1) of this section whose benefit is not in pay status as of the deemed distribution date and whose benefit has a de minimis actuarial present value ($5,000 or less) as of the deemed distribution date under the missing participant lump sum assumptions is such value.

(3) *No lump sum.* The designated benefit of a missing participant not described in paragraph (a)(1) or (a)(2) of this section who, as of the deemed distribution date, cannot elect an immediate lump sum under the plan is the actuarial present value of the missing participant's benefit as of the deemed distribution date under the missing participant annuity assumptions.

(4) *Elective lump sum.* The designated benefit of a missing participant not described in paragraph (a)(1), (a)(2), or (a)(3) of this section is the greater of the amounts determined under the methodologies of paragraph (a)(1) or (a)(3) of this section.

(b) *Assumptions.* When the plan administrator uses the missing participant annuity assumptions or the missing participant lump sum assumptions for purposes of determining the designated benefit under paragraph (a) of this section, the plan administrator must value the most valuable benefit, as determined under paragraph (b)(1) of this section, using the assumptions described in paragraph (b)(2) or (b)(3) of this section (whichever is applicable).

(1) *Most valuable benefit.* For a missing participant whose benefit is in pay status as of the deemed distribution date, the most valuable

benefit is the pay status benefit. For a missing participant whose benefit is not in pay status as of the deemed distribution date, the most valuable benefit is the benefit payable at the age on or after the deemed distribution date (beginning with the participant's earliest early retirement age and ending with the participant's normal retirement age) for which the present value as of the deemed distribution date is the greatest. The present value as of the deemed distribution date with respect to any age is determined by multiplying:

(i) The monthly (or other periodic) benefit payable under the plan; by

(ii) The present value (determined as of the deemed distribution date using the missing participant annuity assumptions) of a $1 monthly (or other periodic) annuity beginning at the applicable age.

(2) *Participant.* A missing participant who is a participant, and whose benefit is not in pay status as of the deemed distribution date, is assumed to be married to a spouse the same age, and the form of benefit that must be valued is the qualified joint and survivor annuity benefit that would be payable under the plan. If the participant's benefit is in pay status as of the deemed distribution date, the form and beneficiary of the participant's benefit are the form of benefit and beneficiary of the pay status benefit.

(3) *Beneficiary.* A missing participant who is a beneficiary, and whose benefit is not in pay status as of the deemed distribution date, is assumed not to be married, and the form of benefit that must be valued is the survivor benefit that would be payable under the plan. If the beneficiary's benefit is in pay status as of the deemed distribution date, the form and beneficiary of the beneficiary's benefit are the form of benefit and beneficiary of the pay status benefit.

(4) *Examples.* See Appendix A to this part for examples illustrating the provisions of this section.

(c) *Missed payments.* In determining the designated benefit, the plan administrator must include the value of any payments that were due before the deemed distribution date but that were not made.

(d) *Payment of designated benefits.* Payment of designated benefits must be made in accordance with § 4050.6 and will be deemed made on the deemed distribution date. [Amended 11/7/97 by 62 FR 60424.]

>>>→ *Caution: Reg. Secs. 4050.1—4050.12 as in effect before January 22, 2018, apply to the PBGC's payment of missing participant benefits attributable to prior plan terminations (i.e., terminations prior to calendar year 2018).*

[¶ 15,530F]

§ 4050.6 **Payment and required documentation.** (a) *Time of payment and filing.* The plan administrator must pay designated benefits, and file the information and certifications (of the plan administrator and the plan's enrolled actuary) specified in the missing participant forms and instructions, by the time the post-distribution certification is due. Except as otherwise provided in the missing participant forms and instructions, the plan administrator must submit the designated benefits, information, and certifications with the post-distribution certification.

(b) *Late charges.* (1) *Interest on late payments.* Except as provided in paragraph (b)(2) of this section, if the plan administrator does not pay a designated benefit by the time specified in paragraph (a) of this section, the plan administrator must pay interest as assessed by the PBGC for the period beginning on the deemed distribution date and ending on the date when the payment is received by the PBGC. Interest will be assessed at the rate provided for late premium payments in § 4007.7 of this chapter. Interest assessed under this paragraph will be deemed paid in full if payment of the amount assessed is received by the PBGC within 30 days after the date of a PBGC bill for such amount.

(2) *Assessment of interest and penalties.* The PBGC will assess interest for late payment of a designated benefit or a penalty for late

filing of information only to the extent paid or filed beyond the time provided in § 4041.29(b).

(c) *Supplemental information.* Within 30 days after the date of a written request from the PBGC, a plan administrator required to provide the information and certifications described in paragraph (a) of this section must file supplemental information, as requested, for the purpose of verifying designated benefits, determining benefits to be paid by the PBGC under this part, and substantiating diligent searches.

(d) *Filing with the PBGC.* (1) *Method and date of filing.* The PBGC applies the rules in subpart A of part 4000 of this chapter to determine permissible methods of filing with the PBGC under this part. The PBGC applies the rules in subpart C of part 4000 of this chapter to determine the date that a submission under this part was filed with the PBGC.

(2) *Where to file.* See Sec. 4000.4 of this chapter for information on where to file.

(3) *Computation of time.* The PBGC applies the rules in subpart D of part 4000 of this chapter to compute any time period for filing under this part. However, for purposes of determining the amount of an interest charge under Sec. 4050.6(b) or Sec. 4050.12(c)(2)(iii), the rule in Sec. 4000.43(a) of this chapter governing periods ending on weekends or Federal holidays does not apply.

[Amended 11/7/97 by 62 FR 60424 and 10/28/2003 by 68 FR 61344]

[¶ 15,530G]

§ 4050.7 **Benefits of missing participants—in general.** (a) *If annuity purchased.* If a plan administrator distributes a missing participant's benefit by purchasing an irrevocable commitment from an insurer, and the missing participant (or his or her beneficiary or estate) later contacts the PBGC, the PBGC will inform the person of the identity of the insurer, the relevant policy number, and (to the extent known) the amount or value of the benefit.

(b) *If designated benefit paid.* If the PBGC locates or is contacted by a missing participant (or his or her beneficiary or estate) for whom a plan administrator paid a designated benefit to the PBGC, the PBGC will pay benefits in accordance with § § 4050.8 through 4050.10 (subject to the limitations and special rules in § § 4050.11 and 4050.12).

(c) *Examples.* See Appendix B to this part for examples illustrating the provisions of § § 4050.8 through 4050.10. [Amended 11/7/97 by 62 FR 60424.]

[¶ 15,530H]

§ 4050.8 **Automatic lump sum.** This section applies to a missing participant whose designated benefit was determined under § 4050.5(a)(1) (mandatory lump sum) or § 4050.5(a)(2) (de minimis lump sum).

(a) *General rule.* (1) *Benefit paid.* The PBGC will pay a single sum benefit equal to the designated benefit plus interest at the designated benefit interest rate from the deemed distribution date to the date on which the PBGC pays the benefit.

(2) *Payee.* Payment will be made—

(i) To the missing participant, if located;

(ii) If the missing participant died before the deemed distribution date, and if the plan so provides, to the missing participant's beneficiary or estate; or

(iii) If the missing participant dies on or after the deemed distribution date, to the missing participant's estate.

(b) *De minimis annuity alternative.* If the guaranteed benefit form for a missing participant whose designated benefit was determined under § 4050.5(a)(2) (de minimis lump sum) (or the guaranteed benefit form for a beneficiary of such a missing participant) would provide for the election of an annuity, the missing participant (or the beneficiary) may elect to receive an annuity. If such an election is made—

(1) The PBGC will pay the benefit in the elected guaranteed benefit form, beginning on the annuity starting date elected by the missing participant (or the beneficiary), which may not be before the later of the date of the election or the earliest date on which the missing participant (or the beneficiary) could have begun receiving benefits under the plan; and

(2) The benefit paid will be actuarially equivalent to the designated benefit, i.e., each monthly (or other periodic) benefit payment will equal the designated benefit divided by the present value (determined as of the deemed distribution date under the missing participant lump sum assumptions) of a $1 monthly (or other periodic) annuity beginning on the annuity starting date. [Amended 11/7/97 by 62 FR 60424.]

[¶ 15,530I]

§ 4050.9 **Annuity or elective lump sum—living missing participant.** This section applies to a missing participant whose designated benefit was determined under § 4050.5(a)(3) (no lump sum) or § 4050.5(a)(4) (elective lump sum) and who is living on the date as of which the PBGC begins paying benefits.

(a) *Missing participant whose benefit was not in pay status as of the deemed distribution date.* The PBGC will pay the benefit of a missing participant whose benefit was not in pay status as of the deemed distribution date as follows.

(1) *Time and form of benefit.* The PBGC will pay the missing participant's benefit in the guaranteed benefit form, beginning on the annuity starting date elected by the missing participant (which may not be before the later of the date of the election or the earliest date on which the missing participant could have begun receiving benefits under the plan).

(2) *Amount of benefit.* The PBGC will pay a benefit that is actuarially equivalent to the unloaded designated benefit, i.e., each monthly (or other periodic) benefit payment will equal the unloaded designated benefit divided by the present value (determined as of the deemed distribution date under the missing participant annuity assumptions) of a $1 monthly (or other periodic) annuity beginning on the annuity starting date.

(b) *Missing participant whose benefit was in pay status as of the deemed distribution date.* The PBGC will pay the benefit of a missing participant whose benefit was in pay status as of the deemed distribution date as follows.

(1) *Time and form of benefit.* The PBGC will pay the benefit in the form that was in pay status, beginning when the missing participant is located.

(2) *Amount of benefit.* The PBGC will pay the monthly (or other periodic) amount of the pay status benefit, plus a lump sum equal to the payments the missing participant would have received under the plan, plus interest on the missed payments (at the plan rate up to the deemed distribution date and thereafter at the designated benefit interest rate) to the date as of which the PBGC pays the lump sum.

(c) *Payment of lump sum.* If a missing participant whose designated benefit was determined under § 4050.5(a)(4) (elective lump sum) so elects, the PBGC will pay his or her benefit in the form of a single sum. This election is not effective unless the missing participant's spouse consents (if such consent would be required under section 205 of ERISA). The single sum equals the designated benefit plus interest (at the designated benefit interest rate) from the deemed distribution date to the date as of which the PBGC pays the benefit. [Amended 11/7/97 by 62 FR 60424.]

[¶ 15,530J]

§ 4050.10 **Annuity or elective lump sum—beneficiary of deceased missing participant.** This section applies to a beneficiary of a deceased missing participant whose designated benefit was determined under § 4050.5(a)(3) (no lump sum) or § 4050.5(a)(4) (elective lump sum) and whose benefit is not payable under § 4050.9.

(a) *If deceased missing participant's benefit was not in pay status as of the deemed distribution date.* The PBGC will pay a benefit with respect to a deceased missing participant whose benefit was not in pay status as of the deemed distribution date as follows.

(1) *General rule.*

(i) *Beneficiary.* The PBGC will pay a benefit to the surviving spouse of a missing participant who was a participant (unless the surviving spouse has properly waived a benefit in accordance with section 205 of ERISA).

(ii) *Form and amount of benefit.* The PBGC will pay the survivor benefit in the form of a single life annuity. Each monthly (or other periodic) benefit payment will equal 50 percent of the quotient that results when the unloaded designated benefit is divided by the present value (determined as of the deemed distribution date under the missing participant annuity assumptions, and assuming that the missing participant survived to the deemed distribution date) of a $1 monthly (or other periodic) joint and 50 percent survivor annuity beginning on the annuity starting date, under which reduced payments (at the 50 percent level) are made only after the death of the missing participant during the life of the spouse (and not after the death of the spouse during the missing participant's life).

(iii) *Time of benefit.* The PBGC will pay the survivor benefit beginning at the time elected by the surviving spouse (which may not be before the later of the date of the election or the earliest date on which the surviving spouse could have begun receiving benefits under the plan).

(2) *If missing participant died before deemed distribution date.* Notwithstanding the provisions of paragraph (a)(1) of this section, if a beneficiary of a missing participant who died before the deemed distribution date establishes to the PBGC's satisfaction that he or she is the proper beneficiary or would have received benefits under the plan in a form, at a time, or in an amount different from the benefit paid under paragraph (a)(1)(ii) or (a)(1)(iii) of this section, the PBGC will make payments in accordance with the facts so established, but only in the guaranteed benefit form.

(3) *Elective lump sum.* Notwithstanding the provisions of paragraphs (a)(1) and (a)(2) of this section, if the beneficiary of a missing participant whose designated benefit was determined under §4050.5(a)(4) (elective lump sum) so elects, the PBGC will pay his or her benefit in the form of a single sum. The single sum will be equal to the actuarial present value (determined as of the deemed distribution date under the missing participant annuity assumptions) of the death benefit payable on the annuity starting date, plus interest (at the designated benefit interest rate) from the deemed distribution date to the date as of which the PBGC pays the benefit.

(b) *If deceased missing participant's benefit was in pay status as of the deemed distribution date.* The PBGC will pay a benefit with respect to a deceased missing participant whose benefit was in pay status as of the deemed distribution date as follows.

(1) *Beneficiary.* The PBGC will pay a benefit to the beneficiary (if any) of the benefit that was in pay status as of the deemed distribution date.

(2) *Form and amount of benefit.* The PBGC will pay a monthly (or other periodic) amount equal to the monthly (or other periodic) amount, if any, that the beneficiary would have received under the form of payment in effect, plus a lump sum payment equal to the payments the beneficiary would have received under the plan after the missing participant's death and before the date as of which the benefit is paid under paragraph (b)(4) of this section, plus interest on the missed payments (at the plan rate up to the deemed distribution date and thereafter at the designated benefit interest rate) to the date as of which the benefit is paid under paragraph (b)(4) of this section.

(3) *Lump sum payment to estate.* The PBGC will make a lump sum payment to the missing participant's estate equal to the payments that the missing participant would have received under the plan for the period before the missing participant's death, plus interest on the missed payments (at the plan rate up to the deemed distribution date and thereafter at the designated benefit interest rate) to the date when the lump sum is paid. Notwithstanding the preceding sentence, if a beneficiary of a missing participant other than the estate establishes to the PBGC's satisfaction that the beneficiary is entitled to the lump sum payment, the PBGC will pay the lump sum to such beneficiary.

(4) *Time of benefit.* The PBGC will pay the survivor benefit beginning when the beneficiary is located.

(5) *Spouse deceased.* If the PBGC locates the estate of the deceased missing participant's spouse under circumstances where a benefit would have been paid under this paragraph (b) if the spouse had been located while alive, the PBGC will pay to the spouse's estate a lump sum payment computed in the same manner as provided for in paragraph (b)(2) of this section based on the period from the missing participant's death to the death of the spouse. [Amended 11/7/97 by 62 FR 60424.]

[¶ 15,530K]

§4050.11 **Limitations.** (a) *Exclusive benefit.* The benefits provided for under this part will be the only benefits payable by the PBGC to missing participants or to beneficiaries based on the benefits of deceased missing participants.

(b) *Limitation on benefit value.* The total actuarial present value of all benefits paid with respect to a missing participant under §§4050.8 through 4050.10, determined as of the deemed distribution date, will not exceed the missing participant's designated benefit.

(c) *Guaranteed benefit.* If a missing participant or his or her beneficiary establishes to the PBGC's satisfaction that the benefit under §§4050.8 through 4050.10 (based on the designated benefit actually paid to the PBGC) is less than the minimum benefit in this paragraph (c), the PBGC will instead pay the minimum benefit. The minimum benefit is the lesser of:

(1) The benefit as determined under the PBGC's rules for paying guaranteed benefits in trusteed plans under subparts A and B of part 4022 of this chapter (treating the deemed distribution date as the termination date for this purpose); or

(2) The benefit based on the designated benefit that should have been paid under §4050.5.

(d) *Limitation on annuity starting date.* A missing participant (or his or her survivor) may not elect an annuity starting date after the later of—

(1) The required beginning date under section 401(a)(9) of the Code; or

(2) The date when the missing participant (or the survivor) is notified of his or her right to a benefit. [Amended 11/7/97 by 62 FR 60424.]

[¶ 15,530L]

§4050.12 **Special rules.** (a) *Missing participants located quickly.* Notwithstanding the provisions of §§4050.8 through 4050.10, if the PBGC or the plan administrator locates a missing participant within 30 days after the PBGC receives the missing participant's designated benefit, the PBGC may in its discretion return the missing participant's designated benefit to the plan administrator, and the plan administrator must make distribution to the individual in such manner as the PBGC will direct.

(b) *Qualified domestic relations orders.* Plan administrators must and the PBGC will take the provisions of qualified domestic relations orders (QDROs) under section 206(d)(3) of ERISA or section 414(p) of the Code into account in determining designated benefits and benefit payments by the PBGC, including treating an alternate payee under an applicable QDRO as a missing participant or as a beneficiary of a missing participant, as appropriate, in accordance with the terms of the QDRO. For purposes of calculating the amount of the designated benefit of an alternate payee, the plan administrator must use the assumptions for a missing participant who is a beneficiary under §4050.5(b).

(c) *Employee contributions.* (1) *Mandatory employee contributions.* Notwithstanding the provisions of §4050.5, if a missing participant made mandatory contributions (within the meaning of section 4044(a)(2) of ERISA), the missing participant's designated benefit may not be less than the sum of the missing participant's mandatory contributions and interest to the deemed distribution date at the plan's rate or the rate under section 204(c) of ERISA (whichever produces the greater amount).

(2) *Voluntary employee contributions.* (i) *Applicability.* This paragraph (c)(2) applies to any employee contributions that were not mandatory (within the meaning of section 4044(a)(2) of ERISA) to which a missing participant is entitled in connection with the termination of a defined benefit plan.

(ii) *Payment to PBGC.* A plan administrator, in accordance with the missing participant forms and instructions, must pay the employee contributions described in paragraph (c)(2)(i) of this section (together with any earnings thereon) to the PBGC, and must file Schedule MP with the PBGC, by the time the designated benefit is due under § 4050.6. Any such amount must be in addition to the designated benefit and must be separately identified.

(iii) *Payment by PBGC.* In addition to any other amounts paid by the PBGC under §§ 4050.8 through 4050.10, the PBGC will pay any amount paid to it under paragraph (c)(2)(ii) of this section, with interest at the designated benefit interest rate from the date of receipt by the PBGC to the date of payment by the PBGC, in the same manner as described in § 4050.8 (automatic lump sums), except that if the missing participant died before the deemed distribution date and there is no beneficiary, payment will be made to the missing participant's estate.

(d) *Residual assets.* The PBGC will determine, in a manner consistent with the purposes of this part and section 4050 of ERISA, how the provisions of this part apply to any distribution (to participants and beneficiaries who cannot be located) of residual assets remaining after the satisfaction of plan benefits (as defined in § 4041.2 of this chapter) in connection with the termination of a defined benefit plan. Unless the PBGC otherwise determines, the payment of residual assets for a participant or beneficiary who cannot be located, and the submission to the PBGC of the related Schedule MP (or amended Schedule MP), must be made no earlier than the date when the post-distribution certification is filed with the PBGC, and no later than the later of—

(1) The 30th day after the date on which all residual assets have been distributed to all participants and beneficiaries other than those who cannot be located and for whom payment of residual assets is made to the PBGC, and

(2) The date when the post-distribution certification is filed with the PBGC.

(e) *Sufficient distress terminations.* In the case of a plan undergoing a distress termination (under section 4041(c) of ERISA) that is sufficient for at least all guaranteed benefits and that distributes its assets in the manner described in section 4041(b)(3) of ERISA, the benefit assumed to be payable by the plan for purposes of determining the amount of the designated benefit under § 4050.5 is limited to the title IV benefit plus any benefit to which funds under section 4022(c) of ERISA have been allocated.

(f) *Similar rules for later payments.* If the PBGC determines that one or more persons should receive benefits (which may be in addition to benefits already provided) in order for a plan termination to be valid (e.g., upon audit of the termination), and one or more of such individuals cannot be located, the PBGC will determine, in a manner consistent with the purposes of this part and section 4050 of ERISA, how the provisions of this part apply to such benefits.

(g) *Discretionary extensions.* Any deadline under this part may be extended in accordance with the rules described in § 4041.30 of this chapter.

(h) *Payments beginning after required beginning date.* If the PBGC begins paying an annuity under § 4050.9(a) or 4050.10(a) to a participant or a participant's spouse after the required beginning date under section 401(a)(9)(C) of the Code, the PBGC will pay to the participant or the spouse (or their respective estates) or both, as appropriate, the lump sum equivalent of the past annuity payments the participant and spouse would have received if the PBGC had begun making payments on the required beginning date. The PBGC will also pay lump sum equivalents under this paragraph (g) if the PBGC locates the estate of the participant or spouse after both are deceased. (Nothing in this paragraph (g) will increase the total value of the benefits payable with respect to a missing participant.) [Amended 11/7/97 by 62 FR 60424.]

[¶ 15,530M]

§ 4050.12 **Appendix A to Part 4050—Examples of Designated Benefit Determinations for Missing Participants Under § 4050.5 in Plans with Deemed Distributions Dates On and After August 17, 1998.** The calculation of the designated benefit under § 4050.5 is illustrated by the following examples.

Example 1. Plan A provides that any participant whose benefit has a value at distribution of $3,500 or less will be paid a lump sum, and that no other lump sums will be paid. P, Q, and R are missing participants.

(1) As of the deemed distribution date, the value of P's benefit is $3,000 under plan A's assumptions. Under § 4050.5(a)(1), the plan administrator pays the PBGC $3,000 as P's designated benefit.

(2) As of the deemed distribution date, the value of Q's benefit is $5,200 under plan A's assumptions and $4,700 under the missing participant lump sum assumptions. Under § 4050.5(a)(2), the plan administrator pays the PBGC $4,700 as Q's designated benefit.

(3) As of the deemed distribution date, the value of R's benefit is $4,900 under plan A's assumptions, $3,600 under the missing participant lump sum assumptions, and $4,950 under the missing participant annuity assumptions. Under § 4050.5(a)(3), the plan administrator pays the PBGC $4,950 as R's designated benefit.

Example 2. Plan B provides for a normal retirement age of 65 and permits early commencement of benefits at any age between 60 and 65, with benefits reduced by 5 percent for each year before age 65 that the benefit begins. The qualified joint and 50 percent survivor annuity payable under the terms of the plan requires in all cases a 16 percent

reduction in the benefit otherwise payable. The plan does not provide for elective lump sums.

(1) M is a missing participant who separated from service under plan B with a deferred vested benefit. M is age 50 at the deemed distribution date, and has a normal retirement benefit of $1,000 per month payable at age 65 in the form of a single life annuity. M's benefit as of the deemed distribution date has a value greater than $5,000 using either plan assumptions or the missing participant lump sum assumptions. Accordingly, M's designated benefit is to be determined under § 4050.5(a)(3).

(2) For purposes of determining M's designated benefit, M is assumed to be married to a spouse who is also age 50 on the deemed distribution date. M's monthly benefit in the form of the qualified joint and survivor annuity under the plan varies from $840 at age 65 (the normal retirement age) ($1,000 × (1-.16)) to $630 at age 60 (the earliest retirement age) ($1,000 × (1-5 × (.05)) × (1-.16)).

(3) Under § 4050.5(a)(3), M's benefit is to be valued using the missing participant annuity assumptions. The select and ultimate interest rates on Plan B's deemed distribution date are 7.50 percent for the first 20 years and 5.75 percent thereafter. Using these rates and the blended mortality table described in paragraph (2) of the definition of "missing participant annuity assumptions" in § 4050.2, the plan administrator determines that the benefit commencing at age 60 is the most valuable benefit (i.e., the benefit at age 60 is more valuable than the benefit at ages 61, 62, 63, 64 or 65). The present value as of the deemed distribution date of each dollar of annual benefit (payable monthly as a joint and 50 percent survivor annuity) is $5.4307 if the benefit begins at

age 60. (Because a new spouse may succeed to the survivor benefit, the mortality of the spouse during the deferral period is ignored.) Thus, without adjustment (loading) for expenses, the value of the benefit

beginning at age 60 is $41,056 (12 × $630 × 5.4307). The designated benefit is equal to this value plus an expense adjustment of $300, or a total of $41,356. [Amended 11/7/97 by 62 FR 60424.]

[¶ 15,530N]

§ 4050.12 **Appendix B to Part 4050—Examples of Benefit Payments for Missing Participants Under §§ 4050.8 Through 4050.10.** The provisions of §§ 4050.8 through 4050.10 are illustrated by the following examples.

Example 1. Participant M from Plan B (see Example 2 in Appendix A of this part) is located. M's spouse is ten years younger than M. M elects to receive benefits in the form of a joint and 50 percent survivor annuity commencing at age 62.

(1) M's designated benefit was $41,356. The unloaded designated benefit was $41,056. As of Plan B's deemed distribution date (and using the missing participant annuity assumptions), the present value per dollar of annual benefit (payable monthly as a joint and 50 percent survivor annuity commencing at age 62 and reflecting the actual age of M's spouse) is $4.7405. Thus, the monthly benefit to M at age 62 is $722 ($41,056 / (4.7405 × 12)). M's spouse will receive $361 (50 percent of $722) per month for life after the death of M.

(2) If M had instead been found to have died on or after the deemed distribution date, and M's spouse wanted benefits to commence when M would have attained age 62, the same calculation would be performed to arrive at a monthly benefit of $361 to M's spouse.

Example 2. Participant P is a missing participant from Plan C, a plan that allows elective lump sums upon plan termination. Plan C's adminis-

trator pays a designated benefit of $10,000 to the PBGC on behalf of P, who was age 30 on the deemed distribution date.

(1) P's spouse, S, is located and has a death certificate showing that P died on or after the deemed distribution date with S as spouse. S is the same age as P, and would like survivor benefits to commence immediately, at age 55 (as permitted by the plan). S's benefit is the survivor's share of the joint and 50 percent survivor annuity which is actuarially equivalent, as of the deemed distribution date, to $9,700 (the unloaded designated benefit).

(2) The select and ultimate interest rates on Plan C's deemed distribution date were 7.50 percent for the first 20 years and 5.75 percent thereafter. Using these rates and the blended mortality table described in paragraph (2) of the definition of "missing participant annuity assumptions" in § 4050.2, the present value as of the deemed distribution date of each dollar of annual benefit (payable monthly as a joint and 50 percent survivor annuity) is $2.4048 if the benefit begins when S and P would have been age 55. Thus, the monthly benefit to S commencing at age 55 is $168 (50 percent of $9,700 / (2.4048 × 12)). Since P could have elected a lump sum upon plan termination, S may elect a lump sum. S's lump sum is the present value as of the deemed distribution date (using the missing participant annuity assumptions) of the monthly benefit of $168, accumulated with interest at the designated benefit interest rate to the date paid. [Amended 11/7/97 by 62 FR 60424.]

>>→ *Caution: Reg. Secs. 4050.101—4050.407 are effective January 22, 2018 and generally applicable to plans terminating on or after January 1, 2018.*

Subpart A—Single-Employer Plans Covered by Title IV

[¶ 15,530P]

§ 4050.101 **Purpose and scope.** (a) *In general.* This subpart describes PBGC's missing participants program for single-employer defined benefit retirement plans covered by title IV of ERISA. The missing participants program is a program to hold retirement benefits for missing participants and beneficiaries in terminated retirement plans and to help them find and receive the benefits being held for them. For a plan to which this subpart applies, this subpart describes what the plan must do upon plan termination if it has missing participants or beneficiaries who are entitled to distributions. This subpart applies to a plan only if it is a single-employer defined benefit plan that—

(1) Is described in section 4021(a) of ERISA and not in any paragraph of section 4021(b) of ERISA and

(2) Terminates in a standard termination or in a distress termination described in section 4041(c)(3)(B)(i) or (ii) of ERISA ("sufficient distress termination").

(b) *Plans that terminate but do not close out.* This subpart does not apply to a plan that terminates but does not close out, such as a plan that terminates in a distress termination described in section 4041(c)(3)(B)(iii) of ERISA ("insufficient distress termination").

(c) *Individual account plans.* This subpart does not apply to an individual account plan under section 3(34) of ERISA, even if it is described in the same plan document as a plan to which this subpart applies. This subpart also does not apply to a plan to the extent that it is treated as an individual account plan under section 3(35)(B) of ERISA. For example, this subpart does not apply to employee contributions (or interest or earnings thereon) held as an individual account. (Subpart B deals with individual account plans.)

[¶ 15,530Q]

§ 4050.102 **Definitions.** The following terms are defined in § 4001.2 of this chapter: Annuity, Code, ERISA, insurer, irrevocable commitment, PBGC, person, and plan administrator. In addition, for purposes of this subpart:

Accrual cessation date for a participant under a subpart A plan means the date the participant stopped accruing benefits under the terms of the plan.

Accumulated single sum means, with respect to a missing distributee, the distributee's benefit transfer amount accumulated at the missing participants interest rate from the benefit determination date to the date when PBGC makes or commences payment to or with respect to the distributee.

Benefit determination date with respect to a subpart A plan means the single date selected by the plan administrator for valuing benefits under § 4050.103(d); this date must be during the period beginning on the first day a distribution is made pursuant to closeout of the plan to a distributee who is not a missing distributee and ending on the last day such a distribution is made.

Benefit transfer amount for a missing distributee of a subpart A plan means the amount determined by the plan administrator under § 4050.103(d) in the close-out of the plan.

Close-out or *close out* with respect to a subpart A plan means the process of the final distribution or transfer of assets pursuant to the termination of the plan.

De minimis means, with respect to the value of a benefit (or other amount), that the value does not exceed the amount specified under section 203(e)(1) of ERISA and section 411(a)(11)(A) of the Code (without regard to plan provisions).

Distributee means, with respect to a subpart A plan, a participant or beneficiary entitled to a distribution under the plan pursuant to the close-out of the plan.

Missing, with respect to a distributee under a subpart A plan, means that any one or more of the following three conditions exists upon close-out of the plan.

(1) The plan administrator does not know with reasonable certainty the location of the distributee.

(2) Under the terms of the plan, the distributee's benefit is to be paid in a lump sum without the distributee's consent, and the distributee has not responded to a notice about the distribution of the lump sum.

(3) Under the terms of the plan and any election made by the distributee, the distributee's benefit is to be paid in a lump sum, but the distributee does not accept the lump sum. For this purpose, a lump sum paid by check is not accepted if the check remains uncashed after—

(i) A "cash-by" date prescribed (on the check or in an accompanying notice) that is at least 45 days after the issuance of the check, or

(ii) If no such "cash-by" date is so prescribed, the check's stale date.

Missing participants forms and instructions means the forms and instructions provided by PBGC for use in connection with the missing participants program.

Missing participants interest rate means, for each month, the applicable federal mid-term rate (as determined by the Secretary of the Treasury pursuant to section 1274(d)(1)(C)(ii) of the Code) for that month, compounded monthly.

Normal retirement date for a participant under a subpart A plan means the normal retirement date of the participant under the terms of the plan.

Pay-status or *pay status* means one of the following (according to context):

(1) With respect to a benefit, that payment of the benefit has actually started before the benefit determination date; or

(2) With respect to a distributee, that payment of the distributee's benefit has actually started before the benefit determination date.

PBGC missing participants assumptions means the actuarial assumptions prescribed in §§ 4044.51 through 4044.57 of this chapter with the following modifications:

(1) The present value is determined as of the benefit determination date instead of the plan termination date.

(2) The mortality assumption is a fixed blend of 50 percent of the healthy male mortality rates in § 4044.53(c)(1) of this chapter and 50 percent of the healthy female mortality rates in § 4044.53(c)(2) of this chapter.

(3) No adjustment is made for loading expenses under § 4044.52(d) of this chapter.

(4) The interest assumption used is the assumption applicable to valuations occurring in January of the calendar year in which the benefit determination date occurs.

(5) The assumed payment form of a benefit not in pay status is a straight life annuity.

(6) Pre-retirement death benefits are disregarded.

(7) Notwithstanding the expected retirement age (XRA) assumptions in §§ 4044.55 through 4044.57 of this chapter,—

(i) In the case of a participant who is not in pay status and whose normal retirement date is on or after the benefit determination date, benefits are assumed to commence at the XRA, determined using the high retirement rate category under Table II–C of Appendix D to part 4044 of this chapter;

(ii) In the case of a participant who is not in pay status and whose normal retirement date is before the benefit determination date, benefits are assumed to commence on the participant's normal retirement date (or accrual cessation date if later);

(iii) In the case of a participant who is in pay status, benefits are assumed to commence on the date on which benefits actually commenced; and

(iv) In the case of a beneficiary, benefits are assumed to commence on the benefit determination date or, if later, the earliest date the beneficiary can begin to receive benefits.

Plan lump sum assumptions means, with respect to a subpart A plan, the following:

(1) If the plan specifies actuarial assumptions and methods to be used to calculate a lump sum distribution, such actuarial assumptions and methods, or

(2) Otherwise, the actuarial assumptions specified under section 205(g)(3) of ERISA and section 417(e)(3) of the Code, determined as of the benefit determination date, including use of the missing participants interest rate to calculate the present value as of the benefit determination date of a payment or payments missed in the past.

QDRO means a qualified domestic relations order as defined in section 206(d)(3) of ERISA and section 414(p) of the Code.

Qualified survivor of a participant or beneficiary under a subpart A plan means, for any benefit with respect to the participant or beneficiary,—

(1) A person who survives the participant or beneficiary and is entitled under applicable provisions of a QDRO to receive the benefit;

(2) A person that is identified by the plan in a submission to PBGC by the plan as being entitled under applicable plan provisions (including elections, designations, and waivers consistent with such provisions) to receive the benefit; or

(3) If no such person is so entitled, a survivor of the participant or beneficiary who is the participant's or beneficiary's living—

(i) Spouse, or if none,

(ii) Child, or if none,

(iii) Parent, or if none,

(iv) Sibling.

Subpart A plan or *plan* means a plan to which this subpart A applies, as described in § 4050.101.

[¶ 15,530R]

§ 4050.103 **Duties of plan administrator**. (a) *Providing for benefits.* For each distributee who is missing upon closeout of a subpart A plan, the plan administrator must provide for the distributee's plan benefits either—

(1) By purchasing an irrevocable commitment from an insurer, or

(2) By—

(i) Determining the distributee's benefit transfer amount under paragraph (d) of this section, and

(ii) Transferring to PBGC as described in this subpart A an amount equal to the distributee's benefit transfer amount.

(b) *Diligent search.* For each distributee whose location the plan administrator does not know with reasonable certainty upon close-out of a subpart A plan, the plan administrator must have conducted a diligent search as described in § 4050.104.

(c) *Filing with PBGC.* For each distributee who is missing upon closeout of a subpart A plan, the plan administrator must file with PBGC as described in § 4050.105.

(d) *Benefit transfer amount.* The benefit transfer amount for a missing distributee is the amount determined by the plan administrator as of the benefit determination date using whichever one of the following three methods applies:

(1) *De minimis.* If the single sum actuarial equivalent of the distributee's benefits (including any payments missed in the past) determined using plan lump sum assumptions is de minimis, then the missing distributee's benefit transfer amount is equal to that single sum.

(2) *Non-de minimis; single sum payment cannot be elected.* If the single sum actuarial equivalent of the distributee's benefits (including any payments missed in the past) determined using plan lump sum assumptions is not de minimis, and a single sum payment cannot be elected, then the missing distributee's benefit transfer amount is the present value of the distributee's accrued benefit determined using PBGC missing participants assumptions, plus

(i) For a missing distributee not in pay status whose normal retirement date (or accrual cessation date if later) precedes the benefit

determination date, the aggregate value of payments of the straight life annuity that would have been payable beginning on the normal retirement date (or accrual cessation date if later), accumulated at the missing participants interest rate from the date each payment would have been made to the benefit determination date, assuming that the distributee survived to the benefit determination date, as determined by the plan administrator; or

(ii) For a missing distributee in pay status, the aggregate value of payments of the pay status annuity due but not made, accumulated at the missing participants interest rate from each payment due date to the benefit determination date, assuming that the distributee survived to the benefit determination date.

(3) *Non-de minimis; single sum payment can be elected.* If the single sum actuarial equivalent of the distributee's benefits (including any payments missed in the past) determined using plan lump sum assumptions is not de minimis, and a single sum payment can be elected, then the missing distributee's benefit transfer amount is the greater of the amounts determined using the methodology in paragraph (d)(1) or (d)(2) of this section.

[¶ 15,530S]

§ 4050.104 **Diligent search**. (a) *Search requirement.* The plan administrator of a subpart A plan must, within the time frame described in paragraph (d) of this section, have diligently searched for each distributee of the plan whose location the plan administrator does not know with reasonable certainty upon close-out, using one of the following two methods:

(1) For any distributee, regardless of the size of the distributee's benefit, the commercial locator service method described in paragraph (b) of this section; or

(2) For a distributee whose normal retirement benefit is not more than $50 per month, the records search method described in paragraph (c) of this section.

(b) *Commercial locator service method*—

(1) *In general.* Using the commercial locator service method means paying a commercial locator service to search for information to locate a distributee.

(2) *Meaning of "commercial locator service".* For purposes of this section, a commercial locator service is a business that holds itself out as a finder of lost persons for compensation using information from a database maintained by a consumer reporting agency (as defined in 15 U.S.C. 1681a(f)).

(c) *Records search method*—

(1) *In general.* Using the records search method means searching for information to locate a distributee by doing all of the following to the extent reasonably feasible and affordable:

(i) Searching the records of the plan for information to locate the distributee.

(ii) Searching the records of the plan's contributing sponsor that is the most recent employer of the distributee for information to locate the distributee.

(iii) Searching the records of each retirement or welfare plan of the plan's contributing sponsor in which the distributee was a participant for information to locate the distributee.

(iv) Contacting each beneficiary of the distributee identified from the records referred to in paragraphs (c)(1)(i), (ii), and (iii) of this section for information to locate the distributee.

(v) Using an internet search method for which no fee is charged, such as a search engine, a network database, a public record database (such as those for licenses, mortgages, and real estate taxes) or a "social media" website.

(2) *Limits on method.* For purposes of this section—

(i) Searching is not feasible to the extent that, as a practical matter, it is thwarted by legal or practical lack of access to records, and

(ii) Searching is not affordable to the extent that the cost of searching (including the value of labor) is more than a reasonable fraction of the benefit of the distributee being searched for. In no event would searching need to be pursued beyond the point where the cost equals the value of the benefit.

(d) *Time frame.* A search for a distributee under this section must have been made within nine months before a filing is made under § 4050.105 identifying the distributee as a missing distributee.

[¶ 15,530T]

§ 4050.105 **Filing with PBGC.** (a) *What to file.* The plan administrator of a subpart A plan must file with PBGC the information specified in the missing participants forms and instructions and, for a missing distributee referred to in § 4050.103(a)(2), payment of—

(1) The benefit transfer amount for the missing distributee;

(2) If the benefit transfer amount is paid more than 90 days after the benefit determination date, interest on the benefit transfer amount computed at the missing participants interest rate for the period beginning on the 90th day after the benefit determination date and ending on the date the benefit transfer amount is paid to PBGC; and

(3) Any fee provided for in the missing participants forms and instructions.

(b) *When to file.* The plan administrator must file the information and payments referred to in paragraph (a) of this section in accordance with the missing participants forms and instructions. Payment of a benefit transfer amount will, if considered timely made for purposes of this paragraph (b), be considered timely made for purposes of part 4041 of this chapter.

(c) *Place, method and date of filing; time periods.* (1) For rules about where to file, see § 4000.4 of this chapter.

(2) For rules about permissible methods of filing with PBGC under this subpart, see subpart A of part 4000 of this chapter.

(3) For rules about the date that a submission under this subpart was filed with PBGC, see subpart C of part 4000 of this chapter.

(4) For rules about any time period for filing under this subpart, see subpart D of part 4000 of this chapter.

(d) *Supplemental information.* Within 30 days after a written request by PBGC (or such other time as may be specified in the request), the plan administrator of a subpart A plan required to file under paragraph (a) of this section must file with PBGC supplemental information for any proper purpose under the missing participants program.

(e) *Reliance.* As administrator of the missing participants program, PBGC will rely on determinations made and information reported by plan administrators in connection with the program. This reliance does not affect PBGC's authority as administrator of the title IV insurance program to audit or make inquiries of subpart A plans, including about the amount to which a missing distributee may be entitled.

[¶ 15,530U]

§ 4050.106 **Missing participant benefits.** (a) *In general—*

(1) *Benefit transfer amount not paid.* If a subpart A plan files with PBGC information about an irrevocable commitment provided by the subpart A plan for a missing distributee, PBGC will provide information about the irrevocable commitment to the distributee or another claimant that may be entitled to payment pursuant to the irrevocable commitment.

(2) *Benefit transfer amount paid.* If a subpart A plan pays PBGC a benefit transfer amount for a missing distributee, PBGC will pay benefits with respect to the missing distributee in accordance with this section, subject to the provisions of a QDRO.

(b) *Benefits for missing distributees who are participants.* Paragraphs (c), (d), (e), and (k) of this section describe the benefits

that PBGC will pay to a non-pay status missing participant of a subpart A plan who claims a benefit under the missing participants program.

(c) *De minimis benefit.* If the benefit transfer amount of a participant described in paragraph (b) of this section is de minimis, PBGC will pay the participant a lump sum equal to the accumulated single sum.

(d) *Non-de minimis benefit of unmarried participant.* If the benefit transfer amount of an unmarried participant described in paragraph (b) of this section is not de minimis, PBGC will pay the participant either the annuity described in paragraph (d)(1) of this section, beginning not before age 55, and (if applicable) the make-up amount described in paragraph (d)(2) of this section; or, if the participant could have elected a lump sum under the subpart A plan, and the participant so elects under the missing participants program, the lump sum described in paragraph (d)(3) of this section.

(1) *Annuity.* The annuity described in this paragraph (d)(1) is either—

(i) *Straight life annuity.* A straight life annuity in the amount that the subpart A plan would have paid the participant, starting at the date that PBGC payments start (or, if earlier, the later of the participant's normal retirement date or accrual cessation date), as reported to PBGC by the subpart A plan (including any early retirement subsidies), or through linear interpolation for participants who start payments between integral ages; or

(ii) *Other form of annuity.* At the participant's election, any form of annuity available to the participant under § 4022.8 of this chapter, in an amount that is actuarially equivalent to the straight life annuity in paragraph (d)(1)(i) of this section as of the date that PBGC payments start (or, if earlier, the later of the participant's normal retirement date or accrual cessation date), determined using the actuarial assumptions in § 4022.8(c)(7) of this chapter.

(2) *Make-up amount.* If PBGC begins to pay the annuity under paragraph (d)(1) of this section after the normal retirement date (or accrual cessation date if later), the make-up amount described in this paragraph (d)(2) is a lump sum equal to the aggregate value of payments of the annuity that would have been payable to the participant (in the elected form) beginning on the normal retirement date (or accrual cessation date if later), accumulated at the missing participants interest rate from the date each payment would have been made to the date when PBGC begins to pay the annuity.

(3) *Lump sum.* The lump sum described in this paragraph (d)(3) is equal to the participant's accumulated single sum.

(e) *Non-de minimis benefit of married participant.* If the benefit transfer amount of a married participant described in paragraph (b) of this section is not de minimis, PBGC will pay the participant either the annuity described in paragraph (e)(1) of this section, beginning not before age 55, and (if applicable) the make-up amount described in paragraph (e)(2) of this section; or, if the participant could have elected a lump sum under the subpart A plan, and the participant so elects under the missing participants program with the consent of the participant's spouse, the lump sum described in paragraph (e)(3) of this section.

(1) *Annuity.* The annuity described in this paragraph (e)(1) is either—

(i) *Joint and survivor annuity.* A joint and 50 percent survivor annuity in an amount that is actuarially equivalent to the straight life annuity under paragraph (d)(1)(i) of this section as of the date that PBGC payments start (or, if earlier, the later of the participant's normal retirement date or accrual cessation date), determined using the actuarial assumptions in § 4022.8(c)(7) of this chapter; or

(ii) *Other form of annuity.* At the participant's election, with the consent of the participant's spouse, any form of annuity available to the participant under § 4022.8 of this chapter, in an amount that is actuarially equivalent to the joint and 50 percent survivor annuity under

»»→ *Caution: Reg. Secs. 4050.101—4050.407 are effective January 22, 2018 and generally applicable to plans terminating on or after January 1, 2018.*

paragraph (e)(1)(i) of this section as of the date that PBGC payments start (or, if earlier, the later of the participant's normal retirement date or accrual cessation date), determined using the actuarial assumptions in §4022.8(c)(7) of this chapter.

(2) *Make-up amount.* If PBGC begins to pay the annuity under paragraph (e)(1) of this section after the normal retirement date (or accrual cessation date if later), the make-up amount described in this paragraph (e)(2) is a lump sum equal to the aggregate value of payments of the annuity that would have been payable to the participant beginning on the normal retirement date (or accrual cessation date if later), accumulated at the missing participants interest rate from the date each payment would have been made to the date when PBGC begins to pay the annuity.

(3) *Lump sum.* The lump sum described in this paragraph (e)(3) is equal to the participant's accumulated single sum.

(f) *Benefits with respect to deceased missing distributees who were participants.* Paragraphs (g), (h), (i), (j), and (k) of this section describe the benefits that PBGC will pay with respect to a non-pay status missing participant of a subpart A plan who dies without receiving a benefit under the missing participants program.

(g) *De minimis benefit.* If the benefit transfer amount of a participant described in paragraph (f) of this section is de minimis, PBGC will pay to the qualified survivor(s) of the participant a lump sum equal to the participant's accumulated single sum.

(h) *Non-de minimis benefit;unmarried participant.* In the case of an unmarried participant described in paragraph (f) of this section whose benefit transfer amount is not de minimis,—

(1) *Death before normal retirement date.* If the participant dies before the normal retirement date (or accrual cessation date if later), PBGC will pay no benefits with respect to the participant; and

(2) *Death after normal retirement date.* If the participant dies on or after the normal retirement date (or accrual cessation date if later), PBGC will pay to the participant's qualified survivor(s) an amount equal to the aggregate value of payments of the straight life annuity described in paragraph (d)(1)(i) of this section that would have been payable to the participant from the normal retirement date (or accrual cessation date if later) to the participant's date of death, accumulated at the missing participants interest rate from the date each payment would have been made to the date when PBGC pays the qualified survivor(s).

(i) *Non-de minimis benefit; married participant with living spouse.* In the case of a married participant described in paragraph (f) of this section whose benefit transfer amount is not de minimis and whose spouse survives the participant and claims a benefit under the missing participants program, PBGC will pay the spouse, beginning not before the participant would have reached age 55, the annuity (if any) described in paragraph (i)(1) of this section and the make-up amounts (if applicable) described in paragraph (i)(2) of this section, except that PBGC will pay the spouse, as a lump sum, the small benefit described in paragraph (i)(3) of this section.

(1) *Annuity.* The annuity described in this paragraph (i)(1) is the survivor portion of a joint and 50 percent survivor annuity that is actuarially equivalent as of the assumed starting date (determined using the actuarial assumptions in §4022.8(c)(7) of this chapter) to the straight life annuity in the amount that the subpart A plan would have paid the participant with an assumed starting date of—

(i) The date when the participant would have reached age 55, if the participant died before that date, or

(ii) The participant's date of death, if the participant died between age 55 and the normal retirement date (or accrual cessation date if later), or

(iii) The normal retirement date (or accrual cessation date if later), if the participant died after that date.

(2) *Make-up amounts.* The make-up amounts described in this paragraph (i)(2) are the amounts described in paragraphs (i)(2)(i) and (ii) of this section.

(i) *Payments from participant's death or 55th birthday to commencement of survivor annuity.* The make-up amount described in this paragraph (i)(2)(i) is a lump sum equal to the aggregate value of payments of the survivor portion of the joint and 50 percent survivor annuity described in paragraph (i)(1) of this section that would have been payable to the spouse beginning on the later of the participant's date of death or the date when the participant would have reached age 55, accumulated at the missing participants interest rate from the date each payment would have been made to the date when PBGC pays the spouse.

(ii) *Payments from normal retirement date to participant's death.* The makeup amount described in this paragraph (i)(2)(ii) is a lump sum equal to the aggregate value of payments (if any) of the joint portion of the joint and 50 percent survivor annuity described in paragraph (i)(1) of this section that would have been payable to the participant from the normal retirement date (or accrual cessation date if later) to the participant's date of death thereafter, accumulated at the missing participants interest rate from the date each payment would have been made to the date when PBGC pays the spouse.

(3) *Small benefit.* If the sum of the actuarial present value of the annuity described in paragraph (i)(1) of this section plus the make-up amounts described in paragraph (i)(2) of this section is de minimis, then the lump sum that PBGC will pay the spouse under this paragraph (i)(3) is an amount equal to that sum. For this purpose, the actuarial present value of the annuity is determined using the actuarial assumptions in §4022.8(c)(7) of this chapter as of the date when PBGC pays the spouse.

(j) *Non-de minimis benefit; married participant with deceased spouse.* In the case of a married participant described in paragraph (f) of this section whose benefit transfer amount is not de minimis and whose spouse survives the participant but dies without receiving a benefit under the missing participants program, PBGC will pay to the qualified survivor(s) of the participant's spouse the make-up amount described in paragraph (j)(1) of this section and to the qualified survivor(s) of the participant the make-up amount described in paragraph (j)(2) of this section.

(1) *Payments from participant's death or 55th birthday to spouse's death.* The make-up amount described in this paragraph (j)(1) is a lump sum equal to the aggregate value of payments of the survivor portion of the joint and 50 percent survivor annuity described in paragraph (i)(1) of this section that would have been payable to the spouse from the later of the participant's date of death or the date when the participant would have reached age 55 to the spouse's date of death, accumulated at the missing participants interest rate from the date each payment would have been made to the date when PBGC pays the spouse's qualified survivor(s).

(2) *Payments from normal retirement date to participant's death.* The makeup amount described in this paragraph (j)(2) is a lump sum equal to the aggregate value of payments of the joint portion of the joint and 50 percent survivor annuity described in paragraph (i)(1) of this section that would have been payable to the participant from the normal retirement date (or accrual cessation date if later) to the participant's date of death thereafter, accumulated at the missing participants interest rate from the date each payment would have been made to the date when PBGC pays the participant's qualified survivor(s).

(k) *Benefits under contributory plans.* If a subpart A plan reports to PBGC that a portion of a missing participant's benefit transfer amount represents accumulated contributions as described in section 204(c)(2)(C) of ERISA and section 411(c)(2)(C) of the Code, PBGC will pay with respect to the missing participant at least the amount of accumulated contributions as reported by the subpart A plan, accumulated at the missing participants interest rate from the benefit determination date to the date when PBGC makes payment.

>>→ *Caution: Reg. Secs. 4050.101—4050.407 are effective January 22, 2018 and generally applicable to plans terminating on or after January 1, 2018.*

(l) *Date for determining marital status.* For purposes of this section, whether a participant is married, and if so the identity of the spouse, is determined as of the earlier of—

(1) The date the participant receives or begins to receive a benefit, or

(2) The date the participant dies.

>>→ *Caution: Reg. Secs. 4050.101—4050.407 are effective January 22, 2018 and generally applicable to plans terminating on or after January 1, 2018.*

Subpart B—Defined Contribution Plans

[¶ 15,531F]

§ 4050.201 **Purpose and scope.** (a) *In general.* This subpart describes PBGC's missing participants program for single-employer and multiemployer defined contribution retirement plans. The missing participants program is a program to hold retirement benefits for missing participants and beneficiaries in terminated retirement plans and to help them find and receive the benefits being held for them. For a plan to which this subpart applies, this subpart describes what the plan must do upon plan termination if it elects to use the missing participants program for missing participants and beneficiaries who are entitled to distributions. This subpart applies to a plan only if it is a plan—

(1) That—

(i) Is a defined contribution (individual account) plan described in section 3(34) of ERISA; or

(ii) Is treated as a defined contribution (individual account) plan under section (3)(35) of ERISA (to the extent so treated);

(2) That is described in section 4021(a) of ERISA and not in any paragraph of section 4021(b) of ERISA other than paragraph (1), (5), (12), or (13), including a plan described in section 403(b) of the Code under which benefits are provided through custodial accounts described in section 403(b)(7) of the Code;

(3) That, if it is a transferring plan, pays all benefit transfer amounts to PBGC in money, consistent with plan provisions and applicable law; and

(4) That terminates and closes out.

(b) *Defined contribution plans that are part of defined benefit plans.* This subpart does not fail to apply to a plan merely because the plan is described in the same plan document as a defined benefit plan (to which this subpart does not apply). For example, this subpart may apply to employee contributions (or interest or earnings thereon) held as an individual account under a defined benefit plan.

(c) *Defined contribution plans that are abandoned plans.* This subpart does not fail to apply to a plan merely because the plan is an abandoned plan, as defined in 29 CFR 2578.1.

[¶ 15,531G]

§ 4050.202 **Definitions.** The following terms are defined in § 4001.2 of this chapter: Annuity, Code, ERISA, PBGC, and person. In addition, for purposes of this subpart:

Accumulated single sum means, with respect to a missing distributee, the distributee's benefit transfer amount accumulated at the missing participants interest rate from the date when the subpart B plan pays PBGC the benefit transfer amount for the missing distributee to the date when PBGC makes or commences payment to or with respect to the distributee.

Benefit conversion assumptions means, with respect to an annuity, the applicable mortality table and applicable interest rate under section 205(g)(3) of ERISA and section 417(e)(3) of the Code for January of the calendar year in which PBGC begins paying the annuity.

Benefit transfer amount for a missing distributee in a transferring plan means the amount available for distribution to the distributee in connection with the close-out of the subpart B plan.

Close-out or *close out* with respect to a subpart B plan means the process of the final distribution or transfer of assets pursuant to the termination of the subpart B plan.

De minimis means, with respect to the value of a benefit (or other amount), that the value does not exceed the amount specified under section 203(e)(1) of ERISA and section 411(a)(11)(A) of the Code (without regard to plan provisions).

Distributee means, with respect to a subpart B plan, a participant or beneficiary entitled to a distribution under the plan pursuant to the close-out of the plan, except that a person is not a distributee if the subpart B plan transfers assets to another pension plan (within the meaning of section 3(2) of ERISA) to pay the person's benefits.

Missing, with respect to a distributee under a subpart B plan, means that any one or more of the following three conditions exists upon close-out of the plan.

(1) The plan does not know with reasonable certainty the location of the distributee.

(2) The distributee has not elected a form of distribution in response to a notice about the distribution.

(3) Under the terms of the plan and any election made by the distributee, the distributee's benefit is to be paid in a lump sum, but the distributee does not accept the lump sum. For this purpose, a lump sum paid by check is not accepted if the check remains uncashed after—

(i) A "cash-by" date prescribed (on the check or in an accompanying notice) that is at least 45 days after the issuance of the check, or

(ii) If no such "cash-by" date is so prescribed, the check's stale date.

Missing participants forms and instructions means the forms and instructions provided by PBGC for use in connection with the missing participants program.

Missing participants interest rate means, for each month, the applicable federal mid-term rate (as determined by the Secretary of the Treasury pursuant to section 1274(d)(1)(C)(ii) of the Code) for that month, compounded monthly.

Notifying plan means a subpart B plan that elects notifying plan status in accordance with § 4050.203.

QDRO means a qualified domestic relations order as defined in section 206(d)(3) of ERISA and section 414(p) of the Code.

Qualified survivor of a participant or beneficiary under a subpart B plan means, for any benefit with respect to the participant or beneficiary,—

(1) A person who survives the participant or beneficiary and is entitled under applicable provisions of a QDRO to receive the benefit;

(2) A person that is identified by the plan in a submission to PBGC by the plan as being entitled under applicable plan provisions (including elections, designations, and waivers consistent with such provisions) to receive the benefit; or

(3) If no such person is so entitled, a survivor of the participant or beneficiary who is the participant's or beneficiary's living—

(i) Spouse, or if none,

(ii) Child, or if none,

(iii) Parent, or if none,

(iv) Sibling.

Subpart B plan or *plan* means a plan to which this subpart B applies, as described in § 4050.201.

Transferring plan means a subpart B plan that elects transferring plan status in accordance with § 4050.203.

[¶ 15,531H]

§ 4050.203 **Options and duties of plan.** (a) *Options.* A subpart B plan that is closing out upon plan termination may (but need not) elect, by filing under § 4050.205, that the subpart B plan—

[¶ 15,530V]

§ 4050.107 **PBGC discretion.** PBGC may in appropriate circumstances extend deadlines, excuse noncompliance, and grant waivers with regard to any provision of this subpart to promote the purposes of the missing participants program and title IV of ERISA. Like circumstances will be treated in like manner under this section.

(1) Will be a "transferring plan," that is, will pay a benefit transfer amount to PBGC for each distributee who is missing upon close-out of the plan and will be bound by the provisions of this subpart B to the extent that they apply to transferring plans, or

(2) Will be a "notifying plan," that is, will notify PBGC of the disposition of the benefits of each distributee identified in the filing who is missing upon close-out of the plan and will, with respect to those distributees, be bound by the provisions of this subpart B to the extent that they apply to notifying plans.

(b) *Diligent search—*

(1) *In general.* Except as provided in paragraph (b)(2) of this section, for each distributee whose location the plan does not know with reasonable certainty upon closeout of a subpart B plan, the plan must have conducted a diligent search as described in §4050.204.

(2) *Notifying plans.* For a notifying plan, the requirement of paragraph (b)(1) of this section applies only to distributees identified in the filing with PBGC.

(c) *Filing with PBGC—*

(1) *In general.* Except as provided in paragraph (c)(2) of this section, for each distributee who is missing upon close-out of a subpart B plan, the plan must file with PBGC as described in §4050.205.

(2) *Notifying plans.* For a notifying plan, the requirement of paragraph (c)(1) of this section applies only to distributees identified in the filing with PBGC.

[¶ 15,531I]

§4050.204 **Diligent search**. (a) *Search requirement—*

(1) *In general.* Except as provided in paragraph (a)(2) of this section, a subpart B plan must, within the time frame described in paragraph (b) of this section, have diligently searched for each distributee of the plan whose location the plan does not know with reasonable certainty upon close-out in accordance with regulations and other applicable guidance issued by the Secretary of Labor under section 404 of ERISA.

(2) *Notifying plans.* For a notifying plan, the requirement of paragraph (a)(1) of this section applies only to distributees identified in the filing with PBGC.

(b) *Time frame.* A search for a missing distributee must be made within nine months before a filing is made under §4050.205 identifying the distributee as a missing distributee.

[¶ 15,531J]

§4050.205 **Filing with PBGC**. (a) *What to file.* A subpart B plan must file with PBGC the information specified in the missing participants forms and instructions, and if the plan is a transferring plan, payment of—

(1) The benefit transfer amount for the missing distributee; and

(2) Any fee provided for in the missing participants forms and instructions.

(b) *When to file.* The plan must file the information and payments referred to in paragraph (a) of this section in accordance with the missing participants forms and instructions.

(c) *Place, method and date of filing; time periods.* (1) For rules about where to file, see §4000.4 of this chapter.

(2) For rules about permissible methods of filing with PBGC under this subpart, see subpart A of part 4000 of this chapter.

(3) For rules about the date that a submission under this subpart was filed with PBGC, see subpart C of part 4000 of this chapter.

(4) For rules about any time period for filing under this subpart, see subpart D of part 4000 of this chapter.

(d) *Supplemental information.* Within 30 days after a written request by PBGC (or such other time as may be specified in the request),

the plan administrator of a subpart B plan required to file under paragraph (a) of this section must file with PBGC supplemental information for any proper purpose under the missing participants program.

(e) *Reliance.* As administrator of the missing participants program, PBGC will rely on determinations made and information reported by plans in connection with the program.

[¶ 15,531K]

§4050.206 **Missing participant benefits**. (a) *In general—*

(1) *Notifying plan.* If a notifying plan files with PBGC information about a disposition of benefits made by the subpart B plan for a missing distributee, PBGC will provide information about the disposition of benefits to the distributee or another claimant that may be entitled to the benefits.

(2) *Transferring plan.* If a transferring plan pays PBGC a benefit transfer amount for a missing distributee, PBGC will pay benefits with respect to the missing distributee in accordance with this section, subject to the provisions of a QDRO.

(b) *Benefits for missing distributees who are participants.* Paragraphs (c), (d), and (e) of this section describe the benefits that PBGC will pay to a missing participant of a subpart B plan who claims a benefit under the missing participants program.

(c) *De minimis benefit.* If the benefit transfer amount of a participant described in paragraph (b) of this section is de minimis, PBGC will pay the participant a lump sum equal to the accumulated single sum.

(d) *Non-de minimis benefit of unmarried participant.* If the benefit transfer amount of an unmarried participant described in paragraph (b) of this section is not de minimis, PBGC will pay the participant either the annuity described in paragraph (d)(1) of this section, beginning not before age 55; or, if the participant so elects, the lump sum described in paragraph (d)(2) of this section.

(1) *Annuity.* The annuity described in this paragraph (d)(1) is, at the participant's election, any form of annuity available to the participant under §4022.8 of this chapter, in an amount that is actuarially equivalent, under the benefit conversion assumptions, to the participant's accumulated single sum.

(2) *Lump sum.* The lump sum described in this paragraph (d)(2) is the participant's accumulated single sum.

(e) *Non-de minimis benefit of married participant.* If the benefit transfer amount of a married participant described in paragraph (b) of this section is not de minimis, PBGC will pay the participant either the annuity described in paragraph (e)(1) of this section, beginning not before age 55; or, if the participant so elects with the consent of the participant's spouse, the lump sum described in paragraph (e)(2) of this section.

(1) *Annuity.* The annuity described in this paragraph (e)(1) is either—

(i) *Joint and survivor annuity.* A joint and 50 percent survivor annuity in an amount that is actuarially equivalent, under the benefit conversion assumptions, to the participant's accumulated single sum; or

(ii) *Other form of annuity.* At the participant's election, with the consent of the participant's spouse, any form of annuity available to the participant under §4022.8 of this chapter, in an amount that is actuarially equivalent, under the benefit conversion assumptions, to the participant's accumulated single sum.

(2) *Lump sum.* The lump sum described in this paragraph (e)(2) is the participant's accumulated single sum.

(f) *Benefits with respect to deceased missing distributees who were participants.* Paragraphs (g), (h), and (i) of this section describe the benefits that PBGC will pay with respect to a missing participant of a subpart B plan who dies without receiving a benefit under the missing participants program.

(g) *De minimis benefit.* If the benefit transfer amount of a participant described in paragraph (f) of this section is de minimis, and the participant's qualified survivor claims a benefit under the missing participants program, PBGC will pay the claimant a lump sum equal to the participant's accumulated single sum.

(h) *Non-de minimis benefit; non-spousal qualified survivor.* If the benefit transfer amount of a married or unmarried participant described in paragraph (f) of this section is not de minimis, and the participant's qualified survivor is not the participant's surviving spouse and claims a benefit under the missing participants program, PBGC will pay the claimant a lump sum equal to the participant's accumulated single sum.

(i) *Non-de minimis benefit; surviving spouse is qualified survivor.* If the benefit transfer amount of a married participant described in paragraph (f) of this section is not de minimis, and the participant's qualified survivor is the participant's surviving spouse and claims a benefit under the missing participants program, PBGC will, at the spouse's election, either pay the spouse, beginning not before the participant would have reached age 55, the annuity described in para-

graph (i)(1) of this section; or pay the spouse the lump sum described in paragraph (i)(2) of this section.

(1) *Annuity.* The annuity described in this paragraph (i)(1) is a straight life annuity for the life of the spouse in an amount that is actuarially equivalent, under the benefit conversion assumptions, to the participant's accumulated single sum.

(2) *Lump sum.* The lump sum described in this paragraph (i)(2) is a lump sum equal to the participant's accumulated single sum.

(j) *Date for determining marital status.* For purposes of this section, whether a participant is married, and if so the identity of the spouse, is determined as of the earlier of—

(1) The date the participant receives or begins to receive a benefit, or

(2) The date the participant dies.

[¶ 15,531L]

§ 4050.207 **PBGC discretion.** PBGC may in appropriate circumstances extend deadlines, excuse noncompliance, and grant waivers with regard to any provision of this subpart to promote the purposes of the missing participants program and title IV of ERISA. Like circumstances will be treated in like manner under this section.

Subpart C—Certain Defined Benefit Plans Not Covered by Title IV

[¶ 15,531W]

§ 4050.301 **Purpose and scope.** (a) *In general.* This subpart describes PBGC's missing participants program for small professional service defined benefit retirement plans not covered by title IV of ERISA. The missing participants program is a program to hold retirement benefits for missing participants and beneficiaries in terminated retirement plans and to help them find and receive the benefits being held for them. For a plan to which this subpart applies, this subpart describes what the plan must do upon plan termination if it elects to use the missing participants program for missing participants and beneficiaries who are entitled to distributions. This subpart applies to a plan only if it is a single-employer defined benefit plan that—

(1) Is described in section 4021(a) of ERISA and not in any paragraph of section 4021(b) of ERISA other than paragraph (13), and

(2) Terminates and closes out with sufficient assets to satisfy all liabilities with respect to employees and their beneficiaries.

(b) *Individual account plans.* This subpart does not apply to an individual account plan under section 3(34) of ERISA, even if it is described in the same plan document as a plan to which this subpart applies. This subpart also does not apply to a plan to the extent that it is treated as an individual account plan under section 3(35)(B) of ERISA. For example, this subpart does not apply to employee contributions (or interest or earnings thereon) held as an individual account. (Subpart B deals with individual account plans.)

[¶ 15,531X]

§ 4050.302 **Definitions.** The following terms are defined in § 4001.2 of this chapter: Annuity, Code, ERISA, PBGC, person, and plan administrator. In addition, for purposes of this subpart:

Accrual cessation date for a participant under a subpart C plan means the date the participant stopped accruing benefits under the terms of the plan.

Accumulated single sum means, with respect to a missing distributee, the distributee's benefit transfer amount accumulated at the missing participants interest rate from the benefit determination date to the date when PBGC makes or commences payment to or with respect to the distributee.

Benefit determination date with respect to a subpart C plan means the single date selected by the plan administrator for valuing benefits under § 4050.303(d); this date must be during the period beginning on

the first day a distribution is made pursuant to closeout of the plan to a distributee who is not a missing distributee and ending on the last day such a distribution is made.

Benefit transfer amount for a missing distributee in a transferring plan means the amount determined by the plan administrator under § 4050.303(d) in the close-out of the subpart C plan.

Close-out or *close out* with respect to a subpart C plan means the process of the final distribution or transfer of assets pursuant to the termination of the subpart C plan.

De minimis means, with respect to the value of a benefit (or other amount), that the value does not exceed the amount specified under section 203(e)(1) of ERISA and section 411(a)(11)(A) of the Code (without regard to plan provisions).

Distributee means, with respect to a subpart C plan, a participant or beneficiary entitled to a distribution under the subpart C plan pursuant to the close-out of the subpart C plan, except that a person is not a distributee if the subpart C plan transfers assets to another pension plan (within the meaning of section 3(2) of ERISA) to pay the person's benefits.

Missing, with respect to a distributee under a subpart C plan, means that any one or more of the following three conditions exists upon close-out of the plan.

(1) The plan administrator does not know with reasonable certainty the location of the distributee.

(2) Under the terms of the plan, the distributee's benefit is to be paid in a lump sum without the distributee's consent, and the distributee has not responded to a notice about the distribution of the lump sum.

(3) Under the terms of the plan and any election made by the distributee, the distributee's benefit is to be paid in a lump sum, but the distributee does not accept the lump sum. For this purpose, a lump sum paid by check is not accepted if the check remains uncashed after—

(i) A "cash-by" date prescribed (on the check or in an accompanying notice) that is at least 45 days after the issuance of the check, or

(ii) If no such "cash-by" date is so prescribed, the check's stale date.

Missing participants forms and instructions means the forms and instructions provided by PBGC for use in connection with the missing participants program.

Missing participants interest rate means, for each month, the applicable federal mid-term rate (as determined by the Secretary of the Treasury pursuant to section 1274(d)(1)(C)(ii) of the Code) for that month, compounded monthly.

»»→ Caution: *Reg. Secs. 4050.101—4050.407 are effective January 22, 2018 and generally applicable to plans terminating on or after January 1, 2018.*

Normal retirement date for a participant under a subpart C plan means the normal retirement date of the participant under the terms of the plan.

Notifying plan means a subpart C plan for which the plan administrator elects notifying plan status in accordance with § 4050.303.

Pay-status or *pay status* means one of the following (according to context):

(1) With respect to a benefit, that payment of the benefit has actually started before the benefit determination date; or

(2) With respect to a distributee, that payment of the distributee's benefit has actually started before the benefit determination date.

PBGC missing participants assumptions means the actuarial assumptions prescribed in §§ 4044.51 through 4044.57 of this chapter with the following modifications:

(1) The present value is determined as of the benefit determination date instead of the plan termination date.

(2) The mortality assumption is a fixed blend of 50 percent of the healthy male mortality rates in § 4044.53(c)(1) of this chapter and 50 percent of the healthy female mortality rates in § 4044.53(c)(2) of this chapter.

(3) No adjustment is made for loading expenses under § 4044.52(d) of this chapter.

(4) The interest assumption used is the assumption applicable to valuations occurring in January of the calendar year in which the benefit determination date occurs.

(5) The assumed payment form of a benefit not in pay status is a straight life annuity.

(6) Pre-retirement death benefits are disregarded.

(7) Notwithstanding the expected retirement age (XRA) assumptions in §§ 4044.55 through 4044.57 of this chapter,—

(i) In the case of a participant who is not in pay status and whose normal retirement date is on or after the benefit determination date, benefits are assumed to commence at the XRA, determined using the high retirement rate category under Table II–C of Appendix D to part 4044 of this chapter;

(ii) In the case of a participant who is not in pay status and whose normal retirement date is before the benefit determination date, benefits are assumed to commence on the participant's normal retirement date (or accrual cessation date if later);

(iii) In the case of a participant who is in pay status, benefits are assumed to commence on the date on which benefits actually commenced; and

(iv) In the case of a beneficiary, benefits are assumed to commence on the benefit determination date or, if later, the earliest date the beneficiary can begin to receive benefits.

Plan lump sum assumptions means, with respect to a subpart C plan, the following:

(1) If the plan specifies actuarial assumptions and methods to be used to calculate a lump sum distribution, such actuarial assumptions and methods, or

(2) Otherwise, the actuarial assumptions specified under section 205(g)(3) of ERISA and section 417(e)(3) of the Code, determined as of the benefit determination date, including use of the missing participants interest rate to calculate the present value as of the benefit determination date of a payment or payments missed in the past.

QDRO means a qualified domestic relations order as defined in section 206(d)(3) of ERISA and section 414(p) of the Code.

Qualified survivor of a participant or beneficiary under a subpart C plan means, for any benefit with respect to the participant or beneficiary—

(1) A person who survives the participant or beneficiary and is entitled under applicable provisions of a QDRO to receive the benefit;

(2) A person that is identified by the plan in a submission to PBGC by the plan as being entitled under applicable plan provisions (including elections, designations, and waivers consistent with such provisions) to receive the benefit; or

(3) If no such person is so entitled, a survivor of the participant or beneficiary who is the participant's or beneficiary's living—

(i) Spouse, or if none,

(ii) Child, or if none,

(iii) Parent, or if none,

(iv) Sibling.

Subpart C plan or *plan* means a plan to which this subpart C applies, as described in § 4050.301.

Transferring plan means a subpart C plan for which the plan administrator elects transferring plan status in accordance with § 4050.303.

[¶ 15,531Y]

§ 4050.303 Options and duties of plan administrator.
(a) *Options.* The plan administrator of a subpart C plan that is closing out upon plan termination may (but need not), by filing under § 4050.305, elect that the subpart C plan—

(1) Will be a "transferring plan," that is, will pay a benefit transfer amount to PBGC for each distributee who is missing upon close-out of the subpart C plan and will be bound by the provisions of this subpart C to the extent that they apply to transferring plans, or

(2) Will be a "notifying plan," that is, will notify PBGC of the disposition of the benefits of each distributee identified in the filing who is missing upon close-out of the plan and will, with respect to those distributees, be bound by the provisions of this subpart C to the extent that they apply to notifying plans.

(b) *Diligent search—*

(1) *In general.* Except as provided in paragraph (b)(2) of this section, for each distributee whose location the plan administrator does not know with reasonable certainty upon close-out of a subpart C plan, the plan administrator must have conducted a diligent search as described in § 4050.304.

(2) *Notifying plans.* For a notifying plan, the requirement of paragraph (b)(1) of this section applies only to distributees identified in the filing with PBGC.

(c) *Filing with PBGC—*

(1) *In general.* Except as provided in paragraph (c)(2) of this section, for each distributee who is missing upon close-out of a subpart C plan, the plan administrator must file with PBGC as described in § 4050.305.

(2) *Notifying plans.* For a notifying plan, the requirement of paragraph (c)(1) of this section applies only to distributees identified in the filing with PBGC.

(d) *Benefit transfer amount.* The benefit transfer amount for a missing distributee is the amount determined by the plan administrator as of the benefit determination date using whichever one of the following three methods applies:

(1) *De minimis.* If the single sum actuarial equivalent of the distributee's benefits (including any payments missed in the past) determined using plan lump sum assumptions is de minimis, then the missing distributee's benefit transfer amount is equal to that single sum.

(2) *Non-de minimis; single sum payment cannot be elected.* If the single sum actuarial equivalent of the distributee's benefits (including any payments missed in the past) determined using plan lump sum assumptions is not de minimis, and a single sum payment cannot be elected, then the missing distributee's benefit transfer amount is the present value of the distributee's accrued benefit determined using PBGC missing participants assumptions, plus

(i) For a missing distributee not in pay status whose normal retirement date (or accrual cessation date if later) precedes the benefit determination date, the aggregate value of payments of the straight life annuity that would have been payable beginning on the normal retirement date (or accrual cessation date if later), accumulated at the missing participants interest rate from the date each payment would have been made to the benefit determination date, assuming that the distributee survived to the benefit determination date, as determined by the plan administrator; or

(ii) For a missing distributee in pay status, the aggregate value of payments of the pay status annuity due but not made, accumulated at the missing participants interest rate from each payment due date to the benefit determination date, assuming that the distributee survived to the benefit determination date.

(3) *Non-de minimis; single sum payment can be elected.* If the single sum actuarial equivalent of the distributee's benefits (including any payments missed in the past) determined using plan lump sum assumptions is not de minimis, and a single sum payment can be elected, then the missing distributee's benefit transfer amount is the greater of the amounts determined using the methodology in paragraph (d)(1) or (d)(2) of this section.

[¶ 15,531Z]

§ 4050.304 **Diligent search**. (a) *Search requirement.* For each distributee of a subpart C plan who is described in § 4050.303(b), the plan administrator must, within the time frame described in paragraph (d) of this section, have diligently searched for each distributee of the plan whose location the plan administrator does not know with reasonable certainty upon close out, using one of the following two methods:

(1) For any distributee, regardless of the size of the distributee's benefit, the commercial locator service method described in paragraph (b) of this section; or

(2) For a distributee whose normal retirement benefit is not more than $50 per month, the records search method described in paragraph (c) of this section.

(b) *Commercial locator service method—*

(1) *In general.* Using the commercial locator service method means paying a commercial locator service to search for information to locate a distributee.

(2) *Meaning of "commercial locator service".* For purposes of this section, a commercial locator service is a business that holds itself out as a finder of lost persons for compensation using information from a database maintained by a consumer reporting agency (as defined in 15 U.S.C. 1681a(f)).

(c) *Records search method—*

(1) *In general.* Using the records search method means searching for information to locate a distributee by doing all of the following to the extent reasonably feasible and affordable:

(i) Searching the records of the plan for information to locate the distributee.

(ii) Searching the records of the plan's contributing sponsor that is the most recent employer of the distributee for information to locate the distributee.

(iii) Searching the records of each retirement or welfare plan of the plan's contributing sponsor in which the distributee was a participant for information to locate the distributee.

(iv) Contacting each beneficiary of the distributee identified from the records referred to in paragraphs (c)(1)(i), (ii), and (iii) of this section for information to locate the distributee.

(v) Using an internet search method for which no fee is charged, such as a search engine, a network database, a public record database (such as those for licenses, mortgages, and real estate taxes) or a "social media" website.

(2) *Limits on method.* For purposes of this section—

(i) Searching is not feasible to the extent that, as a practical matter, it is thwarted by legal or practical lack of access to records, and

(ii) Searching is not affordable to the extent that the cost of searching (including the value of labor) is more than a reasonable fraction of the benefit of the distributee being searched for. In no event would searching need to be pursued beyond the point where the cost equals the value of the benefit.

(d) *Time frame.* A search for a distributee under this section must have been made within nine months before a filing is made under § 4050.305 identifying the distributee as a missing distributee.

[¶ 15,532]

§ 4050.305 **Filing with PBGC**. (a) *What to file.* The plan administrator of a subpart C plan must file with PBGC the information specified in the missing participants forms and instructions, and if the plan is a transferring plan, payment of—

(1) The benefit transfer amount for the missing distributee;

(2) If the benefit transfer amount is paid more than 90 days after the benefit determination date, interest on the benefit transfer amount computed at the missing participants interest rate for the period beginning on the 90th day after the benefit determination date and ending on the date the benefit transfer amount is paid to PBGC; and

(3) Any fee provided for in the missing participants forms and instructions.

(b) *When to file.* The plan administrator must file the information and payments referred to in paragraph (a) of this section in accordance with the missing participants forms and instructions.

(c) *Place, method and date of filing; time periods.* (1) For rules about where to file, see § 4000.4 of this chapter.

(2) For rules about permissible methods of filing with PBGC under this subpart, see subpart A of part 4000 of this chapter.

(3) For rules about the date that a submission under this subpart was filed with PBGC, see subpart C of part 4000 of this chapter.

(4) For rules about any time period for filing under this subpart, see subpart D of part 4000 of this chapter.

(d) *Supplemental information.* Within 30 days after a written request by PBGC (or such other time as may be specified in the request), the plan administrator of a subpart C plan required to file under paragraph (a) of this section must file with PBGC supplemental information for any proper purpose under the missing participants program.

(e) *Reliance.* As administrator of the missing participants program, PBGC will rely on determinations made and information reported by plan administrators in connection with the program.

[¶ 15,532A]

§ 4050.306 **Missing participant benefits**. (a) *In general—*

(1) *Notifying plan.* If a notifying plan files with PBGC information about a disposition of benefits made by the subpart C plan for a missing distributee, PBGC will provide information about the disposition of benefits to the distributee or another claimant that may be entitled to the benefits.

(2) *Transferring plan.* If a transferring plan pays PBGC a benefit transfer amount for a missing distributee, PBGC will pay benefits with respect to the missing distributee in accordance with this section, subject to the provisions of a QDRO.

(b) *Benefits for missing distributees who are participants.* Paragraphs (c), (d), (e), and (k) of this section describe the benefits that PBGC will pay to a non-pay status missing participant of a subpart C plan who claims a benefit under the missing participants program.

(c) *De minimis benefit.* If the benefit transfer amount of a participant described in paragraph (b) of this section is de minimis, PBGC will pay the participant a lump sum equal to the accumulated single sum.

(d) *Non-de minimis benefit of unmarried participant.* If the benefit transfer amount of an unmarried participant described in paragraph (b) of this section is not de minimis, PBGC will pay the participant either the annuity described in paragraph (d)(1) of this section, beginning not before age 55, and (if applicable) the make-up amount described in paragraph (d)(2) of this section; or, if the participant could have elected a lump sum under the subpart C plan, and the participant so elects

⋙→ *Caution: Reg. Secs. 4050.101—4050.407 are effective January 22, 2018 and generally applicable to plans terminating on or after January 1, 2018.*

under the missing participants program, the lump sum described in paragraph (d)(3) of this section.

(1) *Annuity.* The annuity described in this paragraph (d)(1) is either—

(i) *Straight life annuity.* A straight life annuity in the amount that the subpart C plan would have paid the participant, starting at the date that PBGC payments start (or, if earlier, the later of the participant's normal retirement date or accrual cessation date), as reported to PBGC by the subpart C plan (including any early retirement subsidies), or through linear interpolation for participants who start payments between integral ages; or

(ii) *Other form of annuity.* At the participant's election, any form of annuity available to the participant under §4022.8 of this chapter, in an amount that is actuarially equivalent to the straight life annuity in paragraph (d)(1)(i) of this section as of the date that PBGC payments start (or, if earlier, the later of the participant's normal retirement date or accrual cessation date), determined using the actuarial assumptions in §4022.8(c)(7) of this chapter.

(2) *Make-up amount.* If PBGC begins to pay the annuity under paragraph (d)(1) of this section after the normal retirement date (or accrual cessation date if later), the make-up amount described in this paragraph (d)(2) is a lump sum equal to the aggregate value of payments of the annuity that would have been payable to the participant (in the elected form) beginning on the normal retirement date (or accrual cessation date if later), accumulated at the missing participants interest rate from the date each payment would have been made to the date when PBGC begins to pay the annuity.

(3) *Lump sum.* The lump sum described in this paragraph (d)(3) is equal to the participant's accumulated single sum.

(e) *Non-de minimis benefit of married participant.* If the benefit transfer amount of a married participant described in paragraph (b) of this section is not de minimis, PBGC will pay the participant either the annuity described in paragraph (e)(1) of this section, beginning not before age 55, and (if applicable) the make-up amount described in paragraph (e)(2) of this section; or, if the participant could have elected a lump sum under the subpart

C plan, and the participant so elects under the missing participants program with the consent of the participant's spouse, the lump sum described in paragraph (e)(3) of this section.

(1) *Annuity.* The annuity described in this paragraph (e)(1) is either—

(i) *Joint and survivor annuity.* A joint and 50 percent survivor annuity in an amount that is actuarially equivalent to the straight life annuity under paragraph (d)(1)(i) of this section as of the date that PBGC payments start (or, if earlier, the later of the participant's normal retirement date or accrual cessation date), determined using the actuarial assumptions in §4022.8(c)(7) of this chapter; or

(ii) *Other form of annuity.* At the participant's election, with the consent of the participant's spouse, any form of annuity available to the participant under §4022.8 of this chapter, in an amount that is actuarially equivalent to the joint and 50 percent survivor annuity under paragraph (e)(1)(i) of this section as of the date that PBGC payments start (or, if earlier, the later of the participant's normal retirement date or accrual cessation date), determined using the actuarial assumptions in §4022.8(c)(7) of this chapter.

(2) *Make-up amount.* If PBGC begins to pay the annuity under paragraph (e)(1) of this section after the normal retirement date (or accrual cessation date if later), the make-up amount described in this paragraph (e)(2) is a lump sum equal to the aggregate value of payments of the annuity that would have been payable to the participant beginning on the normal retirement date (or accrual cessation date if later), accumulated at the missing participants interest rate from the date each payment would have been made to the date when PBGC begins to pay the annuity.

(3) *Lump sum.* The lump sum described in this paragraph (e)(3) is equal to the participant's accumulated single sum.

(f) *Benefits with respect to deceased missing distributees who were participants.* Paragraphs (g), (h), (i), (j), and (k) of this section describe the benefits that PBGC will pay with respect to a non-pay status missing participant of a subpart C plan who dies without receiving a benefit under the missing participants program.

(g) *De minimis benefit.* If the benefit transfer amount of a participant described in paragraph (f) of this section is de minimis, PBGC will pay to the qualified survivor(s) of the participant a lump sum equal to the participant's accumulated single sum.

(h) *Non-de minimis benefit; unmarried participant.* In the case of an unmarried participant described in paragraph (f) of this section whose benefit transfer amount is not de minimis,—

(1) *Death before normal retirement date.* If the participant dies before the normal retirement date (or accrual cessation date if later), PBGC will pay no benefits with respect to the participant; and

(2) *Death after normal retirement date.* If the participant dies on or after the normal retirement date (or accrual cessation date if later), PBGC will pay to the participant's qualified survivor(s) an amount equal to the aggregate value of payments of the straight life annuity described in paragraph (d)(1)(i) of this section that would have been payable to the participant from the normal retirement date (or accrual cessation date if later) to the participant's date of death, accumulated at the missing participants interest rate from the date each payment would have been made to the date when PBGC pays the qualified survivor(s).

(i) *Non-de minimis benefit; married participant with living spouse.* In the case of a married participant described in paragraph (f) of this section whose benefit transfer amount is not de minimis and whose spouse survives the participant and claims a benefit under the missing participants program, PBGC will pay the spouse, beginning not before the participant would have reached age 55, the annuity (if any) described in paragraph (i)(1) of this section and the make-up amounts (if applicable) described in paragraph (i)(2) of this section, except that PBGC will pay the spouse, as a lump sum, the small benefit described in paragraph (i)(3) of this section.

(1) *Annuity.* The annuity described in this paragraph (i)(1) is the survivor portion of a joint and 50 percent survivor annuity that is actuarially equivalent as of the assumed starting date (determined using the actuarial assumptions in §4022.8(c)(7) of this chapter) to the straight life annuity in the amount that the subpart C plan would have paid the participant with an assumed starting date of—

(i) The date when the participant would have reached age 55, if the participant died before that date, or

(ii) The participant's date of death, if the participant died between age 55 and the normal retirement date (or accrual cessation date if later), or

(iii) The normal retirement date (or accrual cessation date if later), if the participant died after that date.

(2) *Make-up amounts.* The make-up amounts described in this paragraph (i)(2) are the amounts described in paragraphs (i)(2)(i) and (ii) of this section.

(i) *Payments from participant's death or 55th birthday to commencement of survivor annuity.* The make-up amount described in this paragraph (i)(2)(i) is a lump sum equal to the aggregate value of payments of the survivor portion of the joint and 50 percent survivor annuity described in paragraph (i)(1) of this section that would have been payable to the spouse beginning on the later of the participant's date of death or the date when the participant would have reached age 55, accumulated at the missing participants interest rate from the date each payment would have been made to the date when PBGC pays the spouse.

⋙→ *Caution: Reg. Secs. 4050.101—4050.407 are effective January 22, 2018 and generally applicable to plans terminating on or after January 1, 2018.*

(ii) *Payments from normal retirement date to participant's death.* The makeup amount described in this paragraph (i)(2)(ii) is a lump sum equal to the aggregate value of payments (if any) of the joint portion of the joint and 50 percent survivor annuity described in paragraph (i)(1) of this section that would have been payable to the participant from the normal retirement date (or accrual cessation date if later) to the participant's date of death thereafter, accumulated at the missing participants interest rate from the date each payment would have been made to the date when PBGC pays the spouse.

(3) *Small benefit.* If the sum of the actuarial present value of the annuity described in paragraph (i)(1) of this section plus the make-up amounts described in paragraph (i)(2) of this section is de minimis, then the lump sum that PBGC will pay the spouse under this paragraph (i)(3) is an amount equal to that sum. For this purpose, the actuarial present value of the annuity is determined using the actuarial assumptions in §4022.8(c)(7) of this chapter as of the date when PBGC pays the spouse.

(j) *Non-de minimis benefit; married participant with deceased spouse.* In the case of a married participant described in paragraph (f) of this section whose benefit transfer amount is not de minimis and whose spouse survives the participant but dies without receiving a benefit under the missing participants program, PBGC will pay to the qualified survivor(s) of the participant's spouse the make-up amount described in paragraph (j)(1) of this section and to the qualified survivor(s) of the participant the make-up amount described in paragraph (j)(2) of this section.

(1) *Payments from participant's death or 55th birthday to spouse's death.* The make-up amount described in this paragraph (j)(1) is a lump sum equal to the aggregate value of payments of the survivor portion of the joint and 50 percent survivor annuity described in paragraph (i)(1) of this section that would have been payable to the spouse from the later of the participant's date of death or the date when the participant would have reached age 55 to the spouse's date of death, accumulated at the missing participants interest rate from the date each payment

would have been made to the date when PBGC pays the spouse's qualified survivor(s).

(2) *Payments from normal retirement date to participant's death.* The makeup amount described in this paragraph (j)(2) is a lump sum equal to the aggregate value of payments of the joint portion of the joint and 50 percent survivor annuity described in paragraph (i)(1) of this section that would have been payable to the participant from the normal retirement date (or accrual cessation date if later) to the participant's date of death thereafter, accumulated at the missing participants interest rate from the date each payment would have been made to the date when PBGC pays the participant's qualified survivor(s).

(k) *Benefits under contributory plans.* If a subpart C plan reports to PBGC that a portion of a missing participant's benefit transfer amount represents accumulated contributions as described in section 204(c)(2)(C) of ERISA and section 411(c)(2)(C) of the Code, PBGC will pay with respect to the missing participant, at least the amount of accumulated contributions as reported by the subpart C plan, accumulated at the missing participants interest rate from the benefit determination date to the date when PBGC makes payment.

(l) *Date for determining marital status.* For purposes of this section, whether a participant is married, and if so the identity of the spouse, is determined as of the earlier of—

(1) The date the participant receives or begins to receive a benefit, or

(2) The date the participant dies.

[¶ 15,532B]

§4050.307 **PBGC discretion.** PBGC may in appropriate circumstances extend deadlines, excuse noncompliance, and grant waivers with regard to any provision of this subpart to promote the purposes of the missing participants program and title IV of ERISA. Like circumstances will be treated in like manner under this section.

⋙→ *Caution: Reg. Secs. 4050.101—4050.407 are effective January 22, 2018 and generally applicable to plans terminating on or after January 1, 2018.*

Subpart D—Multiemployer Plans Covered by Title IV

[¶ 15,532M]

§4050.401 **Purpose and scope.** (a) *In general.* This subpart describes PBGC's missing participants program for multiemployer defined benefit retirement plans covered by title IV of ERISA. The missing participants program is a program to hold retirement benefits for missing participants and beneficiaries in retirement plans that are closing out and to help them find and receive the benefits being held for them. For a plan to which this subpart applies, this subpart describes what the plan must do upon plan termination if it has missing participants or beneficiaries who are entitled to distributions. This subpart applies to a plan only if it is a multiemployer defined benefit plan that—

(1) Is described in section 4021(a) of ERISA and not in any paragraph of section 4021(b) of ERISA, and

(2) Completes the process of closing out under subpart D of PBGC's regulation on Termination of Multiemployer Plans (29 CFR part 4041A).

(b) *Plans that terminate but do not close out.* This subpart does not apply to plans that terminate but do not close out.

(c) *Individual account plans.* This subpart does not apply to an individual account plan under section 3(34) of ERISA, even if it is described in the same plan document as a plan to which this subpart applies. This subpart also does not apply to a plan to the extent that it is treated as an individual account plan under section 3(35)(B) of ERISA. For example, this subpart does not apply to employee contributions (or interest or earnings thereon) held as an individual account. (Subpart B deals with individual account plans.)

[¶ 15,532N]

§4050.402 **Definitions.** The following terms are defined in §4001.2 of this chapter: Annuity, Code, ERISA, insurer, PBGC, person, and plan sponsor. In addition, for purposes of this subpart:

Accrual cessation date for a participant under a subpart D plan means the date the participant stopped accruing benefits under the terms of the plan.

Accumulated single sum means, with respect to a missing distributee, the distributee's benefit transfer amount accumulated at the missing participants interest rate from the benefit determination date to the date when PBGC makes or commences payment to or with respect to the distributee.

Benefit determination date with respect to a subpart D plan means the single date selected by the plan sponsor for valuing benefits under §4050.103(d); this date must be during the period beginning on the first day a distribution is made pursuant to close-out of the plan to a distributee who is not a missing distributee and ending on the last day such a distribution is made.

Benefit transfer amount for a missing distributee of a subpart D plan means the amount determined by the plan sponsor under §4050.403(d) in the close-out of the plan.

Close-out or *close out* with respect to a subpart D plan means the process of the final distribution or transfer of assets in satisfaction of plan benefits.

De minimis means, with respect to the value of a benefit (or other amount), that the value does not exceed the amount specified under section 203(e)(1) of ERISA and section 411(a)(11)(A) of the Code (without regard to plan provisions).

Distributee means, with respect to a subpart D plan, a participant or beneficiary entitled to a distribution under the subpart D plan pursuant to the close-out of the subpart D plan.

»»→ *Caution: Reg. Secs. 4050.101—4050.407 are effective January 22, 2018 and generally applicable to plans terminating on or after January 1, 2018.*

Missing, with respect to a distributee under a subpart D plan, means that any one or more of the following three conditions exists upon close-out of the plan.

(1) The plan sponsor does not know with reasonable certainty the location of the distributee.

(2) Under the terms of the plan, the distributee's benefit is to be paid in a lump sum without the distributee's consent, and the distributee has not responded to a notice about the distribution of the lump sum.

(3) Under the terms of the plan and any election made by the distributee, the distributee's benefit is to be paid in a lump sum, but the distributee does not accept the lump sum. For this purpose, a lump sum paid by check is not accepted if the check remains uncashed after—

(i) A "cash-by" date prescribed (on the check or in an accompanying notice) that is at least 45 days after the issuance of the check, or

(ii) If no such "cash-by" date is so prescribed, the check's stale date.

Missing participants forms and instructions means the forms and instructions provided by PBGC for use in connection with the missing participants program.

Missing participants interest rate means, for each month, the applicable federal mid-term rate (as determined by the Secretary of the Treasury pursuant to section 1274(d)(1)(C)(ii) of the Code) for that month, compounded monthly.

Normal retirement date for a participant under a subpart D plan means the normal retirement date of the participant under the terms of the plan.

Pay-status or *pay status* means one of the following (according to context):

(1) With respect to a benefit, that payment of the benefit has actually started before the benefit determination date; or

(2) With respect to a distributee, that payment of the distributee's benefit has actually started before the benefit determination date.

PBGC missing participants assumptions means the actuarial assumptions prescribed in §§ 4044.51 through 4044.57 of this chapter with the following modifications:

(1) The present value is determined as of the benefit determination date instead of the plan termination date.

(2) The mortality assumption is a fixed blend of 50 percent of the healthy male mortality rates in § 4044.53(c)(1) of this chapter and 50 percent of the healthy female mortality rates in § 4044.53(c)(2) of this chapter.

(3) No adjustment is made for loading expenses under § 4044.52(d) of this chapter.

(4) The interest assumption used is the assumption applicable to valuations occurring in January of the calendar year in which the benefit determination date occurs.

(5) The assumed payment form of a benefit not in pay status is a straight life annuity.

(6) Pre-retirement death benefits are disregarded.

(7) Notwithstanding the expected retirement age (XRA) assumptions in §§ 4044.55 through 4044.57 of this chapter,—

(i) In the case of a participant who is not in pay status and whose normal retirement date is on or after the benefit determination date, benefits are assumed to commence at the XRA, determined using the high retirement rate category under Table II–C of Appendix D to part 4044 of this chapter;

(ii) In the case of a participant who is not in pay status and whose normal retirement date is before the benefit determination date, benefits are assumed to commence on the participant's normal retirement date (or accrual cessation date if later);

(iii) In the case of a participant who is in pay status, benefits are assumed to commence on the date on which benefits actually commenced; and

(iv) In the case of a beneficiary, benefits are assumed to commence on the benefit determination date or, if later, the earliest date the beneficiary can begin to receive benefits.

Plan lump sum assumptions means, with respect to a subpart D plan, the following:

(1) If the plan specifies actuarial assumptions and methods to be used to calculate a lump sum distribution, such actuarial assumptions and methods, or

(2) Otherwise, the actuarial assumptions specified under section 205(g)(3) of ERISA and section 417(e)(3) of the Code, determined as of the benefit determination date, including use of the missing participants interest rate to calculate the present value as of the benefit determination date of a payment or payments missed in the past.

QDRO means a qualified domestic relations order as defined in section 206(d)(3) of ERISA and section 414(p) of the Code.

Qualified survivor of a participant or beneficiary under a subpart D plan means, for any benefit with respect to the participant or beneficiary,—

(1) A person who survives the participant or beneficiary and is entitled under applicable provisions of a QDRO to receive the benefit;

(2) A person that is identified by the plan in a submission to PBGC by the plan as being entitled under applicable plan provisions (including elections, designations, and waivers consistent with such provisions) to receive the benefit; or

(3) If no such person is so entitled, a survivor of the participant or beneficiary who is the participant's or beneficiary's living—

(i) Spouse, or if none,

(ii) Child, or if none,

(iii) Parent, or if none,

(iv) Sibling.

Subpart D plan or *plan* means a plan to which this subpart D applies, as described in § 4050.401.

[¶ 15,532O]

§ 4050.403 **Duties of plan sponsor**. (a) *Providing for benefits.* For each distributee who is missing upon closeout of a subpart D plan, the plan sponsor must provide for the distributee's plan benefits either—

(1) By purchase of an annuity contract from an insurer; or

(2) By—

(i) Determining the distributee's benefit transfer amount under paragraph (e) of this section, and

(ii) Transferring to PBGC as described in this subpart D an amount equal to the distributee's benefit transfer amount.

(b) *Diligent search.* For each distributee whose location the plan sponsor does not know with reasonable certainty upon close-out of a subpart D plan, the plan sponsor must have conducted a diligent search as described in § 4050.404.

(c) *Filing with PBGC.* For each distributee who is missing upon closeout of a subpart D plan, the plan sponsor must file with PBGC as described in § 4050.405.

(d) *Benefit transfer amount.* The benefit transfer amount for a missing distributee is the amount determined by the plan sponsor as of the benefit determination date using whichever one of the following three methods applies:

(1) *De minimis.* If the single sum actuarial equivalent of the distributee's benefits (including any payments missed in the past) determined using plan lump sum assumptions is de minimis, then the missing distributee's benefit transfer amount is equal to that single sum.

(2) *Non-de minimis; single sum payment cannot be elected.* If the single sum actuarial equivalent of the distributee's benefits (including any payments missed in the past) determined using plan lump sum assumptions is not de minimis, and a single sum payment cannot be elected, then the missing distributee's benefit transfer amount is the present value of the distributee's accrued benefit determined using PBGC missing participants assumptions, plus

(i) For a missing distributee not in pay status whose normal retirement date (or accrual cessation date if later) precedes the benefit determination date, the aggregate value of payments of the straight life annuity that would have been payable beginning on the normal retirement date (or accrual cessation date if later), accumulated at the missing participants interest rate from the date each payment would have been made to the benefit determination date, assuming that the distributee survived to the benefit determination date, as determined by the plan sponsor; or

(ii) For a missing distributee in pay status, the aggregate value of payments of the pay status annuity due but not made, accumulated at the missing participants interest rate from each payment due date to the benefit determination date, assuming that the distributee survived to the benefit determination date.

(3) *Non-de minimis; single sum payment can be elected.* If the single sum actuarial equivalent of the distributee's benefits (including any payments missed in the past) determined using plan lump sum assumptions is not de minimis, and a single sum payment can be elected, then the missing distributee's benefit transfer amount is the greater of the amounts determined using the methodology in paragraph (d)(1) or (d)(2) of this section.

[¶ 15,532P]

§ 4050.404 **Diligent search**. (a) *Search requirement.* The plan sponsor of a subpart D plan must, within the time frame described in paragraph (d) of this section, have diligently searched for each distributee of the plan whose location the plan sponsor does not know with reasonable certainty upon close-out, using one of the following two methods:

(1) For any distributee, regardless of the size of the distributee's benefit, the commercial locator service method described in paragraph (b) of this section; or

(2) For a distributee whose normal retirement benefit is not more than $50 per month, the records search method described in paragraph (c) of this section.

(b) *Commercial locator service method—*

(1) *In general.* Using the commercial locator service method means paying a commercial locator service to search for information to locate a distributee.

(2) *Meaning of "commercial locator service".* For purposes of this section, a commercial locator service is a business that holds itself out as a finder of lost persons for compensation using information from a database maintained by a consumer reporting agency (as defined in 15 U.S.C. 1681a(f)).

(c) *Records search method—*

(1) *In general.* Using the records search method means searching for information to locate a distributee by doing all of the following to the extent reasonably feasible and affordable:

(i) Searching the records of the plan for information to locate the distributee.

(ii) Searching the records of the contributing sponsor that is the most recent employer of the distributee for information to locate the distributee.

(iii) Searching the records of each retirement or welfare plan of the contributing sponsor in which the distributee was a participant for information to locate the distributee.

(iv) Contacting each beneficiary of the distributee identified from the records referred to in paragraphs (c)(1)(i), (ii), and (iii) of this section for information to locate the distributee.

(v) Using an internet search method for which no fee is charged, such as a search engine, a network database, a public record database (such as those for licenses, mortgages, and real estate taxes) or a "social media" website.

(2) *Limits on method.* For purposes of this section,—

(i) Searching is not feasible to the extent that, as a practical matter, it is thwarted by legal or practical lack of access to records, and

(ii) Searching is not affordable to the extent that the cost of searching (including the value of labor) is more than a reasonable fraction of the benefit of the distributee being searched for. In no event would searching need to be pursued beyond the point where the cost equals the value of the benefit.

(d) *Time frame.* A search for a distributee under this section must have been made within nine months before a filing is made under § 4050.405 identifying the distributee as a missing distributee.

[¶ 15,532Q]

§ 4050.405 **Filing with PBGC**. (a) *What to file.* The plan sponsor of a subpart D plan must file with PBGC the information specified in the missing participants forms and instructions and, for a missing distributee referred to in § 4050.403(a)(2), payment of—

(1) The benefit transfer amount for the missing distributee;

(2) If the benefit transfer amount is paid more than 90 days after the benefit determination date, interest on the benefit transfer amount computed at the missing participants interest rate for the period beginning on the 90th day after the benefit determination date and ending on the date the benefit transfer amount is paid to PBGC; and

(3) Any fee provided for in the missing participants forms and instructions.

(b) *When to file.* The plan sponsor must file the information and payments referred to in paragraph (a) of this section in accordance with the missing participants forms and instructions. Payment of a benefit transfer amount will, if considered timely made for purposes of this paragraph (b), be considered timely made for purposes of part 4041A of this chapter.

(c) *Place, method and date of filing; time periods.* (1) For rules about where to file, see § 4000.4 of this chapter.

(2) For rules about permissible methods of filing with PBGC under this subpart, see subpart A of part 4000 of this chapter.

(3) For rules about the date that a submission under this subpart was filed with PBGC, see subpart C of part 4000 of this chapter.

(4) For rules about any time period for filing under this subpart, see subpart D of part 4000 of this chapter.

(d) *Supplemental information.* Within 30 days after a written request by PBGC (or such other time as may be specified in the request), the plan sponsor of a subpart D plan required to file under paragraph (a) of this section must file with PBGC supplemental information for any proper purpose under the missing participants program.

(e) *Reliance.* As administrator of the missing participants program, PBGC will rely on determinations made and information reported by plan sponsors in connection with the program. This reliance does not affect PBGC's authority as administrator of the title IV insurance program to audit or make inquiries of subpart D plans, including about the amount to which a missing distributee may be entitled.

[¶ 15,532R]

§ 4050.406 **Missing participant benefits**. (a) *In general—*

(1) *Benefit transfer amount not paid.* If a subpart D plan files with PBGC information about an annuity contract purchased by the subpart D plan from an insurer for a missing distributee, PBGC will provide information about the annuity contract to the distributee or another claimant that may be entitled to payment pursuant to the contract.

(2) *Benefit transfer amount paid.* If a subpart D plan pays PBGC a benefit transfer amount for a missing distributee, PBGC will pay benefits with respect to the missing distributee in accordance with this section, subject to the provisions of a QDRO.

(b) *Benefits for missing distributees who are participants.* Paragraphs (c), (d), (e), and (k) of this section describe the benefits

⫸ *Caution: Reg. Secs. 4050.101—4050.407 are effective January 22, 2018 and generally applicable to plans terminating on or after January 1, 2018.*

that PBGC will pay to a non-pay status missing participant of a subpart D plan who claims a benefit under the missing participants program.

(c) *De minimis benefit.* If the benefit transfer amount of a participant described in paragraph (b) of this section is de minimis, PBGC will pay the participant a lump sum equal to the accumulated single sum.

(d) *Non-de minimis benefit of unmarried participant.* If the benefit transfer amount of an unmarried participant described in paragraph (b) of this section is not de minimis, PBGC will pay the participant either the annuity described in paragraph (d)(1) of this section, beginning not before age 55, and (if applicable) the make-up amount described in paragraph (d)(2) of this section; or, if the participant could have elected a lump sum under the subpart D plan, and the participant so elects under the missing participants program, the lump sum described in paragraph (d)(3) of this section.

(1) *Annuity.* The annuity described in this paragraph (d)(1) is either—

(i) *Straight life annuity.* A straight life annuity in the amount that the subpart D plan would have paid the participant, starting at the date that PBGC payments start (or, if earlier, the later of the participant's normal retirement date or accrual cessation date), as reported to PBGC by the subpart D plan (including any early retirement subsidies), or through linear interpolation for participants who start payments between integral ages; or

(ii) *Other form of annuity.* At the participant's election, any form of annuity available to the participant under §4022.8 of this chapter, in an amount that is actuarially equivalent to the straight life annuity in paragraph (d)(1)(i) of this section as of the date that PBGC payments start (or, if earlier, the later of the participant's normal retirement date or accrual cessation date), determined using the actuarial assumptions in §4022.8(c)(7) of this chapter.

(2) *Make-up amount.* If PBGC begins to pay the annuity under paragraph (d)(1) of this section after the normal retirement date (or accrual cessation date if later), the make-up amount described in this paragraph (d)(2) is a lump sum equal to the aggregate value of payments of the annuity that would have been payable to the participant (in the elected form) beginning on the normal retirement date (or accrual cessation date if later), accumulated at the missing participants interest rate from the date each payment would have been made to the date when PBGC begins to pay the annuity.

(3) *Lump sum.* The lump sum described in this paragraph (d)(3) is equal to the participant's accumulated single sum.

(e) *Non-de minimis benefit of married participant.* If the benefit transfer amount of a married participant described in paragraph (b) of this section is not de minimis, PBGC will pay the participant either the annuity described in paragraph (e)(1) of this section, beginning not before age 55, and (if applicable) the make-up amount described in paragraph (e)(2) of this section; or, if the participant could have elected a lump sum under the subpart

D plan, and the participant so elects under the missing participants program with the consent of the participant's spouse, the lump sum described in paragraph (e)(3) of this section.

(1) *Annuity.* The annuity described in this paragraph (e)(1) is either—

(i) *Joint and survivor annuity.* A joint and 50 percent survivor annuity in an amount that is actuarially equivalent to the straight life annuity under paragraph (d)(1)(i) of this section as of the date that PBGC payments start (or, if earlier, the later of the participant's normal retirement date or accrual cessation date), determined using the actuarial assumptions in §4022.8(c)(7) of this chapter; or

(ii) *Other form of annuity.* At the participant's election, with the consent of the participant's spouse, any form of annuity available to the participant under §4022.8 of this chapter, in an amount that is

actuarially equivalent to the joint and 50 percent survivor annuity under paragraph (e)(1)(i) of this section as of the date that PBGC payments start (or, if earlier, the later of the participant's normal retirement date or accrual cessation date), determined using the actuarial assumptions in §4022.8(c)(7) of this chapter.

(2) *Make-up amount.* If PBGC begins to pay the annuity under paragraph (e)(1) of this section after the normal retirement date (or accrual cessation date if later), the make-up amount described in this paragraph (e)(2) is a lump sum equal to the aggregate value of payments of the annuity that would have been payable to the participant beginning on the normal retirement date (or accrual cessation date if later), accumulated at the missing participants interest rate from the date each payment would have been made to the date when PBGC begins to pay the annuity.

(3) *Lump sum.* The lump sum described in this paragraph (e)(3) is equal to the participant's accumulated single sum.

(f) *Benefits with respect to deceased missing distributees who were participants.* Paragraphs (g), (h), (i), (j), and (k) of this section describe the benefits that PBGC will pay with respect to a non-pay status missing participant of a subpart D plan who dies without receiving a benefit under the missing participants program.

(g) *De minimis benefit.* If the benefit transfer amount of a participant described in paragraph (f) of this section is de minimis, PBGC will pay to the qualified survivor(s) of the participant a lump sum equal to the participant's accumulated single sum.

(h) *Non-de minimis benefit; unmarried participant.* In the case of an unmarried participant described in paragraph (f) of this section whose benefit transfer amount is not de minimis—

(1) *Death before normal retirement date.* If the participant dies before the normal retirement date (or accrual cessation date if later), PBGC will pay no benefits with respect to the participant; and

(2) *Death after normal retirement date.* If the participant dies on or after the normal retirement date (or accrual cessation date if later), PBGC will pay to the participant's qualified survivor(s) an amount equal to the aggregate value of payments of the straight life annuity described in paragraph (d)(1)(i) of this section that would have been payable to the participant from the normal retirement date (or accrual cessation date if later) to the participant's date of death, accumulated at the missing participants interest rate from the date each payment would have been made to the date when PBGC pays the qualified survivor(s).

(i) *Non-de minimis benefit; married participant with living spouse.* In the case of a married participant described in paragraph (f) of this section whose benefit transfer amount is not de minimis and whose spouse survives the participant and claims a benefit under the missing participants program, PBGC will pay the spouse, beginning not before the participant would have reached age 55, the annuity (if any) described in paragraph (i)(1) of this section and the make-up amounts (if applicable) described in paragraph (i)(2) of this section, except that PBGC will pay the spouse, as a lump sum, the small benefit described in paragraph (i)(3) of this section.

(1) *Annuity.* The annuity described in this paragraph (i)(1) is the survivor portion of a joint and 50 percent survivor annuity that is actuarially equivalent as of the assumed starting date (determined using the actuarial assumptions in §4022.8(c)(7) of this chapter) to the straight life annuity in the amount that the subpart D plan would have paid the participant with an assumed starting date of—

(i) The date when the participant would have reached age 55, if the participant died before that date, or

(ii) The participant's date of death, if the participant died between age 55 and the normal retirement date (or accrual cessation date if later), or

(iii) The normal retirement date (or accrual cessation date if later), if the participant died after that date.

>>>→ *Caution: Reg. Secs. 4050.101—4050.407 are effective January 22, 2018 and generally applicable to plans terminating on or after January 1, 2018.*

(2) *Make-up amounts.* The make-up amounts described in this paragraph (i)(2) are the amounts described in paragraphs (i)(2)(i) and (ii) of this section.

(i) *Payments from participant's death or 55th birthday to commencement of survivor annuity.* The make-up amount described in this paragraph (i)(2)(i) is a lump sum equal to the aggregate value of payments of the survivor portion of the joint and 50 percent survivor annuity described in paragraph (i)(1) of this section that would have been payable to the spouse beginning on the later of the participant's date of death or the date when the participant would have reached age 55, accumulated at the missing participants interest rate from the date each payment would have been made to the date when PBGC pays the spouse.

(ii) *Payments from normal retirement date to participant's death.* The makeup amount described in this paragraph (i)(2)(ii) is a lump sum equal to the aggregate value of payments (if any) of the joint portion of the joint and 50 percent survivor annuity described in paragraph (i)(1) of this section that would have been payable to the participant from the normal retirement date (or accrual cessation date if later) to the participant's date of death thereafter, accumulated at the missing participants interest rate from the date each payment would have been made to the date when PBGC pays the spouse.

(3) *Small benefit.* If the sum of the actuarial present value of the annuity described in paragraph (i)(1) of this section plus the make-up amounts described in paragraph (i)(2) of this section is de minimis, then the lump sum that PBGC will pay the spouse under this paragraph (i)(3) is an amount equal to that sum. For this purpose, the actuarial present value of the annuity is determined using the actuarial assumptions in §4022.8(c)(7) of this chapter as of the date when PBGC pays the spouse.

(j) *Non-de minimis benefit; married participant with deceased spouse.* In the case of a married participant described in paragraph (f) of this section whose benefit transfer amount is not de minimis and whose spouse survives the participant but dies without receiving a benefit under the missing participants program, PBGC will pay to the qualified survivor(s) of the participant's spouse the make-up amount described in paragraph (j)(1) of this section and to the qualified survivor(s) of the participant the make-up amount described in paragraph (j)(2) of this section.

(1) *Payments from participant's death or 55th birthday to spouse's death.* The make-up amount described in this paragraph (j)(1) is a lump sum equal to the aggregate value of payments of the survivor portion of the joint and 50 percent survivor annuity described in paragraph (i)(1) of this section that would have been payable to the spouse from the later of the participant's date of death or the date when the participant would have reached age 55 to the spouse's date of death, accumulated at the missing participants interest rate from the date each payment would have been made to the date when PBGC pays the spouse's qualified survivor(s).

(2) *Payments from normal retirement date to participant's death.* The makeup amount described in this paragraph (j)(2) is a lump sum equal to the aggregate value of payments of the joint portion of the joint and 50 percent survivor annuity described in paragraph (i)(1) of this section that would have been payable to the participant from the normal retirement date (or accrual cessation date if later) to the participant's date of death thereafter, accumulated at the missing participants interest rate from the date each payment would have been made to the date when PBGC pays the participant's qualified survivor(s).

(k) *Benefits under contributory plans.* If a subpart D plan reports to PBGC that a portion of a missing participant's benefit transfer amount represents accumulated contributions as described in section 204(c)(2)(C) of ERISA and section 411(c)(2)(C) of the Code, PBGC will pay with respect to the missing participant, at least the amount of accumulated contributions as reported by the subpart D plan, accumulated at the missing participants interest rate from the benefit determination date to the date when PBGC makes payment.

(l) *Date for determining marital status.* For purposes of this section, whether a participant is married, and if so the identity of the spouse, is determined as of the earlier of—

(1) The date the participant receives or begins to receive a benefit, or

(2) The date the participant dies.

[¶ 15,532S]

§4050.407 **PBGC discretion.** PBGC may in appropriate circumstances extend deadlines, excuse noncompliance, and grant waivers with regard to any provision of this subpart to promote the purposes of the missing participants program and title IV of ERISA. Like circumstances will be treated in like manner under this section.

Subtitle D—Liability

[¶ 15,610]

AMOUNTS PAYABLE BY THE CORPORATION

Act Sec. 4061. The corporation shall pay benefits under a single-employer plan terminated under this title subject to the limitations and requirements of subtitle B of this title. The corporation shall provide financial assistance to pay benefits under a multiemployer plan which is insolvent under section 4245 or 4281(d)(2)(A), subject to the limitations and requirements of subtitles B, C, and E of this title. Amounts guaranteed by the corporation under sections 4022 and 4022A shall be paid by the corporation only out of the appropriate fund. The corporation shall make payments under the supplemental program to reimburse multiemployer plans for uncollectible withdrawal liability only out of the fund established under section 4005(e).

Amendment

P.L. 96-364, §403(f):

Amended Sec. 4061 to read as above, effective September 26, 1980. Prior to amendment, Sec. 4061 read as follows:

"The corporation shall pay benefits under a plan terminated under this title subject to the limitations and requirements of subtitle B of this title. Amounts guaranteed by the corporation under section 4022 shall be paid by the corporation out of the appropriate fund."

Regulations

The following regulations were adopted by the Pension Benefit Guaranty Corporation on July 1, 1996 (61 FR 34002). Prior to July 1, 1996, PBGC regulations were under Chapter XXVI of Title 29 of the Code of Federal Regulations. Effective July 1, 1996, PBGC regulations were moved to Chapter XL, and were renumbered and reorganized.

[¶ 15,611]

§4061.1 **Cross-references.** See part 4022 of this chapter regarding benefits payable under terminated single-employer plans and §4281.47

of this chapter regarding financial assistance to pay benefits under insolvent multiemployer plans.

[¶ 15,620]
LIABILITY FOR TERMINATION OF SINGLE-EMPLOYER PLANS UNDER A DISTRESS TERMINATION OR A TERMINATION BY THE CORPORATION

Act Sec. 4062.(a) In General. In any case in which a single-employer plan is terminated in a distress termination under section 4041(c) or a termination otherwise instituted by the corporation under section 4042, any person who is, on the termination date, a contributing sponsor of the plan or a member of such a contributing sponsor's controlled group shall incur liability under this section. The liability under this section of all such persons shall be joint and several. The liability under this section consists of—

(1) liability to the corporation, to the extent provided in subsection (b), and

(2) liability to the trustee appointed under subsection (b) or (c) of section 4042, to the extent provided in subsection (c).

(b) Liability to the Corporation.—

(1) Amount of liability.—

(A) In general. Except as provided in subparagraph (B), the liability to the corporation of a person described in subsection (a) shall be the total amount of the unfunded benefit liabilities (as to the termination date) to all participants and beneficiaries under the plan, together with interest (at a reasonable rate) calculated from the termination date in accordance with regulations prescribed by the corporation.

(B) Special rule in case of subsequent insufficiency. For purposes of subparagraph (A), in any case described in section 4041(c)(3)(C)(ii), actuarial present values shall be determined as of the date of the notice to the corporation (or the finding by the corporation) described in such section.

(2) Payment of liability.—

(A) In general. Except as provided in subparagraph (B), the liability to the corporation under this subsection shall be due and payable to the corporation as of the termination date, in cash or securities acceptable to the corporation.

(B) Special rule. Payment of so much of the liability under paragraph (1)(A) as exceeds 30 percent of the collective net worth of all persons described in subsection (a) (including interest)" shall be made under commercially reasonable terms prescribed by the corporation. The parties involved shall make a reasonable effort to reach the agreement on such commercially reasonable terms. Any such terms prescribed by the corporation shall provide for deferral of 50 percent of any amount of liability otherwise payable for any year under this subparagraph if a person subject to such liability demonstrates to the satisfaction of the corporation that no person subject to such liability has any individual pre-tax profits for such person's fiscal year ending during such year.

(3) Alternative arrangements. The corporation and any person liable under this section may agree to alternative arrangements for the satisfaction of liability to the corporation under this subsection.

(c) Liability to Section 4042 Trustee. —A person described in subsection (a) shall be subject to liability under this subsection to the trustee appointed under subsection (b) or (c). The liability of such person under this subsection shall consist of—

(1) the sum of the shortfall amortization charge (within the meaning of section 303(c)(1) of this Act and 430(d)(1) of the Internal Revenue Code of 1986) with respect to the plan (if any) for the plan year in which the termination date occurs, plus the aggregate total of shortfall amortization installments (if any) determined for succeeding plan years under section 303(c)(2) of this Act and section 430(d)(2) of such Code (which, for purposes of this subparagraph, shall include any increase in such sum which would result if all applications for waivers of the minimum funding standard under section 302(c) of this Act and section 412(c) of such Code which are pending with respect to such plan were denied and if no additional contributions (other than those already made by the termination date) were made for the plan year in which the termination date occurs or for any previous plan year), and

(2) the sum of the waiver amortization charge (within the meaning of section 303(e)(1) of this Act and 430(e)(1) of the Internal Revenue Code of 1986) with respect to the plan (if any) for the plan year in which the termination date occurs, plus the aggregate total of waiver amortization installments (if any) determined for succeeding plan years under section 303(e)(2) of this Act and section 430(e)(2) of such Code.

(d) Definitions.

(1) Collective net worth of persons subject to liability.—

(A) In general. The collective net worth of persons subject to liability in connection with a plan termination consists of the sum of the individual net worths of all persons who—

(i) have individual net worths which are greater than zero, and

(ii) are (as of the termination date) contributing sponsors of the terminated plan or members of their controlled groups.

(B) Determination of net worth. For purposes of this paragraph, the net worth of a person is— .

(i) determined on whatever basis best reflects, in the determination of the corporation, the current status of the person's operations and prospects at the time chosen for determining the net worth of the person, and

(ii) increased by the amount of any transfers of assets made by the person which are determined by the corporation to be improper under the circumstances, including any such transfers which would be inappropriate under title 11, United States Code, if the person were a debtor in a case under chapter 7 of such title.

(C) Timing of determination. For purposes of this paragraph, determinations of net worth shall be made as of a day chosen by the corporation (during the 120-day period ending with the termination date) and shall be computed without regard to any liability under this section.

(2) Pre-tax profits. The term "pre-tax profits" means—

(A) except as provided in subparagraph (B), for any fiscal year of any person, such person's consolidated net income (excluding any extraordinary charges to income and including any extraordinary credits to income) for such fiscal year, as shown on audited financial statements prepared in accordance with generally accepted accounting principles, or

(B) for any fiscal year of an organization described in section 501(c) of the Internal Revenue Code of 1954, the excess of income over expenses (as such terms are defined for such organizations under generally accepted accounting principles),

before provision for or deduction of Federal or other income tax, any contribution to any single-employer plan of which such person is a contributing sponsor at any time during the period beginning on the termination date and ending with the end of such fiscal year, and any amounts required to be paid for such fiscal year under this section. The corporation may by regulation require such information to be filed on such forms as may be necessary to determine the existence and amount of such pre-tax profits.

(e) Treatment of Substantial Cessation of Operations.—

(1) General rule. —Except as provided in paragraphs (3) and (4), if there is a substantial cessation of operations at a facility in any location, the employer shall be treated with respect to any single employer plan established and maintained by the employer covering participants at such facility as if the

employer were a substantial employer under a plan under which more than one employer makes contributions and the provisions of sections 4063, 4064, and 4065 shall apply.

(2) SUBSTANTIAL CESSATION OF OPERATIONS. —For purposes of this subsection:

(A) IN GENERAL. —The term 'substantial cessation of operations' means a permanent cessation of operations at a facility which results in a workforce reduction of a number of eligible employees at the facility equivalent to more than 15 percent of the number of all eligible employees of the employer, determined immediately before the earlier of—

(i) the date of the employer's decision to implement such cessation, or

(ii) in the case of a workforce reduction which includes 1 or more eligible employees described in paragraph (6)(B), the earliest date on which any such eligible employee was separated from employment.

(B) WORKFORCE REDUCTION. —Subject to subparagraphs (C) and (D), the term 'workforce reduction' means the number of eligible employees at a facility who are separated from employment by reason of the permanent cessation of operations of the employer at the facility.

(C) RELOCATION OF WORKFORCE. —An eligible employee separated from employment at a facility shall not be taken into account in computing a workforce reduction if, within a reasonable period of time, the employee is replaced by the employer, at the same or another facility located in the United States, by an employee who is a citizen or resident of the United States.

(D) DISPOSITIONS. —If, whether by reason of a sale or other disposition of the assets or stock of a contributing sponsor (or any member of the same controlled group as such a sponsor) of the plan relating to operations at a facility or otherwise, an employer (the 'transferee employer') other than the employer which experiences the substantial cessation of operations (the 'transferor employer') conducts any portion of such operations, then—

(i) an eligible employee separated from employment with the transferor employer at the facility shall not be taken into account in computing a workforce reduction if—

(I) within a reasonable period of time, the employee is replaced by the transferee employer by an employee who is a citizen or resident of the United States; and

(II) in the case of an eligible employee who is a participant in a single employer plan maintained by the transferor employer, the transferee employer, within a reasonable period of time, maintains a single employer plan which includes the assets and liabilities attributable to the accrued benefit of the eligible employee at the time of separation from employment with the transferor employer; and

(ii) an eligible employee who continues to be employed at the facility by the transferee employer shall not be taken into account in computing a workforce reduction if—

(I) the eligible employee is not a participant in a single employer plan maintained by the transferor employer, or

(II) in any other case, the transferee employer, within a reasonable period of time, maintains a single employer plan which includes the assets and liabilities attributable to the accrued benefit of the eligible employee at the time of separation from employment with the transferor employer.

(3) EXEMPTION FOR PLANS WITH LIMITED UNDERFUNDING. —Paragraph (1) shall not apply with respect to a single employer plan if, for the plan year preceding the plan year in which the cessation occurred—

(A) there were fewer than 100 participants with accrued benefits under the plan as of the valuation date of the plan for the plan year (as determined under section 303(g)(2)); or

(B) the ratio of the market value of the assets of the plan to the funding target of the plan for the plan year was 90 percent or greater.

(4) ELECTION TO MAKE ADDITIONAL CONTRIBUTIONS TO SATISFY LIABILITY.—

(A) IN GENERAL. —An employer may elect to satisfy the employer's liability with respect to a plan by reason of paragraph (1) by making additional contributions to the plan in the amount determined under subparagraph (B) for each plan year in the 7-plan-year period beginning with the plan year in which the cessation occurred. Any such additional contribution for a plan year shall be in addition to any minimum required contribution under section 303 for such plan year and shall be paid not later than the earlier of—

(i) the due date for the minimum required contribution for such year under section 303(j); or

(ii) in the case of the first such contribution, the date that is 1 year after the date on which the employer notifies the Corporation of the substantial cessation of operations or the date the Corporation determines a substantial cessation of operations has occurred, and in the case of subsequent contributions, the same date in each succeeding year.

(B) AMOUNT DETERMINED.—

(i) IN GENERAL. —Except as provided in clause (iii), the amount determined under this subparagraph with respect to each plan year in the 7-plan-year period is the product of—

(I) $\frac{1}{7}$ of the unfunded vested benefits determined under section 4006(a)(3)(E) as of the valuation date of the plan (as determined under section 303(g)(2)) for the plan year preceding the plan year in which the cessation occurred; and

(II) the reduction fraction.

(ii) REDUCTION FRACTION. —For purposes of clause (i), the reduction fraction of a single employer plan is equal to—

(I) the number of participants with accrued benefits in the plan who were included in computing the workforce reduction under paragraph (2)(B) as a result of the cessation of operations at the facility; divided by

(II) the number of eligible employees of the employer who are participants with accrued benefits in the plan, determined as of the same date the determination under paragraph (2)(A) is made.

(iii) LIMITATION. —The additional contribution under this subparagraph for any plan year shall not exceed the excess, if any, of—

(I) 25 percent of the difference between the market value of the assets of the plan and the funding target of the plan for the preceding plan year; over

(II) the minimum required contribution under section 303 for the plan year.

(C) PERMITTED CESSATION OF ANNUAL INSTALLMENTS WHEN PLAN BECOMES SUFFICIENTLY FUNDED. —An employer's obligation to make additional contributions under this paragraph shall not apply to—

(i) the first plan year (beginning on or after the first day of the plan year in which the cessation occurs) for which the ratio of the market value of the assets of the plan to the funding target of the plan for the plan year is 90 percent or greater, or

(ii) any plan year following such first plan year.

(D) COORDINATION WITH FUNDING WAIVERS.—

(i) IN GENERAL. —If the Secretary of the Treasury issues a funding waiver under section 302(c) with respect to the plan for a plan year in the 7-plan-year period under subparagraph (A), the additional contribution with respect to such plan year shall be permanently waived.

(ii) NOTICE. —An employer maintaining a plan with respect to which such a funding waiver has been issued or a request for such a funding waiver is pending shall provide notice to the Secretary of the Treasury, in such form and at such time as the Secretary of the Treasury shall provide, of a cessation of operations to which paragraph (1) applies.

(E) ENFORCEMENT.—

(i) NOTICE. —An employer making the election under this paragraph shall provide notice to the Corporation, in accordance with rules prescribed by the Corporation, of—

(I) such election, not later than 30 days after the earlier of the date the employer notifies the Corporation of the substantial cessation of operations or the date the Corporation determines a substantial cessation of operations has occurred;

(II) the payment of each additional contribution, not later than 10 days after such payment;

(III) any failure to pay the additional contribution in the full amount for any year in the 7-plan-year period, not later than 10 days after the due date for such payment;

(IV) the waiver under subparagraph (D)(i) of the obligation to make an additional contribution for any year, not later than 30 days after the funding waiver described in such subparagraph is granted; and

(V) the cessation of any obligation to make additional contributions under subparagraph (C), not later than 10 days after the due date for payment of the additional contribution for the first plan year to which such cessation applies.

(ii) ACCELERATION OF LIABILITY TO THE PLAN FOR FAILURE TO PAY. —If an employer fails to pay the additional contribution in the full amount for any year in the 7-plan-year period by the due date for such payment, the employer shall, as of such date, be liable to the plan in an amount equal to the balance which remains unpaid as of such date of the aggregate amount of additional contributions required to be paid by the employer during such 7-year-plan period. The Corporation may waive or settle the liability described in the preceding sentence, at the discretion of the Corporation.

(iii) CIVIL ACTION. —The Corporation may bring a civil action in the district courts of the United States in accordance with section 4003(e) to compel an employer making such election to pay the additional contributions required under this paragraph.

(5) DEFINITIONS. —For purposes of this subsection:

(A) ELIGIBLE EMPLOYEE. —The term 'eligible employee' means an employee who is eligible to participate in an employee pension benefit plan (as defined in section 3(2)) established and maintained by the employer.

(B) FUNDING TARGET. —The term 'funding target' means, with respect to any plan year, the funding target as determined under section 4006(a)(3)(E)(iii)(I) for purposes of determining the premium paid to the Corporation under section 4007 for the plan year.

(C) MARKET VALUE. —The market value of the assets of a plan shall be determined in the same manner as for purposes of section 4006(a)(3)(E).

(6) SPECIAL RULES.—

(A) CHANGE IN OPERATION OF CERTAIN FACILITIES AND PROPERTY. —For purposes of paragraphs (1) and (2), an employer shall not be treated as ceasing operations at a qualified lodging facility (as defined in section 856(d)(9)(D) of the Internal Revenue Code of 1986) if such operations are continued by an eligible independent contractor (as defined in section 856(d)(9)(A) of such Code) pursuant to an agreement with the employer.

(B) AGGREGATION OF PRIOR SEPARATIONS. —The workforce reduction under paragraph (2) with respect to any cessation of operations shall be determined by taking into account any separation from employment of any eligible employee at the facility (other than a separation which is not taken into account as workforce reduction by reason of subparagraph (C) or (D) of paragraph (2)) which—

(i) is related to the permanent cessation of operations of the employer at the facility, and

(ii) occurs during the 3-year period preceding such cessation.

(C) NO ADDITION TO PREFUNDING BALANCE. —For purposes of section 303(f)(6)(B) and section 430(f)(6)(B) of the Internal Revenue Code of 1986, any additional contribution made under paragraph (4) shall be treated in the same manner as a contribution an employer is required to make in order to avoid a benefit reduction under paragraph (1), (2), or (4) of section 206(g) or subsection (b), (c), or (e) of section 436 of the Internal Revenue Code of 1986 for the plan year.

Amendments

P.L. 113-235, §1(a), Div. P:

Amended ERISA Sec. 4062 by inserting new subsection (e) to read as above.

Prior to amendment, ERISA Sec. 4062(e) read as follows:

(e) TREATMENT OF SUBSTANTIAL CESSATION OF OPERATIONS. If an employer ceases operations at a facility in any location and, as a result of such cessation of operations, more than 20 percent of the total number of his employees who are participants under a plan established and maintained by him are separated from employment, the employer shall be treated with respect to that plan as if he were a substantial employer under a plan under which more than one employer makes contributions and the provisions of sections 4063, 4064, and 4065 shall apply.

The above amendment shall apply to a cessation of operations or other event at a facility occurring on or after the date of enactment of this Act (December 16, 2014).

P.L. 113-235, §1(b)(2), Div. P:

Provides a transition rule, as follows:

TRANSITION RULE—An employer that had a cessation of operations before the date of enactment of this Act (as determined under subsection 4062(e) of the Employee Retirement Income Security Act of 1974 as in effect before the amendment made by this section), but did not enter into an arrangement with the Pension Benefit Guaranty Corporation to satisfy the requirements of such subsection (as so in effect) before such date of enactment, shall be permitted to make the election under section 4062(e)(4) of such Act (as in effect after the amendment made by this section) as if such cessation had occurred on such date of enactment. Such election shall be made not later than 30 days after such Corporation issues, on or after such date of the enactment, a final administrative determination that a substantial cessation of operations has occurred.

P.L. 109-280, Sec. 107(b)(4):

Amended ERISA Sec. 4062(c) by striking paragraphs (1), (2), and (3) and inserting new paragraphs (1) and (2) to read as above.

Prior to amendment, ERISA Sec. 4062(c) read as follows:

(c) LIABILITY TO SECTION 4042 TRUSTEE.—A person described in subsection (a) shall be subject to liability under this subsection to the trustee appointed under subsection (b) or (c). The liability of such person under this subsection shall consist of—

(1) the outstanding balance of the accumulated funding deficiencies (within the meaning of section 302(a)(2) of this Act and section 412(a) of the Internal Revenue Code of 1986) of the plan (if any) (which, for purposes of this subparagraph, shall include the amount of any increase in such accumulated funding deficiencies of the plan which would result if all pending applications for waivers of the minimum funding standard under section 303 of this Act or section 412(d) of such Code and for extensions of the amortization period under section 304 of this Act or section 412(e) of such Code with respect to such plan were denied and if no additional contributions (other than those already made by the termination date) were made for the plan year in which the termination date occurs or for any previous plan year),

(2) the outstanding balance of the amount of waived funding deficiencies of the plan waived before such date under section 303 of this Act or section 412(d) of such Code (if any), and

(3) the outstanding balance of the amount of decreases in the minimum funding standard allowed before such date under section 304 of this Act or section 412(e) of such Code (if any), together with interest (at a reasonable rate) calculated from the termination date in accordance with regulations prescribed by the corporation. The liability under this subsection shall be due and payable to such trustee as of the termination date, in cash or securities acceptable to such trustee.

The above amendment is effective for plan years beginning after 2007.

P.L. 101-239, §7881(f)(2):

Amended ERISA Sec. 4062(a) by inserting "and" at the end of paragraph (1); by striking paragraph (2); by redesignating paragraph (3) as paragraph (2); and in paragraph (2) (as redesignated) by striking "subsection (d)" and inserting "subsection (c)." Prior to being stricken, paragraph (2) read as follows:

(2) liability to the trust established pursuant to section 4041(c)(3)(B)(ii) or (iii) or section 4042(i) to the extent provided in subsection (c), and

P.L. 101-239, §7881(f)(10)(A):

Amended ERISA Sec. 4062(b)(2)(B) by striking "the liability under paragraph (1)(A)(ii)" and inserting "so much of the liability under paragraph (1)(A) as exceeds 30 percent of the collective net worth of all persons described in subsection (a) (including interest)."

P.L. 101-239, § 7881(f)(10)(B):

Amended P.L. 100-203, § 9312(b)(2)(B)(ii) to read as below.

The above amendments are effective as if included in P.L. 100-203, § 9312.

P.L. 101-239, § 7891(a)(1):

Titles I, III, and IV of ERISA (other than sections 3(37)(E), 301(a)(7), and 308, the last sentence of section 408(d), and sections 414(c), 4001(a)(3)(ii), and 4303) are each amended by striking "Internal Revenue Code of 1954" each place it appears and inserting "Internal Revenue Code of 1986" effective October 22, 1986.

P.L. 100-203, § 9312(b)(1)(A):

Repealed ERISA Sec. 4062(c) effective for (A) plan terminations under section 4041(c) of ERISA with respect to which notices of intent to terminate are provided under section 4041(a)(2) of ERISA after December 17, 1987, and (B) plan terminations with respect to which proceedings are instituted by the Pension Benefit Guaranty Corporation under section 4042 of ERISA after December 17, 1987.

Prior to repeal, ERISA Sec. 4062(c) read as follows:

Act Sec. 4062. (c) Liability to Section 4049 Trust.—

(1) Amount of Liability.—

(A) In General.—In any case in which there is an outstanding amount of benefit commitments under a plan terminated under section 4041(c) or 4042, a person described in subsection (a) shall be subject to liability under this subsection to the trust established under section 4041(c)(3)(B)(ii) or (iii) or section 4042(i) in connection with the terminated plan. Except as provided in subparagraph (B), the liability of such person under this subsection shall consist of the lesser of—

(i) 75 pecent of the total outstanding amount of benefit commitments under the plan, or

(ii) 15 percent of the actuarial present value (determined as of the termination date of the basis of assumptions prescribed by the corporation for purposes of section 4044) of all benefit commitments under the plan.

(B) Special Rule in Case of Subsequent Insufficiency.—For purposes of subparagraph (A)—

(i) Plan Insufficient for Guaranteed Benefits.—In any case described in section 4041(c)(3)(C)(ii), actuarial present values shall be determined as of the date of the notice to the corporation (or the finding by the corporation) described in such section.

(ii) Plans Sufficient for Guaranteed Benefits but Insufficient for Benefit Entitlement.—In any case described in section 4041(c)(3)(C)(i) but not described in section 4041(c)(3)(C)(ii), actuarial present values shall be determined as of the date on which the final distribution of assets is completed.

(2) Payment of Liability.—

(A) General Rule.—Except as otherwise provided in this paragraph, payment of a person's liability under this subsection shall be made for liability payment years under commercially reasonable terms prescribed by the fiduciary designated by corporation pursuant to section 4049(b)(1)(A). Such fiduciary and the liable persons assessed liability under this subsection shall make a reasonable effort to reach agreement on such commercially reasonable terms.

(B) Special Rule for Plans with Low Amounts of Liability.—In any case in which the amount described in paragraph (1)(A) is less than $100,000, the requirements of subparagraph (A) may be satisfied by payment of such liability over 10 liability payment years in equal annual installments (with interest at the rate determined under section 6621(b) of the Internal Revenue Code of 1954). The corporation may, by regulation, increase the dollar amount referred to in this subparagraph as it determines appropriate, taking into account reasonable administrative costs of trusts established under section 4041(c)(3)(B)(ii) or (iii) or section 4042(i).

(C) Deferral of Payments.—The terms of payment provided for under subparagraph (A) or (B) shall also provide for deferral of 75 percent of any amount of liability otherwise payable for any liability payment year if a person subject to such liability demonstrates to the satisfaction of the corporation that no person subject to such liability has any individual pre-tax profits for such person's fiscal year ending during such year. The amount of liability so deferred is payable only after payment in full of any amount of liability under subsection (b) in connection with the termination of the same plan which has been deferred pursuant to terms provided for under subsection (b)(2)(B).

P.L. 100-203, § 9312(b)(1)(B):

Amended ERISA Sec. 4062 by redesignating subsections (d), (e) and (f) as (c), (d) and (e). For the effective date, see Act Sec. 9312(b)(1)(A), above.

P.L. 100-203, § 9312(b)(2)(A):

Amended ERISA Sec. 4062(b)(1)(A) to read as above. For the effective date, see Act Sec. 9312(b)(1)(A), above. Prior to amendment, ERISA Sec. 4062(b)(1)(A) read as follows:

(A) In General.—Except as provided in subparagraph (B), the liability to the corporation of a person described in subsection (a) shall consist of the sum of—

(1) the lesser of—

(I) the total amount of unfunded guaranteed benefits (as of the termination date) of all participants and beneficiaries under the plan, or

(II) 30 percent of the collective net worth of all persons described in subsection (a), and

(ii) the excess (if any) of—

(I) 75 percent of the amount described in clause (i)(I), over

(II) the amount described in clause (i)(II), together with interest (at a reasonable rate) calculated from the termination date in accordance with regulations prescribed by the corporation.

P.L. 100-203, § 9312(b)(2)(B)(ii):

Amended ERISA Sec. 4062(d) by striking out paragraph 3. For the effective date, see Act Sec. 9312(b)(1)(A), above.

P.L. 99-272:

Act Sec. 11011(a) amended ERISA Sec. 4062 by redesignating section (e) as section (f), by striking out sections (a) through (d) and by adding new sections (a)-(e) to read as above. Subsection (f), as redesignated, was amended by Act Sec. 11011(b) to insert "Treatment of substantial cessation of operations.—"after (f).

The above amendments apply to payments made after January 1, 1986 in taxable years ending after that date.

Prior to amendment, ERISA Sec. 4062 read as follows:

LIABILITY OF EMPLOYER

Act Sec. 4062. (a) This section applies to any employer who maintained a single-employer plan at the time it was terminated, but does not apply—

(1) to an employer who maintained a plan with respect to which he paid the annual premium described in section 4006(a)(2)(B) for each of the 5 plan years immediately preceding the plan year during which the plan terminated unless the conditions imposed by the corporation on the payment of coverage under section 4023 do not permit such coverage to apply under the circumstances, or

(2) to the extent of any liability arising out of the insolvency of an insurance company with respect to an insurance contract.

Act Sec. 4062. (b) Any employer to which this section applies shall be liable to the corporation, in an amount equal to the lesser of—

(1) the excess of—

(A) the current value of the plan's benefits guaranteed under this title on the date of termination over

(B) the current value of the plan's assets allocable to such benefits on the date of termination, or

(2) 30 percent of the net worth of the employer determined as of a day, chosen by the corporation but not more than 120 days prior to the date of termination, computed without regard to any liability under this section.

Act Sec. 4062. (c) For purposes of subsection (b)(2) the net worth of an employer is—

(1) determined on whatever basis best reflects, in the determination of the corporation, the current status of the employer's operations and prospects at the time chosen for determining the net worth of the employer, and

(2) increased by the amount of any transfers of assets made by the employer determined by the corporation to be improper under the circumstances, including any such transfers which would be inappropriate under title 11 of the United States Code if the employer were a debtor in a case under chapter 7 of such title.

Act Sec. 4062. (d) For purposes of this section the following rules apply in the case of certain corporate reorganizations:

(I) If an employer ceases to exist by reason of a reorganization which involves a mere change in identity, form, or place of organization, however effected, a successor corporation resulting from such reorganization shall be treated as the employer to whom this section applies.

(2) If an employer ceases to exist by reason of a liquidation into a parent corporation, the parent corporation shall be treated as the employer to whom this section applies.

(3) If an employer ceases to exist by reason of a merger, consolidation, or division, the successor corporation or corporations shall be treated as the employer to whom this section applies.

Act Sec. 4062. (e) If an employer ceases operations at a facility in any location and, as a result of such cessation of operations, more than 20 percent of the total number of his employees who are participants under a plan established and maintained by him are separatd from employment, the employer shall be treated with respect to that plan as if he were a substantial employer under a plan under which more than one employer makes contributions and the provisions of sections 4063, 4064, and 4065 shall apply.

P.L. 96-364, § 403(g):

Amended Sec. 4062(a) by striking out "plan (other than a multiemployer plan)" and substituting "single-employer plan" in its place, effective September 26, 1980.

P.L. 95-598, § 321(b):

Amended Sec. 4062(c), effective October 1, 1979, by substituting "title 11 of the United States Code" for "Bankruptcy Act" and by substituting "a debtor in a case under chapter 7 of such title" for "the subject of a proceeding under that Act."

Regulations

The following regulations were adopted by the Pension Benefit Guaranty Corporation on July 1, 1996 (61 FR 34002). Prior to July 1, 1996, PBGC regulations were under Chapter XXVI of Title 29 of the Code of Federal Regulations. Effective July 1, 1996, PBGC regulations were moved to Chapter XL, and were renumbered and reorganized. Reg. § § 4062.9 and 4062.10 were amended October 28, 2003 (68 FR 61344). Reg. § § 4062.1, 4062.3, and

4062.7 were amended on June 16, 2006 (71 FR 34819), Reg. §§ 4062.8, 4062.9, and 4062.10 were renumbered and redesignated as Reg. §§ 4062.9, 4062.10, and 4062.11, respectively, and a new §§ 4062.8 was added.

[¶ 15,621]

§ 4062.1 **Purpose and scope.** The purpose of this part is to set forth rules for determination and payment of the liability incurred, under section 4062(b) of ERISA, upon termination of any single-employer plan and, to the extent appropriate, determination of the liability incurred with respect to multiple employer plans under sections 4063 and 4064 of ERISA. This part also sets forth rules for determining the amount of liability incurred under section 4063 of ERISA pursuant to the occurrence of a cessation of operations as described by section 4062(e) of ERISA. The provisions of this part regarding the amount of liability to the PBGC that is incurred upon termination of a single-employer plan apply with respect to a plan for which a notice of intent to terminate under section 4041(c) of ERISA is issued or proceedings to terminate under section 4042 of ERISA are instituted after December 17, 1987. Those provisions also apply, to the extent described in paragraph (a) of this section, to the amount of liability for withdrawal from a multiple employer plan after that date.

[Amended 6/16/06 (71 FR 34819)]

[¶ 15,621A]

§ 4062.2 **Definitions.** The following terms are defined in § 4001.2 of this chapter: *benefit liabilities, Code, contributing sponsor, controlled group, ERISA, fair market value, guaranteed benefit, multiple employer plan, notice of intent to terminate, PBGC, person, plan, plan administrator, proposed termination date, single-employer plan,* and *termination date.*

In addition, for purposes of this part, the term *collective net worth of persons subject to liability in connection with a plan termination* means the sum of the individual net worths of all persons that have individual net worths which are greater than zero and that (as of the termination date) are contributing sponsors of the terminated plan or members of their controlled groups, as determined in accordance with section 4062(d)(1) of ERISA and § 4062.4 of this part.

[¶ 15,621B]

§ 4062.3 **Amount and payment of section 4062(b) liability.** (a) *Amount of liability.* (1) *General rule.* Except as provided in paragraph (a)(2) of this section, the amount of section 4062(b) liability is the total amount (as of the termination date) of the unfunded benefit liabilities (within the meaning of section 4001(a)(18) of ERISA) to all participants and beneficiaries under the plan, together with interest calculated from the termination date in accordance with § 4062.7.

(2) *Special rule in case of subsequent finding of inability to pay guaranteed benefits.* In any distress termination proceeding under section 4041(c) of ERISA and part 4041 of this chapter in which (as described in section 4041(c)(3)(C)(ii) of ERISA), after a determination that the plan is sufficient for benefit liabilities or for guaranteed benefits, the plan administrator finds that the plan is or will be insufficient for guaranteed benefits and the PBGC concurs with that finding, or the PBGC makes such a finding on its own initiative, actuarial present values shall be determined as of the date of the notice to, or the finding by, the PBGC of insufficiency for guaranteed benefits.

(b) *Payment of liability.* Section 4062(b) liability is due and payable as of the termination date, in cash or securities acceptable to the PBGC, except that, as provided in § 4062.9(c), the PBGC shall prescribe commercially reasonable terms for payment of so much of such liability as exceeds 30 percent of the collective net worth of persons subject to liability in connection with a plan termination. The PBGC may make alternative arrangements, as provided in § 4062.9(b).

[Amended 6/16/06 (71 FR 34819)]

[¶ 15,621C]

§ 4062.4 **Determinations of net worth and collective net worth.** (a) *General rules.* When a contributing sponsor, or member(s) of a contributing sponsor's controlled group, notifies and submits information to the PBGC in accordance with § 4062.6, the PBGC shall determine the net worth, as of the net worth record date, of that contributing sponsor and any members of its controlled group based on the factors set forth in paragraph (c) of this section and shall include the value of any assets that it determines, pursuant to paragraph (d) of this section, have been improperly transferred. In making such determinations, the PBGC will consider information submitted pursuant to § 4062.6. The PBGC shall then determine the collective net worth of persons subject to liability in connection with a plan termination.

(b) *Partnerships and sole proprietorships.* In the case of a person that is a partnership or a sole proprietorship, net worth does not include the personal assets and liabilities of the partners or sole proprietor, except for the assets included pursuant to paragraph (d) of this section. As used in this paragraph, "personal assets" are those assets which do not produce income for the business being valued or are not used in the business.

(c) *Factors for determining net worth.* A person's net worth is equal to its fair market value and fair market value shall be determined on the basis of the factors set forth below, to the extent relevant; different factors may be considered with respect to different portions of the person's operations.

(1) A bona fide sale of, agreement to sell, or offer to purchase or sell the business of the person made on or about the net worth record date.

(2) A bona fide sale of, agreement to sell, or offer to purchase or sell stock or a partnership interest in the person, made on or about the net worth record date.

(3) If stock in the person is publicly traded, the price of such stock on or about the net worth record date.

(4) The price/earnings ratios and prices of stocks of similar trades or businesses on or about the net worth record date.

(5) The person's economic outlook, as reflected by its earnings and dividend projections, current financial condition, and business history.

(6) The economic outlook for the person's industry and the market it serves.

(7) The appraised value, including the liquidating value, of the person's tangible and intangible assets.

(8) The value of the equity assumed in a plan of reorganization of a person in a case under title 11, United States Code, or any similar law of a state or political subdivision thereof.

(9) Any other factor relevant in determining the person's net worth.

(d) *Improper transfers.* A person's net worth shall include the value of any assets transferred by the person which the PBGC determines were improperly transferred for the purpose, as inferred from all the facts and circumstances, and with the effect of avoiding liability under this part. Assets "improperly transferred" include but are not limited to assets sold, leased or otherwise transferred for less than adequate consideration and assets distributed as gifts, capital distributions and stock redemptions inconsistent with past practices of the employer. The word "transfer" includes but is not limited to sales, assignments, pledges, leases, gifts and dividends.

[¶ 15,621D]

§ 4062.5 **Net worth record date.** (a) *General.* Unless the PBGC establishes an earlier net worth record date pursuant to paragraph (b) of this section, the net worth record date, for all purposes under this part, is the plan's termination date.

(b) *Establishment of an earlier net worth record date.* At any time during a termination proceeding, the PBGC, in order to prevent undue loss to or abuse of the plan termination insurance system, may establish as the net worth record date an earlier date during the 120-day period ending with the termination date.

(c) *Notification.* Whenever the PBGC establishes an earlier net worth record date, it shall immediately give liable person(s) written notification of that fact. The written notice may also include a request for additional information, as provided in § 4062.6(a)(3).

[¶ 15,621E]

§ 4062.6 **Net worth notification and information.** (a) *General*. (1) A contributing sponsor or member of the contributing sponsor's controlled group that believes section 4062(b) liability exceeds 30 percent of the collective net worth of persons subject to liability in connection with a plan termination shall—

(i) So notify the PBGC by the 90th day after the notice of intent to terminate is filed with the PBGC or, if no notice of intent to terminate is filed with the PBGC and the PBGC institutes proceedings under section 4042 of ERISA, within 30 days after the establishment of the plan's termination date in such proceedings; and

(ii) Submit to the PBGC the information specified in paragraph (b) of this section with respect to the contributing sponsor and each member of the contributing sponsor's controlled group (if any)—

(A) By the 120th day after the proposed termination date, or

(B) If no notice of intent to terminate is filed with the PBGC and the PBGC institutes proceedings under section 4042 of ERISA, within 120 days after the establishment of the plan's termination date in such proceedings.

(2) If a contributing sponsor or a member of its controlled group complies with the requirements of paragraph (a)(1) of this section, the PBGC will consider the requirements to be satisfied by all members of that controlled group.

(3) The PBGC may require any person subject to liability—

(i) To submit the information specified in paragraph (b) of this section within a shorter period whenever the PBGC believes that its ability to obtain information or payment of liability is in jeopardy, and

(ii) To submit additional information within 30 days, or a different specified time, after the PBGC's written notification that it needs such information to make net worth determinations.

(4) If a provision of paragraph (b) of this section or a PBGC notice specifies information previously submitted to the PBGC, a person may respond by identifying the previous submission in which the response was provided.

(b) *Net worth information*. The following information specifications apply, individually, with respect to each person subject to liability:

(1) An estimate, made in accordance with § 4062.4, of the person's net worth on the net worth record date and a statement, with supporting evidence, of the basis for the estimate.

(2) A copy of the person's audited (or if not available, unaudited) financial statements for the 5 full fiscal years plus any partial fiscal year preceding the net worth record date. The statements must include balance sheets, income statements, and statements of changes in financial position and must be accompanied by the annual reports, if available.

(3) A statement of all sales and copies of all offers or agreements to buy or sell at least 25 percent of the person's assets or at least 5 percent of the person's stock or partnership interest, made on or about the net worth record date.

(4) A statement of the person's current financial condition and business history.

(5) A statement of the person's business plans, including projected earnings and, if available, dividend projections.

(6) Any appraisal of the person's fixed and intangible assets made on or about the net worth record date.

(7) A copy of any plan of reorganization, whether or not confirmed, with respect to a case under title 11, United States Code, or any similar law of a state or political subdivision thereof, involving the person and occurring within 5 calendar years prior to or any time after the net worth record date.

(c) *Incomplete submission*. If a contributing sponsor and/or members of the contributing sponsor's controlled group do not submit all of the information required pursuant to paragraph (a) of this section (other than the estimate described in paragraph (b)(1) of this section) with respect to each person subject to liability, the PBGC may base determinations of net worth and the collective net worth of persons

subject to liability in connection with a plan termination on any such information that such person(s) did submit, as well as any other pertinent information that the PBGC may have. In general, the PBGC will view information as of a date further removed from the net worth record date as having less probative value than information as of a date nearer to the net worth record date.

[¶ 15,621F]

§ 4062.7 **Calculating interest on liability and refunds of overpayments.** (a) *Interest*. Whether or not the PBGC has granted deferred payment terms pursuant to § 4062.9, the amount of liability under this part includes interest, from the termination date, on any unpaid portion of the liability. Such interest accrues at the rate set forth in paragraph (c) of this section until the liability is paid in full and is compounded daily. When liability under this part is paid in more than one payment, the PBGC will apply each payment to the satisfaction of accrued interest and then to the reduction of principal.

(b) *Refunds*. If a contributing sponsor or member(s) of a contributing sponsor's controlled group pays the PBGC an amount that exceeds the full amount of liability under this part, the PBGC shall refund the excess amount, with interest at the rate set forth in paragraph (c) of this section. Interest on an overpayment accrues from the later of the date of the overpayment or 10 days prior to the termination date until the date of the refund and is compounded daily.

(c) *Interest rate*. The interest rate on liability under this part and refunds thereof is the annual rate prescribed in section 6601(a) of the Code, and will change whenever the interest rate under section 6601(a) of the Code changes.

[Added 6/16/06 (71 FR 34819)]

[¶ 15,621G]

§ 4062.8 **Liability pursuant to section 4062(e).** (a) *Liability amount*. If, pursuant to section 4062(e) of ERISA, an employer ceases operations at a facility in any location and, as a result of such cessation of operations, more than 20% of the total number of the employer's employees who are participants under a plan established and maintained by the employer are separated from employment, the PBGC will determine the amount of liability under section 4063(b) of ERISA to be the amount described in section 4062 of ERISA for the entire plan, as if the plan had been terminated by the PBGC immediately after the date of the cessation of operations, multiplied by a fraction—

(1) The numerator of which is the number of the employer's employees who are participants under the plan and are separated from employment as a result of the cessation of operations; and

(2) The denominator of which is the total number of the employer's current employees, as determined immediately before the cessation of operations, who are participants under the plan.

(b) *Example*. Company X sponsors a pension plan with 50,000 participants of which 20,000 are current employees and 30,000 are retirees or deferred vested participants. On a PBGC termination basis, the plan is underfunded by $80 million. Company X ceases operations at a facility resulting in the separation from employment of 5,000 employees, all of whom are participants in the pension plan. A section 4062(e) event has occurred, and the PBGC will determine the amount of employer liability under section 4063(b) of ERISA. The numerator described in paragraph (a)(1) of this section is 5,000 and the denominator described in paragraph (a)(2) of this section is 20,000. Therefore, the amount of liability under section 4063(b) of ERISA pursuant to section 4062(e) is $20 million (5,000/20,000 × $80 million).

[Added 6/16/06 (71 FR 34819)]

[¶ 15,621H]

§ 4062.9 **Arrangements for satisfying liability.** (a) *General*. The PBGC will defer payment, or agree to other arrangements for the satisfaction, of any portion of liability to the PBGC only when—

(1) As provided in paragraph (b) of this section, the PBGC determines that such action is necessary to avoid the imposition of a severe hardship and that there is a reasonable possibility that the terms so prescribed will be met and the entire liability paid; or

(2) As provided in paragraph (c) of this section, the PBGC determines that section 4062(b) liability exceeds 30 percent of the

collective net worth of persons subject to liability in connection with a plan termination.

(b) *Upon request.* If the PBGC determines that such action is necessary to avoid the imposition of a severe hardship on persons that are or may become liable under section 4062, 4063, or 4064 of ERISA and that there is a reasonable possibility that persons so liable will be able to meet the terms prescribed and pay the entire liability, the PBGC, in its discretion and when so requested in accordance with paragraph (b)(2) of this section, may grant deferred payment or other terms for the satisfaction of such liability.

(1) In determining what, if any, terms to grant, the PBGC shall examine the following factors:

(i) The ratio of the liability to the net worth of the person making the request and (if different) to the collective net worth of persons subject to liability in connection with a plan termination.

(ii) The overall financial condition of persons that are or may become liable, including, with respect to each such person—

(A) The amounts and terms of existing debts;

(B) The amount and availability of liquid assets;

(C) Current and past cash flow; and

(D) Projected cash flow, including a projection of the impact on operations that would be caused by the immediate full payment of the liability.

(iii) The availability of credit from private sector sources to the person making the request and to other liable persons.

(2) A contributing sponsor or member of a contributing sponsor's controlled group may request deferred payment or other terms for the satisfaction of any portion of the liability under section 4062, 4063, or 4064 of ERISA at any time by filing a written request. The request must include the information specified in § 4062.6(b), except that—

(i) If the request is filed one year or more after the net worth record date, references to "the net worth record date" in § 4062.6(b) shall be replaced by "the most recent annual anniversary of the net worth record date"; and

(ii) Information that already has been submitted to the PBGC need not be submitted again.

(c) *Liability exceeding 30 percent of collective net worth.* If the PBGC determines that section 4062(b) liability exceeds 30 percent of the collective net worth of persons subject to the liability, the PBGC will, after making a reasonable effort to reach agreement with such persons, prescribe commercially reasonable terms for payment of so much of the liability as exceeds 30 percent of the collective net worth of such persons. The terms prescribed by the PBGC for payment of that portion of the liability (including interest) will provide for deferral of 50 percent of any amount otherwise payable for any year if a person subject to such liability demonstrates to the satisfaction of the PBGC that no person subject to such liability has any individual pre-tax profits (within the meaning of section 4062(d)(2) of ERISA) for such person's last full fiscal year ending during that year.

(d) *Interest.* Interest on unpaid liability is calculated in accordance with § 4062.7(a).

(e) *Security during period of deferred payment.* As a condition to the granting of deferred payment terms, PBGC may, in its discretion, require that the liable person(s) provide PBGC with such security for its obligations as the PBGC deems adequate.

[Renumbered 6/16/06 (71 FR 34819)]

[¶ 15,621I]

§ 4062.10 **Method and date of filing; where to file.** (a) *Method of filing.* The PBGC applies the rules in subpart A of part 4000 of this chapter to determine permissible methods of filing with the PBGC under this part. Payment of liability must be clearly designated as such and include the name of the plan.

(b) *Filing date.* The PBGC applies the rules in subpart C of part 4000 of this chapter to determine the date that a submission under this part was filed with the PBGC.

(c) *Where to file.* See Sec. 4000.4 of this chapter for information on where to file.

[Amended 10/28/2003 by 68 FR 61344. Renumbered 6/16/06 (71 FR 34819)]

[¶ 15,621J]

§ 4062.11 **Computation of time.** The PBGC applies the rules in subpart D of part 4000 of this chapter to compute any time period under this part. However, for purposes of determining the amount of an interest charge under Sec. 4062.7, the rule in Sec. 4000.43(a) of this chapter governing periods ending on weekends or Federal holidays does not apply.

[Amended 10/28/2003 by 68 FR 61344. Renumbered 6/16/06 (71 FR 34819)]

[¶ 15,630]

LIABILITY OF SUBSTANTIAL EMPLOYER FOR WITHDRAWAL FROM SINGLE-EMPLOYER PLANS UNDER MULTIPLE CONTROLLED GROUPS

Act Sec. 4063. (a) SINGLE-EMPLOYER PLANS WITH TWO OR MORE CONTRIBUTING SPONSORS.—Except as provided in subsection (d), the plan administrator of a single-employer plan which has two or more contributing sponsors at least two of whom are not under common control—

(1) shall notify the corporation of the withdrawal during a plan year of a substantial employer for such plan year from the plan, with 60 days after such withdrawal, and

(2) request that the corporation determine the liability of all persons with respect to the withdrawal of the substantial employer.

The corporation shall, as soon as practicable thereafter, determine whether there is liability resulting from the withdrawal of the substantial employer and notify the liable persons of such liability.

Act Sec. 4063. (b) COMPUTATION OF LIABILITY.—Except as provided in subsection (c), any one or more contributing sponsors who withdraw, during a plan year for which they constitute a substantial employer, from a single-employer plan which has two or more contributing sponsors at least two of whom are not under common control, shall, upon notification of such contributing sponsors by the corporation as provided by subsection (a), be liable, together with the members of their controlled groups, to the corporation in accordance with the provisions of section 4062 and this section. The amount of such employer's liability shall be computed on the basis of an amount determined by the corporation to be the amount described in section 4062 for the entire plan, as if the plan had been terminated by the corporation on the date of the employer's withdrawal, multiplied by a fraction—

(1) the numerator of which is the total amount required to be contributed to the plan by such contributing sponsor for the last 5 years ending prior to the withdrawal, and

(2) the denominator of which is the total amount required to be contributed to the plan by all contributing sponsors for such last 5 years.

In addition to and in lieu of the manner prescribed in the preceding sentence, the corporation may also determine such liability of each such employer on any other equitable basis prescribed by the corporation in regulations. Any amount collected by the corporation under this subsection shall be held in escrow subject to disposition in accordance with the provisions of paragraph (2) and (3) of subsection (c).

Act Sec. 4063. (c)(1) BOND IN LIEU OF PAYMENT OF LIABILITY; 5-YEAR TERMINATION PERIOD.—In lieu of payment of contributing sponsor's liability under this section the contributing sponsor may be required to furnish a bond to the corporation in an amount not exceeding 150 percent of his liability to insure payment of his liability under this section. The bond shall have as surety thereon a corporate surety company which is an acceptable surety on Federal bonds under authority granted by the Secretary of the Treasury under sections 6 through 13 of title 6, United States Code. Any such bond shall be in a form or of a type approved by the Secretary including individual bonds or schedule or blanket forms of bonds which covers a group or class.

(2) If the plan is not terminated under section 4041(c) or 4042 within the 5-year period commencing on the day of withdrawal, the liability of such employer is abated and any payment held in escrow shall be refunded without interest to the employer (or the bond cancelled) in accordance with bylaws or rules prescribed by the corporation.

(3) If the plan terminates under section 4041(c) or 4042 within the 5-year period commencing on the day of withdrawal, the corporation shall—

    (A) demand payment or realize on the bond and hold such amount in escrow for the benefit of the plan;

    (B) treat any escrowed payments under this section as if they were plan assets and apply them in a manner consistent with this subtitle; and

    (c) refund any amount to the contributing sponsor which is not required to meet any obligation of the corporation with respect to the plan.

Act Sec. 4063. (d) ALTERNATE APPROPRIATE PROCEDURE.—The provisions of this subsection apply in the case of a withdrawal described in subsection (a), and the provision of subsections (b) and (c) shall not apply, if the corporation determines that the procedure provided for under this subsection is consistent with the purposes of this section and section 4064 and is more appropriate in the particular case. Upon a showing by the plan administrator of the plan that the withdrawal from the plan by one or more contributing sponsors has resulted, or will result, in a significant reduction in the amount of aggregate contributions to or under the plan by employers, the corporation may—

    (1) require the plan fund to be equitably allocated between those participants no longer working in covered service under the plan as a result of the withdrawal, and those participants who remain in covered service under the plan;

    (2) treat that portion of the plan funds allocable under paragraph (1) to participants no longer in covered service as a plan terminated under section 4042; and

    (3) treat that portion of the plan fund allocable to participants remaining in covered service as a separate plan.

Act Sec. 4063. (e) INDEMNITY AGREEMENT.—The corporation is authorized to waive the application of the provisions of subsections (b), (c), and (d) of this section whenever it determines that there is an indemnity agreement in effect among contributing sponsors under the plan which is adequate to satisfy the purposes of this section and of section 4064.

Amendments

P.L. 99-272:

Act Sec. 11016(a)(5)(A)(i)(I) amended ERISA Sec. 4063(a) by striking out "plan under which more than one employer makes contributions (other than a multiemployer plan)" and inserting "single-employer plan which has two or more contributing sponsors at least two of whom are not under common control."

Act Sec. 11016(a)(5)(A)(i)(II) amended ERISA Sec. 4063(a)(1) by striking out "withdrawal of a substantial employer" and inserting "withdrawal during the plan year of a substantial employer for such plan year."

Act Sec. 11016(a)(5)(A)(i)(III) amended ERISA Sec. 4063(a)(2) by striking out "of such employer" and inserting "of all persons with respect to the withdrawal of the substantial employer."

Act Sec. 11016(a)(5)(A)(i)(IV) amended ERISA Sec. 4063(a) by striking out "whether such employer is liable for any amount under this subtitle with respect to the withdrawal" and inserting "whether there is liability resulting from the withdrawal of the substantial employer."

Act Sec. 11016(a)(5)(A)(i)(V) amended ERISA Sec. 4063(a) by striking out "notify such employer" and inserting "notify the liable persons."

Act Sec. 11016(a)(5)(A)(ii)(I) amended ERISA Sec. 4063(b) by striking out "an employer who withdraws from a plan to which section 4021 applies, during a plan year for which he was a substantial employer, and who is notified by the corporation as provided by subsection (a), shall be liable" and by inserting *"any one or more contributing sponsors who withdraw, during a plan year for which they constitute a substantial employer, from a single-employer plan which has two or more contributing sponsors at least two of whom are not under common control, shall, upon notification of such contributing sponsors by the corporation as provided by subsection (a), be liable, together with the members of their controlled groups."*

Act Sec. 11016(a)(5)(A)(ii)(II) amended ERISA Sec. 4063(b) by striking out "such employer's."

Act Sec. 11016(a)(5)(A)(ii)(III) amended ERISA Sec. 4063(b) by striking out "the employer's withdrawal" and inserting "the withdrawal referred to in subsection (a)(1)."

Act Sec. 11016(a)(5)(A)(ii)(IV) amended ERISA Sec. 4063(b)(1) by striking out "such employer" and inserting "such contributing sponsors."

Act. Sec. 11016(a)(5)(A)(ii)(V) amended ERISA Sec. 4063(b)(2) by striking out "all employers" and inserting "all contributing sponsors."

Act Sec. 11016(a)(5)(A)(ii)(VI) amended ERISA Sec. 4063(b) by striking out "the liability of each such employer" and inserting "such liability."

Act Sec. 11016(a)(5)(A)(iii)(I) amended ERISA Sec. 4063(c)(1) by striking out "In lieu of payment of his liability under this section the employer" and inserting "In lieu of payment of a contributing sponsor's liability under this section the contributing sponsor."

Act Sec. 11016(a)(5)(A)(iii)(II) amended ERISA Sec. 4063(c)(2) by inserting "under section 4041(c) or 4042" after "terminated;" by striking out "of such employer;" and, by striking out "to the employer (or his bond cancelled)" and inserting "(or the bond cancelled)."

Act Sec. 11016(a)(5)(A)(iii)(III) amended ERISA Sec. 4063(c)(3) by inserting "under section 4041(c) or 4042" after "terminates."

Act Sec. 11016(a)(5)(A)(iv)(I) amended ERISA Sec. 4063(d) by striking out "Upon a showing by the plan administrator of a plan (other than a multiemployer plan) that the withdrawal from the plan by any employer or employers has resulted" and inserting "Upon a showing by the plan administrator of the plan that the withdrawal from the plan by one or more contributing sponsors has resulted."

Act Sec. 11016(a)(5)(A)(iv)(II) amended ERISA Sec. 4063(d) by striking out "by employers."

Act Sec. 11016(a)(5)(A)(iv)(III) amended ERISA Sec. 4063(d)(1) by striking out "all other employers" and inserting "the."

Act Sec. 11016(a)(5)(A)(iv) amended ERISA Sec. 4063(d)(2) by striking out "termination" and inserting "plan termination under section 4042."

Act Sec. 11016(a)(5)(A)(v)(I) amended ERISA Sec. 4063(e) by striking out "to any employer or plan administrator."

Act Sec. 11016(a)(5)(A)(v)(II) amended ERISA Sec. 4063(e) by striking out "all other employers" and inserting "contributing sponsors."

Act Sec. 11016(a)(5)(A)(vi) amended the title to ERISA Sec. 4063 by adding at the end "From Single-Employer Plans Under Multiple Controlled Groups."

The above amendments take effect April 7, 1986.

P.L. 96-364, §403(h):

Amended Sec. 4063 by adding "(other than a multiemployer plan)" in the first sentence in subsection (a) and the second sentence in subsection (d), effective September 26, 1980.

Regulations

The following regulations were adopted by the Pension Benefit Guaranty Corporation on July 1, 1996 (61 FR 34002). Prior to July 1, 1996, PBGC regulations were under Chapter XXVI of Title 29 of the Code of Federal Regulations. Effective July 1, 1996, PBGC regulations were moved to Chapter XL, and were renumbered and reorganized. The regulations were revised on June 16, 2006 (71 FR 34819).

[¶ 15,631]

§4063.1 **Cross-references.** (a) Part 4062 of this chapter sets forth rules for determination and payment of the liability incurred, under section 4062(b) of ERISA, upon termination of any single-employer plan and, to the extent appropriate, determination of the liability incurred with respect to multiple employer plans under sections 4063 and 4064 of ERISA. Part 4062 also sets forth rules for determining the

amount of liability incurred under section 4063 of ERISA pursuant to the occurrence of a cessation of operations as described by section 4062(e) of ERISA.

(b) Part 4068 of this chapter includes rules regarding the PBGC's lien under section 4068 of ERISA with respect to liability arising under section 4062, 4063, or 4064.

[¶ 15,640]
LIABILITY ON TERMINATION OF SINGLE-EMPLOYER PLANS UNDER MULTIPLE CONTROLLED GROUPS

Act Sec. 4064. (a) This section applies to all contributing sponsors of a single-employer plan which has two or more contributing sponsors at least two of whom are not under common control at the time such plan is terminated under section 4041(c) or 4042 or who, at any time within the 5 plan years preceding the date of termination, made contributions under the plan.

Act Sec. 4064. (b) The corporation shall determine the liability with respect to each contributing sponsor and each member of its controlled group in a manner consistent with section 4062, except that the amount of liability determined under section 4062(b)(1) with respect to the entire plan shall be allocated to each controlled group by multiplying such amount by a fraction—

(1) the numerator of which is the amount required to be contributed to the plan for the last 5 plan years ending prior to the termination date by persons in such controlled group as contributing sponsors, and

(2) the denominator of which is the total amount required to be contributed to the plan for such last 5 years by all persons as contributing sponsors,

and section 4068(a) shall be applied separately with respect to each controlled group.

The corporation may also determine the liability of each such contributing sponsor and member of its controlled group on any other equitable basis prescribed by the corporation in regulations.

Amendments

P.L. 101-239, §7881(f)(3)(A):

Amended ERISA Sec. 4064(b) by striking "and clauses (i)(II) and (ii) of section 4062(b)(1)(A)" and inserting "and section 4068(a)" effective as if included in P.L. 100-203, §9312(b)(2).

P.L. 100-203, §9312(b)(2)(C)(i):

Amended ERISA Sec. 4064(b) to read as above, effective for (A) plan terminations under section 4041(c) of ERISA with respect to which notices of intent to terminate are provided under section 4041(a)(2) of ERISA after December 17, 1987, and (B) plan terminations with respect to which proceedings are instituted by the Pension Benefit Guaranty Corporation under section 4042 of ERISA after December 17, 1987.

Prior to amendment, ERISA Sec. 4064(b), up to the second sentence, read as follows:

(b) The corporation shall determine the liability with respect to each contributing sponsor and each member of its controlled group in a manner consistent with section 4062, except that—

(1) the amount of the liability determined under section 4062(b)(1) with respect to the entire plan—

(A) shall be determined without regard to clauses (i)(II) and (ii) of section 4062(b)(1)(A), and

(B) shall be allocated to each controlled group by multiplying such amount by a fraction—

(i) the numerator of which is the amount required to be contributed to the plan for the last 5 plan years ending prior to the termination date by persons in such controlled group as contributing sponsors, and

(ii) the denominator of which is the total amount required to be contributed to the plan for such last 5 plan years by all persons as contributing sponsors,

and clauses (i)(II) and (ii) of section 4062(b)(1)(A) shall be applied separately with respect to each such controlled group, and

(2) the amount of the liability determined under section 4062(c)(1) with respect to the entire plan shall be allocated to each controlled group by multiplying such amount by the fraction described in paragraph (1)(B) in connection with such controlled group.

P.L. 99-272, §11016(a)(5)(B)(i)(I), (II) and (ii):

Amended ERISA Sec. 4064(a) by striking out "all employers who maintain a plan under which more than one employer makes contributions (other than a multiemployer plan)" and inserting "all contributing sponsors of a single-employer plan which has two or more contributing sponsors at least two of whom are not under common control."

Amended ERISA Sec. 4064(a) by inserting "under section 4041(c) or 4042" after "terminated."

Amended ERISA Sec. 4064(b) to read as above.

Prior to amendment, ERISA Sec. 4064 read as follows:

Sec. 4064. (b) The corporation shall determine the liability of each such employer in a manner consistent with section 4062 except that the amount of the liability determined under section 4062(b)(1) with respect to the entire plan shall be allocated to each employer by multiplying such amounts by a fraction—

(1) the numerator of which is the amount required to be contributed to the plan by each employer for the last 5 plan years ending prior to the termination, and

(2) the denominator of which is the total amount required to be contributed to the plan by all such employers for such last 5 years, and the limitation described in section 4062(b)(2) shall be applied separately to each employer. The corporation may also determine the liability of each such employer on any other equitable basis prescribed by the corporation in regulations.

Act Sec. 11016(a)(5)(B)(iii) changed the heading of ERISA Sec. 4064 to read as above. Prior to amendment, the heading read as follows:

"Liability of Employers on Termination of Plan Maintained by More Than One Employer."

These amendments take effect on April 7, 1986.

P.L. 96-364, §403(i)

Amended Sec. 4064(a), effective September 26, 1980, by adding "(other than a multiemployer plan)" after "plan under which more than one employer makes contributions".

Regulations

The following regulations were adopted by the Pension Benefit Guaranty Corporation on July 1, 1996 (61 FR 34002). Prior to July 1, 1996, PBGC regulations were under Chapter XXVI of Title 29 of the Code of Federal Regulations. Effective July 1, 1996, PBGC regulations were moved to Chapter XL, and were renumbered and reorganized.

[¶ 15,641]

§4064.1 **Cross-references.** (a) Part 4062, subpart A, of this chapter sets forth rules for determination and payment of the liability incurred under section 4062(b) of ERISA, upon termination of any single-employer plan and, to the extent appropriate, determination of the liability incurred with respect to multiple employer plans under sections 4063 and 4064 of ERISA.

(b) Part 4068 of this chapter includes rules regarding the PBGC's lien under section 4068 of ERISA with respect to liability arising under section 4062, 4063, or 4064.

[¶ 15,650]
ANNUAL REPORT OF PLAN ADMINISTRATOR

Act Sec. 4065. For each plan year for which section 4021 applies to a plan, the plan administrator shall file with the corporation, on a form prescribed by the corporation, an annual report which identifies the plan and plan administrator and which includes—

(1) a copy of each notification required under section 4063 with respect to such year,

(2) a statement disclosing whether any reportable event (described in section 4043(b)) occurred during the plan year except to the extent the corporation waives such requirement, and

(3) in the case of a multiemployer plan, information with respect to such plan which the corporation determines is necessary for the enforcement of subtitle E and requires by regulation, which may include—

(A) a statement certified by the plan's enrolled actuary of—

(i) the value of all vested benefits under the plan as of the end of the plan year, and

(ii) the value of the plan's assets as of the end of the plan year;

(B) a statement certified by the plan sponsor of each claim for outstanding withdrawal liability (within the meaning of section 4001(a)(12)) and its value as of the end of that plan year and as of the end of the preceding plan year; and

(C) the number of employers having an obligation to contribute to the plan and the number of employers required to make withdrawal liability payments.

The report shall be filed within 6 months after the close of the plan year to which it relates. The corporation shall cooperate with the Secretary of the Treasury and the Secretary of Labor in an endeavor to coordinate the timing and content, and possibly obtain the combination, of reports under this section with reports required to be made by plan administrators to such Secretaries.

Amendment

P.L. 96-364, §106:

Amended section 4065(2) to read as above (by adding "except to the extent the corporation waives such requirement, and") and added new section 4065(3), effective September 26, 1980.

Regulations

The following regulations were adopted by the Pension Benefit Guaranty Corporation on July 1, 1996 (61 FR 34002). Prior to July 1, 1996, PBGC regulations were under Chapter XXVI of Title 29 of the Code of Federal Regulations. Effective July 1, 1996, PBGC regulations were moved to Chapter XL, and were renumbered and reorganized. Reg. §4065.3 was amended December 2, 1996 (61 FR 63998), effective January 1, 1997.

[¶ 15,651]

§4065.1 **Purpose and scope.** The purpose of this part is to specify the form and content of the Annual Report required by section 4065 of ERISA. This part applies to all plans covered by title IV of ERISA.

[¶ 15,651A]

§4065.2 **Definitions.** The following terms are defined in §4001.2 of this chapter: *ERISA, IRS, PBGC,* and *plan.*

[¶ 15,651B]

§4065.3 **Filing requirement.** (a) The requirement to report the occurrence of a reportable event under section 4043 of ERISA in the Annual Report is waived. (Added 12/2/96 by 61 FR 63998.)

(b) Plan administrators shall file the Annual Report on IRS/DOL/PBGC Forms 5500, 5500-C, 5500-K or 5500-R, as appropriate, in accordance with the instructions therein. (Approved by the Office of Management and Budget under control number 1212-0026.)

[¶ 15,660]

ANNUAL NOTIFICATION TO SUBSTANTIAL EMPLOYERS

Act Sec. 4066. The plan administrator of each single-employer plan which has at least two contributing sponsors at least two of whom are not under common control shall notify, within 6 months after the close of each plan year, any contributing sponsor of the plan who is described in section 4001(a)(2) that such contributing sponsor (alone or together with members of such contributing sponsor's controlled group) constitutes a substantial employer for that year.

Amendments

P.L. 101-239, §7893(g)(2):

Amended ERISA Sec. 4066 by inserting "any" before "contributing sponsor" the first place it appears, effective April 7, 1986.

P.L. 99-272:

Act Sec. 11016(a)(5)(C) amended ERISA Sec. 4066 to read as above, effective on April 7, 1986.

Prior to amendment, ERISA Sec. 4066 read as follows:

Sec. 4066. The plan administrator of each plan under which contributions are made by more than one employer (other than a multiemployer plan) shall notify, within 6 months after the close of each plan year, any employer making contributions under that plan who is described in section 4001(a)(2) that he is a substantial employer for that year.

P.L. 96-364, §403(j):

Amended Sec. 4066 to read as above by adding "(other than a multiemployer plan)" after "contributions are made by more than one employer."

[¶ 15,661]

RECOVERY OF LIABILITY FOR PLAN TERMINATION

Act Sec. 4067. The corporation is authorized to make arrangements with contributing sponsors and members of their controlled groups who are or may become liable under section 4062, 4063, or 4064 for payment of their liability, including arrangements for deferred payment of amounts of liability to the corporation accruing as of the termination date on such terms and for such periods as the corporation deems equitable and appropriate.

Amendment

P.L. 100-203, §9313(b)(6):

Amended ERISA Sec. 4067 by striking "controlled groups who are" and inserting "controlled groups who are or may become", to read as above, effective with respect to notices of intent to terminate under ERISA Sec. 4041(a)(2) which are provided after December 17, 1987.

P.L. 99-272, §11016(a)(6)(A):

Amended ERISA Sec. 4067 to read as above, effective on April 7, 1986. Additionally the section's title was amended by the striking out of "EMPLOYER."

Prior to amendment, ERISA Sec. 4067 read as follows:

Sec. 4067. The corporation is authorized to make arrangements with employers who are liable under section 4062, 4063, or 4064 for payment of their liability, including arrangements for deferred payment on such terms and for such periods as the corporation deems equitable and appropriate.

Regulations

The following regulations were adopted by the Pension Benefit Guaranty Corporation on July 1, 1996 (61 FR 34002). Prior to July 1, 1996, PBGC regulations were under Chapter XXVI of Title 29 of the Code of Federal Regulations. Effective July 1, 1996, PBGC regulations were moved to Chapter XL, and were renumbered and reorganized.

[¶ 15,661A]

§4067.1 **Cross-reference.** Section 4062.8 of this chapter contains rules on deferred payment and other arrangements for satisfaction of liability to the PBGC after termination of single-employer plans.

[¶ 15,662]

LIEN FOR LIABILITY

Act Sec. 4068. (a) CREATION OF LIEN.—If any person liable to the corporation under section 4062, 4063, or 4064 neglects or refuses to pay, after demand, the amount of such liability (including interest), there shall be a lien in favor of the corporation in the amount of such liability (including interest) upon all property and rights to property, whether real or personal, belonging to such person, except that such lien may not be in an amount in excess of 30 percent of the collective net worth of all persons described in section 4062(a) of this title.

Act Sec. 4068. (b) TERM OF LIEN.—The lien imposed by subsection (a) arises on the date of termination of a plan, and continues until the liability imposed under section 4062, 4063, or 4064 is satisfied or becomes unenforceable by reason of lapse of time.

Act Sec. 4068. (c)(1) PRIORITY.—Except as otherwise provided under this section, the priority of a lien imposed under subsection (a) shall be determined in the same manner as under section 6323 of the Internal Revenue Code of 1986 (as in effect on the date of the enactment of the Single-Employer Pension Plan Amendments Act of 1986). Such section 6323 shall be applied for purposes of this section by disregarding subsection (g)(4) and by substituting—

(A) "lien imposed by section 4068 of the Employee Retirement Income Security Act of 1974" for "lien imposed by section 6321" each place it appears in subsections (a), (b), (c)(1), (c)(4)(B), (d), (e), and (h)(5);

(B) "the corporation" for "the Secretary" in subsections (a) and (b)(9)(C);

(C) "the payment of the amount on which the section 4068(a) lien is based" for "the collection of any tax under this title" in subsection (b)(3);

(D) "a person whose property is subject to the lien" for "the taxpayer" in subsections (b)(8), (c)(2)(A)(i) (the first place it appears), (c)(2)(A)(ii), (c)(2)(B), (c)(4)(B), and (c)(4)(C) (in the matter preceding clause (i));

(E) "such person" for "the taxpayer" in subsections (c)(2)(A)(i) (the second place it appears) and (c)(4)(C)(ii);

(F) "payment of the loan value of the amount on which the lien is based is made to the corporation" for "satisfaction of a levy pursuant to section 6332(b)" in subsection (b)(9)(C);

(G) "section 4068(a) lien" for "tax lien" each place it appears in subsections (c)(1), (c)(2)(A), (c)(2)(B), (c)(3)(B)(iii), (c)(4)(B), (d), and (h)(5); and

(H) "the date on which the lien is first filed" for "the date of the assessment of the tax" in subsection (g)(3)(A).

(2) In a case under title 11 of the United States Code or in insolvency proceedings, the lien imposed under subsection (a) shall be treated in the same manner as a tax due and owing to the United States for purposes of title 11 of the United States Code or section 3713 of title 31 of the United States Code.

(3) For purposes of applying section 6323(a) of the Internal Revenue Code of 1986 to determine the priority between the lien imposed under subsection (a) and a Federal tax lien, each lien shall be treated as a judgment lien arising as of the time notice of such lien is filed.

(4) For purposes of this subsection, notice of the lien imposed by subsection (a) shall be filed in the same manner as under section 6323(f) and (g) of the Internal Revenue Code of 1986.

Act Sec. 4068. (d)(1) CIVIL ACTION; LIMITATION PERIOD.—In any case where there has been a refusal or neglect to pay the liability imposed under section 4062, 4063, or 4064, the corporation may bring civil action in a district court of the United States to enforce the lien of the corporation under this section with respect to such liability or to subject any property, of whatever nature, of the liable person, or in which he has any right, title, or interest to the payment of such liability.

(2) The liability imposed by section 4062, 4063, or 4064 may be collected by a proceeding in court if the proceeding is commenced within 6 years after the date upon which the plan was terminated or prior to the expiration of any period for collection agreed upon in writing by the corporation and the liable person before the expiration of such 6-year period. The period of limitations provided under this paragraph shall be suspended for the period the assets of the liable person are in the control or custody of any court of the United States, or of any State, or of the District of Columbia, and for 6 months thereafter, and for any period during which the liable person is outside the United States if such period of absence is for a continuous period of at least 6 months.

Act Sec. 4068. (e) RELEASE OR SUBORDINATION.—If the corporation determines that release of the lien or subordination of the lien to any other creditor of the liable person would not adversely affect the collection of the liability imposed under section 4062, 4063, or 4064, or that the amount realizable by the corporation from the property to which the lien attaches will ultimately be increased by such release or subordination, and that the ultimate collection of the liability will be facilitated by such release or subordination, the corporation may issue a certificate of release or subordination of the lien with respect to such property, or any part thereof.

Act Sec. 4068. DEFINITIONS. (f) For purposes of this section—

(1) The collective net worth of persons subject to liability in connection with a plan termination shall be determined as provided in section 4062(d)(1).

(2) The term "pre-tax profits" has the meaning provided in section 4062(d)(2).

Amendments

P.L. 101-239, §7881(f)(3)(B):

Amended ERISA Sec. 4068(a), effective as if included in P.L. 100-203, §9312(b)(2), by striking the last sentence which had read:

The preceding provisions of this subsection shall be applied in a manner consistent with the provisions of section 4064(d) relating to treatment of multiple controlled groups.

P.L. 101-239, §7881(f)(10)(C):

Amended ERISA Sec. 4068 by adding a new subsection (f) to read as above. For the effective date, see P.L. 100-203, §9312(b)(2)(B)(i).

P.L. 101-239, §7881(f)(12):

Amended ERISA Sec. 4068(a) by striking "to the extent such amount does not exceed 30 percent of the collective net worth of all persons described in section 4062(a)" the first place it appeared; and by striking "to the extent such amount does not exceed 30 percent of the collective net worth of all persons described in section 4062(a)" the second place it appeared and all that followed and inserting the following: "in the amount of such liability (including interest) upon all property and rights to property, whether real or personal, belonging to such person, except that such lien may not be in an amount in excess of 30 percent of the collective net worth of all persons described in section 4062(a)." For the effective date, see P.L. 100-203, §9312(b)(2)(B)(i).

P.L. 101-239, §7891(a)(1):

Titles I, III, and IV of ERISA (other than sections 3(37)(E), 301(a)(7), and 308, the last sentence of section 408(d), and sections 414(c), 4001(a)(3)(ii), and 4303) are each amended by striking "Internal Revenue Code of 1954" each place it appears and inserting "Internal Revenue Code of 1986", effective October 22, 1986.

P.L. 101-239, §7894(g)(4):

Amended ERISA Sec. 4068(c) by striking "section 3466 of the Revised Statutes (31 U.S.C. 191)" and inserting "section 3713 of title 31 of the United States Code," effective as if included in P.L. 97-258, §3.

P.L 100-203, §9312(b)(2)(B)(i):

Amended ERISA Sec. 4068(a) by striking out "to the extent of an amount equal to the unpaid amount described in section 4062(b)(1)(A)(i)" each place it appears and inserting in lieu thereof "to the extent such amount does not exceed 30 percent of the collective net worth of all persons described in section 4062(a)", effective for (A) plan terminations under section 4041(c) of ERISA with respect to which notices of intent to terminate are provided under section 4041(a)(2) of ERISA after December 17, 1987, and (B) plan terminations with respect to which proceedings are instituted by the Pension Benefit Guaranty Corporation under section 4042 of ERISA after December 17, 1987.

P.L. 100-203, §9312(b)(2)(C)(ii):

Amended ERISA Sec. 4068(a) by adding a new sentence at the end to read as above. For the effective date, see Act Sec. 9312(b)(2)(B)(i), above.

P.L. 99-272, §11016(a)(6)(B)(i):

Amended ERISA Sec. 4068 by striking out "of Employer" in the heading.

Act Sec. 11016(a)(6)(B)(ii) amended ERISA Sec. 4068(a) by striking out "employer or employers" the first place it appeared and inserting "person"; by striking out "neglect or refuse" and inserting "neglects or refuses"; by inserting "to the extent of an amount equal to the unpaid amount described in section 4062(b)(1)(A)(i)" after "liability" and after "corporation" the second place it appears; and, by striking out "employer or employers" and inserting "person."

Act Sec. 11016(a)(6)(B)(iii) amended ERISA Sec. 4068(d)(1) by striking out "employer" and inserting "liable person."

Act Sec. 11016(a)(6)(B)(iv) amended ERISA Sec. 4068(d)(2) by striking out "employer" and inserting "liable person."

Act Sec. 11016(a)(6)(B)(v) amended ERISA Sec. 4068(e) by striking out "employer or employers" and inserting "liable person."

Act Sec. 11016(a)(6)(B)(vi) amended ERISA Sec. 4068 by striking out subsection (c)(1) and inserting a new subsection (c)(1) to read as above. Prior to amendment, ERISA Sec. 4068(c)(1) read as follows:

Sec. 4068. (c)(1) Except as otherwise provided under this section, the priority of the lien imposed under subsection (a) shall be determined in the same manner as under section 6323 of the Internal Revenue Code of 1954. Such section 6323 shall be applied by substituting "lien imposed by sections 4068 of the Employee Retirement Income Security Act of 1974" for "lien imposed by section 6321"; "corporation" for "Secretary or his delegate"; "employer liability lien" for "tax lien"; "employer" for "taxpayer"; "lien arising under section 4068(a) of the Employee Retirement Income Security Act of 1974" for "assessment of the tax"; and "payment of the loan value is made to the corporation" for "satisfaction of a levy pursuant to section 6332(b)"; each place such terms appear.

Act Sec. 11016(c)(14) amended ERISA Sec. 4068(e) by striking out ", with the consent of the board of directors".

These amendments take effect on April 7, 1986.

P.L. 95-598, §321(c):

Amended Sec. 4068(c)(2) effective October 1, 1979, by substituting "a case under title 11 of the United States Code or in" for "the case of bankruptcy or" and by substituting "title 11 of the United States Code" for "the Bankruptcy Act."

Regulations

The following regulations were adopted by the Pension Benefit Guaranty Corporation on July 1, 1996 (61 FR 34002). Prior to July 1, 1996, PBGC regulations were under Chapter XXVI of Title 29 of the Code of Federal Regulations. Effective July 1, 1996, PBGC regulations were moved to Chapter XL, and were renumbered and reorganized.

[¶ 15,662A]

§4068.1 **Purpose; cross-references.** This part contains rules regarding the PBGC's lien under section 4068 of ERISA with respect to liability arising under section 4062, 4063, or 4064 of ERISA.

[¶ 15,662B]

§4068.2 **Definitions.** The following terms are defined in §4001.2 of this chapter: *ERISA, PBGC, person, plan,* and *termination date.*

Collective net worth of persons subject to liability in connection with a plan termination has the meaning in §4062.2.

[¶ 15,662C]

§4068.3 **Notification of and demand for liability.** (a) *Notification of liability.* Except as provided in paragraph (c) of this section, when the PBGC has determined the amount of the liability under part 4062 and whether or not the liability has already been paid, the PBGC shall notify liable person(s) in writing of the amount of the liability. If the full liability has not yet been paid, the notification will include a request for payment of the full liability and will indicate that, as provided in § 4062.8, the PBGC will prescribe commercially reasonable terms for payment of so much of the liability as it determines exceeds 30 percent of the collective net worth of persons subject to liability in connection with a plan termination. In all cases, the notification will include a statement of the right to appeal the assessment of liability pursuant to part 4003.

(b) *Demand for liability.* Except as provided in paragraph (c) of this section, if person(s) liable to the PBGC fail to pay the full liability and no appeal is filed or an appeal is filed and the decision on appeal finds liability, the PBGC will issue a demand letter for the liability—

(1) If no appeal is filed, upon the expiration of time to file an appeal under part 4003; or

(2) If an appeal is filed, upon issuance of a decision on the appeal finding that there is liability under this part.

The demand letter will indicate that, as provided in § 4062.8, the PBGC will prescribe commercially reasonable terms for payment of so much of the liability as it determines exceeds 30 percent of the collective net worth of such persons.

(c) *Special rule.* Notwithstanding paragraphs (a) and (b) of this section, the PBGC may, in any case in which it believes that its ability to assert or obtain payment of liability is in jeopardy, issue a demand letter for the liability under this part immediately upon determining the liability, without first issuing a notification of liability pursuant to paragraph (a) of this section. When the PBGC issues a demand letter under this paragraph, there is no right to an appeal pursuant to part 4003 of this chapter.

[¶ 15,662D]

§ 4068.4 **Lien.** If any person liable to the PBGC under section 4062, 4063, or 4064 of ERISA fails or refuses to pay the full amount of such liability within the time specified in the demand letter issued under § 4068.3, the PBGC shall have a lien in the amount of the liability, including interest, arising as of the plan's termination date, upon all property and rights to property, whether real or personal, belonging to that person, except that such lien may not be in an amount in excess of 30 percent of the collective net worth of all persons described in section 4062(a) of ERISA and part 4062 of this chapter.

[¶ 15,662L]

TREATMENT OF TRANSACTIONS TO EVADE LIABILITY; EFFECT OF CORPORATE REORGANIZATION

Act Sec. 4069.(a) TREATMENT OF TRANSACTIONS TO EVADE LIABILITY. If a principal purpose of any person in entering into any transaction is to evade liability to which such person would be subject under this subtitle and the transaction becomes effective within five years before the termination date of the termination on which such liability would be based, then such person and the members of such person's controlled group (determined as of the termination date) shall be subject to liability under this subtitle in connection with such termination as if such person were a contributing sponsor of the terminated plan as of the termination date. This subsection shall not cause any person to be liable under this subtitle in connection with such plan termination for any increases or improvements in the benefits provided under the plan which are adopted after the date on which the transaction referred to in the preceding sentence becomes effective.

(b) EFFECT OF CORPORATE REORGANIZATION. For purposes of this subtitle, the following rules apply in the case of certain corporate reorganizations:

(1) CHANGE OF IDENTITY, FORM, ETC.. If a person ceases to exist by reason of a reorganization which involves a mere change in identity, form, or place of organization, however effected, a successor corporation resulting from such reorganization shall be, treated as the person to whom this subtitle applies.

(2) LIQUIDATION INTO PARENT CORPORATION. If a person ceases to exist by reason of liquidation into a parent corporation, the parent corporation shall be treated as the person to whom this subtitle applies.

(3) MERGER, CONSOLIDATION, OR DIVISION. If a person ceases to exist by reason of a merger, consolidation, or division, the successor corporation or corporations shall be treated as the person to whom this subtitle applies.

Amendment:

P.L. 99-272:

Act Sec. 11013(a) added new ERISA Sec. 4069 to read as above, effective for transactions which become effective on or after January 1, 1986.

[¶ 15,662R]

ENFORCEMENT AUTHORITY RELATING TO TERMINATIONS OF SINGLE-EMPLOYER PLANS

Act Sec. 4070.(a) IN GENERAL. Any person who is with respect to a single-employer plan a fiduciary, contributing sponsor, member of a contributing sponsor's controlled group, participant, or beneficiary, and is adversely affected by an act or practice of any party (other than the corporation) in violation of any provision of section 4041, 4042, 4062, 4063, 4064, or 4069, or who is an employee organization representing such a participant so adversely affected for purposes of collective bargaining with respect to such plan, may bring an action—

(1) to enjoin such act or practice, or

(2) to obtain other appropriate equitable relief (A) to redress such violation or (B) to enforce such provision.

(b) STATUS OF PLAN AS PARTY TO ACTION AND WITH RESPECT TO LEGAL PROCESS. A single-employer plan may be sued under this section as an entity. Service of summons, subpoena, or other legal process of a court upon a trustee or an administrator of a single-employer plan in such trustee's or administrator's capacity as such shall constitute service upon the plan. If a plan has not designated in the summary plan description of the plan an individual as agent for the service of legal process, service upon any contributing sponsor of the plan shall constitute such service. Any money judgment under this section against a single-employer plan shall be enforceable only against the plan as an entity and shall not be enforceable against any other person unless liability against such person is established in such person's individual capacity.

(c) JURISDICTION AND VENUE. The district courts of the United States shall have exclusive jurisdiction of civil actions under this section. Such actions may be brought in the district where the plan is administered, where the violation took place, or where a defendant resides or may be found, and process may be served in any other district where a defendant resides or may be found. The district courts of the United States shall have jurisdiction, without regard to the amount in controversy or the citizenship of the parties, to grant the relief provided for in subsection (a) in any action.

(d) RIGHT OF CORPORATION TO INTERVENE. A copy of the complaint or notice of appeal in any action under this section shall be served upon the corporation by certified mail. The corporation shall have the right in its discretion to intervene in any action.

(e) AWARDS OF COSTS AND EXPENSES.—

(1) GENERAL RULE. In any action brought under this section, the court in its discretion may award all or a portion of the costs and expenses incurred in connection with such action, including reasonable attorney's fees, to any party who prevails or substantially prevails in such action.

(2) EXEMPTION FOR PLANS. Notwithstanding the preceding provisions of this subsection, no plan shall be required in any action to pay any costs and expenses (including attorney's fees).

(f) LIMITATION ON ACTIONS.—

(1) IN GENERAL. Except as provided in paragraph (3), an action under this section may not be brought after the later of—

(A) 6 years after the date on which the cause of action arose, or

(B) 3 years after the applicable date specified in paragraph (2).

(2) APPLICABLE DATE.—

(A) GENERAL RULE. Except as provided in subparagraph (B), the applicable date specified in this paragraph is the earliest date on which the plaintiff acquired or should have acquired actual knowledge of the existence of such cause of action.

(B) SPECIAL RULE FOR PLAINTIFFS WHO ARE FIDUCIARIES. In the case of a plaintiff who is a fiduciary bringing the action in the exercise of fiduciary duties, the applicable date specified in this paragraph is the date on which the plaintiff became a fiduciary with respect to the plan if such date is later than the date described in subparagraph (A).

(3) CASES OF FRAUD OR CONCEALMENT. In the case of fraud or concealment, the period described in paragraph (1)(B) shall be extended to 6 years after the applicable date specified in paragraph (2).

Amendments

P.L. 101-239, §7881(f)(8):

Amended ERISA Sec. 4070 by striking "4049," effective December 22, 1987.

P.L. 99-272:

Act Sec. 11014(a) added ERISA Sec. 4070 to read as above, effective with respect to terminations pursuant to notices of intent filed with the PBGC on or after January 1, 1986 or proceedings begun on or after that date.

[¶ 15,662U]
PENALTY FOR FAILURE TO TIMELY PROVIDE REQUIRED INFORMATION

Act Sec. 4071. The corporation may assess a penalty, payable to the corporation, against any person who fails to provide any notice or other material information required under this subtitle, subtitle A, B, or C or section 303(k)(4) or 306(g)(4), or any regulations prescribed under any such subtitle or such section, within the applicable time limit specified therein. Such penalty shall not exceed $1,000 for each day for which such failure continues.

Amendment

P.L. 113-97, §102(b)(9):

Amended ERISA 4071 by striking "section 303(k)(4)" and inserting "section 303(k)(4) or 306(g)(4)".

Effective for years beginning after 12-31-2013.

P.L. 110-458, §101(d)(1)(B):

Amended ERISA Sec. 4071 by striking "as section 303(k)(4) or 307(e)" and inserting "or section 303(k)(4),".

The above amendment applies to plan years beginning after 2007.

P.L. 109-280, Sec. 107(b)(5):

Amended ERISA Sec. 4071 by striking "302(f)(4)" and inserting "303(k)(4)."

The above amendment shall apply for plan years beginning after 2007.

P.L. 101-239, §7881(i)(3)(B):

Amended ERISA Sec. 4071 by striking "or subtitle A, B, or C" and inserting ", subtitle A, B, or C as section 302(f)(4) or 307(e)" and by inserting "or such section" after "such subtitle."

P.L. 100-203, §9314(c):

Added ERISA Sec. 4071, to read as above, effective December 22, 1987.

Regulations

The following regulations were adopted by the Pension Benefit Guaranty Corporation on July 10, 1997 (62 FR 36993) and are effective August 11, 1997. Reg. Sec. 4071.3 was amended in interim final regulations on May 13, 2016 (81 FR 29765), removing "$1,100" and adding "$2,063" in its place. Reg. Sec. 4071.3 was amended in final regulations on January 31, 2017 (82 FR 8813). Reg. Sec. 4071.3 was amended in final regulations on January 12, 2018 (83 FR 1555).

[¶ 15,662V]

§4071.1 **Purpose and scope.** This part specifies the maximum daily amount of penalties that may be assessed by the PBGC under ERISA section 4071 for certain failures to provide notices or other material information, as such amount has been adjusted to account for inflation pursuant to the Federal Civil Monetary Penalty Inflation Adjustment Act of 1990, as amended by the Debt Collection Improvement Act of 1996.

[¶ 15,662W]

§4071.2 **Definitions.** The following terms are defined in §4001.2 of this chapter: *ERISA* and *PBGC*.

[¶ 15,662X]

§4071.3 **Penalty amount.** The maximum daily amount of the penalty under section 4071 of ERISA shall be $2,140. [Amended 5/13/2016 by 81 FR 29765, 1/31/2017 by 82 FR 8813, and 1/12/2018 by 83 FR 1555.]

Subtitle E—Special Provisions for Multiemployer Plans

Part 1—Employer Withdrawals

[¶ 15,663]
WITHDRAWAL LIABILITY ESTABLISHED; CRITERIA AND DEFINITIONS

Act Sec. 4201.(a) If an employer withdraws from a multiemployer plan in a complete withdrawal or a partial withdrawal, then the employer is liable to the plan in the amount determined under this part to be the withdrawal liability.

Act Sec. 4201. (b) For purposes of subsection (a)—

(1) The withdrawal liability of an employer to a plan is the amount determined under section 4211 to be the allocable amount of unfunded vested benefits, adjusted—

(A) first, by any de minimis reduction applicable under section 4209,

(B) next, in the case of a partial withdrawal, in accordance with section 4206,

(C) then, to the extent necessary to reflect the limitation on annual payments under section 4219(c)(1)(B), and

(D) finally, in accordance with section 4225.

(2) The term "complete withdrawal" means a complete withdrawal described in section 4203.

(3) The term "partial withdrawal" means a partial withdrawal described in section 4205.

Amendment

P.L. 96-364, §104(2):

Added Sec. 4201, effective September 26, 1980 under ERISA Sec. 4402.

[¶ 15,664]
DETERMINATION AND COLLECTION OF LIABILITY; NOTIFICATION OF EMPLOYER

Act Sec. 4202. When an employer withdraws from a multiemployer plan, the plan sponsor, in accordance with this part, shall—

(1) determine the amount of the employer's withdrawal liability,

(2) notify the employer of the amount of the withdrawal liability, and

(3) collect the amount of the withdrawal liability from the employer.

Amendment

P.L. 96-364, § 104(2):

Added Sec. 4202, effective September 26, 1980 under ERISA Sec. 4402.

[¶ 15,665]
COMPLETE WITHDRAWAL

Act Sec. 4203. (a) DETERMINATIVE FACTORS.—For purposes of this part, a complete withdrawal from a multiemployer plan occurs when an employer—

(1) permanently ceases to have an obligation to contribute under the plan, or

(2) permanently ceases all covered operations under the plan.

Act Sec. 4203. (b) (1) BUILDING AND CONSTRUCTION INDUSTRY.—Notwithstanding subsection (a), in the case of an employer that has an obligation to contribute under a plan for work performed in the building and construction industry, a complete withdrawal occurs only as described in paragraph (2), if—

(A) substantially all the employees with respect to whom the employer has an obligation to contribute under the plan perform work in the building and construction industry, and

(B) the plan—

(i) primarily covers employees in the building and construction industry, or

(ii) is amended to provide that this subsection applies to employers described in this paragraph.

(2) A withdrawal occurs under this paragraph if—

(A) an employer ceases to have an obligation to contribute under the plan, and

(B) the employer—

(i) continues to perform work in the jurisdiction of the collective bargaining agreement of the type for which contributions were previously required, or

(ii) resumes such work within 5 years after the date on which the obligation to contribute under the plan ceases, and does not renew the obligation at the time of the resumption.

(3) In the case of a plan terminated by mass withdrawal (within the meaning of section 4041A(a)(2)), paragraph (2) shall be applied by substituting "3 years" for "5 years" in subparagraph (B)(ii).

Act Sec. 4203. (c) (1) ENTERTAINMENT INDUSTRY.—Notwithstanding subsection (a), in the case of an employer that has an obligation to contribute under a plan for work performed in the entertainment industry, primarily on a temporary or project-by-project basis, if the plan primarily covers employees in the entertainment industry, a complete withdrawal occurs only as described in subsection (b)(2) applied by substituting "plan" for "collective bargaining agreement" in subparagraph (B)(i) thereof.

(2) For purposes of this subsection, the term "entertainment industry" means—

(A) theater, motion picture (except to the extent provided in regulations prescribed by the corporation), radio, television, sound or visual recording, music, and dance, and

(B) such other entertainment activities as the corporation may determine to be appropriate.

(3) The corporation may by regulation exclude a group or class of employers described in the preceding sentence from the application of this subsection if the corporation determines that such exclusion is necessary—

(A) to protect the interest of the plan's participants and beneficiaries, or

(B) to prevent a significant risk of loss to the corporation with respect to the plan.

(4) A plan may be amended to provide that this subsection shall not apply to a group or class of employers under the plan.

Act Sec. 4203. (d) (1) OTHER DETERMINATIVE FACTORS.—Notwithstanding subsection (a), in the case of an employer who—

(A) has an obligation to contribute under a plan described in paragraph (2) primarily for work described in such paragraph, and

(B) does not continue to perform work within the jurisdiction of the plan,

a complete withdrawal occurs only as described in paragraph (3).

(2) A plan is described in this paragraph if substantially all of the contributions required under the plan are made by employers primarily engaged in the long and short haul trucking industry, the household goods moving industry, or the public warehousing industry.

(3) A withdrawal occurs under this paragraph if—

(A) an employer permanently ceases to have an obligation to contribute under the plan or permanently ceases all covered operations under the plan, and

(B) either—

(i) the corporation determines that the plan has suffered substantial damage to its contribution base as a result of such cessation, or

(ii) the employer fails to furnish a bond issued by a corporate surety company that is an acceptable surety for purposes of section 412, or an amount held in escrow by a bank or similar financial institution satisfactory to the plan, in an amount equal to 50 percent of the withdrawal liability of the employer.

(4) If, after an employer furnishes a bond or escrow to a plan under paragraph (3)(B)(ii), the corporation determines that the cessation of the employer's obligation to contribute under the plan (considered together with any cessations by other employers), or cessation of covered operations under the plan, has resulted in substantial damage to the contribution base of the plan, the employer shall be treated as having withdrawn from the plan on the date on which the obligation to contribute or covered operations ceased, and such bond or escrow shall be paid to the plan. The corporation shall not make a determination under this paragraph more than 60 months after the date on which such obligation to contribute or covered operations ceased.

(5) If the corporation determines that the employer has no further liability under the plan either—

(A) because it determines that the contribution base of the plan has not suffered substantial damage as a result of the cessation of the employer's obligation to contribute or cessation of covered operations (considered together with any cessation of contribution obligation, or of covered operations, with respect to other employers), or

(B) because it may not make a determination under paragraph (4) because of the last sentence thereof,

then the bond shall be cancelled or the escrow refunded.

(6) Nothing in this subsection shall be construed as a limitation on the amount of the withdrawal liability of any employer.

Act Sec. 4203. (e) DATE OF COMPLETE WITHDRAWAL.—For purposes of this part, the date of a complete withdrawal is the date of the cessation of the obligation to contribute or the cessation of covered operations.

Act Sec. 4203. (f) (1) SPECIAL LIABILITY WITHDRAWAL RULES FOR INDUSTRIES OTHER THAN CONSTRUCTION AND ENTERTAINMENT INDUSTRIES; PROCEDURES APPLICABLE TO AMEND PLANS.—The corporation may prescribe regulations under which plans in industries other than the construction or entertainment industries may be amended to provide for special withdrawal liability rules similar to the rules described in subsections (b) and (c).

(2) Regulations under paragraph (1) shall permit use of special withdrawal liability rules—

(A) only in industries (or portions thereof) in which, as determined by the corporation, the characteristics that would make use of such rules appropriate are clearly shown, and

(B) only if the corporation determines, in each instance in which special withdrawal liability rules are permitted, that use of such rules will not pose a significant risk to the corporation under this title.

Amendment

P.L. 96-364, § 104(2):

Added Sec. 4203, effective September 26, 1980 under ERISA Sec. 4402.

Regulations

The following regulations were adopted by the Pension Benefit Guaranty Corporation on July 1, 1996 (61 FR 34002). Prior to July 1, 1996, PBGC regulations were under Chapter XXVI of Title 29 of the Code of Federal Regulations. Effective July 1, 1996, PBGC regulations were moved to Chapter XL, and were renumbered and reorganized. Reg. § 4203.4 was amended October 28, 2003 (68 FR 61344).

[¶ 15,666]

§ 4203.1 **Purpose and scope.** (a) *Purpose.* The purpose of this part is to prescribe procedures whereby a multiemployer plan may, pursuant to sections 4203(f) and 4208(e)(3) of ERISA, request the PBGC to approve a plan amendment which establishes special complete or partial withdrawal liability rules.

(b) *Scope.* This part applies to a multiemployer pension plan covered by Title IV of ERISA.

[¶ 15,666A]

§ 4203.2 **Definitions.** The following terms are defined in § 4001.2 of this chapter: *complete withdrawal, employer, ERISA, multiemployer plan, PBGC, person, plan, plan sponsor,* and *plan year.*

[¶ 15,666B]

§ 4203.3 **Plan adoption of special withdrawal rules.** (a) *General rule.* A plan may, subject to the approval of the PBGC, establish by plan amendment special complete or partial withdrawal liability rules. A complete withdrawal liability rule adopted pursuant to this part shall be similar to the rules for the construction and entertainment industries described in section 4203(b) and (c) of ERISA. A partial withdrawal liability rule adopted pursuant to this part shall be consistent with the complete withdrawal rule adopted by the plan. A plan amendment adopted under this part may not be put into effect until it is approved by the PBGC.

(b) *Discretionary provisions of the plan amendment.* A plan amendment adopted pursuant to this part may—

(1) Cover an entire industry or industries, or be limited to a segment of an industry; and

(2) Apply to cessations of the obligation to contribute that occurred prior to the adoption of the amendment.

[¶ 15,666C]

§ 4203.4 **Requests for PBGC approval of plan amendments.** (a) *Filing of request.* (1) *In general.* A plan shall apply to the PBGC for approval of a plan amendment which establishes special complete or partial withdrawal liability rules. The request for approval shall be filed after the amendment is adopted. PBGC approval shall also be required for any subsequent modification of the plan amendment, other than a repeal of the amendment which results in employers being subject to the general statutory rules on withdrawal.

(2) *Method of filing.* The PBGC applies the rules in subpart A of part 4000 of this chapter to determine permissible methods of filing with the PBGC under this part.

[Amended 10/28/2003 by 68 FR 61344]

(b) *Who may request.* The plan sponsor, or a duly authorized representative acting on behalf of the plan sponsor, shall sign and submit the request.

(c) *Where to file.* See Sec. 4000.4 of this chapter for information on where to file.

[Amended 10/28/2003 by 68 FR 61344]

(d) *Information.* Each request shall contain the following information:

(1) The name and address of the plan for which the plan amendment is being submitted, and the telephone number of the plan sponsor or its authorized representative.

(2) A copy of the executed amendment, including the proposed effective date.

(3) A statement certifying that notice of the adoption of the amendment and the request for approval filed under this part has been given to all employers who have an obligation to contribute under the plan and to all employee organizations representing employees covered under the plan.

(4) A statement indicating how the withdrawal rules in the plan amendment would operate in the event of a sale of assets by a contributing employer or the cessation of the obligation to contribute or the cessation of covered operations by all employers.

(5) A copy of the plan's most recent actuarial valuation.

(6) For each of the previous five plan years, information on the number of plan participants by category (active, retired and separate vested) and a complete financial statement. This requirement may be satisfied by the submission for each of those years of Form 5500, including schedule B, or similar reports required under prior law.

(7) A detailed description of the industry to which the plan amendment will apply, including information sufficient to demonstrate the effect of withdrawals on the plan's contribution base, and information establishing industry characteristics which would indicate that withdrawals in the industry do not typically have an adverse effect on the plan's contribution base. Such industry characteristics include the mobility of employees, the intermittent nature of employment, the project-by-project nature of the work, extreme fluctuations in the level of an employer's covered work under the plan, the existence of a consistent pattern of entry and withdrawal by employers, and the local nature of the work performed.

(e) *Supplemental information.* In addition to the information described in paragraph (d) of this section, a plan may submit any other information it believes is pertinent to its request. The PBGC may require the plan sponsor to submit any other information the PBGC determines it needs to review a request under this part.

[¶ 15,666D]

§ 4203.5 **PBGC action on requests.** (a) *General.* The PBGC shall approve a plan amendment providing for the application of special complete or partial withdrawal liability rules upon a determination by the PBGC that the plan amendment—

(1) Will apply only to an industry that has characteristics that would make use of the special withdrawal rules appropriate; and

(2) Will not pose a significant risk to the insurance system.

(b) *Notice of pendency of request.* As soon as practicable after receiving a request for approval of a plan amendment containing all the information required under § 4203.4, the PBGC shall publish a notice of the pendency of the request in the Federal Register. The notice shall contain a summary of the request and invite interested persons to submit written comments to the PBGC concerning the request. The notice will normally provide for a comment period of 45 days.

(c) *PBGC decision on request.* After the close of the comment period, PBGC shall issue its decision in writing on the request for approval of a plan amendment. Notice of the decision shall be published in the Federal Register.

[¶ 15,667]
SALE OF ASSETS

Act Sec. 4204. (a)(1) COMPLETE OR PARTIAL WITHDRAWAL NOT OCCURING AS A RESULT OF SALE AND SUBSEQUENT CESSATION OF OBLIGATION TO CONTRIBUTE TO COVERED OPERATIONS; CONTINUATION OF LIABILITY OF SELLER.—A complete or partial withdrawal of an employer (hereinafter in this section referred to as the "seller") under this section does not occur solely because, as a result of a bona fide, arm's-length sale of assets to an unrelated party (hereinafter in this section referred to as the "purchaser"), the seller ceases covered operations or ceases to have an obligation to contribute for such operations, if—

(A) the purchaser has an obligation to contribute to the plan with respect to the operations for substantially the same number of contribution base units for which the seller had an obligation to contribute to the plan;

(B) the purchaser provides to the plan for a period of 5 plan years commencing with the first plan year beginning after the sale of assets, a bond issued by a corporate surety company that is an acceptable surety for purposes of section 412 of this Act, or an amount held in escrow by a bank or similar financial institution satisfactory to the plan, in an amount equal to the greater of—

(i) the average annual contribution required to be made by the seller with respect to the operations under the plan for the 3 plan years preceding the plan year in which the sale of the employer's assets occurs, or

(ii) the annual contribution that the seller was required to make with respect to the operations under the plan for the last plan year before the plan year in which the sale of the assets occurs, which bond or escrow shall be paid to the plan if the purchaser withdraws from the plan, or fails to make a contribution to the plan when due, at any time during the first 5 plan years beginning after the sale; and

(C) the contract for sale provides that, if the purchaser withdraws in a complete withdrawal, or a partial withdrawal with respect to operations, during such first 5 plan years, the seller is secondarily liable for any withdrawal liability it would have had to the plan with respect to the operations (but for this section) if the liability of the purchaser with respect to the plan is not paid.

(2) If the purchaser—

(A) withdraws before the last day of the fifth plan year beginning after the sale, and

(B) fails to make any withdrawal liability payment when due, then the seller shall pay to the plan an amount equal to the payment that would have been due from the seller but for this section.

(3)(A) If all, or substantially all, of the seller's assets are distributed, or if the seller is liquidated before the end of the 5 plan year period described in paragraph (1)(C), then the seller shall provide a bond or amount in escrow equal to the present value of the withdrawal liability the seller would have had but for this subsection.

(B) If only a portion of the seller's assets are distributed during such period, then a bond or escrow shall be required, in accordance with regulations prescribed by the corporation, in a manner consistent with subparagraph (A).

(4) The liability of the party furnishing a bond or escrow under this subsection shall be reduced, upon payment of the bond or escrow to the plan, by the amount thereof.

Act Sec. 4204. (b)(1) LIABILITY OF PURCHASER.—For the purposes of this part, the liability of the purchaser shall be determined as if the purchaser had been required to contribute to the plan in the year of the sale and the 4 plan years preceding the sale the amount the seller was required to contribute for such operations for such 5 plan years.

(2) If the plan is in reorganization in the plan year in which the sale of assets occurs, the purchaser shall furnish a bond or escrow in an amount equal to 200 percent of the amount described in subsection (a)(1)(B).

Act Sec. 4204. (c) VARIANCE OR EXEMPTIONS FROM CONTINUATION OF LIABILITY OF SELLER; PROCEDURES APPLICABLE.—The corporation may by regulation vary the standards in subparagraphs (B) and (C) of subsection (a)(1) if the variance would more effectively or equitably carry out the purposes of this title. Before it promulgates such regulations, the corporation may grant individual or class variances or exemptions from the requirements of such subparagraphs if the particular case warrants it. Before granting such an individual or class variance or exemption, the corporation—

(1) shall publish notice in the Federal Register of the pendency of the variance or exemption,

(2) shall require that adequate notice be given to interested persons, and

(3) shall afford interested persons an opportunity to present their views.

Act Sec. 4204. (d) "UNRELATED PARTY" DEFINED.—For purposes of this section, the term "unrelated party" means a purchaser or seller who does not bear a relationship to the seller or purchaser, as the case may be, that is described in section 267(b) of the Internal Revenue Code of 1986, or that is described in regulations prescribed by the corporation applying principles similar to the principles of such section.

Amendments

P.L. 101-239, § 7891(a)(1):

Titles I, III, and IV of ERISA (other than sections 3(37)(E), 301(a)(7), and 308, the last sentence of section 408(d), and sections 414(c), 4001(a)(3)(ii), and 4303) are each

amended by striking "Internal Revenue Code of 1954" each place it appears and inserting "Internal Revenue Code of 1986", effective October 22, 1986.

P.L. 96-364, § 104(2):

Added Sec 4204, effective September 26, 1980 under ERISA Sec. 4402.

Regulations

The following regulations were adopted by the Pension Benefit Guaranty Corporation on July 1, 1996 (61 FR 34002). Prior to July 1, 1996, PBGC regulations were under Chapter XXVI of Title 29 of the Code of Federal Regulations. Effective July 1, 1996, PBGC regulations were moved to Chapter XL, and were renumbered and reorganized. Reg. § 4204.11 and Reg. § 4204.21 were amended October 28, 2003 (68 FR 61344). Reg. § 4204.12 was amended on September 11, 2015 (80 FR 54979).

Subpart A—General

[¶ 15,668]

§ 4204.1 **Purpose and scope.** (a) *Purpose.* Under section 4204 of ERISA, an employer that ceases covered operations under a multiemployer plan, or ceases to have an obligation to contribute for such operations, because of a bona fide, arm's-length sale of assets to an unrelated purchaser does not incur withdrawal liability if certain conditions are met. One condition is that the sale contract provide that the seller will be secondarily liable if the purchaser withdraws from the

[¶ 15,666E]

§ 4203.6 **OMB control number.** The collections of information contained in this part have been approved by the Office of Management and Budget under OMB control number 1212-0050.

plan within five years and does not pay its withdrawal liability. Another condition is that the purchaser furnish a bond or place funds in escrow, for a period of five plan years, in a prescribed amount. Section 4204 also authorizes the PBGC to provide for variances or exemptions from these requirements. Subpart B of this part provides variances and exemptions from the requirements for certain sales of assets. Subpart C of this part establishes procedures under which a purchaser or seller may, when the conditions set forth in subpart B are not satisfied or when the parties decline to provide certain financial information to the plan, request the PBGC to grant individual or class variances or exemptions from the requirements.

(b) *Scope.* In general, this part applies to any sale of assets described in section 4204(a)(1) of ERISA. However, this part does not apply to a sale of assets involving operations for which the seller is obligated to contribute to a plan described in section 404(c) of the Code, or a continuation of such a plan, unless the plan is amended to provide that section 4204 applies.

[¶ 15,668A]

§4204.2 **Definitions.** The following terms are defined in §4001.2 of this chapter: *Code, employer, ERISA, IRS, multiemployer plan, PBGC, person, plan, plan administrator, plan sponsor,* and *plan year.*

In addition, for purposes of this part:

Date of determination means the date on which a seller ceases covered operations or ceases to have an obligation to contribute for such operations as a result of a sale of assets within the meaning of section 4204(a) of ERISA.

Net income after taxes means revenue minus expenses after taxes (excluding extraordinary and non-recurring income or expenses), as presented in an audited financial statement or, in the absence of such statement, in an unaudited financial statement, each prepared in conformance with generally accepted accounting principles.

Net tangible assets means tangible assets (assets other than licenses, patents copyrights, trade names, trademarks, goodwill, experimental or organizational expenses, unamortized debt discounts and expenses and all other assets which, under generally accepted accounting principles, are deemed intangible) less liabilities (other than pension liabilities). Encumbered assets shall be excluded from net tangible assets only to the extent of the amount of the encumbrance.

Purchaser means a purchaser described in section 4204(a)(1) of ERISA.

Seller means a seller described in section 4204(a)(1) of ERISA.

Subpart B—Variance of the Statutory Requirements

[¶ 15,668B]

§4204.11 **Variance of the bond/escrow and sale-contract requirements.** (a) *General rule.* A purchaser's bond or escrow under section 4204(a)(1)(B) of ERISA and the sale-contract provision under section 4204(a)(1)(C) are not required if the parties to the sale inform the plan in writing of their intention that the sale be covered by section 4204 of ERISA and demonstrate to the satisfaction of the plan that at least one of the criteria contained in §4204.12 or §4204.13(a) is satisfied.

(b) *Requests after posting of bond or establishment of escrow.* A request for a variance may be submitted at any time. If, after a purchaser has posted a bond or placed money in escrow pursuant to section 4204(a)(1)(B) of ERISA, the purchaser demonstrates to the satisfaction of the plan that the criterion in either §4204.13(a)(1) or (a)(2) is satisfied, then the bond shall be cancelled or the amount in escrow shall be refunded. For purposes of considering a request after the bond or escrow is in place, the words "the year preceding the date of the variance request" shall be substituted for "the date of determination" for the first mention of that term in both §4204.13 (a)(1) and (a)(2). In addition, in determining the purchaser's average net income after taxes under §4204.13(a)(1), for any year included in the average for which the net income figure does not reflect the interest expense incurred with respect to the sale, the purchaser's net income shall be reduced by the amount of interest paid with respect to the sale in the fiscal year following the date of determination.

[Amended 10/28/2003 by 68 FR 61344]

(c) *Information required.* A request for a variance shall contain financial or other information that is sufficient to establish that one of the criteria in §4204.12 or §4204.13(a) is satisfied. A request on the basis of either §4204.13(a)(1) or (a)(2) shall also include a copy of the purchaser's audited (if available) or (if not) unaudited financial statements for the specified time period.

(d) *Limited exemption during pendency of request.* Provided that all of the information required to be submitted is submitted before the first day of the first plan year beginning after the sale, a plan may not, pending its decision on the variance, require a purchaser to post a bond or place an amount in escrow pursuant to section 4204(a)(1)(B). In the event a bond or escrow is not in place pursuant to the preceding sentence, and the plan determines that the request does not qualify for a variance, the purchaser shall comply with section 4204(a)(1)(B) within 30 days after the date on which it receives notice of the plan's decision.

(Approved by the Office of Management and Budget under control number 1212—0021)

(e) *Method and date of issuance.* The PBGC applies the rules in subpart B of part 4000 of this chapter to determine permissible methods of issuance under this subpart. The PBGC applies the rules in subpart C of part 4000 of this chapter to determine the date that an issuance under this subpart was provided.

[Amended 10/28/2003 by 68 FR 61344]

(Approved by the Office of Management and Budget under control number 1212—0021)

[¶ 15,668C]

§4204.12 **De minimis transactions.** The criterion under this section is that the amount of the bond or escrow does not exceed the lesser of $250,000 or two percent of the average total annual contributions made by all employers to the plan, for the purposes of section 431(b)(3)(A) of the Code, for the three most recent plan years ending before the date of determination. For this purpose, "contributions made" shall have the same meaning as the term has under §4211.12(a) of this chapter. [Amended 9/11/15 by 80 FR 54979.]

[¶ 15,668D]

§4204.13 **Net income and net tangible assets tests.** (a) *General.* The criteria under this section are that either—

(1) *Net income test.* The purchaser's average net income after taxes for its three most recent fiscal years ending before the date of determination (as defined in §4204.12), reduced by any interest expense incurred with respect to the sale which is payable in the fiscal year following the date of determination, equals or exceeds 150 percent of the amount of the bond or escrow required under ERISA section 4204(a)(1)(B); or

(2) *Net tangible assets test.* The purchaser's net tangible assets at the end of the fiscal year preceding the date of determination (as defined in §4204.12), equal or exceed—

(i) If the purchaser was not obligated to contribute to the plan before the sale, the amount of unfunded vested benefits allocable to the seller under section 4211 (with respect to the purchased operations), as of the date of determination, or

(ii) If the purchaser was obligated to contribute to the plan before the sale, the sum of the amount of unfunded vested benefits allocable to the purchaser and to the seller under ERISA section 4211 (with respect to the purchased operations), each as of the date of determination.

(b) *Special rule when more than one plan is covered by request.* For the purposes of paragraphs (a)(1) and (a)(2), if the transaction involves the assumption by the purchaser of the seller's obligation to contribute to more than one multiemployer plan, then the total amount of the bond or escrow or of the unfunded vested benefits, as applicable, for all of the plans with respect to which the purchaser has not posted a bond or escrow shall be used to determine whether the applicable test is met.

(c) *Non-applicability of tests in event of purchaser's insolvency.* A purchaser will not qualify for a variance under this subpart pursuant to paragraph (a)(1) or (a)(2) of this section if, as of the earlier of the date of the plan's decision on the variance request or the first day of the first plan year beginning after the date of determination, the purchaser is the subject of a petition under title 11, United States Code, or of a proceeding under similar provisions of state insolvency laws.

Subpart C—Procedures for Individual and Class Variances or Exemptions

[¶ 15,668E]

§ 4204.21 **Requests to PBGC for variances and exemptions**. (a) *Filing of request.* (1) *In general.* If a transaction covered by this part does not satisfy the conditions set forth in subpart B of this part, or if the parties decline to provide to the plan privileged or confidential financial information within the meaning of section 552(b)(4) of the Freedom of Information Act (5 U.S.C. 552), the purchaser or seller may request from the PBGC an exemption or variance from the requirements of section 4204(a)(1)(B) and (C) of ERISA.

(2) *Method of filing.* The PBGC applies the rules in subpart A of part 4000 of this chapter to determine permissible methods of filing with the PBGC under this subpart.

[Amended 10/28/2003 by 68 FR 61344]

(b) *Who may request.* A purchaser or a seller may file a request for a variance or exemption. The request may be submitted by one or more duly authorized representatives acting on behalf of the party or parties. When a contributing employer withdraws from a plan as a result of related sales of assets involving several purchasers, or withdraws from more than one plan as a result of a single sale, the application may request a class variance or exemption for all the transactions.

(c) *Where to file.* See Sec. 4000.4 of this chapter for information on where to file.

[Amended 10/28/2003 by 68 FR 61344]

(d) *Information.* Each request shall contain the following information:

(1) The name and address of the plan or plans for which the variance or exemption is being requested, and the telephone number of the plan administrator of each plan.

(2) For each plan described in paragraph (d)(1) of this section, the nine-digit Employer Identification Number (EIN) assigned by the IRS to the plan sponsor and the three-digit Plan Identification Number (PN) assigned by the plan sponsor to the plan, and, if different, also the EIN and PN last filed with the PBGC. If an EIN or PN has not been assigned, that should be indicated.

(3) The name, address and telephone number of the seller and of its duly authorized representative, if any.

(4) The name, address and telephone number of the purchaser and of its duly authorized representative, if any.

(5) A full description of each transaction for which the request is being made, including effective date.

(6) A statement explaining why the requested variance or exemption would not significantly increase the risk of financial loss to the plan, including evidence, financial or otherwise, that supports that conclusion.

(7) When the request for a variance or exemption is filed by the seller alone, a statement signed by the purchaser indicating its intention that section 4204 of ERISA apply to the sale of assets.

(8) A statement indicating the amount of the purchaser's bond or escrow required under section 4204(a)(1)(B) of ERISA.

(9) The estimated amount of withdrawal liability that the seller would otherwise incur as a result of the sale if section 4204 did not apply to the sale.

(10) A certification that a complete copy of the request has been sent to each plan described in paragraph (d)(1) of this section and each collective bargaining representative of the seller's employees by certified mail, return receipt requested.

(e) *Additional information.* In addition to the information described in paragraph (d) of this section, the PBGC may require the purchaser, the seller, or the plan to submit any other information the PBGC determines it needs to review the request.

(f) *Disclosure of information.* Any party submitting information pursuant to this section may include a statement of whether any of the information is of a nature that its disclosure may not be required under the Freedom of Information Act, 5 U.S.C. 552. The statement should specify the information that may not be subject to disclosure and the grounds therefor.

(Approved by the Office of Management and Budget under control number 1212-0021)

[¶ 15,668F]

§ 4204.22 **PBGC action on requests**. (a) *General.* The PBGC shall approve a request for a variance or exemption if PBGC determines that approval of the request is warranted, in that it—

(1) Would more effectively or equitably carry out the purposes of title IV of ERISA; and

(2) Would not significantly increase the risk of financial loss to the plan.

(b) *Notice of pendency of request.* As soon as practicable after receiving a variance or exemption request containing all the information specified in § 4204.21, the PBGC shall publish a notice of the pendency of the request in the Federal Register. The notice shall provide that any interested person may, within the period of time specified therein, submit written comments to the PBGC concerning the request. The notice will usually provide for a comment period of 45 days.

(c) *PBGC decision on request.* The PBGC shall issue a decision on a variance or exemption request as soon as practicable after the close of the comment period described in paragraph (b) of this section. PBGC's decision shall be in writing, and if the PBGC disapproves the request, the decision shall state the reasons therefor. Notice of the decision shall be published in the Federal Register.

[¶ 15,669]
PARTIAL WITHDRAWALS

Act Sec. 4205. (a) DETERMINATIVE FACTORS.—Except as otherwise provided in this section, there is a partial withdrawal by an employer from a plan on the last day of a plan year if for such plan year—

(1) there is a 70-percent contribution decline, or

(2) there is a partial cessation of the employer's contribution obligation.

Act Sec. 4205. (b) CRITERIA APPLICABLE.—Purposes of subsection (a)—

(1)(A) There is a 70-percent contribution decline for any plan year if during each plan year in the 3-year testing period the employer's contribution base units do not exceed 30 percent of the employer's contribution base units for the high base year.

(B) For purposes of subparagraph (A)—

(i) The term "3-year testing period" means the period consisting of the plan year and the immediately preceding 2 plan years.

(ii) The number of contribution base units for the high base year is the average number of such units for the 2 plan years for which the employer's contribution base units were the highest within the 5 plan years immediately preceding the beginning of the 3-year testing period.

(2)(A) There is a partial cessation of the employer's contribution obligation for the plan year if, during such year—

(i) the employer permanently ceases to have an obligation to contribute under one or more but fewer than all collective bargaining agreement under which the employer has been obligated to contribute under the plan but continues to perform work in the jurisdiction of the collective bargaining agreement of the type for which contributions were previously required or transfers such work to another location, or to an entity or entities owned or controlled by the employer, or

(ii) an employer permanently ceases to have an obligation to contribute under the plan with respect to work performed at one or more but fewer than all of its facilities, but continues to perform work at the facility of the type for which the obligation to contribute ceased.

(B) For purposes of subparagraph (A), a cessation of obligations under a collective bargaining agreement shall not be considered to have occurred solely because, with respect to the same plan, one agreement that requires contributions to the plan has been substituted for another agreement.

Act Sec. 4205. (c) (1) RETAIL FOOD INDUSTRY.—In the case of a plan in which a majority of the covered employees are employed in the retail food industry, the plan may be amended to provide that this section shall be applied with respect to such plan—

(A) by substituting "35 percent" for "70 percent" in subsections (a) and (b), and

(B) by substituting "65 percent" for "30 percent" in subsection (b).

(2) Any amendment adopted under paragraph (1) shall provide rules for the equitable reduction of withdrawal liability in any case in which the number of the plan's contribution base units, in the 2 plan years following the plan year of withdrawal of the employer, is higher than such number immediately after the withdrawal.

(3) Section 4208 shall not apply to a plan which has been amended under paragraph (1).

Act Sec. 4205. (d) CONTINUATION OF LIABILITY OF EMPLOYER FOR PARTIAL WITHDRAWAL UNDER AMENDED PLAN.—In the case of a plan described in section 404(c) of the Internal Revenue Code of 1986, or a continuation thereof, the plan may be amended to provide rules setting forth other conditions consistent with the purposes of this Act under which an employer has liability for partial withdrawal.

Amendment

P.L. 109-280, Sec. 204(b)(1):

Amended ERISA Sec. 4205(b)(2)(A)(i) by inserting "or to an entity or entities owned or controlled by the employer" after "to another location."

The above amendment is effective with respect to work transferred on or after the date of the enactment of the Act (August 17, 2006).

P.L. 101-239, § 7891(a)(1):

Titles I, III, and IV of ERISA (other than sections 3(37)(E), 301(a)(7), and 308, the last sentence of section 408(d), and sections 414(c), 4001(a)(3)(ii), and 4303) are each amended by striking "Internal Revenue Code of 1954" each place it appears and inserting "Internal Revenue Code of 1986".

The above amendment is effective October 22, 1986.

P.L. 96-364, § 104(2):

Added Sec. 4205.

The above amendment is effective September 26, 1980 under ERISA Sec. 4402, except that Sec. 4205(a)(1) does not apply to any plan year beginning before September 26, 1982, and Sec. 4205(a)(2) does not apply with respect to any cessation of contribution obligations occurring before September 26, 1980 (Sec. 108(d) of P.L. 96-364).

[¶ 15,670]
ADJUSTMENT FOR PARTIAL WITHDRAWAL

Act Sec. 4206. (a) The amount of an employer's liability for a partial withdrawal, before the application of sections 4219(c)(1) and 4225, is equal to the product of—

(1) the amount determined under section 4211, and adjusted under section 4209 if appropriate, determined as if the employer had withdrawn from the plan in a complete withdrawal—

(A) on the date of the partial withdrawal, or

(B) in the case of a partial withdrawal described in section 4205(a)(1) (relating to 70-percent contribution decline), on the last day of the first plan year in the 3-year testing period, multiplied by

(2) a fraction which is 1 minus a fraction—

(A) the numerator of which is the employer's contribution base units for the plan year following the plan year in which the partial withdrawal occurs, and

(B) the denominator of which is the average of the employer's contribution base units for—

(i) except as provided in clause (ii), the 5 plan years immediately preceding the plan year in which the partial withdrawal occurs, or

(ii) in the case of a partial withdrawal described in section 4205(a)(1) (relating to 70-percent contribution decline), the 5 plan years immediately preceding the beginning of the 3-year testing period.

Act Sec. 4206. (b)(1) In the case of an employer that has withdrawal liability for a partial withdrawal from a plan, any withdrawal liability of that employer for a partial or complete withdrawal from that plan in a subsequent plan year shall be reduced by the amount of any partial withdrawal liability (reduced by any abatement or reduction of such liability) of the employer with respect to the plan for a previous plan year.

(2) The corporation shall prescribe such regulations as may be necessary to provide for proper adjustments in the reduction provided by paragraph (1) for—

(A) changes in unfunded vested benefits arising after the close of the prior year for which partial withdrawal liability was determined,

(B) changes in contribution base units occurring after the close of the prior year for which partial withdrawal liability was determined, and

(C) any other factors for which it determines adjustment to be appropriate,

so that the liability for any complete or partial withdrawal in any subsequent year (after the application of the reduction) properly reflects the employer's share of liability with respect to the plan.

Amendment

P.L. 96-364, § 104(2):

Added Sec. 4206, effective September 26, 1980 under ERISA Sec. 4402.

Regulations

The following regulations were adopted by the Pension Benefit Guaranty Corporation on July 1, 1996 (61 FR 34002). Prior to July 1, 1996, PBGC regulations were under Chapter XXVI of Title 29 of the Code of Federal Regulations. Effective July 1, 1996, PBGC regulations were moved to Chapter XL, and were renumbered and reorganized. Reg. § 4206.7 was amended on September 11, 2015 (80 FR 54979).

[¶ 15,670A]

§ 4206.1 **Purpose and scope.** (a) *Purpose.* The purpose of this part is to prescribe rules, pursuant to section 4206(b) of ERISA, for adjusting the partial or complete withdrawal liability of an employer that previously partially withdrew from the same multiemployer plan. Section 4206(b)(1) provides that when an employer that has partially withdrawn from a plan subsequently incurs liability for another partial or a complete withdrawal from that plan, the employer's liability for the subsequent withdrawal is to be reduced by the amount of its liability for the prior partial withdrawal (less any waiver or reduction of that prior liability). Section 4206(b)(2) requires the PBGC to prescribe regulations adjusting the amount of this credit to ensure that the liability for the subsequent withdrawal properly reflects the employer's share of liability with respect to the plan. The purpose of the credit is to protect a withdrawing employer from being charged twice for the same unfunded vested benefits of the plan. The reduction in the credit protects the other employers in the plan from becoming responsible for unfunded vested benefits properly allocable to the withdrawing employer. In the interests of simplicity, the rules in this part provide for, generally, a one-step calculation of the adjusted credit under section 4206(b)(2) against the subsequent liability, rather than for separate calculations first of the credit under section 4206(b)(1) and then of the reduction in the credit under paragraph (b)(2) of that section. In cases where the withdrawal liability for the prior partial withdrawal was reduced by an abatement or other reduction of that liability, the adjusted credit is further reduced in accordance with § 4206.8 of this part.

(b) *Scope.* This part applies to multiemployer plans covered under Title IV of ERISA, and to employers that have partially withdrawn from such plans after September 25, 1980 and subsequently completely or partially withdraw from the same plan.

[¶ 15,670B]

§ 4206.2 **Definitions.** The following are defined in § 4001.2 of this chapter: *Code, employer, ERISA, multiemployer plan, PBGC, plan,* and *plan year.*

In addition, for purposes of this part:

Complete withdrawal means a complete withdrawal as described in section 4203 of ERISA.

Partial withdrawal means a partial withdrawal as described in section 4205 of ERISA.

[¶ 15,670C]

§ 4206.3 **Credit against liability for a subsequent withdrawal.** Whenever an employer that was assessed withdrawal liability for a partial withdrawal from a plan partially or completely withdraws from that plan in a subsequent plan year, it shall receive a credit against the new withdrawal liability in an amount greater than or equal to zero, determined in accordance with this part. If the credit determined under §§ 4206.4 through 4206.9 is less than zero, the amount of the credit shall equal zero.

[¶ 15,670D]

§ 4206.4 **Amount of credit in plans using the presumptive method.** (a) *General.* In a plan that uses the presumptive allocation method described in section 4211(b) of ERISA, the credit shall equal the sum of the unamortized old liabilities determined under paragraph (b) of this section, multiplied by the fractions described or determined under paragraph (c) of this section. When an employer's prior partial withdrawal liability has been reduced or waived, this credit shall be adjusted in accordance with § 4206.8.

(b) *Unamortized old liabilities.* The amounts determined under this paragraph are the employer's proportional shares, if any, of the unamortized amounts as of the end of the plan year preceding the withdrawal for which the credit is being calculated, of—

(1) The plan's unfunded vested benefits as of the end of the last plan year ending before September 26, 1980;

(2) The annual changes in the plan's unfunded vested benefits for plan years ending after September 25, 1980, and before the year of the prior partial withdrawal; and

(3) The reallocated unfunded vested benefits (if any), as determined under section 4211(b)(4) of ERISA, for plan years ending before the year of the prior partial withdrawal.

(c) *Employer's allocable share of old liabilities.* The sum of the amounts determined under paragraph (b) are multiplied by the two fractions described in this paragraph in order to determine the amount of the old liabilities that was previously assessed against the employer.

(1) The first fraction is the fraction determined under section 4206(a)(2) of ERISA for the prior partial withdrawal.

(2) The second fraction is a fraction, the numerator of which is the amount of the liability assessed against the employer for the prior partial withdrawal, and the denominator of which is the product of—

(i) The amount of unfunded vested benefits allocable to the employer as if it had completely withdrawn as of the date of the prior partial withdrawal (determined without regard to any adjustments), multiplied by—

(ii) The fraction determined under section 4206(a)(2) of ERISA for the prior partial withdrawal.

[¶ 15,670E]

§ 4206.5 **Amount of credit in plans using the modified presumptive method.** (a) *General.* In a plan that uses the modified presumptive method described in section 4211(c)(2) of ERISA, the credit shall equal the sum of the unamortized old liabilities determined under paragraph (b) of this section, multiplied by the fractions described or determined under paragraph (c) of this section. When an employer's prior partial withdrawal liability has been reduced or waived, this credit shall be adjusted in accordance with § 4206.8.

(b) *Unamortized old liabilities.* The amounts described in this paragraph shall be determined as of the end of the plan year preceding the withdrawal for which the credit is being calculated, and are the employer's proportional shares, if any, of—

(1) The plan's unfunded vested benefits as of the end of the last plan year ending before September 26, 1980, reduced as if those obligations were being fully amortized in level annual installments over 15 years beginning with the first plan year ending on or after such date; and

(2) The aggregate post-1980 change amount determined under section 4211(c)(2)(C) of ERISA as if the employer had completely withdrawn in the year of the prior partial withdrawal, reduced as if those obligations were being fully amortized in level annual installments over the 5-year period beginning with the plan year in which the prior partial withdrawal occurred.

(c) *Employer's allocable share of old liabilities.* The sum of the amounts determined under paragraph (b) are multiplied by the two fractions described in this paragraph in order to determine the amount of old liabilities that was previously assessed against the employer.

(1) The first fraction is the fraction determined under section 4206(a)(2) of ERISA for the prior partial withdrawal.

(2) The second fraction is a fraction, the numerator of which is the amount of the liability assessed against the employer for the prior partial withdrawal, and the denominator of which is the product of—

(i) The amount of unfunded vested benefits allocable to the employer as if it had completely withdrawn as of the date of the prior partial withdrawal (determined without regard to any adjustments), multiplied by—

(ii) The fraction determined under section 4206(a)(2) of ERISA for the prior partial withdrawal.

[¶ 15,670F]

§ 4206.6 **Amount of credit in plans using the rolling-5 method.** In a plan that uses the rolling-5 allocation method described in section 4211(c)(3) of ERISA, the credit shall equal the amount of the liability assessed for the prior partial withdrawal, reduced as if that amount was being fully amortized in level annual installments over the 5-year period beginning with the plan year in which the prior partial withdrawal occurred. When an employer's prior partial withdrawal liability has been reduced or waived, this credit shall be adjusted in accordance with § 4206.8.

[¶ 15,670G]

§ 4206.7 **Amount of credit in plans using the direct attribution method.** In a plan that uses the direct attribution allocation method described in section 4211(c)(4) of ERISA, the credit shall equal the amount of the liability assessed for the prior partial withdrawal, reduced as if that amount was being fully amortized in level annual installments beginning with the plan year in which the prior partial withdrawal occurred, over the greater of 10 years or the amortization period for the resulting base when the combined charge base and the combined credit base are offset under section 431(b)(5) of the Code. When an employer's prior partial withdrawal liability has been reduced or waived, this credit shall be adjusted in accordance with § 4206.8. [Amended 9/11/15 by 80 FR 54979.]

[¶ 15,670H]

§ 4206.8 **Reduction of credit for abatement or other reduction of prior partial withdrawal liability.** (a) *General.* If an employer's withdrawal liability for a prior partial withdrawal has been reduced or waived, the credit determined pursuant to §§ 4206.4 through 4206.7 shall be adjusted in accordance with this section.

(b) *Computation.* The adjusted credit is calculated by multiplying the credit determined under the preceding sections of this part by a fraction—

(1) the numerator of which is the excess of the total partial withdrawal liability of the employer for all partial withdrawals in prior years (excluding those partial withdrawals for which the credit is zero) over the present value of each abatement or other reduction of that prior withdrawal liability calculated as of the date on which that prior partial withdrawal liability was determined; and

(2) the denominator of which is the total partial withdrawal liability of the employer for all partial withdrawals in prior years (excluding those partial withdrawals for which the credit is zero).

[¶ 15,670I]

§ 4206.9 **Amount of credit in plans using alternative allocation methods.** A plan that has adopted an alternative method of allocating unfunded vested benefits pursuant to section 4211(c)(5) of ERISA and part 4211 of this chapter shall adopt, by plan amendment, a method of calculating the credit provided by § 4206.3 that is consistent with the

rules in §§ 4206.4 through 4206.8 for plans using the statutory allocation method most similar to the plan's alternative allocation method.

[¶ 15,670J]

§ 4206.10 **Special rule for 70-percent decline partial withdrawals.** For the purposes of applying the rules in §§ 4206.4 through 4206.9 in any case in which either the prior or subsequent partial withdrawal resulted from a 70-percent contribution decline (or a 35-percent decline in the case of certain retail food industry plans), the first year of the 3-year testing period shall be deemed to be the plan year in which the partial withdrawal occurred.

[¶ 15,671]
REDUCTION OR WAIVER OF COMPLETE WITHDRAWAL LIABILITY

Act Sec. 4207. (a) The corporation shall provide by regulation for the reduction or waiver of liability for a complete withdrawal in the event that an employer who has withdrawn from a plan subsequently resumes covered operations under the plan or renews an obligation to contribute under the plan, to the extent that the corporation determines that reduction or waiver of withdrawal liability is consistent with the purposes of this Act.

Act Sec. 4207. (b) The corporation shall prescribe by regulation a procedure and standards for the amendment of plans to provide alternative rules for the reduction or waiver of liability for a complete withdrawal in the event that an employer who has withdrawn from the plan subsequently resumes covered operations or renews an obligation to contribute under the plan. The rules may apply only to the extent that the rules are consistent with the purposes of this Act.

Amendment:

P.L. 96-364, § 104(2):

Added Sec. 4207, effective September 26, 1980 under ERISA Sec. 4402.

Regulations

The following regulations were adopted by the Pension Benefit Guaranty Corporation on July 1, 1996 (61 FR 34002). Prior to July 1, 1996, PBGC regulations were under Chapter XXVI of Title 29 of the Code of Federal Regulations. Effective July 1, 1996, PBGC regulations were moved to Chapter XL, and were renumbered and reorganized. Reg. § 4207.10 was revised and Reg. § 4207.11 was added October 28, 2003 (68 FR 61344).

[¶ 15,671A]

§ 4207.1 **Purpose and scope.** (a) *Purpose.* The purpose of this part is to prescribe rules, pursuant to section 4207(a) of ERISA, for reducing or waiving the withdrawal liability of certain employers that have completely withdrawn from a multiemployer plan and subsequently resume covered operations under the plan. This part prescribes rules pursuant to which the plan must waive the employer's obligation to make future liability payments with respect to its complete withdrawal and must calculate the amount of the employer's liability for a partial or complete withdrawal from the plan after its reentry into the plan. This part also provides procedures, pursuant to section 4207(b) of ERISA, for plan sponsors of multiemployer plans to apply to PBGC for approval of plan amendments that provide for the reduction or waiver of complete withdrawal liability under conditions other than those specified in section 4207(a) of ERISA and this part.

(b) *Scope.* This part applies to multiemployer plans covered under title IV of ERISA, and to employers that have completely withdrawn from such plans after September 25, 1980, and that have not, as of the date of their reentry into the plan, fully satisfied their obligation to pay withdrawal liability arising from the complete withdrawal.

[¶ 15,671B]

§ 4207.2 **Definitions.** The following terms are defined in § 4001.2 of this chapter: *employer, ERISA, IRS, Multiemployer Act, multiemployer plan, nonforfeitable benefit, PBGC, plan,* and *plan year.*

In addition, for purposes of this part:

Complete withdrawal means a complete withdrawal as described in section 4203 of ERISA.

Eligible employer means the employer, as defined in section 4001(b) of ERISA, as it existed on the date of its initial partial or complete withdrawal, as applicable. An eligible employer shall continue to be an eligible employer notwithstanding the occurrence of any of the following events:

(1) A restoration involving a mere change in identity, form or place of organization, however effected;

(2) A reorganization involving a liquidation into a parent corporation;

(3) A merger, consolidation or division solely between (or among) trades or businesses (whether or not incorporated) of the employer; or

(4) An acquisition by or of, or a merger or combination with another trade or business.

Partial withdrawal means a partial withdrawal as described in section 4205 of ERISA.

Period of withdrawal means the plan year in which the employer completely withdrew from the plan, the plan year in which the employer reentered the plan and all intervening plan years.

[¶ 15,671C]

§ 4207.3 **Abatement.** (a) *General.* Whenever an eligible employer that has completely withdrawn from a multiemployer plan reenters the plan, it may apply to the plan for abatement of its complete withdrawal liability. Applications shall be filed by the date of the first scheduled withdrawal liability payment falling due after the employer resumes covered operations or, if later, the fifteenth calendar day after the employer resumes covered operations. Applications shall identify the eligible employer, the withdrawn employer, if different, the date of withdrawal, and the date of resumption of covered operations. Upon receiving an application for abatement, the plan sponsor shall determine, in accordance with paragraph (b) of this section, whether the employer satisfies the requirements for abatement of its complete withdrawal liability under § 4207.5, § 4207.9, or a plan amendment which has been approved by PBGC pursuant to § 4207.10. If the plan sponsor determines that the employer satisfies the requirements for abatement of its complete withdrawal liability, the provisions of paragraph (c) of this section shall apply. If the plan sponsor determines that the employer does not satisfy the requirements for abatement of its complete withdrawal liability, the provisions of paragraphs (d) and (e) of this section shall apply.

(b) *Determination of abatement.* As soon as practicable after an eligible employer that completely withdrew from a multiemployer plan applies for abatement, the plan sponsor shall determine whether the employer satisfies the requirements for abatement of its complete withdrawal liability under this part and shall notify the employer in writing of its determination and of the consequences of its determination, as described in paragraphs (c) or (d) and (e) of this section, as appropriate. If a bond or escrow has been provided to the plan under § 4207.4, the plan sponsor shall send a copy of the notice to the bonding or escrow agent.

(c) *Effects of abatement.* If the plan sponsor determines that the employer satisfies the requirements for abatement of its complete withdrawal liability under this part, then—

(1) The employer shall have no obligation to make future withdrawal liability payments to the plan with respect to its complete withdrawal;

(2) The employer's liability for a subsequent withdrawal shall be determined in accordance with § 4207.7 or § 4207.8, as applicable;

(3) Any bonds furnished under § 4207.4 shall be cancelled and any amounts held in escrow under § 4207.4 shall be refunded to the employer; and

(4) Any withdrawal liability payments due after the reentry and made by the employer to the plan shall be refunded by the plan without interest.

(d) *Effects of non-abatement.* If the plan sponsor determines that the employer does not satisfy the requirements for abatement of its complete withdrawal liability under this part, then—

(1) The bond or escrow furnished under § 4207.4 shall be paid to the plan within 30 days after the date of the plan sponsor's notice under paragraph (b) of this section;

(2) The employer shall pay to the plan within 30 days after the date of the plan sponsor's notice under paragraph (b) of this section, the amount of its withdrawal liability payment or payments, with respect to which the bond or escrow was furnished, in excess of the bond or escrow;

(3) The employer shall resume making its withdrawal liability payments as they are due to the plan; and

(4) The employer shall be treated as a new employer for purposes of any future application of the withdrawal liability rules in sections 4201-4225 of title IV of ERISA with respect to its participation in the plan after its reentry into the plan, except that in plans using the "direct attribution" method (section 4211(c)(4) of ERISA), the nonforfeitable benefits attributable to service with the employer shall include nonforfeitable benefits attributable to service prior to reentry that were not nonforfeitable at that time.

(e) *Collection of payments due and review of non-abatement determination.* The rules in part 4219, subpart C, of this chapter (relating to overdue, defaulted, and overpaid withdrawal liability) shall apply with respect to all payments required to be made under paragraphs (d)(2) and (d)(3) of this section. For this purpose, a payment required to be made under paragraph (d)(2) shall be treated as a withdrawal liability payment due on the 30th day after the date of the plan sponsor's notice under paragraph (b) of this section.

(1) *Review of non-abatement determination.* A plan sponsor's determination that the employer does not satisfy the requirements for abatement under this part shall be subject to plan review under section 4219(b)(2) of ERISA and to arbitration under section 4221 of ERISA, within the times prescribed by those sections. For this purpose, the plan sponsor's notice under paragraph (b) of this section shall be treated as a demand under section 4219(b)(1) of ERISA.

(2) *Determination of abatement.* If the plan sponsor or an arbitrator determines that the employer satisfies the requirements for abatement of its complete withdrawal liability under this part, the plan sponsor shall immediately refund the following payments (plus interest, except as indicated below, determined in accordance with § 4219.31(d) of this chapter as if the payments were overpayments of withdrawal liability) to the employer in a lump sum:

(i) The amount of the employer's withdrawal liability payment or payments, without interest, due after its reentry and made by the employer.

(ii) The bond or escrow paid to the plan under paragraph (d)(1) of this section.

(iii) The amount of the employer's withdrawal liability payment or payments in excess of the bond or escrow, paid to the plan under paragraph (d)(2) of this section.

(iv) Any withdrawal liability payment made by the employer to the plan pursuant to paragraph (d)(3) of this section after the plan sponsor's notice under paragraph (b) of this section.

[¶ 15,671D]

§ 4207.4 **Withdrawal liability payments during pendency of abatement determination.** (a) *General rule.* An eligible employer that completely withdraws from a multiemployer plan and subsequently reenters the plan may, in lieu of making withdrawal liability payments due after its reentry, provide a bond to, or establish an escrow account for, the plan that satisfies the requirements of paragraph (b) of this section or any plan rules adopted under paragraph (d)

of this section, pending a determination by the plan sponsor under § 4207.3(b) of whether the employer satisfies the requirements for abatement of its complete withdrawal liability. An employer that applies for abatement and neither provides a bond/escrow nor pays its withdrawal liability payments remains eligible for abatement.

(b) *Bond/escrow.* The bond or escrow allowed by this section shall be in an amount equal to 70 percent of the withdrawal liability payments that would otherwise be due. The bond or escrow relating to each payment shall be furnished before the due date of that payment. A single bond or escrow may be provided for more than one payment due during the pendency of the plan sponsor's determination. The bond or escrow agreement shall provide that if the plan sponsor determines that the employer does not satisfy the requirements for abatement of its complete withdrawal liability under this part, the bond or escrow shall be paid to the plan upon notice from the plan sponsor to the bonding or escrow agent. A bond provided under this paragraph shall be issued by a corporate surety company that is an acceptable surety for purposes of section 412 of ERISA.

(c) *Notice of bond/escrow.* Concurrently with posting a bond or establishing an escrow account under paragraph (b) of this section, the employer shall notify the plan sponsor. The notice shall include a statement of the amount of the bond or escrow, the scheduled payment or payments with respect to which the bond or escrow is being furnished, and the name and address of the bonding or escrow agent.

(d) *Plan amendments concerning bond/escrow.* A plan may, by amendment, adopt rules decreasing the amount specified in paragraph (b) of a bond or escrow allowed under this section. A plan amendment adopted under this paragraph may be applied only to the extent that it is consistent with the purposes of ERISA.

[¶ 15,671E]

§ 4207.5 **Requirements for abatement.** (a) *General rule.* Except as provided in § 4207.9 (d) and (e) (pertaining to acquisitions, mergers and other combinations), an eligible employer that completely withdraws from a multiemployer plan and subsequently reenters the plan shall have its liability for that withdrawal abated in accordance with § 4207.3(c) if the employer resumes covered operations under the plan, and the number of contribution base units with respect to which the employer has an obligation to contribute under the plan for the measurement period (as defined in paragraph (b) of this section) after it resumes covered operations exceeds 30 percent of the number of contribution base units with respect to which the employer had an obligation to contribute under the plan for the base year (as defined in paragraph (c) of this section).

(b) *Measurement period.* If the employer resumes covered operations under the plan at least six full months prior to the end of a plan year and would satisfy the test in paragraph (a) based on its contribution base units for that plan year, then the measurement period shall be the period from the date it resumes covered operations until the end of that plan year. If the employer would not satisfy this test, or if the employer resumes covered operations under the plan less than six full months prior to the end of the plan year, the measurement period shall be the first twelve months after it resumes covered operations.

(c) *Base year.* For purposes of paragraph (a) of this section, the employer's number of contribution base units for the base year is the average number of contribution base units for the two plan years in which its contribution base units were the highest, within the five plan years immediately preceding the year of its complete withdrawal.

[¶ 15,671F]

§ 4207.6 **Partial withdrawals after reentry.** (a) *General rule.* For purposes of determining whether there is a partial withdrawal of an eligible employer whose liability is abated under this part upon the employer's reentry into the plan or at any time thereafter, the plan sponsor shall apply the rules in section 4205 of ERISA, as modified by the rules in this section, and section 108 of the Multiemployer Act. A partial withdrawal of an employer whose liability is abated under this part may occur under these rules upon the employer's reentry into the plan. However, a plan sponsor may not demand payment of withdrawal liability for a partial withdrawal occurring upon the employer's reentry before the plan sponsor has determined that the employer's liability for its complete withdrawal is abated under this part and has so notified the employer in accordance with §4207.3(b).

(b) *Partial withdrawal—70-percent contribution decline.* The plan sponsor shall determine whether there is a partial withdrawal described in section 4205(a)(1) of ERISA (relating to a 70-percent contribution decline) in accordance with the rules in section 4205 of ERISA and section 108 of the Multiemployer Act, as modified by the rules in this paragraph, and shall determine the amount of an employer's liability for that partial withdrawal in accordance with the rules in §4207.8(b).

(1) *Definition of "3-year testing period".* For purposes of section 4205(b)(1) of ERISA, the term "3-year testing period" means the period consisting of the plan year for which the determination is made and the two immediately preceding plan years, excluding any plan year during the period of withdrawal.

(2) *Contribution base units for high base year.* For purposes of section 4205(b)(1) of ERISA and except as provided in section 108(d)(3) of the Multiemployer Act, in determining the number of contribution base units for the high base year, if the five plan years immediately preceding the beginning of the 3-year testing period include a plan year during the period of withdrawal, the number of contribution base units for each such year of withdrawal shall be deemed to be the greater of—

(i) The employer's contribution base units for that plan year; or

(ii) The average of the employer's contribution base units for the three plan years preceding the plan year in which the employer completely withdrew from the plan.

(c) *Partial withdrawal—partial cessation of contribution obligation.* The plan sponsor shall determine whether there is a partial withdrawal described in section 4205(a)(2) of ERISA (relating to a partial cessation of the employer's contribution obligation) in accordance with the rules in section 4205 of ERISA, as modified by the rules in this paragraph, and section 108 of the Multiemployer Act. In making this determination, the sponsor shall exclude all plan years during the period of withdrawal. A partial withdrawal under this paragraph can occur no earlier than the plan year of reentry. If the sponsor determines that there was a partial withdrawal, it shall determine the amount of an employer's liability for that partial withdrawal in accordance with the rules in §4207.8(c).

[¶ 15,671G]

§4207.7 **Liability for subsequent complete withdrawals and related adjustments for allocating unfunded vested benefits.** (a) *General.* When an eligible employer that has had its liability for a complete withdrawal abated under this part completely withdraws from the plan, the employer's liability for that subsequent withdrawal shall be determined in accordance with the rules in sections 4201-4225 of title IV, as modified by the rules in this section, and section 108 of the Multiemployer Act. In the case of a combination described in §4207.9(d), the modifications described in this section shall be applied only with respect to that portion of the eligible employer that had previously withdrawn from the plan. In the case of a combination described in §4207.9(e), the modifications shall be applied separately with respect to each previously withdrawn employer that comprises the eligible employer. In addition, when a plan has abated the liability of a reentered employer, if the plan uses either the "presumptive" or the "direct attribution" method (section 4211(b) or (c)(4), respectively) for allocating unfunded vested benefits, the plan shall modify those allocation methods as described in this section in allocating unfunded vested benefits to any employer that withdraws from the plan after the reentry.

(b) *Allocation of unfunded vested benefits for subsequent withdrawal in plans using "presumptive" method.* In a plan using the "presumptive" allocation method under section 4211(b) of ERISA, the amount of unfunded vested benefits allocable to a reentered employer for a subsequent withdrawal shall equal the sum of—

(1) The unamortized amount of the employer's allocable shares of the amounts described in section 4211(b)(1), for the plan years preceding the initial withdrawal, determined as if the employer had not previously withdrawn;

(2) The sum of the unamortized annual credits attributable to the year of the initial withdrawal and each succeeding year ending prior to reentry; and

(3) The unamortized amount of the employer's allocable shares of the amounts described in section 4211(b)(1)(A) and (C) for plan years ending after its reentry. For purposes of paragraph (b)(2), the annual credit for a plan year is the amount by which the employer's withdrawal liability payments for the year exceed the greater of the employer's imputed contributions or actual contributions for the year. The employer's imputed contributions for a year shall equal the average annual required contributions of the employer for the three plan years preceding the initial withdrawal. The amount of the credit for a plan year is reduced by 5 percent of the original amount for each succeeding plan year ending prior to the year of the subsequent withdrawal.

(c) *Allocation of unfunded vested benefits for subsequent withdrawal in plans using "modified presumptive" or "rolling-5" method.* In a plan using either the "modified presumptive" allocation method under section 4211(c)(2) of ERISA or the "rolling-5" method under section 4211(c)(3), the amount of unfunded vested benefits allocable to a reentered employer for a subsequent withdrawal shall equal the sum of—

(1) The amount determined under section 4211(c)(2) or (c)(3) of ERISA, as appropriate, as if the date of reentry were the employer's initial date of participation in the plan; and

(2) The outstanding balance, as of the date of reentry, of the unfunded vested benefits allocated to the employer for its previous withdrawal (as defined in paragraph (c)(2)(i) of this section) reduced as if that amount were being fully amortized in level annual installments, at the plan's funding rate as of the date of reentry, over the period described in paragraph (c)(2)(ii), beginning with the first plan year after reentry.

(i) The outstanding balance of the unfunded vested benefits allocated to an employer for its previous withdrawal is the excess of the amount determined under section 4211(c)(2) or (c)(3) of ERISA as of the end of the plan year in which the employer initially withdrew, accumulated with interest at the plan's funding rate for that year, from that year to the date of reentry, over the withdrawal liability payments made by the employer, accumulated with interest from the date of payment to the date of reentry at the plan's funding rate for the year of entry.

(ii) The period referred to in paragraph (c)(2) for plans using the modified presumptive method is the greater of five years, or the number of full plan years remaining on the amortization schedule under section 4211(c)(2)(B)(i) of ERISA. For plans using the rolling-5 method, the period is five years.

(d) *Adjustments applicable to all employers in plans using "presumptive" method.* In a plan using the "presumptive" allocation method under section 4211(b) of ERISA, when the plan has abated the withdrawal liability of a reentered employer pursuant to this part, the following adjustments to the allocation method shall be made in computing the unfunded vested benefits allocable to any employer that withdraws from the plan in a plan year beginning after the reentry:

(1) The sum of the unamortized amounts of the annual credits of a reentered employer shall be treated as a reallocated amount under section 4211(b)(4) of ERISA in the plan year in which the employer reenters.

(2) In the event that the 5-year period used to compute the denominator of the fraction described in section 4211(b)(2)(E) and (b)(4)(D) of ERISA includes a year during the period of withdrawal of a reentered employer, the contributions for a year during the period of withdrawal shall be adjusted to include any actual or imputed contributions of the employer, as determined under paragraph (b) of this section.

(e) *Adjustments applicable to all employers in plans using "direct attribution" method.* In a plan using the "direct attribution" method under section 4211(c)(4) of ERISA, when the plan has abated the withdrawal liability of a reentered employer pursuant to this part, the following adjustments to the allocation method shall be made in computing the unfunded vested benefits allocable to any employer that withdraws from the plan in a plan year beginning after the reentry:

(1) The nonforfeitable benefits attributable to service with a reentered employer prior to its initial withdrawal shall be treated as benefits that are attributable to service with that employer.

(2) For purposes of section 4211(c)(4)(D)(ii) and (iii) of ERISA, withdrawal liability payments made by a reentered employer shall be treated as contributions made by the reentered employer.

(f) *Plans using alternative allocation methods under section 4211(c)(5).* A plan that has adopted an alternative method of allocating unfunded vested benefits pursuant to section 4211(c)(5) of ERISA and part 4211 of this chapter shall adopt by plan amendment a method of determining a reentered employer's allocable share of the plan's unfunded vested benefits upon its subsequent withdrawal. The method shall treat the reentered employer and other withdrawing employers in a manner consistent with the treatment under the paragraph(s) of this section applicable to plans using the statutory allocation method most similar to the plan's alternative allocation method.

(g) *Adjustments to amount of annual withdrawal liability payments for subsequent withdrawal.* For purposes of section 4219(c)(1)(C)(i)(I) and (ii)(I) of ERISA, in determining the amount of the annual withdrawal liability payments for a subsequent complete withdrawal, if the period of ten consecutive plan years ending before the plan year in which the withdrawal occurs includes a plan year during the period of withdrawal, the employer's number of contribution base units, used in section 4219(c)(1)(C)(i)(I), or the required employer contributions, used in section 4219(c)(1)(C)(ii)(I), for each such plan year during the period of withdrawal shall be deemed to be the greater of—

(1) The employer's contribution base units or the required employer contributions, as applicable, for that year; or

(2) The average of the employer's contribution base units or of the required employer contributions, as applicable, for those plan years not during the period of withdrawal, within the ten consecutive plan years ending before the plan year in which the employer's subsequent complete withdrawal occurred.

[¶ 15,671H]

§ 4207.8 Liability for subsequent partial withdrawals. (a) *General.* When an eligible employer that has had its liability for a complete withdrawal abated under this part partially withdraws from the plan, the employer's liability for that subsequent partial withdrawal shall be determined in accordance with the rules in sections 4201-4225 of ERISA, as modified by the rules in § 4207.7 (b) through (g) of this part and the rules in this section, and section 108 of the Multiemployer Act.

(b) *Liability for a 70-percent contribution decline.* The amount of an employer's liability under section 4206(a) (relating to the calculation of liability for a partial withdrawal), section 4208 (relating to the reduction of liability for a partial withdrawal) and section 4219(c)(1) (relating to the schedule of partial withdrawal liability payments) of ERISA, for a subsequent partial withdrawal described in section 4205(a)(1) of ERISA (relating to a 70-percent contribution decline) shall be modified in accordance with the rules in this paragraph.

(1) *Definition of "3-year testing period".* For purposes of sections 4206(a) and 4219(c)(1) of ERISA, and paragraphs (b)(2)-(b)(4) of this section, the term "3-year testing period" means the period consisting of the plan year for which the determination is made and the two immediately preceding plan years, excluding any plan year during the period of withdrawal.

(2) *Determination date of section 4211 allocable share.* For purposes of section 4206(a)(1)(B) of ERISA, the amount determined under section 4211 shall be determined as if the employer had withdrawn from the plan in a complete withdrawal on the last day of the first plan year in the 3-year testing period or the last day of the plan year in which the employer reentered the plan, whichever is later.

(3) *Calculation of fractional share of section 4211 amount.* For purposes of sections 4206(a)(2)(B)(ii) and 4219(c)(1)(E)(ii) of ERISA, if the five plan years immediately preceding the beginning of the 3-year testing period include a plan year during the period of withdrawal, then, in determining the denominator of the fraction described in

section 4206(a)(2), the employer's contribution base units for each such year of withdrawal shall be deemed to be the greater of—

(i) The employer's contribution base units for that plan year; or

(ii) The average of the employer's contribution base units for the three plan years preceding the plan year in which the employer completely withdrew from the plan.

(4) *Contribution base units for high base year.* If the five plan years immediately preceding the beginning of the 3-year testing period include a plan year during the period of withdrawal, then for purposes of section 4208(a) and (b)(1) of ERISA, the number of contribution base units for the high base year shall be the number of contribution base units determined under paragraph (b)(3) of this section.

(c) *Liability for partial cessation of contribution obligation.* The amount of an employer's liability under section 4206(a) (relating to the calculation of liability for a partial withdrawal) and section 4219(c)(1) (relating to the amount of the annual partial withdrawal liability payments) of ERISA, for a subsequent partial withdrawal described in section 4205(a)(2) of ERISA (relating to a partial cessation of the contribution obligation) shall be modified in accordance with the rules in this paragraph. For purposes of sections 4206(a)(2)(B)(i) and 4219(c)(1)(E)(ii) of ERISA, if the five plan years immediately preceding the plan year in which the partial withdrawal occurs include a plan year during the period of withdrawal, the denominator of the fraction described in section 4206(a)(2) shall be determined in accordance with the rule set forth in paragraph (b)(3) of this section.

[¶ 15,671I]

§ 4207.9 Special rules. (a) *Employer that has withdrawn and reentered the plan before the effective date of this part.* This part shall apply, in accordance with the rules in this paragraph, with respect to an eligible employer that completely withdraws from a multiemployer plan after September 25, 1980, and is performing covered work under the plan on the effective date of this part. Upon the application of an employer described in the preceding sentence, the plan sponsor of a multiemployer plan shall determine whether the employer satisfies the requirements for abatement of its complete withdrawal liability under this part. Pending the plan sponsor's determination, the employer may provide the plan with a bond or escrow that satisfies the requirements of § 4207.4, in lieu of making its withdrawal liability payments due after its application for an abatement determination. The plan sponsor shall notify the employer in writing of its determination and the consequences of its determination as described in § 4207.3 (c) or (d) and (e), as applicable. If the plan sponsor determines that the employer qualifies for abatement, only withdrawal liability payments made prior to the employer's reentry shall be retained by the plan; payments made by the employer after its reentry shall be refunded to the employer, with interest on those made prior to the application for abatement, in accordance with § 4207.3(e)(2). If a bond or escrow has been provided to the plan in accordance with § 4207.4, the plan sponsor shall send a copy of the notice to the bonding or escrow agent. Sections 4207.6 through 4207.8 shall apply with respect to the employer's subsequent complete withdrawal occurring on or after the effective date of this part, or partial withdrawal occurring either before or after that date. This paragraph shall not negate reasonable actions taken by plans prior to the effective date of this part under plan rules implementing section 4207(a) of ERISA that were validly adopted pursuant to section 405 of the Multiemployer Act.

(b) *Employer with multiple complete withdrawals that has reentered the plan before effective date of this part.* If an employer described in paragraph (a) of this section has completely withdrawn from a multiemployer plan on two or more occasions before the effective date of this part, the rules in paragraph (a) of this section shall be applied as modified by this paragraph.

(1) The plan sponsor shall determine whether the employer satisfies the requirements for abatement under § 4207.5 based on the most recent complete withdrawal.

(2) If the employer satisfies the requirements for abatement, the employer's liability with respect to all previous complete withdrawals shall be abated.

(3) If the liability is abated, §§ 4207.6 and 4207.7 shall be applied as if the employer's earliest complete withdrawal were its initial complete withdrawal.

(c) *Employer with multiple complete withdrawals that has not reentered the plan as of the effective date of this part.* If an eligible employer has completely withdrawn from a multiemployer plan on two or more occasions between September 26, 1980 and the effective date of this part and is not performing covered work under the plan on the effective date of this regulation, the rules in this part shall apply, subject to the modifications specified in paragraphs (b)(1)-(b)(3) of this section, upon the employer's reentry into the plan.

(d) *Combination of withdrawn employer with contributing employer.* If a withdrawn employer merges or otherwise combines with an employer that has an obligation to contribute to the plan from which the first employer withdrew, the combined entity is the eligible employer, and the rules of § 4207.5 shall be applied—

(1) By subtracting from the measurement period contribution base units the contribution base units for which the non-withdrawn portion of the employer was obligated to contribute in the last plan year ending prior to the combination;

(2) By determining the base year contribution base units solely by reference to the contribution base units of the withdrawn portion of the employer; and

(3) By using the date of the combination, rather than the date of resumption of covered operations, to begin the measurement period.

(e) *Combination of two or more withdrawn employers.* If two or more withdrawn employers merge or otherwise combine, the combined entity is the eligible employer, and the rules of § 4207.5 shall be applied by combining the number of contribution base units with respect to which each portion of the employer had an obligation to contribute under the plan for its base year. However, the combined number of contribution base units shall not include contribution base units of a withdrawn portion of the employer that had fully paid its withdrawal liability as of the date of the resumption of covered operations.

[¶ 15,671J]

§ 4207.10 **Plan rules for abatement.** (a) *General rule.* Subject to the approval of the PBGC, a plan may, by amendment, adopt rules for the reduction or waiver of complete withdrawal liability under conditions other than those specified in §§ 4207.5 and 4207.9 (c) and (d), provided that such conditions relate to events occurring or factors existing subsequent to a complete withdrawal year. The request for PBGC approval shall be filed after the amendment is adopted. A plan amendment under this section may not be put into effect until it is approved by the PBGC. However, an amendment that is approved by the PBGC may apply retroactively to the date of the adoption of the amendment. PBGC approval shall also be required for any subsequent modification of the amendment, other than repeal of the amendment. Sections 4207.6, 4207.7, and 4207.8 shall apply to all subsequent partial withdrawals after a reduction or waiver of complete withdrawal liability under a plan amendment approved by the PBGC pursuant to this section.

(b) *Who may request.* The plan sponsor, or a duly authorized representative acting on behalf of the plan sponsor, shall sign and submit the request.

(c) *Where to file.* See Sec. 4000.4 of this chapter for information on where to file.

[Amended 10/28/2003 by 68 FR 61344]

(d) *Information.* Each request shall contain the following information:

(1) The name and address of the plan for which the plan amendment is being submitted and the telephone number of the plan sponsor or its duly authorized representative.

(2) The nine-digit Employer Identification Number (EIN) assigned to the plan sponsor by the IRS and the three-digit Plan Identification Number (PN) assigned to the plan by the plan sponsor, and, if different, the EIN and PN last filed with the PBGC. If no EIN or PN has been assigned, that should be indicated.

(3) A copy of the executed amendment, including—

(i) The date on which the amendment was adopted;

(ii) The proposed effective date; and

(iii) The full text of the rules on the reduction or waiver of complete withdrawal liability.

(4) A copy of the most recent actuarial valuation report of the plan.

(5) A statement certifying that notice of the adoption of the amendment and of the request for approval filed under this section has been given to all employers that have an obligation to contribute under the plan and to all employee organizations representing employees covered under the plan.

(e) *Supplemental information.* In addition to the information described in paragraph (d) of this section, a plan may submit any other information that it believes it pertinent to its request. The PBGC may require the plan sponsor to submit any other information that the PBGC determines it needs to review a request under this section.

(f) *Criteria for PBGC approval.* The PBGC shall approve a plan amendment authorized by paragraph (a) of this section if it determines that the rules therein are consistent with the purposes of ERISA. An abatement rule is not consistent with the purposes of ERISA if—

(1) Implementation of the rule would be adverse to the interest of plan participants and beneficiaries; or

(2) The rule would increase the PBGC's risk of loss with respect to the plan.

(Approved by the Office of Management and Budget under control number 1212-0044)

[¶ 15,671K]

§ 4207.11 **Method of filing; method and date of issuance.** (a) *Method of filing.* The PBGC applies the rules in subpart A of part 4000 of this chapter to determine permissible methods of filing with the PBGC under this part.

(b) *Method of issuance.* The PBGC applies the rules in subpart B of part 4000 of this chapter to determine permissible methods of issuance under this part.

(c) *Date of issuance.* The PBGC applies the rules in subpart C of part 4000 of this chapter to determine the date that an issuance under this part was provided.

[Added 10/28/2003 by 68 FR 61344]

[¶ 15,673]
REDUCTION OF PARTIAL WITHDRAWAL LIABILITY

Act Sec. 4208. (a)(1) Obligation of employer for payments for partial withdrawal for plan years beginning after the second consecutive plan year following the partial withdrawal year; criteria applicable; furnishing of bond in lieu of payment of partial withdrawal liability.—If, for any 2 consecutive plan years following the plan year in which an employer has partially withdrawn from a plan under section 4205(a)(1) (referred to elsewhere in this section as the "partial withdrawal year"), the number of contribution base units with respect to which the employer has an obligation to contribute under the plan for each such year is not less than 90 percent of the total number of contribution base units with respect to which the employer had an obligation to contribute under the plan for the high base year (within the meaning of section 4205(b)(1)(B)(ii), then the employer shall have no obligation to make payments with respect to such partial withdrawal (other than delinquent payments) for plan years beginning after the second consecutive plan year following the partial withdrawal year.

(2)(A) For any plan year for which the number of contribution base units with respect to which an employer who has partially withdrawn under section 4205(a)(1) has an obligation to contribute under the plan equals or exceeds the number of units for the highest year determined under paragraph (1) without regard to "90 percent of", the employer may furnish (in lieu of payment of the partial withdrawal liability determined under section 4206) a bond to the plan in the amount determined by the plan sponsor (not exceeding 50 percent of the annual payment otherwise required).

(B) If the plan sponsor determines under paragraph (1) that the employer has no further liability to the plan for the partial withdrawal, then the bond shall be cancelled.

(C) If the plan sponsor determines under paragraph (1) that the employer continues to have liability to the plan for the partial withdrawal, then—

(i) the bond shall be paid to the plan,

(ii) the employer shall immediately be liable for the outstanding amount of liability due with respect to the plan year for which the bond was posted, and

(iii) the employer shall continue to make the partial withdrawal liability payments as they are due.

Act Sec. 4208. (b) OBLIGATION OF EMPLOYER FOR PAYMENTS FOR PARTIAL WITHDRAWAL FOR PLAN YEARS BEGINNING AFTER THE SECOND CONSECUTIVE PLAN YEAR; OTHER CRITERIA APPLICABLE.—If—

(1) for any 2 consecutive plan years following a partial withdrawal under section 4205(a)(1), the number of contribution base units with respect to which the employer has an obligation to contribute for each such year exceeds 30 percent of the total number of contribution base units with respect to which the employer had an obligation to contribute for the high base year (within the meaning of section 4205(b)(1)(B)(ii)), and

(2) the total number of contribution base units with respect to which all employers under the plan have obligations to contribute in each of such 2 consecutive years is not less than 90 percent of the total number of contribution base units for which all employers had obligations to contribute in the partial withdrawal plan year;

then, the employer shall have no obligation to make payments with respect to such partial withdrawal (other than delinquent payments) for plan years beginning after the second such consecutive plan year.

Act Sec. 4208. (c) PRO RATA REDUCTION OF AMOUNT OF PARTIAL WITHDRAWAL LIABILITY PAYMENT OF EMPLOYER FOR PLAN YEAR FOLLOWING PARTIAL WITHDRAWAL YEAR.—In any case in which, in any plan year following a partial withdrawal under section 4205(a)(1), the number of contribution base units with respect to which the employer has an obligation to contribute for such year equals or exceeds 110 percent (or such other percentage as the plan may provide by amendment and which is not prohibited under regulations prescribed by the corporation) of the number of contribution base units with respect to which the employer had an obligation to contribute in the partial withdrawal year, then the amount of the employer's partial withdrawal liability payment for such year shall be reduced pro rata, in accordance with regulations prescribed by the corporation.

Act Sec. 4208.(d)(1) BUILDING AND CONSTRUCTION INDUSTRY; ENTERTAINMENT INDUSTRY.—An employer to whom section 4203(b) (relating to the building and construction industry) applies is liable for a partial withdrawal only if the employer's obligation to contribute under the plan is continued for no more than an insubstantial portion of its work in the craft and area jurisdiction of the collective bargaining agreement of the type for which contributions are required.

(2) An employer to whom section 4203(c) (relating to the entertainment industry) applies shall have no liability for a partial withdrawal except under the conditions and to the extent prescribed by the corporation by regulation.

Act Sec. 4208.(e)(1) REDUCTION OR ELIMINATION OF PARTIAL WITHDRAWAL LIABILITY UNDER ANY CONDITIONS; CRITERIA; PROCEDURES APPLICABLE.—The corporation may prescribe regulations providing for the reduction or elimination of partial withdrawal liability under any conditions with respect to which the corporation determines that reduction or elimination of partial withdrawal liability is consistent with the purposes of this Act.

(2) Under such regulations, reduction of withdrawal liability shall be provided only with respect to subsequent changes in the employer's contributions for the same operations, or under the same collective bargaining agreement, that gave rise to the partial withdrawal, and changes in the employer's contribution base units with respect to other facilities or other collective bargaining agreements shall not be taken into account.

(3) The corporation shall prescribe by regulation a procedure by which a plan may by amendment adopt rules for the reduction or elimination of partial withdrawal liability under any other conditions, subject to the approval of the corporation based on its determination that adoption of such rules by the plan is consistent with the purposes of this Act.

Amendment

P.L. 96-364, § 104(2):

Added Sec. 4208, effective September 26, 1980 under ERISA Sec. 4402.

Regulations

The following regulations were adopted by the Pension Benefit Guaranty Corporation on July 1, 1996 (61 FR 34002). Prior to July 1, 1996, PBGC regulations were under Chapter XXVI of Title 29 of the Code of Federal Regulations. Effective July 1, 1996, PBGC regulations were moved to Chapter XL, and were renumbered and reorganized. Reg. § 4208.9 was amended, and Reg. § 4208.10 was added, on October 28, 2003 (68 FR 61344).

[¶ 15,673A]

§ 4208.1 **Purpose and scope.** (a) *Purpose.* The purpose of this part is to establish rules for reducing or waiving the liability of certain employers that have partially withdrawn from a multiemployer pension plan.

(b) *Scope.* This part applies to multiemployer pension plans covered under title IV of ERISA and to employers that have partially withdrawn from such plans after September 25, 1980, and that have not, as of the date on which they satisfy the conditions for reducing or eliminating their partial withdrawal liability, fully satisfied their obligation to pay that partial withdrawal liability. This rule shall not negate reasonable actions taken by plans prior to the effective date of this part under plan rules implementing section 4208 of ERISA that were validly adopted pursuant to section 405 of the Multiemployer Act.

[¶ 15,673B]

§ 4208.2 **Definitions.** The following terms are defined in § 4001.2 of this chapter: *employer, ERISA, IRS, Multiemployer Act, multiemployer plan, PBGC, plan,* and *plan year.*

In addition, for purposes of this part:

Complete withdrawal means a complete withdrawal as described in section 4203 of ERISA.

Eligible employer means the employer, as defined in section 4001(b) of ERISA, as it existed on the date of its initial partial or complete withdrawal, as applicable. An eligible employer shall continue to be an eligible employer notwithstanding the occurrence of any of the following events:

(1) A restoration involving a mere change in identity, form or place of organization, however effected;

(2) A reorganization involving a liquidation into a parent corporation;

(3) A merger, consolidation or division solely between (or among) trades or businesses (whether or not incorporated) of the employer; or

(4) An acquisition by or of, or a merger or combination with another trade or business.

Partial withdrawal means a partial withdrawal as described in section 4205 of ERISA.

Partial withdrawal year means the third year of the 3-year testing period in the case of a partial withdrawal caused by a 70-percent contribution decline, or the year of the partial cessation in the case of a partial withdrawal caused by a partial cessation of the employer's contribution obligation.

[¶ 15,673C]

§ 4208.3 **Abatement.** (a) *General.* Whenever an eligible employer that has partially withdrawn from a multiemployer plan satisfies the requirements in § 4208.4 for the reduction or waiver of its partial withdrawal liability, it may apply to the plan for abatement of its partial withdrawal liability. Applications shall identify the eligible employer, the withdrawn employer (if different), the date of withdrawal, and the basis for reduction or waiver of its withdrawal liability. Upon receiving a complete application for abatement, the plan sponsor shall determine, in accordance with paragraph (b) of this section, whether the employer satisfies the requirements for abatement of its partial withdrawal liability under § 4208.4. If the plan sponsor determines that the employer satisfies the requirements for abatement of its partial withdrawal liability, the provisions of paragraph (c) of this section shall apply. If the plan sponsor determines that the employer does not satisfy the requirements for abatement of its partial withdrawal liability, the provisions of paragraphs (d) and (e) of this section shall apply.

(b) *Determination of abatement.* Within 60 days after an eligible employer that partially withdrew from a multiemployer plan applies for abatement in accordance with paragraph (a) of this section, the plan sponsor shall determine whether the employer satisfies the requirements for abatement of its partial withdrawal liability under §4208.4 and shall notify the employer in writing of its determination and of the consequences of its determination, as described in paragraphs (c) or (d) and (e) of this section, as appropriate. If a bond or escrow has been provided to the plan under §4208.5 of this part, the plan sponsor shall send a copy of the notice to the bonding or escrow agent.

(c) *Effects of abatement.* If the plan sponsor determines that the employer satisfies the requirements for abatement of its partial withdrawal liability under §4208.4, then—

(1) The employer's partial withdrawal liability shall be eliminated or its annual partial withdrawal liability payments shall be reduced in accordance with §4208.6, as applicable;

(2) The employer's liability for a subsequent withdrawal shall be determined in accordance with §4208.7;

(3) Any bonds furnished under §4208.5 shall be canceled and any amounts held in escrow under §4208.5 shall be refunded to the employer; and

(4) Any withdrawal liability payments originally due and paid after the end of the plan year in which the conditions for abatement were satisfied, in excess of the amount due under this part after that date shall be credited to the remaining withdrawal liability payments, if any, owed by the employer, beginning with the first payment due after the revised payment schedule is issued pursuant to this paragraph. If the credited amount is greater than the outstanding amount of the employer's partial withdrawal liability, the amount remaining after satisfaction of the liability shall be refunded to the employer. Interest on the credited amount at the rate prescribed in part 4219, subpart C, of this chapter (relating to overdue, defaulted, and overpaid withdrawal liability) shall be added if the plan sponsor does not issue a revised payment schedule reflecting the credit or make the required refund within 60 days after receipt by the plan sponsor of a complete abatement application. Interest shall accrue from the 61st day.

(d) *Effects of non-abatement.* If the plan sponsor determines that the employer does not satisfy the requirements for abatement of its partial withdrawal liability under §4208.4, then the employer shall take or cause to be taken the actions set forth in paragraphs (d)(1)-(d)(3) of this section. The rules in part 4219, subpart C, shall apply with respect to all payments required to be made under paragraphs (d)(2) and (d)(3). For this purpose, a payment required under paragraph (d)(2) shall be treated as a withdrawal liability payment due on the 30th day after the date of the plan sponsor's notice under paragraph (b) of this section.

(1) Any bond or escrow furnished under §4208.5 shall be paid to the plan within 30 days after the date of the plan sponsor's notice under paragraph (b) of this section.

(2) The employer shall pay to the plan within 30 days after the date of the plan sponsor's notice under paragraph (b) of this section, the amount of its withdrawal liability payment or payments, with respect to which the bond or escrow was furnished, in excess of the bond or escrow.

(3) The employer shall resume or continue making its partial withdrawal liability payments as they are due to the plan.

(e) *Review of non-abatement determination.* A plan sponsor's determinations that the employer does not satisfy the requirements for abatement under §4208.4 and of the amount of reduction determined under §4208.6 shall be subject to plan review under section 4219(b)(2) of ERISA and to arbitration under section 4221 of ERISA and part 4221 of this chapter, within the times prescribed by those provisions. For this purpose, the plan sponsor's notice under paragraph (b) of this section shall be treated as a demand under section 4219(b)(1) of ERISA. If the plan sponsor upon review or an arbitrator determines that

the employer satisfies the requirements for abatement of its partial withdrawal liability under §4208.4, the plan sponsor shall immediately refund the amounts described in paragraph (e)(1) of this section if the liability is waived, or credit and refund the amounts described in paragraph (e)(2) if the annual payment is reduced.

(1) *Refund for waived liability.* If the employer's partial withdrawal liability is waived, the plan sponsor shall refund to the employer the payments made pursuant to paragraphs (d)(1)-(d)(3) of this section (plus interest determined in accordance with §4219.31(d) of this chapter as if the payments were overpayments of withdrawal liability).

(2) *Credit for reduced annual payment.* If the employer's annual partial withdrawal liability payment is reduced, the plan sponsor shall credit the payments made pursuant to paragraphs (d)(1)-(d)(3) of this section (plus interest determined in accordance with §4219.31(d) of this chapter as if the payments were overpayments of withdrawal liability) to future withdrawal liability payments owed by the employer, beginning with the first payment that is due after the determination, and refund any credit (including interest) remaining after satisfaction of the outstanding amount of the employer's partial withdrawal liability.

[¶ 15,673D]

§4208.4 **Conditions for abatement.** (a) *Waiver of liability for a 70-percent contribution decline.* An employer that has incurred a partial withdrawal under section 4205(a)(1) of ERISA shall have no obligation to make payments with respect to that partial withdrawal (other than delinquent payments) for plan years beginning after the second consecutive plan year in which the conditions of either paragraph (a)(1) or (a)(2) are satisfied for each of the two years:

(1) The number of contribution base units with respect to which the employer has an obligation to contribute under the plan for each year is not less than 90 percent of the total number of contribution base units with respect to which the employer had an obligation to contribute to the plan for the high base year (as defined in paragraph (d) of this section).

(2) The conditions of this paragraph are satisfied if—

(i) The number of contribution base units with respect to which the employer has an obligation to contribute for each year exceeds 30 percent of the total number of contribution base units with respect to which the employer had an obligation to contribute to the plan for the high base year (as defined in paragraph (d) of this section); and

(ii) The total number of contribution base units with respect to which all employers under the plan have obligations to contribute in each of the two years is not less than 90 percent of the total number of contribution base units for which all employers had obligations to contribute in the partial withdrawal year.

(b) *Waiver of liability for a partial cessation of the employer's contribution obligation.* Except as provided in §4208.8, an employer that has incurred partial withdrawal liability under section 4205(a)(2) of ERISA shall have no obligation to make payments with respect to that partial withdrawal (other than delinquent payments) for plan years beginning after the second consecutive plan year in which the employer satisfies the conditions under either paragraph (b)(1) or (b)(2) of this section.

(1) *Partial restoration of withdrawn work.* The employer satisfies the conditions under this paragraph if, for each of two consecutive plan years—

(i) The employer makes contributions for the same facility or under the same collective bargaining agreement that gave rise to the partial withdrawal;

(ii) The employer's contribution base units for that facility or under that agreement exceed 30 percent of the contribution base units with respect to which the employer had an obligation to contribute for that facility or under that agreement for the high base year (as defined in paragraph (d) of this section); and

(iii) The total number of contribution base units with respect to which the employer has an obligation to contribute to the plan equals at least 90 percent of the total number of contribution base units with respect to which the employer had an obligation to contribute under the plan for the high base year (as defined in paragraph (d) of this section).

(2) *Substantial restoration of withdrawn work.* The employer satisfies the conditions under this paragraph if, for each of two consecutive plan years—

(i) The employer makes contributions for the same facility or under the same collective bargaining agreement that gave rise to the partial withdrawal;

(ii) The employer's contribution base units for that facility or under that agreement are not less than 90 percent of the contribution base units with respect to which the employer had an obligation to contribute for that facility or under that agreement for the high base year (as defined in paragraph (d) of this section); and

(iii) The total number of contribution base units with respect to which the employer has an obligation to contribute to the plan equals or exceeds the sum of—

(A) The number of contribution base units with respect to which the employer had an obligation to contribute in the year prior to the partial withdrawal year, determined without regard to the contribution base units for the facility or under the agreement that gave rise to the partial withdrawal; and

(B) 90 percent of the contribution base units with respect to which the employer had an obligation to contribute for that facility or under that agreement in either the year prior to the partial withdrawal year or the high base year (as defined in paragraph (d) of this section), whichever is less.

(c) *Reduction in annual partial withdrawal liability payment*—

(1) *Partial withdrawals under section 4205(a)(1).* An employer shall be entitled to a reduction of its annual partial withdrawal liability payment for a plan year if the number of contribution base units with respect to which the employer had an obligation to contribute during the plan year exceeds the greater of—

(i) 110 percent (or such lower number as the plan may, by amendment, adopt) of the number of contribution base units with respect to which the employer had an obligation to contribute in the partial withdrawal year; or

(ii) The total number of contribution base units with respect to which the employer had an obligation to contribute to the plan for the plan year following the partial withdrawal year.

(2) *Partial withdrawals under section 4205(a)(2).* An employer that resumes the obligation to contribute with respect to a facility or collective bargaining agreement that gave rise to a partial withdrawal, but does not qualify to have that liability waived under paragraph (b) of this section, shall have its annual partial withdrawal liability payment reduced for any plan year in which the total number of contribution base units with respect to which the employer has an obligation to contribute equals or exceeds the sum of—

(i) The number of contribution base units for the reentered facility or agreement during that year; and

(ii) The total number of contribution base units with respect to which the employer had an obligation to contribute to the plan for the year following the partial withdrawal year.

(d) *High base year.* For purposes of paragraphs (a) and (b)(1)(iii) of this section, the high base year contributions are the average of the total contribution base units for the two plan years for which the employer's total contribution base units were highest within the five plan years immediately preceding the beginning of the 3-year testing period defined in section 4205(b)(1)(B)(i) of ERISA, with respect to paragraph (a) of this section, or the partial withdrawal year, with respect to paragraph (b)(1)(iii) of this section. For purposes of paragraphs (b)(1)(ii) and (b)(2) of this section, the high base year contributions are the average number of contribution base units for the facility or under the agreement for the two plan years for which the employer's contribution base units for that facility or under that agreement were highest within the five plan years immediately preceding the partial withdrawal.

[¶ 15,673E]

§ 4208.5 **Withdrawal liability payments during pendency of abatement determination.** (a) *Bond/Escrow.* An employer that has satisfied the requirements of § 4208.4(a)(1) without regard to "90 percent of" or § 4208.4(b) for one year with respect to all partial withdraw-

als it incurred in a plan year may, in lieu of making scheduled withdrawal liability payments in the second year for those withdrawals, provide a bond to, or establish an escrow account for, the plan that satisfies the requirements of paragraph (b) of this section or any plan rules adopted under paragraph (d) of this section, pending a determination by the plan sponsor of whether the employer satisfies the requirements of § 4208.4 (a)(1) or (b) for the second consecutive plan year. An employer that applies for abatement and neither provides a bond/escrow nor makes its withdrawal liability payments remains eligible for abatement.

(b) *Amount of bond/escrow.* The bond or escrow allowed by this section shall be in an amount equal to 50 percent of the withdrawal liability payments that would otherwise be due. The bond or escrow relating to each payment shall be furnished before the due date of that payment. A single bond or escrow may be provided for more than one payment due during the pendency of the plan sponsor's determination. The bond or escrow agreement shall provide that if the plan sponsor determines that the employer does not satisfy the requirements for abatement of its partial withdrawal liability under § 4208.4 (a)(1) or (b), the bond or escrow shall be paid to the plan upon notice from the plan sponsor to the bonding or escrow agent. A bond provided under this paragraph shall be issued by a corporate surety company that is an acceptable surety for purposes of section 412 of ERISA.

(c) *Notice of bond/escrow.* Concurrently with posting a bond or establishing an escrow account under this section, the employer shall notify the plan sponsor. The notice shall include a statement of the amount of the bond or escrow, the scheduled payment or payments with respect to which the bond or escrow is being furnished, and the name and address of the bonding or escrow agent.

(d) *Plan amendments concerning bond/escrow.* A plan may, by amendment, adopt rules decreasing the amount of the bond or escrow specified in paragraph (b) of this section. A plan amendment adopted under this paragraph may be applied only to the extent that it is consistent with the purposes of ERISA. An amendment satisfies this requirement only if it does not create an unreasonable risk of loss to the plan.

(e) *Plan sponsor determination.* Within 60 days after the end of the plan year in which the bond/escrow is furnished, the plan sponsor shall determine whether the employer satisfied the requirements of § 4208.4 (a)(1) or (b) for the second consecutive plan year. The plan sponsor shall notify the employer and the bonding or escrow agent in writing of its determination and of the consequences of its determination, as described in § 4208.3 (c) or (d) and (e), as appropriate.

[¶ 15,673F]

§ 4208.6 **Computation of reduced annual partial withdrawal liability payment.** (a) *Amount of reduced payment.* An employer that satisfies the requirements of § 4208.4 (c)(1) or (c)(2) shall have its annual partial withdrawal liability payment for that plan year reduced in accordance with paragraph (a)(1) or (a)(2) of this section, respectively.

(1) The reduced annual payment amount for an employer that satisfies § 4208.4(c)(1) shall be determined by substituting the number of contribution base units in the plan year in which the requirements are satisfied for the number of contribution base units in the year following the partial withdrawal year in the numerator of the fraction described in section 4206(a)(2)(A) of ERISA.

(2) The reduced annual payment for an employer that satisfies § 4208.4(c)(2) shall be determined by adding the contribution base units for which the employer is obligated to contribute with respect to the reentered facility or agreement in the year in which the requirements are satisfied to the numerator of the fraction described in section 4206(a)(2)(A) of ERISA.

(b) *Credit for reduction.* The plan sponsor shall credit the account of an employer that satisfies the requirements of § 4208.4(c)(1) or (c)(2) with the amount of annual withdrawal liability that it paid in excess of the amount described in paragraph (a)(1) or (a)(2) of this section, as appropriate. The credit shall be applied, a revised payment schedule issued, refund made and interest added, all in accordance with § 4208.3(c)(4).

[¶ 15,673G]

§ 4208.7 Adjustment of withdrawal liability for subsequent withdrawals. The liability of an employer for a partial or complete withdrawal from a plan subsequent to a partial withdrawal from that plan in a prior plan year shall be reduced in accordance with part 4206 of this chapter.

[¶ 15,673H]

§ 4208.8 Multiple partial withdrawals in one plan year. (a) *General rule.* If an employer partially withdraws from the same multiemployer plan on two or more occasions during the same plan year, the rules of § 4208.4 shall be applied as modified by this section.

(b) *Partial withdrawals under section 4205(a)(1) and (a)(2) in the same plan year.* If an employer partially withdraws from the same multiemployer plan as a result of a 70-percent contribution decline and a partial cessation of the employer's contribution obligation in the same plan year, the employer shall not be eligible for abatement under § 4208.4 (b) or (c)(2) or under paragraph (c) of this section. The employer may qualify for abatement under § 4208.4(a) and (c)(1) and under any rules adopted by the plan pursuant to § 4208.9.

(c) *Multiple partial cessations of the employer's contribution obligation.* If an employer permanently ceases to have an obligation to contribute for more than one facility, under more than one collective bargaining agreement, or for one or more facilities and under one or more collective bargaining agreements, resulting in multiple partial withdrawals under section 4205(b)(2)(A) in the same plan year, the abatement rules in § 4208.4(b) shall be applied as modified by this paragraph. If an employer resumes work at all such facilities and under all such collective bargaining agreements, the determination of whether the employer qualifies for elimination of its liability under § 4208.4(b) shall be made by substituting the test set forth in paragraph (c)(1) of this section for that prescribed by § 4208.4 (b)(1)(ii) or (b)(2)(ii), as applicable. If the employer resumes work at or under fewer than all the facilities or collective bargaining agreements described in this paragraph, the employer cannot qualify for elimination of its liability under § 4208.4(b). However, the employer may qualify for a reduction in its partial withdrawal liability pursuant to paragraph (c)(2) of this section.

(1) *Resumption of work at all facilities and under all bargaining agreements.* The test under this paragraph is satisfied if for each of the two consecutive plan years referred to in § 4208.4(b), the employer's total contribution base units for the facilities and under the collective bargaining agreements with respect to which the employer incurred the multiple partial withdrawals exceed 30 percent of the total number of contribution base units with respect to which the employer had an obligation to contribute for those facilities and under those agreements for the base year (as defined in paragraph (d) of this section).

(2) *Resumption at fewer than all facilities or under fewer than all bargaining agreements.* If the employer satisfies the conditions in § 4208.4 (b)(1)(i) and (b)(1)(iii) and paragraph (c)(2)(i) of this section, or the conditions in § 4208.4 (b)(2)(i) and (b)(2)(iii) and paragraph (c)(2)(ii) of this section, as applicable, the employer's withdrawal liability shall be partially waived as set forth in paragraph (c)(2)(iii) of this section.

(i) With respect to a resumption of work under § 4208.4(b)(1), the condition under this paragraph is satisfied if, for the two consecutive plan years referred to in § 4208.4(b)(1), the employer's contribution base units for any reentered facility or agreement exceed 30 percent of the number of contribution base units with respect to which the employer had an obligation to contribute for that facility or under that agreement for the base year (as defined in paragraph (d) of this section).

(ii) With respect to a resumption of work under § 4208.4(b)(2), the condition under this paragraph is satisfied if, for the two consecutive plan years referred to in § 4208.4(b)(2), the employer's contribution base units for any reentered facility or agreement exceed 90 percent of the number of contribution base units with respect to which the employer had an obligation to contribute for that facility or under that agreement for the base year (as defined in paragraph (d) of this section).

(iii) The employer's reduced withdrawal liability and, if any, the reduced annual payments of the liability shall be determined by

adding the average number of contribution base units that the employer is required to contribute for those two consecutive years for that facility(ies) or agreement(s) to the numerator of the fraction described in section 4206(a)(2)(A) of ERISA. The amount of any remaining partial withdrawal liability shall be paid over the schedule originally established starting with the first payment due after the revised payment schedule is issued under § 4208.3(c)(4).

(d) *Base Year.* For purposes of this section, the base year contribution base units for a reentered facility(ies) or under a reentered agreement(s) are the average number of contribution base units for the facility(ies) or under the agreement(s) for the two plan years for which the employer's contribution base units for that facility(ies) or under that agreement(s) were highest within the five plan years immediately preceding the partial withdrawal.

[¶ 15,673I]

§ 4208.9 Plan adoption of additional abatement conditions. (a) *General rule.* A plan may by amendment, subject to the approval of the PBGC, adopt rules for the reduction or waiver of partial withdrawal liability under conditions other than those specified in § 4208.4, provided that such conditions relate to events occurring or factors existing subsequent to a partial withdrawal year. The request for PBGC approval shall be filed after the amendment is adopted. PBGC approval shall also be required for any subsequent modification of the amendment, other than repeal of the amendment. A plan amendment under this section may not be put into effect until it is approved by the PBGC. An amendment that is approved by the PBGC may apply retroactively.

(b) *Who may request.* The plan sponsor, or a duly authorized representative acting on behalf of the plan sponsor, shall sign and submit the request.

(c) *Where to file.* See Sec. 4000.4 of this chapter for information on where to file.

[Amended 10/28/2003 by 68 FR 61344]

(d) *Information.* Each request shall contain the following information:

(1) The name and address of the plan for which the plan amendment is being submitted and the telephone number of the plan sponsor or its duly authorized representative.

(2) The nine-digit Employer Identification Number (EIN) assigned to the plan sponsor by the IRS and the three-digit Plan Identification Number (PIN) assigned to the plan by the plan sponsor, and, if different, also the EIN-PIN last filed with the PBGC. If an EIN-PIN has not been assigned, that should be indicated.

(3) A copy of the executed amendment, including—

(i) the date on which the amendment was adopted;

(ii) the proposed effective date;

(iii) the full text of the rules on the reduction or waiver of partial withdrawal liability; and

(iv) the full text of the rules adjusting the reduction in the employer's liability for a subsequent partial or complete withdrawal, as required by section 4206(b)(1) of ERISA.

(4) A copy of the most recent actuarial valuation report of the plan.

(5) A statement certifying that notice of the adoption of the amendment and of the request for approval filed under this section has been given to all employers that have an obligation to contribute under the plan and to all employee organizations representing employees covered under the plan.

(e) *Supplemental information.* In addition to the information described in paragraph (d) of this section, a plan may submit any other information that it believes is pertinent to its request. The PBGC may require the plan sponsor to submit any other information that the PBGC determines that it needs to review a request under this section.

(f) *Criteria for PBGC approval.* The PBGC shall approve a plan amendment authorized by paragraph (a) of this section if it determines that the rules therein are consistent with the purposes of ERISA. An abatement amendment is not consistent with the purposes of ERISA unless the PBGC determines that—

(1) The amendment is not adverse to the interests of plan participants and beneficiaries in the aggregate; and

(2) The amendment would not significantly increase the PBGC's risk of loss with respect to the plan.

(Approved by the Office of Management and Budget under control no. 1212-0039)

[¶ 15,673J]

§ 4208.10 **Method of filing; method and date of issuance.** (a) *Method of filing.* The PBGC applies the rules in subpart A of part 4000 of this chapter to determine permissible methods of filing with the PBGC under this part.

(b) *Method of issuance.* The PBGC applies the rules in subpart B of part 4000 of this chapter to determine permissible methods of issuance under this part.

(c) *Date of issuance.* The PBGC applies the rules in subpart C of part 4000 of this chapter to determine the date that an issuance under this part was provided.

[Added 10/28/2003 by 68 FR 61344]

[¶ 15,674]
DE MINIMIS RULE

Act Sec. 4209. (a) REDUCTION OF UNFUNDED VESTED BENEFITS ALLOCABLE TO EMPLOYER WITHDRAWN FROM PLAN.—Except in the case of a plan amended under subsection (b), the amount of the unfunded vested benefits allocable under section 4211 to an employer who withdraws from a plan shall be reduced by the smaller of—

(1) ¾ of 1 percent of the plan's unfunded vested obligations (determined as of the end of the plan year ending before the date of withdrawal), or

(2) $50,000,

reduced by the amount, if any, by which the unfunded vested benefits allowable to the employer, determined without regard to this subsection, exceeds $100,000.

Act Sec. 4209. (b) AMENDMENT OF PLAN FOR REDUCTION OF AMOUNT OF UNFUNDED VESTED BENEFITS ALLOCABLE TO EMPLOYER WITHDRAWN FROM PLAN. A plan may be amended to provide for the reduction of the amount determined under section 4211 by not more than the greater of—

(1) the amount determined under subsection (a), or

(2) the lesser of—

(A) the amount determined under subsection (a)(1), or

(B) $100,000,

reduced by the amount, if any, by which the amount determined under section 4211 for the employer, determined without regard to this subsection, exceeds $150,000.

Act Sec. 4209. (c) NONAPPLICABILITY.—This section does not apply—

(1) to an employer who withdraws in a plan year in which substantially all employers withdraw from the plan, or

(2) in any case in which substantially all employers withdraw from the plan during a period of one or more plan years pursuant to an agreement or arrangement to withdraw, to an employer who withdraws pursuant to such agreement or arrangement.

Act Sec. 4209. (d) PRESUMPTION OF EMPLOYER WITHDRAWAL FROM PLAN PURSUANT TO AGREEMENT OR ARRANGEMENT APPLICABLE IN ACTION OR PROCEEDING TO DETERMINE OR COLLECT WITHDRAWAL LIABILITY.—In any action or proceeding to determine or collect withdrawal liability, if substantially all employers have withdrawn from a plan within a period of 3 plan years, an employer who has withdrawn from such plan during such period shall be presumed to have withdrawn from the plan pursuant to an agreement or arrangement, unless the employer proves otherwise by a preponderance of the evidence.

Amendment

P.L. 96-364, § 104(2):

Added Sec. 4209, effective September 26, 1980 under ERISA Sec. 4402.

[¶ 15,675]
NON APPLICABILITY OF WITHDRAWAL LIABILITY FOR CERTAIN TEMPORARY CONTRIBUTION OBLIGATION PERIODS; EXCEPTION

Act Sec. 4210. (a) An employer who withdraws from a plan in complete or partial withdrawal is not liable to the plan if the employer—

(1) first had an obligation to contribute to the plan after the date of the enactment of the Multiemployer Pension Plan Amendments Act of 1980,

(2) had an obligation to contribute to the plan for no more than the lesser of—

(A) 6 consecutive plan years preceding the date on which the employer withdraws, or

(B) the number of years required for vesting under the plan,

(3) was required to make contributions to the plan for each such plan year in an amount equal to less than 2 percent of the sum of all employer contributions made to the plan for each such year, and

(4) has never avoided withdrawal liability because of the application of this section with respect to the plan.

Act Sec. 4210. (b) Subsection (a) shall apply to an employer with respect to a plan only if—

(1) the plan is amended to provide that subsection (a) applies;

(2) the plan provides, or is amended to provide, that the reduction under section 411(a)(3)(E) of the Internal Revenue Code of 1986 applies with respect to the employees of the employer; and

(3) the ratio of the assets of the plan for the plan year preceding the first plan year for which the employer was required to contribute to the plan to the benefit payments made during that plan year was at least 8 to 1.

Amendments

P.L. 109-280, § 204(c)(1):

Amended ERISA Sec. 4210(b) by striking paragraph (1) and by redesignating paragraphs (2) through (4) as paragraphs (1) through (3), respectively.

Prior to amendment, ERISA Sec. 4210(b) read as follows:

(b) Subsection (a) shall apply to an employer with respect to a plan only if –

(1) the plan is not a plan which primarily covers employees in the building and construction industry;

(2) the plan is amended to provide that subsection (a) applies;

(3) the plan provides, or is amended to provide, that the reduction under section 411(a)(3)(E) of the Internal Revenue Code of 1986 applies with respect to the employees of the employer; and

(4) the ratio of the assets of the plan for the plan year preceding the first plan year for which the employer was required to contribute to the plan to the benefit payments made during that plan year was at least 8 to 1.

The above amendment applies to plan withdrawals occurring on or after January 1, 2007.

P.L. 101-239, § 7891(a)(1):

Titles 1, III, and IV of ERISA (other than sections 3(37)(E), 301(a)(7), and 308, the last sentence of section 408(d), and sections 414(c), 4001(a)(3)(ii), and 4303) are each amended by striking "Internal Revenue Code of 1954" each place it appears and inserting "Internal Revenue Code of 1986", effective October 22, 1986.

P.L. 96-364, § 104(2):

Added Sec. 4210, effective September 26, 1980 under ERISA Sec. 4402.

[¶ 15,676]
METHODS FOR COMPUTING WITHDRAWAL LIABILITY

Act Sec. 4211.(a) DETERMINATION OF AMOUNT OF UNFUNDED VESTED BENEFITS ALLOCABLE TO EMPLOYER WITHDRAWN FROM PLAN.—The amount of the unfunded vested benefits allocable to an employer that withdraws from a plan shall be determined in accordance with subsection (b), (c), or (d) of this section.

Act Sec. 4211.(b)(1) FACTORS DETERMINING COMPUTATION OF AMOUNT OF UNFUNDED VESTED BENEFITS ALLOCABLE TO EMPLOYER WITHDRAWN FROM PLAN.—Except as provided in subsections (c) and (d), the amount of unfunded vested benefits allocable to an employer that withdraws is the sum of—

(A) the employer's proportional share of the unamortized amount of the change in the plan's unfunded vested benefits for plan years ending after September 25, 1980, as determined under paragraph (2);

(B) the employer's proportional share, if any, of the unamortized amount of the plan's unfunded vested benefits at the end of the plan year ending before September 26, 1980, as determined under paragraph (3); and

(C) the employer's proportional share of the unamortized amounts of the reallocated unfunded vested benefits (if any) as determined under paragraph (4).

If the sum of the amounts determined with respect to an employer under paragraphs (2), (3), and (4) is negative, the unfunded vested benefits allocable to the employer shall be zero.

(2)(A) An employer's proportional share of the unamortized amount of the change in the plan's unfunded vested benefits for plan years ending after September 25, 1980, is the sum of the employer's proportional shares of the unamortized amount of the change in unfunded vested benefits for each plan year in which the employer has an obligation to contribute under the plan ending—

(i) after such date, and

(ii) before the plan year in which the withdrawal of the employer occurs.

(B) The change in a plan's unfunded vested benefits for a plan year is the amount by which—

(i) the unfunded vested benefits at the end of the plan year exceeds

(ii) the sum of—

(I) the unamortized amount of the unfunded vested benefits for the last plan year ending before September 26, 1980, and

(II) the sum of the unamortized amounts of the change in unfunded vested benefits for each plan year ending after September 25, 1980, and preceding the plan year for which the change is determined.

(C) The unamortized amount of the change in a plan's unfunded vested benefits with respect to a plan year is the change in unfunded vested benefits for the plan year, reduced by 5 percent of such change for each succeeding plan year.

(D) The unamortized amount of the unfunded vested benefits for the last plan year ending before September 26, 1980, is the amount of the unfunded vested benefits as of the end of that plan year reduced by 5 percent of such amount for each succeeding plan year.

(E) An employer's proportional share of the unamortized amount of a change in unfunded vested benefits is the product of—

(i) the unamortized amount of such change (as of the end of the plan year preceding the plan year in which the employer withdraws); multiplied by

(ii) a fraction—

(I) the numerator of which is the sum of the contributions required to be made under the plan by the employer for the year in which such change arose and for the 4 preceding plan years, and

(II) the denominator of which is the sum for the plan year in which such change arose and the 4 preceding plan years of all contributions made by employers who had an obligation to contribute under the plan for the plan year in which such change arose reduced by the contributions made in such years by employers who had withdrawn from the plan in the year in which the change arose.

(3) An employer's proportional share of the unamortized amount of the plan's unfunded vested benefits for the last plan year ending before September 26, 1980, is the product of—

(A) such unamortized amount; multiplied by—

(B) a fraction—

(i) the numerator of which is the sum of all contributions required to be made by the employer under the plan for the most recent 5 plan years ending before September 26, 1980, and

(ii) the denominator of which is the sum of all contributions made for the most recent 5 plan years ending before September 26, 1980, by all employers—

(I) who had an obligation to contribute under the plan for the first plan year ending on or after such date, and

(II) who had not withdrawn from the plan before such date.

(4)(A) AMENDMENT OF MULTIEMPLOYER PLAN FOR DETERMINATION RESPECTING AMOUNT OF UNFUNDED VESTED BENEFITS ALLOCABLE TO EMPLOYER WITHDRAWN FROM PLAN; FACTORS DETERMINING COMPUTATION OF AMOUNT.—An employer's proportional share of the unamortized amount of the reallocated unfunded vested benefits is the sum of the employer's proportional shares of the unamortized amount of the reallocated unfunded vested benefits for each plan year ending before the plan year in which the employer withdrew from the plan.

(B) Except as otherwise provided in regulations prescribed by the corporation, the reallocated unfunded vested benefits for a plan year is the sum of—

(i) any amount which the plan sponsor determines in that plan year to be uncollectible for reasons arising out of cases or proceedings under Title 11, United States Code, or similar proceedings,

(ii) any amount which the plan sponsor determines in that plan year will not be assessed as a result of the operation of section 4209, 4219(c)(1)(B), or section 4225 against an employer to whom a notice described in section 4219 has been sent, and

(iii) any amount which the plan sponsor determines to be uncollectible or unassessible in that plan year for other reasons under standards not inconsistent with regulations prescribed by the corporation.

(C) The unamortized amount of the reallocated unfunded vested benefits with respect to a plan year is the reallocated unfunded vested benefits for the plan year, reduced by 5 percent of such reallocated unfunded vested benefits for each succeeding plan year.

(D) An employer's proportional share of the unamortized amount of the reallocated unfunded vested benefits with respect to a plan year is the product of—

(i) the unamortized amount of the reallocated unfunded vested benefits (as of the end of the plan year preceding the plan year in which the employer withdraws); multiplied by

(ii) the fraction defined in paragraph (2)(E)(ii).

Act Sec. 4211.(c)(1) AMENDMENT OF MULTIEMPLOYER PLAN FOR DETERMINATION RESPECTING AMOUNT OF UNFUNDED VESTED BENEFITS ALLOCABLE TO EMPLOYER WITHDRAWN FROM PLAN; FACTORS DETERMINING COMPUTATION OF AMOUNT.—A multiemployer plan, other than a plan which primarily covers employees in the building and construction industry, may be amended to provide that the amount of unfunded vested benefits allocable to an employer that withdraws from the plan is an amount determined under paragraph (2), (3), (4), or (5) of this subsection, rather than under subsection (b) or (d). A plan described in section 4203(b)(1)(B)(i) (relating to the building and construction industry) may be amended, to the extent provided in regulations prescribed by the corporation, to provide that the amount of the unfunded vested benefits allocable to an employer not described in section 4203(b)(1)(A) shall be determined in a manner different from that provided in subsection (b).

(2)(A) The amount of the unfunded vested benefits allocable to any employer under this paragraph is the sum of the amounts determined under subparagraphs (B) and (C).

(B) The amount determined under this subparagraph is the product of—

(i) the plan's unfunded vested benefits as of the end of the last plan year ending before September 26, 1980, reduced as if those obligations were being fully amortized in level annual installments over 15 years beginning with the first plan year ending on or after such date; multiplied by

(ii) a fraction—

(I) the numerator of which is the sum of all contributions required to be made by the employer under the plan for the last 5 plan years ending before September 26, 1980, and

(II) the denominator of which is the sum of all contributions made for the last 5 plan years ending before September 26, 1980, by all employers who had an obligation to contribute under the plan for the first plan year ending after September 25, 1980, and who had not withdrawn from the plan before such date.

(C) The amount determined under this subparagraph is the product of—

(i) an amount equal to—

(I) the plan's unfunded vested benefits as of the end of the plan year preceding the plan year in which the employer withdraws, less

(II) the sum of the value as of such date of all outstanding claims for withdrawal liability which can reasonably be expected to be collected, with respect to employers withdrawing before such plan year, and that portion of the amount determined under subparagraph (B)(i) which is allocable to employers who have an obligation to contribute under the plan in the plan year preceding the plan year in which the employer withdraws and who also had an obligation to contribute under the plan for the first plan year ending after September 25, 1980; multiplied by

(ii) a fraction—

(I) the numerator of which is the total amount required to be contributed under the plan by the employer for the last 5 plan years ending before the date on which the employer withdraws, and

(II) the denominator of which is the total amount contributed under the plan by all employers for the last 5 plan years ending before the date on which the employer withdraws, increased by the amount of any employer contributions owed with respect to earlier periods which were collected in those plan years, and decreased by any amount contributed by an employer who withdrew from the plan under this part during those plan years.

(D) The corporation may by regulation permit adjustments in any denominator under this section, consistent with the purposes of this title, where such adjustment would be appropriate to ease administrative burdens of plan sponsors in calculating such denominators.

(3) The amount of the unfunded vested benefits allocable to an employer under this paragraph is the product of—

(A) the plan's unfunded vested benefits as of the end of the plan year preceding the plan year in which the employer withdraws, less the value as of the end of such year of all outstanding claims for withdrawal liability which can reasonably be expected to be collected from employers withdrawing before such year; multiplied by

(B) a fraction—

(i) the numerator of which is the total amount required to be contributed by the employer under the plan for the last 5 plan years ending before the withdrawal, and

(ii) the denominator of which is the total amount contributed under the plan by all employers for the last 5 plan years ending before the withdrawal, increased by any employer contributions owed with respect to earlier periods which were collected in those plan years, and decreased by any amount contributed to the plan during those plan years by employers who withdrew from the plan under this section during those plan years.

(4)(A) The amount of the unfunded vested benefits allocable to an employer under this paragraph is equal to the sum of—

(i) the plan's unfunded vested benefits which are attributable to participants' service with the employer (determined as of the end of the plan year preceding the plan year in which the employer withdraws), and

(ii) the employer's proportional share of any unfunded vested benefits which are not attributable to service with the employer or other employers who are obligated to contribute under the plan in the plan year preceding the plan year in which the employer withdraws (determined as of the end of the plan year preceding the plan year in which the employer withdraws).

(B) The plan's unfunded vested benefits which are attributable to participants' service with the employer is the amount equal to the value of nonforfeitable benefits under the plan which are attributable to participants' service with such employer (determined under plan rules not inconsistent with regulations of the corporation) decreased by the share of plan assets determined under subparagraph (C) which is allocated to the employer as provided under subparagraph (D).

(C) The value of plan assets determined under this subparagraph is the value of plan assets allocated to nonforfeitable benefits which are attributable to service with the employers who have an obligation to contribute under the plan in the plan year preceding the plan year in which the employer withdraws, which is determined by multiplying—

(i) the value of the plan assets as of the end of the plan year preceding the plan year in which the employer withdraws, by

(ii) a fraction—

(I) the numerator of which is the value of nonforfeitable benefits which are attributable to service with such employers, and

(II) the denominator of which is the value of all nonforfeitable benefits under the plan as of the end of the plan year.

(D) The share of plan assets, determined under subparagraph (C), which is allocated to the employer shall be determined in accordance with one of the following methods which shall be adopted by the plan by amendment:

(i) by multiplying the value of plan assets determined under subparagraph (C) by a fraction—

(I) the numerator of which is the value of the nonforfeitable benefits which are attributable to service with the employer; and

(II) the denominator of which is the value of the nonforfeitable benefits which are attributable to service with all employers who have an obligation to contribute under the plan in the plan year preceding the plan year in which the employer withdraws:

(ii) by multiplying the value of plan assets determined under subparagraph (C) by a fraction—

(I) the numerator of which is the sum of all contributions (accumulated with interest) which have been made to the plan by the employer for the plan year preceding the plan year in which the employer withdraws and all preceding plan years; and

(II) the denominator of which is the sum of all contributions (accumulated with interest) which have been made to the plan (for the plan year preceding the plan year in which the employer withdraws and all preceding plan years) by all employers who have an obligation to contribute to the plan for the plan year preceding the plan year in which the employer withdraws; or

(iii) by multiplying the value of plan assets under subparagraph (C) by a fraction—

(I) the numerator of which is the amount determined under clause (ii)(I) of this subparagraph, less the sum of benefit payments (accumulated with interest) made to participants (and their beneficiaries) for the plan years described in such clause (ii)(I) which are attributable to service with the employer; and

(II) the denominator of which is the amount determined under clause (ii) (II) of this subparagraph, reduced by the sum of benefit payments (accumulated with interest) made to participants (and their beneficiaries) for the plan years described in such clause (ii) (II) which are attributable to service with respect to the employers described in such clause (ii) (II).

(E) The amount of the plan's unfunded vested benefits for a plan year preceding the plan year in which an employer withdraws, which is not attributable to service with employers who have an obligation to contribute under the plan in the plan year preceding the plan year in which such employer withdraws, is equal to—

(i) an amount equal to—

(I) the value of all nonforfeitable benefits under the plan at the end of such plan year; reduced by

(II) the value of nonforfeitable benefits under the plan at the end of such plan year which are attributable to participants' service with employers who have an obligation to contribute under the plan for such plan year; reduced by

(ii) an amount equal to—

(I) the value of the plan assets as of the end of such plan year; reduced by

(II) the value of plan assets as of the end of such plan year as determined under subparagraph (C); reduced by

(iii) the value of all outstanding claims for withdrawal liability which can reasonably be expected to be collected with respect to employers withdrawing before the year preceding the plan year in which the employer withdraws.

(F) The employer's proportional share described in subparagraph (A) (ii) for a plan year is the amount determined under subparagraph (E) for the employer, but not in excess of an amount which bears the same ratio to the sum of the amounts determined under subparagraph (E) for all employers under the plan as the amount determined under subparagraph (C) for the employer bears to the sum of the amounts determined under subparagraph (C) for all employers under the plan.

(G) The corporation may prescribe by regulation other methods which a plan may adopt for allocating assets to determine the amount of the unfunded vested benefits attributable to service with the employer and to determine the employer's share of unfunded vested benefits not attributable to service with employers who have an obligation to contribute under the plan in the plan year in which the employer withdraws.

(5) (A) The corporation shall prescribe by regulation a procedure by which a plan may, by amendment, adopt any other alternative method for determining an employer's allocable share of unfunded vested benefits under this section, subject to the approval of the corporation based on its determination that adoption of the method by the plan would not significantly increase the risk of loss to plan participants and beneficiaries or to the corporation.

(B) The corporation may prescribe by regulation standard approaches for alternative methods, other than those set forth in the preceding paragraphs of this subsection, which a plan may adopt under subparagraph (A), for which the corporation may waive or modify the approval requirements of subparagraph (A). Any alternative method shall provide for the allocation of substantially all of a plan's unfunded vested benefits among employers who have an obligation to contribute under the plan.

(C) Unless the corporation by regulation provides otherwise, a plan may be amended to provide that a period of more than 5 but not more than 10 plan years may be used for determining the numerator and denominator of any fraction which is used under any method authorized under this section for determining an employer's allocable share of unfunded vested benefits under this section.

(D) The corporation may by regulation permit adjustments in any denominator under this section, consistent with the purposes of this title, where such adjustment would be appropriate to ease administrative burdens of plan sponsors in calculating such denominators.

(E) FRESH START OPTION. —Notwithstanding paragraph (1), a plan may be amended to provide that the withdrawal liability method described in subsection (b) shall be applied by substituting the plan year which is specified in the amendment and for which the plan has no unfunded vested benefits for the plan year ending before September 26, 1980.

Act Sec. 4211. (d) (1) METHOD OF CALCULATING ALLOCABLE SHARE OF EMPLOYER OF UNFUNDED VESTED BENEFITS SET FORTH IN SUBSECTION (c) (3) OF THIS SECTION; APPLICABILITY OF CERTAIN STATUTORY PROVISIONS.—The method of calculating an employer's allocable share of unfunded vested benefits set forth in subsection (c) (3) shall be the method for calculating an employer's allocable share of unfunded vested benefits under a plan to which section 404(c) of the Internal Revenue Code of 1986, or a continuation of such a plan, applies, unless the plan is amended to adopt another method authorized under subsection (b) or (c).

(2) Sections 4204, 4209, 4219(c) (1) (B), and 4225 shall not apply with respect to the withdrawal of an employer from a plan described in paragraph (1) unless the plan is amended to provide that any of such sections apply.

Act Sec. 4211. (e) REDUCTION OF LIABILITY OF WITHDRAWN EMPLOYER IN CASE OF TRANSFER OF LIABILITIES TO ANOTHER PLAN INCIDENT TO WITHDRAWAL OR PARTIAL WITHDRAWAL OF EMPLOYER.—In the case of a transfer of liabilities to another plan incident to an employer's withdrawal or partial withdrawal, the withdrawn employer's liability under this part shall be reduced in an amount equal to the value, as of the end of the last plan year ending on or before the date of the withdrawal, of the transferred unfunded vested benefits.

Act Sec. 4211. (f) COMPUTATIONS APPLICABLE IN CASE OF WITHDRAWAL FOLLOWING MERGER OF MULTIEMPLOYER PLANS.—In the case of a withdrawal following a merger of multiemployer plans, subsection (b), (c), or (d) shall be applied in accordance with regulations prescribed by the corporation; except that, if a withdrawal occurs in the first plan year beginning after a merger of multiemployer plans, the determination under this section shall be made as if each of the multiemployer plans had remained separate plans.

Amendments

P.L. 109-280, § 204(c)(2):

Amended ERISA Sec. 4211(c) (5) by adding at the end a new subparagraph (E) to read as above.

The above amendment applies with respect to plan withdrawals occurring on or after January 1, 2007.

P.L. 101-239, § 7891(a)(1):

Titles I, III, and IV of ERISA (other than sections 3(37) (E), 301(a) (7), and 308, the last sentence of section 408(d), and sections 414(c), 4001(a) (3) (ii), and 4303) are each

amended by striking "Internal Revenue Code of 1954" each place it appears and inserting "Internal Revenue Code of 1986", effective October 22, 1986.

P.L. 98-369, § 558(b):

Amended ERISA Secs. 4211(b) and (c) by striking out "April 28, 1980" each place it appeared and inserting "September 25, 1980" instead and by striking "April 29, 1980" each place it appeared and inserting "September 26, 1980" instead.

P.L. 96-364, § 104(2):

Added Sec. 4211, effective September 26, 1980 under ERISA Sec. 4402.

Regulations

The following regulations were adopted by the Pension Benefit Guaranty Corporation on July 1, 1996 (61 FR 34002). Prior to July 1, 1996, PBGC regulations were under Chapter XXVI of Title 29 of the Code of Federal Regulations. Effective July 1, 1996, PBGC regulations were moved to Chapter XL, and were renumbered and reorganized. Reg. § 4211.22 was amended October 28, 2003 (68 FR 61344). Reg. §§ 4211.2 and 4211.12 were amended and Reg. § 4211.4 was added on December 30, 2008 (73 FR 79628).

Subpart A—General

[¶ 15,678]

§ 4211.1 **Purpose and scope.** (a) *Purpose.* Section 4211 of ERISA provides four methods for allocating unfunded vested benefits to employers that withdraw from a multiemployer plan: the presumptive method (section 4211(b)); the modified presumptive method (section 4211(c) (2)); the rolling-5 method (section 4211(c) (3)); and the direct attribution method (section 4211(c) (4)). With the minor exceptions covered in § 4211.3, a plan determines the amount of unfunded vested benefits allocable to a withdrawing employer in accordance with the presumptive method, unless the plan is amended to adopt an alternative allocative method. Generally, the PBGC must approve the adoption of an alternative allocation method. On September 25, 1984, 49 FR

37686, the PBGC granted a class approval of all plan amendments adopting one of the statutory alternative allocation methods. Subpart C sets forth the criteria and procedures for PBGC approval of nonstatutory alternative allocation methods. Section 4211(c)(5) of ERISA also permits certain modifications to the statutory allocation methods. The PBGC is to prescribe these modifications in a regulation, and plans may adopt them without PBGC approval. Subpart B contains the permissible modifications to the statutory methods. Plans may adopt other modifications subject to PBGC approval under subpart C. Finally, under section 4211(f) of ERISA, the PBGC is required to prescribe rules governing the application of the statutory allocation methods or modified methods by plans following merger of multiemployer plans. Subpart D sets forth alternative allocative methods to be used by merged plans. In addition, such plans may adopt any of the allocation methods or modifications described under subparts B and C in accordance with the rules under subparts B and C.

(b) *Scope.* This part applies to all multiemployer plans covered by title IV of ERISA.

[¶ 15,678A]

§ 4211.2 **Definitions**. The following terms are defined in § 4001.2 of this chapter: *Code, employer, IRS, multiemployer plan, PBGC, plan,* and *plan year.*

In addition, for purposes of this part:

Initial plan year means a merged plan's first complete plan year that begins after the establishment of the merged plan.

Initial plan year unfunded vested benefits means the unfunded vested benefits as of the close of the initial plan year, less the value as of the end of the initial plan year of all outstanding claims for withdrawal liability that can reasonably be expected to be collected from employers that had withdrawn as of the end of the initial plan year.

Merged plan means a plan that is the result of the merger of two or more multiemployer plans.

Merger means the combining of two or more multiemployer plans into one multiemployer plan.

Nonforfeitable benefit means a benefit described in § 4001.2 of this chapter plus, for purposes of this part, any adjustable benefit that has been reduced by the plan sponsor pursuant to section 305(e)(8) of ERISA or section 432(e)(8) of the Code that would otherwise have been includable as a nonforfeitable benefit for purposes of determining an employer's allocable share of unfunded vested benefits. [Added on 12/30/08 by 73 FR 79628.]

Prior plan means the plan in which an employer participated immediately before that plan became a part of the merged plan.

Unfunded vested benefits means an amount by which the value of nonforfeitable benefits under the plan, as defined for purposes of this section, exceeds the value of the assets of the plan.

Withdrawing employer means the employer for whom withdrawal liability is being calculated under section 4201 of ERISA.

Withdrawn employer means an employer who, prior to the withdrawing employer, has discontinued contributions to the plan or covered operations under the plan and whose obligation to contribute has not been assumed by a successor employer within the meaning of section 4204 of ERISA. A temporary suspension of contributions, including a suspension described in section 4218(2) of ERISA, is not considered a discontinuance of contributions.

[¶ 15,678B]

§ 4211.3 **Special rules for construction industry and IRC section 404(c) plans**. (a) *Construction plans.* Except as provided in §§ 4211.11(b) and 4211.21(b), a plan that primarily covers employees in the building and construction industry shall use the presumptive method for allocating unfunded vested benefits.

(b) *Section 404(c) plans.* A plan described in section 404(c) of the Code or a continuation of such a plan shall allocate unfunded vested benefits under the rolling-5 method unless the plan, by amendment, adopts an alternative method or modification.

[¶ 15,678B-5]

§ 4211.4 Contributions for purposes of the numerator and denominator of the allocation fractions.

Each of the allocation fractions used in the presumptive, modified presumptive and rolling-5 methods is based on contributions that certain employers have made to the plan for a five-year period.

(a) The numerator of the allocation fraction, with respect to a withdrawing employer, is based on the "sum of the contributions required to be made" or the "total amount required to be contributed" by the employer for the specified period. For purposes of these methods, this means the amount that is required to be contributed under one or more collective bargaining agreements or other agreements pursuant to which the employer contributes under the plan, other than withdrawal liability payments or amounts that an employer is obligated to pay to the plan pursuant to section 305(e)(7) of ERISA or section 432(e)(7) of the Code (automatic employer surcharge). Employee contributions, if any, shall be excluded from the totals.

(b) The denominator of the allocation fraction is based on contributions that certain employers have made to the plan for a specified period. For purposes of these methods, and except as provided in § 4211.12, "the sum of all contributions made" or "total amount contributed" by employers for a plan year means the amounts considered contributed to the plan for purposes of section 412(b)(3)(A) or section 431(b)(3)(A) of the Code, other than withdrawal liability payments or amounts that an employer is obligated to pay to the plan pursuant to section 305(e)(7) of ERISA or section 432(e)(7) of the Code (automatic employer surcharge). For plan years before section 412 applies to the plan, "the sum of all contributions made" or "total amount contributed" means the amount reported to the IRS or the Department of Labor as total contributions for the plan year; for example, for the plan years in which the plan filed the Form 5500, the amount reported as total contributions on that form. Employee contributions, if any, shall be excluded from the totals. [Added on 12/30/08 by 73 FR 79628.]

Subpart B—Changes Not Subject to PBGC Approval

[¶ 15,678C]

§ 4211.11 **Changes not subject to PBGC approval**. (a) *General rule.* A plan, other than a plan that primarily covers employees in the building and construction industry, may adopt, by amendment, any of the statutory allocation methods and any of the modifications set forth in §§ 4211.12 and 4211.13, without the approval of the PBGC.

(b) *Building and construction industry plans.* A plan that primarily covers employees in the building and construction industry may adopt, by amendment, any of the modifications to the presumptive rule set forth in § 4211.12 without the approval of the PBGC.

[¶ 15,678D]

§ 4211.12 **Modifications to the presumptive, modified presumptive and rolling-5 methods**. (a) *Changing the period for counting contributions.* A plan sponsor may amend a plan to modify the denominators in the presumptive, modified presumptive and rolling-5 methods in accordance with one of the alternatives described in this paragraph. Except as provided in paragraph (a)(4) of this section, any amendment adopted under this paragraph shall be applied consistently to all plan years. Contributions counted for one plan year may be not counted for any other plan year. If a contribution is counted as part of the "total amount contributed" for any plan year used to determine a denominator, that contribution may not also be counted as a contribution owed with respect to an earlier year used to determine the same denominator, regardless of when the plan collected that contribution.

(1) A plan sponsor may amend a plan to provide that "the sum of all contributions made" or "total amount contributed" for a plan year means the amount of contributions that the plan actually received during the plan year, without regard to whether the contributions are treated as made for that plan year under section 412(b)(3)(A) or section 431(b)(3)(A) of the Code.

(2) A plan sponsor may amend a plan to provide that "the sum of all contributions made" or "total amount contributed" for a plan year means the amount of contributions actually received during the plan year, increased by the amount of contributions received during a specified period of time after the close of the plan year not to exceed

the period described in section 412(c)(10) or section 431(c)(8) of the Code and regulations thereunder.

(3) A plan sponsor may amend a plan to provide that "the sum of all contributions made" or "total amount contributed" for a plan year means the amount of contributions actually received during the plan year, increased by the amount of contributions accrued during the plan year and received during a specified period of time after the close of the plan year not to exceed the period described in section 412(c)(10) or section 431(c)(8) of the Code and regulations thereunder.

(4) A plan sponsor may amend a plan to provide that—

(i) For plan years ending before September 26, 1980, "the sum of all contributions made" or "total amount contributed" means the amount of total contributions reported on Form 5500 and, for years before the plan was required to file Form 5500, the amount of total contributions reported on any predecessor reporting form required by the Department of Labor or the IRS; and

(ii) For subsequent plan years, "the sum of all contributions made" or "total amount contributed" means the amount described in § 4211.4(b), or the amount described in paragraph (a)(1), (a)(2) or (a)(3) of this section.

(b) *Excluding contributions of significant withdrawn employers.* Contributions of certain withdrawn employers are excluded from the denominator in each of the fractions used to determine a withdrawing employer's share of unfunded vested benefits under the presumptive, modified presumptive and rolling-5 methods. Except as provided in paragraph (b)(1) of this section, contributions of all employers that permanently cease to have an obligation to contribute to the plan or permanently cease covered operations before the end of the period of plan years used to determine the fractions for allocating unfunded vested benefits under each of those methods (and contributions of all employers that withdrew before September 26, 1980) are excluded from the denominators of the fractions.

(1) The plan sponsor of a plan using the presumptive, modified presumptive or rolling-5 method may amend the plan to provide that only the contributions of significant withdrawn employers shall be excluded from the denominators of the fractions used in those methods.

(2) For purposes of this paragraph (b), "significant withdrawn employer" means—

(i) An employer to which the plan has sent a notice of withdrawal liability under section 4219 of ERISA; or

(ii) A withdrawn employer that in any plan year used to determine the denominator of a fraction contributed at least $250,000 or, if less, 1% of all contributions made by employers for that year.

(3) If a group of employers withdraw in a concerted withdrawal, the plan shall treat the group as a single employer in determining whether the members are significant withdrawn employers under paragraph (b)(2) of this section. A "concerted withdrawal" means a cessation of contributions to the plan during a single plan year—

(i) By an employer association;

(ii) By all or substantially all of the employers covered by a single collective bargaining agreement; or

(iii) By all or substantially all of the employers covered by agreements with a single labor organization.

(c) *"Fresh start" rules under presumptive method.*

(1) The plan sponsor of a plan using the presumptive method (including a plan that primarily covers employees in the building and construction industry) may amend the plan to provide—

(i) A designated plan year ending after September 26, 1980, will substitute for the plan year ending before September 26, 1980, in applying section 4211(b)(1)(B), section 4211(b)(2)(B)(ii)(I), section 4211(b)(2)(D), section 4211(b)(3), and section 4211(b)(3)(B) of ERISA, and

(ii) Plan years ending after the end of the designated plan year in paragraph (c)(1)(i) will substitute for plan years ending after September 25, 1980, in applying section 4211(b)(1)(A), section 4211(b)(2)(A), and section 4211(b)(2)(B)(ii)(II) of ERISA.

(2) A plan amendment made pursuant to paragraph (c)(1) of this section must provide that the plan's unfunded vested benefits for plan years ending after the designated plan year are reduced by the value of all outstanding claims for withdrawal liability that can reasonably be expected to be collected from employers that had withdrawn from the plan as of the end of the designated plan year.

(3) In the case of a plan that primarily covers employees in the building and construction industry, the plan year designated by a plan amendment pursuant to paragraph (c)(1) of this section must be a plan year for which the plan has no unfunded vested benefits.

(d) *"Fresh start" rules under modified presumptive method.*

(1) The plan sponsor of a plan using the modified presumptive method may amend the plan to provide—

(i) A designated plan year ending after September 26, 1980, will substitute for the plan year ending before September 26, 1980, in applying section 4211(c)(2)(B)(i) and section 4211(c)(2)(B)(ii)(I) and (II) of ERISA, and

(ii) Plan years ending after the end of the designated plan year will substitute for plan years ending after September 25, 1980, in applying section 4211(c)(2)(B)(ii)(II) and section 4211(c)(2)(C)(i)(II) of ERISA.

(2) A plan amendment made pursuant to paragraph (d)(1) of this section must provide that the plan's unfunded vested benefits for plan years ending after the designated plan year are reduced by the value of all outstanding claims for withdrawal liability that can reasonably be expected to be collected from employers that had withdrawn from the plan as of the end of the designated plan year. [Amended on 12/30/08 by 73 FR 79628.]

[¶ 15,678E]

§ 4211.13 **Modifications to the direct attribution method.** (a) *Error in direct attribution method.* The unfunded vested benefits allocated to a withdrawing employer under the direct attribution method are the sum of the employer's attributable liability, determined under section 4211(c)(4)(A)(i) and (B) of ERISA, and the employer's share of the plan's unattributable liability, determined under section 4211(c)(4)(E) and allocated to the employer under section 4211(c)(4)(F). Plan sponsors should allocate unattributable liabilities on the basis of the employer's share of the attributable liabilities. However, section 4211(c)(4)(F) of ERISA, which describes the allocation of unattributable liabilities, contains a typographical error. Therefore, plans adopting the direct attribution method shall modify the phrase "as the amount determined under subparagraph (C) for the employer bears to the sum of the amounts determined under subparagraph (C) for all employers under the plan" in section 4211(c)(4)(F) by substituting "subparagraph (B)" for "subparagraph (C)" in both places it appears.

(b) *Allocating unattributable liability based on contributions in period before withdrawal.* A plan that is amended to adopt the direct attribution method may provide that instead of allocating the unattributable liability in accordance with section 4211(c)(4)(F) of ERISA, the employer's share of the plan's unattributable liability shall be determined by multiplying the plan's unattributable liability determined under section 4211(c)(4)(E) by a fraction—

(1) The numerator of which is the total amount of contributions required to be made by the withdrawing employer over a period of consecutive plan years (not fewer than five) ending before the withdrawal; and

(2) The denominator of which is the total amount contributed under the plan by all employers for the same period of years used in paragraph (b)(1) of this section, decreased by any amount contributed by an employer that withdrew from the plan during those plan years.

Subpart C—Changes Subject to PBGC Approval

[¶ 15,678F]

§ 4211.21 **Changes subject to PBGC approval.** (a) *General rule.* Subject to the approval of the PBGC pursuant to this subpart, a plan, other than a plan that primarily covers employees in the building and construction industry, may adopt, by amendment, any allocation method or modification to an allocation method that is not permitted under subpart B of this part.

(b) *Building and construction industry plans.* Subject to the approval of the PBGC pursuant to this subpart, a plan that primarily covers employees in the building and construction industry may adopt, by amendment, any allocation method or modification to an allocation method that is not permitted under § 4211.12 if the method or modification is applicable only to its employers that are not construction industry employers within the meaning of section 4203(b)(1)(A) of ERISA.

(c) *Substantial overallocation not allowed.* No plan may adopt an allocation method or modification to an allocation method that results in a systematic and substantial overallocation of the plan's unfunded vested benefits.

(d) *Use of method prior to approval.* A plan may implement an alternative allocation method or modification to an allocation method that requires PBGC approval before that approval is given. However, the plan sponsor shall assess liability in accordance with this paragraph.

(1) *Demand for payment.* Until the PBGC approves the allocation method or modification, a plan may not demand withdrawal liability under section 4219 of ERISA in an amount that exceeds the lesser of the amount calculated under the amendment or the amount calculated under the allocation method that the plan would be required to use if the PBGC did not approve the amendment. The plan must inform each withdrawing employer of both amounts and explain that the higher amount may become payable depending on the PBGC's decision on the amendment.

(2) *Adjustment of liability.* When necessary because of the PBGC decision on the amendment, the plan shall adjust the amount demanded from each employer under paragraph (c)(1) of this section and the employer's withdrawal liability payment schedule. The length of the payment schedule shall be increased, as necessary. The plan shall notify each affected employer of the adjusted liability and payment schedule and shall collect the adjusted amount in accordance with the adjusted schedule.

[¶ 15,678G]

§ 4211.22 **Requests for PBGC approval.** (a) *Filing of request.* (1) *In general.* A plan shall submit a request for approval of an alternative allocation method or modification to an allocation method to the PBGC in accordance with the requirements of this section as soon as practicable after the adoption of the amendment.

(2) *Method of filing.* The PBGC applies the rules in subpart A of part 4000 of this chapter to determine permissible methods of filing with the PBGC under this subpart.

[Amended 10/28/2003 by 68 FR 61344]

(b) *Who shall submit.* The plan sponsor, or a duly authorized representative acting on behalf of the plan sponsor, shall sign the request.

(c) *Where to submit.* See Sec. 4000.4 of this chapter for information on where to file.

[Amended 10/28/2003 by 68 FR 61344]

(d) *Content.* Each request shall contain the following information:

(1) The name, address and telephone number of the plan sponsor, and of the duly authorized representative, if any, of the plan sponsor.

(2) The name of the plan.

(3) The nine-digit Employer Identification Number (EIN) that the Internal Revenue Service assigned to the plan sponsor and the three-digit Plan Identification Number (PIN) that the plan sponsor assigned to the plan, and, if different, also the EIN-PIN that the plan last filed with the PBGC. If the plan has no EIN-PIN, the request shall so indicate.

(4) The date the amendment was adopted.

(5) A copy of the amendment, setting forth the full text of the alternative allocation method or modification.

(6) The allocation method that the plan currently uses and a copy of the plan amendment (if any) that adopted the method.

(7) A statement certifying that notice of the adoption of the amendment has been given to all employers that have an obligation to contribute under the plan and to all employee organizations that represent employees covered by the plan.

(e) *Additional information.* In addition to the information listed in paragraph (d) of this section, the PBGC may require the plan sponsor to submit any other information that the PBGC determines is necessary for the review of an alternative allocation method or modification to an allocation method.

(Approved by the Office of Management and Budget under control number 1212-0035)

[¶ 15,678H]

§ 4211.23 **Approval of alternative method.** (a) *General.* The PBGC shall approve an alternative allocation method or modification to an allocation method if the PBGC determines that adoption of the method or modification would not significantly increase the risk of loss to plan participants and beneficiaries or to the PBGC.

(b) *Criteria.* An alternative allocation method or modification to an allocation method satisfies the requirements of paragraph (a) of this section if it meets the following three conditions:

(1) The method or modification allocates a plan's unfunded vested benefits, both for the adoption year and for the five subsequent plan years, to the same extent as any of the statutory allocation methods, or any modification to a statutory allocation method permitted under subpart B.

(2) The method or modification allocates unfunded vested benefits to each employer on the basis of either the employer's share of contributions to the plan or the unfunded vested benefits attributable to each employer. The method or modification may take into account differences in contribution rates paid by different employers and differences in benefits of different employers' employees.

(3) The method or modification fully reallocates among employers that have not withdrawn from the plan all unfunded vested benefits that the plan sponsor has determined cannot be collected from withdrawn employers, or that are not assessed against withdrawn employers because of sections 4209, 4219(c)(1)(B) or 4225 of ERISA.

(c) *PBGC action on request.* The PBGC's decision on a request for approval shall be in writing. If the PBGC disapproves the request, the decision shall state the reasons for the disapproval and shall include a statement of the sponsor's right to request a reconsideration of the decision pursuant to part 4003 of this chapter.

[¶ 15,678I]

§ 4211.24 **Special rule for certain alternative methods previously approved.** A plan may not apply to any employer withdrawing on or after November 25, 1987, an allocation method approved by the PBGC before that date that allocates to the employer the greater of the amounts of unfunded vested benefits determined under two different allocation rules. Until a plan that has been using such a method is amended to adopt a valid allocation method, its allocation method shall be deemed to be the statutory allocation method that would apply if it had never been amended.

Subpart D—Allocation Methods for Merged Multiemployer Plans

[¶ 15,678J]

§ 4211.31 **Allocation of unfunded vested benefits following the merger of plans.** (a) *General Rule.* Except as provided in paragraphs (b) through (d) of this section, when two or more multiemployer plans merge, the merged plan shall adopt one of the statutory allocation methods, in accordance with subpart B of this part, or one of the allocation methods prescribed in §§ 4211.32 through 4211.35, and the method adopted shall apply to all employer withdrawals occurring after the initial plan year. Alternatively, a merged plan may adopt its own allocation method in accordance with subpart C of this part. If a merged plan fails to adopt an allocation method pursuant to this subpart or subpart B or C, it shall use the presumptive allocation method prescribed in § 4211.32. In addition, a merged plan may adopt any of the modifications prescribed in § 4211.36 or in subpart B of this part.

(b) *Construction plans.* Except as provided in the next sentence, a merged plan that primarily covers employees in the building and construction industry shall use the presumptive allocation method prescribed in § 4211.32. However, the plan may, with respect to employers that are not construction industry employers within the meaning of section 4203(b)(1)(A) of ERISA, adopt, by amendment, one of the alternative methods prescribed in §§ 4211.33 through 4211.35 or any other allocation method. Any such amendment shall be adopted in accordance with subpart C of this part. A construction plan may, without the PBGC's approval, adopt by amendment any of the modifications set forth in § 4211.36 or any of the modifications to the statutory presumptive method set forth in § 4211.12.

(c) *Section 404(c) plans.* A merged plan that is a continuation of a plan described in section 404(c) of the Code shall use the rolling-5 allocation method prescribed in § 4211.34, unless the plan, by amendment, adopts an alternative method. The plan may adopt one of the statutory allocation methods or one of the allocation methods set forth in §§ 4211.32 through 4211.35 without PBGC approval; adoption of any other allocation method is subject to PBGC approval under subpart B of this plan. The plan may, without the PBGC's approval, adopt by amendment any of the modifications set forth in § 4211.36 or in subpart B of this part.

(d) *Withdrawals before the end of the initial plan year.* For employer withdrawals after the effective date of a merger and prior to the end of the initial plan year, the amount of unfunded vested benefits allocable to a withdrawing employer shall be determined in accordance with § 4211.37.

[¶ 15,678K]

§ 4211.32 **Presumptive method for withdrawals after the initial plan year.** (a) *General rule.* Under this section, the amount of unfunded vested benefits allocable to an employer that withdraws from a merged plan after the initial plan year is the sum (but not less than zero) of—

(1) The employer's proportional share, if any, of the unamortized amount of the plan's initial plan year unfunded vested benefits, as determined under paragraph (b) of this section;

(2) The employer's proportional share of the unamortized amount of the change in the plan's unfunded vested benefits for plan years ending after the initial plan year, as determined under paragraph (c) of this section; and

(3) The employer's proportional share of the unamortized amounts of the reallocated unfunded vested benefits (if any) as determined under paragraph (d) of this section.

(b) *Share of initial plan year unfunded vested benefits.* An employer's proportional share, if any, of the unamortized amount of the plan's initial plan year unfunded vested benefits is the sum of the employer's share of its prior plan's liabilities (determined under paragraph (b)(1) of this section) and the employer's share of the adjusted initial plan year unfunded vested benefits (determined under paragraph (b)(2) of this section), with such sum reduced by five percent of the original amount for each plan year subsequent to the initial year.

(1) *Share of prior plan liabilities.* An employer's share of its prior plan's liabilities is the amount of unfunded vested benefits that would have been allocable to the employer if it had withdrawn on the first day of the initial plan year, determined as if each plan had remained a separate plan.

(2) *Share of adjusted initial plan year unfunded vested benefits.* An employer's share of the adjusted initial plan year unfunded vested benefits equals the plan's initial plan year unfunded vested benefits, less the amount that would be determined under paragraph (b)(1) of this section for each employer that had not withdrawn as of the end of the initial plan year, multiplied by a fraction—

(i) The numerator of which is the amount determined under paragraph (b)(1) of this section; and

(ii) The denominator of which is the sum of the amounts that would be determined under paragraph (b)(1) of this section for each employer that had not withdrawn as of the end of the initial plan year.

(c) *Share of annual changes.* An employer's proportional share of the unamortized amount of the change in the plan's unfunded vested for the plan years ending after the end of the initial plan year is the sum of the employer's proportional shares (determined under paragraph (c)(2) of this section) of the unamortized amount of the change in unfunded vested benefits (determined under paragraph (c)(1) of this section) for each plan year in which the employer has an obligation to contribute under the plan ending after the initial plan year and before the plan year in which the employer withdraws.

(1) *Change in plan's unfunded vested benefits.* The change in a plan's unfunded vested benefits for a plan year is the amount by which the unfunded vested benefits at the end of a plan year, less the value as of the end of such year of all outstanding claims for withdrawal liability that can reasonably be expected to be collected from employers that had withdrawn as of the end of the initial plan year, exceed the sum of the unamortized amount of the initial plan year unfunded vested benefits (determined under paragraph (c)(1)(i) of this section) and the unamortized amounts of the change in unfunded vested benefits for each plan year ending after the initial plan year and preceding the plan year for which the change is determined (determined under paragraph (c)(1)(ii) of this section).

(i) *Unamortized amount of initial plan year unfunded vested benefits.* The unamortized amount of the initial plan year unfunded vested benefits is the amount of those benefits reduced by five percent of the original amount for each succeeding plan year.

(ii) *Unamortized amount of the change.* The unamortized amount of the change in a plan's unfunded vested benefits with respect to a plan year is the change in unfunded vested benefits for the plan year, reduced by five percent of such change for each succeeding plan year.

(2) Employer's proportional share. An employer's proportional share of the amount determined under paragraph (c)(1) of this section is computed by multiplying that amount by a fraction—

(i) The numerator of which is the total amount required to be contributed under the plan (or under the employer's prior plan) by the employer for the plan year in which the change arose and the four preceding full plan years; and

(ii) The denominator of which is the total amount contributed under the plan (or under employer's prior plan) for the plan year in which the change arose and the four preceding full plan years by all employers that had an obligation to contribute under the plan for the plan year in which such change arose, reduced by any amount contributed by an employer that withdrew from the plan in the year in which the change arose.

(d) *Share of reallocated amounts.* An employer's proportional share of the unamortized amounts of the reallocated unfunded vested benefits, if any, is the sum of the employer's proportional shares (determined under paragraph (d)(2) of this section) of the unamortized amount of the reallocated unfunded vested benefits (determined under paragraph (d)(1) of this section) for each plan year ending before the plan year in which the employer withdrew from the plan.

(1) *Unamortized amount of reallocated unfunded vested benefits.* The unamortized amount of the reallocated unfunded vested benefits with respect to a plan year is the sum of the amounts described in paragraphs (d)(1)(i), (d)(1)(ii), and (d)(1)(iii) of this section for the plan year, reduced by five percent of such sum for each succeeding plan year.

(i) *Uncollectible amounts.* Amounts included as reallocable under this paragraph are those that the plan sponsor determines in that plan year to be uncollectible for reasons arising out of cases or proceedings under Title 11, United States Code, or similar proceedings, with respect to an employer that withdrew after the close of the initial plan year.

(ii) *Relief amounts.* Amounts included as reallocable under this paragraph are those that the plan sponsor determines in that plan year will not be assessed as a result of the operation of sections 4209, 4219(c)(1)(B), or 4225 of ERISA with respect to an employer that withdrew after the close of the initial plan year.

(iii) *Other amounts.* Amounts included as reallocable under this paragraph are those that the plan sponsor determines in that plan year to be uncollectible or unassessable for other reasons under standards not inconsistent with regulations prescribed by the PBGC.

(2) *Employer's proportional share.* An employer's proportional share of the amount of the reallocated unfunded vested benefits with respect to a plan year is computed by multiplying the unamortized amount of the reallocated unfunded vested benefits (as of the end of the year preceding the plan year in which the employer withdraws) by the allocation fraction described in paragraph (c)(2) of this section for the same plan year.

[¶ 15,678L]

§ 4211.33 **Modified presumptive method for withdrawals after the initial plan year.** (a) *General rule.* Under this section, the amount of unfunded vested benefits allocable to an employer that withdraws from a merged plan after the initial plan year is the sum of the employer's proportional share, if any, of the unamortized amount of the plan's initial plan year unfunded vested benefits (determined under paragraph (b) of this section) and the employer's proportional share of the unamortized amount of the unfunded vested benefits arising after the initial plan year (determined under paragraph (c) of this section).

(b) *Share of initial plan year unfunded vested benefits.* An employer's proportional share, if any, of the unamortized amount of the plan's initial plan year unfunded vested benefits is the sum of the employer's share of its prior plan's liabilities, as determined under § 4211.32(b)(1), and the employer's share of the adjusted initial plan year unfunded vested benefits, as determined under § 4211.32(b)(2), with such sum reduced as if it were being fully amortized in level annual installments over fifteen years beginning with the first plan year after the initial plan year.

(c) *Share of unfunded vested benefits arising after the initial plan year.* An employer's proportional share of the amount of the plan's unfunded vested benefits arising after the initial plan year is the employer's proportional share (determined under paragraph (c)(2) of this section) of the plan's unfunded vested benefits as of the end of the plan year preceding the plan year in which the employer withdraws, reduced by the amount of the plan's unfunded vested benefits as of the close of the initial plan year (determined under paragraph (c)(1) of this section).

(1) *Amount of unfunded vested benefits.* The plan's unfunded vested benefits as of the end of the plan year preceding the plan year in which the employer withdraws shall be reduced by the sum of—

(i) The value as of that date of all outstanding claims for withdrawal liability that can reasonably be expected to be collected, with respect to employers that withdrew before that plan year; and

(ii) The sum of the amounts that would be allocable under paragraph (b) of this section to all employers that have an obligation to contribute in the plan year preceding the plan year in which the employer withdraws and that also had an obligation to contribute in the first plan year ending after the initial plan year.

(2) *Employer's proportional share.* An employer's proportional share of the amount determined under paragraph (c)(1) of this section is computed by multiplying that amount by a fraction—

(i) The numerator of which is the total amount required to be contributed under the plan (or under the employer's prior plan) by the employer for the last five full plan years ending before the date on which the employer withdraws; and

(ii) The denominator of which is the total amount contributed under the plan (or under each employer's prior plan) by all employers for the last five full plan years ending before the date on which the employer withdraws, increased by the amount of any employer contributions owed with respect to earlier periods that were collected in those plan years, and decreased by any amount contributed by an employer that withdrew from the plan (or prior plan) during those plan years.

[¶ 15,678M]

§ 4211.34 **Rolling-5 method for withdrawals after the initial plan year.** (a) *General rule.* Under this section, the amount of unfunded

vested benefits allocable to an employer that withdraws from a merged plan after the initial plan year is the sum of the employer's proportional share, if any, of the unamortized amount of the plan's initial plan year unfunded vested benefits (determined under paragraph (b) of this section) and the employer's proportional share of the unamortized amount of the unfunded vested benefits arising after the initial plan year (determined under paragraph (c) of this section).

(b) *Share of initial plan year unfunded vested benefits.* An employer's proportional share, if any, of the unamortized amount of the plan's initial plan year unfunded vested benefits is the sum of the employer's share of its prior plan's liabilities, as determined under § 4211.32(b)(1), and the employer's share of the adjusted initial plan year unfunded vested benefits, as determined under § 4211.32(b)(2), with such sum reduced as if it were being fully amortized in level annual installments over five years beginning with the first plan year after the initial plan year.

(c) *Share of unfunded vested benefits arising after the initial plan year.* An employer's proportional share of the amount of the plan's unfunded vested benefits arising after the initial plan year is the employer's proportional share determined under § 4211.33(c).

[¶ 15,678N]

§ 4211.35 **Direct attribution method for withdrawals after the initial plan year.** The allocation method under this section is the allocation method described in section 4211(c)(4) of ERISA.

[¶ 15,678O]

§ 4211.36 **Modifications to the determination of initial liabilities, the amortization of initial liabilities, and the allocation fraction.** (a) *General rule.* A plan using any of the allocation methods described in §§ 4211.32 through 4211.34 may, by plan amendment and without PBGC approval, adopt any of the modifications described in this section.

(b) *Restarting initial liabilities.* A plan may be amended to allocate the initial plan year unfunded vested benefits under § 4211.32(b), § 4211.33(b), or § 4211.34(b) without separately allocating to employers the liabilities attributable to their participation under their prior plans. An amendment under this paragraph must include an allocation fraction under paragraph (d) of this section for determining the employer's proportional share of the total unfunded benefits as of the close of the initial plan year.

(c) *Amortizing initial liabilities.* A plan may by amendment modify the amortization of initial liabilities in either of the following ways:

(1) If two or more plans that use the presumptive allocation method of section 4211(b) of ERISA merge, the merged plan may adjust the amortization of initial liabilities under § 4211.32(b) to amortize those unfunded vested benefits over the remaining length of the prior plans' amortization schedules.

(2) A plan that has adopted the allocation method under § 4211.33 or § 4211.34 may adjust the amortization of initial liabilities under § 4211.33(b) or § 4211.34(b) to amortize those unfunded vested benefits in level annual installments over any period of at least five and not more than fifteen years.

(d) *Changing the allocation fraction.* A plan may by amendment replace the allocation fraction under § 4211.32(b), § 4211.33(b), or § 4211.34(b) with any of the following contribution-based fractions—

(1) A fraction, the numerator of which is the total amount required to be contributed under the merged and prior plans by the withdrawing employer in the 60-month period ending on the last day of the initial plan year, and the denominator of which is the sum for that period of the contributions made by all employers that had not withdrawn as of the end of the initial plan year;

(2) A fraction, the numerator of which is the total amount required to be contributed by the withdrawing employer for the initial plan year and the four preceding full plan years of its prior plan, and the denominator of which is the sum of all contributions made over that period by employers that had not withdrawn as of the end of the initial plan year; or

(3) A fraction, the numerator of which is the total amount required to be contributed to the plan by the withdrawing employer

since the effective date of the merger, and the denominator of which is the sum of all contributions made over that period by employers that had not withdrawn as of the end of the initial plan year.

[¶ 15,678P]

§ 4211.37 **Allocating unfunded vested benefits for withdrawals before the end of the initial plan year**. If an employer withdraws after the effective date of a merger and before the end of the initial plan year, the amount of unfunded vested benefits allocable to the employer shall be determined as if each plan had remained a separate plan. In making this determination, the plan sponsor shall use the allocation method of the withdrawing employer's prior plan and shall compute the employer's allocable share of the plan's unfunded vested benefits as if the day before the effective date of the merger were the end of the last plan year prior to the withdrawal.

[¶ 15,679]
OBLIGATION TO CONTRIBUTE; SPECIAL RULES

Act Sec. 4212. (a) DEFINITION.—For purposes of this part, the term "obligation to contribute" means an obligation to contribute arising—

(1) under one or more collective bargaining (or related) agreements, or

(2) as a result of a duty under applicable labor-management relations law, but does not include an obligation to pay withdrawal liability under this section or to pay delinquent contributions.

Act Sec. 4212. (b) PAYMENTS OF WITHDRAWAL LIABILITY NOT CONSIDERED CONTRIBUTIONS.—Payments of withdrawal liability under this part shall not be considered contributions for purposes of this part.

Act Sec. 4212. (c) TRANSACTIONS TO EVADE OR AVOID LIABILITY.—If a principal purpose of any transaction is to evade or avoid liability under this part, this part shall be applied (and liability shall be determined and collected) without regard to such transaction.

Amendment

P.L. 96-364, § 104(2):

Added Sec. 4212, effective September 26, 1980 under ERISA Sec. 4402.

[¶ 15,680]
ACTUARIAL ASSUMPTIONS, ETC.

Act Sec. 4213. (a) USE BY PLAN ACTUARY IN DETERMINING UNFUNDED VESTED BENEFITS OF A PLAN FOR COMPUTING WITHDRAWAL LIABILITY OF EMPLOYER.—The corporation may prescribe by regulation actuarial assumptions which may be used by a plan actuary in determining the unfunded vested benefits of a plan for purposes of determining an employer's withdrawal liability under this part. Withdrawal liability under this part shall be determined by each plan on the basis of—

(1) actuarial assumptions and methods which, in the aggregate, are reasonable (taking into account the experience of the plan and reasonable expectations) and which, in combination, offer the actuary's best estimate of anticipated experience under the plan, or

(2) actuarial assumptions and methods sets forth in the corporation's regulations for purposes of determining an employer's withdrawal liability.

Act Sec. 4213. (b) FACTORS DETERMINATIVE OF UNFUNDED VESTED BENEFITS OF PLAN FOR COMPUTING WITHDRAWAL LIABILITY OF EMPLOYER.—In determining the unfunded vested benefits of a plan for purposes of determining an employer's withdrawal liability under this part, the plan actuary may—

(1) rely on the most recent complete actuarial valuation used for purposes of section 412 of the Internal Revenue Code of 1986 and reasonable estimates for the interim years of the unfunded vested benefits, and

(2) in the absence of complete data, rely on the data available or on data secured by a sampling which can reasonably be expected to be representative of the status of the entire plan.

Act Sec. 4213. (c) DETERMINATION OF AMOUNT OF UNFUNDED VESTED BENEFITS.—For purposes of this part, the term "unfunded vested benefits" means with respect to a plan, an amount equal to—

(A) the value of nonforfeitable benefits under the plan, less

(B) the value of the assets of the plan.

Amendment

P.L. 96-364, § 104(2):

Added Sec. 4213, effective September 26, 1980 under ERISA Sec. 4402.

P.L. 101-239, § 3111:

Amended ERISA Sec. 4213(b)(1) by striking "Internal Revenue Code of 1954" and inserting "Internal Revenue Code of 1986".

The above amendment is effective as if originally included in the provision of the Tax Reform Act of 1986 to which it relates.

[¶ 15,681]
APPLICATION OF PLAN AMENDMENTS

Act Sec. 4214. (a) No plan rule or amendment adopted after January 31, 1981, under section 4209 or 4211(c) may be applied without the employer's consent with respect to liability for a withdrawal or partial withdrawal which occurred before the date on which the rule or amendment was adopted.

Act Sec. 4214. (b) All plan rules and amendments authorized under this part shall operate and be applied uniformly with respect to each employer, except that special provisions may be made to take into account the creditworthiness of an employer. The plan sponsor shall give notice to all employers who have an obligation to contribute under the plan and to all employee organizations representing employees covered under the plan of any plan rules or amendments adopted pursuant to this section.

Amendment

P.L. 96-364, § 104(2):

Added Sec. 4214, effective September 26, 1980 under ERISA Sec. 4402.

[¶ 15,682]
PLAN NOTIFICATION TO CORPORATION OF POTENTIALLY SIGNIFICANT WITHDRAWALS

Act Sec. 4215. The corporation may, by regulation, require the plan sponsor of a multiemployer plan to provide notice to the corporation when the withdrawal from the plan by any employer has resulted, or will result, in a significant reduction in the amount of aggregate contributions under the plan made by employers.

Amendment

P.L. 96-364, § 104(2):

Added Sec. 4215, effective September 26, 1980 under ERISA Sec. 4402.

[¶ 15,683]
SPECIAL RULES FOR SECTION 404(c) PLANS

Act Sec. 4216. (a) AMOUNT OF WITHDRAWAL LIABILITY; DETERMINATIVE FACTORS.—In the case of a plan described in subsection (b)—

(1) if an employer withdraws prior to a determination described in section 4041A(a)(2), the amount of withdrawal liability to be paid in any year by such employer shall be an amount equal to the greater of—

    (A) the amount determined under section 4219(c)(1)(C)(i), or

    (B) the product of—

      (i) the number of contribution base units for which the employer would have been required to make contributions for the prior plan year if the employer had not withdrawn, multiplied by

      (ii) the contribution rate for the plan year which would be required to meet the amortization schedules contained in section 4243(d)(3)(B)(ii) (determined without regard to any limitation on such rate otherwise provided by this title)

except that an employer shall not be required to pay an amount in excess of the withdrawal liability computed with interest; and

    (2) the withdrawal liability of an employer who withdraws after December 31, 1983, as a result of a termination described in section 4041A(a)(2) which is agreed to by the labor organization that appoints the employee representative on the joint board of trustees which sponsors the plan, shall be determined under subsection (c) if—

    (A) as a result of prior employer withdrawals in any plan year commencing after January 1, 1980, the number of contribution base units is reduced to less than 67 percent of the average number of such units for the calendar years 1974 through 1979; and

    (B) at least 50 percent of the withdrawal liability attributable to the first 33 percent decline described in subparagraph (A) has been determined by the plan sponsor to be uncollectible within the meaning of regulations of the corporation of general applicability; and

    (C) the rate of employer contributions under the plan for each year following the first plan year beginning after the date of enactment of the Multiemployer Pension Plan Amendments Act of 1980 and preceding the termination date equals or exceeds the rate described in section 4243(d)(3).

Act Sec. 4216. (b) COVERED PLANS.—A plan is described in this subsection if—

    (1) it is a plan described in section 404(c) of the Internal Revenue Code of 1986 or a continuation thereof; and

    (2) participation in the plan is substantially limited to individuals who retired prior to January 1, 1976.

Act Sec. 4216. (c)(1) AMOUNT OF LIABILITY OF EMPLOYER; "A YEAR OF SIGNATORY SERVICE" DEFINED.—The amount of an employer's liability under this paragraph is the product of—

    (A) the amount of the employer's withdrawal liability determined without regard to this section, and

    (B) the greater of 90 percent, or a fraction—

      (i) the numerator of which is an amount equal to the portion of the plan's unfunded vested benefits that is attributable to plan participants who have a total of 10 or more years of signatory service, and

      (ii) the denominator of which is an amount equal to the total unfunded vested benefits of the plan.

    (2) For purposes of paragraph (1), the term "a year of signatory service" means a year during any portion of which a participant was employed for an employer who was obligated to contribute in that year, or who was subsequently obligated to contribute.

Amendments

P.L. 96-364, § 104(2):

Added Sec. 4216, effective September 26, 1980 under ERISA Sec. 4402.

[¶ 15,684]
APPLICATION OF PART IN CASE OF CERTAIN PRE-1980 WITHDRAWALS

Act Sec. 4217. (a) For the purpose of determining the amount of unfunded vested benefits allocable to an employer for a partial or complete withdrawal from a plan which occurs after September 25, 1980, and for the purpose of determining whether there has been a partial withdrawal after such date, the amount of contributions, and the number of contribution base units, of such employer properly allocable—

    (1) to work performed under a collective bargaining agreement for which there was a permanent cessation of the obligation to contribute before September 26, 1980, or

    (2) to work performed at a facility at which all covered operations permanently ceased before September 26, 1980, or for which there was a permanent cessation of the obligation to contribute before that date,

shall not be taken into account.

Act Sec. 4217. (b) A plan may, in a manner not inconsistent with regulations, which shall be prescribed by the corporation, adjust the amount of unfunded vested benefits allocable to other employers under a plan maintained by an employer described in subsection (a).

Amendments

P.L. 98-369, § 558(b):

Amended ERISA Sec. 4217(a) by striking out "April 28, 1980" each place it appeared and inserting "September 25, 1980" instead and by striking out "April 29, 1980" each place it appeared and inserting "September 26, 1980" instead.

P.L. 96-364, § 104(2):

Added Sec. 4217, effective September 26, 1980 under ERISA Sec. 4402.

[¶ 15,685]
WITHDRAWAL NOT TO OCCUR MERELY BECAUSE OF CHANGE IN BUSINESS FORM OR SUSPENSION OF CONTRIBUTIONS DURING LABOR DISPUTE

Act Sec. 4218. Notwithstanding any other provision of this part, an employer shall not be considered to have withdrawn from a plan solely because—

(1) an employer ceases to exist by reason of—

    (A) a change in corporate structure described in section 4069(b) or

    (B) a change to an unincorporated form of business enterprise,

if the change causes no interruption in employer contributions or obligations to contribute under the plan, or

(2) an employer suspends contributions under the plan during a labor dispute involving its employees.

For purposes of this part, a successor or parent corporation or other entity resulting from any such change shall be considered the original employer.

Amendments

P.L. 101-239, § 7862(b)(1)(c):

Added new paragraph (8) to P.L. 99-514, § 1879(u), effective September 26, 1980.

P.L. 101-239, § 7893(f):

Amended ERISA Sec. 4218(1)(A) by striking "section 4062(d)" and by inserting "section 4069(b)", effective September 26, 1980.

P.L. 99-514, § 1879(u):

Amended ERISA Sec. 4218(1)(A) by striking "section 4062(d)" and inserting "section 4069(b)."

P.L. 96-364, § 104(2):

Added Sec. 4218, effective September 26, 1980 under ERISA Sec. 4402.

[¶ 15,686]
NOTICE, COLLECTION, ETC., OF WITHDRAWAL LIABILITY

Act Sec. 4219.(a) FURNISHING OF INFORMATION BY EMPLOYER TO PLAN SPONSOR.—An employer shall, within 30 days after a written request from the plan sponsor, furnish such information as the plan sponsor reasonably determines to be necessary to enable the plan sponsor to comply with the requirements of this part.

Act Sec. 4219.(b)(1) NOTIFICATION, DEMAND FOR PAYMENT, AND REVIEW UPON COMPLETE OR PARTIAL WITHDRAWAL BY EMPLOYER.—As soon as practicable after an employer's complete or partial withdrawal, the plan sponsor shall—

    (A) notify the employer of—

        (i) the amount of the liability, and

        (ii) the schedule for liability payments, and

    (B) demand payment in accordance with the schedule.

  (2)(A) No later than 90 days after the employer receives the notice described in paragraph (1), the employer—

    (i) may ask the plan sponsor to review any specific matter relating to the determination of the employer's liability and the schedule of payments,

    (ii) may identify any inaccuracy in the determination of the amount of the unfunded vested benefits allocable to the employer, and

    (iii) may furnish any additional relevant information to the plan sponsor.

  (B) After a reasonable review of any matter raised, the plan sponsor shall notify the employer of—

    (i) the plan sponsor's decision,

    (ii) the basis for the decision, and

    (iii) the reason for any change in the determination of the employer's liability or schedule of liability payments.

Act Sec. 4219.(c)(1)(A)(i) PAYMENT REQUIREMENTS; AMOUNT, ETC.—Except as provided in subparagraphs (B) and (D) of this paragraph and in paragraphs (4) and (5), an employer shall pay the amount determined under section 4211, adjusted if appropriate first under section 4209 and then under section 4206 over the period of years necessary to amortize the amount in level annual payments determined under subparagraph (C), calculated as if the first payment were made on the first day of the plan year following the plan year in which the withdrawal occurs and as if each subsequent payment were made on the first day of each subsequent plan year. Actual payment shall commence in accordance with paragraph (2).

    (ii) The determination of the amortization period described in clause (i) shall be based on the assumptions used for the most recent actuarial valuation for the plan.

  (B) In any case in which the amortization period described in subparagraph (A) exceeds 20 years, the employer's liability shall be limited to the first 20 annual payments determined under subparagraph (C).

  (C)(i) Except as provided in subparagraph (E), the amount of each annual payment shall be the product of—

    (I) the average annual number of contribution base units for the period of 3 consecutive plan years, during the period of 10 consecutive plan years ending before the plan year in which the withdrawal occurs, in which the number of contribution base units for which the employer had an obligation to contribute under the plan is the highest, and

    (II) the highest contribution rate at which the employer had an obligation to contribute under the plan during the 10 plan years ending with the plan year in which the withdrawal occurs.

For purposes of the preceding sentence, a partial withdrawal described in section 4205(a)(1) shall be deemed to occur on the last day of the first year of the 3-year testing period described in section 4205(b)(1)(B)(i).

    (ii)(I) A plan may be amended to provide that for any plan year ending before 1986 the amount of each annual payment shall be (in lieu of the amount determined under clause (i)) the average of the required employer contributions under the plan for the period of 3 consecutive plan years (during the period of 10 consecutive plan years ending with the plan year preceding the plan year in which the withdrawal occurs) for which such required contributions were the highest.

    (II) Subparagraph (B) shall not apply to any plan year to which this clause applies.

    (III) This clause shall not apply in the case of any withdrawal described in subparagraph (D).

    (IV) If under a plan this clause applies to any plan year but does not apply to the next plan year, this clause shall not apply to any plan year after such next plan year.

    (V) For purposes of this clause, the term "required contributions" means, for any period, the amounts which the employer was obligated to contribute for such period (not taking into account any delinquent contribution for any other period).

    (iii) A plan may be amended to provide that for the first plan year ending on or after September 26, 1980, the number "5" shall be substituted for the number "10" each place it appears in clause (i) or clause (ii) (whichever is appropriate). If the plan is so amended, the number "5" shall be increased by one for each succeeding plan year until the number "10" is reached.

  (D) In any case in which a multiemployer plan terminates by the withdrawal of every employer from the plan, or in which substantially all the employers withdraw from a plan pursuant to an agreement or arrangement to withdraw from the plan—

    (i) the liability of each such employer who has withdrawn shall be determined (or redetermined) under this paragraph without regard to subparagraph (B), and

    (ii) notwithstanding any other provision of this part, the total unfunded vested benefits of the plan shall be fully allocated among all such employers in a manner not inconsistent with regulations which shall be prescribed by the corporation.

Withdrawal by an employer from a plan, during a period of 3 consecutive plan years within which substantially all the employers who have an obligation to contribute under the plan withdraw, shall be presumed to be a withdrawal pursuant to an agreement or arrangement, unless the employer proves otherwise by a preponderance of the evidence.

  (E) In the case of a partial withdrawal described in section 4205(a), the amount of each annual payment shall be the product of—

    (i) the amount determined under subparagraph (C) (determined without regard to this subparagraph), multiplied by

    (ii) the fraction determined under section 4206(a)(2).

  (2) Withdrawal liability shall be payable in accordance with the schedule set forth by the plan sponsor under subsection (b)(1) beginning no later than 60 days after the date of the demand notwithstanding any request for review or appeal of determinations of the amount of such liability or of the schedule.

  (3) Each annual payment determined under paragraph (1)(C) shall be payable in 4 equal installments due quarterly, or at other intervals specified by plan rules. If a payment is not made when due, interest on the payment shall accrue from the due date until the date on which the payment is made.

  (4) The employer shall be entitled to prepay the outstanding amount of the unpaid annual withdrawal liability payments determined under paragraph (1)(C), plus accrued interest, if any, in whole or in part, without penalty. If the prepayment is made pursuant to a withdrawal which is later determined to be part of a withdrawal described in paragraph (1)(D), the withdrawal liability of the employer shall not be limited to the amount of the prepayment.

  (5) In the event of a default, a plan sponsor may require immediate payment of the outstanding amount of an employer's withdrawal liability, plus accrued interest on the total outstanding liability from the due date of the first payment which was not timely made. For purposes of this section, the term "default" means—

(A) the failure of an employer to make, when due, any payment under this section, if the failure is not cured within 60 days after the employer receives written notification from the plan sponsor of such failure, and

(B) any other event defined in rules adopted by the plan which indicates a substantial likelihood that an employer will be unable to pay its withdrawal liability.

(6) Except as provided in paragraph (1)(A)(ii), interest under this subsection shall be charged at rates based on prevailing market rates for comparable obligations, in accordance with regulations prescribed by the corporation.

(7) A multiemployer plan may adopt rules for other terms and conditions for the satisfaction of an employer's withdrawal liability if such rules—

(A) are consistent with this Act, and

(B) are not inconsistent with regulations of the corporation.

(8) In the case of a terminated multiemployer plan, an employer's obligation to make payments under this section ceases at the end of the plan year in which the assets of the plan (exclusive of withdrawal liability claims) are sufficient to meet all obligations of the plan, as determined by the corporation.

Act Sec. 4219. (d) APPLICABILITY OF STATUTORY PROHIBITIONS.—The prohibitions provided in section 406(a) do not apply to any action required or permitted under this part or to any arrangement relating to withdrawal liability involving the plan.

Amendments

P.L. 113-235, § 201(a)(7)(B), Div. O:

Amended ERISA Sec. 4219(d) by striking the period at the end and inserting "or to any arrangement relating to withdrawal liability involving the plan." to read as above.

The above amendment is effective on the date of enactment (December 16, 2014).

P.L. 98-369, § 558(b):

Amended ERISA Sec. 4219(c)(1)(C)(iii) by striking out "April 29, 1980" and inserting "September 26, 1980" instead.

P.L. 96-364, § 104(2):

Added Sec. 4219, effective September 26, 1980 under ERISA Sec. 4402.

Regulations

The following regulations were adopted by the Pension Benefit Guaranty Corporation on July 1, 1996 (61 FR 34002). Prior to July 1, 1996, PBGC regulations were under Chapter XXVI of Title 29 of the Code of Federal Regulations. Effective July 1, 1996, PBGC regulations were moved to Chapter XL, and were renumbered and reorganized. Reg. § 4219.17 was amended and Reg. § 4219.19 was added October 28, 2003 (68 FR 61344). Reg. § § 4219.1, 4219.2, and 4219.15 were amended on December 30, 2008 (73 FR 79628).

Subpart A—General

[¶ 15,687]

§ 4219.1 **Purpose and scope.** (a) *Subpart A.* Subpart A of this part describes the purpose and scope of the provisions in this part and defined terms used in this part.

(b) *Subpart B.*

(1) *Purpose.* When a multiemployer plan terminates by the withdrawal of every employer from the plan, or when substantially all employers withdraw from a multiemployer plan pursuant to an agreement or arrangement to withdraw from the plan, section 4219(c)(1)(D)(i) of ERISA requires that the liability of such withdrawing employers be determined (or redetermined) without regard to the 20-year limitation on annual payments established in section 4219(c)(1)(B) of ERISA. In addition, section 4219(c)(1)(D)(ii) requires that, upon the occurrence of a withdrawal described above, the total unfunded vested benefits of the plan be fully allocated among such withdrawing employers in a manner that is not inconsistent with PBGC regulations. Section 4209(c) of ERISA provides that the de minimis reduction established in sections 4209(a) and (b) of ERISA shall not apply to an employer that withdraws in a plan year in which substantially all employers withdraw from the plan, or to an employer that withdraws pursuant to an agreement to withdraw during a period of one or more plan years during which substantially all employers withdraw pursuant to an agreement or arrangement to withdraw. The purpose of subpart B of this part is to prescribe rules, pursuant to sections 4219(c)(1)(D) and 4209(c) of ERISA, for redetermining an employer's withdrawal liability and fully allocating the unfunded vested benefits of a multiemployer plan in either of two mass-withdrawal situations: the termination of a plan by the withdrawal of every employer and the withdrawal of substantially all employers pursuant to an agreement or arrangement to withdraw. Subpart B also prescribes rules for redetermining the liability of an employer without regard to section 4209(a) or (b) when the employer withdraws in a plan year in which substantially all employers withdraw, regardless of the occurrence of a mass withdrawal. (See part 4281 regarding the valuation of unfunded vested benefits to be fully allocated under subpart B, and parts 4041A and 4281 regarding the powers and duties of the plan sponsor of a plan terminated by mass withdrawal.)

(2) *Scope.* Subpart B applies to multiemployer plans covered by title IV of ERISA, with respect to which there is a termination by the withdrawal of every employer (including a plan created by a partition pursuant to section 4233 of ERISA) or a withdrawal of substantially all employers in the plan pursuant to an agreement or arrangement to withdraw from the plan, and to employers that withdraw from such multiemployer plans. The obligations of a plan sponsor of a masswith-

drawal-terminated plan under subpart B shall cease to apply when the plan assets are distributed in full satisfaction of all nonforfeitable benefits under the plan. Subpart B also applies, to the extent appropriate, to multiemployer plans with respect to which there is a withdrawal of substantially all employers in a single plan year and to employers that withdraw from such plans in that plan year.

(c) *Subpart C.* Subpart C establishes the interest rate to be charged on overdue, defaulted and overpaid withdrawal liability under section 4219(c)(6) of ERISA, and authorizes multiemployer plans to adopt alternative rules concerning assessment of interest and related matters. Subpart C applies to multiemployer plans covered under title IV of ERISA, and to employers that have withdrawn from such plans on or after September 26, 1980, except employers with respect to whom section 4221(f) or section 4221(g) of ERISA applies (provided that such employers are in compliance with the provisions of those sections, as applicable). [Amended 12/30/08 by 73 FR 79628.]

[¶ 15,687A]

§ 4219.2 **Definitions.** (a) The following terms are defined in section 4001.2 of this chapter: *employer, ERISA, IRS, mass withdrawal, multiemployer plan, PBGC, plan,* and *plan year.*

(b) For purposes of this part:

Initial withdrawal liability means the amount of withdrawal liability determined in accordance with sections 4201 through 4225 of title IV without regard to the occurrence of a mass withdrawal.

Mass withdrawal liability means the sum of an employer's liability for de minimis amounts, liability for 20-year-limitation amounts, and reallocation liability.

Mass withdrawal valuation date means—

(1) In the case of a termination by mass withdrawal, the last day of the plan year in which the plan terminates; or

(2) in the case of a withdrawal of substantially all employers pursuant to an agreement or arrangement to withdraw, the last day of the plan year as of which substantially all employers have withdrawn.

Nonforfeitable benefit means a benefit described in § 4001.2 of this chapter plus, for purposes of this part, any adjustable benefit that has been reduced by the plan sponsor pursuant to section 305(e)(8) of ERISA and section 432(e)(8) of the Code that would otherwise have been includable as a nonforfeitable benefit.

Reallocation liability means the amount of unfunded vested benefits allocated to an employer in the event of a mass withdrawal.

Reallocation record date means a date selected by the plan sponsor, which shall be not earlier than the date of the plan's actuarial report for the year of the mass withdrawal and not later than one year after the mass withdrawal valuation date.

Redetermination liability means the sum of an employer's liability for de minimis amounts and the employer's liability for 20-year-limitation amounts.

Unfunded vested benefits means the amount by which the present value of a plan's vested nonforfeitable benefits (as defined for purposes of this section) exceeds the value of plan assets (including claims of the plan for unpaid initial withdrawal liability and redetermination liability), determined in accordance with section 4281 of ERISA and part 4281, subpart B. [Amended 12/30/08 by 73 FR 79628.]

(c) For purposes of subpart B—

Withdrawal means a complete withdrawal as defined in section 4203 of ERISA.

Subpart B—Redetermination of Withdrawal Liability Upon Mass Withdrawal

[¶ 15,687B]

§ 4219.11 **Withdrawal liability upon mass withdrawal**. (a) *Initial withdrawal liability*. The plan sponsor of a multiemployer plan that experiences a mass withdrawal shall determine initial withdrawal liability pursuant to section 4201 of ERISA of every employer that has completely or partially withdrawn from the plan and for whom the liability has not previously been determined and, in accordance with section 4202 of ERISA, notify each employer of the amount of the initial withdrawal liability and collect the amount of the initial withdrawal liability from each employer.

(b) *Mass withdrawal liability*. The plan sponsor of a multiemployer plan that experiences a mass withdrawal shall also—

(1) Notify withdrawing employers, in accordance with § 4219.16(a), that a mass withdrawal has occurred;

(2) Within 150 days after the mass withdrawal valuation date, determine the liability of withdrawn employers for de minimis amounts and for 20-year-limitation amounts in accordance with §§ 4219.13 and 4219.14;

(3) Within one year after the reallocation record date, determine the reallocation liability of withdrawn employers in accordance with § 4219.15;

(4) Notify each withdrawing employer of the amount of mass withdrawal liability determined pursuant to this subpart and the schedule for payment of such liability, and demand payment of and collect that liability, in accordance with § 4219.16; and

(5) Notify the PBGC of the occurrence of a mass withdrawal and certify, in accordance with § 4219.17, that determinations of mass withdrawal liability have been completed.

(c) *Extensions of time*. The plan sponsor of a multiemployer plan that experiences a mass withdrawal may apply to the PBGC for an extension of the deadlines contained in paragraph (b) of this section. The PBGC shall approve such a request only if it finds that failure to grant the extension will create an unreasonable risk of loss to plan participants or the PBGC.

[¶ 15,687C]

§ 4219.12 **Employers liable upon mass withdrawal**. (a) *Liability for de minimis amounts*. An employer shall be liable for de minimis amounts to the extent provided in section 4219(c)(1)(D) of ERISA if the employer's initial withdrawal liability was reduced pursuant to section 4209(a) or (b) of ERISA.

(b) *Liability for 20-year-limitation amounts*. An employer shall be liable for 20-year-limitation amounts to the extent provided in section 4219(c)(1)(D) of ERISA.

(c) *Liability for reallocation liability*. An employer shall be liable for reallocation liability if the employer withdrew pursuant to an agreement or arrangement to withdraw from a multiemployer plan from which substantially all employers withdrew pursuant to an agreement or arrangement to withdraw, or if the employer withdrew after the beginning of the second full plan year preceding the termination date from a plan that terminated by the withdrawal of every employer, and, as of the reallocation record date—

(1) The employer has not been completely liquidated or dissolved;

(2) The employer is not the subject of a case or proceeding under title 11, United States Code, or any case or proceeding under similar provisions of state insolvency laws, except that a plan sponsor may determine that such an employer is liable for reallocation liability if the plan sponsor determines that the employer is reasonably expected to be able to pay its initial withdrawal liability and its redetermination liability in full and on time to the plan; and

(3) The plan sponsor has not determined that the employer's initial withdrawal liability or its redetermination liability is limited by section 4225 of ERISA.

(d) *General exclusion*. In the event that a plan experiences successive mass withdrawals, an employer that has been determined to be liable under this subpart for any component of mass withdrawal liability shall not be liable as a result of the same withdrawal for that component of mass withdrawal liability with respect to a subsequent mass withdrawal.

(e) *Free-look rule*. An employer that is not liable for initial withdrawal liability pursuant to a plan amendment adopting section 4210(a) of ERISA shall not be liable for de minimis amounts or for 20-year-limitation amounts, but shall be liable for reallocation liability in accordance with paragraph (c) of this section.

(f) *Payment of initial withdrawal liability*. An employer's payment of its total initial withdrawal liability, whether by prepayment or otherwise, for a withdrawal which is later determined to be part of a mass withdrawal shall not exclude the employer from or otherwise limit the employer's mass withdrawal liability under this subpart.

(g) *Agreement presumed*. Withdrawal by an employer during a period of three consecutive plan years within which substantially all employers withdraw from a plan shall be presumed to be a withdrawal pursuant to an agreement or arrangement to withdraw unless the employer proves otherwise by a preponderance of the evidence.

[¶ 15,687D]

§ 4219.13 *Amount of liability for de minimis amounts*. An employer that is liable for de minimis amounts shall be liable to the plan for the amount by which the employer's allocable share of unfunded vested benefits for the purpose of determining its initial withdrawal liability was reduced pursuant to section 4209(a) or (b) of ERISA. Any liability for de minimis amounts determined under this section shall be limited by section 4225 of ERISA to the extent that section would have been limiting had the employer's initial withdrawal liability been determined without regard to the de minimis reduction.

[¶ 15,687E]

§ 4219.14 **Amount of liability for 20-year-limitation amounts**. An employer that is liable for 20-year-limitation amounts shall be liable to the plan for an amount equal to the present value of all initial withdrawal liability payments for which the employer was not liable pursuant to section 4219(c)(1)(B) of ERISA. The present value of such payments shall be determined as of the end of the plan year preceding the plan year in which the employer withdrew, using the assumptions that were used to determine the employer's payment schedule for initial withdrawal liability pursuant to section 4219(c)(1)(A)(ii) of ERISA. Any liability for 20-year-limitation amounts determined under this section shall be limited by section 4225 of ERISA to the extent that section would have been limiting had the employer's initial withdrawal liability been determined without regard to the 20-year limitation.

[¶ 15,687F]

§ 4219.15 **Determination of reallocation liability**. (a) *General rule*. In accordance with the rules in this section, the plan sponsor shall determine the amount of unfunded vested benefits to be reallocated and shall fully allocate those unfunded vested benefits among all employers liable for reallocation liability.

(b) *Amount of unfunded vested benefits to be reallocated*. For purposes of this section, the amount of a plan's unfunded vested benefits to be reallocated shall be the amount of the plan's unfunded vested benefits, determined as of the mass withdrawal valuation date, adjusted to exclude from plan assets the value of the plan's claims for unpaid initial withdrawal liability and unpaid redetermination liability that are deemed to be uncollectible under § 4219.12(c)(1) or (c)(2).

(c) *Amount of reallocation liability.* An employer's reallocation liability shall be equal to the sum of the employer's initial allocable share of the plan's unfunded vested benefits, as determined under paragraph (c)(1) of this section, plus any unassessable amounts allocated to the employer under paragraph (c)(2), limited by section 4225 of ERISA to the extent that section would have been limiting had the employer's reallocation liability been included in the employer's initial withdrawal liability. If a plan is determined to have no unfunded vested benefits to be reallocated, the reallocation liability of each liable employer shall be zero.

(1) *Initial allocable share.* Except as otherwise provided in rules adopted by the plan pursuant to paragraph (d) of this section, and in accordance with paragraph (c)(3) of this section, an employer's initial allocable share shall be equal to the product of the plan's unfunded vested benefits to be reallocated, multiplied by a fraction—

(i) The numerator of which is the yearly average of the employer's contribution base units during the three plan years preceding the employer's withdrawal; and

(ii) The denominator of which is the sum of the yearly averages calculated under paragraph (c)(1)(i) of this section for each employer liable for reallocation liability. [Amended 12/30/08 by 73 FR 79628.]

(2) *Allocation of unassessable amounts.* If after computing each employer's initial allocable share of unfunded vested benefits, the plan sponsor knows that any portion of an employer's initial allocable share is unassessable as withdrawal liability because of the limitations in section 4225 of ERISA, the plan sponsor shall allocate any such unassessable amounts among all other liable employers. This allocation shall be done by prorating the unassessable amounts on the basis of each such employer's initial allocable share. No employer shall be liable for unfunded vested benefits allocated under paragraph (c)(1) or this paragraph to another employer that are determined to be unassessable or uncollectible subsequent to the plan sponsor's demand for payment of reallocation liability. [Amended 12/30/08 by 73 FR 79628.]

(3) *Contribution base unit.* For purposes of paragraph (c)(1) of this section, a contribution base unit means a unit with respect to which an employer has an obligation to contribute, such as an hour worked or shift worked or a unit of production, under the applicable collective bargaining agreement (or other agreement pursuant to which the employer contributes) or with respect to which the employer would have an obligation to contribute if the contribution requirement with respect to the plan were greater than zero. [Amended 12/30/08 by 73 FR 79628.]

(d) *Plan rules.* Plans may adopt rules for calculating an employer's initial allocable share of the plan's unfunded vested benefits in a manner other than that prescribed in paragraph (c)(1) of this section, provided that those rules allocate the plan's unfunded vested benefits to substantially the same extent the prescribed rules would. Plan rules adopted under this paragraph shall operate and be applied uniformly with respect to each employer. If such rules would increase the reallocation liability of any employer, they may be effective with respect to that employer earlier than three full plan years after their adoption only if the employer consents to the application of the rules to itself. The plan sponsor shall give a written notice to each contributing employer and each employee organization that represents employees covered by the plan of the adoption of plan rules under this paragraph.

[¶ 15,687G]

§ 4219.16 **Imposition of liability.** (a) *Notice of mass withdrawal.* Within 30 days after the mass withdrawal valuation date, the plan sponsor shall give written notice of the occurrence of a mass withdrawal to each employer that the plan sponsor reasonably expects may be a liable employer under § 4219.12. The notice shall include—

(1) The mass withdrawal valuation date;

(2) A description of the consequences of a mass withdrawal under this subpart; and

(3) A statement that each employer obligated to make initial withdrawal liability payments shall continue to make those payments in accordance with its schedule. Failure of the plan sponsor to notify an employer of a mass withdrawal as required by this paragraph shall not

cancel the employer's mass withdrawal liability or waive the plan's claim for such liability.

(b) *Notice of redetermination liability.* Within 30 days after the date as of which the plan sponsor is required under § 4219.11(b)(2) to have determined the redetermination liability of employers, the plan sponsor shall issue a notice of redetermination liability in writing to each employer liable under § 4219.12 for de minimis amounts or 20-year-limitation amounts, or both. The notice shall include—

(1) The amount of the employer's liability, if any, for de minimis amounts determined pursuant to § 4219.13;

(2) The amount of the employer's liability, if any, for 20-year-limitation amounts determined pursuant to § 4219.14;

(3) The schedule for payment of the liability determined under paragraph (f) of this section;

(4) A demand for payment of the liability in accordance with the schedule; and

(5) A statement of when the plan sponsor expects to issue notices of reallocation liability to liable employers.

(c) *Notice of reallocation liability.* Within 30 days after the date as of which the plan sponsor is required under § 4219.11(b)(3) to have determined the reallocation liability of employers, the plan sponsor shall issue a notice of reallocation liability in writing to each employer liable for reallocation liability. The notice shall include—

(1) The amount of the employer's reallocation liability determined pursuant to § 4219.15;

(2) The schedule for payment of the liability determined under paragraph (f) of this section; and

(3) A demand for payment of the liability in accordance with the schedule.

(d) *Notice to employers not liable.* The plan sponsor shall notify in writing any employer that receives a notice of mass withdrawal under paragraph (a) of this section and subsequently is determined not to be liable for mass withdrawal liability or any component thereof. The notice shall specify the liability from which the employer is excluded and shall be provided to the employer not later than the date by which liable employers are to be provided notices of reallocation liability pursuant to paragraph (c) of this section. If the employer is not liable for mass withdrawal liability, the notice shall also include a statement, if applicable, that the employer is obligated to continue to make initial withdrawal liability payments in accordance with its existing schedule for payment of such liability.

(e) *Combined notices.* A plan sponsor may combine a notice of redetermination liability with the notice of and demand for payment of initial withdrawal liability. If a mass withdrawal and a withdrawal described in § 4219.18 occur concurrently, a plan sponsor may combine—

(1) A notice of mass withdrawal with a notice of withdrawal issued pursuant to § 4219.18(d); and

(2) A notice of redetermination liability with a notice of liability issued pursuant to § 4219.18(e).

(f) *Payment schedules.* The plan sponsor shall establish payment schedules for payment of an employer's mass withdrawal liability in accordance with the rules in section 4219(c) of ERISA, as modified by this paragraph. For an employer that owes initial withdrawal liability as of the mass withdrawal valuation date, the plan sponsor shall establish new payment schedules for each element of mass withdrawal liability by amending the initial withdrawal liability payment schedule in accordance with the paragraph (f)(1) of this section. For all other employers, the payment schedules shall be established in accordance with paragraph (f)(2).

(1) *Employers owing initial withdrawal liability as of mass withdrawal valuation date.* For an employer that owes initial withdrawal liability as of the mass withdrawal valuation date, the plan sponsor shall amend the existing schedule of payments in order to amortize the new amounts of liability being assessed, i.e., redetermination liability and reallocation liability. With respect to redetermination liability, the plan sponsor shall add that liability to the total initial withdrawal liability and determine a new payment schedule, in accordance with section

4219(c)(1) of ERISA, using the interest assumptions that were used to determine the original payment schedule. For reallocation liability, the plan sponsor shall add that liability to the present value, as of the date following the mass withdrawal valuation date, of the unpaid portion of the amended payment schedule described in the preceding sentence and determine a new payment schedule of level annual payments, calculated as if the first payment were made on the day following the mass withdrawal valuation date using the interest assumptions used for determining the amount of unfunded vested benefits to be reallocated.

(2) *Other employers.* For an employer that had no initial withdrawal liability, or had fully paid its liability prior to the mass withdrawal valuation date, the plan sponsor shall determine the payment schedule for redetermination liability, in accordance with section 4219(c)(1) of ERISA, in the same manner and using the same interest assumptions as were used or would have been used in determining the payment schedule for the employer's initial withdrawal liability. With respect to reallocation liability, the plan sponsor shall follow the rules prescribed in paragraph (f)(1) of this section.

(g) *Review of mass withdrawal liability determinations.* Determinations of mass withdrawal liability made pursuant to this subpart shall be subject to plan review under section 4219(b)(2) of ERISA and to arbitration under section 4221 of ERISA within the times prescribed by those sections. Matters that relate solely to the amount of, and schedule of payments for, an employer's initial withdrawal liability are not matters relating to the employer's liability under this subpart and are not subject to review pursuant to this paragraph.

(h) *Cessation of withdrawal liability obligations.* If the plan sponsor of a terminated plan distributes plan assets in full satisfaction of all nonforfeitable benefits under the plan, the plan sponsor's obligation to impose and collect liability, and each employer's obligation to pay liability, in accordance with this subpart ceases on the date of such distribution.

(i) *Determination that a mass withdrawal has not occurred.* If a plan sponsor determines, after imposing mass withdrawal liability pursuant to this subpart, that a mass withdrawal has not occurred, the plan sponsor shall refund to employers all payments of mass withdrawal liability with interest, except that a plan sponsor shall not refund payments of liability for de minimis amounts to an employer that remains liable for such amounts under §4219.18. Interest shall be credited at the interest rate prescribed in subpart C and shall accrue from the date the payment was received by the plan until the date of the refund.

[¶ 15,687H]

§4219.17 **Filings with PBGC.** (a) *Filing requirements.* (1) *In general.* The plan sponsor shall file with PBGC a notice that a mass withdrawal has occurred and separate certifications that determinations of redetermination liability and reallocation liability have been made and notices provided to employers in accordance with this subpart.

(2) *Method of filing.* The PBGC applies the rules in subpart A of part 4000 of this chapter to determine permissible methods of filing with the PBGC under this subpart.

(3) *Computation of time.* The PBGC applies the rules in subpart D of part 4000 of this chapter to compute any time period under this subpart for filing with the PBGC.

[Amended 10/28/2003 by 68 FR 61344]

(b) *Who shall file.* The plan sponsor or a duly authorized representative acting on behalf of the plan sponsor shall sign and file the notice and the certifications.

(c) *When to file.* A notice of mass withdrawal for a plan from which substantially all employers withdraw pursuant to an agreement or arrangement to withdraw shall be filed with the PBGC no later than 30 days after the mass withdrawal valuation date. A notice of mass withdrawal termination shall be filed within the time prescribed for the filing of that notice in part 4041A, subparts A and B, of this chapter. Certifications of liability determinations shall be filed with the PBGC no

later than 30 days after the date on which the plan sponsor is required to have provided employers with notices pursuant to §4219.16.

(d) *Where to file.* See Sec. 4000.4 of this chapter for information on where to file.

[Amended 10/28/2003 by 68 FR 61344]

(e) *Date of filing.* The PBGC applies the rules in subpart C of part 4000 of this chapter to determine the date that a submission under this subpart was filed with the PBGC.

[Amended 10/28/2003 by 68 FR 61344]

(f) *Contents of notice of mass withdrawal.* If a plan terminates by the withdrawal of every employer, a notice of termination filed in accordance with part 4041A, subparts A and B, of this chapter shall satisfy the requirements for a notice of mass withdrawal under this subpart. If substantially all employers withdraw from a plan pursuant to an agreement or arrangement to withdraw, the notice of mass withdrawal shall contain the following information:

(1) The name of the plan.

(2) The name, address and telephone number of the plan sponsor and of the duly authorized representative, if any, of the plan sponsor.

(3) The nine-digit Employer Identification Number (EIN) assigned by the IRS to the plan sponsor and the three-digit Plan Identification Number (PIN) assigned by the plan sponsor to the plan, and, if different, the EIN or PIN last filed with the PBGC. If no EIN or PIN has been assigned, the notice shall so indicate.

(4) The mass withdrawal valuation date.

(5) A description of the facts on which the plan sponsor has based its determination that a mass withdrawal has occurred, including the number of contributing employers withdrawn and the number remaining in the plan, and a description of the effect of the mass withdrawal on the plan's contribution base.

(g) *Contents of certifications.* Each certification shall contain the following information:

(1) The name of the plan.

(2) The name, address and telephone number of the plan sponsor and of the duly authorized representative, if any, of the plan sponsor.

(3) The nine-digit Employer Identification Number (EIN) assigned by the IRS to the plan sponsor and the three-digit Plan Identification Number (PIN) last assigned by the plan sponsor to the plan, and, if different, the EIN or PIN filed with the PBGC. If no EIN or PIN has been assigned, the notice shall so indicate.

(4) Identification of the liability determination to which the certification relates.

(5) A certification, signed by the plan sponsor or a duly authorized representative, that the determinations have been made and the notices given in accordance with this subpart.

(6) For reallocation liability certifications—

(i) A certification, signed by the plan's actuary, that the determination of unfunded vested benefits has been done in accordance with part 4281, subpart B; and

(ii) A copy of plan rules, if any, adopted pursuant to §4219.15(d).

(h) *Additional information.* In addition to the information described in paragraph (g) of this section, the PBGC may require the plan sponsor to submit any other information the PBGC determines it needs in order to monitor compliance with this subpart.

[¶ 15,687I]

§4219.18 **Withdrawal in a plan year in which substantially all employers withdraw.** (a) *General rule.* An employer that withdraws in a plan year in which substantially all employers withdraw from the plan shall be liable to the plan for de minimis amounts if the employer's initial withdrawal liability was reduced pursuant to section 4209(a) or (b) of ERISA.

(b) *Amount of liability.* An employer's liability for de minimis amounts under this section shall be determined pursuant to §4219.13.

(c) *Plan sponsor's obligations.* The plan sponsor of a plan that experiences a withdrawal described in paragraph (a) shall—

(1) Determine and collect initial withdrawal liability of every employer that has completely or partially withdrawn, in accordance with sections 4201 and 4202 of ERISA;

(2) Notify each employer that is or may be liable under this section, in accordance with paragraph (d) of this section;

(3) Within 90 days after the end of the plan year in which the withdrawal occurred, determine, in accordance with paragraph (b) of this section, the liability of each withdrawing employer that is liable under this section;

(4) Notify each liable employer, in accordance with paragraph (e) of this section, of the amount of its liability under this section, demand payment of and collect that liability; and

(5) Certify to the PBGC that determinations of liability have been completed, in accordance with paragraph (g) of this section.

(d) *Notice of withdrawal.* Within 30 days after the end of a plan year in which a plan experiences a withdrawal described in paragraph (a), the plan sponsor shall notify in writing each employer that is or may be liable under this section. The notice shall specify the plan year in which substantially all employers have withdrawn, describe the consequences of such withdrawal under this section, and state that an employer obligated to make initial withdrawal liability payments shall continue to make those payments in accordance with its schedule.

(e) *Notice of liability.* Within 30 days after the determination of liability, the plan sponsor shall issue a notice of liability in writing to each liable employer. The notice shall include—

(1) The amount of the employer's liability for de minimis amounts;

(2) A schedule for payment of the liability, determined under § 4219.16(f); and

(3) A demand for payment of the liability in accordance with the schedule.

(f) *Review of liability determinations.* Determinations of liability made pursuant to this section shall be subject to plan review under section 4219(b)(2) of ERISA and to arbitration under section 4221 of ERISA, subject to the limitations contained in § 4219.16(g).

(g) *Notice to the PBGC.* No later than 30 days after the notices of liability under this section are required to be provided to liable employers, the plan sponsor shall file with the PBGC a notice. The notice shall include the items described in § 4219.17(g)(1) through (g)(3), as well as the information listed below. In addition, the PBGC may require the plan sponsor to submit any further information that the PBGC determines it needs in order to monitor compliance with this section.

(1) The plan year in which the withdrawal occurred.

(2) A description of the effect of the withdrawal, including the number of contributing employers that withdrew in the plan year in which substantially all employers withdrew, the number of employers remaining in the plan, and a description of the effect of the withdrawal on the plan's contribution base.

(3) A certification, signed by the plan sponsor or duly authorized representative, that determinations have been made and notices given in accordance with this section.

[¶ 15,687J]

§ 4219.19 **Method and date of issuance; computation of time.** The PBGC applies the rules in subpart B of part 4000 of this chapter to determine permissible methods of issuance under this subpart. The PBGC applies the rules in subpart C of part 4000 of this chapter to determine the date that an issuance under this subpart was provided. The PBGC applies the rules in subpart D of part 4000 of this chapter to compute any time period for issuances to third parties under this subpart.

[Added 10/28/2003 by 68 FR 61344]

[¶ 15,687J-1]

§ 4219.20 **Information collection.** The information collection requirements contained in §§ 4219.16, 4219.17, and 4219.18 have been

approved by the Office of Management and Budget under control number 1212-0034.

Subpart C—Overdue, Defaulted, and Overpaid Withdrawal Liability

[¶ 15,687K]

§ 4219.31 **Overdue and defaulted withdrawal liability; overpayment.** (a) *Overdue withdrawal liability payment.* Except as otherwise provided in rules adopted by the plan in accordance with § 4219.33, a withdrawal liability payment is overdue if it is not paid on the date set forth in the schedule of payments established by the plan sponsor.

(b) *Default.*

(1) Except as provided in paragraph (c)(1), "default" means—

(i) The failure of an employer to pay any overdue withdrawal liability payment within 60 days after the employer receives written notification from the plan sponsor that the payment is overdue; and

(ii) Any other event described in rules adopted by the plan which indicates a substantial likelihood that an employer will be unable to pay its withdrawal liability.

(2) In the event of a default, a plan sponsor may require immediate payment of all or a portion of the outstanding amount of an employer's withdrawal liability, plus interest. In the event that the plan sponsor accelerates only a portion of the outstanding amount of an employer's withdrawal liability, the plan sponsor shall establish a new schedule of payments for the remaining amount of the employer's withdrawal liability.

(c) *Plan review or arbitration of liability determination.* The following rules shall apply with respect to the obligation to make withdrawal liability payments during the period for plan review and arbitration and with respect to the failure to make such payments:

(1) A default as a result of failure to make any payments shall not occur until the 61st day after the last of—

(i) Expiration of the period described in section 4219(b)(2)(A) of ERISA;

(ii) If the employer requests review under section 4219(b)(2)(A) of ERISA of the plan's withdrawal liability determination or the schedule of payments established by the plan, expiration of the period described in section 4221(a)(1) of ERISA for initiation of arbitration; or

(iii) If arbitration is timely initiated either by the plan, the employer or both, issuance of the arbitrator's decision.

(2) Any amounts due before the expiration of the period described in paragraph (c)(1) shall be paid in accordance with the schedule established by the plan sponsor. If a payment is not made when due under the schedule, the payment is overdue and interest shall accrue in accordance with the rules and at the same rate set forth in § 4219.32.

(d) *Overpayments.* If the plan sponsor or an arbitrator determines that payments made in accordance with the schedule of payments established by the plan sponsor have resulted in an overpayment of withdrawal liability, the plan sponsor shall refund the overpayment, with interest, in a lump sum. The plan sponsor shall credit interest on the overpayment from the date of the overpayment to the date on which the overpayment is refunded to the employer at the same rate as the rate for overdue withdrawal liability payments, as established under § 4219.32 or by the plan pursuant to § 4219.33.

[¶ 15,687L]

§ 4219.32 **Interest on overdue, defaulted and overpaid withdrawal liability.** (a) *Interest assessed.* The plan sponsor of a multiemployer plan—

(1) Shall assess interest on overdue withdrawal liability payments from the due date, as defined in paragraph (d) of this section, until the date paid, as defined in paragraph (e); and

(2) In the event of a default, may assess interest on any accelerated portion of the outstanding withdrawal liability from the due date, as defined in paragraph (d) of this section, until the date paid, as defined in paragraph (e).

(b) *Interest rate.* Except as otherwise provided in rules adopted by the plan pursuant to §4219.33, interest under this section shall be charged or credited for each calendar quarter at an annual rate equal to the average quoted prime rate on short-term commercial loans for the fifteenth day (or next business day if the fifteenth day is not a business day) of the month preceding the beginning of each calendar quarter, as reported by the Board of Governors of the Federal Reserve System in Statistical Release H.15 ("Selected Interest Rates").

(c) *Calculation of interest.* The interest rate under paragraph (b) of this section is the nominal rate for any calendar quarter or portion thereof. The amount of interest due the plan for overdue or defaulted withdrawal liability, or due the employer for overpayment, is equal to the overdue, defaulted, or overpaid amount multiplied by:

(1) For each full calendar quarter in the period from the due date (or date of overpayment) to the date paid (or date of refund), one-fourth of the annual rate in effect for that quarter;

(2) For each full calendar month in a partial quarter in that period, one-twelfth of the annual rate in effect for that quarter; and

(3) For each day in a partial month in that period, one-three-hundred-sixtieth of the annual rate in effect for that month.

(d) *Due date.* Except as otherwise provided in rules adopted by the plan, the due date from which interest accrues shall be, for an overdue withdrawal liability payment and for an amount of withdrawal liability in default, the date of the missed payment that gave rise to the delinquency or the default.

(e) *Date paid.* Any payment of withdrawal liability shall be deemed to have been paid on the date on which it is received.

[¶ 15,687M]

§4219.33 **Plan rules concerning overdue and defaulted withdrawal liability.** Plans may adopt rules relating to overdue and defaulted withdrawal liability, provided that those rules are consistent with ERISA. These rules may include, but are not limited to, rules for determining the rate of interest to be charged on overdue, defaulted and overpaid withdrawal liability (provided that the rate reflects prevailing market rates for comparable obligations); rules providing reasonable grace periods during which late payments may be made without interest; additional definitions of default which indicate a substantial likelihood that an employer will be unable to pay its withdrawal liability; and rules pertaining to acceleration of the outstanding balance on default. Plan rules adopted under this section shall be reasonable. Plan rules shall operate and be applied uniformly with respect to each employer, except that the rules may take into account the creditworthiness of an employer. Rules which take into account the creditworthiness of an employer shall state with particularity the categories of creditworthiness the plan will use, the specific differences in treatment accorded employers in different categories, and the standards and procedures for assigning an employer to a category.

[¶ 15,688]
APPROVAL OF AMENDMENTS

Act Sec. 4220.(a) AMENDMENT OF COVERED MULTIEMPLOYER PLAN; PROCEDURES APPLICABLE.—Except as provided in subsection (b), if an amendment to a multiemployer plan authorized by any preceding section of this part is adopted more than 36 months after the effective date of this section, the amendment shall be effective only if the corporation approves the amendment, or, within 90 days after the corporation receives notice and a copy of the amendment from the plan sponsor, fails to disapprove the amendment.

Act Sec. 4220. (b) AMENDMENT RESPECTING METHODS FOR COMPUTING WITHDRAWAL LIABILITY.—An amendment permitted by section 4211(c)(5) may be adopted only in accordance with that section.

Act Sec. 4220. (c) CRITERIA FOR DISAPPROVAL BY CORPORATION.—The corporation shall disapprove an amendment referred to in subsection (a) or (b) of this section only if the corporation determines that the amendment creates an unreasonable risk of loss to plan participants and beneficiaries or to the corporation.

Amendment

P.L. 96-364, §104(2):

Added Sec. 4220, effective September 26, 1980 under ERISA Sec. 4402.

Regulations

The following regulations were adopted by the Pension Benefit Guaranty Corporation on July 1, 1996 (61 FR 34002). Prior to July 1, 1996, PBGC regulations were under Chapter XXVI of Title 29 of the Code of Federal Regulations. Effective July 1, 1996, PBGC regulations were moved to Chapter XL, and were renumbered and reorganized. Reg. §4220.3 was amended October 28, 2003 (68 FR 61344).

[¶ 15,688A]

§4220.1 **Purpose and scope.** (a) *General.* This part establishes procedures under which a plan sponsor shall request the PBGC to approve a plan amendment under section 4220 of ERISA. This part applies to all multiemployer plans covered by title IV of ERISA that adopt amendments pursuant to the authorization of sections 4201-4219 of ERISA (except for amendments adopted pursuant to section 4211(c)(5)). (The covered amendments are set forth in paragraph (b) of this section.) The subsequent modification of a plan amendment adopted by authorization of those sections is also covered by this part. This part does not, however, cover a plan amendment that merely repeals a previously adopted amendment, returning the plan to the statutorily prescribed rule.

(b) *Covered amendments.* Amendments made pursuant to the following sections of ERISA are covered by this part:

(1) Section 4203(b)(1)(B)(ii).

(2) Section 4203(c)(4).

(3) Section 4205(c)(1).

(4) Section 4205(d).

(5) Section 4209(b).

(6) Section 4210(b)(2).

(7) Section 4211(c)(1).

(8) Section 4211(c)(4)(D).

(9) Section 4211(d)(1).

(10) Section 4211(d)(2).

(11) Section 4219(c)(1)(C)(ii)(I).

(12) Section 4219(c)(1)(C)(iii).

(c) *Exception.* Submission of a request for approval under this part is not required for a plan amendment for which the PBGC has published a notice in the Federal Register granting class approval.

[¶ 15,688B]

§4220.2 **Definitions.** The following terms are defined in §4001.2 of this chapter: *employer, ERISA, IRS, multiemployer plan, PBGC, plan,* and *plan sponsor.*

[¶ 15,688C]

§4220.3 **Requests for PBGC approval.** (a) *Filing of request.* (1) *In general.* A request for approval of an amendment filed with the PBGC in accordance with this section shall constitute notice to the PBGC for purposes of the 90-day period specified in section 4220 of ERISA. A request is treated as filed on the date on which a request containing all information required by paragraph (d) of this section is received by the PBGC. Subpart C of part 4000 of this chapter provides rules for determining when the PBGC receives a submission.

(2) *Method of filing.* The PBGC applies the rules in subpart A of part 4000 of this chapter to determine permissible methods of filing with the PBGC under this part.

[Amended 10/28/2003 by 68 FR 61344]

Reg. §4220.3(a)(2)　**¶15,688C**

(b) *Who may request.* The plan sponsor, or a duly authorized representative acting on behalf of a plan sponsor, shall sign and submit the request.

(c) *Where to file.* See Sec. 4000.4 of this chapter for information on where to file.

[Amended 10/28/2003 by 68 FR 61344]

(d) *Information.* Each request filed shall contain the following information:

(1) The name of the plan for which the amendment is being submitted, and the name, address and the telephone number of the plan sponsor or its duly authorized representative.

(2) The nine-digit Employer Identification Number (EIN) assigned by the IRS to the plan sponsor and the three-digit Plan Identification Number (PIN) assigned by the plan sponsor to the plan, and, if different, the EIN or PIN last filed with PBGC. If no EIN or PIN has been assigned, that fact must be indicated.

(3) A copy of the amendment as adopted, including its proposed effective date.

(4) A copy of the most recent actuarial valuation of the plan.

(5) A statement containing a certification that notice of the adoption of the amendment has been given to all employers who have an obligation to contribute under the plan and to all employee organizations representing employees covered by the plan.

(6) Any other information that the plan sponsor believes to be pertinent to its request.

(e) *Supplemental information.* The PBGC may require a plan sponsor to submit any other information that the PBGC determines to be necessary to review a request under this part. The PBGC may suspend the running of the 90-day period pursuant to § 4220.4(c), pending the submission of the supplemental information.

(f) *Computation of time.* The PBGC applies the rules in subpart D of part 4000 of this chapter to compute any time period under this part.

[Amended 10/28/2003 by 68 FR 61344]

(Approved by the Office of Management and Budget under control number 1212-0031)

[¶ 15,688D]

§ 4220.4 **PBGC action on requests.** (a) *General.* Upon receipt of a complete request, the PBGC shall notify the plan sponsor in writing of the date of commencement of the 90-day period specified in section 4220 of ERISA. Except as provided in paragraph (c) of this section, the PBGC shall approve or disapprove a plan amendment submitted to it under this part within 90 days after receipt of a complete request for approval. If the PBGC fails to act within the 90-day period, or within that period notifies the plan sponsor that it will not disapprove the amendment, the amendment may be made effective without the approval of the PBGC.

(b) *Decision on request.* The PBGC's decision on a request for approval shall be in writing. If the PBGC disapproves the plan amendment, the decision shall state the reasons for the disapproval. An approval by the PBGC constitutes its finding only with respect to the issue of risk as set forth in section 4220(c) of ERISA, and not with respect to whether the amendment is otherwise properly adopted in accordance with the terms of ERISA and the plan in question.

(c) *Suspension of the 90-day period.* The PBGC may suspend the running of the 90-day period referred to in paragraph (a) of this section if it determines that additional information is required under § 4220.3(e). When it does so, PBGC's request for additional information will advise the plan sponsor that the running of 90-day period has been suspended. The 90-day period will resume running on the date on which the additional information is received by the PBGC, and the PBGC will notify the plan sponsor of that date upon receipt of the information.

[¶ 15,689]
RESOLUTION OF DISPUTES

Act Sec. 4221.(a)(1) ARBITRATION PROCEEDINGS; MATTERS SUBJECT TO ARBITRATION, PROCEDURES APPLICABLE, ETC.—. Any dispute between an employer and the plan sponsor of a multiemployer plan concerning a determination made under sections 4201 through 4219 shall be resolved through arbitration. Either party may initiate the arbitration proceeding within a 60-day period after the earlier of—

(A) the date of notification to the employer under section 4219(b)(2)(B), or

(B) 120 days after the date of the employer's request under section 4219(b)(2)(A). The parties may jointly initiate arbitration within the 180-day period after the date of the plan sponsor's demand under section 4219(b)(1).

(2) An arbitration proceeding under this section shall be conducted in accordance with fair and equitable procedures to be promulgated by the corporation. The plan sponsor may purchase insurance to cover potential liability of the arbitrator. If the parties have not provided for the costs of the arbitration, including arbitrator's fees, by agreement, the arbitrator shall assess such fees. The arbitrator may also award reasonable attorney's fees.

(3)(A) For purposes of any proceeding under this section, any determination made by a plan sponsor under sections 4201 through 4219 and section 4225 is presumed correct unless the party contesting the determination shows by a preponderance of the evidence that the determination was unreasonable or clearly erroneous.

(B) In the case of the determination of a plan's unfunded vested benefits for a plan year, the determination is presumed correct unless a party contesting the determination shows by a preponderance of evidence that—

(i) the actuarial assumptions and methods used in the determination were, in the aggregate, unreasonable (taking into account the experience of the plan and reasonable expectations), or

(ii) the plan's actuary made a significant error in applying the actuarial assumptions or methods.

Act Sec. 4221.(b)(1) ALTERNATIVE COLLECTION PROCEEDINGS; CIVIL ACTION SUBSEQUENT TO ARBITRATION AWARD; CONDUCT OF ARBITRATION PROCEEDINGS.—. If no arbitration proceeding has been initiated pursuant to subsection (a), the amounts demanded by the plan sponsor under section 4219(b)(1) shall be due and owing on the schedule set forth by the plan sponsor. The plan sponsor may bring an action in a State or Federal court of competent jurisdiction for collection.

(2) Upon completion of the arbitration proceedings in favor of one of the parties, any party thereto may bring an action, no later than 30 days after the issuance of an arbitrator's award, in an appropriate United States district court in accordance with section 4301 to enforce, vacate, or modify the arbitrator's award.

(3) Any arbitration proceedings under this section shall, to the extent consistent with this title, be conducted in the same manner, subject to the same limitations, carried out with the same powers (including subpoena power), and enforced in United States courts as an arbitration proceeding carried out under title 9, United States Code.

Act Sec. 4221. (c) PRESUMPTION RESPECTING FINDING OF FACT BY ARBITRATOR.—In any proceeding under subsection (b), there shall be a presumption, rebuttable only by a clear preponderance of the evidence, that the findings of fact made by the arbitrator were correct.

Act Sec. 4221. (d) PAYMENTS BY EMPLOYER PRIOR AND SUBSEQUENT TO DETERMINATION BY ARBITRATOR; ADJUSTMENTS; FAILURE OF EMPLOYER TO MAKE PAYMENT.— Payments shall be made by an employer in accordance with the determinations made under this part until the arbitrator issues a final decision with respect to the determination submitted for arbitration, with any necessary adjustments in subsequent payments for overpayments or underpayments arising out of the decision of the arbitrator with respect to the determination. If the employer fails to make timely payment in accordance with such final decision, the employer shall be treated as being delinquent in the making of a contribution required under the plan (within the meaning of section 515).

Act Sec. 4221. (e) PROCEDURES APPLICABLE TO CERTAIN DISPUTES.—

(1) IN GENERAL. If—

(A) a plan sponsor of a plan determines that—

(i) a complete or partial withdrawal of an employer has occurred, or

(ii) an employer is liable for withdrawal liability payments with respect to the complete or partial withdrawal of an employer from the plan,

(B) such determination is based in whole or in part on a finding by the plan sponsor under section 4212(c) that a principal purpose of a transaction that occurred before January 1, 1999, was to evade or avoid withdrawal liability under this subtitle, and

(C) such transaction occurred at least 5 years before the date of the complete or partial withdrawal, then the special rules under paragraph (2) shall be used in applying subsections (a) and (d) of this section and section 4219(c) to the employer.

(2) SPECIAL RULES.—

(A) DETERMINATION. Notwithstanding subsection (a)(3)—

(i) a determination by the plan sponsor under paragraph (1)(B) shall not be presumed to be correct, and

(ii) the plan sponsor shall have the burden to establish, by a preponderance of the evidence, the elements of the claim under section 4212(c) that a principal purpose of the transaction was to evade or avoid withdrawal liability under this subtitle.

Nothing in this subparagraph shall affect the burden of establishing any other element of a claim for withdrawal liability under this subtitle.

(B) PROCEDURE. Notwithstanding subsection (d) and section 4219(c), if an employer contests the plan sponsor's determination under paragraph (1) through an arbitration proceeding pursuant to subsection (a), or through a claim brought in a court of competent jurisdiction, the employer shall not be obligated to make any withdrawal liability payments until a final decision in the arbitration proceeding, or in court, upholds the plan sponsor's determination.

Act Sec. 4221. (f) PROCEDURES APPLICABLE TO CERTAIN DISPUTES.—

(1) IN GENERAL. —If—

(A) a plan sponsor of a plan determines that—

(i) a complete or partial withdrawal of an employer has occurred, or

(ii) an employer is liable for withdrawal liability payments with respect to such complete or partial withdrawal, and

(B) such determination is based in whole or in part on a finding by the plan sponsor under section 4212(c) that a principal purpose of any transaction which occurred after December 31, 1998, and at least 5 years (2 years in the case of a small employer) before the date of the complete or partial withdrawal was to evade or avoid withdrawal liability under this subtitle, then the person against which the withdrawal liability is assessed based solely on the application of section 4212(c) may elect to use the special rule under paragraph (2) in applying subsection (d) of this section and section 4219(c) to such person.

(2) SPECIAL RULE. —Notwithstanding subsection (d) and section 4219(c), if an electing person contests the plan sponsor's determination with respect to withdrawal liability payments under paragraph (1) through an arbitration proceeding pursuant to subsection (a), through an action brought in a court of competent jurisdiction for review of such an arbitration decision, or as otherwise permitted by law, the electing person shall not be obligated to make the withdrawal liability payments until a final decision in the arbitration proceeding, or in court, upholds the plan sponsor's determination, but only if the electing person—

(A) provides notice to the plan sponsor of its election to apply the special rule in this paragraph within 90 days after the plan sponsor notifies the electing person of its liability by reason of the application of section 4212(c); and

(B) if a final decision in the arbitration proceeding, or in court, of the withdrawal liability dispute has not been rendered within 12 months from the date of such notice, the electing person provides to the plan, effective as of the first day following the 12-month period, a bond issued by a corporate surety company that is an acceptable surety for purposes of section 412 of this Act, or an amount held in escrow by a bank or similar financial institution satisfactory to the plan, in an amount equal to the sum of the withdrawal liability payments that would otherwise be due under subsection (d) and section 4219(c) for the 12-month period beginning with the first anniversary of such notice. Such bond or escrow shall remain in effect until there is a final decision in the arbitration proceeding, or in court, of the withdrawal liability dispute, at which time such bond or escrow shall be paid to the plan if such final decision upholds the plan sponsor's determination.

(3) DEFINITION OF SMALL EMPLOYER. —For purposes of this subsection—

(A) IN GENERAL. —The term 'small employer' means any employer which, for the calendar year in which the transaction referred to in paragraph (1)(B) occurred and for each of the 3 preceding years, on average—

(i) employs not more than 500 employees, and

(ii) is required to make contributions to the plan for not more than 250 employees.

(B) CONTROLLED GROUP. —Any group treated as a single employer under subsection (b)(1) of section 4001, without regard to any transaction that was a basis for the plan's finding under section 4212, shall be treated as a single employer for purposes of this subparagraph.

(4) ADDITIONAL SECURITY PENDING RESOLUTION OF DISPUTE. —If a withdrawal liability dispute to which this subsection applies is not concluded by 12 months after the electing person posts the bond or escrow described in paragraph (2), the electing person shall, at the start of each succeeding 12month period, provide an additional bond or amount held in escrow equal to the sum of the withdrawal liability payments that would otherwise be payable to the plan during that period.

(5) The liability of the party furnishing a bond or escrow under this subsection shall be reduced, upon the payment of the bond or escrow to the plan, by the amount thereof.

Amendments

P.L. 110-458, § 105(b)(2):

Amended ERISA Sec. 4221 by striking subsection (e) and by redesignating subsections (f) and (g) as subsections (e) and (f), respectively.

Prior to being stricken, ERISA Sec. 4221(e) read as follows:

ERISA Sec. 4221(e)—

FURNISHING OF INFORMATION BY PLAN SPONSOR TO EMPLOYER RESPECTING COMPUTATION OF WITHDRAWAL LIABILITY OF EMPLOYER; FEES. - If any employer requests in writing that the plan sponsor make available to the employer general information necessary for the employer to compute its withdrawal liability with respect to the plan (other than information which is unique to that employer), the plan sponsor shall furnish the information to the employer without charge. If any employer requests in writing that the plan sponsor make an estimate of such employer's potential withdrawal liability with respect to the plan or to provide information unique to that employer, the plan sponsor may require the employer to pay the reasonable cost of making such estimate or providing such information.

The above amendment applies to plan years beginning after December 31, 2007.

P.L. 109-280, § 204(d)(1):

Amended ERISA Sec. 4221 by adding at the end a new paragraph (g) to read as above.

The above amendment applies to any person that receives a notification under ERISA Sec. 4219(b)(1) on or after the date of enactment of this Act with respect to a transaction that occurred after December 31, 1998.

P.L. 108-218, § 202(a):

Added subsection (f).

Act Sec. 202(b) provides:

Effective Date.—The amendments made by this section shall apply to any employer that receives a notification under section 4219(b)(1) of the Employee Retirement Income Security Act of 1974 (29 U.S.C. 1399(b)(1)) after October 31, 2003.

P.L. 96-364, § 104(2):

Added Sec. 4221, effective September 26, 1980 under ERISA Sec. 4402.

Regulations

The following regulations were adopted by the Pension Benefit Guaranty Corporation on July 1, 1996 (61 FR 34002). Prior to July 1, 1996, PBGC regulations were under Chapter XXVI of Title 29 of the Code of Federal Regulations. Effective July 1, 1996, PBGC regulations were moved to Chapter XL, and were renumbered and reorganized. Reg. §4221.4, Reg. §4221.6, Reg. §4221.12, Reg. §4221.13, and Reg. §4221.14 were amended October 28, 2003 (68 FR 61344).

[¶ 15,689A]

§4221.1 **Purpose and scope.** (a) *Purpose.* The purpose of this part is to establish procedures for the arbitration, pursuant to section 4221 of ERISA, of withdrawal liability disputes arising under sections 4201 through 4219 and 4225 of ERISA.

(b) *Scope.* This part applies to arbitration proceedings initiated pursuant to section 4221 of ERISA and this part on or after September 26, 1985. On and after the effective date, any plan rules governing arbitration procedures (other than a plan rule adopting a PBGC-approved arbitration procedure in accordance with §4221.14) are effective only to the extent that they are consistent with this part and adopted by the arbitrator in a particular proceeding.

[¶ 15,689B]

§4221.2 **Definitions.** The following terms are defined in §4001.2 of this chapter: *ERISA, IRS, multiemployer plan, PBGC, plan,* and *plan sponsor.*

In addition, for purposes of this part:

Arbitrator means an individual or panel of individuals selected according to this part to decide a dispute concerning withdrawal liability.

Employer means an individual, partnership, corporation or other entity against which a plan sponsor has made a demand for payment of withdrawal liability pursuant to section 4219(b)(1) of ERISA.

Party or parties means the employer and the plan sponsor involved in a withdrawal liability dispute.

Withdrawal liability dispute means a dispute described in §4221.1(a) of this chapter.

[¶ 15,689C]

§4221.3 **Initiation of arbitration.** (a) *Time limits—in general.* Arbitration of a withdrawal liability dispute may be initiated within the time limits described in section 4221(a)(1) of ERISA.

(b) *Waiver or extension of time limits.* Arbitration shall be initiated in accordance with this section, notwithstanding any inconsistent provision of any agreement entered into by the parties before the date on which the employer received notice of the plan's assessment of withdrawal liability. The parties may, however, agree at any time to waive or extend the time limits for initiating arbitration.

(c) *Establishment of timeliness of initiation.* A party that unilaterally initiates arbitration is responsible for establishing that the notice of initiation of arbitration was timely received by the other party. If arbitration is initiated by agreement of the parties, the date on which the agreement to arbitrate was executed establishes whether the arbitration was timely initiated.

(d) *Contents of agreement or notice.* If the employer initiates arbitration, it shall include in the notice of initiation a statement that it disputes the plan sponsor's determination of its withdrawal liability and is initiating arbitration. A copy of the demand for withdrawal liability and any request for reconsideration, and the response thereto, shall be attached to the notice. If a party other than an employer initiates arbitration, it shall include in the notice a statement that it is initiating arbitration and a brief description of the questions on which arbitration is sought. If arbitration is initiated by agreement, the agreement shall include a brief description of the questions submitted to arbitration. In no case is compliance with formal rules of pleading required.

(e) *Effect of deficient agreement or notice.* If a party fails to object promptly in writing to deficiencies in an initiation agreement or a notice of initiation of arbitration, it waives its right to object.

[¶ 15,689D]

§4221.4 **Appointment of the arbitrator.** (a) *Appointment of and acceptance by arbitrator.* The parties shall select the arbitrator within 45 days after the arbitration is initiated, or within such other period as is mutually agreed after the initiation of arbitration, and shall mail to the designated arbitrator a notice of his or her appointment. The notice of appointment shall include a copy of the notice or agreement initiating arbitration, a statement that the arbitration is to be conducted in accordance with this part, and a request for a written acceptance by the arbitrator. The arbitrator's appointment becomes effective upon his or her written acceptance, stating his or her availability to serve and making any disclosures required by paragraph (b) of this section. If the arbitrator does not accept in writing within 15 days after the notice of appointment is mailed or delivered to him or her, he or she is deemed to have declined to act, and the parties shall select a new arbitrator in accordance with paragraph (d) of this section.

(b) *Disclosure by arbitrator and disqualification.* Upon accepting the appointment, the arbitrator shall disclose to the parties any circumstances likely to affect his or her impartiality, including any bias or any financial or personal interest in the result of the arbitration and any past or present relationship with the parties or their counsel. If any party determines that the arbitrator should be disqualified because of the information disclosed, that party shall notify all other parties and the arbitrator no later than 10 days after the arbitrator makes the disclosure required by this paragraph (but in no event later than the commencement of the hearing under §4221.6). The arbitrator shall then withdraw, and the parties shall select another arbitrator in accordance with paragraph (d) of this section.

(c) *Challenge and withdrawal.* After the arbitrator has been selected, a party may request that he or she withdraw from the proceedings at any point before a final award is rendered on the ground that he or she is unable to render an award impartially. The request for withdrawal shall be served on all other parties and the arbitrator by hand or by certified or registered mail (or by any other method that includes verification or acknowledgment of receipt and meets (if applicable) the requirements of Sec. 4000.14 of this chapter) and shall include a statement of the circumstances that, in the requesting party's view, affect the arbitrator's impartiality and a statement that the requesting party has brought these circumstances to the attention of the arbitrator and the other parties at the earliest practicable point in the proceedings. If the arbitrator determines that the circumstances adduced are likely to affect his or her impartiality and have been presented in a timely fashion, he or she shall withdraw from the proceedings and notify the parties of the reasons for his or her withdrawal. The parties shall then select a new arbitrator in accordance with paragraph (d) of this section.

[Amended 10/28/2003 by 68 FR 61344]

(d) *Filling vacancies.* If the designated arbitrator declines his or her appointment or, after accepting his or her appointment, is disqualified, resigns, dies, withdraws, or is unable to perform his or her duties at any time before a final award is rendered, the parties shall select another arbitrator to fill the vacancy. The selection shall be made, in accordance with the procedure used in the initial selection, within 20 days after the parties receive notice of the vacancy. The matter shall then be reheard by the newly chosen arbitrator, who may, in his or her discretion, rely on all or any portion of the record already established.

(e) *Failure to select arbitrator.* If the parties fail to select an arbitrator within the time prescribed by this section, either party or both may seek the designation and appointment of an arbitrator in a United States district court pursuant to the provisions of title 9 of the United States Code.

[¶ 15,689E]

§4221.5 **Powers and duties of the arbitrator.** (a) *Arbitration hearing.* Except as otherwise provided in this part, the arbitrator shall conduct the arbitration hearing under §4221.6 in the same manner, and shall possess the same powers, as an arbitrator conducting a proceeding under title 9 of the United States Code.

(1) *Application of the law.* In reaching his or her decision, the arbitrator shall follow applicable law, as embodied in statutes, regulations, court decisions, interpretations of the agencies charged with the enforcement of ERISA, and other pertinent authorities.

(2) *Prehearing discovery.* The arbitrator may allow any party to conduct prehearing discovery by interrogatories, depositions, requests for the production of documents, or other means, upon a showing that the discovery sought is likely to lead to the production of relevant evidence and will not be disproportionately burdensome to the other parties. The arbitrator may impose appropriate sanctions if he or she determines that a party has failed to respond to discovery in good faith or has conducted discovery proceedings in bad faith or for the purpose of harassment. The arbitrator may, at the request of any party or on his or her own motion, require parties to give advance notice of expert or other witnesses that they intend to introduce.

(3) *Admissibility of evidence.* The arbitrator determines the relevance and materiality of the evidence offered during the course of the hearing and is the judge of the admissibility of evidence offered. Conformity to legal rules of evidence is not necessary. To the extent reasonably practicable, all evidence shall be taken in the presence of the arbitrator and the parties. The arbitrator may, however, consider affidavits, transcripts of depositions, and similar documents.

(4) *Production of documents or other evidence.* The arbitrator may subpoena witnesses or documents upon his or her own initiative or upon request by any party after determining that the evidence is likely to be relevant to the dispute.

(b) *Prehearing conference.* If it appears that a prehearing conference will expedite the proceedings, the arbitrator may, at any time before the commencement of the arbitration hearing under §4221.6, direct the parties to appear at a conference to consider settlement of the case, clarification of issues and stipulation of facts not in dispute, admission of documents to avoid unnecessary proof, limitations on the number of expert or other witnesses, and any other matters that could expedite the disposition of the proceedings.

(c) *Proceeding without hearing.* The arbitrator may render an award without a hearing if the parties agree and file with the arbitrator such evidence as the arbitrator deems necessary to enable him or her to render an award under §4221.8.

[¶ 15,689F]

§4221.6 **Hearing.** (a) *Time and place of hearing established.* Unless the parties agree to proceed without a hearing as provided in §4221.5(c), the parties and the arbitrator shall, no later than 15 days after the written acceptance by the arbitrator is mailed to the parties, establish a date and place for the hearing. If agreement is not reached within the 15-day period, the arbitrator shall, within 10 additional days, choose a location and set a hearing date. The date set for the hearing may be no later than 50 days after the mailing date of the arbitrator's written acceptance.

(b) *Notice.* After the time and place for the hearing have been established, the arbitrator shall serve a written notice of the hearing on the parties by hand, by certified or registered mail, or by any other method that includes verification or acknowledgment of receipt and meets (if applicable) the requirements of Sec. 4000.14 of this chapter.

[Amended 10/28/2003 by 68 FR 61344]

(c) *Appearances.* The parties may appear in person or by counsel or other representatives. Any party that, after being duly notified and without good cause shown, fails to appear in person or by representative at a hearing or conference, or fails to file documents in a timely manner, is deemed to have waived all rights with respect thereto and is subject to whatever orders or determinations the arbitrator may make.

(d) *Record and transcript of hearing.* Upon the request of either party, the arbitrator shall arrange for a record of the arbitration hearing to be made by stenographic means or by tape recording. The cost of making the record and the costs of transcription and copying are costs of the arbitration proceedings payable as provided in §4221.10(b) except that, if only one party requests that a transcript of the record be made, that party shall pay the cost of the transcript.

(e) *Order of hearing.* The arbitrator shall conduct the hearing in accordance with the following rules:

(1) *Opening.* The arbitrator shall open the hearing and place in the record the notice of initiation of arbitration or the initiation agreement. The arbitrator may ask for statements clarifying the issues involved.

(2) *Presentation of claim and response.* The arbitrator shall establish the procedure for presentation of claim and response in such a manner as to afford full and equal opportunity to all parties for the presentation of their cases.

(3) *Witnesses.* All witnesses shall testify under oath or affirmation and are subject to cross-examination by opposing parties. If testimony of an expert witness is offered by a party without prior notice to the other party, the arbitrator shall grant the other party a reasonable time to prepare for cross-examination and to produce expert witnesses on its own behalf. The arbitrator may on his or her own initiative call expert witnesses on any issue raised in the arbitration. The cost of any expert called by the arbitrator is a cost of the proceedings payable as provided in §4221.10(b).

(f) *Continuance of hearing.* The arbitrator may, for good cause shown, grant a continuance for a reasonable period. When granting a continuance, the arbitrator shall set a date for resumption of the hearing.

(g) *Filing of briefs.* Each party may file a written statement of facts and argument supporting the party's position. The parties' briefs are due no later than 30 days after the close of the hearing. Within 15 days thereafter, each party may file a reply brief concerning matters contained in the opposing brief. The arbitrator may establish a briefing schedule and may reduce or extend these time limits. Each party shall deliver copies of all of its briefs to the arbitrator and to all opposing parties.

[¶ 15,689G]

§4221.7 **Reopening of proceedings.** (a) *Grounds for reopening.* At any time before a final award is rendered, the proceedings may be reopened, on the motion of the arbitrator or at the request of any party, for the purpose of taking further evidence or rehearing or rearguing any matter, if the arbitrator determines that—

(1) The reopening is likely to result in new information that will have a material effect on the outcome of the arbitration;

(2) Good cause exists for the failure of the party that requested reopening to present such information at the hearing; and

(3) The delay caused by the reopening will not be unfairly injurious to any party.

(b) *Comments on and notice of reopening.* The arbitrator shall allow all affected parties the opportunity to comment on any motion or request to reopen the proceedings. If he or she determines that the proceedings should be reopened, he or she shall give all parties written notice of the reasons for reopening and of the schedule of the reopened proceedings.

[¶ 15,689H]

§4221.8 **Award.** (a) *Form.* The arbitrator shall render a written award that—

(1) States the basis for the award, including such findings of fact and conclusions of law (which need not be explicitly designated as such) as are necessary to resolve the dispute;

(2) Adjusts (or provides a method for adjusting) the amount or schedule of payments to be made after the award to reflect overpayments or underpayments made before the award was rendered or requires the plan sponsor to refund overpayments in accordance with §4219.31(d); and

(3) Provides for an allocation of costs in accordance with §4221.10.

(b) *Time of award.* Except as provided in paragraphs (c), (d), and (e) of this section, the arbitrator shall render the award no later than 30 days after the proceedings close. The award is rendered when filed or served on the parties as provided in §4221.13. The award is final when the period for seeking modification or reconsideration in accordance with § 4221.9(a) has expired or the arbitrator has rendered a revised award in accordance with § 4221.9(c).

(c) *Reopened proceedings.* If the proceedings are reopened in accordance with § 4221.7 after the close of the hearing, the arbitrator shall render the award no later than 30 days after the date on which the reopened proceedings are closed.

(d) *Absence of hearing.* If the parties have chosen to proceed without a hearing, the arbitrator shall render the award no later than 30 days after the date on which final statements and proofs are filed with him or her.

(e) *Agreement for extension of time.* Notwithstanding paragraphs (b), (c), and (d), the parties may agree to an extension of time for the arbitrator's award in light of the particular facts and circumstances of their dispute.

(f) *Close of proceedings.* For purposes of paragraphs (b) and (c) of this section, the proceedings are closed on the date on which the last brief or reply brief is due or, if no briefs are to be filed, on the date on which the hearing or rehearing closes.

(g) *Publication of award.* After a final award has been rendered, the plan sponsor shall make copies available upon request to the PBGC and to all companies that contribute to the plan. The plan sponsor may impose reasonable charges for copying and postage.

[¶ 15,689I]

§ 4221.9 **Reconsideration of award.** (a) *Motion for reconsideration and objections.* A party may seek modification or reconsideration of the arbitrator's award by filing a written motion with the arbitrator and all opposing parties within 20 days after the award is rendered. Opposing parties may file objections to modification or reconsideration within 10 days after the motion is filed. The filing of a written motion for modification or reconsideration suspends the 30-day period under section 4221(b)(2) of ERISA for requesting court review of the award. The 30-day statutory period again begins to run when the arbitrator denies the motion pursuant to paragraph (c) of this section or renders a revised award.

(b) *Grounds for modification or reconsideration.* The arbitrator may grant a motion for modification or reconsideration of the award only if—

(1) There is a numerical error or a mistake in the description of any person, thing, or property referred to in the award; or

(2) The arbitrator has rendered an award upon a matter not submitted to the arbitrator and the matter affects the merits of the decision; or

(3) The award is imperfect in a matter of form not affecting the merits of the dispute.

(c) *Decision of arbitrator.* The arbitrator shall grant or deny the motion for modification or reconsideration, and may render an opinion to support his or her decision within 20 days after the motion is filed with the arbitrator, or within 30 days after the motion is filed if an objection is also filed.

[¶ 15,689J]

§ 4221.10 **Costs.** The costs of arbitration under this part shall be borne by the parties as follows:

(a) *Witnesses.* Each party to the dispute shall bear the costs of its own witnesses.

(b) *Other costs of arbitration.* Except as provided in § 4221.6(d) with respect to a transcript of the hearing, the parties shall bear the other costs of the arbitration proceedings equally unless the arbitrator determines otherwise. The parties may, however, agree to a different allocation of costs if their agreement is entered into after the employer has received notice of the plan's assessment of withdrawal liability.

(c) *Attorneys' fees.* The arbitrator may require a party that initiates or contests an arbitration in bad faith or engages in dilatory, harassing, or other improper conduct during the course of the arbitration to pay reasonable attorneys' fees of other parties.

[¶ 15,689K]

§ 4221.11 **Waiver of rules.** Any party that fails to object in writing in a timely manner to any deviation from any provision of this part is deemed to have waived the right to interpose that objection thereafter.

[¶ 15,689L]

§ 4221.12 **Calculation of periods of time.** The PBGC applies the rules in subpart D of part 4000 of this chapter to compute any time period under this part.

[Amended 10/28/2003 by 68 FR 61344]

[¶ 15,689M]

§ 4221.13 **Filing and issuance rules.** (a) *Method and date of filing.* The PBGC applies the rules in subpart A of part 4000 of this chapter to determine permissible methods of filing with the PBGC under this part. The PBGC applies the rules in subpart C of part 4000 of this chapter to determine the date that a submission under this part was filed with the PBGC.

(b) *Where to file.* See Sec. 4000.4 of this chapter for information on where to file.

(c) *Method and date of issuance.* The PBGC applies the rules in subpart B of part 4000 of this chapter to determine permissible methods of issuance under this part. The PBGC applies the rules in subpart C of part 4000 of this chapter to determine the date that an issuance under this part was provided.

[Amended 10/28/2003 by 68 FR 61344]

[¶ 15,689N]

§ 4221.14 **PBGC-approved arbitration procedures.** (a) *Use of PBGC-approved arbitration procedures.* In lieu of the procedures prescribed by this part, an arbitration may be conducted in accordance with an alternative arbitration procedure approved by the PBGC in accordance with paragraph (c) of this section. A plan may by plan amendment require the use of a PBGC-approved procedure for all arbitrations of withdrawal liability disputes, or the parties may agree to the use of a PBGC-approved procedure in a particular case.

(b) *Scope of alternative procedures.* If an arbitration is conducted in accordance with a PBGC-approved arbitration procedure, the alternative procedure shall govern all aspects of the arbitration, with the following exceptions:

(1) The time limits for the initiation of arbitration may not differ from those provided for by § 4221.3.

(2) The arbitrator shall be selected after the initiation of the arbitration.

(3) The arbitrator shall give the parties opportunity for prehearing discovery substantially equivalent to that provided by § 4221.5(a)(2).

(4) The award shall be made available to the public to at least the extent provided by § 4221.8(g).

(5) The costs of arbitration shall be allocated in accordance with § 4221.10.

(c) *Procedure for approval of alternative procedures.* The PBGC may approve arbitration procedures on its own initiative by publishing an appropriate notice in the Federal Register. The sponsor of an arbitration procedure may request PBGC approval of its procedures by submitting an application to the PBGC. The application shall include:

(1) A copy of the procedures for which approval is sought;

(2) A description of the history, structure and membership of the organization that sponsors the procedures; and

(3) A discussion of the reasons why, in the sponsoring organization's opinion, the procedures satisfy the criteria for approval set forth in this section.

[Amended 10/28/2003 by 68 FR 61344]

(d) *Criteria for approval of alternative procedures.* The PBGC shall approve an application if it determines that the proposed procedures will be substantially fair to all parties involved in the arbitration of a withdrawal liability dispute and that the sponsoring organization is neutral and able to carry out its role under the procedures. The PBGC may request comments on the application by publishing an appropriate notice in the Federal Register. Notice of the PBGC's decision on the application shall be published in the Federal Register. Unless the notice of approval specifies otherwise, approval will remain effective until revoked by the PBGC through a Federal Register notice.

[¶ 15,690]
REIMBURSEMENTS FOR UNCOLLECTIBLE WITHDRAWAL LIABILITY

Act Sec. 4222.(a) REQUIRED SUPPLEMENTAL PROGRAM TO REIMBURSE FOR PAYMENTS DUE FROM EMPLOYERS UNCOLLECTIBLE AS A RESULT OF EMPLOYER INVOLVEMENT IN BANKRUPTCY CASE OR PROCEEDINGS; PROGRAM PARTICIPATION, PREMIUMS, ETC.—By May 1, 1982, the corporation shall establish by regulation a supplemental program to reimburse multiemployer plans for withdrawal liability payments which are due from employers and which are determined to be uncollectible for reasons arising out of cases or proceedings involving the employers under title 11, United States Code, or similar cases or proceedings. Participation in the supplemental program shall be on a voluntary basis, and a plan which elects coverage under the program shall pay premiums to the corporation in accordance with a premium schedule which shall be prescribed from time to time by the corporation. The premium schedule shall contain such rates and bases for the application of such rates as the corporation considers to be appropriate.

Act Sec. 4222. (b) DISCRETIONARY SUPPLEMENTAL PROGRAM TO REIMBURSE FOR PAYMENTS DUE FROM EMPLOYERS UNCOLLECTIBLE FOR OTHER APPROPRIATE REASONS.— The corporation may provide under the program for reimbursement of amounts of withdrawal liability determined to be uncollectible for any other reasons the corporation considers appropriate.

Act Sec. 4222. (c) PAYMENT OF COST OF PROGRAM.—The cost of the program (including such administrative and legal costs as the corporation considers appropriate) may be paid only out of premiums collected under such program.

Act Sec. 4222. (d) TERMS AND CONDITIONS, LIMITATIONS, ETC., OF SUPPLEMENTAL PROGRAM.—The supplemental program may be offered to eligible plans on such terms and conditions, and with such limitations with respect to the payment of reimbursements (including the exclusion of de minimis amounts of uncollectible employer liability, and the reduction or elimination of reimbursements which cannot be paid from collected premiums) and such restrictions on withdrawal from the program, as the corporation considers necessary and appropriate.

Act Sec. 4222. (e) ARRANGEMENTS BY CORPORATION WITH PRIVATE INSURERS FOR IMPLEMENTATION OF PROGRAM; ELECTION OF COVERAGE BY PARTICIPATING PLANS WITH PRIVATE INSURERS.—The corporation may enter into arrangements with private insurers to carry out in whole or in part the program authorized by this section and may require plans which elect coverage under the program to elect coverage by those private insurers.

Amendment:

P.L. 96-364, §104(2):

Added Sec. 4222, effective September 26, 1980 under ERISA Sec. 4402.

[¶ 15,691]
WITHDRAWAL LIABILITY PAYMENT FUND

Act Sec. 4223.(a) ESTABLISHMENT OF OR PARTICIPATION IN FUND BY PLAN SPONSORS.—The plan sponsors of multiemployer plans may establish or participate in a withdrawal liability payment fund.

Act Sec. 4223. (b) DEFINITION.—For purposes of this section, the term "withdrawal liability payment fund", and the term "fund", mean a trust which—

(1) is established and maintained under section 501(c)(22) of the Internal Revenue Code of 1986,

(2) maintains agreements which cover a substantial portion of the participants who are in multiemployer plans which (under the rules of the trust instrument) are eligible to participate in the fund,

(3) is funded by amounts paid by the plans which participate in the fund, and

(4) is administered by a Board of Trustees, and in the administration of the fund there is equal representation of—

(A) trustees representing employers who are obligated to contribute to the plans participating in the fund, and

(B) trustees representing employees who are participants in plans which participate in the fund.

Act Sec. 4223.(c)(1) PAYMENTS TO PLAN; AMOUNT, CRITERIA, ETC.—If an employer withdraws from a plan which participates in a withdrawal liability payment fund, then, to the extent provided in the trust, the fund shall pay to that plan—

(A) the employer's unattributable liability,

(B) the employer's withdrawal liability payments which would have been due but for section 4208, 4209, 4219, or 4225,

(C) the employer's withdrawal liability payments to the extent they are uncollectible.

(2) The fund may provide for the payment of the employer's attributable liability if the fund—

(A) provides for the payment of both the attributable and the unattributable liability of the employer in a single payment, and

(B) is subrogated to all rights of the plan against the employer.

(3) For purposes of this section, the term—

(A) "attributable liability" means the excess, if any, determined under the provisions of a plan not inconsistent with regulations of the corporation, of—

(i) the value of vested benefits accrued as a result of service with the employer, over

(ii) the value of plan assets attributed to the employer, and

(B) "unattributable liability" means the excess of withdrawal liability over attributable liability.

Such terms may be further defined, and the manner in which they shall be applied may be prescribed, by the corporation by regulation.

(4)(A) The trust of a fund shall be maintained for the exclusive purpose of paying—

(i) any amount described in paragraph (1) and paragraph (2), and

(ii) reasonable and necessary administrative expenses in connection with the establishment and operation of the trust and the processing of claims against the fund.

(B) The amounts paid by a plan to a fund shall be deemed a reasonable expense of administering the plan under sections 403(c)(1) and 404(a)(1)(A)(ii), and the payments made by a fund to a participating plan shall be deemed services necessary for the operation of the plan within the meaning of section 408(b)(2) or within the meaning of section 4975(d)(2) of the Internal Revenue Code of 1986.

Act Sec. 4223.(d)(1) APPLICATION OF PAYMENTS BY PLAN.—For purposes of this part—

(A) only amounts paid by the fund to a plan under subsection (c)(1)(A) shall be credited to withdrawal liability otherwise payable by the employer, unless the plan otherwise provides, and

(B) any amounts paid by the fund under subsection (c) to a plan shall be treated by the plan as a payment of withdrawal liability to such plan.

(2) For purposes of applying provisions relating to the funding stand ard accounts (and minimum contribution requirements), amounts paid from the plan to the fund shall be applied to reduce the amount treated as contributed to the plan.

Act Sec. 4223. (e) SUBROGATION OF FUND TO RIGHTS OF PLAN.—The fund shall be subrogated to the rights of the plan against the employer that has withdrawn from the plan for amounts paid by a fund to a plan under—

(1) subsection (c)(1)(A), to the extent not credited under subsection (d)(1)(A), and

(2) subsection (c)(1)(C).

Act Sec. 4223. (f) Discharge of rights of fiduciary of fund; standards applicable, etc.—Notwithstanding any other provision of this Act, a fiduciary of the fund shall discharge the fiduciary's duties with respect to the fund in accordance with the standards for fiduciaries prescribed by this Act (to the extent not inconsistent with the purposes of this section), and in accordance with the documents and instruments governing the fund insofar as such documents and instruments are consistent with the provisions of this Act (to the extent not inconsistent with the purposes of this section). The provisions of the preceding sentence shall supersede any and all State laws relating to fiduciaries insofar as they may now or hereafter relate to a fund to which this section applies.

Act Sec. 4223. (g) Prohibition on payments from fund to plan where certain labor negotiations involve employer withdrawn or partially withdrawn from plan and continuity of labor organization representing employees continues.—No payments shall be made from a fund to a plan on the occasion of a withdrawal or partial withdrawal of an employer from such plan if the employees representing the withdrawn contribution base units continue, after such withdrawal, to be represented under section 9 of the National Labor Relations Act (or other applicable labor laws) in negotiations with such employer by the labor organization which represented such employees immediately preceding such withdrawal.

Act Sec. 4223. (h) Purchase of insurance by employer—Nothing in this section shall be construed to prohibit the purchase of insurance by an employer from any other person, to limit the circumstances under which such insurance would be payable, or to limit in any way the terms and conditions of such insurance.

Act Sec. 4223. (i) Promulgation of regulations for establishment and maintenence of fund.—The corporation may provide by regulation rules not inconsistent with this section governing the establishment and maintenance of funds, but only to the extent necessary to carry out the purposes of this part (other than section 4222).

Amendments:

P.L. 101-239, § 7891(a)(1):

Titles I, III, and IV of ERISA (other than sections 3(37)(E), 301(a)(7), and 308, the last sentence of section 408(d), and sections 414(c), 4001(a)(3)(ii), and 4303) are each amended by striking "Internal Revenue Code of 1954" each place it appears and inserting "Internal Revenue Code of 1986", effective October 22, 1986.

P.L. 96-364, § 104(2):

Added Sec. 4223, effective September 26, 1980 under ERISA Sec. 4402.

[¶ 15,692]
ALTERNATIVE METHOD OF WITHDRAWAL LIABILITY PAYMENTS

Act Sec. 4224. A multiemployer plan may adopt rules providing for other terms and conditions for the satisfaction of an employer's withdrawal liability if such rules are consistent with this Act and with such regulations as may be prescribed by the corporation.

Amendment

P.L. 96-364, § 104(2):

Added Sec. 4224, effective September 26, 1980 under ERISA Sec. 4402.

[¶ 15,696]
LIMITATION ON WITHDRAWAL LIABILITY

Act Sec. 4225. (a)(1) Unfunded vested benefits allocable to employer in bona fide sale of assets of employer in arms-length transaction to unrelated party; maximum amount; determinative factors.—In the case of bona fide sale of all or substantially all of the employer's assets in an arm's-length transaction to an unrelated party (within the meaning of section 4204(d)), the unfunded vested benefits allocable to an employer (after the application of all sections of this part having a lower number designation than this section), other than an employer undergoing reorganization under title 11, United States Code, or similar provisions of State law, shall not exceed the greater of—

(A) a portion (determined under paragraph (2)) of the liquidation or dissolution value of the employer (determined after the sale or exchange of such assets), or

(B) in the case of a plan using the attributable method of allocating withdrawal liability, the unfunded vested benefits attributable to employees of the employer.

(2) For purposes of paragraph (1), the portion shall be determined in accordance with the following table:

If the liquidation or distribution value of the employer after the sale or exchange is—	The portion is—
Not more than $5,000,000	30 percent of the amount.
More than $5,000,000, but not more than $10,000,000,	$1,500,000, plus 35 percent of the amount in excess of $5,000,000.
More than $10,000,000, but not more than $15,000,000,	$3,250,000, plus 40 percent of the amount in excess of $10,000,000.
More than $15,000,000, but not more than $17,500,000,	$5,250,000, plus 45 percent of the amount in excess of $15,000,000.
More than $17,500,000, but not more than $20,000,000,	$6,375,000, plus 50 percent of the amount in excess of $17,500,000.
More than $20,000,000, but not more than $22,500,000,	$7,625,000, plus 60 percent of the amount in excess of $20,000,000.
More than $22,500,000, but not more than $25,000,000,	$9,125,000, plus 70 percent of the amount in excess of $22,500,000.
More than $25,000,000.	$10,875,000, plus 80 percent of the amount in excess of $25,000,000.

Act Sec. 4225. (b) Unfunded vested benefits allocable to insolvent employer undergoing liquidation or dissolution; maximum amount; determinative factors.—In the case of an insolvent employer undergoing liquidation or dissolution, the unfunded vested benefits allocable to that employer shall not exceed an amount equal to the sum of—

(1) 50 percent of the unfunded vested benefits allocable to the employer (determined without regard to this section), and

(2) that portion of 50 percent of the unfunded vested benefits allocable to the employer (as determined under paragraph (1)) which does not exceed the liquidation or dissolution value of the employer determined—

(A) as of the commencement of liquidation or dissolution, and

(B) after reducing the liquidation or dissolution value of the employer by the amount determined under paragraph (1).

Act Sec. 4225. (c) Property not subject to enforcement of liability; precondition.—To the extent that the withdrawal liability of an employer is attributable to his obligation to contribute to or under a plan as an individual (whether as a sole proprietor or as a member of a partnership), property which may be exempt from the estate under section 522 of title 11, United States Code, or under similar provisions of law, shall not be subject to enforcement of such liability.

Act Sec. 4225. (d) Insolvency of employer; liquidation or dissolution value of employer.—For purposes of this section—

(1) an employer is insolvent if the liabilities of the employer, including withdrawal liability under the plan (determined without regard to subsection (b)), exceed the assets of the employer (determined as of the commencement of the liquidation or dissolution), and

(2) the liquidation or dissolution value of the employer shall be determined without regard to such withdrawal liability.

Act Sec. 4225. (e) One or more withdrawals of employer attributable to same sale, liquidation, or dissolution.—In the case of one or more withdrawals of an employer attributable to the same sale, liquidation, or dissolution, under regulations prescribed by the corporation—

(1) all such withdrawals shall be treated as a single withdrawal for the purpose of applying this section, and

(2) the withdrawal liability of the employer to each plan shall be an amount which bears the same ratio to the present value of the withdrawal liability payments to all plans (after the application of the preceding provisions of this section) as the withdrawal liability of the employer to such plan (determined without regard to this section) bears to the withdrawal liability of the employer to all such plans (determined without regard to this section).

Amendments

P.L. 109-280, §204(a)(1):

Amended ERISA Sec. 4225(a)(2) by striking the table contained therein and inserting a new table to read as above.

Prior to amendment, ERISA Sec. 4225(a)(2) read as follows:

For purposes of paragraph (1), the portion shall be determined in accordance with the following table:

If the liquidation or dissolution value of the employer after the sale or exchange is—	The portion is—
Not more than $2,000,000	30 percent of the amount.
More than $2,000,000, but not more than $4,000,000, ...	$600,000, plus 35 percent of the amount in excess of $2,000,000.
More than $4,000,000, but not more than $6,000,000, ...	$1,300,000, plus 40 percent of the amount in excess of $4,000,000.
More than $6,000,000, but not more than $7,000,000, ...	$2,100,000, plus 45 percent of the amount in excess of $6,000,000.

If the liquidation or dissolution value of the employer after the sale or exchange is—	The portion is—
More than $7,000,000, but not more than $8,000,000, ...	$2,550,000, plus 50 percent of the amount in excess of $7,000,000.
More than $8,000,000, but not more than $9,000,000, ...	$3,050,000, plus 60 percent of the amount in excess of $8,000,000.
More than $9,000,000, but not more than $10,000,000, ...	$3,650,000, plus 70 percent of the amount in excess of $9,000,000.
More than $10,000,000.	$4,350,000, plus 80 percent of the amount in excess of $10,000,000.

The above amendment applies to sales occurring on or after January 1, 2007.

P.L. 109-280, §204(a)(2):

Amended ERISA Sec. 4225(a)(1) by amending subparagraph (B) to read as above.

Prior to amendment, ERISA Sec. 4225(a)(1) read as follows:

(B) the unfunded vested benefits attributable to employees of the employer.

The above amendment applies to sales occurring on or after January 1, 2007.

P.L. 96-364, §104(2):

Added Sec. 4225, effective September 26, 1980 under ERISA Sec. 4402.

Part 2—Merger or Transfer of Plan Assets or Liabilities

[¶ 15,700]
MERGERS AND TRANSFERS BETWEEN MULTIEMPLOYER PLANS

Act Sec. 4231.(a) AUTHORITY OF PLAN SPONSOR.—Unless otherwise provided in regulations prescribed by the corporation, a plan sponsor may not cause a multiemployer plan to merge with one or more multiemployer plans, or engage in a transfer of assets and liabilities to or from another multiemployer plan, unless such merger or transfer satisfies the requirements of subsection (b).

Act Sec. 4231. (b) CRITERIA.—A merger or transfer satisfies the requirements of this section if—

(1) in accordance with regulations of the corporation, the plan sponsor of a multiemployer plan notifies the corporation of a merger with or transfer of plan assets or liabilities to another multiemployer plan at least 120 days before the effective date of the merger or transfer;

(2) no participant's or beneficiary's accrued benefit will be lower immediately after the effective date of the merger or transfer than the benefit immediately before that date;

(3) the benefits of participants and beneficiaries are not reasonably expected to be subject to suspension under section 4245; and

(4) an actuarial valuation of the assets and liabilities of each of the affected plans has been performed during the plan year preceding the effective date of the merger or transfer, based upon the most recent data available as of the day before the start of that plan year, or other valuation of such assets and liabilities performed under such standards and procedures as the corporation may prescribe by regulation.

Act Sec. 4231. (c) ACTIONS NOT DEEMED VIOLATIONS OF SECTION 1106(A) OR (B)(2) OF THIS TITLE.—The merger of multiemployer plans or the transfer of assets or liabilities between multiemployer plans, shall be deemed not to constitute a violation of the provisions of section 406(a) or section 406(b)(2) if the corporation determines that the merger or transfer otherwise satisfies the requirements of this section.

Act Sec. 4231. (d) NATURE OF PLAN TO WHICH LIABILITIES ARE TRANSFERRED.—A plan to which liabilities are transferred under this section is a successor plan for purposes of section 4022A(b)(2)(B).

Act Sec. 4231. (e) FACILITATED MERGERS.—

(1) IN GENERAL. —When requested to do so by the plan sponsors, the corporation may take such actions as it deems appropriate to promote and facilitate the merger of two or more multiemployer plans if it determines, after consultation with the Participant and Plan Sponsor Advocate selected under section 4004, that the transaction is in the interests of the participants and beneficiaries of at least one of the plans and is not reasonably expected to be adverse to the overall interests of the participants and beneficiaries of any of the plans. Such facilitation may include training, technical assistance, mediation, communication with stakeholders, and support with related requests to other government agencies.

(2) FINANCIAL ASSISTANCE. —In order to facilitate a merger which it determines is necessary to enable one or more of the plans involved to avoid or postpone insolvency, the corporation may provide financial assistance (within the meaning of section 4261) to the merged plan if—

(A) one or more of the multiemployer plans participating in the merger is in critical and declining status (as defined in section 305(b)(4));

(B) the corporation reasonably expects that—

(i) such financial assistance will reduce the corporation's expected long-term loss with respect to the plans involved; and

(ii) such financial assistance is necessary for the merged plan to become or remain solvent;

(C) the corporation certifies that its ability to meet existing financial assistance obligations to other plans will not be impaired by such financial assistance; and

(D) such financial assistance is paid exclusively from the fund for basic benefits guaranteed for multiemployer plans.

Not later than 14 days after the provision of such financial assistance, the corporation shall provide notice of such financial assistance to the Committee on Education and the Workforce of the House of Representatives, the Committee on Ways and Means of the House of Representatives, the Committee on Finance of the Senate, and the Committee on Health, Education, Labor, and Pensions of the Senate.

Amendment

P.L. 113-235, §121(a), Div. O:

Amended ERISA Sec. 4231 by adding at the end a new paragraph (e) to read as above.

The above amendment shall apply with respect to plan years beginning after December 31, 2014.

P.L. 96-364, §104(2):

Added Sec. 4231 effective September 26, 1980 under ERISA Sec. 4402.

Regulations

The following regulations were adopted by the Pension Benefit Guaranty Corporation on July 1, 1996 (61 FR 34002). Prior to July 1, 1996, PBGC regulations were under Chapter XXVI of Title 29 of the Code of Federal Regulations. Effective July 1, 1996, PBGC regulations were moved to Chapter XL, and were renumbered and reorganized. Amendments to regulations ERISA Secs. 4231.1—4231.10 were published on May 4, 1998 (63 FR 24421). Reg. § 4231.8 was amended October 28, 2003 (68 FR 61344) and May 28, 2014 (79 FR 30459). Reg. § § 4231.2 and 4231.6 were amended on September 11, 2015 (80 FR 54979).

[¶ 15,700A]

§ 4231.1 **Purpose and scope.** (a) *Purpose.* The purpose of this part is to prescribe notice requirements under section 4231 of ERISA for mergers and transfers of assets or liabilities among multiemployer pension plans. This part also interprets the other requirements of section 4231 and prescribes special rules for de minimis mergers and transfers. The collections of information in this part have been approved by the Office of Management and Budget under OMB control number 1212-0022.

(b) *Scope.* This part applies to mergers and transfers among multiemployer plans where all of the plans immediately before and immediately after the transaction are multiemployer plans covered by title IV of ERISA.

[¶ 15,700B]

§ 4231.2 **Definitions.** The following terms are defined in Sec. 4001.2 of this chapter: *Code, EIN, ERISA, fair market value, IRS, multiemployer plan, PBGC, plan, plan year,* and *PN.*

In addition, for purposes of this part:

Actuarial valuation means a valuation of assets and liabilities performed by an enrolled actuary using the actuarial assumptions used for purposes of determining the charges and credits to the funding standard account under section 304 of ERISA and section 431 of the Code. [Amended 9/11/15 by 80 FR 54979.]

Certified change of collective bargaining representative means a change of collective bargaining representative certified under the Labor-Management Relations Act of 1947, as amended, or the Railway Labor Act, as amended.

Fair market value of assets has the same meaning as the term has for minimum funding purposes under section 304 of ERISA and section 431 of the Code. [Amended 9/11/15 by 80 FR 54979.]

Merger means the combining of two or more plans into a single plan. For example, a consolidation of two plans into a new plan is a merger.

Significantly affected plan means a plan that—

(1) Transfers assets that equal or exceed 15 percent of its assets before the transfer,

(2) Receives a transfer of unfunded accrued benefits that equal or exceed 15 percent of its assets before the transfer,

(3) Is created by a spinoff from another plan, or

(4) Engages in a merger or transfer (other than a de minimis merger or transfer) either—

(i) After such plan has terminated by mass withdrawal under section 4041A(a)(2) of ERISA, or

(ii) With another plan that has so terminated.

Transfer and transfer of assets or liabilities mean a diminution of assets or liabilities with respect to one plan and the acquisition of these assets or the assumption of these liabilities by another plan or plans (including a plan that did not exist prior to the transfer). However, the shifting of assets or liabilities pursuant to a written reciprocity agreement between two multiemployer plans in which one plan assumes liabilities of another plan is not a transfer of assets or liabilities. In addition, the shifting of assets between several funding media used for a single plan (such as between trusts, between annuity contracts, or between trusts and annuity contracts) is not a transfer of assets or liabilities.

Unfunded accrued benefits means the excess of the present value of a plan's accrued benefits over the fair market value of its assets, determined on the basis of the actuarial valuation required under Sec. 4231.5(b).

[¶ 15,700C]

§ 4231.3 **Requirements for mergers and transfers.** (a) *General requirements.* A plan sponsor may not cause a multiemployer plan to merge with one or more multiemployer plans or transfer assets or liabilities to or from another multiemployer plan unless the merger or transfer satisfies all of the following requirements:

(1) No participant's or beneficiary's accrued benefit is lower immediately after the effective date of the merger or transfer than the benefit immediately before that date.

(2) Actuarial valuations of the plans that existed before the merger or transfer have been performed in accordance with Sec. 4231.5.

(3) For each plan that exists after the transaction, an enrolled actuary—

(i) Determines that the plan meets the applicable plan solvency requirement set forth in Sec. 4231.6; or

(ii) Otherwise demonstrates that benefits under the plan are not reasonably expected to be subject to suspension under section 4245 of ERISA.

(4) The plan sponsor notifies the PBGC of the merger or transfer in accordance with Sec. 4231.8.

(b) *Compliance determination.* If a plan sponsor requests a determination that a merger or transfer that may otherwise be prohibited by section 406(a) or (b)(2) of ERISA satisfies the requirements of section 4231 of ERISA, the plan sponsor must submit the information described in Sec. 4231.9 in addition to the information required by Sec. 4231.8. PBGC may request additional information if necessary to determine whether a merger or transfer complies with the requirements of section 4231 and this part. Plan sponsors are not required to request a compliance determination. Under section 4231(c) of ERISA, if the PBGC determines that the merger or transfer complies with section 4231 of ERISA and this part, the merger or transfer will not constitute a violation of the prohibited transaction provisions of section 406(a) and (b)(2) of ERISA.

(c) *Certified change in bargaining representative.* Transfers of assets and liabilities pursuant to a certified change in bargaining representative are governed by section 4235 of ERISA. Plan sponsors involved in such transfers are not required to comply with this part. However, under section 4235(f)(1) of ERISA, the plan sponsors of the plans involved in the transfer may agree to a transfer that complies with sections 4231 and 4234 of ERISA. Plan sponsors that elect to comply with sections 4231 and 4234 must comply with the rules in this part.

[¶ 15,700D]

§ 4231.4 **Preservation of accrued benefits.** Section 4231(b)(2) of ERISA and Sec. 4231.3(a)(1) require that no participant's or beneficiary's accrued benefit may be lower immediately after the effective date of the merger or transfer than the benefit immediately before the merger or transfer. A plan that assumes an obligation to pay benefits for a group of participants satisfies this requirement only if the plan contains a provision preserving all accrued benefits. The determination of what is an accrued benefit must be made in accordance with section 411 of the Code and the regulations thereunder.

[¶ 15,700E]

§ 4231.5 **Valuation requirement.** (a) *In general.* For a plan that is not a significantly affected plan, or that is a significantly affected plan only because the merger or transfer involves a plan that has terminated by mass withdrawal under section 4041A(a)(2) of ERISA, the actuarial valuation requirement under section 4231(b)(4) of ERISA and Sec. 4231.3(a)(2) is satisfied if an actuarial valuation has been performed for the plan based on the plan's assets and liabilities as of a date not more than three years before the date on which the notice of the merger or transfer is filed.

(b) *Significantly affected plans.* For a significantly affected plan, other than a plan that is a significantly affected plan only because the merger or transfer involves a plan that has terminated by mass withdrawal under section 4041A(a)(2) of ERISA, the actuarial valuation requirement under section 4231(b)(4) of ERISA and Sec. 4231.3(a)(2) is satisfied only if an actuarial valuation has been performed for the plan based on the plan's assets and liabilities as of a date not earlier than the first day of the last plan year ending before the proposed effective date of the transaction. The valuation must separately identify assets, contributions, and liabilities being transferred and must be based on the actuarial assumptions and methods that are expected to be used for the plan for the first plan year beginning after the transfer.

[¶ 15,700F]

§ 4231.6 **Plan solvency tests.** (a) *In general.* For a plan that is not a significantly affected plan, the plan solvency requirement of section 4231(b)(3) of ERISA and Sec. 4231.3(a)(3)(i) is satisfied if—

(1) The expected fair market value of plan assets immediately after the merger or transfer equals or exceeds five times the benefit payments for the last plan year ending before the proposed effective date of the merger or transfer; or

(2) In each of the first five plan years beginning on or after the proposed effective date of the merger or transfer, expected plan assets plus expected contributions and investment earnings equal or exceed expected expenses and benefit payments for the plan year.

(b) *Significantly affected plans.* The plan solvency requirement of section 4231(b)(3) of ERISA and Sec. 4231.3(a)(3)(i) is satisfied for a significantly affected plan if all of the following requirements are met:

(1) Expected contributions equal or exceed the estimated amount necessary to satisfy the minimum funding requirement of section 412(a) of the Code (including reorganization funding, if applicable) for the five plan years beginning on or after the proposed effective date of the transaction.

(2) The expected fair market value of plan assets immediately after the transaction equal or exceed the total amount of expected benefit payments for the first five plan years beginning on or after the proposed effective date of the transaction.

(3) Expected contributions for the first plan year beginning on or after the proposed effective date of the transaction equal or exceed expected benefit payments for that plan year.

(4) Expected contributions for the amortization period equal or exceed unfunded accrued benefits plus expected normal costs. The actuary may select as the amortization period either—

(i) The first 25 plan years beginning on or after the proposed effective date of the transaction, or

(ii) The amortization period for the resulting base when the combined charge base and the combined credit base are offset under section 431(b)(5) of the Code. [Amended 9/11/15 by 80 FR 54979.]

(c) *Rules for determinations.* In determining whether a transaction satisfies the plan solvency requirements set forth in this section, the following rules apply:

(1) Expected contributions after a merger or transfer must be determined by assuming that contributions for each plan year will equal contributions for the last full plan year ending before the date on which the notice of merger or transfer is filed with the PBGC. Contributions must be adjusted, however, to reflect—

(i) The merger or transfer,

(ii) Any change in the rate of employer contributions that has been negotiated (whether or not in effect), and

(iii) Any trend of changing contribution base units over the preceding five plan years or other period of time that can be demonstrated to be more appropriate.

(2) Expected normal costs must be determined under the funding method and assumptions expected to be used by the plan actuary for purposes of determining the minimum funding requirement under section 431 of the Code (which requires that each such assumption be reasonable). If the plan uses an aggregate funding method, normal costs must be determined under the entry age normal method. [Amended 9/11/15 by 80 FR 54979.]

(3) Expected benefit payments must be determined by assuming that current benefits remain in effect and that all scheduled increases in benefits occur.

(4) The expected fair market value of plan assets immediately after the merger or transfer must be based on the most recent data available immediately before the date on which the notice is filed.

(5) Expected investment earnings must be determined using the same interest assumption to be used for determining the minimum funding requirement under section 431 of the Code. [Amended 9/11/15 by 80 FR 54979.]

(6) Expected expenses must be determined using expenses in the last plan year ending before the notice is filed, adjusted to reflect any anticipated changes.

(7) Expected plan assets for a plan year must be determined by adjusting the most current data on fair market value of plan assets to reflect expected contributions, investment earnings, benefit payments and expenses for each plan year between the date of the most current data and the beginning of the plan year for which expected assets are being determined.

[¶ 15,700G]

§ 4231.7 **De minimis mergers and transfers.** (a) *Special plan solvency rule.* The determination of whether a de minimis merger or transfer satisfies the plan solvency requirement in Sec. 4231.6(a) may be made without regard to any other de minimis mergers or transfers that have occurred since the last actuarial valuation.

(b) *De minimis merger defined.* A merger is de minimis if the present value of accrued benefits (whether or not vested) of one plan is less than 3 percent of the fair market value of the other plan's assets.

(c) *De minimis transfer defined.* A transfer of assets or liabilities is de minimis if—

(1) The fair market value of the assets transferred, if any, is less than 3 percent of the fair market value of all the assets of the transferor plan;

(2) The present value of the accrued benefits transferred (whether or not vested) is less than 3 percent of the fair market value of all the assets of the transferee plan; and

(3) The transferee plan is not a plan that has terminated under section 4041A(a)(2) of ERISA.

(d) *Value of assets and benefits.* For purposes of paragraphs (b) and (c) of this section, the value of plan assets and accrued benefits may be determined as of any date prior to the proposed effective date of the transaction, but not earlier than the date of the most recent actuarial valuation.

(e) *Aggregation required.* In determining whether a merger or transfer is de minimis, the assets and accrued benefits transferred in previous de minimis mergers and transfers within the same plan year must be aggregated as described in paragraphs (e)(1) and (e)(2) of this section. For the purposes of those paragraphs, the value of plan assets may be determined as of the date during the plan year on which the total value of the plan's assets is the highest.

(1) A merger is not de minimis if the total present value of accrued benefits merged into a plan, when aggregated with all prior de minimis mergers of and transfers to that plan effective within the same plan year, equals or exceeds 3 percent of the value of the plan's assets.

(2) A transfer is not de minimis if, when aggregated with all previous de minimis mergers and transfers effective within the same plan year—

(i) The value of all assets transferred from a plan equals or exceeds 3 percent of the value of the plan's assets; or

(ii) The present value of all accrued benefits transferred to a plan equals or exceeds 3 percent of the plan's assets.

[¶ 15,700H]

§ 4231.8 **Notice of merger or transfer.** (a) *Filing of request.* (1) *When to file.* Except as provided in paragraph (f) of this section, a notice of a proposed merger or transfer must be filed not less than 120 days, or not less than 45 days in the case of a merger for which a compliance determination under § 4231.9 is not requested, before the effective date of the transaction. For purposes of this part, the effective date of a merger or transfer is the earlier of—[Amended 5/28/14 by 79 FR 30459.]

Reg. § 4231.8(a)(1)   ¶ 15,700H

(i) The date on which one plan assumes liability for benefits accrued under another plan involved in the transaction; or

(ii) The date on which one plan transfers assets to another plan involved in the transaction.

(2) *Method of filing.* The PBGC applies the rules in subpart A of part 4000 of this chapter to determine permissible methods of filing with the PBGC under this part.

(3) *Computation of time.* The PBGC applies the rules in subpart D of part 4000 of this chapter to compute any time period for filing under this part.

[Amended 10/28/2003 by 68 FR 61344]

(b) *Who must file.* The plan sponsors of all plans involved in a merger or transfer, or the duly authorized representative(s) acting on behalf of the plan sponsors, must jointly file the notice required by this section.

(c) *Where to file.* See Sec. 4000.4 of this chapter for information on where to file.

[Amended 10/28/2003 by 68 FR 61344]

(d) *Date of filing.* The PBGC applies the rules in subpart C of part 4000 of this chapter to determine the date that a submission under this part was filed with the PBGC. For purposes of paragraph (a) of this section, the notice is not considered filed until all of the information required by paragraph (e) of this section has been submitted.

[Amended 10/28/2003 by 68 FR 61344]

(e) *Information required.* Each notice must contain the following information:

(1) For each plan involved in the merger or transfer—

(i) The name of the plan;

(ii) The name, address and telephone number of the plan sponsor and of the plan sponsor's duly authorized representative, if any; and

(iii) The plan sponsor's EIN and the plan's PN and, if different, the EIN or PN last filed with the PBGC. If no EIN or PN has been assigned, the notice must so indicate.

(2) Whether the transaction being reported is a merger or transfer, whether it involves any plan that has terminated under section 4041A(a)(2) of ERISA, whether any significantly affected plan is involved in the transaction (and, if so, identifying each such plan), and whether it is a de minimis transaction as defined in Sec. 4231.7 (and, if so, including an enrolled actuary's certification to that effect).

(3) The proposed effective date of the transaction.

(4) A copy of each plan provision stating that no participant's or beneficiary's accrued benefit will be lower immediately after the effective date of the merger or transfer than the benefit immediately before that date.

(5) For each plan that exists after the transaction, one of the following statements, certified by an enrolled actuary:

(i) A statement that the plan satisfies the applicable plan solvency test set forth in Sec. 4231.6, indicating which is the applicable test.

(ii) A statement of the basis on which the actuary has determined that benefits under the plan are not reasonably expected to be subject to suspension under section 4245 of ERISA, including the supporting data or calculations, assumptions and methods.

(6) For each plan that exists before a transaction (unless the transaction is de minimis and does not involve any plan that has terminated under section 4041A(a)(2) of ERISA), a copy of the most recent actuarial valuation report that satisfies the requirements of Sec. 4231.5.

(7) For each significantly affected plan that exists after the transaction, the following information used in making the plan solvency determination under Sec. 4231.6(b):

(i) The present value of the accrued benefits and fair market value of plan assets under the valuation required by Sec. 4231.5(b), allocable to the plan after the transaction.

(ii) The fair market value of assets in the plan after the transaction (determined in accordance with Sec. 4231.6(c)(4)).

(iii) The expected benefit payments for the plan in the first plan year beginning on or after the proposed effective date of the transaction (determined in accordance with Sec. 4231.6(c)(3)).

(iv) The contribution rates in effect for the plan for the first plan year beginning on or after the proposed effective date of the transaction.

(v) The expected contributions for the plan in the first plan year beginning on or after the proposed effective date of the transaction (determined in accordance with Sec. 4231.6(c)(1)).

(f) *Waiver of notice.* The PBGC may waive the notice requirements of this section and section 4231(b)(1) of ERISA if—

(1) A plan sponsor demonstrates to the satisfaction of the PBGC that failure to complete the merger or transfer in less than the applicable notice period set forth in paragraph (a) of this section will cause harm to participants or beneficiaries of the plans involved in the transaction; [Amended 5/28/14 by 79 FR 30459.]

(2) The PBGC determines that the transaction complies with the requirements of section 4231 of ERISA; or

(3) The PBGC completes its review of the transaction.

[¶ 15,700I]

§ 4231.9 **Request for compliance determination.** (a) *General.* The plan sponsor(s) of one or more plans involved in a merger or transfer, or the duly authorized representative(s) acting on behalf of the plan sponsor(s), may file a request for a determination that the transaction complies with the requirements of section 4231 of ERISA. The request must contain the information described in paragraph (b) or (c) of this section, as applicable.

(1) *The place of filing.* The request must be delivered to the address set forth in Sec. 4231.8(c).

(2) *Single request permitted for all de minimis transactions.* Because the plan solvency test for de minimis mergers and transfers is based on the most recent valuation (without adjustment for intervening de minimis transactions), a plan sponsor may submit a single request for a compliance determination covering all de minimis mergers or transfers that occur between one plan valuation and the next. However, the plan sponsor must still notify PBGC of each de minimis merger or transfer separately, in accordance with Sec. 4231.8. The single request for a compliance determination may be filed concurrently with any one of the notices of a de minimis merger or transfer.

(b) *Contents of request.* (1) *General.* A request for a compliance determination concerning a merger or transfer that is not de minimis must contain—

(i) A copy of the merger or transfer agreement;

(ii) A summary of the required calculations, including a complete description of assumptions and methods, on which the enrolled actuary based each certification that a plan involved in the merger or transfer satisfied a plan solvency test described in Sec. 4231.6; and

(iii) For each significantly affected plan, other than a plan that is a significantly affected plan only because the merger or transfer involves a plan that has terminated by mass withdrawal under section 4041A(a)(2) of ERISA, copies of all actuarial valuations performed within the 5 years preceding the date of filing the notice required under Sec. 4231.8.

(2) *De minimis merger or transfer.* A request for a compliance determination concerning a de minimis merger or transfer must contain one of the following statements for each plan that exists after the transaction, certified by an enrolled actuary:

(i) A statement that the plan satisfies one of the plan solvency tests set forth in Sec. 4231.6(a), indicating which test is satisfied.

(ii) A statement of the basis on which the actuary has determined that benefits under the plan are not reasonably expected to be subject to suspension under section 4245 of ERISA, including supporting data or calculations, assumptions and methods.

[¶ 15,700J]

§4231.10 **Actuarial calculations and assumptions.** (a) *Most recent valuation.* All calculations required by this part must be based on the most recent actuarial valuation as of the date of filing the notice, updated to show any material changes.

(b) *Assumptions.* All calculations required by this part must be based on methods and assumptions that are reasonable in the aggregate, based on generally accepted actuarial principles.

(c) *Updated calculations.* If the actual effective date of the merger or transfer is more than one year after the date the notice is filed with the PBGC, PBGC may require the plans involved to provide updated calculations and representations based on the actual effective date of the transaction.

[¶ 15,701]

TRANSFERS BETWEEN A MULTIEMPLOYER PLAN AND A SINGLE-EMPLOYER PLAN

Act Sec. 4232. (a) GENERAL AUTHORITY.—A transfer of assets or liabilities between, or a merger of, a multiemployer plan and a single-employer plan shall satisfy the requirements of this section.

Act Sec. 4232. (b) ACCRUED BENEFIT OF PARTICIPANT OR BENEFICIARY NOT LOWER IMMEDIATELY AFTER EFFECTIVE DATE OF TRANSFER OR MERGER.—No accrued benefit of a participant or beneficiary may be lower immediately after the effective date of a transfer or merger described in subsection (a) than the benefit immediately before that date.

Act Sec. 4232. (c)(1) LIABILITY OF MULTIEMPLOYER PLAN TO CORPORATION WHERE SINGLE-EMPLOYER PLAN TERMINATES WITHIN 60 MONTHS AFTER EFFECTIVE DATE OF TRANSFER; AMOUNT OF LIABILITY, EXEMPTION, ETC.—Except as provided in paragraphs (2) and (3), a multiemployer plan which transfers liabilities to a single-employer plan shall be liable to the corporation if the single-employer plan terminates within 60 months after the effective date of the transfer. The amount of liability shall be the lesser of—

(A) the amount of the plan asset insufficiency of the terminated single-employer plan, less 30 percent of the net worth of the employer who maintained the single-employer plan, determined in accordance with section 4062 or 4064, or

(B) the value, on the effective date of the transfer, of the unfunded benefits transferred to the single-employer plan which are guaranteed under section 4022.

(2) A multiemployer plan shall be liable to the corporation as provided in paragraph (1) unless, within 180 days after the corporation receives an application (together with such information as the corporation may reasonably require for purposes of such application) from the multiemployer plan sponsor for a determination under this paragraph—

(A) the corporation determines that the interests of the plan participants and beneficiaries and of the corporation are adequately protected, or

(B) fails to make any determination regarding the adequacy with which such interests are protected with respect to such transfer of liabilities.

If, after the receipt of such application, the corporation requests from the plan sponsor additional information necessary for the determination, the running of the 180-day period shall be suspended from the date of such request until the receipt by the corporation of the additional information requested. The corporation may by regulation prescribe procedures and standards for the issuance of determinations under this paragraph. This paragraph shall not apply to any application submitted less than 180 days after the date of enactment of the Multiemployer Pension Plan Amendments Act of 1980.

(3) A multiemployer plan shall not be liable to the corporation as provided in paragraph (1) in the case of a transfer from the multiemployer plan to a single-employer plan of liabilities which accrued under a single-employer plan which merged with the multiemployer plan, if the value of liabilities transferred to the single-employer plan does not exceed the value of the liabilities for benefits which accrued before the merger, and the value of the assets transferred to the single-employer plan is substantially equal to the value of the assets which would have been in the single-employer plan if the employer had maintained and funded it as a separate plan under which no benefits accrued after the date of the merger.

(4) The corporation may make equitable arrangements with multiemployer plans which are liable under this subsection for satisfaction of their liability.

Act Sec. 4232. (d) GUARANTEE OF BENEFITS UNDER SINGLE-EMPLOYER PLAN.—Benefits under a single-employer plan to which liabilities are transferred in accordance with this section are guaranteed under section 4022 to the extent provided in that section as of the effective date of the transfer and the plan is a successor plan.

Act Sec. 4232. (e)(1) TRANSFER OF LIABILITIES BY MULTIEMPLOYER PLAN TO SINGLE-EMPLOYER PLAN.—Except as provided in paragraph (2), a multiemployer plan may not transfer liabilities to a single-employer plan unless the plan sponsor of the plan to which the liabilities would be transferred agrees to the transfer.

(2) In the case of a transfer described in subsection (c)(3), paragraph (1) of this subsection is satisfied by the advance agreement to the transfer by the employer who will be obligated to contribute to the single-employer plan.

Act Sec. 4232. (f)(1) ADDITIONAL REQUIREMENTS BY CORPORATION FOR PROTECTION OF INTEREST OF PLAN PARTICIPANTS, BENEFICIARIES AND CORPORATION; APPROVAL BY CORPORATION OF TRANSFER OF ASSETS OR LIABILITIES TO SINGLE-EMPLOYER PLAN FROM PLAN IN REORGANIZATION; COVERED TRANSFERS IN CONNECTION WITH TERMINATION.—The corporation may prescribe by regulation such additional requirements with respect to the transfer of assets or liabilities as may be necessary to protect the interests of plan participants and beneficiaries and the corporation.

(2) Except as otherwise determined by the corporation, a transfer of assets or liabilities to a single-employer plan from a plan in reorganization under section 4241 is not effective unless the corporation approves such transfer.

(3) No transfer to which this section applies, in connection with a termination described in section 4041A(a)(2) shall be effective unless the transfer meets such requirements as may be established by the corporation to prevent an increase in the risk of loss to the corporation.

Amendment

P.L. 96-364, §104(2):

Added Sec. 4232, effective September 26, 1980 under ERISA Sec. 4402.

[¶ 15,702]

PARTITIONS OF ELIGIBLE MULTIEMPLOYER PLANS

Act Sec. 4233. (a)(1) Upon the application by the plan sponsor of an eligible multiemployer plan for a partition of the plan, the corporation may order a partition of the plan in accordance with this section. The corporation shall make a determination regarding the application not later than 270 days after the date such application was filed (or, if later, the date such application was completed) in accordance with regulations promulgated by the corporation.

(2) Not later than 30 days after submitting an application for partition of a plan under paragraph (1), the plan sponsor of the plan shall notify the participants and beneficiaries of such application, in the form and manner prescribed by regulations issued by the corporation.

Act Sec. 4233. (b) For purposes of this section, a multiemployer plan is an eligible multiemployer plan if—

(1) the plan is in critical and declining status (as defined in section 305(b)(4));

(2) the corporation determines, after consultation with the Participant and Plan Sponsor Advocate selected under section 4004, that the plan sponsor has taken (or is taking concurrently with an application for partition) all reasonable measures to avoid insolvency, including the maximum benefit suspensions under section 305(e)(9), if applicable;

(3) the corporation reasonably expects that—

(A) a partition of the plan will reduce the corporation's expected long-term loss with respect to the plan; and

(B) a partition of the plan is necessary for the plan to remain solvent;

(4) the corporation certifies to Congress that its ability to meet existing financial assistance obligations to other plans (including any liabilities associated with multiemployer plans that are insolvent or that are projected to become insolvent within 10 years) will not be impaired by such partition; and

(5) the cost to the corporation arising from such partition is paid exclusively from the fund for basic benefits guaranteed for multiemployer plans.

Act Sec. 4233. (c) The corporation's partition order shall provide for a transfer to the plan referenced in subsection (d)(1) of the minimum amount of the plan's liabilities necessary for the plan to remain solvent.

Act Sec. 4233.(d)(1) The plan created by the partition order is a successor plan to which section 4022A applies.

(2) The plan sponsor of an eligible multiemployer plan prior to the partition and the administrator of such plan shall be the plan sponsor and the administrator, respectively, of the plan created by the partition order.

(3) In the event an employer withdraws from the plan that was partitioned within ten years following the date of the partition order, withdrawal liability shall be computed under section 4201 with respect to both the plan that was partitioned and the plan created by the partition order. If the withdrawal occurs more than ten years after the date of the partition order, withdrawal liability shall be computed under section 4201 only with respect to the plan that was partitioned (and not with respect to the plan created by the partition order).

Act Sec. 4233.(e)(1) For each participant or beneficiary of the plan whose benefit was transferred to the plan created by the partition order pursuant to a partition, the plan that was partitioned shall pay a monthly benefit to such participant or beneficiary for each month in which such benefit is in pay status following the effective date of such partition in an amount equal to the excess of—

(A) the monthly benefit that would be paid to such participant or beneficiary for such month under the terms of the plan (taking into account benefit suspensions under section 305(e)(9) and any plan amendments following the effective date of such partition) if the partition had not occurred, over

(B) the monthly benefit for such participant or beneficiary which is guaranteed under section 4022A.

(2) In any case in which a plan provides a benefit improvement (as defined in section 305(e)(9)(E)(vi)) that takes effect after the effective date of the partition, the plan shall pay to the corporation for each year during the 10-year period following the partition effective date, an annual amount equal to the lesser of—

(A) the total value of the increase in benefit payments for such year that is attributable to the benefit improvement, or

(B) the total benefit payments from the plan created by the partition for such year.

Such payment shall be made at the time of, and in addition to, any other premium imposed by the corporation under this title.

(3) The plan that was partitioned shall pay the premiums imposed by the corporation under this title with respect to participants whose benefits were transferred to the plan created by the partition order for each year during the 10-year period following the partition effective date.

Act Sec. 4233. (f) Not later than 14 days after the partition order, the corporation shall provide notice of such order to the Committee on Education and the Workforce of the House of Representatives, the Committee on Ways and Means of the House of Representatives, the Committee on Finance of the Senate, the Committee on Health, Education, Labor, and Pensions of the Senate, and any affected participants or beneficiaries.

Amendment

P.L. 113-235, § 122(a), Div. O:

Amended ERISA Sec. 4233 to read as above.

The above amendment shall apply with respect to plan years beginning after December 31, 2014.

Prior to amendment, ERISA Sec. 4233 read as follows:

PARTITION

(a) AUTHORITY OF CORPORATION.—The corporation may order the partition of a multiemployer plan in accordance with this section.

(b) AUTHORITY OF PLAN SPONSOR UPON APPLICATION TO CORPORATION FOR PARTITION ORDER; PROCEDURES APPLICABLE TO CORPORATION.—A plan sponsor may apply to the corporation for an order partitioning a plan. The corporation may not order the partition of a plan except upon notice to the plan sponsor and the participants and beneficiaries whose vested benefits will be affected by the partition of the plan, and upon finding that—

(1) a substantial reduction in the amount of aggregate contributions under the plan has resulted or will result from a case or proceeding under title 11, United States Code, with respect to an employer;

(2) the plan is likely to become insolvent;

(3) contributions will have to be increased significantly in reorganization to meet the minimum contribution requirement and prevent insolvency; and

(4) partition would significantly reduce the likelihood that the plan will become insolvent.

(c) AUTHORITY OF CORPORATION NOTWITHSTANDING PENDENCY OF PARTITION PROCEEDING.— The corporation may order the partition of a plan notwithstanding the pendency of a proceeding described in subsection (b)(1).

(d) SCOPE OF PARTITION ORDER.—The corporation's partition order shall provide for a transfer or no more than the nonforfeitable benefits directly attributable to service with the employer referred to in subsection (b)(1) and an equitable share of assets.

(e) NATURE OF PLAN CREATED BY PARTITION.—The plan created by the partition is—

(1) a successor plan to which section 4022A applies, and

(2) a terminated multiemployer plan to which section 4041A(d) applies, with respect to which only the employer described in subsection (b)(1) has withdrawal liability, and to which section 4068 applies.

(f) AUTHORITY OF CORPORATION TO OBTAIN DECREE PARTITIONING PLAN AND APPOINTED TRUSTEE FOR TERMINATED PORTION OF PARTITIONED PLAN.—The corporation may proceed under section 4042(c) through (h) for a decree partitioning a plan and appointing a trustee for the terminated portion of a partitioned plan. The court may order the partition of a plan upon making the findings described in subsection (b)(1) through (4), and subject to the conditions set forth in subsections (c) through (e).

P.L. 96-364, § 104(2):

Added Sec. 4233, effective September 26, 1980 under ERISA Sec. 4402.

Final Regulations

Interim final Reg. §§4233.1—4233.17 and Appendix A to Part 4233—Model Notices were adopted by the Pension Benefit Guaranty Corporation (PBGC) and published in the Federal Register on June 19, 2015 (80 FR 35220). The PBGC has finalized Reg. §§4233.1—4233.17 and Appendix A to Part 4233—Model Notices and made minor amendments to Reg. §§4233.4, 4233.6, 4233.7, 4233.8, 4233.10, 4233.12, and 4233.13 on December 23, 2015 (80 FR 79687).

[¶ 15,702A]

§4233.1 **Purpose and scope.** The purpose of this part is to prescribe rules governing applications for partition under section 4233 of ERISA, and related notice requirements.

[¶ 15,702B]

§4233.2 **Definitions.** The following terms are defined in §4001.2 of this chapter: ERISA, IRS, multiemployer plan, PBGC, plan, and plan sponsor. In addition, the following terms are defined for purposes of this part:

Advocate means the Participant and Plan Sponsor Advocate under section 4004 of ERISA.

Application for partition means a plan sponsor's application for partition under section 4233 of ERISA and this part.

Application for a suspension of benefits means a plan sponsor's application for a suspension of benefits to the Secretary of the Treasury (Treasury) under section 305(e)(9)(G) of ERISA.

Completed application means an application for partition for which PBGC has made a determination under §4233.10 that the application contains all required information and satisfies the requirements described in §§4233.4 through 4233.9.

Effective date of partition means the date upon which a partition is effective and which is set forth in a partition order.

Financial assistance means financial assistance from PBGC under section 4261 of ERISA.

Insolvent has the same meaning as insolvent under section 4245(b) of ERISA.

Interested party means, with respect to a plan—

(1) Each participant in the plan;

(2) Each beneficiary of a deceased participant;

(3) Each alternate payee under an applicable qualified domestic relations order, as defined in section 206(d)(3) of ERISA;

(4) Each employer that has an obligation to contribute under the plan; and

(5) Each employee organization that currently has a collective bargaining agreement pursuant to which the plan is maintained.

Original plan means an eligible multiemployer plan under 4233(b) of ERISA that is partitioned upon the issuance of a partition order under section 4233(c) of ERISA.

Partition order means a formal PBGC order of partition under section 4233 of ERISA and § 4233.14.

Proposed partition means a proposed partition as structured and described by the plan sponsor in an application for partition.

Remain solvent has the same meaning as "avoid insolvency" in section 305(e)(9)(D)(iv) of ERISA and the regulations thereunder, with respect to the determinations made by PBGC under sections 4233(b)(3) and 4233(c) of ERISA.

Residual benefit means, with respect to a participant or beneficiary whose benefit was partially transferred to a successor plan pursuant to a partition order, the portion of the benefit payable under the original plan, the amount of which is equal to the difference between the benefit defined in section 4233(e)(1)(A) of ERISA, and the successor plan benefit. The residual benefit as of the effective date of the partition is not subject to a separate guarantee under section 4022A of ERISA.

Successor plan means the plan created by a partition order under section 4233(c) of ERISA.

Successor plan benefit means, with respect to a participant or beneficiary whose benefit was wholly or partially transferred from an original plan to a successor plan, the portion of the accrued nonforfeitable monthly benefit which would be guaranteed under section 4022A as of the effective date of the partition, calculated under the terms of the original plan without reflecting any changes relating to a benefit suspension under section 305(e)(9) of ERISA. The payment of a successor plan benefit is subject to the limitations and conditions contained in sections 4022A(a)-(f) of ERISA.

[¶ 15,702C]

§ 4233.3 **Application filing requirements.** (a) *Method of filing.* PBGC applies the rules in part 4000, subpart A of this chapter to determine permissible methods of filing with PBGC under this part, and the rules in part 4000, subpart D of this chapter to determine the computation of time.

(b) *Who may file.* An application for partition under section 4233 of ERISA must be submitted by the plan sponsor. The application must be signed and dated by an authorized trustee who is a current member of the board of trustees, and must include the following statement under penalties of perjury: "Under penalties of perjury, I declare that I have examined this application, including accompanying documents, and, to the best of my knowledge and belief, the application contains all the relevant facts relating to the application, and such facts are true, correct, and complete." A stamped signature or faxed signature is not permitted.

(c) *Where to file.* See § 4000.4 of this chapter for information on where to file.

[¶ 15,702D]

§ 4233.4 **Information to be filed.** (a) *General.* An application for partition must include the information specified in § 4233.5 (plan information), § 4233.6 (partition information), § 4233.7 (actuarial and financial information), § 4233.8 (participant census data), and § 4233.9 (financial assistance information). If any of the information is not included, the application may not be considered complete. [Amended 12/23/2015 (80 FR 79687).]

(b) Additional information. (1) PBGC may require a plan sponsor to submit additional information necessary to make a determination on an application under this part and any information PBGC may need to calculate or verify the amount of financial assistance necessary for a partition. Any additional information must be submitted by the date specified in PBGC's request.

(2) PBGC may suspend the running of the 270-day review period (described in § 4233.10) pending the submission of any addi-

tional information requested by PBGC, or upon the issuance of a conditional determination under § 4233.12(c).

(c) *Duty to amend and supplement application.* During any time in which an application is pending final action by PBGC, the plan sponsor must promptly notify PBGC in writing of any material fact or representation contained in or relating to the application, or in any supporting documents, that is no longer accurate, or any material fact or representation omitted from the application or supporting documents, that the plan sponsor discovers.

[¶ 15,702E]

§ 4233.5 **Plan information.** An application for partition must include the following information with respect to the plan:

(a) The name of the plan, Employer Identification Number (EIN), and three-digit Plan Number (PN).

(b) The name, address, and telephone number of the plan sponsor and the plan sponsor's duly authorized representative, if any.

(c) The most recent trust agreement, including all amendments adopted since the last restatement.

(d) The most recent plan document, including all amendments adopted since the last restatement.

(e) The most recent summary plan description (SPD), and all summaries of material modification (SMM) issued since the effective date of the most recent SPD.

(f) The most recent rehabilitation plan (or funding improvement plan, if applicable), including all subsequent amendments and updates, and the percentage of total contributions received under each schedule of the rehabilitation plan for the most recent plan year available.

(g) A copy of the plan's most recent IRS determination letter.

(h) A copy of the plan's most recent Form 5500 (Annual Report Form) and all schedules and attachments (including the audited financial statement).

(i) A current listing of employers who have an obligation to contribute to the plan, and the approximate number of participants for whom each employer is currently making contributions.

(j) A schedule of withdrawal liability payments collected in each of the most recent five plan years.

[¶ 15,702F]

§ 4233.6 **Partition information.** An application for partition must include the following information with respect to the proposed partition:

(a) A detailed description of the proposed partition, including the proposed structure, proposed effective date, and any larger integrated transaction of which the proposed partition is a part (including, but not limited to, an application for suspension of benefits under section 305(e)(9)(G), or a merger under section 4231 of ERISA). With respect to coordinated applications for partition and suspension of benefits, proposed effective dates for both transactions must satisfy the requirements of section 305(e)(9)(D)(v) of ERISA. [Amended 12/23/2015 (80 FR 79687).]

(b) A narrative description of the events that led to the plan sponsor's decision to submit an application for partition (and, if applicable, application for suspension of benefits).

(c) A narrative description of significant risks and assumptions relating to the proposed partition and the projections provided in support of the application.

(d) If applicable, a copy of the plan sponsor's application for suspension of benefits (including all attachments and exhibits). If the plan sponsor intends to apply for a suspension of benefits with Treasury, but has not yet submitted an application to Treasury, a draft of the application may be filed, which must be supplemented by filing a copy of the completed application within the timeframe established in § 4233.10(d).

(e) A detailed description of all measures the plan sponsor has taken (or is taking) to avoid insolvency, and any measures the plan sponsor considered taking but did not take, including the factor(s) the plan sponsor considered in making these determinations. Include all relevant documentation relating to the plan sponsor's determination that it has taken (or is taking) measures to avoid insolvency.

(f) A detailed description of the estimated benefit amounts the plan sponsor has determined are necessary to be partitioned for the plan to remain solvent, including the following information:

(1) The estimated number of participants and beneficiaries whose benefits (or any portion thereof) would be transferred, including the number of retirees receiving payments (if any), terminated vested participants (if any), and active participants (if any).

(2) Supporting data, calculations, assumptions, and a description of the methodology used to determine the estimated benefit amounts.

(3) If applicable, a description of any classifications or specific group(s) of participants and beneficiaries whose benefits (or any portion thereof) the plan sponsor proposes to transfer, and the plan sponsor's rationale or basis for selecting those classifications or groups.

(g) A copy of the draft notice of application for partition described in § 4233.11.

[¶ 15,702G]

§ 4233.7 **Actuarial and financial information.** (a) *Required information.* An application for partition must include the following plan actuarial and financial information:

(1) A copy of the plan's most recent actuarial report and copies of the actuarial reports for the two preceding plan years.

(2) A copy of the plan actuary's most recent certification of critical and declining status, including a detailed description of the assumptions used in the certification, the basis for the projection of future contributions, withdrawal liability payments, investment return assumptions, and any other assumption that may have a material effect on projections.

(3) A detailed statement of the basis for the conclusion that the plan will not remain solvent without a partition and, if applicable, suspension of benefits, including supporting data, calculations, assumptions, and a description of the methodology. Include as an exhibit annual cash flow projections for the plan without partition (or suspension, if applicable) through the projected date of insolvency. Annual cash flow projections must reflect the following information:

(i) Market value of assets as of the beginning of the year.

(ii) Contributions and withdrawal liability payments.

(iii) Benefit payments organized by participant status (*e.g.*, active, retiree, terminated vested, beneficiary). [Revised 12/23/2015 (80 FR 79687).]

(iv) Administrative expenses.

(v) Market value of assets at year end.

(4) A long-term projection reflecting reduced benefit disbursements at the PBGC-guarantee level after insolvency, and a statement of the present value of all future financial assistance without a partition (using the interest and mortality assumptions applicable to the valuation of plans terminated by mass withdrawal as specified in § 4281.13 of this chapter and other reasonable actuarial assumptions, including retirement age, form of benefit payment, and administrative expenses, certified by an enrolled actuary).

(5) A detailed statement of the basis for the conclusion that the original plan will remain solvent if the application for partition, and, if applicable, the application for suspension of benefits, is granted, including supporting data, calculations, assumptions, and a description of the methodology, which must be consistent with section 305(e)(9)(D)(iv) and the regulations thereunder (including any adjustment to the cash flows in the initial year to incorporate recent actual fund activity required to be included under that section). Annual cash flow projections for the original plan with partition (and suspension, if applicable) must be included as an exhibit and must reflect the following information:

(i) Market value of assets as of the beginning of the year.

(ii) Contributions and withdrawal liability payments.

(iii) Benefit payments organized by participant status (*e.g.*, active, retiree, terminated vested, beneficiary). [Revised 12/23/2015 (80 FR 79687).]

(iv) Administrative expenses.

(v) Market value of assets at year end.

(6) If applicable, a copy of the plan actuary's certification under section 305(e)(9)(C)(i) of ERISA.

(7) The plan's projected insolvency date with benefit suspension alone (if applicable), including supporting data.

(8) A long-term projection reflecting benefit disbursements from the successor plan (organized by participant status (*e.g.*, active, retiree, terminated vested, beneficiary)), and a statement of the present value of all future financial assistance to be paid as a result of a partition (using the interest and mortality assumptions applicable to the valuation of plans terminated by mass withdrawal as specified in § 4281.13 of this chapter and other reasonable actuarial assumptions, including retirement age, form of benefit payment, and administrative expenses, certified by an enrolled actuary). [Revised 12/23/2015 (80 FR 79687).]

(9) A long-term projection of pre-partition benefit disbursements from the original plan reflecting reduced benefit disbursements at the PBGC-guarantee level beginning on the proposed effective date of the partition (using a closed group valuation and no accruals after the proposed effective date of partition, and organized separately by participant status groupings (*e.g.*, active, retiree, terminated vested, beneficiary)). [Added 12/23/2015 (80 FR 79687).]

(10) A long-term projection of pre-partition benefit disbursements from the original plan reflecting the maximum benefit suspensions permissible under section 305(e)(9) of ERISA beginning on the proposed effective date of the partition (using an open group valuation and organized separately by participant status groupings (*e.g.*, active, retiree, terminated vested, beneficiary)). [Added 12/23/2015 (80 FR 79687).]

(b) *Additional projections.* PBGC may ask the plan for additional projections based on assumptions that it specifies.

(c) *Actuarial calculations and assumptions.* (1) *General.* All calculations required by this part must be performed by an enrolled actuary.

(2) *Assumptions.* All calculations required by this part must be consistent with calculations used for purposes of an application for suspension of benefits under section 305(e)(9) of ERISA, and based on methods and assumptions each of which is reasonable (taking into account the experience of the plan and reasonable expectations), and which, in combination, offer the actuary's best estimate of anticipated experience under the plan. Any change(s) in assumptions from the most recent actuarial valuation, and critical and declining status certification, must be disclosed and must be accompanied by a statement explaining the reason(s) for any change(s) in assumptions.

(3) *Updates.* PBGC may, in its discretion, require updated calculations and representations based on the actual effective date of a partition, revised actuarial assumptions, or for other good cause.

[¶ 15,702H]

§ 4233.8 **Participant census data.** An application for partition must include a copy of the census data used for the projections described in § 4233.7(a)(3) and (5), including:

(a) Participant type (retiree, beneficiary, disabled, terminated vested, active, alternate payee).

(b) Date of birth.

(c) Gender.

(d) Credited service for guarantee calculation (*i.e.*, number of years of participation).

(e) Vested accrued monthly benefit before benefit suspension under section 305(e)(9) of ERISA.

(f) Vested accrued monthly benefit after benefit suspension under section 305(e)(9) of ERISA.

(g Monthly benefit guaranteed by PBGC (determined under the terms of the original plan without respect to benefit suspensions).

(h) Benefit commencement date (for participants in pay status and others for which the reported benefit is not payable at Normal Retirement Date).

(i) For each participant in pay status—

(1) Form of payment, and

(2) Data relevant to the form of payment, including:

(i) For a joint and survivor benefit, the beneficiary's benefit amount (before and after suspension) and the beneficiary's date of birth;

(ii) For a Social Security level income benefit, the date of any change in the benefit amount, and the benefit amount after such change;

(iii) For a 5-year certain or 10-year certain benefit (or similar benefit), the relevant defined period.

(iv) For a form of payment not otherwise described in this section, the data necessary for the valuation of the form of payment, including the benefit amount before and after suspension.

(j) If an actuarial increase for postponed retirement applies or if the form of annuity is a Social Security level income option, the monthly vested benefit payable at normal retirement age in normal form of annuity.

[Revised 12/23/2015 (80 FR 79687).]

[¶ 15,702I]

§ 4233.9 **Financial assistance information.** (a) *Required information.* An application for partition must include the estimated amount of annual financial assistance requested from PBGC for the first year the plan receives financial assistance if partition is approved.

(b) *Additional information.* PBGC may ask the plan for additional information in accordance with § 4233.4(b)(1).

[¶ 15,702J]

§ 4233.10 **Initial review.** (a) *Determination on completed application.* PBGC will make a determination on an application not later than 270 days after the date such application is deemed completed.

(b) *Incomplete application.* If the application is incomplete, PBGC will issue a written notice to the plan sponsor describing the information missing from the application no later than 14 calendar days after the submission of such application. [Revised 12/23/2015 (80 FR 79687).]

(c) *Complete application.* Upon making a determination that an application is complete (*i.e.*, the application includes all the information specified in §§ 4233.5 through 4233.9), PBGC will issue a written notice to the plan sponsor no later than 14 calendar days after the submission of such application. The date of the written notice will mark the beginning of PBGC's 270-day review period under section 4233(a)(1) of ERISA, and the plan sponsor's 30-day notice period under 4233(a)(2) of ERISA. [Revised 12/23/2015 (80 FR 79687).]

(d) *Special rule for coordinated applications for partition and benefit suspension.* For a plan requiring both partition and benefit suspensions to remain solvent, PBGC's initial determination that a partition application is complete will be conditioned on the plan sponsor's filing of an application for benefit suspensions with Treasury within 30 days after receiving written notice from PBGC under paragraph (c) of this section. Such a plan is permitted, but not required, to issue a combined notice under § 4233.13(b).

(e) *Informal consultation.* Nothing in this subsection precludes a plan sponsor from contacting PBGC on an informal basis to discuss a potential partition application.

[¶ 15,702K]

§ 4233.11 **Notice of application for partition.** (a) *When to file.* Not later than 30 days after receipt of the written notice described in § 4233.10(c) that an application for partition is complete, the plan sponsor must provide notice of such application to each interested party and PBGC, in accordance with the rules in part 4000, subpart B of this chapter.

(b) *Form of notice.* The notice must be readable and written in a matter calculated to be understood by the average plan participant. The Model Notices in Appendix A to this part (when properly completed) are examples of notices meeting the requirements of this section.

(c) *Information required.* A notice of completed application for partition must include the following information:

(1) *Identifying information.* The name of the plan, the name, address, and phone number of the plan sponsor, the Employer Identification Number (EIN), and three-digit Plan Number (PN).

(2) *Relevant partition application dates.* A brief statement that the plan sponsor has submitted an application for partition to PBGC, the date of the completed application under § 4233.10(c), and a statement that PBGC must issue its decision not later than 270 days after the date on which PBGC notified the plan sponsor that the application was complete.

(3) *Application for suspension of benefits.* If applicable, a statement of whether the plan sponsor has submitted an application for suspension of benefits under section 305(e)(9)(G) of ERISA, and, if so, information on how to obtain a copy of the application and notice required by section 305(e)(9)(F) of ERISA.

(4) *Description of statutory partition provisions.* A brief description of the requirements under section 4233 of ERISA, and other related statutory requirements, including:

(i) The interrelationship between the partition rules under section 4233 of ERISA and suspensions of benefits under section 305(e)(9) of ERISA (if applicable).

(ii) The multiemployer guarantee under section 4022A of ERISA.

(iii) The eligibility requirements for a partition under section 4233(b) of ERISA, including the Advocate consultation requirement.

(5) *Impact of partition on interested parties.* A brief description of how the proposed partition may impact affected participants, beneficiaries, and alternate payees including:

(i) A statement describing the benefit payment obligations of the original plan and the successor plan.

(ii) A statement explaining that the Board of Trustees of the original plan will also administer the successor plan, but the successor plan will be funded solely by PBGC financial assistance payments.

(6) *Partition application contents summary.* A brief summary of the content of the plan sponsor's application for partition, including the following information:

(i) The plan's critical and declining status and projected insolvency date.

(ii) A statement that the plan sponsor has taken (or is taking) all reasonable measures to avoid insolvency, including the maximum benefit suspensions under section 305(e)(9), if applicable.

(iii) If known, a brief statement on the proposed total estimated amount and percentage of liabilities to be partitioned.

(iv) If known, a brief statement summarizing the proposed class or classes of participants whose benefits would be partially or wholly transferred if the application for partition is granted, including a summary of the factors considered by the plan sponsor in preparing its application.

(7) *Contact information for plan sponsor.* The name, address, and telephone number of the plan sponsor or other person designated by the plan sponsor to answer inquiries concerning the application for partition.

(8) *Contact information for PBGC.* Multiemployer Program Division, PBGC, 1200 K Street, NW., Washington, DC 20005-4026, *Multiemployerprogram@pbgc.gov.*

(9) *Contact information for Participant and Plan Sponsor Advocate.* PBGC Participant and Plan Sponsor Advocate, 1200 K Street NW., Washington, DC 20005-4026, *Advocate@pbgc.gov.*

(d) *Model notice.* The appendix to this section contains two model notices—one for plan sponsors that submit coordinated applications for partition with PBGC and for benefit suspensions with Treasury, and one for plans sponsors who apply for partition only. The model notices are intended to assist plan sponsors in discharging their notice obligations under section 4233(a)(2) of ERISA and this part. Use of the model notices is not mandatory, but will be deemed to satisfy the requirements of section 4233(a)(2) of ERISA and this part.

(e) *Foreign languages.* The plan sponsor of a plan that covers the numbers or percentages in § 2520.104b-10(e) of this title of participants literate only in the same non-English language must, for any notice to interested parties—

(1) Include a prominent legend in that common non-English language advising them how to obtain assistance in understanding the notice; or

(2) Provide the notice in that common non-English language to those interested parties literate only in that language.

[¶ 15,702L]

§ 4233.12 **PBGC action on application for partition.** (a) *Review period.* Except as provided in paragraph (c) of this section, PBGC will approve or deny an application for partition submitted to it under this part within 270 days after the date PBGC issued a notice to the plan sponsor of the completed application under § 4233.10(c).

(b) *Determination on application.* PBGC may approve or deny an application at its discretion. PBGC will notify the plan sponsor in writing of PBGC's decision on an application. If PBGC denies the application, PBGC's written decision will state the reason(s) for the denial. If PBGC approves the application, PBGC will issue a partition order under section 4233(c) of ERISA and § 4233.14.

(c) *Conditional determination on application.* At the request of a plan sponsor, PBGC may, in its discretion, issue an approval of an application conditioned on Treasury issuing a final authorization to suspend under section 305(e)(9)(H)(vi) of ERISA and any other terms and conditions set forth in the conditional approval. The conditional approval will include a written statement of preliminary findings, conclusions, and conditions. The conditional approval is not a final agency action. The proposed partition will only become effective upon satisfaction of the required conditions, and the issuance of an order of partition under section 4233(c) of ERISA. [Revised 12/23/2015 (80 FR 79687).]

(d) *Final agency action.* Except as provided in paragraph (c) of this section, PBGC's decision on an application for partition under this section is a final agency action for purposes of judicial review under the Administrative Procedure Act (5 U.S.C. 701 *et seq.*).

[¶ 15,702M]

§ 4233.13 **Coordinated application process for partition and benefit suspension.** (a) *Interagency coordination.* For a plan sponsor that has requested a conditional approval of a partition pursuant to § 4233.12(c), PBGC may render either a conditional approval or a final denial of the application on an expedited basis, provided that the plan sponsor has submitted a completed application to PBGC as prescribed by § 4233.10. PBGC will consult with Treasury and the Department of Labor in the course of reviewing an application for partition.

(1) If PBGC denies the application for partition, it will notify the plan sponsor in writing of PBGC's decision in accordance with § 4233.12(b), and will notify Treasury to allow it to take appropriate action on the benefit suspension application.

(2) If PBGC grants a conditional approval of partition, it will notify the plan sponsor in writing of PBGC's decision in accordance with § 4233.12(c), and will provide Treasury with a copy of PBGC's decision along with PBGC's record of the decision.

(3) If Treasury does not issue the final authorization to suspend, PBGC's conditional approval under § 4233.12(c) will be null and void. [Revised 12/23/2015 (80 FR 79687).]

(4) If Treasury issues a final authorization to suspend, PBGC will issue a final partition order under § 4233.14 and section 4233(c) of ERISA. The effective date of a final partition order must satisfy the requirements of section 305(e)(9)(D)(v) of ERISA. [Revised 12/23/2015 (80 FR 79687).]

(b) *Combined notice.* A plan sponsor submitting an application for benefit suspensions under section 305(e)(9) of ERISA with Treasury, and a partition under section 4233 of ERISA with PBGC, may combine the PBGC model notice for coordinated applications provided at Appendix A with the Treasury model notice in Appendix A of Rev. Proc. 2015-34 in satisfaction of the notice requirement of this part.

[¶ 15,702N]

§ 4233.14 **Partition order.** (a) *General Provisions.* The partition order will describe the liabilities to be transferred to the successor plan under section 4233(c) of ERISA, and the manner in which financial assistance will be provided by PBGC under section 4261 of ERISA. The partition order will also set forth PBGC's findings and conclusions on an application for partition, the effective date of partition, the obligations and responsibilities of the plan sponsor to the original plan and successor plan, and such other information as PBGC may deem appropriate.

(b) *Terms and conditions.* The partition order will set forth the terms and conditions of the partition and will incorporate by reference the applicable requirements under sections 4233(d) and 4233(e) of ERISA.

(1) The plan sponsors of the original plan and the successor plan must amend the original plan and successor plan, respectively, to reflect the benefits payable to participants and beneficiaries as a result of the partition order.

(2) The plan sponsors of the original plan and successor plan must maintain a written record of the respective plans' compliance with the terms of the partition order, section 4233 of ERISA, and this part.

[¶ 15,702O]

§ 4233.15 **Nature and operation of successor plan.** (a) *Nature of plan.* The plan created by the partition order is a successor plan to which section 4022A applies, and an insolvent plan under section 4245 of ERISA.

(b) *Treatment of plan.* The successor plan will be treated as a terminated multiemployer plan to which section 4041A(d) of ERISA applies because there are no contributing employers with an obligation to contribute within the meaning of section 4212 of ERISA as of the effective date of the partition. The treatment of the successor plan as a terminated plan under this paragraph will not be taken into account for purposes of determining the withdrawal liability of contributing employers to the original plan under sections 4201 and 4233(d)(3) of ERISA.

(c) *Administration of plan.* The plan sponsor of the original plan and the administrator of such plan will be the plan sponsor and the administrator, respectively, of the successor plan. PBGC will retain the right to remove and replace the plan sponsor of the successor plan pursuant to section 4042(b)(2) of ERISA.

[¶ 15,702P]

§ 4233.16 **Coordination of benefits under original plan and successor plan.** (a) *Successor plan benefits.* Subject to the limitations contained in section 4022A of ERISA, the only benefit amounts payable under a successor plan are successor plan benefits as defined in § 4233.2.

(b) *Guarantee of successor plan benefit.* When a participant's or beneficiary's benefit is partially or wholly transferred to a successor plan, the PBGC guarantee applicable to such benefit becomes payable under the successor plan. The benefit remaining in the original plan as of the effective date of the partition, if any, is not subject to a new guarantee, and any increase in the PBGC guarantee amount payable under the original plan will arise solely, if at all, due to an increase in the accrued benefit under a plan amendment following the effective date of the partition, or an additional accrual attributable to service after the effective date of the partition.

(c) *PBGC financial assistance.* Subject to the conditions contained in section 4261 of ERISA, PBGC will provide financial assistance to the successor plan in an amount sufficient to enable the successor plan to pay only the PBGC-guaranteed amount transferred to the successor plan pursuant to the partition order, and reasonable and necessary administrative expenses if approved by PBGC. The receipt of benefits payable under a successor plan receiving financial assistance from PBGC will be treated as the receipt of guaranteed benefits under section 4022A.

(d) *Payment of monthly benefits.* The plan sponsors of an original plan and a successor plan may, but are not required to, pay monthly benefits payable under the original plan and successor plan, respectively, in a single monthly payment pursuant to a written cost-sharing or expense allocation agreement between the plans.

[¶ 15,702Q]

§ 4233.17 **Continuing jurisdiction.** (a) PBGC will continue to have jurisdiction over the original plan and the successor plan to carry out the purposes, terms, and conditions of the partition order, section 4233 of ERISA, and this part.

(b) PBGC may, upon providing notice to the plan sponsor, make changes to the partition order in response to changed circumstances consistent with section 4233 of ERISA and this part.

[¶ 15,702R]

§ 4233.17 **Appendix A to Part 4233—Model Notices**
NOTICE OF APPLICATION FOR PARTITION FOR [INSERT PLAN NAME]

[For plans filing an application for partition only]

[Insert Date]

This notice is to inform you that, on [*insert Date*], [*insert Plan Sponsor's Name*] ("Board of Trustees") filed a complete application with the Pension Benefit Guaranty Corporation ("PBGC") requesting approval for a partition of the [*insert Pension Fund name, Employer Identification Number, and three-digit Plan Number*] (the "Plan").

What is partition?

A multiemployer plan that is in critical and declining status may apply to PBGC for an order that separates (*i.e.*, partitions) and transfers the PBGC-guaranteed portion of certain participants' and beneficiaries' benefits to a newly-created successor plan. The total amount transferred from the original plan to the successor plan is the minimum amount needed to keep the original plan solvent. While the Board of Trustees will administer the successor plan, PBGC will provide financial assistance to the successor plan to pay the transferred benefits.

PBGC guarantees benefits up to a legal limit. However, if the PBGC-guaranteed amount payable by the successor plan is less than the benefit payable under the original plan, Federal law requires the original plan to pay the difference. Therefore, partition will *not* change the total amount payable to any participant or beneficiary.

What are the rules for partition?

Federal law permits, but does not require, PBGC to approve an application for partition. PBGC generally will make a decision on the application for partition within 270 days. A plan is eligible for partition if certain requirements are met, including:

1. The pension plan is in critical and declining status. A plan is in critical and declining status if it is in critical status (which generally means the plan's funded percentage is less than 65%) and is projected to run out of money within 15 years (or 20 years if there are twice as many inactive as active participants, or if the plan's funded percentage is less than 80%).

2. PBGC determines, after consulting with the PBGC Participant and Plan Sponsor Advocate, that the Board of Trustees has taken (or is taking) all reasonable measures to avoid insolvency. Reasonable measures may include contribution increases or reductions in the rate of benefit accruals.

3. PBGC determines that: (1) Providing financial assistance in a partition will be significantly less than providing financial assistance in the event the plan becomes insolvent; and (2) partition is necessary for the plan to remain solvent.

4. PBGC certifies to Congress that its ability to meet existing financial assistance obligations to other multiemployer plans (including plans that are insolvent or projected to become insolvent within 10 years) will not be impaired by the partition.

5. The cost of the partition is paid exclusively from PBGC's multiemployer insurance fund.

Why is partition needed?

The Plan is in critical and declining status, is [*insert funded percentage*] funded, and is projected to become insolvent by [*insert expected insolvency date*]. The Board of Trustees asserts that it has taken reasonable measures to avoid insolvency, but has determined that

these measures are insufficient and that the proposed partition is necessary for the Plan to avoid insolvency.

[*Insert brief statement of the amount of liabilities the Board of Trustees proposes to partition and indicate whether it is the minimum amount needed for the Plan to remain solvent.*][*If applicable, insert brief statement summarizing the proposed classes of participants and beneficiaries whose benefits will be partially or wholly transferred if the application is granted, and a summary of the factors considered.*] If instead the Plan is allowed to become insolvent, the benefits of *all* participants and beneficiaries whose benefits exceed the PBGC-guaranteed amount would be reduced to the PBGC-guaranteed amount.

What is PBGC's multiemployer plan guarantee?

Federal law sets the maximum that PBGC may guarantee. For multiemployer plan benefits, PBGC guarantees a monthly benefit payment equal to 100 percent of the first $11 of the Plan's monthly benefit accrual rate, plus 75 percent of the next $33 of the accrual rate, times each year of credited service. The PBGC's maximum guarantee, therefore, is $35.75 per month times a participant's years of credited service.

PBGC guarantees vested pension benefits payable at normal retirement age, early retirement benefits, and certain survivor benefits, if the participant met the eligibility requirements for a benefit before plan termination or insolvency. A benefit or benefit increase that has been in effect for less than 60 months is not eligible for PBGC's guarantee. PBGC also does not guarantee benefits above the normal retirement benefit, disability benefits not in pay status, or non-pension benefits, such as health insurance, life insurance, death benefits, vacation pay, or severance pay.

How will I know when PBGC has made a decision on the application for partition?

If PBGC approves the Board of Trustees' application for partition, PBGC will issue a notice to affected participants and beneficiaries whose benefits will be transferred to the successor plan no later than 14 days after it issues the order of partition. You may also visit *www.pbgc.gov/MPRA* for a list of applications for partition received by PBGC and the status of those applications.

Your Rights To Receive Information About Your Plan and its Benefits

Your plan's Summary Plan Description ("SPD") will include information on the procedures for claiming benefits, which will apply to both the original and successor plans until the Plan provides you a new SPD. You also have the legal right to request documents from the original plan to help you understand the partition and your rights such as:

• The plan document, trust agreement, and other documents governing the Plan (*e.g.*, collective bargaining agreements);

• The latest SPD and summaries of material modification;

• The Plan's Form 5500 annual reports, including audited financial statements, filed with the U.S. Department of Labor during the last six years;

• The Plan's annual funding notices for the last six years;

• Actuarial reports (including reports submitted in support of the application for partition) furnished to the Plan within the last six years;

• The Plan's current rehabilitation plan, including contribution schedules; and

• Any quarterly, semi-annual or annual financial reports prepared for the Plan by an investment manager, fiduciary or other advisor and furnished to the Plan within the last six years.

If your benefits are transferred to the successor plan, you will be furnished a successor plan SPD within 120 days of the partition; and the plan document, trust agreement, and other documents governing the successor plan will be available for review following the partition.

The plan administrator must respond to your request for these documents within 30 days, and may charge you the cost per page for the least expensive means of reproducing documents, but cannot charge more than 25 cents per page. The Plan's Form 5500 annual reports are also available free of charge at *http://www.dol.gov/ ebsa/5500main.html.* Some of the documents also may be available for examination, without charge, at the plan administrator's office, your worksite, or union hall.

Plan Contact Information

For more information about this Notice, you may contact:

[Insert Name of Plan Administrator, address, email address, and phone number]

PBGC Contact Information

Multiemployer Program Division, PBGC, 1200 K Street NW., Washington, DC 20005-4026

Email: *Multiemployerprogram@pbgc.gov*

Phone: (202) 326-4000 x6535

PBGC Participant and Plan Sponsor Advocate Contact Information

Constance Donovan, PBGC, 1200 K Street NW., Washington, DC 20005-4026

Email: *Advocate@pbgc.gov*.

Phone: (202) 326-4488

NOTICE OF APPLICATION FOR PARTITION FOR [INSERT PLAN NAME]

[For plans filing coordinated applications for partition and suspension of benefits]

[Insert Date]

This notice is to inform you that, on [*insert Date*], [*insert Plan Sponsor's Name*] ("Board of Trustees") filed a complete application with the Pension Benefit Guaranty Corporation ("PBGC") requesting approval for a partition of the [*insert Pension Fund name, Employer Identification Number, and three-digit Plan Number*] (the "Plan"). [*Insert statement that the plan sponsor has submitted an application for suspension of benefits under section 305(e)(9)(G) of ERISA, and identify how to obtain a copy of the application and notice required by section 305(e)(9)(F) of ERISA.*]

What is partition?

A multiemployer plan that is in critical and declining status may apply to PBGC for an order that separates (*i.e.*, partitions) and transfers the PBGC-guaranteed portion of certain participants' and beneficiaries' benefits to a newly-created successor plan. The total amount transferred from the original plan to the successor plan is the minimum amount needed to keep the original plan solvent. While the Board of Trustees will administer the successor plan, PBGC will provide financial assistance to the successor plan to pay the transferred benefits.

PBGC guarantees benefits up to a legal limit. However, if the PBGC-guaranteed amount payable by the successor plan is less than the benefit payable under the original plan after taking into account benefit reductions or any plan amendments after the effective date of the partition, Federal law requires the original plan to pay the difference. Therefore, partition will *not* further change the total amount payable to any participant or beneficiary.

What are the rules for partition?

Federal law permits, but does not require, PBGC to approve an application for partition. PBGC generally will make a decision on the application for partition within 270 days. A plan is eligible for partition if certain requirements are met, including:

1. The pension plan is in critical and declining status. A plan is in critical and declining status if it is in critical status (which generally means the plan's funded percentage is less than 65%) and is projected to run out of money within 15 years (or 20 years if there are at least twice as many inactive as active participants, or if the plan's funded percentage is less than 80%).

2. PBGC determines, after consulting with the PBGC Participant and Plan Sponsor Advocate, that the Board of Trustees has taken (or is taking) all reasonable measures to avoid insolvency, including reducing benefits to the maximum allowed under the law.

3. PBGC determines that: (1) Providing financial assistance in a partition will be significantly less than providing financial assistance in the event the plan becomes insolvent; and (2) partition is necessary for the plan to remain solvent.

4. PBGC certifies to Congress that its ability to meet existing financial assistance obligations to other multiemployer plans (including plans that are insolvent or projected to become insolvent within 10 years) will not be impaired by the partition.

5. The cost of the partition is paid exclusively from PBGC's multiemployer insurance fund.

Why are partition and benefit reductions needed?

The Plan is in critical and declining status, is [*insert funded percentage*] funded, and is projected to become insolvent by [*insert expected insolvency date*]. The Board of Trustees has taken reasonable measures to avoid insolvency, but has determined that these measures are insufficient and that the proposed partition and reduction of benefits combined are necessary for the Plan to avoid insolvency.

[*Insert brief statement of the amount of liabilities the Board of Trustees proposes to partition and indicate whether it is the minimum amount needed for the Plan to remain solvent.*][*If applicable, insert brief statement summarizing the proposed classes of participants and beneficiaries whose benefits will be partially or wholly transferred if the application is granted, and a summary of the factors considered.*] If instead the Plan is allowed to become insolvent, the benefits of *all* participants and beneficiaries whose benefits exceed the PBGC-guaranteed amount would be reduced to the PBGC-guaranteed amount.

What is PBGC's multiemployer plan guarantee?

Federal law sets the maximum that PBGC may guarantee. For multiemployer plan benefits, PBGC guarantees a monthly benefit payment equal to 100 percent of the first $11 of the Plan's monthly benefit accrual rate, plus 75 percent of the next $33 of the accrual rate, times each year of credited service. PBGC's maximum guarantee, therefore, is $35.75 per month times a participant's years of credited service.

PBGC guarantees vested pension benefits payable at normal retirement age, early retirement benefits, and certain survivor benefits, if the participant met the eligibility requirements for a benefit before plan termination or insolvency. A benefit or benefit increase that has been in effect for less than 60 months is not eligible for PBGC's guarantee. PBGC also does not guarantee benefits above the normal retirement benefit, disability benefits not in pay status, or non-pension benefits, such as health insurance, life insurance, death benefits, vacation pay, or severance pay.

How will I know when PBGC has made a decision on the application for partition?

If PBGC approves the Board of Trustees' application for partition, PBGC will issue a notice to affected participants and beneficiaries whose benefits will be transferred to the successor plan no later than 14 days after it issues the order of partition. You may also visit *www.pbgc.gov/MPRA* for a list of applications for partition received by PBGC and the status of those applications.

How do I obtain information on the application for approval to reduce benefits?

The application for approval of the proposed reduction of benefits will be publicly available within 30 days after the Treasury Department receives the application. *See www.treasury.gov* for a copy of the application, instructions on how to send comments on the application, and how to contact the Treasury Department for further information and assistance.

Your Rights To Receive Information About Your Plan and its Benefits

Your Plan's Summary Plan Description ("SPD") will include information on the procedures for claiming benefits, which will apply to both the original and successor plans until the Plan provides you a new SPD. You also have the legal right to request documents from the original plan to help you understand the partition and your rights such as:

• The plan document, trust agreement, and other documents governing the Plan (*e.g.*, collective bargaining agreements);

• The latest SPD and summaries of material modification;

• The Plan's Form 5500 annual reports, including audited financial statements, filed with the U.S. Department of Labor during the last six years;

• The Plan's annual funding notices for the last six years;

• Actuarial reports (including reports submitted in support of the application for partition) furnished to the Plan within the last six years;

• The Plan's current rehabilitation plan, including contribution schedules; and

• Any quarterly, semi-annual or annual financial reports prepared for the Plan by an investment manager, fiduciary or other advisor and furnished to the Plan within the last six years.

If your benefits are transferred to the successor plan, you will be furnished a successor plan SPD within 120 days of the partition; and the plan document, trust agreement, and other documents governing the successor plan will be available for review following the partition.

The plan administrator must respond to your request for these documents within 30 days, and may charge you the cost per page for the least expensive means of reproducing documents, but cannot charge more than 25 cents per page. The Plan's Form 5500 annual reports are also available free of charge at *http://www.dol.gov/ebsa/5500main.html.* Some of the documents also may be available for examination, without charge, at the plan administrator's office, your worksite, or union hall.

Plan Contact Information

For more information about this Notice, you may contact:

[Insert Name of Plan Administrator, address, email address, and phone number]

PBGC Contact Information

Multiemployer Program Division, PBGC, 1200 K Street NW., Washington, DC 20005–4026

Email: *Multiemployerprogram@pbgc.gov*

Phone: (202) 326–4000 x6535

PBGC Participant and Plan Sponsor Advocate Contact Information

Constance Donovan, PBGC, 1200 K Street

NW., Washington, DC 20005–4026

Email: *Advocate@pbgc.gov*

Phone: (202) 326–4488

[¶ 15,703]
ASSET TRANSFER RULES

Act Sec. 4234. (a) APPLICABILITY AND SCOPE.—A transfer of assets from a multiemployer plan to another plan shall comply with asset-transfer rules which shall be adopted by the multiemployer plan and which—

(1) do not unreasonably restrict the transfer of plan assets in connection with the transfer of plan liabilities, and

(2) operate and are applied uniformly with respect to each proposed transfer, except that the rules may provide for reasonable variations taking into account the potential financial impact of a proposed transfer on the multiemployer plan.

Plan rules authorizing asset transfers consistent with the requirements of section 4232(c)(3) shall be considered to satisfy the requirements of this subsection.

Act Sec. 4234. (b) EXEMPTION OF DE MINIMIS TRANSFERS.—The corporation shall prescribe regulations which exempt de minimis transfers of assets from the requirements of this part.

Act Sec. 4234. (c) WRITTEN RECIPROCITY AGREEMENTS.—This part shall not apply to transfers of assets pursuant to written reciprocity agreements, except to the extent provided in regulations prescribed by the corporation.

Amendment

P.L. 96-364, §104(2):

Added Sec. 4234, effective September 26, 1980 under ERISA Sec. 4402.

[¶ 15,704]
TRANSFERS PURSUANT TO CHANGE IN BARGAINING REPRESENTATIVE

Act Sec. 4235. (a) AUTHORITY TO TRANSFER FROM OLD PLAN TO NEW PLAN PURSUANT TO EMPLOYEE PARTICIPATION IN ANOTHER MULTIEMPLOYER PLAN AFTER CERTIFIED CHANGE OF REPRESENTATIVE.—In any case in which an employer has completely or partially withdrawn from a multiemployer plan (hereafter in this section referred to as the "old plan") as a result of a certified change of collective bargaining representative occurring after September 25, 1980, if participants of the old plan who are employed by the employer will, as a result of that change, participate in another multiemployer plan (hereafter in this section referred to as the "new plan"), the old plan shall transfer assets and liabilities to the new plan in accordance with this section.

Act Sec. 4235. (b)(1) NOTIFICATION BY EMPLOYER OF PLAN SPONSOR OF OLD PLAN; NOTIFICATION BY PLAN SPONSOR OF OLD PLAN OF EMPLOYER AND PLAN SPONSOR OF NEW PLAN; APPEAL BY NEW PLAN TO PREVENT TRANSFER; FURTHER PROCEEDINGS.—The employer shall notify the plan sponsor of the old plan of a change in multiemployer plan participation described in subsection (a) no later than 30 days after the employer determines that the change will occur.

(2) The plan sponsor of the old plan shall—

(A) notify the employer of—

(i) the amount of the employer's withdrawal liability determined under part 1 with respect to the withdrawal,

(ii) the old plan's intent to transfer to the new plan the nonforfeitable benefits of the employees who are no longer working in covered service under the old plan as a result of the change of bargaining representative, and

(iii) the amount of assets and liabilities which are to be transferred to the new plan, and

(B) notify the plan sponsor of the new plan of the benefits, assets, and liabilities which will be transferred to the new plan.

(3) Within 60 days after receipt of the notice described in paragraph (2)(B), the new plan may file an appeal with the corporation to prevent the transfer. The transfer shall not be made if the corporation determines that the new plan would suffer substantial financial harm as a result of the transfer. Upon notification described in paragraph (2), if—

(A) the employer fails to object to the transfer within 60 days after receipt of the notice described in paragraph (2)(A), or

(B) the new plan either—

(i) fails to file such an appeal, or

(ii) the corporation, pursuant to such an appeal, fails to find that the new plan would suffer substantial financial harm as a result of the transfer described in the notice under paragraph (2)(B) within 180 days after the date on which the appeal is filed,

then the plan sponsor of the old plan shall transfer the appropriate amount of assets and liabilities to the new plan.

Act Sec. 4235. (c) REDUCTION OF AMOUNT OF WITHDRAWAL LIABILITY OF EMPLOYER UPON TRANSFER OF APPROPRIATE AMOUNT OF ASSETS AND LIABILITIES BY PLAN SPONSOR OF OLD PLAN TO NEW PLAN.—If the plan sponsor of the old plan transfers the appropriate amount of assets and liabilities under this section to the new plan, then the amount of the employer's withdrawal liability (as determined under section 4201(b) without regard to such transfer and this section) with respect to the old plan shall be reduced by the amount by which—

(1) the value of the unfunded vested benefits allocable to the employer which were transferred by the plan sponsor of the old plan to the new plan, exceeds

(2) the value of the assets transferred.

Act Sec. 4235. (d) ESCROW PAYMENTS BY EMPLOYER UPON COMPLETE OR PARTIAL WITHDRAWAL AND PRIOR TO TRANSFER.—In any case in which there is a complete or partial withdrawal described in subsection (a), if—

(1) the new plan files an appeal with the corporation under subsection (b)(3), and

(2) the employer is required by section 4219 to begin making payments of withdrawal liability before the earlier of—

(A) the date on which the corporation finds that the new plan would not suffer substantial financial harm as a result of the transfer, or

(B) the last day of the 180-day period beginning on the date on which the new plan files its appeal, then the employer shall make such payments into an escrow held by a bank or similar financial institution satisfactory to the old plan. If the transfer is made, the amounts paid into the escrow shall be returned to the employer. If the transfer is not made, the amounts paid into the escrow shall be paid to the old plan and credited against the employer's withdrawal liability.

Act Sec. 4235. (e)(1) PROHIBITION ON TRANSFER OF ASSETS TO NEW PLAN BY PLAN SPONSOR OF OLD PLAN; EXEMPTIONS.—Notwithstanding subsection (b), the plan sponsor shall not transfer any assets to the new plan if—

(A) the old plan is in reorganization (within the meaning of section 4241(a)), or

(B) the transfer of assets would cause the old plan to go into reorganization (within the meaning of section 4241(a)).

(2) In any case in which a transfer of assets from the old plan to the new plan is prohibited by paragraph (1), the plan sponsor of the old plan shall transfer—

(A) all nonforfeitable benefits described in subsection (b)(2), if the value of such benefits does not exceed the withdrawal liability of the employer with respect to such withdrawal, or

(B) such nonforfeitable benefits having a value equal to the withdrawal liability of the employer, if the value of such benefits exceeds the withdrawal liability of the employer.

Act Sec. 4235. (f)(1) AGREEMENT BETWEEN PLAN SPONSORS OF OLD PLAN AND NEW PLAN TO TRANSFER IN COMPLIANCE WITH OTHER STATUTORY PROVISIONS; REDUCTION OF WITHDRAWAL LIABILITY OF EMPLOYER FROM OLD PLAN; AMOUNT OF WITHDRAWAL LIABILITY OF EMPLOYER TO NEW PLAN.—Notwithstanding subsections (b) and (e), the plan sponsors of the old plan and the new plan may agree to a transfer of assets and liabilities that complies with sections 4231 and 4234, rather than this section, except that the employer's liability with respect to the withdrawal from the old plan shall be reduced under subsection (c) as if assets and liabilities had been transferred in accordance with this section.

(2) If the employer withdraws from the new plan within 240 months after the effective date of a transfer of assets and liabilities described in this section, the amount of the employer's withdrawal liability to the new plan shall be the greater of—

(A) the employer's withdrawal liability determined under part 1 with respect to the new plan, or

(B) the amount by which the employer's withdrawal liability to the old plan was reduced under subsection (c), reduced by 5 percent for each 12-month period following the effective date of the transfer and ending before the date of the withdrawal from the new plan.

Act Sec. 4235. (g) DEFINITIONS.—For purposes of this section—

(1) "appropriate amount of assets" means the amount by which the value of the nonforfeitable benefits to be transferred exceeds the amount of the employer's withdrawal liability to the old plan (determined under part 1 without regard to section 4211(e)), and

(2) "certified change of collective bargaining representative" means a change of collective bargaining representative certified under the Labor-Management Relations Act, 1947, or the Railway Labor Act.

Amendments

P.L. 98-369, §558(b):

Amended ERISA Sec. 4235(a) by striking out "April 28, 1980" and inserting "September 25, 1980" instead.

P.L. 96-364, §104(2):

Added Sec. 4235, September 26, 1980 under ERISA Sec. 4402.

Part 3—Insolvent Plans

[¶ 15,706]
[ERISA Sec. 4241—Repealed]
REORGANIZATION STATUS

Act Sec. 4241. Amendments

P.L. 113-235, §108(a)(1), Div. O:

Amended ERISA by repealing ERISA Sec. 4241.

Prior to the repeal, ERISA Sec. 4241 read as follows:

(a) REORGANIZATION INDEX OF PLAN FOR PLAN YEAR GREATER THAN ZERO.—A multiemployer plan is in reorganization for a plan year if the plan's reorganization index for that year is greater than zero.

(b)(1) DETERMINATION OF REORGANIZATION INDEX OF PLAN FOR PLAN YEAR; APPLICABLE FACTORS, DEFINITIONS, ETC.—A plan's reorganization index for any plan year is the excess of—

(A) the vested benefits charge for such year, over

(B) the net charge to the funding standard account for such year.

(2) For purposes of this part, the net charge to the funding standard account for any plan year is the excess (if any) of—

(A) the charges to the funding standard account for such year under section 412(b)(2) of the Internal Revenue Code of 1986, over

(B) the credits to the funding standard account under section 412(b)(3)(B) of such Code.

(3) For purposes of this part, the vested benefits charge for any plan year is the amount which would be necessary to amortize the plan's unfunded vested benefits as of the end of the base plan year in equal annual installments—

(A) over 10 years, to the extent such benefits are attributable to persons in pay status, and

(B) over 25 years, to the extent such benefits are attributable to other participants.

(4)(A) The vested benefits charge for a plan year shall be based on an actuarial valuation of the plan as of the end of the base plan year, adjusted to reflect—

(i) any—

(I) decrease of 5 percent or more in the value of plan assets, or increase of 5 percent or more in the number of persons in pay status, during the period beginning on the first day of the plan year following the base plan year and ending on the adjustment date, or

(II) at the election of the plan sponsor, actuarial valuation of the plan as of the adjustment date or any later date not later than the last day of the plan year for which the determination is being made,

(ii) any change in benefits under the plan which is not otherwise taken into account under this subparagraph and which is pursuant to any amendment—

(I) adopted before the end of the plan year for which the determination is being made, and

(II) effective after the end of the base plan year and on or before the end of the plan year referred to in subclause (I), and

(iii) any other event (including an event described in subparagraph (B)(i)(I)) which, as determined in accordance with regulations prescribed by the Secretary, would substantially increase the plan's vested benefit charge.

(B)(i) In determining the vested benefits charge for a plan year following a plan year in which the plan was not in reorganization, any change in benefits which—

(I) results from the changing of a group of participants from one benefit level to another benefit level under a schedule of plan benefits as a result of changes in a collective bargaining agreement, or

(II) results from any other change in a collective bargaining agreement,

shall not be taken into account except to the extent provided in regulations prescribed by the Secretary of the Treasury.

(ii) Except as otherwise determined by the Secretary of the Treasury, in determining the vested benefits charge for any plan year following any plan year in which the plan was in reorganization, any change in benefits—

(I) described in clause (i)(I), or

(II) described in clause (i)(II) as determined under regulations prescribed by the Secretary of the Treasury, shall, for purposes of subparagraph (A)(ii), be treated as a change in benefits pursuant to an amendment to a plan.

(5)(A) For purposes of this part, the base plan year for any plan year is—

(i) if there is a relevant collective bargaining agreement, the last plan year ending at least 6 months before the relevant effective date, or

(ii) if there is no relevant collective bargaining agreement, the last plan year ending at least 12 months before the beginning of the plan year.

(B) For purposes of this part, a relevant collective bargaining agreement is a collective bargaining agreement—

(i) which is in effect for at least 6 months during the plan year, and

(ii) which has not been in effect for more than 36 months as of the end of the plan year.

(C) For purposes of this part, the relevant effective date is the earliest of the effective dates for the relevant collective bargaining agreements.

(D) For purposes of this part, the adjustment date is the date which is—

(i) 90 days before the relevant effective date, or

(ii) if there is no relevant effective date, 90 days before the beginning of the plan year.

(6) For purposes of this part, the term "person in pay status" means—

(A) a participant or beneficiary on the last day of the base plan year who, at any time during such year, was paid an early, late, normal, or disability retirement benefit (or a death benefit related to a retirement benefit), and

(B) to the extent provided in regulations prescribed by the Secretary of the Treasury, any other person who is entitled to such a benefit under the plan.

(7) For purposes of paragraph (3)—

(A) in determining the plan's unfunded vested benefits, plan assets shall first be allocated to the vested benefits attributable to persons in pay status, and

(B) the vested benefits charge shall be determined without regard to reductions in accrued benefits under section 4244A which are first effective in the plan year.

(8) For purposes of this part, any outstanding claim for withdrawal liability shall not be considered a plan asset, except as otherwise provided in regulations prescribed by the Secretary of the Treasury.

(9) For purposes of this part, the term "unfunded vested benefits" means with respect to a plan, an amount (determined in accordance with regulations prescribed by the Secretary of the Treasury) equal to—

(A) the value of nonforfeitable benefits under the plan, less

(B) the value of assets of the plan.

(c) PAYMENT OF BENEFITS TO PARTICIPANTS.—Except as provided in regulations prescribed by the corporation, while a plan is in reorganization a benefit with respect to a participant (other than a death benefit) which is attributable to employer contributions and which has a value of more than $1,750 may not be paid in a form other than an annuity which (by itself or in combination with social security, railroad retirement, or workers' compensation benefits) provides substantially level payments over the life of the participant.

(d) TERMINATED MULTIEMPLOYER PLANS.—Any multiemployer plan which terminates under section 4041A(a)(2) shall not be considered in reorganization after the last day of the plan year in which the plan is treated as having terminated.

The above amendment shall apply with respect to plan years beginning after December 31, 2014.

P.L. 101-239, § 7891(a)(1):

Titles I, III, and IV of ERISA (other than sections 3(37)(E), 301(a)(7), and 308, the last sentence of section 408(d), and sections 414(c), 4001(a)(3)(ii), and 4303) are each amended by striking "Internal Revenue Code of 1954" each place it appears and inserting "Internal Revenue Code of 1986", effective October 22, 1986.

P.L. 96-364, § 104(2):

Added Sec. 4241 effective on or after the earlier of the date on which the last collective bargaining agreement providing contributions under the plan, which was in effect on September 26, 1980, expires, without regard to extensions agreed to on or after September 26, 1980 or September 26, 1983 under ERISA Sec. 4402.

[¶ 15,708]
[ERISA Sec. 4242—Repealed]

NOTICE OF REORGANIZATION AND FUNDING REQUIREMENTS

Act Sec. 4242. Amendment

P.L. 113-235, § 108(a)(1), Div. O:

Amended ERISA by repealing ERISA Sec. 4242.

Prior to the repeal, ERISA Sec. 4242 read as follows:

(a)(1) If—

(A) a multiemployer plan is in reorganization for a plan year, and

(B) section 4243 would require an increase in contributions for such plan year,

the plan sponsor shall notify the persons described in paragraph (2) that the plan is in reorganization and that, if contributions to the plan are not increased, accrued benefits under the plan may be reduced or an excise tax may be imposed (or both such reduction and imposition may occur).

(2) The persons described in this paragraph are—

(A) each employer who has an obligation to contribute under the plan (within the meaning of section 4201(h)(5)), and

(B) each employee organization which, for purposes of collective bargaining, represents plan participants employed by such an employer.

(3) The determination under paragraph (1)(B) shall be made without regard to the overburden credit provided by section 4244.

(b) The corporation may prescribe additional or alternative requirements for assuring, in the case of a plan with respect to which notice is required by subsection (a)(1), that the persons described in subsection (a)(2)—

(1) receive appropriate notice that the plan is in reorganization,

(2) are adequately informed of the implications of reorganization status, and

(3) have reasonable access to information relevant to the plan's reorganization status.

The above amendment shall apply with respect to plan years beginning after December 31, 2014.

P.L. 96-364, § 104(2):

Added Sec. 4242 effective on or after the earlier of the date on which the last collective bargaining agreement providing contributions under the plan, which was in effect on September 26, 1980, expires, without regard to extensions agreed to on or after September 26, 1980 or September 26, 1983 under ERISA Sec. 4402.

[¶ 15,709]
[ERISA Sec. 4243—Repealed]

MINIMUM CONTRIBUTION REQUIREMENT

Act Sec. 4243. Amendments

P.L. 113-235, § 108(a)(1), Div. O:

Amended ERISA by repealing ERISA Sec. 4243.

Prior to the repeal, ERISA Sec. 4243 read as follows:

(a)(1) MAINTENANCE OF FUNDING STANDARD ACCOUNT; AMOUNT OF ACCUMULATED FUNDING DEFICIENCY.—For any plan year for which a plan is in reorganization—

(A) the plan shall continue to maintain its funding standard account while it is in reorganization, and

(B) the plan's accumulated funding deficiency under section 304(a) for such plan year shall be equal to the excess (if any) of — (i) the sum of the minimum contribution requirement for such plan year (taking into account any overburden credit under section 4244(a)) plus the plan's accumulated funding deficiency for the preceding plan year (determined under this section if the plan was in reorganization during such year or under section 304(a) if the plan was not in reorganization), over

(ii) amounts considered contributed by employers to or under the plan for the plan year (increased by any amount waived under subsection (f) for the plan year).

(2) For purposes of paragraph (1), withdrawal liability payments (whether or not received) which are due with respect to withdrawals before the end of the base plan year shall be considered amounts contributed by the employer to or under the plan if, as of the adjustment date, it was reasonable for the plan sponsor to anticipate that such payments would be made during the plan year.

(b)(1) DETERMINATION OF AMOUNT; APPLICABLE FACTORS.—Except as otherwise provided in this section, for purposes of this part the minimum contribution requirement for a plan year in which a plan is in reorganization is an amount equal to the excess of—

(A) the sum of—

(i) the plan's vested benefits charge for the plan year, and

(ii) the increase in normal cost for the plan year determined under the entry age normal funding method which is attributable to plan amendments adopted while the plan was in reorganization, over

(B) the amount of the overburden credit (if any) determined under section 4244 for the plan year.

(2) If the plan's current contribution base for the plan year is less than the plan's valuation contribution base for the plan year, the minimum contribution requirement for such plan year shall be equal to the product of the amount determined under paragraph (1) (after any adjustment required by this part other than this paragraph) and a fraction—

(A) the numerator of which is the plan's current contribution base for the plan year, and

(B) the denominator of which is the plan's valuation contribution base for the plan year.

(3)(A) If the vested benefits charge for a plan year of a plan in reorganization is less than the plan's cash-flow amount for the plan year, the plan's minimum contribution requirement for the plan year is the amount determined under paragraph (1) (determined before the application of paragraph (2)) after substituting the term "cash-flow amount" for the term "vested benefits charge" in paragraph (1)(A).

(B) For purposes of subparagraph (A), a plan's cash-flow amount for a plan year is an amount equal to—

(i) the amount of the benefits payable under the plan for the base plan year, plus the amount of the plan's administrative expenses for the base plan year, reduced by

(ii) the value of the available plan assets for the base plan year determined under regulations prescribed by the Secretary of the Treasury,

adjusted in a manner consistent with section 4241(b)(4).

(c)(1) CURRENT CONTRIBUTION BASE; VALUATION CONTRIBUTION BASE.—For purposes of this part, a plan's current contribution base for a plan year is the number of contribution base units with respect to which contributions are required to be made under the plan for that plan year, determined in accordance with regulations prescribed by the Secretary of the Treasury.

(2)(A) Except as provided in subparagraph (B), for purposes of this part a plan's valuation contribution base is the number of contribution base units for which contributions were received for the base plan year—

(i) adjusted to reflect declines in the contribution base which have occurred (or could reasonably be anticipated) as of the adjustment date for the plan year referred to in paragraph (1),

(ii) adjusted upward (in accordance with regulations prescribed by the Secretary of the Treasury) for any contribution base reduction in the base plan year caused by a strike or lockout or by unusual events, such as fire, earthquake, or severe weather conditions, and

(iii) adjusted (in accordance with regulations prescribed by the Secretary of the Treasury) for reductions in the contribution base resulting from transfers of liabilities.

(B) For any plan year—

(i) in which the plan is insolvent (within the meaning of section 4245(b)(1)), and

(ii) beginning with the first plan year beginning after the expiration of all relevant collective bargaining agreements which were in effect in the plan year in which the plan became insolvent,

the plan's valuation contribution base is the greater of the number of contribution base units for which contributions were received for the first or second plan year preceding the first plan year in which the plan is insolvent, adjusted as provided in clause (ii) or (iii) of subparagraph (A).

(d)(1) MAXIMUM AMOUNT; AMOUNT OF FUNDING STANDARD REQUIREMENT; APPLICABILITY TO PLAN AMENDMENTS INCREASING BENEFITS.—Under regulations prescribed by the Secretary of the Treasury, the minimum contribution requirement applicable to any plan for any plan year which is determined under subsection (b) (without regard to subsection (b)(2)) shall not exceed an amount which is equal to the sum of—

(A) the greater of—

(i) the funding standard requirement for such plan year, or

(ii) 107 percent of—

(I) if the plan was not in reorganization in the preceding plan year, the funding standard requirement for such preceding plan year, or

(II) if the plan was in reorganization in the preceding plan year, the sum of the amount determined under this subparagraph for the preceding plan year and the amount (if any) determined under subparagraph (B) for the preceding plan year, plus

(B) if for the plan year a change in benefits is first required to be considered in computing the charges under section 412(b)(2)(A) or (B) of the Internal Revenue Code of 1986, the sum of—

(i) the increase in normal cost for a plan year determined under the entry age normal funding method due to increases in benefits described in section 4241(b)(4)(A)(ii) (determined without regard to section 4241(b)(4)(B)(i)), and

(ii) the amount necessary to amortize in equal annual installments the increase in the value of vested benefits under the plan due to increases in benefits described in clause (i) over—

(I) 10 years, to the extent such increase in value is attributable to persons in pay status, or

(II) 25 years, to the extent such increase in value is attributable to other participants.

(2) For purposes of paragraph (1), the funding standard requirement for any plan year is an amount equal to the net charge to the funding standard account for such plan year (as defined in section 4241(b)(2)).

(3)(A) In the case of a plan described in section 4216(b), if a plan amendment which increases benefits is adopted after January 1, 1980—

(i) paragraph (1) shall apply only if the plan is a plan described in subparagraph (B), and

(ii) the amount under paragraph (1) shall be determined without regard to paragraph (1)(B).

(B) A plan is described in this subparagraph if—

(i) the rate of employer contributions under the plan for the first plan year beginning on or after the date on which an amendment increasing benefits is adopted, multiplied by the valuation contribution base for that plan year, equals or exceeds the sum of—

(I) the amount that would be necessary to amortize fully, in equal annual installments, by July 1, 1986, the unfunded vested benefits attributable to plan provisions in effect on July 1, 1977 (determined as of the last day of the base plan year); and

(II) the amount that would be necessary to amortize fully, in equal annual installments, over the period described in subparagraph (C), beginning with the first day of the first plan year beginning on or after the date on which the amendment is adopted, the unfunded vested benefits (determined as of the last day of the base plan year) attributable to each plan amendment after July 1, 1977; and

(ii) the rate of employer contributions for each subsequent plan year is not less than the lesser of—

(I) the rate which when multiplied by the valuation contribution base for that subsequent plan year produces the annual amount that would be necessary to complete the amortization schedule described in clause (i), or

(II) the rate for the plan year immediately preceding such subsequent plan year, plus 5 percent of such rate.

(C) The period determined under this subparagraph is the lesser of—

(i) 12 years, or

(ii) a period equal in length to the average of the remaining expected lives of all persons receiving benefits under the plan.

(4) Paragraph (1) shall not apply with respect to a plan, other than a plan described in paragraph (3), for the period of consecutive plan years in each of which the plan is in reorganization, beginning with a plan year in which occurs the earlier of the date of the adoption or the effective date of any amendment of the plan which increases benefits with respect to service performed before the plan year in which the adoption of the amendment occurred.

(e) ADJUSTMENT OF VESTED BENEFITS CHARGE.—In determining the minimum contribution requirement with respect to a plan for a plan year under subsection (b), the vested benefits charge may be adjusted to reflect a plan amendment reducing benefits under section 412(c)(8) of the Internal Revenue Code of 1986.

(f)(1) WAIVER OF ACCUMULATED FUNDING DEFICIENCY.—The Secretary of the Treasury may waive any accumulated funding deficiency under this section in accordance with the provisions of section 302(c).

(2) Any waiver under paragraph (1) shall not be treated as a waived funding deficiency (within the meaning of section 302(c)(3)).

(g) STATUTORY METHODS APPLICABLE FOR DETERMINATIONS.—For purposes of making any determination under this part, the requirements of section 304(c)(3) shall apply.

The above amendment shall apply with respect to plan years beginning after December 31, 2014.

P.L. 109-280, § 107(b)(6):

Amended ERISA Sec. 4243(a)(1)(B) by striking "302(a)" and inserting "304(a)", and, in clause (i), by striking "302(a)" and inserting "304(a)".

Prior to amendment, ERISA Sec. 4243(a)(1)(B) read as follows:

(B) the plan's accumulated funding deficiency under section 302(a) for such plan year shall be equal to the excess (if any) of—

(i) the sum of the minimum contribution requirement for such plan year (taking into account any overburden credit under section 4244(a)) plus the plan's accumulated funding deficiency for the preceding plan year (determined under this section if the plan was in reorganization during such year or under section 302(a) if the plan was not in reorganization), over

(ii) amounts considered contributed by employers to or under the plan for the plan year (increased by any amount waived under subsection (f) for the plan year).

The above amendment applies to plan years beginning after 2007.

P.L. 109-280, § 107(b)(7) and (8):

Amended ERISA Sec. 4243(f)(1) by striking "303(a)" and inserting "302(c)"; and amended 4243(f)(2) by striking "303(c)" and inserting "303(c)(3)".

Prior to amendment, ERISA Sec. 4243(f) read as follows:

(1) WAIVER OF ACCUMULATED FUNDING DEFICIENCY.—The Secretary of the Treasury may waive any accumulated funding deficiency under this section in accordance with the provisions of section 303(a).

(2) Any waiver under paragraph (1) shall not be treated as a waived funding deficiency (within the meaning of section 303(c)).

The above amendments apply to plan years beginning after 2007.

P.L. 109-280, § 107(b)(9):

Amended ERISA Sec. 4243(g) by striking "302(c)(3)" and inserting "304(c)(3)".

Prior to amendment, ERISA Sec. 4243(g) read as follows:

(g) STATUTORY METHODS APPLICABLE FOR DETERMINATIONS.—For purposes of making any determination under this part, the requirements of section 302(c)(3) shall apply.

The above amendment applies to plan years beginning after 2007.

P.L. 101-239, § 7891(a)(1):

Titles I, III, and IV of ERISA (other than sections 3(37)(E), 301(a)(7), and 308, the last sentence of section 408(d), and sections 414(c), 4001(a)(3)(ii), and 4303) are each amended by striking "Internal Revenue Code of 1954" each place it appears and inserting "Internal Revenue Code of 1986", effective October 22, 1986.

P.L. 96-364, § 104(2):

Added Sec. 4243 effective on or after the earlier of the date on which the last collective bargaining agreement providing contributions under the plan, which was in effect on September 26, 1980, expires, without regard to extensions agreed to on or after September 26, 1980 or September 26, 1983 under ERISA Sec. 4402.

[¶ 15,710]
[ERISA Sec. 4244—Repealed]

OVERBURDEN CREDIT AGAINST MINIMUM CONTRIBUTION REQUIREMENT

Act Sec. 4244. Amendment

P.L. 113-235, § 108(a)(1), Div. O:

Amended ERISA by repealing ERISA Sec. 4244.

Prior to the repeal, ERISA Sec. 4244 read as follows:

(a) APPLICABILITY OF OVERBURDEN CREDIT TO DETERMINATIONS.—For purposes of determining the minimum contribution requirement under section 4243 (before the application of section 4243(b)(2) or (d)) the plan sponsor of a plan which is overburdened for the plan year shall apply an overburden credit against the plan's minimum contribution requirement for the plan year (determined without regard to section 4243(b)(2) or (d) and without regard to this section).

(b) DETERMINATION OF OVERBURDEN STATUS OF PLAN.—A plan is overburdened for a plan year if—

(1) the average number of pay status participants under the plan in the base plan year exceeds the average of the number of active participants in the base plan year and the 2 plan years preceding the base plan year, and

(2) the rate of employer contributions under the plan equals or exceeds the greater of—

(A) such rate for the preceding plan year, or

(B) such rate for the plan year preceding the first year in which the plan is in reorganization.

(c) AMOUNT OF OVERBURDEN CREDIT.—The amount of the overburden credit for a plan year is the product of—

(1) one-half of the average guaranteed benefit paid for the base plan year, and

(2) the overburden factor for the plan year.

The amount of the overburden credit for a plan year shall not exceed the amount of the minimum contribution requirement for such year (determined without regard to this section).

(d) AMOUNT OF OVERBURDEN FACTOR.—For purposes of this section, the overburden factor of a plan for the plan year is an amount equal to—

(1) the average number of pay status participants for the base plan year, reduced by

(2) the average of the number of active participants for the base plan year and for each of the 2 plan years preceding the base plan year.

(e) DEFINITIONS; DETERMINATIVE FACTORS.—For purposes of this section—

(1) The term "pay status participant" means, with respect to a plan, a participant receiving retirement benefits under the plan.

(2) The number of active participants for a plan year shall be the sum of—

(A) the number of active employees who are participants in the plan and on whose behalf contributions are required to be made during the plan year;

(B) the number of active employees who are not participants in the plan but who are in an employment unit covered by a collective bargaining agreement which requires the employees' employer to contribute to the plan, unless service in such employment unit was never covered under the plan or a predecessor thereof, and

(C) the total number of active employees attributed to employers who made payments to the plan for the plan year of withdrawal liability pursuant to part 1, determined by dividing—

(i) the total amount of such payments, by

(ii) the amount equal to the total contributions received by the plan during the plan year divided by the average number of active employees who were participants in the plan during the plan year.

The Secretary of the Treasury shall by regulation provide alternative methods of determining active participants where (by reason of irregular employment, contributions on a unit basis, or otherwise) this paragraph does not yield a representative basis for determining the credit.

(3) The term "average number" means, with respect to pay status participants for a plan year, a number equal to one-half the sum of—

(A) the number with respect to the plan as of the beginning of the plan year, and

(B) the number with respect to the plan as of the end of the plan year.

(4) The average guaranteed benefit paid is 12 times the average monthly pension payment guaranteed under section 4022A(c)(1) determined under the provisions of the plan in effect at the beginning of the first plan year in which the plan is in reorganization and without regard to section 4022A(c)(2).

(5) The first year in which the plan is in reorganization is the first of a period of 1 or more consecutive plan years in which the plan has been in reorganization not taking into account any plan years the plan was in reorganization prior to any period of 3 or more consecutive plan years in which the plan was not in reorganization.

(f)(1) ELIGIBILITY OF PLAN FOR OVERBURDEN CREDIT FOR PLAN YEAR.—Notwithstanding any other provision of this section, a plan is not eligible for an overburden credit for a plan year if the Secretary of the Treasury finds that the plan's current contribution base for the plan year was reduced, without a corresponding reduction in the plan's unfunded vested benefits attributable to pay status participants, as a result of a change in an agreement providing for employer contributions under the plan.

(2) For purposes of paragraph (1), a complete or partial withdrawal of an employer (within the meaning of part 1) does not impair a plan's eligibility for an overburden credit, unless the Secretary of the Treasury finds that a contribution base reduction described in paragraph (1) resulted from a transfer of liabilities to another plan in connection with the withdrawal.

(g) OVERBURDEN CREDIT WHERE 2 OR MORE MULTIEMPLOYER PLANS MERGE.—Notwithstanding any other provision of this section, if 2 or more multiemployer plans merge, the amount of the overburden credit which may be applied under this section with respect to the plan resulting from the merger for any of the 3 plan years ending after the effective date of the merger shall not exceed the sum of the used overburden credit for each of the merging plans for its last plan year ending before the effective date of the merger. For purposes of the preceding sentence, the used overburden credit is that portion of the credit which does not exceed the excess of the minimum contribution requirement (determined without regard to any overburden requirement under this section) over the employer contributions required under the plan.

The above amendment shall apply with respect to plan years beginning after December 31, 2014.

P.L. 96-364, § 104(2):

Added Sec. 4244 effective on or after the earlier of the date on which the last collective bargaining agreement providing contributions under the plan, which was in effect on September 26, 1980, expires, without regard to extensions agreed to on or after September 26, 1980 or September 26, 1983 under ERISA Sec. 4402.

[¶ 15,712]
[ERISA Sec. 4244A—Repealed]
ADJUSTMENTS IN ACCRUED BENEFITS

Act Sec. 4244A. Amendments

P.L. 113-235, § 108(a)(1), Div. O:

Amended ERISA by repealing ERISA Sec. 4244A.

Prior to the repeal, ERISA Sec. 4244A read as follows:

(a)(1) AMENDMENT OF MULTIEMPLOYER PLAN IN REORGANIZATION TO REDUCE OR ELIMINATE ACCRUED BENEFITS ATTRIBUTABLE TO EMPLOYER CONTRIBUTIONS INELIGIBLE FOR GUARANTEE OF CORPORATION; ADJUSTMENT OF VESTED BENEFITS CHARGE TO REFLECT PLAN AMENDMENT.—Notwithstanding sections 203 and 204, a multiemployer plan in reorganization may be amended in accordance with this section, to reduce or eliminate accrued benefits attributable to employer contributions which, under section 4022A(b), are not eligible for the corporation's guarantee. The preceding sentence shall only apply to accrued benefits under plan amendments (or plans) adopted after March 26, 1980, or under collective bargaining agreements entered into after March 26, 1980.

(2) In determining the minimum contribution requirement with respect to a plan for a plan year under section 4243(b), the vested benefits charge may be adjusted to reflect a plan amendment reducing benefits under this section or section 412(c)(8) of the Internal Revenue Code of 1986, but only if the amendment is adopted and effective no later than 2 Â¿½ months after the end of the plan year, or within such extended period as the Secretary of the Treasury may prescribe by regulation under section 412(c)(10) of such Code.

(b)(1) REDUCTION OF ACCRUED BENEFITS; NOTICE BY PLAN SPONSORS TO PLAN PARTICIPANTS AND BENEFICIARIES.—Accrued benefits may not be reduced under this section unless—

(A) notice has been given, at least 6 months before the first day of the plan year in which the amendment reducing benefits is adopted, to—

(i) plan participants and beneficiaries,

(ii) each employer who has an obligation to contribute (within the meaning of section 4212(a)) under the plan, and

(iii) each employee organization which, for purposes of collective bargaining, represents plan participants employed by such an employer,

that the plan is in reorganization and that, if contributions under the plan are not increased, accrued benefits under the plan will be reduced or an excise tax will be imposed on employers;

(B) in accordance with regulations prescribed by the Secretary of the Treasury—

(i) any category of accrued benefits is not reduced with respect to inactive participants to a greater extent proportionally than such category of accrued benefits is reduced with respect to active participants,

(ii) benefits attributable to employer contributions other than accrued benefits and the rate of future benefit accruals are reduced at least to an extent equal to the reduction in accrued benefits of inactive participants, and

(iii) in any case in which the accrued benefit of a participant or beneficiary is reduced by changing the benefit form or the requirements which the participant or beneficiary must satisfy to be entitled to the benefit, such reduction is not applicable to—

(I) any participant or beneficiary in pay status on the effective date of the amendment, or the beneficiary of such a participant, or

(II) any participant who has attained normal retirement age, or who is within 5 years of attaining normal retirement age, on the effective date of the amendment, or the beneficiary of any such participant; and

(C) the rate of employer contributions for the plan year in which the amendment becomes effective and for all succeeding plan years in which the plan is in reorganization equals or exceeds the greater of—

(i) the rate of employer contributions, calculated without regard to the amendment, for the plan year in which the amendment becomes effective, or

(ii) the rate of employer contributions for the plan year preceding the plan year in which the amendment becomes effective.

(2) The plan sponsors shall include in any notice required to be sent to plan participants and beneficiaries under paragraph (1) information as to the rights and remedies of plan participants and beneficiaries as well as how to contact the Department of Labor for further information and assistance where appropriate.

(c) RECOUPMENT BY PLAN OF EXCESS BENEFIT PAYMENT.—A plan may not recoup a benefit payment which is in excess of the amount payable under the plan because of an amendment retroactively reducing accrued benefits under this section.

(d)(1)(A) AMENDMENT OF PLAN TO INCREASE OR RESTORE ACCRUED BENEFITS PREVIOUSLY REDUCED OR RATE OF FUTURE BENEFIT ACCRUALS; CONDITIONS, APPLICABLE FACTORS, ETC.—A plan which has been amended to reduce accrued benefits under this section may be amended to increase or restore accrued benefits, or the rate of future benefit accruals, only if the plan is amended to restore levels of previously reduced accrued benefits of inactive participants and of participants who are within 5 years of attaining normal retirement age to at least the same extent as any such increase in accrued benefits or in the rate of future benefit accruals.

(B) For purposes of this subsection, in the case of a plan which has been amended under this section to reduce accrued benefits—

(i) an increase in a benefit, or in the rate of future benefit accruals, shall be considered a benefit increase to the extent that the benefit, or the accrual rate, is thereby increased above the highest benefit level, or accrual rate, which was in effect under the terms of the plan before the effective date of the amendment reducing accrued benefits, and

(ii) an increase in a benefit, or in the rate of future benefit accruals, shall be considered a benefit restoration to the extent that the benefit, or the accrual rate, is not thereby increased above the highest benefit level, or accrual rate, which was in effect under the terms of the plan immediately before the effective date of the amendment reducing accrued benefits.

(2) If a plan is amended to partially restore previously reduced accrued benefit levels, or the rate of future benefit accruals, the benefits of inactive participants shall be restored in at least the same proportions as other accrued benefits which are restored.

(3) No benefit increase under a plan may take effect in a plan year in which an amendment reducing accrued benefits under the plan, in accordance with this section, is adopted or first becomes effective.

(4) A plan is not required to make retroactive benefit payments with respect to that portion of an accrued benefit which was reduced and subsequently restored under this section.

(e) DEFINITIONS.—For purposes of this section, "inactive participant" means a person not in covered service under the plan who is in pay status under the plan or who has a nonforfeitable benefit under the plan.

(f) PROMULGATION OF RULES; CONTESTS, ETC.—The Secretary of the Treasury may prescribe rules under which, notwithstanding any other provision of this section, accrued benefit reductions or benefit increases for different participant groups may be varied equitably to reflect variations in contribution rates and other relevant factors reflecting differences in negotiated levels of financial support for plan benefit obligations.

The above amendment shall apply with respect to plan years beginning after December 31, 2014.

P.L. 101-239, §7891(a)(1):

Titles I, III, and IV of ERISA (other than sections 3(37)(E), 301(a)(7), and 308, the last sentence of section 408(d), and sections 414(c), 4001(a)(3)(ii), and 4303) are each amended by striking "Internal Revenue Code of 1954" each place it appears and inserting "Internal Revenue Code of 1986", effective October 22, 1976.

P.L. 96-364, §104(2):

Added Sec. 4244A effective on or after the earlier of the date on which the last collective bargaining agreement providing contributions under the plan, which was in effect on September 26, 1980, expires, without regard to extensions agreed to on or after September 26, 1980 or September 26, 1983 under ERISA Sec. 4402.

[¶ 15,713]
INSOLVENT PLANS

Act Sec. 4245. (a) SUSPENSION OF PAYMENTS OF BENEFITS; CONDITIONS, AMOUNT, ETC.—Notwithstanding sections 203 and 204, in any case in which benefit payments under an insolvent multiemployer plan exceed the resource benefit level, any such payments of benefits which are not basic benefits shall be suspended, in accordance with this section, to the extent necessary to reduce the sum of such payments and the payments of such basic benefits to the greater of the resource benefit level or the level of basic benefits, unless an alternative procedure is prescribed by the corporation under section 4022A(g)(5).

Act Sec. 4245. (b) DETERMINATION OF INSOLVENCY STATUS FOR PLAN YEAR; DEFINITIONS.—For purposes of this section, for a plan year—

(1) a multiemployer plan is insolvent if the plan's available resources are not sufficient to pay benefits under the plan when due for the plan year, or if the plan is determined to be insolvent under subsection (d);

(2) "resource benefit level" means the level of monthly benefits determined under subsections (c)(1) and (3) and (d)(3) to be the highest level which can be paid out of the plan's available resources;

(3) "available resources" means the plan's cash, marketable assets, contributions, withdrawal liability payments, and earnings, less reasonable administrative expenses and amounts owed for such plan year to the corporation under section 4261(b)(2); and

(4) "insolvency year" means a plan year in which a plan is insolvent.

Act Sec. 4245. (c)(1) DETERMINATION BY PLAN SPONSOR OF PLAN IN CRITICAL STATUS AS DESCRIBED IN SUBSECTION 305(B)(2) OF RESOURCE BENEFIT LEVEL OF PLAN FOR EACH INSOLVENCY YEAR; UNIFORM APPLICATION OF SUSPENSION OF BENEFITS; ADJUSTMENTS OF BENEFIT PAYMENTS.—The plan sponsor of a plan in critical status as described in subsection 305(b)(2) shall determine in writing the plan's resource benefit level for each insolvency year, based on the plan sponsor's reasonable projection of the plan's available resources and the benefits payable under the plan.

(2)(A) The suspension of benefit payments under this section shall, in accordance with regulations prescribed by the Secretary of the Treasury, apply in substantially uniform proportions to the benefits of all persons in pay status under the plan, except that the Secretary of the Treasury may prescribe rules under which benefit suspensions for different participant groups may be varied equitably to reflect variations in contribution rates and other relevant factors including differences in negotiated levels of financial support for plan benefit obligations.

(B) For purposes of this paragraph—

(i) the term 'person in pay status' means—

(I) a participant or beneficiary on the last day of the base plan year who, at any time during such year, was paid an early, late, normal, or disability retirement benefit (or a death benefit related to a retirement benefit), and

(II) to the extent provided in regulations prescribed by the Secretary of the Treasury, any other person who is entitled to such a benefit under the plan.

(ii) the base plan year for any plan year is—

(I) if there is a relevant collective bargaining agreement, the last plan year ending at least 6 months before the relevant effective date, or

(II) if there is no relevant collective bargaining agreement, the last plan year ending at least 12 months before the beginning of the plan year.

(iii) a relevant collective bargaining agreement is a collective bargaining agreement—

(I) which is in effect for at least 6 months during the plan year, and

(II) which has not been in effect for more than 36 months as of the end of the plan year.

(iv) the relevant effective date is the earliest of the effective dates for the relevant collective bargaining agreements.

(3) Notwithstanding paragraph (2), if a plan sponsor determines in writing a resource benefit level for a plan year which is below the level of basic benefits, the payment of all benefits other than basic benefits must be suspended for that plan year.

(4)(A) If, by the end of an insolvency year, the plan sponsor determines in writing that the plan's available resources in that insolvency year could have supported benefit payments above the resource benefit level for that insolvency year, the plan sponsor shall distribute the excess resources to the participants and beneficiaries who received benefit payments from the plan in that insolvency year, in accordance with regulations prescribed by the Secretary of the Treasury.

(B) For purposes of this paragraph, the term "excess resources" means available resources above the amount necessary to support the resource benefit level, but no greater than the amount necessary to pay benefits for the plan year at the benefit levels under the plan.

(5) If, by the end of an insolvency year, any benefit has not been paid at the resource benefit level, amounts up to the resource benefit level which were unpaid shall be distributed to the participants and beneficiaries, in accordance with regulations prescribed by the Secretary of the Treasury, to the extent possible taking into account the plan's total available resources in that insolvency year.

(6) Except as provided in paragraph (4) or (5), a plan is not required to make retroactive benefit payments with respect to that portion of a benefit which was suspended under this section.

Act Sec. 4245.(d)(1) APPLICABILITY AND DETERMINATIONS RESPECTING PLAN ASSETS; TIME FOR DETERMINATIONS OF RESOURCE BENEFIT LEVEL AND LEVEL OF BASIC BENEFITS.—As of the end of the first plan year in which a plan is in critical status as described in subsection 305(b)(2), and at least every 3 plan years thereafter (unless the plan is no longer in critical status as described in subsection 305(b)(2)), the plan sponsor shall compare the value of plan assets for that plan year with the total amount of benefit payments made under the plan for that plan year. Unless the plan sponsor determines that the value of plan assets exceeds 3 times the total amount of benefit payments, the plan sponsor shall determine whether the plan will be insolvent in any of the next 5 plan years. If the plan sponsor makes such a determination that the plan will be insolvent in any of the next 5 plan years, the plan sponsor shall make the comparison under this paragraph at least annually until the plan sponsor makes a determination that the plan will not be insolvent in any of the next 5 plan years.

(2) If, at any time, the plan sponsor of a plan in critical status as described in subsection 305(b)(2) reasonably determines, taking into account the plan's recent and anticipated financial experience, that the plan's available resources are not sufficient to pay benefits under the plan when due for the next plan year, the plan sponsor shall make such determination available to interested parties.

(3) The plan sponsor of a plan in critical status as described in subsection 305(b)(2) shall determine in writing for each insolvency year the resource benefit level and the level of basic benefits no later than 3 months before the insolvency year.

(4) For purposes of this subsection, the value of plan assets shall be the value of the available plan assets determined under regulations prescribed by the Secretary of the Treasury.

Act Sec. 4245.(e)(1) NOTICE, ETC., REQUIREMENTS OF PLAN SPONSOR IN CRITICAL STATUS AS DESCRIBED IN SUBSECTION 305(B)(2) REGARDING INSOLVENCY AND REGARDING INSOLVENCY AND RESOURCE BENEFIT LEVELS.—If the plan sponsor of a plan in critical status as described in subsection 305(b)(2) determines under subsection (d)(1) or (2) that the plan may become insolvent (within the meaning of subsection (b)(1)), the plan sponsor shall—

(A) notify the Secretary of the Treasury, the parties described in section 101(f)(1) of that determination, and

(B) inform the parties described in section 101(f)(1) that if insolvency occurs certain benefit payments will be suspended, but that basic benefits will continue to be paid.

(2) No later than 2 months before the first day of each insolvency year, the plan sponsor of a plan in critical status as described in subsection 305(b)(2) shall notify the Secretary of the Treasury, the corporation, and the parties described in paragraph (1)(B) of the resource benefit level determined in writing for that insolvency year.

(3) In any case in which the plan sponsor anticipates that the resource benefit level for an insolvency year may not exceed the level of basic benefits, the plan sponsor shall notify the corporation.

(4) Notice required by this subsection shall be given in accordance with regulations prescribed by the corporation, except that notice to the Secretary of the Treasury shall be given in accordance with regulations prescribed by the Secretary of the Treasury.

(5) The corporation may prescribe a time other than the time prescribed by this section for the making of a determination or the filing of a notice under this section.

Act Sec. 4245.(f)(1) FINANCIAL ASSISTANCE FROM CORPORATION; CONDITIONS AND CRITERIA APPLICABLE.—If the plan sponsor of an insolvent plan, for which the resource benefit level is above the level of basic benefits, anticipates that, for any month in an insolvency year, the plan will not have funds sufficient to pay basic benefits, the plan sponsor may apply for financial assistance from the corporation under section 4261.

(2) A plan sponsor who has determined a resource benefit level for an insolvency year which is below the level of basic benefits shall apply for financial assistance from the corporation under section 4261.

Act Sec. 4245. (g) Subsections (a) and (c) shall not apply to a plan that, for the plan year, is operating under section 305(e)(9), regarding benefit suspensions by certain multiemployer plans in critical and declining status.

Amendments

P.L. 113-235, §108(a)(2)(A), Div. O:

Amended ERISA Sec. 4245 by striking "reorganization" each place it appears and inserting "critical status, as described in subsection 305(b)(2)."

The above amendment shall apply with respect to plan years beginning after December 31, 2014.

P.L. 113-235, §108(a)(2)(B)(i)-(iii), Div. O:

Amended ERISA Sec. 4245(c)(2) by striking "The suspension" and inserting "(A) The suspension"; by striking "(within the meaning of section 4241(b)(6))"; and by adding at the end a new paragraph (B) to read as above.

The above amendment shall apply with respect to plan years beginning after December 31, 2014.

P.L. 113-235, §108(a)(2)(C), Div. O:

Amended ERISA Sec. 4245(d) in paragraph (1), by striking "(determined in accordance with section 4243(b)(3)(B)(ii))"; and by adding at the end a new paragraph (4) to read as above.

The above amendment shall apply with respect to plan years beginning after December 31, 2014.

P.L. 113-235, §108(a)(2)(D)(i)-(ii), Div. O:

Amended ERISA Sec. 4245(e)(1), in subparagraph (A), by striking "the corporation, the parties described in section 4242(a)(2), and the plan participants and beneficiaries" and inserting "the parties described in section 101(f)(1)" and, in subparagraph (B), by striking "section 4242(a)(2) and the plan participants and beneficiaries" and inserting "section 101(f)(1)".

The above amendment shall apply with respect to plan years beginning after December 31, 2014.

P.L. 113-235, §108(a)(2)(E), Div. O:

Amended ERISA Sec. 4245 by adding at the end a new paragraph (g) to read as above.

The above amendment shall apply with respect to plan years beginning after December 31, 2014.

P.L. 109-280, §203(a)(1)-(2):

Amended ERISA Sec. 4245(d)(1) by striking "3 plan years" the second place it appears and inserting "5 plan years" and by adding at the end a new sentence to read as above.

Prior to amendment, ERISA Sec. 4245(d)(1) read as follows:

(d)(1) APPLICABILITY AND DETERMINATIONS RESPECTING PLAN ASSETS; TIME FOR DETERMINATIONS OF RESOURCE BENEFIT LEVEL AND LEVEL OF BASIC BENEFITS.—As of the end of the first plan year in which a plan is in reorganization, and at least every 3 plan years thereafter (unless the plan is no longer in reorganization), the plan sponsor shall compare the value of plan assets (determined in accordance with section 4243(b)(3)(B)(ii)) for that plan year with the total amount of benefit payments made under the plan for that plan year. Unless the plan sponsor determines that the value of plan assets exceeds 3 times the total amount of benefit payments, the plan sponsor shall determine whether the plan will be insolvent in any of the next 3 plan years.

The above amendments apply with respect to determinations made in plan years beginning after 2007.

P.L. 96-364, §104(2):

Added Sec. 4245, effective on or after the earlier of the date on which the last collective bargaining agreement provided contributions under the plan, which was in effect on September 26, 1980, expires, without regard to extensions agreed to on or after September 26, 1980 or September 26, 1983 under ERISA Sec. 4402.

Regulations

The following regulations were adopted by the Pension Benefit Guaranty Corporation on July 1, 1996 (61 FR 34002). Prior to July 1, 1996, PBGC regulations were under Chapter XXVI of Title 29 of the Code of Federal Regulations. Effective July 1, 1996, PBGC regulations were moved to Chapter XL, and were renumbered and reorganized. Reg. §§4245.3—4245.8 were amended October 28, 2003 (68 FR 61344).

[¶ 15,713A]

§4245.1 **Purpose and scope.** (a) *Purpose.* The purpose of this part is to prescribe notice requirements pertaining to insolvent multiemployer plans that are in reorganization.

(b) *Scope.* This part applies to multiemployer plans in reorganization covered by title IV of ERISA, other than plans that have terminated by mass withdrawal under section 4041A(a)(2) of ERISA.

[¶ 15,713B]

§4245.2 **Definitions.** The following terms are defined in §4001.2 of this chapter: *employer, ERISA, IRS, multiemployer plan, nonforfeitable benefit, PBGC, person, plan,* and *plan year.*

In addition, for purposes of this part:

Actuarial valuation means a report submitted to the plan in connection with a valuation of plan assets and liabilities, which, in the case of a plan covered by subparts C and D of part 4281, shall be performed in accordance with subpart B of part 4281.

Available resources means, for a plan year, available resources as described in section 4245(b)(3) of ERISA.

Benefits subject to reduction means those benefits accrued under plan amendments (or plans) adopted after March 26, 1980, or under collective bargaining agreements entered into after March 26, 1980, that are not eligible for the PBGC's guarantee under section 4022A(b) of ERISA.

Financial assistance means financial assistance from the PBGC under section 4261 of ERISA.

Insolvency benefit level means the greater of the resource benefit level or the benefit level guaranteed by the PBGC for each participant and beneficiary in pay status.

Insolvency year means insolvency year as described in section 4245(b)(4) of ERISA.

Insolvent means that a plan is unable to pay benefits when due during the plan year. A plan terminated by mass withdrawal is not insolvent unless it has been amended to eliminate all benefits that are subject to reduction under section 4281(c) of ERISA, or, in the absence of an amendment, no benefits under the plan are subject to reduction under section 4281(c) of ERISA.

Reasonably expected to enter pay status means, with respect to plan participants and beneficiaries, persons (other than those in pay status) who, according to plan records, are disabled, have applied for benefits, or have reached or will reach during the applicable period the normal retirement age under the plan, and any others whom it is reasonable for the plan sponsor to expect to enter pay status during the applicable period.

Reorganization means reorganization under section 4241(a) of ERISA.

Resource benefit level means resource benefit level as described in section 4245(b)(2) of ERISA.

[¶ 15,713C]

§ 4245.3 **Notice of insolvency.** (a) *Requirement of notice.* A plan sponsor of a multiemployer plan in reorganization that determines under section 4245(b)(1), (d)(1) or (d)(2) of ERISA that the plan's available resources are or may be insufficient to pay benefits when due for a plan year shall so notify the PBGC and the interested parties, as defined in paragraph (e) of this section. A single notice may cover more than one plan year. The notices shall be delivered in the manner and within the time prescribed in this section and shall contain the information described in § 4245.4.

[Amended 10/28/2003 by 68 FR 61344]

(b) *When delivered.* A plan sponsor shall mail or otherwise deliver the notices of insolvency no later than 30 days after it determines that the plan is or may become insolvent, as described in paragraph (a) of this section. However, the notice to participants and beneficiaries in pay status may be delivered concurrently with the first benefit payment made more than 30 days after the determination of insolvency.

(c) *Delivery to PBGC.* (1) *Method of filing.* The PBGC applies the rules in subpart A of part 4000 of this chapter to determine permissible methods of filing the notice of insolvency with the PBGC under this part.

(2) *Filing date.* The PBGC applies the rules in subpart C of part 4000 of this chapter to determine the date that a notice of insolvency under this part was filed with the PBGC.

[Amended 10/28/2003 by 68 FR 61344]

(d) *Delivery to interested parties.* (1) *Method of issuance.* The PBGC applies the rules in subpart B of part 4000 of this chapter to determine permissible methods of issuance of the notice of insolvency to interested parties. In addition to the methods permitted under subpart B of part 4000, the plan sponsor may notify interested parties, other than participants and beneficiaries who are in pay status when the notice is required to be delivered, by posting the notice at participants' work sites or publishing the notice in a union newsletter or in a newspaper of general circulation in the area or areas where participants reside. Notice to a participant shall be deemed notice to that participant's beneficiary or beneficiaries.

(2) *Issuance date.* The PBGC applies the rules in subpart C of part 4000 of this chapter to determine the date that the notice of insolvency was issued.

[Amended 10/28/2003 by 68 FR 61344]

(e) *Interested parties.* For purposes of this part, the term "interested parties" means—

(1) Employers required to contribute to the plan;

(2) Employee organizations that, for collective bargaining purposes, represent plan participants employed by such employers; and

(3) Plan participants and beneficiaries.

[¶ 15,713D]

§ 4245.4 **Contents of notice of insolvency.** (a) *Notice to the PBGC.* A notice of insolvency required to be filed with the PBGC pursuant to § 4245.3 shall contain the information set forth below:

(1) The name of the plan.

(2) The name, address and telephone number of the plan sponsor and of the plan sponsor's duly authorized representative, if any.

(3) The nine-digit Employer Identification Number (EIN) assigned by the IRS to the plan sponsor and the three-digit Plan Identifi-

cation Number (PIN) assigned by the plan sponsor to the plan, and, if different, the EIN or PIN last filed with the PBGC. If no EIN or PIN has been assigned, the notice shall so indicate.

(4) The IRS key district that has jurisdiction over determination letters with respect to the plan.

(5) The case number assigned to the plan by the PBGC. If the plan has no case number, the notice shall state whether the plan has previously filed a notice of insolvency with the PBGC and, if so, the date on which the notice was filed.

(6) The plan year or years for which the plan sponsor has determined that the plan is or may become insolvent.

(7) A copy of the plan document, including the last restatement of the plan and all subsequent amendments in effect, or to become effective, during the insolvency year or years. However, if a copy of the plan document was submitted to the PBGC with a previous notice of insolvency or notice of insolvency benefit level, only subsequent plan amendments need be submitted, and the notice shall state when the copy of the plan document was filed.

(8) A copy of the most recent actuarial valuation for the plan and a copy of the most recent Schedule B (Form 5500) filed for the plan, if the Schedule B contains more recent information than the actuarial valuation. If the actuarial valuation or Schedule B was previously submitted to the PBGC, it may be omitted, and the notice shall state the date on which the document was filed and that the information is still accurate and complete.

(9) The estimated amount of annual benefit payments under the plan (determined without regard to the insolvency) for each insolvency year.

(10) The estimated amount of the plan's available resources for each insolvency year.

(11) A certification, signed by the plan sponsor (or a duly authorized representative), that notices of insolvency have been given to all interested parties in accordance with the requirements of this part.

(b) *Notices to interested parties.* A notice of insolvency required under § 4245.3 to be given to interested parties, as defined in § 4245.3(e), shall contain the information set forth below:

(1) The name of the plan.

(2) The plan year or years for which the plan sponsor has determined that the plan is or may become insolvent.

(3) The estimated amount of annual benefit payment under the plan (determined without regard to the insolvency) for each insolvency year.

(4) The estimated amount of the plan's available resources for each insolvency year.

(5) A statement that, during the insolvency year, benefits above the amount that can be paid from available resources or the level guaranteed by the PBGC, whichever is greater, will be suspended, with a brief explanation of which benefits are guaranteed by the PBGC. The following statement may be included as an explanation of PBGC-guaranteed benefits:

Should the plan become insolvent, each participant's benefit guaranteed by the Pension Benefit Guaranty Corporation (PBGC) is determined as follows. Each participant's nonforfeitable monthly benefit payable under the plan at retirement is computed. This benefit is then divided by the participant's years of credited service under the plan. Of the resulting figure (the accrual rate), the first $5 is guaranteed at 100%. Any additional amount (up to $15) is either 75% or 65% guaranteed, depending on the past funding practices of the plan. Any remaining amount that exceeds $20 is not guaranteed. The PBGC guarantees the payment of a monthly benefit equal to this adjusted accrual rate times years of credited service. The PBGC does not guarantee benefits or benefit increases that have been in effect for fewer than 60 months before the plan becomes insolvent or is amended to reduce accrued benefits.

(6) The name, address, and telephone number of the plan administrator or other person designated by the plan sponsor to answer inquiries concerning benefits during the plan's insolvency.

[Amended 10/28/2003 by 68 FR 61344]

[¶ 15,713E]

§ 4245.5 Notice of insolvency benefit level. (a) *Requirement of notice.* Except as provided in paragraph (b) of this section, for each insolvency year the plan sponsor shall notify the PBGC and the interested parties, as defined in § 4245.3(e), of the level of benefits expected to be paid during the year (the "insolvency benefit level"). These notices shall be delivered in the manner and within the time prescribed in this section and shall contain the information described in § 4245.6.

[Amended 10/28/2003 by 68 FR 61344]

(b) *Waiver of notice to certain interested parties.* The notice of insolvency benefit level required under this section need not be given to interested parties, other than participants and beneficiaries who are in pay status or are reasonably expected to enter pay status during the insolvency year, for an insolvency year immediately following the plan year in which a notice of insolvency was required to be delivered pursuant to § 4245.3, provided that the notice of insolvency was in fact delivered.

(c) *When delivered.* The plan sponsor shall mail or otherwise deliver the required notices of insolvency benefit level no later than 60 days before the beginning of the insolvency year, except that if the determination of insolvency is made fewer than 120 days before the beginning of the insolvency year, the notices shall be delivered within 60 days after the date of the plan sponsor's determination.

(d) *Delivery to PBGC.* (1) *Method of filing.* The PBGC applies the rules in subpart A of part 4000 of this chapter to determine permissible methods of filing a notice of insolvency benefit level with the PBGC under this part.

(2) *Filing date.* The PBGC applies the rules in subpart C of part 4000 of this chapter to determine the date that a notice of insolvency benefit level under this part was filed with the PBGC.

[Amended 10/28/2003 by 68 FR 61344]

(e) *Delivery to interested parties.* (1) *Method of issuance.* The PBGC applies the rules in subpart B of part 4000 of this chapter to determine permissible methods of issuance of the notice of insolvency benefit levels to interested parties. In addition to the methods permitted under subpart B of part 4000, the plan sponsor may notify interested parties, other than participants and beneficiaries who are in pay status or reasonably expected to enter pay status during the insolvency year for which the notice is given, by posting the notice at participants' work sites or publishing the notice in a union newsletter or in a newspaper of general circulation in the area or areas where participants reside. Notice to a participant shall be deemed notice to that participant's beneficiary or beneficiaries.

(2) *Issuance date.* The PBGC applies the rules in subpart C of part 4000 of this chapter to determine the date that the notice of insolvency benefit levels was issued.

[Amended 10/28/2003 by 68 FR 61344]

[¶ 15,713F]

§ 4245.6 Contents of notice of insolvency benefit level. (a) *Notice to the PBGC.* A notice of insolvency benefit level required to be filed with the PBGC pursuant to § 4245.5(a) shall contain the information set forth below, except as provided in the next sentence. The information required in paragraphs (a)(7) to (a)(10) need be submitted only if it is different from the information submitted to the PBGC with the notice of insolvency filed for that insolvency year (see § 4245.4 (a)(7) to (a)(10)) or the notice of insolvency benefit level filed for a prior year. When any information is omitted under this exception, the notice shall so state and indicate when the notice of insolvency or prior notice of insolvency benefit level was filed.

(1) The name of the plan.

(2) The name, address and telephone number of the plan sponsor and of the plan sponsor's authorized representative, if any.

(3) The nine-digit Employer Identification Number (EIN) assigned by the IRS to the plan sponsor and the three-digit Plan Identification Number (PIN) assigned by the plan sponsor to the plan, and, if different, the EIN or PIN last filed with the PBGC. If no EIN or PIN has been assigned, the notice shall so indicate.

(4) The IRS key district that has jurisdiction over determination letters with respect to the plan.

(5) The case number assigned to the plan by the PBGC.

(6) The plan year for which the notice is filed.

(7) A copy of the plan document, including any amendments, in effect during the insolvency year.

(8) A copy of the most recent actuarial valuation for the plan and a copy of the most recent Schedule B (Form 5500) filed for the plan, if the Schedule B contains more recent information than the actuarial valuation.

(9) The estimated amount of annual benefit payments under the plan (determined without regard to the insolvency) for the insolvency year.

(10) The estimated amount of the plan's available resources for the insolvency year.

(11) The estimated amount of the annual benefit payments guaranteed by the PBGC for the insolvency year.

(12) The amount of financial assistance, if any, requested from the PBGC.

(13) A certification, signed by the plan sponsor (or a duly authorized representative), that notices of insolvency benefit level have been given to all interested parties in accordance with the requirements of this part.

When financial assistance is requested, the PBGC may require the plan sponsor to submit additional information necessary to process the request.

(b) *Notices to interested parties other than participants in or entering pay status.* A notice of insolvency benefit level required by § 4245.5(a) to be delivered to interested parties, as defined in § 4245.3(e), other than a notice to a participant or beneficiary who is in pay status or is reasonably expected to enter pay status during the insolvency year, shall include the information set forth below:

(1) The name of the plan.

(2) The plan year for which the notice is issued.

(3) The estimated amount of annual benefit payments under the plan (determined without regard to the insolvency) for the insolvency year.

(4) The estimated amount of the plan's available resources for the insolvency year.

(5) The amount of financial assistance, if any, requested from the PBGC.

[Amended 10/28/2003 by 68 FR 61344]

(c) *Notices to participants and beneficiaries in or entering pay status.* A notice of insolvency benefit level required by § 4245.5(a) to be delivered to participants and beneficiaries who are in pay status or are reasonably expected to enter pay status during the insolvency year for which the notice is given, shall include the following information:

(1) The name of the plan.

(2) The plan year for which the notice is issued.

(3) A statement of the monthly benefit expected to be paid to the participant or beneficiary during the insolvency year.

(4) A statement that in subsequent plan years, depending on the plan's available resources, this benefit level may be increased or decreased but will not fall below the level guaranteed by the PBGC, and that the participant or beneficiary will be notified in advance of the new benefit level if it is less than his full nonforfeitable benefit under the plan.

(5) The name, address, and telephone number of the plan administrator or other person designated by the plan sponsor to answer inquiries concerning benefits during the plan's insolvency.

[¶ 15,713G]

§ 4245.7 PBGC address. See Sec. 4000.4 of this chapter for information on where to file.

[Amended 10/28/2003 by 68 FR 61344]

(Approved by the Office of Management and Budget under control number 1212-0033)

[¶ 15,713H]   [Added 10/28/2003 by 68 FR 61344]

§ 4245.8 Computation of time. The PBGC applies the rules in subpart D of part 4000 of this chapter to compute any time period for filing or issuance under this part.

Part 4—Financial Assistance

[¶ 15,714]
FINANCIAL ASSISTANCE

Act Sec. 4261. (a) AUTHORITY; PROCEDURE APPLICABLE; AMOUNT.—If, upon receipt of an application for financial assistance under section 4245(f) or section 4281(d), the corporation verifies that the plan is or will be insolvent and unable to pay basic benefits when due, the corporation shall provide the plan financial assistance in an amount sufficient to enable the plan to pay basic benefits under the plan.

Act Sec. 4261. (b)(1) CONDITIONS; REPAYMENT TERMS.—Financial assistance shall be provided under such conditions as the corporation determines are equitable and are appropriate to prevent unreasonable loss to the corporation with respect to the plan.

(2) A plan which has received financial assistance shall repay the amount of such assistance to the corporation on reasonable terms consistent with regulations prescribed by the corporation.

Act Sec. 4261. (c) ASSISTANCE PENDING FINAL DETERMINATION OF APPLICATION.—Pending determination of the amount described in subsection (a), the corporation may provide financial assistance in such amounts as it considers appropriate in order to avoid undue hardship to plan participants and beneficiaries.

Amendment

P.L. 96-364, § 104(2):

Added Sec. 4261 effective September 26, 1980 under ERISA Sec. 4402.

Regulations

The following regulations were adopted by the Pension Benefit Guaranty Corporation on July 1, 1996 (61 FR 34002). Prior to July 1, 1996, PBGC regulations were under Chapter XXVI of Title 29 of the Code of Federal Regulations. Effective July 1, 1996, PBGC regulations were moved to Chapter XL, and were renumbered and reorganized.

[¶ 15,714A]

§ 4261.1 Cross-reference. See § 4281.47 for procedures for applying to the PBGC for financial assistance under section 4261 of ERISA.

Part 5—Benefits After Termination

[¶ 15,715]
BENEFITS UNDER CERTAIN TERMINATED PLANS

Act Sec. 4281. (a) AMENDMENT OF PLAN BY PLAN SPONSOR TO REDUCE BENEFITS, AND SUSPENSION OF BENEFIT PAYMENTS.—Notwithstanding sections 203 and 204, the plan sponsor of a terminated multiemployer plan to which section 4041A(d) applies shall amend the plan to reduce benefits, and shall suspend benefit payments, as required by this section.

Act Sec. 4281. (b)(1) DETERMINATIONS RESPECTING VALUE OF NONFORFEITABLE BENEFITS UNDER TERMINATED PLAN AND VALUE OF ASSETS OF PLAN.—The value of nonforfeitable benefits under a terminated plan referred to in subsection (a), and the value of the plan's assets, shall be determined in writing, in accordance with regulations prescribed by the corporation, as of the end of the plan year during which section 4041A(d) becomes applicable to the plan, and each plan year thereafter.

(2) For purposes of this section, plan assets include outstanding claims for withdrawal liability (within the meaning of section 4001(a)(12)).

Act Sec. 4281. (c)(1) AMENDMENT OF PLAN BY PLAN SPONSOR TO REDUCE BENEFITS FOR CONSERVATION OF ASSETS; FACTORS APPLICABLE.—If, according to the determination made under subsection (b), the value of nonforfeitable benefits exceeds the value of the plan's assets, the plan sponsor shall amend the plan to reduce benefits under the plan to the extent necessary to ensure that the plan's assets are sufficient, as determined and certified in accordance with regulations prescribed by the corporation, to discharge when due all of the plan's obligations with respect to nonforfeitable benefits.

(2) Any plan amendment required by this subsection shall, in accordance with regulations prescribed by the Secretary of the Treasury—

(A) reduce benefits only to the extent necessary to comply with paragraph (1);

(B) reduce accrued benefits only to the extent that those benefits are not eligible for the corporation's guarantee under section 4022A(b);

(C) comply with the rules for and limitations on benefit reductions under a plan in reorganization, as prescribed in section 4244A, except to the extent that the corporation prescribes other rules and limitations in regulations under this section; and

(D) take effect no later than 6 months after the end of the plan year for which it is determined that the value of nonforfeitable benefits exceeds the value of the plan's assets.

Act Sec. 4281. (d)(1) SUSPENSION OF BENEFIT PAYMENTS; DETERMINATIVE FACTORS; POWERS AND DUTIES OF PLAN SPONSOR; RETROACTIVE BENEFIT PAYMENTS.—In any case in which benefit payments under a plan which is insolvent under paragraph (2)(A) exceed the resource benefit level, any such payments which are not basic benefits shall be suspended, in accordance with this subsection, to the extent necessary to reduce the sum of such payments and such basic benefits to the greater of the resource benefit level or the level of basic benefits, unless an alternative procedure is prescribed by the corporation in connection with a supplemental guarantee program established under section 4022A(g)(2).

(2) For purposes of this subsection, for a plan year—

(A) a plan is insolvent if—

(i) the plan has been amended to reduce benefits to the extent permitted by subsection (c), and

(ii) the plan's available resources are not sufficient to pay benefits under the plan when due for the plan year; and

(B) "resource benefit level" and "available resources" have the meanings set forth in paragraphs (2) and (3), respectively, of section 4245(b).

(3) The plan sponsor of a plan which is insolvent (within the meaning of paragraph (2)(A)) shall have the powers and duties of the plan sponsor of a plan in reorganization which is insolvent (within the meaning of section 4245(b)(1)), except that regulations governing the plan sponsor's exercise of those powers and duties under this section shall be prescribed by the corporation, and the corporation shall prescribe by regulation notice requirements which assure that plan participants and beneficiaries receive adequate notice of benefit suspensions.

(4) A plan is not required to make retroactive benefit payments with respect to that portion of a benefit which was suspended under this subsection, except that the provisions of section 4245(c)(4) and (5) shall apply in the case of plans which are insolvent under paragraph (2)(A), in connection with the plan year during which such section 4041A(d) first became applicable to the plan and every year thereafter, in the same manner and to the same extent as such provisions apply to insolvent plans in reorganization under section 4245, in connection with insolvency years under such section 4245.

Amendment

P.L. 96-364, § 104(2):

Added Sec. 4281, effective September 26, 1980 under ERISA Sec. 4402.

Regulations

The following regulations were adopted by the Pension Benefit Guaranty Corporation on July 1, 1996 (61 FR 34002). Prior to July 1, 1996, PBGC regulations were under Chapter XXVI of Title 29 of the Code of Federal Regulations. Effective July 1, 1996, PBGC regulations were moved to Chapter XL, and were renumbered and reorganized. Reg. §§ 4281.13 and 4281.14 were amended July 15, 1998 (63 FR 38305), effective August 17, 1998. Reg. § 4281.14 was revised December 14, 2006 (71 FR 75117), effective February 27, 2007. Reg. § 4281.15 was removed and reserved July 15, 1998 (63 FR 38305), effective August 17, 1998. Reg. § 4281.3, Reg. § 4281.32, Reg. § 4281.43, and Reg. § 4281.45 were amended October 28, 2003 (68 FR 61344). Reg. § 4281.14 was revised on July 12, 2006 (71 FR 39205). Reg. §§ 4281.43, 4281.44, 4281.46, and 4281.47 were amended May 28, 2014 (79 FR 30459). Reg. §§ 4281.3, 4281.43, and 4281.47 were amended on September 17, 2015 (80 FR 55742). Reg. § 4281.3 was corrected on September 25, 2015 (80 FR 57717).

Subpart A—General Provisions

[¶ 15,715A]

§ 4281.1 **Purpose and scope**. (a) *General*. (1) *Purpose*. When a multiemployer plan terminates by mass withdrawal under section 4041A(a)(2) of ERISA, the plan's assets and benefits must be valued annually under section 4281(b) of ERISA, and plan benefits may have to be reduced or suspended to the extent provided in section 4281(c) or (d). This part implements the provisions of section 4281 and provides rules for applying for financial assistance from the PBGC under section 4261 of ERISA. The plan valuation rules in this part also apply to the determination of reallocation liability under section 4219(c)(1)(D) of ERISA and subpart B of part 4219 of this chapter for multiemployer plans that undergo mass withdrawal (with or without termination).

(2) *Scope*. This part applies to multiemployer plans covered by Title IV of ERISA that have terminated by mass withdrawal under section 4041A(a)(2) of ERISA (including plans created by partition pursuant to section 4233 of ERISA). Subpart B of this part also applies to covered multiemployer plans that have undergone mass withdrawal without terminating.

(b) *Subpart B*. Subpart B establishes rules for determining the value of multiemployer plan benefits and assets, including outstanding claims for withdrawal liability, for plans required to perform annual valuations under section 4281(b) of ERISA or allocate unfunded vested benefits under section 4219(c)(1)(D) of ERISA.

(c) *Subpart C*. Subpart C sets forth procedures under which the plan sponsor of a terminated plan shall amend the plan to reduce benefits subject to reduction in accordance with section 4281(c) of ERISA and § 4041A.24(b) of this chapter. Subpart C applies to a plan for which the annual valuation required by § 4041A.24(a) indicates that the value of nonforfeitable benefits under the plan exceeds the value of the plan's assets (including claims for withdrawal liability) if, at the end of the plan year for which that valuation was done, the plan provided any benefits subject to reduction. Benefit reductions required to be made under subpart C shall not apply to accrued benefits under plans or plan amendments adopted on or before March 26, 1980, or under collective bargaining agreements entered into on or before March 26, 1980.

(d) *Subpart D*. Subpart D sets forth the procedures under which the plan sponsor of an insolvent plan must suspend benefit payments and issue insolvency notices in accordance with section 4281(d) of ERISA and § 4041A.25(c) and (d) of this chapter. Subpart D applies to a plan that has been amended under section 4281(c) of ERISA and subpart C of this part to eliminate all benefits subject to reduction and to a plan that provided no benefits subject to reduction as of the date on which the plan terminated.

[¶ 15,715B]

§ 4281.2 **Definitions**. The following terms are defined in section 4001.2 of this chapter: *annuity, employer, ERISA, fair market value, IRS, insurer, irrevocable commitment, mass withdrawal, multiemployer plan, nonforfeitable benefit, normal retirement age, PBGC, person, plan, plan administrator,* and *plan year*.

In addition, for purposes of this part:

Available resources means, for a plan year, available resources as described in section 4245(b)(3) of ERISA.

Benefits subject to reduction means those benefits accrued under plan amendments (or plans) adopted after March 26, 1980, or under collective bargaining agreements entered into after March 26, 1980, that are not eligible for the PBGC's guarantee under section 4022A(b) of ERISA.

Financial assistance means financial assistance from the PBGC under section 4261 of ERISA.

Insolvency benefit level means the greater of the resource benefit level or the benefit level guaranteed by the PBGC for each participant and beneficiary in pay status.

Insolvency year means insolvency year as described in section 4245(b)(4) of ERISA.

Insolvent means that a plan is unable to pay benefits when due during the plan year. A plan terminated by mass withdrawal is not insolvent unless it has been amended to eliminate all benefits that are subject to reduction under section 4281(c), or, in the absence of an amendment, no benefits under the plan are subject to reduction under section 4281(c) of ERISA.

Pro rata means that the required benefit reduction or payment shall be allocated among affected participants in the same proportion that each such participant's nonforfeitable benefits under the plan bear to all nonforfeitable benefits of those participants under the plan.

Reasonably expected to enter pay status means, with respect to plan participants and beneficiaries, persons (other than those in pay status) who, according to plan records, are disabled, have applied for benefits, or have reached or will reach during the applicable period the normal retirement age under the plan, and any others whom it is reasonable for the plan sponsor to expect to enter pay status during the applicable period.

Resource benefit level means resource benefit level as described in section 4245(b)(2) of ERISA.

Valuation date means the last day of the plan year in which the plan terminates and the last day of each plan year thereafter.

[¶ 15,715C]

§ 4281.3 **Filing and issuance rules**. (a) *Method of filing*. The PBGC applies the rules in subpart A of part 4000 of this chapter to determine permissible methods of filing with the PBGC under this part.

⟫→ *Caution: Reg. § 4281.3(b), as revised, applies to filings made on or after January 1, 2016.*

(b) *Method of issuance*. For rules on method of issuance to interested parties, see § 4281.32(c) for notices of benefit reductions, § 4281.43(c) for notices of insolvency, and § 4281.45(c) for notices of insolvency benefit level. [Revised 9/17/15 by 80 FR 55742 and corrected 9/25/15 by 80 FR 57717.]

(c) *Date of filing*. The PBGC applies the rules in subpart C of part 4000 of this chapter to determine the date that a submission under this part was filed with the PBGC.

(d) *Date of issuance*. The PBGC applies the rules in subpart C of part 4000 of this chapter to determine the date that an issuance under this part was provided.

(e) *Where to file*. See Sec. 4000.4 of this chapter for information on where to file.

(f) *Computation of time*. The PBGC applies the rules in subpart D of part 4000 of this chapter to compute any time period for filing or issuance under this part.

[Amended 10/28/2003 by 68 FR 61344]

[Amended 7/12/06 by 71 FR 39205]

[¶ 15,715D]

§ 4281.4 **Collection of information**. The collection of information requirements contained in this part have been approved by the Office of Management and Budget under control number 1212-0032.

Subpart B—Valuation of Plan Benefits and Plan Assets

[¶ 15,715E]

§ 4281.11 **Valuation dates**. (a) *Annual valuations of mass-with-drawal-terminated plans.* The valuation dates for the annual valuation required under section 4281(b) of ERISA shall be the last day of the plan year in which the plan terminates and the last day of each plan year thereafter.

(b) *Valuations related to mass withdrawal reallocation liability.* The valuation date for determining the value of unfunded vested benefits (for purposes of allocation) under section 4219(c)(1)(D) of ERISA shall be—

(1) If the plan terminates by mass withdrawal, the last day of the plan year in which the plan terminates; or

(2) If substantially all the employers withdraw from the plan pursuant to an agreement or arrangement to withdraw from the plan, the last day of the plan year as of which substantially all employers have withdrawn from the plan pursuant to the agreement or arrangement.

[¶ 15,715F]

§ 4281.12 **Benefits to be valued**. (a) *Form of benefit.* The plan sponsor shall determine the form of each benefit to be valued, without regard to the form of benefit valued in any prior year, in accordance with the following rules:

(1) If a benefit is in pay status as of the valuation date, the plan sponsor shall value the form of benefit being paid.

(2) If a benefit is not in pay status as of the valuation date but a valid election with respect to the form of benefit has been made on or before the valuation date, the plan sponsor shall value the form of benefit so elected.

(3) If a benefit is not in pay status as of the valuation date and no valid election with respect to the form of benefit has been made on or before the valuation date, the plan sponsor shall value the form of benefit that, under the terms of the plan or applicable law, is payable in the absence of a valid election.

(b) *Timing of benefit.* The plan sponsor shall value benefits whose starting date is subject to election—

(1) By assuming that the starting date of each benefit is the earliest date, not preceding the valuation date, that could be elected; or

(2) By using any other assumption that the plan sponsor demonstrates to the satisfaction of the PBGC is more reasonable under the circumstances.

[¶ 15,715G]

§ 4281.13 **Benefit valuation methods**. *General rule.* Except as otherwise provided in § 4281.16 (regarding plans that are closing out), the plan sponsor shall value benefits as of the valuation date by—

(a) Using the interest assumptions described in Table I of appendix B to part 4044 of this chapter;

(b) Using the mortality assumptions described in § 4281.14;

(c) Using interpolation methods, where necessary, at least as accurate as linear interpolation;

(d) Applying valuation formulas that accord with generally accepted actuarial principles and practices; and

(e) Adjusting the values to reflect the loading for expenses in accordance with appendix C to part 4044 of this chapter (substituting the term "benefits" for the term "benefit liabilities (as defined in 29 U.S.C. § 1301(a)(16))").

[¶ 15,715H]

§ 4281.14 **Mortality assumptions**. (a) *General rule.* Subject to paragraph (b) of this section (regarding certain death benefits), the plan

administrator shall use the mortality factors prescribed in paragraphs (c), (d), (e), and (f) of this section to value benefits under Sec. 4281.13.

(b) *Certain death benefits.* If an annuity for one person is in pay status on the valuation date, and if the payment of a death benefit after the valuation date to another person, who need not be identifiable on the valuation date, depends in whole or in part on the death of the pay status annuitant, then the plan administrator shall value the death benefit using—

(1) The mortality rates that are applicable to the annuity in pay status under this section to represent the mortality of the pay status annuitant; and

(2) The mortality rates applicable to annuities not in pay status and to deferred benefits other than annuities, under paragraph (c) of this section, to represent the mortality of the death beneficiary.

(c) *Mortality rates for healthy lives.* The mortality rates applicable to annuities in pay status on the valuation date that are not being received as disability benefits, to annuities not in pay status on the valuation date, and to deferred benefits other than annuities, are,—

(1) For male participants, the rates in Table 1 of Appendix A to part 4044 of this chapter projected from 1994 to the calendar year in which the valuation date occurs plus 10 years using Scale AA from Table 2 of Appendix A to part 4044 of this chapter; and

(2) For female participants, the rates in Table 3 of Appendix A to part 4044 of this chapter projected from 1994 to the calendar year in which the valuation date occurs plus 10 years using Scale AA from Table 4 of Appendix A to part 4044 of this chapter.

(d) *Mortality rates for disabled lives (other than Social Security disability).* The mortality rates applicable to annuities in pay status on the valuation date that are being received as disability benefits and for which neither eligibility for, nor receipt of, Social Security disability benefits is a prerequisite, are,—

(1) For male participants, the lesser of—

(i) The rate determined from Table 1 of Appendix A to part 4044 of this chapter projected from 1994 to the calendar year in which the valuation date occurs plus 10 years using Scale AA from Table 2 of Appendix A to part 4044 of this chapter and setting the resulting table forward three years, or

(ii) The rate in Table 5 of Appendix A to part 4044 of this chapter.

(2) For female participants, the lesser of—

(i) The rate determined from Table 3 of Appendix A to part 4044 of this chapter projected from 1994 to the calendar year in which the valuation date occurs plus 10 years using Scale AA from Table 4 of Appendix A to part 4044 of this chapter and setting the resulting table forward three years, or

(ii) The rate in Table 6 of Appendix A to part 4044 of this chapter.

(e) *Mortality rates for disabled lives (Social Security disability).* The mortality rates applicable to annuities in pay status on the valuation date that are being received as disability benefits and for which either eligibility for, or receipt of, Social Security disability benefits is a prerequisite, are—

(1) For male participants, the rates in Table 5 of Appendix A to part 4044 of this chapter; and

(2) For female participants, the rates in Table 6 of Appendix A to part 4044 of this chapter.

(f) *Contingent annuitant mortality during deferral period.* If a participant's joint and survivor benefit is valued as a deferred annuity, the mortality of the contingent annuitant during the deferral period will be disregarded.

[Revised 12/14/2006 (71 FR 75117).]

[¶ 15,715I]

§ 4281.15 **[Reserved.]**

[¶ 15,715J]

§ 4281.16 **Benefit valuation methods—plans closing out**. (a) *Applicability.* For purposes of the annual valuation required by section 4281(b) of ERISA, the plan sponsor shall value the plan's benefits in accordance with paragraph (b) of this section if,—

(1) *Plans closed out before valuation*. Before the time when the valuation is performed, the plan has satisfied in full all liabilities for payment of nonforfeitable benefits, in a manner consistent with the terms of the plan and applicable law, by the purchase of one or more nonparticipating irrevocable commitments from one or more insurers, with respect to all benefits payable as annuities, and by the payment of single-sum cash distributions, with respect to benefits not payable as annuities; or

(2) *Plans to be closed out after valuation*. As of the time when the valuation is performed, the plan sponsor reasonably expects that the plan will close out before the next annual valuation date and the plan sponsor has a currently exercisable bid or bids to provide the irrevocable commitment(s) described in paragraph (a)(1) of this section and the total cost of the irrevocable commitment(s) under the bid, plus the total amount of the single-sum cash distributions described in paragraph (a)(1), does not exceed the value of the plan's assets, exclusive of outstanding claims for withdrawal liability, as determined under this subpart.

(b) *Valuation rule*. The present value of nonforfeitable benefits under this section is the total amount of single-sum cash distributions made or to be made plus the cost of the irrevocable commitment(s) purchased or to be purchased in order to satisfy in full all liabilities of the plan for nonforfeitable benefits.

[¶ 15,715K]

§ 4281.17 **Asset valuation methods—in general**. (a) *General rule*. The plan sponsor shall value plan assets as of the valuation date, using the valuation methods prescribed by this section and § 4281.18 (regarding outstanding claims for withdrawal liability), and deducting administrative liabilities in accordance with paragraph (c) of this section.

(b) *Assets other than withdrawal liability claims*. The plan sponsor shall value any plan asset (other than an outstanding claim for withdrawal liability) by such method or methods as the plan sponsor reasonably believes most accurately determine fair market value.

(c) *Adjustment for administrative liabilities*. In determining the total value of plan assets, the plan sponsor shall subtract all plan liabilities, other than liabilities to pay benefits. For this purpose, any obligation to repay financial assistance received from the PBGC under section 4261 of ERISA is a plan liability other than a liability to pay benefits. The obligation to repay financial assistance shall be valued by determining the value of the scheduled payments in the same manner as prescribed in § 4281.18(a) for valuing claims for withdrawal liability.

[¶ 15,715L]

§ 4281.18 **Outstanding claims for withdrawal liability**. (a) *Value of claim*. The plan sponsor shall value an outstanding claim for withdrawal liability owed by an employer described in paragraph (b) of this section in accordance with paragraphs (a)(1) and (a)(2) of this section:

(1) If the schedule of withdrawal liability payments provides for one or more series of equal payments, the plan sponsor shall value each series of payments as an annuity certain in accordance with the provisions of § 4281.13.

(2) If the schedule of withdrawal liability payments provides for one or more payments that are not part of a series of equal payments as described in paragraph (a)(1) of this section, the plan sponsor shall value each such unequal payment as a lump-sum payment in accordance with the provisions of § 4281.13.

(b) *Employers neither liquidated nor in insolvency proceedings*. The plan sponsor shall value an outstanding claim for withdrawal liability under paragraph (a) of this section if, as of the valuation date—

(1) The employer has not been completely liquidated or dissolved; and

(2) The employer is not the subject of any case or proceeding under title 11, United States Code, or any case or proceeding under similar provisions of state insolvency laws; except that the claim for withdrawal liability of an employer that is the subject of a proceeding described in this paragraph (b)(2) shall be valued under paragraph (a)

of this section if the plan sponsor determines that the employer is reasonably expected to be able to pay its withdrawal liability in full and on time.

(c) *Claims against other employers*. The plan sponsor shall value at zero any outstanding claim for withdrawal liability owed by an employer that does not meet the conditions set forth in paragraph (b) of this section.

Subpart C—Benefit Reductions

[¶ 15,715M]

§ 4281.31 **Plan amendment**. The plan sponsor of a plan described in § 4281.31 shall amend the plan to eliminate those benefits subject to reduction in excess of the value of benefits that can be provided by plan assets. Such reductions shall be effected by a pro rata reduction of all benefits subject to reduction or by elimination or pro rata reduction of any category of benefit. Benefit reductions required by this section shall apply only prospectively. An amendment required under this section shall take effect no later than six months after the end of the plan year for which it is determined that the value of nonforfeitable benefits exceeds the value of the plan's assets.

[¶ 15,715N]

§ 4281.32 **Notices of benefit reductions**. (a) *Requirement of notices*. A plan sponsor of a multiemployer plan under which a plan amendment reducing benefits is adopted pursuant to section 4281(c) of ERISA shall so notify the PBGC and plan participants and beneficiaries whose benefits are reduced by the amendment. The notices shall be delivered in the manner and within the time prescribed, and shall contain the information described, in this section. The notice required in this section shall be filed in lieu of the notice described in section 4244A(b)(2) of ERISA.

(b) *When delivered*. The plan sponsor shall mail or otherwise deliver the notices of benefit reduction no later than the earlier of—

(1) 45 days after the amendment reducing benefits is adopted; or

(2) The date of the first reduced benefit payment.

(c) *Method of issuance to interested parties*. The PBGC applies the rules in subpart B of part 4000 of this chapter to determine permissible methods of issuance of the notice of benefit reduction to interested parties. In addition to the methods permitted under subpart B of part 4000, the plan sponsor may notify interested parties, other than participants and beneficiaries who are in pay status when the notice is required to be delivered or who are reasonably expected to enter pay status before the end of the plan year after the plan year in which the amendment is adopted, by posting the notice at participants' work sites or publishing the notice in a union newsletter or in a newspaper of general circulation in the area or areas where participants reside. Notice to a participant shall be deemed notice to that participant's beneficiary or beneficiaries.

[Amended 10/28/2003 by 68 FR 61344]

(d) *Contents of notice to the PBGC*. A notice of benefit reduction required to be filed with the PBGC pursuant to paragraph (a) of this section shall contain the following information:

(1) The name of the plan.

(2) The name, address, and telephone number of the plan sponsor and of the plan sponsor's duly authorized representative, if any.

(3) The nine-digit Employer Identification Number (EIN) assigned by the IRS to the plan sponsor and the three-digit Plan Number (PN) assigned by the plan sponsor to the plan, and, if different, the EIN or PN last filed with the PBGC. If no EIN or PN has been assigned, the notice shall so state.

(4) The case number assigned by the PBGC to the filing of the plan's notice of termination pursuant to part 4041A, subpart B, of this chapter.

(5) A statement that a plan amendment reducing benefits has been adopted, listing the date of adoption and the effective date of the amendment.

(6) A certification, signed by the plan sponsor or its duly authorized representative, that notice of the benefit reductions has been given to all participants and beneficiaries whose benefits are reduced by the plan amendment, in accordance with the requirements of this section.

(e) *Contents of notice to participants and beneficiaries.* A notice of benefit reductions required under paragraph (a) of this section to be given to plan participants and beneficiaries whose benefits are reduced by the amendment shall contain the following information:

(1) The name of the plan.

(2) A statement that a plan amendment reducing benefits has been adopted, listing the date of adoption and the effective date of the amendment.

(3) A summary of the amendment, including a description of the effect of the amendment on the benefits to which it applies.

(4) The name, address, and telephone number of the plan administrator or other person designated by the plan sponsor to answer inquiries concerning benefits.

[¶ 15,715O]

§ 4281.33 **Restoration of benefits.** (a) *General.* The plan sponsor of a plan that has been amended to reduce benefits under this subpart shall amend the plan to restore those benefits before adopting any amendment increasing benefits under the plan. A plan is not required to make retroactive benefit payments with respect to any benefit that was reduced and subsequently restored in accordance with this section.

(b) *Notice to the PBGC.* The plan sponsor shall notify the PBGC in writing of any restoration under this section. The notice shall include the information specified in § 4281.32(d)(1) through (d)(4); a statement that a plan amendment restoring benefits has been adopted, the date of adoption, and the effective date of the amendment; and a certification,

signed by the plan sponsor or its duly authorized representative, that the amendment has been adopted in accordance with this section.

Subpart D—Benefit Suspensions

[¶ 15,715P]

§ 4281.41 **Benefit suspensions.** If the plan sponsor determines that the plan is or is expected to be insolvent for a plan year, the plan sponsor shall suspend benefits to the extent necessary to reduce the benefits to the greater of the resource benefit level or the level of guaranteed benefits.

[¶ 15,715Q]

§ 4281.42 **Retroactive payments.** (a) *Erroneous resource benefit level.* If, by the end of a year in which benefits were suspended under § 4281.41, the plan sponsor determines in writing that the plan's available resources in that year could have supported benefit payments above the resource benefit level determined for that year, the plan sponsor may distribute the excess resources to each affected participant and beneficiary who received benefit payments that year on a pro rata basis. The amount distributed to each participant under this paragraph may not exceed the amount that, when added to benefit payments already made, brings the total benefit for the plan year up to the total benefit provided under the plan.

(b) *Benefits paid below resource benefit level.* If, by the end of a plan year in which benefits were suspended under § 4281.41, any benefit has not been paid at the resource benefit level, amounts up to the resource benefit level that were unpaid shall be distributed to each affected participant and beneficiary on a pro rata basis to the extent possible, taking into account the plan's total available resources in that year.

[¶ 15,715R]

§ 4281.43 **Notices of insolvency.** [Amended 5/28/14 by 79 FR 30459.]

>>→ *Caution: Reg. § 4281.43(a), as revised, applies to filings made on or after January 1, 2016.*

(a) *Requirement of notices of insolvency.* A plan sponsor that determines that the plan is, or is expected to be, insolvent for a plan year shall file with the PBGC and issue to plan participants and beneficiaries notices of insolvency. Once notices of insolvency have been filed with the PBGC and issued to plan participants and beneficiaries, no notice of insolvency needs to be issued for subsequent insolvency years. Notices shall be delivered in the manner and within the time prescribed in this section and shall contain the information described in § 4281.44. [Revised 9/17/15 by 80 FR 55742.]

(b) *Notices of insolvency—when delivered.* Except as provided in the next sentence, the plan sponsor shall mail or otherwise deliver the notices of insolvency no later than 30 days after the plan sponsor determines that the plan is or may be insolvent. However, the notice to plan participants and beneficiaries in pay status may be delivered concurrently with the first benefit payment made after the determination of insolvency. [Redesignated 5/28/14 by 79 FR 30459.]

(c) *Notices of insolvency—method of issuance to interested parties.* The PBGC applies the rules in subpart B of part 4000 of this chapter to determine permissible methods of issuance of the notice of insolvency. In addition to the methods permitted under subpart B of part 4000, the plan sponsor may notify interested parties, other than participants and beneficiaries who are in pay status when the notice is required to be delivered, by posting the notice at participants' work sites or publishing the notice in a union newsletter or in a newspaper of general circulation in the area or areas where participants reside. Notice to a participant shall be deemed notice to that participant's beneficiary or beneficiaries. [Amended 10/28/2003 by 68 FR 61344. Redesignated 5/28/14 by 79 FR 30459.]

(d) *Annual updates—when delivered.* [Removed 5/28/14 by 79 FR 30459.]

(f) *Annual updates—method of issuance.* [Removed 5/28/14 by 79 FR 30459.]

[¶ 15,715S]

§ 4281.44 **Contents of notices of insolvency.** [Amended 5/28/14 by 79 FR 30459.]

(a) *Notice of insolvency to the PBGC.* A notice of insolvency required under § 4281.43(a) to be filed with the PBGC shall contain the following information:

(1) The name of the plan.

(2) The name, address, and telephone number of the plan sponsor and of the plan sponsor's duly authorized representative, if any.

(3) The nine-digit Employer Identification Number (EIN) assigned by the IRS to the plan sponsor and the three-digit Plan Number (PN) assigned by the plan sponsor to the plan, and, if different, the EIN or PN last filed with the PBGC. If no EIN or PN has been assigned, the notice shall so state.

(4) The case number assigned by the PBGC to the filing of the plan's notice of termination pursuant to part 4041A, subparts A and B, of this chapter. [Redesignated 5/28/14 by 79 FR 30459.]

(5) The plan year for which the plan' sponsor has determined that the plan is or may be insolvent. [Redesignated 5/28/14 by 79 FR 30459.]

(6) A copy of the plan document currently in effect, i.e., a copy of the last restatement of the plan and all subsequent amendments. However, if a copy of the plan document was submitted to the PBGC with a previous filing, only subsequent plan amendments need be submitted, and the notice shall state when the copy of the plan document was filed. [Redesignated 5/28/14 by 79 FR 30459.]

(7) A copy of the most recent actuarial valuation for the plan (i.e., the most recent report submitted to the plan in connection with a valuation of plan assets and liabilities, which shall be performed in accordance with subpart B of this part). If the actuarial valuation was previously submitted to the PBGC, it may be omitted, and the notice shall state the date on which the document was filed and that the information is still accurate and complete. [Redesignated 5/28/14 by 79 FR 30459.]

(8) The estimated amount of annual benefit payments under the plan (determined without regard to the insolvency) for the insolvency year. [Redesignated 5/28/14 by 79 FR 30459.]

(9) The estimated amount of the plan's available resources for the insolvency year. [Redesignated 5/28/14 by 79 FR 30459.]

(10) The estimated amount of the annual benefits guaranteed by the PBGC for the insolvency year. [Redesignated 5/28/14 by 79 FR 30459.]

(11) A statement indicating whether the notice of insolvency is the result of an insolvency determination under §4041A.25(a) or (b). [Redesignated 5/28/14 by 79 FR 30459.]

(12) A certification, signed by the plan sponsor or its duly authorized representative, that notices of insolvency have been given to all plan participants and beneficiaries in accordance with this part. [Redesignated 5/28/14 by 79 FR 30459.]

(b) *Notice of insolvency to participants and beneficiaries.* A notice of insolvency required under §4281.43(a) to be issued to plan participants and beneficiaries shall contain the following information:

(1) The name of the plan.

(2) A statement of the plan year for which the plan sponsor has determined that the plan is or may be insolvent.

(3) A statement that benefits above the amount that can be paid from available resources or the level guaranteed by the PBGC, whichever is greater, will be suspended during the insolvency year, with a brief explanation of which benefits are guaranteed by the PBGC.

(4) The name, address, and telephone number of the plan administrator or other person designated by the plan sponsor to answer inquiries concerning benefits.

(c) *Annual update to the PBGC.* [Removed 5/28/14 by 79 FR 30459.]

(d) *Annual updates to participants and beneficiaries.* [Removed 5/28/14 by 79 FR 30459.]

§4281.45 **Notices of insolvency benefit level.** (a) *Requirement of notices.* For each insolvency year, the plan sponsor shall issue a notice of insolvency benefit level to the PBGC and to plan participants and beneficiaries in pay status or reasonably expected to enter pay status during the insolvency year. The notices shall be delivered in the manner and within the time prescribed in this section and shall contain the information described in §4281.46.

(b) *When delivered.* The plan sponsor shall mail or otherwise deliver the notices of insolvency benefit level no later than 60 days before the beginning of the insolvency year. A plan sponsor that determines under §4041A.25(b) that the plan is or may be insolvent for a plan year shall mail or otherwise deliver the notices of insolvency benefit level by the later of 60 days before the beginning of the insolvency year or 60 days after the date of the plan sponsor's determination under §4041A.25(b).

(c) *Method of issuance.* The notices of insolvency benefit level shall be delivered to the PBGC and to plan participants and beneficiaries in pay status or reasonably expected to enter pay status during the insolvency year. The PBGC applies the rules in subpart B of part 4000 of this chapter to determine permissible methods of issuance of the notice of insolvency benefit levels to interested parties. [Amended 10/28/2003 by 68 FR 61344]

⋙→ Caution: Reg. §4281.47(b), as revised, applies to filings made on or after January 1, 2016.

(b) *When, how, and where to apply.* When the plan sponsor determines a resource benefit level that is less than guaranteed benefits, it shall apply for financial assistance at the same time that it submits its notice of insolvency benefit level pursuant to § 4281.45. When the plan sponsor determines an inability to pay guaranteed benefits for any month, it shall apply for financial assistance within 15 days after making that determination. Application to the PBGC for financial assistance shall be made in accordance with the rules in subpart A of part 4000 of this chapter. See §4000.4 of this chapter for information on where to apply. [Revised 9/17/15 by 80 FR 55742.]

(c) *Contents of application—resource benefit level below level of guaranteed benefits.* A plan sponsor applying for financial assistance because the plan's resource benefit level is below the level of guaran-

§4281.46 **Contents of notices of insolvency benefit level.** (a) *Notice to the PBGC.* A notice of insolvency benefit level required by §4281.45(a) to be filed with the PBGC shall contain the information specified in §4281.44(a)(1) through (4) and (a)(6) through (10) and: [Amended 5/28/14 by 79 FR 30459.]

(1) The insolvency year for which the notice is being filed.

(2) The amount of financial assistance, if any, requested from the PBGC. (When financial assistance is requested, the plan sponsor shall submit an application in accordance with §4281.47.)

(3) A statement indicating whether the notice of insolvency benefit level is the result of an insolvency determination under §4041A.25(a) or (b).

(4) A certification, signed by the plan sponsor or its duly authorized representative, that a notice of insolvency benefit level has been sent to all plan participants and beneficiaries in pay status or reasonably expected to enter pay status during the insolvency year, in accordance with this part.

(b) *Notice to participants in or entering pay status.* A notice of insolvency benefit level required by §4281.45(a) to be delivered to plan participants and beneficiaries in pay status or reasonably expected to enter pay status during the insolvency year for which the notice is given, shall contain the following information:

(1) The name of the plan.

(2) The insolvency year for which the notice is being sent.

(3) The monthly benefit that the participant or beneficiary may expect to receive during the insolvency year.

(4) A statement that in subsequent plan years, depending on the plan's available resources, this benefit level may be increased or decreased but not below the level guaranteed by the PBGC, and that the participant or beneficiary will be notified in advance of the new benefit level if it is less than the participant's full nonforfeitable benefit under the plan.

(5) The amount of the participant's or beneficiary's monthly nonforfeitable benefit under the plan.

(6) The amount of the participant's or beneficiary's monthly benefit that is guaranteed by the PBGC.

(7) The name, address, and telephone number of the plan administrator or other person designated by the plan sponsor to answer inquiries concerning benefits.

§4281.47 **Application for financial assistance.** (a) *General.* If the plan sponsor determines that the plan's resource benefit level for an insolvency year is below the level of benefits guaranteed by PBGC or that the plan will be unable to pay guaranteed benefits when due for any month during the year, the plan sponsor shall apply to the PBGC for financial assistance pursuant to section 4261 of ERISA. The application shall be filed within the time prescribed in paragraph (b) of this section. When the resource benefit level is below the guarantee level, the application shall contain the information set forth in paragraph (c) of this section. When the plan is unable to pay guaranteed benefits for any month, the application shall contain the information set forth in paragraph (d) of this section.

teed benefits shall file an application that includes the information specified in §4281.44(a)(1) through (a)(4) and: [Amended 5/28/14 by 79 FR 30459.]

(1) The insolvency year for which the application is being filed.

(2) A participant data schedule showing each participant and beneficiary in pay status or reasonably expected to enter pay status during the year for which financial assistance is requested, listing for each—

(i) Name;

(ii) Sex;

(iii) Date of birth;

(iv) Credited service;

(v) Vested accrued monthly benefit;

Reg. §4281.47(c)(2)(v) ¶15,715V

(vi) Monthly benefit guaranteed by PBGC;

(vii) Benefit commencement date; and

(viii) Type of benefit.

(d) *Contents of application—unable to pay guaranteed benefits for any month.* A plan sponsor applying for financial assistance because the plan is unable to pay guaranteed benefits for any month shall file an application that includes the data described in §4281.44(a)(1) through

(a)(5), the month for which financial assistance is requested, and the plan's available resources and guaranteed benefits payable in that month. The participant data schedule described in paragraph (c)(2) of this section shall be submitted upon the request of the PBGC.

(e) *Additional information.* The PBGC may request any additional information that it needs to calculate or verify the amount of financial assistance necessary as part of the conditions of granting financial assistance pursuant to section 4261 of ERISA.

Part 6—Enforcement

[¶ 15,716]
CIVIL ACTIONS

Act Sec. 4301.(a)(1) PERSONS ENTITLED TO MAINTAIN ACTIONS.—A plan fiduciary, employer, plan participant, or beneficiary, who is adversely affected by the act or omission of any party under this subtitle with respect to a multiemployer plan, or an employee organization which represents such a plan participant or beneficiary for purposes of collective bargaining, may bring an action for appropriate legal or equitable relief, or both.

(2) Notwithstanding paragraph (1), this section does not authorize an action against the Secretary of the Treasury, the Secretary of Labor, or the corporation.

Act Sec. 4301. (b) FAILURE OF EMPLOYER TO MAKE WITHDRAWAL LIABILITY PAYMENT WITHIN PRESCRIBED TIME.—In any action under this section to compel an employer to pay withdrawal liability, any failure of the employer to make any withdrawal liability payment within the time prescribed shall be treated in the same manner as a delinquent contribution (within the meaning of section 515).

Act Sec. 4301. (c) JURISDICTION OF FEDERAL AND STATE COURTS.—The district courts of the United States shall have exclusive jurisdiction of an action under this section without regard to the amount in controversy, except that State courts of competent jurisdiction shall have concurrent jurisdiction over an action brought by a plan fiduciary to collect withdrawal liability.

Act Sec. 4301. (d) VENUE AND SERVICE OF PROCESS.—An action under this section may be brought in the district where the plan is administered or where a defendant resides or does business, and process may be served in any district where a defendant resides, does business, or may be found.

Act Sec. 4301. (e) COSTS AND EXPENSES.—In any action under this section, the court may award all or a portion of the costs and expenses incurred in connection with such action, including reasonable attorney's fees, to the prevailing party.

Act Sec. 4301. (f) TIME LIMITATIONS.—An action under this section may not be brought after the later of—

(1) 6 years after the date on which the cause of action arose, or

(2) 3 years after the earliest date on which the plaintiff acquired or should have acquired actual knowledge of the existence of such cause of action; except that in the case of fraud or concealment, such action may be brought not later than 6 years after the date of discovery of the existence of such cause of action.

Act Sec. 4301. (g) SERVICE OF COMPLAINT ON CORPORATION; INTERVENTION BY CORPORATION.—A copy of the complaint in any action under this section or section 4221 shall be served upon the corporation by certified mail. The corporation may intervene in any such action.

Amendment:

P. L. 96-364, §104(2):

Added Sec. 4301 effective September 26, 1980 under ERISA Sec. 4402.

[¶ 15,717]
PENALTY FOR FAILURE TO PROVIDE NOTICE

Act Sec. 4302. Any person who fails, without reasonable cause, to provide a notice required under this subtitle or any implementing regulations shall be liable to the corporation in an amount up to $100 for each day for which such failure continues. The corporation may bring a civil action against any such person in the United States District Court for the District of Columbia or in any district court of the United States within the jurisdiction of which the plan assets are located, the plan is administered, or a defendant resides or does business, and process may be served in any district where a defendant resides or does business, or may be found.

Amendment

P. L. 96-364, §104(2):

Added Sec. 4302 effective September 26, 1980 under ERISA Sec. 4402.

Regulations

The following regulations were adopted by the Pension Benefit Guaranty Corporation on July 10, 1997 (62 FR 36993) and are effective August 11, 1997. Reg. Sec. 4302.3 was amended in interim final regulations on May 13, 2016 (81 FR 29765), removing "$110" and adding "$275" in its place. Reg. Sec. 4302.3 was amended in final regulations on January 31, 2017 (82 FR 8813). Reg. Sec. 4302.3 was amended in final regulations on January 12, 2018 (83 FR 1555).

[¶ 15,717A]

§4302.1 **Purpose and scope.** This part specifies the maximum daily amount of penalties for which a person may be liable to the PBGC under ERISA section 4302 for certain failures to provide multiemployer plan notices, as such amount has been adjusted to account for inflation pursuant to the Federal Civil Monetary Penalty Inflation Adjustment Act of 1990, as amended by the Debt Collection Improvement Act of 1996.

[¶ 15,717B]

§4302.2 **Definitions.** The following terms are defined in §4001.2 of this chapter: *ERISA, multiemployer plan,* and *PBGC.*

[¶ 15,717C]

§4302.3 **Penalty amount.** The maximum daily amount of the penalty under section 4302 of ERISA shall be $285. [Amended 5/13/2016 by 81 FR 29765, 1/31/2017 by 82 FR 8813, and 1/12/2018 by 83 FR 1555.]

[¶ 15,718]
ELECTION OF PLAN STATUS

Act Sec. 4303.(a) AUTHORITY, TIME, AND CRITERA.—Within one year after the date of the enactment of the Multiemployer Pension Plan Amendments Act of 1980, a multiemployer plan may irrevocably elect, pursuant to procedures established by the corporation, that the plan shall not be treated as a multiemployer plan for any purpose under this Act or the Internal Revenue Code of 1954, if for each of the last 3 plan years ending prior to the effective date of the Multiemployer Pension Plan Amendments Act of 1980—

(1) the plan was not a multiemployer plan because the plan was not a plan described in section 3(37)(A)(iii) of this Act and section 414(f)(1)(C) of the Internal Revenue Code of 1954 (as such provisions were in effect on the day before the date of the enactment of the Multiemployer Pension Plan Amendments Act of 1980); and

(2) the plan had been identified as a plan that was not a multiemployer plan in substantially all its filings with the corporation, the Secretary of Labor and the Secretary of the Treasury.

Act Sec. 4303. (b) REQUIREMENTS.—An election described in subsection (a) shall be effective only if—

(1) the plan is amended to provide that it shall not be treated as a multiemployer plan for all purposes under this Act and the Internal Revenue Code of 1954, and

(2) written notice of the amendment is provided to the corporation within 60 days after the amendment is adopted.

Act Sec. 4303. (c) EFFECTIVE DATE.—An election described in subsection (a) shall be treated as being effective as of the date of the enactment of the Multiemployer Pension Plan Amendments Act of 1980.

Amendment:

P.L. 96-364, § 105:

Added new section 4303, effective September 26, 1980, except that the prior definition of multiemployer plan will continue for plan years beginning before enactment.

Subtitle F—Transition Rules and Effective Dates

[¶ 15,719]
AMENDMENTS TO INTERNAL REVENUE CODE OF 1954

Act Sec. 4401. (a) Section 404 of the Internal Revenue Code of 1986 (relating to deduction for contributions of an employer to employees' trust or annuity plan in compensation under a deferred-payment plan) is amended by adding at the end thereof the following new subsection:

[Code Sec. 404(g)]

"(g) CERTAIN EMPLOYER LIABILITY PAYMENTS CONSIDERED AS CONTRIBUTIONS. For purposes of this section any amount paid by an employer under section 4062, 4063, or 4064 of the Employee Retirement Income Security Act of 1974 shall be treated as a contribution to which this section applies by such employer to or under a stock bonus, pension, profit-sharing, or annuity plan."

Act Sec. 4401. (b) Section 6511(d) of the Internal Revenue Code of 1986 (relating to special rules applicable to income taxes) is amended by adding at the end thereof the following new paragraph:

[Code Sec. 6511(d)(8)]

"(8) SPECIAL PERIOD OF LIMITATION WITH RESPECT TO AMOUNTS INCLUDED IN INCOME SUBSEQUENTLY RECAPTURED UNDER QUALIFIED PLAN TERMINATION. If the claim for credit or refund relates to an overpayment of tax imposed by subtitle A on account of the recapture, under section 4045 of the Employee Retirement Income Security Act of 1974, of amounts included in income for a prior taxable year, the 3-year period of limitation prescribed in subsection (a) shall be extended, for purposes of permitting a credit or refund of the amount of the recapture, until the date which occurs one year after the date on which such recaptured amount is paid by the taxpayer.".

[The above amendments to the Internal Revenue Code of 1986 are incorporated in place in the "Internal Revenue Code—Regulations."]

Amendments

P.L. 101-239, § 7891(a)(1):

Titles I, III, and IV of ERISA (other than sections 3(37)(E), 301(a)(7), and 308, the last sentence of section 408(d), and sections 414(c), 4001(a)(3)(ii), and 4303) are each amended by striking "Internal Revenue Code of 1954" each place it appears and inserting "Internal Revenue Code of 1986," effective October 22, 1986.

P.L. 96-364, § 108(a):

Renumbered Sec. 4081 to Sec. 4401, effective September 26, 1980.

[¶ 15,720]
EFFECTIVE DATE; SPECIAL RULES

Act Sec. 4402. (a) The provisions of this title take effect on the date of enactment of this Act.

Act Sec. 4402. (b) Notwithstanding the provisions of subsection (a), the corporation shall pay benefits guaranteed under this title with respect to any plan—

(1) which is not a multiemployer plan,

(2) which terminates after June 30, 1974, and before the date of enactment of this Act,

(3) to which section 4021 would apply if that section were effective beginning on July 1, 1974, and

(4) with respect to which a notice is filed with the Secretary of Labor and received by him not later than 10 days after the date of enactment of this Act, except that, for reasonable cause shown, such notice may be filed with the Secretary of Labor and received by him not later than October 31, 1974, stating that the plan is a plan described in paragraphs (1), (2), and (3).

The corporation shall not pay benefits guaranteed under this title with respect to a plan described in the preceding sentence unless the corporation finds substantial evidence that the plan was terminated for a reasonable business purpose and not for the purpose of obtaining the payment of benefits by the corporation under this title or for the purpose of avoiding the liability which might be imposed under subtitle D if the plan terminated on or after the date of enactment of this Act. The provisions of subtitle D do not apply in the case of such a plan which terminates before the date of enactment of this Act. For purposes of determining whether a plan is a plan described in paragraph (2), the provisions of section 4048 shall not apply, but the corporation shall make the determination on the basis of the date on which benefits ceased to accrue on or any other reasonable basis consistent with the purposes of this subsection.

Act Sec. 4402. (c)(1) Except as provided in paragraphs (2), (3), and (4), the corporation shall not pay benefits guaranteed under this title with respect to a multiemployer plan which terminates before August 1, 1980. Whenever the corporation exercises the authority granted under paragraph (2) or (3), the corporation shall notify the Committee on Education and Labor and the Committee on Ways and Means of the House of Representatives, and the Committee on Labor and Public Welfare and the Committee on Finance of the Senate.

(2) The corporation may, in its discretion, pay benefits guaranteed under this title with respect to a multiemployer plan which terminates after the date of enactment of this Act and before August 1, 1980, if—

(A) the plan was maintained during the 60 months immediately preceding the date on which the plan terminates, and

(B) the corporation determines that the payment by the corporation of benefits guaranteed under this title with respect to that plan will not jeopardize the payments the corporation anticipates it may be required to make in connection with benefits guaranteed under this title with respect to multiemployer plans which terminate after July 31, 1980.

(3) Notwithstanding any provision of section 4021 or 4022 which would prevent such payments, the corporation, in carrying out its authority under paragraph (2), may pay benefits guaranteed under this title with respect to a multiemployer plan described in paragraph (2) in any case in which those benefits would otherwise not be payable if—

(A) the plan has been in effect for at least 5 years.

(B) the plan has been in substantial compliance with the funding requirements for a qualified plan with respect to the employees and former employees in those employment units on the basis of which the participating employers have contributed to the plan for the preceding 5 years, and

(C) the participating employers and employees organization or organizations had no reasonable recourse other than termination.

(4) If the corporation determines, under paragraph (2) or (3), that it will pay benefits guaranteed under this title with respect to a multiemployer plan which terminates before August 1, 1980, the corporation—

(A) may establish requirements for the continuation of payments which commenced before January 2, 1974, with respect to retired participants under the plan,

(B) may not, notwithstanding any other provision of this title, make payments with respect to any participant under such a plan who, on January 1, 1974, was receiving payment of retirement benefits, in excess of the amounts and rates payable with respect to such participant on that date,

(C) shall review from time to time payments made under the authority granted to it by paragraphs (2) and (3), and reduce or terminate such payments to the extent necessary to avoid jeopardizing the ability of the corporation to make payments of benefits guaranteed under this title in connection with multiemployer plans which terminate after July 31, 1980, without increasing premium rates for such plans.

Act Sec. 4402. (d) Notwithstanding any other provision of this title, guaranteed benefits payable by the corporation pursuant to its discretionary authority under this section shall continue to be paid at the level guaranteed under section 4022, without regard to any limitation on payment under subparagraph (C) of subsection (c)(4).

Act Sec. 4402.(e)(1) Except as provided in paragraphs (2), (3), and (4), the amendments to this Act made by the Multiemployer Pension Plan Amendments Act of 1980 shall take effect on the date of the enactment of that Act.

(2)(A) Except as provided in this paragraph, part 1 of subtitle E, relating to withdrawal liability, takes effect on September 26, 1980.

(B) For purposes of determining withdrawal liability under part 1 of subtitle E, an employer who has withdrawn from a plan shall be considered to have withdrawn from a multiemployer plan if, at the time of the withdrawal, the plan was a multiemployer plan as defined in section 4001(a)(3) as in effect at the time of the withdrawal.

(3) Sections 4241 through 4245, relating to multiemployer plan reorganization, shall take effect, with respect to each plan, of the first day of the first plan year beginning on or after the earlier of—

(A) the date on which the last collective bargaining agreement providing for employer contributions under the plan, which was in effect on the date of the enactment of the Multiemployer Pension Plan Amendments Act of 1980, expires, without regard to extensions agreed to on or after the date of the enactment of that Act, or

(B) 3 years after the date of the enactment of the Multiemployer Pension Plan Amendments Act of 1980.

(4) Section 4235 shall take effect on September 26, 1980.

Act Sec. 4402.(f)(1) In the event that before the date of enactment of the Multiemployer Pension Plan Amendments Act of 1980, the corporation has determined that—

(A) an employer has withdrawn from a multiemployer plan under section 4063, and

(B) the employer is liable to the corporation under such section,

the corporation shall retain the amount of liability paid to it or furnished in the form of a bond and shall pay such liability to the plan in the event the plan terminates in accordance with section 4041A(a)(2) before the earlier of September 26, 1980, or the day after the 5-year period commencing on the date of such withdrawal.

(2) In any case in which the plan is not so terminated within the period described in paragraph (1), the liability of the employer is abated and any payment held in escrow shall be refunded without interest to the employer or the employer's bond shall be cancelled.

Act Sec. 4402.(g)(1) In any case in which an employer or employers withdrew from a multiemployer plan before the effective date of part 1 of subtitle E, the corporation may—

(A) apply section 4063(d), as in effect before the amendments made by the Multiemployer Penson Plan Amendments Act of 1980, to such plan,

(B) assess liability against the withdrawn employer with respect to the resulting terminated plan,

(C) guarantee benefits under the terminated plan under section 4022, as in effect before such amendments, and

(D) if necessary, enforce such action through suit brought under section 4003.

(2) The corporation shall use the revolving fund used by the corporation with respect to basic benefits guaranteed under section 4022A in guaranteeing benefits under a terminated plan described in this subsection.

Act Sec. 4402.(h)(1) In the case of an employer who entered into a collective bargaining agreement—

(A) which was effective on January 12, 1979, and which remained in effect through May 15, 1982, and

(B) under which contributions to a multiemployer plan were to cease on January 12, 1982,

any withdrawal liability incurred by the employer pursuant to part 1 of subtitle E as a result of the complete or partial withdrawal of the employer from the multiemployer plan before January 16, 1982, shall be void.

(2) In any case in which—

(A) an employer engaged in the grocery wholesaling business—

(i) had ceased all covered operations under a multiemployer plan before June 30, 1981, and had relocated its operations to a new facility in another State, and

(ii) had notified a local union representative on May 14, 1980, that the employer had tentatively decided to discontinue operations and relocate to a new facility in another State, and

(B) all State and local approvals with respect to construction of and commencement of operations at the new facility had been obtained, a contract for construction had been entered into, and construction of the new facility had begun before September 26, 1980,

any withdrawal liability incurred by the employer pursuant to part 1 of subtitle E as a result of the complete or partial withdrawal of the employer from the multiemployer plan before June 30, 1981, shall be void.

Act Sec. 4402. (i) The preceding provisions of this section shall not apply with respect to amendments made to this title in provisions enacted after the date of the enactment of the Tax Reform Act of 1986.

Amendments

P.L. 112-141, §40234(b)(2)(A):

Amended ERISA Sec. 4402(c)(4) by striking subparagraph (C), and by redesignating subparagraph (D) as subparagraph (C). Prior to amendment, subparagraph (C) read as follows:

"(C) may not make any payments with respect to benefits guaranteed under this title in connection with such a plan which are derived, directly or indirectly, from amounts borrowed under section 4005(c), and"

The above amendment is effective on the date of enactment (July 6, 2012).

P.L. 112-141, §40234(b)(2)(B):

Amended ERISA Sec. 4402(d) by striking "or (D)".

The above amendment is effective on the date of enactment (July 6, 2012).

P.L. 101-239, §7862(a):

Amended ERISA Sec. 4402(h)(1) by striking "January 12, 1982" the second place it appeared and inserting "January 16, 1982" effective July 18, 1984.

P.L. 101-239, §7894(h)(5):

Amended ERISA Sec. 4402 by adding new subsection (i) to read as above.

P.L. 99-514, §1852(i):

Added new Sec. 4402(h) to read as above, effective July 18, 1984.

P.L. 98-360, § 558(b):

Amended ERISA Secs. 4402(e) and (f)(1) by striking out "April 29, 1980" each place it appeared and inserting "September 26, 1980" instead.

P.L. 96-364, § 108:

Renumbered old sections 4081 and 4082 as 4401 and 4402. Amended section 4402(d) to read as above, struck out section 4402(e) and added new sections 4402(e), (f) and (g), effective September 26, 1980.

Prior to amendment, sections 4402(d) and (e) read:

"(d) The corporation shall present to the Committee on Education and Labor of the House of Representatives and the Committee on Human Resources and the Committee on Finance of the Senate a report which comprehensively addresses the anticipated financial condition of the program relating to mandatory coverage of multiemployer plans, including possible events which might cause the corporation to experience serious financial difficulty after July 1, 1979. Such report shall include an explanation of any alternative courses of action which might be taken by the corporation to insure proper coverage of multi-employer plans and the proper financing of the program relating to such plans. If the report contains recommendations for amendments to this title, such recommendations shall be fully explained, and shall be accompanied by explanations of other options for legislative change considered and rejected by the corporation. The report shall be presented by July 1, 1978."

"(e) Notwithstanding any provision of title IV of this Act to the contrary, the annual insurance premium payable to the Pension Benefit Guaranty Corporation for coverage of basic benefits guaranteed under section 4022 of this Act by plans that are not multiemployer plans shall be $2.60 for each participant in the plan. This subsection shall be effective for plan years beginning on or after January 1, 1978, and the premium prescribed by this subsection shall be deemed to be the rate imposed by title IV of this Act for non-multiemployer plans until the rate schedule for such plans is revised pursuant to the procedure set out in section 4006 of this Act."

P.L. 96-293:

Amended Secs. 4082(c)(1), 4082(c)(2), and 4082(c)(4) by substituting "August 1, 1980," for "July 1, 1980," each place it appeared.

Amended Secs. 4082(c)(2)(B) and 4082(c)(4)(D) by substituting "July 31, 1980," for June 30, 1980," each place it appeared.

P.L. 96-239:

Amended Secs. 4082(c)(1), 4082(c)(2), and 4082(c)(4) by substituting "July 1, 1980," for "May 1, 1980," each place it appeared.

Amended Secs. 4082(c)(2)(B) and 4082(c)(4)(D) by substituting "June 30, 1980," for "April 30, 1980," each place it appeared.

P.L. 96-24:

Amended Secs. 4082(c)(1), 4082(c)(2), and 4082(c)(4) by substituting "May 1, 1980" for "July 1, 1979" each place it appeared.

Amended Secs. 4082(c)(2)(B) and 4082(c)(4)(D) by substituting "April 30, 1980" for "June 30, 1979" each place it appeared.

P.L. 95-214:

Amended Secs. 4082(c)(1), 4082(c)(2) and 4082(c)(4) by substituting "July 1, 1979" for "January 1, 1978" each place it appeared.

Amended Secs. 4082(c)(2)(B) and 4082(c)(4)(D) by substituting "June 30, 1979" for "December 31, 1977" each place it appeared.

Added Sec. 4082(d), effective December 19, 1977.

Added Sec. 4082(e), effective December 19, 1977.

Regulations

The following regulations were adopted by the Pension Benefit Guaranty Corporation on July 1, 1996 (61 FR 34002). Prior to July 1, 1996, PBGC regulations were under Chapter XXVI of Title 29 of the Code of Federal Regulations. Effective July 1, 1996, PBGC regulations were moved to Chapter XL, and were renumbered and reorganized. PBGC Reg. Sec. 4902.9 was amended June 14, 2001, 66 FR 32221. Reg. § 4901.6, Reg. § 4901.11, Reg. § 4901.15, Reg. § 4901.33, Reg. § 4902.3, Reg. § 4902.5, Reg. § 4902.6, Reg. § 4902.7, Reg. § 4903.2, and Reg. § 4907.170 were amended, and Reg. § 4902.10 was added, on October 28, 2003 (68 FR 61344). Reg. § 4904.1 was removed on February 13, 2004 (69 FR 7120). Reg. § 4901.2, Reg. § 4901.11, Reg. § 4902.1, Reg. § 4902.2, Reg. § 4902.3, Reg. § 4902.4, Reg. § 4902.6, and Reg. § 4902.7 were amended on June 8, 2009 (74 FR 27080), effective July 8, 2009. Reg. § 4902.9 and Reg. § 4902.10 were redesignated as Reg. § 4902.10 and Reg. § 4902.12, and newly redesignated Reg. § 4902.10 was revised on June 8, 2009 (74 FR 27080), effective July 8, 2009. New Reg. § 4902.9 and Reg. § 4902.11 were added on June 8, 2009 (74 FR 27080), effective July 8, 2009. Reg. § 4902.7 was corrected on June 25, 2009 (74 FR 30212). PBGC regulations on debt collection—Reg. § 4903.1 through Reg. § 4903.33—were revised and replaced on November 5, 2010 (75 FR 68203). Reg. § 4901.3, Reg. § 4901.4, Reg. § 4901.5, Reg. § 4901.14, Reg. § 4901.15, and Reg. § 4901.31 were amended on June 13, 2017 (82 FR 26990).

Subpart A—General

[¶ 15,720A]

§ 4901.1 **Purpose and scope.** This part contains the general rules of the PBGC implementing the Freedom of Information Act. This part sets forth generally the categories of records accessible to the public, the types of records subject to prohibitions or restrictions on disclosure, and the procedure whereby members of the public may obtain access to and inspect and copy information from records in the custody of the PBGC.

[¶ 15,720B]

§ 4901.2 **Definitions.** In addition to terminology in part 4001 of this chapter, as used in this part—

Agency, person, party, rule, rulemaking, order, and *adjudication* have the meanings attributed to these terms by the definitions in 5 U.S.C. 551, except where the context demonstrates that a different meaning is intended, and except that for purposes of the Freedom of Information Act the term agency as defined in 5 U.S.C. 551 includes any executive department, military department, Government corporation, Government controlled corporation, or other establishment in the executive branch of the Government (including the Executive Office of the President) or any independent regulatory agency.

FOIA means the Freedom of Information Act, as amended (5 U.S.C. 552).

Working day means any weekday excepting Federal holidays.

[¶ 15,720C]

§ 4901.3 **Electronic reading room.** The PBGC will maintain an electronic reading room on its Web site, www.pbgc.gov, where persons may inspect in an electronic format all records made available for such purposes under this part. [Revised 6/13/2017 by 82 FR 26990.]

[¶ 15,720D]

§ 4901.4 **Information maintained in electronic reading room.** The PBGC shall make available for public inspection in an electronic format without formal request—[Revised 6/13/2017 by 82 FR 26990.]

(a) *Information published in the Federal Register.* Copies of Federal Register documents published by the PBGC, and copies of Federal Register indexes;

(b) *Information in PBGC publications.* Copies of informational material, such as press releases, pamphlets, and other material ordinarily made available to the public without cost as part of a public information program;

(c) *Rulemaking proceedings.* All papers and documents made a part of the official record in administrative proceedings conducted by the PBGC in connection with the issuance, amendment, or revocation of rules and regulations or determinations having general applicability or legal effect with respect to members of the public or a class thereof (with a register being kept to identify the persons who inspect the records and the times at which they do so);

(d) Except to the extent that deletion of identifying details is required to prevent a clearly unwarranted invasion of personal privacy (in which case the justification for the deletion shall be fully explained in writing)—

(1) *Adjudication proceedings.* Final opinions, orders, and (except to the extent that an exemption provided by FOIA must be asserted in the public interest to prevent a clearly unwarranted invasion of personal privacy or violation of law or to ensure the proper discharge of the functions of the PBGC) other papers and documents made a part of the official record in adjudication proceedings conducted by the PBGC; [Amended 6/13/2017 by 82 FR 26990.]

(2) *Policy statements and interpretations.* Statements of policy and interpretations affecting a member of the public which have been adopted by the PBGC and which have not been published in the Federal Register; [Amended 6/13/2017 by 82 FR 26990.]

(3) *Staff manuals and instructions.* Administrative staff manuals and instructions to staff issued by the PBGC that affect any member of the public; [Amended 6/13/2017 by 82 FR 26990.]

(4) *Frequently requested records.* Records that have been released under 5 U.S.C. 552(a)(3) and have been the subject of three or more requests; and [Added 6/13/2017 by 82 FR 26990.]

(5) *Other records.* Records that have been released under 5 U.S.C. 552(a)(3) and that PBGC determines, because of the nature of the records' subject matter, have become or are likely to become the subject of subsequent requests for substantially the same records; and [Added 6/13/2017 by 82 FR 26990.]

(e) *Indexes to certain records.* Current indexes (updated at least quarterly) identifying materials described in paragraph (a)(2) of FOIA and paragraph (d) of this section.

[¶ 15,720E]

§ 4901.5 **Disclosure of other information.** (a) *In general.* Upon the request of any person submitted in accordance with subpart B of this part, the disclosure officer shall make any document (or portion thereof) from the records of the PBGC in the custody of any official of the PBGC available for inspection and copying unless PBGC reasonably foresees that disclosure would harm an interest protected by an exemption under the provisions of subsection (b) of FOIA and subpart C of this part or disclosure is otherwise prohibited by law. The subpart B procedures must be used for records that are not made available in the PBGC's electronic reading room under § 4901.4 and may be used for records that are available in the electronic reading room. Records that could be produced only by manipulation of existing information (such as computer analyses of existing data), thus creating information not previously in being, are not records of the PBGC and are not required to be furnished under FOIA. [Amended 6/13/2017 by 82 FR 26990.]

(b) *Discretionary disclosure.* Notwithstanding the applicability of an exemption under subsection (b) of FOIA and subpart C of this part (other than an exemption under paragraph (b)(1) or (b)(3) of FOIA and § 4901.21(a)(2) and (a)(3)), the disclosure officer may (subject to 18 U.S.C. 1905 and § 4901.21(a)(1)) make any document (or portion thereof) from the records of the PBGC available for inspection and copying if the disclosure officer determines that disclosure furthers the public interest and does not impede the discharge of any of the functions of the PBGC.

[¶ 15,720E-1]

§ 4901.6 **Filing rules; computation of time.** (a) *Filing rules.* (1) *Where to file.* See Sec. 4000.4 of this chapter for information on where to file a submission under this part with the PBGC.

(2) *Method of filing.* The PBGC applies the rules in subpart A of part 4000 of this chapter to determine permissible methods of filing with the PBGC under this part.

(3) *Date of filing.* The PBGC applies the rules in subpart C of part 4000 of this chapter to determine the date that a submission under this part was filed with the PBGC.

(b) *Computation of time.* The PBGC applies the rules in subpart D of part 4000 of this chapter to compute any time period under this part.

[Added 10/28/2003 by 68 FR 61344]

Subpart B—Procedure for Formal Requests

[¶ 15,720F]

§ 4901.11 **Submittal of requests for access to records.** A request to inspect or copy any record subject to this subpart shall be submitted to the Disclosure Officer, Pension Benefit Guaranty Corporation. Such a request may be sent to the Disclosure Officer or made in person between the hours of 9 a.m. and 4 p.m. on any working day in the Office of the General Counsel, PBGC, 1200 K Street, NW., Suite 11101, Washington, DC 20005-4026. To expedite processing, the request should be prominently identified as a "FOIA request."

[Amended 10/28/2003 by 68 FR 61344. Amended 6/8/2009 by 74 FR 27080, effective July 8, 2009.]

[¶ 15,720G]

§ 4901.12 **Description of information requested.** (a) *In general.* Each request should reasonably describe the record or records sought in sufficient detail to permit identification and location with a reasonable amount of effort. So far as practicable, the request should specify the subject matter of the record, the place where and date or approximate date when made, the person or office that made it, and any other pertinent identifying details.

(b) *Deficient descriptions.* If the description is insufficient to enable a professional employee familiar with the subject area of the request to locate the record with a reasonable amount of effort, the disclosure officer will notify the requester and, to the extent possible, indicate the additional information required. Every reasonable effort shall be made to assist a requester in the identification and location of the record or records sought. Records will not be withheld merely because it is difficult to find them.

(c) *Requests for categories of records.* Requests calling for all records falling within a reasonably specific category will be regarded as reasonably described within the meaning of this section and paragraph (a)(3) of FOIA if the PBGC is reasonably able to determine which records come within the request and to search for and collect them without unduly interfering with PBGC operations. If PBGC operations would be unduly disrupted, the disclosure officer shall promptly notify the requester and provide an opportunity to confer in an attempt to reduce the request to manageable proportions.

[¶ 15,720H]

§ 4901.13 **Receipt by agency of request.** The disclosure officer shall note the date and time of receipt on each request for access to records. A request shall be deemed received and the period within which action on the request shall be taken, as set forth in § 4901.14 of this part, shall begin on the next business day following such date, except that a request shall be deemed received only if and when the PBGC receives—

(a) A sufficient description under § 4901.12;

(b) Payment or assurance of payment if required under § 4901.33(b); and

(c) The requester's consent to pay substantial search, review, and/or duplication charges under subpart D of this part if the PBGC determines that such charges may be substantial and so notifies the requester. Consent may be in the form of a statement that costs under subpart D will be acceptable either in any amount or up to a specified amount. To avoid possible delay, a requester may include such a statement in a request.

[¶ 15,720I]

§ 4901.14 **Action on request.** (a) *Time for action.* Promptly and in any event within 10 working days after receipt of a disclosure request (subject to extension under § 4901.16), the disclosure officer shall take action with respect to each requested item (or portion of an item) under either paragraph (b), (c), or (d) of this section. When responding to a request under paragraph (b), (c), or (d) of this section, the disclosure officer will notify the requester of the requester's right to seek assistance from the PBGC's FOIA Public Liaison and will provide information about how to contact the FOIA Public Liaison. [Amended 6/13/2017 by 82 FR 26990.]

(b) *Request granted.* If the disclosure officer determines that the request should be granted, the requester shall be so advised and the records shall be promptly made available to the requester.

(c) *Request denied.* If the disclosure officer determines that the request should be denied, the requester shall be so advised in writing with a brief statement of the reasons for the denial, including a reference to the specific exemption(s) authorizing the denial and an explanation of how each such exemption applies to the matter withheld. The denial shall also include the name and title or position of the person(s) responsible for the denial, outline the appeal procedure available, and notify the requester of the right to seek dispute resolution services from the PBGC's FOIA Public Liaison or the Office of Government Information Services. [Amended 6/13/2017 by 82 FR 26990.]

(d) *Records not promptly located.* As to records that are not located in time to make an informed determination, the disclosure officer may deny the request and so advise the requester in writing with an explanation of the circumstances and notice of the requester's right to seek dispute resolution services from the PBGC's FOIA Public Liaison or the Office of Government Information Services. The denial shall also include the name and title or position of the person(s) responsible for the denial, outline the appeal procedure available, and advise the requester that the search or examination will be continued and that the denial may be withdrawn, modified, or confirmed when processing of the request is completed. [Amended 6/13/2017 by 82 FR 26990.]

[¶ 15,720J]

§ 4901.15 **Appeals from denial of requests**. (a) *Submittal of appeals*. If a disclosure request is denied in whole or in part by the disclosure officer, the requester may file a written appeal within 90 days from the date of the denial or, if later (in the case of a partial denial), 90 days from the date the requester receives the disclosed material. The appeal shall state the grounds for appeal and any supporting statements or arguments, and shall be addressed to the General Counsel, Pension Benefit Guaranty Corporation. See Sec. 4000.4 of this chapter for information on where to file. To expedite processing, the words "FOIA appeal" should appear prominently on the request. [Amended 10/28/2003 by 68 FR 61344 and 6/13/2017 by 82 FR 26990.]

(b) *Receipt and consideration of appeal*. The General Counsel shall note the date and time of receipt on each appeal and notify the requester thereof. Promptly and in any event within 20 working days after receipt of an appeal (subject to extension under § 4901.16), the General Counsel shall issue a decision on the appeal.

(1) The General Counsel may determine de novo whether the denial of disclosure was in accordance with FOIA and this part.

(2) If the denial appealed from was under § 4901.14(d), the General Counsel shall consider any supplementary determination by the disclosure officer in deciding the appeal.

(3) Unless otherwise ordered by the court, the General Counsel may act on an appeal notwithstanding the pendency of an action for judicial relief in the same matter and, if no appeal has been filed, may treat such an action as the filing of an appeal.

(c) *Decision on appeal*. As to each item (or portion of an item) whose nondisclosure is appealed, the General Counsel shall either—

(1) Grant the appeal and so advise the requester in writing, in which case the records with respect to which the appeal is granted shall be promptly made available to the requester; or

(2) Deny the appeal and so advise the requester in writing with a brief statement of the reasons for the denial, including a reference to the specific exemption(s) authorizing the denial, an explanation of how each such exemption applies to the matter withheld, and notice of the provisions for judicial review in paragraph (a)(4) of FOIA. The General Counsel's decision shall be the final action of the PBGC with respect to the request.

(d) *Records of appeals*. Copies of both grants and denials of appeals shall be collected in one file available in the PBGC's public reference room under § 4901.4(d)(1) and indexed under § 4901.4(e).

[¶ 15,720K]

§ 4901.16 **Extensions of time**. In unusual circumstances (as described in subparagraph (a)(6)(B) of FOIA), the time to respond to a disclosure request under § 4901.14(a) or an appeal under § 4901.15(b) may be extended as reasonably necessary to process the request or appeal. The disclosure officer (with the prior approval of the General Counsel) or the General Counsel, as appropriate, shall notify the requester in writing within the original time period of the reasons for the extension and the date when a response is expected to be sent. The maximum extension for responding to a disclosure request shall be 10 working days, and the maximum extension for responding to an appeal shall be 10 working days minus the amount of any extension on the request to which the appeal relates.

[¶ 15,720L]

§ 4901.17 **Exhaustion of administrative remedies**. If the disclosure officer fails to make a determination to grant or deny access to requested records, or the General Counsel does not make a decision on appeal from a denial of access to PBGC records, within the time prescribed (including any extension) for making such determination or decision, the requester's administrative remedies shall be deemed

exhausted and the requester may apply for judicial relief under FOIA. However, since a court may allow the PBGC additional time to act as provided in FOIA, processing of the request or appeal shall continue and the requester shall be so advised.

Subpart C—Restrictions on Disclosure

[¶ 15,720M]

§ 4901.21 **Restrictions in general**. (a) *Records not disclosable*. Records shall not be disclosed to the extent prohibited by—

(1) 18 U.S.C. 1905, dealing in general with commercial and financial information;

(2) Paragraph (b)(1) of FOIA, dealing in general with matters of national defense and foreign policy; or

(3) Paragraph (b)(3) of FOIA, dealing in general with matters specifically exempted from disclosure by statute, including information or documentary material submitted to the PBGC pursuant to sections 4010 and 4043 of ERISA.

(b) *Records disclosure of which may be refused*. Records need not (but may, as provided in § 4901.5(b)) be disclosed to the extent provided by—

(1) Paragraph (b)(2) of FOIA, dealing in general with internal agency personnel rules and practices;

(2) Paragraph (b)(4) of FOIA, dealing in general with trade secrets and commercial and financial information;

(3) Paragraph (b)(5) of FOIA, dealing in general with inter-agency and intra-agency memoranda and letters;

(4) Paragraph (b)(6) of FOIA, dealing in general with personnel, medical, and similar files;

(5) Paragraph (b)(7) of FOIA, dealing in general with records or information compiled for law enforcement purposes;

(6) Paragraph (b)(8) of FOIA, dealing in general with reports on financial institutions; or

(7) Paragraph (b)(9) of FOIA, dealing in general with information about wells.

[¶ 15,720N]

§ 4901.22 **Partial disclosure**. If an otherwise disclosable record contains some material that is protected from disclosure, the record shall not for that reason be withheld from disclosure if deletion of the protected material is feasible. This principle shall be applied in particular to identifying details the disclosure of which would constitute an unwarranted invasion of personal privacy.

[¶ 15,720O]

§ 4901.23 **Record of concern to more than one agency**. If the release of a record in the custody of the PBGC would be of concern not only to the PBGC but also to another Federal agency, the record will be made available by the PBGC only if its interest in the record is the primary interest and only after coordination with the other interested agency. If the interest of the PBGC in the record is not primary, the request will be transferred promptly to the agency having the primary interest, and the requester will be so notified.

[¶ 15,720P]

§ 4901.24 **Special rules for trade secrets and confidential commercial or financial information submitted to the PBGC**. (a) *Application*. To the extent permitted by law, this section applies to a request for disclosure of a record that contains information that has been designated by the submitter in good faith in accordance with paragraph (b) of this section or a record that the PBGC has reason to believe contains such information, unless—

(1) Access to the information is denied;

(2) The information has been published or officially made available to the public;

(3) Disclosure of the information is required by law other than FOIA; or

(4) The designation under paragraph (b) of this section appears obviously frivolous, except that in such a case the PBGC will notify the submitter in writing of a determination to disclose the information

Reg. § 4901.24(a)(4) **¶ 15,720P**

within a reasonable time before the disclosure date (which shall be specified in the notice).

(b) *Designation by submitter.* To designate information as being subject to this section, the submitter shall, at the time of submission or by a reasonable time thereafter, assert that information being submitted is confidential business information and designate, with appropriate markings, the portion(s) of the submission to which the assertion applies. Any designation under this paragraph shall expire 10 years after the date of submission unless a longer designation period is requested and reasonable justification is provided therefor.

(c) *Notification to submitter of disclosure request.* When disclosure of information subject to this section may be made, the disclosure officer or (where disclosure may be made in response to an appeal) the General Counsel shall promptly notify the submitter, describing (or providing a copy of) the information that may be disclosed, and afford the submitter a reasonable period of time to object in writing to the requested disclosure. (The notification to the submitter may be oral or written; if oral, it will be confirmed in writing.) When a submitter is notified under this paragraph, the requester shall be notified that the submitter is being afforded an opportunity to object to disclosure.

(d) *Objection of submitter.* A submitter's statement objecting to disclosure should specify all grounds relied upon for opposing disclosure of any portion(s) of the information under subsection (b) of FOIA and, with respect to the exemption in paragraph (b)(4) of FOIA, demonstrate why the information is a trade secret or is commercial or financial information that is privileged or confidential. Facts asserted should be certified or otherwise supported. (Information provided pursuant to this paragraph may itself be subject to disclosure under FOIA.) Any timely objection of a submitter under this paragraph shall be carefully considered in determining whether to grant a disclosure request or appeal.

(e) *Notification to submitter of decision to disclose.* If the disclosure officer or (where disclosure is in response to an appeal) the General Counsel decides to disclose information subject to this section despite the submitter's objections, the disclosure officer (or General Counsel) shall give the submitter written notice, explaining briefly why the information is to be disclosed despite those objections, describing the information to be disclosed, and specifying the date when the information will be disclosed to the requester. The notification shall, to the extent permitted by law, be provided a reasonable number of days before the disclosure date so specified, and a copy shall be provided to the requester.

(f) *Notification to submitter of action to compel disclosure.* The disclosure officer or the General Counsel shall promptly notify the submitter if a requester brings suit seeking to compel disclosure.

Subpart D—Fees

[¶ 15,720Q]

§ 4901.31 **Charges for services.** (a) *Generally.* Pursuant to the provisions of FOIA, as amended, charges will be assessed to cover the direct costs of searching for, reviewing, and/or duplicating records requested under FOIA from the PBGC, except where the charges are limited or waived under paragraph (b) or (d) of this section, according to the fee schedule in § 4901.32 of this part. No charge will be assessed if the costs of routine collection and processing of the fee would be equal to or greater than the fee itself. Except as provided in paragraph (e) of this section, no charge for searching (or in the case of a requester described under 5 U.S.C. 552(a)(4)(A)(ii)(II), for duplication) will be assessed if PBGC has failed to comply with any time limit under 5 U.S.C. 552(a)(6). [Amended 6/13/2017 by 82 FR 26990.]

(1) "Direct costs" means those expenditures which the PBGC actually incurs in searching for and duplicating (and in the case of commercial requesters, reviewing) documents to respond to a request under FOIA and this part. Direct costs include, for example, the salary of the employee performing work (i.e., the basic rate of pay plus benefits) or an established average pay for a homogeneous class of personnel (e.g., all administrative/clerical or all professional/executive), and the cost of operating duplicating machinery. Not included in direct costs are overhead expenses such as costs of space, and heating or lighting the facility in which the records are stored.

(2) "Search" means all time spent looking for material that is responsive to a request under FOIA and this part, including page-by-page or line-by-line identification of materials within a document, if required, and may be done manually or by computer using existing programming. "Search" should be distinguished from "review" which is defined in paragraph (a)(3) of this section.

(3) "Review" means the process of examining documents located in response to a request under FOIA and this part to determine whether any portion of any document located is permitted or required to be withheld. It also includes processing any documents for disclosure, e.g., doing all that is necessary to excise them and otherwise prepare them for release. Review does not include time spent resolving general legal or policy issues regarding the application of exemptions.

(4) "Duplication" means the process of making a copy of a document necessary to respond to a request under FOIA and this part, in a form that is reasonably usable by the requester. Copies can take the form of paper copy, microform, audio-visual materials, or machine readable documentation (e.g., magnetic tape or disk), among others.

(b) *Categories of requesters.* Requesters who seek access to records under FOIA and this part are divided into four categories: commercial use requesters, educational and noncommercial scientific institutions, representatives of the news media, and all other requesters. The PBGC will determine the category of a requester and charge fees according to the following rules.

(1) *Commercial use requesters.* When records are requested for commercial use, the PBGC will assess charges, as provided in this subpart, for the full direct costs of searching for, reviewing for release, and duplicating the records sought. Fees for search and review may be charged even if the record searched for is not found or if, after it is found, it is determined that the request to inspect it may be denied under the provisions of subsection (b) of FOIA and this part.

(i) "Commercial use" request means a request from or on behalf of one who seeks information for a use or purpose that furthers the commercial, trade, or profit interests of the requester or the person on whose behalf the request is made.

(ii) In determining whether a request properly belongs in this category, the PBGC will look to the use to which a requester will put the documents requested. Moreover, where the PBGC has reasonable cause to doubt the use to which a requester will put the records sought, or where that use is not clear from the request itself, the PBGC will require the requester to provide clarification before assigning the request to this category.

(2) *Educational and noncommercial scientific institution requesters.* When records are requested by an educational or noncommercial scientific institution, the PBGC will assess charges, as provided in this subpart, for the full direct cost of duplication only, excluding charges for the first 100 pages.

(i) "Educational institution" means a preschool, a public or private elementary or secondary school, an institution of graduate higher education, an institution of undergraduate higher education, an institution of professional education, and an institution of vocational education, which operates a program or programs of scholarly research.

(ii) "Noncommercial scientific institution" means an institution that is not operated on a "commercial" basis as that term is defined in paragraph (b)(1)(i) of this section, and which is operated solely for the purpose of conducting scientific research the results of which are not intended to promote any particular product or industry.

(iii) To be eligible for inclusion in this category, requesters must show that the request is being made as authorized by and under the auspices of a qualifying institution and that the records are not sought for a commercial use, but are sought in furtherance of scholarly (if the request is from an educational institution) or scientific (if the request is from a noncommercial scientific institution) research.

(3) *Requesters who are representatives of the news media.* When records are requested by representatives of the news media, the PBGC will assess charges, as provided in this subpart, for the full direct cost of duplication only, excluding charges for the first 100 pages.

(i) "Representative of the news media" means any person actively gathering news for an entity that is organized and operated to publish or broadcast news to the public. The term "news" means information that is about current events or that would be of current interest to the public. Examples of news media entities include television or radio stations broadcasting to the public at large, and publishers of periodicals (but only in those instances when they can qualify as disseminators of "news") who make their products available for purchase or subscription by the general public. These examples are not intended to be all-inclusive. "Freelance" journalists may be regarded as working for a news organization if they can demonstrate a solid basis for expecting publication through that organization, even though not actually employed by it.

(ii) To be eligible for inclusion in this category, the request must not be made for a commercial use. A request for records supporting the news dissemination function of the requester who is a representative of the news media shall not be considered to be a request that is for a commercial use.

(4) *All other requesters.* When records are requested by requesters who do not fit into any of the categories in paragraphs (b)(1) through (b)(3) of this section, the PBGC will assess charges, as provided in this subpart, for the full direct cost of searching for and duplicating the records sought, with the exceptions that there will be no charge for the first 100 pages of duplication and the first two hours of manual search time (or its cost equivalent in computer search time). Notwithstanding the preceding sentence, there will be no charge for search time in the event of requests under the Privacy Act of 1974 from subjects of records filed in the PBGC's systems of records for the disclosure of records about themselves. Search fees, where applicable, may be charged even if the record searched for is not found.

(c) *Aggregation of requests.* If the PBGC reasonably believes that a requester or group of requesters is attempting to break a request down into a series of requests for the purpose of evading the assessment of fees, the PBGC will aggregate any such requests and charge accordingly. In no case will the PBGC aggregate multiple requests on unrelated subjects from one requester.

(d) *Waiver or reduction of charges.* Circumstances under which searching, review, and duplication facilities or services may be made available to the requester without charge or at a reduced charge are set forth in § 4901.34 of this part.

(e) *Unusual or exceptional circumstances.* Notwithstanding paragraph (a) of this section, if PBGC fails to comply with a time limit under 5 U.S.C. 552(a)(6), PBGC may nevertheless assess a charge for searching (or in the case of a requester described under 5 U.S.C. 552(a)(4)(A)(ii)(II), for duplication) if either paragraph (e)(1) or (2) of this section applies: [Added 6/13/2017 by 82 FR 26990.]

(1) PBGC has determined that unusual circumstances apply and that more than 5,000 pages are necessary to respond to the request, provided that:

(i) PBGC has provided timely written notice of this determination to the requester; and

(ii) PBGC has discussed with the requester—or made three or more goodfaith attempts to do so—via written mail, electronic mail, or telephone how the requester could effectively limit the scope of the request.

(2) A court has determined that exceptional circumstances exist (as defined in 5 U.S.C. 552(a)(6)(C)) and has issued an order excusing PBGC's failure to comply with the time limit.

[¶ 15,720R]

§ 4901.32 **Fee schedule**. (a) *Charges for searching and review of records.* Charges applicable under this subpart to the search for and review of records will be made according to the following fee schedule:

(1) *Search and review time.* (i) Ordinary search and review by custodial or clerical personnel, $1.75 for each one-quarter hour or fraction thereof of employee worktime required to locate or obtain the records to be searched and to make the necessary review; and (ii) search or review requiring services of professional or supervisory personnel to locate or review requested records, $4.00 for each one-quarter hour or fraction thereof of professional or supervisory personnel worktime.

(2) *Additional search costs.* If the search for a requested record requires transportation of the searcher to the location of the records or transportation of the records to the searcher, at a cost in excess of $5.00, actual transportation costs will be added to the search time cost.

(3) *Search in computerized records.* Charges for information that is available in whole or in part in computerized form will include the cost of operating the central processing unit (CPU) for that portion of operating time that is directly attributable to searching for records responsive to the request, personnel salaries apportionable to the search, and tape or printout production or an established agency-wide average rate for CPU operating costs and operator/programmer salaries involved in FOIA searches. Charges will be computed at the rates prescribed in paragraphs (a) and (b) of this section.

(b) *Charges for duplication of records.* Charges applicable under this subpart for obtaining requested copies of records made available for inspection will be made according to the following fee schedule and subject to the following conditions.

(1) *Standard copying fee.* $0.15 for each page of record copies furnished. This standard fee is also applicable to the furnishing of copies of available computer printouts as stated in paragraph (a)(3) of this section.

(2) *Voluminous material.* If the volume of page copy desired by the requester is such that the reproduction charge at the standard page rate would be in excess of $50, the person desiring reproduction may request a special rate quotation from the PBGC.

(3) *Limit of service.* Not more than 10 copies of any document will be furnished.

(4) *Manual copying by requester.* No charge will be made for manual copying by the requesting party of any document made available for inspection under the provisions of this part. The PBGC shall provide facilities for such copying without charge at reasonable times during normal working hours.

(5) *Indexes.* Pursuant to paragraph (a)(2) of FOIA copies of indexes or supplements thereto which are maintained as therein provided but which have not been published will be provided on request at a cost not to exceed the direct cost of duplication.

(c) *Other charges.* The scheduled fees, set forth in paragraphs (a) and (b) of this section, for furnishing records made available for inspection and duplication represent the direct costs of furnishing the copies at the place of duplication. Upon request, single copies of the records will be mailed, postage prepaid, free of charge. Actual costs of transmitting records by special methods such as registered, certified, or special delivery mail or messenger, and of special handling or packaging, if required, will be charged in addition to the scheduled fees.

[¶ 15,720S]

§ 4901.33 **Payment of fees**. (a) *Medium of payment.* Payment of the applicable fees as provided in this subsection shall be made in cash, by U.S. postal money order, or by check payable to the PBGC. Postage stamps will not be accepted in lieu of cash, checks, or money orders as payment for fees specified in the schedule. Cash should not be sent by mail.

(b) *Advance payment or assurance of payment.* Payment or assurance of payment before work is begun or continued on a request may be required under the following rules.

(1) Where the PBGC estimates or determines that charges allowable under the rules in this subpart are likely to exceed $250, the PBGC may require advance payment of the entire fee or assurance of payment, as follows:

(i) Where the requester has a history of prompt payment of fees under this part, the PBGC will notify the requester of the likely cost and obtain satisfactory assurance of full payment; or

(ii) Where the requester has no history of payment for requests made pursuant to FOIA and this part, the PBGC may require the requester to make an advance payment of an amount up to the full estimated charges.

(2) Where the requester has previously failed to pay a fee charged in a timely fashion (i.e., within 30 days of the date of the billing), the PBGC may require the requester to pay the full amount owed plus any applicable interest as provided in paragraph (c) of this section (or demonstrate that he has, in fact, paid the fee) and to make an advance payment of the full amount of the estimated fee.

(c) *Late payment interest charges.* The PBGC may assess late payment interest charges on any amounts unpaid by the 31st day after the date a bill is sent to a requester. Interest will be assessed at the rate prescribed in 31 U.S.C. 3717 and will accrue from the date the bill is sent.

[Amended 10/28/2003 by 68 FR 61344]

[¶ 15,720T]

§ 4901.34 **Waiver or reduction of charges**. (a) The disclosure officer may waive or reduce fees otherwise applicable under this subpart when disclosure of the information is in the public interest because it is likely to contribute significantly to public understanding of the operations or activities of the government and is not primarily in the commercial interest of the requester. A fee waiver request shall set forth full and complete information upon which the request for waiver is based.

(b) The disclosure officer may reduce or waive fees applicable under this subpart when the requester has demonstrated his inability to pay such fees.

[¶ 15,720U]

§ 4902.1 **Purpose and Scope**. (a) *Procedures.* Sections 4902.3 through 4902.7 establish procedures under which—

(1) An individual may—

(i) Determine whether PBGC maintains any system of records that contains a record pertaining to the individual;

(ii) Obtain access to the individual's record upon request;

(iii) Make a request to amend the individual's record; and

(iv) Appeal a denial of a request to amend the individual's record; and

(2) PBGC will make an initial determination of a request to amend an individual's record.

(b) *Fees.* Section 4902.8 prescribes the fees for making copies of an individual's record.

(c) *Privacy Act provisions.* Section 4902.9 summarizes the Privacy Act (5 U.S.C. 552a) provisions for which PBGC claims an exemption for certain systems of records.

(d) *Exemptions.* Sections 4902.10 through 4902.11 set forth those systems of records that are exempted from certain disclosure and other provisions of the Privacy Act, and the reasons for the exemptions.

[Revised 6/8/2009 by 74 FR 27080.]

[¶ 15,720V]

§ 4902.2 **Definitions**. In addition to terminology in part 4001 of this chapter, as used in this part:

Record means any item, collection, or grouping of information about an individual that is maintained by an agency, including, but not limited to, his or her education, financial transactions, medical history, and criminal or employment history and that contains his or her name, or the identifying number, symbol, or other identifying particular assigned to the individual, such as a finger or voice print or a photograph.

System of records means a group of any records under the control of any agency from which information is retrieved by the name of the individual or by some identifying number, symbol, or other identifying particular assigned to the individual.

Working day means any weekday excepting Federal holidays.

[¶ 15,720W]

§ 4902.3 **Procedures for determining existence of and requesting access to records**. (a) Any individual may submit a request to the Disclosure Officer, Pension Benefit Guaranty Corporation, for the pur-

pose of learning whether a system of records maintained by the PBGC contains any record pertaining to the requestor or obtaining access to such a record. Such a request may be sent to the Disclosure Officer or made in person between the hours of 9 a.m. and 4 p.m. on any working day. Current information on how to make a request, including the Disclosure Officer's mailing address and location, can be obtained on PBGC's Web site, *http://www.pbgc.gov.*

[Amended 10/28/2003 by 68 FR 61344 and 6/8/2009 by 74 FR 27080.]

(b) Each request submitted pursuant to paragraph (a) of this section shall include the name of the system of records to which the request pertains and the requester's full name, home address and date of birth, and shall prominently state the words, "Privacy Act Request." If this information is insufficient to enable the PBGC to identify the record in question, or to determine the identity of the requester (to ensure the privacy of the subject of the record), the disclosure officer shall request such further identifying data as the disclosure officer deems necessary to locate the record or to determine the identity of the requester.

[Amended 10/28/2003 by 68 FR 61344]

(c) Unless the request is only for notification of the existence of a record and such notification is required under the Freedom of Information Act (5 U.S.C. 552), the requester shall be required to provide verification of his or her identity to the PBGC as set forth in paragraph (c) (1) or (2) of this section, as appropriate.

(1) If the request is made by mail, the requester shall submit a notarized statement establishing his or her identity.

(2) If the request is made in person, the requester shall show identification satisfactory to the disclosure officer, such as a driver's license, employee identification, annuitant identification or Medicare card.

(d) The disclosure officer shall respond to the request in writing within 10 working days after receipt of the request or of such additional information as may be required under paragraph (b) of this section. If a request for access to a record is granted, the response shall state when the record will be made available.

[¶ 15,720X]

§ 4902.4 **Disclosure of record to an individual**. (a) When the disclosure officer grants a request for access to records under § 4902.3, such records shall be made available when the requester is advised of the determination or as promptly thereafter as possible. At the requester's option, the record will be made available for the requester's inspection and copying at the PBGC, between the hours of 9 a.m. and 4 p.m. on any working day, or a copy of the record will be mailed to the requester. Current information on where the records may be inspected and copied can be obtained on PBGC's Web site, *http://www.pbgc.gov..*

[Amended 6/8/2009 by 74 FR 27080.]

(b) If the requester desires to be accompanied by another individual during the inspection and/or copying of the record, the requester shall, either when the record is made available or at any earlier time, submit to the disclosure officer a signed statement identifying such other individual and authorizing such other individual to be present during the inspection and/or copying of the record.

[¶ 15,720Y]

§ 4902.5 **Procedures for requesting amendment of a record**. (a) Any individual about whom the PBGC maintains a record contained in a system of records may request that the record be amended. Such a request shall be submitted in the same manner described in § 4902.3(a).

(b) Each request submitted under paragraph (a) of this section shall include the information described in § 4902.3(b) and a statement specifying the changes to be made in the record and the justification therefor. The disclosure officer may request further identifying data as described in § 4902.3(b).

(c) An individual who desires assistance in the preparation of a request for amendment of a record shall submit such request for assistance in writing to the Deputy General Counsel, Pension Benefit Guaranty Corporation. The Deputy General Counsel shall respond to such request as promptly as possible.

[Amended 10/28/2003 by 68 FR 61344]

§ 4902.6 **Action on request for amendment of a record**. (a) Within 20 working days after receipt by the PBGC of a request for amendment of a record under § 4902.5, unless for good cause shown the Director of the PBGC extends such 20-day period, the disclosure officer shall notify the requester in writing whether and to what extent the request shall be granted. To the extent that the request is granted, the disclosure officer shall cause the requested amendment to be made promptly.

[Amended 6/8/2009 by 74 FR 27080.]

(b) When a request for amendment of a record is denied in whole or in part, the denial shall include a statement of the reasons therefor, the procedures for appealing such denial, and a notice that the requester has a right to assistance in preparing an appeal of the denial.

(c) An individual who desires assistance in preparing an appeal of a denial under this section shall submit a request to the Deputy General Counsel, Pension Benefit Guaranty Corporation. The Deputy General Counsel shall respond to the request as promptly as possible, but in no event more than 30 days after receipt.

[Amended 10/28/2003 by 68 FR 61344]

§ 4902.7 **Appeal of a denial of a request for amendment of a record**. (a) An appeal from a denial of a request for amendment of a record under Sec. 4902.6 shall be submitted, within 45 days of receipt of the denial, to the General Counsel, Pension Benefit Guaranty Corporation, unless the record subject to such request is one maintained by the Office of the General Counsel, in which event the appeal shall be submitted to the Director or Director's designee, Pension Benefit Guaranty Corporation. The appeal shall state in detail the basis on which it is made and shall clearly state "Privacy Act Request" on the first page. In addition, the submission shall clearly state "Privacy Act Request" on the envelope (for mail, hand delivery, or commercial delivery), in the subject line (for e-mail), or on the cover sheet (for fax).

[Amended 10/28/2003 by 68 FR 61344 and 6/8/2009 by 74 FR 27080. Corrected 6/25/2009 by 74 FR 30212.]

(b) Within 30 working days after the receipt of the appeal, unless for good cause shown the Director of Operations of the PBGC extends such 30-day period, the General Counsel or, where appropriate, the Director or Director's designee, shall issue a decision in writing granting or denying the appeal in whole or in part. To the extent that the appeal is granted, the General Counsel or, where appropriate, the Director or Director's designee, shall cause the requested amendment to be made promptly. To the extent that the appeal is denied, the decision shall include the reasons for the denial and a notice of the requester's right to submit a brief statement setting forth reasons for disputing the denial of appeal, to seek judicial review of the denial pursuant to 5 U.S.C. 552a(g)(1)(A), and to obtain further information concerning the provisions for judicial review under that section.

[Amended 6/8/2009 by 74 FR 27080. Corrected 6/25/2009 by 74 FR 30212.]

(c) An individual whose appeal has been denied in whole or in part may submit a brief summary statement setting forth reasons for disputing such denial. Such statement shall be submitted within 30 days of receipt of the denial of the appeal to the Disclosure Officer. Any such statement shall be made available by the PBGC to anyone to whom the record is subsequently furnished and may also be accompanied, at the discretion of the PBGC, by a brief statement summarizing the PBGC's reasons for refusing to amend the record. The PBGC shall also provide copies of the individual's statement of dispute to all prior recipients of the record with respect to whom an accounting of the disclosure of the record was maintained pursuant to 5 U.S.C. 552a(c)(1).

(d) To request further information concerning the provisions for judicial review, an individual shall submit such request in writing to the Deputy General Counsel, who shall respond to such request as promptly as possible.

§ 4902.8 **Fees**. When an individual requests a copy of his or her record under § 4902.4, charges for the copying shall be made according to the following fee schedule:

(a) *Standard copying fee*. There shall be a charge of $0.15 per page of record copies furnished. Where the copying fee is less than $1.50, it shall not be assessed.

(b) *Voluminous material*. If the volume of page copy desired by the requester is such that the reproduction charge at the standard page rate would be in excess of $50, the individual desiring reproduction may request a special rate quotation from the PBGC.

(c) *Manual copying by requester*. No charge will be made for manual copying by the requester of any document made available for inspection under § 4902.4. The PBGC shall provide facilities for such copying without charge between the hours of 9 a.m. and 4 p.m. on any working day.

§ 4902.9 **Privacy Act provisions for which PBGC claims an exemption**. Subsections 552a(j) and (k) of title 5, U.S.C., authorize PBGC to exempt systems of records meeting certain criteria from various other subsections of section 552a. This section contains a summary of the Privacy Act provisions for which PBGC claims an exemption for the systems of records discussed in this part pursuant to, and to the extent permitted by, subsections 552a(j) and (k):

(a) Subsection (c)(3) of 5 U.S.C. 552a requires an agency to make available to the individual named in the records an accounting of each disclosure of records.

(b) Subsection (c)(4) of 5 U.S.C. 552a requires an agency to inform any person or other agency to which a record has been disclosed of any correction or notation of dispute the agency has made to the record in accordance with subsection (d) of the Privacy Act.

(c) Subsections (d)(1) through (4) of 5 U.S.C. 552a require an agency to permit an individual to gain access to records about the individual, to request amendment of such records, to request a review of an agency decision not to amend such records, and to provide a statement of disagreement about a disputed record to be filed and disclosed with the disputed record.

(d) Subsection (e)(1) of 5 U.S.C. 552a requires an agency to maintain in its records only such information about an individual that is relevant and necessary to accomplish a purpose required by statute or executive order of the President.

(e) Subsection (e)(2) of 5 U.S.C. 552a requires an agency to collect information to the greatest extent practicable directly from the subject individual when the information may result in adverse determinations about an individual's rights, benefits, and privileges under federal programs.

(f) Subsection (e)(3) of 5 U.S.C. 552a requires an agency to inform each person whom it asks to supply information of the authority under which the information is sought, whether disclosure is mandatory or voluntary, the principal purpose(s) for which the information will be used, the routine uses that may be made of the information, and the effects of not providing the information.

(g) Subsection (e)(4)(G) and (H) of 5 U.S.C. 552a requires an agency to publish a **Federal Register** notice of its procedures whereby an individual can be notified upon request whether the system of records contains information about the individual, how to gain access to any record about the individual contained in the system, and how to contest its content.

(h) Subsection (e)(5) of 5 U.S.C. 552a requires an agency to maintain its records with such accuracy, relevance, timeliness, and completeness as is reasonably necessary to ensure fairness to the individual in making any determination about the individual.

(i) Subsection (e)(8) of 5 U.S.C. 552a requires an agency to make reasonable efforts to serve notice on an individual when any record on such individual is made available to any person under compulsory legal process when such process becomes a matter of public record.

(j) Subsection (f) of 5 U.S.C. 552a requires an agency to establish procedures whereby an individual can be notified upon request if any system of records named by the individual contains a record pertaining to the individual, obtain access to the record, and request amendment.

(k) Subsection (g) of 5 U.S.C. 552a provides for civil remedies if an agency fails to comply with the access and amendment provisions of subsections (d)(1) and (d)(3), and with other provisions of the Privacy Act, or any rule promulgated thereunder, in such a way as to have an adverse effect on an individual.

[Added 6/8/2009 by 74 FR 27080.]

[¶ 15,721B-1]

§ 4902.10 **Specific exemption: Personnel Security Investigation Records.** (a) *Exemption.* Under the authority granted by 5 U.S.C. 552a(k)(5), PBGC hereby exempts the system of records entitled "PBGC-12, Personnel Security Investigation Records—PBGC" from the provisions of 5 U.S.C. 552a (c)(3), (d), (e)(1), (e)(4)(G), (H), and (I), and (f), to the extent that the disclosure of such material would reveal the identity of a source who furnished information to PBGC under an express promise of confidentiality or, before September 27, 1975, under an implied promise of confidentiality.

(b) *Reasons for Exemption.* The reasons for asserting this exemption are to insure the gaining of information essential to determining suitability and fitness for PBGC employment or for work for PBGC as a contractor or as an employee of a contractor, access to information, and security clearances, to insure that full and candid disclosures are obtained in making such determinations, to prevent subjects of such determinations from thwarting the completion of such determinations, and to avoid revealing the identities of persons who furnish information to PBGC in confidence.

[Amended June 14, 2001, 66 FR 32221, and 6/8/2009 by 74 FR 27080.]

[¶ 15,721B-2]

§ 4902.11 **Specific exemptions: Office of Inspector General Investigative File System.** (a) *Criminal Law Enforcement.* (1) *Exemption.* Under the authority granted by 5 U.S.C. 552a(j)(2), PBGC hereby exempts the system of records entitled "PBGC-17, Office of Inspector General Investigative File System—PBGC" from the provisions of 5 U.S.C. 552a (c)(3), (c)(4), (d)(1) through (4), (e)(1) through (3), (e)(4)(G) and (H), (e)(5), (e)(8), (f), and (g) because the system contains information pertaining to the enforcement of criminal laws.

(2) *Reasons for exemption.* The reasons for asserting this exemption are:

(i) Disclosure to the individual named in the record pursuant to subsections (c)(3), (c)(4), or (d)(1) through (4) could seriously impede or compromise the investigation by alerting the target(s), subjecting a potential witness or witnesses to intimidation or improper influence, and leading to destruction of evidence.

(ii) Application of subsection (e)(1) is impractical because the relevance of specific information might be established only after considerable analysis and as the investigation progresses. Effective law enforcement requires the Office of Inspector General to keep information that may not be relevant to a specific Office of Inspector General investigation, but which may provide leads for appropriate law enforcement and to establish patterns of activity that might relate to the jurisdiction of the Office of Inspector General and/or other agencies.

(iii) Application of subsection (e)(2) would be counterproductive to performance of a criminal investigation because it would alert the individual to the existence of an investigation.

(iv) Application of subsection (e)(3) could discourage the free flow of information in a criminal law enforcement inquiry.

(v) The requirements of subsections (e)(4)(G) and (H), and (f) do not apply because this system is exempt from the provisions of subsection (d). Nevertheless, PBGC has published notice of its notification, access, and contest procedures because access is appropriate in some cases.

(vi) Although the Office of Inspector General endeavors to maintain accurate records, application of subsection (e)(5) is impractical because maintaining only those records that are accurate, relevant, timely, and complete and that assure fairness in determination is contrary to established investigative techniques. Information that may initially appear inaccurate, irrelevant, untimely, or incomplete may, when collated and analyzed with other available information, become more pertinent as an investigation progresses.

(vii) Application of subsection (e)(8) could prematurely reveal an ongoing criminal investigation to the subject of the investigation.

(viii) The provisions of subsection (g) do not apply to this system if an exemption otherwise applies.

(b) *Other Law Enforcement.* (1) *Exemption.* Under the authority granted by 5 U.S.C. 552a(k)(2), PBGC hereby exempts the system of records entitled "PBGC-17, Office of Inspector General Investigative File System—PBGC" from the provisions of 5 U.S.C. 552a(c)(3), (d)(1) through (4), (e)(1), (e)(4)(G) and (H), and (f) for the same reasons as stated in paragraph (a)(2) of this section, that is, because the system contains investigatory material compiled for law enforcement purposes other than material within the scope of subsection 552a(j)(2).

(2) *Reasons for exemption.* The reasons for asserting this exemption are because the disclosure and other requirements of the Privacy Act could substantially compromise the efficacy and integrity of the Office of Inspector General operations. Disclosure could invade the privacy of other individuals and disclose their identity when they were expressly promised confidentiality. Disclosure could interfere with the integrity of information which would otherwise be subject to privileges (see, e.g., 5 U.S.C. 552(b)(5)), and which could interfere with other important law enforcement concerns (see, e.g., 5 U.S.C. 552(b)(7)).

(c) *Federal Civilian or Contract Employment.* (1) Exemption. Under the authority granted by 5 U.S.C. 552a(k)(5), PBGC hereby exempts the system of records entitled "PBGC-17, Office of Inspector General Investigative File System—PBGC" from the provisions of 5 U.S.C. 552a(c)(3), (d)(1) through (4), (e)(1), (e)(4)(G) and (H), and (f) because the system contains investigatory material compiled for the purpose of determining eligibility or qualifications for federal civilian or contract employment.

(2) *Reason for exemption.* The reason for asserting this exemption is to protect from disclosure the identity of a confidential source when an express promise of confidentiality has been given to obtain information from sources who would otherwise be unwilling to provide necessary information.

[Added 6/8/2009 by 74 FR 27080.]

[¶ 15,721B-3]

§ 4902.12 **Filing rules; computation of time.** (a) *Filing rules.* (1) *Where to file.* See Sec. 4000.4 of this chapter for information on where to file a submission under this part with the PBGC.

(2) *Method of filing.* The PBGC applies the rules in subpart A of part 4000 of this chapter to determine permissible methods of filing with the PBGC under this part.

(3) *Date of filing.* The PBGC applies the rules in subpart C of part 4000 of this chapter to determine the date that a submission under this part was filed with the PBGC.

(b) *Computation of time.* The PBGC applies the rules in subpart D of part 4000 of this chapter to compute any time period for filing under this part.

[Added 10/28/2003 by 68 FR 61344. Redesignated 6/8/2009 by 74 FR 27080.]

Subpart A—General Provisions

[¶ 15,721C]

§ 4903.1 **What definitions apply to this part?.** The following terms are defined in § 4001.2 of this chapter: Code, PBGC, and Person. In addition, for purposes of this part:

Administrative offset or offset means withholding funds payable by the United States (including funds payable by the United States on behalf of a state government) to, or held by the United States for, a person to satisfy a debt owed by the person. The term "administrative offset" can include, but is not limited to, the offset of Federal salary, vendor, retirement, and Social Security benefit payments. The terms "centralized administrative offset" and "centralized offset" refer to the process by which the Treasury Department's Financial Management Service offsets Federal payments through the Treasury Offset Program.

Administrative wage garnishment means the process by which a Federal agency orders a non-Federal employer to withhold amounts from a debtor's wages to satisfy a debt, as authorized by 31 U.S.C. 3720D, 31 CFR 285.11, and this part.

Agency or Federal agency means an executive department or agency; a military department; the United States Postal Service; the Postal Regulatory Commission; any nonappropriated fund instrumentality described in 5 U.S.C. 2105(c); the United States Senate; the United States House of Representatives; any court, court administrative office, or instrumentality in the judicial or legislative branches of the Government; or a Government corporation.

Creditor agency means any Federal agency that is owed a debt.

Debt means any amount of money, funds or property that has been determined by an appropriate official of the Federal Government to be owed to the United States government, including government-owned corporations, by a person. As used in this part, the term "debt" can include a debt owed to PBGC, but does not include debts arising under the Internal Revenue Code of 1986 (26 U.S.C. 1 *et seq.*).

Debtor means a person who owes a debt to the United States.

Delinquent debt means a debt that has not been paid by the date specified in the agency's initial written demand for payment or applicable agreement or instrument (including a post-delinquency payment agreement) unless other satisfactory payment arrangements have been made.

Disposable pay has the same meaning as that term is defined in 5 CFR 550.1103.

Employee or *Federal employee* means a current employee of PBGC or other Federal agency, including a current member of the uniformed services, including the Army, Navy, Air Force, Marine Corps, Coast Guard, Commissioned Corps of the National Oceanic and Atmospheric Administration, Commissioned Corps of the Public Health Service, the National Guard, and the reserve forces of the uniformed services.

FCCS means the Federal Claims Collection Standards, 31 CFR parts 900-904.

Financial Management Service (FMS) means the Treasury Department bureau that is responsible for the centralized collection of delinquent debts through the offset of Federal payments and other means.

Payment agency or *Federal payment agency* means any Federal agency that transmits payment requests in the form of certified payment vouchers, or other similar forms, to a disbursing official for disbursement. The payment agency may be the agency that employs the debtor. In some cases, PBGC may be both the creditor agency and payment agency.

Salary offset means a type of administrative offset to collect a debt under Section 5514 of Title 5 of the United States Code and 5 CFR part 550, subpart K by deduction(s) at one or more officially established pay intervals from the current pay account of an employee with or without his or her consent.

Tax debt means a debt arising under the Code.

Tax refund offset means the reduction by the IRS of a tax overpayment payable to a taxpayer by the amount of past-due, legally enforceable debt owed by that taxpayer to a Federal agency pursuant to Treasury regulations.

[¶ 15,721D]

§ 4903.2 **What do these regulations cover?** (a) *Scope.*. This part provides procedures for the collection of debts owed to PBGC, other than those subject to recoupment (29 CFR 4022, subpart E). This part also provides procedures for collection of other debts owed to the United States when a request for offset of a payment, for which PBGC is the payment agency, is received by PBGC from another agency (for example, when a PBGC employee owes a student loan debt to the United States Department of Education).

(b) *Applicability.*

(1) This part applies to PBGC when collecting a debt owed to PBGC; to persons who owe debts to PBGC; to persons controlled by or controlling persons who owe debts to a Federal agency, and to Federal

agencies requesting offset of a payment issued by PBGC as a payment agency (including salary payments to PBGC employees).

(2) This part does not apply to debts owed to PBGC being collected through recoupment under subpart E of part 4022 of this chapter. Benefits paid by PBGC generally will not be offset, subject to limited exceptions (*e.g.,* in certain fiduciary breach situations).

(3) This part does not apply to tax debts, to any debt based in whole or in part on conduct in violation of the antitrust laws, nor to any debt for which there is an indication of fraud or misrepresentation, as described in § 900.3 of the FCCS, unless the debt is returned by the Department of Justice to PBGC for handling.

(4) Nothing in this part precludes the use of other statutory or regulatory authority to collect or dispose of any debt. *See,* for example, 5 U.S.C. 5705, Advancements and Deductions, which authorizes PBGC to recover travel advances by offset of up to 100 percent of a Federal employee's accrued pay. *See, also,* 5 U.S.C. 4108, governing the collection of training expenses.

(5) To the extent that provisions of laws, other regulations, and PBGC enforcement policies differ from the provisions of this part, those provisions of law, other regulations, and PBGC enforcement policies apply to the remission or mitigation of fines, penalties, and forfeitures, and to debts arising under ERISA, rather than the provisions of this part.

(c) *Additional policies and procedures.*. PBGC may, but is not required to, promulgate additional policies and procedures consistent with this part, the FCCS, and other applicable law, policies, and procedures.

(1) PBGC does not intend this regulation to prohibit PBGC from demanding the return of specific property or the payment of its value.

(2) The failure of PBGC to comply with any provision in this regulation will not serve as a defense to the existence of the debt.

(d) *Duplication not required.*. Nothing in this part requires PBGC to duplicate notices or administrative proceedings required by contract, this part, or other laws or regulations.

(e) *Use of multiple collection remedies allowed.*. PBGC and other Federal agencies may simultaneously use multiple collection remedies to collect a debt, except as prohibited by law. This part is intended to promote aggressive debt collection, using for each debt all available and appropriate collection remedies. To provide PBGC with flexibility in determining which remedies will be most efficient in collecting the particular debt, these remedies are not listed in any prescribed order.

[¶ 15,721E]

§ 4903.3 **Do these regulations adopt the Federal Claims Collection Standards (FCCS)?**. This part adopts and incorporates all provisions of FCCS. This part also supplements the FCCS by prescribing procedures consistent with FCCS, as necessary and appropriate for PBGC operations.

[¶ 15,721F]

§ 4903.4 **What rules apply for purposes of filing with PBGC, determining dates of filings, and computation of time?**. (a) *How and where to file.*. PBGC applies the rules in subpart A of part 4000 of this chapter to determine permissible methods of filing with PBGC under this part. *See* § 4000.4 of this chapter for information on where to file.

(b) *Date of filing.*. PBGC applies the rules in subpart C of part 4000 of this chapter to determine the date that a submission under this part was filed with PBGC.

(c) *Computation of time.*. PBGC applies the rules of subpart D of part 4000 of this chapter to compute any time period under this part.

Subpart B—Procedures To Collect Debts Owed to PBGC

[¶ 15,721G]

§ 4903.5 **What notice will PBGC send to a debtor when collecting a debt owed to PBGC?**. (a) *Notice requirements.*. PBGC will collect debts owed to PBGC. PBGC will promptly send at least one written notice to a debtor informing the debtor of the consequences of failing to pay or otherwise resolve a debt owed to PBGC. The notice(s) will be sent to the debtor at the most current address of the debtor in PBGC's records. Generally, before starting the collection actions described in §§ 4903.6 and 4903.10 through 4903.18 of this part, PBGC will send no more than two written notices to the debtor. The notice will explain why the debt is owed to PBGC, the amount of the debt, how a debtor may pay the debt or make alternate repayment arrangements, how a debtor may review non-privileged documents related to the debt, how a debtor may dispute the debt, the collection remedies available to PBGC if the debtor refuses or otherwise fails to pay the debt, and other consequences to the debtor if the debt is not paid. Except as otherwise provided in paragraph (b) of this section, the written notice(s) will explain to the debtor:

(1) The nature and amount of the debt, and the facts giving rise to the debt;

(2) How interest, penalties, and administrative costs are added to the debt, the date by which payment must be made to avoid such charges, and that such assessments must be made unless excused in accordance with 31 CFR 901.9 (see § 4903.6 of this part);

(3) The date by which payment should be made to avoid the enforced collection actions described in paragraph (a)(6) of this section;

(4) PBGC's willingness to discuss alternative payment arrangements and how the debtor may enter into a written agreement to repay the debt under terms acceptable to PBGC (see § 4903.7 of this part);

(5) The name, address, and telephone number of a contact person or office within PBGC;

(6) PBGC's intention to enforce collection by taking one or more of the following actions if the debtor fails to pay or otherwise resolve the debt:

(i) *Offset.*. Offset the debtor's receipt of Federal payments, including income tax refunds, salary, certain benefit payments (such as Social Security), Federal retirement (*i.e.,* CSRS or FERS), vendor, travel reimbursements and advances, and other Federal payments (see §§ 4903.11 through 4903.13 of this part);

(ii) *Private collection agency.*. Refer the debt to a private collection agency (see § 4903.16 of this part);

(iii) *Credit bureau reporting.*. Report the debt to a credit bureau (see § 4903.15 of this part);

(iv) *Administrative wage garnishment.*. Garnish the debtor's wages through administrative wage garnishment (see § 4903.14 of this part);

(v) *Litigation.*. Whether PBGC will initiate litigation under 29 U.S.C. 1302 to collect the debt or refer the debt to the Department of Justice to initiate litigation to collect the debt (see § 4903.17 of this part);

(vi) *Treasury Department's Financial Management Service.*. Refer the debt to the Financial Management Service for collection (see § 4903.10 of this part);

(7) That debts over 180 days delinquent must be referred to the Financial Management Service for the collection actions described in paragraph (a)(6) of this section (see § 4903.10 of this part);

(8) How the debtor may inspect and copy non-privileged records related to the debt;

(9) How the debtor may request a review of PBGC's determination that the debtor owes a debt to PBGC and present evidence that the debt is not delinquent or legally enforceable (see §§ 4903.11(c) and 4903.12(c) of this part);

(10) How a debtor who is an individual may request a hearing if PBGC intends to garnish the debtor's private sector (*i.e.,* non-Federal) wages (see § 4903.14(a) of this part), including:

(i) The method and time period for requesting a hearing;

(ii) That a request for a hearing, timely filed on or before the 15th business day following the date of the mailing of the notice, will stay the commencement of administrative wage garnishment, but not other collection procedures; and

(iii) The name and address of the office to which the request for a hearing should be sent.

(11) How a debtor who is an individual and a Federal employee subject to Federal salary offset may request a hearing (see § 4903.13(e) of this part), including:

(i) The method and time period for requesting a hearing;

(ii) That a request for a hearing, timely filed on or before the 15th day following receipt of the notice, will stay the commencement of salary offset, but not other collection procedures;

(iii) The name and address of the office to which the request for a hearing should be sent;

(iv) That PBGC will refer the debt to the debtor's employing agency or to the Financial Management Service to implement salary offset, unless the employee files a timely request for a hearing;

(v) That a final decision on the hearing, if requested, will be issued at the earliest practicable date, but not later than 60 days after the filing of the request for a hearing, unless the employee requests and the hearing official grants a delay in the proceedings;

(vi) That any knowingly false or frivolous statements, representations, or evidence may subject the Federal employee to penalties under the False Claims Act (31 U.S.C. 3729-3731) or other applicable statutory authority, and criminal penalties under 18 U.S.C. 286, 287, 1001, and 1002, or other applicable statutory authority;

(vii) That unless prohibited by contract or statute, amounts paid on or deducted for the debt which are later waived or found not owed to the United States will be promptly refunded to the employee; and

(viii) That proceedings with respect to such debt are governed by 5 U.S.C. 5514 and 31 U.S.C. 3716.

(12) How the debtor may request a waiver of the debt, if applicable. *See,* for example, § 4903.6 and § 4903.13(f) of this part.

(13) How the debtor's spouse may claim his or her share of a joint income tax refund by filing Form 8379 with the Internal Revenue Service (*see http://www.irs.gov*);

(14) How the debtor may exercise other rights and remedies, if any, available to the debtor under statutory or regulatory authority under which the debt arose.

(15) That certain debtors and, if applicable, persons controlled by or controlling such debtors, may be ineligible for Federal Government loans, guaranties and insurance, grants, cooperative agreements or other Federal funds (see 28 U.S.C. 3201(e); 31 U.S.C. 3720B, 31 CFR 285.13, and § 4903.18(a) of this part); and

(16) That the debtor should advise PBGC of a bankruptcy proceeding of the debtor or another person liable for the debt being collected.

(b) *Exceptions to notice requirements.*. PBGC may omit from a notice to a debtor one or more of the provisions contained in paragraphs (a)(6) through (a)(16) of this section if PBGC, in consultation with its legal counsel, determines that any provision is not legally required given the collection remedies to be applied to a particular debt.

(c) *Respond to debtors; comply with FCCS.*. PBGC should respond promptly to communications from debtors and comply with other FCCS provisions applicable to the administrative collection of debts. *See* 31 CFR part 901.

[¶ 15,721H]

§ 4903.6 **How will PBGC add interest, penalty charges, and administrative costs to a debt owed to PBGC?**. (a) *Assessment and notice.*. PBGC will assess interest, penalties and administrative costs on PBGC debts in accordance with the provisions of 31 U.S.C. 3717, 31 CFR 901.9 and other applicable requirements. Administrative costs, including the costs of processing and handling a delinquent debt, will be determined by PBGC. PBGC will explain in the notice to the debtor how interest, penalties, costs, and other charges are assessed, unless the requirements are included in a contract or other legally binding agreement.

(b) *Waiver of interest, penalties, and administrative costs.*. Unless otherwise required by law, regulation, or contract, PBGC will not charge interest if the amount due on the debt is paid within 30 days of the date from which the interest accrues. *See* 31 U.S.C. 3717(d). To the extent permitted by law, PBGC may waive interest, penalties, and administrative costs, or any portion thereof, in appropriate circumstances consistent with the FCCS.

(c) *Accrual during suspension of debt collection.*. In most cases, interest, penalties and administrative costs will continue to accrue during any period when collection has been suspended for any reason (for example, when the debtor has requested a hearing). PBGC may suspend accrual of any or all of these charges in appropriate circumstances consistent with the FCCS.

[¶ 15,721I]

§ 4903.7 **When will PBGC allow a debtor to pay a debt owed to PBGC in installments instead of a lump sum?**. If a debtor is financially unable to pay the debt in a lump sum, PBGC may accept payment of a debt in regular installments, in accordance with the provisions of 31 CFR 901.8.

[¶ 15,721J]

§ 4903.8 **When will PBGC compromise a debt owed to PBGC?**. If PBGC cannot collect the full amount of a debt owed to PBGC, PBGC may compromise the debt in accordance with the provisions of 31 CFR part 902.

[¶ 15,721K]

§ 4903.9 **When will PBGC suspend or terminate debt collection on a debt owed to PBGC?**. If, after pursuing all appropriate means of collection, PBGC determines that a debt owed to PBGC is uncollectible, PBGC may suspend or terminate debt collection activity in accordance with the provisions of 31 CFR part 903. Termination of debt collection activity by PBGC does not discharge the indebtedness.

[¶ 15,721L]

§ 4903.10 **When will PBGC transfer a debt owed to PBGC to the Treasury Department's Financial Management Service for collection?**. (a) PBGC will transfer a debt owed to PBGC that is more than 180 days delinquent to the Financial Management Service for debt collection services, a process known as "cross-servicing." *See* 31 U.S.C. 3711(g) and 31 CFR 285.12. PBGC may transfer debts owed to PBGC that are delinquent 180 days or less to the Financial Management Service in accordance with the procedures described in 31 CFR 285.12. The Financial Management Service takes appropriate action to collect or compromise the transferred PBGC debt, or to suspend or terminate collection action thereon, in accordance with the statutory and regulatory requirements and authorities applicable to the debt owed to PBGC and the collection action to be taken. See 31 CFR 285.12(b) and 285.12(c)(2). Appropriate action can include, but is not limited to, contact with the debtor, referral of the debt owed to PBGC to the Treasury Offset Program, private collection agencies, or the Department of Justice; reporting of the debt to credit bureaus, and/or administrative wage garnishment.

(b) At least 60 days prior to transferring a debt owed to PBGC to the Financial Management Service, PBGC will send notice to the debtor as required by § 4903.5 of this part. PBGC will certify to the Financial Management Service that the debt is valid, delinquent, legally enforceable, and that there are no legal bars to collection. In addition, PBGC will certify its compliance with all applicable due process and other requirements as described in this part and other Federal laws. See 31 CFR 285.12(i) regarding the certification requirement.

(c) As part of its debt collection process, the Financial Management Service uses the Treasury Offset Program to collect debts owed to PBGC by administrative and tax refund offset. *See* 31 CFR 285.12(g). Under the Treasury Offset Program, before a Federal payment is disbursed, the Financial Management Service compares the name and taxpayer identification number (TIN) of the payee with the names and TINs of debtors that have been submitted by Federal agencies and states to the Treasury Offset Program database. If there is a match, the Financial Management Service (or, in some cases, another Federal disbursing agency) offsets all or a portion of the Federal payment, disburses any remaining payment to the payee, and pays the offset amount to the creditor agency. Federal payments eligible for offset include, but are not limited to, income tax refunds, salary, travel

advances and reimbursements, retirement and vendor payments, and Social Security and other benefit payments.

[¶ 15,721L-1]

§ 4903.11 **How will PBGC use administrative offset (offset of non-tax Federal payments) to collect a debt owed to PBGC?**.
(a) *Centralized administrative offset through the Treasury Offset Program.*

(1) In most cases, the Financial Management Service uses the Treasury Offset Program to collect debts owed to PBGC by the offset of Federal payments. *See* § 4903.10(c) of this part. If not already transferred to the Financial Management Service under § 4903.10 of this part, PBGC will refer debt over 180 days delinquent to the Treasury Offset Program for collection by centralized administrative offset. *See* 31 U.S.C. 3716(c)(6); 31 CFR part 285, subpart A; and 31 CFR 901.3(b). PBGC may refer to the Treasury Offset Program for offset any debt owed to PBGC that has been delinquent for 180 days or less.

(2) At least 60 days prior to referring a debt owed to PBGC to the Treasury Offset Program, in accordance with paragraph (a)(1) of this section, PBGC will send notice to the debtor in accordance with the requirements of § 4903.5 of this part. PBGC will certify to the Financial Management Service, that the debt is valid, delinquent, and legally enforceable, and that there are no legal bars to collection by offset. In addition, PBGC will certify its compliance with the requirements in this part.

(b) *Non-centralized administrative offset for debts owed to PBGC.*

(1) When centralized administrative offset through the Treasury Offset Program is not available or appropriate, PBGC may collect past-due, legally enforceable debts owed to PBGC through non-centralized administrative offset. See 31 CFR 901.3(c). In these cases, PBGC may offset a payment internally or make an offset request directly to a Federal payment agency.

(2) At least 30 days prior to offsetting a payment internally or requesting a Federal payment agency to offset a payment, PBGC will send notice to the debtor in accordance with the requirements of § 4903.5 of this part. When referring a debt owed to PBGC for offset under this paragraph (b), PBGC will certify that the debt is valid, delinquent, and legally enforceable, and that there are no legal bars to collection by offset. In addition, PBGC will certify its compliance with these regulations concerning administrative offset. *See* 31 CFR 901.3(c)(2)(ii).

(c) *Administrative review.*. The notice described in § 4903.5 of this part will explain to the debtor how to request an administrative review of PBGC's determination that the debtor owes a debt to PBGC and how to present evidence that the debt is not delinquent or legally enforceable. In addition to challenging the existence and amount of the debt owed to PBGC, the debtor may seek a review of the terms of repayment. In most cases, PBGC will provide administrative review based upon the written record, including documentation provided by the debtor. PBGC may provide the debtor with a reasonable opportunity for an oral hearing when the debtor requests reconsideration of the debt owed to PBGC, and PBGC determines that the question of the indebtedness cannot be resolved by review of the documentary evidence. Unless otherwise required by law, an oral hearing under this section is not required to be a formal evidentiary hearing. PBGC will carefully document all significant matters discussed at the hearing. PBGC may suspend collection through administrative offset and/or other collection actions pending the resolution of a debtor's dispute.

(d) *Procedures for expedited offset.*. Under the circumstances described in 31 CFR 901.3(b)(4)(iii), PBGC may offset against a payment to be made to the debtor prior to sending a notice to the debtor, as described in § 4903.5 of this part, or completing the procedures described in paragraph (b)(2) and (c) of this section. PBGC will give the debtor notice and an opportunity for review as soon as practicable and promptly refund any money ultimately found not to have been owed to the Government.

[¶ 15,721L-2]

§ 4903.12 **How will PBGC use tax refund offset to collect a debt owed to PBGC?**. (a) *Tax refund offset.*. In most cases, the Financial Management Service uses the Treasury Offset Program to collect debts owed to PBGC by the offset of tax refunds and other Federal payments. *See* § 4903.10(c) of this part. If not already transferred to the Financial Management Service under § 4903.10 of this part, PBGC will refer to the Treasury Offset Program any past-due, legally enforceable debt for collection by tax refund offset. *See* 26 U.S.C. 6402(d), 31 U.S.C. 3720A and 31 CFR 285.2.

(b) *Notice.*. At least 60 days prior to referring a debt owed to the Treasury Offset Program, PBGC will send notice to the debtor in accordance with the requirements of § 4903.5 of this part. PBGC will certify to the Financial Management Service's Treasury Offset Program that the debt is past due and legally enforceable in the amount submitted, and that the PBGC has made reasonable efforts to obtain payment of the debt as described in 31 CFR 285.2(d). In addition, PBGC will certify its compliance with all applicable due process and other requirements described in this part and other Federal laws. *See* 31 U.S.C. 3720A(b) and 31 CFR 285.2.

(c) *Administrative review.*. The notice described in § 4903.5 of this part will provide the debtor with at least 60 days prior to the initiation of tax refund offset to request an administrative review as described in § 4903.11(c) of this part. PBGC may suspend collection through tax refund offset and/or other collection actions pending the resolution of the debtor's dispute.

[¶ 15,721L-3]

§ 4903.13 **How will PBGC offset a Federal employee's salary to collect a debt owed to PBGC?.** (a) *Federal salary offset.*

(1) Salary offset is used to collect debts owed to the United States or PBGC by Federal employees. If a Federal employee owes PBGC a debt, PBGC may offset the employee's Federal salary to collect the debt in the manner described in this section. For information on how a Federal agency other than PBGC may collect debt from the salary of a PBGC employee, see §§ 4903.21 and 4903.22, subpart C, of this part.

(2) Nothing in this part requires PBGC to collect a debt in accordance with the provisions of this section if Federal law allows other means to collect. *See,* for example, 5 U.S.C. 5705 (travel advances not used for allowable travel expenses are recoverable from the employee or his estate by setoff against accrued pay and other means) and 5 U.S.C. 4108 (recovery of training expenses).

(3) PBGC may use the administrative wage garnishment procedure described in § 4903.14 of this part to collect from an individual's non-Federal wages a debt owed to PBGC.

(b) *Centralized salary offset through the Treasury Offset Program.*. As described in § 4903.10(a) of this part, PBGC will refer debts owed to PBGC to the Financial Management Service for collection by administrative offset, including salary offset, through the Treasury Offset Program. When possible, PBGC will attempt salary offset through the Treasury Offset Program before applying the procedures in paragraph (c) of this section. *See* 5 CFR 550.1108 and 550.1109.

(c) *Non-centralized salary offset for debts owed to PBGC.*. When centralized salary offset through the Treasury Offset Program is not available or appropriate, PBGC may collect delinquent debts owed to PBGC through non-centralized salary offset. *See* 5 CFR 550.1109. In these cases, PBGC may offset a payment internally or make a request directly to a Federal payment agency to offset a salary payment to collect a delinquent debt owed to PBGC by a Federal employee. Thirty (30) days prior to offsetting internally or requesting a Federal agency to offset a salary payment, PBGC will send notice to the debtor in accordance with the requirements of § 4903.5 of this part. When referring a debt owed to PBGC for offset, PBGC will certify to the payment agency that the debt is valid, delinquent and legally enforceable in the amount stated, and there are no legal bars to collection by salary offset. In addition, PBGC will certify that all due process and other prerequisites to salary offset have been met. See 5 U.S.C. 5514, 31 U.S.C. 3716(a), and this section for a description of the due process and other prerequisites for salary offset.

(d) *When prior notice not required.*. PBGC is not required to provide prior notice to an employee when the following adjustments are made by PBGC to a PBGC employee's pay:

(1) Any adjustment to pay arising out of any employee's election of coverage or a change in coverage under a Federal benefits program requiring periodic deductions from pay if the amount to be recovered was accumulated over 4 pay periods or less;

(2) A routine intra-agency adjustment of pay that is made to correct an overpayment of pay attributable to clerical or administrative errors or delays in processing pay documents, if the overpayment occurred within the 4 pay periods preceding the adjustment, and, at the time of such adjustment, or as soon thereafter as practicable, the individual is provided written notice of the nature and the amount of the adjustment and the point of contact for contesting such adjustment; or

(3) Any adjustment to collect a debt amounting to $50 or less, if, at the time of such adjustment, or as soon thereafter as practicable, the individual is provided written notice of the nature and the amount of the adjustment and a point of contact for contesting such adjustment.

(e) *Administrative review—*

(1) *Request for administrative review.*. A Federal employee who has received a notice that his or her debt will be collected by means of salary offset may request administrative review concerning the existence or amount of the debt owed to PBGC. The Federal employee also may request administrative review concerning the amount proposed to be deducted from the employee's pay each pay period. The employee must send any request for administrative review in writing to the office designated in the notice described in § 4903.5. *See* § 4903.5(a)(11). The request must be received by the designated office on or before the 15th day following the employee's receipt of the notice. The employee must sign the request and specify whether an oral hearing is requested. If an oral hearing is requested, the employee must explain why the matter cannot be resolved by review of the documentary evidence alone. All travel expenses incurred by the Federal employee in connection with an in-person hearing will be borne by the employee. *See* 31 CFR 901.3(a)(7).

(2) *Failure to submit timely request for administrative review.*. If the employee fails to submit a request for administrative review within the time period described in paragraph (e)(1) of this section, salary offset may be initiated. However, PBGC may accept a late request for administrative review if the employee can show that the late request was the result of circumstances beyond the employee's control or because of a failure to receive actual notice of the filing deadline.

(3) *Reviewing official.*. PBGC must obtain the services of a reviewing official who is not under the supervision or control of the Director of the PBGC. PBGC may enter into interagency support agreements with other agencies to provide reviewing officials.

(4) *Notice of administrative review.*. After the employee requests administrative review, the designated reviewing official will inform the employee of the form of the review to be provided. For oral hearings, the notice will set forth the date, time and location of the hearing. For determinations based on review of written records, the notice will notify the employee of the date by which he or she should submit written arguments to the designated reviewing official. The reviewing official will give the employee reasonable time to submit documentation in support of the employee's position. The reviewing official will schedule a new hearing date if requested by both parties. The reviewing official will give both parties reasonable notice of the time and place of a rescheduled hearing.

(5) *Oral hearing.*. The reviewing official will conduct an oral hearing if the official determines that the matter cannot be resolved by review of documentary evidence alone. The hearing need not take the form of an evidentiary hearing, but may be conducted in a manner determined by the reviewing official, including but not limited to:

(i) Informal conferences (in person or electronically) with the reviewing official, in which the employee and agency representative will be given a reasonable opportunity to present evidence, witnesses and argument;

(ii) Informal meetings with an interview of the employee by the reviewing official; or

(iii) Formal written submissions, with an opportunity for oral presentation.

(6) *Determination based on review of written record.*. If the reviewing official determines that an oral hearing is not necessary, the official will make the determination based upon a review of the available written record, including any documentation submitted by the employee in support of his or her position. *See* 31 CFR 901.3(a)(7).

(7) *Failure to appear or submit documentary evidence.*. In the absence of good cause shown (for example, excused illness), if the employee fails to appear at an oral hearing or fails to submit documentary evidence as required for administrative review, the employee will have waived the right to administrative review, and salary offset may be initiated. Further, the employee will have been deemed to admit the existence and amount of the debt owed to PBGC as described in the notice of intent to offset. If PBGC's representative fails to appear at an oral hearing, the reviewing official will proceed with the hearing as scheduled, and make his or her determination based upon the oral testimony presented and the documentary evidence submitted by both parties.

(8) *Burden of proof.*. PBGC will have the initial burden to prove the existence and amount of the debt owed to PBGC. Thereafter, if the employee disputes the existence or amount of the debt, the employee must prove by a preponderance of the evidence that no such debt exists or that the amount of the debt is incorrect. In addition, the employee may present evidence that the proposed terms of the repayment schedule are unlawful, would cause a financial hardship to the employee, or that collection of the debt may not be pursued due to operation of law.

(9) *Record.*. The reviewing official will maintain a summary record of any hearing provided by this part. Witnesses will testify under oath or affirmation in oral hearings. See 31 CFR 901.3(a)(7).

(10) *Date of decision.*. The reviewing official will issue a written opinion stating the official's decision, based upon documentary evidence and information developed during the administrative review, as soon as practicable after the review, but not later than 60 days after the date on which the request for review was received by PBGC. If the employee (or the parties jointly) requests a delay in the proceedings, the deadline for the decision may be postponed by the number of days by which the review was postponed. When a decision is not timely rendered, PBGC will waive interest and penalties applied to the debt owed to PBGC for the period beginning with the date the decision is due and ending on the date the decision is issued.

(11) *Content of decision.*. The written decision will include:

(i) A statement of the facts presented to support the origin, nature, and amount of the debt owed to PBGC;

(ii) The reviewing official's findings, analysis, and conclusions; and

(iii) The terms of any repayment schedules, if applicable.

(12) *Final agency action.*. The reviewing official's decision will be final.

(f) *Waiver not precluded.*. Nothing in this part precludes an employee from requesting waiver of an overpayment under 5 U.S.C. 5584 or 8346(b), 32 U.S.C. 716, or other statutory authority. PBGC may grant such waivers when it would be against equity and good conscience or not in the United States' best interest to collect such debts, in accordance with those authorities, 5 CFR 550.1102(b)(2).

(g) *Salary offset process—*

(1) *Determination of disposable pay.*. PBGC will implement salary offset when requested to do so by PBGC, as described in paragraph (c) of this section, or another agency, as described in § 4903.21 of this part. If the debtor is not employed by PBGC, the agency employing the debtor will determine the amount of the employee's disposable pay and will implement salary offset upon request.

(2) *When salary offset begins.*. Deductions will begin within three official pay periods following receipt of the creditor agency's request for offset or after a decision has been issued following a request for a hearing.

(3) *Amount of salary offset.*. The amount to be offset from each salary payment will be up to 15 percent of a debtor's disposable pay, subject to the requirements of 15 U.S.C. 1673, as follows:

(i) If the amount of the debt is equal to or less than 15 percent of the disposable pay, such debt generally will be collected in a lump sum payment;

(ii) Installment deductions will be made over a period of no greater than the anticipated period of employment. An installment deduction will not exceed 15 percent of the disposable pay from which the deduction is made unless the employee has agreed in writing to the deduction of a greater amount, or the creditor agency has determined that smaller deductions are appropriate based on the employee's ability to pay.

(4) *Final salary payment.*. After the employee has separated either voluntarily or involuntarily from the payment agency, the payment agency may make a lump sum deduction exceeding 15 percent of disposable pay from any final salary or other payments pursuant to 31 U.S.C. 3716 in order to satisfy a debt owed to PBGC.

(h) *Payment agency's responsibilities.*

(1) As required by 5 CFR 550.1109, if the employee separates from the payment agency from which PBGC has requested salary offset, the payment agency must certify the total amount of its collection and notify PBGC and the employee of the amounts collected. If the payment agency knows that the employee is entitled to payments from the Civil Service Retirement Fund and Disability Fund, the Federal Employee Retirement System, or other similar payments, it must provide written notification to the agency responsible for making such payments that the debtor owes a debt to PBGC, the amount of the debt, and that PBGC has complied with the provisions of this section. PBGC must submit a properly certified claim to the agency responsible for making such payments before the collection can be made.

(2) If the employee is already separated from employment and all payments due from his or her former payment agency have been made, PBGC may request that money due and payable to the employee from the Civil Service Retirement Fund and Disability Fund, the Federal Employee Retirement System, or other similar funds, be administratively offset to collect the debt. Generally, PBGC will collect such monies through the Treasury Offset Program as described in § 4903.10(c) of this part.

(3) When an employee transfers to another agency, PBGC should resume collection with the employee's new payment agency in order to continue salary offset.

[¶ 15,721L-4]

§ 4903.14 **How will PBGC use administrative wage garnishment to collect a debt owed to PBGC from a debtor's wages?.** (a) PBGC is authorized to collect debts owed to PBGC from an individual debtor's wages by means of administrative wage garnishment in accordance with the requirements of 31 U.S.C. 3720D and 31 CFR 285.11. This part adopts and incorporates all of the provisions of 31 CFR 285.11 concerning administrative wage garnishment, including the hearing procedures described in 31 CFR 285.11(f). PBGC may use administrative wage garnishment to collect a delinquent debt unless the debtor is making timely payments under an agreement to pay the debt in installments (*see* § 4903.7 of this part). Thirty (30) days prior to initiating an administrative wage garnishment, PBGC will send notice to the debtor in accordance with the requirements of § 4903.5 of this part, including the requirements of § 4903.5(a)(10) of this part. For debts referred to the Financial Management Service under § 4903.10 of this part, PBGC may authorize the Financial Management Service to send a notice informing the debtor that administrative wage garnishment will be initiated and how the debtor may request a hearing as described in § 4903.5(a)(10) of this part. If a debtor makes a timely request for a hearing, administrative wage garnishment will not begin until a hearing is held and a decision is sent to the debtor. PBGC will determine whether the matter requires an oral hearing or if a determination based upon review of the written record is sufficient. PBGC will provide the debtor with a reasonable opportunity for an oral hearing when it determines that the issues in dispute cannot be resolved by a review of the documentary evidence. *See* 31 CFR 285.11(f)(1)-(4). Even if a debtor's hearing request is not timely, PBGC may suspend collection by administrative wage garnishment in accordance with the provisions of 31 CFR 285.11(f)(5). All travel expenses incurred by the debtor in connection with an in-person hearing will be borne by the debtor.

(b) This section does not apply to Federal salary offset, the process by which PBGC collects debts owed to PBGC from the salaries of Federal employees (*see* § 4903.13 of this part).

[¶ 15,721L-5]

§ 4903.15 **How will PBGC report debts owed to PBGC to credit bureaus?.** PBGC will report delinquent debts owed to PBGC to credit bureaus in accordance with the provisions of 31 U.S.C. 3711(e), 31 CFR 901.4, and the Office of Management and Budget Circular A-129, "Policies for Federal Credit Programs and Non-tax Receivables." At least 60 days prior to reporting a delinquent debt to a consumer reporting agency, PBGC will send notice to the debtor in accordance with the requirements of § 4903.5 of this part. PBGC may authorize the Financial Management Service to report to credit bureaus those delinquent debts owed to the PBGC that have been transferred to the Financial Management Service under § 4903.10 of this part.

[¶ 15,721L-6]

§ 4903.16 **How will PBGC refer debts owed to PBGC to private collection agencies?.** PBGC will transfer delinquent debts owed to PBGC to the Financial Management Service to obtain debt collection services provided by private collection agencies. See § 4903.10 of this part.

[¶ 15,721L-7]

§ 4903.17 **When will PBGC refer debts owed to PBGC to the Department of Justice?**

PBGC may initiate litigation pursuant to 29 U.S.C. 1302 with delinquent debts on which aggressive collection activity has been taken in accordance with this part and that should not be compromised, and on which collection activity should not be suspended or terminated. Alternatively, PBGC may refer debts owed to PBGC having a principal balance over $100,000, or such higher amount as authorized by the Attorney General, to the Department of Justice for approval of any compromise of a debt or suspension or termination of collection activity. See §§ 4903.8 and 4903.9 of this part; 31 CFR 902.1, 903.1, and part 904. PBGC may authorize the Financial Management Service to refer to the Department of Justice for litigation those delinquent debts that have been transferred to the Financial Management Service under § 4903.10 of this part.

[¶ 15,721L-8]

§ 4903.18 **Will a debtor who owes a debt to PBGC or another Federal agency, and persons controlled by or controlling such debtors, be ineligible for Federal loan assistance, grants, cooperative agreements, or other sources of Federal funds?.** (a) Delinquent debtors are ineligible for and barred from obtaining Federal loans or loan insurance or guaranties. As required by 31 U.S.C. 3720B and 31 CFR 901.6, PBGC will not extend financial assistance in the form of a loan, loan guarantee, or loan insurance to any person delinquent on a debt owed to a Federal agency. PBGC may issue standards under which it may determine that persons controlled by or controlling such delinquent debtors are similarly ineligible in accordance with 31 CFR 285.13(c)(2). This prohibition does not apply to disaster loans. PBGC may extend credit after the delinquency has been resolved. *See* 31 CFR 285.13.

(b) This section does not apply to loans provided to multi-employer pension plans pursuant to 29 U.S.C. 1431, 29 CFR 4261.1 and 4281.47.

(c) A debtor who has a judgment lien against the debtor's property for a debt to the United States is not eligible to receive grants, loans or funds directly or indirectly from the United States until the judgment is paid in full or otherwise satisfied. This prohibition does not apply to funds to which the debtor is entitled as beneficiary. PBGC may promulgate regulations to allow for waivers of this ineligibility. *See* 28 U.S.C. 3201(e).

[¶ 15,721L-9]

§ 4903.19 **How does a debtor request a special review based on a change in circumstances such as catastrophic illness, divorce,**

death, or disability?. (a) *Material change in circumstances..* A debtor who owes a debt to PBGC may, at any time, request a special review by PBGC of the amount of any offset, administrative wage garnishment, or voluntary payment, based on materially changed circumstances beyond the control of the debtor such as, but not limited to, catastrophic illness, divorce, death, or disability.

(b) *Inability to pay..* For purposes of this section, in determining whether an involuntary or voluntary payment would prevent the debtor from meeting essential subsistence expenses (*e.g.,* costs incurred for food, housing, clothing, transportation, and medical care), the debtor must submit a detailed statement and supporting documents for the debtor, his or her spouse, and dependents, indicating:

(1) Income from all sources;

(2) Assets;

(3) Liabilities;

(4) Number of dependents;

(5) Expenses for food, housing, clothing, and transportation;

(6) Medical expenses;

(7) Exceptional expenses, if any; and

(8) Any additional materials and information that PBGC may request relating to ability or inability to pay the amount(s) currently required.

(c) *Alternative payment arrangement..* If the debtor requests a special review under this section, the debtor must submit an alternative proposed payment schedule and a statement to PBGC, with supporting documents, showing why the current offset, garnishment or repayment schedule imposes an extreme financial hardship on the debtor. PBGC will evaluate the statement and documentation and determine whether the current offset, garnishment, or repayment schedule imposes extreme financial hardship on the debtor. PBGC will notify the debtor in writing of such determination, including, if appropriate, a revised offset, garnishment, or payment schedule. If the special review results in a revised offset, garnishment, or repayment schedule, PBGC will notify the appropriate Federal agency or other persons about the new terms.

[¶ 15,721L-10]

§ 4903.20 **Will PBGC issue a refund if money is erroneously collected on a debt?.** PBGC will promptly refund to a debtor any amount collected on a debt owed to PBGC when the debt is waived or otherwise found not to be owed to the United States, or as otherwise required by law.

Subpart C—Procedures for Offset of PBGC Payments To Collect Debts Owed to Other Federal Agencies

[¶ 15,721L-11]

§ 4903.21 **How do other Federal agencies use the offset process to collect debts from payments issued by PBGC?.** (a) *Offset of PBGC payments to collect debts owed to other Federal agencies.*

(1) In most cases, Federal agencies submit debts to the Treasury Offset Program to collect delinquent debts from payments issued by PBGC and other Federal agencies, a process known as "centralized offset." When centralized offset is not available or appropriate, any Federal agency may ask PBGC (when acting as a "payment agency") to collect a debt owed to such agency by offsetting funds payable to a debtor by PBGC, including salary payments issued to PBGC employees. This section and § 4903.21 of this subpart C apply when a Federal agency asks PBGC to offset a payment issued by PBGC to a person who owes a debt to the United States.

(2) This subpart C does not apply to debts owed to PBGC. *See* §§ 4903.11 through 4903.13 of this part for offset procedures applicable to debts owed to PBGC.

(3) This subpart C does not apply to the collection of non-PBGC debts through tax refund offset. See 31 CFR 285.2 for tax refund offset procedures.

(4) Benefits paid by PBGC generally will not be offset, subject to limited exceptions (*e.g.,* in certain fiduciary breach situations).

(b) *Administrative offset (including salary offset); certification..* PBGC will initiate a requested offset only upon receipt of written certification from the creditor agency that the debtor owes the past-due, legally enforceable debt in the amount stated, and that the creditor agency has fully complied with all applicable due process and other requirements contained in 31 U.S.C. 3716, 5 U.S.C. 5514, and the creditor agency's regulations, as applicable. Offsets will continue until the debt is paid in full or otherwise resolved to the satisfaction of the creditor agency.

(c) *Where a creditor agency makes requests for offset.*. Requests for offset under this section must be sent to PBGC, ATTN: Chief Financial Officer, 1200 K Street, NW., Washington, DC 20005.

(d) *Incomplete certification.*. PBGC will return an incomplete debt certification to the creditor agency with notice that the creditor agency must comply with paragraph (b) of this section before action will be taken to collect a debt from a payment issued by PBGC.

(e) *Review.*. PBGC is not authorized to review the merits of the creditor agency's determination with respect to the amount or validity of the debt certified by the creditor agency.

(f) *When PBGC will not comply with offset request.*. PBGC will comply with the offset request of another agency unless PBGC determines, in consultation with that agency, that the offset would not be in the best interests of the United States, or would otherwise be contrary to law.

(g) *Multiple debts.*. When two or more creditor agencies are seeking offsets from payments made to the same person, or when two or more debts are owed to a single creditor agency, PBGC may determine the order in which the debts will be collected or whether one or more debts should be collected by offset simultaneously.

(h) *Priority of debts owed to PBGC.*. For purposes of this section, debts owed to PBGC generally take precedence over debts owed to other agencies. PBGC may determine whether to pay debts owed to other agencies before paying a debt owed to PBGC. PBGC will determine the order in which the debts will be collected based on the best interests of the United States.

[¶ 15,721L-12]

§ 4903.22 **What does PBGC do upon receipt of a request to offset the salary of a PBGC employee to collect a debt owed by the employee to another Federal agency?**. (a) *Notice to a PBGC employee.*. When PBGC receives proper certification of a debt owed by one of its employees, PBGC will send a written notice to the employee indicating that a certified debt claim has been received from the creditor agency, the amount of the debt claimed to be owed by the creditor agency, the date deductions from salary will begin, and the amount of such deductions. PBGC will begin deductions from the employee's pay at the next officially established pay interval.

(b) *Amount of deductions from a PBGC employee's salary.* The amount deducted under § 4903.21(b) of this part will be the lesser of the amount of the debt certified by the creditor agency or an amount up to 15 percent of the debtor's disposable pay so long as that amount does not exceed limitations imposed by 15 U.S.C. 1673. Deductions will continue until PBGC knows that the debt is paid in full or until otherwise instructed by the creditor agency. Alternatively, the amount offset may be an amount agreed upon, in writing, by the debtor and the creditor agency. *See* § 4903.13(g) (salary offset process).

(c) *When the debtor is no longer employed by PBGC.* (1) *Offset of final and subsequent payments.*. If a PBGC employee retires or resigns or if his or her employment ends before collection of the debt is complete, PBGC will continue to offset, under 31 U.S.C. 3716, up to 100 percent of an employee's subsequent payments until the debt is paid or otherwise resolved. Such payments include a debtor's final salary payment, lump-sum leave payment, and other payments payable to the debtor by PBGC. *See* 31 U.S.C. 3716 and 5 CFR 550.1104(l) and 550.1104(m).

(2) *Notice to the creditor agency.*. If the employee is separated from PBGC before the debt is paid in full, PBGC will certify to the creditor agency the total amount of its collection. If PBGC knows that the employee is entitled to payments from the Civil Service Retirement and Disability Fund, Federal Employee Retirement System, or other similar payments, PBGC will provide written notice to the agency

making such payments that the debtor owes a debt (including the amount) and that the provisions of 5 CFR 550.1109 have been fully complied with. The creditor agency is responsible for submitting a certified claim to the agency responsible for making such payments before collection may begin. Generally, creditor agencies will collect such monies through the Treasury Offset Program as described in § 4903.10(c) of this part.

(3) *Notice to the debtor.*. PBGC will provide to the debtor a copy of any notices sent to the creditor agency under paragraph (c)(2) of this section.

(d) *When the debtor transfers to another Federal agency. (1) Notice to the creditor agency.*. If the debtor transfers to another Federal agency before the debt is paid in full, PBGC will notify the creditor agency and will certify the total amount of its collection on the debt. PBGC will provide a copy of the certification to the creditor agency. The creditor agency is responsible for submitting a certified claim to the debtor's new employing agency before collection may begin.

(2) *Notice to the debtor.*. PBGC will provide to the debtor a copy of any notices and certifications sent to the creditor agency under paragraph (d)(1) of this section.

(e) *Request for hearing official.*. PBGC will provide a hearing official upon the creditor agency's request with respect to a PBGC employee. *See* 5 CFR 550.1107(a).

Subpart D—Salary Offset [Reserved]

[¶ 15,721M-1]

§ 4904.1 **Outside employment and other activity**. (a)-(e) [Removed on February 13, 2004, 69 FR 7120].

[¶ 15,721M-2]

§ 4905.1 **Purpose and scope**. (a) *Purpose*. This part sets forth the rules and procedures to be followed when a PBGC employee or former employee is requested or served with compulsory process to appear as a witness or produce documents in a proceeding in which the PBGC is not a party, if such appearance arises out of, or is related to, his or her employment with the PBGC. It provides a centralized decisionmaking mechanism for responding to such requests and compulsory process.

(b) *Scope*. (1) This part applies when, in a judicial, administrative, legislative, or other proceeding, a PBGC employee or former employee is requested or served with compulsory process to provide testimony concerning information acquired in the course of performing official duties or because of official status and/or to produce material acquired in the course of performing official duties or contained in PBGC files.

(2) This part does not apply to:

(i) Proceedings in which the PBGC is a party;

(ii) Congressional requests or subpoenas for testimony or documents; or

(iii) Appearances by PBGC employees in proceedings that do not arise out of, or relate to, their employment with PBGC (e.g., outside activities that are engaged in consistent with applicable standards of ethical conduct).

[¶ 15,721M-3]

§ 4905.2 **Definitions**. For purposes of this part:

Appearance means testimony or production of documents or other material, including an affidavit, deposition, interrogatory, declaration, or other required written submission.

Compulsory Process means any subpoena, order, or other demand of a court or other authority (e.g., an administrative agency or a state or local legislative body) for the appearance of a PBGC employee or former employee.

Employee means any officer or employee of the PBGC, including a special government employee.

Proceeding means any proceeding before any federal, state, or local court; federal, state, or local agency; state or local legislature; or other authority responsible for administering regulatory requirements or adjudicating disputes or controversies, including arbitration, mediation, and other similar proceedings.

Special government employee means an employee of the PBGC who is retained, designated, appointed or employed to perform, with or without compensation, for not to exceed one hundred and thirty days during any three hundred and sixty-five consecutive days, temporary duties either on a full-time or intermittent basis (18 U.S.C. 202).

[¶ 15,721M-4]

§ 4905.3 **General**. No PBGC employee or former employee may appear in any proceeding to which this part applies to testify and/or produce documents or other material unless authorized under this part.

[¶ 15,721M-5]

§ 4905.4 **Appearances by PBGC employees**. (a) Whenever a PBGC employee or former employee is requested or served with compulsory process to appear in a proceeding to which this part applies, he or she will promptly notify the General Counsel.

(b) The General Counsel or his or her designee will authorize an appearance by a PBGC employee or former employee if, and to the extent, he or she determines that such appearance is in the interest of the PBGC.

(1) In determining whether an appearance is in the interest of the PBGC, the General Counsel or his or her designee will consider relevant factors, including:

(i) What, if any, objective of the PBGC (and, where relevant, any federal agency, if the United States is a party) would be promoted by the appearance;

(ii) Whether the appearance would unnecessarily interfere with the employee's official duties;

(iii) Whether the appearance would result in the appearance of improperly favoring one litigant over another; and

(iv) Whether the appearance is appropriate under applicable substantive and procedural rules.

(2) If the General Counsel or his or her designee concludes that compulsory process is essentially a request for PBGC record information, it will be treated as a request under the Freedom of Information Act, as amended, in accordance with part 4901 of this chapter, except to the extent that the Privacy Act of 1974, as amended, and part 4902 of this chapter govern disclosure of a record maintained on an individual.

(c) If, in response to compulsory process in a proceeding to which this part applies, the General Counsel or his or her designee has not authorized an appearance by the return date, the employee or former employee shall appear at the stated time and place (unless advised by the General Counsel or his or her designee that process either was not validly issued or served or has been withdrawn), accompanied by a PBGC attorney, produce a copy of this part of the regulations, and respectfully decline to provide any testimony or produce any documents or other material. When the demand is under consideration, the employee shall respectfully request that the court or other authority stay the demand pending the employee's receipt of instructions from the General Counsel.

[¶ 15,721M-6]

§ 4905.5 **Requests for authenticated copies of PBGC records**. The PBGC will grant requests for authenticated copies of PBGC records, for purposes of admissibility under 28 U.S.C. 1733 and Rule 44 of the Federal Rules of Civil Procedure, for records that are to be disclosed pursuant to this part or part 4901 of this chapter. Appropriate fees will be charged for providing authenticated copies of PBGC records, in accordance with part 4901, subpart D, of this chapter.

[¶ 15,721M-7]

§ 4905.6 **Penalty**. A PBGC employee who testifies or produces documents or other material in violation of a provision of this part of the regulations shall be subject to disciplinary action.

[¶ 15,721N-1]

§ 4907.101 **Purpose**. This part effectuates section 119 of the Rehabilitation, Comprehensive Services, and Developmental Disabilities Amendments of 1978, which amended section 504 of the Rehabilitation Act of 1973 to prohibit discrimination on the basis of handicap in programs or activities conducted by Executive agencies or the United States Postal Service.

[¶ 15,721N-2]

§ 4907.102 **Application**. This part applies to all programs or activities conducted by the agency.

[¶ 15,721N-3]

§ 4907.103 **Definitions**. For purposes of this part, the term—

Assistant Attorney General means the Assistant Attorney General, Civil Rights Division, United States Department of Justice.

Auxiliary aids means services or devices that enable persons with impaired sensory, manual, or speaking skills to have an equal opportunity to participate in, and enjoy the benefits of, programs or activities conducted by the agency. For example, auxiliary aids useful for persons with impaired vision include readers, brailled materials, audio recordings, telecommunications devices and other similar services and devices. Auxiliary aids useful for persons with impaired hearing include telephone handset amplifiers, telephones compatible with hearing aids, telecommunication devices for deaf persons (TDD's), interpreters, notetakers, written materials, and other similar services and devices.

Complete complaint means a written statement that contains the complainant's name and address and describes the agency's alleged discriminatory action in sufficient detail to inform the agency of the nature and date of the alleged violation of section 504. It shall be signed by the complainant or by someone authorized to do so on his or her behalf. Complaints filed on behalf of classes or third parties shall describe or identify (by name, if possible) the alleged victims of discrimination.

Facility means all or any portion of buildings, structures, equipment, roads, walks, parking lots, rolling stock or other conveyances, or other real or personal property.

Handicapped person means any person who has a physical or mental impairment that substantially limits one or more major life activities, has a record of such an impairment, or is regarded as having such an impairment.

As used in this definition, the phrase:

(1) Physical or mental impairment includes—

(i) Any physiological disorder or condition, cosmetic disfigurement, or anatomical loss affecting one or more of the following body systems: Neurological; musculoskeletal; special sense organs; respiratory, including speech organs; cardiovascular; reproductive; digestive; genitourinary; hemic and lymphatic; skin; and endocrine; or

(ii) Any mental or psychological disorder, such as mental retardation, organic brain syndrome, emotional or mental illness, and specific learning disabilities. The term "physical or mental impairment" includes, but is not limited to, such diseases and conditions as orthopedic, visual, speech, and hearing impairments, cerebral palsy, epilepsy, muscular dystrophy, multiple sclerosis, cancer, heart disease, diabetes, mental retardation, emotional illness, and drug addiction and alcoholism.

(2) Major life activities includes functions such as caring for one's self, performing manual tasks, walking, seeing, hearing, speaking, breathing, learning, and working.

(3) Has a record of such an impairment means has a history of, or has been misclassified as having, a mental or physical impairment that substantially limits one or more major life activities.

(4) Is regarded as having an impairment means—

(i) Has a physical or mental impairment that does not substantially limit major life activities but is treated by the agency as constituting such a limitation;

(ii) Has a physical or mental impairment that substantially limits major life activities only as a result of the attitudes of others toward such impairment; or

(iii) Has none of the impairments defined in subparagraph (1) of this definition but is treated by the agency as having such an impairment.

Historic preservation programs means programs conducted by the agency that have preservation of historic properties as a primary purpose.

Historic properties means those properties that are listed or eligible for listing in the National Register of Historic Places or properties designated as historic under a statute of the appropriate State or local government body.

Qualified handicapped person means—

(1) With respect to preschool, elementary, or secondary education services provided by the agency, a handicapped person who is a member of a class of persons otherwise entitled by statute, regulation, or agency policy to receive education services from the agency.

(2) With respect to any other agency program or activity under which a person is required to perform services or to achieve a level of accomplishment, a handicapped person who meets the essential eligibility requirements and who can achieve the purpose of the program or activity without modifications in the program or activity that the agency can demonstrate would result in a fundamental alteration in its nature;

(3) With respect to any other program or activity, a handicapped person who meets the essential eligibility requirements for participation in, or receipt of benefits from, that program or activity; and

(4) Qualified handicapped person is defined for purposes of employment in 29 CFR 1613.702(f), which is made applicable to this part by § 4907.140.

Section 504 means section 504 of the Rehabilitation Act of 1973 (Pub. L. 93-112, 87 Stat. 394 (29 U.S.C. 794)), as amended by the Rehabilitation Act Amendments of 1974 (Pub. L. 93-516, 88 Stat. 1617), and the Rehabilitation, Comprehensive Services, and Developmental Disabilities Amendments of 1978 (Pub. L. 95-602, 92 Stat. 2955). As used in this part, section 504 applies only to programs or activities conducted by Executive agencies and not to federally assisted programs.

Substantial impairment means a significant loss of the integrity of finished materials, design quality, or special character resulting from a permanent alteration.

[¶ 15,721N-4]

§§ 4907.104-4907.109 **[Reserved.]**

[¶ 15,721N-10]

§ 4907.110 **Self-evaluation**. (a) The agency shall, by August 24, 1987, evaluate its current policies and practices, and the effects thereof, that do not or may not meet the requirements of this part, and, to the extent modification of any such policies and practices is required, the agency shall proceed to make the necessary modifications.

(b) The agency shall provide an opportunity to interested persons, including handicapped persons or organizations representing handicapped persons, to participate in the self-evaluation process by submitting comments (both oral and written).

(c) The agency shall, until three years following the completion of the self-evaluation, maintain on file and make available for public inspection:

(1) a description of areas examined and any problems identified, and

(2) a description of any modifications made.

[¶ 15,721N-11]

§ 4907.111 **Notice**. The agency shall make available to employees, applicants, participants, beneficiaries, and other interested persons such information regarding the provisions of this part and its applicability to the programs or activities conducted by the agency, and make such information available to them in such manner as the head of the agency finds necessary to apprise such persons of the protections against discrimination assured them by section 504 and this regulation.

[¶ 15,721N-12]

§§ 4907.112-4907.129 **[Reserved.]**

[¶ 15,721N-30]

§ 4907.130 **General prohibitions against discrimination**. (a) No qualified handicapped person shall, on the basis of handicap, be excluded from participation in, be denied the benefits of, or otherwise be subjected to discrimination under any program or activity conducted by the agency.

(b)(1) The agency, in providing any aid, benefit, or service, may not, directly or through contractual, licensing, or other arrangements, on the basis of handicap—

(i) Deny a qualified handicapped person the opportunity to participate in or benefit from the aid, benefit, or service;

(ii) Afford a qualified handicapped person an opportunity to participate in or benefit from the aid, benefit, or service that is not equal to that afforded others;

(iii) Provide a qualified handicapped person with an aid, benefit, or service that is not as effective in affording equal opportunity to obtain the same result, to gain the same benefit, or to reach the same level of achievement as that provided to others;

(iv) Provide different or separate aid, benefits, or services to handicapped persons or to any class of handicapped persons than is provided to others unless such action is necessary to provide qualified handicapped persons with aid, benefits, or services that are as effective as those provided to others;

(v) Deny a qualified handicapped person the opportunity to participate as a member of planning or advisory boards; or

(vi) Otherwise limit a qualified handicapped person in the enjoyment of any right, privilege, advantage, or opportunity enjoyed by others receiving the aid, benefit, or service.

(2) The agency may not deny a qualified handicapped person the opportunity to participate in programs or activities that are not separate or different, despite the existence of permissibly separate or different programs or activities.

(3) The agency may not, directly or through contractual or other arrangements, utilize criteria or methods of administration the purpose or effect of which would—

(i) Subject qualified handicapped persons to discrimination on the basis of handicap; or

(ii) Defeat or substantially impair accomplishment of the objectives of a program or activity with respect to handicapped persons.

(4) The agency may not, in determining the site or location of a facility, make selections the purpose or effect of which would—

(i) Exclude handicapped persons from, deny them the benefits of, or otherwise subject them to discrimination under any program or activity conducted by the agency; or

(ii) Defeat or substantially impair the accomplishment of the objectives of a program or activity with respect to handicapped persons.

(5) The agency, in the selection of procurement contractors, may not use criteria that subject qualified handicapped persons to discrimination on the basis of handicap.

(6) The agency may not administer a licensing or certification program in a manner that subjects qualified handicapped persons to discrimination on the basis of handicap, nor may the agency establish requirements for the programs or activities of licensees or certified entities that subject qualified handicapped persons to discrimination on the basis of handicap. However, the programs or activities of entities that are licensed or certified by the agency are not, themselves, covered by this part.

(c) The exclusion of nonhandicapped persons from the benefits of a program limited by Federal statute or Executive Order to handicapped persons or the exclusion of a specific class of handicapped persons from a program limited by Federal statute or Executive Order to a different class of handicapped persons is not prohibited by this part.

(d) The agency shall administer programs and activities in the most integrated setting appropriate to the needs of qualified handicapped persons.

[¶ 15,721N-31]

§§ 4907.131-4907.139 **[Reserved.]**

[¶ 15,721N-40]

§ 4907.140 **Employment**. No qualified handicapped person shall, on the basis of handicap, be subjected to discrimination in employment under any program or activity conducted by the agency. The definitions, requirements, and procedures of section 501 of the Rehabilitation Act of 1973 (29 U.S.C. 791), as established by the Equal Employment Opportunity Commission in 29 CFR part 1613, shall apply to employment in federally-conducted programs or activities.

[¶ 15,721N-41]
§§ 4907.141-4907.148 **[Reserved.]**

[¶ 15,721N-49]
§ 4907.149 **Program accessibility: Discrimination prohibited**. Except as otherwise provided in § 4907.150, no qualified handicapped person shall, because the agency's facilities are inaccessible to or unusable by handicapped persons, be denied the benefits of, be excluded from participation in, or otherwise be subjected to discrimination under any program or activity conducted by the agency.

[¶ 15,721N-50]
§ 4907.150 **Program accessibility: Existing facilities.** (a) *General.* The agency shall operate each program or activity so that the program or activity, when viewed in its entirety, is readily accessible to and usable by handicapped persons. This paragraph does not—

(1) Necessarily require the agency to make each of its existing facilities accessible to and usable by handicapped persons;

(2) In the case of historic preservation programs, require the agency to take any action that would result in a substantial impairment of significant historic features of an historic property; or

(3) Require the agency to take any action that it can demonstrate would result in a fundamental alteration in the nature of a program or activity or in undue financial and administrative burdens. In those circumstances where agency personnel believe that the proposed action would fundamentally alter the program or activity or would result in undue financial and administrative burdens, the agency has the burden of proving that compliance with § 4907.150(a) would result in such alteration or burdens. The decision that compliance would result in such alteration or burdens must be made by the agency head or his or her designee after considering all agency resources available for use in the funding and operation of the conducted program or activity, and must be accompanied by a written statement of the reasons for reaching that conclusion. If an action would result in such an alteration or such burdens, the agency shall take any other action that would not result in such an alteration or such burdens but would nevertheless ensure that handicapped persons receive the benefits and services of the program or activity.

(b) *Methods—*

(1) *General.* The agency may comply with the requirements of this section through such means as redesign of equipment, reassignment of services to accessible buildings, assignment of aides to beneficiaries, home visits, delivery of services at alternate accessible sites, alteration of existing facilities and construction of new facilities, use of accessible rolling stock, or any other methods that result in making its programs or activities readily accessible to and usable by handicapped persons. The agency is not required to make structural changes in existing facilities where other methods are effective in achieving compliance with this section. The agency, in making alterations to existing buildings, shall meet accessibility requirements to the extent compelled by the Architectural Barriers Act of 1968, as amended (42 U.S.C. 4151-4157), and any regulations implementing it. In choosing among available methods for meeting the requirements of this section, the agency shall give priority to those methods that offer programs and activities to qualified handicapped persons in the most integrated setting appropriate.

(2) *Historic preservation programs.* In meeting the requirements of § 4907.150(a) in historic preservation programs, the agency shall give priority to methods that provide physical access to handicapped persons. In cases where a physical alteration to an historic property is not required because of § 4907.150(a)(2) or (a)(3), alternative methods of achieving program accessibility include—

(i) Using audio-visual materials and devices to depict those portions of an historic property that cannot otherwise be made accessible;

(ii) Assigning persons to guide handicapped persons into or through portions of historic properties that cannot otherwise be made accessible; or

(iii) Adopting other innovative methods.

(c) *Time period for compliance.* The agency shall comply with the obligations established under this section by October 21, 1986, except that where structural changes in facilities are undertaken, such changes shall be made by August 22, 1989, but in any event as expeditiously as possible.

(d) *Transition plan.* In the event that structural changes to facilities will be undertaken to achieve program accessibility, the agency shall develop, by February 23, 1987 a transition plan setting forth the steps necessary to complete such changes. The agency shall provide an opportunity to interested persons, including handicapped persons or organizations representing handicapped persons, to participate in the development of the transition plan by submitting comments (both oral and written). A copy of the transition plan shall be made available for public inspection. The plan shall, at a minimum—

(1) Identify physical obstacles in the agency's facilities that limit the accessibility of its programs or activities to handicapped persons;

(2) Describe in detail the methods that will be used to make the facilities accessible;

(3) Specify the schedule for taking the steps necessary to achieve compliance with this section and, if the time period of the transition plan is longer than one year, identify steps that will be taken during each year of the transition period; and

(4) Indicate the official responsible for implementation of the plan.

[¶ 15,721N-51]
§ 4907.151 **Program accessibility: New construction and alterations**. Each building or part of a building that is constructed or altered by, on behalf of, or for the use of the agency shall be designed, constructed, or altered so as to be readily accessible to and usable by handicapped persons. The definitions, requirements, and standards of the Architectural Barriers Act (42 U.S.C. 4151-4157), as established in 41 CFR 101-19.600 to 101-19.607, apply to buildings covered by this section.

[¶ 15,721N-52]
§§ 4907.152-4907.159 **[Reserved.]**

[¶ 15,721N-60]
§ 4907.160 **Communications**. (a) The agency shall take appropriate steps to ensure effective communication with applicants, participants, personnel of other Federal entities, and members of the public.

(1) The agency shall furnish appropriate auxiliary aids where necessary to afford a handicapped person an equal opportunity to participate in, and enjoy the benefits of, a program or activity conducted by the agency.

(i) In determining what type of auxiliary aid is necessary, the agency shall give primary consideration to the requests of the handicapped person.

(ii) The agency need not provide individually prescribed devices, readers for personal use or study, or other devices of a personal nature.

(2) Where the agency communicates with applicants and beneficiaries by telephone, telecommunication devices for deaf person (TDD's) or equally effective telecommunication systems shall be used.

(b) The agency shall ensure that interested persons, including persons with impaired vision or hearing, can obtain information as to the existence and location of accessible services, activities, and facilities.

(c) The agency shall provide signage at a primary entrance to each of its inaccessible facilities, directing users to a location at which they can obtain information about accessible facilities. The international symbol for accessibility shall be used at each primary entrance of an accessible facility.

(d) This section does not require the agency to take any action that it can demonstrate would result in a fundamental alteration in the nature of a program or activity or in undue financial and administrative burdens. In those circumstances where agency personnel believe that the proposed action would fundamentally alter the program or activity or would result in undue financial and administrative burdens, the agency has the burden of proving that compliance with §4907.160 would result in such alteration or burdens. The decision that compliance would result in such alteration or burdens must be made by the agency head or his or her designee after considering all agency resources available for use in the funding and operation of the conducted program or activity, and must be accompanied by a written statement of the reasons for reaching that conclusion. If an action required to comply with this section would result in such an alteration or such burdens, the agency shall take any other action that would not result in such an alteration or such burdens but would nevertheless ensure that, to the maximum extent possible, handicapped persons receive the benefits and services of the program or activity.

[¶ 15,721N-61]

§4907.161-§4907.169 **[Reserved.]**

[¶ 15,721N-70]

§4907.170 **Compliance procedures.** (a) Except as provided in paragraph (b) of this section, this section applies to all allegations of discrimination on the basis of handicap in programs or activities conducted by the agency.

(b) The agency shall process complaints alleging violations of section 504 with respect to employment according to the procedures established by the Equal Employment Opportunity Commission in 29 CFR part 1613 pursuant to section 501 of the Rehabilitation Act of 1973 (29 U.S.C. 791).

(c) The Equal Opportunity Manager shall be responsible for coordinating implementation of this section.

(1) *Where to file.* See Sec. 4000.4 of this chapter for information on where to file complaints under this part.

(2) *Method of filing.* The PBGC applies the rules in subpart A of part 4000 of this chapter to determine permissible methods of filing with the PBGC under this part.

(3) *Date of filing.* The PBGC applies the rules in subpart C of part 4000 of this chapter to determine the date that a submission under this part was filed with the PBGC.

(4) *Computation of time.* The PBGC applies the rules in subpart D of part 4000 of this chapter to compute any time period under this part.

[Amended 10/28/2003 by 68 FR 61344]

(d) The agency shall accept and investigate all complete complaints for which it has jurisdiction. All complete complaints must be filed within 180 days of the alleged act of discrimination. The agency may extend this time period for good cause.

(e) If the agency receives a complaint over which it does not have jurisdiction, it shall promptly notify the complainant and shall make reasonable efforts to refer the complaint to the appropriate government entity.

(f) The agency shall notify the Architectural and Transportation Barriers Compliance Board upon receipt of any complaint alleging that a building or facility that is subject to the Architectural Barriers Act of 1968, as amended (42 U.S.C. 4151-4157), or section 502 of the Rehabilitation Act of 1973, as amended (29 U.S.C. 792), is not readily accessible to and usable by handicapped persons.

(g) Within 180 days of the receipt of a complete complaint for which it has jurisdiction, the agency shall notify the complainant of the results of the investigation in a letter containing—

(1) Findings of fact and conclusions of law;

(2) A description of a remedy for each violation found; and

(3) A notice of the right to appeal.

(h) Appeals of the findings of fact and conclusions of law or remedies must be filed by the complainant within 90 days of receipt from the agency of the letter required by §4907.170(g). The agency may extend this time for good cause.

(i) Timely appeals shall be accepted and processed by the head of the agency.

(j) The head of the agency shall notify the complainant of the results of the appeal within 60 days of the receipt of the request. If the head of the agency determines that additional information is needed from the complainant, he or she shall have 60 days from the date of receipt of the additional information to make his or her determination on the appeal.

(k) The time limits cited in paragraphs (g) and (j) of this section may be extended with the permission of the Assistant Attorney General.

(l) The agency may delegate its authority for conducting complaint investigations to other Federal agencies, except that the authority for making the final determination may not be delegated to another agency.

[¶ 15,721N-71]

§§4907.171-4907.999 **[Reserved.]**

Economic Growth and Tax Relief Reconciliation Act of 2001

P.L. 107-16

Signed on June 7, 2001

[Reproduced below are sections of the Economic Growth and Tax Relief Reconciliation Act of 2001 which did not amend any sections of the Internal Revenue Code of 1986 or the Employee Retirement Income Security Act of 1974 (ERISA).]

[¶15,721R]

ACT SEC. 1. SHORT TITLE; REFERENCES; TABLE OF CONTENTS.

(a) SHORT TITLE. This Act may be cited as the "Economic Growth and Tax Relief Reconciliation Act of 2001".

(b) AMENDMENT OF 1986 CODE. Except as otherwise expressly provided, whenever in this Act an amendment or repeal is expressed in terms of an amendment to, or repeal of, a section or other provision, the reference shall be considered to be made to a section or other provision of the Internal Revenue Code of 1986.

* * *

[¶15,721R-1]

ACT SEC. 620. ELIMINATION OF USER FEE FOR REQUESTS TO IRS REGARDING PENSION PLANS.

(a) ELIMINATION OF CERTAIN USER FEES. The Secretary of the Treasury or the Secretary's delegate shall not require payment of user fees under the program established under section 10511 of the Revenue Act of 1987 for requests to the Internal Revenue Service for determination letters with respect to the qualified status of a pension benefit plan maintained solely by one or more eligible employers or any trust which is part of the plan. The preceding sentence shall not apply to any request—

    (1) made after the later of—

        (A) the fifth plan year the pension benefit plan is in existence; or

        (B) the end of any remedial amendment period with respect to the plan beginning within the first 5 plan years; or

    (2) made by the sponsor of any prototype or similar plan which the sponsor intends to market to participating employers.

(b) PENSION BENEFIT PLAN. For purposes of this section, the term "pension benefit plan" means a pension, profit-sharing, stock bonus, annuity, or employee stock ownership plan.

(c) ELIGIBLE EMPLOYER. For purposes of this section, the term "eligible employer" means an eligible employer (as defined in section 408(p)(2)(C)(i)(I) of the Internal Revenue Code of 1986) which has at least one employee who is not a highly compensated employee (as defined in section 414(q)) and is participating in the plan. The determination of whether an employer is an eligible employer under this section shall be made as of the date of the request described in subsection (a).

(d) DETERMINATION OF AVERAGE FEES CHARGED. For purposes of any determination of average fees charged, any request to which subsection (a) applies shall not be taken into account.

(e) EFFECTIVE DATE. The provisions of this section shall apply with respect to requests made after December 31, 2001.

* * *

[¶15,721R-2]

ACT SEC. 634. MODIFICATION TO MINIMUM DISTRIBUTION RULES.

The Secretary of the Treasury shall modify the life expectancy tables under the regulations relating to minimum distribution requirements under sections 401(a)(9), 408(a)(6) and (b)(3), 403(b)(10), and 457(d)(2) of the Internal Revenue Code to reflect current life expectancy.

* * *

[¶15,721R-3]

ACT SEC. 636. PROVISIONS RELATING TO HARDSHIP DISTRIBUTIONS.

(a) SAFE HARBOR RELIEF.—

    (1) IN GENERAL. The Secretary of the Treasury shall revise the regulations relating to hardship distributions under section 401(k)(2)(B)(i)(IV) of the Internal Revenue Code of 1986 to provide that the period an employee is prohibited from making elective and employee contributions in order for a distribution to be deemed necessary to satisfy financial need shall be equal to 6 months.

    (2) EFFECTIVE DATE. The revised regulations under this subsection shall apply to years beginning after December 31, 2001.

* * *

Subtitle D—Increasing Portability for Participants

* * *

[¶15,721R-4]

ACT SEC. 645. TREATMENT OF FORMS OF DISTRIBUTION.

* * *

(b) REGULATIONS.—

* * *

(3) SECRETARY DIRECTED. Not later than December 31, 2003, the Secretary of the Treasury is directed to issue regulations under section 411(d)(6) of the Internal Revenue Code of 1986 and section 204(g) of the Employee Retirement Income Security Act of 1974, including the regulations required by the amendment made by this subsection. Such regulations shall apply to plan years beginning after December 31, 2003, or such earlier date as is specified by the Secretary of the Treasury.

* * *

Subtitle E—Strengthening Pension Security and Enforcement

PART I—GENERAL PROVISIONS

* * *

[¶ 15,721R-5]

ACT SEC. 655. PROTECTION OF INVESTMENT OF EMPLOYEE CONTRIBUTIONS TO 401(k) PLANS.

(a) IN GENERAL. Section 1524(b) of the Taxpayer Relief Act of 1997 is amended to read as follows:

"(b) EFFECTIVE DATE.—

"(1) IN GENERAL. Except as provided in paragraph (2), the amendments made by this section shall apply to elective deferrals for plan years beginning after December 31, 1998.

"(2) NONAPPLICATION TO PREVIOUSLY ACQUIRED PROPERTY. The amendments made by this section shall not apply to any elective deferral which is invested in assets consisting of qualifying employer securities, qualifying employer real property, or both, if such assets were acquired before January 1, 1999.".

• • *TAXPAYER RELIEF ACT OF 1997 ACT SEC. 1524(b) BEFORE AMENDMENT*——————————————————————

ACT SEC. 1524. DIVERSIFICATION OF SECTION 401(k) PLAN INVESTMENTS.

* * *

(b) EFFECTIVE DATE. The amendments made by this section shall apply to elective deferrals for plan years beginning after December 31, 1998.

(b) EFFECTIVE DATE. The amendment made by this section shall apply as if included in the provision of the Taxpayer Relief Act of 1997 to which it relates.

* * *

[¶ 15,721R-6]

ACT SEC. 657. AUTOMATIC ROLLOVERS OF CERTAIN MANDATORY DISTRIBUTIONS.

* * *

(c) FIDUCIARY RULES.—

* * *

(2) REGULATIONS.—

(A) AUTOMATIC ROLLOVER SAFE HARBOR. Not later than 3 years after the date of enactment of this Act, the Secretary of Labor shall prescribe regulations providing for safe harbors under which the designation of an institution and investment of funds in accordance with section 401(a)(31)(B) of the Internal Revenue Code of 1986 is deemed to satisfy the fiduciary requirements of section 404(a) of the Employee Retirement Income Security Act of 1974 (29 U.S.C. 1104(a)).

(B) USE OF LOW-COST INDIVIDUAL RETIREMENT PLANS. The Secretary of the Treasury and the Secretary of Labor may provide, and shall give consideration to providing, special relief with respect to the use of low-cost individual retirement plans for purposes of transfers under section 401(a)(31)(B) of the Internal Revenue Code of 1986 and for other uses that promote the preservation of assets for retirement income purposes.

* * *

[¶ 15,721R-7]

ACT SEC. 658. CLARIFICATION OF TREATMENT OF CONTRIBUTIONS TO MULTIEMPLOYER PLAN.

(a) NOT CONSIDERED METHOD OF ACCOUNTING. For purposes of section 446 of the Internal Revenue Code of 1986, a determination under section 404(a)(6) of such Code regarding the taxable year with respect to which a contribution to a multiemployer pension plan is deemed made shall not be treated as a method of accounting of the taxpayer. No deduction shall be allowed for any taxable year for any contribution to a multiemployer pension plan with respect to which a deduction was previously allowed.

(b) REGULATIONS. The Secretary of the Treasury shall promulgate such regulations as necessary to clarify that a taxpayer shall not be allowed an aggregate amount of deductions for contributions to a multiemployer pension plan which exceeds the amount of such contributions made or deemed made under section 404(a)(6) of the Internal Revenue Code of 1986 to such plan.

(c) EFFECTIVE DATE. Subsection (a), and any regulations promulgated under subsection (b), shall be effective for years ending after the date of the enactment of this Act.

* * *

[¶15,721R-8]

ACT SEC. 663. REPEAL OF TRANSITION RULE RELATING TO CERTAIN HIGHLY COMPENSATED EMPLOYEES.

(a) IN GENERAL. Paragraph (4) of section 1114(c) of the Tax Reform Act of 1986 is hereby repealed.

• • *TAX REFORM ACT OF 1986 ACT SEC. 1114(c)(4) BEFORE REPEAL*————————————————————————

ACT SEC. 1114. DEFENITION OF HIGHLY COMPENSATED EMPLOYEE.

* * *

(c) EFFECTIVE DATE.—

* * *

(4) SPECIAL RULE FOR DETERMINING HIGHLY COMPENSATED EMPLOYEES. For purposes of sections 401(k) and 401(m) of the Internal Revenue Code of 1986, in the case of an employer incorporated on December 15, 1924, if more than 50 percent of its employees in the top-paid group (within the meaning of section 414(q)(4) of such Code) earn less than $25,000 (indexed at the same time and in the same manner as under section 415(d) of such Code), then the highly compensated employees shall include employees described in section 414(q)(1)(C) of such Code determined without regard to the level of compensation of such employees.

(b) EFFECTIVE DATE. The repeal made by subsection (a) shall apply to plan years beginning after December 31, 2001.

[¶15,721R-9]

ACT SEC. 664. EMPLOYEES OF TAX-EXEMPT ENTITIES.

(a) IN GENERAL. The Secretary of the Treasury shall modify Treasury Regulations section 1.410(b)-6(g) to provide that employees of an organization described in section 403(b)(1)(A)(i) of the Internal Revenue Code of 1986 who are eligible to make contributions under section 403(b) of such Code pursuant to a salary reduction agreement may be treated as excludable with respect to a plan under section 401(k) or (m) of such Code that is provided under the same general arrangement as a plan under such section 401(k), if—

(1) no employee of an organization described in section 403(b)(1)(A)(i) of such Code is eligible to participate in such section 401(k) plan or section 401(m) plan; and

(2) 95 percent of the employees who are not employees of an organization described in section 403(b)(1)(A)(i) of such Code are eligible to participate in such plan under such section 401(k) or (m).

(b) EFFECTIVE DATE. The modification required by subsection (a) shall apply as of the same date set forth in section 1426(b) of the Small Business Job Protection Act of 1996.

TITLE IX—COMPLIANCE WITH CONGRESSIONAL BUDGET ACT

[¶15,721R-10]

ACT SEC. 901. SUNSET OF PROVISIONS OF ACT.

(a) IN GENERAL. All provisions of, and amendments made by, this Act shall not apply—

(1) to taxable, plan, or limitation years beginning after December 31, 2012, or

(2) in the case of title V, to estates of decedents dying, gifts made, or generation skipping transfers, after December 31, 2012.

(b) APPLICATION OF CERTAIN LAWS. The Internal Revenue Code of 1986 and the Employee Retirement Income Security Act of 1974 shall be applied and administered to years, estates, gifts, and transfers described in subsection (a) as if the provisions and amendments described in subsection (a) had never been enacted.

Amendments

P.L. 111-312, §101(a):

Amended Section 901 of the Economic Growth and Tax Relief Reconciliation Act of 2001 by striking "December 31, 2010" both places it appears and inserting "December 31, 2012."

The above amendment shall take effect as if included in the enactment of the Economic Growth and Tax Relief Reconciliation Act of 2001.

Age Discrimination in Employment Act of 1967, As Amended

(Act of December 6, 1967, P.L. 90-202, 81 Stat. 609, 29 U.S.C., 1964 Ed., Supplement IV, Chapter 14, Sections 621-634, effective June 12, 1968, as amended by P.L. 93-259, effective May 1, 1974, and as further amended by P.L. 95-256, effective January 1, 1979; by P.L. 97-248, effective January 1, 1983; by P.L. 98-459, effective October 9, 1984; by P.L. 99-509, effective January 1, 1988; by P.L. 99-592, effective January 1, 1987; by P.L. 101-239, effective December 19, 1989; by P.L. 101-433, effective November 5, 1990; by P.L. 101-521, effective November 5, 1990; and by P.L. 102-166, effective November 21, 1991.)

[¶15,731]

SEC. 1. TITLE OF ACT.

This Act may be cited as the "Age Discrimination in Employment Act of 1967."

[¶15,732]

SEC. 2. STATEMENT OF FINDINGS AND PURPOSE.

(a) The Congress hereby finds and declares that—

(1) in the face of rising productivity and affluence, older workers find themselves disadvantaged in their efforts to retain employment, and especially to regain employment when displaced from jobs;

(2) the setting of arbitrary age limits regardless of potential for job performance has become a common practice, and certain otherwise desirable practices may work to the disadvantage of older persons;

(3) the incidence of unemployment, especially long-term unemployment with resultant deterioration of skill, morale, and employer acceptability is, relative to the younger ages, high among older workers; their numbers are great and growing; and their employment problems grave;

(4) the existence in industries affecting commerce of arbitrary discrimination in employment because of age burdens commerce and the free flow of goods in commerce.

(b) It is therefore the purpose of this chapter to promote employment of older persons based on their ability rather than age; to prohibit arbitrary age discrimination in employment; to help employers and workers find ways of meeting problems arising from the impact of age on employment.

[¶15,733]

SEC. 3. EDUCATION AND RESEARCH PROGRAM.

(a) The Secretary of Labor shall undertake studies and provide information to labor unions, management, and the general public concerning the needs and abilities of older workers, and their potentials for continued employment and contribution to the economy. In order to achieve the purposes of this chapter, the Secretary of Labor shall carry on a continuing program of education and information, under which he may, among other measures—

(1) undertake research, and promote research, with a view to reducing barriers to the employment of older persons, and the promotion of measures for utilizing their skills;

(2) publish and otherwise make available to employers, professional societies, the various media of communication, and other interested persons the findings of studies and other materials for the promotion of employment;

(3) foster through the public employment service system and through cooperative effort the development of facilities of public and private agencies for expanding the opportunities and potentials of older persons;

(4) sponsor and assist State and community informational and educational programs.

(b) Not later than six months after the effective date of this chapter, the Secretary shall recommend to the Congress any measures he may deem desirable to change the lower or upper age limits set forth in section 12.

[¶15,734]

SEC. 4. PROHIBITION OF AGE DISCRIMINATION.

(a) It shall be unlawful for an employer—

(1) to fail or refuse to hire or to discharge any individual or otherwise discriminate against any individual with respect to his compensation, terms, conditions, or privileges of employment, because of such individual's age;

(2) to limit, segregate, or classify his employees in any way which would deprive or tend to deprive any individual of employment opportunities or otherwise adversely affect his status as an employee, because of such individual's age; or

(3) to reduce the wage rate of any employee in order to comply with this chapter.

(b) It shall be unlawful for an employment agency to fail or refuse to refer for employment, or otherwise to discriminate against, any individual because of such individual's age, or to classify or refer for employment any individual on the basis of such individual's age.

(c) It shall be unlawful for a labor organization—

(1) to exclude or to expel from its membership, or otherwise to discriminate against, any individual because of his age;

(2) to limit, segregate, or classify its membership, or to classify or fail or refuse to refer for employment any individual, in any way which would deprive or tend to deprive any individual of employment opportunities, or would limit such employment opportunities or otherwise adversely affect his status as an employee or as an applicant for employment, because of such individual's age;

(3) to cause or attempt to cause an employer to discriminate against an individual in violation of this section.

(d) It shall be unlawful for an employer to discriminate against any of his employees or applicants for employment, for an employment agency to discriminate against any individual, or for a labor organization to discriminate against any member thereof or applicant for membership, because such individual, member or applicant for membership has opposed any practice made unlawful by this section, or because such individual, member, or applicant for membership has made a charge, testified, assisted, or participated in any manner in an investigation, proceeding, or litigation under this chapter.

(e) It shall be unlawful for an employer, labor organization, or employment agency to print or publish, or cause to be printed or published, any notice or advertisement relating to employment by such an employer or membership in or any classification or referral for employment by such a labor organization, or relating to any classification or referral for employment by such an employment agency, indicating any preference, limitation, specification, or discrimination, based on age.

(f) It shall not be unlawful for an employer, employment agency, or labor organization—

(1) to take any action otherwise prohibited under subsections (a), (b), (c), or (e) of this section where age is a bona fide occupational qualification reasonably necessary to the normal operation of the particular business, or where the differentiation is based on reasonable factors other than age, or where

such practices involve an employee in a workplace in a foreign country, and compliance with such subsections would cause such employer, or a corporation controlled by such employer, to violate the laws of the country in which such workplace is located.

(2) to take any action otherwise prohibited under subsection (a), (b), (c), or (e) of this section—

(A) to observe the terms of a bona fide seniority system that is not intended to evade the purposes of this chapter, except that no such seniority system shall require or permit the involuntary retirement of any individual specified by section 12(a) because of the age of such individual; or

(B) to observe the terms of a bona fide employee benefit plan—

(i) where, for each benefit or benefit package, the actual amount of payment made or cost incurred on behalf of an older worker is no less than that made or incurred on behalf of a younger worker, as permissible under section 1625.10, title 29, Code of Federal Regulations (as in effect on June 22, 1989); or

(ii) that is a voluntary early retirement incentive plan consistent with the relevant purpose or purposes of this chapter.

Notwithstanding clause (i) or (ii) of subparagraph (B), no such employee benefit plan or voluntary early retirement incentive plan shall excuse the failure to hire any individual, and no such employee benefit plan shall require or permit the involuntary retirement of any individual specified by section 12(a), because of the age of such individual. An employer, employment agency, or labor organization acting under subparagraph (A), or under clause (i) or (ii) of subparagraph (B), shall have the burden of proving that such actions are lawful in any civil enforcement proceeding brought under this chapter; or

(3) to discharge or otherwise discipline an individual for good cause.

(g) [Repealed]

(h)(1) If an employer controls a corporation whose place of incorporation is in a foreign country, any practice by such corporation prohibited under this section shall be presumed to be such practice by such employer.

(2) The prohibitions of this section shall not apply where the employer is a foreign person not controlled by an American employer.

(3) For the purpose of this subsection the determination of whether an employer controls a corporation shall be based upon the—

(A) interrelation of operations,

(B) common management,

(C) centralized control of labor relations, and

(D) common ownership or financial control,

of the employer and the corporation.

(i)(1) Except as otherwise provided in this subsection, it shall be unlawful for an employer, an employment agency, a labor organization, or any combination thereof to establish or maintain an employee pension benefit plan which requires or permits—

(A) in the case of a defined benefit plan, the cessation of an employee's benefit accrual, or the reduction of the rate of an employee's benefit accrual, because of age, or

(B) in the case of a defined contribution plan, the cessation of allocations to an employee's account, or the reduction of the rate at which amounts are allocated to an employee's account, because of age.

(2) Nothing in this section shall be construed to prohibit an employer, employment agency, or labor organization from observing any provision of an employee pension benefit plan to the extent that such provision imposes (without regard to age) a limitation on the amount of benefits that the plan provides or a limitation on the number of years of service or years of participation which are taken into account for purposes of determining benefit accrual under the plan.

(3) In the case of any employee who, as of the end of any plan year under a defined benefit plan, has attained normal retirement age under such plan—

(A) if distribution of benefits under such plan with respect to such employee has commenced as of the end of such plan year, then any requirement of this subsection for continued accrual of benefits under such plan with respect to such employee during such plan year shall be treated as satisfied to the extent of the actuarial equivalent of in-service distribution of benefits, and

(B) if distribution of benefits under such plan with respect to such employee has not commenced as of the end of such year in accordance with section 206(a)(3) of the Employee Retirement Income Security Act of 1974 and section 401(a)(14)(C) of the Internal Revenue Code of 1986, and the payment of benefits under such plan with respect to such employee is not suspended during such plan year pursuant to section 203(a)(3)(B) of the Employee Retirement Income Security Act of 1974 or section 411(a)(3)(B) of the Internal Revenue Code of 1986, then any requirement of this subsection for continued accrual of benefits under such plan with respect to such employee during such plan year shall be treated as satisfied to the extent of any adjustment in the benefit payable under the plan during such plan year attributable to the delay in the distribution of benefits after the attainment of normal retirement age.

The provisions of this paragraph shall apply in accordance with regulations of the Secretary of the Treasury. Such regulations shall provide for the application of the preceding provisions of this paragraph to all employee pension benefit plans subject to this subsection and may provide for the application of such provisions, in the case of any such employee, with respect to any period of time within a plan year.

(4) Compliance with the requirements of this subsection with respect to an employee pension benefit plan shall constitute compliance with the requirements of this section relating to benefit accrual under such plan.

(5) Paragraph (1) shall not apply with respect to any employee who is a highly compensated employee (within the meaning of section 414(q) of the Internal Revenue Code of 1986) to the extent provided in regulations prescribed by the Secretary of the Treasury for purposes of precluding discrimination in favor of highly compensated employees within the meaning of subchapter D of chapter 1 of the Internal Revenue Code of 1986.

(6) A plan shall not be treated as failing to meet the requirements of paragraph (1) solely because the subsidized portion of any early retirement benefit is disregarded in determining benefit accruals or it is a plan permitted by subsection (m) of this section.

(7) Any regulations prescribed by the Secretary of the Treasury pursuant to clause (v) of section 411(b)(1)(H) of the Internal Revenue Code of 1986 and subparagraphs (C) and (D) of section 411(b)(2) of such Code shall apply with respect to the requirement of this subsection in the same manner and to the same extent as such regulations apply with respect to the requirements of such sections 411(b)(1)(H) and 411(b)(2).

(8) A plan shall not be treated as failing to meet the requirements of this section solely because such plan provides a normal retirement age described in section 3(24)(B) of the Employee Retirement Income Security Act of 1974 and section 411(a)(8)(B) of the Internal Revenue Code of 1986.

(9) For purposes of this subsection—

(A) The terms "employee pension benefit plan", "defined benefit plan", "defined contribution plan", and "normal retirement age" have the meanings provided such terms in section 3 of the Employee Retirement Income Security Act of 1974 (29 U.S.C. 1002).

(B) The term "compensation" has the meaning provided by section 414(s) of the Internal Revenue Code of 1986.

(10) SPECIAL RULES RELATING TO AGE.—

    (A) COMPARISON TO SIMILARLY SITUATED YOUNGER INDIVIDUAL.—

        (i) IN GENERAL. —A plan shall not be treated as failing to meet the requirements of paragraph (1) if a participant's accrued benefit, as determined as of any date under the terms of the plan, would be equal to or greater than that of any similarly situated, younger individual who is or could be a participant.

        (ii) SIMILARLY SITUATED. —For purposes of this subparagraph, a participant is similarly situated to any other individual if such participant is identical to such other individual in every respect (including period of service, compensation, position, date of hire, work history, and any other respect) except for age.

        (iii) DISREGARD OF SUBSIDIZED EARLY RETIREMENT BENEFITS. —In determining the accrued benefit as of any date for purposes of this clause, the subsidized portion of any early retirement benefit or retirement-type subsidy shall be disregarded.

        (iv) ACCRUED BENEFIT. —For purposes of this subparagraph, the accrued benefit may, under the terms of the plan, be expressed as an annuity payable at normal retirement age, the balance of a hypothetical account, or the current value of the accumulated percentage of the employee's final average compensation.

    (B) APPLICABLE DEFINED BENEFIT PLANS.—

        (i) INTEREST CREDITS.—

            (I) IN GENERAL. —An applicable defined benefit plan shall be treated as failing to meet the requirements of paragraph (1) unless the terms of the plan provide that any interest credit (or an equivalent amount) for any plan year shall be at a rate which is not greater than a market rate of return. A plan shall not be treated as failing to meet the requirements of this subclause merely because the plan provides for a reasonable minimum guaranteed rate of return or for a rate of return that is equal to the greater of a fixed or variable rate of return.

            (II) PRESERVATION OF CAPITAL. —An interest credit (or an equivalent amount) of less than zero shall in no event result in the account balance or similar amount being less than the aggregate amount of contributions credited to the account.

            (III) MARKET RATE OF RETURN. —The Secretary of the Treasury may provide by regulation for rules governing the calculation of a market rate of return for purposes of subclause (I) and for permissible methods of crediting interest to the account (including fixed or variable interest rates) resulting in effective rates of return meeting the requirements of subclause (I). In the case of a governmental plan (as defined in the first sentence of section 414(d) of the Internal Revenue Code of 1986), a rate of return or a method of crediting interest established pursuant to any provision of Federal, State, or local law (including any administrative rule or policy adopted in accordance with any such law) shall be treated as a market rate of return for purposes of subclause (I) and a permissible method of crediting interest for purposes of meeting the requirements of subclause (I), except that this sentence shall only apply to a rate of return or method of crediting interest if such rate or method does not violate any other requirement of this Act.

        (ii) SPECIAL RULE FOR PLAN CONVERSIONS. —If, after June 29, 2005, an applicable plan amendment is adopted, the plan shall be treated as failing to meet the requirements of paragraph (1)(H) unless the requirements of clause (iii) are met with respect to each individual who was a participant in the plan immediately before the adoption of the amendment.

        (iii) RATE OF BENEFIT ACCRUAL. —Subject to clause (iv), the requirements of this clause are met with respect to any participant if the accrued benefit of the participant under the terms of the plan as in effect after the amendment is not less than the sum of—

            (I) the participant's accrued benefit for years of service before the effective date of the amendment, determined under the terms of the plan as in effect before the amendment, plus

            (II) the participant's accrued benefit for years of service after the effective date of the amendment, determined under the terms of the plan as in effect after the amendment.

        (iv) SPECIAL RULES FOR EARLY RETIREMENT SUBSIDIES. —For purposes of clause (iii)(I), the plan shall credit the accumulation account or similar amount with the amount of any early retirement benefit or retirement-type subsidy for the plan year in which the participant retires if, as of such time, the participant has met the age, years of service, and other requirements under the plan for entitlement to such benefit or subsidy.

        (v) APPLICABLE PLAN AMENDMENT. —For purposes of this subparagraph—

            (I) IN GENERAL. —The term 'applicable plan amendment' means an amendment to a defined benefit plan which has the effect of converting the plan to an applicable defined benefit plan.

            (II) SPECIAL RULE FOR COORDINATED BENEFITS. —If the benefits of 2 or more defined benefit plans established or maintained by an employer are coordinated in such a manner as to have the effect of the adoption of an amendment described in subclause (I), the sponsor of the defined benefit plan or plans providing for such coordination shall be treated as having adopted such a plan amendment as of the date such coordination begins.

            (III) MULTIPLE AMENDMENTS. —The Secretary of the Treasury shall issue regulations to prevent the avoidance of the purposes of this subparagraph through the use of 2 or more plan amendments rather than a single amendment.

            (IV) APPLICABLE DEFINED BENEFIT PLAN. —For purposes of this subparagraph, the term 'applicable defined benefit plan' has the meaning given such term by section 203(f)(3) of the Employee Retirement Income Security Act of 1974.

        (vi) TERMINATION REQUIREMENTS. —An applicable defined benefit plan shall not be treated as meeting the requirements of clause (i) unless the plan provides that, upon the termination of the plan—

            (I) if the interest credit rate (or an equivalent amount) under the plan is a variable rate, the rate of interest used to determine accrued benefits under the plan shall be equal to the average of the rates of interest used under the plan during the 5-year period ending on the termination date, and

(II) the interest rate and mortality table used to determine the amount of any benefit under the plan payable in the form of an annuity payable at normal retirement age shall be the rate and table specified under the plan for such purpose as of the termination date, except that if such interest rate is a variable rate, the interest rate shall be determined under the rules of subclause (I).

(C) CERTAIN OFFSETS PERMITTED. —A plan shall not be treated as failing to meet the requirements of paragraph (1) solely because the plan provides offsets against benefits under the plan to the extent such offsets are allowable in applying the requirements of section 401(a) of the Internal Revenue Code of 1986.

(D) PERMITTED DISPARITIES IN PLAN CONTRIBUTIONS OR BENEFITS. —A plan shall not be treated as failing to meet the requirements of paragraph (1) solely because the plan provides a disparity in contributions or benefits with respect to which the requirements of section 401(l) of the Internal Revenue Code of 1986 are met.

(E) INDEXING PERMITTED.—

(i) IN GENERAL. —A plan shall not be treated as failing to meet the requirements of paragraph (1) solely because the plan provides for indexing of accrued benefits under the plan.

(ii) PROTECTION AGAINST LOSS. —Except in the case of any benefit provided in the form of a variable annuity, clause (i) shall not apply with respect to any indexing which results in an accrued benefit less than the accrued benefit determined without regard to such indexing.

(iii) INDEXING. —For purposes of this subparagraph, the term 'indexing' means, in connection with an accrued benefit, the periodic adjustment of the accrued benefit by means of the application of a recognized investment index or methodology.

(F) EARLY RETIREMENT BENEFIT OR RETIREMENT-TYPE SUBSIDY. —For purposes of this paragraph, the terms 'early retirement benefit' and 'retirement-type subsidy' have the meaning given such terms in section 203(g)(2)(A) of the Employee Retirement Income Security Act of 1974.

(G) BENEFIT ACCRUED TO DATE. —For purposes of this paragraph, any reference to the accrued benefit shall be a reference to such benefit accrued to date.

(j) It shall not be unlawful for an employer which is a State, a political subdivision of a State, an agency or instrumentality of a State or a political subdivision of a State, or an interstate agency to fail or refuse to hire or to discharge any individual because of such individual's age if such action is taken—

(1) with respect to the employment of an individual as a firefighter or as a law enforcement officer, the employer has complied with section 3(d)(2) of the Age Discrimination in Employment Amendments of 1996 if the individual was discharged after the date described in such section, and the individual has attained—

(A) the age of hiring or retirement, respectively, in effect under applicable State or local law on March 3, 1983, or

(B)(i) if the individual was not hired, the age of hiring in effect on the date of such failure or refusal to hire under applicable State or local law after September 30, 1996 [the date of enactment of the Age Discrimination in Employment Amendments of 1996]; or

(ii) if applicable State or local law was enacted after September 30, 1996 [the date of enactment of the Age Discrimination in Employment Amendments of 1996], and the individual was discharged, the higher of—

(I) the age of retirement in effect on the date of such discharge under such law; and

(II) age 55; and

(2) pursuant to a bona fide hiring or retirement plan that is not a subterfuge to evade the purposes of this chapter.

(k) A seniority system or employee benefit plan shall comply with this Act regardless of the date of adoption of such system or plan.

(l) Notwithstanding clause (i) or (ii) of subsection (f)(2)(B)—

(1)(A) It shall not be a violation of subsection (a), (b), (c), or (e) solely because—

(i) an employee pension benefit plan (as defined in section 3(2) of the Employee Retirement Income Security Act of 1974 (29 U.S.C. 1002(2))) provides for the attainment of a minimum age as a condition of eligibility for normal or early retirement benefits; or

(ii) a defined benefit plan (as defined in section 3(35) of such Act) provides for—

(I) payments that constitute the subsidized portion of an early retirement benefit; or

(II) social security supplements for plan participants that commence before the age and terminate at the age (specified by the plan) when participants are eligible to receive reduced or unreduced old-age insurance benefits under title II of the Social Security Act (42 U.S.C. 401 et seq.), and that do not exceed such old-age insurance benefits.

(B) A voluntary early retirement incentive plan that—

(i) is maintained by—

(I) a local educational agency (as defined in section 9101 of the Elementary and Secondary Education Act of 1965 (20 U.S.C. 7801), or

(II) an education association which principally represents employees of 1 or more agencies described in subclause (I) and which is described in section 501(c) (5) or (6) of the Internal Revenue Code of 1986 and exempt from taxation under section 501(a) of such Code, and

(ii) makes payments or supplements described in subclauses (I) and (II) of subparagraph (A)(ii) in coordination with a defined benefit plan (as so defined) maintained by an eligible employer described in section 457(e)(1)(A) of such Code or by an education association described in clause (i)(II),

shall be treated solely for purposes of subparagraph (A)(ii) as if it were a part of the defined benefit plan with respect to such payments or supplements. Payments or supplements under such a voluntary early retirement incentive plan shall not constitute severance pay for purposes of paragraph (2).

(2)(A) It shall not be a violation of subsection (a), (b), (c) or (e) solely because following a contingent event unrelated to age—

(i) the value of any retiree health benefits received by an individual eligible for an immediate pension;

(ii) the value of any additional pension benefits that are made available solely as a result of the contingent event unrelated to age and following which the individual is eligible for not less than an immediate and unreduced pension; or

(iii) the values described in both clauses (i) and (ii)

are deducted from severance pay made available as a result of the contingent event unrelated to age.

(B) For an individual who receives immediate pension benefits that are actuarially reduced under subparagraph (A)(i), the amount of the deduction available pursuant to subparagraph (A)(i) shall be reduced by the same percentage as the reduction in the pension benefits.

(C) For purposes of this paragraph, severance pay shall include that portion of supplemental unemployment compensation benefits (as described in section 501(c)(17) of the Internal Revenue Code of 1986) that—

(i) constitutes additional benefits of up to 52 weeks;

(ii) has the primary purpose and effect of continuing benefits until an individual becomes eligible for an immediate and unreduced pension; and

(iii) is discontinued once the individual becomes eligible for an immediate and unreduced pension.

(D) For purposes of this paragraph and solely in order to make the deduction authorized under this paragraph, the term "retiree health benefits" means benefits provided pursuant to a group health plan covering retirees, for which (determined as of the contingent event unrelated to age)—

(i) the package of benefits provided by the employer for the retirees who are below age 65 is at least comparable to benefits provided under title XVIII of the Social Security Act (42 U.S.C. 1395 et seq.);

(ii) the package of benefits provided by the employer for the retirees who are age 65 and above is at least comparable to that offered under a plan that provides a benefit package with one-fourth the value of benefits provided under title XVIII of such Act

(iii) the package of benefits provided by the employer is as described in clauses (i) and (ii).

(E)(i) If the obligation of the employer to provide retiree health benefits is of limited duration, the value for each individual shall be calculated at a rate of $3,000 per year for benefit years before age 65, and $750 per year for benefit years beginning at age 65 and above.

(ii) If the obligation of the employer to provide retiree health benefits is of unlimited duration, the value for each individual shall be calculated at a rate of $48,000 for individuals below age 65, and $24,000 for individuals age 65 and above.

(iii) The values described in clauses (i) and (ii) shall be calculated based on the age of the individual as of the date of the contingent event unrelated to age. The values are effective on the date of enactment of this subsection [October 16, 1990], and shall be adjusted on an annual basis, with respect to a contingent event that occurs subsequent to the first year after the date of enactment of this subsection [October 16, 1990], based on the medical component of the Consumer Price Index for all-urban consumers published by the Department of Labor.

(iv) If an individual is required to pay a premium for retiree health benefits, the value calculated pursuant to this subparagraph shall be reduced by whatever percentage of the overall premium the individual is required to pay.

(F) If an employer that has implemented a deduction pursuant to subparagraph (A) fails to fulfill the obligation described in subparagraph (E), any aggrieved individual may bring an action for specific performance of the obligation described in subparagraph (E). The relief shall be in addition to any other remedies provided under Federal or State law.

(3) It shall not be a violation of subsection (a), (b), (c), or (e) solely because an employer provides a bona fide employee benefit plan or plans under which long-term disability benefits received by a individual are reduced by any pension benefits (other than those attributable to employee contributions)—

(A) paid to the individual that the individual voluntarily elects to receive; or

(B) for which an individual who has attained the later of age 62 or normal retirement age is eligible.

(m) Notwithstanding subsection (f)(2)(B) of this section, it shall not be a violation of subsection (a), (b), (c), or (e) of this section solely because a plan of an institution of higher education (as defined in section 1001 of title 20) offers employees who are serving under a contract of unlimited tenure (or similar arrangement providing for unlimited tenure) supplemental benefits upon voluntary retirement that are reduced or eliminated on the basis of age, if—

(1) such institution does not implement with respect to such employees any age-based reduction or cessation of benefits that are not such supplemental benefits, except as permitted by other provisions of this Act;

(2) such supplemental benefits are in addition to any retirement or severance benefits which have been offered generally to employees serving under a contract of unlimited tenure (or similar arrangement providing for unlimited tenure), independent of any early retirement or exit-incentive plan, within the preceding 365 days; and

(3) any employee who attains the minimum age and satisfies all non-age-based conditions for receiving a benefit under the plan has an opportunity lasting not less than 180 days to elect to retire and to receive the maximum benefit that could then be elected by a younger but otherwise similarly situated employee, and the plan does not require retirement to occur sooner than 180 days after such election.

Amendments

P.L. 110-458, Act Sec. 123(a), amended ADEA Sec. 4(i)(10)(B)(i)(III) by adding the last sentence.

The above amendment is effective as if included in the provisions of the Pension Protection Act of 2006 to which such amendment relates [generally, periods beginning on or after June 29, 2005].

P.L. 109-280, §701(c) amended ADEA Sec. 4(i) to add paragraph (10) to read as above.

P.L. 109-280, §701(e) provides:

SEC. 701(e). EFFECTIVE DATE.—

(1) IN GENERAL.—

The amendments made by this section shall apply to periods beginning on or after June 29, 2005.

(2) PRESENT VALUE OF ACCRUED BENEFIT.—

The amendments made by subsections (a)(2) and (b)(2) shall apply to distributions made after the date of the enactment of this Act.

(3) VESTING AND INTEREST CREDIT REQUIREMENTS.—

In the case of a plan in existence on June 29, 2005, the requirements of clause (i) of section 411(b)(5)(B) of the Internal Revenue Code of 1986, clause (i) of section 204(b)(5)(B) of the Employee Retirement Income Security Act of 1974, and clause (i) of section 4(i)(10)(B) of the Age Discrimination in Employment Act of 1967 (as added by this Act) and the requirements of 203(f)(2) of the Employee Retirement Income Security Act of 1974 and section 411(a)(13)(B) of the Internal Revenue Code of 1986 (as so added) shall, for purposes of applying the amendments made by subsections (a) and (b), apply to years beginning after December 31, 2007, unless

the plan sponsor elects the application of such requirements for any period after June 29, 2005, and before the first year beginning after December 31, 2007.

(4) SPECIAL RULE FOR COLLECTIVELY BARGAINED PLANS.—

In the case of a plan maintained pursuant to 1 or more collective bargaining agreements between employee representatives and 1 or more employers ratified on or before the date of the enactment of this Act, the requirements described in paragraph (3) shall, for purposes of applying the amendments made by subsections (a) and (b), not apply to plan years beginning before—

(A) the earlier of

(i) the date on which the last of such collective bargaining agreements terminates (determined without regard to any extension thereof on or after such date of enactment), or

(ii) January 1, 2008, or

(B) January 1, 2010.

(5) CONVERSIONS.—

The requirements of clause (ii) of section 411(b)(5)(B) of the Internal Revenue Code of 1986, clause (ii) of section 204(b)(5)(B) of the Employee Retirement Income Security Act of 1974, and clause (ii) of section 4(i)(10)(B) of the Age Discrimination in Employment Act of 1967 (as added by this Act), shall apply to plan amendments adopted after, and taking effect after, June 29, 2005, except that the plan sponsor may elect to have such amendments apply to plan amendments adopted before, and taking effect after, such date.

P.L. 109-280, §1104(a)(2) amended ADEA Sec. 4(l)(1) by inserting "(A)" after "(1)", by redesignating subparagraphs (A) and (B) as clauses (i) and (ii), respectively, by redesignating clauses (i) and (ii) of subparagraph (B) (as in effect before the amendments made by subparagraph (B)) as subclauses (I) and (II), respectively, and by adding at the end subparagraph (B) to read as above.

P.L. 109-280, § 1104(d) provides:

ACT SEC. 1104(d). EFFECTIVE DATES.—

(1) IN GENERAL.—

The amendments made by this Act shall take effect on the date of the enactment of this Act (August 17, 2006).

* * *

(4) CONSTRUCTION.—

Nothing in the amendments made by this section shall alter or affect the construction of the Internal Revenue Code of 1986, the Employee Retirement Income Security Act of 1974, or the Age Discrimination in Employment Act of 1967 as applied to any plan, arrangement, or conduct to which such amendments do not apply.

P.L. 105-244, Act Sec. 941(b) amended ADEA Sec. 4(i)(6), by inserting "or it is a plan permitted by subsection (m)" following "benefit accruals".

P.L. 105-244, Act Sec. 941(a) amended ADEA Sec. 4(j)(1) to read as above.

P.L. 105-244, Act Sec. 941(a) added ADEA Sec. 4(m).

P.L. 101-521, Act Sec. (1) amended ADEA Sec. 4(1)(2)(A), as added by P.L. 101-433, by striking "and" at the end of clause (i), by striking the comma at the end of clause (ii) and inserting "; or" and by inserting new clause (iii) to read as above, effective November 5, 1990. See also Act Sec. 105, below.

P.L. 101-521, Act Sec. (2) amended ADEA Sec. 4(1)(2)(D), as added by P.L. 101-433, by inserting "and solely in order to make the deduction authorized under this paragraph" after "For purposes of this paragraph," by striking "and" at the end of clause (i), by striking the period at the end of clause (ii) and inserting "; or" and by inserting new clause (iii) to read as above, effective November 5, 1990. See also Act Sec. 105, below.

P.L. 101-433, Sec. 103(1) amended ADEA Sec. 4(f) by striking paragraph (2) and inserting new paragraph (2) to read as above, effective with respect to any employee benefits established or modified after October 16, 1990, and other conduct occurring after April 14, 1991. See also Act Sec. 105, below. Prior to amendment, paragraph (2) read as follows:

"(2) to observe the terms of a bona fide seniority system or any bona fide employee benefit plan such as a retirement, pension, or insurance plan, which is not a subterfuge to evade the purposes of this Act, except that no such employee benefit plan shall excuse the failure to hire any individual or permit the involuntary retirement of any individual specified by section 12(a) of this Act because of the age of such individual;"

P.L. 101-433, Sec. 103(2) redesignated ADEA Sec. 4(i) [the second (i)] as (j), effective with respect to any employee benefits established or modified after October 16, 1990, and other conduct occurring after April 14, 1991. See also Act Sec. 105, below.

P.L. 101-433, Sec. 103(3) amended ADEA Sec. 4 by adding new paragraph (k) to read as above, effective with respect to any employee benefits established or modified after October 16, 1990, and other conduct occurring after April 14, 1991. See also Act Sec. 105, below.

P.L. 101-433, Sec. 103(3) amended ADEA Sec. 4 by adding new paragraph (l) to read as above, effective with respect to any employee benefits established or modified after October 16, 1990, and other conduct occurring after April 14, 1991. See also Act Sec. 105, below.

P.L. 101-433, Act. Sec. 105 provides:

SEC. 105. EFFECTIVE DATE.—(a) IN GENERAL.—Except as otherwise provided in this section, this title and the amendments made by this title shall apply only to—

(1) any employee benefit established or modified on or after the date of enactment of this Act; and

(2) other conduct occurring more than 180 days after the date of enactment of this Act.

(b) COLLECTIVELY BARGAINED AGREEMENTS.—With respect to any employee benefits provided in accordance with a collective bargaining agreement—

(1) that is in effect as of the date of enactment of this Act;

(2) that terminates after such date of enactment;

(3) any provision of which was entered into by a labor organization (as defined by section 6(d)(4) of the Fair Labor Standards Act of 1938 (29 U.S.C. 206(d)(4))); and

(4) that contains any provision that would be superseded (in whole or part) by this title and the amendments made by this title, but for the operation of this section,

this title and the amendments made by this title shall not apply until the termination of such collective bargaining agreement or June 1, 1992, whichever occurs first.

(c) STATES AND POLITICAL SUBDIVISIONS.—

(1) IN GENERAL.—With respect to any employee benefits provided by an employer—

(A) that is a State or political subdivision of a State or any agency or instrumentality of a State or political subdivision of a State; and

(B) that maintained an employee benefit plan at any time between June 23, 1989, and the date of enactment of this Act that would be superseded (in whole or part) by this title and the amendments made by this title but for the operation of this subsection, and which plan may be modified only through a change in applicable State or local law,

this title and the amendments made by this title shall not apply until the date that is 2 years after the date of enactment of this Act.

(2) ELECTION OF DISABILITY COVERAGE FOR EMPLOYEES HIRED PRIOR TO EFFECTIVE DATE.—

(A) IN GENERAL.—An employer that maintains a plan described in paragraph (1)(B) may, with regard to disability benefits provided pursuant to such a plan—

(i) following reasonable notice to all employees, implement new disability benefits that satisfy the requirements of the Age Discrimination in Employment Act of 1967 (as amended by this title); and

(ii) then offer to each employee covered by a plan described in paragraph (1)(B) the option to elect such new disability benefits in lieu of the existing disability benefits, if—

(I) the offer is made and reasonable notice provided no later than the date that is 2 years after the date of enactment of this Act; and

(II) the employee is given up to 180 days after the offer in which to make the election.

(B) PREVIOUS DISABILITY BENEFITS.—If the employee does not elect to be covered by the new disability benefits, the employer may continue to cover the employee under the previous disability benefits even though such previous benefits do not otherwise satisfy the requirements of the Age Discrimination in Employment Act of 1967 (as amended by this title).

(C) ABROGATION OF RIGHT TO RECEIVE BENEFITS.—An election of coverage under the new disability benefits shall abrogate any right the electing employee may have had to receive existing disability benefits. The employee shall maintain any years of service accumulated for purposes of determining eligibility for the new benefits.

(3) STATE ASSISTANCE.—The Equal Employment Opportunity Commission, the Secretary of Labor, and the Secretary of the Treasury shall, on request, provide to States assistance in identifying and securing independent technical advice to assist in complying with this subsection.

(4) DEFINITIONS.—For purposes of this subsection:

(A) EMPLOYER AND STATE.—The terms "employer" and "State" shall have the respective meanings provided such terms under subsections (b) and (i) of section 11 of the Age Discrimination in Employment Act of 1967 (29 U.S.C. 630).

(B) DISABILITY BENEFITS.—The term "disability benefits" means any program for employees of a State or political subdivision of a State that provides long-term disability benefits, whether on an insured basis in a separate employee benefit plan or as part of an employee pension benefit plan.

(C) REASONABLE NOTICE.—The term "reasonable notice" means, with respect to notice of new disability benefits described in paragraph (2)(A) that is given to each employee, notice that—

(i) is sufficiently accurate and comprehensive to appraise the employee of the terms and conditions of the disability benefits, including whether the employee is immediately eligible for such benefits; and

(ii) is written in a manner calculated to be understood by the average employee eligible to participate.

(d) DISCRIMINATION IN EMPLOYEE PENSION BENEFIT PLANS.—Nothing in this title, or the amendments made by this title, shall be construed as limiting the prohibitions against discrimination that are set forth in section 4(j) of the Age Discrimination in Employment Act of 1967 (as redesignated by section 103(2) of this Act).

(e) CONTINUED BENEFIT PAYMENTS.—Notwithstanding any other provision of this section, on and after the effective date of this title and the amendments made by this title (as determined in accordance with subsections (a), (b), and (c)), this title and the amendments made by this title shall not apply to a series of benefit payments made to an individual or the individual's representative that began prior to the effective date and that continue after the effective date pursuant to an arrangement that was in effect on the effective date, except that no substantial modification to such arrangement may be made after the date of enactment of this Act if the intent of the modification is to evade the purposes of this Act.

P.L. 101-239, § 6202(b)(3)(C) amended ADEA Sec. 4(g) by striking section 4(g) effective for items and services furnished after December 19, 1989.

P.L. 99-592, Sec. 2(a), amended ADEA Sec. 4(g)(1) by striking out "through 69" each place it appears and inserting in lieu thereof "or older." Sec. 2(b) amended ADEA Sec. 4(g) by striking out "(g)(1)" and inserting in lieu thereof "(h)(1)." It should be noted that these amendments had already been made by P.L. 99-272.

P.L. 99-592, Sec. 3(a), added ADEA Sec. 4(i). P.L. 99-509 also added an ADEA Sec. 4(i). ADEA Sec. 4(i), as added by P.L. 99-592, had been designated as Sec 4(i)[j]. Sec. 3(b) provides that the amendment made by Sec. 3(a), which adds the measure in Sec. 4(i)[j] concerning firefighters and law enforcement officers, is repealed December 31, 1993.

P.L. 99-592, Sec. 7, provides:

"SEC. 7. EFFECTIVE DATE; APPLICATION OF AMENDMENTS.—(a) IN GENERAL.—Except as provided in subsection (b), this Act and the amendments made by this Act shall take effect on January 1, 1987, except that with respect to any employee who is subject to a collective-bargaining agreement—

"(1) which is in effect on June 30, 1986,

"(2) which terminates after January 1, 1987,

"(3) any provision of which was entered into by a labor organization (as defined by section 6(d)(4) of the Fair Labor Standards Act of 1938 (29 U.S.C. 206(d)(4)), and

"(4) which contains any provision that would be superseded by such amendments, but for the operation of this section, such amendments shall not apply until the termination of such collective bargaining agreement or January 1, 1990, whichever occurs first.

"(b) EFFECT ON EXISTING CAUSES OF ACTION.—The amendments made by sections 3 and 4 of this Act shall not apply with respect to any cause of action arising under the Age Discrimination in Employment Act of 1967 as in effect before January 1, 1987."

P.L. 99-592, Sec. 5, provides:

"SEC. 5. STUDY AND PROPOSED GUIDELINES RELATING TO POLICE OFFICERS AND FIREFIGHTERS.—(a) STUDY.—Not later than 4 years after the date of enactment of this Act, the Secretary of Labor and the Equal Employment Opportunity Commission, jointly, shall—

"(1) conduct a study—

"(A) to determine whether physical and mental fitness tests are valid measurements of the ability and competency of police officers and firefighters to perform the requirements of their jobs,

"(B) if such tests are found to be valid measurements of such ability and competency, to determine which particular types of tests most effectively measure such ability and compentency, and

"(C) to develop recommendations with respect to specific standards that such tests, and the administration of such tests should satisfy, and

"(2) submit a report to the Speaker of the House of Representatives and the President pro tempore of the Senate that includes—

"(A) a description of the results of such study, and

"(B) a statement of the recommendations developed under paragraph (1)(C).

"(b) CONSULTATION REQUIREMENT.—The Secretary of Labor and the Equal Employment Opportunity Commission shall, during the conduct of the study required under subsection (a) and prior to the development of recommendations under paragraph (1)(C), consult with the United States Fire Administration, the Federal Emergency Management Agency, organizations representing law enforcement officers, firefighters, and their employers, and organizations representing older Americans.

"(c) PROPOSED GUIDELINES.—Not later than 5 years after the date of the enactment of this Act, the Equal Employment Opportunity Commission shall propose, in accordance with subchapter II of chapter 5 of title 5 of the United States Code, guidelines for the administration and use of physical and mental fitness tests to measure the ability and competency of police officers and firefighters to perform the requirements of their jobs."

P.L. 99-509, Sec. 9201, added ADEA Sec. 4(i). The relevant portion of Sec. 9204 of P.L. 99-509, concerning effective dates and regulations, provides as follows:

"SEC. 9204. EFFECTIVE DATE; REGULATIONS.—

"(a) APPLICABILITY TO EMPLOYEES WITH SERVICE AFTER 1988.—

"(1) IN GENERAL.—The amendments made by sections 9201 and 9202 shall apply only with respect to plan years beginning on or after January 1, 1988, and only to employees who have 1 hour of service in any plan year to which such amendments apply.

"(2) SPECIAL RULE FOR COLLECTIVELY BARGAINED PLANS.—In the case of a plan maintained pursuant to 1 or more collective bargaining agreements between employee representatives and 1 or more employers ratified before March 1, 1986, paragraph (1) shall be applied to benefits pursuant to, and individuals covered by, any such agreement by substituting for 'January 1, 1988' the date of the commencement of the first plan year beginning on or after the earlier of—

"(A) the later of—

"(i) January 1, 1988, or

"(ii) the date on which the last of such collective bargaining agreements terminates (determined without regard to any extension thereof after February 28, 1986), or

"(B) January 1, 1990.

* * *

"(c) PLAN AMENDMENTS.—If any amendment made by this subtitle requires an amendment to any plan, such plan amendment shall not be required to be made before the first plan year beginning on or after January 1, 1989, if—

"(1) during the period after such amendment takes effect and before such first plan year, the plan is operated in accordance with the requirements of such amendment, and

"(2) such plan amendment applies retroactively to the period after such amendment takes effect and such first plan year. A pension plan shall not be treated as failing to provide definitely determinable benefits or contributions, or to be operated in accordance with the provisions of the plan, merely because it operates in accordance with this subsection.

"(d) INTERAGENCY COORDINATION.—The regulations and rulings issued by the Secretary of Labor, the regulations and rulings issued by the Secretary of the Treasury, and the regulations and rulings issued by the Equal Employment Opportunity Commission pursuant to the amendments made by this subtitle shall each be consistent with the others. The Secretary of Labor, the Secretary of the Treasury, and the Equal Employment Opportunity Commission shall each consult with the other to the extent necessary to meet the requirements of the preceding sentence.

"(e) FINAL REGULATIONS.—The Secretary of Labor, the Secretary of the Treasury, and the Equal Employment Opportunity Commission shall each issue before February 1, 1988, such final regulations as may be necessary to carry out the amendments made by this subtitle."

P.L. 99-272, Sec. 9201(b)(1) amended ADEA Sec. 4(g)(1) by striking out "through 69" each place it appeared and inserting "or older" in its place. P.L. 99-272, Sec. 9201(b)(3) redesignated the second subsection (g), added by P.L. 98-459, Sec. 802(b)(2), as subsection (h).

P.L. 98-459, Sec. 802(b)(1) amended ADEA Sec. 4(f)(1) to read as above, effective October 9, 1984. Sec. 802(b)(2) added new ADEA Sec. 4(g) to read as above, effective October 9, 1984. Sec. 4(g) was later redesignated 4(h) by P.L. 99-272.

P.L. 98-369, Sec. 2301(b) amended Sec. 4(g), effective January 1, 1985, (1) by inserting ", and any employee's spouse aged 65 through 69," after "aged 65 through 69"; and (2) by inserting ", and the spouse of such employee," after "same conditions as any employee".

P.L. 97-248; Sec. 116(a), added Sec. 4(g), effective January 1, 1983.

Prior to amendment by P.L. 95-256, Sec. 4(f)(2) read as follows: "(2) to observe the terms of a bona fide seniority system or any bona fide employee benefit plan such as a retirement, pension, or insurance plan, which is not a subterfuge to evade the purposes of this Act, except that no such employee benefit plan shall excuse the failure to hire any individual; or".

.90 Committee Report on P.L. 109-280 (Pension Protection Act of 2006)

For the Committee Report on P.L. 109-280 on cash balance and other hybrid plans, see ¶ 12,200.035.

For the Committee Report on P.L. 109-280 on voluntary early retirement incentive and employment retention plans maintained by local educational agencies and other entities, see ¶ 13,153.018.

[¶15,735]

SEC. 5. STUDY BY SECRETARY OF LABOR.

(a)(1) The Secretary of Labor is directed to undertake an appropriate study of institutional and other arrangements giving rise to involuntary retirement, and report his findings and any appropriate legislative recommendations to the President and to the Congress. Such study shall include—

(A) an examination of the effect of the amendment made by section 3(a) of the Age Discrimination in Employment Act Amendments of 1978 in raising the upper age limitation established by section 12(a) of this Act to 70 years of age;

(B) a determination of the feasibility of eliminating such limitation;

(C) a determination of the feasibility of raising such limitation above 70 years of age; and

(D) an examination of the effect of the exemption contained in section 12(c), relating to certain executive employees, and the exemption contained in section 12(d), relating to tenured teaching personnel.

(2) The Secretary may undertake the study required by paragraph (1) of this subsection directly or by contract or other arrangement.

(b) The report required by subsection (a) of this section shall be transmitted to the President and to the Congress as an interim report not later than January 1, 1981, and in final form not later than January 1, 1982.

Amendments

Prior to amendment by P.L. 95-256, entire Sec. 5 read as follows: "Sec. 5. The Secretary of Labor is directed to undertake an appropriate study of institutional and other arrangements giving rise to involuntary retirement, and report his findings and any appropriate legislative recommendations to the President and to the Congress."

[¶15,736]

SEC. 6. ADMINISTRATION.

The Secretary shall have the power—

(a) to make delegations, to appoint such agents and employees, and to pay for technical assistance on a fee for service basis, as he deems necessary to assist him in the performance of his functions under this chapter;

(b) to cooperate with regional, State, local, and other agencies, and to cooperate with and furnish technical assistance to employers, labor organizations, and employment agencies to aid in effectuating the purposes of this chapter.

[¶15,737]

SEC. 7. RECORDKEEPING, INVESTIGATION AND ENFORCEMENT.

(a) The Equal Employment Opportunity Commission shall have the power to make investigations and require the keeping of records necessary or appropriate for the administration of this chapter in accordance with the powers and procedures provided in sections 9 and 11 of the Fair Labor Standards Act of 1938, as amended (29 U.S.C. 209 and 211).

(b) The provisions of this chapter shall be enforced in accordance with the powers, remedies, and procedures provided in section 11(b), 16 (except for subsection (a) thereof), and 17 of the Fair Labor Standards Act of 1938, as amended (29 U.S.C. 211(b), 216, 217), and subsection (c) of this section. Any act prohibited under section 4 of this Act shall be deemed to be a prohibited act under section 15 of the Fair Labor Standards Act of 1938, as amended (29 U.S.C. 215). Amounts owing to a person as a result of a violation of this chapter shall be deemed to be unpaid minimum wages or unpaid overtime compensation for purposes of sections 16 and 17 of the Fair Labor Standards Act of 1938, as amended (29 U.S.C. 216, 217): Provided, That liquidated damages shall be payable only in cases of willful violations of this chapter. In any action brought to enforce this Act the court shall have jurisdiction to grant such legal or equitable relief as may be appropriate to effectuate the purposes of this chapter, including without limitation judgments compelling employment, reinstatement or promotion, or enforcing the liability for amounts deemed to be unpaid minimum wages or unpaid overtime compensation under this section. Before instituting any action under this section, the Equal Employment Opportunity Commission shall attempt to eliminate the discriminatory practice or practices alleged, and to effect voluntary compliance with the requirements of this Act through informal methods of conciliation, conference, and persuasion.

(c)(1) Any person aggrieved may bring a civil action in any court of competent jurisdiction for such legal or equitable relief as will effectuate the purposes of this Act: Provided, That the right of any person to bring such action shall terminate upon the commencement of an action by the Equal Employment Opportunity Commission to enforce the right of such employee under this Act.

(c)(2) In an action brought under paragraph (1), a person shall be entitled to a trial by jury of any issue of fact in any such action for recovery of amounts owing as a result of a violation of this Act, regardless of whether equitable relief is sought by any party in such action.

(d)(1) No civil action may be commenced by an individual under this section until 60 days after a charge alleging unlawful discrimination has been filed with the Equal Employment Opportunity Commission. Such a charge shall be filed—

(A) within 180 days after the alleged unlawful practice occurred;

(B) in a case to which section 14(b) applies, within 300 days after the alleged unlawful practice occurred, or within 30 days after receipt by an individual of notice of termination of proceedings under State law, whichever is earlier.

(2) Upon receiving such a charge, the Commission shall promptly notify all persons named in such charge as prospective defendants in the action and shall promptly seek to eliminate any alleged unlawful practice by informal methods of conciliation, conference, and persuasion.

(3) For purposes of this section, an unlawful practice occurs, with respect to discrimination in compensation in violation of this Act, when a discriminatory compensation decision or other practice is adopted, when a person becomes subject to a discriminatory compensation decision or other practice, or when a person is affected by application of a discriminatory compensation decision or other practice, including each time wages, benefits, or other compensation is paid, resulting in whole or in part from such a decision or other practice.

>>>→ *Caution: [The statute of limitations under Sec. 7(e) has been extended under P.L. 100-283—See Historical Comment.]*

(e) Section 10 of the Portal-to-Portal Act of 1947 shall apply to actions under this chapter. If a charge filed with the Commission under this Act is dismissed or the proceedings of the Commission are otherwise terminated by the Commission, the Commission shall notify the person aggrieved. A civil action may be brought under this section by a person defined in section 11(a) against the respondent named in the charge within 90 days after the date of the receipt of such notice.

(f)(1) An individual may not waive any right or claim under this chapter unless the waiver is knowing and voluntary. Except as provided in paragraph (2), a waiver may not be considered knowing and voluntary unless at a minimum—

(A) the waiver is part of an agreement between the individual and the employer that is written in a manner calculated to be understood by such individual, or by the average individual eligible to participate;

(B) the waiver specifically refers to rights or claims arising under this chapter;

(C) the individual does not waive rights or claims that may arise after the date the waiver is executed;

(D) the individual waives rights or claims only in exchange for consideration in addition to anything of value to which the individual already is entitled;

(E) the individual is advised in writing to consult with an attorney prior to executing the agreement;

(F)(i) the individual is given a period of at least 21 days within which to consider the agreement; or

(ii) if a waiver is requested in connection with an exit incentive or other employment termination program offered to a group or class of employees, the individual is given a period of at least 45 days within which to consider the agreement;

(G) the agreement provides that for a period of at least 7 days following the execution of such agreement, the individual may revoke the agreement, and the agreement shall not become effective or enforceable until the revocation period has expired;

(H) if a waiver is requested in connection with an exit incentive or other employment termination program offered to a group or class of employees, the employer (at the commencement of the period specified in subparagraph (F)) informs the individual in writing in a manner calculated to be understood by the average individual eligible to participate, as to—

(i) any class, unit, or group of individuals covered by such program, any eligibility factors for such program, and any time limits applicable to such programs; and

(ii) the job titles and ages of all individuals eligible or selected for the program, and the ages of all individuals in the same job classification or organizational unit who are not eligible or selected for the program.

(2) A waiver in settlement of a charge filed with the Equal Employment Opportunity Commission, or an action filed in court by the individual or the individual's representative, alleging age discrimination of a kind prohibited under section 4 or 15 may not be considered knowing and voluntary unless at a minimum—

(A) subparagraphs (A) through (E) of paragraph (1) have been met; and

(B) the individual is given a reasonable period of time within which to consider the settlement agreement.

(3) In any dispute that may arise over whether any of the requirements, conditions, and circumstances set forth in subparagraph (A), (B), (C), (D), (E), (F), (G), or (H) of paragraph (1), or subparagraph (A) or (B) of paragraph (2), have been met, the party asserting the validity of a waiver shall have the burden of proving in a court of competent jurisdiction that a waiver was knowing and voluntary pursuant to paragraph (1) or (2).

(4) No waiver agreement may affect the Commission's rights and responsibilities to enforce this Act. No waiver may be used to justify interfering with the protected right of an employee to file a charge or participate in an investigation or proceeding conducted by the Commission.

Amendments

P.L. 111-2, Sec. 4, amended ADEA Sec. 7(d) as follows: (1) in the first sentence by redesignating paragraphs (1) and (2) as subparagraphs (A) and (B), respectively; and by striking "(d)" and inserting "(d)(1)"; (2) in the third sentence, by striking "Upon" and inserting "(2) Upon"; and (3) by adding subparagraph (3) to read as above.

The above amendments take effect as if enacted on May 28, 2007 and apply to all claims of discrimination in compensation under title VII of the Civil Rights Act of 1964 (42 U.S.C. 2000e et seq.), the Age Discrimination in Employment Act of 1967 (29 U.S.C. 621 et seq.), title I and section 503 of the Americans with Disabilities Act of 1990, and sections 501 and 504 of the Rehabilitation Act of 1973, that are pending on or after that date.

P.L. 102-166, Sec. 115, amended ADEA Sec. 7(e) by eliminating the text of paragraph (2), deleting references to paragraphs (1) and (2), and deleting a reference to Sec. 6 of the Portal-to-Portal Act to read as above, effective November 21, 1991. Prior to amendment, Sec. 7(e) read as follows:

"(e)(1) Sections 6 and 10 of the Portal-to-Portal Act of 1947 shall apply to actions under this Act.

(2) For the period during which the Secretary is attempting to effect voluntary compliance with requirements of this Act through informal methods of conciliation, conference, and persuasion pursuant to subsection (b), the statute of limitations as provided in section 6 of the Portal-to-Portal Act of 1947 shall be tolled, but in no event for a period in excess of one year."

P.L. 101-433, Sec. 201, amended ADEA Sec. 7 by adding a new subsection (f) to read as above, effective for waivers other than those that occur before October 16, 1990.

P.L. 101-433, Act Sec. 202(B), provides:

(b) RULE ON WAIVERS.—Effective on the date of enactment of this Act, the rule on waivers issued by the Equal Employment Opportunity Commission and contained in section 1627.16(c) of title 29, Code of Federal Regulations, shall have no force and effect.

P.L. 100-283, approved by the President on April 12, 1988, temporarily extended the statute of limitations under Sec. 7(e) although it did not directly amend the section. The Act provides as follows:

SECTION 1. SHORT TITLE.

This Act may be cited as the "Age Discrimination Claims Assistance Act of 1988."

SEC. 2. FINDINGS.

The Congress finds that—

(1) the Equal Employment Opportunity Commission (hereafter in this Act referred to as the "Commission") has failed to process an undetermined number of charges filed under the Age Discrimination in Employment Act of 1967 (29 U.S.C. 621-634) before the running of the statute of limitations applicable to bringing civil actions in the Federal courts under such Act, and

(2) many persons who filed such charges with the Commission have lost the right to bring civil actions with respect to the unlawful practices alleged in such charges.

SEC. 3. EXTENSION OF STATUTE OF LIMITATIONS.

Notwithstanding section 7(e) of the Age Discrimination in Employment Act of 1967 (29 U.S.C. 626(e)), a civil action may be brought under section 7 of such Act by the Commission or an aggrieved person, during the 540-day period beginning on the date of enactment of this Act (April 12, 1988) if—

(1) with respect to the alleged unlawful practice on which the claim in such civil action is based, a charge was timely filed under such Act with the Commission after December 31, 1983,

(2) the Commission did not, within the applicable period set forth in section 7(e) either—

(A) eliminate such alleged unlawful practice by informal methods of conciliation, conference, and persuasion, or

(B) notify such persons, in writing, of the disposition of such charge and of the right of such person to bring a civil action on such claim,

(3) the statute of limitations applicable under such section 7(e) to such claim ran before the date of enactment of this Act, and

(4) a civil action on such claim was not brought by the Commission or such person before the running of the statute of limitations.

SEC. 4. NOTICE OF STATUTE OF LIMITATIONS.

(a) NOTICE REGARDING CLAIMS FOR WHICH STATUTE OF LIMITATIONS IS EXTENDED.—Not later than 60 days after the date of enactment of this Act (April 12, 1988), the Commission shall provide the notice specified in subsection (b) to each person who has filed a charge to which section 3 applies.

(b) CONTENTS OF NOTICE.—The notice required to be provided under subsection (a) to a person shall be in writing and shall include the following information:

(1) The rights and benefits to which such person is entitled under the Age Discrimination in Employment Act of 1967.

(2) The date (which is 540 days after the date of the enactment of this Act [April 12, 1988]) on which the statute of limitations applicable to such person's claim will run.

(3) That such person may bring a civil action on such claims before the date specified in paragraph (2).

SEC. 5. REPORTS.

(a) CONTENTS OF REPORTS.—For each 180-day period in the 540-day period beginning on the date of enactment of this Act (April 12, 1988), the Commission shall submit a written report that includes all of the following information:

(1) The number of persons who have claims to which section 3 applies and the dates charges based on such claims were filed with the Commission.

(2) The number of persons to whom notice was provided in accordance with section 4(a) and the date the notice was provided.

(3) With respect to alleged unlawful practices on which claims affected by section 3 are based, the number of such alleged unlawful practices that the Commission has attempted to eliminate by informal methods of conciliation, conference, and persuasion in the 180-day period for which the report is submitted.

(4) The number of alleged unlawful practices referred to in paragraph (3) that were so eliminated in such period.

(5) The number of civil actions filed by the Commission on behalf of persons to whom notice was sent under section 4.

(b) SUBMISSION OF REPORTS.—Each report required by subsection (a) shall be submitted by the Commission to—

(1) the Committee on Education and Labor, and the Select Committee on Aging, of the House of Representatives, and

(2) the Committee on Labor and Human Resources, and the Special Committee on Aging, of the Senate,

not later than 30 days after the expiration of the 180-day period for which such report is required.

Prior to amendment by P.L. 95-256, Sec. 7(d) read as follows:

"(d) No civil action may be commenced by any individual under this section until the individual has given the Secretary not less than sixty days' notice of an intent to file such action. Such notice shall be filed—

"(1) within one hundred and eighty days after the alleged unlawful practice occurred, or

"(2) in a case to which section 14(b) applies, within three hundred days after the alleged unlawful practice occurred or within thirty days after receipt by the individual of notice of termination of proceedings under State law, whichever is earlier.

"Upon receiving a notice of intent to sue, the Secretary shall promptly notify all persons named therein as prospective defendants in the action and shall promptly seek to eliminate any alleged unlawful practice by informal methods of conciliation, conference, and persuasion."

[¶ 15,738]

SEC. 8. NOTICES TO BE POSTED.

Every employer, employment agency, and labor organization shall post and keep posted in conspicuous places upon its premises a notice to be prepared or approved by the Equal Employment Opportunity Commission setting forth information as the Commission deems appropriate to effectuate the purposes of this chapter.

[¶ 15,739]

SEC. 9. RULES AND REGULATIONS.

In accordance with the provisions of subchapter II of chapter 5 of title 5, the Equal Employment Opportunity Commission may issue such rules and regulations as he may consider necessary or appropriate for carrying out this chapter, and may establish such reasonable exemptions to and from any or all provisions of this chapter as it may find necessary and proper in the public interest.

Amendments

P.L. 101-433, Act Sec. 104 provides:

SEC. 104. RULES AND REGULATIONS.—Notwithstanding section 9 of the Age Discrimination in Employment Act of 1967 (29 U.S.C. 628), the Equal Employment Opportunity Commission may issue such rules and regulations as the Commission may consider necessary or appropriate for carrying out this title, and the amendments made by this title, only after consultation with the Secretary of the Treasury and the Secretary of Labor.

[¶ 15,740]

SEC. 10. CRIMINAL PENALTIES.

Whoever shall forcibly resist, oppose, impede, intimidate, or interfere with a duly authorized representative of the Equal Employment Opportunity Commission while it is engaged in the performance of duties under this chapter shall be punished by a fine of not more than $500 or by imprisonment for not more than one year, or by both: Provided, however, That no person shall be imprisoned under this section except when there has been a prior conviction hereunder.

[¶ 15,741]

SEC. 11. DEFINITIONS.

For the purposes of this chapter—

(a) The term "person" means one or more individuals, partnerships, associations, labor organizations, corporations, business trusts, legal representatives, or any organized groups of persons.

(b) The term "employer" means a person engaged in an industry affecting commerce who has twenty or more employees for each working day in each of twenty or more calendar weeks in the current or preceding calendar year: Provided, That prior to June 30, 1968, employers having fewer than fifty employees shall not be considered employers. The term also means (1) any agent of such a person, and (2) a State or political subdivision of a State and any agency or instrumentality of a State or a political subdivision of a State, and any interstate agency, but such term does not include the United States, or a corporation wholly owned by the Government of the United States.

(c) The term "employment agency" means any person regularly undertaking with or without compensation to procure employees for an employer and includes an agent of such a person; but shall not include an agency of the United States.

(d) The term "labor organization" means a labor organization engaged in an industry affecting commerce, and any agent of such an organization, and includes any organization of any kind, any agency, or employee representation committee, group, association, or plan so engaged in which employees participate and which exists for the purpose, in whole or in part, of dealing with employers concerning grievances, labor disputes, wages, rates of pay, hours, or other terms or conditions of employment, and any conference, general committee, joint or system board, or joint council so engaged which is subordinate to a national or international labor organization.

(e) A labor organization shall be deemed to be engaged in an industry affecting commerce if (1) it maintains or operates a hiring hall or hiring office which procures employees for an employer or procures for employees opportunities to work for an employer, or (2) the number of its members (or, where it is a labor organization composed of other labor organizations or their representatives, if the aggregate number of the members of such other labor organization) is fifty or more prior to July 1, 1968, or twenty-five or more on or after July 1, 1968, and such labor organization—

(1) is the certified representative of employees under the provisions of the National Labor Relations Act, as amended, or the Railway Labor Act, as amended; or

(2) although not certified, is a national or international labor organization or a local labor organization recognized or acting as the representative of employees of an employer or employers engaged in an industry affecting commerce; or

(3) has chartered a local labor organization or subsidiary body which is representing or actively seeking to represent employees of employers within the meaning of paragraph (1) or (2); or

(4) has been chartered by a labor organization representing or actively seeking to represent employees within the meaning of paragraph (1) or (2) as the local or subordinate body through which such employees may enjoy membership or become affiliated with such labor organization; or

(5) is a conference, general committee, joint or system board, or joint council subordinate to a national or international labor organization, which includes a labor organization engaged in an industry affecting commerce within the meaning of any of the preceding paragraphs of this subsection.

(f) The term "employee" means an individual employed by any employer except that the term "employee" shall not include any person elected to public office in any State or political subdivision of any State by the qualified voters thereof, or any person chosen by such officer to be on such officer's personal staff, or an appointee on the policy-making level or an immediate adviser with respect to the exercise of the constitutional or legal powers of the office. The exemption set forth in the preceding sentence shall not include employees subject to the civil service laws of a State government, governmental agency, or political subdivision. The term "employee" includes any individual who is a citizen of the United States employed by an employer in a workplace in a foreign country.

(g) The term "commerce" means trade, traffic, commerce, transportation, transmission, or communication among the several States; or between a State and any place outside thereof; or within the District of Columbia, or a possession of the United States; or between points in the same State but through a point outside thereof.

(h) The term "industry affecting commerce" means any activity, business, or industry in commerce or in which a labor dispute would hinder or obstruct commerce or the free flow of commerce and includes any activity or industry "affecting commerce" within the meaning of the Labor-Management Reporting and Disclosure Act of 1959.

(i) The term "State" includes a State of the United States, the District of Columbia, Puerto Rico, the Virgin Islands, American Samoa, Guam, Wake Island, the Canal Zone, and Outer Continental Shelf lands defined in the Outer Continental Shelf Lands Act.

(j) The term "firefighter" means an employee, the duties of whose position are primarily to perform work directly connected with the control and extinguishment of fires or the maintenance and use of firefighting apparatus and equipment, including an employee engaged in this activity who is transferred to a supervisory or administrative position.

(k) The term "law enforcement officer" means an employee, the duties of whose position are primarily the investigation, apprehension, or detention of individuals suspected or convicted of offenses against the criminal laws of a State, including an employee engaged in this activity who is transferred to a supervisory or administrative position. For the purpose of this subsection, "detention" includes the duties of employees assigned to guard individuals incarcerated in any penal institution.

(l) The term "compensation, terms, conditions, or privileges of employment" encompasses all employee benefits, including such benefits provided pursuant to a bona fide employee benefit plan.

Amendments

P.L. 101-433, Sec. 102:

Amended ADEA Sec. 11 by adding new subsection (l) to read as above, effective with respect to any employee benefits established or modified after October 16, 1990 and other conduct occurring after April 14, 1991. See also Act Sec. 105 under Historical Comment to Act Sec. 104.

P.L. 99-592, Sec. 4, added ADEA Secs. 11(j) and 11(k). The amendment is generally effective on January 1, 1987. For additional details on the effective date, see the Historical comment following ADEA Sec. 4.

P.L. 98-459, sec. 801(a) amended ADEA Sec. 11(f) to read as above, by adding a new sentence at the end, effective October 9, 1984.

Prior to amendment by P.L. 95-256, Secs. 11(b), 11(c) and 11(f) read as follows:

"(b) The term 'employer' means a person engaged in an industry affecting commerce who has twenty-five or more employees for each working day in each of twenty or more calendar weeks in the current or preceding calendar year: *Provided,* That prior to June 30, 1968, employers having fewer than fifty employees shall not be considered employers. The term also means any agent of such a person, but such term does not include the United States, a corporation wholly owned by the Government of the United States, or a State or political subdivision thereof."

"(c) The term 'employment agency' means any person regularly undertaking with or without compensation to procure employees for an employer and includes an agent of such a person; but shall not include an agency of the United States, or an agency of a State or political subdivision of a State, except that such term shall include the United States Employment Service and the system of State and local employment services receiving Federal assistance.

"(f) The term 'employee' means an individual employed by an employer."

[¶15,742]

SEC. 12. AGE LIMITATION.

(a) The prohibitions in this chapter shall be limited to individuals who are at least 40 years of age.

(b) In the case of any personnel action affecting employees or applicants for employment which is subject to the provisions of section 15 of this Act, the prohibitions established in section 15 of this title shall be limited to individuals who are at least 40 years of age.

(c)(1) Nothing in this chapter shall be construed to prohibit compulsory retirement of any employee who has attained 65 years of age and who, for the 2-year period immediately before retirement, is employed in a bona fide executive or a high policy-making position, if such employee is entitled to an immediate nonforfeitable annual retirement benefit from a pension, profit-sharing, savings, or deferred compensation plan, or any combination of such plans, of the employer of such employee, which equals, in the aggregate, at least $44,000.

(c)(2) In applying the retirement benefit test of paragraph (1) of this subsection, if any such retirement benefit is in a form other than a straight life annuity (with no ancillary benefits), or if employees contribute to any such plan or make rollover contributions, such benefit shall be adjusted in accordance with regulations prescribed by the Equal Employment Opportunity Commission, after consultation with the Secretary of the Treasury, so that the benefit is the equivalent of a straight life annuity (with no ancillary benefits) under a plan to which employees do not contribute and under which no rollover contributions are made.

Amendments

P.L. 101-239, §6202(b)(3)(C) amended ADEA Sec. 12(a) by striking "except the provisions of section 4(g))", effective for items and services furnished after December 19, 1989.

P.L. 99-592, Sec. 2(c)(1), amended ADEA Sec. 12(a) by striking out "but less than seventy years of age" after the words "40 years of age." Sec. 2(c) amended ADEA sec. 12(c)(2) by striking out "but not seventy years of age," after the words "65 years of age." The amendment is generally effective on January 1, 1987. For greater details on the effective date, see the Historical comment with respect to P.L. 99-592 following Sec. 4 of the ADEA.

P.L. 99-592, Sec. 6(a), added ADEA Sec. 12(d). The provision is generally effective on January 1, 1987. Additional details relating to the effective date of P.L. 99-592 are in the Historical comment following Sec. 4 of the ADEA. Sec. 6(b) of the Act provides that the amendment of Sec. 6(a), adding ADEA Sec. 12(d), relating to college professors, is repealed on December 31, 1993.

P.L. 99-592, Sec. 6(c), provides:

"(c) STUDY REQUIRED.—(1) The Equal Employment Opportunity Commission shall, not later than 12 months after the date of enactment of this Act, [October 31, 1987], enter into an agreement with the National Academy of Sciences for the conduct of a study to analyze the potential consequences of the elimination of mandatory retirement on institutions of higher education.

"(2) The study required by paragraph (1) of this subsection shall be conducted under the general supervision of the National Academy of Sciences by a study panel composed of 9 members. The study panel shall consist of—

"(A) 4 members who shall be administrators at institutions of higher education selected by the National Academy of Sciences after consultation with the American Council of Education, the Association of American Universities, and the National Association of State Universities and Land Grant Colleges;

"(B) 4 members who shall be teachers or retired teachers at institutions of higher education (who do not serve in an administrative capacity at such institutions), selected by the National Academy of Sciences after consultation with the American Federation of Teachers, the National Education Association, the American Association of University Professors, and the American Association of Retired Persons; and

"(C) one member selected by the National Academy of Sciences.

"(3) The results of the study shall be reported, with recommendations, to the President and to the Congress not later than 5 years after the date of enactment of this Act [October 31, 1991].

"(4) The expenses of the study required by this subsection shall be paid from funds available to the Equal Employment Opportunity Commission.

P.L. 99-272, Sec. 9201(b)(2) amended ADEA Sec. 12(a) by inserting "(except the provisions of section 4(g))" after "Act."

P.L. 98-459, sec. 802(c)(1) amended ADEA Sec. 12(c)(1) by striking out "$27,000" and inserting "$44,000" instead, effective October 9, 1984 except that the amendment does not apply with respect to any individual who retires or is compelled to retire before October 9, 1984.

P.L. 95-256 added Sec. 12(d), effective January 1, 1979, automatically repealed July 1, 1982. Prior to repeal, the provision read as follows: "(d) Nothing in this Act shall be construed to prohibit compulsory retirement of any employee who has attained 65 years of age but not 70 years of age, and who is serving under a contract of unlimited tenure (or similar arrangement providing for unlimited tenure) at an institution of higher education (as defined by section 1201(a) of the Higher Education Act of 1965)."

[¶15,743]

SEC. 13. ANNUAL REPORT.

The Equal Employment Opportunity Commission shall submit annually in January a report to the Congress covering his activities for the preceding year and including such information, data, and recommendations for further legislation in connection with the matters covered by this chapter as he may find advisable. Such report shall contain an evaluation and appraisal by the Commission of the effect of the minimum and maximum ages established by this chapter, together with its recommendations to the Congress. In making such evaluation and appraisal, the Commission shall take into consideration any changes which may have occurred in the general age level of the population, the effect of the chapter upon workers not covered by its provisions, and such other factors as it may deem pertinent.

[¶15,744]

SEC. 14. FEDERAL-STATE RELATIONSHIP.

(a) Nothing in this chapter shall affect the jurisdiction of any agency of any State performing like functions with regard to discriminatory employment practices on account of age except that upon commencement of action under this chapter such action shall supersede any State action.

(b) In the case of an alleged unlawful practice occurring in a State which has a law prohibiting discrimination in employment because of age and establishing or authorizing a State authority to grant or seek relief from such discriminatory practice, no suit may be brought under section 7 of this Act before the expiration of sixty days after proceedings have been commenced under the State law, unless such proceedings have been earlier terminated: Provided, That such sixty-day period shall be extended to one hundred and twenty days during the first year after the effective date of such State law. If any requirement for the commencement of such proceedings is imposed by a State authority other than a requirement of the filing of a written and signed statement of the facts upon which the proceeding is based, the proceeding shall be deemed to have been commenced for the purposes of this subsection at the time such statement is sent by registered mail to the appropriate State authority.

[¶15,745]

SEC. 15. FEDERAL EMPLOYEES.

(a) All personnel actions affecting employees or applicants for employment who are at least 40 years of age (except personnel actions with regard to aliens employed outside the limits of the United States) in military departments as defined in section 102 of title 5, [United States Code], in executive agencies as defined in section 105 of title 5 [United States Code], (including employees and applicants for employment who are paid from nonappropriated funds), in the United States Postal Service and the Postal Rate Commission, in those units in the government of the District of Columbia having positions in the competitive service, and in those units of the legislative and judicial branches of the Federal Government having positions in the competitive service, and in the Library of Congress shall be made free from any discrimination based on age.

(b) Except as otherwise provided in this subsection, the Equal Employment Opportunity Commission is authorized to enforce the provisions of subsection (a) through appropriate remedies, including reinstatment or hiring of employees with or without backpay, as will effectuate the policies of this section. The Equal Employment Opportunity Commission shall issue such rules, regulations, orders, and instructions as it deems necessary and appropriate to carry out its responsibilities under this section. The Equal Employment Opportunity Commission shall—

(1) be responsible for the review and evaluation of the operation of all agency programs designed to carry out the policy of this section, periodically obtaining and publishing (on at least a semi-annual basis) progress reports from each such department, agency, or unit referred to in subsection (a) of this section;

(2) consult with and solicit the recommendations of interested individuals, groups, and organizations relating to nondiscrimination in employment on account of age; and

(3) provide for the acceptance and processing of complaints of discrimination in Federal employment on account of age.

The head of each such department, agency, or unit shall comply with such rules, regulations, orders, and instructions of the Equal Employment Opportunity Commission which shall include a provision that an employee or applicant for employment shall be notified of any final action taken on any complaint of discrimination filed by him thereunder. Reasonable exemptions to the provisions of this section may be established by the Commission but only when the Commission has established a maximum age requirement on the basis of a determination that age is a bona fide occupational qualification necessary to the performance of the duties of the position. With respect to employment in the Library of Congress, authorities granted in this subsection to the Equal Employment Opportunity Commission shall be exercised by the Librarian of Congress.

(c) Any persons aggrieved may bring a civil action in any Federal district court of competent jurisdiction for such legal or equitable relief as will effectuate the purposes of this chapter.

(d) When the individual has not filed a complaint concerning age discrimination with the Commission, no civil action may be commenced by the individual under this section until the individual has given the Commission not less than thirty days' notice of an intent to file such action. Such notice shall be filed within one hundred and eighty days after the alleged unlawful practice occurred. Upon receiving a notice of intent to sue, the Commission shall promptly notify all persons named therein as prospective defendants in the action and take any appropriate action to assure the elimination of any unlawful practice.

(e) Nothing contained in this section shall relieve any Government agency or official of the responsibility to assure nondiscrimination on account of age in employment as required under any provision of Federal law.

(f) Any personnel action of any department, agency or other entity referred to in subsection (a) of this section shall not be subject to, or affected by, any provision of this Act, other than the provisions of sections 7(d)(3) and 12(b) of this Act and the provisions of this chapter.

(g)(1) The Equal Employment Opportunity Commission shall undertake a study relating to the effects of the amendments made to this section by the Age Discrimination in Employment Act Amendments of 1978, and the effects of section 12(b) of this Act.

(g)(2) The Equal Employment Opportunity Commission shall transmit a report to the President and to the Congress containing the findings of the Commission resulting from the study of the Commission under paragraph (1) of this subsection. Such report shall be transmitted no later than January 1, 1980.

Amendments

P.L. 111-2, Sec. 5(c)(2), amended ADEA Sec. 15(f) by striking "of section" and inserting "of sections 7(d)(3) and."

The above amendment takes effect as if enacted on May 28, 2007 and applies to all claims of discrimination in compensation under title VII of the Civil Rights Act of 1964 (42 U.S.C. 2000e et seq.), the Age Discrimination in Employment Act of 1967 (29 U.S.C. 621 et seq.), title I and section 503 of the Americans with Disabilities Act of 1990, and sections 501 and 504 of the Rehabilitation Act of 1973, that are pending on or after that date.

P.L. 95-256 amended Sec. 15(a) by adding "who are at least 40 years of age" after the word "employment."

P.L. 93-259 added Section 15(a) through (e) as a new provision.

[¶15,746]

SEC. 16. EFFECTIVE DATE.

This Act shall become effective one hundred and eighty days after enactment, except (a) that the Secretary of Labor may extend the delay in effective date of any provision of this Act up to an additional ninety days thereafter if he finds that such time is necessary in permitting adjustments to the provisions hereof, and (b) that on or after the date of enactment the Secretary of Labor is authorized to issue such rules and regulations as may be necessary to carry out its provisions.

Amendments

Prior to amendment by P.L. 93-259, Sec. 16 was designated as Section 15 of the Age Discrimination in Employment Act.

[¶15,747]

SEC. 17. APPROPRIATIONS.

There are hereby authorized to be appropriated such sums as may be necessary to carry out this chapter.

Amendments

Prior to amendment by P.L. 95-256, Sec. 17 contained an annual appropriation limit of $5,000,000.

Prior to amendment by P.L. 93-259, Sec. 17 was designated Sec. 16.

Age Discrimination in Employment Regulations
(Equal Employment Opportunity Commission)

[¶ 15,750]

Equal Employment Opportunity Commission regulations under the Age Discrimination in Employment Act.—Reproduced below are excerpts from the regulations promulgated by the EEOC on the Age Discrimination in Employment Act. Reg. § 1625.6 (46 FR 47724) relates to bona fide occupational qualifications. Reg. § 1625.7 (46 FR 47724) concerns differentiations based on factors other than age. Reg. § 1625.8 (46 FR 47724) discusses bona fide seniority systems. Reg. § 1625.9 (46 FR 47724) reflects the EEOC's interpretation of ADEA Sec. 4(f)(2)'s prohibition against involuntary retirement because of age. Pursuant to ADEA Sec. 12(c), an executive may be subject to compulsory retirement, if, among other requirements, he is entitled to an annual retirement benefit of at least $27,000. Reg. § 1625.10 (formerly Reg. § 860.120) relates costs and benefits under employee benefit plans. Reg. § 1625.12 (44 FR 66791) sets forth the EEOC's interpretative statements regarding the exemption. Reg. § 1627.17 (44 FR 66791) indicates how the $27,000 annual retirement benefit is to be calculated under specified circumstances. Reg. § 1625.20 is a final and interim rule on group health insurance benefits for employees age 65-69, which awaits OMB approval and publication in the Federal Register. Reg. § 1625.21 (61 FR 15378), added April 8, 1996, discusses age limitations for apprenticeship programs. The recordkeeping requirements are set forth in Reg. § § 1627.2—1627.11 (44 FR 38459). Former Reg. § 1627.16(c), allowing unsupervised waivers, was removed by 57 FR 4158 on February 4, 1992. Former Reg. § 1625.13 on age limitations for apprentices was removed by 61 FR 15378 on April 8, 1996 (having been replaced by Reg. § 1625.21).

Reg. § § 1625.8, 1625.9(c) and (d), 1625.10(f), and 1625.12(a) were amended by 53 FR 5971 on February 29, 1988. Reg. § 1625.23 was added by 65 FR 77437 on December 11, 2000.

Subpart C (Administrative Exemptions) consisting of former Reg. § § 1627.15 and 1627.16, was redesignated as Subpart C under Part 1625 and the regulations were renumbered as § § 1625.30 and 1625.31 by 72 FR 72938 on December 26, 2007. Newly redesignated § 1625.31 was amended and new Reg. § 1625.32 and an Appendix to § 1625.32 was added by 72 FR 72938 on December 26, 2007. § 1625.31 was amended by 74 FR 63981 on December 7, 2009. § 1625.7 was amended by 77 FR 19080 on March 30, 2012.

Reg. § 1625.22(g)(3) was revised by 79 FR 13546 on March 11, 2014. Reg. § 1625.21 was corrected/revised by 80 FR 60539 on October 7, 2015.

Also previously reproduced here was Reg. § 860.120(f)(1)(iv)(B) which stated that the ADEA permits employers to cease contributions and accruals to pension and retirement plans for employees who continue to work past normal retirement age. It was rescinded pursuant to *American Association of Retired Persons, et al. v. EEOC* (CCH PENSION PLAN GUIDE ¶ 23,723K). The notice of rescission was published in the *Federal Register* on March 18, 1987 (52 FR 8448), (CCH PENSION PLAN GUIDE ¶ 23,725A).

EQUAL EMPLOYMENT
OPPORTUNITY COMMISSION

29 CFR Parts 1625 and 1627

Age Discrimination in Employment; Final
Interpretations

[¶ 15,750A]

§ 1625.1 Definitions. The Equal Employment Opportunity Commission is hereinafter referred to as the "Commission". The terms "person", "employer", "employment agency", "labor organization", and "employee" shall have the meanings set forth in Section 11 of the Age Discrimination in Employment Act of 1967, as amended, 29 U.S.C. 621 *et seq.,* hereinafter referred to as the "Act". References to "employers" in this part state principles that are applicable not only to employers but also to labor organizations and to employment agencies.

[¶ 15,750B]

§ 1625.6 Bona fide occupational qualifications. (a) Whether occupational qualifications will be deemed to be "bona fide" to a specific job and "reasonably necessary to the normal operation of the particular business," will be determined on the basis of all the pertinent facts surrounding each particular situation. It is anticipated that this concept of a bona fide occupational qualification will have limited scope and application. Further, as this is an exception to the Act it must be narrowly construed.

(b) An employer asserting a BFOQ defense has the burden of proving that (1) the age limit is reasonably necessary to the essence of the business, and either (2) that all or substantially all individuals excluded from the job involved are in fact disqualified, or (3) that some of the individuals so excluded possess a disqualifying trait that cannot be ascertained except by reference to age. If the employer's objective in asserting a BFOQ is the goal of public safety, the employer must prove that the challenged practice does indeed effectuate that goal and that there is no acceptable alternative which would better advance it or equally advance it with less discriminatory impact.

(c) Many State and local governments have enacted laws or administrative regulations which limit employment opportunities based on age. Unless these laws meet the standards for the establishment of a valid bona fide occupational qualification under section 4(f)(1) of the Act, they will be considered in conflict with and effectively superseded by the ADEA.

[¶ 15,750C]

§ 1625.7 Differentiations based on reasonable factors other than age. (a) Section 4(f)(1) of the Act provides that

* * * it shall not be unlawful for an employer, employment agency, or labor organization * * * to take any action otherwise prohibited under paragraphs (a), (b), (c), or (e) of this section * * * where the differentiation is based on reasonable factors other than age * * *.

(b) When an employment practice uses age as a limiting criterion, the defense that the practice is justified by a reasonable factor other than age is unavailable. [Amended 3/30/12 by 77 FR 19080.]

(c) Any employment practice that adversely affects individuals within the protected age group on the basis of older age is discriminatory unless the practice is justified by a "reasonable factor other than age." An individual challenging the allegedly unlawful practice is responsible for isolating and identifying the specific employment practice that allegedly causes any observed statistical disparities. [Amended 3/30/12 by 77 FR 19080.]

(d) Whenever the "reasonable factors other than age" defense is raised, the employer bears the burdens of production and persuasion to demonstrate the defense. The "reasonable factors other than age" provision is not available as a defense to a claim of disparate treatment. [Amended 3/30/12 by 77 FR 19080.]

(e)(1) A reasonable factor other than age is a non-age factor that is objectively reasonable when viewed from the position of a prudent employer mindful of its responsibilities under the ADEA under like circumstances. Whether a differentiation is based on reasonable factors other than age must be decided on the basis of all the particular facts and circumstances surrounding each individual situation. To establish the RFOA defense, an employer must show that the employment practice was both reasonably designed to further or achieve a legitimate business purpose and administered in a way that reasonably achieves that purpose in light of the particular facts and circumstances that were known, or should have been known, to the employer.

(2) Considerations that are relevant to whether a practice is based on a reasonable factor other than age include, but are not limited to:

(i) The extent to which the factor is related to the employer's stated business purpose;

(ii) The extent to which the employer defined the factor accurately and applied the factor fairly and accurately, including the extent to which managers and supervisors were given guidance or training about how to apply the factor and avoid discrimination;

(iii) The extent to which the employer limited supervisors' discretion to assess employees subjectively, particularly where the criteria that the supervisors were asked to evaluate are known to be subject to negative age-based stereotypes;

(iv) The extent to which the employer assessed the adverse impact of its employment practice on older workers; and

(v) The degree of the harm to individuals within the protected age group, in terms of both the extent of injury and the numbers of persons adversely affected, and the extent to which the employer took steps to reduce the harm, in light of the burden of undertaking such steps.

(3) No specific consideration or combination of considerations need be present for a differentiation to be based on reasonable factors other than age. Nor does the presence of one of these considerations automatically establish the defense. [Amended 3/30/12 by 77 FR 19080.]

(f) A differentiation based on the average cost of employing older employees as a group is unlawful except with respect to employee benefit plans which qualify for the section 4(f)(2) exception to the Act.

[¶ 15,750D]

§1625.8 Bona fide seniority systems. Section 4(f)(2) of the Act provides that

* * * It shall not be unlawful for an employer, employment agency, or labor organization * * * to observe the terms of a bona fide seniority system * * * which is not a subterfuge to evade the purposes of this Act except that no such seniority system * * * shall require or permit the involuntary retirement of any individual specified by section 12(a) of this Act because of the age of such individual. * * *

(a) Though a seniority system may be qualified by such factors as merit, capacity, or ability, any bona fide seniority system must be based on length of service as the primary criterion for the equitable allocation of available employment opportunities and prerogatives among younger and older workers.

(b) Adoption of a purported seniority system which gives those with longer service lesser rights, and results in discharge or less favored treatment to those within the protection of the Act, may, depending upon the circumstances, be a "subterfuge to evade the purposes" of the Act.

(c) Unless the essential terms and conditions of an alleged seniority system have been communicated to the affected employees and can be shown to be applied uniformly to all of those affected, regardless of age, it will not be considered a bona fide seniority system within the meaning of the Act.

(d) It should be noted that seniority systems which segregate, classify, or otherwise discriminate against individuals on the basis of race, color, religion, sex, or national origin, are prohibited under Title VII of the Civil Rights Act of 1964, where that Act otherwise applies. The "bona fides" of such a system will be closely scrutinized to ensure that such a system is, in fact, bona fide under the ADEA. (Amended by 53 FR 5971 on February 29, 1988 and by 53 FR 15673 on May 3, 1988.)

[¶ 15,750E]

§1625.9 Prohibition of involuntary retirement. (a)(1) As originally enacted in 1967, section 4(f)(2) of the Act provided: "It shall not be unlawful * * * to observe the terms of a bona fide seniority system or any bona fide employee benefit plan such as a retirement, pension, or insurance plan, which is not a subterfuge to evade the purposes of this Act, except that no such employee benefit plan shall excuse the failure to hire any individual * * *." The Department of Labor interpreted the provision as "Authoriz[ing]involuntary retirement irrespective of age; *Provided,* That such retirement is pursuant to the terms of a retirement or pension plan meeting the requirements of section 4(f)(2)." The Department took the position that in order to meet the requirements of section 4(f)(2), the involuntary retirement provision had to be (i) contained in a bona fide pension or retirement plan, (ii) required by the terms of the plan and not optional, and (iii) essential to the plan's economic survival or to some other legitimate business purpose—i.e., the provision was not in the plan as the result of arbitrary discrimination on the basis of age.

(2) As revised by the 1978 amendments, section 4(f)(2) was amended by adding the following clause at the end: "and no such seniority system or employee benefit plan shall require or permit the involuntary retirement of an individual specified by section 12(a) of this Act because of the age of such individual * * *." The Conference Committee Report expressly states that this amendment is intended "to make absolutely clear one of the original purposes of this provision, namely, that the exception does not authorize an employer to require or permit involuntary retirement of an employee within the protected age group on account of age" (H.R. Rept. No. 95-950, p. 8).

(b)(1) The amendment applies to all new and existing seniority systems and employee benefit plans. Accordingly, any system or plan provision requiring or permitting involuntary retirement is unlawful, regardless of whether the provision antedates the 1967 Act or the 1978 amendments.

(2) Where lawsuits pending on the date of enactment (April 6, 1978) or filed thereafter challenge involuntary retirements which occurred either before or after that date, the amendment applies.

(c)(1) The amendment protects all individuals covered by section 12(a) of the Act. Section 12(a) was amended in October of 1986 by the Age

Discrimination in Employment Amendments of 1986, Pub. L. 99-592, 100 Stat. 3342 (1986), which removed the age 70 limit. Section 12(a) provides that the Act's prohibitions shall be limited to individuals who are at least forty years of age. Accordingly, unless a specific exemption applies, an employer can no longer force retirement or otherwise discriminate on the basis of age against an individual because (s)he is 70 or older.

(2) The amendment to section 12(a) of the Act became effective on January 1, 1987, except with respect to any employee subject to a collective bargaining agreement containing a provision that would be superseded by such amendment that was in effect on June 30, 1986, and which terminates after January 1, 1987. In that case, the amendment is effective on the termination of the agreement or January 1, 1990, whichever comes first.

(d) Neither section 4(f)(2) nor any other provision of the Act makes it unlawful for a plan to permit individuals to elect early retirement at a specified age at their own option. Not is it unlawful for a plan to require early retirement for reasons other than age. (Amended by 53 FR 5971 on February 29, 1988).

[¶ 15,750F]

§1625.10 Costs and benefits under employee benefit plans. (a)(1) *General.* Section 4(f)(2) of the Act provides that it is not unlawful for an employer, employment agency, or labor organization "to observe the terms of * * * any bona fide employee benefit plan such as a retirement, pension, or insurance plan, which is not a subterfuge to evade the purposes of this Act, except that no such employee benefit plan shall excuse the failure to hire any individual and no such * * * employee benefit plan shall require or permit the involuntary retirement of any individual specified by section 12(a) of this Act because of the age of such individuals." The legislative history of this provision indicates that its purpose is to permit age-based reductions in employee benefit plans where such reductions are justified by significant cost considerations. Accordingly, section 4(f)(2) does not apply, for example, to paid vacations and uninsured paid sick leave, since reductions in these benefits would not be justified by significant cost considerations. Where employee benefit plans do meet the criteria in section 4(f)(2), benefit levels for older workers may be reduced to the extent necessary to achieve approximate equivalency in cost for older and younger workers. A benefit plan will be considered in compliance with the statute where the actual amount of payment made, or cost incurred, in behalf of an older worker is equal to that made or incurred in behalf of a younger worker, even though the older worker may thereby receive a lesser amount of benefits or insurance coverage. Since section 4(f)(2) is an exception from the general nondiscrimination provisions of the Act, the burden is on the one seeking to invoke the exception to show that every element has been clearly and unmistakably met. The exception must be narrowly construed. The following sections explain three key elements of the exception: (i) What a "bona fide employee benefit plan" is; (ii) what it means to "observe the terms" of such a plan; and (iii) what kind of plan, or plan provision, would be considered "a subterfuge to evade the purposes of [the] Act." There is also a discussion of the application of the general rules governing all plans with respect to specific kinds of employee benefit plans.

(2) *Relation of section 4(f)(2) to sections 4(a), 4(b) and 4(c).* Sections 4(a), 4(b) and 4(c) prohibit specified acts of discrimination on the basis of age. Section 4(a) in particular makes it unlawful for an employer to "discriminate against any individual with respect to his compensation, terms, conditions, or privileges of employment, because of such individual's age * * *." Section 4(f)(2) is an exception to this general prohibition. Where an employer under an employee benefit plan provides the same level of benefits to older workers as to younger workers, there is no violation of section 4(a), and accordingly the practice does not have to be justified under section 4(f)(2).

(b) *"Bona fide employee benefit plan".* Section 4(f)(2) applies only to bona fide employee benefit plans. A plan is considered "bona fide" if its terms (including cessation of contributions or accruals in the case of retirement income plans) have been accurately described in writing to all employees and if it actually provides the benefits in accordance with the terms of the plan. Notifying employees promptly of the provisions and changes in an employee benefit plan is essential if they are to know how the plan affects them. For these purposes, it would be sufficient under the ADEA for employers to follow the disclosure requirements of ERISA and the regulations thereunder. The plan must actually provide the benefits its provisions describe, since otherwise the notification of the provisions to employees is misleading and inaccurate. An "employee benefit plan" is a plan, such as a retirement, pension, or insurance plan, which provides employees with what are frequently referred to as "fringe benefits." The term does not refer to wages or salary in cash; neither section 4(f)(2) nor any other section of the Act excuses the payment of lower wages or salary to older employees on account of age. Whether or not any particular employee benefit plan may lawfully provide lower benefits to older employees on account of age depends on whether all of the elements of the exception have been met. An "employee-pay-all" employee benefit plan is one of the "terms, conditions, or privileges of employment" with respect to which discrimination on the basis of age is forbidden under section 4(a)(1). In such a plan, benefits for older workers may be reduced only to the extent and according to the same principles as apply to other plans under section 4(f)(2).

(c) *"To observe the terms" of a plan*. In order for a bona fide employee benefit plan which provides lower benefits to older employees on account of age to be within the section 4(f)(2) exception, the lower benefits must be provided in "observ[ance of] the terms of" the plan. As this statutory text makes clear, the section 4(f)(2) exception is limited to otherwise discriminatory actions which are actually prescribed by the terms of a bona fide employee benefit plan. Where the employer, employment agency, or labor organization is not required by the express provisions of the plan to provide lesser benefits to older workers, section 4(f)(2) does not apply. Important purposes are served by this requirement. Where a discriminatory policy is an express term of a benefit plan, employees presumably have some opportunity to know of the policy and to plan (or protest) accordingly. Moreover, the requirement that the discrimination actually be prescribed by a plan assures that the particular plan provision will be equally applied to all employees of the same age. Where a discriminatory provision is an optional term of the plan, it permits individual, discretionary acts of discrimination, which do not fall within the section 4(f)(2) exception.

(d) *"Subterfuge"*. In order for a bona fide employee benefit plan which prescribes lower benefits for older employees on account of age to be within the section 4(f)(2) exception, it must not be "a subterfuge to evade the purposes of [the] Act." In general, a plan or plan provision which prescribes lower benefits for older employees on account of age is not a "subterfuge" within the meaning of section 4(f)(2), provided that the lower level of benefits is justified by age-related cost considerations. (The only exception to this general rule is with respect to certain retirement plans. See paragraph (f)(4) of this section.) There are certain other requirements that must be met in order for a plan not to be a subterfuge. These requirements are set forth below.

(1) *Cost data—General*. Cost data used in justification of a benefit plan which provides lower benefits to older employees on account of age must be valid and reasonable. This standard is met where an employer has cost data which show the actual cost to it of providing the particular benefit (or benefits) in question over a representative period of years. An employer may rely [on] cost data for its own employees over such a period, or on cost data for a larger group of similarly situated employees. Sometimes, as a result of experience rating or other causes, an employer incurs costs that differ significantly from costs for a group of similarly situated employees. Such an employer may not rely on cost data for the similarly situated employees where such reliance would result in significantly lower benefits for its own older employees. Where reliable cost information is not available, reasonable projections made from existing cost data meeting the standard set forth above will be considered acceptable.

(2) *Cost data—Individual benefit basis and "benefit package" basis*. Cost comparisons and adjustments under section 4(f)(2) must be made on a benefit-by-benefit basis or on a "benefit package" basis, as described below.

(i) *Benefit-by-benefit basis*. Adjustments made on a benefit-by-benefit basis must be made in the amount or level of a specific form of benefit for a specific event or contingency. For example, higher group term life insurance costs for older workers would justify a corresponding reduction in the amount of group term life insurance coverage for older workers, on the basis of age. However, a benefit-by-benefit approach would not justify the substitution of one form of benefit for another, even though both forms of benefit are designed for the same contingency, such as death. See paragraph (f)(1) of this section.

(ii) *"Benefit package" basis*. As an alternative to the benefit-by-benefit basis, cost comparisons and adjustments under section 4(f)(2) may be made on a limited "benefit package" basis. Under this approach, subject to the limitations described below, cost comparisons and adjustments can be made with respect to section 4(f)(2) plans in the aggregate. This alternative basis provides greater flexibility than a benefit-by-benefit basis in order to carry out the declared statutory purpose "to help employers and workers find ways of meeting problems arising from the impact of age on employment." A "benefit package" approach is an alternative approach consistent with this purpose and with the general purpose of section 4(f)(2) only if it is not used to reduce the cost to the employer or the favorability to the employees of overall employee benefits for older employees. A "benefit package" approach used for either of these purposes would be a subterfuge

to evade the purposes of the Act. In order to assure that such a "benefit package" approach is not abused and is consistent with the legislative intent, it is subject to the limitations described in paragraph (f), which also includes a general example.

(3) *Cost data—Five year maximum basis*. Cost comparisons and adjustments under section 4(f)(2) may be made on the basis of age brackets of up to 5 years. Thus a particular benefit may be reduced for employees of any age within the protected age group by an amount no greater than that which could be justified by the additional cost to provide them with the same level of the benefit as younger employees within a specified five-year age group immediately preceding theirs. For example, where an employer chooses to provide unreduced group term life insurance benefits until age 60, benefits for employees who are between 60 and 65 years of age may be reduced only to the extent necessary to achieve approximate equivalency in costs with employees who are 55 to 60 years old. Similarly, any reductions in benefit levels for 65 to 70 year old employees cannot exceed an amount which is proportional to the additional costs for their coverage over 60 to 65 year old employees.

(4) *Employee contributions in support of employee benefit plans—*

(i) *As a condition of employment*. An older employee within the protected age group may not be required as a condition of employment to make greater contributions than a younger employee in support of an employee benefit plan. Such a requirement would be in effect a mandatory reduction in take-home pay, which is never authorized by section 4(f)(2), and would impose an impediment to employment in violation of the specific restrictions in section 4(f)(2).

(ii) *As a condition of participation in a voluntary employee benefit plan*. An older employee within the protected age group may be required as a condition of participation in a voluntary employee benefit plan to make a greater contribution than a younger employee only if the older employee is not thereby required to bear a greater proportion of the total premium cost (employer-paid and employee-paid) than the younger employee. Otherwise the requirement would discriminate against the older employee by making compensation in the form of an employer contribution available on less favorable terms than for the younger employee and denying that contribution altogether to an older employee unwilling or unable to meet the less favorable terms. Such discrimination is not authorized by section 4(f)(2). This principle applies to three different contribution arrangements as follows:

(A) *Employee-pay-all plans*. Older employees, like younger employees, may be required to contribute as a condition of participation up to the full premium cost for their age.

(B) *Non-contributory ("employer-pay-all") plans*. Where younger employees are not required to contribute any portion of the total premium cost, older employees may not be required to contribute any portion.

(C) *Contributory plans*. In these plans employers and participating employees share the premium cost. The required contributions of participants may increase with age so long as the *proportion* of the total premium required to be paid by the participants does not increase with age.

(iii) *As an option in order to receive an unreduced benefit*. An older employee may be given the option, as an individual, to make the additional contribution necessary to receive the same level of benefits as a younger employee (provided that the contemplated reduction in benefits is otherwise justified by section 4(f)(2)).

(5) *Forfeiture clauses*. Clauses in employee benefit plans which state that litigation or participation in any manner in a formal proceeding by an employee will result in the forfeiture of his rights are unlawful insofar as they may be applied to those who seek redress under the Act. This is by reason of section 4(d) which provides that it is unlawful for an employer, employment agency, or labor organization to discriminate against any individual because such individual "has made a charge, testified, assisted, or participated in any manner in an investigation, proceeding, or litigation under this Act."

(6) *Refusal to hire clauses*. Any provision of an employee benefit plan which requires or permits the refusal to hire an individual specified in section 12(a) of the Act on the basis of age is a subterfuge to evade the purposes of the Act and cannot be excused under section 4(f)(2).

(7) *Involuntary retirement clauses.* Any provision of an employee benefit plan which requires or permits the involuntary retirement of any individual specified in section 12(a) of the Act on the basis of age is a subterfuge to evade the purpose of the Act and cannot be excused under section 4(f)(2).

(e) *Benefits provided by the Government.* An employer does not violate the Act by permitting certain benefits to be provided by the Government, even though the availability of such benefits may be based on age. For example, it is not necessary for an employer to provide health benefits which are otherwise provided to certain employees by Medicare. However, the availability of benefits from the Government will not justify a reduction in employer-provided benefits if the result is that, taking the employer-provided and Government-provided benefits together, an older employee is entitled to a lesser benefit of any type (including coverage for family and/or dependents) than a similarly situated younger employee. For example, the availability of certain benefits to an older employee under Medicare will not justify denying an older employee a benefit which is provided to younger employees and is not provided to the older employee by Medicare.

(f) *Application of section 4(f)(2) to various employee benefit plans.*

(1) *Benefit-by-benefit approach.* This portion of the interpretation discusses how a benefit-by-benefit approach would apply to four of the most common types of employee benefit plans.

(i) *Life insurance.* It is not uncommon for life insurance coverage to remain constant until a specified age, frequently 65, and then be reduced. This practice will not violate the Act (even if reductions start before age 65), provided that the reduction for an employee of a particular age is no greater than is justified by the increased cost of coverage for that employee's specific age bracket encompassing no more than five years. It should be noted that a total denial of life insurance, on the basis of age, would not be justified under a benefit-by-benefit analysis. However, it is not unlawful for life insurance coverage to cease upon separation from service.

(ii) *Long-term disability.* Under a benefit-by-benefit approach, where employees who are disabled at younger ages are entitled to long-term disability benefits, there is no cost-based justification for denying such benefits altogether, on the basis of age, to employees who are disabled at older ages. It is not unlawful to cut off long-term disability benefits and coverage on the basis of some non-age factor, such as recovery from disability. Reductions on the basis of age in the level or duration of benefits available for disability are justifiable only on the basis of age-related cost considerations as set forth elsewhere in this section. An employer which provides long-term disability coverage to all employees may avoid any increases in the cost to it that such coverage for older employees would entail by reducing the level of benefits available to older employees. An employer may also avoid such cost increases by reducing the duration of benefits available to employees who become disabled at older ages, without reducing the level of benefits. In this connection, the Department would not assert a violation where the level of benefits is not reduced and the duration of benefits is reduced in the following manner:

(A) With respect to disabilities which occur at age 60 or less, benefits cease at age 65.

(B) With respect to disabilities which occur after age 60, benefits cease 5 years after disablement. Cost data may be produced to support other patterns of reduction as well.

(iii) *Retirement plans.* (A) *Participation.* No employee hired prior to normal retirement age may be excluded from a defined contribution plan. With respect to defined benefit plans not subject to the Employee Retirement Income Security Act (ERISA), Pub. L. 93-406, 29 U.S.C. 1001, 1003(a) and (b), an employee hired at an age more than 5 years prior to normal retirement age may not be excluded from such a plan unless the exclusion is justifiable on the basis of cost considerations as set forth elsewhere in this section. With respect to defined benefit plans subject to ERISA, such an exclusion would be unlawful in any case. An employee hired less than 5 years prior to normal retirement age may be excluded from a defined benefit plan, regardless of whether or not the plan is covered by ERISA. Similarly, any employee hired after normal retirement age may be excluded from a defined benefit plan.

(2) *"Benefit Package" Approach*

A "benefit package" approach to compliance under section 4(f)(2) offers greater flexibility than a benefit-by-benefit approach by permitting deviations from a benefit-by-benefit approach so long as the overall result is no lesser cost to the employer *and* no less favorable benefits for employees. As previously noted, in order to assure that such an approach is used for the benefit of older workers and not to their detriment, and is otherwise

consistent with the legislative intent, it is subject to limitations as set forth below:

(i) *A benefit package approach shall apply only to employee benefit plans which fall within section 4(f)(2).*

(ii) *A benefit package approach shall not apply to a retirement or pension plan.* The 1978 legislative history sets forth specific and comprehensive rules governing such plans, which have been adopted above. These rules are not tied to actuarially significant cost considerations but are intended to deal with the special funding arrangements of retirement or pension plans. Variations from these special rules are therefore not justified by variations from the cost-based benefit-by-benefit approach in other benefit plans, nor may variations from the special rules governing pension and retirement plans justify variations from the benefit-by-benefit approach in other benefit plans.

(iii) *A benefit package approach shall not be used to justify reductions in health benefits greater than would be justified under a benefit-by-benefit approach.* Such benefits appear to be of particular importance to older workers in meeting "problems arising from the impact of age" and were of particular concern to Congress. Therefore, the "benefit package" approach may not be used to reduce health insurance benefits by more than is warranted by the increase in the cost to the employer of those benefits alone. Any greater reduction would be a subterfuge to evade the purpose of the Act.

(iv) *A benefit reduction greater than would be justified under a benefit-by-benefit approach must be offset by another benefit available to the same employees.* No employees may be deprived because of age of one benefit without an offsetting benefit being made available to them.

(v) *Employers who wish to justify benefit reductions under a benefit package approach must be prepared to produce data to show that those reductions are fully justified.* Thus employers must be able to show that deviations from a benefit-by-benefit approach do not result in lesser cost to them or less favorable benefits to their employees. A general example consistent with these limitations may be given. Assume two employee benefit plans, providing Benefit "A" and Benefit "B." Both plans fall within section 4(f)(2), and neither is a retirement or pension plan subject to special rules. Both benefits are available to all employees. Age-based cost increases would justify a 10% decrease in both benefits on a benefit-by-benefit basis. The affected employees would, however, find it more favorable—that is, more consistent with meeting their needs—for no reduction to be made in Benefit "A" and a greater reduction to be made in Benefit "B." This "trade-off" would not result in reduction in health benefits. The "trade-off" may therefore be made. The details of the "trade-off" depend on data on the relative cost to the employer of the two benefits. If the data show that Benefit "A" and Benefit "B" cost the same, Benefit "B" may be reduced up to 20% if Benefit "A" is unreduced. If the data show that Benefit "A" costs only half as much as Benefit "B," however, Benefit "B" may be reduced up to only 15% if Benefit "A" is unreduced, since a greater reduction in Benefit "B" would result in an impermissible reduction in total benefit costs.

(g) *Relation of ADEA to State laws.* The ADEA does not preempt State age discrimination in employment laws. However, the failure of the ADEA to preempt such laws does not affect the issue of whether section 514 of the Employee Retirement Income Security Act (ERISA) preempts State laws which related to employee benefit plans. [Redesignated Reg. § 1625.10 by 52 FR 23811 on June 25, 1987].

[¶ 15,750H]

§1625.12 Exemption for bona fide executive or high policymaking employees. (a) Section 12(c)(1) of the Act, added by the 1978 amendments and as amended in 1984 and 1986, provides: "Nothing in this Act shall be construed to prohibit compulsory retirement of any employee who has attained 65 years of age, and who, for the 2-year period immediately before retirement, is employed in a bona fide executive or higher policymaking position, if such employee is entitled to an immediate nonforfeitable annual retirement benefit from a pension, profit-sharing, savings, or deferred compensation plan, or any combination of such plans, of the employer of such employee which equals, in the aggregate, at least $44,000."

(b) Since this provision is an exemption from the non-discrimination requirements of the Act, the burden is on the one seeking to invoke the exemption to show that every element has been clearly and unmistakably met. Moreover, as with other exemptions from the Act, this exemption must be narrowly construed.

(c) An employee within the exemption can lawfully be forced to retire on account of age at age 65 or above. In addition, the employer is free to retain such employees, either in the same position or status or in a different position or status. For example, an employee who falls within the exemption may be offered a position of lesser status or a part-time position. An employee who accepts such a new status or position, however, may not be treated any less favorably, on account of age, than any similarly situated younger employee.

(d)(1) In order for an employee to qualify as a "bona fide executive," the employer must initially show that the employee satisfies the definition of a bona fide executive set forth in §541.1 of this chapter. Each of the requirements in paragraphs (a) through (e) of §541.1 must be satisfied, regardless of the level of the employee's salary or compensation.

(2) Even if an employee qualifies as an executive under the definition in §541.1 of this chapter, the exemption from the ADEA may not be claimed unless the employee also meets the further criteria specified in the Conference Committee Report in the form of examples (see H.R. Rept. No. 95-950, p. 9). The examples are intended to make clear that the exemption does not apply to middle-management employees, no matter how great their retirement income, but only to a very few top level employees who exercise substantial executive authority over a significant number of employees and a large volume of business. As stated in the Conference Report (H.R. Rept. No. 95-950, p. 9):

"Typically the head of a significant and substantial local or regional operation of a corporation [or other business organization], such as a major production facility or retail establishment, but not the head of a minor branch, warehouse or retail store, would be covered by the term "bona fide executive." Individuals at higher levels in the corporate organizational structure who possess comparable or greater levels of responsibility and authority as measured by established and recognized criteria would also be covered.

"The heads of major departments or divisions of corporations [or other business organizations] are usually located at corporate or regional headquarters. With respect to employees whose duties are associated with corporate headquarters operations, such as finance, marketing, legal, production and manufacturing (or in a corporation organized on a product line basis, the management of product lines), the definition would cover employees who head those divisions.

"In a large organization the immediate subordinates of the heads of these divisions sometimes also exercise executive authority, within the meaning of this exemption. The conferees intend the definition to cover such employees if they possess responsibility which is comparable to or greater than that possessed by the head of a significant and substantial local operation who meets the definition."

(e) The phrase "high policymaking position," according to the Conference Report (H.R. Rept. No. 95-950, p. 10), is limited to "* * * certain top level employees who are not 'bona fide executives' * * *." Specifically, these are:

"* * * individuals who have little or no line authority but whose position and responsibility are such that they play a significant role in the development of corporate policy and effectively recommend the implementation thereof.

"For example, the chief economist or the chief research scientist of a corporation typically has little line authority. His duties would be primarily intellectual as opposed to executive or managerial. His responsibility would be to evaluate significant economic or scientific trends and issues, to develop and recommend policy direction to the top executive officers of the corporation, and he would have a significant impact on the ultimate decision on such policies by virtue of his expertise and direct access to the decisionmakers. Such an employee would meet the definition of a 'high policymaking' employee."

On the other hand, as this description makes clear, the support personnel of a "high policymaking" employeee would not be subject to the exemption even if they supervise the development, and draft the recommendation, of various policies submitted by their supervisors.

(f) In order for the exemption to apply to a particular employee, the employee must have been in a "bona fide executive or high policymaking position," as those terms are defined in this section, for the two-year period immediately before retirement. Thus, an employee who holds two or more different positions during the two-year period is subject to the exemption only if each such job is an executive or high policymaking position.

(g) The Conference Committee Report expressly states that the exemption is not applicable to Federal employees covered by section 15 of the Act (H.R. Rept. No. 95-950, p. 10).

(h) The "annual retirement benefit," to which covered employees must be entitled, is the sum of amounts payable during each one-year period from the date on which such benefits first become receivable by the retiree. Once established, the annual period upon which calculations are based may not be changed from year to year.

(i) The annual retirement benefit must be immediately available to the employee to be retired pursuant to the exemption. For purposes of deter-

mining compliance, "immediate" means that the payment of plan benefits (in a lump sum or the first of a series of periodic payments) must occur not later than 60 days after the effective date of the retirement in question. The fact that an employee will receive benefits only after expiration of the 60-day period will not preclude his retirement pursuant to the exemption, if the employee could have elected to receive benefits within that period.

(j)(1) The annual retirement benefit must equal, in the aggregate, at least $27,000. The manner of determining whether this requirement has been satisfied is set forth in §1627.17(c).

(2) In determining whether the aggregate annual retirement benefit equals at least $27,000, the only benefits which may be counted are those authorized by and provided under the terms of a pension, profitsharing, savings, or deferred compensation plan. (Regulations issued pursuant to section 12(c)(2) of the Act, regarding the manner of calculating the amount of qualified retirement benefits for purposes of the exemption, are set forth in §1627.17 of this Chapter.)

(k)(1) The annual retirement benefit must be "nonforfeitable." Accordingly, the exemption may not be applied to any employee subject to plan provisions which could cause the cessation of payments to a retiree or result in the reduction of benefits to less than $27,000 in any one year. For example, where a plan contains a provision under which benefits would be suspended if a retiree engages in litigation against the former employer, or obtains employment with a competitor of the former employer, the retirement benefit will be deemed to be forfeitable. However, retirement benefits will not be deemed forfeitable solely because the benefits are discontinued or suspended for reasons permitted under section 411(a)(3) of the Internal Revenue Code.

(2) An annual retirement benefit will not be deemed forfeitable merely because the minimum statutory benefit level is not guaranteed against the possibility of plan bankruptcy or is subject to benefit restrictions in the event of early termination of the plan in accordance with Treasury Regulation 1.401-4(c). However, as of the effective date of the retirement in question, there must be at least a reasonable expectation that the plan will meet its obligations.

* * *

[¶ 15,750I]

§1625.21 **Apprenticeship programs.** All apprenticeship programs, including those apprenticeship programs created or maintained by joint labor-management organizations, are subject to the prohibitions of sec. 4 of the Age Discrimination in Employment Act of 1967, as amended, 29 U.S.C. 623. Age limitations in apprenticeship programs are valid only if excepted under sec. 4(f)(1) of the Act, 29 U.S.C. 623(f)(1), or exempted by the Commission under sec. 9 of the Act, 29 U.S.C. 628, in accordance with the procedures set forth in 29 CFR 1625.30. [Corrected/revised by 80 FR 60539 on October 7, 2015.]

[¶ 15,750J]

§1625.22 **Waivers of rights and claims under the ADEA.**
(a) *Introduction.*

(1) Congress amended the ADEA in 1990 to clarify the prohibitions against discrimination on the basis of age. In Title II of OWBPA, Congress addressed waivers of rights and claims under the ADEA, amending section 7 of the ADEA by adding a new subsection (f).

(2) Section 7(f)(1) of the ADEA expressly provides that waivers may be valid and enforceable under the ADEA only if the waiver is "knowing and voluntary". Sections 7(f)(1) and 7(f)(2) of the ADEA set out the minimum requirements for determining whether a waiver is knowing and voluntary.

(3) Other facts and circumstances may bear on the question of whether the waiver is knowing and voluntary, as, for example, if there is a material mistake, omission, or misstatement in the information furnished by the employer to an employee in connection with the waiver.

(4) The rules in this section apply to all waivers of ADEA rights and claims, regardless of whether the employee is employed in the private or public sector, including employment by the United States Government.

(b) *Wording of Waiver Agreements.*

(1) Section 7(f)(1)(A) of the ADEA provides, as part of the minimum requirements for a knowing and voluntary waiver, that:

The waiver is part of an agreement between the individual and the employer that is written in a manner calculated to be understood by such individual, or by the average individual eligible to participate.

(2) The entire waiver agreement must be in writing.

(3) Waiver agreements must be drafted in plain language geared to the level of understanding of the individual party to the agreement or individuals eligible to participate. Employers should take into account such factors as the level of comprehension and education of typical participants. Consideration of these factors usually will require the limitation or elimination of technical jargon and of long, complex sentences.

(4) The waiver agreement must not have the effect of misleading, misinforming, or failing to inform participants and affected individuals. Any advantages or disadvantages described shall be presented without either exaggerating the benefits or minimizing the limitations.

(5) Section 7(f)(1)(H) of the ADEA, relating to exit incentive or other employment termination programs offered to a group or class of employees, also contains a requirement that information be conveyed "in writing in a manner calculated to be understood by the average participant." The same standards applicable to the similar language in section 7(f)(1)(A) of the ADEA apply here as well.

(6) Section 7(f)(1)(B) of the ADEA provides, as part of the minimum requirements for a knowing and voluntary waiver, that "the waiver specifically refers to rights or claims under this Act." Pursuant to this subsection, the waiver agreement must refer to the Age Discrimination in Employment Act (ADEA) by name in connection with the waiver.

(7) Section 7(f)(1)(E) of the ADEA requires that an individual must be "advised in writing to consult with an attorney prior to executing the agreement."

(c) *Waiver of future rights.*

(1) Section 7(f)(1)(C) of the ADEA provides that:

A waiver may not be considered knowing and voluntary unless at a minimum . . . the individual does not waive rights or claims that may arise after the date the waiver is executed.

(2) The waiver of rights or claims that arise following the execution of a waiver is prohibited. However, section 7(f)(1)(C) of the ADEA does not bar, in a waiver that otherwise is consistent with statutory requirements, the enforcement of agreements to perform future employment-related actions such as the employee's agreement to retire or otherwise terminate employment at a future date.

(d) *Consideration.*

(1) Section 7(f)(1)(D) of the ADEA states that:

A waiver may not be considered knowing and voluntary unless at a minimum * * * the individual waives rights or claims only in exchange for consideration in addition to anything of value to which the individual already is entitled.

(2) "Consideration in addition" means anything of value in addition to that to which the individual is already entitled in the absence of a waiver.

(3) If a benefit or other thing of value was eliminated in contravention of law or contract, express or implied, the subsequent offer of such benefit or thing of value in connection with a waiver will not constitute "consideration" for purposes of section 7(f)(1) of the ADEA. Whether such elimination as to one employee or group of employees is in contravention of law or contract as to other employees, or to that individual employee at some later time, may vary depending on the facts and circumstances of each case.

(4) An employer is not required to give a person age 40 or older a greater amount of consideration than is given to a person under the age of 40, solely because of that person's membership in the protected class under the ADEA.

(e) *Time periods.*

(1) Section 7(f)(1)(F) of the ADEA states that:

A waiver may not be considered knowing and voluntary unless at a minimum * * *

(i) The individual is given a period of at least 21 days within which to consider the agreement; or

(ii) If a waiver is requested in connection with an exit incentive or other employment termination program offered to a group or class of employees, the individual is given a period of at least 45 days within which to consider the agreement.

(2) Section 7(f)(1)(G) of the ADEA states:

A waiver may not be considered knowing and voluntary unless at a minimum . . . the agreement provides that for a period of at least 7 days following the execution of such agreement, the individual may revoke the agreement, and the agreement shall not become effective or enforceable until the revocation period has expired.

(3) The term "exit incentive or other employment termination program" includes both voluntary and involuntary programs.

(4) The 21 or 45 day period runs from the date of the employer's final offer. Material changes to the final offer restart the running of the 21 or 45 day period; changes made to the final offer that are not material do not restart the running of the 21 or 45 day period. The parties may agree that changes, whether material or immaterial, do not restart the running of the 21 or 45 day period.

(5) The 7 day revocation period cannot be shortened by the parties, by agreement or otherwise.

(6) An employee may sign a release prior to the end of the 21 or 45 day time period, thereby commencing the mandatory 7 day revocation period. This is permissible as long as the employee's decision to accept such shortening of time is knowing and voluntary and is not induced by the employer through fraud, misrepresentation, a threat to withdraw or alter the

offer prior to the expiration of the 21 or 45 day time period, or by providing different terms to employees who sign the release prior to the expiration of such time period. However, if an employee signs a release before the expiration of the 21 or 45 day time period, the employer may expedite the processing of the consideration provided in exchange for the waiver.

(f) *Informational requirements.*

(1) *Introduction.*

(i) Section 7(f)(1)(H) of the ADEA provides that:

A waiver may not be considered knowing and voluntary unless at a minimum . . . if a waiver is requested in connection with an exit incentive or other employment termination program offered to a group or class of employees, the employer (at the commencement of the period specified in subparagraph (F)) [which provides time periods for employees to consider the waiver] informs the individual in writing in a manner calculated to be understood by the average individual eligible to participate, as to:

(i) Any class, unit, or group of individuals covered by such program, any eligibility factors for such program, and any time limits applicable to such program; and

(ii) The job titles and ages of all individuals eligible or selected for the program, and the ages of all individuals in the same job classification or organizational unit who are not eligible or selected for the program.

(ii) Section 7(f)(1)(H) of the ADEA addresses two principal issues: to whom information must be provided, and what information must be disclosed to such individuals.

(iii)(A) Section 7(f)(1)(H) of the ADEA references two types of "programs" under which employers seeking waivers must make written disclosures: "exit incentive programs" and "other employment termination programs." Usually an "exit incentive program" is a voluntary program offered to a group or class of employees where such employees are offered consideration in addition to anything of value to which the individuals are already entitled (hereinafter in this section, "additional consideration") in exchange for their decision to resign voluntarily and sign a waiver. Usually "other employment termination program" refers to a group or class of employees who were involuntarily terminated and who are offered additional consideration in return for their decision to sign a waiver.

(B) The question of the existence of a "program" will be decided based upon the facts and circumstances of each case. A "program" exists when an employer offers additional consideration for the signing of a waiver pursuant to an exit incentive or other employment termination (e.g., a reduction in force) to two or more employees. Typically, an involuntary termination program is a standardized formula or package of benefits that is available to two or more employees, while an exit incentive program typically is a standardized formula or package of benefits designed to induce employees to sever their employment voluntarily. In both cases, the terms of the programs generally are not subject to negotiation between the parties.

(C) Regardless of the type of program, the scope of the terms "class," "unit," "group," "job classification," and "organizational unit" is determined by examining the "decisional unit" at issue. (See paragraph (f)(3) of this section, "The Decisional Unit.")

(D) A "program" for purposes of the ADEA need not constitute an "employee benefit plan" for purposes of the Employee Retirement Income Security Act of 1974 (ERISA). An employer may or may not have an ERISA severance plan in connection with its OWBPA program.

(iv) The purpose of the informational requirements is to provide an employee with enough information regarding the program to allow the employee to make an informed choice whether or not to sign a waiver agreement.

(2) *To whom must the information be given.* The required information must be given to each person in the decisional unit who is asked to sign a waiver agreement.

(3) *The decisional unit.*

(i)(A) The terms "class," "unit," or "group" in section 7(f)(1)(H)(i) of the ADEA and "job classification or organizational unit" in section 7(f)(1)(H)(ii) of the ADEA refer to examples of categories or groupings of employees affected by a program within an employer's particular organizational structure. The terms are not meant to be an exclusive list of characterizations of an employer's organization.

(B) When identifying the scope of the "class, unit, or group," and "job classification or organizational unit," an employer should consider its organizational structure and decision-making process. A "decisional unit" is that portion of the employer's organizational structure from which the employer chose the persons who would be offered consideration for the signing of a waiver and those who would not be offered consideration for the signing of a waiver. The term "decisional unit" has been developed to reflect the process by which an employer chose certain employees for a program and ruled out others from that program.

(ii)(A) The variety of terms used in section 7(f)(1)(H) of the ADEA demonstrates that employers often use differing terminology to describe their organizational structures. When identifying the population of the decisional unit, the employer acts on a case-by-case basis, and thus the determination of the appropriate class, unit, or group, and job classification or organizational unit for purposes of section 7(f)(1)(H) of the ADEA also must be made on a case-by-case basis.

(B) The examples in paragraph (f)(3)(iii), of this section demonstrate that in appropriate cases some subgroup of a facility's work force may be the decisional unit. In other situations, it may be appropriate for the decisional unit to comprise several facilities. However, as the decisional unit is typically no broader than the facility, in general the disclosure need be no broader than the facility. "Facility" as it is used throughout this section generally refers to place or location. However, in some circumstances terms such as "school," "plant," or "complex" may be more appropriate.

(C) Often, when utilizing a program an employer is attempting to reduce its workforce at a particular facility in an effort to eliminate what it deems to be excessive overhead, expenses, or costs from its organization at that facility. If the employer's goal is the reduction of its workforce at a particular facility and that employer undertakes a decision-making process by which certain employees of the facility are selected for a program, and others are not selected for a program, then that facility generally will be the decisional unit for purposes of section 7(f)(1)(H) of the ADEA.

(D) However, if an employer seeks to terminate employees by exclusively considering a particular portion or subgroup of its operations at a specific facility, then that subgroup or portion of the workforce at that facility will be considered the decisional unit.

(E) Likewise, if the employer analyzes its operations at several facilities, specifically considers and compares ages, seniority rosters, or similar factors at differing facilities, and determines to focus its workforce reduction at a particular facility, then by the nature of that employer's decision-making process the decisional unit would include all considered facilities and not just the facility selected for the reductions.

(iii) The following examples are not all-inclusive and are meant only to assist employers and employees in determining the appropriate decisional unit. Involuntary reductions in force typically are structured along one or more of the following lines:

(A) *Facility-wide:* Ten percent of the employees in the Springfield facility will be terminated within the next ten days;

(B) *Division-wide:* Fifteen of the employees in the Computer Division will be terminated in December;

(C) *Department-wide:* One-half of the workers in the Keyboard Department of the Computer Division will be terminated in December;

(D) *Reporting:* Ten percent of the employees who report to the Vice President for Sales, wherever the employees are located, will be terminated immediately;

(E) *Job Category:* Ten percent of all accountants, wherever the employees are located, will be terminated next week.

(iv) In the examples in paragraph (f)(3)(iii) of this section, the decisional units are, respectively:

(A) The Springfield facility;

(B) The Computer Division;

(C) The Keyboard Department;

(D) All employees reporting to the Vice President for Sales; and

(E) All accountants.

(v) While the particular circumstances of each termination program will determine the decisional unit, the following examples also may assist in determining when the decisional unit is other than the entire facility:

(A) A number of small facilities with interrelated functions and employees in a specific geographic area may comprise a single decisional unit;

(B) If a company utilizes personnel for a common function at more than one facility, the decisional unit for that function (i.e., accounting) may be broader than the one facility;

(C) A large facility with several distinct functions may comprise a number of decisional units; for example, if a single facility has distinct internal functions with no employee overlap (i.e., manufacturing, accounting, human resources), and the program is confined to a distinct function, a smaller decisional unit may be appropriate.

(vi)(A) For purposes of this section, higher level review of termination decisions generally will not change the size of the decisional unit unless the reviewing process alters its scope. For example, review by the Human Resources Department to monitor compliance with discrimination laws does

not affect the decisional unit. Similarly, when a regional manager in charge of more than one facility reviews the termination decisions regarding one of those facilities, the review does not alter the decisional unit, which remains the one facility under consideration.

(B) However, if the regional manager in the course of review determines that persons in other facilities should also be considered for termination, the decisional unit becomes the population of all facilities considered. Further, if, for example, the regional manager and his three immediate subordinates jointly review the termination decisions, taking into account more than one facility, the decisional unit becomes the populations of all facilities considered.

(vii) This regulatory section is limited to the requirements of section 7(f)(1)(H) and is not intended to affect the scope of discovery or of substantive proceedings in the processing of charges of violation of the ADEA or in litigation involving such charges.

(4) *Presentation of information.*

(i) The information provided must be in writing and must be written in a manner calculated to be understood by the average individual eligible to participate.

(ii) Information regarding ages should be broken down according to the age of each person eligible or selected for the program and each person not eligible or selected for the program. The use of age bands broader than one year (such as "age 20-30") does not satisfy this requirement.

(iii) In a termination of persons in several established grade levels and/or other established subcategories within a job category or job title, the information shall be broken down by grade level or other subcategory.

(iv) If an employer in its disclosure combines information concerning both voluntary and involuntary terminations, the employer shall present the information in a manner that distinguishes between voluntary and involuntary terminations.

(v) If the terminees are selected from a subset of a decisional unit, the employer must still disclose information for the entire population of the decisional unit. For example, if the employer decides that a 10% RIF in the Accounting Department will come from the accountants whose performance is in the bottom one-third of the Division, the employer still must disclose information for all employees in the Accounting Department, even those who are the highest rated.

(vi) An involuntary termination program in a decisional unit may take place in successive increments over a period of time. Special rules apply to this situation. Specifically, information supplied with regard to the involuntary termination program should be cumulative, so that later terminees are provided ages and job titles or job categories, as appropriate, for all persons in the decisional unit at the beginning of the program and all persons terminated to date. There is no duty to supplement the information given to earlier terminees so long as the disclosure, at the time it is given, conforms to the requirements of this section.

(vii) The following example demonstrates one way in which the required information could be presented to the employees. (This example is not presented as a prototype notification agreement that automatically will comply with the ADEA. Each information disclosure must be structured based upon the individual case, taking into account the corporate structure, the population of the decisional unit, and the requirements of section 7(f)(1)(H) of the ADEA): Example: Y Corporation lost a major construction contract and determined that it must terminate 10% of the employees in the Construction Division. Y decided to offer all terminees $20,000 in severance pay in exchange for a waiver of all rights. The waiver provides the section 7(f)(1)(H) of the ADEA information as follows:

(A) The decisional unit is the Construction Division.

(B) All persons in the Construction Division are eligible for the program. All persons who are being terminated in our November RIF are selected for the program.

(C) All persons who are being offered consideration under a waiver agreement must sign the agreement and return it to the Personnel Office within 45 days after receiving the waiver. Once the signed waiver is returned to the Personnel Office, the employee has 7 days to revoke the waiver agreement.

(D) The following is a listing of the ages and job titles of persons in the Construction Division who were and were not selected for termination and the offer of consideration for signing a waiver:

Job Title	Age	No. Selected	No. not selected
(1) Mechanical Engineers, I	25	21	48
	26	11	73
	63	4	18
	64	3	11
(2) Mechanical Engineers, II	28	3	10
	29	11	17
	Etc., for all ages		

Job Title	Age	No. Selected	No. not selected
(3) Structural Engineers, I	21	5	8
	Etc., for all ages		
(4) Structural Engineers, II	23	2	4
	Etc., for all ages		
(5) Purchasing Agents	26	10	11
	Etc., for all ages		

(g) *Waivers settling charges and lawsuits.*

(1) Section 7(f)(2) of the ADEA provides that:

A waiver in settlement of a charge filed with the Equal Employment Opportunity Commission, or an action filed in court by the individual or the individual's representative, alleging age discrimination of a kind prohibited under section 4 or 15 may not be considered knowing and voluntary unless at a minimum:

(A) Subparagraphs (A) through (E) of paragraph (1) have been met; and

(B) The individual is given a reasonable period of time within which to consider the settlement agreement.

(2) The language in section 7(f)(2) of the ADEA, "discrimination of a kind prohibited under section 4 or 15" refers to allegations of age discrimination of the type prohibited by the ADEA.

(3) The standards set out in paragraphs (b), (c), and (d) of this section for complying with the provisions of section 7(f)(1) (A)-(E) of the ADEA also will apply for purposes of complying with the provisions of section 7(f)(2)(A) of the ADEA. [Amended by 79 FR 13546 on March 11,2014.]

(4) The term "reasonable time within which to consider the settlement agreement" means reasonable under all the circumstances, including whether the individual is represented by counsel or has the assistance of counsel.

(5) However, while the time periods under section 7(f)(1) of the ADEA do not apply to subsection 7(f)(2) of the ADEA, a waiver agreement under this subsection that provides an employee the time periods specified in section 7(f)(1) of the ADEA will be considered "reasonable" for purposes of section 7(f)(2)(B) of the ADEA.

(6) A waiver agreement in compliance with this section that is in settlement of an EEOC charge does not require the participation or supervision of EEOC.

(h) *Burden of proof.* In any dispute that may arise over whether any of the requirements, conditions, and circumstances set forth in section 7(f) of the ADEA, subparagraph (A), (B), (C), (D), (E), (F), (G), or (H) of paragraph (1), or subparagraph (A) or (B) of paragraph (2), have been met, the party asserting the validity of a waiver shall have the burden of proving in a court of competent jurisdiction that a waiver was knowing and voluntary pursuant to paragraph (1) or (2) of section 7(f) of the ADEA.

(i) *EEOC's enforcement powers.*

(1) Section 7(f)(4) of the ADEA states:

No waiver agreement may affect the Commission's rights and responsibilities to enforce [the ADEA]. No waiver may be used to justify interfering with the protected right of an employee to file a charge or participate in an investigation or proceeding conducted by the Commission.

(2) No waiver agreement may include any provision prohibiting any individual from:

(i) Filing a charge or complaint, including a challenge to the validity of the waiver agreement, with EEOC, or

(ii) Participating in any investigation or proceeding conducted by EEOC.

(3) No waiver agreement may include any provision imposing any condition precedent, any penalty, or any other limitation adversely affecting any individual's right to:

(i) File a charge or complaint, including a challenge to the validity of the waiver agreement, with EEOC, or

(ii) Participate in any investigation or proceeding conducted by EEOC.

(j) *Effective date of this section.*

(1) This section is effective July 6, 1998.

(2) This section applies to waivers offered by employers on or after the effective date specified in paragraph (j)(1) of this section.

(3) No inference is to be drawn from this section regarding the validity of waivers offered prior to the effective date.

(k) *Statutory authority.* The regulations in this section are legislative regulations issued pursuant to section 9 of the ADEA and Title II of OWBPA.

[FR Doc. 98-14908 Filed 6-4-98; 8:45 am]

[¶ 15,750K]

§1625.23 Waivers of rights and claims: Tender back of consideration.

(a) An individual alleging that a waiver agreement, covenant not to sue, or other equivalent arrangement was not knowing and voluntary under the ADEA is not required to tender back the consideration given for that agreement before filing either a lawsuit or a charge of discrimination with EEOC or any state or local fair employment practices agency acting as an EEOC referral agency for purposes of filing the charge with EEOC. Retention of consideration does not foreclose a challenge to any waiver agreement, covenant not to sue, or other equivalent arrangement; nor does the retention constitute the ratification of any waiver agreement, covenant not to sue, or other equivalent arrangement.

(b) No ADEA waiver agreement, covenant not to sue, or other equivalent arrangement may impose any condition precedent, any penalty, or any other limitation adversely affecting any individual's right to challenge the agreement. This prohibition includes, but is not limited to, provisions requiring employees to tender back consideration received, and provisions allowing employers to recover attorneys' fees and/or damages because of the filing of an ADEA suit. This rule is not intended to preclude employers from recovering attorneys' fees or costs specifically authorized under federal law.

(c) *Restitution, recoupment, or setoff.*

(1) Where an employee successfully challenges a waiver agreement, covenant not to sue, or other equivalent arrangement, and prevails on the merits of an ADEA claim, courts have the discretion to determine whether an employer is entitled to restitution, recoupment or setoff (hereinafter, "reduction") against the employee's monetary award. A reduction never can exceed the amount recovered by the employee, or the consideration the employee received for signing the waiver agreement, covenant not to sue, or other equivalent arrangement, whichever is less.

(2) In a case involving more than one plaintiff, any reduction must be applied on a plaintiff-by-plaintiff basis. No individual's award can be reduced based on the consideration received by any other person.

(d) No employer may abrogate its duties to any signatory under a waiver agreement, covenant not to sue, or other equivalent arrangement, even if one or more of the signatories or the EEOC successfully challenges the validity of that agreement under the ADEA [Added 12-11-00 by 65 FR 77437].

Subpart C—Administrative Exemptions

[¶ 15,750P]

§1625.30 Administrative exemptions; procedures.

(a) Section 9 of the Act provides that, "In accordance with the provisions of subchapter II of chapter 5, of title 5, United States Code, the Secretary of Labor * * * may establish such reasonable exemptions to and from any or all provisions of this Act as he may find necessary and proper in the public interest."

(b) The authority conferred on the Commission by section 9 of the Act to establish reasonable exemptions will be exercised with caution and due regard for the remedial purpose of the statute to promote employment of older persons based on their ability rather than age and to prohibit arbitrary age discrimination in employment. Administrative action consistent with this statutory purpose may be taken under this section, with or without a request therefor, when found necessary and proper in the public interest in accordance with the statutory standards. No formal procedures have been prescribed for requesting such action. However, a reasonable exemption from the Act's provisions will be granted only if it is decided, after notice published in the FEDERAL REGISTER giving all interested persons an opportunity to present data, views, or arguments, that a strong and affirmative showing has been made that such exemption is in fact necessary and proper in the public interest. Request for such exemption shall be submitted in writing to the Commission.

[Redesignated 12-26-07 by 72 FR 72938.]

[¶ 15,750Q]

§1625.31 Special employment programs.

(a) Pursuant to the authority contained in section 9 of the Act and in accordance with the procedure provided therein and in §1625.30(b) of this part, it has been found necessary and proper in the public interest to exempt from all prohibitions of the Act all activities and programs under Federal contracts or grants, or carried out by the public employment services of the several States, designed exclusively to provide employment for, or to encourage the employment of, persons with special employment problems, including employment activities and programs under the Manpower Development and Training Act of 1962, Pub. L. No. 87-415, 76 Stat. 23 (1962), as amended, and the Economic Opportunity Act of 1964, Pub. L. No. 88-452, 78 Stat. 508 (1964), as amended, for persons among the long-term unemployed, individuals with disabilities, members of minority groups, older workers, or youth. Questions concerning the application of this exemption shall be referred to the Commission for decision. [Amended 12-7-09 by 74 FR 63981.]

(b) Any employer, employment agency, or labor organization the activities of which are exempt from the prohibitions of the Act under paragraph (a) of this section shall maintain and preserve records containing the same information and data that is required of employers, employment agencies, and labor organizations under §§ 1627.3, 1627.4, and 1627.5, respectively.

[Redesignated 12-26-07 by 72 FR 72938.]

[¶ 15,750R]

§ 1625.32 Coordination of retiree health benefits with Medicare and State health benefits. (a) *Definitions.*

(1) *Employee benefit plan* means an employee benefit plan as defined in 29 U.S.C. 1002(3).

(2) *Medicare* means the health insurance program available pursuant to Title XVIII of the Social Security Act, 42 U.S.C. 1395 *et seq.*

(3) *Comparable State health benefit plan* means a State-sponsored health benefit plan that, like Medicare, provides retired participants who have attained a minimum age with health benefits, whether or not the type, amount or value of those benefits is equivalent to the type, amount or value of the health benefits provided under Medicare.

(b) *Exemption.* Some employee benefit plans provide health benefits for retired participants that are altered, reduced or eliminated when the participant is eligible for Medicare health benefits or for health benefits under a comparable State health benefit plan, whether or not the participant actually enrolls in the other benefit program. Pursuant to the authority contained in section 9 of the Act, and in accordance with the procedures provided therein and in § 1625.30(b) of this part, it is hereby found necessary and proper in the public interest to exempt from all prohibitions of the Act such coordination of retiree health benefits with Medicare or a comparable State health benefit plan.

(c) *Scope of Exemption.* This exemption shall be narrowly construed. No other aspects of ADEA coverage or employment benefits other than those specified in paragraph (b) of this section are affected by the exemption. Thus, for example, the exemption does not apply to the use of eligibility for Medicare or a comparable State health benefit plan in connection with any act, practice or benefit of employment not specified in paragraph (b) of this section. Nor does it apply to the use of the age of eligibility for Medicare or a comparable State health benefit plan in connection with any act, practice or benefit of employment not specified in paragraph (b) of this section.

[Added 12-26-07 by 72 FR 72938.]

[¶ 15,750S]

Appendix to § 1625.32— Questions and Answers Regarding Coordination of Retiree Health Benefits With Medicare and State Health Benefits

Q1. Why is the Commission issuing an exemption from the Act?

A1. The Commission recognizes that while employers are under no legal obligation to offer retiree health benefits, some employers choose to do so in order to maintain a competitive advantage in the marketplace—using these and other benefits to attract and retain the best talent available to work for their organizations. Further, retiree health benefits clearly benefit workers, allowing such individuals to acquire affordable health insurance coverage at a time when private health insurance coverage might otherwise be cost prohibitive. The Commission believes that it is in the best interest of both employers and employees for the Commission to pursue a policy that permits employers to offer these benefits to the greatest extent possible.

Q2. Does the exemption mean that the Act no longer applies to retirees?

A2. No. Only the practice of coordinating retiree health benefits with Medicare (or a comparable State health benefit plan) as specified in paragraph (b) of this section is exempt from the Act. In all other contexts, the Act continues to apply to retirees to the same extent that it did prior to the issuance of this section.

Q3. May an employer offer a "carve-out plan" for retirees who are eligible for Medicare or a comparable State health plan?

A3. Yes. A "carve-out plan" reduces the benefits available under an employee benefit plan by the amount payable by Medicare or a comparable State health plan. Employers may continue to offer such "carve-out plans"

and make Medicare or a comparable State health plan the primary payer of health benefits for those retirees eligible for Medicare or the comparable State health plan.

Q4. Does the exemption also apply to dependent and/or spousal health benefits that are included as part of the health benefits provided for retired participants?

A4. Yes. Because dependent and/or spousal health benefits are benefits provided to the retired participant, the exemption applies to these benefits, just as it does to the health benefits for the retired participant. However, dependent and/or spousal benefits need not be identical to the health benefits provided for retired participants. Consequently, dependent and/or spousal benefits may be altered, reduced or eliminated pursuant to the exemption whether or not the health benefits provided for retired participants are similarly altered, reduced or eliminated.

Q5. Does the exemption address how the ADEA may apply to other acts, practices or employment benefits not specified in the rule?

A5. No. The exemption only applies to the practice of coordinating employer-sponsored retiree health benefits with eligibility for Medicare or a comparable State health benefit program. No other aspects of ADEA coverage or employment benefits other than those retiree health benefits are affected by the exemption.

Q6. Does the exemption apply to existing, as well as to newly created, employee benefit plans?

A6. Yes. The exemption applies to all retiree health benefits that coordinate with Medicare (or a comparable State health benefit plan) as specified in paragraph (b) of this section, whether those benefits are provided for in an existing or newly created employee benefit plan.

Q7. Does the exemption apply to health benefits that are provided to current employees who are at or over the age of Medicare eligibility (or the age of eligibility for a comparable State health benefit plan)?

A7. No. The exemption applies only to retiree health benefits, not to health benefits that are provided to current employees. Thus, health benefits for current employees must be provided in a manner that comports with the requirements of the Act. Moreover, under the laws governing the Medicare program, an employer must offer to current employees who are at or over the age of Medicare eligibility the same health benefits, under the same conditions, that it offers to any current employee under the age of Medicare eligibility.

[Added 12-26-07 by 72 FR 72938.]

29 CFR Part 1627—Records to Be Made or Kept Relating to Age; Notices to Be Posted

* * *

Subpart B—Records to Be Made or Kept Relating to Age; Notices to Be Posted

[¶ 15,751]

§ 1627.2 Forms of records. No particular order or form of records is required by the regulations in this Part 1627. It is required only that the records contain in some form the information specified. If the information required is available in records kept for other purposes, or can be obtained readily by recomputing or extending data recorded in some other form, no further records are required to be made or kept on a routine basis by this Part 1627.

[¶ 15,752]

§ 1627.3 Records to be kept by employers. (a) Every employer shall make and keep for three years payroll or other records for each of his employees which contain: (1) Name; (2) Address; (3) Date of birth; (4) Occupation; (5) Rate of pay; and (6) Compensation earned each week.

(b)(1) Every employer who, in the regular course of his business, makes, obtains, or uses, any personnel or employment records related to the following, shall, except as provided in subparagraphs (3) and (4) of this paragraph, keep them for a period of 1 year from the date of the personnel action to which any records relate:

* * *

(2) Every employer shall keep on file any employee benefit plans such as pension and insurance plans, as well as copies of any seniority systems and merit systems which are in writing, for the full period the plan or system is in effect, and for at least 1 year after its termination. If the plan or system is not in writing, a memorandum fully outlining the terms of such plan or system and the manner in which it has been communicated to the affected employees, together with notations relating to any changes or revisions thereto, shall be kept on file for a like period.

* * *

(4) When an enforcement action is commenced under section 7 of the Act regarding a particular applicant or employee, the Commission or its authorized representative may require the employer to retain any record required to be kept under subparagraph (1), (2), or (3) of this paragraph which is relative to such action until the final disposition thereof.

* * *

[¶ 15,753]

§ 1627.6 Availability of records for inspection. (a) *Place records are to be kept*. The records required to be kept by this part shall be kept safe and accessible at the place of employment or business at which the individual to whom they relate is employed or has applied for employment or membership, or at one or more established central recordkeeping offices.

(b) *Inspection of records*. All records required by this part to be kept shall be made available for inspection and transcription by authorized representatives of the Commission during business hours generally observed by the office at which they are kept or in the community generally. Where records are maintained at a central recordkeeping office pursuant to paragraph (a) of this section, such records shall be made available at the office at which they would otherwise be required to be kept within 72 hours following request from the Commission or its authorized representative.

[¶ 15,754]

§ 1627.7 Transcriptions and reports. Every person required to maintain records under the Act shall make such extension, recomputation or transcriptions of his records and shall submit such reports concerning actions taken and limitations and classifications of individuals set forth in records as the Commission or its authorized representative may request in writing.

[¶ 15,755]

§ 1627.10 Notices to be posted. Every employer, employment agency, and labor organization which has an obligation under the Age Discrimination in Employment Act of 1967 shall post and keep posted in conspicuous places upon its premises the notice pertaining to the applicability of the Act prescribed by the Commission or its authorized representative. Such a notice must be posted in prominent and accessible places where it can readily be observed by employees, applicants for employment and union members.

[¶ 15,756]

§ 1627.11 Petitions for recordkeeping exceptions. (a) *Submission of petitions for relief*. Each employer, employment agency, or labor organization who for good cause wishes to maintain records in a manner other than required in this part, or to be relieved of preserving certain records for the period or periods prescribed in this part, may submit in writing a petition to the Commission requesting such relief setting forth the reasons therefor and proposing alternative recordkeeping or record-retention procedures.

(b) *Action on petitions*. If, on review of the petition and after completion of any necessary or appropriate investigation supplementary thereto, the Commission shall find that the alternative procedure proposed, if granted, will not hamper or interfere with the enforcement of the Act, and will be of equivalent usefulness in its enforcement, the Commission may grant the petition subject to such conditions as it may determine appropriate and subject to revocation. Whenever any relief granted to any person is sought to be revoked for failure to comply with the conditions of the Commission, that person shall be notified in writing of the facts constituting such failure and afforded an opportunity to achieve or demonstrate compliance.

(c) *Compliance after submission of petitions*. The submission of a petition or any delay of the Commission in acting upon such petition shall not relieve any employer, employment agency, or labor organization from any obligations to comply with this part. However, the Commission shall give notice of the denial of any petition with due promptness.

Subpart D—Statutory Exemption

[¶ 15,758A]

§ 1627.17 Calculating the amount of qualified retirement benefits for purposes of the exemption for bona fide executives or high policymaking employees. (a) Section 12(c)(1) of the Act, added by the 1978 amendments and amended in 1984 and 1986, provides: "Nothing in this Act shall be construed to prohibit compulsory retirement of any em-

ployee who has attained 65 years of age, and who, for the 2-year period immediately before retirement, is employed in a bona fide executive or high policymaking position, if such employee is entitled to an immediate nonforfeitable annual retirement benefit from a pension, profitsharing, savings, or deferred compensation plan, or any combination of such plans, of the employer of such employee, which equals, in the aggregate, at least $44,000." The Commission's interpretative statements regarding this exemption are set forth in section 1625 of this chapter.

(b) Section 12(c)(2) of the Act provides:

In applying the retirement benefit test of paragraph (a) of this subsection, if any such retirement benefit is in a form other than a straight life annuity (with no ancillary benefits), or if employees contribute to any such plan or make rollover contributions, such benefit shall be adjusted in accordance with regulations prescribed by the Commission, after consultation with the Secretary of the Treasury, so that the benefit is the equivalent of a straight life annuity (with no ancillary benefits) under a plan to which employees do not contribute and under which no rollover contributions are made.

(c)(1) The requirement that an employee be entitled to the equivalent of a $27,000 straight life annuity (with no ancillary benefits) is satisfied in any case where the employee has the option of receiving, during each year of his or her lifetime following retirement, an annual payment of at least $27,000, or periodic payments on a more frequent basis which, in the aggregate, equal at least $27,000 per year: *Provided, however,* That the portion of the retirement income figure attributable to Social Security, employee contributions, rollover contributions and contributions of prior employers is excluded in the manner described in paragraph (e) of this section. (A retirement benefit which excludes these amounts is sometimes referred to herein as a "qualified" retirement benefit.)

(2) The requirement is also met where the employee has the option of receiving, upon retirement, a lump sum payment with which it is possible to purchase a single life annuity (with no ancillary benefits) yielding at least $27,000 per year as adjusted.

(3) The requirement is also satisfied where the employee is entitled to receive, upon retirement, benefits whose aggregate value, as of the date of the employee's retirement, with respect to those payments which are scheduled to be made within the period of life expectancy of the employee, is $27,000 per year as adjusted.

(4) Where an employee has one or more of the options described in paragraphs (c)(1)-(3) of this section, but instead selects another option (or options), the test is also met. On the other hand, where an employee has no choice but to have certain benefits provided after his or her death, the value of these benefits may not be included in this determination.

(5) The determination of the value of those benefits which may be counted towards the $27,000 requirement must be made on the basis of reasonable actuarial assumptions with respect to mortality and interest. For purposes of excluding from this determination any benefits which are available only after death, it is not necessary to determine the life expectancy of each person on an individual basis. A reasonable actuarial assumption with respect to mortality will suffice.

(6) The benefits computed under paragraphs (c)(1), (2) and (3) of this section shall be aggregated for purposes of determining whether the $27,000 requirement has been met.

(d) The only retirement benefits which may be counted towards the $27,000 annual benefit are those from a pension, profit-sharing, savings, or deferred compensation plan, or any combination of such plans. Such plans include, but are not limited to, stock bonus, thrift and simplified employee pensions. The value of benefits from any other employee benefit plans, such as health or life insurance, may not be counted.

(e) In calculating the value of a pension, profit-sharing, savings, or deferred compensation plan (or any combination of such plans), amounts attributable to Social Security, employee contributions, contributions of prior employers, and rollover contributions must be excluded. Specific rules are set forth below.

(1) *Social Security*. Amounts attributable to Social Security must be excluded. Since these amounts are readily determinable, no specific rules are deemed necessary.

(2) *Employee contributions*. Amounts attributable to employee contributions must be excluded. The regulations governing this requirement are based on section 411(c) of the Internal Revenue Code and Treasury Regulations thereunder (§ 1.411(c)-(1)), relating to the allocation of accrued benefits between employer and employee contributions. Different calculations are needed to determine the amount of employee contributions, depending upon whether the retirement income plan is a defined contribution plan or a defined benefit plan. Defined contribution plans (also referred to as individual account plans) generally provide that each participant has an individual account and the participant's benefits are based solely on the account balance. No set benefit is promised in defined contribution plans, and the final amount is a result not only of the actual contributions, but also of other

factors, such as investment gains and losses. Any retirement income plan which is not an individual account plan is a defined benefit plan. Defined benefit plans generally provide a definitely determinable benefit, by specifying either a flat monthly payment or a schedule of payments based on a formula (frequently involving salary and years of service), and they are funded according to actuarial principles over the employee's period of participation.

(i) *Defined contribution plans.* (A) *Separate accounts maintained.* If a separate account is maintained with respect to an employee's contributions and all income, expenses, gains and losses attributable thereto, the balance in such an account represents the amount attributable to employee contributions.

(B) *Separate accounts not maintained.* If a separate account is not maintained with respect to an employee's contributions and the income, expenses, gains and losses attributable thereto, the proportion of the total benefit attributable to employee contributions is determined by multiplying that benefit by a fraction—

(1) The numerator of which is the total amount of the employee's contributions under the plan (less withdrawals), and

(2) The denominator of which is the sum of the numerator and the total contributions made under the plan by the employer on behalf of the employee (less withdrawals).

Example: A defined contribution plan does not maintain separate accounts for employee contributions. An employee's annual retirement benefit under the plan is $40,000. The employee has contributed $96,000 and the employer has contributed $144,000 to the employee's individual account; no withdrawals have been made. The amount of the $40,000 annual benefit attributable to employee contributions is $40,000 × $96,000/$96,000 + $144,000 = $16,000. Hence the employer's share of the $40,000 annual retirement benefit is $40,000 minus $16,000 or $24,000—too low to fall within the exemption.

(ii) *Defined benefit plans.* (A) *Separate accounts maintained.* If a separate account is maintained with respect to an employee's contributions and all income, expenses, gains and losses attributable thereto, the balance in such an account represents the amount attributable to employee contributions.

(B) *Separate accounts not maintained.* If a separate account is not maintained with respect to an employee's contributions and the income, expenses, gains and losses attributable thereto, all of the contributions made by an employee must be converted actuarially to a single life annuity (without ancillary benefits) commencing at the age of forced retirement. An employee's accumulated contributions are the sum of all contributions (mandatory and, if not separately accounted for, voluntary) made by the employee, together with interest on the sum of all such contributions compounded annually at the rate of 5 percent per annum from the time each such contribution was made until the date of retirement. *Provided, however,* That prior to the date any plan became subject to section 411(c) of the Internal Revenue Code, interest will be credited at the rate (if any) specified in the plan. The amount of the employee's accumulated contribution described in the previous sentence must be multiplied by an "appropriate conversion factor" in order to convert it to a single life annuity (without

ancillary benefits) commencing at the age of actual retirement. The appropriate conversion factor depends upon the age of retirement. In accordance with Rev. Rul. 76-47, 1976-2 C.B. 109, the following conversion factors shall be used with respect to the specified retirement ages:

Retirement age:	Conversion factor percent
65 through 66	10
67 through 68	11
69	12

Example: An employee is scheduled to receive a pension from a defined benefit plan of $50,000 per year. Over the years he has contributed $150,000 to the plan, and at age 65 this amount, when contributions have been compounded at appropriate annual interest rates, is equal to $240,000. In accordance with Rev. Rul. 76-47, 10 percent is an appropriate conversion factor. When the $240,000 is multiplied by this conversion factor, the product is $24,000, which represents that part of the $50,000 annual pension payment which is attributable to employee contributions. The difference—$26,000—represents the employer's contribution, which is too low to meet the test in the exemption.

(3) *Contributions of prior employers.* Amounts attributable to contributions of prior employers must be excluded.

(i) *Current employer distinguished from prior employers.* Under the section 12(c) exemption, for purposes of excluding contributions of prior employers, a prior employer is every previous employer of the employee except those previous employers which are members of a "controlled group of corporations" with, or "under common control" with, the employer which forces the employee to retire, as those terms are used in sections 414(b) and 414(c) of the Internal Revenue Code, as modified by section 414(h) (26 U.S.C. 414(b), (c) and (h)).

(ii) *Benefits attributable to current employer and to prior employers.* Where the current employer maintains or contributes to a plan plan which is separate from plans maintained or contributed to by prior employers, the amount of the employee's benefit attributable to those prior employers can be readily determined. However, where the current employer maintains or contributes to the same plan as prior employers, the following rule shall apply. The benefit attributable to the current employer shall be the total benefit received by the employee, reduced by the benefit that the employee would have received from the plan if he or she had never worked for the current employer. For purposes of this calculation, it shall be assumed that all benefits have always been vested, even if benefits accrued as a result of service with a prior employer had not in fact been vested.

(4) *Rollover contributions.* Amounts attributable to rollover contributions must be excluded. For purposes of § 1627.17(e), a rollover contribution (as defined in sections 402(a)(5), 403(a)(4), 408(d)(3) and 409(b)(3)(C) of the Internal Revenue Code) shall be treated as an employee contribution. These amounts have already been excluded as a result of the computations set forth in § 1627.17(e)(2). Accordingly, no separate calculation is necessary to comply with this requirement.

[¶ 15,759]

[**Reserved.** Reg. § § 860.110 and 860.120 formerly appeared at this paragraph. However, 29 CFR Part 860 was rendered obsolete and removed from the Code of Federal Regulations (52 FR 23812) on June 25, 1987. Reg. § 860.120 was redesignated within Part 1625 as Reg. § 1625.10 (CCH PENSION PLAN GUIDE, ¶ 15,750F).]

Criminal Code

[¶16,201]

SEC. 664. THEFT OR EMBEZZLEMENT FROM EMPLOYEE BENEFIT PLAN

Any person who embezzles, steals, or unlawfully and willfully abstracts or converts to his own use or to the use of another, any of the moneys, funds, securities, premiums, credits, property, or other assets of any employee welfare benefit plan or employee pension benefit plan, or of any fund connected therewith, shall be fined under this title, or imprisoned not more than five years, or both.

As used in this section, the term "any employee welfare benefit plan or employee pension benefit plan" means any employee benefit plan subject to any provision of Title I of the Employee Retirement Income Security Act of 1974.

.01 Historical Comment.

P.L. 103-322 amended Sec. 664 by substituting "fined under this title" for "fined not more than $10,000," effective September 13, 1994. P.L. 93-406 amended Sec. 664, effective January 1, 1975, except that in the case of a plan which has a plan year which begins before January 1, 1975, and ends after December 31, 1974, the Secretary of Labor may postpone by regulation the effective date of the repeal of any provision of the Welfare and Pension Plans Disclosure Act until the beginning of the first plan year of the plan which begins after January 1, 1975. Prior to the amendment, the language which reads "any employee benefit plan subject to any provision of Title I of the Employee Retirement Security Act of 1974" read "any such plan subject to the provisions of the Welfare and Pension Plans Disclosure Act."

Source: P.L. 87-420, approved March 20, 1962, effective June 18, 1962.

[¶16,202]

SEC. 1027. FALSE STATEMENTS AND CONCEALMENT OF FACTS IN RELATION TO DOCUMENTS REQUIRED BY THE EMPLOYEE RETIREMENT INCOME SECURITY ACT OF 1974

Whoever, in any document required by Title I of the Employee Retirement Income Security Act of 1974 (as amended from time to time) to be published, or kept as part of the records of any employee welfare benefit plan or employee pension benefit plan, or certified to the administrator of any such plan, makes any false statement or representation of fact, knowing it to be false, or knowingly conceals, covers up, or fails to disclose any fact the disclosure of which is required by such title or is necessary to verify, explain, clarify or check for accuracy and completeness any report required by such title to be published or any information required by such title to be certified, shall be fined under this title, or imprisoned not more than five years, or both.

.01 Historical Comment.

P.L. 103-322 amended Sec. 1027 by substituting "fined under this title" for "fined not more than $10,000," effective September 13, 1994. P.L. 93-406 amended Sec. 1027 effective January 1, 1975, except that in the case of a plan which has a plan year which begins before January 1, 1975 and ends after December 31, 1974, the Secretary of Labor may postpone by regulation the effective date of the repeal of any provision of the Welfare and Pension Plans Disclosure Act until the beginning of the first plan year of the plan which begins after January 1, 1975. Prior to amendment, the heading of Section 1027 read "False Statements and Concealment of Facts in Relation to Documents Required by the Welfare and Pension Plans Disclosure Act." After amendment "Welfare and Pension Plans Disclosure Act" was sticken and replaced by "Employee Retirement Income Security Act of 1974." Wherever the word "title" appears in the present section, the word "Act" formerly appeared. The words "Whoever, in any document required by title I of the Employee Retirement Income Security Act of 1974 (as amended from time to time)" formerly read "Whoever, in any document required by the Welfare and Pension Plans Disclosure Act (as amended from time to time)."

Source: P.L. 87-420, approved March 20, 1962, effective June 18, 1962.

[¶16,203]

SEC. 1954. OFFER, ACCEPTANCE, OR SOLICITATION TO INFLUENCE OPERATIONS OF EMPLOYEE BENEFIT PLAN

Whoever being—

(1) an administrator, officer, trustee, custodian, counsel, agent, or employee of any employee welfare benefit plan or employee pension benefit plan; or

(2) an officer, counsel, agent, or employee of an employer or an employer any of whose employees are covered by such plan; or

(3) an officer, counsel, agent, or employee of an employee organization any of whose members are covered by such plan; or

(4) a person who, or an officer, counsel, agent, or employee of an organization which, provides benefit plan services to such plan

receives or agrees to receive or solicits any fee, kickback, commission, gift, loan, money, or thing of value because of or with intent to be influenced with respect to, any of his actions, decisions, or other duties relating to any question or matter concerning such plan or any person who directly or indirectly gives or offers, or promises to give or offer, any fee, kickback, commission, gift, loan, money, or thing of value prohibited by this section, shall be fined under this title or imprisoned not more than three years, or both: *Provided,* That this section shall not prohibit the payment to or acceptance by any person of bona fide salary, compensation, or other payments made for goods or facilities actually furnished or for services actually performed in the regular course of his duties as such person, administrator, officer, trustee, custodian, counsel, agent, or employee of such plan, employer, employee organization, or organization providing benefit plan services to such plan.

As used in this section, the term (a) "any employee welfare benefit plan" or "employee pension benefit plan" means any employee welfare benefit plan or employee pension benefit plan, respectively, subject to any provision of Title I of the Employee Retirement Income Security Act of 1974 and (b) "employee organization" and "administrator" as defined respectively in sections 3(4) and 3(16) of the Employee Retirement Income Security Act of 1974.

.01 Historical Comment.

P.L. 103-322 amended Sec. 1954 by substituting "fined under this title" for "fined not more than $10,000," effective September 13, 1994. P.L. 93-406 amended Sec. 1954, effective January 1, 1975, except that in the case of a plan which has a plan year which begins before January 1, 1975 and ends after December 31, 1974, the Secretary may postpone by regulation the effective date of the repeal of any provision of the Welfare and Pension Plans Disclosure Act until the beginning of the first plan year of the plan which begins after January 1, 1975. Section 1954 was amended by striking out "any plan subject to the provisions of the Welfare and Pension Plans Disclosure Act, as amended" and inserting in lieu thereof "any employee welfare benefit plan or employee pension benefit plan, respectively, subject to any provision of title I of the Employee Retirement Income Security Act of 1974"; and by striking out "sections 3(3) and 5(b)(1) and (2) of the Welfare and Pension Plans Disclosure Act, as amended" and inserting in lieu thereof "sections 3(4) and (3)(16) of the Employee Retirement Income Security Act of 1974".

P.L. 91-452, Title II, Sec. 225, effective October 31, 1970. Section 1954 was amended by striking "(a) Whoever" and inserting in lieu thereof "Whoever" and by striking subsection (b) thereof.

Source: P.L. 87-420, approved March 20, 1962, effective September 16, 1962.

[¶ 16,301]

Labor Standards

The Fair Labor Standards Act (FLSA) establishes minimum wage, overtime pay, recordkeeping, and other employment standards affecting employee and employers in the private sector and in federal, state, and local governments.

Generally, every employer must pay to each employee a specified minimum wage. Discrimination in employee compensation based on sex is expressly prohibited.

The Patient Protection and Affordable Care Act (PPACA) added four sections to the FLSA regarding health insurance coverage and employment conditions.

Excerpted from the FLSA are the following United States Code (USC) sections:

1. minimum wage (29 USC § 206);

2. reasonable break time for nursing mothers (29 USC § 207(r));

3. automatic enrollment for employees of large employers (29 USC § 218A);

4. notice to employees (29 USC § 218B); and

5. protections for employees (29 USC § 218C).

Text of Excerpted Fair Labor Standards Act Section

MINIMUM WAGES

[The Federal Minimum Wage]

§ 206(a) Every employer shall pay to each of his employees who in any workweek is engaged in commerce or in the production of goods for commerce, or is employed in an enterprise engaged in commerce or in the production of goods for commerce, wages at the following rates:

(1) except as otherwise provided in this section, not less than—(A) $5.85 an hour, beginning on the 60th day after the date of enactment of the Fair Minimum Wage Act of 2007; (B) $6.55 an hour, beginning 12 months after that 60th day; and (C) $7.25 an hour, beginning 24 months after that 60th day;

[Homeworkers in Puerto Rico and Virgin Islands]

(2) if such employee is a homeworker in Puerto Rico or the Virgin Islands, not less than the minimum piece rate prescribed by regulation or order; or, if no such minimum piece rate is in effect, any piece rate adopted by such employer which shall yield, to the proportion or class of employees prescribed by regulation or order, not less than the applicable minimum hourly wage rate. Such minimum piece rates or employer piece rates shall be commensurate with, and shall be paid in lieu of, the minimum hourly wage rate applicable under the provisions of this section. The Secretary of Labor, or his authorized representative, shall have power to make such regulations or orders as are necessary or appropriate to carry out any of the provisions of this paragraph, including the power without limiting the generality of the foregoing, to define any operation or occupation which is performed by such home work employees in Puerto Rico or the Virgin Islands; to establish minimum piece rates for any operation or occupation so defined; to prescribe the method and procedure for ascertaining and promulgating minimum piece rates; to prescribe standards for employer piece rates, including the proportion or class of employees who shall receive not less than the minimum hourly wage rate; to define the term "home worker"; and to prescribe the conditions under which employers, agents, contractors, and subcontractors shall cause goods to be produced by home workers;

[Seamen of American Vessels]

(3) if such employee is employed as a seaman on an American vessel not less than the rate which will provide to the employee, for the period covered by the wage payment, wages equal to compensation at the hourly rate prescribed by paragraph (1) of this subsection for all hours during such period when he was actually on duty (including periods aboard ship when the employee was on watch or was, at the direction of a superior officer, performing work or standing by, but not including off-duty periods which are provided pursuant to the employment agreement); or

[Agricultural Employees]

(4) if such employee is employed in agriculture, not less than the minimum wage rate in effect under paragraph (1) after December 31, 1977.

[Coverage Under 1966 Amendments]

(b) Every employer shall pay to each of his employees (other than an employee to whom subsection (a)(5) applies) who in any workweek is engaged in commerce or in the production of goods for commerce, or is employed in an enterprise engaged in commerce or in the production of goods for commerce, and who in such workweek is brought within the purview of this section by the amendments made to this Act by the Fair Labor Standards Amendments of 1966, title IX of the Education Amendments of 1972, or the Fair Labor Standards Amendments of 1974, wages at the following rate: Effective after December 31, 1977, not less than the minimum wage rate in effect under subsection (a)(1).

[Other Workers in Puerto Rico and Virgin Islands]

(c)(1) The rate or rates provided by subsection (a)(1) shall be applicable in the case of any employee in Puerto Rico who is employed by—

(A) the United States,

(B) an establishment that is a hotel, motel or restaurant,

(C) any other retail or service establishment that employs such employee primarily in connection with the preparation or offering of food or beverages for human consumption, either on the premises, or by such services as catering, banquet, box lunch, or curb or counter service, to the public, to employees, or to members or guests of members of clubs, or

(D) any other industry in which the average hourly wage is greater than or equal to $4.65 an hour.

(2) In the case of any employee in Puerto Rico who is employed in an industry in which the average hourly wage in not less than $4.00 but not more than $4.64, the minimum wage rate applicable to such employee shall be increased on April 1, 1990, and each April 1 thereafter through April 1, 1994, by equal amounts (rounded to the nearest 5 cents) so that the highest minimum wage rate prescribed in subsection (a)(1) shall apply on April 1, 1994.

(3) In the case of an employee in Puerto Rico who is employed in an industry in which the average hourly wage is less than $4.00, except as provided in paragraph (4), the minimum wage rate applicable to such employee shall be increased on April 1, 1990, and each April 1 thereafter through April 1, 1995, by equal amounts (rounded to the nearest 5 cents) so that the highest minimum wage rate prescribed in subsection (a)(1) shall apply on April 1, 1995.

(4) In the case of any employee of the Commonwealth of Puerto Rico, or a municipality or other governmental entity of the Commonwealth, in which the average hourly wage is less than $4.00 an hour and who was brought under the coverage of this section pursuant to an amendment made by the Fair Labor Standards Amendments of 1985 (Public Law 99-150), the minimum wage rate applicable to such employee shall be increased on April 1, 1990, and each

April 1 thereafter through April 1, 1996, by equal amounts (rounded to the nearest 5 cents) so that the highest minimum wage rate prescribed in subsection (a)(1) shall apply on April 1, 1996.

[Equal Pay for Equal Work]

(d)(1) No employer having employees subject to any provisions of this section shall discriminate, within any establishment in which such employees are employed, between employees on the basis of sex by paying wages to employees in such establishment at a rate less than the rate at which he pays wages to employees of the opposite sex in such establishment for equal work on jobs the performance of which requires equal skill, effort, and responsibility, and which are performed under similar working conditions, except where such payment is made pursuant to (i) a seniority system; (ii) a merit system; (iii) a system which measures earnings by quantity or quality of production; or (iv) a differential based on any other factor other than sex: *Provided,* That an employer who is paying a wage rate differential in violation of this subsection shall not, in order to comply with the provisions of this subsection, reduce the wage rate of any employee.

(2) No labor organization, or its agents, representing employees of an employer having employees subject to any provisions of this section shall cause or attempt to cause such an employer to discriminate against an employee in violation of paragraph (1) of this subsection.

(3) For purposes of administration and enforcement, any amounts owing to any employee which have been withheld in violation of this subsection shall be deemed to be unpaid minimum wages or unpaid overtime compensation under this Act.

(4) As used in this subsection, the term "labor organization" means any organization of any kind, or any agency or employee representation committee or plan, in which employees participate and which exists for the purpose, in whole or in part, of dealing with employers concerning grievances, labor disputes, wages, rates of pay, hours of employment, or conditions of work.

[Contract Services to Federal Government]

(e)(1) Notwithstanding the provisions of section 13 of this Act (except subsections (a)(1) and (f) thereof), every employer providing any contract services (other than linen supply services) under a contract with the United States or any subcontract thereunder shall pay to each of his employees whose rate of pay is not governed by the Service Contract Act of 1965 (41 U.S.C. 351-357) or to whom subsection (a)(1) of this section is not applicable, wages at rates not less than the rates provided for in subsection (b) of this section.

(2) Notwithstanding the provisions of section 13 of this Act (except subsections (a)(1) and (f) thereof) and the provisions of the Service Contract Act of 1965, every employer in an establishment providing linen supply services to the United States under a contract with the United States or any subcontract thereunder shall pay to each of his employees in such establishment wages at rates not less than those prescribed in subsection (b), except that if more than 50 per centum of the gross annual dollar volume of sales made or business done by such establishment is derived from providing such linen supply services under any such contracts or subcontracts, such employer shall pay to each of his employees in such establishment wages at rates not less than those prescribed in subsection (a)(1) of this section.

[Domestic Workers]

(f) Any employee—

(1) who in any workweek is employed in domestic service in a household shall be paid wages at a rate not less than the wage rate in effect under section 6(b) unless such employee's compensation for such service would not because of section 209(g) of the Social Security Act constitute wages for the purposes of title II of such Act, or

(2) who in any workweek—

(A) is employed in domestic service in one or more households, and

(B) is so employed for more than 8 hours in the aggregate, shall be paid wages for such employment in such workweek at a rate not less than the wage rate in effect under section 6(b).

[Opportunity Wage]

(g)(1) In lieu of the rate prescribed by subsection (a)(1), any employer may pay any employee of such employer, during the first 90 consecutive days after such employee is initially employed by such employer, a wage which is not less than $4.25 an hour.

(2) In lieu of the rate prescribed by subsection (a)(1), the Governor of Puerto Rico, subject to the approval of the Financial Oversight and Management Board established pursuant to section 101 of the Puerto Rico Oversight, Management, and Economic Stability Act, may designate a time period not to exceed four years during which employers in Puerto Rico may pay employees who are initially employed after the date of enactment of such Act a wage which is not less than the wage described in paragraph (1). Notwithstanding the time period designated, such wage shall not continue in effect after such Board terminates in accordance with section 209 of such Act.

(3) No employer may take any action to displace employees (including partial displacements such as reduction in hours, wages, or employment benefits) for purposes of hiring individuals at the wage authorized in paragraph (1) or (2).

(4) Any employer who violates this subsection shall be considered to have violated section 15(a)(3) (29 U.S.C. 215(a)(3)).

(5) This subsection shall only apply to an employee who has not attained the age of 20 years, except in the case of the wage applicable in Puerto Rico, 25 years, until such time as the Board described in paragraph (2) terminates in accordance with section 209 of the Act described in such paragraph.

MAXIMUM HOURS

[Overtime Pay—Coverage Under Pre-1966 Provisions]

§207(a)(1) Except as otherwise provided in this section, no employer shall employ any of his employees who in any workweek is engaged in commerce or in the production of goods for commerce, or is employed in an enterprise engaged in commerce or in the production of goods for commerce, for a workweek longer than forty hours unless such employee receives compensation for his employment in excess of the hours above specified at a rate not less than one and one-half times the regular rate at which he is employed.

[Overtime Pay—Coverage Under 1966 Amendments]

(2) No employer shall employ any of his employees who in any workweek is engaged in commerce or in the production of goods for commerce, or is employed in an enterprise engaged in commerce or in the production of goods for commerce, and who in such workweek is brought within the purview of this subsection by the amendments made to this Act by the Fair Labor Standards Amendments of 1966.

(A) for a workweek longer than forty-four hours during the first year from the effective date of the Fair Labor Standards Amendments of 1966,

(B) for a workweek longer than forty-two hours during the second year from such date, or

(C) for a workweek longer than forty hours after the expiration of the second year from such date,

unless such employee receives compensation for his employment in excess of the hours above specified at a rate not less than one and one-half times the regular rate at which he is employed.

[Guaranteed Employment and Wholesale Petroleum Distributor Exemptions]

(b) No employer shall be deemed to have violated subsection (a) by employing any employee for a workweek in excess of that specified in such subsection without paying the compensation for overtime employment prescribed therein if such employee is so employed—

(1) in pursuance of an agreement, made as a result of collective bargaining by representatives of employees certified as bona fide by the National Labor Relations Board, which provides that no employee shall be employed more than one thousand and forty hours during any period of twenty-six consecutive weeks; or

(2) in pursuance of an agreement, made as a result of collective bargaining by representatives of employees certified as bona fide by the National Labor Relations Board, which provides that during a specified period of fifty-two consecutive weeks the employee shall be employed not more than two thousand two hundred and forty hours and shall be guaranteed not less than one thousand eight hundred and forty hours (or not less than forty-six weeks at the normal number of hours worked per week, but not less than thirty hours per week) and not more than two thousand and eighty hours of employment for which he shall receive compensation for all hours guaranteed or worked at rates not less than those applicable under the agreement to the work performed and for all hours in excess of the guaranty which are also in excess of the maximum workweek applicable to such employee under subsection (a) or two thousand and eighty in such period at rates not less than one and one-half times the regular rate at which he is employed; or

(3) by an independently owned and controlled local enterprise (including an enterprise with more than one bulk storage establishment) engaged in the wholesale or bulk distribution of petroleum products if—

(A) the annual gross volume of sales of such enterprise is less than $1,000,000 exclusive of excise taxes,

(B) more than 75 per centum of such enterprise's annual dollar volume of sales is made within the State in which such enterprise is located, and

(C) not more than 25 per centum of the annual dollar volume of sales of such enterprise is to customers who are engaged in the bulk distribution of such products for resale,

and such employee receives compensation for employment in excess of forty hours in any workweek at a rate not less than one and one-half times the minimum wage rate applicable to him under section 6,

and if such employee receives compensation for employment in excess of twelve hours in any workday, or for employment in excess of fifty-six hours in any workweek, as the case may be, at a rate not less than one and one-half times the regular rate at which he is employed.

[Seasonal Industry Exemption]

(c) [Repealed.]

[Processing of Agricultural Products Exemption]

(d) [Repealed.]

[Payments Excluded from "Regular Rate"]

(e) As used in this section the "regular rate" at which an employee is employed shall be deemed to include all remuneration for employment paid to, or on behalf of, the employee, but shall not be deemed to include—

(1) sums paid as gifts; payments in the nature of gifts made at Christmas time or on other special occasions, as a reward for service, the amounts of which are not measured by or dependent on hours worked, production, or efficiency;

(2) payments made for occasional periods when no work is performed due to vacation, holiday, illness, failure of the employer to provide sufficient work, or other similar cause; reasonable payments for traveling expenses, or other expenses, incurred by an employee in the furtherance of his employer's interests and properly reimbursable by the employer; and other similar payments to an employee which are not made as compensation for his hours of employment;

(3) sums paid in recognition of services performed during a given period if either, (a) both the fact that payment is to be made and the amount of the payment are determined at the sole discretion of the employer at or near the end of the period and not pursuant to any prior contract, agreement, or promise causing the employee to expect such payments regularly; or (b) the payments are made pursuant to a bona fide profit-sharing plan or trust or bona fide thrift or savings plan, meeting the requirements of the Secretary of Labor set forth in appropriate regulations which he shall issue, having due regard among other relevant factors, to the extent to which the amounts paid to the employee are determined without regard to hours of work, production, or efficiency; or (c) the payments are talent fees (as such talent fees are defined and delimited by regulations of the Secretary) paid to performers, including announcers, on radio and television programs;

(4) contributions irrevocably made by an employer to a trustee or third person pursuant to a bona fide plan for providing old-age, retirement, life, accident, or health insurance or similar benefits for employees;

(5) extra compensation provided by a premium rate paid for certain hours worked by the employee in any day or workweek because such hours are hours worked in excess of eight in a day or in excess of the maximum workweek applicable to such employee under subsection (a) or in excess of the employee's normal working hours or regular working hours, as the case may be;

(6) extra compensation provided by a premium rate paid for work by the employee on Saturdays, Sundays, holidays, or regular days of rest, or on the sixth or seventh day of the workweek, where such premium rate is not less than one and one-half times the rate established in good faith for like work performed in nonovertime hours on other days;

(7) extra compensation provided by a premium rate paid to the employee, in pursuance of an applicable employment contract or collective-bargaining agreement, for work outside of the hours established in good faith by the contract or agreement as the basic, normal, or regular workday (not exceeding eight hours) or workweek (not exceeding the maximum workweek applicable to such employee under subsection (a), where such premium rate is not less than one and one-half times the rate established in good faith by the contract or agreement for like work performed during such workday or workweek; or

(8) [Worker Economic Opportunity Act]

any value or income derived from employer-provided grants or rights provided pursuant to a stock option, stock appreciation right, or bona fide employee stock purchase program which is not otherwise excludable under any of the paragraphs (1) through (7) if—

(A) grants are made pursuant to a program, the terms and conditions of which are communicated to participating employees either at the beginning of the employee's participation in the program or at the time of the grant;

(B) in the case of stock options and stock appreciation rights, the grant or right cannot be exercisable for a period of at least 6 months after the time of grant (except that grants or rights may become exercisable because of an employee's death, disability, retirement, or a change in corporate ownership, or other circumstances permitted by regulation), and the exercise price is at least 85 percent of the fair market value of the stock at the time of grant;

(C) exercise of any grant or right is voluntary; and

(D) any determinations regarding the award of, and the amount of, employer-provided grants or rights that are based on performance are—

(i) made based upon meeting previously established performance criteria (which may include hours of work, efficiency, or productivity) of any business unit consisting of at least 10 employees or of a facility, except that, any determination may be based on length of service or minimum schedule of hours or days of work; or

(ii) made based upon the best performance (which may include any criteria) of one or more employees in a given period so long as the determination is in the sole discretion of the employer and not pursuant to any prior contract.

[Guaranteed Weekly Pay for Variable Hours]

(f) No employer shall be deemed to have violated subsection (a) by employing any employee for a workweek in excess of the maximum workweek applicable to such employee under subsection (a) if such employee is employed pursuant to a bona fide individual contract, or pursuant to an agreement made as a result of collective bargaining by representatives of employees, if the duties of such employee necessitate irregular hours of work, and the contract or agreement (1) specifies a regular rate of pay of not less than the minimum hourly rate provided in subsection (a) or (b) of section 6 (whichever may be applicable) and compensation at not less than one and one-half times such rate for all hours worked in excess of such maximum workweek, and (2) provides a weekly guaranty of pay for not more than sixty hours based on the rates so specified.

[Overtime Computed on Piece, Hourly or Basic Rates]

(g) No employer shall be deemed to have violated subsection (a) by employing any employee for a workweek in excess of the maximum workweek applicable to such employee under such subsection if, pursuant to an agreement or understanding arrived at between the employer and the employee before performance of the work, the amount paid to the employee for the number of hours worked by him in such workweek in excess of the maximum workweek applicable to such employee under such subsection—

(1) in the case of an employee employed at piece rates, is computed at piece rates not less than one and one-half times the bona fide piece rates applicable to the same work when performed during nonovertime hours; or

(2) in the case of an employee performing two or more kinds of work for which different hourly or piece rates have been established, is computed at rates not less than one and one-half times such bona fide rates applicable to the same work when performed during nonovertime hours; or

(3) is computed at a rate not less than one and one-half times the rate established by such agreement or understanding as the basic rate to be used in computing overtime compensation thereunder; *Provided,* That the rate so established shall be authorized by regulation by the Secretary of Labor as being substantially equivalent to the average hourly earnings of the employee, exclusive of overtime premiums, in the particular work over a representative period of time;

and if (i) the employee's average hourly earnings for the workweek exclusive of payments described in paragraphs (1) through (7) of subsection (e) are not less than the minimum hourly rate required by applicable law, and (ii) extra overtime compensation is properly computed and paid on other forms of additional pay required to be included in computing the regular rate.

[Credits Against Overtime Pay]

(h)(1) Except as provided in paragraph (2), sums excluded from the regular rate pursuant to subsection (e) shall not be creditable toward wages required under section 6 or overtime compensation required under this section.

(2) Extra compensation paid as described in paragraphs (5), (6), and (7) of subsection (e) shall be creditable toward overtime compensation payable pursuant to this section.

[Exemption for Retail and Service Establishments]

(i) No employer shall be deemed to have violated subsection (a) by employing any employee of a retail or service establishment for a workweek in excess of the applicable workweek specified therein, if (1) the regular rate of pay of such employee is in excess of one and one-half times the minimum hourly rate applicable to him under section 6, and (2) more than half his compensation for a representative period (not less than one month) represents commissions on goods or services. In determining the proportion of compensation representing commissions, all earnings resulting from the application of a bona fide commission rate shall be deemed commissions on goods or services without regard to whether the computed commissions exceed the draw or guarantee.

[Hospital Employees]

(j) No employer engaged in the operation of a hospital or an establishment which is an institution primarily engaged in the care of the sick, the aged, or the mentally ill or defective who reside on the premises shall be deemed to have violated subsection (a) if, pursuant to an agreement or understanding arrived at between the employer and the employee before performance of the work, a work period of fourteen consecutive days is accepted in lieu of the workweek of seven consecutive days for purposes of overtime computation and if, for his employment in excess of eight hours in any workday and in excess of eighty hours in such fourteen-day period, the employee receives compensation at a rate not less than one and one-half times the regular rate at which he is employed.

[Police and Firemen]

(k) No public agency shall be deemed to have violated subsection (a) with respect to the employment of any employee in fire protection activities or any employee in law enforcement activities (including security personnel in correctional institutions) if—

(1) in a work period of 28 consecutive days the employee receives for tours of duty which in the aggregate exceed the lesser of (A) 216 hours, or (B) the average number of hours (as determined by the Secretary pursuant to section 6(c)(3) of the Fair Labor Standards Amendments of 1974) in tours of duty of employees engaged in such activities in work periods of 28 consecutive days in calendar year 1975; or

(2) in the case of such an employee to whom a work period of at least 7 but less than 28 days applies, in his work period the employee receives for tours of duty which in the aggregate exceed a number of hours which bears the same ratio to the number of consecutive days in his work period as 216 hours (or if lower, the number of hours referred to in clause (B) of paragraph (1)) bears to 28 days,

compensation at a rate not less than one and one-half times the regular rate at which he is employed.

[Domestic Service]

(l) No employer shall employ any employee in domestic service in one or more households for a workweek longer than forty hours unless such employee receives compensation for such employment in accordance with subsection (a).

[Tobacco Workers]

(m) For a period or periods of not more than fourteen workweeks in the aggregate in any calendar year, any employer may employ any employee for a workweek in excess of that specified in subsection (a) without paying the compensation for overtime employment prescribed in such subsection, if such employee—

(1) is employed by such employer—

(A) to provide services (including stripping and grading) necessary and incidental to the sale or auction of green leaf tobacco of type 11, 12, 13, 14, 21, 22, 23, 24, 31, 35, 36, or 37 (as such types are defined by the Secretary of Agriculture), or in auction sale, buying, handling, stemming, redrying, packing, and storing of such tobacco,

(B) in auction sale, buying, handling, sorting, grading, packing, or storing green leaf tobacco of type 32 (as such type is defined by the Secretary of Agriculture), or

(C) in auction sale, buying, handling, stripping, sorting, grading, sizing, packing, or stemming prior to packing, of perishable cigar leaf tobacco of type 41, 42, 43, 44, 45, 46, 51, 52, 53, 54, 55, 61, or 62 (as such types are defined by the Secretary of Agriculture); and

(2) receives for—

(A) such employment by such employer which is in excess of ten hours in any workday, and

(B) such employment by such employer which is in excess of forty-eight hours in any workweek,

compensation at a rate not less than one and one-half times the regular rate at which he is employed.

An employer who receives an exemption under this subsection shall not be eligible for any other exemption under this section.

[Local Transportation]

(n) In the case of an employee of an employer engaged in the business of operating a street, suburban or interurban electric railway, or local trolley or motorbus carrier (regardless of whether or not such railway or carrier is public or private or operated for profit or not for profit) in determining the hours of employment of such an employee to which the rate prescribed by subsection (a) applies there shall be excluded the hours such employee was employed in charter activities by such employer if (1) the employee's employment in such activities was pursuant to an agreement or understanding with his employer arrived at before engaging in such employment, and (2) if employment in such activities is not part of such employee's regular employment.

[Compensatory Time]

[Rate of Compensation]

(o)(1) Employees of a public agency which is a State, a political subdivision of a State, or an interstate governmental agency may receive, in accordance with this subsection and in lieu of overtime compensation, compensatory time off at a rate not less than one and one-half hours for each hour of employment for which overtime compensation is required by this section.

[Provision of Compensatory Time]

(2) A public agency may provide compensatory time under paragraph (1) only—

(A) pursuant to—

(i) applicable provisions of a collective bargaining agreement, memorandum of understanding, or any other agreement between the public agency and representatives of such employees; or

(ii) in the case of employees not covered by subclause (i), an agreement or understanding arrived at between the employer and employee before the performance of the work; and

(B) if the employee has not accrued compensatory time in excess of the limit applicable to the employee prescribed by paragraph (3).

In the case of employees described in clause (A)(ii) hired prior to April 15, 1986, the regular practice in effect on April 15, 1986, with respect to compensatory time off for such employees in lieu of the receipt of overtime compensation, shall constitute an agreement or understanding under such clause (A)(ii). Except as provided in the previous sentence, the provision of compensatory time off to such employees for hours worked after April 14, 1986, shall be in accordance with this subsection.

[Limit on Hours of Compensatory Time]

(3)(A) If the work of an employee for which compensatory time may be provided included work in a public safety activity, an emergency response activity, or a seasonable activity, the employee engaged in such work may accrue not more than 480 hours of compensatory time for hours worked after April 15, 1986. If such work was any other work, the employee engaged in such work may accrue not more than 250 hours of compensatory time for hours worked after April 15, 1986. Any such employee who, after April 15, 1986, has accrued 480 or 240 hours, as the case may be, of compensatory time off shall, for additional overtime hours of work, be paid overtime compensation.

[Compensation for Accrued Compensatory Time]

(B) If compensation is paid to an employee for accrued compensatory time off, such compensation shall be paid at the regular rate earned by the employee at the time the employee receives such payment.

[Termination of Employment]

(4) An employee who has accrued compensatory time off authorized to be provided under paragraph (1) shall, upon termination of employment, be paid for the unused compensatory time at a rate of compensation not less than—

(A) the average regular rate received by such employee during the last 3 years of the employee's employment, or

(B) the final regular rate received by such employee, whichever is higher.

[Use of Accrued Compensatory Time]

(5) An employee of a public agency which is a State, political subdivision of a State, or an interstate government agency—

(A) who has accrued compensatory time off authorized to be provided under paragraph (1), and

(B) who has requested the use of such compensatory time, shall be permitted by the employee's employer to use such time within a reasonable period after making the request if the use of the compensatory time does not unduly disrupt the operations of the public agency.

[Compensatory Time for Court Reporters]

(6) The hours an employee of a public agency performs court reporting transcript preparation duties shall not be considered as hours worked for the purposes of subsection (a) if—

(A) such employee is paid at a per-page rate which is not less than—

(i) the maximum rate established by State law or local ordinance for the jurisdiction of such public agency,

(ii) the maximum rate otherwise established by a judicial or administrative officer and in effect on July 1, 1995, or

(iii) the rate freely negotiated between the employee and the party requesting the transcript, other than the judge who presided over the proceedings being transcribed, and

(B) the hours spent performing such duties are outside of the hours such employee performs other work (including hours for which the agency requires the employee's attendance) pursuant to the employment relationship with such public agency.

For the purposes of this section, the amount paid such employee in accordance with subparagraph (A) for the performance of court reporting transcript preparation duties, shall not be considered in the calculation of the regular rate at which such employee is employed.

[Definitions]

(7) For purposes of this subsection—

(A) the term "overtime compensation" means the compensation required by subsection (a), and

(B) the terms "compensatory time" and "compensatory time off" mean hours during which an employee is not working, which are not counted as hours worked during the applicable workweek or other work period for purposes of overtime compensation, and for which the employee is compensated at the employee's regular rate.

[Substitution for Another Employee]

(p)(1) If an individual who is employed by a State, political subdivision of a State, or an interstate governmental agency in fire protection or law enforcement activities (including activities of security personnel in correctional institutions) and who, solely at such individual's option, agrees to be employed on a special detail by a separate or independent employer in fire protection, law enforcement, or related activities, the hours such individual was employed by such separate and independent employer shall be excluded by the public agency employing such individual in the calculation of the hours for which the employee is entitled to overtime compensation under this section if the public agency—

(A) requires that its employees engaged in fire protection, law enforcement, or security activities be hired by a separate and independent employer to perform the special detail,

(B) facilitates the employment of such employees by a separate and independent employer, or

(C) otherwise affects the condition of employment of such employees by a separate and independent employer.

[Occasional or Sporadic Employment]

(2) If an employee of a public agency which is a State, political subdivision of a State, or an interstate governmental agency undertakes, on an occasional or sporadic basis and solely at the employee's option, part-time employment for the public agency which is in a different capacity from any capacity in which the employee is regularly employed with the public agency, the hours such employee was employed in performing the different employment shall be excluded by the public agency in the calculation of the hours for which the employee is entitled to overtime compensation under this section.

[Employee Substitution]

(3) If an individual who is employed in any capacity by a public agency which is a State, political subdivision of a State, or an interstate governmental agency, agrees, with the approval of the public agency and solely at the option of such individual, to substitute during scheduled work hours for another individual who is employed by such agency in the same capacity, the hours such employee worked as a substitute shall be excluded by the public agency in the calculation of the hours for which the employee is entitled to overtime compensation under this section.

[Employees Receiving Remedial Education]

(q) Any employer may employ any employee for a period or periods of not more than 10 hours in the aggregate in any workweek in excess of the maximum workweek specified in subsection (a) without applying the compensation for overtime employment prescribed in such subsection, if during such period or periods the employee is receiving remedial education that is—

(1) provided to employees who lack a high school diploma or educational attainment at the eighth grade level;

(2) designed to provide reading and other basic skills at an eighth grade level or below; and

(3) does not include job specific training.

[Reasonable Break Time for Nursing Mothers]

(r)(1) An employer shall provide—

(A) a reasonable break time for an employee to express breast milk for her nursing child for 1 year after the child's birth each time such employee has need to express the milk; and

(B) a place, other than a bathroom, that is shielded from view and free from intrusion from co-workers and the public, which may be used by an employee to express breast milk.

(2) An employer shall not be required to compensate an employee receiving reasonable break time under paragraph (1) for any work time spent for such purpose.

(3) An employer that employs less than 50 employees shall not be subject to the requirements of this subsection, if such requirements would impose an undue hardship by causing the employer significant difficulty or expense when considered in relation to the size, financial resources, nature, or structure of the employer's business.

(4) Nothing in this subsection shall preempt a State law that provides greater protections to employees than the protections provided for under this subsection.

[Limited Insurance Adjuster Exemption]

(s)(1) The provisions of this section shall not apply for a period of 2 years after the occurrence of a major disaster to any employee—

(A) employed to adjust or evaluate claims resulting from or relating to such major disaster, by an employer not engaged, directly or through an affiliate, in underwriting, selling, or marketing property, casualty, or liability insurance policies or contracts;

(B) who receives from such employer on average weekly compensation of not less than $591.00 per week or any minimum weekly amount established by the Secretary, whichever is greater, for the number of weeks such employee is engaged in any of the activities described in subparagraph (C); and

(C) whose duties include any of the following:

(i) interviewing insured individuals, individuals who suffered injuries or other damages or losses arising from or relating to a disaster, witnesses, or physicians;

(ii) inspecting property damage or reviewing factual information to prepare damage estimates;

(iii) evaluating and making recommendations regarding coverage or compensability of claims or determining liability or value aspects of claims;

(iv) negotiating settlements; or

(v) making recommendations regarding litigation.

(2) The exemption in this subsection shall not affect the exemption provided by section 13(a)(1).

(3) For purposes of this subsection—

(A) the term 'major disaster' means any disaster or catastrophe declared or designated by any State or Federal agency or department;

(B) the term 'employee employed to adjust or evaluate claims resulting from or relating to such major disaster' means an individual who timely secured or secures a license required by applicable law to engage in and perform the activities described in clauses (i) through (v) of paragraph (1)(C) relating to a major disaster, and is employed by an employer that maintains worker compensation insurance coverage or protection for its employees, if required by applicable law, and withholds applicable Federal, State, and local income and payroll taxes from the wages, salaries and any benefits of such employees; and

(C) the term 'affiliate' means a company that, by reason of ownership or control of 25 percent or more of the outstanding shares of any class of voting securities of one or more companies, directly or indirectly, controls, is controlled by, or is under common control with, another company.

[Health Benefits Enrollment]

AUTOMATIC ENROLLMENT FOR EMPLOYEES OF LARGE EMPLOYERS [Repealed]

§218A [Repealed.]

2015 Amendment.—Section 604 of P.L. 114-74, effective November 2, 2015, repealed section 18A. Prior to the amendment, it read as follows:

"In accordance with regulations promulgated by the Secretary, an employer to which this Act applies that has more than 200 full-time employees and that offers employees enrollment in 1 or more health benefits plans shall automatically enroll new full-time employees in one of the plans offered (subject to any waiting period authorized by law) and to continue the enrollment of current employees in a health benefits plan offered through the employer. Any automatic enrollment program shall include adequate notice and the opportunity for an employee to opt out of any coverage the individual or employee were automatically enrolled in. Nothing in this section shall be construed to supersede any State law which establishes, implements, or continues in effect any standard or requirement relating to employers in connection with payroll except to the extent that such standard or requirement prevents an employer from instituting the automatic enrollment program under this section."

2010 Amendment.—Section 1511 of P.L. 111-148, effective March 23, 2010, added section 18A.

NOTICE TO EMPLOYEES

§218B(a) IN GENERAL. In accordance with regulations promulgated by the Secretary, an employer to which this Act applies, shall provide to each employee at the time of hiring (or with respect to current employees, not later than March 1, 2013), written notice—

(1) informing the employee of the existence of an Exchange, including a description of the services provided by such Exchange, and the manner in which the employee may contact the Exchange to request assistance;

(2) if the employer plan's share of the total allowed costs of benefits provided under the plan is less than 60 percent of such costs, that the employee may be eligible for a premium tax credit under section 36B of the Internal Revenue Code of 1986 and a cost sharing reduction under section 1402 of the Patient Protection and Affordable Care Act if the employee purchases a qualified health plan through the Exchange; and

(3) if the employee purchases a qualified health plan through the Exchange, the employee may lose the employer contribution (if any) to any health benefits plan offered by the employer and that all or a portion of such contribution may be excludable from income for Federal income tax purposes.

(b) EFFECTIVE DATE. Subsection (a) shall take effect with respect to employers in a State beginning on March 1, 2013.

2011 Amendment.—Section 1858(c) of P.L. 112-10, effective March 1, 2013, amended section 18B(a)(3).

2010 Amendment.—Section 1512 of P.L. 111-148, effective March 1, 2013, added section 18B.

PROTECTIONS FOR EMPLOYEES

§218C(a) PROHIBITION. No employer shall discharge or in any manner discriminate against any employee with respect to his or her compensation, terms, conditions, or other privileges of employment because the employee (or an individual acting at the request of the employee) has—

(1) received a credit under section 36B of the Internal Revenue Code of 1986 or a subsidy under section 1402 of this Act;

(2) provided, caused to be provided, or is about to provide or cause to be provided to the employer, the Federal Government, or the attorney general of a State information relating to any violation of, or any act or omission the employee reasonably believes to be a violation of, any provision of this title (or an amendment made by this title);

(3) testified or is about to testify in a proceeding concerning such violation;

(4) assisted or participated, or is about to assist or participate, in such a proceeding; or

(5) objected to, or refused to participate in, any activity, policy, practice, or assigned task that the employee (or other such person) reasonably believed to be in violation of any provision of this title (or amendment), or any order, rule, regulation, standard, or ban under this title (or amendment).

(b) COMPLAINT PROCEDURE.—

(1) IN GENERAL. An employee who believes that he or she has been discharged or otherwise discriminated against by any employer in violation of this section may seek relief in accordance with the procedures, notifications, burdens of proof, remedies, and statutes of limitation set forth in section 2087(b) of title 15, United States Code.

(2) NO LIMITATION ON RIGHTS. Nothing in this section shall be deemed to diminish the rights, privileges, or remedies of any employee under any Federal or State law or under any collective bargaining agreement. The rights and remedies in this section may not be waived by any agreement, policy, form, or condition of employment.

2010 Amendment.—Section 1558 of P.L. 111-148, effective March 23, 2010, added section 18C.

National Credit Union Administration Regulations

[¶ 16,400]

National Credit Union Administration Regulations: Employee Retirement Benefit Plans.—The following regulations authorize federal credit unions to act as trustees and custodians of certain qualified retirement plans and individual retirement accounts.

The regulations were published in the *Federal Register* of June 17, 1975 (40 FR 25582). The regulations were amended effective July 7, 1978 (43 FR 29270), October 6, 1981 (46 FR 49107), and December 13, 1983 (48 FR 55423). The regulations were further amended, by interim final regulations, to permit federal credit unions to become trustees or custodians of Education IRAs and Roth IRAs. Savings Incentive Match Plan for Employees (SIMPLE) accounts and Medical Savings Accounts (MSAs) were not specifically addressed in the regulations because SIMPLE accounts are already covered by the NCUA regulations regarding IRAs and amendments regarding MSAs will be considered more thoroughly by the NCUA at a later time. The interim final regulations were effective March 24, 1998 (63 FR 14025) and were later adopted, September 29, 1998, as final regulations without any changes except to make the interim final rules retroactively effective as of January 1, 1998 in order to protect those federal credit unions that began acting as trustees of Roth IRAs and Education IRAs between January 1, 1998 and March 23, 1998. The final regulations adopting the interim amendments were published in the *Federal Reg* ister on September 30, 1998 (63 FR 52146), and were revised by 65 FR 10933, March 1, 2000.

As to Section 701.19, proposed rules were issued on December 20, 2001 (66 FR 65662) and September 25, 2002 (67 FR 60184), and a final rule was issued on April 30, 2003 (68 FR 23025), effective May 30, 2003. The final rule is set forth at ¶ 16,401 below; the preamble to the final rule is set forth at ¶ 24,806K.

The introductory comments to the regulations provide in part: "BYLAW CHANGE—In order for a Federal credit union to establish Keogh and IRA trust accounts under the new regulations, it will be necessary for the board of directors to adopt new bylaw provisions. The Administrator will provide all Federal credit unions with preapproved amendments and the procedure and forms necessary for this purpose.

"The new provisions will serve two purposes. First, they expressly provide for the issuance of shares in either revocable or irrevocable trusts, including specific reference to shares issued pursuant to pension plans authorized by regulation. Secondly, the new provisions eliminate problems which have resulted from the present language in Article XVII. Therefore, even though the bylaw changes are directly tied in with the new pension regulations, they are also designed to relieve restrictions imposed by the present bylaw provisions which affect all Federal credit unions, whether or not they intend to offer Keogh or IRA accounts."

Reg. Sec. 721.3 (¶ 16,401F), Reg. Sec. 724.1(¶ 16,402) and Reg. Sec. 724.2 (¶ 16,402A) were amended on July 29, 2004 (69 FR 45237). The corresponding regulation preamble is set forth at ¶ 24,806N.

Reg. Sec. 721.3(l) was redesignated Reg. Sec. 721.3(m) on May 31, 2012 (77 FR 31981).

Reg. Sec. 745.9-1 (¶ 16,403) was amended on December 30, 2003 (68 FR 75114). Reg. Sec. 745.9-2 was added on March 23, 2006 (71 FR 14636).

Reg. Sec. 745.9-2 (a) (¶ 16,403A) was amended on June 18, 2010 (75 FR 34619).

[¶ 16,401]

§ 701.19 Benefits for Employees of Federal Credit Unions.

(a) *General authority*. A federal credit union may provide employee benefits, including retirement benefits, to its employees and officers who are compensated in conformance with the Act and the bylaws, individually or collectively with other credit unions. The kind and amount of these benefits must be reasonable given the federal credit union's size, financial condition, and the duties of the employees.

(b) *Plan trustees and custodians*. Where a federal credit union is the benefit plan trustee or custodian, the plan must be authorized and maintained in accordance with the provisions of part 724 of this chapter. Where the benefit plan trustee or custodian is a party other than a federal credit union, the benefit plan must be maintained in accordance with applicable laws governing employee benefit plans, including any applicable rules and regulations issued by the Secretary of Labor, the Secretary of the Treasury, or any other federal or state authority exercising jurisdiction over the plan.

(c) *Investment authority*. A federal credit union investing to fund an employee benefit plan obligation is not subject to the investment limitations of the Act and part 703 or, as applicable, part 704, of this chapter and may purchase an investment that would otherwise be impermissible if the investment is directly related to the federal credit union's obligation or potential obligation under the employee benefit plan and the federal credit union holds the investment only for as long as it has an actual or potential obligation under the employee benefit plan.

(d) *Defined benefit plans*. Under paragraph (c) of this section, a federal credit union may invest to fund a defined benefit plan if the investment meets the conditions provided in that paragraph. If a federal credit union invests to fund a defined benefit plan that is not subject to the fiduciary responsibility provisions of part 4 of the Employee Retirement Income Security Act of 1974, it should diversify its investment portfolio to minimize the risk of large losses unless it is clearly prudent not to do so under the circumstances.

(e) *Liability insurance*. No federal credit union may occupy the position of a fiduciary, as defined in the Employee Retirement Income Security Act of 1974 and the rules and regulations issued by the Secretary of Labor, unless it has obtained appropriate liability insurance as described and permitted by Section 410(b) of the Employee Retirement Income Security Act of 1974.

(f) *Definitions*. For this section, defined benefit plan has the same meaning as in 29 U.S.C. 1002(35) and employee benefit plan has the same meaning as in 29 U.S.C. 1002(3).

[¶ 16,401A]

§ 701.35 Share, share draft and share certificate accounts.

(a) Federal credit unions may offer share, share draft, and share certificate accounts in accordance with section 107(6) of the Act (12 U.S.C. 1757(6)) and the board of directors may declare dividends on such accounts as provided in section 117 of the Act, (12 U.S.C. 1763).

(b) A Federal credit union shall accurately represent the terms and conditions of its share, share draft, and share certificate accounts in all advertising, disclosures, or agreements, whether written or oral.

(c) A Federal credit union may, consistent with this section, parts 707 and 740 of this subchapter, other federal law, and its contractual obligations, determine the types of fees or charges and other matters affecting the opening, maintaining and closing of a share, share draft or share certificate account. State laws regulating such activities are not applicable to federal credit unions.

(d) For purposes of this section, "state law" means the constitution, statutes, regulations, and judicial decisions of any state, the District of Columbia, the several territories and possessions of the United States, and the Commonwealth of Puerto Rico.

[¶ 16,401F]

§ 721.3 What categories of activities are preapproved as incidental powers necessary or requisite to carry on a credit union's business?

* * *

(m) *Trustee or custodial services*. Trustee or custodial services are services in which you are authorized to act under any written trust instrument or custodial agreement created or organized in the United States and forming part of a tax-advantaged savings plan, as authorized under the Internal Revenue Code. These services may include acting as a trustee or custodian for member retirement, education and health savings accounts. [Amended by 69 FR 45237, 7/29/04, and by 77 FR 31981, 5/31/12.]

[¶ 16,402]

§ 724.1 Federal credit unions acting as trustees and custodians of certain tax-advantaged savings plans.

A federal credit union is authorized to act as trustee or custodian, and may receive reasonable compensation for so acting, under any written trust instrument or custodial agreement created or organized in the United States and forming part of a tax-advantaged savings plan which qualifies or qualified for specific tax treatment under sections 223, 401(d), 408, 408A and 530 of the Internal Revenue Code (26 U.S.C. 223, 401(d), 408, 408A and 530), for its members or groups of its members, provided the funds of such plans are invested in share accounts or share certificate accounts of the Federal credit union. Federal credit unions located in a territory, including the trust territories, or a possession of the United States, or the Commonwealth of Puerto Rico, are also authorized to act as trustee or custodian for such plans, if authorized under sections 223, 401(d), 408, 408A and 530 of the Internal Revenue Code as applied to the territory or possession under similar provisions of territorial law. All funds held in a trustee or custodial capacity must be maintained in accordance with applicable laws and rules and regulations as may be promulgated by the Secretary of Labor, the Secretary of the Treasury, or any other authority exercising jurisdiction over such trust or custodial accounts. The federal credit union shall maintain individual records for each participant which show in detail all transactions relating to the funds of each participant or beneficiary. [Amended by 63 FR 14025, 3/24/98. Revised by 65 FR 10933, 3/1/00. Amended by 69 FR 45237, 7/29/04.]

[¶ 16,402A]

§724.2 Self-directed plans.

A federal credit union may facilitate transfers of plan funds to assets other than share and share certificates of the credit union, provided the conditions of §724.1 are met and the following additional conditions are met:

(a) All contributions of funds are initially made to a share or share certificate account in the Federal credit union;

(b) Any subsequent transfer of funds to other assets is solely at the direction of the member and the Federal credit union exercises no investment discretion and provides no investment advice with respect to plan assets (i.e., the credit union performs only custodial duties); and

(c) The member is clearly notified of the fact that National Credit Union Share Insurance Fund coverage is limited to funds held in share or share certificate accounts of NCUSIF-insured credit unions. [Amended by 69 FR 45237, 7/29/04.]

[¶ 16,402B]

§724.3 Appointment of successor trustee or custodian.

Any plan operated pursuant to this part shall provide for the appointment of a successor trustee or custodian by a person, committee, corporation or organization other than the Federal credit union or any person acting in his capacity as a director, employee or agent of the Federal credit union upon notice from the Federal credit union or the Board that the Federal credit union is unwilling or unable to continue to act as trustee or custodian.

[¶ 16,403]

§745.9-1 IRA/Keogh accounts.

(a) For purposes of this section, trust refers to an irrevocable trust.

(b) All trust interests (as defined in 745.2(d)(4)), for the same beneficiary, deposited in an account and established pursuant to valid trust agreements created by the same settlor (grantor) shall be added together and insured up to $100,000 in the aggregate, separately from other accounts of the trustee of such trust funds or the settlor or beneficiary of such trust arrangements.

(c) This section applies to trust interests created in Coverdell Education Savings Accounts, formerly Education IRAs, established in connection with section 530 of the Internal Revenue Code (26 U.S.C. 530). [51 FR 37560, Oct. 23, 1986, as amended at 65 FR 34924, June 1, 2000; 68 FR 75114, Dec. 30, 2003]

[¶ 16,403A]

§745.9-2 Retirement and other employee benefit plan accounts.

(a) Pass-through share insurance. Any shares of an employee benefit plan in an insured credit union shall be insured on a "pass-through" basis, in the amount of up to the SMSIA for the non-contingent interest of each plan participant, in accordance with §745.2 of this part. An insured credit union that is not "well capitalized" or "adequately capitalized" as those terms are defined in 12 U.S.C. 1790d(c), may not accept employee benefit plan deposits. The terms "employee benefit plan" and "pass-through share insurance" are given the same meaning in this section as in 12 U.S.C. 1787(k)(4). [Amended by 75 FR 34619, 6/18/10.]

(b) Treatment of contingent interests. In the event that participants' interests in an employee benefit plan are not capable of evaluation in accordance with the provisions of this section, or an account established for any such plan includes amounts for future participants in the plan, payment by the NCUA with respect to all such interests shall not exceed the SMSIA in the aggregate.

(c)(1) Certain retirement accounts. Shares in an insured credit union made in connection with the following types of retirement plans shall be aggregated and insured in the amount of up to $250,000 (which amount shall be subject to inflation adjustments as provided under section 11(a)(1)(F) of the Federal Deposit Insurance Act, except that $250,000 shall be substituted for $100,000 wherever such term appears in such section) per account:

(c)(1)(i) Any individual retirement account described in section 408(a) (IRA) of the Internal Revenue Code (26 U.S.C. 408(a)) or similar provisions of law applicable to a U.S. territory or possession;

(c)(1)(ii) Any individual retirement account described in section 408A (Roth IRA) of the Internal Revenue Code (26 U.S.C. 408A) or similar provisions of law applicable to a U.S. territory or possession; and

(c)(1)(iii) Any plan described in section 401(d) (Keogh account) of the Internal Revenue Code (26 U.S.C. 401(d)) or similar provisions of law applicable to a U.S. territory or possession.

(2) Insurance coverage for the accounts enumerated in paragraph (c)(1) of this section is based on the present vested ascertainable interest of a participant or designated beneficiary. For insurance purposes, IRA and Roth IRA accounts will be combined together and insured in the aggregate up to $250,000 (which amount shall be subject to inflation adjustments as provided under section 11(a)(1)(F) of the Federal Deposit Insurance Act, except that $250,000 shall be substituted for $100,000 wherever such term appears in such section). A Keogh account will be separately insured from an IRA account, Roth IRA account or, where applicable, aggregated IRA and Roth IRA accounts. [71 FR 14636, Mar. 23, 2006]

[¶ 16,404]

Appendix to Part 745—Examples of Insurance Coverage Afforded Accounts in Credit Unions Insured by the National Credit Union Share Insurance Fund

* * *

E. How Are Trust Accounts and Retirement Accounts Insured?

* * *

* * * Although credit unions may serve as trustees or custodians for self-directed IRA, Roth IRA and Keogh accounts, once the funds in those accounts are taken out of the credit union, they are no longer insured.

[Added June 1, 2000, by 65 FR 34921. Amended October 29, 2009 (74 FR 55747).]

* * *

[¶16,421]

Public Health Service Act

The Health Insurance Portability and Accountability Act of 1996 (HIPAA) (P.L. 104-191) made important changes to the Public Health Service Act (PHSA) (P.L. 78-410), assuring portability, availability, and renewability of health insurance coverage in the group and individual markets. A new Title XXVII (Assuring Portability, Availability, and Renewability of Health Insurance Coverage) was added to the PHSA by Act Sec. 102(a) of HIPAA, and was amended by Act Sec. 111(a) of HIPAA.

The Patient Protection and Affordable Care Act (P.L. 111-148) and the Health Care and Education Reconciliation Act of 2010 (P.L. 111-152) made significant changes to Title XXVII of the PHSA, extending some portability rules to the individual market, eliminating preexisting condition provisions, expanding dependent coverage rules, and making other health insurance market reforms. Note that the changes included the renumbering of several PHSA sections, including:

- sections 2704 through 2707 were redesignated as sections 2725 through 2728, respectively;
- sections 2711 through 2713 were redesignated as sections 2731 through 2733, respectively; and
- sections 2721 through 2723 were redesignated as sections 2735 through 2737, respectively.

Also note that Act Sec. 1563 of the Patient Protection and Affordable Care Act further redesignated some of these redesignated sections and made other conforming amendments.

Excerpted from Title XXVII of the PHSA are the following sections (42 USC 300gg et seq.):

1. fair health insurance premiums (§ 2701);
2. guaranteed availability of coverage (§ 2702);
3. guaranteed renewability of coverage (§ 2703);
4. prohibition of preexisting condition exclusions or other discrimination based on health status (§ 2704);
5. prohibiting discrimination against individual participants and beneficiaries based on health status (§ 2705);
6. non-discrimination in health care (§ 2706);
7. comprehensive health insurance coverage (§ 2707);
8. prohibition on excessive waiting periods (§ 2708);
9. coverage for individuals participating in approved clinical trials (§ 2709);
10. disclosure of information (§ 2709 [§ 2710]);
11. no lifetime or annual limits (§ 2711);
12. prohibition on rescissions (§ 2712);
13. coverage of preventive health services (§ 2713);
14. extension of dependent coverage (§ 2714);
15. development and utilization of uniform explanation of coverage documents and standardized definitions (§ 2715);
16. provision of additional information (§ 2715A);
17. prohibition on discrimination in favor of highly compensated individuals (§ 2716);
18. ensuring the quality of care (§ 2717);
19. bringing down the cost of health care coverage (§ 2718);
20. appeals process (§ 2719);
21. patient protections (§ 2719A);
22. exclusion of certain plans (§ 2722);
23. enforcement (§ 2723);
24. preemption, state flexibility, and construction (§ 2724);
25. standards relating to benefits for mothers and newborns (§ 2725);
26. parity in mental health and substance use disorder benefits (§ 2726);
27. required coverage for reconstructive surgery following mastectomies (§ 2727);
28. coverage of dependent students on medically necessary leave of absence (§ 2728);
29. guaranteed availability of coverage for employers in the group market (§ 2731);
30. guaranteed renewability of coverage for employers in the group market (§ 2732);
31. guaranteed availability of individual health insurance coverage to certain individuals with prior group coverage (§ 2741);
32. guaranteed renewability of individual health insurance coverage (§ 2742);
33. certification of coverage (§ 2743);
34. state flexibility in individual market reforms (§ 2744);
35. relief for high risk pools (§ 2745);
36. preemption, state flexibility, and construction (§ 2746);
37. general exceptions (§ 2747);
38. standards relating to benefits for mothers and newborns (§ 2751);
39. required coverage for reconstructive surgery following mastectomies (§ 2752);
40. prohibition of health discrimination on the basis of genetic information (§ 2753);
41. enforcement (§ 2761);
42. preemption and application (§ 2762);

43. general exceptions (§ 2763);

44. coverage of dependent students on medically necessary leave of absence [§ 2753];

45. definitions (§ 2791);

46. regulations (§ 2792);

47. health insurance consumer information (§ 2793);

48. ensuring that consumers get value for their dollars (§ 2794); and

49. uniform fraud and abuse referral format [§ 2794].

The Patient Protection and Affordable Care Act (P.L. 111-148) and the Health Care and Education Reconciliation Act of 2010 (P.L. 111-152) added Title XXXII to the PHSA. All the sections (§ 3201 through § 3210) of new Title XXXII are reproduced below.

Text of Excerpted Fair Labor Standards Act Section

TITLE XXVII—REQUIREMENTS RELATING TO HEALTH INSURANCE COVERAGE

PART A—INDIVIDUAL AND GROUP MARKET REFORMS

PART A—INDIVIDUAL AND GROUP MARKET REFORMS

2010 Amendments:

Sec. 1001(1) of the "Patient Protection and Affordable Care Act" (P.L. 111–148), effective for plan years beginning on or after Sept. 23, 2010, amended part A of title XXVII heading by substituting "PART A—INDIVID-UAL AND GROUP MARKET REFORMS" (in bold type) for "Part A—Group Market Reforms".

History:

Sec. 102(a) of the "Health Insurance Portability and Accountability Act of 1996" (P.L. 104–191), sec. 1001(1) of the "Patient Protection and Affordable Care Act" (P.L. 111–148).

SUBPART I—GENERAL REFORM

2010 Amendments:

Sec. 1201(1) of the "Patient Protection and Affordable Care Act" (P.L. 111–148), effective for plan years beginning on or after Jan. 1, 2014, amended heading of first subpart in part A of title XXVII by substituting "Subpart I—General Reform" (in bold type) for "Subpart 1—Portability, Access, and Renewability Requirements".

History:

Sec. 102(a) of the "Health Insurance Portability and Accountability Act of 1996" (P.L. 104–191), sec. 1201(1) of the "Patient Protection and Affordable Care Act" (P.L. 111–148).

Sec. 2701. Fair Health Insurance Premiums

[42 U.S.C. 300gg]

(a) [3] PROHIBITING DISCRIMINATORY PREMIUM RATES.—

(1) IN GENERAL. With respect to the premium rate charged by a health insurance issuer for health insurance coverage offered in the individual or small group market—

(A) such rate shall vary with respect to the particular plan or coverage involved only by—

(i) whether such plan or coverage covers an individual or family;

(ii) rating area, as established in accordance with paragraph (2);

(iii) age, except that such rate shall not vary by more than 3 to 1 for adults (consistent with section 2707(c)); and

(iv) tobacco use, except that such rate shall not vary by more than 1.5 to 1; and

(B) such rate shall not vary with respect to the particular plan or coverage involved by any other factor not described in subparagraph (A).

(2) RATING AREA.—

(A) IN GENERAL. Each State shall establish 1 or more rating areas within that State for purposes of applying the requirements of this title.

(B) SECRETARIAL REVIEW. The Secretary shall review the rating areas established by each State under subparagraph (A) to ensure the adequacy of such areas for purposes of carrying out the requirements of this title. If the Secretary determines a State's rating areas are not adequate, or that a State does not establish such areas, the Secretary may establish rating areas for that State.

(3) PERMISSIBLE AGE BANDS. The Secretary, in consultation with the National Association of Insurance Commissioners, shall define the permissible age bands for rating purposes under paragraph (1)(A)(iii).

(4) APPLICATION OF VARIATIONS BASED ON AGE OR TOBACCO USE. With respect to family coverage under a group health plan or health insurance coverage, the rating variations permitted under clauses (iii) and (iv) of paragraph (1)(A) shall be applied based on the portion of the premium that is attributable to each family member covered under the plan or coverage.

(5) SPECIAL RULE FOR LARGE GROUP MARKET. If a State permits health insurance issuers that offer coverage in the large group market in the State to offer such coverage through the State Exchange (as provided for under section 1312(f)(2)(B) of the Patient Protection and Affordable Care Act), the provisions of this subsection shall apply to all coverage offered in such market (other than self-insured group health plans offered in such market) in the State.

2010 Amendments:

Sec. 1201(4) of the "Patient Protection and Affordable Care Act" (P.L. 111–148), effective for plan years beginning on or after Jan. 1, 2014, added new sec. 2701.

Sec. 10103(a) of the "Patient Protection and Affordable Care Act" (P.L. 111–148), effective Mar. 23, 2010, amended sec. 2701(a)(5) by inserting "(other than self-insured group health plans offered in such market)" after "such market".

---

[3] There are no subsections following subsection (a) in section 2701.

History:

Sec. 1201(4), sec. 10103(a) of the "Patient Protection and Affordable Care Act" (P.L. 111–148).

Sec. 2702. Guaranteed Availability of Coverage

[42 U.S.C. 300gg–1]

(a) GUARANTEED ISSUANCE OF COVERAGE IN THE INDIVIDUAL AND GROUP MARKET. Subject to subsections (b) through (e)[4], each health insurance issuer that offers health insurance coverage in the individual or group market in a State must accept every employer and individual in the State that applies for such coverage.

(b) ENROLLMENT.—

(1) RESTRICTION. A health insurance issuer described in subsection (a) may restrict enrollment in coverage described in such subsection to open or special enrollment periods.

(2) ESTABLISHMENT. A health insurance issuer described in subsection (a) shall, in accordance with the regulations promulgated under paragraph (3), establish special enrollment periods for qualifying events (under section 603 of the Employee Retirement Income Security Act of 1974).

(3) REGULATIONS. The Secretary shall promulgate regulations with respect to enrollment periods under paragraphs (1) and (2).

(c) SPECIAL RULES FOR NETWORK PLANS.—

(1) IN GENERAL. In the case of a health insurance issuer that offers health insurance coverage in the group and individual market through a network plan, the issuer may—

(A) limit the employers that may apply for such coverage to those with eligible individuals who live, work, or reside in the service area for such network plan; and

(B) within the service area of such plan, deny such coverage to such employers and individuals if the issuer has demonstrated, if required, to the applicable State authority that—

(i) it will not have the capacity to deliver services adequately to enrollees of any additional groups or any additional individuals because of its obligations to existing group contract holders and enrollees, and

(ii) it is applying this paragraph uniformly to all employers and individuals without regard to the claims experience of those individuals, employers and their employees (and their dependents) or any health status-related factor relating to such individuals[5] employees and dependents.

(2) 180-DAY SUSPENSION UPON DENIAL OF COVERAGE. An issuer, upon denying health insurance coverage in any service area in accordance with paragraph (1)(B), may not offer coverage in the group or individual market within such service area for a period of 180 days after the date such coverage is denied.

(d) APPLICATION OF FINANCIAL CAPACITY LIMITS.—

(1) IN GENERAL. A health insurance issuer may deny health insurance coverage in the group or individual market if the issuer has demonstrated, if required, to the applicable State authority that—

(A) it does not have the financial reserves necessary to underwrite additional coverage; and

(B) it is applying this paragraph uniformly to all employers and individuals in the group or individual market in the State consistent with applicable State law and without regard to the claims experience of those individuals, employers and their employees (and their dependents) or any health status-related factor relating to such individuals, employees and dependents.

(2) 180-DAY SUSPENSION UPON DENIAL OF COVERAGE. A health insurance issuer upon denying health insurance coverage in connection with group health plans in accordance with paragraph (1) in a State may not offer coverage in connection with group health plans in the group or individual market in the State for a period of 180 days after the date such coverage is denied or until the issuer has demonstrated to the applicable State authority, if required under applicable State law, that the issuer has sufficient financial reserves to underwrite additional coverage, whichever is later. An applicable State authority may provide for the application of this subsection on a service-area-specific basis.

2010 Amendments:

Sec. 1201(4) of the "Patient Protection and Affordable Care Act" (P.L. 111–148), effective for plan years beginning on or after Jan. 1, 2014, added new sec. 2702.

Sec. 1563(c)(8) of the "Patient Protection and Affordable Care Act" (P.L. 111–148) (formerly sec. 1562(c)(8) of such Act, renumbered sec. 1563(c)(8) by sec. 10107(b)(1) of such Act), effective Mar. 23, 2010, amended sec 2702 by adding at the end new subsections (c) and (d), which were transferred from former sec. 2731.

History:

Secs. 1201(4), 1563(c)(8), formerly Sec. 1562(c)(8), renumbered Sec. 1563(c)(8), Sec. 10107(b)(1) of the "Patient Protection and Affordable Care Act" (P.L. 111–148).

Sec. 2703. Guaranteed Renewability of Coverage

[42 U.S.C. 300gg–2]

(a) IN GENERAL. Except as provided in this section, if a health insurance issuer offers health insurance coverage in the individual or group market, the issuer must renew or continue in force such coverage at the option of the plan sponsor or the individual, as applicable.

(b) GENERAL EXCEPTIONS. A health insurance issuer may nonrenew or discontinue health insurance coverage offered in connection with a health insurance coverage offered in the group or individual market based only on one or more of the following:

(1) NONPAYMENT OF PREMIUMS. The plan sponsor, or individual, as applicable, has failed to pay premiums or contributions in accordance with the terms of the health insurance coverage or the issuer has not received timely premium payments.

---

[4] So in original.

[5] So in original. Probably should be followed by a comma.

(2) FRAUD. The plan sponsor, or individual, as applicable, has performed an act or practice that constitutes fraud or made an intentional misrepresentation of material fact under the terms of the coverage.

(3) VIOLATION OF PARTICIPATION OR CONTRIBUTION RATES. In the case of a group health plan, the plan sponsor has failed to comply with a material plan provision relating to employer contribution or group participation rules, pursuant to applicable State law.

(4) TERMINATION OF COVERAGE. The issuer is ceasing to offer coverage in such market in accordance with subsection (c) and applicable State law.

(5) MOVEMENT OUTSIDE SERVICE AREA. In the case of a health insurance issuer that offers health insurance coverage in the market through a network plan, there is no longer any enrollee in connection with such plan who lives, resides, or works in the service area of the issuer (or in the area for which the issuer is authorized to do business) and, in the case of the small group market, the issuer would deny enrollment with respect to such plan under section 2711(c)(1)(A).[6]

(6) ASSOCIATION MEMBERSHIP CEASES. In the case of health insurance coverage that is made available in the small or large group market (as the case may be) only through one or more bona fide associations, the membership of an employer in the association (on the basis of which the coverage is provided) ceases but only if such coverage is terminated under this paragraph uniformly without regard to any health status-related factor relating to any covered individual.

(c) REQUIREMENTS FOR UNIFORM TERMINATION OF COVERAGE.—

(1) PARTICULAR TYPE OF COVERAGE NOT OFFERED. In any case in which an issuer decides to discontinue offering a particular type of group or individual health insurance coverage, coverage of such type may be discontinued by the issuer in accordance with applicable State law in such market only if—

(A) the issuer provides notice to each plan sponsor or individual, as applicable, provided coverage of this type in such market (and participants and beneficiaries covered under such coverage) of such discontinuation at least 90 days prior to the date of the discontinuation of such coverage;

(B) the issuer offers to each plan sponsor or individual, as applicable, provided coverage of this type in such market, the option to purchase all (or, in the case of the large group market, any) other health insurance coverage currently being offered by the issuer to a group health plan or individual health insurance coverage[7] in such market; and

(C) in exercising the option to discontinue coverage of this type and in offering the option of coverage under subparagraph (B), the issuer acts uniformly without regard to the claims experience of those sponsors or individuals, as applicable, or any health status-related factor relating to any participants or beneficiaries covered or new participants or beneficiaries who may become eligible for such coverage.

(2) DISCONTINUANCE OF ALL COVERAGE.—

(A) IN GENERAL. In any case in which a health insurance issuer elects to discontinue offering all health insurance coverage in the individual or group market, or all markets, in a State, health insurance coverage may be discontinued by the issuer only in accordance with applicable State law and if—

(i) the issuer provides notice to the applicable State authority and to each plan sponsor or individual, as applicable, (and participants and beneficiaries covered under such coverage) of such discontinuation at least 180 days prior to the date of the discontinuation of such coverage; and

(ii) all health insurance issued or delivered for issuance in the State in such market (or markets) are discontinued and coverage under such health insurance coverage in such market (or markets) is not renewed.

(B) PROHIBITION ON MARKET REENTRY. In the case of a discontinuation under subparagraph (A) in a market, the issuer may not provide for the issuance of any health insurance coverage in the market and State involved during the 5-year period beginning on the date of the discontinuation of the last health insurance coverage not so renewed.

(d) EXCEPTION FOR UNIFORM MODIFICATION OF COVERAGE. At the time of coverage renewal, a health insurance issuer may modify the health insurance coverage for a product offered to a group health plan—

(1) in the large group market; or

(2) in the small group market if, for coverage that is available in such market other than only through one or more bona fide associations, such modification is consistent with State law and effective on a uniform basis among group health plans with that product.

(e) APPLICATION TO COVERAGE OFFERED ONLY THROUGH ASSOCIATIONS. In applying this section in the case of health insurance coverage that is made available by a health insurance issuer in the small or large group market to employers only through one or more associations, a reference to "plan sponsor" is deemed, with respect to coverage provided to an employer member of the association, to include a reference to such employer.

2010 Amendments:

Sec. 1201(4) of the "Patient Protection and Affordable Care Act" (P.L. 111–148), effective for plan years beginning on or after Jan. 1, 2014, added new sec. 2703.

Sec. 1563(c)(9) of the "Patient Protection and Affordable Care Act" (P.L. 111–148) (formerly sec. 1562(c)(9) of such Act, renumbered sec. 1563(c)(9) by sec. 10107(b)(1) of such Act), effective Mar. 23, 2010, amended sec. 2703

by adding at the end new subsections (b) to (e), which were transferred from former sec. 2732.

History:

Secs. 1201(4), 1563(c)(9), formerly Sec. 1562(c)(9), renumbered Sec. 1563(c)(9), Sec. 10107(b)(1) of the "Patient Protection and Affordable Care Act" (P.L. 111–148).

Sec. 2704. Prohibition of Preexisting Condition Exclusions Or Other Discrimination Based on Health Status[8]

[42 U.S.C. 300gg–3]

(a) IN GENERAL. A group health plan and a health insurance issuer offering group or individual health insurance coverage may not impose any preexisting condition exclusion with respect to such plan or coverage.

(b) DEFINITIONS. For purposes of this part—

---

[6] Section 2711 was renumbered 2731.

[7] Section 1563(c)(9)(C)(i)(III)(bb) (relating to conforming amendments–originally designated as section 1562 and redesignated as section 1563 by section 10107(b)(1)) of Public Law 111–148, which directed the insertion of "or individual health insurance coverage" in subsec. (c)(1)(B) of former section 2732, but did not specify where to make the insertion, was executed by inserting such language after "group health plan" to reflect the probable intent of Congress. Such subsec. (c)(1)(B) was subsequently transferred to this section.

[8] Although this version of section 2704 is generally effective for plan years beginning on or after Jan. 1, 2014, the provisions of this version, as they apply to enrollees who are under 19 years of age, are effective for plan years beginning on or after Sept. 23, 2010.

(1) PREEXISTING CONDITION EXCLUSION.—

(A) IN GENERAL. The term "preexisting condition exclusion" means, with respect to coverage, a limitation or exclusion of benefits relating to a condition based on the fact that the condition was present before the date of enrollment for such coverage, whether or not any medical advice, diagnosis, care, or treatment was recommended or received before such date.

(B) TREATMENT OF GENETIC INFORMATION. Genetic information shall not be treated as a condition described in subsection (a)(1)[9] in the absence of a diagnosis of the condition related to such information.

(2) ENROLLMENT DATE. The term "enrollment date" means, with respect to an individual covered under a group health plan or health insurance coverage, the date of enrollment of the individual in the plan or coverage or, if earlier, the first day of the waiting period for such enrollment.

(3) LATE ENROLLEE. The term "late enrollee" means, with respect to coverage under a group health plan, a participant or beneficiary who enrolls under the plan other than during—

(A) the first period in which the individual is eligible to enroll under the plan, or

(B) a special enrollment period under subsection (f).

(4) WAITING PERIOD. The term "waiting period" means, with respect to a group health plan and an individual who is a potential participant or beneficiary in the plan, the period that must pass with respect to the individual before the individual is eligible to be covered for benefits under the terms of the plan.

(c) RULES RELATING TO CREDITING PREVIOUS COVERAGE.—

(1) CREDITABLE COVERAGE DEFINED. For purposes of this title, the term "creditable coverage" means, with respect to an individual, coverage of the individual under any of the following:

(A) A group health plan.

(B) Health insurance coverage.

(C) Part A or part B of title XVIII of the Social Security Act.

(D) Title XIX of the Social Security Act, other than coverage consisting solely of benefits under section 1928.

(E) Chapter 55 of title 10, United States Code.

(F) A medical care program of the Indian Health Service or of a tribal organization.

(G) A State health benefits risk pool.

(H) A health plan offered under chapter 89 of title 5, United States Code.

(I) A public health plan (as defined in regulations).

(J) A health benefit plan under section 5(e) of the Peace Corps Act (22 U.S.C. 2504(e)).

Such term does not include coverage consisting solely of coverage of excepted benefits (as defined in section 2791(c)).

(2) NOT COUNTING PERIODS BEFORE SIGNIFICANT BREAKS IN COVERAGE.—

(A) IN GENERAL. A period of creditable coverage shall not be counted, with respect to enrollment of an individual under a group or individual health plan, if, after such period and before the enrollment date, there was a 63-day period during all of which the individual was not covered under any creditable coverage.

(B) WAITING PERIOD NOT TREATED AS A BREAK IN COVERAGE. For purposes of subparagraph (A) and subsection (d)(4), any period that an individual is in a waiting period for any coverage under a group or individual health plan (or for group health insurance coverage) or is in an affiliation period (as defined in subsection (g)(2)) shall not be taken into account in determining the continuous period under subparagraph (A).

(C) TAA-ELIGIBLE INDIVIDUALS. In the case of plan years beginning before January 1, 2014—

(i) TAA PRE-CERTIFICATION PERIOD RULE. In the case of a TAA-eligible individual, the period beginning on the date the individual has a TAA-related loss of coverage and ending on the date that is 7 days after the date of the issuance by the Secretary (or by any person or entity designated by the Secretary) of a qualified health insurance costs credit eligibility certificate for such individual for purposes of section 7527 of the Internal Revenue Code of 1986 shall not be taken into account in determining the continuous period under subparagraph (A).

(ii) DEFINITIONS. The terms "TAA-eligible individual" and "TAA-related loss of coverage" have the meanings given such terms in section 2205(b)(4).

(3) METHOD OF CREDITING COVERAGE.—

(A) STANDARD METHOD. Except as otherwise provided under subparagraph (B), for purposes of applying subsection (a)(3),[10] a group health plan, and a health insurance issuer offering group or individual health insurance coverage, shall count a period of creditable coverage without regard to the specific benefits covered during the period.

(B) ELECTION OF ALTERNATIVE METHOD. A group health plan, or a health insurance issuer offering group or individual health insurance, may elect to apply subsection (a)(3)[11] based on coverage of benefits within each of several classes or categories of benefits specified in regulations rather than as provided under subparagraph (A). Such election shall be made on a uniform basis for all participants and beneficiaries. Under such election a group or individual health plan or issuer shall count a period of creditable coverage with respect to any class or category of benefits if any level of benefits is covered within such class or category.

(C) PLAN NOTICE. In the case of an election with respect to a group health plan under subparagraph (B) (whether or not health insurance coverage is provided in connection with such plan), the plan shall—

---

[9] Subsection (a) was struck out and a new subsection (a) was added by Pub. L. 111–148 which does not contain paragraphs.

[10] Subsection (a) was struck out and a new subsection (a) was added by Pub. L. 111–148 which does not contain paragraphs.

[11] Subsection (a) was struck out and a new subsection (a) was added by Pub. L. 111–148 which does not contain paragraphs.

(i) prominently state in any disclosure statements concerning the plan, and state to each enrollee at the time of enrollment under the plan, that the plan has made such election, and

(ii) include in such statements a description of the effect of this election.

(D) ISSUER NOTICE. In the case of an election under subparagraph (B) with respect to health insurance coverage offered by an issuer in the individual or group group[12] market, the issuer—

(i) shall prominently state in any disclosure statements concerning the coverage, and to each employer at the time of the offer or sale of the coverage, that the issuer has made such election, and

(ii) shall include in such statements a description of the effect of such election.

(4) ESTABLISHMENT OF PERIOD. Periods of creditable coverage with respect to an individual shall be established through presentation of certifications described in subsection (e) or in such other manner as may be specified in regulations.

(d) EXCEPTIONS.—

(1) EXCLUSION NOT APPLICABLE TO CERTAIN NEWBORNS. Subject to paragraph (4), a group health plan, and a health insurance issuer offering group or individual health insurance coverage, may not impose any preexisting condition exclusion in the case of an individual who, as of the last day of the 30-day period beginning with the date of birth, is covered under creditable coverage.

(2) EXCLUSION NOT APPLICABLE TO CERTAIN ADOPTED CHILDREN. Subject to paragraph (4), a group health plan, and a health insurance issuer offering group or individual health insurance coverage, may not impose any preexisting condition exclusion in the case of a child who is adopted or placed for adoption before attaining 18 years of age and who, as of the last day of the 30-day period beginning on the date of the adoption or placement for adoption, is covered under creditable coverage. The previous sentence shall not apply to coverage before the date of such adoption or placement for adoption.

(3) EXCLUSION NOT APPLICABLE TO PREGNANCY. A group health plan, and health insurance issuer offering group or individual health insurance coverage, may not impose any preexisting condition exclusion relating to pregnancy as a preexisting condition.

(4) LOSS IF BREAK IN COVERAGE. Paragraphs (1) and (2) shall no longer apply to an individual after the end of the first 63-day period during all of which the individual was not covered under any creditable coverage.

(e) CERTIFICATIONS AND DISCLOSURE OF COVERAGE.—

(1) REQUIREMENT FOR CERTIFICATION OF PERIOD OF CREDITABLE COVERAGE.—

(A) IN GENERAL. A group health plan, and a health insurance issuer offering group or individual health insurance coverage, shall provide the certification described in subparagraph (B)—

(i) at the time an individual ceases to be covered under the plan or otherwise becomes covered under a COBRA continuation provision,

(ii) in the case of an individual becoming covered under such a provision, at the time the individual ceases to be covered under such provision, and

(iii) on the request on behalf of an individual made not later than 24 months after the date of cessation of the coverage described in clause (i) or (ii), whichever is later.

The certification under clause (i) may be provided, to the extent practicable, at a time consistent with notices required under any applicable COBRA continuation provision.

(B) CERTIFICATION. The certification described in this subparagraph is a written certification of—

(i) the period of creditable coverage of the individual under such plan and the coverage (if any) under such COBRA continuation provision, and

(ii) the waiting period (if any) (and affiliation period, if applicable) imposed with respect to the individual for any coverage under such plan.

(C) ISSUER COMPLIANCE. To the extent that medical care under a group health plan consists of group health insurance coverage, the plan is deemed to have satisfied the certification requirement under this paragraph if the health insurance issuer offering the coverage provides for such certification in accordance with this paragraph.

(2) DISCLOSURE OF INFORMATION ON PREVIOUS BENEFITS. In the case of an election described in subsection (c)(3)(B) by a group health plan or health insurance issuer, if the plan or issuer enrolls an individual for coverage under the plan and the individual provides a certification of coverage of the individual under paragraph (1)—

(A) upon request of such plan or issuer, the entity which issued the certification provided by the individual shall promptly disclose to such requesting plan or issuer information on coverage of classes and categories of health benefits available under such entity's plan or coverage, and

(B) such entity may charge the requesting plan or issuer for the reasonable cost of disclosing such information.

(3) REGULATIONS. The Secretary shall establish rules to prevent an entity's failure to provide information under paragraph (1) or (2) with respect to previous coverage of an individual from adversely affecting any subsequent coverage of the individual under another group health plan or health insurance coverage.

(f) SPECIAL ENROLLMENT PERIODS.—

(1) INDIVIDUALS LOSING OTHER COVERAGE. A group health plan, and a health insurance issuer offering group health insurance coverage in connection with a group health plan, shall permit an employee who is eligible, but not enrolled, for coverage under the terms of the plan (or a dependent of such an employee if the dependent is eligible, but not enrolled, for coverage under such terms) to enroll for coverage under the terms of the plan if each of the following conditions is met:

(A) The employee or dependent was covered under a group health plan or had health insurance coverage at the time coverage was previously offered to the employee or dependent.

---

[12] So in law. See amendment made by section 1563(c)(1)(A)(ii)(II) (relating to conforming amendments–originally designated as section 1562 and redesignated as section 1563 by section 10107(b)(1)) of Public Law 111–148.

(B) The employee stated in writing at such time that coverage under a group health plan or health insurance coverage was the reason for declining enrollment, but only if the plan sponsor or issuer (if applicable) required such a statement at such time and provided the employee with notice of such requirement (and the consequences of such requirement) at such time.

(C) The employee's or dependent's coverage described in subparagraph (A)—

(i) was under a COBRA continuation provision and the coverage under such provision was exhausted; or

(ii) was not under such a provision and either the coverage was terminated as a result of loss of eligibility for the coverage (including as a result of legal separation, divorce, death, termination of employment, or reduction in the number of hours of employment) or employer contributions toward such coverage were terminated.

(D) Under the terms of the plan, the employee requests such enrollment not later than 30 days after the date of exhaustion of coverage described in subparagraph (C)(i) or termination of coverage or employer contribution described in subparagraph (C)(ii).

(2) FOR DEPENDENT BENEFICIARIES.—

(A) IN GENERAL. If—

(i) a group health plan makes coverage available with respect to a dependent of an individual,

(ii) the individual is a participant under the plan (or has met any waiting period applicable to becoming a participant under the plan and is eligible to be enrolled under the plan but for a failure to enroll during a previous enrollment period), and

(iii) a person becomes such a dependent of the individual through marriage, birth, or adoption or placement for adoption,

the group health plan shall provide for a dependent special enrollment period described in subparagraph (B) during which the person (or, if not otherwise enrolled, the individual) may be enrolled under the plan as a dependent of the individual, and in the case of the birth or adoption of a child, the spouse of the individual may be enrolled as a dependent of the individual if such spouse is otherwise eligible for coverage.

(B) DEPENDENT SPECIAL ENROLLMENT PERIOD. A dependent special enrollment period under this subparagraph shall be a period of not less than 30 days and shall begin on the later of—

(i) the date dependent coverage is made available, or

(ii) the date of the marriage, birth, or adoption or placement for adoption (as the case may be) described in subparagraph (A)(iii).

(C) NO WAITING PERIOD. If an individual seeks to enroll a dependent during the first 30 days of such a dependent special enrollment period, the coverage of the dependent shall become effective—

(i) in the case of marriage, not later than the first day of the first month beginning after the date the completed request for enrollment is received;

(ii) in the case of a dependent's birth, as of the date of such birth; or

(iii) in the case of a dependent's adoption or placement for adoption, the date of such adoption or placement for adoption.

(3) SPECIAL RULES FOR APPLICATION IN CASE OF MEDICAID AND CHIP.—

(A) IN GENERAL. A group health plan, and a health insurance issuer offering group health insurance coverage in connection with a group health plan, shall permit an employee who is eligible, but not enrolled, for coverage under the terms of the plan (or a dependent of such an employee if the dependent is eligible, but not enrolled, for coverage under such terms) to enroll for coverage under the terms of the plan if either of the following conditions is met:

(i) TERMINATION OF MEDICAID OR CHIP COVERAGE. The employee or dependent is covered under a Medicaid plan under title XIX of the Social Security Act or under a State child health plan under title XXI of such Act and coverage of the employee or dependent under such a plan is terminated as a result of loss of eligibility for such coverage and the employee requests coverage under the group health plan (or health insurance coverage) not later than 60 days after the date of termination of such coverage.

(ii) ELIGIBILITY FOR EMPLOYMENT ASSISTANCE UNDER MEDICAID OR CHIP. The employee or dependent becomes eligible for assistance, with respect to coverage under the group health plan or health insurance coverage, under such Medicaid plan or State child health plan (including under any waiver or demonstration project conducted under or in relation to such a plan), if the employee requests coverage under the group health plan or health insurance coverage not later than 60 days after the date the employee or dependent is determined to be eligible for such assistance.

(B) COORDINATION WITH MEDICAID AND CHIP.—

(i) OUTREACH TO EMPLOYEES REGARDING AVAILABILITY OF MEDICAID AND CHIP COVERAGE.—

(I) IN GENERAL. Each employer that maintains a group health plan in a State that provides medical assistance under a State Medicaid plan under title XIX of the Social Security Act, or child health assistance under a State child health plan under title XXI of such Act, in the form of premium assistance for the purchase of coverage under a group health plan, shall provide to each employee a written notice informing the employee of potential opportunities then currently available in the State in which the employee resides for premium assistance under such plans for health coverage of the employee or the employee's dependents. For purposes of compliance with this subclause, the employer may use any State-specific model notice developed in accordance with section 701(f)(3)(B)(i)(II) of the Employee Retirement Income Security Act of 1974 (29 U.S.C. 1181(f)(3)(B)(i)(II)).

(II) OPTION TO PROVIDE CONCURRENT WITH PROVISION OF PLAN MATERIALS TO EMPLOYEE. An employer may provide the model notice applicable to the State in which an employee resides concurrent with the furnishing of materials notifying the employee of health plan eligibility, concurrent with materials provided to the employee in connection with an open season or election process conducted under the plan, or concurrent with the furnishing of the summary plan description as provided in section 104(b) of the Employee Retirement Income Security Act of 1974.

(ii) DISCLOSURE ABOUT GROUP HEALTH PLAN BENEFITS TO STATES FOR MEDICAID AND CHIP ELIGIBLE INDIVIDUALS. In the case of an enrollee in a group health plan who is covered under a Medicaid plan of a State under title XIX of the Social Security Act or under a State child health plan under title XXI of such Act, the plan administrator of the group health plan shall disclose to the State, upon request, information about the benefits available under the group health plan in sufficient specificity, as determined under regulations of the Secretary of Health and Human Services in consultation with the Secretary that require use of the model coverage coordination disclosure form developed under section 311(b)(1)(C) of the

Children's Health Insurance[13] Reauthorization Act of 2009, so as to permit the State to make a determination (under paragraph (2)(B), (3), or (10) of section 2105(c) of the Social Security Act or otherwise) concerning the cost-effectiveness of the State providing medical or child health assistance through premium assistance for the purchase of coverage under such group health plan and in order for the State to provide supplemental benefits required under paragraph (10)(E) of such section or other authority.

(g) Use of Affiliation Period by HMOs as Alternative to Preexisting Condition Exclusion.—

(1) In general. A health maintenance organization which offers health insurance coverage in connection with a group health plan and which does not impose any preexisting condition exclusion allowed under subsection (a) with respect to any particular coverage option may impose an affiliation period for such coverage option, but only if—

(A) such period is applied uniformly without regard to any health status-related factors; and

(B) such period does not exceed 2 months (or 3 months in the case of a late enrollee).

(2) Affiliation period.—

(A) Defined. For purposes of this title, the term "affiliation period" means a period which, under the terms of the health insurance coverage offered by the health maintenance organization, must expire before the health insurance coverage becomes effective. The organization is not required to provide health care services or benefits during such period and no premium shall be charged to the participant or beneficiary for any coverage during the period.

(B) Beginning. Such period shall begin on the enrollment date.

(C) Runs concurrently with waiting periods. An affiliation period under a plan shall run concurrently with any waiting period under the plan.

(3) Alternative methods. A health maintenance organization described in paragraph (1) may use alternative methods, from those described in such paragraph, to address adverse selection as approved by the State insurance commissioner or official or officials designated by the State to enforce the requirements of this part for the State involved with respect to such issuer.

2011 Amendments:

Sec. 242(a)(3), (4) of the "Trade Adjustment Assistance Extension Act of 2011", Title II of P.L. 112–40, applicable to plan years beginning after Feb. 12, 2011, subject to transitional rules, amended sec. 2701(c)(2)(C) (as in effect for plan years beginning before Jan. 1, 2014) and sec. 2704(c)(2)(C) (as in effect for plan years beginning on or after Jan. 1, 2014) by striking "February 13, 2011" and inserting "January 1, 2014".

2010 Amendments:

Sec. 1201(2) of the "Patient Protection and Affordable Care Act" (P.L. 111–148), effective for plan years beginning on or after Jan. 1, 2014, except that the provisions of sec. 2704 of the Public Health Service Act (as amended by such sec. 1201(2)), as they apply to enrollees who are under 19 years of age, shall become effective for plan years beginning on or after Sept. 23, 2010, amended sec. 2701 by redesignating such section as sec. 2704, substituting "PROHIBITION OF PREEXISTING CONDITION EXCLUSIONS OR OTHER DISCRIMINATION BASED ON HEALTH STATUS" (in bold type) for "INCREASED PORTABILITY THROUGH LIMITATION ON PREEXISTING CONDITION EXCLUSIONS" (in bold type) in section heading, and amending subsection (a).

Prior to amendment sec. 2704(a) read as follows:

"(a) Limitation on Preexisting Condition Exclusion Period; Crediting for Periods of Previous Coverage.—Subject to subsection (d), a group health plan, and a health insurance issuer offering group health insurance coverage, may, with respect to a participant or beneficiary, impose a preexisting condition exclusion only if—

"(1) such exclusion relates to a condition (whether physical or mental), regardless of the cause of the condition, for which medical advice, diagnosis, care, or treatment was recommended or received within the 6-month period ending on the enrollment date;

"(2) such exclusion extends for a period of not more than 12 months (or 18 months in the case of a late enrollee) after the enrollment date; and

"(3) the period of any such preexisting condition exclusion is reduced by the aggregate of the periods of creditable coverage (if any, as defined in subsection (c)(1)) applicable to the participant or beneficiary as of the enrollment date."

Sec. 1563(c)(1) of the "Patient Protection and Affordable Care Act" (P.L. 111–148) (formerly sec. 1562(c)(1) of such Act, renumbered sec. 1563(c)(1) by sec. 10107(b)(1) of such Act), effective Mar. 23, 2010, amended sec. 2704 by making the following changes:

in subsection (c)(2), by substituting "group or individual health plan" for "group health plan" wherever appearing;

in subsection (c)(3), by substituting "group or individual health insurance" for "group health insurance" wherever appearing;

in subsection (c)(3)(D), by substituting "individual or group" for "small or large";

in subsection (d), by substituting "group or individual health insurance" for "group health insurance" wherever appearing;

in subsection (e)(1)(A), by substituting "group or individual health insurance" for "group health insurance".

Sec. 114(c) of the "Omnibus Trade Act of 2010" (P.L. 111–344), applicable to plan years beginning after Dec. 31, 2010, amended sec. 2701(c)(2)(C) by striking "January 1, 2011" and inserting "February 13, 2011".

History:

Sec. 102(a) of the "Health Insurance Portability and Accountability Act of 1996" (P.L. 104–191), sec. 311(b)(2) of the "Children's Health Insurance Program Reauthorization Act of 2009" (P.L. 111–3), sec. 1899D(c) of the "American Recovery and Reinvestment Act of 2009" (P.L. 111–5), secs. 1201(2), 1563(c)(1), formerly sec. 1562(c)(1), renumbered sec. 1563(c)(1), sec. 10107(b)(1) of the "Patient Protection and Affordable Care Act" (P.L. 111–148), sec. 114(c) of the "Omnibus Trade Act of 2010" (P.L. 111–344), sec. 242(a)(3), (4) of the "Trade Adjustment Assistance Extension Act of 2011", Title II of P.L. 112–40.

Sec. 2705. Prohibiting Discrimination Against Individual Participants and Beneficiaries Based on Health Status

[42 U.S.C. 300gg–4]

(a) In General. A group health plan and a health insurance issuer offering group or individual health insurance coverage may not establish rules for eligibility (including continued eligibility) of any individual to enroll under the terms of the plan or coverage based on any of the following health status-related factors in relation to the individual or a dependent of the individual:

(1) Health status.

(2) Medical condition (including both physical and mental illnesses).

(3) Claims experience.

---

[13] So in original. Probably should be followed by the word "Program".

(4) Receipt of health care.

(5) Medical history.

(6) Genetic information.

(7) Evidence of insurability (including conditions arising out of acts of domestic violence).

(8) Disability.

(9) Any other health status-related factor determined appropriate by the Secretary.

(b) IN PREMIUM CONTRIBUTIONS.—

(1) IN GENERAL. A group health plan, and a health insurance issuer offering group or individual health insurance coverage, may not require any individual (as a condition of enrollment or continued enrollment under the plan) to pay a premium or contribution which is greater than such premium or contribution for a similarly situated individual enrolled in the plan on the basis of any health status-related factor in relation to the individual or to an individual enrolled under the plan as a dependent of the individual.

(2) CONSTRUCTION. Nothing in paragraph (1) shall be construed—

(A) to restrict the amount that an employer or individual may be charged for coverage under a group health plan except as provided in paragraph (3) or individual health coverage, as the case may be; or

(B) to prevent a group health plan, and a health insurance issuer offering group health insurance coverage, from establishing premium discounts or rebates or modifying otherwise applicable copayments or deductibles in return for adherence to programs of health promotion and disease prevention.

(3) NO GROUP-BASED DISCRIMINATION ON BASIS OF GENETIC INFORMATION.—

(A) IN GENERAL. For purposes of this section, a group health plan, and health[14] insurance issuer offering group or individual health insurance coverage, may not adjust premium or contribution amounts for the group covered under such plan on the basis of genetic information.

(B) RULE OF CONSTRUCTION. Nothing in subparagraph (A) or in paragraphs (1) and (2) of subsection (d) shall be construed to limit the ability of a health insurance issuer offering group or individual health insurance coverage to increase the premium for an employer based on the manifestation of a disease or disorder of an individual who is enrolled in the plan. In such case, the manifestation of a disease or disorder in one individual cannot also be used as genetic information about other group members and to further increase the premium for the employer.

(c) GENETIC TESTING.—

(1) LIMITATION ON REQUESTING OR REQUIRING GENETIC TESTING. A group health plan, and a health insurance issuer offering health insurance coverage in connection with a group health plan, shall not request or require an individual or a family member of such individual to undergo a genetic test.

(2) RULE OF CONSTRUCTION. Paragraph (1) shall not be construed to limit the authority of a health care professional who is providing health care services to an individual to request that such individual undergo a genetic test.

(3) RULE OF CONSTRUCTION REGARDING PAYMENT.—

(A) IN GENERAL. Nothing in paragraph (1) shall be construed to preclude a group health plan, or a health insurance issuer offering health insurance coverage in connection with a group health plan, from obtaining and using the results of a genetic test in making a determination regarding payment (as such term is defined for the purposes of applying the regulations promulgated by the Secretary under part C of title XI of the Social Security Act and section 264 of the Health Insurance Portability and Accountability Act of 1996, as may be revised from time to time) consistent with subsection (a).

(B) LIMITATION. For purposes of subparagraph (A), a group health plan, or a health insurance issuer offering health insurance coverage in connection with a group health plan, may request only the minimum amount of information necessary to accomplish the intended purpose.

(4) RESEARCH EXCEPTION. Notwithstanding paragraph (1), a group health plan, or a health insurance issuer offering health insurance coverage in connection with a group health plan, may request, but not require, that a participant or beneficiary undergo a genetic test if each of the following conditions is met:

(A) The request is made pursuant to research that complies with part 46 of title 45, Code of Federal Regulations, or equivalent Federal regulations, and any applicable State or local law or regulations for the protection of human subjects in research.

(B) The plan or issuer clearly indicates to each participant or beneficiary, or in the case of a minor child, to the legal guardian of such beneficiary, to whom the request is made that—

(i) compliance with the request is voluntary; and

(ii) non-compliance will have no effect on enrollment status or premium or contribution amounts.

(C) No genetic information collected or acquired under this paragraph shall be used for underwriting purposes.

(D) The plan or issuer notifies the Secretary in writing that the plan or issuer is conducting activities pursuant to the exception provided for under this paragraph, including a description of the activities conducted.

(E) The plan or issuer complies with such other conditions as the Secretary may by regulation require for activities conducted under this paragraph.

(d) PROHIBITION ON COLLECTION OF GENETIC INFORMATION.—

(1) IN GENERAL. A group health plan, and a health insurance issuer offering health insurance coverage in connection with a group health plan, shall not request, require, or purchase genetic information for underwriting purposes (as defined in section 2791).

(2) PROHIBITION ON COLLECTION OF GENETIC INFORMATION PRIOR TO ENROLLMENT. A group health plan, and a health insurance issuer offering health insurance coverage in connection with a group health plan, shall not request, require, or purchase genetic information with respect to any individual prior to such individual's enrollment under the plan or coverage in connection with such enrollment.

---

[14] So in original. Probably should be preceded by "a".

(3) INCIDENTAL COLLECTION. If a group health plan, or a health insurance issuer offering health insurance coverage in connection with a group health plan, obtains genetic information incidental to the requesting, requiring, or purchasing of other information concerning any individual, such request, requirement, or purchase shall not be considered a violation of paragraph (2) if such request, requirement, or purchase is not in violation of paragraph (1).

(e) APPLICATION TO ALL PLANS. The provisions of subsections (a)(6), (b)(3), (c), and (d) and subsection (b)(1) and section 2704 with respect to genetic information, shall apply to group health plans and health insurance issuers without regard to section 2735(a).[15]

(f) GENETIC INFORMATION OF A FETUS OR EMBRYO. Any reference in this part to genetic information concerning an individual or family member of an individual shall—

(1) with respect to such an individual or family member of an individual who is a pregnant woman, include genetic information of any fetus carried by such pregnant woman; and

(2) with respect to an individual or family member utilizing an assisted reproductive technology, include genetic information of any embryo legally held by the individual or family member.

(j) [16] PROGRAMS OF HEALTH PROMOTION OR DISEASE PREVENTION.—

(1) GENERAL PROVISIONS.—

(A) GENERAL RULE. For purposes of subsection (b)(2)(B), a program of health promotion or disease prevention (referred to in this subsection as a "wellness program") shall be a program offered by an employer that is designed to promote health or prevent disease that meets the applicable requirements of this subsection.

(B) NO CONDITIONS BASED ON HEALTH STATUS FACTOR. If none of the conditions for obtaining a premium discount or rebate or other reward for participation in a wellness program is based on an individual satisfying a standard that is related to a health status factor, such wellness program shall not violate this section if participation in the program is made available to all similarly situated individuals and the requirements of paragraph (2) are complied with.

(C) CONDITIONS BASED ON HEALTH STATUS FACTOR. If any of the conditions for obtaining a premium discount or rebate or other reward for participation in a wellness program is based on an individual satisfying a standard that is related to a health status factor, such wellness program shall not violate this section if the requirements of paragraph (3) are complied with.

(2) WELLNESS PROGRAMS NOT SUBJECT TO REQUIREMENTS. If none of the conditions for obtaining a premium discount or rebate or other reward under a wellness program as described in paragraph (1)(B) are based on an individual satisfying a standard that is related to a health status factor (or if such a wellness program does not provide such a reward), the wellness program shall not violate this section if participation in the program is made available to all similarly situated individuals. The following programs shall not have to comply with the requirements of paragraph (3) if participation in the program is made available to all similarly situated individuals:

(A) A program that reimburses all or part of the cost for memberships in a fitness center.

(B) A diagnostic testing program that provides a reward for participation and does not base any part of the reward on outcomes.

(C) A program that encourages preventive care related to a health condition through the waiver of the copayment or deductible requirement under group[17] health plan for the costs of certain items or services related to a health condition (such as prenatal care or well-baby visits).

(D) A program that reimburses individuals for the costs of smoking cessation programs without regard to whether the individual quits smoking.

(E) A program that provides a reward to individuals for attending a periodic health education seminar.

(3) WELLNESS PROGRAMS SUBJECT TO REQUIREMENTS. If any of the conditions for obtaining a premium discount, rebate, or reward under a wellness program as described in paragraph (1)(C) is based on an individual satisfying a standard that is related to a health status factor, the wellness program shall not violate this section if the following requirements are complied with:

(A) The reward for the wellness program, together with the reward for other wellness programs with respect to the plan that requires satisfaction of a standard related to a health status factor, shall not exceed 30 percent of the cost of employee-only coverage under the plan. If, in addition to employees or individuals, any class of dependents (such as spouses or spouses and dependent children) may participate fully in the wellness program, such reward shall not exceed 30 percent of the cost of the coverage in which an employee or individual and any dependents are enrolled. For purposes of this paragraph, the cost of coverage shall be determined based on the total amount of employer and employee contributions for the benefit package under which the employee is (or the employee and any dependents are) receiving coverage. A reward may be in the form of a discount or rebate of a premium or contribution, a waiver of all or part of a cost-sharing mechanism (such as deductibles, copayments, or coinsurance), the absence of a surcharge, or the value of a benefit that would otherwise not be provided under the plan. The Secretaries of Labor, Health and Human Services, and the Treasury may increase the reward available under this subparagraph to up to 50 percent of the cost of coverage if the Secretaries determine that such an increase is appropriate.

(B) The wellness program shall be reasonably designed to promote health or prevent disease. A program complies with the preceding sentence if the program has a reasonable chance of improving the health of, or preventing disease in, participating individuals and it is not overly burdensome, is not a subterfuge for discriminating based on a health status factor, and is not highly suspect in the method chosen to promote health or prevent disease.

(C) The plan shall give individuals eligible for the program the opportunity to qualify for the reward under the program at least once each year.

(D) The full reward under the wellness program shall be made available to all similarly situated individuals. For such purpose, among other things:

(i) The reward is not available to all similarly situated individuals for a period unless the wellness program allows—

(I) for a reasonable alternative standard (or waiver of the otherwise applicable standard) for obtaining the reward for any individual for whom, for that period, it is unreasonably difficult due to a medical condition to satisfy the otherwise applicable standard; and

(II) for a reasonable alternative standard (or waiver of the otherwise applicable standard) for obtaining the reward for any individual for whom, for that period, it is medically inadvisable to attempt to satisfy the otherwise applicable standard.

(ii) If reasonable under the circumstances, the plan or issuer may seek verification, such as a statement from an individual's physician, that a health status factor makes it unreasonably difficult or medically inadvisable for the individual to satisfy or attempt to satisfy the otherwise applicable standard.

---

[15] Section 2735 was renumbered section 2722.

[16] So in law. There are no subsections (g)-(i).

[17] So in original. Probably should be preceded by "a".

(E) The plan or issuer involved shall disclose in all plan materials describing the terms of the wellness program the availability of a reasonable alternative standard (or the possibility of waiver of the otherwise applicable standard) required under subparagraph (D). If plan materials disclose that such a program is available, without describing its terms, the disclosure under this subparagraph shall not be required.

(k) EXISTING PROGRAMS. Nothing in this section shall prohibit a program of health promotion or disease prevention that was established prior to the date of enactment of this section and applied with all applicable regulations, and that is operating on such date, from continuing to be carried out for as long as such regulations remain in effect.

(l) WELLNESS PROGRAM DEMONSTRATION PROJECT.—

(1) IN GENERAL. Not later than July 1, 2014, the Secretary, in consultation with the Secretary of the Treasury and the Secretary of Labor, shall establish a 10-State demonstration project under which participating States shall apply the provisions of subsection (j) to programs of health promotion offered by a health insurance issuer that offers health insurance coverage in the individual market in such State.

(2) EXPANSION OF DEMONSTRATION PROJECT. If the Secretary, in consultation with the Secretary of the Treasury and the Secretary of Labor, determines that the demonstration project described in paragraph (1) is effective, such Secretaries may, beginning on July 1, 2017 expand such demonstration project to include additional participating States.

(3) REQUIREMENTS.—

(A) MAINTENANCE OF COVERAGE. The Secretary, in consultation with the Secretary of the Treasury and the Secretary of Labor, shall not approve the participation of a State in the demonstration project under this section unless the Secretaries determine that the State's project is designed in a manner that—

(i) will not result in any decrease in coverage; and

(ii) will not increase the cost to the Federal Government in providing credits under section 36B of the Internal Revenue Code of 1986 or cost-sharing assistance under section 1402 of the Patient Protection and Affordable Care Act.

(B) OTHER REQUIREMENTS. States that participate in the demonstration project under this subsection—

(i) may permit premium discounts or rebates or the modification of otherwise applicable copayments or deductibles for adherence to, or participation in, a reasonably designed program of health promotion and disease prevention;

(ii) shall ensure that requirements of consumer protection are met in programs of health promotion in the individual market;

(iii) shall require verification from health insurance issuers that offer health insurance coverage in the individual market of such State that premium discounts—

(I) do not create undue burdens for individuals insured in the individual market;

(II) do not lead to cost shifting; and

(III) are not a subterfuge for discrimination;

(iv) shall ensure that consumer data is protected in accordance with the requirements of section 264(c) of the Health Insurance Portability and Accountability Act of 1996 (42 U.S.C. 1320d–2 note); and

(v) shall ensure and demonstrate to the satisfaction of the Secretary that the discounts or other rewards provided under the project reflect the expected level of participation in the wellness program involved and the anticipated effect the program will have on utilization or medical claim costs.

(m) REPORT.—

(1) IN GENERAL. Not later than 3 years after the date of enactment of the Patient Protection and Affordable Care Act, the Secretary, in consultation with the Secretary of the Treasury and the Secretary of Labor, shall submit a report to the appropriate committees of Congress concerning—

(A) the effectiveness of wellness programs (as defined in subsection (j)) in promoting health and preventing disease;

(B) the impact of such wellness programs on the access to care and affordability of coverage for participants and non-participants of such programs;

(C) the impact of premium-based and cost-sharing incentives on participant behavior and the role of such programs in changing behavior; and

(D) the effectiveness of different types of rewards.

(2) DATA COLLECTION. In preparing the report described in paragraph (1), the Secretaries shall gather relevant information from employers who provide employees with access to wellness programs, including State and Federal agencies.

(n) REGULATIONS. Nothing in this section shall be construed as prohibiting the Secretaries of Labor, Health and Human Services, or the Treasury from promulgating regulations in connection with this section.

2010 Amendments:

Sec. 1201(4) of the "Patient Protection and Affordable Care Act" (P.L. 111–148), effective for plan years beginning on or after Jan. 1, 2014, added new sec. 2705.

Sec. 1201(3) of the "Patient Protection and Affordable Care Act" (P.L. 111–148), effective for plan years beginning on or after Jan. 1, 2014, amended sec. 2705 by adding new subsections (b) to (f), which were transferred from former sec. 2702.

History:

Sec. 1201(3), (4) of the "Patient Protection and Affordable Care Act" (P.L. 111–148).

Sec. 2706. Non-Discrimination in Health Care

[42 U.S.C. 300gg–5]

(a) PROVIDERS. A group health plan and a health insurance issuer offering group or individual health insurance coverage shall not discriminate with respect to participation under the plan or coverage against any health care provider who is acting within the scope of that provider's license or certification under applicable State law. This section shall not require that a group health plan or health insurance issuer contract with any health care provider willing to abide by the terms and conditions for participation established by the plan or issuer. Nothing in this section shall be construed as preventing a group health plan, a health insurance issuer, or the Secretary from establishing varying reimbursement rates based on quality or performance measures.

(b) INDIVIDUALS. The provisions of section 1558 of the Patient Protection and Affordable Care Act[18] (relating to non-discrimination) shall apply with respect to a group health plan or health insurance issuer offering group or individual health insurance coverage.

2010 Amendments:

Sec. 1201(4) of the "Patient Protection and Affordable Care Act" (P.L. 111–148), effective for plan years beginning on or after Jan. 1, 2014, added new sec. 2706.

History:

Sec. 1201(4) of the "Patient Protection and Affordable Care Act" (P.L. 111–148).

Sec. 2707. Comprehensive Health Insurance Coverage

[42 U.S.C. 300gg–6]

(a) COVERAGE FOR ESSENTIAL HEALTH BENEFITS PACKAGE. A health insurance issuer that offers health insurance coverage in the individual or small group market shall ensure that such coverage includes the essential health benefits package required under section 1302(a) of the Patient Protection and Affordable Care Act.

(b) COST-SHARING UNDER GROUP HEALTH PLANS. A group health plan shall ensure that any annual cost-sharing imposed under the plan does not exceed the limitations provided for under paragraph (1) of section 1302(c)[19].

(c) CHILD-ONLY PLANS. If a health insurance issuer offers health insurance coverage in any level of coverage specified under section 1302(d) of the Patient Protection and Affordable Care Act, the issuer shall also offer such coverage in that level as a plan in which the only enrollees are individuals who, as of the beginning of a plan year, have not attained the age of 21.

(d) DENTAL ONLY. This section shall not apply to a plan described in section 1302(d)(2)(B)(ii)(I)[20].

2014 Amendments:

Sec. 213(b) of the "Protecting Access to Medicare Act of 2014" (P.L. 113–93), effective as if included in the enactment of the Patient Protection and Affordable Care Act (P.L. 111–148), i.e. effective for plan years beginning on or after Jan. 1, 2014, amended sec. 2707(b) by striking "paragraphs (1) and (2)" and inserting "paragraph (1)".

2010 Amendments:

Sec. 1201(4) of the "Patient Protection and Affordable Care Act" (P.L. 111–148), effective for plan years beginning on or after Jan. 1, 2014, added new sec. 2707.

History:

Sec. 1201(4) of the "Patient Protection and Affordable Care Act" (P.L. 111–148), sec. 213(b) of the "Protecting Access to Medicare Act of 2014" (P.L. 113–93).

Sec. 2708. Prohibition on Excessive Waiting Periods

[42 U.S.C. 300gg–7]

A group health plan and a health insurance issuer offering group health insurance coverage shall not apply any waiting period (as defined in section 2704(b)(4)) that exceeds 90 days.

2010 Amendments:

- Sec. 1201(4) of the "Patient Protection and Affordable Care Act" (P.L. 111–148), effective for plan years beginning on or after Jan. 1, 2014, added new sec. 2708.

Sec. 10103(b) of the "Patient Protection and Affordable Care Act" (P.L. 111–148), effective Mar. 23, 2010, amended sec. 2708 by striking out "or individual" after "offering group".

History:

Sec. 1201(4), sec. 10103(b) of the "Patient Protection and Affordable Care Act" (P.L. 111–148).

Sec. 2709. Coverage for Individuals Participating in Approved Clinical Trials[21]

[42 U.S.C. 300gg–8]

(a) COVERAGE.—

(1) IN GENERAL. If a group health plan or a health insurance issuer offering group or individual health insurance coverage provides coverage to a qualified individual, then such plan or issuer—

(A) may not deny the individual participation in the clinical trial referred to in subsection (b)(2);

(B) subject to subsection (c), may not deny (or limit or impose additional conditions on) the coverage of routine patient costs for items and services furnished in connection with participation in the trial; and

(C) may not discriminate against the individual on the basis of the individual's participation in such trial.

(2) ROUTINE PATIENT COSTS.—

(A) INCLUSION. For purposes of paragraph (1)(B), subject to subparagraph (B), routine patient costs include all items and services consistent with the coverage provided in the plan (or coverage) that is typically covered for a qualified individual who is not enrolled in a clinical trial.

(B) EXCLUSION. For purposes of paragraph (1)(B), routine patient costs does not include—

(i) the investigational item, device, or service, itself;

(ii) items and services that are provided solely to satisfy data collection and analysis needs and that are not used in the direct clinical management of the patient; or

(iii) a service that is clearly inconsistent with widely accepted and established standards of care for a particular diagnosis.

---

[18] Probably means section 18C of the Fair Labor Standards Act, which was added by such section 1558.

[19] Probably means section 1302(c) of the Patient Protection and Affordable Care Act.

[20] Probably should be "section 1311(d)(2)(B)(ii)(I) of the Patient Protection and Affordable Care Act".

[21] This section 2709 was enacted by Pub. L. 111–148, Sec. 10103(c). Another section 2709 is set out infra.

(3) USE OF IN-NETWORK PROVIDERS. If one or more participating providers is participating in a clinical trial, nothing in paragraph (1) shall be construed as preventing a plan or issuer from requiring that a qualified individual participate in the trial through such a participating provider if the provider will accept the individual as a participant in the trial.

(4) USE OF OUT-OF-NETWORK. Notwithstanding paragraph (3), paragraph (1) shall apply to a qualified individual participating in an approved clinical trial that is conducted outside the State in which the qualified individual resides.

(b) QUALIFIED INDIVIDUAL DEFINED. For purposes of subsection (a), the term "qualified individual" means an individual who is a participant or beneficiary in a health plan or with coverage described in subsection (a)(1) and who meets the following conditions:

(1) The individual is eligible to participate in an approved clinical trial according to the trial protocol with respect to treatment of cancer or other life-threatening disease or condition.

(2) Either—

(A) the referring health care professional is a participating health care provider and has concluded that the individual's participation in such trial would be appropriate based upon the individual meeting the conditions described in paragraph (1); or

(B) the participant or beneficiary provides medical and scientific information establishing that the individual's participation in such trial would be appropriate based upon the individual meeting the conditions described in paragraph (1).

(c) LIMITATIONS ON COVERAGE. This section shall not be construed to require a group health plan, or a health insurance issuer offering group or individual health insurance coverage, to provide benefits for routine patient care services provided outside of the plan's (or coverage's) health care provider network unless out-of-network benefits are otherwise provided under the plan (or coverage).

(d) APPROVED CLINICAL TRIAL DEFINED.—

(1) IN GENERAL. In this section, the term "approved clinical trial" means a phase I, phase II, phase III, or phase IV clinical trial that is conducted in relation to the prevention, detection, or treatment of cancer or other life-threatening disease or condition and is described in any of the following subparagraphs:

(A) FEDERALLY FUNDED TRIALS. The study or investigation is approved or funded (which may include funding through in-kind contributions) by one or more of the following:

(i) The National Institutes of Health.

(ii) The Centers for Disease Control and Prevention.

(iii) The Agency for Health Care Research and Quality.

(iv) The Centers for Medicare & Medicaid Services.

(v) cooperative[22] group or center of any of the entities described in clauses (i) through (iv) or the Department of Defense or the Department of Veterans Affairs.

(vi) A qualified non-governmental research entity identified in the guidelines issued by the National Institutes of Health for center support grants.

(vii) Any of the following if the conditions described in paragraph (2) are met:

(I) The Department of Veterans Affairs.

(II) The Department of Defense.

(III) The Department of Energy.

(B) The study or investigation is conducted under an investigational new drug application reviewed by the Food and Drug Administration.

(C) The study or investigation is a drug trial that is exempt from having such an investigational new drug application.

(2) CONDITIONS FOR DEPARTMENTS. The conditions described in this paragraph, for a study or investigation conducted by a Department, are that the study or investigation has been reviewed and approved through a system of peer review that the Secretary determines—

(A) to be comparable to the system of peer review of studies and investigations used by the National Institutes of Health, and

(B) assures unbiased review of the highest scientific standards by qualified individuals who have no interest in the outcome of the review.

(e) LIFE-THREATENING CONDITION DEFINED. In this section, the term "life-threatening condition" means any disease or condition from which the likelihood of death is probable unless the course of the disease or condition is interrupted.

(f) CONSTRUCTION. Nothing in this section shall be construed to limit a plan's or issuer's coverage with respect to clinical trials.

(g) APPLICATION TO FEHBP. Notwithstanding any provision of chapter 89 of title 5, United States Code, this section shall apply to health plans offered under the program under such chapter.

(h) PREEMPTION. Notwithstanding any other provision of this Act, nothing in this section shall preempt State laws that require a clinical trials policy for State regulated health insurance plans that is in addition to the policy required under this section.

2010 Amendments:

Sec. 10103(c) of the "Patient Protection and Affordable Care Act" (P.L. 111–148), effective Mar. 23, 2010, added new sec. 2709.

History:

Sec. 10103(c) of the "Patient Protection and Affordable Care Act" (P.L. 111–148).

Sec. 2709. Disclosure of Information[23]

[42 U.S.C. 300gg–9]

(a) DISCLOSURE OF INFORMATION BY HEALTH PLAN ISSUERS. In connection with the offering of any health insurance coverage to a small employer or an individual, a health insurance issuer—

---

[22] So in original. Probably should be preceded by "A".

[23] This section 2709 was originally section 2713. It was renumbered section 2733 by Pub. L. 111–148, Sec. 1001(3). It was then amended and renumbered section 2709 by Pub. L. 111–148, Sec.

1563(c)(10) (originally Sec. 1562(c)(10); renumbered Sec. 1563(c)(10) by Pub. L. 111–148, Sec. 10107(b)(1)). Another section 2709 is set out supra.

(1) shall make a reasonable disclosure to such employer,,[24] or individual, as applicable, as part of its solicitation and sales materials, of the availability of information described in subsection (b), and

(2) upon request of such a[25] employer, or individual, as applicable,,[26] or individual, as applicable, provide such information.

(b) INFORMATION DESCRIBED.—

(1) IN GENERAL. Subject to paragraph (3), with respect to a health insurance issuer offering health insurance coverage to a[27] employer, or individual, as applicable,,[28] information described in this subsection is information concerning—

(A) the provisions of such coverage concerning issuer's right to change premium rates and the factors that may affect changes in premium rates; and

(B) the benefits and premiums available under all health insurance coverage for which the employer, or individual, as applicable, is qualified.

(2) FORM OF INFORMATION. Information under this subsection shall be provided to employers, or individuals, as applicable, in a manner determined to be understandable by the average employer, or individual, as applicable,,[29] and shall be sufficient to reasonably inform employers, or individuals, as applicable, of their rights and obligations under the health insurance coverage.

(3) EXCEPTION. An issuer is not required under this section to disclose any information that is proprietary and trade secret information under applicable law.

2010 Amendments:

Sec. 1001(3) of the "Patient Protection and Affordable Care Act" (P.L. 111–148), effective for plan years beginning on or after Sept. 23, 2010, renumbered sec. 2713 as sec. 2733.

Sec. 1563(c)(10) of the "Patient Protection and Affordable Care Act" (P.L. 111–148) (formerly sec. 1562(c)(10) of such Act, renumbered sec. 1563(c)(10) by sec. 10107(b)(1) of such Act), effective Mar. 23, 2010, amended sec. 2733 by making the following changes:

in subsection (a), by substituting "small employer or an individual" for "small employer";

in subsection (a)(1), by inserting ", or individual, as applicable," after "employer" each place that such appears;

in subsection (a)(2), by substituting "employer, or individual, as applicable," for "small employer";

in subsection (b)(1), by substituting "employer, or individual, as applicable," for "small employer";

in subsection (b)(1)(A), by adding "and" at the end;

in subsection (b)(1), by striking subparagraphs (B) and (C);

in subsection (b)(1)(D), by inserting ", or individual, as applicable," after "employer";

in subsection (b)(1), by redesignating subparagraph (D) as (B);

in subsection (b)(2), by substituting "employers, or individuals, as applicable," for "small employers" wherever appearing and substituted "employer, or individual, as applicable," for "small employer";

by redesignating sec. 2733 as sec. 2709.

Prior to amendment sec. 2733(b)(1)(B), (C) read as follows:

"(B) the provisions of such coverage relating to renewability of coverage;

"(C) the provisions of such coverage relating to any preexisting condition exclusion; and".

History:

Sec. 102(a) of the "Health Insurance Portability and Accountability Act of 1996" (P.L. 104–191), secs. 1001(3), 1563(c)(10), formerly sec. 1562(c)(10), renumbered sec. 1563(c)(10), sec. 10107(b)(1) of the "Patient Protection and Affordable Care Act" (P.L. 111–148).

SUBPART II—IMPROVING COVERAGE

SUBPART II—IMPROVING COVERAGE

2010 Amendments:

Sec. 1001(5) of the "Patient Protection and Affordable Care Act" (P.L. 111–148), effective for plan years beginning on or after Sept. 23, 2010, added subpart II of part A of title XXVII heading.

History:

Sec. 1001(5) of the "Patient Protection and Affordable Care Act" (P.L. 111–148).

Sec. 2711. No Lifetime Or Annual Limits

[42 U.S.C. 300gg–11]

(a) PROHIBITION.—

(1) IN GENERAL. A group health plan and a health insurance issuer offering group or individual health insurance coverage may not establish—

(A) lifetime limits on the dollar value of benefits for any participant or beneficiary; or

(B) except as provided in paragraph (2), annual limits on the dollar value of benefits for any participant or beneficiary.

(2) ANNUAL LIMITS PRIOR TO 2014. With respect to plan years beginning prior to January 1, 2014, a group health plan and a health insurance issuer offering group or individual health insurance coverage may only establish a restricted annual limit on the dollar value of benefits for any participant or beneficiary with respect to the scope of benefits that are essential health benefits under section 1302(b) of the Patient Protection and Affordable Care Act, as determined by the Secretary. In defining the term "restricted annual limit" for purposes of the preceding sentence, the Secretary shall ensure that access to needed services is made available with a minimal impact on premiums.

(b) PER BENEFICIARY LIMITS. Subsection (a) shall not be construed to prevent a group health plan or health insurance coverage from placing annual or lifetime per beneficiary limits on specific covered benefits that are not essential health benefits under section 1302(b) of the Patient Protection and Affordable Care Act, to the extent that such limits are otherwise permitted under Federal or State law.

2010 Amendments:

Sec. 1001(5) of the "Patient Protection and Affordable Care Act" (P.L. 111–148), effective for plan years beginning on or after Sept. 23, 2010, added new sec. 2711.

Sec. 10101(a) of the "Patient Protection and Affordable Care Act" (P.L. 111–148), effective Mar. 23, 2010, amended sec. 2711.

Prior to amendment sec. 2711 read as follows:

---

[24] So in law.
[25] So in original. Probably should be preceded by "an".
[26] So in original.

[27] So in original. Probably should be preceded by "an".
[28] So in original.
[29] So in law.

"Sec. 2711. NO LIFETIME OR ANNUAL LIMITS. [42 U.S.C. 300gg–11]

"(a) In General.—A group health plan and a health insurance issuer offering group or individual health insurance coverage may not establish—

"(1) lifetime limits on the dollar value of benefits for any participant or beneficiary; or

"(2) unreasonable annual limits (within the meaning of section 223 of the Internal Revenue Code of 1986) on the dollar value of benefits for any participant or beneficiary.

"(b) Per Beneficiary Limits.—Subsection (a) shall not be construed to prevent a group health plan or health insurance coverage that is not required to provide essential health benefits under section 1302(b) of the Patient Protection and Affordable Care Act from placing annual or lifetime per beneficiary limits on specific covered benefits to the extent that such limits are otherwise permitted under Federal or State law."

History:

Secs. 1001(5), 10101(a) of the "Patient Protection and Affordable Care Act" (P.L. 111–148).

Sec. 2712. Prohibition on Rescissions

[42 U.S.C. 300gg–12]

A group health plan and a health insurance issuer offering group or individual health insurance coverage shall not rescind such plan or coverage with respect to an enrollee once the enrollee is covered under such plan or coverage involved, except that this section shall not apply to a covered individual who has performed an act or practice that constitutes fraud or makes an intentional misrepresentation of material fact as prohibited by the terms of the plan or coverage. Such plan or coverage may not be cancelled except with prior notice to the enrollee, and only as permitted under section 2702(c)[30] or 2742(b).

2010 Amendments:

Sec. 1001(5) of the "Patient Protection and Affordable Care Act" (P.L. 111–148), effective for plan years beginning on or after Sept. 23, 2010, added new sec. 2712.

History:

Sec. 1001(5) of the "Patient Protection and Affordable Care Act" (P.L. 111–148).

Sec. 2713. Coverage of Preventive Health Services

[42 U.S.C. 300gg–13]

(a) In General. A group health plan and a health insurance issuer offering group or individual health insurance coverage shall, at a minimum provide coverage for and shall not impose any cost sharing requirements for—

(1) evidence-based items or services that have in effect a rating of "A" or "B" in the current recommendations of the United States Preventive Services Task Force;

(2) immunizations that have in effect a recommendation from the Advisory Committee on Immunization Practices of the Centers for Disease Control and Prevention with respect to the individual involved; and[31]

(3) with respect to infants, children, and adolescents, evidence-informed preventive care and screenings provided for in the comprehensive guidelines supported by the Health Resources and Services Administration.

(4) with respect to women, such additional preventive care and screenings not described in paragraph (1) as provided for in comprehensive guidelines supported by the Health Resources and Services Administration for purposes of this paragraph.[32]

(5) for the purposes of this Act, and for the purposes of any other provision of law, the current recommendations of the United States Preventive Service Task Force regarding breast cancer screening, mammography, and prevention shall be considered the most current other than those issued in or around November 2009.

Nothing in this subsection shall be construed to prohibit a plan or issuer from providing coverage for services in addition to those recommended by United States Preventive Services Task Force or to deny coverage for services that are not recommended by such Task Force.

(b) Interval.—

(1) In General. The Secretary shall establish a minimum interval between the date on which a recommendation described in subsection (a)(1) or (a)(2) or a guideline under subsection (a)(3) is issued and the plan year with respect to which the requirement described in subsection (a) is effective with respect to the service described in such recommendation or guideline.

(2) Minimum. The interval described in paragraph (1) shall not be less than 1 year.

(c) Value-Based Insurance Design. The Secretary may develop guidelines to permit a group health plan and a health insurance issuer offering group or individual health insurance coverage to utilize value-based insurance designs.

2010 Amendments:

Sec. 1001(5) of the "Patient Protection and Affordable Care Act" (P.L. 111–148), effective for plan years beginning on or after Sept. 23, 2010, added new sec. 2713.

History:

Sec. 1001(5) of the "Patient Protection and Affordable Care Act" (P.L. 111–148).

Sec. 2714. Extension of Dependent Coverage

[42 U.S.C. 300gg–14]

(a) In General. A group health plan and a health insurance issuer offering group or individual health insurance coverage that provides dependent coverage of children shall continue to make such coverage available for an adult child until the child turns 26 years of age. Nothing in this section shall require a health plan or a health insurance issuer described in the preceding sentence to make coverage available for a child of a child receiving dependent coverage.

(b) Regulations. The Secretary shall promulgate regulations to define the dependents to which coverage shall be made available under subsection (a).

(c) Rule of Construction. Nothing in this section shall be construed to modify the definition of "dependent" as used in the Internal Revenue Code of 1986 with respect to the tax treatment of the cost of coverage.

---

[30] So in original. Probably should be "2703(b)".
[31] So in original. The word "and" probably should not appear.

[32] So in original. The period should probably be a semicolon.

2010 Amendments:

Sec. 1001(5) of the "Patient Protection and Affordable Care Act" (P.L. 111–148), effective for plan years beginning on or after Sept. 23, 2010, added new sec. 2714.

Sec. 2301(b) of the "Health Care and Education Reconciliation Act of 2010" (P.L. 111–152), effective Mar. 30, 2010, amended sec. 2714(a) by striking out "(who is not married)" after "adult child".

History:

Sec. 1001(5) of the "Patient Protection and Affordable Care Act" (P.L. 111–148), sec. 2301(b) of the "Health Care and Education Reconciliation Act of 2010" (P.L. 111–152).

Sec. 2715. Development and Utilization of Uniform Explanation of Coverage Documents and Standardized Definitions

[42 U.S.C. 300gg–15]

(a) IN GENERAL. Not later than 12 months after the date of enactment of the Patient Protection and Affordable Care Act, the Secretary shall develop standards for use by a group health plan and a health insurance issuer offering group or individual health insurance coverage, in compiling and providing to applicants, enrollees, and policyholders or certificate holders a summary of benefits and coverage explanation that accurately describes the benefits and coverage under the applicable plan or coverage. In developing such standards, the Secretary shall consult with the National Association of Insurance Commissioners (referred to in this section as the "NAIC"), a working group composed of representatives of health insurance-related consumer advocacy organizations, health insurance issuers, health care professionals, patient advocates including those representing individuals with limited English proficiency, and other qualified individuals.

(b) REQUIREMENTS. The standards for the summary of benefits and coverage developed under subsection (a) shall provide for the following:

(1) APPEARANCE. The standards shall ensure that the summary of benefits and coverage is presented in a uniform format that does not exceed 4 pages in length and does not include print smaller than 12-point font.

(2) LANGUAGE. The standards shall ensure that the summary is presented in a culturally and linguistically appropriate manner and utilizes terminology understandable by the average plan enrollee.

(3) CONTENTS. The standards shall ensure that the summary of benefits and coverage includes—

(A) uniform definitions of standard insurance terms and medical terms (consistent with subsection (g)) so that consumers may compare health insurance coverage and understand the terms of coverage (or exception to such coverage);

(B) a description of the coverage, including cost sharing for—

(i) each of the categories of the essential health benefits described in subparagraphs (A) through (J) of section 1302(b)(1) of the Patient Protection and Affordable Care Act; and

(ii) other benefits, as identified by the Secretary;

(C) the exceptions, reductions, and limitations on coverage;

(D) the cost-sharing provisions, including deductible, coinsurance, and co-payment obligations;

(E) the renewability and continuation of coverage provisions;

(F) a coverage facts label that includes examples to illustrate common benefits scenarios, including pregnancy and serious or chronic medical conditions and related cost sharing, such scenarios to be based on recognized clinical practice guidelines;

(G) a statement of whether the plan or coverage—

(i) provides minimum essential coverage (as defined under section 5000A(f) of the Internal Revenue Code 1986); and

(ii) ensures that the plan or coverage share of the total allowed costs of benefits provided under the plan or coverage is not less than 60 percent of such costs;

(H) a statement that the outline is a summary of the policy or certificate and that the coverage document itself should be consulted to determine the governing contractual provisions; and

(I) a contact number for the consumer to call with additional questions and an Internet web address where a copy of the actual individual coverage policy or group certificate of coverage can be reviewed and obtained.

(c) PERIODIC REVIEW AND UPDATING. The Secretary shall periodically review and update, as appropriate, the standards developed under this section.

(d) REQUIREMENT TO PROVIDE.—

(1) IN GENERAL. Not later than 24 months after the date of enactment of the Patient Protection and Affordable Care Act, each entity described in paragraph (3) shall provide, prior to any enrollment restriction, a summary of benefits and coverage explanation pursuant to the standards developed by the Secretary under subsection (a) to—

(A) an applicant at the time of application;

(B) an enrollee prior to the time of enrollment or reenrollment, as applicable; and

(C) a policyholder or certificate holder at the time of issuance of the policy or delivery of the certificate.

(2) COMPLIANCE. An entity described in paragraph (3) is deemed to be in compliance with this section if the summary of benefits and coverage described in subsection (a) is provided in paper or electronic form.

(3) ENTITIES IN GENERAL. An entity described in this paragraph is—

(A) a health insurance issuer (including a group health plan that is not a self-insured plan) offering health insurance coverage within the United States; or

(B) in the case of a self-insured group health plan, the plan sponsor or designated administrator of the plan (as such terms are defined in section 3(16) of the Employee Retirement Income Security Act of 1974).

(4) NOTICE OF MODIFICATIONS. If a group health plan or health insurance issuer makes any material modification in any of the terms of the plan or coverage involved (as defined for purposes of section 102 of the Employee Retirement Income Security Act of 1974) that is not reflected in the most recently provided summary of benefits and coverage, the plan or issuer shall provide notice of such modification to enrollees not later than 60 days prior to the date on which such modification will become effective.

(e) PREEMPTION. The standards developed under subsection (a) shall preempt any related State standards that require a summary of benefits and coverage that provides less information to consumers than that required to be provided under this section, as determined by the Secretary.

(f) FAILURE TO PROVIDE. An entity described in subsection (d)(3) that willfully fails to provide the information required under this section shall be subject to a fine of not more than $1,000 for each such failure. Such failure with respect to each enrollee shall constitute a separate offense for purposes of this subsection.

(g) DEVELOPMENT OF STANDARD DEFINITIONS.—

(1) IN GENERAL. The Secretary shall, by regulation, provide for the development of standards for the definitions of terms used in health insurance coverage, including the insurance-related terms described in paragraph (2) and the medical terms described in paragraph (3).

(2) INSURANCE-RELATED TERMS. The insurance-related terms described in this paragraph are premium, deductible, co-insurance, co-payment, out-of-pocket limit, preferred provider, non-preferred provider, out-of-network co-payments, UCR (usual, customary and reasonable) fees, excluded services, grievance and appeals, and such other terms as the Secretary determines are important to define so that consumers may compare health insurance coverage and understand the terms of their coverage.

(3) MEDICAL TERMS. The medical terms described in this paragraph are hospitalization, hospital outpatient care, emergency room care, physician services, prescription drug coverage, durable medical equipment, home health care, skilled nursing care, rehabilitation services, hospice services, emergency medical transportation, and such other terms as the Secretary determines are important to define so that consumers may compare the medical benefits offered by health insurance and understand the extent of those medical benefits (or exceptions to those benefits).

2010 Amendments:

Sec. 1001(5) of the "Patient Protection and Affordable Care Act" (P.L. 111–148), effective for plan years beginning on or after Sept. 23, 2010, added new sec. 2715.

Sec. 10101(b) of the "Patient Protection and Affordable Care Act" (P.L. 111–148), effective Mar. 23, 2010, amended sec. 2715(a) by substituting

"and providing to applicants, enrollees, and policyholders or certificate holders" for "and providing to enrollees".

History:

Secs. 1001(5), 10101(b) of the "Patient Protection and Affordable Care Act" (P.L. 111–148).

Sec. 2715A. Provision of Additional Information

[42 U.S.C. 300gg–15a]

A group health plan and a health insurance issuer offering group or individual health insurance coverage shall comply with the provisions of section 1311(e)(3) of the Patient Protection and Affordable Care Act, except that a plan or coverage that is not offered through an Exchange shall only be required to submit the information required to the Secretary and the State insurance commissioner, and make such information available to the public.

2010 Amendments:

Sec. 10101(c) of the "Patient Protection and Affordable Care Act" (P.L. 111–148), effective Mar. 23, 2010, added new sec. 2715A.

History:

Sec. 10101(c) of the "Patient Protection and Affordable Care Act" (P.L. 111–148).

Sec. 2716. Prohibition on Discrimination in Favor of Highly Compensated Individuals

[42 U.S.C. 300gg–16]

(a) IN GENERAL. A group health plan (other than a self-insured plan) shall satisfy the requirements of section 105(h)(2) of the Internal Revenue Code of 1986 (relating to prohibition on discrimination in favor of highly compensated individuals).

(b) RULES AND DEFINITIONS. For purposes of this section—

(1) CERTAIN RULES TO APPLY. Rules similar to the rules contained in paragraphs (3), (4), and (8) of section 105(h) of such Code shall apply.

(2) HIGHLY COMPENSATED INDIVIDUAL. The term "highly compensated individual" has the meaning given such term by section 105(h)(5) of such Code.

2010 Amendments:

Sec. 1001(5) of the "Patient Protection and Affordable Care Act" (P.L. 111–148), effective for plan years beginning on or after Sept. 23, 2010, added new sec. 2716.

Sec. 10101(d) of the "Patient Protection and Affordable Care Act" (P.L. 111–148), effective Mar. 23, 2010, amended sec. 2716.

Prior to amendment sec. 2716 read as follows:

"Sec. 2716. PROHIBITION OF DISCRIMINATION BASED ON SALARY. [42 U.S.C. 300gg–16]

"(a) In General.—The plan sponsor of a group health plan (other than a self-insured plan) may not establish rules relating to the health insurance coverage eligibility (including continued eligibility) of any full-time em-

ployee under the terms of the plan that are based on the total hourly or annual salary of the employee or otherwise establish eligibility rules that have the effect of discriminating in favor of higher wage employees.

"(b) Limitation.—Subsection (a) shall not be construed to prohibit a plan sponsor from establishing contribution requirements for enrollment in the plan or coverage that provide for the payment by employees with lower hourly or annual compensation of a lower dollar or percentage contribution than the payment required of similarly situated employees with a higher hourly or annual compensation."

History:

Secs. 1001(5), 10101(d) of the "Patient Protection and Affordable Care Act" (P.L. 111–148).

Sec. 2717. Ensuring the Quality of Care

[42 U.S.C. 300gg–17]

(a) QUALITY REPORTING.—

(1) IN GENERAL. Not later than 2 years after the date of enactment of the Patient Protection and Affordable Care Act, the Secretary, in consultation with experts in health care quality and stakeholders, shall develop reporting requirements for use by a group health plan, and a health insurance issuer offering group or individual health insurance coverage, with respect to plan or coverage benefits and health care provider reimbursement structures that—

(A) improve health outcomes through the implementation of activities such as quality reporting, effective case management, care coordination, chronic disease management, and medication and care compliance initiatives, including through the use of the medical homes model as defined for purposes of section 3602[33] of the Patient Protection and Affordable Care Act, for treatment or services under the plan or coverage;

(B) implement activities to prevent hospital readmissions through a comprehensive program for hospital discharge that includes patient-centered education and counseling, comprehensive discharge planning, and post discharge reinforcement by an appropriate health care professional;

(C) implement activities to improve patient safety and reduce medical errors through the appropriate use of best clinical practices, evidence based medicine, and health information technology under the plan or coverage; and

(D) implement wellness and health promotion activities.

(2) REPORTING REQUIREMENTS.—

(A) IN GENERAL. A group health plan and a health insurance issuer offering group or individual health insurance coverage shall annually submit to the Secretary, and to enrollees under the plan or coverage, a report on whether the benefits under the plan or coverage satisfy the elements described in subparagraphs (A) through (D) of paragraph (1).

(B) TIMING OF REPORTS. A report under subparagraph (A) shall be made available to an enrollee under the plan or coverage during each open enrollment period.

(C) AVAILABILITY OF REPORTS. The Secretary shall make reports submitted under subparagraph (A) available to the public through an Internet website.

(D) PENALTIES. In developing the reporting requirements under paragraph (1), the Secretary may develop and impose appropriate penalties for non-compliance with such requirements.

(E) EXCEPTIONS. In developing the reporting requirements under paragraph (1), the Secretary may provide for exceptions to such requirements for group health plans and health insurance issuers that substantially meet the goals of this section.

(b) WELLNESS AND PREVENTION PROGRAMS. For purposes of subsection (a)(1)(D), wellness and health promotion activities may include personalized wellness and prevention services, which are coordinated, maintained or delivered by a health care provider, a wellness and prevention plan manager, or a health, wellness or prevention services organization that conducts health risk assessments or offers ongoing face-to-face, telephonic or web-based intervention efforts for each of the program's participants, and which may include the following wellness and prevention efforts:

(1) Smoking cessation.

(2) Weight management.

(3) Stress management.

(4) Physical fitness.

(5) Nutrition.

(6) Heart disease prevention.

(7) Healthy lifestyle support.

(8) Diabetes prevention.

(c) PROTECTION OF SECOND AMENDMENT GUN RIGHTS.—

(1) WELLNESS AND PREVENTION PROGRAMS. A wellness and health promotion activity implemented under subsection (a)(1)(D) may not require the disclosure or collection of any information relating to—

(A) the presence or storage of a lawfully-possessed firearm or ammunition in the residence or on the property of an individual; or

(B) the lawful use, possession, or storage of a firearm or ammunition by an individual.

(2) LIMITATION ON DATA COLLECTION. None of the authorities provided to the Secretary under the Patient Protection and Affordable Care Act or an amendment made by that Act shall be construed to authorize or may be used for the collection of any information relating to—

(A) the lawful ownership or possession of a firearm or ammunition;

(B) the lawful use of a firearm or ammunition; or

(C) the lawful storage of a firearm or ammunition.

(3) LIMITATION ON DATABASES OR DATA BANKS. None of the authorities provided to the Secretary under the Patient Protection and Affordable Care Act or an amendment made by that Act shall be construed to authorize or may be used to maintain records of individual ownership or possession of a firearm or ammunition.

(4) LIMITATION ON DETERMINATION OF PREMIUM RATES OR ELIGIBILITY FOR HEALTH INSURANCE. A premium rate may not be increased, health insurance coverage may not be denied, and a discount, rebate, or reward offered for participation in a wellness program may not be reduced or withheld under any health benefit plan issued pursuant to or in accordance with the Patient Protection and Affordable Care Act or an amendment made by that Act on the basis of, or on reliance upon—

(A) the lawful ownership or possession of a firearm or ammunition; or

(B) the lawful use or storage of a firearm or ammunition.

(5) LIMITATION ON DATA COLLECTION REQUIREMENTS FOR INDIVIDUALS. No individual shall be required to disclose any information under any data collection activity authorized under the Patient Protection and Affordable Care Act or an amendment made by that Act relating to—

(A) the lawful ownership or possession of a firearm or ammunition; or

(B) the lawful use, possession, or storage of a firearm or ammunition.

(d) REGULATIONS. Not later than 2 years after the date of enactment of the Patient Protection and Affordable Care Act, the Secretary shall promulgate regulations that provide criteria for determining whether a reimbursement structure is described in subsection (a).

---

[33] So in original. Probably should be "3502".

(e) STUDY AND REPORT. Not later than 180 days after the date on which regulations are promulgated under subsection (c),[34] the Government Accountability Office shall review such regulations and conduct a study and submit to the Committee on Health, Education, Labor, and Pensions of the Senate and the Committee on Energy and Commerce of the House of Representatives a report regarding the impact the activities under this section have had on the quality and cost of health care.

2010 Amendments:

Sec. 1001(5) of the "Patient Protection and Affordable Care Act" (P.L. 111–148), effective for plan years beginning on or after Sept. 23, 2010, added new sec. 2717.

Sec. 10101(e) of the "Patient Protection and Affordable Care Act" (P.L. 111–148), effective Mar. 23, 2010, amended sec. 2717 by making the following changes:

by redesignating subsections (c) and (d) as subsections (d) and (e), respectively;

by adding new subsection (c).

History:

Secs. 1001(5), 10101(e) of the "Patient Protection and Affordable Care Act" (P.L. 111–148).

Sec. 2718. Bringing Down the Cost of Health Care Coverage

[42 U.S.C. 300gg–18]

(a) CLEAR ACCOUNTING FOR COSTS. A health insurance issuer offering group or individual health insurance coverage (including a grandfathered health plan) shall, with respect to each plan year, submit to the Secretary a report concerning the ratio of the incurred loss (or incurred claims) plus the loss adjustment expense (or change in contract reserves) to earned premiums. Such report shall include the percentage of total premium revenue, after accounting for collections or receipts for risk adjustment and risk corridors and payments of reinsurance, that such coverage expends—

(1) on reimbursement for clinical services provided to enrollees under such coverage;

(2) for activities that improve health care quality; and

(3) on all other non-claims costs, including an explanation of the nature of such costs, and excluding Federal and State taxes and licensing or regulatory fees.

The Secretary shall make reports received under this section available to the public on the Internet website of the Department of Health and Human Services.

(b) ENSURING THAT CONSUMERS RECEIVE VALUE FOR THEIR PREMIUM PAYMENTS.—

(1) REQUIREMENT TO PROVIDE VALUE FOR PREMIUM PAYMENTS.—

(A) REQUIREMENT. Beginning not later than January 1, 2011, a health insurance issuer offering group or individual health insurance coverage (including a grandfathered health plan) shall, with respect to each plan year, provide an annual rebate to each enrollee under such coverage, on a pro rata basis, if the ratio of the amount of premium revenue expended by the issuer on costs described in paragraphs (1) and (2) of subsection (a) to the total amount of premium revenue (excluding Federal and State taxes and licensing or regulatory fees and after accounting for payments or receipts for risk adjustment, risk corridors, and reinsurance under sections 1341, 1342, and 1343 of the Patient Protection and Affordable Care Act) for the plan year (except as provided in subparagraph (B)(ii)), is less than—

(i) with respect to a health insurance issuer offering coverage in the large group market, 85 percent, or such higher percentage as a State may by regulation determine; or

(ii) with respect to a health insurance issuer offering coverage in the small group market or in the individual market, 80 percent, or such higher percentage as a State may by regulation determine, except that the Secretary may adjust such percentage with respect to a State if the Secretary determines that the application of such 80 percent may destabilize the individual market in such State.

(B) REBATE AMOUNT.—

(i) CALCULATION OF AMOUNT. The total amount of an annual rebate required under this paragraph shall be in an amount equal to the product of—

(I) the amount by which the percentage described in clause (i) or (ii) of subparagraph (A) exceeds the ratio described in such subparagraph; and

(II) the total amount of premium revenue (excluding Federal and State taxes and licensing or regulatory fees and after accounting for payments or receipts for risk adjustment, risk corridors, and reinsurance under sections 1341, 1342, and 1343 of the Patient Protection and Affordable Care Act) for such plan year.

(ii) CALCULATION BASED ON AVERAGE RATIO. Beginning on January 1, 2014, the determination made under subparagraph (A) for the year involved shall be based on the averages of the premiums expended on the costs described in such subparagraph and total premium revenue for each of the previous 3 years for the plan.

(2) CONSIDERATION IN SETTING PERCENTAGES. In determining the percentages under paragraph (1), a State shall seek to ensure adequate participation by health insurance issuers, competition in the health insurance market in the State, and value for consumers so that premiums are used for clinical services and quality improvements.

(3) ENFORCEMENT. The Secretary shall promulgate regulations for enforcing the provisions of this section and may provide for appropriate penalties.

(c) DEFINITIONS. Not later than December 31, 2010, and subject to the certification of the Secretary, the National Association of Insurance Commissioners shall establish uniform definitions of the activities reported under subsection (a) and standardized methodologies for calculating measures of such activities, including definitions of which activities, and in what regard such activities, constitute activities described in subsection (a)(2). Such methodologies shall be designed to take into account the special circumstances of smaller plans, different types of plans, and newer plans.

(d) ADJUSTMENTS. The Secretary may adjust the rates described in subsection (b) if the Secretary determines appropriate on account of the volatility of the individual market due to the establishment of State Exchanges.

(e) STANDARD HOSPITAL CHARGES. Each hospital operating within the United States shall for each year establish (and update) and make public (in accordance with guidelines developed by the Secretary) a list of the hospital's standard charges for items and services provided by the hospital, including for diagnosis-related groups established under section 1886(d)(4) of the Social Security Act.

---

[34] So in original. Probably should be "(d),".

2010 Amendments:

Sec. 1001(5) of the "Patient Protection and Affordable Care Act" (P.L. 111–148), effective for plan years beginning on or after Sept. 23, 2010, added new sec. 2718.

Sec. 10101(f) of the "Patient Protection and Affordable Care Act" (P.L. 111–148), effective Mar. 23, 2010, amended sec. 2718.

Prior to amendment sec. 2718 read as follows:

"Sec. 2718. BRINGING DOWN THE COST OF HEALTH CARE COVERAGE. [42 U.S.C. 300gg–18]

"(a) Clear Accounting for Costs.—A health insurance issuer offering group or individual health insurance coverage shall, with respect to each plan year, submit to the Secretary a report concerning the percentage of total premium revenue that such coverage expends—

"(1) on reimbursement for clinical services provided to enrollees under such coverage;

"(2) for activities that improve health care quality; and

"(3) on all other non-claims costs, including an explanation of the nature of such costs, and excluding State taxes and licensing or regulatory fees.

The Secretary shall make reports received under this section available to the public on the Internet website of the Department of Health and Human Services.

"(b) Ensuring That Consumers Receive Value for Their Premium Payments.—

"(1) Requirement to provide value for premium payments.— A health insurance issuer offering group or individual health insurance coverage shall, with respect to each plan year, provide an annual rebate to each enrollee under such coverage, on a pro rata basis, in an amount that is equal to the amount by which premium revenue expended by the issuer on activities described in subsection (a)(3) exceeds—

"(A) with respect to a health insurance issuer offering coverage in the group market, 20 percent, or such lower percentage as a State may by regulation determine; or

"(B) with respect to a health insurance issuer offering coverage in the individual market, 25 percent, or such lower percentage as a State may by regulation determine, except that such percentage shall be adjusted to the extent the Secretary determines that the application of such percentage with a State may destabilize the existing individual market in such State.

"(2) Consideration in setting percentages.—In determining the percentages under paragraph (1), a State shall seek to ensure adequate participation by health insurance issuers, competition in the health insurance market in the State, and value for consumers so that premiums are used for clinical services and quality improvements.

"(3) Termination.—The provisions of this subsection shall have no force or effect after December 31, 2013.

"(c) Standard Hospital Charges.—Each hospital operating within the United States shall for each year establish (and update) and make public (in accordance with guidelines developed by the Secretary) a list of the hospital's standard charges for items and services provided by the hospital, including for diagnosis-related groups established under section 1886(d)(4) of the Social Security Act.

"(d) Definitions.—The Secretary, in consultation with the National Association of Insurance Commissions, shall establish uniform definitions for the activities reported under subsection (a)."

History:

Secs. 1001(5), 10101(f) of the "Patient Protection and Affordable Care Act" (P.L. 111–148).

Sec. 2719. Appeals Process

[42 U.S.C. 300gg–19]

(a) INTERNAL CLAIMS APPEALS.—

(1) IN GENERAL. A group health plan and a health insurance issuer offering group or individual health insurance coverage shall implement an effective appeals process for appeals of coverage determinations and claims, under which the plan or issuer shall, at a minimum—

(A) have in effect an internal claims appeal process;

(B) provide notice to enrollees, in a culturally and linguistically appropriate manner, of available internal and external appeals processes, and the availability of any applicable office of health insurance consumer assistance or ombudsman established under section 2793 to assist such enrollees with the appeals processes; and

(C) allow an enrollee to review their file, to present evidence and testimony as part of the appeals process, and to receive continued coverage pending the outcome of the appeals process.

(2) ESTABLISHED PROCESSES. To comply with paragraph (1)—

(A) a group health plan and a health insurance issuer offering group health coverage shall provide an internal claims and appeals process that initially incorporates the claims and appeals procedures (including urgent claims) set forth at section 2560.503–1 of title 29, Code of Federal Regulations, as published on November 21, 2000 (65 Fed. Reg. 70256), and shall update such process in accordance with any standards established by the Secretary of Labor for such plans and issuers; and

(B) a health insurance issuer offering individual health coverage, and any other issuer not subject to subparagraph (A), shall provide an internal claims and appeals process that initially incorporates the claims and appeals procedures set forth under applicable law (as in existence on the date of enactment of this section), and shall update such process in accordance with any standards established by the Secretary of Health and Human Services for such issuers.

(b) EXTERNAL REVIEW. A group health plan and a health insurance issuer offering group or individual health insurance coverage—

(1) shall comply with the applicable State external review process for such plans and issuers that, at a minimum, includes the consumer protections set forth in the Uniform External Review Model Act promulgated by the National Association of Insurance Commissioners and is binding on such plans; or

(2) shall implement an effective external review process that meets minimum standards established by the Secretary through guidance and that is similar to the process described under paragraph (1)—

(A) if the applicable State has not established an external review process that meets the requirements of paragraph (1); or

(B) if the plan is a self-insured plan that is not subject to State insurance regulation (including a State law that establishes an external review process described in paragraph (1)).

(c) SECRETARY AUTHORITY. The Secretary may deem the external review process of a group health plan or health insurance issuer, in operation as of the date of enactment of this section, to be in compliance with the applicable process established under subsection (b), as determined appropriate by the Secretary.

2010 Amendments:

Sec. 1001(5) of the "Patient Protection and Affordable Care Act" (P.L. 111–148), effective for plan years beginning on or after Sept. 23, 2010, added new sec. 2719.

Sec. 10101(g) of the "Patient Protection and Affordable Care Act" (P.L. 111–148), effective Mar. 23, 2010, amended sec. 2719.

Prior to amendment sec. 2719 read as follows:

"Sec. 2719. APPEALS PROCESS. [42 U.S.C. 300gg–19]

" A group health plan and a health insurance issuer offering group or individual health insurance coverage shall implement an effective appeals process for appeals of coverage determinations and claims, under which the plan or issuer shall, at a minimum—

"(1) have in effect an internal claims appeal process;

"(2) provide notice to enrollees, in a culturally and linguistically appropriate manner, of available internal and external appeals processes, and the availability of any applicable office of health insurance consumer assistance or ombudsman established under section 2793 to assist such enrollees with the appeals processes;

"(3) allow an enrollee to review their file, to present evidence and testimony as part of the appeals process, and to receive continued coverage pending the outcome of the appeals process; and

"(4) provide an external review process for such plans and issuers that, at a minimum, includes the consumer protections set forth in the Uniform External Review Model Act promulgated by the National Association of Insurance Commissioners and is binding on such plans."

History:

Secs. 1001(5), 10101(g) of the "Patient Protection and Affordable Care Act" (P.L. 111–148).

Sec. 2719A. Patient Protections

[42 U.S.C. 300gg–19a]

(a) CHOICE OF HEALTH CARE PROFESSIONAL. If a group health plan, or a health insurance issuer offering group or individual health insurance coverage, requires or provides for designation by a participant, beneficiary, or enrollee of a participating primary care provider, then the plan or issuer shall permit each participant, beneficiary, and enrollee to designate any participating primary care provider who is available to accept such individual.

(b) COVERAGE OF EMERGENCY SERVICES.—

(1) IN GENERAL. If a group health plan, or a health insurance issuer offering group or individual health insurance issuer,[35] provides or covers any benefits with respect to services in an emergency department of a hospital, the plan or issuer shall cover emergency services (as defined in paragraph (2)(B))—

(A) without the need for any prior authorization determination;

(B) whether the health care provider furnishing such services is a participating provider with respect to such services;

(C) in a manner so that, if such services are provided to a participant, beneficiary, or enrollee—

(i) by a nonparticipating health care provider with or without prior authorization; or

(ii)(I) such services will be provided without imposing any requirement under the plan for prior authorization of services or any limitation on coverage where the provider of services does not have a contractual relationship with the plan for the providing of services that is more restrictive than the requirements or limitations that apply to emergency department services received from providers who do have such a contractual relationship with the plan; and

(II) if such services are provided out-of-network, the cost-sharing requirement (expressed as a copayment amount or coinsurance rate) is the same requirement that would apply if such services were provided in-network;[36]

(D) without regard to any other term or condition of such coverage (other than exclusion or coordination of benefits, or an affiliation or waiting period, permitted under section 2701[37] of this Act, section 701 of the Employee Retirement Income Security Act of 1974, or section 9801 of the Internal Revenue Code of 1986, and other than applicable cost-sharing).

(2) DEFINITIONS. In this subsection:

(A) EMERGENCY MEDICAL CONDITION. The term "emergency medical condition" means a medical condition manifesting itself by acute symptoms of sufficient severity (including severe pain) such that a prudent layperson, who possesses an average knowledge of health and medicine, could reasonably expect the absence of immediate medical attention to result in a condition described in clause (i), (ii), or (iii) of section 1867(e)(1)(A) of the Social Security Act.

(B) EMERGENCY SERVICES. The term "emergency services" means, with respect to an emergency medical condition—

(i) a medical screening examination (as required under section 1867 of the Social Security Act) that is within the capability of the emergency department of a hospital, including ancillary services routinely available to the emergency department to evaluate such emergency medical condition, and

(ii) within the capabilities of the staff and facilities available at the hospital, such further medical examination and treatment as are required under section 1867 of such Act to stabilize the patient.

(C) STABILIZE. The term "to stabilize", with respect to an emergency medical condition (as defined in subparagraph (A)), has the meaning give[38] in section 1867(e)(3) of the Social Security Act (42 U.S.C. 1395dd(e)(3)).

(c) ACCESS TO PEDIATRIC CARE.—

(1) PEDIATRIC CARE. In the case of a person who has a child who is a participant, beneficiary, or enrollee under a group health plan, or health insurance coverage offered by a health insurance issuer in the group or individual market, if the plan or issuer requires or provides for the designation of a participating primary care provider for the child, the plan or issuer shall permit such person to designate a physician (allopathic or osteopathic) who specializes in pediatrics as the child's primary care provider if such provider participates in the network of the plan or issuer.

(2) CONSTRUCTION. Nothing in paragraph (1) shall be construed to waive any exclusions of coverage under the terms and conditions of the plan or health insurance coverage with respect to coverage of pediatric care.

---

[35] So in original. Probably should be "coverage,".

[36] So in original. The word "and" probably should appear.

[37] Section 2701 was renumbered section 2704 effective for plan years beginning on or after Jan. 1, 2014.

[38] So in original. Probably should be "given".

(d) PATIENT ACCESS TO OBSTETRICAL AND GYNECOLOGICAL CARE.—

(1) GENERAL RIGHTS.—

(A) DIRECT ACCESS. A group health plan, or health insurance issuer offering group or individual health insurance coverage, described in paragraph (2) may not require authorization or referral by the plan, issuer, or any person (including a primary care provider described in paragraph (2)(B)) in the case of a female participant, beneficiary, or enrollee who seeks coverage for obstetrical or gynecological care provided by a participating health care professional who specializes in obstetrics or gynecology. Such professional shall agree to otherwise adhere to such plan's or issuer's policies and procedures, including procedures regarding referrals and obtaining prior authorization and providing services pursuant to a treatment plan (if any) approved by the plan or issuer.

(B) OBSTETRICAL AND GYNECOLOGICAL CARE. A group health plan or health insurance issuer described in paragraph (2) shall treat the provision of obstetrical and gynecological care, and the ordering of related obstetrical and gynecological items and services, pursuant to the direct access described under subparagraph (A), by a participating health care professional who specializes in obstetrics or gynecology as the authorization of the primary care provider.

(2) APPLICATION OF PARAGRAPH. A group health plan, or health insurance issuer offering group or individual health insurance coverage, described in this paragraph is a group health plan or coverage that—

(A) provides coverage for obstetric or gynecologic care; and

(B) requires the designation by a participant, beneficiary, or enrollee of a participating primary care provider.

(3) CONSTRUCTION. Nothing in paragraph (1) shall be construed to—

(A) waive any exclusions of coverage under the terms and conditions of the plan or health insurance coverage with respect to coverage of obstetrical or gynecological care; or

(B) preclude the group health plan or health insurance issuer involved from requiring that the obstetrical or gynecological provider notify the primary care health care professional or the plan or issuer of treatment decisions.

2010 Amendments:

Sec. 10101(h) of the "Patient Protection and Affordable Care Act" (P.L. 111–148), effective Mar. 23, 2010, added new sec. 2719A. The direction to add the section in title XVIII was executed to title XXVII, as the probable intent of Congress.

History:

Sec. 10101(h) of the "Patient Protection and Affordable Care Act" (P.L. 111–148).

Sec. 2722. [39] Exclusion of Certain Plans

[42 U.S.C. 300gg–21]

(a) LIMITATION ON APPLICATION OF PROVISIONS RELATING TO GROUP HEALTH PLANS.—

(1) IN GENERAL. The requirements of subparts 1 and 2[40] shall apply with respect to group health plans only—

(A) subject to paragraph (2), in the case of a plan that is a nonfederal governmental plan, and

(B) with respect to health insurance coverage offered in connection with a group health plan (including such a plan that is a church plan or a governmental plan).

(2) TREATMENT OF NONFEDERAL GOVERNMENTAL PLANS.—

(A) ELECTION TO BE EXCLUDED. Except as provided in subparagraph (D) or (E), if the plan sponsor of a nonfederal governmental plan which is a group health plan to which the provisions of subparts 1 and 2 [656] otherwise apply makes an election under this subparagraph (in such form and manner as the Secretary may by regulations prescribe), then the requirements of such subparts insofar as they apply directly to group health plans (and not merely to group health insurance coverage) shall not apply to such governmental plans for such period except as provided in this paragraph.

(B) PERIOD OF ELECTION. An election under subparagraph (A) shall apply—

(i) for a single specified plan year, or

(ii) in the case of a plan provided pursuant to a collective bargaining agreement, for the term of such agreement.

An election under clause (i) may be extended through subsequent elections under this paragraph.

(C) NOTICE TO ENROLLEES. Under such an election, the plan shall provide for—

(i) notice to enrollees (on an annual basis and at the time of enrollment under the plan) of the fact and consequences of such election, and

(ii) certification and disclosure of creditable coverage under the plan with respect to enrollees in accordance with section 2701(e).[41]

(D) ELECTION NOT APPLICABLE TO REQUIREMENTS CONCERNING GENETIC INFORMATION. The election described in subparagraph (A) shall not be available with respect to the provisions of subsections (a)(1)(F), (b)(3), (c), and (d) of section 2702 and the provisions of sections 2701[42] and 2702(b)[43] to the extent that such provisions apply to genetic information.

(E) ELECTION NOT APPLICABLE. The election described in subparagraph (A) shall not be available with respect to the provisions of subparts I and II.

---

[39] This section 2722 was originally section 2721. It was renumbered section 2735 by Pub. L. 111–148, Sec. 1001(4), effective for plan years beginning on or after Sept. 23, 2010. It was then amended and renumbered section 2722 by Pub. L. 111–148, Sec. 1563(a), (c)(12) (originally Sec. 1562(a), (c)(12); renumbered Sec. 1563(a), (c)(12) by Pub. L. 111–148, Sec. 10107(b)(1)). Although Pub. L. 111–148, Sec. 1563(c)(12)(D), did not expressly direct that this section be moved so as to appear in numerical order, it has been so moved as the probable intent of Congress. There are no sections between 2719A and 2722. This section was originally preceded by a heading "Subpart 4—Exclusion of Plans; Enforcement; Preemption". Although Pub. L. 111–148, Sec. 1563(c)(11), directed that subpart 4 be redesignated as subpart 2, this direction was executed by striking out the subpart 4 designation and heading entirely, as the probable intent of Congress.

There are conflicting amendments made to provisions of this section by section 1563(a) and section 1563(c)(12)(B) (relating to conforming amendments–originally designated as section 1562 and redesignated as section 1563 by section 10107(b)(1)) of Public Law 111–148. The amendments reflected here are from section 1563(a) of such Public Law, which render the global amendment made by subsection (c)(12)(B) unexecutable.

[40] The references to "subparts 1 and 2" probably should read "subparts I and II".

[41] Section 2701 was renumbered section 2704 effective for plan years beginning on or after Jan. 1, 2014.

[42] Section 2701 was renumbered section 2704 effective for plan years beginning on or after Jan. 1, 2014.

[43] Section 2702 was transferred to subsecs. (b)-(f) of section 2705 effective for plan years beginning on or after Jan. 1, 2014.

(b) EXCEPTION FOR CERTAIN BENEFITS. The requirements of subparts 1 and 2[44] shall not apply to any individual coverage or any group health plan (or group health insurance coverage) in relation to its provision of excepted benefits described in section 2791(c)(1).

(c) EXCEPTION FOR CERTAIN BENEFITS IF CERTAIN CONDITIONS MET.—

(1) LIMITED, EXCEPTED BENEFITS. The requirements of subparts 1 and 2 [657] shall not apply to any individual coverage or any group health plan (and group health insurance coverage offered in connection with a group health plan) in relation to its provision of excepted benefits described in section 2791(c)(2) if the benefits—

(A) are provided under a separate policy, certificate, or contract of insurance; or

(B) are otherwise not an integral part of the plan.

(2) NONCOORDINATED, EXCEPTED BENEFITS. The requirements of subparts 1 and 2 [657] shall not apply to any individual coverage or any group health plan (and group health insurance coverage offered in connection with a group health plan) in relation to its provision of excepted benefits described in section 2791(c)(3) if all of the following conditions are met:

(A) The benefits are provided under a separate policy, certificate, or contract of insurance.

(B) There is no coordination between the provision of such benefits and any exclusion of benefits under any group health plan maintained by the same plan sponsor.

(C) Such benefits are paid with respect to an event without regard to whether benefits are provided with respect to such an event under any group health plan maintained by the same plan sponsor or, with respect to individual coverage, under any health insurance coverage maintained by the same health insurance issuer[45].

(3) SUPPLEMENTAL EXCEPTED BENEFITS. The requirements of this part shall not apply to any individual coverage or any group health plan (and group health insurance coverage) in relation to its provision of excepted benefits described in section 27971(c)(4)[46] if the benefits are provided under a separate policy, certificate, or contract of insurance.

(d) TREATMENT OF PARTNERSHIPS. For purposes of this part—

(1) TREATMENT AS A GROUP HEALTH PLAN. Any plan, fund, or program which would not be (but for this subsection) an employee welfare benefit plan and which is established or maintained by a partnership, to the extent that such plan, fund, or program provides medical care (including items and services paid for as medical care) to present or former partners in the partnership or to their dependents (as defined under the terms of the plan, fund, or program), directly or through insurance, reimbursement, or otherwise, shall be treated (subject to paragraph (2)) as an employee welfare benefit plan which is a group health plan.

(2) EMPLOYER. In the case of a group health plan, the term "employer" also includes the partnership in relation to any partner.

(3) PARTICIPANTS OF GROUP HEALTH PLANS. In the case of a group health plan, the term "participant" also includes—

(A) in connection with a group health plan maintained by a partnership, an individual who is a partner in relation to the partnership, or

(B) in connection with a group health plan maintained by a self-employed individual (under which one or more employees are participants), the self-employed individual,

if such individual is, or may become, eligible to receive a benefit under the plan or such individual's beneficiaries may be eligible to receive any such benefit.

2010 Amendments:

Sec. 1001(4) of the "Patient Protection and Affordable Care Act" (P.L. 111–148), effective for plan years beginning on or after Sept. 23, 2010, renumbered sec. 2721 as sec. 2735.

Sec. 1563(a) of the "Patient Protection and Affordable Care Act" (P.L. 111–148) (formerly sec. 1562(a) of such Act, renumbered sec. 1563(a) by sec. 10107(b)(1) of such Act), effective Mar. 23, 2010, amended sec. 2735 by making the following changes:

by striking subsection (a);

in subsection (b)(1), by substituting "1 and 2" for "1 through 3";

in subsection (b)(2)(A), by substituting "subparagraph (D) or (E)" for "subparagraph (D)" and "1 and 2" for "1 through 3";

in subsection (b)(2), by adding at the end new subparagraph (E);

in subsection (c), by substituting "1 and 2 shall not apply to any individual coverage or any group" for "1 through 3 shall not apply to any group";

in subsection (d)(1), by substituting "1 and 2 shall not apply to any individual coverage or any group" for "1 through 3 shall not apply to any group";

in subsection (d)(2), by substituting "1 and 2 shall not apply to any individual coverage or any group" for "1 through 3 shall not apply to any group";

in subsection (d)(2)(C), by inserting "or, with respect to individual coverage, under any health insurance coverage maintained by the same health insurance issuer" before the period at the end (although Congress did not specify where in subsection (d)(2)(C) such language should be inserted, such language was inserted before the period at the end, as the probable intent of Congress);

in subsection (d)(3), by substituting "any individual coverage or any group" for "any group".

Sec. 1563(c)(12) of the "Patient Protection and Affordable Care Act" (P.L. 111–148) (formerly sec. 1562(c)(12) of such Act, renumbered sec. 1563(c)(12) by sec. 10107(b)(1) of such Act), effective Mar. 23, 2010, amended sec. 2735 by making the following changes:

by striking subsection (a) (this amendment was duplicative of an amendment made by section 1563(a) of such Act);

by substituting "subpart 1" for "subparts 1 through 3" wherever appearing (this amendment could not be executed, as the phrase to be struck out did not appear in text after execution of amendments by section 1563(a) of such Act);

by redesignating subsections (b) through (e) as subsections (a) through (d), respectively;

by redesignating sec. 2735 as sec. 2722.

Prior to being struck out, subsection (a) read as follows:

"(a) Exception for Certain Small Group Health Plans.— The requirements of subparts 1 and 3 shall not apply to any group health plan (and health insurance coverage offered in connection with a group health plan) for any plan year if, on the first day of such plan year, such plan has less than 2 participants who are current employees."

---

[44] The references to "subparts 1 and 2" probably should read "subparts I and II".

[45] Section 1563 (relating to conforming amendments–originally designated as section 1562 and redesignated as section 1563 by section 10107(b)(1)) of Public Law 111–148 provides for an amendment to insert "or, with respect to individual coverage, under any health insurance coverage maintained by the same health insurance issuer". Such amendment did not specify where to insert this new language, however, it was carried out by inserting this new language before the period at the end in order to reflect the probable intent of Congress.

[46] So in original. Probably should be "2791(c)(4)".

History:

Sec. 102(a) of the "Health Insurance Portability and Accountability Act of 1996" (P.L. 104–191), sec. 604(b)(1) of the "Newborns' and Mothers' Health Protection Act of 1996", Title VI of the "Departments of Veterans Affairs and Housing and Urban Development, and Independent Agencies Appropria-tions Act, 1997" (P.L. 104–204), sec. 102(c) of the "Genetic Information Nondiscrimination Act of 2008" (P.L. 110–233), secs. 1001(4), sec. 1563(a), (c)(12), formerly sec. 1562(a), (c)(12), renumbered sec. 1563(a), (c)(12), sec. 10107(a), (b)(1) of the "Patient Protection and Affordable Care Act" (P.L. 111–148).

Sec. 2723. Enforcement[47]

[42 U.S.C. 300gg–22]

(a) STATE ENFORCEMENT.—

(1) STATE AUTHORITY. Subject to section 2723,[48] each State may require that health insurance issuers that issue, sell, renew, or offer health insurance coverage in the State in the individual or group market meet the requirements of this part with respect to such issuers.

(2) FAILURE TO IMPLEMENT PROVISIONS. In the case of a determination by the Secretary that a State has failed to substantially enforce a provision (or provisions) in this part with respect to health insurance issuers in the State, the Secretary shall enforce such provision (or provisions) under subsection (b) insofar as they relate to the issuance, sale, renewal, and offering of health insurance coverage in connection with group health plans or individual health insurance coverage in such State.

(b) SECRETARIAL ENFORCEMENT AUTHORITY.—

(1) LIMITATION. The provisions of this subsection shall apply to enforcement of a provision (or provisions) of this part only—

(A) as provided under subsection (a)(2); and

(B) with respect to individual health insurance coverage or group health plans that are non-Federal governmental plans.

(2) IMPOSITION OF PENALTIES. In the cases described in paragraph (1)—

(A) IN GENERAL. Subject to the succeeding provisions of this subsection, any non-Federal governmental plan that is a group health plan and any health insurance issuer that fails to meet a provision of this part applicable to such plan or issuer is subject to a civil money penalty under this subsection.

(B) LIABILITY FOR PENALTY. In the case of a failure by—

(i) a health insurance issuer, the issuer is liable for such penalty, or

(ii) a group health plan that is a non-Federal governmental plan which is—

(I) sponsored by 2 or more employers, the plan is liable for such penalty, or

(II) not so sponsored, the employer is liable for such penalty.

(C) AMOUNT OF PENALTY.—

(i) IN GENERAL. The maximum amount of penalty imposed under this paragraph is $100 for each day for each individual with respect to which such a failure occurs.

(ii) CONSIDERATIONS IN IMPOSITION. In determining the amount of any penalty to be assessed under this paragraph, the Secretary shall take into account the previous record of compliance of the entity being assessed with the applicable provisions of this part and the gravity of the violation.

(iii) LIMITATIONS.—

(I) PENALTY NOT TO APPLY WHERE FAILURE NOT DISCOVERED EXERCISING REASONABLE DILIGENCE. No civil money penalty shall be imposed under this paragraph on any failure during any period for which it is established to the satisfaction of the Secretary that none of the entities against whom the penalty would be imposed knew, or exercising reasonable diligence would have known, that such failure existed.

(II) PENALTY NOT TO APPLY TO FAILURES CORRECTED WITHIN 30 DAYS. No civil money penalty shall be imposed under this paragraph on any failure if such failure was due to reasonable cause and not to willful neglect, and such failure is corrected during the 30-day period beginning on the first day any of the entities against whom the penalty would be imposed knew, or exercising reasonable diligence would have known, that such failure existed.

(D) ADMINISTRATIVE REVIEW.—

(i) OPPORTUNITY FOR HEARING. The entity assessed shall be afforded an opportunity for hearing by the Secretary upon request made within 30 days after the date of the issuance of a notice of assessment. In such hearing the decision shall be made on the record pursuant to section 554 of title 5, United States Code. If no hearing is requested, the assessment shall constitute a final and unappealable order.

(ii) HEARING PROCEDURE. If a hearing is requested, the initial agency decision shall be made by an administrative law judge, and such decision shall become the final order unless the Secretary modifies or vacates the decision. Notice of intent to modify or vacate the decision of the administrative law judge shall be issued to the parties within 30 days after the date of the decision of the judge. A final order which takes effect under this paragraph shall be subject to review only as provided under subparagraph (E).

(E) JUDICIAL REVIEW.—

(i) FILING OF ACTION FOR REVIEW. Any entity against whom an order imposing a civil money penalty has been entered after an agency hearing under this paragraph may obtain review by the United States district court for any district in which such entity is located or the United States

---

[47] This section 2723 was originally section 2722. It was renumbered section 2736 by Pub. L. 111–148, Sec. 1001(4), effective for plan years beginning on or after Sept. 23, 2010. It was then amended and renumbered section 2723 by Pub. L. 111–148, Sec. 1563(c)(13) (originally Sec. 1562(c)(13); renumbered Sec. 1563(c)(13) by Pub. L. 111–148, Sec. 10107(b)(1)). Although Pub. L. 111–148, Sec. 1563(c)(13)(D), did not expressly direct that this section be moved so as to appear in numerical order, it has been so moved as the probable intent of Congress.

[48] So in original. Probably should be "2724,".

District Court for the District of Columbia by filing a notice of appeal in such court within 30 days from the date of such order, and simultaneously sending a copy of such notice by registered mail to the Secretary.

(ii) CERTIFICATION OF ADMINISTRATIVE RECORD. The Secretary shall promptly certify and file in such court the record upon which the penalty was imposed.

(iii) STANDARD FOR REVIEW. The findings of the Secretary shall be set aside only if found to be unsupported by substantial evidence as provided by section 706(2)(E) of title 5, United States Code.

(iv) APPEAL. Any final decision, order, or judgment of the district court concerning such review shall be subject to appeal as provided in chapter 83 of title 28 of such Code.

(F) FAILURE TO PAY ASSESSMENT; MAINTENANCE OF ACTION.—

(i) FAILURE TO PAY ASSESSMENT. If any entity fails to pay an assessment after it has become a final and unappealable order, or after the court has entered final judgment in favor of the Secretary, the Secretary shall refer the matter to the Attorney General who shall recover the amount assessed by action in the appropriate United States district court.

(ii) NONREVIEWABILITY. In such action the validity and appropriateness of the final order imposing the penalty shall not be subject to review.

(G) PAYMENT OF PENALTIES. Except as otherwise provided, penalties collected under this paragraph shall be paid to the Secretary (or other officer) imposing the penalty and shall be available without appropriation and until expended for the purpose of enforcing the provisions with respect to which the penalty was imposed.

(3) ENFORCEMENT AUTHORITY RELATING TO GENETIC DISCRIMINATION.—

(A) GENERAL RULE. In the cases described in paragraph (1), notwithstanding the provisions of paragraph (2)(C), the succeeding subparagraphs of this paragraph shall apply with respect to an action under this subsection by the Secretary with respect to any failure of a health insurance issuer in connection with a group health plan, to meet the requirements of subsection (a)(1)(F), (b)(3), (c), or (d) of section 2702 or section 2701[49] or 2702(b)(1)[50] with respect to genetic information in connection with the plan.

(B) AMOUNT.—

(i) IN GENERAL. The amount of the penalty imposed under this paragraph shall be $100 for each day in the noncompliance period with respect to each participant or beneficiary to whom such failure relates.

(ii) NONCOMPLIANCE PERIOD. For purposes of this paragraph, the term "noncompliance period" means, with respect to any failure, the period—
(I) beginning on the date such failure first occurs; and
(II) ending on the date the failure is corrected.

(C) MINIMUM PENALTIES WHERE FAILURE DISCOVERED. Notwithstanding clauses (i) and (ii) of subparagraph (D):

(i) IN GENERAL. In the case of 1 or more failures with respect to an individual—
(I) which are not corrected before the date on which the plan receives a notice from the Secretary of such violation; and
(II) which occurred or continued during the period involved;
the amount of penalty imposed by subparagraph (A) by reason of such failures with respect to such individual shall not be less than $2,500.

(ii) HIGHER MINIMUM PENALTY WHERE VIOLATIONS ARE MORE THAN DE MINIMIS. To the extent violations for which any person is liable under this paragraph for any year are more than de minimis, clause (i) shall be applied by substituting "$15,000" for "$2,500" with respect to such person.

(D) LIMITATIONS.—

(i) PENALTY NOT TO APPLY WHERE FAILURE NOT DISCOVERED EXERCISING REASONABLE DILIGENCE. No penalty shall be imposed by subparagraph (A) on any failure during any period for which it is established to the satisfaction of the Secretary that the person otherwise liable for such penalty did not know, and exercising reasonable diligence would not have known, that such failure existed.

(ii) PENALTY NOT TO APPLY TO FAILURES CORRECTED WITHIN CERTAIN PERIODS. No penalty shall be imposed by subparagraph (A) on any failure if—
(I) such failure was due to reasonable cause and not to willful neglect; and
(II) such failure is corrected during the 30-day period beginning on the first date the person otherwise liable for such penalty knew, or exercising reasonable diligence would have known, that such failure existed.

(iii) OVERALL LIMITATION FOR UNINTENTIONAL FAILURES. In the case of failures which are due to reasonable cause and not to willful neglect, the penalty imposed by subparagraph (A) for failures shall not exceed the amount equal to the lesser of—
(I) 10 percent of the aggregate amount paid or incurred by the employer (or predecessor employer) during the preceding taxable year for group health plans; or
(II) $500,000.

(E) WAIVER BY SECRETARY. In the case of a failure which is due to reasonable cause and not to willful neglect, the Secretary may waive part or all of the penalty imposed by subparagraph (A) to the extent that the payment of such penalty would be excessive relative to the failure involved.

2010 Amendments:

Sec. 1001(4) of the "Patient Protection and Affordable Care Act" (P.L. 111–148), effective for plan years beginning on or after Sept. 23, 2010, renumbered sec. 2722 as sec. 2736.

Sec. 1563(c)(13) of the "Patient Protection and Affordable Care Act" (P.L. 111–148) (formerly sec. 1562(c)(13) of such Act, renumbered sec. 1563(c)(13) by sec. 10107(b)(1) of such Act), effective Mar. 23, 2010, amended sec. 2736 by making the following changes:

---

[49] Section 2701 was renumbered section 2704 effective for plan years beginning on or after Jan. 1, 2014.

[50] Section 2702 was transferred to subsecs. (b)-(f) of section 2705 effective for plan years beginning on or after Jan. 1, 2014.

in subsection (a)(1), by substituting "individual or group market" for "small or large group markets";

in subsection (a)(2), by inserting "or individual health insurance coverage" after "group health plans";

in subsection (b)(1)(B), by inserting "individual health insurance coverage or" after "respect to";

by redesignating sec. 2736 as sec. 2723.

History:

Sec. 102(a) of the "Health Insurance Portability and Accountability Act of 1996" (P.L. 104–191), sec. 102(a)(5) of the "Genetic Information Nondiscrimination Act of 2008" (P.L. 110–233), secs. 1001(4), sec. 1563(c)(13), formerly sec. 1562(c)(13), renumbered sec. 1563(c)(13), sec. 10107(b)(1) of the "Patient Protection and Affordable Care Act" (P.L. 111–148).

Sec. 2724. Preemption; State Flexibility; Construction[51]

[42 U.S.C. 300gg–23]

(a) CONTINUED APPLICABILITY OF STATE LAW WITH RESPECT TO HEALTH INSURANCE ISSUERS.—

(1) IN GENERAL. Subject to paragraph (2) and except as provided in subsection (b), this part and part C insofar as it relates to this part shall not be construed to supersede any provision of State law which establishes, implements, or continues in effect any standard or requirement solely relating to health insurance issuers in connection with individual or group health insurance coverage except to the extent that such standard or requirement prevents the application of a requirement of this part.

(2) CONTINUED PREEMPTION WITH RESPECT TO GROUP HEALTH PLANS. Nothing in this part shall be construed to affect or modify the provisions of section 514 of the Employee Retirement Income Security Act of 1974 with respect to group health plans.

(b) SPECIAL RULES IN CASE OF PORTABILITY REQUIREMENTS.—

(1) IN GENERAL. Subject to paragraph (2), the provisions of this part relating to health insurance coverage offered by a health insurance issuer supersede any provision of State law which establishes, implements, or continues in effect a standard or requirement applicable to imposition of a preexisting condition exclusion specifically governed by section 701[52] which differs from the standards or requirements specified in such section.

(2) EXCEPTIONS. Only in relation to health insurance coverage offered by a health insurance issuer, the provisions of this part do not supersede any provision of State law to the extent that such provision—

(i) [53] substitutes for the reference to "6-month period" in section 2701(a)(1) a reference to any shorter period of time;

(ii) [661] substitutes for the reference to "12 months" and "18 months" in section 2701(a)(2) a reference to any shorter period of time;

(iii) [661] substitutes for the references to "63" days in sections 2701(c)(2)(A) and 2701(d)(4)(A) a reference to any greater number of days;

(iv) [661] substitutes for the reference to "30-day period" in sections 2701(b)(2) and 2701(d)(1) a reference to any greater period;

(v) [661] prohibits the imposition of any preexisting condition exclusion in cases not described in section 2701(d) or expands the exceptions described in such section;

(vi) [661] requires special enrollment periods in addition to those required under section 2701(f); or

(vii) [661] reduces the maximum period permitted in an affiliation period under section 2701(g)(1)(B).

(c) RULES OF CONSTRUCTION. Nothing in this part (other than section 2704[54]) shall be construed as requiring a group health plan or health insurance coverage to provide specific benefits under the terms of such plan or coverage.

(d) DEFINITIONS. For purposes of this section—

(1) STATE LAW. The term "State law" includes all laws, decisions, rules, regulations, or other State action having the effect of law, of any State. A law of the United States applicable only to the District of Columbia shall be treated as a State law rather than a law of the United States.

(2) STATE. The term "State" includes a State (including the Northern Mariana Islands), any political subdivisions of a State or such Islands, or any agency or instrumentality of either.

2010 Amendments:

Sec. 1001(4) of the "Patient Protection and Affordable Care Act" (P.L. 111–148), effective for plan years beginning on or after Sept. 23, 2010, renumbered sec. 2723 as sec. 2737.

Sec. 1563(c)(14) of the "Patient Protection and Affordable Care Act" (P.L. 111–148) (formerly sec. 1562(c)(14) of such Act, renumbered sec. 1563(c)(14) by sec. 10107(b)(1) of such Act), effective Mar. 23, 2010, amended sec. 2737 by making the following changes:

in subsection (a)(1), by inserting "individual or" before "group health insurance";

by redesignating sec. 2737 as sec. 2724.

History:

Sec. 102(a) of the "Health Insurance Portability and Accountability Act of 1996" (P.L. 104–191), sec. 604(b)(2) of the "Newborns' and Mothers' Health Protection Act of 1996", Title VI of the "Departments of Veterans Affairs and Housing and Urban Development, and Independent Agencies Appropriations Act, 1997" (P.L. 104–204), secs. 1001(4), sec. 1563(c)(14), formerly sec. 1562(c)(14), renumbered sec. 1563(c)(14), sec. 10107(b)(1) of the "Patient Protection and Affordable Care Act" (P.L. 111–148).

Sec. 2725. Standards Relating To Benefits for Mothers and Newborns

[42 U.S.C. 300gg–25]

(a) REQUIREMENTS FOR MINIMUM HOSPITAL STAY FOLLOWING BIRTH.—

(1) IN GENERAL. A group health plan, and a health insurance issuer offering group or individual health insurance coverage, may not—

(A) except as provided in paragraph (2)—

---

[51] This section 2724 was originally section 2723. It was renumbered section 2737 by Pub. L. 111–148, Sec. 1001(4), effective for plan years beginning on or after Sept. 23, 2010. It was then amended and renumbered section 2724 by Pub. L. 111–148, Sec. 1563(c)(14) (originally Sec. 1562(c)(14); renumbered Sec. 1563(c)(14) by Pub. L. 111–148, Sec. 10107(b)(1)). Although Pub. L. 111–148, Sec. 1563(c)(14)(B), did not expressly direct that this section be moved so as to appear in numerical order, it has been so moved as the probable intent of Congress.

[52] So in original. Probably should be "2701". Section 2701 was renumbered section 2704 effective for plan years beginning on or after Jan. 1, 2014.

[53] Clauses (i) through (vii) probably should be redesignated as subparagraphs (A) through (G). See section 102(a) of Public Law 104–191 (110 Stat. 1971).

[54] Section 2704 was renumbered section 2725.

(i) restrict benefits for any hospital length of stay in connection with childbirth for the mother or newborn child, following a normal vaginal delivery, to less than 48 hours, or

(ii) restrict benefits for any hospital length of stay in connection with childbirth for the mother or newborn child, following a cesarean section, to less than 96 hours, or

(B) require that a provider obtain authorization from the plan or the issuer for prescribing any length of stay required under subparagraph (A) (without regard to paragraph (2)).

(2) EXCEPTION. Paragraph (1)(A) shall not apply in connection with any group health plan or health insurance issuer in any case in which the decision to discharge the mother or her newborn child prior to the expiration of the minimum length of stay otherwise required under paragraph (1)(A) is made by an attending provider in consultation with the mother.

(b) PROHIBITIONS. A group health plan, and a health insurance issuer offering group or individual health insurance coverage, may not—

(1) deny to the mother or her newborn child eligibility, or continued eligibility, to enroll or to renew coverage under the terms of the plan or coverage, solely for the purpose of avoiding the requirements of this section;

(2) provide monetary payments or rebates to mothers to encourage such mothers to accept less than the minimum protections available under this section;

(3) penalize or otherwise reduce or limit the reimbursement of an attending provider because such provider provided care to an individual participant or beneficiary in accordance with this section;

(4) provide incentives (monetary or otherwise) to an attending provider to induce such provider to provide care to an individual participant or beneficiary in a manner inconsistent with this section; or

(5) subject to subsection (c)(3), restrict benefits for any portion of a period within a hospital length of stay required under subsection (a) in a manner which is less favorable than the benefits provided for any preceding portion of such stay.

(c) RULES OF CONSTRUCTION.—

(1) Nothing in this section shall be construed to require a mother who is a participant or beneficiary—

(A) to give birth in a hospital; or

(B) to stay in the hospital for a fixed period of time following the birth of her child.

(2) This section shall not apply with respect to any group health plan, or any health insurance issuer offering group or individual health insurance coverage, which does not provide benefits for hospital lengths of stay in connection with childbirth for a mother or her newborn child.

(3) Nothing in this section shall be construed as preventing a group health plan or health insurance issuer from imposing deductibles, coinsurance, or other cost-sharing in relation to benefits for hospital lengths of stay in connection with childbirth for a mother or newborn child under the plan (or under health insurance coverage offered in connection with a group health plan), except that such coinsurance or other cost-sharing for any portion of a period within a hospital length of stay required under subsection (a) may not be greater than such coinsurance or cost-sharing for any preceding portion of such stay.

(d) NOTICE. A group health plan under this part shall comply with the notice requirement under section 711(d) of the Employee Retirement Income Security Act of 1974 with respect to the requirements of this section as if such section applied to such plan.

(e) LEVEL AND TYPE OF REIMBURSEMENTS. Nothing in this section shall be construed to prevent a group health plan or a health insurance issuer offering group or individual health insurance coverage from negotiating the level and type of reimbursement with a provider for care provided in accordance with this section.

(f) PREEMPTION; EXCEPTION FOR HEALTH INSURANCE COVERAGE IN CERTAIN STATES.—

(1) IN GENERAL. The requirements of this section shall not apply with respect to health insurance coverage if there is a State law (as defined in section 2723(d)(1)[55]) for a State that regulates such coverage that is described in any of the following subparagraphs:

(A) Such State law requires such coverage to provide for at least a 48-hour hospital length of stay following a normal vaginal delivery and at least a 96-hour hospital length of stay following a cesarean section.

(B) Such State law requires such coverage to provide for maternity and pediatric care in accordance with guidelines established by the American College of Obstetricians and Gynecologists, the American Academy of Pediatrics, or other established professional medical associations.

(C) Such State law requires, in connection with such coverage for maternity care, that the hospital length of stay for such care is left to the decision of (or required to be made by) the attending provider in consultation with the mother.

(2) CONSTRUCTION. Section 2723(a)(1)[56] shall not be construed as superseding a State law described in paragraph (1).

2010 Amendments:

Sec. 1001(2) of the "Patient Protection and Affordable Care Act" (P.L. 111–148), effective for plan years beginning on or after Sept. 23, 2010, renumbered sec. 2704 as sec. 2725.

Sec. 1563(c)(3) of the "Patient Protection and Affordable Care Act" (P.L. 111–148) (formerly sec. 1562(c)(3) of such Act, renumbered sec. 1563(c)(3) by sec. 10107(b)(1) of such Act), effective Mar. 23, 2010, amended sec. 2725 by making the following changes:

in subsection (a)(1), by substituting "health insurance issuer offering group or individual health insurance coverage" for "health insurance issuer offering group health insurance coverage";

in subsection (b), by substituting "health insurance issuer offering group or individual health insurance coverage" for "health insurance issuer offering group health insurance coverage in connection with a group health plan";

in subsection (b)(1), by substituting "plan or coverage" for "plan";

in subsection (c)(2), by substituting "health insurance issuer offering group or individual health insurance coverage" for "group health insurance coverage offered by a health insurance issuer";

in subsection (c)(3), by substituting "health insurance issuer" for "issuer";

in subsection (e), by substituting "health insurance issuer offering group or individual health insurance coverage" for "health insurance issuer offering group health insurance coverage".

History:

Sec. 604(a)(3) of the "Newborns' and Mothers' Health Protection Act of 1996", Title VI of the "Departments of Veterans Affairs and Housing and Urban Development, and Independent Agencies Appropriations Act, 1997" (P.L. 104–204), secs. 1001(2), 1563(c)(3), formerly sec. 1562(c)(3), renum-

---

[55] So in original. Probably should be "2724(d)(1)".

[56] So in original. Probably should be "2724(a)(1)".

bered sec. 1563(c)(3), sec. 10107(b)(1) of the "Patient Protection and Affordable Care Act" (P.L. 111–148).

Sec. 2726. Parity in Mental Health and Substance Use Disorder Benefits

[42 U.S.C. 300gg–26]

(a) IN GENERAL.—

(1) AGGREGATE LIFETIME LIMITS. In the case of a group health plan or a health insurance issuer offering group or individual health insurance coverage that provides both medical and surgical benefits and mental health or substance use disorder benefits—

(A) NO LIFETIME LIMIT. If the plan or coverage does not include an aggregate lifetime limit on substantially all medical and surgical benefits, the plan or coverage may not impose any aggregate lifetime limit on mental health or substance use disorder benefits.

(B) LIFETIME LIMIT. If the plan or coverage includes an aggregate lifetime limit on substantially all medical and surgical benefits (in this paragraph referred to as the "applicable lifetime limit"), the plan or coverage shall either—

(i) apply the applicable lifetime limit both to the medical and surgical benefits to which it otherwise would apply and to mental health and substance use disorder benefits and not distinguish in the application of such limit between such medical and surgical benefits and mental health and substance use disorder benefits; or

(ii) not include any aggregate lifetime limit on mental health or substance use disorder benefits that is less than the applicable lifetime limit.

(C) RULE IN CASE OF DIFFERENT LIMITS. In the case of a plan or coverage that is not described in subparagraph (A) or (B) and that includes no or different aggregate lifetime limits on different categories of medical and surgical benefits, the Secretary shall establish rules under which subparagraph (B) is applied to such plan or coverage with respect to mental health and substance use disorder benefits by substituting for the applicable lifetime limit an average aggregate lifetime limit that is computed taking into account the weighted average of the aggregate lifetime limits applicable to such categories.

(2) ANNUAL LIMITS. In the case of a group health plan or a health insurance issuer offering group or individual health insurance coverage that provides both medical and surgical benefits and mental health or substance use disorder benefits—

(A) NO ANNUAL LIMIT. If the plan or coverage does not include an annual limit on substantially all medical and surgical benefits, the plan or coverage may not impose any annual limit on mental health or substance use disorder benefits.

(B) ANNUAL LIMIT. If the plan or coverage includes an annual limit on substantially all medical and surgical benefits (in this paragraph referred to as the "applicable annual limit"), the plan or coverage shall either—

(i) apply the applicable annual limit both to medical and surgical benefits to which it otherwise would apply and to mental health and substance use disorder benefits and not distinguish in the application of such limit between such medical and surgical benefits and mental health and substance use disorder benefits; or

(ii) not include any annual limit on mental health or substance use disorder benefits that is less than the applicable annual limit.

(C) RULE IN CASE OF DIFFERENT LIMITS. In the case of a plan or coverage that is not described in subparagraph (A) or (B) and that includes no or different annual limits on different categories of medical and surgical benefits, the Secretary shall establish rules under which subparagraph (B) is applied to such plan or coverage with respect to mental health and substance use disorder benefits by substituting for the applicable annual limit an average annual limit that is computed taking into account the weighted average of the annual limits applicable to such categories.

(3) FINANCIAL REQUIREMENTS AND TREATMENT LIMITATIONS.—

(A) IN GENERAL. In the case of a group health plan or a health insurance issuer offering group or individual health insurance coverage that provides both medical and surgical benefits and mental health or substance use disorder benefits, such plan or coverage shall ensure that—

(i) the financial requirements applicable to such mental health or substance use disorder benefits are no more restrictive than the predominant financial requirements applied to substantially all medical and surgical benefits covered by the plan (or coverage), and there are no separate cost sharing requirements that are applicable only with respect to mental health or substance use disorder benefits; and

(ii) the treatment limitations applicable to such mental health or substance use disorder benefits are no more restrictive than the predominant treatment limitations applied to substantially all medical and surgical benefits covered by the plan (or coverage) and there are no separate treatment limitations that are applicable only with respect to mental health or substance use disorder benefits.

(B) DEFINITIONS. In this paragraph:

(i) FINANCIAL REQUIREMENT. The term "financial requirement" includes deductibles, copayments, coinsurance, and out-of-pocket expenses, but excludes an aggregate lifetime limit and an annual limit subject to paragraphs (1) and (2).

(ii) PREDOMINANT. A financial requirement or treatment limit is considered to be predominant if it is the most common or frequent of such type of limit or requirement.

(iii) TREATMENT LIMITATION. The term "treatment limitation" includes limits on the frequency of treatment, number of visits, days of coverage, or other similar limits on the scope or duration of treatment.

(4) AVAILABILITY OF PLAN INFORMATION. The criteria for medical necessity determinations made under the plan with respect to mental health or substance use disorder benefits (or the health insurance coverage offered in connection with the plan with respect to such benefits) shall be made available by the plan administrator (or the health insurance issuer offering such coverage) in accordance with regulations to any current or potential participant, beneficiary, or contracting provider upon request. The reason for any denial under the plan (or coverage) of reimbursement or payment for services with respect to mental health or substance use disorder benefits in the case of any participant or beneficiary shall, on request or as otherwise required, be made available by the plan administrator (or the health insurance issuer offering such coverage) to the participant or beneficiary in accordance with regulations.

(5) OUT-OF-NETWORK PROVIDERS. In the case of a plan or coverage that provides both medical and surgical benefits and mental health or substance use disorder benefits, if the plan or coverage provides coverage for medical or surgical benefits provided by out-of-network providers, the plan or coverage shall

provide coverage for mental health or substance use disorder benefits provided by out-of-network providers in a manner that is consistent with the requirements of this section.

(6) COMPLIANCE PROGRAM GUIDANCE DOCUMENT.—

(A) IN GENERAL. Not later than 12 months after the date of enactment of the Helping Families in Mental Health Crisis Reform Act of 2016, the Secretary, the Secretary of Labor, and the Secretary of the Treasury, in consultation with the Inspector General of the Department of Health and Human Services, the Inspector General of the Department of Labor, and the Inspector General of the Department of the Treasury, shall issue a compliance program guidance document to help improve compliance with this section, section 712 of the Employee Retirement Income Security Act of 1974, and section 9812 of the Internal Revenue Code of 1986, as applicable. In carrying out this paragraph, the Secretaries may take into consideration the 2016 publication of the Department of Health and Human Services and the Department of Labor, entitled "Warning Signs - Plan or Policy Non-Quantitative Treatment Limitations (NQTLs) that Require Additional Analysis to Determine Mental Health Parity Compliance".

(B) EXAMPLES ILLUSTRATING COMPLIANCE AND NONCOMPLIANCE.—

(i) IN GENERAL. The compliance program guidance document required under this paragraph shall provide illustrative, de-identified examples (that do not disclose any protected health information or individually identifiable information) of previous findings of compliance and noncompliance with this section, section 712 of the Employee Retirement Income Security Act of 1974, or section 9812 of the Internal Revenue Code of 1986, as applicable, based on investigations of violations of such sections, including—

(I) examples illustrating requirements for information disclosures and nonquantitative treatment limitations; and

(II) descriptions of the violations uncovered during the course of such investigations.

(ii) NONQUANTITATIVE TREATMENT LIMITATIONS. To the extent that any example described in clause (i) involves a finding of compliance or noncompliance with regard to any requirement for nonquantitative treatment limitations, the example shall provide sufficient detail to fully explain such finding, including a full description of the criteria involved for approving medical and surgical benefits and the criteria involved for approving mental health and substance use disorder benefits.

(iii) ACCESS TO ADDITIONAL INFORMATION REGARDING COMPLIANCE. In developing and issuing the compliance program guidance document required under this paragraph, the Secretaries specified in subparagraph (A)—

(I) shall enter into interagency agreements with the Inspector General of the Department of Health and Human Services, the Inspector General of the Department of Labor, and the Inspector General of the Department of the Treasury to share findings of compliance and noncompliance with this section, section 712 of the Employee Retirement Income Security Act of 1974, or section 9812 of the Internal Revenue Code of 1986, as applicable; and

(II) shall seek to enter into an agreement with a State to share information on findings of compliance and noncompliance with this section, section 712 of the Employee Retirement Income Security Act of 1974, or section 9812 of the Internal Revenue Code of 1986, as applicable.

(C) RECOMMENDATIONS. The compliance program guidance document shall include recommendations to advance compliance with this section, section 712 of the Employee Retirement Income Security Act of 1974, or section 9812 of the Internal Revenue Code of 1986, as applicable, and encourage the development and use of internal controls to monitor adherence to applicable statutes, regulations, and program requirements. Such internal controls may include illustrative examples of nonquantitative treatment limitations on mental health and substance use disorder benefits, which may fail to comply with this section, section 712 of the Employee Retirement Income Security Act of 1974, or section 9812 of the Internal Revenue Code of 1986, as applicable, in relation to nonquantitative treatment limitations on medical and surgical benefits.

(D) UPDATING THE COMPLIANCE PROGRAM GUIDANCE DOCUMENT. The Secretary, the Secretary of Labor, and the Secretary of the Treasury, in consultation with the Inspector General of the Department of Health and Human Services, the Inspector General of the Department of Labor, and the Inspector General of the Department of the Treasury, shall update the compliance program guidance document every 2 years to include illustrative, de-identified examples (that do not disclose any protected health information or individually identifiable information) of previous findings of compliance and noncompliance with this section, section 712 of the Employee Retirement Income Security Act of 1974, or section 9812 of the Internal Revenue Code of 1986, as applicable.

(7) ADDITIONAL GUIDANCE.—

(A) IN GENERAL. Not later than 12 months after the date of enactment of the Helping Families in Mental Health Crisis Reform Act of 2016, the Secretary, the Secretary of Labor, and the Secretary of the Treasury shall issue guidance to group health plans and health insurance issuers offering group or individual health insurance coverage to assist such plans and issuers in satisfying the requirements of this section, section 712 of the Employee Retirement Income Security Act of 1974, or section 9812 of the Internal Revenue Code of 1986, as applicable.

(B) DISCLOSURE.—

(i) GUIDANCE FOR PLANS AND ISSUERS. The guidance issued under this paragraph shall include clarifying information and illustrative examples of methods that group health plans and health insurance issuers offering group or individual health insurance coverage may use for disclosing information to ensure compliance with the requirements under this section, section 712 of the Employee Retirement Income Security Act of 1974, or section 9812 of the Internal Revenue Code of 1986, as applicable, (and any regulations promulgated pursuant to such sections, as applicable).

(ii) DOCUMENTS FOR PARTICIPANTS, BENEFICIARIES, CONTRACTING PROVIDERS, OR AUTHORIZED REPRESENTATIVES. The guidance issued under this paragraph shall include clarifying information and illustrative examples of methods that group health plans and health insurance issuers offering group or individual health insurance coverage may use to provide any participant, beneficiary, contracting provider, or authorized representative, as applicable, with documents containing information that the health plans or issuers are required to disclose to participants, beneficiaries, contracting providers, or authorized representatives to ensure compliance with this section, section 712 of the Employee Retirement Income Security Act of 1974, or section 9812 of the Internal Revenue Code of 1986, as applicable, compliance with any regulation issued pursuant to such respective section, or compliance with any other applicable law or regulation. Such guidance shall include information that is comparative in nature with respect to—

(I) nonquantitative treatment limitations for both medical and surgical benefits and mental health and substance use disorder benefits;

(II) the processes, strategies, evidentiary standards, and other factors used to apply the limitations described in subclause (I); and

(III) the application of the limitations described in subclause (I) to ensure that such limitations are applied in parity with respect to both medical and surgical benefits and mental health and substance use disorder benefits.

(C) NONQUANTITATIVE TREATMENT LIMITATIONS. The guidance issued under this paragraph shall include clarifying information and illustrative examples of methods, processes, strategies, evidentiary standards, and other factors that group health plans and health insurance issuers offering group or individual health insurance coverage may use regarding the development and application of nonquantitative treatment limitations to ensure compliance with this section, section 712 of the Employee Retirement Income Security Act of 1974, or section 9812 of the Internal Revenue Code of 1986, as applicable, (and any regulations promulgated pursuant to such respective section), including—

(i) examples of methods of determining appropriate types of nonquantitative treatment limitations with respect to both medical and surgical benefits and mental health and substance use disorder benefits, including nonquantitative treatment limitations pertaining to—

(I) medical management standards based on medical necessity or appropriateness, or whether a treatment is experimental or investigative;

(II) limitations with respect to prescription drug formulary design; and

(III) use of fail-first or step therapy protocols;

(ii) examples of methods of determining—

(I) network admission standards (such as credentialing); and

(II) factors used in provider reimbursement methodologies (such as service type, geographic market, demand for services, and provider supply, practice size, training, experience, and licensure) as such factors apply to network adequacy;

(iii) examples of sources of information that may serve as evidentiary standards for the purposes of making determinations regarding the development and application of nonquantitative treatment limitations;

(iv) examples of specific factors, and the evidentiary standards used to evaluate such factors, used by such plans or issuers in performing a nonquantitative treatment limitation analysis;

(v) examples of how specific evidentiary standards may be used to determine whether treatments are considered experimental or investigative;

(vi) examples of how specific evidentiary standards may be applied to each service category or classification of benefits;

(vii) examples of methods of reaching appropriate coverage determinations for new mental health or substance use disorder treatments, such as evidence-based early intervention programs for individuals with a serious mental illness and types of medical management techniques;

(viii) examples of methods of reaching appropriate coverage determinations for which there is an indirect relationship between the covered mental health or substance use disorder benefit and a traditional covered medical and surgical benefit, such as residential treatment or hospitalizations involving voluntary or involuntary commitment; and

(ix) additional illustrative examples of methods, processes, strategies, evidentiary standards, and other factors for which the Secretary determines that additional guidance is necessary to improve compliance with this section, section 712 of the Employee Retirement Income Security Act of 1974, or section 9812 of the Internal Revenue Code of 1986, as applicable.

(D) PUBLIC COMMENT. Prior to issuing any final guidance under this paragraph, the Secretary shall provide a public comment period of not less than 60 days during which any member of the public may provide comments on a draft of the guidance.

(b) CONSTRUCTION. Nothing in this section shall be construed—

(1) as requiring a group health plan or a health insurance issuer offering group or individual health insurance coverage to provide any mental health or substance use disorder benefits; or

(2) in the case of a group health plan or a health insurance issuer offering group or individual health insurance coverage that provides mental health or substance use disorder benefits, as affecting the terms and conditions of the plan or coverage relating to such benefits under the plan or coverage, except as provided in subsection (a).

(c) EXEMPTIONS.—

(1) SMALL EMPLOYER EXEMPTION. This section shall not apply to any group health plan and a health insurance issuer offering group or individual health insurance coverage for any plan year of a small employer (as defined in section 2791(e)(4), except that for purposes of this paragraph such term shall include employers with 1 employee in the case of an employer residing in a State that permits small groups to include a single individual).

(2) COST EXEMPTION.—

(A) IN GENERAL. With respect to a group health plan or a health insurance issuer offering group or individual health insurance coverage, if the application of this section to such plan (or coverage) results in an increase for the plan year involved of the actual total costs of coverage with respect to medical and surgical benefits and mental health and substance use disorder benefits under the plan (as determined and certified under subparagraph (C)) by an amount that exceeds the applicable percentage described in subparagraph (B) of the actual total plan costs, the provisions of this section shall not apply to such plan (or coverage) during the following plan year, and such exemption shall apply to the plan (or coverage) for 1 plan year. An employer may elect to continue to apply mental health and substance use disorder parity pursuant to this section with respect to the group health plan (or coverage) involved regardless of any increase in total costs.

(B) APPLICABLE PERCENTAGE. With respect to a plan (or coverage), the applicable percentage described in this subparagraph shall be—

(i) 2 percent in the case of the first plan year in which this section is applied; and

(ii) 1 percent in the case of each subsequent plan year.

(C) DETERMINATIONS BY ACTUARIES. Determinations as to increases in actual costs under a plan (or coverage) for purposes of this section shall be made and certified by a qualified and licensed actuary who is a member in good standing of the American Academy of Actuaries. All such determinations shall be in a written report prepared by the actuary. The report, and all underlying documentation relied upon by the actuary, shall be maintained by the group health plan or health insurance issuer for a period of 6 years following the notification made under subparagraph (E).

(D) 6-MONTH DETERMINATIONS. If a group health plan (or a health insurance issuer offering coverage in connection with a group health plan)[57] seeks an exemption under this paragraph, determinations under subparagraph (A) shall be made after such plan (or coverage) has complied with this section for the first 6 months of the plan year involved.

---

[57] In section 1563 (relating to conforming amendments–originally designated as section 1562 and redesignated as section 1563 by section 10107(b)(1)) of Public Law 111–148, Congress may have intended to replace the parenthetical with a reference to both group and individual health insurance. The Congression intent is unclear.

(E) NOTIFICATION.—

(i) IN GENERAL. A group health plan (or a health insurance issuer offering coverage in connection with a group health plan) [664] that, based upon a certification described under subparagraph (C), qualifies for an exemption under this paragraph, and elects to implement the exemption, shall promptly notify the Secretary, the appropriate State agencies, and participants and beneficiaries in the plan of such election.

(ii) REQUIREMENT. A notification to the Secretary under clause (i) shall include—

(I) a description of the number of covered lives under the plan (or coverage) involved at the time of the notification, and as applicable, at the time of any prior election of the cost-exemption under this paragraph by such plan (or coverage);

(II) for both the plan year upon which a cost exemption is sought and the year prior, a description of the actual total costs of coverage with respect to medical and surgical benefits and mental health and substance use disorder benefits under the plan; and

(III) for both the plan year upon which a cost exemption is sought and the year prior, the actual total costs of coverage with respect to mental health and substance use disorder benefits under the plan.

(iii) CONFIDENTIALITY. A notification to the Secretary under clause (i) shall be confidential. The Secretary shall make available, upon request and on not more than an annual basis, an anonymous itemization of such notifications, that includes—

(I) a breakdown of States by the size and type of employers submitting such notification; and

(II) a summary of the data received under clause (ii).

(F) AUDITS BY APPROPRIATE AGENCIES. To determine compliance with this paragraph, the Secretary may audit the books and records of a group health plan or health insurance issuer relating to an exemption, including any actuarial reports prepared pursuant to subparagraph (C), during the 6 year period following the notification of such exemption under subparagraph (E). A State agency receiving a notification under subparagraph (E) may also conduct such an audit with respect to an exemption covered by such notification.

(d) SEPARATE APPLICATION TO EACH OPTION OFFERED. In the case of a group health plan that offers a participant or beneficiary two or more benefit package options under the plan, the requirements of this section shall be applied separately with respect to each such option.

(e) DEFINITIONS. For purposes of this section—

(1) AGGREGATE LIFETIME LIMIT. The term "aggregate lifetime limit" means, with respect to benefits under a group health plan or health insurance coverage, a dollar limitation on the total amount that may be paid with respect to such benefits under the plan or health insurance coverage with respect to an individual or other coverage unit.

(2) ANNUAL LIMIT. The term "annual limit" means, with respect to benefits under a group health plan or health insurance coverage, a dollar limitation on the total amount of benefits that may be paid with respect to such benefits in a 12-month period under the plan or health insurance coverage with respect to an individual or other coverage unit.

(3) MEDICAL OR SURGICAL BENEFITS. The term "medical or surgical benefits" means benefits with respect to medical or surgical services, as defined under the terms of the plan or coverage (as the case may be), but does not include mental health or substance use disorder benefits.

(4) MENTAL HEALTH BENEFITS. The term "mental health benefits" means benefits with respect to services for mental health conditions, as defined under the terms of the plan and in accordance with applicable Federal and State law.

(5) SUBSTANCE USE DISORDER BENEFITS. The term "substance use disorder benefits" means benefits with respect to services for substance use disorders, as defined under the terms of the plan and in accordance with applicable Federal and State law.

2016 Amendments:

Sec. 13001(a), (b) of the "Helping Families in Mental Health Crisis Reform Act of 2016" (div. B of the "21st Century Cures Act" (P.L. 114–255)), effective Dec. 13, 2016, amended sec. 2726 by making the following changes:

(1) in sec. 2726(a), by adding at the end new par. (6);

(2) in sec. 2726(a), by adding at the end new par. (7).

2010 Amendments:

Sec. 1001(2) of the "Patient Protection and Affordable Care Act" (P.L. 111–148), effective for plan years beginning on or after Sept. 23, 2010, renumbered sec. 2705 as sec. 2726.

Sec. 1563(c)(4) of the "Patient Protection and Affordable Care Act" (P.L. 111–148) (formerly sec. 1562(c)(4) of such Act, renumbered sec. 1563(c)(4) by sec. 10107(b)(1) of such Act), effective Mar. 23, 2010, amended sec. 2726 by making the following changes:

in subsection (a), by substituting "or a health insurance issuer offering group or individual health insurance coverage" for "(or health insurance coverage offered in connection with such a plan)" wherever appearing;

in subsection (b), by substituting "or a health insurance issuer offering group or individual health insurance coverage" for "(or health insurance coverage offered in connection with such a plan)" wherever appearing;

in subsection (c)(1), by substituting "and a health insurance issuer offering group or individual health insurance coverage" for "(and group health insurance coverage offered in connection with a group health plan)";

in subsection (c)(2), by substituting "or a health insurance issuer offering group or individual health insurance coverage" for "(or health insurance coverage offered in connection with such a plan)" wherever appearing.

History:

Sec. 703(a) of the "Mental Health Parity Act of 1996", Title VII of the "Departments of Veterans Affairs and Housing and Urban Development, and Independent Agencies Appropriations Act, 1997" (P.L. 104–204), sec. 701(b) of the "Departments of Labor, Health and Human Services, and Education, and Related Agencies Appropriations Act, 2002" (P.L. 107–116), sec. 2(b) of the "Mental Health Parity Reauthorization Act of 2002" (P.L. 107–313), sec. 2(b) of the "Mental Health Parity Reauthorization Act of 2003" (P.L. 108–197), sec. 302(c) of the "Working Families Tax Relief Act of 2004" (P.L. 108–311), sec. 1(b) of P.L. 109–151, sec. 115(c) of the "Tax Relief and Health Care Act of 2006" (P.L. 109–432), sec. 401(c) of the "Heroes Earnings Assistance and Relief Tax Act of 2008" (P.L. 110–245), sec. 512(b), (g)(2) of the "Paul Wellstone and Pete Domenici Mental Health Parity and Addiction Equity Act of 2008", Subtitle B of Title V of the "Tax Extenders and Alternative Minimum Tax Relief Act of 2008", Division C of P.L. 110–343, secs. 1001(2), 1563(c)(4), formerly sec. 1562(c)(4), renumbered sec. 1563(c)(4), sec. 10107(b)(1) of the "Patient Protection and Affordable Care Act" (P.L. 111–148), sec. 13001(a), (b) of the "Helping Families in Mental Health Crisis Reform Act of 2016" (div. B of the "21st Century Cures Act" (P.L. 114–255)).

Sec. 2727. Required Coverage for Reconstructive Surgery Following Mastectomies

[42 U.S.C. 300gg–27]

The provisions of section 713 of the Employee Retirement Income Security Act of 1974 shall apply to group health plans, and and[58] health insurance issuers offering group or individual health insurance coverage, as if included in this subpart.

2010 Amendments:

Sec. 1001(2) of the "Patient Protection and Affordable Care Act" (P.L. 111–148), effective for plan years beginning on or after Sept. 23, 2010, renumbered sec. 2706 as sec. 2727.

Sec. 1563(c)(5) of the "Patient Protection and Affordable Care Act" (P.L. 111–148) (formerly sec. 1562(c)(5) of such Act, renumbered sec. 1563(c)(5) by sec. 10107(b)(1) of such Act), effective Mar. 23, 2010, amended sec. 2727 by substituting "and health insurance issuers offering group or individual health insurance coverage" for "health insurance issuers providing health insurance coverage in connection with group health plans".

History:

Sec. 903(a) of the "Women's Health and Cancer Rights Act of 1998", Title IX of the ``Departments of Labor, Health and Human Services, and Education, and Related Agencies Appropriations Act, 1999, sec. 101(f) of Division A of the "Omnibus Consolidated and Emergency Supplemental Appropriations Act, 1999" (P.L. 105–277), secs. 1001(2), 1563(c)(5), formerly sec. 1562(c)(5), renumbered sec. 1563(c)(5), sec. 10107(b)(1) of the "Patient Protection and Affordable Care Act" (P.L. 111–148).

Sec. 2728. Coverage of Dependent Students on Medically Necessary Leave of Absence

[42 U.S.C. 300gg–28]

(a) MEDICALLY NECESSARY LEAVE OF ABSENCE. In this section, the term "medically necessary leave of absence" means, with respect to a dependent child described in subsection (b)(2) in connection with a group health plan or individual health insurance coverage, a leave of absence of such child from a postsecondary educational institution (including an institution of higher education as defined in section 102 of the Higher Education Act of 1965), or any other change in enrollment of such child at such an institution, that—

(1) commences while such child is suffering from a serious illness or injury;

(2) is medically necessary; and

(3) causes such child to lose student status for purposes of coverage under the terms of the plan or coverage.

(b) REQUIREMENT TO CONTINUE COVERAGE.—

(1) IN GENERAL. In the case of a dependent child described in paragraph (2), a group health plan, or a health insurance issuer that offers group or individual health insurance coverage, shall not terminate coverage of such child under such plan or health insurance coverage due to a medically necessary leave of absence before the date that is the earlier of—

(A) the date that is 1 year after the first day of the medically necessary leave of absence; or

(B) the date on which such coverage would otherwise terminate under the terms of the plan or health insurance coverage.

(2) DEPENDENT CHILD DESCRIBED. A dependent child described in this paragraph is, with respect to a group health plan or individual health insurance coverage, a beneficiary under the plan who—

(A) is a dependent child, under the terms of the plan or coverage, of a participant or beneficiary under the plan or coverage; and

(B) was enrolled in the plan or coverage, on the basis of being a student at a postsecondary educational institution (as described in subsection (a)), immediately before the first day of the medically necessary leave of absence involved.

(3) CERTIFICATION BY PHYSICIAN. Paragraph (1) shall apply to a group health plan or individual health insurance coverage only if the plan or issuer of the coverage has received written certification by a treating physician of the dependent child which states that the child is suffering from a serious illness or injury and that the leave of absence (or other change of enrollment) described in subsection (a) is medically necessary.

(c) NOTICE. A group health plan, and a health insurance issuer that offers group or individual health insurance coverage, shall include, with any notice regarding a requirement for certification of student status for coverage under the plan or coverage, a description of the terms of this section for continued coverage during medically necessary leaves of absence. Such description shall be in language which is understandable to the typical plan participant.

(d) NO CHANGE IN BENEFITS. A dependent child whose benefits are continued under this section shall be entitled to the same benefits as if (during the medically necessary leave of absence) the child continued to be a covered student at the institution of higher education and was not on a medically necessary leave of absence.

(e) CONTINUED APPLICATION IN CASE OF CHANGED COVERAGE. If—

(1) a dependent child of a participant or beneficiary is in a period of coverage under a group health plan or individual health insurance coverage, pursuant to a medically necessary leave of absence of the child described in subsection (b);

(2) the manner in which the participant or beneficiary is covered under the plan changes, whether through a change in health insurance coverage or health insurance issuer, a change between health insurance coverage and self-insured coverage, or otherwise; and

(3) the coverage as so changed continues to provide coverage of beneficiaries as dependent children,

this section shall apply to coverage of the child under the changed coverage for the remainder of the period of the medically necessary leave of absence of the dependent child under the plan in the same manner as it would have applied if the changed coverage had been the previous coverage.

2010 Amendments:

Sec. 1001(2) of the "Patient Protection and Affordable Care Act" (P.L. 111–148), effective for plan years beginning on or after Sept. 23, 2010, renumbered sec. 2707 as sec. 2728.

Sec. 1563(c)(6) of the "Patient Protection and Affordable Care Act" (P.L. 111–148) (formerly sec. 1562(c)(6) of such Act, renumbered sec. 1563(c)(6) by sec. 10107(b)(1) of such Act), effective Mar. 23, 2010, amended sec. 2728 by making the following changes:

in subsection (a), by substituting "individual health insurance coverage" for "health insurance coverage offered in connection with such plan";

in subsection (b)(1), by substituting "or a health insurance issuer that offers group or individual health insurance coverage" for "or a health insurance issuer that provides health insurance coverage in connection with a group health plan";

in subsection (b)(2), by substituting "individual health insurance coverage" for "health insurance coverage offered in connection with the plan";

---

[58] So in law.

in subsection (b)(3), by substituting "individual health insurance coverage" for "health insurance coverage offered by an issuer in connection with such plan";

in subsection (c), by substituting "health insurance issuer that offers group or individual health insurance coverage" for "health insurance issuer providing health insurance coverage in connection with a group health plan";

in subsection (e)(1), by substituting "individual health insurance coverage" for "health insurance coverage offered in connection with such a plan".

History:

Sec. 2(b)(1) of "Michelle's Law" (P.L. 110–381), secs. 1001(2), 1563(c)(6), formerly sec. 1562(c)(6), renumbered sec. 1563(c)(6), sec. 10107(b)(1) of the "Patient Protection and Affordable Care Act" (P.L. 111–148).

PART B—INDIVIDUAL MARKET RULES

SUBPART 1—PORTABILITY, ACCESS, AND RENEWABILITY REQUIREMENTS

Sec. 2741. Guaranteed Availability of Individual Health Insurance Coverage To Certain Individuals With Prior Group Coverage

[42 U.S.C. 300gg–41]

(a) GUARANTEED AVAILABILITY.—

(1) IN GENERAL. Subject to the succeeding subsections of this section and section 2744, each health insurance issuer that offers health insurance coverage (as defined in section 2791(b)(1)) in the individual market in a State may not, with respect to an eligible individual (as defined in subsection (b)) desiring to enroll in individual health insurance coverage—

(A) decline to offer such coverage to, or deny enrollment of, such individual; or

(B) impose any preexisting condition exclusion (as defined in section 2701(b)(1)(A)[59]) with respect to such coverage.

(2) SUBSTITUTION BY STATE OF ACCEPTABLE ALTERNATIVE MECHANISM. The requirement of paragraph (1) shall not apply to health insurance coverage offered in the individual market in a State in which the State is implementing an acceptable alternative mechanism under section 2744.

(b) ELIGIBLE INDIVIDUAL DEFINED. In this part, the term "eligible individual" means an individual—

(1)(A) for whom, as of the date on which the individual seeks coverage under this section, the aggregate of the periods of creditable coverage (as defined in section 2701(c)[60]) is 18 or more months and (B) whose most recent prior creditable coverage was under a group health plan, governmental plan, or church plan (or health insurance coverage offered in connection with any such plan);

(2) who is not eligible for coverage under (A) a group health plan, (B) part A or part B of title XVIII of the Social Security Act, or (C) a State plan under title XIX of such Act (or any successor program), and does not have other health insurance coverage;

(3) with respect to whom the most recent coverage within the coverage period described in paragraph (1)(A) was not terminated based on a factor described in paragraph (1) or (2) of section 2712(b)[61] (relating to nonpayment of premiums or fraud);

(4) if the individual had been offered the option of continuation coverage under a COBRA continuation provision or under a similar State program, who elected such coverage; and

(5) who, if the individual elected such continuation coverage, has exhausted such continuation coverage under such provision or program.

(c) ALTERNATIVE COVERAGE PERMITTED WHERE NO STATE MECHANISM.—

(1) IN GENERAL. In the case of health insurance coverage offered in the individual market in a State in which the State is not implementing an acceptable alternative mechanism under section 2744, the health insurance issuer may elect to limit the coverage offered under subsection (a) so long as it offers at least two different policy forms of health insurance coverage both of which—

(A) are designed for, made generally available to, and actively marketed to, and enroll both eligible and other individuals by the issuer; and

(B) meet the requirement of paragraph (2) or (3), as elected by the issuer.

For purposes of this subsection, policy forms which have different cost-sharing arrangements or different riders shall be considered to be different policy forms.

(2) CHOICE OF MOST POPULAR POLICY FORMS. The requirement of this paragraph is met, for health insurance coverage policy forms offered by an issuer in the individual market, if the issuer offers the policy forms for individual health insurance coverage with the largest, and next to largest, premium volume of all such policy forms offered by the issuer in the State or applicable marketing or service area (as may be prescribed in regulation) by the issuer in the individual market in the period involved.

(3) CHOICE OF 2 POLICY FORMS WITH REPRESENTATIVE COVERAGE.—

(A) IN GENERAL. The requirement of this paragraph is met, for health insurance coverage policy forms offered by an issuer in the individual market, if the issuer offers a lower-level coverage policy form (as defined in subparagraph (B)) and a higher-level coverage policy form (as defined in subparagraph (C)) each of which includes benefits substantially similar to other individual health insurance coverage offered by the issuer in that State and each of which is covered under a method described in section 2744(c)(3)(A) (relating to risk adjustment, risk spreading, or financial subsidization).

(B) LOWER-LEVEL OF COVERAGE DESCRIBED. A policy form is described in this subparagraph if the actuarial value of the benefits under the coverage is at least 85 percent but not greater than 100 percent of a weighted average (described in subparagraph (D)).

(C) HIGHER-LEVEL OF COVERAGE DESCRIBED. A policy form is described in this subparagraph if—

(i) the actuarial value of the benefits under the coverage is at least 15 percent greater than the actuarial value of the coverage described in subparagraph (B) offered by the issuer in the area involved; and

(ii) the actuarial value of the benefits under the coverage is at least 100 percent but not greater than 120 percent of a weighted average (described in subparagraph (D)).

---

[59] Section 2701 was renumbered section 2704 effective for plan years beginning on or after Jan. 1, 2014.

[60] Section 2701 was renumbered section 2704 effective for plan years beginning on or after Jan. 1, 2014.

[61] Section 2712 was transferred to subsecs. (b)-(e) of section 2703.

(D) WEIGHTED AVERAGE. For purposes of this paragraph, the weighted average described in this subparagraph is the average actuarial value of the benefits provided by all the health insurance coverage issued (as elected by the issuer) either by that issuer or by all issuers in the State in the individual market during the previous year (not including coverage issued under this section), weighted by enrollment for the different coverage.

(4) ELECTION. The issuer elections under this subsection shall apply uniformly to all eligible individuals in the State for that issuer. Such an election shall be effective for policies offered during a period of not shorter than 2 years.

(5) ASSUMPTIONS. For purposes of paragraph (3), the actuarial value of benefits provided under individual health insurance coverage shall be calculated based on a standardized population and a set of standardized utilization and cost factors.

(d) SPECIAL RULES FOR NETWORK PLANS.—

(1) IN GENERAL. In the case of a health insurance issuer that offers health insurance coverage in the individual market through a network plan, the issuer may—

(A) limit the individuals who may be enrolled under such coverage to those who live, reside, or work within the service area for such network plan; and

(B) within the service area of such plan, deny such coverage to such individuals if the issuer has demonstrated, if required, to the applicable State authority that—

(i) it will not have the capacity to deliver services adequately to additional individual enrollees because of its obligations to existing group contract holders and enrollees and individual enrollees, and

(ii) it is applying this paragraph uniformly to individuals without regard to any health status-related factor of such individuals and without regard to whether the individuals are eligible individuals.

(2) 180-DAY SUSPENSION UPON DENIAL OF COVERAGE. An issuer, upon denying health insurance coverage in any service area in accordance with paragraph (1)(B), may not offer coverage in the individual market within such service area for a period of 180 days after such coverage is denied.

(e) APPLICATION OF FINANCIAL CAPACITY LIMITS.—

(1) IN GENERAL. A health insurance issuer may deny health insurance coverage in the individual market to an eligible individual if the issuer has demonstrated, if required, to the applicable State authority that—

(A) it does not have the financial reserves necessary to underwrite additional coverage; and

(B) it is applying this paragraph uniformly to all individuals in the individual market in the State consistent with applicable State law and without regard to any health status-related factor of such individuals and without regard to whether the individuals are eligible individuals.

(2) 180-DAY SUSPENSION UPON DENIAL OF COVERAGE. An issuer upon denying individual health insurance coverage in any service area in accordance with paragraph (1) may not offer such coverage in the individual market within such service area for a period of 180 days after the date such coverage is denied or until the issuer has demonstrated, if required under applicable State law, to the applicable State authority that the issuer has sufficient financial reserves to underwrite additional coverage, whichever is later. A State may provide for the application of this paragraph on a service-area-specific basis.

(e) [62] MARKET REQUIREMENTS.—

(1) IN GENERAL. The provisions of subsection (a) shall not be construed to require that a health insurance issuer offering health insurance coverage only in connection with group health plans or through one or more bona fide associations, or both, offer such health insurance coverage in the individual market.

(2) CONVERSION POLICIES. A health insurance issuer offering health insurance coverage in connection with group health plans under this title shall not be deemed to be a health insurance issuer offering individual health insurance coverage solely because such issuer offers a conversion policy.

(f) [668] CONSTRUCTION. Nothing in this section shall be construed—

(1) to restrict the amount of the premium rates that an issuer may charge an individual for health insurance coverage provided in the individual market under applicable State law; or

(2) to prevent a health insurance issuer offering health insurance coverage in the individual market from establishing premium discounts or rebates or modifying otherwise applicable copayments or deductibles in return for adherence to programs of health promotion and disease prevention.

Sec. 2742. Guaranteed Renewability of Individual Health Insurance Coverage
[42 U.S.C. 300gg-42]

(a) IN GENERAL. Except as provided in this section, a health insurance issuer that provides individual health insurance coverage to an individual shall renew or continue in force such coverage at the option of the individual.

(b) GENERAL EXCEPTIONS. A health insurance issuer may nonrenew or discontinue health insurance coverage of an individual in the individual market based only on one or more of the following:

(1) NONPAYMENT OF PREMIUMS. The individual has failed to pay premiums or contributions in accordance with the terms of the health insurance coverage or the issuer has not received timely premium payments.

(2) FRAUD. The individual has performed an act or practice that constitutes fraud or made an intentional misrepresentation of material fact under the terms of the coverage.

(3) TERMINATION OF PLAN. The issuer is ceasing to offer coverage in the individual market in accordance with subsection (c) and applicable State law.

(4) MOVEMENT OUTSIDE SERVICE AREA. In the case of a health insurance issuer that offers health insurance coverage in the market through a network plan, the individual no longer resides, lives, or works in the service area (or in an area for which the issuer is authorized to do business) but only if such coverage is terminated under this paragraph uniformly without regard to any health status-related factor of covered individuals.

---

[62] So in law. Probably should redesignate the second subsection (e) and subsection (f) as subsections (f) and (g), respectively. See section 111(a) of Pub. L. 104–191 (110 Stat. 1978).

(5) ASSOCIATION MEMBERSHIP CEASES. In the case of health insurance coverage that is made available in the individual market only through one or more bona fide associations, the membership of the individual in the association (on the basis of which the coverage is provided) ceases but only if such coverage is terminated under this paragraph uniformly without regard to any health status-related factor of covered individuals.

(c) REQUIREMENTS FOR UNIFORM TERMINATION OF COVERAGE.—

(1) PARTICULAR TYPE OF COVERAGE NOT OFFERED. In any case in which an issuer decides to discontinue offering a particular type of health insurance coverage offered in the individual market, coverage of such type may be discontinued by the issuer only if—

(A) the issuer provides notice to each covered individual provided coverage of this type in such market of such discontinuation at least 90 days prior to the date of the discontinuation of such coverage;

(B) the issuer offers to each individual in the individual market provided coverage of this type, the option to purchase any other individual health insurance coverage currently being offered by the issuer for individuals in such market; and

(C) in exercising the option to discontinue coverage of this type and in offering the option of coverage under subparagraph (B), the issuer acts uniformly without regard to any health status-related factor of enrolled individuals or individuals who may become eligible for such coverage.

(2) DISCONTINUANCE OF ALL COVERAGE.—

(A) IN GENERAL. Subject to subparagraph (C), in any case in which a health insurance issuer elects to discontinue offering all health insurance coverage in the individual market in a State, health insurance coverage may be discontinued by the issuer only if—

(i) the issuer provides notice to the applicable State authority and to each individual of such discontinuation at least 180 days prior to the date of the expiration of such coverage, and

(ii) all health insurance issued or delivered for issuance in the State in such market are discontinued and coverage under such health insurance coverage in such market is not renewed.

(B) PROHIBITION ON MARKET REENTRY. In the case of a discontinuation under subparagraph (A) in the individual market, the issuer may not provide for the issuance of any health insurance coverage in the market and State involved during the 5-year period beginning on the date of the discontinuation of the last health insurance coverage not so renewed.

(d) EXCEPTION FOR UNIFORM MODIFICATION OF COVERAGE. At the time of coverage renewal, a health insurance issuer may modify the health insurance coverage for a policy form offered to individuals in the individual market so long as such modification is consistent with State law and effective on a uniform basis among all individuals with that policy form.

(e) APPLICATION TO COVERAGE OFFERED ONLY THROUGH ASSOCIATIONS. In applying this section in the case of health insurance coverage that is made available by a health insurance issuer in the individual market to individuals only through one or more associations, a reference to an "individual" is deemed to include a reference to such an association (of which the individual is a member).

Sec. 2743. Certification of Coverage

[42 U.S.C. 300gg–43]

The provisions of section 2701(e)[63] shall apply to health insurance coverage offered by a health insurance issuer in the individual market in the same manner as it applies to health insurance coverage offered by a health insurance issuer in connection with a group health plan in the small or large group market.

Sec. 2744. State Flexibility in Individual Market Reforms

[42 U.S.C. 300gg–44]

(a) WAIVER OF REQUIREMENTS WHERE IMPLEMENTATION OF ACCEPTABLE ALTERNATIVE MECHANISM.—

(1) IN GENERAL. The requirements of section 2741 shall not apply with respect to health insurance coverage offered in the individual market in the State so long as a State is found to be implementing, in accordance with this section and consistent with section 2762(b), an alternative mechanism (in this section referred to as an "acceptable alternative mechanism")—

(A) under which all eligible individuals are provided a choice of health insurance coverage;

(B) under which such coverage does not impose any preexisting condition exclusion with respect to such coverage;

(C) under which such choice of coverage includes at least one policy form of coverage that is comparable to comprehensive health insurance coverage offered in the individual market in such State or that is comparable to a standard option of coverage available under the group or individual health insurance laws of such State; and

(D) in a State which is implementing—

(i) a model act described in subsection (c)(1),

(ii) a qualified high risk pool described in subsection (c)(2), or

(iii) a mechanism described in subsection (c)(3).

(2) PERMISSIBLE FORMS OF MECHANISMS. A private or public individual health insurance mechanism (such as a health insurance coverage pool or programs, mandatory group conversion policies, guaranteed issue of one or more plans of individual health insurance coverage, or open enrollment by one or more health insurance issuers), or combination of such mechanisms, that is designed to provide access to health benefits for individuals in the individual market in the State in accordance with this section may constitute an acceptable alternative mechanism.

(b) APPLICATION OF ACCEPTABLE ALTERNATIVE MECHANISMS.—

(1) PRESUMPTION.—

(A) IN GENERAL. Subject to the succeeding provisions of this subsection, a State is presumed to be implementing an acceptable alternative mechanism in accordance with this section as of July 1, 1997, if, by not later than April 1, 1997, the chief executive officer of a State—

---

[63] Section 2701 was renumbered section 2704 effective for plan years beginning on or after Jan. 1, 2014.

(i) notifies the Secretary that the State has enacted or intends to enact (by not later than January 1, 1998, or July 1, 1998, in the case of a State described in subparagraph (B)(ii)) any necessary legislation to provide for the implementation of a mechanism reasonably designed to be an acceptable alternative mechanism as of January 1, 1998,[64] (or, in the case of a State described in subparagraph (B)(ii), July 1, 1998); and

(ii) provides the Secretary with such information as the Secretary may require to review the mechanism and its implementation (or proposed implementation) under this subsection.

(B) DELAY PERMITTED FOR CERTAIN STATES.—

(i) EFFECT OF DELAY. In the case of a State described in clause (ii) that provides notice under subparagraph (A)(i), for the presumption to continue on and after July 1, 1998, the chief executive officer of the State by April 1, 1998—

(I) must notify the Secretary that the State has enacted any necessary legislation to provide for the implementation of a mechanism reasonably designed to be an acceptable alternative mechanism as of July 1, 1998; and

(II) must provide the Secretary with such information as the Secretary may require to review the mechanism and its implementation (or proposed implementation) under this subsection.

(ii) STATES DESCRIBED. A State described in this clause is a State that has a legislature that does not meet within the 12-month period beginning on the date of enactment of this Act[65].

(C) CONTINUED APPLICATION. In order for a mechanism to continue to be presumed to be an acceptable alternative mechanism, the State shall provide the Secretary every 3 years with information described in subparagraph (A)(ii) or (B)(i)(II) (as the case may be).

(2) NOTICE. If the Secretary finds, after review of information provided under paragraph (1) and in consultation with the chief executive officer of the State and the insurance commissioner or chief insurance regulatory official of the State, that such a mechanism is not an acceptable alternative mechanism or is not (or no longer) being implemented, the Secretary—

(A) shall notify the State of—

(i) such preliminary determination, and

(ii) the consequences under paragraph (3) of a failure to implement such a mechanism; and

(B) shall permit the State a reasonable opportunity in which to modify the mechanism (or to adopt another mechanism) in a manner so that may be an acceptable alternative mechanism or to provide for implementation of such a mechanism.

(3) FINAL DETERMINATION. If, after providing notice and opportunity under paragraph (2), the Secretary finds that the mechanism is not an acceptable alternative mechanism or the State is not implementing such a mechanism, the Secretary shall notify the State that the State is no longer considered to be implementing an acceptable alternative mechanism and that the requirements of section 2741 shall apply to health insurance coverage offered in the individual market in the State, effective as of a date specified in the notice.

(4) LIMITATION ON SECRETARIAL AUTHORITY. The Secretary shall not make a determination under paragraph (2) or (3) on any basis other than the basis that a mechanism is not an acceptable alternative mechanism or is not being implemented.

(5) FUTURE ADOPTION OF MECHANISMS. If a State, after January 1, 1997, submits the notice and information described in paragraph (1), unless the Secretary makes a finding described in paragraph (3) within the 90-day period beginning on the date of submission of the notice and information, the mechanism shall be considered to be an acceptable alternative mechanism for purposes of this section, effective 90 days after the end of such period, subject to the second sentence of paragraph (1).

(c) PROVISION RELATED TO RISK.—

(1) ADOPTION OF NAIC MODELS. The model act referred to in subsection (a)(1)(D)(i) is the Small Employer and Individual Health Insurance Availability Model Act (adopted by the National Association of Insurance Commissioners on June 3, 1996) insofar as it applies to individual health insurance coverage or the Individual Health Insurance Portability Model Act (also adopted by such Association on such date).

(2) QUALIFIED HIGH RISK POOL. For purposes of subsection (a)(1)(D)(ii), a "qualified high risk pool" described in this paragraph is a high risk pool that—

(A) provides to all eligible individuals health insurance coverage (or comparable coverage) that does not impose any preexisting condition exclusion with respect to such coverage for all eligible individuals, and

(B) provides for premium rates and covered benefits for such coverage consistent with standards included in the NAIC Model Health Plan for Uninsurable Individuals Act (as in effect as of the date of the enactment of this title).

(3) OTHER MECHANISMS. For purposes of subsection (a)(1)(D)(iii), a mechanism described in this paragraph—

(A) provides for risk adjustment, risk spreading, or a risk spreading mechanism (among issuers or policies of an issuer) or otherwise provides for some financial subsidization for eligible individuals, including through assistance to participating issuers; or

(B) is a mechanism under which each eligible individual is provided a choice of all individual health insurance coverage otherwise available.

Sec. 2745. Relief for High Risk Pools

[42 U.S.C. 300gg–45]

(a) SEED GRANTS TO STATES. The Secretary shall provide from the funds appropriated under subsection (d)(1)(A) a grant of up to $1,000,000 to each State that has not created a qualified high risk pool as of the date of enactment of the State High Risk Pool Funding Extension Act of 2006 for the State's costs of creation and initial operation of such a pool.

(b) GRANTS FOR OPERATIONAL LOSSES.—

(1) IN GENERAL. In the case of a State that has established a qualified high risk pool that—

(A) restricts premiums charged under the pool to no more than 200 percent of the premium for applicable standard risk rates;

(B) offers a choice of two or more coverage options through the pool; and

---

[64] So in original. The comma probably should not appear.

[65] Probably means the date of enactment of Pub. L. 104–191, which was approved Aug. 21, 1996.

(C) has in effect a mechanism reasonably designed to ensure continued funding of losses incurred by the State in connection with operation of the pool after the end of the last fiscal year for which a grant is provided under this paragraph;

the Secretary shall provide, from the funds appropriated under paragraphs (1)(B)(i) and (2)(A) of subsection (d) and allotted to the State under paragraph (2), a grant for the losses incurred by the State in connection with the operation of the pool.

(2) ALLOTMENT. Subject to paragraph (4), the amounts appropriated under paragraphs (1)(B)(i) and (2)(A) of subsection (d) for a fiscal year shall be allotted and made available to the States (or the entities that operate the high risk pool under applicable State law) that qualify for a grant under paragraph (1) as follows:

(A) An amount equal to 40 percent of such appropriated amount for the fiscal year shall be allotted in equal amounts to each qualifying State that is one of the 50 States or the District of Columbia and that applies for a grant under this subsection.

(B) An amount equal to 30 percent of such appropriated amount for the fiscal year shall be allotted among qualifying States that apply for such a grant so that the amount allotted to such a State bears the same ratio to such appropriated amount as the number of uninsured individuals in the State bears to the total number of uninsured individuals (as determined by the Secretary) in all qualifying States that so apply.

(C) An amount equal to 30 percent of such appropriated amount for the fiscal year shall be allotted among qualifying States that apply for such a grant so that the amount allotted to a State bears the same ratio to such appropriated amount as the number of individuals enrolled in health care coverage through the qualified high risk pool of the State bears to the total number of individuals so enrolled through qualified high risk pools (as determined by the Secretary) in all qualifying States that so apply.

(3) SPECIAL RULE FOR POOLS CHARGING HIGHER PREMIUMS. In the case of a qualified high risk pool of a State which charges premiums that exceed 150 percent of the premium for applicable standard risks, the State shall use at least 50 percent of the amount of the grant provided to the State to carry out this subsection to reduce premiums for enrollees.

(4) LIMITATION FOR TERRITORIES. In no case shall the aggregate amount allotted and made available under paragraph (2) for a fiscal year to States that are not the 50 States or the District of Columbia exceed $1,000,000.

(c) BONUS GRANTS FOR SUPPLEMENTAL CONSUMER BENEFITS.—

(1) IN GENERAL. In the case of a State that is one of the 50 States or the District of Columbia, that has established a qualified high risk pool, and that is receiving a grant under subsection (b)(1), the Secretary shall provide, from the funds appropriated under paragraphs (1)(B)(ii) and (2)(B) of subsection (d) and allotted to the State under paragraph (3), a grant to be used to provide supplemental consumer benefits to enrollees or potential enrollees (or defined subsets of such enrollees or potential enrollees) in qualified high risk pools.

(2) BENEFITS. A State shall use amounts received under a grant under this subsection to provide one or more of the following benefits:

(A) Low-income premium subsidies.

(B) A reduction in premium trends, actual premiums, or other cost-sharing requirements.

(C) An expansion or broadening of the pool of individuals eligible for coverage, such as through eliminating waiting lists, increasing enrollment caps, or providing flexibility in enrollment rules.

(D) Less stringent rules, or additional waiver authority, with respect to coverage of pre-existing conditions.

(E) Increased benefits.

(F) The establishment of disease management programs.

(3) ALLOTMENT; LIMITATION. The Secretary shall allot funds appropriated under paragraphs (1)(B)(ii) and (2)(B) of subsection (d) among States qualifying for a grant under paragraph (1) in a manner specified by the Secretary, but in no case shall the amount so allotted to a State for a fiscal year exceed 10 percent of the funds so appropriated for the fiscal year.

(4) RULE OF CONSTRUCTION. Nothing in this subsection shall be construed to prohibit a State that, on the date of the enactment of the State High Risk Pool Funding Extension Act of 2006, is in the process of implementing a program to provide benefits of the type described in paragraph (2), from being eligible for a grant under this subsection.

(d) FUNDING.—

(1) APPROPRIATION FOR FISCAL YEAR 2006. There are authorized to be appropriated for fiscal year 2006—

(A) $15,000,000 to carry out subsection (a); and

(B) $75,000,000, of which, subject to paragraph (4)—

(i) two-thirds of the amount appropriated shall be made available for allotments under subsection (b)(2); and

(ii) one-third of the amount appropriated shall be made available for allotments under subsection (c)(3).

(2) AUTHORIZATION OF APPROPRIATIONS FOR FISCAL YEARS 2007 THROUGH 2010. There are authorized to be appropriated $75,000,000 for each of fiscal years 2007 through 2010, of which, subject to paragraph (4)—

(A) two-thirds of the amount appropriated for a fiscal year shall be made available for allotments under subsection (b)(2); and

(B) one-third of the amount appropriated for a fiscal year shall be made available for allotments under subsection (c)(3).

(3) AVAILABILITY. Funds appropriated for purposes of carrying out this section for a fiscal year shall remain available for obligation through the end of the following fiscal year.

(4) REALLOTMENT. If, on June 30 of each fiscal year for which funds are appropriated under paragraph (1)(B) or (2), the Secretary determines that all the amounts so appropriated are not allotted or otherwise made available to States, such remaining amounts shall be allotted and made available under subsection (b) among States receiving grants under subsection (b) for the fiscal year based upon the allotment formula specified in such subsection.

(5) NO ENTITLEMENT. Nothing in this section shall be construed as providing a State with an entitlement to a grant under this section.

(e) APPLICATIONS. To be eligible for a grant under this section, a State shall submit to the Secretary an application at such time, in such manner, and containing such information as the Secretary may require.

(f) ANNUAL REPORT. The Secretary shall submit to Congress an annual report on grants provided under this section. Each such report shall include information on the distribution of such grants among States and the use of grant funds by States.

(g) DEFINITIONS. In this section:

(1) QUALIFIED HIGH RISK POOL.—

(A) [66] IN GENERAL. The term "qualified high risk pool" has the meaning given such term in section 2744(c)(2), except that a State may elect to meet the requirement of subparagraph (A) of such section (insofar as it requires the provision of coverage to all eligible individuals) through providing for the enrollment of eligible individuals through an acceptable alternative mechanism (as defined for purposes of section 2744) that includes a high risk pool as a component.

(2) STANDARD RISK RATE. The term "standard risk rate" means a rate—

(A) determined under the State high risk pool by considering the premium rates charged by other health insurers offering health insurance coverage to individuals in the insurance market served;

(B) that is established using reasonable actuarial techniques; and

(C) that reflects anticipated claims experience and expenses for the coverage involved.

(3) STATE. The term "State" means any of the 50 States and the District of Columbia and includes Puerto Rico, the Virgin Islands, Guam, American Samoa, and the Northern Mariana Islands.

SUBPART 2—OTHER REQUIREMENTS

Sec. 2751. Standards Relating To Benefits for Mothers and Newborns

[42 U.S.C. 300gg–51]

(a) IN GENERAL. The provisions of section 2704[67] (other than subsections (d) and (f)) shall apply to health insurance coverage offered by a health insurance issuer in the individual market in the same manner as it applies to health insurance coverage offered by a health insurance issuer in connection with a group health plan in the small or large group market.

(b) NOTICE REQUIREMENT. A health insurance issuer under this part shall comply with the notice requirement under section 711(d) of the Employee Retirement Income Security Act of 1974 with respect to the requirements referred to in subsection (a) as if such section applied to such issuer and such issuer were a group health plan.

(c) PREEMPTION; EXCEPTION FOR HEALTH INSURANCE COVERAGE IN CERTAIN STATES.—

(1) IN GENERAL. The requirements of this section shall not apply with respect to health insurance coverage if there is a State law (as defined in section 2723(d)(1)[68]) for a State that regulates such coverage that is described in any of the following subparagraphs:

(A) Such State law requires such coverage to provide for at least a 48-hour hospital length of stay following a normal vaginal delivery and at least a 96-hour hospital length of stay following a cesarean section.

(B) Such State law requires such coverage to provide for maternity and pediatric care in accordance with guidelines established by the American College of Obstetricians and Gynecologists, the American Academy of Pediatrics, or other established professional medical associations.

(C) Such State law requires, in connection with such coverage for maternity care, that the hospital length of stay for such care is left to the decision of (or required to be made by) the attending provider in consultation with the mother.

(2) CONSTRUCTION. Section 2762(a) shall not be construed as superseding a State law described in paragraph (1).

Sec. 2752. Required Coverage for Reconstructive Surgery Following Mastectomies

[42 U.S.C. 300gg–52]

The provisions of section 2706[69] shall apply to health insurance coverage offered by a health insurance issuer in the individual market in the same manner as they apply to health insurance coverage offered by a health insurance issuer in connection with a group health plan in the small or large group market.

Sec. 2753. [70] Prohibition of Health Discrimination on the Basis of Genetic Information

[42 U.S.C. 300gg–53]

(a) PROHIBITION ON GENETIC INFORMATION AS A CONDITION OF ELIGIBILITY.—

(1) IN GENERAL. A health insurance issuer offering health insurance coverage in the individual market may not establish rules for the eligibility (including continued eligibility) of any individual to enroll in individual health insurance coverage based on genetic information.

(2) RULE OF CONSTRUCTION. Nothing in paragraph (1) or in paragraphs (1) and (2) of subsection (e) shall be construed to preclude a health insurance issuer from establishing rules for eligibility for an individual to enroll in individual health insurance coverage based on the manifestation of a disease or disorder in that individual, or in a family member of such individual where such family member is covered under the policy that covers such individual.

(b) PROHIBITION ON GENETIC INFORMATION IN SETTING PREMIUM RATES.—

(1) IN GENERAL. A health insurance issuer offering health insurance coverage in the individual market shall not adjust premium or contribution amounts for an individual on the basis of genetic information concerning the individual or a family member of the individual.

(2) RULE OF CONSTRUCTION. Nothing in paragraph (1) or in paragraphs (1) and (2) of subsection (e) shall be construed to preclude a health insurance issuer from adjusting premium or contribution amounts for an individual on the basis of a manifestation of a disease or disorder in that individual, or in a family member of such individual where such family member is covered under the policy that covers such individual. In such case, the manifestation of a

---

[66] So in original. No subpar. (B) has been enacted.

[67] Section 2704 was renumbered section 2725.

[68] So in original. Probably should be "2724(d)(1)".

[69] Section 2706 was renumbered section 2727.

[70] Another section designated as section 2753 appears at the end of part B.

disease or disorder in one individual cannot also be used as genetic information about other individuals covered under the policy issued to such individual and to further increase premiums or contribution amounts.

(c) PROHIBITION ON GENETIC INFORMATION AS PREEXISTING CONDITION.—

(1) IN GENERAL. A health insurance issuer offering health insurance coverage in the individual market may not, on the basis of genetic information, impose any preexisting condition exclusion (as defined in section 2701(b)(1)(A)[71]) with respect to such coverage.

(2) RULE OF CONSTRUCTION. Nothing in paragraph (1) or in paragraphs (1) and (2) of subsection (e) shall be construed to preclude a health insurance issuer from imposing any preexisting condition exclusion for an individual with respect to health insurance coverage on the basis of a manifestation of a disease or disorder in that individual.

(d) GENETIC TESTING.—

(1) LIMITATION ON REQUESTING OR REQUIRING GENETIC TESTING. A health insurance issuer offering health insurance coverage in the individual market shall not request or require an individual or a family member of such individual to undergo a genetic test.

(2) RULE OF CONSTRUCTION. Paragraph (1) shall not be construed to limit the authority of a health care professional who is providing health care services to an individual to request that such individual undergo a genetic test.

(3) RULE OF CONSTRUCTION REGARDING PAYMENT.—

(A) IN GENERAL. Nothing in paragraph (1) shall be construed to preclude a health insurance issuer offering health insurance coverage in the individual market from obtaining and using the results of a genetic test in making a determination regarding payment (as such term is defined for the purposes of applying the regulations promulgated by the Secretary under part C of title XI of the Social Security Act and section 264 of the Health Insurance Portability and Accountability Act of 1996, as may be revised from time to time) consistent with subsection[72] (a) and (c).

(B) LIMITATION. For purposes of subparagraph (A), a health insurance issuer offering health insurance coverage in the individual market may request only the minimum amount of information necessary to accomplish the intended purpose.

(4) RESEARCH EXCEPTION. Notwithstanding paragraph (1), a health insurance issuer offering health insurance coverage in the individual market may request, but not require, that an individual or a family member of such individual undergo a genetic test if each of the following conditions is met:

(A) The request is made pursuant to research that complies with part 46 of title 45, Code of Federal Regulations, or equivalent Federal regulations, and any applicable State or local law or regulations for the protection of human subjects in research.

(B) The issuer clearly indicates to each individual, or in the case of a minor child, to the legal guardian of such child, to whom the request is made that—

(i) compliance with the request is voluntary; and

(ii) non-compliance will have no effect on enrollment status or premium or contribution amounts.

(C) No genetic information collected or acquired under this paragraph shall be used for underwriting purposes.

(D) The issuer notifies the Secretary in writing that the issuer is conducting activities pursuant to the exception provided for under this paragraph, including a description of the activities conducted.

(E) The issuer complies with such other conditions as the Secretary may by regulation require for activities conducted under this paragraph.

(e) PROHIBITION ON COLLECTION OF GENETIC INFORMATION.—

(1) IN GENERAL. A health insurance issuer offering health insurance coverage in the individual market shall not request, require, or purchase genetic information for underwriting purposes (as defined in section 2791).

(2) PROHIBITION ON COLLECTION OF GENETIC INFORMATION PRIOR TO ENROLLMENT. A health insurance issuer offering health insurance coverage in the individual market shall not request, require, or purchase genetic information with respect to any individual prior to such individual's enrollment under the plan in connection with such enrollment.

(3) INCIDENTAL COLLECTION. If a health insurance issuer offering health insurance coverage in the individual market obtains genetic information incidental to the requesting, requiring, or purchasing of other information concerning any individual, such request, requirement, or purchase shall not be considered a violation of paragraph (2) if such request, requirement, or purchase is not in violation of paragraph (1).

(f) GENETIC INFORMATION OF A FETUS OR EMBRYO. Any reference in this part to genetic information concerning an individual or family member of an individual shall—

(1) with respect to such an individual or family member of an individual who is a pregnant woman, include genetic information of any fetus carried by such pregnant woman; and

(2) with respect to an individual or family member utilizing an assisted reproductive technology, include genetic information of any embryo legally held by the individual or family member.

SUBPART 3—GENERAL PROVISIONS [674] Section 605(a)(3) of Public Law 104–204 (110 Stat. 2941) adds this subpart designation and heading to part B.

Sec. 2761. Enforcement

[42 U.S.C. 300gg–61]

(a) STATE ENFORCEMENT.—

(1) STATE AUTHORITY. Subject to section 2762, each State may require that health insurance issuers that issue, sell, renew, or offer health insurance coverage in the State in the individual market meet the requirements established under this part with respect to such issuers.

---

[71] Section 2701 was renumbered section 2704 effective for plan years beginning on or after Jan. 1, 2014.

[72] So in original. Probably should be "subsections".

(2) FAILURE TO IMPLEMENT REQUIREMENTS. In the case of a State that fails to substantially enforce the requirements set forth in this part with respect to health insurance issuers in the State, the Secretary shall enforce the requirements of this part under subsection (b) insofar as they relate to the issuance, sale, renewal, and offering of health insurance coverage in the individual market in such State.

(b) SECRETARIAL ENFORCEMENT AUTHORITY. The Secretary shall have the same authority in relation to enforcement of the provisions of this part with respect to issuers of health insurance coverage in the individual market in a State as the Secretary has under section 2722(b)(2),[73] and section 2722(b)(3)[74] with respect to violations of genetic nondiscrimination provisions, in relation to the enforcement of the provisions of part A with respect to issuers of health insurance coverage in the small group market in the State.

Sec. 2762. Preemption and Application

[42 U.S.C. 300gg–62]

(a) IN GENERAL. Subject to subsection (b), nothing in this part (or part C insofar as it applies to this part) shall be construed to prevent a State from establishing, implementing, or continuing in effect standards and requirements unless such standards and requirements prevent the application of a requirement of this part.

(b) RULES OF CONSTRUCTION.—

(1) Nothing in this part (or part C insofar as it applies to this part) shall be construed to affect or modify the provisions of section 514 of the Employee Retirement Income Security Act of 1974 (29 U.S.C. 1144).

(2) Nothing in this part (other than section 2751) shall be construed as requiring health insurance coverage offered in the individual market to provide specific benefits under the terms of such coverage.

(c) APPLICATION OF PART A PROVISIONS.—

(1) IN GENERAL. The provisions of part A shall apply to health insurance issuers providing health insurance coverage in the individual market in a State as provided for in such part.

(2) CLARIFICATION. To the extent that any provision of this part conflicts with a provision of part A with respect to health insurance issuers providing health insurance coverage in the individual market in a State, the provisions of such part A shall apply.

2010 Amendments:

Sec. 1563(c)(15) of the "Patient Protection and Affordable Care Act" (P.L. 111–148) (formerly sec. 1562(c)(15) of such Act, renumbered sec. 1563(c)(15) by sec. 10107(b)(1) of such Act), effective Mar. 23, 2010, amended sec. 2762 by making the following changes:

in the section heading, by inserting "AND APPLICATION" (in bold type) after "PREEMPTION" (in bold type) in section catchline;

by adding at the end new subsection (c).

History:

Sec. 111(a) of the "Health Insurance Portability and Accountability Act of 1996" (P.L. 104–191), secs. 605(a)(2), (b)(3) of the "Newborns' and Mothers' Health Protection Act of 1996", Title VI of the "Departments of Veterans Affairs and Housing and Urban Development, and Independent Agencies Appropriations Act, 1997" (P.L. 104–204), sec. 1563(c)(15), formerly sec. 1562(c)(15), renumbered sec. 1563(c)(15), sec. 10107(b)(1) of the "Patient Protection and Affordable Care Act" (P.L. 111–148).

Sec. 2763. General Exceptions

[42 U.S.C. 300gg–63]

(a) EXCEPTION FOR CERTAIN BENEFITS. The requirements of this part shall not apply to any health insurance coverage in relation to its provision of excepted benefits described in section 2791(c)(1).

(b) EXCEPTION FOR CERTAIN BENEFITS IF CERTAIN CONDITIONS MET. The requirements of this part shall not apply to any health insurance coverage in relation to its provision of excepted benefits described in paragraph (2), (3), or (4) of section 2791(c) if the benefits are provided under a separate policy, certificate, or contract of insurance.

Sec. 2753. Coverage of Dependent Students on Medically Necessary Leave of Absence[75]

[42 U.S.C. 300gg–54]

The provisions of section 2707 shall apply to health insurance coverage offered by a health insurance issuer in the individual market in the same manner as they apply to health insurance coverage offered by a health insurance issuer in connection with a group health plan in the small or large group market.

PART C—DEFINITIONS; MISCELLANEOUS PROVISIONS

Sec. 2791. Definitions

[42 U.S.C. 300gg–91]

(a) GROUP HEALTH PLAN.—

(1) DEFINITION. The term "group health plan" means an employee welfare benefit plan (as defined in section 3(1) of the Employee Retirement Income Security Act of 1974) to the extent that the plan provides medical care (as defined in paragraph (2)) and including items and services paid for as medical care) to employees or their dependents (as defined under the terms of the plan) directly or through insurance, reimbursement, or otherwise. Except for purposes of part C of title XI of the Social Security Act (42 U.S.C. 1320d et seq.), such term shall not include any qualified small employer health reimbursement arrangement (as defined in section 9831(d)(2) of the Internal Revenue Code of 1986).

(2) MEDICAL CARE. The term "medical care" means amounts paid for—

(A) the diagnosis, cure, mitigation, treatment, or prevention of disease, or amounts paid for the purpose of affecting any structure or function of the body,

---

[73] So in original. Probably should be "2723(b)(2)".

[74] So in original. Probably should be "2723(b)(3)".

[75] The placement of section 2753 at the end of subpart 3 is so in law. See amendment made by section 2(b)(2) of Public Law 110–381 122 Stat. 4084). Section 102(b)(1)(A) of Public Law 110–233 redesignated subpart 3 of part B as subpart 2. Also, another section designated as section 2753 was added by section 102(b)(1)(B) of such Public Law (122 Stat. 893).

(B) amounts paid for transportation primarily for and essential to medical care referred to in subparagraph (A), and

(C) amounts paid for insurance covering medical care referred to in subparagraphs (A) and (B).

(3) TREATMENT OF CERTAIN PLANS AS GROUP HEALTH PLAN FOR NOTICE PROVISION. A program under which creditable coverage described in subparagraph (C), (D), (E), or (F) of section 2701(c)(1) is provided shall be treated as a group health plan for purposes of applying section 2701(e).[76]

(b) DEFINITIONS RELATING TO HEALTH INSURANCE.—

(1) HEALTH INSURANCE COVERAGE. The term "health insurance coverage" means benefits consisting of medical care (provided directly, through insurance or reimbursement, or otherwise and including items and services paid for as medical care) under any hospital or medical service policy or certificate, hospital or medical service plan contract, or health maintenance organization contract offered by a health insurance issuer.

(2) HEALTH INSURANCE ISSUER. The term "health insurance issuer" means an insurance company, insurance service, or insurance organization (including a health maintenance organization, as defined in paragraph (3)) which is licensed to engage in the business of insurance in a State and which is subject to State law which regulates insurance (within the meaning of section 514(b)(2) of the Employee Retirement Income Security Act of 1974). Such term does not include a group health plan.

(3) HEALTH MAINTENANCE ORGANIZATION. The term "health maintenance organization" means—

(A) a Federally qualified health maintenance organization (as defined in section 1301(a)),

(B) an organization recognized under State law as a health maintenance organization, or

(C) a similar organization regulated under State law for solvency in the same manner and to the same extent as such a health maintenance organization.

(4) GROUP HEALTH INSURANCE COVERAGE. The term "group health insurance coverage" means, in connection with a group health plan, health insurance coverage offered in connection with such plan.

(5) INDIVIDUAL HEALTH INSURANCE COVERAGE. The term "individual health insurance coverage" means health insurance coverage offered to individuals in the individual market, but does not include short-term limited duration insurance.

(c) EXCEPTED BENEFITS. For purposes of this title, the term "excepted benefits" means benefits under one or more (or any combination thereof) of the following:

(1) BENEFITS NOT SUBJECT TO REQUIREMENTS.—

(A) Coverage only for accident, or disability income insurance, or any combination thereof.

(B) Coverage issued as a supplement to liability insurance.

(C) Liability insurance, including general liability insurance and automobile liability insurance.

(D) Workers' compensation or similar insurance.

(E) Automobile medical payment insurance.

(F) Credit-only insurance.

(G) Coverage for on-site medical clinics.

(H) Other similar insurance coverage, specified in regulations, under which benefits for medical care are secondary or incidental to other insurance benefits.

(2) BENEFITS NOT SUBJECT TO REQUIREMENTS IF OFFERED SEPARATELY.—

(A) Limited scope dental or vision benefits.

(B) Benefits for long-term care, nursing home care, home health care, community-based care, or any combination thereof.

(C) Such other similar, limited benefits as are specified in regulations.

(3) BENEFITS NOT SUBJECT TO REQUIREMENTS IF OFFERED AS INDEPENDENT, NONCOORDINATED BENEFITS.—

(A) Coverage only for a specified disease or illness.

(B) Hospital indemnity or other fixed indemnity insurance.

(4) BENEFITS NOT SUBJECT TO REQUIREMENTS IF OFFERED AS SEPARATE INSURANCE POLICY. Medicare supplemental health insurance (as defined under section 1882(g)(1) of the Social Security Act), coverage supplemental to the coverage provided under chapter 55 of title 10, United States Code, and similar supplemental coverage provided to coverage under a group health plan.

(d) OTHER DEFINITIONS.—

(1) APPLICABLE STATE AUTHORITY. The term "applicable State authority" means, with respect to a health insurance issuer in a State, the State insurance commissioner or official or officials designated by the State to enforce the requirements of this title for the State involved with respect to such issuer.

(2) BENEFICIARY. The term "beneficiary" has the meaning given such term under section 3(8) of the Employee Retirement Income Security Act of 1974.

(3) BONA FIDE ASSOCIATION. The term "bona fide association" means, with respect to health insurance coverage offered in a State, an association which—

(A) has been actively in existence for at least 5 years;

(B) has been formed and maintained in good faith for purposes other than obtaining insurance;

(C) does not condition membership in the association on any health status-related factor relating to an individual (including an employee of an employer or a dependent of an employee);

(D) makes health insurance coverage offered through the association available to all members regardless of any health status-related factor relating to such members (or individuals eligible for coverage through a member);

---

[76] Section 2701 was renumbered section 2704 effective for plan years beginning on or after Jan. 1, 2014.

(E) does not make health insurance coverage offered through the association available other than in connection with a member of the association; and

(F) meets such additional requirements as may be imposed under State law.

(4) COBRA CONTINUATION PROVISION. The term "COBRA continuation provision" means any of the following:

(A) Section 4980B of the Internal Revenue Code of 1986, other than subsection (f)(1) of such section insofar as it relates to pediatric vaccines.

(B) Part 6 of subtitle B of title I of the Employee Retirement Income Security Act of 1974, other than section 609 of such Act.

(C) Title XXII of this Act.

(5) EMPLOYEE. The term "employee" has the meaning given such term under section 3(6) of the Employee Retirement Income Security Act of 1974.

(6) EMPLOYER. The term "employer" has the meaning given such term under section 3(5) of the Employee Retirement Income Security Act of 1974, except that such term shall include only employers of two or more employees.

(7) CHURCH PLAN. The term "church plan" has the meaning given such term under section 3(33) of the Employee Retirement Income Security Act of 1974.

(8) GOVERNMENTAL PLAN.—

(A) The term "governmental plan" has the meaning given such term under section 3(32) of the Employee Retirement Income Security Act of 1974 and any Federal governmental plan.

(B) FEDERAL GOVERNMENTAL PLAN. The term "Federal governmental plan" means a governmental plan established or maintained for its employees by the Government of the United States or by any agency or instrumentality of such Government.

(C) NON-FEDERAL GOVERNMENTAL PLAN. The term "non-Federal governmental plan" means a governmental plan that is not a Federal governmental plan.

(9) HEALTH STATUS-RELATED FACTOR. The term "health status-related factor" means any of the factors described in section 2702(a)(1).[77]

(10) NETWORK PLAN. The term "network plan" means health insurance coverage of a health insurance issuer under which the financing and delivery of medical care (including items and services paid for as medical care) are provided, in whole or in part, through a defined set of providers under contract with the issuer.

(11) PARTICIPANT. The term "participant" has the meaning given such term under section 3(7) of the Employee Retirement Income Security Act of 1974.

(12) PLACED FOR ADOPTION DEFINED. The term "placement", or being "placed", for adoption, in connection with any placement for adoption of a child with any person, means the assumption and retention by such person of a legal obligation for total or partial support of such child in anticipation of adoption of such child. The child's placement with such person terminates upon the termination of such legal obligation.

(13) PLAN SPONSOR. The term "plan sponsor" has the meaning given such term under section 3(16)(B) of the Employee Retirement Income Security Act of 1974.

(14) STATE. The term "State" means each of the several States, the District of Columbia, Puerto Rico, the Virgin Islands, Guam, American Samoa, and the Northern Mariana Islands.

(15) FAMILY MEMBER. The term "family member" means, with respect to any individual—

(A) a dependent (as such term is used for purposes of section 2701(f)(2)[78]) of such individual; and

(B) any other individual who is a first-degree, second-degree, third-degree, or fourth-degree relative of such individual or of an individual described in subparagraph (A).

(16) GENETIC INFORMATION.—

(A) IN GENERAL. The term "genetic information" means, with respect to any individual, information about—

(i) such individual's genetic tests,

(ii) the genetic tests of family members of such individual, and

(iii) the manifestation of a disease or disorder in family members of such individual.

(B) INCLUSION OF GENETIC SERVICES AND PARTICIPATION IN GENETIC RESEARCH. Such term includes, with respect to any individual, any request for, or receipt of, genetic services, or participation in clinical research which includes genetic services, by such individual or any family member of such individual.

(C) EXCLUSIONS. The term "genetic information" shall not include information about the sex or age of any individual.

(17) GENETIC TEST.—

(A) IN GENERAL. The term "genetic test" means an analysis of human DNA, RNA, chromosomes, proteins, or metabolites, that detects genotypes, mutations, or chromosomal changes.

(B) EXCEPTIONS. The term "genetic test" does not mean—

(i) an analysis of proteins or metabolites that does not detect genotypes, mutations, or chromosomal changes; or

(ii) an analysis of proteins or metabolites that is directly related to a manifested disease, disorder, or pathological condition that could reasonably be detected by a health care professional with appropriate training and expertise in the field of medicine involved.

(18) GENETIC SERVICES. The term "genetic services" means—

(A) a genetic test;

---

[77] Section 2702 was transferred to subsecs. (b)-(f) of section 2705.

[78] Section 2701 was renumbered section 2704 effective for plan years beginning on or after Jan. 1, 2014.

(B) genetic counseling (including obtaining, interpreting, or assessing genetic information); or

(C) genetic education.

(19) UNDERWRITING PURPOSES. The term "underwriting purposes" means, with respect to any group health plan, or health insurance coverage offered in connection with a group health plan—

(A) rules for, or determination of, eligibility (including enrollment and continued eligibility) for benefits under the plan or coverage;

(B) the computation of premium or contribution amounts under the plan or coverage;

(C) the application of any pre-existing condition exclusion under the plan or coverage; and

(D) other activities related to the creation, renewal, or replacement of a contract of health insurance or health benefits.

(20) QUALIFIED HEALTH PLAN. The term "qualified health plan" has the meaning given such term in section 1301(a) of the Patient Protection and Affordable Care Act.

(21) EXCHANGE. The term "Exchange" means an American Health Benefit Exchange established under section 1311 of the Patient Protection and Affordable Care Act.

(e) DEFINITIONS RELATING TO MARKETS AND SMALL EM-PLOYERS. For purposes of this title:

(1) INDIVIDUAL MARKET.—

(A) IN GENERAL. The term "individual market" means the market for health insurance coverage offered to individuals other than in connection with a group health plan.

(B) TREATMENT OF VERY SMALL GROUPS.—

(i) IN GENERAL. Subject to clause (ii), such terms[79] includes coverage offered in connection with a group health plan that has fewer than two participants as current employees on the first day of the plan year.

(ii) STATE EXCEPTION. Clause (i) shall not apply in the case of a State that elects to regulate the coverage described in such clause as coverage in the small group market.

(2) LARGE EMPLOYER. The term "large employer" means, in connection with a group health plan with respect to a calendar year and a plan year, an employer who employed an average of at least 51 employees on business days during the preceding calendar year and who employs at least 2 employees on the first day of the plan year.

(3) LARGE GROUP MARKET. The term "large group market" means the health insurance market under which individuals obtain health insurance coverage (directly or through any arrangement) on behalf of themselves (and their dependents) through a group health plan maintained by a large employer.

(4) SMALL EMPLOYER. The term "small employer" means, in connection with a group health plan with respect to a calendar year and a plan year, an employer who employed an average of at least 1 but not more than 50 employees on business days during the preceding calendar year and who employs at least 1 employees[80] on the first day of the plan year.

(5) SMALL GROUP MARKET. The term "small group market" means the health insurance market under which individuals obtain health insurance coverage (directly or through any arrangement) on behalf of themselves (and their dependents) through a group health plan maintained by a small employer.

(6) APPLICATION OF CERTAIN RULES IN DETERMINATION OF EMPLOYER SIZE. For purposes of this subsection—

(A) APPLICATION OF AGGREGATION RULE FOR EMPLOYERS. all[81] persons treated as a single employer under subsection (b), (c), (m), or (o) of section 414 of the Internal Revenue Code of 1986 shall be treated as 1 employer.

(B) EMPLOYERS NOT IN EXISTENCE IN PRECEDING YEAR. In the case of an employer which was not in existence throughout the preceding calendar year, the determination of whether such employer is a small or large employer shall be based on the average number of employees that it is reasonably expected such employer will employ on business days in the current calendar year.

(C) PREDECESSORS. Any reference in this subsection to an employer shall include a reference to any predecessor of such employer.

(7) STATE OPTION TO EXTEND DEFINITION OF SMALL EMPLOYER. Notwithstanding paragraphs (2) and (4), nothing in this section shall prevent a State from applying this subsection by treating as a small employer, with respect to a calendar year and a plan year, an employer who employed an average of at least 1 but not more than 100 employees on business days during the preceding calendar year and who employs at least 1 employee on the first day of the plan year.

2016 Amendments:

Sec. 18001(c)(1) of the "Increasing Choice, Access, and Quality in Health Care for Americans Act" (div. C of the "21st Century Cures Act" (P.L. 114–255)), effective for plan years beginning after Dec. 31, 2016, amended sec. 2791(a)(1) by adding at the end the following: "Except for purposes of part C of title XI of the Social Security Act (42 U.S.C. 1320d et seq.), such term shall not include any qualified small employer health reimbursement arrangement (as defined in section 9831(d)(2) of the Internal Revenue Code of 1986).".

2015 Amendments:

Sec. 2(b) of the "Protecting Affordable Coverage for Employees Act" (P.L. 114–60), effective Oct. 7, 2015, amended sec. 2791 by making the following changes:

(1) in sec. 2791(e)(2), by striking "101" and inserting "51";

(2) in sec. 2791(e)(4), by striking "100" and inserting "50";

(3) sec. 2791(e), by adding at the end new par. (7).

2010 Amendments:

Sec. 1563(b) of the "Patient Protection and Affordable Care Act" (P.L. 111–148) (formerly sec. 1562(b) of such Act, renumbered sec. 1563(b) by sec. 10107(b)(1) of such Act), effective Mar. 23, 2010, amended sec. 2791(d) by adding at the end new paragraphs (20) and (21).

Sec. 1563(c)(16) of the "Patient Protection and Affordable Care Act" (P.L. 111–148) (formerly sec. 1562(c)(16) of such Act, renumbered sec. 1563(c)(16) by sec. 10107(b)(1) of such Act), effective Mar. 23, 2010, amended sec. 2791(e) by making the following changes:

---

[79] So in original. Probably should be "term".
[80] So in original.

[81] So in original. Probably should be capitalized.

in paragraph (2), by substituting "101" for "51";

in paragraph (4), by substituting "at least 1" for "at least 2" wherever appearing and substituting "100" for "50".

History:

Sec. 102(a) of the "Health Insurance Portability and Accountability Act of 1996" (P.L. 104–191), sec. 102(a)(4) of the "Genetic Information Nondis-

crimination Act of 2008" (P.L. 110–233), sec. 1563(b), (c)(16), formerly sec. 1562(b), (c)(16), renumbered sec. 1563(b), (c)(16), sec. 10107(b)(1) of the "Patient Protection and Affordable Care Act" (P.L. 111–148), sec. 2(b) of the "Protecting Affordable Coverage for Employees Act" (P.L. 114–60), sec. 18001(c)(1) of the "Increasing Choice, Access, and Quality in Health Care for Americans Act" (div. C of the "21st Century Cures Act" (P.L. 114–255)).

Sec. 2792. Regulations

[42 U.S.C. 300gg–92]

The Secretary, consistent with section 104 of the Health Care Portability and Accountability Act of 1996, may promulgate such regulations as may be necessary or appropriate to carry out the provisions of this title. The Secretary may promulgate any interim final rules as the Secretary determines are appropriate to carry out this title.

Sec. 2793. Health Insurance Consumer Information

[42 U.S.C. 300gg–93]

(a) IN GENERAL. The Secretary shall award grants to States to enable such States (or the Exchanges operating in such States) to establish, expand, or provide support for—

(1) offices of health insurance consumer assistance; or

(2) health insurance ombudsman programs.

(b) ELIGIBILITY.—

(1) IN GENERAL. To be eligible to receive a grant, a State shall designate an independent office of health insurance consumer assistance, or an ombudsman, that, directly or in coordination with State health insurance regulators and consumer assistance organizations, receives and responds to inquiries and complaints concerning health insurance coverage with respect to Federal health insurance requirements and under State law.

(2) CRITERIA. A State that receives a grant under this section shall comply with criteria established by the Secretary for carrying out activities under such grant.

(c) DUTIES. The office of health insurance consumer assistance or health insurance ombudsman shall—

(1) assist with the filing of complaints and appeals, including filing appeals with the internal appeal or grievance process of the group health plan or health insurance issuer involved and providing information about the external appeal process;

(2) collect, track, and quantify problems and inquiries encountered by consumers;

(3) educate consumers on their rights and responsibilities with respect to group health plans and health insurance coverage;

(4) assist consumers with enrollment in a group health plan or health insurance coverage by providing information, referral, and assistance; and

(5) resolve problems with obtaining premium tax credits under section 36B of the Internal Revenue Code of 1986.

(d) DATA COLLECTION. As a condition of receiving a grant under subsection (a), an office of health insurance consumer assistance or ombudsman program shall be required to collect and report data to the Secretary on the types of problems and inquiries encountered by consumers. The Secretary shall utilize such data to identify areas where more enforcement action is necessary and shall share such information with State insurance regulators, the Secretary of Labor, and the Secretary of the Treasury for use in the enforcement activities of such agencies.

(e) FUNDING.—

(1) INITIAL FUNDING. There is hereby appropriated to the Secretary, out of any funds in the Treasury not otherwise appropriated, $30,000,000 for the first fiscal year for which this section applies to carry out this section. Such amount shall remain available without fiscal year limitation.

(2) AUTHORIZATION FOR SUBSEQUENT YEARS. There is authorized to be appropriated to the Secretary for each fiscal year following the fiscal year described in paragraph (1), such sums as may be necessary to carry out this section.

2010 Amendments:

Sec. 1002 of the "Patient Protection and Affordable Care Act" (P.L. 111–148), effective for fiscal years beginning with fiscal year 2010, and also effective Mar. 23, 2010 (see sec. 1004 of such Act), added new sec. 2793.

History:

Sec. 1002 of the "Patient Protection and Affordable Care Act" (P.L. 111–148).

Sec. 2794. Ensuring That Consumers Get Value for Their Dollars[82]

[42 U.S.C. 300gg–94]

(a) INITIAL PREMIUM REVIEW PROCESS.—

(1) IN GENERAL. The Secretary, in conjunction with States, shall establish a process for the annual review, beginning with the 2010 plan year and subject to subsection (b)(2)(A), of unreasonable increases in premiums for health insurance coverage.

(2) JUSTIFICATION AND DISCLOSURE. The process established under paragraph (1) shall require health insurance issuers to submit to the Secretary and the relevant State a justification for an unreasonable premium increase prior to the implementation of the increase. Such issuers shall prominently post such information on their Internet websites. The Secretary shall ensure the public disclosure of information on such increases and justifications for all health insurance issuers.

---

[82] There are two sections 2794s'. Sections 1003 and 6603 of Public Law 111–148 add new section 2794s' to the end of part C of title XXVII.

(b) CONTINUING PREMIUM REVIEW PROCESS.—

(1) INFORMING SECRETARY OF PREMIUM INCREASE PATTERNS. As a condition of receiving a grant under subsection (c)(1), a State, through its Commissioner of Insurance, shall—

(A) provide the Secretary with information about trends in premium increases in health insurance coverage in premium rating areas in the State; and

(B) make recommendations, as appropriate, to the State Exchange about whether particular health insurance issuers should be excluded from participation in the Exchange based on a pattern or practice of excessive or unjustified premium increases.

(2) MONITORING BY SECRETARY OF PREMIUM INCREASES.—

(A) IN GENERAL. Beginning with plan years beginning in 2014, the Secretary, in conjunction with the States and consistent with the provisions of subsection (a)(2), shall monitor premium increases of health insurance coverage offered through an Exchange and outside of an Exchange.

(B) CONSIDERATION IN OPENING EXCHANGE. In determining under section 1312(f)(2)(B) of the Patient Protection and Affordable Care Act whether to offer qualified health plans in the large group market through an Exchange, the State shall take into account any excess of premium growth outside of the Exchange as compared to the rate of such growth inside the Exchange.

(c) GRANTS IN SUPPORT OF PROCESS.—

(1) PREMIUM REVIEW GRANTS DURING 2010 THROUGH 2014. The Secretary shall carry out a program to award grants to States during the 5-year period beginning with fiscal year 2010 to assist such States in carrying out subsection (a), including—

(A) in reviewing and, if appropriate under State law, approving premium increases for health insurance coverage;

(B) in providing information and recommendations to the Secretary under subsection (b)(1); and

(C) in establishing centers (consistent with subsection (d)) at academic or other nonprofit institutions to collect medical reimbursement information from health insurance issuers, to analyze and organize such information, and to make such information available to such issuers, health care providers, health researchers, health care policy makers, and the general public.

(2) FUNDING.—

(A) IN GENERAL. Out of all funds in the Treasury not otherwise appropriated, there are appropriated to the Secretary $250,000,000, to be available for expenditure for grants under paragraph (1) and subparagraph (B).

(B) FURTHER AVAILABILITY FOR INSURANCE REFORM AND CONSUMER PROTECTION. If the amounts appropriated under subparagraph (A) are not fully obligated under grants under paragraph (1) by the end of fiscal year 2014, any remaining funds shall remain available to the Secretary for grants to States for planning and implementing the insurance reforms and consumer protections under part A.

(C) ALLOCATION. The Secretary shall establish a formula for determining the amount of any grant to a State under this subsection. Under such formula—

(i) the Secretary shall consider the number of plans of health insurance coverage offered in each State and the population of the State; and

(ii) no State qualifying for a grant under paragraph (1) shall receive less than $1,000,000, or more than $5,000,000 for a grant year.

(d) MEDICAL REIMBURSEMENT DATA CENTERS.—

(1) FUNCTIONS. A center established under subsection (c)(1)(C) shall—

(A) develop fee schedules and other database tools that fairly and accurately reflect market rates for medical services and the geographic differences in those rates;

(B) use the best available statistical methods and data processing technology to develop such fee schedules and other database tools;

(C) regularly update such fee schedules and other database tools to reflect changes in charges for medical services;

(D) make health care cost information readily available to the public through an Internet website that allows consumers to understand the amounts that health care providers in their area charge for particular medical services; and

(E) regularly publish information concerning the statistical methodologies used by the center to analyze health charge data and make such data available to researchers and policy makers.

(2) CONFLICTS OF INTEREST. A center established under subsection (c)(1)(C) shall adopt by-laws that ensures that the center (and all members of the governing board of the center) is independent and free from all conflicts of interest. Such by-laws shall ensure that the center is not controlled or influenced by, and does not have any corporate relation to, any individual or entity that may make or receive payments for health care services based on the center's analysis of health care costs.

(3) RULE OF CONSTRUCTION. Nothing in this subsection shall be construed to permit a center established under subsection (c)(1)(C) to compel health insurance issuers to provide data to the center.

2010 Amendments:

Sec. 1003 of the "Patient Protection and Affordable Care Act" (P.L. 111–148), effective for plan years beginning on or after Sept. 23, 2010, added new sec. 2794.

Sec. 10101(i) of the "Patient Protection and Affordable Care Act" (P.L. 111–148), effective Mar. 23, 2010, amended sec. 2794 by making the following changes:

in subsec. (c)(1)(A), by striking "and" at the end;

in subsec. (c)(1)(B), by striking the period and inserting "; and";

in subsection (c)(1), by adding at the end new subparagraph (C);

by adding at the end new subsection (d).

History:

Sec. 1003, sec. 10101(i) of the "Patient Protection and Affordable Care Act" (P.L. 111–148).

Sec. 2794. Uniform Fraud and Abuse Referral Format[83]

[42 U.S.C. 300gg–95]

The Secretary shall request the National Association of Insurance Commissioners to develop a model uniform report form for private health insurance issuer[84] seeking to refer suspected fraud and abuse to State insurance departments or other responsible State agencies for investigation. The Secretary shall request that the National Association of Insurance Commissioners develop recommendations for uniform reporting standards for such referrals.

2010 Amendments:

Sec. 6603 of the "Patient Protection and Affordable Care Act" (P.L. 111–148), effective Mar. 23, 2010, added new sec. 2794.

History:

Sec. 6603 of the "Patient Protection and Affordable Care Act" (P.L. 111–148).

⋙→ *Caution: Note: Effective January 1, 2011, section 8002(a)(1) of Public Law 111–148 provides for an amendment to add at the end of the Public Health Service Act a new title XXXII as follows:*

[TITLE XXXII—COMMUNITY LIVING ASSISTANCE SERVICES AND SUPPORTS (REPEALED)]

[TITLE XXXII—COMMUNITY LIVING ASSISTANCE SERVICES AND SUPPORTS (REPEALED)][1]

---

[83] There are two sections 2794's. Sections 1003 and 6603 of Public Law 111–148 add new section 2794's to the end of part C of title XXVII.

[84] So in original. Probably should be "issuers".

[1] Title XXXII, which consisted of secs. 3201 to 3210 [42 U.S.C. 300ll to 300ll-9], and which related to community living assistance services and supports, was added by sec. 8002(a)(1) of the "Community Living Assistance Services and Supports Act" ("CLASS Act"), Title VIII of the "Patient Protection and Affordable Care Act" (P.L. 111–148), effective Jan. 1, 2011, and was repealed by sec. 642(a) of the "American Taxpayer Relief Act of 2012" (P.L. 112–240), effective Jan. 2, 2013.

Uniformed Services Employment and Reemployment Rights Act of 1994

P.L. 103-353

Signed on October 22, 1994

[¶16,451]

CHAPTERS 43—EMPLOYMENT AND REEMPLOYMENT RIGHTS OF MEMBERS OF THE ARMED FORCES

* * *

[¶16,452]

Act SEC. 4317. Health plans. (a)(1)(A) Subject to paragraphs (2) and (3), in any case in which a person (or the person's dependents) has coverage under a health plan in connection with the person's position of employment, including a group health plan (as defined in section 607(1) of the Employee Retirement Income Security Act of 1974), and such person is absent from such position of employment by reason of service in the uniformed services, the plan shall provide that the person may elect to continue such coverage as provided in this subsection. The maximum period of coverage of a person and the person's dependents under such an election shall be the lesser of —

(i) the 24-month period beginning on the date on which the person's absence begins; or

(ii) the day after the date on which the person fails to apply for or return to a position of employment, as determined under section 4312(e).

(B) A person who elects to continue health-plan coverage under this paragraph may be required to pay not more than 102 percent of the full premium under the plan (determined in the same manner as the applicable premium under section 4980B(f)(4) of the Internal Revenue Code of 1986) associated with such coverage for the employer's other employees, except that in the case of a person who performs service in the uniformed services for less than 31 days, such person may not be required to pay more than the employee share, if any, for such coverage.

(C) In the case of a health plan that is a multiemployer plan, as defined in section 3(37) of the Employee Retirement Income Security Act of 1974, any liability under the plan for employer contributions and benefits arising under this paragraph shall be allocated—

(i) by the plan in such manner as the plan sponsor shall provide; or

(ii) if the sponsor does not provide—

(I) to the last employer employing the person before the period served by the person in the uniformed services, or

(II) if such last employer is no longer functional, to the plan.

(b)(1) Except as provided in paragraph (2), in the case of a person whose coverage under a health plan was terminated by reason of service in the uniformed services, an exclusion or waiting period may not be imposed in connection with the reinstatement of such coverage upon reemployment under this chapter if an exclusion or waiting period would not have been imposed under a health plan had coverage of such person by such plan not been terminated as a result of such service. This paragraph applies to the person who is reemployed and to any individual who is covered by such plan by reason of the reinstatement of the coverage of such person.

(2) Paragraph (1) shall not apply to the coverage of any illness or injury determined by the Secretary of Veterans Affairs to have been incurred in, or aggravated during, performance of service in the uniformed services.

.01 Historical Comment

P.L. 103-353, §2(a), Oct. 13, 1994, 108 Stat. 3161, as amended by
P.L. 108-454, December 10, 2004.

[¶16,453]

Act SEC. 4318. Employee pension benefit plans. (a)(1)(A) Except as provided in subparagraph (B), in the case of a right provided pursuant to an employee pension benefit plan (including those described in sections 3(2) and 3(33) of the Employee Retirement Income Security Act of 1974), or a right provided under any Federal or State law governing pension benefits for governmental employees, the right to pension benefits of a person reemployed under this chapter shall be determined under this section.

(B) In the case of benefits under the Thrift Savings Plan, the rights of a person reemployed under this chapter shall be those rights provided in section 6432b of title 5. The first sentence of this subparagraph shall not be construed to affect any other right or benefit under this chapter.

(2)(A) A person reemployed under this chapter shall be treated as not having incurred a break in service with the employer or employers maintaining the plan by reason of such person's period or periods of service in the uniformed services.

(B) Each period served by a person in the uniformed services shall, upon reemployment under this chapter, be deemed to constitute service with the employer or employers maintaining the plan for the purpose of determining the nonforfeitability of the person's accrued benefits and for purpose of determining the accrual of benefits under the plan.

(b)(1) An employer reemploying a person under this chapter shall, with respect to a period of service described in subsection (a)(2)(B), be liable to an employee pension benefit plan for funding any obligation of the plan to provide the benefits described in subsection (a)(2) and shall allocate the amount of any employer contribution for the person in the same manner and to the same extent the allocation occurs for other employees during the period of service. For purposes of determining the amount of such liability and any obligation of the plan, earnings and forfeitures shall not be included. For purposes of determining the amount of such liability and for purposes of section 515 of the Employee Retirement Income Security Act of 1974 or any similar Federal or State law governing pension benefit for governmental employees, service in the uniformed services that is deemed under subsection (a) to be service with the employer shall be deemed to be service with the employer under the terms of the plan or any applicable collective bargaining agreement. In the case of a multiemployer plan, as defined in section 3(37) of the Employee Retirement Income Security Act of 1974, any liability of the plan described in this paragraph shall be allocated.

(A) by the plan in such manner as the sponsor maintaining the plan provider; or

(B) if the sponsor does not provide—

(i) to the last employer employing the person before the period served by the person in the uniformed services, or

(ii) if such last employer is no longer functional, to the plan.

(2) A person reemployed under this chapter shall be entitled to accrued benefits pursuant to subsection (a) that are contingent on the making of, or derived from, employee contributions or elective deferrals (as defined in section 402(g)(3) of the Internal Revenue Code of 1966) only to the extent the person makes payment to the plan with respect to such contributions or deferrals. No such payment may exceed the amount the person would have been permitted or required to contribute had the person remained continuously employed by the employer throughout the period of service described in

subsection (a)(2)(B). Any payment to the plan described in this paragraph shall be made during the period beginning with the date of reemployment and whose duration is three times the period of the person's service in the uniformed services, not to exceed five years.

(3) For purposes of computing an employer's liability under paragraph (1) or the employee's contributions under paragraph (2), the employee's compensation during the period of service described in subsection (a)(2)(B) shall be computed—

(A) at the rate the employee would have received but for the period of service described in subsection (a)(2)(B), or

(B) in the case that the determination of such rate is not reasonably certain, on the basis of the employee's average rate of compensation during the 12-month period immediately preceding such period (or, if shorter, the period of employment immediately preceding such period).

(C) Any employer who reemploys a person under this chapter and who is an employer contributing to a multiemployer plan, as defined in section 3(37) of the Employee Retirement Income Security Act of 1974, under which benefits are or may be payable to such person by reason of the obligations set forth in this chapter, shall, within 30 days after the date of such reemployment, provide information, in writing, of such reemployment to the administrator of such plan.

.01 Historical Comment
P.L. 103-353, Sec. 8(h) provides:

(h) EMPLOYER PENSION BENEFIT PLANS.—(1) Nothing in this Act shall be construed to relieve an employer of an obligation to provide contributions to a pension plan (or provide pension benefits), or to relieve the obligation of a pension plan to provide pension benefits, which is required by the provisions of chapter 43 of title 38, United States Code, in effect on the day before this Act takes effect.

(2) If any employee pension benefit plan is not in compliance with section 4318 of such title or paragraph (1) of this subsection on the date of enactment of this Act, such plan shall have two years to come into compliance with such section and paragraph.

Final Regulations

Reproduced below are relevant sections of the final Department of Labor regulations that implement the Uniformed Services Employment and Reemployment Rights Act (USERRA). The regulations were published in the *Federal Register* on March 10, 2005 (70 FR 12105).

[¶ 16,453A]

1002.1 PART 1002

SUBPART A——INTRODUCTION TO THE REGULATIONS UNDER THE UNIFORMED SERVICES EMPLOYMENT AND REEMPLOYMENT RIGHTS ACT OF 1994

GENERAL PROVISIONS

§ 1002.1 What is the purpose of this part?

§ 1002.2 Is USERRA a new law?

§ 1002.3 When did USERRA become effective?

§ 1002.4 What is the role of the Secretary of Labor under USERRA?

§ 1002.5 What definitions apply to USERRA?

§ 1002.6 What types of service in the uniformed services are covered by USERRA?

§ 1002.7 How does USERRA relate to other laws, public and private contracts, and employer practices?

SUBPART B——ANTI-DISCRIMINATION AND ANTI-RETALIATION

PROTECTION FROM EMPLOYER DISCRIMINATION AND RETALIATION

§ 1002.18 What status or activity is protected from employer discrimination by USERRA?

§ 1002.19 What activity is protected from employer retaliation by USERRA?

§ 1002.20 Does USERRA protect an individual who does not actually perform service in the uniformed services?

§ 1002.21 Do the Act's prohibitions against discrimination and retaliation apply to all employment positions?

§ 1002.22 Who has the burden of proving discrimination or retaliation in violation of USERRA?

§ 1002.23 What must the individual show to carry the burden of proving that the employer discriminated or retaliated against him or her?

SUBPART C——ELIGIBILITY FOR REEMPLOYMENT

GENERAL ELIGIBILITY REQUIREMENTS FOR REEMPLOYMENT

§ 1002.32 What criteria must the employee meet to be eligible under USERRA for reemployment after service in the uniformed services?

§ 1002.33 Does the employee have to prove that the employer discriminated against him or her in order to be eligible for reemployment?

COVERAGE OF EMPLOYERS AND POSITIONS

§ 1002.34 Which employers are covered by USERRA?

§ 1002.35 Is a successor in interest an employer covered by USERRA?

§ 1002.36 Can an employer be liable as a successor in interest if it was unaware that an employee may claim reemployment rights when the employer acquired the business?

§ 1002.37 Can one employee be employed in one job by more than one employer?

§ 1002.38 Can a hiring hall be an employer?

§ 1002.39 Are States (and their political subdivisions), the District of Columbia, the Commonwealth of Puerto Rico, and United States territories, considered employers?

§ 1002.40 Does USERRA protect against discrimination in initial hiring decisions?

§ 1002.41 Does an employee have rights under USERRA even though he or she holds a temporary, parttime, probationary, or seasonal employment position?

§ 1002.42 What rights does an employee have under USERRA if he or she is on layoff, on strike, or on a leave of absence?

§ 1002.43 Does an individual have rights under USERRA even if he or she is an executive, managerial, or professional employee?

§ 1002.44 Does USERRA cover an independent contractor?

COVERAGE OF SERVICE IN THE UNIFORMED SERVICES

§ 1002.54 Are all military fitness examinations considered "service in the uniformed services?"

§ 1002.55 Is all funeral honors duty considered "service in the uniformed services?"

§ 1002.56 What types of service in the National Disaster Medical System are considered "service in the uniformed services?"

§ 1002.57 Is all service as a member of the National Guard considered "service in the uniformed services?"

§ 1002.58 Is service in the commissioned corps of the Public Health Service considered "service in the uniformed services?"

§ 1002.59 Are there any circumstances in which special categories of persons are considered to perform "service in the uniformed services?"

§ 1002.60 Does USERRA cover an individual attending a military service academy?

§ 1002.61 Does USERRA cover a member of the Reserve Officers Training Corps?

§ 1002.62 Does USERRA cover a member of the Commissioned Corps of the National Oceanic and Atmospheric Administration, the Civil Air Patrol, or the Coast Guard Auxiliary?

ABSENCE FROM A POSITION OF EMPLOYMENT NECESSITATED BY REASON OF SERVICE IN THE UNIFORMED SERVICES

§ 1002.73 Does service in the uniformed services have to be an employee's sole reason for leaving an employment position in order to have USERRA reemployment rights?

§ 1002.74 Must the employee begin service in the uniformed services immediately after leaving his or her employment position in order to have USERRA reemployment rights?

REQUIREMENT OF NOTICE

§ 1002.85 Must the employee give advance notice to the employer of his or her service in the uniformed services?

§ 1002.86 When is the employee excused from giving advance notice of service in the uniformed services?

§ 1002.87 Is the employee required to get permission from his or her employer before leaving to perform service in the uniformed services?

§ 1002.88 Is the employee required to tell his or her civilian employer that he or she intends to seek reemployment after completing uniformed service before the employee leaves to perform service in the uniformed services?

PERIOD OF SERVICE

§ 1002.99 Is there a limit on the total amount of service in the uniformed services that an employee may perform and still retain reemployment rights with the employer?

§ 1002.100 Does the fiveyear service limit include all absences from an employment position that are related to service in the uniformed services?

§ 1002.101 Does the fiveyear service limit include periods of service that the employee performed when he or she worked for a previous employer?

§ 1002.102 Does the fiveyear service limit include periods of service that the employee performed before USERRA was enacted?

§ 1002.103 Are there any types of service in the uniformed services that an employee can perform that do not count against USERRA's fiveyear service limit?

§ 1002.104 Is the employee required to accommodate his or her employer's needs as to the timing, frequency or duration of service?

APPLICATION FOR REEMPLOYMENT

§ 1002.115 Is the employee required to report to or submit a timely application for reemployment to his or her preservice employer upon completing the period of service in the uniformed services?

§ 1002.116 Is the time period for reporting back to an employer extended if the employee is hospitalized for, or convalescing from, an illness or injury incurred in, or aggravated during, the performance of service?

§ 1002.117 Are there any consequences if the employee fails to report for or submit a timely application for reemployment?

§ 1002.118 Is an application for reemployment required to be in any particular form?

§ 1002.119 To whom must the employee submit the application for reemployment?

§ 1002.120 If the employee seeks or obtains employment with an employer other than the pre service employer before the end of the period within which a reemployment application must be filed, will that jeopardize reemployment rights with the preservice employer?

§ 1002.121 Is the employee required to submit documentation to the employer in connection with the application for reemployment?

§ 1002.122 Is the employer required to reemploy the employee if documentation establishing the employee's eligibility does not exist or is not readily available?

§ 1002.123 What documents satisfy the requirement that the employee establish eligibility for reemployment after a period of service of more than thirty days?

CHARACTER OF SERVICE

§ 1002.134 What type of discharge or separation from service is required for an employee to be entitled to reemployment under USERRA?

§ 1002.135 What types of discharge or separation from uniformed service will make the employee ineligible for reemployment under USERRA?

§ 1002.136 Who determines the characterization of service?

§ 1002.137 If the employee receives a disqualifying discharge or release from uniformed service and it is later upgraded, will reemployment rights be restored?

§ 1002.138 If the employee receives a retroactive upgrade in the characterization of service, will that entitle him or her to claim back wages and benefits lost as of the date of separation from service?

EMPLOYER STATUTORY DEFENSES

§ 1002.139 Are there any circumstances in which the preservice employer is excused from its obligation to reemploy the employee following a period of uniformed service? What statutory defenses are available to the employer in an action or proceeding for reemployment benefits?

SUBPART D——RIGHTS, BENEFITS, AND OBLIGATIONS OF PERSONS ABSENT FROM EMPLOYMENT DUE TO SERVICE IN THE UNIFORMED SERVICES

FURLOUGH AND LEAVE OF ABSENCE

§ 1002.149 What is the employee's status with his or her civilian employer while performing service in the uniformed services?

§ 1002.150 Which nonseniority rights and benefits is the employee entitled to during a period of service?

§ 1002.151 If the employer provides full or partial pay to the employee while he or she is on military leave, is the employer required to also provide the nonseniority rights and benefits ordinarily granted to similarly situated employees on furlough or leave of absence?

§ 1002.152 If employment is interrupted by a period of service in the uniformed services, are there any circumstances under which the employee is not entitled to the nonseniority rights and benefits ordinarily granted to similarly situated employees on furlough or leave of absence?

§ 1002.153 If employment is interrupted by a period of service in the uniformed services, is the employee permitted upon request to use accrued vacation, annual or similar leave with pay during the service? Can the employer require the employee to use accrued leave during a period of service?

HEALTH PLAN COVERAGE

§ 1002.163 What types of health plans are covered by USERRA?

§ 1002.164 What health plan coverage must the employer provide for the employee under USERRA?

§ 1002.165 How does the employee elect continuing health plan coverage?

§ 1002.166 How much must the employee pay in order to continue his or her health plan coverage?

§ 1002.167 What actions may a plan administrator take if the employee does not elect or pay for continuing coverage in a timely manner?

§ 1002.168 If the employee's coverage was terminated at the beginning of or during service, does his or her coverage have to be reinstated upon reemployment?

§ 1002.169 Can the employee elect to delay reinstatement of health plan coverage until a date after the date he or she is reemployed?

§ 1002.170 In a multiemployer health plan, how is liability allocated for employer contributions and benefits arising under USERRA's health plan provisions?

§ 1002.171 How does the continuation of health plan coverage apply to a multiemployer plan that provides health plan coverage through a health benefits account system?

SUBPART E——REEMPLOYMENT RIGHTS AND BENEFITS

PROMPT REEMPLOYMENT

§ 1002.180 When is an employee entitled to be reemployed by his or her civilian employer?

§ 1002.181 How is "prompt reemployment" defined?

REEMPLOYMENT POSITION

§ 1002.191 What position is the employee entitled to upon reemployment?

§ 1002.192 How is the specific reemployment position determined?

§ 1002.193 Does the reemployment position include elements such as seniority, status, and rate of pay?

§ 1002.194 Can the application of the escalator principle result in adverse consequences when the employee is reemployed?

§ 1002.195 What other factors can determine the reemployment position?

§ 1002.196 What is the employee's reemployment position if the period of service was less than 91 days?

§ 1002.197 What is the reemployment position if the employee's period of service in the uniformed services was more than 90 days?

§ 1002.198 What efforts must the employer make to help the employee become qualified for the reemployment position?

§ 1002.199 What priority must the employer follow if two or more returning employees are entitled to reemployment in the same position?

SENIORITY RIGHTS AND BENEFITS

§ 1002.210 What seniority rights does an employee have when reemployed following a period of uniformed service?

§ 1002.211 Does USERRA require the employer to use a seniority system?

§ 1002.212 How does a person know whether a particular right or benefit is a senioritybased right or benefit?

§ 1002.213 How can the employee demonstrate a reasonable certainty that he or she would have received the seniority right or benefit if he or she had remained continuously employed during the period of service?

DISABLED EMPLOYEES

§ 1002.225 Is the employee entitled to any specific reemployment benefits if he or she has a disability that was incurred in, or aggravated during, the period of service?

§ 1002.226 If the employee has a disability that was incurred in, or aggravated during, the period of service, what efforts must the employer make to help him or her become qualified for the reemployment position?

RATE OF PAY

§ 1002.236 How is the employee's rate of pay determined when he or she returns from a period of service?

PROTECTION AGAINST DISCHARGE

§ 1002.247 Does USERRA provide the employee with protection against discharge?

§ 1002.248 What constitutes cause for discharge under USERRA?

PENSION PLAN BENEFITS

§ 1002.259 How does USERRA protect an employee's pension benefits?

§ 1002.260 What pension benefit plans are covered under USERRA?

§ 1002.261 Who is responsible for funding any plan obligation to provide the employee with pension benefits?

§ 1002.262 When is the employer required to make the plan contribution that is attributable to the employee's period of uniformed service?

§ 1002.263 Does the employee pay interest when he or she makes up missed contributions or elective deferrals?

§ 1002.264 Is the employee allowed to repay a previous distribution from a pension benefits plan upon being reemployed?

§ 1002.265 If the employee is reemployed with his or her preservice employer, is the employee's pension benefit the same as if he or she had remained continuously employed?

§ 1002.266 What are the obligations of a multiemployer pension benefit plan under USERRA?

§ 1002.267 How is compensation during the period of service calculated in order to determine the employee's pension benefits, if benefits are based on compensation?

SUBPART F——COMPLIANCE ASSISTANCE, ENFORCEMENT AND REMEDIES

COMPLIANCE ASSISTANCE

§ 1002.277 What assistance does the Department of Labor provide to employees and employers concerning employment, reemployment, or other rights and benefits under USERRA?

INVESTIGATION AND REFERRAL

§ 1002.288 How does an individual file a USERRA complaint?

§ 1002.289 How will VETS investigate a USERRA complaint?

§ 1002.290 Does VETS have the authority to order compliance with USERRA?

§ 1002.291 What actions may an individual take if the complaint is not resolved by VETS?

§ 1002.292 What can the Attorney General do about the complaint?

ENFORCEMENT OF RIGHTS AND BENEFITS AGAINST A STATE OR PRIVATE EMPLOYER

§ 1002.303 Is an individual required to file his or her complaint with VETS?

§ 1002.304 If an individual files a complaint with VETS and VETS' efforts do not resolve the complaint, can the individual pursue the claim on his or her own?

§ 1002.305 What court has jurisdiction in an action against a State or private employer?

§ 1002.306 Is a National Guard civilian technician considered a State or Federal employee for purposes of USERRA?

§ 1002.307 What is the proper venue in an action against a State or private employer?

§ 1002.308 Who has legal standing to bring an action under USERRA?

§ 1002.309 Who is a necessary party in an action under USERRA?

§ 1002.310 How are fees and court costs charged or taxed in an action under USERRA?

§ 1002.311 Is there a statute of limitations in an action under USERRA?

§ 1002.312 What remedies may be awarded for a violation of USERRA?

§ 1002.313 Are there special damages provisions that apply to actions initiated in the name of the United States?

§ 1002.314 May a court use its equity powers in an action or proceeding under the Act?

ATHORITY: section 4331(a) of USERRA (Pub. L. 103353, 108 Stat. 3150, 38 U.S.C. 4331(a)).

SUBPART A—INTRODUCTION TO THE REGULATIONS UNDER THE UNIFORMED SERVICES EMPLOYMENT AND REEMPLOYMENT RIGHTS ACT OF 1994

GENERAL PROVISIONS

§ 1002.1 What is the purpose of this part?

This part implements the Uniformed Services Employment and Reemployment Rights Act of 1994 ("USERRA" or "the Act"). 38 U.S.C. 43014334. USERRA is a law that establishes certain rights and benefits for employees, and duties for employers. USERRA affects employment, reemployment, and retention in employment, when employees serve or have served in the uniformed services. There are five subparts to these regulations. Subpart A gives an introduction to the USERRA regulations. Subpart B describes USERRA's antidiscrimination and antiretaliation provisions. Subpart C explains the steps that must be taken by a uniformed service member who wants to return to his or her previous civilian employment. Subpart D describes the rights, benefits, and obligations of persons absent from employment due to service in the uniformed services, including rights and obligations related to health plan coverage. Subpart E describes the rights, benefits, and obligations of the returning veteran or service member. Subpart F explains the role of the Department of Labor in enforcing and giving assistance under USERRA. These regulations implement USERRA as it applies to States, local governments, and private employers. Separate regulations published by the Federal Office of Personnel Management implement USERRA for Federal executive agency employers and employees.

§ 1002.2 Is USERRA a new law?

USERRA is the latest in a series of laws protecting veterans' employment and reemployment rights going back to the Selective Training and Service Act of 1940. USERRA's immediate predecessor was commonly referred to as the Veterans' Reemployment Rights Act (VRRA), which was enacted as section 404 of the Vietnam Era Veterans' Readjustment Assistance Act of 1974. In enacting USERRA, Congress emphasized USERRA's continuity with the VRRA and its intention to clarify and strengthen that law. Congress also emphasized that Federal laws protecting veterans' employment and reemployment rights for the past fifty years had been successful and that the large body of case law that had developed under those statutes remained in full force and effect, to the extent it is consistent with USERRA. USERRA authorized the Department of Labor to publish regulations implementing the Act for State, local government, and private employers. USERRA also authorized the Office of Personnel Management to issue regulations implementing the Act for Federal executive agencies (other than some Federal intelligence agencies). USERRA established a separate program for employees of some Federal intelligence agencies.

§ 1002.3 When did USERRA become effective?

USERRA became law on October 13, 1994. USERRA's reemployment provisions apply to members of the uniformed services seeking civilian reemployment on or after December 12, 1994. USERRA's antidiscrimination and antiretaliation provisions became effective on October 13, 1994.

§ 1002.4 What is the role of the Secretary of Labor under USERRA?

(a) USERRA charges the Secretary of Labor (through the Veterans' Employment and Training Service) with providing assistance to any person with respect to the employment and reemployment rights and benefits to which such person is entitled under the Act. More information about the Secretary's role in providing this assistance is contained in Subpart F.

(b) USERRA also authorizes the Secretary of Labor to issue regulations implementing the Act with respect to States, local governments, and private employers. These regulations are issued under this authority.

(c) The Secretary of Labor delegated authority to the Assistant Secretary for Veterans' Employment and Training for administering the veterans' reemployment rights program by Secretary's Order 183 (February 3, 1983) and for carrying out the functions and authority vested in the Secretary pursuant to USERRA by memorandum of April 22, 2002 (67 FR 31827).

§ 1002.5 What definitions apply to USERRA?

(a) *Attorney General*

means the Attorney General of the United States or any person designated by the Attorney General to carry out a responsibility of the Attorney General under USERRA.

(b) *Benefit, benefit of employment, or rights and benefits*

means any advantage, profit, privilege, gain, status, account, or interest (other than wages or salary for work performed) that accrues to the employee because of an employment contract, employment agreement, or employer policy, plan, or practice. The term includes rights and benefits under a pension plan, health plan, or employee stock ownership plan, insurance coverage and awards, bonuses, severance pay, supplemental unemployment benefits, vacations, and the opportunity to select work hours or the location of employment.

(c) *Employee*

means any person employed by an employer. The term also includes any person who is a citizen, national or permanent resident alien of the United States who is employed in a workplace in a foreign country by an employer that is an entity incorporated or organized in the United States, or that is controlled by an entity organized in the United States. "Employee" includes the former employees of an employer.

(d)(1) *Employer,*

except as provided below in paragraphs (2) and (3), means any person, institution, organization, or other entity that pays salary or wages for work performed, or that has control over employment opportunities, including—

(i) a person, institution, organization, or other entity to whom the employer has delegated the performance of employmentrelated responsibilities, except in the case that such entity has been delegated functions that are purely ministerial in nature, such as maintenance of personnel files or the preparation of forms for submission to a government agency;

(ii) the Federal Government;

(iii) a State;

(iv) any successor in interest to a person, institution, organization, or other entity referred to in this definition; and,

(v) a person, institution, organization, or other entity that has denied initial employment in violation of 38 U.S.C. 4311, USERRA's antidiscrimination and antiretaliation provisions.

(2) In the case of a National Guard technician employed under 32 U.S.C. 709, the term "employer" means the adjutant general of the State in which the technician is employed.

(3) An employee pension benefit plan as described in section 3(2) of the Employee Retirement Income Security Act of 1974 (ERISA)(29 U.S.C. 1002(2)) is considered an employer for an individual that it does not actually employ only with respect to the obligation to provide pension benefits.

(e) *Health plan*

means an insurance policy, insurance contract, medical or hospital service agreement, membership or subscription contract, or other arrangement under which health services for individuals are provided or the expenses of such services are paid.

(f) *National Disaster Medical System (NDMS)*

is an agency within the Federal Emergency Management Agency, Department of Homeland Security, established by the National Disaster Medical System (NDMS) is an agency within the Federal Emergency Management Agency, Department of Homeland Security, established by the Public Health Security and Bioterrorism Preparedness and Response Act of 2002, P.L. 107188 . *The NDMS* provides medicalrelated assistance to respond to the needs of victims of public health emergencies. Participants in the NDMS are volunteers who serve as intermittent Federal employees when activated. For purposes of USERRA coverage only, these persons are treated as members of the uniformed services when they are activated to provide assistance in response to a public health emergency or to be present for a short period of time when there is a risk of a public health emergency, or when they are participating in authorized training. *See* 42 U.S.C. 300hh11(e).

(g) *Notice*

when the employee is required to give advance notice of service, means any written or verbal notification of an obligation or intention to perform service in the uniformed services provided to an employer by the employee who will perform such service, or by the uniformed service in which the service is to be performed.

(h) *Qualified*

with respect to an employment position, means having the ability to perform the essential tasks of the position.

(i) *Reasonable efforts*

in the case of actions required of an employer, means actions, including training provided by an employer that do not place an undue hardship on the employer.

(j) *Secretary*

means the Secretary of Labor or any person designated by the Secretary of Labor to carry out an activity under USERRA and these regulations, unless a different office is expressly indicated in the regulation.

(k) *Seniority*

means longevity in employment together with any benefits of employment that accrue with, or are determined by, longevity in employment.

(l) *Service in the uniformed services*

means the performance of duty on a voluntary or involuntary basis in a uniformed service under competent authority. Service in the uniformed services includes active duty, active and inactive duty for training, National Guard duty under Federal statute, and a period for which a person is absent from a position of employment for an examination to determine the fitness of the person to perform such duty. The term also includes a period for which a person is absent from employment to perform funeral honors duty as authorized by law (10 U.S.C. 12503 or 32 U.S.C. 115). The Public Health Security and Bioterrorism Preparedness and Response Act of 2002, P.L. 107188, provides that service as an intermittent disasterresponse appointee upon activation of the National Disaster Medical System (NDMS) or as a participant in an authorized training program is deemed "service in the uniformed services." 42 U.S.C. 300hh11(e)(3).

(m) *State*

means each of the several States of the United States, the District of Columbia, the Commonwealth of Puerto Rico, Guam, the Virgin Islands, and other territories of the United States (including the agencies and political subdivisions thereof); however, for purposes of enforcement of rights under 38 U.S.C. 4323, a political subdivision of a State is a private employer.

(n) *Undue hardship*

in the case of actions taken by an employer, means an action requiring significant difficulty or expense, when considered in light of—

(1) the nature and cost of the action needed under USERRA and these regulations;

(2) the overall financial resources of the facility or facilities involved in the provision of the action; the number of persons employed at such facility; the effect on expenses and resources, or the impact otherwise of such action upon the operation of the facility;

(3) the overall financial resources of the employer; the overall size of the business of an employer with respect to the number of its employees; the number, type, and location of its facilities; and,

(4) the type of operation or operations of the employer, including the composition, structure, and functions of the work force of such employer; the geographic separateness, administrative, or fiscal relationship of the facility or facilities in question to the employer.

(o) *Uniformed services*

means the Armed Forces; the Army National Guard and the Air National Guard when engaged in active duty for training, inactive duty training, or fulltime National Guard duty; the commissioned corps of the Public Health Service; and any other category of persons designated by the President in time of war or national emergency. For purposes of USERRA coverage only, service as an intermittent disaster response appointee of the NDMS when federally activated or attending authorized training in support of their Federal mission is deemed "service in the uniformed services," although such appointee is not a member of the "uniformed services" as defined by USERRA.

§ 1002.6 What types of service in the uniformed services are covered by USERRA?

USERRA's definition of "service in the uniformed services" covers all categories of military training and service, including duty performed on a voluntary or involuntary basis, in time of peace or war. Although most often understood as applying to National Guard and reserve military personnel, USERRA also applies to persons serving in the active components of the Armed Forces. Certain types of service specified in 42 U.S.C. 300hh11 by members of the National Disaster Medical System are covered by USERRA.

§ 1002.7 How does USERRA relate to other laws, public and private contracts, and employer practices?

(a) USERRA establishes a floor, not a ceiling, for the employment and reemployment rights and benefits of those it protects. In other words, an employer may provide greater rights and benefits than USERRA requires, but no employer can refuse to provide any right or benefit guaranteed by USERRA.

(b) USERRA supersedes any State law (including any local law or ordinance), contract, agreement, policy, plan, practice, or other matter that reduces, limits, or eliminates in any manner any right or benefit provided by USERRA, including the establishment of additional prerequisites to the exercise of any USERRA right or the receipt of any USERRA benefit. For example, an employment contract that determines seniority based only on actual days of work in the place of employment would be superseded by USERRA, which requires that seniority credit be given for periods of absence from work due to service in the uniformed services.

(c) USERRA does not supersede, nullify or diminish any Federal or State law (including any local law or ordinance), contract, agreement, policy, plan, practice, or other matter that establishes an employment right or benefit that is more beneficial than, or is in addition to, a right or benefit provided under the Act. For example, although USERRA does not require an employer to pay an employee for time away from work performing service, an employer policy, plan, or practice that provides such a benefit is permissible under USERRA.

(d) If an employer provides a benefit that exceeds USERRA's requirements in one area, it cannot reduce or limit other rights or benefits provided by USERRA. For example, even though USERRA does not require it, an employer may provide a fixed number of days of paid military leave per year to employees who are members of the National Guard or Reserve. The fact that it provides such a benefit, however, does not permit an employer to refuse to provide an unpaid leave of absence to an employee to perform service in the uniformed services in excess of the number of days of paid military leave.

SUBPART B—ANTI-DISCRIMINATION AND ANTI-RETALIATION

PROTECTION FROM EMPLOYER DISCRIMINATION AND RETALIATION

§ 1002.18 What status or activity is protected from employer discrimination by USERRA?

An employer must not deny initial employment, reemployment, retention in employment, promotion, or any benefit of employment to an individual on the basis of his or her membership, application for membership, performance of service, application for service, or obligation for service in the uniformed services.

§ 1002.19 What activity is protected from employer retaliation by USERRA?

An employer must not retaliate against an individual by taking any adverse employment action against him or her because the individual has taken an action to enforce a protection afforded any person under USERRA; testified or otherwise made a statement in or in connection with a proceeding under USERRA; assisted or participated in a USERRA investigation: or, exercised a right provided for by USERRA.

§ 1002.20 Does USERRA protect an individual who does not actually perform service in the uniformed services?

Yes. Employers are prohibited from taking actions against an individual for any of the activities protected by the Act, whether or not he or she has performed service in the uniformed services.

§ 1002.21 Do the Act's prohibitions against discrimination and retaliation apply to all employment positions?

The prohibitions against discrimination and retaliation apply to all covered employers (including hiring halls and potential employers, see sections 1002.36 and .38) and employment positions, including those that are for a brief, nonrecurrent period, and for which there is no reasonable expectation that the employment position will continue indefinitely or for a significant period. However, USERRA's reemployment rights and benefits do not apply to such brief, nonrecurrent positions of employment.

§ 1002.22 Who has the burden of proving discrimination or retaliation in violation of USERRA?

The individual has the burden of proving that a status or activity protected by USERRA was one of the reasons that the employer took action against him or her, in order to establish that the action was discrimination or retaliation in violation of USERRA. If the individual succeeds in proving that the status or activity protected by USERRA was one of the reasons the employer took action against him or her, the employer has the burden to prove the affirmative defense that it would have taken the action anyway.

§ 1002.23 What must the individual show to carry the burden of proving that the employer discriminated or retaliated against him or her?

(a) In order to prove that the employer discriminated or retaliated against the individual, he or she must first show that the employer's action was motivated by one or more of the following:

(1) membership or application for membership in a uniformed service;

(2) performance of service, application for service, or obligation for service in a uniformed service;

(3) action taken to enforce a protection afforded any person under USERRA;

(4) testimony or statement made in or in connection with a USERRA proceeding;

(5) assistance or participation in a USERRA investigation; or,

(6) exercise of a right provided for by USERRA.

(b) If the individual proves that the employer's action was based on one of the prohibited motives listed in paragraph (a) of this section, the employer has the burden to prove the affirmative defense that the action would have been taken anyway absent the USERRAprotected status or activity.

SUBPART C—ELIGIBILITY FOR REEMPLOYMENT

GENERAL ELIGIBILITY REQUIREMENTS FOR REEMPLOYMENT

§ 1002.32 What criteria must the employee meet to be eligible under USERRA for reemployment after service in the uniformed services?

(a) In general, if the employee has been absent from a position of civilian employment by reason of service in the uniformed services, he or she will be eligible for reemployment under USERRA by meeting the following criteria:

(1) the employer had advance notice of the employee's service;

(2) the employee has five years or less of cumulative service in the uniformed services in his or her employment relationship with a particular employer;

(3) the employee timely returns to work or applies for reemployment; and,

(4) the employee has not been separated from service with a disqualifying discharge or under other than honorable conditions.

(b) These general eligibility requirements have important qualifications and exceptions, which are described in detail in §§ 1002.73 through 1002.138. If the employee meets these eligibility criteria, then he or she is eligible for reemployment unless the employer establishes one of the defenses described in § 1002.139. The employment position to which the employee is entitled is described in §§ 1002.191through 1002.199.

§ 1002.33 Does the employee have to prove that the employer discriminated against him or her in order to be eligible for reemployment?

No. The employee is not required to prove that the employer discriminated against him or her because of the employee's uniformed service in order to be eligible for reemployment.

COVERAGE OF EMPLOYERS AND POSITIONS

§ 1002.34 Which employers are covered by USERRA?

(a) USERRA applies to all public and private employers in the United States, regardless of size. For example, an employer with only one employee is covered for purposes of the Act.

(b) USERRA applies to foreign employers doing business in the United States. A foreign employer that has a physical location or branch in the United States (including U.S. territories and possessions) must comply with USERRA for any of its employees who are employed in the United States.

(c) An American company operating either directly or through an entity under its control in a foreign country must also comply with USERRA for all its foreign operations, unless compliance would violate the law of the foreign country in which the workplace is located.

§ 1002.35 Is a successor in interest an employer covered by USERRA?

USERRA's definition of "employer" includes a successor in interest. In general, an employer is a successor in interest where there is a substantial continuity in operations, facilities, and workforce from the former employer. The determination whether an employer is a successor in interest must be made on a casebycase basis using a multifactor test that considers the following:

(a) whether there has been a substantial continuity of business operations from the former to the current employer;

(b) whether the current employer uses the same or similar facilities, machinery, equipment, and methods of production;

(c) whether there has been a substantial continuity of employees;

(d) whether there is a similarity of jobs and working conditions;

(e) whether there is a similarity of supervisors or managers; and,

(f) whether there is a similarity of products or services.

§ 1002.36 Can an employer be liable as a successor in interest if it was unaware that an employee may claim reemployment rights when the employer acquired the business?

Yes. In order to be a successor in interest, it is not necessary for an employer to have notice of a potential reemployment claim at the time of merger, acquisition, or other form of succession.

§ 1002.37 Can one employee be employed in one job by more than one employer?

Yes. Under USERRA, an employer includes not only the person or entity that pays an employee's salary or wages, but also includes a person or entity that has control over his or her employment opportunities, including a person or entity to whom an employer has delegated the performance of employmentrelated responsibilities. For example, if the employee is a security guard hired by a security company and he or she is assigned to a work site, the employee may report both to the security company and to the site owner. In such an instance, both employers share responsibility for compliance with USERRA. If the security company declines to assign the employee to a job because of a uniformed service obligation (for example, National Guard duties), then the security company could be in violation of the reemployment requirements and the antidiscrimination provisions of USERRA. Similarly, if the employer at the work site causes the employee's removal from the job position because of his or her uniformed service obligations, then the work site employer could be in violation of the reemployment requirements and the antidiscrimination provisions of USERRA.

§ 1002.38 Can a hiring hall be an employer?

Yes. In certain occupations (for example, longshoreman, stagehand, construction worker), the employee may frequently work for many different employers. A hiring hall operated by a union or an employer association typically assigns the employee to the jobs. In these industries, it may not be unusual for the employee to work his or her entire career in a series of shortterm job assignments. The definition of "employer" includes a person, institution, organization, or other entity to which the employer has delegated the performance of employmentrelated responsibilities. A hiring hall therefore is considered the employee's employer if the hiring and job assignment functions have been delegated by an employer to the hiring hall. As the employer, a hiring hall has reemployment responsibilities to its employees. USERRA's antidiscrimination and antiretaliation provisions also apply to the hiring hall.

§ 1002.39 Are States (and their political subdivisions), the District of Columbia, the Commonwealth of Puerto Rico, and United States territories, considered employers?

Yes. States and their political subdivisions, such as counties, parishes, cities, towns, villages, and school districts, are considered employers under USERRA. The District of Columbia, the Commonwealth of Puerto Rico, Guam, the Virgin Islands, and territories of the United States, are also considered employers under the Act.

§ 1002.40 Does USERRA protect against discrimination in initial hiring decisions?

Yes. The Act's definition of employer includes a person, institution, organization, or other entity that has denied initial employment to an individual in violation of USERRA's anti discrimination provisions. An employer need not actually employ an individual to be his or her "employer" under the Act, if it has denied initial employment on the basis of the individual's membership, application for membership, performance of service, application for service, or obligation for service in the uniformed services. Similarly, the employer would be liable if it denied initial employment on the basis of the individual's action taken to enforce a protection afforded to any person under USERRA, his or her testimony or statement in connection with any USERRA proceeding, assistance or other participation in a USERRA investigation, or the exercise of any other right provided by the Act. For example, if the individual has been denied initial employment because of his or her obligations as a member of the National Guard or Reserves, the company or entity denying employment is an employer for purposes of USERRA. Similarly, if an entity withdraws an offer of employment because the individual is called upon to fulfill an obligation in the uniformed services, the entity withdrawing the employment offer is an employer for purposes of USERRA.

§ 1002.41 Does an employee have rights under USERRA even though he or she holds a temporary, parttime, probationary, or seasonal employment position?

USERRA rights are not diminished because an employee holds a temporary, parttime, probationary, or seasonal employment position. However, an employer is not required to reemploy an employee if the employment he or she left to serve in the uniformed services was for a brief, nonrecurrent period and there is no reasonable expectation that the employment would have continued indefinitely or for a significant period. The employer bears the burden of proving this affirmative defense.

§ 1002.42 What rights does an employee have under USERRA if he or she is on layoff, on strike, or on a leave of absence?

(a) If an employee is laid off with recall rights, on strike, or on a leave of absence, he or she is an employee for purposes of USERRA. If the employee is on layoff and begins service in the uniformed services, or is laid off while performing service, he or she may be entitled to reemployment on return if the employer would have recalled the employee to employment during the period of service. Similar principles apply if the employee is on strike or on a leave of absence from work when he or she begins a period of service in the uniformed services.

(b) If the employee is sent a recall notice during a period of service in the uniformed services and cannot resume the position of employment because of the service, he or she still remains an employee for purposes of the Act. Therefore, if the employee is otherwise eligible, he or she is entitled to reemployment following the conclusion of the period of service even if he or she did not respond to the recall notice.

(c) If the employee is laid off before or during service in the uniformed services, and the employer would not have recalled him or her during that period of service, the employee is not entitled to reemployment following the period of service simply because he or she is a covered employee. Reemployment rights under USERRA cannot put the employee in a better position than if he or she had remained in the civilian employment position.

§ 1002.43 Does an individual have rights under USERRA even if he or she is an executive, managerial, or professional employee?

Yes. USERRA applies to all employees. There is no exclusion for executive, managerial, or professional employees.

§ 1002.44 Does USERRA cover an independent contractor?

(a) No. USERRA does not provide protections for an independent contractor.

(b) In deciding whether an individual is an independent contractor, the following factors need to be considered:

(1) the extent of the employer's right to control the manner in which the individual's work is to be performed;

(2) the opportunity for profit or loss that depends upon the individual's managerial skill;

(3) any investment in equipment or materials required for the individual's tasks, or his or her employment of helpers;

(4) whether the service the individual performs requires a special skill;

(5) the degree of permanence of the individual's working relationship; and,

(6) whether the service the individual performs is an integral part of the employer's business.

(c) No single one of these factors is controlling, but all are relevant to determining whether an individual is an employee or an independent contractor.

COVERAGE OF SERVICE IN THE UNIFORMED SERVICES

§ 1002.54 Are all military fitness examinations considered "service in the uniformed services?"

Yes. USERRA's definition of "service in the uniformed services" includes a period for which an employee is absent from a position of employment for the purpose of an examination to determine his or her fitness to perform duty in the uniformed services. Military fitness examinations can address more than physical or medical fitness, and include evaluations for mental, educational, and other types of fitness. Any examination to determine an employee's fitness for service is covered, whether it is an initial or recurring examination. For example, a periodic medical examination required of a Reserve component member to determine fitness for continued service is covered.

§ 1002.55 Is all funeral honors duty considered "service in the uniformed services?"

(a) USERRA's definition of "service in the uniformed services" includes a period for which an employee is absent from employment for the purpose of performing authorized funeral honors duty under 10 U.S.C. 12503 (members of Reserve ordered to perform funeral honors duty) or 32 U.S.C. 115 (Member of Air or Army National Guard ordered to perform funeral honors duty).

(b) Funeral honors duty performed by persons who are not members of the uniformed services, such as members of veterans' service organizations, is not "service in the uniformed services."

§ 1002.56 What types of service in the National Disaster Medical System are considered "service in the uniformed services?"

Under a provision of the Public Health Security and Bioterrorism Preparedness and Response Act of 2002, 42 U.S.C. 300hh 11(e)(3), "service in the uniformed services" includes service performed as an intermittent disasterresponse appointee upon activation of the National Disaster Medical System or participation in an authorized training program, even if the individual is not a member of the uniformed services.

§ 1002.57 Is all service as a member of the National Guard considered "service in the uniformed services?"

The National Guard has a dual status. It is a Reserve component of the Army, or, in the case of the Air National Guard, of the Air Force. Simultaneously, it is a State military force subject to callup by the State Governor for duty not subject to Federal control, such as emergency duty in cases of floods or riots. National Guard members may perform service under either Federal or State authority, but only Federal National Guard service is covered by USERRA.

(a) National Guard service under Federal authority is protected by USERRA. Service under Federal authority includes active duty performed under Title 10 of the United States Code. Service under Federal authority also includes duty under Title 32 of the United States Code, such as active duty for training, inactive duty training, or fulltime National Guard duty.

(b) National Guard service under authority of State law is not protected by USERRA. However, many States have laws protecting the civilian job rights of National Guard members who serve under State orders. Enforcement of those State laws is not covered by USERRA or these regulations.

§ 1002.58 Is service in the commissioned corps of the Public Health Service considered "service in the uniformed services?"

Yes. Service in the commissioned corps of the Public Health Service (PHS) is "service in the uniformed services" under USERRA.

§ 1002.59 Are there any circumstances in which special categories of persons are considered to perform "service in the uniformed services?"

Yes. In time of war or national emergency the President has authority to designate any category of persons as a "uniformed service" for purposes of USERRA. If the President exercises this authority, service as a member of that category of persons would be "service in the uniformed services" under USERRA.

§ 1002.60 Does USERRA cover an individual attending a military service academy?

Yes. Attending a military service academy is considered uniformed service for purposes of USERRA. There are four service academies: The United States Military Academy (West Point, New York), the United States Naval Academy (Annapolis, Maryland), the United States Air Force Academy (Colorado Springs, Colorado), and the United States Coast Guard Academy (New London, Connecticut).

§ 1002.61 Does USERRA cover a member of the Reserve Officers Training Corps?

Yes, under certain conditions.

(a) Membership in the Reserve Officers Training Corps (ROTC) or the Junior ROTC is not "service in the uniformed services." However, some Reserve and National Guard enlisted members use a college ROTC program as a means of qualifying for commissioned officer status. National Guard and Reserve members in an ROTC program may at times, while participating in that program, be receiving active duty and inactive duty training service credit with their unit. In these cases, participating in ROTC training sessions is considered "service in the uniformed services," and qualifies a person for protection under USERRA's reemployment and anti discrimination provisions.

(b) Typically, an individual in a College ROTC program enters into an agreement with a particular military service that obligates such individual to either complete the ROTC program and accept a commission or, in case he or she does not successfully complete the ROTC program, to serve as an enlisted member. Although an individual does not qualify for reemployment protection, except as specified in (a) above, he or she is protected under USERRA's antidiscrimination provisions because, as a result of the agreement, he or she has applied to become a member of the uniformed service and has incurred an obligation to perform future service.

§ 1002.62 Does USERRA cover a member of the Commissioned Corps of the National Oceanic and Atmospheric Administration, the Civil Air Patrol, or the Coast Guard Auxiliary?

No. Although the Commissioned Corps of the National Oceanic and Atmospheric Administration (NOAA) is a "uniformed service" for some purposes, it is not included in USERRA's definition of this term. Service in the Civil Air Patrol and the Coast Guard Auxiliary similarly is not considered "service in the uniformed services" for purposes of USERRA. Consequently, service performed in the Commissioned Corps of the National Oceanic and Atmospheric Administration (NOAA), the Civil Air Patrol, and the Coast Guard Auxiliary is not protected by USERRA.

ABSENCE FROM A POSITION OF EMPLOYMENT NECESSITATED BY REASON OF SERVICE IN THE UNIFORMED SERVICES

§ 1002.73 Does service in the uniformed services have to be an employee's sole reason for leaving an employment position in order to have USERRA reemployment rights?

No. If absence from a position of employment is necessitated by service in the uniformed services, and the employee otherwise meets the Act's eligibility requirements, he or she has reemployment rights under USERRA, even if the employee uses the absence for other purposes as well. An employee is not required to leave the employment position for the sole purpose of performing service in the uniformed services. For example, if the employee is required to report to an out of State location for military training and he or she spends offduty time during that assignment moonlighting as a security guard or visiting relatives who live in that State, the employee will not lose reemployment rights simply because he or she used some of the time away from the job to do something other than attend the military training. Also, if an employee receives advance notification of a mobilization order, and leaves his or her employment position in order to prepare for duty, but the mobilization is cancelled, the employee will not lose any reemployment rights.

§ 1002.74 Must the employee begin service in the uniformed services immediately after leaving his or her employment position in order to have USERRA reemployment rights?

No. At a minimum, an employee must have enough time after leaving the employment position to travel safely to the uniformed service site and arrive fit to perform the service. Depending on the specific circumstances, including the duration of service, the amount of notice received, and the location of the service, additional time to rest, or to arrange affairs and report to duty, may be necessitated by reason of service in the uniformed services. The following examples help to explain the issue of the period of time between leaving civilian employment and beginning of service in the uniformed services:

(a) If the employee performs a full overnight shift for the civilian employer and travels directly from the work site to perform a full day of uniformed service, the employee would not be considered fit to perform the uniformed service. An absence from that work shift is necessitated so that the employee can report for uniformed service fit for duty.

(b) If the employee is ordered to perform an extended period of service in the uniformed services, he or she may require a reasonable period of time off from the civilian job to put his or her personal affairs in order, before beginning the service. Taking such time off is also necessitated by the uniformed service.

(c) If the employee leaves a position of employment in order to enlist or otherwise perform service in the uniformed services and, through no fault of his or her own, the beginning date of the service is delayed, this delay does not terminate any reemployment rights.

REQUIREMENT OF NOTICE

§ 1002.85 Must the employee give advance notice to the employer of his or her service in the uniformed services?

(a) Yes. The employee, or an appropriate officer of the uniformed service in which his or her service is to be performed, must notify the employer that the employee intends to leave the employment position to perform service in the uniformed services, with certain exceptions described below. In cases in which an employee is employed by more than one employer, the employee, or an appropriate office of the uniformed service in which his or her service is to be performed, must notify each employer that the employee intends to leave the employment position to perform service in the uniformed services, with certain exceptions described below.

(b) The Department of Defense USERRA regulations at 32 C.F.R. 104.3 provide that an "appropriate officer" can give notice on the employee's behalf. An "appropriate officer" is a commissioned, warrant, or noncommissioned officer authorized to give such notice by the military service concerned.

(c) The employee's notice to the employer may be either verbal or written. The notice may be informal and does not need to follow any particular format.

(d) Although USERRA does not specify how far in advance notice must be given to the employer, an employee should provide notice as far in advance as is reasonable under the circumstances. In regulations promulgated by the Department of Defense under USERRA, 32 C.F.R. § 104.6(a)(2)(i)(B), the Defense Department "strongly recommends that advance notice to civilian employers be provided at least 30 days prior to departure for uniformed service when it is feasible to do so."

§ 1002.86 When is the employee excused from giving advance notice of service in the uniformed services?

The employee is required to give advance notice of pending service unless giving such notice is prevented by military necessity, or is otherwise impossible or unreasonable under all the circumstances.

(a) Only a designated authority can make a determination of "military necessity," and such a determination is not subject to judicial review. Guidelines for defining "military necessity" appear in regulations issued by the Department of Defense at 32 C.F.R. 104.3. In general, these regulations cover situations where a mission, operation, exercise or requirement is classified, or could be compromised or otherwise adversely affected by public knowledge. In certain cases, the Secretary of Homeland Security, in consultation with the Secretary of Defense, can make a determination that giving of notice by intermittent disasterresponse appointees of the National Disaster Medical System is precluded by "military necessity." *See* 42 U.S.C. § 300hh11(e)(3)(B).

(b) It may be impossible or unreasonable to give advance notice under certain circumstances. Such circumstances may include the unavailability of the employee's employer or the employer's representative, or a requirement that the employee report for uniformed service in an extremely short period of time.

§ 1002.87 Is the employee required to get permission from his or her employer before leaving to perform service in the uniformed services?

No. The employee is not required to ask for or get his or her employer's permission to leave to perform service in the uniformed services. The employee is only required to give the employer notice of pending service.

§ 1002.88 Is the employee required to tell his or her civilian employer that he or she intends to seek reemployment after completing uniformed service before the employee leaves to perform service in the uniformed services?

No. When the employee leaves the employment position to begin a period of service, he or she is not required to tell the civilian employer that he or she intends to seek reemployment after completing uniformed service. Even if the employee tells the employer before entering or completing uniformed service that he or she does not intend to seek reemployment after completing the uniformed service, the employee does not forfeit the right to reemployment after completing service. The employee is not required to decide in advance of leaving the civilian employment position whether he or she will seek reemployment after completing uniformed service.

PERIOD OF SERVICE

§ 1002.99 Is there a limit on the total amount of service in the uniformed services that an employee may perform and still retain reemployment rights with the employer?

Yes. In general, the employee may perform service in the uniformed services for a cumulative period of up to five (5) years and retain reemployment rights with the employer. The exceptions to this rule are described below.

§ 1002.100 Does the fiveyear service limit include all absences from an employment position that are related to service in the uniformed services?

No. The fiveyear period includes only the time the employee spends actually performing service in the uniformed services. A period of absence from employment before or after performing service in the uniformed services does not count against the fiveyear limit. For example, after the employee completes a period of service in the uniformed services, he or she is provided a certain amount of time, depending upon the length of service, to report back to work or submit an application for reemployment. The period between completing the uniformed service and reporting back to work or seeking reemployment does not count against the fiveyear limit.

§ 1002.101 Does the fiveyear service limit include periods of service that the employee performed when he or she worked for a previous employer?

No. An employee is entitled to a leave of absence for uniformed service for up to five years with each employer for whom he or she works. When the employee takes a position with a new employer, the fiveyear period begins again regardless of how much service he or she performed while working in any previous employment relationship. If an employee is employed by more than one employer, a separate fiveyear period runs as to each employer independently, even if those employers share or codetermine the employee's terms and conditions of employment.

§ 1002.102 Does the fiveyear service limit include periods of service that the employee performed before USERRA was enacted?

It depends. USERRA provides reemployment rights to which an employee may become entitled beginning on or after December 12, 1994, but any uniformed service performed before December 12, 1994, that was counted against the service limitations of the previous law (the Veterans Reemployment Rights Act), also counts against USERRA's fiveyear limit.

§ 1002.103 Are there any types of service in the uniformed services that an employee can perform that do not count against USERRA's fiveyear service limit?

(a) USERRA creates the following exceptions to the fiveyear limit on service in the uniformed services:

(1) Service that is required beyond five years to complete an initial period of obligated service. Some military specialties require an individual to serve more than five years because of the amount of time or expense involved in training. If the employee works in one of those specialties, he or she has reemployment rights when the initial period of obligated service is completed;

(2) If the employee was unable to obtain orders releasing him or her from service in the uniformed services before the expiration of the fiveyear period, and the inability was not the employee's fault;

(3) (i) Service performed to fulfill periodic National Guard and Reserve training requirements as prescribed by 10 U.S.C. 10147 and 32 U.S.C. 502(a) and 503; and,

(ii) Service performed to fulfill additional training requirements determined and certified by a proper military authority as necessary for the employee's professional development, or to complete skill training or retraining;

(4) Service performed in a uniformed service if he or she was ordered to or retained on active duty under:

(i) 10 U.S.C. 688 (involuntary active duty by a military retiree);

(ii) 10 U.S.C. 12301(a) (involuntary active duty in wartime);

(iii) 10 U.S.C. 12301(g) (retention on active duty while in captive status);

(iv) 10 U.S.C. 12302 (involuntary active duty during a national emergency for up to 24 months);

(v) 10 U.S.C. 12304 (involuntary active duty for an operational mission for up to 270 days);

(vi) 10 U.S.C. 12305 (involuntary retention on active duty of a critical person during time of crisis or other specific conditions);

(vii) 14 U.S.C. 331 (involuntary active duty by retired Coast Guard officer);

(viii) 14 U.S.C. 332 (voluntary active duty by retired Coast Guard officer);

(ix) 14 U.S.C. 359 (involuntary active duty by retired Coast Guard enlisted member);

(x) 14 U.S.C. 360 (voluntary active duty by retired Coast Guard enlisted member);

(xi) 14 U.S.C. 367 (involuntary retention of Coast Guard enlisted member on active duty); and

(xii) 14 U.S.C. 712 (involuntary active duty by Coast Guard Reserve member for natural or manmade disasters).

(5) Service performed in a uniformed service if the employee was ordered to or retained on active duty (other than for training) under any provision of law because of a war or national emergency declared by the President or the Congress, as determined by the Secretary concerned;

(6) Service performed in a uniformed service if the employee was ordered to active duty (other than for training) in support of an operational mission for which personnel have been ordered to active duty under 10 U.S.C. 12304, as determined by a proper military authority;

(7) Service performed in a uniformed service if the employee was ordered to active duty in support of a critical mission or requirement of the uniformed services as determined by the Secretary concerned; and,

(8) Service performed as a member of the National Guard if the employee was called to respond to an invasion, danger of invasion, rebellion, danger of rebellion, insurrection, or the inability of the President with regular forces to execute the laws of the United States.

(b) Service performed to mitigate economic harm where the employee's employer is in violation of its employment or reemployment obligations to him or her.

§ 1002.104 Is the employee required to accommodate his or her employer's needs as to the timing, frequency or duration of service?

No. The employee is not required to accommodate his or her employer's interests or concerns regarding the timing, frequency, or duration of uniformed service. The employer cannot refuse to reemploy the employee because it believes that the timing, frequency or duration of the service is unreasonable. However, the employer is permitted to bring its concerns over the timing, frequency, or duration of the employee's service to the attention of the appropriate military authority. Regulations issued by the Department of Defense at 32 CFR 104.4 direct military authorities to provide assistance to an employer in addressing these types of employment issues. The military authorities are required to consider requests from employers of National Guard and Reserve members to adjust scheduled absences from civilian employment to perform service.

APPLICATION FOR REEMPLOYMENT

§ 1002.115 Is the employee required to report to or submit a timely application for reemployment to his or her preservice employer upon completing the period of service in the uniformed services?

Yes. Upon completing service in the uniformed services, the employee must notify the preservice employer of his or her intent to return to the employment position by either reporting to work or submitting a timely application for reemployment. Whether the employee is required to report to work or submit a timely application for reemployment depends upon the length of service, as follows:

(a) *Period of service less than 31 days or for a period of any length for the purpose of a fitness examination.* If the period of service in the uniformed services was less than 31 days, or the employee was absent from a position of employment for a period of any length for the purpose of an examination to determine his or her fitness to perform service, the employee must report back to the employer not later than the beginning of the first full regularlyscheduled work period on the first full calendar day following the completion of the period of service, and the expiration of eight hours after a period allowing for safe transportation from the place of that service to the employee's residence. For example, if the employee completes a period of service and travel home, arriving at ten o'clock in the evening, he or she cannot be required to report to the employer until the beginning of the next full regularlyscheduled work period that begins at least eight hours after arriving home, i.e., no earlier than six o'clock the next morning. If it is impossible or unreasonable for the employee to report within such time period through no fault of his or her own, he or she must report to the employer as soon as possible after the expiration of the eighthour period.

(b) *Period of service more than 30 days but less than 181 days.* If the employee's period of service in the uniformed services was for more than 30 days but less than 181 days, he or she must submit an application for reemployment (written or verbal) with the employer not later than 14 days after completing service. If it is impossible or unreasonable for the employee to apply within 14 days through no fault of his or her own, he or she must submit the application not later than the next full calendar day after it becomes possible to do so.

(c) *Period of service more than 180 days.* If the employee's period of service in the uniformed services was for more than 180 days, he or she must submit an application for reemployment (written or verbal) not later than 90 days after completing service.

§ 1002.116 *Is the time period for reporting back to an employer extended if the employee is hospitalized for, or convalescing from, an illness or injury incurred in, or aggravated during, the performance of service?*

Yes. If the employee is hospitalized for, or convalescing from, an illness or injury incurred in, or aggravated during, the performance of service, he or she must report to or submit an application for reemployment to the employer at the end of the period necessary for recovering from the illness or injury. This period may not exceed two years from the date of the completion of service, except that it must be extended by the minimum time necessary to accommodate circumstances beyond the employee's control that make reporting within the period impossible or unreasonable. This period for recuperation and recovery extends the time period for reporting to or submitting an application for reemployment to the employer, and is not applicable following reemployment.

§ 1002.117 *Are there any consequences if the employee fails to report for or submit a timely application for reemployment?*

(a) If the employee fails to timely report for or apply for reemployment, he or she does not automatically forfeit entitlement to USERRA's reemployment and other rights and benefits. Rather, the employee becomes subject to the conduct rules, established policy, and general practices of the employer pertaining to an absence from scheduled work.

(b) If reporting or submitting an employment application to the employer is impossible or unreasonable through no fault of the employee, he or she may report to the employer as soon as possible (in the case of a period of service less than 31 days) or submit an application for reemployment to the employer by the next full calendar day after it becomes possible to do so (in the case of a period of service from 31 to 180 days), and the employee will be considered to have timely reported or applied for reemployment.

§ 1002.118 *Is an application for reemployment required to be in any particular form?*

An application for reemployment need not follow any particular format. The employee may apply orally or in writing. The application should indicate that the employee is a former employee returning from service in the uniformed services and that he or she seeks reemployment with the preservice employer. The employee is permitted but not required to identify a particular reemployment position in which he or she is interested.

§ 1002.119 *To whom must the employee submit the application for reemployment?*

The application must be submitted to the preservice employer or to an agent or representative of the employer who has apparent responsibility for receiving employment applications. Depending upon the circumstances, such a person could be a personnel or human resources officer, or a firstline supervisor. If there has been a change in ownership of the employer, the application should be submitted to the employer's successorininterest.

§ 1002.120 *If the employee seeks or obtains employment with an employer other than the pre service employer before the end of the period within which a reemployment application must be filed, will that jeopardize reemployment rights with the preservice employer?*

No. The employee has reemployment rights with the preservice employer provided that he or she makes a timely reemployment application to that employer. The employee may seek or obtain employment with an employer other than the preservice employer during the period of time within which a reemployment application must be made, without giving up reemployment rights with the preservice employer. However, such alternative employment during the application period should not be of a type that would constitute cause for the employer to discipline or terminate the employee following reemployment. For instance, if the employer forbids employees from working concurrently for a direct competitor during employment, violation of such a policy may constitute cause for discipline or even termination.

§ 1002.121 *Is the employee required to submit documentation to the employer in connection with the application for reemployment?*

Yes, if the period of service exceeded 30 days and if requested by the employer to do so. If the employee submits an application for reemployment after a period of service of more than 30 days, he or she must, upon the request of the employer, provide documentation to establish that:

(a) the reemployment application is timely;

(b) the employee has not exceeded the fiveyear limit on the duration of service (subject to the exceptions listed at § 1002.103); and,

(c) the employee's separation or dismissal from service was not disqualifying.

§ 1002.122 *Is the employer required to reemploy the employee if documentation establishing the employee's eligibility does not exist or is not readily available?*

Yes. The employer is not permitted to delay or deny reemployment by demanding documentation that does not exist or is not readily available. The employee is not liable for administrative delays in the issuance of military documentation. If the employee is reemployed after an absence from employment for more than 90 days, the employer may require that he or she submit the documentation establishing entitlement to reemployment before treating the employee as not having had a break in service for pension purposes. If the documentation is received after reemployment and it shows that the employee is not entitled to reemployment, the employer may terminate employment and any rights or benefits that the employee may have been granted.

§ 1002.123 *What documents satisfy the requirement that the employee establish eligibility for reemployment after a period of service of more than thirty days?*

(a) Documents that satisfy the requirements of USERRA include the following:

(1) DD (Department of Defense) 214 Certificate of Release or Discharge from Active Duty;

(2) (2) Copy of duty orders prepared by the facility where the orders were fulfilled carrying an endorsement indicating completion of the described service;

(3) Letter from the commanding officer of a Personnel Support Activity or someone of comparable authority;

(4) Certificate of completion from military training school;

(5) Discharge certificate showing character of service; and,

(6) Copy of extracts from payroll documents showing periods of service;

(7) Letter from National Disaster Medical System (NDMS) Team Leader or Administrative Officer verifying dates and times of NDMS training or Federal activation .

(b) The types of documents that are necessary to establish eligibility for reemployment will vary from case to case. Not all of these documents are available or necessary in every instance to establish reemployment eligibility.

CHARACTER OF SERVICE

§ 1002.134 *What type of discharge or separation from service is required for an employee to be entitled to reemployment under USERRA?*

USERRA does not require any particular form of discharge or separation from service. However, even if the employee is otherwise eligible for reemployment, he or she will be disqualified if the characterization of service falls within one of four categories. USERRA requires that the employee not have received one of these types of discharge.

§ 1002.135 *What types of discharge or separation from uniformed service will make the employee ineligible for reemployment under USERRA?*

Reemployment rights are terminated if the employee is:

(a) separated from uniformed service with a dishonorable or bad conduct discharge;

(b) separated from uniformed service under other than honorable conditions, as characterized by regulations of the uniformed service;

(c) a commissioned officer dismissed as permitted under 10 U.S.C. 1161(a) by sentence of a general courtmartial; in commutation of a sentence of a general courtmartial; or, in time of war, by order of the President; or,

(d) a commissioned officer dropped from the rolls under 10 U.S.C. 1161(b) due to absence without authority for at least three months; separation by reason of a sentence to confinement adjudged by a courtmartial; or, a sentence to confinement in a Federal or State penitentiary or correctional institution.

§ 1002.136 *Who determines the characterization of service?*

The branch of service in which the employee performs the tour of duty determines the characterization of service.

§ 1002.137 *If the employee receives a disqualifying discharge or release from uniformed service and it is later upgraded, will reemployment rights be restored?*

Yes. A military review board has the authority to prospectively or retroactively upgrade a disqualifying discharge or release. A retroactive upgrade would restore reemployment rights providing the employee otherwise meets the Act's eligibility criteria.

§ 1002.138 *If the employee receives a retroactive upgrade in the characterization of service, will that entitle him or her to claim back wages and benefits lost as of the date of separation from service?*

No. A retroactive upgrade allows the employee to obtain reinstatement with the former employer, provided the employee otherwise meets the Act's eligibility criteria. Back pay and other benefits such as pension plan credits attributable to the time period between discharge and the retroactive upgrade are not required to be restored by the employer in this situation.

EMPLOYER STATUTORY DEFENSES

§ 1002.139 *Are there any circumstances in which the preservice employer is excused from its obligation to reemploy the employee following a period of uniformed service? What statutory defenses are available to the employer in an action or proceeding for reemployment benefits?*

(a) Even if the employee is otherwise eligible for reemployment benefits, the employer is not required to reemploy him or her if the employer establishes that its circumstances have so changed as to make reemployment impossible or unreasonable. For example, an employer may be excused from reemploying the employee where there has been an intervening reduction in force that would have included that employee. The employer may not, however, refuse to reemploy the employee on the basis that another employee was hired to fill the reemployment position during the employee's absence, even if reemployment might require the termination of that replacement employee;

(b) Even if the employee is otherwise eligible for reemployment benefits, the employer is not required to reemploy him or her if it establishes that assisting the employee in becoming qualified for reemployment would impose an undue hardship, as defined in § 1002.5(n) and discussed in § 1002.198, on the employer; or,

(c) Even if the employee is otherwise eligible for reemployment benefits, the employer is not required to reemploy him or her if it establishes that the employment position vacated by the employee in order to perform service in the uniformed services was for a brief, nonrecurrent period and there was

no reasonable expectation that the employment would continue indefinitely or for a significant period.

(d) The employer defenses included in this section are affirmative ones, and the employer carries the burden to prove by a preponderance of the evidence that any one or more of these defenses is applicable.

SUBPART D—RIGHTS, BENEFITS, AND OBLIGATIONS OF PERSONS ABSENT FROM EMPLOYMENT DUE TO SERVICE IN THE UNIFORMED SERVICES

FURLOUGH AND LEAVE OF ABSENCE

§ 1002.149 *What is the employee's status with his or her civilian employer while performing service in the uniformed services?*

During a period of service in the uniformed services, the employee is deemed to be on furlough or leave of absence from the civilian employer. In this status, the employee is entitled to the nonseniority rights and benefits generally provided by the employer to other employees with similar seniority, status, and pay that are on furlough or leave of absence. Entitlement to these nonseniority rights and benefits is not dependent on how the employer characterizes the employee's status during a period of service. For example, if the employer characterizes the employee as "terminated" during the period of uniformed service, this characterization cannot be used to avoid USERRA's requirement that the employee be deemed on furlough or leave of absence, and therefore entitled to the nonseniority rights and benefits generally provided to employees on furlough or leave of absence.

§ 1002.150 *Which nonseniority rights and benefits is the employee entitled to during a period of service?*

(a) The nonseniority rights and benefits to which an employee is entitled during a period of service are those that the employer provides to similarly situated employees by an employment contract, agreement, policy, practice, or plan in effect at the employee's workplace. These rights and benefits include those in effect at the beginning of the employee's employment and those established after employment began. They also include those rights and benefits that become effective during the employee's period of service and that are provided to similarly situated employees on furlough or leave of absence.

(b) If the nonseniority benefits to which employees on furlough or leave of absence are entitled vary according to the type of leave, the employee must be given the most favorable treatment accorded to any comparable form of leave when he or she performs service in the uniformed services. In order to determine whether any two types of leave are comparable, the duration of the leave may be the most significant factor to compare. For instance, a two-day funeral leave will not be "comparable" to an extended leave for service in the uniformed service. In addition to comparing the duration of the absences, other factors such as the purpose of the leave and the ability of the employee to choose when to take the leave should also be considered.

(c) As a general matter, accrual of vacation leave is considered to be a nonseniority benefit that must be provided by an employer to an employee on a military leave of absence only if the employer provides that benefit to similarly situated employees on comparable leaves of absence.

§ 1002.151 *If the employer provides full or partial pay to the employee while he or she is on military leave, is the employer required to also provide the nonseniority rights and benefits ordinarily granted to similarly situated employees on furlough or leave of absence?*

Yes. If the employer provides additional benefits such as full or partial pay when the employee performs service, the employer is not excused from providing other rights and benefits to which the employee is entitled under the Act.

§ 1002.152 *If employment is interrupted by a period of service in the uniformed services, are there any circumstances under which the employee is not entitled to the nonseniority rights and benefits ordinarily granted to similarly situated employees on furlough or leave of absence?*

If employment is interrupted by a period of service in the uniformed services and the employee knowingly provides written notice of intent not to return to the position of employment after service in the uniformed services, he or she is not entitled to those nonseniority rights and benefits. The employee's written notice does not waive entitlement to any other rights to which he or she is entitled under the Act, including the right to reemployment after service.

§ 1002.153 *If employment is interrupted by a period of service in the uniformed services, is the employee permitted upon request*

to use accrued vacation, annual or similar leave with pay during the service? Can the employer require the employee to use accrued leave during a period of service?

(a) If employment is interrupted by a period of service, the employee must be permitted upon request to use any accrued vacation, annual, or similar leave with pay during the period of service, in order to continue his or her civilian pay. However, the employee is not entitled to use sick leave that accrued with the civilian employer during a period of service in the uniformed services, unless the employer allows employees to use sick leave for any reason, or allows other similarly situated employees on comparable furlough or leave of absence to use accrued paid sick leave. Sick leave is usually not comparable to annual or vacation leave; it is generally intended to provide income when the employee or a family member is ill and the employee is unable to work.

(b) The employer may not require the employee to use accrued vacation, annual, or similar leave during a period of service in the uniformed services.

HEALTH PLAN COVERAGE

§ 1002.163 What types of health plans are covered by USERRA?

(a) USERRA defines a health plan to include an insurance policy or contract, medical or hospital service agreement, membership or subscription contract, or arrangement under which the employee's health services are provided or the expenses of those services are paid.

(b) USERRA covers group health plans as defined in the Employee Retirement Income Security Act of 1974 (ERISA) at 29 U.S.C. 1191b(a). USERRA applies to group health plans that are subject to ERISA, and plans that are not subject to ERISA, such as those sponsored by State or local governments or religious organizations for their employees.

(c) USERRA covers multiemployer plans maintained pursuant to one or more collective bargaining agreements between employers and employee organizations. USERRA applies to multiemployer plans as they are defined in ERISA at 29 U.S.C. 1002(37). USERRA contains provisions that apply specifically to multiemployer plans in certain situations.

§ 1002.164 What health plan coverage must the employer provide for the employee under USERRA?

If the employee has coverage under a health plan in connection with his or her employment, the plan must permit the employee to elect to continue the coverage for a certain period of time as described below:

(a) When the employee is performing service in the uniformed services, he or she is entitled to continuing coverage for himself or herself (and dependents if the plan offers dependent coverage) under a health plan provided in connection with the employment. The plan must allow the employee to elect to continue coverage for a period of time that is the lesser of:

(1) the 24-month period beginning on the date on which the employee's absence for the purpose of performing service begins; or,

(2) the period beginning on the date on which the employee's absence for the purpose of performing service begins, and ending on the date on which he or she fails to return from service or apply for a position of employment as provided under sections 1002.115-123 of these regulations.

(b) USERRA does not require the employer to establish a health plan if there is no health plan coverage in connection with the employment, or, where there is a plan, to provide any particular type of coverage.

(c) USERRA does not require the employer to permit the employee to initiate new health plan coverage at the beginning of a period of service if he or she did not previously have such coverage.

§ 1002.165 How does the employee elect continuing health plan coverage?

USERRA does not specify requirements for electing continuing coverage. Health plan administrators may develop reasonable requirements addressing how continuing coverage may be elected, consistent with the terms of the plan and the Act's exceptions to the requirement that the employee give advance notice of service in the uniformed services. For example, the employee cannot be precluded from electing continuing health plan coverage under circumstances where it is impossible or unreasonable for him or her to make a timely election of coverage.

§ 1002.166 How much must the employee pay in order to continue health plan coverage?

(a) If the employee performs service in the uniformed service for fewer than 31 days, he or she cannot be required to pay more than the regular employee share, if any, for health plan coverage.

(b) If the employee performs service in the uniformed service for 31 or more days, he or she may be required to pay no more than 102% of the full premium under the plan, which represents the employer's share plus the employee's share, plus 2% for administrative costs.

(c) USERRA does not specify requirements for methods of paying for continuing coverage. Health plan administrators may develop reasonable procedures for payment, consistent with the terms of the plan.

§ 1002.167 What actions may a plan administrator take if the employee does not elect or pay for continuing coverage in a timely manner?

The actions a plan administrator may take regarding the provision or cancellation of an employee's continuing coverage depend on whether the employee is excused from the requirement to give advance notice, whether the plan has established reasonable rules for election of continuation coverage, and whether the plan has established reasonable rules for the payment for continuation coverage.

(a) *No notice of service and no election of continuation coverage:.* If an employer provides employment-based health coverage to an employee who leaves employment for uniformed service without giving advance notice of service, the plan administrator may cancel the employee's health plan coverage upon the employee's departure from employment for uniformed service. However, in cases in which an employee's failure to give advance notice of service was excused under the statute because it was impossible, unreasonable, or precluded by military necessity, the plan administrator must reinstate the employee's health coverage retroactively upon his or her election to continue coverage and payment of all unpaid amounts due, and the employee must incur no administrative reinstatement costs. In order to qualify for an exception to the requirement of timely election of continuing health care, an employee must first be excused from giving notice of service under the statute.

(b) *Notice of service but no election of continuing coverage:.* Plan administrators may develop reasonable requirements addressing how continuing coverage may be elected. Where health plans are also covered under the Consolidated Omnibus Budget Reconciliation Act of 1985, 26 U.S.C. 4980B (COBRA), it may be reasonable for a health plan administrator to adopt COBRA-compliant rules regarding election of continuing coverage, as long as those rules do not conflict with any provision of USERRA or this rule. If an employer provides employment-based health coverage to an employee who leaves employment for uniformed service for a period of service in excess of 30 days after having given advance notice of service but without making an election regarding continuing coverage, the plan administrator may cancel the employee's health plan coverage upon the employee's departure from employment for uniformed service, but must reinstate coverage without the imposition of administrative reinstatement costs under the following conditions:

(1) Plan administrators who have developed reasonable rules regarding the period within which an employee may elect continuing coverage must permit retroactive reinstatement of uninterrupted coverage to the date of departure if the employee elects continuing coverage and pays all unpaid amounts due within the periods established by the plan;

(2) In cases in which plan administrators have not developed rules regarding the period within which an employee may elect continuing coverage, the plan must permit retroactive reinstatement of uninterrupted coverage to the date of departure upon the employee's election and payment of all unpaid amounts at any time during the period established in section 1002.164(a).

(c) *Election of continuation coverage without timely payment:.* Health plan administrators may adopt reasonable rules allowing cancellation of coverage if timely payment is not made. Where health plans are covered under COBRA, it may be reasonable for a health plan administrator to adopt COBRA-compliant rules regarding payment for continuing coverage, as long as those rules do not conflict with any provision of USERRA or this rule.

§ 1002.168 If the employee's coverage was terminated at the beginning of or during service, does his or her coverage have to be reinstated upon reemployment?

(a) If health plan coverage for the employee or a dependent was terminated by reason of service in the uniformed services, that coverage must be reinstated upon reemployment. An exclusion or waiting period may not be imposed in connection with the reinstatement of coverage upon reemployment, if an exclusion or waiting period would not have been imposed had coverage not been terminated by reason of such service.

(b) USERRA permits a health plan to impose an exclusion or waiting period as to illnesses or injuries determined by the Secretary of Veterans Affairs to have been incurred in, or aggravated during, performance of service in the uniformed services. The determination that the employee's illness or injury was incurred in, or aggravated during, the performance of service may only be made by the Secretary of Veterans Affairs or his or her representative. Other coverage, for injuries or illnesses that are not servicer-related (or for the employee's dependents, if he or she has dependent coverage), must be reinstated subject to paragraph (a) of this section.

§ 1002.169 Can the employee elect to delay reinstatement of health plan coverage until a date after the date he or she is reemployed?

USERRA requires the employer to reinstate health plan coverage upon request at reemployment. USERRA permits but does not require the employer to allow the employee to delay reinstatement of health plan coverage until a date that is later than the date of reemployment.

§ 1002.170 In a multiemployer health plan, how is liability allocated for employer contributions and benefits arising under USERRA's health plan provisions?

Liability under a multiemployer plan for employer contributions and benefits in connection with USERRA's health plan provisions must be allocated either as the plan sponsor provides, or, if the sponsor does not provide, to the employee's last employer before his or her service. If the last employer is no longer functional, liability for continuing coverage is allocated to the health plan.

§ 1002.171 How does the continuation of health plan benefits apply to a multiemployer plan that provides health plan coverage through a health benefits account system?

(a) Some employees receive health plan benefits provided pursuant to a multiemployer plan that utilizes a health benefits account system in which an employee accumulates prospective health benefit eligibility, also commonly referred to as "dollar bank," "credit bank," and "hour bank" plans. In such cases, where an employee with a positive health benefits account balance elects to continue the coverage, the employee may further elect either option below:

(1) The employee may expend his or her health account balance during an absence from employment due to service in the uniformed services in lieu of paying for the continuation of coverage as set out in section 1002.166. If an employee's health account balance becomes depleted during the applicable period provided for in section 1002.164(a), the employee must be permitted, at his or her option, to continue coverage pursuant to section 1002.166. Upon reemployment, the plan must provide for immediate reinstatement of the employee as required by section 1002.168, but may require the employee to pay the cost of the coverage until the employee earns the credits necessary to sustain continued coverage in the plan.

(2) The employee may pay for continuation coverage as set out in section 1002.166, in order to maintain intact his or her account balance as of the beginning date of the absence from employment due to service in the uniformed services. This option permits the employee to resume usage of the account balance upon reemployment.

(b) Employers or plan administrators providing such plans should counsel employees of their options set out in this subsection.

SUBPART E—REEMPLOYMENT RIGHTS AND BENEFITS

PROMPT REEMPLOYMENT

§ 1002.180 When is an employee entitled to be reemployed by his or her civilian employer?

The employer must promptly reemploy the employee when he or she returns from a period of service if the employee meets the Act's eligibility criteria as described in Subpart C of these regulations.

§ 1002.181 How is "prompt reemployment" defined?

"Prompt reemployment" means as soon as practicable under the circumstances of each case. Absent unusual circumstances, reemployment must occur within two weeks of the employee's application for reemployment. For example, prompt reinstatement after a weekend National Guard duty generally means the next regularly scheduled working day. On the other hand, prompt reinstatement following several years of active duty may require more time, because the employer may have to reassign or give notice to another employee who occupied the returning employee's position.

REEMPLOYMENT POSITION

§ 1002.191 What position is the employee entitled to upon reemployment?

As a general rule, the employee is entitled to reemployment in the job position that he or she would have attained with reasonable certainty if not

for the absence due to uniformed service. This position is known as the escalator position. The principle behind the escalator position is that, if not for the period of uniformed service, the employee could have been promoted (or, alternatively, demoted, transferred, or laid off) due to intervening events. The escalator principle requires that the employee be reemployed in a position that reflects with reasonable certainty the pay, benefits, seniority, and other job perquisites, that he or she would have attained if not for the period of service. Depending upon the specific circumstances, the employer may have the option, or be required, to reemploy the employee in a position other than the escalator position.

§ 1002.192 How is the specific reemployment position determined?

In all cases, the starting point for determining the proper reemployment position is the escalator position, which is the job position that the employee would have attained if his or her continuous employment had not been interrupted due to uniformed service. Once this position is determined, the employer may have to consider several factors before determining the appropriate reemployment position in any particular case. Such factors may include the employee's length of service, qualifications, and disability, if any. The reemployment position may be either the escalator position; the preservice position; a position comparable to the escalator or preservice position; or, the nearest approximation to one of these positions.

§ 1002.193 Does the reemployment position include elements such as seniority, status, and rate of pay?

(a) Yes. The reemployment position includes the seniority, status, and rate of pay that an employee would ordinarily have attained in that position given his or her job history, including prospects for future earnings and advancement. The employer must determine the seniority rights, status, and rate of pay as though the employee had been continuously employed during the period of service. The seniority rights, status, and pay of an employment position include those established (or changed) by a collective bargaining agreement, employer policy, or employment practice. The sources of seniority rights, status, and pay include agreements, policies, and practices in effect at the beginning of the employee's service, and any changes that may have occurred during the period of service. In particular, the employee's status in the reemployment position could include opportunities for advancement, general working conditions, job location, shift assignment, rank, responsibility, and geographical location.

(b) If an opportunity for promotion, or eligibility for promotion, that the employee missed during service is based on a skills test or examination, then the employer should give him or her a reasonable amount of time to adjust to the employment position and then give a skills test or examination. No fixed amount of time for permitting adjustment to reemployment will be deemed reasonable in all cases. However, in determining a reasonable amount of time to permit an employee to adjust to reemployment before scheduling a makeup test or examination, an employer may take into account a variety of factors, including but not limited to the length of time the returning employee was absent from work, the level of difficulty of the test itself, the typical time necessary to prepare or study for the test, the duties and responsibilities of the reemployment position and the promotional position, and the nature and responsibilities of the service member while serving in the uniformed service. If the employee is successful on the makeup exam and, based on the results of that exam, there is a reasonable certainty that he or she would have been promoted, or made eligible for promotion, during the time that the employee served in the uniformed service, then the promotion or eligibility for promotion must be made effective as of the date it would have occurred had employment not been interrupted by uniformed service.

§ 1002.194 Can the application of the escalator principle result in adverse consequences when the employee is reemployed?

Yes. The Act does not prohibit lawful adverse job consequences that result from the employee's restoration on the seniority ladder. Depending on the circumstances, the escalator principle may cause an employee to be reemployed in a higher or lower position, laid off, or even terminated. For example, if an employee's seniority or job classification would have resulted in the employee being laid off during the period of service, and the layoff continued after the date of reemployment, reemployment would reinstate the employee to layoff status. Similarly, the status of the reemployment position requires the employer to assess what would have happened to such factors as the employee's opportunities for advancement, working conditions, job location, shift assignment, rank, responsibility, and geographical location, if he or she had remained continuously employed. The reemployment position may involve transfer to another shift or location, more or less strenuous working conditions, or changed opportunities for advancement, depending upon the application of the escalator principle.

§ 1002.195 What other factors can determine the reemployment position?

Once the employee's escalator position is determined, other factors may allow, or require, the employer to reemploy the employee in a position other than the escalator position. These factors, which are explained in §§ 1002.196 through 1002.199, are:

(a) the length of the employee's most recent period of uniformed service;

(b) the employee's qualifications; and,

(c) whether the employee has a disability incurred or aggravated during uniformed service.

§ 1002.196 What is the employee's reemployment position if the period of service was less than 91 days?

Following a period of service in the uniformed services of less than 91 days, the employee must be reemployed according to the following priority:

(a) The employee must be reemployed in the escalator position. He or she must be qualified to perform the duties of this position. The employer must make reasonable efforts to help the employee become qualified to perform the duties of this position.

(b) If the employee is not qualified to perform the duties of the escalator position after reasonable efforts by the employer, the employee must be reemployed in the position in which he or she was employed on the date that the period of service began. The employee must be qualified to perform the duties of this position. The employer must make reasonable efforts to help the employee become qualified to perform the duties of this position.

(c) If the employee is not qualified to perform the duties of the escalator position or the preservice position, after reasonable efforts by the employer, he or she must be reemployed in any other position that is the nearest approximation first to the escalator position and then to the preservice position. The employee must be qualified to perform the duties of this position. The employer must make reasonable efforts to help the employee become qualified to perform the duties of this position.

§ 1002.197 What is the reemployment position if the employee's period of service in the uniformed services was more than 90 days?

Following a period of service of more than 90 days, the employee must be reemployed according to the following priority:

(a) The employee must be reemployed in the escalator position or a position of like seniority, status, and pay. He or she must be qualified to perform the duties of this position. The employer must make reasonable efforts to help the employee become qualified to perform the duties of this position.

(b) If the employee is not qualified to perform the duties of the escalator position or a like position after reasonable efforts by the employer, the employee must be reemployed in the position in which he or she was employed on the date that the period of service began or in a position of like seniority, status, and pay. The employee must be qualified to perform the duties of this position. The employer must make reasonable efforts to help the employee become qualified to perform the duties of this position.

(c) If the employee is not qualified to perform the duties of the escalator position, the preservice position, or a like position, after reasonable efforts by the employer, he or she must be reemployed in any other position that is the nearest approximation first to the escalator position and then to the preservice position. The employee must be qualified to perform the duties of this position. The employer must make reasonable efforts to help the employee become qualified to perform the duties of this position.

§ 1002.198 What efforts must the employer make to help the employee become qualified for the reemployment position?

The employee must be qualified for the reemployment position. The employer must make reasonable efforts to help the employee become qualified to perform the duties of this position. The employer is not required to reemploy the employee on his or her return from service if he or she cannot, after reasonable efforts by the employer, qualify for the appropriate reemployment position.

(a)(1) "Qualified" means that the employee has the ability to perform the essential tasks of the position. The employee's inability to perform one or more nonessential tasks of a position does not make him or her unqualified.

(2) Whether a task is essential depends on several factors, and these factors include but are not limited to:

(i) the employer's judgment as to which functions are essential;

(ii) written job descriptions developed before the hiring process begins;

(iii) the amount of time on the job spent performing the function;

(iv) the consequences of not requiring the individual to perform the function;

(v) the terms of a collective bargaining agreement;

(vi) the work experience of past incumbents in the job; and/or

(vii) the current work experience of incumbents in similar jobs.

(b) Only after the employer makes reasonable efforts, as defined in § 1002.5(i), may it determine that the employee is not qualified for the reemployment position. These reasonable efforts must be made at no cost to the employee.

§ 1002.199 What priority must the employer follow if two or more returning employees are entitled to reemployment in the same position?

If two or more employees are entitled to reemployment in the same position and more than one employee has reported or applied for employment in that position, the employee who first left the position for uniformed service has the first priority on reemployment in that position. The remaining employee (or employees) is entitled to be reemployed in a position similar to that in which the employee would have been reemployed according to the rules that normally determine a reemployment position, as set out in §§ 1002.196 through 1002.197.

SENIORITY RIGHTS AND BENEFITS

§ 1002.210 What seniority rights does an employee have when reemployed following a period of uniformed service?

The employee is entitled to the seniority and senioritybased rights and benefits that he or she had on the date the uniformed service began, plus any seniority and senioritybased rights and benefits that the employee would have attained if he or she had remained continuously employed. In determining entitlement to seniority and senioritybased rights and benefits, the period of absence from employment due to or necessitated by uniformed service is not considered a break in employment. The rights and benefits protected by USERRA upon reemployment include those provided by the employer and those required by statute. For example, under USERRA, a reemployed service member would be eligible for leave under the Family and Medical Leave Act of 1993, 29 U.S.C. 26012654 (FMLA), if the number of months and the number of hours of work for which the service member was employed by the civilian employer, together with the number of months and the number of hours of work for which the service member would have been employed by the civilian employer during the period of uniformed service, meet FMLA's eligibility requirements. In the event that a service member is denied FMLA leave for failing to satisfy the FMLA's hours of work requirement due to absence from employment necessitated by uniformed service, the service member may have a cause of action under USERRA but not under the FMLA.

§ 1002.211 Does USERRA require the employer to use a seniority system?

No. USERRA does not require the employer to adopt a formal seniority system. USERRA defines seniority as longevity in employment together with any employment benefits that accrue with, or are determined by, longevity in employment. In the absence of a formal seniority system, such as one established through collective bargaining, USERRA looks to the custom and practice in the place of employment to determine the employee's entitlement to any employment benefits that accrue with, or are determined by, longevity in employment.

§ 1002.212 How does a person know whether a particular right or benefit is a senioritybased right or benefit?

A senioritybased right or benefit is one that accrues with, or is determined by, longevity in employment. Generally, whether a right or benefit is senioritybased depends on three factors:

(a) whether the right or benefit is a reward for length of service rather than a form of shorterterm compensation for work performed;

(b) whether it is reasonably certain that the employee would have received the right or benefit if he or she had remained continuously employed during the period of service; and,

(c) whether it is the employer's actual custom or practice to provide or withhold the right or benefit as a reward for length of service. Provisions of an employment contract or policies in the employee handbook are not controlling if the employer's actual custom or practice is different from what is written in the contract or handbook.

§ 1002.213 How can the employee demonstrate a reasonable certainty that he or she would have received the seniority right or benefit if he or she had remained continuously employed during the period of service?

A reasonable certainty is a high probability that the employee would have received the seniority or senioritybased right or benefit if he or she had been continuously employed. The employee does not have to establish that he or she would have received the benefit as an absolute certainty. The employee can demonstrate a reasonable certainty that he or she would have received the seniority right or benefit by showing that other employees with seniority similar to that which the employee would have had if he or she had remained continuously employed received the right or benefit. The employer cannot withhold the right or benefit based on an assumption that a series of unlikely events could have prevented the employee from gaining the right or benefit.

DISABLED EMPLOYEES

§ 1002.225 Is the employee entitled to any specific reemployment benefits if he or she has a disability that was incurred in, or aggravated during, the period of service?

Yes. A disabled service member is entitled, to the same extent as any other individual, to the escalator position he or she would have attained but for uniformed service. If the employee has a disability incurred in, or aggravated during, the period of service in the uniformed services, the employer must make reasonable efforts to accommodate that disability and to help the employee become qualified to perform the duties of his or her reemployment position. If the employee is not qualified for reemployment in the escalator position because of a disability after reasonable efforts by the employer to accommodate the disability and to help the employee to become qualified, the employee must be reemployed in a position according to the following priority. The employer must make reasonable efforts to accommodate the employee's disability and to help him or her to become qualified to perform the duties of one of these positions:

(a) a position that is equivalent in seniority, status, and pay to the escalator position; or,

(b) a position that is the nearest approximation to the equivalent position, consistent with the circumstances of the employee's case, in terms of seniority, status, and pay. A position that is the nearest approximation to the equivalent position may be a higher or lower position, depending on the circumstances.

§ 1002.226 If the employee has a disability that was incurred in, or aggravated during, the period of service, what efforts must the employer make to help him or her become qualified for the reemployment position?

(a) USERRA requires that the employee be qualified for the reemployment position regardless of any disability. The employer must make reasonable efforts to help the employee to become qualified to perform the duties of this position. The employer is not required to reemploy the employee on his or her return from service if he or she cannot, after reasonable efforts by the employer, qualify for the appropriate reemployment position.

(b) "Qualified" has the same meaning here as in § 1002.198.

RATE OF PAY

§ 1002.236 How is the employee's rate of pay determined when he or she returns from a period of service?

The employee's rate of pay is determined by applying the same escalator principles that are used to determine the reemployment position, as follows:

(a) If the employee is reemployed in the escalator position, the employer must compensate him or her at the rate of pay associated with the escalator position. The rate of pay must be determined by taking into account any pay increases, differentials, step increases, merit increases, or periodic increases that the employee would have attained with reasonable certainty had he or she remained continuously employed during the period of service. In addition, when considering whether merit or performance increases would have been attained with reasonable certainty, an employer may examine the returning employee's own work history, his or her history of merit increases, and the work and pay history of employees in the same or similar position. For example, if the employee missed a merit pay increase while performing service, but qualified for previous merit pay increases, then the rate of pay should include the merit pay increase that was missed. If the merit pay increase that the employee missed during service is based on a skills test or examination, then the employer should give the employee a reasonable amount of time to adjust to the reemployment position and then give him or her the skills test or examination. No fixed amount of time for permitting adjustment to reemployment will be deemed reasonable in all cases. However, in determining a reasonable amount of time to permit an employee to adjust to reemployment before scheduling a makeup test or examination, an employer may take into account a variety of factors, including but not limited to the length of time the returning employee was absent from work, the level of difficulty of the test itself, the typical time necessary to prepare or study for the test, the duties and responsibilities of the reemployment position and the promotional position, and the nature and responsibilities of the service member while serving in the uniformed

service. The escalator principle also applies in the event a pay reduction occurred in the reemployment position during the period of service. Any pay adjustment must be made effective as of the date it would have occurred had the employee's employment not been interrupted by uniformed service.

(b) If the employee is reemployed in the preservice position or another position, the employer must compensate him or her at the rate of pay associated with the position in which he or she is reemployed. As with the escalator position, the rate of pay must be determined by taking into account any pay increases, differentials, step increases, merit increases, or periodic increases that the employee would have attained with reasonable certainty had he or she remained continuously employed during the period of service.

PROTECTION AGAINST DISCHARGE

§ 1002.247 Does USERRA provide the employee with protection against discharge?

Yes. If the employee's most recent period of service in the uniformed services was more than 30 days, he or she must not be discharged except for cause -

(a) for 180 days after the employee's date of reemployment if his or her most recent period of uniformed service was more than 30 days but less than 181 days; or,

(b) for one year after the date of reemployment if the employee's most recent period of uniformed service was more than 180 days.

§ 1002.248 What constitutes cause for discharge under USERRA?

The employee may be discharged for cause based either on conduct or, in some circumstances, because of the application of other legitimate nondiscriminatory reasons.

(a) In a discharge action based on conduct, the employer bears the burden of proving that it is reasonable to discharge the employee for the conduct in question, and that he or she had notice, which was express or can be fairly implied, that the conduct would constitute cause for discharge.

(b) If, based on the application of other legitimate nondiscriminatory reasons, the employee's job position is eliminated, or the employee is placed on layoff status, either of these situations would constitute cause for purposes of USERRA. The employer bears the burden of proving that the employee's job would have been eliminated or that he or she would have been laid off.

PENSION PLAN BENEFITS

§ 1002.259 How does USERRA protect an employee's pension benefits?

On reemployment, the employee is treated as not having a break in service with the employer or employers maintaining a pension plan, for purposes of participation, vesting and accrual of benefits, by reason of the period of absence from employment due to or necessitated by service in the uniformed services.

(a) Depending on the length of the employee's period of service, he or she is entitled to take from one to ninety days following service before reporting back to work or applying for reemployment (See § 1002.115). This period of time must be treated as continuous service with the employer for purposes of determining participation, vesting and accrual of pension benefits under the plan.

(b) If the employee is hospitalized for, or convalescing from, an illness or injury incurred in, or aggravated during, service, he or she is entitled to report to or submit an application for reemployment at the end of the time period necessary for him or her to recover from the illness or injury. This period, which may not exceed two years from the date the employee completed service, except in circumstances beyond his or her control, must be treated as continuous service with the employer for purposes of determining the participation, vesting and accrual of pension benefits under the plan.

§ 1002.260 What pension benefit plans are covered under USERRA?

(a) The Employee Retirement Income Security Act of 1974 (ERISA) defines an employee pension benefit plan as a plan that provides retirement income to employees, or defers income to a period extending to or beyond the termination of employment. Any such plan maintained by the employer or employers is covered under USERRA. USERRA also covers certain pension plans not covered by ERISA, such as those sponsored by a State, government entity, or church for its employees.

(b) USERRA does not cover pension benefits under the Federal Thrift Savings Plan; those benefits are covered under 5 U.S.C. 8432b.

§ 1002.261 Who is responsible for funding any plan obligation to provide the employee with pension benefits?

With the exception of multiemployer plans, which have separate rules discussed below, the employer is liable to the pension benefit plan to fund any obligation of the plan to provide benefits that are attributable to the employee's period of service. In the case of a defined contribution plan, once the employee is reemployed, the employer must allocate the amount of its makeup contribution for the employee, if any; his or her makeup employee contributions, if any; and his or her elective deferrals, if any; in the same manner and to the same extent that it allocates the amounts for other employees during the period of service. In the case of a defined benefit plan, the employee's accrued benefit will be increased for the period of service once he or she is reemployed and, if applicable, has repaid any amounts previously paid to him or her from the plan and made any employee contributions that may be required to be made under the plan.

§ 1002.262 When is the employer required to make the plan contribution that is attributable to the employee's period of uniformed service?

(a) The employer is not required to make its contribution until the employee is reemployed. For employer contributions to a plan in which the employee is not required or permitted to contribute, the employer must make the contribution attributable to the employee's period of service no later than ninety days after the date of reemployment, or when plan contributions are normally due for the year in which the service in the uniformed services was performed, whichever is later. If it is impossible or unreasonable for the employer to make the contribution within this time period, the employer must make the contribution as soon as practicable.

(b) If the employee is enrolled in a contributory plan he or she is allowed (but not required) to make up his or her missed contributions or elective deferrals. These makeup contributions or elective deferrals must be made during a time period starting with the date of reemployment and continuing for up to three times the length of the employee's immediate past period of uniformed service, with the repayment period not to exceed five years. Makeup contributions or elective deferrals may only be made during this period and while the employee is employed with the postservice employer.

(c) If the employee's plan is contributory and he or she does not make up his or her contributions or elective deferrals, he or she will not receive the employer match or the accrued benefit attributable to his or her contribution because the employer is required to make contributions that are contingent on or attributable to the employee's contributions or elective deferrals only to the extent that the employee makes up his or her payments to the plan. Any employer contributions that are contingent on or attributable to the employee's makeup contributions or elective deferrals must be made according to the plan's requirements for employer matching contributions.

(d) The employee is not required to make up the full amount of employee contributions or elective deferrals that he or she missed making during the period of service. If the employee does not make up all of the missed contributions or elective deferrals, his or her pension may be less than if he or she had done so.

(e) Any vested accrued benefit in the pension plan that the employee was entitled to prior to the period of uniformed service remains intact whether or not he or she chooses to be reemployed under the Act after leaving the uniformed service.

(f) An adjustment will be made to the amount of employee contributions or elective deferrals the employee will be able to make to the pension plan for any employee contributions or elective deferrals he or she actually made to the plan during the period of service.

§ 1002.263 Does the employee pay interest when he or she makes up missed contributions or elective deferrals?

No. The employee is not required or permitted to make up a missed contribution in an amount that exceeds the amount he or she would have been permitted or required to contribute had he or she remained continuously employed during the period of service.

§ 1002.264 Is the employee allowed to repay a previous distribution from a pension benefits plan upon being reemployed?

Yes, provided the plan is a defined benefit plan. If the employee received a distribution of all or part of the accrued benefit from a defined benefit plan in connection with his or her service in the uniformed services before he or she became reemployed, he or she must be allowed to repay the withdrawn amounts when he or she is reemployed. The amount the employee must repay includes any interest that would have accrued had the monies not been withdrawn. The employee must be allowed to repay these amounts during a time period starting with the date of reemployment and continuing for up to three times the length of the employee's immediate past period of uniformed service, with the repayment period not to exceed five years (or such longer time as may be agreed to between the employer and the employee), provided the employee is employed with the postservice employer during this period.

§ 1002.265 If the employee is reemployed with his or her preservice employer, is the employee's pension benefit the same as if he or she had remained continuously employed?

The amount of the employee's pension benefit depends on the type of pension plan.

(a) In a noncontributory defined benefit plan, where the amount of the pension benefit is determined according to a specific formula, the employee's benefit will be the same as though he or she had remained continuously employed during the period of service.

(b) In a contributory defined benefit plan, the employee will need to make up contributions in order to have the same benefit as if he or she had remained continuously employed during the period of service.

(c) In a defined contribution plan, the benefit may not be the same as if the employee had remained continuously employed, even though the employee and the employer make up any contributions or elective deferrals attributable to the period of service, because the employee is not entitled to forfeitures and earnings or required to experience losses that accrued during the period or periods of service.

§ 1002.266 What are the obligations of a multiemployer pension benefit plan under USERRA?

A multiemployer pension benefit plan is one to which more than one employer is required to contribute, and which is maintained pursuant to one or more collective bargaining agreements between one or more employee organizations and more than one employer. The Act uses ERISA's definition of a multiemployer plan. In addition to the provisions of USERRA that apply to all pension benefit plans, there are provisions that apply specifically to multiemployer plans, as follows:

(a) The last employer that employed the employee before the period of service is responsible for making the employer contribution to the multiemployer plan, if the plan sponsor does not provide otherwise. If the last employer is no longer functional, the plan must nevertheless provide coverage to the employee.

(b) An employer that contributes to a multiemployer plan and that reemploys the employee pursuant to USERRA must provide written notice of reemployment to the plan administrator within 30 days after the date of reemployment. The returning service member should notify the reemploying employer that he or she has been reemployed pursuant to USERRA. The 30day period within which the reemploying employer must provide written notice to the multiemployer plan pursuant to this subsection does not begin until the employer has knowledge that the employee was reemployed pursuant to USERRA.

(c) The employee is entitled to the same employer contribution whether he or she is reemployed by the preservice employer or by a different employer contributing to the same multiemployer plan, provided that the preservice employer and the postservice employer share a common means or practice of hiring the employee, such as common participation in a union hiring hall.

§ 1002.267 How is compensation during the period of service calculated in order to determine the employee's pension benefits, if benefits are based on compensation?

In many pension benefit plans, the employee's compensation determines the amount of his or her contribution or the retirement benefit to which he or she is entitled.

(a) Where the employee's rate of compensation must be calculated to determine pension entitlement, the calculation must be made using the rate of pay that the employee would have received but for the period of uniformed service.

(b)(1) Where the rate of pay the employee would have received is not reasonably certain, such as where compensation is based on commissions earned, the average rate of compensation during the 12month period prior to the period of uniformed service must be used.

(2) Where the rate of pay the employee would have received is not reasonably certain and he or she was employed for less than 12 months prior to the period of uniformed service, the average rate of compensation must be derived from this shorter period of employment that preceded service.

SUBPART F—COMPLIANCE ASSISTANCE, ENFORCEMENT AND REMEDIES

COMPLIANCE ASSISTANCE

§ 1002.277 What assistance does the Department of Labor provide to employees and employers concerning employment, reemployment, or other rights and benefits under USERRA?

The Secretary, through the Veterans' Employment and Training Service (VETS), provides assistance to any person or entity with respect to employment and reemployment rights and benefits under USERRA. This assistance includes a wide range of compliance assistance outreach activities, such as responding to inquiries; conducting USERRA briefings and Webcasts; issuing news releases; and, maintaining the elaws USERRA Advisor (located at *http://www.dol.gov/elaws/userra.htm*), the eVETS Resource Advisor and other webbased materials (located at http://www.dol.gov/vets), which are designed to increase awareness of the Act among affected persons, the media, and the general public. In providing such assistance, VETS may request the assistance of other Federal and State agencies, and utilize the assistance of volunteers.

INVESTIGATION AND REFERRAL

§ 1002.288 How does an individual file a USERRA complaint?

If an individual is claiming entitlement to employment rights or benefits or reemployment rights or benefits and alleges that an employer has failed or refused, or is about to fail or refuse, to comply with the Act, the individual may file a complaint with VETS or initiate a private legal action in a court of law (see § 1002.303 below). A complaint may be filed with VETS either in writing, using VETS Form 1010, or electronically, using VETS Form e1010 (instructions and the forms can be accessed at http://www.dol.gov/elaws/vets/userra/1010.asp). A complaint must include the name and address of the employer, a summary of the basis for the complaint, and a request for relief.

§ 1002.289 How will VETS investigate a USERRA complaint?

(a) In carrying out any investigation, VETS has, at all reasonable times, reasonable access to and the right to interview persons with information relevant to the investigation. VETS also has reasonable access to, for purposes of examination, the right to copy and receive any documents of any person or employer that VETS considers relevant to the investigation.

(b) VETS may require by subpoena the attendance and testimony of witnesses and the production of documents relating to any matter under investigation. In case of disobedience of or resistance to the subpoena, the Attorney General may, at VETS' request, apply to any district court of the United States in whose jurisdiction such disobedience or resistance occurs for an order enforcing the subpoena. The district courts of the United States have jurisdiction to order compliance with the subpoena, and to punish failure to obey a subpoena as a contempt of court. This paragraph does not authorize VETS to seek issuance of a subpoena to the legislative or judicial branches of the United States.

§ 1002.290 Does VETS have the authority to order compliance with USERRA?

No. If VETS determines as a result of an investigation that the complaint is meritorious, VETS attempts to resolve the complaint by making reasonable efforts to ensure that any persons or entities named in the complaint comply with the Act. If VETS' efforts do not resolve the complaint, VETS notifies the person who submitted the complaint of:

(a) the results of the investigation; and,

(b) the person's right to proceed under the enforcement of rights provisions in 38 U.S.C. 4323 (against a State or private employer), or 38 U.S.C. 4324 (against a Federal executive agency or the Office of Personnel Management (OPM)).

§ 1002.291 What actions may an individual take if the complaint is not resolved by VETS?

If an individual receives a notification from VETS of an unsuccessful effort to resolve his or her complaint relating to a State or private employer, the individual may request that VETS refer the complaint to the Attorney General.

§ 1002.292 What can the Attorney General do about the complaint?

(a) If the Attorney General is reasonably satisfied that an individual's complaint is meritorious, meaning that he or she is entitled to the rights or benefits sought, the Attorney General may appear on his or her behalf and act as the individual's attorney, and initiate a legal action to obtain appropriate relief.

(b) If the Attorney General determines that the individual's complaint does not have merit, the Attorney General may decline to represent him or her.

ENFORCEMENT OF RIGHTS AND BENEFITS AGAINST A STATE OR PRIVATE EMPLOYER

§ 1002.303 Is an individual required to file his or her complaint with VETS?

No. The individual may initiate a private action for relief against a State or private employer if he or she decides not to apply to VETS for assistance.

§ 1002.304 If an individual files a complaint with VETS and VETS' efforts do not resolve the complaint, can the individual pursue the claim on his or her own?

Yes. If VETS notifies an individual that it is unable to resolve the complaint, the individual may pursue the claim on his or her own. The individual may choose to be represented by private counsel whether or not the Attorney General decides to represent him or her as to the complaint.

§ 1002.305 What court has jurisdiction in an action against a State or private employer?

(a) If an action is brought against a State or private employer by the Attorney General, the district courts of the United States have jurisdiction over the action. If the action is brought against a State by the Attorney General, it must be brought in the name of the United States as the plaintiff in the action.

(b) If an action is brought against a State by a person, the action may be brought in a State court of competent jurisdiction according to the laws of the State.

(c) If an action is brought against a private employer or a political subdivision of a State by a person, the district courts of the United States have jurisdiction over the action.

(d) An action brought against a State Adjutant General, as an employer of a civilian National Guard technician, is considered an action against a State for purposes of determining which court has jurisdiction.

§ 1002.306 Is a National Guard civilian technician considered a State or Federal employee for purposes of USERRA?

A National Guard civilian technician is considered a State employee for USERRA purposes, although he or she is considered a Federal employee for most other purposes.

§ 1002.307 What is the proper venue in an action against a State or private employer?

(a) If an action is brought by the Attorney General against a State, the action may proceed in the United States district court for any district in which the State exercises any authority or carries out any function.

(b) If an action is brought against a private employer, or a political subdivision of a State, the action may proceed in the United States district court for any district in which the employer maintains a place of business.

§ 1002.308 Who has legal standing to bring an action under USERRA?

An action may be brought only by the United States or by the person, or representative of a person, claiming rights or benefits under the Act. An employer, prospective employer or other similar entity may not bring an action under the Act.

§ 1002.309 Who is a necessary party in an action under USERRA?

In an action under USERRA only an employer or a potential employer, as the case may be, is a necessary party respondent. In some circumstances, such as where terms in a collective bargaining agreement need to be interpreted, the court may allow an interested party to intervene in the action.

§ 1002.310 How are fees and court costs charged or taxed in an action under USERRA?

No fees or court costs may be charged or taxed against an individual if he or she is claiming rights under the Act. If the individual obtains private counsel for any action or proceeding to enforce a provision of the Act, and prevails, the court may award reasonable attorney fees, expert witness fees, and other litigation expenses.

§ 1002.311 *Is there a statute of limitations in an action under USERRA?*

USERRA does not have a statute of limitations, and it expressly precludes the application of any State statute of limitations. At least one court, however, has held that the fouryear general Federal statute of limitations, 28 U.S.C. 1658, applies to actions under USERRA. *Rogers v. City of San Antonio*, 2003 WL 1566502 (W.D. Texas), *reversed on other grounds*, 392 F.3d 758 (5th Cir. 2004). *But see Akhdary v. City of Chattanooga*, 2002 WL 32060140 (E.D. Tenn.). In addition, if an individual unreasonably delays asserting his or her rights, and that unreasonable delay causes prejudice to the employer, the courts have recognized the availability of the equitable doctrine of *laches* to bar a claim under USERRA. Accordingly, individuals asserting rights under USERRA should determine whether the issue of the applicability of the Federal statute of limitations has been resolved and, in any event, act promptly to preserve their rights under USERRA.

§ 1002.312 *What remedies may be awarded for a violation of USERRA?*

In any action or proceeding the court may award relief as follows:

(a) The court may require the employer to comply with the provisions of the Act;

(b) The court may require the employer to compensate the individual for any loss of wages or benefits suffered by reason of the employer's failure to comply with the Act;

(c) The court may require the employer to pay the individual an amount equal to the amount of lost wages and benefits as liquidated damages, if the court determines that the employer's failure to comply with the Act was willful. A violation shall be considered to be willful if the employer either knew or showed reckless disregard for whether its conduct was prohibited by the Act.

(d) Any wages, benefits, or liquidated damages awarded under paragraphs (b) and (c) of this section are in addition to, and must not diminish, any of the other rights and benefits provided by USERRA (such as, for example, the right to be employed or reemployed by the employer).

§ 1002.313 *Are there special damages provisions that apply to actions initiated in the name of the United States?*

Yes. In an action brought in the name of the United States, for which the relief includes compensation for lost wages, benefits, or liquidated damages, the compensation must be held in a special deposit account and must be paid, on order of the Attorney General, directly to the person. If the compensation is not paid to the individual because of the Federal Government's inability to do so within a period of three years, the compensation must be converted into the Treasury of the United States as miscellaneous receipts.

§ 1002.314 *May a court use its equity powers in an action or proceeding under the Act?*

Yes. A court may use its full equity powers, including the issuance of temporary or permanent injunctions, temporary restraining orders, and contempt orders, to vindicate the rights or benefits guaranteed under the Act.

[¶ 16,453B]

1002 PART 1002—REGULATIONS UNDER THE UNIFORMED SERVICES EMPLOYMENT AND REEMPLOYMENT RIGHTS ACT OF 1994

Appendix to Part 1002—Your Rights Under USERRA

Pursuant to 38 U.S.C. 4334(a), each employer shall provide to persons entitled to rights and benefits under USERRA a notice of the rights, benefits, and obligations of such persons and such employers under USERRA. The requirement for the provision of notice under this section may be met by the posting of one of the following notices where employers customarily place notices for employees. The following texts are provided by the Secretary of Labor to employers pursuant to 38 U.S.C. 4334(b). Text A is appropriate for use by employers in the private sector and for State government employers. Text B is appropriate for use by Federal Executive Agencies.

Text A—For Use by Private Sector and State Government Employers
Your Rights Under USERRA

The Uniformed Services Employment and Reemployment Rights Act

USERRA protects the job rights of individuals who voluntarily or involuntarily leave employment positions to undertake military service or certain types of service in the National Disaster Medical System. USERRA also prohibits employers from discriminating against past and present members of the uniformed services, and applicants to the uniformed services.

Reemployment Rights

You have the right to be reemployed in your civilian job if you leave that job to perform service in the uniformed service and:

• You ensure that your employer receives advance written or verbal notice of your service;

• You have five years or less of cumulative service in the uniformed services while with that particular employer;

• You return to work or apply for reemployment in a timely manner after conclusion of service; and

• You have not been separated from service with a disqualifying discharge or under other than honorable conditions.

If you are eligible to be reemployed, you must be restored to the job and benefits you would have attained if you had not been absent due to military service or, in some cases, a comparable job.

Right To Be Free From Discrimination and Retaliation

If you:

• Are a past or present member of the uniformed service;

• Have applied for membership in the uniformed service;

or

• Are obligated to serve in the uniformed service; then an employer may not deny you

• Initial employment;

• Reemployment;

• Retention in employment;

• Promotion; or

• Any benefit of employment.

because of this status.

In addition, an employer may not retaliate against anyone assisting in the enforcement of USERRA rights, including testifying or making a statement in connection with a proceeding under USERRA, even if that person has no service connection.

Health Insurance Protection

• If you leave your job to perform military service, you have the right to elect to continue your existing employer-based health plan coverage for you and your dependents for up to 24 months while in the military.

• Even if you don't elect to continue coverage during your military service, you have the right to be reinstated in your employer's health plan when you are reemployed, generally without any waiting periods or exclusions (e.g., pre-existing condition exclusions) except for service-connected illnesses or injuries.

Enforcement

• The U.S. Department of Labor, Veterans' Employment and Training Service (VETS) is authorized to investigate and resolve complaints of USERRA violations.

For assistance in filing a complaint, or for any other information on USERRA, contact VETS at 1-866-4-USA-DOL or visit its Web site at *http://frwebgate.access.gpo.gov/cgi-bin/leaving.cgi?from=leavingFR.html&log=linklog&to=http://www.dol.gov/vets* An interactive online USERRA Advisor can be viewed at *http://frwebgate.access.gpo.gov/cgi-bin/leaving.cgi?from=leavingFR.html&log=linklog&to=http://www.dol.gov/elaws/userra.htm.*

• If you file a complaint with VETS and VETS is unable to resolve it, you may request that your case be referred to the Department of Justice for representation.

• You may also bypass the VETS process and bring a civil action against an employer for violations of USERRA.

The rights listed here may vary depending on the circumstances. The text of this notice was prepared by VETS, and may be viewed on the Internet at this address: *http://frwebgate.access.gpo.gov/cgi-bin/leaving.cgi?from=leavingFR.html&log=linklog&to=http://www.dol.gov/vets/programs/userra/poster.htm.*

Federal law requires employers to notify employees of their rights under USERRA, and employers may meet this requirement by displaying the text of this notice where they customarily place notices for employees.

Text B—For Use by Federal Executive Agencies
Your Rights Under USERRA

The Uniformed Services Employment and Reemployment Rights Act

USERRA protects the job rights of individuals who voluntarily or involuntarily leave employment positions to undertake military service or certain types of service in the National Disaster Medical System. USERRA also prohibits employers from discriminating against past and present members of the uniformed services, and applicants to the uniformed services.

Reemployment Rights

You have the right to be reemployed in your civilian job if you leave that job to perform service in the uniformed service and:

• You ensure that your employer receives advance written or verbal notice of your service;

• You have five years or less of cumulative service in the uniformed services while with that particular employer;

• You return to work or apply for reemployment in a timely manner after conclusion of service; and

• You have not been separated from service with a disqualifying discharge or under other than honorable conditions.

If you are eligible to be reemployed, you must be restored to the job and benefits you would have attained if you had not been absent due to military service or, in some cases, a comparable job.

Right To Be Free From Discrimination and Retaliation

If you:

• Are a past or present member of the uniformed service;

• Have applied for membership in the uniformed service; or

• Are obligated to serve in the uniformed service; then an employer may not deny you

  • Initial employment;

  • Reemployment;

  • Retention in employment;

  • Promotion; or

  • Any benefit of employment.

because of this status.

In addition, an employer may not retaliate against anyone assisting in the enforcement of USERRA rights, including testifying or making a statement in connection with a proceeding under USERRA, even if that person has no service connection.

Health Insurance Protection

• If you leave your job to perform military service, you have the right to elect to continue your existing employer-based health plan coverage for you and your dependents for up to 24 months while in the military.

• Even if you don't elect to continue coverage during your military service, you have the right to be reinstated in your employer's health plan when you are reemployed, generally without any waiting periods or exclusions (e.g., pre-existing condition exclusions) except for service-connected illnesses or injuries.

Enforcement

• The U.S. Department of Labor, Veterans' Employment and Training Service (VETS) is authorized to investigate and resolve complaints of USERRA violations.

For assistance in filing a complaint, or for any other information on USERRA, contact VETS at 1-866-4-USA-DOL or visit its Web site at *http:// frwebgate.access.gpo.gov/cgi-bin/leaving.cgi?from=leavingFR.html&log=linklog&to=http://www.dol.gov/vets* An interactive online USERRA Advisor can be viewed at *http:// frwebgate.access.gpo.gov/cgi-bin/leaving.cgi?from=leavingFR.html&log=linklog&to=http://www.dol.gov/elaws/ userra.htm.*

• In some cases involving USERRA claims against Federal executive agencies, a complaint filed with VETS before September 30, 2007, may be transferred to the Office of Special Counsel for investigation and resolution pursuant to a demonstration project established under Section 204 of the Veterans Benefits Improvement Act of 2004, Public Law 108-454 (Dec. 10, 2004).

• If VETS is unable to resolve a complaint that has not been transferred for investigation under the demonstration project, you may request that your case be referred to the Office of Special Counsel for representation.

• You may also bypass the VETS process and bring a civil action against an employer for violations of USERRA.

The rights listed here may vary depending on the circumstances. The text of this notice was prepared by VETS, and may be viewed on the Internet at this address: *http://frwebgate.access.gpo.gov/cgi-bin/leaving.cgi?from=leavingFR.html&log=linklog&to=http://www.dol.gov/vets/* programs/userra/poster.htm. Federal law requires employers to notify employees of their rights under USERRA, and employers may meet this requirement by displaying the text of this notice where they customarily place notices for employees.

U.S. Department of Labor, Veterans' Employment and Training Service, 1-866-487-2365.

Bankruptcy Abuse Prevention and Consumer Protection Act of 2005

P.L. 109-8

Signed on April 20, 2005

[Reproduced below are excerpts from the Bankruptcy Abuse Prevention and Consumer Protection Act of 2005 (P.L. 109-8) that pertain to pensions and employee benefits.]

TITLE II—ENHANCED CONSUMER PROTECTION

SUBTITLE C—OTHER CONSUMER PROTECTIONS

[¶16,456]

ACT SEC. 224. PROTECTION OF RETIREMENT SAVINGS IN BANKRUPTCY. (a) *In general.* Section 522 of title 11, United States Code, is amended—

(1) in subsection (b)—

(A) in paragraph (2)—

(i) in subparagraph (A), by striking 'and' at the end;

(ii) in subparagraph (B), by striking the period at the end and inserting '; and';

(iii) by adding at the end the following:

'(C) retirement funds to the extent that those funds are in a fund or account that is exempt from taxation under section 401, 403, 408, 408A, 414, 57, or 501(a) of the Internal Revenue Code of 1986.'; and

(iv) by striking '(2)(A) any property' and inserting:

'(3) Property listed in this paragraph is—

'(A) any property';

(B) by striking paragraph (1) and inserting:

'(2) Property listed in this paragraph is property that is specified under subsection (d), unless the State law that is applicable to the debtor under paragraph (3)(A) specifically does not so authorize.';

(C) by striking '(b) Notwithstanding' and inserting '(b)(1) Notwithstanding';

(D) by striking 'paragraph (2)' each place it appears and inserting 'paragraph (3)';

(E) by striking 'paragraph (1)' each place it appears and inserting 'paragraph (2)';

(F) by striking 'Such property is—'; and

(G) by adding at the end the following:

'(4) For purposes of paragraph (3)(C) and subsection (d)(12), the following shall apply:

'(A) If the retirement funds are in a retirement fund that has received a favorable determination under section 7805 of the Internal Revenue Code of 1986, and that determination is in effect as of the date of the filing of the petition in a case under this title, those funds shall be presumed to be exempt from the estate.

'(B) If the retirement funds are in a retirement fund that has not received a favorable determination under such section 7805, those funds are exempt from the estate if the debtor demonstrates that—

'(i) no prior determination to the contrary has been made by a court or the Internal Revenue Service; and

'(ii)(I) the retirement fund is in substantial compliance with the applicable requirements of the Internal Revenue Code of 1986; or

'(II) the retirement fund fails to be in substantial compliance with the applicable requirements of the Internal Revenue Code of 1986 and the debtor is not materially responsible for that failure.

'(C) A direct transfer of retirement funds from 1 fund or account that is exempt from taxation under section 401, 403, 408, 408A, 414, 457, or 501(a) of the Internal Revenue Code of 1986, under section 401(a)(31) of the Internal Revenue Code of 1986, or otherwise, shall not cease to qualify for exemption under paragraph (3)(C) or subsection (d)(12) by reason of such direct transfer.

'(D)(i) Any distribution that qualifies as an eligible rollover distribution within the meaning of section 402(c) of the Internal Revenue Code of 1986 or that is described in clause (ii) shall not cease to qualify for exemption under paragraph (3)(C) or subsection (d)(12) by reason of such distribution.

'(ii) A distribution described in this clause is an amount that—

'(I) has been distributed from a fund or account that is exempt from taxation under section 401, 403, 408, 408A, 414, 457, or 501(a) of the Internal Revenue Code of 1986; and

'(II) to the extent allowed by law, is deposited in such a fund or account not later than 60 days after the distribution of such amount.'; and

(2) in subsection (d)—

(A) in the matter preceding paragraph (1), by striking 'subsection (b)(1)' and inserting 'subsection (b)(2)'; and

(B) by adding at the end the following:

'(12) Retirement funds to the extent that those funds are in a fund or account that is exempt from taxation under section 401, 403, 408, 408A, 414, 457, or 501(a) of the Internal Revenue Code of 1986.'.

(b) *Automatic stay.* Section 362(b) of title 11, United States Code, is amended—

(1) in paragraph (17), by striking 'or' at the end;

(2) in paragraph (18), by striking the period and inserting a semicolon; and

(3) by inserting after paragraph (18) the following:

'(19) under subsection (a), of withholding of income from a debtor's wages and collection of amounts withheld, under the debtor's agreement authorizing that withholding and collection for the benefit of a pension, profit-sharing, stock bonus, or other plan established under section 401, 403, 408, 408A, 414, 457, or 501(c) of the Internal Revenue Code of 1986, that is sponsored by the employer of the debtor, or an affiliate, successor, or predecessor of such employer—

ACT SEC. 224.   ¶16,456

'(A) to the extent that the amounts withheld and collected are used solely for payments relating to a loan from a plan under section 408(b)(1) of the Employee Retirement Income Security Act of 1974 or is subject to section 72(p) of the Internal Revenue Code of 1986; or

'(B) a loan from a thrift savings plan permitted under subchapter III of chapter 84 of title 5, that satisfies the requirements of section 8433(g) of such title; but nothing in this paragraph may be construed to provide that any loan made under a governmental plan under section 414(d), or a contract or account under section 403(b), of the Internal Revenue Code of 1986 constitutes a claim or a debt under this title;'.

(c) *Exceptions to discharge.* Section 523(a) of title 11, United States Code, as amended by section 215, is amended by inserting after paragraph (17) the following:

'(18) owed to a pension, profit-sharing, stock bonus, or other plan established under section 401, 403, 408, 408A, 414, 457, or 501(c) of the Internal Revenue Code of 1986, under—

'(A) a loan permitted under section 408(b)(1) of the Employee Retirement Income Security Act of 1974, or subject to section 72(p) of the Internal Revenue Code of 1986; or

'(B) a loan from a thrift savings plan permitted under subchapter III of chapter 84 of title 5, that satisfies the requirements of section 8433(g) of such title; but nothing in this paragraph may be construed to provide that any loan made under a governmental plan under section 414(d), or a contract or account under section 403(b), of the Internal Revenue Code of 1986 constitutes a claim or a debt under this title; or'.

(d) *Plan contents.* Section 1322 of title 11, United States Code, is amended by adding at the end the following:

'(f) A plan may not materially alter the terms of a loan described in section 362(b)(19) and any amounts required to repay such loan shall not constitute 'disposable income' under section 1325.'.

(e) *Asset limitation.* (1) *Limitation.* Section 522 of title 11, United States Code, is amended by adding at the end the following:

'(n) For assets in individual retirement accounts described in section 408 or 408A of the Internal Revenue Code of 1986, other than a simplified employee pension under section 408(k) of such Code or a simple retirement account under section 408(p) of such Code, the aggregate value of such assets exempted under this section, without regard to amounts attributable to rollover contributions under section 402(c), 402(e)(6), 403(a)(4), 403(a)(5), and 403(b)(8) of the Internal Revenue Code of 1986, and earnings thereon, shall not exceed $1,000,000 in a case filed by a debtor who is an individual, except that such amount may be increased if the interests of justice so require.'.

(2) *Adjustment of dollar amounts.* Paragraphs (1) and (2) of section 104(b) of title 11, United States Code, are amended by inserting '522(n),' after '522(d),'.

[¶16,457]

ACT SEC. 225 PROTECTION OF EDUCATION SAVINGS IN BANKRUPTCY. (a) *Exclusions.* Section 541 of title 11, United States Code, is amended—

(1) in subsection (b)—

(A) in paragraph (4), by striking 'or' at the end;

(B) by redesignating paragraph (5) as paragraph (9); and

(C) by inserting after paragraph (4) the following:

'(5) funds placed in an education individual retirement account (as defined in section 530(b)(1) of the Internal Revenue Code of 1986) not later than 365 days before the date of the filing of the petition in a case under this title, but—

'(A) only if the designated beneficiary of such account was a child, stepchild, grandchild, or stepgrandchild of the debtor for the taxable year for which funds were placed in such account;

'(B) only to the extent that such funds—

'(i) are not pledged or promised to any entity in connection with any extension of credit; and

'(ii) are not excess contributions (as described in section 4973(e) of the Internal Revenue Code of 1986); and

'(C) in the case of funds placed in all such accounts having the same designated beneficiary not earlier than 720 days nor later than 365 days before such date, only so much of such funds as does not exceed $5,000;

'(6) funds used to purchase a tuition credit or certificate or contributed to an account in accordance with section 529(b)(1)(A) of the Internal Revenue Code of 1986 under a qualified State tuition program (as defined in section 529(b)(1) of such Code) not later than 365 days before the date of the filing of the petition in a case under this title, but—

'(A) only if the designated beneficiary of the amounts paid or contributed to such tuition program was a child, stepchild, grandchild, or stepgrandchild of the debtor for the taxable year for which funds were paid or contributed;

'(B) with respect to the aggregate amount paid or contributed to such program having the same designated beneficiary, only so much of such amount as does not exceed the total contributions permitted under section 529(b)(6) of such Code with respect to such beneficiary, as adjusted beginning on the date of the filing of the petition in a case under this title by the annual increase or decrease (rounded to the nearest tenth of 1 percent) in the education expenditure category of the Consumer Price Index prepared by the Department of Labor; and

'(C) in the case of funds paid or contributed to such program having the same designated beneficiary not earlier than 720 days nor later than 365 days before such date, only so much of such funds as does not exceed $5,000;'; and

(2) by adding at the end the following:

'(e) In determining whether any of the relationships specified in paragraph (5)(A) or (6)(A) of subsection (b) exists, a legally adopted child of an individual (and a child who is a member of an individual's household, if placed with such individual by an authorized placement agency for legal adoption by such individual), or a foster child of an individual (if such child has as the child's principal place of abode the home of the debtor and is a member of the debtor's household) shall be treated as a child of such individual by blood.'.

(b) *Debtor's duties.* Section 521 of title 11, United States Code, as amended by section 106, is amended by adding at the end the following:

'(c) In addition to meeting the requirements under subsection (a), a debtor shall file with the court a record of any interest that a debtor has in an education individual retirement account (as defined in section 530(b)(1) of the Internal Revenue Code of 1986) or under a qualified State tuition program (as defined in section 529(b)(1) of such Code).'.

* * *

Amendments

The above amendment is effective December 22, 2010.

P.L. 111-327, §2(a)(22):

Act Sec. 2(a)(22) amends Act Sec. 225(a)(1)(C)(6)(B) by striking "section 529(b)(7)" and inserting "section 529(b)(6)".

TITLE III.—DISCOURAGING BANKRUPTCY ABUSE

[¶16,458]

ACT SEC. 323 EXCLUDING EMPLOYEE BENEFIT PLAN PARTICIPANT CONTRIBUTIONS AND OTHER PROPERTY FROM THE ESTATE. Section 541(b) of title 11, United States Code, as amended by section 225, is amended by adding after paragraph (6), as added by section 225(a)(1)(C), the following:

'(7) any amount—

'(A) withheld by an employer from the wages of employees for payment as contributions—

'(i) to—

'(I) an employee benefit plan that is subject to title I of the Employee Retirement Income Security Act of 1974 or under an employee benefit plan which is a governmental plan under section 414(d) of the Internal Revenue Code of 1986;

'(II) a deferred compensation plan under section 457 of the Internal Revenue Code of 1986; or

'(III) a tax-deferred annuity under section 403(b) of the Internal Revenue Code of 1986; except that such amount under this subparagraph shall not constitute disposable income as defined in section 1325(b)(2); or

'(ii) to a health insurance plan regulated by State law whether or not subject to such title; or

'(B) received by an employer from employees for payment as contributions—

'(i) to—

'(I) an employee benefit plan that is subject to title I of the Employee Retirement Income Security Act of 1974 or under an employee benefit plan which is a governmental plan under section 414(d) of the Internal Revenue Code of 1986;

'(II) a deferred compensation plan under section 457 of the Internal Revenue Code of 1986; or

'(III) a tax-deferred annuity under section 403(b) of the Internal Revenue Code of 1986; except that such amount under this subparagraph shall not constitute disposable income, as defined in section 1325(b)(2); or

'(ii) to a health insurance plan regulated by State law whether or not subject to such title;'.

* * *

[¶16,459]

ACT SEC. 329. CLARIFICATION OF POSTPETITION WAGES AND BENEFITS. Section 503(b)(1)(A) of title 11, United States Code, is amended to read as follows:

'(A) the actual, necessary costs and expenses of preserving the estate including—

'(i) wages, salaries, and commissions for services rendered after the commencement of the case; and

'(ii) wages and benefits awarded pursuant to a judicial proceeding or a proceeding of the National Labor Relations Board as back pay attributable to any period of time occurring after commencement of the case under this title, as a result of a violation of Federal or State law by the debtor, without regard to the time of the occurrence of unlawful conduct on which such award is based or to whether any services were rendered, if the court determines that payment of wages and benefits by reason of the operation of this clause will not substantially increase the probability of layoff or termination of current employees, or of nonpayment of domestic support obligations, during the case under this title;'.

* * *

[¶16,459A]

ACT SEC. 331. LIMITATION ON RETENTION BONUSES, SEVERANCE PAY, AND CERTAIN OTHER PAYMENTS. Section 503 of title 11, United States Code, is amended by adding at the end the following:

'(c) Notwithstanding subsection (b), there shall neither be allowed, nor paid—

'(1) a transfer made to, or an obligation incurred for the benefit of, an insider of the debtor for the purpose of inducing such person to remain with the debtor's business, absent a finding by the court based on evidence in the record that—

'(A) the transfer or obligation is essential to retention of the person because the individual has a bona fide job offer from another business at the same or greater rate of compensation;

'(B) the services provided by the person are essential to the survival of the business; and

'(C) either—

'(i) the amount of the transfer made to, or obligation incurred for the benefit of, the person is not greater than an amount equal to 10 times the amount of the mean transfer or obligation of a similar kind given to nonmanagement employees for any purpose during the calendar year in which the transfer is made or the obligation is incurred; or

'(ii) if no such similar transfers were made to, or obligations were incurred for the benefit of, such nonmanagement employees during such calendar year, the amount of the transfer or obligation is not greater than an amount equal to 25 percent of the amount of any similar transfer or obligation made to or incurred for the benefit of such insider for any purpose during the calendar year before the year in which such transfer is made or obligation is incurred;

'(2) a severance payment to an insider of the debtor, unless—

'(A) the payment is part of a program that is generally applicable to all full-time employees; and

'(B) the amount of the payment is not greater than 10 times the amount of the mean severance pay given to nonmanagement employees during the calendar year in which the payment is made; or

'(3) other transfers or obligations that are outside the ordinary course of business and not justified by the facts and circumstances of the case, including transfers made to, or obligations incurred for the benefit of, officers, managers, or consultants hired after the date of the filing of the petition.'.

ACT SEC. 331.   ¶16,459A

[¶16,459B]

ACT SEC. 332. FRAUDULENT INVOLUNTARY BANKRUPTCY. (a) *Short title.* This section may be cited as the 'Involuntary Bankruptcy Improvement Act of 2005'.

(b) *Involuntary cases.* Section 303 of title 11, United States Code, is amended by adding at the end the following:

'(k)(1) If—

'(A) the petition under this section is false or contains any materially false, fictitious, or fraudulent statement;

'(B) the debtor is an individual; and

'(C) the court dismisses such petition, the court, upon the motion of the debtor, shall seal all the records of the court relating to such petition, and all references to such petition.

'(2) If the debtor is an individual and the court dismisses a petition under this section, the court may enter an order prohibiting all consumer reporting agencies (as defined in section 603(f) of the Fair Credit Reporting Act (15 U.S.C. 1681a(f))) from making any consumer report (as defined in section 603(d) of that Act) that contains any information relating to such petition or to the case commenced by the filing of such petition.

'(3) Upon the expiration of the statute of limitations described in section 3282 of title 18, for a violation of section 152 or 157 of such title, the court, upon the motion of the debtor and for good cause, may expunge any records relating to a petition filed under this section.'.

(c) *Bankruptcy fraud.* Section 157 of title 18, United States Code, is amended by inserting ', including a fraudulent involuntary bankruptcy petition under section 303 of such title' after 'title 11'.

* * *

Amendments	The above amendment is effective December 22, 2010.

P.L. 111-327, §2(a)(9):

Act Sec. 2(a)(9) amends Act Sec. 332(b) by redesignating subsection (l) as subsection (k).

TITLE IV.—GENERAL AND SMALL BUSINESS BANKRUPTCY PROVISIONS

SUBTITLE B—SMALL BANKRUPTCY PROVISIONS

[¶16,459C]

ACT SEC. 446. DUTIES WITH RESPECT TO A DEBTOR WHO IS A PLAN ADMINISTRATOR OF AN EMPLOYEE BENEFIT PLAN. (a) *In general.* Section 521(a) of title 11, United States Code, as amended by sections 106 and 304, is amended—

(1) in paragraph (5), by striking 'and' at the end;

(2) in paragraph (6), by striking the period at the end and inserting '; and'; and

(3) by adding after paragraph (6) the following:

'(7) unless a trustee is serving in the case, continue to perform the obligations required of the administrator (as defined in section 3 of the Employee Retirement Income Security Act of 1974) of an employee benefit plan if at the time of the commencement of the case the debtor (or any entity designated by the debtor) served as such administrator.'.

(b) *Duties of trustees.* Section 704(a) of title 11, United States Code, as amended by sections 102 and 219, is amended—

(1) in paragraph (10), by striking 'and' at the end; and

(2) by adding at the end the following:

'(11) if, at the time of the commencement of the case, the debtor (or any entity designated by the debtor) served as the administrator (as defined in section 3 of the Employee Retirement Income Security Act of 1974) of an employee benefit plan, continue to perform the obligations required of the administrator; and'.

(c) *Conforming amendment.* Section 1106(a)(1) of title 11, United States Code, is amended to read as follows:

'(1) perform the duties of the trustee, as specified in paragraphs (2), (5), (7), (8), (9), (10), and (11) of section 704;'.

* * *

TITLE XIII.—TECHNICAL AMENDMENTS

[¶16,459D]

ACT SEC. 1202. ADJUSTMENT OF DOLLAR AMOUNTS. Section 104(b) of title 11, United States Code, as amended by this Act, is further amended—

(1) by inserting '101(19A),' after '101(18),' each place it appears;

(2) by inserting '522(f)(3) and 522(f)(4),' after '522(d),' each place it appears;

(3) by inserting '541(b), 547(c)(9),' after '523(a)(2)(C),' each place it appears;

(4) in paragraph (1), by striking 'and 1325(b)(3)' and inserting '1322(d), 1325(b), and 1326(b)(3) of this title and section 1409(b) of title 28'; and

(5) in paragraph (2), by striking 'and 1325(b)(3) of this title' and inserting '1322(d), 1325(b), and 1326(b)(3) of this title and section 1409(b) of title 28'.

* * *

[¶16,459E]

ACT SEC. 1208. ALLOWANCE OF ADMINISTRATIVE EXPENSES. Section 503(b)(4) of title 11, United States Code, is amended by inserting 'subparagraph (A), (B), (C), (D), or (E) of' before 'paragraph (3)'.

[¶16,459F]

ACT SEC. 1209. EXCEPTIONS TO DISCHARGE. Section 523 of title 11, United States Code, as amended by sections 215 and 314, is amended—

(1) by transferring paragraph (15), as added by section 304(e) of Public Law 103-394 (108 Stat. 4133), so as to insert such paragraph after subsection (a)(14A);

(2) in subsection (a)(9), by striking 'motor vehicle' and inserting 'motor vehicle, vessel, or aircraft'; and

(3) in subsection (e), by striking 'a insured' and inserting 'an insured'.

* * *

TITLE XIV.—PREVENTING CORPORATE BANKRUPTCY ABUSE

[¶16,459G]

ACT SEC. 1401. EMPLOYEE WAGE AND BENEFIT PRIORITIES. Section 507(a) of title 11, United States Code, as amended by section 212, is amended—

(1) in paragraph (4) by striking '90' and inserting '180', and

(2) in paragraphs (4) and (5) by striking '$4,000' and inserting '$10,000'.

[¶16,459H]

ACT SEC. 1402. FRAUDULENT TRANSFERS AND OBLIGATIONS. Section 548 of title 11, United States Code, is amended—

(1) in subsections (a) and (b) by striking 'one year' and inserting '2 years',

(2) in subsection (a)—(A) by inserting '(including any transfer to or for the benefit of an insider under an employment contract)' after 'transfer' the 1st place it appears, and

(B) by inserting '(including any obligation to or for the benefit of an insider under an employment contract)' after 'obligation' the 1st place it appears, and

(3) in subsection (a)(1)(B)(ii)—

(A) in subclause (II) by striking 'or' at the end,

(B) in subclause (III) by striking the period at the end and inserting '; or', and

(C) by adding at the end the following:

'(IV) made such transfer to or for the benefit of an insider, or incurred such obligation to or for the benefit of an insider, under an employment contract and not in the ordinary course of business.'.

(4) by adding at the end the following:

'(e)(1) In addition to any transfer that the trustee may otherwise avoid, the trustee may avoid any transfer of an interest of the debtor in property that was made on or within 10 years before the date of the filing of the petition, if—

'(A) such transfer was made to a self-settled trust or similar device;

'(B) such transfer was by the debtor;

'(C) the debtor is a beneficiary of such trust or similar device; and

'(D) the debtor made such transfer with actual intent to hinder, delay, or defraud any entity to which the debtor was or became, on or after the date that such transfer was made, indebted.

'(2) For the purposes of this subsection, a transfer includes a transfer made in anticipation of any money judgment, settlement, civil penalty, equitable order, or criminal fine incurred by, or which the debtor believed would be incurred by—

'(A) any violation of the securities laws (as defined in section 3(a)(47) of the Securities Exchange Act of 1934 (15 U.S.C. 78c(a)(47))), any State securities laws, or any regulation or order issued under Federal securities laws or State securities laws; or

'(B) fraud, deceit, or manipulation in a fiduciary capacity or in connection with the purchase or sale of any security registered under section 12 or 15(d) of the Securities Exchange Act of 1934 (15 U.S.C. 78l and 78o(d)) or under section 6 of the Securities Act of 1933 (15 U.S.C. 77f).'.

* * *

[¶16,459I]

ACT SEC. 1403. PAYMENT OF INSURANCE BENEFITS TO RETIRED EMPLOYEES. Section 1114 of title 11, United States Code, is amended—

(1) by redesignating subsection (l) as subsection (m), and

(2) by inserting after subsection (k) the following:

'(l) If the debtor, during the 180-day period ending on the date of the filing of the petition—

'(1) modified retiree benefits; and

'(2) was insolvent on the date such benefits were modified; the court, on motion of a party in interest, and after notice and a hearing, shall issue an order reinstating as of the date the modification was made, such benefits as in effect immediately before such date unless the court finds that the balance of the equities clearly favors such modification.'.

* * *

[¶16,459J]

ACT SEC. 1406. EFFECTIVE DATE; APPLICATION OF AMENDMENTS. (a) *Effective date.* Except as provided in subsection (b), this title and the amendments made by this title shall take effect on the date of the enactment of this Act.

(b) *Application of amendments.* (1) *In general.* ***except as provided in paragraph (2), the amendments made by this title shall apply only with respect to cases commenced under title 11 of the United States Code on or after the date of the enactment of this Act.

(2) *Avoidance period.* The amendment made by section 1402(1) shall apply only with respect to cases commenced under title 11 of the United States Code more than 1 year after the date of the enactment of this Act.

TITLE XV—GENERAL EFFECTIVE DATE; APPLICATION OF AMENDMENTS

[¶16,459K]

ACT SEC. 1501. EFFECTIVE DATE; APPLICATION OF AMENDMENTS. (a) *Effective date.* Except as otherwise provided in this Act, this Act and the amendments made by this Act shall take effect 180 days after the date of enactment of this Act.

(b) *Application of amendments.* (1) *In general.* Except as otherwise provided in this Act and paragraph (2), the amendments made by this Act shall not apply with respect to cases commenced under title 11, United States Code, before the effective date of this Act.

(2) *Certain limitation applicable to debtors.* The amendments made by sections 308, 322, and 330 shall apply with respect to cases commenced under title 11, United States Code, on or after the date of the enactment of this Act.

[¶16,459L]

ACT SEC. 1502. TECHNICAL CORRECTIONS. (a) *Conforming amendments to Title 11 of the United States Code.* Title 11 of the United States Code, as amended by the preceding provisions of this Act, is amended—

  (1) in section 507—

    (A) in subsection (a)—

      (i) in paragraph (5)(B)(ii) by striking 'paragraph (3)' and inserting 'paragraph (4)'; and

      (ii) in paragraph (8)(D) by striking 'paragraph (3)' and inserting 'paragraph (4)';

    (B) in subsection (b) by striking 'subsection (a)(1)' and inserting 'subsection (a)(2)'; and

    (C) in subsection (d) by striking 'subsection (a)(3)' and inserting 'subsection (a)(1)';

  (2) in section 523(a)(1)(A) by striking '507(a)(2)' and inserting '507(a)(3)';

  (3) in section 752(a) by striking '507(a)(1)' and inserting '507(a)(2)';

  (4) in section 766—

    (A) in subsection (h) by striking '507(a)(1)' and inserting '507(a)(2)'; and

    (B) in subsection (i) by striking '507(a)(1)' each place it appears and inserting '507(a)(2)';

  (5) in section 901(a) by striking '507(a)(1)' and inserting '507(a)(2)';

  (6) in section 943(b)(5) by striking '507(a)(1)' and inserting '507(a)(2)';

  (7) in section 1123(a)(1) by striking '507(a)(1), 507(a)(2)' and inserting '507(a)(2), 507(a)(3)';

  (8) in section 1129(a)(9)—

    (A) in subparagraph (A) by striking '507(a)(1) or 507(a)(2)' and inserting '507(a)(2) or 507(a)(3)'; and

    (B) in subparagraph (B) by striking '507(a)(3)' and inserting '507(a)(1)';

  (9) in section 1226(b)(1) by striking '507(a)(1)' and inserting '507(a)(2)'; and

  (10) in section 1326(b)(1) by striking '507(a)(1)' and inserting '507(a)(2)'.

  (b) *Related conforming amendment.* Section 6(e) of the Securities Investor Protection Act of 1970 (15 U.S.C. 78fff(e)) is amended by striking '507(a)(1)' and inserting '507(a)(2)'.

Katrina Emergency Tax Relief Act

[¶16,460]

P.L. 109-73

Signed on September 21, 2005

[Reproduced below are excerpts from the Katrina Emergency Tax Relief Act (P.L. 109-73) that pertain to pensions and employee benefits. The Act provides emergency tax relief for victims of Hurricane Katrina.]

[¶16,460A]

ACT SEC. 1. SHORT TITLE, ETC. (a) *Short title*. This Act may be cited as the "Katrina Emergency Tax Relief Act of 2005".

* * *

[¶16,460B]

ACT SEC. 2. HURRICANE KATRINA DISASTER AREA. For purposes of this Act—

(1) *Hurricane Katrina disaster area*. The term "Hurricane Katrina disaster area" means an area with respect to which a major disaster has been declared by the President before September 14, 2005, under section 401 of the Robert T. Stafford Disaster Relief and Emergency Assistance Act by reason of Hurricane Katrina.

(2) *Core disaster area*. The term "core disaster area" means that portion of the Hurricane Katrina disaster area determined by the President to warrant individual or individual and public assistance from the Federal Government under such Act.

TITLE I.—SPECIAL RULES FOR USE OF RETIREMENT FUNDS FOR RELIEF RELATING TO HURRICANE KATRINA

[¶16,460C]

⋙→ *Caution: Sec. 101, below, was repealed by the Gulf Opportunity Zone Act (P.L. 109-135), Act Sec. 201(b)(4), effective December 21, 2005.*

ACT SEC. 101. TAX-FAVORED WITHDRAWALS FROM RETIREMENT PLANS FOR RELIEF RELATING TO HURRICANE KATRINA. (a) *In general*. Section 72(t) of the Internal Revenue Code of 1986 shall not apply to any qualified Hurricane Katrina distribution.

(b) *Aggregate dollar limitation.—*

(1) *In general*. For purposes of this section, the aggregate amount of distributions received by an individual which may be treated as qualified Hurricane Katrina distributions for any taxable year shall not exceed the excess (if any) of—

(A) $100,000, over

(B) the aggregate amounts treated as qualified Hurricane Katrina distributions received by such individual for all prior taxable years.

(2) *Treatment of plan distributions*. If a distribution to an individual would (without regard to paragraph (1)) be a qualified Hurricane Katrina distribution, a plan shall not be treated as violating any requirement of the Internal Revenue Code of 1986 merely because the plan treats such distribution as a qualified Hurricane Katrina distribution, unless the aggregate amount of such distributions from all plans maintained by the employer (and any member of any controlled group which includes the employer) to such individual exceeds $100,000.

(3) *Controlled group*. For purposes of paragraph (2), the term "controlled group" means any group treated as a single employer under sub-section (b), (c), (m), or (o) of section 414 of such Code.

(c) *Amount distributed may be repaid.—*

(1) *In general*. Any individual who receives a qualified Hurricane Katrina distribution may, at any time during the 3-year period beginning on the day after the date on which such distribution was received, make one or more contributions in an aggregate amount not to exceed the amount of such distribution to an eligible retirement plan of which such individual is a beneficiary and to which a rollover contribution of such distribution could be made under section 402(c), 403(a)(4), 403(b)(8), 408(d)(3), or 457(e)(16) of such Code, as the case may be.

(2) *Treatment of repayments of distributions from eligible retirement plans other than IRAs*. For purposes of such Code, if a contribution is made pursuant to paragraph (1) with respect to a qualified Hurricane Katrina distribution from an eligible retirement plan other than an individual retirement plan, then the taxpayer shall, to the extent of the amount of the contribution, be treated as having received the qualified Hurricane Katrina distribution in an eligible rollover distribution (as defined in section 402(c)(4) of such Code) and as having transferred the amount to the eligible retirement plan in a direct trustee to trustee transfer within 60 days of the distribution.

(3) *Treatment of repayments for distributions from IRAs*. For purposes of such Code, if a contribution is made pursuant to paragraph (1) with respect to a qualified Hurricane Katrina distribution from an individual retirement plan (as defined by section 7701(a)(37) of such Code), then, to the extent of the amount of the contribution, the qualified Hurricane Katrina distribution shall be treated as a distribution described in section 408(d)(3) of such Code and as having been transferred to the eligible retirement plan in a direct trustee to trustee transfer within 60 days of the distribution.

(d) *Definitions*.—For purposes of this section—

(1) *Qualified Hurricane Katrina distribution* . Except as provided in subsection (b), the term "qualified Hurricane Katrina distribution" means any distribution from an eligible retirement plan made on or after August 25, 2005, and before January 1, 2007, to an individual whose principal place of abode on August 28, 2005, is located in the Hurricane Katrina disaster area and who has sustained an economic loss by reason of Hurricane Katrina.

(2) *Eligible retirement plan*. The term "eligible retirement plan" shall have the meaning given such term by section 402(c)(8)(B) of such Code.

(e) *Income inclusion spread over 3 year period for qualified Hurricane Katrina distributions.—*

(1) *In general*. In the case of any qualified Hurricane Katrina distribution, unless the taxpayer elects not to have this subsection apply for any taxable year, any amount required to be included in gross income for such taxable year shall be so included ratably over the 3-taxable year period beginning with such taxable year.

ACT SEC. 101.   ¶16,460C

(2) *Special rule.* For purposes of paragraph (1), rules similar to the rules of subparagraph (E) of section 408A(d)(3) of such Code shall apply.

(f) *Special rules.*—

(1) *Exemption of distributions from trustee to trustee transfer and withholding rules.* For purposes of sections 401(a)(31), 402(f), and 3405 of such Code, qualified Hurricane Katrina distributions shall not be treated as eligible rollover distributions.

(2) *Qualified Hurricane Katrina distributions treated as meeting plan distribution requirements.* For purposes of such Code, a qualified Hurricane Katrina distribution shall be treated as meeting the requirements of sections 401(k)(2)(B)(i), 403(b)(7)(A)(ii), 403(b)(11), and 457(d)(1)(A) of such Code.

[¶16,460D]

»»→ *Caution: Sec. 102, below, was repealed by the Gulf Opportunity Zone Act (P.L. 109-135), Act Sec. 201(b)(4), effective December 21, 2005.*

ACT SEC. 102. RECONTRIBUTIONS OF WITHDRAWALS FOR HOME PURCHASES CANCELLED DUE TO HURRICANE KATRINA. (a) *Recontributions.*—

(1) *In general.* Any individual who received a qualified distribution may, during the period beginning on August 25, 2005, and ending on February 28, 2006, make one or more contributions in an aggregate amount not to exceed the amount of such qualified distribution to an eligible retirement plan (as defined in section 402(c)(8)(B) of the Internal Revenue Code of 1986) of which such individual is a beneficiary and to which a rollover contribution of such distribution could be made under section 402(c), 403(a)(4), 403(b)(8), or 408(d)(3) of such Code, as the case may be.

(2) *Treatment of repayments.* Rules similar to the rules of paragraphs (2) and (3) of section 101(c) of this Act shall apply for purposes of this section.

(b) *Qualified distribution defined.* For purposes of this section, the term "qualified distribution" means any distribution—

(1) described in section 401(k)(2)(B)(i)(IV), 403(b)(7)(A)(ii) (but only to the extent such distribution relates to financial hardship), 403(b)(11)(B), or 72(t)(2)(F) of such Code,

(2) received after February 28, 2005, and before August 29, 2005, and

(3) which was to be used to purchase or construct a principal residence in the Hurricane Katrina disaster area, but which was not so purchased or constructed on account of Hurricane Katrina.

[¶16,460E]

»»→ *Caution: Sec. 103, below, was repealed by the Gulf Opportunity Zone Act (P.L. 109-135), Act Sec. 201(b)(4), effective December 21, 2005.*

ACT SEC. 103. LOANS FROM QUALIFIFED PLANS FOR RELIEF RELATING TO HURRICANE KATRINA. (a) *Increase in limit on loans not treated as distributions.* In the case of any loan from a qualified employer plan (as defined under section 72(p)(4) of the Internal Revenue Code of 1986) to a qualified individual made after the date of enactment of this Act and before January 1, 2007—

(1) clause (i) of section 72(p)(2)(A) of such Code shall be applied by substituting "$100,000" for "$50,000", and

(2) (2) clause (ii) of such section shall be applied by substituting "the present value of the nonforfeitable accrued benefit of the employee under the plan" for "one-half of the present value of the nonforfeitable accrued benefit of the employee under the plan".

(b) *Delay of repayment.* In the case of a qualified individual with an outstanding loan on or after August 25, 2005, from a qualified employer plan (as defined in section 72(p)(4) of such Code)—

(1) if the due date pursuant to subparagraph (B) or (C) of section 72(p)(2) of such Code for any repayment with respect to such loan occurs during the period beginning on August 25, 2005, and ending on December 31, 2006, such due date shall be delayed for 1 year,

(2) any subsequent repayments with respect to any such loan shall be appropriately adjusted to reflect the delay in the due date under paragraph (1) and any interest accruing during such delay, and

(3) in determining the 5-year period and the term of a loan under subparagraph (B) or (C) of section 72(p)(2) of such Code, the period described in paragraph (1) shall be disregarded.

(c) *Qualified individual.* For purposes of this section, the term "qualified individual" means an individual whose principal place of abode on August 28, 2005, is located in the Hurricane Katrina disaster area and who has sustained an economic loss by reason of Hurricane Katrina.

[¶16,460F]

»»→ *Caution: Sec. 104, below, was repealed by the Gulf Opportunity Zone Act (P.L. 109-135), Act Sec. 201(b)(4), effective December 21, 2005.*

ACT SEC. 104. PROVISIONS RELATING TO PLAN AMENDMENTS. (a) *In general.* If this section applies to any amendment to any plan or annuity contract, such plan or contract shall be treated as being operated in accordance with the terms of the plan during the period described in subsection (b)(2)(A).

(b) *Amendments to which section applies.*—

(1) *In general.* This section shall apply to any amendment to any plan or annuity contract which is made—

(A) pursuant to any amendment made by this title, or pursuant to any regulation issued by the Secretary of the Treasury or the Secretary of Labor under this title, and

(B) on or before the last day of the first plan year beginning on or after January 1, 2007, or such later date as the Secretary of the Treasury may prescribe.

In the case of a governmental plan (as defined in section 414(d) of the Internal Revenue Code of 1986), subparagraph (B) shall be applied by substituting the date which is 2 years after the date otherwise applied under subparagraph (B).

(2) *Conditions.* This section shall not apply to any amendment unless—

(A) during the period—

(i) beginning on the date the legislative or regulatory amendment described in paragraph (1)(A) takes effect (or in the case of a plan or contract amendment not required by such legislative or regulatory amendment, the effective date specified by the plan), and

(ii) ending on the date described in paragraph (1)(B) (or, if earlier, the date the plan or contract amendment is adopted),

the plan or contract is operated as if such plan or contract amendment were in effect; and

(B) (iii) such plan or contract amendment applies retroactively for such period.

TITLE II.—EMPLOYMENT RELIEF

[¶16,460G]

ACT SEC. 201. WORK OPPORTUNITY TAX CREDIT FOR HURRICANE KATRINA EMPLOYEES. (a) *In general.* For purposes of section 51 of the Internal Revenue Code of 1986, a Hurricane Katrina employee shall be treated as a member of a targeted group.

(b) *Hurricane Katrina Employee.* For purposes of this section, the term "Hurricane Katrina employee" means—

(1) any individual who on August 28, 2005, had a principal place of abode in the core disaster area and who is hired during the 2-year period beginning on such date for a position the principal place of employment of which is located in the core disaster area, and

(2) any individual who on such date had a principal place of abode in the core disaster area, who is displaced from such abode by reason of Hurricane Katrina, and who is hired during the period beginning on such date and ending on December 31, 2005.

(c) *Reasonable identification acceptable.* In lieu of the certification requirement under subparagraph (A) of section 51(d)(12) of such Code, an individual may provide to the employer reasonable evidence that the individual is a Hurricane Katrina employee, and subparagraph (B) of such section shall be applied as if such evidence were a certification described in such subparagraph.

(d) *Special rules for determining credit.* For purposes of applying subpart F of part IV of subchapter A of chapter 1 of such Code to wages paid or incurred to any Hurricane Katrina employee—

(1) section 51(c)(4) of such Code shall not apply, and

(2) section 51(i)(2) of such Code shall not apply with respect to the first hire of such employee as a Hurricane Katrina employee, unless such employee was an employee of the employer on August 28, 2005.

[¶16,460H]

⪢→ *Caution: Sec. 202, below, was repealed by the Gulf Opportunity Zone Act (P.L. 109-135), Act Sec. 201(b)(4), effective December 21, 2005.*

ACT SEC. 202. EMPLOYEE RETENTION CREDIT FOR EMPLOYERS AFFECTED BY HURRICANE KATRINA. (a) *In general.* In the case of an eligible employer, there shall be allowed as a credit against the tax imposed by chapter 1 of the Internal Revenue Code of 1986 for the taxable year an amount equal to 40 percent of the qualified wages with respect to each eligible employee of such employer for such taxable year. For purposes of the preceding sentence, the amount of qualified wages which may be taken into account with respect to any individual shall not exceed $6,000.

(b) *Definitions.* For purposes of this section—

(1) *Eligible employer.* The term "eligible employer" means any employer—

(A) which conducted an active trade or business on August 28, 2005, in a core disaster area, and

(B) with respect to whom the trade or business described in subparagraph (A) is inoperable on any day after August 28, 2005, and before January 1, 2006, as a result of damage sustained by reason of Hurricane Katrina.

(2) *Eligible employee.* The term "eligible employee" means with respect to an eligible employer an employee whose principal place of employment on August 28, 2005, with such eligible employer was in a core disaster area.

(3) *Qualified wages.* The term "qualified wages" means wages (as defined in section 51(c)(1) of such Code, but without regard to section 3306(b)(2)(B) of such Code) paid or incurred by an eligible employer with respect to an eligible employee on any day after August 28, 2005, and before January 1, 2006, which occurs during the period—

(A) beginning on the date on which the trade or business described in paragraph (1) first became inoperable at the principal place of employment of the employee immediately before Hurricane Katrina, and

(B) ending on the date on which such trade or business has resumed significant operations at such principal place of employment.

Such term shall include wages paid without regard to whether the employee performs no services, performs services at a different place of employment than such principal place of employment, or performs services at such principal place of employment before significant operations have resumed.

(c) *Credit not allowed for large businesses.* The term "eligible employer" shall not include any trade or business for any taxable year if such trade or business employed an average of more than 200 employees on business days during the taxable year.

(d) *Certain rules to apply.* For purposes of this section, rules similar to the rules of sections 51(i)(1), 52, and 280C(a) of such Code shall apply.

(e) *Employee not taken into account more than once.* An employee shall not be treated as an eligible employee for purposes of this section for any period with respect to any employer if such employer is allowed a credit under section 51 of such Code with respect to such employee for such period.

(f) *Credit to be part of general business credit.* The credit allowed under this section shall be added to the current year business credit under section 38(b) of such Code and shall be treated as a credit allowed under subpart D of part IV of subchapter A of chapter 1 of such Code.

TITLE III.—CHARITABLE GIVING INCENTIVES

[¶16,460I]

ACT SEC. 303. INCREASE IN STANDARD MILEAGE RATE FOR CHARITABLE USE OF VEHICLES. Notwithstanding section 170(i) of the Internal Revenue Code of 1986, for purposes of computing the deduction under section 170 of such Code for use of a vehicle described in subsection (f)(12)(E)(i) of such section for provision of relief related to Hurricane Katrina during the period beginning on August 25, 2005, and ending on December 31, 2006, the standard mileage rate shall be 70 percent of the standard mileage rate in effect under section 162(a) of such Code at the time of such use. Any increase under this section shall be rounded to the next highest cent.

ACT SEC. 303. ¶16,460I

[¶ 16,460J]

ACT SEC. 304. MILEAGE REIMBURSEMENTS TO CHARITABLE VOLUNTEERS EXCLUDED FROM GROSS INCOME. (a) *In general.* For purposes of the Internal Revenue Code of 1986, gross income of an individual for taxable years ending on or after August 25, 2005, does not include amounts received, from an organization described in section 170(c) of such Code, as reimbursement of operating expenses with respect to use of a passenger automobile for the benefit of such organization in connection with providing relief relating to Hurricane Katrina during the period beginning on August 25, 2005, and ending on December 31, 2006. The preceding sentence shall apply only to the extent that the expenses which are reimbursed would be deductible under chapter 1 of such Code if section 274(d) of such Code were applied—

> (1) by using the standard business mileage rate in effect under section 162(a) at the time of such use, and

> (2) as if the individual were an employee of an organization not described in section 170(c) of such Code.

(b) *Application to volunteer services only.* Subsection (a) shall not apply with respect to any expenses relating to the performance of services for compensation.

(c) *No double benefit.* No deduction or credit shall be allowed under any other provision of such Code with respect to the expenses excludable from gross income under subsection (a).

* * *

TITLE IV.—ADDITIONAL TAX RELIEF PROVISIONS

[¶ 16,460K]

ACT SEC. 403. REQUIRED EXERCISE OF AUTHORITY UNDER SECTION 7508A FOR TAX RELIEF RELATING TO HURRICANE KATRINA. (a) *Authority includes suspension of payment of employment and excise taxes.* Subparagraphs (A) and (B) of section 7508(a)(1) of the Internal Revenue Code of 1986 are amended to read as follows:

"(A) Filing any return of income, estate, gift, employment, or excise tax;

"(B) Payment of any income, estate, gift, employment, or excise tax or any installment thereof or of any other liability to the United States in respect thereof;".

⫸→ *Caution: Sec. 403(b), below, was repealed by the Gulf Opportunity Zone Act (P.L. 109-135), Act Sec. 201(b)(4), effective December 21, 2005.*

(b) *Application with respect to Hurricane Katrina.* In the case of any taxpayer determined by the Secretary of the Treasury to be affected by the Presidentially declared disaster relating to Hurricane Katrina, any relief provided by the Secretary of the Treasury under section 7508A of the Internal Revenue Code of 1986 shall be for a period ending not earlier than February 28, 2006, and shall be treated as applying to the filing of returns relating to, and the payment of, employment and excise taxes.

(c) *Effective date.* The amendment made by subsection (a) shall apply for any period for performing an act which has not expired before August 25, 2005.

* * *

[¶ 16,460L]

⫸→ *Caution: Sec. 407, below, was repealed by the Gulf Opportunity Zone Act (P.L. 109-135), Act Sec. 201(b)(4), effective December 21, 2005.*

ACT SEC. 407. SECRETARIAL AUTHORITY TO MAKE ADJUSTMENTS REGARDING TAXPAYER AND DEPENDENCY STATUS. With respect to taxable years beginning in 2005 or 2006, the Secretary of the Treasury or the Secretary's delegate may make such adjustments in the application of the internal revenue laws as may be necessary to ensure that taxpayers do not lose any deduction or credit or experience a change of filing status by reason of temporary relocations by reason of Hurricane Katrina. Any adjustments made under the preceding sentence shall ensure that an individual is not taken into account by more than one taxpayer with respect to the same tax benefit.

* * *

Pension Protection Act of 2006

[¶16,465]

P.L. 109-280

Signed on August 17, 2006

[Reproduced below are provisions of the Pension Protection Act pertaining to pensions and employee benefits that did not amend the Internal Revenue Code or ERISA. Sections that amended the Internal Revenue Code are reflected in the "Code and Regulations" divisions starting at ¶ 11,000. Sections which amended ERISA are reflected in the "Labor Laws and Regulations" division starting at ¶ 14,110—CCH.]

[¶16,465A]

ACT SEC. 1. SHORT TITLE AND TABLE OF CONTENTS.

(a) SHORT TITLE. This Act may be cited as the "Pension Protection Act of 2006".

* * *

[¶16,465B]

ACT SEC. 104. SPECIAL RULES FOR MULTIPLE EMPLOYER PLANS OF CERTAIN COOPERATIVES.

(a) GENERAL RULE. Except as provided in this section, if a plan in existence on July 26, 2005, was an eligible cooperative plan or an eligible charity plan for its plan year which includes such date, the amendments made by this subtitle and subtitle B shall not apply to plan years beginning before the earlier of—

(1) the first plan year for which the plan ceases to be an eligible cooperative plan or eligible charity plan, or

(2) January 1, 2017.

(b) INTEREST RATE. In applying section 302(b)(5)(B) of the Employee Retirement Income Security Act of 1974 and section 412(b)(5)(B) of the Internal Revenue Code of 1986 (as in effect before the amendments made by this subtitle and subtitle B) to an eligible cooperative plan or an eligible charity plan for plan years beginning after December 31, 2007, and before the first plan year to which such amendments apply, the third segment rate determined under section 303(h)(2)(C)(iii) of such Act and section 430(h)(2)(C)(iii) of such Code (as added by such amendments) shall be used in lieu of the interest rate otherwise used.

(c) ELIGIBLE COOPERATIVE PLAN DEFINED. For purposes of this section, a plan shall be treated as an eligible cooperative plan for a plan year if the plan is maintained by more than 1 employer and at least 85 percent of the employers are—

(1) rural cooperatives (as defined in section 401(k)(7)(B) of such Code without regard to clause (iv) thereof), or

(2) organizations which are—

(A) cooperative organizations described in section 1381(a) of such Code which are more than 50-percent owned by agricultural producers or by cooperatives owned by agricultural producers, or

(B) more than 50-percent owned, or controlled by, one or more cooperative organizations described in subparagraph (A).

A plan shall also be treated as an eligible cooperative plan for any plan year for which it is described in section 210(a) of the Employee Retirement Income Security Act of 1974 and is maintained by a rural telephone cooperative association described in section 3(40)(B)(v) of such Act.

(d) ELIGIBLE CHARITY PLAN DEFINED. (1) IN GENERAL. For purposes of this section, a plan shall be treated as an eligible charity plan for a plan year if the plan is maintained by more than one employer (determined without regard to section 414(c) of the Internal Revenue Code) and 100 percent of the employers are described in section 501(c)(3) of such Code.

(2) ELECTION NOT TO BE AN ELIGIBLE CHARITY PLAN. A plan sponsor may elect for a plan to cease to be treated as an eligible charity plan for plan years beginning after December 31, 2013. Such election shall be made at such time and in such form and manner as shall be prescribed by the Secretary of the Treasury. Any such election may be revoked only with the consent of the Secretary of the Treasury.

(3) ELECTION TO USE FUNDING OPTIONS AVAILABLE TO OTHER PLAN SPONSORS

(A) A plan sponsor that makes the election described in paragraph (2) may elect for a plan to apply the rules described in subparagraphs (B), (C), and (D) for plan years beginning after December 31, 2013. Such election shall be made at such time and in such form and manner as shall be prescribed by the Secretary of the Treasury. Any such election may be revoked only with the consent of the Secretary of the Treasury.

(B) Under the rules described in this subparagraph, for the first plan year beginning after December 31, 2013, a plan has—

(i) an 11-year shortfall amortization base,

(ii) a 12-year shortfall amortization base, and

(iii) a 7-year shortfall amortization base.

(C) Under the rules described in this subparagraph, section 303(c)(2)(A) and (B) of the Employee Retirement Income Security Act of 1974, and section 430(c)(2)(A) and (B) of the Internal Revenue Code of 1986 shall be applied by—

(i) in the case of an 11-year shortfall amortization base, substituting '11-plan-year period' for '7-plan-year period' wher ever such phrase appears, and

(ii) in the case of a 12-year shortfall amortization base, substituting '12-plan-year period' for '7-plan-year period' wher ever such phrase appears.

(D) Under the rules described in this subparagraph, section 303(c)(7) of the Employee Retirement Income Security Act of 1974 and section 430(c)(7) of the Internal Revenue Code of 1986 shall apply to a plan for which an election has been made under subparagraph (A). Such provisions shall apply in the following manner:

(i) The first plan year beginning after December 31, 2013, shall be treated as an election year, and no other plan years shall be so treated.

(ii) All references in section 303(c)(7) of such Act and section 430(c)(7) of such Code to 'February 28, 2010' or 'March 1, 2010' shall be treated as references to 'February 28, 2013' or 'March 1, 2013', respectively.

(E) For purposes of this paragraph, the 11-year amortization base is an amount, determined for the first plan year beginning after December 31, 2013, equal to the unamortized principal amount of the shortfall amortization base (as defined in section 303(c)(3) of the Employee Retirement Income Security Act of 1974 and section 430(c)(3) of the Internal Revenue Code of 1986) that would have applied to the plan for the first plan beginning after December 31, 2009, if—

(i) the plan had never been an eligible charity plan,

(ii) the plan sponsor had made the election described in section 303(c)(2)(D)(i) of the Employee Retirement Income Security Act of 1974 and in section 430(c)(2)(D)(i) of the Internal Revenue Code of 1986 to have section 303(c)(2)(D)(i) of such Act and section 430(c)(2)(D)(iii) of such Code apply with respect to the shortfall amortization base for the first plan year beginning after December 31, 2009, and

(iii) no event had occurred under paragraph (6) or (7) of section 303(c) of such Act or paragraph (6) or (7) of section 430(c) of such Code that, as of the first day of the first plan year beginning after December 31, 2013, would have modified the shortfall amortization base or the shortfall amortization installments with re spect to the first plan year beginning after December 31, 2009.

(F) For purposes of this paragraph, the 12-year amortization base is an amount, determined for the first plan year beginning after December 31, 2013, equal to the unamortized principal amount of the shortfall amortization base (as defined in section 303(c)(3) of the Employee Retirement Income Security Act of 1974 and section 430(c)(3) of the Internal Revenue Code of 1986) that would have applied to the plan for the first plan beginning after December 31, 2010, if—

(i) the plan had never been an eligible charity plan,

(ii) the plan sponsor had made the election described in section 303(c)(2)(D)(i) of the Employee Retirement Income Security Act of 1974 and in section 430(c)(2)(D)(i) of the Internal Revenue Code of 1986 to have section 303(c)(2)(D)(i) of such Act and section 430(c)(2)(D)(iii) of such Code apply with respect to the shortfall amortization base for the first plan year beginning after De cember 31, 2010, and

(iii) no event had occurred under paragraph (6) or (7) of section 303(c) of such Act or paragraph (6) or (7) of section 430(c) of such Code that, as of the first day of the first plan year beginning after December 31, 2013, would have modified the shortfall amortization base or the shortfall amortization installments with respect to the first plan year beginning after December 31, 2010.

(G) For purposes of this paragraph, the 7-year shortfall amortization base is an amount, determined for the first plan year beginning after December 31, 2013, equal to—

(i) the shortfall amortization base for the first plan year beginning after Decem ber 31, 2013, without regard to this para graph, minus

(ii) the sum of the 11-year shortfall amortization base and the 12-year shortfall amortization base.

(4) RETROACTIVE ELECTION. Not later than December 31, 2014, a plan sponsor may make a one-time, irrevocable, retroactive election to not be treated as an eligible charity plan. Such election shall be effective for plan years beginning after December 31, 2007, and shall be made by providing reasonable notice to the Secretary of the Treasury.

Amendments

P.L. 113-97, § 103(b)(2):

Amended section 104(d) of the Pension Protection Act of 2006 by striking "For purposes of" and inserting "(1) IN GENERAL – For purposes of" and by adding at the end paragraphs (2)-(4) to read as above.

Effective on the date of enactment of the Cooperative and Small Employer Pension Flexibility Act.

P.L. 111-192, § 202(b):

Amended section 104 of the Pension Protection Act of 2006 by striking "eligible cooperative plan" wherever it appears in subsections (a) and (b)

and inserting "eligible cooperative plan or an eligible charity plan", and by adding subsection (d) to read as above.

The amendments above shall apply to plan years beginning after December 31, 2007, except that a plan sponsor may elect to apply such amendments to plan years beginning after December 31, 2008. Any such election shall be made at such time, and in such form and manner, as shall be prescribed by the Secretary of the Treasury, and may be revoked only with the consent of the Secretary of the Treasury.

[¶16,465C]

ACT SEC. 105. TEMPORARY RELIEF FOR CERTAIN PBGC SETTLEMENT PLANS.

(a) GENERAL RULE. Except as provided in this section, if a plan in existence on July 26, 2005, was a PBGC settlement plan as of such date, the amendments made by this subtitle and subtitle B shall not apply to plan years beginning before January 1, 2014.

(b) INTEREST RATE. In applying section 302(b)(5)(B) of the Employee Retirement Income Security Act of 1974 and section 412(b)(5)(B) of the Internal Revenue Code of 1986 (as in effect before the amendments made by this subtitle and subtitle B), to a PBGC settlement plan for plan years beginning after December 31, 2007, and before January 1, 2014, the third segment rate determined under section 303(h)(2)(C)(iii) of such Act and section 430(h)(2)(C)(iii) of such Code (as added by such amendments) shall be used in lieu of the interest rate otherwise used.

(c) PBGC SETTLEMENT PLAN. For purposes of this section, the term "PBGC settlement plan" means a defined benefit plan (other than a multiemployer plan) to which section 302 of such Act and section 412 of such Code apply and—

(1) which was sponsored by an employer which was in bankruptcy, giving rise to a claim by the Pension Benefit Guaranty Corporation of not greater than $150,000,000, and the sponsorship of which was assumed by another employer that was not a member of the same controlled group as the bankrupt sponsor and the claim of the Pension Benefit Guaranty Corporation was settled or withdrawn in connection with the assumption of the sponsorship, or

(2) which, by agreement with the Pension Benefit Guaranty Corporation, was spun off from a plan subsequently terminated by such Corporation under section 4042 of the Employee Retirement Income Security Act of 1974.

[¶16,465D]

ACT SEC. 106. SPECIAL RULES FOR PLANS OF CERTAIN GOVERNMENT CONTRACTORS.

(a) GENERAL RULE. Except as provided in this section, if a plan is an eligible government contractor plan, this subtitle and subtitle B shall not apply to plan years beginning before the earliest of—

(1) the first plan year for which the plan ceases to be an eligible government contractor plan,

(2) the effective date of the Cost Accounting Standards Pension Harmonization Rule, or

(3) January 1, 2011.

(b) INTEREST RATE. In applying section 302(b)(5)(B) of the Employee Retirement Income Security Act of 1974 and section 412(b)(5)(B) of the Internal Revenue Code of 1986 (as in effect before the amendments made by this subtitle and subtitle B) to an eligible government contractor plan for plan years beginning after December 31, 2007, and before the first plan year to which such amendments apply, the third segment rate determined under section 303(h)(2)(C)(iii) of such Act and section 430(h)(2)(C)(iii) of such Code (as added by such amendments) shall be used in lieu of the interest rate otherwise used.

(c) ELIGIBLE GOVERNMENT CONTRACTOR PLAN DEFINED. For purposes of this section, a plan shall be treated as an eligible government contractor plan if it is maintained by a corporation or a member of the same affiliated group (as defined by section 1504(a) of the Internal Revenue Code of 1986), whose primary source of revenue is derived from business performed under contracts with the United States that are subject to the Federal Acquisition Regulations (Chapter 1 of Title 48, C.F.R.) and that are also subject to the Defense Federal Acquisition Regulation Supplement (Chapter 2 of Title 48, C.F.R.), and whose revenue derived from such business in the previous fiscal year exceeded $5,000,000,000, and whose pension plan costs that are assignable under those contracts are subject to sections 412 and 413 of the Cost Accounting Standards (48 C.F.R. 9904.412 and 9904.413).

(d) COST ACCOUNTING STANDARDS PENSION HARMONIZATION RULE. The Cost Accounting Standards Board shall review and revise sections 412 and 413 of the Cost Accounting Standards (48 C.F.R. 9904.412 and 9904.413) to harmonize the minimum required contribution under the Employee Retirement Income Security Act of 1974 of eligible government contractor plans and government reimbursable pension plan costs not later than January 1, 2010. Any final rule adopted by the Cost Accounting Standards Board shall be deemed the Cost Accounting Standards Pension Harmonization Rule.

* * *

[¶16,465D-3]

ACT SEC. 107. APPLICATION OF EXTENDED AMORTIZATION PERIODS TO PLANS WITH DELAYED EFFECTIVE DATE.

(a) IN GENERAL. If the plan sponsor of a plan to which section 104, 105, or 106 of this Act applies elects to have this section apply for any eligible plan year (in this section referred to as an 'election year'), section 302 of the Employee Retirement Income Security Act of 1974 and section 412 of the Internal Revenue Code of 1986 (as in effect before the amendments made by this subtitle and subtitle B) shall apply to such year in the manner described in subsection (b) or (c), whichever is specified in the election. All references in this section to 'such Act' or 'such Code' shall be to such Act or such Code as in effect before the amendments made by this subtitle and subtitle B.

(b) APPLICATION OF 2 AND 7 RULE. In the case of an election year to which this subsection applies –

(1) 2-YEAR LOOKBACK FOR DETERMINING DEFICIT REDUCTION CONTRIBUTIONS FOR CERTAIN PLANS. For purposes of applying section 302(d)(9) of such Act and section 412(l)(9) of such Code, the funded current liability percentage (as defined in subparagraph (C) thereof) for such plan for such plan year shall be such funded current liability percentage of such plan for the second plan year preceding the first election year of such plan.

(2) CALCULATION OF DEFICIT REDUCTION CONTRIBUTION. For purposes of applying section 302(d) of such Act and section 412(l) of such Code to a plan to which such sections apply (after taking into account paragraph (1)) –

(A) in the case of the increased unfunded new liability of the plan, the applicable percentage described in section 302(d)(4)(C) of such Act and section 412(l)(4)(C) of such Code shall be the third segment rate described in sections 104(b), 105(b), and 106(b) of this Act, and

(B) in the case of the excess of the unfunded liability over the increased unfunded new liability, such applicable percentage shall be determined without regard to this section.

(c) APPLICATION OF 15-YEAR AMORTIZATION. In the case of an election year to which this subsection applies, for purposes of applying section 302(d) of such Act and section 412(l) of such Code –

(1) . in the case of the increased unfunded new liability of the plan, the applicable percentage described in section 302(d)(4)(C) of such Act and section 412(l)(4)(C) of such Code for any pre-effective date plan year beginning with or after the first election year shall be the ratio of –

(A) the annual installments payable in each year if the increased unfunded new liability for such plan year were amortized over 15 years, using an interest rate equal to the third segment rate described in sections 104(b), 105(b), and 106(b) of this Act, to

(B) the increased unfunded new liability for such plan year, and

(2) in the case of the excess of the unfunded new liability over the increased unfunded new liability, such applicable percentage shall be determined without regard to this section.

(d) ELECTION. (1) IN GENERAL. The plan sponsor of a plan may elect to have this section apply to not more than 2 eligible plan years with respect to the plan, except that in the case of a plan to which section 106 of this Act applies, the plan sponsor may only elect to have this section apply to 1 eligible plan year.

(2) AMORTIZATION SCHEDULE. Such election shall specify whether the rules under subsection (b) or (c) shall apply to an election year, except that if a plan sponsor elects to have this section apply to 2 eligible plan years, the plan sponsor must elect the same rule for both years.

(3) OTHER RULES. Such election shall be made at such time, and in such form and manner, as shall be prescribed by the Secretary of the Treasury, and may be revoked only with the consent of the Secretary of the Treasury.

(e) DEFINITIONS. For purposes of this section –

(1) ELIGIBLE PLAN YEAR. For purposes of this subparagraph, the term "eligible plan year" means any plan year beginning in 2008, 2009, 2010, or 2011, except that a plan year beginning in 2008 shall only be treated as an eligible plan year if the due date for the payment of the minimum required contribution for such plan year occurs on or after the date of the enactment of this clause.

(2) PRE-EFFECTIVE DATE PLAN YEAR. The term "pre-effective date plan year" means, with respect to a plan, any plan year prior to the first year in which the amendments made by this subtitle and subtitle B apply to the plan.

(3) INCREASED UNFUNDED NEW LIABILITY. The term "increased unfunded new liability" means, with respect to a year, the excess (if any) of the unfunded new liability over the amount of unfunded new liability determined as if the value of the plan's assets determined under subsection 302(c)(2) of such Act and section 412(c)(2) of such Code equaled the product of the current liability of the plan for the year multiplied by the funded current liability percentage (as defined in section 302(d)(8)(B) of such Act and 412(l)(8)(B) of such Code) of the plan for the second plan year preceding the first election year of such plan.

(4) OTHER DEFINITIONS. The terms "unfunded new liability" and "current liability" shall have the meanings set forth in section 302(d) of such Act and section 412(l) of such Code.

P.L. 111-192, §202(a):

Amended the Pension Protection Act of 2006 by redesignating section 107 as section 108 and by inserting after section 106, new section 107 to read as above.

The amendment shall take effect as if included in the Pension Protection Act of 2006.

[¶16,465D-5]

ACT SEC. 107. TECHNICAL AND CONFORMING AMENDMENTS.

* * *

(c) AMENDMENTS TO REORGANIZATION PLAN NO. 4 OF 1978. Section 106(b)(ii) of Reorganization Plan No. 4 of 1978 (ratified and affirmed as law by Public Law 98-532 (98 Stat. 2705)) is amended by striking "302(c)(8)" and inserting "302(d)(2)", by striking "304(a) and (b)(2)(A)" and inserting "304(d)(1), (d)(2), and (e)(2)(A)", and by striking "412(c)(8), (e), and (f)(2)(A)" and inserting "412(c)(2) and 431(d)(1), (d)(2), and (e)(2)(A)".

* * *

(e) EFFECTIVE DATE. —The amendments made by this section shall apply to plan years beginning after 2007.

P.L. 111-192, § 202(a):

Amended the Pension Protection Act of 2006 by redesignating section 107 as section 108.

The amendment shall take effect as if included in the Pension Protection Act of 2006.

[¶16,465E]

ACT SEC. 115. MODIFICATION OF TRANSITION RULE TO PENSION FUNDING REQUIREMENTS.

(a) IN GENERAL. In the case of a plan that—

(1) was not required to pay a variable rate premium for the plan year beginning in 1996,

(2) has not, in any plan year beginning after 1995, merged with another plan (other than a plan sponsored by an employer that was in 1996 within the controlled group of the plan sponsor); and

(3) is sponsored by a company that is engaged primarily in the interurban or interstate passenger bus service,

the rules described in subsection (b) shall apply for any plan year beginning after December 31, 2007.

(b) MODIFIED RULES. The rules described in this subsection are as follows:

(1) For purposes of section 430(j)(3) of the Internal Revenue Code of 1986 and section 303(j)(3) of the Employee Retirement Income Security Act of 1974, the plan shall be treated as not having a funding shortfall for any plan year.

(2) For purposes of—

(A) determining unfunded vested benefits under section 4006(a)(3)(E)(iii) of such Act, and

(B) determining any present value or making any computation under section 412 of such Code or section 302 of such Act,

the mortality table shall be the mortality table used by the plan.

(3) Section 430(c)(5)(B) of such Code and section 303(c)(5)(B) of such Act (relating to phase-in of funding target for exemption from new shortfall amortization base) shall each be applied by substituting "2012" for "2011" therein and by substituting for the table therein the following:

In the case of a plan year beginning in calendar year:	The applicable percentage is:
2008	90 percent
2009	92 percent
2010	94 percent
2011	96 percent.

(c) DEFINITIONS. Any term used in this section which is also used in section 430 of such Code or section 303 of such Act shall have the meaning provided such term in such section. If the same term has a different meaning in such Code and such Act, such term shall, for purposes of this section, have the meaning provided by such Code when applied with respect to such Code and the meaning provided by such Act when applied with respect to such Act.

(d) SPECIAL RULE FOR 2006 AND 2007.—

(1) IN GENERAL. Section 769(c)(3) of the Retirement Protection Act of 1994, as added by section 201 of the Pension Funding Equity Act of 2004, is amended by striking "and 2005" and inserting ", 2005, 2006, and 2007".

(2) EFFECTIVE DATE. The amendment made by paragraph (1) shall apply to plan years beginning after December 31, 2005.

(e) CONFORMING AMENDMENT.—

(1) Section 769 of the Retirement Protection Act of 1994 is amended by striking subsection (c).

(2) The amendment made by paragraph (1) shall take effect on December 31, 2007, and shall apply to plan years beginning after such date.

* * *

[¶16,465E-5]

ACT SEC. 201. FUNDING RULES FOR MULTIEMPLOYER DEFINED BENEFIT PLANS.

* * *

(b) SHORTFALL FUNDING METHOD.—

(1) IN GENERAL. —A multiemployer plan meeting the criteria of paragraph (2) may adopt, use, or cease using, the shortfall funding method and such adoption, use, or cessation of use of such method, shall be deemed approved by the Secretary of the Treasury under section 302(d)(1) of the Employee Retirement Income Security Act of 1974 and section 412(d)(1) of the Internal Revenue Code of 1986.

(2) CRITERIA. A multiemployer pension plan meets the criteria of this clause if—

(A) the plan has not used the shortfall funding method during the 5-year period ending on the day before the date the plan is to use the method under paragraph (1); and

(B) the plan is not operating under an amortization period extension under section 304(d) of such Act and did not operate under such an extension during such 5-year period.

(3) SHORTFALL FUNDING METHOD DEFINED. —For purposes of this subsection, the term "shortfall funding method" means the shortfall funding method described in Treasury Regulations section 1.412(c)(1)-2 (26 CFR 1.412(c)(1)-2).

(4) BENEFIT RESTRICTIONS TO APPLY. —The benefit restrictions under section 302(c)(7) of such Act and section 412(c)(7) of such Code shall apply during any period a multiemployer plan is on the shortfall funding method pursuant to this subsection.

(5) USE OF SHORTFALL METHOD NOT TO PRECLUDE OTHER OPTIONS. —Nothing in this subsection shall be construed to affect a multiemployer plan's ability to adopt the shortfall funding method with the Secretary's permission under otherwise applicable regulations or to affect a multiemployer plan's right to change funding methods, with or without the Secretary's consent, as provided in applicable rules and regulations.

* * *

(d) EFFECTIVE DATE.—

(1) IN GENERAL. —The amendments made by this section shall apply to plan years beginning after 2007.

(2) SPECIAL RULE FOR CERTAIN AMORTIZATION EXTENSIONS. —If the Secretary of the Treasury grants an extension under section 304 of the Employee Retirement Income Security Act of 1974 and section 412(e) of the Internal Revenue Code of 1986 with respect to any application filed with the Secretary of the Treasury on or before June 30, 2005, the extension (and any modification thereof) shall be applied and administered under the rules of such sections as in effect before the enactment of this Act, including the use of the rate of interest determined under section 6621(b) of such Code.

[¶16,465F]

ACT SEC. 206. SPECIAL RULE FOR CERTAIN BENEFITS FUNDED UNDER AN AGREEMENT APPROVED BY THE PENSION BENEFIT GUARANTY CORPORATION.

In the case of a multiemployer plan that is a party to an agreement that was approved by the Pension Benefit Guaranty Corporation prior to June 30, 2005, and that—

(1) increases benefits, and

(2) provides for special withdrawal liability rules under section 4203(f) of the Employee Retirement Income Security Act of 1974 (29 U.S.C. 1383),

the amendments made by sections 201, 202, 211, and 212 of this Act shall not apply to the benefit increases under any plan amendment adopted prior to June 30, 2005, that are funded pursuant to such agreement if the plan is funded in compliance with such agreement (and any amendments thereto).

* * *

[¶16,465G]

ACT SEC. 214. EXEMPTION FROM EXCISE TAXES FOR CERTAIN MULTIEMPLOYER PENSION PLANS.

(a) IN GENERAL. Notwithstanding any other provision of law, no tax shall be imposed under subsection (a) or (b) of section 4971 of the Internal Revenue Code of 1986 with respect to any accumulated funding deficiency of a plan described in subsection (b) of this section for any taxable year beginning before the earlier of—

(1) the taxable year in which the plan sponsor adopts a rehabilitation plan under section 305(e) of the Employee Retirement Income Security Act of 1974 and section 432(e) of such Code (as added by this Act); or

(2) the taxable year that contains January 1, 2009.

(b) PLAN DESCRIBED. A plan described under this subsection is a multiemployer pension plan—

(1) with less than 100 participants;

(2) with respect to which the contributing employers participated in a Federal fishery capacity reduction program;

(3) with respect to which employers under the plan participated in the Northeast Fisheries Assistance Program; and

(4) with respect to which the annual normal cost is less than $100,000 and the plan is experiencing a funding deficiency on the date of enactment of this Act.

* * *

[¶16,465I]

ACT SEC. 301. EXTENSION OF REPLACEMENT OF 30-YEAR TREASURY RATES.

* * *

(c) PLAN AMENDMENTS. Clause (ii) of section 101(c)(2)(A) of the Pension Funding Equity Act of 2004 is amended by striking "2006" and inserting "2008".

* * *

[¶16,465J]

ACT SEC. 402. SPECIAL FUNDING RULES FOR CERTAIN PLANS MAINTAINED BY COMMERCIAL AIRLINES.

(a) IN GENERAL. The plan sponsor of an eligible plan may elect to either—

(1) have the rules of subsection (b) apply, or

(2) have section 303 of the Employee Retirement Income Security Act of 1974 and section 430 of the Internal Revenue Code of 1986 applied to its first taxable year beginning in 2008 by amortizing the shortfall amortization base for such taxable year over a period of 10 plan years (rather than 7 plan years) beginning with such plan year and by using, in determining the funding target for each of the 10 plan years during such period, an interest rate of 8.25 percent (rather than the segment rates calculated on the basis of the corporate bond yield curve).

ACT SEC. 402. ¶16,465J

(b) ALTERNATIVE FUNDING SCHEDULE.—

(1) IN GENERAL. If an election is made under subsection (a)(1) to have this subsection apply to an eligible plan and the requirements of paragraphs (2) and (3) are met with respect to the plan—

(A) in the case of any applicable plan year beginning before January 1, 2008, the plan shall not have an accumulated funding deficiency for purposes of section 302 of the Employee Retirement Income Security Act of 1974 and sections 412 and 4971 of the Internal Revenue Code of 1986 if contributions to the plan for the plan year are not less than the minimum required contribution determined under subsection (e) for the plan for the plan year, and

(B) in the case of any applicable plan year beginning on or after January 1, 2008, the minimum required contribution determined under sections 303 of such Act and 430 of such Code shall, for purposes of sections 302 and 303 of such Act and sections 412, 430, and 4971 of such Code, be equal to the minimum required contribution determined under subsection (e) for the plan for the plan year.

(2) ACCRUAL RESTRICTIONS.—

(A) IN GENERAL. The requirements of this paragraph are met if, effective as of the first day of the first applicable plan year and at all times thereafter while an election under this section is in effect, the plan provides that—

(i) the accrued benefit, any death or disability benefit, and any social security supplement described in the last sentence of section 411(a)(9) of such Code and section 204(b)(1)(G) of such Act, of each participant are frozen at the amount of such benefit or supplement immediately before such first day, and

(ii) all other benefits under the plan are eliminated,

but only to the extent the freezing or elimination of such benefits would have been permitted under section 411(d)(6) of such Code and section 204(g) of such Act if they had been implemented by a plan amendment adopted immediately before such first day.

(B) INCREASES IN SECTION 415 LIMITS. If a plan provides that an accrued benefit of a participant which has been subject to any limitation under section 415 of such Code will be increased if such limitation is increased, the plan shall not be treated as meeting the requirements of this section unless, effective as of the first day of the first applicable plan year (or, if later, the date of the enactment of this Act) and at all times thereafter while an election under this section is in effect, the plan provides that any such increase shall not take effect. A plan shall not fail to meet the requirements of section 411(d)(6) of such Code and section 204(g) of such Act solely because the plan is amended to meet the requirements of this subparagraph.

(3) RESTRICTION ON APPLICABLE BENEFIT INCREASES.—

(A) IN GENERAL. The requirements of this paragraph are met if no applicable benefit increase takes effect at any time during the period beginning on July 26, 2005, and ending on the day before the first day of the first applicable plan year.

(B) APPLICABLE BENEFIT INCREASE. For purposes of this paragraph, the term "applicable benefit increase" means, with respect to any plan year, any increase in liabilities of the plan by plan amendment (or otherwise provided in regulations provided by the Secretary) which, but for this paragraph, would occur during the plan year by reason of—

(i) any increase in benefits,

(ii) any change in the accrual of benefits, or

(iii) any change in the rate at which benefits become nonforfeitable under the plan.

(4) EXCEPTION FOR IMPUTED DISABILITY SERVICE. Paragraphs (2) and (3) shall not apply to any accrual or increase with respect to imputed service provided to a participant during any period of the participant's disability occurring on or after the effective date of the plan amendment providing the restrictions under paragraph (2) (or on or after July 26, 2005, in the case of the restrictions under paragraph (3)) if the participant—

(A) was receiving disability benefits as of such date, or

(B) was receiving sick pay and subsequently determined to be eligible for disability benefits as of such date.

(c) DEFINITIONS. For purposes of this section—

(1) ELIGIBLE PLAN. The term "eligible plan" means a defined benefit plan (other than a multiemployer plan) to which sections 302 of such Act and 412 of such Code applies which is sponsored by an employer—

(A) which is a commercial airline passenger airline, or

(B) the principal business of which is providing catering services to a commercial passenger airline.

(2) APPLICABLE PLAN YEAR. The term "applicable plan year" means each plan year to which the election under subsection (a)(1) applies under subsection (d)(1)(A).

(d) ELECTIONS AND RELATED TERMS.—

(1) YEARS FOR WHICH ELECTION MADE.—

(A) ALTERNATIVE FUNDING SCHEDULE. If an election under subsection (a)(1) was made with respect to an eligible plan, the plan sponsor may select either a plan year beginning in 2006 or a plan year beginning in 2007 as the first plan year to which such election applies. The election shall apply to such plan year and all subsequent years. The election shall be made—

(i) not later than December 31, 2006, in the case of an election for a plan year beginning in 2006, or

(ii) not later than December 31, 2007, in the case of an election for a plan year beginning in 2007.

(B) 10 YEAR AMORTIZATION. An election under subsection (a)(2) shall be made not later than December 31, 2007.

(C) ELECTION OF NEW PLAN YEAR FOR ALTERNATIVE FUNDING SCHEDULE. In the case of an election under subsection (a)(1), the plan sponsor may specify a new plan year in such election and the plan year of the plan may be changed to such new plan year without the approval of the Secretary of the Treasury.

(2) MANNER OF ELECTION. A plan sponsor shall make any election under subsection (a) in such manner as the Secretary of the Treasury may prescribe. Such election, once made, may be revoked only with the consent of such Secretary.

(e) MINIMUM REQUIRED CONTRIBUTION. In the case of an eligible plan with respect to which an election is made under subsection (a)(1)—

¶16,465J   ACT SEC. 402.

(1) IN GENERAL. In the case of any applicable plan year during the amortization period, the minimum required contribution shall be the amount necessary to amortize the unfunded liability of the plan, determined as of the first day of the plan year, in equal annual installments (until fully amortized) over the remainder of the amortization period. Such amount shall be separately determined for each applicable plan year.

(2) YEARS AFTER AMORTIZATION PERIOD. In the case of any plan year beginning after the end of the amortization period, section 302(a)(2)(A) of such Act and section 412(a)(2)(A) of such Code shall apply to such plan, but the prefunding balance and funding standard carryover balance as of the first day of the first of such years under section 303(f) of such Act and section 430(f) of such Code shall be zero.

(3) DEFINITIONS. For purposes of this section—

(A) UNFUNDED LIABILITY. The term "unfunded liability" means the unfunded accrued liability under the plan, determined under the unit credit funding method.

(B) AMORTIZATION PERIOD. The term "amortization period" means the 17-plan year period beginning with the first applicable plan year.

(4) OTHER RULES. In determining the minimum required contribution and amortization amount under this subsection—

(A) the provisions of section 302(c)(3) of such Act and section 412(c)(3) of such Code, as in effect before the date of enactment of this section, shall apply,

(B) a rate of interest of 8.85 percent shall be used for all calculations requiring an interest rate, and

(C) the value of plan assets shall be equal to their fair market value.

(5) SPECIAL RULE FOR CERTAIN PLAN SPINOFFS. For purposes of subsection (b), if, with respect to any eligible plan to which this subsection applies—

(A) any applicable plan year includes the date of the enactment of this Act,

(B) a plan was spun off from the eligible plan during the plan year but before such date of enactment,

the minimum required contribution under paragraph (1) for the eligible plan for such applicable plan year shall be an aggregate amount determined as if the plans were a single plan for that plan year (based on the full 12-month plan year in effect prior to the spin-off). The employer shall designate the allocation of such aggregate amount between such plans for the applicable plan year.

(f) SPECIAL RULES FOR CERTAIN BALANCES AND WAIVERS. In the case of an eligible plan with respect to which an election is made under subsection (a)(1)—

(1) FUNDING STANDARD ACCOUNT AND CREDIT BALANCES. Any charge or credit in the funding standard account under section 302 of such Act or section 412 of such Code, and any prefunding balance or funding standard carryover balance under section 303 of such Act or section 430 of such Code, as of the day before the first day of the first applicable plan year, shall be reduced to zero.

(2) WAIVED FUNDING DEFICIENCIES. Any waived funding deficiency under sections 302 and 303 of such Act or section 412 of such Code, as in effect before the date of enactment of this section, shall be deemed satisfied as of the first day of the first applicable plan year and the amount of such waived funding deficiency shall be taken into account in determining the plan's unfunded liability under subsection (e)(3)(A). In the case of a plan amendment adopted to satisfy the requirements of subsection (b)(2), the plan shall not be deemed to violate section 304(b) of such Act or section 412(f) of such Code, as so in effect, by reason of such amendment or any increase in benefits provided to such plan's participants under a separate plan that is a defined contribution plan or a multiemployer plan.

(g) OTHER RULES FOR PLANS MAKING ELECTION UNDER THIS SECTION.—

(1) SUCCESSOR PLANS TO CERTAIN PLANS. If—

(A) an election under paragraph (1) or (2) of subsection (a) is in effect with respect to any eligible plan, and

(B) the eligible plan is maintained by an employer that establishes or maintains 1 or more other defined benefit plans (other than any multiemployer plan), and such other plans in combination provide benefit accruals to any substantial number of successor employees,

the Secretary of the Treasury may, in the Secretary's discretion, determine that any trust of which any other such plan is a part does not constitute a qualified trust under section 401(a) of the Internal Revenue Code of 1986 unless all benefit obligations of the eligible plan have been satisfied. For purposes of this paragraph, the term "successor employee" means any employee who is or was covered by the eligible plan and any employees who perform substantially the same type of work with respect to the same business operations as an employee covered by such eligible plan.

(2) SPECIAL RULES FOR TERMINATIONS.—

* * *

(B) TERMINATION PREMIUM. In applying section 4006(a)(7)(A) of the Employee Retirement Income Security Act of 1974 to an eligible plan during any period in which an election under subsection (a)(1) is in effect—

(i) "$2,500" shall be substituted for "$1,250" in such section if such plan terminates during the 5-year period beginning on the first day of the first applicable plan year with respect to such plan, and

(ii) such section shall be applied without regard to subparagraph (B) of section 8101(d)(2) of the Deficit Reduction Act of 2005 (relating to special rule for plans terminated in bankruptcy).

The substitution described in clause (i) shall not apply with respect to any plan if the Secretary of Labor determines that such plan terminated as a result of extraordinary circumstances such as a terrorist attack or other similar event.

(3) LIMITATION ON DEDUCTIONS UNDER CERTAIN PLANS. Section 404(a)(7)(C)(iv) of the Internal Revenue Code of 1986, as added by this Act, shall not apply with respect to any taxable year of a plan sponsor of an eligible plan if any applicable plan year with respect to such plan ends with or within such taxable year.

(4) NOTICE. In the case of a plan amendment adopted in order to comply with this section, any notice required under section 204(h) of such Act or section 4980F(e) of such Code shall be provided within 15 days of the effective date of such plan amendment. This subsection shall not apply to any plan unless such plan is maintained pursuant to one or more collective bargaining agreements between employee representatives and 1 or more employers.

* * *

(i) EXTENSION OF SPECIAL RULE FOR ADDITIONAL FUNDING REQUIREMENTS. In the case of an employer which is a commercial passenger airline, section 302(d)(12) of the Employee Retirement Income Security Act of 1974 and section 412(l)(12) of the Internal Revenue Code of 1986, as in effect before the date of the enactment of this Act, shall each be applied—

(1) by substituting "January 1, 2008" for "December 28, 2005" in subparagraph (D)(i) thereof, and

(2) without regard to subparagraph (D)(ii).

(j) EFFECTIVE DATE. Except as otherwise provided in this section, the provisions of and amendments made by this section shall apply to plan years ending after the date of the enactment of this Act.

* * *

Amendments

P.L. 110-28, §6614(a):

Amended Section 402(i)(1) of the Pension Protection Act of 2006 by striking "December 28, 2007" and inserting "January 1, 2008".

The above amendment takes effect as if included in section 402 of the Pension Protection Act of 2006.

P.L. 110-28, §6615(a):

Amended Section 402(a)(2) of the Pension Protection Act of 2006 by inserting "and by using, in determining the funding target for each of the 10 plan years during such period, an interest rate of 8.25 percent (rather than the segment rates calculated on the basis of the corporate bond yield curve)" after "such plan year".

The above amendment takes effect as if included in the provisions of the Pension Protection Act of 2006 to which such amendment relates.

[¶16,465K]

ACT SEC. 411. DIRECTOR OF THE PENSION BENEFIT GUARANTY CORPORATION.

* * *

(c) JURISDICTION OF NOMINATION.—

(1) IN GENERAL. The Committee on Finance of the Senate and the Committee on Health, Education, Labor, and Pensions of the Senate shall have joint jurisdiction over the nomination of a person nominated by the President to fill the position of Director of the Pension Benefit Guaranty Corporation under section 4002 of the Employee Retirement Income Security Act of 1974 (29 U.S.C. 1302) (as amended by this Act), and if one committee votes to order reported such a nomination, the other shall report within 30 calendar days, or be automatically discharged.

(2) RULEMAKING OF THE SENATE. This subsection is enacted by Congress—

(A) as an exercise of rulemaking power of the Senate, and as such it is deemed a part of the rules of the Senate, but applicable only with respect to the procedure to be followed in the Senate in the case of a nomination described in such sentence, and it supersedes other rules only to the extent that it is inconsistent with such rules; and

(B) with full recognition of the constitutional right of the Senate to change the rules (so far as relating to the procedure of the Senate) at any time, in the same manner and to the same extent as in the case of any other rule of the Senate.

(d) TRANSITION. The term of the individual serving as Executive Director of the Pension Benefit Guaranty Corporation on the date of enactment of this Act shall expire on such date of enactment. Such individual, or any other individual, may serve as interim Director of such Corporation until an individual is appointed as Director of such Corporation under section 4002 of the Employee Retirement Income Security Act of 1974 (29 U.S.C. 1302) (as amended by this Act).

* * *

[¶16,465L]

ACT SEC. 501. DEFINED BENEFIT PLAN FUNDING NOTICE.

* * *

(c) MODEL NOTICE. Not later than 1 year after the date of the enactment of this Act, the Secretary of Labor shall publish a model version of the notice required by section 101(f) of the Employee Retirement Income Security Act of 1974. The Secretary of Labor may promulgate any interim final rules as the Secretary determines appropriate to carry out the provisions of this subsection.

(d) EFFECTIVE DATE.—

(1) IN GENERAL. —The amendments made by this section shall apply to plan years beginning after December 31, 2007, except that the amendment made by subsection (b) shall apply to plan years beginning after December 31, 2006.

(2) TRANSITION RULE. —Any requirement under section 101(f) of the Employee Retirement Income Security Act of 1974 (as amended by this section) to report the funding target attainment percentage or funded percentage of a plan with respect to any plan year beginning before January 1, 2008, shall be treated as met if the plan reports—

(A) in the case of a plan year beginning in 2006, the funded current liability percentage (as defined in section 302(d)(8) of such Act) of the plan for such plan year, and

(B) in the case of a plan year beginning in 2007, the funding target attainment percentage or funded percentage as determined using such methods of estimation as the Secretary of the Treasury may provide.

* * *

[¶16,465L-1]

ACT SEC. 502. ACCESS TO MULTIEMPLOYER PLAN INFORMATION.

(a) FINANCIAL INFORMATION WITH RESPECT TO MULTIEMPLOYER PLANS.—

* * *

(3) REGULATIONS.—

The Secretary shall prescribe regulations under section 101(k)(2) of the Employee Retirement Income Security Act of 1974 (as added by paragraph (1)) not later than 1 year after the date of the enactment of this Act.

[¶16,465M]

ACT SEC. 503. ADDITIONAL ANNUAL REPORTING REQUIREMENTS.

(a) ADDITIONAL ANNUAL REPORTING REQUIREMENTS WITH RESPECT TO DEFINED BENEFIT PLANS.—

* * *

(2) GUIDANCE BY SECRETARY OF LABOR.—

Not later than 1 year after the date of enactment of this Act, the Secretary of Labor shall publish guidance to assist multiemployer defined benefit plans to—

(A) identify and enumerate plan participants for whom there is no employer with an obligation to make an employer contribution under the plan; and

(B) report such information under section 103(f)(2)(D) of the Employee Retirement Income Security Act of 1974 (as added by this section).

* * *

(e) MODEL FORM. Not later than 1 year after the date of the enactment of this Act, the Secretary of Labor shall publish a model form for providing the statements, schedules, and other material required to be provided under section 101(f) of the Employee Retirement Income Security Act of 1974, as amended by this section. The Secretary of Labor may promulgate any interim final rules as the Secretary determines appropriate to carry out the provisions of this subsection.

(f) EFFECTIVE DATE. —The amendments made by this section shall apply to plan years beginning after December 31, 2007.

* * *

[¶16,465N]

ACT SEC. 507. NOTICE OF FREEDOM TO DIVEST EMPLOYER SECURITIES.

* * *

(c) MODEL NOTICE. The Secretary of the Treasury shall, within 180 days after the date of the enactment of this subsection, prescribe a model notice for purposes of satisfying the requirements of the amendments made by this section.

(d) EFFECTIVE DATES.—

(1) IN GENERAL. —The amendments made by this section shall apply to plan years beginning after December 31, 2006.

(2) TRANSITION RULE. —If notice under section 101(m) of the Employee Retirement Income Security Act of 1974 (as added by this section) would otherwise be required to be provided before the 90th day after the date of the enactment of this Act, such notice shall not be required to be provided until such 90th day.

* * *

[¶16,465O]

ACT SEC. 508. PERIODIC PENSION BENEFIT STATEMENTS.

* * *

(b) MODEL STATEMENTS.—

(1) IN GENERAL. The Secretary of Labor shall, within 1 year after the date of the enactment of this section, develop 1 or more model benefit statements that are written in a manner calculated to be understood by the average plan participant and that may be used by plan administrators in complying with the requirements of section 105 of the Employee Retirement Income Security Act of 1974.

(2) INTERIM FINAL RULES. The Secretary of Labor may promulgate any interim final rules as the Secretary determines appropriate to carry out the provisions of this subsection.

* * *

[¶16,465P]

ACT SEC. 601. PROHIBITED TRANSACTION EXEMPTION FOR PROVISION OF INVESTMENT ADVICE.

* * *

(b) AMENDMENTS TO INTERNAL REVENUE CODE OF 1986.—

* * *

(3) DETERMINATION OF FEASIBILITY OF APPLICATION OF COMPUTER MODEL INVESTMENT ADVICE PROGRAMS FOR INDIVIDUAL RETIREMENT AND SIMILAR PLANS.—

(A) SOLICITATION OF INFORMATION. As soon as practicable after the date of the enactment of this Act, the Secretary of Labor, in consultation with the Secretary of the Treasury, shall—

(i) solicit information as to the feasibility of the application of computer model investment advice programs for plans described in subparagraphs (B) through (F) (and so much of subparagraph (G) as relates to such subparagraphs) of section 4975(e)(1) of the Internal Revenue Code of 1986, including soliciting information from—

(I) at least the top 50 trustees of such plans, determined on the basis of assets held by such trustees, and

(II) other persons offering computer model investment advice programs based on nonproprietary products, and

(ii) shall on the basis of such information make the determination under subparagraph (B).

The information solicited by the Secretary of Labor under clause (i) from persons described in subclauses (I) and (II) of clause (i) shall include information on computer modeling capabilities of such persons with respect to the current year and preceding year, including such capabilities for investment accounts maintained by such persons.

ACT SEC. 601.   ¶16,465P

(B) DETERMINATION OF FEASIBILITY. The Secretary of Labor, in consultation with the Secretary of the Treasury, shall, on the basis of information received under subparagraph (A), determine whether there is any computer model investment advice program which may be utilized by a plan described in subparagraph (A)(i) to provide investment advice to the account beneficiary of the plan which—

(i) utilizes relevant information about the account beneficiary, which may include age, life expectancy, retirement age, risk tolerance, other assets or sources of income, and preferences as to certain types of investments,

(ii) takes into account the full range of investments, including equities and bonds, in determining the options for the investment portfolio of the account beneficiary, and

(iii) allows the account beneficiary, in directing the investment of assets, sufficient flexibility in obtaining advice to evaluate and select investment options.

The Secretary of Labor shall report the results of such determination to the committees of Congress referred to in subparagraph (D)(ii) not later than December 31, 2007.

(C) APPLICATION OF COMPUTER MODEL INVESTMENT ADVICE PROGRAM.—

(i) CERTIFICATION REQUIRED FOR USE OF COMPUTER MODEL.—

(I) RESTRICTION ON USE. Subclause (II) of section 4975(f)(8)(B)(i) of the Internal Revenue Code of 1986 shall not apply to a plan described in subparagraph (A)(i).

(II) RESTRICTION LIFTED IF MODEL CERTIFIED. If the Secretary of Labor determines under subparagraph (B) or (D) that there is a computer model investment advice program described in subparagraph (B), subclause (I) shall cease to apply as of the date of such determination.

(ii) CLASS EXEMPTION IF NO INITIAL CERTIFICATION BY SECRETARY. If the Secretary of Labor determines under subparagraph (B) that there is no computer model investment advice program described in subparagraph (B), the Secretary of Labor shall grant a class exemption from treatment as a prohibited transaction under section 4975(c) of the Internal Revenue Code of 1986 to any transaction described in section 4975(d)(17)(A) of such Code with respect to plans described in subparagraph (A)(i), subject to such conditions as set forth in such exemption as are in the interests of the plan and its account beneficiary and protective of the rights of the account beneficiary and as are necessary to—

(I) ensure the requirements of sections 4975(d)(17) and 4975(f)(8) (other than subparagraph (C) thereof) of the Internal Revenue Code of 1986 are met, and

(II) ensure the investment advice provided under the investment advice program utilizes prescribed objective criteria to provide asset allocation portfolios comprised of securities or other property available as investments under the plan.

If the Secretary of Labor solicits any information under subparagraph (A) from a person and such person does not provide such information within 60 days after the solicitation, then, unless such failure was due to reasonable cause and not wilful neglect, such person shall not be entitled to utilize the class exemption under this clause.

(D) SUBSEQUENT DETERMINATION.—

(i) IN GENERAL. If the Secretary of Labor initially makes a determination described in subparagraph (C)(ii), the Secretary may subsequently determine that there is a computer model investment advice program described in subparagraph (B). If the Secretary makes such subsequent determination, then the class exemption described in subparagraph (C)(ii) shall cease to apply after the later of—

(I) the date which is 2 years after such subsequent determination, or

(II) the date which is 3 years after the first date on which such exemption took effect.

(ii) REQUESTS FOR DETERMINATION. Any person may request the Secretary of Labor to make a determination under this subparagraph with respect to any computer model investment advice program, and the Secretary of Labor shall make a determination with respect to such request within 90 days. If the Secretary of Labor makes a determination that such program is not described in subparagraph (B), the Secretary shall, within 10 days of such determination, notify the Committee on Ways and Means and the Committee on Education and the Workforce of the House of Representatives and the Committee on Finance and the Committee on Health, Education, Labor, and Pensions of the Senate of such determination and the reasons for such determination.

(E) EFFECTIVE DATE. The provisions of this paragraph shall take effect on the date of the enactment of this Act.

* * *

(c) COORDINATION WITH EXISTING EXEMPTIONS. Any exemption under section 408(b) of the Employee Retirement Income Security Act of 1974 and section 4975(d) of the Internal Revenue Code of 1986 provided by the amendments made by this section shall not in any manner alter existing individual or class exemptions, provided by statute or administrative action.

* * *

[¶16,465Q]

ACT SEC. 625. CLARIFICATION OF FIDUCIARY RULES.

(a) IN GENERAL. Not later than 1 year after the date of the enactment of this Act, the Secretary of Labor shall issue final regulations clarifying that the selection of an annuity contract as an optional form of distribution from an individual account plan to a participant or beneficiary—

(1) is not subject to the safest available annuity standard under Interpretive Bulletin 95-1 (29 C.F.R. 2509.95-1), and

(2) is subject to all otherwise applicable fiduciary standards.

(b) EFFECTIVE DATE. This section shall take effect on the date of enactment of this Act.

[¶16,465R]

ACT SEC. 701. BENEFIT ACCRUAL STANDARDS.

* * *

(d) NO INFERENCE. Nothing in the amendments made by this section shall be construed to create an inference with respect to—

(1) the treatment of applicable defined benefit plans or conversions to applicable defined benefit plans under sections 204(b)(1)(H) of the Employee Retirement Income Security Act of 1974, 4(i)(1) of the Age Discrimination in Employment Act of 1967, and 411(b)(1)(H) of the Internal Revenue Code of 1986, as in effect before such amendments, or

(2) the determination of whether an applicable defined benefit plan fails to meet the requirements of sections 203(a)(2), 204(c), or 204(g) of the Employee Retirement Income Security Act of 1974 or sections 411(a)(2), 411(c), or 417(e) of such Code, as in effect before such amendments, solely because the present value of the accrued benefit (or any portion thereof) of any participant is, under the terms of the plan, equal to the amount expressed as the balance in a hypothetical account or as an accumulated percentage of the participant's final average compensation.

For purposes of this subsection, the term "applicable defined benefit plan" has the meaning given such term by section 203(f)(3) of the Employee Retirement Income Security Act of 1974 and section 411(a)(13)(C) of such Code, as in effect after such amendments.

(e) EFFECTIVE DATE.—

(1) IN GENERAL. —The amendments made by this section shall apply to periods beginning on or after June 29, 2005.

(2) PRESENT VALUE OF ACCRUED BENEFIT. —The amendments made by subsections (a)(2) and (b)(2) shall apply to distributions made after the date of the enactment of this Act.

(3) VESTING AND INTEREST CREDIT REQUIREMENTS. —In the case of a plan in existence on June 29, 2005, the requirements of clause (i) of section 411(b)(5)(B) of the Internal Revenue Code of 1986, clause (i) of section 204(b)(5)(B) of the Employee Retirement Income Security Act of 1974, and clause (i) of section 4(i)(10)(B) of the Age Discrimination in Employment Act of 1967 (as added by this Act) and the requirements of 203(f)(2) of the Employee Retirement Income Security Act of 1974 and section 411(a)(13)(B) of the Internal Revenue Code of 1986 (as so added) shall, for purposes of applying the amendments made by subsections (a) and (b), apply to years beginning after December 31, 2007, unless the plan sponsor elects the application of such requirements for any period after June 29, 2005, and before the first year beginning after December 31, 2007.

(4) SPECIAL RULE FOR COLLECTIVELY BARGAINED PLANS. —In the case of a plan maintained pursuant to 1 or more collective bargaining agreements between employee representatives and 1 or more employers ratified on or before the date of the enactment of this Act, the requirements described in paragraph (3) shall, for purposes of applying the amendments made by subsections (a) and (b), not apply to plan years beginning before—

(A) the earlier of—

(i) the date on which the last of such collective bargaining agreements terminates (determined without regard to any extension thereof on or after such date of enactment), or

(ii) January 1, 2008, or

(B) January 1, 2010.

(5) CONVERSIONS. —The requirements of clause (ii) of section 411(b)(5)(B) of the Internal Revenue Code of 1986, clause (ii) of section 204(b)(5)(B) of the Employee Retirement Income Security Act of 1974, and clause (ii) of section 4(i)(10)(B) of the Age Discrimination in Employment Act of 1967 (as added by this Act), shall apply to plan amendments adopted after, and taking effect after, June 29, 2005, except that the plan sponsor may elect to have such amendments apply to plan amendments adopted before, and taking effect after, such date.

* * *

[¶16,465S]

ACT SEC. 702. REGULATIONS RELATING TO MERGERS AND ACQUISITIONS.

The Secretary of the Treasury or his delegate shall, not later than 12 months after the date of the enactment of this Act, prescribe regulations for the application of the amendments made by, and the provisions of, this title in cases where the conversion of a plan to an applicable defined benefit plan is made with respect to a group of employees who become employees by reason of a merger, acquisition, or similar transaction.

[¶16,465T]

ACT SEC. 811. PENSIONS AND INDIVIDUAL RETIREMENT ARRANGEMENT PROVISIONS OF ECONOMIC GROWTH AND TAX RELIEF RECONCILIATION ACT OF 2001 MADE PERMANENT.

Title IX of the Economic Growth and Tax Relief Reconciliation Act of 2001 shall not apply to the provisions of, and amendments made by, subtitles A through F of title VI of such Act (relating to pension and individual retirement arrangement provisions).

* * *

[¶16,465U]

ACT SEC. 823. CLARIFICATION OF MINIMUM DISTRIBUTION RULES FOR GOVERNMENTAL PLANS.

The Secretary of the Treasury shall issue regulations under which a governmental plan (as defined in section 414(d) of the Internal Revenue Code of 1986) shall, for all years to which section 401(a)(9) of such Code applies to such plan, be treated as having complied with such section 401(a)(9) if such plan complies with a reasonable good faith interpretation of such section 401(a)(9).

* * *

[¶16,465V]

ACT SEC. 825. ELIGIBILITY FOR PARTICIPATION IN RETIREMENT PLANS.

An individual shall not be precluded from participating in an eligible deferred compensation plan by reason of having received a distribution under section 457(e)(9) of the Internal Revenue Code of 1986, as in effect prior to the enactment of the Small Business Job Protection Act of 1996.

[¶16,465W]

ACT SEC. 826. MODIFICATIONS OF RULES GOVERNING HARDSHIPS AND UNFORESEEN FINANCIAL EMERGENCIES.

Within 180 days after the date of the enactment of this Act, the Secretary of the Treasury shall modify the rules for determining whether a participant has had a hardship for purposes of section 401(k)(2)(B)(i)(IV) of the Internal Revenue Code of 1986 to provide that if an event (including the occurrence of a medical expense) would constitute a hardship under the plan if it occurred with respect to the participant's spouse or dependent (as defined in section 152 of such Code), such event shall, to the extent permitted under a plan, constitute a hardship if it occurs with respect to a person who is a beneficiary under the plan with respect to the participant. The Secretary of the Treasury shall issue similar rules for purposes of determining whether a participant has had—

(1) a hardship for purposes of section 403(b)(11)(B) of such Code; or

(2) an unforeseen financial emergency for purposes of sections 409A(a)(2)(A)(vi), 409A(a)(2)(B)(ii), and 457(d)(1)(A)(iii) of such Code.

* * *

[¶16,465X]

ACT SEC. 830. DIRECT PAYMENT OF TAX REFUNDS TO INDIVIDUAL RETIREMENT PLANS.

(a) IN GENERAL. The Secretary of the Treasury (or the Secretary's delegate) shall make available a form (or modify existing forms) for use by individuals to direct that a portion of any refund of overpayment of tax imposed by chapter 1 of the Internal Revenue Code of 1986 be paid directly to an individual retirement plan (as defined in section 7701(a)(37) of such Code) of such individual.

(b) EFFECTIVE DATE. The form required by subsection (a) shall be made available for taxable years beginning after December 31, 2006.

* * *

[¶16,465Y]

ACT SEC. 861. EXTENSION TO ALL GOVERNMENTAL PLANS OF CURRENT MORATORIUM ON APPLICATION OF CERTAIN NONDISCRIMINATION RULES APPLICABLE TO STATE AND LOCAL PLANS.

(a) IN GENERAL.—

* * *

(2) Subparagraph (G) of section 401(k)(3) of such Code and paragraph (2) of section 1505(d) of the Taxpayer Relief Act of 1997 (Public Law 105-34; 111 Stat. 1063) are each amended by striking "maintained by a State or local government or political subdivision thereof (or agency or instrumentality thereof)".

• • **TAXPAYER RELIEF ACT OF 1997 ACT SEC. 1505(d)(2) BEFORE AMENDMENT**————————————

ACT SEC. 1505. EXTENSION OF MORATORIUM ON APPLICATION OF CERTAIN NONDISCRIMINATION RULES TO STATE AND LOCAL GOVERNMENTS.

* * *

(d) EFFECTIVE DATES.—

* * *

(2) TREATMENT FOR YEARS BEGINNING BEFORE DATE OF ENACTMENT.—A governmental plan (within the meaning of section 414(d) of the Internal Revenue Code of 1986) maintained by a State or local government or political subdivision thereof (or agency or instrumentality thereof) shall be treated as satisfying the requirements of sections 401(a)(3), 401(a)(4), 401(a)(26), 401(k), 401(m), 403(b)(1)(D) and (b)(12), and 410 of such Code for all taxable years beginning before the date of enactment of this Act.

————————————————————

* * *

(c) EFFECTIVE DATE. The amendments made by this section shall apply to any year beginning after the date of the enactment of this Act.

* * *

[¶16,465Z]

ACT SEC. 865. GRANDFATHER RULE FOR CHURCH PLANS WHICH SELF-ANNUITIZE.

(a) IN GENERAL. In the case of any plan year ending after the date of the enactment of this Act, annuity payments provided with respect to any account maintained for a participant or beneficiary under a qualified church plan shall not fail to satisfy the requirements of section 401(a)(9) of the Internal Revenue Code of 1986 merely because the payments are not made under an annuity contract purchased from an insurance company if such payments would not fail such requirements if provided with respect to a retirement income account described in section 403(b)(9) of such Code.

(b) QUALIFIED CHURCH PLAN. For purposes of this section, the term "qualified church plan" means any money purchase pension plan described in section 401(a) of such Code which—

(1) is a church plan (as defined in section 414(e) of such Code) with respect to which the election provided by section 410(d) of such Code has not been made, and

(2) was in existence on April 17, 2002.

* * *

[¶16,465Z-1]

ACT SEC. 1001. REGULATIONS ON TIME AND ORDER OF ISSUANCE OF DOMESTIC RELATIONS ORDERS.

Not later than 1 year after the date of the enactment of this Act, the Secretary of Labor shall issue regulations under section 206(d)(3) of the Employee Retirement Security Act of 1974 and section 414(p) of the Internal Revenue Code of 1986 which clarify that—

(1) a domestic relations order otherwise meeting the requirements to be a qualified domestic relations order, including the requirements of section 206(d)(3)(D) of such Act and section 414(p)(3) of such Code, shall not fail to be treated as a qualified domestic relations order solely because—

(A) the order is issued after, or revises, another domestic relations order or qualified domestic relations order; or

(B) of the time at which it is issued; and

(2) any order described in paragraph (1) shall be subject to the same requirements and protections which apply to qualified domestic relations orders, including the provisions of section 206(d)(3)(H) of such Act and section 414(p)(7) of such Code.

[¶16,465Z-2]

ACT SEC. 1002. ENTITLEMENT OF DIVORCED SPOUSES TO RAILROAD RETIREMENT ANNUITIES INDEPENDENT OF ACTUAL ENTITLEMENT OF EMPLOYEE.

(a) IN GENERAL. Section 2 of the Railroad Retirement Act of 1974 (45 U.S.C. 231a) is amended—

　(1) in subsection (c)(4)(i), by striking "(A) is entitled to an annuity under subsection (a)(1) and (B)"; and

　(2) in subsection (e)(5), by striking "or divorced wife" the second place it appears.

(b) EFFECTIVE DATE. The amendments made by this section shall take effect 1 year after the date of the enactment of this Act.

[¶16,465Z-2a]

ACT SEC. 1003. EXTENSION OF TIER II RAILROAD RETIREMENT BENEFITS TO SURVIVING FORMER SPOUSES PURSUANT TO DIVORCE AGREEMENTS.

(a) IN GENERAL. Section 5 of the Railroad Retirement Act of 1974 (45 U.S.C. 231d) is amended by adding at the end the following:

"(d) Notwithstanding any other provision of law, the payment of any portion of an annuity computed under section 3(b) to a surviving former spouse in accordance with a court decree of divorce, annulment, or legal separation or the terms of any court-approved property settlement incident to any such court decree shall not be terminated upon the death of the individual who performed the service with respect to which such annuity is so computed unless such termination is otherwise required by the terms of such court decree."

(b) EFFECTIVE DATE. The amendment made by this section shall take effect 1 year after the date of the enactment of this Act.

* * *

[¶16,465Z-3]

ACT SEC. 1101. EMPLOYEE PLANS COMPLIANCE RESOLUTION SYSTEM.

(a) IN GENERAL. The Secretary of the Treasury shall have full authority to establish and implement the Employee Plans Compliance Resolution System (or any successor program) and any other employee plans correction policies, including the authority to waive income, excise, or other taxes to ensure that any tax, penalty, or sanction is not excessive and bears a reasonable relationship to the nature, extent, and severity of the failure.

(b) IMPROVEMENTS. The Secretary of the Treasury shall continue to update and improve the Employee Plans Compliance Resolution System (or any successor program), giving special attention to—

　(1) increasing the awareness and knowledge of small employers concerning the availability and use of the program;

　(2) taking into account special concerns and circumstances that small employers face with respect to compliance and correction of compliance failures;

　(3) extending the duration of the self-correction period under the Self-Correction Program for significant compliance failures;

　(4) expanding the availability to correct insignificant compliance failures under the Self-Correction Program during audit; and

　(5) assuring that any tax, penalty, or sanction that is imposed by reason of a compliance failure is not excessive and bears a reasonable relationship to the nature, extent, and severity of the failure.

[¶16,465Z-4]

ACT SEC. 1102. NOTICE AND CONSENT PERIOD REGARDING DISTRIBUTIONS.

* * *

(b) NOTIFICATION OF RIGHT TO DEFER.—

　(1) IN GENERAL. The Secretary of the Treasury shall modify the regulations under section 411(a)(11) of the Internal Revenue Code of 1986 and under section 205 of the Employee Retirement Income Security Act of 1974 to provide that the description of a participant's right, if any, to defer receipt of a distribution shall also describe the consequences of failing to defer such receipt.

　(2) EFFECTIVE DATE.—

　　(A) IN GENERAL. The modifications required by paragraph (1) shall apply to years beginning after December 31, 2006.

　　(B) REASONABLE NOTICE. A plan shall not be treated as failing to meet the requirements of section 411(a)(11) of such Code or section 205 of such Act with respect to any description of consequences described in paragraph (1) made within 90 days after the Secretary of the Treasury issues the modifications required by paragraph (1) if the plan administrator makes a reasonable attempt to comply with such requirements.

[¶16,465Z-5]

ACT SEC. 1103. REPORTING SIMPLIFICATION.

(a) SIMPLIFIED ANNUAL FILING REQUIREMENT FOR OWNERS AND THEIR SPOUSES.—

　(1) IN GENERAL. The Secretary of the Treasury shall modify the requirements for filing annual returns with respect to one-participant retirement plans to ensure that such plans with assets of $250,000 or less as of the close of the plan year need not file a return for that year.

　(2) ONE-PARTICIPANT RETIREMENT PLAN DEFINED. For purposes of this subsection, the term "one-participant retirement plan" means a retirement plan with respect to which the following requirements are met:

　　(A) on the first day of the plan year—

　　　(i) the plan covered only one individual (or the individual and the individual's spouse) and the individual owned 100 percent of the plan sponsor (whether or not incorporated), or

　　　(ii) the plan covered only one or more partners (or partners and their spouses) in the plan sponsor;

(B) the plan meets the minimum coverage requirements of section 410(b) of the Internal Revenue Code of 1986 without being combined with any other plan of the business that covers the employees of the business;

(C) the plan does not provide benefits to anyone except the individual (and the individual's spouse) or the partners (and their spouses);

(D) the plan does not cover a business that is a member of an affiliated service group, a controlled group of corporations, or a group of businesses under common control; and

(E) the plan does not cover a business that uses the services of leased employees (within the meaning of section 414(n) of such Code).

For purposes of this paragraph, the term "partner" includes a 2-percent shareholder (as defined in section 1372(b) of such Code) of an S corporation.

(3) OTHER DEFINITIONS. Terms used in paragraph (2) which are also used in section 414 of the Internal Revenue Code of 1986 shall have the respective meanings given such terms by such section.

(4) EFFECTIVE DATE. The provisions of this subsection shall apply to plan years beginning on or after January 1, 2007.

(b) SIMPLIFIED ANNUAL FILING REQUIREMENT FOR PLANS WITH FEWER THAN 25 PARTICIPANTS. In the case of plan years beginning after December 31, 2006, the Secretary of the Treasury and the Secretary of Labor shall provide for the filing of a simplified annual return for any retirement plan which covers less than 25 participants on the first day of a plan year and which meets the requirements described in subparagraphs (B), (D), and (E) of subsection (a)(2).

* * *

[¶16,465Z-6]

ACT SEC. 1107. PROVISIONS RELATING TO PLAN AMENDMENTS.

(a) IN GENERAL. If this section applies to any pension plan or contract amendment—

(1) such pension plan or contract shall be treated as being operated in accordance with the terms of the plan during the period described in subsection (b)(2)(A), and

(2) except as provided by the Secretary of the Treasury, such pension plan shall not fail to meet the requirements of section 411(d)(6) of the Internal Revenue Code of 1986 and section 204(g) of the Employee Retirement Income Security Act of 1974 by reason of such amendment.

(b) AMENDMENTS TO WHICH SECTION APPLIES.—

(1) IN GENERAL. This section shall apply to any amendment to any pension plan or annuity contract which is made—

(A) pursuant to any amendment made by this Act or pursuant to any regulation issued by the Secretary of the Treasury or the Secretary of Labor under this Act, and

(B) on or before the last day of the first plan year beginning on or after January 1, 2009.

In the case of a governmental plan (as defined in section 414(d) of the Internal Revenue Code of 1986), this paragraph shall be applied by substituting "2011" for "2009".

(2) CONDITIONS. This section shall not apply to any amendment unless—

(A) during the period—

(i) beginning on the date the legislative or regulatory amendment described in paragraph (1)(A) takes effect (or in the case of a plan or contract amendment not required by such legislative or regulatory amendment, the effective date specified by the plan), and

(ii) ending on the date described in paragraph (1)(B) (or, if earlier, the date the plan or contract amendment is adopted), the plan or contract is operated as if such plan or contract amendment were in effect; and

(B) such plan or contract amendment applies retroactively for such period.

Genetic Information Nondiscrimination Act of 2008

[¶ 16,467]

P.L. 110-233

Signed May 21, 2008

[Reproduced below are provisions of the Genetic Information Nondiscrimination Act of 2008 pertaining to pensions and employee benefits that did not amend the Internal Revenue Code or ERISA. Sections that amended the Internal Revenue Code are reflected in the "Code and Regulations" divisions starting at ¶ 11,000. Sections which amended ERISA are reflected in the "Labor Laws and Regulations" division starting at ¶ 14,110 – CCH.]

[¶ 16,467A]

ACT SEC. 101. AMENDMENTS TO EMPLOYEE RETIREMENT INCOME SECURITY ACT OF 1974.

* * *

(f) Regulations and Effective Date—

(1) REGULATIONS—. The Secretary of Labor shall issue final regulations not later than 12 Months after the date of enactment of this Act to carry out the amendments made by this section.

* * *

[¶ 16,467B]

ACT SEC. 103. AMENDMENTS TO THE INTERNAL REVENUE CODE OF 1986.

* * *

(f) Regulations and Effective Date—

(1) REGULATIONS—. The Secretary of the Treasury shall issue final regulations or other guidance not later than 12 months after the date of the enactment of this Act to carry out the amendments made by this section.

* * *

[¶ 16,468]

ACT SEC. 15345. HEARTLAND, HABITAT, HARVEST, AND HORTICULTURE ACT OF 2008

P.L. 110-246

[Effective on May 22, 2008]

* * *

ACT SEC. 15345. TEMPORARY TAX RELIEF FOR KIOWA COUNTY, KANSAS AND SURROUNDING AREA.

(a) IN GENERAL.—Subject to the modifications described in this section, the following provisions of or relating to the Internal Revenue Code of 1986 shall apply to the Kansas disaster area in addition to the areas to which such provisions otherwise apply:

* * *

(7) Section 1400Q of such Code (relating to special rules for use of retirement funds).

* * *

(b) KANSAS DISASTER AREA.—

For purposes of this section, the term "Kansas disaster area" means an area with respect to which a major disaster has been declared by the President under section 401 of the Robert T. Stafford Disaster Relief and Emergency Assistance Act (FEMA-1699-DR, as in effect on the date of the enactment of this Act) by reason of severe storms and tornados beginning on May 4, 2007, and determined by the President to warrant individual or individual and public assistance from the Federal Government under such Act with respect to damages attributable to such storms and tornados.

(c) REFERENCES TO AREA OR LOSS.—

(1) AREA.—

Any reference in such provisions to the Katrina disaster area or the Gulf Opportunity Zone shall be treated as a reference to the Kansas disaster area.

(2) LOSS.—

Any reference in such provisions to any loss or damage attributable to Hurricane Katrina shall be treated as a reference to any loss or damage attributable to the May 4, 2007, storms and tornados.

(d) REFERENCES TO DATES, ETC.—

* * *

(5) SPECIAL RULES FOR USE OF RETIREMENT FUNDS.—Section 1400Q of such Code—

(A) by substituting "qualified Recovery Assistance distribution" for "qualified hurricane distribution" each place it appears,

(B) by substituting "on or after May 4, 2007, and before January 1, 2009" for "on or after August 25, 2005, and before January 1, 2007" in subsection (a)(4)(A)(i),

(C) by substituting "May 4, 2007" for "August 28, 2005" in subsections (a)(4)(A)(i) and (c)(3)(B),

(D) disregarding clauses (ii) and (iii) of subsection (a)(4)(A),

(E) by substituting "qualified storm distribution" for "qualified Katrina distribution" each place it appears,

(F) by substituting "after November 4, 2006, and before May 5, 2007" for "after February 28, 2005, and before August 29, 2005" in subsection (b)(2)(B)(ii),

(G) by substituting "the Kansas disaster area (as defined in section 15345(b) of the Food, Conservation, and Energy Act of 2008) but which was not so purchased or constructed on account of the May 4, 2007, storms and tornados" for "the Hurricane Katrina disaster area, but not so purchased or constructed on account of Hurricane Katrina" in subsection (b)(2)(B)(iii),

(H) by substituting "beginning on May 4, 2007, and ending on the date which is 5 months after the date of the enactment of the Heartland, Habitat, Harvest, and Horticulture Act of 2008" for "beginning on August 25, 2005, and ending on February 28, 2006" in subsection (b)(3)(A),

(I) by substituting "qualified storm individual" for "qualified Hurricane Katrina individual" each place it appears,

(J) by substituting "December 31, 2008" for "December 31, 2006" in subsection (c)(2)(A),

(K) by substituting "beginning on the date of the enactment of the Food, Conservation, and Energy Act of 2008 and ending on December 31, 2008" for "beginning on September 24, 2005, and ending on December 31, 2006" in subsection (c)(4)(A)(i),

(L) by substituting "May 4, 2007" for "August 25, 2005" in subsection (c)(4)(A)(ii), and

(M) by substituting "January 1, 2009" for "January 1, 2007" in subsection (d)(2)(A)(ii).

* * *

Emergency Economic Stabilization Act Of 2008

[¶ 16,469]

P.L. 110-343

Effective October 3, 2008

[Reproduced below are provisions of the Emergency Economic Stabilization Act of 2008 pertaining to pensions and employee benefits that did not amend the Internal Revenue Code or ERISA. Sections that amended the Internal Revenue Code are reflected in the "Code and Regulations" divisions starting at ¶ 11,000. Sections which amended ERISA are reflected in the "Labor Laws and Regulations" division starting at ¶ 14,110 – CCH.]

[¶ 16,469A]

TITLE V—ADDITIONAL TAX RELIEF AND OTHER TAX PROVISIONS

Subtitle A—General Provisions

* * *

ACT SEC. 504 INCOME AVERAGING FOR AMOUNTS RECEIVED IN CONNECTION WITH THE EXXON VALDEZ LITIGATION.

(a) Income Averaging of Amounts Received From the Exxon Valdez Litigation- For purposes of section 1301 of the Internal Revenue Code of 1986—

(1) any qualified taxpayer who receives any qualified settlement income in any taxable year shall be treated as engaged in a fishing business (determined without regard to the commercial nature of the business), and

(2) such qualified settlement income shall be treated as income attributable to such a fishing business for such taxable year.

(b) Contributions of Amounts Received to Retirement Accounts—

(1) IN GENERAL. Any qualified taxpayer who receives qualified settlement income during the taxable year may, at any time before the end of the taxable year in which such income was received, make one or more contributions to an eligible retirement plan of which such qualified taxpayer is a beneficiary in an aggregate amount not to exceed the lesser of—

(A) $100,000 (reduced by the amount of qualified settlement income contributed to an eligible retirement plan in prior taxable years pursuant to this subsection), or

(B) the amount of qualified settlement income received by the individual during the taxable year.

(2) TIME WHEN CONTRIBUTIONS DEEMED MADE—. For purposes of paragraph (1), a qualified taxpayer shall be deemed to have made a contribution to an eligible retirement plan on the last day of the taxable year in which such income is received if the contribution is made on account of such taxable year and is made not later than the time prescribed by law for filing the return for such taxable year (not including extensions thereof).

(3) TREATMENT OF CONTRIBUTIONS TO ELIGIBLE RETIREMENT PLANS—. For purposes of the Internal Revenue Code of 1986, if a contribution is made pursuant to paragraph (1) with respect to qualified settlement income, then—

(A) except as provided in paragraph (4)—

(i) to the extent of such contribution, the qualified settlement income shall not be included in taxable income, and

(ii) for purposes of section 72 of such Code, such contribution shall not be considered to be investment in the contract,

(B) the qualified taxpayer shall, to the extent of the amount of the contribution, be treated—

(i) as having received the qualified settlement income—

(I) in the case of a contribution to an individual retirement plan (as defined under section 7701(a)(37) of such Code), in a distribution described in section 408(d)(3) of such Code, and

(II) in the case of any other eligible retirement plan, in an eligible rollover distribution (as defined under section 402(f)(2) of such Code), and

(ii) as having transferred the amount to the eligible retirement plan in a direct trustee to trustee transfer within 60 days of the distribution,

(C) section 408(d)(3)(B) of the Internal Revenue Code of 1986 shall not apply with respect to amounts treated as a rollover under this paragraph, and

(D) section 408A(c)(3)(B) of the Internal Revenue Code of 1986 shall not apply with respect to amounts contributed to a Roth IRA (as defined under section 408A(b) of such Code) or a designated Roth contribution to an applicable retirement plan (within the meaning of section 402A of such Code) under this paragraph.

(4) SPECIAL RULE FOR ROTH IRAS AND ROTH 401(K)S—. For purposes of the Internal Revenue Code of 1986, if a contribution is made pursuant to paragraph (1) with respect to qualified settlement income to a Roth IRA (as defined under section 408A(b) of such Code) or as a designated Roth contribution to an applicable retirement plan (within the meaning of section 402A of such Code), then—

(A) the qualified settlement income shall be includible in taxable income, and

(B) for purposes of section 72 of such Code, such contribution shall be considered to be investment in the contract.

(5) ELIGIBLE RETIREMENT PLAN. For purpose of this subsection, the term `eligible retirement plan' has the meaning given such term under section 402(c)(8)(B) of the Internal Revenue Code of 1986.

(c) Treatment of Qualified Settlement Income Under Employment Taxes—

(1) SECA—. For purposes of chapter 2 of the Internal Revenue Code of 1986 and section 211 of the Social Security Act, no portion of qualified settlement income received by a qualified taxpayer shall be treated as self-employment income.

(2) FICA—. For purposes of chapter 21 of the Internal Revenue Code of 1986 and section 209 of the Social Security Act, no portion of qualified settlement income received by a qualified taxpayer shall be treated as wages.

(d) QUALIFIED TAXPAYER—. For purposes of this section, the term `qualified taxpayer' means—

(1) any individual who is a plaintiff in the civil action In re Exxon Valdez, No. 89-095-CV (HRH) (Consolidated) (D. Alaska); or

(2) any individual who is a beneficiary of the estate of such a plaintiff who—

ACT SEC. 15345.   ¶ 16,469A

(A) acquired the right to receive qualified settlement income from that plaintiff; and

(B) was the spouse or an immediate relative of that plaintiff.

(e) QUALIFIED SETTLEMENT INCOME. For purposes of this section, the term `qualified settlement income' means any interest and punitive damage awards which are—

(1) otherwise includible in taxable income, and

(2) received (whether as lump sums or periodic payments) in connection with the civil action In re Exxon Valdez, No. 89-095-CV (HRH) (Consolidated) (D. Alaska) (whether pre-or post-judgment and whether related to a settlement or judgment).

[¶16,469B]

TITLE VII—DISASTER RELIEF

Subtitle A—Heartland and Hurricane Ike Disaster Relief

* * *

Act Sec. 702 TEMPORARY TAX RELIEF FOR AREAS DAMAGED BY 2008 MIDWESTERN SEVERE STORMS, TORNADOS, AND FLOODING.

* * *

(b) Midwestern Disaster Area—

(1) IN GENERAL—. For purposes of this section and for applying the substitutions described in subsections (d) and (e), the term `Midwestern disaster area' means an area—

(A) IN GENERAL—. with respect to which a major disaster has been declared by the President on or after May 20, 2008, and before August 1, 2008, under section 401 of the Robert T. Stafford Disaster Relief and Emergency Assistance Act by reason of severe storms, tornados, or flooding occurring in any of the States of Arkansas, Illinois, Indiana, Iowa, Kansas, Michigan, Minnesota, Missouri, Nebraska, and Wisconsin, and

(B) determined by the President to warrant individual or individual and public assistance from the Federal Government under such Act with respect to damages attributable to such severe storms, tornados, or flooding.

* * *

(c) References—

(1) AREA—. Any reference in such provisions to the Hurricane Katrina disaster area or the Gulf Opportunity Zone shall be treated as a reference to any Midwestern disaster area and any reference to the Hurricane Katrina disaster area or the Gulf Opportunity Zone within a State shall be treated as a reference to all Midwestern disaster areas within the State.

(2) ITEMS ATTRIBUTABLE TO DISASTER—. Any reference in such provisions to any loss, damage, or other item attributable to Hurricane Katrina shall be treated as a reference to any loss, damage, or other item attributable to the severe storms, tornados, or flooding giving rise to any Presidential declaration described in subsection (b)(1)(A).

(3) APPLICABLE DISASTER DATE—. For purposes of applying the substitutions described in subsections (d) and (e), the term `applicable disaster date' means, with respect to any Midwestern disaster area, the date on which the severe storms, tornados, or flooding giving rise to the Presidential declaration described in subsection (b)(1)(A) occurred.

(d) MODIFICATIONS TO 1986 CODE—. The following provisions of the Internal Revenue Code of 1986 shall be applied with the following modifications:

* * *

(10) SPECIAL RULES FOR USE OF RETIREMENT FUNDS—. (A) SECTION 1400Q—. by substituting `qualified Disaster Recovery Assistance distribution' for `qualified hurricane distribution' each place it appears,

(B) by substituting `on or after the applicable disaster date and before January 1, 2010' for `on or after August 25, 2005, and before January 1, 2007' in subsection (a)(4)(A)(i),

(C) by substituting `the applicable disaster date' for `August 28, 2005' in subsections (a)(4)(A)(i) and (c)(3)(B),

(D) by disregarding clauses (ii) and (iii) of subsection (a)(4)(A) thereof,

(E) by substituting `qualified storm damage distribution' for `qualified Katrina distribution' each place it appears,

(F) by substituting `after the date which is 6 months before the applicable disaster date and before the date which is the day after the applicable disaster date' for `after February 28, 2005, and before August 29, 2005' in subsection (b)(2)(B)(ii),

(G) by substituting `the Midwestern disaster area, but not so purchased or constructed on account of severe storms, tornados, or flooding giving rise to the designation of the area as a disaster area' for `the Hurricane Katrina disaster area, but not so purchased or constructed on account of Hurricane Katrina' in subsection (b)(2)(B)(iii),

(H) by substituting `beginning on the applicable disaster date and ending on the date which is 5 months after the date of the enactment of the Heartland Disaster Tax Relief Act of 2008' for `beginning on August 25, 2005, and ending on February 28, 2006' in subsection (b)(3)(A),

(I) by substituting `qualified storm damage individual' for `qualified Hurricane Katrina individual' each place it appears, (J) by substituting `December 31, 2009' for `December 31, 2006' in subsection (c)(2)(A),

(J) by substituting `December 31, 2009' for `December 31, 2006' in subsection (c)(2)(A),

(K) by disregarding subparagraphs (C) and (D) of subsection (c)(3) thereof,

(L) by substituting `beginning on the date of the enactment of the Heartland Disaster Tax Relief Act of 2008 and ending on December 31, 2009' for `beginning on September 24, 2005, and ending on December 31, 2006' in subsection (c)(4)(A)(i),

(M) by substituting `the applicable disaster date' for `August 25, 2005' in subsection (c)(4)(A)(ii), and

(N) by substituting `January 1, 2010' for `January 1, 2007' in subsection (d)(2)(A)(ii).

* * *

Worker, Retiree, And Employer Recovery Act Of 2008

[¶16,470]

P.L. 110-458

Signed December 23, 2008

[Reproduced below are provisions of the Worker, Retiree, and Employer Recovery Act of 2008 pertaining to pensions and employee benefits that did not amend the Internal Revenue Code or ERISA. Sections that amended the Internal Revenue Code are reflected in the "Code and Regulations" divisions starting at ¶ 11,000. Sections which amended ERISA are reflected in the "Labor Laws and Regulations" division starting at ¶ 14,110 – CCH..]

[¶16,470A]

ACT SEC. 1. SHORT TITLE; ETC.

1(a) SHORT TITLE. -

This Act may be cited as the "Worker, Retiree, and Employer Recovery Act of 2008".

* * *

[¶16,470B]

ACT SEC. 100. REFERENCES IN TITLE.

For purposes of this title:

100(1) AMENDMENT OF 1986 CODE. —

The term "1986 Code" means the Internal Revenue Code of 1986.

100(2) AMENDMENT OF ERISA. —

The term "ERISA" means the Employee Retirement Income Security Act of 1974.

100(3) 2006 ACT. —

The term "2006 Act" means the Pension Protection Act of 2006.

* * *

[¶16,470C]

ACT SEC. 101. AMENDMENTS RELATED TO TITLE I.

* * *

101(c)(3) AMENDMENTS TO 2006 ACT. —

Sections 103(c)(2)(A)(ii) and 113(b)(2)(A)(ii) of the 2006 Act are each amended —

101(c)(3)(A) by striking "subsection" and inserting "section", and

101(c)(3)(B) by striking "subparagraph" and inserting "paragraph".

* * *

101(d) AMENDMENTS RELATED TO SECTIONS 107 AND 114. —

* * *

101(d)(3) AMENDMENT TO 2006 ACT. —

Section 114 of the 2006 Act is amended by adding at the end the following new subsection:

"(g) EFFECTIVE DATES. —

"(1) IN GENERAL. —The amendments made by this section shall apply to plan years beginning after 2007.

"(2) EXCISE TAX. —The amendments made by subsection (e) shall apply to taxable years beginning after 2007, but only with respect to plan years described in paragraph (1) which end with or within any such taxable year.".

* * *

[¶16,470D]

ACT SEC. 102. AMENDMENTS RELATED TO TITLE II.

102(a) AMENDMENT RELATED TO SECTIONS 201 AND 211. —

Section 201(b)(2)(A) of the 2006 Act is amended by striking "has not used" and inserting "has not adopted, or ceased using,".

102(b) AMENDMENTS RELATED TO SECTIONS 202 AND 212. —

* * *

102(b)(3) AMENDMENTS TO 2006 ACT. —

102(b)(3)(A) Section 212(b)(2) of the 2006 Act is amended by striking "Section 4971(c)(2) of such Code" and inserting "Section 4971(e)(2) of such Code".

102(b)(3)(B) Section 212(e)(1) of the 2006 Act is amended by inserting ", except that the amendments made by subsection (b) shall apply to taxable years beginning after 2007, but only with respect to plan years beginning after 2007 which end with or within any such taxable year" before the period at the end.

102(b)(3)(C) Section 212(e)(2) of the 2006 Act is amended by striking "section 305(b)(3) of the Employee Retirement Income Security Act of 1974" and inserting "section 432(b)(3) of the Internal Revenue Code of 1986".

[¶16,470E]

ACT SEC. 103. AMENDMENTS RELATED TO TITLE III.

103(a) AMENDMENT RELATED TO SECTION 301. —

Clause (ii) of section 101(c)(2)(A) of the Pension Funding Equity Act of 2004, as amended by section 301(c) of the 2006 Act, is amended by striking "2008" and inserting "2009".

* * *

[¶16,470F]

ACT SEC. 104. AMENDMENTS RELATED TO TITLE IV.

* * *

104(b) AMENDMENT RELATED TO SECTION 402. -

Section 402(c)(1)(A) of the 2006 Act is amended by striking "commercial airline" and inserting "commercial".

* * *

[¶16,470G]

ACT SEC. 105. AMENDMENTS RELATED TO TITLE V.

* * *

105(c) AMENDMENTS RELATED TO SECTION 503. -

* * *

105(c)(2) AMENDMENTS TO 2006 ACT. -

Section 503(e) of the 2006 Act is amended by striking "section 101(f)" and inserting "section 104(d)".

[¶16,470H]

ACT SEC. 106. AMENDMENTS RELATED TO TITLE VI.
106(a) AMENDMENTS RELATED TO SECTION 601. -

* * *

106(a)(3) AMENDMENT TO 2006 ACT. -

Section 601(b)(4) of the 2006 Act is amended by striking "section 4975(c)(3)(B)" and inserting "section 4975(e)(3)(B)".

[¶16,470I]

ACT SEC. 107. AMENDMENTS RELATED TO TITLE VII.

* * *

107(c) AMENDMENTS TO 2006 ACT. -

107(c)(1) Section 701(d)(2) of the 2006 Act is amended by striking "204(g)" and inserting "205(g)".

107(c)(2) Section 701(e) of the 2006 Act is amended -

107(c)(2)(A) by inserting "on or" after "period" in paragraph (3),

107(c)(2)(B) in paragraph (4) -

107(c)(2)(B)(i) by inserting "the earlier of" after "before" in the matter preceding subparagraph (A), and

107(c)(2)(B)(ii) by striking "earlier" and inserting "later" in subparagraph (A),

107(c)(2)(C) by inserting "on or" before "after" each place it appears in paragraph (5), and

107(c)(2)(D) by adding at the end the following new paragraph:

"(6) SPECIAL RULE FOR VESTING REQUIREMENTS. —The requirements of section 203(f)(2) of the Employee Retirement Income Security Act of 1974 and section 411(a)(13)(B) of the Internal Revenue Code of 1986 (as added by this Act) —

"(A) shall not apply to a participant who does not have an hour of service after the effective date of such requirements (as otherwise determined under this subsection); and

"(B) in the case of a plan other than a plan described in paragraph (3) or (4), shall apply to plan years ending on or after June 29, 2005.".

[¶16,470J]

ACT SEC. 109. AMENDMENTS RELATED TO TITLE IX.

* * *

109(c) AMENDMENTS RELATED TO SECTION 903. -

* * *

109(d) AMENDMENTS RELATED TO SECTION 906. -

109(d)(1) Section 906(b)(1)(B)(ii) of the 2006 Act is amended by striking "paragraph (1)" and inserting "paragraph (10)".

* * *

[¶16,470J-1]

ACT SEC. 110. AMENDMENTS RELATED TO TITLE X.
110(a) AMENDMENTS TO RAILROAD RETIREMENT ACT. -

110(a)(1) Section 14(b) of the Railroad Retirement Act of 1974 (45 U.S.C. 231m(b)) is amended by adding at the end the following:

"(3)(A) Payments made pursuant to paragraph (2) of this subsection shall not require that the employee be entitled to an annuity under section 2(a)(1) of this Act: Provided, however, That where an employee is not entitled to such an annuity, payments made pursuant to paragraph (2) may not begin before the month in which the following three conditions are satisfied:

"(i) The employee has completed ten years of service in the railroad industry or, five years of service all of which accrues after December 31, 1995.

"(ii) The spouse or former spouse attains age 62.

"(iii) The employee attains age 62 (or if deceased, would have attained age 62).

"(B) Payments made pursuant to paragraph (2) of this subsection shall terminate upon the death of the spouse or former spouse, unless the court document provides for termination at an earlier date. Notwithstanding the language in a court order, that portion of payments made pursuant to paragraph (2) which represents payments computed pursuant to section 3(f)(2) of this Act shall not be paid after the death of the employee.

"(C) If the employee is not entitled to an annuity under section 2(a)(1) of this Act, payments made pursuant to paragraph (2) of this subsection shall be computed as though the employee were entitled to an annuity.".

110(a)(2) Subsection (d) of section 5 of the Railroad Retirement Act (45 U.S.C. 231d) is repealed.

110(b) EFFECTIVE DATES. -

110(b)(1) SUBSECTION (a)(1). -

The amendment made by subsection (a)(1) shall apply with respect to payments due for months after August 2007. If, prior to the effective date of such amendment, payment pursuant to paragraph (2) of section 14(b) of the Railroad Retirement Act of 1974 (45 U.S.C. 231m(b)) was terminated because of the employee's death, payment to the former spouse may be reinstated for months after August 2007.

110(b)(2) SUBSECTION (a)(2). -

The amendment made by subsection (a)(2) shall take effect upon the date of the enactment of this Act.

[¶16,470K]

ACT SEC. 111. AMENDMENTS RELATED TO TITLE XI.

111(a) AMENDMENT RELATED TO SECTION 1104. -

Section 1104(d)(1) of the 2006 Act is amended by striking "Act" the first place it appears and inserting "section".

* * *

[¶16,470L]

ACT SEC. 112. EFFECTIVE DATE.

Except as otherwise provided in this subtitle, the amendments made by this subtitle shall take effect as if included in the provisions of the 2006 Act to which the amendments relate.

[¶16,470M]

ACT SEC. 123. DETERMINATION OF MARKET RATE OF RETURN FOR GOVERNMENTAL PLANS.

123(a) AMENDMENT OF ADEA. -

Section 4(i)(10)(B)(i)(III) of the Age Discrimination in Employment Act of 1967 (29 U.S.C. 623(i)(10)(B)(i)(III)) is amended by adding at the end the following: "In the case of a governmental plan (as defined in the first sentence of section 414(d) of the Internal Revenue Code of 1986), a rate of return or a method of crediting interest established pursuant to any provision of Federal, State, or local law (including any administrative rule or policy adopted in accordance with any such law) shall be treated as a market rate of return for purposes of subclause (I) and a permissible method of crediting interest for purposes of meeting the requirements of subclause (I), except that this sentence shall only apply to a rate of return or method of crediting interest if such rate or method does not violate any other requirement of this Act.".

123(b) EFFECTIVE DATE. -

The amendment made by this section shall take effect as if included in the provisions of the Pension Protection Act of 2006 to which such amendment relates.

* * *

[¶16,470N]

ACT SEC. 125. ROLLOVER OF AMOUNTS RECEIVED IN AIRLINE CARRIER BANKRUPTCY TO ROTH IRAS.

125(a) GENERAL RULE. -

If a qualified airline employee receives any airline payment amount and transfers any portion of such amount to a Roth IRA within 180 days of receipt of such amount (or, if later, within 180 days of the date of the enactment of this Act), then such amount (to the extent so transferred) shall be treated as a qualified rollover contribution described in section 408A(e) of the Internal Revenue Code of 1986, and the limitations described in section 408A(c)(3) of such Code shall not apply to any such transfer.

125(b) DEFINITIONS AND SPECIAL RULES. -

For purposes of this section -

125(b)(1) AIRLINE PAYMENT AMOUNT. -

125(b)(1)(A) IN GENERAL. -

The term "airline payment amount" means any payment of any money or other property which is payable by a commercial passenger airline carrier to a qualified airline employee -

125(b)(1)(A)(i) under the approval of an order of a Federal bankruptcy court in a case filed after September 11, 2001, and before January 1, 2007, and

125(b)(1)(A)(ii) in respect of the qualified airline employee's interest in a bankruptcy claim against the carrier, any note of the carrier (or amount paid in lieu of a note being issued), or any other fixed obligation of the carrier to pay a lump sum amount.

The amount of such payment shall be determined without regard to any requirement to deduct and withhold tax from such payment under sections 3102(a) and 3402(a).

125(b)(1)(B) EXCEPTION. -

An airline payment amount shall not include any amount payable on the basis of the carrier's future earnings or profits.

125(b)(2) QUALIFIED AIRLINE EMPLOYEE. -

The term "qualified airline employee" means an employee or former employee of a commercial passenger airline carrier who was a participant in a defined benefit plan maintained by the carrier which -

125(b)(2)(A) is a plan described in section 401(a) of the Internal Revenue Code of 1986 which includes a trust exempt from tax under section 501(a) of such Code, and

125(b)(2)(B) was terminated or became subject to the restrictions contained in paragraphs (2) and (3) of section 402(b) of the Pension Protection Act of 2006.

125(b)(3) REPORTING REQUIREMENTS. -

If a commercial passenger airline carrier pays 1 or more airline payment amounts, the carrier shall, within 90 days of such payment (or, if later, within 90 days of the date of the enactment of this Act), report —

125(b)(3)(A) to the Secretary of the Treasury, the names of the qualified airline employees to whom such amounts were paid, and

125(b)(3)(B) to the Secretary and to such employees, the years and the amounts of the payments.

Such reports shall be in such form, and contain such additional information, as the Secretary may prescribe.

125(c) EFFECTIVE DATE. -

This section shall apply to transfers made after the date of the enactment of this Act with respect to airline payment amounts paid before, on, or after such date.

[¶16,470O]

ACT SEC. 126. DETERMINATION OF ASSET VALUE FOR SPECIAL AIRLINE FUNDING RULES.

126(a) IN GENERAL. -

Section 402(e)(4)(C) of the 2006 Act is amended to read as follows:

"(C) the value of plan assets shall be determined under sections 303(g)(3) of such Act and 430(g)(3) of such Code.".

126(b) EFFECTIVE DATE. -

The amendment made by this section shall apply to plan years beginning after December 31, 2007.

* * *

[¶16,470O-1]

ACT SEC. 203. TEMPORARY MODIFICATION OF APPLICATION OF LIMITATION ON BENEFIT ACCRUALS.

In the case of the first plan year beginning during the period beginning on October 1, 2008, and ending on September 30, 2009, sections 206(g)(4)(A) of the Employee Retirement Income Security Act of 1974 (29 U.S.C. 1056(g)(4)(A)) and 436(e)(1) of the Internal Revenue Code of 1986 shall be applied by substituting the plan's adjusted funding target attainment percentage for the preceding plan year for such percentage for such plan year but only if the adjusted funding target attainment percentage for the preceding plan year is greater.

[¶16,470P]

ACT SEC. 204. TEMPORARY DELAY OF DESIGNATION OF MULTIEMPLOYER PLANS AS IN ENDANGERED OR CRITICAL STATUS.

204(a) IN GENERAL. -

Notwithstanding the actuarial certification under section 305(b)(3) of the Employee Retirement Income Security Act of 1974 and section 432(b)(3) of the Internal Revenue Code of 1986, if a plan sponsor of a multiemployer plan elects the application of this section, then, for purposes of section 305 of such Act and section 432 of such Code —

204(a)(1) the status of the plan for its first plan year beginning during the period beginning on October 1, 2008, and ending on September 30, 2009, shall be the same as the status of such plan under such sections for the plan year preceding such plan year, and

204(a)(2) in the case of a plan which was in endangered or critical status for the preceding plan year described in paragraph (1), the plan shall not be required to update its plan or schedules under section 305(c)(6) of such Act and section 432(c)(6) of such Code, or section 305(e)(3)(B) of such Act and section 432(e)(3)(B) of such Code, whichever is applicable, until the plan year following the first plan year described in paragraph (1).

If section 305 of the Employee Retirement Income Security Act of 1974 and section 432 of the Internal Revenue Code of 1986 did not apply to the preceding plan year described in paragraph (1), the plan actuary shall make a certification of the status of the plan under section 305(b)(3) of such Act and section 432(b)(3) of such Code for the preceding plan year in the same manner as if such sections had applied to such preceding plan year.

204(b) EXCEPTION FOR PLANS BECOMING CRITICAL DURING ELECTION. -

If -

204(b)(1) an election was made under subsection (a) with respect to a multiemployer plan, and

204(b)(2) such plan has, without regard to such election, been certified by the plan actuary under section 305(b)(3) of such Act and section 432(b)(3) of such Code to be in critical status for the first plan year described in subsection (a)(1), then such plan shall be treated as a plan in critical status for such plan year for purposes of applying section 4971(g)(1)(A) of such Code, section 302(b)(3) of such Act (without regard to the second sentence thereof), and section 412(b)(3) of such Code (without regard to the second sentence thereof).

204(c) ELECTION AND NOTICE. -

204(c)(1) ELECTION. -

An election under subsection (a) shall -

204(c)(1)(A) be made at such time and in such manner as the Secretary of the Treasury or the Secretary's delegate may prescribe and, once made, may be revoked only with the consent of the Secretary, and

204(c)(1)(B) if the election is made —

204(c)(1)(B)(i) before the date the annual certification is submitted to the Secretary or the Secretary's delegate under section 305(b)(3) of such Act and section 432(b)(3) of such Code, be included with such annual certification, and

204(c)(1)(B)(ii) after such date, be submitted to the Secretary or the Secretary's delegate not later than 30 days after the date of the election.

204(c)(2) NOTICE TO PARTICIPANTS. —

204(c)(2)(A) IN GENERAL. —

Notwithstanding section 305(b)(3)(D) of such Act and section 431(b)(3)(D) of such Code, if the plan is neither in endangered nor critical status by reason of an election made under subsection (a) -

204(c)(2)(A)(i) the plan sponsor of a multiemployer plan shall not be required to provide notice under such sections, and

204(c)(2)(A)(ii) the plan sponsor shall provide to the participants and beneficiaries, the bargaining parties, the Pension Benefit Guaranty Corporation, and the Secretary of Labor a notice of the election and such other information as the Secretary of the Treasury (in consultation with the Secretary of Labor) may require -

204(c)(2)(A)(ii)(I) if the election is made before the date the annual certification is submitted to the Secretary or the Secretary's delegate under section 305(b)(3) of such Act and section 432(b)(3) of such Code, not later than 30 days after the date of the certification, and

204(c)(2)(A)(ii)(II) if the election is made after such date, not later than 30 days after the date of the election.

204(c)(2)(B) NOTICE OF ENDANGERED STATUS. -

Notwithstanding section 305(b)(3)(D) of such Act and section 431(b)(3)(D) of such Code, if the plan is certified to be in critical status for any plan year but is in endangered status by reason of an election made under subsection (a), the notice provided under such sections shall be the notice which would have been provided if the plan had been certified to be in endangered status.

[¶16,470Q]

ACT SEC. 205. TEMPORARY EXTENSION OF THE FUNDING IMPROVEMENT AND REHABILITATION PERIODS FOR MULTIEMPLOYER PENSION PLANS IN CRITICAL AND ENDANGERED STATUS FOR 2008 OR 2009.

205(a) IN GENERAL. -

If the plan sponsor of a multiemployer plan which is in endangered or critical status for a plan year beginning in 2008 or 2009 (determined after application of section 204) elects the application of this section, then, for purposes of section 305 of the Employee Retirement Income Security Act of 1974 and section 432 of the Internal Revenue Code of 1986 -

205(a)(1) except as provided in paragraph (2), the plan's funding improvement period or rehabilitation period, whichever is applicable, shall be 13 years rather than 10 years, and

205(a)(2) in the case of a plan in seriously endangered status, the plan's funding improvement period shall be 18 years rather than 15 years.

205(b) DEFINITIONS AND SPECIAL RULES. -

For purposes of this section -

205(b)(1) ELECTION. -

An election under this section shall be made at such time, and in such manner and form, as the Secretary of Labor or the Secretary's delegate may prescribe.

205(b)(2) DEFINITIONS. -

Any term which is used in this section which is also used in section 305 of the Employee Retirement Income Security Act of 1974 and section 432 of the Internal Revenue Code of 1986 shall have the same meaning as when used in such sections.

205(c) EFFECTIVE DATE. -

This section shall apply to plan years beginning after December 31, 2007.

American Recovery and Reinvestment Act Of 2009

[¶16,471]

P.L. 111-5

Signed February 17, 2009

[Reproduced below are provisions of the American Recovery and Reinvestment Act of 2009 pertaining to pensions and employee benefits that did not amend the Internal Revenue Code or ERISA. Sections that amended the Internal Revenue Code are reflected in the "Code and Regulations" divisions starting at ¶ 11,000. Sections which amended ERISA are reflected in the "Labor Laws and Regulations" division starting at ¶ 14,110 – CCH.]

[¶16,471A]

ACT SEC. 1000. SHORT TITLE; ETC.

1000(a) SHORT TITLE. -

This Act may be cited as the "American Recovery and Reinvestment Act of 2009".

* * *

[¶16,471B]

ACT SEC. 1899E. CONTINUED QUALIFICATION OF FAMILY MEMBERS AFTER CERTAIN EVENTS.

* * *

1899E(b) CONFORMING AMENDMENT. —

Section 173(f) of the Workforce Investment Act of 1998 (29 U.S.C. 2918(f)) is amended by adding at the end the following:

"(8) CONTINUED QUALIFICATION OF FAMILY MEMBERS AFTER CERTAIN EVENTS. —In the case of eligible coverage months beginning before January 1, 2011-

"(A) MEDICARE ELIGIBILITY. —In the case of any month which would be an eligible coverage month with respect to an eligible individual but for paragraph (7)(B)(i), such month shall be treated as an eligible coverage month with respect to such eligible individual solely for purposes of determining the eligibility of qualifying family members of such individual under this subsection. This subparagraph shall only apply with respect to the first 24 months after such eligible individual is first entitled to the benefits described in paragraph (7)(B)(i).

"(B) DIVORCE. —In the case of the finalization of a divorce between an eligible individual and such individual's spouse, such spouse shall be treated as an eligible individual for purposes of this subsection for a period of 24 months beginning with the date of such finalization, except that the only qualifying family members who may be taken into account with respect to such spouse are those individuals who were qualifying family members immediately before such finalization.

"(C) DEATH. —In the case of the death of an eligible individual -

"(i) any spouse of such individual (determined at the time of such death) shall be treated as an eligible individual for purposes of this subsection for a period of 24 months beginning with the date of such death, except that the only qualifying family members who may be taken into account with respect to such spouse are those individuals who were qualifying family members immediately before such death, and

"(ii) any individual who was a qualifying family member of the decedent immediately before such death shall be treated as an eligible individual for purposes [of] this subsection for a period of 24 months beginning with the date of such death, except that no qualifying family members may be taken into account with respect to such individual.".

1899E(c) EFFECTIVE DATE. - The amendments made by this section shall apply to months beginning after December 31, 2009.

[¶16,471C]

ACT SEC. 1899I. SURVEY AND REPORT ON ENHANCED HEALTH COVERAGE TAX CREDIT PROGRAM.

1899I(a) SURVEY. -

1899I(a)(1) IN GENERAL. -The Secretary of the Treasury shall conduct a biennial survey of eligible individuals (as defined in section 35(c) of the Internal Revenue Code of 1986) relating to the health coverage tax credit under section 35 of the Internal Revenue Code of 1986 (hereinafter in this section referred to as the "health coverage tax credit").

1899I(a)(2) INFORMATION OBTAINED. —The survey conducted under subsection (a) shall obtain the following information:

1899I(a)(2)(A) HCTC PARTICIPANTS. -In the case of eligible individuals receiving the health coverage tax credit (including individuals participating in the health coverage tax credit program under section 7527 of such Code, hereinafter in this section referred to as the "HCTC program") -

1899I(a)(2)(A)(i) demographic information of such individuals, including income and education levels,

1899I(a)(2)(A)(ii) satisfaction of such individuals with the enrollment process in the HCTC program,

1899I(a)(2)(A)(iii) satisfaction of such individuals with available health coverage options under the credit, including level of premiums, benefits, deductibles, cost-sharing requirements, and the adequacy of provider networks, and

1899I(a)(2)(A)(iv) any other information that the Secretary determines is appropriate.

1899I(a)(2)(B) NON-HCTC PARTICIPANTS. - In the case of eligible individuals not receiving the health coverage tax credit -

1899I(a)(2)(B)(i) demographic information of each individual, including income and education levels,

1899I(a)(2)(B)(ii) whether the individual was aware of the health coverage tax credit or the HCTC program,

1899I(a)(2)(B)(iii) the reasons the individual has not enrolled in the HCTC program, including whether such reasons include the burden of the process of enrollment and the affordability of coverage,

1899I(a)(2)(B)(iv) whether the individual has health insurance coverage, and, if so, the source of such coverage, and

1899I(a)(2)(B)(v) any other information that the Secretary determines is appropriate.

1899I(a)(3) REPORT. - Not later than December 31 of each year in which a survey is conducted under paragraph (1) (beginning in 2010), the Secretary of the Treasury shall report to the Committee on Finance and the Committee on Health, Education, Labor, and Pensions of the Senate and the Committee on Ways and Means, the Committee on Education and Labor, and the Committee on Energy and Commerce of the House of Representatives the findings of the most recent survey conducted under paragraph (1).

1899I(b) REPORT. - Not later than October 1 of each year (beginning in 2010), the Secretary of the Treasury (after consultation with the Secretary of Health and Human Services, and, in the case of the information required under paragraph (7), the Secretary of Labor) shall report to the Committee on Finance and the Committee on Health, Education, Labor, and Pensions of the Senate and the Committee on Ways and Means, the Committee on Education and Labor, and the Committee on Energy and Commerce of the House of Representatives the following information with respect to the most recent taxable year ending before such date:

1899I(b)(1) In each State and nationally -

1899I(b)(1)(A) the total number of eligible individuals (as defined in section 35(c) of the Internal Revenue Code of 1986) and the number of eligible individuals receiving the health coverage tax credit,

1899I(b)(1)(B) the total number of such eligible individuals who receive an advance payment of the health coverage tax credit through the HCTC program,

1899I(b)(1)(C) the average length of the time period of the participation of eligible individuals in the HCTC program, and

1899I(b)(1)(D) the total number of participating eligible individuals in the HCTC program who are enrolled in each category of coverage as described in section 35(e)(1) of such Code, with respect to each category of eligible individuals described in section 35(c)(1) of such Code.

1899I(b)(2) In each State and nationally, an analysis of -

1899I(b)(2)(A) the range of monthly health insurance premiums, for self-only coverage and for family coverage, for individuals receiving the health coverage tax credit, and

1899I(b)(2)(B) the average and median monthly health insurance premiums, for self-only coverage and for family coverage, for individuals receiving the health coverage tax credit, with respect to each category of coverage as described in section 35(e)(1) of such Code.

1899I(b)(3) In each State and nationally, an analysis of the following information with respect to the health insurance coverage of individuals receiving the health coverage tax credit who are enrolled in coverage described in subparagraphs (B) through (H) of section 35(e)(1) of such Code:

1899I(b)(3)(A) Deductible amounts.

1899I(b)(3)(B) Other out-of-pocket cost-sharing amounts.

1899I(b)(3)(C) A description of any annual or lifetime limits on coverage or any other significant limits on coverage services, or benefits.

The information required under this paragraph shall be reported with respect to each category of coverage described in such subparagraphs.

1899I(b)(4) In each State and nationally, the gender and average age of eligible individuals (as defined in section 35(c) of such Code) who receive the health coverage tax credit, in each category of coverage described in section 35(e)(1) of such Code, with respect to each category of eligible individuals described in such section.

1899I(b)(5) The steps taken by the Secretary of the Treasury to increase the participation rates in the HCTC program among eligible individuals, including outreach and enrollment activities.

1899I(b)(6) The cost of administering the HCTC program by function, including the cost of subcontractors, and recommendations on ways to reduce administrative costs, including recommended statutory changes.

1899I(b)(7) The number of States applying for and receiving national emergency grants under section 173(f) of the Workforce Investment Act of 1998 (29 U.S.C. 2918(f)), the activities funded by such grants on a State-by-State basis, and the time necessary for application approval of such grants.

[¶16,471D]

ACT SEC. 1899L. GAO STUDY AND REPORT.

1899L(a) STUDY. - The Comptroller General of the United States shall conduct a study regarding the health insurance tax credit allowed under section 35 of the Internal Revenue Code of 1986.

1899L(b) REPORT. - Not later than March 1, 2010, the Comptroller General shall submit a report to Congress regarding the results of the study conducted under subsection (a). Such report shall include an analysis of -

1899L(b)(1) the administrative costs -

1899L(b)(1)(A) of the Federal Government with respect to such credit and the advance payment of such credit under section 7527 of such Code, and

1899L(b)(1)(B) of providers of qualified health insurance with respect to providing such insurance to eligible individuals and their qualifying family members,

1899L(b)(2) the health status and relative risk status of eligible individuals and qualifying family members covered under such insurance,

1899L(b)(3) participation in such credit and the advance payment of such credit by eligible individuals and their qualifying family members, including the reasons why such individuals did or did not participate and the effect of the amendments made by this part on such participation, and

1899L(b)(4) the extent to which eligible individuals and their qualifying family members -

1899L(b)(4)(A) obtained health insurance other than qualifying health insurance, or

1899L(b)(4)(B) went without health insurance coverage.

1899L(c) ACCESS TO RECORDS. -

For purposes of conducting the study required under this section, the Comptroller General and any of his duly authorized representatives shall have access to, and the right to examine and copy, all documents, records, and other recorded information —

1899L(c)(1) within the possession or control of providers of qualified health insurance, and

1899L(c)(2) determined by the Comptroller General (or any such representative) to be relevant to the study.

The Comptroller General shall not disclose the identity of any provider of qualified health insurance or any eligible individual in making any information obtained under this section available to the public.

1899L(d) DEFINITIONS. -

Any term which is defined in section 35 of the Internal Revenue Code of 1986 shall have the same meaning when used in this section.

[¶16,471E]

ACT SEC. 3001. PREMIUM ASSISTANCE FOR COBRA BENEFITS.

3001(a) PREMIUM ASSISTANCE FOR COBRA CONTINUATION COVERAGE FOR INDIVIDUALS AND THEIR FAMILIES. -

3001(a)(1) PROVISION OF PREMIUM ASSISTANCE. -

3001(a)(1)(A) REDUCTION OF PREMIUMS PAYABLE. -

In the case of any premium for a period of coverage beginning on or after the date of the enactment of this Act for COBRA continuation coverage with respect to any assistance eligible individual, such individual shall be treated for purposes of any COBRA continuation provision as having paid the amount of such premium if such individual pays (or a person other than such individual's employer pays on behalf of such individual) 35 percent of the amount of such premium (as determined without regard to this subsection).

3001(a)(1)(B) PLAN ENROLLMENT OPTION. -

3001(a)(1)(B)(i) IN GENERAL. -

Notwithstanding the COBRA continuation provisions, an assistance eligible individual may, not later than 90 days after the date of notice of the plan enrollment option described in this subparagraph, elect to enroll in coverage under a plan offered by the employer involved, or the employee organization involved (including, for this purpose, a joint board of trustees of a multiemployer trust affiliated with one or more multiemployer plans), that is different than coverage under the plan in which such individual was enrolled at the time the qualifying event occurred, and such coverage shall be treated as COBRA continuation coverage for purposes of the applicable COBRA continuation coverage provision.

3001(a)(1)(B)(ii) REQUIREMENTS. -

An assistance eligible individual may elect to enroll in different coverage as described in clause (i) only if -

3001(a)(1)(B)(ii)(I) the employer involved has made a determination that such employer will permit assistance eligible individuals to enroll in different coverage as provided for [in] this subparagraph;

3001(a)(1)(B)(ii)(II) the premium for such different coverage does not exceed the premium for coverage in which the individual was enrolled at the time the qualifying event occurred;

3001(a)(1)(B)(ii)(III) the different coverage in which the individual elects to enroll is coverage that is also offered to the active employees of the employer at the time at which such election is made; and

3001(a)(1)(B)(ii)(IV) the different coverage is not -

3001(a)(1)(B)(ii)(IV)(aa) coverage that provides only dental, vision, counseling, or referral services (or a combination of such services);

3001(a)(1)(B)(ii)(IV)(bb) a flexible spending arrangement (as defined in section 106(c)(2) of the Internal Revenue Code of 1986); or

3001(a)(1)(B)(ii)(IV)(cc) coverage that provides coverage for services or treatments furnished in an on-site medical facility maintained by the employer and that consists primarily of first-aid services, prevention and wellness care, or similar care (or a combination of such care).

3001(a)(1)(C) PREMIUM REIMBURSEMENT. -

For provisions providing the balance of such premium, see section 6432 of the Internal Revenue Code of 1986, as added by paragraph (12).

3001(a)(2) LIMITATION OF PERIOD OF PREMIUM ASSISTANCE. -

3001(a)(2)(A) IN GENERAL. -

Paragraph (1)(A) shall not apply with respect to any assistance eligible individual for months of coverage beginning on or after the earlier of -

3001(a)(2)(A)(i) the first date that such individual is eligible for coverage under any other group health plan (other than coverage consisting of only dental, vision, counseling, or referral services (or a combination thereof), coverage under a flexible spending arrangement (as defined in section 106(c)(2) of the Internal Revenue Code of 1986), or coverage of treatment that is furnished in an on-site medical facility maintained by the employer and that consists primarily of first-aid services, prevention and wellness care, or similar care (or a combination thereof)) or is eligible for benefits under title XVIII of the Social Security Act, or

3001(a)(2)(A)(ii) the earliest of -

3001(a)(2)(A)(ii)(I) the date which is 15 months after the first day that paragraph (1)(A) applies with respect to such individual,

3001(a)(2)(A)(ii)(II) the date following the expiration of the maximum period of continuation coverage required under the applicable COBRA continuation coverage provision, or

3001(a)(2)(A)(ii)(III) the date following the expiration of the period of continuation coverage allowed under paragraph (4)(B)(ii).

3001(a)(2)(B) TIMING OF ELIGIBILITY FOR ADDITIONAL COVERAGE. -

For purposes of subparagraph (A)(i), an individual shall not be treated as eligible for coverage under a group health plan before the first date on which such individual could be covered under such plan.

3001(a)(2)(C) NOTIFICATION REQUIREMENT. -

An assistance eligible individual shall notify in writing the group health plan with respect to which paragraph (1)(A) applies if such paragraph ceases to apply by reason of subparagraph (A)(i). Such notice shall be provided to the group health plan in such time and manner as may be specified by the Secretary of Labor.

3001(a)(3) ASSISTANCE ELIGIBLE INDIVIDUAL. -

For purposes of this section, the term "assistance eligible individual" means any qualified beneficiary if -

3001(a)(3)(A) such qualified beneficiary is eligible for COBRA continuation coverage related to a qualifying event occurring during the period that begins with September 1, 2008, and ends with May 31, 2010,

3001(a)(3)(B) such qualified beneficiary elects such coverage, and

3001(a)(3)(C) the qualifying event with respect to the COBRA continuation coverage consists of the involuntary termination of the covered employee's employment and occurred during such period or consists of a reduction of hours followed by such an involuntary termination of employment during such period (as described in paragraph (17)(C)).

3001(a)(4) EXTENSION OF ELECTION PERIOD AND EFFECT ON COVERAGE. —

3001(a)(4)(A) IN GENERAL. -

For purposes of applying section 605(a) of the Employee Retirement Income Security Act of 1974, section 4980B(f)(5)(A) of the Internal Revenue Code of 1986, section 2205(a) of the Public Health Service Act, and section 8905a(c)(2) of title 5, United States Code, in the case of an individual who does not have an election of COBRA continuation coverage in effect on the date of the enactment of this Act but who would be an assistance eligible individual if such election were so in effect, such individual may elect the COBRA continuation coverage under the COBRA continuation coverage provisions containing such sections during the period beginning on the date of the enactment of this Act and ending 60 days after the date on which the notification required under paragraph (7)(C) is provided to such individual.

3001(a)(4)(B) COMMENCEMENT OF COVERAGE; NO REACH-BACK. -

Any COBRA continuation coverage elected by a qualified beneficiary during an extended election period under subparagraph (A) -

3001(a)(4)(B)(i) shall commence with the first period of coverage beginning on or after the date of the enactment of this Act, and

3001(a)(4)(B)(ii) shall not extend beyond the period of COBRA continuation coverage that would have been required under the applicable COBRA continuation coverage provision if the coverage had been elected as required under such provision.

3001(a)(4)(C) PREEXISTING CONDITIONS. -

With respect to a qualified beneficiary who elects COBRA continuation coverage pursuant to subparagraph (A), the period -

3001(a)(4)(C)(i) beginning on the date of the qualifying event, and

3001(a)(4)(C)(ii) ending with the beginning of the period described in subparagraph (B)(i), shall be disregarded for purposes of determining the 63-day periods referred to in section 701(c)(2) of the Employee Retirement Income Security Act of 1974, section 9801(c)(2) of the Internal Revenue Code of 1986, and section 2701(c)(2) of the Public Health Service Act.

3001(a)(5) EXPEDITED REVIEW OF DENIALS OF PREMIUM ASSISTANCE. -

In any case in which an individual requests treatment as an assistance eligible individual and is denied such treatment by the group health plan, the Secretary of Labor (or the Secretary of Health and Human Services in connection with COBRA continuation coverage which is provided other than pursuant to part 6 of subtitle B of title I of the Employee Retirement Income Security Act of 1974), in consultation with the Secretary of the Treasury, shall provide for expedited review of such denial. An individual shall be entitled to such review upon application to such Secretary in such form and manner as shall be provided by such Secretary. Such Secretary shall make a determination regarding such individual's eligibility within 15 business days after receipt of such individual's application for review under this paragraph. Either Secretary's determination upon review of the denial shall be de novo and shall be the final determination of such Secretary. A reviewing court shall grant deference to such Secretary's determination. The provisions of this paragraph, paragraphs (1) through (4), and paragraph (7) shall be treated as provisions of title I of the Employee Retirement Income Security Act of 1974 for purposes of part 5 of subtitle B of such title. In addition to civil actions that may be brought to enforce applicable provisions of such Act or other laws, the appropriate Secretary or an affected individual may bring a civil action to enforce such determinations and for appropriate relief. In addition, such Secretary may assess a penalty against a plan sponsor or health insurance issuer of not more than $110 per day for each failure to comply with such determination of such Secretary after 10 days after the date of the plan sponsor's or issuer's receipt of the determination.

3001(a)(6) DISREGARD OF SUBSIDIES FOR PURPOSES OF FEDERAL AND STATE PROGRAMS. -

Notwithstanding any other provision of law, any premium reduction with respect to an assistance eligible individual under this subsection shall not be considered income or resources in determining eligibility for, or the amount of assistance or benefits provided under, any other public benefit provided under Federal law or the law of any State or political subdivision thereof.

3001(a)(7) NOTICES TO INDIVIDUALS. -

3001(a)(7)(A) GENERAL NOTICE. -

3001(a)(7)(A)(i) IN GENERAL. -

In the case of notices provided under section 606(a)(4) of the Employee Retirement Income Security Act of 1974 (29 U.S.C. 1166(4)), section 4980B(f)(6)(D) of the Internal Revenue Code of 1986, section 2206(4) of the Public Health Service Act (42 U.S.C. 300bb-6(4)), or section 8905a(f)(2)(A) of title 5, United States Code, with respect to individuals who, during the period described in paragraph (3)(A), have a qualifying event relating to COBRA continuation coverage, the requirements of such sections shall not be treated as met unless such notices include an additional notification to the recipient of -

3001(a)(7)(A)(i)(I) the availability of premium reduction with respect to such coverage under this subsection, and

3001(a)(7)(A)(i)(II) the option to enroll in different coverage if the employer permits assistance eligible individuals to elect enrollment in different coverage (as described in paragraph (1)(B)).

3001(a)(7)(A)(ii) ALTERNATIVE NOTICE. -

In the case of COBRA continuation coverage to which the notice provision under such sections does not apply, the Secretary of Labor, in consultation with the Secretary of the Treasury and the Secretary of Health and Human Services, shall, in consultation with administrators of the group health plans (or other entities) that provide or administer the COBRA continuation coverage involved, provide rules requiring the provision of such notice.

3001(a)(7)(A)(iii) FORM. -

The requirement of the additional notification under this subparagraph may be met by amendment of existing notice forms or by inclusion of a separate document with the notice otherwise required.

3001(a)(7)(B) SPECIFIC REQUIREMENTS. -

Each additional notification under subparagraph (A) shall include —

3001(a)(7)(B)(i) the forms necessary for establishing eligibility for premium reduction under this subsection,

3001(a)(7)(B)(ii) the name, address, and telephone number necessary to contact the plan administrator and any other person maintaining relevant information in connection with such premium reduction,

3001(a)(7)(B)(iii) a description of the extended election period provided for in paragraph (4)(A),

3001(a)(7)(B)(iv) a description of the obligation of the qualified beneficiary under paragraph (2)(C) to notify the plan providing continuation coverage of eligibility for subsequent coverage under another group health plan or eligibility for benefits under title XVIII of the Social Security Act and the penalty provided under section 6720C of the Internal Revenue Code of 1986 for failure to so notify the plan,

3001(a)(7)(B)(v) a description, displayed in a prominent manner, of the qualified beneficiary's right to a reduced premium and any conditions on entitlement to the reduced premium, and

3001(a)(7)(B)(vi) a description of the option of the qualified beneficiary to enroll in different coverage if the employer permits such beneficiary to elect to enroll in such different coverage under paragraph (1)(B).

3001(a)(7)(C) NOTICE IN CONNECTION WITH EXTENDED ELECTION PERIODS. -

In the case of any assistance eligible individual (or any individual described in paragraph (4)(A)) who became entitled to elect COBRA continuation coverage before the date of the enactment of this Act, the administrator of the group health plan (or other entity) involved shall provide (within 60 days after the date of enactment of this Act) for the additional notification required to be provided under subparagraph (A) and failure to provide such notice shall be treated as a failure to meet the notice requirements under the applicable COBRA continuation provision.

3001(a)(7)(D) MODEL NOTICES. -

Not later than 30 days after the date of enactment of this Act -

3001(a)(7)(D)(i) the Secretary of the Labor, in consultation with the Secretary of the Treasury and the Secretary of Health and Human Services, shall prescribe models for the additional notification required under this paragraph (other than the additional notification described in clause (ii)), and

3001(a)(7)(D)(ii) in the case of any additional notification provided pursuant to subparagraph (A) under section 8905a(f)(2)(A) of title 5, United States Code, the Office of Personnel Management shall prescribe a model for such additional notification.

3001(a)(8) REGULATIONS. -

The Secretary of the Treasury may prescribe such regulations or other guidance as may be necessary or appropriate to carry out the provisions of this subsection, including the prevention of fraud and abuse under this subsection, except that the Secretary of Labor and the Secretary of Health and Human Services may prescribe such regulations (including interim final regulations) or other guidance as may be necessary or appropriate to carry out the provisions of paragraphs (5), (7), and (9).

3001(a)(9) OUTREACH. -

The Secretary of Labor, in consultation with the Secretary of the Treasury and the Secretary of Health and Human Services, shall provide outreach consisting of public education and enrollment assistance relating to premium reduction provided under this subsection. Such outreach shall target employers, group health plan administrators, public assistance programs, States, insurers, and other entities as determined appropriate by such Secretaries. Such outreach shall include an initial focus on those individuals electing continuation coverage who are referred to in paragraph (7)(C). Information on such premium reduction, including enrollment, shall also be made available on websites of the Departments of Labor, Treasury, and Health and Human Services.

3001(a)(10) DEFINITIONS. -

For purposes of this section -

3001(a)(10)(A) ADMINISTRATOR. -

The term "administrator" has the meaning given such term in section 3(16)(A) of the Employee Retirement Income Security Act of 1974.

3001(a)(10)(B) COBRA CONTINUATION COVERAGE. -

The term "COBRA continuation coverage" means continuation coverage provided pursuant to part 6 of subtitle B of title I of the Employee Retirement Income Security Act of 1974 (other than under section 609), title XXII of the Public Health Service Act, section 4980B of the Internal Revenue Code of 1986 (other than subsection (f)(1) of such section insofar as it relates to pediatric vaccines), or section 8905a of title 5, United States Code, or under a State program that provides comparable continuation coverage. Such term does not include coverage under a health flexible spending arrangement under a cafeteria plan within the meaning of section 125 of the Internal Revenue Code of 1986.

3001(a)(10)(C) COBRA CONTINUATION PROVISION. -

The term "COBRA continuation provision" means the provisions of law described in subparagraph (B).

3001(a)(10)(D) COVERED EMPLOYEE. -

The term "covered employee" has the meaning given such term in section 607(2) of the Employee Retirement Income Security Act of 1974.

3001(a)(10)(E) QUALIFIED BENEFICIARY. -

The term "qualified beneficiary" has the meaning given such term in section 607(3) of the Employee Retirement Income Security Act of 1974.

3001(a)(10)(F) GROUP HEALTH PLAN. -

The term "group health plan" has the meaning given such term in section 607(1) of the Employee Retirement Income Security Act of 1974.

3001(a)(10)(G) STATE. -

The term "State" includes the District of Columbia, the Commonwealth of Puerto Rico, the Virgin Islands, Guam, American Samoa, and the Commonwealth of the Northern Mariana Islands.

3001(a)(10)(H) PERIOD OF COVERAGE. -

Any reference in this subsection to a period of coverage shall be treated as a reference to a monthly or shorter period of coverage with respect to which premiums are charged with respect to such coverage.

3001(a)(11) REPORTS. -

3001(a)(11)(A) INTERIM REPORT. -

The Secretary of the Treasury shall submit an interim report to the Committee on Education and Labor, the Committee on Ways and Means, and the Committee on Energy and Commerce of the House of Representatives and the Committee on Health, Education, Labor, and Pensions and the Committee on Finance of the Senate regarding the premium reduction provided under this subsection that includes -

3001(a)(11)(A)(i) the number of individuals provided such assistance as of the date of the report; and

3001(a)(11)(A)(ii) the total amount of expenditures incurred (with administrative expenditures noted separately) in connection with such assistance as of the date of the report.

3001(a)(11)(B) FINAL REPORT. -

As soon as practicable after the last period of COBRA continuation coverage for which premium reduction is provided under this section, the Secretary of the Treasury shall submit a final report to each Committee referred to in subparagraph (A) that includes —

3001(a)(11)(B)(i) the number of individuals provided premium reduction under this section;

3001(a)(11)(B)(ii) the average dollar amount (monthly and annually) of premium reductions provided to such individuals; and

3001(a)(11)(B)(iii) the total amount of expenditures incurred (with administrative expenditures noted separately) in connection with premium reduction under this section.

3001(a)(12) COBRA PREMIUM ASSISTANCE. -

* * *

3001(a)(12)(B) SOCIAL SECURITY TRUST FUNDS HELD HARMLESS. -

In determining any amount transferred or appropriated to any fund under the Social Security Act, section 6432 of the Internal Revenue Code of 1986 shall not be taken into account.

3001(a)(12)(E) SPECIAL RULE. -

3001(a)(12)(E)(i) IN GENERAL. -

In the case of an assistance eligible individual who pays, with respect to the first period of COBRA continuation coverage to which subsection (a)(1)(A) applies or the immediately subsequent period, the full premium amount for such coverage, the person to whom such payment is payable shall -

3001(a)(12)(E)(i)(I) make a reimbursement payment to such individual for the amount of such premium paid in excess of the amount required to be paid under subsection (a)(1)(A); or

3001(a)(12)(E)(i)(II) provide credit to the individual for such amount in a manner that reduces one or more subsequent premium payments that the individual is required to pay under such subsection for the coverage involved.

3001(a)(12)(E)(ii) REIMBURSING EMPLOYER. -

A person to which clause (i) applies shall be reimbursed as provided for in section 6432 of the Internal Revenue Code of 1986 for any payment made, or credit provided, to the employee under such clause.

3001(a)(12)(E)(iii) PAYMENT OR CREDITS. -

Unless it is reasonable to believe that the credit for the excess payment in clause (i)(II) will be used by the assistance eligible individual within 180 days of the date on which the person receives from the individual the payment of the full premium amount, a person to which clause (i) applies shall make the payment required under such clause to the individual within 60 days of such payment of the full premium amount. If, as of any day within the 180-day period, it is no longer reasonable to believe that the credit will be used during that period, payment equal to the remainder of the credit outstanding shall be made to the individual within 60 days of such day.

* * *

3001(a)(16) RULES RELATED TO 2009 EXTENSION. -

3001(a)(16)(A) ELECTION TO PAY PREMIUMS RETROACTIVELY AND MAINTAIN COBRA COVERAGE. -

In the case of any premium for a period of coverage during an assistance eligible individual's transition period, such individual shall be treated for purposes of any COBRA continuation provision as having timely paid the amount of such premium if -

3001(a)(16)(A)(i) such individual was covered under the COBRA continuation coverage to which such premium relates for the period of coverage immediately preceding such transition period, and

3001(a)(16)(A)(ii) such individual pays, the amount of such premium, after the application of paragraph (1)(A), by the latest of —

3001(a)(16)(A)(ii)(I) 60 days after the date of the enactment of this paragraph,

3001(a)(16)(A)(ii)(II) 30 days after the date of provision of the notification required under subparagraph (D)(ii), or

3001(a)(16)(A)(ii)(III) the end of the period described in section 4980B(f)(2)(B)(iii) of the Internal Revenue Code of 1986.

3001(a)(16)(B) REFUNDS AND CREDITS FOR RETROACTIVE PREMIUM ASSISTANCE ELIGIBILITY. -

In the case of an assistance eligible individual who pays, with respect to any period of COBRA continuation coverage during such individual's transition period, the premium amount for such coverage without regard to paragraph (1)(A), rules similar to the rules of paragraph (12)(E) shall apply.

3001(a)(16)(C) TRANSITION PERIOD. -

3001(a)(16)(C)(i) IN GENERAL. -

For purposes of this paragraph, the term "transition period" means, with respect to any assistance eligible individual, any period of coverage if -

3001(a)(16)(C)(i)(I) such assistance eligible individual experienced an involuntary termination that was a qualifying event prior to the date of enactment of the Department of Defense Appropriations Act, 2010; and

3001(a)(16)(C)(i)(II) paragraph (1)(A) applies to such period by reason of the amendment made by section 1010(b) of the Department of Defense Appropriations Act, 2010.

3001(a)(16)(C)(ii) CONSTRUCTION. -

Any period during the period described in subclauses (I) and (II) of clause (i) for which the applicable premium has been paid pursuant to subparagraph (A) shall be treated as a period of coverage referred to in such paragraph, irrespective of any failure to timely pay the applicable premium (other than pursuant to subparagraph (A)) for such period.

3001(a)(16)(D) NOTIFICATION. -

3001(a)(16)(D)(i) IN GENERAL. -

In the case of an individual who was an assistance eligible individual at any time on or after October 31, 2009, or experiences a qualifying event (consisting of termination of employment) relating to COBRA continuation coverage on or after such date, the administrator of the group health plan (or other entity) involved shall provide an additional notification with information regarding the amendments made by section 1010 of the Department of Defense Appropriations Act, 2010, within 60 days after the date of the enactment of such Act or, in the case of a qualifying event occurring after such date of enactment, consistent with the timing of notifications under paragraph (7)(A).

3001(a)(16)(D)(ii) TO INDIVIDUALS WHO LOST ASSISTANCE. -

In the case of an assistance eligible individual described in subparagraph (A)(i) who did not timely pay the premium for any period of coverage during such individual's transition period or paid the premium for such period without regard to paragraph (1)(A), the administrator of the group health plan (or other entity) involved shall provide to such individual, within the first 60 days of such individual's transition period, an additional notification with information regarding the amendments made by section 1010 of the Department of Defense Appropriations Act, 2010, including information on the ability under subparagraph (A) to make retroactive premium payments with respect to the transition period of the individual in order to maintain COBRA continuation coverage.

3001(a)(16)(D)(iii) APPLICATION OF RULES. -

Rules similar to the rules of paragraph (7) shall apply with respect to notifications under this subparagraph.

3001(a)(17) SPECIAL RULES IN CASE OF INDIVIDUALS LOSING COVERAGE BECAUSE OF A REDUCTION OF HOURS. -

3001(a)(17)(A) NEW ELECTION PERIOD. -

3001(a)(17)(A)(i) IN GENERAL. -

For the purposes of the COBRA continuation provisions, in the case of an individual described in subparagraph (C) who did not make (or who made and discontinued) an election of COBRA continuation coverage on the basis of the reduction of hours of employment, the involuntary termination of employment of such individual on or after the date of the enactment of this paragraph shall be treated as a qualifying event.

3001(a)(17)(A)(ii) COUNTING COBRA DURATION PERIOD FROM PREVIOUS QUALIFYING EVENT. -

In any case of an individual referred to in clause (i), the period of such individual's continuation coverage shall be determined as though the qualifying event were the reduction of hours of employment.

3001(a)(17)(A)(iii) CONSTRUCTION. -

Nothing in this paragraph shall be construed as requiring an individual referred to in clause (i) to make a payment for COBRA continuation coverage between the reduction of hours and the involuntary termination of employment.

3001(a)(17)(A)(iv) PREEXISTING CONDITIONS. -

With respect to an individual referred to in clause (i) who elects COBRA continuation coverage pursuant to such clause, rules similar to the rules in paragraph (4)(C) shall apply.

3001(a)(17)(B) NOTICES. -

In the case of an individual described in subparagraph (C), the administrator of the group health plan (or other entity) involved shall provide, during the 60-day period beginning on the date of such individual's involuntary termination of employment, an additional notification described in paragraph (7)(A), including information on the provisions of this paragraph. Rules similar to the rules of paragraph (7) shall apply with respect to such notification.

3001(a)(17)(C) INDIVIDUALS DESCRIBED. -

Individuals described in this subparagraph are individuals who are assistance eligible individuals on the basis of a qualifying event consisting of a reduction of hours occurring during the period described in paragraph (3)(A) followed by an involuntary termination of employment insofar as such involuntary termination of employment occurred on or after the date of the enactment of this paragraph.

3001(a)(18) RULES RELATED TO APRIL AND MAY 2010 EXTENSION. -

In the case of an individual who, with regard to coverage described in paragraph (10)(B), experiences a qualifying event related to a termination of employment on or after April 1, 2010 and prior to the date of the enactment of this paragraph, rules similar to those in paragraphs (4)(A) and (7)(C) shall apply with respect to all continuation coverage, including State continuation coverage programs.

3001(b) ELIMINATION OF PREMIUM SUBSIDY FOR HIGH-INCOME INDIVIDUALS. -

3001(b)(1) RECAPTURE OF SUBSIDY FOR HIGH-INCOME INDIVIDUALS. -

If -

3001(b)(1)(A) premium assistance is provided under this section with respect to any COBRA continuation coverage which covers the taxpayer, the taxpayer's spouse, or any dependent (within the meaning of section 152 of the Internal Revenue Code of 1986, determined without regard to subsections (b)(1), (b)(2), and (d)(1)(B) thereof) of the taxpayer during any portion of the taxable year, and

3001(b)(1)(B) the taxpayer's modified adjusted gross income for such taxable year exceeds $125,000 ($250,000 in the case of a joint return),

then the tax imposed by chapter 1 of such Code with respect to the taxpayer for such taxable year shall be increased by the amount of such assistance.

3001(b)(2) PHASE-IN OF RECAPTURE. -

3001(b)(2)(A) IN GENERAL. -

In the case of a taxpayer whose modified adjusted gross income for the taxable year does not exceed $145,000 ($290,000 in the case of a joint return), the increase in the tax imposed under paragraph (1) shall not exceed the phase-in percentage of such increase (determined without regard to this paragraph).

3001(b)(2)(B) PHASE-IN PERCENTAGE. -

For purposes of this subsection, the term "phase-in percentage" means the ratio (expressed as a percentage) obtained by dividing -

3001(b)(2)(B)(i) the excess of [sic]described in subparagraph (B) of paragraph (1), by

3001(b)(2)(B)(ii) $20,000 ($40,000 in the case of a joint return).

3001(b)(3) OPTION FOR HIGH-INCOME INDIVIDUALS TO WAIVE ASSISTANCE AND AVOID RECAPTURE. -

Notwithstanding subsection (a)(3), an individual shall not be treated as an assistance eligible individual for purposes of this section and section 6432 of the Internal Revenue Code of 1986 if such individual —

3001(b)(3)(A) makes a permanent election (at such time and in such form and manner as the Secretary of the Treasury may prescribe) to waive the right to the premium assistance provided under this section, and

3001(b)(3)(B) notifies the entity to whom premiums are reimbursed under section 6432(a) of such Code of such election.

3001(b)(4) MODIFIED ADJUSTED GROSS INCOME. -

For purposes of this subsection, the term "modified adjusted gross income" means the adjusted gross income (as defined in section 62 of the Internal Revenue Code of 1986) of the taxpayer for the taxable year increased by any amount excluded from gross income under section 911, 931, or 933 of such Code.

3001(b)(5) CREDITS NOT ALLOWED AGAINST TAX, ETC. -

For purposes [of] determining regular tax liability under section 26(b) of such Code, the increase in tax under this subsection shall not be treated as a tax imposed under chapter 1 of such Code.

3001(b)(6) REGULATIONS. -

The Secretary of the Treasury shall issue such regulations or other guidance as are necessary or appropriate to carry out this subsection, including requirements that the entity to whom premiums are reimbursed under section 6432(a) of the Internal Revenue Code of 1986 report to the Secretary, and to each assistance eligible individual, the amount of premium assistance provided under subsection (a) with respect to each such individual.

3001(b)(7) EFFECTIVE DATE. -

The provisions of this subsection shall apply to taxable years ending after the date of the enactment of this Act.

* * *

Amendments

P.L. 111-157, §3(a):

Amended Section 3001(a)(3)(A) of division B of the American Recovery and Reinvestment Act of 2009 by striking "March 31, 2010" and inserting "May 31, 2010".

The above amendment takes effect as if included in the provisions of section 3001 of division B of the American Recovery and Reinvestment Act of 2009 [effective generally for premiums for a period of coverage beginning on or after February 17, 2009. –CCH].

P.L. 111-157, §3(b):

Amended Section 3001(a) of division B of the American Recovery and Reinvestment Act of 2009 by adding at the end paragraph (18) to read as above.

The above amendment takes effect as if included in the provisions of section 3001 of division B of the American Recovery and Reinvestment Act of 2009 [effective generally for premiums for a period of coverage beginning on or after February 17, 2009. –CCH].

P.L. 111-144, §3(a):

Amended Section 3001(a)(3)(A) of division B of the American Recovery and Reinvestment Act of 2009 by striking "February 28, 2010" and inserting "March 31, 2010".

The above amendment takes effect as if included in the provision of section 3001 of division B of the American Recovery and Reinvest- ment Act of 2009 to which it relates [effective generally for premiums for a period of coverage beginning on or after February 17, 2009.— CCH].

P.L. 111-144, §3(b)(1)(A):

Amended Section 3001(a)(3)(C) of division B of the American Recovery and Reinvestment Act of 2009 by inserting before the period at the end the following: "or consists of a reduction of hours followed by such an involuntary termination of employment during such period (as described in paragraph (17)(C))".

The above amendment applies to periods of coverage beginning after the date of the enactment of this Act [March 2, 2010.—CCH].

P.L. 111-144, §3(b)(1)(B):

Amended Section 3001(a) of division B of the American Recovery and Reinvestment Act of 2009 by adding at the end paragraph (17) to read as above.

The above amendment applies to periods of coverage beginning after the date of the enactment of this Act [March 2, 2010.—CCH].

P.L. 111-144, §3(b)(2)(A):

Amended Section 3001(a)(16)(A) of division B of the American Recovery and Reinvestment Act of 2009 by striking clause (ii) and inserting new clause (ii) to read as above. Prior to amendment, Section 3001(a)(16)(A)(ii) read as follows:

"such individual pays, not later than 60 days after the date of the enactment of this paragraph (or, if later, 30 days after the date of provision of the notification required under subparagraph (D)(ii)), the amount of such premium, after the application of paragraph (1)(A).".

The above amendment takes effect as if included in the amendments made by section 1010 of division B of the Department of Defense Appropriations Act, 2010 [i.e., as if included in the provision of section 3001 of division B of the American Recovery and Reinvestment Act of 2009 to which it relates (effective generally for premiums for a period of coverage beginning on or after February 17, 2009).—CCH].

P.L. 111-144, §3(b)(2)(B):

Amended Section 3001(a)(16)(C)(i) of division B of the American Recovery and Reinvestment Act of 2009 by striking subclause (I) and inserting new clause (I) to read as above. Prior to amendment, Section 3001(a)(16)(C)(i)(I) read as follows:

"such period begins before the date of the enactment of this paragraph, and".

The above amendment takes effect as if included in the amendments made by section 1010 of division B of the Department of Defense Appropriations Act, 2010 [i.e., as if included in the provision of section 3001 of division B of the American Recovery and Reinvestment Act of 2009 to which it relates (effective generally for premiums for a period of coverage beginning on or after February 17, 2009).—CCH].

P.L. 111-144, §3(b)(3):

Amended Section 3001(a)(2)(A)(ii)(I) of division B of the American Recovery and Reinvestment Act of 2009 by striking "of the first month".

The above amendment takes effect on the date of enactment of this Act [March 2, 2010.—CCH].

P.L. 111-144, §3(b)(4):

Amended Section 3001(a)(5) of division B of the American Recovery and Reinvestment Act of 2009 by adding at the end the following:

"In addition to civil actions that may be brought to enforce applicable provisions of such Act or other laws, the appropriate Secretary or an affected individual may bring a civil action to enforce such determinations and for appropriate relief. In addition, such Secretary may assess a penalty against a plan sponsor or health insurance issuer of not more than $110 per day for each failure to comply with such determination of such Secretary after 10 days after the date of the plan sponsor's or issuer's receipt of the determination.".

The above amendment takes effect on the date of enactment of this Act [March 2, 2010.—CCH].

P.L. 111-118, §1010(a):

Amended Section 3001(a)(3)(A) of division B of the American Recovery and Reinvestment Act of 2009 by striking "December 31, 2009" and inserting "February 28, 2010".

The above amendment takes effect as if included in section 3001 of division B of the American Recovery and Reinvestment Act of 2009.

P.L. 111-118, §1010(b):

Amended Section 3001(a)(2)(A)(ii)(I) of division B of the American Recovery and Reinvestment Act of 2009 by striking "9 months" and inserting "15 months".

The above amendment takes effect as if included in section 3001 of division B of the American Recovery and Reinvestment Act of 2009.

P.L. 111-118, §1010(c):

Amended Section 3001(a) of division B of the American Recovery and Reinvestment Act of 2009 by adding at the end paragraph (16) to read as above.

The above amendment takes effect as if included in section 3001 of division B of the American Recovery and Reinvestment Act of 2009.

P.L. 111-118, §1010(d)(1)(A):

Amended Section 3001(a)(3)(A) of division B of the American Recovery and Reinvestment Act of 2009 by striking "at any time" and inserting "such qualified beneficiary is eligible for COBRA continuation coverage related to a qualifying event occurring".

The above amendment takes effect as if included in section 3001 of division B of the American Recovery and Reinvestment Act of 2009.

P.L. 111-118, §1010(d)(1)(B):

Amended Section 3001(a)(3)(A) of division B of the American Recovery and Reinvestment Act of 2009 by striking ", such qualified beneficiary is eligible for COBRA continuation coverage".

The above amendment takes effect as if included in section 3001 of division B of the American Recovery and Reinvestment Act of 2009.

P.L. 111-118, §1010(d)(2):

Amended Section 3001(a)(7)(A)[i] of division B of the American Recovery and Reinvestment Act of 2009 by striking "become entitled to elect COBRA continuation coverage" and inserting "have a qualifying event relating to COBRA continuation coverage".

The above amendment takes effect as if included in section 3001 of division B of the American Recovery and Reinvestment Act of 2009.

P.L. 111-118, §1010(e):

EFFECTIVE DATE.- The amendments made by this section shall take effect as if included in the provisions of section 3001 of division B of the American Recovery and Reinvestment Act of 2009 to which they relate.

P.L. 111-118, §1010(f):

(f) EMERGENCY DESIGNATIONS-

(1) IN GENERAL.- Amounts in this section are designated as emergency requirements and necessary to meet emergency needs pursuant to sections 403 and 423(b) of S. Con. Res. 13 (111th Congress), the concurrent resolution on the budget for fiscal year 2010.

(2) PAYGO.- All applicable provisions in this section are designated as an emergency for purposes of pay-as-you-go principles.

[¶16,471F]

SEC. 7001. EXECUTIVE COMPENSATION AND CORPORATE GOVERNANCE.

Section 111 of the Emergency Economic Stabilization Act of 2008 (12 U.S.C. 5221) is amended to read as follows:

"SEC. 111. EXECUTIVE COMPENSATION AND CORPORATE GOVERNANCE.

"(a) DEFINITIONS. —For purposes of this section, the following definitions shall apply:

"(1) SENIOR EXECUTIVE OFFICER. —The term 'senior executive officer' means an individual who is 1 of the top 5 most highly paid executives of a public company, whose compensation is required to be disclosed pursuant to the Securities Exchange Act of 1934, and any regulations issued thereunder, and non-public company counterparts.

"(2) GOLDEN PARACHUTE PAYMENT. —The term 'golden parachute payment' means any payment to a senior executive officer for departure from a company for any reason, except for payments for services performed or benefits accrued.

"(3) TARP RECIPIENT. —The term 'TARP recipient' means any entity that has received or will receive financial assistance under the financial assistance provided under the TARP.

"(4) COMMISSION. —The term 'Commission' means the Securities and Exchange Commission.

"(5) PERIOD IN WHICH OBLIGATION IS OUTSTANDING; RULE OF CONSTRUCTION.—For purposes of this section, the period in which any obligation arising from financial assistance provided under the TARP remains outstanding does not include any period during which the Federal Government only holds warrants to purchase common stock of the TARP recipient.

"(b) EXECUTIVE COMPENSATION AND CORPORATE GOVERNANCE. —

"(1) ESTABLISHMENT OF STANDARDS. —During the period in which any obligation arising from financial assistance provided under the TARP remains outstanding, each TARP recipient shall be subject to —

"(A) the standards established by the Secretary under this section; and

"(B) the provisions of section 162(m)(5) of the Internal Revenue Code of 1986, as applicable.

"(2) STANDARDS REQUIRED. —The Secretary shall require each TARP recipient to meet appropriate standards for executive compensation and corporate governance.

"(3) SPECIFIC REQUIREMENTS. —The standards established under paragraph (2) shall include the following:

"(A) Limits on compensation that exclude incentives for senior executive officers of the TARP recipient to take unnecessary and excessive risks that threaten the value of such recipient during the period in which any obligation arising from financial assistance provided under the TARP remains outstanding.

"(B) A provision for the recovery by such TARP recipient of any bonus, retention award, or incentive compensation paid to a senior executive officer and any of the next 20 most highly-compensated employees of the TARP recipient based on statements of earnings, revenues, gains, or other criteria that are later found to be materially inaccurate.

"(C) A prohibition on such TARP recipient making any golden parachute payment to a senior executive officer or any of the next 5 most highly-compensated employees of the TARP recipient during the period in which any obligation arising from financial assistance provided under the TARP remains outstanding.

"(D)(i) A prohibition on such TARP recipient paying or accruing any bonus, retention award, or incentive compensation during the period in which any obligation arising from financial assistance provided under the TARP remains outstanding, except that any prohibition developed under this paragraph shall not apply to the payment of long-term restricted stock by such TARP recipient, provided that such long-term restricted stock —

"(I) does not fully vest during the period in which any obligation arising from financial assistance provided to that TARP recipient remains outstanding;

"(II) has a value in an amount that is not greater than 1/3 of the total amount of annual compensation of the employee receiving the stock; and

"(III) is subject to such other terms and conditions as the Secretary may determine is in the public interest.

"(ii) The prohibition required under clause (i) shall apply as follows:

"(I) For any financial institution that received financial assistance provided under the TARP equal to less than $25,000,000, the prohibition shall apply only to the most highly compensated employee of the financial institution.

"(II) For any financial institution that received financial assistance provided under the TARP equal to at least $25,000,000, but less than $250,000,000, the prohibition shall apply to at least the 5 most highly-compensated employees of the financial institution, or such higher number as the Secretary may determine is in the public interest with respect to any TARP recipient.

"(III) For any financial institution that received financial assistance provided under the TARP equal to at least $250,000,000, but less than $500,000,000, the prohibition shall apply to the senior executive officers and at least the 10 next most highly-compensated employees, or such higher number as the Secretary may determine is in the public interest with respect to any TARP recipient.

"(IV) For any financial institution that received financial assistance provided under the TARP equal to $500,000,000 or more, the prohibition shall apply to the senior executive officers and at least the 20 next most highly-compensated employees, or such higher number as the Secretary may determine is in the public interest with respect to any TARP recipient.

"(iii) The prohibition required under clause (i) shall not be construed to prohibit any bonus payment required to be paid pursuant to a written employment contract executed on or before February 11, 2009, as such valid employment contracts are determined by the Secretary or the designee of the Secretary.

"(E) A prohibition on any compensation plan that would encourage manipulation of the reported earnings of such TARP recipient to enhance the compensation of any of its employees.

"(F) A requirement for the establishment of a Board Compensation Committee that meets the requirements of subsection (c).

"(4) CERTIFICATION OF COMPLIANCE. —The chief executive officer and chief financial officer (or the equivalents thereof) of each TARP recipient shall provide a written certification of compliance by the TARP recipient with the requirements of this section —

"(A) in the case of a TARP recipient, the securities of which are publicly traded, to the Securities and Exchange Commission, together with annual filings required under the securities laws; and

"(B) in the case of a TARP recipient that is not a publicly traded company, to the Secretary.

"(c) BOARD COMPENSATION COMMITTEE. —

"(1) ESTABLISHMENT OF BOARD REQUIRED. —Each TARP recipient shall establish a Board Compensation Committee, comprised entirely of independent directors, for the purpose of reviewing employee compensation plans.

"(2) MEETINGS. —The Board Compensation Committee of each TARP recipient shall meet at least semiannually to discuss and evaluate employee compensation plans in light of an assessment of any risk posed to the TARP recipient from such plans.

"(3) COMPLIANCE BY NON-SEC REGISTRANTS. —In the case of any TARP recipient, the common or preferred stock of which is not registered pursuant to the Securities Exchange Act of 1934, and that has received $25,000,000 or less of TARP assistance, the duties of the Board Compensation Committee under this subsection shall be carried out by the board of directors of such TARP recipient.

"(d) LIMITATION ON LUXURY EXPENDITURES. —The board of directors of any TARP recipient shall have in place a company-wide policy regarding excessive or luxury expenditures, as identified by the Secretary, which may include excessive expenditures on —

"(1) entertainment or events;

"(2) office and facility renovations;

"(3) aviation or other transportation services; or

"(4) other activities or events that are not reasonable expenditures for staff development, reasonable performance incentives, or other similar measures conducted in the normal course of the business operations of the TARP recipient.

"(e) SHAREHOLDER APPROVAL OF EXECUTIVE COMPENSATION. —

"(1) ANNUAL SHAREHOLDER APPROVAL OF EXECUTIVE COMPENSATION. —Any proxy or consent or authorization for an annual or other meeting of the shareholders of any TARP recipient during the period in which any obligation arising from financial assistance provided under the TARP remains outstanding shall permit a separate shareholder vote to approve the compensation of executives, as disclosed pursuant to the compensation disclosure rules of the Commission (which disclosure shall include the compensation discussion and analysis, the compensation tables, and any related material).

"(2) NONBINDING VOTE. —A shareholder vote described in paragraph (1) shall not be binding on the board of directors of a TARP recipient, and may not be construed as overruling a decision by such board, nor to create or imply any additional fiduciary duty by such board, nor shall such vote be construed to restrict or limit the ability of shareholders to make proposals for inclusion in proxy materials related to executive compensation.

"(3) DEADLINE FOR RULEMAKING. —Not later than 1 year after the date of enactment of the American Recovery and Reinvestment Act of 2009, the Commission shall issue any final rules and regulations required by this subsection.

"(f) REVIEW OF PRIOR PAYMENTS TO EXECUTIVES. —

"(1) IN GENERAL. —The Secretary shall review bonuses, retention awards, and other compensation paid to the senior executive officers and the next 20 most highly-compensated employees of each entity receiving TARP assistance before the date of enactment of the American Recovery and Reinvestment Act of 2009, to determine whether any such payments were inconsistent with the purposes of this section or the TARP or were otherwise contrary to the public interest.

"(2) NEGOTIATIONS FOR REIMBURSEMENT. —If the Secretary makes a determination described in paragraph (1), the Secretary shall seek to negotiate with the TARP recipient and the subject employee for appropriate reimbursements to the Federal Government with respect to compensation or bonuses.

"(g) NO IMPEDIMENT TO WITHDRAWAL BY TARP RECIPIENTS. —Subject to consultation with the appropriate Federal banking agency (as that term is defined in section 3 of the Federal Deposit Insurance Act), if any, the Secretary shall permit a TARP recipient to repay any assistance previously provided under the TARP to such financial institution, without regard to whether the financial institution has replaced such funds from any other source or to any waiting period, and when such assistance is repaid, the Secretary shall liquidate warrants associated with such assistance at the current market price.

"(h) REGULATIONS. —The Secretary shall promulgate regulations to implement this section.".

* * *

FAA MODERNIZATION AND REFORM ACT OF 2012

[¶16,473]

P.L. 112-95

Signed February 14, 2012

[Reproduced below are provisions of the FAA Modernization and Reform Act of 2012, pertaining to rollovers of amounts received in airline carrier bankruptcies, that did not amend the Internal Revenue Code or ERISA.]

[¶16,473A]

ACT SEC. 1106. TITLE XI—AIRPORT AND AIRWAY TRUST FUND PROVISIONS AND RELATED TAXES

ACT SEC. 1106. ROLLOVER OF AMOUNTS RECEIVED IN AIRLINE CARRIER BANKRUPTCY.

(a) General Rules.—

(1) Rollover of airline payment amount.—

If a qualified airline employee receives any airline payment amount and transfers any portion of such amount to a traditional IRA within 180 days of receipt of such amount (or, if later, within 180 days of the date of the enactment of this Act), then such amount (to the extent so transferred) shall be treated as a rollover contribution described in section 402(c) of the Internal Revenue Code of 1986. A qualified airline employee making such a transfer may exclude from gross income the amount transferred, in the taxable year in which the airline payment amount was paid to the qualified airline employee by the commercial passenger airline carrier.

(2) Transfer of amounts attributable to airline payment amount following rollover to roth ira.—

A qualified airline employee who has contributed an airline payment amount to a Roth IRA that is treated as a qualified rollover contributon pursuant to section 125 of the Worker, Retiree, and Employer Recovery Act of 2008, may transfer to a traditional IRA, in a trustee-to-trustee transfer, all or any part of the contribution (together with any net income allocable to such contribution), and the transfer to the traditional IRA will be deemed to have been made at the time of the rollover to the Roth IRA, if such transfer is made within 180 days of the date of the enactment of this Act. A qualified airline employee making such a transfer may exclude from gross income the airline payment amount previously rolled over to the Roth IRA, to the extent an amount attributable to the previous rollover was transferred to a traditional IRA, in the taxable year in which the airline payment amount was paid to the qualified airline employee by the commercial passanger airline carrier. No amount so transferred to a traditional IRA may be treated as a qualified rollover contribution with respect to a Roth IRA within the 5-taxable year period beginning with the taxable year in which such transfer was made.

(3) Extension of time to file claim for refund.—

A qualified airline employee who excludes an amount from gross income in a prior taxable year under paragraph (1) or (2) may reflect such exclusion in a claim for refund filed within the period of limitation under section 6511(a) of such Code (or, if later, April 15, 2015).

(4) Overall limitation on amounts transferred to traditional iras.—

(A) In general.—

The aggregate amount of airline payment amounts which may be transferred to 1 or more traditional IRAs under paragraphs (1) and (2) with respect to any qualified employee for any taxable year shall not exceed the excess (if any) of—

(i) 90 percent of the aggregate airline payment amounts received by the qualified airline employee during the taxable year and all preceding taxable years, over

(ii) the aggregate amount of such transfers to which paragraphs (1) and (2) applied for all preceding taxable years.

(B) Special rules.—

For purposes of applying the limitation under subparagraph (A)—

(i) any airline payment amount received by the surviving spouse of any qualified employee, and any amount transferred to a traditional IRA by such spouse under subsection (d), shall be treated as an amount received or transferred by the qualified employee, and

(ii) any amount transferred to a traditional IRA which is attributable to net income described in paragraph (2) shall not be taken into account.

(5) Covered executives not eligible to make transfers.—

Paragraphs (1) and (2) shall not apply to any transfer by a qualified airline employee (or any transfer authorized under subsection (d) by a surviving spouse of the qualified airline employee) if at any time during the taxable year of the transfer or any preceding taxable year the qualified airline employee held a position described in subparagraph (A) or (B) of section 162(m)(3) with the commercial passenger airline carrier from whom the airline payment amount was received.

(b) Treatment of Airline Payment Amounts and Transfers for Employment Taxes.—

For purposes of chapter 21 of the Internal Revenue Code of 1986 and section 209 of the Social Security Act, an airline payment amount shall not fail to be treated as a payment of wages by the commercial passenger airline carrier to the qualified airline employee in the taxable year of payment because such amount is excluded from the qualified airline employee's gross income under subsection (a).

(c) Definitions and Special Rules.—

For purposes of this section—

(1) Airline payment amount.—

(A) In general.—

The term "airline payment amount" means any payment of any money or other property which is payable by a commercial passenger airline carrier to a qualified airline employee-

(i) under the approval of an order of a Federal bankruptcy court in a case filed after September 11, 2001, and before January 1, 2007, or filed on November 29, 2011, and

(ii) in respect of the qualified airline employee's interest in a bankruptcy claim against the carrier, any note of the carrier (or amount paid in lieu of a note being issued), or any other fixed obligation of the carrier to pay a lump sum amount.

The amount of such payment shall be determined without regard to any requirement to deduct and withhold tax from such payment under sections 3102(a) of the Internal Revenue Code of 1986 and 3402(a) of such Code.

(B) Exception.—

An airline payment amount shall not include any amount payable on the basis of the carrier's future earnings or profits.

¶16,473   ACT SEC. 1106.

(2) Qualified airline employee.—

The term "qualified airline employee" means an employee or former employee of a commercial passenger airline carrier who was a participant in a defined benefit plan maintained by the carrier which—

(A) is a plan described in section 401(a) of the Internal Revenue Code of 1986 which includes a trust exempt from tax under section 501(a) of such Code, and

(B) was terminated, became subject to the restrictions contained in paragraphs (2) and (3) of section 402(b) of the Pension Protection Act of 2006, or was frozen effective November 1, 2012.

(3) Traditional IRA.—

The term "traditional IRA" means an individual retirement plan (as defined in section 7701(a)(37) of the Internal Revenue Code of 1986) which is not a Roth IRA.

(4) Roth IRA.—

The term "Roth IRA" has the meaning given such term by section 408A(b) of such Code.

(d) Surviving Spouse.—

If a qualified airline employee died after receiving an airline payment amount, or if an airline payment amount was paid to the surviving spouse of a qualified airline employee in respect of the qualified airline employee, the surviving spouse of the qualified airline employee may take all actions permitted under section 125 of the Worker, Retiree and Employer Recovery Act of 2008, or under this section, to the same extent that the qualified airline employee could have done had the qualified airline employee survived.

(e) Effective Date.—

This section shall apply to transfers made after the date of the enactment of this Act with respect to airline payment amounts paid before, on, or after such date.

Amendments

P.L. 113-243, § 1(a):

Amended section 1106(a)(3) of the FAA Modernization and Reform Act of 2012 by striking "2013" and inserting "2015".

Effective on the date of enactment [12/18/2014.—CCH].

P.L. 113-243, § 1(b)(1)-(2):

Amended section 1106(c) of the FAA Modernization and Reform Act of 2012 (1) in paragraph (1)(A)(i) by inserting "or filed on November 29, 2011," after "2007,"; and (2) in paragraph (2)(B), (A) by striking "terminated or" and inserting "terminated,"; and (B) by inserting ", or was frozen effective November 1, 2012" after "Pension Protection Act of 2006".

Effective on the date of enactment [12/18/2014.—CCH].

MOVING AHEAD FOR PROGRESS IN THE 21ST CENTURY ACT

[¶16,474]

P.L. 112-141

Signed July 6, 2012

[Reproduced below are provisions of the Moving Ahead for Progress in the 21st Century Act, pertaining to pensions and employee benefits, that did not amend the Internal Revenue Code or ERISA.]

[¶16,474A]

ACT SEC. 40231. DIVISION D—FINANCE

* * *

TITLE II—REVENUE PROVISIONS

* * *

Subtitle B—Pension Provisions

* * *

ACT SEC. 40231. PENSION BENEFIT GUARANTY CORPORATION GOVERNANCE IMPROVEMENT.

* * *

(f) Study Regarding Governance Structures.—

(1) In general.—Not later than 90 days after the date of enactment of this Act, the Pension Benefit Guaranty Corporation shall enter into a contract with the National Academy of Public Administration to conduct the study described in paragraph (2) with respect to the Pension Benefit Guaranty Corporation.

(2) Content of study.—The study conducted under paragraph (1) shall include—

(A) a review of the governance structures of governmental and nongovernmental organizations that are analogous to the Pension Benefit Guaranty Corporation; and

(B) recommendations regarding—

(i) the ideal size and composition of the board of directors of the Pension Benefit Guaranty Corporation;

(ii) procedures to select and remove members of such board;

(iii) qualifications and term lengths of members of such board; and

(iv) policies necessary to enhance Congressional oversight and transparency of such board and to mitigate potential conflicts of interest of the members of such board.

(3) Submission to Congress.—Not later than 1 year after the initiation of the study under paragraph (1), the National Academy of Public Administration shall submit the results of the study to the Committees on Health, Education, Labor, and Pensions and Finance of the Senate and the Committees on Education and the Workforce and Ways and Means of the House of Representatives.

* * *

[¶16,474B]

ACT SEC. 40233. Moving Ahead For Progress in the 21st Century

ACT SEC. 40233. QUALITY CONTROL PROCEDURES FOR THE PENSION BENEFIT GUARANTY CORPORATION.

(a) Annual Peer Review of Insurance Modeling Systems.— The Pension Benefit Guaranty Corporation shall contract with a capable agency or organization that is independent from the Corporation, such as the Social Security Administration, to conduct an annual peer review of the Corporation's Single-Employer Pension Insurance Modeling System and the Corporation's Multiemployer Pension Insurance Modeling System. The board of directors of the Corporation shall designate the agency or organization with which any such contract is entered into. The first of such annual peer reviews shall be initiated no later than 3 months after the date of enactment of this Act

(b) Policies and Procedures Relating to the Policy, Research, and Analysis Department.—The Pension Benefit Guaranty Corporation shall—

(1) develop written quality review policies and procedures for all modeling and actuarial work performed by the Corporation's Policy, Research, and Analysis Department; and

(2) conduct a record management review of such Department to determine what records must be retained as Federal records.

(c) Report Relating to OIG Recommendations.—Not later than 2 months after the date of enactment of this Act, the Pension Benefit Guaranty Corporation shall submit to Congress a report, approved by the board of directors of the Corporation, setting forth a timetable for addressing the outstanding recommendations of the Office of the Inspector General relating to the Policy, Research, and Analysis Department and the Benefits Administration and Payment Department.

COOPERATIVE AND SMALL EMPLOYER CHARITY PENSION FLEXIBILITY ACT

[¶16,475]

P.L. 113-97

Signed April 7, 2014

[Reproduced below are provisions of the Cooperative and Small Employer Charity Pension Flexibility Act, pertaining to pensions and employee benefits, that did not amend the Internal Revenue Code or ERISA.]

[¶16,475A]

ACT SEC. 103.

* * *

¶16,474   ACT SEC. 40231.

TITLE I—AMENDMENTS TO EMPLOYEE RETIREMENT INCOME SECURITY ACT OF 1974 AND OTHER PROVISIONS

* * *

SEC. 103. ELECTIONS.

* * *

(c) Deemed Election.—For purposes of the Internal Revenue Code of 1986, sections 4(b)(2) and 4021(b)(3) of the Employee Retirement Income Security Act of 1974, and all other purposes, a plan shall be deemed to have made an irrevocable election under section 410(d) of the Internal Revenue Code of 1986 if—

(1) the plan was established before January 1, 2014;

(2) the plan falls within the definition of a CSEC plan;

(3) the plan sponsor does not make an election under section 210(f)(3)(A) of the Employee Retirement Income Security Act of 1974 and section 414(y)(3)(A) of the Internal Revenue Code of 1986, as added by this Act; and

(4) the plan, plan sponsor, administrator, or fiduciary remits one or more premium payments for the plan to the Pension Benefit Guaranty Corporation for a plan year beginning after December 31, 2013.

(d) Effective Date.—The amendments made by this section shall apply as of the date of enactment of this Act.

* * *

[¶16,475B]

ACT SEC. 105. SEC. 105. SPONSOR EDUCATION AND ASSISTANCE.

(a) Definition.—In this section, the term "CSEC plan" has the meaning given that term in subsection (f)(1) of section 210 of the Employee Retirement Income Security Act of 1974 (29 U.S.C. 1060(f)(1)) (as added by this Act).

(b) Education.—The Participant and Plan Sponsor Advocate established under section 4004 of the Employee Retirement Income Security Act of 1974 (29 U.S.C. 1304) shall make itself available to assist CSEC plan sponsors and participants as part of the duties it performs under the general supervision of the Board of Directors under section 4004(b) of such Act (29 U.S.C. 1304(b)).

CONSOLIDATED AND FURTHER CONTINUING APPROPRIATIONS ACT, 2015

[¶16,476]

P.L. 113-235

Signed December 16, 2014

[Reproduced below are provisions of the Consolidated and Further Continuing Appropriations Act, 2015, pertaining to pensions and employee benefits, that did not amend the Internal Revenue Code or ERISA.]

[¶16,476A]

ACT SEC. 1. DIVISION M—EXPATRIATE HEALTH COVERAGE CLARIFICATION ACT OF 2014

SEC. 1. SHORT TITLE.

This division may be cited as the "Expatriate Health Coverage Clarification Act of 2014".

[¶16,476B]

ACT SEC. 2.SEC. 2. SENSE OF CONGRESS.

It is the sense of Congress that—

(1) American expatriate health insurance companies should be permitted to compete on a level playing field in the global marketplace;

(2) the global competitiveness of American companies should be encouraged; and

(3) in implementing the health insurance provider fee under section 9010 of the Patient Protection and Affordable Care Act (Public Law 111–148; 26 U.S.C. 4001 note prec.) and other provisions of such Act and title I and subtitle B of title II of the Health Care and Education Reconciliation Act of 2010 (Public Law 111–152), the Secretary of the Treasury, Secretary of Health and Human Services, and Secretary of Labor should continue to recognize the unique and multinational features of expatriate health plans and the United States companies that operate such plans and the competitive pressures of such plans and companies.

[¶16,476C]

ACT SEC. 3.SEC. 3. TREATMENT OF EXPATRIATE HEALTH PLANS UNDER ACA.

(a) IN GENERAL.

Subject to subsection (b), the provisions of (including any amendment made by) the Patient Protection and Affordable Care Act (Public Law 111–148) and of title I and subtitle B of title II of the Health Care and Education Reconciliation Act of 2010 (Public Law 111–152) shall not apply with respect to—

(1) expatriate health plans;

(2) employers with respect to such plans, solely in their capacity as plan sponsors for such plans; or

(3) expatriate health insurance issuers with respect to coverage offered by such issuers under such plans.

(b) MINIMUM ESSENTIAL COVERAGE AND REPORTING REQUIREMENTS.

(1) IN GENERAL.

For the purpose of section 5000A(f) of the Internal Revenue Code of 1986, and any other section of the Internal Revenue Code of 1986 that incorporates the definition of minimum essential coverage under such section 5000A(f) by reference:

(A) An expatriate health plan offered to primary enrollees who are described in subsections (d)(3)(A) and (d)(3)(B) of this section shall be treated as an eligible employer sponsored plan under 5000A(f)(2) of such Code.

(B) An expatriate health plan offered to primary enrollees who are described in subsection (d)(3)(C) of this section shall be treated as a plan in the individual market under section 5000A(f)(1)(C) of such Code. This subparagraph shall apply solely for the purposes of sections 36B, 5000A, and 6055 of such Code.

(2) EXCEPTION.

Subsection (a) shall not apply with respect to section 6055 of the Internal Revenue Code of 1986, or sections 4980H and 6056 of such Code in the case of an applicable large employer (as defined in section 4980H of such Code), except that statements furnished to individuals may be provided through electronic media and the primary insured shall be deemed to have consented to receive the statements under such sections in electronic form, unless the individual explicitly refuses such consent. Notwithstanding subsection (a), section 4980I of the Internal Revenue Code of 1986 shall continue to apply with respect to applicable employer-sponsored coverage (as defined in such section) of a qualified expatriate described in section 3(d)(3)(A)(i) who is assigned (rather than transferred) to work in the United States.

(c) QUALIFIED EXPATRIATES, SPOUSES, AND DEPENDENTS NOT UNITED STATES HEALTH RISK.

(1) IN GENERAL.

For purposes of section 9010 of the Patient Protection and Affordable Care Act (26 U.S.C. 4001 note prec.), for calendar years after 2015, a qualified expatriate (and any spouse, dependent, or any other individual enrolled in the plan) enrolled in an expatriate health plan shall not be considered a United States health risk.

(2) SPECIAL RULE.

Notwithstanding paragraph (1), the fee under section 9010 of such Act for each of calendar years 2014 and 2015 with respect to any expatriate health insurance issuer shall be the amount which bears the same ratio to the fee amount determined by the Secretary of the Treasury with respect to such issuer under such section for each such year (determined without regard to this paragraph) as—

(A) the amount of premiums taken into account under such section with respect to such issuer for each such year, less the amount of premiums for expatriate health plans taken into account under such section with respect to such issuer for each such year, bears to

(B) the amount of premiums taken into account under such section with respect to such issuer for each such year.

(d) DEFINITIONS.

In this section:

(1) EXPATRIATE HEALTH INSURANCE ISSUER.

The term "expatriate health insurance issuer" means a health insurance issuer that issues expatriate health plans.

(2) EXPATRIATE HEALTH PLAN.

The term "expatriate health plan" means a group health plan, health insurance coverage offered in connection with a group health plan, or health insurance coverage offered to a group of individuals described in paragraph (3)(C) (which may include spouses, dependents, and other individuals enrolled in the plan) that meets each of the following standards:

(A) Substantially all of the primary enrollees in such plan or coverage are qualified expatriates with respect to such plan or coverage. In applying the previous sentence, an individual shall not be considered a primary enrollee if the individual is not a national of the United States and the individual resides in the country of which the individual is a citizen.

(B) Substantially all of the benefits provided under the plan or coverage are not excepted benefits described in section 9832(c) of the Internal Revenue Code of 1986.

(C) The plan or coverage provides coverage for inpatient hospital services, outpatient facility services, physician services, and emergency services (comparable to such emergency services coverage described in and offered under section 8903(1) of title 5, United States Code for plan year 2009)—

(i) in the case of individuals described in paragraph (3)(A), both in the United States and in the country or countries from which the individual was transferred or assigned (accounting for flexibility needed with existing coverage), and such other country or countries as the Secretary of Health and Human Services, in consultation with the Secretary of the Treasury and the Secretary of Labor, may designate (after taking into account the barriers and prohibitions to providing health care services in the countries as designated);

(ii) in the case of individuals described in paragraph (3)(B), in the country or countries in which the individual is present in connection with the individual's employment, and such other country or countries as the Secretary of Health and Human Services, in consultation with the Secretary of the Treasury and the Secretary of Labor, may designate; or

(iii) in the case of individuals described in paragraph (3)(C), in the country or countries as the Secretary of Health and Human Services, in consultation with the Secretary of the Treasury and the Secretary of Labor, may designate.

(D) The plan sponsor reasonably believes that the benefits provided by the expatriate health plan satisfy a standard at least actuarially equivalent to the level provided for in section 36B(c)(2)(C)(ii) of the Internal Revenue Code of 1986.

(E) If the plan or coverage provides dependent coverage of children, the plan or coverage makes such dependent coverage available for adult children until the adult child turns 26 years of age, unless such individual is the child of a child receiving dependent coverage.

(F) The plan or coverage—

(i) is issued by an expatriate health plan issuer, or administered by an administrator, that together with any other person in the expatriate health plan issuer's or administrator's controlled group (as described in section 9010 of the Patient Protection and Affordable Care Act (and the regulations promulgated thereunder)), has licenses to sell insurance in more than two countries, and, with respect to such plan, coverage, or company in the controlled group—

(I) maintains network provider agreements that provide for direct claims payments, directly or through third party contracts, with health care providers in eight or more countries;

(II) maintains call centers, directly or through third party contracts, in three or more countries and accepts calls from customers in eight or more languages;

(III) processes (in the aggregate together with other plans or coverage it issues or administers) at least $1,000,000 in claims in foreign currency equivalents each year;

(IV) makes available (directly or through third party contracts) global evacuation/repatriation coverage; and

(V) maintains legal and compliance resources in three or more countries; and

(ii) offers reimbursements for items or services under such plan or coverage in the local currency in eight or more countries.

(G) The plan or coverage, and the plan sponsor or expatriate health insurance issuer with respect to such plan or coverage, satisfies the provisions of title XXVII of the Public Health Service Act (42 U.S.C. 300gg et seq.), chapter 100 of the Internal Revenue Code of 1986, and part 7 of subtitle B of title I of the Employee Retirement Income Security Act of 1974 (29 U.S.C. 1181 et seq.), which would otherwise apply to such a plan or coverage, and sponsor or issuer, if not for the enactment of the Patient Protection and Affordable Care Act and title I and subtitle B of title II of the Health Care and Education Reconciliation Act of 2010.

(3) QUALIFIED EXPATRIATE.

The term "qualified expatriate" means a primary insured, or individual otherwise described in subparagraph (C)—

(A)(i) whose skills, qualifications, job duties, or expertise is of a type that has caused his or her employer to transfer or assign him or her to the United States for a specific and temporary purpose or assignment tied to his or her employment; and

(ii) in connection with such transfer or assignment, is reasonably determined by the plan sponsor to require access to health insurance and other related services and support in multiple countries, and is offered other multinational benefits on a periodic basis (such as tax equalization, compensation for cross border moving expenses, or compensation to enable the expatriate to return to their home country);

(B) who is working outside of the United States for a period of at least 180 days in a consecutive 12-month period that overlaps with the plan year; or

(C) who is a member of a group of similarly situated individuals—

(i) that is formed for the purpose of traveling or relocating internationally in service of one or more of the purposes listed in section 501(c)(3) or 501(c)(4) of the Internal Revenue Code of 1986, or similarly situated organizations or groups (such as students or religious missionaries);

(ii) that is not formed primarily for the sale of health insurance coverage; and

(iii) that the Secretary of Health and Human Services, in consultation with the Secretary of the Treasury and the Secretary of Labor, determines requires access to health insurance and other related services and support in multiple countries.

(4) UNITED STATES.

The term "United States" means the 50 States, the District of Columbia, and Puerto Rico.

ACT SEC. 3.   ¶16,476C

(5) MISCELLANEOUS TERMS.

(A) GROUP HEALTH PLAN; HEALTH INSURANCE COVERAGE; HEALTH INSURANCE ISSUER; PLAN SPONSOR.

The terms "group health plan", "health insurance coverage", "health insurance issuer", and "plan sponsor" have the meanings given those terms in section 2791 of the Public Health Service Act (42 U.S.C. 300gg–91).

(B) TRANSFER.

The term "transfer" means an employer has transferred an employee to perform services for a branch of the same employer or a parent, affiliate, franchise, or subsidiary thereof.

(e) REGULATIONS.

The Secretary of the Treasury, the Secretary of Health and Human Services, and the Secretary of Labor may promulgate regulations necessary to carry out this Act, including such rules as may be necessary to prevent inappropriate expansion of the application of the exclusions under this Act from applicable laws and regulations, and to amend existing annual reporting requirements or procedures to include applicable qualified expatriate health insurers' total number of expatriate plan enrollees.

(f) EFFECTIVE DATE.

Unless otherwise specified, this Act shall take effect on the date of enactment of this Act, and shall apply only to expatriate health plans issued or renewed on or after July 1, 2015.

[¶16,476D]

ACT SEC. 131. DIVISION O—MULTIEMPLOYER PENSION REFORM

SEC. 131. PREMIUM INCREASES FOR MULTIEMPLOYER PLANS.

* * *

(c) REPORT. —In addition to any other report required by section 4022A(f), not later than June 1, 2016, the Pension Benefit Guaranty Corporation shall submit to Congress a report that includes—

(1) an analysis of whether the premium levels enacted under the amendment made by subsection (a) are sufficient for the Pension Benefit Guaranty Corporation to meet its projected mean stochastic basic benefit guarantee obligations for the ten- and twenty-year periods beginning with 2015, including an explanation of the assumptions underlying this analysis; and

(2) if the analysis under paragraph (1) concludes that the premium levels are insufficient to meet such obligations (or are in excess of the levels sufficient to meet such obligations), a proposed schedule of revised premiums sufficient to meet (but not exceed) such obligations.

[¶16,476E]

ACT SEC. 201. SEC. 201. CONDITIONS, LIMITATIONS, DISTRIBUTION AND NOTICE REQUIREMENTS, AND APPROVAL PROCESS FOR BENEFIT SUSPENSIONS UNDER MULTIEMPLOYER PLANS IN CRITICAL AND DECLINING STATUS.

* * *

(8) GUIDANCE. —Not later than 180 days after the date of the enactment of this Act, the Secretary of the Treasury, in consultation with the Pension Benefit Guaranty Corporation and the Secretary of Labor, shall publish appropriate guidance to implement section 305(e)(9) of the Employee Retirement Income Security Act of 1974 (29 U.S.C. 1085(e)(9)).

[¶16,476F]

ACT SEC. 1. DIVISION P—OTHER RETIREMENT-RELATED MODIFICATIONS

SEC. 1. SUBSTANTIAL CESSATION OF OPERATIONS.

* * *

(c) DIRECTION TO THE CORPORATION. —The Pension Benefit Guaranty Corporation shall not take any enforcement, administrative, or other action pursuant to section 4062(e) of the Employee Retirement Income Security Act of 1974, or in connection with an agreement settling liability arising under such section, that is inconsistent with the amendment made by this section, without regard to whether the action relates to a cessation or other event that occurs before, on, or after the date of the enactment of this Act, unless such action is in connection with a settlement agreement that is in place before June 1, 2014. The Pension Benefit Guaranty Corporation shall not initiate a new enforcement action with respect to section 4062(e) of such Act that is inconsistent with its enforcement policy in effect on June 1, 2014.

DISASTER TAX RELIEF AND AIRPORT AND AIRWAY EXTENSION ACT OF 2017

[¶16,477]

P.L. 115-63

Signed on September 29, 2017

[Reproduced below are excerpts from the Disaster Tax Relief and Airport and Airway Extension Act of 2017 (P.L. 115-63) that pertain to pensions and employee benefits.]

[¶16,477A]

ACT SEC. 501. DEFINITIONS.

(a) HURRICANE HARVEY DISASTER ZONE AND DISASTER AREA. For purposes of this title—

(1) HURRICANE HARVEY DISASTER ZONE. The term "Hurricane Harvey disaster zone" means that portion of the Hurricane Harvey disaster area determined by the President to warrant individual or individual and public assistance from the Federal Government under the Robert T. Stafford Disaster Relief and Emergency Assistance Act by reason of Hurricane Harvey.

(2) HURRICANE HARVEY DISASTER AREA. The term "Hurricane Harvey disaster area" means an area with respect to which a major disaster has been declared by the President before September 21, 2017, under section 401 of such Act by reason of Hurricane Harvey.

(b) HURRICANE IRMA DISASTER ZONE AND DISASTER AREA. For purposes of this title—

(1) HURRICANE IRMA DISASTER ZONE. The term "Hurricane Irma disaster zone" means that portion of the Hurricane Irma disaster area determined by the President to warrant individual or individual and public assistance from the Federal Government under such Act by reason of Hurricane Irma.

(2) HURRICANE IRMA DISASTER AREA. The term "Hurricane Irma disaster area" means an area with respect to which a major disaster has been declared by the President before September 21, 2017, under section 401 of such Act by reason of Hurricane Irma.

(c) HURRICANE MARIA DISASTER ZONE AND DISASTER AREA. For purposes of this title—

(1) HURRICANE MARIA DISASTER ZONE. The term "Hurricane Maria disaster zone" means that portion of the Hurricane Maria disaster area determined by the President to warrant individual or individual and public assistance from the Federal Government under such Act by reason of Hurricane Maria.

(2) HURRICANE MARIA DISASTER AREA. The term "Hurricane Maria disaster area" means an area with respect to which a major disaster has been declared by the President before September 21, 2017, under section 401 of such Act by reason of Hurricane Maria.

[¶16,477B]

ACT SEC. 502. SPECIAL DISASTER-RELATED RULES FOR USE OF RETIREMENT FUNDS.

(a) TAX-FAVORED WITHDRAWALS FROM RETIREMENT PLANS.—

(1) IN GENERAL. Section 72(t) of the Internal Revenue Code of 1986 shall not apply to any qualified hurricane distribution.

(2) AGGREGATE DOLLAR LIMITATION.—

(A) IN GENERAL. For purposes of this subsection, the aggregate amount of distributions received by an individual which may be treated as qualified hurricane distributions for any taxable year shall not exceed the excess (if any) of—

(i) $100,000, over

(ii) the aggregate amounts treated as qualified hurricane distributions received by such individual for all prior taxable years.

(B) TREATMENT OF PLAN DISTRIBUTIONS. If a distribution to an individual would (without regard to subparagraph (A)) be a qualified hurricane distribution, a plan shall not be treated as violating any requirement of the Internal Revenue Code of 1986 merely because the plan treats such distribution as a qualified hurricane distribution, unless the aggregate amount of such distributions from all plans maintained by the employer (and any member of any controlled group which includes the employer) to such individual exceeds $100,000.

(C) CONTROLLED GROUP. For purposes of subparagraph (B), the term "controlled group" means any group treated as a single employer under subsection (b), (c), (m), or (o) of section 414 of the Internal Revenue Code of 1986.

(3) AMOUNT DISTRIBUTED MAY BE REPAID.—

(A) IN GENERAL. Any individual who receives a qualified hurricane distribution may, at any time during the 3-year period beginning on the day after the date on which such distribution was received, make one or more contributions in an aggregate amount not to exceed the amount of such distribution to an eligible retirement plan of which such individual is a beneficiary and to which a rollover contribution of such distribution could be made under section 402(c), 403(a)(4), 403(b)(8), 408(d)(3), or 457(e)(16), of the Internal Revenue Code of 1986, as the case may be.

(B) TREATMENT OF REPAYMENTS OF DISTRIBUTIONS FROM ELIGIBLE RETIREMENT PLANS OTHER THAN IRAS. For purposes of the Internal Revenue Code of 1986, if a contribution is made pursuant to subparagraph (A) with respect to a qualified hurricane distribution from an eligible retirement plan other than an individual retirement plan, then the taxpayer shall, to the extent of the amount of the contribution, be treated as having received the qualified hurricane distribution in an eligible rollover distribution (as defined in section 402(c)(4) of such Code) and as having transferred the amount to the eligible retirement plan in a direct trustee to trustee transfer within 60 days of the distribution.

(C) TREATMENT OF REPAYMENTS FOR DISTRIBUTIONS FROM IRAS. For purposes of the Internal Revenue Code of 1986, if a contribution is made pursuant to subparagraph (A) with respect to a qualified hurricane distribution from an individual retirement plan (as defined by section 7701(a)(37) of such Code), then, to the extent of the amount of the contribution, the qualified hurricane distribution shall be treated as a distribution described in section 408(d)(3) of such Code and as having been transferred to the eligible retirement plan in a direct trustee to trustee transfer within 60 days of the distribution.

(4) DEFINITIONS. For purposes of this subsection—

(A) QUALIFIED HURRICANE DISTRIBUTION. Except as provided in paragraph (2), the term "qualified hurricane distribution" means—

(i) any distribution from an eligible retirement plan made on or after August 23, 2017, and before January 1, 2019, to an individual whose principal place of abode on August 23, 2017, is located in the Hurricane Harvey disaster area and who has sustained an economic loss by reason of Hurricane Harvey,

(ii) any distribution (which is not described in clause (i)) from an eligible retirement plan made on or after September 4, 2017, and before January 1, 2019, to an individual whose principal place of abode on September 4, 2017, is located in the Hurricane Irma disaster area and who has sustained an economic loss by reason of Hurricane Irma, and

(iii) any distribution (which is not described in clause (i) or (ii)) from an eligible retirement plan made on or after September 16, 2017, and before January 1, 2019, to an individual whose principal place of abode on September 16, 2017, is located in the Hurricane Maria disaster area and who has sustained an economic loss by reason of Hurricane Maria.

(B) ELIGIBLE RETIREMENT PLAN. The term "eligible retirement plan" shall have the meaning given such term by section 402(c)(8)(B) of the Internal Revenue Code of 1986.

(5) INCOME INCLUSION SPREAD OVER 3-YEAR PERIOD.—

(A) IN GENERAL. In the case of any qualified hurricane distribution, unless the taxpayer elects not to have this paragraph apply for any taxable year, any amount required to be included in gross income for such taxable year shall be so included ratably over the 3-taxable-year period beginning with such taxable year.

(B) SPECIAL RULE. For purposes of subparagraph (A), rules similar to the rules of subparagraph (E) of section 408A(d)(3) of the Internal Revenue Code of 1986 shall apply.

(6) SPECIAL RULES.—

(A) EXEMPTION OF DISTRIBUTIONS FROM TRUSTEE TO TRUSTEE TRANSFER AND WITHHOLDING RULES. For purposes of sections 401(a)(31), 402(f), and 3405 of the Internal Revenue Code of 1986, qualified hurricane distributions shall not be treated as eligible rollover distributions.

(B) QUALIFIED HURRICANE DISTRIBUTIONS TREATED AS MEETING PLAN DISTRIBUTION REQUIREMENTS. For purposes the Internal Revenue Code of 1986, a qualified hurricane distribution shall be treated as meeting the requirements of sections 401(k)(2)(B)(i), 403(b)(7)(A)(ii), 403(b)(11), and 457(d)(1)(A) of such Code.

(b) RECONTRIBUTIONS OF WITHDRAWALS FOR HOME PURCHASES.—

(1) RECONTRIBUTIONS.—

(A) IN GENERAL. Any individual who received a qualified distribution may, during the period beginning on August 23, 2017, and ending on February 28, 2018, make one or more contributions in an aggregate amount not to exceed the amount of such qualified distribution to an eligible retirement plan (as defined in section 402(c)(8)(B) of the Internal Revenue Code of 1986) of which such individual is a beneficiary and to which a rollover contribution of such distribution could be made under section 402(c), 403(a)(4), 403(b)(8), or 408(d)(3), of such Code, as the case may be.

(B) TREATMENT OF REPAYMENTS. Rules similar to the rules of subparagraphs (B) and (C) of subsection (a)(3) shall apply for purposes of this subsection.

(2) QUALIFIED DISTRIBUTION. For purposes of this subsection, the term "qualified distribution" means any distribution—

(A) described in section 401(k)(2)(B)(i)(IV), 403(b)(7)(A)(ii) (but only to the extent such distribution relates to financial hardship), 403(b)(11)(B), or 72(t)(2)(F), of the Internal Revenue Code of 1986,

(B) received after February 28, 2017, and before September 21, 2017, and

(C) which was to be used to purchase or construct a principal residence in the Hurricane Harvey disaster area, the Hurricane Irma disaster area, or the Hurricane Maria disaster area, but which was not so purchased or constructed on account of Hurricane Harvey, Hurricane Irma, or Hurricane Maria.

(c) LOANS FROM QUALIFIED PLANS.—

(1) INCREASE IN LIMIT ON LOANS NOT TREATED AS DISTRIBUTIONS. In the case of any loan from a qualified employer plan (as defined under section 72(p)(4) of the Internal Revenue Code of 1986) to a qualified individual made during the period beginning on the date of the enactment of this Act and ending on December 31, 2018—

(A) clause (i) of section 72(p)(2)(A) of such Code shall be applied by substituting "$100,000" for "$50,000", and

(B) clause (ii) of such section shall be applied by substituting "the present value of the nonforfeitable accrued benefit of the employee under the plan" for "one-half of the present value of the nonforfeitable accrued benefit of the employee under the plan".

(2) DELAY OF REPAYMENT. In the case of a qualified individual with an outstanding loan on or after the qualified beginning date from a qualified employer plan (as defined in section 72(p)(4) of the Internal Revenue Code of 1986)—

(A) if the due date pursuant to subparagraph (B) or (C) of section 72(p)(2) of such Code for any repayment with respect to such loan occurs during the period beginning on the qualified beginning date and ending on December 31, 2018, such due date shall be delayed for 1 year,

(B) any subsequent repayments with respect to any such loan shall be appropriately adjusted to reflect the delay in the due date under paragraph (1) and any interest accruing during such delay, and

(C) in determining the 5-year period and the term of a loan under subparagraph (B) or (C) of section 72(p)(2) of such Code, the period described in subparagraph (A) shall be disregarded.

(3) QUALIFIED INDIVIDUAL. For purposes of this subsection—

(A) IN GENERAL. The term "qualified individual" means any qualified Hurricane Harvey individual, any qualified Hurricane Irma individual, and any qualified Hurricane Maria individual.

(B) QUALIFIED HURRICANE HARVEY INDIVIDUAL. The term "qualified Hurricane Harvey individual" means an individual whose principal place of abode on August 23, 2017, is located in the Hurricane Harvey disaster area and who has sustained an economic loss by reason of Hurricane Harvey.

(C) QUALIFIED HURRICANE IRMA INDIVIDUAL. The term "qualified Hurricane Irma individual" means an individual (other than a qualified Hurricane Harvey individual) whose principal place of abode on September 4, 2017, is located in the Hurricane Irma disaster area and who has sustained an economic loss by reason of Hurricane Irma.

(D) QUALIFIED HURRICANE MARIA INDIVIDUAL. The term "qualified Hurricane Maria individual" means an individual (other than a qualified Hurricane Harvey individual or a qualified Hurricane Irma individual) whose principal place of abode on September 16, 2017, is located in the Hurricane Maria disaster area and who has sustained an economic loss by reason of Hurricane Maria.

(4) QUALIFIED BEGINNING DATE. For purposes of this subsection, the qualified beginning date is—

(A) in the case of any qualified Hurricane Harvey individual, August 23, 2017,

(B) in the case of any qualified Hurricane Irma individual, September 4, 2017, and

(C) in the case of any qualified Hurricane Maria individual, September 16, 2017.

(d) PROVISIONS RELATING TO PLAN AMENDMENTS.—

(1) IN GENERAL. If this subsection applies to any amendment to any plan or annuity contract, such plan or contract shall be treated as being operated in accordance with the terms of the plan during the period described in paragraph (2)(B)(i).

(2) AMENDMENTS TO WHICH SUBSECTION APPLIES.—

(A) IN GENERAL. This subsection shall apply to any amendment to any plan or annuity contract which is made—

(i) pursuant to any provision of this section, or pursuant to any regulation issued by the Secretary or the Secretary of Labor under any provision of this section, and

(ii) on or before the last day of the first plan year beginning on or after January 1, 2019, or such later date as the Secretary may prescribe.

In the case of a governmental plan (as defined in section 414(d) of the Internal Revenue Code of 1986), clause (ii) shall be applied by substituting the date which is 2 years after the date otherwise applied under clause (ii).

(B) CONDITIONS. This subsection shall not apply to any amendment unless—

(i) during the period—

(I) beginning on the date that this section or the regulation described in subparagraph (A)(i) takes effect (or in the case of a plan or contract amendment not required by this section or such regulation, the effective date specified by the plan), and

(II) ending on the date described in subparagraph (A)(ii) (or, if earlier, the date the plan or contract amendment is adopted),

the plan or contract is operated as if such plan or contract amendment were in effect, and

(ii) such plan or contract amendment applies retroactively for such period.

¶ 16,830 TEXT OF ERISA REORGANIZATION PLAN

Following is the text of Reorganization Plan No. 4 of 1978 (the ERISA Reorganization Plan).

Prepared by the President and transmitted to the Senate and the House of Representatives in Congress assembled, August 10, 1978, pursuant to the provisions of chapter 9 of title 5 of the United States Code.

EMPLOYEE RETIREMENT INCOME SECURITY ACT TRANSFERS

Section 101. Transfer to the Secretary of the Treasury

Except as otherwise provided in sections 104 and 106 of this Plan, all authority of the Secretary of Labor to issue the following described documents pursuant to the statutes hereinafter specified is hereby transferred to the Secretary of the Treasury:

(a) regulations, rulings, opinions, variances and waivers under Parts 2 and 3 of subtitle B of title I and subsection 1012(c) of title II of the Employee Retirement Income Security Act of 1974 (29 U.S.C. 1001 note) (hereinafter referred to as "ERISA"), *except* for sections and subsections 201, 203(a)(3)(B), 209, and 301(a) of ERISA;

(b) such regulations, ruling, and opinions which are granted to the Secretary of Labor under Sections 404, 410, 411, 412, and 413 of the Internal Revenue Code of 1954, as amended, (hereinafter referred to as the "Code"), *except* for subsection 411(a)(3)(B) of the Code and the definitions of "collectively bargained plan" and "collective bargaining agreement" contained in subsections 404(a)(1)(B) and (a)(1)(C), 410(b)(2)(A) and (b)(2)(B), and 413(a)(1) of the Code; and

(c) regulations, rulings, and opinions under subsections 3(19), 3(22), 3(23), 3(24), 3(25), 3(27), 3(28), 3(29), 3(30), and 3(31) of subtitle A of title I of ERISA.

Section 102. Transfers to the Secretary of Labor

Except as otherwise provided in section 105 of this plan, all authority of the Secretary of the Treasury to issue the following described documents pursuant to the statutes hereinafter specified is hereby transferred to the Secretary of Labor:

(a) regulations, rulings, opinions, and exemptions under section 4975 of the Code, *except* for (i) subsections 4975(a), (b), (c)(3), (d)(3), (e)(1), and (e)(7) of the Code; (ii) to the extent necessary for the continued enforcement of subsections 4975(a) and (b) by the Secretary of the Treasury, subsections 4975(f)(1), (f)(2), (f)(4), (f)(5), and (f)(6) of the Code; and (iii) exemptions with respect to transactions that are exempted by subsection 404(c) of ERISA from the provisions of part 4 of subtitle B of title I of ERISA; and

(b) regulations, rulings, and opinions under subsection 2003(c) of ERISA, *except* for subsection 2003(c)(1)(B).

Section 103. Coordination Concerning Certain Fiduciary Actions

In the case of fiduciary actions which are subject to part 4 of subtitle B of title I of ERISA, the Secretary of the Treasury shall notify the Secrtary of Labor prior to the time of commencing any proceeding to determine whether the action violates the exclusive benefit rule of subsection 401(a) of the Code, but not later than prior to issuing a preliminary notice of intent to disqualify under that rule, and the Secretary of the Treasury shall not issue a determination that a plan or trust does not satisfy the requirements of subsection 401(a) by reason of the exclusive benefit rule of subsection 401(a), unless within 90 days after the date on which the Secretary of the Treasury notifies the Secretary of Labor of pending action, the Secretary of Labor certifies that he has no objection to the disqualification or the Secretary of Labor fails to respond to the Secretary of the Treasury. The requirements of this paragraph do not apply in the case of any termination or jeopardy assessment under section 6851 or 6861 of the Code that has been approved in advance by the Commissioner of Internal Revenue, or as delegated, the Assistant Commissioner for Employee Plans and Exempt Organizations.

Section 104. Enforcement by the Secretary of Labor

The transfers provided for in section 101 of this plan shall not affect the ability of the Secretary of Labor, subject to the provisions of title III of ERISA relating to jurisdiction, administration, and enforcement, to engage in enforcement under section 502 of ERISA or to exercise the authority set forth under title III of ERISA, including the ability to make interpretations necessary to engage in such enforcement or to exercise such authority. However, in bringing such actions and in exercising such authority with respect to parts 2 and 3 of subtitle B of title I of ERISA and any definitions for which the authority of the Secretary of Labor is transferred to the Secretary of the Treasury as provided in section 101 of this plan, the Secretary of Labor shall be bound by the regulations, rulings, opinions, variances, and waivers issued by the Secretary of the Treasury.

Section 105. Enforcement by the Secretary of the Treasury

The transfers provided for in section 102 of this plan shall not affect the ability of the Secretary of the Treasury, subject to the provisions of title III of ERISA relating to jurisdiction, administration, and enforcement, (a) to audit plans and employers and to enforce the excise tax provisions of subsections 4975(a) and 4975(b) of the Code, to exercise the authority set forth in subsections 502(b)(1) and 502(h) of ERISA, or to exercise the authority set forth in title III of ERISA, including the ability to make interpretations necessary to audit, to enforce such taxes, and to exercise such authority; and (b) consistent with the coordination requirements under section 103 of this plan, to disqualify, under section 401 of the Code, a plan subject to part 4 of subtitle B of title I of ERISA, including the ability to make the interpretations necessary to make such disqualification. However, in enforcing such excise taxes and, to the extent applicable, in disqualifying such plans the Secretary of the Treasury shall be bound by the regulations, rulings, opinions, and exemptions issued by the Secretary of Labor pursuant to the authority transferred to the Secretary of Labor as provided in section 102 of this plan.

Section 106. Coordination for Section 101 Transfers

(a) The Secretary of the Treasury shall not exercise the functions transferred pursuant to section 101 of this plan to issue in proposed or final form any of the documents described in subsection (b) of this Section in any case in which such documents would significantly impact on or substantially affect collectively bargained plans unless, within 100 calendar days after the Secretary of the Treasury notifies the Secratary of Labor of such proposed action, the Secretary of Labor certifies that he has no objection or he fails to respond to the Secretary of the Treasury. The fact of such a notification, except for such notification for documents described in subsection (b)(iv) of this Section, from the Secretary of the Treasury to the Secretary of Labor shall be announced by the Secretary of Labor to the public within ten days following the date of receipt of the notification by the Secretary of Labor.

(b) The documents to which this Section applies are:

(i) amendments to regulations issued pursuant to subsections 202(a)(3), 203(b)(2) and (3)(A), 204(b)(3)(A), (C), and (E), and 210(a)(2) of ERISA, and subsections 410(a)(3) and 411(a)(5), (6)(A), and (b)(3)(A), (C), and (E), 413(b)(4) and (c)(3) and 414(f) of the Code;

(ii) regulations issued pursuant to subsections 204(b)(3)(D), 302(d)(2), and 304(d)(1), (d)(2) and (e)(2)(A) of ERISA, and subsections 411(b)(3)(D), 412(c)(2) and 413(d)(1), (d)(2), and (e)(2)(A) of the Code; and

(iii) revenue rulings (within the meaning of 26 CFR section 601.201(a)(6)), revenue procedures, and similar publications, if the rulings, procedures and publications are issued under one of the statutory provisions listed in (i) and (ii) of this subsection; and

(iv) rulings (within the meaning of 26 CFR section 601.201(a)(2)) issued prior to the issuance of a published regulation under one of the statutory provisions listed in (i) and (ii) of this subsection and not issued under a published Revenue Ruling.

(c) For those documents described in subsections (b)(i), (b)(ii) and (b)(iii) of this section, the Secretary of Labor may request the Secretary of the Treasury to initiate the actions described in this section 106 of this plan.

Section 107. Evaluation

On or before January 31, 1980, the President will submit to both Houses of the Congress an evaluation of the extent to which this reorganization plan has alleviated the problems associated with the present administrative structure under ERISA, accompanied by specific legislative recommendations for a long-term administrative structure under ERISA.

Section 108. Incidental Transfers

So much of the personnel, property, records, and unexpended balances of appropriations, allocations and other funds employed, used, held, available, or to be made available in connection with the functions transferred under this plan, as the Director of the Office of Management and Budget shall determine, shall be transferred to the appropriate agency, or component at such time or times as the Director of the Office of Management and Budget shall provide, except that no such unexpended balances transferred shall be used for purposes other than those for which the appropriation was originally made. The Director of the Office of Management and Budget shall provide for terminating the affairs of any agencies abolished herein and for such further measures and dispositions as such Director deems necessary to effectuate the purposes of this reorganization plan.

Section 109. Effective Date

The provisions of this reorganization plan shall become effective at such time or times, on or before April 30, 1979, as the President shall specify, but not sooner than the earliest time allowable under section 906 of title 5 United States Code. [The provisions of the Reorganization Plan went into effect on December 31, 1978, under Executive Order 12108, December 18, 1978 (44 FR 1065)].

Amendments

P.L. 109-280, §107(c):

Amended Section 106(b)(ii) of Reorganization Plan No. 4 of 1978 by striking "302(c)(8)" and inserting "302(d)(2)", by striking "304(a) and (b)(2)(A)" and inserting "304(d)(1), (d)(2), and (e)(2)(A)", and by striking "412(c)(8), (e), and (f)(2)(A)" and inserting "412(c)(2) and 431(d)(1), (d)(2), and (e)(2)(A)".

The above amendment is effective is effective for plan years beginning after 2007.

Proposed Regulations—Internal Revenue Code

¶ 20,118B

Proposed regulations: Individual retirement plans: Annual reporting requirements.—Reproduced below is the text of proposed regulations that require annual reporting of information relating to individual retirement plans. The regulations affect trustees of individual retirement accounts and issuers of individual retirement annuities as well as individuals who own or benefit from such plans. In particular, the proposed regulations reflect changes made by Internal Revenue Service News Release IR-83-88 (CCH Pension Plan Guide, ¶ 17,019G) and the Tax Reform Act of 1984.

The proposed regulations were published in the *Federal Register* on November 16, 1984 (49 FR 45450).

DEPARTMENT OF THE TREASURY

Internal Revenue Service

[26 CFR Part 1]

[EE-65-83]

Annual Information Reports of Trustees and Issuers of Individual Retirement Plans

Notice of Proposed Rulemaking

AGENCY: Internal Revenue Service, Treasury.

ACTION: Notice of proposed rulemaking.

SUMMARY: This document contains proposed regulations that require annual reporting of information relating to individual retirement plans. The regulations reflect changes made to the applicable reporting requirements by both News Release IR-83-88 and the Tax Reform Act of 1984. The regulations affect trustees of individual retirement accounts and issuers of individual retirement annuities (including accounts and annuities that are simplified employee pensions), and individuals who oen or benefit from such individual retirement plans.

DATES: Written comments and requests for a public hearing must be delivered or mailed by January 15, 1985. The amendments are proposed to be effective for reports relating to calendar years beginning after 1982.

ADDRESS: Send comments and requests for a public hearing to: Commissioner of Internal Revenue, Attention: CC:LR:T

(EE-65-83), 1111 Constitution Avenue, N.W., Washington, D.C. 20224.

FOR FURTHER INFORMATION CONTACT: Philip R. Bosco of the Employee Plans and Exempt Organization Division, Office of the Chief Counsel, Internal Revenue Service, 1111 Constitution Avenue, N.W., Washington, D.C. 20224 (Attention: CC:LR:T), 202-566-3430 (not a toll-free number).

SUPPLEMENTARY INFORMATION:

Background

Section 408 of the Internal Revenue Code of 1954 defines various individual retirement plans, including individual retirement accounts, individual retirement annuities, and simplified employee pensions. Section 408(i) of the Code provides that the trustee of an individual retirement account or the issuer of an individual retirement annuity (including an account or annuity that is a simplified employee pension) shall make such reports regarding the status of an account or annuity as the Secretary may require under regulations.

Section 1.408-5(c)(1) of the Income Tax Regulations (26 CFR Part 1) under section 408 of the Code requires that an annual report must be furnished to each participant, i.e., the individual for whose benefit the account was established or in whose name the annuity was purchased (or the beneficiary of such individual). The report must contain the following information for transactions occurring during the calendar year: the amount of contributions; the amount of distributions; in the case of an endowment contract, the amount of the premium paid allocable to the cost of life insurance; and the name and address of the trustee or issuer. The report must be furnished on or before June 30 following the calendar year for which the report is required. Paragraph (c)(2) of § 1.408-5 provides that the Commissioner may require the annual report to be filed with the Service at the time the Commissioner specifies.

On June 28, 1983, the Service issued News Release IR-83-88 relating to the filing requirement permissible under § 1.408-5(c)(2). Beginning with the 1983 calendar year, the annual reports required by § 1.408-5 must also be filed with the Service. New Form 5498, Individual Retirement Arrangement Information, has been developed for this purpose. The form, a copy of which may be utilized to satisfy the existing reporting requirement of § 1.408-5, must contain the following information for transactions occurring during the calendar year: the amount of contributions (exclusive of rollover contributions for calendar years after 1983); the amount of rollover contributions (for calendar years after 1983); and the name and address of the trustee or issuer. For the 1983 calendar year, the form must be filed with the Service, and the annual report furnished to the participant, on or before June 30, 1984. Finally, IR-83-88 stated that, for calendar year 1984, the form must be

filed with the Service on or before February 28, 1985, and the annual report must be furnished to the participant on or before June 30, 1985.

On July 18, 1984, section 147 of the Tax Reform Act of 1984 (Pub. L. 98-369) amended section 408(i) to provide that the information reports required by such section identify the taxable year to which individual retirement plan contributions relate. This amendment is effective for contributions made after December 31, 1984.

The proposed regulations contained in this document amend § 1.408-5 to conform such section to both the new filing requirements announced in News Release IR-83-88 and the new reporting requirement added by the Tax Reform Act of 1984. The amendments are to be issued under the authority contained in sections 408(i) and 7805 of the Code (88 Stat. 964, 26 U.S.C. 408(i); 68A Stat. 917, 26 U.S.C. 7805, respectively).

As proposed, the regulations necessarily modify the requirements of IR-83-88 for calendar years 1984 and thereafter. Beginning with calendar year 1984, Form 5498 shall be filed with the Service and the statement to the participant shall be furnished to such person on or before May 31 following the calendar year for which such reports are required. For calendar year 1984, this is a change of the due dates originally announced in IR-83-88. Beginning with calendar year 1985, both Form 5498 and the statement to the participant must report, as the amount of contributions for the calendar year, the amount of contributions made during or after the calendar year that relate to such calendar year. Also beginning with calendar year 1985, both Form 5498 and the statement to the participant must report, in the case of an endowment contract premium allocable to the cost of life insurance, that amount of the premium paid either during or after the calendar year that relates to such calendar year.

Finally, the proposed regulations contain special transitional requirements for the 1985 calendar year reports. For that calendar year both Form 5498 and the statement to the participant must report, as a separate entry, the amount of contributions made during 1985 that relate to 1984. This requirement also applies to the statement to the participant in the case of an endowment contract premium allocable to the cost of life insurance paid during 1985 that relates to 1984.

Special Analysis

The Commissioner of Internal Revenue has determined that these proposed rules are not major rules as defined in either Executive Order 12291 or the Treasury and OMB implementation of that Order dated April 29, 1983. Accordingly, a Regulatory Impact Analysis is not required.

Although this document is a notice of proposed rulemaking that solicits public comments, the Internal Revenue Service has concluded that the regulations proposed herein are interpretative and that the notice and public procedure requirements of 5 U.S.C. 553 do not apply. Accordingly, these proposed regulations do not constitute regulations subject to the Regulatory Flexibility Act (5 U.S.C. Chapter 6).

Comments and Request for a Public Hearing

Before adopting these proposed regulations, consideration will be given to any written comments that are submitted (preferably seven copies) to the Commissioner of Internal Revenue. All comments will be available for public inspection and copying. A public hearing will be held upon written request to the Commissioner by any person who has submitted written comments. If a public hearing is held, notice of the time and place will be published in the *Federal Register.*

The collection of information requirements contained in this notice of proposed rulemaking have been submitted to the Office of Management and Budget (OMB) for review under section 3504(h) of the Paperwork Reduction Act of 1980. Comments on these requirements should be sent to the Office of Information and Regulatory Affairs of OMB, Attention: Desk Office for Internal Revenue Service, New Executive Office Building, Washington, D.C. 20503. The Internal Revenue Service requests that persons submitting comments on these requirements to OMB also send copies of those comments to the Service.

Drafting Information

The principal author of these proposed regulations is Philip R. Bosco of the Employee Plans and Exempt Organizations Division of the Office of Chief Counsel, Internal Revenue Service. However, personnel from other offices of the Internal Revenue Service and Treasury Department participated in developing the regulations, on matters of both substance and style.

List of Subjects in 26 CFR §§ 1.401-1—1.425-1

Employee benefit plans, pensions, individual retirement accounts.

Proposed amendments to the regulations

The proposed amendments to 26 CFR Part 1 are as follows:

Section 1.408-5 is amended by revising the section to read as follows:

§ 1.408-5 Annual reports by trustees and issuers.

(a) *Requirement and form of report.* The trustee of an individual retirement account or the issuer of an individual retirement annuity (including an account or annuity that is a simplified employee pension) shall make annual calendar year reports on Form 5498 concerning the status of the account or annuity. The report shall contain the following information for transactions occurring during or after the calendar year that relate to such calendar year:

(1) The name, address and identifying number of the trustee or issuer;

(2) The name, address, and identifying number of the participant (the individual on whose behalf the account is established or in whose name the annuity is purchased (or the beneficiary of the individual or owner));

(3) The amount of contributions (exclusive of rollover contributions) made during or after the calendar year that relate to such calendar year;

(4) The amount of rollover contributions made during the calendar year;

(5) In the case of an endowment contract, the amount of the premium allocable to the cost of life insurance paid either during or after the calendar year that relates to such calendar year; and

(6) Such other information as the Commissioner may require.

(b) *Manner and time for filing.* The report on Form 5498 shall be filed, accompanied by transmittal Form 1096, with the appropriate Internal Revenue Service Center. The report shall be filed on or before May 31 following the calendar year for which the report is required.

(c) *Statement of participants.* (1) Each trustee or issuer required to file Form 5498 under this section shall furnish the participant a statement containing the information required to be furnished on Form 5498 plus the value of the account or annuity at the end of the calendar year. A copy of Form 5498, containing the additional information specified in the previous sentence, may be used to satisfy the statement requirement of this paragraph. If a copy of Form 5498 is not used to satisfy the statement requirement of this paragraph, the statement shall contain the following language: "This information is being furnished to the Internal Revenue Service."

(2) Each statement required by this paragraph to be furnished to participants shall be furnished to such person on or before May 31 following the calendar year for which the report on Form 5498 is required.

(d) *Penalties.* Section 6693 prescribes penalties for failure to file an annual report required by this section.

(e) *Effective date.* In general, this section applies to reports for calendar years beginning with 1983. For additional requirements relating to the 1985 calendar year reports, see paragraph (f) of this section. For special requirements relating to the 1983 and 1984 calendar year reports, see paragraph (g) of this section. For requirements relating to pre-1983 calendar year reports, see 26 C.F.R. § 1.408-5 (1983).

(f) *Reports for calendar year 1985.* For calendar year 1985, both Form 5498 and the statement to the participant must report, as a separate entry, the amount of contributions made during the 1985 calendar year that relate to the 1984 calendar year. This also applies, in the case of the statement to the participant, to endowment contract premiums allocable to the cost of life insurance that are paid during the 1985 calendar year but that relate to the 1984 calendar year.

(g) *Reports for calendar years 1983 and 1984.* (1) For calendar years 1983 and 1984, neither Form 5498 nor the statement to the participant need identify the calendar year to which a contribution relates. The form and statement need only report the amount of contributions actually made during the calendar year. This also applies to endowment contract premiums allocable to the cost of life insurance and paid during the calendar year.

(2) For calendar years 1983 and 1984, Form 5498 need not report (but the statement to the participant must report), in the case of an endowment contract, the amount of !he premium allocable to the cost of life insurance paid during the calendar year.

(3) For calendar year 1983, neither Form 5498 nor the statement to the participant need separately report rollover contributions made during the calendar year. Rollover contributions are to be aggregated with the amount of other contributions made during the calendar year.

(4) For calendar year 1983, the statement to the participant need not contain the language required by paragraph (c)(1) of this section.

(5) For calendar year 1983, Form 5498 shall be filed, and the statement to the participant shall be furnished, on or before June 30, 1984.

(h) *Related reports by trustees and issuers.* See § 1.408-7 for reports relating to distributions from individual retirement plans.

(signed) Roscoe L. Egger, Jr.

Commissioner of Internal Revenue

[¶ 20,118C Reserved.—Proposed regulations relating to the deduction of employer liability payments were formerly reproduced at this point. The final regulations are at ¶ 11,869A.]

¶ 20,118D

Proposed regulations: Limits on contributions to and reserves of welfare benefit funds maintained pursuant to a collective bargaining agreement: Cross reference to temporary regulations.—The Internal Revenue Service has issued temporary regulations relating to contributions to and reserves of welfare benefit funds maintained pursuant to a collective bargaining agreement. The text of those temporary regulations (¶ 12,970) serves as the common document for this notice of proposed rulemaking which follows.

These regulations appeared in the *Federal Register* on July 3, 1985.

AGENCY: Internal Revenue Service, Treasury.

ACTION: Notice of proposed rulemaking by cross reference to temporary regulations.

SUMMARY: In the Rules and Regulations portion of this issue of the Federal Register, the Internal Revenue Service is issuing temporary regulations relating to contributions to and reserves of welfare benefit funds maintained pursuant to a collective bargaining agreement. The text of those temporary regulations [CCH PENSION PLAN GUIDE, ¶ 12,970] also serves as the comment document for this notice of proposed rulemaking.

DATES: Written comments and requests for a public hearing must be delivered or mailed by September 3, 1985. The regulations are proposed to be effective for contributions paid or accrued after December 31, 1985.

ADDRESS: Send comments and requests for a public hearing to Commissioner of Internal Revenue, Attn: CC:LR:T (EE-66-84), 1111 Constitution Avenue N.W., Washington D.C. 20224.

FOR FURTHER INFORMATION CONTACT: John T. Ricotta of the Employee Plans and Exempt Organizations Division, Office of Chief Counsel, Internal Revenue Service, 1111 Constitution Ave., N. W., Washington, D.C. 20224, Attention: CC:LR:T (EE-66-84), telephone: 202-566-4396 (not a toll-free number).

SUPPLEMENTARY INFORMATION:

Background

The temporary regulations provide guidance concerning the limits on contributions to and the reserves of welfare benefit funds maintained pursuant to a collective bargaining agreement under section 419A(f)(5) of the Internal Revenue Code of 1954 (Code), as added to the Code by section 511 of the Tax Reform Act of 1984 (26 U.S.C. §419A). The proposed regulations are issued under the authority contained in section 7805 of the Code (26 U.S.C. §7805). For the text of the temporary regulations, see F.R. Doc. [—] published in the Rules and Regulations portion of this issue of the FEDERAL REGISTER.

Special Analysis

The Commissioner of Internal Revenue has determined that this proposed rule is not a major rule as defined in Executive Order 12291 and that a Regulatory Impact Analysis is therefore not required. Although this document is a notice of proposed rulemaking which solicits public comment, the Internal Revenue has concluded that the regulations proposed herein are interpretative and that the notice and public procedure requirements of 5 U.S.C. 553 do not apply. Accordingly, these proposed regulations do not constitute regulations subject to the Regulatory Flexibility Act (5 U.S.C. Chapter 6).

Comments and Requests for a Public Hearing

Before adopting the temporary regulations referred to in this document as final regulations, consideration will be given to any written comments that are submitted (preferably 8 copies) to the Commissioner of Internal Revenue. All comments will be available for public inspection and copying. A public hearing will be held upon written request to the Commissioner by any person who has submitted written comments. If a public hearing is held, notice of the time and place will be published in the FEDERAL REGISTER.

List of Subjects in 26 CFR §§ 1.401-0—1.425-1

Income Taxes, Employee Benefit Plans, Pensions, Stock Options, Individual Retirement Accounts, Employee Stock Ownership Plans.

M. Eddie Heironimus

Acting Commissioner of Internal Revenue

[**¶ 20,118E Reserved.**—Proposed regulations requiring employers filing information returns on certain forms to use magnetic media instead of paper forms were formerly reproduced at this point. The final regulations appear at ¶ 13,649D.]

[**¶ 20,118F Reserved.**—Proposed regulations which include new unisex annuity tables used to compute the portion of an amount received as an annuity that is includible in gross income were formerly reproduced at this point. The final regulations appear at ¶ 11,194—11,197, 11,199, 11,201, and 11,803.]

¶ 20,118G

Proposed regulations: Employee achievement awards: Tax Reform Act of 1986.—Reproduced below is the text of proposed regulations that would amend the regulations (¶ 11,357) on the excludability and deductibility of certain employee awards. These amendments, if adopted, will provide guidance needed to comply with the Tax Reform Act of 1986.

The proposed regulations were established in the *Federal Register* on January 9, 1989 (54 FR 627).

DEPARTMENT OF THE TREASURY

Internal Revenue Service

26 CFR Part 1

[IA-111-86]

Income Tax; Taxable Years Beginning After December 31, 1986; Changes With Respect to Prizes and Awards and Employee Achievement Awards

AGENCY: Internal Revenue Service.

ACTION: Notice of proposed rulemaking.

SUMMARY: This document contains proposed amendments to the regulations relating to the excludability of certain prizes and awards and to the deductibility of certain employee awards. Changes to the applicable tax law were made by the Tax Reform Act of 1986. These amendments, if adopted, will provide the public with the guidance needed to comply with the Act.

DATES: Written comments and requests for a public hearing must be delivered or mailed by March 10, 1989. The amendments are proposed to be effective after December 31, 1986.

ADDRESS: Send comments and requests for a public hearing to: Commissioner of Internal Revenue, Internal Revenue Service, 1111 Constitution Avenue, NW., Washington, DC 20224; Attention: CC:CORP:T:R, IA-111-86.

FURTHER INFORMATION CONTACT: Johnnel St. Germain of the Office of Assistant Chief Counsel (Income Tax and Accounting), Internal Revenue Service, 1111 Constitution Avenue, NW., Washington, DC 20224; Attention: CC:CORP:T:R, IA-111-86. Telephone 202-566-4509 (not a toll-free call).

SUPPLEMENTARY INFORMATION:

Paperwork Reduction Act

The collections of information contained in this notice of proposed rulemaking have been submitted to the Office of Management and Budget for review in accordance with the Paperwork Reduction Act of 1980 (44 U.S.C. 3504(h)). Comments on the collections of information should be sent to the Office of Information and Regulatory Affairs, Office of Management and Budget, Washington, DC 20503, attention: Desk Officer for the Internal Revenue Service. Copies of comments should also be sent to the Internal Revenue Service at the address previously specified.

The collections of information in this regulation are in 26 CFR 1.74-1(c). This information is required by the Internal Revenue Service in order to verify that the proper amount of income is reported by taxpayers on their returns of tax. The likely respondents are individuals.

Estimated total annual reporting burden: 1,275 hours.

Estimated average annual burden per respondent: 15 minutes.

Estimated number of respondents: 5,100.

Background

This document contains proposed amendments to the Income Tax Regulations (26 CFR Part 1) under sections 74, 102, and 274 of the Internal Revenue Code (Code). The amendments are proposed to conform the regulations to section 122 of the Tax Reform Act of 1986 (Pub. L. 99-514). The proposed amendments, if adopted, will be issued under the authority contained in section 7805 of the Code (68A Stat. 917; 26 U.S.C. 7805).

General Information

Prior to the 1986 Code, section 74 stated that prizes and awards, other than certain types of fellowship grants and scholarships, were includible in gross income unless they were made primarily in recognition of religious, charitable, scientific, educational, artistic, literary, or civic achievement. To qualify for the exclusion, the recipient must have been selected without any action on his part and could not be required to render substantial services as a condition to receiving the prize or award.

Within the context of a business relationship, prizes and awards that would otherwise be includible in a recipient's gross income were excludable if they qualified as gifts under section 102. In general, section 274(b) disallowed an employer a business deduction for gifts to an employee to the extent that the total cost of all gifts of cash, tangible personal property, and other items to the same individual during the taxable year exceeded $25. A special exception to the $25 limitation was allowed for items of tangible personal property awarded to an employee for length of service, safety achievement, or productivity. The employer could deduct the cost of such an award up to $400. If the item was provided under a qualified award plan, the deductibility limitation was increased to $1600, provided the average cost of all plan awards made during the year did not exceed $400. A de minimis fringe benefit under section 132(e) was, and continues to be, excludable from gross income and is not subject to the requirements imposed upon prizes and awards under sections 74 and 274.

Explanation of Provisions

These proposed amendments relate to the includability of certain prizes and awards and to the deductibility of certain employee awards and reflect the substantial changes made by the Tax Reform Act of 1986 (the Act) to sections 74, 102 and 274 of the Internal Revenue Code (Code). Changes to the applicable sections of the Code and regulations, amended or newly incorporated by this document, are effective for awards made after December 31, 1986.

Under the Act, the section 74(b) exclusion for prizes or awards received in recognition of charitable achievement is available only if the payor transfers the prize or award to one or more entities described in paragraph (1) and/or (2) of section 170(c) pursuant to the direction of the recipient.

Section 1.74-1(c) of the proposed regulations requires that recipients of prizes and awards clearly designate, in writing, within 45 days of the date the item is granted that they wish to have the prize or award transferred to one or more qualifying donee organizations. The proposed regulations set forth requirements which, in certain instances, determine whether a qualifying designation has been made.

Section 1.74-1(d) of the proposed regulations clarifies that the exclusion under section 74(b) will not be available unless the prize or award is transferred by the payor to one or more qualified donee organizations before the recipient, or any person other than the grantor or a qualified donee organization, uses the item. In general, a transfer may be accomplished by any method that results in receipt of the prize or award by, or on behalf of, one or more qualified donee organizations.

Section 1.74-1(e) further clarifies the requirements of section 74(b) by defining certain terms. Definitions are included which determine what constitutes a "qualified donee organization," when a "disqualifying use" has taken place, and when an item is considered "granted."

Section 1.74-1(f) provides that neither the payor nor the recipient of the prize or award may claim a charitable contribution deduction for the value of any prize or award for which an exclusion is allowed under section 74(b).

All of the requirements of section 74(b) in existence prior to passage of the Act remain in effect and must be met in order for the award recipient to be eligible for the exclusion. Accordingly, rules and regulations governing these additional requirements, to the extent they are not inconsistent with the proposed regulations, will remain in effect.

New Code section 74(c) excludes certain employee achievement awards from gross income. The exclusion applies, subject to certain limitations, to the value of awards made by the employer for safety achievement or length of service achievement. The amount of the exclusion generally corresponds with the deduction given the employer under new section 274(j) for these "employee achievement awards." Thus, in general, the employee must include these awards in income to the extent that the fair market value of the award, or, if greater, the cost of the award to the employer, exceeds the amount deductible under section 274(j). The exclusion allows an employee to exclude the full fair market value of the award where the cost of the award is fully deductible by the employer.

Section 1.74-2(d) of the proposed regulations provides special rules for employee achievement awards applicable to sole-proprietors and tax-exempt employers.

Section 1.74-2(e) clarifies that an employee award, whether or not an employee achievement award, may be excludible from gross income as a de minimis fringe benefit under section 132(e).

Section 102(c) of the Code clarifies that, with the exception of employee achievement awards under section 74(c) and de minimis fringe benefits under section 132(e), an employee shall not exclude from gross income any amount transferred to the employee (or for the employee's benefit) by, or on behalf of, the employer in the form of a gift, bequest, devise, or inheritance. Therefore, while awards satisfying the requirements of section 74(c) and de minimis fringe benefits qualifying under section 132(e) will be excluded from gross income under those sections, no amounts (except in certain narrowly defined circumstances) transferred by, or on behalf of, an individual's employer will be excludable from gross income under section 102.

Section 1.102-1(f)(2) of the proposed regulations provides that for purposes of section 102(c), extraordinary transfers to the natural objects of one's bounty will not be considered transfers for the benefit of an employee if it can be shown that the transfer was not made in recognition of the transferee's employment. Thus, the rules set out in *Comm. v. Duberstein,* 363 U.S. 278 (1960), formerly applicable in the determination of whether all property transferred inter-vivos from an employer to an employee constitutes a gift, will only be applicable where the transferee employee would be the natural object of the employer's bounty.

From an employer's perspective, the Act substantially modifies an employer's ability to deduct the cost of certain employee awards. New section 274(j) defines deductible "employee achievement awards" to include only those awards made for length of service or safety achievement. In addition, an employee achievement award must be an item of tangible personal property awarded as part of a meaningful presentation and made under conditions and circumstances that do not create a significant likelihood of the payment of disguised compensation.

Section 274(j) also establishes a limit on the amount that may be deducted by an employer. The annual deduction limitation per employee is $400 for employee achievement awards that are not awarded as part of a qualified award plan. The annual deduction limitation per employee is $1,600 for employee achievement awards that are awarded as part of a qualified award plan. In no event may an employer deduct more than $1,600 per employee for all employee achievement awards made during the year. An award is not a qualified plan award where the average cost of all employee achievement awards made by the employer pursuant to a plan exceeds $400 during the taxable year.

Section 1.274-8(b) of the proposed regulations clarifies that the $1,600 deduction limitation applies in the aggregate, so that the $1,600 limitation for qualified plan awards and the $400 limitation for employee achievement awards that are not qualified plan awards cannot be added together to allow deductions exceeding $1,600 for employee achievement awards made to an employee in a taxable year.

Section 1.274-8(c)(2) of the proposed regulations provides that tangible personal property does not include cash or any gift certificate other than a nonnegotiable gift certificate conferring only the right to receive tangible personal property. The proposed regulations also give examples of what will be considered to create a significant likelihood of the payment of disguised compensation. For example, the providing of employee achievement awards in a manner that discriminates in favor of highly paid employees will be considered to be a payment of disguised compensation.

Section 1.274-8(c)(5) of the proposed regulations defines a "qualified plan award" as an employee achievement award presented pursuant to an established written award plan or program of the employer that does not discriminate as to eligibility or benefits.

Section 1.274-8(d)(1) of the proposed regulations states that the deduction limitations shall apply to a partnership as well as to each member of the partnership. Paragraph (d)(2) provides that the cost of length of service achievement awards (other than awards excludable under section 132(e)) may only be deducted by the employer if the employee has at least 5 years of service with the employer and has not received a length of service achievement award during that year or any of the 4 prior years. In addition, this paragraph clarifies that although a retirement award will be treated as having been provided for length of service achievement, it may also qualify for treatment as a de minimis fringe benefit under section 132(e) of the Code. Paragraph (d)(3) provides guidance with respect to safety achievement awards. An employer may deduct the cost of safety achievement awards only when presented to no more than 10 percent of an employer's eligible employees. Eligible employees include any employee who has worked for the employer in full time capacity for at least one year and who is not a manager, administrator, clerical employee, or other professional employee. Special rules clarify that in the case where more than 10 percent of an employer's eligible employees receive a safety achievement award, no award will be considered to be awarded for safety achievement if it cannot be determined that the award was presented before the 10 percent limitation was exceeded.

The Act specifically excludes awards qualifying as de minimis fringe benefits under section 132(e) from the requirements for length of service achievement and safety achievement. As a result, employers are not required to consider section 132(e) awards in determining whether employee achievement awards comply with the 5 year limitations for length of service achievement and the 10 percent eligible employee limitations for safety achievement.

Special Analyses

The Commissioner of Internal Revenue has determined that this proposed rule is not a major rule as defined in Executive Order 12291. Accordingly, a Regulatory Impact Analysis is not required. The Internal Revenue Service has concluded that although this document is a notice of proposed rulemaking that solicits public comment, the regulations proposed herein are interpretative and the notice and public procedure requirements of 5 U.S.C. 553 do not apply. Accordingly, no Regulatory Flexibility Analysis is required for this rule.

Comments and Requests for a Public Hearing

Before adopting these proposed regulations, consideration will be given to any written comments that are submitted (preferably eight copies) to the Commissioner of Internal Revenue. All comments will be available for public inspection and copying. A public hearing will be held upon written request to the Commissioner by any person who has submitted written comments. If a public hearing is held, notice of time and place will he published in the **Federal Register.**

Drafting Information

The principal author of these proposed regulations is Christopher J. Wilson, formerly of the Legislation and Regulations Division of the Office of Chief Counsel, Internal Revenue Service. However, personnel from other offices of the Internal Revenue Service and Treasury Department participated in developing the regulations, on matters of both substance and style.

List of Subjects in 26 CFR Parts §§ 1.61-1—1.281-4

Income taxes, Taxable income, Deductions, Exemptions.

Proposed Amendments to the Regulations

The proposed amendments to 26 CFR Part 1 are as follows:

[* * *]

§ 1.274-3 [Amended].

Par. 6. Section 1.274-3 is amended as follows:

(a) The last sentence of paragraph (b)(1) is amended by substituting "subsections (b) and (c) of section 74" for "section 74(b)".

(b) The language "recipient, or" at the end of paragraph (b)(2)(ii) is replaced by the language "recipient."

(c) Subdivisions (iii) and (iv) of paragraph (b)(2) are removed.

(d) The first, second, and fourth sentences of the flush material immediately following subdivision (iv) are removed and the last sentence is amended by substituting "sections 61, 74, 102, and 132" for "sections 61, 74, and 102".

(e) Paragraph (d) is removed and paragraphs (e), (f), and (g) are redesignated as paragraphs (d), (e), and (f).

§ 1.274-8 [Redesignated as § 1.274-9].

Par. 7. Section 1.274-8 is redesignated as § 1.274-9 and a new § 1.274-8 is added immediately following § 1.274-7 to read as set forth below.

§ 1.274-8 Disallowance of certain employee achievement award expenses.

(a) *In general.* No deduction is allowable under section 162 or 212 for any portion of the cost of an employee achievement award (as defined in section 274(j)(3)(A)) in excess of the deduction limitations of section 274(j)(2).

(b) *Deduction limitations.* The deduction for the cost of an employee achievement award made by an employer to an employee: (1) Which is not a qualified plan award, when added to the cost to the employer for all other employee achievement awards made to such employee during the taxable year which are not qualified plan awards, shall not exceed $400, and (2) which is a qualified plan award, when added to the cost to the employer for all other employee achievement awards made to such employee during the taxable year (including employee achievement awards which are not qualified plan awards), shall not exceed $1,600. Thus, the $1,600 limitation is the maximum amount that may be deducted by an employer for all employee achievement awards granted to any one employee during the taxable year.

(c) *Definitions*—(1) *Employee achievement award.* The term "employee achievement award", for purposes of this section, means an item of tangible personal property that is transferred to an employee by reason of the employee's length of service or safety achievement. The item must be awarded as part of a meaningful presentation, and under conditions and circumstances that do not create a significant likelihood of the payment of disguised compensation. For purposes of section 274(j), an award made by a sole proprietorship to the sole proprietor is not an award made to an employee.

(2) *Tangible personal property.* For purposes of this section, the term "tangible personal property" does not include cash or a certificate (other than a nonnegotiable certificate conferring only the right to receive tangible personal property). If a certificate entitles an employee to receive a reduction of the balance due on his account with the issuer of the certificate, the certificate is a negotiable certificate and is not tangible personal property for purposes of this section. Other items that will not be considered to be items of tangible personal property include vacations, meals, lodging, tickets to theater and sporting events, and stocks, bonds, and other securities.

(3) *Meaningful presentation.* Whether an award is presented as part of a meaningful presentation is determined by a facts and circumstances test. While the presentation need not be elaborate, it must be a ceremonious observance emphasizing the recipient's achievement in the area of safety or length of service.

(4) *Disguised compensation.* An award will be considered disguised compensation if the conditions and circumstances surrounding the award create a significant likelihood that it is payment of compensation. Examples include the making of employee achievement awards at the time of annual salary adjustments or as a substitute for a prior program of awarding cash bonuses, the providing of employee achievement awards in a manner that discriminates in favor of highly paid employees, or, with respect to awards the cost of which would otherwise be fully deductible by the employer under the deduction limitations of section 274(j)(2), the making of an employee achievement award the cost of which to the employer is grossly disproportionate to the fair market value of the item.

(5) *Qualified plan awards*—(i) *In general.* Except as provided in paragraph (c)(5)(ii) of this section, the term "qualified plan award" means an employee achievement award that is presented pursuant to an established written plan or program that does not discriminate in terms of eligibility or benefits in favor of highly compensated employees. See section 414(q) of the Code for the definition of highly compensated employees. Whether an award plan is established shall be determined from all the facts and circumstances of the particular case, including the frequency and timing of any changes to the plan. Whether or not an award plan is discriminatory shall be determined from all the facts and circumstances of the particular case. An award plan may fail to qualify because it is discriminatory in its actual operation even though the written provisions of the award plan are nondiscriminatory.

(ii) *Items not treated as qualified plan awards.* No award presented by an employer during the taxable year will be considered a qualified plan award if the average cost of all employee achievement awards presented during the taxable year by the taxpayer under any plan described in paragraph (c)(5)(i) of this section exceeds $400. The average cost of employee achievement awards shall be computed by dividing (A) the sum of the costs to the employer for all employee achievement awards (without regard to the deductibility of those costs) by (B) the total number of employee achievement awards presented. For purposes of the preceding sentence, employee achievement awards of nominal value shall not be taken into account in the computation of average cost. An employee achievement award that costs the employer $50 or less shall be considered to be an employee achievement award of nominal value.

(d) *Special rules*—(1) *Partnerships.* Where employee achievement awards are made by a partnership, the deduction limitations of section 274(j)(2) shall apply to the partnership as well as to each member thereof.

(2) *Length of service awards.*—An item shall not be treated as having been provided for length of service achievement if the item is presented for less than 5 years employment with the taxpayer or if the award recipient received a length of service achievement award (other than an award excludable under section 132(e)(1)) during that year or any of the prior 4 calendar years. An award presented upon the occasion of a recipient's retirement is a length of service award subject to the rules of this section. However, under appropriate circumstances, a traditional retirement award will be treated as a de minimis fringe. For example, assume that an employer provides a gold watch to each employee who completes 25 years of service with the employer. The value of the gold watch is excluded from gross income as a de minimis fringe. However, if the employer provides a gold watch to an employee who has not completed lengthy service with the employer or on an occasion other than retirement, the value of the watch is not excludable from gross income under section 132(e).

(3) *Safety achievement awards*—(i) *In general.* An item shall not be treated having been provided for safety achievement if—

(A) During the taxable year, employee achievement awards (other than awards excludable under section 132(e)(1)) for safety achievement have previously been awarded by the taxpayer to more than 10 percent of the eligible employees of the taxpayer, or

(B) Such item is awarded to a manager, administrator, clerical employee, or other professional employee.

(ii) *"Eligible employee" defined.* An eligible employee is one not described in paragraph (d)(3)(i)(B) of this section and who has worked in a full-time capacity for the taxpayer for a minimum of one year immediately preceding the date on which the safety achievement award is presented.

(iii) *Special rules.* Where safety achievement awards are presented to more than 10 percent of the taxpayer's eligible employees, only those awards presented to eligible employees before 10 percent of the taxpayer's eligible employees are exceeded shall be treated as having been provided for safety achievement. Where the only safety achievement awards presented by an employer consist of items that are presented at one time during the calendar year, then, if safety achievement awards are presented to more than 10 percent of the taxpayer's eligible employees, the taxpayer may deduct an amount equal to the product of the cost of the item (subject to the applicable deduction limitation) and 10 percent of the taxpayer's eligible employees. Except as provided in the preceding sentence, no award shall be treated as having been provided for safety achievement except to the extent that it can be reasonably demonstrated that that award was made before the 10 percent limitation was exceeded.

Lawrence B. Gibbs,

Commissioner of Internal Revenue.

[FR Doc. 89-368 Filed 1-6-89; 8:45 am]

[¶ 20,118H Reserved.—Proposed regulations on the minimum participation standards under Code Sec. 401(a)(26) were formerly reproduced at this paragraph. They were withdrawn by the IRS and replaced by new proposed regulations published in the *Federal Register* dated May 14, 1990 (55 FR 19935) and corrected on June 22, 1990 (55 FR 25673). The new proposed regulations appear at ¶ 20,121B.]

¶ 20,118I

Proposed regulations: Fringe benefits: Nondiscrimination rules.—Reproduced below are proposed regulations regarding cafeteria plans. The proposals may be relied upon by taxpayers as current working authority. The proposals affect accident and health plans, group-term life insurance and other welfare benefit plans. Note: Q-6 has been republished and A-6(c) and A-6(d) have been revised in proposed regulations reproduced at ¶ 20,227. Q-6 was also republished and A-6(b)(2), A-6(c) and A-6(d) amended in proposed regulations reproduced at ¶ 20,247. Additionally, A-6(f) has been withdrawn and replaced by Temp. Reg. § 1.125-4T(j) at ¶ 11,288E. A-6(c), A-6(c), and A-6(d) were again amended in proposed regulations reproduced at ¶ 20,258. The revised proposed regulations were published in the *Federal Register* on November 7, 1997 (62 FR 60196), March 23, 2000 (65 FR 15587), and January 10, 2001 (66 FR 1923).

Proposed regulations on compliance with Code Sec. 89 nondiscrimination rules, which were issued along with the proposals under Code Sec. 125, have been removed because Code Sec. 89 was retroactively repealed by P.L. 101-140.

The proposed regulations were published in the Federal Register on March 7, 1989 (54 FR 9460), and withdrawn on August 6, 2007 (72 FR 43938).

[¶ 20,119 Reserved.—Proposed Reg. §§1.406-1 and 1.407-1, relating to plans of certain subsidiaries, were formerly reproduced at this point. The final regulations appear at ¶ 11,961 and 12,011.]

[¶ 20,120 Reserved.—Proposed Reg. §§1.46-1, 1.50A-1, 1.72-17, 1.72-17A, 1.401-13, 1.401-14, 1.401(e)-1, 1.401(e)-2, 1.401(e)-3, 1.401(e)-4, 1.401(e)-5, 1.401(e)-6, 1.404(e)-1 and 1.404(e)-1A, relating to contributions to pension, profit-sharing, etc., plans on behalf of self-employed individuals and shareholder-employees were formerly reproduced at this point. The final regulations appear at ¶ 11,207, 11,207A, 11,713, 11,724, 11,724A, 11,724B, 11,724C, 11,724D, 11,724E, 11,868, and 11,869.]

¶ 20,121

Proposed regulations: Treatment of certain lump sum distributions.—Reproduced below are proposed amendments to conform regulations under sections 62, 72, 101, 122, 402, 403, 405, 652, and 1304 of the Internal Revenue Code of 1954 to the provisions of the Employee Retirement Income Security Act (P.L. 93-406), relating to taxation of certain lump sum distributions. The proposed regulations will provide a method of computing the capital gain portion of a lump sum distribution and will impose a separate tax on the ordinary income portion of a lump sum distribution. The ordinary income portion of a distribution to a recipient will be deductible from gross income equal to the amount of the ordinary income portion of the distribution included in the recipient's gross income. The proposed changes also provide a special method for computing tax on a distribution which includes an annuity contract. Under the proposed changes, a distribution to multiple recipients cannot qualify as a lump sum distribution unless the amount of the distribution is otherwise includible in the income of the individual in respect of whom the distribution was made under the judicial doctrines of assignment of income or constructive receipt. Finally, the proposed regulations redefine "active participation," as it relates to an employee in a particular plan who receives a lump sum distribution.

The proposed regulations were published in the Federal Register of April 30, 1975 at 40 F.R. 18798. Official corrections, published in the Federal Register of May 23, 1975 (40 F.R. 22548), have been made in place in the proposed regulations.

Notice is hereby given that the regulations set forth in tentative form [below] are proposed to be prescribed by the Commissioner of Internal

Revenue, with the approval of the Secretary of the Treasury or his delegate. Prior to the final adoption of such regulations, consideration will be given to any comments pertaining thereto which are submitted in writing (preferably six copies) to the Commissioner of Internal Revenue, Attention: CC:LR:T, Washington, D.C. 20224, by June 16, 1975. Pursuant to 26 CFR 601.601(b), designations of material as confidential or not to be disclosed, contained in such comments, will not be accepted. Thus, a person submitting written comments should not include therein material that he considers to be confidential or inappropriate for disclosure to the public. It will be presumed by the Internal Revenue Service that every written comment submitted to it in response to this notice of proposed rule making is intended by the person submitting it to be subject in its entirety to public inspection and copying in accordance with the procedures of 26 CFR 601.702(d)(9). Any person submitting written comments who desires an opportunity to comment orally at a public hearing on these proposed regulations should submit his request, in writing, to the Commissioner by June 16, 1975. In such case, a public hearing will be held, and notice of the time, place, and date will be published in a subsequent issue of the Federal Register unless the person or persons who have requested a hearing withdraw their requests for a hearing before notice of the hearing has been filed with the Office of the Federal Register. The proposed regulations are to be issued under the authority contained in sections 402(a)(2), 402(e) and 7805 of the Internal Revenue Code of 1954 (88 Stat. 990, 987 and 68A Stat. 917; 26 U.S.C. 402(a)(2), 402(e), 7805).

(Signed) Donald C. Alexander

Commissioner of Internal Revenue

Preamble

This document proposes amendments to the Income Tax Regulations (26 CFR Part 1) in order to conform the regulations under sections 62, 72, 101, 122, 402, 403, 405, 652, and 1304 of the Internal Revenue Code of 1954 to the provisions of section 2005 of the Employee Retirement Income Security Act of 1974 (Public Law 93-406, 88 Stat. 987), relating to taxation of certain lump sum distributions.

The amendments proposed relating to sections 62, 72, 101, 122, 403, 405, 652, and 1304 of the Code merely conform the regulations under those sections to the changes in the taxation of a lump sum distribution under section 402 of the Code, as amended by section 2005(a) of the Act.

Under section 402(a)(2) of the Code, as amended, a method of computing the capital gain portion of a lump sum distribution is provided. In general, the capital gain portion of a lump sum distribution will be an amount equal to the product of the total taxable amount of the lump sum distribution and a fraction, the numerator of which is the number of calendar years of active participation before January 1, 1974, and the denominator of which is the total number of calendar years of active participation.

Under section 402(e)(1) of the Code, as amended, a separate tax is imposed on the ordinary income portion of a lump sum distribution.

Under section 402(e)(2) of the Code, as amended, a special rule is provided for computing the separate tax on the ordinary income portion of a lump sum distribution if there have been one or more lump sum distributions after December 31, 1973, made with respect to the recipient within the 6-taxable-year period ending on the last day of the taxable year of the recipient in which the distribution is made.

Under section 402(e)(3) of the Code, as amended, a deduction is allowed from gross income equal to the amount of the ordinary income portion of the distribution included in the recipient's gross income.

Under section 402(e)(4) of the Code, as amended, definitions and special rules are provided for computing the separate tax, including the definition of a lump sum distribution and the computation of the ordinary income portion of a lump sum distribution.

Under proposed § 1.402(e)-2(c)(1), a special method for computing the separate tax on a distribution including an annuity contract is provided. In such a case, the adjusted total taxable amount must be determined. For taxable years beginning before January 1, 1975, the adjusted total taxable amount is defined as the sum of the total taxable amount of the lump sum distribution for the taxable year, and the current actuarial value of annuity contracts distributed to the recipient reduced by the portion of the net amount contributed by the employee which is allocable to the annuity contract. For taxable years beginning after December 31, 1974, the adjusted total taxable amount is defined as the sum of the total taxable amount of the lump sum distribution for the taxable year, and the current actuarial value of annuity contracts distributed to the recipient reduced by the excess of the net amount contributed by the employee over the cash and other property distributed.

Under proposed § 1.402(e)-2(d)(1) a distribution to multiple recipients (except a payment or distribution solely to two or more trusts) cannot qualify as a lump sum distribution unless the amount of the distribution is otherwise includible in the income of the individual in respect of whom the distribution was made under the judicial doctrines of assignment of income or constructive receipt of income.

Under proposed § 1.402(e)-2(d)(3), the term "active participation" is defined so that active participation commences with the first month in which an employee becomes a participant under the plan and ends with the earliest of (1) the month in which the employee receives a lump sum distribution under the plan, (2) in the case of an employee without regard to section 401(e)(1), the month in which the employee separates from the service of the employer, (3) the month in which the employee dies, or (4) in the case of a self-employed individual who receives a lump sum distribution on account of disability, the first month in which he becomes disabled.

It is contemplated that upon adoption of the proposed amendments the Temporary Income Tax Regulations under section 402(e)(4)(B) (§ 11.402(e)(4)(B-1) will be revoked.

Proposed amendments to the regulations

In order to conform the Income Tax Regulations (26 CFR Part 1) to the provisions of section 2005 of the Employee Retirement Income Security Act of 1974 (Public Law 93-406, 88 Stat. 987), such regulations are amended as follows:

[INCOME TAX REGULATIONS]

Paragraph 1. Section 1.62 is amended by adding a new paragraph (11) at the end thereof and revising the historical note. These added and revised provisions read as follows:

* * *

[Asterisks represent 1954 Code Sec. 62 as amended by sec. 7(b), Self-Employed Individuals Tax Retirement Act 1962 (76 Stat. 828); sec. 213(b) Rev. Act 1964 (78 Stat. 52); sec. 2005(c)(9) Employee Retirement Income Security Act 1974 (88 Stat. 992)]

Par. 2 Reserved. Proposed Reg. § 1.62-1(c)(14), on the deduction for the ordinary income portion of lump-sum distributions, was formerly reproduced at this point. The final regulation appears at ¶ 11,181.

Par. 3. Subdivision (i) of § 1.72-4(a)(1) is amended by deleting "72(o)" and inserting in lieu thereof "72(n)". As amended, § 1.724(a)(1)(i) reads as follows:

§ 1.72-4 Exclusion ratio.

(a) *General rule.* (1)(i) To determine the proportionate part of the total amount received each year as an annuity which is excludable from the gross income of a recipient in the taxable year of receipt (other than amounts received under (A) certain employee annuities described in section 72(d) and § 1.72-13, or (B) certain annuities described in section 72(n) and § 1.122-1), an exclusion ratio is to be determined for each contract. In general, this ratio is determined by dividing the investment in the contract as found under § 1.72-6 by the expected return under such contract as found under § 1.72-5. Where a single consideration is given for a particular contract which provides for two or more annuity elements, an exclusion ratio shall be determined for the contract as a whole by dividing the investment in such contract by the aggregate of the expected returns under all the annuity elements provided thereunder. However, where the provisions of paragraph (b)(3) of § 1.72-2 apply to payments received under such a contract, see paragraph (b)(3) of § 1.72-6.

Par. 4. Section 1.72-13(e)(3) is amended by deleting "72(o)" and inserting in lieu thereof "72(n)". As amended § 1.72-13(e)(3) reads as follows:

§ 1.72-13 Special rule for employee contributions recoverable in three years.

* * *

(e) *Inapplicability of section 72(d) and this section.* Section 72(d) and this section do not apply to: * * *

(3) Amounts paid to an annuitant under chapter 73 of title 10 of the United States Code with respect to which section 72(n) and § 1.122-1 apply.

Par. 5. Section 1.101 is amended by revising subsection (b)(2)(B) and the historical note. As amended, these revised provisions read as follows:

* * *

[Asterisks represent 1954 Code Sec. 101 as amended by sec. 23(d), Technical Amendments Act 1958 (72 Stat. 1622); sec. 7(c), Self-Employed Individuals Tax Retirement Act 1962 (80 Stat. 32); sec. 101(j)(1), Tax Reform Act 1969 (Public Law 91-172, 83 Stat. 655); sec. 2005(c)(15), Employee Retirement Income Security Act 1974 (88 Stat. 992)]

Par. 6. Paragraph (d) of §1.101-2 is amended by revising subparagraph (3)(i) and examples (2), (3), and (4) of subparagraph (ii) to read as follows:

§1.101-2 Employees' death benefits.

* * *

(d) *Nonforfeitable rights.* * * *

(3)(i) Notwithstanding the rule stated in subparagraph (d)(1) of this paragraph and illustrated in subparagraph (2) of this section, the exclusion from gross income provided by section 101(b) applies to a lump sum distribution (as defined in section 402(e)(4)(A) and the regulations thereunder) with respect to which the deceased employee possessed, immediately before his death, a nonforfeitable right to receive the amounts while living (see section 101(b)(2)(B)(i) and (ii)). See paragraph (d)(4) of this section relating to the exclusion of amounts which are received under annuity contracts purchased by certain exempt organizations and with respect to which the deceased employee possessed, immediately before his death, a nonforfeitable right to receive the amounts while living.

(ii) The application of the provisions of paragraph (d)(3)(i) of this section may be illustrated by the following examples:

Example (2). The trustee of the X Corporation noncontributory, "qualified," profit-sharing plan is required under the provisions of the plan to pay to the beneficiary of B, an employee of the X Corporation who died on July 1, 1974, the benefit due on account of the death of B. The provisions of the profit-sharing plan give each participating employee, in case of termination of employment, a 10 percent vested interest in the amount accumulated in his account for each of the first 10 years of participation in the plan, but, in case of death, the entire balance to the credit of the participant's account is to be paid to his beneficiary. At the time of B's death he had been a participant for five years. The accumulation in his account was $8,000 and the amount which would have been distributable to him in the event of termination of employment was $4,000 (50 percent of $8,000). After his death, $8,000 is paid to his beneficiary in a lump sum. (it may he noted that these are the same facts as in example (5) of subparagraph (2) of this paragraph except that the employee has been a participant for five years instead of three and the plan is a "qualified" plan.) It is immaterial that the employee had a nonforfeitable right to $4,000 because the payment of the $8,000 to the beneficiary is the payment of a lump sum distribution to which subdivision (i) of this subparagraph applies. Assuming no other death benefits are involved, the beneficiary may exclude $5,000 of the $8,000 payment from gross income.

Example (3). The facts are the same as in example (2) except that the beneficiary is entitled to receive only the $4,000 to which the employee had a nonforfeitable right and elects, 30 days after B's death, to receive it over a period of ten years. Because the distribution is not a lump sum distribution and because B's interest is nonforfeitable, no exclusion from gross income is allowable with respect to the $4,000.

Example (4). The X Corporation instituted a trust, forming part of a "qualified" profit-sharing plan for its employees, the cost thereof being borne entirely by the corporation. The plan provides, in part, that if an employee leaves the employ of the corporation, either voluntarily or involuntarily, before retirement, 10 percent of the account balance provided for the employee in the trust fund will be paid to the employee for each of the first 10 years of service. The plan further provides that if an employee dies before reaching retirement age, his beneficiary will receive a percentage of the account balance provided for the employee in the trust fund, on the same basis as shown in the preceding sentence. A, an employee of the X Corporation for 5 years, died before attaining retirement age while in the employ of the corporation. At the time of his death, $15,000 was the account balance provided for him in the trust fund. His beneficiary receives $7,500 in a lump sum, an amount equal to 50 percent of the account balance provided for A's retirement. The beneficiary may exclude from gross income (assuming no other death benefits are involved) $5,000 of the $7,500, since the latter amount constitutes a lump sum distribution to which subdivision (i) of this subparagraph applies.

Par. 7. Section 1.122 is amended by deleting "72(o)" in section 122(b)(2) and inserting in lieu thereof "72(n)". As amended, §1.122(b)(2) reads as follows:

* * *

[Asterisks represent 1954 Code Sec. 122 as added by Sec. 1(a)(1), Act of Mar. 8, 1966 (80 Stat. 32); as amended by sec. 2005(c)(10), Employed Retirement Income Security Act 1974 (88 Stat. 992)]

Par. 8. Section 1.122-1 is amended by deleting "72(o)" each place it appears and inserting in lieu thereof "72(n)". As amended, §1.122-1(b)(2)(ii) and examples (2) and (3) of §1.122-1(d) read as follows:

§1.122-1 Applicable rules relating to certain reduced uniformed services retirement pay.

* * *

(b) *Rule applicable after December 31, 1965*

(2)

(ii) Upon the death of a member or former member of the uniformed services, where the "consideration for the contract" (as described in paragraph (b)(2)(iii) of this section) has not been excluded in whole or in part from gross income under section 122(b) and (b)(2)(i) of this section, the survivor of such member who is receiving an annuity under chapter 73 of title 10 of the United States Code shall, after December 31, 1965, exclude from gross income under section 72(n) and this subdivision such annuity payments received after December 31, 1965, until there has been so excluded annuity payments equalling the portion of the "consideration for the contract" not previously excluded under paragraph (b)(2)(i) of this section.

* * *

(d) *Examples.* The rules discussed in paragraph (a) of this section may be illustrated by the following examples:

* * *

Example (2). Assume the facts in Example (1) except that A retires on disability resulting from active service and his disability is rated at 40 percent. The entire amount of disability retirement pay, prior to and including 1966, is excludable from gross income under sections 104(a)(4) and 105(d), and in 1966, section 122(a). Assume further that A attains retirement age on December 31, 1966, dies on January 1, 1967, and his widow then begins receiving a survivor annuity under the Retired Serviceman's Family Protection Plan (10 U.S.C. 1431). A's widow may exclude from gross income in 1967 and 1968 under section 72(n) and paragraph (b)(2)(ii) of this section, the $1,800 of "consideration for the contract" i.e., the reductions in 1963, 1964, and 1965 to provide the survivor annuity. Thus, A's widow will exclude all of the survivor annuity she receives in 1967 ($1,350) and $450 of the $1,350 annuity received in 1968. In addition, if A had not attained retirement age at the time of his death, his widow would, under section 101 and paragraph (a)(2) of §1.101-2, exclude up to $5,000 subject to the limitations of paragraph (b)(2)(ii) of this section.

Example (3). Assume, in the previous example, that A dies on January 1, 1965, and his widow then begins receiving a survivor annuity. Assume further that A's widow is entitled to exclude under section 72(b) $1,000 of the $1,350 she received in 1965. Under section 72(n) and paragraph (b)(2)(ii) of this section, A's widow for 1966 will exclude the $200 remaining consideration for the contract ($1,200 – $1,000) and will include $1,150 of the survivor annuity in gross income.

* * *

Par. 9. Section 1.402(a) is amended by revising subparagraph (2) and the historical note. As amended, these revised provisions read as follows:

* * *

[Asterisks represent 1954 Code Sec. 402(a) as amended by Sec. 4(c) Self-Employed Individuals Tax Retirement Act 1962 (76 Stat. 825); sec. 221(c)(1), Rev. Act 1964 (78 Stat. 75); sec. 2005(b)(1), Employee Retirement Income Security Act 1974 (88 Stat. 990)]

Par. 10. Section 1.402(a)-1 is amended by revising paragraphs (a)(1)(ii), (a)(1)(iii), (a)(2), (a)(5), (a)(6), (a)(7), (a)(9), and (b)(1) to read as follows:

§1.402(a)-1 Taxability of beneficiary under a trust which meets the requirements of section 401(a).

(a) *In general.* (1) * * *

(ii) The provisions of section 402(a) relate only to distribution by a trust which is described in section 401(a) and which is exempt under section 501(a) for the taxable year of the trust in which the distribution is made. With three exceptions, the distribution from such an exempt trust when received or made available is taxable to the distributee or recipient to the extent provided in section 72 (relating to annuities).

First, for taxable years beginning before January 1, 1964, section 72(e)(3) (relating to the treatment of certain lump sums), as in effect before such date, shall not apply to such distributions. For taxable years beginning after December 31, 1963, such distributions may be taken into account in computations under sections 1301 through 1305 (relating to income averaging). For treatment of such total distributions, see paragraph (a)(6) of this section. Secondly, if the taxable year ends after December 31, 1969 and begins before January 1, 1974, the portion of the distribution treated as long-term capital gain is subject to the limitation under section 402(a)(5), as in effect on December 31, 1973. Thirdly, for taxable years beginning after December 31, 1973, a certain portion, described in section 402(a)(2), of a lump sum distribution, as defined in section 402(e)(4)(A) is taxable as long-term capital gain and a certain portion, described in section 402(e)(4)(E), may be taxable under section 402(e). For the treatment of such lump sum distributions, see paragraph (a)(9) of this section. Under certain circumstances, an amount representing the unrealized appreciation in the value of the securities of the employer is excludable from gross income for the year of distribution. For the rules relating to such exclusion, see paragraph (b) of this section. Furthermore, the exclusion provided by section 105(b) is applicable to a distribution from a trust described in section 401(a) and exempt under section 501(a) if such distribution constitutes wages or payments in lieu of wages for a period during which an employee is absent from work on account of a personal injury or sickness. See § 1.72-15 for the rules relating to the tax treatment of accident or health benefits received under a plan to which section 72 applies.

(iii) Except as provided in paragraph (b) of this section, a distribution of property (other than an annuity contract) by a trust described in section 401(a) and exempt under section 501(a) shall be taken into account by the recipient at its fair market value. For valuation of an annuity contract, see § 1.402(e)-2(c)(1)(ii)(F).

(2) If a trust described in section 401(a) and exempt under section 501(a) purchases an annuity contract for an employee and distributes it to the employee in a year for which the trust is exempt, and the contract contains a cash surrender value which may be available to an employee by surrendering the contract, such cash surrender value will not be considered income to the employee unless and until the contract is surrendered. For the rule as to nontransferability of annuity contracts issued after 1962, see paragraph (b)(1) of § 1.401-9. However, the distribution of an annuity contract must be treated as a lump sum distribution under section 402(e) for purposes of determining the separate tax imposed under section 402(e)(1)(A). If, however, the contract distributed by such exempt trust is a retirement income, endowment, or other life insurance contract and is distributed after October 26, 1956, the entire cash value of such contract at the time of distribution must be included in the distributee's income in accordance with the provisions of section 402(a), except to the extent that, within 60 days after the distribution of such contract, (i) all or any portion of such value is irrevocably converted into a contract under which no part of any proceeds payable on death at any time would be excludable under section 101(a) (relating to life insurance proceeds), or (ii) such contract is treated as a rollover contribution under section 402(a)(5), as in effect after December 31, 1973. If the contract distributed by such trust is a transferable annuity contract issued after 1962, or a retirement income, endowment, or other life insurance contract which is distributed after 1962 (whether or not transferable), then notwithstanding the preceding sentence the entire cash value of the contract is includible in the distributee's gross income, unless within such 60 days such contract is also made nontransferable.

(5) If pension or annuity payments or other benefits are paid or made available to the beneficiary of a deceased employee or a deceased retired employee by a trust described in section 401(a) which is exempt under section 501(a), such amounts are taxable in accordance with the rules of section 402(a) and this section. In case such amounts are taxable under section 72, the "investment in the contract" shall be determined by reference to the amount contributed by the employee and by applying the applicable rules of sections 72 and 101(b)(2)(D). In case the amounts paid to, or includible in the gross income of, the beneficiaries of the deceased employee or deceased retired employee constitute a distribution to which paragraph (6) or (9) (whichever applies) of this section is applicable the extent to which the distribution is taxable is determined by reference to the contributions of the employee, by reference to any prior distributions which were excludable from gross income as a return of employee contributions, and by applying the applicable rules of sections 72 and 101(b).

(6) This subparagraph applies in the case of a total distribution made in a taxable year of the distributee or payee ending before January 1, 1970.

(i) If the total distributions payable with respect to any employee under a trust described in section 401(a) which in the year of distribution is exempt under section 501(a) are paid to, or includible in the gross income of, the distributee within one taxable year of the distributee on account of the employee's death or other separation from the service, or death after such separation from service, the amount of such distribution, to the extent it exceeds the net amount contributed by the employee, shall be considered a gain from the sale or exchange of a capital asset held for more than six months. The total distributions payable are includible in the gross income of the distributee within one taxable year if they are made available to such distributee and the distributee fails to make a timely election under section 72(h) to receive an annuity in lieu of such total distributions. The "net amount contributed by the employee" is the amount actually contributed by the employee plus any amounts considered to be contributed by the employee under the rules of section 72(f), 101(b), and paragraph (a)(3) of this section, reduced by any amounts theretofore distributed to him which were excludable from gross income as a return of employee contributions. See, however, paragraph (b) of this section for rules relating to the exclusion of amounts representing net unrealized appreciation in the value of securities of the employer corporation. In addition, all or part of the amount otherwise includible in gross income under this paragraph by a nonresident alien individual in respect of a distribution by the United States under a qualified pension plan may be excludable from gross income under section 402(a)(4). For rules relating to such exclusion, see paragraph (c) of this section. For additional rules relating to the treatment of total distributions described in this subdivision in the case of a nonresident alien individual, see sections 871 and 1441 and the regulations thereunder.

(7) The capital gains treatment provided by section 402(a)(2), as in effect for taxable years beginning before January 1, 1974, and subparagraph (a)(6) of this section is not applicable to distributions paid during such years to a distributee to the extent such distributions are attributable to contributions made on behalf of an employee while he was a self-employed individual in the business with respect to which the plan was maintained. For the taxation of such amounts, see § 1.72-18. For the rules for determining the amount attributable to contributions on behalf of an employee while he was self-employed, see paragraphs (b)(4) and (c)(2) of such section.

* * *

(9) For taxable years beginning after December 31, 1973, in the case of a lump sum distribution (as defined in section 402(e)(4)(A)) made to a recipient which is an individual, estate, or trust, so much of the total taxable amount (as defined in section 402(e)(4)(D) and § 1.402(e)-2(d)(2)) of such lump sum distribution as is equal to the product of such total taxable amount multiplied by a fraction—

(i) The numerator of which is the number of calendar years of active participation (as determined under § 1.402(e)-2(d)(3)(ii)) by the employee in such plan before January 1, 1974, and

(ii) The denominator of which is the number of calendar years of active participation (as determined under § 1.402(e)-2(d)(3)(ii)) by the employee in such plan, shall be treated as gain from the sale or exchange of a capital asset held for more than six months. For purposes of this subparagraph, in the case of an individual who at no time during his participation under the plan is an employee within the meaning of section 401(c)(1), determination of whether any distribution is a lump sum distribution shall be made without regard to the requirement that an election be made under section 402(e)(4)(B) and § 1.402(e)-3.

(b) *Distributions including securities of the employer corporation*—(1) *In general.* (i) If a trust described in section 401(a) which is exempt under section 501(a) makes a distribution to a distributee, and such distribution includes securities of the employer corporation, the amount of any net unrealized appreciation in such securities shall be excluded from the distributee's income in the year of such distribution to the following extent:

(A) If the distribution constitutes a total distribution to which the regulations of paragraph (a)(6) of this section are applicable, or if the distribution would constitute a lump sum distribution as defined in section 402(e)(4)(A) (without regard to section 402(e)(4)(H)), the amount to be excluded is the entire net unrealized appreciation attributable to that part of the distribution which consists of securities of the employer corporation; and

(B) If the distribution is other than a total distribution to which paragraph (a)(6) of this section is applicable, or if the distribution is other than a lump sum distribution as defined in section 402(e)(4)(A) (without regard to section 402(e)(4)(H)), the amount to be excluded is that portion of the net unrealized appreciation in the securities of the employer corporation which is attributable to the amount considered to be contributed by the employee to the purchase of such securities.

The amount of net unrealized appreciation which is excludable under the regulations of (b)(1)(i)(A) and (B) of this section shall not be included in the basis of the securities in the hands of the distributee at the time of distribution for purposes of determining gain or loss on their subsequent disposition. Further, the amount of net unrealized appreciation which is not included in the basis of the securities in the hands of the distributee at the time of distribution shall be considered as a gain from the sale or exchange of a capital asset held for more than six months to the extent that such appreciation is realized in a subsequent taxable transaction. However, if the net gain realized by the distributee in a subsequent taxable transaction exceeds the amount of the net unrealized appreciation at the time of distribution, such excess shall constitute a long-term or short-term capital gain depending upon the holding period of the securities in the hands of the distributee.

(ii) (A) For purposes of section 402(a) and of this section, the term "securities" means only shares of stock and bonds or debentures issued by a corporation with interest coupons or in registered form, and the term "securities of the employer corporation" includes securities of a parent or subsidiary corporation (as defined in subsections (e) and (f) of section 425) of the employer corporation.

(B) For purposes of this paragraph, for taxable years beginning after December 31, 1973, the term "distributee means recipient".

Par. 11. Section 1.402(e) is amended to read as follows:

* * *

[Asterisks represent 1954 Code Sec. 402]

Par. 12. There are added immediately after § 1.402(e)-1 the following new sections:

§ 1.402(e)-2 Treatment of certain lump sum distributions made after 1973.

(a) *In general.* (1) *Tax imposed; deduction allowed.* For a taxable year, at the election of the recipient of a lump sum distribution, the ordinary income portion of such distribution is subject to the tax imposed by section 402(e)(1)(A) (hereinafter referred to as the "separate tax") and, under section 402(e)(3), an amount equal to such portion is allowable as a deduction from gross income (see section 62 (11), as added by sec. 2005(c)(9) of Pub. L. No. 93-406, and the regulations thereunder) to the extent such portion is included in the gross income of the taxpayer for such year. The separate tax imposed by section 402(e)(1)(A) is an addition to the tax otherwise imposed under chapter 1 of the Code and may be elected whether or not the tax otherwise imposed by such chapter is computed under part I of subchapter Q of such chapter (relating to income averaging). This section applies with respect to distributions or payments made, or made available, to a recipient after December 31, 1973, in taxable years of the recipient beginning after that date.

(2) *Cross references—*(i) *Computation; ordinary method.* Paragraph (b) of this section provides rules with respect to a distribution which is not a multiple distribution, and does not include an annuity contract.

(ii) *Computation; special method (distribution including an annuity contract).* Paragraph (c)(1) of this section provides rules with respect to a distribution which is not a multiple distribution and which includes an annuity contract.

(iii) *Computation; special method (multiple distribution).* Paragraph (c)(2) of this section provides rules with respect to a distribution which is a multiple distribution.

(iv) *Lump sum distribution.* For the definition of the term "lump sum distribution", see paragraph (d)(1) of this section.

(v) *Total taxable amount.* For the definition of the term "total taxable amount," see paragraph (d)(2) of this section.

(vi) *Ordinary income portion.* For the definition of the term "ordinary income portion," see paragraph (d)(3) of this section.

(vii) *Multiple distribution.* For the definition of the term "multiple distribution," see paragraph (c)(2)(ii)(E) of this section.

(viii) *Election.* For rules relating to the election of lump sum distribution treatment under this section, see § 1.402(e)-3.

(b) *Ordinary method—*(1) *In general.* In the case of a distribution which is not included in a multiple distribution, and which does not include an annuity contract, if the recipient elects (under § 1.402(e)-3) to treat such distribution as a lump sum distribution under this section, the tax imposed by section 402(e)(1)(A) for the recipient's taxable year is an amount equal to the initial separate tax determined under subparagraph (2) of this paragraph) for such taxable year, multiplied by a fraction—

(i) The numerator of which is the ordinary income portion (determined under paragraph (d)(3) of this section) of such lump sum distribution for such taxable year, and

(ii) The denominator of which is the total taxable amount (determined under paragraph (d)(2) of this section) of such lump sum distribution for such taxable year.

(2) *Computation of initial separate tax.* For purposes of subparagraph (1) of this paragraph, the initial separate tax is an amount equal to 10 times the tax which would be imposed by section 1(c) (relating to unmarried individuals (other than surviving spouses and heads of households)) if the recipient were an individual referred to in such section and the taxable income referred to in such section were an amount equal to one-tenth of the excess of—

(i) The total taxable amount (determined under paragraph (d)(2) of this section) of the lump sum distribution, over

(ii) The minimum distribution allowance (determined under paragraph (b)(3) of this section).

(3) *Computation of minimum distribution allowance.* For purposes of paragraph (b)(2)(ii) of this section, the minimum distribution allowance is the lesser of—

(i) $10,000, or

(ii) One-half of the total taxable amount of the lump sum distribution for the taxable year,

reduced (but not below zero) by 20 percent of the excess (if any) of such total taxable amount over $20,000.

(4) *Example.* The application of this paragraph is illustrated by the following example:

Example. (i) On December 22, 1975, A separates from the service of the M Corporation and receives a lump sum distribution of $65,000 from the M Corporation's contributory qualified plan. A's contributions to the plan as an employee were $15,000. A has been an active participant in the plan since February 20, 1966. A and his wife, B, are each age 50. Neither received an annuity contract from a qualified plan in 1974 or 1975. Neither received a lump sum distribution in 1974. A and B file a joint return for the calendar year 1975. Their income for 1975 consists of A's salary of $15,000 from the M Corporation and of $5,000 from the N Corporation. Their deductions for 1975 (other than deductions attributable to the distribution) consist of itemized deductions of $3,000. Their average base period income (determined under section 1302(b)(1)) for the four preceding taxable years (1971 through 1974) is $14,000. Assuming there are no changes in the applicable tax law after 1974, A and B's income tax liability for 1975 is computed as follows.

(ii) A and B's gross income for 1975 is $70,000, computed by adding the total taxable amount of the lump sum distribution (determined under paragraph (d)(2) of this section) to their otherwise computed gross income [$15,000 + $5,000 + ($65,000 – $15,000)]. Their adjusted gross income for 1975 is $40,000 [$70,000 – ($10,000 + $20,000)] computed by reducing their gross income by the sum of the lump sum distribution deduction allowed by section 402(e)(3) with respect to the ordinary income portion of the distribution [$50,000 x 24/120] and the deduction allowed by section 1202 with respect to the capital gains portion of the distribution [($50,000 × 96/120) x 0.5]. A and B's joint taxable income is $35,500 (their itemized deductions are $3,000 and their personal exemptions total $1,500). A and B choose to apply the income averaging rules of section 1301 for 1975. Thus, A and B's income tax liability not including the separate tax on the ordinary income portion of the distribution is $8,828.

(iii) The minimum distribution allowance with respect to A's distribution is $4,000 [$10,000 – (($50,000 – $20,000) × 0.2)]. The initial separate tax on A's distribution is 10 times the tax imposed by section 1(c), computed as if the taxable income therein described were

$$\frac{\$4,600 \qquad [\$50,000 - \$4,000].}{10}$$

Thus, A's initial separate tax is $8,160. The separate tax on A's distribution is computed by multiplying the initial separate tax and the quotient of the ordinary income portion divided by the total taxable amount. Thus, the separate tax on A's distribution is $1,632 [$8,160 × $10,000/$50,000].

(iv) A and B's total income tax liability for 1975 is the sum of the income tax as otherwise determined and the separate tax. Thus, A and B's total income tax liability for 1975 is $10,460 [$8,828 + $1,632].

(c) *Special method*—(1) *Computation of separate tax on distribution including annuity contract and lump sum distribution*—(i) *Computation.* In the case of a distribution which is not included in a multiple distribution and which includes an annuity contract, if the recipient elects (under §1.402(e)-3) to treat the portion of such distribution not consisting of an annuity contract as a lump sum distribution under this section, the separate tax imposed by section 402(e)(l)(A) of the recipient's taxable year is the excess (if any) of the adjusted separate tax over the tax attributable to the annuity contract (determined under paragraph (c)(1)(iii) of this section).

(ii) *Definitions.* For purposes of this section—

(A) *Adjusted separate tax.* The adjusted separate tax is an amount equal to the adjusted initial separate tax multiplied by a fraction—

(*1*) The numerator of which is the ordinary income portion of the distribution, and

(*2*) The denominator of which is the total taxable amount (determined under paragraph (d)(2) of this section) of the lump sum distribution.

(B) *Adjusted initial separate tax.* The adjusted initial separate tax is an amount equal to 10 times the tax which would be imposed by section 1(c) (relating to unmarried individuals (other than surviving spouses and heads of households)) if the recipient were an individual referred to in such section and the taxable income referred to in such section were an amount equal to one-tenth of the excess of—

(*1*) the adjusted total taxable amount of the lump sum distribution, over

(*2*) the adjusted minimum distribution allowance.

(C) *Adjusted total taxable amount.* (*1*) For taxable years beginning before January 1, 1975, the adjusted total taxable amount is the sum of—

(*i*) The excess (if any) of the current actuarial value of annuity contracts distributed to the recipient, over the portion of the net amount contributed by the employee which is allocable to the contract, and

(*ii*) The total taxable amount (determined under paragraph (d)(2) of this section) of the lump sum distribution for the taxable year. For purposes of (c)(1)(ii)(C)(*1*)(*i*) of this section (*1*), the net amount contributed by the employee which is allocable to the contract is an amount equal to the amounts considered contributed by the employee under the plan (determined by applying sections 72(f) and 101(b), and paragraph (b) of §1.72-16) reduced by any amount theretofore distributed to the employee which were [sicl not includible in his gross income multiplied by a fraction, the numerator of which is the current actuarial value of the contract, and the denominator of which is the sum of such current actuarial value and the value of other property (including cash) distributed.

(*2*) For taxable years beginning after December 31, 1974, the adjusted total taxable amount is the sum of—

(*i*) The current actuarial value of annuity contracts distributed to the recipient, reduced by the excess, if any, of the net amount contributed by the employee (as defined in paragraph (d)(2)(ii)(A) of this section) over the cash and other property distributed, and

(*ii*) The total taxable amount (determined under paragraph (d)(2) of this section) of the lump sum distribution for the taxable year.

(D) *Adjusted ordinary income portion.* The adjusted ordinary income portion of a lump sum distribution is the amount which would be computed under (3) of paragraph (d)(3) of this section if "adjusted total taxable amount" is substituted for "total taxable amount" in such subparagraph.

(E) *Adjusted minimum distribution allowance.* The adjusted minimum distribution allowance is the lesser of—

(*1*) $10,000, or

(*2*) one-half of the adjusted total taxable amount of the lump sum distribution for the taxable year,

reduced (but not below zero) by 20 percent of the excess (if any) of the adjusted total taxable amount over $20,000.

(F) *Current actuarial value.* The current actuarial value of an annuity contract is the greater of—

(*1*) The cash value of the annuity contract (determined without regard to any loans under the contract) on the date of distribution, or

(*2*) The amount determined under the appropriate tables contained in publication No. 861, entitled "Annuity Factors for Lump Sum Distributions."

(iii) *Tax attributable to an annuity contract.* For purposes of subdivision (i) of this subparagraph, the tax attributable to an annuity contract is the product of—

(A) The quotient of the adjusted ordinary income portion (determined under paragraph (c)(1)(ii)(D) of this section) of the lump sum distribution divided by the adjusted total taxable amount (determined under paragraph (c)(1)(ii)(C) of this section), and

(B) 10 times the tax which would be imposed by section 1(c) (relating to unmarried individuals (other than surviving spouses and heads of households)) if the recipient were an individual referred to in such section and the taxable income were an amount equal to one-tenth of the excess of—

(*1*) The current actuarial value of the annuity contract, over

(*2*) The adjusted minimum distribution allowance multiplied by a fraction—

(*i*) The numerator of which is the current actuarial value of the annuity contract, and

(*ii*) The denominator of which is the adjusted total taxable amount (determined under paragraph (c)(1)(ii) of this section).

(iv) *Examples.* The application of this subparagraph is illustrated by the following examples:

Example (1). (i) On December 29, 1975, A separates from the service of the M Corporation and receives a distribution of the balance to the credit of his account under the M Corporation's noncontributory qualified plan. The distribution consists of cash of $44,000, and an annuity contract with a current actuarial value of $6,000. A has been a participant in the plan since March 26, 1966. A and his wife, B, are each age 50. Neither received a previous distribution from a qualified plan. A and B file a joint return for 1975. Their income for 1975, other than the distribution, consists of A's salary from the M Corporation of $15,000 and of $5,000 from the N Corporation. Their deductions (other than deductions attributable to the distribution) consist of itemized deductions of $3,000. They are not otherwise permitted to use income averaging for 1975 under section 1301. Assuming there are no changes in the applicable tax law after 1974, A and B's income tax liability for 1975 is computed as follows.

(ii) A and B's gross income for 1975 is $64,000, computed by adding the total taxable amount (determined under paragraph (d)(2) of this section) of the lump sum distribution to their otherwise computed gross income [$15,000 + $5,000 + $44,000]. Their adjusted gross income for 1975 is $37,600 [$64,000 – ($8,800 + $17,600)], computed by reducing their gross income by the sum of the lump sum distribution deduction allowed by section 4o2(e)(3) with respect to the ordinary income portion of the distribution [$44,000 × 24/120] and the deduction allowed by section 1202 with respect to the capital gains portion of the distribution [($44,000 × 96/120) × 0.51. A and B's taxable income for 1975 is $33.100 (their itemized deductions are $3,000 and their personal exemptions total $1,500).

Thus, A and B's income tax liability not including the separate tax on the ordinary income portion of the distribution is $9,122.

(iii) The adjusted total taxable amount of A's distribution is the sum of the current actuarial value of the annuity contract distributed and the total taxable amount of the lump sum distribution. Thus, the adjusted total taxable amount of A's distribution is $50,000 [$6,000 + $44,000]. The adjusted minimum distribution allowance with respect to A's distribution is the lesser of $10,000 or Y2 of the adjusted total taxable amount, reduced by 20 percent of the excess (if any) of the adjusted total taxable amount over $20,000. Thus, the adjusted minimum distribution allowance with respect to A's distribution is $4000 [$10,000 – (($50,000 – $20,000) x 0.2)1. The adjusted initial separate tax on A's distribution is computed by multiplying 10 times the tax imposed by section 1(c) computed as if the taxable income therein described were $4,600 [($50,000 – $4,000)/10]. Thus, A's adjusted initial separate tax is $3,160. The adjusted separate tax on A's distribution is computed by multiplying the adjusted initial separate tax by the quotient of the ordinary income portion divided by tide total taxable amount. Thus, the adjusted separate tax on A's distribution is $1,632 ($8,160 × $8,800/$44,000). The tax attributable to the annuity contract is 10 times the tax that would be imposed by section 1(c) computed as if the taxable income of a person described therein were

$552   [$6,000 – ($4,000 × ($6,000/$50,000))]
_____
                    10

multiplied by the quotient described in the second preceding sentence. Thus, the tax attributable to the annuity contract is $156 [$778 × $8,800/$44,000]. The separate tax on A's distribution is computed by reducing the adjusted separate tax by the tax attributable to the annuity contract. Thus, the separate tax on A's distribution is $1,476 [$1,632 – $156].

(iv) A and B's total income tax liability for 1975 is the sum of their income tax liability, as otherwise determined, and the separate tax. Thus A and B's total income tax liability for 1975 is $10,598 [$9,122 + $1,476].

Example (2). (i) Assume the same facts as in example (1) except that the M Corporation's qualified plan is contributory and that A's contributions under the plan as an employee were $1,760, and the current actuarial value of the annuity contract which is distributed is $5,760.

(ii) A and B's gross income for 1975 is $62,240. computed by adding the total taxable amount (determined tinder paragraph (d)(2) of this section) of the lump sum distribution to their otherwise computed gross income [$15,000 + $5,000 + ($44.000 – $1.760)]. Their adjusted gross income for 1975 is $36,896 [$62,240 – ($8,448 + $16,896)1, computed by reducing their gross income by the sum of the lump sum distribution deduction allowed by section 402 (e)(3) with respect to the ordinary income portion of the distribution [$42,240 x 24/120] and the deduction allowed by section 1202 with respect to the capital gains portion of the distribution. [($42,240 × 96/120) x 0.5]. A and B's taxable income for 1975 is $32,396 (their itemized deductions are $3,000 and their personal exemptions total $1,500). Thus A and B's income tax liability not including the separate tax on the ordinary income portion of the distribution is $8,826.

(iii) The adjusted total taxable amount of A's distribution is the sum of the current actuarial value of the annuity contract distributed and the total taxable amount of the lump sum distribution. Thus, the adjusted total taxable amount of A's distribution is $48,000 [$5,760 + ($44,000 – $1,760)]. The adjusted minimum distribution allowance with respect to A's distribution is the lesser of $10,000 or 1/2 of the adjusted total taxable amount, reduced by 20 percent of the excess of the adjusted total taxable amount over $20,000. Thus, the adjusted minimum distribution allowance with respect to A's distribution is $4,400 [$10,000 – (($48,000 – $20,000) × 0.2)1. The adjusted initial separate tax on A's distribution is 10 times the tax imposed by section 1(c) computed as if the taxable income therein described were

$$ \$4,360 \qquad \frac{[(\$48,000 - \$4,400)]}{10} $$

Thus, A's adjusted initial separate tax is $7,656. The adjusted separate tax on A's distribution is computed by multiplying the adjusted initial separate tax by the quotient of the ordinary income portion divided by the total taxable amount. Thus, the adjusted separate tax on A's distribution is $1,531 [$7,656 x $8,448/$42,240I. The tax attributable to the annuity contract is 10 times the tax that would be imposed by section 1(c) computed as if the taxable income of a person therein described were

$$ \$523 \qquad \frac{[\$5,760 - (\$4,400 \ x \ (\$5,760/\$48,000))]}{10} $$

multiplied by the quotient described in the second preceding sentence. Thus, the tax attributable to the annuity contract is $147 [$735 × $8,443/$42,240]. The separate tax on A's distribution is computed by reducing the adjusted separate tax by the tax attributable to the annuity contract. Thus, the separate tax on A's distribution is $1,384 [$1,531 – $147].

(iv) A and B's total income tax liability for 1975 is the sum of their income tax liability, as otherwise determined, and the separate tax. Thus A and B's total income tax liability for 1975 is $10,210 [$1,384 + $8,826].

Example (3). (i) On December 7, 1974 C separates from the service of P Corporation and receives a distribution of the balance to the credit of his account under the P Corporations contributory qualified plan. The distribution consists of cash of $44,000, and an annuity contract with a current actuarial value of $6,000. C has been a participant in the plan since February 20. 1965. C's contributions under the plan as an employee were $2.000. C and his wife, D, are each age 50. Neither received a previous distribution from a qualified plan. C and D file a joint return for 1974. Their income for 1974, other than the distribution, consists of C's salary from the P Corporation of $20,000. Their deductions (other than deductions attributable to the distribution) consist of itemized deductions of $3,000. They are not otherwise permitted to use income averaging for 1974 under section 1301. C and D's income tax liability for 1974 is computed as follows.

(ii) C and D's gross income for 1974 is $62,240, computed by adding the total taxable amount (determined under paragraph (d)(2) of this section) of the lump sum distribution to their otherwise computed gross income [$20,000 + ($44,000 – $1,760)] Their adjusted gross income for 1974 is $39,008 [$62,240 – ($4,224 + $19,008)], computed by reducing their gross income by the sum of the lump sum distribution deduction allowed by section 402(e)(3) with respect to the ordinary income portion of the distribution [$42,240 × 12/120] and the deduction allowed by section 1202 with respect to the capital gains portion of the distribution [($42,240 × 108/120) × 0.5]. C and D's taxable income for 1974 is $34,508 (their itemized deductions are $3,000 and their personal exemptions total $1,500). C and D's income tax liability for 1974 not including the separate tax on the ordinary income portion of the distribution is $9,713.

(iii) The adjusted total taxable amount of C's distribution is the sum of the current actuarial value of the annuity contract distributed and the total taxable amount of the lump sum distribution. Thus, the adjusted total taxable amount of C's distribution is $48.000 [($6,000 – $240) + ($44,000 – $1,760)]. The adjusted minimum distribution allowance with respect to C's distribution is the lesser of $10,000 or ½ of the adjusted total taxable amount, reduced by 20 percent of the excess of the adjusted total taxable amount over $20,000. Thus, the adjusted minimum distribution allowance with respect to C's distribution is $4,400 [$10,000 – (($48,000 – $20,000) × 0.2)]. The adjusted initial separate tax on C's distribution is 10 times the tax imposed by section 1(c) computed as if the taxable income therein described were

$$ \$4,360 \qquad \frac{[(\$48,000 - \$4,400)]}{10} $$

Thus, C's adjusted 10 initial separate tax is $7,656. The adjusted separate tax on C's distribution is computed by multiplying the adjusted initial separate tax by the quotient of the ordinary income portion divided by the total taxable amount Thus, the adjusted separate tax on C's distribution is $766 ($7,656 x $4,224/$42,240). The tax attributable to the annuity contract is 10 times the tax imposed by section 1(c) computed as if the taxable income therein described were

$$ \$360 \qquad \frac{[\$5,760 - (\$4,400 \times (\$5,760/\$48,000))]}{10} $$

multiplied by the quotient described in the second preceding sentence. Thus, the amount attributable to the annuity contract is $74 [$735 × ($4,224/$42,240)]. The separate tax on C's distribution is computed by reducing the adjusted separate tax by the tax attributable to the annuity contract. Thus, the separate tax on C's distribution is $692 ($766 – $74).

(iv) C and D's total income tax liability for 1974 is the sum of their income tax liability, as otherwise determined, and the separate tax. Thus, C and D's total income tax liability for 1974 is $10,405 [$9,713 + $692].

(2) *Computation of separate tax in case of multiple distribution—(i) Computation.* In the case of a payment or distribution which is included in a multiple distribution, the separate tax imposed on such multiple distribution by section 402(e)(1)(A) for the recipient's taxable year is the excess (if any) of the modified separate tax, over the sum of

(A) The aggregate amount of the separate tax imposed by section 402(e)(1)(A) paid during the lookback period, and

(B) The modified tax attributable to the annuity contract.

(ii) *Definitions.* For purposes of this section—(A) *Modified separate tax.* The term "modified separate tax" means an amount equal to the modified initial separate tax multiplied by a fraction

(1) The numerator of which is the sum of the ordinary income portions of the lump sum distributions made within the lookback period, and

(2) The denominator of which is the sum of the total taxable amounts of the lump sum distributions made within the lookback period.

(B) *Modified initial separate tax.* The modified initial separate tax is an amount equal to 10 times the tax which would be imposed by section 1(c) (relating to unmarried individuals (other than surviving spouses and heads of households)) if the recipient were an individual referred to in such section and the taxable income referred to in such section were an amount equal to one-tenth of the excess of—

(1) The modified total taxable amount of the lump sum distribution. over

(2) The modified minimum distribution allowance.

(C) *Modified total taxable amount.* The modified total taxable amount is the sum of the total taxable amounts (determined under paragraph (d)(2) of this section) of the distributions made during the lookback period and, in the case of a distribution made during such period to which subparagraph (C)(1) of this section applied, the amount specified in paragraph (C)(1)(ii) (C)(1)(i) or (2)(i) of this paragraph, which ever is applicable.

(D) *Modified minimum distribution allowance.* The modified minimum distribution allowance is the lesser of

(1) $10,000, or

(2) one-half of the modified total taxable amount, reduced (but not below zero) by 20 percent of the excess of the modified total taxable amount over $20,000.

(E) *Multiple distribution.* A distribution or payment received during a taxable year of the recipient which begins with or within a lookback period and after December 31, 1973, is included in a multiple distribution for such lookback period if—

(*1*) Any part of such distribution or payment (i) is treated as a lump sum distribution under this section or (ii) consists of a contract which would constitute all or a part of a lump sum distribution (determined without regard to section 402(e)(4)(B) and § 1.402(e)-3), except for the fact that it is an annuity contract, and

(*2*) a distribution or payment received in another such taxable year is treated as a lump sum distribution under this section. For purposes of this subdivision (E), if the recipient of a lump sum distribution is a trust and if a beneficiary of such trust is an employee with respect to the plan under which the distribution is made, or treated as the owner of such trust for purposes of subpart E of part I of subchapter J of chapter 1 of the Code (relating to grantors and others treated as substantial owners), then such employee or owner shall be treated as the sole recipient of the lump sum distribution. For purposes of this subdivision (E), the term "an employee with respect to the plan under which the distribution is made" means an individual who immediately before the distribution is made, is a participant in the plan under which the distribution is made.

(F) *Lookback period.* The lookback period with respect to any recipient is a period of 6 consecutive taxable years ending on the last day of the taxable year of the recipient in which a payment or distribution which is a multiple distribution is made.

(iii) *Modified tax attributable to an annuity contract.* For purposes of subdivision (i) of this subparagraph, the modified tax attributable to an annuity contract is equal to the product of—

(A) The quotient of the sum of the ordinary income portions (determined under paragraph (d)(3)) of the lump sum distributions received during the lookback period divided by the sum of the total taxable amounts (determined under paragraph (d)(2)) of the distributions made during the lookback period, and

(B) 10 times the tax which would be imposed by section 1(c) (relating to unmarried individuals (other than surviving spouses and heads of households)) if the recipient were an individual referred to in such section and the taxable income were an amount equal to one-tenth of the excess of—

(*1*) The sum of the amounts described in paragraph C (1)(ii)(C)(1)(i) or (2)(i) of this section in respect of the annuity contracts distributed during the lookback period, over

(2) the modified minimum distribution allowance multiplied by a fraction—

(i) The numerator of which is the sum of the amounts described in paragraph C(2)(iii)(B) in (1) of this section, and

(ii) the denominator of which is the modified total taxable amount (determined under paragraph (C)(2)(ii)(C) of this section).

(iv) The application of this subparagraph is illustrated by the following examples:

Example (1). (i) On December 7, 1976, A separates from the service of N Corporation and receives a distribution of the balance to the credit of his account under the N Corporation's noncontributory qualified plan. The distribution consists of cash of $4,000 and an annuity contract with a current actuarial value of $6,000. A has been a participant in the plan since October 13, 1967. A and his wife, B, are each age 50. A and B file a joint return for 1976. Their income for 1976, other than the distribution, consists of A's salary from N Corporation of $25,000 and interest income of $3,000. Their deductions (other than deductions attributable to the distribution) consist of itemized deductions of $2,100. They are not otherwise permitted to use income averaging for 1976 under section 1301. A received a distribution in 1975 from the M

Corporation and elected lump sum treatment for such distribution. The ordinary income portion of such distribution was $10,000; the total taxable amount of such distribution was $50,000; the adjusted ordinary income portion and the adjusted total taxable amount of such distribution are the same as the ordinary income portion and the total taxable amount; and they paid a separate tax on such distribution of $1,632. Assuming there are no changes in the applicable tax law after 1974, A and B's income tax liability for 1976 is computed as follows:

(ii) A and B's gross income for 1976 is $32,000, computed by adding the total taxable amount (determined under paragraph (d)(2) of this section) of the lump sum distribution to their otherwise computed gross income [$25,000 + $3,000 + $4,000]. Their adjusted gross income for 1976 is $29,400 [$32,000 – ($1,200 + $1,400)], computed by reducing their gross income by the sum of the lump sum distribution deduction allowed by section 402(e)(3) with respect to the ordinary income portion of the distribution [$4,000 × 36/120] and the deduction allowed by section 1202 with respect to the capital gains portion of the distribution [($4,000 × (84/120)) × 0.5]. A and B's taxable income for 1976 is $25,800 (their itemized deductions are $2,100 and their personal exemptions total $1,500). Thus, A and B's income tax liability for 1976, not including the separate tax on the ordinary income portion of the distribution, is $6,308.

(iii) The adjusted total taxable amount of A's distribution for 1976 is the sum of the current actuarial value of the annuity contract distributed and the total taxable amount of the lump sum distribution. Thus, the adjusted total taxable amount of A's 1976 distribution is $10,000 [$6,000 + $4,000]. The modified total taxable amount is $60,000 [$50,000 + $10,000]. The modified minimum distribution allowance with respect to A's 1976 distribution is the lesser of $10,000 or 1/2 of the modified total taxable amount, reduced by 20 percent of the excess (if any) of the modified total taxable amount over $20,000. Thus, the modified minimum distribution allowance with respect to A's 1976 distribution is $2,000 [$10,000 – (($60,000 – $20,000) × 0.2)]. The modified initial separate tax on A's 1976 distribution is computed by multiplying 10 times the tax imposed by section 1(c) computed as if the taxable income therein described were $5,800

$$\frac{[(\$60,000 - \$2,000)]}{10}$$

Thus, A's modified initial separate tax is $10,680. The modified separate tax on A's 1976 distribution is computed by multiplying the modified initial separate tax by the quotient of the sum of the ordinary income portions of the lump sum distributions received during the lookback period divided by the sum of the total taxable amounts of each lump sum distribution made during such period. Thus, the modified separate tax on A's 1976 distribution is $2,215 [$10,680 × ($10,000 + $1,200)/ ($50,000 + $4,000)]. The modified tax attributable to the annuity contract is 10 times the tax imposed by section 1(c) computed as if the taxable income of a person described therein were $580

$$\frac{[\$6,000 - ((\$6,000/\$60,000) \times \$2,000)]}{10}$$

multiplied by the quotient described in the second preceding sentence. Thus, the modified tax attributable to the annuity contract is $170 [$820 × ($10,000 + $1,200)/($50,000 + $4,000)]. The separate tax on A's 1976 distribution is computed by reducing the modified separate tax by the sum of the separate tax paid during the lookback period, and the modified tax attributable to the annuity contract. Thus, the separate tax on A's 1976 distribution is $413 [$2,215 ($1,632 + $170)].

(iv) A and B's total income tax liability for 1976 is the sum of their income tax liability as otherwise determined, and the separate tax. Thus, A and B's total income tax liability for 1976 is $6,721 [$6,308 + $413].

Example (2). (i) Assume the same facts as in example (1) except that the N Corporation's qualified plan was contributory and that A's contributions under the plan as an employee were $800, and the current actuarial value of the annuity contract which is distributed is $4,800.

(ii) A and B's gross income for 1976 is $31,200, computed by adding the total taxable amount (determined under paragraph (d)(2) of this section) of the lump sum distribution to their otherwise computed gross income [$25,000 + $3,000 + ($4,000 – $800)]. Their adjusted gross income for 1976 is $29,120 [$31,200 – ($960 + $1,120)] computed by reducing their gross income by the sum of the lump sum distribution deduction allowed by section 402(e)(3) with respect to the ordinary income portion of the distribution [$3,200 × 36/120] and the deduction allowed by section 1202 with respect to the capital gains portion of the distribution [($3,200 × 84/120) × 0.5]. A and B's taxable income for 1976 is $25,520, their itemized taxable deductions are $2,100 and their personal exemptions total $1,500. Thus, A and B's income tax liability for 1976, not including the separate tax on the ordinary income portion of the distribution, is $6,207.

(iii) The adjusted total taxable amount of A's distribution for 1976 is the sum of the current actuarial value of the annuity contract distributed and the total taxable amount of the lump sum distribution. Thus, the adjusted total taxable amount of A's 1976 distribution is $8,000 [$4,800 + ($4,000 – $800)]. The modified total taxable amount is $58,000 [$50,000 + $8,000]. The modified minimum distribution allowance with respect to A's 1976 distribution is the lesser of $10,000 or ½ of the modified total taxable amount reduced by the excess, if any, of such modified total taxable amount over $20,000. Thus, the modified minimum distribution allowance with respect to A's 1976 distribution is $2,400 [$10,000 – [(($8,000 + $50,000) – $20,000) × 0.2]]. The modified initial separate tax on A's 1976 distribution is 10 times the tax imposed by section 1(c) computed as if the taxable income therein described were $5,560

$$\left[\frac{(\$58,000 - \$2,400)\ \$2,000)]}{10} \right]$$

Thus, A's modified initial separate tax is $10,176. The modified separate tax on A's 1976 distribution is computed by multiplying the modified initial separate tax by the quotient of the sum of the ordinary income portions of each lump sum distribution received during the lookback period divided by the sum of the total taxable amounts of each lump sum distribution made during such period. Thus, the modified separate tax on A's 1976 distribution is $2,096 [$10,176 × ($10,000 + $960)/ ($50,000 + $3,200)]. The modified tax attributable to the annuity contract is 10 times the tax imposed by section 1(c) computed as if the taxable income therein described were $460

$$\$4,800 - \left[\frac{(\$2,400 \times (\$4,800/\$58,000))}{10} \right]$$

multiplied by the quotient described in the second preceding sentence. Thus, the modified tax attributable to the annuity contract is $133 [$644 × ($10,000 + $960)/($50,000 + $3,200)]. The separate tax on A's 1976 distribution is computed by reducing the modified separate tax by the sum of the separate tax paid during the lookback period, and the modified tax attributable to the annuity contract. Thus, the separate tax on A's 1976 distribution is $331 [$2,096 – ($1,632 + $133)].

(iv) A and B's total income tax liability for 1976 is the sum of their income tax liability as otherwise determined, and the separate tax. Thus, A and B's total income tax liability for 1976 is $6,538 [$6,207 + $331].

Example (3). (i) Assume the same facts as in example (1) except that the distribution on December 7, 1976, from the N Corporation's non-contributory qualified plan consists only of an annuity contract with a current actuarial value of $6,000.

(ii) A and B's gross income for 1976 is $28,000, computed by adding the total taxable amount (determined under paragraph (d)(2) of this section) of the lump sum distribution to their otherwise computed gross income [$25,000 + $3,000 + 0]. Their adjusted gross income for 1976 is $28,000 [$28,000 – ($0 + $0)], computed by reducing their gross income by the sum of the lump sum distribution deduction allowed by section 402(e)(3) with respect to the ordinary income portion of the distribution [$0 × 36/120] and the deduction allowed by section 1202 with respect to the capital gains portion of the distribution [($0 x 84/120) × 0.5]. Their taxable income for 1976 is $24,000 (their itemized deductions are $2,100 and their personal exemptions total $1,500). Thus, A and B's income tax liability for 1976, not including the separate tax on the distribution, is $5,804.

(iii) The adjusted total taxable amount of A's distribution for 1976 is the sum of the current actuarial value of the annuity contract distributed and the total taxable amount of the lump sum distribution. Thus, the adjusted total taxable amount of A's 1976 distribution is $6,000 [$6,000 + $0]. The modified total taxable amount is $56,000 [$6,000 + $50,000]. The modified minimum distribution allowance with respect to A's 1976 distribution is the lesser of $10,000 or 1/2 of the modified total taxable amount, reduced by 20 percent of the excess (if any) of the modified total taxable amount over $20,000. Thus, the modified minimum distribution allowance with respect to A's 1976 distribution is $2,800 [$10,000 – (($56,000 – $20,000) × 0.2)]. The modified initial separate tax on A's 1976 distribution is computed by multiplying 10 times the tax imposed by section 1(c) computed as if the taxable income therein described were $5,320

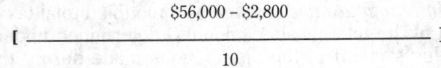

$$\left[\frac{\$56,000 - \$2,800}{10} \right]$$

Thus, A's modified initial separate tax is $9,672. The modified separate tax on A's 1976 distribution is computed by multiplying the modified initial separate tax by the quotient of she sum of the ordinary income portions of the lump sum distributions received during the lookback period divided by the sum of the total taxable amounts of each lump sum distribution made during such period. Thus, the modified separate tax on A's 1976 distribution is $1,934 [$9,672 × ($10,000 + $0)/($50,000 + $0)]. The modified tax attributable to the annuity contract is 10 times the tax imposed by section 1(c) computed as if the taxable income of a person described therein were $570

$$\frac{[(\$6,000 - ((\$6,000/\$56,000) \times \$2,800))]}{10}$$

multiplied by the quotient described in the second preceding sentence. Thus, the modi-fied tax attributable to the annuity contract is $161 [$805 × ($10,000 + $0)/($50,000 + $0)]. The separate tax on A's 1976 distribution is computed by reducing the modified separate tax by the sum of the separate tax paid during the lookback period, and the modified tax attributable to the annuity contract. Thus, the separate tax on A's 1976 distribution is $141 [$1,934 – ($1,632 + $161)].

(iv) A and B's total income tax liability for 1976 is the sum of their income tax liability as otherwise determined, and the separate tax. Thus, A and B's total income tax liability for 1976 is $5,945 [$5,804 + $141].

Example (4). (i) Assume the same facts as in example (3) except that the N Corporation's qualified plan was contributory and that A's contributions under the plan as an employee were $2,000.

(ii) A and B's gross income for 1976 is $28,000, computed by adding the total taxable amount (determined under paragraph (d)(2) of this section) of the lump sum distribution to their otherwise computed gross income [$25,000 + $3,000 + 0]. Their adjusted gross income for 1976 is $28,000 [$28,000 – ($0 + $0)], computed by reducing their gross income by the sum of the lump sum distribution deduction allowed by section 402(e)(3) with respect to the ordinary income portion of the distribution [$0 × 36/120] and the deduction allowed by section 1202 with respect to the capital gains portion of the distribution [($0 × 84/120) × 0.5]. Their taxable income for 1976 is $24,400 (their itemized deductions are $2,100 and their personal exemptions total $1,500). Thus, A and B's income tax liability for 1976, not including the separate tax on the distribution is $5,804.

(iii) The adjusted total taxable amount of A's distribution for 1976 is the sum of the current actuarial value of the annuity contract distributed, reduced by the excess of the net amount contributed by the employee over the cash and other property distributed, and the total taxable amount of the lump sum distribution. Thus, the adjusted total taxable amount of A's 1976 distribution is $4,000 [($6,000 – $2,000) + $0]. The modified total taxable amount is $54,000 [$50,000 + $4,000.] The modified minimum distribution allowance with respect to A's 1976 distribution is the lesser of $10,000 or 1/2 of the modified total taxable amount, reduced by 20 percent of the excess (if any) of the modified total taxable amount over $20,000. Thus, the modified minimum distribution allowance with respect to A's 1976 distribution is $3,200 [$10,000 – (($54,000 – $20,000) × 0.2)]. The modified initial separate tax on A's 1976 distribution is computed by multiplying 10 times the tax imposed by section 1(c) computed as if the taxable income therein described were $5,080

$$\frac{[\$54,000 - \$3,200]}{10}$$

Thus, A's modified initial separate tax is $9,168. The modified separate tax on A's 1976 distribution is computed by multiplying the modified initial separate tax by the quotient of the sum of the ordinary income portions of the lump sum distribution received during the lookback period divided by the sum of the total taxable amounts of each lump sum distribution made during such period. Thus, the modified separate tax on A's 1976 distribution is $1,833 [$9,168 × ($10,000 + $0)/($50,000 + $0)]. The modified tax attributable to the annuity contract is 10 times the tax imposed by section 1(c) computed as if the taxable income therein described were $376

$$\frac{[\$4,000 - ((\$4,000/\$54,000) \times \$3,200)]}{10}$$

multiplied by the quotient described in the second preceding sentence. Thus, the modified tax attributable to the annuity contract is $105 [$526

× ($10,000 + $0)/($50,000 + $0)]. The separate tax on A's 1976 distribution is computed by reducing the modified separate tax by the sum of the separate tax paid during the lookback period, and the modified tax attributable to the annuity contract. Thus, the separate tax on A's 1976 distribution is $96 [$1,833 − ($1,632 + $105)].

(iv) A and B's total income tax liability for 1976 is the sum of their income tax liability as otherwise determined and the separate tax. Thus, A and B's total income tax liability for 1976 is $5,900 [$5,804 + $96].

(d) *Definitions.* For purposes of this section and §1.402(e)-3—(1) *Lump sum distribution.* (i) For taxable years of a recipient beginning after December 31, 1973, the term "lump sum distribution" means the distribution or payment within one taxable year of the recipient of the balance under the plan to the credit of an employee which becomes payable, or is made available, to the recipient—

(A) On account of the employee's death,

(B) After the employee attains age 59 ½,

(C) In the case of an employee who at no time during his participation in the plan was an employee within the meaning of section 401(c)(1), on account of the employee's separation from the service, or

(D) In the case of an employee within the meaning of section 401(c)(1), after the employee has become disabled within the meaning of section 72(m)(7) and paragraph (f) of §1.72-17,

from a trust forming part of a plan described in section 401(a) and which is exempt from tax under section 501(a) or from a plan described in section 403(a). Although periodic payments made under an annuity contract distributed under a plan described in the preceding sentence are taxed under section 72, solely for purposes of determining the adjusted total taxable amount or the modified total taxable amount, an annuity contract distributed from a plan described in the preceding sentence shall be treated as a lump sum distribution.

(ii) (A) A distribution or payment is not a lump sum distribution unless it constitutes the balance to the credit of the employee at the time the distribution or payment commences. For purposes of the preceding sentence, the time at which a distribution or payment commences shall be the date on which the requirements of subdivision (A), (B), (C), or (D) (whichever is applicable) of paragraph (d)(1)(i) of this section are satisfied, disregarding any previous distribution which constituted the balance to the credit of the employee.

(B) A distribution made before the death of an employee (for example, annuity payments received by the employee after retirement) will not preclude an amount paid on account of the death of the employee from being treated as a lump sum distribution by the recipient. Further, if a distribution or payment constitutes the balance to the credit of the employee, such distribution or payment shall not be treated as other than a lump sum distribution merely because an additional amount, attributable to the last or a subsequent year of service, is credited to the account of the employee and distributed.

(C) The application of this subdivision may be illustrated by the following example:

Example. A, an individual who is a calendar year taxpayer, retires from services with the M Corporation on October 31, 1975 after attaining age 59-1/2. A begins to receive monthly annuity payments under the M Corporation's qualified plan on November 1, 1975. On February 3, 1976, A takes the balance to his credit under the M Corporation's plan in lieu of any future annuity payments. The balance to the credit of A under the M Corporation's plan is distributed to him on February 3, 1976, and as of such date he had not previously received any amount constituting a lump sum distribution. Such payments and distributions are not to be treated as a lump sum distribution because they are not paid within 1 taxable year of the recipient.

(iii) A payment or distribution described in paragraph (d)(1)(i) of this section which is made to more than one person (except a payment or distribution made solely to two or more trusts), shall not be treated as a lump sum distribution, unless the entire amount paid or distributed is included in the income of the employee in respect of whom the payment or distribution is made. Thus, for example, a distribution of the balance to the credit of the employee after the death of the employee made to the surviving spouse and his children cannot be treated as a lump sum distribution by the surviving spouse and children. However, a distribution to the employee's estate can be treated as a lump sum distribution even though the estate subsequently distributes the amount received to the surviving spouse and children.

(iv) The term "balance to the credit of the employee" does not include United States Retirement Plan Bonds held by a trust to the credit of an employee. Thus, a distribution or payment by a plan

described in subdivision (i) of this subparagraph may constitute a lump sum distribution with respect to an employee even though the trust retains retirement plan bonds registered in the name of such employee. Similarly, the proceeds of a retirement plan bond received as a part of the balance to the credit of an employee will not be entitled to be treated as a lump sum distribution. See section 405(e) and paragraph (a)(4) of §1.405-3.

(v) The term "balance to the credit of the employee" includes any amount to the credit of the employee under any plan which is required to be aggregated under the provisions of section 402(e)(4)(C) and paragraph (e)(1) of this section.

(vi) The term "balance to the credit of the employee" does not include any amount which has been placed in a separate account for the funding of medical benefits described in section 401(h) as defined in paragraph (a) of §1.401-14. Thus, a distri-bution or payment by a plan described in subdivision (i) of this subparagraph may constitute the "balance to the credit of the employee" with respect to an employee even though the trust retains amounts attributable to the funding of medical benefits described in section 401(h).

(vii) The term "balance to the credit of the employee" includes any amount which is not forfeited under the plan as of the close of the taxable year of the recipient within which the distribution is made except that in the case of an employee who has separated from the service and incurs a break in service (within the meaning of section 411), such term does not include an amount which is forfeited at the close of the plan year, beginning with or within such taxable year, by reason of such break in service.

(viii) The balance to the credit of the employee is includible in the gross income of the recipient if the recipient fails to make a timely election under section 72(h) to receive an annuity in lieu of such balance.

(2) *Total taxable amount.* (i) The term "total taxable amount" means, with respect to a lump sum distribution described in the first sentence of paragraph (d)(1)(i) of this section, the amount of such lump sum distribution which exceeds the sum of—

(A) The net amount contributed by the employee, and

(B) The net unrealized appreciation attributable to that part of the distribution which consists of the securities of the employer corporation so distributed.

(ii) For purposes of paragraph (d)(2)(i)(A) of this section, the term "net amount contributed by the employee" means—

(A) For taxable years beginning after December 31, 1974, the amount actually contributed by the employee plus any amounts considered to be contributed by the employee under the rules of sections 72(f) and 101(b), and paragraph (b) of §1.72-16, reduced by any amounts theretofore distributed to him which were excludable from gross income as a return of employee contributions.

(B) For taxable years beginning before January 1, 1975, an amount equal to the product of the amounts considered contributed by the employee under the plan (determined by applying section 72(f) and 101(b), and paragraph (b) of §1.72-16) reduced by any amounts theretofore distributed to the employee which were not includible in his gross income, multiplied by a fraction—

(i) The numerator of which is the excess, if any, of the sum of the current actuarial value of the annuity contract distributed and the value of the other property (including cash) distributed, over such current actuarial value, and

(ii) The denominator of which is the sum of the current actuarial value of the annuity contract distributed and the value of other property (including cash) distributed.

(iii) The provisions of this subparagraph may be illustrated by the following examples:

Example (1). A, age 60, receives a lump sum distribution from the N Corporation's noncontributory qualified plan on November 24, 1975. The distribution of $25,000 consists of cash and M Corporation securities with net unrealized appreciation of $15,000. The total taxable amount of the distribution to A is $10,000.

Example (2). B, age 60, receives a lump sum distribution from the N Corporation's contributory qualified plan on December 29, 1975. The distribution consists of $25,000 in cash. B's contributions under the plan as an employee are $5,000. The total taxable amount of the distribution to B is $20,000.

Example (3). W receives a lump sum distribution on April 1, 1975, from the M Corporation's noncontributory qualified plan as beneficiary of H on account of H's death. The distribution consists of $25,000 in cash. The total taxable amount of distribution to W is $20,000 if W is otherwise allowed a $5,000 exclusion under section 101(b).

(3) *Ordinary income portion* (i) The ordinary income portion of a lump sum distribution is the product of the total taxable amount of the lump sum distribution, multiplied by a fraction—

(A) the numerator of which is the number of calendar years of active participation by the employee in the plan after December 31, 1973, under which the lump sum distribution is made, and

(B) the denominator of which is the total number of calendar years of active participation by the employee in such plan.

(ii) For purposes of computing the fraction described in subdivision (i) of this subparagraph, the number of calendar years of active participation shall be the number of calendar months during the period beginning with the first month in which the employee became a participant under the plan and ending with the earliest of—

(A) The month in which the employee receives a lump sum distribution under the plan,

(B) In the case of an employee who is not an employee within the meaning of section 401(c)(1), the month in which the employee separates from the service,

(C) The month in which the employee dies, or

(D) In the case of an employee within the meaning of section 401(c)(1) who receives a lump sum distribution on account of disability, the first month in which he becomes disabled within the meaning of section 72(m)(?) and paragraph (f) of § 1.72-17.

In computing the month. of active participation, in the case of active participation before January 1, 1974, a pout of a calendar year in which the employee was an active participant under the plan shall be counted as 12 months, and in the case of active participation after December 31, 1973 a part of a calendar month in which an individual is an active participant under the plan shall be counted as 1 month. Thus, for example, if A, an individual, became an active participant under a plan on December 31, 1965, and continued to be an active participant under the plan until May 7, 1976, A has 108 (12 × 9) months of active participation under the plan before January 1, 1974, and A has 29 (12 + 12 + 5) months of active participation after December 31, 1973. For special rule[s] in case of aggregation of plans, see paragraph (e)(1)(ii) of this section.

(4) *Employee; employer.* The term "employee" includes an employee within the meaning of section 401(c)(1) and the employer of such individual is the person treated as his employer under section 401(c)(4).

(5) *Securities.* The terms "securities" and "securities of the employer corporation shall have the meanings provided in sections 402(a)(3)(A) and 402(a)(3)(B), respectively.

(e) *Special rules—(1) Aggregation. (i) Aggregation of trusts and plans—*(A) For purposes of determining the balance to the credit of an employee, all trusts described in section 401(a) and which are exempt from tax under section 501(a) and which are part of a plan shall be treated as a single trust; all pension plans described in section 401(a) maintained by an employer shall be treated as a single plan; all profit-sharing plans described in section 401(a) maintained by an employer shall he treated as a single plan; and all stock bonus plans described in section 401(a) maintained by an employer shall be treated as a single plan. For purposes of this subdivision (i), an annuity contract shall be considered to be a trust.

(B) Trusts which are not described in section 401(a) or which are not exempt from tax under section 501(a), and annuity contracts which do not satisfy the requirements of section 404(a)(2) shall not be taken into account for purposes of subdivision (i) of this subparagraph.

(ii) *Computation of ordinary income portion.* The ordinary income portion of a distribution from two or more plans (which are treated as a single plan under subdivision (i) of this subparagraph) shall be computed by aggregating all of the amounts which would constitute the ordinary income portion of a lump sum distribution if each plan maintained by the employer were not subject to the application of subdivision (i) of this subparagraph.

(iii) *Examples.* The application of this subparagraph is illustrated by the following examples:

Example (1). M Corporation maintains a qualified profit-sharing plan and a qualified defined benefit pension plan. A, who has participated in each plan for 5 years and is age 55, separates from the service on December 5, 1975. On December 5, 1975, A receives a distribution of the balance to the credit of his account under the profit-sharing plan.

Payment of his pension benefits, however, will not commence until he attains age 65. A is entitled to treat his profit-sharing distribution as a lump sum distribution.

Example (2). Assume the same facts as in example (1) except bat instead of a profit-sharing plan, M Corporation maintains a qualified money purchase pension plan. A is not entitled to have the amount received from the money purchase pension plan treated as a lump sum distribution.

Example (3). Assume the same facts as in example (2) except that the trust forming part of the defined benefit pension maintained by M Corporation is not a qualified trust. A is entitled to have the amount received from the money purchase plan treated as a lump sum distribution.

Example (4). N Corporation maintains profit-sharing plan X and profit-scaring plan Y which plans are qualified and are noncontributory. A is a participant in each plan. A has been a participant in the profit-sharing plan X since October 13, 1966 and a participant in profit-sharing plan Y since its inception on May 9, 1968. A, age 55, separates from the service on December 5, 1975. He receives the balance to his credit from each plan upon separation. He receives $50,000 from profit-sharing plan X and $60,000 from profit-sharing plan Y. The ordinary income portion of his distribution from the N Corporation plans is $25,000 [($50,000 × (24/120)) + ($60,000 × (24/96))].

(2) *Community property laws.* (i) Except as provided in paragraph (e)(2)(ii) of this section, the provisions of this section shall be applied without regard to community property laws.

(ii) In applying the provisions of section 402(e)(3), relating to the allowance of a deduction from gross income of the ordinary income portion of a lump sum distribution, community property laws shall not be disregarded. Thus, for example, if A, a married individual subject to the community property laws of a jurisdiction, receives a lump sum distribution of which the ordinary income portion is $10,000, and he and his wife, B, file separate returns for the taxable year, generally, one half of the total taxable amount of the lump sum distribution is includible in A's gross income, and he will be entitled to a deduction under section 402(e)(3) of $5,000. In this case, the other half of the total taxable amount is includible in B's gross income, and she will be entitled to a deduction of $5,000. The entire amount of the lump sum distribution, however, must be taken into account by A in computing the separate tax imposed by section 402(e)(1)(A).

(3) *Minimum period of service.* For purposes of computing the separate tax imposed by section 402(e)(1)(A), no amount distributed or paid to an employee may be treated as a lump sum distribution under section 402(e>4)(A) and this section unless he has been a participant in the plan for at least 5 full taxable years of such employee (preceding his taxable year in which such amount is distributed or paid). Thus, for example, if an amount, which would otherwise be a lump sum distribution, is distributed to A, an employee who has completed only 4 of his taxable years of participation in the plan before the first day of the taxable year in which the amount is distributed, A is not. entitled to use the provisions of section 402(e) to compute the tax on the ordinary income portion of the amount distribution. If the amount were distributed to A's beneficiary on account of A's death, however, Ax beneficiary could treat the distribution as a lump sum distribution under section 402(e) and this section.

(4) *Amounts subject to penalty.* Section 402(e) and this section do not apply to an amount described in section 72(m)(5)(A)(ii) and § 1.72-17(e)(1)(i)(b) to the extent the provisions of section 72(m)(5) apply to such amount.

(5) *Distributions including securities of the employer corporation.* For rules relating to distributions including securities of the employer corporation, see § 1.402(a)-1(b).

(6) *Liability for tax.* (i) Except as provided in subdivision (ii) of this subparagraph the recipient shall be liable for the tax imposed by section 402(e)(1)(A).

(ii) (A) In any case in which the recipient of a lump sum distribution is a trust, if a beneficiary of such trust is—

(1) An employee with respect to the plan under which the distribution is made, or

(2) Treated as the owner of such trust for purposes of subpart E of part I of subchapter J of chapter 1 of the Code (relating to grantors and others treated as substantial owners),

then such employee or the owner shall be treated as the sole recipient of the lump sum distribution. For purposes of (1) of this subdivision, the term "an employee with respect to the plan under which the distribution is made" means an individual who immediately before the distribution is made, is a participant in the plan under which the distribution is made.

(B)(1) In any case in which a lump sum distribution is made within a taxable year with respect to an individual only to two or more trusts, if a beneficiary of any one of such trusts is not treated as the sole recipient of the distribution by reason of the application of (A) of this subdivision (ii) the separate tax imposed by section 402(e)(1). (A) shall be computed as if the distribution were made to a single recipient consisting of all of such trusts, but the liability for such separate tax shall be allocated among the trusts according to the relative portions of the total taxable amount of the distribution received by each trust.

(2) In any case in which a lump sum distribution is made in a succeeding taxable year in a lookback period with respect to a trust described in (1) of this subdivision (B), the separate tax imposed by section 402[(e)](1)(A) shall be computed as if the amount described in section 402(e)(2)(A) (relating to the amount of tax imposed by section 402(e)(1)(A) paid with respect to other distributions in a lookback period) includes the separate tax determined in (1) of this subdivision (B) (without regard to the allocation described therein).

(7) *Change in exempt status of trust.* For principles applicable in making appropriate adjustments if the trust was not exempt for one or more years before the year of distribution, see § 1.402(a)-1(a)(1)(iv).

(f) *Reporting—(1) Information required.* An employer who maintains a, plan described in section 401(a) or 403(a), under which a distribution or payment which may be treated as a lump sum distribution is made in a taxable year of the recipient beginning after December 31, 1973, shall communicate (or cause to be communicated) in writing, to the recipient on Form 1099 R the following information (where applicable):

(i) The gross amount of such distribution (including the value of any United States retirement plan bonds distributed to or held for the recipient);

(ii) The total taxable amount of such distribution;

(iii) The ordinary income portion and capital gain element of such distribution;

(iv) The net amount contributed by the employee (within the meaning of paragraph (d)(2)(ii) of this section);

(v) The portions of such distribution excludable from the gross income of the recipient under paragraph (c) of § 1.72-16 and paragraph (b) of § 1.402(a)-1;

(vi) The value of any United States retirement plan bonds distributed to or held for the recipient in excess of the net amount contributed by the employee (within the meaning of paragraph (d)(2)(ii) of this section) included in the basis of such bonds;

(vii) The current actuarial value of any annuity contract distributed as part of the balance to the credit of the employee in excess of the net amount contributed by the employee (within the meaning of paragraph (d)(2)(ii) of this section) considered to be an investment in the contract;

(viii) The net unrealized appreciation on any securities of the employer corporation.

(2) *Alternate method of communication.* The obligation of the employer to communicate the information described in subparagraph (1) of this paragraph to the recipient shall be satisfied if the fiduciary of the trust or the payer of such distribution communicates the information to the recipient.

(3) *Taxable year of recipient.* The report required by this paragraph may be prepared, at the option of the employer as if the taxable year of each employee were the calendar year.

(4) *Failure to satisfy requirements.* In the event that the requirements of this paragraph are not satisfied, the information required to be furnished under this paragraph shall be furnished as part of the return required to be filed under section 6058 and the regulations thereunder.

§ *1.402(e)-3 Election to treat an amount as a lump sum distribution.*

* * *

(a) *In general.* For purposes of sections 402, 403, and this section, an amount which is described in section 402(e)(4)(A) and which is not an annuity contract may be treated as a lump sum distribution under section 402(e)(4)(A) only if the taxpayer elects for ?he taxable year to have all such amounts received during such year so treated. Not more than one election may be made under this section with respect to an employee after such employee has attained age 59V2.

(b) *Taxpayers eligible to make the election.* Individuals, estates, and trusts are the only taxpayers eligible to make the election provided by this section. In the case of a lump sum distribution made with respect to an employee to 2 or more trusts, the election provided by this section shall be made by the employee or by the personal representative of a deceased employee.

(c) *Procedure for making election—(1) Time and scope of election.* An election under this section shall be made for each taxable year to which such election is to apply. The election shall be made before the expiration of the period (including extensions thereof) prescribed in section 6511 for making a claim for credit or refund of the assessed tax imposed by chapter 1 of subtitle A of the Code for such taxable year.

(2) *Manner of making election.* An election by the taxpayer with respect to a tax-able year shall be made by filing Form 4972 as a part of the taxpayer's income tax return or amended return for the taxable year.

(3) *Revocation of election.* An election made pursuant to this section may be revoked within the time prescribed in subparagraph (1) of this paragraph for making an election, only if there is filed, within such time, an amended income tax return for such taxable year, which includes a statement revoking the election and is accompanied by payment of any tax attributable to the revocation. If an election for a taxable year is revoked, another election may be made for that taxable year under paragraphs (c)(1) and (2) of this section.

(4) Eject of election on subsequent distribution. An election made pursuant to this section shall be an election to treat an annuity contract distributed after December 31, 1973, in a lookback period (as defined in § 1.402(e)-2(c)(2)(iii)(F)) beginning after such date as a lump sum distribution in the taxable year of the recipient in which such contract is distributed.

Par. 13. Section 1.403(a) is amended by amending paragraph (A)(2)(iii) thereof and by revising the historical note. As amended, these revised provisions read as follows:

§ *1.403(a) Statutory provisions; taxation of employee annuities; qualified annuity plan.*

* * *

[Asterisks represent 1954 Code Sec. 403(a) as amended by Sec. 23(b), Technical Amendments Act 1958 (72 Stat. 1622); sec. 4(d), Self-Employed Individuals Tax Retirement Act 1962 (76 Stat. 825); sec. 232(e)(4), Rev. Act 1964 (78 Stat. 111); sec. 2005 (b)(2), Employee Retirement Income Security Act 1974 (88 Stat. 991)]

Par. 14. Section 1.403(a)-1(b)(1) and (2) are amended to read as follows:

§ *1.403(a)-1 Taxability of beneficiary under a qualified annuity plan.*

* * *

(b) The amounts received by or made available to any employee referred to in paragraph (a) of this section under an annuity contract shall be included in the gross income of the employee for the taxable year in which received on made available, as provided in section 72 (relating to annuities), except that—

(1) For taxable years beginning before January 1, 1970, certain total distributions described in section 403(a)(2) (as in effect for such years) are taxable as long-term capital gains (see § 1.403(a)-2 for rules applicable to such amounts), and

(2) For taxable years beginning after December 31, 1973, a portion of a lump sum distribution (as defined by section 402 (e)(4)(A)) is treated as long-term capital gains (see paragraph (d) of § 1.403(a)-2 for rules applicable to such portion and see § 1.402(e)-2 for the computation of the separate tax on the portion of a lump sum distribution not treated as long-term capital gains).

For taxable years beginning before January 1, 1964, section 72(e)(3) (relating to treatment of certain lump sums), as in effect before such date, shall not apply to an amount described in this paragraph. For taxable years beginning after December 31, 1963, such amounts may be taken into account in computations under section 1301 through 1305 (relating to income averaging)

* * *

Par. 15. Section 1.403(a)-2(a)(1) and (b) are amended; (c) is revised, (d) and (e) are added to read as follows:

§ *1.403(a)-2. Capital gains treatment for certain distributions.*

(a) For taxable years beginning before January 1, 1970, if the total amounts payable with respect to any employee for whom an annuity contract has been purchased by an employer under a plan which—

(1) Is a plan described in section 403(a)(1) and § 1.403(a)-1, and

* * *

(b) For taxable years beginning before January 1, 1970—

(1) The term "total amounts" means the balance to the credit of an employee with respect to all annuities under the annuity plan which becomes payable to the payee by reason of the employee's death or other separation from the service, or by reason of his death after separation from the service. If an employee commences to receive annuity payments on retirement and then a lump sum payment is made to his widow upon his death, the capital gains treatment applies to the lump sum payment, but it does not apply to amounts received before the time the "total amounts" become payable. However, if the total amount to the credit of the employee at the time of his death or other separation from the service or death after separation from the service is paid or includible in the gross income of the payee within one taxable year of the payee, such amount is entitled to the capital gains treatment notwithstanding that in a later taxable year an additional amount is credited to the employee and paid to the payee.

* * *

(c) For taxable years beginning before January 1, 1970, the provisions of this section are not applicable to any amounts paid to a payee to the extent such amounts are attributable to contributions made on behalf of an employee while he was a self-employed individual in the business with respect to which the plan was established. For the taxation of such amounts, see § 1.72-18. For such years for the rules for determining the amount attributable to contributions on behalf of an employee while he was self-employed, see paragraphs (b)(4) and (c)(2) of such section.

(d) For taxable years ending after December 31, 1969, and beginning before January 1, 1974, the portion of the total amounts described in paragraph (b)(1) of this section treated as gain from the sale or exchange of a capital asset held for more than six months is subject to the limitation of section 403(a)(2)(C), as in effect on December 31, 1973.

(e) For taxable years beginning after December 31, 1973—

(1) If a lump sum distribution (as defined in section 402(e)(4)(A) and the regulations thereunder) is received by, or made available to, the recipient under an annuity contract described in subparagraph (2)(i) of this paragraph, the ordinary income portion (as defined in section 402(e)(4)(E) and the regulations thereunder) of such distribution shall be taxable in accordance with the provisions of section 402(e) and the regulations thereunder and the portion of such distribution determined under paragraph (3) of this section shall be treated in accordance with the provisions of subparagraph (2) of this section.

(2) If—

(i) An annuity contract is purchased by an employer for an employee under a plan described in section 403(a)(1) and § 1.403 (a)-1,

(ii) Such plan requires that refunds of contributions with respect to annuity contracts purchased under the plan be used to reduce subsequent premiums on the contracts under the plan, and

(iii) A lump sum distribution (as define in section 402(e)(4)(A) and the regulations' thereunder) is paid to the recipient, the amount described in paragraph (e)(3) of this section shall be treated as gain from the sale or exchange of a capital asset held for more than 6 months.

(3) For purposes of paragraph (e)(2) of this section, the portion of a lump sum distribution treated as gain from the sale or exchange of a capital asset held for more than 6 months is an amount equal to the total taxable amount of the lump sum distribution (as defined in section 402(e)(4) (D) and the regulations thereunder) multiplied by a fraction—

(i) The numerator of which is the number of calendar years of active participation (as determined under § 1.402(e)-2(d)(3)(ii)) by the employee in such plan before January 1, 1974, and

(ii) The denominator of which is the number of calendar years of active participation (as determined under § 1.402(e)-2 (d)(3)(ii)) by the employee in such plan.

(4) For the purposes of this paragraph—

(i) In the case of an employee who is an employee without regard to section 401(c) (1), the determination of whether or not an amount is a lump sum distribution shall be made without regard to the requirements of section 402(e)(4)(B) and § 1.402(e)-3.

(ii) No distribution to any taxpayer other than an individual, estate, or trust may be treated as a lump sum distribution under this section.

Par. 16. Section 1.405 is amended by deleting "Section 72(n) and section 402(a)(2)" in subsection (e) and inserting in lieu thereof "Subsection(a)(2) and (e) of section 402"

and revising the historical note. These amended, and revised provisions read as follows:

* * *

[Asterisks represent 1954 Code] Sec. 405 as added by sea 5, Self-Employed Individuals Tax Retirement Act 1962 (76 Stat. 826) and as amended by Sec. 106(d)(5), Social Security Amendments 1965 (79 Stat. 337); sea 515(c)(1) Tax Reform Act 1969 (83 Stat. 654); sec. 2005(c)(11) Employee Retirement Income Security Act 1974 (88 Stat. 992)1

Par. 17. Paragraph (4) of § 1.405-3(a) is revised to read as follows:

§ 1.405.3 Taxation of retirement bonds.

(a) In general. * * *

(4) The provisions of section 402(a)(2) and (e) are not applicable to a retirement bond. In general, section 402(a)(2) provides for capital gains treatment of a portion of a lump sum distribution as defined in section 402(e)(4)(A) and section 402(e) provides a special I0year averaging of the ordinary income portion of much a lump sum distribution. The proceeds of a retirement bond received upon redemption will not be entitled to such capital gains treatment or 10-year averaging even though the bond is received as part of, or as the entire, balance to the credit of the employee. Nor will such a bond be taken into consideration in determining the balance to the credit of the employee. Thus, a distribution by a qualified trust may constitute a lump sum distribution for purposes of section 402(a)(2) and (e) even though the trust retains retirement bonds registered in the name of the employee.

Par. 18. Section 1.652(b)-1is amended by deleting "72(n)" and inserting in lieu thereof "402(a)(2)". As amended, § 1.652(b)-1 reads as follows:

§ 1.652(b)-1 Character of amounts.

In determining the gross income of a beneficiary, the amounts includible under § 1.652(a)-1 have the same character in the hands of the beneficiary as in the hands of the trust. For example, to the extent that the amounts specified in § 1.652(a)-1 consist of income exempt from tax under section 103, such amounts are not included in the beneficiary's gross income. Similarly, dividends distributed to a beneficiary retain their original character in the beneficiary's hands for purposes of determining the availability to the beneficiary of the dividends received credit under section 34 (for dividends received on or before December 31, 1964) and the dividend exclusion under section 116. Also, to the extent that the amounts specified in § 1.652(a)-1 consist of "earned income" in the hands of the trust under the provisions of section 1348 such amount shall be treat-A under section 1348 as "earned income" in the hands of the beneficiary. Similarly, to the extent the amounts specified in § 1.652(a)-1 consist of an amount received as a part of a lump sum distribution from a qualified plan and to which the provisions of section 402(a)(2) would apply in the hands of the trust, such amount shall be treated as subject to such section in the hands of the beneficiary except where such amount is deemed under section 666(a) to have been distributed in a preceding taxable year of the trust and the partial tax described in section 668 (a)(2) is determined under section 668 (b)(1)(B). The tax treatment of amounts determined under § 1.652(a)-1 depends upon the beneficiary's status with respect to them, not upon the status of the trust. Thus, if a beneficiary is deemed to have received foreign income of a foreign trust, the includibility of such income in his gross income depends upon his taxable status with respect to that income.

Par. 19. Section 1.1304 is amended by deleting paragraph (b)(2) and redesignating paragraphs (3), (4), (5), and (6) as paragraphs (2), (3), (4), and (5), respectively, and revising the historical note. These amended and revised provisions read as follows:

* * *

[[Asterisks represent 1954 Code]Sec. 1304 as amended by sec. 232(a), Rev. Act 1964 (78 Stat. 105); secs. 311(c) and (d), 515 (c)(4), 802(c)(5), and 803(d)(8), Tax Reform Act 1969 (83 Stat. 537, 646, 678, 684); sec. 2005(c)(6) Employee Retirement Income Security Act 1974 (88 Stat. 991)]

Par. 20. Paragraph (a) of § 1.1304-2 is amended to read as follows:

§ 1.1304-2 Provisions inapplicable if income averaging is chosen.

(a) Provisions inapplicable. If a taxpayer chooses the benefits of income averaging for any taxable year, pursuant to section 1304(a) and

§ 1.1304-1, the following sections of the Code will not apply for such year: * * *

(2) In taxable years beginning before January 1, 1974, section 72(n)(2) (relating to limitation of tax in case of certain distributions with respect to contributions by self-employed individuals).

* * *

[Temporary income tax regulations under the Employee Retirement Income Security Act of 1974]

Par. 21. Section 11.402(e)(4)(B)-1 is revoked.

[¶ 20,121A Reserved.—Proposed regulations under Code Secs. 401(a)(4) and 410(b) were formerly reproduced here. The final regulations are reproduced at ¶ 11,720W-14 and 12,165.]

[¶ 20,121B Reserved.—Proposed regulations relating to minimum participation requirements under Code Sec. 401(a)(26) were formerly reproduced here. The final regulations are now at ¶ 11,720Z-31 through ¶ 11,720Z-40.]

[¶ 20,121C Reserved.—Proposed rules relating to the $200,000 compensation limit under Code Sec. 401(a)(17) were formerly reproduced here. The final regulations are at ¶ 11,720Z-11.]

¶ 20,121D

Proposed regulations: Compensation: Definition.—Temporary and proposed regulations have been issued by the IRS to provide guidance with respect to definitions of compensation.

The temporary and proposed regulations were published in the Federal Register on May 14, 1990 (55 FR 19945).

AGENCY: Internal Revenue Service, Treasury.

ACTION: Notice of proposed rulemaking by cross-reference to temporary regulations.

SUMMARY: In the Rules and Regulations portion of this issue of the Federal Register, the Internal Revenue Service is issuing temporary regulations relating to the scope and meaning of the term "compensation" in section 414(s) of the Internal Revenue Code of 1986. They reflect changes made by the Tax Reform Act of 1986 (TRA '86) and by the Technical and Miscellaneous Revenue Act of 1988 (TAMRA). The text of those temporary regulations also serves as the text for this Notice of Proposed Rulemaking. These regulations will provide the public with guidance necessary to comply with the law and will affect sponsors of, and participants in, pension, profit-sharing and stock bonus plans, and certain other employee benefit plans.

DATES: Written comments must be received by July 13, 1990. Requests to speak (with outlines of oral comments) at a public hearing scheduled for Wednesday, September 26, 1990, at 10:00 a.m., and continuing at 10:00 a.m. each day, if necessary, on Thursday, September 27, 1990, and Friday, September 28, 1990, must received by Wednesday, September 12, 1990. See the notice of hearing published elsewhere in this issue of the Federal Register.

ADDRESSES: Send comments and requests to speak (with outlines of oral comments) at the public hearing to: Internal Revenue Service, P.O. Box 7604, Ben Franklin Station, Attn: CC:CORP:T:R (EE-129-86), Room 4429, Washington, D.C. 20044.

FOR FURTHER INFORMATION CONTACT: Concerning the regulation, Marjorie Hoffman, Office of the Assistant Chief Counsel (Employee Benefits and Exempt Organizations), at 202-343-6954 (not a toll-free number). Concerning the hearing, Carol Savage, Regulations Unit, at 202-343-0232 or 202-343-0232 or 202-566-3935 (not toll free numbers).

SUPPLEMENTARY INFORMATION:

Background

The temporary regulations in the Rules and Regulations portion of this issue of the Federal Register amend 26 CFR by amending § 1.414(s)-1T and § 1.415-2(d) to provide guidance with respect to definitions of compensation within the meaning of section 414(s) and section 415(c)(3) of the Internal Revenue Code (Code). The regulations are proposed to be issued under the authority contained in sections 414(s) and 7805 of the Code (100 Stat. 2453, 68A Stat. 917; 26

U.S.C. 414(s), 7805). For the text of the temporary regulations, see T.D. 8301 published in the Rules and Regulations portion of this issue of the Federal Register.

Special analyses

It has been determined that these proposed rules are not major rules as defined in Executive order 12291. Therefore, a Regulatory Impact Analysis is not required. It has been determined that section 553(b) of the Administrative Procedure Act (5 U.S.C. Chapter 5) and the Regulatory Flexibility Act (5 U.S.C. Chapter 6) do not apply to these regulations, and therefore, an initial Regulatory Flexibility Analysis is not required. Pursuant to section 7805(f) of the Internal Revenue Code, the proposed regulations are being sent to the Administrator of the Small Business Administration for comment on their impact on small business.

Comments and requests for public hearing

Before adopting these proposed regulations, consideration will be given to any written comments that are submitted (preferably a signed original and eight copies) to the Commissioner of Internal Revenue. All comments will be available for public inspection and copying in their entirety. Because the Treasury Department expects to issue final regulations on this matter as soon as possible, a public hearing will be held at 10:00 a.m. on September 26, 1990, and continued, if necessary, on September 27 and 28, 1990, in the I.R.S. Auditorium, Seventh Floor, 7400 Corridor, Internal Revenue Building, 1111 Constitution Ave., N.W., Washington, D.C. Comments must be received by July 13, 1990. Requests to speak (with outlines of oral comments) must be received by Wednesday, September 12, 1990. See the notice of hearing published elsewhere in this issue of the Federal Register.

Drafting information

The principal author of these proposed regulations is Marjorie Hoffman, Office of the Assistant Chief Counsel (Employee Benefits and Exempt Organizations). However, other personnel from the Service and Treasury Department participated in their development.

List of Subjects

26 CFR 1.401-0—1.425-1

Employee benefit plans, Employee stock ownership plans, Income taxes, Individual retirement accounts, Pensions, Stock options.

[¶ 20,122 Reserved.—Proposed Reg. §§ 1.7476-1, 1.7476-2, and 301.7476-1, relating to notification of interested parties regarding qualification of certain retirement plans, were formerly reported at this point. The final regulations now appear at ¶ 13,913, 13,914 and 13,916.]

[¶ 20,123 Reserved.—Proposed Reg. § 1.7476-3 relating to notice of determination was formerly reported at this point. The final regulation now appears at ¶ 13,915.]

[¶ 20,124 Reserved.—Proposed Reg. § 54.4975-9, relating to the definition of "fiduciary," was formerly reported at this point. The final regulation now appears at ¶ 13,647.]

[¶ 20,125 Reserved.—Proposed Reg. §§ 20.2039-1(a) and 20.2039-2(d), relating to the exclusion of annuity interests created by community property laws, were formerly reported at this point. The final regulations now appear at ¶ 13,501 and 13,502.]

[¶ 20,126 Reserved.—Proposed Reg. § 1.514(b)-1, relating to the definition of debt-financed property and the determination of interest on a refund of taxes on property acquired for prospective exempt use, was formerly reported at this point. The final regulation now appears at ¶ 13,233.]

[¶ 20,127 Reserved.—The discussion draft of proposed Reg. § 1.61-16 and proposed amendments of Reg. § 1.61-2 relating to treatment of fringe benefits was withdrawn in the Federal Register of December 28, 1976 (41 FR 56334). The announcement of the withdrawal appears in a Treasury Department News Release at ¶ 17,070T.]

[¶ 20,128 Reserved.—Proposed Reg. §§ 1.512(a)-1 and 1.512(a)-4, relating to the treatment of unrelated business income of war veteran organizations, were formerly reproduced at this point. The final regulations appear at ¶ 13,211 and 13,212B.]

[¶ 20,129 Reserved.—Proposed Reg. §§ 1.414(f)-1 and 1.414(g)-1, concerning the definitions of "multiemployer plan" and "plan administrator," were formerly reproduced at this point. The final regulations appear at ¶ 12,361 and ¶ 12,362.]

[¶ 20,130 Reserved.—Proposed Reg. § 1.401(a)-11, relating to qualified joint and survivor annuities, was formerly reproduced at this point. The final regulation appears at ¶ 11,719.]

[¶ 20,131 Reserved.—Proposed Reg. §§ 1.410(a)-1—1.410(a)-6, 1.410(b)-1, 1.410(d)-1, 1.413-1(a) and 1.413-2(a), relating to minimum participation standards, were formerly reproduced at this point. Reg. §§ 1.413-1(a) and 1.413-2(a) were renumbered §§ 1.413-1(b) and 1.413-2(b). The final regulations appear at ¶ 12,156—12,161, 12,163, 12,171, 12,311, and 12,312.]

[¶ 20,132 Reserved.—Proposed Reg. § 1.401(a)-14, relating to the commencement of benefits under qualified trusts, was formerly reproduced at this point. The final regulation appears at ¶ 11,720.]

[¶ 20,133 Reserved.—Proposed Reg. §§ 1.401-5 and 1.401(b)-1, relating to certain retroactive amendments of employee plans, were formerly reproduced at this point. The final regulations appear at ¶ 11,705 and 11,721.]

[¶ 20,134 Reserved.—Proposed Reg. § 1.401(a)-15, relating to the requirement that plan benefits are not decreased on account of certain social security increases, was formerly reproduced at this point. The final regulation appears at ¶ 11,720A.]

[¶ 20,135 Reserved.—Proposed Reg. § 1.401-12, relating to nonbank trustees of pension and profit-sharing trusts benefiting owner-employees, was formerly reproduced at this point. The final regulation appears at ¶ 11,712.]

[¶ 20,136 Reserved.—Proposed regulations §§ 1.401-8 and 1.401-8A, relating to custodial accounts and annuity contracts under qualified pension, profit-sharing, and stock bonus plans, were formerly reproduced at this point. The final regulations appear at ¶ 11,707A and 11,708.]

[¶ 20,137 Reserved.—Proposed regulations under Code Secs. 401(a)-19, 404(a), 406, 407, 411, and 805, relating to minimum vesting standards, were formerly reproduced at this point. The final regulations appear at ¶ 11,700A, 11,720O, 11,859, 12,211—12,231, 12,311, 12,312, and 13,302.]

[¶ 20,137A Reserved.—Proposed regulations under Code Secs. 2039 and 2517, relating to the estate and gift tax treatment of amounts payable under qualified employee retirement plans, were formerly reproduced at this point. The final regulations appear at ¶ 13,502, 13,502A, 13,502B, 13,502C and 13,521.]

¶ 20,137B

Proposed regulations relating to individual retirement plans and simplified employee pensions.—Reproduced below is the text of proposed regulations under Code Secs. 62, 219, 220, 404, 408, 409, 2503, 3121, 3306, 4973, 4974, and 6693, relating to individual retirement plans and simplified employee pensions (SEPs.) The proposed regulations were filed with the *Federal Register* on July 13, 1981 and published on July 14, 1981.

Proposed Reg. § 1.408(b)(4)(ii) was withdrawn on July 11, 2014 by 79 FR 40031. See ¶ 17,203Y-30.

DEPARTMENT OF THE TREASURY

Internal Revenue Service

26 CFR Parts 1, 25, 31, 54, and 301

[EE-7-78]

Individual Retirement Plans and Simplified Employee Pensions

AGENCY: Internal Revenue Service, Treasury.

ACTION: Notice of proposed rulemaking.

SUMMARY: This document contains proposed regulations relating to individual retirement plans and simplified employee pensions. Changes to the applicable law were made by the Employee Retirement Income Security Act of 1974, the Tax Reform Act of 1976, the Revenue Act of 1978 and the Technical Corrections Act of 1979. The regulations would provide the public with the guidance needed to comply with these Acts

and would affect institutions which sponsor individual retirement plans and simplified employee pensions. The regulations also affect employers and individuals who use these plans for retirement income.

DATES: Written comments and requests for a public hearing must be delivered or mailed by September 14, 1981. The amendments would have varying effective dates. The provisions relating to spousal individual retirement plans are generally effective for taxable years beginning after December 31, 1976. The provisions relating to simplified employee pensions are generally effective for taxable years beginning after December 31, 1978. The provisions defining "active participant" for individuals covered by defined benefit offset plans are effective for taxable years beginning after December 31, 1980.

ADDRESS: Send comments and requests for a public hearing to: Commissioner of Internal Revenue, Attention: CC:LR:T (EE-7-78), Washington, D.C. 20224.

FOR FURTHER INFORMATION CONTACT: William D. Gibbs of the Employee Plans and Exempt Organizations Division, Office of the

Chief Counsel, Internal Revenue Service, 1111 Constitution Avenue, N.W., Washington, D.C. 20224 (Attention: CC:LR:T) (202-566-3430) (not a toll-free number).

SUPPLEMENTARY INFORMATION:

Background

This document contains proposed amendments to the Income Tax Regulations (26 CFR Part 1), the Gift Tax Regulations (26 CFR Part 31), the Regulations on Pension Excise Taxes (26 CFR Part 54) and the Procedure and Administration Regulations (26 CFR Part 301) under section 62, 219, 220, 404, 408, 409, 2503, 3121, 3306, 4973, 4974,, and 6693 of the Internal Revenue Code of 1954. These amendments are proposed to conform the regulations to section 2002(d) of the Employee Retirement Income Security Act of 1974 (88 Stat. 966), section 1501 of the Tax Reform Act of 1976 (90 Stat. 1734), section 152, 156(c) and 157 of the Revenue Act of 1978 (90 Stat. 1734), sections 152, 156(c) and 157 of the Revenue Act of 1978 (92 Stat. 2797, 2802, 2803), and sections 101(a)(10), (101)(a)(14)(A), 101(a)(B), and 101(a)(14)(E)(ii) of the Technical Corrections Act of 1979 (94 Stat. 201-205). These regulations are to be issued under the authority contained in section 7805 of the Internal Revenue Code of 1954 (68A Stat. 917; 26 U.S.C. 7805).

On August 8, 1980, the Federal Register published final regulations relating to individual retirement plans under the Income Tax Regulations (26 CFR Part 1) under section 219, 409, 409 and under the Pension Excise Taxes (26 CFR Part 54) under section 4974 (45 FR 52782). Also, because of subsequent statutory provisions, some of the proposed regulations published on February 21, 1975 (40 FR 7661) were withdrawn in connection with those final regulations. The preamble to those final regulations indicated that regulations under other statutory provisions relating to retirement plans would be reproposed at a later date. This document contains these reproposed amendments, other than those relating to the rollover rules under Code sections 402 and 403. The Service intends to repropose these rules at a later date in connection with the regulations under Code sections 402(a) (5), (6) and (7), and 403(a) (4), (6) and (8).

Spousal Individual Retirement Plans

Internal Revenue Code section 220 allows an individual to deduct amounts contributed to an individual retirement plan maintained for the individual's benefit and an individual retirement plan maintained for the benefit of the individual's non-employed spouse. The proposed regulations set forth the type of funding arrangements which must be used and additional limitations and restrictions the individual and spouse must meet in order for the individual to obtain this deduction.

Simplified Employees Pensions

Internal Revenue Code section 408(k) sets forth rules for simplified employee pension ("SEP's"). The proposed regulations, §§ 1.408-7 through -9, indicate to employers and sponsoring institutions what requirements these arrangements must meet. Section 1.404(h)-1 of the proposed regulations sets forth the special deduction limitations for employers under Code section 404(h). Section 1.219-1(d)(4) and 1.219-3 of the proposed regulations set forth the rules governing the inclusion/deduction rules for employees for employer contributions to SEP's.

An employee will be allowed to deduct an employer contribution to a simplified employee pension. In general, the maximum amount the employee will be allowed to deduct is the lesser of 15 percent of compensation includible in gross income or $7,500. Proposed § 1.219-3 makes it clear that the deduction and the compensation are computed separately with respect to each employer's arrangement. Thus, an employee who has two or more employers can use only the compensation from the employer maintaining the simplified employee pension arrangement in computing the section 219(b)(7) limitation. On the other hand, if two or more employers of an employee each maintain a simplified employee will be allowed to deduct each employer's contribution, up to the compensation and dollar limit applied separately to each employer. Special limitations apply to certain related employers under Code section 414(b) and (c) and to self-employed individuals.

Certain rules have been included to make SEP arrangements more administrable by employers and the Service. Under proposed § 1.408-7(d)(1)(iii) and employer is not required to make a contribution to the SEP of an otherwise eligible employee who receives less than $200 compensation for a calendar year. This relieves employers of the burden of setting up SEP's to which very shall amounts of money will be contributed (the maximum deductible contribution would equal $30 (15% or $200)). This rule was published by the Service in Announcement 80-112, 1980-36 I.R.B. 35.

Further, under proposed § 1.408-7(d)(2), employers may execute necessary documents on behalf of employees who are unwilling or unable to execute those documents or whom the employer is unable to locate. This remedial rule prevents an employer's SEP arrangement from being disqualified because of a recalcitrant employee or one who has left the employer's service and is unable to be located by the employer. (See also proposed § 1.408-9(c) for possible reporting requirements in this instance.) Comments are requested as to what alternative remedial action, in lieu of execution on behalf of employees, employer would wish to take to avoid disqualification of their SEP arrangements. Comments also are requested on this proposed rule as to whether in a particular State there is any law that would preclude this action by the employer on the employee's behalf.

Employer contributions which exceed the amounts called for under the written allocation formula for the SEP arrangement are treated as if made to the employee's individual retirement account or individual retirement annuity, maintained outside the employee's SEP. It is contemplated that the employer, when it discovers the erroneous contribution, will notify the employee of the amount of the non-SEP contribution made in excess of the allocation formula. Because this amount may result in an excess contribution when made the employee may wish to take appropriate action in order to avoid IRA penalties. The normal IRA rules under Code section 219 apply in such a situation. This rule is proposed in order to prevent the entire SEP arrangement from being disqualified due to an inadvertent error on the part of the employer, such as an incorrect calculation of employee compensation. Under Code section 408(k), the entire SEP arrangement could be disqualified on account of the excess contribution. This rule is proposed to provide relief in such cases. See proposed § 1.408-7(f) and the example of how the rule would operate in a particular case.

Proposed § 1.408-7(c)(2) contains a special rule clarifying the relationship between SEP's and salary reduction agreements. This rule makes it clear that employer contributions to an employee's individual retirement account or annuity that are made under a salary reduction agreement between the employer and employee are not treated as employer contributions to an employee's simplified employee pension. Thus, if the employee may elect either an contribution or current compensation, the contribution is treated as an employee contribution and, therefore, is not eligible for the favorable SEP arrangement rules.

Similarly, other contributions such as voluntary contributions made by the employee, or on behalf of the employee by the employer as the agent for the employee (such as by payroll withholding), are treated as employee contributions.

Even though the employer picks the institution or substantially influences the employee's choice of the institution to which the employer makes the SEP contribution and which serves as trustee or sponsor for the employee's DEP, the SEP arrangement remains qualified under the Code. Further, this action by the employer is not a prohibition on withdrawal of funds within the meaning of Code section 408(k)(4)(B). The employer should, however, be aware that the Department of Labor may require special reporting for such action. (See 29 CFR 2520.104-48 (1980) and 29 CFR 2520.104-49 (1981).)

Proposed § 1.408-9 contains reporting requirements for SEP's. Employer who use the Service's Model Simplified Employee Pension Arrangement (Form 5305-SEP) and furnish the Model to their employees will satisfy the disclosure requirements relating to adoption of the SEP arrangement. Further, if the employer reports the amount of the SEP contribution on an employee's W-2, the annual reporting requirements will be satisfied. The Department of Labor also has reporting requirements for SEP's, which are in addition to the requirements of the Internal Revenue Service. (See 29 CFR 2520.104-48 (1980) and 29 CFR 2520.104-49 (1981).)

Employers who failed to make required contributions on behalf of employees for calendar year 1979 because the employees were no longer employed at the end of the employer's taxable year may make such "make up" contributions before January 1, 1981. This conforms to Announcement 80-112, 1980-36 I.R.B. 35. This relief is given because employers may not have anticipated the rules contained in that announcement and § 1.408-7(d)(1), (2) and (3), relating to which employees are entitled to receive an allocation. It is expected that employers who make such contributions will comply with the reporting requirements of § 1.408-9(b) and file amended tax returns. Likewise, employees who receive such contributions are expected to file amended tax returns.

Other Amendments

Conforming and technical amendments made by the Tax Reform Act of 1976, the Revenue Act of 1978, and the Technical Corrections Act of

1979 have been made to the regulations under Code sections 62, 219, 220, 404, 408, 409, 415, 3121, 3306, 4973, 4974, and 6693.

Also, regulations are proposed which define "active participant" under section 219(b)(2) for individuals who are covered with Federal or State benefits such as social security benefits. These rules were requested by commentators at the public hearing held July 19, 1979, on the reproposed active participant rules, and in other written comments on those proposed regulations published in the **Federal Register** on March 23, 1979 (44 FR 17754). This proposed rule allows employees to make IRA contributions when, in effect, they get no benefit from their employers' plans.

Regulatory Flexibility Act

Although this document is a notice of proposed rulemaking which solicits public comment, the Internal Revenue Service has concluded that the regulations proposed herein are interpretative and that the notice and public procedure requirements of 5 U.S.C. 553 do not apply. Accordingly, these proposed regulations do not constitute regulations subject to the Regulatory Flexibility Act (5 U.S.C. chapter 6).

Comments and Requests for a Public Hearing

Before adopting these proposed regulations, consideration will be given to any written comments that are submitted (preferably six copies) to the Commissioner of Internal Revenue. All comments will be available for public inspection and copying. A public hearing will be held upon written request to the Commissioner by any person who has submitted written comments. If a public hearing is held, notice of the time and place will be published in the **Federal Register**.

Drafting Information

The principal author of these proposed regulations is William D. Gibbs of the Employee Plans and Exempt Organizations Division of the Office of Chief Counsel, Internal Revenue Service. However, personnel from other offices of the Internal Revenue Service and Treasury Department participated in developing the regulation, both on matters of substance and style.

Proposed Amendments to the Regulations

The proposed amendments to 26 CFR Parts 1, 25, 31, 54, and 301 are as follows:

Income Tax Regulations (26 CFR Part 1)

PART 1—INCOME TAX; TAXABLE YEARS BEGINNING AFTER DECEMBER 31, 1953

Paragraph 1. Section 1.62-1 is amended by revising paragraphs (c)(13) to read as follows:

§ 1.62-1 Adjusted gross income.

* * *

(c) * * *

(13) Deductions allowed by sections 219 and 220 for contributions to an individual retirement account described in section 408(a), for an individual retirement annuity described in section 408(b), or for a retirement bond described in section 409;

Par. 2. Section 1.219-1 is revised by adding: (1) a new subdivision (iv) to paragraph (b)(2), and (2) new paragraphs (d) and (e) to read as follows:

§ 1.219-1 Deduction for retirement savings.

* * *

(b) *Limitations and restrictions.* * * *

(2) *Restrictions.* * * *

(iv) *Alternative deduction.* No deduction is allowed under subsection (a) for the taxable year if the individual claims the deduction allowed by section 220 (relating to retirement savings for certain married individuals) for the taxable year.

* * *

(d) *Time when contributions deemed made*—(1) *Taxable years beginning before January 1, 1978.* For taxable years beginning before January 1, 1977, a taxpayer must make a contribution to an individual retirement plan during a taxable year in order to receive a deduction for such taxable year. For taxable years beginning after December 31, 1976, and before January 1, 1978, a taxpayer shall be deemed to have made a contribution on the last day of the preceding taxable year if the contribution is made on account of such taxable year and is made not

later than 45 days after the end of such taxable year. A contribution made not later than 45 days after the end of a taxable year shall be treated as made on account of such taxable year if the individual specifies in writing to the trustee, insurance company, or custodian that the amounts contributed are for such taxable year.

(2) *Taxable years beginning after December 31, 1977.* For taxable years beginning after December 31, 1977, a taxpayer shall be deemed to have made a contribution on the last day of the preceding taxable year if the contribution is made on account of such taxable year and is made not later than the time prescribed by law for filing the return for such taxable year (including extensions thereof). A contribution made not later than the time prescribed by law for filing the return for a taxable year (including extensions thereof) shall be treated as made on account of such taxable year if it is irrevocably specified in writing to the trustee, insurance company, or custodian that the amounts contributed are for such taxable year.

(3) *Time when individual retirement plan must be established.* For purposes of this paragraph, an individual retirement plan need not be established until the contribution is made.

(4) *Year of inclusion in income.* Any amount paid by an employer to an individual retirement account, for an individual retirement annuity or for an individual retirement bond (including an individual retirement account or individual retirement annuity maintained as part of a simplified employee pension plan) shall be included in the gross income of the employee for the taxable year for which the contribution is made.

(e) *Excess contributions treated as contribution made during subsequent year for which there is an unused limitation*—(1) *In general.* If for the taxable year the maximum amount allowable as a deduction under this section exceeds the amount contributed, then the taxpayer, whether or not a deduction is actually claimed, shall be treated as having made an additional contribution for the taxable year in an amount equal to the lesser of—

(i) The amount of such excess, or

(ii) The amount of the excess contributions for such taxable year (determined under section 4973(b)(2) without regard to subparagraph (C) thereof).

(2) *Amount contributed.* For purposes of this paragraph, the amount contributed—

(i) Shall be determined without regard to this paragraph, and

(ii) Shall not include any rollover contribution.

(3) *special rule where excess deduction was allowed for closed year.* Proper reduction shall be made in the amount allowable as a deduction by reason of this paragraph for any amount allowed as a deduction under this section or section 220 for a prior taxable year for which the period for assessing a deficiency has expired if the amount so allowed exceeds the amount which should have been allowed for such prior taxable year.

(4) *Effective date.* (i) This paragraph shall apply to the determination of deductions for taxable years beginning after December 31, 1975.

(ii) If, but for this subdivision, an amount would be allowable as a deduction by reason of section 219(c)(5) for a taxable year beginning before January 1, 1978, such amount shall be allowable only for the taxpayer's first taxable year beginning in 1978.

(5) *Examples.* The provisions of this paragraph may be illustrated by the following examples. (Assume in each example, unless otherwise stated, that it is less than age 70 ½ and is not covered by a simplified employee pension or a plan described in section 219(b)(2).)

Example (1). (i) B, a calendar-year taxpayer, earns $8,000 in compensation includible in gross income for 1979. On December 1, 1979, B establishes an individual retirement account (IRA) and contributes $1,500 to the account. B does not withdraw any money from the IRA after the initial contribution. Under section 219(b)(i), the maximum amount that B can deduct for 1979 is 15% of $8,000 or $1,200. B has an excess contribution for 1979 of $300.

(ii) For 1980, B has compensation includible in gross income of $12,000. B makes a $1,000 contribution to his IRA for 1980.

(iii) Although B made only a $1,000 contribution to his IRA for 1980, under the rules contained in this paragraph, B is treated as having made an additional contribution of $300 for 1980 and will be allowed to deduct $1,300 as his 1980 IRA contribution.

Example (2). (i) For 1979, the facts are the same as in *Example (1).*

(ii) For 1980, B has compensation includible in gross income of $12,000. B makes a $1,500 contribution to his IRA for 1980.

(iii) B will be allowed a $1,500 deduction for 1980 (the amount of his contribution). B will not be allowed a deduction for the $300 excess contribution made in 1979 because the maximum amount allowable for 1980 does not exceed the amount contributed.

Example (3). (i) For 1979, the facts are the same as in *Example (1).*

(ii) For 1980, B has compensation includible in gross income of $12,000. B makes a $1,400 contribution to his IRA for 1980.

(iii) For 1980, B will be allowed to deduct his contribution of $1,400 and $100 of the excess contribution made for 1979. He will not be allowed to deduct the remaining $200 of the excess contribution made for 1979 because that would make his deduction for 1980 more than $1,500, his allowable deduction for 1980.

(iv) For 1981, B has compensation includible in gross income of $15,000. B makes a $1,300 contribution to his IRA for 1981.

(v) B will be allowed to deduct the remaining $200 and his $1,300 contribution for 1981.

Example (4). (i) For 1979, the facts are the same as in *Example (1).*

(ii) For 1980, B has compensation includible in gross income of $12,000. B makes a $1,000 contribution to his IRA for 1980. B is allowed to deduct the $300 excess contribution for 1980 but fails to do so on his return. Consequently, B deducts only $1,000 for 1980.

(iii) Under no circumstances will B be allowed to deduct the $300 excess contribution made for 1979 for any taxable year after 1980 because B is treated as having made the contribution for 1980.

Example (5). (i) For 1979, the facts are the same as *Example (1).*

(ii) For 1980, B has compensation includible in gross income of $15,000 and is an active participant in a plan described in section 219(b)(2)(A).

(iii) B will not be allowed to deduct for 1980 the $300 excess contribution for 1979 because the maximum amount allowable as a deduction under sections 219(b)(1) and 219(b)(2) is $0.

Par. 3. Section 1.219-2 is amended by: (1) revising the first sentence of paragraph (b)(1); (2) renumbering paragraph (b)(2), (3), and (4) as paragraph (b)(3), (4) and (5), respectively, and adding a new paragraph (b)(2) before the renumbered paragraph (b)(3), (4) and (5); (3) revising paragraph (f) and (4) adding new examples (3), (4) and (5) after *Example (2)* in paragraph (h). These revised and added provisions read as follows:

§ 1.219-2 Definition of active participant.
* * * * *

(b) *Defined benefit plans*—(1) *In general.* Except as provided in subparagraphs (2), (3), (4) and (5) of this paragraph, an individual is an active participant in a defined benefit plan if for any portion of the plan year ending with or within such individual's taxable year he is not excluded under the eligibility provisions of this plan. * * *

(2) *Special rule for offset plans.* For taxable years beginning after December 31, 1980, an individual who satisfies the eligibility requirements of a plan under which benefits are offset by Social Security or Railroad Retirement benefits is not considered an active participant by virtue of participation in such plan for a particular plan year if such individual's compensation for the calendar year during which such plan year ends does not exceed the offset plan's breakpoint compensation amount for such plan year. Breakpoint compensation is the maximum compensation determined for the plan for a plan year that any participant could earn and have a projected benefit from the offset plan of $0. For purposes of determining the projected plan benefit, the following assumptions are made: plan participation begins at age 25 and maximum credited service is earned for participation from age 25 to age 65 regardless of the participant's actual participation; plan benefits, including the offset, are based on W-2 earnings from the employer for such calendar year regardless of the definition of compensation on which plan benefits are based; and the projected Social Security Primary Insurance Amount (PIA) is computed under a formula that the Commissioner may, from time to time, prescribe for this purpose.

* * * * *

(f) *Certain individuals not active participants*—(1) *Election out of plan.* For purposes of this section, an individual who elects pursuant to the plan not to participate in the plan will be considered to be ineligible for participation for the period to which the election applies, in the case of a defined benefit plan, such as an election shall be effective no earlier than the first plan year commencing after the date of the election.

(2) *Members of reserve components.* A member of a reserve component of the armed forces (as defined in section 261(a) of Title 10 of the United States Code) is not considered to be an active participant in a plan described in section 219(b)(2)(A)(iv) for a taxable year solely because he is a member of a reserve component unless he has served in excess of 90 days on active duty (other than military duty for training) during the year.

(3) *Volunteer firefighters.* An individual whose participation in a plan described in section 219(b)(2)(A)(iv) is based solely upon his activity as a volunteer firefighter and whose accrued benefit as of the beginning of the taxable year is not more than an annual benefit of $1,800 (when expressed as a single life annuity commencing at age 65) is not considered to be an active participant in such a plan for the taxable year.

* * * * *

(h) *Examples.* * * *

Example (3). (i) For plan year X the annual projected Social Security PIA is determined as follows:

Compensation range[1]	PIA formula[1]
$0 to $1,626	PIA = $1,484.
$1,627 to $2,160	PIA = .90 (compensation).
$2,161 to $13,020	PIA = .32 (compensation) + $1,253.
$13,021 to $22,900	PIA = 15 (compensation) + $3,466.
$22,901 and over	PIA = $6,901.

[1] These numbers are for illustrative purposes only.

(ii) V is a defined benefit plan which provides a normal retirement benefit of 1.5% of high five-year average earnings excluding overtime pay, minus 2% of Social Security PIA, the difference multiplied by years of plan participation up to a maximum of 30 years. V provides that individuals commence plan participation on their date of employment. Normal retirement age is 62. V's breakpoint compensation for the plan year ending in year X can be determined as follows:

I. *Determine V's projected benefits:*

An individual credited with 40 years of service (from age 25 to 65) would have a projected benefit of:

(30) (1.5% (compensation) –2% (PIA))

or

45% (compensation) –60% (PIA).

Note that in the determination of the projected benefit, the normal retirement age is assumed to be age 65 rather than the actual normal retirement age of 62, the participant is assumed to have 40 years of credited service, and the plan definition of compensation is assumed to be the same as is used to compute the Social Security benefit.

II. *Determine V's formula compensation changepoints.* The formula compensation changepoints are amounts where the projected benefit formula, expressed in terms of compensation, changes:

Since V's benefit formula applies uniformly to all compensation, the compensation changepoints are determined by the PIA portion only, and are

a. $1,626,

b. 2,160.

c. 13,020.

d. 22,900.

III. *Determine which of the formula compensation changepoints first produces a projected benefit greater than 0.* This can be done by testing the projected benefit for compensation amounts equal to V's compensation changepoints:

a. Formula compensation changepoint equal to $1,626.

i. Projected benefit = 45% × 1,626 – 60% × 1.464 = 0.

V's compensation breakpoint, therefore, exceeds $1,626.

b. Formula compensation changepoint equal to $2,160.

i. Projected benefit = 45% × 2,160 – 60% × (90 × 2,160) = 0.

V's compensation breakpoint, therefore, exceeds $2,160.

c. Formula compensation changepoint equal to $13,020.

i. Projected benefit = 45% × 13,020 – 60% × (.32 × 13,020 + 1,253) = 2,607.

V's compensation breakpoint is, therefore, in the compensation range $2,161 to $13,020.

IV. *Determine V's compensation breakpoint within the $2,161 to $13,020 compensation range.*

V's compensation breakpoint can be determined by finding the greatest compensation that will result in a projected benefit of 0 for this compensation range:

a. 45% × compensation – 60% × (.32 × compensation + 1,253) = 0.

b. Eliminate the parentheses in equation a by multiplying each of the terms within the parentheses by – 60%. 45% × compensation – 19.2% × compensation – 751.80 = 0.

c. Add 751.80 to both sides of equation in b and combine the first two terms. 25.8% × compensation = 751.80.

d. Dividing both sides of the equation in c by 25.8%, V's breakpoint compensation for 1979 = $2,914.

V. Therefore, individuals whose W-2 earnings from the employer do not exceed $2,914 in year X are not considered active participants by virtue of participating in Plan V.

Example (4). For year X the annual projected Social Security PIA is determined as in *Example (3).*

T is defined benefit plan which provides a normal retirement benefit equal to 20% of final average earnings plus 10% of such earnings in excess of $2,000 minus 45% of PIA, the net result reduced pro-rata for participation less than 15 years. Participation commences upon attainment of age 20. Normal retirement age is 65.

I. *Determine T's projected benefit for year X.*

An individual credited with 40 years of service (from age 25 to 65) would have projected benefit of:

20% of compensation plus 10% of compensation in excess of $2,000, if any

minus

45% of PIA

II. *Determine T's formula compensation changepoints.*

$2,000 is a formula compensation changepoint, in addition to the four PIA changepoints, since T's benefit formula changes at this compensation amount. The five formula compensation changepoints are:

a. $1,626.

b. 2,000.

c. 2,160.

d. 13,020.

e. 22,900.

III. *Determine which of T's formula compensation changepoints first produces a projected benefit greater than 0.*

a. Compensation changepoint equal to $1,626.

i. Projected benefit = 20% × 1,626 + 10% × 0 – 45% × 1.424 = 0.

T's compensation changepoint, therefore, exceeds $1,626.

b. Compensation changepoint equal to $2,000.

i. Projected benefit = 20% × 2,000 + 10% × 0 – 45% × (.90 × 2,000) = 0.

T's compensation changepoint, therefore, exceeds $2,000.

c. Compensation changepoint equal to $2,160.

i. Projected benefit = 20% × 2,160 + 10% × (2,160 – 2,000) – 45% × (.90 × 2,160) = 0.

T's compensation breakpoint, therefore, exceeds $2,160.

d. Compensation changepoint equal to $13,020.

i. Projected benefit = 20% × 13,020 + 10% (13,020 – 2,000) – 45% × (.32 × 13,020 + 1.253) = 1,267.

T's compensation breakpoint, therefore, in the compensation range $2,160 to $13,020.

IV. *Determine T's breakpoint compensation within the $2,160 to $13,020 range.*

T's compensation breakpoint can be determined by finding the greatest compensation that will result in a projected benefit of 0 for this range:

a. 20% × comp. + 10% × (comp. – 2,000) – 45% × (.32 × comp. + 1.253) = 0.

b. Eliminating both parenthesis in equation a. by multiplying each of the terms within by the appropriate percentage.

20% × comp. + 10% × comp. – 200 – 14.4% × comp. – 563.85 = 0.

c. Add 763.85 to both sides of equation and combine remaining terms in equation b.

15.6% × comp. = 763.85.

d. Dividing each side of equation c. by 15.6%, T's breakpoint compensation for year X = $4,896.

V. Therefore, individuals whose W-2 earnings do not exceed $4,896 in year X are not considered active participants by virtue of participating in Plan T.

Example (5). Assume the same facts as *Example (4),* except that T also provides a minimum monthly benefit of $100 for participants with 15 or more years of plan participation. There is no compensation amount which will produce a projected benefit of $0. Therefore, all individuals who satisfy T's eligibility requirements are considered active participants.

Par. 4. There are added after § 1.219-2 the following new sections:

§ 1.219-3 Limitation on simplified employee pension deductions.

(a) *General rule*—(1) *In general.* Under section 219(b)(7), if an employer contribution is made on behalf of an employee to a simplified employee pension described in section 408(k), the limitations of this action, and not section 219(b)(1) and § 1.219-1(b)(1), shall apply for purposes of computing the maximum allowable deduction for that individual employee. The other rules of section 219 and § § 1.219-1 and 1.219-2 apply for purposes of computing an individual's deduction except as modified by this section.

(2) *Employer limitation.* The maximum deduction limitation under section 219(a) for an employee with respect to an employer contribution to the employee's simplified employee pension under that employer's arrangement cannot exceed an amount equal to the lesser of—

(i) 15 percent of the employee's compensation from that employer (determined without regard to the employer contribution to the simplified employee pension) includible in the employee's gross income for the taxable year, or

(ii) The amount contributed by that employer to the employee's simplified employee pension and included in gross income (but not in excess of $7,500).

(3) *Special rules*—(i) *Compensation.* Compensation referred to in paragraph (a)(2)(i) has the same meaning as under § 1.219-1(c)(1) except that it includes only the compensation from the employer making the contribution to the simplified employee pension. Thus, if an individual earns $50,000 from employer A and $20,000 from employer B and employer B contributes $4,000 to a simplified employee pension on behalf of the individual, the maximum amount the individual will be able to deduct under section 219(b)(7) is 15 percent of $20,000, or $3,000.

(ii) *Special rule for officers, shareholders, and owner-employees.* In the case of an employee who is an officer, shareholder, or owner-employee described in section 408(k)(3) with respect to a particular employer, the $7,500 amount referred to in paragraph (a)(2)(ii) shall be reduced by the amount of tax taken into account with respect to such individual under section 408(k)(3)(D).

(iii) *More than one employer arrangement.* Except as provided in paragraph (c), below, the maximum deduction under paragraph (a)(2) for an individual who receives simplified employee pension contributions under two or more employers' simplified employee pension arrangements cannot exceed the sum of the maximum deduction limitations computed separately for that individual under each such employer's arrangement.

(iv) *Section 408 rules.* Under section 408(j), for purposes of applying the $7,500 limitations under section 408(a)(1), (b)(1), (b)(2)(B) and (d)(5) (§ 1.408-2(b)(1), § 1.408-3(b)(2) and § 1.408-4(h)(3)(i), respectively), the $7,500 limitations shall be applied separately with respect to each employer's contributions to a individual's simplified employee pension.

(b) *Limitations not applicable to SEP contributions*—(1) *Active participant.* The limitations on coverage by certain other plans in section 219(b)(2) and § 1.219-1(b)(2)(i) shall not apply with respect to the employer contribution to a simplified employee pension. Thus, an employee is allowed a deduction for an employer's contribution to a simplified employee pension even though he is an active participant in an employer's qualified plan.

(2) *Contributions to simplified employee pensions after age 70 ½.* The denial of deductions for contributions after age 70 ½ contained in

section 219(b)(3) and § 1.219-1(b)(2)(ii) shall not apply with respect to the employer contribution to a simplified employee pension.

(c) *Multiple employer, etc. limitations*—(1) *Section 414(b) and (c) employers*. In the case of a controlled group of employers within the meaning of section 414(b) or (c), the maximum deduction limitation for an employee under paragraph (a)(2) shall be computed by treating such employers as one employer maintaining a single simplified pension arrangement and by treating the compensation of that employee from such employers as if from one employer. Thus, for example, for a particular employee the 15 percent limitation on compensation would be determined with regard to the compensation from all employers within such group. Further, the maximum deduction with respect to such group could not exceed $7,500.

(2) *Self-employed individuals*. In the case of an employee who is a self-employed individual within the meaning of section 401(c)(1) with respect to more than one trade or business, the maximum deduction limitation for such an employee under paragraph (a)(2) shall not exceed the lesser of the sum of such limitation applied separately with respect to the simplified employee pension arrangement of each trade or business or such limitation determined by treating such trades or businesses as if they constituted a single employer.

(d) *Additional deduction for employee contributions*. If the maximum allowable deduction for an individual employee determined under paragraph (a) for employer contributions to that individual's simplified employee pensions is less than $1,500, the individual shall be entitled to an additional deduction for contributions to individual retirement programs maintained on his behalf. The additional deduction shall equal the excess, if any, of the section 219(b)(1) and § 1.219-1(b)(1) maximum deduction limitation over the maximum deduction limitation determined under paragraph (a). For purpose of determining the compensation limit of section 219(b)(1), employer simplified employee pension contributions shall not be taken into account. Thus, for example, if $1,000 is deductible by individual A for employer contributions under a simplified employee pension arrangement and A's compensation, not including the $1,000 SEP contribution, is $10,000, than A would be entitled to an additional deduction of $500.

(e) *Examples*. The provisions of this section may be illustrated by the following examples:

Example (1). Corporation X is a calendar-year, cash basis taxpayer. It adopts a simplified employee pension agreement in 1980 and wishes to contribute the maximum amount on behalf of each employee for 1980. Individual E is a calendar-year taxpayer who is employed solely by Corporation X in 1980. Beginning in June 1980, Corporation X pays $100 each month into a simplified employee pension maintained on behalf of E. X makes a total payment to E's simplified employee pension during the year of $700. E's other compensation from X for the year totals $15,000. The maximum amount which E will be allowed to deduct as a simplified employee pension contribution is 15% of $15,000, or $2,250. Therefore, X may make an additional contribution for 1980 to E's simplified employee pension of $1,550. X makes this additional contribution to E's simplified employee pension in February of 1981. E's total compensation for 1980 includible in gross income is $15,000 ♦ $2,250 or $17,250.

Example (2). (i) Corporation G is a calendar-year taxpayer which does not maintain an integrated plan as defined in section 408(k)(3)(E). It adopts a simplified employee pension agreement for 1980. It wishes to contribute 15% of compensation on behalf of each employee reduced by its tax under section 3111(a). The corporation has 4 employees, A, B, C, and D. D is a shareholder. The compensation for these employees for 1980 is as follows:

A ✓ $10,000

B ✓ 20,000

C ✓ 30,000

D ✓ 60,000

(ii) The amount of money which the corporation will be allowed to contribute on behalf of each employee under this allocation formula and the amount of the employer contribution each employee will be allowed to deduct is set forth in the following table:

Employee	Compensation	Lesser of $7500 or 15% of Comp.	3111(a)[1] Tax	SEP[2] Contribution	Sec. 219(b)(7) deduction
A	$10,000	$1,500	$508.00	$992.00	$992.00
B	20,000	3,000	1,016.00	1,984.00	1,984.00
C	30,000	4,500	1,315.72	1,184.28	1,184.28
D	60,000	7,500	1,315.72	6,184.28	6,184.28

[1] The section 3111(a) tax is computed by multiplying compensation up to the taxable wage base ($25,900 for 1980) by the tax rate (5.08% for 1980).
[2] Simplified Employee Pension.

Example (3). Corporations A and B are calendar year taxpayers. Corporations A and B are not members of a controlled group of employers within the meaning of section 414(b) or (c). Individual M is employed full-time by Corporation A and part-time by Corporation B. Corporation A adopts a simplified employee pension agreement for calendar year 1980 and agrees to contribute 15% of compensation for each participant. M is a participant under Corporation A's simplified employee pension agreement and earns $15,000 for 1980 from Corporation A before A's contribution to his simplified employee pension. M also earns $5,000 as a part-time employee of Corporation B for 1980. Corporation A contributes $2,500 to M's simplified employee pension. The maximum amount that M will be allowed to deduct under Section 219(b)(7) for 1980 is 15% of $15,000 or $2,250. The remaining $250 is an excess contribution because M cannot consider the compensation earned from Corporation B under § 1.219-3(a)(3)(i).

Example (4). Individual P is employed by Corporation H and Corporation O. Corporation H and O are not members of a controlled group of employers within the meaning of section 414(b) or (c). Both Corporation H and Corporation O maintain a simplified employee pension arrangement and contribute 15 percent of compensation on behalf of each employee. P earns $50,000 from Corporation H and $60,000 from Corporation O. Corporation H and O each contributes $7,500 under its simplified employee pension arrangement to an individual retirement account maintained on behalf of P. P will be allowed to deduct $15,000 for employer contributions to simplified employee pensions because each employer has a simplified employee pension arrangement and the SEP contributions by Corporation H and O do not exceed the applicable $7,500 ← 15 percent limitation.

§ 1.220-1 Deduction for retirement savings for certain married individuals.

(a) *In general*. Subject to the limitations and restrictions of paragraphs (c), (d) and (e) and the special rules of paragraph (f) of this section, there shall be allowed a deduction under section 62 from gross income of amounts paid for the taxable year of an individual by or on behalf of such individual for the benefit of himself and his spouse to an individual retirement account described in section 408(a), for an individual retirement annuity described in section 408(b), or for an individual retirement bond described in section 409. The amounts contributed to an individual retirement account, for an individual retirement annuity, or for an individual retirement bond by or on behalf of an individual for the benefit of himself and his spouse shall be deductible only by such individual. The first sentence of this paragraph shall apply only in the case of a contribution of cash; a contribution of property other than cash is not allowable as a deduction. In the case of an individual retirement bond, a deduction will not be allowed if the bond is redeemed within 12 months of its issue date.

(b) *Definitions*—(1) *Compensation*. For purposes of this section, the term "compensation" has the meaning set forth in § 1.219-1(c)(1).

(2) *Active participant*. For purposes of this section, the term "active participant" has the meaning set forth in § 1.219-2.

(3) *Individual retirement subaccount*. For purposes of this section, the term individual retirement subaccount is that part of an individual retirement account maintained for the exclusive benefit of the individual or the individual's spouse and which meets the following requirements:

(i) The individual or spouse for whom the subaccount is maintained has exclusive control over the subaccount after deposits have been made,

(ii) The subaccount, by itself, meets the requirements of section 408(a), except that it is not a separate trust,

(iii) The trustee or custodian maintains records indicating the ownership of the funds, and

(iv) The individual and spouse do not jointly own the individual retirement account of which the subaccount is a part.

(c) *Types of funding arrangements permitted.* The deduction under paragraph (a) of this section shall be allowed only if one of the following types of funding arrangements is used:

(1) A separate individual retirement account, individual retirement annuity, or individual retirement bond is established or purchased for the benefit of the individual and a separate individual retirement account, individual retirement annuity or individual retirement bond is established or purchased for the individual's spouse.

(2) A single individual retirement account described in section 408(a) is established or purchased and such account has an individual retirement subaccount for the benefit of the individual and an individual retirement subaccount for the benefit of the spouse. The single individual retirement account cannot be owned jointly by the husband and wife.

(3) An individual retirement account described in section 408(c) is maintained by an employer or employee association and such account has arrangements described in subparagraphs (1) or (2).

(d) *Maximum deduction.* The amount allowable as a deduction under section 220(a) to an individual for any taxable year may not exceed—

(1) Twice the amount paid (including prior excess contributions) to the account, subaccount, annuity, or for the bond, established for the individual or for the spouse to or for which the lesser amount was paid for the taxable year.

(2) An amount equal to 15 percent of the compensation includible in the individual's gross income for the taxable year, or

(3) $1,750

whichever is the smallest amount.

(e) *Limitations and restrictions*—(1) *Alternative deduction.* No deduction is allowable under section 220(a) for the taxable year if the individual claims the deduction allowed by section 219(a) for the taxable year.

(2) *Individual or spouse covered by certain other plans.* No deduction is allowable under section 220(a) to an individual for the taxable year if for any part of such year—

(i) He or his spouse was an active participant (as defined in §1.219-2), or

(ii) Amounts were contributed by his employer, or his spouse's employer, on the individual's or spouse's behalf for an annuity contract described in section 403(b) (whether or not his, or his spouse's, rights in such contract are nonforfeitable).

(3) *Contributions after age 70 ½.* No deduction is allowable under section 220(a) with respect to any payment which is made for a taxable year of an individual if either the individual or his spouse has attained age 70 ½ before the close of such taxable year.

(4) *Recontributed amounts.* No deduction is allowable under section 220(a) for any taxable year of an individual with respect to a rollover contribution described in section 402(a)(5), 402(a)(7), 403(a)(4), 403(b)(8), 408(d)(3), or 409(b)(3)(C).

(5) *Amounts contributed under endowment contracts.* The rules for endowment contracts under section 220 are the same as the provisions for such contracts under §1.219-1(b)(3).

(6) *Employed spouses.* No deduction is allowable under section 220(a) if the spouse of the individual has any compensation (as defined in §1.219-1(c)(1) determined without regard to section 911) for the taxable year of such spouse ending with or within the taxable year of the individual.

(f) *Special rules*—(1) *Community property.* Section 220 is to be applied without regard to any community property laws.

(2) *Time when contributions deemed made.* The time when contributions are deemed made is determined in the same manner as under section 219(c)(3). See §1.219-1(d).

(g) *Excess contributions treated as contribution made during subsequent year for which there is an unused limitation*—(1) *In general.* If for the taxable year the maximum amount allowable as a deduction under this section exceeds the amount contributed, then the taxpayer, whether or not a deduction is actually claimed, shall be treated as

having made an additional contribution for the taxable year in an amount equal to the lesser of—

(i) The amount of such excess, or

(ii) The amount of the excess contributions for such taxable year (determined under section 4973(b)(2) without regard to subparagraph (C) thereof).

For purposes of computing the maximum deduction under section 220(b)(1), the excess contribution for a previous year shall be treated as made for the current year.

(2) *Amount contributed.* For purposes of this paragraph, the amount contributed—

(i) Shall be determined without regard to this paragraph, and

(ii) Shall not include any rollover contribution.

(3) *Special rule where excess contribution was allowed for closed year.* Proper reduction shall be made in the amount allowable as a deduction by reason of this paragraph for any amount allowed as a deduction under this section or section 219 for a prior taxable year for which the period for assessing a deficiency has expired if the amount so allowed exceeds the amount which should have been allowed for such prior taxable year.

(4) *Examples.* The provisions of this paragraph may be illustrated by the following examples:

Example (1). (i) H, a calendar-year taxpayer, earns $10,000 in compensation includible in gross income for 1979. H is married to W, also a calander-year taxpayer, who has no compensation for 1979. For 1979, neither H nor W is covered by certain other plans within the meaning of section 220(b)(3). On November 24, 1979, H establishes an individual retirement account (IRA) for himself and an individual retirement account for W. H contributes $850 to each account. Neither H nor W withdraws any money from either account after the initial contribution. Under section 220(b)(1) the maximum amount that H can deduct for 1979 is 15 percent of the compensation includible in his gross income or $1,500. H has made an excess contribution of $200 for 1979.

(ii) for 1980, H has compensation includible in gross income of $12,000. W has no compensation for 1980. For 1980, neither H nor W is covered by certain other plans, within the meaning of section 220(b)(3). No contributions are made to the IRA of H or W for 1980.

(iii) Although H made no contributions to either his or W's IRA for 1980, under the rules contained in this paragraph, H is treated as having made an additional contribution of $100 to his IRA and $100 to W's IRA for 1980 and will be allowed to deduct $200 as his 1980 IRA contribution.

Example (2). (i) For 1979, the facts are the same as in *Example (1).*

(ii) For 1980, H has compensation of $15,000 includible in gross income and is not covered by any other plans within the meaning of section 219(b)(2). W also goes to work in 1980 and has compensation of $6,000, but is not covered by certain other plans within the meaning of section 219(b)(2). H will not be treated as having made a deductible contribution of a previous year's excess contribution within the meaning of section 220(c)(6) because W has compensation for 1980. However, both H and W now meet the deduction standards of section 219 and each will be treated as having made a deductible contribution of $100 to their separate IRA's for 1980 under section 219(c)(5).

Example (3). (i) For 1979, the facts are the same as in *Example (1).*

(ii) For 1980, H has compensation of $15,000 includible in gross income and is covered by certain other plans within the meaning of section 220(b)(3). W has no compensation for 1980 and is not covered by certain other plans within the meaning of section 220(b)(3). H will not be treated as having made a deductible contribution of a previous year's excess contribution within the meaning of section 219(c)(5) or 220(c)(6) because H is covered by other plans for 1980 and has no allowable deduction under section 219 or 220.

(iii) W will not be treated as having made a deductible contribution of a previous year's excess contribution within the meaning of section 219(c)(5) because W has no compensation for 1980 and thus no allowable deduction under section 219.

(h) *Effective date.* (1) This section is effective for taxable years beginning after December 31, 1976.

(2) If, but for this subparagraph, an amount would be allowable as a deduction by reason of section 220(c)(6) and paragraph (g) for a taxable year beginning before January 1, 1978, such amount shall be allowable only for the taxpayer's first taxable year beginning in 1978.

Par. 5. There is added after § 1.404(e)-1A the following new section:

§ *1.404(h)(1) Special rules for simplified employee pensions.*

(a) *In general.* (1) Employer contributions to a simplified employee pension shall be treated as if they are made to a plan subject to the requirements of section 404. Employer contributions to a simplified employee pension are subject to the limitations of subparagraphs (2), (3), (4) and (5). For purposes of this paragraph participants means those employees who satisfy the age, service and other requirements to participate in a simplified employee pension. For purposes of this paragraph, "compensation" means all of the compensation paid by the employer except either that for which a deduction is allowable under section 404(h) for simplified employee pension or that for which a deduction is allowable under a plan that qualifies under section 401(a), including a plan that qualifies under section 404(a)(2) or 405.

(2) Employer contributions made for a calendar year are deductible for the taxable year of the employer with which or within which the calendar year ends.

(3) Contributions made within 3 ½ months after the close of a calendar year are treated as if they were made on the last day of such calendar year if they are made on account of such calendar year.

(4) The amount deductible for a taxable year for a simplified employee pension shall not exceed 15 percent of the compensation paid to the employees who are participants during the calendar year ending with or within the taxable year.

(5) The excess of the amount contributed over the amount deductible for a taxable year shall be deductible in the succeeding taxable years in order of time subject to the 15 percent limit of subparagraph (4).

(b) *Effect on stock bonus and profit-sharing trust.* For any taxable year for which the employer has a deduction under section 404(h)(1), the otherwise applicable limitations in section 404(a)(3)(A) shall be reduced by the amount of the allowable deductions under section 404(h)(1) with respect to participants in the stock bonus or profit-sharing trust.

(c) *Effect on limit on deductions.* For any taxable year for which the employer has an allowable deduction under section 404(h)(1), the otherwise applicable 25 percent limitations in section 404(a)(7) shall be reduced by the amount of the allowable deductions under section 404(h)(1) with respect to participants in the stock bonus or profit-sharing trust.

(d) *Effect on self-employed individuals or shareholder-employee.* The limitations described in paragraphs (1), (2)(A), and (4) of section 404(e) or described in section 1379(b)(1) for any taxable year shall be reduced by the amount of the allowable deductions under section 404(h)(1) with respect to an employee within the meaning of section 401(c)(1) or a shareholder-employee (as defined in section 1379(d)).

(e) *Examples.* The provisions of this section may be illustrated by the following examples:

Example (1). Corporation X is a calendar-year taxpayer. On January 2, 1980, it adopts a simplified employee pension arrangement. At the end of 1980, if determines that it has paid $230,000 to all of its employees. Eight of its employees met its eligibility provisions for contributions to simplified employee pensions and their compensation totaled $140,000 before any contributions were made to their simplified employee pensions. Corporation X will be allowed to deduct its contributions to its employees' simplified employee pensions, not to exceed 15% of $140,000 or $21,000.

Example (2). Corporation Y is a calendar-year taxpayer which maintains a simplified employee pension agreement and a profit-sharing plan. The corporation has 100 employees. For the taxable year of 1980, it makes contributions to the simplified employee pensions of 75 of its employees. These contributions are 10 percent of compensation received in 1980. These same 75 employees are also participants in the corporation's profit-sharing plan. These 75 employees had total compensation paid during 1980 of $1,125,000. The corporation can deduct $112,500 under section 404(h) as its contributions to the simplified employee pension agreement. The corporation must reduce the otherwise applicable allowable deduction for contributions to the profit-sharing plan on behalf of these employees by the $112,500.

Example (3). Corporation Z is a calendar-year taxpayer which maintains a simplified employee pension arrangement and a profit-sharing plan. The corporation has 100 employees. For the taxable year of 1980, it makes contributions to the simplified employee pensions of 75 of its employees. These contributions are 10 percent of compensation received in 1980. Twenty-five of these employees are also participants in the corporation's profit-sharing plan. Each of these 75 employees had

compensation for the year of $15,000, or total compensation of $1,125,000. The corporation deducts $112,500 under section 404(h) as its contribution to the simplified employee pension arrangement. The corporation must reduce the otherwise applicable allowable deduction for contributions to the profit-sharing plan on behalf of the 25 employees by $37,500, the amount contributed to the simplified employee pensions on behalf of employees covered by the profit-sharing plan.

Example (4). Corporation K is a taxpayer with a taxable year of December 1—November 30. On December 15, 1979, it adopts a simplified employee pension arrangement for its employees. It would like to make contributions to the plan on behalf of its employees for calendar year 1979. In order to make contributions to its employees' simplified employee pensions for calendar year 1979, the corporation must make the contributions by April 15, 1980. In order to receive a deduction for its taxable year ending November 30, 1980, for the contributions for calendar year 1979, the corporation must make the contributions by April 15, 1980.

Par. 6. Section 1.408-2 is amended by revising paragraph (c)(3) to read as follows:

§ *1.408-2 Individual retirement accounts.*

* * * * *

(c) * * *

(3) *Special requirement.* There must be a separate accounting for the interest of each employee or member (or spouse of an employee or member).

* * * * *

Par. 7. Section 1.408-3 is revised by adding new paragraphs (b)(6) and (f). These added provisions read as follows:

§ *1.408-3 Individual retirement annuities.*

* * * * *

(b) * * *

(6) *Flexible premium.* (i) In the case of annuity contracts issued after November 6, 1978, the premiums under such contracts are not fixed. See paragraph (f) for the definition of an annuity contract under which "the premiums are not fixed."

(ii) In the case of a fixed premium individual retirement annuity or individual retirement endowment contract issued before November 7, 1978, the issuer of such contract may offer the holder of the contract the option of exchanging such contract for a flexible premium contract. If such an exchange is made before January 1, 1981, the exchange shall not constitute a distribution and shall be nontaxable.

* * * * *

(f) *Flexible premium annuity contract*—(1) *In general.* A flexible premium retirement annuity contract shall be considered a contract under which "the premiums are not fixed" if it provides the following.

(i) At no time after the initial premium for the contract has been paid is there a specified renewal premium required.

(ii) The contract must allow for the continuance of the contract (as a paid-up annuity) under its nonforfeiture provision if premium payments cease altogether.

(iii) The contract, if being continued on a paid-up basis (*i.e.*, if it has not been terminated by a payment in cash), will be reinstated at any date prior to its maturity date upon payment of a premium to the insurer.

(2) *Exceptions.* (i) The insurer may require that if a premium is remitted, it will be accepted only if the amount remitted is some stated amount, not in excess of $50.

(ii) The contract may provide that if no premiums have been received under the contract for two (2) full years and the paid-up annuity benefit at maturity of the plan stipulated in the contract arising from the premium paid prior to such two-year period would be less than $20 a month, the insurer may, at its option, terminate the contract by payment in cash of the then present value of the paid-up benefit (computed on the same basis specified in the contract for determining the paid-up benefit).

(3) *Permissible provisions.* A flexible premium contract will not be considered to have fixed premiums merely because—

(i) A maximum limit (which may be expressed as a multiple of the premium paid in the first year of the contract) is placed on the amount of the premium that the insurer will accept in any year,

(ii) An annual charge is made against the policy value,

(iii) A fee (which may be composed of a flat dollar amount plus an amount equal to the required premium tax imposed by the state government) is charged upon the acceptance of each premium by the insurer, or

(iv) The contract requires a level annual premium for a supplementary benefit, such as a waiver of premium benefit.

Par. 8. Section 1.408-4 is amended by: (1) Adding new paragraphs (b)(3), (b)(4)(ii), and (c)(3)(ii); and (2) adding a new paragraph (h). These added provisions read as follows:

§ *1.408-4 Treatment of distributions from individual retirement arrangements.*

* * * * *

(b) *Rollover Contribution.* * * *

(3) *To section 403(b) contract.*

Paragraph (a)(1) of this section does not apply to any amount paid or distributed from an individual retirement account or individual retirement annuity to the individual for whose benefit the account or annuity is maintained if—

(i) The entire amount received (including money and other property) represents the entire interest in the account or the entire value of the annuity,

(ii) No amount in the account and no part of the value of the annuity is attributable to any source other than a rollover contribution from an annuity contract described in section 403(b) and any earnings on such rollover,

(iii) The entire amount thereof is paid into an annuity contract described in section 403(b) (for the benefit of such individual) not later than the 60th day after the receipt of the payment or distribution, and

(iv) The distribution or transfer is made in a taxable year beginning after December 31, 1978.

(4) * * *

(ii) [Withdrawn on July 11, 2014 by 79 FR 40031.]

(c) * * *

(3) *Time of inclusion.* * * *

(ii) For taxable years beginning after December 31, 1976, the amount of net income determined under subparagraph (2) is includible in the gross income of the individual in the taxable year in which such excess contribution is made. The amount of net income thus distributed is subject to the tax imposed by section 408(f)(1) for the year includible in gross income.

(h) *Certain deductions of excess contributions after due date of return for taxable year*—(1) *general rule.* In the case of any individual, if the aggregate contributions (other than valid rollover contributions) paid for any taxable year to an individual retirement account or for an individual retirement annuity do not exceed $1,750, section 408(d)(1) shall not apply to the distribution of any such contribution to the extent that such contribution exceeds the amount allowable as a deduction under section 219 or 220 for the taxable year for which the contribution was paid—

(i) If such distribution is received after the date described in section 408(d)(4),

(ii) But only to the extent that no deduction has been allowed under section 219 or 220 with respect to such excess contribution.

(2) *Excess rollover contribution attributable to erroneous information.* If the taxpayer reasonably relies on information supplied pursuant to subtitle F of the Internal Revenue Code of 1954 for determining the amount of a rollover contribution, but such information was erroneous, subparagraph (1) of this paragraph shall be applied by increasing the dollar limit set forth therein by that portion of the excess contribution which was attributable to such information.

(3) *Special rule for contributions to simplified employee pension.* If employer contributions on behalf of the individual are paid for the taxable year to a simplified employee pension, the dollar limitation of subparagraph (1) shall be the lesser of the amount of such contributions or $7,500. See § 1.219-3(a)(3)(iv) for a special rule where there is more than one employer.

(4) *Effective date.* (1) Subparagraphs (1) and (2) of this paragraph shall apply to distributions in taxable years beginning after December 31, 1975.

(ii) In the case of contributions for taxable years beginning before January 1, 1978, paragraph (5) of section 408(d) of the Internal Reve-

nue Code of 1954 shall be applied as if such paragraph did not contain any dollar limitation.

(4) *Examples.* The provisions of this paragraph may be illustrated by the following examples:

Example (1). T, a calendar-year taxpayer, had been a participant in a government pension plan for 6 years prior to separation from service on July 31, 1976. The plan required T to make mandatory contributions and as of July 31, 1976, these mandatory contributions totaled $6,000. Upon T's separation from service, she was given the option of receiving back all of her mandatory contributions or leaving them with the plan. T elected to receive her mandatory contributions and attempted to roll over these amounts into an individual retirement account (IRA) in August of 1976. The trustee of the IRA accepted these funds and IRA was established. In March of 1977, T discovered that the funds she received from the government plan did not qualify for rollover treatment because they were employee contributions and withdrew all of the money from her IRA. T will not have to include any of the money withdrawn from the IRA in gross income for 1977 because the transitional rule of paragraph (h)(3)(ii) permits the withdrawal of all contributions which have not been allowed as deductions under section 219 or 220 made to IRA's for taxable years beginning before January 1, 1978, regardless of the amount of the contribution.

Example (2). (i) On April 1, 1980, A, a calendar-year taxpayer, receives a lump sum distribution satisfying the requirements of section 402(e)(4)(A) and (C) under the plan of A's employer. The distribution consists of $50,000 case. A made contributions under the plan totaling $8,000, and has received no prior distributions under the plan. However, on the form furnished to A by the employer on account of the distribution, A's contributions under the plan are listed as totaling only $4,500. A reasonably relied on this information.

(ii) A desires to establish an individual retirement account (as described in section 408(a)) with the cash received in the distribution. A desires to contribute the maximum amount permitted under the rollover rules. Under sections 402(a)(5)(B) and 402(a)(5)(D)(ii), A determines that the maximum rollover amount is $45,500, the total of the distribution ($50,000), less the amount listed as A's contributions under the plan ($4,500). The actual maximum rollover amount is $42,000, the total of the distribution ($50,000), less A's actual contribution under the plan ($8,000).

(iii) On May 23, 1980, A contributes $45,500 to an individual retirement account as a rollover contribution.

(iv) On May 1, 1981, A's employer furnishes A a corrected statement indicating that A's contributions under the plan were $8,000. On June 1, 1981, A withdraws $3,500 from the individual retirement account to correct the mistaken contribution. A will not have to include the $3,500 withdrawn from the individual retirement account due to erroneous information furnished by the employer and reasonably relied upon by A and thus falls under the exception provided in section 408(d)(5)(B) to section 406(d)(1).

Par 9. Section 1.406-6 is amended by removing paragraph (d)(4)(xi) and adding a new paragraph (b) to read as follows:

§ *1.408-6 Disclosure statements for individual retirement arrangements.*

* * *

(b) *Disclosure statements for spousal individual retirement arrangements.* The trustee of an individual retirement account and the issuer of an individual retirement annuity shall furnish to the benefited individual of a spousal individual retirement arrangement a disclosure statement in accordance with paragraph (d). In the case of a spousal individual retirement arrangement that uses subaccounts, the benefited individual includes both the working and non-working spouse.

Par. 10. There are added after § 1.408-6 the following new sections:

§ *1.408-7 Simplified employee pension.*

(a) *In general.* The term "simplified employee pension" means an individual retirement account or individual retirement annuity described in section 408(a), (b) or (c) with respect to which the requirements of paragraphs (b), (d), (e), (g), and (h) of this section are met and the requirements of § 1.408-8 are met with respect to any calendar year.

(b) *Establishment of simplified employee pension.* In order to establish a simplified employee pension, the employer must execute a written instrument (hereinafter referred to as the simplified employee pension arrangement) within the time prescribed for making deductible contributions. This instrument shall include: the name of the employer, the requirements for employee participation, the signature of a responsible official, and the definite allocation formula specified in section 408(k)(5) and paragraph (f) of this section.

(c) *Variation in contribution*—(1) *Permitted variations.* An employer's total contributions to its employees' simplified employee pensions may vary annually at the employer's discretion.

(2) *Salary reduction.* Contributions made to a simplified employee pension under an arrangement under which the contribution will be made only if the employee receives a reduction in compensation or forgoes a compensation increase shall be treated as employer contributions to a simplified employee pension only if the arrangement precludes an individual election by the employee. If there is an individual election, then the contribution shall be treated as an employee contribution.

(d) *Participation requirements*—(1) *Age and service requirements.* This paragraph is satisfied with respect to a simplified employee pension arrangement for a calendar year only if for such year the employer contributes to the simplified employee pension on behalf of each individual who is an employee at any time during the calendar year who has—

(i) Attained age 25,

(ii) Performed service for the employer during at least 3 of the immediately preceding 5 calendar years, and

(iii) Received at least $200 compensation from the employer for the calendar year.

(2) *Execution of documents.* The employer may execute any necessary documents on behalf of an employee who is entitled to a contribution to a simplified employee pension if the employee is unable or unwilling to execute such documents or the employer is unable to locate the employee.

(3) *Required employment.* An employer may not require that an employee be employed as of a particular date in order to receive a contribution for a calendar year.

(4) *Nonresident aliens and employees covered by collective-bargaining agreements.* An employer may exclude from participation in the simplified employee pension arrangement employees described in section 410(b)(2)(A) or 410(b)(2)(C).

(5) *Example.* The provisions of this paragraph may be illustrated by the following example:

Example. Corporation X maintains a simplified employee pension arrangement for its employees. Individual J worked for Corporation X while in graduate school in 1976, 1977, and 1978, J began to work for corporation X on a full-time basis. J earned $5,000 from Corporation X for 1979. J became 25 on December 31, 1979. Corporation X must make a contribution to a simplified employee pension maintained on behalf of J for 1979 because as of December 31, 1979, J had met the minimum age requirement of section 408(k)(2), had performed service for Corporation X in 3 of the 5 calendar years preceding 1979, and met the minimum compensation requirements of paragraph (d)(1)(iii).

(e) *Requirement of written allocation formula*—(1) *Requirement of definite written allocation formula.* Employer contributions to a simplified employee pension must be made under a definite written allocation formula which specifies—

(i) The requirements which an employee must satisfy to share in an allocation, and

(ii) The manner in which the amount allocated to each employee's account is computed.

(2) *Employer may vary formula.* An employer may vary the definite written allocation formula from year to year provided the simplified employee pension arrangement is amended by the permissible date for making contributions to indicate the new formula.

(f) *Treatment of contributions which exceed the written allocation formula*—

(1) *General rule.* To the extent that employer contributions do not satisfy § 1.408—7(e)(1), the contributions shall be deemed to be contributions which are not made under a simplified employee pension arrangement except for purposes of section 408(a)(1), (b)(2)(B) and (d)(5). These contribution shall be deemed made to an individual retirement account or individual retirement annuity not maintained as part of a simplified employee pension arrangement.

(2) *Example.* This paragraph is illustrated by the following example:

Example. (i) Assume that in 1979 Corporation X adopts a simplified employee pension arrangement ("SEP Arrangement"). The arrange-

ment calls for Corporation X to contribute the same percentage of each participant's compensation exclusive of SEP contributions to a simplified employee pension (Allocation Compensation). X has three employees, A, B, and C, who satisfy the participation requirements of the SEP Arrangement. The compensation, the contributions to the individual simplified employee pension ("SEP") for A, B and C and the varying treatment of the contributions are set forth as follows:

Employee	Gross income	Net compensation before contribution	SEP-IRA contribution	Ratio of SEP-IRA contributions to net compensation (percent)
A	$110,000	$10,000	$1,000	10
B	11,500	10,000	1,500	15
C	57,500	50,000	7,500	15
Totals	80,000	$70,000	$10,000	

(ii) Under the special rule of this paragraph, because only 10 percent of compensation was allocated to A, and the allocation formula provides that the same percentage will be allocated to each participant, a certain portion of the contribution to B and C under the SEP shall be deemed made to IRA's that are not part of the SEP Arrangement.

(iii) To determine A's and B's Allocation Compensation the respective total compensation included in A's and B's gross income must be divided by 1.10 (1 plus the percentage of Allocation Compensation contributed to A under the SEP Arrangement). The excess of compensation included in gross income over Allocation Compensation is considered as a contribution under the SEP. The following table shows the result of this calculation:

Employee	Gross income	Allocation compensation[1]	SEP-IRA contribution	Deemed IRA contribution[2]
A	$11,000	$10,000	$1,000	$0
B	11,500	10,455	1,045	455
C	57,500	52,273	5,227	2,273
Totals	80,000	72,728	7,272	2,728

[1] Gross income divided by 1.10.
[2] Also included in Allocation Compensation.

(iv) Under section 404(h) for purposes of computing Corporation X's deduction, only the $7,272 is considered as a contribution to a SEP Arrangement described in section 409(k) under the special rule. The allowable 404(h) deduction equals $10,900 (15% of the excess of total compensation of $80,000 over the SEP contribution of $7,272 or 15% of $72,728). The other $2,728 is payment of compensation and subject to the deduction rules of section 162 or 212. Similarly, the $2,728 would not be considered as an employer SEP contribution for purposes of exemption from FICA and FUTA taxes under sections 3121 and 3306.

(v) The effect of treating the $2,273 as a contribution to SEP's for purposes of section 408(a)(1), (b)(2)(B) and (d)(5) is to not disqualify the individual retirement arrangement of C for accepting non-SEP contributions in excess of $1,500 and to allow C to withdraw the excess contribution of $2,273 without including that amount in income under section 404(d)(1).

(g) *Permitted withdrawals.* A simplified employee pension meets the requirements of this paragraph only if—

(1) Employer contributions thereto are not conditioned on the retention in such pension of any portion of the amount contributed, and

(2) There is no prohibition imposed by the employer on withdrawals from the simplified employee pension.

See section 408(d) for rules concerning the taxation of withdrawals from individual retirement accounts and annuities. See section 408(f)(1) for penalties for premature withdrawals from individual retirement accounts and annuities.

(h) *Section 401(j) plan.* The requirements of this paragraph are met with respect to a simplified employee pension for a calendar year unless the employer maintains during any part of such year a plan—

(1) Some or all of the active participants in which are employees (within the meaning of section 4012(c)(1)) or shareholder-employees (as defined in section 1379(d)), and

(2) To which section 401(j) applies.

§ 1.408-8 Nondiscrimination requirements for simplified employee pensions.

(a) *In general.* The requirements of this section are met with respect to a simplified employee pension for a calendar year if for such year the contributions made by the employer to simplified employee pensions of its employees do not discriminate in favor of any employee who is—

(1) An officer,

(2) A shareholder, within the meaning of paragraph (b)(2),

(3) A self-employed individual, or

(4) Highly compensated.

(b) *Special rules.* (1) For purposes of this section, employees described in subparagraph (A) or (C) of section 410 (b)(2) shall be excluded from consideration.

(2) An individual shall be considered a shareholder if he owns (with the application of section 318) more than 10 percent of the value of the stock of the employer.

(c) *Contributions must bear a uniform relationship to total compensation*—(1) *General rule.* Contributions shall be considered discriminatory unless employer contributions to its employees' simplified employee pensions bear a uniform relationship to the total compensation (not in excess of the first $100,000) of each employee maintaining a simplified employee pension. A rate of contribution which decreases as compensation increases shall be considered uniform.

(2) *Definition of compensation.* For purposes of this section, the term "compensation" has the meaning set forth in § 1.219-1, and is determined without regard to the employer contributions to the simplified employee pension arrangement.

(3) *Example.* The provisions of this paragraph may be illustrated by the following example:

Example. Corporation X maintains a simplified employee pension arrangement which allocates employer contributions in the manner described below. First, contributions made by June 30 of each year are allocated in proportion to compensation paid from January 1 to June 30. Second, contributions made between July 1 and December 31 are allocated in proportion to compensation paid during the same period.

In 1980, the salaries paid, and contributions allocated are shown below:

Participant	Compensation[1]	Allocation[2]	Compensation[3]	Allocation[4]
A	10,000	500	10,000	1,000
B	10,000	500	1,000	100
C	10,000	500	15,000	1,500

[1] Jan. 1, 1980 to June 30, 1980.
[2] June 30, 1980.
[3] July 1, 1980 to Dec. 31, 1980.
[4] Dec. 31, 1980.

For 1980, A, B, and C received allocations equal to 7.5 percent, 5.45 percent, and 8 percent of compensation, respectively. These contributions are discriminatory because they do not bear a uniform relationship to total compensation.

(d) *Treatment of certain contributions and taxes*—(1) *General rule.* (i) Except as provided in this paragraph, employer contributions do not meet the requirements of this section unless such contributions meet the requirements of this section without taking into account contributions or benefits under Chapter 2 of the Internal Revenue Code (relating to tax on self-employment income), Chapter 21 (relating to Federal Insurance Contribution Act), Title II of the Social Security Act, or any other Federal or State law ("Social Security Taxes"). If the employer does not maintain an integrated plan at any time during the taxable year, taxes paid under section 3111(a) (relating to tax on employers) with respect to an employe may, for purposes of this section, be taken into account as a contribution by the employer to an employee's simplified employee pension. If contributions are made to the simplified employee pension of an owner-employee, the preceding sentence shall not apply unless paid by an such owner-employees under section 1401(a), and the taxes which would be payable under section 3111(a) by such owner-employees but for paragraphs (4) and (5) of section 1402(c), are taken into account as contributions by the employer on behalf of such owner-employee. The amount of such taxes shall be determined in a manner consistent with § 1.401-12(h)(3).

(ii) If contributions are made to the simplified employee pension of a self-employed individual who is not an owner-employee, the arrangement may be integrated. In such a case, the portion of the earned income of such individual which does not exceed the maximum amount which may be treated as self-employment income under section 1402(b)(1) shall be treated as "wages" under section 3121(a)(1) subject to the tax imposed by section 3111(a) and such tax shall be taken into account as employer contributions.

(iii) An employer may take into account as contributions amounts not in excess of such Social Security taxes. Thus, an employer may integrate using a rate less than the maximum rate of tax under section 3111(a) or compensation less than the maximum amount specified as wages under section 3121(a).

(2) *Integrated plan defined.* For purposes of subparagraph (1), the term "integrated plan" means a plan which meets the requirements on section 401(a), 403(a), or 405(a) but would not meet such requirements if contributions or benefits under Chapter 2 (relating to tax on self-employment income), Chapter 21 (relating to Federal Insurance Contributions Act), Title II of the Social Security Act, or any other Federal or State law were not taken into account.

(e) *Examples.* The provisions of this section may be illustrated by the following examples:

Example (1). Corporation M adopts a simplified employee pension arrangement. The corporation would like to contribute 7.5% of an employee's first $10,000 in compensation and 5% of all compensation above $10,000. The simplified employee pension arrangement which Corporation M adopts will not be considered discriminatory within the meaning of paragraph (c) of this section because the rate of contribution decreases as compensation increases.

Example (2). Corporation L adopts a simplified employee pension plan. It wishes to contribute to the simplified employee pension of each employee who is currently performing service. The corporation would like to contribute to the simplified employee pensions 5% of the total compensation of each employee who has completed up to 5 years of service and 7% of the total compensation of each employee who has completed more than 5 years of service. The simplified employee pension plan which Corporation L adopts will be considered discriminatory within the meaning of paragraph (c) of this section because the employer contributions do not bear a uniform relationship to each employee's total compensation.

§ 1.408-9 Reports for simplified employee pensions.

(a) *Information to be furnished upon adoption of plan.* (1) An employer who adopts a definite written allocation formula for making contributions to an employee's simplified employee pension shall furnish the employee in writing the following information:

(i) A notice that the simplified employee pension arrangement has been adopted,

(ii) The requirements which an employee must meet in order to receive a contribution under the agreement,

(iii) The basis upon which the employer's contribution will be allocated to employees, and

(iv) Such other information that the Commissioner may require.

(2) The information in subparagraph (1) must be furnished to an employee no later than a reasonable time after the later of the time the employee becomes employed or the time of the adoption of the simplified employee pension arrangement.

(3) The Commissioner may relieve employers from furnishing any or all of the information specified in subparagraph (1).

(b) *Information to be furnished for a calendar year.* (1) For each calendar year, the employer shall furnish to the employee a written statement indicating the amount of employer contributions made to the employee's individual retirement account or individual retirement annuity under the simplified employee pension arrangement. This requirement is satisfied if the information is on the employee's W-2 for the calendar year for which the contribution is made. Amounts described in § 1.408-7(f)(1) which are not considered made under the simplified employee pension arrangement should not be included.

(2) The information required to be furnished by subparagraph (1) shall be furnished to the employee no later than the later of 30 days after the contribution or January 31 following the calendar year for which the contribution was made.

(c) The Internal Revenue Service may require reports to be filed with the Service with respect to employees who cannot be located by the employer (see § 1.408-7(d)(2)). Such reports shall include such information and shall be filed in the time and manner as the Commissioner specifies.

(d) *Effective date.* The provisions of this section are effective for calendar years beginning after December 31, 1978.

Par. 11. Section 1.409-1 is amended by adding "or 220" after 219 each place it appears and by revising paragraph (c) to read as follows:

§ 1.409-1 Retirement bonds.

* * * * *

(c) *Rollover.* The first sentence of paragraph (b)(1) of this section shall not apply in any case in which a retirement bond is redeemed by the registered owner before the close of the taxable year in which he attains the age of 70 ½ if he transfers the entire amount of the proceeds of such redemption to—

(1) An individual retirement account described in section 408(a) or an individual retirement annuity described in section 408(b) (other than an endowment contract described in § 1.408-3(e)), or

(2) An employees' trust which is described in section 401(a) which is exempt from tax under section 501(a), an annuity plan described in section 403 (a), or an annuity contract described in section 403(b), for the benefit of the registered owner,

on or before the 60th day after the day on which he received the proceeds of such redemption. This paragraph does not apply in the case of a transfer to an employees' trust or such an annuity plan unless no part of the value of such proceeds is attributable to any source other than a rollover contribution from such an employees' trust or annuity plan (other than an annuity plan or a trust forming part of a plan under which the individual was an employee within the meaning of section 401(c)(1) at the time contributions were made on his behalf under the plan). This paragraph does not apply in the case of a transfer to an annuity contract described in section 403(b) unless no part of the value of such proceeds is attributable to any source other than a rollover contribution from such annuity contract.

Par. 12. Section 1.415-8 is amended by adding at the end thereof new paragraph (i).

§ 1.415-8 Combining and aggregating plans.

* * * * *

(i) *Special aggregation rule for simplified employee pension.* For purposes of section 415 and this section, any contribution made by an employer to a simplified employee pension (as defined in section 408(k)) of an individual for a calendar year shall be treated as an employer contribution to a defined contribution plan maintained by that employer. This paragraph shall apply to taxable years beginning after December 31, 1980.

Gift Tax Regulations

26 CFR Part 25

PART 25—GIFT TAX; GIFTS MADE AFTER DECEMBER 31, 1954

Par. 13. There is added after § 25.2503-4 the following new section:

§ 25.2503-5 Individual retirement plan for spouse.

(a) *In general.* For purposes of section 2503(b), and payment made by an individual for the benefit of his or her spouse—

(1) To individual retirement account described in section 408(a).

(2) To an individual retirement subaccount described in § 1.220-1(b)(3),

(3) For an individual retirement annuity described in section 408(b), or

(4) For a retirement bond described in section 409,

shall not be considered a gift of a future interest in property to the extent that such payment is allowable as a deduction under section 220 for the taxable year for which the contribution is made. Thus, for example, if individual A paid $900 to an individual retirement account for 1980 on behalf of A's spouse, B, of which $875 was deductible, $875 would not be a gift of a future interest.

(b) *Effective date.* Paragraph (a) of this section is effective for transfers made after December 31, 1976.

Employment Tax Regulations

26 CFR Part 31

PART 31—EMPLOYMENT TAXES; APPLICABLE ON AND AFTER JANUARY 1, 1955

Par. 14. Section 31.3121(a)(5)-1 is amended by adding at the end thereof a new paragraph (d). This new paragraph reads as follows:

§ 31.3121(a)(5)-1 Payments from or to certain tax-exempt trusts, or under or to certain annuity plans or bond purchase plans.

* * * * *

(d) *Payments to a simplified employee pension.* The term "wages" does not include any payment made after December 31, 1978 by an employer on behalf of an employee to a simplified employee pension described in section 408(k) if at the time of the payment it is reasonable to believe that the employee will be entitled to a deduction under section 219 for such payment.

Par. 15. Section 31.3306(b)(5)-1 is amended by adding at the end thereof a new paragraph (d). This new paragraph reads as follows:

§ 31.3306(b)(5)-1 Payments from or to certain tax-exempt trusts, or under or to certain annuity plans or bond purchase plans.

* * * * *

(d) *Payments to a simplified employee pension.* The term "wages" does not include any payment made after December 31, 1978 by an employer on behalf of an employee to a simplified employee pension described in section 40B(k) if at the time of the payment it is reasonable to believe that the employee will be entitled to a deduction under section 219 for such payment.

Pension Excise Tax Regulations

26 CFR Part 54

PART 54—PENSION EXCISE TAXES

Par. 16. There is inserted in the appropriate place the following new section:

§ 54.4973-1 Excess contributions to certain accounts, contracts and bonds.

(a) *In general.* Under section 4973, in the case of an individual retirement account (described in section 408(a)), an individual retirement annuity (described in section 498(b)), a custodial account treated as an annuity contract under section 403(b)(7)(A), or an individual retirement bond described in section 409. a tax equal to 6 percent of the amount of excess contributions (as defined in paragraph (c) or (d) of this section) to such account, annuity or bond is imposed.

(b) *Individual liable for tax—(1) Individual retirement plans.* In the case of an individual retirement account, individual retirement annuity or individual retirement bond the tax imposed by section 4973 shall be paid by the individual to whom a deduction is or would be allowed with respect to contributions for the taxable year under section 219 (determined without regard to subsection (b)(1) thereof) or section 220 (determined without regard to subsection (b)(1) thereof), whichever is appropriate.

(2) *Custodial accounts under section 403(b)(7)(A).* In the case of a custodial account treated as an annuity contract under section 403(b)(7)(A), the tax imposed by section 4973 shall be paid by the individual for whose benefit the account is maintained.

(c) *Excess contributions defined for individual retirement plans.* For purposes of section 4973, in the case of individual retirement accounts, individual retirement annuities, or individual retirement bonds, the term "excess contributions" means the sum of—

(1) The excess (if any) of—

(i) The amount contributed for the taxable year to the accounts or for the annuities or bonds (other than a valid rollover contribution described in section 402(a)(5), 402(a)(7), 403(a)(4), 403(b)(8), 408(d)(3), 409(b)(3)(C)), over

(ii) The amount allowable as a deduction under section 219 or 220 for such contributions, and

(2) The amount determined under his subsection for the preceding taxable year, reduced by the sum of—

(i) The distributions out of the account for the taxable year which were included in the gross income of the payee under section 408(d)(1).

(ii) The distributions out of the account for the taxable bear to which section 408(d)(5) applies. and

(iii) The excess (if any) of the minimum amount allowable as a deduction under section 219 or 220 for the taxable year over the amount contributed (determined without regard to sections 219(c)(5) and 220(c)(6)) to the accounts or for the annuities or bonds for the taxable year. For purposes of this paragraph, any contribution which is distributed from the individual retirement account, individual retirement annuity, or bond in a distribution to which section 408(d)(4) applies shall be treated as an amount not contributed.

(d) *Excess contributions defined for custodial accounts under section 403(b)(7)(A).* For purposes of section 4973, in the case of a custodial account referred to in paragraph (b)(2) of this section, the term "excess contributions" means the sum of—

(1) The excess (if any) of the amount contributed for the taxable year to such account (other than a valid rollover contribution described in section 403(b)(8), 408(d)(3)(A)(iii), or 409(b)(3)(C)), over the lesser of the amount excludable from gross income under section 403(b) or the amount permitted to be contributed under the limitations contained in section 415 (or under whichever such section is applicable, if only one is applicable), and

(2) The amount determined under this subsection for the preceding taxable year, reduced by—

(i) The excess (if any) of the lesser of (A) the amount excludable from gross income under section 403(b) or (B) the amount permitted to be contributed under the limitations contained in section 415 over the amount contributed to the account for the taxable year (or under whichever such section is applicable, if only one is applicable), and

(ii) The sum of the distributions out of the account (for the taxable year) which are included in gross income under section 72(e).

(e) *Special rules.* (1) The tax imposed by section 4973 cannot exceed 6 percent of the value (determined as of the close of the individuals taxable year) of the account, annuity or bond.

(2) In the case of an endowment contract described in section 408(b), the tax imposed by section 4973 is not applicable to any amount allocate under §1.219-1(b)(3) to the cost of life insurance under the contract.

(f) *Examples.* The provisions of this section may be illustrated by the following examples;

Example (1). On April 20, 1979, A, a single individual, establishes an individual retirement account (IRA) and contributes $1,500. On January 11, 1980, A determines he has compensation for 1979 within the meaning of section 219(c) and the regulations thereafter of $8,000. Under section 219. the maximum amount allowable as a deduction for retirement savings available to A is $1,200. On April 15, 1980, A files his income tax return for 1979 taking a deduction of $1,200 for his contribution to his IRA, and as of such date there had been no distribution from the IRA. Under section 4973. A would have $300 of excess contribution in his account for 1979 [($1,500-$1,200) + 0] and A would be liable for an excise tax of $18 on such excess contribution.

Example (2) Assume the same facts as in Example (1). Assume further that on July 1, 1980. A contributes $1,500 to his account. On January 9, 1981, A determines that he has compensation for 1980 of $12,000. Under section 219, the maximum amount allowable to A as a deduction for retirement savings is $1,500 for 1980. On April 15, 1981. A files his income tax return for 1980 taking a deduction of $1,500 for his contribution to his IRA. As of such date, there had been no distribution from the account. Under section 4973, A would have $300 of excess contributions in his IRA for 1980 ($1,500 - $1,500) + ($300 - $ 0)] and would be liable for an excise tax of $18 on such excess contribution.

Example (3) Assume the same facts as in Example (1) and (2). Assume further that on July 1, 1981, A contributes $1,000 to his account. On January 9, 1982, A determines that he has compensation for 1981 of $15,000. Under section 219, the maximum amount allowable as a deduction to A as a deduction for retirement savings is $1,500 for 1981. On April 15, 1982. A files his income tax return for 1981 taking a deduction of $1,000 for his 1981 contribution to his IRA and an additional deduction of $300 under section 219(c)(5). A will have no excess contributions in his IRA for 1981 because he made no excess contributions for 1981 and the previous year's excess contribution has been eliminated by the underutilization (section 4973(b)(2)(C)) of 1981's allowable contribution.

Example (4) Assume the same facts as in Examples (1) and (2). Assume further that on July 1, 1981, A contributes $1,500 to his account. On December 1, 1981, A withdraws $300 from his IRA. On January 9. 1982. A determines that he has compensation for 1981 of $15,000. Under section 219. the maximum amount allowable as a deduction to A as a deduction for retirement savings is $1,500 for 1981.

On April 15, 1982, A files his income tax return for 1981 taking a deduction of $1,500 for his 1981 contribution to his IRA. A will have no excess contributions in his IRA for 1981 because he made no excess contributions for 1981 and the previous year's excess contribution has been eliminated in a distribution described in section 408(d)(5).

Example (5) On February 1, 1979, H, an individual, establishes an IRA for himself and one for his nonworking spouse W. He contributes $875 to his account and $775 to his wife's account. On January 31, 1980. H determines that he has compensation for 1979 within the meaning of section 220(c) and the regulations thereunder of $20,000. Under Section 220(b)(1). the maximum amount allowable as a deduction for retirement savings to A is $1,550. On April 15, 1980. H files a Joint income tax return for 1979 and takes a deduction of $1,550 for his contribution to the IRA of himself and his spouse. As of such date, there had been no distribution from either IRA. Under section 4973, H would have $100 of excess contributions in his account for 1979 [($1,650 – $1,550) + 0] and H would be liable for an excise tax of $6 on such excess contribution.

Example (6) Assume the same facts as in Example (5). Assume further that on June 1, 1980, H contributes $875 to his account and $875 to his wife's account. On January 31, 1981, H determines that he has compensation for 1980 within the meaning of section 220(c) and the regulations thereunder of $20,000. Under section 220(b)(1), the maximum amount allowable as a deduction for retirement savings is $1,750. On April 15, 1981, H files his income tax return for 1980 taking a deduction of $1,750 for his contribution to the individual retirement account of himself and his wife. As of such date, there had been no distribution from either account. Under section 4973, H would have $100 of excess contributions in his account for 1980 and would be liable for an excise tax of $6 for such excess contribution.

Example (7) Assume the same facts as in Example (5). Assume further that on June 1, 1980, A contributes $1,000 to his account and nothing to his wife's account. On January 31, 1981, A determines that he has compensation for 1980 within the meaning of section 219(c) of $22,000. On April 15, 1981, H files his income tax return for 1980 and takes a $1,000 deduction under section 219(a) for the 1980 contribution to his IRA and a $100 deduction under section 219(c)(5) for the 1979 excess contribution Under section 4973. H would have $0 excess contributions for 1980 because the previous year's excess contribution has been eliminated under section 4973(b)(2)(C).

Example (8) On March 1, 1979, a custodial account under section 403(b)(7)(A) is established for the benefit of T who is otherwise eligible to have such an account established and a contribution of $7,000 is made to such account by A's employer which is a tax-exempt organization described in section 501(c)(3). The amount excludible from T's gross income in 1979 under section 403(b) is $4,000 and the amount permitted to be contributed for 1979 under section 415 is $5,000. Under section 4973, T would have an excess contribution of $3,000 [($7,000 – $4,000) + 0] in his account for 1979 and would be liable for an excise tax of $180.

Par. 17. A new paragraph (d) is added to §54.474-1 to read as follows.

§54.4974-1 Excise tax on accumulations in individual retirement accounts or annuities.

* * *

(d) *Waiver of tax in certain cases*—(1) In general. If the payee described in section 4974(a) establishes to the satisfaction of the Commissioner that—

(i) The shortfall described in section 4974(a) in the amount distributed during any taxable year was due to reasonable error, and

(ii) Reasonable steps are being taken to remedy the shortfall, the tax imposed by section 4974(a) may be waived.

(2) *Reasonable error.* Examples of reasonable error leading to an underdistribution include: erroneous advice from the sponsoring organization or other pension advisors or organizations which misled the payee, attempts by the payee to apply the required formula which led to a miscalculation, or misunderstanding of the formula.

Procedure and Administration Regulations

26 CFR Part 301

PART 301—PROCEDURE AND ADMINISTRATION

Par. 18. Section 301.6693-1 is revised by changing its title, adding after paragraph (a)(2) a new paragraph (a)(3), and amending paragraph (e). Section 301.6693-1, as revised, reads as follows:

§ 301.6693-1 Penalty for failure to provide reports and documents concerning individual retirement accounts, individual retirement annuities and simplified employee pensions.

(a) *In general.* * * *

(3) *Simplified employee pensions.* An employer who makes a contribution on behalf of an employee to a simplified employee pension who fails to furnish or file a report or any other document required under section 408(1) or § 1.406-9 within the time and in the manner prescribed for furnishing or filing such item shall pay a penalty of $10 for each failure unless it is shown that such failure is due to reasonable cause.

* * *

(e) *Effective date.* This section shall take effect on January 1, 1975, except for paragraph (a)(3) which is effective for years beginning after December 31, 1978.

Roscoe L. Egger, Jr.,

Commissioner of Internal Revenue.

[FR Doc. 81-20505 filed 7-13-81; 8:45 am]

[¶ **20,137C Reserved.**—Formerly reproduced at this paragraph were proposed regulations relating to disclosures of returns and return information to officers and employees of the Labor Department and the Pension Benefit Guaranty Corporation. The regulations were finalized on September 9, 1983, by T.D. 7911 and appear at ¶ 13,763.]

¶ 20,137D

Proposed regulations: Qualified joint and survivor annuities: *BBS Associates, Inc. v. Commissioner.*—Reproduced below are proposed regulations that are designed to conform the rules on qualified joint and survivor annuities with the holdings of the Tax Court and the U.S. Court of Appeals for the Third Circuit in *BBS Associates, Inc. v. Commissioner.* The proposed regulations were published in the Federal Register on October 27, 1982 (47 FR 47600).

DEPARTMENT OF THE TREASURY INTERNAL REVENUE SERVICE

[26 CFR Part 1]

[EE-52-78]

QUALIFIED JOINT AND SURVIVOR ANNUITY

NOTICE OF PROPOSED RULEMAKING

AGENCY: Internal Revenue Service, Treasury.

ACTION: Notice of proposed rulemaking.

SUMMARY: This document contains proposed regulations relating to qualified joint and survivor annuities required to be provided under certain retirement plans. Changes to the present regulations are being made to conform them to *BBS Associates, Inc. v. Commissioner of Internal Revenue,* 74 T.C. 1118 (1980), *aff'd* No. 80-2851 (3d Cir. July 29, 1981) and to simplify them. The regulations would affect sponsors of, administrators of and participants in certain retirement plans.

DATES: Written comments and requests for a public hearing must be delivered or mailed by December 27, 1982. The regulations are generally effective for plan years beginning after December 31, 1975.

ADDRESS: Send comments and requests for a public hearing to: Commissioner of Internal Revenue, Attention: CC:LR:T (EE-52-78), Washington, D.C. 20224.

FOR FURTHER INFORMATION CONTACT: William D. Gibbs of the Employee Plans and Exempt Organizations Division, Office of the Chief Counsel, Internal Revenue Service, 1111 Constitution Avenue, N.W., Washington, D.C. 20224 (Attention: CC:LR:T) (202-566-3430) (not a toll-free number).

SUPPLEMENTARY INFORMATION:

Background

This document contains proposed amendments to the Income Tax Regulations (26 CFR Part 1) under section 401(a)(11) of the Internal Revenue Code of 1954. These amendments are proposed to conform the regulations to *BBS Associates, Inc. v. Commissioner of Internal Revenue,* 74 T.C. 1118 (1980), *aff'd.* No. 80-2851 (3d Cir. July 29, 1981) and to simplify them. These regulations are to be issued under the authority contained in section 7805 of the Internal Revenue Code of 1954 (68A Stat. 917; 26 U.S.C. 7805).

Qualified Joint and Survivor Annuity

Section 401(a)(11) provides that if a trust provides for the payment of benefits in the form of an annuity, such trust must provide for the payment of annuity benefits in a form having the effect of a qualified joint and survivor annuity in order for the trust to be qualified under section 401.

The existing regulations under section 401(a)(11) interpret this provision to require a plan offering a life annuity benefit as a benefit option to provide that the automatic form of benefit payment be a qualified joint and survivor annuity.

The Tax Court and the Court of Appeals for the Third Circuit rejected the Service's interpretation in *BBS Associates, Inc. v. Commis-* *sioner of Internal Revenue,* 74 T.C. 1118 (1980), *aff'd.* No. 80-2851 (3d Cir. July 29, 1981). The court held that sections 401(a)(11)(A) and 401(a)(11)(E) do not require that the automatic form of benefit distribution be a qualified joint and survivor annuity merely because a plan offers a life annuity as an optional form of benefit. The court also held that *Example 1* of § 1.401(a)-11(a)(3), which illustrated the Service's position, was invalid.

In Notice 82-4, 1982-8 I.R.B. 36, the Service stated that it would not file a petition for a writ of certiorari in the *BBS* case and that the invalidated regulations would be amended.

This notice of proposed rulemaking conforms § 1.401(a)-11 to the *BBS* decision. The proposed regulations require that, in order for a plan to qualify under section 401(a), if the plan offers benefits payable as a life annuity, such life annuity benefits must be paid in the form of a qualified joint and survivor annuity unless the participant elects otherwise.

Approval of Benefit Options

The court also held in the *BBS* decision that section 401(a)(11) was not violated by a plan provision requiring administrative committee consent before forms of benefit payment other than a lump sum could be elected. The proposed regulations clarify that such a procedure is permissible. However, it is made clear that such a procedure can not result in the denial of benefit payments required by section 401(a)(11). The regulations illustrate a method whereby a plan may use an administrative committee and satisfy the requirements of section 401(a)(11).

Changes to Simplify Administration

The proposed changes to the regulations under section 401(a)(11) also include several changes that are intended to ease the administrative burdens of complying with the joint and survivor annuity requirements.

The regulations require the plan administrator, to provide certain information to participants concerning their ability to elect out of a joint and survivor annuity and to elect an early survivor annuity. The proposed amendments make it clear that it is permissible to provide this information by posting it, as opposed to mailing or hand delivering it to individual plan participants.

The regulations currently allow defined contribution plans to satisfy the requirement that election of an early survivor annuity be permitted by automatically paying a survivor benefit equal to the vested portion of the account balance. The proposed amendments allow defined benefit plans to adopt a similar procedure if the plan pays a survivor benefit equal to the present value of the vested benefit.

Executive Order 12291 and Regulatory Flexibility Act

The Commissioner has determined than this proposed regulation is not a major regulation for purposes of Executive Order 12291. Accordingly, a regulatory impact analysis is not required.

Although this document is a notice of proposed rulemaking which solicits public comments, the Internal Revenue Service has concluded that the regulations proposed herein are interpretative and that the notice and public procedure requirements of 5 U.S.C. 553 do not apply. Accordingly, these proposed regulations do not constitute regulations subject to the Regulatory Flexibility Act (5 U.S.C. chapter 6).

Comments and Requests for a Public Hearing

Before adopting these proposed regulations, consideration will be given to any written comments that are submitted (preferably six copies) to the Commissioner of Internal Revenue. All comments will be available for public inspection and copying. A public hearing will be held upon written request to the Commissioner by any person who has submitted written comments. If a public hearing is held, notice of the time and place will be published in the Federal Register.

Drafting Information

The principal author of these proposed regulations is William D. Gibbs of the Employee Plans and Exempt Organizations Division of the Office of Chief Counsel, Internal Revenue Service. However, personnel from other offices of the Internal Revenue Service and Treasury Department participated in developing the regulation, both on matters of substance and style.

List of Subjects in 26 CFR §§ 1.401-0—1.425-1

Income taxes, Employee benefit plan, Pensions, Stock options, Individual retirement accounts, Employee stock ownership plans.

Proposed amendments to the regulations

The proposed amendments to 26 CFR Part 1 are as follows:

Section 1.401(a)-(11) is amended by—

1. Striking out in paragraphs (a)(1)(i), (ii) and (iii) "such benefits" and inserting in lieu thereof "life annuity benefits".

2. Revising paragraph (a)(3) *Example* (1).

3. Revising paragraph (c)(2)(i)(C).

4. Revising the first two sentences of paragraph (c)(3)(ii).

5. Revising paragraph (d)(1) and adding a new paragraph (d)(5).

These revised and added provisions read as follows:

§ *1.401(a)-11 Qualified joint and survivor annuities.*

(a) *General rule—* * * *

(3) *Illustrations* * * *

Example (1). The X Corporation Defined Contribution Plan was established in 1960. As in effect on January 1, 1974, the plan provided that, upon his retirement, a participant could elect to receive the balance of his individual account in the form of (1) a lump-sum cash payment, (2) a lump-sum distribution consisting of X Corporation stock, (3) five equal annual cash payments, (4) a life annuity, or (5) a combination of options (1) through (4). The plan also provided that, if a participant did not elect another form of distribution, the balance of his individual account would be distributed to him in the form of a lump-sum cash payment upon his retirement. Assume that section 401(a)(11) and this section became applicable to the plan as of its plan year beginning January 1, 1976, with respect to persons who were active participants in the plan as of such date (see paragraph (f) of this section). If the X Corporation Defined Contribution Plan continues to allow the life annuity payment option, it must be amended to provide that if a participant elects a life annuity option the life annuity benefit will be paid in a form having the effect of a qualified joint and survivor annuity, except to the extent that the participant elects another form of

benefit payment. However, the plan can continue to provide that, if no election is made, the balance will be paid as a lump-sum cash payment. If the trust is not so amended, it will fail to qualify under section 401(a).

* * *

(c) *Elections.* * * *

(2) *Election of early survivor annuity*—(i) *In general.* * * *

(C) A plan is not required to provide an election under this subparagraph if—

(*1*) The plan provides that an early survivor annuity is the only form of benefit payable under the plan with respect to a married participant who dies while employed by an employer maintaining the plan,

(*2*) in the case of a defined contribution plan, the plan provides a survivor benefit at least equal in value to the vested portion of the participant's account balance, if the participant dies while in active service with an employer maintaining the plan, or

(*3*) in the case of a defined benefit plan, the plan provides a survivor benefit at least equal in value to the present value of the vested portion of the participant's accrued benefit (determined immediately prior to death), if the participant dies while in active service with an employer maintaining the plan. Any present values must be determined in accordance with actuarial assumptions or factors specified in the plan.

* * *

(3) *Information to be provided by plan administrator.* * * *

(ii) The method or methods used to provide the information described in subdivision (i) of this subparagraph may vary. Posting which meets the requirements of § 1.7476-2(c)(1) may be used; see § 1.7476-2(c)(i) for examples of other methods which may be used. * * *

(d) *Permissible additional plan provisions*— (1) *In general.* A plan will not fail to meet the requirements of section 401(a)(11) and this section merely because it contains one or more of the provisions described in paragraph (d)(2) through (5) of this section.

* * *

(5) *Benefit option approval by third party.* (i) A plan may provide that optional forms of benefit payment elected by a participant are subject to the approval of an administrative committee or similar third party. However, the administrative committee cannot deny a participant any of the benefits required by section 401(a)(11). For example, if a plan offers a life annuity option, the committee may deny the participant a qualified joint and survivor annuity only by denying the participant access to all life annuity options without knowledge of whether the participant wishes to receive a qualified joint and survivor annuity. Alternatively, if the committee knows which form of life annuity the participant has chosen before it makes its decision, the committee cannot withhold its consent for payment of a qualified joint and survivor annuity even though it denies all other life annuity options.

(ii) The provisions of this subparagraph may be illustrated by the following example:

Example. Plan M provides that the automatic form of benefit payout will be a single sum distribution. The plan also permits, subject to approval by the administrative committee, the election of several optional forms of life annuity. On the election form that is reviewed by the administrative committee the participant indicates whether any life annuity option is preferred, without indicating the particular life annuity chosen. Thus, the committee approves or disapproves the election without knowledge of whether a qualified joint and survivor annuity will be elected. The administrative committee approval provision in Plan M does not cause the plan to fail to satisfy this section. On the other hand, if the form indicates which form of life annuity is preferred, committee disapproval of any election of the qualified joint and survivor annuity would cause the plan to fail to satisfy this section.

* * *

(signed) Roscoe L. Egger, Jr.

Commissioner of Internal Revenue

¶ 20,137E

Proposed regulations on minimum funding standards and the excise taxes imposed for failure to meet the funding standards.— Reproduced below are proposed regulations relating to the minimum funding requirements under Code Sec. 412 and the excise taxes imposed under Code Sec. 4971 for failure to meet the minimum funding standards. The proposed regulations address issues affecting funding standard accounts, such as charges and credits, amortization amounts, the treatment of interest, unreasonable assumptions or funding methods, and plan termination. Also discussed are questions relating to money purchase plans, bond valuation elections, frequency of actuarial valuations, timing of contributions, and alternative minimum funding standard accounts.

The proposed regulations were published in the *Federal Register* on December 1, 1982 (47 FR 54093).

NOTICE OF PROPOSED RULEMAKING

AGENCY: Internal Revenue Service, Treasury.

ACTION: Notice of proposed rulemaking.

SUMMARY: This document contains proposed regulations relating to the minimum funding requirements for employee pension benefit plans, and to excise taxes for failure to meet the minimum funding standards. Changes to the applicable tax law were made by the Employee Retirement Income Security Act of 1974. The regulations would provide the public with guidance needed to comply with that Act and would affect all pension plans subject to the provisions of the Act.

DATES: Written comments and requests for public hearing must be delivered or mailed by January 28, 1983. The proposed amendments would apply generally for plan years beginning after 1975, but earlier (or later) in the case of some plans as provided for meeting the minimum funding requirements under the Act. The proposed rules pertaining to the frequency of actuarial valuations, and to the time for making contributions, generally would not be effective prior to the publication of final regulations.

ADDRESS: Send comments and requests for a public hearing to: Commissioner of Internal Revenue, Attention: CC:LR:T (EE-99-78), Washington, D.C. 20224.

FOR FURTHER INFORMATION CONTACT: Eric A. Raps of the Employee Plans and Exempt Organizations Division, Office of the Chief Counsel, Internal Revenue Service, 1111 Constitution Avenue, N.W., Washington, D.C. 20224 (Attention: CC:LR T) (202-566-6212, not a toll-free call).

SUPPLEMENTARY INFORMATION:

Background

This document contains proposed amendments to the Income Tax Regulations (26 CFR Part 1) under section 412 of the Internal Revenue Code of 1954. These amendments are proposed to conform the regulations to section 1013(a) of the Employee Retirement Income Security Act of 1974 (ERISA) (88 Stat. 914). The proposed amendments would also apply for purposes of sections 302 and 305 of ERISA (88 Stat. 869, 873).

The proposed amendments would be issued under the authority of section 302(b)(4), (b)(5), (c)(2)(B), (c)(9) and (c)(10) of ERISA (88 Stat. 870, 871, and 872; 29 U.S.C. 1082) and sections 412(b)(4), (b)(5), (c)(2)(B), (c)(9) and (c)(10) and 7805 of the Internal Revenue Code of 1954 (88 Stat. 915, 916, and 917; 68A Stat. 917; 26 U.S.C. 412(b)(4), (b)(5), (c)(2)(B), (c)(9), and (c)(10) and 7805).

This document also contains proposed amendments to the Income Tax Regulations (26 CFR Part 1) and the Pension Excise Tax Regulations (26 CFR Part 54) under section 413(b)(6) and (c)(5) and section 4971 of the Internal Revenue Code of 1954. These regulations are proposed primarily to conform the regulations to section 1013(b) of the Employee Retirement income Security Act of 1974 (ERISA) (88 Stat. 920). They are to be issued under the authority of section 413(b)(6) and (c)(5) and section 7805 of the Internal Revenue Code of 1954 (88 Stat. 924, 925, 68A Stat. 917; 26 U.S.C. 413(b)(6) and (c)(5), 7805).

The proposed regulations do not reflect changes to the second-level excise tax made by the Act of Dec. 24, 1980, Pub. L. 96-596 (94 Stat. 3469), or amendments to sections 412 and 4971 made by the Multiemployer Pension Plan Amendments Act of 1980, Pub. L 96-364 (94 Stat. 1208).

Purpose and Scope

The proposed amendments address the remaining statutory provisions not yet addressed by regulations relating to the minimum funding requirements with respect to which either regulatory guidance is required by law or interpretative assistance would be helpful in applying the law. These proposed amendments, together with proposed or final regulations previously issued under section 412 of the Code, generally constitute the regulatory guidance to be provided with respect to the minimum funding requirements, with the exception of rules relating to mergers. However, comments noting additional issues with respect to which regulatory guidance might be helpful will be considered along with comments addressing issues that arise under the proposed amendments.

The provisions under section 4971 of the Code contain sanctions for enforcing the minimum funding requirements. The sanctions are two excise taxes. The initial tax is 5 percent of an accumulated funding deficiency, and an additional tax of 100 percent is imposed if the deficiency is not corrected. Generally, the employer responsible for contributing to the plan is liable for these taxes.

Section 3002(b) of ERISA provides special rules regarding the section 4971 taxes and coordination of matters regarding these taxes with the Secretary of Labor.

Funding Standard Account

Under section 412(b) of the Code, a plan must maintain a funding standard account. The mechanics for reflecting charges and credits to the account appear in section 412(b)(2) and (3). The proposed amendments address a number of key issues arising under the funding standard account provisions.

Money Purchase Plans

Under the proposed amendments, a money purchase pension plan is, like other plans, required to maintain a funding standard account. However, the accounting under such a plan for funding purposes is limited to charges for the contribution required under the formula provided by the plan, credits for amounts actually contributed, and charges and credits to amortize certain bases.

Normally, the need to create an amortization base does not exist under a money purchase plan. However, such a base would be created, for example, with the issuance of a waiver of the minimum funding standard for a plan.

Combining and Offsetting

The proposed amendments would provide rules, as required under section 412(b)(4) of the Code, for combining and offsetting amortization amounts determined under the funding standard account. The proposed method for combining and offsetting these amounts is described in the legislative history of ERISA. (See H.R. Rep. No. 93-807, 93rd Cong., 2d Sess. 86-87 (1974), 1974-3 C.B. Supp. 321-322.)

Treatment of Interest

The proposed amendments would provide rules, as required by section 412(b)(5) of the Code, for treating interest charges and credits under the funding standard account.

Generally under the proposed amendments, charges and credits are made as of an assumed accounting date under the plan. There must be an interest charge or credit, as the case may be, for the period between this assumed date and the end of the plan year.

A contribution made during the "grace period" between the last day of a plan year and the day determined under section 412(c)(10) is treated as having been made on the last day of the plan year.

Retroactive Changes

The proposed amendments provide for reflecting in the funding standard account retroactive changes required by the Commissioner to adjust for the use of unreasonable assumptions or funding methods.

Plan Termination

The proposed amendments relating to the effect of plan termination on the funding standard account are substantially identical to the provisions of Rev. Rul. 79-237, 1979-2 C.B. 190.

Bond Valuation Election

The proposed amendments would provide rules, as required by section 412(c)(2)(B) of the Code, for the election of a special valuation rule applicable to bonds and other evidences of indebtedness. The proposed amendments would be substantially identical to temporary regulations published in 1974 with respect to the bond valuation election. However, the proposed amendments would clarify the temporary rules by providing that certain convertible debt instruments are treated as debt until converted into equity securities. The rules concerning valuation of convertible debt would be effective only for debt instruments acquired after the date on which the proposal is adopted as a final regulation. For debt instruments acquired before that date, a valuation method will be considered acceptable if it is applied on a consistent basis.

Actuarial Valuation

The proposed amendments would provide rules, as required by section 412(c)(9) of the Code, relating to the frequency of actuarial valuations for plans. These rules would identify situations in which valuations may be required more frequently than once every 3 years.

Comments are requested as to the appropriateness of requiring more frequent valuations under the situations described in the proposed amendments. Comments are also requested as to any additional circumstances where valuations should be required more frequently than once every 3 years. The rules also would describe how the funding standard account is to be maintained for years when there is no valuation.

Timing of Contributions

The proposed amendments would provide rules, as required by section 412(c)(10) of the Code, relating to the time for making contributions for purposes of section 412. Unlike the temporary regulations published in 1976, these rules would not contain an automatic six-month extension of the two and one-half month grace period set forth as a general rule under the statute for meeting the minimum funding requirements. The Commissioner may approve applications for an extension of the grace period of up to six months. This more restrictive approach would be applied prospectively from a date after the publication of final regulations. However, a transitional rule is provided to phase in the two and one-half month period over the first three plan years following a date after publication of final regulations, and extensions may be approved by the Commissioner.

Alternative Funding Standard Account

The proposed amendments contain rules that would apply to plans maintaining the alternative minimum funding standard account. These rules would reflect section 412(g)(1) by limiting the use of the alternative account to plans using a funding method that requires contributions in all years at least equal to those required under the entry age normal funding method. Thus, only plans that use the entry age normal funding method may use the alternative account.

Allocation of Excise Tax Liability

The proposed amendments would contain rules to allocate excise tax liability under section 4971 of more than one employer, but they would permit allocation in a reasonable manner that is not inconsistent with the rules provided.

Under the proposed amendments, the tax liability of each employer would generally be based on the obligation of each employer to contribute to the plan. To the extent that a funding deficiency would be attributable to the delinquent contribution of an individual employer, that employer would be liable for the tax. To the extent that a funding deficiency is not attributable to a delinquent contribution, each employer would share liability in proportion to its share of required contributions to the plan.

Allocations for Related Employers

The general rules for allocating tax liability would not apply to certain related employers. To the extent that an accumulated funding deficiency is attributable to related employers, those employers would be jointly and severally liable for the excise tax with respect to that deficiency. This rule would apply to related employers maintaining a plan of their own or in conjunction with other employers.

Employer Withdrawal

The proposed amendments would generally provide that an employer withdrawing from a plan remains liable for tax imposed with respect to the portion of an accumulated funding deficiency attributable to that employer for years before withdrawal. The remaining employers would be liable for the tax attributable to the accumulated funding deficiency for years after an employer's withdrawal, even if the deficiency is attributable to prior years.

Temporary Regulations Superseded

The proposed amendments contain rules that would supersede the following temporary regulations: § 11.412(c)-7, relating to the election to treat certain retroactive plan amendments as made on the first day of the plan year; § 11.412(c)-11, relating to the election with respect to bonds; and § 11.412(c)-12, relating to the extension of time to make contributions to satisfy requirements of section 412.

Executive Order 12291 and Regulatory Flexibility Act

The Commissioner of Internal Revenue has determined that this proposed regulation is not a major regulation for purposes of Executive Order 12291. Accordingly, a regulatory impact analysis is not required.

Although this document is a notice of proposed rule making which solicits public comments, the Internal Revenue Service has concluded that the regulations proposed herein are interpretative and that the

notice and public procedure requirements of 5 U.S.C. 553 do not apply. Accordingly, these proposed regulations do not constitute regulations subject to the Regulatory Flexibility Act (5 U.S.C. chapter 6).

Comments and Requests for a Public Hearing

Before adopting these proposed regulations, consideration will be given to any written comments that are submitted (preferably eight copies) to the Commissioner of Internal Revenue. It is requested that persons submitting comments use professional letterhead stationery only if the comment represents the position of the firm or a named client, rather than the views of the writer. All comments are available for public inspection and copying. A public hearing will be held upon written request to the Commissioner by any person who has submitted written comments. If a public hearing is held, notice of the time and place will be published in the *Federal Register*.

Drafting Information

The principal author of these proposed regulations is Joel E. Horowitz of the Employee Plans and Exempt Organizations Division of the Office of Chief Counsel, Internal Revenue Service. However, personnel from other offices of the Internal Revenue Service and Treasury Department participated in developing the regulations, both on matters of substance and style.

List of Subjects in 26 CFR §§ 1.401-0—1.425-1

Income taxes, Employee benefit plans, Pensions.

Proposed amendments to the regulations

The proposed amendments to 26 CFR Parts 1, 11, and 54 are as follows:

Income Tax Regulations

(26 CFR Part 1)

Paragraph 1. The Income Tax Regulations, 26 CFR Part 1, are amended by adding the following new sections immediately after § 1.411(d)-3:

§ 1.412(a)-1 General scope of minimum funding standard requirements.

(a) *General rule.* Section 412 of the Code provides minimum funding requirements for plans that include a trust qualified under section 401(a) and for plans that meet the requirements of section 403(a) or section 405(a). Generally, such plans include defined benefit pension plans, money purchase pension plans (including target benefit plans), qualified annuity plans, and qualified bond purchase plans. The minimum funding requirements continue to apply to any plan that was qualified under, or was determined to have met the requirements of, these sections for any plan year beginning on or after the effective date described in paragraph (d) of this section for the plan. Also, under section 302 of the Employee Retirement Income Security Act of 1974 ("ERISA"), the minimum funding requirements apply to employee pension benefit plans described in section 301(a) of that Act. The regulations prescribed under this section and the following sections with respect to section 412 also apply for purposes of sections 302 and 305 of ERISA. These topics are among those discussed in the following sections: maintenance of a funding standard account (including rules for combining and offsetting amounts to be amortized, rules for computing interest on amounts charged and credited to the account, rules relating to the treatment of gains and losses, and rules relating to retroactive changes in the funding standard account required by the Commissioner), § 1.412(b)-1; amortization of experience gains in connection with group deferred annuity contracts, § 1.412(b)-2; funding standard account adjustments for plan mergers and spinoffs, § 1.412(b)-3; plan terminations, § 1.412(b)-4; election of the alternative amortization method of funding, § 1.412(b)-5; determinations to be made under funding method, § 1.412(c)(1)-2; valuation of plan assets and reasonable valuation methods, § 1.412(c)(2); bond valuation election, § 1.412(c)(2)-2; reasonable funding methods, § 1.412(c)(3)-1 and -2; certain changes in accrued liability, § 1.412(c)(4)-1; changes in funding method or plan year, § 1.412(c)(5)-1; full funding and the full funding limitation, § 1.412(c)(6)-1 and § 1.412(c)(7)-1; retroactive plan amendment, § 1.412(c)(8)-1; frequency of actuarial valuations, § 412(c)(9)-1; time for making contributions to satisfy section 412, § 1.412(c)(10)-1; and maintenance of an alternative funding standard account, § 1.412(g)-1.

(b) *Exceptions.* See section 412(h) for a list of plans not subject to the requirements of section 412. These excepted plans include profit-sharing or stock bonus plans; certain insurance contract, government, and church plans; and certain plans that do not provide for employer contributions.

(c) *Failure to meet minimum funding standards.* A plan fails to meet the minimum funding standards for a plan year if, as of the end of that year, there is an accumulated funding deficiency as defined in section 412(a) and §54.4971-1(d). See regulations to taxes for failure to meet the minimum funding standards.

(d) *Effective date*—(1) *In general.* Unless otherwise provided, this section and the following sections providing regulations under section 412 apply to any plan year to which section 412 applies. For a plan in existence on January 1, 1974, section 412 generally applies to plan years beginning in 1976. However, this time is extended by special transitional rules under section 1017(c)(2) of ERISA for such existing plans under collective bargaining agreements. For a plan not in existence on January 1, 1974, section 412 generally applies for plan years beginning after September 2, 1974.

(2) *date when plan is in existence.* See §1.410(a)-2(c) for rules concerning the date when a plan is considered to be in existence.

(3) *Early application of section 412.* See §1.410(a)-2(d) for rules permitting plans in existence on January 1, 1974, to elect to have section 412, as well as other provisions added by section 1013 of ERISA, apply to plan year beginning after September 4, 1974, and before the effective date of the provision otherwise applicable to the plan.

(4) *Transitional rule.* The regulations issued under sections §1.412(b)-1, §1.412)b)-3, §1.412(b)-4, §1.41'2(c)(2)-2, §1.412(c)(4)-1, §1.412(c)(5)-1, §1.412(c)(6)-1, §1.412(c)(7)-1, §1.412(c)(8)-1, §1.412(c)(9)-1, §1.412 (c)(10)-1, and §1.412(g)-1, unless otherwise indicated are effective with respect to a particular plan when section 412 first applies to that plan. However, for plan years beginning on or before [INSERT DATE 60 DAYS AFTER PUBLICATION OF THESE REGULATIONS AS A TREASURY DECISION IN THE FEDERAL REGISTER] the plan may rely on the prior published position of the Internal Revenue Service with respect to the application of section 412. Other effective dates are included in §1.412(b)-2, §1.412(c)(1)-2, §1.412(c)(2)-1, §1.412(c)(3)-2 and §1.412(i)-1.

§1.412(b)-1 Funding standard account.

(a) *General rule.* Generally, for each single plan subject to the minimum funding standards there must be maintained a funding standard account as prescribed by section 412(b). (See §1.414(1)-1(b)(1) for definition of "single plan".) Such an account for a money purchase pension plan reflects charges for contributions required under the plan, credits for amounts contributed, and charges and credits for amortization bases described in paragraph (b)(3) of this section,.

(b) *Definitions and special rules.*—(1) *Accounting date*—(i) *In general.* Each charge or credit to the funding standard account is charged or credited as of an accounting date. The accounting date for an item depends on the nature of the item and must be consistent with the computation of the amount of that item.

(ii) *Specific accounting dates.* The accounting date for each individual charge for normal cost or any charge or credit for the amortization of an amortization base is the date as of which the charge or credit is computed as due during the plan year. The last day of the plan year is the accounting date for any credit described in section 412(b)(3)(C). The first day of the plan year is the accounting date for any credit described in section 412(b)(3)(D) or for any accumulated funding deficiency or credit balance existing as of the end of the prior plan year. The accounting date for each contribution is made or, if made during the period described in section 412(c)(10) the last day of the plan year. Further, any contribution made must be credited as of the accounting date.

(2) *Valuation rate.* The term "valuation rate" means the assumed interest rate used to value plan liabilities.

(3) *Amortization base.* For purposes of this section, the term "amortization base" means any amount established under section 412(b)(2)(B), (C), or (D) to be amortized as a charge to the funding standard account, under section 412(b)(3)(B) to be amortized as a credit to the funding standard account, any other base resulting from a combination of offset of bases or any shortfall gain or loss base under §1.412(c)(1)-2. Any base required by the Commissioner to be established pursuant to any approved change in funding method is also an amortization base. Each amortization base established under one of the provisions enumerated above with respect to a particular year is referred to as an "individual base."

(4) *Amortization period.* The amortization period for a base is the period of years stated in section 412(b)(2) or (3) over which a particular base is to be amortized. See §1.412(c)(1)-2(g)(2) and (h)(2) for amortization periods under the shortfall method. See section 412(b)(2)

and (3) for amortization periods for bases described in those sections. See paragraph (d) of this section for amortization periods of bases resulting from a combination or offset of bases. If the number of years in the amortization period is not an integer, the charge or credit in the last year will not be for the entire amortization amount but will be for the outstanding balance of the base at the time of the charge or credit.

(5) *Outstanding balance.* The outstanding balance of a base as of the end of a plan year equals the difference between two amounts:

(i) The first amount is the outstanding balance of the base as of the beginning of the plan year (or, if later, the date as of which the base is required to be established) increased by interest at the valuation rate.

(ii) The second amount is the charge (or credit) for that year for the base increased by interest at the valuation rate. For purposes of testing the basic funding formula in §1.412(c)(3)-1(b)(1) the outstanding balance of amortizable bases must be computed as of the valuation date (the same date as of which the present value of future benefits and the present value of normal costs over the future working lifetime of participants are determined), rather than as of the end of the plan year. In testing the basic funding formula, the outstanding balance as of a valuation date equals the difference two amounts. The first amount is the outstanding balance as of the preceding valuation date (or, if later, the date as of which the base is required to be established) increased by interest at the valuation rate. The second amount is the charge (or credit) for the plan year preceding the plan year to which the current valuation refers increased by interest at the valuation rate.

(6) *Remaining amortization period.* The remaining amortization period for an amortization base is the difference between the amortization period and the number of years (including whole and fractional years) for which the base has been reduced by charging or crediting the funding standard account, as the case may be, with the amortization payment for each year.

(7) *Amortization amount.* The amortization amount is the amount of the charge or credit to the funding standard account required with respect to an amortization base for a plan year.

(8) *True and absolute values.* See §1.404(a)-14(b)(4) for a definition of the terms "absolute value."

(9) *Immediate gain type funding method.* A funding method is an immediate gain type method if, under the method—

(i) The accrued liability may be determined solely from the computations with respect to the liabilities;

(ii) The accrued liability is an integral part of the funding method; and

(iii) The accrued liability is the excess of the present value, as of any valuation date, of the projected future benefit costs for all plan participants and beneficiaries over the present value of future contributions for the normal cost of all current plan participants.

Examples of the immediate gain type of funding method are the unit credit method, the entry-age normal cost method, and the individual level premium method.

(10) *Spread gain type funding method.* A funding method is a spread gain type method if it is not an immediate gain type method. Examples of the spread gain type of funding method are the aggregate cost method, the frozen initial liability cost method and the attained age normal cost method.

(11) *Actual unfunded liability for immediate gain funding methods.*—(1) *In general.* For a funding method of the immediate gain type, the actual unfunded liability as of any valuation date is the excess, if any, of the accrued liability over the actuarial value of assets as of that date.

(ii) *Accrued liability.* The accrued liability is equal to the present value of future benefits less the present value of future normal costs. Generally, for purposes of computing costs for a plan year and gains and losses for a plan year, the normal cost for the plan year to which the valuation refers is considered to be a future normal cost and is not included in the accrued liability.

(iii) *Actuarial value of assets.* The value of assets must be determined in a manner consistent with section 412(c)(2) of the Code and §1.412(c)(2)-1. Furthermore, for the purposes of computing costs for a plan year and gains and losses for a plan year, the assets must be treated in a manner that is consistent with the method of calculation of the accrued liability. If, in determining the accrued liability, the normal cost for the plan year to which valuation refers is treated as a future normal cost, then the assets used to compute the unfunded accrued liability should not include contributions that are credited to the funding standard account for the plan year to which the valuation refers or for any plan year thereafter.

(12) *Actual unfunded liability for spread gain funding methods.* For a funding method of the spread gain type that maintains an unfunded liability, the actual unfunded liability equals the expected unfunded liability.

(13) *Expected unfunded liability.* The expected unfunded liability as of any valuation date is determined as:

(i) The actual unfunded liability as of the prior valuation date increased with interest at the valuation rate to this later valuation date, plus

(ii) Normal costs representing accrued liabilities that were not included in determining the accrued liability as of the prior valuation date (*i.e.*, such costs as of the prior valuation date) but that are included (*i.e.*, are not considered future normal costs) in determining the accrued liability as of this later valuation date, plus interest at the valuation rate from the date as of which the normal costs were assumed payable to this valuation date, minus

(iii) The amount considered contributed by the employer to or under the plan for the plan year that was not included in the calculation of the actual unfunded liability as of the prior valuation date and was included in the calculation of the actual unfunded liability as of this later valuation date, plus interest at the valuation rate from the date on which the contribution was made if during the plan year, or under section 412(C)(10) was deemed to have been made if made after the plan year, to this later valuation date.

(14) *Plan year to which a valuation refers.* The plan year for which the funding standard account is charged with the first normal cost determined by a valuation is the plan year to which the valuation refers. See also § 1.412(c)(9)-1(b) concerning the date of a valuation.

(c) *Establishment and maintenance of amortization bases.*—(1) *Immediate gain type funding methods.* Under a plan using an immediate gain type funding method, a new amortization base must be established to reflect each change in unfunded past service liability arising from a plan amendment, net experience gain or loss, and change in unfunded past service liability arising from a change in funding method or actuarial assumptions.

(2) *Spread gain type funding methods*—(i) *In general.* Under a plan using a spread gain type funding method, amortization bases may be established to reflect changes in unfunded past service liability arising from plan amendments or changes in actuarial assumptions. Alternatively, these changes in unfunded liability may be reflected in the normal cost. Whether these changes are reflected in amortization bases or in the normal cost is part of the funding method. Thus, any change from past practice constitutes a change in funding method and must be approved under section 412(c)(5). Furthermore, the method must treat increases and decreases due to any type of event consistently.

(ii) *Experience gain or loss.* An amortization base may not be established to reflect a new experience gain or loss under a plan using a spread gain type funding method.

(3) *Special amortization bases.* Any amortization base established to amortize a waived funding deficiency under section 412(b)(2)(C) must continue to maintained regardless of the type of funding method used by the plan. Also see § 1.412(b)-1(d)(1).

(d) *Combining and offsetting amounts to be amortized*—(1) *In general.* Under section 412(b)(4), individual bases, with the exception of bases under section 412(b)(2)(C), may be combined and offset to form a

single base. This single base is computed under the provisions of paragraph (d) that follow. However, any number of amortization bases having the same remaining amortization period may be combined and offset simply by adding the outstanding balances of the individual bases, using true rather than absolute values, without regard to the computations under paragraph (d) of this section that follow. Bases under section 412(b)(2)(C) may not be combined with any bases not established under section 412(b)(2)(C).

(2) *Combine outstanding balances of bases for charges and for credits.* Except as provided in subparagraph (1) the outstanding balances of any individual bases established for the purpose of charging the funding standard account may be combined as of any date by adding the outstanding balance of each base to be combined as of that date. Likewise, the outstanding balances of any bases for crediting the account may be combined.

(3) *Determine remaining amortization period of each combined base.* The remaining amortization period of a combined base is determined as follows:

(i) Add the amortization amounts, based on the same mode of payment, for the individual bases being combined. Amortization amounts are of the same mode of payment if they are charged or credited on the same day of the plan year, or on the same days if charged or credited in installments during the plan year.

(ii) Divide the outstanding balance of the combined base by the combined amortization amount determined under subdivision (i).

(iii) Compute the period of years for which the amount determined under subdivision (ii) provides an annuity certain of $1 per year at the valuation rate. This number, the remaining amortization period, must be computed in terms of fractional years, if necessary. Standard present value tables may be used together with linear interpolation.

(iv) As an alternative, the amortization period may be rounded to the next lowest integer (if charge bases) or next highest integer (if credit bases) and the amortization amount must then be recomputed by dividing the outstanding balance of the combined based by the present value of annuity certain of $1 per year at the valuation rate for the rounded amortization period.

(4) *Offset.* Combined bases may be offset only if all charge and credit bases have been combined (except those that may not be combined pursuant to subparagraph (1)). The combined charge base and the combined credit base are offset by subtracting the lesser outstanding balance from the greater outstanding balance. The difference between these two outstanding balances is amortized over the remaining amortization period for the greater of the two outstanding balances, whether for charges or for credits. The amortization amount (charge or credit) for this offset base is the level amount payable for each plan year to reduce the outstanding balance of the base to zero over the remaining amortization period at the valuation rate. However, see paragraph (d)(3)(iv) of this section concerning an alternative method of computing the remaining amortization period.

(5) *Example.* Assume that at the beginning of a plan year the actuary for a plan decides to combine and offset the amortization bases as reflected in the plan's funding standard account. No funding deficiency of the plan has been waived. All amortization amounts are due at the end of the plan year. The valuation rate is 5 percent. Based on pertinent information from the plan records, all amortization bases, A and B for charges and C and D for credits, are combined and offset as follows:

Base	Outstanding balance (beginning of year)	Amortization amount (due end of year)	Remaining amortization period
(i) *Individual bases.*			
A	$165,468	$10,000	36
B	8,863	1,000	12
C	(4,153)	(500)	11
D	(30,745)	(2,000)	30
(i) *Combined bases.*			
AB	$174,331	$11,000	32.23
CD	(34,898)	(2,500)	24.53
(i) *Offset base.*			
ABCD	$139,433	$8,798	32.23

(iv) The outstanding balanes of the charge and credit bases were combined in step (ii) by adding the outstanding balances of the like bases (165,468 + 8,863 = 174,331 and 4,153 + 30,745 = 34,898). The charge and credit base amortization amounts were similarly computed (10,000 + 1,000 = 11,000 and 500 + 2,000 = 2,500). The remaining amortization periods were derived from standard present value tables and linear interpolation as the amount having a present value at the 5 percent valuation rate for a $1 per year annuity certain equal to the ration of the outstanding balance to the amortization amount.

(v) The combined bases were offset in step (iii) by subtracting base CD from AB to obtain the $139,433 outstanding balance, using the 32.23 remaining amortization period for base AB, and computing the

$8,798 amortization amount as the level annual amount necessary to amortize the base fully over 32.23 years. (Alternatively, the amortization period may be rounded to 32 years. The amortization charge corresponding to that amortization period is $8,823.)

(e) *Interest.*—(1) *General rule.* The funding standard account is charged or credited with interest at the valuation rate for the time between the accounting date for the item giving rise to the interest charge or credit and the end of the plan year.

(2) *Change of interest rate.* A change of the assumed interest rate under a plan does not affect the outstanding balance or the remaining amortization period of any existing base. However, the amortization amount for each base is increased to reflect an increase in interest and decrease to reflect a decrease in interest so that the present value of future amortization amounts equal the outstanding balance of the base. This chane is made in addition to creating any new base required by § 1.412(b)-1(c).

(f) *Gains and losses.*—(1) *Amortization requirements*—(i) *Immediate gain type funding method.* A plan that uses an immediate gain type of funding method separately amortizes experience gains and losses over the period prescribed in section 412(b)(2)(B)(iv) and (3)(B)(ii). The first year of the amortization of an experience gain or less determined as of particular valuation date is the plan year to which the valuation refers.

(ii) *Spread gain type funding method.* A plan that uses a spread gain type of funding method spreads experience gains and losses over future periods as part of the plan's normal cost. These gains and losses are reflected in the amount charged to the funding standard account under section 412(b)(2)(A) and are not separately amortized.

(2) *Amount of experience gain or loss.*—(i) *In general.* For an immediate gain type of funding method the experience gain determined as of a valuation late is the excess of the expected unfunded liability described in § 1.412(b)-1(b)(13) over the actual unfunded liability described in § 1.412(b)-1(b)(11). The experience loss is the excess of the actual unfunded liability described in § 1.412(b)-1(b)(11) over the expected unfunded liability described in § 1.412(b)-1(b)(13).

(ii) *Special rule.* Paragraph (f)(2)(ii) of this section applies to an immediate gain funding method if there are no other amortization charges (under section 412(b)(2(B), (C), or (D)) or credits (under section 412(b)(3)(B) for the first plan year in which the loss will be amortized. The experience loss as of the valuation date is the sum of—

(A) The actual unfunded liability as of the valuation date, plus

(B) Any credit balance (or minus any funding deficiency) in the funding standard account as of the first day of the first plan year in which the loss will be amortized adjusted with interest at the valuation rate to the valuation date.

(g) *Certain retroactive changes required by Commissioner.* Under section 412(c)(3), all costs liabilities, rates of interest, and other factors under the plan must be determined on the basis on actuarial assumptions and methods which, in th aggregate, are reasonable. Assumptions and methods are established in the first Schedule B (Form 5500) that is filed with respect to a plan year and may not be changed for that plan year. However, upon a determination by the Commissioner that the the actuarial asssumptions and methods used by a plan are not reasonable in the aggregate, the Commissioner may require certain retroactive adjustments to the funding standard account of the plan. The funding standard account must reflect these changes as required by the Commissioner.

(h) *Reasonable actuarial assumptions.*—(1) *In general.* The determination whether actuarial assumptions are reasonable in the aggregate is generally based upon the experience under the plan, unless it is established that past experience is not likely to recur and thus is not a good indication of future experience. In addition, assumptions may be considered unreasonable in the circumstances described in paragraphs (h)(2)-(4) of this section.

(2) *Noncounterbalancing assumptions.* Assumptions may be considered unreasonable if an assumption used by the plan is not yet reflected in the experience of the plan, is not reasonable under the circumstances of the plan, and is not counterbalanced by another assumption. For example, isn a plan with one participant who has not yet attained the normal retirement age, an assumption of an unreasonable annuity purchase rate could be counter balanced by a change in the plan interest rate.

(3) *Inconsistent with benefit structure.* As assumptions may be unreasonable if use of an assumption is inconsistent with the benefit structure of the plan. For example, a plan which provides benefits not based on compensation may not assume a salary increase if it spreads the present value of future normal costs over the present value of future compensation.

(4) *Inconsistent assumptions.* Assumptions may be considered unreasonable in the aggregate if one plan assumption is inconsistent with other assumptions used by the plan. For example, an assumption which projects benefits based on a salary increase of 5-percent per year may cause assumptions to be unreasonable in the aggregate in a plan which spreads normal costs over future years' compensation using an assumption of 8-percent annual compensation increases.

Par. 2. The Income Tax Regulations, 26 CFR Part 1, are amended by adding the following new sections after § 1.412(b)-2.

§ 1.412(b)-3 Funding standard account adjustments for plan mergers and spinoffs. [RESERVED]

§ 1.412(b)-4 Plan termination and plan years of less than twelve months.

(a) *General rules.* The minimum funding standard under section 412 applies to a plan under the end of the plan year in which the plan terminates. Therefore, the funding standard account (or the alternative funding standard account, as the case may be) must be maintained until the end of the plan year in which the plan terminates even though the plan terminates before the last day of the plan year.

(b) *Defined benefit plan.* In the case of a defined benefit plan, the charges and credits to the funding standard account are adjusted ratably to reflect the portion of the plan year before the date of plan termination. Similarly, annual charges and adjusted for a short plan year. However, this ratable adjustment is not made for credits under section 412(b)(2)(C), and (D), for interest charges and credits under section 412(b)(5), and for credits under section 412(c)(6).

(c) *Money purchase pension plans*—(1) *General rule for termination.* In the case of a money purchase pension plan, the minimum funding standard requires the funding standard account to be charged with the entire amount of any contribution due on or before the date of plan termination however, it does not require a charge for contributions due after that date.

(2) *General rule for short plan year.* In the case of a money purchase pension plan, the minimum funding standard requires the funding standard account to be charged with the entire amount of any contribution due as of a date within a short plan year.

(3) *Due date of contributions.* For the purposes of paragraphs (c)(1) and (2) of this section, a contribution is due as of the earlier of—

(i) The date specified in the plan, or

(ii) The date as of which the contribution is required to be allocated.

(4) *Date for allocation of contribution.* For purposes of paragraph (c)(3)(ii) of this section, a contribution is required to be allocated as of a date if all the requirements for the allocation have been satisfied as of that date.

(d) *Date of plan termination*—(1) *Title IV plans.* In the case of a plan subject to Title IV of ERISA, the date of plan termination is generally the date described in section 40489 of ERISA. However, if that date precedes the tenth day after the date on which notice of intent to terminate is filed, and if any contributions made or required by Code section 412 to avoid an accumulated funding deficiency for the period ending on such tenth day would increase any participant's benefits upon termination (taking benefits guaranteed by the Pension Benefit Guaranty Corporation into account), the date of termination will be the tenth day after the date on which notice of intent to terminate is filed.

(2) *Other plans.* In the case of a plan not subject to Title IV of ERISA, the date of plan termination occurs no earlier than the date on which the actions necessary to effect the plan termination are taken. The determination of this date is based on the facts and circumstances of each case.

(e) *Partial terminations.* This section does not apply to a partial plan termination within the meaning of section 411(d)(3)(A).

(f) *Funding excise taxes.* See § 54.4971-3(d) of the Pension Excise Tax Regulations (26 CFR Part 54) for the effect of plan termination on an employer's liability for taxes imposed by section 4971(a) and (b).

Par. 3. The Income Tax Regulations, 26 CFR Part 1, are amended by adding the following new section after § 1.412(c)(2)-1:

§ 1.412(c)(2)-2 Bond valuation election.

(a) *Scope of election.*—(1) *In general.* The election described in section 412(c)(2)(B) with respect to bonds generally applies to all bonds and evidences of indebtedness including those acquired by merger. The election applies only to defined benefit plans. A defined contribution plan must value bonds and other evidences of indebtedness on the basis of fair market value.

(2) *Exception.* The election does not apply to bonds or evidences of indebtedness at any time that they are in default as to principal or interest.

(3) *Convertible debt.* For purposes of this section, a debut instrument which is convertible into an equity security and acquired after [THE DATE 90 DAYS AFTER THE DATE ON WHICH § 1.412(c)(2)-2 IS ADOPTED AS A TREASURY DECISION] is treated as an evidence of indebtedness until the conversion occurs.

(b) *Effect of election.*—(1) *In general.* The effect of the election is that bonds and other evidences of indebtedness included among the plan assets are valued on an amortized basis rather than on a fair market value basis.

(2) *Amount amortized.*—(i) *In general.* The amount amortized with respect to a bond or other evidence of indebtedness is generally the difference between its initial cost when acquired by the plan and its redemption value at the end of the amortization period. In the case of a bond or other evidence of indebtedness that was acquired by the plan in a plan year before the plan year for which the election was made, the amortized value for each year must be determined as though the election had always been in effect with respect to the bond or other evidence of indebtedness.

(ii) *Spinoffs.* The amount amortized after a spinoff is based on the initial cost to the plan which acquired the bond or other evidence of indebtedness and not the value to the plan after the spinoff.

(iii) *Mergers.* The amount amortized after a merger is based on the cost of the plan which first elected to value the bonds and other evidences of indebtedness on an amortized basis. In the case of a bond or other evidence of indebtedness that was acquired by any merging plan before the election was first made with respect to the bond or other evidence of indebtedness, the premium or discount shall be amortized as provided in paragraph (b)(2)(i).

(3) *Amortization period.* The amortization period is the time from the date on which the plan acquires the bond or other evidence of indebtedness to its maturity date (or, in the case of a debt instrument that is callable prior to maturity, the earliest call date).

(c) *Effect of default.* Once the election is made, it applies to each debt instrument held or acquired that is not in default as to principal or interest. While in default, the instrument is subject to the fair market value requirements of section 412(c)(2)(A).

(d) *Manner of making election.* The plan administrator makes the election by preparing a statement that the election described in section 412(c)(2)(B) is being made and by filing the statement attached to the annual return required under section 6058 for the first plan year for which the election is to apply.

(e) *Revocation of election.*—(1) *Effect.* Once consent to the revocation of the election is obtained as prescribed in paragraph (e)(2) of this section, all plan assets are valued under section 412(c)(2)(A).

(2) *Consent.* Consent for the revocation of the election must be obtained in the manner prescribed by the Commissioner for obtaining permission to change funding methods under section 412(c)(5) and § 1.412(c)(5)-1.

(3) *Mergers.* A plan which has acquired a bond or other evidence of indebtedness by merger must obtain the consent of the Commissioner to value bonds and other evidences of indebtedness on a basis other than amortized value if an election under section 412(c)(2)(B) with respect to the asset acquired had been made prior to the merger.

Par. 4. The Income Tax Regulations, 26 CFR Part 1, are amended by adding the following new sections after § 1.412(c)(3)-2:

§ 1.412(c)(4)-1 Certain changes in accrued liability.

(a) *In general.* In the case of immediate gain type funding methods, section 412(c)(4) treats certain increases and decreases in the accrued liability under a plan as an experience gain or loss. Plans using a spread gain type of funding method will reflect the gain or loss in determining the normal cost under the plan. Under section 412(b)(2) and (3), plans which are valued using a funding method of the immediate gain type will amortize the amount treated as an experience gain or loss in equal amounts over the period described in section 412(b). See § 1.412(b)-1(b)(9) and (10) for examples of spread gain type and immediate gain type funding methods.

(b) *Applicable changes.* A change treated as an experience gain or loss under section 412(c)(4) includes an increase or decrease in accrued liability caused by:

(1) A change in benefits under the Social Security Act,

(2) A change in other retirement benefits created under Federal or State law,

(3) A change in the definition of "wages" under section 3121, or

(4) A change in the amount of wages under section 3121 that are taken into account for purposes of section 401(a)(5) and the regulations thereunder.

§ 1.412(c)(5)-1 Change in plan year or funding method.

Approval given under section 412(c)(5) authorizes a change in plan year or funding method. Written requests for approval are to be submitted, as directed by the Commissioner, to Commissioner of Internal Revenue, Attention: OP:E:A:P, 1111 Constitution Avenue, N.W., Washington, D.C. 29224, Such a request must be submitted before the close of the plan year of which the change is to be effective unless an extension of time for filing request is granted.

§ 1.412(c)(6)-1 Full funding and full funding limitation.

(a) *In general.* This section provides rules relating to full funding and the full funding limitation under section 412(c)(6) and (7). The full funding limitation for a plan year is the excess, if any, of the accrued liability under the plan plus the normal cost of the plan year over the value of the plan's assets.

(b) *Valuation.*—(1) *Timing rule.* For purposes of this section, assets and accrued liabilities are to be valued at the usual time used by the plan for valuations.

(2) *Interest adjustments.* If the valuation is performed before the end of the plan year, the assets and accrued liabilities (including normal cost) are projected to the end of the plan year. The projection is based on the valuation rate.

(c) *Calculation of accrued liability.* The accrued liability of a plan is determined under the funding method used by the plan. However, if the funding method used by the plan is not an immediate gain method and, thus, does not directly calculate an accrued liability, the calculation of the accrued liability is made under the entry age normal funding method.

(d) *Calculation of normal cost.* In general the normal cost is the normal cost determined under the funding method used by the plan. However, if under paragraph (c) accrued liability is calculated under the entry age normal cost method, then the normal cost is also calculated under the entry age normal cost method.

(e) *Calculation of assets.* The value of plan assets used to determine the full funding limitation is the lesser of the fair market value of the assets or the actuarial value of the assets, if different. The value of plan assets must be reduced by any credit balance existing on the first day of the plan year.

(f) *Effect of full funding on deduction limits.* See § 404(a)-14(k) for provisions relating to the effect of the full funding limitation on the maximum deductible contribution limitations and 10-year amortization bases under section 404(a).

(g) *Effect of the full funding limitation on the funding standard account.*—(1) *General rule.* If, as of the end of any plan year, the accumulated funding deficiency (calculated without regard to any credit balance for the plan year or any contributions made for that plan year) exceeds the full funding limitation of section 412(c)(7) calculated as the valuation date and projected, if necessary, to the end of the plan year, then the following adjustments are made:

(i) The amount of such excess is credited to the funding standard account for the plan year.

(ii) As of the end of that plan year, all the amounts described in paragraphs (2)(B), (C), (D), and (3)(B) of section 412(b) which are required to be amortized shall be considered fully amortized.

(2) *Example.* The principles of section 412(c)(6) and of paragraph (e) of this section are illustrated in the following example:

Example. Assume that a single employer plan is established on January 1, 1976, with a calendar plan year. The funding method is the accrued benefit cost method (unit credit method), the interest assumption is 5 percent, and both the normal cost and the amortization charges and credits are calculated on the basis of payment at the beginning of the year. The annual charge to the funding standard account due to the amortization (over 30 years) of the initial past service liability is $200, and the annual credit due to the amortization (over 15 years) of a 1979 experience gain is $10. A valuation is performed as of January 1, 1985, to determine costs for the 1985 plan year. There was a credit balance of $100 in the funding standard account on December 31, 1984. As of January 1, 1985, plan assets (determined in accordance with section 412(c)(7)(B) and reduced by the $100 credit balance as of January 1, 1985) were $10,400; the accrued liability under the plan was $10,000; the normal cost (for the 1985 plan year) was $1,200; and the 1985 employer contribution (made as of January 1, 1985) was $1,000. The accumulated funding deficiency (calculated ignoring the credit balance and employer contribution) as of December 31, 1985, is $1,459.50, determined as the excess of charges of $1,470 ($1,200 normal cost, plus $200 amortization charge, plus $70 interest) over the credits of $10.50 ($10 amortization credit,

plus, $.50 interest). The full limitation as of the valuation date (January 1, 1985) is $800, determined as the excess of the sum of the accrued liability ($10,000) plus normal cost ($1,200) over the adjusted plan assets ($10,400). The value of this $800 as of the end of the year (i.e., December 31, 1985) is $800 plus $40 interest, or $840.00. The excess, as of the end of the 1985 plan year, of the accumulated funding deficiency over the full funding limitation is thus $1,459.50 minus $840.00, or $619.50. The funding standard account is charged and credited as follows:

Charges	
Normal cost	$1,200.00
Amortization charge	200.00
Interest	70.00
Total	$1,470.00

Credits	
Credit balance	$100.00
Contribution	1,000.00
Amortization credit	10.00
Interest	55.50
Sec. 412(c)(6) credit	619.50
Total	$1,784.50

Credit balance December 31, 1985	$314.50

§ 1.412(c)(7)-1 Full funding limitation.

See § 1.412(c)(6)-1 for rules relating both to full funding under section 412(c)(6) and to the full funding limitation under section 412(c)(7).

§ 1.412(c)(8)-1 Election to treat certain retroactive plan amendments as made on first day of a plan year.

The function of the Secretary of Labor described in section 412(c)(8) was transferred to the Secretary of Treasury as of December 31, 1978, by Reorganization Plan No. 4 of 1978, 197901 C.B. 480. Therefore, the material described in section 412(c)(8) now must be filed as directed by the Secretary of Treasury.

§ 1.412(c)(9)-1 Frequency of actuarial valuations.

(a) *Required valuation.* Section 412(c)(9) requires an actuarial valuation not less frequently than once every three years. Paragraph (b) of this section provides general rules for performing valuations. Paragraph (d) describes certain situations in which the Commissioner may require an actuarial valuation more frequently than once every three years. These rules may be waived at the discretion of the Commissioner and do not apply to mutiemployer plans within the meaning of section 414(f).

(b) *General rules for valuations.*—(1) *Dates of valuation.* Except as provided by the Commissioner, the valuation must be as of a date within the plan year to which the valuation refers or within the one month prior to that year. All assets and liabilities must be valued as of the same date. The valuation must us data as of the valuation data; it is not permissible to use adjusted data from a prior or subsequent year.

(2) *Use of prior valuations.* A plan may not use a valuation for any subsequent plan year if that valuation was not also used for the year to which it refers. Also, a prior valuation may not be used if the plan has used any subsequent valuation for another plan year.

(c) *Funding standard account rules for years when there is no valuation.*—(1) *Amortization of bases.* After an amortization amount of that base is charged or credit in each plan year, whether or not a valuation is performed for the year, until the outstanding balance of the base is zero. However, see § 1.412(c)(6)-1 for rules for years after a full funding limitation credit and § 1.412(b)-1 for combining and offsetting bases.

(2) *Normal cost.* If valuations are performed less frequently than every year, then any valuation computes the normal cost for the year to which the valuation refers and for subsequent years until another valuation applies. In those subsequent years, the normal cost is—

(i) If the funding method computes normal cost as a level dollar amount, the same dollar amount as for the year to which the valuation refers;

(ii) If the funding method computes normal cost as a level percentage pay, the same percentage of current pay as for the year to which the valuation refers, or

(iii) If the funding method computes normal cost as an amount equal to the present value of benefits accruing under the method for the year, under any reasonable method.

The rules in subdivisions (i) and (ii) apply whether the funding method computes normal cost on either an individual or an aggregate basis.

(d) *Situations when more frequent valuations are required.*—(1) *Amendments is increasing actuarial costs*—(i) *General rule.* A valuation is required for any plan year when a plan amendment first increases the actuarial costs of a plan. For this purpose, actuarial costs consist of the plan's normal costs under section 412(b)(2)(A), amortization charges under section 412(b)(2)(B), and amortization credits under section 412(b)(3)(B).

(ii) *Exception.* No valuation will be required under paragraph (d)(1)(i) of this section if two conditions are met: first, the plan actuary estimates that the cost increase attributable to the amendment is less than 5 percent of the actuarial cost determined without regard to the amendment; and second, the actuary files a signed statement to that effect with the annual return required under section 6058 for the year of the amendment.

(2) *Certain changes in number of participants*—(i) *General rule.* A valuation is required for a plan year when the actual number of plan participants that would be considered in the current valuations differs from the number of participants that were considered in the prior valuation by more than 20 percent of that number.

(ii) *Exception.* Notwithstanding subdivision (i), no valuation will be required merely because of a change in the number of estimated participants under a plan that determines normal cost as a level percentage of payroll (on either an individual or aggregate basis) or as a level dollar amount per individual.

(iii) *Plans using shortfall method.* No valuation will be required merely because of a change in the number of estimated participants under a plan which uses the shortfall method described in § 1.412(c)(1)-2. However, a valuation is required for a plan year if the estimated units of service or production ("estimated base units" under § 1.412(c)(1)-2(e)) for the prior plan exceeds the actual number of units of service or production for that plan year be more than 20 percent.

(3) *Change in actuarial funding method or assumptions.* A valuation is required for any plan year with respect to which a change in the funding method or actuarial assumptions of a plan is made.

(4) *Mergers and spinoffs*— (i) *General rule.* A valuation is required for any plan merger or spinoff occurs.

(ii) *Safe harbor for mergers.* In the case of a merger, no valuation will be required under paragraph (d)(4) of this section if the *de minimis* rule in § 1.414(l)-1(h) is satisfied.

(iii) *Safe harbor for spinoffs.* In the case of a spinoff, no valuation will be required under paragraph (d)(4) of this section if the present value of all the benefits being spun off from the plan during the plan year is less than 3 percent of the plan's assets as of the beginning of the year.

(5) *Change in average age of participant s*— (i) *General rule.* A valuation is required for any plan year with respect to which the average age of plan participants changes significantly, within the meaning of subdivisions (i) and (iii), from the average age of plan participants at the last valuation.

(ii) *Rule for large plans.* For a plan with 100 or more participants, an increase or decrease in average age of more than two years is a significant change.

(iii) *Rule for small plans.* For a plan with fewer than 100 participants, an increase or decrease in average age of more than four years is a significant change.

(6) *Alternative minimum funding standard account.* A valuation is required for each year for which the plan uses the alternative minimum funding standard account.

(7) *Deductibility considerations.* A valuation is required when it appears that the full funding limitation has been reached for purposes of determining the maximum deductible contribution limitations of section 404(a).

(8) *Other situations.* The Commissioner may require valuations in other situations as the facts and circumstances warrant.

§ 1.412(c)(10)-1 Time for making contributions to satisfy section 412.

(a) *General rule.* Under section 412(c)(10), a contribution made after the end of a plan year but no later than two and one-half months after the end of that year is deemed to have been made on the last day of that year.

(b) *Extension of general rule*—(1) *Plan years ending before* [*90 DAYS AFTER PUBLICATION DATE OF FINAL REGULATIONS*]. For plan years ending before [90 DAYS AFTER PUBLICATION OF FINAL REGULATIONS], for purposes of section 412 a contribution for such a plan year that is made not later than eight and one-half months after the end of that plan year is deemed to have been made on the last day of that year.

(2) *Plan years ending on or after* [*90 DAYS AFTER PUBLICATION OF FINAL REGULATIONS*]—(I) *Transitional rule.* The two and one-half month period provided in section 412(c)(10) and § 1.410(c)(10)-1(a) is extended for each of the first three plan years ending after [90 DAYS AFTER PUBLICATION OF FINAL REGULATIONS]. For the first plan year ending after [90 DAYS AFTER PUBLICATION OF FINAL REGULATIONS], a contribution made not later then eight and one-half months after the end of that plan year is deemed to have been made on the last day of that year. For the second year, the two and one-half month period is extended to six and one-half months, and for the third year, the two and one-half period is extended to four and one-half months.

(ii) *Extensions of general and transitional periods.* The time for making contributions under the general rule described in paragraph (a) and transitional rule of paragraph (b)(2)(i) of this section may be extended to a date not beyond eight and one-half months after the end of the plan year. Extensions of the two and one-half month period and transitional years' periods are granted on an individual basis by the Commissioner. A request for extension should be submitted to the Commissioner of Internal Revenue, 1111 Constitution Avenue, N.W., Washington, D.C. 20224 (Attention OP:E:A).

(c) *Effect on section 404.* The rules of this section, relating to the timing of contributions for purposes of section 412, operate independently from the rules under section 404(a)(6), relating to the timing of contributions for purposes of claiming a deduction under section 404.

§ 1.412(g)-1 Alternative maximum funding standard account.

(a) *In general.* A plan that maintains an alternative minimum funding standard account (" ASA ") for any plan year under section 412(g) must satisfy the requirements of this section. To use the ASA, a plan must use a funding method that requires contributions for all years that are not less than those required under the entry age normal cost method of funding. A funding method does not affect cost of plan benefits but only the incidence of contributions in different years. Thus, any funding method that requires a contribution in one year that exceeds that required by the entry age normal method (EAN) for that year must require a lesser contribution in another year. Hence, only a plan which uses the EAN cost method may use the ASA.

(b) *Special rules*—(1) *Dual accounting.* While maintaining an ASA, a plan must maintain the funding standard account under section 412(b) for each plan year.

(2) *Change of method.* For any plan year, the choice of whether to use the ASA is independent of whether the ASA or funding standard

account was used in the prior year. Any change from the choice made in the prior year does not require approval of the Commissioner. Further, a plan which has filed for a plan year the actuarial report described in section 6059(b) using the ASA to determine its minimum funding requirement may change to use the funding standard account to determine the funding requirement for that year. However, a plan may not switch to the ASA for a plan year after having filed the actuarial report for that year using the funding standard account.

(3) *PBGC Valuation.* In determining charges and credits to the ASA under paragraphs (b) and (c) of this section (other than the amount in paragraph (c)(2)(i)), a plan must value its assets and liabilities on a termination basis as provided in regulations issued by the Pension Benefit Guaranty Corporation (PBGC) under sections 4041 and 4062 of the Employee Retirement Income Security Act of 1974 ("ERISA") for plans placed in trusteeship by PBGC.

(4) *Cumulative nature of account.* When the ASA is used for a plan year after a plan year for which the ASA was not used, the credit balance and charge balance as of the first day of the year equal zero. However, during any continuous period of years for which the ASA is used, the credit or charge balance as of the end of any ASA year are carried forward as beginning balances in the next ASA year.

(c) *Charges*—(1) *In general.* The GSA is charged with the amounts described in paragraph (c) of this section.

(2) *Normal cost.* The ASA is charged with the normal cost of the plan for a plan year. This amount is the normal cost for that plan year computed—

(i) Under the method of funding and actuarial assumptions used for purposes of maintaining the plan's funding standard account or, if less,

(ii) As the present value of benefits expected, on a termination basis, to accrue during the plan year.

(3) *Unfunded accrued benefits.* The ASA is charged with the unfunded accrued benefits of the plan for a plan year. This amount is the excess of—

(i) The present value of accrued benefits under the plan, determined as of the valuation date for the plan year, over

(ii) The fair market value of plan assets, determined as of the valuation date for the plan year.

Because fair market value is used, any election to value evidences of indebtedness at amortized value does not apply in computing this value.

(4) *Credit balance from prior plan year.* The ASA is charged as of the first day of a plan year with any ASA credit balance carried forward from the prior plan year.

(5) *Interest.* The ASA is charged with interest on the amounts charged to the ASA under paragraph (b)(2), (b)(3) and (b)(4) of this section, as generally prescribed for the funding standard account under § 1.412(b)-1(e).

(d) *Credits*—(1) *In general.* The ASA is credited with the amounts described in paragraph (d) of this section.

(2) *Employer contributions.* The ASA is credited with the amount of contributions made by the employer to the plan for the plan year.

(3) *Interest.* The ASA is credited with the interest on the amount credited under paragraph (d)(2) of this section, determined as of the end of the plan year as generally prescribed for the funding standard account under § 1.412(b)-1(e).

Par. 5. The Income Tax Regulations, 26 CFR Part 1, are further amended by adding new paragraphs (f) and (g) of § 1.413-1 to read as follows:

§ 1.413-1 Special rules for collectively bargained plans.

* * *

(f) *Minimum funding standard.* The minimum funding standard for a collectively bargained plan shall be determined as if all participants in the plan were employed by a single employer.

(g) *Liability for funding tax.* See § 54.4971-3 of the Pension Excise Tax Regulations, 26 CFR Part 54, for rules under section 413(b)(6), relating to liability for excise tax on failure to meet minimum funding standards with respect to collectively bargained plans.

* * *

Par. 6. The Income Tax Regulations, 26 CFR Part 1, are further amended by adding new paragraphs (e) and (f) of § 1.413-2 to read as follows:

§ 1.413-2 Special rules for plans maintained by more than one employer.

* * *

(e) *Minimum funding standard.* The minimum funding standard for a plan maintained by more than one employer shall be determined as if all participants in the plan were employed by a single employer.

(f) *Liability for funding tax.* See § 54.4971-3 of the Pension Excise Tax Regulations, 26 CFR Part 54, for rules under section 413(c)(5), relating to liability for excise tax on failure to meet minimum funding standards with respect to plans maintained by more than one employer.

Temporary Income Tax Regulations under the Employee Retirement Income Security Act of 1974

(26 CFR Part 54)

Par. 7. The Temporary Regulations under the Employee Retirement Income Security Act of 1974, 26 CFR Part 11, are amended by removing the following sections: § 11.412(c)-7, § 11.412(c)-11, and § 11.412(c)-12.

Pension Excise Tax Regulations

(26 CFR Part 54)

Par. 8. The Pension Excise Tax Regulations, 26 CFR Part 54, are amended by adding in the appropriate place the following new sections:

§ 54.4971-1 General rules relating to excise tax on failure to meet minimum funding standards.

(a) *Scope.* This section and §§ 54.4971-1 and 54.4971-3 provide rules for the imposition of tax on a failure to meet the minimum funding standards of section 412. General rules appear in this section. Operational rules and special definitions appear in § 54.4971-2 Rules relating to tax liability appear in § 54.4971-3.

(b) *Initial tax*—(1) *General rule.* Section 4971(a) imposes an initial tax on an employer who maintains a plan to which section 412 applies for each taxable year in which there is an accumulated funding deficiency as of the end of the plan year ending with or within such taxable year.

(2) *Amount of tax.* The initial tax is 5 percent of the accumulated funding deficiency determined under section 412 as of the end of the plan year ending with or within the taxable year of the employer.

(c) *Additional tax.* [Reserved]

(d) *Accumulated funding deficiency*—(1) *In general.* The accumulated funding deficiency of a plan for a plan year is the lesser of the amounts described in paragraphs (d)(2) and (d)(3). Paragraph (d)(3) only applies for a year if the actuarial report described in section 6059(b) was filed using the alternative funding standard account for that year.

(2) *Funding standard account method.* The accumulated funding deficiency under this subparagraph is equal to the excess, as of the end of the plan year, of the total charges to the funding standard account under section 412 for all plan years to which section 412 applies over the total credits to that account under section 412 for those years.

(3) *Alternative funding standard account method.* The accumulated funding deficiency under this subparagraph is equal to the excess, as of the end of the plan year, of the total charges to the alternative minimum funding standard account under section 412(g) for that plan years over the total credits to the account under section 412(g) for that year.

§ 54.4971-2 Operational rules and special definitions relating to excise tax on failure to meet minimum funding standards.

(a) *Correction*—(1) *General rule.* To correct an accumulated funding deficiency for a plan year, a contribution must be made to the plan that reduces the deficiency, as of the end of that plan year, to zero. To reduce the deficiency to zero, the contribution must include interest at the plan's actuarial valuation rate for the period between the end of the plan year and the date of the contribution.

(2) *Corrective effect of certain retroactive amendments.* Certain retroactive plan amendments that meet the requirements of section 412(c)(8) may reduce an accumulated funding deficiency for a plan year to zero.

(3) *Optional corrective actions when employers withdraw from certain plans.* See § 54.4971-3(e)(2) for correcting deficiencies attributable to certain withdrawing employers.

(b) *No deduction.* Under section 275(a)(6), no deduction is allowed for a tax imposed under section 4971(a) or (b).

(c) *Waiver of imposition of tax.* Under section 3002(b) of the Employee Retirement Income Security Act of 1974 (ERISA), the Commissioner may waive the imposition of the additional tax under section 4971(b) in appropriate cases. This authority does not extend to the imposition of the initial tax under section 4971(a).

(d) *Notification of the Secretary of Labor*—(1) *In general.* Except as provided in paragraph (d)(2) of this section, before issuing a notice of deficiency with respect to the tax imposed under section 4971(a) or (b), the Commissioner must notify the Secretary of Labor that the Internal Revenue Servicer proposes to assess the tax. The purpose of this notice is to give the Secretary of labor a reasonable opportunity to obtain a correction of the accumulated funding deficiency or to comment on the imposition of the tax. (See section 4971(d) and section 3002(b) of ERISA.) The Commissioner may issue a notice of deficiency with respect to the tax imposed under section 4971(a) or (b) 60 days after the mailing of the notice of proposed deficiency to the Secretary of Labor. Any action taken by the Secretary of Labor will not affect the imposition of the 5-percent initial tax imposed by section 4971(a). See paragraph (c) of this section, however, concerning the Commissioner's authority to waive the 100-percent additional tax imposed by section 4971(b).

(2) *Jeopardy assessments.* The Commissioner may determine that the assessment or collection of the tax imposed under section 4971(a) or (b) will be jeopardized by delay. If the Commissioner makes this determination, the Internal Revenue Service may immediately assess a deficiency under section 6861 without prior notice to the Secretary of Labor. Abatement of the assessment may be granted upon correction of the deficiency. See section 6861 and § 301.6861-1 concerning abatement of assessments.

(e) *Requests for investigation with respect to tax imposed under section 4971.* Under section 3002(b) of ERISA, upon receiving a written request from the Secretary of Labor or from the Pension Benefit Guaranty Corporation, the Commissioner will investigate whether the taxes under section 4971(a) and (b) should be imposed on any employer referred to in the request.

§ 54.4971-3 Rules relating to liability for excise tax on failure to meet minimum funding standards.

(a) *General rule*—(1) *One employer.* An excise tax imposed under section 4971(a) or (b) with respect to a plan to or under which only one employer is responsible for contributing must be paid by that employer.

(2) *More than one employer.* An excise tax imposed under section 4971(a) or (b) with respect to a plan to or under which more than one employer is responsible for contributing must be allocated between these employers under paragraph (b) of this section.

(3) *Related employers.* Related corporations, trades, and businesses described in section 414(b) and (c) are "related employers" for purposes of this section. All related employers are treated as one employer for purposes of paragraph (b) of this section. The tax liability of each such related employer is determined separately by allocations under paragraph (c) of this section.

(b) *Allocation of tax liability*—(1) *In general.* Section 413(b)(6) and (c)(5) and section 414(b) and (c) discuss liability for tax under section 4971(a) or (b) with respect to collectively bargained plans and plans of more than one employer. Each employer's tax liability relates to an accumulated funding deficiency under a plan. However, the funding deficiency is determined with respect to a plan as a whole, not with respect to individual employers adopting the plan. Therefore, the deficiency must be allocated among employers adopting or maintaining the plan to determine their individual liability for a tax. Except as otherwise provided in paragraphs (c) and (d) of this section, this liability must be determined in a reasonable manner that is not inconsistent with the requirements of this paragraph (b).

(2) *Failure of individual employer to meet obligation under plan or contract*—(i) *Single delinquency.* An accumulated funding deficiency may be attributable, in whole or in part, to a delinquent contribution, that is, the failure of an individual employer to contribute to the plan as required by its terms or by the terms of a collectively bargained agreement pursuant to which the plan is maintained. To the extent that an accumulated funding deficiency is attributable to a delinquent contribution, the delinquent employer is solely liable for the resulting tax imposed under section 4971(a) or (b).

(ii) *Multiple delinquency.* If an accumulated funding deficiency is attributable to more than one delinquent employer, liability for tax is allocated in proportion to each employer's share of the delinquency.

(iii) *Further liability.* A delinquent employer may also be liable for the portion of tax determined by an allocation under paragraph (b)(3) of this section.

(3) *Failure of employers in the aggregate to avoid accumulated funding deficiency*—(1) *Aggregate failure.* An accumulated funding deficiency may be attributable, in whole or in part, to the failure of employers in the aggregate to contribute to the plan a sufficient amount to avoid an accumulated funding deficiency. To the extent that a deficiency for a plan year is not attributable to a delinquent contribution for that year, the deficiency is attributable to an aggregate failure described in this subparagraph (3). Thus, for example, if 10 percent of the deficiency results from a delinquent contribution described in paragraph (b)(2) of this section 90 percent results from failures described in this subparagraph (3). The allocation of tax liability to an individual employer for such an aggregate failure to avoid an accumulated funding deficiency is made under paragraph (b)(3)(ii) of this section.

(ii) *Allocation rule for aggregate failure.* An individual employer's liability for tax attributable to an aggregate failure described in this subparagraph (3) is the product of the tax attributable to the aggregate failure times a fraction. The numerator of this fraction is the contribution the employer is required to make for the plan year under the plan or under the collectively bargained agreement pursuant to which the plan is maintained. The denominator of this fraction is the total contribution all employers are required to make for the plan year under the plan or under the collectively bargained agreement pursuant to which the plan is maintained. Thus, for example, if an employer is responsible for one-half of a plan's required contribution and 90 percent of an accumulated funding deficiency arises under this subparagraph (3), that employer is liable under this subparagraph (3) for 45 percent of the tax under section 4971(a) or (b), as the case may be, with respect to that deficiency.

(c) *Allocation rules for related employers*—(1) *In general.* To the extent that an accumulated funding deficiency is attributable to related employers, those employers are jointly and severally liable for an excise tax imposed under section 4971(a) or (b) with respect to that deficiency.

(2) *Plans not solely maintained by related employers.* A plan that is not solely maintained by related employers first allocates tax liability under paragraph (b) of this section by treating the related employers as a single employer. The related employers are jointly and severally liable for the tax liability so allocated to any of the related employers.

(d) *Effect of plan termination on employer's tax liability.* No tax is imposed under section 4971(a) for years after the plan year in which a plan terminates. An employer is liable only for unpaid 5-percent initial taxes under section 4971(a) and any additional tax which has been imposed under section 4971(b).

(e) *Effect of employer withdrawal from plan*—(1) *General rule.* An employer that withdraws from a plan remains liable for tax imposed with respect to the portion of an accumulated funding deficiency attributable to that employer for plan years before withdrawal.

(2) *Years subsequent to withdrawal.* For any plan year with an accumulated funding deficiency, the tax is allocated between the employers responsible for contributing to the plan for that plan year in accordance with paragraphs (b) or (c) even if the deficiency in that year is attributable to an uncorrected deficiency from a prior year.

(f) *Examples.* The provisions of paragraphs (a)-(c) of this section may be illustrated by the following examples:

Example (1). Employers W, X, Y, and Z maintain a collectively bargained plan. Y and Z are related employers under paragraph (a)(3). W and X are each unrelated to any other employer. For plan year 1982, the employers are obligated, under the collectively bargained agreement, to contribute the following amount: W—$10x; X—$20x; Y—$30x; Z—$40x. As of the last date for making plan contributions, there is a delinquency of $10x attributable to W and $30x attributable to Y. Under paragraph (b)(2)(ii), W is liable for 10/40 of the tax imposed for 1982. Under paragraphs (b)(2)(ii) and (c)(2), Y and Z are jointly and severally liable for 30/40 of the tax.

Example (2). Assume the same facts as in Example (1). For plan year 1983, the minimum funding requirement is $145x. Contributions totalling $110x are made for 1983 in the amounts provided by the agreement: W—$15x; X—$20x; Y—$30x; Z—$45x. Under paragraph (b)(3)(i) of this section, there is an aggregate failure to avoid an accumulated funding deficiency, as the minimum funding requirement exceeds plan contributions by $35x. The tax attributable to the aggregate failure is allocated under paragraphs (b)(3)(ii) and (c)(2) as follows: W is liable for 15/110, or 13.6 percent of the tax; X is liable for 20/110, or 18.2 percent. Y and Z are jointly and severally liable for 75/110, or 68.2 percent.

Example (3). Assume the same facts as in Example (1). For 1984, the minimum funding requirement is $210x and employers are obligated under the agreement to contribute $130x: W—$15x; X—$25x; Y—$30x; Z—$60x. There is a funding deficiency due in part to a delinquency attributable to Y. Under paragraph (b)(3)(i), the remaining deficiency is an aggregate failure. Under paragraphs (b)(2)(i) and (c), Y and Z are jointly and severally liable for the 23 percent (30/130) of the excise tax attributable to the delinquency. The remaining 76.9 percent of the tax is allocated as follows: W—15/130 (11.5 percent) of the 76.9 percent; X—25/130 (19.2 percent) of the aggregate failure tax; Y and Z, combined under paragraph (c)(2)—90/130 (69.2 percent) of the aggregate failure tax. Y and Z are jointly and severally liable for approximately 76.3 percent of the total tax under section 4971 for the year: 23.1 percent attributable to Y's delinquency and 53.2 percent (69.2 × 76.9 attributable to the aggregate failure under paragraph (b)(3).

Roscoe L. Egger, Jr.

Commissioner.

[FR Doc. 82-32582 Filed 11-30-82; 8:45 am]

[¶ 20,137F Reserved.—Proposed regulations providing rules governing the deductibility by employers of expenses for awards to employees formerly were reproduced here. The final regulations are at ¶ 11,357.]

¶ 20,137G

Proposed regulations: Affiliated service groups: Two or more separate service organizations.—Reproduced below are proposed regulations prescribing rules for determining whether two or more separate service groups constitute an affiliated service group. The proposed regulations were published in the *Federal Register* on February 28, 1983 (48 FR 8293).

Affiliated Service Groups; Proposed Rulemaking

AGENCY: Internal Revenue Service, Treasury.

ACTION: Notice of proposed rulemaking.

SUMMARY: This document contains proposed regulations prescribing rules for determining whether two or more separate service organizations constitute an affiliated service group, and detailing how certain requirements are satisfied by a qualified retirement plan maintained by a member of an affiliated service group. Changes to the applicable tax law were made by the Miscellaneous Revenue Act of 1980. The regulations would provide the public with additional guidance needed to comply with that Act and would affect all employers that maintain qualified retirement plans and that are members of an affiliated service group.

DATES: Written comments and requests for a public hearing must be delivered or mailed by April 29, 1983. For plans that were not in existence on November 30 1980, the amendments is proposed to be effective for plan years ending after that date. For plans in existence on

November 30, 1980, the amendments is proposed to be effective for plan years beginning after that date.

ADDRESS: Send comments and requests for a public hearing to: Commissioner of Internal Revenue, Attention: CC:LR:T (EE-3-81), Washington, D.C. 20224.

FOR FURTHER INFORMATION CONTACT: Patricia K. Keesler of the Employee Plans and Exempt Organizations Division, Office of Chief Counsel, Internal Revenue Service, 1111 Constitution Avenue, NW., Washington, D.C. 20224 (Attention: CC:LR:T) (202/566-3430) (not a toll-free number).

SUPPLEMENTARY INFORMATION:

Background

This document contains proposed amendments to the Income Tax Regulations (26 CFR Part 1) under section 414(m) of the Internal Revenue Code of 1954. These amendments are proposed to conform the regulations to section 201 of the Miscellaneous Revenue Act of 1980 (94 Stat. 3526) and section 5 of Pub. L. 96-613 (94 Stat. 3580).

These regulations do not reflect amendments made to section 414(m) under the Tax Equity and Fiscal Responsibility Act of 1982. These regulations are to be issued under the authority contained in section 414(m) and in section 7805 of the Internal Revenue Code of 1954 (94 Stat. 3526, 94 Stat. 3580, 68A Stat. 917; 26 U.S.C. 414(m), 7805).

Statutory Provisions

Section 414(m)(1) of the Code provides that, for purposes of certain employee benefit requirements listed in section 414(m)(4), except to the extent otherwise provided in regulations, all employees of the members of an affiliated service group shall be treated as employed by a single employer.

Section 414(m)(2) defines an affiliated service group as a First Service Organization and one or more of the following: (A) Any service organization (A Organization) that is a shareholder or partner in the First Service Organization and that regularly performs services for the First Service Organization or is regularly associated with the First Service Organization in performing services for third persons; and (B) any other organization (B Organization) if a significant portion of the business of that organization is the performance of services for the First Service Organization, for A Organizations, or both, of a type historically performed by employees in the service field of the First Service Organization or the A Organizations, and ten percent or more of the interests in the organization is held by persons who are officers, highly compensated employees, or owners of the First Service Organization or of the A Organizations.

Section 414(m)(3) defines a service organization as an organization the principal business of which is the performance of services.

Section 414(m)(5)(A) provides that the term "organization" means a corporation, partnership, or other organization. Section 414(m)(5)(B) provides that principles of section 267(c) apply in determining ownership.

Section 414(m)(6) provides that the Secretary of the Treasury or his delegate shall prescribe such regulations as may be necessary to prevent the avoidance of the employee benefit requirements listed in section 414(m)(4) through the use of separate service organizations.

Prior Guidelines

Initial guidelines under section 414(m) were set forth in Revenue Ruling 81-105, 1981-1 C.B. 256. Rev. Rul. 81-105 provided illustrations of how the provisions of section 414(m) operate by way of three examples. The rules set forth in Rev. Rul. 81-105 remain operative and are not affected by the promulgation of these proposed regulations.

Revenue Procedure 81-12, 1981-1 C.B. 652, prescribes procedures for (1) obtaining a ruling on whether two or more organizations are members of an affiliated service group, and (2) obtaining determination letters on the qualification, under section 401(a) or 403(a), of an employee's pension, profit-sharing, stock bonus, annuity, or bond purchase plan established by a member or of an affiliated service group.

Administrative Exemptions

Several parties have expressed concern that aggregation may be required under the rules of section 414(m)(2)(A) and (B) in situations where there has been no attempt to avoid the employee benefit requirements listed in section 414(m)(4).

Those parties noted that an organization qualifies as an A Organization whenever it is a shareholder or partner in the First Service Organization and regularly performs services for the First Service Organization or is regularly associated with the First Service Organization in performing services for third persons. Thus, aggregation will be required regardless of how small the interest is that the A Organization holds in the First Service Organization, irrespective of whether the services performed by the A Organization are of a type historically performed by employees in the service field of the First Service Organization, and even if the services performed for the First Service Organization only constitute an insignificant portion of the business of the A Organization.

However, section 414(m)(1) grants authority to promulgate regulations that specify when all the employees of an affiliated service group will not be treated as employed by a single employer. Accordingly, proposed Treasury Regulation § 1.414(m)-1(c) provides that a corporation, other than a professional service corporation, will not be treated as a First Service Organization for purposes of section 414(m)(2)(A). Professional service corporations are not excepted from treatment as First Service Organizations for purposes of section 414(m)(2)(A) be-

cause the legislative history indicates that such corporations were intended to be covered. A special definition of professional service corporations is provided in the proposed regulation.

A corporation will still be treated as a First Service Organization for purposes of section 414(m)(2)(B). Thus, two corporations, neither of which is a professional service organization, will be aggregated only if one of the corporations satisfies the more stringent tests to be classified as a B Organization.

However, the Commissioner may determine that, in practice, the exception in the A Organization test for corporations, other than professional service corporations, results in an avoidance of the requirements of section 414(m) that circumvents Congressional intent. If such avoidance is found in a significant number of cases, this exception may be removed from the regulations.

Similarly, several parties have mentioned that aggregation may be required under section 414(m)(2)(B) whenever the owner of the potential B Organization acquires an interest in the First Service Organization (or in an A Organization), even though this interest is minimal and even though the owner does not have any other significant connection with the First Service Organization (*i.e.*, the owner is not an officer or highly compensated employee of the First Service Organization).

Pursuant to the authority contained in section 414(m)(1), a special rule is provided for determining whether ten percent or more of the interests in the potential B Organization is held by officers, highly compensated employees, or owners of the First Service Organization (or of an A Organization). For this purpose, the interests held by persons who are owners of the First Service Organization and the B Organization (but who are not also officers or highly compensated employees of the First Service Organization), will be taken into account as owners of the First Service Organization only if they hold, in the aggregate, three percent or more of the interests in such First Service Organization.

There may be other situations, not covered by the special rules of the regulations, where aggregation should not be required although the organizations are described in the literal language of either section 414(m)(2)(A) or (B). Comments are solicited from the public as to what these rules should be.

Significant Portion

Proposed Treasury Regulation § 1.414(m)-2(c)(2) provides that the determination of whether providing services for the First Service Organization, for one or more A Organizations determined with respect to the First Service Organization, or for both, is a significant portion of the business of the potential B Organization will generally be based on the facts and circumstances. However, two specific rules are provided.

A safe harbor rule is provided under which the performance of services for the First Service Organization, for one or more A Organizations, or for both, will not be considered a significant portion of the business of a potential B Organization if the Service Receipts Percentage is less than five percent. The Service Receipts Percentage is the ratio of the gross receipts of the organization derived from performing services for the First Service Organization, for one or more A Organizations, or for both, to the total gross receipts of the organization derived from performing services. This ratio is the greater of the ratio for the year for which the determination is being made or for the three year period including that year and the two preceding years (or the period of existence of the organizations, if less).

Except for a situation described in the preceding paragraph, the performance of services for the First Service Organization, for one or more A Organizations, or for both, will be considered a significant portion of the business of the potential B Organization if the Total Receipts Percentage is ten percent or more. The Total Receipts Percentage is calculated in the same manner as the Service Receipts Percentage, except that gross receipts in the denominator are determined without regard to whether they were derived from performing services.

Comments from the public are requested regarding these significant portion tests.

Historically Performed

Proposed Treasury Regulation § 1.414(m)-2(c)(3) provides that services will be considered of a type historically performed by employees in a particular service field if it was not unusual for the services to be performed by employees of organizations in that service field in the United States on December 13, 1980 (the date of enactment of section 414(m)).

Constructive Ownership

Proposed Treasury Regulation § 1.414(m)-2(d)(2) provides that in determining ownership for purposes of section 414(m), an individual's interest under a plan that qualifies under section 401(a) will be taken into account. Comments from the public are requested concerning appropriateness of this rule in cases in which the investment in employer securities by the plan results from an independent decision of the plan trustee.

Organization

Proposed Treasury Regulation § 1.414(m)-2(e) provides that the term "organization" includes a sole proprietorship. The proposed regulations do not consider the impact of sections 414(b) (controlled group of corporations) or 414(c) (group of trades or businesses under common control) on the definition of "organization" in § 1.414(m)-2(e)(1). Specifically, the regulations do not consider the situation in which a particular organization is potentially part of both an affiliated service group and either a controlled group of corporations or a group of trades or businesses under common control. In such a situation, issues arise as to the order in which the determinations are made as to what constitutes a single employer. For example, whereas an individual corporation may be a service organization, the controlled group of which that corporation is a part may not be a service organization (or vice versa). Comments from the public are requested regarding the treatment of a controlled group of corporations or a group of trades or businesses under common control in this respect.

Service Organization

Proposed Treasury Regulation § 1.414(m)-2(f) provides that the principal business of an organization will be considered the performance of services if capital is not a material income-producing factor for the organization. The test for determining whether or not capital is a material income-producing factor is similar to the test in Treasury Regulation § 1.1348-3(a)(3)(ii), as in effect on February 28, 1983.

Numerous fields are listed in proposed Treasury Regulation § 1.414(m)-2(f) as being service fields. Organizations engaged in a field not listed therein and in which capital is a material income-producing factor will not be considered to be service organizations until the first day of the first plan year beginning at least 180 days after the date of the publication of an official document (such as a revenue ruling) giving notice to the contrary. The Commissioner of Internal Revenue is granted authority to determine that certain organizations, or types of organizations, should not be considered as being subject to the requirements of section 414(m) even though the organizations are engaged in a field listed in the proposed regulation. Comments are requested from the public as to examples of organizations that should or should not be considered as being service organizations subject to the provisions of section 414(m).

Multiple Affiliated Service Groups

Proposed Treasury Regulation § 1.414(m)-2(g) provides rules for multiple affiliated service groups. Two or more affiliated service groups will not be aggregated simply because an organization is an A Organization or a B Organization with respect to each affiliated service group. However, if an organization is a First Service Organization with respect to two or more A Organizations or two or more B Organizations, or both, all of the organizations will be considered to constitute a single affiliated service group.

Special Qualification Requirements

Pursuant to the authority granted in section 414(m)(6), proposed Treasury Regulation § 1.414(m)-3(b) provides that if a plan maintained by a member of an affiliated service group covers an employee described in section 401(c)(1) (self-employed individual), an owner-employee (as described in section 401(c)(3)), or a shareholder-employee (as described in section 1379(d)), the plan must also satisfy the special requirements relating to plans that cover those types of employees, to the extent those requirements apply, even though that individual is not employed by the member maintaining the plan. This provision only applies if such an employee's earned income or compensation received as a shareholder-employee is taken into account in computing contributions or benefits under the plan.

Multiple Employer Plans

Proposed Treasury Regulation § 1.414(m)-3(c) provides that if a plan maintained by a member of an affiliated service group covers an individual who is not an employee of that member, but who is an employee of another member of that affiliated service group, the plan will be considered to be maintained by more than one employer for purposes of several provisions of section 413(c) (relating to plans maintained by more than one employer). This rule allows a member of the affiliated service group to deduct contributions on behalf of individuals who are not employed by that member.

However, this multiple employer plan rule does not apply in the case of a controlled group of corporations (as described in section 414(b)) or a group of trades or businesses under common control (as described in section 414(c)). Those situations will be governed by the special rules of section 414(b) or (c), respectively.

Discrimination

Proposed Treasury Regulation § 1.414(m)-3(d) provides that in testing for discrimination under section 401(a)(4) (requiring that contributions or benefits do not discriminate in favor of employees who are officers, shareholders, or highly compensated) all of the compensation paid to an individual must be considered in determining the contributions or benefits on behalf of the individual under a plan maintained by a member of an affiliated service group without regard to the percentage of the organization employing the individual owned by the member maintaining the plan.

Effective Dates

In the case of a plan that was not in existence on November 30, 1980, section 414(m) applies to plan years ending after that date. In the case of a plan that was in existence on November 30, 1980, section 414(m) applies to plan years beginning after that date.

Proposed Treasury Regulation § 1.414(m)-4(b)(1) provides that a defined contribution plan in existence on November 30, 1980 that fails to satisfy the requirements for qualification under section 401(a) solely because of the application of section 414(m) will be treated as continuing to satisfy the requirements of section 401(a) after the effective date of section 414(m) if the plan is terminated and all amounts are distributed to participants within 180 days after the latest of:

(i) [the date of the publication of this regulation in the *Federal Register* as a Treasury decision]

(ii) The date on which notice of the final determination with respect to a request for a determination letter is issued by the Internal Revenue Service, such request is withdrawn, or such request is finally disposed of by the Internal Revenue Service, provided the request for a determination letter was pending on [the date of the publication of this regulation in the *Federal Register* as a Treasury decision] or, in the case of a request for a determination letter on the plan termination, was made within 60 days after [the date of the publication of this regulation in the *Federal Register* as a Treasury decision], or

(iii) If a petition is timely filed with the United States Tax Court for a declaratory judgment under section 7476 with respect to the final determination (or the failure of the Internal Revenue Service to make a final determination) in response to such request, the date on which the decision of the United States Tax Court in such proceeding becomes final.

Proposed Treasury Regulation § 1.414(m)-4(b)(2) provides that a defined benefit plan in existence on November 30, 1980 that fails to satisfy the requirements for qualification under section 401(a) solely because of the application of section 414(m) will be treated as continuing to satisfy the requirements of section 401(a) after the effective date of section 414(m) if the plan is terminated and all amounts are distributed within the same period as that provided for defined contribution plans. However, deductions for contributions to the plan for plan years after the effective date of section 414(m) are limited to those necessary to satisfy the minimum funding standards of section 412.

Reliance on Proposed Regulations

Pending the adoption of final regulations, taxpayers may rely on the rules contained in this notice of proposed rulemaking and the Internal Revenue Service will issue determination, opinion, and ruling letters based on these rules. If any provisions of the final regulations are less favorable to taxpayers than these proposed rules, those provisions only will be effective for periods after adoption of final regulations.

Comments and Requests for a Public Hearing

Before adopting these proposed regulations, consideration will be given to any written comments that are submitted (preferably seven copies) to the Commissioner of Internal Revenue. All comments will be available for public inspection and copying. A public hearing will be held upon written request to the Commissioner by any person who has submitted written comments. If a public hearing is held, notice of the time and place will be published in the *Federal Register*.

Executive Order 12291 and Regulatory Flexibility Act

The Commissioner has determined that this proposed regulation is not a major regulation for purposes of Executive Order 12291. Accordingly, a regulatory impact analysis is not required.

Although this document is a notice of proposed rulemaking which solicits public comments, the Internal Revenue Service has concluded that the regulations proposed herein are interpretative and that the notice and public procedure requirements of 5 U.S.C. 553 do not apply. Accordingly, these proposed regulations do not constitute regulations subject to the Regulatory Flexibility Act (5 U.S.C. chapter 6).

Drafting Information

The principal authors of these proposed regulations are Kirk F. Maldonado and Mary M. Levontin of the Employee Plans and Exempt Organizations Division of the Office of Chief Counsel, Internal Revenue Service and Treasury Department, participated in developing these regulations, both on matters of substance and style.

List of Subjects in 26 CFR §§ 1.401-0—1.425-1

Income taxes, Employee benefit plans, Pensions.

Proposed Amendments to the Regulations

PART 1—[AMENDED]

The proposed amendments to 26 CFR Part 1 are as follows:

§ 1.105-11 [Amended]

Paragraph 1. Paragraph (f) of § 1.105-11 is amended by striking out "section 414(b) and (c)" and inserting in lieu thereof "section 414(b), (c), or (m)."

Par. 2. The following new sections are added at the appropriate place:

§ 1.414(m)-1. Affiliated service groups.

(a) *In general.* Section 414(m) provides rules that require, in some circumstances, employees of separate organizations to be treated as if they were employed by a single employer for purposes of certain employee benefit requirements. For other rules requiring aggregation of employees of different organizations, see section 414(b) (relating to controlled groups of corporations) and section 414(c) (relating to trades or businesses under common control). If aggregation is required under either of the preceding provisions and also under section 414(m), the requirements with respect to all of the applicable provisions must be satisfied.

(b) *Aggregation.* Except as provided in paragraph (c), all the employees of the members of an affiliated service group shall be treated as if they were employed by a single employer for purposes of the employee benefit reuirements listed in § 1.414(m)-3.

(c) *Aggregation not required.* Pursuant to the authority contained in section 414(m)(1), a corporation, other than a professional service corporation, shall not be treated as a First Service Organization (see § 1.414(m)-2) for purposes of section 414(m)(2)(A). Also, a special rule is provided in § 1.414(m)-2(c)(4) for determining ownership under section 414(m)(2)(B). For purposes of this paragraph, a professional service corporation is a corporation that is organized under state law for the principal purpose of providing professional services and has at least one shareholder who is licensed or otherwise legally authorized to render the type of services for which the corporation is organized. "Professional services" means the services performed by certified or other public accountants, actuaries, architects, attorneys, chiropodists, chiropractors, medical doctors, dentists, professional engineers, optometrists, osteopaths, podiatrists, psychologists, and veterinarians. The Commissioner may expand the list of services in the preceding sentence. However, no such expansion will be effective with respect to any organization until the first day of the first plan year beginning at least 180 days after the publication of such change.

§ 1.414(m)-2 Definitions.

(a) *Affiliated service group.* "Affiliated service group" means a group consisting of a service organization (First Service Organization) and

(1) One or more A Organizations described in paragraph (b), or

(2) One or more B Organizations described in paragraph (c), or

(3) One or more A Organizations described in paragraph (b) and one or more B Organizations described in paragraph (c).

(b) *A Organizations*—(1) *General rule.* A service organization is an A Organization if it:

(i) Is a partner or shareholder in the First Service Organization (regardless of the percentage interest it owns in the First Service Organization but determined with regard to the constructive ownership rules of paragraph (d)); and

(ii) Regularly performs services for the First Service Organization, or is regularly associated with the First Service Organization in performing services for third persons. It is not necessary that any of the employees of the organization directly perform services for the First Service Organization; it is sufficient that the organization is regularly associated with the First Service Organization in performing services for third persons.

(2) *Regularly performs services for.* The determination of whether a service organization regularly performs services for the First Service Organization or is regularly associated with the First Service Organization in performing services for third persons shall be made on the basis of the facts and circumstances. One factor that is relevant in making this determination is the amount of the earned income that the organization derives from performing services for the First Service Organization, or from performing services for persons in association with the First Service Organization.

(3) *Examples.* The provisions of this paragraph may be illustrated by the following examples.

Example (1). A Organization. (i) Attorney N is incorporated, and the corporation is a partner in a law firm. Attorney N and his corporation are regularly associated with the law firm in performing services for third persons.

(ii) Considering the law firm as a First Service Organization, the corporation is an A Organization because it is a partner in the law firm and it is regularly associated with the law firm in performing services for third persons. Accordingly, the corporation and the law firm constitute an affiliated service group.

Example (2). Corporation. (i) Corporation F is a service organization that is a shareholder in Corporation G, another service organization. F regularly provides services for G. Neither corporation is a professional service corporation within the meaning of subsection (1)(c).

(ii) Neither corporation may be considered a First Service Organization for purposes of this paragraph and, thus, aggregation will not be required by operation of the A Organization test. However, G or F may be treated as a First Service Organization and the other organization may be a B Organization under the rules of subsection (2)(c).

Example (3). Regularly associated with (i) R, S & T is a law partnership with offices in numerous cities. The office in the city of D is incorporated, and the corporation is a partner in the law firm. All of the employees of the corporation work directly for the corporation, and none of them work directly for any of the other offices of the law firm.

(ii) Considering the law firm as a First Service Organization, the corporation is an A Organization because it is a partner in the First Service Organization and is regularly associated with the law firm in performing services for third persons. Accordingly, the corporation and the law firm constitute an affiliated service group.

(c) *B Organizations*—(1) *General rule.* An organization is a B Organization if:

(i) A significant portion of the business of the organization is the performance of services for the First Service Organization, for one or more A Organizations determined with respect to the First Service Organization, or for both.

(ii) Those services are of a type historically performed by employees in the service field of the First Service Organization or the A Organizations, and

(iii) Ten percent or more of the interests in the organization is held, in the aggregate, by persons who are designated group members (as defined in subparagraph (4)) of the First Service Organization or of the A Organizations, determined using the constructive ownership rules of paragraph (d).

(2) *Significant portion*—(i) *General rule.* Except as provided in paragraphs (c)(2)(ii) and (iii), the determination of whether providing services for the First Service Organization, for one or more A Organizations, or for both, is a significant portion of the business of an organization will be based on the facts and circumstances. Wherever it appears in this paragraph (c)(2), "one or more A organizations" means one or more A organizations determined with respect to the First Service Organization.

(ii) *Service Receipts safe harbor.* The performance of services for the First Service Organizations, for one or more A Organizations, or for both, will not be considered a significant portion of the business of an organization if the Service Receipts Percentage is less than five percent.

(iii) *Total Receipts threshold test.* The performance of services for the First Service Organization, for one or more A Organizations, or for both, will be considered a significant portion of the business of an organization if the Total Receipts Percentage is ten percent or more.

(iv) *Service Receipts Percentage.* The Service Receipts Percentage is the ratio of the gross receipts of the organization derived from performing services for the First Service Organization, for one or more A Organizations, or for both, to the total gross receipts of the organization derived from performing services. This ratio is the greater of the ratio for the year for which the determination is being made or for the three year period including that year and the two preceding years (or the period of the organization's existence, if less).

(v) *Total Receipts Percentage.* The Total Receipts Percentage is calculated in the same manner as the Service Receipts Percentage, except that gross receipts in the denominator are determined without regard to whether they were derived from performing services.

(3) *Historically performed.* Services will be considered of a type historically performed by employees in a particular service field if it was not unusual for the services to be performed by employees of organizations in that service field (in the United States) on December 13, 1980.

(4) *Designated group*—(i) *Definition.* "Designated group" members are the officers, the highly compensated employees, and the common owners of an organization (as defined in paragraph (c)(4)(ii)). However, even though a person is not a common owner, the interests the person holds in the potential B Organization will be taken into account if the person is an officer or a highly compensated employee of the First Service Organization or of an A Organization.

(ii) *Common owner.* A person who is an owner of a First Service Organization or of an A Organization is a common owner if at least three percent of the interests in the organization is, in the aggregate, held by persons who are owners of the potential B organization (determined using the constructive ownership rules of paragraph (d)).

(5) *Owner.* The term "owner" includes organizations that have an ownership interest described in paragraph (c).

(6) *Aggregation of ownership interests.* It is not necessary that a single designated group member of the First Service Organization or of an A Organization own ten percent or more of the interests, determined using the constructive ownership rules of paragraph (d), in the organization for the organization to be a B Organization. It is sufficient that the sum of the interests, determined using the constructive ownership rules of paragraph (d), held by all of the designated group members of the First Service Organization, and the designated group members of the A Organizations, is ten percent or more of the interests in the organizations.

(7) *Non-service organization.* An organization may be a B Organization even though it does not qualify as a service organization under paragraph (f).

(8) *Examples.* The provisions of this paragraph may be illustrated by the following examples.

Example (1). B Organization. (i) R is a service organization that has 11 partners. Each partner of R owns one percent of the stock in Corporation D. The corporation provides services to the partnership of a type historically performed by employees in the service field of the partnership. A significant portion of the business of the corporation consists of providing services to the partnership.

(ii) Considering the partnership as a First Service Organization, the corporation is a B organization because a significant portion of the business of the corporation is the performance of services for the partnership of a type historically performed by employees in the service field of the partnership, and more than ten percent of the interests in the corporation is held, in the aggregate, by the designated group members (consisting of the 11 common owners of the partnership). Accordingly, the corporation and the partnership constitute an affiliated service group.

(iii) A similar result would be obtained if no more than 8 percent of the 11 percent ownership in Corporation D were held by highly compensated employees of R who were not owners of R (even though no one group of the three preceding groups held 10 percent or more of the stock of Corporation D).

Example (2). Other aggregation rules. (i) C, an individual, is a 60 percent partner in D, a service organization, and regularly performs services for D. C is also an 80 percent partner in F. A significant portion

¶20,137G

of the gross receipts of F are derived from providing services to D of a type historically performed by employees in the service field of D.

(ii) Viewing D as a First Service Organization, F is a B Organization because a significant portion of gross receipts of F are derived from performing services for D of a type historically performed by employees in that service field, and more than ten percent of the interest in F is held by the designated group member C (who is a common owner of D). Accordingly, D and F constitute an affiliated service group. Additionally, the employees of D and F are aggregated under the rules of section 414(c). Thus, any plan maintained by a member of the affiliated service group must satisfy the aggregation rules of sections 414(c) and 414(m).

Example (3). Common owner. (i) Corporation T is a service organization. The sole function of Corporation W is to provide services to Corporation T of a type historically performed by employees in the service field of Corporation T. Individual C owns all of the stock of Corporation W and two percent of the stock of Corporation T. C is not an officer or a highly compensated employee of Corporation T.

(ii) Considering Corporation T as a First Service Organization, Corporation W is not a B Organization because it is not 10 percent owned by designated group members. Because C owns less than 3 percent of Corporation T, C is not a common owner of T.

Example (4). B Organization. (i) Individual M owns one-third of an employee benefit consulting firm. M also owns one-third of an insurance agency. A significant portion of the business of the consulting firm consists of assisting the insurance agency in developing employee benefit packages for sale to third persons and providing services to the insurance company in connection with employee benefit programs sold to other clients of the insurance agency. Additionally, the consulting firm frequently provides services to clients who have purchased insurance arrangements from the insurance company for the employee benefit plans they maintain. The insurance company frequently refers clients to the consulting firm to assist them in the design of their employee benefit plans. The percentage of the total gross receipts of the consulting firm that represent gross receipts from the performance of these services for the insurance agency is 20 percent.

(ii) Considering the insurance agency as a First Service Organization, the consulting firm is a B Organization because a significant portion of the business of the consulting firm (as determined under the Total Receipts Percentage Test) is the performance of services for the insurance agency of a type historically performed by employees in the service field of insurance, and more than 10 percent of the interests in the consulting firm is held by owners of the insurance agency. Thus, the insurance agency and the consulting firm constitute an affiliated service group.

Example (5). B Organization. (i) Attorney T is incorporated, and the corporation is a 6% shareholder in a law firm (which is also incorporated). All of the work of Corporation T is performed for the law firm.

(ii) Under the principles of section 267(c), T is deemed to own the shares of the law firm owned by T Corporation. Thus, T is a common owner of the law firm. Considering the law firm as a First Service Organization, Corporation T is a B Organization because a significant portion of the business of Corporation T consists of performing services for the law firm of a type historically performed by employees, and 100 percent of Corporation T is owned by a common owner of the law firm.

Example (6). Significant portion. (i) The income of Corporation X is derived from both performing services and other business activities. The amount of its receipts derived from performing services for, and its total receipts derived from, Corporation Z and the total for all other customers is set forth below.

		Origin of income	Corpora-tion Z	All customers
Year 1	. . . .	Services	$4	$100
		Total		120
Year 2	. . . .	Services	9	150
		Total		180
Year 3	. . . .	Services	42	200
		Total		240

(ii) In year 1 (the first year of existence of Corporation X), the Service Receipts Percentage for Corporation X (for its business with Corporation Z) is less than five percent ($4/$100, or 4%). Thus performing services for Corporation Z will not be considered a significant portion of the business of Corporation X.

(iii) In year 2, the Service Receipts Percentage is the greater of the ratio for that year ($9/$150, or 6%) or for years 1 and 2 combined ($13/$250, or 5.2%), which is six percent. The Total Receipts Percentage is the greater of the ratio for that year ($9/$180, or 5%) or for years 1 and 2 combined ($13/$300, or 4.3%), which is five percent. Because the Service Receipts Percentage is greater than five percent and the Total Receipts Percentage is less than ten percent, whether performing services for Corporation Z constitutes a significant portion of the business of Corporation X is determined by the facts and circumstances.

(iv) In year 3, the Service Receipts Percentage is the greater of the ratio for that year ($42/$200, or 21%) or for years 1, 2, and 3 combined ($55/$450, or 12.2%), which is 21 percent. The Total Receipts Percentage is the greater of the ratio for that year ($42/$240, or 17.5%) or for years 1, 2, and 3 combined ($55/$540, or 10.1%), which is 17.5 percent. Because the Total Receipts Percentage is greater than ten percent and the Service Receipts Percentage is not less than five percent, a significant portion of the business of Corporation X is considered to be the performance of services for Corporation Z.

(d) *Ownership*—(1) *Constructive ownership.* Except as otherwise provided in the regulations under section 414(m), the principles of section 267(c) (relating to constructive ownership of stock) shall apply in determining ownership for purposes of section 414(m). Accordingly, the rules of section 267(c) shall apply to partnership interests as well as to stock.

(2) *Qualified plans.* In determining ownership for purposes of section 414(m), an individual's interest under a plan that qualifies under section 401(a) will be taken into account.

(3) *Special rules.* For purposes of section 414(m):

(i) Stock or partnership interests owned, directly or indirectly, by or for a corporation, partnership, estate, or trust shall be considered as being owned proportionately by or for its shareholders, partners, or beneficiaries;

(ii) An individual shall be considered as owning the stock or partnership interests owned, directly or indirectly, by or for his family;

(iii) An individual owning (otherwise than by the application of paragraph (d)(3)(ii)) any stock in a corporation or interest in a partnership shall be considered as owning the stock or partnership interests owned, directly or indirectly, by or for his partner;

(iv) The family of an individual shall include only his brothers and sisters (whether by the whole or half blood), spouse, ancestors, and lineal descendants; and

(v) Stock or partnership interests constructively owned by a person by reason of the application of paragraph (d)(3)(i) shall, for the purpose of applying paragraph (d)(3)(i), (ii), or (iii), be treated as actually owned by such person, but stock or partnership interests constructively owned by an individual by reason of the application of paragraph (d)(3)(ii) or (iii) shall not be treated as owned by him for the purpose of again applying either of such subdivisions in order to make another the constructive owner of such stock or partnership interests.

(4) *Examples.* The provisions of this paragraph may be illustrated by the following examples.

Example (1). Constructive ownership. (i) Individual K is incorporated as K Corporation, and K Corporation is a partner in a management consulting firm K & F. K regularly performs services for the management consulting firm K & F. The secretarial services for the consulting firm are performed by Corporation M. A significant portion of the business of the secretarial corporation, M, consists of providing services to the consulting firm. All of the stock of the secretarial corporation, M, is owned by individual K.

(ii) Considering the consulting firm as a First Service Organization, Corporation K is an A Organization because it is a partner in the consulting firm and regularly performs services for the firm or is regularly associated with the firm in performing services for third persons.

(iii) Under the principles of section 267(c), individual K is deemed to own the partnership interest in the consulting firm that is held by K Corporation. Thus, K is considered to be an owner of the consulting firm.

(iv) Considering the consulting firm as a First Service Organization, the secretarial corporation is a B Organization because a significant portion of its business consists of performing services for the consulting firm or for Corporation K of a type historically performed by employees in the service field of management consulting, and at least ten percent of the interests in the secretarial corporation, M, is held by individual K, an owner of the consulting firm.

Example (2). Constructive ownership. (i) J is the office manager and highly compensated employee of an accounting partnership, H & H.

The secretarial services for the partnership are provided by Corporation W. J owns fifty percent of the stock of the secretarial corporation. A significant portion of the business of the secretarial corporation consists of providing services to the partnership.

(ii) Considering the partnership as a First Service Organization, the secretarial corporation is a B Organization because a significant portion of the business of the secretarial corporation is the performance of services for the partnership of a type historically performed by employees of accounting firms, and more than ten percent of the interests in the corporation is held by a highly compensated employee of the partnership.

(iii) Under the principles of section 267(c), the result would be the same, for example, if the stock were held (instead of by J) by the spouse of J, the children of J, the parents or grandparents of J, a trust for the benefit of J's children, or by a combination of such relatives.

Example (3). Qualified plan. (i) T is the chief executive officer of W Corporation, which is the consulting firm. T is also a participant in the W Corporation Profit-Sharing Plan, which qualifies under section 401(a). T's account balance in the plan is $150,000, and it consists of 25 percent of the stock of X Corporation. The sole function of X Corporation is to provide secretarial services to W Corporation.

(ii) Considering W Corporation as a First Service Organization, X Corporation is a B Organization because a significant portion of the business of X Corporation consists of providing secretarial services to W Corporation, secretarial services are of a type historically performed by employees in the field of consulting, and 25 percent of the stock of X Corporation is considered to be owned by T, a highly compensated employee of W Corporation, using the principles of section 267(c). Accordingly, W Corporation and X Corporation constitute an affiliated service group.

(e) *Organization*—(1) *General rule.* The term "organization" includes a sole proprietorship, partnership, corporation, or any other type of entity regardless of its ownership format.

(2) *Special rule.* [Reserved]

(f) *Service organization*—(1) *Noncapital intensive organizations.* The principal business of an organization will be considered the performance of services if capital is not a material income-producing factor for the organization, even though the organization is not engaged in a field listed in subparagraph (2). Whether capital is a material income-producing factor must be determined by reference to all the facts and circumstances of each case. In general, capital is a material income-producing factor if a substantial portion of the gross income of the business is attributable to the employment of capital in the business, as reflected, for example, by a substantial investment in inventories, plant, machinery, or other equipment. Additionally, capital is a material income-producing factor for banks and similar institutions. However, capital is not a material income-producing factor if the gross income of the business consists principally of fees, commissions, or other compensation for personal services performed by an individual.

(2) *Specific fields.* Regardless of whether subparagraph (1) applies, an organization engaged in any one or more of the following fields is a service organization:

(i) Health;

(ii) Law;

(iii) Engineering;

(iv) Architecture;

(v) Accounting;

(vi) Actuarial science;

(vii) Performing arts;

(viii) Consulting; and

(ix) Insurance.

Notwithstanding the preceding sentence, an organization will not be considered to be performing services merely because it is engaged in the manufacture or sale of equipment or supplies used in the above fields, or merely because it is engaged in performing research or publishing in the above fields. An organization will not be considered to be a service organization under this subparagraph (2) merely because an employee provides one of the enumerated services to the organization or to other employees of the organization unless the organization is also engaged in the performance of the same services for third parties.

(3) *Other organizations.* Organizations engaged in performing services and that are not described in subparagraph (1) or (2) shall not be

considered to be service organizations. The Commissioner may expand the list of fields contained in subparagraph (2). However, no such expansion will be effective until the first day of the first plan year beginning at least 180 days after the publication of such change.

(4) *Exempted organizations.* The Commissioner may determine that certain organizations, or types of organizations, should not be considered as subject to the requirements of section 414(m), even though the organizations are described in subparagraph (1) or (2).

(g) *Multiple affiliated service groups*—(1) *Multiple First Service Organizations.* Two or more affiliated service groups will not be aggregated simply because an organization is an A Organization or a B Organization with respect to each affiliated service group.

(2) *Multiple A or B Organizations.* If an organization is a First Service Organization with respect to two or more A Organizations or two or more B Organizations, or both, all of the organizations shall be considered to constitute a single affiliated service group.

(3) The provisions of this paragraph may be illustrated by the following examples.

Example (1).—Multiple First Service Organizations. (i) Corporation P provides secretarial service to numerous dentists in a medical building, each of whom maintains his own separate unincorporated practice. Dentist T owns 20 percent of the secretarial corporation and accounts for 20 percent of its gross receipts. Dentist W owns 25 percent of the corporation and accounts for 25 percent of its gross receipts.

(ii) Considering Dentist T as a First Service Organization, the secretarial corporation, P, is a B Organization because 20 percent of the gross receipts of the corporation are derived from performing services for Dentist T of a type historically performed by employees of dentists, and 20 percent of the interests in the corporation is owned by Dentist T. Accordingly, Dentist T and the corporation constitute an affiliated service group.

(iii) Considering Dentist W as a First Service Organization, the secretarial corporation, P, is a B Organization, because 25 percent of the gross receipts of the corporation are derived from performing services for Dentist W of a type historically performed by employees of dentists, and 25 percent of the interests in the corporation is owned by Dentist W. Accordingly, Dentist W and the corporation constitute an affiliated service group. However, this affiliated service group does not include Dentist T even though the secretarial corporation, P, is a B Organization with respect to both dentists. Thus, there are two affiliated service groups.

Example (2).— Multiple B Organizations. (i) Doctor N is incorporated as Corporation N. Secretarial services are provided to Corporation N by Corporation Q. Corporation N owns 20 percent of the interests in the secretarial corporation and provides 20 percent of its gross receipts. Nursing services are provided to Corporation N by Corporation R. Corporation N owns 25 percent of the interests in the nursing corporation and provides 25 percent of its gross receipts.

(ii) Considering Corporation N as a First Service Organization, the secretarial corporation, Q, is a B Organization because 20 percent of the gross receipts of the secretarial corporation, Q, are derived from performing services for Corporation N of a type historically performed by employees of doctors, and 20 percent of the secretarial corporation is owned by the owner of Corporation N. Accordingly, Corporation N and the secretarial corporation, Q, constitute an affiliated service group.

(iii) Considering Corporation N as a First Service Organization, the nursing corporation, R, is a B Organization because 25 percent of the gross receipts of the nursing corporation, R, are derived from performing services for Corporation N of a type historically performed by employees of doctors, and 25 percent of the nursing corporation is owned by the owner of Corporation N. Accordingly, Corporation N and the nursing corporation constitute an affiliated service group.

(iv) For purposes of section 414(m), there will be considered to be one affiliated service group consisting of Corporation N, the secretarial corporation, Q, and the nursing corporation, R.

§ 1.414(m)-3 Employee benefit requirements.

(a) *Employee benefit requirements affected.* All of the employees of the members of an affiliated service group shall be treated as employed by a single employer for purposes of the following employee benefit requirements:

(1) Sections 401(a)(3) and 410 (relating to minimum participation requirements);

(2) Section 401(a)(4) (requiring that contributions or benefits do not discriminate in favor of employees who are officers, shareholders, or highly compensated);

(3) Sections 401(a)(7) and 411 (relating to minimum vesting standards);

(4) Sections 401(a)(16) and 415 (relating to limitations on contributions and benefits);

(5) Section 408(k) (relating to simplified employee pensions);

(6) Section 105(h) (relating to self-insured medical reimbursement plans);

(7) Section 125 (relating to cafeteria plans); and

(8) Pursuant to the authority granted in section 414(m)(6), section 401(a)(10) (relatingg to plans providing contributions or benefits to owner-employees).

(b) *Special requirements.* If a plan maintained by a member of an affiliated service group covers an employee described in section 401(c)(1) (self-employed individual), an owner-employee within the meaning of section 401(c)(3), or a shareholder-employee within the meaning of section 1379(d), the plan must also satisfy the following requirements to the extent they apply:

(1) Section 401(a)(9) (relating to special distribution requirements for plans benefiting self-employed individuals);

(2) Section 401(a)(10) (relating to special requirements for plans benefiting owner-employees);

(3) Section 401(a)(17) (relating to a limitation on the compensation base of plans benefiting self-employed individuals or shareholder-employees); and

(4) Section 401(a)(18) (relating to special requirements for defined benefit plans benefiting self-employed individuals or shareholder-employees).

Pursuant to the authority granted in section 414(m)(6), a plan that covers a self-employed individual, an owner-employee, or a shareholder-employee will be subject to the preceding requirements, even though that individual is not employed by the member of the affiliated service group maintaining the plan. These requirements apply only if the earned income of the self-employed individual or owner-employee or the compensation received as a shareholder-employee is taken into account in computing contributions or benefits under the plan.

(c) *Multiple employer plans*—(1) *General rule.* If a plan maintained by a member of an affiliated service group covers an individual who is not an employee of that member, but who is an employee of another member of that affiliated service group, the plan will be considered to be maintained by the member that does employ that individual. Thus, the plan will be considered to be maintained by more than one employer for purposes of section 413(c)(2) (relating to the exclusive benefit rule), (4) (relating to funding), (5) (relating to liability for funding tax), and (6) (relating to deductions). Therefore, a member of an affiliated service group may deduct contributions on behalf of individuals who are not employees of that member, if the individuals are employed by another member of that affiliated service group.

(2) *Special rule.* The multiple employer plan rule contained in paragraph (c)(1) shall not apply in the case of a controlled group of corporations (as described in section 414(b)) or a group of trades or businesses under common control (as described in section 414(c)).

(d) *Discrimination.* In testing for discrimination under section 401(a)(4) (requiring that contributions or benefits do not discriminate in favor of employees who are officers, shareholders, or highly compensated), all of the compensation paid to an employee must be considered in determining the contributions or benefits under a plan maintained by a member of an affiliated service group, without regard to the percentage of the organization employing the individual owned by the member maintaining the plan.

(e) *Example.* The provisions of this section may be illustrated by the following example.

(1) T is incorporated and Corporation T is a partner in a service organization. Corporation T employs only its sole shareholder and maintains a retirement plan. W and Z, the other partners in the service organization, are not incorporated. Each partner has a one-third interest in the service organization. The partnership has eight common law employees.

(2) Considering the partnership as a First Service Organization, Corporation T is an A Organization because it is a partner in the First Service Organization and regularly performs services for the partnership or is regularly associated with the partnership in performing

services for third persons. Accordingly, the partnership and Corporation T constitute an affiliated service group.

(3) If the retirement plan maintained by Corporation T covers any of the common law employees of the partnership, it will be benefiting individuals who are not employees of the member of the affiliated service group maintaining the plan (Corporation T). As such, the plan will be considered to be maintained by more than one employer, and will be subject to the rules of section 413(c)(2), (4), (5), and (6) and the regulations thereunder. Thus, contributions by Corporation T on behalf of these individuals will not fail to be deductible under section 404 merely because they are not employees of Corporation T. In testing for discrimination under section 401(a)(4), all of the compensation paid to the employees of the partnership must be taken into account in determining their contributions or benefits under the plan, without regard to the percentage of the partnership owned by Corporation T.

(4) If the plan maintained by Corporation T covers partners W and Z, the plan must also satisfy the requirements listed in paragraph (b), to the extent they are applicable.

§ 1.414(m)-4 Effective dates.

(a) *Effective dates*—(1) *New plans.* In the case of a plan that was not in existence on November 30, 1980, section 414(m) and the regulations thereunder apply to plan years ending after November 30, 1980.

(2) *Existing plans.* In the case of a plan in existence on November 30, 1980, section 414(m) and the regulations thereunder shall apply to plan years beginning after November 30, 1980.

(b) *Frozen plans*—(1) *Defined contribution plans.* In the case of a defined contribution plan in existence on November 30, 1980, that fails to satisfy the requirements of section 401(a) solely because of the application of section 414(m), the trust shall be treated as continuing to satisfy the requirements of section 401(a) after the effective date of section 414(m) if the plan is terminated and all amounts are distributed to the participants within 180 days after the latest of:

(i) [The date of the publication of this regulation in the *Federal Register* as a Treasury decision],

(ii) The date on which notice of the final determination with respect to a request for a determination letter is issued by the Internal Revenue Service, such request is withdrawn, or such request is finally disposed of by the Internal Revenue Service, provided the request for a determination letter was pending on [the date of the publication of this regulation in the *Federal Register* as a Treasury decision] or, in the case of a request for a determination letter on the plan termination, was made within 60 days after the [date of the publication of this regulation in the *Federal Register* as a Treasury decision].

(iii) If a petition is timely filed with the United States Tax Court for a declaratory judgment under section 7476 with respect to the final determination (or the failure of the Internal Revenue Service to make a final determination) in response to such request, the date on which the decision of the United States Tax Court in such proceeding becomes final.

(2) *Defined benefit plans.* In the case of a defined benefit plan in existence on November 30, 1980, that fails to satisfy the requirements of section 401(a) solely because of the application of section 414(m), the trust shall be treated as continuing to satisfy the requirements of section 414(m) if the plan is terminated within 180 days after the latest of the dates determined in a manner consistent with paragraph (b)(1). However, deductions for contributions to the plan for plan years after the effective date of section 414(m) are limited to those necessary to satisfy the minimum funding standards of section 412.

§ 1.415-8 [Amended]

Par. 3. Paragraph (c) of §1.415-8 is amended by adding "or by an affiliated service group (within the meaning of section 414(m)" before the words "is deemed maintained."

Roscoe L. Egger, Jr.,

Commissioner of Internal Revenue.

[FR Doc. 83-5045 Filed 2-25-83; 8:45 am]

[¶ 20,137H Reserved.—Proposed Regs. §§ 1.401(b)-1 and 1.416-1, relating to top-heavy pension, profit-sharing, and stock bonus plans were formerly reproduced at this point. The final regulations appear at ¶ 11,721 and 12,503.]

¶ 20,137I

Proposed regulations: Multiemployer plans.—Reproduced below were proposed regulations relating, in the case of multiemployer plans, to the return of employer contributions or withdrawal liability overpayments which were made due to a mistake of fact or law. The proposed regulations were published in the *Federal Register* on March 11, 1983 (48 FR 10374). Final regulations, which were published in the *Federal Register* on July 22, 2002 (67 FR 47692), are reproduced at ¶ 11,720W-12. The preamble appears at ¶ 23,194.

¶ 20,137J

Proposed regulation: Personal service corporations: Reallocation of income, deductions, credits and exclusions.—Following are proposed regulations relating to the reallocation of income, deductions, credits, and exclusions between a personal service corporation and its employee-owners if the corporation was formed primarily to avoid or evade federal income taxes. The proposed regulations were published in the *Federal Register* on March 31, 1983 (48 FR 13438).

DEPARTMENT OF THE TREASURY

Internal Revenue Service

26 CFR Part 1

[LR-188-82]

Personal Service Corporations; Proposed Income Tax Regulations

AGENCY: Internal Revenue Service, Treasury.

ACTION: Notice of proposed rulemaking.

SUMMARY: This document provides proposed regulations relating to the reallocation of income, deductions, credits and exclusions between a personal service corporation and its employee-owners if the corporation was formed or availed primarily to evade or avoid Federal income taxes. Changes to the applicable tax law were made by section 250 of the Tax Equity and Fiscal Responsibility Act of 1982 (TEFRA), which added new section 269A to the Internal Revenue Code of 1954. These regulations would affect all employee-owners and their personal service corporations if the personal service corporation provides substantially all of its services for or on behalf of one other entity, but only if the corporation was formed or availed of primarily to evade or avoid

Federal income taxes. These regulations would provide affected persons with the guidance to comply with the law.

DATES: Written comments and requests for a public hearing must be delivered or mailed by May 31, 1983. The regulations provided by this document are proposed to be generally effective for taxable years of personal service corporations beginning after December 31, 1982.

ADDRESS: Send comments and requests for a public hearing to: Commissioner of Internal Revenue, Attention: CC:LR:T (LR-188-82) Washington, D.C. 20224.

FOR FURTHER INFORMATION CONTACT: Phoebe A. Mix or Philip R. Bosco of Legislation and Regulations Division, Office of Chief Counsel, Internal Revenue Service, 1111 Constitution Avenue, N.W., Washington, D.C. 20224, Attention: CC:LR:T, (202) 566-3238, not a toll-free call.

SUPPLEMENTARY INFORMATION:

Background

Section 269A was added to the Internal Revenue Code by the Tax Equity and Fiscal Responsibility Act of 1982. Section 269A permits the Secretary to allocate all income, deductions, credits, exclusions, and other tax benefits between a personal service corporation and its employee-owners in order to prevent the avoidance or evasion of Federal income taxes or to reflect clearly the income of the personal service corporation or any of its employee-owners if substantially all of the services are performed for one other entity and if the principal purpose for forming, or availing of, the corporation is the avoidance or evasion of Federal income taxes. Avoidance or evasion of Federal income taxes may be either the reduction of income of an employee-owner through the use of the corporation or the securing of one or more tax benefits that would not otherwise be available. These regulations define benefits that would not otherwise be available as benefits that would not be available to a taxpayer providing services as an unincorporated individual.

These regulations also provide a safe-harbor, excluding from the application of section 269A those situations in which the Federal income tax liability of each employee-owner is reduced by not more than 10 percent of $2,500, whichever is less.

Prior to "parity" between qualified retirement plans of corporations and those of noncorporate employers (effective generally for taxable years beginning after December 31, 1983), an employee-owner can make larger contributions to a corporate qualified retirement plan than could have been made to a Keogh or H.R. 10 plan had the corporation not been in existence. For corporations in existence before the date of enactment of TEFRA (September 3, 1982), qualified retirement plans available to corporations generally will not be taken into account for purposes of determining the corporation's principal purpose. Thus, a corporation created principally to take advantage of the higher contributions to corporate plans may still have an impermissible purpose if its principal purpose (other than qualified retirement plan benefit) was to reduce income or secure one or more tax benefits. If a corporation is found to have an impermissible principal purpose, the contributions to the qualified retirement plan will neither be reallocated to the employee-owner nor reduced as a result of reallocation of other income to the employee-owner. For corporations formed after the date of enactment of TEFRA, this protection is not available for contributions or benefits that would not have been available to the employee-owner absent the corporation. In that case, contributions to a qualified retirement plan will be considered in determining the corporation's principal purpose and may be reallocated or reduced through application of section 269A.

Section 269A does not override other sections of the Code or existing tax law principles. Nothing in these regulations, including the safe-harbor provision, precludes application of any other Code section (*e.g.,* sections 61 or 482) or principle of tax law (*e.g.,* assignment of income doctrine) to reallocate or reapportion income, deductions, credits or any other tax benefits if such reallocation is necessary to reflect the true earner of the income.

The regulations provide guidance regarding certain specific section 269A issues determined to be of major interest. No inference should be drawn regarding issues not included in the regulations, or as to why some issues, and not others, are addressed.

Special Analysis

The Commissioner of Internal Revenue has determined that these proposed regulations are not a major rule as defined in Executive Order 12291. Accordingly, a Regulatory Impact Analysis is not required. Although this document is a notice of proposed rulemaking that solicits public comment, the Internal Revenue Service has concluded that the notice and public procedure requirements of 5 U.S.C. 553 do not apply because the rules proposed are interpretative. Accordingly, a Regulatory Flexibility Analysis is not required.

Comments and Requests for a Public Hearing

Before adopting these proposed regulations, consideration will be given to any written comments that are submitted (preferably seven copies) to the Commissioner of Internal Revenue. All comments will be available for public inspection and copying. A public hearing will be held upon written request to the Commissioner by any person who has submitted written comments. If a public hearing is held, notice of the time and place will be published in the Federal Register.

Drafting Information

The principal authors of these proposed regulations are Phoebe A. Mix and Philip R. Bosco of the Legislation and Regulations Division of the Office of Chief Counsel, Internal Revenue Service. However, personnel from other offices of the Internal Revenue Service and Treasury participated in developing the regulations, both on matters of substance and style.

List of Subjects in 26 CFR 1.296A-1

Income taxes, Personal service corporations.

PART I—[AMENDED]

Proposed Amendments to the Regulations

The Income Tax Regulations (26 CFR Part 1) are proposed to be amended by adding the new § 1.269A-1, in the appropriate place:

§ 1.269A Personal service corporations.

(a) *In general.* Section 269A permits the Internal Revenue Service to reallocate income and tax benefits between personal service corporations and their employee-owners to prevent evasion or avoidance of Federal income taxes or to reflect clearly the income of the personal service corporation or any of its employee-owners, if:

(1) Substantially all of the services of the personal service corporation are performed for or on behalf of one other entity, and

(2) The principal purpose for which the corporation was formed or availed of is the evasion or avoidance of Federal income tax. Such purpose is evidenced when use of the corporation either reduces the income of any employee-owner, or secures for any employee-owner one or more tax benefits which would not otherwise be available.

(b) *Definitions.* For purposes of section 269A and the regulations thereunder, the following definitions will apply:

(1) *Personal service corporation.* The term "personal service corporation" means a corporation the principal activity of which is the performance of personal services that are substantially performed by employee-owners.

(2) *Employee-owner.* The term "employee-owner" means an employee who owns, directly or indirectly, on any day of the corporation's taxable year, more than 10 percent of the outstanding stock of the personal service corporation. Section 318 will apply to determine indirect stock ownership, except that "5 per cent" is to be substituted for "50 percent" in section 318(a)(2)(C).

(3) *Entity.* The term "entity" means a corporation, partnership, or other entity. All persons related to such entity will be treated as one entity. A related person is a related person within the meaning of section 103(b)(6)(C).

(4) *Not otherwise be available.* The term "not otherwise be available" refers to any tax benefit that would not be available to an employee-owner had such employee-owner performed the personal services in an individual capacity.

(5) *Qualified employer plan.* The term "qualified employer plan" means a qualified employer plan as defined in section 219(e)(3).

(6) *Tax benefits.* The term "tax benefits" means any expense, deduction, credit, exclusion or other allowance which would not otherwise be available. The term includes, but is not limited to: multiple surtax exemptions being claimed by the owners of a single integrated business operation conducted through multiple corporate entities, accumulation of income by the corporation, the corporate dividends received deduction under section 213, deferral of income of an employee-owner through the use of a corporation with a fiscal year or accounting method differing from that of such employee-owner, the use of multiple classes of stock to deflect income to taxpayers in lower tax brackets, group-term life insurance (section 79), certain accident and health plans (section 105 and 106), certain employee death benefits (section 101), meals and lodging furnished for the convenience of the employer (section 119), and qualified transportation expenses (section 124). Except as otherwise provided in paragraph (d)(2)(ii) of this section, the term "tax benefits" does not include contributions to a qualified employer plan.

(c) *Safe harbor.* In general, a personal service corporation will be deemed not to have been formed or availed of for the principal purpose of avoiding or evading Federal income taxes if the Federal income tax liability of the employee-owner is reduced in a 12 month period by more than the lesser of (1) $2,500 or (2) 10 percent of the Federal income tax liability of the employee-owner that would have resulted in that 12 month period had the employee-owner performed the personal services in an individual capacity. For purposes of the computation required by this paragraph, and current corporate tax liability incurred for that 12 month period by the personal service corporation will be considered to be the tax liability of the employee-owners in proportion to the employee-owners stock holding in the personal service corporation.

(d) *Special rules relating to qualified employer plans.*—(1) *In general.* Contributions to, and benefits under, qualified employer plans will not be taken into account in determining the presence or absence of a principal purpose of the personal service corporation for purposes of paragraph (c) of this section, except as provided in this paragraph.

(2) *Taxable years beginning before January 1, 1984.* For taxable years beginning before January 1, 1984.

(i) *Corporations in existence on or before September 3, 1982.* For corporations in existence on or before September 3, 1982, the general rule provided in paragraph (d)(1) of this section will apply unless:

(A) The corporation adopts a new qualified employer plan after September 3, 1982, that has a plan year differing from either the taxable year of the corporation or the calendar year, or

(B) The corporation changes the plan year of an existing qualified employer plan, or its taxable year, after September 3, 1982, in a manner that would extend the period during which section 416 (relating to restrictions on "top heavy" plans), or section 269A (if this (B) did not apply) would be inapplicable to such corporation.

If (A) or (B) applies, the corporation will be treated as a corporation formed after September 3, 1982 for purposes of this paragraph.

(ii) *Corporations formed after September 3, 1982.* For corporations formed after September 3, 1982, contributions to, and benefits under, a qualified employer plan that are in excess of those that would have been available to an employee-owner performing the personal services in an individual capacity are to be taken into account in determining the principal purpose of the personal service corporation and will be considered to be tax benefits.

(e) *Effective dates.*—(1) *In general.* In general, section 269A and this section are effective for taxable years of personal service corporations beginning after December 31, 1982. Taxable years of employee-owners generally are not considered for purposes of this paragraph.

(2) *Exceptions.* If a personal service corporation changes its taxable year or qualified employer plan year after September 3, 1982, in a manner that would delay the effective date of section 416 (relating to restrictions on top-heavy plans), or section 269A (but for this (2)), section 269A will be applied to the corporation and its employee-owners on the earlier of the first day of the first taxable year of the corporation or any of its employee-owners beginning after December 31, 1982.

(f) *Effect on section 269A on other sections.* Nothing in section 269A or the regulations thereunder, including the safe harbor provided in paragraph (c) of this section, precludes application with respect to personal service corporations or their employee-owners of any other Code section (*e.g.,* sections 61 or 482) or tax law principle (*e.g.,* assignment of income doctrine) to reallocate or reapportion income, deductions, credits, etc., so as to reflect the true earner of income.

Roscoe L. Egger, Jr.,

Commissioner of Internal Revenue.

[¶ 20,137K Reserved.—Proposed regulations relating to uniform premium rates for group-term life insurance were formerly reproduced here. The final regulations appear at ¶ 11,231 and 11,233.]

[¶ 20,137L Reserved.—Proposed regulations relating to tables for valuing annuities, life estates, terms for years, remainders, and reversions for purposes of federal income, estate, and gift taxation were formerly reproduced here. The final regulations appear at ¶ 11,252, 12,365, 13,497, 13,498, and 13,498A.]

[¶ 20,137M Reserved.—Proposed regulations relating to the definition of brother-sister controlled group of corporations or businesses were formerly reproduced at this paragraph. The final regulations are at ¶ 12,355 and 12,358.]

[¶ 20,137N Reserved.—Formerly reproduced at this paragraph were proposed regulations on transactions in which property is transferred in connection with the performance of services under Code Sec. 83. The IRS withdrew the regulations when it later issued proposed regulations on Code Sec. 83 in 1994. See ¶ 20,203.]

¶ 20,137O

Proposed regulations: IRAs: SEPs: QVECs: Changes made by ERTA.—Reproduced below are proposed regulations reflecting changes relating to IRAs, SEPs and QVECs made by the Economic Recovery Tax Act of 1981 under Code Secs. 219, 408, 415, 2039 and 6652.

The proposed regulations were published in the *Federal Register* on January 23, 1984 (49 FR 2794). The proposed revision of Reg. § 1.409-1(b)(2)(i) was withdrawn on January 8, 1996 (61 FR 552).

Note that these regulations were proposed prior to changes made by the Tax Reform Act of 1986.

[4830-01]

[Final draft of 9/14/82]

DEPARTMENT OF THE TREASURY

Internal Revenue Service

[26 CFR Parts 1, 20, 25, and 301]

[EE-148-81]

Individual Retirement Plans, Simplified Employee Pensions, and Qualified Voluntary Employee Contributions

AGENCY: Internal Revenue Service, Treasury.

ACTION: Notice of proposed rulemaking.

SUMMARY: This document contains proposed regulations relating to individual retirement plans, simplified employee pensions, and qualified voluntary employee contributions. Changes to the applicable law were made by the Economic Recovery Tax Act of 1981. The regulations would provide the public with the guidance needed to comply with the Act. The regulations would affect: institutions which sponsor individual retirement plans and simplified employee pensions, employers and individuals who use individual retirement plans and simplified employee pensions for retirement income, employers who maintain plans which accept qualified voluntary employee contributions and employees who make qualified voluntary employee contributions.

DATES: Written comments and requests for a public hearing must be delivered or mailed by March 23, 1984. The regulations would be

generally effective for taxable years beginning after December 31, 1981.

ADDRESS: Send comments and requests for a public hearing to: Commissioner of Internal Revenue, Attention: CC:LR:T (EE-148-81), Washington, D.C. 20224.

FOR FURTHER INFORMATION CONTACT: William D. Gibbs of the Employee Plans and Exempt Organizations Division, Office of the Chief Counsel, Internal Revenue Service, 1111 Constitution Avenue, N.W., Washington, D.C. 20224 (Attention: CC:LR:T) (202-566-3430) (not a toll-free number).

SUPPLEMENTARY INFORMATION:

Background

This document contains proposed amendments to the Income Tax Regulations (26 CFR Part 1), the Estate Tax Regulations (26 CFR Part 20), the Gift Tax Regulations (26 CFR Part 25), and the Procedure and Administration Regulations (26 CFR Part 301) under sections 219, 408, 409, 415, 2039, 2517, and 6652 of the Internal Revenue Code of 1954. These amendments are proposed to conform the regulations to sections 311 (except subsection (b)) and 314(b) of the Economic Recovery Tax Act of 1981 (95 Stat. 274, 286). These regulations are to be issued under the authority contained in section 7805 of the Internal Revenue Code of 1954 (68A Stat. 917; 26 U.S.C. 7805).

Individual Retirement Plans

Section 219, as amended by the Economic Recovery Tax Act of 1981, allows an individual a deduction of up to the lesser of $2,000 or compensation includible in gross income for contributions to an individual retirement plan. Unlike old section 219, an individual is allowed this deduction whether or not he is an "active participant" in an employer's plan. The deduction for individual retirement plan contributions is reduced, however, by amounts which the employee contributes to an employer's plan and treats as qualified voluntary employee contributions. The remainder of the individual retirement plan rules are similar to those under prior law.

Spousal Individual Retirement Accounts

Code section 220 was deleted by the Economic Recovery Tax Act of 1981. In its place is new section 219(c), which allows an individual and his nonworking spouse to contribute up to the lesser of compensation includible in the working spouse's gross income or $2,250 to individual retiremnt accounts. The spouses must file a joint return to obtain this additional $250 deduction. No deduction is allowed if the spouse for whose benefit the individual retirement plan is maintained has attained age 70 ½ before the close of the taxable year.

There is no requirement, as under old law, that equal amounts be contributed to the individual retirement accounts of both spouses. However, no more than $2,000 may be contributed to the individual retirement account of either spouse.

Simplified Employee Pensions

The Economic Recovery Tax Act of 1981 increased the maximum deduction for contributions to simplified employee pensions to the lesser of 15% of compensation from the employer maintaining the simplified employee pension arrangement or the amount contributed by the employer to the simplified employee pension and included in gross income (but not in excess of $15,000). An employer may also contribute and deduct the lesser of $2,000 or compensation includible in gross income regardless of the employer's contribution to the simplified employee pension.

Qualified Voluntary Employee Contributions

Section 219, as amended by the Economic Recovery Tax Act of 1981, allows an individual a deduction for qualified voluntary employee contributions (QVEC's). QVEC's are voluntary contributions made by an individual as an employee under an employer's plan. The employer's plan must allow employees to make contributions which may be treated as QVEC's.

The maximum amount which can be deducted as a QVEC is the lesser of $2,000 or the compensation includible in gross income from the employer which maintains the plan which accepts the QVEC's.

Proposed § 1.219(a)-5(a) sets forth the type of plans which can accept qualified voluntary employee contributions.

Proposed § 1.219(a)-5(c) sets forth the rules a plan must follow to receive qualified voluntary employee contributions.

Additional rules for QVEC's are set forth in proposed § 1.219(a)-5(d), (e), and (f).

The reporting rules for qualified voluntary employee contributions are in proposed § 1.219(e)-5(g). This provision gives the Commissioner discretionary authority to modify the reporting requirements for these contributions. Any such modification of the reporting requirements would be subject to review by the Office of Management and Budget under the Paperwork Reduction Act of 1980.

Other Amendments

Conforming and technical amendments made by the Economic Recovery Tax Act of 1981 have been made to the regulations under Code sections 408, 409, 415, 2039, 2517, and 6652.

Although the Treasury Department stopped selling retirement bonds in early 1982, the regulations contain references to Code sections 405 and 409. These references apply to retirement bonds sold through early 1982 and to retirement bonds that may be sold subsequently.

These proposed regulations do not reflect amendments made to the Code by the Tax Equity and Fiscal Responsibility Act of 1982. These proposed regulations reflect certain changes in the applicable statutory provisions made by the Technical Corrections Act of 1982.

Executive Order 12291 And Regulatory Flexibility Act

The Commissioner has determined that this proposed regulation is not a major regulation for purposes of Executive Order 12291. Accordingly, a regulatory impact analysis is not required.

Although this document is a notice of proposed rulemaking which solicits public comment, the Internal Revenue Service has concluded that the regulations proposed herein are interpretative and that the notice and public procedure requirements of 5 U.S.C. 553 do not apply.

Accordingly, these proposed regulations do not constitute regulations subject to the Regulatory Flexibility Act (5 U.S.C. chapter 6).

Comments and Requests for a Public Hearing

Before adopting these proposed regulations, consideration will be given to any written comments that are submitted (preferably seven copies) to the Commissioner of Internal Revenue. All comments will be available for public inspection and copying. A public hearing will be held upon written request to the Commissioner by any person who has submitted written comments. If a public hearing is held, notice of the time and place will be published in the FEDERAL REGISTER.

The collection of information requirements contained in this notice of proposed rulemaking have been submitted to the Office of Management and Budget (OMB) for review under section 3504(h) of the Paperwork Reduction Act of 1980. Comments on these requirements should be sent to the Office of Information and Regulatory Affairs of OMB, Attention: Desk Office for Internal Revneue Service, New Executive Office Building, Washington, D.C. 20503. The Internal Revenue Service requests that persons submitting comments on these requirements to OMB also send copies of those comments to the Service.

Drafting Information

The principal author of these proposed regulations is William D. Gibbs of the Employee Plans and Exempt Organizations Division of the Office of Chief Counsel, Internal Revenue Service. However, personnel from other offices of the Internal Revenue Service and Treasury Department participated in developing the regulation, both on matters of substance and style.

List of Subjects in 26 CFR §§ 1.61-1—1.281-4

Income taxes, Taxable income, Deductions, Exemptions.

List of Subjects in 26 CFR §§ 1.401-0—1.425-1

Income taxes, Employee benefit plan, Pensions, Stock options, Individual retirement accounts, Employee stock ownership plans.

List of Subjects in 26 CFR Part 20

Estate taxes.

List of Subjects in 26 CFR Part 25

Gift taxes.

List of Subjects in 26 CFR Part 301

Administrative practice and procedure, Bankruptcy, Courts, Crime, Employment taxes, Estate taxes, Excise taxes, Gift taxes, Income taxes, Investigations, Law enforcement, Penalties, Pensions, Statistics, Taxes, Disclosure of information, Filing requirements.

Proposed amendments to the regulations

The proposed amendments to 26 CFR Parts 1, 20, 25, and 301 are as follows:

Income Tax Regulations [26 CFR Part 1]

Paragraph 1. There are added after proposed § 1.219-3, 46 FR 36202 (1981), the following new sections 1.219(a)-1 through 1.219(a)-6:

§ 1.219(a)-1 Deduction for contributions to individual retirement plans and employer plans under the Economic Recovery Tax Act of 1981.

(a) *In general.* Under section 219, as amended by the Economic Recovery Tax Act of 1981, an individual is allowed a deduction from gross income for amounts paid on his behalf to an individual retirement plan or to certain employer retirement plans. The following table indicates the location of the rules for deductions on behalf of individuals to individual retirement plans or employer plans.

§ 1.219(a)-2: Individual retirement plans.

§ 1.219(a)-3: Spousal individual retirement accounts.

§ 1.219(a)-4: Simplified employee pensions.

§ 1.219(a)-5: Employer plans.

§ 1.219(a)-6: Divorced individuals.

(b) *Definitions.* The following is a list of terms and their definitions to be used for purposes of this section and §§ 1.219(a)-2 through 1.219(a)-6:

(1) *Individual retirement plan.* The term "individual retirement plan" means an individual retirement account described in section 408(a), an individual retirement annuity described in section 408(b), and a retirement bond described in section 409.

(2) *Simplified employee pension.* The term "simplified employee pension" has the meaning set forth in § 1.408-7(a).

(3) *Compensation.* The term "compensation" means wages, salaries, professional fees, or other amounts derived from or received for personal service actually rendered (including, but not limited to, commissions paid salesmen, compensation for services on the basis of a percentage of profits, commissions on insurance premiums, tips, and bonuses), but does not include amounts derived from or received as earnings or profits from property (including, but not limited to, interest and dividends) or amounts not includible in gross income such as amounts excluded under section 911. Compensation includes earned income, as defined in section 401(c)(2), reduced by amounts deductible under sections 404 and 405. Compensation does not include amounts received as deferred compensation, including any pension or annuity payment. Compensation does not include unemployment compensation within the meaning of section 85(c).

(4) *Qualified voluntary employee contribution.* The term "qualified voluntary employee contribution" means any employee contribution which is not a mandatory contribution within the meaning of section 411(c)(2)(C) made by an individual as an employee under qualified employer plan or government plan, which plan allows an employee to make such contribution, and which the individual has not designated as a contribution other than a qualified voluntary employee contribution. Thus, if employee contributions are required as a condition of plan participation, they are mandatory contributions within the meaning of section 411(c)(2)(C) and cannot be treated as qualified voluntary employee contributions.

(5) *Qualified retirement contribution.* The term "qualified retirement contribution" means any amount paid in cash for the taxable year by or on behalf of an individual for his benefit to an individual retirement plan and any qualified voluntary employee contribution paid in cash by the individual for the taxable year.

(6) *Deductible employee contribution.* The term "deductible employee contribution" means any qualified voluntary employee contribution made after December 31, 1981, in a taxable year beginning after such date and allowable as a deduction under section 219(a) for such taxable year.

(7) *Qualified employer plan.* The term "qualified employer plan" means—

(i) A plan described in section 401(a) which includes a trust exempt from tax under section 501(a),

(ii) An annuity plan described in section 403(a),

(iii) A qualified bond purchase plan described in section 405(a), and

(iv) A plan under which amounts are contributed by an individual's employer for an annuity contract described in section 403(b).

(8) *Government plan.* The term "government plan" means any retirement plan, whether or not qualified, established and maintained for its employees by the United States, by a State or political subdivision thereof, or by an agency or instrumentality of any of the foregoing.

(c) *Effective date.* This section and §§ 1.219(a)-2 through 1.219(a)-6 are effective **for taxable years of individuals beginning after December 31, 1981.**

§ 1.219(a)-2 Deduction for contributions to individual retirement plans under the Economic Recovery Tax Act of 1981.

(a) *In general.* Subject to the limitations and restrictions of paragraph (b) and the special rules of paragraph (c)(3) of this section, there shall be allowed a deduction under section 62 from gross income of amounts paid for the taxable year of an individual by or on behalf of such individual to an individual retirement plan. The deduction described in the preceding sentence shall be allowed only to the individual on whose behalf such individual retirement plan is maintained and only in the case of a contribution of cash. No deduction is allowable under this section for a contribution of property other than cash. In the case of a retirement bond, no deduction is allowed if the bond is redeemed within 12 months of its issue date.

(b) *Limitations and restrictions*—(1) *Maximum deduction.* The amount allowable as a deduction for contributions to an individual retirement plan to an individual for any taxable year cannot exceed the lessor of—

(i) $2,000, or

(ii) An amount equal to the compensation includible in the individual's gross income for the taxable year, reduced by the amount of the individual's qualified voluntary employee contributions for the taxable year.

(2) *Contributions after age 70 ½.* No deduction is allowable for contributions to an individual retirement plan to an individual for the taxable year of the individual if he has attained the age of 70 ½ before the close of such taxable year.

(3) *Rollover contributions.* No deduction is allowable under § 1.219(a)-2(a) for any taxable year of an individual with respect to a rollover contribution described in section 402(a)(5), 402(a)(7), 403(a)(4), 403(b)(8), 405(d)(3), 408(d)(3), or 409(b)(3)(C).

(4) *Amounts contributed under endowment contracts.* (i) For any taxable year, no deduction is allowable under § 1.219(a)-2(a) for amounts paid under an endowment contract described in § 1.408-3(e) which is allocable under subdivision (ii) of this subparagraph to the cost of life insurance.

(ii) For any taxable year, the cost of current life insurance protection under an endowment contract described in paragraph (b)(4)(i) of this section is the product of the net premium cost, as determined by the commissioner, and the excess, if any, of the death benefit payable under the contract during the policy year beginning in the taxable year over the cash value of the contract at the end of such policy year.

(c) *Special rules*—(1) *Separate deduction for each individual.* The maximum deduction allowable for contributions to an individual retirement plan is computed separately for each individual. Thus, if a husband and wife each has compensation of $15,000 for the taxable year, the maximum amount allowable as a deduction on their joint return is $4,000. See § 1.219(a)-3 for the maximum deduction for a spousal individual retirement plan when one spouse has no compensation.

(2) *Community property.* Section 219 is to be applied without regard to any community property laws. Thus, if, for example, a husband and wife live in a community property jurisdiction, the husband has compensation of $30,000 for the taxable year, and the wife has no compensation for the taxable year, then the maximum amount allowable as a deduction for contributions to an individual retirement plan, other than a spousal individual retirement plan, is $2,000.

(3) *Employer contributions.* For purposes of this chapter, any amount paid by an employer to an individual retirement plan of an employee (other than a self-employed individual who is an employee within the meaning of section 401(c)(1)) constitutes the payment of compensation to the employee. The payment is includible in the employee's gross income, whether or not a deduction for such payment is allowable under section 219 to this employee. An employer will be entitled to a deduction for compensation paid to an employee for amounts the employer contributes on the employee's behalf to an individual retirement plan if such deduction is otherwise allowable under section 162. See § 1.404(h)-1 for certain limitations on this deduction in the case of employer contributions to a simplified employee pension.

(4) *Year of inclusion in income.* Any amount paid by an employer to an individual retirement plan (including an individual retirement account or individual retirement annuity maintained as part of a simplified employee pension arrangement) shall be included in the gross income of the employee for the taxable year for which the contribution was made.

(5) *Time when contributions deemed made.* A taxpayer shall be deemed to have made a contribution on the last day of the preceding taxable year if the contribution is made on account of the taxable year which includes such last day and is made not later than the time prescribed by law for filing the return for such taxable year (including extensions thereof). A contribution made not later than the time prescribed by law for filing the return for a taxable year (including extensions thereof) shall be treated as made on account of such taxable year if it is irrevocably specified in writing to the trustee, insurance company, or custodian that the amounts contributed are for such taxable year.

(d) *Excess contributions treated as contribution made during subsequent year for which there is an unused limitation*—(1) *In general.* This paragraph sets forth rules for the possible deduction of excess contributions made to an individual retirement plan for the taxable years following the taxable year of the excess contribution. If for a taxable year subsequent to the taxable year for which the excess contribution was made, the maximum amount allowable as a deduction for contributions to an individual retirement plan exceeds the amount contributed, then the taxpayer, whether or not a deduction is actually claimed, shall be treated as having made an additional contribution for the taxable year in an amount equal to the lesser of—

(i) The amount of such excess, or

(ii) The amount of the excess contributions for such taxable year (determined under section 4973(b)(2) without regard to subparagraph (C) thereof).

(2) *Amount contributed.* For purposes of this paragraph, the amount contributed—

(i) Shall be determined without regard to this paragraph, and

(ii) Shall not incude any rollover contribution.

(3) *Special rule where excess deduction was allowed for closed year.* Proper reduction shall be made in the amount allowable as a deduction by reason of this paragraph for any amount allowed as a deduction for contributions to an individual retirement plan for a prior taxable year for which the period for assessing a deficiency has expired if the amount so allowed exceeds the amount which should have been allowed for such prior taxable year.

(4) *Excise tax consequences.* See section 4973 and the regulations thereunder for the excise tax applicable to excess contributions made to individual retirement plans.

(5) *Examples.* The provisions of this paragraph may be illustrated by the following examples. (Assume in each example, unless otherwise stated, that T is less than age 70 ½ and is not married.)

Example (1). (i) T, a calendar-year taxpayer, earns $1,500 in compensation includible in gross income for 1982. On December 1, 1982, T establishes an individual retirement account (IRA) and contributes $2,000 to the account. T does not withdraw any money from the IRA after the initial contribution. Under section 219(b)(1), the maximum amount that T can deduct for 1982 is $1,500. T has an excess contribution for 1982 of $500.

(ii) For 1983, T has compensation includible in gross income of $12,000. T makes a $1,000 contribution to his IRA for 1983.

(iii) Although T made only a $1,000 contribution to his IRA for 1983, under the rules contained in this paragraph, T is treated as having made an additional contribution of $500 for 1983 and will be allowed to deduct $1,500 as his 1983 IRA contribution.

Example (2). (i) For 1982, the facts are the same as in *Example (1).*

(ii) For 1983, T has compensation includible in gross income of $12,000. T makes a $2,000 contribution to his IRA for 1983.

(iii) T will be allowed a $2,000 deduction for 1983 (the amount of his contribution). T will not be allowed a deduction for the $500 excess contribution made in 1982 because the maximum amount allowable for 1983 does not exceed the amount contributed.

Example (3). (i) For 1982, the facts are the same as in *Example (1).*

(ii) For 1983, T has compensation includible in gross income of $12,000. T makes a $1,800 contribution to his IRA for 1983.

(iii) For 1983, T will be allowed to deduct his contribution of $1,800 and $200 of the excess contribution made for 1982. He will not be allowed to deduct the remaining $300 of the excess contribution made for 1982 because his deduction for 1983 would then exceed $2,000, his allowable deduction for 1983.

(iv) For 1984, T has compensation includible in gross income of $15,000. T makes a $1,300 contribution to his IRA for 1984.

(v) T will be allowed to deduct both his $1,300 contribution for 1984 and the remaining $300 contribution made for 1982.

Example (4). (i) For 1982, the facts are the same as in *Example (1).*

(ii) For 1983, T has compensation includible in gross income of $12,000. T makes a $1,000 contribution to his IRA for 1983. T is allowed to deduct the $500 excess contribution for 1983 but fails to do so on his return. Consequently, T deducts ony $1,000 for 1983.

(iii) Under no circumstances will T be allowed to deduct the $500 excess contribution made for 1982 for any taxable year after 1983 because T is treated as having made the contribution for 1983.

Example (5). (i) For 1982, the facts are the same as in *Example (1).*

(ii) For 1983, T has no compensation includible in gross income.

(iii) T will not be allowed to deduct for 1983 the $500 excess contribution for 1982 because the maximum amount allowable as a deduction under section 219(b)(1) is $0.

§ 1.219(a)-3 Deduction for retirement savings for certain married individuals.

(a) *In general.* Subject to the limitations and restrictions of paragraphs (c) and (d) and the special rules of paragraph (e) of this section, there shall be allowed a deduction under section 62 from gross income of amounts paid for the taxable year of an individual by or on behalf of such individual for the benefit of his spouse to an individual retirement plan. The amounts contributed to an individual retirement plan by or on behalf of an individual for the benefit of his spouse shall be deductible only by such individual and only in the case of a contribution of cash. No deduction is allowable under this section for a contribution of property other than cash. In the case of an individual retirement bond, no deduction is allowed if the bond is redeemed within 12 months of its issue date.

(b) *Definition of compensation.* For purposes of this section, the term "compensation" has the meaning set forth in § 1.219(a)-1(b)(3).

(c) *Maximum deduction.* The amount allowable as a deduction under this section to an individual for any taxable year may not exceed the smallest of—

(1) $2,000,

(2) An amount equal to the compensation includible in the individual's gross income for the taxable year less the amount allowed as a deduction under section 219(a) (determined without regard to contributions to a simplified employee pension allowed under section 219(b)(2)), § 1.219(a)-2 and § 1.219(a)-5 for the taxable year, or

(3) $2,250 less the amount allowed as a deduction under section 219(a) (determined without regard to contributions to a simplified employee pension allowed under section 219(b)(2)), § 1.219(a)-2 and § 1.219(a)-5 for the taxable year.

(d) *Limitations and restrictions*—(1) *Requirement to file joint return.* No deduction is allowable under this section for a taxable year unless the individual and his spouse file a joint return under section 6013 for the taxable year.

(2) *Employed spouses.* No deduction is allowable under this section if the spouse of the individual has any compensation for the taxable year of such spouse ending with or within the taxable year of the individual. For purposes of this subparagraph, compensation has the meaning set forth in § 1.219(a)-1(b)(3), except that compensation shall include amounts excluded under section 911.

(3) *Contributions after age 70 ½.* No deduction is allowable under this section with respect to any payment which is made for a taxable year of an individual if the individual for whose benefit the individual retirement plan is maintained has attained age 70 ½ before the close of such taxable year.

(4) *Recontributed amounts.* No deduction is allowable under this section for any taxable year of an individual with respect to a rollover contribution described in section 402(a)(5), 402(a)(7), 403(a)(4), 403(b)(8), 405(d)(3), 408(d)(3), or 409(b)(3)(C).

(5) *Amounts contributed under endowment contracts.* The rules for endowment contracts under this section are the same as the provisions for such contracts under § 1.219(a)-2(b)(4).

(e) *Special rules*—(1) *Community Property.* This section is to be applied without regard to any community property laws.

(2) *Time when contributions deemed made.* The time when contributions are deemed made is determined under section 219(f)(3). See § 1.219(a)-2(c)(5).

§ 1.219(a)-4 Deduction for contributions to simplified employee pensions.

(a) *General rule*—(1) *In general.* Under section 219(b)(2), if an employer contribution is made on behalf of an employee to a simplified employee pension described in section 408(k), the limitations of this section, and not section 219(b)(1) and § 1.219(a)-2, shall apply for purposes of computing the maximum allowable deduction with respect to that contribution for that individual employee.

(2) *Employer limitation.* The maximum deduction under section 219(b)(2) for an employee with respect to an employer contribution to the employee's simplified employee pension under that employer's arrangement cannot exceed an amount equal to the lesser of—

(i) 15 percent of the employee's compensation from the employer (determined without regard to the employer contribution to the simplified employee pension) includible in the employee's gross income for the taxable year, or

(ii) The amount contributed by that employer to the employee's simplified employee pension and included in gross income (but not in excess of $15,000).

(3) *Special rules*—(i) *Compensation.* Compensation referred to in paragraph (a)(2)(i) has the same meaning as under § 1.219(a)-1(b)(3) except that it includes only the compensation from the employer making the contribution to the simplified employee pension. Thus, if an individual earns $50,000 from employer A and $20,000 from employer B and employer B contributes $4,000 to a simplified employee pension on behalf of the individual, the maximum amount the individual will be

able to deduct under section 219(b)(2) is 15 percent of $20,000, or $3,000.

(ii) *Special rule for officers, shareholders, and owner-employees.* In the case of an employee who is an officer, shareholder, or owner-employee described in section 408(k)(3) with respect to a particular employer, the $15,000 amount referred to in paragraph (a)(2)(ii) shall be reduced by the amount of tax taken into account with respect to such individual under section 408(k)(3)(D).

(iii) *More than one employer arrangement.* Except as provided in paragraph (c), below, the maximum deduction under paragraph (a)(2) for an individual who receives simplified employee pension contributions under two or more employers' simplified employee pension arrangements cannot exceed the sum of the maximum deduction limitations computed separately for that individual under each such employer's arrangement.

(iv) *Section 408 rules.* Under section 408(j), the limitations under section 408(a)(1) and (b)(2)(B) (§ 1.408-2(b)(1) and § 1.408-3(b)(2)), shall be applied separately with respect to each employer's contributions to an individual's simplified employee pension.

(4) *Additional deduction for individual retirement plan and qualified voluntary employee contribution.* The deduction under this paragraph is in addition to any deduction allowed under section 219(a) to the individual for qualified retirement contributions.

(b) *Contributions to simplified employee pensions after age 70 ½.* The denial of deductions for contributions after age 70 ½ contained in section 219(d)(1) and § 1.219(a)-2(b)(2) shall not apply with respect to employer contributions to a simplified employee pension.

(c) *Multiple employer, etc. limitations—(1) Section 414(b), (c) and (m) employers.* In the case of a controlled group of employers within the meaning of section 414(b) or (c) or employers aggregated under section 414(m), the maximum deduction limitation for an employee under paragraph (a)(2) shall be computed by treating such employers as one employer maintaining a single simplified employee pension arrangement and by treating the compensation of that employee from such employers as if from one employer. Thus, for example, for a particular employee the 15 percent limitation on compensation would be determined with regard to the compensation from all employers within such group. Further, the maximum deduction with respect to contributions made by employers included within such group could not exceed $15,000.

(2) *Self-employed individuals.* In the case of an employee who is a self-employed individual within the meaning of section 401(c)(1) with respect to more than one trade or business, the maximum deduction limitation for such an employee under paragraph (a)(2) shall not exceed the lesser of the sum of such limitation applied separately with respect to the simplified employee pension arrangement of each trade or business or such limitation determined by treating such trades or businesses as if they constituted a single employer.

(d) *Examples.* The provisions of this section may be illustrated by the following examples:

Example (1). Corporation X is a calendar-year, cash-basis taxpayer. It adopts a simplified employee pension agreement in 1982 and wishes to contribute the maximum amount on behalf of each employee for 1982. Individual E is a calendar-year taxpayer who is employed solely by Corporation X in 1982. Beginning in June, 1982, Corporation X pays $100 each month into a simplified employee pension maintained on behalf of E. X makes a total payment to E's simplified employee pension during the year of $700. E's other compensation from X for the year totals $15,000. The maximum amount which E will be allowed to deduct as a simplified employee pension contribution is 15% of $15,000, or $2,250. Therefore, X may make an additional contribution for 1982 to E's simplified employee pension of $1,550. X makes this additional contribution to E's simplified employee pension in February of 1983. E's total compensation includible in gross income for 1982 is $15,000 + $2,250 or $17,250.

Example (2). (i) Corporation G is a calendar-year taxpayer which adopts a simplified employee pension agreement for 1982. It does not maintain an integrated plan as defined in section 408(k)(3)(E). It wishes to contribute 15% of compensation on behalf of each employee reduced by its tax under section 3111(a). The corporation has 4 employees, A, B, C, and D. D is a shareholder. The compensation for these employees for 1982 is as follows:

A = $10,000

B = 20,000

C = 30,000

D = 120,000

(ii) The amount of money which the corporation will be allowed to contribute on behalf of each employee under this allocation formula and the amount of the employer contribution each employee will be allowed to deduct is set forth in the following table:

Employee	Compensation	Lesser of $15,000 or 15% of Comp.	3111(a)[1] Tax	SEP[2] Contribution	Sec. 219 (b)(2) Deduction
A	$10,000	$1,500	$540.00	$960.00	$960.00
B	20,000	3,000	1,080.00	1,920.00	1,920.00
C	30,000	4,500	1,620.00	2,880.00	2,880.00
D	120,000	15,000	1,749.60	13,250.40	13,250.40

[1] The section 3111(a) tax is computed by multiplying compensation up to the taxable wage base ($32,400 for 1982) by the tax rate (5.40% for 1982).
[2] Simplified Employee Pension.

Example (3). Corporations A and B are calendar year taxpayers. Corporations A and B are not aggregated employers under section 414(b), (c) or (m). Individual M is employed full-time by Corporation A and part-time by Corporation B. Corporation A adopts a simplified employee pension agreement for calendar year 1982 and agrees to contribute 15% of compensation for each participant. M is a participant under Corporation A's simplified employee pension agreement and earns $15,000 for 1982 from Corporation A before A's contribution to his simplified employee pension. M also earns $5,000 as a part-time employee of Corporation B for 1982. Corporation A contributes $2,500 to M's simplified employee pension. The maximum amount that M will be allowed to deduct under section 219(b)(2) for 1982 is 15% of $15,000 or $2,250. In addition, M would be allowed to deduct the remaining $250 under section 219(a) for qualified retirement contributions.

Example (4). Individual P is employed by Corporation H and Corporation O. Corporations H and O are not aggregated employers under section 414(b), (c) or (m). Both Corporation H and Corporation O maintain a simplified employee pension arrangement and contribute 15 percent of compensation on behalf of each employee, up to a maximum of $15,000. P earns $100,000 from Corporation H and $120,000 from Corporation O. Corporation H and O each contribute $15,000 under its simplified employee pension arrangement to an individual retirement account maintained on behalf of P. P will be allowed to deduct $30,000 for employer contributions to simplified employee pensions because each employer has a simplified employee pension arrangement and the SEP contributions by Corporation H and O do not exceed the applicable $15,000-15 percent limitation with respect to compensation received

from each employer. In addition, P would be allowed to deduct $2,000 under section 219(a) for qualified retirement contributions.

§ 1.219(a)-5 Deduction for employee contributions to employer plans.

(a) *Deduction allowed.* In the case of an individual, there is allowed as a deduction amounts contributed in cash to a qualified employer plan or government plan (as defined, respectively, in paragraphs (b)(7) and (b)(8) of § 1.219(a)-1) and designated as qualified voluntary employee contributions. If an employee transfers an amount of cash from one account in a plan to the qualified voluntary employee contribution account, such transfer is a distribution for purposes of sections 72, 402 and 403, and the amounts are considered recontributed as qualified voluntary employee contributions. No deduction will be allowed for a contribution of property other than cash.

(b) *Limitations—(1) Maximum amount of deduction.* The amount allowable as a deduction under paragraph (a) to any individual for any taxable year shall not exceed the lesser of $2,000 or an amount equal to the compensation (from the employer who maintains the plan) includible in the individual's gross income for such taxable year.

(2) *Contributions after age 70 ½.* No deduction is allowable for contributions under paragraph (a) to an individual for the taxable year of the individual if he has attained the age of 70 ½ before the close of such taxable year.

(3) *Rollover contributions.* No deduction is allowable under paragraph (a) for any taxable year of an individual with respect to a rollover

contribution described in section 402(a)(5), 402(a)(7), 403(a)(4), 403(b)(8), 405(d)(3), 408(d)(3), or 409(b)(3)(C).

(c) *Rules for plans accepting qualified voluntary employee contributions*—(1) *Plan provision, etc.* (i) No plan may receive qualified voluntary employee contributions unless the plan document provides for acceptance of voluntary contributions. No plan may receive qualified voluntary employee contributions unless either the plan document provides for acceptance of qualified voluntary employee contributions or the employer or the plan administrator manifests an intent to accept such contributions. Such intention must be communicated to the employees. Any manner of communication that satisfies § 1.7476-2(c)(1) shall satisfy the requirements of this subparagraph.

(ii) If the plan document provides for the acceptance of voluntary contributions, but does not specifically provide for acceptance of qualified voluntary employee contributions, the plan qualification limitation on voluntary contributions (the limit of 10 percent of the employee's cumulative compensation less prior voluntary contributions) would apply to both qualified voluntary employee contributions and other voluntary contributions. On the other hand, if the plan document provides for acceptance of both qualified voluntary employee contributions and other voluntary contributions, the plan qualification limitation on voluntary contributions would apply only to the contributions other than the qualified voluntary employee contributions.

(2) *Plans accepting only qualified voluntary employee contributions.* A qualified pension plan or stock bonus plan may be established that provides only for qualified voluntary employee contributions. Similarly, a government plan may be established that provides only for qualified voluntary employee contributions. A plan that provides only for qualified voluntary employee contributions would not satisfy the qualification requirements for a profit-sharing plan.

(3) *Recordkeeping provisions.* Separate accounting for qualified voluntary employee contributions that are deductible under this section is not required as a condition for receiving qualified voluntary employee contributions. However, failure to properly account for such contributions may result in adverse tax consequences to employees upon subsequent plan distributions and reporting and recordkeeping penalties for employers. See section 72(o) for rules for accounting for such contributions.

(4) *Status as employee.* An amount will not be considered as a qualified voluntary employee contribution on behalf of an individual unless the individual is an employee of the employer at some time during the calendar year for which the voluntary contribution is made. See section 415(c) concerning the effect of a nondeductible voluntary employee contribution on plan qualification.

(5) *Contribution before receipt of compensation.* A plan may allow an individual to make a qualified voluntary employee contribution greater than the amount he has received in compensation from the employer at the time the contribution is made. However, see paragraph (f) of this section.

(d) *Designations, procedures, etc.*—(1) *Plan procedures.* (i) A plan which accepts qualified voluntary employee contributions may adopt procedures by which an employee can designate the character of the employee's voluntary contributions as either qualified voluntary employee contributions or other employee contributions. Such procedures may, but need not, be in the plan document.

(ii) In the absence of such plan procedures, all voluntary employee contributions shall be deemed to be qualified voluntary employee contributions unless the employee notifies the employer that the contributions are not qualified voluntary employee contributions. Such notification must be received by April 15 following the calendar year for which such contributions were made. If such notification is not received, contributions are deemed to be qualified voluntary employee contributions for the prior year.

(2) *Characterization procedures, etc.* (i) The plan procedures may allow an employee to elect whether or not an employee contribution is to be treated as a qualified voluntary employee contribution or as other voluntary contributions. This election can be required either prior to or after the contribution is made. If a contribution may be treated under such procedures as a qualified voluntary employee contribution or other voluntary contribution for a calendar year and the employee has not by April 15 of the subsequent calendar year designated the character of the contribution, the contribution must be treated as a qualified voluntary employee contribution for the calendar year. An employer may allow the election to be irrevocable or revocable. A procedure allowing revocable elections may limit the time within which an election may be revoked. The revocation of an election after April 15 following the calendar year for which the contribution was made is

deemed to be ineffective in changing the character of employee contributions.

(ii) For purposes of this section, if the plan procedures allow employees to make contributions on account of the immediately preceding calendar year, a taxpayer shall be deemed to have made a qualified voluntary employee contribution to such plan on the last day of the preceding calendar year if the contribution is on account of such year and is made by April 15 of the calendar year or such earlier time as provided by the plan procedure.

(e) *Nondiscrimination requirements*—(1) *General rule.* Plans subject to the nondiscrimination requirements of section 401(a)(4) which accept qualified voluntary employee contributions must permit such contributions in a nondiscriminatory manner in order to satisfy section 401(a)(4). If a plan permits participants to make qualified voluntary employee contributions, the opportunity to make such contributions must be reasonably available to a nondiscriminatory group of employees. The availability standard will be satisfied if a nondiscriminatory group of employees is eligible to make qualified voluntary employee contributions under the terms of the plan and if a nondiscriminatory group of employees actually has the opportunity to make qualified voluntary employee contributions when plan restrictions are taken into account.

(2) *Eligible employees.* A nondiscriminatory group of employees is eligible to make qualified voluntary employee contributions under the terms of the plan if the group either meets the percentage requirements of section 410(b)(1)(A) or comprises a classification of employees that does not discriminate in favor of employees who are officers, shareholders, or highly compensated, as provided in section 410(b)(1)(B).

(3) *Plan restrictions.* In some cases, an employee may not be permitted to make qualified voluntary employee contributions until a plan restriction (such as making a certain level of mandatory employee contributions) is satisfied. In this case, it is necessary to determine whether a nondiscriminatory group of employees actually has the opportunity to make qualified voluntary employee contributions. For this purpose, only employees who have satisfied the plan restriction will be considered to have the opportunity to make deductible contributions. Thus, for example, if a plan requires an employee to make mandatory contributions of 6 percent of compensation in order to make qualified voluntary employee contributions and if only a small percentage of employees make the 6 percent mandatory contributions, then the group of employees who have the opportunity to make qualified voluntary employee contributions may not satisfy either test under section 410(b). A similar rule is applicable to integrated plans: employees who are not permitted to make qualified voluntary employee contributions to such a plan because they earn less than the integration level amount will be considered as employees who do not have the opportunity to make qualified voluntary employee contributions.

(4) *Permissible contributions.* If the availability standards are met, and if the qualified voluntary employee contributions permitted are not higher, as a percentage of compensation, for officers, shareholders or highly compensated employees than for other participants, the qualified voluntary employee contribution feature will meet the requirement that contributions or benefits not discriminate in favor of employees who are officers, shareholders, or highly compensated. This is so because the contributions are made by the employee, not the employer.

(5) *Acceptable contributions.* A plan may accept qualified voluntary employee contributions in an amount less than the maximum deduction allowable to an individual.

(f) *Excess qualified voluntary employee contributions.* Voluntary employee contributions which exceed the amount allocable as a deduction under paragraph (b) of this section will be treated as nondeductible voluntary employee contributions to the plan. See § 1.415-6(b)(8).

(g) *Reports*—(1) *Requirements.* Each employer who maintains a plan which accepts qualified voluntary employee contributions must furnish to each employee—

(i) A report showing the amount of qualified voluntary employee contributions the employee made for the calendar year, and

(ii) A report showing the amount of withdrawals made by the employee of qualified voluntary employee contributions during the calendar year.

(2) *Times.* (i) The report required by paragraph (g)(1)(i) of this section must be furnished by the later of January 31 following the year for which the contribution was made or the time the contribution is made.

(ii) The report required by paragraph (g)(1)(ii) of this section must be furnished by January 31 following the year of withdrawal.

(3) *Authority for additional reports.* The Commissioner may require additional reports to be given to individuals or to be filed with the Service. Such reports shall be furnished at the time and in the manner that the Commissioner specifies.

(4) *Authority to modify reporting requirements.* The Commissioner may, in his discretion, modify the reporting requirements of this paragraph. Such modification may include: the matters to be reported, the forms to be used for the reports, the time when the reports must be filed or furnished, who must receive the reports, the substitution of the plan administrator for the employer as the person required to file or furnish the reports, and the deletion of some or all of the reporting requirements. The Commissioner may, in his discretion, relieve employers from making the reports required by section 219(f)(4) and this paragraph (g). This discretion includes the ability to relieve categories of employers (but not individual employers) from furnishing or filing any report required by section 219(f)(4) and this paragraph (g).

(5) *Effective date.* This paragraph shall apply to reports for calendar years after 1982.

§ 1.219(a)-6 Alternative deduction for divorced individuals.

(a) *In general.* A divorced individual may use the provisions of this section rather than § 1.219(a)-2 in computing the maximum amount he may deduct as a contribution to an individual retirement plan. A divorced individual is not required to use the provisions of this section; he may use the provisions of § 1.219(a)-2 in computing the maximum amount he may deduct as a contribution to an individual retirement plan.

(b) *Individuals who may use this section.* An individual may compute the deduction for a contribution to an individual retirement plan under this section if—

(1) An individual retirement plan was established for the benefit of the individual at least five years before the beginning of the calendar year in which the decree of divorce or separate maintenance was issued, and

(2) For at least three of the former spouse's most recent five taxable years ending before the taxable year in which the decree was issued, such former spouse was allowed a deduction under section 219(c) (or the corresponding provisions of prior law) for contributions to such individual retirement plan.

(c) *Limitations*—(1) *Amount of deduction.* An individual who computes his deduction for contributions to an individual retirement plan under this section may deduct the smallest of—

(i) The amount contributed to the individual retirement plan for the taxable year,

(ii) $1,125, or

(iii) The sum of the amount of compensation includible in the individual's gross income for the taxable year and any qualifying alimony received by the individual during the taxable year.

(2) *Contributions after age 70 ½.* No deduction is allowable for contributions to an individaul retirement plan to an individual for the taxable year of the individual if he has attained the age of 70 ½ before the close of such taxable year.

(3) *Rollover contributions.* No deduction is allowable under this section for any taxable year of an individual with respect to a rollover contribution described in section 402(a)(5), 402(a)(7), 403(a)(4), 403(b)(8), 405(d)(3), 408(d)(3), or 409(b)(3)(C).

(d) *Qualifying alimony.* For purposes of this section, the term "qualifying alimony" means amounts includible in the individual's gross income under section 71(a)(1) (relating to a decree of divorce or separate maintenance).

Par. 2. Section 1.408-2 is amended by revising paragraph (b)(1) to read as follows:

§ 1.408-2 Individual retirement accounts.

* * *

(b) * * *

(1) *Amount of acceptable contributions.* Except in the case of a contribution to a simplified employee pension described in section 408(k) and a rollover contribution described in section 408(d)(3), 402(a)(5), 402(a)(7), 403(a)(4), 403(b)(8), 405(d)(3), or 409(b)(3)(C), the trust instrument must provide that contributions may not be accepted by the trustee for the taxable year in excess of $2,000 on behalf

of any individual for whom the trust is maintained. An individual retirement account maintained as a simplified employee pension may provide for the receipt of up to the limits specified in section 408(j) for a calendar year.

* * *

Par. 3. Section 1.408-3 is amended by revision paragraph (b)(2) to read as follows:

§ 1.408-3 Individual retirement annuities.

* * *

(b) * * *

(2) *Annual premium.* Except in the case of a contribution to a simplified employee pension described in section 408(k), the annual premium on behalf of any individual for the annuity cannot exceed $2,000. Any refund of premiums must be applied before the close of the calendar year following the year of the refund toward the payment of future premiums or the purchase of additional benefits. An individual retirement annuity maintained as a simplified employee pension may provide for an annual premium of up to the limits specified in section 408(j).

* * *

Par. 4. There is added after proposed § 1.408-9, 46 FR 36209 (1981), the following new section 1.408-10:

§ 1.408-10 Investment in collectibles.

(a) *In general.* The acquisition by an individual retirement account or by an individually-directed account under a plan described in section 401(a) of any collectble shall be treated (for purposes of sections 402 and 408) as a distribution from such account in an amount equal to the cost to such account of such collectible.

(b) *Collectible defined.* For purposes of this section, the term "collectible" means—

(1) Any work of art,

(2) Any rug or antique,

(3) Any metal or gem,

(4) Any stamp or coin,

(5) Any alcoholic beverage,

(6) Any musical instrument,

(7) Any historical objects (documents, clothes, etc.), or

(8) Any other tangible personal property which the Commissioner determines is a "collectible" for purposes of this section.

(c) *Individually-directed account.* For purposes of this section, the term "individually-directed account" means an account under a plan that provides for individual accounts and that has the effect of permitting a plan participant to invest or control the manner in which the account will be invested.

(d) *Acquisition.* For purposes of this section, the term acquisition includes a purchase, exchange, contribution, or any method by which an individual retirement account or individually-directed account may directly or indirectly acquire a collectible.

(e) *Cost.* For purposes of this section, cost means fair market value.

(f) *Premature withdrawal penalty.* The ten percent penalty described in sections 72(m)(5) and 408(f)(1) shall apply in the case of a deemed distribution from an individual retirement account described in paragraph (a) of this section.

(g) *Amounts subsequently distributed.* When a collectible is actually distributed from an individual retirement account or an individually-directed account, any amounts included in gross income because of this section shall not be included in gross income at the time when the collectible is actually distributed.

(h) *Effective date.* This section applies to property acquired after December 31, 1981, in taxable years ending after such date.

* * *

Par. 6. Section 1.415-1 is amended by removing paragraph (c) and paragraph (f)(3).

Par. 7. Section 1.415-2 is amended by removing paragraph (b)(8).

Par. 8. Section 1.415-6 is amended by: (1) Revising paragraph (b)(3) to read as set forth below, (2) removing paragraph (b)(7)(iv), and (3) adding a new paragraph (b)(8) to read as set forth below.

§ 1.415-6 Limitation for defined contribution plans.

* * *

(b) *Annual additions.* * * *

(3) *Employee contributions.* For purposes of subparagraph (1)(ii) of this paragraph, the term "annual additions" includes, to the extent employee contributions would otherwise be taken into account under this section as an annual addition, mandatory employee contributions (as defined in section 411(c)(2)(C) and the regulations thereunder) as well as voluntary employee contributions. The term "annual additions" does not include—

(i) Rollover contributions (as defined in sections 402(a)(5), 403(a)(4), 403(b)(8), 405(d)(3), 408(d)(3) and 409(b)(3)(C)),

(ii) Repayments of loans made to a participant from the plan,

(iii) Repayments of amounts described in section 411(a)(7)(B) (in accordance with section 411(a)(7)(C)) and section 411(a)(3)(D) (see § 1.411(a)-7(d)(6)(iii)(B)),

(iv) The direct transfer of employee contributions from one qualified plan to another,

(v) Employee contributions to a simplified employee pension allowable as a deduction under section 219(a), or

(vi) Deductible employee contributions within the meaning of section 72(o)(5).

However, the Commissioner may in an appropriate case, considering all of the facts and circumstances, treat transactions between the plan and the employee or certain allocations to participants' accounts as giving rise to annual additions.

* * *

(8) *Qualified voluntary employee contributions.* This subparagraph provides rules for qualified voluntary employee contributions that are eligible for the deduction under section 219(a). This subparagraph is applicable only if the total of such contributions for the year is not in excess of $2,000. If such contributions are not deductible under section 219, and result in an annual addition that causes the section 415 limits to be exceeded, they will not be treated as annual additions to the extent that the portion of the contribution exceeding the limitation (and earnings thereon) is returned to the employee as soon as administratively feasible after the employer knows or has reason to know that such contributions are not deductible employee contributions within the meaning of section 72(o)(5).

* * *

Par. 9. Section 1.415-7 is amended by: (1) Removing paragraph (c)(2)(iii), (2) redesignating paragraph (c)(2)(iv) as paragraph (c)(2)(iii), and (3) removing paragraph (i).

Estate Tax Regulations

[26 CFR Part 20]

Par. 10. Section 20.2039-2 is amended by adding a new subdivision (ix) to paragraph (c)(1) to read as follows:

§ 20.2039-2 Annuities under "qualified plans" and section 403(b) annuity contracts.

* * *

(c) *Amounts excludable from the gross estate.*

(1) * * *

(ix) Any deductible employee contributions (within the meaning of section 72(o)(5)) are considered amounts contributed by the employer.

Par. 11. Section 20.2039-4 is amended by adding a new paragraph (h) to read as follows:

§ 20.2039-4 Lump sum distributions from "qualified plans;" decedents dying after December 31, 1978.

* * *

(h) *Accumulated deductible employee contributions.* For purposes of this section, a lump sum distribution includes an amount attributable to accumulated deductible employee contributions (as defined in section 72(o)(5)(B)) in any qualified plan taken into account for purposes of determining whether any distribution from that qualified plan is a lump sum distribution as determined under paragraph (b) of this section. Thus, amounts attributable to accumulated deductible employee contributions in a qualified plan under which amounts are payable in a lump sum distribution are not excludable from the decedent's gross estate under § 20.2039-2, unless the recipient makes the section 402(a)/403(c) taxation election with respect to a lump sum distribution payable from that qualified plan.

Gift Tax Regulations

[26 CFR Part 25]

Par. 12. Section 25.2517-1 is amended by adding a new subdivision (viii) to paragraph (c)(1) to read as follows:

§ 25.2517-1 Employees' annuities.

* * *

(c) *Limitation on amount excludable from gift.*

(1) * * *

(vii) Any deductible employee contributions (within the meaning of section 72(o)(5)) are considered amounts contributed by the employer.

* * *

Procedure and Administration Regulations

[26 CFR Part 301]

Par. 13. There is added after § 301.6652-3 the following new section:

§ 301.6652-4 Failure to file information with respect to qualified voluntary employee contributions.

(a) *Failure to make annual reports to employees.* In the case of a failure to make an annual report required by § 1.219(a)-5(g) which contains the information required by such section on the date prescribed therefore, there shall be paid (on notice and demand by the Secretary and in the same manner as tax) by the person failing to make such annual report an amount equal to $25 for each participant with respect to when there was a failure to make such report, multiplied by the number of years during which such failure continues.

(b) *Limitation.* The total amount imposed under this section on any person shall not exceed $10,000 with respect to any calendar year.

(signed) Roscoe L. Egger, Jr.

Commissioner of Internal Revenue

[¶ 20,137P Reserved.—Proposed Regs. §§ 53.4941(e)-1, 53.4961-1, 53.4961-2, 53.4963-1, 53.4971-1, 53.4975-1, 141.4975-13 and 301.7422-1, relating to second-tier excise taxes were formerly reproduced at this point. The final regulations appear at ¶ 13,584, 13,593F, 13,593G, 13,597F, 13,600D, 13,642, 13,648 and 13,905.]

¶ 20,137Q

Proposed regulations: Tax treatment of cafeteria plans.— The IRS issued proposed regulations on the tax treatment of cafeteria plans that were set forth in a question and answer format. Note: Q&A-21 was replaced by a new Q&A-21 in proposed regulations at ¶ 20,137R. Additional Q&As providing transition rules in accordance with changes made by the Tax Reform Act of 1984 also appeared at that paragraph. In addition, Q-8 was republished and A-8 was revised in proposed regulations reproduced at ¶ 20,227. A-8 was also amended in proposed regulations reproduced at ¶ 20,247 and in proposed regulations reproduced at ¶ 20,258. The revised proposed regulations were published in the *Federal Register* on November 7, 1997 (62 FR 60196), March 23, 2000 (65 FR 15587), and January 10, 2001 (66 FR 1923).

The proposed regulations were published in the *Federal Register* on May 7, 1984 (49 FR 19321), and withdrawn on August 6, 2007 (72 FR 43938). See proposed regulations at ¶ 20,262B.

¶ 20,137R

Proposed regulations: Cafeteria plans: Transition rules.— The IRS issued proposed regulations that amended portions of previously issued proposed regulations (¶ 20,137Q) relating to the tax treatment of cafeteria plans. The proposed regulations also provided transition rules relieving certain cafeteria plans from requirements of the earlier proposed regulations. The proposed regulations were published in the Federal Register on December 31, 1984 (49 FR 50733), and withdrawn on August 6, 2007 (72 FR 43938). See proposed regulations at ¶ 20,262B

Back reference: ¶ 9100.

¶ 20,137S

Proposed regulations: Taxation of fringe benefits.—Reproduced below is the text of proposed regulations concerning the treatment of taxable and nontaxable fringe benefits. The proposed regulations were published in the *Federal Register* on February 20, 1985 (50 FR 7073). The proposed regulations were also issued as temporary regulations under T.D. 8009 and are reproduced at ¶ 11,172A, 11,289N, 11,306, 13,530A, 13,551, 13,576, and 13,648E. Portions of the proposed regulations dealing with Temp. Reg. §§1.132-1T Q/A 4a, 1.274-5T, and 1.274-6T have been withdrawn to reflect the repeal of the contemporaneous recordkeeping requirements (¶ 23,694E). Proposed regulations which are also temporary regulations, contain the new rules on the substantiation of business expenses (¶ 20,137U).

DEPARTMENT OF THE TREASURY

Internal Revenue Service

26 CFR Parts 1, 31, and 54

[LR-216-84]

Taxation of Fringe Benefits; Withdrawal of Previous Notice of Proposed Rulemaking and Notice of Proposed Rulemaking by Cross-Reference to Temporary Regulations

AGENCY: Internal Revenue Service, Treasury.

ACTION: Withdrawal of previous notice of proposed rulemaking and notice of proposed rulemaking by cross-reference to temporary regulations.

SUMMARY: This document withdraws the notice of proposed rulemaking by cross-reference to temporary regulations that was published in the *Federal Register* on January 7, 1985 (50 FR 836), relating to the taxation of fringe benefits. Temporary regulations also published on January 7, 1985 (50 FR 747) served as the comment document for the withdrawn notice of rulemaking. In the Rules and Regulations portion of this issue of the *Federal Register,* the Internal Revenue Service is amending those temporary regulations. The text of the temporary regulations, as amended, serves as the comment document for a new notice of proposed rulemaking contained in this document.

DATES: Written comments must be delivered or mailed by April 8, 1985. The regulations are proposed to be effective as of January 1, 1985. One amendment that is published elsewhere in this issue of the *Federal Register* is proposed to be effective as of March 22, 1985.

ADDRESS: Send comments to: Commissioner of Internal Revenue, Attention: CC:LR:T (LR-216-84), Washington, D.C. 20224.

FOR FURTHER INFORMATION CONTACT: Annette J. Guarisco of the Legislation and Regulations Division, Office of Chief Counsel, Internal Revenue Service, 1111 Constitution Avenue, NW., Washington, D.C. 20224, Attention CC:LR:T (202) 566-3918 (not toll-free call).

SUPPLEMENTARY INFORMATION:

Background

Temporary regulations published in the *Federal Register* on January 7, 1985 (50 FR 747) amended Parts 1, 31, and 54 of Title 26 of the Code of Federal Regulations, relating to the taxation of fringe benefits. Those temporary regulations are amended by a Treasury decision published in the Rules and Regulations portion of this issue of the *Federal Register.*

The regulations as amended provide guidance on the treatment of taxable and nontaxable fringe benefits, including the valuation of taxable fringe benefits for purposes of income and employment tax withholding. In particular, the regulations provide special rules for valuing employer-provided automobiles, use of employer-provided automobiles or other vehicles for commuting, flights on employer-provided airplanes, and free or discounted flights on commercial airlines. In addition, the regulations provide guidance concerning when and in what manner employers must collect and pay income and employment taxes.

Sections 61, 3121, 3231, 3306, 3401, and 3501 of the Internal Revenue Code of 1954 (Code) were amended, and sections 132 and 4977 were added to the Code, by section 531 of the Tax Reform Act of 1984 (98 Stat. 877). The regulations are to be issued under the authority contained in sections 132 and 7805 of the Code (98 Stat. 878; 68A Stat. 917). The preamble to the temporary regulations published on January

7, 1985, and the preamble to the amendments published in this issue of the *Federal Register* contain a detailed explanation of the provisions of the regulations. The temporary regulations, as amended, will remain in effect until superseded by final regulations which are proposed to be based on the temporary regulations.

Comments

Before adopting these proposed regulations, consideration will be given to any written comments that are submitted (preferably eight copies) to the Commissioner of Internal Revenue. All comments will be available for public inspection and copying. Comments submitted with respect to the withdrawn notice of proposed rulemaking remain on file and need not be resubmitted. Notice of the time and place of the public hearing is published in this *Federal Register.*

Comments are invited concerning the administrability and appropriateness of the special rules contained in the temporary regulations relating to valuing employer-provided automobiles, use of employer-provided automobiles or other vehicles for commuting, flights on employer-provided airplanes, and free or discounted flights on commercial airlines. In particular, comments are requested on the manner in which employers and employees should elect to use these special valuation rules, including any necessary reporting requirements.

To use the special rule for valuing the availability of an employer-provided vehicle for commuting, the employer must require the employee to commute in the vehicle for bona fide noncompensatory business reasons. Examples of these reasons may include:

(1) The availability of an employee to respond at any time to a radio dispatch or similar call (for example, a utility company truck equipped with tools necessary to respond to a power emergency),

(2) The elimination of a significant expense for the employer because of the need to provide security for, or to garage, the vehicle (for example, the danger of vandalism in the case of a vehicle parked overnight on a construction site), and

(3) The attendant public benefit derived from such requirement (for example, a police automobile parked in public view). Suggestions of other reasons are invited.

Comments are requested relating to the allocation by employers of the income attributable to personal use of vehicles that are available to more than one employee during a period. Comments are invited concerning the appropriateness of requiring employers to allocate income attributable to personal use or, in the alternative, providing that employees may determine, together with their employer, the allocation of income attributable to personal use.

Comments are also requested concerning the definition of "officer" for purposes of determining whether an employee is a "key employee." In particular, comments are invited regarding the circumstances under which employees of certain employers, such as banks and thrift institutions, should or should not be considered officers.

Comments are also requested relating to the need for special rules for valuing other taxable fringe benefits, such as the use of an employer-subsidized eating facility that does not meet the statutory exclusion requirements, because for example, it is not available on a nondiscriminatory basis to all employees or it derives revenue that normally equals or exceeds the costs of operating the facility. In addition, comments are invited concerning the need for a special rule for valuing the use of an employer-operated athletic facility that is not eligible for an exclusion from income because, for example, substantially all the use of the facility is not by employees and their spouses and dependent children. Comments should also focus on the need for special rules for valuing international flights on employer-provided airplanes and use of employer-provided automobiles in foreign countries.

Comments are also requested relating to the definition of "employee" for purposes of the section 4977 election concerning the line-of-business restriction in section 132. Specifically, comments are requested as to whether, and to what extent, retirees should be included in the definition of employee.

Comments are also requested concerning the circumstances under which retirees should be treated as officers, owners, or highly compensated employees for purposes of the nondiscrimination rules contained in section 132.

The collection of information requirements contained in these regulations have been submitted to the Office of Management and Budget (OMB) in accordance with the requirements of the Paperwork Reduction Act of 1980. Comments on those requirements should be sent to the Office of Information and Regulatory Affairs of OMB, Attention: Desk Officer for Internal Revenue Service, New Executive Office Building, Washington, D.C. 20503. The Internal Revenue Service requests that persons submitting comments on these requirements to OMB also send copies to the Service.

Special Analyses

The Commissioner of Internal Revenue has determined that this proposed rule is not a major rule as defined in Executive Order 12291. Accordingly, a Regulatory Impact Analysis is not required.

Although this document is a notice of proposed rulemaking that solicits public comments, the Internal Revenue Service has concluded that the regulations proposed herein are interpretative and that the notice and public procedure requirements of 5 U.S.C. 553 do not apply. Accordingly, no Regulatory Flexibility Analysis is required by Chapter 6 of Title 5, United States Code.

Drafting Information

The principal author of these regulations is Annette J. Guarisco of the Legislation and Regulations Division of the Office of Chief Counsel, Internal Revenue Service. However, personnel from other offices of the Internal Revenue Service and Treasury Department participated in developing the regulations, on matters of both substance and style.

List of Subjects

26 CFR 1.61-1.281-4

Income taxes, Taxable income, Deductions, Exemptions.

26 CFR Part 31

Employment taxes, Income taxes, Lotteries, Railroad Retirement, Social Security, Unemployment tax, Withholding.

26 CFR Part 54

Excise taxes, Pensions.

The notice of proposed rulemaking by cross-reference to temporary regulations that was published in the *Federal Register* on January 7, 1985 (50 FR 836), relating to the taxation of fringe benefits, is hereby withdrawn. The withdrawn notice of proposed rulemaking is superseded by the notice of proposed rulemaking by cross-reference to temporary regulations that is contained in this document.

Roscoe L. Egger, Jr.,

Commissioner of Internal Revenue.

[FR Doc. 85-4138 Filed 2-15-85; 8:45 am]

[The proposed regulations were also issued as temporary regulations and are reproduced at ¶ 11,172A, 11,289N, 11,306, 13,530A, and 13,648E.]

¶ 20,137T

Proposed regulations: Cost recovery deductions and investment tax credit: Automobiles used in trade or business: Use of "listed property" for business and personal purposes.—Reproduced below is the text of proposed regulations relating to the limitation on the amount of cost recovery deductions and investment tax credit allowed to taxpayers who purchase passenger automobiles for use in a trade or business or for use in the production of income, and to the limitations on cost recovery deductions and the investment tax credit allowed to taxpayers who use "listed property" for both business and personal purposes. The proposed regulations, which are also temporary regulations, were published in the *Federal Register* on February 20, 1985 (50 FR 7071). Temporary regulations which serve as the text for these proposals are at ¶ 11,357G, 11,357H and 11,358A—11,358D. Portions of the proposed regulations dealing with Temp. Reg. §§1.132-1T Q/A 4a, 1.274-5T, and 1.274-6T have been withdrawn to reflect the repeal of the contemporaneous recordkeeping requirements (¶ 23,694E). Proposed regulations, which are also temporary regulations, contain the new rules on the substantiation of business expenses (¶ 20,137V).

DEPARTMENT OF THE TREASURY

Internal Revenue Service

26 CFR Part 1

[LR-145-84]

Limitation on Amount of Depreciation and Investment Tax Credit for Luxury Automobiles; Limitation When Certain Property Is Used For Personal Purposes

AGENCY: Internal Revenue Service, Treasury.

ACTION: Withdrawal of previous notice of proposed rulemaking and notice of proposed rulemaking by cross-reference to temporary regulations.

SUMMARY: This document withdraws the notice of proposed rulemaking by cross-reference to temporary regulations that was published in the *Federal Register* on October 24, 1984 (49 FR 42743), relating to the limitation on the amount of cost recovery deductions and investment tax credit allowed to taxpayers who purchase passenger automobiles for use in a trade or business or for use in the production of income, and to the limitations on cost recovery deductions and the investment tax credit allowed to taxpayers who use "listed property" for both business and personal purposes. The text of temporary income tax regulations under sections 274 and 280F of the Internal Revenue Code of 1954, also published on that date (49 FR 41701), served as the comment document for the withdrawn notice of proposed rulemaking. In the Rules and Regulations portion of this issue of the *Federal Register,* the Internal Revenue Service is amending the temporary regulations under sections 274 and 280F that were published on October 24, 1984, and issuing a new temporary regulation under section 274. The text of the new and amended temporary regulations serves as

the comment document for a new notice of proposed rulemaking contained in this document.

DATES: Proposed effective dates. The regulations relating to the limitations on the investment tax credit and recovery deductions are proposed to be effective in general for "listed property" placed in service or leased after June 18, 1984. Those regulations would not apply to certain property acquired or leased pursuant to a binding contract in effect on June 18, 1984. The regulations relating to substantiation requirements for the use of "listed property" are proposed to be effective for taxable years beginning after December 31, 1984.

Dates for comments. Written comments must be delivered or mailed by April 8, 1985.

ADDRESS: Send comments to: Commissioner of Internal Revenue. Attention: CC:LR:T (LR-145-84), Washington, D.C. 20224.

FOR FURTHER INFORMATION CONTACT: George T. Magnatta (with respect to cost recovery deduction questions) (202-566-6456), Michel A. Dazé (with respect to investment tax credit or leasing questions) (202-566-3829), or Cynthia E. Grigsby (with respect to definitional or substantiation questions) (202-566-3935), of the Legislation and Regulations Division, Office of the Chief Counsel, Internal Revenue Service, 1111 Constitution Avenue, NW., Washington, D.C. 20224 (Attention: CC:LR:T).

SUPPLEMENTARY INFORMATION:

Background

Temporary regulations published in the *Federal Register* on October 24, 1984 (49 FR 42701) amended the Income Tax Regulations (26 CFR Part 1) to reflect amendments to section 274 of the Internal Revenue Code of 1954, relating to substantiation requirements, and the addition to the Code of section 280F, relating to limitations on cost recovery deductions and the investment tax credit for certain property. Those temporary regulations are amended and a new temporary regulation under section 274 is added by a Treasury decision published in the Rules and Regulations portion of this issue of the *Federal Register*. The preamble to the temporary regulations published on October 24, 1984, and the preamble to the amendments published in this issue of the *Federal Register* contain a detailed explanation of the provisions of the regulations. The temporary regulations, as amended, will remain in effect until superseded by final regulations which are proposed to be based on the temporary regulations and issued under the authority contained in sections 280F and 7805 of the Internal Revenue Code of 1954 (98 Stat. 494, 26 U.S.C. 280F; 68A Stat. 917, 26 U.S.C. 7805).

Comments

Before these proposed amendments are adopted, consideration will be given to any written comments that are submitted (preferably eight copies) to the Commissioner of Internal Revenue. All comments will be available for public inspection and copying. Comments submitted with respect to the withdrawn notice or proposed rulemaking remain on file and need not be resubmitted.

Certain types of vehicles are excluded from the definition of "passenger automobile" including, *inter alia,* any truck or van, if the regulations so specify. Comments are invited as to the types of trucks or vans that should be excluded from the definition of "passenger automobile."

Comments are also invited with respect to the manner of allocating the use of "listed property" between the business and personal use of the property. Specifically, the Internal Revenue Service is interested in suggestions as to whether different measures of business and personal use other than those provided in the temporary regulations are appropriate.

The temporary regulations (§ 1.274-6T) published in this issue of the *Federal Register* prescribed certain methods that a taxpayer may use to satisfy the "adequate contemporaneous record" requirement of section 274(d)(4). For example, if an employer provides an automobile for use by an employee who spends most of a normal business day using the automobile in connection with the employer's business, the employer may treat the automobile as used 70 percent for business and 30 percent for personal purposes. The employer must also determine an amount to be included in the employee's income for the availability of the automobile for personal use. It is thought that the employee should have the opportunity to document a greater amount of business use and thus reduce the amount of the taxable fringe benefit. Comments are requested as to whether the regulations should require an employer to notify an employee if the employer is using one of the methods prescribed in § 1.274-6T. Comments are also welcome on whether the regulations should establish a procedure for employers and employees to elect the same method at the beginning of each calendar year.

In the case of a fleet of vehicles owned or leased by an employer and used by employees for most of a normal business day in connection with the employer's trade or business, the Service is considering an alternative method for the employer to satisfy its "adequate contemporaneous record" requirement. In lieu of using the percentages prescribed in § 1.274-6T(b)(3) of the temporary regulations, an employer would be able to establish different percentages for direct use of a vehicle in the employer's trade or business and personal use by employees by a method similar to the following:

(1) The employer would identify a class of at least 100 vehicles that are physically similar and that are used in a similar fashion.

(2) In each taxable year, the employer would choose a random sample of the class of vehicles using accepted sampling techniques.

(3) The sample size would preferably be at least 250 vehicles, or one-half the class in the case of fleets of less than 500 vehicles, and

(4) The percentage of average business use of the vehicles in the sample would apply to the class if determined from records of actual use kept for these vehicles. Comments are invited with respect to this alternative method of satisfying the "adequate contemporaneous record" requirement.

A public hearing had been scheduled to be held on February 5, 1985, at the national office of the Internal Revenue Service. That hearing is postponed and will be rescheduled at a later time in order to provide the public an opportunity to consider the amendments proposed by this notice. Notice of the time and place of the hearing is published in this *Federal Register*.

The collection of information requirements contained in the temporary regulations have been submitted to the Office of Management and Budget (OMB) for review under Section 3504(h) of the Paperwork Reduction Act. Comments on these requirements should be sent to the Office of Information and Regulatory Affairs of OMB, Attention: Desk Officer for Internal Revenue Service, New Executive Office Building, Washington, D.C. 20503. The Internal Revenue Service requests that persons submitting comments on the requirements to OMB also send copies of those comments to the Service.

Executive Order 12291 and Regulatory Flexibility Act

The Commissioner of Internal Revenue has determined that this proposed rule is not a major rule as defined in Executive Order 12291 and that a Regulatory Impact Analysis is therefore not required.

Although this document is a notice of proposed rulemaking which solicits public comment, the Internal Revenue Service has concluded that the regulations proposed herein are interpretative and that the notice and public procedure requirements of 5 U.S.C. 553 do not apply. Accordingly, these proposed regulations do not constitute regulations subject to the Regulatory Flexibility Act (5 U.S.C. Chapter 6).

List of Subjects in 26 CFR §§ 1.61-1—1.281-4.

Income taxes, Taxable income, Deductions, Exemptions. The notice of proposed rulemaking by cross-reference to temporary regulations that was published in the *Federal Register* on October 24, 1984 (49 FR 42743), relating to the limitation on the amount of cost recovery deductions and investment tax credit allowed for passenger automobiles and to the limitations on cost recovery deductions and the investment tax credit allowed for "listed property", is hereby withdrawn. The withdrawn notice of proposed rulemaking is superseded by the notice of proposed rulemaking by cross-reference to temporary regulations that is contained in this document.

Roscoe L. Egger, Jr.,

Commissioner of Internal Revenue.

[FR Doc. 85-4137 Filed 2-15-85; 8:45 am]

¶ 20,137U

Proposed regulations: Taxation of fringe benefits.—Reproduced below is the text of proposed regulations dealing with rules for valuing the commuting use of employer-provided vehicles and rules relating to working condition fringe exclusions. The proposed regulations were published in the *Federal Register* on November 6, 1985 (50 FR 46087). The proposed regulations were also issued as temporary regulations under T.D. 8061 and are reproduced at ¶ 11,172A and 11,289N.

[4830-01]

[Final draft of 9-18-85]

DEPARTMENT OF THE TREASURY

Internal Revenue Service

[26 CFR PART 1]

[LR-216-84]

Taxation of Fringe Benefits; Notice of Proposed Rulemaking

AGENCY: Internal Revenue Service, Treasury.

ACTION: Notice of proposed rulemaking by cross-reference to temporary regulations.

SUMMARY: In the Rules and Regulations portion of this issue of the FEDERAL REGISTER, the Internal Revenue Service is issuing temporary income tax regulations under section 61 and 132. The temporary regulations under section 61 provide rules for valuation of the commuting use of employer-provided vehicles. The temporary regulations under section 132 provide rules relating to working condition fringe exclusions. The text of the temporary regulations serves as the comment document for the notice of proposed rulemaking contained in this document.

DATES: Proposed effective date: The regulations are generally proposed to be effective as of January 1, 1985.

Dates for comments and requests for a public hearing: Written comments and requests for a public hearing must be delivered or mailed by January 5, 1986.

ADDRESS: Send comments and requests for a public hearing to Commissioner of Internal Revenue, 1111 Constitution Ave., N.W., Washington, D.C. 20224 Attention: CC:LR:T (LR-216-84).

FOR FURTHER INFORMATION CONTACT: Annette J. Guarisco of the Legislation and Regulations Division, Office of Chief Counsel, Internal Revenue Service, (202) 566-3918 (not a toll-free number).

SUPPLEMENTARY INFORMATION:

Background

The temporary regulations in the Rules and Regulations portion of this issue of the *Federal Register* amend Part 1 of Title 26 of the Code of Federal Regulations. The temporary regulations are designated by a "T" following their section citation. The final regulations, which this document proposes to base on those temporary regulations, would amend Part 1 of Title 26 of the Code of Federal Regulations.

Section 61 was amended and section 132 was added to the Internal Revenue Code of 1954 ("Code") by section 531 of the Tax Reform Act of 1984 (Pub. Law 98-369, 98 Stat. *877*). Section 274(d) of the Code was amended by section 179 of the Tax Reform Act of 1984 (99 Stat. 494) and section 1(a) of the Repeal of Contemporaneous Recordkeeping Requirements (Pub. Law 99-44, 99 Stat. 77). Because of the relationship between sections 274(d) and 132 of the Code, the temporary regulations under section 132 are amended.

Comments and Requests for a Public Hearing

Before these proposed amendments are adopted, consideration will be given to any written comments that are submitted (preferably eight copies) to the Commissioner of Internal Revenue. All comments will be available for public inspection and copying.

A public hearing will be held upon written request to the Commissioner by any person who has submitted written comments. If a public hearing is held, notice of the time and place will be published in the *Federal Register*.

The collection of information requirements contained in the temporary regulations have been submitted to the Office of Management and Budget (OMB) for review under the Paperwork Reduction Act of 1980. Comments on those requirements should be sent to the Office of Information and Regulatory Affairs, Attention: Desk Officer for Internal Revenue Service, New Executive Office Building, Washington, D.C. 20503. The Internal Revenue Service requests that persons submitting comments on the requirements to OMB also send copies of those comments to the Service.

Executive Order 12291 and Regulatory Flexibility Act

The Commissioner of Internal Revenue has determined that this proposed rule is not a major rule as defined in Executive Order 12291 and that a Regulatory Impact Analysis is therefore not required.

Although this document is a notice of proposed rulemaking which solicits public comments, the Internal Revenue Service has concluded that the regulations proposed herein are interpretative and that the notice and public procedure requirements of 5 U.S.C. 553 do not apply. Accordingly, these proposed regulations do not constitute regulations subject to the Regulatory Flexibility Act (5 U.S.C. Chapter 6).

Drafting Information

The principal author of this document is Annette J. Guarisco of the Legislation and Regulations Division of the Office of Chief Counsel, Internal Revenue Service. However, personnel from other offices of the Internal Revenue Service and Treasury Department participated in developing the regulations on matters of both substance and style.

List of Subjects in 26 CFR §§ 1.61-1—1.281-4

Income taxes, Taxable income, Deductions, Exemptions.

Roscoe L. Egger, Jr.

Commissioner of Internal Revenue

¶ 20,137V

Proposed regulations: Taxation of fringe benefits.—Reproduced below is the text of proposed regulations concerning rules for the substantiation of deductions or credit claims with respect to traveling away from home, certain entertainment expenditures, business-related gifts, and "listed property". The proposed regulations were published in the *Federal Register* on November 6, 1985 (50 FR 46088). The proposed regulations were also issued as temporary regulations under T.D. 8061 and are reproduced at ¶ 11,306, ¶ 11,357G, and ¶ 11,357H.

IRS Proposed Reg. § 1.274-5(k) and (l) as originally proposed here were re-proposed in 2008 IRS proposed regulations (REG-106897-08, 73 FR 32500, June 9, 2008). The corresponding provisions of the below proposed regulations were withdrawn.

[4830-01]

[Final Draft of 9-17-85]

DEPARTMENT OF THE TREASURY

Internal Revenue Service

[26 CFR Parts 1 and 602]

[LR-145-84]

Limitation on Amount of Depreciation and Investment Tax Credit for Luxury Automobiles; Limitation When Certain Property Is Used for Personal Purposes

Notice of Proposed Rulemaking

AGENCY: Internal Revenue Service, Treasury.

ACTION: Notice of proposed rulemaking by cross-reference to temporary regulations.

SUMMARY: In the Rules and Regulations portion of this issue of the *Federal Register,* the Internal Revenue Service is issuing temporary income tax regulations under section 274 and amending other temporary regulations under sections 162 and 280F. The temporary regulations under section 274 provide rules for the substantiation of any deduction or credit claimed with respect to traveling away from home, certain entertainment expenditures, business-related gifts, and "listed property." The amendment to the temporary regulations under section 162 relate to the deductibility of certain expenses incurred by employers and employees with respect to noncash fringe benefits. The amendments to the temporary regulations under section 280F provide new limitations on the deductions of lessees of passenger automobiles. The text of the new and amended temporary regulations serves as the comment document for the notice of proposed rulemaking contained in this document.

DATES: Proposed effective dates: The regulations under section 162 are proposed to be effective as of January 1, 1985. The regulations under section 274 relating to the substantiation of deductions and credits claimed with respect to certain business expenditures are proposed to be effective generally for taxable years beginning after December 31, 1985. The amendments relating to the limitations on the deductions of lessees of passenger automobiles are proposed to be effective generally for automobiles leased after April 2, 1935.

Dates for comments and requests for a public hearing: Written comments and requests for a public hearing must be delivered or mailed by January 5, 1986.

ADDRESS: Send comments and requests for a public hearing to Commissioner of Internal Revenue, Attention: CC:LR:T (LR-145-84), Washington, D.C. 20224.

FOR FURTHER INFORMATION CONTACT: Michel A. Daz'e of the Legislation and Regulations Division, Office of the Chief Counsel, Internal Revenue Service, 1111 Constitution Avenue, N.W., Washington, D.C. 20224 (202-566-6456, not a toll-free call).

SUPPLEMENTARY INFORMATION:

Background

The temporary regulations published in the Rules and Regulations portion of this issue of the *Federal Register* amend the Income Tax Regulations (26 CFR Part 1) to reflect amendments to section 274 of the Internal Revenue Code of 1954, relating to substantiation requirements, and to section 280F relating to limitations on cost recovery deductions and the investment tax credit allowed for passenger automobiles. The temporary regulations issued under section 274 reflect amendments to section 274(d) by section 179 of the Tax Reform Act of 1984 (Pub. L. 98-369, 98 Stat. 494) and by sections 1(a) and 2 of the Repeal of Contemporaneous Recordkeeping Requirements (Pub. L. 99-44, 99 Stat. 77). The amendments to the temporary regulations under section 280F reflect amendments to that section by section 4 of Public Law 99-44. The preamble to the temporary regulations contains an explanation of the provisions of those regulations. The temporary regulations will remain in effect until superseded by final regulations which are proposed to be based on the temporary regulations.

Before amendment by the Tax Reform Act of 1984 and Public Law 99-44, section 274(d) required that any deduction for expenses incurred for (1) traveling away from home, (2) entertainment, amusement, or recreation activities or the use of a facility in connection with those activities, or (3) business-related gifts be substantiated by adequate records or sufficient evidence corroborating a taxpayer's own statement. Section 274(d) did not apply to vehicles when used in local travel. Instead, the more general substantiation standards under section 162 were applicable. As amended, section 274(d) requires, for taxable years beginning after December 31, 1985, that any deduction or credit claimed for the expenses described above and for expenses incurred with respect to "listed property" be substantiated by adequate records or sufficient evidence corroborating a taxpayer's own statement. Section 274(d) will then apply to vehicles used in local travel.

First adopted by Treasury decision in 1962, § 1.274-5 of the Income Tax Regulations reflects the addition of section 274(d) to the Code. Amendments to § 1.274-5 are proposed to conform the regulations to the 1984 Act and to Public Law 99-44. For the convenience of taxpayers who must comply with the section 274(d) substantiation requirements, the proposed amendments are incorporated into § 1.274-5 and published in full in the format of a temporary regulation. New material is indicated by underlining.

Comments and Requests for a Public Hearing

Before these proposed amendments are adopted, consideration will be given to any written comments that are submitted (preferably eight copies) to the Commissioner of Internal Revenue. All comments will be available for public inspection and copying.

Comments are invited, however, on only those portions of new temporary § 1.274-5T that are amendments to § 1.274-5 to reflect the recent legislation. Specifically, comments are invited on the following provisions that are included among those amendments:

Paragraph (b)(6), the elements of an expenditure or use with respect to listed property,

Paragraph (c)(2)(ii)(C), substantiation of business use,

Paragraph (c)(3)(ii), sampling rule for the substantiation of business use,

Paragraph (c)(6)(i)(C), aggregation of business use,

Paragraph (d)(2) and (3), disclosure on tax returns of certain information with respect to the use of listed property,

Paragraph (e), substantiation of working condition fringe exclusions and certain employee deductions, and

Paragraph (k), other vehicles that may be designated as qualified nonpersonal use vehicles.

Comments are also invited on the provisions of § 1.162-25T and § 1.274-6T and the amendments to the temporary regulations under section 280F. Comments have been received previously on the limitations applicable to lessees contained in § 1.280F-5T of those temporary regulations. The comments have pointed out that separate limitations are not applicable to lessees to whom lessors have elected to pass through the investment credit. The Internal Revenue Service intends to issue an announcement in the near future providing separate limitations for these lessees.

In the case of a fleet of vehicles owned or leased by an employer and used by employees in connection with the employer's business, the Service is considering an alternative method for the employer to satisfy its substantiation requirements. An employer would be able to establish the business use of each vehicle in the fleet and the personal use by an employee by a method similar to the following:

(1) The employer would identify a class of at least 100 vehicles that are physically similar and that are used in a similar fashion,

(2) No vehicle in the class would have a fair market value greater than $16,500,

(3) At the beginning of each taxable year, the employer would select from the class a random sample using accepted sampling techniques,

(4) The sample size would preferably be at least 250 vehicles, or one-half the class in the case of fleets of less than 500 vehicles (but in no event less than 50 vehicles),

(5) The taxpayer would determine the business use of each vehicle in the sample from adequate records maintained for each vehicle, and

(6) The average of the business use of each vehicle in the sample would be the business use of each vehicle in the class.

Comments are invited with respect to this alternative method of satisfying the substantiation requirements of section 274(d).

A public hearing will be held upon written request to the Commissioner by any person who submits written comments. If a public hearing is held, notice of the time and place will be published in the FEDERAL REGISTER.

The collection of information requirements contained in the temporary regulations have been submitted to the office of Management and Budget (OMB) for review under section 3504(b) of the Paperwork Reduction Act. Comments on these requirements should be sent to the Office of Information and Regulatory Affairs, Attention: Desk Officer for Internal Revenue Service, New Executive Office Building, Washington, D.C. 20503. The Internal Revenue Service requests that persons submitting comments on the requirements to OMB also send copies of those comments to the Service.

Executive Order 12291 and Regulatory Flexibility Act

The Commissioner of Internal Revenue has determined that this proposed rule is not a major rule as defined in Executive Order 12291 and that a Regulatory Impact Analysis is therefore not required.

Although this document is a notice of proposed rulemaking which solicits public comment, the Internal Revenue Service has concluded that the regulations proposed herein are interpretative and that the notice and public procedure requirements of 5 U.S.C. 553 do not apply. Accordingly, these proposed regulations do not constitute regulations subject to the Regulatory Flexibility Act (5 U.S.C. Chapter 6).

Drafting Information

The principal author of this document is Michel A. Dazé of the Legislation and Regulations Division of the Office of Chief Counsel, Internal Revenue Service. However, personnel from other offices of the Internal Revenue Service and Treasury Department participated in developing the regulations on matters of both substance and style.

List of Subjects

26 CFR §§ 1.61-1—1.281-4

Income taxes, Taxable income, Deductions, Exemptions.

List of Subjects

26 CFR Part 602

Reporting and recordkeeping requirements.

Roscoe L. Egger, Jr.

Commissioner of Internal Revenue

[¶ 20,137W Reserved.—Proposed regulations relating to taxation of fringe benefits, were formerly reproduced at this point. The final regulations are at ¶ 11,172, 11,172A, 11,176, 11,289N-1—11,289N-8, 11,289O-11,289O-8.]

[¶ 20,137X Reserved.—Proposed regulations relating to certain restrictions on an employee's right to receive optional forms of benefit under qualified plans were formerly reproduced here. The final regulations appear at ¶ 11,716E and 12,233.]

¶ 20,137Y

Proposed regulations: Employee benefit provisions of the Tax Reform Act of 1984.—Following is the text of proposed regulations on the employee benefit provisions of the Tax Reform Act of 1984. The proposed regulations concern vacation pay, the economic performance requirement for certain employee benefits, group-term life insurance, welfare benefit plans, unfunded deferred benefits, requirements for exempt organizations, rollovers, distributions, the estate tax exclusion, collective bargaining agreements, ESOPs, and treatment of employer and employee benefit associations. The proposed regulations were also issued as temporary regulations under T.D. 8073 and are reproduced at ¶ 11,209, ¶ 11,234, ¶ 11,289S, ¶ 11,304A, ¶ 11,751A, ¶ 11,851A, ¶ 11,859A, ¶ 11,865A, ¶ 11,867, ¶ 11,870, ¶ 12,905, ¶ 12,969, ¶ 13,154E, ¶ 13,194, ¶13,212C, ¶ 13,383, ¶ 13,502D, ¶ 13,648C, ¶ 13,648G. The effective dates of the temporary regulations and the introductory material preceding the temporary regulations are at ¶ 23,073. The proposed regulations were published in the *Federal Register* on February 4, 1986 (51 FR 4391). The IRS withdrew the proposed regulation relating to Code Sec. 512 UBTI requirements and replaced it with a new proposed regulation on February 6, 2014 (79 FR 7110).

[4830-01]

[Final Draft of 9-27-85]

DEPARTMENT OF THE TREASURY

Internal Revenue Service

[26 CFR Parts 1, 20, 54, 301 and 602]

[EE-96-85]

Effective Dates And Other Issues Arising Under The Employee Benefit Provisions Of The Tax Reform Act Of 1984

NOTICE OF PROPOSED RULEMAKING

AGENCY: Internal Revenue Service, Treasury.

ACTION: Notice of proposed rulemaking by cross reference to temporary regulations.

SUMMARY: In the Rules and Regulations portion of this issue of the *Federal Register,* the Internal Revenue Service is issuing temporary regulations relating to effective dates and certain other issues arising under the employee benefit provisions of the Tax Reform Act of 1984. The text of those temporary regulations also serves as the comment document for this notice of proposed rulemaking.

DATES: Written comments and requests for a public hearing must be delivered or mailed by April 7, 1986. The regulations are proposed to be effective on varying date provided in the temporary regulations.

ADDRESS: Send comments and requests for a public hearing to Commissioner of Internal Revenue, Attn: CC:LR:T (EE-96-85), 1111 Constitution Avenue N.W., Washington, D.C. 20224.

FOR FURTHER INFORMATION CONTACT: John T. Ricotta of the Employee Plans and Exempt Organizations Division, Office of Chief Counsel, Internal Revenue Service, 1111 Constitution Ave., N.W., Washington, D.C. 20224, Attention: CC:LR:T (EE-96-85), telephone: 202-566-3544 (not a toll-free number).

SUPPLEMENTARY INFORMATION:

Background

The temporary regulations provide guidance concerning the economic performance requirement for certain employee benefits under section 461(h) of the Internal Revenue Code of 1954 (Code), as added by section 91 of the Tax Reform Act of 1984 (Act) (P.L. 98-369, 98 Stat. 598); the transitional rule for vested accrued vacation pay under section 463 of the Code, as amended by section 91(i) of the Act (P.L. 98-369, 98 Stat. 609); the treatment of group-term life insurance purchased for employees under section 79 of the Code, as amended by section 223 of the Act (P.L. 98-369, 98 Stat. 775); the treatment of funded welfare benefit plans under sections 419 and 419A of the Code, as added by section 511 of the Act (P.L. 98-369, 98 Stat. 854); the treatment of unfunded deferred benefits under sections 404(b) and 162 of the Code, as amended by section 512 of the Act (P.L. 98-369, 98 Stat. 862); additional requirements for tax-exempt status of certain organizations under section 505 of the Code, as added by section 513 of the Act (P.L.

98-369, 98 Stat. 863); rollovers of partial distributions under sections 402 and 403 of the Code, as amended by section 522 of the Act (P.L. 98-369, 98 Stat. 868); distributions where substantially all contributions are employee contributions under section 72 of the Code, as amended by section 523 of the Act (P.L. 98-369, 98 Stat. 871); repeal of the estate tax exclusion for qualified plan benefits under section 2039 of the Code, as amended by section 525 of the Act (P.L. 98-369, 98 Stat. 873); determination of whether there is a collective bargaining agreement under section 7701(a)(46) of the Code, as added by section 526(c) of the Act (P.L. 98-369, 98 Stat. 881); nonrecognition of gain on stock sold to an employee stock ownership plan (ESOP) under section 1042 of the Code, as added by section 541 of the Act (P.L. 98-369, 98 Stat. 887); deductibility of dividends relating to ESOPs under sections 404 and 3405 of the Code, as amended by section 542 of the Act (P.L. 98-369, 98 Stat. 890); exclusion of interest on ESOP loans under section 133 of the Code, as added by section 543 of the Act (P.L. 98-369, 98 Stat. 894); treatment of an employer and an employee benefit association as related under section 1239 of the Code, as amended by section 557 of the Act (P.L. 98-369, 98 Stat. 898); and technical corrections to the pension provisions of the Tax Equity and Fiscal Responsibility Act of 1982 under sections 713 and 715 of the Act (P.L. 98-369, 98 Stat. 955, 966). The proposed regulations are issued under the authority contained in section 7805 of the Code (26 U.S.C. § 7805). For the text of the temporary regulations, see F.R. Doc. (—) published in the Rules and Regulations portion of this issue of the Federal Register.

Special Analysis

The Commissioner of Internal Revenue has determined that this proposed rule is not a major rule as defined in Executive Order 12291 and that a Regulatory Impact Analysis is therefore not required. Although this document is a notice of proposed rulemaking which solicits public comment, the Internal Revenue Service has concluded that the regulations proposed herein are interpretative and that the notice and public procedure requirements of 5 U.S.C. 553 do not apply. Accordingly, these proposed regulations do not constitute regulations subject to the Regulatory Flexibility Act (5 U.S.C. Chapter 6).

Comments and Requests for a Public Hearing

Before the adoption of these proposed regulations, consideration will be given to any written comments that are submitted (preferably eight copies) to the Commissioner of Internal Revenue. All comments will be available for public inspection and copying. A public hearing will be held upon written request to the Commissioner by any person who has submitted written comments. If a public hearing is held, notice of the time and place will be published in the Federal Register. The collection of information requirements contained herein have been submitted to the Office of Management and Budget (OMB) for review under section 3504(h) of the Paperwork Reduction Act. Comments on the requirements should be sent to the Office of Information and Regulatory Affairs, of OMB, Attention: Desk Officer for Internal Revenue Service, New Executive Office Building, Washington, D.C. 20503. The Internal Revenue Service requests persons submitting comments to OMB also to send copies of the comments to the Service.

Roscoe L. Egger, Jr.

Commissioner of Internal Revenue

¶ 20,137Z

Proposed regulations: Mortality table: Deferred payments of life insurance proceeds: Exclusion from gross income of deferred payments.—Following is the text of proposed regulations on the mortality table to be used in determining the extent to which deferred payments of life insurance proceeds are excluded from gross income. The proposed regulations were also issued as temporary regulations under T.D. 8161 and are reproduced at ¶ 11,256D. The introductory material preceding the temporary regulations is at ¶ 23,077. The proposed regulations were published in the *Federal Register* on September 21, 1987 (52 FR 35447).

DEPARTMENT OF THE TREASURY

Internal Revenue Service

[26 CFR Part 1]

[LR-I35-86]

Mortality Table Used to Determine Exclusion for Deferred Payments of Life Insurance Proceeds

Notice of Proposed Rulemaking

AGENCY: Internal Revenue Service, Treasury.

ACTION: Notice of proposed rulemaking by cross-reference to temporary regulations.

SUMMARY: In the Rules and Regulations portion of this issue of the FEDERAL REGISTER, the Internal Revenue Service is issuing temporary regulations that prescribe the mortality table to be used in determining the extent to which deferred payments of life insurance proceeds are excluded from gross income. The text of the temporary regulations also serves as the comment document for this notice of proposed rulemaking.

DATES: Written comments and requests for a public hearing must be delivered or mailed by [60 DAYS AFTER DATE OF PUBLICATION OF THIS DOCUMENT IN THE FEDERAL REGISTER]. The regulations are proposed to be effective on October 23, 1986, and to apply to amounts received with respect to deaths occurring after October 22, 1986, in taxable years ending after October 22, 1986.

ADDRESS: Send comments and requests for a public hearing to: Commissioner of Internal Revenue, Attention: CC:LR:T (LR-135-86), Washington, D.C. 20224.

FOR FURTHER INFORMATION CONTACT: Sharon L. Hall of the Legislation and Regulations Division, Office of Chief Counsel, Internal Revenue Service, 1111 Constitution Avenue, N.W., Washington, D.C. 20224 (Attention: CC:LR:T), (202) 566-3288 (not a toll-free call).

SUPPLEMENTARY INFORMATION

Background

The temporary regulations (designated by a "T" following the section citation) in the Rules and Regulations section of this issue of the FEDERAL REGISTER amend the Income Tax Regulations (26 CFR Part 1) to provide rules under sections 101(d) of the Internal Revenue Code of 1986, as amended by section 1001(b) of the Tax Reform Act of 1986 (100 Stat. 2387). This document proposes to adopt those temporary regulations as final regulations. Accordingly, the text of the temporary regulations serves as the comment document for this notice of proposed rulemaking. The preamble to the temporary regulations provides a discussion of the proposed and temporary rules.

For the text of the temporary regulations, see FR Doc. (T.D. 8161) published in the Rules and Regulations section of this issue of the FEDERAL REGISTER.

Special Analysis

The Commissioner of Internal Revenue has determined that this proposed rule is not a major rule as defined in Executive Order 12291 and that a regulatory impact analysis therefore is not required. Although this document is a notice of proposed rulemaking that solicits public comment, the Internal Revenue Service has concluded that the regulations proposed herein are interpretative and that the notice and public procedure requirements of 5 U.S.C. 553 do not apply. Accordingly, these proposed regulations do not constitute regulations subject to the Regulatory Flexibility Act (5 U.S.C. chapter 6).

Comments and Requests for a Public Hearing

Before these proposed regulations are adopted, consideration will be given to any written comments that are submitted (preferably eight copies) to the Commissioner of Internal Revenue. All comments will be available for public inspection and copying. A public hearing will be held upon written request to the Commissioner by any person who has submitted written comments. If a public hearing is held, notice of the time and place will be published in the FEDERAL REGISTER.

Drafting Information

The principal author of these proposed regulations is Sharon L. Hall of the Legislation and Regulations Division of the Office of Chief Counsel, Internal Revenue Service. However, personnel from other offices of the Internal Revenue Service and Treasury Department participated in developing the regulations on matters of both substance and style.

List of Subjects in 26 CFR §§ 1.61-1—1.281-4

Income taxes, Taxable income, Deductions, Exemptions.

(signed) Lawrence B. Gibbs

Commissioner of Internal Revenue

[¶ 20,138 Reserved.—**Proposed regulations relating to employees of organizations under common control were formerly reproduced at this paragraph. The final regulations are at ¶ 12,353—12,358.**]

[¶ 20,138A Reserved.—**A notice of proposed rulemaking by cross-reference to temporary regulations related to notice, election, and consent rules under the Retirement Equity Act of 1984 was formerly reproduced at this paragraph. The temporary regulations were removed by T.D. 8219 (53 FR 31837).**]

[¶ 20,138B Reserved.—**Proposed and temporary regulations under Code Sec. 401 relating to effective dates, transitional rules, restrictions on distributions, and other issues arising under the Retirement Equity Act of 1984 were formerly reproduced here. The temporary regulations, which served as the text of the proposed regulations, were removed by T.D. 8219 (53 FR 31837).**]

[¶ 20,138C Reserved.—**Proposed regulations relating to cash or deferred arrangements under Code Sec. 401(k) and new nondiscrimination rules for employee contributions and matching contributions made to employee plans were formerly reproduced here. The final regulations now appear at ¶ 11,720J, 11,730, 11,731, 11,732, 11,732A, 11,732B, 11,751, 11,755-3, 11,755-4, 12,214, 12,233V, 12,406, 12,503, 13,648K and 13,648K-1.**]

[¶ 20,139 Reserved.—**Proposed Reg. § 1.408-2(b)(2)(ii), relating to certain trustees of individual retirement accounts, was formerly reproduced here. The final regulation appears at ¶ 12,054.**]

[¶ 20,140 Reserved.—**Proposed Reg. § 31.3401(a)-1, relating to federal income tax withholding on remuneration paid in the form of wage continuation payments, was formerly reproduced at this point. The final regulation appears at ¶ 13,551.**]

[¶ 20,141 Reserved.—**Proposed Reg. § 1.408-1(d)(4) (redesignated as Reg. § 1.408-6(d)(4) by T.D. 7714), relating to individual retirement account disclosure statements, was formerly reproduced at this point. The final regulation appears at ¶ 12,058.**]

[¶ 20,142 Reserved.—**Proposals to conform the regulations to provisions of section 101(j) of the Tax Reform Act of 1969 (83 Stat. 526) and section 2003(b) of the Pension Reform Act of 1974 were formerly reported at this point. The final regulations now appear at ¶ 11,252, 11,701, 11,712, 13,161, 13,162, 13,181—13,189, 13,502 and 13,521.**]

[¶ 20,142A Reserved.—Proposed regulations relating to the minimum participation standards for qualified retirement plans were formerly reproduced at this point. The final regulations are at ¶ 12,156 and 12,163.]

[¶ 20,142B Reserved.—Proposed Regs. §§31.3401(a)(12)-1 and 301.6693-1, prescribing withholding tax rules for individual retirement plans and penalties for failure to furnish information in connection with such plans, were formerly reproduced at this point. The final regulations appear at ¶ 13,553 and 13,852.]

[¶ 20,142C Reserved.—Proposed regs. §§1.401(k)-1 and 1.402(a)-1(d), relating to cash or deferred arrangements, were formerly reproduced here. The final regulations now appear at ¶ 11,721, 11,730, 11,731, and 11,751.]

[¶ 20,142D Reserved.—Proposed Reg. §§1.401(a)-50 and 1.501(a)-1, relating to treatment of Puerto Rican retirement income plans, were formerly reproduced at this point. The final regulations appear at ¶ 11,720V and 13,161.]

[¶ 20,142E Reserved.—Proposed Reg. §§1.127-1, 1.127-2, 31.3121(a)(18)-1, 31.3306(b)(13)-1 and 31.3401(a)(19)-1, relating to educational assistance programs, were formerly reproduced at this point. The final regulations appear at ¶ 11,289A, 11,289B, 13,534M, and 13,553G.]

[¶ 20,142F Reserved.—Formerly reproduced at this paragraph were proposed regulations relating to the limitation of benefits in the event of an early termination of certain qualified plans. The proposed regulations were finalized by T.D. 7934 on January 9, 1984, and appear at ¶ 11,704.]

[¶ 20,142G Reserved.—Formerly reproduced at this paragraph were proposed regulations on withholding from amounts paid under accident or health plans. The proposed regulations were finalized by T.D. 7888 on April 22, 1983 (48 FR 17586) and appear at ¶ 13,551.]

¶ 20,142H

Proposed regulations: Withholding social security tax from sick pay.—Following are proposed regulations that relate to withholding of social security or railroad retirement taxes from sick pay. The regulations that are being proposed are also issued as temporary regulations and are reproduced at ¶ 13,535. Temp. Reg. §32.2, which relates to withholding of railroad retirement taxes, is not reproduced because it is not pertinent to the PENSION PLAN GUIDE.

These regulations appeared in the *Federal Register* on July 6, 1982.

DEPARTMENT OF THE TREASURY

Internal Revenue Service

26 CFR Part 31

[LR-23-82]

Withholding Social Security or Railroad Retirement Tax from Sick Pay

AGENCY: Internal Revenue Service, Treasury.

ACTION: Notice of proposed rulemaking by cross-reference to temporary regulations.

SUMMARY: In the Rules and Regulations portion of this *Federal Register,* the Internal Revenue Service is publishing temporary regulations that relate to withholding social security or railroad retirement tax from sick pay. The text of those temporary regulations also serves as the comment document for this proposed rulemaking.

DATES: Written comments and requests for a public hearing must be delivered by September 7, 1982. The regulations are proposed to be effective with respect to sick pay payments made on or after January 1, 1982.

ADDRESS: Send comments and requests for a public hearing to: Commissioner of Internal Revenue, Attention: CC:LR:T (LR-23-82), Washington, D.C. 20224.

FOR FURTHER INFORMATION CONTACT: Pamela F. Olson of the Legislation and Regulations Division, Office of the Chief Counsel, Internal Revenue Service, 1111 Constitution Avenue, N.W., Washington, D.C. 20224 (Attention: CC:LR:T) (202-566-3459).

SUPPLEMENTARY INFORMATION:

Background

The temporary regulations in the Rules and Regulations portion of this issue of the *Federal Register* add a new Part 32 to Title 26 of the Code of Federal Regulations. The final regulations, which this document proposes be based on those temporary regulations, would be added to Part 31 of Title 26 of the Code of Federal Regulations. Section 32.1 would become §31.3121(a)(2)-2, §32.2 would become §31.3231(e)-2, and Part 32 would be deleted.

The regulations would require an employer or third party making a payment on account of sickness or accident disability on or after January 1, 1982, to withhold, deposit, and pay the applicable social security or railroad retirement taxes based on the amount of the payment and provide a receipt of the amount of any such payment to the employee pursuant to section 6051. The regulations would allow third parties to transfer to the employer liability for paying the employer portion of the tax and responsibility for providing a receipt to the employee if they promptly (1) withhold the employee share of the tax, (2) deposit such portion pursuant to section 6302, and (3) notify the employer for whom services are normally rendered of the amount of the payment. Notification of the employer would be considered to be prompt if such notice is mailed on or before the required date for the deposit of the employee share of the tax by the third party. For purposes of the employer's paying the employer portion of the tax, payment to the employee would be deemed to have been made on the date that the employer receives notice of such payment from the third party.

The proposed regulations define "employer for whom services are normally rendered" as the last employer for whom the employee worked. Alternatives to this rule were considered for multiemployer plans. These alternatives included (1) allowing each plan to establish its own definition of "employer for whom services are normally rendered," (2) allocating the burden among all of the employers for whom the employee performed services over some period prior to the disability, (3) defining "employer for whom services are normally rendered" as the employer for whom the employee worked the most hours over some period prior to the disability, and (4) providing no definition of "employer for whom services are normally rendered." All of these alternatives were rejected in favor of the last employer rule because it was believed to be the rule which was most feasible administratively for the multiemployer plans, the employers, and the Service. For purposes of multiemployer plans which have purchased insurance to provide benefits to covered employees, the trust fund would be considered to be the third party making payments on account of sickness or accident disability provided the insurer withholds and deposits the tax imposed on the employee and notifies the plan of the payments. In order to relieve itself of liability, any such notified multiemployer plan which would itself be treated as the third party payer must, within 6 days of receipt of notification from the insurance company, notify the last employer for whom the employee worked.

The proposed regulations would not apply to a payment which is made under a workmen's compensation law, the Railroad Retirement Act, the Railroad Unemployment Insurance Act for days of sickness related to on-the-job injury, or which is unrelated to absence from work, is made after the expiration of six calendar months following the

¶20,142A

last calendar month in which the employee worked, or is attributable to a contribution by the employee.

The proposed regulations would allow a third party to request and rely on certain information from the employer in order to avoid overpayment of tax with respect to any employee receiving a payment on account of sickness or accident disability.

Employees of State and local governments may or may not be participants in the social security system. State and local governments that have elected to become part of the social security system do so by means of an agreement with the Secretary of Health and Human Services. Under these agreements, State governments make contributions equivalent to the social security tax which are deposited in Federal Reserve banks and accounted for to the Social Security Administration. Third parties making payments to employees of State and local governments should, therefore, contact the State or local government to determine the proper procedures to follow to insure correct and timely deposits and accurate wage reports.

The regulations are necessary because of the amendments made to section 3121(a) and 3231(e) by Pub. L. 97-123 (95 Stat. 1659). These statutory changes are effective with respect to payments made on or after January 1, 1982, on account of sickness or accident disability. These regulations are proposed to be issued under the authority contained in sections 3121(a) and 3231(e) (95 Stat. 1662 and 1663; 26 U. S. C. 3121(a) and 3231(e)) and 7805 (68A Stat. 917; 26 U. S. C. 7805) of the Internal Revenue Code of 1954.

Non-Applicability of Executive Order 12291

The Treasury Department has determined that this proposed regulation is not subject to review under Executive Order 12291 or the Treasury and OMB implementation of the Order dated April 28, 1982.

Regulatory Flexibility Act

Although this document is a notice of proposed rulemaking which solicits public comment, the Internal Revenue Service has concluded that the regulations proposed herein are interpretative and that the notice and public procedure requirements of 5 U. S. C. 553 do not apply. Accordingly, these proposed regulations do not constitute regulations subject to the Regulatory Flexibility Act (5 U. S. C. Chapter 6).

Comments and Requests for a Public Hearing

Before adopting these proposed regulations, consideration will be given to any written comments that are submitted (preferably six copies) to the Commissioner of Internal Revenue. All comments will be available for public inspection and copying. A public hearing will be held upon written request to the Commissioner by any person who has submitted written comments. If a public hearing is held, notice of the time and place will be published in the *Federal Register*.

Roscoe L. Egger, Jr.

Commissioner of Internal Revenue.

[FR Doc. 82-18185; Filed 6-30-82; 4:00 pm]

[¶ 20,142I Reserved.—Proposed Reg. §§ 20.20394(d) and (e), relating to the method for receiving an estate tax exclusion for lump-sum distributions from qualified plans, were formerly reproduced at this point. The final regulations appear at ¶ 13,502B.]

¶ 20,142J

Proposed regulations: Reclassification of investment arrangements: Multiple classes of ownership.—Reproduced below is the text of proposed regulations that relate to the classification for tax purposes of investment arrangements with multiple classes of ownership. The proposed regulations clarify that certain investment arrangements would be classified as associations or partnerships rather than trusts.

The proposed regulations were published in the *Federal Register* on May 2, 1984 (49 FR 18741).

DEPARTMENT OF THE TREASURY

Internal Revenue Service

26 CFR Part 301

[LR-68-84]

Classification of Investment Arrangements With Multiple Classes of Ownership

AGENCY: Internal Revenue Service, Treasury.

ACTION: Notice of proposed rulemaking.

SUMMARY: This document contains proposed regulations relating to the classification for federal tax purposes of investment arrangements with multiple classes of ownership. The proposed regulations are designed to clarify the meaning of the term "fixed investment trust" and the application of the classification rules to investment arrangements with multiple classes of ownership. The regulations would provide guidance to taxpayers and Internal Revenue Service personnel.

DATES: *Proposed effective date.* The amendments to the regulations are proposed to apply with respect to arrangements, any interests in which are initially issued after April 27, 1984.

Date for comments. Written comments must be delivered or mailed by July 2, 1984.

Date for public hearing. A public hearing on the proposed regulations will be held on July 31, 1984; for further information, see the notice of public hearing published elsewhere in this issue of the *Federal Register*. [CCH PENSION PLAN GUIDE, ¶ 23,653E].

ADDRESS: Send comments to Commissioner of Internal Revenue. Attention: CC:LR:T [LR-68-84], Washington, D.C. 20224.

FOR FURTHER INFORMATION CONTACT: Cynthia Grigsby of the Legislation and Regulations Division, Office of the Chief Counsel, Internal Revenue Service, 1111 Constitution Avenue NW., Washington. D.C. 20224 (Attention: CC:LR:T) (202-566-3935).

SUPPLEMENTARY INFORMATION:

Background

This document contains proposed amendments to the Regulations on Procedure and Administration (26 CFR Part 301) under section 7701 of the Internal Revenue Code of 1954. The proposed amendments relate to the definition of the term "trust" for federal tax purposes. These amendments to the regulations are proposed to be issued under the authority contained in section 7805 of the Internal Revenue Code of 1954 (68A Stat. 917; 26 U.S.C. 7805).

Explanation of Amendments

Existing § 301.7701-4(c) of the Regulations on Procedure and Administration provides guidance as to the classification for federal tax purposes of certain "investment" trusts. Under that regulation an entity of the type "commonly known as a fixed investment trust" is classified as a trust or an association (taxable as a corporation), depending upon the existence of a power under the agreement to vary the investment of the certificate holders. The question has been raised whether the rules for fixed investment trusts apply to an investment arrangement under which investors may choose among different classes of ownership with varying investment attributes.

The entities commonly known as fixed investment trusts at the time that the existing regulations were first promulgated in 1945 has only one class of certificates, with each certificate representing an undivided interest in trust property. "The investor [in a fixed trust] * * * has a beneficial undivided interest in specific deposited securities or property. * * * In the fixed trust * * * only one class of security is issued—the certificate of beneficial interest which is, in form, a receipt issued by the trustee for the deposited property" [Investment Trusts and Investment Companies, H.R. Doc. No. 567, 76th Cong., 3d Sess. 8-9 (1940) (footnote omitted).]The purpose of a fixed investment trust was to provide a convenient vehicle to enable investors to acquire undivided beneficial interests in a diversified investment portfolio. Thus, entities with multiple classes of ownership were not commonly known as fixed investment trusts at the time that the regulations were promulgated.[1]

---

[1] In *Commissioner v. Chase National Bank,* 122 F.2d 540 (2d Cir. 1941). the court held that a trust having certificates with detachable coupons evidencing the bearer's rights to receive semiannual distributions from the trust paid out of dividends and other income from stocks held by the trust was a fixed investment trust. The court found, however, that the purpose underlying the arrangement was to enable investors to acquire undivided beneficial interests in the stocks held in the arrangement. 122 F.2d at 541. The detachable coupons were a convenience to facilitate distributions and there was no apparent intention for the coupons to be detached and actively traded prior to their maturity. Thus, there was no intention to create a second class of ownership.

Consequently, the "fixed investment trust" rules were not intended to apply to such entities. In contrast, at the time the regulations were issued, multiple classes of ownership, such as preferred and common stock, often were associated with "management companies." H.R. Doc. No. 567 at 8-9. A "management trust," which is one type of management company, is classified for tax purposes as an association taxable as a corporation. Treas. Reg. § 301.7701-4(c).

In recent months new arrangements have been created that are claimed to be fixed investment trusts. In one such arrangement, a mortgage pool was formed to allow various groups of investors with different investment objectives to join together in a financial arrangement in which different rights and risks associated with a pool of mortgages are allocated among three classes of certificates. The first class of certificates provides for a priority in distributions from the pool and represents a short term interest while the second and third classes of certificates represent interests with longer maturities. The owner of a certificate in any of the three classes is not entitled to distributions of principal and interest on any specific mortgage or mortgages, but merely the right to certain distributions from the pool. Because there are multiple classes of ownership, this arrangement is not a fixed investment trust. Moreover, a significant objective of the arrangement is to shift to the first class of certificate holders the risk that mortgages in the pool will be prepaid, so that the holders of the second and third classes of certificates will have "call protection" (freedom from premature termination of their interests on account of prepayments.) This arrangement was not intended to protect and conserve property for the beneficiaries. Rather, the certificate holders, through this arrangement, associated together to fulfill their diverse profit-making objectives. The certificate holders must be viewed, therefore, as association in a joint enterprise for the conduct of business for profit, and the arrangement is classified as an association or a partnership under § 301.7701-2 of the regulations.

A second new type of arrangement provides a vehicle for investors to divide the income and appreciation elements inherent in a share of common stock. In this arrangement, a custodian accepts shares of stock in a single corporation and issues to the depositor one certificate for each share deposited. The certificate is perforated and can be separated by the depositor into two parts, with one part representing the right to receive an amount referable to the current value of the share of stock and the right to dividends from the stock, and the other part representing the right to the future appreciation on the share above the amount allocated to holders of the first part. The purpose of the arrangement is to allow investors to separate the certificate, retain the portion that suits their objectives and sell the other portion in the market. Buying one of the two parts enables investors to fulfill their specific profit-making objectives. Although only one type or class of certificate is issued by the custodian, the effect of the arrangement is to create two classes of interests. Thus, the arrangement is not a fixed investment trust. Moreover, as with the type of arrangement described above, the investors have associated together to divide the burdens and benefits inherent in the contributed shares and must be viewed as associates with an objective to carry on a business and divide the gains therefrom. Thus, this arrangement is also classified as an association or a partnership under § 301.7701-2 of the regulations.

In a third type of arrangement, a custodian holds one or more issues of bonds and issues certificates representing the right to specific interest or principal payments on the bonds. Although this arrangement is similar to the described above, it is distinguishable in that the division of the property is only between the bonds and specific interest coupons thereon. In section 1232B of the Code, Congress has provided a method for taxing transactions involving such "stripped bonds" and "stripped coupons." Thus, it would be inconsistent with section 1232B to treat typical "coupon stripping" arrangements in which bonds are held by a custodian and interests in specifically identifiable stripped coupons or bonds are sold as either associations or partnerships.

The proposed amendments to the regulations clarify the meaning of "fixed investment trust" under the regulations. The existing regulations, in focusing on the power of the trustee to vary the investment of the certificate holders, reflect the issue that was of primary concern at the time the regulations were drafted. With the development of multiple class investment arrangements, however, there is a need for further elaboration on the definition of the term "fixed investment trust" and the essential elements of this type of entity. In providing this definition, the proposed amendments impose a limitation not expressly stated in the existing regulations, and thus it was decided that the amendments should be prospective from April 27, 1984. The proposed rules for classification will apply to investment arrangements, any interests in which are initially issued after April 27, 1984.

Special Analyses

The Commissioner of Internal Revenue has determined that this proposed rule is not a major rule as defined in Executive Order 12291 and that a Regulatory Impact Analysis is therefore not required.

Although this document is a notice of proposed rulemaking that solicits public comments, the Internal Revenue Service has concluded that the regulations proposed therein are interpretative and that the notice and public procedure requirements of 5 U.S.C. 553 do not apply. Accordingly, no Regulatory Flexibility Analysis is required by chapter 6 of title 5, United States Code.

Comments and Public Hearing

Before adoption of these proposed regulations, consideration will be given to any written comments that are submitted (preferably seven copies) to the Commissioner of Internal Revenue. All comments will be available for public inspection and copying.

A public hearing on the proposed regulations will be held on July 31, 1984. For further information about the public hearing, see the notice of hearing that appears elsewhere in this issue of the **Federal Register.**

Drafting Information

The principal author of these proposed regulations is Paul A. Francis of the Legislation and Regulations Division of the Office of Chief Counsel, Internal Revenue Service. However, personnel from other offices of the Internal Revenue Service and Treasury Department participated in developing the regulations, on matters of both substance and style.

List of Subjects in 26 CFR Part 301

Administrative practice and procedure, Bankruptcy, Courts, Crime, Employment taxes, Estate taxes, Excise taxes, Gift taxes, Income taxes, Investigations, Law enforcement, Penalties, Pensions, Statistics, Taxes, Disclosure of information, Filing requirements.

Proposed Amendments to the Regulations

PART 301—[AMENDED]

Accordingly, it is proposed to amend 26 CFR Part 301 as follows: Paragraph (c) of § 301.7701-4 is revised to read as follows:

§ 301.7701-4 Trusts.

* * *

(c) *Certain investment trusts*—(1) An "investment" trust of the type commonly known as a management trust is an association, and a trust of the type commonly known as a fixed investment trust is an association if there is power under the trust agreement to vary the investment of the certificate holders. See *Commissioner v. North American Bond Trust,* 122 F.2d 545 (2d Cir. 1941), *cert. denied* 314 U.S. 701 (1942). However, if there is no power under the trust agreement to vary the investment of the certificate holders, such fixed investment trust shall be classified as a trust.

(2) A trust commonly known as a fixed investment trust is an arrangement in which legal title to property is conveyed to a trustee for the benefit of a group of investors. Each investor in such a trust has an undivided beneficial interest in the property held in trust, typically represented by certificates of beneficial interest issued to the investor; there is only one class of ownership interest. An arrangement having more than one class of ownership interest is not a fixed investment trust because an investor, rather than having an undivided beneficial interest in each asset of the trust, has a participating interest that differs from the interest held by an investor of another class. Because an arrangement with multiple classes of ownership enable investors to fulfill varying profit-making objectives through the division of rights and the sharing of risks in certain assets, the arrangement is considered to have associates and an objective to carry on business and divide the gains therefrom. Such an arrangement, therefore, is classified as an association or a partnership under § 301.7701-2.

(3) The requirement that a fixed investment trust have only one class of undivided interests has no application to mere custodial arrangements formed to allow investors to own specifically identifiable stripped coupons or stripped bonds within the meaning of section 1232B.

(4) The provisions of paragraph (c)(2) of this section may be illustrated by the following examples:

Example (1). A corporation purchases a portfolio of residential mortgages (or participations in residential mortgages) and transfers the mortgages to a bank under a custody agreement. At the same time, the bank as custodian delivers to the corporation certificates evidencing rights to payments from the pooled mortgages; the corporation sells the certificates to the public. The custodian holds legal title to the mortgages in the pool for the benefit of the certificate holders but has no power to reinvest proceeds attributable to the mortgages in the pool or to vary investments in the pool in any other manner. There are two classes of certificates. Holders of class A certificates are entitled to all payments of mortgage principal, both scheduled and prepaid, until their certificates are retired; holders of class B certificates receive payments of principal only after all class A certificates have been retired. This arrangement has two classes of ownership and is therefore, not a fixed investment trust, such an arrangement is considered to have associates and an objective to carry on business for profit and divide the gains there from. Therefore, it is classified as an association or a partnership under § 301.7701-2.

Example (2). A promoter formed a trust in which shareholders of a publicly traded corporation could deposit their stock. For each share of stock deposited with the trust, the participant receives a certificate that can be separated into two parts. One part represents the right to dividends and the value of the underlying stock up to a specified amount, the other part represents the right to appreciation above the specified amount. The two parts are traded separately on the open market. There are two classes of ownership in this arrangement and it is, therefore, not a fixed investment trust. Such an arrangement is considered to have associates and an objective to carry on business for profit and divide the gains therefrom. Therefore, it is classified as an association or a partnership under § 301.7701-2.

* * *

Roscoe L. Egger, Jr.,

Commissioner of Internal Revenue.

[FR Doc. 84-11865 Filed 4-27-84; 4:57 am]

[¶ 20,143 Reserved.—§ 1.1441-2(a) and 1.1441-2(b)(2)(ii) were previously reproduced at this paragraph. The regulations were removed by subsequently proposed regulations that are at ¶ 20,216.]

[¶ 20,144 Reserved.—Proposed Reg. §§ 54.4975-7, 54.4975-11, and 54.4975-12, relating to employee stock ownership plans, were formerly reproduced at this point. The final regulations appear at ¶ 13,644, 13,647B, and 13,647C.]

[¶ 20,145 Reserved.—Proposed Reg. §§ 54.4975-6 and 54.4975-15, relating to exemption from excise tax for provision of services and office space to plans, were formerly reported at this point. The final regulations now appear at ¶ 13,643 and 13,647B.]

[¶ 20,146 Reserved.—Proposed Reg. §§ 1.46-7 and 1.46-8 were formerly reproduced at this point. Some of the proposals were revised and adopted as final regulations and appear at ¶ 11,123 and 11,124.]

¶ 20,146A

Proposed regulations: Election to treat no portion of a lump sum distribution from an employee benefit plan as long-term capital gain: Election to treat pre-1974 plan participation as post-1973 participation ("the 402(e)(4)(L) election").—Reproduced below is the text of proposed regulations under Code Secs. 402 and 403 relating to the taxation of lump sum distributions from qualified pension, profit-sharing, stock bonus and annuity plans which conform to previously proposed amendments (40 FR 18798, PENSION PLAN GUIDE, ¶ 20,121) to the Tax Reform Act of 1976. The proposed regulations were published in the Federal Register of May 31, 1979 (44 FR 31228).

DEPARTMENT OF THE TREASURY

Internal Revenue Service

[26 CFR Part 1]

[EE-16-78]

Income Tax; Election to Treat Pre-1974 Plan Participation as Post-1973 Participation

AGENCY: Internal Revenue Service, Treasury.

ACTION: Notice of proposed rulemaking.

SUMMARY: This document contains proposed regulations relating to the election to treat no portion of a lump sum distribution from an employee benefit plan as long-term capital gain. Changes in the applicable tax law were made by the Tax Reform Act of 1976. The regulations would provide the public with the guidance needed to comply with that Act and would affect any recipient of a lump sum distribution.

DATES: Written comments and requests for a public hearing must be delivered or mailed by July 30, 1979. The amendments are proposed to be effective for distributions received in taxable years of the recipient beginning after December 31, 1975.

ADDRESS: Send comments and requests for a public hearing to: Commissioner of Internal Revenue, Attention:

CC:LR:T:EE-16-78, Washington, D. C. 20224.

FOR FURTHER INFORMATION CONTACT:

Richard L. Johnson of the Employee Plans and Exempt Organizations Division, Office of the Chief Counsel, Internal Revenue Service, 1111 Constitution Avenue, NW., Washington, D. C. 20224. Attention: CC:LR:T, 202-566-3544 (Not a toll-free number).

SUPPLEMENTARY INFORMATION:

Background

On April 30, 1975, the Federal Register published at 40 FR 18798 proposed amendments to the Income Tax Regulations (26 CFR Part 1) under sections 402(a), 402(e), 403(a) and other sections of the Internal Revenue Code of 1954, relating to the taxation of lump sum distributions from qualified pension, profit-sharing, stock bonus and annuity plans. A correction notice was published in the Federal Register on May 23, 1975, at 40 FR 22548. The amendments were proposed to conform the regulations to section 2005 of the Employee Retirement Income Security Act of 1974 (88 Stat. 987). Proposed amendments contained in paragraphs 1 and 2 of the appendix to that notice of proposed rulemaking were adopted by Treasury decision 7399 published in the Federal Register on February 3, 1976, at 41 FR 5099. The remainder of the amendments proposed in the appendix to the notice of proposed rulemaking of April 30, 1975, have not yet been adopted.

This document contains further proposed amendments to the Income Tax Regulations (26 CFR Part 1) under Code sections 402(a)(2), 402(e) and 403(a)(2) to conform the regulations to Code section 402(e)(4)(L), as added by section 1512 of the Tax Reform Act of 1976 (90 Stat. 1742). The proposed regulations are to be issued under the authority contained in sections 402(e)(4)(L) and 7805 of the Internal Revenue Code of 1954 (90 Stat. 1742, 68A Stat. 917; 26 U. S. C. 402(e)(4)(L), 7805).

Pre-1974 and Post-1973 Plan Participation

Under Code section 402(a)(2) or 403(a)(2), a portion of a lump sum distribution from a qualified pension, profit sharing, stock bonus or annuity plan is taxable as long-term capital gain. If the employee has been a participant in the plan for at least 5 years, and if the recipient is eligible to make the required election, the portion of the distribution not taxable as long-term capital gain is taxable under the 10-year averaging provisions of Code section 402(e). The portion of a lump sum distribution taxable as long-term capital gain is determined by taking into account the number of calendar years of participation by the employee in the plan before January 1, 1974. The portion taxable under Code section 402(e) represents participation in the plan after December 31, 1973.

Ordinary Income Election

Under Code section 402(e)(4)(L), a recipient may elect, under certain circumstances, to treat all calendar years of the employee's participation in all plans before January 1, 1974, as calendar years of participation after December 31, 1973. In such a case, no portion of the lump sum distribution is taxable as long-term capital gain. If the distribution is otherwise eligible for application of Code section 402(e), the total taxable amount of the distribution is taxable under the 10-year averaging pro. visions.

Comments and Requests for a Public Hearing

Before adopting these proposed regulations, consideration will be given to any written comments that are submitted (preferably eight copies) to the Commissioner of Internal Revenue. All comments will be available for public inspection and copying. A public hearing will be held upon written request to the Commissioner by any person who has submitted written comments. If a public hearing is held, notice of the time and place will be published in the Federal Register.

Drafting Information

The principal author of these proposed regulations is Richard L. Johnson of the Employee Plans and Exempt Organizations Division of the Office of Chief Counsel, Internal Revenue Service. However, personnel from other offices of the Internal Revenue Service and Treasury Department participated in developing the regulation, both on matters of substance and style.

Proposed Amendments to the Regulations

The proposed amendments to the regulations are as follows:

Paragraph 1. Section 1.402(a)-1(a)(9), as set forth in paragraph 10 of the appendix to the notice of proposed rulemaking of April 30, 1975, is revised by adding a new sentence at the end thereof to read as follows:

§ 1.402(a)-1 Taxability of beneficiary under a trust which meets the requirements of section 401(a).

(a) *In general.* * * *

(9) * * * In the case of a lump sum distribution received by or made available to a recipient in a taxable year of the recipient beginning after December 31, 1975, the recipient may elect, in accordance with section 402(e)(4)(L) and § 1.402(e)-14, to treat all calendar years of an employee's active participation in all plans in which the employee has been an active participant as years of active participation after December 31, 1973. If a recipient makes the election, no portion of any distribution received by or made available to the recipient with respect to the employee (whether in the recipient's taxable year for which the election is made, or thereafter) is taxable to the recipient as long-term capital gain under section 402(a)(2) and this subparagraph.

Par. 2. Section 1.402(e)-2(d)(3) as set forth in paragraph 12 of the appendix to the notice of proposed rulemaking of April 30, 1975, is revised by adding a new subdivision (iii) to read as follows:

§ 1.402(e)-2 Treatment of certain lump sum distributions made after 1973.

* * *

(d) *Definitions.* * * *

(3) *Ordinary income portion.* * * *

(iii) In the case of a lump sum distribution received in a taxable year of the recipient beginning after December 31, 1975, the recipient may elect, in accordance with section 402(e)(4)(L) and § 1.402(e)-14, to treat all calendar years of an employee's active participation in all plans in which the employee has been an active participant as years of active participation after December 31, 1973. If a recipient makes the election, the ordinary income portion of any lump sum distribution received by the recipient with respect to the employee (whether in the recipient's taxable year for which the election is made, or thereafter) is equal to the total taxable amount of the distribution.

* * *

Par. 3. The following new section is added in the appropriate place:

§ 1.402(e)-14 Election to treat pre-1974 participation as post-1973 participation (the "402(e)(4)(L) election").

(a) *In general.* Under section 402(e)(4)(L) and this section, the recipient of a lump sum distribution may elect to treat all calendar years of an employee's active participation in all plans in which the employee has been an active participant as years of active participation after December 31, 1973. This election is the "402(e)(4)(L) election." For rules relating to the treatment of distributions made on behalf of an employee with respect to whom the election is made, see § 1.402(a)-1(a)(9) (relating to the capital gains portion of a lump sum distribution) and § 1.402(e)-2(d)(3)(iii) (relating to the ordinary income portion of a lump sum distribution). For purposes of this section the

term "lump sum distribution" means a lump sum distribution as defined in section 402(e)(4)(A), without regard to section 402(e)(4)(B).

(b) *Taxpayers not eligible to make the election.* A taxpayer may not make the 402(e)(4)(L) election with respect to a lump sum distribution made on behalf of an employee, if—

(1) The taxpayer received a prior lump sum distribution made on behalf of the employee in a taxable year of the employee (or in a year that would have been a taxable year of the employee, but for the death of the employee) beginning after December 31, 1975, and

(2) A portion of that prior lump sum distribution was treated as long-term capital gain under section 402(a)(2) or 403(a)(2).

(c) *Time and scope of election—*(1) *In general.* The 402(e)(4)(L) election shall be made for the first lump sum distribution made with respect to an employee to which the election is to apply. The election does not apply to a lump sum distribution received by the recipient with respect to an other employee. The 402(e)(4)(L) election is irrevocable. A revocation under § 1.402(e)-3 of the election to apply the separate tax to a lump sum distribution will not revoke a 402(e)(4)(L) election.

(2) *Application of separate tax.* Nothing in this section 402(e)(4)(L) and this section changes the requirements which must be satisfied in order for a lump sum distribution to be eligible for application of the separate tax under section 402(e). Accordingly, a lump sum distribution is not taxable under section 402(e) merely because the 402(e)(4)(L) election is made with respect to, or otherwise applies to, the distribution.

(3) *Example.* The provisions of subparagraph (2) of this paragraph may be illustrated by the following example:

Example. (i) A, a calendar year taxpayer aged 59 ½, separates from the service of A's employer, the M Corporation, on October 31, 1976. On December 15, 1976, A receives a distribution of the balance to A's credit under the M Corporation qualified profit sharing plan. A has been an active participant in the plan since January 1, 1971. The distribution is a lump sum distribution within the meaning of section 402(e)(4)(A) which satisfies the requirements of section 402(e)(4)(C), relating to the aggregation of certain trusts and plans, and section 402(e)(4)(H), relating to a minimum period of participation in the plan.

(ii) A makes the 402(e)(4)(L) election with respect to the distribution. Under section 402(e)(4)(L), all years of A's active participation in all plans in which A has been an active participant are treated as years of active participation after December 31, 1973. Accordingly, no portion of the distribution is taxable as long-term capital gain under section 402(a)(2), and the total taxable amount of the distribution is "ordinary income" for purposes of section 402(e). A also makes the section 402(e)(4)(B) election for A's taxable year in which A receives the distribution. Accordingly, the total taxable amount of the distribution is taxable under the 10-year averaging provisions of section 402(e) (the separate tax).

(iii) On January 15, 1977, A receives a distribution of the balance of A's credit under the M Corporation-qualified pension plan. A has been an active participant in the plan since January 1, 1958. The distribution is a lump sum distribution within the meaning of section 402(e)(4)(A) which satisfies the requirements of section 402 (e)(4)(C), relating to the aggregation of certain trusts and plans, and section 402 (e)(4)(H), relating to a minimum period of participation in the plan. No portion of the distribution is taxable as long-term capital gain under section 402(a)(2) because A made the 402(e)(4)(L) election with respect to A's 1976 distribution. In addition, no portion of the distribution is taxable under the 10-year averaging provisions of section 402(e) because A made a prior election under section 402(e)(4)(B) with respect to a distribution made on A's behalf and after A was age 59 ½ (the 1976 distribution).

(d) *Manner of making election.* The 402 (e)(4)(L) election shall be made in the manner indicated on the form filed pursuant to section 402(e)(4)(B) and § 1.402(e)-3 (c)(2) before the expiration of the period prescribed in § 1.402(e)-3 for making the election to apply the separate tax to the ordinary income portion of a lump sum distribution.

(e) *Effective date.* Taxpayers eligible under this section to make the 402(e)(4)(L) election may make the election with respect to a lump sum distribution received after December 31, 1975, and in a taxable year of the recipient beginning after that date.

Par. 4. Section 1.403(a)-2(e)(3), as set forth in paragraph 15 of the appendix to the notice of proposed rulemaking of April 30, 1975, is revised by adding, immediately after subdivision (ii) thereof, a new sentence to read as follows:

§ 1.403(a)-2 Capital gains treatment for certain distributions.

* * *

(e) * * *

(3) * * *

(i) * * *

(ii) * * *

In the case of a lump sum distribution received by or made available to a recipient in a taxable year of the recipient beginning after December 31, 1975, the recipient may elect, in accordance with section 402(e)(4)(L), and § 1.402(e)-14, to treat all calendar years of an em-

ployee's active participation in all plans in which the employee has been an active participant as years of active participation after December 31, 1973. If a recipient makes the election, no portion of any distribution received by or made available to the recipient with respect to the employee (whether in the recipient's taxable year for which the election is made, or thereafter) is taxable to the recipient as long-term capital gain under section 403(a)(2) and this subparagraph.

* * *

Jerome Kurtz,

Commissioner of Internal Revenue.

[FR Doc. 79-16949 Filed 5-30-79; 8:45am]

[¶ 20,146B Reserved.—Proposed Reg. § 1.46-9, relating to investment credit employee stock ownership plans (TRASOPs) that provide for an extra one-half percent credit, was formerly reproduced at this point. The final regulation now appears at ¶ 11,124A.]

[¶ 20,147 Reserved.—Proposed Reg. § 54.4975-14, relating to the election to pay an excise tax for certain pre-1975 prohibited transactions, was formerly reported at this point. The final regulation now appears at ¶ 13,647A.]

[¶ 20,148 Reserved.—Proposed Reg. § 1.401(a)-13, relating to assignment or alienation of benefits, was formerly reported at this point. The final regulations appear at ¶ 11,719B.]

[¶ 20,149 Reserved.—Proposed Regs. §§ 1.79-1(b)(1)(ii), 1.79-1(b)(ii)(a) and 1.79-3(d), relating to the qualification of group-term life insurance coverage for favorable tax treatment and which were formerly reported at this point, were withdrawn by the IRS.]

¶ 20,149A

Proposed regulations: Continuation coverage of group health plans. The IRS issued proposed regulations relating to the requirement that a group health plan offer continuation coverage to people who would otherwise lose coverage as the result of a "qualifying event." The proposed regulations were published in the *Federal Register* on June 15, 1987 (52 FR 22716).

The final regulations were published in the Federal Register on February 3, 1999 (64 FR 5160). The preamble to the final regulations is at ¶ 23,152. The final regulations are at ¶ 13,648W-5, ¶ 13,648W-6, ¶ 13,648W-7, ¶ 13,648W-8, ¶ 13,648W-9, ¶ 13,648W-10, ¶ 13,648W-11, ¶ 13,648W-12, ¶ 13,648W-13.

¶ 20,149B

Proposed regulations: Affiliated service groups: Employee leasing.—Reproduced below is the text of proposed regulations which prescribe rules for determining: (1) when a management organization and the organization for which the management organization performs management services constitute an affiliated service group; (2) when leased employees are treated as employees of the lessee organization for purposes of certain employee benefit provisions; and (3) when arrangements involving separate organizations, employee leasing, or other arrangements will be ignored in order to prevent the avoidance of certain employee benefit requirements.

These regulations appeared in the *Federal Register* on August 27, 1987.

[NOTE: Reg. §§ 1.414(m)-5; 1.414(m)-6; 1.414(n)-1 through 1.414(n)-4; 1.414(o)-1(c) through 1.414(o)-1(k)(1); 1.414(o)-1(k)(3); and 1.414(o)(k)(4) were withdrawn by the IRS on April 27, 1993 (58 F.R. 25587).]

DEPARTMENT OF THE TREASURY

Internal Revenue Service

26 CFR Part 1

[EE-111-82]

Affiliated Service Groups, Employee Leasing, and Other Arrangements

AGENCY: Internal Revenue Service, Treasury.

ACTION: Notice of proposed rulemaking.

SUMMARY: This document provides proposed regulations prescribing rules for determining: (1) When a management organization and the organization for which the management organization performs management services constitute an affiliated service group; (2) when leased employees are treated as employees of the lessee organization for purposes of certain employee benefit provisions; and (3) when arrangements involving separate organizations, employee leasing, or other arrangements will be ignored in order to prevent the avoidance of certain employee benefit requirements.

Changes to the applicable tax law were made by the Tax Equity and Fiscal Responsibility Act of 1982, the Tax Reform Act of 1984, and the Tax Reform Act of 1986. The regulations provide the public with guidance needed to comply with those Acts and would affect employers that maintain, and participants in, qualified plans.

DATES: Written comments and requests for a public hearing must be delivered or mailed by October 26, 1987. The regulations provided by this document are proposed to be generally effective for tax years beginning after December 31, 1983.

ADDRESS: Send comments and requests for a public hearing to: Commissioner of Internal Revenue, Attention: CC:LR:T (EE-111-82), Washington, DC 20224.

FOR FURTHER INFORMATION CONTACT: Michael Garvey of the Employee Plans and Exempt Organizations Division, Office of Chief Counsel, Internal Revenue Service, 1111 Constitution Avenue, NW., Washington, DC 20224, Attention: CC:LR:T, (202) 566-3903, not a toll-free call.

SUPPLEMENTARY INFORMATION:

Background

This document contains proposed amendments to the Income Tax Regulations (26 CFR Part 1) under sections 414(m)(5), 414(n), and 414(o) of the Internal Revenue Code. These amendments are proposed to conform the regulations to sections 246 and 248 of the Tax Equity and Fiscal Responsibility Act of 1982 (26 U.S.C. 414(m)(5), 414(n)), section 526 of the Tax Reform Act of 1984 (26 USC 414(n)(2), 414(o)), and section 1146 of the Tax Reform Act of 1986 (26 U.S.C. 414(n), 414(o)). Other sections of the Tax Reform Act of 1986 that relate to section 414(n) are not reflected in this document.

Organizations Performing Management Functions

Section 414(m)(5) of the Code expands the definition of an affiliated service group that is to be treated as a single employer under section 414(m) for purposes of certain employee benefit requirements. Pursuant to section 414(m)(5), an affiliated service group includes a management organization and a recipient organization (i.e., the organization (and related organizations) for which the management organization performs management functions). An organization is a management organization if the principal business of the organization is the performing of, on a regular and continuing basis, management functions for a recipient organization.

Employee Leasing

Section 414(n) provides that, under certain circumstances, an individual ("leased employee") who performs services for a person ("recipient") through another person ("leasing organization") shall be treated as the employee of the recipient for purposes of certain employee benefit requirements. If the services being provided by an individual to a recipient are pursuant to an agreement between the recipient and the leasing organization, and the individual performs such services for the recipient on a substantially full-time basis for a period of at least one year, and the services are of a type historically performed by employees, then the individual is a leased employee and, therefore, shall be treated as an employee of the recipient.

Section 414(n)(5) provides, however, that if the leasing organization maintains a safe-harbor plan with respect to a leased employee, such individual will generally not be treated as an employee of the recipient. Section 414(n)(5), as originally enacted, required that a safe-harbor plan must be a qualified money purchase pension plan with provision for nonintegrated employer contributions of at least 7 ½ percent, immediate participation, and full and immediate vesting.

The Tax Reform Act of 1986 amended several provisions relating to sections 414(n) and 414(o). These amendments include the following:

(1) The definition of a safe-harbor plan under section 414(n)(5) has been amended to require a contribution rate of 10 percent and to require that the plan must cover all employees of the leasing organization (other than employees who perform substantially all of their services for the leasing organization (and not for recipients) and employees whose compensation from the leasing organization is less than $1,000 during the plan year and during each of the 3 prior plan years).

(2) Under section 414(n)(5), a leased employee will be treated as an employee of the recipient, regardless of the existence of a safe-harbor plan, if more than 20 percent of the recipient's nonhighly compensated workforce are leased employees (as specially defined for this purpose).

(3) A recordkeeping exception from the section 414(n) employee leasing provisions is provided under section 414(o) in the case of an employer that has no section 416(g) top-heavy plans and that uses the services of nonemployees only for an insignificant percentage of the employer's total workload.

(4) The scope of the section 414(n) employee leasing provisions has been expanded to include a number of non-pension employee benefit requirements (listed under section 414(n)(3)), including group-term life insurance, accident and health plans, qualified group legal services, cafeteria plans, etc. In addition, the employee leasing provisions will apply to these non-pension employee benefit requirements regardless of the existence of a safe-harbor plan.

Except for the amendments relating to the non-pension employee benefit requirements, the proposed regulations reflect the Tax Reform Act of 1986 amendments described above. Guidance relating to the non-pension employee benefit requirements, and other relevant amendments made by the Tax Reform Act of 1986, will be forthcoming.

Avoidance of Certain Employee Benefits Requirements

Section 414(o) provides that the Secretary shall prescribe such regulations as may be necessary to prevent the avoidance of any employee benefit requirement listed in sections 414(m)(4) or 414(n)(3) through the use of separate organizations, employee leasing, or other arrangements. Specifically, the Secretary has the authority to provide rules in addition to the rules contained in sections 414(m) and 414(n).

Pursuant to section 414(o), the proposed regulations provide rules relating to several arrangements that may result in the avoidance of the listed employee benefit requirements. These arrangements include the leasing of certain owners, the leasing of certain managers, the creation of successive organizations in time, expense sharing arrangements, plans maintained by certain corporate directors, and plans covering certain five-percent owners.

Effective Data

The amendments made to section 414 by the Tax Equity and Fiscal Responsibility Act of 1982 are effective for tax years of a recipient or of a member of an affiliated service group that begin after December 31, 1983.

The amendments made to section 414 by the Tax Reform Act of 1984 are effective as of July 18, 1984. The regulations promulgated under section 414(o), however, are variously effective for (1) plan years beginning more than six months after this document is published in

the *Federal Register*, (2) plan years beginning more than sixty days after this document is published in the *Federal Register* as a Treasury decision, and (3) plan years beginning during or after the first tax year of a recipient beginning after December 31, 1983. (To the extent that the regulations under section 414(o) aggregate plans for purposes of section 415 that were not previously aggregated, the rules of § 1.415-10 apply.)

The amendments made to section 414 by the Tax Reform Act of 1986 are generally effective with respect to services performed after December 31, 1986. The recordkeeping exception from section 414(n), provided under section 414(o), and certain clarifying amendments under section 414(n) are effective as if originally enacted as part of the section 414 amendments made by the Tax Equity and Fiscal Responsibility Act of 1982. The section 414(n)(3) amendments relating to the non-pension employee benefit requirements are generally effective when section 89 applies to such non-pension employee benefits (see section 1151(k) of the Tax Reform Act of 1986).

Special Analysis

The Commissioner of Internal Revenue has determined this rule is not a major rule as defined in Executive Order 12291. Therefore, a Regulatory Impact Analysis is not required. Although this document is a notice of proposed rulemaking that solicits public comment, the Internal Revenue Service has concluded that the regulations proposed are interpretative and that the notice and public procedure requirements of 5 U.S.C. 553(b) do not apply. Accordingly, these proposed regulations do not constitute regulations subject to the Regulatory Flexibility Act (5 U.S.C. chapter 6).

Comments and Requests for a Public Hearing

Before adopting these proposed regulations, consideration will be given to any written comments that are submitted (preferably eight copies) to the Commissioner or Internal Revenue. All comments will be available for public inspection and copying. A public hearing will be held upon written request to the Commissioner by any person who has submitted written comments. If a public hearing is held, notice of the time and place will be published in the *Federal Register*.

Drafting Information

The principal author of these proposed regulations is Philip R. Bosco of the Employee Plans and Exempt Organizations Division of the Office of Chief Counsel, Internal Revenue Service. However, personnel from other offices of the Internal Revenue Service and Treasury participated in developing the regulations, both on matters of substance and style.

List of Subjects in 26 CFR 1.401—1-1.425-1

Employee benefit plans, Pensions.

Proposed Amendment to the Regulations

The Income Tax Regulations (26 CFR Part 1) are proposed to be amended as follows:

Paragraph 1. The authority citation for Part 1 is amended by adding the following citation:

Authority: 26 U.S.C. 7805. * * * Section 1.414(n)-1 also issued under 26 U.S.C. 414(n). Section 1.414(o)-1 also issued under 26 U.S.C. 414(o).

Par. 2. The following new sections are added immediately following § 1.414(m)-4 and read as follows:

§ 1.414(m)-5 Organizations performing management functions. [Withdrawn.]

* * *

§ 1.414(m)-6 Application of section 414(o) to section 414(m). [Withdrawn.]

* * *

§ 1.414(n)-1 Employee leasing. [Withdrawn.]

* * *

§ 1.414(n)-2 Qualified plan coverage of leased employees. [Withdrawn.]

* * *

§ 1.414(n)-3 Employee benefit requirements, recordkeeping, and effective dates. [Withdrawn.]

* * *

§ 1.414(n)-4 Application of section 414(o) to section 414(n). [Withdrawn.]

* * *

§ 1.414(o)-1 Avoidance of employee benefit requirements through the use of separate organizations, employee leasing, or other arrangements.

(a) *In general.* (1) Pursuant to section 414(o), this section provides rules, in addition to the rules contained in sections 414(m) and 414(n) and the regulations thereunder, to prevent the avoidance of any employee benefit requirement listed in either § 1.414(m)-3 or § 1.414(n)-3, through the use of separate organizations, employee leasing, or other arrangements.

(2) For the definition of the terms "person" and "leased employee", see § 1.414(n)-1(b). For the definition of the term "organization", see § 1.414(m)-5(a)(2). For the definition of the terms "management functions" and "management activities or services", see § 1.414(m)-5(c).

(3) For purposes of this section, the term "plan" means a stock bonus, pension, or profit-sharing plan qualified under section 401(a) or a simplified employee pension under section 408(k).

(4) For purposes of this section, the term "employee" includes a "self-employed individual" as defined in section 401(c)(1).

(5) For purposes of this section, the term "maintained", when used in the context of a plan maintained by any person, means "maintained at any time."

(6) For purposes of this section, services performed for a person other than as an employee of such person means services performed directly or indirectly for such person.

(b) *Services performed by leased owners—* (1) *In general.* (i) If an individual is a leased owner with respect to a recipient, then for purposes of determining whether any qualified plan actually maintained by the recipient and whether any qualified plan maintained by a leasing organization in which the leased owner is a participant (or in which the leased owner has or had an accrued benefit) satisfies the employee benefit requirements of section 1.41 4(n)-3(a) (except for paragraph (a)(6) of that section) for a plan year, the leased owner's interest in the leasing organization's qualified plan attributable to services performed by the leased owner for the recipient is to be treated as provided under a separate qualified plan maintained by the recipient covering only the leased owner and the leased owner is to be treated as an employee of the recipient. If a separate qualified plan is treated as maintained by the recipient with respect to a leased owner and such leased owner also participates in a qualified plan actually maintained by the recipient, the leased owner's interest in the leasing organization's qualified plan attributable to the leased owner's performance of services for the recipient that is treated as provided to the leased owner under a separate qualified plan of the recipient is to be treated as provided to the leased owner under the qualified plan actually maintained by the recipient for purposes of determining whether such qualified plan satisfies the applicable employee benefit requirements. If either the separate qualified plan for the leased owner that is treated as maintained by the recipient or any qualified plan that is actually maintained by the recipient fails to satisfy any of the applicable employee benefit requirements, then except as provided in paragraphs (b)(1)(ii) and (b)(1)(iii) of this section, the following qualified plans shall be treated as not satisfying such requirements: any qualified plan actually maintained by the recipient in which the leased owner is a participant (or has or had an accrual benefit) and any qualified plan that is actually maintained by a leasing organization in which the leased owner has an interest that is attributable to the leased owner's performance of services for the recipient.

(ii) The Commissioner will not apply paragraph (b)(1)(i) of this section so as to disqualify a plan actually maintained by a recipient unless the Commissioner determines that, taking into account all the facts and circumstances, the disqualification of a leasing organization's plan would be ineffective as a means of securing compliance with the applicable employee benefit requirements. For example, it may be appropriate to disqualify the recipient's plan where a leasing organization's plan was terminated or substantial assets were removed therefrom in a year for which the statute of limitations has run with respect to the employer, employee, or trust.

(iii) If pursuant to paragraph (b)(1)(i) of this section, more than one leasing organization plan is subject to disqualification and at least one of the plans would not be disqualified if another plan or plans were disqualified first, all affected plan sponsors may, by agreement, elect the plan or plans subject to disqualification, provided that such election is not inconsistent with the purposes of this paragraph (b), such as where the plan or plans elected were terminated or substantial assets were removed therefrom in a year for which the statute of limitations has run with respect to the employer, employee, or trust. In the absence of such an election, the Commissioner, taking into account all the facts and circumstances, shall have the discretion to determine which plan or plans shall be disqualified.

(2) *Leased owner.* (i) For purposes of this paragraph (b), an individual is a "leased owner" with respect to a recipient if during the plan year of a plan maintained by a leasing organization the individual (A) performs any services for a recipient other than as an employee of the recipient and (B) is, at the time such services are performed, a five-percent owner of the recipient. The fact that an individual may also perform services as an employee of the recipient does not affect his status as a leased owner. If an individual becomes a leased owner with respect to a recipient, such individual is from that point on always to be considered a leased owner with respect to the recipient, notwithstanding anything in this paragraph (b) to the contrary, even if subsequently all services performed by the individual for the recipient are performed as an employee of the recipient.

(ii) Except as provided in paragraph (b)(2)(iii) of this section, and notwithstanding the first sentence of paragraph (b)(2)(i) of this section to the contrary, an individual is not a leased owner with respect to a recipient for purposes of a plan year of a plan maintained by a leasing organization if, during each calendar year containing at least one day of such plan year, less than 25 percent of his total hours actually worked for substantial compensation are for all recipients with respect to which he is a leased owner (but for the application of this paragraph (b)(2)(ii)) and less than 25 percent of his total compensation is derived from performing services for all such recipients. For purposes of this paragraph (b)(2)(ii), performing services for the recipient includes services performed as an employee of the recipient and in any other capacity. For purposes of this paragraph (b)(2)(ii), the term "compensation" means (A) with respect to services performed as a common-law employee, compensation reportable on Form W-2, and (B) with respect to services performed other than as a common-law employee, earned income as defined in section 401(c)(2). See section 414(s) for the definition of "compensation" for years beginning after December 31, 1986.

(iii) Paragraph (b)(2)(ii) of this section does not apply to an individual who (A) is a leased owner with respect to a recipient pursuant to the application of the first sentence of paragraph (b)(2)(i) of this section, and (B) performs professional services (as defined in § 1.414(m)-1(c)) for the recipient, whether or not as an employee of the recipient, during the plan year of the plan maintained by the leasing organization, of the same type as the professional services performed by the recipient for third parties.

(3) *Recipient.* For purposes of this paragraph (b), the term "recipient" has the same meaning as in paragraphs (b)(2) and (b)(6) of § 1.414(n)-1, except that "leased owner" is substituted for "leased employee".

(4) *Leasing organization.* For purposes of this paragraph (b), the term "leasing organization" has the same meaning as in § 1.414(n)-1(b)(1), except that "leased owner" is substituted for "leased employee" and that "or provided" is added after "provides".

(5) *Five-percent owner.* For purposes of this paragraph (b), an individual is a 5-percent owner of a recipient if such individual is a 5-percent owner (as defined in section 416(i)) of any person included in the recipient.

(6) *Contributions, benefit, etc., provided to a leased owner.* For purposes of this paragraph (b), a leased owner's interest in a leasing organization (as defined in § 1.414(n)-2(b)(1)(ii) and in a leasing organization's qualified plan, as defined in § 1.414(n)-2(b)(1)(i), to the extent attributable to services for the recipient by the leased owner, is, for purposes of the applicable employee benefit requirements, treated as provided by the recipient or under a plan of the recipient. For rules relating to the application of this requirement, see paragraph (b)(2) of § 1.414(n)-2.

(7) *Effect on employee rules.* To the extent that a leased owner performs services for a recipient other than in the capacity of an employee, a leased owner is not an employee of the recipient and may not be actually covered by a plan of the recipient. Such leased owner may, however, qualify as a leased employee under section 414(n) and the regulations thereunder.

[NOTE: Reg. § 1.414(o)-1(c) through 1.414(o)-1(k)(1) withdrawn.]

* * *

(k) *Effective dates.* * * *.

(2) The provisions of paragraph (b) of this section are effective for tax years of recipients beginning after December 31, 1983. Therefore, the provisions of paragraph (b) apply to plan years beginning during and after the first tax year of a recipient beginning after December 31, 1983. For purposes of applying paragraph (b) of this section to plan years beginning during and after the first tax year of a recipient beginning after December 31, 1983, contributions, forfeitures and bene-

fits provided during any plan year beginning prior to the first tax year of a recipient beginning after December 31, 1983, shall be taken into account if they would have been taken into account had paragraph (b) been effective for such prior plan year.

[NOTE: Reg. § 1.414(o)-1(k)(3) and 1.414(o)-1(k)(4) withdrawn.]

* * *

James I. Owens,

Acting Commissioner.

[FR Doc. 87-19579 Filed 8-26-87; 8:45 a.m.]

¶ 20,149C

Proposed regulations: Benefit accruals beyond normal retirement age: Employee benefit plans: Minimum vesting standards: Plan qualification.—Reproduced below is the text of proposed regulations relating to the requirement for the continued accrual of benefits beyond normal retirement age under employee pension benefit plans as provided for in the Omnibus Budget Reconciliation Act of 1986. The proposed regulations were published in the *Federal Register* on April 11, 1988 (53 FR 11876).

DEPARTMENT OF THE TREASURY

Internal Revenue Service

26 CFR Part 1

[EE-184-86]

Income Taxes; Continued Accruals Beyond Normal Retirement Age

AGENCY: Internal Revenue Service, Treasury.

ACTION: Notice of proposed rulemaking.

SUMMARY: This document contains proposed regulations relating to the requirement for continued accruals beyond normal retirement age under employee pension benefit plans. Changes to the applicable tax law were made by the Omnibus Budget Reconciliation Act of 1986. These regulations will provide the public with guidance needed to comply with the minimum participation and vesting standards and affect employers maintaining employee retirement plans.

DATES: Written comments and request for a public hearing must be delivered or mailed by June 10, 1988. These amendments generally apply to plan years beginning after December 31, 1987, except as otherwise specified in the Omnibus Budget Reconciliation Act of 1986.

ADDRESS: Send comments and requests for a public hearing to: Commissioner of Internal Revenue, Attention: CC:LR:T (EE-184-86) Washington, D.C. 20224.

FOR FURTHER INFORMATION CONTACT: Michael C. Garvey of the Employee Benefits and Exempt Organizations Division, Office of Chief Counsel, Internal Revenue Service, 1111 Constitution Avenue N.W., Washington, D.C. 20224 (Attention: CC:LR:T) (202-566-6271) (not a toll-free number).

SUPPLEMENTARY INFORMATION:

Background

This document contains proposed amendments to the Income Tax Regulations (26 CFR Part 1) under sections 410 and 411 of the Internal Revenue Code of 1986. These amendments are proposed to conform the regulations to sections 9201 through 9204, Subtitle C (Older Americans Pension benefits) of Title IX of the Omnibus Budget Reconciliation Act of 1986 (Pub. L. 99-509) (OBRA 1986) (100 Stat. 1874, 1973).

Explanation of Provisions

Section 9202(b)(1) of OBRA 1986 added subparagraph (H) to section 411(b)(1) of the Internal Revenue Code (Code) to provide rules for continued benefit accruals under defined benefit plans without regard to the attainment of any age. Section 9202 (b)(2) of OBRA 1986 redesignated paragraphs (2) and (3) of Code section 411(b) as paragraphs (3) and (4) and added a new paragraph (2) to Code section 411(b) to provide rules for allocations to the accounts of employees in defined contribution plans without regard to the attainment of any age.

Effective with respect to plan years beginning after December 31, 1987, section 411(b)(1)(H)(i) provides the general rule that a defined benefit plan will not be treated as meeting the minimum vesting standards of section 411 (and, accordingly, will not constitute a qualified plan under section 401(a)) if under the plan an employee's benefit accrual is ceased, or the rate of an employee's benefit accrual is reduced, because of the attainment of any age. Effective for plan years beginning after December 31, 1987, section 411(b)(2) provides that a defined contribution plan will not be treated as satisfying the minimum vesting standards of section 411 (and, accordingly, will not constitute a qualified plan under section 401(a)) if allocations to an employee's account are ceased, or the rate of allocations to an employee's account is reduced, because of the attainment of any age.

The proposed regulations provide that reductions or cessations of account allocations or benefit accruals that are based on factors other than age will not affect the qualification of the plan under section 411(b)(1)(H) or (b)(2). The proposed regulations also provide that benefits under a defined benefit plan may accrue at different rates without violating section 411(b)(1)(H), provided the difference in the rate of benefit accrual is determined without regard to the attainment of any age.

Section 411(b)(1)(H)(ii) provides that a plan will not be treated as failing to satisfy the general rule in section 411(b)(1)(H)(i) merely because the plan contains a limitation (determined without regard to age) on the maximum number of years of service or participation that are taken into account in determining benefits under the plan or merely because the plan contains a limitation on the amount of benefits an employee will receive under the plan. The proposed regulations provide that these limitations are permitted in both defined benefit plans and defined contributions plans (including target benefit plans).

Section 411(b)(1)(H)(iii) provides that, with respect to an employee who, as of the end of a plan year, has attained normal retirement age under a defined benefit plan, certain adjustments may be made to the benefit accrual for the plan year if the plan distributes benefits to the employee or if the plan adjusts the amount of the benefits payable to take into account delayed payment. The continued benefit accrual rules of section 411(b)(1)(H) operate in conjunction with the suspension of benefit payment rules under section 203(a)(3)(B) of the Employee Retirement Income Security Act of 1974 (ERISA) and the proposed regulations do not change the rules relating to the suspension of pension benefit payments under section 203(a)(3)(B) of ERISA and the regulations thereunder issued by the Department of Labor. However, the proposed regulations provide rules under which benefit accruals required under section 411(b)(1)(H)(i) may be reduced or offset either by the value of actuarial adjustments in an employee's normal retirement benefit or by the value of benefit distributions made to an employee.

Section 411(b)(1)(H)(iv) provides that a defined benefit plan will not be treated as failing to satisfy the general rule of section 411(b)(1)(H)(i) merely because the subsidized portion of an early retirement benefit provided under the plan (whether provided on a permanent or temporary basis) is disregarded in determining benefit accruals under the plan. The proposed regulations also provide that a plan will not be treated as failing to satisfy the general rule of section 411(b)(1)(H)(i) merely because a social security supplemental benefit or a qualified disability benefit is disregarded in determining benefit accruals under the plan.

The proposed regulations provide that the rate of an employee's benefit accrual under a defined benefit plan or the rate of allocations to an employee's account under a defined contribution plan will be considered to be reduced on account of the attainment of a specified age if optional forms of benefits, ancillary benefits or other benefits, rights or features under a plan that are provided with respect to benefits or allocations prior to such age are not provided (on terms that are at least as favorable to employees) with respect to benefits or allocations after such age. Thus, for example, under the proposed regulations, a plan may not make a lump sum option available only with respect to benefits or allocations attributable to service prior to a specified age. Similarly, a plan may not use actuarial assumptions that are less favorable to employees for determining lump sum benefits payable after a specified age than are used for determining lump sum benefits payable prior to such age. However, the proposed regulations provide that the accrual rate under a defined benefit plan will not be considered to be reduced merely because the subsidized portion of an early retirement benefit, a qualified disability benefit or a social security supplemental benefit provided under the plan ceases to be provided to an employee or is provided on a reduced basis to an employee by a plan on account of the employee's attainment of a specified age.

Section 411(b)(1)(H)(v) and (b)(2)(D) provide that the Secretary shall prescribe regulations coordinating the requirements of section 411(b)(1)(H) and (b)(2) with the requirements of sections 411(a), 404, 410, 415 and the antidiscrimination provisions of subchapter D of Chapter 1 (Code sections 401 through 425). The proposed regulations provide that no allocation to the account of an employee in a defined contribution plan and no benefit accrual on behalf of an employee in a defined benefit plan are required under section 411(b)(1)(H) or (b)(2) if such allocation or benefit accrual would cause the plan to (1) exceed the section 415 limitations on benefits and contributions, or (2) discriminate in favor of highly compensated employees within the meaning of section 401(a)(4).

Section 9203(a)(2) of OBRA 1986 amended Code section 410(a)(2) to provide that a plan will not constitute a qualified plan under section 401(a) if the plan excludes from participation (on the basis of age) an employee who has attained a specified age. The proposed regulations provide that, effective for plan years beginning after December 31, 1987, a plan may not apply a maximum age provision to any employee who has at least one hour of service for the employer on or after January 1, 1988, regardless of when the employee first performed an hour of service for the employer.

In the case of an employee who was ineligible to participate in a plan before the effective date of amended Code section 410(a)(2) because of a maximum age condition and who is eligible to participate in the plan on or after the effective date of such section, hours of service and years of service credited to the employee before the first plan year beginning on or after January 1, 1988, shall be taken into account in accordance with section 411 and the regulations thereunder and in accordance with 29 CFR Part 2530 for purposes of determining the employee's nonforfeitable right to the employee's accrued benefit. However, with respect to an employee described in the preceding sentence, hours of service and years of service credited to the employee before the first plan year beginning on or after January 1, 1988, are not required to be taken into account for purposes of determining the employee's accrued benefit under the plan for plan years beginning on or after January 1, 1988. See, also, section 411(a)(4) and § 1.411(a)-5 for rules relating to service that must be taken into account in determining an employee's nonforfeitable right to the employee's accrued benefit.

Section 9203(b)(2) of OBRA 1986 amended Code section 411(a)(8)(B) to provide rules relating to the determination of a participant's normal retirement age under a defined benefit plan and a defined contribution plan. Because section 203(e) of the pending Technical Corrections Act of 1987 (H.R. 2636) would change the definition of normal retirement age from the definition now set forth in section 411(a)(8)(B) (as amended by OBRA 1986), the proposed regulations do not set forth any rules under section 411(a)(8)(B) (as amended by OBRA 1986).

Section 9202(b) of OBRA 1986 amended Code section 411(B)(2)(C) to require the Secretary to provide by regulations for the application of the continued allocation rules of section 411(b)(2) to target benefit plans. The proposed regulations do not provide detailed special rules applicable to target benefit plans. Target benefit plans are subject to the rules applicable to defined contribution plans. The Commissioner will prescribe such additional rules relating to the continued allocation of contributions and accrual of benefits under target benefit plans as may be necessary or appropriate.

Effective Date

Section 9204(a)(1) of OBRA 1986 provides that the amendments made with regard to section 411(b)(1)(H) and (b)(2) "shall apply only with respect to plan years beginning on or after January 1, 1988, and only to employees who have 1 hour of service in any plan year to which such amendments apply." The proposed regulations provide that section 411(b)(1)(H) and (b)(2) does not apply to an employee who does not have at least 1 hour of service for the employer in a plan year beginning on or after January 1, 1988.

However, the proposed regulations provide that section 411(b)(1)(H) and (b)(2) applies with respect to all years of service completed by an employee who has at least 1 hour of service in a plan year beginning on or after January 1, 1988. Accordingly, under section 411(b)(1)(H)(i), the proposed regulations provide that, for plan years beginning on or after January 1, 1988, in determining the benefit payable under a defined benefit plan to a participant who has at least 1 hour of service in a plan year beginning on or after January 1, 1988, the plan does not satisfy section 411(a) if the plan disregards, because of the participant's attainment of any age, any year of service completed by the participant or any compensation earned by the participant after attaining such age, including years of service completed and compensation earned before the first plan year beginning on or after January 1,

1988. Under the proposed regulations, section 411(b)(2) does not require allocations to the accounts of employees under a defined contribution plan for any plan year beginning before January 1, 1988. However, the proposed regulations provide that, for plan years beginning on or after January 1, 1988, in determining the allocation to the account of a participant (who has at least 1 hour of service in a plan year beginning on or after January 1, 1988) under a defined contribution plan that determines allocations under a service related allocation formula, the plan does not satisfy section 411(a) if the plan disregards, because of the participant's attainment of any age, any year of service completed by the participant.

Under the proposed regulations, a defined benefit plan and a defined contribution plan will not be treated as impermissibly disregarding, because of the participant's attainment of any age, a year of service completed by the participant before the first plan year beginning before January 1, 1988, merely because the participant was not eligible under the plan to make mandatory or voluntary employee contributions (as well as contributions under a cash or deferred arrangement described in section 401(k)) for such year.

Title I of ERISA and OBRA 1986

Under section 101 of Reorganization Plan No. 4 of 1978 (43 FR 47713), the Secretary of the Treasury has jurisdiction over the subject matter addressed in the OBRA 1986 regulations. Therefore, under section 104 of the Reorganization Plan, these regulations apply when the Secretary of Labor exercises authority under Title I of ERISA (as amended, including the amendments made by Title IX of OBRA 1986 and the amendments by the Tax Reform Act of 1986). Thus, the requirements also apply to employee plans subject to Part 2 of Title I of ERISA.

Under section 9201 of OBRA 1986, these regulations also apply for purposes of applying comparable provisions under section 4(i)(7) of the Age Discrimination in Employment Act of 1967 (29 U.S.C. 623) as amended. No interference is intended under the proposed regulations as to the application of the Age Discrimination in Employment Act of 1967, as in effect prior to its amendment by OBRA 1986, to employees who are not credited with at least 1 hour of service in a plan year beginning on or after January 1, 1988.

Reliance on These Proposed Regulations

Taxpayers may rely on these proposed regulations for guidance pending the issuance of final regulations. Because these regulations are generally effective for plan years beginning after 1987, the Service will apply these proposed regulations in issuing rulings and in examining returns with respect to taxpayers and plans. If future guidance is more restrictive, such guidance will be applied without retroactive effect.

Time of Plan Amendments

The proposed regulations provide rules relating to the postponement of the deadline for amending plans to comply with the provisions of OBRA 1986. Plan amendments required to conform the plan to the changes contained in OBRA 1986 need not be made until the dates specified in section 1140 of the Tax Reform Act of 1986 (in general, the last day of the first plan year commencing on or after January 1, 1989). This deferred amendment date is available only if: (1) The plan is operated in accordance with the applicable provisions of OBRA 1986 for the period beginning with the effective date of the provision with respect to the plan; (2) the plan amendments adopted are retroactive to such effective date; and (3) the plan amendments adopted are consistent with plan operation during the retroactive effective period.

Special Analyses

The Commissioner of Internal Revenue has determined that this proposed rule is not a major rule as defined in Executive Order 12291 and that a regulatory impact analysis is not required.

Although this document is a notice of proposed rulemaking which solicits public comments, the Internal Revenue Service has concluded that the regulations proposed herein are interpretative and that the notice and public procedure requirements of 5 U.S.C. 553 do not apply. Accordingly, these proposed regulations do not constitute regulations subject to the Regulatory Flexibility Act (5 U.S.C. Chapter 6).

Comments and Requests for a Public Hearing

Before adopting these proposed regulations, consideration will be given to any written comments that are submitted (preferably eight copies) to the Commissioner of Internal Revenue. All comments will be available for public inspection and copying. A public hearing will be held upon written request to the Commissioner by any person who has submitted comments. If a public hearing is held, notice of the time and place will be published in the *Federal Register*.

Drafting Information

The principal author of these proposed regulations is Michael C. Garvey of the Employee Benefits and Exempt Organizations Division of the Office of Chief Counsel, Internal Revenue Service. However, personnel from other offices of the Internal Revenue Service and Treasury Department participated in developing the regulations, both on matters of substance and style.

List of Subjects in 26 CFR 1.401-0-1.425-1

Income taxes, Employee benefits plans, Pensions.

Proposed Amendments to the Regulations

The proposed amendments to 26 CFR Part 1 are as follows:

PART 1—[AMENDED]

Income Tax Regulations

Paragraph 1. The authority citation for Part 1 is amended by adding the following citation:

Authority: 26 U.S.C. 7805 * * * Section 1.411(b)-2 is also issued under 26 U.S.C. 411(b)(1)(H) and 411(b)(2).

Par. 2. A new § 1.410(a)-4A is added immediately after § 1.410(a)-4 to read as follows:

§ 1.410(a)-4A. Maximum age conditions after 1987.

(a) *Maximum age conditions.* Under section 410(a)(2), a plan is not a qualified plan (and a trust forming a part of such plan is not a qualified trust) if the plan, either directly or indirectly, excludes any employee from participation on the basis of attaining a maximum age.

(b) *Effective date and transitional rule.* If a plan contains a provision that excludes an employee from participation on the basis of attaining a maximum age, the provision may not be applied in a plan year beginning on or after January 1, 1988, to any employee (regardless of when the employee first performed an hour of service for the employer) who is credited with at least 1 hour of service on or after January 1, 1988. For purposes of determining when such an employee (who is not otherwise ineligible to participate in the plan) must become eligible to participate in the plan under section 410(a)(1)(A)(ii), section 410(a)(1)(B) and the provisions of the plan, hours of service and years of service credited to the employee before the first plan year beginning on or after January 1, 1988, are taken into account in accordance with section 410 and the regulations thereunder and in accordance with 29 CFR Part 2530. Any employee who would be eligible to participate in the plan taking such service into account and whose entry date would be prior to the first day of the first plan year beginning on or after January 1, 1988, must participate in the plan as of the first day of such plan year.

(c) *Examples.* The provisions of this section may be illustrated by the following examples:

Example (1). Employer X maintains a defined benefit plan that uses a 12-month period beginning July 1 and ending June 30 as its plan year and that specifies a normal retirement age of 65. The plan provides that each employee of X is eligible to become a participant in the plan on the first entry date on or after the employee completes 1 year of service for X. The plan has 2 entry dates, July 1 and January 1. However, prior to the plan year beginning July 1, 1988, the plan contained a provision that excluded from participation any employee first hired within 5 years of attaining the plan's specified normal retirement age of 65. Employee A was hired by X on August 1, 1986 at age 62. A completes 1 year of service for X by August 1, 1987. If A performs at least one hour of service for X on or after January 1, 1988, the plan, in order to meet the requirements of section 410(a)(2), may not apply the maximum age provision to A on or after July 1, 1988, and A must be eligible to become a participant in the plan in accordance with the other eligibility rules contained in the plan, taking into account A's service with X performed prior to July 1, 1988 to the extent required under the terms of the plan or under section 410 and the regulations thereunder and under regulations in 29 CFR Part 2530. Accordingly, if A is still employed by X on July 1, 1988, A must become a participant in the plan on that date.

Example (2). Employer Y maintains a defined benefit plan that uses the calendar year as its plan year and that specifies a normal retirement age of 65. Employee B is first hired by Y in 1988 when B is age 66. In order for the plan to meet the requirements of section 410(a)(2), B may

not be excluded from plan participation on the basis of B having attained a specified age.

Par. 3. Section 1.411(a)-1 is amended by revising paragraph (a)(3) to read as follows:

§ 1.411(a)-1. Minimum vesting standards; general rules.

(a) *In general.* * * *

(3) The plan satisfies the requirements of—

(i) Section 411(a)(2) and § 1.411(a)-3 (relating to vesting in accrued benefit derived from employer contributions),

(ii) In the case of a defined benefit plan, section 411(b)(1) and (3) (see §§ 1.411(b)-1 and 1.411(b)-2, relating to accrued benefit requirements, separate accounting and accruals and allocations after a specified age), and

(iii) In the case of a defined contribution plan, section 411(b)(2) and (3) (see §§ 1.411(b)-1(e)(2) and 1.411(b)-2, relating to accruals and allocations after a specified age and separate accounting).

* * *

Par. 4. Section 1.411(a)-7 is amended by adding a new paragraph (b)(3) to read as follows:

§ 1.411(a)-7. Definitions and special rules.

* * *

(b) *Normal retirement age.* * * *

(3) *Effect of Omnibus Budget Reconciliation Act of 1986 (OBRA).* [Reserved]

* * *

Par. 5. A new § 1.411(b)-2 is added after § 1.411(b)-1 to read as follows:

§ 1.411(b)-2. Accruals and allocations after a specified age.

(a) *In general.* Section 411(b)(1)(H) provides that a defined benefit plan does not satisfy the minimum vesting standards of section 411(a) if, under the plan, benefit accruals on behalf of a participant are discontinued or the rate of benefit accrual on behalf of a participant is reduced because of the participant's attainment of any age. Section 411(b)(2) provides that a defined contribution plan does not satisfy the minimum vesting standards of section 411(a) if, under the plan, allocations to a participant's account are reduced or discontinued or the rate of allocations to a participant's account is reduced because of the participant's attainment of any age. A defined benefit plan is not considered to discontinue benefit accruals or reduce the rate of benefit accrual on behalf of a participant because of the attainment of any age in violation of section 411(b)(1)(H) and a defined contribution plan is not considered to reduce or discontinue allocations to a participant's account or reduce the rate of allocations to a participant's account because of the attainment of any age in violation of section 411(b)(2) solely because of a positive correlation between increased age and a reduction or discontinuance in benefit accruals or account allocations under a plan. Thus, for example, if a defined benefit plan or a defined contribution plan provides for reduced or discontinued benefit accruals or account allocations on behalf of participants who have completed a specified number of years of credited service, the plan will not thereby fail to satisfy section 411(b)(1)(H) or (b)(2) solely because of a positive correlation between increased age and completion of the specified number of years of credited service. See paragraph (b)(2) of this section for rules relating to benefit and service limitations under defined benefit plans and paragraph (c)(2) of this section for rules relating to limitations on allocations under defined contribution plans. Also, if benefit accruals or the rate of benefit accrual on behalf of a participant in a defined benefit plan or allocations or the rate of allocations to the account of a participant in a defined contribution plan are reduced or discontinued under the plan and the reason for the reduction or discontinuance is neither directly nor indirectly related to the participant's attainment of a specified age, the plan does not thereby fail to satisfy the requirements of section 411(b)(1)(H) or (b)(2). Thus, for example, if a defined benefit plan is amended to cease or reduce the rate of benefit accrual for all plan participants, such cessation or reduction does not fail to satisfy the requirements of section 411(b)(1)(H).

(b) *Defined benefit plans—(1) In general.* (i) A defined benefit plan does not satisfy the minimum vesting standards of section 411(a) if, either directly or indirectly, because of the attainment of any age—

(A) A participant's accrual of benefits is discontinued or the rate of a participant's accrual of benefits is decreased, or

(B) A participant's compensation after the attainment of such age is not taken into account in determining the participant's accrual of benefits.

(ii) In determining whether a defined benefit plan satisfies paragraph (b)(1)(i) of this section, the subsidized portion of an early retirement benefit (whether provided on a temporary or permanent basis), a social security supplement (as defined in § 1.411(a)-7(c)(4)(ii)) and a qualified disability benefit (as defined in § 1.411(a)-7(c)(3)) are disregarded in determining the rate of a participant's accrual of benefits under the plan.

(iii) The provisions of paragraph (b)(1)(i) of this section may be illustrated by the following example. In the example, assume that the participant completes the hours of service in a plan year required under the plan to accrue a full benefit for the plan year.

Example. Employer X maintains a defined benefit plan that provides a normal retirement benefit of 1% of a participant's average annual compensation, multiplied by the participant's years of credited service under the plan. Normal retirement age under the plan is age 65. The plan contains no limitations (other than the limitations imposed by section 415) on the maximum amount of benefits the plan will pay to any participant or on the maximum number of years of credited service taken into account under the plan for purposes of determining the amount of any participant's normal retirement benefit. Participant A became a participant in the plan at age 25 and worked continuously for X until A retired at age 70. The plan will satisfy the requirements of section 411(b)(1)(H) and paragraph (b)(2) of this section if, under the plan's benefit formula, upon A's retirement, A has an accrued normal retirement benefit of at least 45% of A's average annual compensation (1% per year × 45 years).

(2) *Benefit and service limitations*—(i) *In general.* A defined benefit plan does not fail to satisfy section 411(b)(1)(H) and paragraph (b) of this section solely because the plan limits the amount of benefits a participant may accrue under the plan or limits the number of years of service or years of participation taken into account for purposes of determining the accrual of benefits under the plan (credited service). For this purpose, a limitation that is expressed as a percentage of compensation (whether averaged over a participant's total years of credited service for the employer or over a shorter period) and a limitation of the type described in section 401(a)(5)(D) are treated as permissible limitations on the amount of benefits a participant may accrue under the plan. However, in applying a limitation on the number of years of credited service that are taken into account under a plan, the plan may not take into account any year of service that is disregarded in determining the accrual of benefits under the plan (prior to the effective date of section 411(b)(1)(H) and this section) because of the attainment of any age.

(ii) *Limitation not based on age.* Any limitation on the amount of benefits a participant may accrue under the plan and any limitation on the number of years of credited service taken into account under the plan may not be based, directly or indirectly, on the attainment of any age. A limitation that is determined by reference to age or that is not determinable except by reference to age is considered a limitation directly based on age. Thus, a plan provision that, for purposes of benefit accrual, disregards years of service completed after a participant becomes eligible to receive social security benefits is considered a limitation directly based on age. Similarly, a plan provision that, for purposes of benefit accrual, disregards years of service completed after the sum of a participant's age and the participant's number of years of credited service equals a specified number, is considered a limitation directly based on age. Whether a limitation is indirectly based on age is determined with reference to all the facts and circumstances.

(iii) *Examples.* The provisions of paragraph (b)(2) of this section may be illustrated by the following examples. In each example, assume that the participant completes the hours of service in a plan year required under the plan to accrue a full benefit for the plan year.

Example (1). Assume the same facts as in the example set forth in paragraph (b)(1)(ii) of this section, except that the plan provides that not more than 35 years of credited service will be taken into account in determining a participant's normal retirement benefit under the plan. Upon A's retirement at age 70, A will have a normal retirement benefit under the plan's benefit formula of 35% of A's average annual compensation (1% per year × 35 years). The plan will not fail to satisfy the requirements of section 411(b)(1)(H) and this paragraph (b) merely because the plan provides that the final 10 years of A's service under the plan is not taken into account in determining A's normal retirement benefit. The result would be the same if the plan provided that no participant could accrue a normal retirement benefit in excess of 35% of the participant's average annual compensation.

Example (2). Employer Y maintains a defined benefit plan that provides a normal retirement benefit of 50% of a participant's final average compensation. Normal retirement age under the plan is age 65. Other than the limitations imposed by section 415, the plan contains no provision that limits the accrual of the benefit payable to a participant who has less than a specified number of years of credited service for Y. Participant A is hired by Y at age 66 and commences participation in the plan at age 67. Under the plan's benefit formula, if A completes one year of credited service under the plan, A will be entitled to receive (subject to the limitations of section 415) a normal retirement benefit equal to 50% of A's final average compensation.

(3) *Different rates of benefit accrual*—(i) *In general.* A defined benefit plan does not fail to satisfy the requirements of section 411(b)(1)(H) and paragraph (b) of this section solely because the plan provides for the accrual of benefits at different rates with respect to participants under the plan. Accordingly, a plan under which a participant's accrued benefit is determined in accordance with the fractional rule described in section 411(b)(1)(C) and § 1.411(b)-1(b)(3) will not fail to satisfy the requirements of section 411(b)(1)(H) and paragraph (b) of this section solely because the rate at which a participant's normal retirement benefit accrues differs depending on the number of years of credited service a participant would have between the date of commencement of participation and the attainment of normal retirement age. In addition, a plan will not be treated as failing to satisfy section 411(b)(1)(H) and paragraph (b) of this section solely because the plan's benefit formula provides, on a uniform and consistent basis, a normal retirement benefit equal to, for example, 2% of average annual compensation multiplied by a participant's first 15 years of credited service and 1% of average annual compensation multiplied by a participant's years of credited service in excess of 15 years. The preceding sentence applies regardless of when the participant's normal retirement age occurs.

(ii) *Differences not based on age.* Any differences in the rate of benefit accrual described in paragraph (b)(3)(i) of this section may not be based, directly or indirectly, on the attainment of any age.

(4) *Certain adjustments for delayed retirement*—(i) *In general.* Under section 411(b)(1)(H)(iii), a plan may provide that benefit accruals that would otherwise be required under section 411(b)(1)(H)(i) and paragraph (b) of this section for a plan year are reduced (but not below zero) as set forth in paragraph (b)(4)(ii) and (iii) of this section. This paragraph (b)(4) applies for a plan year to a participant who, as of the end of the plan year, has attained normal retirement age under the plan.

(ii) *Distribution of benefits.* (A) A plan may provide that the benefit accrual otherwise required under section 411(b)(1)(H)(i) and paragraph (b) of this section for a plan year is reduced (but not below zero) by the actuarial equivalent of total plan benefit distributions (as determined under this paragraph (b)(4)(ii)) made to the participant by the close of the plan year.

(B) The plan benefit distributions described in this paragraph (b)(4)(ii) are limited to distributions made to the participant during plan years and periods with respect to which section 411(b)(1)(H)(i) and this section apply (including plan years and periods beginning before January 1, 1988) for which the plan could (without regard to section 401(a)(9) and the regulations thereunder) provide for the suspension of the participant's plan benefits in accordance with section 203(a)(3)(B) of the Employee Retirement Income Security Act of 1974 (ERISA) and regulations issued thereunder by the Department of Labor.

(C) For purposes of determining the total amount of plan benefit distributions that may be taken into account under this paragraph (b)(4)(ii) as of the close of a plan year, distributions shall be disregarded to the extent the total amount of distributions made to the participant by the close of the plan year exceeds the total amount of the distributions the participant would have received by the close of the plan year if the distributions had been made in accordance with the plan's normal form of benefit distribution. Accordingly, the plan is required to accrue a benefit for the plan year on behalf of a participant in accordance with the plan's benefit formula, taking into account all of the participant's years of credited service, reduced (but not below the participant's normal retirement benefit for the prior plan year) by the actuarial equivalent of total benefit distributions (taken into account under this paragraph (b)(4)(ii)) made to the participant by the close of the plan year. If, by the close of the plan year, the actuarial equivalent of total plan benefit distributions made to the participant and taken into account under this paragraph (b)(4)(ii) is greater than the total benefit accruals required under section 411(b)(1)(H)(i) and paragraph (b) of this section for the plan years during which such distributions were made, the plan is not required under section 411(b)(1)(H)(i) and paragraph (b) of this section to accrue any benefit on behalf of the participant for the plan year.

(iii) *Adjustment in benefits payable.* (A) A plan may provide that the benefit accrual otherwise required under section 411(b)(1)(H)(i) and paragraph (b) of this section for the plan year is reduced (but not below zero) by the amount of any actuarial adjustment under the plan in the benefit payable for the plan year with respect to the participant because of a delay in the payment of plan benefits after the participant's attainment of normal retirement age.

(B) For purposes of paragraph (b)(4)(iii)(A) of this section, the actuarial adjustment may be taken into account for a plan year only to the extent it is made to the greater of the participant's retirement benefit as of the close of the prior plan year, including any actuarial adjustment made under the plan for the prior plan year, and the participant's normal retirement benefit as of the close of the prior plan year determined by including benefit accruals required by section 411(b)(1)(H)(i) and paragraph (b) of this section. If the retirement benefit, as actuarially adjusted for the plan year in accordance with this paragraph (b)(4)(iii) for delayed payment, exceeds the normal retirement benefit, as determined by including benefit accruals required for the plan year by section 411(b)(1)(H)(i) and paragraph (b) of this section, the plan shall be required to provide the retirement benefit, as actuarially adjusted in accordance with this paragraph (b)(4)(iii) under the plan. Notwithstanding the provisions of this paragraph (b)(4)(iii)(B), in the case of a plan that suspends benefit payments in accordance with section 203(a)(3)(B) of the Employee Retirement Income Security Act of 1974 and the regulations issued thereunder by the Department of Labor, the plan does not fail to satisfy the requirements of section 411(b)(1)(H) and paragraph (b) of this section solely because the plan provides that the retirement benefit to which a participant is entitled as of the close of a plan year ending after the participant attains normal retirement age under the plan is the greater of the benefit payable at normal retirement age (not including benefit accruals otherwise required by section 411(b)(1)(H) and paragraph (b) of this section) actuarially adjusted under the plan to the close of the plan year for delayed payment, and the retirement benefit determined under the plan as of the close of the plan year determined by section 411(b)(1)(H) and paragraph (b) of this section and determined without regard to any offset that would otherwise be applicable under this paragraph (b)(4)(iii).

(iv) *Examples.* The provisions of paragraph (b)(4) of this section may be illustrated by the following examples. In each example, assume that the participant completes the hours of service in a plan year required under the plan to accrue a full benefit for the plan year and assume that the participant is not married unless otherwise specified.

Example (1). Employer Y maintains a defined benefit plan that provides a normal retirement benefit of $20 per month multiplied by the participant's years of credited service. The plan contains no limit on the number of years of credited service taken into account for purposes of determining the normal retirement benefit provided by the plan. Participant A attains normal retirement age of 65 and continues in the full time service of Y. At age 65, A has 30 years of credited service under the plan and could receive a normal retirement benefit of $600 per month ($20 × 30 years) if A retires. The plan provides for the suspension of A's normal retirement benefit (in accordance with section 203(a)(3)(B) of the Employee Retirement Income Security Act of 1974 (ERISA) and regulations issued by the Department of Labor) during the period of A's continued employment with Y. Accordingly, the plan does not provide for an actuarial adjustment of A's normal retirement benefit because of delayed payment and the plan does not pay A's normal retirement benefit while A remains in the full time service of Y. If A retires at age 67, after completing two additional years of credited service for Y, A must receive additional accruals for the two years of credited service completed after attaining normal retirement age in order for the plan to satisfy section 411(b)(1)(H)(i). Accordingly, A is entitled to receive a normal retirement benefit of $640 per month ($20 × 32 years).

Example (2). Assume the same facts as in *Example (1),* except that the plan provides that at the time A's normal retirement benefit becomes payable, the amount of A's normal retirement benefit (determined as of A's normal retirement age and each year thereafter) will be actuarially increased for delayed retirement. The plan offsets this actuarial increase against benefit accruals in plan years ending after A's attainment of normal retirement age, as permitted by paragraph (b)(4)(iii) of this section. Accordingly, the plan does not provide for the suspension of normal retirement benefits (in accordance with section 203(a)(3)(B) of ERISA and regulations thereunder issued by the Department of Labor). Under section 411(b)(1)(H), the plan must provide A with a benefit of at least $620 per month after A completes 31 years of credited service for Y. However, under paragraph (b)(4)(iii) of this

section, the plan is not required to provide A with a benefit accrual for A's additional year of credited service for Y because, under the plan, A will be entitled to receive, upon retirement at age 66 after completing 1 additional year of credited service for Y, an actuarially increased benefit of $672 per month. This monthly benefit of $672 is the greater of A's normal retirement benefit at normal retirement age ($20 × 30 years = $600) actuarially adjusted for delayed payment and A's normal retirement benefit ($20 × 31 years = $620) determined by taking into account A's year of credited service after attaining normal retirement age. Under the plan, A will be entitled to receive, upon retirement at age 67 after completing 2 additional years of credited service for Y after attaining normal retirement age, an actuarially increased benefit of $756 per month. This monthly benefit of $756 is the greater of A's actuarially adjusted normal retirement benefit at age 66 ($672) actuarially adjusted to $756 for delayed payment to age 67 and A's normal retirement benefit ($20 × 32 years = $640) determined by taking into account A's years of credited service after attaining normal retirement age.

Example (3). Assume the same facts as in *Example (1),* except that the plan neither provides for the suspension of normal retirement benefit payments (in accordance with section 203(a)(3)(B) of ERISA and regulations thereunder issued by the Department of Labor) nor provides for an actuarial increase in benefit payments because of delayed payment of benefits. Consequently, the plan provides that the normal retirement benefit will be paid to a participant, beginning at age 65 (normal retirement age) even though the participant remains in the service of Y and offsets the value of the benefit distributions against benefit accruals in plan years ending after the participant's attainment of normal retirement age, as permitted by paragraph (b)(4)(ii) of this section. Participant B (who remains in the full time service of Y) receives 12 monthly benefit payments prior to attainment of age 66. The total monthly benefit payments of $7,200 ($600 × 12 payments) have an actuarial value at age 66 of $7,559 (reflecting interest and mortality) which would produce a monthly benefit of $72 commencing at age 66. The benefit accrual for the year of credited service B completed after attaining normal retirement age is $20 per month ($20 × 1 year). Because the actuarial value (determined as a monthly benefit of $72) of the benefit payments made during the one year of credited service after B's attainment of normal retirement age exceeds the benefit accrual for the one year of credited service after B's attainment of normal retirement age, the plan is not required to accrue benefits on behalf of B for the one year of credited service after B's attainment of normal retirement age and the plan is not required to increase B's monthly benefit payment of $600 at age 66.

Assume B receives 24 monthly benefit payments prior to B's retirement at age 67. The total monthly benefit payments of $14,400 ($600 × 24 payments) have an actuarial value at age 67 of $15,839 (reflecting interest and mortality) which would produce a monthly benefit payment of $156 commencing at age 67. The benefit accrual for the two years of credited service B completed after attaining normal retirement age is $40 per month ($20 × 2 years). Because the actuarial value (determined as a monthly benefit of $156) of the benefit payments made during the two years of credited service after B's normal retirement age exceeds the benefit accrual for the two years of credited service after B's normal retirement age ($20 × 2 years = $40), the plan is not required to accrue benefits on behalf of B for the second year of credited service B completed after attaining normal retirement age and the plan is not required to increase B's monthly benefit payment of $600.

Example (4). Assume that Employer Z maintains a defined benefit plan that provides a normal retirement benefit of 2% of the average of a participant's high three consecutive years of compensation multiplied by the participant's years of credited service under the plan. The plan contains no limit on the number of years of credited service taken into account for purposes of determining the normal retirement benefit provided by the plan. Participant C, who has attained normal retirement age (age 65) under the plan, continues in the full time service of Z. At normal retirement age, C has average compensation of $20,000 for C's high three consecutive years and has 10 years of credited service under the plan. Thus, at normal retirement age, C is entitled to receive an annual normal retirement benefit of $4,000 ($20,000 × .02 × 10 years). Assume further that the plan provides for the suspension of N's normal retirement benefit (in accordance with section 203(a)(3)(B) of ERISA and regulations issued thereunder by the Department of Labor) during the period of C's continued employment with Z. Accordingly, the plan does not provide for the actuarial increase of C's normal retirement benefit because of delayed payment and the plan does not pay C's normal retirement benefit while C remains in the full time service of Z. At age 70, when C retires, C has average annual compensation for C's high three consecutive years of $35,000. Under section 411(b)(1)(H), C must be credited with 15 years of credited service for

Z and C's increased compensation after attaining normal retirement age must be taken into account for purposes of determining C's normal retirement benefit. At age 70, C is entitled to receive an annual normal retirement benefit of $10,500 ($35,000 × .02 × 15 years).

Example (5). Assume the same facts as in *Example (4),* except that the payment of C's retirement benefit is not suspended (in accordance with section 203(a)(3)((B) of ERISA and regulations issued thereunder by the Department of Labor) and, accordingly, the plan provides that retirement benefits that commence after a participant's normal retirement age will be actuarially increased for late retirement. The plan offsets this actuarial increase against benefit accruals in plan years ending after C's attainment of normal retirement age, as permitted by paragraph (b)(4)(iii) of this section. Under this provision, at the close of each plan year after C's attainment of normal retirement age, C's

retirement benefit is actuarially increased. Under this provision, the actuarial increase for the plan year is made to the greater of C's normal retirement benefit at the close of the prior plan year (including previous actuarial adjustments) and C's normal retirement benefit at the close of the prior plan year determined by including all benefit accruals. Accordingly, at the close of each plan year, C is entitled to receive an annual normal retirement benefit equal to the greater of C's normal retirement benefit (adjusted actuarially under the plan from the benefit to which C was entitled at the close of the prior plan year) determined at the close of the plan year and C's normal retirement benefit determined at the close of the plan year by taking into account C's years of credited service and benefit accruals after C's attainment of normal retirement age. The foregoing is illustrated in the following table with respect to certain years of credited service performed by C after attaining normal retirement age 65.

Age	Years of credited service	Average compensation for high three consecutive years	Normal retirement benefit with additional accruals (.02 × column 2 × column 3)	Retirement benefit, as actuarially increased under the plan from the benefit at prior age (column 6)	Normal retirement benefit to which C is entitled (greater of column 4 and column 5)
1	2	3	4	5	6
65	10	$20,000	$4,000	N/A	$4,000
66	11	21,000	4,620	$4,482	4,620
67	12	29,000	6,960	5,192	6,960
68	13	30,000	7,800	7,848	7,848
69	14	33,000	9,240	8,880	9,240
70	15	35,000	10,500	10,494	10,500

Example (6). Assume the same facts as in *Example (4),* except that C does not retire at age 70, but continues in the full time service of Z. Upon C's attainment of age 70, the plan commences benefit payments to C. The annual benefit paid to C in the first plan year is $10,500 ($35,000 × .02 × 15 years). In determining the annual benefit payable to C in each subsequent plan year, the plan offsets the value of benefit distributions made to the participant by the close of the prior plan year against benefit accruals in plan years during which such distributions were made, as permitted by paragraph (b)(4)(ii) of this section. Ac-

cordingly, for each subsequent plan year, C is entitled under the plan to receive benefit payments based on C's benefit (at the close of the prior plan year) determined under the plan formula by taking into account all of C's years of credited service, reduced (but not below C's normal retirement benefit for the prior plan year) by the value of total benefit distributions made to C by the close of the prior plan year. The foregoing is illustrated in the following table with respect to certain years of credited service performed by C while benefits were being distributed to C.

Years of benefit distributions	Years of credited service (as of close of the year)	Average compensation for high three years	Normal retirement benefit with additional accruals (.02 × column 2 × column 3)	Suspendible benefit distributions made during the year
1	2	3	4	5
N/A	15	$35,000	$10,500	N/A
1	16	35,000	11,200	$10,500
2	17	45,000	15,300	10,500
3	18	50,000	18,000	12,091

Years of benefit distributions	Cumulative suspendible benefit distributions made as of close of the year	Annual benefit that is actuarial equivalent of cumulative suspendible benefit distributions made as of close of the year	Retirement benefit to which C is entitled at close of the year (column 4 − column 7, but not less than column 8 for prior year)
1	6	7	8
N/A	N/A	N/A	$10,500
1	$10,500	$1,472	10,500
2	21,000	3,209	12,091
3	33,091	5,510	12,490

(c) *Defined contribution plans*—(1) *In general.* A defined contribution plan (including a target benefit plan described in § 1.410(a)-4(a)(1)) does not satisfy the minimum vesting standards of section 411(a) if, either directly or indirectly, because of the attainment of any age—

(i) The allocation of employer contributions or forfeitures to the accounts of participants is discontinued, or

(ii) The rate at which the allocation of employer contributions or forfeitures is made to the accounts of participants is decreased.

(2) *Limitations on allocations.* (i) A defined contribution plan (including a target benefit plan described in § 1.410(a)-4(a)(1)) does not fail to satisfy the minimum vesting standards of section 411(a) solely because the plan limits the total amount of employer contributions and forfeitures that may be allocated to a participant's account (for a particular plan year or for the participant's total years of credited service under the plan) or solely because the plan limits the total number of years of credited service for which a participant's account may receive alloca-

tions of employer contributions and forfeitures. The limitations described in the preceding sentence may not be applied with respect to the allocation of gains, losses or income of the trust to the account of a participant. Furthermore, a defined contribution plan (including a target benefit plan) does not fail to satisfy section 411(a) solely because the plan limits the number of years of credited service that may be taken into account for purposes of determining the amount of, or the rate at which, employer contributions and forfeitures are allocated to a participant's account for a particular plan year. However, in applying a credited service limitation described in this paragraph (c)(2)(i), the plan may not take into account any year of service (prior to the effective date of section 411(b)(2) and paragraph (c) of this section) that is disregarded in determining allocations to a participant's account because of the participant's attainment of any age.

(ii) Any limitation described in paragraph (c)(2)(i) of this section may not be based, directly or indirectly, on the attainment of any age.

¶20,149C

The provisions of paragraph (b)(2)(ii) of this section shall also apply for purposes of this paragraph (c).

(iii) The Commissioner shall provide such additional rules as may be necessary or appropriate with respect to the application of section 411(b)(2) and this section to target benefit plans.

(d) *Benefits and forms of benefits subject to requirements —*(1) *General rule.* Except as provided in paragraph (d)(2) of this section, section 411(b)(1)(H) and (b)(2) and paragraphs (b) and (c) of this section apply to all benefits (and forms of benefits) provided under a defined benefit plan and a defined contribution plan, including accrued benefits, benefits described in section 411(d)(6), ancillary benefits and other rights and features provided under the plan. Accordingly, except as provided in paragraph (d)(2) of this section, benefit accruals under a defined benefit plan and allocations under a defined contribution plan will be considered to be reduced on account of the attainment of a specified age if optional forms of benefits, ancillary benefits, or other rights or features under the plan provided with respect to benefits or allocations attributable to credited service prior to the attainment of such age are not provided (on at least as favorable a basis to participants) with respect to benefits or allocations attributable to credited service after such age. Thus, for example, a plan may not provide a lump sum payment only with respect to benefits attributable to years of credited service before the attainment of a specified age. Similarly, except as provided in paragraph (d)(2) of this section, if an optional form of benefit is available under the plan at a specified age, the availability of such form of benefit, or the method for determining the manner in which such benefit is paid, may not, directly or indirectly, be denied or provided on terms less favorable to participants because of the attainment of any higher age. Similarly, if the method for determining the amount or the rate of the subsidized portion of a joint and survivor annuity or the subsidized portion of a preretirement survivor annuity is less favorable with respect to participants who have attained a specified age than with respect to participants who have not attained such age, benefit accruals or account allocations under the plan will be considered to be reduced on account of the attainment of such age.

(2) *Special rule for certain benefits.* A plan will not fail to satisfy section 411(b)(1)(H) or paragraph (b) of this section merely because the following benefits, or the manner in which such benefits are provided under the plan, vary because of the attainment of any higher age.

(i) The subsidized portion of an early retirement benefit (whether provided on a temporary or permanent basis),

(ii) A qualified disability benefit (as defined in §1.411(a)-7(c)(3)); and

(iii) A social security supplement (as defined in §1.411(a)-7(c)(4)(ii)).

(e) *Coordination with certain provisions.* Notwithstanding section 441(b)(1)(H), (b)(2) and the preceding paragraphs of this section, the following rules shall apply.

(1) *Section 415 limitations.* No allocation to the account of a participant in a defined contribution plan (including a target benefit plan described in §1.410(a)-4(a)(1)) shall be required for a limitation year by section 411(b)(2) and no benefit accrual with respect to a participant in a defined benefit plan shall be required for a limitation year by section 411(b)(1)(H)(i) to the extent that the allocation of accrual would cause the plan to exceed the limitations of section 415(b), (c), or (e) applicable to the participant for the limitation year.

(2) *Prohibited discrimination.* (i) No allocation to the account of a highly compensated employee in a defined contribution plan (including a target benefit plan) shall be required for a plan year by section 411(b)(2) to the extent the allocation would cause the plan to discriminate in favor of highly compensated employees within the meaning of section 401(a)(4).

(ii) No benefit accrual on behalf of a highly compensated employee in a defined benefit plan shall be required for a plan year by section 411(b)(1)(H)(i) to the extent such benefit accrual would cause the plan to discriminate in favor of highly compensated employees within the meaning of section 410(a)(4).

(iii) The Commissioner may provide additional rules relating to prohibited discrimination in favor of highly compensated employees.

(3) *Permitted disparity.* In the case of a plan that would fail to satisfy section 401(a)(4) except for the application of section 401(a), no allocation to the account of a participant in a defined contribution plan and no benefit accrual on behalf of a participant in a defined benefit plan shall be required under section 411(b)(1)(H) or (b)(2) for a plan year to the extent such allocation or accrual would cause the plan to fail to satisfy

the requirements of section 401(1) and the regulations thereunder for the plan year.

(f) *Effective dates*—(1) *Noncollectively bargained plans*—(i) *In general.* Except as otherwise provided in paragraph (f)(2) of this section, section 411(b)(1)(H) and (b)(2) and paragraphs (b) and (c) of this section are effective for plan years beginning on or after January 1, 1988, with respect to a participant who is credited with at least 1 hour of service in a plan year beginning on or after January 1, 1988. Section 411(b)(1)(H) and (b)(2) and paragraphs (b) and (c) of this section are not effective with respect to a participant who is not credited with at least 1 hour of service in a plan year beginning on or after January 1, 1988.

(ii) *Defined benefit plans.* In the case of a participant who is credited with at least 1 hour of service in a plan year beginning on or after January 1, 1988, section 411(b)(1)(H) and paragraph (b) of this section are effective with respect to all years of service completed by the participant, including years of service completed before the first plan year beginning on or after January 1, 1998. Accordingly, in the case of a participant described in the preceding sentence, a defined benefit plan does not satisfy section 411(b)(1)(H) and paragraph (b) of this section for a plan year beginning on or after January 1, 1988, if the plan disregards, because of the participant's attainment of any age, any year of service completed by the participant or any compensation earned by the participant after attaining such age. However, a defined benefit plan is not required under section 411(b)(1)(H) and paragraph (b) of this section to take into account for benefit accrual purposes any year of service completed before an employee becomes a participant in the plan. See paragraph (b)(2) of this section for rules relating to benefit and service limitations that may be imposed by a defined benefit plan.

(iii) *Defined contribution plans.* Section 411(b)(2) and paragraph (c) of this section are not applicable with respect to allocations of employer contributions or forfeitures to the accounts of participants under a defined contribution plan for a plan year beginning before January 1, 1988. However, in the case of a defined contribution plan under which allocations to the accounts of participants for a plan year are determined on the basis of an allocation formula that takes into account service or compensation for the employer during prior plan years, section 411(b)(2) and paragraph (c) of this section are effective for plan years beginning on or after January 1, 1988, with respect to all years of service completed by the participant, including years of service completed before the first plan year beginning on or after January 1, 1988. Accordingly, in the case of a participant who has at least 1 hour of service in a plan year beginning on or after January 1, 1988, a defined contribution plan containing an allocation formula described in the preceding sentence does not satisfy section 411(b)(2) and paragraph (c) of this section with respect to allocations for a plan year beginning on or after January 1, 1988, if the plan disregards, because of the participant's attainment of any age, any year of service completed by the participant. See paragraph (c)(2) of this section for the rules relating to limitations on allocations to the accounts of participants that may be imposed by a defined contribution plan.

(iv) *Employee contributions.* In applying paragraph (f)(1)(i), (ii) and (iii) of this section to plan years beginning on or after January 1, 1988, a year of service completed before the first plan year beginning on or after January 1, 1988, will not be treated as being disregarded under a plan on account of a participant's attainment of a specified age solely because such year of service is disregarded under the plan because the participant was not eligible to make voluntary or mandatory employee contributions (as well as contributions under a cash or deferred arrangement described in section 401(k)) under the plan for such year. A plan is not required to permit a participant to make voluntary or mandatory employee contributions (as well as contributions under a cash or deferred arrangement described in section 401(k)) for a plan year beginning before January 1, 1988, in order to satisfy section 411(b)(1)(H) or (b)(2) or paragraph (b) or (c) of this section for a plan year beginning on or after January 1, 1988.

(v) *Hour of service.* For purposes of this paragraph (f)(1), one hour of service means one hour of service recognized under the plan or required to be recognized under the plan by section 410 (relating to minimum participation standards) or section 411 (relating to minimum vesting standards). In the case of a plan that does not determine service on the basis of hours of service, one hour of service means any service recognized under the plan or required to be recognized under the plan by section 410 (relating to minimum participation standards) or section 411 (relating to minimum vesting standards).

(vi) *Examples.* The provisions of paragraph (f)(1) of this section may be illustrated by the following examples. In each example, assume that the participant completes the hours of service in a plan year required under the plan to accrue a full benefit or receive an allocation for the plan year.

¶20,149C

Example (1). Employer X maintains a noncontributory defined benefit plan (that is not a collectively bargained plan) that provides a normal retirement benefit equal to 1% of a participant's average annual compensation for the participant's three consecutive years of highest compensation, multiplied by the participant's years of credited service under the plan. The plan contains no limit on the number of years of credited service taken into account for purposes of determining the normal retirement benefit provided by the plan. The plan uses the calendar year as its plan year. The plan specifies a normal retirement age of 65 and provides (prior to January 1, 1988) that no compensation earned and no service performed by a participant after attainment of normal retirement age will be taken into account in determining the participant's normal retirement benefit. Participant A attains normal retirement age on December 15, 1985. A continues in the full time service of X and has at least 1 hour of service for X during the plan year beginning on January 1, 1988. As of the plan year ending December 31, 1985, A had 35 years of credited service under the plan. In accordance with the plan provisions in effect prior to January 1, 1988, A's service and compensation during the 1986 and 1987 plan years is not taken into account in determining A's normal retirement benefit for those plan years. Beginning on January 1, 1988, the plan provisions that compensation earned and years of service completed after normal retirement age are not taken into account in determining a participant's normal retirement benefit may not be applied to A. Thus, as of the plan year beginning January 1, 1988, A's normal retirement benefit under the plan must be determined without regard to those provisions. Accordingly, beginning on January 1, 1988, the plan is required to take into account A's service for X and A's compensation from X during the 1986 and 1987 plan years for purposes of determining A's normal retirement benefit in order to satisfy section 411(b)(1)(H) and paragraph (b) of this section.

Example (2). Assume the same facts as in *Example (1)*, except that the plan provides that, in determining a participant's normal retirement benefit under the plan (a) not more than 35 years of credited service will be taken into account and (b) no compensation earned after 35 years of credited service have been completed will be taken into account. Accordingly, the plan is not required to take into account A's service for X or A's compensation from X during the 1986 and 1987 plan years for purposes of determining A's normal retirement benefit in order to satisfy section 411(b)(1)(H) and paragraph (b) of this section.

Example (3). Assume the same facts as in *Example (1)*, except that A retires on December 5, 1987 and does not perform any hours of service for X after A's retirement. Accordingly, the plan is not required to take into account A's service for X and A's compensation from X during the 1986 and 1987 plan years for purposes of determining A's normal retirement benefit in order to satisfy section 411(b)(1)(H) and paragraph (b) of this section.

Example (4). Assume the same facts as in *Example (1)*, except that the plan requires, as a condition to accruing benefits attributable to employer contributions under the plan, that a participant make employee contributions under the plan. The plan provides that a participant is not eligible to make employee contributions in a plan year beginning after the plan year in which the participant attains normal retirement age under the plan. Accordingly, A does not make employee contributions during the 1986 and 1987 plan years and, therefore, does not accrue in those plan years a benefit attributable to employer contributions. The plan is not required to take into account A's service for X and A's compensation from X during the 1986 and 1987 plan years in order to satisfy section 411(b)(1)(H) and paragraph (b) of this section. In addition, the plan is not required to permit A to make employee contributions to the plan for the 1986 and 1987 plan years in order to satisfy section 411(b)(1)(H) and paragraph (b) of this section.

Example (5). Employer Y maintains a profit-sharing plan (that is not a collectively bargained plan). The plan is the only qualified plan maintained by Y and uses the calendar year as its plan year. The formula under the plan for allocating employer contributions and forfeitures to the accounts of participants contains a years of service factor. Pursuant to the allocation formula containing the years of service factor, employer contributions and forfeitures for the plan year are allocated among the accounts of participants on the basis of one unit for each full $200 of compensation for the participant for the plan year and one unit for each year of credited service for Y completed by the participant. The plan contains no limit on the number of years of credited service taken into account for purposes of determining the allocation to the account of a participant for the plan year under the plan's allocation formula. The plan specifies a normal retirement age of 65 and provides (prior to January 1, 1988) that no service performed by a participant in a plan year beginning after the attainment of normal retirement age will be taken into account in determining the allocation to the participant's account for a plan year. Participant B attains normal retirement age on December 15, 1985. B continues in the full time service of Y and has at least 1 hour of service for Y during the plan year beginning January 1, 1988. As of the plan year ending December 31, 1985, B had 35 years of credited service under the plan. In accordance with the plan provisions in effect prior to January 1, 1988, B's service during the 1986 and 1987 plan year is not taken into account in determining the allocation of employer contributions and forfeitures to B's account for the 1986 and 1987 plan years. As of the plan year beginning January 1, 1988, the plan provision that years of service in plan years beginning after attainment of normal retirement age are not taken into account in determining the allocation of employer contributions and forfeitures to the accounts of participants may not be applied to B. Thus, the allocation of employer contributions and forfeitures to B's account for the 1988 plan year must be determined under the allocation formula contained in the plan without regard to that provision. Accordingly, the plan is required to take into account B's service for Y during the 1986 and 1987 plan years for purposes of determining the allocation of employer contributions and forfeitures to B's account for the 1988 plan year in order to satisfy section 411(b)(2) and paragraph (c) of this section. However, the plan is not required to provide any additional allocations to B's account under the plan for the 1986 or 1987 plan year in order to satisfy section 411(b)(2) and paragraph (c) of this section.

Example (6). Assume the same facts as in *Example (5)*, except that the plan provides that, in determining the allocation of employer contributions and forfeitures to the account of a participant for a plan year, not more than 35 years of credited service for Y will be taken into account. Accordingly, the plan is not required to take into account B's service for Y during the 1986 or 1987 plan years for purposes of determining the allocation of employer contributions and forfeitures to B's account for the 1988 plan year under the allocation formula contained in the plan.

(2) *Collectively bargained plans*. (i) In the case of a plan maintained pursuant to 1 or more collective bargaining agreements between employee representatives and 1 or more employers, ratified before March 1, 1986, section 411(b)(1)(H) and (b)(2) is effective for benefits provided under, and employees covered by, any such agreement with respect to plan years beginning on or after the later of—

(A) January 1, 1988, or

(B) The date on which the last of such collective bargaining agreements terminates (determined without regard to any extension of any such agreement occurring on or after March 1, 1986).

However, notwithstanding the preceding sentence, section 411(b)(1)(H) and (b)(2) shall be effective for benefits provided under, and employees covered by, any agreement described in this paragraph (f)(2)(i) no later than with respect to the first plan year beginning on or after January 1, 1990.

(ii) The effective date provisions of paragraph (f)(1) of this section shall apply in paragraph (f)(2)(i) of this section, except that the effective date determined under paragraph (f)(2)(i) of this section shall be substituted for the effective date determined under paragraph (f)(1) of this section.

(iii) In accordance with the provisions of paragraph (f)(2)(i) of this section, a plan described therein may be subject to different effective dates under section 411(b)(1)(H) and (b)(2) for employees who are covered by a collective bargaining agreement and employees who are not covered by a collective bargaining agreement.

(iv) For purposes of paragraph (f)(2)(i) of this section, the service crediting rules of paragraph (f)(1) of this section shall apply to a plan described in paragraph (f)(2)(i) of this section, except that in applying such rules the effective date determined under paragraph (f)(2)(i) of this section shall be substituted for the effective date determined under paragraph (f)(1) of this section. See paragraph (f)(1)(v) of this section for rules relating to the recognition of an hour of service.

(3) *Amendments to plans*. (i) Except as provided in paragraph (f)(3)(ii) of this section, plan amendments required by section 411(b)(1)(H) and (b)(2) (the applicable sections) shall not be required to be made before the first plan year beginning on or after January 1, 1989, if the following requirements are met—

(A) The plan is operated in accordance with the requirements of the applicable section for all periods before the first plan year beginning on or after January 1, 1989, for which such section is effective with respect to the plan; and

(B) Such plan amendments are adopted no later than the last day of the first plan year beginning on or after January 1, 1989, and are made effective retroactively for all periods for which the applicable section is effective with respect to the plan.

(ii) In the case of a collectively bargained plan described in paragraph (f)(2)(i) of this section that satisfies the requirements of paragraph (f)(3)(i) of this section (as modified by this paragraph (f)(3)(ii)), paragraph (f)(3)(i) shall be applied by substituting for "the first plan year beginning on or after January 1, 1989, "the first plan year beginning on or after the later of—

(A) January 1, 1989, or

(B) The date on which the last of such collective bargaining agreements terminates (determined without regard to any extension of any such agreement occurring on or after March 1, 1986).

However, notwithstanding the preceding sentence, section 411(b)(1)(H) and (b)(2) shall be applicable to plans described in this paragraph (f)(3)(ii) no later than the first plan year beginning on or after January 1, 1990.

Par. 6. Section 1.411(c)-1 is amended by revising paragraph (f)(2) to read as follows:

§ 1.411(c)-1 Allocation of accrued benefits between employer and employee contributions.

* * *

(f) *Suspension of benefits, etc.* * * *

(2) *Employment after retirement.* Except as permitted by paragraph (f)(1) of this section, a defined benefit plan must make an actuarial adjustment to an accrued benefit the payment of which is deferred past normal retirement age. See, also, section 411(b)(1)(H) (relating to continued accruals after normal retirement age) and § 1.411(b)-2.

Lawrence B. Gibbs,

Commissioner of Internal Revenue.

[FR Doc. 88-7880 Filed 4-8-88; 8:45 am]

[¶ 20,150 Reserved.—Proposed Reg. § 1.414(e)-1, relating to the definition of "church plan", was formerly reproduced at this point. The final regulation is ¶ 12,360.]

[¶ 20,150A Reserved.—Proposed regulations relating to the exclusion of certain disability payments from gross income were formerly reproduced at this paragraph. The regulations were withdrawn by the Internal Revenue Service in a withdrawal notice on January 13, 1987 (52 FR 2724).]

[¶ 20,150B Reserved.—Proposed regulations relating to the requirements for the filing of returns by employee plans were formerly reproduced at this paragraph. The final regulations appear at ¶ 13,649A, 13,650A, 13,651, 13,662, 13,789 and 13.905.]

¶ 20,150C

Proposed regulations on 26 CPR Part 301.—Reproduced below is the text of proposed regulations which clarify the significance, for classification purposes, of a power in the limited partners to remove a general partner, and provide that references in the classification rules to the Uniform Limited Partnership Act refer to that Act both as originally promulgated and as revised in 1976.

The proposed regulations were published in the *Federal Register* on October 27, 1980 (45 FR 70909).

DEPARTMENT OF THE TREASURY

Internal Revenue Service

26 CFR Part 301

[LR-232-78]

Revision of Rules on Tax Classification of Limited Partnerships in Light of Certain Recent Legislative Developments

AGENCY: Internal Revenue Service, Treasury.

ACTION: Notice of proposed rulemaking.

SUMMARY: This document contains proposed regulations relating to the classification, for federal tax purposes, of limited partnerships. The proposed regulations provide that references in the classification rules to the Uniform Limited Partnership Act (ULPA) refer to that Act both as originally promulgated and as revised in 1976. The proposed regulations also clarify the significance, for classification purposes, of a power in the limited partners to remove a general partner.

DATES: Written comments and requests for a public hearing must be delivered or mailed by December 26, 1980. The amendments are proposed to be effective for taxable years beginning after 1953.

ADDRESS: Send comments and requests for a public hearing to: Commissioner of Internal Revenue, Attention: CC:LR:T (LR-232-78), Washington, D.C. 20224.

FOR FURTHER INFORMATION CONTACT: Paul A. Francis (202-566-6640).

SUPPLEMENTARY INFORMATION:

Background

This document contains proposed amendments to the Regulations on Procedure and Administration (26 CFR Part 301) under section 7701 of the Internal Revenue Code of 1954. These regulations are proposed to make clear the application of certain tax classification rules to limited partnerships and are to be issued under the authority contained in section 7805 of the Internal Revenue Code of 1954 (68A Stat. 917; 26 U.S.C. 7805).

References to the ULPA

For federal tax purposes various entities may be classified as associations (which are taxable as corporations), partnerships, or trusts. Section 7701(a)(2) and (3) of the Code and §§ 301.7701-1 through 301.7701-4 of the Regulations on Procedure and Administration set forth the definitions and rules that control the tax classification of entities. Section 301.7701-2 provides that the classification of an entity depends upon the presence or absence of corporate characteristics. That section also includes certain special rules for determining whether an entity organized under a statute corresponding to the ULPA possesses or lacks the corporate characteristics of continuity of life, centralization of management, and limited liability.

The National Conference of Commissioners on Uniform State Laws revised the ULPA in 1976. The proposed regulations provide that references in § 301.7701-2 to the ULPA shall be deemed to refer to that Act both as originally promulgated and as revised in 1976. Thus, the same classification rules will apply to entities organized under a statute corresponding to the revised ULPA as apply to entities organized under a statute corresponding to the original ULPA.

Power to Remove General Partner

The proposed regulations provide that all the facts and circumstances must be taken into account in determining whether the characteristic of centralized management is found in a limited partnership whose limited partners may remove the general partner. The proposed regulations note that a substantially restricted removal power would not itself cause the partnership to possess centralized management.

Comments and Requests for a Public Hearing

Before adopting these proposed regulations, consideration will be given to any written comments that are submitted (preferably six copies) to the Commissioner of Internal Revenue. All comments will be available for public inspection and copying. A public hearing will be held upon written request to the Commissioner by any person who has submitted written comments. If a public hearing is held, notice of the time and place will be published in the *Federal Register*.

Drafting Information

The principal author of these proposed regulations was Paul A. Francis of the Legislation and Regulations Division of the Office of

Chief Counsel, Internal Revenue Service. However, personnel from other offices of the Internal Revenue Service and Treasury Department participated in developing the regulation, both on matters of substance and style.

Proposed amendments to the regulations

For the reasons stated, it is proposed to amend §301.7701-2 of the Regulations on Procedure and Administration (26 CFR Part 301) by adding a new subparagraph (5) at the end of paragraph (a) and by adding two new sentences at the end of paragraph (c)(4). These added provisions read as follows:

§301.7701-2 Associations.

(a) *Characteristics of corporations.*

* * *

(5) All references in this section to the Uniform Limited Partnership Act shall be deemed to refer both to the original Uniform Limited Partnership Act (adopted in 1916) and to the revised Uniform Limited Partnership Act (adopted by the National Conference of Commissioners on Uniform State Laws in 1976).

* * *

(e) *Centralization of management.*

* * *

(4) * * * Furthermore, if all or a specified group of the limited partners may remove a general partner, all the facts and circumstances must be taken into account in determining whether the partnership possesses centralized management. A substantially restricted right of the limited partners to remove the general partner (*e. g.,* in the event of the general partner's gross negligence, self-dealing, or embezzlement) will not itself cause the partnership to possess centralized management.

* * *

Jerome Kurtz,

Commissioner of Internal Revenue.

[¶ 20,150D Reserved.—Proposed regulations relating to the tax treatment of insurance provided to employees under policies that are not underwritten on a group basis were formerly reproduced at this paragraph. The regulations were withdrawn by the Internal Revenue Service in a withdrawal notice on January 13, 1987 (52 FR 2724).]

¶ 20,150E

Proposed regulations: Incentive stock options.—The IRS issued proposed regulations that explain the incentive stock option (ISO) rules enacted by the Economic Recovery Tax Act of 1981. The proposed regulations set forth the requirements for receiving special tax treatment for ISOs, the conditions that must be met for an option to qualify as an incentive stock option, and the rules for converting existing options to ISOs.

The proposed regulations were published in the *Federal Register* on February 7, 1984 (49 FR 4504). They were withdrawn by the IRS on June 9, 2003 (see ¶ 20,260W).

For statutory options granted on or before June 9, 2003, taxpayers may rely on these 1984 proposed regulations, the 2003 proposed regulations (¶ 20,260W), or on final regulations in T.D. 9144 issued on August 3, 2004 (see ¶ 23,220), until the earlier of January 1, 2006, or the first regularly scheduled stockholders meeting of the granting corporation occurring six months after August 3, 2004.

[¶ 20,151 Reserved.—Proposed Regs. §§301.6110-1 through 301.6110-7, relating to public inspection of written determinations, were formerly reproduced at this point. The final regulations appear at ¶ 13,786A—13,786G.]

[¶ 20,151A Reserved.—Proposed amendments to regulations clarifying that a partnership would lack the continuity of life if dissolution of the partnership occurred due not only to the retirement, death or insanity of a general partner but also from other types of withdrawal from the partnership by a general partner were formerly reproduced here. The final amendments are reproduced at ¶ 13,922.]

[¶ 20,152 Reserved.—Proposed Regs. §§1.401(a)-12 and 1.414(l)-1, relating to mergers and consolidations of retirement plans and transfers of plan assets or liabilities, were formerly reproduced here. The final regulations appear at ¶ 11,719A and 12,364.]

[¶ 20,153 Reserved.—Proposed amendments to Reg. §54.4975-11, relating to requirements for stock ownership plans, were formerly reproduced at this point. The final regulations appear at ¶ 13,647B.]

[¶ 20,153A Reserved.—Proposed regulations on procedure and administration relating to the disclosure of returns and return information to various government departments and agencies were formerly reproduced at this point. The final regulations are at ¶ 13,761—13,763.]

[¶ 20,154 Reserved.]

[¶ 20,155 Reserved.—Proposed Reg. §§1.83-6(e) and (f) and 1.83-7(c), relating to the reporting requirements for nonqualified stock options, formerly reproduced at this point, have been withdrawn. The notice of withdrawal was published in the *Federal Register* on June 27, 1983 (48 FR 29538).]

[¶ 20,156 Reserved.—Proposed regulations on public inspection of written determinations were formerly reported at this point. The final regulations are at ¶ 13,786F.]

[¶ 20,157 Reserved.—Proposed regulations on group-term life insurance were formerly reproduced at this point. The final regulations are at ¶ 11,172, 13,511, 13,721 and 13,733.]

[¶ 20,157A Reserved.—Proposed regulations on the requirements for filing an actuarial report were formerly reproduced at this point. The final regulations are at ¶ 13,750B and 13,845.]

[¶ 20,157B Reserved.—Proposed Reg. §301.6109-1, which modified the current information and reporting requirements for certain grantor trusts, was formerly reproduced here. The proposed regulation was pubished in the *Federal Register* of October 24, 1980 (45 FR 70478). The final regulation is reproduced at ¶ 13,782.]

[¶ 20,158 Reserved.—Proposed Reg. §§301.6057-1, 301.6057-2, 301.6057-3, and 301.6690-1, concerning annual report information relating to plan participants who separate from service with vested retirement benefits, were formerly reproduced here. The proposed regulations were published in the *Federal Register* of January 20, 1978 (43 FR 2892). The final regulations are reproduced at ¶ 13,733, 13,734, 13,803 and 13,883.]

[¶ 20,158A Reserved.—Proposed Reg. §§1.422-2 and 1.424-2 concerning qualified stock options granted after May 20, 1976 were formerly reproduced at this point. The final regulations appear at ¶ 13,122 and 13,142.]

[¶ 20,158B Reserved.—Proposed regulations on the definition of employee stock purchase plans and the coverage requirements of employee stock purchase plans were formerly reproduced at this point. The final regulations are at ¶ 13,132.]

[¶ 20,158C Reserved.—Proposed Reg. §1.412(c)(3)-1, concerning reasonable funding methods designed to assure the equitable character and financial soundness of plans that must meet the minimum funding requirements of ERISA, formerly was reproduced here. The final regulations are reported at ¶ 12,250M.]

¶ 20,159

Proposed regulations on tax treatment of compensatory payments which are deferred under certain nonqualified compensation reduction plans or arrangements.—The proposed regulations would provide that if a taxpayer (whether or not an employee) individually chooses to have payment of some portion of his current compensation or an amount of an increase in compensation deferred and paid in a later year, the amount will nevertheless be treated as received by the taxpayer in the earlier taxable year.

The proposed regulations were published in the *Federal Register* of February 3, 1978 (43 FR 4638).

DEPARTMENT OF THE TREASURY

Internal Revenue Service

[26 CFR Part 1]

[LR-194-77]

Amounts Payments of Which are Deferred Under Certain Compensation Reduction Plans or Arrangements

Notice of Proposed Rulemaking

AGENCY: Internal Revenue Service, Treasury.

ACTION: Notice of proposed rulemaking.

SUMMARY: This document contains proposed regulations relating to the tax treatment of amounts of compensatory payments which are deferred under certain nonqualified compensation reduction plans or arrangements. The regulations would reflect a change in the Internal Revenue Service position relating to these plans or arrangements and provide the public with needed guidance.

DATES: Written comments and requests for a public hearing must be delivered or mailed by April 4, 1978. The amendments are proposed to be effective in the case of compensatory payments which the taxpayer has chosen to defer if the amount would have been payable, but for the taxpayer's exercise of the option to defer receipt, on or after a date 30 days following publication of this regulation as a Treasury decision in the FEDERAL REGISTER.

ADDRESS: Send comments and requests for a public hearing to: Commissioner of Internal Revenue, Attention: CC:LR:T (LR-194-77), Washington, D.C. 20224.

FOR FURTHER INFORMATION CONTACT: William E. Mantle of the Legislation and Regulations Division, Office of the Chief Counsel, Internal Revenue Service, 1111 Constitution Avenue, N.W., Washington, D.C. 20224 (Attention: CC:LR:T) (202-566-3734).

SUPPLEMENTARY INFORMATION:

Background

This document contains a proposed amendment to the Income Tax Regulations (26 CFR Part 1) under section 61 of the Internal Revenue Code of 1954. The amendment is proposed in order to change the Internal Revenue Service position on certain nonqualified compensation reduction plans or arrangements and is to be issued under the authority contained in section 7805 of the Internal Revenue Code of 1954 (68A Stat. 917; 26 U.S.C. 7805).

General Rule

The new regulation provides that if a taxpayer (whether or not an employee) individually chooses to have payment of some portion of his current compensation or an amount of an increase in compensation deferred and paid in a later year, the amount will nevertheless be treated as received by the taxpayer in the earlier taxable year. The taxpayer's exercise of the option to defer payment must be under a plan or arrangement other than one described in section 401(a), 403(a) or (b), or 405(a) of the Internal Revenue Code of 1954 (relating respectively to qualified pension, profit-sharing, and stock bonus plans; taxation of employee annuities; and qualified bond purchase plans).

Definition of Compensation

Under the proposed amendment, a taxpayer's compensation includes, in addition to basic or regular compensation fixed by contract, statute, or otherwise, a supplement, such as a bonus, and increases in basic or regular compensation.

Exception

An exception to the general rule is proposed to provide that it does not apply to the amount of any payment which the taxpayer has chosen to defer under an existing plan or arrangement if the amount would have been payable, but for the taxpayer's exercise of the option to defer receipt, before a date 30 days following publication of this regulation as a Treasury decision in the FEDERAL REGISTER.

Effect on Present IRS Published Positions

If this regulation is published as a Treasury decision, Rev. Rul. 67-449, 1967-2 C.B. 173, Rev. Rul. 68-86, 1968-1 C.B. 184, Rev. Rul. 69-650, 1969-2 C.B. 106, and Rev. Rul. 71-419, 1971-2 C.B. 220 would no longer be applied and present Service acquiescences in the decisions in *James F. Oates,* 18 T.C. 570 (1952) and *Ray S. Robinson*, 44 T.C. 20 (1965) would be reconsidered. Further, it would be necessary to examine the facts and circumstances of cases similar to those described in several other published revenue rulings (such as Examples (1) and (3) of Rev. Rul. 60-31, 1960-1 C.B. 174, Rev. Rul. 68-99, 1968-1 C.B. 193, and Rev. Rul. 72-25, 1972-1 C.B. 127) to determine whether the deferral of payment of compensation was in fact at the individual option of the taxpayer who earned the compensation.

On September 7, 1977, the Service announced in IR-1881 that it had suspended the issuance of rulings dealing with the income tax treatment of certain nonqualified deferred compensation plans established by State and local governments and other employers pending completion of a review of this area. The plans reviewed permit the employee to individually elect to defer a portion of his or her salary. This proposed amendment represents conclusions reached as a result of this review.

Comments and Requests for a Public Hearing

Before adopting these proposed regulations, consideration will be given to any written comments that are submitted (preferably six copies) to the Commissioner of Internal Revenue. All comments will be available for public inspection and copying. A public hearing will be held upon written request to the Commissioner by any person who has submitted written comments. If a public hearing is held, notice of the time and place will be published in the FEDERAL REGISTER.

Drafting Information

The principal author of these proposed regulations was William E. Mantle of the Legislation and Regulations Division of the Office of Chief Counsel, Internal Revenue Service. However, personnel from other offices of the Internal Revenue Service and Treasury Department participated in developing the regulation, both on matters of substance and style.

Proposed Amendments to the Regulations

26 CFR Part 1 is amended by adding a new § 1.61-16 immediately after § 1.61-15. The new section reads as follows:

§ 1.61-16 Amounts payments of which are deferred under certain compensation reduction plans or arrangements.—(a) In general. Except as otherwise provided in paragraph (b) of this section, if under a plan or arrangement (other than a plan or arrangement described in section 401(a), 403(a) or (b), or 405(a)) payment of an amount of a taxpayer's basic or regular compensation fixed by contract, statute, or otherwise (or supplements to such compensation, such as bonuses, or increases in such compensation) is, at the taxpayer's individual option, deferred to a taxable year later than that in which such amount would have been payable but for his exercise of such option, the amount shall be treated as received by the taxpayer in such earlier taxable year. For purposes of this paragraph, it is immaterial that the taxpayer's rights in the amount payment of which is so deferred become forfeitable by reason of his exercise of the option to defer payment.

(b) *Exception.* Paragraph (a) of this section shall not apply to an amount payment of which is deferred as described in paragraph (a) under a plan or arrangement in existence on February 3, 1978 if such amount would have been payable, but for the taxpayer's exercise of the option, at any time prior to [date 30 days following publication of this section as a Treasury decision]. For purposes of this paragraph, a plan or arrangement in existence on February 3, 1978 which is significantly amended after such date will be treated as a new plan as of the date of such amendment. Examples of significant amendments would be extension of coverage to an additional class of taxpayers or an increase in the maximum percentage of compensation subject to the taxpayer's option.

S.B. Wolfe

Acting Commissioner of Internal Revenue

¶ 20,159A

Proposed regulations: Payment of excise tax: Reversion of qualified plan assets to employer.—Reproduced below is the text of proposed regulations regarding the payment of the excise tax by employers receiving (directly or indirectly) reversions of qualified plan assets required by the Tax Reform Act of 1986. The regulations that are proposed are also issued as temporary regulations and are reproduced at ¶ 13,649B.

The proposed regulations were published in the *Federal Register* on April 3, 1987.

DEPARTMENT OF THE TREASURY

Internal Revenue Service

[26 CFR Parts 54 and 602]

[EE-151-86]

Payment of Excise Tax On Reversion of Qualified Plan Assets to Employer

Notice of Proposed Rulemaking

AGENCY: Internal Revenue Service, Treasury.

ACTION: Notice of proposed rulemaking by cross-reference to temporary regulations.

SUMMARY: This document provides regulations regarding the payment of the excise tax by employers receiving (directly or indirectly) reversions of qualified plan assets required by the Tax Reform Act of 1986. In the Rules and Regulations portion of this FEDERAL REGISTER, the Internal Revenue Service is issuing temporary regulations relating to the payment of the excise tax; the text of these temporary regulations also serves as the comment document for this notice of proposed rulemaking.

DATES: Written comments and requests for a public hearing must be delivered or mailed by June 1, 1987. These amendments are proposed to be applicable to reversions occurring after December 31, 1985.

ADDRESS: Please mail or deliver comments to: Commissioner of Internal Revenue, Attention: CC:LR:T (EE-151-86), 1111 Constitution Avenue, N.W., Washington, D.C. 20224.

FOR FURTHER INFORMATION CONTACT: Suzanne K. Tank of the Employee Plans and Exempt Organizations Division, Office of Chief Counsel, Internal Revenue Service, 1111 Constitution Avenue, N.W., Washington, D.C. 20224 (Attention: CC:LR:T) (202-566-3938, not a toll-free number).

SUPPLEMENTARY INFORMATION:

Background

The temporary regulations in the Rules and Regulations portion of this issue of the FEDERAL REGISTER amend Part 54 of the Code of Federal Regulations. New § 54.6011-1T [CCH PENSION PLAN GUIDE, ¶ 13,649B] and new § 54.6071-1T [CCH PENSION PLAN GUIDE, ¶ 13,649C] are added to Part 54 of Title 26 of the Code of Federal Regulations. When § 54.6011-1T is promulgated as final regulations, § 54.6011-1 will be revised to reflect the new provision. For the text of the temporary regulations, see FR Doc. 87-7306 (TD 8133) published in the Rules and Regulations portion of this issue of the FEDERAL REGISTER. The preamble to the temporary regulations [CCH PENSION PLAN GUIDE, ¶ 23,725B] explains this addition to the Pension Excise Tax Regulations.

Nonapplicability of Executive Order 12291

The Commissioner of Internal Revenue has determined that this proposed rule is not a major rule as defined in Executive Order 12291 and that a regulatory impact analysis therefore is not required.

Regulatory Flexibility Act

The Secretary of the Treasury has certified that this rule will not have a significant impact on a substantial number of small entities. First, most small businesses maintain defined contribution plans. The regulations do not generally affect defined contribution plans. Hence, small businesses would not generally be affected by the regulation. Second, very few businesses with defined benefit plans will be terminating their plans and receiving a reversion in any calendar quarter or year. A Regulatory Flexibility Analysis, therefore, is not required under the Regulatory Flexibility Act (5 U.S.C. 605(b)).

Paperwork Reduction Act

The collection of information requirements contained in this regulation have been submitted to the Office of Management and Budget (OMB) for review under section 3504(h) of the Paperwork Reduction Act of 1980. Comments on these requirements should be sent to the Office of Information and Regulatory Affairs of OMB, Attention: Desk Officer for Internal Revenue Service, New Executive Office Building, Washington, D.C. 20503. The Internal Revenue Service requests that persons submitting comments on the requirements to OMB also send copies of these comments to the Service.

Drafting Information

The principal author of these proposed regulations is Suzanne K. Tank of the Employee Plans and Exempt Organizations Division of the Office of Chief Counsel, Internal Revenue Service. However, personnel from other offices of the Internal Revenue Service and the Treasury Department participated in developing the regulations, on matters of both substance and style.

Comments and Requests for a Public Hearing

Before adoption of these proposed regulations, consideration will be given to any written comments that are submitted (preferably eight copies) to the Commissioner of Internal Revenue. All comments will be available for public inspection and copying. A public hearing will be held upon written request to the Commissioner by any person who has submitted written comments. If a public hearing is held, notice of the time and place will be published in the FEDERAL REGISTER.

Lawrence B. Gibbs,

Commissioner of Internal Revenue.

¶ 20,159B

Fringe benefits: Employer-provided vehicle and fuel: Personal use: Valuation.—The IRS has updated previous guidance concerning the valuation of an employee's personal use of employer-provided fuel when an employer-provided automobile is valued under the automobile lease valuation rule. The proposals affect employees receiving this fringe benefit.

The proposed regulations were filed with the *Federal Register* on October 8, 1992, and published in the *Federal Register* on October 9, 1992 (57 FR 46525).

DEPARTMENT OF THE TREASURY

Internal Revenue Service

26 CFR Part 1

[EE-101-91]

RIN 1545-AQ28

Taxation of Fringe Benefits and Exclusions From Gross Income of Certain Fringe Benefits

AGENCY: Internal Revenue Service, Treasury.

ACTION: Notice of proposed rulemaking

SUMMARY: This document contains proposed amendments relating to the taxation and valuation of fringe benefits under section 61 of the Internal Revenue Code. These proposed amendments update previous guidance concerning the valuation of an employee's personal use of employer-provided fuel when an employer-provided automobile is valued pursuant to the automobile lease valuation rule. The proposed regulations affect employees receiving this fringe benefit and provide guidance to employers and employees to help determine their federal tax liability.

DATES: Written comments and requests for a public hearing must be received by November 9, 1992.

ADDRESSES: Send comments and requests for a public hearing to: Internal Revenue Service, P.O. Box 7604, Ben Franklin Station, Attention: CC:CORP:T:R (EE-l0l-91), Room 5228, Washington, D.C. 20044.

FOR FURTHER INFORMATION CONTACT: Marianna Dyson, at 202-622-4606 (not a toll-free number).

SUPPLEMENTARY INFORMATION:

Background

This document contains proposed amendments to the Income Tax Regulations (26 CFR part 1) under section 61 of the Internal Revenue Code of 1986 (Code). The amendments pertain to the valuation of employer-provided fuel under the automobile lease valuation rule of § 1.61-21(d) of the regulations.

Explanation of Provisions

The final fringe benefit regulations issued in July 1989 and effective for benefits furnished on or after January 1, 1989, provide that in valuing the personal use of automobiles under § 1.61-21(d) of the regulations, the Annual Lease Values do not include the fair market value of fuel provided by the employer. Thus, fuel consumed for any personal miles driven must be valued separately for inclusion in income. Section 1.61-21(d)(3)(ii)(A).

Under § 1.61-21(d)(3)(ii)(B), employer-paid fuel provided *in kind* to employees for personal use may be valued at fair market value or, in the alternative, at 5.5 cents per mile. If the cost of the fuel is reimbursed by or charged to an employer, the value of the fuel is its fair market value, which is generally the amount of the actual reimbursement or amount charged, provided the purchase of the fuel is at arm's-length. Section 1.61-21(d)(3)(ii)(C).

For employers with fleets of at least 20 automobiles, § 1.61-21(d)(3)(ii)(D) sets forth two additional methods for valuing fuel for personal use. The general method provides that employers who reimburse employees for the cost of fuel or allow employees to charge the employer for the cost of fuel may value the fuel by reference to the employer's "fleet-average cents-per-mile fuel cost." The fleet-average cents-per-mile fuel cost is equal to the fleet-average per-gallon fuel cost divided by the fleet-average miles-per-gallon rate. The average per-gallon fuel cost and the miles-per-gallon rate are determined by averaging the per-gallon fuel costs and miles-per-gallon rates of a representative sample of the automobiles in the fleet equal to the greater of ten percent of the automobiles in the fleet or 20 automobiles for a representative period. Section 1.61-21(d)(3)(ii)(D).

In lieu of calculating the "fleet-average cents-per-mile fuel cost" under the general method of paragraph (d)(3)(ii)(D) of § 1.61-21, employers with fleets of at least 20 automobiles that use the fleet-average

valuation rule of paragraph (d)(5)(D) may use the 5.5 cents-per-mile option of paragraph (d)(3)(ii)(B), if determining the amount of the actual reimbursement or the amount charged for the purchase of fuel would impose unreasonable administrative burdens on the employer ("the alternative method").

In no event, however, may an employer with a fleet of at least 20 automobiles use either the general or alternative method of paragraph (d)(3)(ii)(D) of § 1.61-21 unless the requirements of paragraph (d)(5)(v)(D) are also met. This paragraph contains the rules for using a fleet-average value in calculating the Annual Lease Values of the automobiles in the fleet. In particular, it specifies that the fair market value of each vehicle in the fleet may not exceed $16,500 (as adjusted pursuant to section 280F(d)(7) of the Code).

For calendar years prior to 1991, Notice 89-110, 1989-2 C.B. 447, expanded the availability of the 5.5 cents-per-mile option to employers with fleets of at least 20 automobiles that satisfy the requirements of paragraph (d)(5)(v)(D), regardless of whether they are actually using the fleet-average valuation rule of paragraph (d)(5)(v). Notice 91-41, 1991-51 I.R.B. 63, provides that the 5.5 cents-per-mile option as provided in Notice 89-110 is available in calendar year 1991.

Notice 89-110 did not eliminate the requirement that the employer must demonstrate that it is using the 5.5 cents-per-mile option because determining the amount of the actual reimbursement or the amount charged for the purchase of fuel would impose unreasonable administrative burdens on the employer. As a practical matter, however, it is believed that fleet operators with at least 20 automobiles would have little difficulty in demonstrating the existence of unreasonable administrative burdens.

The proposed amendments to § 1.61-21(d)(3)(ii) provide that, for calendar year 1992, employers with fleets of at least 20 automobiles may continue to use the 5.5 cents-per-mile rate as provided in Notice 89-110 and extended in Notice 91-41. In addition, the proposed amendments provide that employers with fleets of at least 20 automobiles may value fuel that is reimbursed by or charged to the employer by reference to the alternative cents-per-mile rate without regard to the rules in paragraph (d)(5)(v)(D) concerning the value of automobiles in the fleet, and without the necessity of demonstrating the existence of administrative burdens.

Finally, the proposed amendments provide that for calendar years subsequent to 1992 the Service will announce the appropriate cents-per-mile rate for valuing fuel that is provided in kind or that is reimbursed by or charged to employers with fleets of at least 20 automobiles. The announcement will appear in the annual revenue procedure concerning the optional standard mileage rates used in computing deductible costs of operating a passenger automobile for business.

The rules under paragraph (d)(3)(ii) of § 1.61-21, as amended by this Notice, will enable employers with fleets of at least 20 automobiles to value the personal use of employer-paid fuel in any of the following ways: (1) fuel provided in kind may be valued at fair market value based on all the facts and circumstances; (2) fuel that is provided in kind may be valued at the cents-per-mile rate applicable to the particular year; (3) fuel, the cost of which is reimbursed by or charged to the employer, may be valued based on the amount of the actual reimbursement or the amount charged; (4) fuel, the cost of which is reimbursed by or charged to the employer, may be valued based on the fleet-average cents-per-mile fuel cost; or (5) fuel, the cost of which is reimbursed by or charged to the employer, may be valued based on the applicable cents-per-mile rate without regard to the fair market value of any automobile in the fleet or the administrative burdens requirement.

The amendments are proposed to be effective for benefits provided in calendar years beginning after December 31, 1992. However, because of the number of inquiries the Service has received from taxpayers expressing uncertainty as to the scope of the guidance in Notice 89-110 concerning employer-provided fuel, the amendments may be relied upon as if they had been included in the final regulations published on July 6, 1989.

Special Analyses

It has been determined that these rules are not major rules as defined in Executive Order 12291. Therefore, a Regulatory Impact

Analysis is not required. It has also been determined that section 553(b) of the Administrative Procedure Act (5 U.S.C. chapter 5) and the Regulatory Flexibility Act (5 U.S.C. chapter 6) do not apply to these regulations, and, therefore, an initial Regulatory Flexibility Analysis is not required. Pursuant to section 7805(f) of the Internal Revenue Code, these regulations will be submitted to the Chief Counsel for Advocacy of the Small Business Administration for comment on their impact on small business.

Comments and Requests to Appear at a Public Hearing

Before adopting these proposed regulations, consideration will be given to any written comments that are submitted (preferably a signed original and eight copies) to the Internal Revenue Service. All comments will be available for public inspection and copying in their entirety. A public hearing will be held upon written request to the Commissioner by any person who has submitted written comments. Written comments and requests for a hearing must be received by November 9, 1992. If a public hearing is held, notice of the time and place will be published in the Federal Register.

Drafting Information

The principal author of these regulations is Marianna Dyson, Office of the Associate Chief Counsel (Employee Benefits and Exempt Organizations), Internal Revenue Service. However, personnel from other offices of the Service and Treasury Department participated in their development.

Par. 2. Section 1.61-21 is amended by revising paragraphs (d)(3)(ii)(A), (B), and (D) as follows:

* * *

(d) * * *

(3) * * *

(ii) *Fuel excluded*—(A) *In general*. The Annual Lease Values do not include the fair market value of fuel provided by the employer, whether fuel is provided in kind or its cost is reimbursed by or charged to the employer. Thus, if an employer provides fuel for the employee's personal use, the fuel must be valued separately for inclusion in income.

(B) *Valuation of fuel provided in kind*. Fuel provided in kind may be valued at fair market value based on all the facts and circumstances or, in the alternative, may be valued at 5.5 cents per mile for all miles driven by the employee in calendar years 1989 through 1992. For subsequent calendar years, the applicable cents-per-mile rate is the amount specified in the annual Revenue Procedure concerning the optional standard mileage rates used in computing deductible costs of operating a passenger automobile for business. However, fuel provided in kind may not be valued at the alternative cents-per-mile rate for miles driven outside the United States, Canada, or Mexico.

* * *

(D) *Additional methods available to employers with fleets of at least 20 automobiles*— (*1*) *Fleet-average cents-per-mile fuel cost*. If an employer with a fleet of at least 20 automobiles (regardless of whether the requirements of paragraph (d)(5)(v)(D) of this section are met) reimburses employees for the cost of fuel or allows employees to charge the employer for the cost of fuel, the fair market value of fuel provided to those automobiles may be determined by reference to the employer's fleet-average cents-per-mile fuel cost. The fleet-average cents-per-mile fuel cost is equal to the fleet-average per-gallon fuel cost divided by the fleet-average miles-per-gallon rate. The averages described in the preceding sentence must be determined by averaging the per-gallon fuel costs and miles-per-gallon rates of a representative sample of the automobiles in the fleet equal to the greater of ten percent of the automobiles in the fleet or 20 automobiles for a representative period, such as a two-month period.

(*2*) *Alternative cents-per-mile method*. In lieu of determining the fleet-average cents-per-mile fuel cost under paragraph (d)(3)(ii)(D)(*1*) of this section, an employer with a fleet of at least 20 automobiles may value the fuel provided for these automobiles by reference to the cents-per-mile rate set forth in paragraph (d)(3)(ii)(B) of this section (regardless of whether the requirements of paragraph (d)(5)(v)(D) of this section are met).

* * *

[¶ 20,160 Reserved.—Proposed regulations on custodial accounts for regulated investment company stock were formerly reproduced at this paragraph. The regulations were withdrawn by the Internal Revenue Service in a withdrawal notice on January 13, 1987 (51 FR 2724).]

[¶ 20,161 Reserved.—Proposed Reg. §§1.404(a)-2A, 1.6033-2, 1.6047-1, 301.6058-1, and 301.6652-3 on annual returns for employee retirement benefit plans were formerly reproduced at this point. The final regulations appear at ¶ 11,853, 13,662, 13,691, 13,745, and 13,803.]

[¶ 20,161A Reserved.—Proposed regulations on amortization of experience gains by plans funded by group deferred annuity contracts formerly appeared at this point. The final regulations appear at ¶ 12,250C.]

[¶ 20,162 Reserved.—Proposed regulations on the deduction limitations on contributions to defined benefit pension plans formerly appeared at this point. The final regulations appear at ¶ 11,864A.]

¶ 20,162A

Foreign deferred compensation plans: Qualified funded plans: Qualified reserve plans: Deductions or reductions of earnings and profits or accumulated profits: Elections.—The IRS has issued proposed regulations dealing with limitations on deductions and reductions in earnings and profits (or accumulated profits) with respect to certain foreign deferred compensation plans maintained by certain foreign corporations or by foreign branches of domestic corporations. Proposed regulations that were issued on April 8, 1985 have been withdrawn.

These regulations appeared in the *Federal Register* on May 7, 1993.

DEPARTMENT OF THE TREASURY

Internal Revenue Service

26 CFR Part 1

[EE-14-81]

RIN 1545-AD81

AGENCY: Internal Revenue Service, Treasury.

ACTION: Withdrawal of previous proposed rules and notice of proposed rulemaking.

SUMMARY: This document contains proposed regulations relating to the limitations on deductions and adjustments to earnings and profits (or accumulated profits) with respect to certain foreign deferred compensation plans. These new proposed regulations reflect changes to the applicable law made by the Act of December 28, 1980, as amended by the Technical Corrections Act of 1982, by the Tax Reform Act of 1986, and by the Technical and Miscellaneous Revenue Act of 1988. The new proposed regulations will affect employers (and shareholders of employers) that provide deferred compensation directly or indirectly to foreign employees and will provide the public and Internal Revenue Service personnel with the guidance needed to comply with section 404A of the Internal Revenue Code of 1986. These new proposed regulations supersede the prior proposed regulations published in the Federal Register on April 8, 1985 (50 FR 13821).

DATES: Written comments must be received by [*INSERT DATE THAT IS 60 DAYS AFTER THE DATE OF PUBLICATION OF THESE PROPOSED REGULATIONS IN THE FEDERAL REGISTER*]. Requests to speak (with outlines of oral comments) at a public hearing scheduled for October 5, 1993, at 10:00 a.m., must be received by

September 14, 1993. See notice of hearing published elsewhere in this issue of the Federal Register.

ADDRESSES: Send comments, requests to appear at the public hearing, and outlines of comments to be presented to: Internal Revenue Service, P.O. Box 7604, Ben Franklin Station, Attention: CC:CORP:T:R (EE-14-81), Room 5228, Washington, D.C. 20044.

FOR FURTHER INFORMATION CONTACT: Concerning the proposed regulations, Elizabeth A. Purcell, Office of the Associate Chief Counsel (Employee Benefits and Exempt Organizations) at (202) 622-6080 (not a toll-free number). Concerning the hearing, Carol Savage, Regulations Unit, at (202) 622-8452 (not a toll-free number).

SUPPLEMENTARY INFORMATION:

Statutory Authority

This document contains proposed amendments to the Income Tax Regulations (26 CFR part 1) under sections 404A and 7805(a) of the Internal Revenue Code (Code).

Paperwork Reduction Act

The collection of information requirement contained in this notice of proposed rulemaking has been submitted to the Office of Management and Budget for review in accordance with the Paperwork Reduction Act of 1980 (44 U.S.C. 3504(h)). Comments on the collection of information should be sent to the Office of Management and Budget, Attention: Desk Officer for the Department of the Treasury, Office of Information and Regulatory Affairs, Washington, D.C. 20503, with copies to the Internal Revenue Service, Attention: IRS Reports Clearance Officer T:FP, Washington, D.C. 20224.

The collection of information requirement in these regulations is in §§ 1.404A-5, 1.404A-6 and 1.404A-7. This information is required by the Internal Revenue Service to determine accurately the correct deductions and reductions in earnings and profits for foreign deferred compensation. The likely respondents are businesses or other for-profit institutions.

These estimates are an approximation of the average time expected to be necessary for a collection of information. They are based on such information as is available to the Internal Revenue Service. Individual respondents may require greater or less time, depending on their particular circumstances. The estimated total annual reporting burden is 633,200 hours. The estimated annual reporting burden per respondent varies from 5 hours to 1,000 hours, depending on individual circumstances, with an estimated average of 506 hours. The estimated number of respondents is 1,250. The estimated annual frequency: once.

Background

On April 8, 1985, the Internal Revenue Service published in the Federal Register proposed amendments to the Income Tax Regulations under section 404A of the Internal Revenue Code of 1954 (now 1986) (50 FR 13821). Comments were requested and received, and a public hearing was held on September 20, 1985. After consideration of the comments received, the Service has determined that, rather than promulgate final regulations, it is more appropriate to withdraw the original proposed regulations and propose new regulations. This determination is based on a number of factors, including the number of significant substantive changes made to the prior proposed rules, changes to the underlying statute and other relevant Code provisions, and a need to reorganize the regulations. For a general discussion of section 404A and description of the prior proposed regulations, see the preamble to the prior proposed regulations published in the Federal Register on April 8, 1985.

The significant differences (or, where appropriate, the significant similarities) between these new proposed regulations and the prior proposed regulations are discussed, section by section, in the remainder of this preamble. Prior proposed § 1.404A-1 remains new proposed § 1.404A-1. However, the rules found in § 1.404A-2 of the prior proposed regulations are now incorporated in new proposed §§ 1.404A-6 and 1.404A-7. Prior proposed §§ 1.404A-3, 1.404A-4, 1.404A-5 and 1.404A-6 are redesignated §§ 1.404A-2, 1.404A-3, 1.404A-4 and 1.404A-5, respectively.

§ 1.404A-1: General rules concerning deductions and adjustments to earnings and profits for foreign deferred compensation plans.

90-percent test

As a condition to electing treatment as a qualified foreign plan, section 404A(e)(2) requires that 90 percent or more of the amounts taken into account for a taxable year under the plan be attributable to services performed by nonresident aliens, the compensation for which

is not subject to United States federal income tax. Prior proposed § 1.404A-1(c) provided that, in determining whether the 90-percent test is satisfied, accrued benefits may be calculated under any reasonable method. It also provided that the rules for calculating the present value of accrued benefits at normal retirement age (except for the actuarial assumption safe harbor) under § 1.416-1 (concerning the determination whether a retirement plan is top-heavy) are presumed to be reasonable for this purpose.

Many commentators suggested that these rules for calculating accrued benefits for purposes of the 90-percent test are extremely burdensome and disproportionately expensive. They also suggested that the calculations require a degree of precision and accuracy that in many cases is unwarranted by the circumstances (i.e., where very few plan participants are United States citizens or residents and little compensation of the plan participants is subject to United States federal income tax). To give taxpayers in those cases a less burdensome and less expensive means of demonstrating compliance with the 90-percent requirement, a safe harbor provision has been provided in paragraph (c)(2) of new proposed § 1.404A-1. It provides that the 90-percent requirement of § 1.404A-1(a)(3) will be deemed satisfied with respect to a plan if the participants' benefits under the plan increase generally in proportion to their compensation taken into account under the plan, and the sum of (1) the compensation of United States citizens and residents taken into account under the plan, and (2) any other compensation subject to United States federal income tax taken into account under the plan, does not exceed five percent of all compensation taken into account under the plan for the plan year. This safe harbor provision does not apply, however, if the Commissioner determines that a significant purpose of the plan is to provide benefits not otherwise eligible for tax benefits under the Internal Revenue Code for participants who are United States citizens or residents. An example is provided in new proposed § 1.404A-1(c)(4) to illustrate the application of this safe harbor provision.

Termination indemnity plans

Many commentators suggested that the regulations be revised to provide specifically that certain termination indemnity plans are considered deferred compensation plans for purposes of section 404A. The laws of many countries require employers to maintain termination indemnity plans to pay termination benefits. Some of these termination indemnities are payable solely upon involuntary discharge (other than by reason of mandatory retirement) and thus may be viewed as dismissal wage plans under United States tax principles. However, other termination indemnity plans are akin to deferred compensation plans. For example, one commentator noted that, in one European country, employers are required by law to provide severance benefits equal to one month's pay (final pay) for each year of service. These benefits are fully vested and payable upon all events of termination, including retirement.

Because the provisions of termination indemnity plans may vary widely, paragraph (iii) of the definition of deferred compensation in paragraph (e) of new proposed § 1.404A-1 provides guidelines for determining whether such a plan provides deferred compensation. A termination indemnity plan is considered to provide deferred compensation if: (1) a major purpose of the plan is to provide for the payment of retirement benefits, (2) it has a benefit formula providing for payment based at least in part upon length of service, (3) it provides for the payment of benefits to employees (or their beneficiaries) after the employee's retirement, death or other termination of employment, and (4) it meets such other requirements as may be prescribed by the Commissioner with respect to termination indemnity plans. An example is provided under the definition of deferred compensation in paragraph (e) of new proposed § 1.404A-1 to illustrate this provision. Any plan that meets these requirements is treated as providing deferred compensation, whether or not it is called a termination indemnity plan.

Equivalent of a trust

Section 404A(b)(5)(A) provides that, in order for a contribution to be taken into account in the case of a qualified funded plan, it must be paid to a trust or the "equivalent of a trust". The reference to the equivalent of a trust recognizes that, in some foreign countries, the common law concept of a trust does not exist. Thus, in those countries, the arrangement used to fund deferred compensation benefits for purposes of section 404A(b)(5)(A) must be functionally equivalent to a trust. The essential function of a trust in the context of a United States deferred compensation plan is to provide an entity separate from an employer through which deferred compensation benefits may be secured and liabilities funded. The four elements necessary to accomplish this function are provided in the definition of "equivalent of a trust" in paragraph (e) of new proposed § 1.404A-1. These elements have been revised to allow an employer some latitude to insulate corpus and income from the claims of an employer's creditors, and to remove the concept of legal and beneficial ownership. Finally, the concept of fiduciary duty has been replaced with legally enforceable duty.

Some commentators urged the Service to endorse as the equivalent of a trust the so-called "Security Contract" or "Security Concept" developed in Germany. As explained by those commentators, the Security Contract combines a book reserve commitment by an employer with a pledge and guaranty. First, an employer establishes a book reserve for its pension liabilities for which it receives a tax deduction under German law. It then establishes a wholly-owned subsidiary to which it transfers assets to fund its pension liabilities. As such, the corpus and income of the subsidiary are separately identifiable from an employer's general assets. This arrangement, without more, would not satisfy the requirements of the equivalent of a trust because the assets held by the subsidiary are not protected from the claims of an employer's creditors in the event of bankruptcy or receivership. Under the Security Contract concept, however, the subsidiary also pledges its assets irrevocably to a custodian who then gives a guaranty to the employees up to the assets pledged to the custodian in the event an employer declares bankruptcy or goes into receivership. The custodian's guaranty is intended to place a prior lien on the assets pledged and protect them from the claims of an employer's creditors in the event of bankruptcy or receivership.

As one commentator asserted, however, it is unclear under German law that the arrangement provides such protection. According to that commentator, in the event of bankruptcy or receivership, the German Pension Guaranty Corporation is required by law to settle an employer's book reserve commitment. The Pension Guaranty Corporation then becomes a non-privileged creditor in the bankruptcy process and exercises any rights the employees have under the plan. As a non-privileged creditor, the Pension Guaranty Corporation is not entitled to all the assets pledged to the custodian, but is limited to a percentage of employer assets that is consistent with its general bankruptcy quota. Thus, it appears that the subsidiary's assets may be subject to the claims of an employer's creditors before all claims of the Pension Guaranty Corporation, exercising the rights of the employees under the plan, are settled.

Until the Service is satisfied that the corpus and income of the subsidiary are to be used to satisfy the claims of the employees and their beneficiaries (or those exercising their rights under the plan) before those of an employer's creditors, the Service cannot endorse this arrangement as the equivalent of a trust.

Exclusive means for deduction or reduction in earnings and profits

For foreign plans that fail to satisfy the requirements of section 404A, section 404 governs deductions for deferred compensation expense. For plans that are not qualified under section 401, section 404(a)(5) generally provides that the employer's deduction for contributions is delayed until amounts attributable to the employer's contribution are includible in the plan participant's gross income. In addition, under section 404(a)(5), deductions are denied altogether unless separate accounts are maintained for each participant. The Service took this position with respect to a foreign plan in Private Letter Ruling 7904042 (Oct. 25, 1978), available in the Freedom of Information Reading Room, Room 1569, Internal Revenue Service, 1111 Constitution Avenue, N.W., Washington, D.C. 20224. This position is reflected, in part, in paragraph (a) of new proposed § 1.404A-1.

Prior proposed § 1.404A-1(e) provided that earnings and profits (or accumulated profits) may be reduced with respect to payments by an employer to a funded foreign deferred compensation plan that are not deductible under section 404(a) even where an election under section 404A has not been made. Upon reexamination of the Congressional intent underlying the enactment of section 404A, however, the Service now believes that the position reflected in the prior proposed regulations is inconsistent with the purposes of section 404A (and the limitations thereunder). Thus, in accordance with the Secretary's section 404A(h) authority to prescribe regulations necessary to carry out the purposes of section 404A, paragraph (a) of new proposed § 1.404A-1 provides that section 404A provides the exclusive means by which an employer may reduce earnings and profits for deferred compensation in situations other than those in which a reduction of earnings and profits is permitted under section 404. See also the discussion below of the relevance of sections 61, 671 through 679, and 1001 in this context.

Request for comments concerning foreign corporations that are not controlled

The Service is considering whether simplified or alternative methods of determining allowable earnings and profits reductions under section 404A might be appropriate for foreign corporations that are not controlled. Suggestions are invited on this matter.

§ 1.404A-2: Rules for qualified funded plans.

Substantiality of payments to trust

A commentator suggested that the focus of the flush language of paragraph (b) of prior proposed § 1.404A-3 (requiring a trust to have "substantiality") should be on the substantiality of payments to a trust (or the equivalent of a trust) rather than on the substantiality of a trust (or the equivalent of a trust), because the determination with respect to the latter can be made under the standards set forth in prior proposed § 1.404A-1(g)(9). Accordingly, new proposed § 1.404A-2(b)(2)(i) provides that employer contributions must have substance. For example, contributions may not be made in the form of a promissory note. This also means that the contributions must be accumulated in the trust (or the equivalent of a trust) in order to be distributed as benefits under a deferred compensation plan. Whether contributions are being accumulated in the trust (or the equivalent of a trust) to be distributed as benefits will depend on the facts and circumstances. The example in paragraph (b)(5) of new proposed § 1.404A-2 reflects this change.

Exclusive benefit rule

Section 404A(b)(5)(A) provides that, in the case of a qualified funded plan, a contribution is taken into account only if it is paid to a trust (or the equivalent of a trust) that meets the requirements of section 401(a)(2). Section 401(a)(2) provides generally that it must be impossible, at any time prior to the satisfaction of all liabilities with respect to employees and their beneficiaries under the trust, for any part of the corpus or income to be used for, or diverted to, purposes other than the exclusive benefit of the employees or their beneficiaries. Thus, in effect, section 404A(b)(5)(A) reemphasizes, with regard to qualified funded plans, the general rule found in section 404A(e) that any "qualified foreign plan" must be for the exclusive benefit of an employer's employees or their beneficiaries. (As stated in the Senate Finance Committee Report, "[f]irst, the plan must be for the exclusive benefit of an employer's employees or their beneficiaries." S. Rep. No. 1039, 96th Cong., 2d Sess. 13 (1980).)

To reflect this emphasis, new proposed § 1.404A-2(b)(2) provides that one important factor that is taken into account in determining whether a trust has or has not been operated in a manner consistent with the exclusive benefit rule is whether it has not or has been involved in a transaction that would be described in section 4975(c)(1) if the plan were the type of plan subject to those rules. For example, a loan from the trust to an employer, on any terms, ordinarily would be a circumstance that strongly suggests noncompliance with section 404A(b)(5)(A). Similarly, a sale, exchange, or lease of any property between the trust and an employer would generally violate this provision. These rules, as set forth in new proposed § 1.404A-2(b)(2), apply prospectively.

Contributions deemed made before payment

Paragraph (c) of new proposed § 1.404A-2 clarifies the circumstances under which a payment made after the last day of an employer's taxable year is deemed to have been made on that last day.

Frequency of actuarial valuations

The new proposed regulations generally continue the requirement in the prior proposed regulations that an actuarial valuation be made no less frequently than once every three years for a qualified funded plan. However, for interim years, they require a reasonable actuarial determination to be made of whether the full funding limit in § 1.404A-5(c)(2) applies to the plan, and provide that the Commissioner may require an actuarial valuation in interim years under appropriate circumstances. It is anticipated that the Commissioner will not exercise this authority except in situations similar to those described in § 1.412(c)(9)-1(d) of the proposed regulations.

Shareholder-level consequences

A sentence in paragraph (d)(1) of prior proposed § 1.404A-3 provided that, where a foreign corporation maintained a qualified funded plan, the deductible amount was taken into account for the shareholder's taxable year in which or with which an employer's taxable year ended. This sentence has been deleted because section 404A does not govern the time at which adjustments to earnings and profits of a foreign employer corporation for a particular year are taken into account at the shareholder level.

§ 1.404A-3: Rules for qualified reserve plans.

The new proposed regulations have modified in several ways the guidance on the calculation of the amount that may be taken into account under a qualified reserve plan. First, the presentation has been changed in order to parallel the components of net periodic pension cost used in Statement of Financial Accounting Standards No. 87 "Employer's Accounting for Pensions" (1985), available from the Financial Accounting Standards Board, 401 Merritt 7, Norwalk, CT 06856. Thus, the amount taken into account for a year is based on the sum of a type of "service cost", "interest cost" and the amortization of the increase or decrease in the reserve from other sources. As part of this change, the steps for determining the actuarial gain or loss have been made explicit. In addition, as discussed below, certain increases or decreases in the reserve that were subject to amortization under the old proposed regulations are now included in the reasonable addition to the reserve.

Ten-Year amortization

Section 404A(c)(4) provides for the spreading over ten years of certain increases and decreases in reserves on account of various events including a catch-all category of "such other factors as may be prescribed by regulations". The Senate Finance Committee Report includes two suggestions of possible items that could be included in this category: "adjustments in the reserve resulting from changes in levels of compensation on which benefits depend or the vesting in one year of a benefit which was accrued in a prior year." S. Rep. No. 1039, 96th Cong. 2d. Sess. 14 (1980).

Some commentators criticized the rule in paragraph (d) of prior proposed § 1.404A-4 providing for the amortization of changes in the reserve arising from these two sources. They suggested that the ten-year amortization requirement for increases or decreases to the reserve on account of changes in the level of compensation upon which plan benefits depend, and for vesting of benefits accrued in prior years, was unnecessary because those items are ongoing costs of the plan that are specifically contemplated by the plan and will arise periodically as each participant's circumstances dictate. Thus, those increases or decreases can be expected to occur regularly in the aggregate and will not create the "bunching" that section 404A(c)(4) was designed to avoid.

The new proposed regulations respond to commentators' concerns by incorporating certain increases in the reserve (as described below) into the definition of the reasonable addition to a reserve, subject to an anti-abuse rule. The effect of this change is to allow immediate recognition, rather than ten-year amortization, of these changes. Under normal circumstances this immediate recognition will not result in significant bunching of income or deductions. Further, to the extent bunching occurs, abuse potential is limited because the bunching is the result of a deferral of deductions rather than the recognition of these items. Finally, as discussed below, for taxable years beginning after December 31, 1986, the indirect foreign tax credit is determined using post-1986 earnings and profits (i.e., aggregated for all post-1986 years). Use of a multi-year earnings and profits pool diminishes the effect of bunching on the foreign tax credit.

The increases in reserve that are now included in the reasonable addition to the reserve are those increases that result from expected changes in compensation and from the increase in vesting for employees whose liabilities were included in the reserve as of the beginning of the year. Thus, for example, the reasonable addition to the reserve may reflect an expected increase in compensation of five percent and expected changes in the vesting percentage in the current year for all employees in the reserve as of the beginning of the year. By contrast, any increase in reserve that results from compensation changes that are greater than expected or from the inclusion of newly-vested employees who were not included in the prior year's reserve are categorized as actuarial losses subject to ten-year amortization.

§ 1.404A-4: United States and foreign law limitations on amounts taken into account for qualified foreign plans.

§ 404A(d) limitation—pooling of earnings and profits

Section 404A(d)(3) provides that, in determining the earnings and profits (and accumulated profits) of any foreign corporation with respect to a qualified foreign plan, the amount determined under section 404A with respect to any plan for any taxable year must not exceed the amount allowed as a deduction under the appropriate foreign law for such taxable year. As the legislative history makes clear, this limitation was imposed in response to "the possibilities for distortion of a taxpayer's indirect foreign tax credit which are presented by the present annual system for determining the amount of the foreign taxes paid by a subsidiary which are attributable to dividends paid to U.S. shareholders." S. Rep. No. 1039, 96th Cong., 2d Sess. 15 (1980). The legislative history further makes clear that "[t]his potential for distortion might be eliminated if the indirect credit were computed with reference to the subsidiary's accumulated foreign taxes and undistributed accumulated profits for all years." Id.

Section 1202(a) of the Tax Reform Act of 1986 amended section 902 to provide for computation of the indirect foreign tax credit by pooling all post-1986 earnings and profits and all post-1986 creditable foreign taxes. These amendments to section 902 prevent the distortion at which section 404A(d)(3) was aimed. Section 1012(b)(4) of the Technical and Miscellaneous Revenue Act of 1988 added specific regulatory authority to section 404A(d)(3) (retroactive to enactment of the Tax Reform Act of 1986), to take this change in the law into account. Accordingly, pursuant to that grant of regulatory authority, new proposed § 1.404A-4 provides that, for taxable years beginning after December 31, 1986, the reduction of earnings and profits of a foreign corporation with respect to a qualified foreign plan is determined without regard to the tax deduction under foreign law for that year. This new rule allows any amount that is disallowed for a year (because the foreign tax deduction for that year is greater than the amount allowed under section 404A(b) or (c)) to be carried forward to a future year, in which it may increase the amount allowable under section 404A.

Section 404A(d) limitation

Section 404A(d)(1) provides that the annual amount allowable under section 404A "shall equal" the lesser of the cumulative United States amount or the cumulative foreign amount, reduced by the aggregate amount. Prior proposed § 1.404A-5 (a) provided that the annual amount allowable "shall not exceed" these cumulative amounts. The new proposed regulations adopt the language of the statute. See new proposed § 1.404A-4 (b).

Foreign currency rules

One commentator requested guidance with respect to a number of foreign currency issues. Sections 985-989 were subsequently enacted by the Tax Reform Act of 1986. These sections, effective for taxable years beginning after December 31, 1986, address many of the problems identified by the commentator. Paragraph (d)(1) in new proposed § 1.404A-4 clarifies that, for taxable years beginning after December 31, 1986, income or loss of foreign branches and earnings and profits (or deficits in earnings and profits) of foreign corporations are determined in functional currency as defined in section 985. For taxable years beginning before January 1, 1987, paragraph (d)(2) in new proposed § 1.404A-4 provides that the rules in effect for those taxable years determine the amount of income or loss or earnings and profits (or deficit in earnings and profits) for the foreign branch or subsidiary. A new paragraph (d)(3) provides special rules for those circumstances where the net worth method of accounting is used.

§ 1.404A-5: Additional limitations on amounts taken into account for qualified foreign plans.

New proposed § 1.404A-5 clarifies the evidentiary requirements and rules on actuarial assumptions. No significant changes are made to the rules in prior proposed § 1.404A-6, which are now contained in new proposed § 1.404A-5.

§ 1.404A-6: Elections under section 404A and other changes in accounting method.

Time and manner for making elections

Paragraph (b)(5) of prior proposed § 1.404A-2 provided that elections made under section 404A must be made no later than the time prescribed by law for filing the United States tax return for a United States taxpayer's taxable year. For a qualified foreign plan maintained by a foreign corporation, the regulations have been modified to conform the filing requirements to the general rules applicable to tax accounting elections on behalf of foreign corporations under section 964. For example, under the new proposed regulations, a section 404A election need not be made before the United States shareholder's tax liability is affected by the earnings and profits of the foreign corporation. Such an effect on the United States shareholder's tax liability may occur as the result of any of the following: a dividend distribution, an income inclusion under section 951(a), a section 1248 transaction, a section 864(e) basis adjustment by earnings and profits, or an inclusion in income of the earnings of a qualified electing fund under section 1293(a)(1).

The prior proposed regulations provided that, in order for "protective" or "Method (2)" elections to be effective, taxpayers who made those elections had to file amended returns no later than 90 days after the date on which the final regulations were published in the Federal Register. See Ann. 81-114, Ann. 81-148 and Ann. 82-128, reproduced as an appendix to this preamble. Otherwise, the elections would have no effect. Numerous commentators suggested that the 90-day period is inadequate for taxpayers to evaluate the final regulations, collect the required data, make the appropriate actuarial calculations, decide whether the election is beneficial, and file the required returns. Thus, the deadlines for perfecting retroactive elections and making or perfecting certain other elections in new proposed § 1.404A-7 have generally been extended to 365 days after the publication of final regulations.

Single plan

As originally proposed, § 1.404A-2(b)(6)(i) provided that an election may be made with respect to each plan that qualifies as a "single plan". The term "single plan" has for this purpose the same definition as it has in § 1.414(l)-1(b). Commentators asked for an illustration of the application of this single plan rule to an existing deferred compensation plan that is split into two single plans for purposes of section 404A. Thus, a new example has been added in paragraph (a)(2) of new proposed § 1.404A-6.

Section 481(a) adjustment

New proposed § 1.404A-6(a) addresses the adoption of methods of accounting and changes in methods of accounting with respect to a foreign deferred compensation plan for which an election under section 404A has been made. It clarifies, for example, that an initial election with respect to a pre-existing plan, termination of an election, revocation of an election, and a change in actuarial funding method, constitute changes in methods of accounting under section 446(e) and section 481(a). To compute the section 481(a) adjustment upon a change in method of accounting under section 404A, § 1.404A-6(f)(6) of the prior proposed regulations required a historical computation. Taxpayers were to compute contributions, deductions or reductions in earnings and profits from the establishment of the plan to the first day of the first year in which a section 404A election was made. Commentators argued that this historical approach was unduly burdensome.

The new proposed regulations respond to commentators' concerns by generally replacing the historical computation requirement with a "snapshot" approach to determining the amount of the section 481(a) adjustment for purposes of section 404A. As illustrated below, the snapshot approach is adopted in the proposed regulations in an effort to reduce substantially taxpayers' recordkeeping and compliance burdens.

The snapshot approach is generally intended to compare (i) the extent to which an employer has accelerated deductions (or reductions in earnings and profits) under its old method of accounting for deferred compensation with (ii) the acceleration (if any) that would have been allowed under its new method of accounting. In the interest of avoiding historical calculations and other complexities, the snapshot approach generally attempts to compare the old and new methods of accounting based, to the extent possible, on actual reserve or fund balances existing at the time of the change. These balances generally have been reduced for amounts actually paid to plan participants and beneficiaries. However, amounts actually paid to participants and beneficiaries would be the same under both an employer's old method and its new method of accounting. Therefore, deductions attributable to such payments can be eliminated from consideration in determining both the old and the new method amounts that are compared.

In other words, in the case of both the old method and the new method of accounting, the extent of acceleration is measured by reference to a common baseline: the amount actually paid to plan participants and beneficiaries (i.e., a pay-as-you-go method). Thus, the snapshot approach generally measures the extent to which an employer, under its old method of accounting, has claimed deductions (or reductions in earnings and profits) that exceed the amount actually paid to plan participants and beneficiaries as of the change in accounting method. This amount (generally referred to as the "Old Method Closing Amount") is then compared to the deductions (or reductions in earnings and profits) in excess of the amount actually paid to plan participants and beneficiaries that the employer would have claimed for the same period under its new method of accounting (generally referred to as the "New Method Opening Amount"). The section 481(a) adjustment is equal to the difference between the Old Method Closing Amount and the New Method Opening Amount. The comparison is based on the status of the plan as of the beginning of the year of a change in accounting method.

To illustrate, if the employer has used a funded method of accounting for deferred compensation, the Old Method Closing Amount equals the amount of the fund balance as of the beginning of the year that the accounting method is changed. In determining the amount of the section 481(a) adjustment for purposes of section 404A, this fund balance is compared with a New Method Opening Amount. The New Method Opening Amount will depend on which new method of accounting the employer elects. If the employer makes a qualified funded plan election, the New Method Opening Amount generally will equal the amount of the fund balance, adjusted as appropriate to reflect the

limitations in section 404A(b) and (d) on prior contributions to the fund that could have been taken into account under section 404A. If, however, the employer makes a qualified reserve plan election, the New Method Opening Amount generally will be the amount of the reserve under section 404A(c). Alternatively, if the new method of accounting is a non-section 404A method (i.e., a pay-as-you-go method), the New Method Opening Amount generally will be zero.

As the foregoing discussion indicates, the new method will not necessarily be a section 404A method (a qualified funded plan method or qualified reserve plan method), and the old method will not necessarily be a non-section 404A method. The section 481(a) adjustment and the proposed snapshot approach to computing the adjustment apply whether the employer is changing to or from a section 404A method or from one section 404A method to another. For example, assume that a foreign branch has a qualified funded plan with a trust fund balance of 15 of functional currency (as defined in section 985(b)). Assume that this fund balance resulted from FC10 of deductible contributions to the fund under section 404A, plus FC5 of net investment income earned within the fund. Under the snapshot approach, the Old Method Closing Amount upon a change to qualified reserve plan treatment is FC15. Assuming that the reserve under the qualified reserve plan method is FC20 as of the date of the method change, the New Method Opening Amount is FC20, and the amount of the section 481(a) adjustment under section 404A is a negative FC5.

By using the amount of the fund balance in determining both the Old Method Closing Amount and the New Method Opening Amount, the proposed regulations require consideration of both the deductions previously taken by the employer and the accumulated net income (or inside build-up) of a fund in calculating the amount of the section 481(a) adjustment for purposes of section 404A. The Service believes that, in addition to permitting the adoption of a simplified method for determining the section 481(a) adjustment, consideration of a fund's accumulated net income under the snapshot approach avoids additional complexities that might result from the application of sections 61 and 1001 at the time of an election under section 404A. For example, consider an employer that makes a qualified funded plan election after having used a funded method of accounting for a foreign deferred compensation plan that is not a qualified funded plan. Ordinarily, the value of the fund (which is used to satisfy the employer's plan liabilities) will exceed the employer's contributions to the fund (net of the fund's previous payments to plan participants and beneficiaries). If the snapshot method were not applied, arguably sections 61 and 1001 would result in a recognition of income (or increase in earnings and profits) by the employer at the time of the election equal to the excess of the value of the fund over the employer's basis in the fund. This result is consistent with the treatment of a change in method of accounting that consists of a qualified funded plan election as involving a change in the status of the fund from a grantor trust (defined and treated in accordance with sections 671 through 679) to a non-grantor trust (treated in a manner analogous to the treatment of a trust under a section 401(a) tax-qualified plan). The Service solicits comments from interested parties on this analysis and on the utility of the snapshot approach in reducing taxpayer burden.

Effect of section 404A(d)(1) limits on section 481(a) adjustment computation

Since the limitations of section 404A(d)(1) are part of the section 404A method of accounting under the new proposed regulations, the snapshot section 481(a) adjustment calculation must take into account the cumulative foreign amount limitation in section 404A(d) and new proposed § 1.404A-4. This is a departure from § 1.404A-6(f)(9) in the prior proposed regulations. The snapshot approach includes a simplified method to make this adjustment in computing the section 481(a) adjustment. More specifically, paragraph (g) of new proposed § 1.404A-6 allows taxpayers to use the snapshot approach to compute the initial cumulative United States and foreign law limitations under section 404A(d) as of the beginning of a year of change in method of accounting. The rules to initialize the cumulative United States amount, cumulative foreign amount and the aggregate amount rely on the constant relationship between these three amounts (i.e., the aggregate amount always equals the lesser of the two cumulative amounts).

Section 481(a) adjustment period

As required by section 404A(g)(5), the period for taking into account the section 481(a) adjustment arising from an election or a re-election under section 404A is 15 years. Additionally, new proposed § 1.404A-6(e)(2)(iii) provides for a six-year section 481(a) adjustment period for a change in method of accounting arising from the termination or revocation of an election under section 404A, and for any other change in accounting method under section 404A. This new paragraph also requires netting of any section 481(a) adjustment remaining from a previous change in method in determining the amount to be taken into account during the six-year section 481(a) adjustment period. The example in new proposed § 1.404A-6(e)(4) illustrates this netting rule.

Examples in the new proposed regulations illustrate the principle under section 446(e) and its underlying administrative procedures that the District Director may modify a taxpayer's calculated section 481(a) adjustment under section 404A if the District Director (1) determines that the taxpayer used an erroneous method of accounting in an open year prior to the year in which the taxpayer's qualified funded plan or qualified reserve plan election is effective, and (2) requires the taxpayer to change its erroneous method of accounting in that earlier open year. For example, if a taxpayer erroneously deducted FC100 for amounts accrued under a reserve plan in an open year prior to the effective date of a qualified reserve plan election under section 404A, the District Director could require the taxpayer to change its method of accounting in that earlier open year and to take a positive FC100 section 481(a) adjustment into account entirely in that earlier open year (rather than permitting the positive FC100 amount to be netted against any New Method Opening Amount under the snapshot approach and spread prospectively over a 15-year section 481(a) adjustment period). See section 2.02 of Rev. Proc. 92-20, 1992-1 C.B. 685.

§ 1.404A-7: Effective date and retroactive application.

Prior proposed § 1.404A-2(c), relating to retroactive elections, has been moved to § 1.404A-7. This change was made because the rules relating to retroactive elections are relatively discrete and thus logically should be set apart from the general election rules. Because the importance of these rules will greatly diminish within a few years, their placement at the end of the regulations will improve the clarity of the remainder of the regulations for the future. Other specific changes to the retroactive election rules are discussed below.

All-or-nothing rule

Many commentators criticized the rule in paragraph (c)(2)(ii) of prior proposed § 1.404A-2 as an improper interpretation of section 2(e)(2) of the Act of December 28, 1980 (Pub. L. 96-603). Prior proposed § 1.404A-2(c)(2)(i) provided that a taxpayer could elect, during its "open period," for section 404A to apply to a qualified foreign plan maintained by a foreign subsidiary. However, prior proposed § 1.404A-2(c)(2)(i) conditioned that election for any plan on a taxpayer electing to apply section 404A with respect to all written plans of every foreign subsidiary (whether or not wholly owned) that defer the receipt of compensation and that satisfy the requirements of section 404A(e)(1) and (2). Commentators argued that the "all-or-nothing rule" of section 2(e)(2) of the Act of December 28, 1980, simply provides that a taxpayer may elect to have section 404A apply for certain prior years, and that such an election must be made for all of a taxpayer's foreign subsidiaries. It does not, however, require that a taxpayer make an election under section 404A for any of its foreign subsidiaries' plans. According to this view, once the election is made to have section 404A apply to the foreign subsidiaries for prior years, the consequences of making or not making an election under section 404A will be determined as though section 404A had been in effect for those years.

After further consideration, the proposed regulations adopt the commentators' view of section 2(e)(2) of the Act of December 28, 1980. Thus, if a taxpayer makes an election to have section 404A apply retroactively to its foreign subsidiaries during its open period, the election to have section 404A apply must be made for all of a taxpayer's foreign subsidiaries (whether or not wholly owned) during a taxpayer's open period. Accordingly, if a taxpayer elects to have section 404A apply during a taxpayer's open period, it may not rely on any other law or rule of law to reduce earnings and profits (or accumulated profits) of any foreign subsidiary with respect to deferred compensation expenses, regardless of whether the taxpayer elects to apply section 404A to any specific deferred compensation plan. Paragraph (b) of new § 1.404A-7 reflects this view, and paragraph (c)(5) illustrates this rule with an example.

Making, perfecting and revoking retroactive elections

New proposed § 1.404A-7 provides rules for making, perfecting and revoking retroactive effective date elections as well as retroactive plan-by-plan elections for qualified foreign plans maintained by foreign subsidiaries and for qualified funded plans maintained by foreign branches. Taxpayers are afforded 365 days after publication of the final regulations to decide whether to perfect or revoke retroactive elections or to make, revoke or re-elect in intervals of six or more years, effective for taxable years in the open period (as defined in new proposed § 1.404A-7(g)(6)) and continuing after taxable years beginning after December 31, 1979. Taxpayers must file amended returns and attach statements in order to perfect a retroactive election and to conform all items to the treatment consistent with election or revocation. If the amended returns and statements are not timely filed, the retroactive elections will be deemed revoked.

Alternative to contemporaneous evidence requirement

Many commentators criticized the rule in prior proposed § 1.404A-2(c)(4)(iii) prohibiting a retroactive election if a taxpayer was unable to calculate the requisite section 481(a) adjustment based upon actual data, because, in effect, it unduly restricted taxpayers' ability to make retroactive elections. The commentators were concerned that many taxpayers would lack "actual data", and thus be unable to make the election, and that, even if such data were technically available, its retrieval would be prohibitively burdensome. After further consideration, the Service has altered this requirement. Accordingly, new proposed § 1.404A-7(f) provides that the section 481(a) adjustment must be made based upon contemporaneous substantiation quality data. If contemporaneous substantiation quality data is not readily available, however, the adjustment may be based on data which are combinations of actual contemporaneous evidence and reasonable actuarial backward projections of substantiation quality data.

For the convenience of taxpayers, Ann. 81-114, 1981 I.R.B. 21, Ann. 81-148, 1981-39 I.R.B. 15, and Ann. 82-128, 1982-39 I.R.B. 103, concerning Method (1) and Method (2) elections, are reproduced below.

Appendix

Announcement 81-114, 1981-28 I.R.B. 21

This announcement provides guidance relating to section 404A of the Internal Revenue Code. Until proposed regulations are published, taxpayers may rely on the guidance provided below.

Section 404A, added by the Act of December 28, 1980, Pub. L. 96-603 (1981-5 I.R.B. 31), allows taxpayers to make certain elections concerning deductions for amounts paid or accrued by an employer under qualified foreign plans. The two types of qualified foreign plans are qualified funded plans and qualified reserve plans. A qualified foreign plan is any written plan which defers the receipt of compensation and which satisfies two requirements. First, the plan must be for the exclusive benefit of the employer's employees or their beneficiaries. Second, 90 percent or more of the amounts taken into account for the taxable year under the plan must be attributable to services performed by nonresident aliens, the compensation for which is not subject to federal income tax. In addition, the employer must properly elect to have section 404A apply to such plan. If an employer does not make such an election, deductions (or reductions in earnings and profits) are allowed only as provided under section 404 for plans and trusts meeting the requirements of that section.

The rules of section 404A are applicable for taxable years beginning after December 31, 1979, and for certain prior years to the extent the taxpayer elects to have the provisions of section 404A of the Code apply retroactively. Pending the issuance of regulations relating to such elections, the elections referred to in section 404A(e)(3) and (f)(2) of the Code may be made either by (1) claiming the permissible deduction or credit on the taxpayer's income tax return for the first taxable year ending on or after December 31, 1980, including extensions (or an amended return that is filed no later than the end of the extended time period prescribed in section 6081, whether or not such time is actually extended for filing the taxpayer's return), or (2) attaching a statement of election to the taxpayer's income tax return within the time period described in the first method. If the election is made by attaching a statement of election under method (2), the taxpayer's current return would not include deductions or in the case of foreign subsidiaries, take into account reductions in earnings and profits that relate to foreign deferred compensation plans. Deductions or credits consistent with the election would be included on an amended return, to be filed no later than the deadline (described below) for revoking the election. Under either method, the taxpayer must attach to the return a list of plans with respect to which the elections are made. Method (1) or method (2) may also be used for the elections described in section 2(e) of Pub. L. 96-603. When method (2) is used in connection with section 2(e) of Pub. L. 96-603, taxpayers need not amend past returns until regulations are issued.

A taxpayer must determine the amount deductible under section 404A(d) based, in part, on the cumulative foreign amount as defined in section 404A(d)(2)(B). No deduction is allowable under section 404A unless the cumulative foreign amount is established in one of the documents described in section 404A(g)(2)(A)(i), (ii) or (iii) of the Code. Section 404A(g)(2)(A)(iii) authorizes the Secretary to promulgate regulations that would accept certain unspecified statements or evidence as being sufficient to establish the amount of the deduction under foreign law. Until such time as regulations are promulgated under section 404A(g)(2)(A)(iii), the requirements of that section will be considered to be satisfied by a statement prepared at or before the time the return is filed, which lists separately for each plan the cumulative foreign amount and which states that such cumulative foreign amount has been determined pursuant to the requirements of the appropriate foreign tax law. The statement must be prepared by the U.S. taxpayer or a person authorized to practice before the Service. While a taxpayer need not attach any of these documents to its tax return, the taxpayer must furnish the documents for examination upon request of the Internal Revenue Service.

Taxpayers that have made the elections described in section 404A and/or section 2 (e) of Pub. L. 96-603 under method (2) need not prepare the statement, described in the immediately preceding paragraph, until they amend their returns. In addition, taxpayers that have made the election described in section 404A for taxable years beginning after December 31, 1979, under Method (1), and have made the election described in section 2 (e) of Pub. L. 96-603 under method (2) will satisfy section 404A(g)(2)(A)(iii) if the cumulative foreign amount in the statement reflects the aggregate foreign deductions allowed under foreign law for taxable years commencing after December 31, 1979.

Taxpayers that have already made an election, referred to in this announcement, that does not conform with the requirements stated herein may perfect that election on an amended return filed by the later of September 23, 1981 or by the due date of the taxpayer's income tax return for the first taxable year beginning after December 31, 1979, including extensions. These taxpayers may also satisfy section 404A(g)(2)(A)(iii), to the extent applicable as previously described in this announcement, by preparing the required statement within the same time limits for perfecting the elections under sections 404A(e)(3) and (f)(2).

The qualified reserve plan election, including any retroactive election described in section 2(e)(2) of Pub. L. 96-603, may be revoked on an amended return for the first taxable year ending on or after December 31, 1980, without the consent of the Commissioner until 90 days after the publication of final regulations regarding such elections. Similarly, the qualified foreign plan election and the retroactive election described in section 2(e)(3) may be revoked within the same period.

It is anticipated that the effective date of the final regulations generally will be for taxable years beginning after December 31, 1979, and such prior years as may be affected by an election under section 2(e) of Pub. L. 96-603. Accordingly, taxpayers may be required to amend their tax returns to the extent that deductions or credits claimed are inconsistent with final regulations.

Announcement 81-148, 1981-39 I.R.B. 15

On June 24, 1981, the Internal Revenue Service issued Announcement 81-114, 1981-28 I.R.B. 21. The announcement was intended to provide pre-regulation guidance to taxpayers concerning recent legislation under section 404A. Taxpayers have expressed concern with respect to a statement in that announcement, with respect to reductions of earnings and profits if section 404A is not elected. Announcement 81-114 is clarified as follows:

The decision not to elect section 404A will not affect the computation of earnings and profits with respect to contributions to plans as allowed under prior law. In the case of an accrued liability to a reserve plan, however, such accrued liability reduces earnings and profits only as provided in section 404A with respect to the taxable years described in section 2 (e) of Pub. L. 96-603, 1980-2 C.B. 684.

Announcement 82-128, 1982-39 I.R.B. 103

Taxpayers that are interested in making the elections referred to in section 404A(e)(3) and (f)(2) of the Internal Revenue Code may continue to use the "method (1)" or "method (2)" election described in Announcement 81-114, 1981-28 I.R.B. 21 for taxable years beginning after December 31, 1979, until further guidance is made available. Pending the issuance of regulations under section 404A, qualified foreign plans must comply with the reporting requirements and other rules contained in Announcement 81-114.

Effective dates

The amendments are proposed generally to apply to taxable years beginning after December 31, 1979. The prohibited transaction rules in § 1.404A-2 (a) are proposed to be effective May 6, 1993. If a taxpayer elected pursuant to section 2(e)(2) of the Act of December 28, 1980, the amendments are proposed to apply to certain prior taxable years beginning after December 31, 1970.

Special Analyses

It has been determined that these proposed rules are not major rules as defined in Executive Order 12291. Therefore, a Regulatory Impact Analysis is not required. It has also been determined that section 553(b) of the Administrative Procedure Act (5 U.S.C. chapter 5) and the Regulatory Flexibility Act (5 U.S.C. chapter 6) do not apply to these proposed regulations and, therefore, an initial Regulatory Flexibility Analysis is not required. Pursuant to section 7805(f) of the Internal Revenue Code, these proposed regulations will be submitted to the Chief Counsel for Advocacy of the Small Business Administration for comment on their impact on small business.

Comments and Requests to Appear at the Public Hearing

Before adopting these proposed regulations, consideration will be given to any written comments that are submitted (preferably a signed original and eight copies) to the Commissioner of Internal Revenue. All comments will be available for public inspection and copying in their entirety. Because the Treasury Department expects to issue final regulations on this matter as soon as possible, a public hearing will be held at 10:00 a.m. on October 5, 1993, in Room 2615, Internal Revenue Building, 1111 Constitution Ave., N.W., Washington, D.C. Written comments must be received by July 6, 1993. Requests to speak (with outlines of oral comments) at the public hearing must be received by September 14, 1993. See notice of hearing published elsewhere in this issue of the Federal Register.

Drafting Information

The principal author of these proposed regulations is Elizabeth A. Purcell of the Office of the Associate Chief Counsel (Employee Benefits and Exempt Organizations), Internal Revenue Service. However, personnel from other offices of the Service and Treasury Department participated in their development.

List of Subjects in 26 CFR 1.401-0 Through 1.419A-2T

Bonds, Employee benefit plans, Income taxes, Pensions, Reporting and recordkeeping requirements, Securities, Trusts and trustees.

Withdrawal of Proposed Amendments

The proposed amendments to 26 CFR part 1, relating to §§ 1.404A-0, 1.404A-1, 1.404A-2, 1.404A-3, 1.404A-4, 1.404A-5 and 1.404A-6, published in the **Federal Register** for April 8, 1985 (50 FR 13821), are withdrawn.

Proposed Amendments to the Regulations

Accordingly, the proposed amendments to 26 CFR part 1 are added to read as follows:

PART 1—INCOME TAX; TAXABLE YEARS BEGINNING AFTER DECEMBER 31, 1953

Paragraph 1. The authority citation for part 1 is amended by adding the following citations to read as follows:

Authority: 26 U.S.C. 7805 * * * §§ 1.404A-1, 1.404A-2, 1.404A-3, 1.404A-4, 1.404A-5, 1.404A-6 and 1.404A-7 also issued under 26 U.S.C. 404A. * * *

Par. 2. Sections 1.404A-0 through 1.404A-7 are added as follows:

§ 1.404A-0. Table of Contents, EE-14-81, 5/6/93.

This section 1.404A-0 lists the major headings that appear in §§ 1.404A-1 through 1.404A-7.

§ 1.404A-1 General rules concerning deductions and adjustments to earnings and profits for foreign deferred compensation plans.

(a) In general.

(b) 90-percent test.

(1) Reserve plans.

(2) Funded plans.

(c) Calculation of 90 percent amounts.

(1) In general.

(2) Safe harbor.

(3) Anti-abuse rule.

(4) Example.

(d) Deductions and reductions of earnings and profits.

(e) Definitions.

Actuarial present value.

Aggregate amount.

Appropriate foreign tax law.

Authorized officer.

Carryover contributions.

Change in method of accounting.

Closing year.

Contributions accumulated to pay deferred compensation.

Contributions to a trust.

Controlled foreign corporation.

Cumulative foreign amount.

Cumulative limitation.

Cumulative United States amount.

Deductible limit

Deductions.

Deferred compensation

Earnings and profits.

Employer.

Equivalent of a trust.

Erroneous deduction.

Exclusive benefit.

Fixed or determinable benefits.

Full funding limitation.

Functional currency.

Funded method.

Initial aggregate amount.

Initial Cumulative foreign amount.

Initial Cumulative United States amount.

Initial section 404A(d) amounts.

Liability.

Majority domestic corporate shareholders.

Method of accounting.

Method (1) election.

Method (2) election.

New Method Opening Amount.

Noncontrolled foreign corporation.

Nonqualified individual.

Nonqualified plan.

Old Method Closing Amount.

Open period.

Open years.

Opening reserve.

Opening year.

Pay-as-you-go method.

Period of adjustment.

Permitted plan year.

Plan year.

Primary evidence.

Prior deduction.

Protective election.

Qualified business unit.

Qualified foreign plan.

Qualified funded plan.

Qualified reserve plan.

Reasonable actuarial assumptions.

Reductions in earnings and profits.

Reserve method.

Retirement annuity.

Retroactive effective date election.

Retroactive period

Retroactive plan-by-plan election.

Revocation of election.

Secondary evidence.

Separate funding entity.

Short taxable year.

Single plan.

Substantial risk of forfeiture.

Substantiation quality data.

Taxable year of a controlled foreign corporation.

Taxable year of a noncontrolled foreign corporation.

Taxpayer.

Termination of election.

Transition period.

Trust.

Unit credit method.

United States tax significance.

Written plan.

(f) Application of other Code requirements.

(1) Deductibility requirement.

(2) Section 461 requirements.

1.404A-2 Rules for qualified funded plans.

(a) In general.

(b) Payment to a trust.

(1) Contribution requirements.

(2) Trust requirements.

(3) Retirement annuity.

(4) Effect of reversion of overfunded contributions.

(5) Example.

(c) Contribution deemed made before payment.

(1) Time of payment to trust.

(2) Time of designation.

(3) Irrevocable designation.

(d) Limitation for qualified funded plans.

(1) Plans with fixed or determinable benefits.

(2) Plans without fixed or determinable benefits.

(3) Limitations where more than one type of plan is maintained.

(4) Carryover contributions.

(5) Additional rules.

(e) Examples.

1.404A-3 Rules for qualified reserve plans.

(a) Amounts taken into account with respect to qualified reserve plans.

(1) General rule.

(2) Amounts less than zero.

(3) Exclusive rules for qualified reserve plans.

(b) Reasonable addition to a reserve for liabilities.

(1) General rule.

(2) Unit credit method required.

(3) Timing of valuation.

(4) Permissible actuarial assumptions.

(c) Ten-year amortization for certain changes in reserves.

(1) Actuarial valuation.

(2) Expected value of reserve.

(3) Special rule for certain cost of living adjustments.

(4) Anti-abuse rule.

(d) Examples.

1.404A-4 United States and foreign law limitations on amounts taken into account for qualified foreign plans.

(a) In general.

(b) Cumulative limitation.

(c) Special rule for foreign corporations in pre-pooling years.

(d) Rules relating to foreign currency.

(1) Taxable years beginning after December 31, 1986.

(2) Taxable years beginning before January 1, 1987.

(3) Special rules for the net worth method of accounting.

(e) Maintenance of more than one type of qualified foreign plan by an employer.

(f) United States and foreign law limitations not applicable.

(g) Definitions.

(1) Cumulative United States amount.

(2) Cumulative foreign amount.

(3) Appropriate foreign tax law.

(4) Aggregate amount.

(h) Examples.

1.404A-5 Additional limitations on amounts taken into account for qualified foreign plans.

(a) Restrictions for nonqualified individuals.

(1) General rule.

(2) Determination of service attribution.

(b) Records to be provided by taxpayer.

(1) In general.

(2) Primary evidence.

(3) Additional requirements.

(4) Secondary evidence.

(5) Foreign language.

(6) Additional information required by District Director.

(7) Authorized officer to complete documents.

(8) Transitional rules.

(c) Actuarial requirements.

(1) Reasonable actuarial assumptions.

(2) Full funding limitation.

1.404A-6 Elections under section 404A and changes in methods of accounting.

(a) Elections, changes in accounting methods, and changes in plan years.

(1) In general.

(2) Single plan.

(b) Initial elections under section 404A.

(1) In general.

(2) Time for making election.

(3) Manner in which election is to be made.

(4) Other requirements for election.

(c) Termination of election when a plan ceases to be a qualified foreign plan.

(1) In general.

(2) Rules for changing method of accounting upon termination of election.

(d) Other changes in methods of accounting and changes in plan year.

(1) Application for consent.

(2) Procedures for other changes in method of accounting.

(3) Plan year.

(e) Application of section 481.

(1) In general.

(2) Period of adjustment.

(3) Allocation and source.

(4) Example.

(f) Computation of section 481(a) adjustment.

(1) In general.

(2) Old Method Closing Amount.

(3) New Method Opening Amount.

(4) Definitions and special rules.

(5) Examples.

(g) Initial section 404A (d) amounts.

(1) In general.

(2) Computation of amounts.

(3) Example.

§ 1.404A-7 Effective date, retroactive elections, and transition rules.

(a) In general.

(1) Effective date.

(2) Overview of retroactive elections for taxable years beginning before January 1, 1980.

(3) Overview of special transition rules for election, revocation, and re-election.

(b) Retroactive effective date elections for foreign subsidiaries.

(1) In general.

(2) Time and manner to make, perfect, or revoke election.

(3) Requirement to amend returns.

(c) Retroactive plan-by-plan elections for foreign subsidiaries.

(1) In general.

(2) Time and manner to make, perfect, or revoke election.

(3) Requirement to amend returns.

(4) Revocation after initial election and re-election permitted.

(5) Examples.

(d) Retroactive plan-by-plan qualified funded plan elections for plans of foreign branches.

(1) In general.

(2) Amounts allowed as a deduction.

(3) Definitions.

(4) Time and manner to make, perfect, or revoke election.

(5) Examples.

(e) Special transition rules for election, revocation and re-election.

(1) In general.

(2) Time and manner initially to elect, revoke and re-elect.

(3) Revocation after initial election and re-election permitted.

(4) Example.

(f) Special data rules for retroactive elections.

(1) Retroactive calculation of section 481(a) adjustments.

(2) Determination of reasonable addition to a reserve in interim years.

(3) Protective elections.

(g) Definitions and special rules.

(1) Method (1) election.

(2) Protective or Method (2) election.

(3) Open years of the taxpayer.

(4) Retroactive period.

(5) Transition period.

(6) Open period.

[Reg. § 1.404A-0.]

§ 1.404A-1. *General rules concerning deductions and adjustments to earnings and profits for foreign deferred compensation plans*, EE-14-81, 5/6/93.

(a) *In general.* Section 404A provides the exclusive means by which an employer may take a deduction or reduce earnings and profits for deferred compensation in situations other than those in which a deduction or reduction of earnings and profits is permitted under section 404. A deduction or reduction of earnings and profits is permitted under section 404A for amounts paid or accrued by an employer under a foreign deferred compensation plan, in the taxable year in which the amounts are properly taken into account under §§ 1.404A-1 through 1.404A-7, if each of the following requirements is satisfied:

(1) The plan is a written plan maintained by the employer that provides deferred compensation.

(2) The plan is maintained for the exclusive benefit of the employer's employees or their beneficiaries.

(3) 90 percent or more of the amounts taken into account under the plan are attributable to services performed by nonresident aliens, the compensation for which is not subject to United States federal income tax.

(4) An election under § 1.404A-6 or 1.404A-7 is made to treat the plan as either a qualified funded plan or a qualified reserve plan and to select a plan year.

(b) *90-percent test*—(1) *Reserve plans.* Paragraph (a)(3) of this section is not satisfied by a reserve plan unless 90 percent or more of the actuarial present value of the total vested benefits (i.e., benefits not subject to substantial risk of forfeiture) accrued under the plan is attributable to services performed by nonresident aliens, the compensation for which is not subject to United States federal income tax.

(2) *Funded plans*—(i) *Individual account plans.* Paragraph (a)(3) of this section is not satisfied by a funded plan with individual accounts unless 90 percent or more of the amounts allocated to individual accounts (as described in section 414(i)) under the plan are allocated to the accounts of nonresident aliens and are attributable to services the compensation for which is not subject to United States federal income tax.

(ii) *Plans without individual accounts.* Paragraph (a)(3) of this section is not satisfied by a funded plan not described in paragraph (b)(2)(i) of this section unless 90 percent or more of the actuarial present value of the total benefits accrued under the plan is attributable to services performed by nonresident aliens the compensation for which is not subject to United States federal income tax.

(c) *Calculation of 90 percent amounts*—(1) *In general.* In determining whether the tests described in paragraphs (b)(1) and (b)(2)(ii) of this section are satisfied, accrued benefits and the actuarial present values of accrued benefits may be calculated under any reasonable method. See § 1.404A-5(a) for rules describing the calculation of accrued benefits attributable to services for which the compensation is subject to United States federal income tax.

(2) *Safe harbor.* The requirement of paragraph (a)(3) of this section will be deemed satisfied with respect to a plan if—

(i) The participants' benefits under the plan increase generally in proportion to their compensation taken into account under the plan; and

(ii) The sum of the following amounts does not exceed five percent of all compensation taken into account under the plan for the plan year—

(A) The compensation of United States citizens and residents taken into account under the plan; and

(B) Any other compensation subject to United States federal income tax taken into account under the plan.

(3) *Anti-abuse rule.* Notwithstanding paragraph (c)(2) of this section, the requirement of paragraph (a)(3) of this section will not be deemed satisfied under paragraph (c)(2) of this section if the Commissioner determines that a significant purpose of the plan is to secure benefits not otherwise eligible for tax benefits under the Internal Revenue Code to participants who are United States citizens or residents.

(4) *Example.* The principles of paragraphs (c)(2) and (c)(3) of this section are illustrated by the following example:

Example. A foreign branch of a domestic corporation maintains a deferred compensation plan under which benefits are based upon a participant's average compensation for the last five consecutive years of employment. The significant purposes of the plan do not include the

provision of benefits otherwise unavailable under the Code to participants who are United States citizens or residents. The foreign branch maintains its books and records in its functional currency (FC). The taxpayer's taxable year and the plan year are coterminous with the calendar year. During the plan year in question, the compensation taken into account under the plan for all plan participants totals FC200 million. Of the FC200 million, FC6 million of the compensation taken into account under the plan is compensation for United States citizens and residents or otherwise subject to United States federal income tax. Because the FC6 million is less than five percent of all compensation taken into account under the plan for the plan year, the 90-percent requirement of paragraph (a)(3) of this section is deemed satisfied for this taxable year.

(d) *Deductions and reductions of earnings and profits.* Deductions and reductions of earnings and profits for amounts paid by an employer to a plan that provides deferred compensation that does not meet the requirements of paragraph (a) of this section are governed exclusively by section 404, without regard to whether the plan benefits foreign employees.

(e) *Definitions.* The following definitions apply for purposes of section 404A and §§ 1.404A-1 through 1.404A-7:

Actuarial present value. "Actuarial present value" is defined in § 1.401(a)(4)-12.

Aggregate amount. "Aggregate amount" is defined in § 1.404A-4(g)(4).

Appropriate foreign tax law. "Appropriate foreign tax law" is defined in § 1.404A-4(g)(3).

Authorized officer. "Authorized officer" is defined in § 1.404A-5(b)(7).

Carryover contributions. "Carryover contributions" are defined in § 1.404A-2(d)(4).

Change in method of accounting. "Change in method of accounting" is defined in § 1.404A-6(a).

Closing year. "Closing year" is defined in § 1.404A-6(f)(4)(ii).

Contributions accumulated to pay deferred compensation. "Contributions accumulated to pay deferred compensation" are defined in § 1.404A-2(b)(2).

Contributions to a trust. "Contributions to a trust" are defined in § 1.404A-2(b)(1).

Controlled foreign corporation. "Controlled foreign corporation" means a controlled foreign corporation as defined in sections 953(c)(1)(B) and 957.

Cumulative foreign amount. "Cumulative foreign amount" is defined in § 1.404A-4(g)(2).

Cumulative limitation. "Cumulative limitation" is defined in § 1.404A-4(b).

Cumulative United States amount. "Cumulative United States amount" is defined in § 1.404A-4(g)(1).

Deductible limit. "Deductible limit" is defined in § 1.404A-2(d)(1)(i).

Deductions. "Deductions" are defined in § 1.404A-1(f)(1).

Deferred compensation—(i) *In general.* "Deferred compensation" means any item the deductibility of which is determined by reference to section 404, without regard to whether section 404 permits a deduction and without regard to whether elections are made under § 1.404A-6 or 1.404A-7. Deferred compensation, as described in the preceding sentence, does not include deferred benefits described in section 404(b)(2)(B).

(ii) *Social security.* A plan under which a foreign government (including a political subdivision, agency or instrumentality thereof) makes a contribution or a direct payment to a participant (or the participant's beneficiary) does not provide deferred compensation to the extent of such contributions or payments. Thus, for example, a foreign country's social security system generally will not be considered as providing deferred compensation. However, the fact that employers are required to maintain the plan by reason of foreign law, or the fact that the plan supplements social security benefits provided by a foreign country, or provides benefits in lieu of such social security benefits, does not prevent a plan from providing deferred compensation.

(iii) *Termination indemnity plans.* The determination of whether a plan (including a termination indemnity plan) provides deferred compensation must generally be made under paragraph (i) of this definition in light of all of the facts and circumstances. Benefits paid under a plan, including a plan denominated a termination indemnity plan will generally be treated as deferred compensation if—

(A) A major purpose of the plan is to provide for the payment of retirement benefits;

(B) The plan has a benefit formula providing for payment based at least in part upon length of service;

(C) The plan provides for the payment of benefits to employees (or their beneficiaries) after the employee's retirement, death or other termination of employment; and

(D) It meets such other requirements as may be prescribed by the Commissioner in guidance of general applicability with respect to termination indemnity plans.

(iv) *Example.* The definition of deferred compensation is illustrated by the following example:

Example. A domestic corporation maintains a branch operation in foreign country F. F requires that all employers doing business in its country provide benefits to employees under a termination indemnity plan insured by F's government. The plan provides for payments to employees who terminate employment for any reason, including retirement, death, voluntary resignation and discharge for cause (other than for gross misconduct) and permits withdrawals for certain hardship conditions. Upon separation, the employee (or his or her beneficiary) receives an amount equal to the accumulation on the employer's books of one-thirteenth of his or her annual salary for each year of employment, with specified adjustments for interest and inflation. This termination indemnity plan provides deferred compensation as described in paragraph (e) of this section.

Earnings and profits. "Earnings and profits" means earnings and profits computed in accordance with sections 312 and 964(a) and, for taxable years beginning after December 31, 1986, section 986 and the regulations thereunder; and for purposes of section 902 in taxable years beginning before January 1, 1987, accumulated profits within the meaning of section 902(c) as in effect on the day before the enactment of the Tax Reform Act of 1986.

Employer. "Employer" means a person that maintains a plan for the payment of deferred compensation for services provided to it by its employees. "Employer" for purposes of the acceleration of the section 481(a) adjustment is defined in § 1.404A-6(e)(2)(iv).

Equivalent of a trust. "Equivalent of a trust" means a fund—

(i) The corpus and income of which is separately identifiable and segregated, through a separate legal entity, from the general assets of the employer;

(ii) The corpus and income of which is not subject, under the applicable foreign law, to the claims of the employer's creditors prior to the claims of employees and their beneficiaries under the plan;

(iii) The corpus and income of which, by law or by contract, cannot at any time prior to the satisfaction of all liabilities with respect to employees under the plan be used for, or diverted to, any purpose other than providing benefits under the plan; and

(iv) The corpus and income of which is held by a person who has a legally enforceable duty to operate the fund prudently.

Erroneous deduction. "Erroneous deduction" is defined in § 1.404A-7(d)(3)(ii).

Exclusive benefit. "Exclusive benefit" has the same meaning as in §§ 1.401-2 and 1.413-1(d).

Fixed or determinable benefits. "Fixed or determinable benefits" are defined in § 1.404A-2(d)(1)(i).

Full funding limitation. "Full funding limitation" is defined in § 1.404A-5(c)(2).

Functional currency. "Functional currency" (abbreviated as FC) means the functional currency of a taxpayer or a qualified business unit determined in accordance with section 985(b) and the regulations thereunder, or, for taxable years beginning before January 1, 1987, the currency in which the employer's books and records were maintained for United States tax purposes.

Funded method. "Funded method" is defined in § 1.404A-6(f)(2)(iv).

Initial aggregate amount. "Initial aggregate amount" is defined in § 1.404A-6(g)(2)(iii).

Initial Cumulative foreign amount. "Initial Cumulative foreign amount" is defined in § 1.404A-6(g)(2)(ii).

Initial Cumulative United States amount. "Initial Cumulative United States amount" is defined in § 1.404A-6(g)(2)(i).

Initial section 404A(d) amounts. "Initial section 404A(d) amounts" are defined in § 1.404A-6(g).

Liability. "Liability" is defined in § 1.404A-1(f)(2).

Majority domestic corporate shareholders. "Majority domestic corporate shareholders" are defined in § 1.404A-6(c)(2)(ii)(C).

Method of accounting. "Method of accounting" is defined in § 1.404A-6(a)(1).

Method (1) election. "Method (1) election" is defined in § 1.404A-7(g)(1).

Method (2) election. "Method (2) election" is defined in § 1.404A-7(g)(2).

New Method Opening Amount. "New Method Opening Amount" is defined in § 1.404A-6(f)(3).

Noncontrolled foreign corporation. "Noncontrolled foreign corporation" means a foreign corporation other than a controlled foreign corporation.

Nonqualified individual. "Nonqualified individual" is defined in § 1.404A-5(a)(1).

Nonqualified plan. "Nonqualified plan" is defined in § 1.404A-6(f)(3)(iii).

Old Method Closing Amount. "Old Method Closing Amount" is defined in § 1.404A-6(f)(2).

Open period. "Open period" is defined in § 1.404A-7(g)(6).

Open years. "Open years" are defined in § 1.404A-7(g)(3).

Opening reserve. "Opening reserve" is defined in § 1.404A-6(f)(3)(i).

Opening year. "Opening year" is defined in § 1.404A-6(f)(4)(i).

Pay-as-you-go method. "Pay-as-you-go method" is defined in § 1.404A-6(f)(2)(iii).

Period of adjustment. "Period of adjustment" is defined in § 1.404A-6(e)(2).

Permitted plan year. "Permitted plan year" means the plan year of a plan providing deferred compensation ending with or within the employer's taxable year.

Plan year. "Plan year" means the annual accounting period of a plan providing deferred compensation.

Primary evidence. "Primary evidence" is defined in § 1.404A-5(b)(2).

Prior deduction. "Prior deduction" is defined in § 1.404A-7(d)(3)(i).

Protective election. "Protective election" is defined in § 1.404A-7(g)(2).

Qualified business unit. "Qualified business unit" is defined in section 989(a).

Qualified foreign plan. "Qualified foreign plan" means a plan that meets the requirements of paragraph (a) of this section.

Qualified funded plan. "Qualified funded plan" means a qualified foreign plan for which an election has been made under § 1.404A-6 or 1.404A-7 by the taxpayer to treat the plan as a qualified funded plan.

Qualified reserve plan. "Qualified reserve plan" means a qualified foreign plan for which an election has been made by the taxpayer under § 1.404A-6 or 1.404A-7 to treat the plan as a qualified reserve plan.

Reasonable actuarial assumptions. "Reasonable actuarial assumptions" are defined in § 1.404A-5(c).

Reductions in earnings and profits. "Reductions in earnings and profits" are defined in § 1.404A-1(f)(1).

Reserve method. "Reserve method" is defined in § 1.404A-6(f)(2)(ii).

Retirement annuity. "Retirement annuity" is defined in § 1.404A-2(b)(3).

Retroactive effective date election. "Retroactive effective date election" is defined in § 1.404A-7(b)(1).

Retroactive period. "Retroactive period" is defined in § 1.404A-7(g)(4).

Retroactive plan-by-plan election. "Retroactive plan-by-plan election" is defined in § 1.404A-7(c)(1) and (d)(1).

Revocation of election. "Revocation of election" is defined in § 1.404A-6(d)(1).

Secondary evidence. "Secondary evidence" is defined in § 1.404A-5(b)(4).

Separate funding entity. "Separate funding entity" is defined in § 1.404A-6(f)(4)(iii).

Short taxable year. "Short taxable year" is defined in § 1.404A-7(d)(2).

Single plan. "Single plan" is defined in § 1.404A-6(a)(2).

Substantial risk of forfeiture. "Substantial risk of forfeiture" is defined in § 1.404A-3(b)(2).

Substantiation quality data. "Substantiation quality data" means less than precise data that is nevertheless the best data available for the plan year at reasonable expense.

Taxable year of a controlled foreign corporation. "Taxable year of a controlled foreign corporation" means the taxable year as defined in sections 441(b) and 7701(a)(23), subject to section 898.

Taxable year of a noncontrolled foreign corporation. "Taxable year of a noncontrolled foreign corporation" means the taxable year as defined in sections 441(b) and 7701(a)(23).

Taxpayer. "Taxpayer" is defined in section 7701(a)(14).

Termination of election. "Termination of election" is defined in § 1.404A-6(c)(1).

Transition period. "Transition period" is defined in § 1.404A-7(g)(5).

Trust. "Trust" means a trust (as defined in § 301.7701-4(a) of this chapter) or the equivalent of a trust.

Unit credit method. "Unit credit method" is defined in § 1.404A-3(b)(2).

United States tax significance. "United States tax significance" is defined in § 1.404A-6(b)(2)(ii).

Written plan. "Written plan" means a plan that is defined by plan instruments or required under the law of a foreign country, or both. An insurance contract can constitute a written plan.

(f) *Application of other Code requirements*—(1) *Deductibility requirement*—(i) *In general.* In order to deduct amounts under section 404A, amounts contributed to a qualified funded plan or properly added to a reserve with respect to a qualified reserve plan must otherwise be deductible. The standards under section 404 are to be used in determining whether an amount would otherwise be deductible for this purpose. Thus, amounts may be taken into account under section 404A only to the extent that they are ordinary and necessary expenses during the taxable year in carrying on a trade or business and are compensation for personal services actually rendered before the end of the year. Similarly, in order to reduce earnings and profits under section 404A by amounts contributed to a qualified funded plan or properly added to a reserve with respect to a qualified reserve plan, earnings and profits must otherwise be able to be reduced by such amounts under the general principles of sections 312, 901, 902, 960, and 964.

(ii) *Capitalization requirements.* In determining if an amount would otherwise be deductible (or able to be used to reduce earnings and profits) for purposes of paragraph (g)(1)(i) of this section, the fact that the amount is required to be capitalized (e.g., under section 263A) is ignored. Additionally, while section 404A and §§ 1.404A-1 through 1.404A-7 refer generally to permissible deductions or reductions of earnings and profits for deferred compensation, those references are intended to refer both to situations under which amounts may be taken into account as deductions or reductions of earnings and profits and to situations under which amounts may be taken into account through inclusion in the basis of inventory or through capitalization.

(2) *Section 461 requirements.* In determining whether any amount of deferred compensation may be taken into account under section 404A by an accrual method taxpayer, the conditions for accrual under section 461 must be met with respect to the amount by the last day of the taxable year. For this purpose, an amount determined under §§ 1.404A-1 through 1.404A-7 establishes the fact of the liability and determines the amount of the liability with reasonable accuracy. See § 1.461-4(d)(2)(iii), which generally provides that the economic performance requirement of section 461(h) is satisfied to the extent that any amount is otherwise properly taken into account under §§ 1.404A-1 through 1.404A-7. [Reg. § 1.404A-1.]

§ 1.404A-2. Rules for qualified funded plans, EE-14-81, 5/6/93.

(a) *In general.* Except as provided in this section and in §§ 1.404A-4 and 1.404A-5, the amount taken into account for a taxable year with respect to a qualified funded plan is the amount of the contributions paid by the employer to the trust in that year (regardless of whether the employer uses an accrual method of accounting). Accretions in a trust are not considered contributions to a plan.

(b) *Payment to a trust*—(1) *Contribution requirements.* Contributions paid under a qualified funded plan may not be taken into account unless they are—

(i) Paid to a trust which is operated in accordance with the requirements of section 401(a)(2);

(ii) Paid for a retirement annuity under which retirement benefits are provided and which is for the exclusive benefit of the employer's employees or their beneficiaries; or

(iii) Paid directly to a participant or beneficiary (rather than a trust).

(2) *Trust requirements*—(i) *General rule.* A contribution does not satisfy paragraph (b)(1)(i) of this section unless it is accumulated in the trust for the purpose of being distributed as deferred compensation. Whether a contribution is being accumulated in the trust for the purpose of being distributed as deferred compensation depends on the facts and circumstances. For purposes of paragraph (b)(1)(i) of this section, the fact that a trust has been (or has not been) involved in transactions that would be described in section 4975(c)(1) (and not exempted under section 4975(c)(2) or 4975(d)), e.g., contributions made in the form of a promissory note, if the plan were subject to section 4975(c)(1), is an important factor in determining whether the trust is not (or is) considered to be operated in accordance with the requirements of section 401(a)(2). In addition, a contribution to a trust does not satisfy paragraph (b)(1)(i) of this section unless it has substance.

(ii) *Effective date.* The section 4975(c)(1) factor in determining compliance with section 401(a)(2) provided in this paragraph (b)(2) is taken into account for all transactions entered into after May 6, 1993.

(3) *Retirement annuity.* A retirement annuity means a retirement annuity (as defined in section 404(a)(2)) except that the retirement annuity need not be part of a plan that meets the requirements of section 401(a) or 401(d). Notwithstanding the preceding sentence, the retirement annuity described therein need not be issued by an insurance company qualified to do business in a State in the United States if the taxpayer(s) and/or sponsoring employer(s) of the plan have shifted the risk of making payments under the plan to an entity that is qualified to do business in the country (or countries) where the plan is maintained.

(4) *Effect of reversion of overfunded contributions.* If any portion of a contribution to a trust may revert to the benefit of the employer before the satisfaction of all liabilities to employees or their beneficiaries covered by the trust, no amount of the contribution may be taken into account under this section.

(5) *Example.* The principles of paragraph (b) of this section are illustrated by the following example:

Example. A foreign subsidiary of a domestic corporation maintains a deferred compensation plan for its employees. The foreign subsidiary makes annual contributions under the plan to a trust. Each year after the contribution is made to the trust, the trustee lends the contribution back to the foreign subsidiary maintaining the plan. The foreign subsidiary executes promissory notes obligating it to repay the borrowed funds (at a reasonable rate of interest) to the trust and to pay any benefits due under the plan. Notwithstanding that the taxpayer may have designated the plan as a qualified funded plan, amounts may not be taken into account under section 404A with respect to contributions to the trust because the loans cause the trust to fail the requirements of section 401(a)(2). Even if the loans do not cause the trust to violate section 401(a)(2), the portion of any contribution that is loaned to the foreign subsidiary could not be taken into account because, to the extent of the loan (or loans), the contribution lacks substance and is not accumulated in the trust.

(c) *Contribution deemed made before payment*—(1) *Time of payment to trust.* Regardless of whether an employer uses the cash or an accrual method of accounting, for purposes of this section, a contribution to a trust that is paid after the close of an employer's taxable year is deemed to have been paid on the last day of that taxable year if—

(i) The payment is made on account of the taxable year and is made not later than the 15th day of the ninth month after the close of the taxable year;

(ii) The payment is treated by the plan in the same manner that the plan would treat a payment actually received on the last day of the taxable year; and

(iii) Either—

(A) The employer notifies the plan administrator or trustee in writing that the payment to the plan is designated on account of the taxable year;

(B) The taxpayer claims the payment as a deduction on its tax return for the taxable year; or

(C) The employer reduces earnings and profits with respect to the payment.

(2) *Time of designation.* Any designation of a payment pursuant to paragraph (c)(1)(iii)(A) of this section must occur not later than the time described in paragraph (c)(1)(i) of this section.

(3) *Irrevocable designation.* After a payment has been designated or claimed on a return in the manner provided in paragraph (c)(1)(iii)(A) of this section as being on account of a taxable year, the designation or claim may not be retracted or changed.

(d) *Limitation for qualified funded plans*— (1) *Plans with fixed or determinable benefits*—(i) *Limit on amount taken into account.* Contributions made to a qualified funded plan under which the benefits are fixed or determinable are not taken into account under this section to the extent they exceed the amount that would be taken into account under section 404(a)(1)(A)(ii) and (iii) (determined without regard to the last sentence of paragraph (A) of section 404(a)(1) and without regard to whether the trust is exempt under section 501(a)). Benefits are considered fixed or determinable for this purpose if either benefits under or contributions to the plan are definitely determinable within the meaning of §1.401-1(b)(1)(i). The limit described in the first sentence of this paragraph (d)(1)(i) is determined on the basis of the permitted plan year of the qualified foreign plan. Thus, the limit for the employer's taxable year is the limit for the plan year ending with or within the employer's taxable year.

(ii) *Actuarial valuation requirements.* In determining the amount to be taken into account under this section, an actuarial valuation must be made not less frequently than once every three years. However, an actuarial valuation must be made for the first plan year of the plan for which an election under §1.404A-6 is in effect. For interim years, a reasonable actuarial determination of whether the full funding limit in §1.404A-5(c)(2) applies to the qualified funded plan must be made. The Commissioner may require a full actuarial valuation in an interim year under appropriate circumstances. See §1.404A-6 for rules on changes in methods of accounting.

(2) *Plans without fixed or determinable benefits.* Contributions made to a qualified funded plan under which the benefits are not fixed or determinable may not be taken into account under this section to the extent they exceed the limitations of section 404(a)(3) (determined without regard to whether the payment is made to a trust that is exempt under section 501(a)).

(3) *Limitations where more than one type of plan is maintained.* Where payments are made for a taxable year to more than one type of qualified funded plan, the amounts that may be taken into account for the taxable year with respect to the payments are subject to the limitations of section 404(a)(7). The amount that is taken into account under this paragraph (d)(3) is determined without regard to whether the payment satisfies the minimum funding standard described in section 412.

(4) *Carryover contributions.* In the event that the aggregate amount of contributions paid during an employer's taxable year in which an election under section 404A is in effect (reduced by an amount described in section 404A(g)(1)) exceeds the amount that may be taken into account under section 404A(a) and this section (computed without regard to section 404A(d) and §1.404A-4), the excess contributions are treated as an amount paid in the succeeding taxable year with respect to that qualified foreign plan. A carryover contribution is also taken into account in determining whether a carryover contribution exists for a succeeding taxable year.

(5) *Additional rules.* The Commissioner may prescribe additional rules for determining the amount that may be taken into account under this paragraph (d) in guidance of general applicability.

(e) *Examples.* The principles of this section are illustrated by the following examples:

Example 1. A qualified funded plan under which benefits are not fixed or determinable is maintained by a foreign branch of a domestic corporation. The foreign branch computes its income in units of local currency, the FC. The taxpayer's taxable year and the plan year are coterminous with the calendar year. The plan was established in 1985, and the taxpayer made an election to apply section 404A, a qualified funded plan election as described in §1.404A-6. For the 1985 taxable year, the employer made a FC25,000 contribution under the plan, and FC15,000 of that contribution could be taken into account under paragraph (d)(2) of this section. The cumulative foreign amount for the 1985 taxable year was FC20,000. The amount of the excess contribution carried forward was FC10,000 (FC25,000–FC15,000), because the amount of the carryover contribution is determined without regard to section 404A(d) and §1.404A-4.

Example 2. Assume the same facts as in *Example 1*, except that the entire FC25,000 contribution made under the plan may be taken into account under paragraph (d)(2) of this section. The amount of the excess contribution carried forward was zero, even though the cumulative United States amount may have exceeded the cumulative foreign amount for the taxable year, because the amount of the excess contribution is determined without regard to section 404A(d) and §1.404A-4.

Example 3. P, a domestic corporation, owns all of the one class of stock of foreign corporation S. The taxable year for P is the calendar year. The taxable year for S is the fiscal year beginning on June 1. S made a contribution to its qualified funded plan on February 15, 1983, and notified the plan's trustee in writing that S designated the contribution as a payment on account of S's preceding taxable year (ending May 31, 1982). The contribution is taken into account in computing S's earnings and profits for S's taxable year ending May 31, 1982.

[Reg. §1.404A-2.]

§ 1.404A-3. Rules for qualified reserve plans, EE-14-81, 5/6/93.

(a) *Amounts taken into account with respect to qualified reserve plans*—(1) *General rule.* Except as provided in §§1.404A-4 and 1.404A-5, the amount taken into account for a taxable year with respect to a qualified reserve plan equals the sum of—

(i) The reasonable addition during the permitted plan year to a reserve for liabilities under the plan as described in paragraph (b) of this section; and

(ii) The amortization of certain increases or decreases in the plan reserve over ten years, as described in paragraph (c) of this section.

(2) *Amounts less than zero.* If the amount to be taken into account under this section is less than zero, that amount must be treated as an increase in income and earnings and profits for the taxable year.

(3) *Exclusive rules for qualified reserve plans.* No amounts may be taken into account with respect to a qualified reserve plan except as provided for in this section. Thus, for example, no deduction is allowed for benefit payments from the reserve. Similarly, no amount may be taken into account for any payments made by the employer that are used either to reinsure the liabilities or benefits under a qualified reserve plan or to fund separately all or a portion of the benefits under a qualified reserve plan. These amounts may, however, be taken into account as contributions to a qualified funded plan to the extent the requirements of §1.404A-2 are satisfied.

(b) *Reasonable addition to a reserve for liabilities*—(1) *General rule.* Except as provided in §1.404A-7(f)(2), the reasonable addition to a reserve for a plan year equals the increase in the reserve, determined under the unit credit method as described in paragraph (b)(2) of this section, that arises from the passage of time and from additional service and expected changes in compensation in the current plan year for employees who were included in the reserve as of the end of the prior plan year. Thus, the reasonable addition to the reserve includes an element of interest on the reserve as of the beginning of the plan year (less the interest on the benefit payments during the plan year) and the actuarial present value of the expected increase in vested benefits accrued during the current plan year for employees who were included in the reserve as of the end of the prior plan year, determined without reference to any plan amendment during the plan year.

(2) *Unit credit method required.* The reserve for the employer's liability must be determined under the unit credit method. Thus, the reserve must be the actuarial present value of the employer's liability, taking into account service and compensation only through the valuation date. In determining the reserve under this section, benefits that are subject to a substantial risk of forfeiture may not be taken into account. The term "substantial risk of forfeiture" has the meaning stated in section 83, except that the term "property" in all events includes benefits accrued under a qualified reserve plan.

(3) *Timing of valuation.* The determination of the reserve and the reasonable addition to the reserve must be made as of the last day of the plan year.

(4) *Permissible actuarial assumptions*—(i) *Interest rates*—(A) *In general.* Notwithstanding any other provision of §§1.404A-1 through 1.404A-7, no amount may be taken into account under section 404A with respect to a qualified reserve plan unless the rate (or rates) of interest for the plan that are selected by the employer are within the permissible range. The interest rate selected by the employer for the plan under this paragraph must remain in effect for that plan until the first plan year for which that rate is no longer within the permissible range. At that time, a new rate of interest must be selected by the employer from within the permissible range applicable at that time.

(B) *Permissible range.* For purposes of this paragraph (b)(4), the term "permissible range" means a rate of interest that is not more than 1.2 and not less than the product of 0.8 multiplied by the average rate of interest for the highest quality long-term corporate bonds denominated in the functional currency of the qualified business unit of the employer whose books reflect the plan's liabilities for the 15-year period ending on the last day before the beginning of the employer's taxable year. If there is no market in long-term corporate bonds denominated in the relevant functional currency, or if the qualified business unit computes its income or earnings and profits in dollars under § 1.985-3, the employer must use a rate that can be demonstrated clearly to reflect income, based on all relevant facts and circumstances, including appropriate rates of inflation and commercial practices.

(ii) *Plan benefits.* Except as otherwise provided by the Commissioner, changes in plan benefits or applicable foreign law that become effective (whether or not retroactively) in a future plan year may not be taken into account until the plan year the change is effective. Notwithstanding the above, the reserve calculation may take into account cost-of-living adjustments that are part of the employee's vested accrued benefit, using assumptions regarding cost-of-living adjustments that are consistent with the interest rate assumptions described in paragraph (b)(4)(i) of this section and the terms of the plan. Thus, for example, a cost-of-living adjustment that does not require any future service on the part of the employee and is not subject to employer discretion may be taken into account.

(c) *Ten-year amortization for certain changes in reserves*—(1) *Actuarial valuation.* Each plan year an actuarial valuation must be made as of the end of the plan year, comparing the actual reserve with the expected value of the reserve. Any difference between the actual reserve determined as of the end of the plan year and the expected value of the reserve as of that date must be amortized in level amounts of principal over ten years, beginning in the plan year of the actuarial valuation. This amortization applies regardless of whether the difference is attributable to changes in employee population, changes in plan provisions, or changes in actuarial assumptions.

(2) *Expected value of reserve.* The expected value of the reserve as of the end of the plan year is equal to the sum of the reserve as of the end of the prior plan year plus the reasonable addition to the reserve for the plan year described in paragraph (b) of this section less the benefit payments during the plan year. Thus, the expected value of the reserve is generally determined on the basis of the plan in effect and the actuarial assumptions used as of the end of the prior plan year, but, because it includes the reasonable addition to the reserve, includes the effect of expected changes in compensation, service and vesting during the current plan year.

(3) *Special rule for certain cost of living adjustments.* Notwithstanding the general rule that the increase in liability from a plan amendment is amortized over ten years, if under foreign law a shorter period for amortization is required, that shorter period shall be substituted for ten years in this paragraph (c) if the amendment is a cost of living adjustment that either—

(i) Relates primarily to retirees; or

(ii) Is for employees of a foreign corporation in a taxable year beginning before [*INSERT DATE THAT IS 90 DAYS AFTER THE DATE OF PUBLICATION OF FINAL REGULATIONS IN THE FEDERAL REGISTER*].

(4) *Anti-abuse rule.* The Commissioner may reclassify any item included by a taxpayer as a reasonable addition to a reserve as instead subject to amortization over ten years if the Commissioner determines that the taxpayer's classification of that item circumvents the intent of section 404A(c)(4). Thus, for example, if the Commissioner determines that the vesting provisions of the plan cause the increase in vested benefits to be unreasonably large in a single plan year, the reasonable addition under paragraph (b) of this section must be calculated without recognizing any changes in vesting for the plan year.

(d) *Examples.* The principles of this section are illustrated by the following examples:

Example 1. S, a foreign subsidiary of P, a domestic corporation, contributes funds to an irrevocable trust which is used to pay benefits provided under S's reserve plan. The trust does not satisfy the requirements of section 401(a), 404(a)(4), or 404(a)(5). The funds are not used to provide benefits in addition to those provided by the reserve plan. In 1984, the year the plan was adopted, S elected to treat the plan as a qualified reserve plan. In 1984, S also contributed an amount to the irrevocable trust. The fact that S contributed an amount to the trust has no effect on the computation of the amount that S is entitled to take into account under this section in 1984 (or in any other year). Furthermore, no additional amount may be taken into account for the amount of the contribution to the trust beyond the amount permitted to be taken into account under this section.

Example 2. (a) Employer Y hired 10,000 employees in 1980, each of whom was age 40 at the beginning of the year and earned FC10,000. The employees immediately commenced participation in the plan. The plan provided that the accrued benefit at the end of X years equaled: (X multiplied by one percent) multiplied by the highest one year's compensation. The plan vesting was 20 percent per year starting after two years of service with the employer. Under the plan, once an employee was vested in a benefit, the benefit could not be forfeited for any reason other than the death of the employee. Employees who terminate employment for reasons other than death or retirement receive an immediate single sum distribution in an amount equal to the actuarial present value (calculated at eight percent interest) of the vested accrued benefit (where the actuarial present value and the vested accrued benefit are determined as of the end of the prior plan year). Reserves and expected increases in the reserve were determined using eight percent interest, five percent assumed compensation increases, the UP-84 mortality table and assuming no pre-retirement terminations other than death. However as set forth in the relevant data below, the actual experience differed from these assumptions (e.g., the actual compensation did not increase five percent each year and the mortality and termination experience were different than assumed).

Year	End of Year Age
1980	41
1981	42
1982	43
1983	44
1984	45

Year	Compensation for Each Employee
1980	10,000
1981	10,000
1982	10,000
1983	12,000
1984	12,000

Year	Benefit Payments
1980	0
1981	0
1982	0
1983	369
1984	6,396

Number of Deaths	Number of Terminations	Number of Employees Remaining
16	5	9,979
18	5	9,956
20	5	9,931
25	5	9,901
30	25	9,846

End of Year Accrued Benefit for Each Employee	End of Year Vested Accrued Benefit for Each Employee
100	0
200	0
300	60
480	192
600	360

End of Year Actuarial Factor	End of Year Reserve for Vested Benefits
1.049706	0
1.136328	0
1.230380	733,134
1.332564	2,533,194
1.443638	5,117,062

(b) *Computation of amounts taken into account for 1980.* The amount taken into account for 1980 was zero because there was no reasonable addition to the reserve (i.e., no increase in the reserve on account of the passage of time, additional service or expected changes in compensation for employees who were included in the reserve at the end of the prior year) and there were no amounts that are subject to ten-year amortization under paragraph (c) of this section.

(c) *Computation of amounts taken into account for 1981.* There was no amount taken into account for 1981 for the same reason as in 1980.

(d) *Computation of amount taken into account for 1982.* The amount taken into account in 1982 was the sum of the reasonable addition to the reserve determined under paragraph (b) of this section and the amortization of certain increases in the plan reserve over ten years determined under paragraph (c) of this section. There was no reasonable addition to the reserve (i.e., no increase in the reserve on account of the passage of time, additional service or expected changes in compensation for employees who were included in the reserve at the end of the prior year) for the 1982 year because no employee was included in the reserve as of the end of 1981. There were no benefits paid during 1981. Thus, the expected value of the reserve at the end of 1982 was zero. However, the actual value of the reserve at the end of 1982 was FC733,134 (9,931 employees × 60 × 1.230380). The difference between the expected and actual values of the reserve was taken into account over ten years beginning in 1982. Thus, the total amount taken into account for 1982 was FC73,313.

(e) *Computation of amount taken into account for 1983.* Using the employee data as of the end of 1982 and the expected rate of compensation increase for 1983, each employee's accrued benefit was expected to be 420 (10,500 × 4 years × .01) as of the end of 1983. 40 percent of this accrued benefit, or 168, was expected to be vested. Thus, the expected increase in each employee's vested accrued benefit was 108 (the difference between 168 and the vested accrued benefit as of the end of the prior year (60) for those employees who were included in the reserve as of the end of the prior year). There were 9,931 employees included in the reserve as of the end of the prior year and 9,931 × p_{43} were expected to be in the reserve as of the end of 1983. The actuarial present value factor for a deferred annuity of FC1 commencing at age 65 payable monthly is 1.332564. Thus, the actuarial present value of the expected increase in vested accrued benefits as of the end of the year was FC1,425,212 (9,931 employees × p_{43} × 108 × 1.332564). The reasonable addition to the reserve also included an element of interest on the reserve as of the end of the prior year equal to FC58,651 (8 percent × 733,134) that is offset by the interest attributable to the actual benefits paid during the year (FC15, which is interest on the benefits paid during the year (FC369) from the date of payment through the end of the year). Thus, the reasonable addition to the reserve for 1983

was FC1,483,848 (1,425,212 + 58,651 – 15) and the expected reserve at the end of the year was FC2,216,613 (733,134 + 1,483,848 – 369). The actual reserve at the end of 1983 is FC2,533,194, so there was an actuarial loss of FC316,581 (2,533,194 – 2,216,613) which was amortized over 10 years beginning in 1983. Thus, the total amount taken into account in 1983 was FC1,588,819 (1,483,848 + 73,313 + 10 percent of 316,581).

(f) *Computation of amount taken into account for 1984.* Using the employee data as of the end of 1983 and the expected rate of compensation increase for 1984, each employee's accrued benefit was expected to be 630 (12,600 × 5 years × .01) as of the end of 1984. 60 percent of this accrued benefit, or 378, was expected to be vested. Thus, the expected increase in each employee's vested accrued benefit was 186 (the difference between 378 and the vested accrued benefit as of the end of the prior year (192) for those employees who were included in the reserve as of the end of the prior year). There were 9,901 employees included in the reserve as of the end of the prior year and 9,901 × p_{44} were expected to be in the reserve as of the end of 1984. The actuarial present value factor for a deferred annuity of FC1 commencing at age 65 payable monthly is 1.443638. Thus, the actuarial present value of the expected increase in vested accrued benefits as of the end of the year was FC2,650,355 (9,901 employees × p_{44} × 186 × 1.443638). The reasonable addition to the reserve also included an element of interest on the reserve as of the end of the prior year equal to FC202,656 (8 percent × 2,533,194), offset by interest attributable to the actual benefits paid during the year (FC256, which is interest on the benefits paid during the year (FC6,396) from the date of payment through the end of the year). Thus, the reasonable addition to the reserve for 1984 was FC2,852,755 (2,650,355 + 202,656 – 256) and the expected reserve at the end of the year is FC5,379,553 (2,533,194 + 2,852,755 – 6,396). The actual reserve at the end of 1984 was FC5,117,062, so there was an actuarial gain of FC262,491 (5,379,553 – 5,117,062) which was amortized over 10 years beginning in 1984. Thus, the total amount taken into account in 1984 was FC2,931,477 (2,852,755 + 73,313 + 31,658 – 10 percent of 262,491).

(g) *Alternative computation method.* The amounts taken into account for 1982, 1983 and 1984 may also be illustrated as follows—

1982

Worksheet for Calculating Amount Taken Into Account For Qualified Reserve Plans Under § 404A

(1)	Reserve at end of Prior Year	0
(2)	Interest on (1) to end of Current Year	0
(3)	Present Value of the Expected Increase in Vested Accrued Benefits for employees who were included in the reserve as of the end of the prior year.	0
(4)	Benefit Payments during current year	0
(5)	Interest on (4) from date of payment through end of Current year	0
(6)	Reasonable addition to the reserve (2) + (3) – (5)	0
(7)	Expected value of reserve (1) + (6) – (4)	0
(8)	Actual value of reserve	733,134
(9)	Amount to be amortized (8) – (7)	733,134
(10)	Remaining 10 Percent Bases from Prior Years (original amounts) (Item 12 from Prior Year)	0
(11)	10 percent Bases whose 10 years ended last year	0
(12)	(9) + (10) – (11)	733,134
(13)	10 percent of (12)	73,313
(14)	Amount Taken Into Account for Current Year [(6) + (13)]	73,313

1983

Worksheet For Calculating Amount Taken Into Account For Qualified Reserve Plans Under § 404A

(1)	Reserve at end of Prior Year	733,134
(2)	Interest on (1) to end of Current Year	58,651
(3)	Present Value of the Expected Increase in Vested Accrued Benefits for employees who were included in the reserve as of the end of the prior year	1,425,212
(4)	Benefit Payments during current year	369
(5)	Interest on (4) from date of payment through end of Current year	15
(6)	Reasonable addition to the reserve (2) + (3) – (5)	1,483,848

(7)	Expected value of reserve (1) + (6) − (4)	2,216,613
(8)	Actual value of reserve	2,533,194
(9)	Amount to be amortized (8) − (7)	316,581
(10)	Remaining 10 Percent Bases from Prior Years (original amounts) (Item 12 from Prior Year) ...	733,134
(11)	10 percent Bases whose 10 years ended last year	0
(12)	(9) + (10) − (11)	1,049,715
(13)	10 percent of (12)	104,971
(14)	Amount Taken Into Account for Current Year [(6) + (13)]	1,588,819

1984

Worksheet For Calculating Amount Taken Into Account For Qualified Reserve Plans Under
§ 404A

(1)	Reserve at end of Prior Year	2,533,194
(2)	Interest on (1) to end of Current Year	202,656
(3)	Present Value of the Expected Increase in Vested Accrued Benefits for employees who were included in the reserve as of the end of the prior year.	2,650,355
(4)	Benefit Payments during current year	6,396
(5)	Interest on (4) from date of payment through end of Current year	256
(6)	Reasonable addition to the reserve (2) + (3) − (5)	2,852,755
(7)	Expected value of reserve (1) + (6) − (4)	5,379,553
(8)	Actual value of reserve	5,117,062
(9)	Amount to be amortized (8) − (7)	(262,491)
(10)	Remaining 10 Percent Bases from Prior Years (original amounts) (Item 12 from Prior Year) ...	1,049,715
(11)	10 percent Bases whose 10 years ended last year	0
(12)	(9) + (10) − (11)	787,224
(13)	10 percent of (12)	78,722
(14)	Amount Taken Into Account for Current Year [(6) + (13)]	2,931,477

Example 3. (a) The facts are the same as in *Example 2*, except that the interest rate used to determine the reserve as of the end of 1984 has been decreased to 7%.

(b) The amount taken into account for 1984 under the alternative calculation method is determined as follows:

1984

Worksheet For Calculating Amount Taken Into Account For Qualified Reserve Plans Under
§ 404A

(1)	Reserve at end of Prior Year	2,533,194
(2)	Interest on (1) to end of Current Year	202,656
(3)	Present Value of the Expected Increase in Vested Accrued Benefits for employees who were included in the reserve as of the end of the prior year.	3,402,637
(4)	Benefit Payments during current year	6,396
(5)	Interest on (4) from date of payment through end of Current year	256
(6)	Reasonable addition to the reserve (2) + (3) − (5)	3,605,037
(7)	Expected value of reserve (1) + (6) − (4)	6,131,835
(8)	Actual value of reserve	6,569,498
(9)	Amount to be amortized (8) − (7)	437,663
(10)	Remaining 10 Percent Bases from Prior Years (original amounts) (Item 12 from Prior Year) ...	1,049,715
(11)	10 percent Bases whose 10 years ended last year	0
(12)	(9) + (10) − (11)	1,487,378
(13)	10 percent of (12)	148,738
(14)	Amount Taken Into Account for Current Year [(6) + (13)]	3,753,775

[Reg. § 1.404A-3.]

§ 1.404A-4. United States and foreign law limitations on amounts taken into account for qualified foreign plans, EE-14-81, 5/6/93.

(a) *In general.* Section 404A(d) and this section place two limits on the amount taken into account for a taxable year with respect to a qualified foreign plan under section 404A(b) and (c) and §§ 1.404A-2 and 1.404A-3. First, as set forth in paragraph (b) of this section, the cumulative amounts that are or have been taken into account under section 404A through the end of the current year may not exceed the cumulative amounts deductible under foreign law in that period. Because the foreign law deduction is cumulative, however, amounts previously disallowed under this rule are taken into account in later years as the amount deductible under foreign law increases. Second, for taxable years beginning before January 1, 1987, or such later year determined under section 902(c)(3)(A), the rule in paragraph (c) of this section further limits the amount taken into account during those taxable years. Because section 404A(d) and this section apply solely to amounts that would otherwise be taken into account under § 1.404A-2 or 1.404A-3, these limitations are applied without regard to amounts taken into account under section 481 (i.e., without regard to the portion of a section 481(a) adjustment that is taken into account during any taxable year within the section 481(a) adjustment period, as defined in § 1.404A-6(e)(2)). See § 1.404A-6, however, for rules applying the section 404A(d) limitations to the calculation of the section 481(a) adjustment.

(b) *Cumulative limitation.* The amount taken into account with respect to a qualified foreign plan for any taxable year equals—

(1) The lesser of—

(i) The cumulative United States amount; or

(ii) The cumulative foreign amount;

(2) Reduced by the aggregate amount.

(c) *Special rule for foreign corporations in pre-pooling years.* For a taxable year of a foreign corporation beginning before January 1, 1987, or such later year determined under section 902(c)(3)(A), the reduction in earnings and profits determined under paragraph (b) of this section with respect to a qualified foreign plan may not exceed the amount allowed as a deduction under the appropriate foreign tax laws for such taxable year. See *Example 3* of paragraph (h) of this section for an illustration of this rule.

(d) *Rules relating to foreign currency*—(1) *Taxable years beginning after December 31, 1986.* For taxable years beginning after December 31, 1986, the cumulative United States amount, the cumulative foreign amount, and the aggregate amount must be computed in the employer's functional currency. See generally section 964 and sections 985 through 989 for rules applicable to determining and translating into dollars the amount of income or loss of foreign branches and earnings and profits (or deficits in earnings and profits) of foreign corporations.

(2) *Taxable years beginning before January 1, 1987.* For taxable years beginning before January 1, 1987, the cumulative United States amount, the cumulative foreign amount, and the aggregate amount must be computed in the currency in which the foreign branch or foreign subsidiary kept its books and records. See Rev. Rul. 75-106, 1975-1 C.B. 31 (see § 601.601(d)(2)(ii)(*b*) of this chapter), for rules for determining the amount of income or loss of foreign branches using a net worth method of accounting. See Rev. Rul. 75-107, 1975-1 C.B. 32 (see § 601.601(d)(2)(ii)(*b*) of this chapter), for rules for determining the amount of income or loss of foreign branches using a profit and loss method of accounting. See sections 312, 902, and 1248 and the regulations thereunder for rules for determining the earnings and profits of noncontrolled foreign corporations. See section 964 and the regulations thereunder for rules for determining the earnings and profits of foreign corporations for purposes of subpart F.

(3) *Special rules for the net worth method of accounting.* For purposes of § 1.964-1(e)(4), an amount of deduction that is accrued but not paid at the end of the employer's taxable year with respect to a qualified funded plan must be treated as a short-term liability. In the case of a qualified reserve plan, for purposes of § 1.964-1(e), the amount of the reserve taken into account as a liability on the balance sheet as of the beginning of the taxable year must be limited to the aggregate amount, and the amount of the reserve taken into account as a liability on the balance sheet as of the close of the taxable year must be limited to the sum of the aggregate amount and the amount taken into account for the taxable year. For purposes of § 1.964-1(e)(4), each annual increase in the aggregate amount must be treated as a long-term liability incurred on the last day of the employer's taxable year to which the increase relates. As of the close of each taxable year, a portion of the aggregate amount equal to the amount of benefits expected to be paid during the succeeding taxable year must be reclassified as a short-term liability. The reclassified amount must be allocated to the annual increases in the aggregate amount on a first-in-first-out basis. Similar

rules apply for purposes of determining the amount of reserve taken into account by a foreign branch using the net worth method of accounting for taxable years beginning before January 1, 1987, and by a qualified business unit that uses the United States dollar approximate separate transactions method of accounting under § 1.985-3 in a taxable year beginning after December 31, 1986.

(e) *Maintenance of more than one type of qualified foreign plan by an employer.* In determining the deduction or reduction in earnings and profits when an employer maintains one plan for purposes of foreign law that is treated as two separate plans for purposes of § 1.404A-6(a)(2), the cumulative United States amount for each plan must be combined for purposes of paragraphs (a) and (b) of this section. See *Example 5* of paragraph (h) of this section for an illustration of this rule.

(f) *United States and foreign law limitations not applicable.* The limitations set forth in this section do not apply to the adjustments required by section 481, section 446(e) and section 2(e)(3)(A) of Public Law 96-603.

(g) *Definitions*—(1) *Cumulative United States amount.* The term "cumulative United States amount" means (with respect to a qualified foreign plan) the amount determined under section 404A (without regard to section 404A(d)) for the taxable year of the employer and for all consecutive prior taxable years for which an election under section 404A was in effect for the plan plus the "initial section 404A amount" within the meaning of § 1.404A-6(g)(2)(i).

(2) *Cumulative foreign amount.* The term "cumulative foreign amount" means (with respect to a qualified foreign plan) the cumulative amount allowed as a deduction under the appropriate foreign tax law for the taxable year of the employer and for all consecutive prior taxable years for which an election under section 404A was in effect for the plan plus the initial section 404A amount within the meaning of § 1.404A-6(g)(2)(ii).

(3) *Appropriate foreign tax law.* The appropriate foreign tax law is the income tax law of the country (other than the United States) that is the principal place of business of the qualified business unit of the employer whose books reflect the plan liabilities.

(4) *Aggregate amount.* The term "aggregate amount" means (with respect to a qualified foreign plan) amounts permitted to be taken into account under section 404A(d)(1) for all consecutive prior taxable years for which an election under section 404A was in effect for the plan plus the initial section 404A amount required by § 1.404A-6(g)(2)(iii).

(h) *Examples.* The principles of this section are illustrated by the following examples:

Example 1. X, a foreign subsidiary of a domestic corporation, maintains its main office in foreign country *A*, and a branch, *Y*, in foreign country *B*. The functional currency of *X* is the FC. *Y*'s functional currency is the local currency, LC. *X* maintains a qualified foreign plan for the benefit of *X*'s employees in *B*. In the year the plan was adopted, a section 404A election was made for the plan. The appropriate foreign tax law is the tax law of *B* because all the employees covered by the plan are in *B* and plan liabilities are accounted for on *Y*'s books. The tax law of *B* permits *X* to deduct contributions to the plan. The cumulative amount allowed as a deduction under the tax law of *B* is LC80. The cumulative United States amount with respect to the plan is LC100. Therefore, the cumulative limitation is LC80. The earnings and profits of *X* include the profit and loss for *Y* (reflecting a reduction for contributions to the plan, computed in LC and translated into FC under the principles of section 987).

Example 2. A qualified reserve plan is maintained by a foreign branch of a domestic corporation. The foreign branch computes its income under the profit and loss method of Rev. Rul. 75-107, 1975-1 C.B. 32 (see § 601.601(d)(2)(ii)(*b*) of this chapter), in units of the local currency, the FC. The foreign branch established the qualified reserve plan in 1985 and the taxpayer made the elections described in § 1.404A-6. The taxpayer's taxable year and the plan year is the calendar year. The assumed amounts taken into account under section 404A and appropriate foreign tax law for selected years and the computations under this section which follow from the amounts, in units of FC, are shown in the following table—

		1985	1986	1987	1988
(1)	Amount determined with respect to the plan under section 404A for the taxable year without regard to section 404A(d)	800,000	900,000	300,000	1,000,000
(2)	Cumulative United States amount	800,000	1,700,000	2,000,000	3,000,000
(3)	Cumulative foreign amount	1,000,000	1,600,000	2,000,000	2,200,000
(4)	Lesser of cumulative United States or cumulative foreign amount	800,000	1,600,000	2,000,000	2,200,000

		1985	1986	1987	1988
(5)	Reduced by aggregate amount (cumulative sum of (6) for prior years)	(0)	(800,000)	(1,600,000)	(2,000,000)
		800,000	800,000	400,000	200,000
(6)	Amount taken into account for the taxable year	800,000	800,000	400,000	200,000

Example 3. Assume the same facts as in *Example 2* for all taxable years, except that the qualified reserve plan is maintained by a foreign subsidiary of a domestic corporation. The foreign subsidiary computes its earnings and profits in units of the local currency, the FC. The foreign subsidiary's taxable year and the plan year are calendar years.

The assumed amounts taken into account under section 404A and appropriate foreign law for selected years, and the computations under this section which follow from the amounts, in units of FC, are shown in the following table—

		1985	1986	1987	1988
(1)	Amount determined with respect to the plan under section 404A for the taxable year without regard to section 404A(d)	800,000	900,000	300,000	1,000,000
(2)	Amount allowed as a deduction under the appropriate foreign tax laws for the taxable year	1,000,000	600,000	400,000	200,000
(3)	Cumulative United States amount	800,000	1,700,000	2,000,000	3,000,000
(4)	Cumulative foreign amount	1,000,000	1,600,000	2,000,000	2,200,000
(5)	Lesser of cumulative United States or cumulative foreign amount	800,000	1,600,000	2,000,000	2,200,000
(6)	Reduced by aggregate amount (cumulative sum of (7) or (8), whichever is applicable, for prior years)	(0)	(800,000)	(1,400,000)	(2,000,000)
		800,000	800,000	600,000	200,000
(7)	Amount taken into account for taxable years before 1987 (lesser of (2) and (6))	800,000	600,000	n/a	n/a
(8)	Amount taken into account for taxable years after 1986 (same as (6))	n/a	n/a	600,000	200,000

Example 4. Z, a domestic corporation, maintains a retirement plan for employees employed in its foreign branch office. The foreign branch computes its income under the profit and loss method Rev. Rul. 75-107, 1975-1 C.B. 32 (see § 601.601(d)(2)(ii)(*b*) of this chapter), in units of local currency, the FC. The plan is a combination book reserve and funded plan, but is considered a single plan under foreign law. The total retirement benefits that a participant is eligible to receive is the sum of the benefits provided by the qualified reserve plan and the qualified funded plan. Pursuant to § 1.404A-6, in the year the plan was adopted, *Z* made a separate qualified reserve plan and funded plan election with respect to each portion of the foreign plan. The assumed deductions under section 404A and appropriate foreign law for selected years, and the computations under this section which follow from the deductions, are shown in the following table—

		Qualified funded plan 1984	Qualified funded plan 1985	Qualified reserve plan 1984	Qualified reserve plan 1985	Combined amount—qualified foreign plans 1984	Combined amount—qualified foreign plans 1985
(1)	Amount determined with respect to the qualified foreign plans under section 404A for the taxable year without regard to section 404A(d)	40,000	90,000	30,000	80,000		
(2)	Amount allowed as a deduction under the appropriate foreign tax laws for the taxable year					60,000	185,000
(3)	Cumulative United States amount	40,000	130,000	30,000	110,000		
(4)	Combined cumulative United States amount (cumulative sum of (3))					70,000	240,000
(5)	Cumulative foreign amount (cumulative sum of (2))					60,000	245,000
(6)	Aggregate amount					0	60,000
(7)	Lesser of combined cumulative United States amount or cumulative foreign amount ((4) or (5))					60,000	240,000
(9)	Reduced by the aggregate amount for the qualified funded and reserve plan (cumulative sum of (10) for prior years)					(0)	(60,000)
(10)	Amount taken into account for taxable year					60,000	180,000

Example 5. A qualified reserve plan is maintained by *M*, the foreign subsidiary of *N*, a domestic corporation. *M* computes its earnings and profits in units of the local currency, the FC. The taxable years of *M* and *N* and the plan year are the calendar year. *M* established the qualified reserve plan in 1984 and *N* made the elections described in § 1.404A-6. In that year, the reasonable addition to the plan reserve under § 1.404A-3 was FC750,000. However, the amount allowed as a deduction under the appropriate foreign tax laws for the taxable year was FC650,000. The difference between the amount taken into account under § 1.404A-3 and the deduction under the appropriate foreign tax laws, FC100,000, could not be taken into account for any succeeding taxable year under § 1.404A-3, but it may later reduce *M*'s earnings and profits pursuant to paragraph (a) of this section.

[Reg. § 1.404A-4.]

§ 1.404A-5. Additional limitations on amounts taken into account for qualified foreign plans, EE-14-81, 5/6/93.

(a) *Restrictions for nonqualified individuals—*(1) *General rule.* Notwithstanding any other provisions of §§ 1.404A-1 through 1.404A-7, no amount may be taken into account under section 404A for any contribution or amount accrued that is attributable to services performed either in the current or in a prior taxable year—

(i) By a citizen or resident of the United States who is a highly compensated [employee] (within the meaning of section 414(q)) (or, for taxable years beginning before January 1, 1989, by a citizen or resident of the United States who is an officer, shareholder, or highly compensated (within the meaning of § 1.410(b)-1(d)); or

(ii) In the United States, the compensation for which is subject to tax under chapter 1 of subtitle A of the Internal Revenue Code.

(2) *Determination of service attribution*— (i) *Not limited to actual service*. Service performed by individuals described in paragraph (a)(1)(i) of this section includes service credited to those individuals. Service performed in the United States includes service credited in relation (directly or indirectly) to any United States service.

(ii) *Amounts attributable to service performed in the United States*. The accrued benefit attributable to services described in this paragraph (a) is the excess, if any, of the total accrued benefit over the accrued benefit determined without credit for time spent performing services described in this paragraph (a) and without regard to the compensation levels for that time.

(b) *Records to be provided by taxpayer*—(1) *In general*. Notwithstanding any other provisions of §§ 1.404A-1 through 1.404A-7, no amount may be taken into account under section 404A for any contribution or amount accrued unless the taxpayer attaches a statement to its United States income tax return for any taxable year for which a qualified foreign plan maintained by an employer has United States tax significance. This statement must specify the name and type of qualified foreign plan; the cumulative United States amount, the cumulative foreign amount, and the aggregate amount with respect to the plan; the name and country of organization of the employer; and any other information the Commissioner may prescribe by forms and accompanying instructions or by revenue procedure.

(2) *Primary evidence*. The statement described in paragraph (b)(1) of this section and any required forms must be completed in good faith with all of the information called for and with the calculations referenced in paragraph (b)(1) of this section. Except as provided in paragraph (b)(4) of this section, one of the following documents must be attached to the United States income tax return—

(i) A statement from the foreign tax authorities specifying the amount of the deduction allowed in computing taxable income under the appropriate foreign tax law for the relevant year or years with respect to the qualified foreign plan; or

(ii) If the return under the appropriate foreign tax law shows the deduction for plan contributions or plan reserves as a separate identifiable item, a copy of the foreign tax return for the relevant year or years with respect to the qualified foreign plan.

(3) *Additional requirements*. The statement or return attached pursuant to paragraph (b)(2) of this section may be either the original, a duplicate original, a duly certified or authenticated copy, or a sworn copy. If only a sworn copy of a receipt or return is attached, there must be kept readily available for comparison on request the original, a duplicate original, or a duly certified or authenticated copy.

(4) *Secondary evidence*. Where the statement or return described in paragraph (b)(2)(i) or (b)(2)(ii) of this section is not available, all of the following information must be attached to the United States income tax return—

(i) A certified statement setting forth the cumulative foreign amount for each taxable year to which section 404A applies;

(ii) The excerpts from the employer's books and records showing either the change in the reserve or contributions made with respect to the plan for the taxable year to which section 404A applies; and

(iii) The computations of the foreign deduction relating to the plan to be established by data such as excerpts from the foreign law, assessment notices, or other documentary evidence.

(5) *Foreign language*. If the relevant returns, books, records or computations are not maintained in the English language, the taxpayer must furnish, upon request, a certified translation that is satisfactory to the District Director.

(6) *Additional information required by District Director*. If the taxpayer upon request of the District Director fails, without justification, to furnish any additional information that is significant, the provisions of section 982 will apply.

(7) *Authorized officer to complete documents*. The documents required by this section and by §§ 1.404A-6 and 1.404A-7 must be signed by an authorized officer of the taxpayer (as defined in section 6062 or 6063) who must verify under penalty of perjury that the statement and all other documents submitted are true and correct to his knowledge and belief.

(8) *Transitional rule—good faith effort*. For taxable years ending before [*INSERT DATE THAT IS 90 DAYS AFTER THE DATE OF*

PUBLICATION OF FINAL REGULATIONS IN THE FEDERAL REGISTER] a taxpayer will be treated as satisfying this paragraph (b) if it makes a good faith effort to provide reasonable documentation.

(c) *Actuarial requirements*—(1) *Reasonable actuarial assumptions*. Except as otherwise specifically provided in §§ 1.404A-2 and 1.404A-3 and this paragraph (c), in the case of a qualified reserve plan or a qualified funded plan under which benefits are fixed or determinable, no amount may be taken into account under section 404A unless costs, liabilities, rates of interest, and other factors under the plan are determined on the basis of actuarial assumptions and methods each of which is reasonable (taking into account the experience of the plan and reasonable expectations), or which, in the aggregate, result in an amount being taken into account that is equivalent to that which would be determined if each such assumption and method were reasonable, and that, in combination, offer the actuary's best estimate of anticipated experience under the plan. For plan years beginning before January 1, 1988, the preceding sentence is satisfied if costs, liabilities, rates of interest, and other factors under the plan are determined on the basis of actuarial assumptions and methods that are reasonable in the aggregate (taking into account the experience of the plan and reasonable expectations) and that, in combination, offer the actuary's best estimate of anticipated experience under the plan. Except to the extent required under that paragraph, the interest rate determined under § 1.404A-3(b)(4) may not be considered in determining whether other actuarial assumptions are reasonable in the aggregate for this purpose.

(2) *Full funding limitation*. Notwithstanding any other provisions of §§ 1.404A-1 through 1.404A-7, no amount may be taken into account under section 404A if the amount causes the assets in the trust (in the case of a qualified funded plan) or if taking into account the amount causes the amount of the reserve (in the case of a qualified reserve plan) to exceed the amount described in section 412(c)(7)(A)(i). [Reg. § 1.404A-5.]

§ 1.404A-6. Elections under section 404A and changes in methods of accounting, EE-14-81, 5/6/93.

(a) *Elections, changes in accounting methods, and changes in plan years*—(1) *In general*—(i) *Methods of accounting*. An election under section 404A with respect to a qualified foreign plan constitutes the adoption of a method of accounting if the election is made in the taxable year in which the plan is adopted. Any election under section 404A with respect to a pre-existing plan, however, constitutes a change in method of accounting requiring the Commissioner's consent under section 446(e) and an adjustment under section 481(a). Additionally, any other change in the method used to determine the amount taken into account under section 404A(a), as well as the revocation of any election under section 404A, constitutes a change in accounting method subject to the consent and adjustment requirements of sections 446(e) and 481(a). This section provides procedures for obtaining the Commissioner's consent to make certain changes in methods of accounting under section 404A. Additionally, § 1.404A-7 provides special procedural rules applicable (along with the rules under this section) for retroactive and transition-period elections under section 404A.

(ii) *Changes not involving accounting methods*. Any change in treatment, adjustment, or correction described in § 1.446-1(e)(2)(ii)(b) (e.g., correction of computational errors) is not a change in accounting method. While a retroactive qualified funded plan election under § 1.404A-7(c) constitutes a change in method of accounting, a mere election to apply the effective date of section 404A under § 1.404A-7(b) retroactively does not necessarily result in a change in accounting method. Additionally, a retroactive election for funded foreign branch plans under § 1.404A-7(d) will not be treated as a change in method of accounting, except to the extent that the taxpayer took erroneous deductions under its method of accounting prior to the beginning of its open period. Finally, a change of actuarial assumptions will not be treated as a change in method of accounting for purposes of this section.

(2) *Single plan*—(i) *General rule*. Except as otherwise provided, the rules of this section regarding elections, revocations, and re-elections, and the adoption or change of a plan year, apply separately (i.e., on a plan-by-plan basis) to each plan that qualifies as a single plan (as defined in § 1.414(l)-1(b)). For purposes of this definition, a separate reserve maintained by an employer exclusively for its liability under a plan is considered a plan asset that is available exclusively to pay benefits to employees who are covered by the plan and to their beneficiaries. Although a plan may be treated as a reserve plan under foreign law, this treatment is not binding for purposes of section 404A and this section.

(ii) *Example*. The principles of this paragraph (a)(2) are illustrated by the following example:

Example. S is a wholly-owned foreign subsidiary of P, a domestic corporation. S maintains a deferred compensation plan under local law to provide benefits to its employees upon retirement based upon years of service and the highest five-year average salary. S decided to account for 70 percent of its deferred compensation liabilities through an unfunded book reserve (Plan One), and to account for the remaining 30 percent through a trust equivalent (Plan Two). All of the assets of Plan One and Plan Two were available for payment of liabilities under their respective plans, and were only available for payment of liabilities under their respective plans. Thus, when deferred compensation was paid to S's employees, within the meaning of this paragraph (a)(2), 70 percent of the amount was paid by check drawn against the general assets of S and 30 percent of the amount paid was paid by check drawn on the assets of the trust equivalent. Pursuant to this section, P made a qualified reserve plan election for Plan One, which it defined as a plan of deferred compensation with liability for 70 percent of the amount of deferred compensation owing to each employee under S's deferred compensation plan. In addition, it made a qualified funded plan election for Plan Two, which it defined as a plan of deferred compensation with liability for the remaining 30 percent. Because S's reserve for its liability was treated as a plan asset with respect to 70 percent of the liability and the assets of the trust, Plan One met the requirements of a "single plan" under § 1.414(l)-1(b), and Plan Two was a separate "single plan". Thus, S could take into account only 70 percent of its liability to each employee under its deferred compensation plan when calculating the reasonable additions to the reserve under section 404A(c) for Plan One. Similarly, the full funding limitation and other calculations with respect to Plan Two may only be made with respect to 30 percent of S's liability to each employee under the foreign deferred compensation plan.

(b) *Initial elections under section 404A*—(1) *In general.* The Commissioner's consent to elect initially under section 404A to treat a single plan as a qualified funded plan or as a qualified reserve plan is granted automatically if the taxpayer complies with the requirements of this paragraph (b). Except as provided in § 1.404A-7, an initial election under this section with respect to any qualified foreign plan may be made only for a taxable year beginning after December 31, 1979.

(2) *Time for making election*—(i) *Foreign branch plans.* Except as provided in § 1.404A-7, the initial election for a qualified foreign plan maintained by a foreign branch must be made no later than the time prescribed by law for filing the United States return (including extensions) for the first taxable year for which the election is to be effective.

(ii) *Foreign corporation plans.* Except as provided in § 1.404A-7, the initial election for a qualified foreign plan maintained by a foreign corporation must be made no later than the time allowed for making elections under §§ 1.964-1 and 1.964-1T. Thus, the election under section 404A may be deferred until the earnings and profits of the foreign corporation have United States tax significance, as defined in §§ 1.964-1 and 1.964-1T. United States tax significance may occur in a number of ways, including, for example, a dividend distribution, an income inclusion under section 951(a), a section 1248 transaction, a step-up of basis by earnings and profits for purposes of valuing assets for interest allocation purposes under section 864(e), or an inclusion in income of the earnings of a qualified electing fund under section 1293(a)(1).

(3) *Manner in which election is to be made*—(i) *Foreign branch plans.* In the case of a qualified foreign plan maintained by a domestic corporation, the initial election must be made by the taxpayer by attaching a list of plans for which section 404A treatment is desired to a return filed within the time prescribed in paragraph (b)(2)(i) of this section.

(ii) *Controlled foreign corporation plans.* If a qualified foreign plan is maintained by a controlled foreign corporation, the initial election under this section must be made in the manner prescribed by §§ 1.964-1 and 1.964-1T and must include a list of all plans for which the election is made.

(iii) *Noncontrolled foreign corporation plans.* If a qualified foreign plan is maintained by a noncontrolled foreign corporation, the initial election under this section must be made in the manner prescribed by §§ 1.964-1 and 1.964-1T and must include a list of all plans for which the election is made, as if the noncontrolled foreign corporation were a controlled foreign corporation. In applying the rules of §§ 1.964-1 and 1.964-1T, the term "majority domestic corporate shareholders" is substituted for the term "controlling United States shareholders" wherever it appears in §§ 1.964-1 and 1.964-1T. The term "majority domestic corporate shareholders" has the meaning set forth in § 1.985-2(c)(3)(i).

(4) *Other requirements for election.* For each plan listed, pursuant to paragraph (b)(3) of this section, the taxpayer must designate whether it elects to treat the plan as a qualified funded plan or qualified reserve

plan, and must designate a plan year. Additionally, for each plan listed, the taxpayer must disclose the amount of any section 481(a) adjustment, as well as the initial cumulative United States amount, the initial cumulative foreign amount, and the initial aggregate amount defined in paragraph (g) of this section. See § 1.404A-5(b) for rules on additional information required, signing and verifying required statements, and notices and forms necessary to elect under section 404A. Additionally, see § 1.404A-7(d)(1) for required agreement to assessment of tax for retroactive elections for funded foreign branch plans.

(c) *Termination of election when a plan ceases to be a qualified foreign plan*—(1) *In general.* An election under section 404A with respect to a foreign deferred compensation plan is terminated if at any time on or after the first day of the first taxable year for which the election is effective the plan ceases to be a qualified foreign plan by reason of a failure to satisfy the conditions of section 404A(e)(1) or (2). Thus, for example, the election is terminated (subject to the consent of the Commissioner) if more than 10 percent of the amounts taken into account under the plan are attributable to services performed by employees subject to United States federal income tax. As used in this section, the term "termination" refers only to situations under which a plan ceases to be a qualified foreign plan by reason of a failure to satisfy the conditions of section 404(e)(1) or (2). Thus, the term is distinguished from a voluntary revocation of an election (i.e., under paragraph (d)(1) of this section), which also causes a plan to cease to be a qualified foreign plan. Upon termination of an election under section 404A, a change in method of accounting is required. The conditional advance consent of the Commissioner is granted for this change in method of accounting. This conditional consent may be withdrawn, however, if the District Director determines that tax avoidance was a purpose of the termination or if the procedures in paragraph (c)(2) of this section are not satisfied.

(2) *Rules for changing method of accounting upon termination of election*—(i) *Time for making change*—(A) *Foreign branch plans.* Except as provided in § 1.404A-7, in the case of a plan of a foreign branch the change in method of accounting required upon termination of a section 404A election must be made no later than the time prescribed by law for filing the United States return (including extensions) for the taxable year in which the plan ceases to satisfy the requirements of section 404A(e)(1) or (2).

(B) *Foreign corporation plans.* Except as provided in § 1.404A-7, in the case of a plan of a foreign corporation the change in method of accounting required upon termination of a section 404A election shall be made no later than the first year after the termination in which the earnings and profits of the foreign corporation have United States tax significance, as defined in §§ 1.964-1 and 1.964-1T. See paragraph (b)(2)(ii) of this section for United States tax significance examples.

(ii) *Procedures for changing method of accounting upon termination of election*—(A) *Foreign branch plans.* The change in method of accounting required upon termination of a section 404A election with respect to a foreign branch plan must be made by attaching a statement to the return described in paragraph (c)(2)(i)(A) of this section disclosing the amount of any section 481(a) adjustment (required under paragraph (e) of this section and computed in accordance with paragraph (f) of this section) arising upon the change.

(B) *Controlled foreign corporation plans.* The change in method of accounting required upon termination of a section 404A election with respect to a controlled foreign corporation plan must be made in the manner prescribed by §§ 1.964-1 and 1.964-1T and must include disclosure of the amount of any section 481(a) adjustment (required under paragraph (e) of this section and computed in accordance with paragraph (f) of this section) arising upon the change.

(C) *Noncontrolled foreign corporation plans.* The change in method of accounting required upon termination of a section 404A election with respect to a noncontrolled foreign corporation plan must be made in the manner prescribed by §§ 1.964-1 and 1.964-1T and must include disclosure of the amount of any section 481(a) adjustment (required under paragraph (e) of this section and computed in accordance with paragraph (f) of this section) arising upon the change. In applying the rules of §§ 1.964-1 and 1.964-1T, the term "majority domestic corporate shareholders" is substituted for the term "controlling United States shareholders" wherever it appears in §§ 1.964-1 and 1.964-1T. The term "majority domestic corporate shareholders" has the meaning set forth in § 1.985-2(c)(3)(i).

(d) *Other changes in methods of accounting and changes in plan year*—(1) *Application for consent.* Except as provided in paragraph (c) of this section or in § 1.404A-7, once an initial election under section 404A is effective with respect to a plan, the taxpayer must separately apply to obtain the express consent of the Commissioner prior to changing any method of accounting with respect to a foreign deferred compensation plan. Application for the consent of the Commissioner is required whether or not the method being changed is proper or permitted under the Internal Revenue Code and regulations thereunder. Any change in method of accounting not described in this paragraph (d)(1) must be made in accordance with the requirements of section 446(e) and the regulations thereunder. The procedures prescribed in this paragraph (d), however, are the exclusive procedures for making the following changes in method of accounting—

(i) Revocation of a section 404A election;

(ii) Re-election under section 404A following termination or revocation of a section 404A election;

(iii) Changing the treatment of a plan from a qualified funded plan to a qualified reserve plan (or the converse); or

(iv) Changing the actuarial funding method used to determine costs under a qualified funded plan.

(2) *Procedures for other changes in method of accounting*—(i) *Foreign branch plans.* To request consent to a change in method of accounting described in paragraph (d)(1) of this section, the taxpayer must file an application on Form 3115 with the Commissioner generally within 180 days after the beginning of the taxable year in which the change is requested to be effective. In the case of a revocation of an election under section 404A, however, the 180-day period in the preceding sentence is extended to the time prescribed by law for filing the United States return for the taxable year of the change.

(ii) *Foreign corporation plans.* For a controlled foreign corporation or a noncontrolled foreign corporation, a request for consent to revocation or to another change in method of accounting must be made in accordance with the rules of §§ 1.964-1 and 1.964-1T.

(3) *Plan year.* A taxpayer must secure the consent of the Commissioner to change the plan year of a qualified foreign plan. Termination or revocation of a section 404A election will not effect a change in the plan year of the plan.

(e) *Application of section 481*—(1) *In general.* A change in method described in this section constitutes a change in method of accounting to which section 481 applies. Except as otherwise provided in this paragraph and in paragraph (f) of this section, this adjustment must be made in accordance with section 481 and the regulations thereunder in those circumstances. For purposes of section 481(a)(2), any change in method described in this section is considered a change in method of accounting initiated by the taxpayer.

(2) *Period of adjustment*—(i) *In general.* The section 481(a) adjustment period is determined under the rules of this paragraph (e)(2).

(ii) *Election or re-election.* In the case of an election or a re-election following termination or revocation, the section 481(a) adjustment required by paragraph (e)(1) of this section must be taken into account ratably over a 15-year period, beginning with the first taxable year for which the election or re-election is effective. This section 481(a) adjustment period also applies to a change from a qualified funded plan to a qualified reserve plan.

(iii) *Termination or revocation of election and all other changes in method.* The adjustment required by paragraph (e)(1) of this section for

all changes in method (other than those described in paragraph (e)(2)(ii) of this section), including changes in election from a qualified reserve plan to a qualified funded plan, must be taken into account ratably over a six-year period, beginning with the first taxable year for which the change is effective. If an unamortized section 481(a) adjustment amount (e.g., from a previous change) remains at the end of a change in method of accounting to which this paragraph (e)(2)(iii) applies, the net amount of all of the section 481(a) adjustments must be taken into account ratably over this six-year section 481(a) adjustment period.

(iv) *Acceleration of section 481(a) adjustment.* If the employer ceases to engage in the relevant trade or business at any time prior to the expiration of the applicable section 481(a) adjustment period provided in paragraph (e)(2)(ii) or (e)(2)(iii) of this section, the employer must take into account, in the taxable year of cessation, the balance of any section 481(a) adjustment not previously taken into account in computing taxable income (in the case of a branch) or earnings and profits (in the case of a foreign corporation). For purposes of this paragraph (e)(2)(iv), whether or not an employer ceases to engage in the trade or business is to be determined under administrative procedures issued under § 1.446-1(e). In applying those procedures, "employer" is to be defined in the same manner as "taxpayer" is defined under those procedures.

(3) *Allocation and source.* The amount of any net negative section 481(a) adjustment determined under this section and taken into account for a taxable year must be allocated and apportioned under § 1.861-8 in the same manner as a deduction or reduction in earnings and profits under section 404A. Any net positive section 481(a) adjustment that is taken into account for a taxable year first must be reduced by directly allocating to such adjustment the employer's section 404A expense that is subject to apportionment (including any amount that otherwise would be capitalized); to the extent a net positive section 481(a) adjustment exceeds the amount of the employer's section 404A expense for the taxable year, such excess must be sourced or otherwise classified in the same manner as section 404A deductions or reductions in earnings and profits are allocated and apportioned.

(4) *Example.* The principles of this paragraph (e) are illustrated by the following example:

Example. X, a domestic corporation, made an initial election under section 404A to treat an existing deferred compensation plan maintained by its foreign branch as a qualified reserve plan, effective beginning in *X*'s 1985 taxable year. *X*'s foreign branch maintains its books and records in FC, the functional currency. Previously, *X* had consistently used a permissible method of accounting with respect to the plan. The section 481(a) adjustment arising from *X*'s change in accounting method upon its section 404A election was a negative FC150,000. Beginning with its 1985 taxable year, *X* took into account a negative FC10,000 each year (FC150,000/15). Effective beginning in *X*'s 1988 taxable year, *X* received the Commissioner's express consent to change from a qualified reserve plan to a qualified funded plan. The section 481(a) adjustment attributable solely to the 1988 change was a positive FC132,000. Beginning with its 1988 taxable year, and for each of the five succeeding taxable years, *X* took into account a positive FC2,000, as computed below.

Negative 1985 section 481(a) adjustment	(FC150,000)
Less: 1985, 1986 & 1987 amounts taken into account	30,000
Subtotal	(120,000)
Positive 1988 section 481(a) adjustment	132,000
Net positive section 481(a) adjustment	12,000
Section 481(a) adjustment period	÷ 6
Net amount taken into account annually during section 481(a) adjustment period	FC2,000

(f) *Computation of section 481(a) adjustment*—(1) *In general.* For purposes of section 404A, except as provided in § 1.404A-7(f)(1)(ii)(C), the amount of the section 481(a) adjustment required under paragraph (e)(1) of this section equals—

(i) The Old Method Closing Amount; less

(ii) The New Method Opening Amount.

(2) *Old Method Closing Amount*—(i) *In general.* Except as otherwise provided in paragraph (f)(2)(ii), (iii), or (iv) of this section (or as otherwise prescribed by the Commissioner), the Old Method Closing Amount equals—

(A) The total of all past deductions taken with respect to liabilities under the plan; plus

(B) The net income earned directly or indirectly by any separate funding entity (e.g., account or trust) with respect to the plan, but only to the extent that such net income has not previously been taken into account in determining taxable income (in the case of a foreign branch) or earnings and profits (in the case of a foreign corporation); minus

(C) The total of all past payments under the plan made to plan participants and beneficiaries by the employer, the trust, or the separate funding entity.

(ii) *Taxpayer formerly using a reserve method*—(A) *In general.* If a taxpayer has consistently taken amounts with respect to the plan into account under a reserve method, the Old Method Closing Amount equals the closing reserve balance at the end of the closing year calculated under the taxpayer's reserve method. For purposes of the preceding sentence, a reserve method means a method of accrual based on the actuarial present value of expected future plan benefits.

(B) *Former qualified reserve plan.* To request the Commissioner's consent in the case of a former qualified reserve plan, the closing reserve balance must be adjusted for any unamortized increases or decreases to the reserve described in §1.404A-3(c) that have not yet been taken into account. For example, if the closing reserve balance is FC100,000, but FC10,000 of the closing reserve balance consists of an unamortized increase in the reserve that has not previously been taken into account due to the ten-year amortization requirements of §1.404A-3(c), the Old Method Closing Amount is FC90,000.

(iii) *Taxpayer formerly using pay-as-you-go method.* If the taxpayer has consistently taken amounts into account with respect to the plan based only on actual payments of plan benefits to participants and beneficiaries, the Old Method Closing Amount equals zero.

(iv) *Taxpayer formerly using a funded method*—(A) *Payment to separate funding entity.* If the taxpayer has consistently taken amounts into account with respect to the plan based only on actual payments to a separate funding entity and on payments by the employer (but not by the funding entity) to plan participants or beneficiaries, the Old Method Closing Amount equals the balance in the separate funding entity at the end of the closing year, including amounts attributable, directly or indirectly, to net investment income that has not previously been taken into account in determining taxable income (in the case of a foreign branch) or earnings and profits (in the case of a foreign corporation).

(B) *Former qualified funded plan.* In the case of a former qualified funded plan, the Old Method Closing Amount generally equals the amount described in paragraph (f)(2)(iv)(A) of this section, adjusted, however, by—

(*1*) Reducing the amount properly to reflect any net limitations under section 404A(b) and (g) (e.g., the full funding limitation for a qualified funded plan) that were applied in determining amounts taken into account under the former section 404A method of accounting; and

(*2*) Increasing the amount properly to reflect any amounts that are not paid during the closing year but that are permitted to be taken into account in the closing year under section 404A(b)(2) (relating to payments made after the close of the taxable year).

(v) *Section 404A(d) limitation.* In computing the Old Method Closing Amount upon the termination or revocation of an election under section 404A, the limitations of section 404A(d) and §1.404A-4 must be taken into account. Thus, if the Old Method Closing Amount is determined under paragraph (f)(2)(ii)(B) or (f)(2)(iv)(B) of this section, the amount otherwise determined under those paragraphs shall be reduced by applying the section 404A(d) and §1.404A-4 limitations to the extent the cumulative United States amount under §1.404A-4 exceeds the cumulative foreign amount under §1.404A-4.

(3) *New Method Opening Amount*—(i) *Qualified reserve plan.* In the case of an election to treat a plan as a qualified reserve plan, the New Method Opening Amount equals the balance of the reserve as of the end of the last day of the closing year, calculated under the rules of section 404A(c) and §1.404A-3 based on plan information and data as of that date. The New Method Opening Amount must be reduced (or increased) for any unamortized increases (or decreases) to the reserve described in section 404A(c)(4) and §1.404A-3(c).

(ii) *Qualified funded plan.* In the case of an election to be treated as a qualified funded plan, the New Method Opening Amount equals the amount of funds in the trust as of the beginning of the first day of the opening year, adjusted as necessary to take into account the rules of section 404A(b) and (g). If the separate funding entity does not qualify as a trust under §1.404A-1(e), the New Method Opening Amount in the case of a qualified funded plan is zero because there is no balance in a trust as defined in §1.404A-1(e).

(iii) *Nonqualified plan.* In the case of any plan that ceases to be a qualified foreign plan (either by reason of the termination or revocation of a section 404A election), the New Method Opening Amount is zero.

(iv) *Section 404A(d) limitation.* In computing the New Method Opening Amount upon an election under section 404A, the limitation on deductions of section 404A(d) and §1.404A-4 must be taken into account. Thus, if the New Method Opening Amount is determined under paragraph (f)(2)(i) or (f)(2)(ii) of this section, the amount otherwise determined must be reduced to the extent the cumulative United States amount computed under §1.404A-4 exceeds the cumulative foreign amount computed under §1.404A-4. See paragraph (g) of this section for initialization of amounts taken into account under section 404A(d).

(4) *Definitions and special rules*—(i) *Opening year.* For purposes of this section, the opening year is the first taxable year for which the new method of accounting is effective with respect to a plan. For example, in the case of an election to treat a foreign corporation plan as a qualified reserve plan beginning in 1989, the opening year is 1989, even though the election may not be made until 1994 pursuant to paragraph (b)(2)(ii) of this section.

(ii) *Closing year.* For purposes of this section, the closing year is the taxable year immediately preceding the opening year.

(iii) *Separate funding entity.* A separate funding entity described in paragraphs (f)(2)(i)(B) and (f)(2)(iv) of this section is any entity that satisfies the first requirement in the definition of the equivalent of a trust in §1.404A-1(e) (segregation in a separate legal entity) and, in practice, also satisfies the third requirement in that definition (dedication to payment of plan benefits) with respect to benefits under the relevant plan.

(iv) *Special rules for certain foreign corporation plans.* In the case of a foreign corporation's plan for which no method has been used for some or all prior taxable years because no calculation of earnings and profits has been necessary for those years (see, e.g., paragraph (b)(2)(ii) of this section), the employer may assume that the old method has been consistent with any method actually used consistently in immediately prior years. If no calculation of earnings and profits has been made for prior years, in determining the Old Method Closing Amount, the taxpayer may assume the method used was a method described in paragraph (f)(2)(iii) of this section. This assumed method used in the calculation of the Old Method Closing Amount must actually be used by the taxpayer for all the prior taxable years to the extent reductions of earnings and profits for those years are ever determined with respect to the plan.

(v) *Reference to rules applicable in the case of failure to consider net investment income in computing section 481(a) adjustment.* The treatment of net investment income earned by a funding vehicle that has not previously taken into account by the taxpayer in determining taxable income (in the case of a foreign branch) or earnings and profits (in the case of a foreign corporation), and that is not properly considered (as required under paragraphs (f)(2)(i)(B) and (f)(2)(iv)(A) of this section) in determining the amount of the section 481(a) adjustment for purposes of section 404A, is determined under other applicable provisions, which may include sections 61, 671 through 679, and 1001.

(vi) *Certain section 481(a) adjustments treated as carryover contributions.* In the case of an election for a plan to be treated as a qualified funded plan, any net positive section 481(a) adjustment is treated as a carryover contribution (within the meaning of §1.404A-2(d)(4)) to the extent that the adjustment is attributable to limits (that would be taken into account under §1.404A-2(d)(4)) on the amounts previously contributed to the trust under the plan that could be taken into account under section 404A.

(5) *Examples.* The principles of paragraph (f) of this section are illustrated by the following examples:

Example 1. Nonqualified reserve plan to qualified reserve plan. A foreign subsidiary of a domestic corporation established an irrevocable balance sheet reserve for pension expenses in 1981. The subsidiary maintains its books and records in FC, the functional currency. From 1981 through 1987, the taxpayer reduced earnings and profits of the foreign subsidiary by FC150,000, the amount of the pension liability which had accrued under the plan. This method of accounting was never challenged or changed by the District Director prior to the expiration of the statute of limitations for the 1981 through 1987 taxable years. Through December 31, 1987, the last day of the closing year, actual pension payments totalled FC15,000. For the 1988 taxable year, the taxpayer made an election for the plan to be treated as a qualified reserve plan. The reserve calculated under section 404A as of the first day of the 1988 taxable year, the opening year, and based upon employee census data as of that date, was FC175,000. The Old Method Closing Amount was FC135,000 (FC150,000 less FC15,000). The New Method Opening Amount was FC175,000. The section 481(a) adjustment was a negative FC40,000 (FC135,000 less FC175,000). This adjustment is to be taken into account over the 15-year section 481(a) adjustment period prescribed in paragraph (e)(2)(ii) of this section.

Example 2. Nonqualified reserve plan to qualified reserve plan. Assume the same facts as in *Example 1,* except that the reserve calculated under section 404A as of the first day of the 1988 taxable year and based upon employee census data as of that date was FC75,000. The Old Method Closing Amount was FC135,000 (FC150,000 less FC15,000). The New Method Opening Amount was FC75,000. The section 481(a) adjustment was a positive FC60,000 (FC135,000 less FC75,000). This adjustment is to be taken into account over the 15-year section 481(a) adjustment period prescribed in paragraph (e)(2)(ii) of this section.

Example 3. Nonqualified funded plan to qualified reserve plan. M, a domestic corporation, wholly owns N, a foreign corporation. N maintains its books and records in FC, the local currency. From 1981 through 1988, N maintained a nonqualified funded plan. During this period, N contributed FC55,000 to the separate funding entity administering the plan and reduced earnings and profits by FC55,000. The separate funding entity realized net income of FC17,000 from investment of plan assets and paid nothing to participants. None of the FC17,000 net investment income earned in the separate funding entity was taken into account in computing N's earnings and profits. As of the last day of N's 1988 taxable year, the closing year, the plan's fund balance was FC72,000, comprised of FC55,000 (excess contributions) and FC17,000 (investment income). The reserve calculated under section 404A as of the first day of the 1989 taxable year, the opening year, was FC100,000. Effective for M's 1989 taxable year, M elected under section 404A to treat N's funded plan as a qualified reserve plan. The Old Method Closing Amount was FC72,000. The New Method Opening Amount was FC100,000; thus, if, in the future, N pays FC100,000 to plan participants or beneficiaries, that FC100,000 will not again reduce N's earnings and profits. The section 481(a) adjustment was a negative FC28,000 (FC72,000 less FC100,000). However, if the District Director later challenges and requires N to change its method of accounting for foreign deferred compensation used in determining its 1981 through 1988 earnings and profits in a taxable year prior to the 1989 taxable year, the section 481(a) adjustment could be changed from a negative FC28,000 to a negative FC100,000. Pursuant to the administrative procedures under section 446(e), the District Director, upon challenging the treatment of foreign deferred compensation in years prior to 1989, could require any necessary positive section 481(a) adjustment to be taken into account in one taxable year.

Example 4. Nonqualified funded plan to qualified funded plan. Y, a domestic corporation, wholly owns X, a foreign corporation. X maintains its books and records in FC, the local currency. From 1981 through 1988, X maintained a nonqualified funded plan. During this period, X reduced earnings and profits by contributions of FC55,000 to the plan. The plan paid participants FC30,000. As of the last day of Y's

1988 taxable year, the plan's fund balance was FC29,000, comprised of FC25,000 (net contributions) and FC4,000 (interest income that was never previously taken into account in determining earnings and profits). Effective for Y's 1989 taxable year, Y elected under section 404A to treat X's funded plan as a qualified funded plan. The Old Method Closing Amount was FC29,000. The New Method Opening Amount was FC29,000. The section 481(a) adjustment was zero (FC29,000 less FC29,000). See *Example 3*, however, for the effects on the section 481(a) adjustment of a successful challenge to X's method of accounting for foreign deferred compensation in years prior to 1989 by the District Director.

Example 5. Z, the wholly owned foreign subsidiary of Y, a domestic corporation, has maintained a reserve plan for its employees, beginning in 1981. Z maintains its books and records in FC, the local currency. Effective for 1984, Y elected under section 404A to treat the plan as a qualified reserve plan. The only section 481(a) adjustment required was to take into account the limitation under section 404A(d). In 1981 through 1983, prior to the section 404A election, Z's earnings and profits were reduced by additions to the reserve. This method of accounting was never challenged or changed by the District Director prior to the expiration of the statute of limitations for the 1981 through 1983 taxable years. Thus, the Old Method Closing Amount equaled the balance in the reserve, which was FC300. To compute the New Method Opening Amount, the opening reserve took into account the lesser of the cumulative United States amount (FC300) or the cumulative foreign amount (FC90) as of the first day of 1984, the opening year. Thus, the New Method Opening Amount was FC90. The section 481(a) adjustment was therefore a positive FC210 (FC300—FC90); 1/15 of this amount, FC14 (FC210/15), is being taken into account as an increase in earnings and profits each year over the 15-year section 481(a) adjustment period that began in 1984.

Example 6. Nonqualified reserve plan to qualified reserve plan. Assume the same facts as in *Example 5* for all taxable years and the annual United States reduction, foreign reduction, cumulative United States amount, cumulative foreign amount and the section 481(a) adjustment shown below. The total annual reduction (or increase) in Z's earnings and profits was as follows—

	1984	1985	1986	1987	1988	1989	1990
Amount determined under U.S. law with respect to the plan under section 404A for the taxable year without regard to section 404A(d)	FC(40)	FC(50)	FC(60)	FC(70)	FC(80)	FC(90)	FC(100)
Amount allowed as a deduction for the taxable year under the appropriate foreign tax laws	(70)	(260)	(50)	(40)	(30)	(20)	(10)
Cumulative U.S. amount	(340)	(390)	(450)	(520)	(600)	(690)	(790)
Cumulative foreign amount	(160)	(420)	(470)	(510)	(540)	(560)	(570)
Lesser of cumulative U.S. or foreign amount	(160)	(390)	(450)	(510)	(540)	(560)	(570)
Reduced by the aggregate amount . . .	90	160	390	440	510	540	560
	(70)	(230)	(60)	(70)	(30)	(20)	(10)
Amount taken into account for the taxable year*	(70)	(230)	(50)	(70)	(30)	(20)	(10)
Positive section 481 adjustment	14	14	14	14	14	14	14
Total increase (reduction) in earnings and profits taken into account for the taxable year	FC(56)	FC(216)	FC(36)	FC(56)	FC(16)	FC(6)	FC(4)

(g) *Initial section 404A(d) amounts*—(1) *In general.* By making an election under section 404A, a taxpayer adopts section 404A(d) as part of its method of accounting. Section 1.404A-4 provides rules to apply the limitations of section 404A(d) in taxable years when an election under section 404A is in effect. This paragraph (g) provides rules to compute initial amounts under section 404A(d) in the opening year. These rules are based on the rules to compute the New Method Opening Amount in paragraph (f)(3) of this section.

(2) *Computation of amounts.* As of the first day of the opening year, the initial section 404A(d) amounts are as follows:

(i) The initial cumulative United States amount equals the New Method Opening Amount without regard to any reduction under paragraph (f)(3)(iv) of this section.

(ii) The initial cumulative foreign amount equals the New Method Opening Amount computed as though the appropriate foreign tax law were the new method of accounting and without regard to paragraph (f)(3)(iv) of this section.

(iii) The initial aggregate amount equals the lesser of—

(A) The initial cumulative United States amount; and

(B) The initial cumulative foreign amount.

(3) *Example.* The principles of paragraph (g) of this section are illustrated by the following example:

Example. A foreign subsidiary of a domestic corporation maintains its books and records in FC, the local currency. The subsidiary established a funded deferred compensation plan in 1983 but reduced earnings and profits on a pay-as-you-go basis. The plan year and the taxable year of the domestic corporation and the subsidiary are the calendar year. For the 1990 taxable year, the domestic corporation elected to treat the plan as a qualified reserve plan. The balance in the separate funding entity as of January 1, 1990, the first day of the opening year, was FC90,000. The initial United States cumulative amount (the opening reserve) was FC150,000. The initial foreign cumulative amount (the balance in the separate funding entity) was FC90,000. The initial aggre-

---

* The limitation in §1.404A-4(c) applies to taxable years 1984, 1985 and 1986. In 1986, the amount deductible under the appropriate foreign tax law was less than the lower of (1) the cumulative U.S. amount, or, (2) the cumulative foreign amount (then reduced by the aggregate amount).

gate amount was FC90,000 (the lesser of FC90,000 or FC150,000). Since the subsidiary reduced earnings and profits on the pay-as-you-go method, the Old Method Closing Amount was zero. The section 481(a) adjustment was a negative FC90,000 (zero less FC90,000 (the lesser of FC150,000 or FC90,000)).

[Reg. § 1.404A-6.]

§ 1.404A-7. Effective date, retroactive elections, and transition rules, EE-14-81, 5/6/93.

(a) *In general*—(1) *Effective date.* Except as otherwise provided in this section, section 404A applies to taxable years beginning after December 31, 1979.

(2) *Overview of retroactive elections for taxable years beginning before January 1, 1980*— (i) *Plans of foreign subsidiaries.* Section 2(e)(2) of Public Law 96-603 permitted a taxpayer to make section 404A apply retroactively for all of its foreign subsidiaries. Paragraph (b) of this section describes and provides the time and manner to make, perfect, or revoke this retroactive effective date election. If a retroactive effective date election was made, the taxpayer was also eligible to make a qualified funded plan election or a qualified reserve plan election effective retroactively for any of its subsidiaries' plans that met the requirements of § 1.404A-1(a) (other than paragraph (4) thereof) for the relevant period. Paragraph (c) of this section describes and provides the time and manner to make, perfect, or revoke these retroactive plan-by-plan elections for foreign subsidiaries.

(ii) *Plans of foreign branches.* Section 2(e)(3) of Public Law 96-603 permitted a taxpayer to make a qualified funded plan election retroactively for any plans maintained by a foreign branch that met the requirements of § 1.404A-1(a) (other than paragraph (4) thereof) for the relevant period. Paragraph (d) of this section describes and provides the time and manner to make this retroactive plan-by-plan qualified funded plan election for plans maintained by foreign branches.

(3) *Overview of special transition rules for election, revocation, and re-election.* Paragraph (e) of this section provides the time and manner to make and revoke qualified funded plan and qualified reserve plan elections for a taxpayer's transition period.

(b) *Retroactive effective date elections for foreign subsidiaries*—(1) *In general.* Section 2(e)(2) of Public Law 96-603 permitted a taxpayer to make section 404A effective during the taxpayer's open period. If the election was made, the taxpayer accepted section 404A (including, for example, § 1.404A-1(d)) as the operative law for all foreign subsidiaries (whether or not controlled foreign corporations) during the taxpayer's entire open period. If the election was made, section 404A applies to all distributions from accumulated profits (or earnings and profits) earned after December 31, 1970 (unless the election is revoked pursuant to paragraph (b)(3) of this section, if applicable). If accumulated profits were earned prior to January 1, 1971, a change in method of accounting is required for the foreign subsidiary's taxable year that ends with or within the first taxable year in the taxpayer's open period. A section 481(a) adjustment is required for amounts taken into account prior to the beginning of the foreign subsidiary's year of change and must be computed applying the rules of § 1.404A-6(f).

(2) *Time and manner to make, perfect, or revoke election.* The retroactive effective date election described in paragraph (b)(1) of this section is not effective unless the election was actually made no later than the time prescribed by law for filing the United States return for the first taxable year ending on or after December 31, 1980, including extensions (whether or not the time was actually extended for filing the taxpayer's return), and unless the taxpayer perfects the election by filing a statement indicating the taxpayer's agreement to perfect the election with an amended return for the first taxable year ending on or after December 31, 1980, on or before [*INSERT DATE THAT IS 365 DAYS AFTER THE DATE OF PUBLICATION OF FINAL REGULATIONS IN THE* FEDERAL REGISTER]. In order to be effective, the perfection must be made in the manner provided in § 1.404A-6(b)(3)(ii) or (iii). An election that is not perfected is considered retroactively revoked.

(3) *Requirement to amend returns*—(i) *In general.* In addition to the amended return required by paragraph (b)(2) of this section, the taxpayer must file any other amended United States returns that are necessary to conform the treatment of all items affected by the election or revocation to the treatment consistent with the election or revocation within the time period described in paragraph (b)(2) of this section. If no adjustments are necessary, the amended return required by paragraph (b)(2) of this section must contain a statement to that effect.

(ii) *Required statements.* All amended returns required by this paragraph (b)(3) must be accompanied by a statement containing—

(A) The open years, open period and retroactive period of the taxpayer;

(B) The taxable year for which the election is perfected or revoked;

(C) A statement that the election (or elections) are perfected or revoked pursuant to the authority contained in § 1.404A-7; and

(D) A signature and verification as provided in § 1.404A-5(b)(7).

(c) *Retroactive plan-by-plan elections for foreign subsidiaries*—(1) *In general.* Any taxpayer that makes a retroactive effective date election described in paragraph (a)(2)(i) of this section under the rules of paragraph (b) of this section may, at its option, also elect to treat any foreign plan of a subsidiary that met the requirements of § 1.404A-1(a) (other than paragraph (4) thereof) for the relevant period as a qualified funded plan or as a qualified reserve plan under section 404A, beginning in any taxable year of the foreign subsidiary that ends with or within the taxpayer's open period (or for any earlier taxable year beginning after December 31, 1971, for which earnings and profits of the subsidiary had no United States tax significance). Alternatively, the taxpayer may decide to make no such plan-by-plan election with respect to any particular plan or plans of any of its foreign subsidiaries. Rules similar to those contained in § 1.404A-6 (including, where applicable, the requirement to obtain the consent of the Commissioner) are used to effect such plan-by-plan elections. If the plan existed in a taxable year beginning prior to the first year for which the election was effective, a change in method of accounting is required for the year of the election. The year of change for purposes of computing the section 481(a) adjustment is the first year that the election is effective.

(2) *Time and manner to make, perfect, or revoke election.* A taxpayer that is eligible to make a plan-by-plan election described in paragraph (c)(1) of this section may make or perfect such an election by attaching a statement to that effect on an amended return for the year that the election is to be effective on or before [*INSERT DATE THAT IS 365 DAYS AFTER THE DATE OF PUBLICATION OF FINAL REGULATIONS IN THE* FEDERAL REGISTER]. In order to be effective, the perfection of a plan-by-plan election must be made in the manner provided in § 1.404A-6(b)(3)(ii) or (iii). An election that is not perfected is considered retroactively revoked. Any election made or perfected under this paragraph (c) will continue in effect for taxable years beginning after the taxpayer's open period, unless revoked under paragraph (c)(4) or (e) of this section or § 1.404A-6.

(3) *Requirement to amend returns.* In addition to the amended return required by paragraph (c)(2) of this section, the taxpayer must file any other amended United States returns that are necessary to conform the treatment of all items affected by the election or revocation to the treatment consistent with the election or revocation. All amended returns must be accompanied by the statement described in paragraph (b)(3)(ii) of this section (substituting "made, perfected, or revoked" for "perfected or revoked" where applicable) and all of the information required by § 1.404A-6(b)(4) (and § 1.404A-6(c)(2)(ii), if applicable, in the case of a termination). If no adjustments are necessary, the amended return required by paragraph (c)(2) of this section must contain a statement to that effect.

(4) *Revocation after initial election and re-election permitted.* Any taxpayer that makes an initial election for any plan under paragraph (c)(2) of this section may, under the rules of that paragraph, revoke the election for any taxable year after the sixth consecutive taxable year for which the election is effective, and may re-elect for any taxable year after the sixth consecutive taxable year for which the election is not in effect (regardless of whether the election is not in effect due to revocation or termination of the election as defined in § 1.404A-6(c)(1)). The consecutive changes in method of accounting described in the first sentence of this paragraph (c)(3) must be made under the rules in § 1.404A-6 regarding the section 481(a) adjustment period. The Commissioner may approve a letter ruling request (see § 601.201 of this chapter) to shorten the six-year waiting period upon a showing of extraordinary circumstances.

(5) *Examples.* The principles of paragraphs (b) and (c) of this section are illustrated by the following examples:

Example 1. P, a domestic corporation, wholly owns two foreign subsidiaries, *S* and *T*. *S* and *T* maintain their books and records in FC, the local currency. Since 1978, *S* and *T* have maintained unfunded pension plans for their respective employees. *S* maintained two plans, Plan 1 and Plan 2, and *T* maintained one plan. The plan years and the taxable years of all three corporations are the calendar year.

(i) For 1978 and 1979, *P* reduced the earnings and profits of *S* and *T* by the amount of the pension liability that had accrued under the plans as follows—

Taxable year	S's Plan 1	S's Plan 2	T's plan
1978	FC30,000	FC5,000	FC70,000
1979	50,000	15,000	80,000
Total reduction in earnings and profits	FC80,000	FC20,000	FC150,000
Total reduction in earnings and profits			
S	FC100,000		
T	FC150,000		

(ii) In 1981, *P* made a retroactive effective date election pursuant to section 2(e)(2) of Public Law 96-603 and paragraph (b) of this section for taxable years beginning after December 31, 1977, and ending before January 1, 1980, *P*'s open period. Thus, with respect to its open period, *P* has made section 404A the operative law for all distributions of earnings and profits (or accumulated profits) earned after December 31, 1970 for *S* and *T*. The consequences of making or not making the retroactive plan-by-plan election under section 404A for each foreign plan will be determined as though section 404A had been in effect for those years. Accordingly, earnings and profits of *S* and *T* may not be reduced with respect to amounts accrued under their respective plans unless the plans met the requirements of § 1.404A-1(a) for those years in the open period.

(iii) *P* made a retroactive plan-by-plan election to treat *S*'s Plan 1 as a qualified reserve plan for *P*'s retroactive period. The amount taken into account under § 1.404A-3 for *S*'s Plan 1 calculated under section 404A was FC25,000 for 1978 and FC35,000 for 1979. No election under

section 404A was made for *S*'s Plan 2 or for *T*'s plan. Thus, no amount of the accrued but unpaid pension liability attributable to *S*'s Plan 2 or to *T*'s plan may reduce *S*'s or *T*'s respective 1978 and 1979 earnings and profits. *P* amended its tax returns for 1978 and 1979 to reflect the correct reduction of earnings and profits of FC25,000 and FC35,000 with respect to *S*'s Plan 1 and no reduction for those years with respect to *S*'s Plan 2 or *T*'s plan. Since *S*'s and *T*'s plans were established during the open period, no section 481(a) adjustment is required.

Example 2. Q, a domestic corporation, has wholly owned *R*, a foreign subsidiary, since *R*'s formation in 1968. *R* maintains its books and records in FC, the local currency. Since 1968, *R* maintained an unfunded pension plan for its employees. The plan year and the taxable year of both corporations is the calendar year. *R*, since 1968, used a method of accounting under which it reduced earnings and profits by its accrued pension liability.

(i) *R*'s earnings and profits were earned and distributed to *Q* as follows—

Taxable year	Earnings and profits	Distribution of earnings and profits
1968	FC10,000	
1969	20,000	
1970	20,000	
Subtotal		50,000
1971	30,000	
1972	30,000	
1973	30,000	
1974	30,000	
1975	30,000	FC200,000
Subtotal		150,000
1976	40,000	
1977	40,000	
1978	40,000	
1979	40,000	
1980	40,000	
1981	50,000	
Subtotal		250,000
Total	FC450,000	

(ii) In 1981, *Q* made a retroactive effective date election pursuant to section 2(e)(2) of Public Law 96-603 and paragraph (b)(1) of this section for its open period. As of December 31, 1980, *Q*'s open period included the taxable years 1975 through 1979. Thus, with respect to those taxable years, *Q* has made section 404A the operative law for *R*. The consequences of making or not making the retroactive plan-by-plan election under section 404A for *R*'s foreign plan will be determined as though section 404A had been in effect for those taxable years. Thus, the earnings and profits of *R* may not be reduced with respect to amounts accrued under *R*'s plan, unless the plan met the requirements of § 1.404A-1(a) for those taxable years.

Q made a retroactive plan-by-plan election to treat *R*'s plan as a qualified reserve plan effective beginning in 1971. Of the distribution of FC200,000 to *Q* in 1975, section 404A applies to FC150,000, because these accumulated profits (or earnings and profits) were earned in taxable years beginning after December 31, 1970 and were also distributed in 1975, within *Q*'s open period. However, section 404A does not apply to the FC50,000 distribution made from accumulated profits earned before December 31, 1970. Since *R*'s plan was established before *Q*'s open period, a section 481(a) adjustment is required. This section 481(a) adjustment must be taken into account in determining earnings and profits beginning with the 1971 year of change.

(d) *Retroactive plan-by-plan qualified funded plan elections for certain plans of foreign branches*—(1) *In general.* Section 2(e)(3) of Public Law 96-603 permitted a taxpayer to make a qualified funded plan election retroactively for any plans maintained by a foreign branch that met the requirements of § 1.404A-1(a) (other than paragraph (4) thereof) for the relevant period. As a condition of making this election, a taxpayer is

required to agree to the assessment of all deficiencies (including interest thereon) arising during those taxable years within the open period (even those taxable years that are not open years as defined in paragraph (g)(4) of this section) to the extent that the deficiencies arise from erroneous deductions claimed by the taxpayer with respect to all of the taxpayer's foreign branches that maintained a deferred compensation plan. For a taxpayer that agrees to the assessment of tax in an election under this paragraph (d), a change in method of accounting is necessary (and a section 481(a) adjustment is required in accordance with the provisions of § 1.404A-6) with respect to any erroneous deductions claimed by the taxpayer under its method of accounting in taxable years ending prior to the beginning of the open period. For such a change in method of accounting, the year of change is the first taxable year in the open period, and the method of accounting to which the taxpayer is required to change is the method permitted during the open period under this paragraph (d).

(2) *Amounts allowed as a deduction.* If an election under section 2(e)(3) of Public Law 96-603 was made under the rules of this paragraph (d), the aggregate of the taxpayer's prior deductions is allowed as a deduction ratably over a 15-year period, beginning with the taxpayer's first taxable year beginning after December 31, 1979. A fractional part of a year which is a taxable year (as defined in sections 441(b) and 7701(a)(23)) is a taxable year for purposes of the 15-year period.

(3) *Definitions*—(i) *Prior deduction*—(A) *In general.* The term "prior deduction" means a deduction with respect to a qualified funded plan (i.e., a plan that met the requirements of § 1.404A-1(a) for the relevant period, and with respect to which a qualified funded plan election was

made under the rules of this paragraph (d)) maintained by a foreign branch of a taxpayer for a taxable year beginning before January 1, 1980—

(*1*) That the taxpayer claimed;

(*2*) That was not allowable under the law in effect prior to the enactment of section 404A;

(*3*) With respect to which, on December 1, 1980, the assessment of a deficiency was not barred by any law or rule of law; and

(*4*) That would have been allowable if section 404A applied to taxable years beginning before January 1, 1980.

(B) *Application of section 404A(d)*. Because the prior deductions are limited by the amounts that may be taken into account under section 404A, the computation of those prior deductions for the relevant taxable years is subject to the limitations described in section 404A(d) and § 1.404A-4. However, once the aggregate of prior deductions is calculated, the aggregate, or any portion thereof permitted to be taken into account over the 15-year period of paragraph (d)(2) of this section, is not subject to the limitations prescribed by section 404A(d) and § 1.404A-4.

(ii) *Erroneous deduction*. The term "erroneous deduction" means an amount that is not deductible under section 404(a) (including section 404(a)(5)), that was deducted on a taxpayer's income tax return with respect to a foreign deferred compensation plan.

(4) *Time and manner to make, perfect, or revoke election*—(i) *In general*. A plan-by-plan election described in paragraph (d)(1) of this section is not effective unless the election was actually made no later than the time prescribed by law for filing the United States return for the first taxable year ending on or after December 31, 1980, including extensions (whether or not the time was actually extended for filing the taxpayer's return), and unless the taxpayer perfects the election by

	1977	1978	1979	Total
Amount deducted on tax return	FC100	FC100	FC100	FC300
Amount deductible under section 404(a)	20	20	20	FC60
Amount deductible under section 404A	90	90	90	FC270

(ii) The assessment (including interest) for the open years 1977 through 1979 is based on adjustments to the erroneous deductions of FC240 (FC300 less FC60).

(iii) The amount of the prior deductions taken into account ratably over 15 years as provided in paragraph (d)(2) of this section, beginning in 1981, is a negative FC210 (FC60 less FC270).

(iv) No section 481(a) adjustment is required because *X* took no deductions with respect to the plan prior to the beginning of its open period.

Example 2. (i) *Z*, a domestic corporation, maintained a nonqualified funded foreign branch plan for its foreign employees, beginning in its 1965 (calendar) taxable year. In 1981, *Z* made a retroactive effective date election and a retroactive plan-by-plan election to treat this plan as a qualified funded plan. As of December 31, 1980, *Z*'s 1965 taxable year was closed, but its 1978 taxable year was open. The amounts deducted on *Z*'s tax returns, the amount deductible under sections 404(a) and 404A (expressed in FC, the local currency) are as follows—

	1965	1978	Total
Amount deducted on tax return	FC20	FC80	FC100
Amount deductible under section 404(a)	5	6	FC11
Amount deductible under section 404A	10	40	FC60

(ii) Under paragraph (d)(1) of this section, *Z* agreed to an assessment of deficiencies for its 1978 taxable year based on its FC74 (FC80—FC6) of erroneous deductions as defined in paragraph (d)(3)(ii) of this section.

(iii) The FC34 (FC40—FC6) of prior deductions is permitted to be taken into account as a deduction over the 15-year period beginning with its 1980 taxable year as provided in paragraph (d)(2) of this section.

(iv) Additionally, because *Z* took erroneous deductions under its method of accounting prior to the beginning of its open period, it is required to change to the method of accounting permitted during the open period, and must take a section 481(a) adjustment (determined under the snapshot method of § 1.404A-6(f)) into account over the 15-year section 481(a) adjustment period of § 1.404A-6(e)(2)(ii) beginning in its 1978 year of change. See paragraph (d)(1) of this section.

filing a statement indicating the taxpayer's agreement to perfect the election with an amended return for the first taxable year ending on or after December 31, 1980, on or before [*INSERT DATE THAT IS 365 DAYS AFTER THE DATE OF PUBLICATION OF FINAL REGULATIONS IN THE FEDERAL REGISTER*]. In order to be effective, the perfection must be made in the manner provided in § 1.404A-6(b)(3)(ii) or (iii). An election that is not perfected is considered retroactively revoked. Any election under this paragraph (d) will continue in effect for taxable years beginning after the taxpayer's open period, unless revoked under paragraph (e) of this section or § 1.404A-6.

(ii) *Requirement to amend returns*. In addition to the amended return required by paragraph (d)(4)(i) of this section, the taxpayer must file any other amended United States returns that are necessary to conform the treatment of all items affected by the election or revocation to the treatment consistent with the election or revocation under this paragraph (d) within the time period described in paragraph (d)(4)(i) of this section. All amended returns must be accompanied by the statement described in paragraph (b)(3)(ii) of this section and all of the information required by § 1.404A-6(b)(4) (and § 1.404A-6(c)(2)(ii), if applicable, in the case of a termination). If no adjustments are necessary, the amended return required by paragraph (d)(4)(i) of this section must contain a statement to that effect.

(5) *Examples*. The principles of this paragraph (d) are illustrated by the following examples:

Example 1. (i) During its open taxable years 1977 through 1979, *X*, a domestic corporation, maintained a nonqualified funded plan for the employees of its foreign branch. In 1981, *X* made a retroactive effective date election and a retroactive plan-by-plan election to treat this plan as a qualified funded plan. The amounts deducted on *X*'s tax returns, the amount deductible under sections 404(a) and 404A (expressed in FC, the local currency) are as follows—

Example 3. A foreign branch which computes its income under the profit and loss method of Rev. Rul. 75-107, 1975-1 C.B. 32 (see § 601.601(d)(2)(ii)(*b*) of this chapter), in units of local currency, the FC, maintains a qualified funded plan. In 1980, the taxpayer was eligible to make the elections described in this section, and did so during the 1980 taxable year. The amount determined under paragraph (d)(3)(i) of this section after taking into account the limitations prescribed [by]§ 1.404A-4(a) for the open period was FC1,500,000. For the 1980 taxable year, and as provided in paragraph (d) of this section, FC100,000 of the prior deductions were deductible. The prior deductions allowed to be taken into account in the 1980 through 1994 taxable years are determined without regard to, and thus are not subject to, the limitations prescribed by § 1.404A-4(a).

(e) *Special transition rules for election, revocation and re-election*—(1) *In general*. This paragraph (e) provides the time and manner for making and revoking qualified funded plan and qualified reserve plan elections for a taxpayer's transition period. A taxpayer may make an election, revoke an election, and re-elect to treat any plan that met the requirements of § 1.404A-1(a) (other than paragraph (4) thereof) for the relevant period as a qualified funded plan or a qualified reserve plan under this paragraph (e) for the transition period without regard to whether a retroactive election is made under paragraph (b), (c), or (d) of this section. However, an election made under paragraph (c) or (d) of this section is deemed to continue in effect for taxable years beginning after December 31, 1979, unless revoked under paragraph (c)(4) of this section or this paragraph (e) or terminated or revoked under § 1.404A-6(f). See paragraphs (c)(2) and (d)(4)(i) of this section.

(2) *Time and manner initially to elect and revoke*—(i) *In general*. Taxpayers that wish to make an election under this paragraph (e) may have, but were not required to have, made a Method (1) or Method (2) election for the taxable year for which an election is made under this paragraph. Those taxpayers that wish to make (or perfect) an election under this paragraph (e) must attach a statement to that effect on an amended return for the year the election is to be effective on or before [*INSERT DATE THAT IS 365 DAYS AFTER THE DATE OF PUBLICATION OF FINAL REGULATIONS IN THE FEDERAL REGISTER*]. An election previously made that is not perfected is considered retroactively revoked.

(ii) *Requirement to amend returns*. In addition to the amended return required by paragraph (e)(2)(i) of this section, the taxpayer must file any other amended United States returns that are necessary to conform the treatment of all items affected by the election or revocation to the treatment consistent with the election or revocation under this paragraph (e) within the time period described in paragraph (e)(2)(i) of this section. All amended returns must be accompanied by the statement described in paragraph (b)(3)(ii) of this section (substituting "made, perfected, or revoked" for "perfected or revoked" where applicable) and all of the information required by §1.404A-6(b)(4) (and §1.404A-6(c)(2)(ii), if applicable, in the case of a termination). If no adjustments are necessary, the amended return required by paragraph (e)(2)(i) of this section must contain a statement to that effect.

(3) *Revocation after initial election and re-election permitted.* Any taxpayer that makes an initial election for any plan under paragraph (e)(2) of this section may, under the rules of that paragraph, revoke the election for any taxable year after the sixth consecutive taxable year for which the election is effective, and may re-elect for any taxable year after the sixth consecutive taxable year for which the election is not in effect (whether the election is not in effect due to either revocation or

Plan-by-plan election
effective
1971—1974
1982—1987

(ii) A section 481(a) adjustment is required for the years of change 1975, 1982 and 1988.

(f) *Special data rules for retroactive elections—*(1) *Retroactive calculation of section 481(a) adjustments—*(i) *General rule.* Retroactive elections may be made only if the taxpayer calculates the section 481(a) adjustment required by §1.404A-6 based on substantiation quality data. Substantiation quality data generally must be current as of the date of the change in method of accounting. Nevertheless, if contemporaneous substantiation quality data is not readily available, the taxpayer may calculate the section 481(a) adjustment based on backward projections to earlier years from the first taxable year beginning before January 1, 1980, for which sufficient contemporaneous substantiation quality data is readily available. However, such projections must satisfy the substantiation requirements in paragraph (f)(1)(ii) of this section. Furthermore, the taxpayer may not use any of the approaches provided for under this paragraph (f) if circumstances indicate that the overall result is a material distortion of the amounts allowable.

(ii) *Substantiation requirement for retroactive reserves—*(A) *In general.* Although reasonable actuarial estimates and projections may be used, the calculation of the opening balance of the reserve for the first year for which a qualified reserve plan election under paragraph (c)(1) of this section is effective must nonetheless be based on some actual contemporaneous evidence. Thus, the opening balance may be based on actual aggregate covered payroll, the actual number of covered employees, or a contemporaneous actuarial valuation that used reasonable actuarial methods. For example, if the taxpayer has contemporaneous records of the number of covered employees and the aggregate covered payroll, it may estimate other actuarial information, such as average age and marital status, based on reasonable actuarial methods (e.g., using substantiation quality data as of another date and adjusting for actual or expected changes for the interim years). The resulting combination of actual contemporaneous evidence and reasonably estimated data may be used to calculate the opening reserve. If a contemporaneous actuarial valuation is used as the basis of an opening reserve, the results of the valuation must be adjusted to reflect any difference between the actuarial method used in that actuarial valuation and the unit credit method, as required by section 404A(c) and §1.404A-3(b).

(B) *Interpolation.* In cases where a taxpayer can meet the substantiation requirement of paragraph (f)(1)(ii)(A) of this section for some years, but cannot meet that requirement in intervening years (including the year of the change in method of accounting), the taxpayer may interpolate a reserve balance for the intervening years based on reasonable actuarial methods. In the absence of evidence to the contrary, it is assumed that a pro rata allocation of amounts to those intervening years is a reasonable actuarial method. This paragraph (f)(1)(ii)(B) does not authorize any interpolation for years in which other evidence indicates that it would cause a material distortion (such as a year during which the work force was on strike and no deferred compensation benefits were accrued). In addition, this paragraph (f)(1)(ii)(B) does not authorize extrapolation of reserve balances to years that are not intervening years between years that meet the substantiation requirements of paragraph (f)(1)(ii)(A) of this section.

(C) *Extrapolation.* If the first year for which the taxpayer is able to meet the substantiation requirements of paragraph (f)(1)(ii)(A) of this section ("the substantiation year") is later than the year of the change

termination of the election as defined in §1.404A-6(c)(1)). The consecutive changes in method of accounting described in the first sentence of this paragraph (e)(3) must be made under the rules in §1.404A-6 regarding the section 481(a) adjustment period. The Commissioner may approve a letter ruling request to shorten the six-year waiting period upon a showing of extraordinary circumstances.

(4) *Example.* The principles of paragraph (e)(3) of this section are illustrated by the following example:

Example. (i) *L,* a domestic corporation, has wholly owned foreign subsidiary *M,* since *M*'s formation in 1971. *M* maintained a funded plan for its employees from 1971 through 1991. The taxable year of *L* and *M* is the calendar year. In 1981, *L* made a Method (2) election. Within 365 days after the publication of the final regulations in the Federal Register, *L* perfected its retroactive effective date election for all its foreign subsidiaries. *L*'s election terminated in 1975 due to its plan's violation of the requirements of section 404A(e)(2). Additionally, *L* perfected, revoked and re-elected on a plan-by-plan basis its election for *M*'s plan, as follows—

Plan-by-plan election
terminated or revoked
1975—1981
1988—1993

in method of accounting, a taxpayer may use the approach described in this paragraph (f)(1)(ii)(C) to determine the section 481(a) adjustments described in §1.404A-6(f) in years prior to the substantiation year. Under this approach, the taxpayer's closing balance under its prior method as of the date of the change in the method of accounting is compared with the opening balance in the substantiation year. If the closing balance exceeds the opening balance, the excess is the amount to be used in calculating the adjustment under section 481, as required by §1.404A-6. However, if the closing balance of the taxpayer's reserve under its method used for years prior to the election under section 404A is less than the opening balance for the substantiation year, the opening balance as of the date of the change in method in accounting is assumed to be equal to the closing balance. Thus, if the closing balance is less than the opening balance for the substantiation year, there is no adjustment under section 481. In such a case, the difference between the opening balance as of the date of the change in method of accounting and the opening balance for the substantiation year is allocated to the years prior to the substantiation year based on reasonable actuarial methods using all available information.

(2) *Determination of reasonable addition to a reserve in interim years.* In the case of a qualified reserve plan that is using the interpolation option of paragraph (f)(1)(ii)(B) of this section or that is described in the last sentence in paragraph (f)(1)(ii)(C) of this section, none of the increase in the reserve in the intervening year is considered a reasonable addition to the reserve under §1.404A-3(b). Thus, the entire amount of the increase must be considered an amount to be amortized over ten years under §1.404A-3(c).

(3) *Protective elections.* For those taxpayers that relied on the prior position of the Internal Revenue Service by making a Method (1) election under which the section 481(a) adjustment was computed in a manner inconsistent with this section or by making a Method (2) election under which no section 481(a) adjustment was reflected in the original return, appropriate adjustments required by section 404A and its underlying regulations must be made on an amended return filed no later than [*INSERT DATE THAT IS 365 DAYS AFTER THE DATE OF PUBLICATION OF FINAL REGULATIONS IN THE FEDERAL REGISTER*] for the first year the election is effective and for all subsequent affected years for which a return has been filed. If no adjustments are necessary, an amended return should be filed for the first year stating that no adjustments are necessary.

(g) *Definitions and special rules—*(1) *Method (1) election.* The term "Method (1) election" means an election that was made under Method (1) (as defined in Ann. 81-114, 1981-28 I.R.B. 21) (see §601.601(d)(2)(ii)(*b*) of this chapter) by claiming the deduction or credit allowable under section 404A on the taxpayer's income tax return for the first taxable year ending on or after December 31, 1980, including extensions (or an amended return filed no later than the end of the extended time period prescribed in section 6081, whether or not such time was actually extended for filing the taxpayer's return).

(2) *Protective or Method (2) election.* The term "protective election" or "Method (2) election" means an election that was made under Method (2) (as defined in Ann. 81-114, 1981-28 I.R.B. 21) (see §601.601(d)(2)(ii)(*b*) of this chapter) without claiming deductions attributable to a qualified foreign plan on the taxpayer's income tax return (or, in the case of foreign subsidiaries, without taking into account reductions of earnings and profits).

(3) *Open years of the taxpayer.* The term "open years of the taxpayer" means open taxable years beginning after December 31, 1971, and for which, on December 31, 1980, the making of a refund, or the assessment of a deficiency, was not barred by any law or rule of law.

(4) *Retroactive period.* The term "retroactive period" means a taxpayer's taxable years (whether or not the making of a refund, or the assessment of a deficiency, was barred by any law or rule of law for any taxable year) in the following range—

(i) Any taxable year selected by the taxpayer between taxable years beginning after December 31, 1970 and before January 1, 1980 (the beginning taxable year); and

(ii) The last taxable year beginning before January 1, 1980 (the ending taxable year).

(5) *Transition period.* The term "transition period" means taxable years beginning after December 31, 1979, and before [*INSERT THE DATE OF PUBLICATION OF FINAL REGULATIONS IN THE FEDERAL REGISTER*].

(6) *Open period.* For purposes of this section, the term "open period" means, with respect to any taxpayer, all taxable years beginning after December 31, 1971, and beginning before January 1, 1980, and for which, on December 31, 1980, the making of a refund, or the assessment of a deficiency, was not barred by any law or rule of law. [Reg. § 1.404A-7.]

¶ 20,162B

Proposed regulations: Required distribution rules: Qualified plans: IRAs: Trust as beneficiary.—The IRS has issued proposed regulations under Code Sec. 401(a)(9) that make changes to the required distribution rules that apply if a trust is named as beneficiary of an employee's benefit under a qualified plan or IRA. The proposed regulations amend the existing proposed rules that were issued in 1987 (CCH PENSION PLAN GUIDE ¶ 20,163B) and, like the existing proposed rules, may be relied on until final regulations are issued.

The proposed regulations were published in the *Federal Register* on December 30, 1997 (62 FR 67780). The proposed regulations were amended March 25, 1998 (63 FR 14391).

DEPARTMENT OF THE TREASURY

Internal Revenue Service

26 CFR Part 1

[REG-209463-82]

RIN 1545-AV82

Required Distributions from Qualified Plans and Individual Retirement Plans

AGENCY: Internal Revenue Service (IRS), Treasury.

ACTION: Notice of proposed rulemaking.

SUMMARY: This document contains amendments to the existing proposed regulations under section 401(a)(9) that make changes to the rules that apply if a trust is named as a beneficiary of an employee's benefit under a retirement plan. These proposed regulations will affect administrators of, participants in, and beneficiaries of qualified plans, institutions which sponsor and individuals who administer individual retirement plans, individuals who use individual retirement plans, simplified employee pensions and SIMPLE Savings Plans for retirement income and beneficiaries of individual retirement plans; and employees for whom amounts are contributed to section 403(b) annuity contracts, custodial accounts, or retirement income accounts and beneficiaries of such contracts and accounts.

DATES: Written comments and requests for a public hearing must be received by March 30, 1998.

ADDRESSES: Send submissions to CC:DOM:CORP:R (REG-209463-82), room 5226, Internal Revenue Service, POB 7604, Ben Franklin Station, Washington, DC 20044. Submissions may be hand delivered between the hours of 8 a.m. and 5 p.m. to CC:DOM:CORP:R (REG-209463-82), Courier's Desk, Internal Revenue Service, 1111 Constitution Avenue NW., Washington, DC. Alternatively, taxpayers may submit comments electronically via the Internet by selecting the "Tax Regs" option on the IRS Home Page, or by submitting comments directly to the IRS Internet site at http://www.irs.ustreas.gov/prod/tax_regs/comments.html

FOR FURTHER INFORMATION CONTACT: Thomas Foley at (202) 622-6030 (not a toll-free number).

SUPPLEMENTARY INFORMATION:

Paperwork Reduction Act

The collection of information contained in this notice of proposed rulemaking has been submitted to the Office of Management and Budget for review in accordance with the Paperwork Reduction Act of 1995 (44 U.S.C. 3507(d)). Comments on the collection of information should be sent to the **Office of Management and Budget**, Attn: Desk Officer for the Department of the Treasury, Office of Information and Regulatory Affairs, Washington, DC 20503, with copies to the **Internal Revenue Service**, Attn: IRS Reports Clearance Officer, T:FP, Washington, DC 20224. Comments on the collection of information should be received by March 2, 1998. Comments are specifically requested concerning:

Whether the proposed collection of information is necessary for the proper performance of the functions of the **Internal Revenue Service**, including whether the information will have practical utility;

The accuracy of the estimated burden associated with the proposed collection of information (see below);

How the quality, utility, and clarity of the information to be collected may be enhanced;

How the burden of complying with the proposed collection of information may be minimized, including through the application of automated collection techniques or other forms of information technology; and

Estimates of capital or start-up costs and costs of operation, maintenance, and purchase of services to provide information.

The collection of information in this proposed regulation is in Question and Answer D-7 of § 1.401(a)(9)-1. This information is required for a taxpayer who wants to name a trust and treat the underlying beneficiaries of the trust as designated beneficiaries of the taxpayer's benefit under a retirement plan or an individual retirement plan ("IRA"). The taxpayer must provide a copy of the trust instrument or IRA trustee, custodian, or issuer, or provide a list of all the beneficiaries of the trust, certify that, to the best of the taxpayer's knowledge, this list is correct and complete, and agree to provide a copy of the trust instrument upon demand. In addition, other related requirements for the beneficiaries of the trust to be treated as designated beneficiaries must be satisfied. If the trust instrument is amended at any time in the future, the taxpayer must, within a reasonable time, provide a copy of each such amendment, or provide corrected certifications to the extent that the amendment changes the information previously certified. In addition, by the end of the ninth month after the death of the taxpayer, the trustee of the trust must provide a copy of the trust to the plan administrator or IRA trustee, custodian, or issuer, or provide a list of all the beneficiaries of the trust, certify that, to the best of the taxpayer's knowledge, this list is correct and complete, and agrees to provide a copy of the trust instrument upon demand. The collection of information is required to obtain a benefit. The likely respondents are individuals or households.

Estimated total annual reporting hours is 333 hours.

The estimated average burden per respondent is 20 minutes.

The estimated total number of respondents is 1,000.

An agency may not conduct or sponsor, and a person is not required to respond to, a collection of information unless it displays a valid control number assigned by the Office of Management and Budget.

Books or records relating to a collection of information must be retained as long as their contents may become material in the administration of any internal revenue law. Generally, tax returns and tax return information are confidential, as required by 26 U.S.C. 6103.

Background

On July 27, 1987, Proposed Regulations (EE-113-82) under sections 401(a)(9), 403(b), 408, and 4974 of the Internal Revenue Code of 1986 were published in the **Federal Register** (52 FR 28070) Those proposed regulations provide guidance for complying with the rules relating to required distributions from qualified plans, individual retirement plans, and section 403(b) annuity contracts, custodial accounts, and retirement income accounts. This document contains amendments to proposed § 1.401(a)(9)-1 (hereinafter referred to as the Existing Proposed Regulations) that was included in EE-113-82. Specifically this document contains amendments to Q&As D-5 and Q&A D-6 of the

Existing Proposed Regulations which prescribe specific requirements that must be met when a trust is named as a beneficiary of an employee's benefit under a plan, and adds a new Q&A D-7 to the Existing Proposed Regulations. Proposed §§ 1.408-8 and 1.403(b)-2 (also included in EE-113-82) provide that the provisions of proposed § 1.401(a)(9)-1 generally apply to individual retirement plans, and section 403(b) annuity contracts, custodial accounts, and retirement income accounts. Accordingly, these amendments and additions also generally apply to such plans, contracts, and accounts.

The amendments and additions to the Existing Proposed Regulations in these proposed regulations are issued in response to comments and questions received regarding the Existing Proposed Regulations with respect to section 401(a)(9). Treasury and the IRS continue to welcome additional comments concerning the Existing Proposed Regulations and the other sections of EE-113-82.

As in the case of the Existing Proposed Regulations and the other sections of EE-113-82, taxpayers may rely on these proposed regulations for guidance pending the issuance of final regulations. If, and to the extent, future guidance is more restrictive than the guidance in these proposed regulations, the future guidance will be applied without retroactive effect.

Explanation of provisions

Overview

Section 401(a)(9)(A) provides that, in order for a plan to be qualified under section 401(a), distributions of each employee's interest in the plan must commence no later than the "required beginning date" for the employee and must be distributed over a period not to exceed the joint lives or joint life expectancy of the employee and the employee's designated beneficiary. Section 401(a)(9)(B) provides that if distribution does not commence prior to death in accordance with section 401(a)(9)(A), distributions of the employee's interest must be made within 5 years of the employee's death or, generally, commence within one year of the employee's death and be made over the life or life expectancy of the designated beneficiary.

Section 401(a)(9)(E) defines the term "designated beneficiary" as an individual designated as a beneficiary by the employee. The Existing Proposed Regulations provide that, for purposes of section 401(a)(9), only individuals may be designated beneficiaries. A beneficiary who is not an individual, such as the employee's estate, may not be a designated beneficiary for purposes of determining the minimum required distribution, but nevertheless may be designated as the employee's beneficiary under the plan. If a beneficiary who is not an individual is designated to receive an employee's benefit after death, the employee is treated as having no designated beneficiary when determining the required minimum distribution. In that case, under section 401(a)(9), distributions commencing before death must be made over the employee's single life or life expectancy and distributions commencing after death must be made within 5 years of the employee's death.

However, the Existing Proposed Regulations provide that if a trust is named as a beneficiary of an employee's benefit under the plan, the underlying beneficiaries of the trust may be treated as designated beneficiaries for purposes of section 401(a)(9) if certain requirements are satisfied. In response to comments, these proposed regulations modify these trust beneficiary requirements as explained below by:

• Permitting the designated beneficiary of a revocable trust to be treated as the designated beneficiary for purposes of determining the minimum distribution under section 401(a)(9), provided that the trust becomes irrevocable upon the death of the employee.

• Providing relief from the requirement that the plan be provided with a copy of the trust document if certain certification requirements are met.

Irrevocability of trust

The Existing Proposed Regulations generally provide that a trust must be irrevocable as of the employee's required beginning date in order for the beneficiaries of the trust to be treated as designated beneficiaries under the plan for purposes of determining the distribution period under section 401(a)(9)(A). Commentators have indicated that most trusts established for estate planning purposes and designated as the beneficiary of an employee's plan benefits are revocable instruments prior to the death of the employee. In response to those comments, these proposed regulations provide that a trust named as beneficiary of an employee's interest in a retirement plan be permitted to be revocable while the employee is alive, provided that it becomes irrevocable, by its terms, upon the death of the employee. The requirements in the Existing Proposed Regulations that the trust be valid under state law (or would be but for the fact that there is no corpus)

and that the beneficiaries be identifiable from the trust instrument are retained.

Information to Plan Administrator

In order to permit the plan administrator to substantiate that the requirements for treating the beneficiaries of the trust as designated beneficiaries under the plan are satisfied, the Existing Proposed Regulations require that a copy of the trust instrument be provided to the plan administrator by the earlier of the required beginning date or the date of the employee's death. In response to comments, this proposed regulation permits an alternative method of substantiation.

As under the Existing Proposed Regulations, a copy of the trust instrument may be provided to the plan administrator. However, because the trust need not be irrevocable, under this method, the employee must also agree that if the trust instrument is amended at any time in the future, the employee will, within a reasonable time, provide a copy of each such amendment.

Alternatively, the employee may provide a list of all of the beneficiaries of the trust (including contingent beneficiaries) with a description of the portion to which they are entitled and any conditions on their entitlement, and certify that, to the best of the employee's knowledge, this list is correct and complete and that the other requirements for the beneficiaries of the trust to be treated as designated beneficiaries are satisfied. Under the second method, the employee must also agree to provide corrected certifications to the extent that the amendment changes the information previously certified. Finally, the employee must agree to provide a copy of the trust instrument to the plan administrator upon demand.

In addition, these proposed regulations provide that, if the minimum required distributions after death are determined by treating the beneficiaries of the trust as designated beneficiaries, a final certification as to the beneficiaries of the trust instrument must be provided to the plan administrator by the end of the ninth month after the death of the employee. This rule applies even if a copy of the trust instrument were provided to the plan administrator before the employee's death. Alternatively, an updated trust instrument may be provided.

The proposed regulations also provide that a plan will not fail to satisfy section 401(a)(9) merely because the terms of the actual trust instrument are inconsistent with the information in the certifications or trust instruments previously provided to the plan administrator if the plan administrator reasonably relies on the information provided in the certifications or trust instruments. However, the minimum required distributions for years after the year in which the discrepancy is discovered must be determined based on the actual terms of the trust instrument. For those years, the minimum required distribution will be determined by treating the beneficiaries of the employee as having been changed in the year in which the year the discrepancy was discovered to conform to the corrected information and by applying the change in beneficiary provisions found under the Existing Proposed Regulations. However, for purposes of determining the amount of the excise tax under section 4974 (including application of a waiver, if any, for reasonable error under section 4974), the minimum required distribution is determined for any year based on the actual terms of the trust in effect during the year.

Special Analyses

It has been determined that this notice of proposed rulemaking is not a significant regulatory action as defined in EO 12866. Therefore, a regulatory assessment is not required. It also has been determined that section 553(b) of the Administrative Procedure Act (5 U.S.C. chapter 5) does not apply to these regulations. Moreover, it hereby certified that the regulations in this document will not have a significant economic impact on a substantial number of small entities. This certification is based on the fact that the reporting burden is primarily on the plan participant to supply the information rather than on the entity maintaining the retirement plan and the fact that the number of participants per plan to whom the burden applies is insignificant. Accordingly, a regulatory flexibility analysis under the Regulatory Flexibility Act (5 U.S.C. chapter 6) is not required. Pursuant to section 7805(f) of the Internal Revenue Code, this notice of proposed rulemaking will be submitted to the Chief Counsel for Advocacy of the Small Business Administration for comment on its impact on small business.

Comments and Requests for a Public Hearing

Before these proposed regulations are adopted as final regulations, consideration will be given to any written comments (preferably a signed original and eight (8) copies) or comments transmitted via Internet that are submitted timely to the IRS. All comments will be available for public inspection and copying. A public hearing may be scheduled if requested in writing by a person that timely submits written comments. If a public hearing is scheduled, notice of the date, time, and place for the hearing will be published in the **Federal Register**.

Drafting Information

The principal author of these regulations is Cheryl Press, Office of the Associate Chief Counsel (Employee Benefits and Exempt Organizations), IRS. However, other personnel from the IRS and Treasury Department participated in their development.

List of Subjects in 26 CFR Part 1

Income taxes, Reporting and recordkeeping requirements.

Amendments to the Previously Proposed Regulations

Accordingly, 26 CFR part 1 is proposed to be amended as follows:

PART 1—INCOME TAXES

Paragraph 1. The authority citation for part 1 continues to read in part as follows:

Authority: 26 U.S.C. 7805 ***

Par. 2. Section 1.401(a)(9)-1, as proposed to be added at 52 FR 28075, July 27, 1987, is amended by:

1. Revising Q&A D-5

2. Revising Q&A D-6.

3. Adding Q&A D-7

The additions and revisions read as follows:

§ 1.401(a)(9)-1 *Required distributions from trust and plans.*

*****

D. Determination of the Designated Beneficiary.

*****

D-5. Q. If a trust is named as a beneficiary of an employee, will the beneficiaries of the trust with respect to the trust's interest in the employee's benefit be treated as having been designated as beneficiaries of the employee under the plan for purposes of determining the distribution period under section 401(a)(9)(A)(ii)?

A. (a) Pursuant to D-2A of this section, only an individual may be a designated beneficiary for purposes of determining the distribution period under section 401(a)(9)(A)(ii). Consequently, a trust itself may not be the designated beneficiary even though the trust is named as a beneficiary. However, if the requirements of paragraph (b) of this D-5 are met, distributions made to the trust will be treated as paid to the beneficiaries of the trust with respect to the trust's interest in the employee's benefit, and the beneficiaries of the trust will be treated as having been designated as beneficiaries of the employee under the plan for purposes of determining the distribution period under section 401(a)(9)(A)(ii). If, as of any date on or after the employee's required beginning date, a trust is named as a beneficiary of the employee and the requirements in paragraph (b) of this D-5 are not met, the employee will be treated as not having a designated beneficiary under the plan for purposes of section 401(a)(9)(A)(ii). Consequently, for calendar years beginning after that date, distribution must be made over the employee's life (or over the period which would have been the employee's remaining life expectancy determined as if no beneficiary had been designated as of the employee's required beginning date). [Amended by 63 FR 14391, March 25, 1998.]

(b) The requirements of this paragraph (b) are met if, as of the later of the date on which the trust is named as a beneficiary of the employee, or the employee's required beginning date, and as of all subsequent periods during which the trust is named as a beneficiary, the following requirements are met:

(1) The trust is a valid trust under state law, or would be but for the fact that there is no corpus.

(2) The trust is irrevocable or will, by its terms, become irrevocable upon the death of the employee.

(3) The beneficiaries of the trust who are beneficiaries with respect to the trust's interest in the employee's benefit are identifiable from the trust instrument within the meaning of D-2 of this section.

(4) The documentation described in D-7 of this section has been provided to the plan administrator.

(c) In the case of payments to a trust having more than one beneficiary, see E-5 of this section for the rules for determining the designated

beneficiary whose life expectancy will be used to determine the distribution period. If the beneficiary of the trust named as beneficiary is another trust, the beneficiaries of the other trust will be treated as having been designated as beneficiaries of the employee under the plan for purposes of determining the distribution period under section 401(a)(9)(A)(ii), provided that the requirements of paragraph (b) of this D-5 are satisfied with respect to such other trust in addition to the trust named as beneficiary. [Amended by 63 FR 14391, March 25, 1998.]

D-6. Q. If a trust is named as a beneficiary of an employee, will the beneficiaries of the trust with respect to the trust's interest in the employee's benefit be treated as designated beneficiaries under the plan with respect to the employee for purposes of determining the distribution period under section 401(a)(9)(B)(iii) and (iv)?

A. (a) If a trust is named as a beneficiary of an employee and the requirements of paragraph (b) of D-5 of this section are satisfied as of the date of the employee's death or, in the case of the documentation described in D-7 of this section, by the end of the ninth month beginning after the employee's date of death, then distributions to the trust for purposes of section 401(a)(9) will be treated as being paid to the appropriate beneficiary of the trust with respect to the trust's interest in the employee's benefit, and all beneficiaries of the trust with respect to the trust's interest in the employee's benefit will be treated as designated beneficiaries of the employee under the plan for purposes of determining the distribution period under section 401(a)(9)(B)(iii) and (iv). If the beneficiary of the trust named as beneficiary is another trust, the beneficiaries of the other trust will be treated as having been designated as beneficiaries of the employee under the plan for purposes of determining the distribution period under section 401(a)(9)(B)(iii) and (iv), provided that the requirements of paragraph (b) of D-5 of this section are satisfied with respect to such other trust in addition to the trust named as beneficiary. If a trust is named as a beneficiary of an employee and if the requirements of paragraph (b) of D-5 of this section are not satisfied as of the dates specified in the first sentence of this paragraph, the employee will be treated as not having a designated beneficiary under the plan. Consequently, distribution must be made in accordance with the five-year rule in section 401(a)(9)(B)(ii). [Amended by 63 FR 14391, March 25, 1998.]

(b) The rules of D-5 of this section and this D-6 also apply for purposes of applying the provisions of section 401(a)(9)(B)(iv)(II) if a trust is named as a beneficiary of the employee's surviving spouse. In the case of payments to a trust having more than one beneficiary, see E-5 of this section for the rules for determining the designated beneficiary whose life expectancy will be used to determine the distribution period.

D-7. Q. If a trust is named as a beneficiary of an employee, what documentation must be provided to the plan administrator so that the beneficiaries of the trust who are beneficiaries with respect to the trust's interest in the employee's benefit are identifiable to the plan administrator?

A. (a) *Required distributions commencing before death.* In order to satisfy the requirement of paragraph (b)(4) of D-5 of this section for distributions required under section 401(a)(9) to commence before the death of an employee, the employee must comply with either paragraph (a)(1) or (2) of this D-7:

(1) The employee provides to the plan administrator a copy of the trust instrument and agrees that if the trust instrument is amended at any time in the future, the employee will, within a reasonable time, provide to the plan administrator a copy of each such amendment.

(2) The employee—

(i) Provides to the plan administrator a list of all of the beneficiaries of the trust (including contingent and remainderman beneficiaries with a description of the conditions on their entitlement);

(ii) Certifies that, to the best of the employee's knowledge, this list is correct and complete and that the requirements of paragraphs (b)(1), (2), and (3) of D-5 of this section are satisfied;

(iii) Agrees to provide corrected certifications to the extent that an amendment changes any information previously certified; and

(iv) Agrees to provide a copy of the trust instrument to the plan administrator upon demand. [Amended by 63 FR 14391, March 25, 1998.]

(b) *Required distributions after death.* In order to satisfy the documentation requirement of this D-7 for required distributions after death, by the end of the ninth month beginning after the death of the employee, the trustee of the trust must either

(1) Provide the plan administrator with a final list of all of the beneficiaries of the trust (including contingent and remainderman beneficiaries with a description of the conditions on their entitlement) as of the date of death; certify that, to the best of the trustee's knowledge, this list is correct and complete and that the requirements of paragraph (b)(1), (2), and (3) of D-5 of this section are satisfied as of the date of death; and agree to provide a copy of the trust instrument to the plan administrator upon demand; or

(2) Provide the plan administrator with a copy of the actual trust document for the trust that is named as a beneficiary of the employee under the plan as of the employee's date of death. [Amended by 63 FR 14391, March 25, 1998.]

(c) *Relief for discrepancy between trust instrument and employee certifications or earlier trust instruments.* (1) If required distributions are determined based on the information provided to the plan administrator in certifications or trust instruments described in paragraph (a)(1), (a)(2) or (b) of this D-7, a plan will not fail to satisfy section 401(a)(9) merely because the actual terms of the trust instrument are inconsistent with the information in those certifications or trust instruments previously provided to the plan administrator, but only if the plan administrator reasonably relied on the information provided and the

minimum required distributions for calendar years after the calendar year in which the discrepancy is discovered are determined based on the actual terms of the trust instrument. For purposes of determining whether the plan satisfies section 401(a)(9) for calendar years after the calendar year in which the discrepancy is discovered, if the actual beneficiaries under the trust instrument are different from the beneficiaries previously certified or listed in the trust instrument previously provided to the plan administrator, or the trust instrument specifying the actual beneficiaries does not satisfy the other requirements of paragraph (b) of D-5 of this section, the minimum required distribution will be determined by treating the beneficiaries of the employee as having been changed in the calendar year in which the discrepancy was discovered to conform to the corrected information and by applying the change in beneficiary provisions of E-5 of this section.

(2) For purposes of determining the amount of the excise tax under section 4974, the minimum required distribution is determined for any year based on the actual terms of the trust in effect during the year. [Amended by 63 FR 14391, March 25, 1998.]

*****

Michael P. Dolan

Deputy Commissioner of Internal Revenue

[¶ 20,163 Reserved.—Proposed regulations on defined benefit plans for self-employed individuals and shareholder-employees formerly were reproduced at this paragraph. The final regulations appear at ¶ 11,720C and 11,729—11,729E.]

[¶ 20,163A Reserved.—Proposed regulations relating to the limitations on deductions and adjustments to earnings and profits with respect to certain foreign deferred compensation plans formerly were reproduced at this paragraph. These proposals were withdrawn by the IRS on May 9, 1993 (57 FR 27219) and replaced by new proposed regulations which appear at ¶ 20,162A.]

¶ 20,163B

Proposed regulations: Required distribution rules: Qualified plans: IRAs: Tax-sheltered annuities: Custodial accounts: Retirement income accounts: Minimum distribution incidental benefit requirement.—Reproduced below is the text of proposed regulations relating to required distributions from qualified plans, individual retirement plans, Code Sec. 403(b) annuity contracts, custodial accounts, and retirement income accounts.

The proposed regulations were published in the *Federal Register* on July 27, 1987 (52 FR 28070). On December 30, 1997, the IRS issued proposed regulations, amending Q&As D-5 and D-6 and adding Q&A D-7 (see ¶ 20,162B).

DEPARTMENT OF THE TREASURY

Internal Revenue Service

[26 CFR Part 1]

[26 CFR Part 54]

[EE-113-82]

Required Distributions From Qualified Plans And Individual Retirement Plans Notice Of Proposed Rulemaking

AGENCY: Internal Revenue Service, Treasury.

ACTION: Notice of proposed rulemaking.

SUMMARY: This document contains proposed regulations relating to required distributions from qualified plans, individual retirement plans, and section 403(b) annuity contracts, custodial accounts, and retirement income accounts. Changes to the applicable tax law were made by the Tax Reform Act of 1986, the Tax Reform Act of 1984 and the Tax Equity and Fiscal Responsibility Act of 1982. These regulations will provide the public with guidance necessary to comply with the law and will affect administrators of, participants in, and beneficiaries of qualified plans; institutions which sponsor and individuals who administer individual retirement plans, individuals who use individual retirement plans and simplified employee pensions for retirement income and beneficiaries of individual retirement plans; and employees for whom accounts are contributed to section 403(b) annuity contracts, custodial accounts, or retirement income accounts and beneficiaries of such contracts and accounts.

DATES: Written comments and requests for a public hearing must be delivered or mailed by September 25, 1987. These amendments generally apply to calendar years beginning after December 31, 1984, except as otherwise specified in the applicable Act.

ADDRESS: Send comments and requests for a public hearing to: Commissioner of Internal Revenue, Attention: CC:LR:T (EE-113-82) Washington, D.C. 20224.

FOR FURTHER INFORMATION CONTACT: Marjorie Hoffman of the Employee Plans and Exempt Organizations Division, Office of the Chief Counsel, Internal Revenue Service, 111 Constitution Avenue,

N.W., Washington, D.C. 20224 (Attention: CC:LR:T) (202-566-3903) (not a toll-free number).

SUPPLEMENTARY INFORMATION:

Background

This document contains proposed amendments to the Income Tax Regulations (26 CFR Part 1) and to the Pension Excise Taxes Regulations (26 CFR Part 54) under sections 401, 403, 408, and 4974 of the Internal Revenue Code of 1986. These amendments are proposed to conform the regulations to sections 1121 and 1852 of the Tax Reform Act of 1986 (TRA of 1986) (100 Stat. 2464 and 2864), sections 521 and 713 of the Tax Reform Act of 1984 (TRA of 1984) (98 Stat. 865 and 955), and sections 242 and 243 of the Tax Equity and Fiscal Responsibility Act of 1982 (TEFRA) (96 Stat. 521).

Description of Distribution Rules

The basic principles of these regulations are illustrated by the following description of the rules for distributions made from an individual retirement account before the IRA owner's death. (Special rules in the regulations apply to distributions made after the IRA owner's death.) A distribution must be made for the year in which the IRA owner attains age 70 ½ (the 70 ½ year) and for each year thereafter. Essentially, the minimum distribution for each year is determined by dividing the account balance by the lesser of the applicable life expectancy or the applicable divisor. All calculations are based on calendar years.

The minimum distribution for the 70 ½ year must be made by April 1 of the following year. A further distribution must be made by December 31 of each year after the 70 ½ year. Thus, if no distribution is made in the calendar year in which the IRA owner attains age 70 ½, distributions for two years must be calculated and made in the year after the 70 ½ year (one by April 1 and one by December 31).

In general, the account balance used to determine the minimum distribution for a calendar year is the account balance as of the close of business on the last day of the previous calendar year. The account balance as of the close of business on the last day of the calendar year preceding the 70 ½ year is therefore used to determine the minimum distribution that must be made for the 70 ½ year, even if the actual distribution is made in the year following the 70 ½ year. However, if the distribution for the 70 ½ year is deferred until the first quarter of the subsequent year (January 1 through April 1), the account balance used to determine the second minimum distribution that must be made in that year is calculated by subtracting from the account balance as of the close of business on the last day of the 70 ½ year any distribution made in the first quarter of the subsequent year in order to satisfy the minimum distribution requirement for the 70 ½ year.

The applicable divisor is the divisor under the table in Q&A-4 of 1.401(a)(9)-2 used for purposes of satisfying the minimum distribution incidental benefit requirement. If the IRA has only one beneficiary other than the IRA owner, the applicable life expectancy is the joint life and last survivor expectancy of the IRA owner and the beneficiary. To determine this life expectancy, the first step is to determine the ages of the IRA owner and beneficiary as of their attained ages on their birthdays in the 70 ½ year. The individual's life expectancy may or may not be recalculated. If life expectancy is not recalculated, the applicable life expectancy for years after the 70 ½ year is the initial joint life and last survivor expectancy reduced by one for each subsequent calendar year.

If life expectancy is recalculated, the method of recalculation depends on whether the beneficiary is the IRA owner's spouse. If the spouse is the beneficiary, the applicable life expectancy for each year subsequent to the 70 ½ year is the joint life and last survivor expectancy of the IRA owner and spouse based on their attained ages on their birthdays in each subsequent year. If the beneficiary is not the IRA owner's spouse, the method of recalculation is explained in Question and Answer E-8 of § 1.401(a)(9)-1 and the examples therein. Also, as explained in Question and Answer E-8, if either life expectancy is being recalculated, distributions may be accelerated upon the death of the individual whose life expectancy is being recalculated.

In general, the rules applicable to minimum distributions from qualified plans are identical to those for IRAs. However, the employee's benefit under the plan is used in place of the account balance as of December 31 of the preceding calendar year. As explained in Question and Answer F-5 of § 1.401(a)(9)-1, the benefit is valued as of the last valuation date in the previous calendar year and is adjusted for contributions and forfeitures allocated and distributions made after that date.

The regulations also contain rules for special situations that affect the amount of the required minimum distribution from an IRA or a qualified plan, examples of which are the following:

1. *Multiple beneficiaries and changes in beneficiaries.* See Question and Answer E-5 of § 1.401(a)(9)-1.

2. *Death of the IRA owner (or employee) after the date distributions are required to commence.* See Questions and Answers B-4 through B-6 of § 1.401(a)(9)-1.

3. *Death of the IRA owner (or employee) before the date on which distributions are required to commence.* See Questions and Answers C-1 through C-6 of § 1.401(a)(9)-1.

4. *Distribution in the form of an annuity.* See Questions and Answers F-3 and F-4 of § 1.401(a)(9)-1.

5. *A trust being named as a beneficiary.* See Questions and Answers D-5 and D-6 of § 1.401(a)(9)-1.

6. *Rollovers or transfers from one IRA (or plan) to another.* See Questions and Answers G-1 through G-5 of § 1.401(a)(9)-1.

7. *A division of the benefit (or IRA) into separate accounts with or without different beneficiaries for each account.* See Questions and Answers H-1 through H-2A of § 1.401(a)(9)-1.

8. *A portion of an employee's benefit being payable to an alternate payee pursuant to a qualified domestic relations order.* See Question and Answer H-4 of § 1.401(a)(9)-1.

Simplification of Required Distribution Rules

The Service is concerned that the regulations implementing the required distribution rules for qualified plans, IRAs, and tax-sheltered annuity contracts not cause practitioners, plan and IRA administrators, and taxpayers unnecessary difficulty. These statutory rules reflect an important policy objective. However, due to the inherent difficulty of the statutory rules, we believe that these regulations should provide as certain and simple rules as possible. In the preparation of these proposed regulations, the Service reviewed all available materials to identify issues that required resolution. The proposed regulations thus address as many of these issues as possible. Furthermore, the proposed regulations attempt to simplify compliance with the required distribution rules in several ways (e.g., by integrating the incidental benefit distribution requirement into the required distribution rules and by providing two alternative methods for calculating the distribu-

tions for 1985 and 1986 that must be made by the end of 1987). These efforts have added to the length of the proposed regulations, but should provide administrators and taxpayers with important certainty as to the requirements and thus should simplify compliance with the statutory rules.

Because of the time that many administrators will need to implement the required distributions rules, it is important that practitioners, administrators, and taxpayers provide the Service with comments on the proposed regulations at the earliest possible time. In particular, the Service specifically requests that comments consider further simplification to the rules contained in the proposed regulations, including alternative methods of complying with the statutory rules (including administrative safe harbors, particularly for IRAs). The Service will promptly review any comments and proposed alternatives so that any necessary modifications to these regulations applicable for 1987 can be announced well in advance of the end of 1987.

Transition Rules

Transition rules for determining the amounts of the minimum distributions required for qualified plans and IRAs for calendar years 1985, 1986, and 1987 are contained in Questions and Answers I-1 through I-15 of § 1.401(a)(9)-1 and Questions and Answers B-1 through B-11 of § 1.408-8. In accordance with Notice 86-14, 1986-48 IRB 10, these transition rules provide that minimum distributions for calendar years 1985 and 1986 are not required to be made from qualified plans and IRAs until December 31, 1987.

Incidental Benefit Requirement

Section 401(a)(9)(G), added by section 1852 of TRA of 1986 and effective for years after 1984, provides that distributions must be made in accordance with the incidental benefit requirements in order to satisfy section 401(a)(9). Section 403(b)(10), as added, and section 408(a)(6) and (b)(3), as amended by section 1852 of TRA of 1986, provide that requirements similar to the incidental benefit requirements of section 401(a) apply to annuity contracts, custodial accounts, and retirement income accounts described in section 403(b) and to IRAs.

Section 1.401(a)(9)-2 provides rules for satisfying the minimum distribution incidental benefit requirement (MDIB requirement). § 1.401(a)-1 is proposed to be amended to incorporate the provisions of § 1.401(a)(9)-2 and the existing incidental benefit requirement in § 1.401-1(b)(1)(i) and (ii). For calendar years before 1989, the rules in existing revenue rulings continue to apply for purposes of determining whether distributions satisfy the MDIB requirement. For calendar year after 1988, revised MDIB requirements apply for purposes of determining whether distributions satisfy this requirement. For calendar years before 1989, the MDIB requirement will also be satisfied if distributions are made in accordance with the revised requirements.

The revised requirements provide objective rules for determining whether the amount distributed for a calendar year satisfies the MDIB requirement. These revised requirements have been developed to be integrated with the other minimum distribution requirements in section 401(a)(9). Consequently, taxpayers can apply both of these requirements, which are designed to work together, to determine on an annual basis whether plan distributions for a year are acceptable. The example in Question and Answer F-3A of 1.401(a)(9)-1 illustrate how these requirements work together.

Essentially, the revised rules provide that, where the spouse is not the designated beneficiary, the amount of the payments to be made to the employee before death must be determined in accordance with the principles of section 401(a)(9) using a hypothetical individual not more than 10 years younger than the employee as the employee's designated beneficiary. Where the distribution is in the form of a joint and survivor annuity, the revised rules were developed using an interest rate of eight percent. In general, if an employee's spouse is the employee's beneficiary, the MDIB requirement will be satisfied if distributions are made in accordance with section 401(a)(9), without regard to the MDIB requirement.

While these new objective rules are based on the principles in the existing rulings, they reach different results in certain cases. Thus, on an individual basis the operation of the new rules may require more or less to be distributed for a calendar year depending on the circumstances, such as the date the employee separated from service and the earliest retirement date under the plan.

Existing revenue rulings continue to provide guidance with respect to the application of the incidental benefit requirements to pre-retirement distributions in the form of permissible nonretirement benefits such as life, accident, or health insurance.

Amount to Be Distributed by the Required Beginning Date

As indicated above in the description of the distribution rules, the amount required to be distributed by an employee's or IRA owner's required beginning date is treated as the amount required to be distributed for the immediately preceding year, the year the employee or IRA owner attained age 70 ½ or retired, whichever is applicable. Under section 401(a)(9) as amended by TEFRA, distributions were required to commence by the end of the taxable year in which an employee either retired or attained age 70 ½. Under TRA of 1984, the date by which distribution must commence was extended to the April 1 of the calendar year following the calendar year in which the employee either attains age 70 ½ or retires. The required commencement date was not extended to the end of the calendar year following the calendar year in which the employee either attains age 70 ½ or retires. Thus, the extension to April 1 is merely an extension of the time to make the distribution previously required under TEFRA to be made by the end of the year in which the employee either attains age 70 ½ or retires. This extension was intended to solve the administrative problems that a plan would have faced if it were required to make a December 31 distribution to an employee who retires in December. There is no indication that the extension to April 1 for the first distribution was intended to provide a full additional year of tax deferral. Thus, the distribution for the calendar year after the employee attains age 70 ½ (or retires if applicable) must still be made by the end of that year.

When Distributions Have Begun in Accordance With Section 401(a)(9)(A)

Section 401(a)(9) provides different rules for determining the minimum distributions required after an employee's death depending on whether or not distributions have begun in accordance with section 401(a)(9) before the employee's death. Question and Answer B-5 of § 1.401(a)(9)-1 generally provides that distributions are not treated as having begun until the employee's required beginning date even though payments were made before that date. However, Question and Answer B-5 provides an exception for certain distributions in the form of an annuity which commence before the required beginning date.

This interpretation was adopted because it is more administrable than other possible interpretations and places the least burden on plan administrators. If another interpretation had been adopted, additional rules would be required to determine when distributions made before the required beginning date are in accordance with section 401(a)(9)(A)(ii), placing both a burden on plan administrators to conform earlier distributions to such rules and on the Service to administer the additional rules. Further other interpretations considered would have provided that distributions commencing under a distribution option before the required beginning date would be required to be made in accordance with section 401(a)(9) both before and after the required beginning date in order to satisfy section 401(a)(9). This interpretation would have reduced the flexibility in choosing benefit options which plans may provide to employees without violating section 401(a)(9).

Use of Unisex Annuity Tables

The unisex expected return multiples in Table V and VI of § 1.72-9 as amended by Treasury Decision 8115 published in the Federal Register on December 19, 1986 (51 F.R. 45690) must be used to compute life expectancies for purposes of determining required distribution under section 401(a)(9). Thus, these tables must be used for determining the amount of minimum distributions required for calendar years after 1984. The July 1, 1986 effective date, provided in Treasury Decision 8115 for using these tables does not apply to § 1.401(a)(9)-1.

Designated Beneficiaries

In general, designated beneficiaries who may be taken into account under section 401(a)(9) are limited to those individuals who are designated as beneficiaries under the plan. Question and Answer D-2 of § 1.401(a)(9)-1 further provides that a beneficiary under the plan is an individual who is entitled to a portion of an employee's benefit, contingent on the employee's death or another specified event. Thus, a distribution such as that described in Rev. Rul. 72-240, 1972-1 CB 108, will not satisfy section 401(a) unless the same individual is both the beneficiary under the plan and the person whose life is being used to measure the payment period under the survivor portion of the joint and survivor annuity.

Amendment of Qualified Plans

Although minimum distributions are required to be made from qualified plans under section 401(a)(9) in order to retain a plan's tax-qualified status for calendar years after 1984, a plan will not be disqualified solely because it is not amended for section 401(a)(9) and the regulations thereunder prior to the amendment period contained in section 1140 of TRA of 1986 if the plan amendments are adopted retroactively to the effective date of section 401(a)(9) and the regulations thereunder. See Question and Answer A-4 of § 1.401 (a)(9)-1. However, distributions must satisfy the distribution requirements in section 401(a)(9) and the regulations thereunder in operation beginning with calendar year 1985 notwithstanding the absence of plan provisions.

Amendment of IRAs

In general, the minimum distribution rules in section 401(a)(9) and § 1.401(a)(9)-1 will apply to IRAs, beginning with calendar year 1985. The minimum distribution incidental benefit requirement in § 1.401(a)(9)-2 will apply to distributions from IRAs, beginning with calendar year 1989. The trust instrument or custodial agreement for an IRA with a favorable opinion letter need not be amended to provide the distribution rules in section 408(a)(6) and (b)(3) and these regulations until the later of December 31, 1988, or such time as the Commissioner prescribes. See Question and Answer B-5 of § 1.408-8. (The date prescribed by the Commissioner will be established after the Service has published sample language for IRAs, including IRAs used for funding simplified employee pensions (SEPs), that, if adopted, will satisfy section 408(a)(6) and (b)(3).) Existing IRAs or newly established IRAs, established by executing Form 5305 or Form 5305A, may be the current (Rev. 11-83) editions of those forms until such time as the Commissioner prescribes. An IRA which does not have a favorable opinion letter and which is not established by executing Form 5305 or Form 5305A will satisfy 408(a)(6) and 408(b)(3) until the date as of which IRAs with a favorable opinion letter must be amended if such IRA contains the statutory provisions in section 401(a)(9) applicable to IRAs. Notwithstanding the absence of trust provisions, Question and Answer B-5 of § 1.408-8 provides that distributions must satisfy the additional distribution requirements in 1.408-8 in operation.

Reliance on these Proposed Regulations

Taxpayers may rely on these proposed regulations for guidance pending the issuance of final regulations. Because these regulations are generally effective for calendar years after 1984, the Service will apply the questions and answers in these proposed regulations in issuing determination letters, opinion letters, and other rulings and in auditing returns with respect to taxpayers and plans. If future guidance is more restrictive, such guidance will be applied without retroactive effect.

PART 1—[AMENDED]

Index for Proposed Regulations

The following index is provided to assist taxpayers in using these proposed regulations.

§ 54.4974-2. Excise tax on accumulations in qualified retirement plans.

Special Analyses

The Commissioner of Internal Revenue has determined that this proposed rule is not a major rule as defined in Executive Order 12291 and that a regulatory impact analysis is not required.

Although this document is a notice of proposed rulemaking which solicits public comments, the Internal Revenue Service has concluded that the regulations proposed herein are interpretative and that the notice and public procedure requirements of 5 U. S. C. 553 do not apply. Accordingly, these proposed regulations do not constitute regulations subject to the Regulatory Flexibility Act (5 U. S. C. chapter 6).

Comments And Request For A Public Hearing

Before adopting these proposed regulations, consideration will be given to any written comments that are submitted (preferably eight copies) to the Commissioner of Internal Revenue. All comments will be available for public inspection and copying. A public hearing will be held upon written request to the Commissioner by any person who has submitted comments. If a public hearing is held, notice of the time and place will be published in the Federal Register. The collection of information requirements contained herein have been submitted to the Office of Management and Budget (OMB) for review under section 3504(h) of the Paperwork Reduction Act. Comments on the requirements should be sent to the Office of Information and Regulatory Affairs, of OMB, Attention: Desk Officer for Internal Revenue Service, New Executive Office Building, Washington, D. C. 20503. The Internal Revenue Service requests persons submitting copies of the comments to OMB also to send copies of the comments to the Service.

Drafting Information

The principal author of these proposed regulations is Marjorie Hoffman of the Employee Plans and Exempt Organizations Division of the Office of Chief Counsel, Internal Revenue Service. However, personnel from other offices of the Internal Revenue Service and Treasury Department participated in developing the regulation, both on matters of substance and style.

LIST OF SUBJECTS IN

26 CFR 1.401-0-1.425-1

Income taxes, Employee benefit

plans, Pensions.

26 CFR Part 54

Excise taxes

Proposed amendments to the regulations

The proposed amendments to 26 CFR Parts 1 and 54 are as follows:

Income Tax Regulations

(26 CFR Part 1)

Paragraph 1. The authority citation for Part 1 is amended by adding the following citation:

Authority: 26 U.S.C. 7805 * * * Section 1.401(a)(9)-1 is also issued under 26 U. S. C. § § 401(a)(9), 408(a)(6), 408(b)(3), and 403(b)(10). Section 1.408-8 is also issued under 26 U.S.C. § § 408(a)(6) and 408(b)(3). Section 1.403(b)-2 is also issued under 26 U.S.C. 403(b)(10).

Par. 2. Section 1.401(a)-1 is amended by adding a new paragraph (c) to read as follows:

§ 1.401(a)-1 Post-ERISA qualified plans and qualified trusts; in general.

* * * * *

(c) *Incidental death benefit requirement.* In order for a pension, stock bonus, or profit-sharing plan to be a qualified plan under section 401(a), distributions under the plan must satisfy the incidental death benefit requirement. Section 1.401-1(b)(1), a pre-ERISA regulation, and § 1.401(a)(9)-2 provide rules applicable to this requirement.

Par. 3. There are added § § 1.401(a)(9)-1 and 1.401(a)(9)-2 after § 1.401(a)-2 to read as follows:

§ 1.401(a)(9)-1 Required distributions from trusts and plans.

The following questions and answers relate to the distribution rules for qualified plans provided in section 401(a)(9) of the Internal Revenue Code of 1986 and section 401(a)(9) of the Internal Revenue Code of 1954, as amended by section 521 of the Tax Reform Act of 1984 (Pub. L. 98-369) (TRA of 1984) and by section 1121 and 1852 of the Tax Reform Act of 1986 (TRA of 1986) (Pub. L. 99-514):

Table of Contents

A. In general.

B. Distributions commencing before an employee's death.

C. Distributions commencing after an employee's death.

D. Determination of the designated beneficiary.

E. Determination of life expectancy.

F. Determination of the amount which must be distributed each year.

G. Rollovers and transfers.

H. Special rules

I. Transitional rules.

J. Election under section 242(b)(2) of TEFRA.

A. *In General*

A-1. Q. What plans are subject to the new distributions rules in section 401(a)(9) of the Internal Revenue Code of 1986, as amended by section 521 of the Tax Reform Act of 1984, and by sections 1121 and 1852 of the Tax Reform Act of 1986, and the regulations thereunder?

A. All stock bonus, pension, and profit-sharing plans qualified under section 401(a) and annuity contracts described in section 403(a) are subject to the distribution rules in section 401(a)(9) of the Internal Revenue Code of 1986 and section 401(a)(9) of the Internal Revenue Code of 1954 as amended by section 521 of the Tax Reform Act of 1984 (TRA of 1984), and by sections 1121 and 1852 of the Tax Reform Act of 1986 (TRA of 1986) and the regulations thereunder. See § 1.403(b)-2 for the distribution rules applicable to annuity contracts or custodial accounts described in section 403(b), and see § 1.408-8 for the distribution rules applicable to individual retirement plans described in section 408. See also section 457(d)(2)(A) for distribution rules applicable to certain deferred compensation plans.

A-2. Q. Which employee account balances and benefits held under qualified trusts and plans are subject to the distribution rules of section 401(a)(9) of the Internal Revenue Code of 1986 and section 401(a)(9) of the Internal Revenue Code of 1954, as amended?

A. The distribution rules of section 401(a)(9) of the Internal Revenue Code of 1986 and 401(a)(9) of the Internal Revenue Code of 1954, as amended, apply to all account balances and benefits in existence on or after January 1, 1985. The new rules apply to such balances and benefits even though the employee has retired or died, or distributions have commenced prior to that time. However, section 521(e)(4) and (5) of TRA of 1984 provided delayed effective dates for governmental plans and plans maintained pursuant to collective bargaining agreements. Also see J-1 through J-5 concerning designations made pursuant to section 242(b)(5) of the Tax Equity and Fiscal Responsibility Act of 1982 (TEFRA).

A-3. Q. What specific provisions must a plan contain in order to satisfy section 401(a)(9)?

A. (a) *Required provisions.* In order to satisfy section 401(a)(9), the plan must include several written provisions reflecting section 401(a)(9). First, the plan must generally set forth the statutory rules of section 401(a)(9), including the incidental death benefit requirement in section 401 (a)(9)(G). Second, the plan must provide that distributions will be made in accordance with the regulations under section 401(a)(9), including § 1.401(a)(9)-2. The plan document must also provide that the provisions reflecting section 401(a)(9) override any distribution options in the plan inconsistent with section 401(a)(9). Finally, the plan must include any other provisions reflecting section 401(a)(9) as are prescribed by the Commissioner.

(b) *Optional provisions.* The plan may also include written provisions regarding any optional provisions governing plan distributions that do not conflict with section 401(a)(9) and the regulations thereunder.

(b) *Absence of optional provisions.* (1) Plan distributions will be required to be made under the default provisions set forth in this section unless the plan document contains optional provisions that override such default provisions. (2) For example, if distributions have not commenced to the employee at the time of the employee's death, distributions after the death of an employee are to be made automatically in accordance with the default provisions in C-4(a) unless the plan either (i) specifies in accordance with C-4(b) the method under which distributions will be made or (ii) provides for elections by the employee (or beneficiary) (in accordance with C-4(c)) and such elections are made by the employee or beneficiary. (3) Similarly, life expectancies of employees and spouses of employees automatically will be recalculated pursuant to E-7(a) unless the plan either (i) specifies in accordance with E-7(b) that life expectancies of employees and spouses of employees will not be calculated or (ii) provides for elections by the employee (or spouse) in accordance with E-7(c) (in which case life expectancy will not be recalculated if there is such an election or if a plan default provision so provides).

A-4. Q. When must plans be amended to satisfy section 401(a)(9) and how must they operate prior to such amendment?

A. (a) *Form requirements before 1989.* A plan will not be disqualified solely because it is not amended for section 401(a)(9) and the regulations thereunder prior to the end of the amendment period contained in section 1140 of TRA of 1986 if the plan amendments are adopted retroactively to the effective date of section 401(a)(9) and the regulations thereunder.

(b) *Operational requirements before 1989.* For plan years beginning in calendar years after 1984, a plan must satisfy section 401(a)(9) and the applicable regulations in operation in order to meet the qualification requirements of section 401(a). Therefore, distributions for calendar years after 1984 must be made in accordance with the provisions of section 401(a)(9) and the regulations thereunder notwithstanding any provisions of the plan to the contrary. For plan years before the plan year in which the plan is required to be amended pursuant to paragraph (a), the plan will not fail to satisfy either the requirement that a plan be operated in accordance with its terms or the requirement that a pension plan provide definitely determinable benefits (or the requirement that a profit-sharing plan provide a definite predetermined formula for distributing the funds accumulated under the plan) merely because distributions are made to comply with section 401(a)(9) and the regulations thereunder rather than in accordance with the terms of the plan.

(c) *Default provisions.* For calendar years ending in plan years before the plan year in which the plan is required to be amended pursuant to paragraph (a), notwithstanding A-3(b), a plan will not be subject to the default provisions in this section if benefits are distributed in accordance with this section in a reasonable and consistent manner. For example, for purposes of determining pursuant to C-4 whether the five-year rule in section 401(a)(9)(B)(ii) or the exception to the five-year rule in section 401(a)(9)(B)(iii) and (iv) applies, a plan does not have to make distributions in accordance with the default provisions in C-4(a) if the plan administrator establishes a consistent policy of either (1) distributing benefits under one method or the other or (2) distributing benefits pursuant to an election by an employee or beneficiary (or in the absence of an election under one method or the other). Similarly, for purposes of determining whether or not the life expectancies of an employee and the employee's spouse will be recalculated pursuant to section 401(a)(9)(D) and E-7, a plan does not have to recalculate life expectancies of employees or their spouses if the plan administrator establishes a policy of either not recalculating such life expectancies or of allowing elections by employees or spouses. In the latter case, a plan does not have to recalculate the employee or the employee's spouse's life expectancy if the employee or spouse elects not to recalculate life expectancy (or in the absence of an election, of not recalculating life expectancies). However, if a plan administrator adopts a policy of not distributing in accordance with one of the default provisions, when the plan is amended to comply with section 401(a)(9), the amendment must be consistent with the policy established.

A-5. Q. To what extent will a plan be treated as failing to satisfy the qualification requirements of section 401(a) if the plan in operation fails to make distributions in accordance with section 401(a)(9)?

A. A plan will not satisfy the qualification requirements of section 401(a) with respect to a plan year unless all distributions required under section 401(a)(9) are made for the calendar year ending with or within such plan year. Notwithstanding the preceding sentence, for plan years beginning after December 31, 1988, a plan will not fail to satisfy the qualification requirements of section 401(a) because there are isolated instances when the minimum distribution requirements of section 401(a)(9) are not satisfied in operation. However, a pattern or regular practice of failing to meet the minimum distribution requirements of section 401(a)(9) with respect to one or more employees will not be considered an isolated instance even if each instance is de minimis.

B. *Distributions commencing before an employee's death.*

B-1. Q. In the case of distributions before an employee's death, how must the employee's entire interest be distributed in order to satisfy section 401(a)(9)(A)?

A. (a) In order to satisfy section 401 (a)(9)(A), the entire interest of each employee (1) must be distributed to such employee not later than the required beginning date, or (2) must be distributed, beginning not later than the required beginning date, over the life of such employee or over the lives of such employee and the designated beneficiary (or over a period not extending beyond life expectancy of such employee or the joint life and last survivor expectancy of such employee and the designated beneficiary).

(b) See 13-2 and 13-3 for the definition of required beginning date. See D-1 through D-4 for the determination of the designated beneficiary of the employee. See E-1 and E-3 through E-8 for the rules for calculating the life expectancy of the employee (and the designated beneficiary). See F-1 through F-7 for the rules for determining the amount of the minimum distribution to be made each year.

B-2. Q. For purposes of section 401(a)(9)(C), what does the term "required beginning date" mean?

A. (a) For an employee who attains age 70 ½ after December 31, 1987 (i.e., age 70 after June 30, 1987), the term "required beginning date" means April 1 of the calendar year following the year in which the employee attains age 70 ½.

(b) For an employee who attains age 70 ½ before January 1, 1988 (i. e., age 70 before July 1, 1987) and is not a "5-percent owner" (as defined in paragraph (d)), the term "required beginning date" means April 1 of the calendar year following the later of (1) the calendar year in which the employee attains age 70 ½ or (2) the calendar year in which the employee retires.

(c) For an employee who attains age 70 ½ before January 1, 1988 and is a "5-percent owner" (as defined in paragraph (d)), the term "required beginning date" means April 1 of the calendar year following the later of (1) the calendar year in which the employee attains age 70 ½, or (2) the earlier of (i) the calendar year with or within which ends the plan year in which the employee becomes a "5-percent owner," or (ii) the calendar year in which the employee retires.

(d) (1) An employee is treated as a "5-percent owner" for purposes of this Q&A, if such employee is a "5-percent owner" (as defined in section 416(i)) at any time during the plan year ending with or within the calendar year in which such owner attains age 66 ½ or any subsequent plan year. Once an employee is described in this subparagraph, distributions must continue to such employee even if such employee ceases to own more than 5 percent of the employer in a subsequent year.

(2) The determination of whether or not an employee is a 5-percent owner will be made in accordance with section 416 but will be made without regard to whether the plan is top-heavy.

(3) An employee's required beginning date is determined under paragraph (c) if the employee is a 5-percent owner during any plan year beginning after December 31, 1979. For example, if an employee attains age 66 ½ within calendar year 1980 and is a 5-percent owner during the plan year ending within calendar year 1980, but is not a 5-percent owner at any time during any other plan year, the employee is considered a 5-percent owner and the employee's required beginning date is determined under paragraph (c) and this paragraph.

B-3. Q. When does an employee attain age 70 ½?

A. An employee attains age 70 ½ as of the date six months after the 70th anniversary of the employee's birth. For example, if an employee's date of birth was June 30, 1919, the 70th anniversary of such employee's birth is June 30, 1989. Such employee attains age 70 ½ on December 30, 1989. Consequently, such employee's required beginning date is April 1, 1990. However, if the employee's date of birth was July 1, 1919, the 70th anniversary of such employee's birth would be July 1, 1989. Such employee would then attain age 70 ½ on January 1, 1990.

B-3A. Q. Must distributions made before the employee's required beginning date satisfy section 401(a)(9)?

A. Lifetime distributions made before the employee's required beginning date for calendar years before the employee's first distribution calendar year, as defined in F-1, need not be made in accordance with section 401(a)(9). However, if distributions commence under a particular distribution option, such as in the form of an annuity, before the employee's required beginning date for the employee's first distribution calendar year, the distribution option will fail to satisfy section 401(a)(9) at the time distributions commence if, under the particular distribution option, distributions to be made for the employee's first distribution calendar year or any subsequent distribution calendar year will not satisfy section 401(a)(9).

B-4. Q. if distributions have begun to an employee before the employee's death (in accordance with section 401(a)(9)(A)(ii)), how must distributions be made after an employee's death?

A. Section 401(a)(9)(B)(i) provides that if the distribution of the employee's interest has begun in accordance with section 401(a)(9)(A)(ii) and the employee dies before his entire interest has been distributed to him, the remaining portion of such interest must be distributed at least as rapidly as under the distribution method being used under section 401(a)(9)(A)(ii) as of the date of his death. As explained further in D-3, in the case of distributions which began before the employee's death and which are being paid over the lives of the employee and a designated beneficiary (or over a period not exceeding the joint life and last survivor expectancy), the designated beneficiary whose life or life expectancy was being used to determine the period described in section 401(a)(9)(A)(ii) must be the beneficiary of such remaining portion unless otherwise provided in E-5.

B-5. Q. For purposes of section 401(a)(9)(B), when are distributions considered to have begun to the employee in accordance with section 401(a)(9)(A)(ii)?

A. (a) *General rule.* Except as provided in paragraph (b), distributions are treated as having begun to the employee in accordance with section 401(a)(9)(A)(ii) on the employee's required beginning date, even though payments may actually have been made before that date. For example, if employee A upon retirement in 1990 at age 65 ½ begins receiving installment distributions from a profit-sharing plan over a period not exceeding the joint life and last survivor expectancy of A and A's beneficiary, benefits are not treated as having begun in accordance with section 401(a)(9)(A)(ii) until April 1, 1996 (the April 1 following the calendar year in which A attains age 70 ½). Consequently, if such employee dies before April 1, 1996 (A's required beginning date), distributions to be made after A's death must be made in accordance with section 401(a)(9)(B)(ii) or (iii) and (iv). This is the case even though the plan has distributed the minimum distribution for the first distribution calendar year (as defined in F-1) before A's death.

(b) *Annuities.* If distributions irrevocably (except for acceleration) commence to an employee on a date before the employee's required beginning date over a period permitted under section 401(a)(9)(A)(ii) and the distribution form is an annuity under which distributions are made in accordance with the provisions of F-3 (and if applicable F-4), distributions will be considered to have begun on the actual commencement date in accordance with section 401(a)(9)(A)(ii) even if the employee dies before the employee's required beginning date. Thus,

pursuant to section 401(a)(9)(B)(i), after the employee's death, the remaining portion of the employee's interest must continue to be distributed at least as rapidly as under the method of distribution in effect as of the employee's date of death and the rules in section 401(a)(9)(B)(ii) or (iii) and (iv) do not apply. See D-3 and E-1 for special rules for determining the employee's designated beneficiary and for determining life expectancy.

(c) *Cross reference.* See F-3A for rules for satisfying the requirement that the employee's remaining interest be distributed at least as rapidly as under the method being used under section 401(a)(9)(A)(ii) as of the date of the employee's death.

C. *Distributions commencing after an employee's death.*

C-1. Q. In the case in which an employee dies before distributions are treated as having begun to the employee for purposes of section 401(a)(9)(A)(ii), how must the employee's entire interest be distributed in order to satisfy section 401(a)(9)?

A. (a) In the case in which an employee dies before distributions are treated as having begun to an employee in accordance with section 401(a)(9)(A)(ii), section 401(a)(9)(B) provides two methods for distributing the employee's interest. In order to satisfy section 401(a)(9), distributions must be made under one of these two methods. The first method (the five-year rule in section 401(a)(9)(B)(ii)) requires that the entire interest of the employee be distributed within 5 years of the employee's death regardless of to whom or to what entity the distribution is made. The second method (the exception to the five-year rule in section 401(a)(9)(B)(iii)) requires that any portion of an employee's interest which is payable to (or for the benefit of) a designated beneficiary be distributed, commencing within one year of the employee's death, over the life of such beneficiary (or over a period not extending beyond the life expectancy of such beneficiary). Section 401(a)(9)(B)(iv) provides special rules where the designated beneficiary is the surviving spouse of the employee, including a special commencement date for distribution under section 401(a)(9)(B)(iii) to the surviving spouse.

(b) See C-2 to determine when the five-year period in section 401(a)(9)(B)(ii) ends. See C-3 to determine when distribution under the exception to the five-year rule in section 401(a)(9)(13)(iii) and (iv) must commence. See C-4 for the rules for determining which of the methods described in paragraph (a) applies. See D-1, D-2, and D-4 in order to determine the designated beneficiary under section 401(a)((9)(B)(iii) and (iv). See E-2 through E-8 for the rules for calculating the designated beneficiary's life expectancy. See F-l through F-7 for the rules for determining the amount of the minimum distribution to be distributed each year.

C-2. Q. As of what date must the employee's entire interest be distributed in order to satisfy the five-year rule in section 401(a)(9)(B)(ii)?

A. In order to satisfy the five-year rule in section 401(a)(9)(B)(ii), the employee's entire interest must be distributed as of December 31 of the calendar year which contains the fifth anniversary of the date of the employee's death. For example, if an employee dies on January 1 1990, the entire interest must be distributed by December 31, 1995, in order to satisfy the five-year rule in section 401(a)(9)(B)(ii).

C-3. Q. When are distributions required to commence in order to satisfy the exception to the five-year rule in section 401(a)(9)(B)(iii) and (iv)?

A. (a) *Nonspousal beneficiary.* In order to satisfy the rule in section 401(a)(B)(iii) (the exception to the five-year rule for nonspouse beneficiaries), if the designated beneficiary is not the employee's surviving spouse, distributions must commence on or before December 31 of the calendar year immediately following the calendar year in which the employee died. This rule also applies to the distribution of the entire remaining benefit if, as of the employee's date of death, an individual is designated as a beneficiary in addition to the employee's surviving spouse. See H-2 and H-2A, however, if the employee's benefit is divided into separate accounts (or segregated shares, in the case of a defined benefit plan).

(b) *Spousal beneficiary.* In order to satisfy the rule in section 401(a)(9)(B)(iii) and (iv), if the designated beneficiary is the employee's surviving spouse, distributions must commence on or before the later of (1) December 31 of the calendar year immediately following the calendar year in which the employee died and (2) December 31 of the calendar year in which the employee would have attained age 70 ½.

C-4. Q. How is it determined whether the five-year rule in section 401(a)(9)(B)(ii) or the exception to the five-year rule in section 401(a)(9)(B)(iii) and (iv) applies to a distribution?

A. (a) *No plan provision.* If a plan does not adopt an optional provision specifying the methods of distribution after the death of an employee, distribution must be made as follows:

(1) In the case in which the surviving spouse of an employee is a beneficiary of the employee, distributions are to be made in accordance with the exception to the five-year rule in section 401(a)(9)(B)(iii) and (iv).

(2) In all other cases, distributions are to be made in accordance with the five-year rule in section 401(a)(9)(B)(ii).

(b) *Optional methods.* The plan may adopt a provision specifying which of the two methods apply to distributions after the death of an employee. For example, the plan may specify that distribution in every case will be made in accordance with the exception to the five-year rule in section 401(a)(9)(B) (iii) and (iv). Further, a plan need not have the same method of distribution for the benefits of all employees, e.g., a plan may have one method of distribution for benefits of employees whose beneficiaries are not surviving spouses and another method of distribution for the benefits of employees whose beneficiaries are surviving spouses, so long as there is a single method with respect to the benefit of each employee. (If an employee's benefit is divided into separate accounts, see H-2 and H-2A).

(c) *Employee Elections.* A plan may adopt a provision that permits employees (or beneficiaries) to elect on an individual basis whether the five-year rule in section 401(a)(9)(B)(ii) or the exception to the five-year rule in section 401(a)(9)(B)(iii) and (iv) applies to distributions. In operation, such an election must be made no later than the earlier of (1) December 31 of the calendar year in which distribution would be required to commence in order to satisfy the requirements for the exception to the five-year rule in section 401(a)(9)(B)(iii) and (iv) (see C-3 for the determination of such calendar year), or (2) December 31 of the calendar year which contains the fifth anniversary of the date of death of the employee. As of such date, the election must be irrevocable with respect to the beneficiary (and all subsequent beneficiaries) and must apply to all subsequent years. If a plan provides for elections, the plan may also specify, pursuant to paragraph (b), which method of distribution applies if neither the employee nor the beneficiary makes the election. If neither the employee nor the beneficiary elects a method and the plan does not specify which rule applies, distribution must be made in accordance with paragraph (a).

(d) *Other requirements.* A plan must satisfy other distribution requirements under the Code. For example, plan distributions must satisfy the survivor annuity requirements of sections 401(a)(11) and 417, except as otherwise provided in this section. These requirements may mandate a particular method of distribution to a surviving spouse. Any plan provision described in paragraphs (b) and (c), or method of distribution elected pursuant to paragraph (c), must satisfy these other distribution rules.

C-5. Q. If the employee's surviving spouse is the employee's designated beneficiary and such spouse dies after the employee, but before distributions have begun to the surviving spouse under section 401(a)(9)(B)(iii) and (iv), how is the employee's interest to be distributed?

A. Pursuant to section 401(a)(9)(B)(iv)(II), if the surviving spouse dies after the employee, but before distributions to such spouse have begun under section 401(a)(9)(B)(iii) and (iv), the five-year rule in section 401(a)(9)(B)(ii) and the exception to the five-year rule in section 401(a)(9)(B)(iii) are to be applied as if the surviving spouse were the employee. In applying this rule, the date of death of the surviving spouse shall be substituted for the date of death of the employee. However, in such case, the rules in section 401(a)(9)(B)(iv) are not available to the surviving spouse of the deceased employee's surviving spouse.

C-6. For purposes of section 401(a)(9)(B)(iv)(II), when are distributions considered to have begun to the surviving spouse?

A. (a) *General rule.* Except as otherwise provided in paragraph (b), distributions are considered to have begun to the surviving spouse of an employee, for purposes of section 401(a)(9)(B)(iv)(II), on the date, determined in accordance with C-3, on which distributions are required to commence to the surviving spouse, even though payments have actually been made before that date. See paragraph (b) for special rule for annuities.

(b) *Annuity.* If distributions commence irrevocably (except for acceleration) to the surviving spouse of an employee over a period permitted under section 401(a)(9)(B)(iii)(II) before the date on which distributions are required to commence and the distribution form is an annuity under which distributions are made as of the date distributions commence in accordance wit's the provisions of F-3 (and F-4 if applicable),

distributions will be considered to have begun on the actual commencement date for purposes of section 401(a)(9)(B)(iv)(II). Consequently, in such case, section 401(a)(9)(B)(ii) and (iii) will not apply upon the death of the surviving spouse as though the surviving spouse were the employee even if the spouse dies before the date, determined in accordance with C-3, on which distributions are required to commence to the surviving spouse. Instead, the annuity distributions must continue to be made, in accordance with the provisions of F-3 or F-4, at least as rapidly as under the method of distribution being used as of the date of the surviving spouse's death. The rules of F-3A shall apply in determining whether distributions are being made at least as rapidly as under the method of distribution being used as of the date of the surviving spouse's death.

D. *Determination of the designated beneficiary.*

D-1. Q. Must an employee (or the employee's spouse) make an affirmative election specifying a beneficiary for a person to be a designated beneficiary under section 401(a)(9)(E)?

A. No. A person's status as designated beneficiary is not dependent upon being selected by an employee (or by the employee's surviving spouse, in the case of certain distributions under section 401(a)(9)(B)(iv)(II)). Thus, for example, if the terms of the plan specify the beneficiary, then whoever is so specified is the designated beneficiary and is treated for purposes of section 401(a)(9) as having been designated by the employee (or the employee's surviving spouse). The choice of beneficiary is subject to the requirements of sections 401(a)(11), 414(p), and 417.

D-2. Q. May an individual who is not designated as a beneficiary under the plan be considered a designated beneficiary for purposes of determining the minimum distribution required under section 401(a)(9)?

A. (a)(1) Except to the extent provided in E-5 with respect to former beneficiaries, designated beneficiaries are only individuals who are designated as beneficiaries under the plan. An individual may be designated as a beneficiary under the plan either by the terms of the plan or, if the plan provides, by an affirmative election by the employee (or the employee's surviving spouse) specifying the beneficiary. A beneficiary designated as such under the plan is an individual who is entitled to a portion of an employee's benefit, contingent on the employee's death or another specified event. For example, if a distribution is in the form of a joint and survivor annuity over the life of the employee and another individual, the plan does not satisfy section 401(a)(9) unless such other individual is a designated beneficiary under the plan. A designated beneficiary need not be specified by name in the plan or by the employee to the plan in order to be a designated beneficiary so long as the individual who is to be the beneficiary is identifiable under the plan as of the employee's required beginning date, or as of the date of the employee's death (in the case of distributions governed by section 401(a)(9)(B)(iii) and (iv)), and at all subsequent times. The members of a class of beneficiaries capable of expansion or contraction will be treated as being identifiable if it is possible at the applicable time to identify the class member with the shortest life expectancy. The fact that an employee's interest under the plan passes to a certain individual under applicable state law does not make such individual a designated beneficiary unless such individual is designated as a beneficiary under the plan.

(2) This paragraph (a) is illustrated by the following example.

Example. Employee X attains age 70½ in calendar year 1990. As of April 1, 1991, X designates as his beneficiaries under the plan his spouse and his children. X does not specify them by name. Even though X did not specify his spouse and his children by name, they are identifiable based on their relationship to X as of his required beginning date. Further, it is irrelevant that additional children of X may be born after his required beginning date and thus that the class of beneficiaries is capable of expansion.

(b) See E-5 for the rules which apply if there is a change in beneficiaries under the plan with respect to an employee.

D-2A. Q. May a person other than an individual be considered to be a designated beneficiary for purposes of section 401(a)(9)?

A. (a) No. Only individuals may be designated beneficiaries for purposes of section 401(a)(9). A person who is not an individual, such as the employee's estate, may not be a designated beneficiary. However, see D-5 and D-6 for special rules which apply to trusts.

(b) Except as otherwise provided in D-5, D-6, and E-5(e)(1), if a person other than an individual is designated as a beneficiary of an employee's benefit, the employee will be treated as having no designated beneficiary for purposes of section 401(a)(9). In such case, distribution under section 401(a)(9)(A)(ii) must be made over the employee's life or over a period not exceeding the employee's life expectancy. Further, in such case, if upon the employee's death section 401(a)(9)(B)(i) does not apply, distribution must be made in accordance with the 5-year rule in section 401(a)(9)(B)(ii).

D-3. Q. For purposes of calculating the distribution period described in section 401(a)(9)(A)(ii) (for distributions before death), when is the designated beneficiary determined?

A. (a) *General rule required beginning date.* For purposes of calculating the distribution period described in section 401(a)(9)(A)(ii) (for distributions before death), except as otherwise provided in paragraphs (b) through (d), the designated beneficiary will be determined as of the employee's required beginning date. If, as of that date, there is no designated beneficiary under the plan to receive the employee's benefit upon the employee's death, the distribution period described in section 401(a)(9)(A)(ii) is limited to the employee's life (or a period not extending beyond the employee's life expectancy). (If there is a beneficiary (other than a beneficiary whose rights are contingent on the death of another beneficiary) who is not designated in accordance with D-2, there is deemed to be no designated beneficiary for purposes of section 401(a)(9)(A)(ii).)

(b) *Exception for first distribution year.* Except to the extent that B-5(b) is applicable, if a designated beneficiary is added or replaces another designated beneficiary during the calendar year in which the employee's required beginning date occurs, but on or before the employee's required beginning date (January 1 through April 1 of such calendar year), the designated beneficiary of the employee for purposes of calculating the minimum distribution for the employee's first distribution calendar year (as defined in F-1) may be determined as of any date after December 31 of the employee's first distribution calendar year and before the employee's required beginning date. Thus, e.g., for purposes of determining the minimum distribution for the employee's first distribution calendar year, either designated beneficiary may be used to determine the joint life and last survivor expectancy of the employee and designated beneficiary. However, for purposes of determining the minimum distribution for subsequent distribution calendar years (including the distribution calendar year in which the employee's required beginning date occurs), the designated beneficiary will be determined as of the employee's required beginning date.

(c) *Annuity form.* If annuity payments commence to an employee (either on or before the employee's required beginning date), the employee's designated beneficiary may be determined as of any date during the 90 days before the date on which the annuity payments commence.

(d) *Multiple and substitute beneficiaries.* Notwithstanding anything in this D-3 to the contrary, the rules in E-5 apply if more than one beneficiary is designated with respect to an employee as of the applicable date (in paragraphs (a), (b), or (c)), on which the employee's designated beneficiary is determined or if a beneficiary is added or replaces another beneficiary (due to death or any other reason) after such date.

D-4. Q. For purposes of calculating the distribution period described in section 401(a)(9)(B)(iii) or (iv) (for distributions beginning after death in accordance with the exception to the five-year rule), when is the designated beneficiary determined?

A. (a) *Employee.* Except as provided in paragraph (b), for purposes of calculating the distribution period described in section 401(a)(9)(B)(iii) or (iv), the designated beneficiary will be determined as of the employee's date of death. If, as of the date of the employee's death, there is no designated beneficiary under the plan with respect to that employee, distribution must be made in accordance with the five-year rule in section 401(a)(9)(B)(ii). (If there is a beneficiary (other than a beneficiary whose rights are contingent on the death of another beneficiary) who is not designated in accordance with D-2, there is deemed to be no designated beneficiary for purposes of section 401(a)(9)(B)(iii) and (iv).)

(b) *Surviving spouse.* As provided in C-5, in the case in which the employee's spouse is the designated beneficiary as of the date of the employee's death for distributions under section 401(a)(9)(B)(iii) and the surviving spouse dies after the employee and before the date on which distributions have begun to the spouse under section 401(a)(9)(B)(iii) and (iv), the rule in section 401(a)(9)(B)(iv)(II) will apply. Thus the relevant designated beneficiary for determining the distribution period is the designated beneficiary of the surviving spouse. Such designated beneficiary will be determined as of the surviving spouse's date of death (rather than the employee's date of death). If, as of the date of the surviving spouse's death, there is no designated beneficiary under the plan with respect to that surviving spouse, distribution must be made in accordance with the 5-year rule in

section 401(a)(9)(B)(ii). (If there is a beneficiary (other than a beneficiary whose rights are contingent on the death of another beneficiary) who is not designated in accordance with D-2, there is deemed to be no designated beneficiary for purposes of section 401(a)(9)(B)(iii).)

(c) *Multiple beneficiaries.* Notwithstanding anything in this D-4 to the contrary, the rules in E-5 apply if more than one beneficiary is designated with respect to an employee as of the date determined in accordance with paragraphs (a) and (b) on which the designated beneficiary is to be determined.

D-5. Q. In the case in which a trust is named as a beneficiary of an employee, are the beneficiaries of the trust with respect to the trust's interest in the employee's benefit treated as having been designated as beneficiaries of the employee under the plan for purposes of determining the distribution period under section 401(a)(9)(A)(ii)?

A. (a) In the case in which a trust is named as a beneficiary of an employee, all beneficiaries of the trust with respect to the trust's interest in the employee's benefit are treated as having been designated as beneficiaries of the employee under the plan for purposes of determining the distribution period under section 401(a)(9)(A)(ii) if, as of the later of the date on which the trust is named as a beneficiary of the employee, or the employee's required beginning date, and as of all subsequent periods during which the trust is named as a beneficiary, the following requirements are met.

(1) The trust is a valid trust under state law, or would be but for the fact that there is no corpus.

(2) The trust is irrevocable.

(3) The beneficiaries of the trust who are beneficiaries with respect to the trust's interest in the employee's benefit are identifiable from the trust instrument within the meaning of D-2.

(4) A copy of the trust instrument is provided to the plan.

(b) Pursuant to D-2A, only an individual may be a designated beneficiary. Consequently, a trust itself may not be the designated beneficiary even though the trust is named as a beneficiary. However, if the requirements in paragraph (a) are met, for purposes of section 401(a)(9), distributions made to the trust will be treated as paid to the beneficiaries of the trust with respect to the trust's interest in the employee's benefit. If, as of any date on or after the employee's required beginning date, a trust is named as a beneficiary of the employee and the requirements in paragraph (a) are not met, the employee will be treated as not having a designated beneficiary under the plan for purposes of section 401(a)(9)(A)(ii). Consequently, for calendar years subsequent to such date, distribution must be made over the employee's life (or over the period which would have been the employee's remaining life expectancy determined as if no beneficiary had been designated as of the employee's required beginning date). In the case of payments to a trust having more than one beneficiary, see E-5 for the rules for determining the designated beneficiary whose life expectancy will be used to determine the distribution period.

D-6. Q. In the case in which a trust is named as a beneficiary of an employee, are beneficiaries of the trust with respect to the trust's interest in the employee's benefit treated as designated beneficiaries under the plan with respect to the employee for purposes of determining the distribution period under section 401(a)(9)(B)(iii) and (iv)?

A. (a) In the case in which a trust is named as a beneficiary of an employee, all beneficiaries of the trust with respect to the trust's interest in the employee's benefit are treated as designated beneficiaries of the employee under the plan for purposes of determining the distribution period under section 401(a)(9)(B)(iii) and (iv) if the requirements in paragraph (a) of D-5 are satisfied as of the date of the employee's death. If the requirements in paragraph (a) of D-5 are satisfied as of the date of the employee's death, distributions to the trust for purposes of section 401(a)(9) will be treated as being paid to the appropriate beneficiary of the trust with respect to the trust's interest in the employee's benefit. However, if a trust is named as a beneficiary of an employee and if, as of the date of the employee's death, the requirements of D-5 are not satisfied, the employee will be treated as not having a designated beneficiary under the plan. Consequently, distribution must be made in accordance with the five-year rule in section 401(a)(9)(B)(ii).

(b) The rules of D-5 and this D-6 also apply for purposes of applying the provisions of section 401(a)(9)(B)(iv)(II) if a trust is named as a beneficiary of the employee's surviving spouse.

E. Determination of life expectancy.

E-1. Q. For required distributions under section 401(a)(9)(A), what age (or ages) is used to calculate the employee's life expectancy (or the joint life and last survivor expectancy of the employee and a designated beneficiary)?

A. (a) Except as otherwise provided in paragraph (b), for required distributions under section 401(a)(9)(A), life expectancies are calculated using the employee's (and the designated beneficiary's) attained age as of the employee's birthday (and the designated beneficiary's birthday) in the calendar year in which the employee attains age 70 ½. If life expectancy is being recalculated pursuant to E-6 through E-8, the life expectancy of the employee or spouse (or the joint life and last survivor expectancy of the employee and spouse) will be recalculated using the employee's (and the spouse's) attained age as of the employee's birthday (and the surviving spouse's birthday) in each succeeding calendar year in which recalculation is provided for purposes of calculating the minimum distribution for that distribution calendar year.

(b) If, pursuant to B-2(b), an employee's required beginning date is April 1 of the calendar year following the calendar year in which the employee retires or becomes a 5-percent owner, such calendar year is substituted in paragraph (a) for the calendar year in which the employee attains age 70 ½.

(c) If, in accordance with B-5(b), annuity payments commence to an employee before the employee's required beginning date, the calendar year in which the annuity payments commence is substituted in paragraph (a) for the calendar year in which the employee attains age 70 ½.

E-2. Q. In the case of any distribution under section 401(a)(9)(B)(iii) and (iv) what age is used to calculate the beneficiary's life expectancy?

A. (a) In the case of any distribution under section 401(a)(9)(B)(iii) and (iv), the life expectancy of any designated beneficiary is calculated based on the beneficiary's attained age as of the beneficiary's birthday in the calendar year in which distributions are required to commence to such beneficiary in order to satisfy section 401(a)(9)(B)(iii) and (iv). For example, if an unmarried participant (A) dies at age 50 on January 31, 1987, A's designated beneficiary is A's brother (B), and B will receive A's interest over B's life expectancy, the date on which distributions are required to commence to B in order to satisfy section 401(a)(9)(B)(iii) is December 31, 1988 (see C-3). Therefore, B's life expectancy is calculated based on B's attained age as of B's birthday in calendar year 1988. This rule also applies to a designated beneficiary of a surviving spouse where such surviving spouse is treated as the employee for purposes of applying section 401(a)(9)(B)(iii). If the life expectancy of the surviving spouse is being recalculated pursuant to E-6 through E-8, the life expectancy of the surviving spouse will be recalculated using the surviving spouse's attained age as the surviving spouse's birthday in each succeeding calendar year in which recalculation is provided, for purposes of calculating the minimum distribution for that distribution calendar year.

(b) If distribution under section 401(a)(9)(B)(iii) and (iv) commences irrevocably (except for acceleration) over a period described in section 401(a)(9)(B)(iii)(II) in a calendar year prior to the calendar year in which distributions are required to commence and distribution is an annuity under which distributions are made in accordance with the provisions of F-3 (and if applicable F-4), the designated beneficiary's life expectancy (where applicable) is based on the designated beneficiary's attained age as of the designated beneficiary's birthday in the calendar year in which distribution commences.

(c) If a designated beneficiary of the employee, other than the employee's surviving spouse, dies after the employee but before the designated beneficiary's birthday in the calendar year in which life expectancy is determined under paragraphs (a) and (b), such beneficiary will be treated as being alive on such date for purposes of calculating the designated beneficiary's life expectancy. (See C-5 for the special rule which applies if the surviving spouse lies after the employee but before the date on which distributions have begun to the surviving spouse.)

E-3 & 4. Q. What life expectancies must be used for purposes of determining required distributions under section 401(a)(9)?

A. Life expectancies for purposes of determining required distributions under section 401(a)(9) must be computed by use of the expected return multiples in Tables V and VI of § 1.72-9.

E-5. Q. If an employee has more than one designated beneficiary or if a designated beneficiary is added or replaces another designated beneficiary after the date for determining the designated beneficiary, which designated beneficiary's life expectancy will be used to determine the distribution period?

A. (a) *General rule.* (1) Except as otherwise provided in paragraph (f), if more than one individual is designated as a beneficiary with respect to an employee as of the applicable date for determining the designated beneficiary, the designated beneficiary with the shortest life expectancy will be the designated beneficiary for purposes of determining the distribution period. However, except as otherwise provided in D-5, D-6, and paragraph (e)(1) of this E-5, if a person other than an individual is designated as a beneficiary, the employee will be treated as not having any designated beneficiaries for purposes of section 401(a)(9) even if there are also individuals designated as beneficiaries. The date for determining the designated beneficiary (under D-3 or D-4, whichever is applicable) is the applicable date. The period described in section 401(a)(9)(A)(ii) (for distributions commencing before the employee's death) or section 401(a)(9)(B)(iii) (for distributions over a life expectancy commencing after the employee's death), whichever is applicable, is the distribution period.

(2) See H-2 for special rules which apply if an employee's benefit under a plan is divided into separate accounts (or segregated shares in the case of a defined benefit plan) and the beneficiaries with respect to a separate account differ from the beneficiaries of another separate account.

(b) *Contingent beneficiary.* Except as provided in paragraph (e)(1), if a beneficiary's entitlement to an employee's benefit is contingent on an event other than the employee's death (e.g., death of another beneficiary), such contingent beneficiary is considered to be a designated beneficiary for purposes of determining which designated beneficiary has the shortest life expectancy under paragraph (a).

(c) *New beneficiary.* (1) Except as provided in paragraph (e)(2) (in the case of the death of a beneficiary), if, after the applicable date for determining the designated beneficiary, a new designated beneficiary with a life expectancy shorter than the life expectancy of the designated beneficiary whose life expectancy is being used to determined [*sic*] the distribution period is added or replaces a designated beneficiary, the new designated beneficiary is treated as the designated beneficiary for purposes of determining the distribution period. In such case, the new beneficiary's life expectancy will be used to calculate the distribution period in subsequent calendar years. In determining the beneficiary with the shorter life expectancy, the life expectancies will be calculated as of the applicable birthdays in the calendar year specified in and in the manner provided in E-1 through E-4. Consequently, the old distribution period must be replaced by a new distribution period. The new distribution period equals the period which would have been the remaining joint life and last survivor expectancy of the employee and the designated beneficiary if the new designated beneficiary had been designated as of the applicable date. If, instead, the new designated beneficiary has a life expectancy longer than the life expectancy of the designated beneficiary whose life expectancy is being used to determine the distribution period, the life expectancy of the old designated beneficiary will continue to be used for purposes of determining the distribution period even though such old designated beneficiary is no longer a beneficiary under the plan.

(2) If a new beneficiary who is not an individual is added or replaces a designated beneficiary after the applicable date, unless otherwise provided in D-5 and D-6, the employee will be treated as not having designated a beneficiary. Further, except as provided in paragraph (e)(2) in the case of the death of a designated beneficiary, if at any point in time after the applicable date there is no beneficiary designated with respect to the employee, the employee will also be treated as not having a designated beneficiary. In either case, the new distribution period described in subparagraph (1) will equal the period which would have been the employee's remaining life expectancy if no beneficiary had been designated as of the applicable date.

(3) Any adjustment described in this paragraph will only affect distributions for calendar years after the calendar year in which the new designated beneficiary is added or replaces the prior beneficiary, or there is no beneficiary designated with respect to the employee.

(d) *Recalculation for spouse.* For purposes of determining the distribution period in accordance with paragraph (a) or (c)(1), if any designated beneficiary involved is the employee's spouse and the life expectancy of the spouse is being recalculated, the life expectancy of the spouse as recalculated will be compared in each calendar year to the remaining life expectancy of the other applicable designated beneficiary or beneficiaries, not recalculated, and the shortest life expectancy will be used for determining the minimum distribution required for that calendar year.

(e) *Death contingency.* (1) If a beneficiary's entitlement to an employee's benefit is contingent on the death of a prior beneficiary, such contingent beneficiary will not be considered a beneficiary for purposes of determining who is the designated beneficiary with the shortest life expectancy under paragraph (a) or whether a beneficiary who is not an individual is a beneficiary. This rule does not apply if the death occurs prior to the applicable date for determining the designated beneficiary.

(2) If the designated beneficiary whose life expectancy is being used to calculate the distribution period dies on or after the applicable date, such beneficiary's remaining life expectancy will be used to determine the distribution period whether or not a beneficiary with a shorter life expectancy receives the benefits. However, in accordance with E-8, if the designated beneficiary is the employee's spouse, the spouse's life expectancy is being recalculated, and the spouse dies, the spouse does not have any remaining life expectancy; therefore, in the calendar year following the spouse's death, the spouse's life expectancy will be reduced to zero.

(3) This paragraph is illustrated by the following example:

Example. The designated beneficiary of an unmarried participant (X) as of X's required beginning date on April 1, 1988, is X's sister (A), but X has specified that, in the event of A's death, X's brother (B) will become the beneficiary. A's life expectancy as of A's birthday in calendar year 1987 is 25 years. B's life expectancy as of B's birthday in calendar year 1987 is 10 years. On X's required beginning date, A is the designated beneficiary because B entitlement to benefits is contingent on A's death. A dies on May 1, 1988. A's remaining life expectancy will continue to be used to determine the distribution period with respect to X for purposes of determining the minimum distribution for the 1988 distribution calendar year and each succeeding distribution calendar year. This is true even though, upon A's death, B will become X's beneficiary and B's life expectancy as of B's birthday in calendar year 1987 is shorter than A's life expectancy as of A's birthday in that calendar year. However, if B's entitlement was not contingent on A's death but was contingent for another reason, B would be the designated beneficiary for purposes of determining the period described in section 401(a)(9)(A)(ii), even during the period in which his entitlement is contingent, because B's life expectancy, as of B's birthday in calendar year 1987, is shorter than A's life expectancy, as of A's birthday in that calendar year.

(f) *Designations by beneficiaries.* If the plan provides (or allows the employee to specify) that, after the employee's death any person or persons have the discretion to change the beneficiaries of the employee, then, for purposes of determining the distribution period for both distributions before and after the employee's death, the employee will be treated as not having designated a beneficiary. However, such discretion will not be found to exist merely because the employee's surviving spouse may designate a beneficiary for distributions pursuant to section 401(a)(9)(B)(iv)(II).

E-6. Q. After life expectancy has been determined as of the date provided in E-1 or E-2, may life expectancy be recalculated?

A. Pursuant to section 401(a)(9)(D), after life expectancy has been determined as of the date provided in E-1 and E-2, life expectancy of an employee and the employee's spouse (other than in the case of a life annuity) may be recalculated in accordance with E-7 and E-8 but not more frequently than annually.

E-7. Q. How is it determined whether or not the life expectancies of the employee and the employee's spouse will be recalculated pursuant to section 401(a)(9)(D)?

A. (a) If the plan does not adopt an optional provision specifying whether life expectancies will be determined with or without regard to the permissive recalculation rule of section 401(a)(9)(D) and the employee or spouse has not made an election pursuant to paragraph (c), the life expectancy of the employee or spouse (or the joint life and last survivor expectancy of the employee and spouse) must be recalculated annually as provided in section 401(a)(9)(D) for purposes of determining all distributions required under section 401(a)(9).

(b) The plan may adopt a provision specifying whether life expectancies will be determined with or without regard to the permissive recalculation rule of section 401(a)(9)(D). The life expectancy of the employee may be recalculated even though the life expectancy of the spouse is not recalculated and, correspondingly, the life expectancy of the spouse may be recalculated even though the life expectancy of the employee is not recalculated.

(c) The plan may adopt a provision that permits the employee (or spouse, in the case of distributions described in section 401(a)(9)(B)(iii) and (iv)) to elect the applicability or inapplicability of section 401(a)(9)(D). If such election is permitted, the employee (or spouse) must elect whether or not life expectancy will be recalculated no later than the time of the first required distribution under section 401(a)(9). As of the date of the first required distribution under section 401(a)(9), a method (either recalculation of life expectancy or no recalculation of life expectancy) which is in effect with respect to an employee (or spouse) must be irrevocable with respect to the employee (or spouse) and must apply to all subsequent years. The plan

may specify, pursuant to paragraph (b), whether or not life expectancy will be recalculated in the event that the employee (or spouse) fails to make the election. Absent such a plan provision, the life expectancy of the employee (and the spouse) must be recalculated annually pursuant to paragraph (a) in the event that the employee (or spouse) fails to make the election.

E-8 Q. How are life expectancies recalculated annually under section 401(a)(9)(D)?

A. (a) An employee's life expectancy (or the joint life and last survivor expectancy of the employee and spouse) is recalculated annually by redetermining the employee's life expectancy (or the joint life and last survivor expectancy of the employee and spouse) in each distribution calendar year using the employee's (and spouse's) attained age as of the employee's birthday (and the spouse's birthday) in that distribution calendar year. Upon the death of the employee (or the employee's spouse), the recalculated life expectancy of the employee (or the employee's spouse) will be reduced to zero in the calendar year following the calendar year of death. In any calendar year in which the last applicable life expectancy is reduced to zero, the plan must distribute the employee's entire remaining interest prior to the last day of such year in order to satisfy section 401(a)(9).

(b) If the designated beneficiary is not the employee's spouse (or if the spouse's life expectancy is not being recalculated) and the life expectancy of the employee is being recalculated annually, the applicable life expectancy for determining the minimum distribution for each distribution calendar year will be determined by recalculating the employee's life expectancy but not recalculating the beneficiary's life expectancy. Such applicable life expectancy is the joint life and last survivor expectancy using the employee's attained age as of the employee's birthday in the distribution calendar year and an adjusted age of the designated beneficiary. The adjusted age of the designated beneficiary is determined as follows: First, the beneficiary's applicable life expectancy is calculated based on the beneficiary's attained age as of the beneficiary's birthday in the calendar year described in E-1, reduced by one for each calendar year which has elapsed since that calendar year. The age (rounded if necessary to the higher age) in Table V of § 1.72-9 is then located which corresponds to the designated beneficiary's applicable life expectancy. Such age is the adjusted age of the designated beneficiary. As provided in paragraph (a), upon the death of the employee, the life expectancy of the employee is reduced to zero in the calendar year following the calendar year of the employee's death. Thus, for determining the minimum distribution for such calendar year and subsequent calendar years, the applicable life expectancy is the applicable life expectancy of the designated beneficiary determined under this paragraph.

(c) This Question and Answer is illustrated by the following examples:

Example 1. (a) A participant in a qualified profit-sharing plan retires on January 1, 1987. The benefit for determining the 1987 calendar year minimum distribution (determined in accordance with F-5) is $100,000. As of the participant's birthday in calendar year 1987, the participant, who was born December 31, 1916 is age 71. The participant's spouse died some years earlier and the participant designates his brother as his sole beneficiary on his retirement date and his brother is still designated as his sole beneficiary as of April 1, 1988. As of his brother's birthday in calendar year 1987, his brother, who was born on July 2, 1920, is age 67. The plan does not provide that life expectancies will not be recalculated and does not permit employees to elect not to recalculate life expectancy. Thus, pursuant to E-7(a), the life expectancy of the participant will be recalculated.

(b) For calendar year 1987, the payment that is to be made pursuant to section 401(a)(9) is the benefit of $100,000 divided by the joint and last survivor life expectancy of the participant and his brother calculated using their ages as of their birthdays in calendar year 1987. Pursuant to Table VI of § 1.72-9, such joint life and last survivor expectancy is 21.7 years. The payment required for 1987 is therefore $4,608.30 ($100,000 divided by 21.7). $4,608.30 is distributed on April 1, 1988.

(c) The benefit for determining the 1988 minimum distribution (determined in accordance with F-5) before adjustment for the distribution on April 1, 1987 is $109,515.71. The amount of the minimum distribution for 1988 distributed on April 1, 1988 is then subtracted from that amount. (109,515.71 − 4,608.30 = 104,907.41.) Thus, $104,907.41 is the benefit to be used to determine the 1988 minimum distribution. The minimum payment for 1988 is determined by dividing the benefit of $104,907.41 by a recalculated joint life and last survivor expectancy of the participant and his brother. Such joint life and last survivor expectancy is recalculated as follows:

(1)	Life expectancy of brother (using age as of birthday in calendar year 1987, from Table V of § 1.72-9)	=	18.4	years
(2)	Number of years elapsed since calendar year 1987	=	1	year
(3)	Remaining period of life expectancy of brother, (1) – (2)	=	17.4	years
(4)	Age in Table V of § 1.72-9 corresponding to life expectancy of 17.4 years (rounding to higher age)	=	69	
(5)	Age of participant (age determined as of birthday in calendar year 1988)	=	72	
(6)	Joint life and last survivor expectancy using the age in (4) and (5) from Table VI of § 1.72-9	=	20.3	

The minimum payment for 1988 is therefore $5,167.85 ($104,907.41 divided by 20.3). This must be paid by December 31, 1988, to the participant.

(d) The benefit for determining the 1989 minimum distribution (determined in accordance with F-5) is $109,714.00. The minimum payment for 1989 is determined by dividing the benefit of $109,714.00 by the recalculated joint life and last survivor expectancy of the participant and his brother; such joint life and last survivor expectancy is recalculated as follows:

(1)	Life expectancy of brother (using age as of birthday in calendar year 1987 from Table V of § 1.72-9)	=	18.4	years
(2)	Number of years elapsed since 1987	=	2	years
(3)	Remaining period of life expectancy of brother (1) – (2) .	=	16.4	years
(4)	Age in Table V of § 1.72-9 corresponding to life expectancy of 16.4 years rounding to higher age)	=	70	
(5)	Age of participant (age determined using age as of birthday in calendar year 1989)	=	73	
(6)	Joint life and last survivor expectancy using the ages in (4) and (5) from Table VI of § 1.72-9 years	=	19.4	

The minimum payment for 1989 is therefor $5,655.36 ($109,714.00 divided by 19A). This must be paid by December 31, 1989, to the participant.

Example 2. Assume the same facts as in Example 1, except that the participant dies in 1988 after the participant's required beginning date. The recalculation of life expectancy for the participant and the calculation of the minimum payment for 1988 will be the same as in Example 1. The participant's life expectancy is not reduced to zero until the calendar year following the year of death. The calculation of the minimum payment for 1989 is as follows:

(1)	Life expectancy of brother (using age as of birthday in calendar year 1988 from Table V of § 1.79-9)	=	18.4 years
(2)	Number of elapsed years since 1987	=	2 years
(3)	Remaining period, (1) – (2)	=	16.4 years
(4)	Benefit for determining 1989 minimum distribution . . .	=	$109,714.00
(5)	Minimum payment for 1989, (4) divided by (3)	=	$ 6,689.88

Example 3. Assume the same facts in Example 1, except the brother (rather than the participant) dies in 1988 after the participant's required beginning date. The redetermination of life expectancy for the participant and the calculation of the minimum payment for 1988 and 1989 will be the same as in Example 1; the brother's life expectancy was fixed at the time benefits commenced and is used even after the brother dies.

F. *Determination of the amount which must be distributed each year.*

F-1. Q. If an employee's benefit is in the form of an individual account, what is the amount required to be distributed for each calendar year in the case of either (1) distributions to an employee before death over a period described in section 401(a)(9)(A)(ii) or (2) to a beneficiary after the employee's death over a period described in section 401(a)(9)(B)(iii)?

A. (a) *General rule.* If an employee's benefit is in the form of an individual account and is to be distributed over (1) a period not extending beyond the life expectancy of the employee or the joint life and last survivor expectancy of the employee and the designated beneficiary (as described in section 401(a)(9)(A)(ii)) or (2) over a period not extending beyond the life expectancy of the designated beneficiary (as described in section 401(a)(9)(B)(iii)), the amount required to be distributed for each calendar year, beginning with the first calendar year for which distributions are required and then for each succeeding calendar year, must at least equal the quotient obtained by dividing the employee's benefit by the applicable life expectancy. The minimum amount which is required to be distributed on or before an employee's required beginning date is always determined under this F-1 and not section 401(a)(9)(A)(i). The amount described in section 401(a)(9)(A)(i) will always exceed the amount determined under this F-1. See paragraph (e) for purchases of annuity contracts. Also, see F-4A and Q&A-4 of § 1.401(a)(9)-2 for additional limits under the minimum distribution incidental benefit requirement on the divisor which must be used to determine the minimum required distribution.

(b) *Distribution calendar year.* A calendar year for which a minimum distribution is required is a distribution calendar year. The first calendar year for which a distribution is required is an employee's first distribution calendar year. In the case of distributions required before death under section 401(a)(9)(A), if an employee's required beginning date is April 1 of the calendar year following the calendar year in which the employee attains age 70 ½, the employee's first distribution calendar year is the year the employee attains age 70 ½. However, if, pursuant to B-2(b), an employee's required beginning date is April 1 of the calendar year following the calendar year in which the employee retires or becomes a 5-percent owner, the calendar year in which the employee retires or becomes a 5-percent owner is the employee's first distribution calendar year. In the case of distributions to be made in accordance with the exception to the five-year rule in section 401(a)(9)(B)(iii) and (iv), the first distribution calendar year is the calendar year containing the date described in C-3(a) or C-3(b), whichever is applicable.

(c) *Time for distributions.* The distribution required to be made on or before the employee's required beginning date shall be treated as the distribution required for the employee's first distribution calendar year (as defined in paragraph (b)). The minimum distribution for other distribution calendar years, including the minimum distribution for the distribution calendar year in which the employee's required beginning date occurs, must be made on or before December 31 of that distribution calendar year.

(d) *Life expectancy.* The applicable life expectancy is the life expectancy (or joint life and last survivor expectancy) determined in accordance with E-1 through E-5, reduced by one for each calendar year which has elapsed since the date on which the life expectancy (or joint and last survivor expectancy) was calculated. However, pursuant to E-6 through E-8, life expectancy is recalculated, the applicable life expectancy will be the life expectancy as so recalculated.

(e) *Annuity contracts.* (1) Instead of satisfying F-1, the minimum distribution requirement may be satisfied by purchase with the employee's benefit of an annuity contract from an insurance company in accordance with F-4. Only a purchase of an annuity contract will insure that distribution can be made over the employee's or a beneficiary's life, or joint lives if applicable.

(2) If an annuity is purchased on or before the date when distributions are required to commence (the required beginning date, in the case of distributions before death, or the date determined under C-3, in the case of distributions after death), distribution under the annuity contract purchased will satisfy section 401(a)(9) if payments under the annuity contract are made in accordance with F-3.

(3) As explained in F-3A(b) with reference to distributions after death which must be made at least as rapidly as under the method used under section 401(a)(9)(A)(ii), unless life expectancy is being recalculated, if the annuity contract is purchased after the date on which distributions are required to commence, the annuity contract purchased may not be a life annuity and must be payable for a term certain not exceeding the remaining applicable life expectancy. The remaining applicable life expectancy is the applicable life expectancy described in paragraph (d) which would have been used, if the annuity contract had not been purchased, to determine the minimum distribution in accordance with paragraphs (a) through (c) for the first distribution calendar year in which the annuity contract is purchased.

(4) If the annuity contract is purchased after the date on which distributions are required to commence and life expectancy is being recalculated, distribution under the contract will satisfy section 401(a)(9) if the contract is a life annuity payable either (i) over the life (or lives) of the individual (or individuals) whose life expectancy is being recalculated (with or without a period certain that meets the requirements of subparagraph (3)) or (ii) for a term certain determined under subparagraph (3).

(5) If an annuity is purchased on or after the employee's required beginning date with a period certain feature, the period certain may not be lengthened after the date of the initial purchase by exchanging the annuity contract for an annuity contract with a longer period certain even if the original period certain was shorter than the maximum permitted.

F-2. Q. If an employee's benefit is in the form of an individual account and in any calendar year the amount distributed exceeds the minimum required, will credit be given in subsequent years for such excess distribution?

A. If, in any calendar year, the amount distributed exceeds the minimum required, no credit will be given in subsequent years for such excess distribution. However, in the case in which the employee's first distribution calendar year is the calendar year immediately preceding the employee's required beginning date, amounts distributed in the employee's first distribution calendar year will be credited toward the distribution required to be made on or before the employee's required beginning date for the employee's first distribution calendar year.

F-3. Q. How must annuity distributions under a defined benefit plan be paid in order to satisfy section 401(a)(9)?

A. (a) In order to satisfy section 401(a)(9), annuity distributions under a defined benefit plan must be paid in periodic payments made at intervals not longer than one year (payment intervals) for a life (or lives), or over a period certain not longer than a life expectancy (or joint life and last survivor expectancy) described in section 401(a)(9)(A)(ii) or section 401(a)(9)(B)(iii), whichever is applicable. The life expectancy (or joint life and last survivor expectancy) for purposes of determining the length of the period certain will be determined in accordance with E-1 through E-5, without recalculation of life expectancy. Once payments have commenced over a period certain, the period certain may not be lengthened even if the period certain is shorter than the maximum permitted. Payments must be either nonincreasing or increase only as follows:

(1) With any percentage increase in a specified and generally recognized cost-of-living index,

(2) To the extent of the reduction in the amount of the employee's payments to provide for a survivor benefit upon death, but only if the beneficiary whose life was being used to determine the period described in section 401(a)(9)(A)(ii) over which payments were being made dies and the payments continue otherwise in accordance with that section over the life of the employee,

(3) To provide cash refunds of employee contributions upon the employee's death, or

(4) Because of an increase in benefits under the plan. Also see FAA for additional requirements for distributions in the form of an annuity which must be satisfied in order for the distribution to satisfy the minimum distribution incidental benefit. If distribution is permitted to be made over the lives of the employee and the designated beneficiary, references to a life annuity herein include a joint and survivor annuity for purposes of section 401(a)(9).

(b) The annuity may be a life annuity with a period certain if the life (or lives, if applicable) and period certain each meet the requirements of paragraph (a).

(c) Distributions under a variable life annuity (or a life annuity with a period certain) will not be found to be increasing merely because the amount of the payments vary with the investment performance of the underlying assets. However, the Commissioner may prescribe additional requirements applicable to such variable life annuities.

(d)(1) If the annuity is a life annuity (or a life annuity with a period certain not exceeding 20 years), the following rule will apply. The first payment which must be made on or before the employee's required beginning date must be the payment which is required for one payment interval. The second payment need not be made until the end of the next payment interval even if that payment interval ends in the next calendar year. Similarly, in the case of distributions commencing after death in accordance with section 401(a)(9)(B)(iii) and (iv), the first payment that must be made on or before the date determined under C-3(a) or (b) (whichever is applicable) must be the payment which is required for one payment interval. Payment intervals are the periods for which payments are received, e.g., bimonthly, monthly, semi-annually, or annually.

(2) If the annuity is a period certain annuity without a life contingency (or is a life annuity with a period certain exceeding 20 years), periodic payments for each distribution calendar year (as defined in F-1(b)) will be combined and treated as an annual amount. Such annual amount must meet the requirements of paragraph (a). The amount which is required to be distributed on or before the employee's required beginning date is the annual amount for the employee's first distribution calendar year (as defined in F-1(b)). The annual amount for other distribution calendar years, including the annual amount which is for the calendar year in which the employee's required beginning date occurs, must be distributed on or before December 31 of the calendar year for which the distribution is required. Similarly, in the case of such distributions commencing after death in accordance with section 401(a)(9)(B)(iii) and (iv), the amount which is required to be distributed on or before the date determined under C-3(a) or (b), whichever is applicable, is the annual amount for the beneficiary's first distribution calendar year.

(3) This paragraph is illustrated by the following examples:

Example (1). A defined benefit plan (Plan X) provides monthly annuity payments of $500 for the life of unmarried participants with a 10 year period certain. An unmarried participant (A) in the plan (Z) attains age 70 ½ in 1990. In order to meet the requirements of this paragraph, the first payment which must be made on or before April 1, 1991 will be $500 and the payments must continue to be made in monthly payments of $500 thereafter for the life and 10 year certain period.

Example (2). The facts are the same as in *Example (1),* except that the annuity is an optional form of payment elected by Z which provides for annuity payments of $700 a month for a 10 year period certain, without a life contingency. In such case, in order to meet the requirements of this paragraph, the monthly payments of $700 a month for each calendar year will be combined and treated as an annual amount of $8,400 a year. On or before April 1, 1987, Z must be paid $8,400, the annual amount for 1986. The annual amount for calendar year 1987 of $8,400 must be distributed on or before December 31, 1987.

(e) If distributions from a defined benefit plan are not in the form of an annuity, the employee's benefit will be treated as an individual account for purposes of determining the minimum distribution. See F-1 to determine the minimum distribution if distribution is being made over life expectancy.

F-3A. Q. How must distributions be made after the employee's death in order to be considered to satisfy the requirement that the employee's remaining interest be distributed at least as rapidly as under the distribution method being used under section 401(a)(9)(A)(ii) as of the date of the employee's death?

A: (a) *General rule.* After the employee's death, the requirement that the employee's remaining interest be distributed at least as rapidly as under the method of distribution being used under section 401(a)(9)(A)(ii) as of the date of the employee's death will be considered to be satisfied if the employee's remaining interest is distributed in accordance with either paragraph (b) or (c).

(b) *Individual account—General rule.* (1) Except as otherwise provided in subparagraph (2), if the employee's benefit is in the form of an individual account and, as of the date of the employee's death, distributions had commenced in accordance with F-1, the employee's remaining interest must continue to be distributed in accordance with F-1. If, before the employee's death, the divisor being used to determine the amount which was required to be distributed was the applicable divisor pursuant to Q&A4 of §1.401(a)(9)-2 rather than the applicable life expectancy determined under F-1, the required distributions after the employee's death may be determined without regard to §1.401(a)(9)-2 using the applicable life expectancy determined under F-1 as the relevant divisor.

(2) *Purchased annuity contract.* (i) The employee's remaining interest will be treated as distributed in accordance with F-1 if it (A) is distributed under an immediate annuity contract that makes payments for a period certain that satisfy F-3 and (B) is purchased at any time with the employee's remaining benefits. The period over which the annuity contract makes payments may not exceed the applicable life expectancy that would have been used to determine the minimum distribution under F-1 for the distribution calendar year in which the annuity is purchased (purchase year). Further, in the purchase year, the amount distributed (when combined with amounts distributed in the purchase year before the immediate annuity contract is purchased) must equal (or exceed) the lesser of (C) the amount required to be distributed for such purchase year under F-1 or (D) the amount of the annual amount for the purchase year determined under F-3(d)(2). If the employee's life expectancy is being recalculated in the purchase year, the applicable life expectancy is the life expectancy (or joint life and last survivor expectancy) as recalculated, in accordance with E-8, after the employee's death.

(ii) If the designated beneficiary is the surviving spouse and the spouse's life expectancy is being recalculated, the annuity contract must satisfy (i) except that it may be a life annuity (with or without a period certain) payable over the remaining life of the surviving spouse.

(c) *Existing annuity.* If, as of the date of the employee's death, the employee's benefit was being distributed as an annuity in accordance with F-3 (and F-4, if applicable), annuity distribution of the employee's remaining benefit must continue to be made (except for acceleration) in accordance with F-3 (and F-4, if applicable) for the remainder of the period under the annuity as of the date of the employee's death.

(d) *Examples.* This F-3A is illustrated by the following examples:

Example (1). (a) An employee (X) was born February 1, 1919. His required beginning date is April 1, 1990. As permitted by the plan, he elects not to recalculate life expectancy. Pursuant to E-1, life expectancy is determined using X's and X's designated beneficiary's attained ages as of their birthdays in calendar year 1989. The joint life and last survivor expectancy using such ages is 22 years under Table VI of §1.72-9. X dies on January 1, 1991 after receiving his minimum distribution from X's account for calendar year 1989 on April 1, 1990, and his minimum distribution from X's account for calendar year 1990 on December 31, 1990. His remaining benefit, determined in accordance with F-5, for purposes of determining the minimum distribution for calendar year 1991 is $20,000. Distribution of his benefit, after his death, must continue to be distributed in accordance with F-1 over the remaining 20 years of the joint life and last survivor expectancy of X and X's designated beneficiary. The minimum distribution for calendar year 1989 is $1,000 ($20,000 divided by 20).

(b) Alternatively, in calendar year 1991, the plan may distribute to X's designated beneficiary an immediate annuity contract purchased with X's remaining benefit which makes payments for a term certain not exceeding 20 years provided that the payments satisfy F-3. Assuming no amount is distributed in 1991 prior to the distribution of the annuity contract, the amount paid under the annuity contract in 1991 must equal or exceed the lesser of (1) $1,000 or (2) the annual amount payable under the annuity contract. If instead of purchasing an annuity in 1991 the plan distributed the $1,000 minimum distribution for calendar year to X's designated beneficiary, the plan may still distribute an immediate annuity in calendar year 1992. However, in such case, any period certain under the annuity contract must be for no more than 19 years.

Example (2). The facts are the same as in *Example (1)* except that Plan B is a defined benefit plan. On April 1, 1990, annuity distributions commence to X under a life annuity for the life of X with a 10 year term certain. After X's death the annuity distributions must continue to be made over the remaining years in the 10 year certain period even though the term certain originally could have been for 22 years and still have satisfied section 401(a)(9)(A)(ii).

F-4. Q. May distributions be made from an annuity contract which is purchased from an insurance company?

A. Yes. Distributions may be made from an annuity contract which is purchased by the plan from an insurance company with the employee's benefit and which makes payments that satisfy the provisions of F-3. However, if the payments actually made under the annuity contract do not meet the requirements of section 401(a)(9), the plan fails to satisfy section 401(a)(9).

F-4A. Q. Must distributions be made in accordance with the minimum distribution incidental benefit requirement under §1.401(a)(9)-2 in order to satisfy section 401(a)(9)?

A. Yes. Section 401(a)(9)(G) provides that any distribution required under the incidental benefit requirements of section 401(a) shall be treated as a distribution required under section 401(a)(9). Consequently, in order to satisfy section 401(a)(9), distributions must be made in accordance with minimum distribution incidental benefit requirement (MDIB requirement) in §1.401(a)(9)-2 in addition to the minimum distribution requirements in this §1.401(a)(9)-1.

(b) This Question and Answer is illustrated by the following example.

Example

(a) Employee (X) is a participant in a qualified profit-sharing plan (Plan A). Plan A provides that life expectancies are not recalculated. X, born December 1, 1918 is age 71 as of his birthday in the calendar year he attains age 70 ½. As of April 1, 1990, X's only beneficiary designated to the plan is his granddaughter (Y), born January 1, 1979. X's benefit under Plan A to be used to determine the minimum distribution for 1989 (determined under F-5) is $25,300.00.

(b) In order to satisfy the MDIB requirement in §1.401(a)(9)-2 and the minimum distribution requirements in this §1.401(a)(9)-1, distribution of X's entire interest must be distributed as follows. Distribution must commence not later than April 1, 1990 (X's required beginning date determined under B-2 and B-3). The distribution for 1989 (X's first distribution calendar year determined under F-1) must be calculated by dividing X's benefit of $25,300 by the lesser of (1) the applicable divisor from the table in Q&A-4 of §1.401(a)(9)-2 and (2) the applicable life expectancy determined under F-1. The applicable divisor from the table in Q&A-4 of §1.401(a)(9)-2 for an employee age 71 is 25.3. The applicable life expectancy is 71.8 (the joint life and last survivor expectancy from Table IV of §1.72-9 of X and Y using their attained ages as of their birthdays in 1989 (the year X obtained age 70 ½) of 71 and 10). Thus, the minimum distribution for 1989 is $1,000 (25,300 divided by 25.3). $1,000 is distributed to X by Plan A on April 1, 1990.

(c) X's benefit to be used to determine the minimum distribution for 1990 (determined under F-5 including the adjustment for the distribution on April 1, 1990) is $26,803.00. The minimum distribution for 1990 must be made by December 31, 1990. The minimum distribution from 1990 is determined by dividing X's benefit of 26,803.00 by the lesser of (1) the applicable divisor from the table in Q&A-4 of §1.401(a)(9)-2 for an employee age 72 and (2) the applicable life expectancy determined under F-1. The applicable divisor from the table in Q&A-4 of §1.401(a)(9)-2 for an employee age 72 is 24.4. The applicable life is 70.8 (71.8 reduced by one, the number of years elapsed since the calendar year X attained age 70 ½). Thus the minimum distribution for 1990 is $1098.48 (26,803.00 divided by 24.4).

F-5. Q. What benefit is used for determining the employee's minimum distribution in the case of an individual account?

A. (a) In the case of an individual account, the benefit used in determining the minimum distribution for a distribution calendar year is the account balance as of the last valuation date in the calendar year immediately preceding any distribution calendar year (valuation calendar year) adjusted as set forth below.

(b) The account balance is increased by the amount of any contributions or forfeitures allocated to the account balance as of dates in the valuation calendar year after the valuation date. Contributions include contributions made after the close of the valuation calendar year which are allocated as of dates in the valuation calendar year.

(c)(1) The account balance is decreased by distributions made in the valuation calendar year after the valuation date.

(2)(i) The following rule applies if any portion of the minimum distribution for the first distribution calendar year is made in the second distribution calendar year (i.e., generally, the distribution calendar year in which the required beginning date as defined in section 401(a)(9)(C) occurs). In such case, for purposes of determining the account balance to be used for determining the minimum distribution for the second distribution calendar year, distributions described in paragraph (c)(1) shall include an additional amount. This additional amount is equal to the amount of any distribution made in the second distribution calendar year on or before the required beginning date that is not in excess (when added to the amounts distributed in the first calendar year) of the amount required to meet the minimum distribution for the first distribution calendar year.

(ii) This paragraph (c)(2) is illustrated by the following example:

Example. (a) Employee (X), born October 1, 1918, is a participant in a qualified defined contribution plan (Plan Z). X attains age 70 ½ in calendar year 1989. X's required beginning date is April 1, 1990. As of the last valuation date under Plan Z in calendar year 1988, which was on December 31, 1988, the value of X's account balance was $24,000. No contributions are made or amounts forfeited after such date which are allocated in calendar year 1988. No rollover amounts are received after such date by Plan Z on X's behalf which were distributed by a qualified plan or IRA in calendar years 1988, 1989, or 1990. The joint life and last survivor expectancy is 24 years. The required minimum distribution for calendar year 1989 is $1,000 ($24,000 divided by 24). That amount is distributed to X on April 1, 1990. On the same date, X elects not to recalculate life expectancy, as permitted by the plan.

(b) The value of X's account balance as of December 31, 1989 (the last valuation date under Plan Z in calendar year 1989) is $26,400. No contributions are made or amounts forfeited after such date which are allocated in calendar year 1989. In order to determine the benefit to be used in calculating the minimum distribution for calendar year 1990, the account balance of $26,400 will be reduced by $1,000, the amount of the minimum distribution for calendar year 1989 made on April 1, 1990. Consequently, the benefit for purposes of determining the minimum distribution for calendar year 1990 is $25,400.

(c) If, instead of $1,000 being distributed to X, $20,000 is distributed, the account balance of $26,400 would still be reduced by $1,000 in order to determine the benefit to be used in calculating the minimum distribution for calendar year 1990. The amount of the distribution made on April 1, 1990, in order to meet the minimum distribution for 1989 would still be $1,000. The remaining $19,000 ($20,000 – $1,000) of the distribution is not the minimum distribution for 1989. Instead, the remaining $19,000 of the distribution satisfies the minimum distribution requirement with respect to X for calendar year 1990. The amount which is required to be distributed for calendar year 1990 is $1,104.35 ($25,400 divided by 23). Consequently, no additional amount is required to be distributed to X in 1990 because $19,000 exceeds $1,105.26. However, pursuant to F-2, the remaining $17,895.65 ($19,000 – $1,104.35) may not be used to satisfy the minimum distribution requirements for calendar year 1991 or any subsequent calendar years.

(d) If an amount is distributed by one plan and rolled over to another plan (receiving plan), G-2 provides additional rules for determining the benefit and minimum distribution under the receiving plan. If an amount is transferred from one plan (transferor plan) to another plan (transferee plan), G-3 and G-4 provide additional rules for determining the minimum distribution and the benefit under both the transferor and transferee plans.

F-6. Q. If a portion of an employee's benefit is not vested as of the employee's required beginning date, how is the determination of the minimum required distribution affected?

A. (a) If the employee's benefit is in the form of an individual account, the benefit used to determine the minimum distribution required for any distribution calendar year will be determined in accordance with F-5 without regard to whether or not any portion of the employee's benefit is not vested. If any portion of the employee's benefit is not vested, distributions will be treated as being paid from the vested portion of the benefit first. If, as of the end of a distribution calendar year (or as of the employee's required beginning date, in the case of the employee's first distribution calendar year), the total amount of the employee's vested benefit is less than the minimum distribution required for the calendar year, only the vested portion of the employee's benefit is required to be distributed by the end of the calendar year (or, if applicable, by the employee's required beginning date). Further, if no portion of the employee's benefit is vested as of that date, no distribution is required as of that date. However, in the calendar year when an amount becomes vested, the amount required to be distributed in such calendar year will include the additional amount. Such additional amount will equal the lesser of (1) the vested portion of the employee's benefit, and (2) the sum of amounts not distributed in prior calendar years because the employee's vested benefit was less than the minimum required distribution. In such case, an adjustment for the additional amount distributed which corresponds to the adjustment described in F-5(c)(2) will be made to the benefit used to determine the minimum distribution for that calendar year.

(b) In the case of annuity distributions from a defined benefit plan, if any portion of the employee's benefit is not vested as of December 31 of a distribution calendar year (or as of the employee's required beginning date in the case of the employee's first distribution calendar year), the portion which is not vested as of such date will be treated as not having accrued for purposes of determining the minimum distribution for that distribution calendar year. When an additional portion of the employee's benefit becomes vested, such portion will be treated as an additional accrual. See F-7 for the rules for distributing benefits which accrue under a defined benefit plan after the employee's required beginning date.

F-7. Q. In the case of annuity distributions under a defined benefit plan, how must additional benefits which accrue after the employee's required beginning date be distributed in order to satisfy section 401(a)(9)?

A. In the case of annuity distributions under a defined benefit plan, if any additional benefits accrue after the employee's required beginning date, distribution of such amount as a separate identifiable component must commence in accordance with F-3 beginning with the first payment interval ending in the calendar year immediately following the calendar year in which such amount accrues.

G. Rollovers and Transfers

G-1. Q. If an amount is distributed by one plan (distributing plan) and is rolled over to another plan, is the benefit or the minimum distribution under the distributing plan affected by the rollover?

A. No. If an amount is distributed by one plan and is rolled over to another plan, the amount distributed is still treated as a distribution by the distributing plan, notwithstanding the rollover.

G-1A. Q. If the amount is distributed by a plan in a distribution calendar year of that plan and rolled over to another plan, what amount will be treated as a minimum distribution required under section 401(a)(9) which may not be rolled over pursuant to section 402(a)(5)(G)?

A. (a) Except as otherwise provided in paragraphs (b) and (c), all amounts distributed in a distribution calendar year will be treated for purposes of section 402(a)(5)(G) as being required under section 401(a)(9) until the total amount distributed in such calendar year exceeds the total amount which is required to be distributed for such distribution calendar year in order to satisfy section 401(a)(9).

(b) In the case of any distribution in an employee's second distribution calendar year, the amounts distributed in such calendar year which will be treated for purposes of section 402(a)(5)(G) as being required under section 401(a)(9) will include the sum of (1) the amount required to be distributed for the second distribution calendar year and (2) the amount required to be distributed for the employee's first distribution calendar year (to the extent such amount is not distributed in the first distribution calendar year).

(c) If in any calendar year the minimum amount required to be distributed under section 401(a)(9) is not distributed, such amount will be treated as an amount which is required to be distributed in the next calendar year for purposes of section 402(a)(5)(G).

(d) If the employee's entire benefit is distributed in the employee's first and second distribution calendar year but before the employee's required beginning date, the amount distributed which will be treated as an amount which is required to be distributed under section 401(a)(9) for purposes of section 402(a)(5)(G) will be determined using the designated beneficiary of the employee, if any, under the plan (or individual retirement plan) receiving the rollover contribution.

G-1B. What are the tax consequences under section 402(a) and 408(d) to an employee who rolls over an amount which is required under section 401(a)(9)?

A. The tax consequences under section 402(a) and 408(d) to an employee who rolls over an amount which is required to be distributed under section 401(a)(9) are as follows:

(a) The amount which is required to be distributed under section 401(a)(9) is taxable under section 72 in the taxable year in which distributed without regard to the rollover.

(b) If the amount which is required to be distributed under section 401(a)(9) is contributed to an individual retirement plan as a rollover contribution, such amount will be treated as a contribution to an individual retirement plan which is not a rollover contribution and thus will be an excess contribution for purposes of section 4973 if the amount is not deductible under section 219 or may not be treated as a nondeductible contribution under section 408(o). Of course, if the amount is an excess contribution, it may be withdrawn with earnings from the account before the due date of the employee's return pursuant to section 408(d)(4) in order to avoid imposition of the excise tax under section 4973.

G-2. Q. If an amount is distributed by one plan (distributing plan) and is rolled over to another plan (receiving plan), how are the benefit and the minimum distribution under the receiving plan affected?

A. (a) Except as otherwise provided in paragraph (b), if an amount is distributed by one plan (distributing plan) and is rolled over to another plan (receiving plan), the benefit of the employee under the receiving plan is increased by the amount rolled over. However, the distribution has no impact on the minimum distribution required to be made by the receiving plan for the calendar year in which the rollover is received. But, if a minimum distribution is required to be made by the receiving plan for the following calendar year, the rollover amount must be considered to be part of the employee's benefit under the receiving plan. Consequently, for purposes of determining any minimum distribution for the calendar year immediately following the calendar year in which the amount rolled over is received by the receiving plan, in the case in which the amount rolled over is received after the last valuation date in the calendar year under the receiving plan, the benefit of the employee as of such valuation date, adjusted in accordance with F-5, will be increased by the rollover amount valued as of the date of receipt. For purposes of calculating the benefit under the receiving plan pursuant to the preceding sentence, if the amount rolled over is received by the receiving plan in a different calendar year from the calendar year in which it is distributed by the distributing plan, the amount rolled over is deemed to have been received by the receiving plan in the calendar year in which it was distributed by the distributing plan.

(b) If an amount is distributed by the distributing plan after the employee's required beginning date under both the distributing plan and the receiving plan, and the designated beneficiary of the employee under the receiving plan is a designated beneficiary with a life expectancy that is longer than the life expectancy of the designated beneficiary under the distributing plan, the following rule will apply. In such case, the receiving plan must separately account for the amount rolled over and treat it as a separate benefit. It must then begin distribution of such separate benefit in the calendar year following the calendar year in which the amount rolled over was distributed by the distributing plan. The separate benefit attributable to the rollover amount must be distributed over a period not exceeding the period (including any adjustments for recalculation under section 401(a)(9)(D), if applicable) used by the distributing plan to determine the employee's minimum distribution with respect to the benefit attributable to the amount rolled over. For purposes of determining the life expectancies or lives used to determine the minimum distribution under the receiving plan, the designated beneficiary under the distributing plan will be the designated beneficiary under the receiving plan (with respect to the benefit attributable to the amount rolled over). If such beneficiary is changed under the receiving plan to a different beneficiary from the designated beneficiary under the distributing plan, or a beneficiary is added who was not a beneficiary under the distributing plan, the rules in E-5 applicable to changes in beneficiaries will be used to determine the period over which distributions must be made by the receiving plan.

G-3. Q. In the case of a transfer of an amount of an employee's benefit from one plan (transferor plan) to another plan (transferee plan), are there any special rules for satisfying the minimum distribution requirement or determining the employee's benefit under the transferor plan?

A. (a) In the case of a transfer of an amount of an employee's benefit from one plan to another, the transfer is not treated as a distribution by the transferor plan for purposes of section 401(a)(9). Instead, the benefit of the employee under the transferor plan is decreased by the amount transferred. However, if any portion of an employee's benefit is transferred in a distribution calendar year with respect to that employee, in order to satisfy section 401(a)(9), the transferor plan must determine the amount of the minimum distribution with respect to that employee for the calendar year of the transfer using the employee's benefit under the transferor plan before the transfer. Additionally, if any portion of an employee's benefit is transferred in the employee's second distribution calendar year but on or before the employee's required beginning date, in order to satisfy section 401(a)(9), the transferor plan must determine the amount of the minimum distribution requirement for the employee's first distribution calendar year based on the employee's benefit under the transferor plan before the transfer. The transferor plan may satisfy the minimum distribution requirement for the calendar year of the transfer (and the prior year if applicable) by segregating the amount which must be distributed from the employee's benefit and not transferring that amount. Such amount may be retained by the transferor plan and distributed on or before the date required or paid to an escrow account which in turn distributes such amount on or before the date required.

(b) For purposes of determining any minimum distribution for the calendar year immediately following the calendar year in which the transfer occurs, in the case of a transfer after the last valuation date for the calendar year of the transfer under the transferor plan, the benefit of the employee as of such valuation date, adjusted in accordance with F-5, will be decreased by the amount transferred valued as of the date transferred.

G-3A. Q. What are the excise tax consequences for an employee (or other distributee) if, before transferring a portion of an employee's benefit in a distribution calendar year, the transferor plan does not satisfy the minimum distribution requirement for the calendar year of the transfer (and, if applicable, the prior calendar year)?

A. If the transferor plan does not satisfy the minimum distribution for the calendar year of transfer (and, if applicable, the prior calendar year) in accordance with G-3, the amount required to be distributed to satisfy the minimum distribution requirement for the calendar year of the transfer (and, if applicable, the prior calendar year) will be treated for purposes of section 4974 as a minimum distribution that was not distributed. Consequently, the payee with respect to such amount will be subject to the excise tax imposed under section 4974.

G-4. Q. If an amount of an employee's benefit is transferred from one plan (transferor plan) to another plan (transferee plan), how are the benefit and the minimum distribution under the transferee plan affected?

A. (a) Except as otherwise provided in paragraph (b), in the case of a transfer from one plan (transferor plan) to another (transferee plan), the general rule is that the benefit of the employee under the transferee plan is increased by the amount transferred. The transfer has no impact on the minimum distribution required to be made by the transferee plan in the calendar year in which the transfer is received. However, if a minimum distribution is required from the transferee plan for the following calendar year, the transferred amount must be considered to be part of the employee's benefit under the transferee plan. Consequently, for purposes of determining any minimum distribution for the calendar year immediately following the calendar year in which the transfer occurs, in the case of a transfer after the last valuation date of the transferee plan in the transfer calendar year, the benefit of the employee under the receiving plan valued as of such valuation date, adjusted in accordance with F-5, will be increased by the amount transferred valued as of the date transferred.

(b) If an amount is transferred after the employee's required beginning date under both the transferor plan and the transferee plan, and

the designated beneficiary of the employee under the transferee plan is a designated beneficiary with a life expectancy that is longer than the life expectancy of the designated beneficiary under the transferor plan, the following rule will apply. The transferee plan must separately account for the amount rolled over and treat it as a separate benefit. The transferee plan must then begin distribution of such separate benefit in the calendar year following the calendar year in which the amount was transferred. This benefit attributable to the transferred amount must be distributed over a period not exceeding the period (including any adjustments for recalculation under section 401(a)(9)(D), if applicable) used by the transferor plan to determine the employee's minimum distribution with respect to the benefit attributable to the amount transferred. For purposes of determining the life expectancies or lives used to determine the minimum distribution under the transferee plan, the designated beneficiary under the transferor plan will be the designated beneficiary under the transferee plan (with respect to the benefit attributable to the amount transferred). If such beneficiary is changed under the transferee plan to a different beneficiary from the designated beneficiary under the transferor plan or a beneficiary is added who was not a beneficiary under the transferor plan, the rules in E-5, applicable to changes in beneficiaries, will be used to determine the period over which distributions must be made by the transferee plan.

G-5. Q. How are a spinoff, merger or consolidation (as defined in §1.414(l)-1) treated for purposes of determining an employee's benefit and minimum distribution under section 401(a)(9)?

A. For purposes of determining an employee's benefit and minimum distribution under section 401(a)(9), a spinoff, a merger, or a consolidation (as defined in §1.414(l)) will be treated as a transfer of the benefits of the employees involved. Consequently, the benefit and minimum distribution of each employee involved under the transferor and transferee plans will be determined in accordance with G-3 and G-4.

H. *Special rules*

H-1. Q. What distribution rules apply if an employee is a participant in more than one plan?

A. If an employee is a participant in more than one plan, the plans in which the employee participates may not be aggregated for purposes of testing whether or not the distribution requirements of section 401(a)(9) are met. The distribution of the benefit of the employee under each plan must separately meet the requirements of section 401(a)(9).

H-2. Q. If an employee's benefit under a plan is divided into separate accounts (or segregated shares in the case of a defined benefit plan), do the distribution rules in section 401(a)(9) and these regulations apply separately to each separate account (or segregated share)?

A. (a) Except as otherwise provided in paragraphs (b) and (c), if an employee's benefit under a plan is divided into separate accounts (or segregated shares in the case of a defined benefit plan), the separate accounts (or segregated shares) will be aggregated for purposes of satisfying the rules in section 401(a)(9). Thus, except as otherwise provided in paragraphs (b) and (c), all separate accounts, including a separate account for nondeductible employee contributions (under section 72(e)(9)) or for qualified voluntary employee contributions (as defined in section 219(e)(2)), will be aggregated for purposes of section 401(a)(9).

(b) If, as of an employee's required beginning date or, in the case of distributions under section 401(a)(9)(B)(ii) or (iii) and (iv), as of the employee's (or spouse's where applicable) date of death, the beneficiaries with respect to a separate account (or segregated share in the case of a defined benefit plan) differ from the beneficiaries with respect to the other separate accounts (or segregate shares) of the employee, such separate account (or segregated share) need not be aggregated with other separate accounts (or segregated shares) in order to determine whether the distributions from such separate account (or segregated share) satisfy section 401(a)(9). Instead, the rules in section 401(a)(9) may separately apply to such separate account (or segregated share). Thus, for example, if the employee designated a different beneficiary for each separate account (or segregated share), each separate account (or segregated share) may be distributed over the joint life (or joint life and last survivor expectancy) of the employee and the designated beneficiary (or the life or life expectancy of the designated beneficiary in the case of any distribution described in section 401(a)(9)(B)(iii) and (iv)) for that separate account (or segregated share). Further, for example, if, in the case of a distribution described in section 401(a)(9)(B)(iii) and (iv), the only designated beneficiary of a separate account (or segregated share) is the employee's surviving spouse, and beneficiaries other than the surviving spouse are designated with respect to the other separate accounts of the employee, distribution of the spouse's separate account (or segregated share) need not commence until the date determined under the first sentence in C-3(b) even if distribution of the other separate accounts (or segregated shares) must commence at an earlier date. Also, for example, in the case of a distribution after the death of an employee to which section 401(a)(9)(B)(i) does not apply, distribution from a separate account (or segregated share) of an employee may be made over a beneficiary's life expectancy in accordance with section 401(a)(9)(B)(iii) and (iv) even though distributions from other separate accounts (or segregated shares) with different beneficiaries are being made in accordance with the five-year rule in section 401(a)(9)(B)(ii).

(c) See G-2 through G-4 for special rules which apply to the distribution from separate accounts maintained because of a transfer or rollover.

H-2A. What is a separate account or segregated share for purposes of section 401(a)(9)?

A. (a) For purposes of section 401(a)(9) a separate account in an individual account is a portion of an employee's benefit determined by an acceptable separate accounting including allocating investment gains and losses, and contributions and forfeitures, on a pro rata basis in a reasonable and consistent matter between such portion and any other benefits. Further, the amounts of each such portion of the benefit will be separately determined for purposes of determining the amount of the minimum distribution in accordance with F-5.

(b) A benefit in a defined benefit plan is separated into segregated shares if it consists of separate identifiable components which may be separately distributed.

H-3. Q. Must a distribution that is required by section 401(a)(9) to be made by the required beginning date to the participant or that is required by section 401(a)(9)(B)(ii) to be made by the required time to a designated beneficiary who is a surviving spouse be made notwithstanding the failure of the participant, or spouse where applicable, to consent to a distribution while a benefit is immediately distributable?

A. Yes. Section 411(a)(11) and section 417(e) (see § 1.411(a)(11)-1T(c)(2) and § 1.417(e)-1T(c)) require participant and spousal consent to certain distributions of plan benefits while such benefits are immediately distributable. If a participant's normal retirement age is later than the required beginning date for the commencement of distributions under section 401(a)(9) and, therefore, benefits are still immediately distributable, the plan must, nevertheless, distribute plan benefits to the participant (or where applicable, to the spouse) in a manner that satisfies the requirements of section 401(a)(9). Section 401(a)(9) must be satisfied even though the participant (or spouse, where applicable) fails to consent to the distribution. In such a case, the plan may distribute in the form of a qualified joint and survivor annuity (QJSA) or in the form of a qualified preretirement survivor annuity (QPSA) and the consent requirements of sections 411(a)(11) and 417(e) are deemed to be satisfied if the plan has made reasonable efforts to obtain consent from the participant (or spouse if applicable) and if the distribution otherwise meets the requirements of section 417. If, because of section 401(a)(11)(B), the plan is not required to distribute in the form of a QJSA to a participant or a QPSA to a surviving spouse, the plan may distribute the minimum amount required at the time required to satisfy section 401(a)(9) and the consent requirements of sections 411(a)(11) and 417(e) are deemed to be satisfied if the plan has made reasonable efforts to obtain consent from the participant (or spouse if applicable) and if the distribution otherwise meets the requirements of section 417.

H-3A. Who is an employee's spouse or surviving spouse for purposes of section 401(a)(9)?

A. Except as otherwise provided in H-4(a) in the case of distributions of a portion of an employee's benefit payable to a former spouse of an employee pursuant to a qualified domestic relations order, for purposes of section 401(a)(9), an individual is a spouse or surviving spouse of an employee if such individual is treated as the employee's spouse under applicable state law as of the following dates, whichever is applicable. Sections 401(a)(11)(D) and 417(d) do not apply for purposes of determining who is an employee's spouse or surviving spouse under section 401(a)(9). In the case of distributions before the death of an employee under section 401(a)(9)(A)(ii), for purposes of determining whether the designated beneficiary's life expectancy may be recalculated, the spouse of the employee is determined as of the employee's required beginning date. In the case of distributions after the death of an employee, for purposes of determining whether, under the exception to the five-year rule in section 401(a)(9)(B)(iii) and (iv), the provisions of clause (iv) apply, the spouse of the employee is determined as of the date of death of the employee.

H-4. Q. In order to satisfy section 401(a)(9), are there any special rules which apply to the distribution of all or a portion of an employee's benefit payable to an alternate payee pursuant to a qualified domestic relations order as defined in section 414(p) (QDRO)?

A. (a) A former spouse to whom all or a portion of the employee's benefit is payable pursuant to a QDRO will be treated as a spouse (including a surviving spouse) of the employee for purposes of section 401(a)(9).

(b)(1) If a QDRO provides that an employee's benefit is to be divided and a portion is to be allocated to an alternate payee, such portion will be treated as a separate account (or segregated share) which separately must satisfy the requirements of section 401(a)(9) and may not be aggregated with other separate accounts (or segregated shares) of the employee for purposes of satisfying section 401(a)(9). Except as otherwise provided in subparagraph (2), distribution of such separate account allocated to an alternate payee pursuant to a QDRO must be made in accordance with section 401(a)(9). For example, in general, distribution of such account will satisfy section 401(a)(9)(A) if such account will be distributed, beginning not later than the employee's required beginning date over the life of the employee or over the lives of the employee and the alternate payee (or over a period not extending beyond the life expectancy of such employee or the joint life and last survivor expectancy of such employee and alternate payee). Distribution of the separate account will not satisfy section 401(a)(9)(A)(ii) if it is distributed over the joint lives of the alternate payee and a designated beneficiary (other than the employee). The determination of whether distribution from such account after the death of the employee to the alternate payee will be made in accordance with section 401(a)(9)(B)(i) or section 401(a)(9)(B)(ii) or (iii) and (iv) will depend on whether distributions have begun as determined under B-5 (which provides, in general, that distributions are not treated as having begun until the employee's required beginning date even though payments may actually have begun before that date). Further, for example, if the alternate payee dies before the date on which the designated beneficiary is determined under D-3 or D-4 and distribution of the separate account allocated to the alternate payee pursuant to the QDRO is to be made to the alternate payee's beneficiary, such beneficiary may be treated as a designated beneficiary for purposes of determining the minimum distribution required from such account if the beneficiary of the alternate payee is an individual and if such beneficiary is a beneficiary under the plan or specified to or in the plan. (Specification in the QDRO will also be treated as specification to the plan.)

(2) Distribution of the separate account allocated to an alternative payee pursuant to a QDRO will satisfy section 401(a)(9)(A) even though distributions are made to the alternate payee rather than the employee if the distribution otherwise meets the requirements of section 401(a)(9)(A). Distribution of the separate account allocated to an alternate payee pursuant to a QDRO will also meet the requirements of section 401(a)(9)(A)(ii) if such account is to be distributed, beginning not later than the employee's required beginning date, over the life of the alternate payee (or over a period not extending beyond the life expectancy of the alternative payee). If the plan permits the employee to elect not to recalculate life expectancies (life expectancies of the employee and the employee's spouse) pursuant to E-7(c), such election is to be made only by the alternate payee for purposes of distributing the separate account allocated to such alternative payee pursuant to the QDRO. Also, if the plan permits the employee to elect whether distribution upon the death of the employee will be made in accordance with the five-year rule in section 401(a)(9)(B)(ii) or the exception to the five-year rule in section 401(a)(9)(B)(iii) and (iv) pursuant to C-4(c), such election is to be made only by the alternate payee for purposes of distributing the separate account allocated to the alternate payee pursuant to the QDRO. If the alternate payee dies after distribution of the separate account allocated to the alternate payee pursuant to a QDRO has begun (determined under B-5), distribution of the remaining portion of that portion of the benefit allocated to the alternate payee must be made at least as rapidly (determined under B-6) as under the method of distributions being used as of the date of the alternate payee's death. As provided in § 1.401(a)(9)-2, distribution of the separate account allocated to an alternate payee pursuant to a QDRO need not satisfy the minimum distribution incidental benefit rule as long as the distribution of such account otherwise satisfies section 401(a)(9).

(c) If a QDRO does not provide that an employee's benefit is to be divided but merely provides that a portion of an employee's benefit (otherwise payable to the employee) is to be paid to an alternate payee, such portion will not be treated as a separate account (or segregated share) of the employee. Instead, such portion will be aggregated with any amount distributed to the employee and will be treated as having been distributed to the employee for purposes of determining whether the minimum distribution requirement has been satisfied with respect to that employee.

H-5. Q. Will a plan fail to qualify as a pension plan within the meaning of section 401(a), solely because the plan permits distributions to commence to an employee on or after April 1 of the calendar year following the calendar year in which the employee attains age 70 ½ even though the employee has not retired or attained the normal retirement age under the plan as of the date on which such distributions commence?

A. No. A plan will not fail to qualify as a pension plan within the meaning of section 401(a), solely because the plan permits distributions to commence to an employee on or after April 1 of the calendar year following the calendar year in which the employee attains age 70 ½ even though the employee has not retired or attained the normal retirement age under the plan as of the date on which such distributions commence. This rule applies without regard to whether or not the employee is a 5-percent owner with respect to the plan year ending in the calendar year in which distributions commence.

H-6. Q. Is the distribution of an annuity contract a distribution for purposes of section 401(a)(9)?

A. No. The distribution of an annuity contract is not a distribution for purposes of section 401(a)(9).

H-7. Will a payment by a plan after the death of an employee fail to be treated as a distribution for purposes of section 401(a)(9) solely because it is made to an estate or a trust?

A. A payment by a plan after the death of an employee will not fail to be treated as a distribution for purposes of section 401(a)(9) solely because it is made to an estate or a trust. As a result, the estate or trust which receives a payment from a plan after the death of an employee need not distribute the amount of such payment to the beneficiaries of the estate or trust in accordance with section 401(a)(9)(B). However, pursuant to D-2A, distribution to the estate must satisfy the five-year rule in section 401(a)(9)(B)(iii) if the distribution to the employee had not begun (as defined in B-5) as of the employee's date of death, and pursuant to D-2A, an estate may not be a designated beneficiary. See D-5 and D-6 for provisions under which beneficiaries of a trust with respect to the trust's interest in an employee's benefit are treated as having been designated as beneficiaries of the employee under the plan.

H-8. Will a plan fail to satisfy section 411 if the plan is amended to eliminate benefit options that do not satisfy section 401(a)(9)?

A. Nothing in section 401(a)(9) permits a plan to eliminate for all participants a benefit option that could not otherwise be eliminated pursuant to section 411(d)(6). However, a plan must provide that, notwithstanding any other plan provisions, it will not distribute benefits under any option that does not satisfy section 401(a)(9). See A-3. Thus, the plan, notwithstanding section 411(d)(6), must prevent participants from electing benefit options that do not satisfy section 401(a)(9).

H-9. Does section 401(a)(4) prevent a plan from distributing benefits in any manner otherwise permitted under section 401(a)(9)?

A. A plan may not distribute benefits to any employee in any manner which results in discrimination prohibited under section 401(a)(4) even if the distribution otherwise satisfies section 401(a)(9).

I. *Transition Rules*

I-1. Q. Are there any special distribution rules for calendar years before 1988?

A. Yes. Minimum distributions required for calendar years 1985 and 1986 are not required to be made until December 31, 1987. Further, there are special rules for determining the amount that is required to be distributed for 1985 and 1986 (and with respect to certain employees for 1987). There are also special rules for determining the first distribution calendar year with respect to certain employees. In the case of an employee whose required beginning date is on or before April 1, 1987 and who is alive on December 31, 1987, see I-2 through I-5. In the case of an employee who dies before January 1, 1988, see I-6 through I-13. See I-14 through I-16 for other special transition rules.

I-2. Q. If an employee's required beginning date (see Q&A B-2 & 3) is on or before April 1, 1987 and such employee is alive on December 31, 1987, what is the first calendar year for which a distribution is required?

A. Except as provided in I-4 (special rule for certain life annuities), the following rules apply for purposes of determining the first distribution calendar year of an employee with a required beginning date on or before April 1, 1987 if such employee is alive on December 31, 1987:

(a) *Pre-1987 required beginning date.* If an employee's required beginning date was on or before April 1, 1986, the first distribution calendar year is 1985. However, under these transition rules, the minimum distribution for 1985 is not required to be made by April 1, 1986, and the minimum distribution for 1986 is not required to be made by December 31, 1986. Instead, the minimum distributions for calendar years 1985 and 1986 are required to be made by December 31, 1987. Thus, the minimum distributions for 1985, 1986, and 1987 must be made by December 31, 1987.

(b) *1987 required beginning date.* If an employee's required beginning date is April 1, 1987, the first distribution calendar year is 1986. However, under these transition rules, the minimum distribution for 1986 is not required to be made by April 1, 1987. Instead, the minimum distribution for 1986 is required to be made by December 31, 1987. Thus, the minimum distribution for 1986 and 1987 must be made by December 31, 1987.

I-3. Q. If (1) the employee is alive on December 31, 1987 and (2) the employee's first distribution calendar year is 1985 or 1986 (as determined under I-2), how is the amount of the minimum required distribution determined for calendar years 1985, 1986, and 1987?

A. (a) *In general.* If (1) the employee is alive on December 31, 1987 and (2) the employee's first distribution calendar year is 1985 or 1986 (as determined under I-2), the amount of the minimum distribution for calendar years 1985, 1986, and 1987 is to be determined under one of the three methods described in paragraphs (b), (c), and (d). The plan administrator is to determine which method, including the credit rules under paragraphs (b)(4) and (c)(3), is to be used. The same method used under this I-3 and I-8 must be used with respect to all such employees covered by the plan. See I-4 for a special amount of distribution rule for certain life annuities.

(b) *Life expectancy method.* Under the life expectancy method, the total amount of the minimum distribution required for calendar years 1985, 1986, and 1987 is determined as follows:

(1) *Designated beneficiary and life expectancy.* The designated beneficiary of the employee will be determined on any date in 1987. The applicable life expectancy (either the life expectancy of the employee or the joint life and last survivor expectancy of the employee and the employee's designated beneficiary, whichever is applicable) is determined using attained ages as of birthdays in 1987. In the case of a beneficiary who is not alive on his birthday in 1987, the beneficiary is treated as being alive on that date for purposes of determining life expectancy.

(2) *Benefit determination.* The benefit of the employee is determined using the account balance as of the last valuation date under the plan in 1986, adjusted in accordance with F-5 with the following further modifications. First, the benefit adjustment for distributions after the valuation date under F-5(c) is not made. Second, the benefit is increased by any distribution made in 1985 or 1986 before the valuation date for which credit is being taken under subparagraph (4).

(3) *Required distribution.* The total amount which must be distributed for calendar years 1985, 1986, and 1987 using the life expectancy method is determined by dividing the benefit determined under subparagraph (2) by the applicable life expectancy determined under subparagraph (1) and multiplying the quotient by:

(i) 2.8, in the case of an employee with respect to whom the first distribution calendar year is 1985, or

(ii) 1.9, in the case of an employee with respect to whom the first distribution calendar year is 1986.

(4) *Credit for distributions.* In determining whether the total amount which must be distributed for calendar years 1985, 1986 and 1987 has been distributed, credit may be taken (as determined by the plan administrator) for any amount distributed in a distribution calendar year of the employee. Consequently, to determine the amount which is required to be distributed in calendar year 1987, the plan administrator may reduce the total amount which must be distributed in 1987 for calendar years 1985, 1986, and 1987 (determined under (3)) by the amounts distributed in:

(i) 1985 and 1986, in the case of an employee with respect to whom the first distribution calendar year is 1985, or

(ii) 1986, in the case of an employee with respect to whom the first distribution calendar year is 1986. However, in the case of distributions before the last valuation date in 1986, credit may only be taken for amounts which were used to increase the benefit pursuant to subparagraph (2).

(c) *Percentage method.* Under the percentage method, the total amount of the minimum distribution required for calendar years 1985, 1986, and 1987 is determined as follows:

(1) *Benefit determination.* The benefit of the employee is determined in the same manner as under paragraph (b)(2).

(2) *Required distribution.* The total amount required to be distributed for calendar years 1985, 1986, and 1987 is the following percentage of the benefit (determined in accordance with subparagraph (1)):

(i) 15%, in the case of an employee with respect to whom the first distribution calendar year is 1985, or

(ii) 10%, in the case of an employee with respect to whom the first distribution calendar year is 1986.

(3) *Credits.* Credits for distributions may be taken in the same manner as under paragraph (b)(4).

(d) *Regular method.* Under the regular method, the sum of the minimum distributions required for each calendar year 1985, 1986, and 1987, calculated separately, is determined under section 401(a)(9) and this section with appropriate adjustments. However, in determining the amount of the minimum distribution required for calendar years 1985, 1986, and 1987, the rule in F-2 does not apply. Also, credit (with an appropriate gross-up) may be taken toward the minimum distribution required for the 1986 or 1987 distribution calendar year for distributions in the 1985 or 1986 distribution calendar years that exceeded the minimum required distribution for such year. If distribution is being made in the form of an annuity and the annuity either is not a life annuity or is a life annuity with a period certain exceeding 20 years, the amount which must be distributed by December 31, 1987 is the aggregate of annual amounts (see F-3(d)(2)) for each calendar year for which a distribution is required before 1988, determined under I-2.

(e) This Q&A is illustrated by the following example:

Example.

(a) An employee (X), born February 1, 1914, is a participant in a profit-sharing plan (Plan Z). X retired December 31, 1979. Consequently his required beginning date occurred on or before April 1, 1986. Thus X's first distribution calendar year is 1985. As of January 1, 1987, X's spouse (Y), born March 1, 1920 is X's only beneficiary under Plan Z. As of December 31, 1986, the last valuation date under Plan Z in 1986, X's benefit is $198,000. In 1985, X received distributions from Plan Z totaling $5,000. In 1986 (before December 31), X received distributions from Plan Z totaling $7,000.

(b) Under the life expectancy method, X's minimum distribution required for 1985, 1986, and 1987 which must be distributed in 1987 by December 31 is determined as follows:

(1)	Benefit under Plan Z as of the last valuation date in 1986.	$198,000
(2)	Distributions in 1985.	$5,000
(3)	Distributions in 1986 before 12/31/86.	$7,000
(4)	Benefit to be used. (sum of (1), (2), and (3))	$210,000
(5)	X's attained age as of X's birthday in 1987.	73
(6)	Y's attained age as of Y's birthday in 1987.	67
(7)	Joint life and last survivor of X and Y (determined under Table VI of 1.72-9 using ages in (5) and (6)).	21
(8)	Benefit ((line 4) divided by the applicable life expectancy (line 7)).	$10,000
(9)	The total amount which must be distributed for 1985, 1986, and 1987. (2.8 × 10,000)	$28,000
(10)	Distribution in 1985 and 1986 for which credit may be taken (Sum of lines (2) and (3)).	$12,000
(11)	Amount required to be distributed in 1987. (Line 9 minus line 10)	$16,000

(c) Under the percentage method, X's minimum distribution required for 1985, 1986, and 1987 which must be distributed in 1987 by December 31 is determined as follows:

(1)	Benefit under Plan Z as of the last valuation date in 1986.	$198,000
(2)	Distributions in 1985.	$5,000
(3)	Distributions in 1986 before 12/31/86.	$7,000
(4)	Benefit to be used (sum of (1), (2), and (3)).	$210,000
(5)	Total amount which must be distributed for 1985, 1986, and 1987 (15% of line (4)).	$31,500
(6)	Distribution in 1985 and 1986 for which credit may be taken (Sum of lines (2) and (3)).	$12,000
(7)	Amount required to be distributed in 1987. (Line 5 minus line 6)	$19,500

I-4. Q. If (a) the employee's benefit is to be distributed in the form of a life annuity (or a life annuity with a period certain not exceeding 20 years), (b) the employee's required beginning date is on or before April 1, 1987, and (c) the employee is alive on December 31, 1987, then as of what date must distributions be made and how is the amount which must be distributed by that date determined?

A. (a) If the three conditions set forth in the question above are satisfied, and if the employee's required beginning date is on or before April 1, 1986, the first period for which a distribution is required is the last payment interval (as defined in F-3) ending on or before April 1, 1986. However, under these transition rules, no distribution is required to be made by April 1, 1986. Instead, distribution of an amount equal to the aggregate of the payments for all payment intervals from the last payment interval ending on or before April 1, 1986 through the last payment interval ending on or before December 31, 1987 must be made by December 31, 1987. Consequently, the total amount that must be distributed by December 31, 1987 will equal the total amount that would have been distributed by December 31, 1987, if annuity payments made in accordance with F-3 had begun on or before April 1, 1986.

(b) If the three conditions set forth above are satisfied and the employee's required beginning date is April 1, 1987, the first period for which a distribution is required is the last payment interval (as defined in F-3) ending on or before April 1, 1987. However, under these transition rules, no distribution is required to be made by April 1, 1987. Instead, distribution of an amount equal to the aggregate of the payments for all payment intervals from the last payment interval ending on or before April 1, 1987 through the last payment interval ending on or before December 31, 1987 must be made by December 31, 1987. Consequently, the total amount which must be distributed by December 31, 1987 will equal the total amount which would have been distributed by December 31, 1987, if annuity payments made in accordance with F-3 had begun on or before April 1, 1987.

(c) In the case of distributions in the form of a joint and survivor annuity, the designated beneficiary for purposes of determining the aggregate amount that is required to be distributed by December 31, 1987 may be determined as of any date during the 90 day period ending on the date on which annuity payments commence but not later than the earlier of (1) the date annuity distributions commence or (2) December 31, 1987.

(d) The provisions of this Question and Answer must be satisfied even if the employee and spouse do not consent to any catch-up distribution required by paragraph (a) or (b). The spouse's consent is not required even if as a result of making distributions required by paragraph (a) or (b), the amount payable after the death of the employee to the employee's surviving spouse is reduced. If (1) the plan has made reasonable efforts to obtain consent from the employee and the employee's spouse, (2) the requirement of section 417 that plan benefits be provided in the form of a qualified joint and survivor annuity is otherwise satisfied, and (3) the distribution otherwise meets the requirement of section 417, then the consent requirements of section 411(a)(11) and 417(e) are deemed to be satisfied with respect to the distribution.

(e) The amount of the catch-up distributions described in paragraphs (a) and (b) may be determined using either the normal form of qualified joint and survivor annuity under the terms of the plan or a benefit option, if any, selected by the employee as long as the distribution satisfies section 401(a)(9). Thus, if the employee has not elected a benefit option, the plan may determine the amount of the catch-up distribution using the qualified joint and survivor option under the plan (as long as such form of benefit provides for distributions that satisfy section 401(a)(9)).

(f) This Question and Answer is illustrated by the following example:

Example.

Plan Y, a defined benefit pension plan, provides that monthly annuity payments are to be made to an unmarried employee (X) for life with a 10 year period certain X's required beginning date is April 1, 1986 but X received no distributions before December 31, 1987. If annuity distributions had begun to X on April 1, 1986, he would have been entitled under the terms of Plan Y to receive a monthly benefit of $100. Thus if annuity distributions had begun on April 1, 1986, by December 31, 1987, the plan would have distributed $2100 to X, an amount equal to the aggregate of the payments for all payment intervals from the last payment interval ending on or before April 1, 1986 through the last payment interval ending on or before December 31, 1987. This is the amount that the plan must distribute to X by December 31, 1987. (Annuity payments made after December 31, 1987 will be adjusted for interest on $2100 due to the delay in commencing distributions.)

I-5. Q. If an employee's required beginning date is on or before April 1, 1987, are there any special rules for determining the minimum distribution for calendar years after 1987?

A. (a) Except as otherwise provided in paragraphs (b) and (c), if an employee's required beginning date is on or before April 1, 1987 and if the employee's benefit is in the form of an individual account, the amount of the minimum distribution required for calendar years after 1987 will be determined in a manner consistent with the use of December 31, 1987 as the employee's required beginning date. Consequently, for example, the employee must elect, if such election is permitted by the plan administrator, no later than December 31 1987 whether or not life expectancy will be recalculated for purposes of determining the minimum distribution required for calendar years after 1987. Further, for example, the designated beneficiary of an employee will be determined as of December 31, 1987 for purposes of determining the minimum distribution required for calendar years after 1987.

(b) If an employee's required beginning date is on or before April 1, 1987 and if the employee's benefit is in the form of an individual account, the following rule applies for determining life expectancies for purposes of determining the minimum distribution for calendar years after 1987. If an employee's life expectancy is being recalculated, the joint life and last-survivor expectancy of the employee and the designated beneficiary (other than the employee's spouse) will be determined using the attained age of the employee as of the employee's birthday in the calendar year for which the minimum distribution is being determined and the attained age of the designated beneficiary as of the beneficiary's birthday in 1987, adjusted in accordance with E-8, for purposes of determining the minimum distribution required for calendar years after 1987. If an employee's life expectancy is not being recalculated, the joint life and last survivor expectancy of the employee and the designated beneficiary will be determined based on the attained ages of the employee and designated beneficiary as of their birthdays in 1987. Such joint life and last survivor expectancy is then reduced by one for each calendar year that has elapsed since 1987. In such case if the designated beneficiary is not alive on his birthday in 1987, such beneficiary will be treated as alive on that date for purposes of determining life expectancy. If the employee's designated beneficiary is the employee's spouse, and the life expectancy of the employee and spouse are being recalculated, the joint life and last survivor expectancy of the employee and spouse will be calculated using their attained ages as of their birthdays in the calendar year for which the minimum distribution is being determined.

(c) If any employee's required beginning date is on or before April 1, 1987 and if an employee's benefit is being distributed in the form of annuity payments, for determining the minimum distribution for calendar years after 1987, the following rules will apply. The designated beneficiary may be determined as of any date during the 90 day period ending on the date on which such annuity payments commence. Life expectancy will be determined using the attained ages of the employee and the employee's designated beneficiary as of their birthdays in the calendar year in which the annuity payments commence.

I-6. Q. If an employee dies before January 1, 1988, are distributions to be made in accordance with section 401(a)(9)(B)(i) or in accordance with section 401(a)(9)(B)(ii) or (iii) and (iv)?

A. (a) *General rule.* If an employee dies before January 1, 1988, distributions must be made in accordance with either the five year rule in section 401(a)(9)(B)(ii) or the exception to the five-year rule in section 401(a)(9)(B)(iii) and (iv), whichever is applicable. (See A-4 and C-4.) If an employee dies before January 1, 1986, and distribution is being made over the life or life expectancy of a designated beneficiary in accordance with section 401(a)(9)(B)(iii) and (iv), see I-7 through I-9 for the rules concerning (1) which calendar year is the first calendar year for which a distribution is required (or in the case of certain life annuities which period is the first payment interval for which a distribution is required), (2) as of what date distributions are required to commence, and (3) how the amount which is required to be distributed by such date is determined.

(b) *Certain distributions treated as having begun.* Except as otherwise provided in paragraph (c), if an employee's required beginning date is (or would have been) on or before April 1, 1987 and such employee dies in calendar year 1985, 1986 or 1987, but on or after the first day of the employee's first distribution calendar year, the plan administrator may, under these transition rules, treat distributions as having begun in accordance with section 401(a)(9)(A)(ii) before the employee died for purposes of section 401(a)(9)(B)(i). The plan administrator may make such determination on an individual by individual basis. Distributions may be treated as having begun for purposes of section 401(a)(9)(B)(i) even though payments were not actually made before the employee died. If, under this transition rule, distributions are treated as having begun before the employee died, distribution of the employee's benefit for calendar years 1985 (if applicable), 1986, 1987, and subsequent calendar years will be made to the employee's beneficiaries over a period described in section 401(a)(9)(A)(i) pursuant to section 401(a)(9)(B)(i) rather than in accordance with section 401(a)(9)(B)(ii) or (iii) and (iv). (See C-4.) If distributions are thus treated as having

begun, the amount any minimum distribution required for calendar years 1985, 1986 or 1987 will be determined in accordance with I-2 through I-5 treating the employee as alive on December 31, 1987. If such amount was not paid to the employee before the employee's death, it must be paid to the beneficiaries of the employee on or before December 31, 1987. Further, in such case, the designated beneficiary of the employee will be determined as of any date in 1987. The applicable life expectancies are determined using birthdays in 1987, and by treating the employee and designated beneficiary as alive. Except as otherwise provided in these transition rules, the employee's life expectancy will not be recalculated. However, if the employee's spouse is a beneficiary, such spouse's life expectancy will be recalculated unless either (1) the plan administrator establishes a policy that spouses' life expectancies are not recalculated or (2) the spouse elects not to have life expectancy recalculated.

(c) *Distributions to the employee's spouse.* Except as otherwise provided in I-9(c) plan distributions must satisfy the survivor requirements of sections 401(a)(11) and 417 notwithstanding the rules in paragraph (b). These requirements may mandate a particular method of distribution to a surviving spouse or require spousal consent. Further, the rules in paragraph (b) allowing a plan administrator to treat distributions as having begun do not apply for purposes of determining under section 401(a)(11) and 417 whether distribution must be in the form of a qualified preretirement survivor annuity or a qualified joint and survivor annuity.

(d) *Example.* This I-6 is illustrated by the following example:

Example.

(a) An employee (X), born May 2, 1915, is a participant in Plan Y (a profit-sharing plan). X retired December 31, 1985. X died March 1, 1986. As of X's date of death, X's sole beneficiary under Plan Y was X's spouse. The plan administrator of Plan Y has established no policy concerning recalculation of life expectancy or of permitting elections of such recalculation. (Thus, any default provisions in this section of the regulations apply.)

(b) If X had survived, X's required beginning date would have been April 1, 1986 and X's first distribution calendar year would have been 1985. Because X died on or after January 1, 1985 and before December 31, 1987, the plan may distribute either (1) to X's spouse in accordance with the exception to the five year rule in section 401(a)(9)(B)(iii) and (iv) or (2) treat distributions as having begun to X before death pursuant to paragraph (b) of this I-6.

(c) If Plan Y distributes to X's spouse in accordance with the exception to the five-year rule in section 401(a)(9)(B)(iii) and (iv), the first distribution calendar year is 1987 and distributions must commence by December 31, 1987. If instead Plan Y treats distributions as having begun, X's first distribution calendar year is 1985. Under these transition rules, minimum distributions for 1985, 1986, and 1987 would then be required to be made by December 31, 1987. In accordance with paragraph (b) of this I-6, X's life expectancy will not be recalculated but, in accordance with E-7(a), X's spouse's life expectancy will be recalculated.

I-7. Q. If an employee died prior to January 1, 1986 and distributions are being made over the life expectancy of a designated beneficiary in accordance with section 401(a)(9)(B)(iii) and (iv), which is the first calendar year for which a distribution is required and when must distribution commence?

A. Except as otherwise provided in I-9 (special rule for certain life annuities), if an employee died prior to January 1, 1986 and distributions are being made over the life expectancy of a designated beneficiary in accordance with section 401(a)(9)(B)(iii) and (iv), the first distribution calendar year for which a minimum distribution is required is the later of (1) the calendar year which contains the required commencement date determined under C-3(a) or (b), whichever is applicable, or (2) calendar year 1985. However, under these transitional rules, if the first distribution calendar year is 1985, the minimum distribution for 1985 is not required to be made by December 31, 1985. Similarly, under these transition rules, if the first (or second) distribution calendar year is 1986, the minimum distribution for 1980 is not required to be made by December 31, 1986. Instead, in such case, the minimum distribution required for 1985 (if applicable), 1986, and 1987 is required to be made by December 31, 1987.

I-8. Q. If (a) distributions after the death of an employee are being made over the life expectancy of a designated beneficiary in accordance with section 401(a)(9)(B)(iii) and (iv), and (b) the first distribution calendar year is 1985 or 1986 (determined under I-3), then how is the amount of the minimum distribution determined for calendar years 1985, 1986, and 1987?

A. (a) *In general.* (1) If the two conditions set forth in the Question are satisfied, the amount of the minimum distribution for calendar years 1985, 1986, and 1987 is to be determined under one of the three methods described in paragraphs (b), (c), and (d). The plan administrator is to determine which method, including the credit rules under paragraph (b)(4) and (c)(3), is to be used. The same method used under this I-8 and I-2 must be used with respect to all such employees.

(2) See I-9 for a special rule for distributions in the form of a life annuity.

(b) *Life expectancy method.* Under the life expectancy method, the total amount of the minimum distribution required for calendar years 1985, 1986, and 1987 is determined as follows:

(1) *Designated beneficiary and life expectancy.* The designated beneficiary of the employee will be determined as of any date in 1987. The applicable life expectancy will be the designated beneficiary's life expectancy using attained age as of his birthday in 1987. In the case of a beneficiary who is not alive on his birthday in 1987, such beneficiary will be treated as being alive on his birthday in 1987 for purposes of determining life expectancy under this transitional rule.

(2) *Benefit determination.* The benefit of the employee is determined using the account balance as of the last valuation date under the plan in 1986, adjusted in accordance with F-5 with the following modifications. First, the benefit adjustment for distributions after the valuation date under F-5(c) is not made. Second, the benefit is increased by any distribution made in 1985 or 1986 before the valuation date described in subparagraph (2) for which credit is being taken under subparagraph (4).

(3) *Required distribution.* The total amount which must be distributed for calendar years 1985, 1986, and 1987 using the life expectancy method will be determined by dividing the benefit determined under subparagraph (2) by the applicable life expectancy determined under subparagraph (1) and multiplying the quotient by:

(i) 2.8, in the case of an employee with respect to whom the first distribution calendar year is 1985, or

(ii) 1.9, in the case of an employee with respect to whom the first distribution calendar year is 1986.

(4) *Credit for distributions.* In determining whether the total amount which must be distributed for calendar years 1985, 1986, and 1987 has been distributed credit may be taken (as determined by the plan administrator) for any amount distributed in a distribution calendar year of the employee (1985 through 1987). Consequently, to determine the amount which is required to be distributed in calendar year 1987, the plan administrator may reduce the total amount which must be distributed in 1987 for calendar years 1985, 1986, and 1987 (determined under subparagraph (3)) by the amounts distributed in:

(i) 1985 and 1986, in the case of an employee with respect to whom the first distribution calendar year is 1985, or

(ii) 1986, in the case of an employee with respect to whom the first distribution calendar year is 1986.

However, in the case of distributions before the last valuation date in 1986, credit may only be taken for amounts which were used to increase the benefit pursuant to subparagraph (2).

(c) *Percentage method.* Under the percentage method, the total amount of the minimum distribution required for calendar years 1985, 1986, and 1987 is determined as follows:

(1) *Benefit determination.* The benefit of the employee is determined in the same manner as under paragraph (b)(2).

(2) *Required distribution.* The total amount required to be distributed for calendar years 1985, 1986, and 1987 is the following percentage of the benefit (determined in accordance with subparagraph (1)):

(i) 15%, in the case of an employee with respect to whom the first distribution calendar year is 1985, or

(ii) 10%, in the case of an employee with respect to whom the first distribution calendar year is 1986.

(3) *Credits.* Credits for distributions may be taken in the same manner as under paragraph (b)(4).

(d) *Regular method.* Under the regular method, the sum of the minimum distributions required for each calendar year 1985, 1986, and 1987, calculated separately, is determined under section 401(a)(9) and this section with appropriate adjustments. However, the rule in F-2 does not apply. Also, credit (with an appropriate gross-up) may be taken toward the minimum required distribution for the 1986 or 1987 distribution calendar year for distributions in 1985 or 1986 distribution calendar years that exceeded the minimum required distribution for

such year. If distribution is being made in the form of an annuity and the annuity is not a life annuity (or is a life annuity with a period certain exceeding 20 years), the amount which must be distributed by December 31, 1987 is the aggregate of annual amounts (see F-3 (d)(2)) for each calendar year for which a distribution is required before 1988, determined under I-2.

I-9. Q. If (a) the employee died prior to January 1, 1986, (b) distribution is to be made in accordance with the exception to the five-year rule in section 401 (a)(9)(B)(iii) and (iv), and (c) the employees benefit is to be distributed in the form of a life annuity (or a life annuity with a period certain not exceeding 20 years), then as of what date must distributions be made, and how is the amount which must be distributed by that date determined?

A. (a) If the three conditions set forth in the Question are satisfied, the first period for which a distribution is required is the last payment interval (as defined in F-5) ending on or before the later of (1) the required commencement date determined under C-3(a) or (b), whichever is applicable, and (2) December 31, 1985. However, if such date is before December 31, 1987, under these transition rules, no distribution is required to be made on such date. Instead, distribution of an amount equal to the aggregate of the payments for all payment intervals from the last payment interval ending on or before that date through the last payment interval ending on or before December 31, 1987 must be made by December 31, 1987. Consequently, the total amount which must be distributed by December 31, 1987 will equal the total amount that which would have been distributed by December 31, 1987 if annuity payments made in accordance with C-3 had begun on or before the later of (1) the required commencement date determined under C-3(a) or (b), whichever is applicable, and (2) December 31, 1985.

(b) The designated beneficiary may be determined as of any date during the 90 day period ending on the earlier of (1) the date annuity distributions commence or (2) December 31, 1987.

(c) The provisions of this Question and Answer must be satisfied even if the surviving spouse does not consent to any catch-up distribution required under paragraph (a), and even if, as a result of such catch-up distribution, the amount payable after December 31, 1987 to the employee's surviving spouse under a qualified preretirement survivor annuity is reduced. In such case, if (1) the plan has made reasonable efforts to obtain consent from the employee's surviving spouse, (2) the requirement of section 417 that plan benefits be provided in the form of a qualified preretirement annuity is otherwise satisfied, and (3) the distribution otherwise meets the requirement of section 417, then the consent requirements of section 417 are deemed to be satisfied with respect to the distribution.

I-10. Q. If an employee died prior to January 1, 1986 and distributions are being made over the life expectancy of a designated beneficiary in accordance with section 401(a)(9)(B)(iii) and (iv), as of what date is the designated beneficiary determined, and what age is used to determine the designated beneficiary's life expectancy, for purposes of determining the minimum distribution for calendar years after 1987?

A. (a) If an employee died prior to January 1, 1986 and distributions are being made over the life expectancy of a designated beneficiary in accordance with section 401(a)(9)(B)(iii) and (iv), the designated beneficiary will be determined as of any date in 1987 for purposes of determining the minimum distribution for calendar years after 1987. The life expectancy of the designated beneficiary (other than the employee's surviving spouse whose life expectancy is being recalculated) will be determined using the attained age of the designated beneficiary as of such beneficiary's birthday in calendar year 1987, reduced by one for each calendar year which has elapsed after 1987. In such case if the designated beneficiary is not alive on his birthday in 1987, such beneficiary will be treated as being alive on that date for purposes of determining life expectancy. If the employee's surviving spouse is a designated beneficiary and such spouse's life expectancy is being recalculated, the life expectancy of spouse will be calculated using the attained age of the spouse as of such spouse's birthday in the calendar year for which the minimum distribution is being determined.

(b) If an employee died prior to January 1, 1986 and distributions are being made over the life expectancy of a designated beneficiary in accordance with section 401(a)(9)(B)(iii) and (iv) in the form of annuity payments, the designated beneficiary will be determined as of any date during the 90 day period ending on the date such annuity payments commence. The designated beneficiary's life expectancy will be determined using the attained age of the designated beneficiary as of such beneficiary's birthday in the calendar year in which the annuity payments commence.

I-11. Q. In the case of the surviving spouse of an employee for whom the first calendar year for which a distribution is required to be made is

1985 or 1986, when must the employee's spouse elect whether or not life expectancy will be recalculated?

A. If an employee for whom the first calendar year for which a distribution is required to be made is calendar year 1985 or 1986, any election, if permitted by the plan administrator, concerning recalculation of life expectancy must be made by December 31, 1987.

I-12. Q. When must the election described in C-4 (concerning whether distribution will be made in accordance with the five year rule in section 401(a)(9)(B)(ii) or the exception to the five-year rule in section 401(a)(9)(B)(iii) and (iv)) be made by a beneficiary otherwise required to make such election on or before December 31, 1985 or December 31, 1986?

A. The election described in C-4 (concerning whether distribution will be made in accordance with the five-year rule in section 401(a)(9)(B)(ii) or the exception to the five year rule in section 401(a)(9)(B)(iii) and (iv)), if otherwise required to have been made on or before December 31, 1985 or December 31, 1986, must, if permitted by the plan administrator, be made by December 31, 1987.

I-13. Q. If an employee died prior to January 1, 1985 and distribution is to be made in accordance with the five-year rule contained in section 401(a)(9)(B)(ii), as of what date must the employee's entire interest be distributed?

A. If an employee died prior to January 1, 1985 and distribution is to be made in accordance with the five-year rule contained in section 401(a)(9)(B)(ii), the employee's entire interest must be distributed as of the later of: (a) December 31 of the calendar year which contains the fifth anniversary of the employee's death or (b) December 31, 1987.

I-14. Q. If any portion of the minimum distribution required for calendar years 1985, 1986, or 1987 (which is required to be distributed by December 31, 1987) is distributed by a plan and rolled over to another plan (receiving plan) before such date, how does receipt of such rollover amount affect the qualification under section 401(a) of the plan accepting it?

A. If any portion of the minimum distribution required for calendar years 1985, 1986, or 1987 which is required to be distributed by December 31, 1987 is distributed by a plan and rolled over to another plan (receiving plan) before such date, under these transitional rules, the qualification under section 401(a) of the receiving plan is not affected by the receipt of such amount. However, see G-1B for the tax consequences to the distributee who rolls over the amount (including, if the amount is rolled over to an individual retirement plan, the rule for avoiding certain tax consequences). Certain tax consequences may be avoided by the distributee who rolls over to another qualified plan in either of two ways: (a) the receiving plan may distribute by December 31, 1987 that portion of the amount rolled over which is the minimum distribution from the distributing plan for calendar years 1985, 1986 or 1987 or (b) the distributing plan may distribute by December 31, 1987 an additional amount equal to that portion of the amount rolled over which is the minimum distribution from such plan for calendar years 1985, 1986 or 1987.

I-15. Q. In the case of a transfer in 1985, 1986, or 1987 of all or a portion of an employee's benefit from one plan (transferor plan) to another plan (transferee plan), is the amount transferred treated as an amount distributed for purposes of section 401(a)(9)?

A. (a) Except as otherwise provided in paragraph (b), in the case of a transfer in 1985, 1986, or 1987 but before [60 days after this notice is published] of all or a portion of an employee's benefit from one plan (transferor plan) to another plan (transferee plan) before the minimum amount required to be distributed by the transferor plan for such calendar year has been distributed, the transferor plan may treat the amount transferred as a distribution for purposes of section 401(a)(9).

(b) If all or a portion of an employee's benefit is transferred from one plan (transferor plan) to another plan (transferee plan) in 1985, 1986, or 1987 before [60 days after this notice is published]and before the minimum amount required to be distributed by the transferor plan for such calendar year has been distributed and the employee is a 5-percent owner (as defined in B-2) with respect to the employer maintaining either the transferor plan or the transferee plan, the transferee plan must distribute by December 31, 1987 any portion of the minimum distribution required to be distributed with respect to the portion of the benefit transferred but not distributed by the transferor plan for calendar years 1985, 1986, or 1987.

(c) In the case of a transfer in 1987 on or after [60 days after this notice is published], the rules in G-3 apply.

I-16. Q. What are the distribution requirements applicable to qualified plans that cover self-employed individuals described in section 401(c)(1) (HR 10 plans) for 1984?

A. For 1984, HR 10 plans are subject to the distribution requirements of section 401(a)(9) as in effect on September 2, 1982 (prior to such section's replacement by section 242(a) of TEFRA). (The after-death distribution rules in section 401(d)(7) applicable to owner-employees in HR 10 plans were repealed by section 237 of TEFRA and were not reinstated for 1984 by TRA of 1984.) An HR 10 plan that does not satisfy section 401(a)(9) (as in effect on September 2, 1982) in 1984 will not be considered to fail to qualify under section 401(a) or 403(a) solely for that reason if, in operation, the aggregate amount distributed by December 31, 1987 equals or exceeds the amount required to satisfy section 401(a)(9) prior to its amendment by TEFRA plus the amount required to satisfy section 401(a)(9) after its amendment by TRA of 1984 for calendar years 1985, 1986, and 1987. Thus, plan amendments to reflect the law for 1984 are not required in order to satisfy the old HR 10 requirement.

I-17. Q. In the case of a plan covering self-employed individuals to which the minimum distribution rules in §1.401-11(e) apply, if the aggregate amounts distributed with respect to an employee in calendar years prior to 1985 for which minimum distributions were required pursuant to §1.401-11(e) exceeded the aggregate amount required for such calendar years, may credit be given for such amount for purposes of satisfying the minimum distribution requirement for calendar years 1985 through 1987?

A. Yes. In the case of a plan covering self-employed individuals to which the minimum distribution rules in ·§1.401-11(e) apply, if the aggregate amounts distributed with respect to an employee in calendar years prior to 1985 for which minimum distributions were required pursuant to §1.401-11(e) exceed the aggregate amount required, credit may be taken for the difference between the aggregate amount distributed in calendar years before 1985 and the aggregate amount required to be distributed for such calendar years. Such excess amount will be treated as an amount distributed in calendar year 1985 for purposes of determining the amount which is required to be distributed by December 31, 1987 under I-3.

J. *Elections under section 242(b)(2) of TEFRA.*

J-1. Q. Is a plan disqualified merely because it pays benefits under a designation made before January 1, 1984, in accordance with section 242(b)(2) of TEFRA?

A. No. Even though the distribution requirements added by TEFRA were retroactively repealed by TRA of 1984, the transitional election rule in section 242(b) was preserved. Notice 83-23, 1983-2 CB 418, provides guidance for distributions permitted by this transitional rule. Satisfaction of the spousal consent requirements of section 417(a) and (e) (added by the Retirement Equity Act of 1984) will not be considered a revocation of the pre-1984 designation under that Notice. However, sections 401(a)(11) and 417 must be satisfied with respect to any distribution subject to such section. The election provided in section 242(b) is hereafter referred to as a section 242(b)(2) election.

J-2 Q. In the case in which an amount is transferred from one plan (transferor plan) to another plan (transferee plan), may the transferee plan distribute the amount transferred in accordance with a section 242(b)(2) election made under either the transferor plan or under the transferee plan?

A. (a) In the case in which an amount is transferred from one plan to another plan, the amount transferred may be distributed in accordance with a section 242(b)(2) election made under the transferor plan if the employee did not elect to have the amount transferred and if the amount transferred is separately accounted for by the transferee plan. However, only the benefit attributable to the amount transferred, plus earnings thereon, may be distributed in accordance with the section 242(b)(2) election made under the transferor plan. If the employee elected to have the amount transferred, the transfer will be treated as a distribution and rollover of the amount transferred for purposes of this J-2 and J-3.

(b) In the case in which an amount is transferred from one plan to another plan, the amount transferred may not be distributed in accordance with a section 242(b)(2) election made under the transferee plan. If a section 242(b)(2) election was made under the transferee plan, the amount transferred must be separately accounted for. If the amount transferred is not separately accounted for under the transferee plan, the section 242(b)(2) election under the transferee plan is revoked and section 401(a)(9) will apply to subsequent distributions by the transferee plan.

(c) A merger, spinoff, or consolidation, as defined in 1.414(l)-1(b), will be treated as a transfer for purposes of the section 242(b)(2) election.

J-3. Q. If an amount is distributed by one plan (distributing plan) and rolled over into another plan (receiving plan), may the receiving plan distribute the amount rolled over in accordance with a section 242(b)(2) election made under either the distributing plan or the receiving plan?

A. No. If an amount is distributed by one plan and rolled over into another plan, the receiving plan must distribute the amount rolled over in accordance with section 401(a)(9) whether or not the employee made a section 242(b)(2) election under the distributing plan. Further, if the amount rolled over was not distributed in accordance with the election, the election under the distributing plan is revoked and section 401(a)(9) will apply to all subsequent distributions by the distributing plan. Finally, if the employee made a section 242(b)(2) election under the receiving plan and such election is still in effect, the amount rolled over must be separately accounted for under the receiving plan and distributed in accordance with section 401(a)(9). If amounts rolled over are not separately accounted for, any section 242(b)(2) election under the receiving plan is revoked and section 401(a)(9) will apply to subsequent distributions by the receiving plan.

J-4. Q. May a section 242(b)(2) election be revoked after the date by which distributions are required to commence in order to satisfy section 401(a)(9) and this section of the regulations?

A. Yes. A section 242(b)(2) election may be revoked after the date by which distributions are required to commence in order to satisfy section 401(a)(9) and this section of the regulations. However, if the section 242(b)(2) election is revoked after the date by which distributions are required to commence in order to satisfy section 401(a)(9) and this section of the regulations and the total amount of the distributions which would have been required to be made prior to the date of the revocation in order to satisfy section 401(a)(9), but for the section 242(b)(2) election, have not been made, the trust must distribute by the end of the calendar year following the calendar year in which the revocation occurs the total amount not yet distributed which was required to have been distributed to satisfy the requirements of section 401(a)(9) and continue distributions in accordance with such requirements. Further, an additional amount may be required to be distributed to satisfy the minimum distribution incidental death benefit requirement. See § 1.401(a)(9)-2.

J-5. Q. May the distribution of amounts otherwise required to be distributed in 1985, 1986, or 1987 before December 31, 1987, pursuant to a section 242(b)(2) election be deferred until December 31, 1987 under the transition rule in I-1 or through J-15?

A. The transition rules in I-1 through I-15 do not apply to distributions to be made pursuant to a section 242(b)(2) election. Failure to make any distribution of an amount specified at the time specified under the method of distribution provided in a section 242(b)(2) election will be treated as a change in the election and thus a revocation of the election. In the event of such a revocation before December 31, 1987, the transition rules in I-1 through I-15 will apply to any distributions otherwise required to be made before December 31, 1987. Accordingly, in the event of such a revocation before December 31, 1987, any distribution otherwise required under section 401(a)(9) and this section of the regulations to be made before December 31, 1987 may be delayed until that date.

§ 1.401(a)(9)-2 Minimum distribution incidental benefit requirement.

Q-1. What is the incidental benefit requirement?

A. The incidental benefit requirement has two components, the minimum distribution incidental benefit requirement (MDIB requirement) and the pre-retirement incidental benefit requirement. The pre-retirement incidental benefit requirement applies to limit pre-retirement distributions in the form of nonretirement benefits such as life, accident, or health insurance. Both the MDIB requirement and the pre-retirement incidental benefit requirement requires that death and other nonretirement benefits payable under a pension, stock bonus, or profit-sharing plan be incidental to the primary purpose of the plan which is to provide retirement benefits (in the case of a pension plan) or deferred compensation (in the case of a profit-sharing plan) to the employee. Thus, the relationship of an employee's total benefits under the plan to the retirement benefits or deferred compensation payable to the employee must be such that the primary purpose of the plan is to provide retirement benefits or deferred compensation to the employee. See § 1.401-1(b)(1). Also, see section 401(a)(9)(G), as added by section 1852(a)(6) of the Tax Reform Act of 1986 (TRA of 1986) which provides that any distribution required to satisfy the incidental benefit requirement is also a required distribution under section 401(a)(9). Further,

see section 403(b)(10), added by section 1852(a)(3)(A) of TRA of 1986, which codified the application of the incidental benefit requirement to annuity contracts and custodial contracts described in section 403(b). See section 408(a)(6) and (b)(3), as amended by section 1852(a)(1) of TRA of 1986, which extends the incidental benefit requirement to distribution from IRAs. Finally, see section 457(d)(2)(A), added by section 1107(a) of TRA of 1986, which provides that an eligible deferred compensation plan must satisfy section 401(a)(9) and thus the incidental benefit requirement.

Q-1A. How is the MDIB requirement satisfied?

A. (a) *Operational requirements.* Distributions under a plan in each calendar year must satisfy the MDIB requirement in order for the plan to be qualified under section 401(a) in operation. If any distributions for a calendar year fail to satisfy the MDIB requirement, the plan will not satisfy section 401(a) for the plan year beginning with or within that calendar year.

(b) *Required plan provisions.* See A-3 of § 1.401(a)(9)-1, which provides that the plan must include certain written provisions reflecting section 401(a)(9). Section 401(a)(9) includes the MDIB requirement.

Q-2. For calendar years beginning before January 1, 1989, how must benefits be distributed in order to satisfy the MDIB requirement?

A. For calendar years beginning before January 1, 1989, distribution of benefits must satisfy either the rules in effect as of [date of publication of this notice] interpreting § 1.401-1(b)(1)(i) or the rules in Q&A-3 through Q&A-7 in order to satisfy the MDIB requirement.

Q-3. For calendar years beginning after December 31, 1988, how must an employee's benefits be distributed in order to satisfy the MDIB requirement?

A. For calendar years beginning after December 31, 1988, distributions of an employee's benefit must commence not later than the employee's required beginning date as defined in section 401(a)(9)(C) and be made in accordance with the rules in Q&A-4 through Q&A-7 in order to satisfy the MDIB requirement. The amount required to be distributed to satisfy the MDIB requirement for a calendar year may be greater than the amount required to satisfy the other minimum distribution requirements in section 401(a)(9). Distributions made before the employee's required beginning date for calendar years before the employee's first distribution calendar year, as defined in F-1 of § 1.401(a)(9)-1, need not be made in accordance with the MDIB requirement. However, if distributions commence under a particular distribution option, such as in the form of an annuity, before the beginning of the employee's first distribution calendar year, the distribution option will fail to satisfy the MDIB requirement at the time distributions commence if, under the particular distribution option, distributions to be made for the employee's first distribution calendar year or any subsequent distribution calendar year will not satisfy the MDIB requirement. The MDIB requirement does not apply to distributions after the employee's death although distributions to be made after the death of the employee must be taken into account in determining whether distributions before the employee's death satisfy the MDIB requirement. Q&A-4 provides rules which apply to nonannuity distributions from an individual account. Q&A-5 provides rules which apply to distributions in the form of an annuity for a period certain without a life contingency. Q&A-6 provides rules which apply to distributions in the form of a life annuity or a joint and survivor annuity. Q&A-7 provides special rules which apply if the employee's beneficiary is the employee's spouse. Q&A-8 provides a special rule for annuity distributions commencing before January 1, 1988.

Q-4. For calendar years after 1988, if an employee's benefit is in the form of an individual account, how must the employee's benefit be distributed in order to satisfy the MDIB requirement?

A. (a) *General rule—*(1) *Explanation of rule.* If an employee's benefit is in the form of an individual account, distribution must be made for each distribution calendar year (determined under F-1 of § 1.401(a)(9)-1) of the employee in accordance with the following rules in order to satisfy the MDIB requirement. The first year for which a distribution must be made to satisfy the MDIB requirement is the employee's first distribution calendar year, determined under F-1 of § 1.401(a)(9)-1. The minimum amount that must be distributed for each distribution calendar year of the employee to satisfy the MDIB requirement is the amount determined by dividing the employee's benefit by the applicable divisor under the table below. The applicable divisor is determined using the attained age of the employee as of the employee's birthday in that distribution calendar year. The employee's benefit must be determined under F-5 of § 1.401(a)(9)-1. As under F-1 of § 1.401(a)(9)-1, the distribution required to be made by the employee's required beginning date is for the employee's first distribution calendar year, and in the case of distributions for other distribution calendar years, the distribution must be made by the end of such calendar year.

(2) *Table for determining applicable divisor*

Age of the employee	Applicable divisor
70	26.2
71	25.3
72	24.4
73	23.5
74	22.7
75	21.8
76	20.9
77	20.1
78	19.2
79	18.4
80	17.6
81	16.8
82	16.0
83	15.3
84	14.5
85	13.8
86	13.1
87	12.4
88	11.8
89	11.1
90	10.5
91	9.9
92	9.4
93	9.8
94	9.3
95	7.8
96	7.3
97	6.9
98	6.5
99	6.1
100	5.7
101	5.3
102	5.0
103	4.7
104	4.4
105	4.1
106	3.8
107	3.6
108	3.3
109	3.1
110	2.8
111	2.6
112	2.4
113	2.2
114	2.0
115 and older	1.8

(b) *Annuity contract.* If an employee's benefit is in the form of an individual account and the employee's benefit is used to purchase an annuity contract from an insurance company, the MDIB requirement is not satisfied unless the annuity distributions under the contract are made in accordance with Q&A-5 or Q&A-6.

Q-5. For calendar years after 1988, if an employee's benefit is being distributed in the form of a period certain annuity without a life contingency (e.g., installment payout), how must the benefit be distributed in order to satisfy the MDIB requirement?

A. (a) *General rule.* If an employee's benefit is being distributed in the form of a period certain annuity without a life contingency, the period certain may not exceed the applicable period determined using the table below. In general, the applicable period is determined using the attained age of the employee as of the employee's birthday in the calendar year in which the annuity payments commence. However, if distributions commence after the end of the employee's first distribution calendar year and on or before the employee's required beginning date, the applicable period is determined using the attained age of the employee as of the employee's birthday in the employee's first distribution calendar year. Further, if distributions commence before January 1 of the employee's first distribution calendar year under a benefit option which provides for distributions in the form of a period certain annuity without a life contingency, the MDIB requirement will not be satisfied as of the date distributions commence unless the benefit option provides that, as of the beginning of the employee's first distribution calendar year, the remaining period under the annuity (including such calendar year) will not exceed the period determined under the table

below using the attained age of the employee as of the employee's birthday in the employee's first distribution calendar year. For example, if distributions commence to an employee (X), born May 5, 1930, on January 1, 1990, and the benefit option provides for distribution in the form of a period certain annuity for 37 years, the MDIB requirement is not satisfied when the distributions commence because the remaining period certain as the beginning of X's first distribution calendar year (year 2000) will be 27 years (37 minus 10) which exceeds 26.2. However, the benefit could provide for an automatic shortening of the period at age 70 ½ to conform to the MDIB requirement. Additionally, the amount of the annuity payments must satisfy F-3 of § 1.401(a)(9)-1 in order to satisfy the MDIB requirement. Of course, if the annuity payments commence after the employee's required beginning date, distributions before the annuity payments commence must satisfy Q&A-4.

(b) *Table*

Age of employee	Maximum period certain
70	26.2
71	25.3
72	24.4
73	23.5
74	22.7
75	21.8
76	20.9
77	20.1
78	19.2
79	18.4
80	17.6
81	16.8
82	16.0
83	15.3
84	14.5
85	13.8
86	13.1
87	12.4
88	11.8
89	11.1
90	10.5
91	9.9
92	9.4
93	8.8
94	8.3
95	7.8
96	7.3
97	6.9
98	6.5
99	6.1
100	5.7
101	5.3
102	5.0
103	4.7
104	4.4
105	4.1
106	3.8
107	3.6
108	3.3
109	3.1
110	2.8
111	2.6
112	2.4
113	2.2
114	2.0
115 and older	1.8

Q-6. For calendar years after 1988, how must distributions in the form of a life (or joint and survivor) annuity be made in order to satisfy the MDIB requirement?

A. (a) *Annuity for employee.* If the employee's benefit is payable in the form of a life annuity for the life of the employee satisfying section 401(a)(9), the MDIB requirement will be satisfied.

(b) *Joint and survivor annuity, nonspouse beneficiary-*(1) *Explanation of rule.* If distributions commence under a distribution option that is in the form of a joint and survivor annuity for the joint lives of the employee and a beneficiary, other than the employee's spouse, the MDIB requirement will not be satisfied as of the date distributions commence unless the distribution option provides that annuity payments to be made to the employee on and after the employee's required beginning date will satisfy the conditions of this paragraph. The periodic annuity payment payable to the survivor must not at any time on and after the employee's required beginning date exceed the applicable percentage of the annuity payment for such period payable to the employee using the table below. Thus, this requirement must be satisfied with respect to any benefit increase after such date, including increases to reflect increases in the cost of living. The applicable percentage is based on the excess of the age of the employee over the age of the beneficiary as of their attained ages as of their birthdays in the employee's first distribution calendar year. If the employee has more than one beneficiary, the applicable percentage will be the percentage using the age of the youngest beneficiary. Further, if a beneficiary replaces another beneficiary under the annuity or a beneficiary is added, and the new beneficiary is younger than the beneficiary being used to determine the applicable percentage, the employee's benefit must be adjusted in the calendar year following the calendar year of the change. The employee's benefit must be adjusted so that the periodic benefit payable to the survivor does not exceed the applicable percentage of the annuity payment for such period payable to the employee using the age of the employee and the new younger beneficiary. Additionally, the amount of the annuity payments must satisfy F-3 of § 1.401(a)(9)-1.

(2) *Table.*

Excess of age of employee over age of beneficiary	Applicable percentage
10 years or less	100%
11	96%
12	93%
13	90%
14	87%
15	84%
16	82%
17	79%
18	77%
19	75%
20	73%
21	72%
22	70%
23	68%
24	67%
25	66%
26	64%
27	63%
28	62%
29	61%
30	60%
31	59%
32	59%
33	58%
34	57%
35	56%
36	56%
37	55%
38	55%
39	54%
40	54%
41	53%
42	53%
43	53%
44 and greater	52%

(3) *Example.* This paragraph is illustrated by the following example.

Example. Distributions commence on January 1, 1993 to an employee (Z), born March 1, 1927, after retirement at age 65. Z's granddaughter (Y), born February 5, 1967, is Z's beneficiary. The distributions are in the form of a joint and survivor annuity for the lives of Z and Y with payments of $500 a month to Z and upon Z's death of $500 a month to Y, *i.e.* the projected monthly payment to Y is 100 percent of the monthly amount payable to Z. There is no provision under the option for a change in the projected payments to Y as of April 1, 1998, Z's required beginning date. Consequently, as of January 1, 1993, the date annuity distributions commence, the plan does not satisfy the MDIB requirement in operation because, as of such date, the distribution option provides that, as of Z's required beginning date, the monthly payment to Y upon Z's death will exceed 54 percent of Z's monthly payment (the maximum percentage for a difference of ages of 40).

(c) *Period certain and annuity features.* If a distribution form includes a life annuity and a period certain, the amount of the annuity payments payable to the employee must satisfy either paragraph (a) or (b),

whichever is applicable, and the period certain may not exceed the period determined under Q&A-4.

Q-7. For calendar years after 1988, if the employee's beneficiary is the employee's spouse, how must distributions be made in order to satisfy the MDIB requirement?

A. (a) *General rule.* If the employee's beneficiary, as of the employee's required beginning date, is the employee's spouse and the distributions satisfy section 401(a)(9) without regard to the MDIB requirement, the distributions to the employee will be deemed to satisfy the MDIB requirement. For example, if an employee's benefit is being distributed in the form of a joint and survivor annuity for the lives of the employee and the employee's spouse and the spouse is the employee's beneficiary, the amount of the periodic payment payable to the spouse may always be 100 percent of the annuity payment payable to the employee. However, under section 401(a)(9) the amount of the payments under the annuity must be nonincreasing unless specifically permitted under F-3 of § 1.401(a)(9)-1. A former spouse to whom all or a portion of an employee's benefit is payable pursuant to a qualified domestic relations order as defined in section 414(p) will be treated as a spouse of the employee for purposes of the MDIB requirement.

(b) *Multiple beneficiaries.* If the employee has more than one beneficiary, the special rule in paragraph (a) will only apply to the portion of the employee's benefit of which the spouse is the sole beneficiary. However, in order for the special requirement in paragraph (a) to apply to the distribution of the portion of the employee's benefit of which the spouse is the sole beneficiary, such portion must be a separate account (or segregated share, in the case of a defined benefit plan), as defined in H-2A of § 1.401(a)(9)-1.

(c) *Changes in beneficiaries.* (1) If, after the employee's required beginning date, the employee's spouse ceases to be the employee's sole beneficiary because the spouse dies before the employee, distributions after the death of the spouse to the employee will continue to satisfy the MDIB requirement if such distributions satisfy section 401(a)(9), without regard to the MDIB requirement. See paragraph (d)(2) if the employee's spouse dies before the employee's required beginning date.

(2) If, after the employee's required beginning date, the employee's spouse ceases to be the employee's sole beneficiary for a reason other than the death of the spouse, if the portion of the employee's benefit of which the employee's spouse is the beneficiary ceases to be maintained as a separate account or segregated share, or the spouse ceases to be the sole beneficiary of such separate account or segregated share for a reason other than the death of the spouse, the following rules apply. In the case of distributions from an individual account not in the form of an annuity, distributions in calendar years following the calendar year in which the spouse ceases to be the beneficiary must satisfy Q&A-4. If distribution is in the form of an annuity for a period certain, the remaining period of the period certain as of the calendar year following the calendar year of the change may not exceed the period which would have remained if annuity payments had commenced in accordance with Q&A-5 on the employee's required beginning date and the spouse was not the beneficiary. If the employee's benefit is being distributed in the form of a joint and survivor annuity, the amount of the periodic payment payable to the employee beginning in the calendar year following the calendar year of the change must be redetermined. The new amount may not exceed the applicable percentage under Q&A-6 using the excess of the age of the employee over the age of the new beneficiary using their attained ages as of their birthdays in the calendar year of the redetermination.

(d) *Change in status—*(1) *After the employee's required beginning date.* If a beneficiary of the employee is the employee's spouse as of the employee's required beginning date, such beneficiary will continue to be treated as a spouse of the employee for purposes of the MDIB requirement for all distribution calendar years of the employee even if such beneficiary ceases to be the employee's spouse by reason of divorce, and such beneficiary remains the employee's sole beneficiary.

(2) *Before the employee's required beginning date.* Generally, the special rule in paragraph (a) only applies if a beneficiary is the employee's spouse as of the employee's required beginning date. However, if distributions commence irrevocably (except for acceleration) to the employee before the employee's required beginning date over a period described in section 401(a)(9)(A)(ii), if the distribution form is an annuity under which distributions are made in accordance with the provisions of F-3 (and F-4, if applicable) of § 1.401(a)(9)-1, and if the employee's beneficiary with respect to the annuity payments is the employee's spouse, the following rules will apply. If the employee's spouse dies before the employee's required beginning date, distributions may continue over any remaining period certain under the annuity even if, as of the beginning of the employee's first distribution

calendar year, such period exceeds the period permitted under Q&A-4. If such beneficiary ceases to be the employee's spouse by reason of divorce, such beneficiary will continue to be treated as a spouse of the employee for purposes of the MDIB requirement if such beneficiary continues to be the employee's beneficiary with respect to the annuity payments after the employee's required beginning date.

Q-8. For calendar years after 1988, is there any special rule for distributions in the form of an annuity that commence prior to January 1, 1989?

A. Yes. If distributions in the form of an annuity (from a defined benefit plan or under an annuity contract purchased from an insurance company) commence in accordance with F-3 (and F-4 if applicable) of § 1.401(a)(9)-1 prior to January 1, 1989, the annuity distributions in each calendar year (including calendar years after 1988) will satisfy the MDIB requirement if distributions are made in accordance with Q&A-2. This rule applies whether the annuity is a life (or joint and survivor) annuity or an annuity for a period certain, or a combination thereof, and without regard to whether the annuity form of payment is irrevocable. This special rule applies to a deferred annuity contract distributed to or owned by the employee prior to January 1, 1989 unless additional contributions are made under the plan by the employer with respect to such contract.

Q-9. Is there a special rule which applies to distributions under a designation of a method of distribution made before January 1, 1984, in accordance with section 242(b)(2) of the Tax Equity and Fiscal Responsibility Act (TEFRA)?

A. Yes. Distributions (including distributions in calendar years after 1988) under a designation of a method of distribution made before January 1, 1984, in accordance with section 242(b)(2) of TEFRA will satisfy the MDIB requirement if such distributions are made in accordance with Q&A-2. However, if the designation is revoked, distributions in calendar years after 1988, except as otherwise provided in Q&A-8, must satisfy the rules in Q&A-3 through Q&A-7. Further, if the revocation occurs in a calendar year after 1988, the trust must distribute by the end of the calendar year following the calendar year in which the revocation occurs the total amount which was required to be distributed under Q&A-3 through Q&A-7 for the calendar years that have elapsed since 1988.

Q-10. Will a plan fail to satisfy section 411 if the plan is amended to eliminate benefit options that do not satisfy the MDIB requirement?

A. Nothing in section 401(a)(9) permits a plan to eliminate for all participants a benefit option that could not otherwise be eliminated pursuant to section 411(d)(6). However, a plan must provide that, notwithstanding any other plan provisions, it will not distribute benefits under any option that does not satisfy section 401(a)(9), including the MDIB requirement. See A-3 of § 1.401(a)(9)-1. Thus, the plan, notwithstanding section 411(d)(6), must prevent participants from electing benefit options that do not satisfy the MDIB requirement.

Q-11. Does the MDIB requirement apply to distributions to an alternate payee pursuant to a qualified domestic relations order as defined in section 414(p)(QDRO)?

A. If a QDRO provides that an employee's benefit is to be divided and a portion allocated to an alternate payee, the MDIB requirement will not apply to the distribution of the portion of the employee's benefit allocated to the alternate payee. However, if the QDRO does not provide that an employee's benefit is to be divided but merely provides that a portion of an employee's benefit (otherwise payable to the employee) is to be paid to an alternate payee, the MDIB requirement will apply to the distribution of the employee's entire benefit (including the portion payable to the alternative payee). Also, see Q&A-7 with respect to distributions to a former spouse pursuant to the QDRO.

Par. 4. There is added the following new section after § 1.403(b)-1 to read as follows:

§ 1.403(b)-2 Required distributions from annuity contracts purchased, or custodial accounts or retirement income accounts established by, a section 501(c)(3) organizations or public schools.

Q-1. Are annuity contracts described in section 403(b)(1), custodial accounts described in section 403(b)(7), and retirement income accounts described in section 403(b)(9) subject to the distribution rules provided in section 401(a)(9)?

A. (a) Yes. Annuity contracts described in section 403(b)(1), custodial accounts described in section 403(b)(7), and retirement income accounts described in section 403(b)(9) are subject to the distribution rules provided in section 401(a)(9) for calendar years after 1986. Hereinafter, annuity contracts described in section 403(b)(1), custodial

accounts described in section 403(b)(7), and retirement income accounts described in section 403(b)(9) will be referred to as section 403(b) contracts.

(b) For purposes of applying the distribution rules in section 401(a)(9), section 403(b) contracts will be treated as individual retirement annuities described in section 408(b) and individual retirement accounts described in section 408(a), respectively (IRAs). Consequently, except as otherwise provided in paragraph (c), the distribution rules in section 401(a)(9) will be applied to section 403(b) contracts in accordance with the provisions in § 1.408-8.

(c) The transitional rule in § 1.401(a)(9)-1 B-2(b) will apply to distributions from section 403(b) contracts even though such transitional rule does not apply to distributions from IRAs. Thus, for an employee who attained 70 ½ before January 1, 1988, the required beginning date is April 1, of the calendar year following the later of (1) the calendar year in which the employed attains 70 ½ or (2) the calendar year in which the employee retires. The concept of 5-percent owner has no application iii the case of employees of employers described in section 403(b)(1)(A).

Q-2. To what benefits under section 403(b) contracts, do the distribution rules provided in section 401(a)(9) and § 1.401(a)(9)-1 apply?

A. (a) The distribution rules provided in section 401(a)(9) and § 1.401(a)(9)-1 apply to all benefits under section 403(b) contracts accruing after December 31, 1986 (post-'86 account balance). The distribution rules provided in section 401(a)(9) and § 1.401(a)(9)-1 do not apply to the value of the account balance under the section 403(b) contract valued as of December 31, 1986, exclusive of subsequent earnings (pre-'87 account balance). Consequently, the post-'86 account balance includes earnings after December 31, 1986, on contributions made before January 1, 1987, in addition to contributions made after December 31, 1986 and earnings thereon. The issuer or custodian of the section 403(b) contract must keep records that enable it to identify the pre-'87 account balance and subsequent changes as set forth in paragraph (b) and provide such information upon request to the relevant employee or beneficiaries with respect to the contract. If the issuer does not keep such records, the entire account balance will be treated as subject to section 401(a)(9).

(b) In applying the distribution rules in section 401(a)(9), only the post-'86 account balance is used to calculate the minimum distribution required for a calendar year. The amount of any distribution required to satisfy the minimum distribution requirement for a calendar year will be treated as being paid from the post-'86 account balance. Any amount distributed in a calendar year in excess of the minimum distribution requirement for a calendar year will be treated as paid from the pre-'87 account balance. The pre-'87 account balance for the next calendar year will be permanently reduced by the deemed distributions from the account.

(c) The pre-'86 account balance and the post-'87 account balance have no relevance for purposes of determining the amount includible in income under section 72.

Q-3. Must the value of the account balance under a section 403(b) contract as of December 31, 1986 be distributed in accordance with the incidental benefit requirement?

A. Distributions of the entire account balance of a section 403(b) contract, including the value of the account balance under the contract or account as of December 31, 1986, must satisfy the minimum distribution incidental benefit requirement (MDIB requirement) in Q&A-2 of § 1.401(a)(9)-2. Distributions required to satisfy the MDIB requirement in Q&A-2 of § 1.401(a)(9)-2 reduce the pre-'87 account balance as set forth in Q&A-2 of this section of the regulations. The MDIB requirement in Q&A-3 through Q&A-7 of § 1.401(a)(9)-2, applicable to calendar years after 1988, need only be satisfied for distributions from the post-'86 account.

Par. 5. There is added the following new section after § 1.408-7 to read as follows:

§ 1.408-8 Distribution requirements for individual retirement plans.

The following questions and answers relate to the distribution rules for IRAs provided in section 408(a)(6) and section 408(b)(3), as added by section 521(b) of the Tax Reform Act of 1984 (Pub. L. 98-369) (TRA of 1984) and amended by section 1852(a) of the Tax Reform Act of 1986 (Pub. L. 99-514) (TRA of 1986).

Table of Contents

A. *General rules.*

A-1. Q. Are individual retirement plans (IRAs) subject to the distribution rules provided in section 401(a)(9) and §1.401(a)(9)-1 for qualified plans?

A. Yes. Except as otherwise provided in this section, IRAs are subject to the distribution rules provided in section 401(a)(9) and §1.401(a)(9)-1 for qualified plans. The distribution rules in §1.408-2 (b)(6) and (7) (as in effect on December 31, 1983) no longer apply to IRAs. For example, (a) the amount of the minimum distribution for each calendar year will be determined in accordance with §1.401(a)(9)-1 F-1 through F-4A, (b) in the event that the individual for whom an IRA is maintained (individual) changes or adds beneficiaries after the distributions are required to commence, the maximum distribution period will be determined in accordance with §1.401(a)(9)-1 E-5, (c) pursuant to §1.401(a)(9)-1 H-1, the rules in section 401(a)(9) apply separately to each IRA maintained for an individual's benefit, and (d) the rules in §1.401(a)(9)-1 E-6 through E-8 concerning recalculation of life expectancy apply to IRAs. However, the effective date and transitional rules for the distribution rules applicable to IRAs are determined under this §1.408-8 and not §1.401(a)(9)-1.

A-2. Q. Are employer contributions under a simplified employee pension (defined in section 408(k)) treated as contributions to an IRA?

A. Yes. IRAs that receive employer contributions under a simplified employee pension (defined in section 408(k)) are treated as IRAs and are, therefore, subject to the distribution rules in this section.

A-3. Q. In the case of distributions from an IRA, what does the term "required beginning date" mean?

A. In the case of distributions from an IRA, the term "required beginning date" means April 1, of the calendar year following the calendar year in which the individual attains age 70 ½. The transition rule in §1.401(a)(9)-1 B-2(b) does not apply to distributions from IRAs.

A-3A. Q. Will an IRA lose its tax-exempt status for failing in operation to make minimum distributions in accordance with section 408(a)(6) and (b)(3).

A. An IRA will not lose its tax-exempt status for isolated instances of failing in operation to make minimum distributions in accordance with section 408(a)(8) and (b)(3). A pattern or regular practice of failing to meet the minimum distribution requirements of section 408(a)(6) and (b)(3) with respect to the individual (or of the individual's beneficiaries) will not be treated as an isolated instance even if each instance is de minimis.

A-4. Q. May an individual's beneficiary elect to treat such beneficiary's entire interest in the trust upon the death of the individual (or the remaining part of such interest if distribution to the beneficiary has commenced) as the beneficiary's own account?

A. (a) In the case of an individual who died before January 1, 1984, the provisions of §1.408-2(b)(7)(ii) (as in effect on December 31, 1983) continue to apply to the distribution of such individual's account. Thus, any beneficiary (whether or not the beneficiary is the individual's surviving spouse) may treat his interest in such individual's account as the beneficiary's own account in accordance with §1.408-2(b)(7)(ii), regardless of whether or not distribution to the beneficiary has commenced.

(b) In the case of an individual dying after December 31, 1983, the only beneficiary of the individual who may elect to treat the beneficiary's entire interest in the trust (or the remaining part of such interest if distribution thereof has commenced to the beneficiary) as the beneficiary's own account is the individual's surviving spouse. If the surviving spouse makes such an election, the spouse's interest in the account would then be subject to the distribution requirements of section 401(a)(9)(A), rather than those of section 401(a)(9)(B). An election will be considered to have been made by the surviving spouse if either of the following occurs: (1) any required amounts in the account (including any amounts that have been rolled over or transferred, in accordance with the requirements of section 408(d)(3)(A)(i), into an individual retirement account or individual retirement annuity for the benefit of such surviving spouse) have not been distributed within the appropriate time period applicable to the decedent under section 401(a)(9)(B), or (2) any additional amounts are contributed to the account (or to the account or annuity to which the surviving spouse has rolled such amounts over, as described in (1) above) which are subject, or deemed to be subject, to the distribution requirements of section 401(a)(9)(A). The result of such an election is that the surviving spouse shall then be considered the individual for whose benefit the trust is maintained.

A-5. Q. How is the benefit determined for purposes of calculating the minimum distribution from an IRA?

A. For purposes of determining the minimum distribution required to he made from an IRA in any calendar year, the account balance of the IRA as of the December 31 of the calendar year immediately preceding the calendar year for which distributions are being made will be substituted in §1.401(a)(9)-1 F-1 for the benefit of the employee. The account balance as of December 31 of such calendar year is the value of the IRA upon close of business on such December 31. However, for purposes of determining the minimum distribution for the second distribution calendar year for an individual, the account balance as of December 31 of such calendar year must be reduced by any distribution (as described in §1.401(a)(9)-1 F-5(c)(2)) made to satisfy the minimum distribution requirements for the individual's first distribution calendar year after such date.

A-6. Q. What rules apply in the case of a rollover to an IRA of an amount distributed by a qualified plan or another IRA?

A. If the surviving spouse of an employee rolls over a distribution from a qualified plan, such surviving spouse may elect to treat the IRA as the spouse's own IRA in accordance with the provisions in A-4. In the event of any other rollover to an IRA of an amount distributed by a qualified plan or another IRA, the rules in §1.401(a)(9)-1 will apply for purposes of determining the account balance for the receiving IRA and the minimum distribution from the receiving IRA. Thus, for example, certain amounts rolled over to a plan must be separately accounted for and the minimum distribution with respect to such amounts must be separately determined, as described in G-2. However, because the value of the account balance is determined as of December 31 of the year preceding the year for which the minimum distribution is being determined and not as of a valuation date in the preceding year, the account balance of the receiving IRA need not be adjusted for the amount received as provided in §1.401(a)(9)-1 G-2(a) in order to determine the minimum distribution for the calendar year following the calendar year in which the amount rolled over is received, unless the amount received is deemed to have been received in the immediately preceding year, pursuant to §1.401(a)(9)-1 G-2(a) or (b)(7). In that case, for purposes of determining the minimum distribution for the calendar year in which such amount is actually received, either the account balance of the receiving IRA as of December 31 of the preceding year must be adjusted by the amount received in accordance with §1.401(a)(9)-1 G-2(a) or the amount received will be treated as a separate account balance, in accordance with §1.401(a)(9)-1 G-2(b).

A-7. Q. What rules apply in the case of a transfer from one IRA to another?

A. In the case of a transfer from one IRA to another IRA, the rules in §1.401(a)(9)-1 G-3 and G-4 will apply for purposes of determining the account balance of, and the minimum distribution from, the IRA involved. Thus, the transferor IRA must distribute in the year of the transfer any amount required with respect to the portion of the account transferred; certain amounts transferred must be separately accounted for by the transferee IRA; and the minimum distribution with respect to such amounts must be separately determined by the transferee IRA. However, for purposes of determining the account balance of the transferee IRA and the transferor IRA, the account balance need not be adjusted for the amount transferred as provided in §1.401(a)(9)-1 G-4(a) in order to calculate the minimum distribution for the calendar year following the calendar year of the transfer, because the account balance is determined as of December 31 of the calendar year immediately preceding the calendar year for which the minimum distribution is being determined.

A-8. Q. Can a qualified trust or plan described in section 401(a) or an annuity described in section 403(a) or 403(b) make a transfer to an IRA that is not a rollover contribution described in section 402(a)(7), 403(a)(4) or 403(b)(8)?

A. (a) No. A qualified trust or plan described in section 401(a) or an annuity described in section 403(a) or 403(b) can not make a transfer to an IRA. However, an IRA may accept a rollover contribution that satisfies the requirements of section 402(a)(5), 402(a)(7), 403(a)(4) or 403(b)(8) even if such contribution is distributed by a qualified trust, plan, or annuity directly to the IRA at the direction of the employee (or the employee's surviving spouse). Such contribution will not be treated as a transfer to an IRA. Instead, such contribution will be treated as though it was distributed by the qualified trust, plan, or annuity to the employee (or the employee's surviving spouse) and subsequently rolled over to an IRA within the requisite 60 day period.

(b) Transfers directly from such a qualified trust or plan described in section 401(a) or annuity described in section 403(a) or 403(b) to an IRA may adversely affect both the qualified status of the trust, plan or annuity from which the transfer is made and the qualified status of the IRA which receives the transfer.

B. *Effective date and transition rules.*

B-1. Q. When are the distribution rules for IRAs in A-1 through A-8 effective?

A. The new distribution rules in A-1 through A-8 are effective for calendar years after calendar year 1984. However, distributions for calendar years 1985 and 1986 are not required to be made until December 31, 1987. If an individual attained age 70 ½ in calendar year 1986 or a prior calendar year and is alive on December 31, 1987, B-2 and B-3 provide special rules for determining the minimum distribution required for calendar years 1985 through 1987, and B-4 provides special rules for determining the minimum distribution required for calendar years after 1987. In the case of an individual who dies before January 1, 1988, B-4 through B-11 provide special rules for determining the minimum distribution required for calendar years 1985 through 1987 and for subsequent calendar years. See B-12 to determine when the IRA trust instrument must be amended. See B-13 to determine when the incidental death benefit rule applies to IRAs.

B-2. Q. If an individual attained age 70 ½ in calendar year 1986 or a prior calendar year and is alive on December 31, 1987, as of what date must the required distributions for calendar years 1985 through 1987 be made?

A. (a) *In general.* This B-2 determines when distributions must be made if an individual attained age 70 ½ in calendar year 1986 or a prior calendar year and is alive on December 31, 1987. Paragraph (d) provides a special rule which applies if distributions under certain annuity contracts which commenced not later than [30 days after publication of this notice].

(b) *70 ½ in a calendar year before 1985.* If an individual attained age 70 ½ in a calendar year prior to 1985, under these transition rules, the minimum distribution for 1985 is not required to be made by December 31, 1985 and the minimum distribution for calendar year 1986 is not required to be made by December 31, 1986. Instead, the minimum distribution for calendar years 1985 and 1986 are required to be made by December 31, 1987. Thus, the minimum distributions for calendar years 1985, 1986, and 1987 must be made by December 31, 1987.

(c) *70 ½ in 1985.* If an individual attained age 70 ½ in calendar year 1985, under these transition rules, the minimum distribution for calendar year 1985 is not required to be made by April 1, 1986, and the minimum distribution for calendar year 1986 is not required to be made by December 31, 1986. Instead, the minimum distributions for calendar years 1985 and 1986 are required to be made by December 31, 1987. Thus, the minimum distributions for calendar years 1985, 1986, and 1987 must be made by December 31, 1987.

(d) *70 ½ in 1986.* If an individual attained age 70 ½ in 1986, the minimum distribution required for calendar year 1986 is not required to be made by April 1, 1987. Instead, the minimum distribution for 1986 is required to be made by December 31, 1987. Thus, the minimum distributions for calendar years 1986 and 1987 must be made by December 31, 1987.

(e) *Certain annuity payments.* In the case of an individual described in paragraph (a) to whom nonincreasing annuity payments from one or more annuity contracts purchased from an insurance company commence not later than August 26, 1987 and to whom such annuity payments continue through December 31, 1987, no additional amount is required under these transition rules to be distributed for 1985, 1986, and 1987 from such annuity contracts. However, this rule only applies if such payments comply with § 1.401(a)(9)-1F-3 and F-4. If such payments commenced after the individual's required beginning date and if the individual has other IRAs (from which annuity payments as described above are not being made), any additional amount required to be distributed from such annuity contracts, under these transition rules, for 1985, 1986, and 1987 must be distributed to the extent available from such other IRAs. In determining whether an additional amount is required to be distributed from another IRA, the cash surrender value of the annuity contract as of the close of business on December 31, 1986 will be treated as the account balance of the annuity contract as of December 31, 1986.

B-3. Q. If (a) the individual attained age 70 ½ in calendar year 1986 or a prior calendar year and (b) the individual is alive on December 31, 1987, then how is the amount of the minimum required distribution from the individual's IRAs determined for calendar years 1985, 1986, and 1987?

A. (a) *In general.* If (1) the individual attained age 70 ½ in calendar year 1986 or a prior calendar year and (2) the individual is alive on December 31, 1987, for calendar years 1985, 1986, and 1987, the amount of the minimum distribution from the individual's IRAs is to be determined under one of the three methods: the life expectancy method, the percentage method, or the regular method. The individual will select which method is to be used. Under the life expectancy method and the percentage method, the total amount of the minimum distribution required for calendar years 1985, 1986, and 1987 is determined by aggregating the account balances under all of an individual's IRAs.

(b) *Life expectancy method.* Under the life expectancy method, the minimum distribution for 1985, 1986, and 1987 is determined as follows:

(1) *Designated beneficiary and life expectancy.* The designated beneficiary with respect to the individual under all IRAs will be determined as of any date in 1987. The beneficiary under all of the individual's IRAs as of such date with the longest life expectancy is the designated beneficiary that must be used to determine the aggregate minimum distribution. The applicable life expectancy (either the life expectancy of the individual or joint life and last survivor expectancy of the individual and the individual's designated beneficiary, whichever is applicable) is determined using ages as of birthdays in 1987. In the case of any beneficiary who is not alive on his birthday in 1987, such beneficiary is treated as being alive on that birthday for purposes of determining life expectancy.

(2) *Account balance.* The account balance is the aggregate of the account balances of all IRAs of the individual as of close of business December 31, 1986 with the following modifications. First, the aggregated account balance is increased by any amounts not reflected in an IRA as of such date due to withdrawal to make a rollover contribution to another IRA. Second, the aggregate account balance is then increased by any amount distributed in 1985 or 1986 for which credit is being taken under subparagraph (4).

(3) *Required distribution.* The total amount which must be distributed for calendar years 1985, 1986, and 1987 is determined by dividing the aggregate account balance determined under subparagraph (2) by the applicable life expectancy and multiplying the quotient by:

(i) 2.8, in the case of an individual with respect to whom the first distribution calendar year is 1985 (or a prior calendar year), or

(ii) 1.9, in the case of an individual with respect to whom the first distribution calendar year is 1986.

(4) *Credits for distributions.* In determining whether the total amount which must be distributed for calendar years 1985, 1986, and 1987 has been distributed, credit may be taken for any amount distributed in a distribution calendar year of the individual after 1984. However, in the case of any distribution in 1985 or 1986, credit may only be taken for amounts which were used to increase the aggregate account balance pursuant to subparagraph (2). See paragraph (e) for a special rule if an individual received excess distributions in a calendar year before 1985.

(c) *Percentage method.* Under the percentage method, the total amount of the minimum distribution required for calendar years 1985, 1986, and 1987 is determined as follows:

(1) *Account balance.* The account balance is determined in the same manner as under paragraph (b)(2).

(2) *Required distribution.* The total aggregate amount required to be distributed from all IRAs of the individual (which may be aggregated pursuant to this paragraph) is the following percentage of the aggregate account balance determined under subparagraph (1):

(i) 15%, in the case of an individual with respect to whom the first distribution calendar year under section 401(a)(9) is 1985, or

(ii) 10%, in the case of an individual with respect to whom the first distribution calendar year is 1986.

(3) *Credit for distributions.* Credits for distributions may be taken in the same manner as under paragraph (b)(4).

(d) *Regular method.* Under the regular method, the sum of the minimum distributions required for calendar years 1985, 1986, and 1987, calculated separately, is determined under section 408(a)(6) and (b)(3) and this section with appropriate adjustments. However, in determining the minimum distribution required for calendar years 1985, 1986, and 1987, the rule in § 1.401(a)(9)-1 F-2 does not apply. Also, credit (with an appropriate gross up) may be taken toward the minimum distribution required for the 1986 or 1987 distribution calendar year for distributions in the 1985 or 1986 distribution calendar years that exceeded the minimum required distribution for such year.

(e) *Credits.* Credit may be taken under the life expectancy method, the percentage method, and the regular method for excess distributions from IRAs in calendar years before 1985 to the extent that the aggregate amount distributed by the end of 1984 by all IRAs of the individual exceeded the aggregate of the minimum amounts required by 1.408-2(b)(6)(v) to have been distributed by the end of 1984. Such excess distributions will be treated as amounts distributed in 1985 for purposes of determining the amount which is required to be distributed by determining the amount which is required to be distributed by December 31, 1987 under each of those methods.

(f) *Example.* This Q&A is illustrated by the following example:

Example.

(a) An individual (X), born March 1, 1915, has three TRAs (IRA 1, IRA 2, and IRA 3) as of January 1, 1987. Each IRA has a different

(1)		Account balances as of December 31, 1986		
	(a)	IRA 1		$53,000.00
	(b)	IRA 2		$25,000.00
	(c)	IRA 3		$24,000.00
(2)		Aggregate account balances of X as of December 31, 1986		$102,000.00
(3)		Distribution in 1985		$3,000.00
(4)		Distribution in 1986 ($1,500 plus $2,500)		$4,000.00
(5)		Account balance to be used to determine minimum distribution (sum of lines 2, 3, and 4)		$109,000.00
(6)		Attained age of beneficiary with longest life expectancy (youngest—X's son) as of birthday in 1987		46.00
(7)		X's attained age as of X's birthday in 1987		72.00
(8)		Joint life and last survivor expectancy of X and X's son (using Table VI of §1.72-9) using ages on lines 6 and 7		37.30
(9)		Account balance (line 5) divided by the applicable life expectancy (line 8)		$2,922.25
(10)		Total amount which must be distributed for 1985, 1986, and 1987 (line 9 multiplied by 2.8)		$8,182.30
(11)		Distributions in 1985 and 1986 for which credit may be taken (sum of lines (3) and (4))		$7,000.00
(12)		Amount required to be distributed in 1987 (line 10 minus line 11)		$1,182.30

(c) Under the percentage method, X's required minimum distribution in 1987 (required to be made by December 31, 1987) is determined as follows:

(1)		Account balances as of December 31, 1986:		
	(a)	IRA 1		$53,000
	(b)	IRA 2		$25,000
	(c)	IRA 3		$24,000
(2)		Aggregate account balances of X as of December 31, 1986		$102,000
(3)		Distribution in 1985		$3,000
(4)		Distribution in 1986 ($1,500 plus $2,500)		$4,000
(5)		Account balance to be used to determine minimum distribution (sum of lines 2, 3, and 4)		$109,000
(6)		Total amount which must be distributed for 1985, 1986, and 1987 (15% of line 5)		$16,350
(7)		Distributions in 1985 and 1986 for which credit may be taken (sum of lines 3 and 4)		$7,000
(8)		Amount required to be distributed in 1987 (line 6 minus line 7)		$9,350

B-4. Q. If an individual attained age 70 ½ in 1986 or in a prior calendar year, are there any special rules for determining the minimum distribution for calendar years after 1987?

A. (a) *Required beginning date.* If an individual attained age 70 ½ in 1986 or in a prior calendar year, the amount of the minimum distribution required for calendar years after 1987 will be determined in a manner consistent with the use of December 31, 1987 as the individual's required beginning date. Consequently, for example, if any election is permitted by the IRA trustee, the individual must elect no later than December 31, 1987 whether or not life expectancy will be recalculated for purposes of determining the minimum distribution required for calendar years after 1987. Further, for example, the designated beneficiary of the individual under each IRA will be determined as of December 31, 1987 for purposes of determining the minimum distribution required for calendar years after 1987.

(b) *Life expectancies.* If an individual attained age 70 ½ in 1986 or in a prior calendar year, for purposes of determining the minimum distribution for calendar years after 1987, life expectancies shall be determined for each IRA as follows. If the individual's designated beneficiary is the individual's spouse, and the life expectancy of the individual and spouse are being recalculated, the joint life and last survivor expectancy of the individual and spouse is calculated using their attained ages as of their birthdays in the calendar year for which the minimum distribution is being determined. If the individual's designated beneficiary is not the individual's spouse and life expectancy is being recalculated, the joint life and last survivor expectancy of the individual and the designated beneficiary (other than the individual's spouse) is determined using the attained age of the individual as of the individual's birthday in the calendar year for which the minimum distribution is being determined and the attained age of the designated beneficiary as of the beneficiary's birthday in 1987, adjusted in accordance with E-8. If an individual's life expectancy is not being recalculated, the joint life and last survivor expectancy of the individual and the designated beneficiary will be determined based on the attained ages of the individual and designated beneficiary as of their birthdays in 1987, reduced by one for each calendar year that has elapsed since 1987. For purposes of this

designated beneficiary. X's spouse, born January 15, 1920 is the sole designated beneficiary of IRA 1. X's daughter, born May 5, 1939, is the sole designated beneficiary of IRA 2. X's son, born April 2, 1941, is the sole designated beneficiary of IRA 3. X's account balance in IRA 1 as of December 31, 1986 is $53,000. X's account balance in IRA 2 as of December 31, 1986 is $25,000. X's account balance in IRA 3 as of December 31, 1986 is $24,000. Distributions in 1985 and 1986 from X's IRAs are as follows: $3,000 from IRA 1 in 1985, $1,500 from IRA 2 in 1986, and $2,500 from IRA 3 in 1986.

(b) Under the life expectancy method, X's required minimum distribution in 1987 (required to be made by December 31, 1987) is determined as follows:

paragraph (b), if the designated beneficiary is not alive of his birthday in 1987, such beneficiary will be deemed to be alive on that date for purposes of determining life expectancy.

(c) *Normal rules.* For years after 1987, the requirement that each IRA separately satisfy the minimum distribution requirement applies. Thus, except as noted in this section, the rules in H-1 through H-2A of §1.401(a)(9)-1 apply.

B-5. Q. If an individual dies before January 1, 1988, are distributions to be made in accordance with section 401(a)(9)(B)(i) or in accordance with section 401(a)(9)(B)(ii) or (iii) and (iv)?

A. If an individual dies prior to January 1, 1988 (including deaths before January 1, 1985), the IRA must be distributed in accordance with section 401(a)(9)(B)(ii) or (iii) and (iv), whichever is applicable (see B-12 and §1.401(a)(9)-1 C-4). If an individual dies prior to January 1, 1986, see B-6 and B-7 for rules concerning which calendar year is the first calendar year for which distributions must be made in accordance with section 401(a)(9), when such distributions are required to commence, and how the amount which is required to be distributed by such date is determined.

B-6. Q. If an individual died prior to January 1, 1986 and distributions are being made over the life expectancy of a designated beneficiary in accordance with section 401(a)(9)(B)(iii) and (iv), what is the first calendar year for which a distribution is required and when must distributions commence?

A. (a) *General rule.* If an individual died prior to January 1, 1986 and distributions are being made over the life expectancy of a designated beneficiary in accordance with section 401(a)(9)(B)(iii) and (iv), the first calendar year for which a minimum distribution under section 401(a)(9) is required is the later of: (1) the calendar year which contains the required commencement date determined under §1.401(a)(9)-1 C-3(a) or (b), whichever is applicable, or (2) calendar year 1985. However, under these transition rules, if the first distribution calendar year for which minimum distributions must be determined in accordance with section 401(a)(9) is 1985, such minimum distribution is not required to be made by December 31, 1985. Similarly, under these transition rules, if the first (or second) distribution calendar year (for which minimum distributions must be determined in accordance with section 401(a)(9)) is 1986, the minimum distribution for 1986 is not required to be made by December 31, 1986. Instead, in such case, the minimum distributions for 1985 (if applicable), 1986, and 1987, must be made by December 31, 1987. Paragraph (b) provides a special rule made by December 31, 1987. Paragraph (b) provides a special rule for certain annuity payments.

(b) *Certain annuity payments.* In the case of a beneficiary described in paragraph (a) to whom nonincreasing annuity payments from one or more annuity contracts purchased from an insurance company commenced not later than [30 days after the publication of this notice]and to whom such annuity payments continue through December 31, 1987, no additional amount is required under these transition rules to be distributed for 1985, 1986, and 1987 from such annuity contracts. However, this rule only applies if such annuity payments comply with § 1.401(a)(9)-1 F-3 and F-4. If such payments commenced after the last day of the distribution calendar year determined under paragraph (a), and if such beneficiary is also the sole beneficiary of other IRAs (from which annuity payments as described above are not being made) that were inherited from the same individual from whom such annuity contracts were inherited, any additional amount required to be distributed from such annuity contract, under these transition rules, for 1985, 1986, and 1987 must be distributed to the extent available from such other IRAs. In determining whether an additional amount is required to be distributed from another IRA, the cash surrender value of the annuity contract as of the close of business December 31, 1986 will be treated as the account balance of the annuity contract as of December 31, 1986.

B-7. Q. If (a) distributions are being made over the life expectancy of a designated beneficiary in accordance with section 401(a)(9)(B)(iii) and (iv) and (b) the first distribution calendar year is 1985 or 1986 (determined under B-6(a)), then how is the amount of the minimum distribution determined for calendar years 1985, 1986, and 1987?

A. (a) *In general.* If the two conditions set forth in the question are met, the amount of the minimum distribution for calendar years 1985, 1986, and 1987 is to be determined under one of three methods, the life and the regular method. Under the life expectancy method and the percentage method, IRAs which were inherited from the same individual and which have the same beneficiaries will be aggregated. The beneficiary (or beneficiaries) of the aggregated IRAs will select which of the three methods is to be used.

(b) *Life expectancy method.* Under the life expectancy method, the minimum distribution for 1985, 1986, and 1987 will then be determined as follows:

(1) *Designated beneficiary and life expectancy.* The designated beneficiary with respect to an individual for IRAs being aggregated will be determined as of any date in 1987. The applicable life expectancy will be the life expectancy of the designated beneficiary using the designated beneficiary's age as of his birthday in 1987. In the case of a beneficiary who is not alive on his birthday in 1987, the beneficiary will be treated as being alive on that date for purposes of determining life expectancy under this transition rule.

(2) *Account balance.* The account balance is the aggregate of the account balances of all the IRAs to be aggregated (determined under paragraph (a)) as of close of business December 31, 1986 with the following modifications. First, the aggregated account balance is increased by any amounts not reflected in an IRA as of such date due to withdrawal to make a rollover contribution to another IRA. Second, the aggregate account balance is then increased by any amount distributed in 1985 or 1986 for which credit is being taken under subparagraph (4).

(3) *Required distribution.* The total amount which must be distributed for calendar years 1985, 1986, and 1987 will be determined by dividing the account balance determined under subparagraph (2) by the applicable life expectancy determined under subparagraph (1) and multiplying the quotient by:

(i) 2.8, in the case of an individual with respect to whom the first distribution calendar year is 1985, or

(ii) 1.9, in the case of an individual with respect to whom the first distribution calendar year is 1986.

(4) *Credit for distributions.* In determining whether the total amount which must be distributed for calendar years 1985, 1986, and 1987 has been distributed, credit may be taken for any amount distributed in a distribution calendar year of the individual after 1984. However, in the case of any distribution in 1985 or 1986, credit may only be taken for amounts which were used to increase the aggregate account balance pursuant to subparagraph (2).

(c) *Percentage method.* Under the percentage method, the total amount of the minimum distribution required for calendar years 1985, 1986, and 1987 is determined as follows:

(1) *Account balance.* The account balance is determined in the same manner as under paragraph (b)(2).

(2) *Required distribution.* The total aggregate amount required to be distributed from all the IRAs to be aggregated determined under paragraph (a) is the following percentage of the aggregate account balance determined under subparagraph (1):

(i) 15%, in the case of an individual with respect to whom the first distribution calendar year is 1985, or

(ii) 10%, in the case of an individual with respect to whom the first distribution calendar year is 1986.

(3) *Credit for distributions.* Credits for distributions may be taken in the same manner as under paragraph (b)(3).

(d) *Regular method.* Under the regular method, the sum of the minimum distributions required for calendar years 1985, 1986, and 1987, calculated separately, is determined under section 408(a)(6) and (b)(3) and this section with the appropriate adjustments. However, the rule in § 1.401(a)(9)-1 F-2 does not apply. Also credit (with an appropriate gross-up) may be taken toward the minimum distributions required for the 1986 or 1987 distribution calendar year for distributions in the 1985 or 1986 distribution calendar years which exceeded the minimum required distribution for such year.

B-8. Q. If distributions are being made with respect to an individual over the life expectancy of a designated beneficiary in accordance with section 401(a)(9)(B)(iii) and (iv), as of what date is the designated beneficiary determined, and as of what date is the life expectancy of the designated beneficiary determined, for purposes of determining the minimum distribution for calendar years after 1987?

A. If distributions are being made over the life expectancy of a designated beneficiary in accordance with section 401(a)(9)(B)(iii) and (iv), the designated beneficiary will be determined as of any date in 1987. The life expectancy of the designated beneficiary (other than an individual's surviving spouse whose life expectancy is being recalculated) will be determined using the attained age of the designated beneficiary as of such beneficiary's birthday in calendar year 1987, reduced by one for each calendar year which has elapsed after 1987. If the designated beneficiary is not alive on his birthday in 1987, such beneficiary will be treated as alive on that date for purposes of determining life expectancy. If the individual's surviving spouse is a designated beneficiary and such spouse's life expectancy is being recalculated, the life expectancy of such spouse will be calculated using the attained age of the spouse as of such spouse's birthday in the calendar year for which the minimum distribution is being determined.

B-9 Q. In the case of an individual's surviving spouse for whom a distribution is required to be made for 1985 or 1986, when must any election concerning recalculation of life expectancy be made by the spouse?

A. In the case of an individual's surviving spouse for whom a distribution is required to be made for 1985 or 1986, any election concerning recalculation of life expectancy must be made by December 31, 1987.

B-10. Q. When must the election described in § 1.401(a)(9)-1 C-4 (concerning whether distribution will be made in accordance with the five-year rule in section 401(a)(9)(B)(ii) or the exception to the five-year rule in section 401(a)(9)(B)(iii)) be made by a beneficiary otherwise required to make such election on or before December 31, 1986?

A. The election described in § 1.401(a)(9)-1 C-4 (concerning whether distribution will be made in accordance with the five-year rule in section 401(a)(9)(B)(ii) or the exception to the five-year rule in section 401(a)(9)(B)(iii)) if otherwise required to make such election on or before December 31, 1986 must be made by December 31, 1987.

B-11. Q. If an individual died prior to January 1, 1985, and distribution is to be made in accordance with the five-year rule contained in section 401(a)(9)(B)(ii), as of what date must the individual's entire interest be distributed?

A. If an individual died prior to January 1, 1985 and distribution is to be made in accordance with the five-year rule contained in section 401(a)(9)(b)(ii), the individual's entire interest must be distributed as of the later of: (a) December 31 of the calendar year which contains the fifth anniversary of the employee's death or (b) December 31, 1987.

B-12. Q. When must the trust instrument for an IRA be amended to provide the distribution rules in section 408(a)(6) or

A. (a) The trust instrument for an IRA with a favorable opinion letter need not be amended until the later of December 31, 1988 or such time as the Commissioner prescribes (after publication of sample language for IRAs, including IRAs used for funding simplified employee pensions (SEPs)). In the case of an existing IRA or a newly established IRA which is established by executing Form 5305 or Form 5305A, the current (Rev. 11-83) editions of those forms may be used until such time as the Commissioner prescribes. Prior to the date when the trust instrument must be amended, an IRA with a favorable opinion letter or an IRA established by executing Form 5305 or Form 5305A will not be considered to fail to be described in section 408(a) or (b) merely because it fails in form to satisfy section 408(a)(6) or (b)(3) and this section of the regulations. However, distributions must satisfy section 408(a)(6) or 408(b)(3) and the regulations thereunder in operation, notwithstanding the absence of provisions in the trust instrument beginning with calendar year 1985.

(b) An IRA which does not have a favorable opinion letter and which is not established by executing Form 5305 or Form 5305A will satisfy section 408(a)(6) and 408(b)(3) until the date prescribed in paragraph (a) as of which IRAs with a favorable opinion letter must be amended if such IRA contains the statutory provisions in section 401(a)(9) applicable to IRAs. Not all provisions in section 401(a)(9) apply to IRAs. For example, pursuant to A-3, the transitional rule in §1.401(a)(9)-1 B-2(b) does not apply to distributions from IRAs.

(c) For calendar years before the calendar year in which IRAs must be amended pursuant to this B-5, an IRA will not be subject to the default provisions of §1.401(a)(9)-1 if distributions under each IRA are otherwise made in accordance with these regulations in a reasonable and consistent manner. For example, for purposes of determining, pursuant to §1.401(a)(9)-1 C-4, whether the exception to the five-year rule in section 401(a)(9)(B)(iii) and (iv) applies, an IRA will be found to comply with section 408(a)(6) or (b)(3) in operation even though distributions are not made in accordance with the default provisions in §1.401(a)(9)-1 C-4(a) if the IRA trustee decides with respect to an IRA to either distribute benefits under one method or the other or distribute benefits pursuant to the election by an individual or the individual's beneficiary (or in the absence of an election, under one or the other of such methods). Similarly, for calendar years before the calendar year in which IRAs must be amended pursuant to B-5, for purposes of determining whether or not the life expectancies off the individual and the individual's spouse will be recalculated pursuant to section 401(a)(9)(D) and §1.401(a)(9)-1 E-7, an IRA will be found to comply with section 408(a)(6) or (b)(3) and this section of the regulations in operation even though the life expectancies of the individual and individual's spouse are not recalculated if the trustee decides not to recalculate such life expectancies, if the IRA trustee allows elections by the individual or spouse and the individual or spouse elects not to recalculate life expectancy, or if the IRA trustee decides not to recalculate life expectancy in the absence of an election to recalculate life expectancy.

B-13. Q. Must distributions from IRAs for calendar years before 1989 satisfy the incidental benefit rule in §1.401(a)(9)-2?

A. No. Distributions from IRAs for calendar years before 1989 are not required to satisfy the incidental benefit rule in §1.401(a)(9)-2. However, for calendar years after 1988, distributions must satisfy the incidental benefit rule in §1.401(a)(9)-2 which applies to calendar years after 1988.

B-14. Q. What are the distribution rules applicable to individual retirement plans (IRAs) in 1984?

A. For calendar year 1984, IRAs arc subject to the distribution requirements of section 408(a)(6) and (7) and section 408(b)(3) and (4), as in effect immediately prior to the enactment of the Tax Reform Act of 1984 (TRA of 1984). With respect to individuals who died prior to January 1, 1984, the law in effect immediately prior to the enactment of TRA of 1984 is the law in effect immediately prior to the enactment of the Tax Equity and Fiscal Responsibility Act (TEFRA). Section 243(b) of (TEFRA) (as amended by section 713(g) of TRA of 1984) denies deductions for contributions to, and rollover treatment for distributions to or from, inherited IRAs (as defined in section 408(d)(3)(c)(ii)) with respect to individuals dying after December 31, 1983.

Pension Excise Tax Regulations (26 CFR Part 54)

Par. 6. The authority citation for Part 54 is amended by adding the following citation:

Authority: 26 U. S. C. 7305 * * * Section 54.4974-2 is also issued under 26 U. S. C. 4974.

Par. 7. There is added the following new section after §54.4974-1 to read as follows:

§54.4974-2. Excise tax on accumulations in qualified retirement plans.

Q-1. Is any tax imposed on a payee under any qualified retirement plan or any eligible deferred compensation plan (as defined in section 457(b)) to whom an amount is required to be distributed for a taxable year if the amount distributed during the taxable year is less than the minimum required distribution?

A. Yes. If the amount distributed to a payee under any qualified retirement plan or any eligible deferred compensation plan (as defined in section 457(b)) for a calendar year is' less than the minimum required distribution for such year, an excise tax is imposed on such payee under section 4974 for the taxable year beginning with or within the calendar year during which the amount is required to be distributed. The tax is equal to 50 percent of the amount by which such minimum required distribution exceeds the actual amount distributed during the calendar year. Section 4974 provides that this tax shall be paid by the payee. For purposes of section 4974, the term "minimum required distribution" means the minimum amount required to be distributed pursuant to section 401(a)(9), 403(b)(10), 408(a)(6), 408(b)(3), or 457(d)(2), as the case may be, and the regulations thereunder. Except as otherwise provided in Q&A-6, the minimum required distribution for a calendar year is the minimum amount required to be distributed during the calendar year. Q&A-6 provides a special rule for amounts required to be distributed by an employee's (or individual's) required beginning date.

Q-2. For purposes of section 4974, what is a qualified retirement plan?

A. For purposes of section 4974, each of the following is a qualified retirement plan:

(a) A plan described in section 401(a) which includes a trust exempt from tax under section 501(a),

(b) An annuity plan described in section 403(a),

(c) An annuity contract, custodial account, or retirement income account described in 403(b),

(d) An individual retirement account described in section 408(a),

(e) An individual retirement annuity described in section 408(b), or

(f) Any other plan, contract account, or annuity that, at any time, has been treated as a plan, account, or annuity described in (a) through (e), whether or not such plan, contract, account, or annuity currently satisfies the applicable qualification requirements.

Q-3. If a payee's interest under a qualified retirement plan is in the form of an individual account, how is the minimum required distribution for a given calendar year determined for purposes of section 4974?

A. (a) *General rule.* If a payee's interest under a qualified retirement plan is in the form of an individual account and distribution of such account is not being made under an annuity contract purchased in accordance with §1.401(a)(9)-1 F-4, the amount of the minimum required distribution for any calendar year for purposes of section 4974 is the minimum amount required to be distributed for such calendar year in order to satisfy the minimum distribution requirements in §§1.401(a)(9)-1 and 1.401(a)(9)-2 as provided in the following (whichever is applicable):

(1) Section 401(a)(9) and §§1.401(a)(9)-1 and 1.401(a)(9)-2 (in the case of a plan described in section 401(a) which includes a trust exempt under section 501(a) or an annuity plan described in section 403(a)),

(2) Section 403(b)(10) and §1.403(b)-2 (in the case of an annuity contract or custodial account described in section 403(b)), or

(3) Section 408(a)(6) or (b)(3) and §1.408-8 (in the case of an individual retirement account or annuity described in section 498(a) or

(b) *Default provisions.* Unless otherwise provided under the qualified retirement plan (or, if applicable, the governing instrument of the qualified retirement plan), the default provisions in §1.401(a)(9)-1 apply in determining the minimum required distribution for purposes of section 4974. For example, if the amount of the minimum required distribution for purposes of section 4974 is to be determined using the life expectancies of the employee (or IRA owner), the employee's spouse (or IRA owner's spouse), or both, the life expectancy of such individuals must be recalculated in order to determine the minimum required distribution unless the exceptions in §1.401(a)(9)-1 E-7 apply. Similarly, if the rules in §1.401(a)(9)-1 C-1 through C-6 (after death distribution rules) apply to a payee, the minimum required distribution for any given calendar year to satisfy the applicable section enumerated in paragraph (a) will be determined using the default provisions in §1.401(a)(9)-1 C-4 unless an exception stated therein applies.

(c) *Five year rule.* If the five-year rule in section 401(a)(9)(3)(ii) applies to the distribution to a payee, no amount is required to be distributed for any calendar year to satisfy the applicable enumerated section in paragraph (a) until the calendar year which contains the date five years after the date of the employee's death. For the calendar year which contains the date five years after the employee's death, the minimum amount required to be distributed to satisfy the applicable enumerated section is the payee's entire remaining interest in the qualified retirement plan.

Q-4. If a payee's interest in a qualified retirement plan is being distributed in the form of an annuity, how is the amount of the minimum required distribution determined for purposes of section 4974?

A. If a payee's interest in a qualified retirement plan is being distributed in the form of an annuity (either directly from the plan, in the case of a defined benefit plan, or under an annuity contract purchased from an insurance company), the amount of the minimum required distribution for purposes of section 4974 will be determined as follows:

(a) *Permissible annuity distribution option.* A permissible annuity distribution option is an annuity contract (or, in the case of annuity distributions from a defined benefit plan, a distribution option) which specifically provides for distributions which, if made as provided, would for every calendar year equal or exceed the minimum amount required to be distributed to satisfy the applicable section enumerated in paragraph (a) of Q-4 for every calendar year. If the annuity contract (or, in the case of annuity distributions from a defined benefit plan, a distribution option) under which distributions to the payee are being made is a permissible annuity distribution option, the minimum required distribution for a given calendar year will equal the amount which the annuity contract (or distribution option) provides is to be distributed for that calendar year.

(b) *Impermissible annuity distribution option.* An impermissible annuity distribution option is an annuity contract (or, in the case of annuity distributions from a defined benefit plan, a distribution option) under which distributions to the payee are being made specifically provides for distributions which, if made as provided, would for any calendar year be less than the minimum amount required to be distributed to satisfy the applicable section enumerated in paragraph (a) of Q-4. If the annuity contract (or, in the case of annuity distributions from a defined benefit plan, the distribution option) under which distributions to the payee are being made is an impermissible annuity distribution option, the minimum required distribution for each calendar year will be determined as follows:

(1) If the qualified retirement plan under which distributions are being made is a defined benefit plan, the minimum amount required to be distributed each year will be the amount which would have been distributed under the plan if the distribution option under which distributions to the payee were being made was the following permissible annuity distribution option:

(i) In the case of distributions commencing before the death of the employee, if there is a designated beneficiary under the impermissible annuity distribution option for purposes of section 401(a)(9), the permissible annuity distribution option is the joint and survivor annuity option under the plan for the lives of the employee and the designated beneficiary which provides for the greatest level amount payable to the employee determined on an annual basis. If the plan does not provide such an option or there is no designated beneficiary under the impermissible distribution option for purposes of section 401(a)(9), the permissible annuity distribution option is the life annuity option under the plan payable for the life of the employee in level amounts with no survivor benefit.

(ii) In the case of distributions commencing after the death of the employee, if there is a designated beneficiary under the impermissible annuity distribution option for purposes of section 401(a)(9), the permissible annuity distribution option is the life annuity option under the plan payable for the life of the designated beneficiary in level amounts. If there is no designated beneficiary, the five year rule in section 401(a)(9)(B)(ii) applies. See subparagraph (3).

The determination of whether or not there is a designated beneficiary and the determination of which designated beneficiary life is to be used in the case of multiple beneficiaries will be made in accordance with § 1.401(a)(9)-1. See D-1 through D-3, D-5, E-1, and E-5 of § 1.401(a)(9)-1. If the defined benefit plan does not provide for distribution in the form of the applicable permissible distribution option, the minimum required distribution for each calendar year will be an amount as determined by the Commissioner.

(2) If the qualified retirement plan under which distributions are being made is a defined contribution plan and the impermissible annuity distribution option is an annuity contract purchased from an insurance company, the minimum amount required to be distributed

each year will be the amount which would have been distributed in the form of an annuity contract under the permissible annuity distribution option under the plan determined in accordance with subparagraph (1) for defined benefit plans. If the defined contribution plan does not provide the applicable permissible annuity distribution option, the minimum required distribution for each calendar year will be the amount which would have been distributed under an annuity described below purchased with the employee's or individual's account used to purchase the annuity contract which is the impermissible annuity distribution option.

(i) In the case of distributions commencing before the death of the employee, if there is a designated beneficiary under the impermissible annuity distribution option for purposes of section 401(a)(9), the annuity is a joint and survivor annuity for the lives of the employee and the designated beneficiary which provides level annual payments and which would have been a permissible annuity distribution option. However, the amount of the periodic payment which would have been payable to the survivor will be the applicable percentage under the table in Q&A-6 of § 1.401(a)(9)-2 of the amount of the periodic payment which would have been payable to the employee or individual. If there is no designated beneficiary under the impermissible distribution option for purposes of section 401(a)(9), the annuity is a life annuity for the life of the employee with no survivor benefit which provides level annual payments and which would have been a permissible annuity distribution option.

(ii) In the case of a distribution commencing after the death of the employee, if there is a designated beneficiary under the impermissible annuity distribution option for purposes of section 401(a)(9), the annuity option is a life annuity for the life of the designated beneficiary which provides level annual payments and which would have been a permissible annuity distribution option. If there is no designated beneficiary, the five year rule in section 401(a)(9)(B)(ii) applies. See subparagraph (3).

The amount of the payments under the annuity contract will be determined using the interest and mortality tables specified in § 20.2031-7 of the Estate Tax Regulations. The determination of whether or not there is a designated beneficiary and the determination of which designated beneficiary's life is to be used in the case of multiple beneficiaries will be made in accordance with § 1.401(a)(9)-1. See D-1 through D-3, D-5, and E-5 of § 1.401(a)(9)-1.

(3) If the five-year rule in section 401(a)(9)(B)(ii) applies to the distribution to the payee under the contract (or distribution option), no amount is required to be distributed to satisfy the applicable enumerated section in paragraph (a) until the calendar year which contains the date five years after the date of the employee's death. For the calendar year which contains the date five years after the employee's death, the minimum amount required to be distributed to satisfy the applicable enumerated section is the payee's entire remaining interest in the annuity contract (or under the plan in the case of distributions from a defined benefit plan).

Q-4A. If there is any remaining benefit with respect to an employee (or IRA owner) after any calendar year in which the entire remaining benefit is required to be distributed under section, what is the amount of the minimum required distribution for each calendar year subsequent to such calendar year?

A. If there is any remaining benefit with respect to an employee (or IRA owner) after the calendar year in which the entire remaining benefit is required to be distributed, the minimum required distribution for each calendar year subsequent to such calendar year is the entire remaining benefit. For example, if there is any remaining benefit with respect to an employee (or IRA owner), for which the minimum required distribution is being determined under paragraph (b) of Q&A-4, after the calendar year in which the life (or lives) described therein expire, the minimum required distribution for each subsequent calendar year is the entire remaining benefit.

Q-5. If a payee has an interest under an eligible deferred compensation plan (as defined in section 457(b)), how is the minimum required distribution for a given taxable year of the payee determined for purposes of section 4974?

A. If a payee has an interest under an eligible deferred compensation plan (as defined in section 457(b)), the minimum required distribution for a given taxable year of the payee determined for purposes of section 4974 is determined under section 457(d).

Q-6. With respect to which calendar year is the excise tax under section 4974 imposed in the case in which the amount not distributed is an amount required to be distributed by April 1 of a calendar year (by the employee's or individual's required beginning date)?

A. In the case in which the amount not paid is an amount required to be paid by April 1 of a calendar year, such amount is a minimum required distribution for the previous calendar year, *i.e.,* for the employee's or the individual's first distribution calendar year. However, the excise tax under section 4974 is imposed for the calendar year containing the last day by which the amount is required to be distributed, *i.e.,* the calendar year containing the employee's or individual's required beginning date, even though the preceding calendar year is the calendar year for which the amount is required to be distributed. Pursuant to F-2 of §1.401(a)(9)-1, amounts distributed in the employee's or individual's first distribution calendar year will reduce the amount required to be distributed in the next calendar year by the employee's or individual's required beginning date. There is also a minimum required distribution for the calendar year which contains the employee's required beginning date. Such distribution is also required to be made during the calendar year which contains the employee's required beginning date.

Q-7. For what taxable years is the excise tax imposed under section 4974 effective?

A. The excise tax imposed under section 4974 as amended by 1121 of the Tax Reform Act of 1986 (TRA '86) is effective for payees' taxable years beginning after December 31, 1988. Consequently, with respect to qualified plans described in section 401(a), annuity contracts and custodial accounts described in section 403(b), and an eligible deferred compensation plans (as defined in section 457(b)), the excise tax imposed under section 4974 only applies for taxable years beginning after December 31, 1988. However, with respect to individual retirement plans described in section 408, an excise tax is also imposed under section 4974 for taxable years beginning before January 1, 1989.

Q-8. Are there any circumstances when the excise tax under section 4974 for a taxable year may be waived?

A. The tax under section 4974(a) may be waived if the payee described in section 4974(a) establishes to the satisfaction of the Commissioner the following:

(a) The shortfall described in section 4974(a) in the amount distributed in any taxable year was due to reasonable error, and

(b) Reasonable steps are being taken to remedy the shortfall.

Lawrence B. Gibbs,

Commissioner of Internal Revenue.

¶ 20,163C

Qualification of plans and trusts: Highly compensated employees: Definitions.—The IRS has issued temporary regulations (¶ 12,364E) that also serve as proposed regulations relating to the scope and meaning of the term "highly compensated employee" in Code Sec. 414(q). The proposed IRS regulations were published in the *Federal Register* on February 1, 1991 (56 FR 3976).

DEPARTMENT OF THE TREASURY

Internal Revenue Service

[26 CFR Part 1]

[EE-129-86]

RIN 1545-A066

Definition of highly compensated employee.

AGENCY: Internal Revenue Service, Treasury.

ACTION: Notice of proposed rulemaking by cross-reference to temporary regulations.

SUMMARY: In the Rules and Regulations portion of this issue of the Federal Register, the Internal Revenue Service is issuing temporary regulations relating to the scope and meaning of the term "highly compensated employee" in section 414(q) of the Internal Revenue Code of 1986. They reflect changes made by the Tax Reform Act of 1986 (TRA '86). The text of those temporary regulations also serves as the text for this Notice of Proposed Rulemaking. These regulations will provide the public with guidance necessary to comply with the law and will affect sponsors of, and participants in, pension, profit-sharing and stock bonus plans, and certain other employee benefit plans.

DATES: Written comments must be reeived by April 2, 1991. Requests to speak (with outlines of oral comments) at a public hearing scheduled for Thursday, May 16, 1991, at 10:00 a.m., and continued, if necessary, on Friday, May 17, 1991, must be received by May 2, 1991. See the notice of hearing published elsewhere in this issue of the Federal Register.

ADDRESSES: Send comments and requests to speak (with outlines of oral comments) at the public hearing to: Internal Revenue Service, P.O. Box 7604, Ben Franklin Station, Attn: CC:CORP:T:R (EE-129-86), Room 4429, Washington, D.C. 20044.

FOR FURTHER INFORMATION CONTACT: Concerning the regulation, Thomas G. Schendt or Rhonda G. Migdail, Office of the Assistant Chief Counsel (Employee Benefits and Exempt Organizations), at 202-633-0849 (not a toll-free number). Concerning the hearing, Robert Boyer, Regulations Unit, at 202-566-3935 (not a toll free number).

SUPPLEMENTARY INFORMATION:

Background

The temporary regulations in the Rules and Regulations portion of this issue of the Federal Register amend 26 CFR by amending §1.414(q)-1T to provide guidance with respect to the definition of a highly compensated employee within the meaning of section 414(q) of the Internal Revenue Code (Code). The regulations are proposed to be issued under the authority contained in sections 414(q) and 7805 of the Code 100 Stat. 2448, 68A Stat. 917; 26 U.S.C. 414(q), 7805. For the text of the temporary regulations, see T.D. 8334 published in the Rules and Regulations portion of this issue of the Federal Register.

Special analyses

It has been determined that these proposed rules are not major rules as defined in Executive Order 12291. Therefore, a Regulatory Impact Analysis is not required. It has been determined that section 553(b) of the Administrative Procedure Act (5 U.S.C. Chapter 5) and the Regulatory Flexibility Act (5 U.S.C. Chapter 6) do not apply to these regulations, and therefore, an initial Regulatory Flexibility Analysis is not required. Pursuant to section 7805(f) of the Internal Revenue Code, the proposed regulations are being sent to the Chief Counsel on Advocacy of the Small Business Administration for comment on their impact on small business.

Comments and requests for public hearing

Before adopting these proposed regulations, consideration will be given to any written comments that are submitted (preferably a signed original and eight copies) to the Commissioner of Internal Revenue. All comments will be available for public inspection and copying in their entirety. Because the Treasury Department expects to issue final regulations on this matter as soon as possible, a public hearing will be held at 10:00 a.m. on May 16, 1991, and continued, if necessary, on Friday, May 17, 1991, in the I.R.S. Auditorium, Seventh Floor, 7400 Corridor, Internal Revenue Building, 1111 Constitution Ave., N.W., Washington, D.C. 20224.

List of Subjects

26 CFR 1.401-0—1.425-1

Employee benefit plans, Employee stock ownership plans, Income taxes, Individual retirement accounts, Pensions, Stock options.

Michael J. Murphy

Acting Commissioner of Internal Revenue

[¶ 20,164 Reserved.—Proposed regulation under Code Sec. 120, relating to the application for recognition as a qualified group legal services plan, was formerly reproduced at this point. The final regulation is at ¶ 11,285.]

¶ 20,164A

Proposed regulations on qualified group legal services plans.—Reproduced below is the text of proposed Reg. §§ 1.1201, 1.1202, and 1.501(c)(20)-1, which provide guidance for complying with the Tax Reform Act of 1976. The proposed regulations were published in the *Federal Register* of April 29, 1980 (45 FR 28360).

DEPARTMENT OF THE TREASURY

Internal Revenue Service

26 CFR Part 1

[EE-5-78]

Income Tax; Qualified Group Legal Services Plans

AGENCY: Internal Revenue Service, Treasury.

ACTION: Notice of proposed rulemaking.

SUMMARY: This document contains proposed regulations relating to qualified group legal services plans. Changes to the applicable tax law were made by the Tax Reform Act of 1976. The regulations would provide the public with the guidance needed to comply with that Act and would affect both employers who establish group legal services plans and employees and their spouses and dependents who receive benefits under these plans.

DATES: Written comments and requests for a public hearing must be delivered or mailed by June 30, 1980. The amendments are generally proposed to be effective for taxable years beginning after December 31, 1976, and ending before January 1, 1982.

ADDRESS: Send comments and requests for a public hearing to: Commissioner of Internal Revenue, Attention: CC:LR:T:EE-5-78, Washington, D.C. 20224.

FOR FURTHER INFORMATION CONTACT: Richard L. Johnson of the Employee Plans and Exempt Organizations Division, Office of the Chief Counsel, Internal Revenue Service, 1111 Constitution Avenue, NW., Washington, D.C. 20224, Attention CC:LR:T:EE-5-78, 202-566-3544 (Not a toll-free number).

SUPPLEMENTARY INFORMATION:

Background

This document contains proposed amendments to the Income Tax Regulations (26 CFR Part 1) under sections 120 and 501(c)(20) of the Internal Revenue Code of 1954, as added by section 2134 of the Tax Reform Act of 1976 (90 Stat. 1926). The amendments are to be issued under the authority contained in sections 120 and 7805 of the Internal Revenue Code of 1954 (90 Stat. 1926, 68A Stat. 917; 26 U. S. C. 120, 7805).

Prepaid Legal Services

Code section 120(a) excludes from the gross income of an employee, and the employee's spouse or dependent, employer contributions made on their behalf to a qualified group legal services plan. The value of legal services provided, or amounts paid for legal services, under the plan are also excluded from gross income.

Qualified Group Legal Services Plans

In order for a group legal services plan to be a qualified plan, the plan must satisfy certain requirements relating principally to nondiscrimination in employer contributions, plan benefits and eligibility for participation, the limitation on employer contributions for participants who are shareholders or owners, and the means by which the plan is funded. If the plan is funded by means of a trust, subject to certain requirements, the trust is exempt from tax.

Deletion of Regulations Under Repealed Code Provision

Existing § 1.120-1 of the Income Tax Regulations provides regulations under Code section 120, relating to statutory subsistence allowance received by police, which was repealed by section 3 of the Technical Amendments Act of 1958 (72 Stat. 1607). This section is being deleted.

Comments and Requests for a Public Hearing

Before adopting these proposed regulations, consideration will be given to any written comments that are submitted (pre-ferably six copies) to the Commissioner of Internal Revenue. All comments will be available for public inspection and copying. A public hearing will be held upon written request to the Commissioner by any person who has submitted written comments. If a public hearing is held, notice of the time and place will be published in the *Federal Register.*

Drafting Information

The principal author of these proposed regulations is Richard L. Johnson of the Employee Plans and Exempt Organizations Division of the Office of Chief Counsel, Internal Revenue Service. However, personnel from other offices of the Internal Revenue Service and Treasury Department participated in developing the regulation, both on matters of substance and style.

Proposed Amendments to the Regulations

The proposed amendments to 26 CFR Part 1 are as follows:

§ 1.120-1 [Deleted]

Paragraph 1. Section 1.120-1, relating to statutory subsistence allowances received by police, is deleted.

Par. 2. New §§ 1.120-1 and 1.120-2 are added in the appropriate place:

§ 1.120-1 Amounts received under a qualified group legal services plan.

(a) *Exclusion from gross income.* The gross income of an employee, or the employee's spouse or dependent, does not include—

(1) Amounts contributed by an employer on behalf of the employee, spouse, or dependent under a qualified group legal services plan described in § 1.120-2,

(2) The value of legal services provided the employee, spouse or dependent under the plan, or

(3) Amounts paid to the employee, spouse or dependent under the plan as reimbursement for the cost of personal legal services provided to the employee, spouse or dependent.

(b) *Definitions.* For rules relating to the meaning of the terms "employee," "employer," "spouse," and "dependent" see paragraph (d)(3) and (4) and paragraph (i) of § 1.120-2.

(c) *Effective date.* This section is effective with respect to employer contributions made on behalf of, and legal services provided to, an employee, spouse or dependent on or after the first day of the period of plan qualification (as determined under § 1.120-3(d)) and in taxable years of the employee, spouse or dependent beginning after December 31, 1976, and ending before January 1, 1982.

§ 1.120-2 Qualified group legal services plan.

(a) *In general.* In general, a qualified group legal services plan is a plan established and maintained by an employer under which the employer provides employees, or their spouses or dependents, personal legal services by prepaying, or providing in advance for, all or part of the legal fees for the services. To be a qualified plan, the plan must satisfy the requirements described in paragraphs (b) through (h) of this section and be recognized as a qualified plan by the Internal Revenue Service. Section 1.120-3 provides rules under which a plan must apply to the Internal Revenue Service for recognition as a qualified plan.

(b) *Separate written plan.* The plan must be a separate written plan of the employer. For purposes of this section—

(1) *Plan.* The term "plan" implies a permanent as distinguished from a temporary program. Thus, although the employer may reserve the right to change or terminate the plan, and to discontinue contributions thereunder, the abandonment of the plan for any reason other than a business necessity soon after it has taken effect will be evidence that the plan from its inception was not a *bona fide* plan for the benefit of employees generally (see paragraph (d) of this section). Such evidence will be given special weight if, for example, a plan is abandoned soon after extensive benefits are provided to persons with respect to whom discrimination in plan benefits is prohibited (see paragraph (e) of this section).

(2) *Separate plan.* The requirement that the plan be a separate plan means that the plan may not provide benefits which are not personal legal services within the meaning of paragraph (c) of this section. For example, the requirement for a separate plan is not satisfied if personal legal services are provided under an employee benefit plan that also provides pension, disability, life insurance, medical or other such non-legal benefits. The requirement for a separate plan does not, however, preclude a single plan from being adopted by more than one employer.

(c) *Personal legal services*—(1) *In general.* In general, benefits under the plan must consist of, or be provided with respect to, only personal legal services that are specified in the plan. The plan must specifically prohibit a diversion or use of any funds of the plan for purposes other than the providing of personal legal services for the participants. In general, a personal legal service is a legal service (within the meaning of subparagraph (3) of this paragraph) provided to a participant employee, spouse or dependent which is not directly connected with or pertaining to—

(i) A trade or business of the employee, spouse or dependent,

(ii) The management, conservation or preservation of property held by the employee, spouse or dependent for the production of income, or

(iii) The production or collection of income by the employee, spouse or dependent.

(2) *Certain personal legal services.* Notwithstanding subparagraph (1) (ii) and (iii) of this paragraph, the following (if legal services within the meaning of subparagraph (3)) are considered personal legal services—

(i) A legal service provided to a participant with respect to securing, increasing or collecting alimony under a decree of divorce (or payments in lieu of alimony) or the division or redivision of community property under the community property laws of the State,

(ii) A legal service provided to a participant as heir or legatee of a decedent, or as beneficiary under a testamentary trust, in protecting or asserting rights to property of a decedent, or

(iii) A legal service provided to a participant with respect to the participant's claim for damages, other than compensatory damages, for personal injury.

(3) *Legal services*—(i) *Services of a lawyer.* In general, a legal service is a service performed by a lawyer if the performing of the service constitutes the practice of law.

(ii) *Services of a person not a lawyer.* A legal service may include a service performed by a person who is not a lawyer, if the service is performed under the direction or control of a lawyer, in conection with a legal service (within the meaning of subdivision (i)) performed by the lawyer, and the fee for the service is included in the legal fee of the lawyer. Examples of services to which this subdivision (ii) may apply are the services of an accountant, a researcher, a paralegal, a law clerk, an investigator or a searcher of title to real property.

(iii) *Court fees.* Amounts payable to a court in connection with the presentation, litigation or appeal from a matter before a court is considered the cost of a legal service. For example, benefits under the plan may be provided with respect to a court filing fee, a fee for service of summons or other process, the cost of a transcript of trial or the posting of bail bond.

(iv) *Other fees or charges.* An amount payable to a competent governmental authority (for example, the United States, a State or any subdivision thereof) is considered the cost of a legal service, if the amount is payable with respect to the filing or registration of a legal document (for example, a deed or will). However, any amount payable directly or indirectly to a governmental authority is not the cost of a legal service, if the amount is in the nature of a tax. For example, although a plan may provide for payment of an amount payable to a county for the filing or registration of a deed to real property, a plan may not provide for payment of an amount in the nature of a tax on the transfer of title to real property.

(4) *Limited initial consultation.* A plan is not other than a qualified plan merely because, in connection with providing personal legal services, the plan provides a specified "limited initial consultation" benefit without restricting the benefit to personal legal services. An "initial consultation" is a consultation, the purpose of which is to determine whether a plan participant is in need of a personal legal service and, if so, whether the required personal legal service may be provided under the plan. An initial consultation must not include document preparation or review, or representation of the participant. An initial consultation benefit is "limited", if under the plan it is limited either in time (*e.g.,* no more than 4 hours of initial consultation during any year) or number (*e.g.,* no more than 4 initial consultations during any year).

(d) *Exclusive benefit*—(1) *In general.* The plan must benefit only employees of the employer, including individuals who are employees within the meaning of paragraph (i) (1) of this section, or the spouses or dependents of employees.

(2) *Plans to which more than one employer contributes.* In the case of a plan to which more than one employer contributes, in determining whether the plan is for the exclusive benefit of an employer's employees, or their spouses or dependents, the employees of any employer who maintains the plan are considered the employees of each employer who maintains the plan.

(3) *Spouses of employees.* In general, for purposes of determining whether a plan is for the exclusive benefit of an employer's employees, or their spouses or dependents, the determination of whether an individual is a spouse of an employee is made at the time the legal services are provided to the individual. The term "spouse" includes a surviving spouse of a deceased employee. Although, in general, the term "spouse" does not include a person legally spearated from an employee under a decree of divorce or separate maintenance, a legal service provided to an employee's former spouse after the issuing of a decree of divorce, annulment or separate maintenance from the employee is considered a service provided to the spouse of an employee, if the service relates to the divorce, annulment or separation. For purposes of this section and § 1.120-1, the term "spouse" includes an individual to whom benefits may be provided under this subparagraph.

(4) *Dependents of employees.* For purposes of determining whether a plan is for the exclusive benefit of an employer's employees, or their spouses or dependents, benefits provided to the following individuals are considered benefits provided to a dependent of an employee:

(i) An individual who is a dependent of an employee within the meaning of section 152 for the taxable year of the employee within which the legal services are provided to the individual;

(ii) An individual who is described in paragraph (h) (2) of this section (relating to certain surviving dependents) at the time the legal services are provided to the individual; or

(iii) An individual who is a dependent of an employee within the meaning of section 152 for the taxable year of the employee ending on the date of the employee's death, under age 21 on the date of the employee's death, and under age 21 at the time the legal services are provided to the individual.

For purposes of this section and § 1.120-1, the term "dependent" means an individual to whom benefits may be provided under this subparagraph.

(5) *Estates of employees.* A plan is for the exclusive benefit of the employer's employees, or their spouses or dependents, notwithstanding that the plan provides benefits to the personal representative of a deceased employee, or spouse or dependent, with respect to the estate of the deceased.

(e) *Prohibited discrimination*—(1) *In general.* The plan must benefit the employer's employees generally. Among those benefited may be employees who are officers, shareholders, self-employed or highly compensated. A plan is not for the benefit of employees generally, however, if the plan discriminates in favor of employees described in the preceding sentence, or their spouses or dependents, in eligibility requirements (see subparagraph (2) of this paragraph) or in contributions or benefits (see subparagraph (3) of this paragraph).

(2) *Eligibility to participate.* A plan need not provide benefits for all employees (or their spouses or dependents). A plan must, however, benefit those employees (or their spouses or dependents) who qualify under a classification of employees set up by the employer which is found by the Internal Revenue Service not to discriminate in favor of employees who are officers, shareholders, self-employed or highly compensated, or their spouses or dependents. In general, this determination shall be made by applying the same standards as are applied under section 410(b) (1) (B) (relating to qualified pension, profit-sharing and stock bonus plans), without regard to section 401 (a) (5). For purposes of making this determination, there shall be excluded from consideration employees not covered by the plan who are included in a unit of employees covered by an agreement which the Secretary of Labor finds to be a collective bargaining agreement between employee representatives and one or more employers, if the Internal Revenue Service finds that group legal services plan benefits were the subject of good faith bargaining between the employee representatives and the employer or employers. For purposes of determining whether such bargaining occurred, it is not material that the employees are not covered by another plan or that the employer's present plan was not considered in the bargaining.

(3) *Contributions and benefits*—(i) *In general.* Employer contributions under the plan or benefits provided under the plan must not discriminate in favor of employees who are officers, shareholders, self-employed or highly compensated, or their spouses or dependents, as against other employees, or their spouses or dependents, covered by the plan. This does not mean that contributions or benefits may not vary. Variations in contributions or benefits may be provided so long as the plan, viewed as a whole for the benefit of employees in general, with all its attendant circumstances, does not discriminate in favor of

those with respect to whom discrimination is prohibited. Thus, contributions or benefits which vary by reason of a formula which takes into account years of service with the employer, or other factors, are not prohibited unless those factors discriminate in favor of employees who are officers, shareholders, self-employed or highly compensated, or their spouses or dependents. Under this subparagraph (3), if a plan covers employees who are highly compensated, and benefits under the plan uniformly increase as compensation increases, the plan is not a qualified plan.

(ii) *Relative utilization of plan benefits.* Not only must a plan not discriminate on its face in employer contributions or plan benefits in favor of employees who are officers, shareholders, self-employed or highly compensated, or their spouses or dependents, the plan also must not discriminate in favor of such employees, or their spouses or dependents, in actual operation. Accordingly, the extent to which such employees, or their spouses or dependents, as a group, utilize plan benefits must be compared to the extent to which all other employees, or their spouses or dependents, as a group, utilize plan benefits. A plan is not other than a qualified plan for a plan year merely because, relative to their number, those employees, or their spouses or dependents, with respect to whom discrimination is prohibited utilize plan benefits to a greater extent than do other employees, or their spouses or dependents. However, a persistent pattern of greater relative utilization of plan benefits by the group of employees who are officers, shareholders, self-employed or highly compensated, or their spouses or dependents, may be evidence that the plan discriminates in favor of such employees and is not for the benefit of employees generally. Such evidence will be considered, together with all other pertinent facts and circumstances, to determine whether the plan improperly discriminates in actual operation.

(f) *Contribution limitation*—(1) *In general.* Under section 120(c)(3), a plan is a qualified plan for a plan year only if no more than 25% of the amount contributed by the employer under the plan for the plan year is contributed on behalf of the limitation class described in subparagraph (2). A plan satisfies the requirements of section 120(c)(3) for a plan year (as determined under the plan) if either—

(i) The plan satisfies the requirements of subparagraph (3), or

(ii) The percentage determined under subparagraph (4) is 25% or less, and the plan is not other than a qualified plan by reason of subparagraph (5).

(2) *Limitation class.* The limitation class consists of—

(i) *Shareholders.* Individuals who, on any day of the plan year, own more than 5% of the total number of shares of outstanding stock of the employer, or

(ii) *Owners.* In the case of an employer's trade or business, which is not incorporated, individuals who on any day of the plan year, own more than 5% of the capital or profits interest in the employer, and

(iii) *Spouses and dependents.* Individuals who are spouses or dependents of shareholders or owners described in subdivision (i) or (ii). For purposes of determining stock ownership, the attribution rules described in paragraph (i)(4) of this section apply. The regulations prescribed under section 414(c) are applicable in determining an individual's interest in the capital or profits of an unincorporated trade or business.

(3) *Disregarding allocation rules*—(i) *Plans providing legal services directly.* If a plan is one under which legal services are provided directly to a participant, the plan will satisfy the requirements of section 120(c)(3), without regard to the allocation rules described in subparagraphs (4) and (5) of this paragraph, if the plan satisfies the following requirement. The plan must provide and be operated so that no legal service may be provided to a member of the limitation class if to provide the service would cause the fair market value of legal services provided to date during the plan year to members of the limitation class to exceed 25% of the fair market value of the legal services provided under the plan to date during the plan year.

(ii) *Plans providing reimbursement for the cost of legal services.* If a plan is one under which a participant is reimbursed for the cost of legal services, the plan will satisfy the requirements of section 120(c)(3), without regard to the allocation rules described in subparagraphs (4) and (5) of this paragraph, if the plan satisfies the following requirement. The plan must provide and be operated so that no amount may be paid to a member of the limitation class if the payment would cause amounts paid to date during the plan year to members of the limitation class to exceed 25% of the amounts paid under the plan to date during the plan year.

(iii) *Limitation class; special rule.* For purposes of this subparagraph (3) an individual is a member of the limitation class only if the individual is a member (within the meaning of subparagraph (2)) on or before the date on which the determination described in subdivision (ii) or (iii) is required to be made.

(iv) *Example.* The provisions of subdivision (iii) of this subparagraph may be illustrated by the following example:

Example. (A) Plan X is a qualified group legal services plan under which plan participants are reimbursed for the cost of personal legal services specified in the plan. The plan includes a provision satisfying the requirements of subdivision (ii) of this subparagraph. The plan year is the calendar year.

(B) A, an individual, is a participant in Plan X. On March 18, 1981, A is paid an amount under the plan. On June 21, 1981, A purchases shares of stock of the employer maintaining the plan. As a result of the purchase A owns more than 5% of the total number of shares of outstanding stock of the employer. Accordingly, under subparagraph (2) of this paragraph, A is a member of the limited class for the plan year 1981. On August 14, 1981, A sells the shares of stock purchased on June 21, 1981, and no longer owns more than 5% of the total number of shares of outstanding stock of the employer. On October 9, 1981, A is paid an additional amount under the plan.

(C) For purposes of the determination required by subdivision (ii) of this subparagraph, if the determination is made for a date after March 17, 1981, and before June 21, 1981, the amount paid to A on March 18, 1981, is not considered an amount paid to a member of the limitation class. If the determination is made for a date after June 20, 1981, the amount paid to A on March 18, 1981, is considered an amount paid to a member of the limitation class. With respect to a determination made for a date after October 8, 1981, the amount paid to A on October 9, 1981, is considered an amount paid to a member of the limitation class.

(4) *Contribution allocation*—(i) *Equal benefits.* In general, if under a plan the same benefits are made available to each participant, the percentage of the amount contributed by the employer for a plan year that is considered contributed on behalf of the limitation class is equal to the number of participants who are members of the limitation class at any time during the plan year, divided by the number of individuals who are participants in the plan at any time during the plan year.

(ii) *Unequal benefits.* In general, if under the plan different benefits are made available to different participants or different classes of participants, the percentage of the amount contributed by the employer for a plan year that is considered contributed on behalf of the limitation class is equal to the fair market value (as of the first day of the plan year) of those benefits available under the plan to participants who are members of the limitation class at any time during the plan year, divided by the fair market value (as of the first day of the plan year) of those benefits available under the plan to all individuals who are participants in the plan at any time during the plan year.

(iii) *Individual premiums.* Notwithstanding subdivision (i) or (ii) of this subparagraph, if benefits are provided under the plan in exchange for the employer's prepayment or payment of a premium, and the amount of the prepayment or premium is determined by taking into account the circumstances of individual participants or classes of participants, the percentage of the amount contributed by the employer for a plan year that is considered contributed on behalf of the limitation class is equal to the sum of the prepayments or premiums paid for the plan year on behalf of participants who are members of the limitation class at any time during the plan year, divided by the sum of the prepayments or premiums paid for the plan year. A prepayment or premium is paid for the plan year if it is paid with respect to legal services provided or made available during the plan year. This subdivision (iii) will apply if, for example, equal benefits are provided each participant under the plan in exchange for the employer's payment of a premium with respect to each participant employee, and the amount of the premium varies, taking into account the employee's income level, the number and ages of the employee's dependents or other such factors.

(5) *Relative utilization of plan benefits*—(i) *Application.* The extent to which members of the limitation class, as a class, utilize plan benefits shall be taken into account in determining the percentage of amounts contributed by the employer that is considered contributed on behalf of the limitation class. The rules described in this subparagraph (5) are in addition to those described in subparagraph (4) of this paragraph, and a plan may be other than a qualified plan by reason of the application of this subparagraph (5), notwithstanding that the percentage determined under subparagraph (4) is 25% or less.

(ii) *Computation.* Under this subparagraph (5), if during any three successive plan years, benefits paid to or with respect to the limitation class (as determined for each plan year) exceed 25% of all benefits paid under the plan during the three years, the plan is not a qualified plan for the next succeeding plan year.

(iii) *Reapplication for recognition as a qualified plan.* A plan that is not a qualified plan for a plan year by reason of this subparagraph (5), may reapply under § 1.120-3 for recognition as a qualified plan for any plan year following the first plan year for which it is not a qualified plan. A plan so reapplying will be recognized as a qualified plan for any plan year for which recognition is sought only if the plan is a qualified plan under this subparagraph (5) for the first plan year for which such recognition is sought and otherwise satisfies the requirements of section 120 and this section.

(g) *Employer contributions*—(1) *In general.* Employer contributions under the plan may be made only—

(i) To insurance companies, or to organizations or persons that provide personal legal services, or indemnification against the cost of personal legal services, in exchange for a prepayment or payment of a premium,

(ii) To organizations or trusts described in section 501(c)(20),

(iii) To organizations described in section 510(c) that are permitted by that section to receive payments from an employer for support of a qualified group legal services plan, except that the organization shall pay or credit the contribution to an organization or trust described in section 501(c)(20),

(iv) As prepayment to providers of legal services under the plan, or

(v) A combination of the above.

(2) *Prepayment required.* For purposes of subparagraph (1)(i) and (iv), employer contributions are considered prepayments or premiums only if a contribution made with respect to benefits reasonably anticipated to be provided under the plan during any month is made on or before the tenth day of the month.

(h) *Employee contributions*—(1) *In general.* A plan is not a qualified plan if it permits participants to contribute under the plan other than as described in subparagraphs (2) and (3) of this paragraph.

(2) *Certain separated employees and surviving spouses and dependents.* A plan will not be other than a qualified plan merely because the plan allows—

(i) A separated former employee,

(ii) A surviving spouse of a deceased employee, or

(iii) An individual who is a dependent of an employee within the meaning of section 152 for the taxable year of the employee ending on the date of the death of the employee, to elect to continue as a participant under the plan on a self-contributory basis for a period not to exceed one year after the separation or death.

(3) *Certain employee contributions in lieu of employer contributions.* This subparagraph (3) applies with respect to a plan that—

(i) Is maintained pursuant to an agreement that the Secretary of Labor finds to be a collective bargaining agreement between employee representatives and one or more employers, and

(ii) Provides that an employer is required to contribute (or contribute in full) on behalf of a participant employee only if the employee completes a minimum number of hours of service with the employer within a stated period ending on or before the date the contribution is otherwise required to be made by the employer.

Such a plan is not other than a qualified plan merely because it permits a participant employee to contribute under the plan an amount not required to he contributed by the employer because the employee fails to complete the minimum number of hours. However, no amount may be contributed by an employee under this subparagraph (3) unless employer contributions on behalf of participant employees are required to be made monthly or more often, and at least one employer contribution is made on behalf of the employee under the plan before the contribution by the employee is made under the plan. In addition, a

plan shall not be a qualified plan for a plan year by reason of this subparagraph (3), if amounts contributed by employees under this subparagraph (3) during the plan year exceed 5% of the total amount contributed wider the plan during the plan year.

(i) *Definitions.* For purposes of this section, § 1.120-1 and § 1.120-3—

(1) *Employee.* The term "employee" includes—

(i) A retired, disabled or, laid-off employee,

(ii) A present employee who is on leave, as, for example, in the Armed Forces of the United States,

(iii) An individual who is self-employed within the meaning of section 401(c)(1), or

(iv) A separated former employee who is covered by the plan by reason of paragraph (h)(2)(i) of this section (relating to employee contributions).

(2) *Employer.* An individual who owns the entire interest in an unincorporated trade or business is treated as his or her own employer. A partnership is treated as the employer of each partner who is an employee within the meaning of section 401(c)(1).

(3) *Officer.* An officer is an individual who is an officer within the meaning of regulations prescribed under section 414(c).

(4) *Shareholder.* The term "shareholder" includes an individual who is a shareholder as determined by the attribution rules under section 1563(d) and (e), without regard to section 1563(e)(3)(C).

(5) *Highly compensated.* The term "highly compensated" has the same meaning as it does for purposes of section 410(b)(1)(B).

Par. 3. There is added in the appropriate place the following new section:

§ *1.501(c)(20)-1 Qualified group legal services plan trust.*

(a) *Qualified group legal services plan.* For purposes of this section, a "qualified group legal services plan" is a plan that satisfies the requirements of section 120(b) and § 1.120-2.

(b) *General requirements for exemption.* Under section 501(c)(20), an organization or trust created or organized in the United States is exempt as provided in section 501(a) if the exclusive function of the organization or trust is to form part of a qualified group legal services plan or plans.

(c) *Exception for trust associated with section 501(c) organization.* As described in section 120(c)(5)(C), employer contributions under a qualified group legal services plan may be paid to an organization described in section 501(c) if that organization is permitted by section 501(c) to receive payments from an employer for support of a qualified group legal services plan. However, that organization must, in turn, pay or credit the contributions to an organization or trust described in section 501(c)(20). In such a case, the organization or trust to which the contributions are finally paid or credited is considered to satisfy the require-ment that the *exclusive* function of the organization or trust be to form part of a qualified group legal services plan or plans, notwithstanding that the organization or trust provides legal services or indemnification against the cost of legal services unassociated with such a qualified plan. This exception applies, however, only if any such legal service or indemnification is provided under a program established and maintained by the organization described in section 501(c) to which the employer contributions under a qualified group legal services plan are first paid under section 120(c)(5)(C). Whether providing legal services or indemnification against the cost of legal services unassociated with a qualified group legal services plan is a permissible activity of an organization described in section 501(c) is determined under the rules under that paragraph of section 501(c) in which the organization is described.

Jerome Kurtz,

Commissioner of Internal Revenue.

[FR Doc. 80-13072 Filed 4-28-80; 8:45 am]

[¶ 20,165 Reserved.—Proposed regulations defining the term "reasonable actuarial method of valuation" for purposes of computing the minimum funding standard for pension plans were formerly reproduced at this point. The final regulations are at ¶ 12,250U.]

[¶ 20,165A Reserved.—Proposed regulations relating to the procedure for electing an alternative amortization method of funding certain pension plans formerly appeared at this point. The final regulations are at ¶ 12,250G.]

¶ 20,165B

Proposed regulations prescribing rules for determining if the vesting schedule of a qualified plan discriminates in favor of employees who are officers, shareholders, or highly compensated.—Reproduced below is the text of proposed Reg. § 1.411(d)-1(c)(2) which modifies previously proposed regulations (CCH Pension Plan Guide, ¶ 20,172). The proposed regulations also withdraw § 1.411(d)-(d) of the previously proposed regulation. The proposed regulations were filed with the *Federal Register* on June 9, 1980.

DEPARTMENT OF THE TREASURY

Internal Revenue Service

[26 CFR Part 1]

[EE-164-78]

Coordination Of Vesting And Discrimination Requirements For Qualified Plans

Notice Of Proposed Rulemaking

AGENCY: Internal Revenue Service, Treasury.

ACTION: Notice of proposed rulemaking.

SUMMARY: This document contains modifications to proposed regulations, published in the FEDERAL REGISTER for April 9, 1980 (45 FR 24201), relating to coordination of vesting and discrimination requirements for qualified pension, etc. plans. These modifications to the proposed regulations have been prepared in response to the comments received on the proposed regulation. The test for determining the existence of discriminatory vesting is reproposed in modified form and the "safe harbors" against a finding of discriminatory vesting are withdrawn.

DATES: A public hearing on the notice of proposed rulemaking published April 9, 1980, has been scheduled for July 10, 1980. A notice of the public hearing was published in the FEDERAL REGISTER on May 2, 1980. Outlines of oral comments for the public hearing must be delivered or mailed by June 26, 1980. Written comments on the modifications set forth in this notice must be delivered or mailed by [60 days after publication of this notice in the FEDERAL REGISTER].

ADDRESS: Send comments to: Commissioner of Internal Revenue, Attention: CC:LR:T (EE-164-78), Washington, D. C. 20224.a favorable advance determination letter. If a plan failed to satisfy these tests, a favorable determination letter was not issued unless the plan adopted the accelerated vesting schedule set forth in the Procedure (so-called "4/40 vesting").

Revenue Procedure 76-11, 1976-1 C.B. 550, was issued pending reconsideration of Revenue Procedure 75-49. That Procedure adopted two new alternative means of satisfying the requirements of section 411(d)(1) in order to secure a favorable advance determination letter, in addition to the tests contained in Revenue Procedure 75-49.

One of the new alternatives contained in Revenue Procedure 76-11 is to establish that the plan had previously received a favorable advance determination letter which had not been revoked, and that the percentage of vesting of each participant under the plan as amended is not less (at every point) than that provided under the vesting schedule of the plan when it received the most recent favorable prior determination letter.

The other new alternative contained in Revenue Procedure 76-11 is a demonstration, on the basis of all of the facts and circumstances that there have not been, and that there is no reason to believe there will be, any discriminatory accruals.

Revenue Procedure 76-11 also provided that a plan could secure a favorable determination letter without regard to whether the vesting is nondiscriminatory.

However, the determination letters processed in this manner contained a caveat to the effect that such letter is not a determination as to whether the vesting provisions of the plan satisfy the nondiscrimination requirements of section 401(a)(4).

The tests of Revenue Procedures 75-49 and 76-11 are applied only with respect to whether a plan could receive a favorable advance determination letter. The determination letter, by its terms, provided that the approval of the plan's qualified status by the Internal Revenue Service did not separate tests for determining discrimination in vesting where necessary with respect to the issuance of a determination letter and with respect to testing the operation of the plan's vesting schedule.

Thus, an employer could receive a favorable advance determination letter, but would have no protection against a finding that the plan's vesting schedule was discriminatory in operation. The proposed rules remove this separate testing of form and operation, and provide that the test for discriminatory vesting shall be made, in both situations, on the basis of the facts and circumstances. Thus, if a plan has a favorable advance determination letter based on the facts and circumstances test of the proposed rules, this determination will protect the plan from a finding of discriminatory vesting in operation, provided the facts and circumstances have not materially changed since the determination letter was issued.

Additionally, plans which currently possess certain types of favorable determination letters will be treated as if their determination letter was processed under the facts and circumstances test contained in the proposed rules. The plans which will be given this treatment are those which received their favorable determination letter based on their satisfying one or more of the following tests:

1. the key employee and/or the turnover test of Revenue Procedure 75-49;

2. the prior letter tests of Revenue Procedure 76-11; or

3. the facts and circumstances test of Revenue Procedure 76-11. Thus, a plan described above would also be protected against a finding of discriminatory vesting in operation, based on its outstanding favorable determination letter, provided the facts and circumstances have not materially changed.

Safe Harbors

Paragraph (d) of proposed regulation § 1.411(d)-1, as published in the FEDERAL REGISTER on April 9, 1980, sets forth two safe harbors against a finding of discriminatory vesting. Both of the safe harbors required the adoption of a vesting schedule substantially more rapid than 4/40 vesting. many of the commentators viewed this as an attempt to require that all plans adopt either one of these accelerated vesting schedules. Because that was not the intent of the proposed rules, the portion of the proposed regulation containing the safe harbors is withdrawn.

However, this deletion should not be interpreted as meaning that 4/40 vesting is a safe harbor. Comments are requested from the public as to the desirability of reinstating a safe harbor and, if so, on what basis.

Test For Discriminatory Vesting

Paragraph (c)(2) of proposed regulation § 1.411(d)-1, as published in the FEDERAL REGISTER on April 9, 1980, sets forth certain factors to be considered in applying the facts and circumstances test for discriminatory vesting. These factors were included simply to reflect current Internal Revenue Service practice and to provide greater guidance to both employers and to Internal Revenue Service personnel. The factors were not intended to create new standards.

Nevertheless, many commentators interpreted the recital of specific factors as substantially increasing their burden of establishing that the plan's vesting schedule is nondiscriminatory. Accordingly, the list of specific factors is deleted in the reproposed test for discriminatory vesting.

The determination of whether the vesting schedule of a plan is discriminatory, under the reproposed rules, shall be made on the basis of the facts and circumstances of each case. The reproposed rules now specifically provide that a plan's vesting schedule is nondiscriminatory if the disparity between the vested benefits provided to the prohibited group and the vested benefits provided to all other employees is reasonable.

Additional Guidance

It is anticipated that additional guidance regarding the application of the facts and circumstances test for discriminatory vesting will be provided in revenue rulings and procedures issued at the time the regulations are published in final form. Accordingly, comments are requested as to whether the following examples are appropriate for this purpose:

Example 1. A plan has the "10 year cliff" vesting schedule described in section 411(a)(2)(A) for all employees. Employment turnover among member of the prohibited group is less than that for all other employees because the prohibited group tends to stay longer with the company. Nevertheless, the present value of the vested benefits for the officers and 5% shareholders (determined using the attribution rules of section 1563(e), without regard to section 1563(e)(3)(C)), is less than the present value of the vested benefits of all other employees. Because the vested benefits provided employees who are not officers or shareholders are greater than that provided officers and shareholders, the plan's vesting schedule is not considered to be discriminatory.

Example 2. The facts are the same as in *Example 1,* except that there has been no comparison of the pr3esent values of the vested benefits of each group of employees. However, it is clear that the class of employees who have bested benefits, considering those employees alone and not any nonvested employees, would satisfy the nondiscriminatory classification test of section 410(b)(1)(B) by covering a reasonable cross section. Because a reasonable cross section of all employees under the plan have bested benefits, the vesting schedule of the plan is not considered to be discriminatory. [When the example is published, specific facts along the lines of Revenue Ruling 70-200, 1970-1 C.B. 101, Revenue Ruling 74-255, 1974-1 C.B. 93, and Revenue Ruling 74-256, 1974-1 C.B. 94, will be included to illustrate the reasonable cross section test.]

Example 3. Company B has a plan that satisfies the minimum participation requirements of section 410. The plan provides for 4/40 vesting. In its six years of operation the plan has always covered five employees. Because of the high rate of employee turnover, the only employee, past or present, to earn vested benefit under the plan is X. X is the sole shareholder of Company B. Absent a showing of other facts and circumstances, the vesting schedule of the plan is discriminatory.

Comments And Public Hearing

Before adopting these proposed regulations, consideration will be given to any written comments that are submitted (preferably eight copies) to the Commissioner of Internal Revenue. All comments will be available for public inspection and copying. As indicated above, a public hearing has already been scheduled on the proposed regulations published April 9, 1980. Anyone wishing to comment on these modifications may do so at the hearing.

Drafting Information

The principal author of this regulation is Kirk F. Maldonado of the Employee Plans and Exempt Organizations Division of the Office of Chief Counsel, Internal Revenue Service. however, personnel from other offices of the Internal Revenue Service and the Treasury Department participated in developing the regulation, both on matters of substance and style.

Proposed Amendments To The Regulations

Accordingly, the notice of proposed rulemaking published in the FEDERAL REGISTER for April 9, 1980 (45 FR 24201) is modified as follows:

1. Paragraph (d) of § 1.411(d)-1, as set forth in the notice of proposed rulemaking published in the FEDERAL REGISTER for April 9, 1980 (45 FR 24201) is withdrawn.

2. Paragraph (c)(2) of § 1.411(d)-1, as set forth in the notice of proposed rulemaking published in the FEDERAL REGISTER for April 9, 1980 (45 FR 24201) is modified to read as follows:

§ *1.411(d)-1 Coordination of vesting and discrimination requirements.*

* * *

(c) *Discriminatory vesting.* * * *

(2) *Test for discriminatory vesting.* The determination of whether there is, or there is reason to believe there will be, discriminatory vesting shall be made on the basis of the facts and circumstances of each case. A reasonable disparity between the vested benefits paid to or accrued by the prohibited group and the vested benefits paid to or accrued by other employees will not result in a finding that there is discriminatory vesting.

Commissioner of Internal Revenue

¶ 20,165C

Proposed regulations: Minimum vesting standards for qualified employee plans.—Reproduced below is the text of proposed regulations relating to the minimum vesting standards for qualified employee plans. The proposed regulations amend current regulations to reflect changes made by the Tax Reform Act of 1986. The proposed regulations were published in the *Federal Register* on January 6, 1988 (53 FR 261). The proposed regulations were also issued as temporary regulations under T.D. 8170 and are reproduced at ¶ 12,158A, 12,162H, 12,162I, 12,213A, 12,214A, and 12,218A. The effective dates of the temporary regulations and the introductory material preceding the temporary regulations are at ¶ 23,079.

DEPARTMENT OF THE TREASURY

Internal Revenue Service

[26 CFR Part 1]

[EE-167-86]

Minimum Vesting Standards

Notice Of Proposed Rulemaking

AGENCY: Internal Revenue Service, Treasury.

ACTION: Notice of proposed rulemaking by cross reference to temporary regulations.

SUMMARY: This document provides proposed regulations relating to the minimum vesting standards for qualified employee plans. Changes to the applicable laws were made by the Tax Reform Act of 1986. These proposed regulations amend the current regulations to reflect the changes. In the Rules and Regulations portion of this issue of the FEDERAL REGISTER, the Internal Revenue Service is issuing temporary regulations relating to the minimum vesting standards. The text of these temporary regulations also serves as the comment document for this notice of proposed rulemaking.

DATES: Written comments and requests for a public hearing must be delivered or mailed by March 7, 1988. The amendments are proposed to be generally effective for plan years beginning after December 31, 1988.

ADDRESS: Send comments and requests for a public hearing to: Commissioner of Internal Revenue, Attention: CC:LR:T (EE-167-86), 1111 Constitution Avenue, N.W., Washington, D.C. 20224.

FOR FURTHER INFORMATION CONTACT: V. Moore of the Employee Plans and Exempt Organizations Division, Office of Chief Counsel, Internal Revenue Service, 1111 Constitution Avenue, N.W., Washington, D.C. 20224 (Attention: CC:LR:T) (202-566-3938, not a toll-free call).

SUPPLEMENTARY INFORMATION:

Background

The temporary regulations in the Rules and Regulations portion of this issue of the FEDERAL REGISTER amend Part 1 of the Code of Federal Regulations. New § 1.410(a)-3T, § 1.410(a)-8T, § 1.410(a)-9T, § 1.411(a)-3T, § 1411(a)-4T, and § 1.411(a)-8T are added to Part 1 of Title 26 of the Code of Federal Regulations. When these temporary regulations are promulgated as final regulations, § 1.410(a)-3, § 1.410(a)-5, § 1.410(a)-7, § 1.411(a)-3, § 1.411(a)-4, and § 1.411(a)-8 will be revised to reflect the new provisions. For the text of the temporary regulations, see T.D. 8170 published in the Rules and Regulations portion of this issue of the FEDERAL REGISTER. The preamble to the temporary regulations explains the amendments to the Income Tax Regulations.

Regulatory Flexibility Act And Executive Order 12291

Although this document is a notice of proposed rulemaking which solicits public comment, the Internal Revenue Service has concluded that the regulations proposed herein are interpretative and that the notice and public procedure requirements of 5 U.S.C. 553 do not apply. Accordingly, these proposed regulations do not constitute regulations subject to the Regulatory Flexibility Act (5 U.S.C. chapter 6).

The Commissioner of Internal Revenue has determined that this proposed rule is not a major rule as defined in Executive Order 12291 and that a regulatory impact analysis therefore is not required.

Comments And Request For A Public Hearing

Before adopting these proposed regulations, consideration will be given to any written comments that are submitted (preferably eight copies) to the Commissioner of Internal Revenue. All comments will be available for public inspection and copying. A public hearing will be held upon written request to the Commissioner by any person who has submitted written comments. If a public hearing is held, notice of the time and place will be published in the FEDERAL REGISTER.

Drafting Information

The principal author of these proposed regulations is V. Moore of the Employee Plans and Exempt Organizations Division of the Office of Chief Counsel. Other offices of the Internal Revenue Service and Treasury Department participated in developing the regulations, both on matters of substance and style.

Lawrence B. Gibbs

Commissioner of Internal Revenue

¶ 20,165D

Proposed regulations: Highly compensated employee: Compensation: Tax Reform Act of 1986.—Reproduced below is the text of proposed regulations on the scope and meaning of the terms "highly compensated employee" in Code Sec. 414(q) and "compensation" in Code Sec. 414(s). They reflect changes made by the Tax Reform Act of 1986. The proposed regulations were also issued as temporary regulations under T.D. 8173 and are reproduced at ¶ 12,364E and 12,364G. The introductory material preceding the temporary regulations is at ¶ 23,080. The proposed regulations were published in the *Federal Register* on February 19, 1988 (53 FR 4999).

DEPARTMENT OF THE TREASURY

Internal Revenue Service

[26 CFR Part 1]

[EE-129-86]

Definitions Of "Highly Compensated Employee" And "Compensation"

Notice Of Proposed Rulemaking

AGENCY: Internal Revenue Service, Treasury.

ACTION: Notice of proposed rulemaking by cross-reference to temporary regulations.

SUMMARY: In the Rules and Regulations portion of this issue of the Federal Register, the Internal Revenue Service is issuing temporary regulations relating to the scope and meaning of the terms "highly compensated employee" in section 414(q) and "compensation" in section 414(s) of the Internal Revenue Code of 1986. They reflect changes made by the Tax Reform Act of 1986 (TRA '86). The text of those temporary regulations also serves as the text for this Notice of Proposed Rulemaking. These regulations will provide the public with guidance necessary to comply with the law and would affect sponsors of, and participants in, pension, profit-sharing and stock bonus plans, and certain other employee benefit plans.

DATES: Written comments and requests for a public hearing must be delivered or mailed [60 DAYS AFTER DATE OF PUBLICATION OF NOTICE OF PROPOSED RULEMAKING]. In general, these regulations apply to years beginning on or after January 1, 1987, except as otherwise specified in TRA '86.

ADDRESS: Send comments and requests for a public hearing to: Commissioner of Internal Revenue, Attention: CC:LR:T (EE-129-86), Washington, D.C. 20224.

FOR FURTHER INFORMATION CONTACT: Nancy J. Marks of the Employee Plans and Exempt Organizations Division, Office of the Chief Counsel, Internal Revenue Service, 1111 Constitution Avenue, N.W., Washington, D.C. 20224 (Attention: CC:LR:T), (202-566-3938) (not a toll-free number).

SUPPLEMENTARY INFORMATION:

Background

The temporary regulations in the Rules and Regulations portion of this issue of the Federal Register amend 26 CFR by adding a new section 1.414(q)-1T under Part 1 to provide guidance with respect to the definitions of highly compensated employee and compensation within the meaning of Code section 414(q) and (s). The regulations are proposed to be issued under the authority contained in sections 414(s) and 7805 of the Code (100 Stat. 2453, 68A Stat. 917; 26 U.S.C. 414(s), 7805). For the text of the temporary regulations, see F.R. Doc. (T.D. —) published in the Rules and Regulations portion of this issue of the Federal Register.

Special Analyses

The Commissioner of Internal Revenue has determined that this proposed rule is not a major rule as defined in Executive Order 12291 and that a regulatory impact analysis is not required.

Although this document is a notice of proposed rulemaking which solicits public comment, the Internal Revenue Service has concluded that the regulations proposed herein are interpretative and that the notice and public procedure requirements of 5 U.S.C. 553 do not apply. Accordingly, these proposed regulations do not constitute regulations subject to the Regulatory Flexibility Act (5 U.S.C. chapter 6).

Comments And Requests For Public Hearing

Before adopting these proposed regulations, consideration will be given to any written comments that are submitted (preferably eight copies) to the Commissioner of Internal Revenue. All comments will be available for public inspection and copying. A public hearing will be held upon written request to the Commissioner by any person who has submitted written comments. If a public hearing is held, notice of the time and place will be published in the FEDERAL REGISTER.

Drafting Information

The principal author of these proposed regulations is Nancy J. Marks of the Employee Plans and Exempt Organizations Division of the Office of Chief Counsel, Internal Revenue Service. However, personnel from other offices of the Internal Revenue Service and Treasury Department participated in developing the regulations, both on matters of substance and style.

List Of Subjects In 26 §§ CFR 1.401-0—1.425-1

Income taxes, Employee benefit plans, Pensions.

Lawrence B. Gibbs,

Commissioner of Internal Revenue.

[¶ 20,166 Reserved.—Proposed regulations under Code Sec. 413, relating to collectively bargained plans and plans maintained by more than one employer were formerly reproduced at this point. The final regulations appear at ¶ 12,311 and 12,312.]

[¶ 20,166A Reserved.—Proposed regulations relating to the permitted disparity in employer contributions and employer-derived benefits for highly compensated employees in employee benefit plans and the determination of whether certain disparities resulted in prohibited discrimination were formerly reproduced here. The final regulations are at ¶ 11,731Q-1—¶ 11,731Q-6.]

[¶ 20,167 Reserved.—Proposed regulations on tax treatment of certain option income of exempt organizations formerly appeared at this point. The final regulations are at ¶ 13,213 and 13,233.]

[¶ 20,168 Reserved.—Proposed regulations requesting comments on temporary TRASOP regulations were formerly reproduced at this paragraph. The temporary regulations were finalized and appear at ¶ 11,124.]

[¶ 20,169 Reserved.—Proposed Reg. §§ 1.219-1(c) and 1.219-2(a)-(i), defining the term "active participant" for purposes of determining who can make deductible contributions to an individual retirement account, were formerly reproduced here. The final regulations appear at ¶ 11,331 and 11,332.]

[¶ 20,170 Reserved.—Proposed regulations relating to excise taxes imposed on excess contributions to Keogh plans were formerly reproduced at this point. The final regulations are at ¶ 13,611.]

[¶ 20,171 Reserved.—Proposed regulations under Code Secs. 401, 403, and 415, relating to limitations on benefits and contributions under qualified plans, were formerly reproduced at this point. The final regulations are at ¶ 11,702, 11,708, 11,715, 11,716, 11,720B, 11,725, 11,803, 11,901, and 12,401—12,410.]

¶ 20,172

Proposed regulations prescribing rules for determining if the vesting schedule of a qualified plan discriminates in favor of employees who are officers, shareholders, or highly compensated.—Reproduced below is the text of proposed Reg. § 1.411(d)-1, which sets forth guidelines for determining if a plan's vesting schedule discriminates in favor of prohibited groups.

The proposed regulations were published in the *Federal Register* of April 9, 1980 (45 FR 24201).

DEPARTMENT OF THE TREASURY

Internal Revenue Service

[26 CFR Part 1]

[EE-164-78]

Coordination Of Vesting And Discrimination Requirements For Qualified Plans

AGENCY: Internal Revenue Service, Treasury.

ACTION: Notice of proposed rulemaking.

SUMMARY: This document contains proposed regulations prescribing rules for determining if the vesting schedule of a qualified plan discriminates in favor of employees who are officers, shareholders, or highly compensated. Changes to the applicable tax law were made by the Employee Retirement Income Security Act of 1974. The regulations would provide the public with additional guidance needed to comply with that Act and would affect all employers maintaining qualified plans.

DATES: Written comments and requests for a public hearing must be delivered or mailed by June 9, 1980. The amendments are proposed to be effective for plan years beginning 30 days after the publication of this regulation in the FEDERAL REGISTER as a Treasury decision.

ADDRESS: Send comments and requests for a public hearing to: Commissioner of Internal Revenue, Attention: CC:LR:T (EE-164-78), Washington, D.C. 20224.

FOR FURTHER INFORMATION CONTACT: Kirk F. Maldonado of the Employee Plans and Exempt Organizations Division, Office of the Chief Counsel, Internal Revenue Service, 1111 Constitution Avenue, N.W., Washington, D.C. 20224 (Attention: CC:LR:T) (202-566-3430) (not a toll-free number).

SUPPLEMENTARY INFORMATION:

Background

This document contains proposed amendments to the Income Tax Regulations (26 CFR Part 1) under section 411(d)(1) of the Internal Revenue Code of 1954. These amendments are proposed to conform the regulations to section 1012(a) of the Employee Retirement Income Security Act of 1974 (88 Stat. 901) and these regulations are to be issued under the authority contained in section 7805 of the Internal Revenue Code of 1954 (68A Stat. 917; 26 U.S.C. 7805).

Statutory Provisions

Section 401(a)(4) of the Code provides that a plan which discriminates in favor of employees who are officers, shareholders, or highly compensated (hereinafter referred to as "prohibited group") is not a qualified plan under section 401(a). Section 411(d)(1) provides that the vesting schedule of a plan which satisfies the requirements of section 411 shall be considered as satisfying any vesting requirements resulting from the application of section 401(a)(4) except in two situations. One situation, as set forth in section 411(d)(1)(A), is a pattern of abuse under the plan which tends to discriminate in favor of the prohibited group (pattern of abuse). The other situation, as detailed in section 411(d)(1)(B), is where there have been, or there is reason to believe there will be, an accrual of benefits or forfeitures tending to discriminate in favor of the prohibited group (hereinafter referred to as "discriminatory vesting").

Prior Guidelines

Initial guidelines under section 411(d)(1) were set forth in Revenue Procedure 75-49, 1975-2 C.B. 584. That procedure established several alternative tests, with respect to vesting, that a plan must satisfy to secure a favorable advance determination letter. If a plan fails to satisfy these tests, a favorable advance determination letter will not be issued unless the plan adopts accelerated vesting (so-called "4/40 vesting").

Revenue Procedure 75-49 was modified in Revenue Procedure 76-11, 1976-1 C.B. 550. That procedure adopted alternative ways of satisfying the requirements of section 411(d)(1) in order to secure a favorable advance determination letter, in addition to the tests contained in Revenue Procedure 75-49.

The tests of Revenue Procedures 75-49 and 76-11 were applied only with respect to whether a plan could receive a favorable advance determination letter. The determination letter by its terms provided that the approval of the plan's qualified status by the Service did not extend to the plan in operation. Therefore, separate tests for determining discrimination in vesting were necessary with respect to the issuance of a determination letter and with respect to testing the operation of the plan's vesting schedule.

In addition, the tests described in Revenue Procedures 75-49 and 76-11 were generally mechanical. Objections were raised by plan administrators and sponsors when they were required to accept 4/40 vesting as a minimum schedule, and yet 4/40 vesting did not reflect the policies of ERISA if applied as a maximum vesting schedule. At the same time, it is recognized that there is a value in allowing safe harbors for plan administrators who seek a determination letter with respect to the qualified status of a plan. Therefore, although a facts and circumstances test more accurately reflects the vesting antidiscrimination provisions of the Code, and the policies of ERISA, it is recognized that some forms of safe harbor are appropriate for certainty purposes.

The rules contained in the proposed regulations attempt to accommodate both goals. On the one hand, a facts and circumstances test is described. This description is amplified by a list of factors which may be included in applying the test. It is anticipated that these factors will offer substantial guidance to plan administrators in reviewing the vesting provisions applicable both with respect to a determination letter application and with respect to the status of a plan in operation. On the other hand, two safe harbor tests are provided which would insulate a plan against a finding of discriminatory vesting under the plan.

After this regulation is adopted, it is anticipated that the tests and vesting schedule contained in Revenue Procedures 75-49 and 76-11 will no longer be applied. While plans having determination letters based on 4/40 vesting need not apply for a new determination letter on the basis of the plan's vesting schedule, plan administrators should be aware that the tests included in these regulations will be applied in testing the operation of each plan's vesting schedule and are cautioned to review each plan accordingly. Because of the guidance to be provided by this regulation after it is adopted, the concerns voiced by plan administrators under prior rules regarding how a plan's operation with respect to vesting would be judged should be alleviated. In addition, when a plan is submitted to the Internal Revenue Service for a determination letter it is anticipated that the rules in these regulations will be applied for purposes of issuing such letters.

Discrimination In Vesting

The proposed rules provide that the determination of whether there is a pattern of abuse or discriminatory vesting under a plan shall be determined on the facts and circumstances of each case. Several criteria are set forth as factors to be used in making such a determination.

Two safe harbors are provided against a finding of discriminatory vesting under the plan. One safe harbor requires full vesting after an employee has three years of service. The other safe harbor requires full vesting after ten years of service, and the sum of the vested percentages for the employee's service prior to the completion of ten years of service must equal or exceed 700.

Comments And Requests For A Public Hearing

Before adopting these proposed regulations, consideration will be given to any written comments that are submitted (preferably eight copies) to the Commissioner of Internal Revenue. All comments will be available for public inspection and copying. A public hearing will be held upon written request to the Commissioner by any person who has submitted written comments. If a public hearing is held, notice of the time and place will be published in the *Federal Register*.

Drafting Information

The principal author of these proposed regulations is Kirk F. Maldonado of the Employee Plans and Exempt Organizations Division of the Office of Chief Counsel, Internal Revenue Service. However, personnel from other offices of the Internal Revenue Service and Treasury Department participated in developing these regulations, both on matters of substance and style.

Proposed amendment to the regulations

It is proposed to amend 26 CFR Part 1 by adding the following new section at the appropriate place.

§ 1.411(d)-1 Coordinaation of vesting and discrimination requirements.

(a) *General rule.* A plan which satisfies the requirements of section 411(a)(2) shall be treated as satisfying any vesting schedule requirements resulting from the appliciation of section 401(a)(4) unless the plan is discriminatory within the meaning of section 411(d)(1) and this section. A plan is discriminatolry if there is a pattern of abuse or there is discriminatory vesting as determined under paragraphs (b) and (c) of this section, respectively. Under section 401(a)(4), a plan which discriminates in favor of employees who are officers, shareholders, or highly compensated (hereinafter referred to as "prohibited group") is not a qualified plan under section 401(a).

(b) *Pattern of abuse*—(1) *Definition.* A plan is discriminatory under section 411(d)(1)(A) and shall not be considered to satisfy the requirements of section 401(a)(4) if there has been a pattern of abuse under the plan tending to discriminate in favor of the prohibited group (hereinafter referred to as "pattern of abuse").

(2) *Test for pattern of abuse.* The determination of whether there has been a pattern of abuse shall be made on the basis of the facts and circumstances of each case. An example of a pattern of abuse is the systematic dismissal of employees before their accrued benefits vest.

(c) *Discriminatory vesting*—(1) *Definition.* A plan is discriminatory under section 411(d)(1)(B) and shall not be considered to satisfy the requirements of section 401(a)(4) if there have been, or there is reason to believe there will be, an accrual of benefits or forfeitures tending to discriminate in favor of the prohibited group by operation of the vesting schedule (hereinafter referred to as "discriminatory vesting").

≫→ *Proposed Reg. § 1.411(d)-1(c)(2) was modified by new Proposed Reg. § 1.414(d)-1(c)(2) at ¶ 20,165B.*

(2) *Test for discriminatory vesting.* Unless paragraph (d) applies, the determination of whether there is, or there is reason to believe there will be, discriminatory vesting shall be made on the basis of the facts and circumstances of each case. An unfavorable comparison based on one of the following factors does not require a finding that there is discriminatory vesting. Factors which are relevant to this determination include, but are not limited to, comparisons between the prohibited group and all other employees covered by the plan of:

(i) The employment turnover rate. The term "employment turnover rate" means the annual rate of turnover for employees.

(ii) The average percentage of vesting of each employee currently employed by the employer maintaining the plan.

(iii) The average percentage of vesting of each employee whose employment is terminated. For purposes of this subparagraph, a "termination of employment" occurs when the employee leaves by reason of a quit, discharge, retirement, or any other means.

(iv) The average number of years remaining for each employee until that employee becomes fully vested.

(v) In the case of a plan amendment which increases the length of service required for any particular level of vesting, the percentage of employees satisfying the new length of service requirement at the time it becomes effective.

≫→ *Proposed Reg. § 1.411(d)-1(d) was withdrawn. See ¶ 20,165B.*

(d) *Safe harbor test*—(1) *General rule.* A plan whose vesting schedule satisfies the requirements of subparagraph (2) or (3) of this paragraph shall be deemed not to be discriminatory under paragraph (c) of this section.

(2) *Three year rule.* A plan satisfies the requirements of this subparagraph if any employee who has completed 3 years of service has a 100% nonforfeitable right to the accrued benefit derived from employer contributions.

(3) *Ten year rule.* A plan satisfies the requirements of this subparagraph if any employee who has completed 10 years of service has a 100% nonforfeitable right to the accrued benefit derived from employer contributions, and the sum of the 10 relevant percentages of the employee's nonforfeitable rights equals or exceeds 700. The relevant percentages to be added are the employee's vested percentage (if any) prior to the completion of the first year of service, and the vested percentages after the completion of each of the first 9 years of service.

(4) *Determination of years of service.* For purposes of this paragraph, the term "years of service" means years of service required to be taken into account for purposes of section 411(a)(2), determined without regard to subparagraphs (A), (B), and (C) of section 411(a)(4).

(5) *Examples.* The rules provided by this paragraph are illustrated by the following examples:

Example (1). (i) Plan A provides that years of service for purposes of vesting are calculated under section 411(a)(2) without regard to subparagraphs (A), (B), and (C) of section 411(a)(4). Under the plan, an employee is 100% vested in the accrued benefit derived from employer contributions after three years of service.

(ii) The vesting schedule of Plan A can be illustrated by the following table:

Completed years of service	Nonforfeitable percentage
less than 1	0
1 but less than 2	0
2 but less than 3	0
3 but less than 4	100
4 but less than 5	100
5 but less than 6	100
6 but less than 7	100
7 but less than 8	100
8 but less than 9	100
9 but less than 10	100
	700

(iii) Plan A satisfies the requirements of subparagraph (2) of this paragraph because an employee is 100% vested after three years of service. Plan A also satisfies the requirements of subparagraph (3) of this paragraph because the sum of the 10 relevant percentages equals 700 and an employee is 100% vested after 10 years of service. Therefore, Plan A is deemed to be nondiscriminatory under paragraph (c) of this section.

Example (2). (i) Plan B provides that years of service for purposes of vesting are calculated under section 411(a)(2), without regard to subparagraphs (A), (B), and (C) of section 411(a)(4). Under the plan, an employee is 20% vested after one year of service, 40% after two years, 60% after three years, 80% after four years, and 100% after five years.

(ii) The vesting schedule of Plan B can be illustrated by the following table:

Completed years of service	Nonforfeitable percentage
less than 1	0
1 but less than 2	20
2 but less than 3	40
3 but less than 4	60
4 but less than 5	80
5 but less than 6	100
6 but less than 7	100
7 but less than 8	100
8 but less than 9	100
9 but less than 10	100
	700

(iii) Plan B does not satisfy the requirements of subparagraph (2) of this paragraph because an employee is not 100% vested after 3 years of service. However, Plan B satisfies the requirements of subparagraph (3) of this paragraph because the sum of the 10 relevant percentages equals 700 and an employee is 100% vested after 10 years of service. Therefore, Plan B is deemed to be nondiscriminatory under paragraph (c) of this section.

Example (3). (i) Plan C provides that years of service for purposes of vesting are calculated under section 411(a)(2), with regard to subparagraphs (A), (B), and (C) of section 411(a)(4). Under the plan, an employee's right to the accrued benefit derived from employer contributions vest as provided in section 411(a)(2)(A).

(ii) The vesting schedule of Plan C can be illustrated by the following table:

Completed years of service	Nonforfeitable percentage
less than 1	0
1 but less than 2	0
2 but less than 3	0
3 but less than 4	0
4 but less than 5	0
5 but less than 6	0
6 but less than 7	0
7 but less than 8	0
8 but less than 9	0
9 but less than 10	0
10 or more	100
	700

(iii) Plan C does not meet the requirements of subparagraph (2) of this paragraph because the employee is not 100% vested after 3 years of service. Plan C does not meet the requirements of subparagraph (3) of this paragraph because the sum of the 10 relevant percentages does not equal 700, although an employee is 100% vested after 10 years of service. Also, Plan C fails to meet the requirements of subparagraph (4) of this paragraph because an employee's service for vesting purposes is calculated using all of the subparagraphs of section 411(a)(4) instead of disregarding subparagraphs (A), (B), and (C) thereof.

(iv) Even though Plan C does not satisfy the requirements of subparagraph (2) or (3) of this paragraph, it may be found to be nondiscriminatory under paragraph (c) of this section if it satisfies the facts and circumstances test set forth in paragraph (c)(2) of this section.

(e) *Defined benefit plans.* A defined benefit plan which satisfies the benefit accrual requirements of section 411(b) shall still be subject to the nondiscrimination requirements of section 401(a)(4) with regard to its benefit accrual rates. Thus, even though a plan satisfies the section 411(b) requirements, the plan may still be discriminatory under section 401(a)(4) with respect to its benefit accruals.

(f) *Effective date.* This section shall apply to plan years beginning 30 days after the publication of this section in the FEDERAL REGISTER as a Treasury decision.

(Signed) Jerome Kurtz

Commissioner of Internal Revenue

[¶ 20,173 Reserved.—Proposed Reg. §§ 301.6104(a)-1 through 301.6104(a)-6, relating to public inspection of applications for tax exemption, applications for determination of the qualification of pension and other plans, and other related material, were formerly reproduced here. The finalized regulations now appear at ¶ 13,771—13,776.]

[¶ 20,174 Reserved.—Proposed regulations amending proposed rulemaking relating to custodial accounts for regulated investment company stock were formerly reproduced at this paragraph. The regulations were withdrawn by the Internal Revenue Service in a withdrawal notice on January 13, 1987 (52 FR 2724).]

[¶ 20,175 Reserved.—Proposed regulations relating to deferred compensation plans maintained by state and local governments and rural electric cooperatives were formerly reproduced at this paragraph. The final regulations are at ¶ 11,251, 11,252, 11,803, and 13,154—13,154C.]

[¶ 20,176 Reserved.—Proposed regulations concerning the diversification requirements for variable annuity, endowment, and life insurance contracts were formerly reproduced here. The final regulations are at ¶ 13,312B.]

¶ 20,177

Proposed regulations: Excess distributions: Excise tax: Qualified plans, IRAs, annuities, custodial accounts.—Reproduced below is the text of a notice of proposed rulemaking relating to the excise tax on excess distributions from qualified plans, individual retirement accounts, 403(b) annuity contracts, custodial accounts, and retirement income accounts. Temporary regulations, which serve as the text for these proposed regulations, appear at ¶ 13,648V. The proposed regulations were published in the *Federal Register* on December 10, 1987 (52 FR 46747).

DEPARTMENT OF THE TREASURY

Internal Revenue Service

26 CFR Parts 54 and 602

[EE-162-86]

Excise Tax on Excess Distributions from Retirement Plans; Proposed Rulemaking

AGENCY: Internal Revenue Service, Treasury.

ACTION: Notice of proposed rulemaking by cross-reference to temporary regulations.

SUMMARY: In the Rules and Regulations portion of this issue of the *Federal Register,* the Internal Revenue Service is issuing temporary regulations relating to the excise tax on excess distributions from retirement plans under section 1133 of the Tax Reform Act of 1986. The text of those temporary regulations also serves as the text for this Notice of Proposed Rulemaking.

DATES: Written comments and requests for a public hearing must be delivered or mailed before February 8, 1988.

ADDRESS: Send comments and requests for a public hearing to: Commissioner of Internal Revenue, Attention: CC:LR:T (EE-162-86), Washington, DC 20224.

FOR FURTHER INFORMATION CONTACT: Marjorie Hoffman of the Employee Plans and Exempt Organizations Division, Office of Chief Counsel, Internal Revenue Service, 1111 Constitution Avenue, NW., Washington, DC 20224, Attention: CC:LR:T (EE-162-86), 202-566-3903 (not a toll-free number).

SUPPLEMENTARY INFORMATION:

Background

The temporary regulations in the Rules and Regulations portion of this issue of the *Federal Register* amend 26 CFR by adding a new § 54.4981A-1T under Part 54 to provide guidance so taxpayers can comply with section 4981A of the Internal Revenue Code. The final regulations which are proposed to be based on the temporary regulations would amend Part 54 of Title 26 of the Code of Federal Regulations by adding similar sections to Part 54 (Pension Excise Tax Regulations). The regulations are proposed to be issued under the authority contained in sections 4981A and 7805 of the Code (100 Stat. 2841, 26 U.S.C. 4981A; 68A Stat. 917, 26 U.S.C. 7805). For the text of the temporary regulations, see F.R. Doc. 87-28401 (T.D. 8165) published in the Rules and Regulations of this issue of the *Federal Register.*

Special Analyses

The Commissioner of Internal Revenue has determined that this proposed rule is not a major rule as defined in Executive Order 12291 and that a Regulatory Impact Analysis is therefore not required. Although this document is a notice of proposed rulemaking which solicits public comment, the Internal Revenue Service has concluded that the regulations proposed herein are interpretative and that the notice and public procedure requirements of 5 U.S.C. 553 do not apply. Accordingly, these proposed regulations do not constitute regulations subject to the Regulatory Flexibility Act (5 U.S.C. Chapter 6).

Comments and Request for Public Hearing

Before adopting these proposed regulations, consideration will be given to any written comments that are submitted (preferably 8 copies) to the Commissioner of Internal Revenue. All comments will be available for public inspection and copying. A public hearing will be held upon written request to the Commissioner by any person who has submitted written comments. If a public hearing is held, notice of the time and place will be published in the *Federal Register.* The collection of information requirements contained herein have been submitted to the Office of Management and Budget (OMB) for review under section 3504(h) of the Paperwork Reduction Act. Comments on the requirements should be sent to the Office of Information and Regulatory Affairs of OMB, Attention: Desk Officer for the Internal Revenue Service, New Executive Office Building, Washington, DC 20503. The Internal Revenue Service requests persons submitting comments to OMB also to send copies of the comments to the Service.

Drafting Information

The principal author of these proposed regulations is Marjorie Hoffman of the Employee Plans and Exempt Organizations Division of the Office of Chief Counsel, Internal Revenue Service. However, personnel from other offices of the Internal Revenue Service and Treasury Department participated in developing the regulations, both on matters of substance and style.

List of Subjects

26 CFR 54

Excise taxes, Pensions.

26 CFR 602

Reporting and recordkeeping requirements.

Lawrence B. Gibbs,

Commissioner of Internal Revenue.

[FR Doc. 87-28402 Filed 12-9-87; 8:45 am]

¶ 20,178

Proposed regulations: Golden parachute payments.—Reproduced below is the text of proposed regulations on golden parachute payments relating to exempt parachute payments, disqualified individuals, changes in corporate ownership or control, and reasonable compensation.

The proposed regulations were published in the *Federal Register* on May 5, 1989 (54 FR 19390).

The proposed regulations were amended by the proposed regulations at ¶ 20,260G, published in the *Federal Register* on February 20, 2002 (67 FR 7630). Under the new proposed regulations, the IRS clarified that the 1989 proposed regulations could be applied to any payments that are contingent on a change in ownership or control occurring prior to January 1, 2004.

AGENCY: Internal Revenue Service, Treasury.

ACTION: Notice of proposed rulemaking.

SUMMARY: This document contains proposed regulations relating to golden parachute payments. Changes to the applicable tax law were made by the Tax Reform Act of 1984, the Tax Reform Act of 1986, and the Technical and Miscellaneous Revenue Act of 1988. The regulations will provide guidance to taxpayers who must comply with section 280G of the Internal Revenue Code of 1986.

DATES: Written comments and requests for a public hearing must be delivered or mailed by July 5, 1989. Generally, these regulations are proposed to be effective for payments made under agreements entered into or renewed after June 14, 1984. These regulations also are proposed to be effective for certain payments under agreements entered into on or before June 14, 1984, and amended or supplemented in significant relevant respect after that date.

ADDRESS: Send comments and requests for a public hearing to: Internal Revenue Service, Attention: CC:CORP:T:R (PS217-84), Room 4429, Washington, D.C. 20024.

FOR FURTHER INFORMATION CONTACT: Stuart G. Wessler, 202-566-6016, or Robert Misner, 202-566-4752 (not toll-free numbers).

SUPPLEMENTARY INFORMATION:

Background

This document contains proposed amendments to the Income Tax Regulations (26 CFR Part 1) under section 280G of the Internal Revenue Code. These amendments are proposed to conform the Income Tax Regulations to section 67 of the Tax Reform Act of 1984 (Pub. L. No. 98-369; 98 Stat. 585), which added sections 280G and 4999 to the Code and amended Code sections 275(a)(6) and 3121(v)(2)(A), and to section 1804(j) of the Tax Reform Act of 1986 (Pub. L. No. 99-514; 100 Stat. 2807) and section 1018(d)(6)-(8) of the Technical and Miscellaneous Revenue Act of 1988 (Pub. L. No. 100-647; 102 Stat. 3581), which amended Code section 280G. These provisions relate to golden parachute payments. Specifically, section 280G denies a deduction for any "excess parachute payment," section 4999 imposes a 20-percent excise tax on the recipient of any excess parachute payment, section 275(a)(6) denies a deduction for the section 4999 excise tax, and section 3121(v)(2)(A) relates to FICA.

Overview of Statutory Provisions

In applying the golden parachute provisions, the first step is to identify payments that constitute "parachute payments." Section 280G(b)(2)(A) defines a "parachute payment" as any payment that meets all of the following four conditions: (a) the payment is in the nature of compensation; (b) the payment is to, or for the benefit of, a disqualified individual; (c) the payment is contingent on a change in the ownership of a corporation, the effective control of a corporation, or the ownership of a substantial portion of the assets of a corporation ("change in ownership or control"); and (d) the payment has (together with other payments described above in (a), (b), and (c) with respect to the same individual) an aggregate present value of at least 3 times the individual's base amount.

For this purpose, an individual's base amount is, in general, the individual's average annualized includible compensation for the most recent 5 taxable years ending before the change in ownership or control.

Section 280G(b)(2)(B) provides that the term "parachute payment" also includes any payment in the nature of compensation to, or for the benefit of, a disqualified individual if the payment is pursuant to an agreement that violates any generally enforced securities laws or regulations ("securities violation parachute payment").

Once payments are identified as "parachute payments", the next step is to determine any "excess" portion of the payments. Section 280G(b)(1) defines the term "excess parachute payment" as an amount equal to the excess of any parachute payment over the portion of the disqualified individual's base amount that is allocated to such payment. For this purpose, the portion of the base amount allocated to a parachute payment is the amount that bears the same ratio to the base amount as the present value of the parachute payment bears to the aggregate present value of all such payments to the same disqualified individual.

Generally, excess parachute payments may be reduced by certain amounts of reasonable compensation. Section 280G(b)(4)(B) provides that except in the case of securities violation parachute payments, the amount of an excess parachute payment is reduced by any portion of the payment that the taxpayer establishes by clear and convincing evidence is reasonable compensation for personal services actually rendered by the disqualified individual before the date of change in ownership or control. Such reasonable compensation is first offset against the portion of the base amount allocated to the payment.

Exempt Payments

Section 280G specifically exempts several types of payments from the definition of the term "parachute payment."

Deductions for payments exempt from the definition of "parachute payment" are not disallowed by section 280G, and such exempt payments are not subject to the 20-percent excise tax of section 4999. In addition, such exempt payments are not taken into account in applying the three-times-base-amount test of section 280G(b)(2)(A)(ii).

Section 280G(b)(5) provides an exemption for payments with respect to certain corporations. Pursuant to that section, the term "parachute payment" does not include any payment made to a disqualified individual with respect to a corporation which, immediately before the change in ownership or control, was a small business corporation (as defined in section 1361(b) but without regard to paragraph (1)(C) thereof). In addition, the term "parachute payment" does not include any payment made with respect to a corporation if, immediately before the change in ownership or control, no stock in the corporation was readily tradable on an established securities market (or otherwise) and certain shareholder approval requirements are met with respect to the payment. For this purpose, stock that is described in section 1504(a)(4) is not treated as being readily tradable on an established securities market if the payment does not adversely affect the shareholder's redemption and liquidation rights. The proposed regulations provide guidance on applying the exemptions contained in section 280G(b)(5).

Section 280G(b)(6) exempts certain payments under a qualified plan. Pursuant to that section, the term "parachute payment" does not include any payment to or from: (a) a plan described in section 401(a) which includes a trust exempt from tax under section 501(a); (b) an annuity plan desecribed in section 403(a); or (c) a simplified employee pension as defined in section 408(k).

Finally, section 280G(b)(4)(A) exempts certain payments of reasonable compensation. Pursuant to that section, except in the case of securities violation parachute payments, the term "parachute payment" does not include the portion of any payment which the taxpayer establishes by clear and convincing evidence is reasonable compensation for personal services to be rendered on or after the date of the change in ownership or control. The proposed regulations provide guidance for rdetermining amounts of reasonable compensation.

Disqualified Individuals

To be a parachute payment, a payment must be made to (or for the benefit of) a "disqualified individual." Section 280G(c) defines the term "disqualified individual" to include any individual who (a) is an employee or independent contractor who performs personal services for a corporation, and (b) is an officer, shareholder, or highly-compensated individual. The proposed regulations provide guidance on who will be treated as an "officer," a "shareholder," and a "highly-compensated individual" for this purpose.

Section 280G(c) provides that a "highly-compensated individual" with respect to a corporation only includes an individual who is (or would be if the individual were an employee) a member of the group consisting of the highest paid 1 percent of the employees of the corporation or, if less, the 250 highest paid employees of the corporation. The proposed regulations provide rules for applying this definition. In addition, the proposed regulations provide that no individual whose annual compensation is less than $75,000 will be treated as a highly compensated individual. The proposed regulations also provide an exception to the definition of "highly-compensated individual" to prevent fees earned by independent service providers (such as independent brokers, attorneys, and investment bankers) from becoming subject to section 280G when they perform services in connection with a change in ownership or control.

With respect to who will be treated as a "shareholder" for purposes of section 280G(c), the proposed regulations provide a *de minimis* rule. Pursuant to this rule, only an individual who owns stock of a corporation having a value that exceeds the lesser of $1 million, or 1 percent of the total value of the outstanding shares of all classes of the corporation's stock, is treated as a disqualified individual with respect to the corporation by reason of stock ownership. For purposes of determining the amount of the stock owned by an individual, the constructive ownership rules of section 318(a) shall apply.

The proposed regulations also limit the number of employees who will be treated as disqualified individuals with respect to a corporation by reason of being "officers" of the corporation. The proposed regulations provide that no more than 50 employees (or, if less, the greater of 3 employees or 10 percent of the employees of the corporation) will be treated as disqualified individuals with respect to a corporation by reason of being an officer of the corporation. In the case of an affiliated group treated as one corporation, the previous sentence will be applied to each member of such group.

Contingent on Change

To be a parachute payment, a payment must be contingent on a change in ownership or control. The proposed regulations provide rules on when a payment will be treated as so "contingent."

In general, a payment will be treated as contingent on a change in ownership or control if the payment would not in fact have been made had no change in ownership or control occurred. A payment generally will be treated as one which would not in fact have been made in the absence of a change in ownership or control unless it is substantially certain, at the time of the change, that the payment would have been made whether or not the change occurred. In addition, a payment

generally is treated as contingent on a change in ownership of control if (a) the payment is contingent on an event that is closely associated with such a change, (b) a change in ownership or control actually occurs, and (c) the event is materially related to the change in ownership or control. Some types of events that are considered closely associated with a change in ownership or control are the onset of a tender offer, the termination of the disqualified individual's employment, and a significant reduction in the disqualified individual's job responsibilities.

Moreover, a payment will be treated as contingent on a change in ownership or control if the change accelerates the time at which the payment is made. However, if it is substantially certain at the time of the change that the payment would have been made whether or not the change occurred, but the payment is treated as contingent on the change solely because the change accelerates the time at which the payment is made, only a portion of the payment will be treated as contingent on the change. In such case, the portion of the payment that will be treated as contingent on the change is the amount by which the amount of the accelerated payment exceeds the present value of the payment absent the acceleration. In addition, if a payment is accelerated by a change in ownership or control and the payment is substantially certain, at the time of the change, to have been made without regard to such change provided that the disqualified individual had continued to perform services for the corporation for a specified period of time, only a portion of the payment is treated as contingent on the change. The proposed regulations provide rules for determining the portion of the payment so treated. The proposed regulations provide that payments made pursuant to an agreement that is entered into after a change in ownership or control will not be treated as contingent on the change. However, for this purpose, an agreement that is executed after a change in ownership or control pursuant to a legally enforceable agreement that was entered into before the change will be considered to have been entered into before the change.

Presumption That Payment Is Contingent on Change

Section 280G(b)(2)(C) provides a presumption that certain payments are contingent on a change in ownership or control. Specifically, this provision provides that any payment pursuant to an agreement (or an amendment of a previous agreement) that is entered into within one year before a change in ownership or control is presumed to be contingent on such change unless the contrary is established by clear and convincing evidence.

The proposed regulations provide that an amendment of a previous agreement triggers this presumption only if the previous agreement is amended "in any significant respect." The proposed regulations also provide that when the presumption is triggered by an amendment, only the portion of a payment that exceeds the amount of such payment that would have been made in the absence of the amendment is presumed, by reason of the amendment, to be contingent on the change in ownership or control.

In addition, the proposed regulations provide that if an agreement is entered into within one year before the date of a change in ownership or control, clear and convincing evidence that the agreement is (a) a nondiscriminatory employee plan or program; (b) a contract that replaces a prior contract entered into by the same parties more than one year before the change in ownership or control (if the new contract meets certain requirements); or (c) a contract between a corporation and a disqualified individual who did not perform services for the corporation prior to the individual's taxable year in which the change in ownership or control occurs (if the contract meets certain requirements); generally will rebut the presumption that payments under the agreement are contingent on the change.

Change in Ownership or Control

The proposed regulations also provide guidance on when a change in ownership or control will be considered to occur. The regulations provide that a change in the ownership of a corporation occurs when any one person, or more than one person acting as a group, acquires ownership of stock of the corporation that, together with stock held by such person or group, has more than 50 percent of the total fair market value or voting power of all of the corporation's outstanding stock. Section 318(a) will apply in determining stock ownership for this purpose.

The proposed regulations provide that a change in the ownership of a substantial portion of the assets of a corporation occurs when any one person, or more than one person acting as a group, acquires (or has acquired during the 12 months ending on the date of the most recent acquisition by such person or persons) assets from the corporation that have a total fair market value equal to or more than one third of the total fair market value of all of the assets of the corporation immediately prior to such acquisition or acquisitions. However, the proposed regulations provide that a transfer of assets by a corporation will not be treated as a change in ownership if the assets are transferred to certain shareholders of the corporation or to an entity at least 50 percent of the total value or voting power of which is owned by the corporation.

Under the proposed regulations, a change in the effective control of a corporation is presumed to occur when either of the following events occurs: (a) any one person, or more than one person acting as a group acquires (or has acquired during the 12 month period ending on the date of the most recent acquisition) ownership of stock of the corporation possessing 20 percent or more of the total voting power of the stock of the corporation; or (b) a majority of the members of the corporation's board of directors is replaced during any 12-month period by directors whose appointment or election is not endorsed by a majority of the members of the corporation's board of directors prior to the appointment or election.

Under the proposed regulations, a taxpayer may rebut the presumption described in the preceding paragraph by establishing that such acquisition or acquisitions of the corporation's stock, or such replacement of the majority of the members of the corporation's board of directors, does not transfer the power to control (directly or indirectly) the management and policies of the corporation from any one person or group to another person or group.

Securities Violation Parachute Payments

The proposed regulation implement section 280G(b)(2)(B) by providing that the term "parachute payment" also includes any payment in the nature of compensation to (or for the benefit of) a disqualified individual if such payment is made (a) pursuant to an agreement that violates any generally enforced federal or state securities law or regulation, and (b) in connection with a potential or actual change in ownership or control. However, a violation will not be taken into account for this purpose if it is merely technical in character or is not materially prejudicial to shareholders or potential shareholders. Generally, a securities violation will be presumed not to exist unless the existence of the violation has been determined or admitted in a civil or criminal action (or an administrative action by a regulatory body charged with enforcing the particular securities law or regulation) which has been resolved by adjudication or consent.

Reasonable Compensation

As previously mentioned, section 280G(b)(4)(A) provides that except in the case of securities violation parachute payments, the amount of a payment treated as a parachute payment shall not include the portion of such payment which the taxpayer establishes by clear and convincing evidence is reasonable compensation for personal services to be rendered on or after the date of the change in ownership or control.

Section 280G(b)(4)(B) provides that except in the case of securities violation parachute payments, the amount of a payment treated as an excess parachute payment is reduced by any portion of the payment that the taxpayer establishes by clear and convincing evidence is reasonable compensation for personal services actually rendered by the disqualified individual before the date of the change in ownership or control. Such reasonable compensation is first offset against the portion of the base amount allocated to the payment.

The proposed regulations provide criteria for determining whether payments are reasonable compensation. In general, whether payments are reasonable compensation is determined on the basis of all the facts and circumstances in the particular case. Factors relevant to such a determination include the nature of the services rendered or to be rendered, the individual's historic compensation for performing such services, and the compensation of individuals performing comparable services in situations where the compensation is not contingent on the change. The proposed regulations also provide that payments made under certain nondiscriminatory employee plans or programs will generally be considered to be clear and convincing evidence that the payments are reasonable compensation.

Generally, clear and convincing evidence of reasonable compensation for personal services to be rendered on or after the change in ownership or control will not exist if the individual does not, in fact, perform the services. However, the proposed regulations provide that damages paid for the breach of an employment contract may be reasonable compensation for such services if certain factors are shown. One of these factors is that the damages must be reduced by mitigation. For this purpose, damages will be treated as being mitigated if the damages are reduced (or any payment of such damages is returned) to the extent of the disqualified individual's earned income during the remainder of the contract term. The proposed regulations do not provide a rule concerning the method of establishing mitigation of

damages in other situations, such as where the disqualified individual does not accept alternative employment during the remainder of the contract term or where the individual and the corporation considered mitigation in determining the amount of a lump-sum settlement agreement, because the Service is concerned about the administrability of such a rule. Accordingly, the Service solicits comment on how a rule which would allow damages to be treated as mitigated in such cases could be administered.

Finally, the proposed regulations provide that for purposes of section 280G, severance payments will not be considered as reasonable compensation.

Issues on Which Comments are Requested

In addition to the issue concerning mitigation of damages, the Service solicits comment on the following issues:

(a) How the present value of a payment to be made in the future should be determined if such value depends on some uncertain future event or condition (and what adjustments, if any, are to be made if the amount of the actual payment differs from the amount used in determining present value). See Q/A-31, Q/A-32, and Q/A-33 of the proposed regulations.

(b) How the special rules of section 280G should interact with special income deferral rules such as those contained in section 83. See Q/A-12 and Q/A-13 of the proposed regulations.

(c) Whether the rules for identifying the disqualified individuals of a corporation (including the rules relating to the time period that should be utilized to determine who the disqualified individuals are and how the compensation for such a time period should be determined) could be simplified. See Q/A-20 and Q/A-21 of the proposed regulations.

(d) How severance payments should be treated. See Q/A-44 of the proposed regulations.

(e) Whether any of the rules contained in the proposed regulations should be given only prospective effect.

Special Analyses

The Commissioner of Internal Revenue has determined that this proposed rule is not a major rule as defined in Executive Order 12291 and that a Regulatory Impact Analysis is therefore not required.

Although this document is a notice of proposed rulemaking which solicits public comments, the Internal Revenue Service has concluded that the regulations proposed herein are interpretative and that the notice and public procedure requirements of 5 U.S.C. 553 do not apply. Accordingly, these proposed regulations do not constitute regulations subject to the Regulatory Flexibility Act (5 U.S.C. Chapter 6).

Comments and Requests for a Public Hearing

Before these proposed regulations are adopted consideration will be given to any written comments that are submitted to the Commissioner of Internal Revenue. All comments will be available for public inspection and copying. A public hearing will be held upon written request to the Commissioner by any person who has submitted written comments. If a public hearing is held, notice of the time and place will be published in the FEDERAL REGISTER.

Drafting Information

The principal author of these proposed regulations is Stuart G. Wessler of the Office of Chief Counsel, Internal Revenue Service. However, personnel from other offices of the Service and Treasury Department participated in their development.

List of Subjects

26 CFR §§ 1.61-1—1.281-4

Income taxes, Taxable income, Deductions, Exemptions.

Proposed amendments to the regulations

The proposed amendments to 26 CFR Part 1 are as follows:

PART 1—INCOME TAX; TAXABLE YEARS BEGINNING AFTER DECEMBER 31, 1986

Paragraph 1. The authority for Part 1 is amended by adding the following citation:

Authority: 26 U.S.C. 7805. * * * Section 1.280G-1 also issued under 26 U.S.C. 280G(b) and (e).

Par. 2. A new § 1.280G-1 is added after § 1.280F-6T to read as follows:

§ 1.280G-1. *Golden parachute payments.*—The following questions and answers relate to the treatment of golden parachute payments under section 280G of the Internal Revenue Code of 1986, as added by section 67 of the Tax Reform Act of 1984 (Pub. L. No. 98-369; 98 Stat. 585) and amended by section 1804(j) of the Tax Reform Act of 1986 (Pub. L. No. 99-514; 100 Stat. 2807) and section 1018(d)(6)-(8) of the Technical and Miscellaneous Revenue Act of 1988 (Pub. L. No. 100-647; 102 Stat. 3581).

The following is a table of contents for this section:

Overview

Q-1: What is the effect of Code section 280G?

A-1: Section 280G disallows a deduction for any "excess parachute payment" paid or accrued. For rules relating to the imposition of a nondeductible 20-percent excise tax on the recipient of any excess parachute payment, see Code sections 4999, 275(a)(6), and 3121(v)(2)(A).

Q-2: What is a "parachute payment" for purposes of section 280G?

A-2: (a) The term "parachute payment" means any payment (other than a payment with respect to certain corporations exempted under Q/A-6

of this section, a payment under a qualified plan exempted under Q/A-8 of this section, or a payment of reasonable compensation exempted under Q/A-9 of this section) that—

(1) Is in the nature of compensation;

(2) Is made or is to be made to (or for the benefit of) a "disqualified individual;"

(3) Is contingent on a change—

(i) In the ownership of a corporation,

(ii) In the effective control of a corporation, or

(iii) In the ownership of a substantial portion of the assets of a corporation; and

(4) Has (together with other payments described in paragraph (a)(1), (2), and (3) of this A-2 with respect to the same disqualified individual) an aggregate present value of at least 3 times the individual's "base amount."

Hereinafter, a change referred to in paragraph (a)(3) of this A-2 is referred to as a "change in ownership or control." For a discussion of the application of paragraph (a)(1), see Q/A-11 through Q/A-14; paragraph (a)(2), Q/A-15 through Q/A-21; paragraph (a)(3), Q/A-22 through Q/A-29; and paragraph (a)(4), Q/A-30 through Q/A-36.

(b) The term "parachute payment" also includes any payment in the nature of compensation to (or for the benefit of) a disqualified individual that is pursuant to an agreement that violates a generally enforced securities law or regulation. This type of parachute payment is referred to in this section as a "securities violation parachute payment." See Q/A-37 for the definition and treatment of securities violation parachute payments.

Q-3: What is an "excess parachute payment" for purposes of section 280G?

A-3: The term "excess parachute payment" means an amount equal to the excess of any parachute payment over the portion of the "base amount" allocated to such payment. Subject to certain exceptions and limitations, an excess parachute payment is reduced by any portion of the payment which the taxpayer establishes by clear and convincing evidence is reasonable compensation for personal services actually rendered by the disqualified individual before the date of the change in ownership or control. For a discussion of the computation of excess parachute payments and their reduction by reasonable compensation, see Q/A-38 through Q/A-44. For a discussion of the nonreduction of a securities violation parachute payment by reasonable compensation, see Q/A-37.

Q-4: What is the effective date of section 280G and this section?

A-4: In general, section 280G and this section apply to payments under agreements entered into or renewed after June 14, 1984. Section 280G and this section also apply to certain payments under agreements entered into on or before June 14, 1984, and amended or supplemented in significant relevant respect after that date. For a discussion of the application of the effective date, see Q/A-47 through Q/A-52.

Exempt Payments

Q-5: Are some types of payments exempt from the definition of the term "parachute payment"?

A-5: Yes. The following four types of payments are exempt from the definition of "parachute payment": (a) payments with respect to a small business corporation (described in Q/A-6 of this section); (b) certain payments with respect to a corporation no stock in which is readily tradable on an established securities market (or otherwise) (described in Q/A-6 of this section); (c) payments to or from a qualified plan (described in Q/A-8 of this section); and (d) certain payments of reasonable compensation (described in Q/A-9 of this section). Deductions for payments exempt from the definition of "parachute payment" are not disallowed by section 280G, and such exempt payments are not subject to the 20-percent excise tax of section 4999. In addition, such exempt payments are not taken into account in applying the three-times-base-amount test of Q/A-30 of this section.

Q-6: Which payments with respect to a corporation referred to in paragraph (a) or (b) of A-5 of this section are exempt from the definition of "parachute payment"?

A-6: (a) The term "parachute payment" does not include—

(1) Any payment to a disqualified individual with respect to a corporation which (immediately before the change in ownership or control) was a small business corporation (as defined in section 1361(b) but without regard to paragraph (1)(C) thereof), or

(2) Any payment to a disqualified individual with respect to a corporation (other than a small business corporation described in paragraph (a)(1) of this A-6) if—

(i) Immediately before the change in ownership or control, no stock in such corporation was readily tradable on an established securities market or otherwise, and

(ii) The shareholder approval requirements described in Q/A-7 of this section are met with respect to such payment.

(b) For purposes of paragraph (a)(1) of this A-6, the members of an affiliated group are not treated as one corporation.

(c) The requirements of paragraph (a)(2)(i) of this A-6 are not met if a substantial portion of the assets of any entity consists (directly or indirectly) of stock in such corporation and any ownership interest in such entity is readily tradable on an established securities market or otherwise. For this purpose, such stock constitutes a substantial portion of the assets of an entity if the total fair market value of the stock is equal to or more than one third of the total fair market value of all of the assets of the entity. If a corporation is a member of an affiliated group (which group is treated as one corporation under A-46 of this section), the requirements of paragraph (a)(2)(i) of this A-6 are not met if any stock in any member of such group is readily tradable on an established securities market or otherwise.

(d) For purposes of paragraph (a)(2)(i) of this A-6, the term "stock" does not include stock described in section 1504(a)(4) if the payment does not adversely affect the redemption and liquidation rights of any shareholder owning such stock.

(e) For purposes of paragraph (a)(2)(i) of this A-6, stock shall be treated as readily tradable if it is regularly quoted by brokers or dealers making a market in such stock.

(f) For purposes of paragraph (a)(2)(i) of this A-6, the term "established securities market" means an established securities market as defined in § 1.897-1(m).

(g) The following examples illustrate the application of this exemption:

Example (1). A small business corporation (within the meaning of paragraph (a)(1) of this section) operates two businesses. The corporation sells the assets of one of its businesses, and these assets represent a substantial portion of the assets of the corporation. Because of the sale, the corporation terminates its employment relationship with persons employed in the business the assets of which are sold. Several of these employees are highly-compensated individuals to whom the owners of the corporation make severance payments in excess of 3 times each employee's base amount. Since the corporation is a small business corporation immediately before the change in ownership or control, the payments are not parachute payments.

Example (2). Assume the same facts as in example (1), except that the corporation is not a small business corporation within the meaning of paragraph (a)(1) of this section. If no stock in the corporation is readily tradable on an established securities market (or otherwise) immediately before the change in ownership or control and the shareholder approval requirements described in Q/A-7 of this section are met, the payments are not parachute payments.

Example (3). Seventy percent of the stock of Corporation S is owned by Corporation P, stock in which is readily tradable on an established securities market. The Corporation S stock represents a substantial portion of the assets of Corporation P. Corporation P sells all of its stock in Corporation S to Corporation X. Because of the sale, Corporation S makes severance payments to several of its highly-compensated individuals in excess of 3 times each individual's base amount. Since stock in Corporation P is readily tradable on an established securities market, the payments are not exempt from the definition of "parachute payments" under this A-6.

Q-7: How are the shareholder approval requirements referred to in paragraph (a)(2)(ii) of A-6 of this section met?

A-7: (a) The shareholder approval requirements referred to in paragraph (a)(2)(ii) of A-6 of this section are met with respect to any payment if—

(1) Such payment was approved by a separate vote of the persons who owned, immediately before the change in ownership or control, more than 75 percent of the voting power of all outstanding stock of the corporation, and

(2) There was adequate disclosure, to all persons entitled to vote under paragraph (a)(1) of this A-7, of all material facts concerning all material payments which (but for Q/A-6 of this section) would be parachute payments with respect to a disqualified individual.

The vote described in paragraph (a)(1) of this A-7 must determine the right of the disqualified individual to receive the payment, or, in the case of a payment made before the vote, the right of the disqualified individual to retain the payment.

(b) Approval of a payment by any shareholder that is not an individual ("entity shareholder") generally must be made by the person authorized by the entity shareholder to approve the payment. However, if a substantial portion of the assets of an entity shareholder consists (directly or indirectly) of stock in the corporation undergoing the change in ownership or control, approval of the payment by that entity shareholder must be made by a separate vote of the persons who hold, immediately before the change in ownership or control, more than 75 percent of the voting power of the entity shareholder. The preceding sentence does not apply if the value of the stock of the corporation owned, directly or indirectly, by or for the entity shareholder does not exceed 1 percent of the total value of the outstanding stock of the corporation. Where approval of a payment by an entity shareholder must be made by a separate vote of the owners of the entity shareholder, the normal voting rights of the entity shareholder determine which owners shall vote.

(c) In determining the persons who comprise the "more than 75 percent" group referred to in paragraph (a)(1) of this A-7, stock is not counted as outstanding stock if the stock is actually owned or constructively owned under section 318(a) by or for a disqualified individual who receives (or is to receive) payments that would be parachute payments if the shareholder approval requirements described in paragraph (a) of this A-7 were not met. Likewise, stock is not counted as outstanding stock if the owner is considered under section 318(a) to own any part of the stock owned directly or indirectly by or for a disqualified individual described in the preceding sentence. However, if all persons who hold voting power in the corporation or the entity shareholder are disqualified individuals or related persons described in either of the two preceding sentences, then stock owned by such persons is counted as outstanding stock.

(d) To be adequate disclosure for purposes of paragraph (a)(2) of this A-7, disclosure must be full and truthful disclosure of the material facts and such additional information as is necessary to make the disclosure not materially misleading at the time the disclosure was made. An omitted fact is considered a material fact if there is a substantial likelihood that a reasonable shareholder would consider it important.

(e) The following examples illustrate the application of this A-7:

Example (1). Corporation S has two shareholders—Corporation P, which owns 76 percent of the stock of Corporation S, and A, an individual, who owns the remaining 24 percent. No stock of Corporation P is readily tradable on an established securities market (or otherwise). Stock of Corporation S represents a substantial portion of the assets of Corporation P. All of the stock of Corporation S is sold to Corporation M. Contingent on the change in ownership of Corporation S, severance payments are made to the officers of Corporation S in excess of 3 times each officer's base amount. If the payments are approved by a separate vote of the persons who hold, immediately before the sale, more than 75 percent of the voting power of the outstanding stock of Corporation P and the disclosure rules of paragraph (a)(2) of this A-7 are compiled [complied] with, the shareholder approval requirements of this A-7 are met, and the payments are exempt from the definition of "parachute payment" pursuant to A-6 of this section [amended on June 20, 1989 (54 FR 25879)].

Example (2). Corporation M is wholly owned by Partnership P, no interest in which is readily tradable on an established securities market (or otherwise). Stock of Corporation M represents a substantial portion of the assets of Partnership P. Partnership P has one general partner and 200 limited partners. None of the limited partners are entitled to vote on issues involving the management of the partnership investments. If the payments are approved by the general partner and the disclosure rules of paragraph (a)(2) of this A-7 are complied with, the shareholder approval requirements of this A-7 are met, and the payments are exempt from the definition of "parachute payment" pursuant to A-6 of this section.

Q-8: Which payments under a qualified plan are exempt from the definition of "parachute payment"?

A-8: The term "parachute payment" does not include any payment to or from—

(a) A plan described in section 401(a) which includes a trust exempt from tax under section 501(a),

(b) An annuity plan described in section 403(a), or

(c) A simplified employee pension (as defined in section 408(k)).

Q-9: Which payments of reasonable compensation are exempt from the definition of "parachute payment"?

A-9: Except in the case of securities violation parachute payments, the term "parachute payment" does not include any payment (or portion thereof) which the taxpayer establishes by clear and convincing evidence is reasonable compensation for personal services to be rendered by the disqualified individual on or after the date of the change in ownership or control. See Q/A-38 through Q/A-44 for rules on determining amounts of reasonable compensation. See Q/A-37 for the definition and treatment of securities violation parachute payments.

Payor of Parachute Payments

Q-10: Who may be the payor of parachute payments?

A-10: Parachute payments within the meaning of Q/A-2 of this section may be paid directly or indirectly by the corporation referred to in paragraph (a)(3) of A-2 of this section, by a person acquiring ownership or effective control of that corporation or ownership of a substantial portion of that corporation's assets, or by any person whose relationship to such corporation or other person is such as to require attribution of stock ownership between the parties under section 318(a).

Payments in the Nature of Compensation

Q-11: What types of payments are in the nature of compensation?

A-11: (a) In general, for purposes of this section, all payments—in whatever form—are payments in the nature of compensation if they arise out of an employment relationship or are associated with the performance of services. For this purpose, the performance of services includes holding oneself out as available to perform services and refraining from performing services (such as under a covenant not to compete or similar arrangement). Payments in the nature of compensation include (but are not limited to) wages and salary, bonuses, severance pay, fringe benefits, and pension benefits and other deferred compensation (including any amount characterized by the parties as interest thereon). However, payments in the nature of compensation do not include attorney's fees or court costs paid or incurred in connection with the payment of any amount described in paragraph (a)(1), (2), and (3) of A-2 of this section.

(b) Transfers of property are treated as payments for purposes of this A-11. See Q/A-12 for rules on determining when such payments are considered made and the amount of such payments. See Q/A-13 for special rules on transfers of nonqualified stock options.

Q-12: If a property transfer to a disqualified individual is a payment in the nature of compensation, when is the payment considered made (or to be made), and how is the amount of the payment determined?

A-12: (a) Except as provided in this A-12 and A-13 of this section, a transfer of property is considered a payment made (or to be made) in the taxable year in which the property transferred is includible in the gross income of the disqualified individual under section 83 and the regulations thereunder. Thus, in general, such a payment is considered made (or to be made) when the property is transferred (as defined in §1.83-3(a)) to the disqualified individual and becomes substantially vested (as defined in §1.83-3(b)) in such individual. In such case, the amount of the payment is determined under section 83 and the regulations thereunder. Thus, in general, the amount of the payment is equal to the excess of the fair market value of the transferred property (determined without regard to any lapse restriction, as defined in §1.83-3(i)) at the time that the property becomes substantially vested, over the amount (if any) paid for the property.

(b) An election made by a disqualified individual under section 83(b) with respect to transferred property will not apply for purposes of this A-12. Thus, even if such an election is made with respect to a property transfer that is a payment in the nature of compensation, the payment is generally considered made (or to be made) when the property is transferred to and becomes substantially vested in such individual.

(c) See Q/A-13 for rules on applying this A-12 to transfers of nonqualified stock options.

(d) *Example.* On January 1, 1986, Corporation M gives to A, a disqualified individual, in connection with his performance of services to Corporation M, a bonus of 100 shares of Corporation M stock. Under the terms of the bonus arrangement A is obligated to return the Corporation M stock to Corporation M unless the earnings of Corporation M double by January 1, 1989, or there is a change in ownership or control of Corporation M before that date. A's rights in the stock are treated as substantially nonvested (within the meaning of §1.83-3(b)) during that period because A's rights in the stock are subject to a substantial risk of forfeiture (within the meaning of §1.83-3(c)) and are nontransferable (within the meaning of §1.83-3(d)). On January 1,

1988, a change in the ownership of Corporation M occurs. On that day, the fair market value of the Corporation M stock is $250 per share. Since A's rights in the Corporation M stock become substantially vested (within the meaning of §1.83-3(b)) on that day, the payment is considered made on that day, and the amount of the payment for purposes of this section is equal to $25,000 (100 × $250). See Q/A-39 for rules relating to the reduction of the excess parachute payment by the portion of the payment which is established to be reasonable compensation for personal services actually rendered before the date of a change in ownership or control.

Q-13: How are nonqualified stock options treated?

A-13: (a) For purposes of this section, if an option to which section 421 (relating generally to certain qualified and other options) does not apply has an ascertainable fair market value (whether or not readily ascertainable as defined in §1.83-7(b)) at the time the option becomes substantially vested (as defined in §1.83-3(b), the option shall be treated as property that is transferred not later than the time at which the option becomes substantially vested. Thus, for purposes of this section, the vesting of such an option is treated as a payment in the nature of compensation. The value of an option with a readily ascertainable fair market value at the time the option vests shall be determined by applying the rules set forth in §1.83-7(b). The value of an option with an ascertainable fair market value at the time the option vests is determined under all the facts and circumstances in the particular case. Factors relevant to such a determination include, but are not limited to: (1) the difference between the option's exercise price and the value of the property subject to the option [at] the time of vesting; (2) the probability of the value of such property increasing or decreasing; and (3) the length of the period during which the option can be exercised. See Q/A-33 for the treatment of options the vesting of which is contingent on a change in ownership or control and that do not have an ascertainable fair market value at the time of vesting.

(b) Any money or other property transferred to the disqualified individual upon the exercise, or as consideration upon the sale or other disposition, of an option described in paragraph (a) of this A-14 after the time such option vests is not treated as a payment in the nature of compensation to the disqualified individual under A-11 of this section. Nonetheless, the amount of the otherwise allowable deduction under section 162 or 212 with respect to such transfer shall be reduced by the amount of the payment described in paragraph (a) of this section treated as an excess parachute payment.

(c) (The issue of whether an option to which section 421 applies will be treated as a payment for purposes of this section at the time of grant or at a later time is reserved for future regulations.)

Q-14: Are payments in the nature of compensation reduced by consideration paid by the disqualified individual?

A-14: Yes. To the extent not otherwise taken into account under Q/A-12 and Q/A-13 of this section, the amount of any payment in the nature of compensation is reduced by the amount of any money or the fair market value of any property (owned by the disqualified individual without restriction) that is (or will be) transferred by the disqualified individual in exchange for the payment. For purposes of the preceding sentence, the fair market value of property is determined as of the date the property is transferred by the disqualified individual.

Disqualified Individuals

Q-15: Who is a "disqualified individual"?

A-15: For purposes of this section, an individual is a disqualified individual with respect to a corporation if, at any time during the "disqualified individual determination period" (as defined in Q/A-20 of this section), the individual is an employee or independent contractor of the corporation and is, with respect to the corporation—

(a) A shareholder (but see Q/A-17),

(b) An officer (see Q/A-18), or

(c) A highly-compensated individual (see Q/A-19).

Q-16: Is a personal service corporation treated as an individual?

A-16: (a) Yes. For purposes of this section, a personal service corporation (as defined in section 269A(b)(1)), or a noncorporate entity that would be a personal service corporation if it were a corporation, is treated as an individual.

(b) *Example.* Corporation N, a personal service corporation (as defined in section 269A(b)(1)), has a single individual as its sole shareholder and employee. Corporation N performs personal services for Corporation M as an independent contractor. The compensation paid to Corporation N by Corporation M puts Corporation N within the group of the highly-compensated individuals of Corporation M as determined under A-18 of this section. Hence, Corporation N is treated as a highly-compensated individual with respect to Corporation M.

Q-17: Are all shareholders of a corporation considered shareholders for purposes of paragraph (a) of A-15 of this section?

A-17: No. Only an individual who owns stock of a corporation having a fair market value that exceeds the lesser of $1 million, or 1 percent of the total fair market value of the outstanding shares of all classes of the corporation's stock, is treated as a disqualified individual with respect to the corporation by reason of stock ownership. An individual who owns a lesser amount of stock may, however, be a disqualified individual with respect to the corporation by reason of being an officer or highly-compensated individual with respect to the corporation. For purposes of determining the amount of stock owned by an individual, the constructive ownership rules of section 318 (a) shall apply.

Q-18: Who is an officer?

A-18: (a) For purposes of this section, whether an individual is an officer with respect to a corporation is determined upon the basis of all the facts and circumstances in the particular case (such as the source of the individual's authority, the term for which the individual is elected or appointed, and the nature and extent of the individual's duties). Generally, the term "officer" means an administrative executive who is in regular and continued service. The term "officer" implies continuity of service and excludes those employed for a special and single transaction. An individual who merely has the title of officer but not the authority of an officer is not considered an officer for purposes of this section. Similarly, an individual who does not have the title of officer but has the authority of an officer is an officer for purposes of this section.

(b) An individual who is an officer with respect to any member of an affiliated group that is treated as one corporation pursuant to Q/A-46 of this section is treated as an officer of such one corporation.

(c) No more than 50 employees (or, if less, the greater of 3 employees, or 10 percent of the employees (rounded up to the nearest integer)) of the corporation (in the case of an affiliated group treated as one corporation, each member of the affiliated group) shall be treated as disqualified individuals with respect to a corporation by reason of being an officer of the corporation. For purposes of the preceding sentence, the number of employees of the corporation is the greatest number of employees the corporation has during the disqualified individual determination period (as defined in Q/A-20 of this section). If the number of officers of the corporation exceeds the number of employees who may be treated as officers under the first sentence of this paragraph (c), then the employees who are treated as officers for purposes of this section are the highest paid 50 employees (or, if less, the greater of 3 employees, or 10 percent of the employees (rounded up to the nearest integer)) of the corporation when ranked on the basis of compensation (as determined under Q/A-21 of this section) paid during the disqualified individual determination period.

Q-19: Who is a "highly-compensated individual"?

A-19: (a) For purposes of this section, a "highly-compensated individual" with respect to a corporation is any individual who is, or would be if the individual were an employee, a member of the group consisting of the lesser of (1) the highest paid 1 percent of the employees of the corporation (rounded up to the nearest integer), or (2) the highest paid 250 employees of the corporation, when ranked on the basis of compensation (as determined under Q/A-21 of this section) paid during the disqualified individual determination period (as defined in Q/A-20 of this section). However, no individual whose annualized compensation during the disqualified individual determination period is less than $75,000 will be treated as a highly-compensated individual.

(b) An individual who is not an employee of the corporation is not treated as a highly-compensated individual with respect to the corporation on account of compensation received for performing services (such as brokerage, legal, or investment banking services) in connection with a change in ownership or control of the corporation, if the services are performed in the ordinary course of the individual's trade or business and the individual performs similar services for a significant number of clients unrelated to the corporation.

(c) In determining the total number of employees of a corporation for purposes of this A-19, employees are not counted if they normally work less than 17 1/2 hours per week (as defined in section 414 (q) (8) (B) and the regulations thereunder) or if they normally work during not more than 6 months during any year (as defined in section 414 (q) (8) (C) and the regulations thereunder). However, an employee who is not counted for purposes of the preceding sentence may still be a highly-compensated individual.

Q-20: What is the "disqualified individual determination period"?

A-20: (a) The "disqualified individual determination period" is the portion of the year of the corporation ending on the date of the change in ownership or control of the corporation (the "change in ownership period") and the twelve month period immediately preceding such change in ownership period. For purpose of this A-20, a corporation may elect to use its taxable year or the calendar year. For this purpose, the taxable year of an affiliated group treated as one corporation pursuant to Q/A-46 of this section is the taxable year of the common parent.

(b) The provisions of this A-20 may be illustrated by the following examples:

Example (1). A change in ownership of Corporation M, a calendar year corporation, takes place on June 12, 1988. The disqualified individual determination period of Corporation M begins on January 1, 1987 and ends on June 12, 1988.

Example (2). Assume the same facts as example (1), except that Corporation M is a fiscal year taxpayer with a taxable year ending on May 31. Corporation M may elect as its disqualified individual determination period either the period beginning on January 1, 1987, and ending on June 12, 1988, or the period beginning on June 1, 1987, and ending on June 12, 1988.

Q-21: How is "compensation" defined?

A-21: (a) For purposes of this section, the term "compensation" is the compensation which was payable by the corporation with respect to which the change in ownership or control occurs ("changed corporation"), by a predecessor entity, or by a related entity. Such compensation shall be determined without regard to sections 125, 402 (a) (8), and 402 (h) (1) (B), and in the case of employer contributions made pursuant to a salary reduction agreement, without regard to section 403 (b). Thus, for example, compensation includes elective or salary reduction contributions to a cafeteria plan, cash or deferred arrangement or tax-sheltered annuity.

(b) For purposes of this section, a "predecessor entity" is any entity which, as a result of a merger, consolidation, purchase or acquisition of property or stock, corporate separation, or other similar business transaction transfers some or all of its employees to the changed corporation or to a related entity or to a predecessor entity of the changed corporation. The term "related entity" includes: (1) all members of a controlled group of corporations (as defined in section 414(b)) that includes the changed corporation or a predecessor entity; (2) all trades or business (whether or not incorporated) that are under common control (as defined in section 414(c)) if such group includes the changed corporation or a predecessor entity; (3) all members of an affiliated service group (as defined in section 414(m)) that includes the changed corporation or a predecessor entity; and (4) any other entities required to be aggregated with the changed corporation or a predecessor entity pursuant to section 414(o) and the regulations thereunder (except leasing organizations as defined in section 414(n)).

(c) For purposes of Q/A-18 and Q/A-19 of this section, compensation that was contingent on the change in ownership or control and that was payable in the year of the change shall not be treated as compensation.

Contingent on Change in Ownership or Control

Q-22: When is a payment "contingent" on a change in ownership or control?

A-22: (a) In general, a payment is treated as "contingent" on a change in ownership or control if the payment would not, in fact, have been made had no change in ownership or control occurred. A payment generally is to be treated as one which would not, in fact, have been made in the absence of a change in ownership or control unless it is substantially certain, at the time of the change, that the payment would have been made whether or not the change occurred. (But see Q/A-23 of this section regarding payments under agreements entered into after a change in ownership or control.) Property that becomes substantially vested (as defined in § 1.83-3 (b)) as a result of a change in ownership or control will not be treated as a payment which was substantially certain to have been made whether or not the change occurred.

(b) A payment is also generally treated as contingent on a change in ownership or control if—

(1) The payment is contingent on an event that is closely associated with a change in ownership or control,

(2) A change in ownership or control actually occurs, and

(3) The event is materially related to the change in ownership or control.

For purposes of paragraph (b) (1) of this A-22, a payment is treated as contingent on an event that is closely associated with a change in ownership or control unless it is substantially certain, at the time of the event, that the payment would have been made whether or not the event occurred. An event is considered closely associated with a change in ownership or control if the event is of a type often preliminary or subsequent to, or otherwise closely associated with, a change in ownership or control. For example, the following events are considered closely associated with a change in the ownership or control of a corporation: the onset of a tender offer with respect to the corporation; a substantial increase in the market price of the corporation's stock that occurs within a short period (but only if such increase occurs prior to a change in ownership or control); the cessation of the listing of the corporation's stock on an established securities market; the acquisition of more than 5 percent of the corporation's stock by a person (or more than one person acting as a group) not in control of the corporation; the voluntary or involuntary termination of the disqualified individual's employment; and a significant reduction in the disqualified individual's job responsibilities. Whether other events will be treated as closely associated with a change in ownership or control will be based on all the facts and circumstances of the particular case. For purposes of paragraph (b)(3) of this A-22, an event will be presumed to be materially related to a change in ownership or control if the event occurs within the period beginning one year before and ending one year after the date of change in ownership or control. If such event occurs outside of the period beginning one year before and ending one year after the date of change in ownership or control, the event will be presumed not to be materially related to the change in ownership or control.

(c) A payment that would in fact have been made had no change in ownership or control occurred is treated as contingent on a change in ownership or control if the change accelerates the time at which the payment is made. Thus, for example, if a change in ownership or control accelerates the time of payment of vested deferred compensation, the payment may be treated as contingent on the change. See Q/A-24 regarding the portion of a payment that is so treated. See also Q/A-8 regarding the exemption for certain payments under qualified plans and Q/A-40 regarding treatment of a payment as reasonable compensation.

(d) A payment is treated as contingent on a change in ownership or control even if the employment or independent contractor relationship of the disqualified individual is not terminated (voluntarily or involuntarily) as a result of the change.

(e) The following examples illustrate the principles of this A-22:

Example (1). A contract between a corporation and A, a disqualified individual, provides that a payment will be made to A if his employment with the corporation is terminated at any time over the succeeding 3 years. Eighteen months later, a change in the ownership of the corporation occurs. Six months after the change in ownership, A's employment is terminated and the payment is made to A. It was not substantially certain, at the time of A's termination, that the payment would have been made had A's employment not been terminated. Termination of employment is considered closely associated with a change in ownership or control. Because the termination occurred within one year after the date of the change in ownership the termination of A's employment is presumed to be materially related to the change in ownership. If this presumption is not rebutted, the payment will be treated as contingent on the change in ownership.

Example (2). A contract between a corporation and a disqualified individual provides that a payment will be made to the individual upon the onset of a tender offer for shares of the corporation's stock. A tender offer is made on December 1, 1988, and the payment is made to the disqualified individual. Although the tender offer is unsuccessful, it leads to a negotiated merger with another entity on June 1, 1989, which results in a change in the ownership of the corporation. It was not substantially certain, at the time of the onset of the tender offer, that the payment would have been made had no tender offer taken place. The onset of a tender offer is considered closely associated with a change in ownership or control. Because the tender offer occurred within one year before the date of the change in ownership of the corporation, the onset of the tender offer is presumed to be materially related to the change in ownership. If this presumption is not rebutted, the payment will be treated as contingent on the change in ownership. If no change in ownership or control had occurred, the payment would not be treated as contingent on a change in ownership or control; however, the payment still could be a parachute payment under Q/A-37 of this section if the contract violated a generally enforced securities law or regulation.

Example (3). A contract between a corporation and a disqualified individual provides that a payment will be made to the individual if the

corporation's level of product sales or profits reaches a specified level. At the time the contract was entered into, the parties had no reason to believe that such an increase in the corporation's level of product sales or profits would be preliminary or subsequent to, or otherwise closely associated with, a change in ownership or control of the corporation. Eighteen months later, a change in the ownership of the corporation occurs and within one year after the date of the change, the corporation's level of product sales or profits reaches the specified level. Under these facts and circumstances (and in the absence of contradictory evidence), the increase in product sales or profits of the corporation is not an event closely associated with the change in ownership or control of the corporation. Accordingly, even if the increase is materially related to the change, the payment will not be treated as contingent on a change in ownership or control.

Q-23: May a payment be treated as contingent on a change in ownership or control if the payment is made under an agreement entered into after the change?

A-23: (a) No. Payments are not treated as contingent on a change in ownership or control if they are made (or to be made) pursuant to an agreement entered into after the change. For this purpose, an agreement that is executed after a change in ownership or control, pursuant to a legally enforceable agreement that was entered into before the change, will be considered to have been entered into before the change. (See Q/A-9 regarding the exemption for reasonable compensation for services rendered on or after a change in ownership or control.)

(b) The following examples illustrate the principles of this A-23:

Example (1). Assume that a disqualified individual is an employee of a corporation. A change in control of the corporation occurs, and thereafter the individual enters into an employment agreement with the acquiring company. Since the agreement is entered into after the change in control occurs, payments to be made under agreement are not treated as contingent on the change.

Example (2). Assume the same facts as in example (1), except that the agreement between the disqualified individual and the acquiring company is executed after the change in control, pursuant to a legally enforceable agreement entered into before the change. Payments to be made under the agreement may be treated as contingent on the change in control pursuant to Q/A-22 of this section. However, see Q/A-9 regarding the exemption from the definition of parachute payment for certain amounts of reasonable compensation.

Q-24: If a payment is treated as contingent on a change in ownership or control, is the full amount of the payment so treated?

A-24: (a) Generally, yes. However, in certain circumstances, described in paragraphs (b) and (c) of this A-24, only a portion of the payment is treated as contingent on the change.

(b) This paragraph (b) applies if it is substantially certain, at the time of the change, that the payment would have been made whether or not the change occurred, but the payment is treated as contingent on the change solely because the change accelerates the time at which the payment is made. In such case, the portion of the payment that is treated as contingent on the change in ownership or control is the amount by which the amount of the accelerated payment exceeds the present value of the payment absent the acceleration. If the amount of such a payment absent the acceleration is not reasonably ascertainable, and the acceleration of the payment does not significantly increase the present value of the payment absent the acceleration, the present value of the payment absent the acceleration shall be treated as equal to the amount of the accelerated payment. For rules on determining present value, see paragraph (d) of this A-24, and Q/A-32 and Q/A-33.

(c)(1) This paragraph (c) applies in the case of a payment that is accelerated by a change in ownership or control and that was substantially certain, at the time of the change, to have been made without regard to the change if the disqualified individual had continued to perform services for the corporation for a specified period of time. In such case, the portion of the payment that is treated as contingent on the change in ownership or control is the lesser of—

(i) The amount of the accelerated payment; or

(ii) The amount by which the amount of the accelerated payment exceeds the present value of the payment that was expected to be made absent the acceleration (determined without regard to the risk of forfeiture for failure to continue to perform services), plus an amount, as determined in paragraph (c) (2) of this A-24, to reflect the lapse of the obligation to continue to perform services.

If the value of the payment that was expected to be made absent the acceleration is not reasonably ascertainable, the future value of such payment shall be deemed to be equal to the amount of the accelerated payment.

(2) The amount reflecting the lapse of the obligation to continue to perform services (described in paragraph (c)(1)(ii) of this A-24) will depend on all of the facts and circumstances. In no event, however, shall such amount be less than 1 percent of the amount of the accelerated payment multiplied by the number of full months between the date that the individual's right to receive the payment is not subject to any requirement or condition which would be treated as resulting in a substantial risk of forfeiture (within the meaning of §1.83-3 (c)) and the date that, absent the acceleration the individual's right to receive the payment would not have been subject to any requirement or condition which would be treated as resulting in a substantial risk of forfeiture.

(d) For purposes of this A-24, the present value of a payment is determined as of the date on which the accelerated payment is made.

(e) The following examples illustrate the principles of this A-24:

Example (1). A corporation and a disqualified individual enter into a contract providing that, if a change in the ownership or control of the corporation occurs, all of the nonforfeitable deferred compensation the individual has earned prior thereto will be paid immediately. The deferred compensation otherwise will be paid when the individual reaches age 60. A change in the ownership of the corporation occurs, and the deferred compensation is immediately paid. Since the payment would have been made in any event when the individual reached age 60, it is substantially certain, at the time of the change, that the payments would have been made whether or not the change occurred. The payment is treated as contingent on the change in ownership or control solely because the change accelerates the time at which the payments are made. Therefore, the portion of the payment treated as contingent on the change is the amount by which the amount of the accelerated payment (*i.e.,* the amount paid to the individual because of the change in ownership or control) exceeds the present value of the payment absent the acceleration (*i.e.,* the value of the deferred compensation at the time of the change in ownership or control, if the compensation had remained nonpayable until age 60).

Example (2). A corporation grants a stock appreciation right to a disqualified individual. After the stock appreciation right vests and becomes exercisable, a change in the ownership of the corporation occurs, and the individual exercises the right. Neither the granting nor the vesting of the stock appreciation right was treated as a payment in the nature of compensation. Even if the change in ownership accelerates the time at which the right is exercised, no portion of the payment received upon exercise of the right is treated as contingent on the change, since the amount of the accelerated payment does not exceed the present value of the payment absent the acceleration.

Example (3). As a result of a change in the effective control of a corporation, a disqualified individual with respect to the corporation receives payment of his vested account balance in a nonqualified individual account plan. Actual interest and other earnings on the plan assets are credited to each account as earned and before distribution. Investment of the plan assets is not restricted in such a manner as would prevent the earning of a market rate of return on the plan assets. The date on which the individual would have received his vested account balance absent the change in control is uncertain, and the rate of earnings on the plan assets is not fixed. Thus, the amount of the payment absent the acceleration is not reasonably ascertainable. Under these facts, acceleration of the payment does not significantly increase the present value of the payment absent the acceleration, and the present value of the payment absent the acceleration shall be treated as equal to the amount of the accelerated payment. Accordingly, no portion of the payment is treated as contingent on the change.

Example (4). As a result of a change in the effective control of a corporation, a disqualified individual with respect to the corporation receives payment of the individual's vested benefits under a nonqualified pension plan which the individual otherwise would have received upon retirement. The amount of the benefits is not actuarially reduced to reflect its earlier payment. The payment is treated as contingent on the change in control solely because the change accelerates the time at which the payment is made. Therefore, the portion of the payment treated as contingent on the change is the amount by which the amount of the accelerated payment exceeds the present value of the payment absent the acceleration.

Example (5). On January 15, 1986, a corporation and a disqualified individual enter into a contract providing for a cash payment of $500,000 to be made to the individual on January 15, 1991. The payment is to be forfeited by the individual if he does not remain employed by the corporation for the entire 5-year period. However, the full amount of the payment is to be made immediately upon a change in the

ownership or control of the corporation during the 5-year period. On January 15, 1989, a change in the ownership of the corporation occurs and the full amount of the payment ($500,000) is made on that date to the individual. Since the payment would have been made in the absence of the change if the individual had continued to perform services for the corporation until the end of the five year period, it is substantially certain, at the time of the change, that the payment would have been made in the absence of the change if the individual had continued to perform services for the corporation for a specified period of time. Therefore, only a portion of the payment is treated as contingent on the change. The portion of the payment that is treated as contingent on the change is the amount by which the amount of the accelerated payment (*i.e.,* $500,000, the amount paid to the individual because of the change in ownership) exceeds the present value of the payment that was expected to have been made absent the acceleration (*i.e.,* $406,838, the present value on January 15, 1989, of a $500,000 payment on January 15, 1991), plus an amount reflecting the lapse of the obligation to continue to perform services. Such amount will depend on all the facts and circumstances but in no event will such amount be less than $115,000 (1% × 23 months × $500,000). Accordingly, the minimum amount of the payment treated as contingent on the change in ownership or control is $208,162 ([$500,000 − $406,838] + $115,000). This result is not changed if the individual actually remains employed until the end of the 5-year period [amended on June 20, 1989 (54 FR 25879)].

Example (6). (i) On January 15, 1986, a corporation gives to a disqualified individual, in connection with his performance of services to the corporation, a bonus of 1,000 shares of the corporation's stock. Under the terms of the bonus arrangement, the individual is obligated to return the stock to the corporation if she terminates her employment for any reason prior to January 15, 1991. However, if there is a change in the ownership or effective control of the corporation prior to January 15, 1991, she ceases to be obligated to return the stock. The individual's rights in the stock are treated as substantially nonvested (within the meaning of §1.83-3 (b)) during that period. On January 15, 1989, a change in the ownership of the corporation occurs. On that day, the fair market value of the stock is $500,000.

(ii) Since the stock would have become substantially vested in the individual in the absence of the change if she had continued to perform services for the corporation through January 15, 1991, it is substantially certain, at the time of the change, that the payment would have been made in the absence of the change if the individual had continued to perform services for the corporation for a specified period of time. Thus, only a portion of the payment is treated as contingent on the change in ownership or control. The portion of the payment that is treated as contingent on the change is the amount by which the amount of the accelerated payment on January 15, 1989 ($500,000), exceeds the present value of the payment that was expected to have been made on January 15, 1991, plus an amount reflecting the lapse of the obligation to continue to perform services. Assuming that, at the time of the change, it cannot be reasonably ascertained what the value of the stock would have been on January 15, 1991, the future value of such stock on January 15, 1991, is deemed to be $500,000, the amount of the accelerated payment. The present value on January 15, 1989, of a $500,000 payment to be made on January 15, 1991, is $406,838. Thus, the portion of the payment treated as contingent on the change is $93,162 ($500,000 − $406,838), plus an amount reflecting the lapse of the obligation to continue to perform services. Such amount will depend on all the facts and circumstances but in no event will such amount be less than $115,000 [1% × 23 months × $500,000] [amended on June 20, 1989 (54 FR 25879)].

Example (7). (i) On January 15, 1986, a corporation grants to a disqualified individual nonqualified stock options to purchase 30,000 shares of the corporation's stock. The options do not have a readily ascertainable fair market value at the time of grant. The options will be forfeited by the individual if he fails to perform personal services for the corporation until January 15, 1989. The options will, however, substantially vest in the individual at an earlier date if there is a change in ownership or control of the corporation. On January 16, 1988, a change in the ownership of the corporation occurs and the options become substantially vested in the individual. On January 16, 1988, the options have an ascertainable fair market value of $600,000.

(ii) At the time of the change, it is substantially certain that the payment of the options to purchase 30,000 shares would have been made in the absence of the change if the individual had continued to perform services for the corporation until January 15, 1989. Therefore, only a portion of the payment is treated as contingent on the change. The portion of the payment that is treated as contingent on the change is the amount by which the amount of the accelerated payment on January 16, 1988 ($600,000) exceeds the present value on January 16, 1988, of the payment that was expected to have been made on January

15, 1989, absent the acceleration, plus an amount reflecting the lapse of the obligation to continue to perform services. Assuming that, at the time of the change, it cannot be reasonably ascertained what the value of the options would have been on January 15, 1989, the value of such options on January 16, 1988, is deemed to be $600,000, the amount of the accelerated payment. The present value on January 16, 1988, of a $600,000 payment to be made on January 15, 1989, is $549,964.13. Thus, the portion of the payment treated as contingent on the change is $50,035.87 ($600,000 – $549,964.13), plus an amount reflecting the lapse of the obligation to continue to perform services. Such amount will depend on all the facts and circumstances but in no event will such amount be less than $66,000 (1% × 11 months × $600,000) [amended on June 20, 1989 (54 FR 25879)].

Example (8). (i) The facts are the same as in example (7), except that the options become substantially vested periodically (absent a change in ownership of control), with one-third of the options vesting on January 15, 1987, 1988, and 1989, respectively. Thus, options to purchase 20,000 shares vest independently of the January 16, 1988, change in ownership and the options to purchase the remaining 10,000 shares vest as a result of the change.

(ii) At the time of the change, it is substantially certain that the payment of the options to purchase 10,000 shares would have been made without regard to the change if the individual had continued to perform services for the corporation until January 15, 1989. Therefore, only a portion of the payment is treated as contingent on the change. The portion of the payment that is treated as contingent on the change is the amount by which the amount of the accelerated payment on January 16, 1988 ($200,000) exceeds the present value on January 16, 1988, of the payment that was expected to have been made on January 15, 1989, absent the acceleration, plus an amount reflecting the lapse of the obligation to continue to perform services. Assuming that, at the time of the change, it cannot be reasonably ascertained what the value of the options would have been on January 15, 1989, the value of such options on January 16, 1988, is deemed to be $200,000, the amount of the accelerated payment. The present value on January 16, 1988, of a $200,000 payment to be made on January 15, 1989, is $183,328.38. Thus, the portion of the payment treated as contingent on the change is $16,671.62 ($200,000 – $183,328.38), plus an amount reflecting the lapse of the obligation to continue to perform services. Such amount will depend on all the facts and circumstances but in no event will such amount be less than $22,000 (1% × 11 months × $200,000) [amended on June 20, 1989 (54 FR 25879)].

Example (9). Assume the same facts as in example (7), except that the option agreement provides that the options will vest either upon the corporation's level of profits reaching a specified level, or if earlier, on the date on which there is a change in ownership or control of the corporation. The corporation's level of profits do not reach the specified level prior to January 16, 1988. In such case, the full amount of the payment, $600,000, is treated as contingent on the change because it was not substantially certain, at the time of the change, that the payment would have been made in the absence of the change if the individual had continued to perform services for the corporation for a specified period of time. See Q/A-39 for rules relating to the reduction of the excess parachute payment by the portion of the payment which is established to be reasonable compensation for personal services actually rendered before the date of a change in ownership or control.

Presumption That Payment Is Contingent on Change

Q-25: Is there a presumption that certain payments are contingent on a change in ownership or control?

A-25: Yes. For purposes of this section, any payment pursuant to—

(a) An agreement entered into within one year before the date of a change in ownership or control, or

(b) An amendment that modifies a previous agreement in any significant respect, if the amendment is made within one year before the date of a change in ownership or control,

is presumed to be contingent on such change unless the contrary is established by clear and convincing evidence. In the case of an amendment described in paragraph (b) of this A-25, only the portion of any payment that exceeds the amount of such payment that would have been made in the absence of the amendment is presumed, by reason of the amendment, to be contingent on the change in ownership or control.

Q-26: How may the presumption described in Q/A-25 of this section be rebutted?

A-26: (a) To rebut the presumption described in Q/A-25 of this section, the taxpayer must establish by clear and convincing evidence that the payment is not contingent on the change in ownership or control.

Whether the payment is contingent on such change is determined on the basis of all the facts and circumstances of the particular case. Factors relevant to such a determination include, but are not limited to: (1) the content of the agreement or amendment; and (2) the circumstances surrounding the execution of the agreement or amendment, such as whether it was entered into at a time when a takeover attempt had commenced and the degree of likelihood that a change in ownership or control would actually occur.

(b) In the case of an agreement described in paragraph (a) of A-25 of this section, clear and convincing evidence that the agreement is one of the three following types will generally rebut the presumption that payments under the agreement are contingent on the change in ownership or control:

(1) A "nondiscriminatory employee plan or program" as defined in paragraph (c) of this A-26;

(2) A contract between a corporation and an individual that replaces a prior contract entered into by the same parties more than one year before the change in ownership or control, if the new contract does not provide for increased payments (apart from normal increases attributable to increased responsibilities or cost of living adjustments), accelerate the payment of amounts due at a future time, or modify (to the individual's benefit) the terms or conditions under which payments will be made; or

(3) A contract between a corporation and an individual who did not perform services for the corporation prior to the individual's taxable year in which the change in ownership or control occurs, if the contract does not provide for payments that are significantly different in amount, timing, terms, or conditions from those provided under contracts entered into by the corporation (other than contracts that themselves were entered into within one year before the change in ownership or control and in contemplation of the change) with individuals performing comparable services.

However, even if the presumption is rebutted with respect to an agreement, payments under the agreement still may be contingent on the change in ownership or control pursuant to Q/A-22 of this section.

(c) For purposes of this section, the term "nondiscriminatory employee plan or program" means: a group term life insurance plan that meets the requirements of section 79(d); an employee benefit plan that meets the requirements of section 89(d) and (e); a self insured medical reimbursement plan that meets the requirements of section 105(h); a qualified group legal services plan (within the meaning of section 120); a cafeteria plan (within the meaning of section 125); an educational assistance program (within the meaning of section 127); and a dependent care assistance program (within the meaning of section 129). Payments under certain other plans are exempt from the definition of "parachute payment" under Q/A-8 of this section.

(d) The following examples illustrate the application of the presumption:

Example (1). A corporation and a disqualified individual who is an employee of the corporation enter into an employment contract. The contract replaces a prior contract entered into by the same parties more than one year before the change and the new contract does not provide for any increased payments other than a cost of living adjustment, does not accelerate the payment of amounts due at a future time, and does not modify (to the individual's benefit) the terms or conditions under which payments will be made. Clear and convincing evidence of these facts rebuts the presumption described in A-25 of this section. However, payments under the contract still may be contingent on the change in ownership or control pursuant to Q/A-22 of this section.

Example (2). Assume the same facts as in example (1), except that the contract is entered into after a tender offer for the corporation's stock had commenced and it was likely that a change in ownership would occur and the contract provides for a substantial bonus payment to the individual upon his signing the contract. The individual has performed services for the corporation for many years, but previous employment contracts between the corporation and the individual did not provide for a similar signing bonus. One month after the contract is entered into, a change in the ownership of the corporation occurs. All payments under the contract are presumed to be contingent on the change in ownership even though the bonus payment would have been legally required even if no change had occurred. Clear and convincing evidence of these facts rebuts the presumption described in A-25 of this section with respect to all of the payments under the contract with the exception of the bonus payment (which is treated as contingent on the change). However, such payments under the contract still may be contingent on the change in ownership or control pursuant to Q/A-22 of this section.

Change in Ownership or Control

Q-27: When does a change in the ownership of a corporation occur?

A-27: (a) For purposes of this section, a change in the ownership or control of a corporation occurs on the date that any one person, or more than one person acting as a group, acquires ownership of stock of the corporation that, together with stock held by such person or group, possesses more than 50 percent of the total fair market value or total voting power of the stock of such corporation. However, if any one person, or more than one person acting as a group, is considered to own more than 50 percent of the total fair market value or total voting power of the stock of a corporation, the acquisition of additional stock by the same person or persons is not considered to cause a change in the ownership of the corporation (or to cause a change in the effective control of the corporation (within the meaning of Q/A-28 of this section)). An increase in the percentage of stock owned by any one person, or persons acting as a group, as a result of a transaction in which the corporation acquires its stock in exchange for property will be treated as an acquisition of stock for purposes of this section.

(b) For purposes of paragraph (a) of this A-27, persons will not be considered to be "acting as a group" merely because they happen to purchase or own stock of the same corporation at the same time, or as a result of the same public offering. However, persons will be considered to be "acting as a group" if they are owners of an entity that enters into a merger, consolidation, purchase or acquisition of stock, or similar business transaction with the corporation.

(c) For purposes of this A-27, section 318(a) shall apply in determining stock ownership.

(d) The following examples illustrate the principles of this A-27:

Example (1). Corporation M has owned stock having a fair market value equal to 19 percent of the value of the stock of Corporation N (an otherwise unrelated corporation) for many years prior to 1986. Corporation M acquires additional stock having a fair market value equal to 15 percent of the value of the stock of Corporation N on January 1, 1986, and an additional 18 percent on February 21, 1987. As of February 21, 1987, Corporation M has acquired stock having a fair market value greater than 50 percent of the value of the stock of Corporation N. Thus, a change in the ownership of Corporation N is considered to occur on February 21, 1987 (assuming that Corporation M did not have effective control of Corporation N immediately prior to the acquisition on that date).

Example (2). All of the corporation's stock is owned by the founders of the corporation. The board of directors of the corporation decides to offer shares of the corporation to the public. After the public offering, the founders of the corporation own a total of 40 percent of the corporation's stock, and members of the public own 60 percent. If no one person (or more than one person acting as a group) owns more than 50 percent of the corporation's stock (by value or voting power) after the public offering, there is no change in the ownership of the corporation.

Example (3). Corporation P merges into Corporation O (a previously unrelated corporation). In the merger, the shareholders of Corporation P receive Corporation O stock in exchange for their Corporation P stock. Immediately after the merger, the former shareholders of Corporation P own stock having a fair market value equal to 60 percent of the value of the stock of Corporation O, and the former shareholders of Corporation O own stock having a fair market value equal to 40 percent of the value of the stock of Corporation O. The former shareholders of Corporation P will be treated as "acting as a group" in their acquisition of Corporation O stock. Thus, a change in the ownership of Corporation O occurs on the date of the merger.

Example (4). A, an individual, owns stock having a fair market value equal to 20 percent of the value of the stock of Corporation Q. On January 1, 1987, Corporation Q acquires in a redemption for cash all of the stock held by shareholders other than A. Thus, A is left as the sole shareholder of Corporation Q. A change in ownership of Corporation Q is considered to occur on January 1, 1987 (assuming that A did not have effective control of Corporation Q immediately prior to the redemption) [amended on June 20, 1989 (54 FR 25879)].

Example (5). Assume the same facts as in example (4), except that A owns stock having a fair market value equal to 51 percent of the value of all the stock of Corporation Q immediately prior to the redemption. There is no change in the ownership of Corporation Q as a result of the redemption.

Q-28: When does a change in the effective control of a corporation occur?

A-28: (a) For purposes of this section, a change in the effective control of a corporation is presumed to occur on the date that either—

(1) Any one person, or more than one person acting as a group, acquires (or has acquired during the 12 month period ending on the date of the most recent acquisition by such person or persons) ownership of stock of the corporation possessing 20 percent or more of the total voting power of the stock of such corporation; or

(2) A majority of members of the corporation's board of directors is replaced during any 12-month period by directors whose appointment or election is not endorsed by a majority of the members of the corporation's board of directors prior to the date of the appointment or election.

This presumption may be rebutted by establishing that such acquisition or acquisitions of the corporation's stock, or such replacement of the majority of the members of the corporation's board of directors, does not transfer the power to control (directly or indirectly) the management and policies of the corporation from any one person (or more than one person acting as a group) to another person (or group). For purposes of this section, in the absence of an event described in paragraph (a)(1) or (2) of this A-28, a change in the effective control of a corporation is presumed not to have occurred.

(b) If any one person, or more than one person acting as a group, is considered to effectively control a corporation (within the meaning of this A-28), the acquisition of additional control of the corporation by the same person or persons is not considered to cause a change in the effective control of the corporation (or to cause a change in the ownership of the corporation within the meaning of Q/A-27 of this section).

(c) For purposes of this A-28, persons will not be considered to be "acting as a group" merely because they happen to purchase or own stock of the same corporation at the same time, or as a result of the same public offering. However, persons will be considered as "acting as a group" if they are owners of an entity that enters into a merger, consolidation, purchase or acquisition of stock, or similar business transaction with the corporation.

(d) Section 318(a) shall apply in determining stock ownership for purposes of this A-28.

(e) The following examples illustrate the principles of this A-28:

Example (1). Shareholder A acquired the following percentages of the voting stock of Corporation M (an otherwise unrelated corporation) on the following dates: 16 percent on January 1, 1985; 10 percent on January 10, 1986; 8 percent on February 10, 1986; 11 percent on March 1, 1987; and 8 percent on March 10, 1987. Thus, on March 10, 1987, A owns a total of 53 percent of M's voting stock. Since A did not acquire 20 percent or more of M's voting stock during any 12-month period, there is no presumption of a change in effective control pursuant to paragraph (a)(1) of this A-28. In addition, under these facts there is a presumption that no change in the effective control of Corporation M occurred. If this presumption is not rebutted (and thus no change in effective control of Corporation M is treated as occurring prior to March 10, 1987), a change in the ownership of Corporation M will be treated as having occurred on March 10, 1987 (pursuant to Q/A-27 of this section) since A had acquired more than 50 percent of Corporation M's voting stock as of that date.

Example (2). A minority group of shareholders of a corporation opposes the practices and policies of the corporation's current board of directors. A proxy contest ensues. The minority group presents its own slate of candidates for the board at the next annual meeting of the corporation's shareholders, and candidates of the minority group are elected to replace a majority of the current members of the board. A change in the effective control of the corporation is presumed to have occurred on the date the election of the new board of directors becomes effective.

Q-29: When does a change in the ownership of a substantial portion of a corporation's assets occur?

A-29: (a) For purposes of this section, a change in the ownership of a substantial portion of a corporation's assets occurs on the date that any one person, or more than one person acting as a group, acquires (or has acquired during the 12-month period ending on the date of the most recent acquisition by such person or persons) assets from the corporation that have a total fair market value equal to or more than one third of the total fair market value of all of the assets of the corporation immediately prior to such acquisition or acquisitions.

(b) A transfer of assets by a corporation is not treated as a change in the ownership of such assets if the assets are transferred to—

(1) A shareholder of the corporation (immediately before the asset transfer) in exchange for or with respect to its stock,

(2) An entity, 50 percent or more of the total value or voting power of which is owned, directly or indirectly, by the corporation,

(3) A person, or more than one person acting as a group, that owns, directly or indirectly, 50 percent or more of the total value or voting power of all the outstanding stock of the corporation, or

(4) An entity, at least 50 percent of the total value or voting power is owned, directly or indirectly, by a person described in paragraph (b)(3) of this A-29.

For purposes of this paragraph (b) (except as otherwise provided), a person's status is determined immediately after the transfer of the assets. For example, a transfer of assets pursuant to a complete liquidation of a corporation, a redemption of a shareholder's interest, or a transfer to a majority-owned subsidiary of the corporation is not treated as a change in the ownership of the assets of the transferor corporation.

(c) For purposes of this A-29, section 318(a) shall apply in determining stock ownership.

(d) The following examples illustrate the principles of this A-29:

Example (1). Corporation M acquires assets having a fair market value of $500,000 from Corporation N (an unrelated corporation) on January 1, 1986. The total fair market value of Corporation N's assets immediately prior to the acquisition was $3 million. Since the value of the assets acquired by Corporation M is less than one third of the fair market value of Corporation N's total assets immediately prior to the acquisition, the acquisition does not represent a change in the ownership of a substantial portion of Corporation N's assets.

Example (2). Assume the same facts as in example (1). Also assume that on November 1, 1986, Corporation M acquires from Corporation N additional assets having a fair market value of $700,000. Thus, Corporation M has acquired from Corporation N assets worth a total of $1.2 million during the 12-month period ending on November 1, 1986. Since $1.2 million is more than one third of the total fair market value of all of Corporation N's assets immediately prior to the earlier of these acquisitions ($3 million), a change in the ownership of a substantial portion of Corporation N's assets is considered to have occurred on November 1, 1986.

Example (3). All of the assets of Corporation P are transferred to Corporation O (an unrelated corporation). In exchange, the shareholders of Corporation P receive Corporation O stock. Immediately after the transfer, the former shareholders of Corporation P own 60 percent of the fair market value of the outstanding stock of Corporation O and the former shareholders of Corporation O own 40 percent of the fair market value of the outstanding stock of Corporation O. Because Corporation O is an entity more than 50 percent of the fair market value of the outstanding stock of which is owned by the former shareholders of Corporation P, the transfer of assets is not treated as a change in ownership of a substantial portion of the assets of Corporation P.

"Three Times Base Amount Test" for Parachute Payments

Q-30: Are all payments that are in the nature of compensation, are made to a disqualified individual, and are contingent on a change in ownership or control, parachute payments?

A-30: (a) No. To determine whether such payments are parachute payments, they must be tested against the individual's "base amount" (as defined in Q/A-34 of this section). To do this, the aggregate present value of all payments in the nature of compensation that are made or to be made to (or for the benefit of) the same disqualified individual and are contingent on the change in ownership or control must be determined. If this aggregate present value equals or exceeds the amount equal to 3 times the individual's base amount, the payments are parachute payments. If this aggregate present value is less than the amount equal to 3 times the individual's base amount, no portion of the payments is a parachute payment. See Q/A-31, Q/A-32, and Q/A-33 for rules on determining present value. Parachute payments that are securities violation parachute payments are not included in the foregoing computation if they are not contingent on a change in ownership or control. See Q/A-37 for the definition and treatment of securities violation parachute payments.

(b) The following examples illustrate the principles of this A-30:

Example (1). A is a disqualified individual with respect to Corporation M. A's base amount is $100,000. Payments totalling $400,000 that are in the nature of compensation and contingent on a change in the ownership of Corporation M are made to A on the date of the change.

The payments are parachute payments since they have an aggregate present value at least equal to 3 times A's base amount of $100,000 (3 × $100,000 = $300,000).

Example (2). Assume the same facts as in example (1), except that the payments contingent on the change in the ownership of Corporation M total $290,000. Since the payments do not have an aggregate present value at least equal to 3 times A's base amount, no portion of the payments is a parachute payment.

Q-31: As of what date is the present value of a payment determined?

A-31: Except as provided in this section, the present value of a payment is determined as of the date on which the change in ownership or control occurs, or, if a payment is made prior to such date, the date on which the payment is made.

Q-32: What discount rate is to be used to determine present value?

A-32: For purposes of this section, present value generally is determined by using a discount rate equal to 120 percent of the applicable Federal rate (determined under section 1274(d) and the regulations thereunder) compounded semiannually. The applicable Federal rate to be used for this purpose is the Federal rate that is in effect on the date as of which the present value is determined. See Q/As 24 and 31. However, for any payment, the corporation and the disqualified individual may elect to use the applicable Federal rate that is in effect on the date that the contract which provides for the payment is entered into, if such election is made in the contract [amended on June 20, 1989 (54 FR 25879) and on July 11, 1989 (54 FR 29061)].

Q-33: If the present value of a payment to be made in the future is contingent on an uncertain future event or condition, how is the present value of the payment determined?

A-33: (a) In certain cases, it may be necessary to apply the 3-times-base-amount test of Q/A-30 of this section or to allocate a portion of the base amount to a payment described in paragraph (a)(1), (2), and (3) of A-2 of this section at a time when the aggregate present value of all such payments cannot be determined with certainty because the time, amount, or right to receive one or more such payments is contingent on the occurrence of an uncertain future event or condition. For example, a disqualified individual's right to receive a payment may be contingent on the involuntary termination of such individual's employment with the corporation. In such a case, a reasonable estimate of the time and amount of the future payment shall be made, and the present value of the payment will be determined on the basis of this estimate. For purposes of making this estimate, an uncertain future event or condition that may reduce the present value of a payment will be taken into account only if the possibility of the occurrence of the event or condition can be determined on the basis of generally accepted actuarial principles or can be otherwise estimated with reasonable accuracy.

(b) Whenever a payment described in paragraph (a) of this A-33 is actually made or becomes certain not to be made, the 3-times-base-amount test described in Q/A-30 of this section shall be reapplied (and the portion of the base amount allocated to previous payments shall be reallocated (if necessary) to such payments) to reflect the actual time and amount of the payment. Whenever the 3-times-base-amount test is applied (or whenever the base amount is allocated), the aggregate present value of the payments received or to be received by the disqualified individual is redetermined as of the date described in A-31 of this section, using the discount rate described in A-32 of this section. This redetermination may affect the amount of any excess parachute payment for a prior taxable year.

(c) The following examples illustrate the principles of this A-33:

Example (1). A, a disqualified individual with respect to Corporation M, has a base amount of $100,000. Under his employment agreement with Corporation M, A is entitled to receive a payment in the nature of compensation in the amount of $250,000 contingent on a change in the ownership of Corporation M. In addition, the agreement provides that if A's employment is terminated within 1 year after the change in ownership, A will receive an additional payment in the nature of compensation in the amount of $150,000, payable 1 year after the date of the change in ownership. A and Corporation M are calendar year taxpayers. A change in the ownership of Corporation M occurs and A receives the first payment of $250,000. At the time Corporation M files its income tax return for the year of the change in ownership, it reasonably estimates that there is a 50-percent probability that, as a result of the change, A's employment will be terminated within 1 year of the date of the change. For purposes of applying the 3-times-base-amount test (and if the first payment is determined to be a parachute payment, for purposes of allocating a portion of A's base amount to that payment), Corporation M shall assume that an additional payment of $75,000 (.5 × $150,000) will be made to A as a result of the change in ownership. The present value of the additional payment is determined under Q/A-31 and Q/A-32 of this section.

Example (2). B, a disqualified individual with respect to Corporation N, has a base amount of $100,000. Under her employment agreement with Corporation N, B is entitled to receive payments in the nature of compensation in the amount of $20,000 per month for a period of 24 months if B terminates employment with Corporation N as a result of a change in ownership of Corporation N. Such monthly payments are to be reduced by the amount of any compensation earned by B from unrelated employers during the 24-month period. B and Corporation N are calendar year taxpayers. On June 1, 1988, there is a change in the ownership of Corporation N. As a result of the change, B voluntarily terminates employment with Corporation N and begins to receive monthly payments under the agreement. Assume that the present value, determined as of June 1, 1988, of a stream of 24-monthly payments of $20,000, is $438,134. At the time Corporation N files its income tax return for 1988, it cannot be determined with reasonable accuracy whether B will earn any compensation from unrelated employers during the 24-month period. Accordingly, the present value of the payments to be received by B ($438,134) exceeds 3 times B's base amount ($300,000) and a portion of each of the 1988 payments will be treated as an excess parachute payment for the 1988 taxable year.

Example (3). Assume the same facts as in example (2), except that in April 1989 B becomes employed by an employer unrelated to Corporation N. At the time Corporation N files its income tax return for 1989, it has become certain that, due to the compensation earned by B from unrelated employers, the present value, determined as of June 1, 1988, of the stream of payments from Corporation N will not exceed $192,060. Because it has been redetermined that the present value of the payments received or to be received by B does not equal or exceed 3 times B's base amount, no portion of the payments made in 1988 or 1989 will be treated as excess parachute payments.

Q-34: What is the "base amount"?

A-34: (a) The base amount of a disqualified individual is the average annual compensation (as defined in Q/A-21 of this section) which was includible in the gross income of such individual for taxable years in the "base period" (or either was excludible from such gross income as "foreign earned income" within the meaning of section 911, or would have been includible in such gross income if such person had been a United States citizen or resident.) See Q/A-35 for the definition of "base period" and for examples of base amount computations.

(b) If the base period of a disqualified individual includes a short taxable year or less than all of a taxable year, compensation for such short or incomplete taxable year must be annualized before determining the average annual compensation for the base period. In annualizing compensation, the frequency with which payments are expected to be made over an annual period must be taken into account. Thus, any amount of compensation for such a short or incomplete taxable year that represents a payment that will not be made more often than once per year is not annualized.

(c) Because the base amount includes only compensation that is includible in gross income, the base amount does not include certain items that constitute parachute payments. For example, payments in the form of untaxed fringe benefits are not included in the base amount but may be treated as parachute payments.

Q-35: What is the "base period"?

A-35: (a) The "base period" of a disqualified individual is the most recent 5 taxable years of the individual ending before the date of the change in ownership or control. However, if the disqualified individual was not an employee or independent contractor of the corporation with respect to which the change in ownership or control occurs (or a predecessor entity or a related entity as defined in A-21 of this section) for this entire 5-year period, the individual's base period is the portion of such 5-year period during which the individual performed personal services for the corporation or predecessor entity or related entity.

(b) The following examples illustrate the principles of Q/A-34 of this section and this Q/A-35:

Example (1). A disqualified individual was employed by a corporation for 2 years and 4 months preceding his taxable year in which a change in ownership or control of the corporation occurs. The individual's includible compensation income from the corporation was $30,000 for the 4-month period, $120,000 for the first full year, and $150,000 for the second full year. The individual's base amount is $120,000

$$\frac{[(3 \times \$30,000) + \$120,000 + \$150,000]}{3}$$

Example (2). Assume the same facts as in example (1), except that the individual also received a $60,000 "sign-up" bonus when his employment with the corporation commenced at the beginning of the 4-month period. The individual's base amount is $140,000

$$\frac{[(\$60,000 + (3 + \$30,000) + \$120,000 + \$150,000]}{3}$$

Since the bonus will not be paid more often than once per year, the amount of the bonus is not increased in annualizing the individual's compensation for the 4-month period.

Q-36: How is the base amount determined in the case of a disqualified individual who did not perform services for the corporation (or a predecessor entity or a related entity as defined in A-21 of this section), prior to the individual's taxable year in which the change in ownership or control occurs?

A-36: (a) In such a case, the individual's base amount is the annualized compensation (as defined in Q/A-21 of this section) which—

(1) Was includible in the individual's gross income for that portion, prior to such change, of the individual's taxable year in which the change occurred (or either was excludible from such gross income as "foreign earned income" within the meaning of section 911, or would have been includible in such gross income if such person had been a United States citizen or resident),

(2) Was not contingent on the change in ownership or control, and

(3) Was not a securities violation parachute payment.

(b) The following examples illustrate the principles of this A-36:

Example (1). On January 1, 1986, A, an individual whose taxable year is the calendar year, enters into a 4-year employment contract with Corporation M as an officer of the corporation. A has not previously performed services for Corporation M (or any predecessor entity or related entity as defined in A-21 of this section). Under the employment contract, A is to receive an annual salary of $120,000 for each of the 4 years that he remains employed by Corporation M with any remaining unpaid balance to be paid immediately in the event that A's employment is terminated without cause. On July 1, 1986, after A has received compensation of $60,000, a change in the ownership of Corporation M occurs. Because of the change, A's employment is terminated without cause, and he receives a payment of $420,000. It is established by clear and convincing evidence that the $60,000 in compensation is not contingent on the change in ownership or control, but the presumption of Q/A-25 of this section is not rebutted with respect to the $420,000 payment. Thus, the payment of $420,000 is treated as contingent on the change in ownership of Corporation M. In this case, A's base amount is $120,000 (2 × $60,000). Since the present value of the payment which is contingent on the change in ownership of Corporation M ($420,000) is more than 3 times A's base amount of $120,000 (3 × $120,000 = $360,000), the payment is a parachute payment.

Example (2). Assume the same facts as in example (1), except that A also receives a "sign-up" bonus of $50,000 from Corporation M on January 1, 1986. It is established by clear and convincing evidence that the bonus is not contingent on the change in ownership. When the change in ownership occurs on July 1, 1986, A has received compensation of $110,000 (the $50,000 bonus plus $60,000 in salary). In this case, A's base amount is $170,000 [$50,000 + (2 × $60,000)]. Since the $50,000 bonus will not be paid more than once per year, the amount of the bonus is not increased in annualizing A's compensation. The present value of the potential parachute payment ($420,000) is less than 3 times A's base amount of $170,000 (3 × $170,000 = $510,000), and therefore no portion of the payment is a parachute payment.

Securities Violation Parachute Payments

Q-37: Must a payment be contingent on a change in ownership or control in order to be a parachute payment?

A-37: (a) No. The term "parachute payment" also includes any payment (other than a payment exempted under Q/A-6 or Q/A-8 of this section) that is in the nature of compensation and is to (or for the benefit of) a disqualified individual, if such payment is made or to be made—

(1) Pursuant to an agreement that violates any generally enforced Federal or State securities laws or regulations, and

(2) In connection with a potential or actual change in ownership or control.

A violation is not taken into account under paragraph (a)(1) of this A-37 if it is merely technical in character or is not materially prejudicial to shareholders or potential shareholders. Moreover, a violation will be presumed not to exist unless the existence of the violation has been determined or admitted in a civil or criminal action (or an administrative action by a regulatory body charged with enforcing the particular securities law or regulation) which has been resolved by adjudication or consent. Parachute payments described in this A-37 are referred to in this section as "securities violation parachute payments."

(b) Securities violation parachute payments that are not contingent on a change in ownership or control within the meaning of Q/A-22 of this section are not taken into account in applying the 3-times-base-amount test of Q/A-30 of this section. Such payments are considered parachute payments regardless of whether such test is met with respect to the disqualified individual. Moreover, the amount of a securities violation parachute payment treated as an excess parachute payment shall not be reduced by the portion of such payment that is reasonable compensation for personal services actually rendered before the date of a change in ownership or control if such payment is not contingent on such change. Likewise, the amount of a securities violation parachute payment shall include the portion of such payment that is reasonable compensation for personal services to be rendered on or after the date of a change in ownership or control if such payment is not contingent on such change.

(c) The rules in paragraph (b) of this A-37 also apply to securities violation parachute payments that are contingent on a change in ownership or control if the application of these rules results in greater total excess parachute payments with respect to the disqualified individual than would result if the payments were treated simply as payments contingent on a change in ownership or control (and hence were taken into account in applying the 3-times-base-amount test and were reduced by, or did not include, any applicable amount of reasonable compensation).

(d) The following examples illustrate the principles of this A-37:

Example (1). A, a disqualified individual with respect to Corporation M, receives two payments in the nature of compensation that are contingent on a change in the ownership or control of Corporation M. The present value of the first payment is equal to A's base amount and is not a securities violation parachute payment. The present value of the second payment is equal to 1.5 times A's base amount and is a securities violation parachute payment. Neither payment includes any reasonable compensation. If the second payment is treated simply as a payment contingent on a change in ownership or control, the amount of A's total excess parachute payments is zero because the aggregate present value of the payments does not equal or exceed 3 times A's base amount. If the second payment is treated as a securities violation parachute payment subject to the rules of paragraph (b) of this A-37, the amount of A's total excess parachute payments is 0.5 times A's base amount. Thus, the second payment is treated as a securities violation parachute payment.

Example (2). Assume the same facts as in example (1), except that the present value of the first payment is equal to 2 times A's base amount. If the second payment is treated simply as a payment contingent on a change in ownership or control, the total present value of the payments is 3.5 times A's base amount, and the amount of A's total excess parachute payments is 2.5 times A's base amount. If the second payment is treated as a securities violation parachute payment, the amount of A's total excess parachute payments is 0.5 times A's base amount. Thus, the second payment is treated simply as a payment contingent on a change in ownership or control.

Example (3). B, a disqualified individual with respect to Corporation N, receives two payments in the nature of compensation that are contingent on a change in the control of Corporation N. The present value of the first payment is equal to 4 times B's base amount and is a securities violation parachute payment. The present value of the second payment is equal to 2 times B's base amount and is not a securities violation parachute payment. B establishes by clear and convincing evidence that the entire amount of the first payment is reasonable compensation for personal services to be rendered after the change in control. If the first payment is treated simply as a payment contingent on a change in ownership or control, it is exempt from the definition of "parachute payment" pursuant to Q/A-9 of this section. Thus, the amount of B's total excess parachute payment is zero because the present value of the second payment does not equal or exceed three times B's base amount. However, if the first payment is treated as a securities violation parachute payment, the amount of B's total excess parachute payments is 3 times B's base amount. Thus, the first payment is treated as a securities violation parachute payment.

Example (4). Assume the same facts as in example (3), except that B does not receive the second payment and B establishes by clear and convincing evidence that the first payment is reasonable compensation for services actually rendered before the change in the control of Corporation N. If the payment is treated simply as a payment contin-

gent on a change in ownership or control, the amount of B's excess parachute payment is zero because the amount treated as an excess parachute payment is reduced by the amount that B establishes as reasonable compensation. However, if the payment is treated as a securities violation parachute payment, the amount of B's excess parachute payment is 3 times B's base amount. Thus, the payment is treated as a securities violation parachute payment.

Computation and Reduction of Excess Parachute Payments

Q-38: How is the amount of an excess parachute payment computed?

A-38: (a) The amount of an excess parachute payment is the excess of the amount of any parachute payment over the portion of the disqualified individual's base amount that is allocated to such payment. For this purpose, the portion of the base amount allocated to any parachute payment is the amount that bears the same ratio to the base amount as the present value of such parachute payment bears to the aggregate present value of all parachute payments made or to be made to (or for the benefit of) the same disqualified individual. Thus, the portion of the base amount allocated to any parachute payment is determined by multiplying the base amount by a fraction, the numerator of which is the present value of such parachute payment and the denominator of which is the aggregate present value of all such payments. See Q/A-31, Q/A-32, and Q/A-33 for rules on determining present value and Q/A-34 for the definition of "base amount".

(b) *Example*. An individual with a base amount of $100,000 is entitled to receive two parachute payments, one of $200,000 and the other of $400,000. The $200,000 payment is made at the time of the change in ownership or control, and the $400,000 payment is to be made at a future date. The present value of the $400,000 payment is $300,000 on the date of the change in ownership or control. The portions of the base amount allocated to these payments are $40,000 ([$200,000/$500,000] × $100,000) and $60,000 ([$300,000/$500,000] × $100,000), respectively. Thus, the amount of the first excess parachute payment is $160,000 ($200,000 – $40,000) and that of the second is $340,000 ($400,000 – $60,000).

Q-39: May the amount of an excess parachute payment be reduced by reasonable compensation for personal services actually rendered before the change in ownership or control?

A-39: (a) Generally, yes. Except in the case of payments treated as securities violation parachute payments, the amount of an excess parachute payment is reduced by any portion of the payment that the taxpayer establishes by clear and convincing evidence is reasonable compensation for personal services actually rendered by the disqualified individual before the date of the change in ownership or control. Services reasonably compensated for by payments that are not parachute payments (either because the payments are not contingent on a change in ownership or control and are not securities violation parachute payments, or because the payments are made pursuant to a contract entered into before June 15, 1984, which has not been renewed, or amended or supplemented in significant relevant respect after June 14, 1984) are not taken into account for this purpose. The portion of any parachute payment that is established as reasonable compensation is first reduced by the portion of the disqualified individual's base amount that is allocated to such parachute payment; any remaining portion of the parachute payment established as reasonable compensation then reduces the excess parachute payment.

(b) Reasonable compensation for personal services to be rendered by the disqualified individual on or after the date of the change in ownership or control is exempt from the definition of "parachute payment" pursuant to Q/A-9 of this section. For rules on determining amounts of reasonable compensation, see Q/A-40 through Q/A-43.

(c) The following examples illustrate the principles of this A-39:

Example (1). Assume that a parachute payment of $600,000 is made to a disqualified individual, and the portion of the individual's base amount that is allocated to the parachute payment is $100,000. Also assume that $300,000 of the $600,000 parachute payment is established as reasonable compensation for personal services actually rendered by the disqualified individual before the date of the change in ownership or control. Before the reasonable compensation is taken into account, the amount of the excess parachute payment is $500,000 ($600,000 – $100,000). In reducing the excess parachute payment by reasonable compensation, the portion of the parachute payment that is established as reasonable compensation ($300,000) is first reduced by the portion of the disqualified individual's base amount that is allocated to the parachute payment ($100,000), and the remainder ($200,000) then reduces the excess parachute payment. Thus, in this case, the excess parachute payment of $500,000 is reduced by $200,000 of reasonable compensation.

Example (2). Assume the same facts as in example (1), except that the full amount of the $600,000 parachute payment is established as reasonable compensation. In this case, the excess parachute payment of $500,000 is reduced to zero by $500,000 of reasonable compensation. As a result, no portion of any deduction for the payment is disallowed by section 280G, and no portion of the payment is subject to the 20-percent excise tax of section 4999.

Determination of Reasonable Compensation

Q-40: How is it determined whether payments are reasonable compensation?

A-40: In general, whether payments are reasonable compensation for personal services actually rendered, or to be rendered, by the disqualified individual is determined on the basis of all the facts and circumstances of the particular case. Factors relevant to such a determination include, but are not limited to, the following:

(a) The nature of the services rendered or to be rendered;

(b) The individual's historic compensation for performing such services; and

(c) The compensation of individuals performing comparable services in situations where the compensation is not contingent on a change in ownership or control.

Q-41: Is any particular type of evidence generally considered clear and convincing evidence of reasonable compensation for personal services?

A-41: Yes. A showing that payments are made under a nondiscriminatory employee plan or program (as defined in Q/A-26 of this section) generally is considered to be clear and convincing evidence that the payments are reasonable compensation. This is true whether the personal services for which the payments are made are actually rendered before, or to be rendered on or after, the date of the change in ownership or control. Q/A-46 of this section (relating to the treatment of an affiliated group as one corporation) does not apply for purposes of this A-41. No determination of reasonable compensation is needed in order for payments under qualified plans to be exempt from the definition of "parachute payment" under Q/A-8 of this section.

Q-42: Is any particular type of evidence generally considered clear and convincing evidence of reasonable compensation for personal services to be rendered on or after the date of a change in ownership or control?

A-42: (a) Yes. If payments are made or to be made to (or on behalf of) a disqualified individual for personal services to be rendered on or after the date of a change in ownership or control, a showing that—

(1) The payments were made or are to be made only for the period the individual actually performs such personal services, and

(2) The individual's annual compensation for such services is not significantly greater than such individual's annual compensation prior to the change in ownership or control, apart from normal increase attributable to increased responsibilities or cost of living adjustments (or is not significantly greater than the annual compensation customarily paid by the employer or by comparable employers to persons performing comparable services),

generally is considered to be clear and convincing evidence that the payments are reasonable compensation for services to be rendered on or after the date of change in ownership or control. However, except as provided in paragraph (b) of this A-42, such clear and convincing evidence will not exist if the individual does not, in fact, perform the services.

(b) If the employment of a disqualified individual is involuntarily terminated before the end of a contract term and the individual is paid damages for the breach of the contract, a showing of the following factors generally is considered clear and convincing evidence that the payment is reasonable compensation for personal services to be rendered on or after the date of change in ownership or control:

(1) The contract was not entered into, amended, or renewed in contemplation of the change in ownership or control;

(2) The compensation the individual would have received under the contract would qualify as reasonable compensation under section 162;

(3) The damages do not exceed the present value (determined as of the date of receipt) of the compensation the individual would have received under the contract if the individual had continued to perform services for the employer until the end of the contract term;

(4) The damages are received because an offer to provide personal services was made by the disqualified individual but was rejected by the employer; and

(5) The damages are reduced by mitigation.

Mitigation will be treated as occurring when such damages are reduced (or any payment of such damages is returned) to the extent of the disqualified individual's earned income (within the meaning of section 911(d)(2)(A)) during the remainder of the period in which the contract would have been in effect. See Q/A-44 for rules regarding damages for a failure to make severance payments.

(c) The following examples illustrate the principles of this A-42:

Example (1). A, a disqualified individual, has a three-year employment contract with Corporation M, a publicly traded corporation. Under this contract, A is to receive a salary for $100,000 for the first year of the contract and, for each succeeding year, an annual salary that is 10 percent higher than his prior year's salary. During the third year of the contract, Corporation N acquires all the stock of Corporation M. Prior to the change in ownership, Corporation N arranges to retain A's services by entering into an employment contract with him that is essentially the same as A's contract with Corporation M. Under the new contract, Corporation N is to fulfill Corporation M's obligations for the third year of the old contract, and, for each of the succeeding years, pay A an annual salary that is 10 percent higher than his prior year's salary. Amounts are payable under the new contract only for the portion of the contract term during which A remains employed by Corporation N. A showing of the facts described above (and in the absence of contradictory evidence) is regarded as clear and convincing evidence that all payments under the new contract are reasonable compensation for personal services to be rendered on or after the date of the change in ownership. Therefore, the payments under this agreement are exempt from the definition of "parachute payment" pursuant to Q/A-9 of this section.

Example (2). Assume the same facts as in example (1), except that the employment contract with Corporation N does not provide that amounts are payable under the contract only for the portion of the term for which A remains employed by Corporation N. Shortly after the change in ownership, and despite A's request to remain employed by Corporation N, A's employment with Corporation N is involuntarily terminated. Shortly thereafter, A obtains employment with Corporation 0. A commences a civil action against Corporation N, alleging breach of the employment contract. In settlement of the litigation, A receives an amount equal to the present value of the compensation A would have received under the contract with Corporation N, reduced by the amount of compensation A otherwise receives from Corporation 0 during the period that the contract would have been in effect. A showing of the facts described above (and in the absence of contradictory evidence) is regarded as clear and convincing evidence that the amount A receives as damages is reasonable compensation for personal services to be rendered on or after the date of the change in ownership. Therefore, the amount received by A is exempt from the definition of "parachute payment" pursuant to Q/A-9 of this section.

Q-43: Is any particular type of payment generally considered reasonable compensation for personal services actually rendered before the date of a change in ownership or control?

A-43: (a) Yes. Payments of compensation earned before the date of a change in ownership or control generally are considered reasonable compensation for personal services actually rendered before the date of a change in ownership or control if they qualify as reasonable compensation under section 162.

Q-44: May severance payments be treated as reasonable compensation?

A-44: No. Severance payments are not treated as reasonable compensation for personal services actually rendered before, or to be rendered on or after, the date of a change in ownership or control. Moreover, any damages paid for a failure to make severance payments are not treated as reasonable compensation for personal services actually rendered before, or to be rendered on or after, the date of such change. For purposes of this section, the term "severance payment" means any payment that is made to (or for the benefit of) a disqualified individual on account of the termination of such individual's employment prior to the end of a contract term, but shall not include any payment that otherwise would be made to (or for the benefit of) such individual upon the termination of such individual's employment, whenever occurring.

Miscellaneous Rules

Q-45: How is the term "corporation" defined?

A-45: For purposes of this section, the term "corporation" has the meaning prescribed by section 7701(a)(3) and shall include a publicly traded partnership treated as a corporation under section 7704(a).

Q-46: How is an affiliated group treated?

A-46: For purposes of this section, and except as otherwise provided in this section, all members of the same affiliated group (as defined in section 1504, determined without regard to section 1504(b)) are treated as one corporation. Rules affected by this treatment of an affiliated group include (but are not limited to) rules relating to exempt payments of certain corporations (Q/A-6, Q/A-7 (except as provided therein)), payor of parachute payments (Q/A-10), disqualified individuals (Q/A-15 through Q/A-21 (except as provided therein)), rebuttal of the presumption that payments are contingent on a change (Q/A-26 except as provided therein), change in ownership or control (Q/A-27, 28, 29), and reasonable compensation (Q/A-42, Q/A-43, and 44).

Effective Date

Q-47: What is the general effective date of section 280G and this section?

A-47: In general, section 280G and this section apply to payments under agreements entered into or renewed after June 14, 1984. Any agreement that is entered into before June 15, 1984, and is renewed after June 14, 1984, is to be treated as a new contract entered into on the day the renewal takes effect. (See Q/A-48 regarding application of section 280G and this section with respect to contracts entered into on or before June 14, 1984, and amended or supplemented after that date.)

Q-48: How is a contract that is cancellable at will treated for purposes of the effective date of section 280G and this section?

A-48: (a) For this purpose, a contract that is terminable or cancellable unconditionally at will by either party to the contract without the consent of the other, or by both parties to the contract, is treated as a new contract entered into on the date any such termination or cancellation, if made, would be effective. However, a contract is not treated as so terminable or cancellable if it can be terminated or cancelled only by terminating the employment relationship or independent contractor relationship of the disqualified individual.

(b) The following examples illustrate the principles of this A-48:

Example (1). Before June 15, 1984, a corporation and a disqualified individual enter into a contract providing for payments to the individual contingent on a change in the ownership or control of the corporation. The corporation may cancel the contract unconditionally at will by giving 3 months notice. Thus, the earliest date that any such cancellation after June 14, 1984, could be effective is September 15, 1984. The contract is treated as a new contract entered into on September 15, 1984, whether or not it is in fact cancelled. Therefore, section 280G and this section apply to all payments made or to be made under the contract in taxable years of the individual that end on or after September 15, 1984.

Example (2). On January 1, 1984, a corporation and a disqualified individual enter into a contract providing for payments to the individual contingent on a change in the ownership or control of the corporation. The corporation has a right to terminate the employment of the individual with or without cause, and the individual has the right to cease working for the corporation; otherwise, the contract is not terminable by either party. Since the contract is terminable only by terminating the employment relationship between the parties, it is not treated as terminable at will. Thus, since the contract was entered into on or before June 14, 1984, no payments under the contract are subject to section 280G or this section.

Q-49: Do section 280G and this section apply to payments under some agreements entered into on or before June 14, 1984, that are not renewed after this date?

A-49: Yes. Section 280G and this section apply to payments under a contract entered into on or before June 14, 1984, if the contract is amended or supplemented after June 14, 1984, in significant relevant respect. For this purpose, a "supplement" to a contract is defined as a new contract entered into after June 14, 1984, that affects the trigger, amount, or time of receipt of a payment under an existing contract.

Q-50: Under what circumstances is a contract considered to be amended or supplemented in significant relevant respect?

A-50: Except as otherwise provided in Q/A-51 of this section, a contract is considered to be amended or supplemented in significant relevant respect if provisions for payments contingent on a change in ownership or control ("parachute provisions"), or provisions in the nature of parachute provisions, are added to the contract, or are amended or supplemented to provide significant additional benefits to the disqualified individual. Thus, for example, a contract generally is treated as amended or supplemented in significant relevant respect if it is amended or supplemented:

(a) To add or modify, to the disqualified individual's benefit, a change in ownership or control trigger;

(b) To increase amounts payable that are contingent on a change in ownership or control (or, where payment is to be made under a formula, to modify the formula to the disqualified individual's advantage); or

(c) To accelerate, in the event of a change in ownership or control, the payment of amounts otherwise payable at a later date.

For purposes of this A-50, a payment will not be treated as being accelerated in the event of a change in ownership or control if the acceleration does not increase the present value of the payment.

Q-51: Will normal adjustments in an employment contract cause the contract to be treated as amended or supplemented in significant relevant respect?

A-51: No. A contract entered into on or before June 14, 1984, will not be treated as amended or supplemented in significant relevant respect merely by reason of normal adjustments in the terms of employment relationship or independent contractor relationship of the disqualified individual. Whether an adjustment in the terms of such a relationship is considered normal for this purpose depends on all of the facts and circumstances of the particular case. Relevant factors include, but are not limited to, the following:

(a) the length of time between the adjustment and the change in ownership or control;

(b) the extent to which the corporation, at the time of the adjustment, viewed itself as a likely takeover candidate;

(c) a comparison of the adjustment with historical practices of the corporation;

(d) the extent of overlap between the group receiving the benefits of the adjustment and those members of that group who are the beneficiaries of pre-June 15, 1984, parachute contracts; and

(e) the size of the adjustment, both in absolute terms and in comparison with the benefits provided to other members of the group receiving the benefits of the adjustment.

Q-52: What are some examples illustrating the principles of Q/A-49, Q/A-50, and Q/A-51 of this section?

A-52: The following examples illustrate these principles:

Example (1). Corporation M grants a nonqualified stock option to a disqualified individual before June 15, 1984. After June 14, 1984, at a time when the option is currently vested and exercisable by the individual regardless of whether a change in ownership or control occurs, Corporation M amends the option to permit the individual to surrender it for cash or other property equal to the fair market value of the stock that would have been received if the option had been exercised (minus the exercise price of the option). Since the individual could have exercised the option and then sold the stock received upon the exercise, the amendment does not provide significant additional benefits to the individual. Hence, the amendment does not cause payments under the option to become subject to section 280G and this section.

Example (2). Corporation N and A, a disqualified individual, enter into an employment contract before June 15, 1984, that provides for a payment, contingent on a change in the ownership or control of Corporation N, equal to 4 times A's base amount. After June 14, 1984, and at a time when Corporation N did not view itself as a likely takeover candidate, Corporation N increases A's annual compensation by 25 percent to reflect additional managerial responsibilities. Such increase is consistent with the historical practices of Corporation N. Although the amount payable to A contingent on a change in ownership is increased, the employment contract is not treated as amended in significant relevant respect because, under these facts (and in the absence of contrary evidence), the amendment to the contract is treated as a normal adjustment in the terms of the employment relationship.

Example (3). Before June 15, 1984, Corporation 0 enters into contracts with disqualified individuals A, B, and C, providing for payments contingent on a change in the ownership of Corporation 0 equal to 4 times each individual's base amount. After June 14, 1984, Corporation 0, consistent with its historical practices, grants identical nonvested stock options to numerous disqualified individuals, including A, B, and C. All of these new options provide that the vesting of all such options will be accelerated if a change in the ownership or control of Corporation 0 occurs. Section 280G and this section apply to payments under the options granted after June 14, 1984. However, the granting of these options does not cause the contracts that were entered into before June 15, 1984, to be treated as amended or supplemented in significant relevant respect because, under these facts (and in the absence of contrary evidence), the granting of options is treated as a normal adjustment in the terms of the employment relationship. [Reg. § 1.280G-1.]

[¶ 20,179 Reserved.—Proposed regulations relating to minimum participation requirements under Code Sec. 401(a)(26) were formerly reproduced here. The final regulations are now at ¶ 11,720Z-32, 11,720Z-34, and 11,720Z-39.]

[¶ 20,180 Reserved.—Introductory material to proposed rulemaking concerning the uniform premium table used to calculate the cost of group-term life insurance coverage was formerly reproduced here. The final regulation is reproduced at ¶ 11,233.]

[¶ 20,181 Reserved.—Amendments to proposed regulations under Code Sec. 410(a)(4) and Code Sec. 410(b), relating to the requirement that contributions or benefits may not discriminate in favor of highly compensated employees and to minimum coverage requirements, were formerly reproduced here. The final regulations are now at ¶ 11,720W-11,720W-13 and 12,163-12,163J.]

[¶ 20,182 Reserved.—Temporary regulations that also served as proposed regulations applying the minimum funding standards to terminated pension plans that were restored by the PBGC were formerly reproduced here. The final regulations are now at ¶ 12,250J.]

[¶ 20,183 Reserved.—Amendments to proposed regulations under Code Sec. 401(a)(4) and Code Sec. 410(b), relating to the requirement that contributions or benefits may not discriminate in favor of highly compensated employees and to minimum coverage requirements, were formerly reproduced here. The final regulations are now at ¶ 11,720W-11,720W-13 and 12,163-12,163J.]

¶ 20,184

Proposed regulations: Employee business expense reimbursements: Reporting and withholding.—The IRS has issued temporary regulations (¶ 11,181, 11,182, 13,551 and 13,551B) that also serve as proposed regulations relating to deductions allowable in computing adjusted gross income that consist of expenses paid or incurred by an employee under a reimbursement or other expense allowance arrangement. The proposed IRS regulations were published in the *Federal Register* on December 17, 1990 (55 FR 51688).

Reg. § 1.62-1T

DEPARTMENT OF THE TREASURY

Internal Revenue Service

26 CFR PART 1

EE-8-89

RIN 1545-AP29

Employee Business Expenses—Reporting and Withholding on Employee Business Expense Reimbursements and Allowances.

AGENCY: Internal Revenue Service, Treasury.

ACTION: Notice of proposed rulemaking by cross-reference to temporary regulations.

SUMMARY: In the Rules and Regulations portions of this issue of the Federal Register, the Internal Revenue Service is issuing a temporary regulation relating to deductions allowable in computing adjusted gross income that consist of expenses paid or incurred by an employee under a reimbursement or other expense allowance arrangement with his or her employer. The text of the temporary regulation also serves as the comment document for this notice of proposed rulemaking.

DATES: Written comments and requests for a public hearing must be delivered or mailed before [Insert date that is 60 days after publication of this document in the Federal Register].

ADDRESSES: Send comments and requests for a public hearing to Internal Revenue Service, P.O. Box 7604, Ben Franklin Station, Attention: CC:CORP:T:R (EE-8-89), Room 4425, Washington, D.C. 20044.

FOR FURTHER INFORMATION CONTACT: Richard Pavel at telephone 202-377-9372 (not a toll-free number).

SUPPLEMENTARY INFORMATION:

Background

The text of the temporary regulation amends 26 CFR by amending paragraphs (c)(2) and (f) of § 1.62-1T with respect to deductions allowable in computing adjusted gross income that consist of expenses paid or incurred by an employee under a reimbursement or other expense allowance arrangement with his or her employer. For the text of the temporary regulation, see T.D. 8324 published in the Rules and Regulations portion of this issue of the Federal Register.

Special Analyses

It has been determined that these proposed rules are not major rules as defined in Executive Order 12291. Therefore, a Regulatory Impact Analysis is not required. It has also been determined that section 553(b) of the Administrative Procedure Act (5 U.S.C. chapter 5) and the Regulatory Flexibility Act (5 U.S.C. chapter 6) do not apply to these regulations, and, therefore, an initial Regulatory Flexibility Analysis is not required. Pursuant to section 7805(f) of the Internal Revenue Code, these regulations will be submitted to the Administrator of the Small Business Administration for comment on their impact on small business.

Comments and Requests for a Public Hearing

Before these proposed regulations are adopted, consideration will be given to any written comments that are submitted (preferably nine copies) to the Internal Revenue Service. All comments will be available for public inspection and copying. A public hearing will be held upon written request to the Internal Revenue Service by any person who also submits written comments. If a public hearing is held, notice of the time and place will be published in the Federal Register.

Drafting Information

The principal author of these regulations is Richard Pavel of the Office of the Assistant Chief Counsel (Employee Benefits and Exempt Organizations), Internal Revenue Service. However, personnel from other offices of the Service and Treasury Department participated in their development.

[¶ 20,185 Reserved.—Proposed regulations relating to employer-provided transportation and transit passes for employees were formerly reproduced here. The final regulations are now at ¶ 11,176 and ¶ 11,2890-6.]

[¶ 20,186 Reserved.—Proposed regulations relating to employer-provided transportation and benefits for volunteers of exempt organizations were formerly reproduced here. The final regulations are now at ¶ 11,172A, 11,176, 11,2890, 11,2890-1 and 11,2890-5.]

¶ 20,187

Proposed regulations: VEBAs: Single geographical locale requirement: Employment-related common bond.—The IRS has issued proposed amendments to regulations under Code Sec. 509(c)(9) which provide supplemental rules, including a safe harbor, that define the geographic area within which unrelated employers must be engaged in the same line of business in order for employees to be members of a tax-exempt voluntary employees' beneficiary association (VEBA). Employees of one or more unrelated employers engaged in the same line of business in the same geographic locale are considered to share an employment-related common bond for purposes of eligibility for membership in a VEBA. The proposed amendments were published in the *Federal Register* on August 7, 1992 (57 FR 34886).

AGENCY: Internal Revenue Service, Treasury.

ACTION: Notice of proposed rulemaking and notice of public hearing.

SUMMARY: This document contains proposed regulations about the qualification of voluntary employees' beneficiary associations (VEBAs) under section 501(c)(9) of the Internal Revenue Code (Code). The proposed regulations supplement the existing regulations with rules for determining whether the membership of an organization consists of employees of employers engaged in the same line of business in the same geographic locale. The proposed regulations will provide the public with guidance necessary to comply with the law in the case of an organization that does not consist exclusively of the employees of a single employer or the members of a single labor union. They will affect entities seeking to sponsor VEBAs covering the employees of more than one unrelated employer, as well as those employees.

DATES: Written comments must be received by October 6, 1992. Requests to speak (with outlines of oral comments) at a public hearing scheduled for December 3, 1992, at 1:00 p.m. must be received by November 12, 1992.

ADDRESSES: Send all submissions to: Internal Revenue Service, P.O. Box 7604, Ben Franklin Station, Attention: CC:CORP:T:R (EE-23-92) Washington, D.C. 20044.

FOR FURTHER INFORMATION CONTACT: Michael J. Roach at 202-622-6060 concerning the regulations; Carol Savage at 202-622-8452 concerning the hearing (not toll-free numbers).

SUPPLEMENTARY INFORMATION:

Background

The existing regulations at § 1.501(c)(9)-2(a)(1) contain general rules for determining when an association qualifies as a voluntary employees' beneficiary association (VEBA) eligible for exemption from income tax under section 501(c)(9) of the Internal Revenue Code. Under those regulations, the members of the association must share an employment-related common bond. The members are deemed to share an employment-related common bond if membership in the association is open only to persons whose eligibility for membership is based on employment by a single employer or affiliated group of employers, or is based on membership in one or more locals of a national or international labor union, or is based on coverage under one or more collective bargaining agreements. In addition, under the existing regulations, employees of one or more employers engaged in the same line of business in the same geographic locale are considered to share an employment-related common bond.

Questions have arisen about the geographic extent of a single "geographic locale." In its report on the Deficit Reduction Act of 1984, Pub. L. No. 98-369, 98 Stat. 494, the House Ways and Means Committee described the effect of the geographic locale restriction affecting VEBAs as follows:

Under [the] standards [prescribed in the regulations], for example, a group of car dealers in the same city or other similarly restricted geographical locale could form a VEBA to provide permissible benefits to their employees.

H.R. Rep. No. 432, Part II, 98th Cong., 2d Sess. 1285.

Administratively, the Internal Revenue Service has treated employers located in any one state as located in the same geographic locale. The Service has also treated a single standard metropolitan statistical area (SMSA), as defined by the Bureau of the Census, as a single geographic locale, even though the boundaries of some SMSAs include portions of more than one state.

In 1986, the United States Court of Appeals for the Seventh Circuit held the geographic locale restriction invalid in *Water Quality Association Employees' Benefit Corp. v. United States*, 795 F.2d 1303 (7th Cir. 1986). The court agreed with the Government's argument that the existence of an employment-related common bond is the essential factor that distinguishes a tax-exempt VEBA from a taxable insurance company, but concluded that restricting VEBAs covering employees of unrelated employers to those employers located in the same geographic locale did not enhance the employment-related bond of the employees participating in the organization.

The preamble to the final regulations published as T.D. 7750, 1981-1 C.B. 338 (46 F.R. 1719 (January 7, 1981)), explains the reason why the Secretary decided to retain the geographic locale restriction despite comments from the public requesting its deletion from the final regulations. In relevant part, the preamble states:

First, section 501(c)(9) provides for the exemption of associations of employees who enjoy some employment related bond. Allowing section 501(c)(9) to be used as a tax-exempt vehicle for offering insurance products to unrelated individuals scattered throughout the country would undermine those provisions of the Internal Revenue Code that prescribe the income tax treatment of insurance companies. Second, it is the position of the Internal Revenue Service that where an organization such as a national trade association or business league exempt from taxation under section 501(c)(6) operates a group insurance program for its members, the organization is engaged in an unrelated trade or business. *See* Rev. Rul. 66-151, 1966-1 C.B. 152; Rev. Rul. 73-386, 1973-2 C.B. 191; Rev. Rul. 78-52, 1978-1 C.B. 166. To allow trade associations to provide insurance benefits through a trust exempt under section 501(c)(9) would simply facilitate circumvention of the unrelated trade or business income tax otherwise applicable to such organizations.

These restrictions are consistent with the history of section 501(c)(9) of the Code. As Kenneth W. Gideon, then Assistant Secretary of the Treasury for Tax Policy, said in testimony before the Subcommittee on Taxation of the Senate Finance Committee on September 10, 1991, the VEBA tax exemption was originally intended to benefit associations formed and managed by employees of a single employer, or of small local groups of employers, to provide certain welfare benefits to their members in situations where such benefits would not otherwise have been available. *Tax Simplification Bills: Hearings on S. 1364, S. 1394, and H.R. 2777 Before the Subcommittee on Taxation of the Senate Committee on Finance*, 102d Cong., 1st Sess., 260-261. In 1928, when the predecessor of section 501(c)(9) of the Code was enacted as section 103(16) of the Revenue Act of 1928, 45 Stat; 791, ch. 852, the prevalent form of "mutual benefit association" that provided welfare benefits to employees was an organization providing benefits to the employees of a single establishment, such as an industrial plant. National Industrial Conference Board, *The Present Status of Mutual Benefit Associations*, 1-2, 50-51 (1931). At the time, there was concern that, although these organizations performed valuable social functions, they might not be able to continue to exist without a tax exemption. By contrast, larger associations covering employees of unrelated employers in different geographic areas are more likely to be viable without a tax exemption, and the benefits they provide are more likely to be available through commercial insurance. *Tax Simplification Bills, supra*, at 260. In general, when Congress exempts a class of organizations from income tax, it is deemed to have referred to the existing organizations of that class at the time the exemption was adopted. *United States v. Cambridge Loan and Building Co.*, 278 U.S. 55, 58 (1928). Thus, the absence of large regional or national organizations among the class of organizations known as VEBAs or "mutual benefit associations" that were dedicated to providing welfare benefits to employees in 1928 is relevant in determining the proper scope of the exemption granted by section 501(c)(9) of the Code.

The factors cited in the preamble to the 1981 regulations for imposing a geographic locale restriction on the membership of VEBAs that include employees of unrelated employers are matters of continuing concern today. Because of these factors and the history of section 501(c)(9), the proposed regulations limit the geographic region within which unrelated employers must be engaged in the same line of business in order for employees of those lines of business to participate in a single VEBA to the minimum area that is consistent with enabling all employees of employers engaged in a particular line of business to participate in an economically feasible VEBA. If VEBA participation were always limited to employees of employers located in the same state or SMSA, however, the diversity of regional population density and employment patterns in the United States could make it infeasible in many cases for benefits to be provided through a VEBA. Accordingly, the proposed regulations afford a safe harbor that treats any three contiguous states as a single geographic locale, and they authorize the Commissioner of Internal Revenue to recognize larger areas as a single geographic locale on a case-by-case basis upon application by an organization seeking recognition as a VEBA. Thus, the Commissioner may recognize an organization as a VEBA under section 501(c)(9), even though its members are employed by unrelated employers engaged in the same line of business located in any number of states, whether or not contiguous. To obtain recognition as a VEBA under this discretionary authority, the applicant must show (1) that it would not be economically feasible to cover employees of employers engaged in that line of business in the states to be included in the proposed VEBA under two or more separate VEBAs, and (2) either that the states to be included are all contiguous, or that there are legitimate reasons supporting the inclusion of those particular states.

During the drafting of these proposed regulations consideration was given to a rule that would allow an area to be treated as a single geographic locale even though it included areas outside the United States. It is not clear, however, whether it is necessary or desirable to include such a rule. Comments are invited about the extent, if any, to which the regulations should allow the inclusion of areas outside the United States in a single geographic locale.

Proposed Effective Date

These regulations are proposed to be effective on August 7, 1992; however, taxpayers may treat the rules as applicable to prior years.

Special Analyses

It has been determined that these rules are not major rules as defined in Executive Order 12291. Therefore, a Regulatory Impact Analysis is not required. It has also been determined that section 553(b) of the Administrative Procedure Act (5 U.S.C. chapter 5) and the Regulatory Flexibility Act (5 U.S.C. chapter 6) do not apply to these proposed regulations and, therefore, an initial Regulatory Flexibility Analysis is not required. Pursuant to section 7805(f) of the Internal Revenue Code, these regulations will be submitted to the Chief Counsel for Advocacy of the Small Business Administration for comment on their impact on small business.

Comments and Public Hearing

Before these proposed regulations are adopted as final regulations, consideration will be given to any written comments that are submitted timely (preferably an original and eight copies) to the Internal Revenue Service. All comments will be available for public inspection and copying.

A public hearing will be held on Thursday, December 3, 1992, at 1:00 p.m. in the Internal Revenue Service Auditorium, Internal Revenue Building, 1111 Constitution Avenue, N.W. Washington, DC. The rules of § 601.601(a)(3) of the "Statement of Procedural Rules" (26 CFR part 601) shall apply to the public hearing.

Persons who have submitted written comments by October 6, 1992, and who also desire to present oral comments at the hearing on the proposed regulations, should submit, not later than November 12, 1992, a request to speak and an outline of the oral comments to be presented at the hearing stating the time they wish to devote to each subject.

Each speaker (or group of speakers representing a single entity) will be limited to 10 minutes for an oral presentation exclusive of the time consumed by the questions from the panel for the government and answers thereto.

Because of controlled access restrictions, attendees cannot be admitted beyond the lobby of the Internal Revenue Building before 12:45 p.m.

An agenda showing the scheduling of the speakers will be made after outlines are received from the persons testifying. Copies of the agenda will be available free of charge at the hearing.

Drafting Information

The principal author of these proposed regulations is Michael J. Roach, Office of the Associate Chief Counsel (Employee Benefits and Exempt Organizations), Internal Revenue Service. However, personnel from other offices of the Service and the Treasury Department participated in their development.

List of Subjects

26 CFR 1.501(a)-1 through 1.505(c)-1T

Income taxes, Nonprofit organizations, Reporting and recordkeeping requirements.

Proposed Amendment to the Regulations

Accordingly, the proposed amendment to 26 CFR part 1 is as follows:

PART 1—INCOME TAX; TAXABLE YEARS BEGINNING AFTER DECEMBER 31, 1953

Paragraph 1. The authority citation for part 1 continues to read in part as follows:

Authority: 26 U.S.C. 7805 * * *

Par. 2. In § 1.501(c)(9)-2, paragraph (a)(1) is amended by adding a sentence between the fourth and fifth sentences, and a new paragraph (d) is added, to read as follows:

(a) * * *

(1) *In general.* * * * (See paragraph (d) of this section for the meaning of geographic locale.) * * *

* * * * *

(d) *Meaning of geographic locale*—(1) *Three-state safe harbor.* An area is a single geographic locale for purposes of paragraph (a)(1) of this section if it does not exceed the boundaries of three contiguous states, *i.e.,* three states each of which shares a land or river border with at least one of the others. For this purpose, Alaska and Hawaii are deemed to be contiguous with each other and with each of the following states: Washington, Oregon, and California.

(2) *Discretionary authority to recognize larger areas as geographic locales.* In determining whether an organization covering employees of employers engaged in the same line of business is a voluntary employees' beneficiary association (VEBA) described in section 501(c)(9), the Commissioner may recognize an area that does not satisfy the three-state safe harbor in paragraph (d)(1) of this section as a single geographic locale if—

(i) It would not be economically feasible to cover employees of employers engaged in that line of business in that area under two or more separate VEBAs each extending over fewer states; and

(ii) Employment characteristics in that line of business, population characteristics, or other regional factors support the particular states included. This paragraph (d)(2)(ii) is deemed satisfied if the states included are contiguous.

(3) *Examples.* The following examples illustrate this paragraph (d).

Example 1. The membership of the W Association is made up of employers whose business consists of the distribution of produce in Virginia, North Carolina, and South Carolina. Because Virginia and South Carolina each share a land border with North Carolina, the three states are contiguous states and form a single geographic locale.

Example 2. The membership of the X Association is made up of employers whose business consists of the retail sale of computer software in Montana, Wyoming, North Dakota, South Dakota, and Nebraska, which are contiguous states. X establishes the X Trust to provide life, sick, accident, or other benefits for the employees of its members. The X Trust applies for recognition of exemption as a VEBA, stating that it intends to permit employees of any employer that is a member of X to join the proposed VEBA. In its application, the X Trust provides summaries of employer data and economic analyses showing that no division of the region into smaller groups of states would enable X to establish two or more separate VEBAs each with enough members to make the formation of those separate VEBAs economically feasible. Furthermore, although some possible divisions of the region into three-state or four-state areas could form an economically feasible VEBA, any such division of the five-state region covered by X would leave employees of X's employer-members located in at least one state without a VEBA. The Commissioner may, as a matter of administrative discretion, recognize the X Trust as a VEBA described in section 501(c)(9) based on its showing that the limited number of employees in each state would make any division of the region into two or more VEBAs economically infeasible.

Example 3. The membership of the Y Association is made up of employers whose business consists of shipping freight by barge on the Mississippi and Ohio Rivers. Some of the members of Y conduct their business out of ports in Louisiana, while others operate out of ports in Arkansas, Missouri, and Ohio. Y establishes the Y Trust to provide life, sick, accident, or other benefits to the employees of its members. The Y Trust applies for recognition of exemption as a VEBA, stating that it intends to permit the employees of any employer that is a member of Y to join the proposed VEBA. In its application, the Y Trust sets forth facts tending to show that there are so few members of Y in each of the four states that any division of those states into two or more separate regions would result in creating VEBAs that would be too small to be economically feasible, that all of the members of Y are engaged in river shipping between inland and Gulf ports that are united by the existence of a natural waterway, and that the labor force engaged in providing transportation by river barge is distinct from that engaged in providing other means of transportation. Even though Ohio, Louisiana, Arkansas, and Missouri are not contiguous, because Ohio does not share a land or river border with any of the other three states, the Commissioner may, as a matter of administrative discretion, recognize the Y Trust as a VEBA described in section 501(c)(9) based on its showing that the establishment of separate VEBAs would not be economically feasible and that the characteristics of the river shipping business justify permitting a VEBA to cover the scattered concentrations of employees in that business located in Louisiana, Arkansas, Missouri, and Ohio.

Example 4. The membership of the Z Association is made up of employers whose business consists of the retail sale of agricultural implements in the states west of the Mississippi River except California, Alaska, and Hawaii. There are 21 states in the region covered by Z. Z establishes the Z1 Trust, the Z2 Trust, and the Z3 Trust to provide life, sick, accident or other benefits to the employees of its members. The trusts cover different subregions which were formed by dividing the Z region into three areas each consisting of seven contiguous states. Each trust applies for recognition of exemption as a VEBA, stating that it intends to permit the employees of any employer that is a member of Z located within its subregion to join its proposed VEBA. Each trust sets forth facts in its application tending to show that four

states within its particular subregion would be needed to create a VEBA large enough to be economically feasible, so that any further division of its seven-state subregion would leave employees of at least some of Z's employer-members located in the subregion in an area too small to support an economically feasible VEBA. The applications contain no justification for the choice of three seven-state subregions. Since the applicants have not shown that it would not be economically feasible to divide the Z region into smaller subregions (*e.g.,* four containing four states and one containing five states), the applicants have not satisfied paragraph (d)(2)(i) of this section, and the Commissioner does not have the discretion to recognize the Z1, Z2, and Z3 Trusts as VEBAs described in section 501(c)(9).

[¶ 20,188 Reserved.—Proposed regulations to delay the effective date of final regulations under Code Secs. 401(a)(4), 410(b), and related nondiscrimination requirements, were formerly reproduced at this paragraph. The final nondiscrimination regulations, as revised, appear at ¶ 11,720W-14, 11,720X-5, 11,720Z-11, 11,731Q, 12,165, 12,364F-11—12,364F-22, and 12,364K.]

[¶ 20,189 Reserved.—Proposed regulations dealing with eligible rollover distributions from qualified retirement plans and tax-free annuities under Code Sec. 403(b) were formerly reproduced at this paragraph. The final regulations now appear at ¶ 11,720Z-50; 11,753-10; 11,755-2F; 11,830-10 and 13,566-10. The introductory material proceding the final regulations is at ¶ 23,122.]

¶ 20,190

Proposed regulations: Valuations: Annuities: Estate tax.—The IRS has issued proposed amendments to regulations under the Code relating to the valuation of annuities, interests for life or a term of years, or remainder or reversionary interests for estate tax purposes. The amendments are required because Code Sec. 7520, added by the Technical and Miscellaneous Revenue Act of 1988, provides a new method of valuing these interests after April 30, 1989. The IRS has included actuarial tables in the proposed amendments. The proposed amendments were published in the *Federal Register* on November 2, 1992 (57 FR 49514).

[¶ 4830-01]

DEPARTMENT OF THE TREASURY

Internal Revenue Service

26 CFR Parts 1, 20, 25 and 602

RIN 1545-AM81

Valuation Tables

AGENCY: Internal Revenue Service, Treasury.

ACTION: Notice of proposed rulemaking.

SUMMARY: This document contains proposed amendments to the regulations under the Internal Revenue Code relating to the valuation of any annuity, any interest for life or a term of years, or any remainder or reversionary interest. These amendments are necessary because section 7520, which provides a new method for valuing these interests after April 30, 1989, was added to the Internal Revenue Code (the Code) by section 5031 of the Technical and Miscellaneous Revenue Act of 1988 (the Act). These proposed regulations would affect all transfers of such interests in property. The proposed regulations do not apply for purposes of section 72 of the Code (relating to the income taxation of life insurance, endowments, and annuities), for purposes of sections 401 through 419A, 457, 3121(v), 3306(r), and 6058 (relating to deferred compensation arrangements), for purposes of section 7872 (relating to income and gift taxation of interest-free and below-market interest rate loans), for purposes of certain property interests under sections 83 and 451, or for purposes of certain transfers under Chapter 14.

DATES: Written comments, requests to appear and outlines of comments to be presented at a public hearing must be received by November 30, 1992.

ADDRESSES: All submissions should be sent to: Internal Revenue Service, P.O. Box 7604, Ben Franklin Station, Attention: CC:CORP:T:R (PS-100-88), Room 5228, Washington, D.C. 20044.

FOR FURTHER INFORMATION CONTACT: William L. Blodgett, telephone 202-622-3090 (not a toll-free number).

SUPPLEMENTARY INFORMATION:

Paperwork Reduction Act

The collection of information contained in this notice of proposed rulemaking has been submitted to the Office of Management and Budget for review in accordance with the Paperwork Reduction Act of 1980 (44 U.S.C. 3504(h)). Comments on the collection of information should be sent to the Office of Management and Budget, Attention: Desk Officer for the Department of the Treasury, Office of Information and Regulatory Affairs, Washington, D.C. 20503, with copies to the Internal Revenue Service, Attn: IRS Reports Clearance Officer T:FP, Washington, D.C. 20224.

The collection of information in this proposed rulemaking is in §§ 20.7520-1 through 20.7520-4. This information is required to compute the present value of any annuity, any interest for life or a term of years, or any remainder or reversionary interest for income, gift, estate, and generation-skipping transfer tax purposes. The likely respondents are individuals, estates, trusts, and nonprofit institutions.

These estimates are an approximation of the average time expected to be necessary for a collection of information. They are based on such information as is available to the Internal Revenue Service. Individual respondents may require greater or less time, depending on their particular circumstances. Estimated total annual reporting burden: 4,500 hours. The estimated annual burden per respondent varies from 30 minutes to one hour, depending on individual circumstances, with an estimated average of 45 minutes. Estimated number of respondents: 6,000. Estimated annual frequency of responses: one.

Background

This document provides proposed regulations (26 CFR 20.7520) for the valuation of certain partial interests in property under section 7520 of the Internal Revenue Code of 1986 (the Code); as added by section 5031 of the Technical and Miscellaneous Revenue Act of 1988 (the Act).

In General

Section 7520 provides that the value of an annuity, an interest for life or a term of years, and a remainder or reversionary interest is to be determined under tables published by the Internal Revenue Service based on a discount rate (rounded to the nearest two-tenths of one percent) equal to 120 percent of the applicable Federal mid-term rate in effect under section 1274(d)(1) for the month in which the valuation date falls. These tables have been published in Internal Revenue Service Publications 1457 "Actuarial Values, Alpha Volume" and 1458 "Actuarial Values, Beta Volume." Those publications also contain special factors to make necessary adjustments for frequency and time of payments when the value of the interest is based upon recurring payments, along with examples of computations. The tables will be revised at least once every 10 years to reflect the most recent mortality experience available. Certain tables contained in those publications are included in these regulations so that taxpayers and their advisers can have more ready access to the tables.

To compute the present value of the property interest being transferred, it is necessary to use the interest rate that is 120 percent of the applicable Federal mid-term rate compounded annually and that is published in the Internal Revenue Bulletin for the month in which the valuation date falls. This rate must be rounded to the nearest two-tenths of one percent. However, if an income, estate, or gift tax charitable deduction is allowable for any part of the property transferred, the transferor may elect to use an interest rate that is 120 percent of the applicable Federal mid-term rate for either of the two months preceding the month in which the valuation date falls.

Section 7520 does not apply for purposes of section 72 of the Code (involving the income taxation of life insurance, endowments, and annuities), for purposes of sections 401 through 419A, 457, 3121(v), 3306(r), and 6058 (relating to deferred compensation arrangements), for purposes of section 7872 (relating to income and gift taxation of interest-free and below-market interest rate loans), for purposes of certain property interests under sections 83 and 451, or for purposes of certain transfers under chapter 14 of the Code.

During the 5 and ½ year period before the enactment of section 7520 of the Code, the present value of an annuity, an interest for life or a term of years, or a remainder or reversionary interest was computed using an interest rate of 10 percent, based on tables contained in regulations under section 2031 (estate tax), section 2512 (gift tax), section 2624 (generation-skipping transfer tax), section 664 (charitable remainder trusts), and section 642 (pooled income funds). The regulations under each of these sections are amended to provide that transfers of such interests with respect to which the valuation date falls on or after May 1, 1989, are valued under section 7520.

The following is a chart that summarizes the periods of time, the interest rates, and the applicable regulation sections under the existing and proposed regulations.

Valuation Period	Interest Rate	Prior Section	Revised Section
	***		
§ 2031:			
Valuation, in general	—	—	20.2031-7
05/01/89 - present	§ 7520	none	20.2031-7(e)
before - 01/01/52	4%	none	20.2031-7A(a)
01/01/52 - 12/31/70	3.5%	none	20.2031-7A(b)
01/01/71 - 11/30/83	6%	20.2031-10	20.2031-7A(c)
12/01/83 - 04/30/89	10%	20.2031-7	20.2031-7A(d)
	***		

With respect to transfers to pooled income funds, the proposed regulations provide rules for determining the rate of return for purposes of valuing charitable remainder gifts in pooled income funds described in section 642. In general, the rate of return for a pooled income fund is equal to the highest annual rate of return of the fund for the 3 taxable years immediately preceding the year in which the transfer of property to the fund is made. For a pooled income fund that has been in existence for less than 3 years, § 1.642(c)-6(b)(2) of the existing regulations provides a deemed rate of return of 9 percent for funds created between December 1, 1983, and April 30, 1989. This deemed rate was 1 percent less than general interest rate of 10 percent that was prescribed by the regulations for that period. Notice 89-60, 1989-1 C.B. 700 (See § 601.601(d)(2)(ii)(b) of the Statement of Procedural Rules), announced a method of determining the deemed rate of return for pooled income funds created after April 30, 1989. Under the Notice, the deemed rate is equal to 1 percent less than the highest average annual rate (120 percent of the applicable Federal mid-term rate rounded to the nearest two-tenths of one percent) for the 3 years preceding the date the fund is created. The proposed regulation provides that the deemed rate for pooled income funds created after April 30, 1989, is 90 percent of the same highest average annual rate for the 3 years preceding the creation of the fund. In the case of funds created in 1989 (after April 30), 1990, 1991, and 1992, the method in the proposed regulation yields the same deemed rate of return as the method in Notice 89-60. Although the proposed regulation applies to pooled income funds created after April 30, 1989, for transfers to pooled income funds created prior to November 2, 1992, a transferor can rely on the Notice.

Transitional Rules

Under section 5031 of the Act, section 7520 is effective where the valuation date with respect to a transfer occurs on or after May 1, 1989. These proposed regulations provide certain transitional rules intended to alleviate any adverse consequences resulting from the statutory change. Several principal provisions of the proposed regulations were announced in Notice 89-24, 1989-1 C.B. 660 (which announced the change from the 10 percent fixed rate of interest to the section 7520 floating rate of interest), and Notice 89-60 (which announced the change in mortality tables) (see § 601.601(d)(2)(ii)(b) of the Statement of Procedural Rules). A transitional rule in the proposed regulation provides that, for valuation dates of transfers after April 30, 1989, and before November 2, 1992, a transferor can rely on Notice 89-24 or Notice 89-60 in valuing the transferred interest. For gift tax purposes, a transitional rule provides that if, after December 31, 1988, but before May 1, 1989, a donor transferred an interest in property, retaining an interest in the same property, and the donor later transferred the

retained interest in the property after April 30, 1989, and before January 1, 1990, the donor may elect to value the transfer of the retained interest under either the 10 percent tables or the section 7520 tables (whichever is more beneficial). For estate tax purposes, a transitional rule provides that a decedent's estate may elect to value the property interest included in the gross estate under either set of tables if the decedent was under a mental incapacity that existed on May 1, 1989, and continued uninterrupted until the decedent's death. For determining the value of the remainder interest in a testamentary charitable remainder unitrust or annuity trust, a transitional rule provides that the interest rate of either 10 percent or the rate under section 7520 may be used if the decedent was mentally incompetent on May 1, 1989, and (1) such incompetency continued uninterrupted until death or (2) the decedent died within 90 days of first regaining competency after April 30, 1989.

Election Requirements

These regulations specify the time and manner of making the election to use the applicable Federal mid-term rate for either of the two months preceding the month in which the valuation date falls when a charitable deduction is allowable for part of the interest transferred. The election must be made with the first income, estate, or gift tax return that is filed after the transfer. Generally, the person required to file the return is also required to make the election. Any election may be revoked if revocation occurs within the period of limitations on assessment and collection under section 6501. If, in addition to the charitable interest, another interest in the same property is transferred and the taxpayer elects to use an interest rate from one of the two preceding months, the taxpayer must use the same rate to determine the value of each interest transferred. A cross-reference is provided in the proposed regulations to § 301.9100-8(a)(1), which provides interim rules for this election, which was enacted under the Technical and Miscellaneous Revenue Act of 1988.

Special Analyses

It has been determined that these proposed rules are not major rules as defined in Executive Order 12291. Therefore, a Regulatory Impact Analysis is not required. It has also been determined that section 553(b) of the Administrative Procedure Act (5 U.S.C. chapter 5) and the Regulatory Flexibility Act (5 U.S.C. chapter 6) do not apply to these regulations, and, therefore, an initial Regulatory Flexibility Analysis is not required. Pursuant to section 7805(f) of the Internal Revenue Code, these proposed regulations will be submitted to the Chief Counsel for Advocacy of the Small Business Administration for comment on their impact on small business.

Comments and Requests for a Public Hearing

Before adopting these proposed regulations, consideration will be given to any written comments that are submitted timely (preferably a signed original and 8 copies) to the Internal Revenue Service. All comments will be available for public inspection and copying in their entirety. See the notice of public hearing published elsewhere in this issue of the **Federal Register.**

Drafting Information

The principal author of these regulations is William L. Blodgett of the Office of Assistant Chief Counsel (Passthroughs and Special Industries), Internal Revenue Service. However, personnel from other offices of the Internal Revenue Service and Treasury Department participated in their development.

List of Subjects

* * *

26 CFR Part 20

Estate taxes, Reporting and recordkeeping requirements.

26 CFR Part 25

* * *

Proposed amendments to the regulations

Accordingly, 26 CFR parts 1, 20, 25, and 602 are proposed to be amended as follows:

Parts 1, 20 and 25 [Amended]

Paragraph 1. In the list below, for each section indicated in the left column, remove the language in the middle column and add the language in the right column:

Section	Remove	Add
* * *		
1.101-2(e)(1)(iii)(*b*)(*3*)	paragraph (f) of	—
1.101-2(e)(2), *Example (1)*(ii)	paragraph (f) of	—
* * *		
1.170A-5(b), *Example 5*, fifth sentence	Table A(1) in § 20.2031-10(f)	§ 20.2031-7A(c)
* * *		
1.414(c)-2(b)(2)(ii), second sentence	or § 20.2031-10 (Estate Tax Regulations), whichever is appropriate,	—
1.414(c)-4(b)(3)(i), last sentence	or § 20.2031-10 (Estate Tax Regulations), whichever is appropriate,	—
* * *		
20.2031-7(a)(2) first and second sentences	paragraph (f)	paragraph (d)(6)
20.2031-7(a)(2)	paragraph (e)	paragraph (d)(5)
20.2031-7(b)(1)	paragraph (b)(1)	paragraph (d)(2)(i)
20.2031-7(b)(2)	paragraph (b)(2)	paragraph (d)(2)(ii)
20.2031-7(b)(2) (in the *Example*)	paragraph (b)(1)	paragraph (d)(2)(i)
20.2031-7(b)(3)(i)	paragraphs (b)(1) or (2)	paragraphs (d)(2)(i) or (ii)
20.2031-7(b)(3)(i)	paragraph (b)(3)(i)	paragraph (d)(2)(iii)(A)
20.2031-7(b)(3)(i) (in the *Example*)	paragraph (b)(2)	paragraph (d)(2)(ii)
20.2031-7(b)(3)(ii)	paragraph (b)(3)(ii)	paragraph (d)(2)(iii)(B)
20.2031-7(c)	paragraph (c)	paragraph (d)(3)
20.2031-7(d)	paragraph (d)	paragraph (d)(4)
20.2031-7(e)	paragraph (f)	paragraph (d)(6)
* * *		
20.2039-2(c)(1)(viii)	through 20.2031-10	—
20.2039-5(c)(1)	through 20.2031-10	—
20.2039-5(c)(2)	through 20.2031-10	—
* * *		

PART 1—INCOME TAX; TAXABLE YEARS BEGINNING AFTER DECEMBER 31, 1953

Par. 2. The authority citation for part 1 continues to read in part: * * *

Authority: 26 U.S.C. 7805 * * *

PART 20—ESTATE TAX; ESTATES OF DECEDENTS DYING AFTER AUGUST 16, 1954

Par. 12. The general authority citation for part 20 is revised to read as follows:

Authority: 26 U.S.C. 7805.

Par. 14. Section 20.2031-0 is added to read as follows:

§ 20.2031-0 Table of contents.

This section lists the section headings that appear in the regulations under section 2031.

§ 20.2031-1 *Definition of gross estate; valuation of property.*

§ 20.2031-2 *Valuation of stocks and bonds.*

§ 20.2031-3 *Valuation of interests in businesses.*

§ 20.2031-4 *Valuation of notes.*

§ 20.2031-5 *Valuation of cash on hand or on deposit.*

§ 20.2031-6 *Valuation of household and personal effects.*

§ 20.2031-7 *Valuation of annuities, life estates, terms for years, remainders, and reversions after April 30, 1989.*

§ 20.2031-7A *Valuation of annuities, life estates, terms for years, remainders, and reversions before May 1, 1989.*

§ 20.2031-8 *Valuation of certain life insurance and annuity contracts; valuation of shares in an open-end investment company.*

§ 20.2031-9 *Valuation of other property.*

Par. 15. Immediately following § 20.2046-1 an undesignated center heading and § 20.2031-7A are added to read as follows:

Actuarial tables applicable before May 1, 1989, § 20.2031-7A Valuation of annuities, life estates, terms for years, remainders, and reversions for estates of decedents who died before May 1, 1989—(a) *Valuation of annuities, life estates, terms for years, remainders, and reversions for estates of decedents who died before January 1, 1952.* Except as otherwise provided in § 20.2031-7(c), if the decedent died before January 1, 1952, the present value of annuities, life estates, terms for years, remainders, and reversions is their present value determined under this section. If the valuation of the interest involved is dependent upon the continuation or termination of one or more lives or upon a term certain concurrent with one or more lives, the factor for the present value is computed on the basis of interest at the rate of 4 percent a year, compounded annually, and life contingencies as to each life involved from values that are based on the Actuaries' or Combined Experience Table of Mortality, as extended. This table and related factors are described in former § 81.10 (as contained in CFR edition revised as of

April 1, 1958). The present value of an interest measured by a term for years is computed on the basis of interest at the rate of 4 percent a year.

(b) *Valuation of annuities, life estates, terms for years, remainders, and reversions for estates of decedents who died after December 31, 1951, and before January 1, 1971.* Except as otherwise provided in § 20.2031-7(c), if the decedent died after December 31, 1951, and before January 1, 1971, the present value of annuities, life estates, terms for years, remainders, and reversions is their present value determined under this section. If the valuation of the interest involved is dependent upon the continuation or termination of one or more lives, or upon a term certain concurrent with one or more lives, the factor for the present value is computed on the basis of interest at the rate of 3 ½ percent a year, compounded annually, and life contingencies as to each life involved are taken from U.S. Life Table 38. This table and related factors are set forth in former § 20.2031-7 (as contained in CFR edition revised as of April 1, 1984). Special factors involving one and two lives may be found in or computed with the use of tables contained in the publication entitled "Actuarial Values for Estate and Gift Tax," Publication Number 11 (Rev. 5-59). A copy of this publication may be purchased from the Superintendent of Documents, United States Printing Office, Washington, D.C. 20402. The present value of an interest measured by a term for years is computed on the basis of interest at the rate of 3 ½ percent a year.

(c) *Valuation of annuities, life estates, terms for years, remainders, and reversions for estates of decedents who died after December 31, 1970, and before December 1, 1983.* Except as otherwise provided in § 20.2031-7(c), if the decedent died after December 31, 1970, and before December 1, 1983, the present value of annuities, life estates, terms for years, remainders, and reversions is their present value determined under this section. If the valuation of the interest involved is dependent upon the continuation of or termination of one or more lives or upon a term certain concurrent with one or more lives, the factor for the present value is computed on the basis of interest at the rate of 6 percent a year, compounded annually, and life contingencies are determined as to each male and female life involved, from values that are set forth in Table LN. Table LN contains values that are taken from the life table for total males and the life table for total females appearing as Tables 2 and 3, respectively in United States Life Tables: 1959-1960, published by the Department of Health and Human Services, Public Health Service. Table LN and related factors are set forth in former § 20.2031-10 (as contained in CFR edition revised as of April 1, 1992). Special factors involving one and two lives may be found in or computed with the use of tables contained in Internal Revenue Service Publication 723E, "Actuarial Values I: Valuation of Last Survivor Charitable Remainders," (12-70), and Publication 723A, "Actuarial Values II: Factors at 6 Percent Involving One and Two Lives," (12-70). A copy of this publication may be purchased from the Superintendent of Documents, United States Printing Office, Washington, D.C. 20402.

Old CFR unit number in § 20.2031-7

§ 20.2031-7 heading
(a)
(a) (1)
(a) (2)
(a) (3)
(b)
(b) (1)
(b) (2)
(b) (3) (i)
(b) (3) (ii)
(c) through (f)

2. The paragraph heading for (d) is revised.

3. Paragraph (d) (1) (i) is revised.

4. Paragraph (d) (1) (iii) is revised.

5. Paragraph (d) (5), third and fourth sentences are revised.

6. The revised provisions read as follows:

§ 20.2031-7A Valuation of annuities, life estates, terms for years, remainders, and reversions before May 1, 1989.

* * * * *

(d) *Valuation of annuities, life estates, terms for years, remainders, and reversions for estates of decedents who died after November 30, 1983, if the valuation date for the gross estate is before May 1, 1989—* (1) *In general.* (i) Except as otherwise provided in § 20.2031-7(c), if the decedent died after November 30, 1983, and the valuation date for the gross estate is before May 1, 1989, the fair market value of annuities, life estates, terms for years, remainders, and reversions is their present value determined under this section. If a decedent died after November 30, 1983, and before August 9, 1984, or, in cases where the valuation date of the decedent's gross estate is before May 1, 1989, if, on December 1, 1983, the decedent was mentally incompetent so that the disposition of the decedent's property could not be changed, and the decedent died on or after December 1, 1983, without having regained competency to dispose of the decedent's property, or if the decedent died within 90 days of the date on which the decedent first regained competency, the fair market value of annuities, life estates, terms for years, remainders, and reversions included in the estate of such decedent is their present value determined under either this section or § 20.2031-7A(c), at the option of the taxpayer. The value of annuities issued by companies regularly engaged in their sale, and of insurance policies on the lives of persons other than the decedent is determined under § 20.2031-8. The fair market value of a remainder interest in a charitable remainder unitrust as defined in § 1.664-3 is its present value determined under § 1.664-4. The fair market value of a life interest or term for years in a charitable remainder unitrust is the fair market value of the property as of the date of valuation less the fair market value of the remainder interest on such date determined under § 1.664-4. The fair market value of the interests in a pooled income fund, as defined in § 1.642(c)-5, is their value determined under § 1.642(c)-6.

* * * * *

(iii) In all examples set forth in this section, the decedent is assumed to have died on or after August 9, 1984, with the valuation date of the decedent's gross estate falling before May 1, 1989, and to have been competent to change the disposition of the property on December 1, 1983.

Par. 16. Section 20.2031-7 is redesignated as § 20.2031-7A paragraph (d) and amended as follows:

1. The following redesignation table indicates the old CFR unit numbers for § 20.2031-7 and the corresponding new CFR unit numbers for § 20.2031-7A(d):

Corresponding new number in § 20.2031-7A

paragraph (d) heading
(d) (1)
(d) (1) (i)
(d) (1) (ii)
(d) (1) (iii)
(d) (2)
(d) (2) (i)
(d) (2) (ii)
(d) (2) (iii) (A)
(d) (2) (iii) (B)
(d) (3) through (d) (6)

* * * * *

(5) *Actuarial computations by the Internal Revenue Service.* * * * Table LN contains values of *lx* taken from the life table for the total population appearing as Table 1 of United States Life Tables: 1969-71, published by the Department of Health and Human Services, Public Health Service. Many special factors involving one and two lives may be found in or computed with the use of tables contained in Internal Revenue Service publication 723E, "Actuarial Values II: Factors at 10 Percent Involving One and Two Lives," (12-83). A copy of this publication may be purchased from the Superintendent of Documents, United States Printing Office, Washington, D.C. 20402 * * *

* * * * *

Par. 17. New § 20.2031-7 is added to read as follows: *§ 20.2031-7 Valuation of annuities, life estates, terms for years, remainders, and reversions after April 30, 1989—*(a) *In general.* Except as otherwise provided in paragraph (c) of this section, the fair market value of annuities, life estates, terms for years, remainders, and reversions for estates of decedents is the present value of such interests determined under paragraph (d) of this section.

(b) *Actuarial computations by the Internal Revenue Service.* The regulations in this and in related sections provide tables with actuarial factors and examples that illustrate how to use the tables to compute the value of annuity, life, and remainder interests in property. These sections also refer to government publications that provide additional tables of factors and examples of computations for more complex situations. Some older publications are no longer available. If the executor of a decedent's estate requires a special factor or computation, the executor may request a ruling on the matter. A request for a ruling must comply with the instructions for requesting a ruling published periodically in the Internal Revenue Bulletin (see § 601.601(d) (2) (ii) (*b*) of this chapter) and include payment of the required user fee.

(c) *Commercial annuities and insurance contracts.* The value of annuities issued by companies regularly engaged in their sale, and of insurance policies on the lives of persons other than the decedent is determined under § 20.2031-8. See § 20.2042-1 with respect to insurance policies on the decedent's life.

(d) *Valuation.* The present value of annuities, life estates, terms for years, remainders, and reversions for estates of decedents who died after April 30, 1989, is determined under paragraph (e) of this section. The present value of annuities, life estates, terms for years, remainders, and reversions for estates of decedents who died before May 1, 1989, is determined under the following sections:

Decedent's Date of Death (or Alternate Valuation Date)		Applicable Section
After	Before	
—	01-01-52	20.2031-7A (a)
12-31-51	01-01-71	20.2031-7A(b)
12-31-70	12-01-83	20.2031-7A(c)
11-30-83	05-01-89	20.2031-7A(d)

(e) *Valuation of annuities, life estates, terms for years, remainders, and reversions for estates of decedents who died after April 30, 1989—*(1) *In general.* Except as otherwise provided in paragraph (c) of this section and § 20.7520-3, if the valuation date for the gross estate of the decedent is after April 30, 1989, the fair market value of annuities, life estates, terms for years, remainders, and reversions is their present value determined by use of the tables in paragraph (e)(6) of this section and the interest rate component described in § 20.7520-1(b)(1). The tables are also contained in Internal Revenue Service Publication 1457, "Actuarial Values, Alpha Volume," (8-89). A copy of this publication may be purchased from the Superintendent of Documents, United States Printing Office, Washington, D.C. 20402. If the valuation date is after April 30, 1989, and before November 2, 1992, a taxpayer can rely on Notice 89-24, 1989-1 C.B. 660, or Notice 89-60, 1989-1 C.B. 700 (See § 601.601(d)(2)(ii)(b) of this chapter).

(2) *Certain Interests*—(i) *Charitable Interests.* The fair market value of a remainder interest in a pooled income fund, as defined in § 1.642(c)-5, is its value determined under § 1.642(c)-6(e). The fair market value of a remainder interest in a charitable remainder annuity trust, as defined in § 1.664-2(a), is its present value determined under § 1.664-2(c). The fair market value of a remainder interest in a charitable remainder unitrust, as defined in § 1.664-3, is its present value determined under § 1.664-4(e). The fair market value of a life interest or term for years in a charitable remainder unitrust is the fair market value of the property as of the date of valuation less the fair market value of the remainder interest on that date determined under § 1.664-4(e).

(ii) *Annuities.* (A) The present value of an annuity may be determined by use of the appropriate table containing remainder factors. If an annuity is payable annually at the end of each year for the life of an individual, the aggregate amount payable annually is multiplied by an annuity factor derived from Table S (remainder factors for one life) in paragraph (e)(6) of this section based on the interest rate component on the valuation date. If an annuity is payable until the death of the survivor of two individuals, the aggregate amount payable annually is multiplied by an annuity factor derived from Table R(2) (remainder factors for two lives) in Publication 1457. A copy of this publication may be purchased from the Superintendent of Documents, United States Government Printing Office, Washington, D.C. 20402. In the case of an annuity that is payable at the end of each year for a term of years, the aggregate amount payable annually is multiplied by an annuity factor derived from Table B (remainder factors for a term of years) in paragraph (e)(6) of this section based on the interest rate component on the valuation date. The annuity factor is obtained by subtracting the remainder factor in Table S, Table R(2), or Table B, whichever is appropriate, under the appropriate interest rate component opposite the number of years nearest the age of the individual or individuals (or the term of years representing the duration of the annuity), from 1.00 and then dividing the result by the appropriate interest rate component expressed as a decimal number. Alternatively, annuity factors for the life of one individual have been published and are contained in column (2) of the appropriate Table S in publication 1457. Annuity factors for a term of years have been published and are contained in column (2) of the appropriate Table B in Publication 1457. If the annuity is payable at the end of semiannual, quarterly, monthly, or weekly periods, the product obtained by multiplying the annuity factor by the aggregate amount payable annually is then multiplied by the applicable adjustment factor set forth in Table K for payments made at the end of the specified periods. The provisions of this paragraph (e) are illustrated by the following example:

Example. At the time of the decedent's death in January 1990, the annuitant, age 72, is entitled to receive an annuity of $15,000 a year payable in equal monthly installments at the end of each period. The rate that is 120 percent of the applicable Federal mid-term rate for January 1990 is 9.57 percent. This rate is rounded to 9.6 percent. Under Table S, the remainder factor at 9.6 percent for an individual aged 72 is .40138. By converting the remainder factor to an annuity factor, as described above, the annuity factor at 9.6 percent for an individual aged 72 is 6.2356 (1.00 minus .40138, divided by .096). Under Table K, the adjustment factor under the column for payments made at the end of each monthly period at the rate of 9.6 percent is 1.0433. The aggregate annual amount, $15,000, is multiplied by the factor 6.2356 and the product multiplied by 1.0433. The present value of the annuity at the date of the decedent's death is, therefore, $97,584 ($15,000 × 6.2356 × 1.0433).

(B) If an annuity is payable at the beginning of annual, semiannual, quarterly, monthly, or weekly periods for one or two lives, the value of the annuity is the sum of the first payment plus the present value of a similar annuity, the first payment of which is not to be made until the end of the payment period, determined as provided in paragraph (e)(2)(ii)(A) of this section. If the first payment of an annuity for a definite number of years is due at the beginning of the payment period, the value of the annuity is computed by multiplying the aggregate amount payable annually by the annuity factor derived from the appropriate Table B, as described in paragraph (e)(2)(ii)(A) of this section, opposite the number of years representing the duration of the annuity. The product so obtained is then multiplied by the adjustment factor in Table J at the appropriate interest rate component for payments made at the beginning of specified periods.

(iii) *Life estates, terms for years, remainders, and reversions.* If the interest to be valued is the right of a person to receive the income of certain property, or to use certain property for the life of one or two individuals, or for a term for years, the present value of the interest is

computed by multiplying the value of the property by the applicable factor representing the income interest. The applicable factor is obtained by subtracting the appropriate remainder factor in Table S (for the life of one individual), Table R(2) (for the lives of two individuals), or Table B (for a term of years), whichever is appropriate, from 1.00. If the interest to be valued is to take effect after the death of one or two individuals, or after a definite number of years, the present value of the interest is computed by multiplying the value of the property by the applicable actuarial factor in Table S, Table R(2), or Table B, whichever is appropriate, corresponding to the applicable Federal mid-term rate (rounded) opposite either the number of years nearest the age of the individual or individuals whose lives measure the interest or the number of years representing the duration of the interest. See § 20.7520-1(c) with respect to the valuation of a qualified annuity interest described in section 2702(b)(1) and a qualified unitrust interest described in section 2702(b)(2).

(iv) *Other Interests.* See § 20.7520-1(c) with respect to the valuation of a qualified annuity interest described in section 2702(b)(1) and a qualified unitrust interest described in section 2702(b)(2). See § 20.2031-7A(d) with respect to the valuation of annuities, life estates, terms for years, remainders, and reversions includible in estates of decedents who died after November 30, 1983, where the valuation date for the gross estate falls before May 1, 1989. See § 20.2031-7A(c) with respect to the valuation of annuities, life estates, terms for years, remainders, and reversions includible in estates of decedents who died after December 31, 1970, and before December 1, 1983. See § 20.2031-7A(b) with respect to the valuation of annuities, life estates, terms for years, remainders, and reversions includible in estates of decedents who died after December 31, 1951, and before January 1, 1971. See § 20.2031-7A(a) with respect to the valuation of annuities, life estates, terms for years, remainders, and reversions includible in estates of decedents who died before January 1, 1952.

(3) *Transitional rule.* If a decedent died after April 30, 1989, and if on May 1, 1989, the decedent was mentally incompetent so that the disposition of the decedent's property could not be changed, and the decedent died without having regained competency to dispose of the decedent's property or died within 90 days of the date on which the decedent first regained competency, the fair market value of annuities, life estates, terms for years, remainders, and reversions included in the estate of the decedent is their present value determined either under this section or under the corresponding section applicable at the time the decedent became mentally incompetent, at the option of the decedent's executor. For example, see § 20.2031-7A(d).

(4) *Publications.* Many actuarial factors not contained in paragraph (e)(6) of this section are contained in Internal Revenue Service Publication 1457, "Actuarial Values, Alpha Volume," (8-89). A copy of this publication may be purchased from the Superintendent of Documents, United States Government Printing Office, Washington, D.C. 20402. If a special factor is required in the case of an actual decedent, the Service will furnish the factor to the executor upon a request for a ruling. The request for a ruling must be accompanied by a recitation of the facts including a statement of the date of birth for each measuring life, the date of the decedent's death, any other applicable dates, and a copy of the will, trust, or other relevant documents. A request for a ruling must comply with the instructions for requesting a ruling published periodically in the Internal Revenue Bulletin (see § 601.601(d)(2)(ii)(b) of this chapter) and include payment of the required user fee.

(5) *Examples.* The provisions of this section are illustrated by the following examples:

Example 1. Annuity payable for an individual's life. Under the terms of A's father's will an annuity of $10,000 a year payable in equal semiannual installments made at the end of each interval to A and, after A's death, to A's estate for the life of B, A's brother. A died in September 1989. For September 1989, the rate that was 120 percent of the applicable Federal mid-term rate was 9.68. This rate is rounded to 9.6 percent. At A's death, B was 45 years seven months old. Under Table S in paragraph (e)(6) of this section, the factor at 9.6 percent for determining the present value of the remainder interest at the death of a person age 46, the number of years nearest B's actual age, is .11013. By converting the factor to an annuity factor, as described in paragraph (e)(2)(ii) of this section, the factor for the present value of an annuity payable until the death of a person age 46 is 9.2695 (1.00 minus .11013, divided by .096). The adjustment factor from Table K in paragraph (e)(6) at an interest rate of 9.6 percent for semiannual annuity payments made at the end of the period is 1.0235. The present value of the annuity at the date of A's death is, therefore, $94,873 ($10,000 × 9.2695 × 1.0235).

Example 2. Annuity payable for a term of years. The decedent, or decedent's estate, was entitled to receive an annuity of $10,000 a year payable in equal quarterly installments at the end of each quarter throughout a term certain. The decedent died in February 1990. For February 1990, the rate that was 120 percent of the applicable Federal mid-term rate was 9.70. This rate is rounded to 9.8. A quarterly payment had just been made prior to the decedent's death and payments were to continue for 5 more years. Under Table B in paragraph (e)(6) of this section for the interest rate of 9.8 percent, the factor for the present value of a remainder interest due after a term of 5 years is .626597. Converting the factor to an annuity factor, as described in paragraph (e)(2)(ii) of this section, the factor for the present value of an annuity for a term of 5 years is 3.8102. The adjustment factor from Table K in paragraph (e)(6) at an interest rate of 9.8 percent for quarterly annuity payments made at the end of the period is 1.0360. The present value of the annuity is, therefore, $39,474 ($10,000 × 3.8102 × 1.0360).

Example 3. Income payable for an individual's life. The decedent or the decedent's estate was entitled to receive the income from a fund of $50,000 during the life of the decedent's elder brother. Upon the brother's death, the remainder is to pass to B. The brother was 31 years old at the time of the decedent's death in October 1989. The rate that was 120 percent of the applicable Federal mid-term rate in October 1989 was 10.10 percent. That rate is rounded to 10.2 percent. Under Table S in paragraph (e)(6) of this section, the remainder factor at 10.2 percent for determining the present value of the remainder interest due

at the death of a person aged 31, the number of years closest to the brother's age at the decedent's death, is .03753. Converting this remainder factor to an income factor, as described in paragraph (e)(2)(iii) of this section, the factor for determining the present value of an income interest for the life of a person aged 31 is .96247. The present value of the decedent's interest at the time of the decedent's death is, therefore, $48,124 ($50,000 × .96247).

Example 4. Remainder payable at an individual's death. The decedent, or the decedent's estate, was entitled to receive certain property worth $50,000 upon the death of the decedent's elder sister, to whom the income was bequeathed for life. The decedent died in February 1990. At the time of the decedent's death, the elder sister was 47 years 5 months old. In February 1990, the rate that was 120 percent of the applicable Federal mid-term rate was 9.70. This rate is rounded to 9.8 percent. Under Table S in paragraph (e)(6) of this section, the remainder factor at 9.8 percent for determining the present value of the remainder interest due at the death of a person aged 47, the number of years nearest the elder sister's actual age at the decedent's death, is .11352. The present value of the remainder interest at the date of the decedent's death is, therefore, $5,676 ($50,000 × .11352).

(6) *Tables.* The following tables must be used in the application of the provisions of this section when the interest rate component, as described in §20.7520-1(b)(1), is between 4.2 and 14 percent.

TABLE B
TERM CERTAIN REMAINDER FACTORS
APPLICABLE AFTER APRIL 30, 1989
INTEREST RATE

Years	4.2%	4.4%	4.6%	4.8%	5.0%	5.2%	5.4%	5.6%	5.8%	6.0%
1	.959693	.957854	.956023	.954198	.952381	.950570	.948767	.946970	.945180	.943396
2	.921010	.917485	.913980	.910495	.907029	.903584	.900158	.896752	.893364	.889996
3	.883887	.878817	.873786	.868793	.863838	.858920	.854040	.849197	.844390	.839619
4	.848260	.841779	.835359	.829001	.822702	.816464	.810285	.804163	.798100	.792094
5	.814069	.806302	.798623	.791031	.783526	.776106	.768771	.761518	.754348	.747258
6	.781257	.772320	.763501	.754801	.746215	.737744	.729384	.721135	.712994	.704961
7	.749766	.739770	.729925	.720230	.710681	.701277	.692015	.682893	.673908	.665057
8	.719545	.708592	.697825	.687242	.676839	.666613	.656561	.646679	.636964	.627412
9	.690543	.678728	.667137	.655765	.644609	.633663	.622923	.612385	.602045	.591898
10	.662709	.650122	.637798	.625730	.613913	.602341	.591009	.579910	.569041	.558395
11	.635997	.622722	.609750	.597071	.584679	.572568	.560729	.549157	.537846	.526788
12	.610362	.596477	.582935	.569724	.556837	.544266	.532001	.520035	.508361	.496969
13	.585760	.571339	.557299	.543630	.530321	.517363	.504745	.492458	.480492	.468839
14	.562150	.547259	.532790	.518731	.505068	.491790	.478885	.466343	.454151	.442301
15	.539491	.524195	.509360	.494972	.481017	.467481	.454350	.441612	.429255	.417265
16	.517746	.502102	.486960	.472302	.458112	.444374	.431072	.418194	.405723	.393646
17	.496877	.480941	.465545	.450670	.436297	.422408	.408987	.396017	.383481	.371364
18	.476849	.460671	.445071	.430028	.415521	.401529	.388033	.375016	.362458	.350344
19	.457629	.441256	.425498	.410332	.395734	.381681	.368153	.355129	.342588	.330513
20	.439183	.422659	.406786	.391538	.376889	.362815	.349291	.336296	.323807	.311805
21	.421481	.404846	.388897	.373605	.358942	.344881	.331396	.318462	.306056	.294155
22	.404492	.387783	.371794	.356494	.341850	.327834	.314417	.301574	.289278	.277505
23	.388188	.371440	.355444	.340166	.325571	.311629	.298309	.285581	.273420	.261797
24	.372542	.355785	.339813	.324586	.310068	.296225	.283025	.270437	.258431	.246979
25	.357526	.340791	.324869	.309719	.295303	.281583	.268525	.256096	.244263	.232999
26	.343115	.326428	.310582	.295533	.281241	.267664	.254768	.242515	.230873	.219810
27	.329285	.312670	.296923	.281998	.267848	.254434	.241715	.229654	.218216	.207368
28	.316012	.299493	.283866	.269082	.255094	.241857	.229331	.217475	.206253	.195630
29	.303275	.286870	.271382	.256757	.242946	.229902	.217582	.205943	.194947	.184557
30	.291051	.274780	.259447	.244997	.231377	.218538	.206434	.195021	.184260	.174110
31	.279319	.263199	.248038	.233776	.220359	.207736	.195858	.184679	.174158	.164255
32	.268061	.252106	.237130	.223069	.209866	.197468	.185823	.174886	.164611	.154957
33	.257256	.241481	.226702	.212852	.199873	.187707	.176303	.165612	.155587	.146186
34	.246887	.231304	.216732	.203103	.190355	.178429	.167270	.156829	.147058	.137912
35	.236935	.221556	.207201	.193801	.181290	.169609	.158701	.148512	.138996	.130105
36	.227385	.212218	.198089	.184924	.172657	.161225	.150570	.140637	.131376	.122741
37	.218220	.203274	.189377	.176454	.164436	.153256	.142856	.133179	.124174	.115793
38	.209424	.194707	.181049	.168373	.156605	.145681	.135537	.126116	.117367	.109239
39	.200983	.186501	.173087	.160661	.149148	.138480	.128593	.119428	.110933	.103056
40	.192882	.178641	.165475	.153302	.142046	.131635	.122004	.113095	.104851	.097222

Years	4.2%	4.4%	4.6%	4.8%	5.0%	5.2%	5.4%	5.6%	5.8%	6.0%
41	.185107	.171112	.158198	.146281	.135282	.125128	.115754	.107098	.099103	.091719
42	.177646	.163900	.151241	.139581	.128840	.118943	.109823	.101418	.093670	.086527
43	.170486	.156992	.144590	.133188	.122704	.113064	.104197	.096040	.088535	.081630
44	.163614	.150376	.138231	.127088	.116861	.107475	.098858	.090947	.083682	.077009
45	.157019	.144038	.132152	.121267	.111297	.102163	.093793	.086124	.079094	.072650
46	.150690	.137968	.126340	.115713	.105997	.097113	.088988	.081557	.074758	.068538
47	.144616	.132153	.120784	.110413	.100949	.092312	.084429	.077232	.070660	.064658
48	.138787	.126583	.115473	.105356	.096142	.087749	.080103	.073136	.066786	.060998
49	.133193	.121248	.110395	.100530	.091564	.083412	.075999	.069258	.063125	.057546
50	.127824	.116138	.105540	.095926	.087204	.079289	.072106	.065585	.059665	.054288
51	.122672	.111243	.100898	.091532	.083051	.075370	.068411	.062107	.056394	.051215
52	.117728	.106555	.096461	.087340	.079096	.071644	.064907	.058813	.053302	.048316
53	.112982	.102064	.092219	.083340	.075330	.068103	.061581	.055695	.050380	.045582
54	.108428	.097763	.088164	.079523	.071743	.064737	.058426	.052741	.047618	.043001
55	.104058	.093642	.084286	.075880	.068326	.061537	.055433	.049944	.045008	.040567
56	.099864	.089696	.080580	.072405	.065073	.058495	.052593	.047296	.042541	.038271
57	.095839	.085916	.077036	.069089	.061974	.055604	.049898	.044787	.040208	.036105
58	.091976	.082295	.073648	.065924	.059023	.052855	.047342	.042412	.038004	.034061
59	.088268	.078826	.070409	.062905	.056212	.050243	.044916	.040163	.035921	.032133
60	.084710	.075504	.067313	.060024	.053536	.047759	.042615	.038033	.033952	.030314

TABLE B
TERM CERTAIN REMAINDER FACTORS
APPLICABLE AFTER APRIL 30, 1989
INTEREST RATE

Years	6.2%	6.4%	6.6%	6.8%	7.0%	7.2%	7.4%	7.6%	7.8%	8.0%
1	.941620	.939850	.938086	.936330	.934579	.932836	.931099	.929368	.927644	.925926
2	.886647	.883317	.880006	.876713	.873439	.870183	.866945	.863725	.860523	.857339
3	.834885	.830185	.825521	.820892	.816298	.811738	.807211	.802718	.798259	.793832
4	.786144	.780249	.774410	.768626	.762895	.757218	.751593	.746021	.740500	.735030
5	.740248	.733317	.726464	.719687	.712986	.706360	.699808	.693328	.686920	.680583
6	.697032	.689208	.681486	.673864	.666342	.658918	.651590	.644357	.637217	.630170
7	.656339	.647752	.639292	.630959	.622750	.614662	.606694	.598845	.591111	.583490
8	.618022	.608789	.599711	.590786	.582009	.573379	.564892	.556547	.548340	.540269
9	.581942	.572170	.562581	.553170	.543934	.534868	.525971	.517237	.508664	.500249
10	.547968	.537754	.527750	.517950	.508349	.498944	.489731	.480704	.471859	.463193
11	.515977	.505408	.495075	.484972	.475093	.465433	.455987	.446750	.437717	.428883
12	.485854	.475007	.464423	.454093	.444012	.434173	.424569	.415196	.406046	.397114
13	.457490	.446436	.435669	.425181	.414964	.405012	.395316	.385870	.376666	.367698
14	.430781	.419582	.408695	.398109	.387817	.377810	.368078	.358615	.349412	.340461
15	.405632	.394344	.383391	.372762	.362446	.352434	.342717	.333285	.324130	.315242
16	.381951	.370624	.359654	.349028	.338735	.328763	.319103	.309745	.300677	.291890
17	.359653	.348331	.337386	.326805	.316574	.306682	.297117	.287867	.278921	.270269
18	.338656	.327379	.316498	.305997	.295864	.286084	.276645	.267534	.258739	.250249
19	.318885	.307687	.296902	.286514	.276508	.266870	.257584	.248638	.240018	.231712
20	.300268	.289179	.278520	.268272	.258419	.248946	.239836	.231076	.222651	.214548
21	.282739	.271785	.261276	.251191	.241513	.232225	.223311	.214755	.206541	.198656
22	.266232	.255437	.245099	.235197	.225713	.216628	.207925	.199586	.191596	.183941
23	.250689	.240073	.229924	.220222	.210947	.202078	.193598	.185489	.177733	.170315
24	.236054	.225632	.215689	.206201	.197147	.188506	.180259	.172387	.164873	.157699
25	.222273	.212060	.202334	.193072	.184249	.175845	.167839	.160211	.152943	.146018
26	.209297	.199305	.189807	.180779	.172195	.164035	.156275	.148895	.141877	.135202
27	.197078	.187317	.178056	.169269	.160930	.153017	.145507	.138379	.131611	.125187
28	.185572	.176049	.167031	.158491	.150402	.142740	.135482	.128605	.122088	.115914
29	.174739	.165460	.156690	.148400	.140563	.133153	.126147	.119521	.113255	.107328
30	.164537	.155507	.146989	.138951	.131367	.124210	.117455	.111079	.105060	.099377
31	.154932	.146154	.137888	.130104	.122773	.115868	.109362	.103233	.097458	.092016
32	.145887	.137362	.129351	.121820	.114741	.108085	.101827	.095942	.090406	.085200
33	.137370	.129100	.121342	.114064	.107235	.100826	.094811	.089165	.083865	.078889
34	.129350	.121335	.113830	.106802	.100219	.094054	.088278	.082867	.077797	.073045
35	.121798	.114036	.106782	.100001	.093663	.087737	.082196	.077014	.072168	.067635
36	.114688	.107177	.100171	.093634	.087535	.081844	.076532	.071574	.066946	.062625
37	.107992	.100730	.093969	.087673	.081809	.076347	.071259	.066519	.062102	.057986

Years	6.2%	6.4%	6.6%	6.8%	7.0%	7.2%	7.4%	7.6%	7.8%	8.0%
38	.101688	.094671	.088151	.082090	.076457	.071219	.066349	.061821	.057609	.053690
39	.095751	.088977	.082693	.076864	.071455	.066436	.061778	.057454	.053440	.049713
40	.090161	.083625	.077573	.071970	.066780	.061974	.057521	.053396	.049573	.046031
41	.084897	.078595	.072770	.067387	.062412	.057811	.053558	.049625	.045987	.042621
42	.079941	.073867	.068265	.063097	.058329	.053929	.049868	.046120	.042659	.039464
43	.075274	.069424	.064038	.059079	.054513	.050307	.046432	.042862	.039572	.036541
44	.070880	.065248	.060074	.055318	.050946	.046928	.043233	.039835	.036709	.033834
45	.066742	.061323	.056354	.051796	.047613	.043776	.040254	.037021	.034053	.031328
46	.062845	.057635	.052865	.048498	.044499	.040836	.037480	.034406	.031589	.029007
47	.059176	.054168	.049592	.045410	.041587	.038093	.034898	.031976	.029303	.026859
48	.055722	.050910	.046522	.042519	.038867	.035535	.032493	.029717	.027183	.024869
49	.052469	.047848	.043641	.039812	.036324	.033148	.030255	.027618	.025216	.023027
50	.049405	.044970	.040939	.037277	.033948	.030922	.028170	.025668	.023392	.021321
51	.046521	.042265	.038405	.034903	.031727	.028845	.026229	.023855	.021699	.019742
52	.043805	.039722	.036027	.032681	.029651	.026907	.024422	.022170	.020129	.018280
53	.041248	.037333	.033796	.030600	.027711	.025100	.022739	.020604	.018673	.016925
54	.038840	.035087	.031704	.028652	.025899	.023414	.021172	.019149	.017322	.015672
55	.036572	.032977	.029741	.026828	.024204	.021842	.019714	.017796	.016068	.014511
56	.034437	.030993	.027900	.025119	.022621	.020375	.018355	.016539	.014906	.013436
57	.032427	.029129	.026172	.023520	.021141	.019006	.017091	.015371	.013827	.012441
58	.030534	.027377	.024552	.022023	.019758	.017730	.015913	.014285	.012827	.011519
59	.028751	.025730	.023032	.020620	.018465	.016539	.014817	.013276	.011899	.010666
60	.027073	.024183	.021606	.019307	.017257	.015428	.013796	.012339	.011038	.009876

TABLE B
TERM CERTAIN REMAINDER FACTORS
APPLICABLE AFTER APRIL 30, 1989
INTEREST RATE

Years	8.2%	8.4%	8.6%	8.8%	9.0%	9.2%	9.4%	9.6%	9.8%	10.0%
1	.924214	.922509	.920810	.919118	.917431	.915751	.914077	.912409	.910747	.909091
2	.854172	.851023	.847892	.844777	.841680	.838600	.835536	.832490	.829460	.826446
3	.789438	.785077	.780747	.776450	.772183	.767948	.763744	.759571	.755428	.751315
4	.729610	.724241	.718920	.713649	.708425	.703250	.698121	.693039	.688003	.683013
5	.674316	.668119	.661989	.655927	.649931	.644001	.638136	.632335	.626597	.620921
6	.623213	.616346	.609566	.602874	.596267	.589745	.583305	.576948	.570671	.564474
7	.575982	.568585	.561295	.554112	.547034	.540059	.533186	.526412	.519737	.513158
8	.532331	.524524	.516846	.509294	.501866	.494560	.487373	.480303	.473349	.466507
9	.491988	.483879	.475917	.468101	.460428	.452894	.445496	.438233	.431101	.424098
10	.454703	.446383	.438230	.430240	.422411	.414738	.407218	.399848	.392624	.385543
11	.420243	.411792	.403526	.395441	.387533	.379797	.372228	.364824	.357581	.350494
12	.388394	.379882	.371571	.363457	.355535	.347799	.340245	.332869	.325666	.318631
13	.358960	.350445	.342147	.334060	.326179	.318497	.311010	.303713	.296599	.289664
14	.331756	.323288	.315052	.307040	.299246	.291664	.284287	.277110	.270127	.263331
15	.306613	.298236	.290103	.282206	.274538	.267092	.259860	.252838	.246017	.239392
16	.283376	.275126	.267130	.259381	.251870	.244589	.237532	.230691	.224059	.217629
17	.261901	.253806	.245976	.238401	.231073	.223983	.217123	.210485	.204061	.197845
18	.242052	.234139	.226497	.219119	.211994	.205113	.198467	.192048	.185848	.179859
19	.223708	.215995	.208561	.201396	.194490	.187832	.181414	.175226	.169260	.163508
20	.206754	.199257	.192045	.185107	.178431	.172007	.165826	.159878	.154153	.148644
21	.191085	.183817	.176837	.170135	.163698	.157516	.151578	.145874	.140395	.135131
22	.176604	.169573	.162834	.156374	.150182	.144245	.138554	.133097	.127864	.122846
23	.163220	.156432	.149939	.143726	.137781	.132093	.126649	.121439	.116452	.111678
24	.150850	.144310	.138065	.132101	.126405	.120964	.115767	.110802	.106058	.101526
25	.139418	.133128	.127132	.121416	.115968	.110773	.105820	.101097	.096592	.092296
26	.128852	.122811	.117064	.111596	.106393	.101441	.096727	.092241	.087971	.083905
27	.119087	.113295	.107794	.102570	.097608	.092894	.088416	.084162	.080119	.076278
28	.110062	.104515	.099258	.094274	.089548	.085068	.080819	.076790	.072968	.069343
29	.101721	.096416	.091398	.086649	.082155	.077901	.073875	.070064	.066456	.063039
30	.094012	.088945	.084160	.079640	.075371	.071338	.067527	.063927	.060524	.057309
31	.086887	.082053	.077495	.073199	.069148	.065328	.061725	.058327	.055122	.052099
32	.080302	.075694	.071358	.067278	.063438	.059824	.056422	.053218	.050202	.047362
33	.074216	.069829	.065708	.061837	.058200	.054784	.051574	.048557	.045722	.043057
34	.068592	.064418	.060504	.056835	.053395	.050168	.047142	.044304	.041641	.039143
35	.063394	.059426	.055713	.052238	.048986	.045942	.043092	.040423	.037924	.035584

Proposed Regulations

Years	8.2%	8.4%	8.6%	8.8%	9.0%	9.2%	9.4%	9.6%	9.8%	10.0%
36	.058589	.054821	.051301	.048013	.044941	.042071	.039389	.036882	.034539	.032349
37	.054149	.050573	.047239	.044130	.041231	.038527	.036005	.033652	.031457	.029408
38	.050045	.046654	.043498	.040560	.037826	.035281	.032911	.030704	.028649	.026735
39	.046253	.043039	.040053	.037280	.034703	.032309	.030083	.028015	.026092	.024304
40	.042747	.039703	.036881	.034264	.031838	.029587	.027498	.025561	.023763	.022095
41	.039508	.036627	.033961	.031493	.029209	.027094	.025136	.023322	.021642	.020086
42	.036514	.033789	.031271	.028946	.026797	.024811	.022976	.021279	.019711	.018260
43	.033746	.031170	.028795	.026605	.024584	.022721	.021002	.019415	.017951	.016600
44	.031189	.028755	.026515	.024453	.022555	.020807	.019197	.017715	.016349	.015091
45	.028825	.026527	.024415	.022475	.020692	.019054	.017548	.016163	.014890	.013719
46	.026641	.024471	.022482	.020657	.018984	.017449	.016040	.014747	.013561	.012472
47	.024622	.022575	.020701	.018986	.017416	.015978	.014662	.013456	.012351	.011338
48	.022756	.020825	.019062	.017451	.015978	.014632	.013402	.012277	.011248	.010307
49	.021031	.019212	.017552	.016039	.014659	.013400	.012250	.011202	.010244	.009370
50	.019437	.017723	.016163	.014742	.013449	.012271	.011198	.010221	.009330	.008519
51	.017964	.016350	.014883	.013550	.012338	.011237	.010236	.009325	.008497	.007744
52	.016603	.015083	.013704	.012454	.011319	.010290	.009356	.008508	.007739	.007040
53	.015345	.013914	.012619	.011446	.010385	.009423	.008552	.007763	.007048	.006400
54	.014182	.012836	.011620	.010521	.009527	.008629	.007817	.007083	.006419	.005818
55	.013107	.011841	.010699	.009670	.008741	.007902	.007146	.006463	.005846	.005289
56	.012114	.010923	.009852	.008888	.008019	.007237	.006532	.005897	.005324	.004809
57	.011196	.010077	.009072	.008169	.007357	.006627	.005971	.005380	.004849	.004371
58	.010347	.009296	.008354	.007508	.006749	.006069	.005458	.004909	.004416	.003974
59	.009563	.008576	.007692	.006901	.006192	.005557	.004989	.004479	.004022	.003613
60	.008838	.007911	.007083	.006343	.005681	.005089	.004560	.004087	.003663	.003284

TABLE B
TERM CERTAIN REMAINDER FACTORS
APPLICABLE AFTER APRIL 30, 1989
INTEREST RATE

Years	10.2%	10.4%	10.6%	10.8%	11.0%	11.2%	11.4%	11.6%	11.8%	12.0%
1	.907441	.905797	.904159	.902527	.900901	.899281	.897666	.896057	.894454	.892857
2	.823449	.820468	.817504	.814555	.811622	.808706	.805804	.802919	.800049	.797194
3	.747232	.743178	.739153	.735158	.731191	.727253	.723343	.719461	.715607	.711780
4	.678069	.673168	.668312	.663500	.658731	.654005	.649321	.644679	.640078	.635518
5	.615307	.609754	.604261	.598827	.593451	.588134	.582873	.577669	.572520	.567427
6	.558355	.552313	.546348	.540457	.534641	.528897	.523225	.517625	.512093	.506631
7	.506674	.500284	.493985	.487777	.481658	.475627	.469682	.463821	.458044	.452349
8	.459777	.453156	.446641	.440232	.433926	.427722	.421617	.415610	.409700	.403883
9	.417221	.410467	.403835	.397322	.390925	.384642	.378472	.372411	.366458	.360610
10	.378603	.371800	.365131	.358593	.352184	.345901	.339741	.333701	.327780	.321973
11	.343560	.336775	.330137	.323640	.317283	.311062	.304974	.299016	.293184	.287476
12	.311760	.305050	.298496	.292094	.285841	.279732	.273765	.267935	.262240	.256675
13	.282904	.276313	.269888	.263623	.257514	.251558	.245749	.240085	.234561	.229174
14	.256719	.250284	.244022	.237927	.231995	.226221	.220601	.215130	.209804	.204620
15	.232957	.226706	.220634	.214735	.209004	.203436	.198026	.192769	.187661	.182696
16	.211395	.205350	.199489	.193804	.188292	.182946	.177761	.172732	.167854	.163122
17	.191828	.186005	.180369	.174914	.169633	.164520	.159570	.154778	.150138	.145644
18	.174073	.168483	.163083	.157864	.152822	.147950	.143241	.138690	.134291	.130040
19	.157961	.152612	.147453	.142477	.137678	.133048	.128582	.124274	.120117	.116107
20	.143340	.138235	.133321	.128589	.124034	.119648	.115424	.111357	.107439	.103667
21	.130073	.125213	.120543	.116055	.111742	.107597	.103612	.099782	.096100	.092560
22	.118033	.113418	.108990	.104743	.100669	.096760	.093009	.089410	.085957	.082643
23	.107108	.102733	.098544	.094533	.090693	.087014	.083491	.080117	.076884	.073788
24	.097195	.093056	.089100	.085319	.081705	.078250	.074947	.071789	.068770	.065882
25	.088198	.084289	.080560	.077003	.073608	.070369	.067278	.064327	.061511	.058823
26	.080035	.076349	.072839	.069497	.066314	.063281	.060393	.057641	.055019	.052521
27	.072627	.069157	.065858	.062723	.059742	.056908	.054213	.051650	.049212	.046894
28	.065905	.062642	.059547	.056609	.053822	.051176	.048665	.046281	.044018	.041869
29	.059804	.056741	.053840	.051091	.048488	.046022	.043685	.041470	.039372	.037383
30	.054269	.051396	.048680	.046111	.043683	.041386	.039214	.037160	.035216	.033378
31	.049246	.046554	.044014	.041617	.039354	.037218	.035201	.033297	.031500	.029802
32	.044688	.042169	.039796	.037560	.035454	.033469	.031599	.029836	.028175	.026609

Years	10.2%	10.4%	10.6%	10.8%	11.0%	11.2%	11.4%	11.6%	11.8%	12.0%
33	.040552	.038196	.035982	.033899	.031940	.030098	.028365	.026735	.025201	.023758
34	.036798	.034598	.032533	.030595	.028775	.027067	.025463	.023956	.022541	.021212
35	.033392	.031339	.029415	.027613	.025924	.024341	.022857	.021466	.020162	.018940
36	.030301	.028387	.026596	.024921	.023355	.021889	.020518	.019235	.018034	.016910
37	.027497	.025712	.024047	.022492	.021040	.019684	.018418	.017236	.016131	.015098
38	.024952	.023290	.021742	.020300	.018955	.017702	.016533	.015444	.014428	.013481
39	.022642	.021096	.019658	.018321	.017077	.015919	.014841	.013839	.012905	.012036
40	.020546	.019109	.017774	.016535	.015384	.014316	.013323	.012400	.011543	.010747
41	.018645	.017309	.016071	.014923	.013860	.012874	.011959	.011111	.010325	.009595
42	.016919	.015678	.014531	.013469	.012486	.011577	.010735	.009956	.009235	.008567
43	015353	.014201	.013138	.012156	.011249	.010411	.009637	.008922	.008260	.007649
44	.013932	.012864	.011879	.010971	.010134	.009362	.008651	.007994	.007389	.006830
45	.012642	.011652	.010740	.009902	.009130	.008419	.007765	.007163	.006609	.006098
46	.011472	.010554	.009711	.008937	.008225	.007571	.006971	.006419	.005911	.005445
47	.010410	.009560	.008780	.008065	.007410	.006809	.006257	.005752	.005287	.004861
48	.009447	.008659	.007939	.007279	.006676	.006123	.005617	.005154	.004729	.004340
49	.008572	.007844	.007178	.006570	.006014	.005506	.005042	.004618	.004230	.003875
50	.007779	.007105	.006490	.005929	.005418	.004952	.004526	.004138	.003784	.003460
51	.007059	.006435	.005868	.005351	.004881	.004453	.004063	.003708	.003384	.003089
52	.006406	.005829	.005306	.004830	.004397	.004005	.003647	.003322	.003027	.002758
53	.005813	.005280	.004797	.004359	.003962	.003601	.003274	.002977	.002708	.002463
54	.005275	.004783	.004337	.003934	.003569	.003238	.002939	.002668	.002422	.002199
55	.004786	.004332	.003922	.003551	.003215	.002912	.002638	.002390	.002166	.001963
56	.004343	.003924	.003546	.003205	.002897	.002619	.002368	.002142	.001938	.001753
57	.003941	.003554	.003206	.002892	.002610	.002355	.002126	.001919	.001733	.001565
58	.003577	.003220	.002899	.002610	.002351	.002118	.001908	.001720	.001550	.001398
59	.003246	.002916	.002621	.002356	.002118	.001905	.001713	.001541	.001387	.001248
60	.002945	.002642	.002370	.002126	.001908	.001713	.001538	.001381	.001240	.001114

TABLE B
TERM CERTAIN REMAINDER FACTORS
APPLICABLE AFTER APRIL 30, 1989
INTEREST RATE

Years	12.2%	12.4%	12.6%	12.8%	13.0%	13.2%	13.4%	13.6%	13.8%	14.0%
1	.891266	.889680	.888099	.886525	.884956	.883392	.881834	.880282	.878735	.877193
2	.794354	.791530	.788721	.785926	.783147	.780382	.777632	.774896	.772175	.769468
3	.707981	.704208	.700462	.696743	.693050	.689383	.685742	.682127	.678536	.674972
4	.630999	.626520	.622080	.617680	.613319	.608996	.604711	.600464	.596254	.592080
5	.562388	.557402	.552469	.547589	.542760	.537982	.533255	.528577	.523949	.519369
6	.501237	.495909	.490648	.485451	.480319	.475249	.470242	.465297	.460412	.455587
7	.446735	.441200	.435744	.430364	.425061	.419831	.414676	.409592	.404580	.399637
8	.398160	.392527	.386984	.381529	.376160	.370876	.365675	.360557	.355518	.350559
9	.354866	.349223	.343680	.338235	.332885	.327629	.322465	.317391	.312406	.307508
10	.316280	.310697	.305222	.299853	.294588	.289425	.284361	.279394	.274522	.269744
11	.281889	.276421	.271068	.265827	.260698	.255676	.250759	.245945	.241232	.236617
12	.251238	.245926	.240735	.235663	.230706	.225862	.221128	.216501	.211979	.207559
13	.223920	.218795	.213797	.208921	.204165	.199525	.194998	.190582	.186273	.182069
14	.199572	.194658	.189873	.185213	.180677	.176258	.171956	.167766	.163685	.159710
15	.177872	.173183	.168626	.164196	.159891	.155705	.151637	.147681	.143835	.140096
16	.158531	.154077	.149757	.145564	.141496	.137549	.133718	.130001	.126393	.122892
17	.141293	.137080	.132999	.129046	.125218	.121510	.117917	.114438	.111066	.107800
18	.125930	.121957	.118116	.114403	.110812	.107341	.103984	.100737	.097598	.094561
19	.112237	.108503	.104899	.101421	.098064	.094824	.091696	.088677	.085762	.082948
20	.100033	.096533	.093161	.089912	.086782	.083767	.080861	.078061	.075362	.072762
21	.089156	.085883	.082736	.079709	.076798	.073999	.071306	.068716	.066224	.063826
22	.079462	.076408	.073478	.070664	.067963	.065370	.062880	.060489	.058193	.055988
23	.070821	.067979	.065255	.062646	.060144	.057747	.055450	.053247	.051136	.049112
24	.063121	.060480	.057953	.055537	.053225	.051014	.048898	.046873	.044935	.043081
25	.056257	.053807	.051468	.049235	.047102	.045065	.043119	.041261	.039486	.037790
26	.050140	.047871	.045709	.043648	.041683	.039810	.038024	.036321	.034698	.033149
27	.044688	.042590	.040594	.038695	.036888	.035168	.033531	.031973	.030490	.029078
28	.039829	.037892	.036052	.034304	.032644	.031067	.029569	.028145	.026793	.025507
29	.035498	.033711	.032017	.030411	.028889	.027444	.026075	.024776	.023544	.022375
30	.031638	.029992	.028435	.026960	.025565	.024244	.022994	.021810	.020689	.019627

Years	12.2%	12.4%	12.6%	12.8%	13.0%	13.2%	13.4%	13.6%	13.8%	14.0%
31	.028198	.026684	.025253	.023901	.022624	.021417	.020277	.019199	.018180	.017217
32	.025132	.023740	.022427	.021189	.020021	.018920	.017881	.016900	.015975	.015102
33	.022399	.021121	.019917	.018785	.017718	.016714	.015768	.014877	.014038	.013248
34	.019964	.018791	.017689	.016653	.015680	.014765	.013905	.013096	.012336	.011621
35	.017793	.016718	.015709	.014763	.013876	.013043	.012261	.011528	.010840	.010194
36	.015858	.014873	.013951	.013088	.012279	.011522	.010813	.010148	.009525	.008942
37	.014134	.013233	.012390	.011603	.010867	.010178	.009535	.008933	.008370	.007844
38	.012597	.011773	.011004	.010286	.009617	.008992	.008408	.007864	.007355	.006880
39	.011227	.010474	.009772	.009119	.008510	.007943	.007415	.006922	.006463	.006035
40	.010007	.009319	.008679	.008084	.007531	.007017	.006538	.006093	.005679	.005294
41	.008919	.008291	.007708	.007167	.006665	.006199	.005766	.005364	.004991	.004644
42	.007949	.007376	.006845	.006354	.005898	.005476	.005085	.004722	.004386	.004074
43	.007084	.006562	.006079	.005633	.005219	.004837	.004484	.004157	.003854	.003573
44	.006314	.005838	.005399	.004993	.004619	.004273	.003954	.003659	.003386	.003135
45	.005628	.005194	.004795	.004427	.004088	.003775	.003487	.003221	.002976	.002750
46	.005016	.004621	.004258	.003924	.003617	.003335	.003075	.002835	.002615	.002412
47	.004470	.004111	.003782	.003479	.003201	.002946	.002711	.002496	.002298	.002116
48	.003984	.003658	.003359	.003084	.002833	.002602	.002391	.002197	.002019	.001856
49	.003551	.003254	.002983	.002734	.002507	.002299	.002108	.001934	.001774	.001628
50	.003165	.002895	.002649	.002424	.002219	.002031	.001859	.001702	.001559	.001428
51	.002821	.002576	.002353	.002149	.001963	.001794	.001640	.001499	.001370	.001253
52	.002514	.002292	.002089	.001905	.001737	.001585	.001446	.001319	.001204	.001099
53	.002241	.002039	.001856	.001689	.001538	.001400	.001275	.001161	.001058	.000964
54	.001997	.001814	.001648	.001497	.001361	.001237	.001124	.001022	.000930	.000846
55	.001780	.001614	.001463	.001327	.001204	.001093	.000991	.000900	.000817	.000742
56	.001586	.001436	.001300	.001177	.001066	.000965	.000874	.000792	.000718	.000651
57	.001414	.001277	.001154	.001043	.000943	.000853	.000771	.000697	.000631	.000571
58	.001260	.001136	.001025	.000925	.000835	.000753	.000680	.000614	.000554	.000501
59	.001123	.001011	.000910	.000820	.000739	.000665	.000600	.000540	.000487	.000439
60	.001001	.000900	.000809	.000727	.000654	.000588	.000529	.000476	.000428	.000385

TABLE J
ADJUSTMENT FACTORS FOR TERM CERTAIN ANNUITIES
PAYABLE AT THE BEGINNING OF EACH INTERVAL
APPLICABLE AFTER APRIL 30, 1989
FREQUENCY OF PAYMENTS

Interest Rate	Annually	Semi Annually	Quarterly	Monthly	Weekly
4.2	1.0420	1.0314	1.0261	1.0226	1.0213
4.4	1.0440	1.0329	1.0274	1.0237	1.0223
4.6	1.0460	1.0344	1.0286	1.0247	1.0233
4.8	1.0480	1.0359	1.0298	1.0258	1.0243
5.0	1.0500	1.0373	1.0311	1.0269	1.0253
5.2	1.0520	1.0388	1.0323	1.0279	1.0263
5.4	1.0540	1.0403	1.0335	1.0290	1.0273
5.6	1.0560	1.0418	1.0348	1.0301	1.0283
5.8	1.0580	1.0433	1.0360	1.0311	1.0293
6.0	1.0600	1.0448	1.0372	1.0322	1.0303
6.2	1.0620	1.0463	1.0385	1.0333	1.0313
6.4	1.0640	1.0478	1.0397	1.0343	1.0323
6.6	1.0660	1.0492	1.0409	1.0354	1.0333
6.8	1.0680	1.0507	1.0422	1.0365	1.0343
7.0	1.0700	1.0522	1.0434	1.0375	1.0353
7.2	1.0720	1.0537	1.0446	1.0386	1.0363
7.4	1.0740	1.0552	1.0458	1.0396	1.0373
7.6	1.0760	1.0567	1.0471	1.0407	1.0383
7.8	1.0780	1.0581	1.0483	1.0418	1.0393
8.0	1.0800	1.0596	1.0495	1.0428	1.0403
8.2	1.0820	1.0611	1.0507	1.0439	1.0413
8.4	1.0840	1.0626	1.0520	1.0449	1.0422
8.6	1.0860	1.0641	1.0532	1.0460	1.0432
8.8	1.0880	1.0655	1.0544	1.0471	1.0442
9.0	1.0900	1.0670	1.0556	1.0481	1.0452

Interest Rate	Annually	Semi Annually	Quarterly	Monthly	Weekly
9.2	1.0920	1.0685	1.0569	1.0492	1.0462
9.4	1.0940	1.0700	1.0581	1.0502	1.0472
9.6	1.0960	1.0715	1.0593	1.0513	1.0482
9.8	1.0980	1.0729	1.0605	1.0523	1.0492
10.0	1.1000	1.0744	1.0618	1.0534	1.0502
10.2	1.1020	1.0759	1.0630	1.0544	1.0512
10.4	1.1040	1.0774	1.0642	1.0555	1.0521
10.6	1.1060	1.0788	1.0654	1.0565	1.0531
10.8	1.1080	1.0803	1.0666	1.0576	1.0541
11.0	1.1100	1.0818	1.0679	1.0586	1.0551
11.2	1.1120	1.0833	1.0691	1.0597	1.0561
11.4	1.1140	1.0847	1.0703	1.0607	1.0571
11.6	1.1160	1.0862	1.0715	1.0618	1.0581
11.8	1.1180	1.0877	1.0727	1.0628	1.0590
12.0	1.1200	1.0892	1.0739	1.0639	1.0600
12.2	1.1220	1.0906	1.0752	1.0649	1.0610
12.4	1.1240	1.0921	1.0764	1.0660	1.0620
12.6	1.1260	1.0936	1.0776	1.0670	1.0630
12.8	1.1280	1.0950	1.0788	1.0681	1.0639
13.0	1.1300	1.0965	1.0800	1.0691	1.0649
13.2	1.1320	1.0980	1.0812	1.0701	1.0659
13.4	1.1340	1.0994	1.0824	1.0712	1.0669
13.6	1.1360	1.1009	1.0836	1.0722	1.0679
13.8	1.1380	1.1024	1.0849	1.0733	1.0688
14.0	1.1400	1.1039	1.0861	1.0743	1.0698

TABLE K
ADJUSTMENT FACTORS FOR ANNUITIES
PAYABLE AT THE END OF EACH INTERVAL
APPLICABLE AFTER APRIL 30, 1989
FREQUENCY OF PAYMENTS

Interest Rate	Annually	Semi Annually	Quarterly	Monthly	Weekly
4.2	1.0000	1.0104	1.0156	1.0191	1.0205
4.4	1.0000	1.0109	1.0164	1.0200	1.0214
4.6	1.0000	1.0114	1.0171	1.0209	1.0224
4.8	1.0000	1.0119	1.0178	1.0218	1.0234
5.0	1.0000	1.0123	1.0186	1.0227	1.0243
5.2	1.0000	1.0128	1.0193	1.0236	1.0253
5.4	1.0000	1.0133	1.0200	1.0245	1.0262
5.6	1.0000	1.0138	1.0208	1.0254	1.0272
5.8	1.0000	1.0143	1.0215	1.0263	1.0282
6.0	1.0000	1.0148	1.0222	1.0272	1.0291
6.2	1.0000	1.0153	1.0230	1.0281	1.0301
6.4	1.0000	1.0158	1.0237	1.0290	1.0311
6.6	1.0000	1.0162	1.0244	1.0299	1.0320
6.8	1.0000	1.0167	1.0252	1.0308	1.0330
7.0	1.0000	1.0172	1.0259	1.0317	1.0339
7.2	1.0000	1.0177	1.0266	1.0326	1.0349
7.4	1.0000	1.0182	1.0273	1.0335	1.0358
7.6	1.0000	1.0187	1.0281	1.0344	1.0368
7.8	1.0000	1.0191	1.0288	1.0353	1.0378
8.0	1.0000	1.0196	1.0295	1.0362	1.0387
8.2	1.0000	1.0201	1.0302	1.0370	1.0397
8.4	1.0000	1.0206	1.0310	1.0379	1.0406
8.6	1.0000	1.0211	1.0317	1.0388	1.0416
8.8	1.0000	1.0215	1.0324	1.0397	1.0425
9.0	1.0000	1.0220	1.0331	1.0406	1.0435
9.2	1.0000	1.0225	1.0339	1.0415	1.0444
9.4	1.0000	1.0230	1.0346	1.0424	1.0454
9.6	1.0000	1.0235	1.0353	1.0433	1.0463
9.8	1.0000	1.0239	1.0360	1.0442	1.0473
10.0	1.0000	1.0244	1.0368	1.0450	1.0482
10.2	1.0000	1.0249	1.0375	1.0459	1.0492
10.4	1.0000	1.0254	1.0382	1.0468	1.0501

Interest Rate	Annually	Semi Annually	Quarterly	Monthly	Weekly
10.6	1.0000	1.0258	1.0389	1.0477	1.0511
10.8	1.0000	1.0263	1.0396	1.0486	1.0520
11.0	1.0000	1.0268	1.0404	1.0495	1.0530
11.2	1.0000	1.0273	1.0411	1.0503	1.0539
11.4	1.0000	1.0277	1.0418	1.0512	1.0549
11.6	1.0000	1.0282	1.0425	1.0521	1.0558
11.8	1.0000	1.0287	1.0432	1.0530	1.0568
12.0	1.0000	1.0292	1.0439	1.0539	1.0577
12.2	1.0000	1.0296	1.0447	1.0548	1.0587
12.4	1.0000	1.0301	1.0454	1.0556	1.0596
12.6	1.0000	1.0306	1.0461	1.0565	1.0605
12.8	1.0000	1.0310	1.0468	1.0574	1.0615
13.0	1.0000	1.0315	1.0475	1.0583	1.0624
13.2	1.0000	1.0320	1.0482	1.0591	1.0634
13.4	1.0000	1.0324	1.0489	1.0600	1.0643
13.6	1.0000	1.0329	1.0496	1.0609	1.0652
13.8	1.0000	1.0334	1.0504	1.0618	1.0662
14.0	1.0000	1.0339	1.0511	1.0626	1.0671

TABLE S
BASED ON LIFE TABLE 80CNSMT
SINGLE LIFE REMAINDER FACTORS
APPLICABLE AFTER APRIL 30, 1989
INTEREST RATE

Age	4.2%	4.4%	4.6%	4.8%	5.0%	5.2%	5.4%	5.6%	5.8%	6.0%
0	.07389	.06749	.06188	.05695	.05261	.04879	.04541	.04243	.03978	.03744
1	.06494	.05832	.05250	.04738	.04287	.03889	.03537	.03226	.02950	.02705
2	.06678	.05999	.05401	.04874	.04410	.03999	.03636	.03314	.03028	.02773
3	.06897	.06200	.05587	.05045	.04567	.04143	.03768	.03435	.03139	.02875
4	.07139	.06425	.05796	.05239	.04746	.04310	.03922	.03578	.03271	.02998
5	.07401	.06669	.06023	.05451	.04944	.04494	.04094	.03738	.03421	.03137
6	.07677	.06928	.06265	.05677	.05156	.04692	.04279	.03911	.03583	.03289
7	.07968	.07201	.06521	.05918	.05381	.04903	.04477	.04097	.03757	.03453
8	.08274	.07489	.06792	.06172	.05621	.05129	.04689	.04297	.03945	.03630
9	.08597	.07794	.07079	.06443	.05876	.05370	.04917	.04511	.04148	.03821
10	.08936	.08115	.07383	.06730	.06147	.05626	.05159	.04741	.04365	.04027
11	.09293	.08453	.07704	.07035	.06436	.05900	.05419	.04988	.04599	.04250
12	.09666	.08807	.08040	.07354	.06739	.06188	.05693	.05248	.04847	.04486
13	.10049	.09172	.08387	.07684	.07053	.06487	.05977	.05518	.05104	.04731
14	.10437	.09541	.08738	.08017	.07370	.06788	.06263	.05791	.05364	.04978
15	.10827	.09912	.09090	.08352	.07688	.07090	.06551	.06064	.05623	.05225
16	.11220	.10285	.09445	.08689	.08008	.07394	.06839	.06337	.05883	.05472
17	.11615	.10661	.09802	.09028	.08330	.07699	.07129	.06612	.06144	.05719
18	.12017	.11043	.10165	.09373	.08656	.08009	.07422	.06890	.06408	.05969
19	.12428	.11434	.10537	.09726	.08992	.08327	.07724	.07177	.06679	.06226
20	.12850	.11836	.10919	.10089	.09337	.08654	.08035	.07471	.06959	.06492
21	.13282	.12248	.11311	.10462	.09692	.08991	.08355	.07775	.07247	.06765
22	.13728	.12673	.11717	.10848	.10059	.09341	.08686	.08090	.07546	.07049
23	.14188	.13113	.12136	.11248	.10440	.09703	.09032	.08418	.07858	.07345
24	.14667	.13572	.12575	.11667	.10839	.10084	.09395	.08764	.08187	.07659
25	.15167	.14051	.13034	.12106	.11259	.10486	.09778	.09130	.08536	.07991
26	.15690	.14554	.13517	.12569	.11703	.10910	.10184	.09518	.08907	.08346
27	.16237	.15081	.14024	.13056	.12171	.11359	.10614	.09930	.09302	.08724
28	.16808	.15632	.14555	.13567	.12662	.11831	.11068	.10366	.09720	.09125
29	.17404	.16208	.15110	.14104	.13179	.12329	.11547	.10827	.10163	.09551
30	.18025	.16808	.15692	.14665	.13721	.12852	.12051	.11313	.10631	.10002
31	.18672	.17436	.16300	.15255	.14291	.13403	.12584	.11827	.11127	.10480
32	.19344	.18090	.16935	.15870	.14888	.13980	.13142	.12367	.11650	.10985
33	.20044	.18772	.17598	.16514	.15513	.14587	.13730	.12936	.12201	.11519
34	.20770	.19480	.18287	.17185	.16165	.15221	.14345	.13533	.12780	.12080
35	.21522	.20215	.19005	.17884	.16846	.15883	.14989	.14159	.13388	.12670
36	.22299	.20974	.19747	.18609	.17552	.16571	.15660	.14812	.14022	.13287
37	.23101	.21760	.20516	.19360	.18286	.17288	.16358	.15492	.14685	.13933

Age	4.2%	4.4%	4.6%	4.8%	5.0%	5.2%	5.4%	5.6%	5.8%	6.0%
38	.23928	.22572	.21311	.20139	.19048	.18032	.17085	.16201	.15377	.14607
39	.24780	.23409	.22133	.20945	.19837	.18804	.17840	.16939	.16097	.15310
40	.25658	.24273	.22982	.21778	.20654	.19605	.18624	.17706	.16847	.16043
41	.26560	.25163	.23858	.22639	.21499	.20434	.19436	.18502	.17627	.16806
42	.27486	.26076	.24758	.23525	.22370	.21289	.20276	.19326	.18434	.17597
43	.28435	.27013	.25683	.24436	.23268	.22172	.21143	.20177	.19270	.18416
44	.29407	.27975	.26633	.25373	.24191	.23081	.22038	.21057	.20134	.19265
45	.30402	.28961	.27608	.26337	.25142	.24019	.22962	.21966	.21028	.20144
46	.31420	.29970	.28608	.27326	.26120	.24983	.23913	.22904	.21951	.21053
47	.32460	.31004	.29632	.28341	.27123	.25975	.24892	.23870	.22904	.21991
48	.33521	.32058	.30679	.29379	.28151	.26992	.25897	.24862	.23883	.22957
49	.34599	.33132	.31746	.30438	.29201	.28032	.26926	.25879	.24888	.23949
50	.35695	.34224	.32833	.31518	.30273	.29094	.27978	.26921	.25918	.24966
51	.36809	.35335	.33940	.32619	.31367	.30180	.29055	.27987	.26973	.26010
52	.37944	.36468	.35070	.33744	.32486	.31292	.30158	.29081	.28057	.27083
53	.39098	.37622	.36222	.34892	.33629	.32429	.31288	.30203	.29170	.28186
54	.40269	.38794	.37393	.36062	.34795	.33590	.32442	.31349	.30308	.29316
55	.41457	.39985	.38585	.37252	.35983	.34774	.33621	.32522	.31474	.30473
56	.42662	.41194	.39796	.38464	.37193	.35981	.34824	.33720	.32666	.31658
57	.43884	.42422	.41028	.39697	.38426	.37213	.36053	.34945	.33885	.32872
58	.45123	.43668	.42279	.40951	.39682	.38468	.37307	.36196	.35132	.34114
59	.46377	.44931	.43547	.42224	.40958	.39745	.38584	.37471	.36405	.35383
60	.47643	.46206	.44830	.43513	.42250	.41040	.39880	.38767	.37699	.36674
61	.48916	.47491	.46124	.44814	.43556	.42350	.41192	.40080	.39012	.37985
62	.50196	.48783	.47427	.46124	.44874	.43672	.42518	.41408	.40340	.39314
63	.51480	.50081	.48736	.47444	.46201	.45006	.43856	.42749	.41684	.40658
64	.52770	.51386	.50054	.48773	.47540	.46352	.45208	.44105	.43043	.42019
65	.54069	.52701	.51384	.50115	.48892	.47713	.46577	.45480	.44422	.43401
66	.55378	.54029	.52727	.51472	.50262	.49093	.47965	.46876	.45824	.44808
67	.56697	.55368	.54084	.52845	.51648	.50491	.49373	.48293	.47248	.46238
68	.58026	.56717	.55453	.54231	.53049	.51905	.50800	.49729	.48694	.47691
69	.59358	.58072	.56828	.55624	.54459	.53330	.52238	.51179	.50154	.49160
70	.60689	.59427	.58205	.57021	.55874	.54762	.53683	.52638	.51624	.50641
71	.62014	.60778	.59578	.58415	.57287	.56193	.55131	.54100	.53099	.52126
72	.63334	.62123	.60948	.59808	.58700	.57624	.56579	.55563	.54577	.53617
73	.64648	.63465	.62315	.61198	.60112	.59056	.58029	.57030	.56059	.55113
74	.65961	.64806	.63682	.62590	.61527	.60492	.59485	.58504	.57550	.56620
75	.67274	.66149	.65054	.63987	.62948	.61936	.60950	.59990	.59053	.58140
76	.68589	.67495	.66429	.65390	.64377	.63390	.62427	.61487	.60570	.59676
77	.69903	.68841	.67806	.66796	.65811	.64849	.63910	.62993	.62097	.61223
78	.71209	.70182	.69179	.68199	.67242	.66307	.65393	.64501	.63628	.62775
79	.72500	.71507	.70537	.69588	.68660	.67754	.66867	.65999	.65151	.64321
80	.73768	.72809	.71872	.70955	.70058	.69180	.68320	.67479	.66655	.65849
81	.75001	.74077	.73173	.72288	.71422	.70573	.69741	.68926	.68128	.67345
82	.76195	.75306	.74435	.73582	.72746	.71926	.71123	.70335	.69562	.68804
83	.77346	.76491	.75654	.74832	.74026	.73236	.72460	.71699	.70952	.70219
84	.78456	.77636	.76831	.76041	.75265	.74503	.73756	.73021	.72300	.71592
85	.79530	.78743	.77971	.77212	.76466	.75733	.75014	.74306	.73611	.72928
86	.80560	.79806	.79065	.78337	.77621	.76917	.76225	.75544	.74875	.74216
87	.81535	.80813	.80103	.79404	.78717	.78041	.77375	.76720	.76076	.75442
88	.82462	.81771	.81090	.80420	.79760	.79111	.78472	.77842	.77223	.76612
89	.83356	.82694	.82043	.81401	.80769	.80147	.79533	.78929	.78334	.77747
90	.84225	.83593	.82971	.82357	.81753	.81157	.80570	.79991	.79420	.78857
91	.85058	.84455	.83861	.83276	.82698	.82129	.81567	.81013	.80466	.79927
92	.85838	.85263	.84696	.84137	.83585	.83040	.82503	.81973	.81449	.80933
93	.86557	.86009	.85467	.84932	.84405	.83884	.83370	.82862	.82360	.81865
94	.87212	.86687	.86169	.85657	.85152	.84653	.84160	.83673	.83192	.82717
95	.87801	.87298	.86801	.86310	.85825	.85345	.84872	.84404	.83941	.83484
96	.88322	.87838	.87360	.86888	.86420	.85959	.85502	.85051	.84605	.84165
97	.88795	.88328	.87867	.87411	.86961	.86515	.86074	.85639	.85208	.84782
98	.89220	.88769	.88323	.87883	.87447	.87016	.86589	.86167	.85750	.85337
99	.89612	.89176	.88745	.88318	.87895	.87478	.87064	.86656	.86251	.85850

Age	4.2%	4.4%	4.6%	4.8%	5.0%	5.2%	5.4%	5.6%	5.8%	6.0%
100	.89977	.89555	.89136	.88722	.88313	.87908	.87506	.87109	.86716	.86327
101	.90326	.89917	.89511	.89110	.88712	.88318	.87929	.87543	.87161	.86783
102	.90690	.90294	.89901	.89513	.89128	.88746	.88369	.87995	.87624	.87257
103	.91076	.90694	.90315	.89940	.89569	.89200	.88835	.88474	.88116	.87760
104	.91504	.91138	.90775	.90415	.90058	.89704	.89354	.89006	.88661	.88319
105	.92027	.91681	.91337	.90996	.90658	.90322	.89989	.89659	.89331	.89006
106	.92763	.92445	.92130	.91816	.91506	.91197	.90890	.90586	.90284	.89983
107	.93799	.93523	.93249	.92977	.92707	.92438	.92170	.91905	.91641	.91378
108	.95429	.95223	.95018	.94814	.94611	.94409	.94208	.94008	.93809	.93611
109	.97985	.97893	.97801	.97710	.97619	.97529	.97438	.97348	.97259	.97170

TABLE S
BASED ON LIFE TABLE 80CNSMT
SINGLE LIFE REMAINDER FACTORS
APPLICABLE AFTER APRIL 30, 1989
INTEREST RATE

Age	6.2%	6.4%	6.6%	6.8%	7.0%	7.2%	7.4%	7.6%	7.8%	8.0%
0	.03535	.03349	.03183	.03035	.02902	.02783	.02676	.02579	.02492	.02413
1	.02486	.02292	.02119	.01963	.01824	.01699	.01587	.01486	.01395	.01312
2	.02547	.02345	.02164	.02002	.01857	.01727	.01609	.01504	.01408	.01321
3	.02640	.02429	.02241	.02073	.01921	.01785	.01662	.01552	.01451	.01361
4	.02753	.02535	.02339	.02163	.02005	.01863	.01735	.01619	.01514	.01418
5	.02883	.02656	.02453	.02269	.02105	.01956	.01822	.01700	.01590	.01490
6	.03026	.02790	.02578	.02387	.02215	.02060	.01919	.01792	.01677	.01572
7	.03180	.02935	.02714	.02515	.02336	.02174	.02027	.01894	.01773	.01664
8	.03347	.03092	.02863	.02656	.02469	.02300	.02146	.02007	.01881	.01766
9	.03528	.03263	.03025	.02810	.02615	.02438	.02278	.02133	.02000	.01880
10	.03723	.03449	.03201	.02977	.02774	.02590	.02423	.02271	.02133	.02006
11	.03935	.03650	.03393	.03160	.02949	.02757	.02583	.02424	.02279	.02147
12	.04160	.03865	.03598	.03356	.03136	.02936	.02755	.02589	.02438	.02299
13	.04394	.04088	.03811	.03560	.03331	.03123	.02934	.02761	.02603	.02458
14	.04629	.04312	.04025	.03764	.03527	.03311	.03113	.02933	.02768	.02617
15	.04864	.04536	.04238	.03968	.03721	.03496	.03290	.03103	.02930	.02773
16	.05099	.04759	.04451	.04170	.03913	.03679	.03466	.03270	.03090	.02926
17	.05333	.04982	.04662	.04370	.04104	.03861	.03638	.03434	.03247	.03075
18	.05570	.05207	.04875	.04573	.04296	.04044	.03812	.03599	.03404	.03225
19	.05814	.05438	.05095	.04781	.04494	.04231	.03990	.03769	.03565	.03378
20	.06065	.05677	.05321	.04996	.04698	.04424	.04173	.03943	.03731	.03535
21	.06325	.05922	.05554	.05217	.04907	.04623	.04362	.04122	.03901	.03697
22	.06594	.06178	.05797	.05447	.05126	.04831	.04559	.04309	.04078	.03865
23	.06876	.06446	.06051	.05688	.05355	.05048	.04766	.04505	.04265	.04042
24	.07174	.06729	.06321	.05945	.05599	.05281	.04987	.04715	.04465	.04233
25	.07491	.07031	.06609	.06219	.05861	.05530	.05224	.04941	.04680	.04438
26	.07830	.07355	.06918	.06515	.06142	.05799	.05481	.05187	.04915	.04662
27	.08192	.07702	.07250	.06832	.06446	.06090	.05759	.05454	.05170	.04906
28	.08577	.08071	.07603	.07171	.06772	.06402	.06059	.05740	.05445	.05170
29	.08986	.08464	.07981	.07534	.07120	.06736	.06380	.06049	.05742	.05456
30	.09420	.08882	.08383	.07921	.07492	.07095	.06725	.06381	.06061	.05763
31	.09881	.09327	.08812	.08335	.07891	.07479	.07095	.06738	.06405	.06095
32	.10369	.09797	.09267	.08774	.08315	.07888	.07491	.07120	.06774	.06451
33	.10885	.10297	.09750	.09241	.08767	.08325	.07913	.07529	.07170	.06834
34	.11430	.10824	.10261	.09736	.09246	.08790	.08363	.07964	.07592	.07243
35	.12002	.11380	.10800	.10259	.09754	.09282	.08841	.08428	.08041	.07679
36	.12602	.11963	.11366	.10809	.10288	.09800	.09344	.08917	.08516	.08140
37	.13230	.12574	.11961	.11387	.10850	.10347	.09876	.09433	.09018	.08628
38	.13887	.13214	.12584	.11994	.11441	.10922	.10436	.09978	.09549	.09145
39	.14573	.13883	.13237	.12630	.12061	.11527	.11025	.10553	.10109	.09690
40	.15290	.14583	.13920	.13297	.12712	.12162	.11644	.11157	.10698	.10266
41	.16036	.15312	.14633	.13994	.13393	.12827	.12294	.11792	.11318	.10871
42	.16810	.16071	.15375	.14720	.14103	.13522	.12973	.12456	.11967	.11505
43	.17614	.16858	.16146	.15475	.14842	.14245	.13682	.13149	.12645	.12169
44	.18447	.17675	.16948	.16261	.15613	.15000	.14421	.13873	.13355	.12864
45	.19310	.18524	.17780	.17078	.16414	.15787	.15192	.14630	.14096	.13591
46	.20204	.19402	.18644	.17926	.17247	.16604	.15995	.15418	.14870	.14350

Age	6.2%	6.4%	6.6%	6.8%	7.0%	7.2%	7.4%	7.6%	7.8%	8.0%
47	.21128	.20311	.19538	.18806	.18112	.17454	.16830	.16238	.15676	.15141
48	.22080	.21249	.20462	.19716	.19007	.18335	.17696	.17090	.16513	.15964
49	.23059	.22214	.21413	.20653	.19930	.19244	.18591	.17970	.17379	.16816
50	.24063	.23206	.22391	.21617	.20881	.20180	.19514	.18879	.18274	.17697
51	.25095	.24225	.23398	.22610	.21861	.21147	.20466	.19818	.19199	.18609
52	.26157	.25275	.24436	.23636	.22874	.22147	.21453	.20791	.20159	.19556
53	.27249	.26357	.25505	.24694	.23919	.23180	.22474	.21799	.21154	.20537
54	.28369	.27466	.26604	.25782	.24995	.24244	.23526	.22839	.22181	.21552
55	.29518	.28605	.27734	.26900	.26103	.25341	.24611	.23912	.23243	.22601
56	.30695	.29774	.28893	.28050	.27242	.26469	.25728	.25019	.24338	.23685
57	.31902	.30973	.30084	.29232	.28415	.27632	.26881	.26161	.25469	.24805
58	.33138	.32203	.31306	.30446	.29621	.28829	.28069	.27339	.26637	.25962
59	.34402	.33461	.32558	.31691	.30859	.30059	.29290	.28550	.27839	.27155
60	.35690	.34745	.33836	.32963	.32124	.31317	.30540	.29792	.29073	.28379
61	.36999	.36050	.35137	.34259	.33414	.32601	.31817	.31062	.30334	.29633
62	.38325	.37374	.36458	.35576	.34726	.33907	.33117	.32356	.31621	.30912
63	.39669	.38717	.37799	.36913	.36060	.35236	.34441	.33674	.32933	.32217
64	.41031	.40078	.39159	.38272	.37415	.36588	.35789	.35016	.34270	.33548
65	.42416	.41464	.40545	.39656	.38798	.37968	.37166	.36390	.35639	.34912
66	.43825	.42876	.41958	.41070	.40211	.39380	.38576	.37797	.37043	.36312
67	.45260	.44315	.43399	.42513	.41655	.40824	.40019	.39238	.38482	.37749
68	.46720	.45779	.44868	.43985	.43129	.42299	.41494	.40713	.39956	.39221
69	.48197	.47263	.46357	.45478	.44625	.43798	.42995	.42215	.41458	.40722
70	.49686	.48760	.47861	.46988	.46140	.45316	.44516	.43738	.42983	.42248
71	.51182	.50265	.49374	.48508	.47666	.46847	.46051	.45276	.44523	.43790
72	.52685	.51778	.50896	.50038	.49203	.48390	.47599	.46829	.46079	.45349
73	.54194	.53298	.52426	.51578	.50751	.49946	.49161	.48397	.47652	.46926
74	.55714	.54832	.53972	.53134	.52317	.51520	.50744	.49986	.49247	.48527
75	.57250	.56382	.55536	.54710	.53904	.53118	.52351	.51601	.50870	.50156
76	.58803	.57951	.57120	.56308	.55515	.54740	.53984	.53245	.52522	.51817
77	.60369	.59535	.58720	.57923	.57144	.56383	.55639	.54912	.54200	.53504
78	.61942	.61126	.60329	.59549	.58787	.58040	.57310	.56596	.55896	.55212
79	.63508	.62713	.61935	.61174	.60428	.59698	.58983	.58283	.57597	.56925
80	.65059	.64285	.63527	.62785	.62058	.61345	.60646	.59961	.59290	.58632
81	.66579	.65827	.65090	.64368	.63659	.62965	.62283	.61615	.60959	.60316
82	.68061	.67332	.66616	.65914	.65226	.64550	.63886	.63235	.62595	.61968
83	.69499	.68793	.68099	.67418	.66749	.66092	.65447	.64813	.64191	.63579
84	.70896	.70213	.69541	.68881	.68233	.67595	.66969	.66353	.65748	.65153
85	.72256	.71596	.70947	.70308	.69681	.69063	.68456	.67859	.67271	.66693
86	.73569	.72931	.72305	.71688	.71081	.70484	.69896	.69318	.68748	.68188
87	.74818	.74204	.73599	.73003	.72417	.71839	.71271	.70711	.70159	.69616
88	.76011	.75419	.74836	.74261	.73695	.73137	.72588	.72046	.71512	.70986
89	.77169	.76599	.76037	.75484	.74938	.74400	.73870	.73347	.72831	.72323
90	.78302	.77755	.77215	.76683	.76158	.75640	.75129	.74625	.74128	.73638
91	.79395	.78870	.78352	.77842	.77337	.76840	.76349	.75864	.75385	.74913
92	.80423	.79920	.79423	.78933	.78449	.77971	.77499	.77033	.76572	.76118
93	.81377	.80894	.80417	.79946	.79481	.79022	.78568	.78120	.77677	.77239
94	.82247	.81784	.81325	.80873	.80425	.79983	.79547	.79115	.78688	.78266
95	.83033	.82586	.82145	.81709	.81278	.80852	.80431	.80014	.79602	.79195
96	.83729	.83298	.82872	.82451	.82034	.81622	.81215	.80812	.80414	.80019
97	.84361	.83944	.83532	.83124	.82721	.82322	.81927	.81537	.81151	.80769
98	.84929	.84525	.84126	.83730	.83339	.82952	.82569	.82190	.81815	.81443
99	.85454	.85062	.84674	.84290	.83910	.83534	.83161	.82792	.82427	.82066
100	.85942	.85561	.85184	.84810	.84440	.84074	.83711	.83352	.82997	.82644
101	.86408	.86037	.85670	.85306	.84946	.84589	.84236	.83886	.83539	.83196
102	.86894	.86534	.86177	.85823	.85473	.85126	.84782	.84442	.84104	.83770
103	.87408	.87060	.86714	.86371	.86032	.85695	.85362	.85031	.84703	.84378
104	.87980	.87644	.87311	.86980	.86653	.86328	.86005	.85686	.85369	.85054
105	.88684	.88363	.88046	.87731	.87418	.87108	.86800	.86494	.86191	.85890
106	.89685	.89389	.89095	.88804	.88514	.88226	.87940	.87656	.87374	.87094
107	.91117	.90858	.90600	.90344	.90089	.89836	.89584	.89334	.89085	.88838
108	.93414	.93217	.93022	.92828	.92634	.92442	.92250	.92060	.91870	.91681
109	.97081	.96992	.96904	.96816	.96729	.96642	.96555	.96468	.96382	.96296

TABLE S
BASED ON LIFE TABLE 80CNSMT
SINGLE LIFE REMAINDER FACTORS
APPLICABLE AFTER APRIL 30, 1989
INTEREST RATE

Age	8.2%	8.4%	8.6%	8.8%	9.0%	9.2%	9.4%	9.6%	9.8%	10.0%
0	.02341	.02276	.02217	.02163	.02114	.02069	.02027	.01989	.01954	.01922
1	.01237	.01170	.01108	.01052	.01000	.00953	.00910	.00871	.00834	.00801
2	.01243	.01172	.01107	.01048	.00994	.00944	.00899	.00857	.00819	.00784
3	.01278	.01203	.01135	.01073	.01016	.00964	.00916	.00872	.00832	.00795
4	.01332	.01253	.01182	.01116	.01056	.01001	.00951	.00904	.00862	.00822
5	.01400	.01317	.01241	.01172	.01109	.01051	.00998	.00949	.00904	.00862
6	.01477	.01390	.01310	.01238	.01171	.01110	.01054	.01002	.00954	.00910
7	.01563	.01472	.01389	.01312	.01242	.01178	.01118	.01064	.01013	.00966
8	.01660	.01564	.01477	.01396	.01322	.01254	.01192	.01134	.01081	.01031
9	.01770	.01669	.01577	.01492	.01414	.01342	.01276	.01216	.01159	.01107
10	.01891	.01785	.01688	.01599	.01517	.01442	.01372	.01308	.01249	.01194
11	.02026	.01915	.01814	.01720	.01634	.01555	.01481	.01414	.01351	.01293
12	.02173	.02056	.01950	.01852	.01761	.01678	.01601	.01529	.01463	.01402
13	.02326	.02204	.02092	.01989	.01895	.01807	.01726	.01651	.01582	.01517
14	.02478	.02351	.02234	.02126	.02027	.01935	.01850	.01771	.01698	.01630
15	.02628	.02495	.02372	.02259	.02155	.02058	.01969	.01886	.01810	.01738
16	.02774	.02635	.02507	.02388	.02279	.02178	.02084	.01997	.01917	.01842
17	.02917	.02772	.02637	.02513	.02399	.02293	.02194	.02103	.02018	.01940
18	.03059	.02907	.02767	.02637	.02517	.02406	.02302	.02207	.02118	.02035
19	.03205	.03046	.02899	.02763	.02637	.02521	.02412	.02312	.02218	.02131
20	.03355	.03188	.03035	.02892	.02760	.02638	.02524	.02419	.02320	.02229
21	.03509	.03334	.03173	.03024	.02886	.02758	.02638	.02527	.02424	.02328
22	.03669	.03487	.03318	.03162	.03017	.02882	.02757	.02640	.02532	.02430
23	.03837	.03646	.03470	.03306	.03154	.03013	.02881	.02759	.02644	.02538
24	.04018	.03819	.03634	.03463	.03303	.03155	.03016	.02888	.02767	.02655
25	.04214	.04006	.03812	.03633	.03465	.03309	.03164	.03029	.02902	.02784
26	.04428	.04210	.04008	.03820	.03644	.03481	.03328	.03186	.03052	.02928
27	.04662	.04434	.04223	.04025	.03841	.03670	.03509	.03360	.03219	.03088
28	.04915	.04677	.04456	.04249	.04056	.03876	.03708	.03550	.03403	.03264
29	.05189	.04941	.04709	.04493	.04291	.04102	.03925	.03760	.03604	.03458
30	.05485	.05226	.04984	.04757	.04546	.04348	.04162	.03988	.03825	.03671
31	.05805	.05535	.05282	.05045	.04824	.04616	.04421	.04238	.04067	.03905
32	.06149	.05867	.05603	.05356	.05124	.04906	.04702	.04510	.04329	.04160
33	.06520	.06226	.05950	.05692	.05449	.05221	.05007	.04806	.04616	.04438
34	.06916	.06609	.06322	.06052	.05799	.05560	.05336	.05125	.04926	.04738
35	.07339	.07020	.06720	.06439	.06174	.05925	.05690	.05469	.05260	.05063
36	.07787	.07455	.07143	.06850	.06573	.06313	.06068	.05836	.05617	.05411
37	.08262	.07917	.07593	.07287	.06999	.06727	.06470	.06228	.05999	.05783
38	.08765	.08407	.08069	.07751	.07451	.07167	.06899	.06646	.06407	.06180
39	.09296	.08925	.08574	.08243	.07931	.07635	.07356	.07092	.06841	.06604
40	.09858	.09472	.09109	.08765	.08440	.08132	.07841	.07565	.07303	.07055
41	.10449	.10050	.09673	.09316	.08978	.08658	.08355	.08067	.07794	.07535
42	.11069	.10656	.10265	.09895	.09544	.09212	.08896	.08596	.08312	.08041
43	.11718	.11291	.10887	.10503	.10140	.09794	.09466	.09154	.08858	.08576
44	.12399	.11958	.11540	.11143	.10766	.10407	.10067	.09743	.09434	.09141
45	.13111	.12656	.12224	.11814	.11423	.11052	.10699	.10362	.10042	.09736
46	.13856	.13387	.12941	.12516	.12113	.11728	.11362	.11013	.10680	.10363
47	.14633	.14150	.13690	.13252	.12835	.12438	.12059	.11697	.11352	.11022
48	.15442	.14945	.14471	.14020	.13589	.13179	.12787	.12412	.12055	.11713
49	.16280	.15769	.15281	.14816	.14373	.13949	.13544	.13157	.12787	.12433
50	.17147	.16622	.16121	.15643	.15186	.14749	.14331	.13931	.13548	.13182
51	.18045	.17507	.16993	.16501	.16030	.15580	.15150	.14737	.14342	.13963
52	.18979	.18427	.17899	.17394	.16911	.16448	.16004	.15579	.15172	.14780
53	.19947	.19383	.18842	.18324	.17828	.17352	.16896	.16458	.16038	.15635
54	.20950	.20372	.19819	.19288	.18779	.18291	.17822	.17372	.16940	.16524
55	.21986	.21397	.20831	.20288	.19767	.19266	.18785	.18322	.17878	.17450
56	.23058	.22457	.21879	.21324	.20791	.20278	.19785	.19310	.18854	.18414
57	.24167	.23554	.22965	.22399	.21854	.21329	.20824	.20338	.19870	.19419
58	.25314	.24690	.24090	.23512	.22956	.22420	.21904	.21407	.20927	.20464
59	.26497	.25863	.25252	.24664	.24097	.23550	.23023	.22515	.22024	.21551

Age	8.2%	8.4%	8.6%	8.8%	9.0%	9.2%	9.4%	9.6%	9.8%	10.0%
60	.27712	.27068	.26448	.25849	.25272	.24716	.24178	.23659	.23158	.22674
61	.28956	.28304	.27674	.27067	.26480	.25913	.25366	.24837	.24325	.23831
62	.30228	.29567	.28929	.28312	.27717	.27141	.26584	.26045	.25524	.25020
63	.31525	.30857	.30211	.29586	.28982	.28397	.27832	.27284	.26754	.26240
64	.32851	.32176	.31522	.30890	.30278	.29685	.29111	.28555	.28016	.27493
65	.34209	.33528	.32868	.32229	.31610	.31010	.30429	.29865	.29317	.28787
66	.35604	.34918	.34253	.33609	.32983	.32377	.31788	.31217	.30663	.30124
67	.37037	.36347	.35678	.35028	.34398	.33786	.33191	.32614	.32053	.31508
68	.38508	.37815	.37142	.36489	.35854	.35237	.34638	.34055	.33488	.32937
69	.40008	.39313	.38638	.37982	.37344	.36724	.36120	.35533	.34961	.34405
70	.41533	.40838	.40162	.39504	.38864	.38241	.37634	.37043	.36468	.35907
71	.43076	.42382	.41705	.41047	.40405	.39780	.39171	.38578	.38000	.37436
72	.44638	.43945	.43269	.42611	.41969	.41344	.40733	.40138	.39558	.38991
73	.46218	.45527	.44854	.44197	.43556	.42931	.42321	.41725	.41143	.40575
74	.47823	.47137	.46466	.45812	.45173	.44549	.43940	.43345	.42763	.42195
75	.49459	.48777	.48112	.47462	.46826	.46205	.45598	.45004	.44424	.43856
76	.51127	.50452	.49793	.49148	.48517	.47900	.47297	.46706	.46129	.45563
77	.52823	.52157	.51505	.50867	.50243	.49632	.49033	.48447	.47873	.47311
78	.54541	.53885	.53242	.52613	.51996	.51392	.50800	.50220	.49652	.49094
79	.56267	.55621	.54989	.54369	.53762	.53166	.52582	.52009	.51448	.50897
80	.57987	.57354	.56733	.56125	.55527	.54941	.54366	.53802	.53248	.52705
81	.59685	.59065	.58457	.57860	.57274	.56699	.56134	.55579	.55035	.54499
82	.61351	.60746	.60151	.59567	.58993	.58429	.57875	.57331	.56796	.56270
83	.62978	.62387	.61806	.61236	.60675	.60123	.59581	.59047	.58523	.58007
84	.64567	.63992	.63426	.62869	.62321	.61783	.61253	.60731	.60218	.59713
85	.66125	.65565	.65014	.64472	.63938	.63413	.62896	.62387	.61886	.61392
86	.67636	.67092	.66557	.66030	.65511	.65000	.64496	.64000	.63511	.63030
87	.69081	.68554	.68034	.67522	.67018	.66520	.66031	.65548	.65071	.64602
88	.70468	.69957	.69453	.68956	.68466	.67983	.67507	.67037	.66574	.66117
89	.71821	.71326	.70838	.70357	.69882	.69414	.68952	.68495	.68045	.67601
90	.73153	.72676	.72204	.71739	.71280	.70827	.70379	.69938	.69502	.69071
91	.74447	.73986	.73532	.73083	.72640	.72202	.71770	.71343	.70921	.70504
92	.75669	.75225	.74787	.74354	.73927	.73504	.73087	.72674	.72267	.71864
93	.76807	.76379	.75957	.75540	.75127	.74719	.74317	.73918	.73524	.73135
94	.77849	.77437	.77030	.76627	.76229	.75835	.75446	.75061	.74680	.74303
95	.78792	.78394	.78001	.77611	.77226	.76845	.76468	.76096	.75727	.75362
96	.79630	.79244	.78863	.78485	.78112	.77742	.77377	.77015	.76657	.76303
97	.80391	.80016	.79646	.79280	.78917	.78559	.78203	.77852	.77504	.77160
98	.81076	.80712	.80352	.79996	.79643	.79294	.78948	.78606	.78267	.77931
99	.81709	.81354	.81004	.80657	.80313	.79972	.79635	.79302	.78971	.78644
100	.82296	.81950	.81609	.81270	.80934	.80602	.80273	.79947	.79624	.79304
101	.82855	.82518	.82185	.81854	.81526	.81201	.80880	.80561	.80245	.79932
102	.83438	.83110	.82785	.82462	.82142	.81826	.81512	.81200	.80892	.80586
103	.84056	.83737	.83420	.83106	.82795	.82487	.82181	.81878	.81577	.81279
104	.84743	.84433	.84127	.83822	.83521	.83221	.82924	.82630	.32338	.82048
105	.85591	.85295	.85001	.84709	.84419	.84132	.83846	.83563	.83282	.83003
106	.86816	.86540	.86266	.85993	.85723	.85454	.85187	.84922	.84659	.84397
107	.88592	.88348	.88105	.87863	.87623	.87384	.87147	.86911	.86676	.86443
108	.91493	.91306	.91119	.90934	.90749	.90566	.90383	.90201	.90020	.89840
109	.96211	.96125	.96041	.95956	.95872	.95788	.95704	.95620	.95537	.95455

TABLE S
BASED ON LIFE TABLE 80CNSMT
SINGLE LIFE REMAINDER FACTORS
APPLICABLE AFTER APRIL 30, 1989
INTEREST RATE

Age	10.2%	10.4%	10.6%	10.8%	11.0%	11.2%	11.4%	11.6%	11.8%	12.0%
0	.01891	.01864	.01838	.01814	.01791	.01770	.01750	.01732	.01715	.01698
1	.00770	.00741	.00715	.00690	.00667	.00646	.00626	.00608	.00590	.00574
2	.00751	.00721	.00693	.00667	.00643	.00620	.00600	.00580	.00562	.00544
3	.00760	.00728	.00699	.00671	.00646	.00622	.00600	.00579	.00560	.00541
4	.00786	.00752	.00721	.00692	.00665	.00639	.00616	.00594	.00573	.00554
5	.00824	.00788	.00755	.00724	.00695	.00668	.00643	.00620	.00598	.00578
6	.00869	.00832	.00796	.00764	.00733	.00705	.00678	.00654	.00630	.00608

Age	10.2%	10.4%	10.6%	10.8%	11.0%	11.2%	11.4%	11.6%	11.8%	12.0%
7	.00923	.00883	.00846	.00811	.00779	.00749	.00720	.00694	.00669	.00646
8	.00986	.00943	.00904	.00867	.00833	.00801	.00771	.00743	.00716	.00692
9	.01059	.01014	.00972	.00933	.00897	.00863	.00831	.00801	.00773	.00747
10	.01142	.01095	.01051	.01009	.00971	.00935	.00901	.00869	.00840	.00812
11	.01239	.01189	.01142	.01098	.01057	.01019	.00983	.00950	.00918	.00889
12	.01345	.01292	.01243	.01197	.01154	.01113	.01075	.01040	.01007	.00975
13	.01457	.01401	.01349	.01300	.01255	.01212	.01172	.01135	.01100	.01067
14	.01567	.01508	.01453	.01402	.01354	.01309	.01267	.01227	.01190	.01155
15	.01672	.01610	.01552	.01498	.01448	.01400	.01356	.01314	.01275	.01238
16	.01772	.01707	.01646	.01589	.01536	.01486	.01439	.01396	.01354	.01315
17	.01866	.01798	.01734	.01674	.01618	.01566	.01516	.01470	.01427	.01386
18	.01958	.01886	.01818	.01755	.01697	.01641	.01590	.01541	.01495	.01452
19	.02050	.01974	.01903	.01837	.01775	.01717	.01662	.01611	.01563	.01517
20	.02143	.02064	.01989	.01919	.01854	.01793	.01735	.01681	.01630	.01582
21	.02238	.02154	.02075	.02002	.01933	.01868	.01807	.01750	.01696	.01646
22	.02336	.02247	.02164	.02087	.02014	.01946	.01882	.01821	.01764	.01711
23	.02438	.02345	.02257	.02176	.02099	.02027	.01959	.01895	.01835	.01778
24	.02550	.02451	.02359	.02273	.02192	.02115	.02044	.01976	.01913	.01853
25	.02673	.02569	.02472	.02381	.02295	.02214	.02138	.02067	.01999	.01936
26	.02811	.02701	.02598	.02502	.02411	.02326	.02246	.02170	.02098	.02031
27	.02965	.02849	.02741	.02639	.02543	.02452	.02367	.02287	.02211	.02140
28	.03134	.03013	.02898	.02790	.02689	.02593	.02503	.02418	.02338	.02262
29	.03322	.03193	.03072	.02958	.02851	.02750	.02654	.02564	.02479	.02398
30	.03527	.03394	.03264	.03143	.03030	.02923	.02821	.02726	.02635	.02550
31	.03753	.03610	.03475	.03348	.03228	.03115	.03008	.02907	.02811	.02720
32	.04000	.03849	.03707	.03573	.03446	.03326	.03213	.03105	.03004	.02907
33	.04269	.04111	.03961	.03819	.03685	.03558	.03438	.03325	.03217	.03115
34	.04561	.04394	.04236	.04087	.03946	.03812	.03685	.03565	.03451	.03342
35	.04877	.04702	.04535	.04378	.04229	.04087	.03953	.03826	.03706	.03591
36	.05215	.05031	.04856	.04690	.04533	.04384	.04242	.04108	.03980	.03859
37	.05578	.05384	.05200	.05025	.04860	.04703	.04553	.04411	.04276	.04148
38	.05965	.05761	.05568	.05385	.05211	.05045	.04888	.04738	.04595	.04460
39	.06379	.06165	.05962	.05770	.05587	.05412	.05247	.05089	.04939	.04795
40	.06820	.06596	.06383	.06181	.05989	.05806	.05631	.05465	.05307	.05155
41	.07288	.07054	.06832	.06620	.06418	.06226	.06042	.05868	.05701	.05541
42	.07784	.07539	.07306	.07085	.06873	.06671	.06479	.06295	.06119	.05952
43	.08308	.08052	.07808	.07576	.07355	.07143	.06941	.06748	.06564	.06387
44	.08861	.08594	.08340	.08097	.07865	.07644	.07432	.07230	.07036	.06851
45	.09445	.09167	.08901	.08648	.08406	.08174	.07953	.07741	.07538	.07343
46	.10060	.09770	.09494	.09230	.08977	.08735	.08503	.08281	.08068	.07865
47	.10707	.10406	.10119	.09843	.09579	.09327	.09085	.08853	.08630	.08417
48	.11386	.11073	.10774	.10487	.10213	.09949	.09697	.09455	.09222	.08999
49	.12094	.11769	.11458	.11160	.10874	.10600	.10337	.10084	.09842	.09609
50	.12831	.12494	.12172	.11862	.11565	.11280	.11006	.10743	.10490	.10247
51	.13600	.13251	.12917	.12596	.12288	.11991	.11706	.11432	.11169	.10915
52	.14405	.14044	.13698	.13366	.13046	.12738	.12442	.12157	.11883	.11619
53	.15247	.14875	.14517	.14172	.13841	.13522	.13215	.12919	.12635	.12360
54	.16124	.15740	.15370	.15014	.14671	.14341	.14023	.13717	.13421	.13136
55	.17039	.16642	.16261	.15893	.15539	.15198	.14868	.14551	.14244	.13948
56	.17991	.17583	.17190	.16811	.16445	.16092	.15752	.15423	.15106	.14799
57	.18984	.18564	.18160	.17769	.17392	.17029	.16677	.16338	.16010	.15692
58	.20018	.19587	.19172	.18770	.18382	.18007	.17645	.17295	.16956	.16628
59	.21093	.20652	.20225	.19812	.19414	.19028	.18655	.18294	.17945	.17606
60	.22206	.21753	.21316	.20893	.20483	.20087	.19703	.19332	.18972	.18624
61	.23353	.22890	.22442	.22009	.21589	.21182	.20788	.20407	.20037	.19678
62	.24532	.24059	.23601	.23158	.22728	.22311	.21907	.21515	.21135	.20767
63	.25742	.25260	.24793	.24339	.23900	.23473	.23060	.22658	.22268	.21890
64	.26987	.26495	.26019	.25556	.25107	.24671	.24248	.23837	.23438	.23050
65	.28271	.27771	.27286	.26815	.26357	.25912	.25480	.25059	.24651	.24254
66	.29601	.29093	.28600	.28120	.27654	.27200	.26760	.26331	.25913	.25507
67	.30978	.30462	.29961	.29474	.29000	.28539	.28090	.27653	.27227	.26813
68	.32401	.31879	.31371	.30877	.30396	.29927	.29471	.29027	.28593	.28171
69	.33863	.33336	.32822	.32322	.31835	.31359	.30896	.30445	.30005	.29576

Age	10.2%	10.4%	10.6%	10.8%	11.0%	11.2%	11.4%	11.6%	11.8%	12.0%
70	.35361	.34829	.34310	.33804	.33311	.32830	.32361	.31903	.31457	.31021
71	.36886	.36349	.35826	.35316	.34818	.34332	.33858	.33394	.32942	.32500
72	.38439	.37899	.37373	.36858	.36356	.35866	.35387	.34919	.34461	.34015
73	.40021	.39479	.38950	.38432	.37927	.37433	.36950	.36478	.36016	.35565
74	.41639	.41096	.40565	.40046	.39538	.39042	.38556	.38081	.37616	.37161
75	.43301	.42758	.42226	.41706	.41198	.40699	.40212	.39734	.39267	.38809
76	.45009	.44467	.43937	.43417	.42908	.42410	.41921	.41443	.40974	.40514
77	.46761	.46221	.45693	.45175	.44667	.44170	.43682	.43203	.42734	.42274
78	.48548	.48013	.47488	.46973	.46468	.45972	.45486	.45009	.44541	.44082
79	.50356	.49826	.49306	.48795	.48294	.47802	.47319	.46845	.46379	.45922
80	.52171	.51647	.51133	.50628	.50132	.49644	.49166	.48695	.48233	.47779
81	.53974	.53457	.52950	.52451	.51961	.51479	.51006	.50541	.50083	.49633
82	.55753	.55245	.54745	.54254	.53771	.53296	.52828	.52369	.51917	.51472
83	.57500	.57001	.56510	.56026	.55551	.55083	.54623	.54170	.53724	.53285
84	.59216	.58726	.58245	.57770	.57304	.56844	.56391	.55945	.55506	.55074
85	.60906	.60428	.59956	.59492	.59034	.58583	.58139	.57702	.57270	.56845
86	.62555	.62088	.61627	.61173	.60725	.60284	.59849	.59420	.58997	.58580
87	.64139	.63683	.63233	.62790	.62352	.61921	.61495	.61076	.60661	.60253
88	.65666	.65221	.64783	.64350	.63923	.63502	.63086	.62675	.62270	.61871
89	.67163	.66730	.66304	.65882	.65466	.65055	.64650	.64249	.63854	.63463
90	.68646	.68226	.67812	.67402	.66998	.66599	.66204	.65814	.65430	.65049
91	.70093	.69686	.69285	.68888	.68496	.68108	.67725	.67347	.66973	.66604
92	.71466	.71073	.70684	.70300	.69920	.69545	.69173	.68806	.68444	.68085
93	.72750	.72370	.71994	.71622	.71254	.70890	.70530	.70174	.69822	.69474
94	.73931	.73562	.73198	.72838	.72481	.72129	.71780	.71434	.71093	.70755
95	.75001	.74644	.74291	.73941	.73595	.73253	.72914	.72579	.72247	.71919
96	.75953	.75606	.75262	.74923	.74586	.74253	.73924	.73598	.73275	.72955
97	.76819	.76481	.76147	.75816	.75489	.75165	.74844	.74526	.74211	.73899
98	.77599	.77270	.76944	.76621	.76302	.75986	.75672	.75362	.75054	.74750
99	.78319	.77998	.77680	.77365	.77053	.76744	.76437	.76134	.75833	.75535
100	.78987	.78673	.78362	.78054	.77748	.77446	.77146	.76849	.76555	.76263
101	.79622	.79315	.79010	.78708	.78409	.78113	.77819	.77528	.77239	.76953
102	.80283	.79983	.79685	.79390	.79097	.78807	.78519	.78234	.77951	.77671
103	.80983	.80690	.80399	.80111	.79825	.79541	.79260	.78981	.78705	.78430
104	.81760	.81475	.81192	.80912	.80633	.80357	.80083	.79810	.79541	.79273
105	.82726	.82451	.82178	.81907	.81638	.81371	.81106	.80843	.80582	.80322
106	.84137	.83879	.83623	.83368	.83115	.82863	.82614	.82366	.82119	.81874
107	.86211	.85981	.85751	.85523	.85297	.85071	.84847	.84624	.84403	.84182
108	.89660	.89481	.89304	.89127	.88950	.88775	.88601	.88427	.88254	.88081
109	.95372	.95290	.95208	.95126	.95045	.94964	.94883	.94803	.94723	.94643

TABLE S
BASED ON LIFE TABLE 80CNSMT
SINGLE LIFE REMAINDER FACTORS
APPLICABLE AFTER APRIL 30, 1989
INTEREST RATE

Age	12.2%	12.4%	12.6%	12.8%	13.0%	13.2%	13.4%	13.6%	13.8%	14.0%
0	.01683	.01669	.01655	.01642	.01630	.01618	.01607	.01596	.01586	.01576
1	.00559	.00544	.00531	.00518	.00506	.00494	.00484	.00473	.00464	.00454
2	.00528	.00513	.00499	.00485	.00473	.00461	.00449	.00439	.00428	.00419
3	.00524	.00508	.00493	.00479	.00465	.00453	.00441	.00429	.00419	.00408
4	.00536	.00519	.00503	.00488	.00473	.00460	.00447	.00435	.00423	.00412
5	.00558	.00540	.00523	.00507	.00492	.00477	.00464	.00451	.00439	.00427
6	.00588	.00569	.00550	.00533	.00517	.00502	.00487	.00473	.00460	.00448
7	.00624	.00604	.00584	.00566	.00549	.00532	.00517	.00502	.00488	.00475
8	.00668	.00646	.00626	.00606	.00588	.00570	.00554	.00538	.00523	.00509
9	.00722	.00699	.00677	.00656	.00636	.00617	.00600	.00583	.00567	.00552
10	.00785	.00761	.00737	.00715	.00694	.00674	.00655	.00637	.00620	.00604
11	.00861	.00835	.00810	.00786	.00764	.00743	.00723	.00704	.00686	.00668
12	.00946	.00918	.00891	.00866	.00843	.00820	.00799	.00779	.00760	.00741
13	.01035	.01006	.00978	.00951	.00927	.00903	.00880	.00859	.00839	.00819
14	.01122	.01091	.01061	.01034	.01007	.00982	.00958	.00936	.00914	.00894
15	.01203	.01171	.01140	.01110	.01082	.01056	.01031	.01007	.00985	.00963
16	.01279	.01244	.01211	.01181	.01151	.01123	.01097	.01072	.01048	.01025

Proposed Regulations

Age	12.2%	12.4%	12.6%	12.8%	13.0%	13.2%	13.4%	13.6%	13.8%	14.0%
17	.01347	.01311	.01276	.01244	.01213	.01184	.01156	.01130	.01104	.01081
18	.01411	.01373	.01336	.01302	.01270	.01239	.01210	.01182	.01155	.01130
19	.01474	.01434	.01396	.01359	.01325	.01293	.01262	.01233	.01205	.01178
20	.01537	.01494	.01454	.01415	.01379	.01345	.01313	.01282	.01252	.01224
21	.01598	.01553	.01510	.01470	.01432	.01396	.01361	.01329	.01298	.01268
22	.01660	.01613	.01568	.01525	.01485	.01446	.01410	.01375	.01343	.01312
23	.01725	.01674	.01627	.01581	.01539	.01498	.01460	.01423	.01388	.01355
24	.01796	.01742	.01692	.01644	.01599	.01556	.01515	.01476	.01439	.01404
25	.01876	.01819	.01765	.01714	.01666	.01621	.01577	.01536	.01497	.01460
26	.01967	.01907	.01850	.01796	.01745	.01696	.01650	.01606	.01565	.01525
27	.02072	.02008	.01948	.01890	.01836	.01784	.01735	.01688	.01644	.01601
28	.02190	.02122	.02057	.01996	.01938	.01883	.01831	.01781	.01734	.01689
29	.02322	.02249	.02181	.02116	.02054	.01996	.01940	.01887	.01836	.01788
30	.02469	.02392	.02319	.02250	.02184	.02122	.02062	.02006	.01952	.01900
31	.02634	.02552	.02475	.02401	.02331	.02264	.02201	.02140	.02083	.02028
32	.02816	.02729	.02647	.02568	.02494	.02423	.02355	.02291	.02229	.02170
33	.03018	.02926	.02838	.02755	.02675	.02600	.02528	.02459	.02393	.02331
34	.03239	.03142	.03048	.02960	.02875	.02795	.02718	.02645	.02575	.02508
35	.03482	.03378	.03279	.03185	.03095	.03009	.02928	.02850	.02775	.02704
36	.03743	.03633	.03528	.03428	.03333	.03242	.03155	.03072	.02992	.02916
37	.04026	.03909	.03798	.03692	.03591	.03494	.03401	.03313	.03228	.03147
38	.04330	.04207	.04089	.03977	.03869	.03767	.03668	.03574	.03484	.03398
39	.04658	.04528	.04403	.04284	.04170	.04061	.03957	.03857	.03762	.03670
40	.05011	.04873	.04741	.04615	.04495	.04379	.04269	.04163	.04061	.03964
41	.05389	.05244	.05104	.04971	.04844	.04721	.04604	.04492	.04384	.04281
42	.05791	.05638	.05491	.05350	.05216	.05086	.04962	.04844	.04729	.04620
43	.06219	.06057	.05902	.05754	.05612	.05475	.05344	.05218	.05098	.04981
44	.06673	.06503	.06340	.06184	.06034	.05890	.05752	.05619	.05491	.05368
45	.07157	.06978	.06806	.06642	.06484	.06332	.06186	.06046	.05911	.05781
46	.07669	.07481	.07301	.07128	.06962	.06802	.06649	.06501	.06358	.06221
47	.08212	.08015	.07826	.07645	.07470	.07302	.07140	.06984	.06834	.06690
48	.08784	.08578	.08380	.08190	.08006	.07830	.07660	.07496	.07338	.07186
49	.09384	.09169	.08961	.08762	.08570	.08384	.08206	.08034	.07868	.07708
50	.10013	.09787	.09570	.09361	.09160	.08966	.08779	.08598	.08424	.08256
51	.10671	.10436	.10209	.09991	.09780	.09577	.09381	.09192	.09009	.08832
52	.11365	.11120	.10883	.10655	.10435	.10222	.10017	.09819	.09628	.09442
53	.12095	.11840	.11593	.11355	.11126	.10904	.10689	.10482	.10282	.10088
54	.12860	.12595	.12338	.12090	.11851	.11619	.11396	.11179	.10970	.10767
55	.13663	.13386	.13120	.12862	.12613	.12372	.12138	.11912	.11694	.11482
56	.14503	.14217	.13940	.13672	.13413	.13162	.12919	.12683	.12456	.12235
57	.15385	.15089	.14801	.14523	.14254	.13994	.13741	.13496	.13259	.13029
58	.16311	.16004	.15706	.15418	.15139	.14868	.14606	.14352	.14105	.13866
59	.17279	.16961	.16654	.16355	.16066	.15786	.15514	.15250	.14994	.14745
60	.18286	.17958	.17640	.17332	.17033	.16743	.16462	.16188	.15922	.15664
61	.19330	.18992	.18665	.18347	.18038	.17738	.17447	.17164	.16889	.16622
62	.20409	.20061	.19724	.19396	.19078	.18768	.18467	.18175	.17891	.17614
63	.21522	.21165	.20818	.20480	.20152	.19833	.19523	.19221	.18928	.18642
64	.22672	.22306	.21949	.21602	.21265	.20937	.20617	.20306	.20003	.19708
65	.23867	.23491	.23125	.22769	.22423	.22085	.21757	.21437	.21125	.20821
66	.25112	.24727	.24353	.23988	.23632	.23286	.22948	.22619	.22299	.21986
67	.26409	.26016	.25633	.25260	.24896	.24541	.24195	.23857	.23528	.23206
68	.27760	.27359	.26968	.26586	.26214	.25851	.25497	.25151	.24814	.24484
69	.29157	.28748	.28350	.27961	.27581	.27211	.26849	.26495	.26150	.25812
70	.30596	.30181	.29775	.29379	.28992	.28614	.28245	.27884	.27532	.27187
71	.32069	.31648	.31236	.30833	.30440	.30055	.29679	.29312	.28952	.28600
72	.33578	.33151	.32733	.32325	.31925	.31535	.31152	.30778	.30412	.30054
73	.35123	.34691	.34269	.33855	.33450	.33054	.32666	.32286	.31914	.31550
74	.36715	.36279	.35852	.35434	.35024	.34623	.34230	.33845	.33468	.33098
75	.38360	.37921	.37491	.37069	.36656	.36250	.35853	.35464	.35082	.34708
76	.40064	.39623	.39190	.38765	.38349	.37941	.37540	.37148	.36762	.36384
77	.41823	.41381	.40947	.40521	.40103	.39692	.39290	.38895	.38507	.38126
78	.43632	.43189	.42755	.42329	.41910	.41499	.41095	.40698	.40309	.39926
79	.45473	.45032	.44599	.44173	.43755	.43344	.42940	.42543	.42153	.41770

Age	12.2%	12.4%	12.6%	12.8%	13.0%	13.2%	13.4%	13.6%	13.8%	14.0%
80	.47333	.46894	.46463	.46040	.45623	.45213	.44811	.44414	.44025	.43642
81	.49191	.48755	.48328	.47907	.47493	.47085	.46684	.46290	.45902	.45520
82	.51034	.50603	.50179	.49762	.49351	.48947	.48549	.48157	.47772	.47392
83	.52852	.52427	.52008	.51595	.51189	.50788	.50394	.50006	.49623	.49246
84	.54648	.54228	.53815	.53407	.53006	.52610	.52221	.51836	.51458	.51084
85	.56426	.56013	.55606	.55205	.54810	.54420	.54035	.53656	.53282	.52913
86	.58169	.57764	.57364	.56970	.56581	.56197	.55818	.55445	.55076	.54713
87	.59850	.59452	.59060	.58673	.58291	.57913	.57541	.57174	.56811	.56453
88	.61476	.61086	.60702	.60322	.59947	.59577	.59212	.58851	.58494	.58142
89	.63078	.62697	.62321	.61950	.61583	.61220	.60862	.60508	.60159	.59813
90	.64674	.64302	.63935	.63573	.63215	.62861	.62511	.62165	.61823	.61485
91	.66238	.65877	.65520	.65167	.64819	.64474	.64133	.63795	.63462	.63132
92	.67730	.67379	.67032	.66689	.66350	.66014	.65682	.65354	.65029	.64708
93	.69130	.68789	.68452	.68119	.67789	.67463	.67140	.66820	.66504	.66191
94	.70421	.70090	.69762	.69438	.69118	.68800	.68486	.68175	.67867	.67563
95	.71594	.71272	.70954	.70639	.70326	.70017	.69712	.69409	.69109	.68812
96	.72638	.72325	.72014	.71707	.71403	.71101	.70803	.70507	.70215	.69925
97	.73590	.73285	.72982	.72682	.72385	.72090	.71799	.71510	.71224	.70941
98	.74448	.74149	.73853	.73560	.73269	.72981	.72696	.72414	.72134	.71856
99	.75240	.74948	.74658	.74371	.74086	.73805	.73525	.73248	.72974	.72702
100	.75974	.75687	.75403	.75121	.74842	.74566	.74292	.74020	.73751	.73484
101	.76669	.76388	.76109	.75833	.75559	.75287	.75018	.74751	.74486	.74223
102	.77393	.77117	.76844	.76573	.76304	.76037	.75773	.75511	.75251	.74993
103	.78158	.77888	.77620	.77355	.77091	.76830	.76571	.76313	.76058	.75805
104	.79007	.78743	.78482	.78222	.77964	.77709	.77455	.77203	.76953	.76705
105	.80065	.79809	.79556	.79304	.79054	.78805	.78559	.78314	.78071	.77829
106	.81631	.81389	.81149	.80911	.80674	.80438	.80204	.79972	.79741	.79511
107	.83963	.83745	.83529	.83313	.83099	.82886	.82674	.82463	.82254	.82045
108	.87910	.87739	.87569	.87400	.87232	.87064	.86897	.86731	.86566	.86401
109	.94563	.94484	.94405	.94326	.94248	.94170	.94092	.94014	.93937	.93860

TABLE 80CNSMT

Age x	1(x)	Age x	1(x)	Age x	1(x)
(1)	(2)	(1)	(2)	(1)	(2)
0	100000	37	95492	74	59279
1	98740	38	95317	75	56799
2	98648	39	95129	76	54239
3	98584	40	94926	77	51599
4	98535	41	94706	78	48878
5	98495	42	94465	79	46071
6	98459	43	94201	80	43180
7	98426	44	93913	81	40208
8	98396	45	93599	82	37172
9	98370	46	93256	83	34095
10	98347	47	92882	84	31012
11	98328	48	92472	85	27960
12	98309	49	92021	86	24961
13	98285	50	91526	87	22038
14	98248	51	90986	88	19235
15	98196	52	90402	89	16598
16	98129	53	89771	90	14154
17	98047	54	89087	91	11908
18	97953	55	88348	92	9863
19	97851	56	87551	93	8032
20	97741	57	86695	94	6424
21	97623	58	85776	95	5043
22	97499	59	84789	96	3884
23	97370	60	83726	97	2939
24	97240	61	82581	98	2185
25	97110	62	81348	99	1598
26	96982	63	80024	100	1150
27	96856	64	78609	101	815
28	96730	65	77107	102	570

Age x	1(x)	Age x	1(x)	Age x	1(x)
29	96604	66	75520	103	393
30	96477	67	73846	104	267
31	96350	68	72082	105	179
32	96220	69	70218	106	119
33	96088	70	68248	107	78
34	95951	71	66165	108	51
35	95808	72	63972	109	33
36	95655	73	61673	110	0

Par. 18. Section 20.2031-10 is removed.

* * *

Shirley D. Peterson

Commissioner of Internal Revenue

[¶ 20,191 Reserved.—Proposed Regulation Sec. 1.514(c)-2, relating to unrelated business income partnerships, was formerly reproduced at this point. The final regulations appear at ¶ 13,234B.]

¶ 20,192

Proposed regulations: Cash or deferred arrangements: Collective bargaining units.—The IRS has issued proposed amendments to final regulations under Code Sec. 401(k) that allow a plan sponsor or administrator of a cash or deferred arrangement to treat portions of the plan that benefit employees of different collective bargaining units as separate plans or as one plan for aggregation purposes. However, disaggregation of a plan covering members of collective bargaining units and employees who are not included in collective bargaining units is still mandatory. The proposed optional disaggregation rules for cash or deferred arrangements also apply to certain multiemployer plans. The proposed amendments were published in the *Federal Register* on January 4, 1993 (58 FR 43).

[4830-01]

DEPARTMENT OF THE TREASURY

Internal Revenue Service

26 CFR Part 1

[EE-42-92]

RIN 1545-AQ77

Certain cash or deferred arrangements under employee plans.

AGENCY: Internal Revenue Service, Treasury.

ACTION: Notice of Proposed Rulemaking.

SUMMARY: This document proposes to amend final regulations under section 401(k). The proposed amendments will affect sponsors of certain cash or deferred arrangements benefiting employees who are members of collective bargaining units.

DATES: Written comments and requests for a public hearing must be received by March 5, 1993.

ADDRESSES: Send written comments and requests for a public hearing to: Internal Revenue Service, P.O. Box 7604, Ben Franklin Station, Attention: CC:CORP:T:R (EE-42-92), Washington, D.C. 20044. In the alternative, comments may be hand delivered to: Internal Revenue Building, Room 5228, 1111 Constitution Ave., N.W., Attention: CC:CORP:T:R (EE-42-92), Washington, D.C.

FOR FURTHER INFORMATION CONTACT: Cheryl Press at 202-622-4688 (not a toll-free number).

SUPPLEMENTARY INFORMATION:

Background

Final regulations under section 401(k) of the Internal Revenue Code (Code) were published in the Federal Register on August 15, 1991 (56 FR 40507). Amendments to the final regulations were published in the Federal Register on December 4, 1991 (56 FR 63420). Corrections to the final regulations were published in the Federal Register on March 25, 1992 (57 FR 10289).

Explanation of Provisions

This document proposes amendments to the final regulations under section 401(k) of the Code. The proposed amendments simplify the application of the regulations to certain plans benefiting employees who are members of collective bargaining units. The amendments modify the definition of the term "plan" to make optional, instead of mandatory, the disaggregation of a plan covering members of more than one collective bargaining unit.

Section 1.401(k)-1(g)(11)(iii)(A) of the final regulations provides that a plan that benefits employees who are included in a unit of employees covered by a collective bargaining agreement and employees who are not included in a collective bargaining unit is treated as comprising separate plans. Furthermore, employees of each collective bargaining unit benefiting under the plan must be treated as covered under a separate plan. Thus, for example, if a plan benefits employees in three categories, employees included in collective bargaining unit A, employees included in unit B, and those not included in any collective bargaining unit, the plan is treated as comprising three separate plans, each of which benefits only one category of employees. Many commentators have suggested that an employer be required instead to treat the portion of the plan that benefits employees included in collective bargaining units as a separate plan from the portion of the plan that benefits other employees.

The proposed amendments adopt the approach suggested by commentators. The portion of a plan that benefits employees who are included in collective bargaining units and the portion that benefits employees who are not included in collective bargaining units must be treated as comprising separate plans. However, further disaggregation of the plan by collective bargaining units is permissive, provided that the combinations of units are determined on a basis that is reasonable and reasonably consistent from year to year. An employer or plan administrator, as appropriate, may therefore treat the entire portion of a plan benefiting members of collective bargaining units as a single plan, may treat the portion benefiting members of each collective bargaining unit as separate plans, or may aggregate the portions benefiting members of any two or more collective bargaining units.

Section 1.401(k)-1(g)(11)(iii)(D) is similarly amended to make permissive the disaggregation of a multiemployer plan by collective bargaining unit. Under the final regulations, only the portion of a multiemployer plan benefiting employees under the same collective bargaining agreement and the same benefit computation formula is treated as a separate plan. Under the proposed amendments, the employer or plan administrator may choose to disaggregate this separate plan further on the basis of collective bargaining units.

Under §§ 1.401(k)-1(a)(7)(i) and 1.402(a)-1(d)(3)(iv) of the final regulations, a collectively bargained plan is only required to satisfy the actual deferral percentage test for plan years beginning after December 31, 1992. The proposed amendments are effective for the same plan years.

The proposed amendments to the regulations change the aggregation rules only for collectively bargained plans. Treasury and the Service anticipate further technical amendments to the regulations under section 401(k) and related provisions. No inference should be drawn from these proposed amendments concerning any other issue under the final regulations, including any other issue involving the treatment of collectively bargained or multiemployer plans.

Comments on the proposed amendments, and on any other issues or problems related to the testing of plans with participants who are members of collective bargaining units, are invited. In particular, comments are invited regarding the aggregation or disaggregation of multiemployer plans by collective bargaining agreement (as opposed to or in addition to collective bargaining unit) or by benefit computation formula.

Special Analyses

It has been determined that these proposed rules are not major rules as defined in Executive Order 12291. Therefore, a Regulatory Impact Analysis is not required. It has also been determined that section 553(b) of the Administrative Procedure Act (5 U.S.C. chapter 5) and the Regulatory Flexibility Act (5 U.S.C. chapter 6) do not apply to these regulations and, therefore, an initial Regulatory Flexibility Analysis is not required. Pursuant to section 7805(f) of the Code, these regulations will be submitted to the Chief Counsel for Advocacy of the Small Business Administration for comment on their impact on small business.

Written Comments

Before adopting these proposed regulations, consideration will be given to any written comments that are submitted timely (preferably a signed original and eight copies) to the Internal Revenue Service. All comments will be available for public inspection and copying in their entirety.

Drafting Information

The principal author of these regulations is Cheryl Press, Office of the Associate Chief Counsel (Employee Benefits and Exempt Organizations), Internal Revenue Service. However, personnel from other offices of the Service and Treasury Department participated in their development.

List of Subjects in 26 CFR 1.401-0 through 1.419A-2T

Bonds, Employee benefit plans, Income taxes, Pensions, Reporting and recordkeeping requirements, Securities, Trusts and trustees.

Proposed Amendments to the Regulations

Accordingly, 26 CFR part 1 is proposed to be amended as follows:

PART I—INCOME TAX; TAXABLE YEARS BEGINNING AFTER DECEMBER 31, 1953

Par. 1. The authority citation for part 1 continues to read, in part, as follows:

Authority: 26 U.S.C. 7805 * * *

Par. 2. Section 1.401(k)-1 is amended by revising paragraphs (g)(11)(iii)(A) and (g)(11)(iii)(D)(2) to read as follows:

§ 1.401(k)-1 *Certain cash or deferred arrangements.*

* * *

(g) * * *

(11) * * *

(iii) * * *

(A) *Plans benefiting collective bargaining unit employees.* A plan that benefits employees who are included in a unit of employees covered by a collective bargaining agreement and employees who are not included in such a collective bargaining unit is treated as comprising separate plans. This paragraph (g)(11)(iii)(A) is generally applied separately with respect to each collective bargaining unit. At the option of the employer, however, two or more separate collective bargaining units can be treated as a single collective bargaining unit, provided that the combinations of units are determined on a basis that is reasonable and reasonably consistent from year to year. Thus, for example, if a plan benefits employees in three categories—employees included in collective bargaining unit A, employees included in collective bargaining unit B, and employees who are not included in any collective bargaining unit—the plan can be treated as comprising three separate plans, each of which benefits only one category of employees. However, if collective bargaining units A and B are treated as a single collective bargaining unit, the plan will be treated as comprising only two separate plans, one benefiting all employees who are included in a collective bargaining unit and another benefiting all other employees. Similarly, if a plan benefits only employees who are included in collective bargaining unit A and collective bargaining unit B, the plan can be treated as comprising two separate plans. However, if collective bargaining units A and B are treated as a single collective bargaining unit, the plan will be treated as a single plan.

* * *

(D) * * *

(2) *Multiemployer plans.* Consistent with section 413(b), the portion of the plan that is maintained pursuant to a collective bargaining agreement (within the meaning of § 1.413-1(a)(2)) is treated as a single plan maintained by a single employer that employs all the employees benefiting under the same benefit computation formula and covered pursuant to that collective bargaining agreement. [As corrected by 58 FR 15312 on March 22, 1993 and Announcement 93-56, I.R.B. 1993-15, 12.] The rules of paragraph (g)(11)(iii)(A) of this section (including the optional aggregation of collective bargaining units) apply to the resulting deemed single plan in the same manner as they would to a single employer plan, except that the plan administrator is substituted for the employer where appropriate and appropriate fiduciary obligations are taken into account. The non-collectively bargained portion of the plan is treated as maintained by one or more employers, depending on whether the non-collective bargaining unit employees who benefit under the plan are employed by one or more employers.

* * *

Shirley D. Peterson

Commissioner of Internal Revenue

[¶ 20,193 Reserved.—Proposed regulations under Code Sec. 401(a)(4) were formerly reproduced at this paragraph. The final regulations appear at ¶ 11,720W-14.]

¶ 20,194

Proposed regulations: Tax-exempt organizations: Unrelated business taxable income: Income from corporate sponsorship.—The IRS has issued proposed regulations giving guidance on whether sponsorship payments received by exempt organizations under Code Sec. 501(a) are unrelated business taxable income, as defined in Code Sec. 512. The proposed regulations also clarify that the allocation rules governing the use of exempt activities apply to sponsorship income.

The proposed regulations were published in the *Federal Register* on January 22, 1993 (58 FR 5687). The proposed amendments were officially withdrawn by IRS on March 1, 2000 (65 FR 11015).

[¶ 20,195 Reserved.—Proposed regulations on minimum coverage requirements under Code Sec. 410(b) were formerly reproduced at this paragraph. The final regulations appear at ¶ 12,165.]

[¶ 20,196 Reserved.—Proposed regulations on the definition of compensation under Code sec. 414(s) were formerly reproduced at this paragraph. The final regulations appear at ¶ 12,364K.]

[¶ 20,197 Reserved.—Proposed regulations on permitted disparity under Code Sec. 401(l) were formerly reproduced at this paragraph. The final regulations appear at ¶ 11,731Q.]

[¶ 20,198 Reserved.—Proposed regulations under Code Sec. 414(a), relating to separate lines of business, were formerly reproduced at this paragraph. The final regulations are at ¶ 12,165, 12,365D, 12,364F-11 through 12,364F-19, and 12,364F-22.]

[¶ 20,199 Reserved.—Proposed regulations relating to payroll reporting and deposit rules for employers were formerly reproduced here. The final regulations are now at ¶ 13,649F.]

[¶ 20,200 Reserved.—Proposed regulations on the compensation limit for qualified plans under Code Sec. 401(a)(17) were formerly reproduced at this paragraph. The final regulations are at ¶ 11,720Z-11.]

[¶ 20,201 Reserved.—Proposed regulations on the $1 million cap on deductible employee renumeration were formerly reproduced at this paragraph. The final regulations are at ¶ 11,307.]

[¶ 20,202 Reserved.—Proposed regulations on the $1 million cap on deductible employee renumeration were formerly reproduced at this paragraph. The final regulations are at ¶ 11,307.]

[¶ 20,203 Reserved.—Proposed Reg. §1.83-6, concerning the elimination of the withholding requirement as a prerequisite to claiming a deduction for property transferred to an employee in connection with the performance of service, formerly was reproduced here. The final regulation is at ¶ 11,246.]

[¶ 20,204 Reserved.—Proposed regulations relating to the financial requirements of nonbank trustees were formerly reproduced at this paragraph. The final regulations are at ¶ 11,725 and ¶ 12,054.]

¶ 20,205

Actuarial assumptions: GATT.—The new interest and mortality rules for valuing lump-sum distributions under GATT have been put into temporary and proposed regulations under Code Sec. 417.

The new regulations explain the time for determining the applicable 30-year Treasury bond interest rate, provide when plans may use an interest rate and/or mortality table that is an alternative to the new applicable interest rate and mortality table, explain the various effective date options a plan has before implementing the new rules, and specify under what circumstances application of the new rules will not result in a reduction of benefits under Code Sec. 411(d)(6).

The temporary and proposed regulations were published in the *Federal Register* on April 5, 1995 (60 FR 17286) and are reproduced at ¶ 12,556 and 12,557.

The regulations were finalized April 7, 1998 (63 FR 16895). The regulations are reproduced at ¶ 12,556 and ¶ 12,557. The preamble is reproduced at ¶ 23,140.

[¶ 20,206 Reserved] .—Proposed regulations regarding the requirement that persons furnish a taxpayer identification number on returns, statements, or other documents under Code Sec. 6109 were formerly reproduced at this paragraph. The final regulations now appear at ¶ 13,782. The introductory material proceding the final regulations is at ¶ 23,128.]

¶ 20,207

Proposed Regulations: Distributions: Consent requirements.—The IRS has proposed regulations regarding the consent requirements for distributions under Code Sec. 411(a)(11) and QJSA's under Code Sec. 417. The proposed regulations, which were also issued as temporary regulations, are structured to allow plan administrators to provide the participant notices required under sections 411(a)(11) and 417 at the same time of providing the notice regarding rollover treatment under Code Sec. 402(f).

The proposed regulations also allow a plan to distribute benefits prior to the expiration of the 30-day time period, provided certain requirements are met and the participant affirmatively elects the earlier distribution after being properly informed. The proposed regulations also delegate authority to the Commissioner of the IRS to provide further guidance on the notice requirements to address the use of electronic media and invites comments on this subject.

The temporary and proposed regulations were published in the *Federal Register* on September 22, 1995 (60 FR 49236) and are reproduced at ¶ 12,219E and 12,557.

The regulations were finalized December 18, 1998 (63 FR 70009). The regulations are reproduced at ¶ 12,219D and ¶ 12,556. The preamble is reproduced at ¶ 23,147.

¶ 20,208

Withholding: Nonpayroll payments.—The IRS has issued final, temporary and proposed regulations regarding the reporting of income taxes withheld on nonpayroll payments under Code Sec. 6011, including withholding on pension, annuities, IRAs and other deferred income subject to withholding. Final regulations were amended to refer to new temporary regulations which were also issued as proposed regulations providing interested persons the opportunity to comment.

The IRS previously issued final regulations removing all nonpayroll withholding taxes from reporting on Form 941, Employer's Quarterly Federal Tax Return (CCH PENSION PLAN GUIDE ¶ 10,728) and requiring those taxes to be reported on Form 945, Annual Return of Withheld Federal Income Tax (CCH PENSION PLAN GUIDE ¶ 10,730). Those regulations were effective December 23, 1993 and provided that if a person was required to file a Form 945 for calendar year 1994, that person was required to continue to file Form 945 annually until a final return was filed, even if the person was no longer liable for withholding income taxes for nonpayroll payments. In response to several comments received, the proposed and temporary regulations provide a person must file a Form 945 only for a calendar year in which the person is required to withhold federal income tax from nonpayroll payments.

The proposed regulations were published in the *Federal Register* on October 16, 1995 and are reproduced with the preamble below. The final and temporary regulations were also published in the *Federal Register* on October 16, 1995 and are at ¶ 13,649F and ¶ 13,649G.

DEPARTMENT OF THE TREASURY

Internal Revenue Service

26 CFR Part 31

RIN 1545-AT86

Reporting of Nonpayroll Withheld Tax Liabilities

AGENCY: Internal Revenue Service (IRS), Treasury.

ACTION: Notice of proposed rulemaking by cross-reference to temporary regulations.

SUMMARY: In the Rules and Regulations section of this issue of the Federal Register, the IRS is issuing temporary regulations relating to the reporting of nonpayroll withheld income taxes under section 6011 of the Internal Revenue Code. The text of the temporary regulations also serves as the text for this notice of proposed rulemaking.

DATES: Written comments and requests for a public hearing must be received by December 15, 1995.

ADDRESSES: Send submissions to: CC:DOM:CORP:T:R (IA-30-95), room 5228, Internal Revenue Service, POB 7604, Ben Franklin Station, Washington, DC 20044. In the alternative, submissions may be hand delivered between the hours of 8 a.m. and 5 p.m. to:

CC:DOM:CORP:T:R (IA-30-95), Courier's Desk, Internal Revenue Service, 1111 Constitution Ave. NW., Washington, D.C.

FOR FURTHER INFORMATION CONTACT: Vincent G. Surabian, (202) 622-6232 (not a toll-free number).

SUPPLEMENTARY INFORMATION:

Paperwork Reduction Act

The collection of information contained in this notice of proposed rulemaking has been submitted to the Office of Management and Budget (OMB) for review in accordance with the Paperwork Reduction Act of 1995 (44 U.S.C. 3507). The collection of information is in §31.6011(a)-4T(b). This information is required by the IRS to monitor compliance with the federal tax rules related to the reporting and deposit of nonpayroll withheld taxes.

Comments on the collection of information should be sent to the Office of Management and Budget, Attn: Desk Officer for the Department of the Treasury, Office of Information and Regulatory Affairs, Washington, DC 20503, with copies to the Internal Revenue Service, Attn: IRS Reports Clearance Officer, PC:FP, Washington, DC 20224. To ensure that comments on the collection of information may be given full consideration during the review by the Office of Management and Budget, comments on the collection of information should be received by December 15, 1995.

An agency may not conduct or sponsor, and a person is not required to respond to, a collection of information unless the collection of information displays a valid control number.

Books or records relating to a collection of information must be retained as long as their contents may become material in the administration of any internal revenue law. Generally, tax returns and tax return information are confidential, as required by 26 U.S.C. 6103.

Estimates of the reporting burden in this Notice of Proposed Rulemaking will be reflected in the burden of Form 945.

Background

The temporary regulations published in the Rules and Regulations section of this issue of the Federal Register contain an amendment to the Regulations on Employment Taxes and Collection of Income Tax at Source (26 CFR part 31). This amendment relates to the reporting of nonpayroll withheld tax liabilities. The temporary regulations change the rule regarding the filing of Form 945, Annual Return of Withheld Federal Income Tax, for a calendar year in which there is no liability.

The text of those temporary regulations also serves as the text of these proposed regulations. The preamble to the temporary regulations explains these proposed regulations.

Special Analyses

It has been determined that this notice of proposed rulemaking is not a significant regulatory action as defined in EO 12866. Therefore, a regulatory assessment is not required. It also has been determined that section 553(b) of the Administrative Procedure Act (5 U.S.C. chapter 5) and the Regulatory Flexibility Act (5 U.S.C. chapter 6) do not apply to these regulations, and, therefore, a Regulatory Flexibility Analysis is not required. Pursuant to section 7805(f) of the Internal Revenue Code, this notice of proposed rulemaking will be submitted to the Chief Counsel for Advocacy of the Small Business Administration for comment on its impact on small business.

Comments and Requests for a Public Hearing

Before these proposed regulations are adopted as final regulations, consideration will be given to any written comments (preferably a signed original and eight (8) copies) that are timely submitted to the IRS. All comments will be available for public inspection and copying. A public hearing may be scheduled if requested in writing by a person that timely submits written comments. If a public hearing is scheduled, notice of the date, time, and place for the hearing will be published in the Federal Register.

Drafting Information

The principal author of these regulations is Vincent G. Surabian, Office of Assistant Chief Counsel (Income Tax and Accounting). However, other personnel from the IRS and Treasury Department participated in their development.

List of Subjects in 26 CFR Part 31

Employment taxes, Income taxes, Penalties, Pensions, Railroad retirement, Reporting and recordkeeping requirements, Social security, Unemployment compensation.

Proposed Amendments to the Regulations

Accordingly, 26 CFR part 31 is proposed to be amended as follows:

PART 31—EMPLOYMENT TAXES AND COLLECTION OF INCOME TAX AT SOURCE

Paragraph 1. The authority citation for part 31 continues to read in part as follows:

Authority: 26 U.S.C. 7805 ***

Par. 2. In §31.6011(a)-4, paragraph (b) is revised to read as follows:

§31.6011(a)-4 Returns of income tax withheld.

*****

(b) [The text of this proposed paragraph (b) is the same as the text of §31.6011(a)-4T(b) [¶ 13,649G] published elsewhere in this issue of the Federal Register].

*****

Margaret Milner Richardson

Commissioner of Internal Revenue

¶ 20,209

ERISA: Notice requirements: Minimum funding standards: Benefit accrual.—The IRS has issued temporary and proposed regulations, in question and answer format, addressing the notice requirements of ERISA Sec. 204(h) when a defined benefit plan or individual account plan that is subject to ERISA's minimum funding standards is amended to provide for a significant reduction in the rate of future benefit accrual. The IRS determined that the guidance in the temporary regulations was needed immediately because issues relating to ERISA Sec. 204(h) arise in connection with a broad range of plan amendments, including amendments prompted by recent changes in the law. The text of the temporary regulation is also the text for the proposed regulation.

The regulations clarify that an amendment to a defined benefit plan that does not affect the annual benefit commencing at normal retirement age does not affect the rate of future benefit accrual. Therefore, a plan administrator need not provide a section 204(h) notice when a plan amendment only affects other forms of payment such as lump sum distributions or benefits commencing at a date other than normal retirement age. The regulations also clarify that a 204(h) notice is only required for an amendment to an individual account plan that significantly reduces the rate of future benefit accrual. The regulations delegate authority to the Commissioner of the IRS to provide a 204(h) notice need not be provided with respect to plan amendments that the Commissioner determines, by published revenue rulings, notices, or other guidance published in the Internal Revenue Bulletin, are necessary or appropriate, as a result of a change in federal law or to maintain compliance with the law. The regulations also provide guidance on to whom the notice must be provided.

The proposed regulations were published in the *Federal Register* on December 15, 1995 (60 FR 66233).

The regulations were finalized December 4, 1998 (63 FR 68678). The regulations are reproduced at ¶ 12,234M. The preamble is reproduced at ¶ 23,146.

DEPARTMENT OF THE TREASURY

Internal Revenue Service

6 CFR Part 1

[EE-34-95]

IN 1545-AT78

Notice of Significant Reduction in the Rate of Future Benefit Accrual.

AGENCY: Internal Revenue Service (IRS), Treasury.

ACTION: Notice of proposed rulemaking by cross-reference to temporary regulations.

SUMMARY: In the Rules and Regulations section of this issue of the Federal Register, the IRS is issuing temporary regulations relating to the requirements of section 204(h) of the Employee Retirement Income Security Act of 1974, as amended (ERISA). Section 204(h) of ERISA applies to defined benefit plans and to individual account plans that are subject to the funding standards of section 302 of ERISA. It requires the plan administrator to give notice of certain plan amendments to participants in the plan and certain other parties. The text of those temporary regulations also serves as the text of these proposed regulations.

DATES: Written comments must be received by March 14, 1996.

ADDRESSES: Send submissions to CC:DOM:CORP:R (EE-34-95), room 5228, Internal Revenue Service, POB 7604, Ben Franklin Station, Washington, DC 20044. In the alternative, submissions may be hand delivered between the hours of 8 a.m. and 5 p.m. to CC:DOM:CORP:R (EE-34-95), Courier's Desk, Internal Revenue Service, 1111 Constitution Avenue NW., Washington DC.

FOR FURTHER INFORMATION CONTACT: Betty J. Clary, (202) 622-6070 (not a toll-free number).

SUPPLEMENTARY INFORMATION:

Paperwork Reduction Act

The collection of information contained in this notice of proposed rulemaking has been submitted to the Office of Management and Budget for review in accordance with the Paperwork Reduction Act of 1995 (44 U.S.C. 3507).

Comments on the collection of information should be sent to the Office of Management and Budget, Attn: Desk Officer for the Department of Treasury, Office of Information and Regulatory Affairs, Washington DC 20503, with copies to the Internal Revenue Service, Attn: IRS Reports Clearance Officer, T:FP, Washington, DC 20224. Comments on the collection of information should be received by February 13, 1996.

An agency may not conduct or sponsor, and a person is not required to respond to, a collection of information unless the collection of information displays a valid control number.

The collection of information is in § 1.411(d)-6T which implements the statutory requirement of section 204(h) of ERISA that a plan administrator provide notice to participants and certain other parties if certain pension plans are amended to provide for a significant reduction in the rate of futurebenefit accrual. This collection of information is required to assure that the rights of participants in plans subject to section 204(h) of ERISA are protected. The likely respondents are small businesses. Responses to this collection of information are required under section 204(h) of ERISA in order for certain amendments to qualified plans to become effective.

These regulations do not involve any issues of confidentiality.

Estimated total annual reporting burden: 15,000 hours.

The estimated annual burden per respondent varies from 1 hour to 40 hours, depending on individual circumstances, with an estimated average of 5 hours.

Estimated number of respondents: 3,000.

Estimated annual frequency of responses: Once.

Background

Temporary regulations in the Rules and Regulations portion of this issue of the Federal Register amend the Income Tax Regulations (26 CFR part 1) (relating to section 411(d)). The text of those temporary regulations also serves as the text of these proposed regulations. The preamble to the temporary regulations explains the temporary regulations.

Special Analyses

It has been determined that this notice of proposed rulemaking is not a significant regulatory action as defined in EO 12866. Therefore, a regulatory assessment is not required. It also has been determined that section 553(b) of the Administrative Procedure Act (5 U.S.C. chapter 5) and the Regulatory Flexibility Act (5 U.S.C. chapter 6) do not apply to these regulations, and, therefore, a Regulatory Flexibility Analysis is not required. Pursuant to section 7805(f) of the Internal Revenue Code, the notice of proposed rulemaking will be submitted to the Chief Counsel for Advocacy of the Small Business Administration for comment on their impact on small business.

Comments and Requests for a Public Hearing

Before these proposed regulations are adopted as final regulations, consideration will be given to any written comments (a signed original and eight (8) copies) that are submitted timely to the IRS. All comments will be available for public inspection and copying. A public hearing may be scheduled if requested in writing by a person that timely submits written comments. If a public hearing is scheduled, notice of the date, time, and place for the hearing will be published in the Federal Register.

Drafting Information

The principal author of these regulations is Betty J. Clary, Office of the Associate Chief Counsel (Employee Benefits and Exempt Organizations), IRS. However, other personnel from the IRS and Treasury Department participated in their development.

List of Subjects in 26 CFR Part 1

Income taxes, Reporting and recordkeeping requirements.

Proposed Amendments to the Regulations

Accordingly, 26 CFR part 1 is proposed to be amended as follows:

PART 1—INCOME TAXES

Paragraph 1. The authority citation for part 1 continues to read, in part, as follows:

Authority: 26 U.S.C. 7805. ***

Section 1.411(d)-6 also issued under Reorganization Plan No. 4 of 1978, 29 U.S.C. 1001nt. ***

Par. 2. Section 1.411(d)-6 is added to read as follows: § 1.411(d)-6 Section 204(h) notice.

[The text of this proposed section is the same as the text of § 1.411(d)-6T [¶ 12,235] published elsewhere in this issue of the Federal Register.]

¶ 20,210

Proposed regulations: Plan Loans; Deemed Distributions.—The IRS has issued proposed regulations that would amend regulations regarding the tax treatment of loans from qualified employer plans to plan participants. The proposed regulations clarify when qualified loans will be deemed distributions from the plan.

Generally, a loan from a qualified employer plan will not be considered a taxable distribution or a prohibited transaction if certain requirements regarding the terms of the loan are met. The requirements include that the loan be evidenced by an enforceable written agreement, the amount of the loan not exceed $50,000, and the repayment period be limited to no more than five years unless the loan is used to purchase a principal residence. The proposed regulations clarify that if a loan fails to satisfy the repayment requirements or the enforceable agreement requirement, the balance then due under the loan is to be treated as a distribution. This may occur at the time the loan is made or at a later date if the loan is not repaid in accordance with the repayment schedule. If, at the time the loan is made, the amount of the loan exceeds the statutory limit, the proposed regulations provide that only the excess amount is a deemed distribution.

The proposed regulations also clarify that principal residence has the same meaning as under Code Sec. 1034 (relating to the taxation of a sale of a residence) and that tracing rules established under Code Sec. 163(h) (relating to interest deductions for indebtedness incurred with respect to the acquisition of a principal residence) will be used to determine whether the exception to the five-year repayment requirement applies.

TRA '86 amended section 72(p) to require that, in order for a loan to not be a distribution, it must require level amortization over the term of the loan. Section 72(p) authorizes regulations to allow exceptions from this requirement. The proposed regulations permit loan repayments to be suspended during a leave of absence of up to one year, if the participant's pay from the employer is insufficient to service the debt, but only if the loan is repaid by the latest date permitted under the Code.

Note: Q&A-19 has been revised and redesignated Q&A-21, and new Q&A-19 and Q&A-20 have been added in amended proposed regulations reproduced at ¶ 20,230. The amended proposed regulations were published in the *Federal Register* on January 2, 1998 (62 FR 42).

The proposed regulations were published in the *Federal Register* on December 21, 1995 (60 FR 66233) and are reproduced with the preamble below.

The regulations were finalized by T.D. 8894 and published in the *Federal Register* on July 31, 2000 (65 FR 46588). The regulations are reproduced at ¶ 11,207A and ¶ 11,210. The preamble is reproduced at ¶ 23,168.

¶ 20,211

Proposed Regulations: Cafeteria Plans: Family and Medical Leave Act.—The IRS has issued proposed additions to proposed regulations under Code Section 125. The additions address how the Family and Medical Leave Act of 1993 (FMLA) affects the operation of cafeteria plans, including flexible spending arrangements, under Code Section 125. FMLA imposes certain obligations on employers to maintain coverage under a group health plan during an employee's FMLA leave and to restore benefits upon the employee's return. The additions to the proposed regulations provide guidance on the cafeteria plan rules that apply to an employee in circumstances to which FMLA and regulations issued by the Department of Labor pertaining to FMLA apply.

The proposed regulations were published in the *Federal Register* on December 21, 1995 (60 FR 66229).

The regulations were finalized by T.D. 8966 and published in the *Federal Register* on October 17, 2001 (66 FR 52675). The regulations are reproduced at ¶ 11,288B-45 and ¶ 11,288B-50. The preamble is reproduced at ¶ 23,186.

¶ 20,212

Proposed Regulations: Allocation of Accrued Benefits: Employer and Employee Contributions.—IRS proposed regulations provide guidance on calculating an employee's accrued benefit derived from the employee's contributions to a qualified defined benefit pension plan. The proposed regulations were published in the *Federal Register* on December 22, 1995 (60 FR 66532) and officially corrected on March 14, 1996.

DEPARTMENT OF THE TREASURY

Internal Revenue Service

26 CFR Part 1

[EE-35-95]

RIN 1545-AT82

Allocation of Accrued Benefits Between Employer and Employee Contributions

AGENCY: Internal Revenue Service (IRS), Treasury.

ACTION: Notice of proposed rulemaking.

SUMMARY: This document contains proposed regulations that provide guidance on calculation of an employee's accrued benefit derived from the employee's contributions to a qualified defined benefit pension plan. These regulations are issued to reflect changes to the applicable law made by the Omnibus Budget Reconciliation Act of 1987 (OBRA '87) and the Omnibus Budget Reconciliation Act of 1989 (OBRA '89). OBRA '87 and OBRA '89 amended the law to change the accumulation of employee contributions and the conversion of those accumulated contributions to employee-derived accrued benefits.

DATES: Written comments and requests for a public hearing must be received by March 21, 1996.

ADDRESSES: Send submissions to: CC:DOM:CORP:R (EE-35-95), room 5228, Internal Revenue Service, POB 7604, Ben Franklin Station, Washington, DC 20044. In the alternative, submissions may be hand delivered between the hours of 8 a.m. and 5 p.m. to: CC:DOM:CORP:R (EE-35-95), Courier's Desk, Internal Revenue Service, 1111 Constitution Avenue, NW., Washington, DC.

FOR FURTHER INFORMATION CONTACT: Concerning the regulations, Janet A. Laufer, (202) 622-4606, concerning submissions, Michael Slaughter, (202) 622-7190 (not toll-free numbers).

SUPPLEMENTARY INFORMATION:

Background

This document contains proposed amendments to regulations containing rules for computing an employee's accrued benefit derived from the employee's contributions to a qualified defined benefit pension plan. The proposed amendments reflect changes made to section 411(c)(2) by the Omnibus Budget Reconciliation Act of 1987, Public Law 100-203 (OBRA '87), and the Omnibus Budget Reconciliation Act of 1989, Public Law 101-239 (OBRA '89). OBRA '87 and OBRA '89 changed the interest rates used to accumulate an employee's contributions to normal retirement age. OBRA '89 also changed the manner in which the accumulated contributions are converted to an annual benefit payable at normal retirement age, and removed a limitation on the employee-derived accrued benefit contained in prior law.

Section 411(c)(1) provides that an employee's accrued benefit derived from employer contributions as of any applicable date is the excess, if any, of the accrued benefit for the employee as of that date over the accrued benefit derived from contributions made by the employee as of that date. Section 411(c)(2)(B) provides that in the case of a defined benefit plan, the accrued benefit derived from contributions made by an employee as of any applicable date is the amount equal to the employee's contributions accumulated to normal retirement age using the interest rate(s) specified in section 411(c)(2)(C), expressed as an actuarially equivalent annual benefit commencing at normal retirement age using an interest rate which would be used by the plan under section 417(e)(3), as of the determination date. If the employee-derived accrued benefit is determined with respect to a benefit other than an annual benefit in the form of a single life annuity (without ancillary benefits) commencing at normal retirement age, section 411(c)(3) requires that the employee-derived accrued benefit be the actuarial equivalent of the benefit determined under section 411(c)(2).

Under section 411(c)(2)(C)(iii)(I), effective for plan years beginning after December 31, 1987, the interest rate used to accumulate an employee's contributions until the determination date is 120 percent of the Federal mid-term rate under section 1274 of the Internal Revenue Code (Code). For the period between the determination date and normal retirement age, section 411(c)(2)(C)(iii)(II) provides that the interest rate used to accumulate an employee's contributions is the interest rate which would be used under the plan under section

417(e)(3) as of the determination date. As noted above, section 411(c)(2)(B) provides that the interest rate which would be used under the plan under section 417(e)(3) as of the determination date also applies for purposes of converting the accumulated contributions to an annual benefit commencing at normal retirement age. The Retirement Protection Act of 1994, Public Law 103-465 (RPA '94) amended section 417(e) to change the applicable interest rate under section 417(e)(3) and to specify the applicable mortality table under that section. Examples contained in §1.411(c)-1(c)(6) of these proposed regulations reflect a plan that has been amended to comply with the interest rate and mortality table specifications enacted in RPA '94.

Explanation of Provisions

1. Conversion calculation

Prior to OBRA '89, section 411(c)(2)(B) specified that the conversion factor to be used for purposes of computing the employee-derived accrued benefit was 10 percent for a straight life annuity commencing at normal retirement age of 65 (i.e., multiply the accumulated contributions by .10), and that for other normal retirement ages the conversion factor was to be determined in accordance with regulations prescribed by the Secretary. Section 1.411(c)-1(c)(2) of the existing regulations provides that for normal retirement ages other than age 65, the conversion factor shall be the factor as determined by the Commissioner.

Rev. Rul. 76-47 (1976-1 C.B. 109) sets forth in tabular form the conversion factors to be used for determining the accrued benefit derived from employee contributions when the normal retirement age under the plan is other than age 65 or when the normal form of benefit is other than a single life annuity (without ancillary benefits). Rev. Rul. 76-47 further provides that where no standard factor is available, a conversion factor must be determined using an interest rate of 5 percent and the UP-1984 mortality table (without age setback).

OBRA '89 deleted the ten percent conversion factor in section 411(c)(2)(B) and replaced it with the requirement that the accumulated contributions at normal retirement age be expressed as an annual benefit commencing at normal retirement age using an interest rate which would be used under the plan under section 417(e)(3) (as of the determination date). This change was effective retroactively to the effective date of the OBRA '87 provision relating to section 411(c)(2)(C) (the first day of the first plan year beginning after December 31, 1987).

To reflect the OBRA '89 amendments, these proposed regulations define *appropriate conversion factor* with respect to an accrued benefit expressed in the form of an annual benefit that is nondecreasing for the life of the participant as the present value of an annuity in the form of that annual benefit commencing at normal retirement age at a rate of $1 per year. This amount is to be computed using the interest rate and mortality table which would be used under the plan under section 417(e)(3) and §1.417(e)-1T. To reflect the post-OBRA '89 conversion factor definition and to conform to common actuarial practice, these proposed regulations would change the *multiplied by* language in §1.411(c)-1(c)(1) to *divided by*.

2. Accumulated contributions

As added by the Employee Retirement Income Security Act of 1974 (ERISA), section 411(c)(2)(C) provided that employee contributions were to be accumulated using a standard interest rate of 5 percent for years beginning on or after the effective date of that section. OBRA '87 changed the interest rate under section 411(c)(2)(C) to 120 percent of the applicable Federal mid-term rate under section 1274 for plan years after 1987. OBRA '89 again amended section 411(c)(2)(C) to provide that 120 percent of the applicable Federal mid-term rate under section 1274 is to be used for accumulating contributions only up to the *determination date*. For the period from the determination date to normal retirement age, the interest rate which would be used under the plan under section 417(e)(3) (as of the determination date) must be used for accumulating contributions for the period from the determination date to normal retirement age. Accordingly, these proposed regulations would amend paragraph (3) of §1.411(c)-1(c) to reflect those rates. As stated above, RPA '94 amended section 417(e)(3) to change the applicable interest rate. See §1.417(e)-1T.

3. Determination date

Section 1.411(c)-1(c)(5)(i) defines the term determination date for purposes of section 411(c)(2)(C)(iii), in a case in which a participant will receive his or her entire accrued benefit derived from employee contributions in any one of the following forms (described in paragraph (c)(5)(ii)): an annuity that is substantially nonincreasing, substantially nonincreasing installment payments for a fixed number of years, or a single sum distribution. In such a case, the term determination date

means the date on which distribution of such benefit commences. For this purpose, an annuity that is nonincreasing except for automatic increases to reflect increases in the consumer price index is considered to be an annuity that is substantially nonincreasing.

Thus, for example, for purposes of section 411(c)(2)(C)(iii), in the case of a distribution of the employee's entire accrued benefit (or the employee's entire employee-derived accrued benefit) in the form of a nonincreasing single life annuity payable commencing either at normal retirement age or at early retirement age, the determination date is the date the annuity commences. Similarly, in the case of a single sum distribution of accumulated employee contributions (i.e., employee contributions plus interest computed at or above the section 411(c) required rates) upon termination of employment with a deferred annuity benefit derived solely from employer contributions, the determination date is the date of distribution of the single sum of accumulated employee contributions.

Alternatively, the plan may provide that the determination date is the annuity starting date, as defined in §1.401(a)-20, Q&A-10.

Under §1.411(c)-1(c)(5)(iii) of these regulations, where a participant will receive a distribution that is not described in paragraph (c)(5)(i), the determination date will be as provided by the Commissioner.

4. Elimination of limitation on employee-derived accrued benefit

Prior to OBRA '89, section 411(c)(2)(E) of the Code limited the accrued benefit derived from employee contributions to the greater of (1) the employee's accrued benefit under the plan, or (2) the sum of the employee's mandatory contributions, without interest. Section 7881(m)(1)(C) of OBRA '89 deleted that provision. Section 7881(m)(1)(D) of OBRA '89 added section 411(a)(7)(D) to the Code, which provides that the accrued benefit of an employee shall not be less than the amount determined under section 411(c)(2)(B) with respect to the employee's accumulated contributions. Accordingly, these proposed regulations delete the rule included in §1.411(c)-1(d) of the existing regulations, which reflects the pre-OBRA '89 rule.

5. Delegation of authority

Section 1.411(c)-1(d) of these proposed regulations provides that the Commissioner may prescribe additional guidance on calculating the accrued benefit derived from employer or employee contributions under a defined benefit plan.

Effective Date

These amendments are proposed to be effective for plan years beginning on or after January 1, 1997. For example, assume that under a plan the employee's date of termination of employment is treated as the determination date, and distribution of the employee's entire employee-derived accrued benefit (as determined under the terms of the plan then in effect) occurs or commences prior to the first day of the plan year beginning in 1997. In that case, with respect to interest credits under section 411(c)(2)(C)(iii) for plan years beginning after 1987, the Service will not treat the plan as having failed to satisfy the requirements of section 411(c), nor will it require that additional amounts be credited in the calculation of the employee-derived accrued benefit in order to satisfy the requirements of section 411(c) after final regulations become effective, merely because the date the employee's employment terminated was treated as the determination date, provided that interest is credited in accordance with section 411(c)(2)(C)(iii)(I) for the period before the date the employee terminated employment and in accordance with section 411(c)(2)(C)(iii)(II) thereafter.

Once amendments to the regulations under §1.411(c)-1 are adopted in final form, the Service will obsolete or modify Rev. Rul. 76-47, Rev. Rul. 78-202 (1978-2 C.B. 124) and Rev. Rul. 89-60 (1989-1 C.B. 113) as necessary or appropriate.

Taxpayers may rely on these proposed regulations for guidance pending the issuance of final regulations.

Special Analyses

It has been determined that this notice of proposed rulemaking is not a significant regulatory action as defined in EO 12866. Therefore, a regulatory assessment is not required. It also has been determined that section 553(b) of the Administrative Procedure Act (5 U.S.C. chapter 5) and the Regulatory Flexibility Act (5 U.S.C. chapter 6) do not apply to these regulations, and, therefore, a Regulatory Flexibility Analysis is not required. Pursuant to section 7805(f) of the Internal Revenue Code, this notice of proposed rulemaking will be submitted to the Chief Counsel for Advocacy of the Small Business Administration for comment on its impact on small business.

Comments and Requests for a Public Hearing

Before these proposed regulations are adopted as final regulations, consideration will be given to any written comments (a signed original and eight (8) copies) that are submitted timely to the IRS. All comments will be available for public inspection and copying. A public hearing may be scheduled if requested in writing by a person that timely submits written comments. If a public hearing is scheduled, notice of the date, time, and place for the hearing will be published in the **Federal Register**.

Drafting Information

The principal author of these regulations is Janet A. Laufer, Office of the Associate Chief Counsel (Employee Benefits and Exempt Organizations). However, other personnel from the IRS and Treasury Department participated in their development.

List of Subjects in 26 CFR Part 1

Income taxes, Reporting and recordkeeping requirements.

Proposed Amendments to the Regulations

Accordingly, 26 CFR part 1 is proposed to be amended as follows:

PART 1—INCOME TAXES

Paragraph 1. The authority citation for part 1 continues to read in part as follows:

Authority: 26 U.S.C. 7805 ***

Par. 2. Section 1.411(c)-1 is amended by:

1. Revising paragraphs (c)(1), (c)(2), (c)(3), (c)(5) and (c)(6).

2. Revising paragraph (d).

3. Adding paragraph (g).

The additions and revisions read as follows:

§ 1.411(c)-1 Allocation of accrued benefits between employer and employee contributions.

***

(c) *Accrued benefit derived from mandatory employee contributions to a defined benefit plan*—(1) *General Rule.* In the case of a defined benefit plan (as defined in section 414(j)), the accrued benefit derived from contributions made by an employee under the plan as of any applicable date in the form of an annual benefit commencing at normal retirement age and nondecreasing for the life of the participant is equal to the amount of the employee's accumulated contributions (determined under paragraph (c)(3) of this section) divided by the appropriate conversion factor with respect to that form of benefit (determined under paragraph (c)(2) of this section). Paragraph (e) of this section provides rules for actuarial adjustments where the benefit is to be determined in a form other than the form described in this paragraph (c)(1).

(2) *Appropriate conversion factor.* For purposes of this paragraph, with respect to a form of annual benefit commencing at normal retirement age described in paragraph (c)(1), the term *appropriate conversion factor* means the present value of an annuity in the form of that annual benefit commencing at normal retirement age at a rate of $1 per year, computed using an interest rate and mortality table which would be used under the plan under section 417(e)(3) and § 1.417(e)-1T (as of the determination date).

(3) *Accumulated contributions.* For purposes of section 411(c) and this section, the term *accumulated contributions* means the total of—

(i) All mandatory contributions made by the employee (determined under paragraph (c)(4) of this section);

(ii) Interest (if any) on such contributions, computed at the rate provided by the plan to the end of the last plan year to which section 411(a)(2) does not apply (by reason of the applicable effective dates);

(iii) Interest on the sum of the amounts determined under paragraphs (c)(3)(i) and (ii) of this section compounded annually at the rate of 5 percent per annum from the beginning of the first plan year to which section 411(a)(2) applies (by reason of the applicable effective date) to the beginning of the first plan year beginning after December 31, 1987;

(iv) Interest on the sum of the amounts determined under paragraphs (c)(3)(i) through (iii) of this section compounded annually at 120 percent of the Federal mid-term rate(s) (as in effect under section 1274(d) of the Internal Revenue Code for the first month of a

plan year) for the period beginning with the first plan year beginning after December 31, 1987 and ending on the determination date; arld

(v) Interest on the sum of the amounts determined under paragraphs (c)(3)(i) through (iv) of this section compounded annually, using an interest rate which would be used under the plan under section 417(e)(3) and § 1.417(e)-1T (as of the determination date), from the determination date to the date on which the employee would attain normal retirement age.

*****

(5) *Determination date*—(i) For purposes of section 411(c) and this section, in a case in which a participant will receive his or her entire accrued benefit derived from employee contributions in any one of the forms described in paragraph (c)(5)(ii), the term *determination date* means the date on which distribution of such benefit commences. Alternatively, in such a case, the plan may provide that the determination date is the annuity starting date with respect to that benefit, as defined in § 1.401(a)-20, Q&A-10.

(ii) Paragraph (c)(5)(i) applies to the following forms: an annuity that is substantially nonincreasing (e.g., an annuity that is nonincreasing except for automatic increases to reflect increases in the consumer price index), substantially nonincreasing installment payments for a fixed number of years, or a single sum distribution.

(iii) In a case in which a participant will receive a distribution that is not described in paragraph (c)(5)(i), the determination date will be as provided by the Commissioner.

(6) *Examples.*

(i) *Facts.* (A) In the following examples, Employer X maintains a qualified defined benefit plan that required mandatory employee contributions for 1987 and prior years, but not for years after 1987. The plan year is the calendar year. The plan provides for a normal retirement age of 65 and for 100 percent vesting in the employer-derived portion of a participant's accrued benefit after 5 years of service.

(B) The terms of the plan provide that the normal form of benefit is a level monthly amount commencing at normal retirement age and payable for the life of the participant. A plan participant who elects not to receive benefits in the form of the qualified joint and survivor annuity provided by the plan may elect to receive a single-sum distribution of the present value of his or her accrued benefit upon termination of employment.

(C) As of January 1, 1995, the plan was amended to provide that, for purposes of computing actuarially equivalent benefits, the single sum is calculated using the unisex version of the 1983 GAM mortality table (as provided in Revenue Ruling 95-6 (1995-1 C.B. 80)), and interest at the rate equal to the annual rate of interest on 30-year Treasury securities for the first calendar month preceding the first day of the plan year during which the annuity starting date occurs √ K√ √ K.

(D) Under the plan, employee contributions are accumulated at 3 percent interest for plan years beginning before 1976, 5 percent interest for plan years beginning after 1975 and before 1988, and interest at 120 percent of the Federal mid-term rate (as in effect under section 1274(d) for the first month of the plan year) for plan years beginning after 1987 until the determination date. Under the plan, the determination date is defined as the annuity starting date. For the period from the determination date until the date on which the employee attains normal retirement age, interest is credited at the interest rate which would be used under the plan under section 417(e)(3) as of the determination date.

(E) A, an unmarried participant, terminates employment with X on January 1, 1997 at age 56 with 15 years of service. As of December 31, 1987, A's total accumulated mandatory employee contributions to the plan, including interest compounded annually at 5 percent for plan years beginning after 1975 and before 1988, equaled $3,021. A receives his or her accrued benefit in the form of an annual single life annuity commencing at normal retirement age. A's annuity starting date is January 1, 2006, and therefore the determination date is January 1, 2006.

(ii) *Annuity at Normal Retirement Age—Determination of Employee-Derived and Total Plan Vested Accrued Benefit.*

Example 1.

For purposes of this example, it is assumed that A's total accrued benefit under the plan in the normal form of benefit commencing at normal retirement age is $2,949 per year. A's benefit, as of January 1, 2006, would be determined as follows:

(A) Determine A's total accrued benefit in the form of an annual single life annuity commencing at normal retirement age under the plan's formula ($2,949 per year payable at age 65).

(B) Determine A's accumulated contributions with interest to January 1, 1997. As of December 31, 1987, A's accumulated contributions with interest under the plan provisions were $3,021. A's employee contributions are accumulated from December 31, 1987 to January 1, 1997 using 120 percent of the Federal mid-term rate under section 1274(d). This rate is 10.61 percent for 1988, 11.11 percent for 1989, 9.57 percent for 1990, 9.78 percent for 1991, 8.10 percent for 1992, 7.63 percent for 1993, 6.40 percent for 1994, and 9.54 percent for 1995. It is assumed for purposes of this example that 120 percent of the Federal mid-term rate is 7.00 percent for each year between 1996 and 2006, and that the 30-year Treasury rate for December 2005 is 8.00 percent. Thus, A's contributions accumulated to January 1, 1997, equal $6,480.

(C) Determine A's accumulated contributions with interest to normal retirement age (January 1, 2006) using, for the 1996 plan year and for years until normal retirement age, 120 percent of the Federal mid-term rate under section 1274(d), which is assumed to be 7.00 percent ($11,913).

(D) Determine the accrued annual annuity benefit derived from A's contributions by dividing A's accumulated contributions determined in paragraph (C) of this *Example 1* by the plan's appropriate conversion factor. The plan's appropriate conversion factor at age 65 is 9.196, and the accrued benefit derived from A's contributions would be $11,913 ÷ 9.196 = $1,295.

(E) Determine the accrued benefit derived from employer contributions as the excess, if any, of the employee's accrued benefit under the plan over the accrued benefit derived from employee contributions ($2,949—$1,295 = $1,654 per year).

(F) Determine the vested percentage of the accrued benefit derived from employer contributions under the plan's vesting schedule (100 percent).

(G) Determine the vested accrued benefit derived from employer contributions by multiplying the accrued benefit derived from employer contributions by the vested percentage ($1,654 x 100 percent = $1,654 per year).

(H) Determine A's vested accrued benefit in the form of an annual single life annuity commencing at normal retirement age by adding the accrued benefit derived from employee contributions and the vested accrued benefit derived from employer contributions, the sum of paragraphs (D) and (G) of this *Example 1* ($1,295 + $1,654 = $2,949 per year).

Example 2.

This example assumes the same facts as *Example 1* except that A's total accrued benefit under the plan in the normal form of benefit commencing at normal retirement age is $1,000 per year. A's benefit, as of January 1, 2006, would be determined as follows:

(A) Determine A's total accrued benefit in the form of an annual single life annuity commencing at normal retirement age under the plan's formula ($1,000 per year payable at age 65).

(B) Determine A's accumulated contributions with interest to January 1, 1997 ($6,480 from paragraph (B) of *Example 1*).

(C) Determine A's accumulated contributions with interest to normal retirement age (January 1, 2006) ($11,913 from paragraph (C) of *Example 1*).

(D) Determine the accrued annual annuity benefit derived from A's contributions by dividing A's accumulated contributions determined in paragraph (C) of this *Example 2* by the plan's appropriate conversion factor ($1,295 from paragraph (D) of *Example 1*).

(E) Determine the accrued benefit derived from employer contributions as the excess, if any, of the employee's accrued benefit under the plan over the accrued benefit derived from employee contributions. Because the accrued benefit derived from employee contributions ($1,295) is greater than the employee's accrued benefit under the plan ($1,000), the accrued benefit derived from employer contributions is zero, and A's vested accrued benefit in the form of an annual single life annuity commencing at normal retirement age is $1,295 per year.

(d) *Delegation to Commissioner.* The Commissioner may prescribe additional guidance on calculating the accrued benefit derived from employee contributions under a defined benefit plan through publication in the Internal Revenue Bulletin of revenue rulings, notices, or other documents (see § 601.601(d)(2) of this chapter).

(e) ***

(f) ***

(g) *Effective date.* Paragraphs (c)(1), (c)(2), (c)(3), (c)(5), (c)(6) and (d) of this section are effective for plan years beginning on or after January 1, 1997.

Commissioner of Internal Revenue

¶ 20,213

Proposed regulations: Labor Organizations; Multiemployer Plans.—The IRS has issued proposed regulations to clarify the requirements for an organization to be exempt from taxes under Code Sec. 501(c)(5) as a labor, agricultural or horticultural organization. The proposed regulations are in reaction to the Second Circuit decision in *Morganbesser v. United States* (CCH PENSION PLAN GUIDE Transfer Binder, August, 1991-June, 1993 ¶ 23,868Y), holding that a multiemployer pension trust established pursuant to a collective bargaining agreement was exempt from tax as a labor organization described in Code Sec. 501(c)(5) even though it did not meet the ERISA requirements for being a qualified plan. Therefore, the IRS could not collect penalties from the trust for failing to satisfy the tax qualifications of ERISA. The IRS believes that this decision is contrary to existing law, and has issued a nonacquiescence reflecting its view that the court erred in its holding (See CCH PENSION PLAN GUIDE ¶ 23,915C). The proposed regulations provide an organization is not an organization described in Code Sec. 501(c)(5) if the principal activity of the organization is to receive, hold, invest, disburse, or otherwise manage funds associated with savings or investment plans or programs, including pension or other retirement savings plans or programs.

The proposed regulations were published in the *Federal Register* on December 21, 1995 (60 FR 66228) and are reproduced with the preamble below.

The regulations were finalized effective December 21, 1995 by T.D. 8726 and were published in the *Federal Register* on July 28, 1997 (62 FR 40447). The regulations are reproduced at ¶ 13,162A. The preamble is reproduced at ¶ 23,135.

¶ 20,214

Proposed regulations: Nonqualified Deferred Compensation Plans; FICA Contributions.—The IRS has proposed regulations relating to the FICA tax treatment of amounts deferred under or paid from certain nonqualified deferred compensation plans.

The proposed regulations define what constitute a nonqualified deferred compensation plan and provide certain administrative relief for applying FICA to such plans. In general, Code Sec. 3121(v) provides any "amount deferred" under a nonqualified deferred compensation plan must be taken into account as wages for FICA purposes as of the later of (1) when the services are performed, rather than when paid, or (2) when there is no substantial risk of forfeiture of the rights to such amount. This special timing rule may result in imposition of FICA tax before the benefit payments under the plan begin, thus accelerating the imposition of FICA tax on benefits under a nonqualified deferred compensation plan. However, the proposed regulations provide various administrative rules to ease the burdens. Note: The proposed effective date has been extended in revised proposed regulations reproduced at ¶ 20,229. The revised proposed regulations were published in the *Federal Register* on December 24, 1997 (62 FR 67304).

The proposed regulations were published in the *Federal Register* on January 25, 1996 (60 FR 2194).

The final regulations were published in the *Federal Register* on January 29, 1999 (64 FR 4542). The regulations are reproduced at ¶ 13,534T and ¶ 13,534U. The preamble is at ¶ 23,150.

¶ 20,215

Proposed regulations: Nonqualified Deferred Plans: FUTA Contributions.—The IRS has issued proposed regulations under Code Sec. 3306(r)(2) relating to when amounts deferred or paid from certain nonqualified deferred compensation plans are taken into account as "wages" for purposes of the employment taxes imposed by the Federal Unemployment Tax Act (FUTA). The rules are substantially similar to rules applicable to the Federal Insurance Contributions Act (FICA) tax treatment of such amounts deferred under Code Sec. 3121(v)(2). As a result, the proposed regulations cross-reference the proposed regulations under Code Sec. 3121(v)(2). Note: The proposed effective date has been extended in revised proposed regulations reproduced at ¶ 20,229. The revised proposed regulations were published in the *Federal Register* on December 24, 1997 (62 FR 67304).

The proposed regulations were published in the *Federal Register* on January 25, 1996 (60 FR 2214.

The final regulations were published in the *Federal Register* on January 29, 1999 (64 FR 4540). The regulations are reproduced at ¶ 13,541K. The preamble is at ¶ 23,151.

¶ 20,216

Proposed regulations: U.S. source income paid to foreign persons: Withholding: Annuities: Taxpayer identification numbers.— Reproduced below are excerpts from proposed regulations under Code Secs. 1441, 6041, and 6109 relating to the withholding of income tax on U.S. income paid to foreign persons and the inclusion of taxpayer identification numbers on withholding certificates. The regulations would require withholding on distributions from certain pension plans and annuities under Code Sec. 1441 rather than Code Sec. 3405.

The proposed regulations were published in the *Federal Register* on April 22, 1996 (61 FR 17614), and officially corrected in the *Federal Register* on August 15, 1996 (61 FR 42401).

The regulations were finalized October 6, 1997 (62 FR 53387, October 14, 1997). The regulations are reproduced at ¶ 13,490A, ¶ 13,491, ¶ 13,492, ¶ 13,493, ¶ 13,681, ¶ 13,682, ¶ 13,684, ¶ 13,685, and ¶ 13,782. The preamble is reproduced at ¶ 23,137.

¶ 20,217

Business organizations: Classifications: Limited liability partnerships.—The Internal Revenue Service has issued proposed regulations that would allow certain organizations to elect what type of business entity they would be for tax purposes. The regulations were developed in response to recent changes in state laws that permit entities such as partnerships to change status to a limited liability corporation or limited liability partnership. The proposed regulations recognize that there has been a significant gap between changes in state laws and the federal government's business classification system and tries to create a workable framework that can accommodate these newly created limited liability entities.

The proposed regulations were published in the *Federal Register* on May 13, 1996, (61 FR 21989).

The regulations were finalized December 17, 1996 and were published in the *Federal Register* on December 18, 1996 (61 FR 66584). The regulations are reproduced at ¶ 13,782, ¶ 13,921, ¶ 13,922, ¶ 13,923, ¶ 13,924, and ¶ 13,926. The preamble is reproduced at ¶ 23,132.

¶ 20,218

Proposed regulations: Eligible rollover distributions: Eligible retirement plans: Disqualification of plans: Individual retirement accounts.—The IRS has issued proposed regulations designed to increase the ability of employees to roll over their benefits to qualified plans. In particular, the regulations expand the circumstances in which plans can accept rollovers without facing disqualification. The regulations also apply to contributions accepted from "conduit IRAs." The proposed regulations were published in the *Federal Register* on September 19, 1996 (61 FR 49279). On December 17, 1998 (63 FR 69584), the proposed regulations were amended at ¶ 20,237.

The final regulations were published in the *Federal Register* on April 21, 2000 (65 FR 21312). The regulations are reproduced at ¶ 11,720Z-50, ¶ 11,753-10, ¶ 11,803, and ¶ 13,566. The preamble is at ¶ 23,163.

¶ 20,219

Proposed regulations: Nonexempt employees' trusts under Code Sec. 402(b): Taxation of trust income: Grantor trusts: Separate trusts: Domestic and foreign trusts.—Reproduced below are regulations proposed under Code Secs. 671 and Code Sec. 1297. The regulations provide that domestic nonexempt employees' trust would be taxed as separate trusts under Code Sec. 641 and that they would not be subject to the grantor trust rules under Code Sec. 671. Therefore, an employer would not be subject to tax on trust income as a grantor owner of such a trust. Furthermore, foreign nonexempt employees' trusts would also escape application of the grantor trust rules under the proposed regulations, but certain significant exceptions would apply. For example, the grantor trust rules would apply to a controlled foreign corporation with a foreign nonexempt employees' trust.

The proposed regulations were published in the *Federal Register* on September 27, 1996 (61 FR 50778).

DEPARTMENT OF THE TREASURY

Internal Revenue Service

26 CFR Part 1

[REG-209826-96]

RIN 1545-AU29

Application of the Grantor Trust Rules to Nonexempt Employees' Trusts

AGENCY: Internal Revenue Service (IRS), Treasury.

ACTION: Notice of proposed rulemaking and notice of public hearing.

SUMMARY: This document contains proposed regulations relating to the application of the grantor trust rules to nonexempt employees' trusts. The proposed regulations clarify that the grantor trust rules generally do not apply to domestic nonexempt employees' trusts, and clarify the interaction between the grantor trust rules, the rules generally governing the taxation of nonqualified deferred compensation arrangements, and the antideferral rules for United States persons holding interests in foreign entities. The proposed regulations affect nonexempt employees' trusts funding deferred compensation arrangements, as well as U.S. persons holding interests in certain foreign corporations and foreign partnerships with deferred compensation arrangements funded through foreign nonexempt employees' trusts. In addition, the proposed regulations affect U.S. persons that have deferred compensation arrangements funded through certain foreign nonexempt employees' trusts. This document also provides notice of a public hearing on these proposed regulations.

DATES: Written comments must be received by December 26, 1996. Requests to speak (with outlines of oral comments to be discussed) at the public hearing scheduled for January 15, 1997, at 10:00 a.m. must be submitted by December 24, 1996.

ADDRESSES: Send submissions to: CC:DOM:CORP:R (REG-209826-96), room 5226, Internal Revenue Service, POB 7604, Ben

Franklin Station, Washington, DC 20044. Submissions may be hand delivered between the hours of 8 a.m. and 5 p.m. to: CC:DOM:CORP:R (REG-209826-96), Courier's Desk, Internal Revenue Service, 1111 Constitution Avenue, NW., Washington, DC. The public hearing will be held in room 2615, Internal Revenue Building, 1111 Constitution Avenue, NW., Washington, DC. Alternatively, taxpayers may submit comments electronically via the Internet by selecting the "Tax Regs" option on the IRS Home Page, or by submitting comments directly to the IRS Internet site at http://www.irs.ustreas.gov/prod/tax_regs/comments.html.

FOR FURTHER INFORMATION CONTACT: Concerning the regulations, James A. Quinn, (202) 622-3060; Linda S. F. Marshall, (202) 622-6030; Kristine K. Schlaman (202) 622-3840; and M. Grace Fleeman (202) 622-3850; concerning submissions and the hearing, Michael Slaughter, (202) 622-7190 (not toll-free numbers).

SUPPLEMENTARY INFORMATION:

Paperwork Reduction Act

The collection of information contained in this notice of proposed rulemaking has been submitted to the Office of Management and Budget for review in accordance with the Paperwork Reduction Act of 1995 (44 U.S.C. 3507(d)). Comments on the collection of information should be sent to the **Office of Management and Budget,** Attn: Desk Officer for the Department of the Treasury, Office of Information and Regulatory Affairs, Washington, DC 20503, with copies to the **Internal Revenue Service,** Attn: IRS Reports Clearance Officer, T:FP, Washington, DC 20224. Comments on the collection of information should be received by November 26, 1996.Comments are specifically requested concerning:

Whether the proposed collection of information is necessary for the proper performance of the functions of the **Internal Revenue Service,** including whether the information will have practical utility;

The accuracy of the estimated burden associated with the proposed collection of information (see below);

How the quality, utility, and clarity of the information to be collected may be enhanced;

How the burden of complying with the proposed collection of information may be minimized, including through the application of automated collection techniques or other forms of information technology; and

Estimates of capital or start-up costs and costs of operation, maintenance, and purchase of services to provide information.

The collection of information in this proposed regulation is in § 1.671-1(h)(3)(iii). This information is required by the IRS to determine accurately the portion of certain foreign employees' trusts properly treated as owned by the employer. This information will be used to notify the Commissioner that certain entities are relying on an exception for reasonable funding. The collection of information is mandatory. The likely respondents are businesses or other for-profit organizations.

Estimated total annual reporting burden: **1,000 hours.**

The estimated annual burden per respondent varies from **.5 hours** to **1.5 hours,** depending on individual circumstances, with an estimated average of **1 hour.**

Estimated number of respondents: **1,000.**

Estimated annual frequency of responses: **On occasion.**

An agency may not conduct or sponsor, and a person is not required to respond to, a collection of information unless the collection of information displays a valid control number assigned by the Office of Management and Budget.

Books or records relating to a collection of information must be retained as long as their contents may become material in the administration of any internal revenue law. Generally, tax returns and tax return information are confidential, as required by 26 U.S.C. 6103.

Background

On May 7, 1993, the IRS issued proposed regulations under section 404A (58 **FR** 27219). The section 404A proposed regulations provide that section 404A is the exclusive means by which an employer may take a deduction or reduce earnings and profits for amounts used to fund deferred compensation in situations other than those in which a deduction or reduction of earnings and profits is permitted under section 404 (the "exclusive means" rule).

The section 404A proposed regulations do not provide rules regarding the treatment of income and ownership of assets of foreign trusts established to fund deferred compensation arrangements, but refer to

"other applicable provisions," including the grantor trust rules of subpart E of the Internal Revenue Code of 1986, as amended. Thus, the 1993 proposed section 404A regulations imply that, if an employer cannot or does not elect section 404A treatment for a foreign trust established to fund the employer's deferred compensation arrangements, the employer may be treated as the owner of the entire trust for purposes of subtitle A of the Code under sections 671 through 679 even though all or part of the trust assets are set aside for purposes of satisfying liabilities under the plan. Conversely, some commentators believe that, for U.S. tax purposes, a foreign employer would not be treated as the owner of any portion of a foreign trust established to fund a section 404A qualified foreign plan even though all or part of the trust assets might be used for purposes other than satisfying liabilities under the plan. A number of different rules, in addition to the grantor trust rules, potentially affect the taxation of foreign trusts established to fund deferred compensation arrangements. These rules include: the nonexempt deferred compensation trust rules of sections 402(b) and 404(a)(5); the partnership rules of subchapter K; and the antideferral rules, which include subpart F and the passive foreign investment company (PFIC) rules (sections 1291 through 1297).

Following publication of the proposed 1993 regulations and enactment of section 956A in August of 1993, comments were received concerning both the asset ownership rules for foreign employees' trusts and the "exclusive means" rule for deductions or reductions in earnings and profits. These proposed regulations address only comments concerning income and asset ownership rules for foreign employees' trusts for federal income tax purposes. A foreign employees' trust is a nonexempt employees' trust described in section 402(b) that is part of a deferred compensation plan, and that is a foreign trust within the meaning of section 7701(a)(31). Comments concerning the "exclusive means" rule will be addressed in future regulations.

Statutory Background

1. Transfers of Property Not Complete for Tax Purposes

In certain situations, assets that are owned by a trust as a legal matter may be treated as owned by another person for tax purposes. Thus, assets may be treated as owned by a pension trust for non-tax legal purposes but not for tax purposes. This occurs, for example, if the person who has purportedly transferred assets to the trust retains the benefits and burdens of ownership. *See, e.g., Frank Lyon Co. v. United States,* 435 U.S. 561 (1978); *Corliss v. Bowers,* 281 U.S. 376 (1930); *Grodt & McKay Realty, Inc. v. Commissioner,* 77 T.C. 1221 (1981); Rev. Proc. 75-21 (1975-1 C.B. 715). If, under these principles, no assets have been transferred to an employees' trust for federal tax purposes, these proposed regulations do not apply.

2. Subpart E—Grantors and others treated as substantial owners

Even if there has been a completed transfer of trust assets, the subpart E rules may apply to treat the grantor as the owner of a portion of the trust for federal income tax purposes. Subpart E of part I of subchapter J, chapter 1 of the Code (sections 671 through 679) taxes income of a trust to the grantor or another person notwithstanding that the grantor or other person may not be a beneficiary of the trust. Under section 671, a grantor or another person includes in computing taxable income and credits those items of income, deduction, and credit against tax that are attributable to or included in any portion of a trust of which that person is treated as the owner.

Sections 673 through 679 set forth the rules for determining when the grantor or another person is treated as the owner of a portion of a trust for federal income tax purposes. Under sections 673 through 678, the grantor trust rules apply only if the grantor or other person has certain powers or interests. For example, section 676 provides that the grantor is treated as the owner of a portion of a trust where, at any time, the power to revest in the grantor title to that portion is exercisable by the grantor or a nonadverse party, or both. A grantor who is the owner of a trust under subpart E is treated as the owner of the trust property for federal income tax purposes. See Rev. Rul. 85-13 (1985-1 C.B. 184). This document is made available by the Superintendent of Documents, U.S. Government Printing Office, Washington, DC 20402.

Section 679 generally applies to a U.S. person who directly or indirectly transfers property to a foreign trust, subject to certain exceptions described below. Section 679 generally treats a U.S. person transferring property to a foreign trust as the owner of the portion of the trust attributable to the transferred property for any taxable year of that person for which there is a U.S. beneficiary of any portion of the trust. In general, a trust is treated as having a U.S. beneficiary for a taxable year of the U.S. transferor unless, under the terms of the trust, no part of the income or corpus of the trust may be paid or accumulated during the taxable year to or for the benefit of a U.S. person, and unless no part of the income or corpus of the trust could be paid to or for the benefit of a U.S. person if the trust were terminated at any time during the taxable year. A U.S. person is treated as having made an indirect transfer to the foreign trust of property if a non-U.S. person acts as a conduit with respect to the transfer or if the U.S. person has sufficient control over the non-U.S. person to direct the transfer by the non-U.S. person rather than itself.

Section 679(a) provides several exceptions from the application of section 679 for certain compensatory trusts. Under these exceptions, section 679 does not apply to a trust described in section 404(a)(4) or section 404A. Pursuant to amendments made in section 1903(b) of the Small Business Job Protection Act of 1996 (SBJPA), section 679 also does not apply to any transfer of property after February 6, 1995, to a trust described in section 402(b).

3. Taxability of beneficiary of nonexempt employees' trust

Section 402(b) provides rules for the taxability of beneficiaries of a nonexempt employees' trust. Under section 402(b)(1), employer contributions to a nonexempt employees' trust generally are included in the gross income of the employee in accordance with section 83. Section 402(b)(2) provides that amounts distributed or made available from a nonexempt employees' trust generally are taxable to the distributee under the rules of section 72 in the taxable year in which distributed or made available. Section 402(b)(4) provides that, under certain circumstances, a highly compensated employee is taxed each year on the employee's vested accrued benefit (other than the employee's investment in the contract) in a nonexempt employees' trust. Under section 402(b)(3), a beneficiary of a nonexempt employees' trust generally is not treated as the owner of any portion of the trust under subpart E. The rules of section 402(b) apply to a beneficiary of a nonexempt employees' trust regardless of whether the trust is a domestic trust or a foreign trust.

4. Employer deduction for contributions to a nonexempt employees' trust

Section 404(a)(5) provides rules regarding the deductibility of contributions to a nonqualified deferred compensation plan. Under section 404(a)(5), any contribution paid by an employer under a deferred compensation plan, if otherwise deductible under chapter 1 of the Code, is deductible only in the taxable year in which an amount attributable to the contribution is includible in the gross income of employees participating in the plan, and only if separate accounts are maintained for each employee. Section 1.404(a)-12(b)(1) clarifies that an employer's deduction for contributions to a nonexempt employees' trust is restricted to the amount of the contribution, and excludes any income received by the trust with respect to contributed amounts.

5. The partnership rules of subchapter K

A partnership is not subject to income taxation. However, a partner must take into account separately on its return its distributive share of the partnership's income, gain, loss, deduction, or credit. A U.S. partner of a foreign partnership is subject to U.S. tax on its distributive share of partnership income. In addition, a foreign partnership may have a controlled foreign corporation (CFC) partner which must take into account its distributive share of partnership income, gain, loss, or deduction in determining its taxable income. These distributive share inclusions of the CFC may result in subpart F income and thus income to a U.S. shareholder of the CFC. If the grantor trust rules do not apply to any portion of a foreign employees' trust, a foreign partnership could fund a foreign employees' trust in excess of the amount needed to meet its obligations to its employees under its deferred compensation plan and yet retain control over the excess amount. As a result, the foreign partnership would not have to include items in taxable income attributable to the excess amount, and consequently the U.S. partner or CFC would not have to include those items in its income.

6. The antideferral rules of subpart F, including section 956A, and PFIC

A U.S. person that owns stock in a foreign corporation generally pays no U.S. tax currently on income earned by the foreign corporation. Instead, the United States defers taxation of that income until it is distributed to the U.S. person. The antideferral rules, however, which include subpart F and the PFIC rules, limit this deferral in certain situations.

Subpart F of part III of Subchapter N (sections 951 through 964) applies to CFCs. A foreign corporation is a CFC if more than 50 percent of the total voting power of all classes of stock entitled to vote, or the total value of the stock in the corporation, is owned by "U.S. shareholders" (defined as U.S. persons who own ten percent or more of the voting power of all classes of stock entitled to vote) on any day during the foreign corporation's taxable year. The United States generally taxes U.S. shareholders of the CFC currently on their pro rata share of

the CFC's subpart F income and sections 956 and 956A amounts. In effect, the U.S. shareholders are treated as having received a distribution out of the earnings and profits (E&P) of the CFC.

The types of income earned by a foreign employees' trust (dividends, interest, income equivalent to interest, rents and royalties, and annuities) are generally subpart F income. The inclusion under section 956 is based on the CFC's investment in U.S. property, which generally includes stock of a U.S. shareholder of the CFC. A U.S. shareholder's section 956A amount for a taxable year is the lesser of two amounts. The first amount is the excess of the U.S. shareholder's pro rata share of the CFC's "excess passive assets" over the portion of the CFC's E&P treated as previously included in gross income by the U.S. shareholder under section 956A. For purposes of section 956A, "passive asset" includes any asset which produces (or is held for the production of) passive income, and generally includes property that produces dividends, interest, income equivalent to interest, rents and royalties, and annuities, subject to exceptions that generally are not relevant in this context. The second amount is the U.S. shareholder's pro rata share of the CFC's "applicable earnings" to the extent accumulated in taxable years beginning after September 30, 1993.

Section 1501(a)(2) of SBJPA repeals section 956A. The repeal is effective for taxable years of foreign corporations beginning after December 31, 1996, and for taxable years of U.S. shareholders with or within which such taxable years of foreign corporations end.

If a CFC employer is not treated for federal income tax purposes as the owner of any portion of a foreign employees' trust under the grantor trust rules, then to the extent that passive assets contributed by a CFC to a nonexempt employees' trust would otherwise result in subpart F consequences for the CFC and its shareholders, the CFC's contribution could allow those consequences to be avoided. For example, a contribution by a CFC of passive assets to its foreign employees' trust could reduce the CFC's subpart F earnings and profits, and its applicable earnings or passive assets for section 956A purposes, and could affect the CFC's increase in investment in U.S. property for purposes of section 956, all of which could affect a U.S. shareholder's pro rata subpart F inclusions for the taxable year.

In contrast to the subpart F rules, the PFIC rules apply to any U.S. person who directly or indirectly owns any stock in a foreign corporation that is a PFIC under either an income or asset test. A foreign corporation, including a CFC, is a PFIC if either (1) 75 percent or more of its gross income for the taxable year is passive income or (2) at least 50 percent of the value of the corporation's assets produce passive income or are held for the production of passive income. For this purpose, passive income generally is the same type of income (dividends, interest, income equivalent to interest, rents and royalties, and annuities) that would be earned by a foreign employees' trust.

Under the PFIC rules, a U.S. person who is a direct or indirect shareholder of a PFIC is subject to a special tax regime upon either disposition of the PFIC's stock or receipt of certain distributions (excess distributions) from the PFIC. A shareholder, however, may avoid the application of this special regime by electing to include its pro rata share of certain of the PFIC's passive income in the year in which the foreign corporation earns it.

If the grantor trust rules did not apply to any portion of a foreign employees' trust, a contribution by a foreign corporation of passive assets to a nonexempt employees' trust would enable a U.S. person to avoid the PFIC rules if those assets would otherwise generate PFIC consequences for the foreign corporation and its shareholders. For example, by transferring passive assets to its nonexempt employees' trust in excess of the amount needed to meet obligations to its employees under its deferred compensation plan while retaining control over the excess amount, a foreign corporation could divest itself of a sufficient amount of passive assets and the passive income they produce to avoid meeting the income and asset tests. Furthermore, a foreign corporation that is a PFIC could minimize income inclusions for a U.S. shareholder that has made an election to include PFIC income currently by transferring income-producing assets to a foreign employees' trust.

Overview of proposed regulations

Under the proposed regulations, an employer is not treated as an owner of any portion of a domestic nonexempt employees' trust described in section 402(b) for federal income tax purposes. Section 404(a)(5) and §1.404(a)-12(b) provide a deduction to the employer solely for contributions to a nonexempt employees' trust, and not for any income of the trust. This rule is inconsistent with treating the employer as owning any portion of a nonexempt employees' trust, which would require the employer to recognize the trust's income that it may not deduct under section 404(a)(5). Accordingly, such a trust is treated as a separate taxable trust that is taxed under the rules of section 641 et seq. The rule in the proposed regulations is consistent with the holdings of a number of private letter rulings with respect to nonexempt employees' trusts and with the Service's treatment of trusts that no longer qualify as exempt under 501(a) (because they are no longer described in section 401(a)) as separate taxable trusts rather than as grantor trusts. See also Rev. Rul. 74-299 (1974-1 C.B. 154). This document is made available by the Superintendent of Documents, U.S. Government Printing Office, Washington, DC 20402.

Under the proposed regulations, an employer generally is not treated as the owner of any portion of a foreign nonexempt employees' trust for federal income tax purposes, except as provided under section 679. The proposed regulations, however, also provide that the grantor trust rules apply to determine whether an employer that is a CFC or a U.S. employer is treated as the owner of a specified "fractional interest" in a foreign employees' trust. This rule applies whether or not the employer elects section 404A treatment for the trust. Under the proposed regulations, this rule also applies in the case of an employer that is a foreign partnership with one or more partners that are U.S. persons or CFCs (U.S.-related partnership). Such an employer is treated as the owner of a portion of a foreign employees' trust under these proposed regulations only if the employer retains a grantor trust power or interest over a foreign employees' trust and has a specified "fractional interest" in the trust.

Under these proposed regulations, the grantor trust rules of subpart E do not apply to a foreign employees' trust with respect to a foreign employer other than a CFC or a U.S.-related foreign partnership, except for cases in which assets are transferred to a foreign employees' trust with a principal purpose of avoiding the PFIC rules. The IRS and Treasury will continue to consider whether these regulations should provide additional antiabuse rules that may be necessary for other purposes, including for purposes of calculating earnings and profits, determining the foreign tax credit limitation, and applying the interest allocation rules of § 1.882-5.

Explanation of provisions

1. § 1.671-1(g): Domestic nonexempt employees' trusts

The proposed regulations provide that an employer is not treated for federal income tax purposes as an owner of any portion of a nonexempt employees' trust described in section 402(b) that is part of a deferred compensation plan, and that is not a foreign trust within the meaning of section 7701(a)(31), regardless of whether the employer has a power or interest described in sections 673 through 677 over any portion of the trust. This rule is analogous to the rule set forth in § 1.641(a)-0, which provides that subchapter J, including the grantor trust rules, does not apply to tax-exempt employees' trusts.

2. § 1.671-1(h): Subpart E rules for certain foreign employees' trusts

The proposed regulations provide Subpart E rules for foreign employees' trusts of CFCs, foreign partnerships, and U.S. employers that apply for all federal income tax purposes. Under the proposed regulations, except as provided under section 679 or the proposed regulations (as described below), an employer is not treated as an owner of any portion of a foreign employees' trust for federal income tax purposes. If an employer is treated as the owner of a portion of a foreign employees' trust for federal income tax purposes as described below, then the employer is considered to own the trust assets attributable to that portion of the trust for all federal income tax purposes. Thus, for example, if an employer is treated as the owner of a portion of a foreign employees' trust for federal income tax purposes as described below, then income of the trust that is attributable to that portion of the trust increases the employer's earnings and profits for purposes of sections 312 and 964.

A foreign employees' trust is a nonexempt employees' trust described in section 402(b) that is part of a deferred compensation plan, and that is a foreign trust within the meaning of section 7701(a)(31). The proposed regulations apply to any foreign employees' trust of a CFC or U.S.-related foreign partnership, whether or not a trust funds a qualified foreign plan (as defined in section 404A(e)). The proposed regulations clarify that the income inclusion and asset ownership rules apply to the entity whose employees or independent contractors are covered under the deferred compensation plan.

A. Plan of CFC employer

The proposed regulations provide that, if a CFC maintains a deferred compensation plan funded through a foreign employees' trust, then, with respect to the CFC, the provisions of subpart E apply to the portion of the trust that is the fractional interest of the trust described in the proposed regulations.

B. Plan of U.S. employer

The proposed regulations provide that if a U.S. person maintains a deferred compensation plan funded through a foreign employees' trust, then, with respect to the U.S. person, the provisions of subpart E apply to the portion of the trust that is the fractional interest of the trust described in the proposed regulations.

C. Plan of U.S.-related foreign partnership employer

The proposed regulations provide that, if a U.S.-related foreign partnership maintains a deferred compensation plan funded through a foreign employees' trust, then, with respect to the U.S.-related foreign partnership, the provisions of subpart E apply to the portion of the trust that is the fractional interest of the trust described in the proposed regulations. The IRS and Treasury solicit comments on whether these regulations should provide a safe harbor rule for a U.S.-related foreign partnership that maintains a deferred compensation plan funded through a foreign employees' trust if U.S. or CFC partnership interests are de minimis. The IRS and Treasury specifically solicit comments concerning the amount of U.S. or CFC partnership interests that would qualify as "de minimis."

D. Plan of non-CFC foreign employer

The proposed regulations provide that a foreign employer that is not a CFC is treated as an owner of a portion of a foreign employees' trust only as provided in the antiabuse rule of § 1.1297-4.

E. Fractional interest

The fractional interest of a foreign employees' trust described above is defined in the proposed regulations as an undivided fractional interest in the trust for which the fraction is equal to the relevant amount determined for the employer's taxable year divided by the fair market value of trust assets determined for the employer's taxable year.

F. Relevant amount

The relevant amount for the employer's taxable year is defined in the proposed regulations as the amount, if any, by which the fair market value of trust assets, plus the fair market value of any assets available to pay plan liabilities (including any amount held under an annuity contract that exceeds the amount that is needed to satisfy the liabilities provided for under the contract) that are held in the equivalent of a trust within the meaning of section 404A(b)(5)(A), exceed the plan's accrued liability, determined using a projected unit credit funding method.

The relevant amount is reduced to the extent the taxpayer demonstrates to the Commissioner that the relevant amount is attributable to amounts that were properly contributed to the trust pursuant to a reasonable funding method, or experience that is favorable relative to any actuarial assumptions used that the Commissioner determines to be reasonable. In addition, if an employer that is a controlled foreign corporation otherwise would be treated as the owner of a fractional interest in a foreign employees' trust, the taxpayer may rely on this rule only if it so indicates on a statement attached to a timely filed Form 5471. The IRS and Treasury solicit comments regarding the most appropriate way in which to extend a filing requirement to partners in U.S.-related foreign partnerships and other affected taxpayers.

G. Plan's accrued liability

Under the proposed regulations, the plan's accrued liability for a taxable year of the employer is computed as of the plan's measurement date for the employer's taxable year. The plan's accrued liability is determined using a projected unit credit funding method, taking into account only liabilities relating to services performed for the employer or a predecessor employer. In addition, the plan's accrued liability is reduced (but not below zero) by any liabilities that are provided for under annuity contracts held to satisfy plan liabilities.

Because CFCs generally are required to determine their taxable income by reference to U.S. tax principles, the definition of a plan's "accrued liability" refers to § 1.412(c)(3)-1. This definition generally is intended to track the method used for calculating pension costs under Statement of Financial Accounting Standards No. 87, Employers' Accounting for Pensions (FAS 87), available from the Financial Accounting Standards Board, 401 Merritt 7, Norwalk, CT 06856. Under the method required to be used to calculate FAS 87's projected benefit obligation (PBO), plan costs are based on projected salary levels. Because many taxpayers already compute PBO annually to determine the pension costs of their nonexempt employees' trusts for financial reporting, the timing, interval and method to compute plan liabilities under § 1.671-1(h) should minimize taxpayer burden. The IRS and Treasury solicit comments regarding the extent to which the proposed regulations conform to existing procedures under FAS 87 and applicable foreign law, and regarding appropriate conforming adjustments.

H. Fair market value of trust assets

Under the proposed regulations, for a taxable year of the employer, the fair market value of trust assets, and the fair market value of retirement annuities or other assets held in the equivalent of a trust, equals the fair market value of those assets, as of the measurement date for the employer's taxable year. The fair market value of these assets is adjusted to include contributions made between the measurement date and the end of the employer's taxable year.

I. De minimis exception

The proposed regulations provide an exception to the general rule for determining the relevant amount. If the relevant amount would not otherwise be greater than the plan's normal cost for the plan year ending with or within the employer's taxable year, then the relevant amount is considered to be zero.

J. Proposed effective date and transition rules

The proposed regulations are proposed to be prospective. For taxable years ending prior to September 27, 1996, employers generally would not be treated for federal income tax purposes as owning the assets of foreign nonexempt employees' trusts (except as provided under section 679), consistent with the rules applying to domestic nonexempt employees' trusts. A transition rule, for purposes of § 1.671-1(h), exempts certain amounts from the application of the proposed regulations. This exemption is phased out over a ten-year period. There is a special transition rule for any foreign corporation that becomes a CFC after September 27, 1996. In addition, there is a special transition rule for certain entities that become U.S.-related foreign partnerships after September 27, 1996.

3. § 1.671-2: General asset ownership rules

The proposed regulations provide that a person who is treated as the owner of any portion of a trust under subpart E is considered to own the trust assets attributable to that portion of the trust for all federal income tax purposes.

4. § 1.1297-4: Subpart E rules for foreign employers that are not controlled foreign corporations

Under the proposed regulations, a foreign employer other than a CFC is not treated as the owner of any portion of a foreign nonexempt employees' trust for purposes of sections 1291 through 1297, except for cases in which a principal purpose for transferring property to the trust is to avoid classification of a foreign corporation as a PFIC (as defined in section 1296) or, if the foreign corporation is classified as a PFIC, in cases in which a principal purpose for transferring property to the trust is to avoid or to reduce taxation of U.S. shareholders of the PFIC under section 1291 or 1293. The effective date of this rule is September 27, 1996.

Income inclusion and related asset ownership rules for foreign welfare benefit plans

The IRS and Treasury solicit comments on the need for (and content of) income inclusion and asset ownership rules for foreign welfare benefit trusts.

Special Analyses

It has been determined that this notice of proposed rulemaking is not a significant regulatory action as defined in Executive Order 12866. Therefore, a regulatory assessment is not required. It is hereby certified that these regulations do not have a significant economic impact on a substantial number of small entities. This certification is based on the fact that these regulations will primarily affect U.S. owners of significant interests in foreign entities, which owners generally are large multinational corporations. This certification is also based on the fact that the burden imposed by the collection of information in the regulation, which is a requirement that certain entities may rely on an exception for reasonable funding only if they indicate such reliance on a statement attached to a timely filed Form 5471, is minimal, and, therefore, the collection of information will not impose a significant economic impact on such entities. Therefore, a Regulatory Flexibility Analysis under the Regulatory Flexibility Act (5 U.S.C. chapter 6) is not required. Pursuant to section 7805(f) of the Internal Revenue Code, this notice of proposed rulemaking will be submitted to the Chief Counsel for Advocacy of the Small Business Administration for comment on its impact on small business.

Comments and Public Hearing

Before these proposed regulations are adopted as final regulations, consideration will be given to any written comments (a signed original and eight (8) copies) that are submitted timely to the IRS. All comments will be available for public inspection and copying.

A public hearing has been scheduled for January 15, 1997, at 10:00 a.m. in room 2615, Internal Revenue Building, 1111 Constitution Avenue, NW., Washington DC. Because of access restrictions, visitors will not be admitted beyond the Internal Revenue Building lobby more than 15 minutes before the hearing starts.

The rules of 26 CFR 601.601(a)(3) apply to the hearing.

Persons that wish to present oral comments at the hearing must submit written comments by December 26, 1996, and submit an outline of the topics to be discussed and the time to be devoted to each topic (signed original and eight (8) copies) by December 24, 1996.

A period of 10 minutes will be allotted to each person for making comments.

An agenda showing the scheduling of the speakers will be prepared after the deadline for receiving outlines has passed. Copies of the agenda will be available free of charge at the hearing.

Drafting Information

The principal authors of these regulations are James A. Quinn of the Office of Assistant Chief Counsel (Passthroughs and Special Industries), Linda S. F. Marshall of the Office of Associate Chief Counsel (Employee Benefits and Exempt Organizations), and Kristine K. Schlaman and M. Grace Fleeman of the Office of Associate Chief Counsel (International). However, other personnel from the IRS and Treasury Department participated in their development.

List of Subjects in 26 CFR Part 1

Income taxes, Reporting and recordkeeping requirements.

Proposed Amendments to the Regulations

Accordingly, 26 CFR part 1 is proposed to be amended as follows:

PART 1—INCOME TAXES

Paragraph 1. The authority citation for part 1 is amended by removing the entry for sections 1.1291-10T, 1.1294-1T, 1.1295-1T, and 1.1297-3T and adding entries in numerical order to read as follows:

Authority: 26 U.S.C. 7805 ***

Section 1.671-1 also issued under 26 U.S.C. 404A(h) and 672(f)(2)(B). ***

Section 1.1291-10T also issued under 26 U.S.C. 1291(d)(2).

Section 1.1294-1T also issued under 26 U.S.C. 1294.

Section 1.1295-1T also issued under 26 U.S.C. 1295.

Section 1.1297-3T also issued under 26 U.S.C. 1297(b)(1).

Section 1.1297-4 also issued under 26 U.S.C. 1297(f). ***

Par. 2. Section 1.671-1 is amended by adding paragraphs (g) and (h) to read as follows:

§ 1.671-1 Grantors and others treated as substantial owners; scope.

*****

(g) *Domestic nonexempt employees' trust*— (1) *General rule.* An employer is not treated as an owner of any portion of a nonexempt employees' trust described in section 402(b) that is part of a deferred compensation plan, and that is not a foreign trust within the meaning of section 7701(a)(31), regardless of whether the employer has a power or interest described in sections 673 through 677 over any portion of the trust. See section 402(b)(3) and § 1.402(b)-1(b)(6) for rules relating to treatment of a beneficiary of a nonexempt employees' trust as the owner of a portion of the trust.

(2) *Example.* The following example illustrates the rules of paragraph (g)(1) of this section:

Example. Employer X provides nonqualified deferred compensation through Plan A to certain of its management employees. Employer X has created Trust T to fund the benefits under Plan A. Assets of Trust T may not be used for any purpose other than to satisfy benefits provided under Plan A until all plan liabilities have been satisfied. Trust T is classified as a trust under § 301.7701-4 of this chapter, and is not a foreign trust within the meaning of section 7701(a)(31). Under § 1.83-3(e), contributions to Trust T are considered transfers of property to participants within the meaning of section 83. On these facts,

Trust T is a nonexempt employees' trust described in section 402(b). Because Trust T is a nonexempt employees' trust described in section 402(b) that is part of a deferred compensation plan, and that is not a foreign trust within the meaning of section 7701(a)(31), Employer X is not treated as an owner of any portion of Trust T.

(h) *Foreign employees' trust*—(1) *General rules.* Except as provided under section 679 or as provided under this paragraph (h)(1), an employer is not treated as an owner of any portion of a foreign employees' trust (as defined in paragraph (h)(2) of this section), regardless of whether the employer has a power or interest described in sections 673 through 677 over any portion of the trust.

(i) *Plan of CFC employer.* If a controlled foreign corporation (as defined in section 957) maintains a deferred compensation plan funded through a foreign employees' trust, then, with respect to the controlled foreign corporation, the provisions of subpart E apply to the portion of the trust that is the fractional interest described in paragraph (h)(3) of this section.

(ii) *Plan of U.S. employer.* If a United States person (as defined in section 7701(a)(30)) maintains a deferred compensation plan that is funded through a foreign employees' trust, then, with respect to the U.S. person, the provisions of subpart E apply to the portion of the trust that is the fractional interest described in paragraph (h)(3) of this section.

(iii) *Plan of U.S.-related foreign partnership employer*—(A) *General rule.* If a U.S.-related foreign partnership (as defined in paragraph (h)(1)(iii)(B) of this section) maintains a deferred compensation plan funded through a foreign employees' trust, then, with respect to the U.S.-related foreign partnership, the provisions of subpart E apply to the portion of the trust that is the fractional interest described in paragraph (h)(3) of this section.

(B) *U.S.-related foreign partnership.* For purposes of this paragraph (h), a U.S.-related foreign partnership is a foreign partnership in which a U.S. person or a controlled foreign corporation owns a partnership interest either directly or indirectly through one or more partnerships.

(iv) *Application of § 1.1297-4 to plan of foreign non-CFC employer.* A foreign employer that is not a controlled foreign corporation may be treated as an owner of a portion of a foreign employees' trust as provided in § 1.1297-4.

(v) *Application to employer entity.* The rules of paragraphs (h)(1)(i) through (h)(1)(iv) of this section apply to the employer whose employees benefit under the deferred compensation plan funded through a foreign employees' trust, or, in the case of a deferred compensation plan covering independent contractors, the recipient of services performed by those independent contractors, regardless of whether the plan is maintained through another entity. Thus, for example, where a deferred compensation plan benefitting employees of a controlled foreign corporation is funded through a foreign employees' trust, the controlled foreign corporation is considered to be the grantor of the foreign employees' trust for purposes of applying paragraph (h)(1)(i) of this section.

(2) *Foreign employees' trust.* A foreign employees' trust is a nonexempt employees' trust described in section 402(b) that is part of a deferred compensation plan, and that is a foreign trust within the meaning of section 7701(a)(31).

(3) *Fractional interest for paragraph (h)(1)*—(i) *In general.* The fractional interest for a foreign employees' trust used for purposes of paragraph (h)(1) of this section for a taxable year of the employer is an undivided fractional interest in the trust for which the fraction is equal to the relevant amount for the employer's taxable year divided by the fair market value of trust assets for the employer's taxable year.

(ii) *Relevant amount*—(A) *In general.* For purposes of applying paragraph (h)(3)(i) of this section, and except as provided in paragraph (h)(3)(iii) of this section, the relevant amount for the employer's taxable year is the amount, if any, by which the fair market value of trust assets, plus the fair market value of any assets available to pay plan liabilities that are held in the equivalent of a trust within the meaning of section 404A(b)(5)(A), exceed the plan's accrued liability. The following rules apply for this purpose:

(*1*) The plan's accrued liability is determined using a projected unit credit funding method that satisfies the requirements of § 1.412(c)(3)-1, taking into account only liabilities relating to services performed through the measurement date for the employer or a predecessor employer.

(*2*) The plan's accrued liability is reduced (but not below zero) by any liabilities that are provided for under annuity contracts held to satisfy plan liabilities.

(*3*) Any amount held under an annuity contract that exceeds the amount that is needed to satisfy the liabilities provided for under the contract (e.g., the value of a participation right under a participating annuity contract) is added to the fair market value of any assets available to pay plan liabilities that are held in the equivalent of a trust.

(*4*) If the relevant amount as determined under this paragraph (h)(3)(ii), without regard to this paragraph (h)(3)(ii)(A)(*4*), is greater than the fair market value of trust assets, then the relevant amount is equal to the fair market value of trust assets.

(B) *Permissible actuarial assumptions for accrued liability.* For purposes of paragraph (h)(3)(ii)(A) of this section, a plan's accrued liability must be calculated using an interest rate and other actuarial assumptions that the Commissioner determines to be reasonable. It is appropriate in determining this interest rate to look to available information about rates implicit in current prices of annuity contracts, and to look to rates of return on high-quality fixed-income investments currently available and expected to be available during the period prior to maturity of the plan benefits. If the qualified business unit computes its income or earnings and profits in dollars pursuant to the dollar approximate separate transactions method under § 1.985-3, the employer must use an exchange rate that can be demonstrated to clearly reflect income, based on all relevant facts and circumstances, including appropriate rates of inflation and commercial practices.

(iii) *Exception for reasonable funding.* The relevant amount does not include an amount that the taxpayer demonstrates to the Commissioner is attributable to amounts that were properly contributed to the trust pursuant to a reasonable funding method, applied using actuarial assumptions that the Commissioner determines to be reasonable, or any amount that the taxpayer demonstrates to the Commissioner is attributable to experience that is favorable relative to any actuarial assumptions used that the Commissioner determines to be reasonable. For this paragraph (h)(3)(iii) to apply to a controlled foreign corporation employer described in paragraph (h)(1)(i) of this section, the taxpayer must indicate on a statement attached to a timely filed Form 5471 that the taxpayer is relying on this rule. For purposes of this paragraph (h)(3)(iii), an amount is considered contributed pursuant to a reasonable funding method if the amount is contributed pursuant to a funding method permitted to be used under section 412 (e.g., the entry age normal funding method) that is consistently used to determine plan contributions. In addition, for purposes of this paragraph (h)(3)(iii), if there has been a change to that method from another funding method, an amount is considered contributed pursuant to a reasonable funding method only if the prior funding method is also a funding method described in the preceding sentence that was consistently used to determine plan contributions. For purposes of this paragraph (h)(3)(iii), a funding method is considered reasonable only if the method provides for any initial unfunded liability to be amortized over a period of at least 6 years, and for any net change in accrued liability resulting from a change in funding method to be amortized over a period of at least 6 years.

(iv) *Reduction for transition amount.* The relevant amount is reduced (but not below zero) by any transition amount described in paragraphs (h)(5), (h)(6), or (h)(7) of this section.

(v) *Fair market value of assets.* For purposes of paragraphs (h)(3)(i) and (ii) of this section, for a taxable year of the employer, the fair market value of trust assets, and the fair market value of other assets held in the equivalent of a trust within the meaning of section 404A(b)(5)(A), equals the fair market value of those assets, as of the measurement date for the employer's taxable year, adjusted to include contributions made after the measurement date and by the end of the employer's taxable year.

(vi) *Annual valuation.* For purposes of determining the relevant amount for a taxable year of the employer, the fair market value of plan assets, and the plan's accrued liability as described in paragraphs (h)(3)(ii) and (iii) of this section, and the normal cost as described in paragraph (h)(4) of this section, must be determined as of a consistently used annual measurement date within the employer's taxable year.

(vii) *Special rule for plan funded through multiple trusts.* In cases in which a plan is funded through more than one foreign employees' trust, the fractional interest determined under paragraph (h)(3)(i) of this section in each trust is determined by treating all of the trusts as if their assets were held in a single trust for which the fraction is determined in accordance with the rules of this paragraph (h)(3).

(4) *De minimis exception.* If the relevant amount is not greater than the plan's normal cost for the plan year ending with or within the employer's taxable year, computed using a funding method and actuarial assumptions as described in paragraph (h)(3)(ii) of this section or

as described in paragraph (h)(3)(iii) of this section if the requirements of that paragraph are met, that are used to determine plan contributions, then the relevant amount is considered to be zero for purposes of applying paragraph (h)(3)(i) of this section.

(5) *General rule for transition amount*—(i) *General rule.* If paragraphs (h)(6) and (h)(7) of this section do not apply to the employer, the transition amount for purposes of paragraph (h)(3)(iv) of this section is equal to the preexisting amount multiplied by the applicable percentage for the year in which the employer's taxable year begins.

(ii) *Preexisting amount.* The preexisting amount is equal to the relevant amount of the trust, determined without regard to paragraphs (h)(3)(iv) and (h)(4) of this section, computed as of the measurement date that immediately precedes September 27, 1996 disregarding contributions to the trust made after the measurement date.

(iii) *Applicable percentage.* The applicable percentage is equal to 100 percent for the employer's first taxable year ending after this document is published as a final regulation in the Federal Register and prior taxable years of the employer, and is reduced (but not below zero) by 10 percentage points for each subsequent taxable year of the employer.

(6) *Transition amount for new CFCs*—(i) *General rule.* In the case of a new controlled foreign corporation employer, the transition amount for purposes of paragraph (h)(3)(iv) is equal to the pre-change amount multiplied by the applicable percentage for the year in which the new controlled foreign corporation employer's taxable year begins.

(ii) *Pre-change amount.* The pre-change amount for purposes of paragraph (h)(6)(i) is equal to the relevant amount of the trust, determined without regard to paragraphs (h)(3)(iv) and (h)(4) of this section and disregarding contributions to the trust made after the measurement date, for the new controlled foreign corporation employer's last taxable year ending before the corporation becomes a new controlled foreign corporation employer.

(iii) *Applicable percentage*—(A) *General rule.* Except as provided in paragraph (h)(6)(iii)(B) of this section, the applicable percentage is equal to 100 percent for a new controlled foreign corporation employer's first taxable year ending after the corporation becomes a controlled foreign corporation. The applicable percentage is reduced (but not below zero) by 10 percentage points for each subsequent taxable year of the new controlled foreign corporation.

(B) *Interim rule.* For any taxable year of a new controlled foreign corporation employer that ends on or before the date this document is published as a final regulation in the **Federal Register,** the applicable percentage is equal to 100 percent. The applicable percentage is reduced by 10 percentage points for each subsequent taxable year of the new controlled foreign corporation employer that ends after the date this document is published as a final regulation in the **Federal Register.**

(iv) *New CFC employer.* For purposes of paragraph (h)(6) of this section, a new controlled foreign corporation employer is a corporation that first becomes a controlled foreign corporation within the meaning of section 957 after September 27, 1996. A new controlled foreign corporation employer includes a corporation that was a controlled foreign corporation prior to, but not on, September 26, 1996 and that first becomes a controlled foreign corporation again after September 27, 1996.

(v) *Anti-stuffing rule.* Notwithstanding paragraph (h)(6)(iii) of this section, if, prior to becoming a controlled foreign corporation, a corporation contributes amounts to a foreign employees' trust with a principal purpose of obtaining tax benefits by increasing the pre-change amount, the applicable percentage with respect to those amounts is 0 percent for all taxable years of the new controlled foreign corporation employer.

(7) *Transition amount for new U.S.-related foreign partnerships*—(i) *General rule.* In the case of a new U.S.-related foreign partnership employer, the transition amount for purposes of paragraph (h)(3)(iv) of this section is equal to the pre-change amount multiplied by the applicable percentage for the year in which the new U.S.-related foreign partnership employer's taxable year begins.

(ii) *Pre-change amount.* The pre-change amount for purposes of paragraph (h)(7)(i) of this section is equal to the relevant amount of the trust, determined without regard to paragraphs (h)(3)(iv) and (h)(4) of this section and disregarding contributions to the trust made after the measurement date, for the entity's last taxable year ending before the entity becomes a new U.S.-related foreign partnership employer.

(iii) *Applicable percentage*—(A) *General rule.* Except as provided in paragraph (h)(7)(iii)(B) of this section, the applicable percentage is equal to 100 percent for a new U.S.-related foreign partnership employer's first taxable year ending after the entity becomes a new U.S.-related foreign partnership employer. The applicable percentage is reduced (but not below zero) by 10 percentage points for each subsequent taxable year of the new U.S.-related foreign partnership employer.

(B) *Interim rule.* For any taxable year of a new U.S.-related foreign partnership employer that ends on or before the date this document is published as a final regulation in the **Federal Register,** the applicable percentage is equal to 100 percent. The applicable percentage is reduced by 10 percentage points for each subsequent taxable year of the new U.S.-related foreign partnership employer that ends after the date this document is published as a final regulation in the **Federal Register.**

(iv) *New U.S.-related foreign partnership employer.* For purposes of paragraph (h)(7) of this section, a new U.S.-related foreign partnership employer is an entity that was a foreign corporation other than a controlled foreign corporation, or that was a foreign partnership other than a U.S.-related foreign partnership, and that changes from this status to a U.S.-related foreign partnership after September 27, 1996. A new U.S.-related foreign partnership employer includes a corporation that was a U.S.-related foreign partnership prior to, but not on, September 27, 1996, and that first becomes a U.S.-related foreign partnership again after September 27, 1996.

(v) *Anti-stuffing rule.* Notwithstanding paragraph (h)(7)(iii) of this section, if, prior to becoming a new U.S.-related foreign partnership employer, an entity contributes amounts to a foreign employees' trust with a principal purpose of obtaining tax benefits by increasing the pre-change amount, the applicable percentage with respect to those amounts is 0 percent for all taxable years of the new U.S.-related foreign partnership employer.

(8) *Examples.* The following examples illustrate the rules of paragraph (h) of this section. In each example, the employer has a power or interest described in sections 673 through 677 over the foreign employees' trust, and the monetary unit is the applicable functional currency (FC) determined in accordance with section 985(b) and the regulations thereunder.

Example 1. (i) Employer X is a controlled foreign corporation (as defined in section 957). Employer X maintains a defined benefit retirement plan for its employees. Employer X's taxable year is the calendar year. Trust T, a foreign employees' trust, is the sole funding vehicle for the plan. Both the plan year of the plan and the taxable year of Trust T are the calendar year.

(ii) As of December 31, 1997, Trust T's measurement date, the fair market value (as described in paragraph (h)(3)(iv) of this section) of Trust T's assets is FC 1,000,000, and the amount of the plan's accrued liability is FC 800,000, which includes a normal cost for 1997 of FC 50,000. The preexisting amount for Trust T is FC 40,000. Thus, the relevant amount for 1997 is FC 160,000 (which is greater than the plan's normal cost for the year). Employer X's shareholder does not indicate on a statement attached to a timely filed Form 5471 that any of the relevant amount qualifies for the exception described in paragraph (h)(3)(iii) of this section. Therefore, the fractional interest for Employer X's taxable year ending on December 31, 1997, is 16 percent. Employer X is treated as the owner for federal income tax purposes of an undivided 16 percent interest in each of Trust T's assets for the period from January 1, 1997 through December 31, 1997. Employer X must take into account a 16 percent pro rata share of each item of income, deduction or credit of Trust T during this period in computing its federal income tax liability.

Example 2. Assume the same facts as in *Example 1,* except that Employer X's shareholder indicates on a statement attached to a timely filed Form 5471 and can demonstrate to the satisfaction of the Commissioner that, in reliance on paragraph (h)(3)(iii) of this section, FC 100,000 of the fair market value of Trust T's assets is attributable to favorable experience relative to reasonable actuarial assumptions used. Accordingly, the relevant amount for 1997 is FC 60,000. Because the plan's normal cost for 1997 is less than FC 60,000, the de minimis exception of paragraph (h)(4) of this section does not apply. Therefore, the fractional interest for Employer X's taxable year ending on December 31, 1997, is 6 percent. Employer X is treated as the owner for federal income tax purposes of an undivided 6 percent interest in each of Trust T's assets for the period from January 1, 1997, through December 31, 1997. Employer X must take into account a 6 percent pro rata share of each item of income, deduction or credit of Trust T during this period in computing its federal income tax liability.

(9) *Effective date.* Paragraphs (g) and (h) of this section apply to taxable years of an employer ending after September 27, 1996.

Par. 3. Section 1.671-2 is amended by adding paragraph (f) to read as follows:

§ 1.671-2 Applicable principles

*****

(f) For purposes of subtitle A of the Internal Revenue Code, a person that is treated as the owner of any portion of a trust under subpart E is considered to own the trust assets attributable to that portion of the trust.

Par. 4. Section 1.1297-4 is added to read as follows:

§ 1.1297-4 Application of subpart E of subchapter J with respect to foreign employees' trusts.

(a) *General rules.* For purposes of part VI of subchapter P, chapter 1 of the Code, a foreign employer that is not a controlled foreign corporation is not treated as the owner of any portion of a foreign employees' trust (as defined in § 1.671-1(h)(2)) except as provided in this paragraph (a), regardless of whether the employer has a power or interest described in sections 673 through 677 over any portion of the trust.

(1) *Principal purpose to avoid classification as a passive foreign investment company.* If a principal purpose for a transfer of property by any person to a foreign employees' trust (as defined in § 1.671-1(h)(2)) is to avoid classification of a foreign corporation as a passive foreign investment company, then the following rule applies. If the foreign employer has a power or interest described in sections 673 through 677 over the trust, then the grantor trust rules of subpart E of part I of subchapter J, chapter 1 of the Code will apply, for purposes of part VI of subchapter P, to a fixed dollar amount in the trust that is equal to the fair market value of the property that is transferred for the purpose of avoiding classification as a passive foreign investment company. Whether a principal purpose for a transfer is the avoidance of classification as a passive foreign investment company will be determined on the basis of all of the facts and circumstances, including whether the amount of assets held by the foreign employees' trust is reasonably related to the plan's anticipated liabilities, taking into account any local law and practice relating to proper funding levels.

(2) *Principal purpose to reduce or eliminate taxation under section 1291 or 1293.* If a principal purpose for a transfer of property by any person to a foreign employees' trust (as defined in § 1.671-1(h)(2)) is to reduce or eliminate taxation under section 1291 or 1293, then the following rule applies. If the foreign employer has a power or interest described in sections 673 through 677 over the trust, then the provisions of subpart E will apply, for purposes of part VI of subchapter P, to a fixed dollar amount in the trust that is equal to the fair market value of the property transferred for the purpose of reducing or eliminating taxation under section 1291 or 1293. Whether a principal purpose for a transfer is to reduce or eliminate taxation under section 1291 or 1293 will be determined on the basis of all the facts and circumstances, including whether the amount of assets held by the foreign employees' trust is reasonably related to the plan's anticipated liabilities, taking into account any local law and practice relating to proper funding levels.

(3) *Application to employer entity.* The rules of this section apply to the employer whose employees benefit under the deferred compensation plan funded through the foreign employees' trust, or, in the case of a deferred compensation plan covering independent contractors, the recipient of services performed by those independent contractors, regardless of whether the plan is maintained through another entity. Thus, for example, where a deferred compensation plan benefitting employees of a foreign employer that is not a controlled foreign corporation is funded through a foreign employees' trust, the foreign employer is considered to be the grantor of the foreign employees' trust for purposes of this paragraph (a).

(b) *Effective date.* This section applies to taxable years of a foreign corporation ending after September 27, 1996.

Commissioner of Internal Revenue

Margaret Milner Richardson

CERTIFIED COPY

Michael L. Slaughter

¶ 20,220

Proposed regulations: Magnetic media filing: Information returns: Form W-2: Form 1099 series: Form 5498.—The IRS has issued proposed regulations regarding the requirements for filing information returns on magnetic media or in other machine-readable form under Code Sec. 6011(e). The proposed regulations, which were also issued as temporary regulations, provide that filers of the Form 1099 series and Form 5498 must now obtain consent from the IRS before filing magnetically. Filers are instructed to use Form 4419 to obtain the necessary consent. Additionally, the regulations state that filers of Form W-2 are now required to file magnetically.

The proposed regulations also provide that magnetic filing will not be required for persons filing less than 250 returns during a calendar year. Further, in keeping with its current administrative practices, the IRS will no longer permit filing on cassette.

The temporary and proposed regulations were published in the *Federal Register* on October 10, 1996 (61 FR 53161) and are reproduced at ¶ 13,649E. The preamble to the temporary regulations is reproduced at ¶ 23,131.

AGENCY: Internal Revenue Service (IRS), Treasury.

ACTION: Notice of proposed rulemaking and notice of public hearing.

SUMMARY: In the Rules and Regulations section of this issue of the **Federal Register,** the IRS is issuing temporary regulations relating to the requirements for filing information returns on magnetic media or in other machine-readable form under section 6011(e) of the Internal Revenue Code. The text of those temporary regulations also serves as the text of the proposed regulations. This document also contains a proposed amendment to § 301.6011-2(g)(2). This document also provides notice of a public hearing on these proposed regulations.

DATES: Written comments must be received by January 8, 1997. Outlines of topics to be discussed at the public hearing scheduled for February 5, 1997, must be received by January 15, 1997.

ADDRESSES: Send submissions to: CC:DOM:CORP:R (REG-209803-95), room 5228, Internal Revenue Service, POB 7604, Ben Franklin Station, Washington, DC 20044. In the alternative, submissions may be hand delivered between the hours of 8 a.m. and 5 p.m. to: CC:DOM:CORP:R (REG-209803-95), Courier's Desk, Internal Revenue Service, 1111 Constitution Ave., NW., Washington, DC. Alternatively, taxpayers may submit comments electronically via the internet by selecting the "Tax Regs" option on the IRS Home Page, or by submitting comments directly to the IRS internet site at http://www.irs.ustreas.gov/prod/tax_regs/comments.html. The public hearing will be held in Room 3313 of the Internal Revenue Building, 1111 Constitution Ave., NW., Washington, DC.

FOR FURTHER INFORMATION CONTACT: Concerning the regulations, Donna Welch, (202) 622-4910; concerning submissions and the hearing, Mike Slaughter, (202) 622-7190 (not toll-free numbers).

SUPPLEMENTARY INFORMATION:

Background

Temporary regulations in the Rules and Regulations portion of this issue of the **Federal Register** amend the Income Tax Regulations (26 CFR part 1) relating to section 6045 and the Procedure and Administration Regulations (26 CFR part 301) relating to section 6011(e). The temporary regulations contain rules relating to the filing requirements of information returns on magnetic media or in other machine-readable form under section 6011(e).

The text of those temporary regulations also serves as the text of these proposed regulations. The preamble to the temporary regulations explains the temporary regulations.

Special Analyses

It has been determined that these proposed regulations are not a significant regulatory action as defined in EO 12866. Therefore, a regulatory assessment is not required.

It is hereby certified that the regulations in this document will not have a significant economic impact on a substantial number of small entities. This certification is based on a determination that these regulations impose no additional reporting or recordkeeping requirement and only prescribe the method of filing information returns that are already required to be filed. Further, these regulations are consistent with the requirements imposed by statute. Section 6011(e)(2)(A) provides that, in prescribing regulations providing standards for determining which returns must be filed on magnetic media or in other machine-readable form, the Secretary shall not require any person to file returns on magnetic media unless the person is required to file at least 250 returns during the calendar year. Consistent with the statutory provision, these regulations do not require information returns to be filed on magnetic media unless 250 or more returns are required to be filed. Further, the economic impact caused by requiring filing on magnetic media should be minimal. If a taxpayer's operations are computerized, reporting in accordance with the regulations should be less costly than filing on paper. If the taxpayer's operations are not computerized, the incremental cost of magnetic media reporting should be minimal in most cases because of the availability of computer service bureaus. In addition, the existing regulations provide that the IRS may waive the magnetic media filing requirements upon a showing of hardship. It is anticipated that the waiver authority will be exercised so as not to unduly burden taxpayers lacking both the necessary data processing facilities and access at a reasonable cost to computer service bureaus. Accordingly, a Regulatory Flexibility Analysis under the Regulatory Flexibility Act (5 U.S.C. chapter 6) is not required.

Pursuant to section 7805(f) of the Internal Revenue Code, these proposed regulations will be submitted to the Chief Counsel for Advocacy of the Small Business Administration for comment on their impact on small business.

Comments and Public Hearing

Before these proposed regulations are adopted as final regulations, consideration will be given to any written comments (a signed original and eight (8) copies) that are submitted timely to the IRS. All comments will be available for public inspection and copying.

A public hearing has been scheduled for February 5, 1997, at 10 am. The hearing will be held in room 3313 of the Internal Revenue Building, 1111 Constitution Ave., NW., Washington, DC. Because of access restrictions, visitors will not be admitted beyond the Internal Revenue Building lobby more than 15 minutes before the hearing starts.

The rules of 26 CFR 601.601(a)(3) apply to the hearing.

Persons who wish to present oral comments at the hearing must submit written comments by January 8, 1997, and submit an outline of the topics to be discussed and the time to be devoted to each topic (signed original and eight (8) copies) by January 15, 1997.

A period of 10 minutes will be allotted to each person for making comments.

An agenda showing the scheduling of the speakers will be prepared after the deadline for receiving outlines has passed. Copies of the agenda will be available free of charge at the hearing.

Drafting Information

The principal author of the regulations is Donna Welch, Office of Assistant Chief Counsel (Income Tax and Accounting). However, other personnel from the IRS and the Treasury Department participated in the development of the regulations.

List of Subjects

26 CFR Part 1

Income taxes, Reporting and recordkeeping requirements.

26 CFR Part 301

Employment taxes, Estate taxes, Excise taxes, Gift taxes, Income taxes, Penalties, Reporting and recordkeeping requirements.

Proposed Amendments to the Regulations

Accordingly, 26 CFR parts 1 and 301 are proposed to be amended as follows:

****

PART 301—PROCEDURE AND ADMINISTRATION

Par. 4. The authority citation for part 301 continues to read in part as follows:

Authority: 26 U.S.C. 7805 * * *

Par. 5. Section 301.6011-2 is amended by revising paragraphs (a)(1), (b)(1) and (2), (c)(1)(i) and (iii), (c)(2), (f) and (g)(2), and by adding (c)(1)(iv), and by removing paragraphs (c)(3) and (4) and the last sentence of paragraph (e). The revisions and additions read as follows:

§ 301.6011-2 Required use of magnetic media.

[The text of paragraphs (a)(1), (b)(1) and (2), (c)(1)(i), (iii), and (iv), (c)(2), (f), and (g)(2) as proposed is the same as the text in § 301.6011-2T(a)(1), (b)(1) and (2), (c)(1)(i), (iii), and (iv), (c)(2), (f), and the first sentence of (g)(2) published elsewhere in this issue of the **Federal Register**].

¶ 20,221

Proposed regulations: Self-employment tax: Limited partners.—Following is the text of proposed regulations defining which partners of a federal tax partnership are considered limited partners for purposes of Sec. 1402(a)(13). The definitions depend on the relationship between the partner, the partnership and the partnership's business, and state law characterizations of an individual as a limited partner are not determinative.

The proposed regulations were published in the *Federal Register* on January 13, 1997 (62 FR 1702). The text, reproduced below, contains amendments to the regulations under Code Sec. 1402 that have been re-proposed by the IRS. The IRS has withdrawn proposed regulations for Code Sec. 1402 issued in 1994 (CCH PENSION PLAN GUIDE ¶ 20,110).

DEPARTMENT OF THE TREASURY

Internal Revenue Service

26 CFR Part 1

RIN 1545-AU24

Definition of Limited Partner for Self-Employment Tax Purposes

AGENCY: Internal Revenue Service (IRS), Treasury.

ACTION: Notice of proposed rulemaking and notice of public hearing.

SUMMARY: This document contains proposed amendments to the regulations relating to the self-employment income tax imposed under section 1402 of the Internal Revenue Code of 1986. These regulations permit individuals to determine whether they are limited partners for purposes of section 1402(a)(13), eliminating the uncertainty in calculating an individual's net earnings from self-employment under existing law. This document also contains a notice of public hearing on the proposed regulations.

DATES: Written comments must be received by April 14, 1997. Requests to speak and outlines of oral comments to be discussed at the public hearing scheduled for May 21, 1997, at 10 a.m. must be received by April 30, 1997.

ADDRESSES: Send submissions to: CC:DOM:CORP:R (REG-209824-96), room 5226, Internal Revenue Service, POB 7604, Ben Franklin Station, Washington, DC 20044. Submissions may be hand delivered between the hours of 8 a.m. and 5 p.m. to: CC:DOM:CORP:R (REG-209824-96), Courier's Desk, Internal Revenue Service, 1111 Constitution Avenue, NW, Washington, DC. Alternatively, taxpayers may submit comments electronically via the Internet by selecting the "Tax Regs" option on the IRS Home Page, or by submitting comments directly to the IRS Internet site at http://www.irs.ustreas.gov/prod/tax-regs/comments.html. The public hearing will be held in the Auditorium, Internal Revenue Service building, 1111 Constitution Avenue, NW, Washington, DC.

FOR FURTHER INFORMATION CONTACT: Concerning the regulation, Robert Honigman, (202) 622-3050; concerning submissions and the hearing, Christina Vasquez, (202) 622-6808 (not toll-free numbers).

SUPPLEMENTARY INFORMATION:

Background

This document contains proposed amendments to the Income Tax Regulations (26 CFR part 1) under section 1402 of the Internal Revenue Code and replaces the notice of proposed rulemaking published in the **Federal Register** on December 29, 1994, at 59 FR 67253, that treated certain members of a limited liability company (LLC) as limited partners for self-employment tax purposes. Written comments responding to the proposed regulations were received, and a public hearing was held on June 23, 1995.

Under the 1994 proposed regulations, an individual owning an interest in an LLC was treated as a limited partner if (1) the individual lacked the authority to make management decisions necessary to conduct the LLC's business (the management test), and (2) the LLC could have been formed as a limited partnership rather than an LLC in the same jurisdiction, and the member could have qualified as a limited partner in the limited partnership under applicable law (the limited partner equivalence test). The intent of the 1994 proposed regulations was to treat owners of an LLC interest in the same manner as similarly situated partners in a state law partnership.

Public comments on the 1994 proposed regulations were mixed. While some commentators were pleased with the proposed regulations for attempting to conform the treatment of LLCs with state law partnerships, others criticized the 1994 proposed regulations based on a variety of arguments.

A number of commentators discussed administrative and compliance problems with the 1994 proposed regulations. For example, it was noted that both the management test and the limited partner equivalence test depend upon legal or factual determinations that may be difficult for taxpayers or the IRS to make with certainty.

Another commentator pointed out that basing the self-employment tax treatment of LLC members on state law limited partnership rules would lead to disparate treatment between members of different LLCs with identical rights based solely on differences in the limited partnership statutes of the states in which the members form their LLC. For example, State A's limited partnership act may allow a limited partner to participate in a partnership's business while State B's limited partnership act may not. Thus, an LLC member, who is not a manager, that participates in the LLC's business would be a limited partner under the proposed regulations if the LLC is formed in State A, but not if the LLC is formed in State B. Commentators asserted that this disparate treatment is inherently unfair for federal tax purposes.

Some commentators argued for a "material participation" test to determine whether an LLC member's distributive share is included in the individual's net earnings from self-employment. The proposed regulations did not contain a participation test. Commentators advocating a participation test stressed that such a test would eliminate uncertainty concerning many LLC members' limited partner status and would better implement the self-employment tax goal of taxing compensation for services.

Other commentators argued for a more uniform approach, stating that a single test should govern all business entities (i.e., partnerships, LLCs, LLPs, sole proprietorships, et al.) whose members may be subject to self-employment tax. These commentators generally recognized, however, that a change in the treatment of a sole proprietorship or an entity that is not characterized as a partnership for federal tax purposes would be beyond the scope of regulations to be issued under section 1402(a)(13).

Finally, some commentators focused on whether the Service would respect the ownership of more than one class of partnership interest for self-employment tax purposes (bifurcation of interests). The proposed regulations treated an LLC member as a limited partner with respect to his or her entire interest (if the member was not a manager and satisfied the limited partner equivalence test), or not at all (if either the management test or limited partner equivalence test was not satisfied). Commentators, however, pointed to the legislative history of section 1402(a)(13) to support their argument that Congress only intended to tax a partner's distributive share attributable to a general partner interest. Under this argument, a partner that holds both a general partner interest and a limited partner interest is only subject to self-employment tax on the distributive share attributable to the partner's general partner interest. This intent also may be inferred from the statutory language of section 1402(a)(13) that the self-employment tax does not apply to ". . . the distributive share of any item of income or loss of a limited partner, as such . . . ." Based on this evidence, these commentators requested that the proposed regulations be revised to allow the bifurcation of interests for self-employment tax purposes.

After considering the comments received, the IRS and Treasury have decided to withdraw the 1994 notice of proposed rulemaking and to re-propose amendments to the Income Tax Regulations (26 CFR part 1) under section 1402 of the Code.

Explanation of Provisions

The proposed regulations contained in this document define which partners of a federal tax partnership are considered limited partners for section 1402(a)(13) purposes. These proposed regulations apply to all entities classified as a partnership for federal tax purposes, regardless of the state law characterization of the entity. Thus, the same standards apply when determining the status of an individual owning an interest in a state law limited partnership or the status of an individual owning an interest in an LLC. In order to achieve this conformity, the proposed

regulations adopt an approach which depends on the relationship between the partner, the partnership, and the partnership's business. State law characterizations of an individual as a "limited partner" or otherwise are not determinative.

Generally, an individual will be treated as a limited partner under the proposed regulations unless the individual (1) has personal liability (as defined in § 301.7701-3(b)(2)(ii) of the Procedure and Administration Regulations) for the debts of or claims against the partnership by reason of being a partner; (2) has authority to contract on behalf of the partnership under the statute or law pursuant to which the partnership is organized; or, (3) participates in the partnership's trade or business for more than 500 hours during the taxable year. If, however, substantially all of the activities of a partnership involve the performance of services in the fields of health, law, engineering, architecture, accounting, actuarial science, or consulting, any individual who provides services as part of that trade or business will not be considered a limited partner.

By adopting these functional tests, the proposed regulations ensure that similarly situated individuals owning interests in entities formed under different statutes or in different jurisdictions will be treated similarly. The need for a functional approach results not only from the proliferation of new business entities such as LLCs, but also from the evolution of state limited partnership statutes. When Congress enacted the limited partner exclusion found in section 1402(a)(13), state laws generally did not allow limited partners to participate in the partnership's trade or business to the extent that state laws allow limited partners to participate today. Thus, even in the case of a state law limited partnership, a functional approach is necessary to ensure that the self-employment tax consequences to similarly situated taxpayers do not differ depending upon where the partnership organized.

The proposed regulations allow an individual who is not a limited partner for section 1402(a)(13) purposes to nonetheless exclude from net earnings from self-employment a portion of that individual's distributive share if the individual holds more than one class of interest in the partnership. Similarly, the proposed regulations permit an individual that participates in the trade or business of the partnership to bifurcate his or her distributive share by disregarding guaranteed payments for services. In each case, however, such bifurcation of interests is permitted only to the extent the individual's distributive share is identical to the distributive share of partners who qualify as limited partners under the proposed regulation (without regard to the bifurcation rules) and who own a substantial interest in the partnership. Together, these rules exclude from an individual's net earnings from self-employment amounts that are demonstrably returns on capital invested in the partnership.

Proposed Effective Date

These regulations are proposed to be effective beginning with the individual's first taxable year beginning on or after the date these regulations are published as final regulations in the **Federal Register**.

Special Analyses

It has been determined that this notice of proposed rulemaking is not a significant regulatory action as defined in EO 12866. Therefore, a regulatory assessment is not required. It also has been determined that section 553(b) of the Administrative Procedure Act (5 U.S.C. chapter 5) does not apply to these regulations, and, because the regulations do not impose a collection of information on small entities, the Regulatory Flexibility Act (5 U.S.C. chapter 6) does not apply. Pursuant to section 7805(f) of the Internal Revenue Code, this notice of proposed rulemaking will be submitted to the Chief Counsel for Advocacy of the Small Business Administration for comment on its impact on small business.

Comments and Public Hearing

Before these proposed regulations are adopted as final regulations, consideration will be given to any written comments (a signed original and eight (8) copies) that are submitted timely to the IRS. All comments will be available for public inspection and copying.

A public hearing has been scheduled for Wednesday, May 21, 1997, at 10 a.m. in the Auditorium, Internal Revenue Service building, 1111 Constitution Avenue, NW, Washington, DC. Because of access restrictions, visitors will not be admitted beyond the Internal Revenue Service building lobby more than 15 minutes before the hearing starts.

The rules of 26 CFR 601.601(a)(3) apply to the hearing.

Persons that wish to present oral comments at the hearing must submit written comments by April 14, 1997, and submit an outline of the topics to be discussed and the time to be devoted to each topic (signed original and eight (8) copies) by April 30, 1997.

A period of 10 minutes will be allotted to each person for making comments.

An agenda showing the scheduling of the speakers will be prepared after the deadline for receiving outlines has passed. Copies of the agenda will be available free of charge at the hearing.

Drafting Information

The principal author of these regulations is Robert Honigman of the Office of Assistant Chief Counsel (Passthroughs & Special Industries). However, other personnel from the IRS and Treasury Department participated in their development.

List of Subjects in 26 CFR Part 1

Income taxes, Reporting and recordkeeping requirements.

Proposed Amendments to the Regulations

Accordingly, 26 CFR part 1 is proposed to be amended as follows:

PART 1—INCOME TAXES

Paragraph 1. The authority citation for part 1 continues to read in part as follows:

Authority: 26 U.S.C. 7805 ***

Par. 2. Section 1.1402(a)-2 is amended by:

1. Revising the first sentence of paragraph (d).

2. Removing the reference "section 702(a)(9)" in the first sentence of paragraph (e) and adding "section 702(a)(8)" in its place.

3. Revising the last sentence of paragraph (f).

4. Revising paragraphs (g) and (h).

5. Adding new paragraphs (i) and (j).

The revisions and additions read as follows:

§ 1.1402(a)-2 *Computation of net earnings from self-employment.*

*****

(d) *** Except as otherwise provided in section 1402(a) and paragraph (g) of this section, an individual's net earnings from self-employment include the individual's distributive share (whether or not distributed) of income or loss described in section 702(a)(8) from any trade or business carried on by each partnership of which the individual is a partner. ***

*****

(f) *** For rules governing the classification of an organization as a partnership or otherwise, see §§ 301.7701-1, 301.7701-2, and 301.7701-3 of this chapter.

(g) *Distributive share of limited partner.* An individual's net earnings from self-employment do not include the individual's distributive share of income or loss as a limited partner described in paragraph (h) of this section. However, guaranteed payments described in section 707(c) made to the individual for services actually rendered to or on behalf of the partnership engaged in a trade or business are included in the individual's net earnings from self-employment.

(h) *Definition of limited partner*—(1) *In general.* Solely for purposes of section 1402(a)(13) and paragraph (g) of this section, an individual is considered to be a limited partner to the extent provided in paragraphs (h)(2), (h)(3), (h)(4), and (h)(5) of this section.

(2) *Limited partner.* An individual is treated as a limited partner under this paragraph (h)(2) unless the individual—

(i) Has personal liability (as defined in § 301.7701-3(b)(2)(ii) of this chapter for the debts of or claims against the partnership by reason of being a partner;

(ii) Has authority (under the law of the jurisdiction in which the partnership is formed) to contract on behalf of the partnership; or

(iii) Participates in the partnership's trade or business for more than 500 hours during the partnership's taxable year.

(3) *Exception for holders of more than one class of interest.* An individual holding more than one class of interest in the partnership who is not treated as a limited partner under paragraph (h)(2) of this section is treated as a limited partner under this paragraph (h)(3) with respect to a specific class of partnership interest held by such individual if, immediately after the individual acquires that class of interest—

(i) Limited partners within the meaning of paragraph (h)(2) of this section own a substantial, continuing interest in that specific class of partnership interest; and,

(ii) The individual's rights and obligations with respect to that specific class of interest are identical to the rights and obligations of that specific class of partnership interest held by the limited partners described in paragraph (h)(3)(i) of this section.

(4) *Exception for holders of only one class of interest.* An individual who is not treated as a limited partner under paragraph (h)(2) of this section solely because that individual participates in the partnership's trade or business for more than 500 hours during the partnership's taxable year is treated as a limited partner under this paragraph (h)(4) with respect to the individual's partnership interest if, immediately after the individual acquires that interest—

(i) Limited partners within the meaning of paragraph (h)(2) of this section own a substantial, continuing interest in that specific class of partnership interest; and

(ii) The individual's rights and obligations with respect to the specific class of interest are identical to the rights and obligations of the specific class of partnership interest held by the limited partners described in paragraph (h)(4)(i) of this section.

(5) *Exception for service partners in service partnerships.* An individual who is a service partner in a service partnership may not be a limited partner under paragraphs (h)(2), (h)(3), or (h)(4) of this section.

(6) *Additional definitions.* Solely for purposes of this paragraph (h)—

(i) A *class of interest* is an interest that grants the holder specific rights and obligations. If a holder's rights and obligations from an interest are different from another holder's rights and obligations, each holder's interest belongs to a separate class of interest. An individual may hold more than one class of interest in the same partnership provided that each class grants the individual different rights or obligations. The existence of a guaranteed payment described in section 707(c) made to an individual for services rendered to or on behalf of a partnership, however, is not a factor in determining the rights and obligations of a class of interest.

(ii) A *service partner* is a partner who provides services to or on behalf of the service partnership's trade or business. A partner is not considered to be a service partner if that partner only provides a de minimis amount of services to or on behalf of the partnership.

(iii) A *service partnership* is a partnership substantially all the activities of which involve the performance of services in the fields of health, law, engineering, architecture, accounting, actuarial science, or consulting.

(iv) A *substantial interest in a class of interest* is determined based on all of the relevant facts and circumstances. In all cases, however, ownership of 20 percent or more of a specific class of interest is considered substantial.

(i) *Example.* The following example illustrates the principles of paragraphs (g) and (h) of this section:

Example. (i) A, B, and C form LLC, a limited liability company, under the laws of State to engage in a business that is not a service partnership described in paragraph (h)(6)(iii) of this section. LLC, classified as a partnership for federal tax purposes, allocates all items of income, deduction, and credit of LLC to A, B, and C in proportion to their ownership of LLC. A and C each contribute $1x for one LLC unit. B contributes $2x for two LLC units. Each LLC unit entitles its holder to receive 25 percent of LLC's tax items, including profits. A does not perform services for LLC; however, each year B receives a guaranteed payment of $6x for 600 hours of services rendered to LLC and C receives a guaranteed payment of $10x for 1000 hours of services rendered to LLC. C also is elected LLC's manager. Under State's law, C has the authority to contract on behalf of LLC.

(ii) *Application of general rule of paragraph (h)(2) of this section.* A is treated as a limited partner in LLC under paragraph (h)(2) of this section because A is not liable personally for debts of or claims against LLC, A does not have authority to contract for LLC under State's law, and A does not participate in LLC's trade or business for more than 500 hours during the taxable year. Therefore, A's distributive share attributable to A's LLC unit is excluded from A's net earnings from self-employment under section 1402(a)(13).

(iii) *Distributive share not included in net earnings from self-employment under paragraph (h)(4) of this section.* B's guaranteed payment of $6x is included in B's net earnings from self-employment under section 1402(a)(13). B is not treated as a limited partner under paragraph (h)(2) of this section because, although B is not liable for debts of or claims against LLC and B does not have authority to contract for LLC under State's law, B does participates in LLC's trade or business for more than 500 hours during the taxable year. Further, B is not treated as a limited partner under paragraph (h)(3) of this section because B does not hold more than one class of interest in LLC. However, B is treated as a limited partner under paragraph (h)(4) of this section because B is not treated as a limited partner under paragraph (h)(2) of this section solely because B participated in LLC's business for more than 500 hours and because A is a limited partner under paragraph (h)(2) of this section who owns a substantial interest with rights and obligations that are identical to B's rights and obligations. In this example, B's distributive share is deemed to be a return on B's investment in LLC and not remuneration for B's service to LLC. Thus, B's distributive share attributable to B's two LLC units is not net earnings from self-employment under section 1402(a)(13).

(iv) *Distributive share included in net earnings from self-employment.* C's guaranteed payment of $10x is included in C's net earnings from self-employment under section 1402(a). In addition, C's distributive share attributable to C's LLC unit also is net earnings from self-employment under section 1402(a) because C is not a limited partner under paragraphs (h)(2), (h)(3), or (h)(4) of this section. C is not

treated as a limited partner under paragraph (h)(2) of this section because C has the authority under State's law to enter into a binding contract on behalf of LLC and because C participates in LLC's trade or business for more than 500 hours during the taxable year. Further, C is not treated as a limited partner under paragraph (h)(3) of this section because C does not hold more than one class of interest in LLC. Finally, C is not treated as a limited partner under paragraph (h)(4) of this section because C has the power to bind LLC. Thus, C's guaranteed payment and distributive share both are included in C's net earnings from self-employment under section 1402(a).

(j) *Effective date.* Paragraphs (d), (e), (f), (g), (h), and (i) are applicable beginning with the individual's first taxable year beginning on or after the date this section is published as a final regulation in the **Federal Register**.

/s/ Margaret Milner Richardson

Commissioner of Internal Revenue

¶ 20,222

IRS proposed regulations: Business expenses: Expense substantiation.—The IRS has issued proposed regulations by cross-reference to final and temporary regulations. Pursuant to the newly released final and temporary regulations regarding the substantiation of business expenses for travel, entertainment, gift or listed property (¶ 11,357G and ¶ 23,133), receipts or other documentary evidence must be produced to substantiate any lodging costs and any other expenditures of $75 or more. The change in the receipt threshold, from $25 to $75, is effective for expenses incurred on or after October 1, 1995. Comments from the public are requested.

The proposed regulations, which were published in the *Federal Register* on March 25, 1997 (62 FR 14051), are reproduced below.

DEPARTMENT OF THE TREASURY

Internal Revenue Service

26 CFR Part 1

[REG-209785-95]

RIN 1545-AT97

Substantiation of Business Expenses for Travel, Entertainment, Gifts and Listed Property

AGENCY: Internal Revenue Service (IRS), Treasury.

ACTION: Notice of proposed rulemaking by cross-reference to temporary regulations.

SUMMARY: In the Rules and Regulations section of this issue of the Federal Register, the IRS is issuing temporary regulations relating to the substantiation requirements for business expenses for travel, entertainment, gifts, or listed property. The text of those temporary regulations also serves as the text of these proposed regulations.

DATES: Written or electronically generated comments and requests for a public hearing must be received by June 23, 1997.

ADDRESSES: Send submissions to CC:DOM:CORP:R (REG-209785-95), room 5228, Internal Revenue Service, P.O. Box 7604, Ben Franklin Station, Washington, DC 20044. In the alternative, submissions may be hand delivered between the hours of 8 a.m. and 5 p.m. to CC:DOM:CORP:R (REG-209785-95), Courier's Desk, Internal Revenue Service, 1111 Constitution Avenue NW., Washington, DC, or electronically, via the IRS Internet site at: http://www.irs.ustreas.gov/prod/tax—regs/comments.html.

FOR FURTHER INFORMATION CONTACT: Concerning the regulations, contact Donna M. Crisalli, (202) 622-4920; concerning submissions, contact Christina Vasquez, (202) 622-7190 (not toll-free numbers).

SUPPLEMENTARY INFORMATION:

Paperwork Reduction Act

The collection of information contained in this notice of proposed rulemaking has been submitted to the Office of Management and Budget for review in accordance with the Paperwork Reduction Act of 1995 (44 U.S.C. 3507). Comments on the collection of information should be sent to the Office of Management and Budget, Attn: Desk Officer for the Department of the Treasury, Office of Information and Regulatory Affairs, Washington, DC 20503, with copies to the Internal Revenue Service, Attn: IRS Reports Clearance Officer, T:FP, Washington, DC 20224. Comments on the collection of information should be received by May 27, 1997.

Comments are specifically requested concerning: Whether the proposed collection of information is necessary for the proper performance of the functions of the Internal Revenue Service, including whether the information will have practical utility;

The accuracy of the estimated burden associated with the proposed collection of information (see below);

How the quality, utility, and clarity of the information to be collected may be enhanced;

How the burden of complying with the proposed collection of information may be minimized, including through the application of automated collection techniques or other forms of information technology; and

Estimates of capital or start-up costs and costs of operation, maintenance, and purchase of service to provide information.

The collection of information in this notice of proposed rulemaking is in Sec. 1.274-5T(c)(2) and (f)(4). This information is required by the IRS as a condition for a taxpayer to deduct certain business expenses or exclude from income certain reimbursed business expenses of employees. This information will be used to determine whether a taxpayer properly qualifies for a deduction or exclusion. The collection of information is required in order to deduct certain business expenses or exclude from income certain reimbursed business expenses of employees. The likely respondents and recordkeepers are individuals, business or other for-profit institutions, state or local governments, federal agencies, and nonprofit institutions.

Estimated total annual reporting and recordkeeping burden: 36,920,000 hours.

The estimated annual burden per respondent or recordkeeper varies from 10 minutes to 20 hours, depending on individual circumstances, with an estimated average of 1.3 hours.

Estimated number of respondents and recordkeepers: 28,400,000.

Estimated annual frequency of responses: On occasion.

An agency may not conduct or sponsor, and a person is not required to respond to, a collection of information unless the collection of information displays a valid control number.

Books or records relating to a collection of information must be retained as long as their contents may become material in the administration of any internal revenue law. Generally, tax returns and tax return information are confidential, as required by 26 U.S.C. 6103.

Special Analyses

It has been determined that this notice of proposed rulemaking is not a significant regulatory action as defined in EO 12866. Therefore, a regulatory assessment is not required. It is hereby certified that these regulations do not have a significant economic impact on a substantial number of small entities. This certification is based on the fact that, by increasing the receipt threshold from $25 to $75, these regulations are expected to reduce the existing recordkeeping requirements of taxpayers, including small entities, from 49,375,000 hours to 36,920,000 hours. The regulations do not otherwise significantly alter the reporting or recordkeeping duties of small entities. Therefore, a Regulatory Flexibility Analysis under the Regulatory Flexibility Act (5 U.S.C. chapter 6) is not required. Pursuant to section 7805(f) of the Internal Revenue Code, this notice of proposed rulemaking will be submitted to the Chief Counsel for Advocacy of the Small Business Administration for comment on its impact on small business.

Comments and Requests for a Public Hearing

Before adopting these proposed regulations as final regulations, consideration will be given to any comments that are submitted timely (and in the manner described in ADDRESSES portion of this preamble) to the IRS. The IRS is considering publishing a revenue procedure implementing Sec. 1.274-5T(f)(4)(ii) of the temporary regulations (that is, prescribing rules under which an employee may make an adequate accounting to his employer by submitting an expense voucher or equivalent without submitting documentary evidence such as receipts) for federal government agencies that use the published procedures. In addition, the IRS is considering whether there are circumstances or conditions under which the IRS could extend these procedures beyond federal government agencies, and requests comments in this regard. The IRS also requests comments on what procedures (such as internal controls) should be required in any rules that permit a taxpayer to satisfy the substantiation requirements of section 274(d) for purposes of deducting business expenses reimbursed to employees who have accounted for their expenses only by means of an expense voucher or equivalent without documentary evidence such as receipts. All comments will be available for public inspection and copying. A public hearing will be scheduled and held upon written request by any person who submits written comments on the proposed rules. Notice of the time and place for the hearing will be published in the Federal Register.

Drafting Information

The principal author of these proposed regulations is Donna M. Crisalli, Office of the Assistant Chief Counsel (Income Tax and Accounting). However, personnel from other offices of the IRS and Treasury Department participated in their development.

List of Subjects in 26 CFR Part 1

Income taxes, Reporting and recordkeeping requirements.

Proposed Amendments to the Regulations

Accordingly, 26 CFR part 1 is proposed to be amended as follows:

PART 1—INCOME TAXES

Paragraph 1. The authority citation for part 1 is amended by adding an entry to read in part as follows:

Authority: 26 U.S.C. 7805 * * *

Section 1.274-5 also issued under 26 U.S.C. 274(d). * * *

Par. 2. Section 1.274-5 is added to read as follows:

Sec. 1.274-5 *Substantiation requirements.*

(a) through (c)(2)(iii)(A) [Reserved]. For further guidance, see Sec. 1.274-5T.

(c)(2)(iii)(B) [The text of paragraph (c)(2)(iii)(B) is the same as the text in Sec. 1.274-5T published elsewhere in this issue of the Federal Register].

(c)(2)(iv) through (f)(3) [Reserved]. For further guidance, see Sec. 1.274-5T.

(f)(4) through (f)(4)(iii) [The text of paragraphs (f)(4) through (f)(4)(iii) is the same as the text in Sec. 1.274-5T published elsewhere in this issue of the Federal Register].

(f)(5) through (1) [Reserved]. For further guidance, see Sec. 1.274-5T.

Margaret Milner Richardson,

Commissioner of Internal Revenue.

¶ 20,223

IRS proposed regulations: Group insurance: Health insurance plans: Insurance portability.—The IRS has issued notice of proposed rulemaking and a request for comments on temporary regulations relating to health insurance portability for group health plans under the Health Insurance Portability and Accountability Act of 1996 (HIPAA). The IRS temporary regulations are being issued at the same time that substantially similar regulations on group health plan portability, access, and renewability requirements added by HIPAA to ERISA and the Public Health Service Act are being issued by the PWBA and the Health Care Financing Administration. The IRS temporary regulations were finalized on 12/30/04.

The proposed regulations, which were published in the *Federal Register* on April 8, 1997 (62 FR 16977), are reproduced below.

[4830-01-u]

DEPARTMENT OF THE TREASURY

Internal Revenue Service

26 CFR Part 54

[Reg-253578-96]

RIN 1545-AV12

Health Insurance Portability for Group Health Plans

AGENCY: Internal Revenue Service (IRS), Treasury.

ACTION: Notice of proposed rulemaking by cross-reference to temporary regulations.

SUMMARY: Elsewhere in this issue of the **Federal Register**, the IRS is issuing temporary regulations relating to group health plan portability, access, and renewability requirements added to the Internal Revenue Code by section 401 of the Health Insurance Portability and Accountability Act of 1996 (HIPAA). The IRS is issuing the temporary regulations at the same time that the Pension and Welfare Benefits Administration of the U.S. Department of Labor and the Health Care Financing Administration of the U.S. Department of Health and Human Services are issuing substantially similar interim final regulations relating to the group health plan portability, access, and renewability requirements added by HIPAA to the Employee Retirement Income Security Act of 1974 and the Public Health Service Act. The temporary regulations provide guidance to employers and group health plans relating to the obligation of plans to comply with new requirements relating to preexisting condition exclusions, discrimination based on health status, access to coverage, and other requirements. The text of those temporary regulations also serves as the text of these proposed regulations.

DATES: Written comments and requests for a public hearing must be received by July 7, 1997.

ADDRESSES: Send submissions to: CC:DOM:CORP:R (REG-253578-96), room 5226, Internal Revenue Service, POB 7604, Ben Franklin Station, Washington, DC 20044. Submissions may be hand delivered to: CC:DOM:CORP:R (REG-253578-96), room 5226, Internal Revenue Service, 1111 Constitution Avenue, NW, Washington, DC.

Alternatively, taxpayers may submit comments electronically via the Internet by selecting the "Tax Regs" option on the IRS Home Page, or by submitting comments directly to the IRS Internet site at http://www.irs.ustreas.gov/prod/tax_regs/comments.html

FOR FURTHER INFORMATION CONTACT: Concerning the regulations, RUSS WEINHEIMER, (202) 622-4695; concerning submissions or to request a hearing, CHRISTINA D. VASQUEZ, 202-622-7180. These are not toll-free numbers.

SUPPLEMENTARY INFORMATION:

Paperwork Reduction Act

The collection of information referenced in this notice of proposed rulemaking has been submitted to the Office of Management and Budget for review in accordance with the Paperwork Reduction Act of 1995 (44 U.S.C. 3507(d)).

An agency may not conduct or sponsor, and a person is not required to respond to, a collection of information unless it displays a valid control number assigned by the Office of Management and Budget.

The collection of information is in §§ 54.9801-3T, 54.9801-4T, 54.9801-5T, 54.9801-6T, and 54.9806-1T (see the temporary regulations published elsewhere in this issue of the **Federal Register**). This information is required by the statute so that participants will be informed about their rights under HIPAA and about the amount of creditable coverage that they have accrued under a group health plan. The likely respondents are business or other for-profit institutions, nonprofit institutions, small businesses or organizations, and Taft-Hartley trusts. Responses to this collection of information are mandatory.

Books or records relating to a collection of information must be retained as long as their contents may become material in the administration of any internal revenue law. Generally tax returns and tax return information are confidential, as required by 26 U.S.C. 6103.

Comments on the collection of information should be sent to the **Office of Management and Budget**, Attn: Desk Officer for the Department of the Treasury, Office of Information and Regulatory Affairs, Washington, DC 20503, with copies to the **Internal Revenue Service**, Attn: IRS Reports Clearance Officer, T:FP, Washington, DC 20224. Comments on the collection of information should be received by June 8, 1997. Comments are specifically requested concerning:

Whether the proposed collection of information is necessary for the proper performance of the functions of the Internal Revenue Service, including whether the information will have practical utility;

The accuracy of the estimated burden associated with the proposed collection of information (see the preamble to the temporary regulations published elsewhere in this issue of the **Federal Register**);

How to enhance the quality, utility, and clarity of the information to be collected;

How to minimize the burden of complying with the proposed collection of information, including the application of automated collection techniques or other forms of information technology; and

Estimates of capital or start-up costs and costs of operation, maintenance, and purchase of services to provide information.

Background

The temporary regulations published elsewhere in this issue of the **Federal Register** add §§ 54.9801-1T through 54.9801-6T, 54.9802-1T, 54.9804-1T, and 54.9806-1T to the Miscellaneous Excise Tax Regulations. These regulations are being published as part of a joint rulemaking with the Department of Labor and the Department of Health and Human Services (the joint rulemaking).

The text of those temporary regulations also serves as the text of these proposed regulations. The preamble to the temporary regulations explains the temporary regulations.

Special Analyses

Pursuant to sections 603(a) and 605(b) of the Regulatory Flexibility Act, it is hereby certified that the collection of information referenced in this notice of proposed rulemaking (see §§ 54.9801-3T, 54.9801-4T, 54.9801-5T, 54.9801-6T and 54.9806-1T of the temporary regulations published elsewhere in this issue of the Federal Register) will not have a significant economic impact on a substantial number of small entities. Although a substantial number of small entities will be subject to the collection of information requirements in these regulations, the requirements will not have a significant economic impact on these entities. The average time required to complete a certification required under these regulations is estimated to be 5 to 12 minutes for all employers. This average is based on the assumption that most employers will automate the certification process. The paperwork requirements other than certifications that are contained in the regulations are estimated to impose less than 10% of the burden imposed by the certifications. Many small employers that maintain group health plans have their plans administered by an insurance company or third party administrators (TPAs). Most insurers and TPAs are expected to automate the certification process and therefore their average time to produce a certificate should be similar to the 5 to 12 minute average estimated for all employers. However, even for small employers that do not automate the certification process, the collection of information requirements in the regulation will not have a significant impact. Even if it is conservatively assumed that their average time to produce a certificate is 3 times as long as the highest estimate for all employers (i.e., 36 minutes per certificate) and that all of their employees are covered by their group health plan and that half of the employees receive a certificate each year, and this figure is then increased by 10% to account for the paperwork burdens apart from the certifications, the average burden per employee is only 20 minutes per year. Thus, for example, for an employer with 10 employees, the annual burden would be 3 hours and 20 minutes per year. At an estimated cost of $11 per hour, this would result in a cost of less than $37 per year for the employer, which is not a significant economic impact.

This regulation is not subject to the Unfunded Mandates Reform Act of 1995 because the regulation is an interpretive regulation. For further information and for analyses relating to the joint rulemaking, see the preamble to the joint rulemaking. Pursuant to section 7805(f) of the Internal Revenue Code, this notice of proposed rulemaking will be submitted to the Chief Counsel for Advocacy of the Small Business Administration for comment on its impact on small business.

Comments and Requests for a Public Hearing

Before these proposed regulations are adopted as final regulations, consideration will be given to any written comments (a signed original and eight (8) copies) that are submitted timely to the IRS. All comments will be available for public inspection and copying. A public hearing may be scheduled if requested in writing by a person that timely submits written comments. If a public hearing is scheduled, notice of the date, time, and place for the hearing will be published in the **Federal Register**.

Drafting Information

The principal author of these proposed regulations is Russ Weinheimer, Office of the Chief Counsel, Employee Benefits and Exempt Organizations. However, other personnel from the IRS and Treasury Department participated in their development. The proposed regulations, as well as the temporary regulations, have been developed in coordination with personnel from the U.S. Department of Labor and U.S. Department of Health and Human Services.

List of Subjects in 26 CFR Part 54

Excise taxes, Health insurance, Pensions, Reporting and recordkeeping requirements.

Proposed Amendments to the Regulations

Accordingly, 26 CFR part 54 is proposed to be amended as follows:

PART 54—PENSION EXCISE TAXES

Paragraph 1. The authority citation for part 54 is amended by adding entries in numerical order to read as follows:

Authority: 26 U.S.C. 7805 * * *

Section 54.9801-1 is also issued under 26 U.S.C. 9806.

Section 54.9801-2 is also issued under 26 U.S.C. 9806.

Section 54.9801-3 is also issued under 26 U.S.C. 9806.

Section 54.9801-4 is also issued under 26 U.S.C. 9806.

Section 54.9801-5 is also issued under 26 U.S.C. 9801(c)(4), 9801(e)(3), and 9806.

Section 54.9801-6 is also issued under 26 U.S.C. 9806.

Section 54.9802-1 is also issued under 26 U.S.C. 9806.

Section 54.9804-1 is also issued under 26 U.S.C. 9806.

Section 54.9806-1 is also issued under 26 U.S.C. 9806. * * *

Par. 2. Sections 54.9801-1, 54.9801-2, 54.9801-3, 54.9801-4, 54.9801-5, 54.9801-6, 54.9802-1, 54.9804-1, and 54.9806-1 are added to read as follows:

[The text of these proposed sections is the same as the text of §§ 54.9801-1T, 54.9801-2T, 54.9801-3T, 54.9801-4T, 54.9801-5T, 54.9801-6T, 54.9802-1T, 54.9804-1T, and 54.9806-1T published elsewhere in this issue of the **Federal Register**].

Margaret Milner Richardson

Commissioner of Internal Revenue

[FR Doc. 97-8267 Filed 4-1-97; 12:48 p.m.]

¶ 20,224

IRS proposed regulations: Residency of trusts: Foreign trusts: Domestic trusts: Exclusions.—The IRS has issued a notice of proposed rulemaking and a request for comments on proposed regulations affecting the determination of the residency of trusts for federal tax purposes. The proposed regulations provide a safe harbor for determining if a trust is foreign or domestic based on which court exercises primary supervision authority over administration (court test), and define key terms for determining the residency of trusts based on the residency of fiduciaries with authority to control substantial decisions of the trust (control test). The proposed regulations reflect changes to the law made by the Small Business Job Protection Act of 1996.

The proposed regulations were published in the *Federal Register* on June 5, 1997 (62 FR 30796).

The final regulations were issued on February 2, 1999 (64 FR 4976). The regulations are reproduced at ¶ 13,925 (IRS Reg. Sec. 301.7701-5) and ¶ 13,927 (IRS Reg. Sec. 301.7701-7). The text of the preamble is reproduced at ¶ 23,153.

¶ 20,225

IRS proposed regulations: Plan amendments: Elimination of optional form of benefit: Age 70 ½ distribution.—The proposed regulations would provide relief from Code Sec. 411(d)(6) for certain plan amendments that eliminate preretirement distribution options commencing after age 70 1/2.

The proposed regulations, which were published in the *Federal Register* on July 2, 1997 (62 FR 35752).

The regulations were finalized June 5, 1998 (63 FR 30621). The regulations are reproduced at ¶ 12,233. The preamble is reproduced at ¶ 23,141.

¶ 20,226

IRS proposed regulations: Remedial amendment period: Disqualifying provisions.—The IRS has issued proposed regulations regarding the remedial amendment period. Under the regulations, the IRS Commissioner will have the authority to designate a plan provision as a disqualifying provision in certain circumstances and will be able to impose limits and additional rules pertaining to amendments that may be made during the remedial amendment period.

The final regulations were issued on February 4, 2000 (65 FR 5432). The proposed regulations, which were published in the *Federal Register* on August 1, 1997 (62 FR 41274), are reproduced below. The proposed regs were also issued as final and temporary regs and are reproduced at ¶ 11,721 and ¶ 11,722, respectively. The preamble to the final and temporary regulations is at ¶ 23,136.

¶ 20,227

IRS proposed regulations: Cafeteria plans: Election of coverage: Revocation of election: Health Insurance Portability and Accountability Act of 1996 (HIPAA).—Reproduced below is the text of proposed regulations that amend portions of previously issued proposed regulations (¶ 20,118I and ¶ 20,137Q) concerning the circumstances under which a cafeteria plan participant may revoke an existing election and make a new election during a period of coverage. The proposed regulations permit a cafeteria plan to allow an employee, during a plan year, to change his or her health coverage election to conform with special enrollment rights provided under the Health Insurance Portability and Accountability Act of 1996 (HIPAA) and for a variety of other "changes in status."

The proposed regulations were published in the *Federal Register* on November 7, 1997 (62 FR 60196), and were withdrawn on August 6, 2007 (72 FR 43938).

¶ 20,228

IRS proposed regulations: Mental Health Parity Act (MHPA): Mental health benefits: Medical/surgical benefits.—The IRS has issued a notice of proposed rulemaking and a request for comments on temporary regulations providing guidance to employers and group health plans relating to the new mental health parity rules, which were added to the Code by the Taxpayer Relief Act of 1997. The IRS temporary regulations, which are generally effective January 1, 1998, are being issued at the same time that the Department of Labor and the Department of Health and Human Services are issuing substantially similar regulations relating to mental health parity requirements added to ERISA and the Public Health Service Act by MHPA.

The proposed regulations, which were published in the *Federal Register* on December 22, 1997 (62 FR 66967), are reproduced below. The preamble to the IRS temporary regulations is at ¶ 23,139, and the temporary regulations are at ¶ 13,968Q-10, ¶ 13,968Q-12, ¶ 13,968Q-16, ¶ 13,968Q-18, ¶ 13,968W-10, ¶ 13,968Y-10, ¶ 13,968U-10, and ¶ 15,050K-1.

The IRS withdrew these proposed regulations on February 2, 2010 (75 FR 5452) and has issued new proposed regulations relating the mental health parity requirements for group health plans (see ¶ 20,262U).

¶ 20,229

IRS proposed regulations: Nonqualified deferred compensation: FICA contributions: FUTA contributions.—The IRS has issued revisions to proposed regulations under Code Sec. 3121(v)(2) and Code Sec. 3306(r)(2) relating to when amounts deferred under or paid from certain nonqualified deferred compensation plans are taken into account as "wages" for purposes of taxes imposed by the Federal Insurance Contributions Act (FICA) and the Federal Unemployment Tax Act (FUTA), respectively. The original proposed regulations were published in the *Federal Register* on January 25, 1996 (CCH PENSION PLAN GUIDE, ¶ 20,214 and ¶ 20,215), with a proposed general effective date of January 1, 1997. The new notice of proposed rulemaking extends the proposed general effective date for both proposed regulations to January 1, 1998.

The proposed revised regulations, which were published in the *Federal Register* on December 24, 1997 (62 FR 67304).

Final FICA and FUTA regulations were published in the *Federal Register* on January 29, 1999 (64 FR 4542 and 64 FR 4540, respectively). For FICA, the regulations are reproduced at ¶ 13,534T and ¶ 13,534U, and the preamble is at ¶ 23,150. For FUTA, the regulations are reproduced at ¶ 13,541K and the preamble is at ¶ 23,151.

¶ 20,230

IRS proposed regulations: Loans from qualified plans: Deemed distributions: Code Sec. 72(p).—The IRS has issued proposed amendments to existing proposed regulations (CCH PENSION PLAN GUIDE ¶ 20,210) that would provide additional guidance concerning the tax treatment of loans from qualified plans to participants that are deemed distributions under Code Sec. 72(p). Under the proposed amended regulations, interest that accrued on the loan would not be included in income and neither the loan nor the interest would increase the participant's tax basis for purposes of Code Sec. 72. Cash repayments made after the loan was deemed distributed would increase the participant's tax basis in the same manner as if the repayments were after-tax contributions.

The regulations are proposed to become effective for loans made on or after the first January 1 that is at least 6 months after the date the regulations are published as final regulations in the *Federal Register*. The original proposed regulations were amended to reflect the same proposed effective date. Taxpayers may rely on the proposed amended regulations for guidance pending the issuance of final regulations.

The proposed regulations, which were published in the *Federal Register* on January 2, 1998 (62 FR 42), are reproduced below.

The regulations were finalized by T.D. 8894 and published in the *Federal Register* on July 31, 2000 (65 FR 46588). The regulations are reproduced at ¶ 11,207A and ¶ 11,210. The preamble is reproduced at ¶ 23,168.

¶ 20,231

IRS proposed regulations: Continuation coverage of group health plans: Disabled beneficiaries: Children: Long-term care services: Medical Savings Accounts (MSAs).—The IRS has issued proposed regulations to provide guidance under Code Sec. 4980B on law changes made by the Health Portability and Accountability Act of 1996 (HIPAA), the Technical and Miscellaneous Revenue Act of 1988 (TAMRA), and the Omnibus Budget Reconciliation Act of 1989 (OBRA '89), relating to the continuation coverage requirements applicable to group health plans. The proposed regulations clarify the disability extension requirements, the maximum coverage period for newborn and adopted children, the method for determining qualified long-term care services, and the continuation coverage applicable to medical savings accounts.

The proposed regulations, which were published in the *Federal Register* on January 7, 1998 (63 FR 708), were adopted on February 3, 1999 by T.D. 8812 (64 FR 5160). Reg. Secs. 54.4980B-0 through 54.4980B-8 were amended, and Reg. Secs. 54.4980B-9 and 54.4980B-10 were added by T.D. 8928 on January 10, 2001 (66 FR 1843). The preamble to the final regulations is reproduced at ¶ 23,174. The regs are reproduced at ¶ 13,648W-5—¶ 13,648W-15.

¶ 20,232

IRS proposed regulations: Widely held fixed investment trust: Tax Exempt organizations: Individual retirement plan: Reporting requirements.—The IRS has issued proposed regulations that define widely held fixed investment trusts and clarify the reporting requirements of trustees and middlemen of these trusts to ensure that beneficial owners of trust interests receive accurate and timely tax reporting information. Information reporting generally is not required for interests held by exempt recipients such as individual retirement plans and organizations that are exempt from taxation under Code Sec. 501(a). However, the proposed regulations provide that exempt recipients may request tax information for a calendar quarter, computed as of the last day of the quarter specified, or for a calendar year, computed as of December 31 of the year specified.

The proposed regulations and excerpts of the preamble, which appeared in the *Federal Register* on August 13, 1998 (63 FR 43354), are reproduced below.

DEPARTMENT OF THE TREASURY

Internal Revenue Service

26 CFR Parts 1 and 301

[REG-209813-96]

RIN 1545-AU15

Reporting Requirements for Widely Held Fixed Investment Trusts

AGENCY: Internal Revenue Service (IRS), Treasury

ACTION: Notice of proposed rulemaking and notice of public hearing.

SUMMARY: This document contains proposed regulations that define widely held fixed investment trusts, clarify the reporting obligations of the trustees of these trusts and the middlemen connected with these trusts, and provide for the communication of necessary tax information to beneficial owners of trust interests. This document also provides notice of a public hearing on these proposed regulations.

DATES: Written comments must be received by [*INSERT DATE 90 DAYS AFTER PUBLICATION OF THIS DOCUMENT IN THE FEDERAL REGISTER*]. Requests to speak (with outlines of oral comments) at a public hearing scheduled for Thursday, November 5, 1998 at 10 a.m. must be submitted by October 15, 1998.

ADDRESSES: Send submissions to: CC:DOM:CORP:R (REG-209813-96), room 5228, Internal Revenue Service, POB 7604, Ben Franklin Station, Washington, DC 20044. In the alternative, submissions may be hand delivered between the hours of 8 a.m. and 5 p.m. to: CC:DOM:CORP:R (REG-209813-96), Courier's Desk, Internal Revenue Building, 1111 Constitution Avenue, NW., Washington, DC. Alternatively, taxpayers may submit comments electronically via the Internet by selecting the "Tax Regs" option on the IRS Home Page, or by submitting comments directly to the IRS Internet site at http://www.irs.ustreas.gov/prod/tax_regs/comments.html. The public hearing will be held in room 2615, Internal Revenue Building, 1111 Constitution Avenue, NW., Washington, DC.

FOR FURTHER INFORMATION CONTACT: Concerning the regulations, Faith Colson, (202) 622-3060; concerning submissions and the hearing, LaNita Van Dyke, (202) 622-7180 (not toll-free numbers).

SUPPLEMENTARY INFORMATION:

Paperwork Reduction Act

The collection of information contained in this notice of proposed rulemaking has been submitted to the Office of Management and Budget for review in accordance with the Paperwork Reduction Act of

1995 (44 U.S.C. 3507(d)). Comments on the collection of information should be sent to the **Office of Management and Budget,** Attn: Desk Officer for the Department of Treasury, Office of Information and Regulatory Affairs, Washington, DC 20503, with copies to the **Internal Revenue Service,** Attn: IRS Reports Clearance Officer, OP:FS:FP, Washington, DC 20224. Comments on the collection of information should be received by [*INSERT DATE 60 DAYS AFTER PUBLICATION OF THIS DOCUMENT IN THE FEDERAL REGISTER*]. Comments are specifically requested concerning:

Whether the proposed collection of information is necessary for the proper performance of the functions of the **Internal Revenue Service,** including whether the information will have practical utility;

The accuracy of the estimated burden associated with the proposed collection of information (see below);

How the quality, utility, and clarity of the information to be collected may be enhanced;

How the burden of complying with the proposed collection of information may be minimized, including through the application of automated collection techniques or other forms of information technology; and

Estimates of capital or start-up costs and costs of operation, maintenance, and purchase of service to provide information.

The collection of information in these proposed regulations is in § 1.671-4 of the Income Tax Regulations. This information is required to enable holders of trust interests to report items of income, deduction, and credit of a widely held fixed investment trust under section 671. This information will be used by the IRS to ensure that those items are reported accurately by beneficial owners of trust interests. The collection of information is mandatory. The likely respondents are businesses and other for-profit institutions.

Estimated total annual reporting burden: 2,400 hours.

Estimated average annual burden hours per respondent: 2 hours.

Estimated number of respondents: 1,200.

Estimated annual frequency of responses: Annually (but more often for a trust providing information to certain persons on request).

An agency may not conduct or sponsor, and a person is not required to respond to, a collection of information unless it displays a valid control number assigned by the Office of Management and Budget.

Books or records relating to the collection of information must be retained as long as their contents may become material in the administration of any internal revenue law. Generally, tax returns and tax return information are confidential, as required by 26 U.S.C. 6103.

Background

This document contains proposed amendments to the Income Tax Regulations (26 CFR part 1) under section 671. The proposed amendments are to be issued under the authority of sections 671, 6034A, 6049(d)(7), and 7805.

A fixed investment trust is an arrangement classified as a trust under § 301.7701-4(c). Beneficial interests in these trusts are divided into units. The Service treats these trusts as grantor trusts under section 671 and the owners of the beneficial interests, or units, as the grantors. See Rev. Rul. 84-10 (1984-1 C.B. 155); Rev. Rul. 70-545 (1970-2 C.B. 7); Rev. Rul. 70-544 (1970-2 C.B. 6); Rev. Rul. 61-175 (1961-2 C.B. 128). Under the proposed regulations, a *widely held fixed investment trust* is a fixed investment trust in which any interest is held by a middleman. For this purpose, the term *middleman* includes, but is not limited to, a custodian of a person's account, a nominee, and a broker holding an interest for a customer in street name. The IRS and Treasury request comments on the application and scope of these definitions, including the appropriateness of a de minimis rule as to the number of middlemen.

Interests in widely held fixed investment trusts are often held in the street name of a middleman, who holds such interests on behalf of the beneficial owners. Thus, trustees frequently do not know the identity of the beneficial owners and are not in a position to communicate necessary tax information directly to such owners. Currently, there are no tax information reporting rules specifically providing for the sharing of tax information among trustees, middlemen, and beneficial owners of these trusts.

On December 21, 1995, final regulations (TD 8633) under section 671, relating to the information reporting requirements of grantor trusts, were published in the **Federal Register** (60 FR 66085). See § 1.671-4. While drafting the final regulations, the IRS and Treasury concluded that special reporting requirements were needed for widely held fixed investment trusts but that such guidance fell outside the scope of the final regulations. The preamble to the final regulations stated that the IRS and Treasury anticipated providing guidance for these trusts in a separate project and invited comments from interested taxpayers and practitioners regarding such guidance.

In developing these proposed regulations, the IRS and Treasury have continued to solicit comments from the public. Comments were received from various industry members and practitioners, and these proposed regulations take such comments into account. The proposed regulations are intended to clarify the reporting requirements of trustees and middlemen and to ensure that beneficial owners of trust interests receive accurate and timely tax reporting information. The IRS and Treasury welcome comments on specific instances of industry practice that differ significantly from the framework of these proposed regulations and on suggestions to tailor the reporting requirements to account for those differences.

Explanation of Provisions

A. *General Framework of Reporting Rules*

The information reporting framework in the proposed regulations is similar to that for regular interests in a real estate mortgage investment conduit. See § 1.6049-7.

Under the proposed regulations, the responsibility for information reporting lies primarily with the person in the ownership chain who holds a unit interest for a beneficial owner and is, therefore, in the best position to communicate with, and provide tax information to, the beneficial owner. Thus, a brokerage firm that holds a unit interest directly for an individual as a middleman will have the primary obligation to report to the IRS and to provide tax information to the individual. Similarly, if a unit interest is held directly by an individual and not through a middleman, the trustee is to report to the IRS and to provide tax information to the individual. Information reporting generally is not required for interests held by *exempt recipients*. Middlemen and trustees, however, are to make trust tax information available upon request to exempt recipients.

Appropriate adjustments may be necessary to other information reporting rules to make them compatible with these proposed regulations.

B. *Trustee or Middleman to Report to the IRS on Form 1099*

Under proposed § 1.671-4(j)(2)(i)(A), a trustee must report to the IRS, on the appropriate Forms 1099, the gross amount of trust income (determined in accordance with proposed § 1.671-4(j)(6)(i)) attributable to a unit interest holder who holds an interest in the trust directly and not through a middleman. Similarly, under proposed § 1.671-4(j)(2)(i)(B), a middleman must report for any unit interest holder on whose behalf or account the middleman holds an interest. (To comply with this requirement, middlemen may request the necessary tax information from the trustee. See the discussion below.) In addition, the trustee or middleman is to report on the appropriate Form 1099 the gross proceeds from the sale or other disposition of a trust asset that is attributable to the unit interest holder. Forms 1099 are not required for any unit interest holder who is an *exempt recipient*, as defined in proposed § 1.671-4(j)(1).

C. *Statements to be Furnished to the Beneficial Owners of Unit Interests*

Every middleman or trustee required to file with the IRS a Form 1099 under these proposed regulations for a unit interest holder must furnish to the unit interest holder a written statement providing the holder with necessary tax reporting information including: (1) the items of income (determined in accordance with proposed § 1.671-4(j)(6)(i)), deduction, and credit of the trust attributable to the unit interest holder; (2) if any trust asset has been sold or otherwise disposed of during the calendar year, the portion of the gross proceeds relating to the trust asset which is attributable to the unit interest holder, the date of sale or disposition of the trust asset, and the percentage of that trust asset that has been sold or disposed of; and (3) any other information necessary for the unit interest holder to accurately report the income, deductions, and credits of the trust attributable to the unit interest as required under section 671.

In addition, to enable unit interest holders to calculate gain or loss on the disposition of a trust asset, if a trust sells or disposes of a trust asset during a particular calendar year, the proposed regulations require the trustee or middleman to include, with the statement to the holder, a schedule showing the portion (expressed as a percentage) of the total fair market value of all the assets held by the trust that the trust asset sold or disposed of represented as of the last day of each quarter that the asset was held by the trust. It is contemplated that, in the absence of more accurate information, this information may be used by the unit interest holder to determine the percentage of the holder's basis in its unit interest that the disposed asset represents, so that the holder may calculate its gain or loss on the disposition of the asset.

The IRS and Treasury welcome comments on whether the approach taken in the proposed regulations to communicate information to enable the holder of a unit interest to calculate its basis in a trust asset is effective, or whether a different approach, which continues to be consistent with the taxation of grantor trusts, would be more effective. In addition, the IRS and Treasury invite comments on whether, for trusts consisting of fungible assets, an approach other than the proposed asset-by-asset approach for reporting sales and determining basis is administratively feasible or whether an aggregate approach would be more appropriate and on the manner in which such an aggregate approach would be applied.

D. *Information to be Furnished to Middlemen by Trusts*

In general, information reporting is not required for unit interests held by *exempt recipients*. To enable such persons to receive necessary trust information, however, § 1.671-4(j)(3)(iii) of the proposed regulations provides that middlemen, exempt recipients, and certain other persons may request from the trust tax information for a calendar quarter, computed as of the last day of the quarter specified, or for a calendar year, computed as of December 31 of the year specified. The tax reporting information the trust is to make available includes: (1) all items of income (determined in accordance with proposed § 1.671-4(j)(6)(i)), deduction, and credit of the trust for the period specified; (2) if any trust asset has been sold or otherwise disposed of during the period specified, the gross proceeds received by the trust for the trust asset, the date of sale or disposition, and the percentage of that trust asset that has been sold or disposed of; (3) the number of units outstanding on the last business day of the period specified; and (4) any other information necessary for the unit interest holder to accurately report the income, deductions, and credits attributable to the portion of the trust treated as owned by the holder, as required under section 671. In addition, if a trust asset is sold or otherwise disposed of during the period specified, the trust must provide a schedule showing the portion (expressed in terms of a percentage) of the total fair market value of all the assets held by the trust that the asset sold or disposed of represented as of the last day of each calendar quarter that the trust held the asset.

E. *Special Rules*

A beneficial owner of a unit interest must report trust items consistent with the owner's method of accounting. See, e.g., Rev. Rul. 84-10. For administrative convenience, and with the intent of being consistent with industry practice, however, the proposed regulations require a trust to provide tax information as if the trust were a taxpayer using the cash receipts and disbursements method of tax accounting (cash method). Although a trust must provide tax information to unit holders as if the trust were a cash method taxpayer, the trust must provide information necessary for such holders to comply with the original issue discount rules and other provisions requiring the inclusion of accrued amounts regardless of the holder's method of accounting. The IRS and Treasury are continuing to study, and welcome comments on, whether to require trusts to provide tax reporting information to accommodate the different methods of accounting used by the beneficial owners of a trust.

In the case of a widely held fixed investment trust that holds a pool of debt instruments subject to section 1272(a)(6)(C)(iii), the proposed regulations require that middlemen, unit interest holders, exempt recipients, and noncalendar-year taxpayers be provided with certain additional information that is necessary for compliance with the market discount rules and, where applicable, section 1272(a)(6) (as amended by section 1004 of the Taxpayer Relief Act of 1997, Public Law 105-34, 111 Stat. 788, 911 (1997)). This additional information includes information necessary to compute (1) the accrual of market discount, including the type of information required under § 1.6049-7(f)(2)(i)(G) in the case of a REMIC regular interest or a collateralized debt obligation not issued with original issue discount; and (2) the accrual of original issue discount and market discount, including the type of information required under § 1.6049-7(f)(2)(ii)(E), (F), (I), and (K) in the case of a REMIC regular interest or a collateralized debt obligation that is issued with original issue discount. The IRS and Treasury request comments on whether similar information reporting requirements, for example, reporting of information necessary to compute the accrual of market discount, should be extended to widely held fixed investment trusts that hold instruments (or pools of instruments) not subject to section 1272(a)(6)(C).

To enable a beneficial owner to comply fully with section 671 and section 67 (where applicable), § 1.671-4(j)(6)(i) of the proposed regulations requires the amount of trust income to be reported by the trustee to be the gross amount of income generated by the trust assets (other than from the sale or other disposition of trust assets). Thus, in the case of a trust that receives a payment net of an expense, the payment must be grossed up to reflect the deducted expense. Trustees must also have, and make available, information regarding the trust's affected expenses (as defined in § 1.67-2T(i)(1)) for the calendar year. In addition, in the case of a unit interest holder that is an affected investor (as defined in § 1.67-2T(h)(1)), the trustee or middleman must provide such unit interest holder with information regarding the holder's proportionate share of the trust's affected expenses for the calendar year.

The proposed regulations also require the trust to separately state any other item that, if taken into account separately by any unit interest holder, could result in an income tax liability for that unit interest holder different from that which would result if the unit interest holder did not take the item into account separately. The IRS and Treasury request comments on whether this requirement is administratively feasible in the context of a widely held fixed investment trust or whether a different approach, also consistent with the taxation of grantor trusts, would be more appropriate.

F. Coordination with Backup Withholding Rules

Section 1.671-4(j)(7) of the proposed regulations contains provisions to coordinate these regulations with the backup withholding rules.

Proposed Effective Date

These regulations are proposed to apply to calendar years beginning on or after the date that final regulations are published in the **Federal Register**.

Special Analyses

It has been determined that this notice of proposed rulemaking is not a significant regulatory action as defined in EO 12866. Therefore, a regulatory assessment is not required. It is hereby certified that these regulations will not have a significant economic impact on a substantial number of small entities. This certification is based on the fact that the regulations generally clarify existing reporting obligations and are expected, for the most part, to have a minimal impact on industry practice. Thus, the regulations will not result in a significant economic impact on any entity subject to the regulations. Further, the reporting burdens in these regulations will fall primarily on large brokerage firms, large banks, and other large entities acting as trustees or middlemen, most of which are not small entities within the meaning of the Regulatory Flexibility Act (5 U.S.C. chapter 6). Thus, a substantial number of small entities will not be affected. Therefore, a Regulatory

Flexibility Analysis under the Regulatory Flexibility Act (5 U.S.C. chapter 6) is not required. Pursuant to section 7805(f) of the Internal Revenue Code, this notice of proposed rulemaking will be submitted to the Chief Counsel for Advocacy of the Small Business Administration for comment on its impact on small business.

Comments and Public Hearing

Before these proposed regulations are adopted as final regulations, consideration will be given to any written comments (a signed original and eight (8) copies) that are submitted timely (in the manner described in the ADDRESSES caption) to the IRS. All comments will be available for public inspection and copying.

A public hearing has been scheduled for Thursday, November 5, 1998 at 10 a.m., in room 2615, Internal Revenue Building, 1111 Constitution Avenue, NW., Washington, DC. Because of access restrictions, visitors will not be admitted beyond the Internal Revenue Building lobby more than 15 minutes before the hearing starts.

The rules of 26 CFR 601.601(a)(3) apply to the hearing.

Persons that wish to present oral comments at the hearing must submit written comments by **[INSERT DATE 90 DAYS AFTER DATE OF PUBLICATION IN THE FEDERAL REGISTER]** and submit an outline of the topics to be discussed and the time to be devoted to each topic (signed original and eight (8) copies) by October 15, 1998.

A period of 10 minutes will be allotted to each person for making comments.

An agenda showing the scheduling of the speakers will be prepared after the deadline for receiving outlines has passed. Copies of the agenda will be available free of charge at the hearing.

Drafting Information

The principal author of these regulations is Faith Colson, Office of Assistant Chief Counsel (Passthroughs and Special Industries). However, other personnel from the IRS and Treasury Department participated in their development.

List of Subjects

26 CFR Part 1

Income taxes, Reporting and recordkeeping requirements

26 CFR Part 301

Employment taxes, Estate taxes, Excise taxes, Gift taxes, Income taxes, Penalties, Reporting and recordkeeping requirements

Proposed Amendments to the Regulations

Accordingly, 26 CFR parts 1 and 301 are proposed to be amended as follows:

PART 1—INCOME TAXES

Paragraph 1. The authority citation for part 1 is amended by adding an entry in numerical order to read as follows:

Authority: 26 U.S.C. 7805 * * * * *

Section 1.671-4 also issued under 26 U.S.C. 671, 26 U.S.C. 6034A, and 26 U.S.C. 6049(d)(7).

Par. 2. Section 1.671-4 is amended by revising paragraph (a) and adding paragraph (j) to read as follows:

§ 1.671-4 Method of reporting.

(a) *Portion of trust treated as owned by the grantor or another person.* Except as otherwise provided in paragraphs (b) and (j) of this section, items of income, deduction, and credit attributable to any portion of a trust which, under the provisions of subpart E (section 671 and following), part I, subchapter J, chapter 1 of the Internal Revenue Code, is treated as owned by the grantor or another person are not reported by the trust on Form 1041, but are shown on a separate statement to be attached to that form. Paragraph (j) of this section provides special reporting rules for widely held fixed investment trusts. Section 301.7701-4(e)(2) of this chapter provides guidance on how the reporting rules in this paragraph (a) apply to an environmental remediation trust.

* * * * *

(j) *Special rules applicable to widely held fixed investment trusts.* The reporting rules contained in this paragraph (j) apply to any widely held fixed investment trust.

(1) *Definitions.* For purposes of this paragraph (j):

Affected expenses. The term *affected expenses* has the meaning given that term by § 1.67-2T(i)(1).

Affected investor. The term *affected investor* has the meaning given that term by § 1.67-2T(h)(1).

Exempt recipient. An *exempt recipient* is any person described in paragraphs (j)(2)(iv)(A) through (R) of this section.

Middleman. A *middleman* is any person who holds an interest in an arrangement classified as a trust under § 301.7701-4(c) of this chapter, and subject to subpart E, part I, subchapter J, chapter 1 of the Internal Revenue Code, on behalf of, or for the account of, another person, or who otherwise acts in a capacity as an intermediary for the account of another person, at any time during the calendar year. A middleman includes, but is not limited to—

(i) A custodian of a person's account, such as a bank, financial institution, or brokerage firm acting as custodian of an account;

(ii) A nominee, including the joint owner of an account or instrument except if the joint owners are husband and wife; and

(iii) A broker (as defined in section 6045(c)(1) and § 1.6045-1(a)(1)) holding an interest for a customer in street name.

Requesting person. A *requesting person* is a person specified in paragraph (j)(3)(iii)(A) of this section who is entitled to request from the trustee the information specified in paragraph (j)(3)(ii) of this section.

Trustee. Trustee means the trustee of a widely held fixed investment trust.

Unit interest holder. A *unit interest holder* is any person who holds a direct or indirect interest, including a beneficial interest, in a widely held fixed investment trust at any time during the calendar year.

Widely held fixed investment trust. A *widely held fixed investment trust* is an arrangement classified as a trust under § 301.7701-4(c) of this chapter, and subject to subpart E, part I, subchapter J, chapter 1 of the Internal Revenue Code, in which any interest is held by a middleman.

(2) *Form 1099 requirement for trustees and middlemen*—(i) *Obligation to file Form 1099 with the Internal Revenue Service.* Except as provided in paragraph (j)(2)(iv) of this section —

(A) Every trustee must file with the Internal Revenue Service the appropriate Forms 1099 reporting the information specified in paragraph (j)(2)(ii) of this section with respect to any unit interest holder who holds an interest in the trust directly and not through a middleman; and

(B) Every middleman must file with the Internal Revenue Service the appropriate Forms 1099, reporting the information specified in paragraph (j)(2)(ii) of this section with respect to any unit interest holder on whose behalf or account the middleman holds an interest in the trust or acts in a capacity as an intermediary.

(ii) *Information to be reported.* The following information must be reported to the Internal Revenue Service on the appropriate Forms 1099—

(A) The name, address, and taxpayer identification number of the unit interest holder;

(B) The name, address, and taxpayer identification number of the person required to file the form;

(C) The amount of trust income (determined in accordance with paragraph (j)(6)(i) of this section) attributable to the unit interest holder for the calendar year for which the return is made;

(D) In the case of the sale or other disposition of a trust asset during the calendar year, the portion of the gross proceeds relating to the trust asset that is attributable to the unit interest holder; and

(E) Any other information required by the Forms 1099.

(iii) *Time and place for filing Forms 1099.* The Forms 1099 required to be filed with the Internal Revenue Service by trustees or middlemen pursuant to paragraph (j)(2)(i) of this section must be filed on or before February 28 of the year following the year for which the Forms 1099 are being filed. The returns must be filed with the appropriate Internal Revenue Service Center, at the address listed in the instructions for the Forms 1099. For extensions of time for filing returns under this section, see § 1.6081-1. For magnetic media filing requirements, see § 301.6011-2 of this chapter.

(iv) *Forms 1099 not required.* A Form 1099 is not required for a unit interest holder that is an exempt recipient. However, if the trustee or middleman backup withholds under section 3406 on payments made to a unit interest holder (because, for example, the unit interest holder has failed to furnish a Form W-9 on request), then the trustee or

middleman is required to make a return under this section, unless the trustee or middleman refunds the amount withheld in accordance with § 31.6413(a)-3 of this chapter. An exempt recipient is generally exempt from information reporting without filing a certificate claiming exempt status unless the provisions of this paragraph (j)(2)(iv) require the unit interest holder to file a certificate. A trustee or middleman may in any case require a unit interest holder not otherwise required to file a certificate under this paragraph (j)(2)(iv) to file a certificate in order to qualify as an exempt recipient. See § 31.3406(h)-3(a)(1)(iii) and (c)(2) of this chapter for the certificate that a unit interest holder must provide if a trustee or middleman requires the certificate in order to treat the unit interest holder as an exempt recipient under this paragraph (j)(2)(iv). A trustee or middleman may treat a unit interest holder as an exempt recipient based upon a properly completed form as described in § 31.3406(h)-3(e)(2) of this chapter, its actual knowledge that the unit interest holder is a person described in this paragraph (j)(2)(iv), or the indicators described in this paragraph (j)(2)(iv). Any unit interest holder who ceases to be an exempt recipient shall, no later than 10 days after such cessation, notify the trustee or middleman in writing when it ceases to be an exempt recipient. For purposes of this paragraph (j)—

(A) *Corporation.* A corporation, as defined in section 7701(a)(3), whether domestic or foreign, is an exempt recipient. In addition, for purposes of this paragraph (j)(2)(iv), the term corporation includes a partnership all of whose members are corporations described in this paragraph (j)(2)(iv), but only if the partnership files with the trustee or middleman a properly completed form as described in § 31.3406(h)-3(e)(2) of this chapter. Absent actual knowledge otherwise, a trustee or middleman may treat a unit interest holder as a corporation (and, therefore, as an exempt recipient) if one of the requirements of paragraph (j)(2)(iv)(A)(*1*), (*2*), (*3*), or (*4*), is met at the time a unit interest holder acquires an interest in the trust.

(*1*) The name of the unit interest holder contains an unambiguous expression of corporate status (that is, Incorporated, Inc., Corporation, Corp., P.C., (but not Company or Co.)) or contains the term *insurance company, indemnity company, reinsurance company,* or *assurance company,* or its name indicates that it is an entity listed as a per se corporation under § 301.7701-2(b)(8)(i) of this chapter.

(*2*) The trustee or middleman has on file a corporate resolution or similar document clearly indicating corporate status. For this purpose, a similar document includes a copy of Form 8832, filed by the unit interest holder to elect classification as an association under § 301.7701-3(c) of this chapter.

(*3*) The trustee or middleman receives a Form W-9 which includes an EIN and a statement from the unit interest holder that it is a domestic corporation.

(*4*) The trustee or middleman receives a withholding certificate described in § 1.1441-1(e)(2)(i), that includes a certification that the person whose name is on the certificate is a foreign corporation.

(B) *Tax exempt organization.* Any organization that is exempt from taxation under section 501(a) is an exempt recipient. A custodial account under section 403(b)(7) shall be considered an exempt recipient under this paragraph. A trustee or middleman may treat an organization as an exempt recipient under this paragraph (j)(2)(iv)(B) without requiring a certificate if the organization's name is listed in the compilation by the Commissioner of organizations for which a deduction for charitable contributions is allowed, if the name of the organization contains an unambiguous indication that it is a tax-exempt organization, or if the organization is known to the trustee or middleman to be a tax-exempt organization.

(C) *Individual retirement plan.* An individual retirement plan as defined in section 7701(a)(37) is an exempt recipient. A trustee or middleman may treat any such plan of which it is the trustee or custodian as an exempt recipient under this paragraph (j)(2)(iv)(C) without requiring a certificate.

(D) *United States.* The United States Government and any wholly-owned agency or instrumentality thereof are exempt recipients. A trustee or middleman may treat a person as an exempt recipient under this paragraph (j)(2)(iv)(D) without requiring a certificate if the name of such person reasonably indicates it is described in this paragraph (j)(2)(iv)(D).

(E) *State.* A State, the District of Columbia, a possession of the United States, a political subdivision of any of the foregoing, a wholly-owned agency or instrumentality of any one or more of the foregoing, and a pool or partnership composed exclusively of any of the foregoing are exempt recipients. A trustee or middleman may treat a person as an exempt recipient under this paragraph (j)(2)(iv)(E) without requiring a certificate if the name of such person reasonably indicates it is described in this paragraph (j)(2)(iv)(E) or if such person is known generally in the community to be a State, the District of Columbia, a possession of the United States or a political subdivision or a wholly-owned agency or instrumentality or any one or more of the foregoing (for example, an account held in the name of "Town of S" or "County of T" may be treated as held by an exempt recipient under this paragraph (j)(2)(iv)(E)).

(F) *Foreign government.* A foreign government, a political subdivision of a foreign government, and any wholly-owned agency or instrumentality of either of the foregoing are exempt recipients. A trustee or middleman may treat a foreign government or a political subdivision thereof as an exempt recipient under this paragraph (j)(2)(iv)(F) without requiring a certificate provided that its name reasonably indicates that it is a foreign government or provided that it is known to the trustee or middleman to be a foreign government or a political subdivision thereof (for example, an account held in the name of the "Government of V" may be treated as held by a foreign government).

(G) *International organization.* An international organization and any wholly-owned agency or instrumentality thereof are exempt recipients. The term *international organization* shall have the meaning ascribed to it in section 7701(a)(18). A trustee or middleman may treat a unit interest holder as an international organization without requiring a certificate if the unit interest holder is designated as an international organization by executive order (pursuant to 22 U.S.C. 288 through 288f).

(H) *Foreign central bank of issue.* A foreign central bank of issue is an exempt recipient. A foreign central bank of issue is a bank which is by law or government sanction the principal authority, other than the government itself, issuing instruments intended to circulate as currency. See § 1.895-1(b)(1). A trustee or middleman may treat a person as a foreign central bank of issue (and, therefore, as an exempt recipient) without requiring a certificate provided that such person is known generally in the financial community as a foreign central bank of issue or if its name reasonably indicates that it is a foreign central bank of issue.

(I) *Securities and commodities dealer.* A dealer in securities, commodities, or notional principal contracts that is registered as such under the laws of the United States or a State or under the laws of a foreign country is an exempt recipient. A trustee or middleman may treat a dealer as an exempt recipient under this paragraph (j)(2)(iv)(I) without requiring a certificate if the person is known generally in the investment community to be a dealer meeting the requirements set forth in this paragraph (j)(2)(iv)(I) (for example, a registered broker-dealer or a person listed as a member firm in the most recent publication of members of the National Association of Securities Dealers, Inc.).

(J) *Real Estate Investment Trust.* A real estate investment trust, as defined in section 856 and § 1.856-1, is an exempt recipient. A trustee or middleman may treat a person as a real estate investment trust (and, therefore, as an exempt recipient) without requiring a certificate if the person is known generally in the investment community as a real estate investment trust.

(K) *Entity registered under the Investment Company Act of 1940.* An entity registered at all times during the taxable year under the Investment Company Act of 1940, as amended (15 U.S.C. 80a-1), (or during such portion of the taxable year that it is in existence), is an exempt recipient. An entity that is created during the taxable year will be treated as meeting the registration requirement of the preceding sentence provided that such entity is so registered at all times during the taxable year for which such entity is in existence. A trustee or middleman may treat such an entity as an exempt recipient under this paragraph (j)(2)(iv)(K) without requiring a certificate if the entity is known generally in the investment community to meet the requirements of the preceding sentence.

(L) *Common trust fund.* A common trust fund, as defined in section 584(a), is an exempt recipient. A trustee or middleman may treat the fund as an exempt recipient without requiring a certificate provided that its name reasonably indicates that it is a common trust fund or provided that it is known to the trustee or middleman to be a common trust fund.

(M) *Financial institution.* A financial institution such as a bank, mutual savings bank, savings and loan association, building and loan association, cooperative bank, homestead association, credit union, industrial loan association or bank, or other similar organization, whether organized in the United States or under the laws of a foreign country is an exempt recipient. A financial institution also includes a clearing organization defined in § 1.163-5(c)(2)(i)(D)(8) and the Bank for International Settlements. A trustee or middleman may treat any person described in the preceding sentence as an exempt recipient

without requiring a certificate if the person's name (including a foreign name, such as "Banco" or "Banque") reasonably indicates the unit interest holder is a financial institution described in the preceding sentence.

(N) *Trust.* A trust which is exempt from tax under section 664(c) (i.e., a charitable remainder annuity trust or a charitable remainder unitrust) or is described in section 4947(a)(1) (relating to certain charitable trusts) is an exempt recipient. A trustee or middleman which is a trustee of the trust may treat the trust as an exempt recipient without requiring a certificate.

(O) *Middlemen.* A middleman, as defined in paragraph (j)(1) of this section, is an exempt recipient.

(P) *Brokers.* A broker, as defined in section 6045(c) and § 1.6045-1(a)(1), is an exempt recipient.

(Q) *Real estate mortgage investment conduit.* A real estate mortgage investment conduit, as defined in section 860D(a), is an exempt recipient.

(R) *A widely held fixed investment trust.* A widely held fixed investment trust, as defined in paragraph (j)(1) of this section, is an exempt recipient.

(3) *Trustee's requirement to furnish information to middlemen, exempt recipients, and noncalendar-year taxpayers—*(i) *In general.* The trustee must cause to be printed in a publication generally read by and available to requesting persons, the name, address, and telephone number of a representative or official of the trust who will provide the information specified in paragraph (j)(3)(ii) of this section to such persons. The trustee must provide the information in the time and manner prescribed in paragraph (j)(3)(iii)(C) of this section to requesting persons who request the information in the manner prescribed in paragraph (j)(3)(iii)(B) of this section.

(ii) *Information required to be reported.* For each calendar quarter or calendar year specified, the trustee must have available and provide, upon request, the following information computed as of the last day of the quarter, or computed as of December 31 of the year specified—

(A) The name of the trust, the name and address of the trustee of the trust, and the employer identification number of the trust;

(B) The Committee on Uniform Security Identification Procedure (CUSIP) number, account number, serial number or other identifying number of the trust;

(C) All items of income (determined in accordance with paragraph (j)(6)(i) of this section), deduction, and credit of the trust, expressed both as a total dollar amount for the trust and as a dollar amount per unit outstanding on the last day of the period requested;

(D) If any trust asset has been sold or otherwise disposed of during the period requested, the gross proceeds received by the trust for the trust asset, the date of sale or disposition of the trust asset, and the percentage of that trust asset that has been sold or disposed of. The trust must also provide a schedule showing the portion (expressed in terms of a percentage) of the total fair market value of all the assets held by the trust that the asset sold or disposed of represented as of the last day of the quarter for each quarter that the asset was held by the trust;

(E) The amount of affected expenses of the trust expressed both as a total dollar amount and as a dollar amount per unit outstanding on the last day of the period requested;

(F) In the case of a widely held fixed investment trust that holds a pool of debt instruments subject to section 1272(a)(6)(C)(iii), the information required by paragraph (j)(6)(ii) of this section;

(G) The number of units outstanding on the last business day of the period requested; and

(H) Any other information necessary for a unit interest holder that is the beneficial owner of a trust interest to properly report the income, deductions, and credits attributable to the portion of the trust treated as owned by the unit interest holder under section 671. For this purpose, the trustee shall separately state any trust item that, if taken into account separately by a unit interest holder, could result in an income tax liability for that unit interest holder different from that which would result if the unit interest holder did not take the item into account separately.

(iii) *Providing and requesting trust information—*(A) *Requesting persons.* The following persons that hold an interest in a trust may request the information specified in paragraph (j)(3)(ii) of this section from that trust—

(*1*) Any middleman;

(*2*) Any broker who holds a unit interest on its own behalf;

(*3*) Any other exempt recipient who holds an interest directly and not through a middleman;

(*4*) Any noncalendar-year unit interest holder who holds a trust interest directly and not through a middleman; and

(*5*) A representative or agent for a person specified in paragraphs (j)(3)(iii)(A)(*1*) through (*4*) of this section.

(B) *Manner of requesting information from the trust.* A requesting person may request the information specified in paragraph (j)(3)(ii) of this section in writing or by telephone. The request must specify the calendar quarters or years for which the information is needed.

(C) *Time and manner of furnishing information*—(*1*) *Manner of furnishing information.* The information specified in paragraph (j)(3)(ii) of this section may be furnished as follows—

(*i*) By telephone;

(*ii*) By written statement sent by first class mail to the address provided by the requesting person;

(*iii*) By causing it to be printed in a publication generally read by and available to requesting persons and by notifying the requesting person in writing or by telephone of the publication in which it will appear, the date on which it will appear, and, if possible, the page on which it will appear; or

(*iv*) By any other method agreed to by the parties.

(*2*) *Time for furnishing the information.* The trustee must furnish, or cause to be furnished, the information specified in paragraph (j)(3)(ii) of this section on or before the later of—

(*i*) The 30th day after the close of the period for which the information was requested; or

(*ii*) The day that is 2 weeks after the receipt of the request.

(4) *Requirement of furnishing statement to unit interest holder*—(i) *In general.* Every trustee or middleman required to file appropriate Forms 1099 under paragraph (j)(2)(i) of this section with respect to a particular unit interest holder must furnish to that unit interest holder (the person whose identifying number is required to be shown on the form) a written statement showing the information required by paragraph (j)(4)(ii) of this section.

(ii) *Information required to be provided on written statement.* The written statement must specify for the calendar year for which the return is made the following information—

(A) The name of the trust and the CUSIP number, account number, serial number, or other identifying number for the trust or unit interest;

(B) The name, address, and taxpayer identification number of the person required to send the statement;

(C) All items of income (determined in accordance with paragraph (j)(6)(i) of this section), deduction, and credit of the trust attributable to the unit interest holder;

(D) If any trust asset is sold, or otherwise disposed of during the calendar year, the portion of the gross proceeds relating to the trust asset that is attributable to the unit interest holder, the date of sale or disposition of the trust asset, and the percentage of that trust asset that has been sold or otherwise disposed of. A schedule showing the portion (expressed in terms of a percentage) of the total fair market value of all the assets held by the trust that the asset sold or disposed of represented as of the last day of the quarter for each quarter that the asset was held by the trust must be included with the statement;

(E) In the case of a unit interest holder that is an affected investor, the affected expenses that are attributable to the unit interest holder;

(F) In the case of a widely held fixed investment trust that holds a pool of debt instruments subject to section 1272(a)(6)(C)(iii), the information required by paragraph (j)(6)(ii) of this section;

(G) Any other information necessary for a unit interest holder to properly report the income, deductions, and credit attributable to the unit interest holder under section 671. For this purpose, the trustee or middleman, as the case may be, shall separately state any trust item that, if taken into account separately by any unit interest holder, could result in an income tax liability for that unit interest holder different from that which would result if the unit interest holder did not take the item into account separately; and

(H) A statement that the items of income, deduction, and credit and other information shown on the statement must be taken into account

in computing the taxable income and credits of the unit interest holder on the income tax return of the unit interest holder.

(iii) *Due date and other requirements with respect to statement required to be furnished to the unit interest holder.* The statement required to be furnished to the unit interest holder under this paragraph (j)(4) for a calendar year must be furnished to the holder after April 30 of that year and on or before March 15 of the year following the year for which the statement is being furnished. The person sending the statement must maintain in its records a copy of the statement furnished to the unit interest holder for a period of 3 years from the due date for furnishing such statement specified in this paragraph (j)(4).

(5) *Requirement that middlemen furnish information to exempt recipients and noncalendar-year taxpayers.* For each calendar quarter or calendar year specified, any exempt recipient listed in paragraph (j)(2)(iv) of this section and any noncalendar-year unit interest holder may request from the middleman who holds the unit interest on behalf of, or for the account of, the unit interest holder, the information listed in paragraph (j)(4)(ii)(A) through (G) of this section computed as of the last day of the calendar quarter specified, or computed as of December 31 of the year specified. The middleman must provide in writing or by telephone the information listed in paragraph (j)(4)(ii)(A) through (G) of this section to any such requester on or before the later of the 45th day after the close of the period for which the information was requested, or that day that is 4 weeks after the receipt of the request.

(6) *Special rules.* For purposes of this paragraph (j):

(i) *Determination of trust income.* Trust income is to be determined in the following manner—

(A) The trust is to be treated as a calendar year taxpayer using the cash receipts and disbursements method of accounting; and

(B) The amount of trust income for the calendar year is the gross amount of income generated by the trust assets (other than from the sale or other disposition of trust assets). Thus, in the case of a trust that receives a payment net of an expense, the payment must be grossed up to reflect the deducted expense.

(ii) *Widely held fixed investment trust holding pool of debt instruments subject to section 1272(a)(6)(C)(iii).* In the case of a widely held fixed investment trust that holds a pool of debt instruments subject to section 1272(a)(6)(C)(iii), requesting persons, unit interest holders, exempt recipients, and noncalendar-year taxpayers must be provided, as required under paragraphs (j)(3)(ii)(F), (j)(4)(ii)(F), and (j)(5), respectively, of this section, information necessary to compute—

(A) The accrual of market discount, including the type of information required under paragraphs §1.6049-7(f)(2)(i)(G) in the case of a REMIC regular interest or a collateralized debt obligation not issued with original issue discount; and

(B) The accrual of original issue discount and market discount, including the type of information required under § 1.6049-7(f)(2)(ii)(E), (F), (I), and (K) in the case of a REMIC regular interest or a collateralized debt obligation that is issued with original issue discount.

(7) *Backup withholding requirements.* Every trustee and middleman filing a Form 1099 under this section shall be considered a payor within the meaning of §31.3406(a)-2 of this chapter. The obligation of a trustee or middleman as payor to backup withhold shall be determined pursuant to section 3406 and the regulations promulgated thereunder.

(8) *Penalties for failure to comply.* Every trustee and middleman who has a reporting obligation under this paragraph (j) and who fails to comply is subject to the penalties provided by sections 6721, 6722, and any other applicable penalty provisions.

(9) *Effective date.* Trustees and middlemen must report in accordance with this paragraph (j) for calendar years beginning on or after the date that the final regulations are published in the **Federal Register**.

Par. 3. Section 1.6049-7 is amended by adding a sentence to the end of paragraph (f)(4) to read as follows:

§ *1.6049-7 Returns of information with respect to REMIC regular interests and collateralized debt obligations.*

*****

(f) *****

(4) ***** For rules regarding a widely held fixed investment trust that holds a pool of debt instruments subject to section 1272(a)(6)(C)(iii), see § 1.671-4(j).

*****

PART 301—PROCEDURE AND ADMINISTRATION

Par. 4. The authority citation for part 301 continues to read in part as follows:

Authority: 26 U.S.C. 7805 *****

Par. 5. Section 301.6109-1 is amended by revising the last sentence of paragraph (a)(2)(i) to read as follows:

§ 301.6109-1 *Identifying numbers.*

(a) *****

(2) ***** (i) ***** If the trustee has not already obtained a taxpayer identification number for the trust, the trustee must obtain a taxpayer identification number for the trust as provided in paragraph (d)(2) of this section in order to report pursuant to § 1.671-4(a), (b)(2)(i)(B), (b)(3)(i), or (j) of this chapter.

*****

Deputy Commissioner of Internal Revenue

Michael P. Dolan

¶ 20,233

IRS proposed regulations: Roth IRAs.—The IRS has issued proposed regulations, explaining the contribution, conversion, distribution, and reporting rules for Roth IRAs. The proposed rules reflect the recent changes made to Roth IRAs by the IRS Restructuring and Reform Act of 1998 (P.L. 105-206). Taxpayers may rely on the proposed regulations for guidance pending the issuance of final regulations. According to the IRS, if future guidance is more restrictive than the guidance issued in these proposed regulations, future guidance will be applied without retroactive effect.

The proposed regulations are set out in a question-and-answer format and are designed to provide guidance to individuals establishing Roth IRAs, beneficiaries under Roth IRAs, and trustees, custodians, and issuers of Roth IRAs.

The proposed regulations were published in the *Federal Register* on September 3, 1998 (63 FR 46937).

The regulations were finalized February 3, 1999 (64 FR 5597). The regulations are reproduced at ¶ 12,097A-0, ¶ 12,097A-1, ¶ 12,097A-2, ¶ 12,097A-3, ¶ 12,097A-4, ¶ 12,097A-5, ¶ 12,097A-6, ¶ 12,097A-7, ¶ 12,097A-8, and ¶ 12,097A-9. The preamble is reproduced at ¶ 23,154.

¶ 20,234

IRS proposed regulations: Section 411(d)(6) Protected Benefits: Qualified Retirement Plan Benefits.—The IRS has issued proposed regulations regarding Code Sec. 411(d)(6) protected qualified retirement plan benefits. The proposed regulations reflect changes made by the Taxpayer Relief Act of 1997 (TRA '97) to the rules under Code Sec. 411(d)(6) regarding qualified retirement plan benefits that are protected from reduction by plan amendment. The proposed regulations change the existing regulations to conform with the TRA '97 rules regarding in-kind distribution requirements for certain employee stock ownership plans. The regulations also specify the time period during which certain plan amendments, for which relief has been granted by TRA '97, may be made without violating the prohibition against plan amendments that reduce accrued benefits.

The proposed regulations, which were published in the *Federal Register* on September 4, 1998 (63 FR 47214), are reproduced below. The proposed regs were also issued as final and temporary regs; those are reproduced at ¶ 12,233 and ¶ 12,233A. The preamble to the final and temporary regulations is at ¶ 23,142.

DEPARTMENT OF THE TREASURY

Internal Revenue Service

26 CFR Part 1

[REG-101363-98]

RIN 1545-AV94

Section 411(d)(6) Protected Benefits (Taxpayer Relief Act of 1997); Qualified Retirement Plan Benefits

AGENCY: Internal Revenue Service (IRS), Treasury.

ACTION: Notice of proposed rulemaking by cross-reference to temporary regulations.

SUMMARY: In the Rules and Regulations section of this issue of the **Federal Register**, the IRS is issuing temporary regulations providing for changes to the rules regarding qualified retirement plan benefits that are protected from reduction by plan amendment, that have been made necessary by the Taxpayer Relief Act of 1997. The text of those temporary regulations also serves as the text of these proposed regulations.

DATES: Written comments and requests for a public hearing must be received by December 3, 1998.

ADDRESSES: Send submissions to: CC:DOM:CORP:R (REG-101363-98), room 5228, Internal Revenue Service, POB 7604, Ben Franklin Station, Washington, DC 20044. Submissions may be hand delivered between the hours of 8 a.m. and 5 p.m. to: CC:DOM:CORP:R (REG-101363-98), Courier's Desk, Internal Revenue Service, 1111 Constitution Avenue NW., Washington, DC. Alternatively, taxpayers may submit comments electronically via the internet by selecting the "Tax Regs" option on the IRS Home Page, or by submitting comments directly to the IRS internet site at http://www.irs.ustreas.gov/prod/tax_regs/comments.html.

FOR FURTHER INFORMATION CONTACT: Concerning the regulations, Linda S. F. Marshall, (202) 622-6030 (not a toll-free call); concerning submissions, Michael Slaughter, (202) 622-7190 (not a toll-free call).

SUPPLEMENTARY INFORMATION:

Background

Temporary regulations in the Rules and Regulations section of this issue of the **Federal Register** amend the Income Tax Regulations (26 CFR part 1) relating to section 411(d)(6), to provide for changes that have been made necessary by the Taxpayer Relief Act of 1997 (TRA '97), Public Law 105-34, 111 Stat. 788 (1997). The temporary regulations change the existing regulations to conform with the TRA '97 rules regarding in-kind distribution requirements for certain employee stock ownership plans, and specify the time period during which certain plan amendments for which relief has been granted by TRA '97 may be made without violating the prohibition against plan amendments that reduce accrued benefits.

The text of those temporary regulations also serves as the text of these proposed regulations. The preamble to the temporary regulations explains the temporary regulations.

Special Analyses

It has been determined that this notice of proposed rulemaking is not a significant regulatory action as defined in EO 12866. Therefore, a regulatory assessment is not required. It also has been determined that section 553(b) of the Administrative Procedure Act (5 U.S.C. chapter 5) does not apply to these regulations, and because the regulation does not impose a collection of information on small entities, the Regulatory Flexibility Act (5 U.S.C. chapter 6) does not apply. Pursuant to section 7805(f) of the Internal Revenue Code, this notice of proposed rulemaking will be submitted to the Chief Counsel for Advocacy of the Small Business Administration for comment on its impact on small business.

Comments and Requests for a Public Hearing

Before these proposed regulations are adopted as final regulations, consideration will be given to any written comments (a signed original and eight (8) copies) that are submitted timely to the IRS. All comments will be available for public inspection and copying. A public hearing may be scheduled if requested in writing by any person that timely submits written comments. If a public hearing is scheduled, notice of the date, time, and place for the hearing will be published in the **Federal Register**.

Drafting Information

The principal author of these regulations is Linda S. F. Marshall, Office of the Associate Chief Counsel (Employee Benefits and Exempt Organizations. However, other personnel from the IRS and Treasury Department participated in their development.

List of Subjects in 26 CFR Part 1

Income taxes, Reporting and recordkeeping requirements.

Proposed Amendments to the Regulations

Accordingly, 26 CFR part 1 is proposed to be amended as follows:

PART 1—INCOME TAXES

Paragraph 1. The authority citation for part 1 continues to read in part as follows:

Authority: 26 U.S.C. 7805 * * *

Par. 2. Section 1.411(d)-4 is amended by:

1. Revising paragraph (d)(1)(ii) of Q&A-2.

2. Adding Q&A-11.

The addition and revisions read as follows:

§ 1.411(d)-4 Section 411(d)(6) protected benefits.

* * * * *

Q&A-2 * * *

(d)(1)(ii) [The text of proposed paragraph (d)(1)(ii) of Q&A-2 is the same as the text of § 1.411(d)-4T Q&A-2(d)(1)(ii) published elsewhere in this issue of the **Federal Register**.]

* * * * *

Q&A-11 [The text of proposed Q&A-11 is the same as the text of § 1.411(d)-4T Q&A-11 published elsewhere in this issue of the **Federal Register**.]

Michael P. Dolan

Deputy Commissioner of Internal Revenue

¶ 20,235

IRS: Proposed regulations: Mileage allowances.—The IRS has issued a proposed regulation which applies the substantiation rules to mileage allowances for business use of an automobile after December 31, 1997, without the limitation that a mileage allowance is available only to the owner of a vehicle. Another proposed regulation authorizes the Commissioner to establish a method under which a taxpayer may use mileage rates to determine the amount of the ordinary and necessary business expenses of using an automobile for local transportation to, from, and at the destination while traveling away from home, in lieu of substantiating the actual costs. Written or electronically generated comments and requests for a public hearing regarding the proposed regs must be received by December 30, 1998. Submissions should be sent to CC:DOM:CORP:R (REG-122488-97), Room 5228, Internal Revenue Service, P.O. Box 7604, Ben Franklin Station, Washington, DC 20044. For information concerning the proposed regulations, contact Edwin B. Cleverdon or Donna M. Crisalli, phone: (202) 622-4920.

The proposed regulations and preamble were published in the *Federal Register* on October 1, 1998 (63 FR 52660).

The final regulations were published in the *Federal Register* on January 26, 2000 (65 FR 4121). IRS Reg. Sec. 1.62-2 is reproduced at ¶ 11,182. IRS Reg. Sec. 1.274-5 is reproduced at ¶ 11,357B. The preamble is reproduced at ¶ 23,158.

¶ 20,236

IRS: Temporary regulations: Health care: Women and newborn children.—The IRS issued temporary regulations relating to minimum hospital length-of-stay requirements imposed on group health plans with respect to mothers and newborns. These regulation were issued at the same time that the Pension and Welfare Benefts Administration and the Health Care Financing Adminstration issued substantially similar interim final regulations (See ¶ 23,143).

The temporary regulations and preamble, which were published in the *Federal Register* on October 27, 1998 (63 FR 57565), were formerly reproduced below.

The regulations were finalized on October 20, 2008 by T.D. 9427 (73 FR 62410). The preamble to the final regulations is reproduced at ¶ 23,257.

¶ 20,237

IRS proposed regulations: Eligible rollover distributions: Eligible retirement plans: Disqualification of plans: Favorable IRS determination letter.—The IRS has issued proposed regulations providing additional guidance regarding the circumstances in which plans could accept rollovers without facing disqualification. The proposed regulations, which amend previously proposed regulations (CCH PENSION PLAN GUIDE ¶ 20,218), clarify that a distributing plan does not need to have a favorable IRS determination letter for the receiving plan administrator to make a reasonable conclusion that a contribution is a valid rollover.

The proposed regulations were published in the *Federal Register* on December 17, 1998 (63 FR 69584).

The final regulations were published in the *Federal Register* on April 21, 2000 (65 FR 21312). The regulations are reproduced at ¶ 11,720Z-50, ¶ 11,753-10, ¶ 11,803, and ¶ 13,566. The preamble is at ¶ 23,163.

¶ 20,238

IRS proposed regulations: Electronic media: Notices: Consent requirements: Code Sec. 402(f): Code Sec. 411(a)(11): Code Sec. 3405(e)(10)(B).—The IRS has issued proposed regulations providing guidelines for the proper electronic transmission of certain notices and consent requirements under Code Sec. 402(f), Code Sec. 411(a)(11), and Code Sec. 3405(e)(10)(B).

The proposed regulations were published in the *Federal Register* on December 18, 1998 (63 FR 70071).

Final regulations were published in the *Federal Register* on February 8, 2000 (65 FR 6001). The regulations are reproduced at ¶ 11,755-2, ¶ 12,219D, and ¶ 13,566-50. The preamble is reproduced at ¶ 23,159.

¶ 20,239

IRS: Qualified plans: Distribution limits: Lookback rule.—The IRS has issued proposed regulations which would eliminate, for all qualified plan distributions, the "lookback rule" pursuant to which the qualified plan benefits of certain participants are deemed to exceed the $5,000 cash-out limit on mandatory distributions. These regulations were issued at the same time IRS issued temporary regulations which served as a portion of the text of these proposed regulations (see ¶ 23,145).

The proposed regulations and preamble were published in the *Federal Register* on December 21, 1998 (63 FR 70356).

Final regulations were published in the *Federal Register* on July 19, 2000 (65 FR 44679). The regulations are reproduced at ¶ 12,217, ¶ 12,219D, and ¶ 12,556. The preamble is reproduced at ¶ 23,167.

¶ 20,240

IRS proposed regulations: Group-term life insurance: Uniform premium table.—The IRS has issued proposed amendments to the regulations under IRS Code Sec. 79, revising the uniform premium table used to calculate the cost of group-term life insurance coverage provided to an employee by an employer. The rules provide guidance to employers who must use the uniform premium table to calculate the cost of group-term insurance includible in their employees' gross income.

The proposed regulations were published in the *Federal Register* on January 13, 1999 (64 FR 2164).

The final regulations were published in the *Federal Register* on June 3, 1999 (64 FR 29788). IRS Reg. Sec. 1.79-(d)(7) is reproduced at ¶ 11,231. IRS Reg. Sec. 1.79-3 is reproduced at ¶ 11,233. The preamble is at ¶ 23,155.

¶ 20,241

IRS proposed regulations: COBRA continuation coverage: Compliance guidance.—The IRS has issued proposed regulations in conjunction with the final rules on COBRA continuation coverage issued on February 3, 1999 (¶ 23,152, ¶ 13,648W-5, ¶ 13,648W-6, ¶ 13,648W-7, ¶ 13,648W-8, ¶ 13,648W-9, ¶ 13,648W-10, ¶ 13,648W-11, ¶ 13,648W-12, and ¶ 13,648W-13). The proposed rules provide plan sponsors and plan administrators with guidance on compliance with the final rules.

The proposed regulations were published in the *Federal Register* on February 3, 1999 (64 FR 5237).

Final regulations became effective on January 10, 2001, the date of their publication in the *Federal Register* (66 FR 1893). The regulations are reproduced at ¶ 13,648W-5, ¶ 13,648W-6, ¶ 13,648W-7, ¶ 13,648W-8, ¶ 13,648W-9, ¶ 13,648W-10, ¶ 13,648W-11, ¶ 13,648W-12 ¶ 13,648W-13 ¶ 13,648W-14, and ¶ 13,648W-15. The preamble is reproduced at ¶ 23,174.

¶ 20,242

IRS proposed regulations: Annuities: Valuation: Actuarial tables.—The IRS has issued proposed regulations to update the mortality tables to reflect the most recent mortality experience available. These regulations will effect the valuation of annuities.

The preamble and portions of the proposed regulations were published in the *Federal Register* on April 30, 1999 (64 FR 23245).

The final regulations were published in the *Federal Register* on June 12, 2000 (65 FR 36907). The regulations are reproduced at ¶ 13,498 and ¶ 13,498A. The preamble is reproduced at ¶ 23,166.

¶ 20,243

IRS Proposed Regulations: Tax liabilities: Compromise: Retirement income: IRA rollover.—The IRS has issued proposed regulations that provide guidance regarding the compromise of tax liabilities to reflect tax law changes made by the IRS Restructuring and Reform Act of 1998. The proposed regulations allow for compromise based on doubt as to liability and/or collectibility. The proposed regulations also provide for compromise where either collection of the liability would create economic hardship or exceptional circumstances exist such that collection of the liability would be detrimental to compliance. The temporary regulations include examples of transactions involving retirement plans and IRAs.

The preamble and the proposed regulations, which were published in the *Federal Register* on July 21, 1999 (64 FR 39106) are reproduced below. The text of the proposed regulations is the same as the text of temporary regulations IRS Reg. Sec. 301.7122-1T, adopted July 21, 1999 by T.D. 8829 (64 FR 39020) (CCH PENSION PLAN GUIDE ¶ 13,866).

DEPARTMENT OF THE TREASURY

Internal Revenue Service

26 CFR Part 301

RIN 1545-AW88

Compromises

AGENCY: Internal Revenue Service (IRS), Treasury.

ACTION: Notice of proposed rulemaking by cross-reference to temporary regulations.

SUMMARY: In the Rules and Regulations section of this issue of the **Federal Register,** the IRS is issuing temporary regulations relating to the compromise of tax liabilities. These regulations provide additional guidance regarding the compromise of internal revenue taxes. The temporary regulations reflect changes to the law made by the Internal Revenue Service Restructuring and Reform Act of 1998 and the Taxpayer bill of Rights II. The text of the temporary regulations also serves as the text of these proposed regulations.

DATE: Written or electronically generated comments and requests for a public hearing must be received by October 19, 1999.

ADDRESSES: Send submissions to: CC:DOM:CORP:R (REG-116991-98), room 5226, Internal Revenue Service, POB 7604, Ben Franklin Station, Washington, DC 20044. Submissions may be hand delivered Monday through Friday between the hours of 8 a.m. and 5 p.m. to: CC:DOM:CORP:R (REG-116991-98), Courier's Desk, Internal Revenue Service, 1111 Constitution Avenue, NW., Washington, DC. Alternatively, taxpayers may submit comments electronically via the Internet by selecting the "Tax Regs" option on the IRS Home Page, or

by submitting comments directly to the IRS Internet site at http://www.irs.gov/prod/tax_regs/comments.html.

FOR FURTHER INFORMATION CONTACT: Concerning the regulations, Carol A. Campbell, (202) 622-3620 (not a toll-free number).

SUPPLEMENTARY INFORMATION:

Background

Temporary regulations in the Rules and Regulations section of this issue of the **Federal Register** amend the Procedure and Administration Regulations (26 CFR part 301) under section 7122 of the Internal Revenue Code. The temporary regulations reflect the amendment of section 7122 by section 3462 of the Internal Revenue Service Restructuring and Reform Act of 1998 ("RRA 1998") Public Law, 105-206, (112 Stat. 685, 764) and by section 503(a) of Taxpayer Bill of Rights II Public Law 104-168, (110 Stat. 1452, 1461).

The text of the temporary regulations also serves as the text of these proposed regulations. The preamble to the temporary regulations explains the regulations.

Special Analyses

It has been determined that this notice of proposed rulemaking is not a significant regulatory action as defined in EO 12866. Therefore, a regulatory assessment is not required. It also has been determined that section 553(b) of the Administrative Procedure Act (5 U.S.C. chapter 5) does not apply to these regulations, and because the regulation does not impose a collection of information on small entities, the Regulatory Flexibility Act (5 U.S.C. chapter 6) does not apply. Pursuant to section 7805(f) of the Internal Revenue Code, this notice of proposed rulemaking will be submitted to the Chief Counsel for Advocacy of the Small Business Administration for comment on its impact on small business.

Comments and Requests for a Public Hearing

Before these proposed regulations are adopted as final regulations, consideration will be given to any written comments (a signed original and eight (8) copies) or electronically generated comments that are submitted timely to the IRS. The IRS generally requests any comments on the clarity of the proposed rule and how it may be made easier to understand.

Section 3462 of RRA 1998 and its legislative history provide for the consideration of factors such as equity, hardship, and public policy in the compromise of tax cases, if such consideration would promote effective tax administration. The legislative history also states that the IRS should use this new compromise authority "to resolve longstanding cases by forgoing penalties and interest which have accumulated as a result of delay in determining the taxpayer's liability." H. Conf. Rep. 599, 105th Cong., 2d Sess. 289 (1998). The text of the temporary regulation provides the authority to compromise cases involving issues of equity, hardship, and public policy, if such a compromise would promote effective tax administration. The temporary regulation provides factors to be considered and examples of cases that could be compromised under this authority when collection of the full amount of the tax liability would create economic hardship. The temporary regulation also provides limited examples of cases that could be compromised when the facts and circumstances presented indicate that collection of the full tax liability would be detrimental to voluntary compliance. The temporary regulation does not contain examples of longstanding cases that could be compromised to promote effective tax administration when penalties and interest have accumulated as the result of delay by the Service in determining the tax liability.

The public is specifically encouraged to make comments or provide examples regarding the particular types of cases or situations in which the Secretary's authority to compromise should be used because: (1) collection of the full amount of tax liability would be detrimental to voluntary compliance or (2) IRS delay in determining the tax liability has resulted in the accumulation of significant interest and penalties. In formulating comments regarding delay in interest and penalty cases, consideration should be given to the possible interplay between cases compromised under this provision and the relief accorded taxpayers under I.R.C. § 6404(e).

All comments will be available for public inspection and copying.

A public hearing may be scheduled if requested in writing by a person that timely submits written comments. If a public hearing is scheduled, notice of the date, time, and place for the hearing will be published in the **Federal Register.**

Drafting Information

The principal author of these regulations is Carol A. Campbell, Office of the Assistant Chief Counsel (General Litigation) CC:EL:GL, IRS. However, other personnel from the IRS and Treasury Department participated in their development.

List of Subjects in 26 CFR Part 301

Employment taxes, Estate taxes, Excise taxes, Gift taxes, Income taxes, Penalties, Reporting and recordkeeping requirements.

Proposed Amendments to the Regulations

Accordingly, 26 CFR Part 301 is proposed to be amended as follows:

PART 301—PROCEDURE AND ADMINISTRATION

Paragraph 1. The authority citation for part 301 continues to read in part as follows:

Authority: 26 U.S.C. 7805 *****

Paragraph 2. Section 301. 7122—1 is added to read as follows:

§ 301.7122-1 Compromises.

[The text of this proposed section is the same as the text of § 301.7122-IT published elsewhere in this issue of the **Federal Register.**]

* * * * *

Charles O. Rossotti

Commissioner of Internal Revenue

¶ 20,244

IRS Proposed Regulations: Deficiency notices: Taxpayers: Addresses.—The IRS has issued a proposed regulation that defines the "last known address" for the purposes of mailing deficiency notices, other types of notices, statements or documents to taxpayers.

The preamble and portions of the proposed regulations reproduced below were published in the *Federal Register* on November 22, 1999 (64 FR 63768).

The final regulations were published in the *Federal Register* on January 12, 2001 (66 FR 2812). The final regulations are reproduced at ¶ 13,786P. The preamble is reproduced at ¶ 23,179.

¶ 20,245

IRS proposed regulations: Fringe benefits: Qualified transportation.—The IRS has issued proposed regulations which provide guidance to employers that provide qualified transportation fringes to employees, explain that there are two categories of qualified transportation fringes for purposes of determining the amount that is excludable from gross income, and clarify the meaning of "significant administrative costs." Note: The IRS has issued a clarification to these proposed regulations. Announcement 2000-78, which contains the clarification, can be found at ¶ 17,097Q-86.

The proposed regulations, which were published in the *Federal Register* January 27, 2000 (65 FR 4388) are reproduced below.

The final regulations were published in the *Federal Register* on January 11, 2001 (66 FR 2241). The final regulation are reproduced at ¶ 11,289O-5 and ¶ 11,289O-9. The preamble is reproduced at ¶ 23,177.

¶ 20,246

IRS proposed regulations: Information returns: Electronic filing: Due date extension.—The IRS has issued proposed regulations which extend by one month the due date for filing certain information returns required by Code Sec. 6041, Code Sec. 6047 and Code Sec. 6052 if the return is filed electronically. The proposed regulations affect Forms W-2, W-3, 1096, and the Form 1099 series.

The proposed regulations, which were published in the *Federal Register* January 27, 2000 (65 FR 4396), are reproduced below.

The final regulations were published in the *Federal Register* on August 18, 2000 (65 FR 50405). Portions of the final regulations are reproduced at ¶ 13,683, ¶ 13,691 and ¶ 13,721. The preamble is reproduced at ¶ 23,170.

¶ 20,247

IRS proposed regulations: Cafeteria plans: Election of coverage: Revocation of election.—The IRS has issued proposed regulations which supplement the final regulations (¶ 23,162) by permitting a mid-year cafeteria plan election change in connection with dependent care assistance and adoption assistance under change in status standards that are specific to dependent care and adoption assistance.

The proposed regulations (formerly reproduced below) were amended by proposed regulations published in the *Federal Register* January 10, 2001 (66 FR 1923). These proposed regulations are reproduced at ¶ 20,258.

The proposed regulations, which were published in the *Federal Register* March 23, 2000 (65 FR 15587), were withdrawn on August 6, 2007 (72 FR 43938) by proposed regulations reproduced at ¶ 20,262B.

¶ 20,248

IRS proposed regulations: Defined contribution plans: Plan amendments: Optional forms of benefit.—The IRS has issued proposed regulations providing relief to defined contribution plans from Code Sec. 411(d)(6), which precludes qualified retirement plan amendments from eliminating optional forms of benefits.

The proposed regulations were published in the *Federal Register* March 29, 2000 (65 FR 16546).

The final regulations were published in the *Federal Register* on September 6, 2000 (65 FR 53901). The final regulations are reproduced at ¶ 12,233. The preamble to the final regulations is reproduced at ¶ 23,171.

¶ 20,249

IRS proposed regulations: Plan loans: Qualified plans: Refinancing: Multiple loans.—The IRS has issued proposed regulations that supplement final regulations (¶ 23,168) issued on plan loans that are deemed to be distributed to a participant. The proposed regs indicate that a refinancing of a plan loan will effectively be treated as a new loan, which is applied to repay the balance of a prior loan, if the new loan replaces the prior and has a later repayment date than the prior loan. The transaction will result in a deemed distribution if the amount of the new loan, when added to the amount of the prior outstanding loan, exceeds the amount limitations of Code Sec. 72(p)(2)(A). This rule does not apply if the prior loan is to be repaid by its original repayment date. A participant may also borrow more than once from a plan. However, a deemed distribution of a loan will occur if two loans have previously been made from the plan during the year.

The proposed regulations were published in the *Federal Register* on July 31, 2000 (65 FR 46677). The final regulations were published in the *Federal Register* on December 3, 2002 (67 FR 71821). The final regulations are reproduced at ¶ 11,210. The preamble to the final regulations is reproduced at ¶ 23,199.

¶ 20,250

IRS proposed regulations: Defined contribution plans: New comparability: Cross-testing: Minimum allocation "gateway" requirement.—The IRS has issued proposed regulations that would, effective for 2002 plan years, permit new comparability defined contribution plans to continue to utilize cross-testing, but that would implement minimum allocation "gateways" that are designed to restrict the disparity in allocation rates between highly compensated and nonhighly compensated employees.

The preamble and final regulations, which were published in the *Federal Register* on June 29, 2001 (66 FR 34535) can be found at ¶ 23,183. The amended portions of the regulations appear at ¶ 11,720W-14.

¶ 20,251

IRS proposed regulations: Employee benefit plan trusts: IRA's: Investment trusts: Fiduciary: Domestic trust status: Control test.—The IRS has issued proposed regulations relating to a safe harbor for certain employee benefit trusts and investment trusts stating that group trusts and certain investment trusts are deemed to satisfy the control test for determining domestic status under IRS Reg. Sec. 301.7701-7 if U. S. trustees control all substantial trust decisions.

The preamble and the proposed regulations were published in the *Federal Register* on October 12, 2000 (65 FR 60821).

The regulations were finalized by T.D. 8962 and published in the *Federal Register* on August 9, 2001 (66 FR 41778). The regulations are reproduced at ¶ 13,927. The preamble is reproduced at ¶ 23,185.

¶ 20,252

IRS proposed regulations: Determination of payee: Information reporting: Joint payees.—The IRS has issued proposed regulations that clarify who is the payee for information reporting purposes if an instrument is made payable to joint payees, provide information reporting requirements for persons making payment on behalf of another person, and clarify that the amount to be reported paid is the gross amount of the payment.

The proposed regulations, which were published in the *Federal Register* October 17, 2000 (65 FR 61292), are reproduced below.

DEPARTMENT OF THE TREASURY

Internal Revenue Service

26 CFR Parts 1, 5f, and 31

[REG-246249-96]

RIN 1545-AW48

Information Reporting Requirements for Certain Payments Made on Behalf of Another Person, Payments to Joint Payees, and Payments of Gross Proceeds from Sales Involving Investment Advisers

AGENCY: Internal Revenue Service (IRS), Treasury.

ACTION: * * * notice of proposed rulemaking; and notice of public hearing.

SUMMARY: * * * This document contains proposed regulations under section 6041 that clarify who is the payee for information reporting purposes if a check or other instrument is made payable to joint payees, provide information reporting requirements for escrow agents and other persons making payments on behalf of another person, and clarify that the amount to be reported paid is the gross amount of the payment. This document also contains proposed regulations under section 6045 that remove investment advisers from the list of exempt recipients. In addition, this document provides notice of a public hearing on these proposed regulations.

DATES: Written or electronic comments must be received by January 17, 2001. Requests to speak (with outlines of oral comments) at a public hearing scheduled for February 7, 2001, at 10 a.m. must be submitted by January 24, 2001.

ADDRESSES: Send submissions to: CC:M&SP:RU (REG-246249-96), room 5226, Internal Revenue Service, POB 7604, Ben Franklin Station, Washington, DC 20044. In the alternative, submissions may be hand delivered Monday through Friday between the hours of 8 a.m. and 5 p.m. to: CC:M&SP:RU (REG-246249-96), Courier's Desk, Internal Revenue Service, 1111 Constitution Avenue, NW., Washington, DC, or sent electronically via the IRS Internet site at http://www.irs.gov/tax_regs/regslist.html. The public hearing will be held in the IRS Auditorium, Seventh Floor, Internal Revenue Service Building, 1111 Constitution Avenue, NW., Washington, DC.

FOR FURTHER INFORMATION CONTACT: Concerning the regulations, Nancy L. Rose, (202) 622-4910; concerning submission of comments, the hearing, and/or to be placed on the building access list to attend the hearing, Guy R. Traynor, (202) 622-7190 (not toll-free numbers).

SUPPLEMENTARY INFORMATION:

Paperwork Reduction Act

The collection of information contained in this notice of proposed rulemaking has been submitted to the Office of Management and Budget for review in accordance with the Paperwork Reduction Act of 1995 (44 U.S.C. 3507(d)). Comments on the collection of information should be sent to the Office of Management and Budget, Attn: Desk Officer for the Department of Treasury, Office of Information and Regulatory Affairs, Washington, DC 20503, with copies to the Internal Revenue Service, Attn: IRS Reports Clearance Officer,W:CAR:MP:FP:S:O, Washington, DC 20224. Comments on the collection of information should be received by December 19, 2000. Comments are specifically requested concerning:

Whether the proposed collection of information is necessary for the proper operation of the functions of the Internal Revenue Service, including whether the information will have practical utility;

The accuracy of the estimated burden associated with the proposed collection of information (see below);

How the quality, utility, and clarity of the information to be collected may be enhanced;

How the burden of complying with the proposed collection of information may be minimized, including through the application of automated collection techniques or other forms of information technology; and

Estimates of capital or start-up costs and costs of operation, maintenance, and purchase of service to provide information.

The collection of information in these proposed regulations is in §§ 1.6041-1(e) and 1.6045-1(c)(3). This information is required to determine if taxpayers have properly reported amounts received as income. The collection of information is mandatory. The likely respondents are businesses and other for-profit institutions.

The estimate of the reporting burden in proposed § 1.6041-1 is reflected in the burden of Form 1099-MISC, Miscellaneous Income, which is currently 14 minutes per form. The estimate of the reporting burden in proposed § 1.6045-1 is reflected in the burden of Form 1099-B, Proceeds of Broker and Barter Exchange Transactions, which is currently 15 minutes per form.

An agency may not conduct or sponsor, and a person is not required to respond to, a collection of information unless it displays a valid control number assigned by the Office of Management and Budget.

Books or records relating to the collection of information must be retained as long as their contents may become material in the administration of any internal revenue law. Generally tax returns and tax return information are confidential, as required by 26 U.S.C. 6103.

Background and Explanation of Provisions

1. *Proposed Regulations Under Section 6041*

Section 6041 provides that all persons engaged in a trade or business that make certain payments in the course of that trade or business to another person of $600 or more in a taxable year must report the amount of the payments and the name and address of the recipient.

Section 3406(a) provides that a payor must withhold tax from reportable payments under certain circumstances, for example, if the payee has failed to furnish a valid taxpayer identification number to the payor in the manner required. "Reportable payments" include payments that are required to be reported under sections 6041 and 6045. Section 3406(b)(3)(A) and (C). The party that is responsible for reporting the payments under sections 6041 and 6045 is also responsible for any backup withholding required under section 3406.

These proposed regulations address certain issues identified by the Commissioner's Information Reporting Program Advisory Committee (IRPAC) and take into account comments and information provided by IRPAC members representing the banking, real estate, insurance, and securities industries.

a. *Payments to Joint Payees*

The proposed regulations clarify the definition of fixed and determinable income in § 1.6041-1(c) when a payment is made payable to joint payees. This issue was discussed in papers presented at IRPAC meetings in May 1994 and May 1995. The regulations provide that a payment made jointly to two or more payees may be fixed and determinable income to one payee even though the payment is not fixed and

determinable income to another payee. For example, when a payment in consideration for services is made payable to joint payees, one of whom is the service provider, an information return must be made showing the service provider as the payee if the payment is fixed and determinable income to the service provider, even if the payment is not fixed and determinable income to the other payee. See, e.g., Situation 2 of Rev. Rul. 70-608 (1970-2 C.B. 286).

b. *Identification of Payor*

A payment reportable under section 6041 may be made by a person on behalf of another person that is the actual source of the funds. Under certain circumstances this so-called middleman, and not the person that provided the funds, is the payor obligated to report the payment under section 6041. See, e.g., Rev. Rul. 93-70 (1993-2 C.B. 294).

Consistent with Rev. Rul. 93-70, the proposed regulations add a new paragraph (e)(1) to § 1.6041-1 that provides that a person that makes a payment on behalf of another person and performs a management or oversight function in connection with, or has a significant economic interest in, the payment must report under section 6041. A management or oversight function is an activity that is more than merely administrative or ministerial. For example, a person that merely writes checks at the direction of others in connection with a transaction, sometimes referred to as a paying agent, is performing only an administrative or ministerial function and is not a payor. In contrast, a person that exercises discretion or supervision in connection with a payment is performing a management or oversight function and is a payor. A significant economic interest in a payment is an economic interest that would be compromised if the payment were not made. For example a bank has a significant economic interest in a payment to a contractor when damage occurs to property securing a mortgage held by the bank. With this standard, which was also discussed in the IRPAC papers of May 1994 and May 1995, the proposed regulations attempt to replace disparate revenue rulings with a consistent and easily administrable rule that can be applied to a variety of factual situations involving middlemen.

Section 1.6041-1(e)(2) of the proposed regulations provides an exception to the general rule of § 1.6041-1(e)(1) by referencing the procedures in Rev. Proc. 84-33 (1984-1 C.B. 502) for an optional method for payors to designate a paying agent to file information returns and backup withhold.

The proposed regulations include examples, derived primarily from revenue rulings and private letter rulings, which are intended to be all-inclusive. Rulings that are factually encompassed by the proposed regulations will be obsoleted. Comments are requested identifying other factually relevant rulings or suggesting appropriate additional examples.

* * *

d. *Revenue Rulings to Become Obsolete*

As discussed above, the proposed regulations apply to the factual situations addressed in the following revenue rulings, which will become obsolete:

* * *

Rev. Rul. 70-608, Situations 1, 2, and 5 (1970-2 C.B. 286)

Rev. Rul. 69-595 (1969-2 C.B. 242)

* * *

2. *Proposed Regulations Under Section 6045*

Section 6045 provides that a broker must file an information return showing the name and address of the broker's customer and other details, such as the amount of the gross proceeds of the transaction, as the Secretary may require. Section 6045(c) defines a broker as a dealer, a barter exchange, or any other person who, for a consideration, regularly acts as a middleman with respect to property or services.

Section 1.6045-1(a)(2) provides that a customer is the person who makes a sale effected by a broker, if the broker acts as (i) an agent for the customer in the sale, (ii) a principal in the sale, or (iii) the party in the sale responsible for paying or crediting the proceeds to the customer. Under § 1.6045-1(h), a broker must treat the person whose name appears on the broker's books and records as the principal.

Section 5f.6045-1(c)(3), also published as proposed regulations (49 FR 22343), provides that no return of information is required with respect to a sale effected for a customer that is an exempt recipient. Among the categories of exempt recipients is a person registered under the Investment Advisers Act of 1940 who regularly acts as a broker (an investment adviser).

Section 5f.6045-1(c)(3)(iii) provides that, in a cash on delivery or similar transaction, only the broker that receives the gross proceeds against delivery of the securities sold is required to report a sale, unless the broker's customer is another broker (a second-party broker) that is an exempt recipient. In that case, only the second-party broker is required to report.

One effect of these provisions is to shift the reporting requirement in a cash on delivery transaction from the broker that receives the gross proceeds against delivery of the securities to an investment adviser.

* * *

Commentators on the proposed regulations objected to the imposition of the reporting obligation under section 6045(a) on investment advisers because (1) investment advisers generally do not have first-hand knowledge that a sale has been completed, and (2) investment advisers generally do not handle the proceeds of a sale and, consequently, cannot comply with the backup withholding requirements of section 3406. Investment adviser reporting issues were also the subject of IRPAC papers presented at meetings in November 1995 and October 1997.

These proposed regulations withdraw the 1984 proposed regulations. In general, they propose to incorporate the provisions of § 5f.6045-1 into § 1.6045-1(c)(3) and (4). The proposed regulations also remove investment advisers from the list of exempt recipients and revise current § 5f.6045-1(c)(4) *Examples 4* and *5* to clarify that, under the revised rules, an investment adviser that initiates a sale on behalf of a customer is required to make a return of information only if the sale relates to an investment account in the investment adviser's name (i.e., the identity of the customer is not disclosed to the account custodian).

Proposed Effective Date

The provisions of these regulations under sections 6041 and 3406 are proposed to be applicable for payments made on or after the beginning of the first calendar year that begins after these regulations are published in the **Federal Register** as final regulations. The provisions of these regulations under section 6045 are proposed to be applicable for sales effected on or after the beginning of the first calendar year that begins after the date these regulations are published in the **Federal Register** as final regulations.

Special Analyses

It has been determined that this notice of proposed rulemaking is not a significant regulatory action as defined in Executive Order 12866. Therefore, a regulatory assessment is not required. It has also been determined that section 553(b) of the Administrative Procedure Act (5 U.S.C. chapter 5) does not apply to these regulations. An initial regulatory flexibility analysis has been prepared for the collection of information in this notice of proposed rulemaking under 5 U.S.C. section 603. The analysis is set forth in this preamble under the heading "Initial Regulatory Flexibility Analysis." Pursuant to section 7805(f) of the Internal Revenue Code, this notice of proposed rulemaking will be submitted to the Chief Counsel for Advocacy of the Small Business Administration for comment on its impact on small business.

Initial Regulatory Flexibility Analysis

The collection of information proposed in § 1.6041-1(e) is needed to clarify the requirements for filing an information return under section 6041 when a person makes a payment on behalf of another person or to joint payees. The objectives of the proposed regulations are to provide uniform, practicable, and administrable rules under section 6041 for persons making payments on behalf of another person or to joint payees. The types of small entities to which the proposed regulations may apply are small businesses. An estimate of the number of small entities affected is not feasible because of the large variety of entities and transactions to which the proposed regulations may apply. However, in 1997 a total of 73,273,621 Forms 1099-MISC were filed with the IRS. The number of 1997 Forms 1099-MISC that related to transactions that involved payments made on behalf of another person or to joint payees cannot be determined. The current estimated reporting burden relating to Form 1099-MISC is 14 minutes per form. No special professional skills are necessary for preparation of the reports or records. There are no known Federal rules that duplicate, overlap, or conflict with these proposed regulations. The regulations proposed are considered to have the least economic impact on small entities of all alternatives considered.

The collection of information in proposed § 1.6045-1(c)(3) will not have a significant economic impact on a substantial number of small entities. The proposed regulations will relieve investment advisers of the requirement to make information returns under section 6045(a),

and few, if any, financial custodians that may be affected by the regulations are small entities.

Comments and Public Hearing

Before these proposed regulations are adopted as final regulations, consideration will be given to any electronic or written comments (a signed original and eight (8) copies) that are submitted timely (in the manner described in the ADDRESSES caption) to the IRS. The IRS and Treasury Department request comments on the clarity of the proposed rules and how they may be made easier to understand. All comments will be available for public inspection and copying.

A public hearing has been scheduled for February 7, 2001, beginning at 10 a.m. in the IRS Auditorium, Seventh Floor, Internal Revenue Building, 1111 Constitution Avenue, NW., Washington, DC. Due to building security procedures, visitors must enter at the 10th Street entrance, located between Constitution and Pennsylvania Avenues, NW. In addition, all visitors must present photo identification to enter the building. Because of access restrictions, visitors will not be admitted beyond the immediate entrance area more than 15 minutes before the hearing starts. For information about having your name placed on the building access list to attend the hearing, see the "FOR FURTHER INFORMATION CONTACT" section of the preamble.

The rules of 26 CFR 601.601(a)(3) apply to the hearing. Persons who wish to present oral comments at the hearing must submit written comments and an outline of the topics to be discussed and the time to be devoted to each topic (signed original and eight (8) copies) by January 24, 2001. A period of 10 minutes will be allotted to each person for making comments. An agenda showing the scheduling of the speakers will be prepared after the deadline for receiving outlines has passed. Copies of the agenda will be available free of charge at the hearing.

Drafting Information

The principal author of these regulations is Donna M. Crisalli, Office of the Associate Chief Counsel (Income Tax & Accounting). However, other personnel from the IRS and Treasury Department participated in their development.

List of Subjects

26 CFR Parts 1 and 5f

Income taxes, Reporting and recordkeeping requirements.

26 CFR Part 31

Employment taxes, Income taxes, Penalties, Railroad retirement, Reporting and recordkeeping requirements, Social security, Unemployment compensation.

Proposed Amendments to the Regulations

Accordingly, under the authority of 26 U.S.C. 7805, the notice of proposed rulemaking (LR-62-84) amending 26 CFR part 1 that was published in the **Federal Register** on May 29, 1984 (49 FR 22343) is withdrawn. In addition, 26 CFR parts 1, 5f, and 31 are proposed to be amended as follows:

PART 1—INCOME TAXES

Paragraph 1. The authority citation for part 1 is amended by adding an entry in numerical order to read in part as follows:

Authority: 26 U.S.C. 7805 * * *

Section 1.6041-1 also issued under 26 U.S.C. 6041(a). * * *

Par. 2. Section 1.6041-1 is amended by:

1. Removing the language "paragraph (g)" in the second sentence of paragraph (b)(1) and adding the language "paragraph (i)" in its place.

2. Adding two sentences after the fourth sentence of paragraph (c).

* * *

4. Adding new paragraphs (e) * * *.

The additions and revisions read as follows:

§ 1.6041-1 Return of information as to payments of $600 or more.

* * * * *

(c) * * * A payment made jointly to two or more payees may be fixed and determinable income to one payee even though the payment is not fixed and determinable income to another payee. For example, property insurance proceeds paid jointly to the owner of damaged property and to a contractor that repairs the property may be fixed and determinable income to the contractor but not fixed and determinable income to the owner. * * *

* * * * *

(e) *Payment made on behalf of another person*—(1) *In general.* A person that makes a payment in the course of its trade or business on behalf of another person is the payor that must make a return of information under this section with respect to that payment if the payment is described in paragraph (a) of this section and, under all the facts and circumstances, that person—

(i) Performs management or oversight functions (i.e., performs more than mere administrative or ministerial functions) in connection with the payment; or

(ii) Has a significant economic interest in the payment. (2) *Optional method to report.* A person that makes a payment on behalf of another person but is not required to make an information return under paragraph (e)(1) of this section may elect to do so pursuant to the procedures established in Rev. Proc. 84-33 (1984-1 C.B. 502) (optional method for a paying agent to report and deposit amounts withheld for payors under the statutory provisions of backup withholding) (see § 601.601(d)(2) of this chapter).

(3) *Examples.* The provisions of this paragraph (e) are illustrated by the following examples:

Example 1. Bank B provides financing to C, a real estate developer, for a construction project. B puts the funds in an escrow account and makes disbursements from the account for labor, materials, services, and other expenses related to the construction project. In connection with the payments, B performs the following functions on behalf of C: approves payments to the general contractor or subcontractors; ensures that loan proceeds are properly applied and that all approved bills are properly paid to avoid mechanics or materialmen's liens; conducts site inspections to determine whether work has been completed (but does not check the quality of the work); evaluates and assesses the cost of the project, including costs of changes; and communicates resulting concerns to C or to the general contractor so that modifications can be made or additional funding obtained. B is performing management or oversight functions in connection with the payment and is subject to the information reporting requirements of section 6041 with respect to payments from the escrow fund.

* * *

* * *

(j) *Effective date.* The provisions of paragraphs (b), (c), (e), and (f) apply to payments made on or after the beginning of the first calendar year that begins after these regulations are published in the **Federal Register** as final regulations.

§ *1.6041-3 Payments for which no return of information is required under Section 6041.* [Amended]

* * *

Par. 4. Section 1.6045-1, as in effect on January 1, 2001, is amended as follows:

* * *

2. Revising paragraphs (c)(3) and (c)(4).

3. Removing the language "5f.6045-1(c)(3)(ii) of this chapter" and adding the language "paragraph (c)(3)(iii) of this section" in its place in each place it appears in paragraph (g)(4) *Examples 1, 4, 5, 6*, and 7(i).

The revisions read as follows:

§ *1.6045-1 Returns of information of brokers and barter exchanges.*

(a) *Definitions.* * * *

(c) * * *

(3) *Exceptions*—(i) *Sales effected for exempt recipients*—(A) *In general.* No return of information is required with respect to a sale effected for a customer that is an exempt recipient under paragraph (c)(3)(i)(B) of this section.

(B) *Exempt recipient defined.* The term *exempt recipient* means—

(*1*) A corporation as defined in section 7701(a)(3), whether domestic or foreign;

(*2*) An organization exempt from taxation under section 501(a) or an individual retirement plan;

* * *

(C) *Exemption certificate.* A broker may treat a person described in paragraph (c)(3)(i)(B) of this section as an exempt recipient based on a properly completed exemption certificate (as provided in § 31.3406(h)-3) of this chapter or on the broker's actual knowledge that the payee is a person described in paragraph (c)(3)(i)(B) of this section. A broker may require an exempt recipient to file a properly completed exemption certificate and may treat an exempt recipient that fails to do so as a recipient that is not exempt.

* * *

(iv) *Cash on delivery transactions.* In the case of a sale of securities through a cash on delivery account, a delivery versus payment account, or other similar account or transaction, only the broker that receives the gross proceeds from the sale against delivery of the securities sold is required to report the sale. If, however, the broker's customer is another broker (second-party broker) that is an exempt recipient, then only the second-party broker is required to report the sale.

(v) *Fiduciaries and partnerships.* No return of information is required with respect to a sale effected by a custodian or trustee in its capacity as such or a redemption of a partnership interest by a partnership provided the sale is otherwise reported by the custodian or trustee on a properly filed Form 1041, or the redemption is otherwise reported by the partnership on a properly filed Form 1065, and all Schedule K-1 reporting requirements are satisfied.

* * *

(xiii) *Effective date.* The provisions of this paragraph (c)(3) apply for sales effected on or after the beginning of the first calendar year that begins after the date these regulations are published in the **Federal Register** as final regulations.

* * *

Robert E. Wenzel

Deputy Commissioner of Internal Revenue

¶ 20,253

IRS proposed regulations: Health Insurance Portability and Accountability Act (HIPAA): Nondiscrimination rules: Group health plans: Eligibility for benefits: Health factors.—The IRS has issued proposed regulations interpreting and providing guidance on the nondiscrimination provisions under HIPAA. The regulations, among other things, explain the application of the provisions to premiums, describe "similarly situated individuals," and clarify that more favorable treatment of individuals with medical needs generally is permitted. The text of the proposed regulations is provided by the text of the IRS temporary regulations issued at the same time as the proposed regulations. The preamble of the temporary regulations is at ¶ 23,181. The text of the temporary regulations is at ¶ 13,968R-10.

The proposed regulations, which were published in the *Federal Register* January 8, 2001 (65 FR 1435), are reproduced below.

DEPARTMENT OF THE TREASURY

Internal Revenue Service

26 CFR Part 54

[REG-114082-00]

RIN 1545-AY32

HIPAA Nondiscrimination

AGENCY: Internal Revenue Service (IRS), Treasury.

ACTION: Notice of proposed rulemaking by cross-reference to temporary regulations.

SUMMARY: Elsewhere in this issue of the **Federal Register,** the IRS is issuing temporary and final regulations governing the provisions prohibiting discrimination based on a health factor for group health plans. The IRS is issuing the temporary and final regulations at the same time that the Pension and Welfare Benefits Administration of the U.S. Department of Labor and the Health Care Financing Administration of the U.S. Department of Health and Human Services are issuing substantially similar interim final regulations governing the provisions prohibiting discrimination based on a health factor for group health plans and issuers of health insurance coverage offered in connection with a group health plan under the Employee Retirement Income Security Act of 1974 and the Public Health Service Act. The temporary regulations provide guidance to employers and group health plans relating to the group health plan nondiscrimination requirements. The text of those temporary regulations also serves as the text of these proposed regulations.

DATES: Written comments and requests for a public hearing must be received by *[INSERT DATE 90 DAYS AFTER PUBLICATION OF THIS DOCUMENT IN THE FEDERAL REGISTER]*.

ADDRESSES: Send submissions to: CC:M & SP:RU (REG-114082-00), room 5226, Internal Revenue Service, POB 7604, Ben Franklin Station, Washington, DC 20044. Submissions may be hand-delivered to: CC:M & SP:RU (REG-114082-00), room 5226, Internal Revenue Service, 1111 Constitution Avenue, NW., Washington, DC.

Alternatively, taxpayers may submit comments electronically via the Internet by selecting the "Tax Regs" option on the IRS Home Page, or by submitting comments directly to the IRS Internet site at:

http://www.irs.gov/tax_regs/regslist.html.

FOR FURTHER INFORMATION CONTACT: Concerning the regulations, Russ Weinheimer at 202-622-6080; concerning submissions of comments or requests for a hearing, Sonya Cruse at 202-622-7190 (not toll-free numbers).

SUPPLEMENTARY INFORMATION:

Paperwork Reduction Act

The collection of information referenced in this notice of proposed rulemaking has been submitted to the Office of Management and Budget for review in accordance with the Paperwork Reduction Act of 1995 (44 U.S.C. 3507(d)).

An agency may not conduct or sponsor, and a person is not required to respond to, a collection of information unless it displays a valid control number assigned by the Office of Management and Budget.

The collections of information are in § 54.9802-1T (see the temporary regulations published elsewhere in this issue of the **Federal Register**). The collections of information are required so that individuals denied enrollment in a group health plan based on one or more health factors will be apprised of their right to enroll in the plan without regard to their health. The likely respondents are business or other for-profit institutions, nonprofit institutions, small businesses or organizations, and Taft-Hartley trusts. Responses to this collection of information are required of plans that have denied enrollment to individuals based on one or more health factors.

Books or records relating to a collection of information must be retained as long as their contents may become material in the administration of any internal revenue law. Generally tax returns and tax return information are confidential, as required by 26 U.S.C. 6103.

Comments on the collection of information should be sent to the **Office of Management and Budget,** Attn: Desk Officer for the Department of the Treasury, Office of Information and Regulatory Affairs, Washington, DC 20503, with copies to the **Internal Revenue Service,** Attn: IRS Reports Clearance Officer, W:CAR:MP:FP:S:O, Washington, DC 20224. Comments on the collection of information should be received by [*INSERT DATE 90 DAYS AFTER PUBLICATION OF THIS DOCUMENT IN THE FEDERAL REGISTER*]. Comments are specifically requested concerning:

• Whether the proposed collection of information is necessary for the proper performance of the functions of the Internal Revenue Service, including whether the information will have practical utility;

• The accuracy of the estimated burden associated with the proposed collection of information (see the preamble to the temporary regulations published elsewhere in this issue of the **Federal Register**);

• How to enhance the quality, utility, and clarity of the information to be collected;

• How to minimize the burden of complying with the proposed collection of information, including the application of automated collection techniques or other forms of information technology; and

• Estimates of capital or start-up costs and costs of operation, maintenance, and purchase of services to provide information.

Background

The temporary regulations published elsewhere in this issue of the **Federal Register** add a new § 54.9802-1T to the Miscellaneous Excise Tax Regulations.[1] When these proposed regulations are published as final regulations, they will supplement the final regulations in § 54.9802-1 being published elsewhere in this issue of the **Federal Register.** The proposed, temporary, and final regulations are being published as part of a joint rulemaking with the Department of Labor and the Department of Health and Human Services (the joint rulemaking).

The text of those temporary regulations also serves as the text of these proposed regulations. The preamble to the temporary regulations explains the temporary regulations.

Special Analyses

This regulation is not subject to the Unfunded Mandates Reform Act of 1995 because the regulation is an interpretive regulation. It has also been determined that section 553(b) of the Administrative Procedure Act (5 U.S.C. chapter 5) does not apply to this regulation. For further information and for analyses relating to the joint rulemaking, see the preamble to the joint rulemaking. Pursuant to section 7805(f) of the Internal Revenue Code, this notice of proposed rulemaking will be submitted to the Chief Counsel for Advocacy of the Small Business Administration for comment on its impact on small business.

Comments and Requests for a Public Hearing

Before these proposed regulations are adopted as final regulations, consideration will be given to any written comments (a signed original and eight (8) copies) that are submitted timely to the IRS. Comments are specifically requested on the clarity of the proposed regulations and how they may be made easier to understand. All comments will be available for public inspection and copying. A public hearing may be scheduled if requested in writing by a person that timely submits written comments. If a public hearing is scheduled, notice of the date, time, and place for the hearing will be published in the **Federal Register.**

Drafting Information

The principal author of these proposed regulations is Russ Weinheimer, Office of the Operating Division Counsel/Associate Chief Counsel (Tax Exempt and Government Entities), IRS. However, other personnel from the IRS and Treasury Department participated in their development. The proposed regulations, as well as the temporary regulations, have been developed in coordination with personnel from the U.S. Department of Labor and the U.S. Department of Health and Human Services.

List of Subjects in 26 CFR Part 54

Excise taxes, Health insurance, Pensions, Reporting and recordkeeping requirements.

Proposed Amendments to the Regulations

Accordingly, 26 CFR part 54 is proposed to be amended as follows:

PART 54—PENSION EXCISE TAXES

Paragraph 1. The authority citation for part 54 continues to read in part as follows:

Authority: 26 U.S.C. 7805 ***

Par. 2. Section 54.9802-1 is amended to read as follows:

§ 54.9802-1 Prohibiting discrimination against participants and beneficiaries based on a health factor.

[The text of the proposed amendments to this section is the same as the text of § 54.9802-1T published elsewhere in this issue of the **Federal Register**].

Robert E. Wenzel

Deputy Commissioner of Internal Revenue

---

[1] A previous § 54.9802-1T was published in the **Federal Register** on April 8, 1997. By operation of section 7805(e) of the Internal Revenue Code, the previous § 54.9802-1T expired on April 8, 2000. Proposed regulations containing the same text as previous § 54.9802-1T were also published on April 8, 1997, and final regulations based on those proposed regulations are being published elsewhere in this issue of the **Federal Register** as § 54.9802-1. The new § 54.9802-1T being published elsewhere in this issue of the **Federal Register** consists almost entirely of new guidance not contained in the previous § 54.9802-1T.

¶ 20,254

IRS proposed regulations: Health Insurance Portability and Accountability Act of 1996 (HIPAA): Nondiscrimination requirements: Grandfathered church plans.—The IRS has issued proposed regulations containing guidance regarding the exception from the nondiscrimination requirements, added by the Health Insurance Portability and Accountability Act of 1996 (HIPAA), applicable to group health plans under Code Sec. 9802(a) and (b), for certain grandfathered church plans.

The proposed regulations were published in the *Federal Register* on January 8, 2001 (66 FR 1437).

The final regulations, which were published in the Federal Register on December 13, 2006 (71 FR 75055), are reproduced at ¶ 13,968R-4 (IRS Reg. Sec. 54.9802-2). The preamble to the final regulations is at ¶ 24,508K.

¶ 20,255

IRS proposed regulations: Pension and Welfare Benefits Administration (PWBA): Bona fide wellness programs: Health Insurance Portability and Accountability Act of 1996 (HIPAA): Nondiscrimination requirements.—The IRS, in conjunction with the PWBA and the Department of Health and Human Services, has issued proposed regulations to establish and elucidate the meaning of "bona fide wellness program" with regard to nondiscrimination provisions of the Code and ERISA, as added by HIPAA.

The proposed regulations were published in the *Federal Register* on January 8, 2001 (66 FR 1421). The PWBA's proposed regulations were at ¶ 20,534H.

The final regulations, which were published in the Federal Register on December 13, 2006 (71 FR 75014), are reproduced at ¶ 13,968R-3 (IRS Reg. Sec. 54.9802-1). The preamble to the final regulations is at ¶ 23,240.

¶ 20,256

IRS proposed regulations: Transfer of excess assets: Defined benefit plans: Funding of retiree health accounts: Minimum cost requirement.—The IRS has issued proposed regulations that clarify the circumstances under which an employer may transfer excess defined benefit plan assets to a retiree health benefit account. The proposed regulations provide that an employer who significantly reduces retiree health coverage during its cost maintenance period does not satisfy the minimum cost requirement of Code Sec. 420(c)(3) and clarify the circumstances under which an employer is considered to have significantly reduced retiree health coverage during the cost maintenance period.

The proposed regulations, which were published in the *Federal Register* January 5, 2001 (66 FR 1066), are reproduced below.

The regulations were finalized by T.D. 8948 and published in the *Federal Register* on June 19, 2001 (66 FR 32897). The regulations are reproduced at ¶ 13,031. The preamble is reproduced at ¶ 23,182.

¶ 20,257

IRS proposed regulations: Third-party contacts: Determination: Tax liability: Collection.—The IRS has issued proposed regulations which amend Code Sec. 7602 to prohibit IRS officers and employees from contacting any person, other than the taxpayer, concerning a determination or collection of the taxpayer's liability without first giving the taxpayer reasonable advance notice that such contacts may be made. Contacts with pension plans that relate to determining the plan's deferred compensation are not considered contacts being made "with respect to" the determination of the plan participants' tax liabilities.

Portions of the preamble of the proposed regulations reproduced below were published in the *Federal Register* on January 2, 2001 (66 FR 77).

DEPARTMENT OF THE TREASURY

Internal Revenue Service

26 CFR Part 301

[REG-104906-99]

RIN 1545-AX04

Third Party Contacts

AGENCY: Internal Revenue Service (IRS), Treasury.

ACTION: Notice of proposed rulemaking.

SUMMARY: This document contains proposed regulations providing guidance on third-party contacts made with respect to the determination or collection of tax liabilities. The proposed regulations reflect changes to section 7602 of the Internal Revenue Code made by section 3417 of the Internal Revenue Service Restructuring and Reform Act of 1998. The proposed regulations potentially affect all taxpayers whose Federal tax liabilities are being determined or collected by the IRS.

DATES: Written and electronic comments and requests for a public hearing must be received by 90 days after the date these proposed regulations are published in the Federal Register.

ADDRESSES: Send submission to: CC:M & SP:RU (REG-104906-99), room 5226, Internal Revenue Service, POB 7604, Ben Franklin Station, Washington, DC 20044. Submissions may be hand delivered Monday through Friday between the hours of 8 a.m. and 5 p.m. to: CC:M & SP:RU (REG-104906-99), Courier's Desk, Internal Revenue Service, 1111 Constitution Avenue, NW., Washington, DC. Alternatively, taxpayers may submit comments electronically via the Internet by selecting the "Tax Regs" option on the IRS Home Page, or by submitting comments directly to the IRS Internet site at http://www.irs.gov/tax_regs/reglist.html.

FOR FURTHER INFORMATION CONTACT: Concerning the regulations, Bryan T. Camp, 202-622-3620 (not a toll-free number); concerning submissions, Sonya Cruse at 202-622-7180 (not a toll-free number).

SUPPLEMENTARY INFORMATION:

Background

This document contains proposed regulations amending the Procedure and Administration Regulations (26 CFR part 301) relating to the exercise by officers and employees of the IRS of the authority given them under section 7602 of the Internal Revenue Code (Code). Section 3417 of the IRS Restructuring and Reform Act of 1998 (RRA 1998), Public Law 105-206 (112 Stat. 685), amends section 7602 to prohibit IRS officers or employees from contacting any person other than the taxpayer with respect to the determination or collection of the taxpayer's liability without first giving the taxpayer reasonable advance notice that such contacts may be made. The section further requires that a record of the persons contacted be provided to the taxpayer both periodically and upon the taxpayer's request. The section sets forth a number of exceptions to its requirements. These proposed regulations interpret and implement the amendments made by section 3417 of RRA 1998.

Explanation of Provisions

Section 3417 of RRA 1998 amended section 7602 to prohibit IRS officers or employees from contacting any person other than the taxpayer with respect to the determination or collection of the taxpayer's liability without giving the taxpayer reasonable advance notice that contacts with persons other than the taxpayer may be made.

Section 3417 was added to the bill by the Senate Finance Committee. In explaining the reasons for its proposal, the Senate Finance Committee expressed a concern that third-party contacts "may have a chilling effect on the taxpayer's business and could damage the taxpayer's reputation in the community," and that taxpayers "should have the opportunity to resolve issues and volunteer information before the IRS contacts third parties." S. Rep. No. 174, 105th Cong., 2nd Sess. 77 (1998). At the same time, the Senate Finance Committee stated that "[c]ontacts with government officials relating to matters such as the location of assets or the taxpayers current address are not restricted by this provision." *Id.*

As originally drafted by the Senate Finance Committee, the third-party contact rule would have prohibited most IRS contacts with third parties prior to taxpayer notification of the specific contact to be made. It contained exceptions for notification of contacts (i) that were authorized by a taxpayer, (ii) that would jeopardize collection, or (iii) with respect to pending criminal investigations. The require ment for specific pre-contact notice was modified by the Conference Committee to require only a generalized notice of IRS intent to contact third parties, followed by post-contact notice of specific contacts. Further, the exceptions were expanded to include situations that might involve reprisal against the third party or any other person. With regard to the general, pre-contact notice, the Conference Report states that "this notice will be provided as part of an existing IRS notice provided to taxpayers." H.R. Rep. No. 599, 105th Cong., 2nd Sess. at 277 (1998).

The provision as enacted and the particular changes made by the Conference Committee to the Senate proposal support an interpretative approach that balances taxpayers' business and reputational interests, articulated as the principal impetus for the Senate proposal, with third parties' privacy interests and the IRS' responsibility to administer the internal revenue laws effectively. The replacement of specific pre-contact identification of intended third-party contacts, as proposed by the Senate, with a general pre-contact notice accompanied by post-contact identification, still enables taxpayers to come forward with information before third parties are contacted. The modifications still allow taxpayers to address business or reputational concerns arising from IRS contact with third parties, but accomplish this result without impeding the ability of the IRS to make those third-party contacts that are necessary to administer the internal revenue laws. The maintenance of the exceptions proposed in the Senate version and the addition of an exception for situations involving potential reprisal express Congressional concern that the business and reputational interests of taxpayers be balanced with the privacy and safety interests of third parties and that certain types of investigations (*i.e.*, those involving jeopardy and potential criminal prosecution) be excepted from the statute.

Accordingly, the proposed regulations attempt to balance among the taxpayer, third party, and governmental interests implicated by the statute. The IRS and Treasury invite public comments on the following specific issues addressed by these proposed regulations, as well as any other issue raised by the new requirements for third-party contacts.

* * *

The Meaning of "with respect to a determination or Collection" of Tax.

Section 7602(c) prohibits IRS employees from contacting any person other than "the" taxpayer "with respect to" the determination or the collection of the tax liability of "such" taxpayer. The term "with respect to" indicates a required nexus between the contact and one of the two enumerated purposes of determining or collecting tax. The use of the words "the" and "such" imply a single affected taxpayer whose liability is being determined. The statute and committee reports do not describe with greater specificity the type of contacts that should be considered "with respect to" the determination or collection of a tax liability, nor how close a nexus must exist between a contact and the purposes described in section 7602(c).

Examination and collection activity is critical to the IRS' mission of "helping [taxpayers] understand and meet their tax responsibilities." Administering the tax laws, however, involves more activities than an individual IRS employee examining a single return selected for audit or collecting unpaid taxes. It also includes: locating taxpayers who may not have fulfilled a filing or payment obligation, monitoring information returns, performing compliance checks to help identify which returns to examine, investigating leads from newspapers and other sources to identify non-filers and underreporters, providing services to taxpayers such as issuing Private Letter Rulings or determining employment status, tracing lost payments, and exchanging information with other taxing authorities and other federal agencies. Moreover, the examination of a single return may significantly affect other taxpayers. **For example, adjustments to items attributable to partnerships or other pass-through entities may significantly affect partners or**

other investors in flow-through entities. Likewise, adjustments on returns of corporate taxpayers may significantly affect the corporations' shareholder liabilities. Broadly stated, almost every third-party contact made by IRS employees could be seen as "with respect to the determination or collection" of tax in that almost every contact may indirectly affect the liability of one or more taxpayers. Not every contact, however, has a direct and immediate nexus to the determination or collection of a particular taxpayer's liability.

The proposed regulations generally provide that a contact must be directly connected to the purpose of determining or collecting an identified taxpayer's liability before the contact is subject to the statute, in contrast to making every contact which may affect a person's liability subject to the statute. An interpretation that requires each IRS employee to report each contact to every taxpayer whose liability could potentially be affected by the contact is overbroad, potentially unadministrable, and could needlessly alarm taxpayers whose returns were not actually being examined and would not in fact be selected for examination. Conversely, an interpretation that a contact was not "with respect to" the determination of liability until a return had been formally selected for examination would unduly elevate administrative concerns over taxpayer business and reputational interests. If a bank is contacted about a particular taxpayer, for example, the reputational concerns caused by the contact do not depend on whether the taxpayer is under formal examination at the time or is merely being screened as part of a process to identify returns for examination. Therefore, although the proposed regulations require a direct connection between the contact and the purpose of examining or collecting a liability of an identified taxpayer's liability before the contact is subject to the statute, they do not require that a formal examination be opened. They instead provide a series of tests and examples to identify classes of contacts which should or should not be subject to the statute under this standard, regardless of whether a formal examination has been opened.

Request for Comments.

The IRS and the Treasury Department are interested in receiving comments on the types of contacts that should be considered to be "with respect to the determination or collection of the liability of such taxpayer" and, when one contact may indirectly affect the liabilities of more than one taxpayer, which taxpayers should receive the general advance notice.

* * *

Special Analyses

This notice of proposed rulemaking is not a significant regulatory action as defined in Executive Order 12866. Therefore, a regulatory assessment is not required. Likewise, section 553(b) of the Administrative Procedure Act (5 U.S.C. chapter 5) does not apply to this regulation, and because the proposed regulations do not impose a collection of information on small entities, the Regulatory Flexibility Act (5 U.S.C. chapter 6) does not apply. Pursuant to section 7805(f) of the Internal Revenue Code, these proposed regulations will be submitted to the Chief Counsel for Advocacy of the Small Business Administration for comment on their impact on small business.

Comments and Requests for a Public Hearing

Before these proposed regulations are adopted as final regulations, consideration will be given to any written comments (a signed original and eight (yes, 8) copies) and electronic comments that are submitted timely to the IRS. The IRS and Treasury Department specifically request comments on the clarity of the proposed regulations and how they can be made easier to understand. All comments will be available for public inspection and copying. A public hearing may be conducted if requested in writing by any person who timely submits written comments. If a public hearing is scheduled, notice of the date, time, and place for the hearing will be published in the **Federal Register**.

Drafting Information

The principal author of these proposed regulations is Bryan T. Camp of the Office of Assistant Chief Counsel (General Litigation). Other personnel from the IRS and Treasury Department have also participated in their drafting and development.

List of Subjects in 26 CFR Part 301

Employment taxes, Estate taxes, Excise taxes, Gift taxes, Income taxes, Penalties, Reporting and recordkeeping requirements.

Proposed Amendments to the Regulations

Accordingly, 26 CFR part 301 is proposed to be amended as follows:

PART 301—PROCEDURES AND ADMINISTRATION

Par. 1. The authority citation for part 301 continues to read in part as follows:

Authority: 26 U.S.C. 7805 * * *

Par. 2. Section 301.7602-2 is added to read as follows:

§ 301.7602-2 Third party contacts.

(a) *In general.* Subject to the exceptions in paragraph (f) of this section, no officer or employee of the Internal Revenue Service (IRS) may contact any person other than the taxpayer with respect to the determination or collection of such taxpayer's tax liability without giving the taxpayer reasonable notice in advance that such contacts may be made. A record of persons so contacted must be made and given to the taxpayer both periodically and upon the taxpayer's request.

(b) *Third-party contact defined.* Contacts subject to section 7602(c) and this regulation shall be called "third-party contacts." A third-party contact is a communication which—

(1) Is initiated by an IRS employee;

(2) Is made to a person other than the taxpayer;

(3) Is made with respect to the determination or collection of the tax liability of such taxpayer;

(4) Discloses the identity of the taxpayer being investigated; and

(5) Discloses the association of the IRS employee with the IRS.

(c) *Elements of third-party contact explained.* (1) *Initiation by an IRS employee*— (i) *Explanation.* For purposes of this section an IRS employee includes all officers and employees of the IRS, the Chief Counsel of the IRS and the National Taxpayer Advocate, as well as any other person who, through a written agreement with the IRS, is subject to disclosure restrictions consistent with section 6103. No inference about the employment or contractual relationship of such other persons with the IRS may be drawn from this regulation for any purpose other than the requirements of section 7602(c). An IRS employee initiates a communication whenever it is the employee who first tries to communicate with a person other than the taxpayer. Returning unsolicited telephone calls or speaking with persons other than the taxpayer as part of an attempt to speak to the taxpayer are not initiations of third-party contacts.

* * *

(2) *Person other than the taxpayer*—(i) *Explanation.* The phrases "person other than the taxpayer" and "third party" are used interchangeably in this section, and do not include—

(A) An officer or employee of the IRS, as defined in paragraph (c)(1)(i) of this section, acting within the scope of his or her employment;

(B) Any computer database or web site regardless of where located and by whom maintained, including databases or web sites maintained on the Internet or in county courthouses, libraries, or any other real or virtual site; or

(C) A current employee, officer, or fiduciary of a taxpayer when acting within the scope of his or her employment or relationship with the taxpayer. Such employee, officer, or fiduciary shall be conclusively presumed to be acting within the scope of his or her employment or relationship during business hours on business premises.

* * *

(3) *With respect to the determination or collection of the tax liability of such taxpayer*—(i) *With respect to.* A contact is "with respect to" the determination or collection of the tax liability of such taxpayer when made for the purpose of either determining or collecting a particular tax liability and when directly connected to that purpose. While a contact made for the purpose of determining a particular taxpayer's tax liability may also affect the tax liability of one or more other taxpayers, such contact is not for that reason alone a contact "with respect to" the determination or collection of those other taxpayers' tax liabilities. Contacts to determine the tax status of a pension plan under Chapter I, Subchapter D (Deferred Compensation), are not "with respect to" the determination of plan participants' tax liabilities. Contacts to determine the tax status of a bond issue under Chapter 1, Subchapter B, Part IV (Tax Exemption Requirements for State and Local Bonds), are not "with respect to" the determination of the bondholders' tax liabilities. Contacts to determine the tax status of an organization under Chapter 1, Subchapter F (Exempt Organizations), are not "with respect to" the determination of the contributors' liabilities, nor are any similar determinations "with respect to" any persons with similar relationships to the taxpayer whose tax liability is being determined or collected.

(ii) *Determination or collection.* A contact is with respect to the "determination or collection" of the tax liability of such taxpayer when made during the administrative determination or collection process. For purposes of this paragraph (c) only, the administrative determination or collection process may include any administrative action to ascertain the correctness of a return, make a return when none has been filed, or determine or collect the tax liability of any person as a transferee or fiduciary under Chapter 71 of title 26.

(iii) *Tax liability.* A "tax liability" means the liability for any tax imposed by Title 26 of the United States Code (including any interest, additional amount, addition to the tax, or assessable penalty) and does not include the liability for any tax imposed by any other jurisdiction nor any liability imposed by other federal statutes.

(iv) *Such taxpayer.* A contact is with respect to the determination or collection of the tax liability of "such taxpayer" when made while determining or collecting the tax liability of a particular, identified taxpayer. Contacts made during an investigation of a particular, identified taxpayer are third-party contacts only as to the particular, identified taxpayer under investigation and not as to any other taxpayer whose tax liabilities might be affected by such contacts.

* * *

(g) *Effective Date.* This section is applicable on the date the final regulations are published in the **Federal Register.**

Charles O. Rossotti

Commissioner of Internal Revenue

¶ 20,258

IRS proposed regulations: Cafeteria plans: Tax treatment: Election of coverage: Revocation of election.—The IRS has issued proposed regulations which amend the text of previously issued proposed regulations (¶ 20,118I, ¶ 20,137Q, and ¶ 20,247) concerning the circumstances under which a cafeteria plan participant may revoke an existing election and make a new election during a period of coverage.

The proposed regulations, which were published in the *Federal Register* January 10, 2001 (66 FR 1923), are reproduced below.

DEPARTMENT OF THE TREASURY

Internal Revenue Service

26 CFR Part 1

REG-209461-79

RIN 1545-AY67

Tax Treatment of Cafeteria Plans

AGENCY: Internal Revenue Service (IRS), Treasury.

ACTION: Partial withdrawal of notice of proposed rulemaking and amendments to notice of proposed rulemaking.

SUMMARY: This document withdraws § 1.125-2 Q & A-6(b),(c), and (d), and amends § 1.125-2 Q & A-6(a) in the notice of proposed

rulemaking relating to cafeteria plans that was published in the **Federal Register** on March 7, 1989. Further, this document amends § 1.125-1 Q & A-8 in the notice of proposed rulemaking relating to cafeteria plans that was published in the Federal Register on May 7, 1984, and amended on November 7, 1997 and March 23, 2000. This withdrawal and amendment are made because of changes made to these rules in the § 1.125-4 final regulations relating to cafeteria plans published elsewhere in this issue of the **Federal Register.**

FOR FURTHER INFORMATION CONTACT: Christine Keller or Janet Laufer at (202) 622-6080 (not a toll-free number).

SUPPLEMENTARY INFORMATION:

DATES: Written or electronically generated comments and requests for a public hearing must be received by **[January 10, 2001]**.

ADDRESSES: Send submissions to: CC:M & SP:RU (REG-209461-79), room 5226, Internal Revenue Service, POB 7604, Ben

Franklin Station, Washington, DC 20044. Submissions may be hand delivered Monday through Friday between the hours of 8 a.m. and 5 p.m. to CC:M & SP:RU (REG-209461-79), Courier's Desk, Internal Revenue Service, 1111 Constitution Avenue, NW., Washington, DC. Alternatively, taxpayers may submit comments electronically via the Internet by selecting the "Tax Regs" option on the IRS Home Page, or by submitting comments directly to the IRS Internet site at http://www.irs.gov/tax_regs/regslist.html.

Background

On March 7, 1989, the IRS issued proposed regulations § 1.125-2 Q & A-6 relating to the circumstances under which participants may revoke existing elections and make new elections under a cafeteria plan. Elsewhere in this issue of the Federal Register the IRS is publishing final regulations under § 1.125-4 that address certain parts of this rule. Accordingly, § 1.125-2 Q & A-6(b), (c), and (d) are withdrawn and § 1.125-2 Q & A-6(a) of this rule is amended.

Further, on May 7, 1984, the IRS issued proposed regulations § 1.125-1 Q & A-8 relating to the requirements that apply to participants' elections under a cafeteria plan. Q & A-8 of these regulations was amended on November 7, 1997 and March 23, 2000 to conform with the § 1.125-4T and § 1.125-4 regulations published on these dates, and is further amended to conform with the final § 1.125-4 regulations published on [**January 10, 2001**].

Partial Withdrawal of Notice of Proposed Rulemaking

Accordingly, under the authority of 26 U.S.C. 7805, § 1.125-2 Q & A-6(b), (c) and (d) in the notice of proposed rulemaking that was published on March 7, 1989 (54 FR 9460) is withdrawn.

List of Subjects in 26 CFR Part 1

Income taxes, Reporting and recordkeeping requirements.

Amendments to Previously Proposed Rules

Accordingly, the proposed rules published on May 7, 1984 (49 FR 19321) and amended on November 7, 1997 (62 FR 60196), and March 23, 2000 (65 FR 15587) and the rules published on March 7, 1989 (54 FR 9460) are amended as follows:

PART 1—INCOME TAXES

Paragraph 1. The authority citation for part 1 continues to read in part as follows:

Authority: 26 U.S.C. 7805 *****

Par. 2. In § 1.125-1, as proposed May 7, 1984 (49 FR 19321) and as amended March 23, 2000 (65 FR 15587), Q & A-8 is amended by removing the last four sentences of A-8 and adding a sentence in their place to read as follows:

§ 1.125-1 Questions and answers relating to cafeteria plan.

*****

Q-8: What requirements apply to participants' elections under a cafeteria plan?

A-8: ***** However, a cafeteria plan may permit a participant to revoke a benefit election after the period of coverage has commenced and make a new election with respect to the remainder of the period of coverage if both the revocation and the new election are permitted under § 1.125-4.

*****

Par. 3. In § 1.125-2, as proposed March 7, 1989 (54 FR 9460) and as amended March 23, 2000 (65 FR 15587), A-6 is amended by removing A-6(b), A-6(c), and A-6(d), redesignating A-6(e) as paragraph A-6(b), removing the last 5 sentences of A-6(a) and adding a sentence in their place to read as follows:

Q-6: In what circumstance may participants revoke existing elections and make new elections under a cafeteria plan?

A-6: *****

(a) ***** However, to the extent permitted under § 1.125-4, the terms of a cafeteria plan may permit a participant to revoke an existing election and to make a new election with respect to the remaining portion of the period of coverage.

*****

Robert E. Wenzel

Deputy Commissioner of Internal Revenue

¶ 20,259

IRS: Proposed regulations: Election: S Corporation: Small business trust.—The IRS has issued proposed regulations which relate to "tiered" S Corporations and the election and tax treatment of small business trusts. The proposed regulations state that a trust described under Code Sec. 401(a) or Code Sec. 501(c)(3), is not a "deferral entity" for purposes of Reg. § 1.444-2T. Therefore, an S Corporation with such a trust may make an election of a taxable year other than the required taxable year.

The preamble and portions of the proposed regulations reproduced below were published in the *Federal Register* on December 29, 2000 (65 FR 82963).

The final regulations were published in the *Federal Register* on May 14, 2002 (67 FR 34388). The regulations are reproduced at ¶ 13,152C. The preamble is at ¶ 23,191.

¶ 20,260

IRS proposed regulations: Excise tax: Excess benefit transactions: Tax exempt organizations: Disqualified persons.—The IRS has issued proposed regulations on excise taxes under Code Sec. 4958 that can be imposed in cases involving excess benefit transactions occurring on or after September 14, 1995 between tax-exempt organizations and disqualified persons.

The text of the proposed regulations is provided by the text of the IRS temporary regulations issued at the same time as the proposed regulations. The preamble of the temporary regulations is at ¶ 23,178. The text of the temporary regulations is at ¶ 13,592A, ¶ 13,592B, ¶ 13,592C, ¶ 13,592D, ¶ 13,592E, ¶ 13,592H and ¶ 13,592I.

The proposed regulations, which were published in the *Federal Register* January 10, 2001 (66 FR 2173), are reproduced below.

DEPARTMENT OF THE TREASURY

Internal Revenue Service

26 CFR Parts 53 and 301

[REG-246256-96]

RIN 1545-AY65

Excise Taxes on Excess Benefit Transactions

AGENCY: Internal Revenue Service (IRS), Treasury.

ACTION: Notice of proposed rulemaking by cross-reference to temporary regulations.

SUMMARY: In the Rules and Regulations section of this issue of the **Federal Register,** the IRS is issuing temporary regulations relating to

the excise taxes on excess benefit transactions under section 4958 of the Internal Revenue Code (Code), as well as certain amendments and additions to existing Income Tax Regulations affected by section 4958. Section 4958 was enacted in section 1311 of the Taxpayer Bill of Rights 2. Section 4958 generally is effective for transactions occurring on or after September 14, 1995.

Section 4958 imposes excise taxes on transactions that provide excess economic benefits to disqualified persons of public charities and social welfare organizations (referred to as applicable tax-exempt organizations). Disqualified persons who benefit from an excess benefit transaction with an applicable tax-exempt organization are liable for a tax of 25 percent of the excess benefit. Such persons are also liable for a tax of 200 percent of the excess benefit if the excess benefit is not corrected by a certain date. Additionally, organization managers who participate in an excess benefit transaction knowingly, willfully, and without reasonable cause, are liable for a tax of 10 percent of the excess benefit. The tax for which participating organization managers are liable cannot exceed $10,000 for any one excess benefit transaction.

DATES: Written comments and requests for a public hearing must be received by April 10, 2001. In addition to any comments addressing substantive issues of the proposed regulations, the IRS and Treasury specifically request comments on the clarity of the proposed rule and how it may be made easier to understand.

ADDRESSES: Send submissions to: CC:M & SP:RU (REG-246256-96), room 5226, Internal Revenue Service, POB 7604, Ben Franklin Station, Washington, DC 20044. Submissions may be hand delivered Monday through Friday between the hours of 8 a.m. and 5 p.m. to: CC:M & SP:RU (REG-246256-96), Courier's Desk, Internal Revenue Service, 1111 Constitution Avenue NW., Washington, DC. Alternatively, taxpayers may submit comments electronically via the Internet by selecting the "Tax Regs" option on the IRS Home Page, or by submitting comments directly to the IRS Internet site at http://www.irs.gov/prod/tax_regs/comments.html. A public hearing will be scheduled if requested.

FOR FURTHER INFORMATION CONTACT: Concerning submissions, Guy Traynor, (202) 622-7180; concerning the regulations, Phyllis D. Haney, (202) 622-4290 (not toll-free numbers).

SUPPLEMENTARY INFORMATION:

Paperwork Reduction Act

The collections of information contained in these proposed regulations have been reviewed and approved by the Office of Management and Budget in accordance with the Paperwork Reduction Act (44 U.S.C. 3507) under control number 1545-1623, in conjunction with the notice of proposed rulemaking published August 4, 1998, 63 FR 41486, REG-246256-96, Failure by Certain Charitable Organizations to Meet Certain Qualification Requirements; Taxes on Excess Benefit Transactions.

An agency may not conduct or sponsor, and a person is not required to respond to, a collection of information unless it displays a valid control number assigned by the Office of Management and Budget.

Books and records relating to the collection of information must be retained as long as their contents may become material in the administration of any internal revenue law. Generally, tax returns and tax return information are confidential, as required by 26 U.S.C. 6103.

Special Analyses

It has been determined that this notice of proposed rulemaking is not a significant regulatory action as defined in Executive Order 12866. Therefore, a regulatory assessment is not required.

An initial regulatory flexibility analysis was prepared as required for the collection of information under 5 U.S.C. 603 in the notice of proposed rulemaking, REG-246256-96, Failure by Certain Charitable Organizations to Meet Certain Qualification Requirements; Taxes on

Excess Benefit Transactions, published August 4, 1998, at 63 FR 41486. The initial analysis was submitted to the Chief Counsel for Advocacy of the Small Business Administration pursuant to section 7805(f) of the Code for comment on its impact on business. The initial analysis continues to apply to this proposed rule. Pursuant to section 7805(f) of the Code, this notice of proposed rulemaking will be submitted to the Chief Counsel for Advocacy of the Small Business Administration for comment on its impact on business.

Comments and Requests for a Public Hearing

Before these proposed regulations are adopted as final regulations, consideration will be given to any comments (a signed original and eight (8) copies) that are submitted timely to the IRS. The IRS and Treasury specifically request comments on the clarity of the proposed rule and how it may be made easier to understand. All comments will be available for public inspection and copying.

A public hearing may be scheduled if requested in writing by a person who timely submits written comments. If a public hearing is scheduled, notice of the date, time, and place will be published in the **Federal Register.**

Drafting Information

The principal author of these regulations is Phyllis D. Haney, Office of Division Counsel/Associate Chief Counsel (Tax-Exempt and Government Entities). However, other personnel from the IRS and Treasury Department participated in their development.

List of Subjects in 26 CFR Part 53

Excise taxes, Foundations, Investments, Lobbying, Reporting and recordkeeping requirements, Trusts and trustees.

26 CFR Part 301

Employment taxes, Estate taxes, Excise taxes, Gift taxes, Income taxes,Penalties, Reporting and recordkeeping requirements.

Accordingly, 26 CFR Parts 53 and 301 are proposed to be amended as follows:

PART 53—FOUNDATION AND SIMILAR EXCISE TAXES

Paragraph 1. The authority citation for part 53 continues to read as follows:

Authority: 26 U.S.C. 7805.

Par. 2. Sections 53.4958-0 through 53.4958-8 are added to read as follows:

[The text of proposed §§ 53.4958-0 through 53.4958-8 is the same as the text of § 53.4958-0T through 53.4958-8T published elsewhere in this issue of the **Federal Register**].

Robert E. Wenzel

Deputy Commissioner of Internal Revenue

¶ 20,260A

IRS proposed regulations: Electronic media: Requests for determination of qualified status: Notice to interested parties.—The IRS has issued proposed regulations, which eliminate the writing requirement for notices to interested parties when a plan sponsor requests a determination of the qualified status of a retirement plan. The proposed regulations provide that notice may be provided by any method that reasonably ensures that all interested parties will receive the notice, including electronically.

The proposed regulations were published in the *Federal Register* on January 17, 2001 (66 FR 3954). The final regulations (¶ 23,193) were published in the *Federal Register* on July 19, 2002 (67 FR 47454).

¶ 20,260B

IRS proposed regulations: Qualified retirement plans: Qualified joint and survivor annuity (QJSA): Waiver of QJSA distribution: Explanation requirements: Retroactive annuity starting date.—The IRS has issued proposed regulations that define how payments are to be made and set conditions for the use of the provision under Code Sec. 417(a)(7)(A), which allows a qualified plan to furnish an explanation concerning a beneficiary's right to elect a payment type other than a QJSA after the date that the annuity payments are to start.

The proposed regulations, which were published in the *Federal Register* January 17, 2001 (66 FR 3916), were finalized on July 16, 2003 (68 FR 41906). See ¶ 23,210.

¶ 20,260C

Proposed regulations: Required distribution rules: Qualified plans: IRAs: Tax-sheltered annuities: Custodial accounts: Retirement income accounts.—The IRS has issued proposed regulations on minimum required distributions from qualified plans, IRAs, Code Sec. 457 plans, and 403(b) plans. The new proposed regulations simplify and modify various minimum distribution rules contained in 1987 proposed regulations (¶ 20,163B).

The proposed regulations, which were published in the *Federal Register* on January 17, 2001 (66 FR 3928) are reproduced below. Modified and corrected by IRS Announcement 2001-18, I.R.B. 2001-10, March 5, 2001 at ¶ 17,097R-14. Final regulations, published in the *Federal Register* on June 15, 2004 (69 FR 33288) are found at ¶ 11,720Y-6 and ¶ 11,720Y-8, with a preamble at ¶ 23,218.

DEPARTMENT OF TREASURY

Internal Revenue Service (IRS)

26 CFR Parts 1 and 54

RIN 1545-AY69, 1545-AY70

[REG-130477-00;REG-130481-00]

Required Distributions from Retirement Plans

AGENCY: Internal Revenue Service (IRS), Treasury.

ACTION: Notice of proposed rulemaking and notice of public hearing.

SUMMARY: This document contains proposed regulations relating to required minimum distributions from qualified plans, individual retirement plans, deferred compensation plans under section 457, and section 403(b) annuity contracts, custodial accounts, and retirement income accounts. These regulations will provide the public with guidance necessary to comply with the law and will affect administrators of, participants in, and beneficiaries of qualified plans; institutions that sponsor and individuals who administer individual retirement plans, individuals who use individual retirement plans for retirement income, and beneficiaries of individual retirement plans; and employees for whom amounts are contributed to section 403(b) annuity contracts, custodial accounts, or retirement income accounts and beneficiaries of such contracts and accounts.

DATES: Written and electronic comments must be received by April 19, 2001. Outlines of topics to be discussed at the public hearing scheduled for June 1, 2001, at 10 a.m. must be received by May 11, 2001.

ADDRESSES: Send submissions to: CC:M&SP:RU (REG-130477-00/REG130481-00) room 5226, Internal Revenue Service, POB 7604, Ben Franklin Station, Washington, DC 20044. Submissions may be hand delivered Monday through Friday between the hours of 8 a.m. and 5 p.m. to: CC:M&SP:RU (REG-130477-00/REG-130481-00), Courier's Desk, Internal Revenue Service, 1111 Constitution Avenue NW, Washington, DC. Alternatively, taxpayers may submit comments electronically via the Internet by selecting the "Tax Regs" option of the IRS Home Page, or by submitting comments directly to the IRS Internet site at: http://www.irs.gov/tax>regs/reglist.html. The public hearing on June 1, 2001, will be held in the IRS Auditorium (7th Floor), Internal Revenue Building, 1111 Constitution Avenue NW, Washington, DC.

FOR FURTHER INFORMATION CONTACT: Concerning the regulations, Cathy A. Vohs, 202-622-6090; concerning submissions and the hearing, and/or to be placed on the building access list to attend the hearing, Guy Traynor, 202-622-7180 (not toll-free numbers).

Paperwork Reduction Act

The collections of information contained in these proposed regulations have been reviewed and approved by the Office of Management and Budget in accordance with the Paperwork Reduction Act (44 U.S.C. 3507) under control number 1545-0996, in conjunction with the notice of proposed rulemaking published on July 27, 1987, 52 FR 28070, REG-EE-113-82, Required Distributions From Qualified Plans and Individual Retirement Plans, and control number 1545-1573, in conjunction with the notice of proposed rulemaking published on December 30, 1997, 62 FR 67780, REG-209463-82, Required Distributions from Qualified Plans and Individual Retirement Plans.

An agency may not conduct or sponsor, and a person is not required to respond to, a collection of information unless it displays a valid control number assigned by the Office of Management and Budget.

Books and records relating to the collection of information must be retained as long as their contents may become material in the administration of any internal revenue law. Generally, tax returns and tax return information are confidential, as required by 26 U.S.C. 6103.

Background

This document contains proposed amendments to the Income Tax Regulations (26 CFR Part 1) and to the Pension Excise Tax Regulations (26 CFR Part 54) under sections 401, 403, 408, and 4974 of the Internal Revenue Code of 1986. It is contemplated that proposed rules similar to those in these proposed regulations applicable to section 401 will be published in the near future for purposes of applying the distribution requirements of section 457(d). These amendments are proposed to

conform the regulations to section 1404 of the Small Business Job Protection Act of 1996 (SBJPA) (110 Stat. 1791), sections 1121 and 1852 of the Tax Reform Act of 1986 (TRA of 1986) (100 Stat. 2464 and 2864), sections 521 and 713 of the Tax Reform Act of 1984 (TRA of 1984) (98 Stat. 865 and 955), and sections 242 and 243 of the Tax Equity and Fiscal Responsibility Act of 1982 (TEFRA) (96 Stat. 521). The regulations provide guidance on the required minimum distribution requirements under section 401(a)(9) for plans qualified under section 401(a). The rules are incorporated by reference in section 408(a)(6) and (b)(3) for individual retirement accounts and annuities (IRAs), section 408A(c)(5) for Roth IRAs, section 403(b)(10) for section 403(b) annuity contracts, and section 457(d) for eligible deferred compensation plans.

For purposes of this discussion of the background of the regulations in this preamble, as well as the explanation of provisions below, whenever the term *employee* is used, it is intended to include not only an employee but also an IRA owner.

Section 401(a)(9) provides rules for distributions during the life of the employee in section 401(a)(9)(A) and rules for distributions after the death of the employee in section 401(a)(9)(B). Section 401(a)(9)(A)(ii) provides that the entire interest of an employee in a qualified plan must be distributed, beginning not later than the employee's required beginning date, in accordance with regulations, over the life of the employee or over the lives of the employee and a designated beneficiary (or over a period not extending beyond the life expectancy of the employee and a designated beneficiary).

Section 401(a)(9)(C) defines required beginning date for employees (other than 5-percent owners and IRA owners) as April 1 of the calendar year following the later of the calendar year in which the employee attains age 70 ½ or the calendar year in which the employee retires. For 5-percent owners and IRA owners, the required beginning date is April 1 of the calendar year following the calendar year in which the employee attains age 70 ½, even if the employee has not retired.

Section 401(a)(9)(D) provides that (except in the case of a life annuity) the life expectancy of an employee and the employee's spouse that is used to determine the period over which payments must be made may be redetermined, but not more frequently than annually.

Section 401(a)(9)(E) provides that the term *designated beneficiary* means any individual designated as a beneficiary by the employee.

Section 401(a)(9)(G) provides that any distribution required to satisfy the incidental death benefit requirement of section 401(a) is a required minimum distribution.

Section 401(a)(9)(B)(i) provides that, if the employee dies after distributions have begun, the employee's interest must be distributed at least as rapidly as under the method used by the employee.

Section 401(a)(9)(B)(ii) and (iii) provides that, if the employee dies before required minimum distributions have begun, the employee's interest must be either: distributed (in accordance with regulations) over the life or life expectancy of the designated beneficiary with the distributions beginning no later than 1 year after the date of the employee's death, or distributed within 5 years after the death of the employee. However, under section 401(a)(9)(B)(iv), a surviving spouse may wait until the date the employee would have attained age 70 ½ to begin taking required minimum distributions.

Comprehensive proposed regulations under section 401(a)(9) were previously published in the **Federal Register** on July 27, 1987, 52 FR 28070. Many of the comments on the 1987 proposed regulations expressed concerns that the required minimum distribution must be satisfied separately for each IRA owned by an individual by taking distributions from each IRA. In response, Notice 88-38 (1988-1 C.B. 524) provided that the amount of the required minimum distribution must be calculated for each IRA, but permitted that amount to be taken from any IRA. Amendments to the 1987 proposed regulations published in the **Federal Register** on December 30, 1997, 62 FR 67780, responded to comments on the use of trusts as beneficiaries. Notice 96-67 (1996-2 C.B. 235) and Notice 97-75 (1997-2 C.B. 337) provided guidance on the changes made to section 401(a)(9) by the SBJPA. The guidance in Notice 88-38, Notice 96-67, and Notice 97-75 is incorporated in these proposed regulations with some modifications.

Even though the distribution requirements added by TEFRA were retroactively repealed by TRA of 1984, the transition election rule in section 242(b) of TEFRA was preserved. Notice 83-23 (1983-2 C.B. 418) continues to provide guidance for distributions permitted by this transition election rule. These proposed regulations retain the additional guidance on the transition rule provided in the 1987 proposed regulations.

As discussed below, in response to extensive comments, the rules for calculating required minimum distributions from individual accounts under the 1987 proposed regulations have been substantially simplified. Certain other 1987 rules have also been simplified and modified, although many of the 1987 rules remain unchanged. In particular, due to the relatively small number of comments on practices with respect to annuity contracts, and the effect of the 1987 proposed regulations on these practices, the basic structure of the 1987 proposed regulation provisions with respect to annuity payments is retained in these proposed regulations. The IRS and Treasury are continuing to study these rules and specifically request updated comments on current practices and issues relating to required minimum distributions from annuity contracts.

Explanation of Provisions

Overview

Many of the comments on the 1987 proposed regulations addressed the rules for required minimum distributions during an employee's life, including calculation of life expectancy and determination of designated beneficiary. In particular, comments raised concerns about the default provisions, election requirements, and plan language requirements. In general, the need to make decisions at age 70 ½, which under the 1987 proposed regulations would bind the employee in future years during which financial circumstances could change significantly, was perceived as unreasonably restrictive. In addition, the determination of life expectancy and designated beneficiary and the resulting required minimum distribution calculation for individual accounts were viewed as too complex.

To respond to these concerns, these proposed regulations would make it much easier for individuals—both plan participants and IRA owners—and plan administrators to understand and apply the minimum distribution rules. The new proposed regulations would make major simplifications to the rules, including the calculation of the required minimum distribution during the individual's lifetime and the determination of a designated beneficiary for distributions after death. The new proposed regulations simplify the rules by

• Providing a simple, uniform table that all employees can use to determine the minimum distribution required during their lifetime. This makes it far easier to calculate the required minimum distribution because employees would

• no longer need to determine their beneficiary by their required beginning date,

• no longer need to decide whether or not to recalculate their life expectancy each year in determining required minimum distributions, and

• no longer need to satisfy a separate incidental death benefit rule.

• Permitting the required minimum distribution during the employee's lifetime to be calculated without regard to the beneficiary's age (except when required distributions can be reduced by taking into account the age of a beneficiary who is a spouse more than 10 years younger than the employee).

• Permitting the beneficiary to be determined as late as the end of the year following the year of the employee's death. This allows

• the employee to change designated beneficiaries after the required beginning date without increasing the required minimum distribution and

• the beneficiary to be changed after the employee's death, such as by one or more beneficiaries disclaiming or being cashed out.

• Permitting the calculation of post-death minimum distributions to take into account an employee's remaining life expectancy at the time of death, thus allowing distributions in all cases to be spread over a number of years after death.

These simplifications would also have the effect of reducing the required minimum distributions for the vast majority of employees.

The uniform distribution period

Under these proposed regulations and the 1987 proposed regulations, for distributions from an individual account, the required minimum distribution is determined by dividing the account balance by the distribution period. For lifetime required minimum distributions, these proposed regulations provide a uniform distribution period for all employees of the same age. The uniform distribution period table is the required minimum distribution incidental benefit (MDIB) divisor table

originally prescribed in § 1.401(a)(9)-2 of the 1987 proposed regulations and now included in A-4 of § 1.401(a)-5 of the new proposed regulations. An exception applies if the employee's sole beneficiary is the employee's spouse and the spouse is more than 10 years younger than the employee. In that case, the employee is permitted to use the longer distribution period measured by the joint life and last survivor life expectancy of the employee and spouse.

These changes provide a simple administrable rule for plans and individuals. Using the MDIB table, most employees will be able to determine their required minimum distribution for each year based on nothing more than their current age and their account balance as of the end of the prior year (which IRA trustees report annually to IRA owners). Under the 1987 proposed regulations, some employees already use the MDIB table to determine required minimum distributions. Under the new proposed regulations, they would continue to do so. For the majority of other employees, required minimum distributions would be reduced as a result of the changes.

For years after the year of the employee's death, the distribution period is generally the remaining life expectancy of the designated beneficiary. The beneficiary's remaining life expectancy is calculated using the age of the beneficiary in the year following the year of the employee's death, reduced by one for each subsequent year. If the employee's spouse is the employee's sole beneficiary at the end of the year following the year of death, the distribution period during the spouse's life is the spouse's single life expectancy. For years after the year of the spouse's death, the distribution period is the spouse's life expectancy calculated in the year of death, reduced by one for each subsequent year. If there is no designated beneficiary as of the end of the year after the employee's death, the distribution period is the employee's life expectancy calculated in the year of death, reduced by one for each subsequent year.

The MDIB table is based on the joint life expectancies of an individual and a survivor 10 years younger at each age beginning at age 70. Allowing the use of this table reflects the fact that an employee's beneficiary is subject to change until the death of the employee and ultimately may be a beneficiary more than 10 years younger than the employee. The proposed regulations would allow lifetime distributions at a rate consistent with this possibility. Consistent with the requirements of section 401(a)(9)(A)(ii), the distribution period after death is measured by the life expectancy of the employee's designated beneficiary in the year following death, or the employee's remaining life expectancy if there is no designated beneficiary. This ensures that the employee's entire benefit is distributed over a period described in section 401(a)(9)(A)(ii), i.e., the life expectancy of the employee or the joint life expectancy of the employee and a designated beneficiary.

The approach in these proposed regulations allowing the use of a uniform lifetime distribution period addresses concerns raised in comments on the 1987 proposed regulations that the rules are too complex. It eliminates the use of two tables and the interaction of the multiple beneficiary and change in beneficiary rules. Finally, it generally eliminates the need to fix the amount of the distribution during the employee's lifetime based on the beneficiary designated on the required beginning date and eliminates the need to elect recalculation or no recalculation of life expectancies at the required beginning date.

Suggestions have been received that the life expectancy table used to calculate required minimum distributions should be revised to reflect recent increases in longevity. These proposed regulations instead provide authority for the Commissioner to issue guidance of general applicability revising the life expectancy tables and the uniform distribution table in the future if it becomes appropriate. While life expectancy has increased in the 14 years since the issuance of the section 72 life expectancy tables, those tables may already overstate the average life expectancy of the class of individuals who are subject to these required minimum distribution rules (qualified plan participants, IRA owners, et al.). That is because those existing section 72 tables were derived from the particular mortality experience of the select population of individuals who purchase individual annuities, as opposed to the population who are subject to the required minimum distribution rules. In any event, as noted earlier, the new proposed uniform distribution period—equal to the joint life expectancy of an individual and a survivor 10 years younger at each age—would lengthen the lifetime distribution period for most employees and beneficiaries. In fact, the new proposed regulations would lengthen that period more for many individuals than would an update to reflect recent increases in longevity. The IRS and Treasury believe that this lengthening of the distribution period for most employees provides further justification for retaining the existing life expectancy tables at this time.

Some commentators suggested that the calculation of required minimum distributions include credit for any distribution in a prior year that exceeded that year's required minimum distribution. However, such a "credit" carryforward would require significant additional data retention and would add substantial complexity to the calculation of required minimum distributions. By using the prior year's ending account balance for calculating required minimum distributions, distribution of amounts in excess of the required minimum distribution has the effect of reducing future required minimum distributions over the remaining distribution period to some extent. Accordingly, these proposed regulations do not provide for a credit carryforward.

Determination of the designated beneficiary

These proposed regulations provide that, generally, the designated beneficiary is determined as of the end of the year following the year of the employee's death rather than as of the employee's required beginning date or date of death, as under the 1987 proposed regulations. Thus, any beneficiary eliminated by distribution of the benefit or through disclaimer (or otherwise) during the period between the employee's death and the end of the year following the year of death is disregarded in determining the employee's designated beneficiary for purposes of calculating required minimum distributions. If, as of the end of the year following the year of the employee's death, the employee has more than one designated beneficiary and the account or benefit has not been divided into separate accounts or shares for each beneficiary, the beneficiary with the shortest life expectancy is the designated beneficiary, consistent with the approach in the 1987 proposed regulations.

This approach for determining the designated beneficiary following the death of an employee after the employee's required beginning date is simpler in several respects than the approach in the 1987 proposed regulations and responds to concerns raised with respect to the effects of beneficiary designation at the required beginning date. Under this approach, the determination of the designated beneficiary and the calculation of the beneficiary's life expectancy generally are contemporaneous with commencement of required distributions to the beneficiary. Any prior beneficiary designation is irrelevant for distributions from individual accounts, unless the employee takes advantage of a lifetime distribution period measured by the joint life expectancy of the employee and a spouse more than 10 years younger than the employee. Further, for an employee with a designated beneficiary, this approach provides the same rules for distributions after the employee's death, regardless of whether death occurs before or after an employee's required beginning date. Finally, in the case of an employee who elects or defaults into recalculation of life expectancy and who dies without a designated beneficiary, the requirement that the employee's entire remaining account balance be distributed in the year after an employee's death has been eliminated and replaced with a distribution period equal to the employee's remaining life expectancy recalculated immediately before death.

Default rule for post-death distributions

As requested by some commentators, these proposed regulations would change the default rule in the case of death before the employee's required beginning date for a nonspouse designated beneficiary from the 5-year rule in section 401(a)(9)(B)(ii) to the life expectancy rule in section 401(a)(9)(B)(iii). Thus, absent a plan provision or election of the 5-year rule, the life expectancy rule would apply in all cases in which the employee has a designated beneficiary. As in the case of death on or after the employee's required beginning date, the designated beneficiary whose life expectancy is used to determine the distribution period would be determined as of the end of the year following the year of the employee's death, rather than as of the employee's date of death (as would have been required under the 1987 proposed regulations). The 5-year rule would apply automatically only if the employee did not have a designated beneficiary as of the end of the year following the year of the employee's death. Finally, in the case of death before the employee's required beginning date, these proposed regulations allow a waiver, unless the Commissioner determines otherwise, of any excise tax resulting from the life expectancy rule during the first five years after the year of the employee's death if the employee's entire benefit is distributed by the end of the fifth year following the year of the employee's death.

Annuity payments

These proposed regulations make several changes to the rules for determining whether annuity payments satisfy section 401(a)(9). The changes are designed to make these rules more administrable without adverse effects on the basic structure and application of the rules. The IRS and Treasury are continuing to study and evaluate whether additional changes would be appropriate for determining whether annuity payments satisfy section 401(a)(9). Some comments were received on the annuity rules in 1987, but updated comments that include a discus-

sion of current industry practices, products, and concerns would be helpful.

These proposed regulations provide that the designated beneficiary for determining the distribution period for annuity payments generally is the beneficiary as of the annuity starting date, even if that date is after the required beginning date. Thus, if annuity payments commence after the required beginning date, the determination of the designated beneficiary is contemporaneous with the annuity starting date and any intervening changes in the beneficiary designation since the required beginning date are ignored. Second, as requested in comments, these regulations extend to all annuity payment streams the rule in the 1987 proposed regulations that allows a life annuity with a period certain not exceeding 20 years to commence on the required beginning date with no makeup for the first distribution calendar year. For this purpose, the regulations clarify that only accruals as of the end of the prior calendar year must be taken into account in calculating the amount of an annuity commencing on the required beginning date. Subsequent accruals are treated as additional accruals that must be taken into account in the next calendar year. Also as requested in comments, the regulations provide that, although additional accruals need to be taken into account in the first payment in the calendar year following the year of the accrual, actual payment in the form of a makeup payment need only be completed by the end of that calendar year.

The permitted increase in annuity payments to an employee upon the death of the survivor annuitant has been expanded to cover the elimination of the survivor portion of a joint and survivor annuity due to a qualified domestic relations order. Further, in response to comments, in the case of an annuity contract purchased from an insurance company, an exception to the nonincreasing-payment requirement in these proposed regulations has been added to accommodate a cash refund upon the employee's death of the amount of the premiums paid for the contract.

One of the rules in the 1987 proposed regulations that the IRS and Treasury are continuing to study and evaluate is the rule providing that if the distributions from a defined benefit plan are not in the form of an annuity, the employee's benefit will be treated as an individual account for purposes of determining required minimum distributions. The IRS and Treasury are continuing to consider whether retention of this rule is appropriate for defined benefit plans. Similarly, the IRS and Treasury are continuing to consider whether the rule permitting the benefit under a defined benefit plan to be divided into segregated shares for purposes of section 401(a)(9) is useful and appropriate for defined benefit plans.

Trust as beneficiary

These proposed regulations retain the provision in the proposed regulations, as amended in 1997, allowing an underlying beneficiary of a trust to be an employee's designated beneficiary for purposes of determining required minimum distributions when the trust is named as the beneficiary of a retirement plan or IRA, provided that certain requirements are met. One of these requirements is that documentation of the underlying beneficiaries of the trust be provided timely to the plan administrator. In the case of individual accounts, unless the lifetime distribution period for an employee is measured by the joint life expectancy of the employee and the employee's spouse, the deadline under these proposed regulations for providing the beneficiary documentation would be the end of the year following year of the employee's death. This is consistent with the deadline for determining the employee's designated beneficiary. Because the designated beneficiary during an employee's lifetime is not relevant for determining lifetime required minimum distributions in most cases under these proposed regulations, the burden of lifetime documentation requirements contained in the previous proposed regulations is significantly reduced.

A significant number of commentators on the 1997 amendment to the proposed regulations requested clarification that a testamentary trust named as an employee's beneficiary is a trust that qualifies for the look-through rule to the underlying beneficiaries, as permitted in the 1997 proposed regulations. These proposed regulations provide examples in which a testamentary trust is named as an employee's beneficiary and the look-through trust rules apply. As previously illustrated in the facts of Rev. Rul. 2000-2, 2000-3 I.R.B. 305, the examples also clarify that remaindermen of a "QTIP" trust must be taken into account as beneficiaries in determining the distribution period for required minimum distributions if amounts are accumulated for their benefit during the life of the income beneficiary under the trust.

Rules for qualified domestic relations orders

These proposed regulations retain the basic rules in the 1987 proposed regulation for a qualified domestic relations order (QDRO).

Thus, for example, the proposed regulations continue to provide that a former spouse to whom all or a portion of the employee's benefit is payable pursuant to a QDRO will be treated as a spouse (including a surviving spouse) of the employee for purposes of section 401(a)(9), including the minimum distribution incidental benefit requirement, regardless of whether the QDRO specifically provides that the former spouse is treated as the spouse for purposes of sections 401(a)(11) and 417. This rule applies regardless of the number of former spouses an employee has who are alternate payees with respect to the employee's retirement benefits. Further, for example, if a QDRO divides the individual account of an employee in a defined contribution plan into a separate account for the employee and a separate account for the alternate payee, the required minimum distribution to the alternate payee during the lifetimee of the employee must nevertheless be determined using the same rules that apply to distribution to the employee. Thus, required minimum distributions to the alternate payee must commence by the employee's required beginning date. However, the required minimum distribution for the alternate payee will be separately determined. The required minimum distributions for the alternate payee during the lifetime of the employee may be determined either using the uniform distribution period discussed above based on the age of the employee in the distribution calendar year, or, if the alternate payee is the employee's former spouse and is more than 10 years younger than the employee, using the joint life expectancy of the employee and the alternate payee.

Election of surviving spouse to treat an inherited IRA as spouse's own IRA

These proposed regulations clarify the rule in the 1987 proposed regulations that allows the surviving spouse of a decedent IRA owner to elect to treat an IRA inherited by the surviving spouse from that owner as the spouse's own IRA. The 1987 proposed regulations provide that this election is deemed to have been made if the surviving spouse contributes to the IRA or does not take the required minimum distribution for a year under section 401(a)(9)(B) as a beneficiary of the IRA. These new proposed regulations clarify that this deemed election is permitted to be made only after the distribution of the required minimum amount for the account, if any, for the year of the individual's death. Further these new proposed regulations clarify that this deemed election is permitted only if the spouse is the sole beneficiary of the account and has an unlimited right to withdrawal from the account. This requirement is not satisfied if a trust is named as beneficiary of the IRA, even if the spouse is the sole beneficiary of the trust. These clarifications make the election consistent with the underlying premise that the surviving spouse could have received a distribution of the entire decedent IRA owner's account and rolled it over to an IRA established in the surviving spouse's own name as IRA owner.

These new proposed regulations also clarify that, except for the required minimum distribution for the year of the individual's death, the spouse is permitted to roll over the post-death required minimum distribution under section 401(a)(9)(B) for a year if the spouse is establishing the IRA rollover account in the name of the spouse as IRA owner. However, if the surviving spouse is age 70 ½ or older, the minimum lifetime distribution required under section 401(a)(9)(A) must be made for the year and, because it is a required minimum distribution, that amount may not be rolled over. These proposed regulations provide that this election by a surviving spouse eligible to treat an IRA as the spouse's own may also be accomplished by redesignating the IRA with the name of the surviving spouse as owner rather than beneficiary.

IRA reporting of required minimum distributions

Because these regulations substantially simplify the calculation of required minimum distributions from IRAs, IRA trustees determining the account balance as of the end of the year can also calculate the following year's required minimum distribution for each IRA. To improve compliance and further reduce the burden imposed on IRA owners and beneficiaries, under the authority provided in section 408(i), these proposed regulations would require the trustee of each IRA to report the amount of the required minimum distribution from the IRA to the IRA owner or beneficiary and to the IRS at the time and in the manner provided under IRS forms and instructions. This reporting would be required regardless of whether the IRA owner is planning to take the required minimum distribution from that IRA or from another IRA, and would indicate that the IRA owner is permitted to take the required minimum distribution from any other IRA of the owner. During year 2001, the IRS will be receiving public comments and consulting with interested parties to assist the IRS in evaluating what form best accommodates this reporting requirement, what timing is appropriate (e.g., the beginning of the calendar year for which the required amount is being calculated), and what effective date would be most appropriate for the reporting requirement. In this context, after

thorough consideration of comments and consultation with interested parties, the IRS intends to develop procedures and a schedule for reporting that provides adequate lead time, and minimizes the reporting burden, for IRA trustees, issuers, and custodians in complying with this new reporting requirement while providing the most useful information to the IRA owners and beneficiaries.

The IRS and Treasury are also considering whether similar reporting would be appropriate for section 403(b) contracts.

Permitted Delays Relative to QDROs and State Insurer Delinquency Proceedings

The regulations permit the required minimum distribution for a year to be delayed to a later year in certain circumstances. Specifically, commentators requested a delay during a period of up to 18 months during which an amount is segregated in connection with the review of a domestic relations order pursuant to section 414(p)(7). Commentators also requested that a delay be permitted while annuity payments under an annuity contract issued by a life insurance company in state insurer delinquency proceedings have been reduced or suspended by reason of state proceedings. These proposed regulations allow delay in these circumstances.

Correction of failures under section 401(a)(9)

The proposed regulations do not set forth the special rule relieving a plan from disqualification for isolated instances of failure to satisfy section 401(a)(9) because all failures for qualified plans and section 403(b) accounts under section 401(a)(9) are now permitted to be corrected through the Employee Plans Compliance Resolution System (EPCRS). See Rev. Proc. 2000-16 (2000-6 I.R.B. 518).

Amendment of Qualified Plans

These regulations are proposed to be effective for distributions for calendar years beginning on or after January 1, 2002. For distributions for calendar years beginning before the effective date of final regulations, plan sponsors can continue to rely on the 1987 proposed regulations, to the extent those proposed regulations are not inconsistent with the changes to section 401(a)(9) made by the Small Business Job Protection Act of 1996 (SBJPA) and guidance related to those changes. Alternatively, for distributions for the 2001 and subsequent calendar years beginning before the effective date of final regulations, plan sponsors are permitted, but not required, to follow these proposed regulations in the operation of their plans by adopting the model amendment set forth below.

The Treasury Department and the IRS are making the model amendment set forth below available to plan sponsors to permit them to apply these proposed regulations in the operation of their plans without violating the requirement that a plan be operated in accordance with its terms. Plan sponsors who adopt the model amendment will have reliance that, during the term of the amendment, operation of their plans in a manner that satisfies the minimum distribution requirements in these proposed regulations will not cause their plans to fail to be qualified. In addition, distributees will have reliance that distributions that are made during the term of the amendment that satisfy the minimum distribution requirements in these proposed regulations. The model amendment may be adopted by plan sponsors, practitioners who sponsor volume submitter specimen plans and sponsors of master and prototype (M&P) plans.

These proposed regulations permit plans to make distributions under either default provisions or under permissible optional provisions. A plan that has been amended by adoption of the model amendment will be treated as operating in conformance with a requirement of the proposed regulations that permits the use of either default or optional provisions if the plan is operated consistently in accordance with either the default rule or a specific permitted alternative, notwithstanding the plan's terms.

The Service will not issue determination, opinion or advisory letters on the basis of the changes in these proposed regulations until the publication of final regulations. Until such time, the IRS will continue to issue such letters on the basis of the 1987 proposed regulations and SBJPA. Although the IRS will not issue determination, opinion or advisory letters with respect to the model amendment, the adoption of the model amendment will not affect a determination letter issued for a plan whose terms otherwise satisfy the 1987 proposed regulations and SBJPA. Plan sponsors should not adopt other amendments to attempt to conform their plans to the changes in these proposed regulations before the publication of final regulations. The IRS intends to publish procedures at a later date that will allow qualified plans to be amended to reflect the regulations under section 401(a)(9) when they are finalized.

Qualified plans are required to be amended for changes in the plan qualification requirements made by GUST by the end of the GUST remedial amendment period under section 401(b), which is generally the end of the first plan year beginning on or after January 1, 2001, or, if applicable, a later date determined under the provisions of section 19 of Rev. Proc. 2000-20 (2000-6 I.R.B. 553). Many plans have been operated in a manner that reflects the changes to section 401(a)(9) made by SBJPA and will have to be amended for these changes by the end of the GUST remedial amendment period. The IRS intends that its procedures for amending qualified plans for the final regulations under section 401(a)(9) will generally avoid the need for plan sponsors, volume submitter practitioners and M&P plan sponsors to request another determination, opinion or advisory letter subsequent to their application for a GUST letter. In addition, to the extent such a subsequent letter is needed or desired, the IRS intends that its procedures will provide that the application for the letter will not have to be submitted prior to the next time the plan is otherwise amended or required to be amended.

The model amendment described above is set forth below: "With respect to distributions under the Plan made in calendar years beginning on or after January 1, 2000 (ALTERNATIVELY, SPECIFY A LATER CALENDAR YEAR FOR WHICH THE AMENDMENT IS TO BE INITIALLY EFFECTIVE), the Plan will apply the minimum distribution requirements of section 401(a)(9) of the Internal Revenue Code in accordance with the regulations under section 401(a)(9) that were proposed in January 2001, notwithstanding any provision of the Plan to the contrary. This amendment shall continue in effect until the end of the last calendar year beginning before the effective date of final regulations under section 401(a)(9) or such other date specified in guidance published by the Internal Revenue Service."

Amendment of IRAs and Effective Date

These regulations are proposed to be effective for distributions for calendar years beginning on or after January 1, 2002. For distributions for the 2001 calendar year, IRA owners are permitted, but not required, to follow these proposed regulations in operation, notwithstanding the terms of the IRA documents. IRA owners may therefore rely on these proposed regulations for distributions for the 2001 calendar year. However, IRA sponsors should not amend their IRA documents to conform their IRAs to the changes in these proposed regulations before the publication of final regulations. The IRS will not issue model IRAs on the basis of the changes in these proposed regulations until the publication of final regulations. Until such time, IRA owners can continue to use the current model IRAs which are based on the 1987 proposed regulations under section 401(a)(9). The IRS will publish procedures at a later date that will allow IRAs to be amended to reflect final regulations under section 401(a)(9).

Proposed Effective Date

The regulations are proposed to be applicable for determining required minimum distributions for calendar years beginning on or after January 1, 2002. For determining required minimum distributions for calendar year 2001, taxpayers may rely on these proposed regulations or on the 1987 proposed regulations. If, and to the extent, future guidance is more restrictive than the guidance in these proposed regulations, the future guidance will be issued without retroactive effect.

Special Analyses

It has been determined that this notice of proposed rulemaking is not a significant regulatory action as defined in Executive Order 12866. Therefore, a regulatory assessment is not required. It also has been determined that section 553(b) of the Administrative Procedure Act (5 U.S.C. chapter 5) does not apply to these regulations, and because the regulation does not impose a collection of information on small entities, the Regulatory Flexibility Act (5 U.S.C. chapter 6) does not apply. Pursuant to section 7805(f) of the Code, these proposed regulations will be submitted to the Chief Counsel for Advocacy of the Small Business Administration for comment on their impact on small business.

Comments and Public Hearing

Before these proposed regulations are adopted as final regulations, consideration will be given to any electronic or written comments (preferably a signed original and eight (8) copies) that are submitted timely to the IRS. In addition to the other requests for comments set forth in this document, the IRS and Treasury also request comments on the clarity of the proposed rule and how it may be made easier to understand. All comments will be available for public inspection and copying.

A public hearing has been scheduled for June 1, 2001, at 10 a.m. in the IRS Auditorium (7th Floor), Internal Revenue Building, 1111 Constitution Avenue NW., Washington, DC. Due to building security procedures, visitors must enter at the 10th street entrance, located between Constitution and Pennsylvania Avenues, NW. In addition, all visitors must present photo identification to enter the building. Because of access restrictions, visitors will not be admitted beyond the immediate entrance area more than 15 minutes before the hearing starts. For information about having your name placed on the building access list to attend the hearing, see the "FOR FURTHER INFORMATION CONTACT" section of this preamble.

The rules of 26 CFR 601.601(a)(3) apply to the hearing.

Persons who wish to present oral comments at the hearing must submit written comments and an outline of the topics to be discussed and the time to be devoted to each topic (signed original and eight (8) copies) by May 11, 2001.

A period of 10 minutes will be allotted to each person for making comments.

An agenda showing the scheduling of the speakers will be prepared after the deadline for receiving outlines has passed. Copies of the agenda will be available free of charge at the hearing.

Drafting Information

The principal authors of these regulations are Marjorie Hoffman and Cathy A. Vohs of the Office of the Division Counsel/Associate Chief Counsel (Tax Exempt and Government Entities). However, other personnel from the IRS and Treasury participated in their development.

List of Subjects

26 CFR Part 1

Income taxes, Reporting and recordkeeping requirements.

26 CFR Part 54

Excise taxes, Pensions, Reporting and recordkeeping requirements.

Adoption of Amendments of the Regulations

Accordingly, 26 CFR part 1 is amended as follows:

PART 1 - INCOME TAXES

Paragraph 1. The authority citation for part 1 is amended by adding entries in numerical order to read in part as follows:

Authority: 26 U.S.C. 7805 * * *

§ 1.401(a)(9)-1 is also issued under 26 U.S.C. 401(a)(9).

§ 1.401(a)(9)-2 is also issued under 26 U.S.C. 401(a)(9).

§ 1.401(a)(9)-3 is also issued under 26 U.S.C. 401(a)(9).

§ 1.401(a)(9)-4 is also issued under 26 U.S.C. 401(a)(9).

§ 1.401(a)(9)-5 is also issued under 26 U.S.C. 401(a)(9).

§ 1.401(a)(9)-6 is also issued under 26 U.S.C. 401(a)(9).

§ 1.401(a)(9)-7 is also issued under 26 U.S.C. 401(a)(9).

§ 1.401(a)(9)-8 is also issued under 26 U.S.C. 401(a)(9). * * *

§ 1.403(b)-2 is also issued under 26 U.S.C. 403(b)(10). * * *

§ 1.408-8 is also issued under 26 U.S.C. 408(a)(6) and (b)(3). * * *

Par. 2. Sections 1.401(a)(9)-0 through 1.401(a)(9)-8 are added to read as follows:

§ 1.401(a)(9)-0 Required minimum distributions; table of contents.

• This table of contents lists the regulations relating to required minimum distributions under section 401(a)(9) of the Internal Revenue Code as follows:

§ 1.401(a)(9)-0 Required minimum distributions; table of contents.

§ 1.401(a)(9)-1 Required minimum distribution requirement in general.

§ 1.401(a)(9)-2 Distributions commencing before an employee's death.

§ 1.401(a)(9)-3 Death before required beginning date.

§ 1.401(a)(9)-4 Determination of the designated beneficiary.

§ 1.401(a)(9)-5 Required minimum distributions from defined contribution plans.

§ 1.401(a)(9)-6 Required minimum distributions from defined benefit plans.

§ *1.401(a)(9)-7 Rollovers and transfers.*

§ *1.401(a)(9)-8 Special rules.*

§ *1.401(a)(9)-1 Required minimum distribution requirement in general.*

Q-1. What plans are subject to the required minimum distribution requirement under section 401(a)(9) and §§ 1.401(a)(9)-1 through 1.401(a)(9)-8?

A-1. All stock bonus, pension, and profit-sharing plans qualified under section 401(a) and annuity contracts described in section 403(a) are subject to the required minimum distribution rules in section 401(a)(9) and §§ 1.401(a)(9)-1 through 1.401(a)(9)-8. See § 1.403(b)-2 for the distribution rules applicable to annuity contracts or custodial accounts described in section 403(b), see § 1.408-8 for the distribution rules applicable to individual retirement plans, see § 1.408A-6 described for the distribution rules applicable to Roth IRAs under section 408A, and see section 457(d)(2)(A) for distribution rules applicable to certain deferred compensation plans for employees of tax exempt organizations or state and local government employees.

Q-2. Which employee account balances and benefits held under qualified trusts and plans are subject to the distribution rules of section 401(a)(9) and §§ 1.401(a)(9)-1 through 1.401(a)(9)-8?

A-2. The distribution rules of section 401(a)(9) apply to all account balances and benefits in existence on or after January 1, 1985. Sections 1.401(a)(9)-1 through 1.401(a)(9)-8 apply for purposes of determining required minimum distributions for calendar years beginning on or after January 1, 2002.

Q-3. What specific provisions must a plan contain in order to satisfy section 401(a)(9)?

A-3. (a) *Required provisions.* In order to satisfy section 401(a)(9), the plan must include several written provisions reflecting section 401(a)(9). First, the plan must generally set forth the statutory rules of section 401(a)(9), including the incidental death benefit requirement in section 401(a)(9)(G). Second, the plan must provide that distributions will be made in accordance with §§ 1.401(a)(9)-1 through 1.401(a)(9)-8. The plan document must also provide that the provisions reflecting section 401(a)(9) override any distribution options in the plan inconsistent with section 401(a)(9). The plan also must include any other provisions reflecting section 401(a)(9) as are prescribed by the Commissioner in revenue rulings, notices, and other guidance published in the Internal Revenue Bulletin. See § 601.601(d)(2)(ii)(b) of this chapter.

(b) *Optional provisions.* The plan may also include written provisions regarding any optional provisions governing plan distributions that do not conflict with section 401(a)(9) and the regulations thereunder.

(c) *Absence of optional provisions.* Plan distributions commencing after an employee's death will be required to be made under the default provision set forth in § 1.401(a)(9)-3 for distributions unless the plan document contains optional provisions that override such default provisions. Thus, if distributions have not commenced to the employee at the time of the employee's death, distributions after the death of an employee are to be made automatically in accordance with the default provisions in A-4(a) of § 1.401(a)(9)-3 unless the plan either specifies in accordance with A-4(b) of § 1.401(a)(9)-3 the method under which distributions will be made or provides for elections by the employee (or beneficiary) in accordance with A-4(c) of § 1.401(a)(9)-3 and such elections are made by the employee or beneficiary.

§ *1.401(a)(9)-2 Distributions commencing before an employee's death.*

Q-1. In the case of distributions commencing before an employee's death, how must the employee's entire interest be distributed in order to satisfy section 401(a)(9)(A)?

A-1. (a) In order to satisfy section 401(a)(9)(A), the entire interest of each employee must be distributed to such employee not later than the required beginning date, or must be distributed, beginning not later than the required beginning date, over the life of the employee or joint lives of the employee and a designated beneficiary or over a period not extending beyond the life expectancy of the employee or the joint life and last survivor expectancy of the employee and the designated beneficiary.

(b) Section 401(a)(9)(G) provides that lifetime distributions must satisfy the incidental death benefit requirements.

(c) The amount required to be distributed for each calendar year in order to satisfy section 401(a)(9)(A) and (G) generally depends on whether a distribution is in the form of distributions under a defined contribution plan or annuity payments under a defined benefit plan. For

the method of determining the required minimum distribution in accordance with section 401(a)(9)(A) and (G) from an individual account under a defined contribution plan, see § 1.401(a)(9)-5. For the method of determining the required minimum distribution in accordance with section 401(a)(9)(A) and (G) in the case of annuity payments from a defined benefit plan or an annuity contract, see § 1.401(a)(9)-6.

Q-2. For purposes of section 401(a)(9)(C), what does the term *required beginning date* mean?

A-2. (a) Except as provided in paragraph (b) of this A-2 with respect to a 5-percent owner, as defined in paragraph (c), the term *required beginning date* means April 1 of the calendar year following the later of the calendar year in which the employee attains age 70 ½, or the calendar year in which the employee retires from employment with the employer maintaining the plan.

(b) In the case of an employee who is a 5-percent owner, the term *required beginning date* means April 1 of the calendar year following the calendar year in which the employee attains age 70 ½.

(c) For purposes of section 401(a)(9), a 5-percent owner is an employee who is a 5-percent owner (as defined in section 416) with respect to the plan year ending in the calendar year in which the employee attains age 70 ½.

(d) Paragraph (b) of this A-2 does not apply in the case of a governmental plan (within the meaning of section 414(d)) or a church plan. For purposes of this paragraph, the term *church plan* means a plan maintained by a church for church employees, and the term *church* means any church (as defined in section 3121(w)(3)(A)) or qualified church-controlled organization (as defined in section 3121(w)(3)(B)).

(e) A plan is permitted to provide that the required beginning date for purposes of section 401(a)(9) for all employees is April 1 of the calendar year following the calendar year in which the employee attained age 70 ½ regardless of whether the employee is a 5-percent owner.

Q-3. When does an employee attain age 70 ½?

A-3. An employee attains age 70 ½ as of the date six calendar months after the 70th anniversary of the employee's birth. For example, if an employee's date of birth was June 30, 1932, the 70th anniversary of such employee's birth is June 30, 2002. Such employee attains age 70 ½ on December 30, 2002. Consequently, if the employee is a 5-percent owner or retired, such employee's required beginning date is April 1, 2003. However, if the employee's date of birth was July 1, 1932, the 70th anniversary of such employee's birth would be July 1, 2002. Such employee would then attain age 70 ½ on January 1, 2003 and such employee's required beginning date would be April 1, 2004.

Q-4. Must distributions made before the employee's required beginning date satisfy section 401(a)(9)?

A-4. Lifetime distributions made before the employee's required beginning date for calendar years before the employee's first distribution calendar year, as defined in A-1(b) of § 1.401(a)(9)-5, need not be made in accordance with section 401(a)(9). However, if distributions commence before the employee's required beginning date under a particular distribution option, such as in the form of an annuity, the distribution option fails to satisfy section 401(a)(9) at the time distributions commence if, under terms of the particular distribution option, distributions to be made for the employee's first distribution calendar year or any subsequent distribution calendar year will fail to satisfy section 401(a)(9).

Q-5. If distributions have begun to an employee before the employee's death (in accordance with section 401(a)(9)(A)(ii)), how must distributions be made after an employee's death?

A-5. Section 401(a)(9)(B)(i) provides that if the distribution of the employee's interest has begun in accordance with section 401(a)(9)(A)(ii) and the employee dies before his entire interest has been distributed to him, the remaining portion of such interest must be distributed at least as rapidly as under the distribution method being used under section 401(a)(9)(A)(ii) as of the date of his death. The amount required to be distributed for each distribution calendar year following the calendar year of death generally depends on whether a distribution is in the form of distributions from an individual account under a defined contribution plan or annuity payments under a defined benefit plan. For the method of determining the required minimum distribution in accordance with section 401(a)(9)(B)(i) from an individual account, see A-5(a) of § 1.401(a)(9)-5 for the calculation of the distribution period that applies when an employee dies after the employee's required beginning date. In the case of annuity payments from a defined benefit plan or an annuity contract, see § 1.401(a)(9)-6.

Q-6. For purposes of section 401(a)(9)(B), when are distributions considered to have begun to the employee in accordance with section 401(a)(9)(A)(ii)?

A-6. (a) *General rule.* Except as otherwise provided in A-10 of §1.401(a)(9)-6, distributions are not treated as having begun to the employee in accordance with section 401(a)(9)(A)(ii) until the employee's required beginning date, without regard to whether payments have been made before that date. For example, if employee A upon retirement in 2002, the calendar year A attains age 65 ½, begins receiving installment distributions from a profit-sharing plan over a period not exceeding the joint life and last survivor expectancy of A and A's beneficiary, benefits are not treated as having begun in accordance with section 401(a)(9)(A)(ii) until April 1, 2008 (the April 1 following the calendar year in which A attains age 70 ½). Consequently, if such employee dies before April 1, 2008 (A's required beginning date), distributions after A's death must be made in accordance with section 401(a)(9)(B)(ii) or (iii) and (iv) and §1.401(a)(9)-4, and not section 401(a)(9)(B)(i). This is the case without regard to whether the plan has distributed the minimum distribution for the first distribution calendar year (as defined in A-1(b) of §1.401(a)(9)-5) before A's death.

(b) If a plan provides, in accordance with A-2(e) of this section, that the required beginning date for purposes of section 401(a)(9) for all employees is April 1 of the calendar year following the calendar year in which the employee attains age 70 ½, an employee who dies after the required beginning date determined under the plan terms is treated as dying after the employee's required beginning date for purposes of A-5(a) of this section even though the employee dies before the April 1 following the calendar year in which the employee retires.

§1.401(a)(9)-3 Death before required beginning date.

Q-1. If an employee dies before the employee's required beginning date, how must the employee's entire interest be distributed in order to satisfy section 401(a)(9)?

A-1. (a) Except as otherwise provided in A-10 of §1.401(a)(9)-6, if an employee dies before the employee's required beginning date (and, thus, generally before distributions are treated as having begun in accordance with section 401(a)(9)(A)(ii)), distribution of the employee's entire interest must be made in accordance with one of the methods described in section 401(a)(9)(B)(ii) or (iii). One method (the five-year rule in section 401(a)(9)(B)(ii)) requires that the entire interest of the employee be distributed within five years of the employee's death regardless of who or what entity receives the distribution. Another method (the life expectancy rule in section 401(a)(9)(B)(iii)) requires that any portion of an employee's interest payable to (or for the benefit of) a designated beneficiary be distributed, commencing within one year of the employee's death, over the life of such beneficiary (or over a period not extending beyond the life expectancy of such beneficiary). Section 401(a)(9)(B)(iv) provides special rules where the designated beneficiary is the surviving spouse of the employee, including a special commencement date for distributions under section 401(a)(9)(B)(iii) to the surviving spouse.

(b) See A-4 of this section for the rules for determining which of the methods described in paragraph (a) applies. See A-3 of this section to determine when distributions under the exception to the five-year rule in section 401(a)(9)(B)(iii) and (iv) must commence. See A-2 of this section to determine when the five-year period in section 401(a)(9)(B)(ii) ends. For distributions using the life expectancy rule in section 401(a)(9)(B)(iii) and (iv), see §1.401(a)(9)-4 in order to determine the designated beneficiary under section 401(a)(9)(B)(iii) and (iv), see §1.401(a)(9)-5 for the rules for determining the required minimum distribution under a defined contribution plan, and see §1.401(a)(9)-6 for required minimum distributions under defined benefit plans.

Q-2. By when must the employee's entire interest be distributed in order to satisfy the five-year rule in section 401(a)(9)(B)(ii)?

A-2. In order to satisfy the five-year rule in section 401(a)(9)(B)(ii), the employee's entire interest must be distributed by the end of the calendar year which contains the fifth anniversary of the date of the employee's death. For example, if an employee dies on January 1, 2002, the entire interest must be distributed by the end of 2007, in order to satisfy the five-year rule in section 401(a)(9)(B)(ii).

Q-3. When are distributions required to commence in order to satisfy the life expectancy rule in section 401(a)(9)(B)(iii) and (iv)?

A-3. (a) *Nonspouse beneficiary.* In order to satisfy the life expectancy rule in section 401(a)(9)(B)(iii), if the designated beneficiary is not the employee's surviving spouse, distributions must commence on or before the end of the calendar year immediately following the calendar year in which the employee died. This rule also applies to the distribu-

tion of the entire remaining benefit if another individual is a designated beneficiary in addition to the employee's surviving spouse. See A-2 and A-3 of §1.401(a)(9)-8, however, if the employee's benefit is divided into separate accounts (or segregated shares, in the case of a defined benefit plan).

(b) *Spousal beneficiary.* In order to satisfy the rule in section 401(a)(9)(B)(iii) and (iv), if the sole designated beneficiary is the employee's surviving spouse, distributions must commence on or before the later of-

(1) The end of the calendar year immediately following the calendar year in which the employee died; and

(2) The end of the calendar year in which the employee would have attained age 70 ½.

Q-4. How is it determined whether the five-year rule in section 401(a)(9)(B)(ii) or the life expectancy rule in section 401(a)(9)(B)(iii) and (iv) applies to a distribution?

A-4. (a) *No plan provision.* If a plan does not adopt an optional provision described in paragraph (b) or (c) of this A-4 specifying the method of distribution after the death of an employee, distribution must be made as follows:

(1) If the employee has a designated beneficiary, as determined under §1.401(a)(9)-4, distributions are to be made in accordance with the life expectancy rule in section 401(a)(9)(B)(iii) and (iv).

(2) If the employee has no designated beneficiary, distributions are to be made in accordance with the five-year rule in section 401(a)(9)(B)(ii).

(b) *Optional plan provisions.* The plan may adopt a provision specifying either that the five-year rule in section 401(a)(9)(B)(ii) will apply to certain distributions after the death of an employee even if the employee has a designated beneficiary or that distribution in every case will be made in accordance with the five-year rule in section 401(a)(9)(B)(ii). Further, a plan need not have the same method of distribution for the benefits of all employees.

(c) *Elections.* A plan may adopt a provision that permits employees (or beneficiaries) to elect on an individual basis whether the five-year rule in section 401(a)(9)(B)(ii) or the life expectancy rule in section 401(a)(9)(B)(iii) and (iv) applies to distributions after the death of an employee who has a designated beneficiary. Such an election must be made no later than the earlier of, the end of the calendar year in which distribution would be required to commence in order to satisfy the requirements for the life expectancy rule in section 401(a)(9)(B)(iii) and (iv) (see A-3 of this section for the determination of such calendar year), or the end of the calendar year which contains the fifth anniversary of the date of death of the employee. As of the date determined under the life expectancy rule, the election must be irrevocable with respect to the beneficiary (and all subsequent beneficiaries) and must apply to all subsequent calendar years. If a plan provides for the election, the plan may also specify the method of distribution that applies if neither the employee nor the beneficiary makes the election. If neither the employee nor the beneficiary elects a method and the plan does not specify which method applies, distribution must be made in accordance with paragraph (a).

Q-5. If the employee's surviving spouse is the employee's designated beneficiary and such spouse dies after the employee, but before distributions have begun to the surviving spouse under section 401(a)(9)(B)(iii) and (iv), how is the employee's interest to be distributed?

A-5. Pursuant to section 401(a)(9)(B)(iv)(II), if the surviving spouse dies after the employee, but before distributions to such spouse have begun under section 401(a)(9)(B)(iii) and (iv), the five-year rule in section 401(a)(9)(B)(ii) and the life expectancy rule in section 401(a)(9)(B)(iii) are to be applied as if the surviving spouse were the employee. In applying this rule, the date of death of the surviving spouse shall be substituted for the date of death of the employee. However, in such case, the rules in section 401(a)(9)(B)(iv) are not available to the surviving spouse of the deceased employee's surviving spouse.

Q-6. For purposes of section 401(a)(9)(B)(iv)(II), when are distributions considered to have begun to the surviving spouse?

A-6. Distributions are considered to have begun to the surviving spouse of an employee, for purposes of section 401(a)(9)(B)(iv)(II), on the date, determined in accordance with A-3 of this section, on which distributions are required to commence to the surviving spouse, even though payments have actually been made before that date. See A-11 of §1.401(a)(9)-6 for a special rule for annuities.

§1.401(a)(9)-4 Determination of the designated beneficiary.

Q-1. Who is a designated beneficiary under section 401(a)(9)(E)?

A-1. A designated beneficiary is an individual who is designated as a beneficiary under the plan. An individual may be designated as a beneficiary under the plan either by the terms of the plan or, if the plan so provides, by an affirmative election by the employee (or the employee's surviving spouse) specifying the beneficiary. A beneficiary designated as such under the plan is an individual who is entitled to a portion of an employee's benefit, contingent on the employee's death or another specified event. For example, if a distribution is in the form of a joint and survivor annuity over the life of the employee and another individual, the plan does not satisfy section 401(a)(9) unless such other individual is a designated beneficiary under the plan. A designated beneficiary need not be specified by name in the plan or by the employee to the plan in order to be a designated beneficiary so long as the individual who is to be the beneficiary is identifiable under the plan as of the date the beneficiary is determined under A-4 of this section. The members of a class of beneficiaries capable of expansion or contraction will be treated as being identifiable if it is possible, as of the date the beneficiary is determined, to identify the class member with the shortest life expectancy. The fact that an employee's interest under the plan passes to a certain individual under applicable state law does not make that individual a designated beneficiary unless the individual is designated as a beneficiary under the plan.

Q-2. Must an employee (or the employee's spouse) make an affirmative election specifying a beneficiary for a person to be a designated beneficiary under section 40l(a)(9)(E)?

A-2. No. A designated beneficiary is an individual who is designated as a beneficiary under the plan whether or not the designation under the plan was made by the employee. The choice of beneficiary is subject to the requirements of sections 401(a)(11), 414(p), and 417.

Q-3. May a person other than an individual be considered to be a designated beneficiary for purposes of section 401(a)(9)?

A-3. (a) No. Only individuals may be designated beneficiaries for purposes of section 401(a)(9). A person that is not an individual, such as the employee's estate, may not be a designated beneficiary, and, if a person other than an individual is designated as a beneficiary of an employee's benefit, the employee will be treated as having no designated beneficiary for purposes of section 401(a)(9). However, see A-5 of this section for special rules which apply to trusts.

(b) If an employee is treated as having no designated beneficiary, for distributions under a defined contribution plan, the distribution period under section 401(a)(9)(A)(ii) after the death of the employee is limited to the period described in A-5(a)(2) of § 1.401(a)(9)-5 (the remaining life expectancy of the employee determined in accordance with A-5(c)(3) of § 1.401(a)(9)-5). Further, in such case, except as provided in A-10 of § 1.401(a)(9)-6, if the employee dies before the employee's required beginning date, distribution must be made in accordance with the 5-year rule in section 401(a)(9)(B)(ii).

Q-4. When is the designated beneficiary determined?

A-4. (a) *General rule.* Except as provided in paragraph (b) and § 1.401(a)(9)-6, the employee's designated beneficiary will be determined based on the beneficiaries designated as of the last day of the calendar year following the calendar year of the employee's death. Consequently, except as provided in § 1.401(a)(9)-6, any person who was a beneficiary as of the date of the employee's death, but is not a beneficiary as of that later date (e.g., because the person disclaims entitlement to the benefit in favor of another beneficiary or because the person receives the entire benefit to which the person is entitled before that date), is not taken into account in determining the employee's designated beneficiary for purposes of determining the distribution period for required minimum distributions after the employee's death.

(b) *Surviving spouse.* As provided in A-5 of § 1.401(a)(9)-3, in the case in which the employee's spouse is the designated beneficiary as of the date described in paragraph (a) of this A-5, and the surviving spouse dies after the employee and before the date on which distributions have begun to the spouse under section 401(a)(9)(B)(iii) and (iv), the rule in section 40l(a)(9)(B)(iv)(II) will apply. Thus, the relevant designated beneficiary for determining the distribution period is the designated beneficiary of the surviving spouse. Such designated beneficiary will be determined as of the last day of the calendar year following the calendar year of surviving spouse's death. If, as of such last day, there is no designated beneficiary under the plan with respect to that surviving spouse, distribution must be made in accordance with the 5-year rule in section 401(a)(9)(B)(ii) and A-2 of § 1.401(a)(9)-3.

(c) *Multiple beneficiaries.* Notwithstanding anything in this A-4 to the contrary, the rules in A-7 of § 1.401(a)(9)-5 apply if more than one beneficiary is designated with respect to an employee as of the date on which the designated beneficiary is to be determined in accordance with paragraphs (a) and (b) of this A-4.

Q-5. If a trust is named as a beneficiary of an employee, will the beneficiaries of the trust with respect to the trust's interest in the employee's benefit be treated as having been designated as beneficiaries of the employee under the plan for purposes of determining the distribution period under section 401(a)(9)?

A-5. (a) Only an individual may be a designated beneficiary for purposes of determining the distribution period under section 401(a)(9). Consequently, a trust is not a designated beneficiary even though the trust is named as a beneficiary. However, if the requirements of paragraph (b) of this A-5 are met, the beneficiaries of the trust will be treated as having been designated as beneficiaries of the employee under the plan for purposes of determining the distribution period under section 401(a)(9).

(b) The requirements of this paragraph (b) are met if, during any period during which required minimum distributions are being determined by treating the beneficiaries of the trust as designated beneficiaries of the employee, the following requirements are met:

(1) The trust is a valid trust under state law, or would be but for the fact that there is no corpus.

(2) The trust is irrevocable or will, by its terms, become irrevocable upon the death of the employee.

(3) The beneficiaries of the trust who are beneficiaries with respect to the trust's interest in the employee's benefit are identifiable from the trust instrument within the meaning of A-1 of this section.

(4) The documentation described in A-6 of this section has been provided to the plan administrator.

(c) In the case of payments to a trust having more than one beneficiary, see A-7 of § 1.401(a)(9)-5 for the rules for determining the designated beneficiary whose life expectancy will be used to determine the distribution period. If the beneficiary of the trust named as beneficiary is another trust, the beneficiaries of the other trust will be treated as having been designated as beneficiaries of the employee under the plan for purposes of determining the distribution period under section 401(a)(9)(A)(ii), provided that the requirements of paragraph (b) of this A-5 are satisfied with respect to such other trust in addition to the trust named as beneficiary.

Q-6. If a trust is named as a beneficiary of an employee, what documentation must be provided to the plan administrator?

A-6. (a) *Required minimum distributions before death.* In order to satisfy the documentation requirement of this A-6 for required minimum distributions under section 401(a)(9) to commence before the death of an employee, the employee must comply with either paragraph (a)(1) or (2) of this A-6:

(1) The employee provides to the plan administrator a copy of the trust instrument and agrees that if the trust instrument is amended at any time in the future, the employee will, within a reasonable time, provide to the plan administrator a copy of each such amendment.

(2) The employee—

(i) Provides to the plan administrator a list of all of the beneficiaries of the trust (including contingent and remaindermen beneficiaries with a description of the conditions on their entitlement);

(ii) Certifies that, to the best of the employee's knowledge, this list is correct and complete and that the requirements of paragraphs (b)(1), (2), and (3) of A-5 of this section are satisfied;

(iii) Agrees that, if the trust instrument is amended at any time in the future, the employee will, within a reasonable time, provide to the plan administrator corrected certifications to the extent that the amendment changes any information previously certified; and

(iv) Agrees to provide a copy of the trust instrument to the plan administrator upon demand.

(b) *Required minimum distributions after death.* In order to satisfy the documentation requirement of this A-6 for required minimum distributions after the death of the employee, by the last day of the calendar year immediately following the calendar year in which the employee died, the trustee of the trust must either -

(1) Provide the plan administrator with a final list of all beneficiaries of the trust (including contingent and remaindermen beneficiaries with a description of the conditions on their entitlement) as of the end of the calendar year following the calendar year of the employee's death; certify that, to the best of the trustee's knowledge, this list is correct and complete and that the requirements of paragraph (b)(1), (2), and

(3) of A-5 of this section are satisfied; and agree to provide a copy of the trust instrument to the plan administrator upon demand; or

(2) Provide the plan administrator with a copy of the actual trust document for the trust that is named as a beneficiary of the employee under the plan as of the employee's date of death.

(c) *Relief for discrepancy between trust instrument and employee certifications or earlier trust instruments.* (1) If required minimum distributions are determined based on the information provided to the plan administrator in certifications or trust instruments described in paragraph (a)(1), (a)(2) or (b) of this A-6, a plan will not fail to satisfy section 401(a)(9) merely because the actual terms of the trust instrument are inconsistent with the information in those certifications or trust instruments previously provided to the plan administrator, but only if the plan administrator reasonably relied on the information provided and the required minimum distributions for calendar years after the calendar year in which the discrepancy is discovered are determined based on the actual terms of the trust instrument.

(2) For purposes of determining the amount of the excise tax under section 4974, the required minimum distribution is determined for any year based on the actual terms of the trust in effect during the year.

§ 1.401(a)(9)-5 Required minimum distributions from defined contribution plans.

Q-1. If an employee's benefit is in the form of an individual account under a defined contribution plan, what is the amount required to be distributed for each calendar year?

A-1. (a) *General rule.* If an employee's accrued benefit is in the form of an individual account under a defined contribution plan, the minimum amount required to be distributed for each distribution calendar year, as defined in paragraph (b) of this A-1, is equal to the quotient obtained by dividing the account (determined under A-3 of this section) by the applicable distribution period (determined under A-4 of this section). However, the required minimum distribution amount will never exceed the entire vested account balance on the date of the distribution. Further, the minimum distribution required to be distributed on or before an employee's required beginning date is always determined under section 401(a)(9)(A)(ii) and this A-1 and not section 401(a)(9)(A)(i).

(b) *Distribution calendar year.* A calendar year for which a minimum distribution is required is a distribution calendar year. If an employee's required beginning date is April 1 of the calendar year following the calendar year in which the employee attains age 70 ½, the employee's first distribution calendar year is the year the employee attains age 70 ½. If an employee's required beginning date is April 1 of the calendar year following the calendar year in which the employee retires, the calendar year in which the employee retires is the employee's first distribution calendar year. In the case of distributions to be made in accordance with the life expectancy rule in § 1.401(a)(9)-3 and in section 401(a)(9)(B)(iii) and (iv), the first distribution calendar year is the calendar year containing the date described in A-3(a) or A-3(b) of § 1.401(a)(9)-3, whichever is applicable.

(c) *Time for distributions.* The distribution required to be made on or before the employee's required beginning date shall be treated as the distribution required for the employee's first distribution calendar year (as defined in paragraph (b) of this A-1). The required minimum distribution for other distribution calendar years, including the required minimum distribution for the distribution calendar year in which the employee's required beginning date occurs, must be made on or before the end of that distribution calendar year.

(d) *Minimum distribution incidental benefit requirement.* If distributions are made in accordance with this section, the minimum distribution incidental benefit requirement of section 401(a)(9)(G) will be satisfied.

(e) *Annuity contracts.* Instead of satisfying this A-1, the required minimum distribution requirement may be satisfied by the purchase of an annuity contract from an insurance company in accordance with A-4 of § 1.401(a)(9)-6 with the employee's entire individual account. If such an annuity is purchased after distributions are required to commence (the required beginning date, in the case of distributions commencing before death, or the date determined under A-3 of § 1.401(a)(9)-3, in the case of distributions commencing after death), payments under the annuity contract purchased will satisfy section 401(a)(9) for distribution calendar years after the calendar year of the purchase if payments under the annuity contract are made in accordance with § 1.401(a)(9)-6. In such a case, payments under the annuity contract will be treated as distributions from the individual account for purposes of determining if the individual account satisfies section 401(a)(9) for the calendar year of the purchase. An employee may also purchase an annuity contract

for a portion of the employee's account under the rules of A-2(c) of § 1.401(a)(9)-8.

Q-2. If an employee's benefit is in the form of an individual account and, in any calendar year, the amount distributed exceeds the minimum required, will credit be given in subsequent calendar years for such excess distribution?

A-2. If, for any distribution calendar year, the amount distributed exceeds the minimum required, no credit will be given in subsequent calendar years for such excess distribution.

Q-3. What is the amount of the account of an employee used for determining the employee's required minimum distribution in the case of an individual account?

A-3. (a) In the case of an individual account, the benefit used in determining the required minimum distribution for a distribution calendar year is the account balance as of the last valuation date in the calendar year immediately preceding that distribution calendar year (valuation calendar year) adjusted in accordance with paragraphs (b) and (c) of this A-3.

(b) The account balance is increased by the amount of any contributions or forfeitures allocated to the account balance as of dates in the valuation calendar year after the valuation date. Contributions include contributions made after the close of the valuation calendar year which are allocated as of dates in the valuation calendar year.

(c)(1) The account balance is decreased by distributions made in the valuation calendar year after the valuation date.

(2)(i) The following rule applies if any portion of the required minimum distribution for the first distribution calendar year is made in the second distribution calendar year (i.e., generally, the distribution calendar year in which the required beginning date occurs). In such case, for purposes of determining the account balance to be used for determining the required minimum distribution for the second distribution calendar year, distributions described in paragraph (c)(1) shall include an additional amount. This additional amount is equal to the amount of any distribution made in the second distribution calendar year on or before the required beginning date that is not in excess (when added to the amounts distributed in the first calendar year) of the amount required to meet the required minimum distribution for the first distribution calendar year.

(ii) This paragraph (c)(2) is illustrated by the following example:

Example. (i) Employee X, born October 1, 1931, is an unmarried participant in a qualified defined contribution plan (Plan Z). After retirement, X attains age 70 ½ in calendar year 2002. X's required beginning date is April 1, 2003. As of the last valuation date under Plan Z in calendar year 2001, which was on December 31, 2001, the value of X's account balance was $25,300. No contributions are made or amounts forfeited after such date which are allocated in calendar year 2001. No rollover amounts are received after such date by Plan Z on X's behalf which were distributed by a qualified plan or IRA in calendar years 2001, 2002, or 2003. The applicable distribution period from the table in A-4(a)(2) for an individual age 71 is 25.3 years. The required minimum distribution for calendar year 2002 is $1,000 ($25,300 divided by 25.3). That amount is distributed to X on April 1, 2003.

(ii) The value of X's account balance as of December 31, 2002 (the last valuation date under Plan Z in calendar year 2002) is $26,400. No contributions are made or amounts forfeited after such date which are allocated in calendar year 2002. In order to determine the benefit to be used in calculating the required minimum distribution for calendar year 2003, the account balance of $26,400 will be reduced by $1,000, the amount of the required minimum distribution for calendar year 2002 made on April 1, 2003. Consequently, the benefit for purposes of determining the required minimum distribution for calendar year 2003 is $25,400.

(iii) If, instead of $1,000 being distributed to X, $20,000 is distributed on April 1 2003, the account balance of $26,400 would still be reduced by $1,000 in order to determine the benefit to be used in calculating the required minimum distribution for calendar year 2003. The amount of the distribution made on April 1, 2003, in order to meet the required minimum distribution for 2002 would still be $1,000. The remaining $19,000 ($20,000 – $1,000) of the distribution is not the required minimum distribution for 2002. Instead, the remaining $19,000 of the distribution is sufficient to satisfy the required minimum distribution requirement with respect to X for calendar year 2003. The amount which is required to be distributed for calendar year 2003 is $1,040.10 ($25,400 divided by 24.4, the applicable distribution period for an individual age 72). Consequently, no additional amount is required to be distributed to X in 2003 because $19,000 exceeds $1,040.10. However, pursuant to A-2 of this section, the remaining $17,959.90

($19,000–$1,040.10) may not be used to satisfy the required minimum distribution requirements for calendar year 2004 or any subsequent calendar years.

(d) If an amount is distributed by one plan and rolled over to another plan (receiving plan), A-2 of § 1.401(a)(9)-7 provides additional rules for determining the benefit and required minimum distribution under the receiving plan. If an amount is transferred from one plan (transferor plan) to another plan (transferee plan), A-3 and A-4 of § 1.401(a)(9)-7 provide additional rules for determining the amount of the required minimum distribution and the benefit under both the transferor and transferee plans.

Q-4. For required minimum distributions during an employee's lifetime, what is the applicable distribution period?

A-4. (a) *General rule*—(1) *Applicable distribution period.* Except as provided in paragraph (b) of this A-4, the applicable distribution period for required minimum distributions for distribution calendar years up to and including the distribution calendar year that includes the employee's date of death is determined using the table in paragraph (a)(2) for the employee's age as of the employee's birthday in the relevant distribution calendar year.

(2) *Table for determining distribution period*—(i) *General rule.* The following table is used for determining the distribution period for lifetime distributions to an employee.

Age of the employee	Distribution period
70	26.2
71	25.3
72	24.4
73	23.5
74	22.7
75	21.8
76	20.9
77	20.1
78	19.2
79	18.4
80	17.6
81	16.8
82	16.0
83	15.3
84	14.5
85	13.8
86	13.1
87	12.4
88	11.8
89	11.1
90	10.5
91	9.9
92	9.4
93	8.8
94	8.3
95	7.8
96	7.3
97	6.9
98	6.5
99	6.1
100	5.7
101	5.3
102	5.0
103	4.7
104	4.4
105	4.1
106	3.8
107	3.6
108	3.3
109	3.1
110	2.8
111	2.6
112	2.4
113	2.2
114	2.0
115 and older	1.8

(ii) *Authority for revised table.* The table in A-4(a)(2)(i) of this section may be replaced by any revised table prescribed by the Commissioner in revenue rulings, notices, or other guidance published in the Internal Revenue Bulletin. See § 601.601(d)(2)(ii)(b) of this chapter.

(b) *Spouse is sole beneficiary.* If the sole designated beneficiary of an employee is the employee's surviving spouse, for required minimum distributions during the employee's lifetime, the applicable distribution period is the longer of the distribution period determined in accordance with paragraph (a) of this A-4 or the joint life expectancy of the employee and spouse using the employee's and spouse's attained ages as of the employee's and the spouse's birthdays in the distribution calendar year. The spouse is sole designated beneficiary for purposes of determining the applicable distribution period for a distribution calendar year during the employee's lifetime if the spouse is the sole beneficiary of the employee's entire interest at all times during the distribution calendar year.

Q-5. For required minimum distributions after an employee's death, what is the applicable distribution period?

A-5. (a) *Death on or after the employee's required beginning date.* If an employee dies on or after distribution has begun as determined under A-6 of § 1.401(a)(9)-2 (generally after the employee's required beginning date), in order to satisfy section 401(a)(9)(B)(i), the applicable distribution period for distribution calendar years after the distribution calendar year containing the employee's date of death is either -

(1) If the employee has a designated beneficiary as of the date determined under A-4 of § 1.401(a)(9)-4, the remaining life expectancy of the employee's designated beneficiary determined in accordance with paragraph (c)(1) or (2) of this A-5; or

(2) If the employee does not have a designated beneficiary as of the date determined under A-4(a) of § 1.401(a)(9)-4, the remaining life expectancy of the employee determined in accordance with paragraph (c)(3) of this A-5.

(b) *Death before an employee's required beginning date.* If an employee dies before distribution has begun as determined under A-5 of § 1.401(a)(9)-2 (generally before the employee's required beginning date), in order to satisfy section 401(a)(9)(B)(iii) or (iv) and the life expectancy rule described in A-1 of §1.401(a)(9)-3, the applicable distribution period for distribution calendar years after the distribution calendar year containing the employee's date of death is the remaining life expectancy of the employee's designated beneficiary, determined in accordance with paragraph (c)(1) or (2) of this A-5.

(c) *Life expectancy*—(1) *Nonspouse designated beneficiary.* The applicable distribution period measured by the beneficiary's remaining life expectancy is determined using the beneficiary's age as of the beneficiary's birthday in the calendar year immediately following the calendar year of the employee's death. In subsequent calendar years the applicable distribution period is reduced by one for each calendar year that has elapsed since the calendar year immediately following the calendar year of the employee's death.

(2) *Spouse designated beneficiary.* If the surviving spouse of the employee is the employee's sole beneficiary, the applicable period is measured by the surviving spouse's life expectancy using the surviving spouse's birthday for each distribution calendar year for which a required minimum distribution is required after the calendar year of the employee's death. For calendar years after the calendar year of the spouse's death, the spouse's remaining life expectancy is the life expectancy of the spouse using the age of the spouse as of the spouse's birthday in the calendar year of the spouse's death. In subsequent calendar years, the applicable distribution period is reduced by one for each calendar year that has elapsed since the calendar year immediately following the calendar year of the spouse's death.

(3) *No designated beneficiary.* The applicable distribution period measured by the employee's remaining life expectancy is the life expectancy of the employee using the age of the employee as of the employee's birthday in the calendar year of the employee's death. In subsequent calendar years the applicable distribution period is reduced by one for each calendar year that has elapsed since the calendar year of death.

Q-6. What life expectancies must be used for purposes of determining required minimum distributions under section 401(a)(9)?

A-6. (a) *General rule.* Unless otherwise prescribed in accordance with paragraph (b) of this A-6, life expectancies for purposes of determining required minimum distributions under section 401(a)(9) must be computed using of the expected return multiples in Tables V and VI of §1.72-9.

(b) *Revised expected return table.* The expected return multiples described in paragraph (a) of this A-6 may be replaced by revised expected return multiples prescribed for use for purposes of determining required minimum distributions under section 401(a)(9) by the Commissioner in revenue rulings, notices, and other guidance published in the Internal Revenue Bulletin. See §601.601(d)(2)(ii)(b) of this chapter.

Q-7. If an employee has more than one designated beneficiary, which designated beneficiary's life expectancy will be used to determine the applicable distribution period?

A-7. (a) *General rule.* (1) Except as otherwise provided in paragraph (c) of this A-7, if more than one individual is designated as a beneficiary with respect to an employee as of any applicable date for determining the designated beneficiary, the designated beneficiary with the shortest life expectancy will be the designated beneficiary for purposes of determining the distribution period. However, except as otherwise provided in A-5 of §1.401(a)(9)-4 and paragraph (c)(1) of this A-7, if a person other than an individual is designated as a beneficiary, the employee will be treated as not having any designated beneficiaries for purposes of section 401(a)(9) even if there are also individuals designated as beneficiaries.

(2) See A-2 of §1.401(a)(9)-8 for special rules which apply if an employee's benefit under a plan is divided into separate accounts (or segregated shares in the case of a defined benefit plan) and the beneficiaries with respect to a separate account differ from the beneficiaries of another separate account.

(b) *Contingent beneficiary.* Except as provided in paragraph (c)(1) of this A-7, if a beneficiary's entitlement to an employee's benefit is contingent on an event other than the employee's death or the death of another beneficiary, such contingent beneficiary is considered to be a designated beneficiary for purposes of determining which designated beneficiary has the shortest life expectancy under paragraph (a) of this A-7.

(c) *Death contingency.* (1) If a beneficiary (subsequent beneficiary) is entitled to any potion of an employee's benefit only if another beneficiary dies before the entire benefit to which that other beneficiary is entitled has been distributed by the plan, the subsequent beneficiary

will not be considered a beneficiary for purposes of determining who is the designated beneficiary with the shortest life expectancy under paragraph (a) of this A-7 or whether a beneficiary who is not an individual is a beneficiary. This rule does not apply if the other beneficiary dies prior to the applicable date for determining the designated beneficiary.

(2) If the designated beneficiary whose life expectancy is being used to calculate the distribution period dies on or after the applicable date, such beneficiary's remaining life expectancy will be used to determine the distribution period whether or not a beneficiary with a shorter life expectancy receives the benefits.

(3) This paragraph (c) is illustrated by the following examples:

Example 1. Employer L maintains a defined contribution plan, Plan W. Unmarried Employee C dies in calendar year 2001 at age 30. As of December 31, 2002, D, the sister of C, is the beneficiary of C's account balance under Plan W. Prior to death C has designated that, if D dies before C's entire account balance has been distributed to D, E, mother of C and D, will be the beneficiary of the account balance. Because E is only entitled, as a beneficiary, to any portion of C's account if D dies before the entire account has been distributed, E is disregarded in determining C's designated beneficiary. Accordingly, even after D's death, D's life expectancy continues to be used to determined the distribution period.

Example 2. (i) Employer M maintains a defined contribution plan, Plan X. Employee A, an employee of M, died in 2001 at the age of 55, survived by spouse, B, who was 50 years old. Prior to A's death, M had established an account balance for A in Plan X. A's account balance is invested only in productive assets. A named the trustee of a testamentary trust (Trust P) established under A's will as the beneficiary of all amounts payable from the A's account in Plan X after A's death. A copy of the Trust P and a list of the trust beneficiaries were provided to the plan administrator of Plan X by the end of the calendar year following the calendar year of A's death. As of the date of *A*'s death, the Trust P was irrevocable and was a valid trust under the laws of the state of *A*'s domicile. A's account balance in Plan X was includible in A's gross estate under §2039.

(ii) Under the terms of Trust P, all trust income is payable annually to B, and no one has the power to appoint Trust P principal to any person other than B. A's children, who are all younger than B, are the sole remainder beneficiaries of the Trust P. No other person has a beneficial interest in Trust P. Under the terms of the Trust P, B has the power, exercisable annually, to compel the trustee to withdraw from A's account balance in Plan X an amount equal to the income earned on the assets held in A's account in Plan X during the calendar year and to distribute that amount through Trust P to B. Plan X contains no prohibition on withdrawal from A's account of amounts in excess of the annual required minimum distributions under section 401(a)(9). In accordance with the terms of Plan X, the trustee of Trust P elects, in order to satisfy section 401(a)(9), to receive annual required minimum distributions using the life expectancy rule in section 401(a)(9)(B)(iii) for distributions over a distribution period equal to B's life expectancy. If B exercises the withdrawal power, the trustee must withdraw from A's account under Plan X the greater of the amount of income earned in the account during the calendar year or the required minimum distribution. However, under the terms of Trust P, and applicable state law, only the portion of the Plan X distribution received by the trustee equal to the income earned by A's account in Plan X is required to be distributed to B (along with any other trust income.)

(iii) Because some amounts distributed from A's account in Plan X to Trust P may be accumulated in Trust P during B's lifetime for the benefit of A's children, as remaindermen beneficiaries of Trust P, even though access to those amounts are delayed until after B's death, A's children are beneficiaries of A's account in Plan X in addition to B and B is not the sole beneficiary of A's account. Thus the designated beneficiary used to determine the distribution period from A's account in Plan X is the beneficiary with the shortest life expectancy. B's life expectancy is the shortest of all the potential beneficiaries of the testamentary trust's interest in A's account in Plan X (including remainder beneficiaries). Thus, the distribution period for purposes of section 401(a)(9)(B)(iii) is B's life expectancy. Because B is not the sole beneficiary of the testamentary trust's interest in A's account in Plan X, the special rule in 401(a)(9)(B)(iv) is not available and the annual required minimum distributions from the account to Trust M must begin no later than the end of the calendar year immediately following the calendar year of A's death.

Example 3. (i) The facts are the same as *Example 2* except that the testamentary trust instrument provides that all amounts distributed from A's account in Plan X to the trustee while B is alive will be paid directly to B upon receipt by the trustee of Trust P.

(ii) In this case, B is the sole beneficiary of A's account in Plan X for purposes of determining the designated beneficiary under section 401(a)(9)(B)(iii) and (iv). No amounts distributed from A's account in Plan X to Trust P are accumulated in Trust P during B's lifetime for the benefit of any other beneficiary. Because B is the sole beneficiary of the testamentary trust's interest in A's account in Plan X, the annual required minimum distributions from A's account to Trust P must begin no later than the end of the calendar year in which A would have attained age 70 ½. rather than the calendar year immediately following the calendar year of A's death.

(d) *Designations by beneficiaries.* (1) If the plan provides (or allows the employee to specify) that, after the end of the calendar year following the calendar year in which the employee died, any person or persons have the discretion to change the beneficiaries of the employee, then, for purposes of determining the distribution period after the employee's death, the employee will be treated as not having designated a beneficiary. However, such discretion will not be found to exist merely because a beneficiary may designate a subsequent beneficiary for distributions of any portion of the employee's benefit after the beneficiary dies.

(2) This paragraph (d) is illustrated by the following example:

Example. The facts are the same as in *Example 1* in paragraph (c)(3) of this A-7, except that, as permitted under the plan, D designates E as the beneficiary of any amount remaining after the death of D rather than C making this designation. E is still disregarded in determining C's designated beneficiary for purposes of section 401(a)(9).

Q-8. If a portion of an employee's individual account is not vested as of the employee's required beginning date, how is the determination of the required minimum distribution affected?

A-8. If the employee's benefit is in the form of an individual account, the benefit used to determine the required minimum distribution for any distribution calendar year will be determined in accordance with A-1 of this section without regard to whether or not all of the employee's benefit is vested. If any portion of the employee's benefit is not vested, distributions will be treated as being paid from the vested portion of the benefit first. If, as of the end of a distribution calendar year (or as of the employee's required beginning date, in the case of the employee's first distribution calendar year), the total amount of the employee's vested benefit is less than the required minimum distribution for the calendar year, only the vested portion, if any, of the employee's benefit is required to be distributed by the end of the calendar year (or, if applicable, by the employee's required beginning date). However, the required minimum distribution for the subsequent distribution calendar year must be increased by the sum of amounts not distributed in prior calendar years because the employee's vested benefit was less than the required minimum distribution (subject to the limitation that the required minimum distribution for that subsequent distribution calendar year will not exceed the vested portion of the employee's benefit). In such case, an adjustment for the additional amount distributed which corresponds to the adjustment described in A-3(c)(2) of this section will be made to the account used to determine the required minimum distribution for that calendar year.

§ 1.401(a)(9)-6 Required minimum distributions as annuity payments.

Q-1. How must annuity distributions under a defined benefit plan be paid in order to satisfy section 401(a)(9)?

A-1. (a) In order to satisfy section 401(a)(9), annuity distributions under a defined benefit plan must be paid in periodic payments made at intervals not longer than one year (payment intervals) for a life (or lives), or over a period certain not longer than a life expectancy (or joint life and last survivor expectancy) described in section 401(a)(9)(A)(ii) or section 401(a)(9)(B)(iii), whichever is applicable. The life expectancy (or joint life and last survivor expectancy) for purposes of determining the length of the period certain will be determined in accordance with A-3 of this section. Once payments have commenced over a period certain, the period certain may not be lengthened even if the period certain is shorter than the maximum permitted. Life annuity payments must satisfy the minimum distribution incidental benefit requirements of A-2 of this section. All annuity payments (life and period certain) also must either be nonincreasing or increase only as follows:

(1) With any percentage increase in a specified and generally recognized cost-of-living index;

(2) To the extent of the reduction in the amount of the employee's payments to provide for a survivor benefit upon death, but only if the beneficiary whose life was being used to determine the period described in section 401(a)(9)(A)(ii) over which payments were being

made dies or is no longer the employee's beneficiary pursuant to a qualified domestic relations order within the meaning of section 414(p);

(3) To provide cash refunds of employee contributions upon the employee's death; or

(4) Because of an increase in benefits under the plan.

(b) The annuity may be a life annuity (or joint and survivor annuity) with a period certain if the life (or lives, if applicable) and period certain each meet the requirements of paragraph (a) of this A-1. For purposes of this section, if distribution is permitted to be made over the lives of the employee and the designated beneficiary, references to life annuity include a joint and survivor annuity.

(c) Distributions under a variable annuity will not be found to be increasing merely because the amount of the payments varies with the investment performance of the underlying assets. However, the Commissioner may prescribe additional requirements applicable to such variable life annuities in revenue rulings, notices, and other guidance published in the Internal Revenue Bulletin. See § 601.601(d)(2)(ii)(b) of this chapter.

(d) (1) Except as provided in (d)(2) of this A-1, annuity payments must commence on or before the employee's required beginning date (within the meaning of A-2 of § 1.401(a)(9)-2). The first payment which must be made on or before the employee's required beginning date must be the payment which is required for one payment interval. The second payment need not be made until the end of the next payment interval even if that payment interval ends in the next calendar year. Similarly, in the case of distributions commencing after death in accordance with section 401(a)(9)(B)(iii) and (iv), the first payment that must be made on or before the date determined under A-3(a) or (b) (whichever is applicable) of § 1.401(a)(9)-3 must be the payment which is required for one payment interval. Payment intervals are the periods for which payments are received, e.g., bimonthly, monthly, semi-annually, or annually. All benefit accruals as of the last day of the first distribution calendar year must be included in the calculation of the amount of the life annuity payments for payment intervals ending on or after the employee's required beginning date.

(2) In the case of an annuity contract purchased after the required beginning date, the first payment interval must begin on or before the purchase date and the payment required for one payment interval must be made no later than the end of such payment interval.

(3) This paragraph (d) is illustrated by the following example:

Example. A defined benefit plan (Plan X) provides monthly annuity payments of $500 for the life of unmarried participants with a 10-year period certain. An unmarried participant (A) in Plan X attains age 70 ½ in 2001. In order to meet the requirements of this paragraph, the first payment which must be made on behalf of A on or before April 1, 2002, will be $500 and the payments must continue to be made in monthly payments of $500 thereafter for the life and 10-year certain period.

(e) If distributions from a defined benefit plan are not in the form of an annuity, the employee's benefit will be treated as an individual account for purposes of determining the required minimum distribution. See § 1.401(a)(9)-5.

Q-2. How must distributions in the form of a life (or joint and survivor) annuity be made in order to satisfy the minimum distribution incidental benefit (MDIB) requirement of section 401(a)(9)(G)?

A-2. (a) *Life annuity for employee.* If the employee's benefit is payable in the form of a life annuity for the life of the employee satisfying section 401(a)(9), the MDIB requirement of section 401(a)(9)(G) will be satisfied.

(b) *Joint and survivor annuity, spouse beneficiary.* If the employee's sole beneficiary, as of the annuity starting date for annuity payments, is the employee's spouse and the distributions satisfy section 401(a)(9) without regard to the MDIB requirement, the distributions to the employee will be deemed to satisfy the MDIB requirement of section 401(a)(9)(G). For example, if an employee's benefit is being distributed in the form of a joint and survivor annuity for the lives of the employee and the employee's spouse and the spouse is the sole beneficiary of the employee, the amount of the periodic payment payable to the spouse may always be 100 percent of the annuity payment payable to the employee regardless of the difference in the ages between the employee and the employee's spouse. However, the amount of the payments under the annuity must be nonincreasing unless specifically permitted under A-1 of this section.

(c) *Joint and survivor annuity, nonspouse beneficiary—*(1) *Explanation of rule.* If distributions commence under a distribution option that is in the form of a joint and survivor annuity for the joint lives of the employee and a beneficiary other than the employee's spouse, the

MDIB requirement will not be satisfied as of the date distributions commence unless the distribution option provides that annuity payments to be made to the employee on and after the employee's required beginning date will satisfy the conditions of this paragraph. The periodic annuity payment payable to the survivor must not at any time on and after the employee's required beginning date exceed the applicable percentage of the annuity payment payable to the employee using the table below. Thus, this requirement must be satisfied with respect to any benefit increase after such date, including increases to reflect

increases in the cost of living. The applicable percentage is based on the excess of the age of the employee over the age of the beneficiary as of their attained ages as of their birthdays in a calendar year. If the employee has more than one beneficiary, the applicable percentage will be the percentage using the age of the youngest beneficiary. Additionally, the amount of the annuity payments must satisfy A-1 of this section.

(2) *Table.*

Excess of age of employee over age of beneficiary	Applicable percentage
10 years or less	100%
11	96%
12	93%
13	90%
14	87%
15	84%
16	82%
17	79%
18	77%
19	75%
20	73%
21	72%
22	70%
23	68%
24	67%
25	66%
26	64%
27	63%
28	62%
29	61%
30	60%
31	59%
32	59%
33	58%
34	57%
35	56%
36	56%
37	55%
38	55%
39	54%
40	54%
41	53%
42	53%
43	53%
44 and greater	52%

(3) *Example.* This paragraph (c) is illustrated by the following example:

Example. Distributions commence on January 1, 2001 to an employee (Z), born March 1, 1935, after retirement at age 65. Z's daughter (Y), born February 5, 1965, is Z's beneficiary. The distributions are in the form of a joint and survivor annuity for the lives of Z and Y with payments of $500 a month to Z and upon Z's death of $500 a month to Y, i.e., the projected monthly payment to Y is 100 percent of the monthly amount payable to Z. There is no provision under the option for a change in the projected payments to Y as of April 1, 2006, Z's required beginning date. Consequently, as of January 1, 2001, the date annuity distributions commence, the plan does not satisfy the MDIB requirement in operation because, as of such date, the distribution option provides that, as of Z's required beginning date, the monthly payment to Y upon Z's death will exceed 60 percent of Z's monthly payment (the maximum percentage for a difference of ages of 30 years).

(d) *Period certain and annuity features.* If a distribution form includes a life annuity and a period certain, the amount of the annuity payments payable to the employee must satisfy paragraph (c) of this A-2, and the period certain may not exceed the period determined under A-3 of this section.

Q-3. How long is a period certain under an annuity contract permitted to extend?

A-3. (a) *Distributions commencing during the employee's life* — (1) *Spouse beneficiary.* If an employee's spouse is the employee's sole beneficiary as of the annuity starting date, the period certain for annuity distributions commencing during the life of an employee with an annuity starting date on or after the employee's required beginning date is not permitted to exceed the joint life and last survivor expectancy of the employee and the spouse using the age of the employee

and spouse as of their birthdays in the calendar year that contains the annuity starting date.

(2) *Nonspouse beneficiary.* If an employee's surviving spouse is not the employee's sole beneficiary as of the annuity starting date, the period certain for any annuity distributions during the life of the employee with an annuity starting date on or after the employee's required beginning date is not permitted to exceed the shorter of the applicable distribution period for the employee (determined in accordance with the table in A-4(a)(2) of §1.401(a)(9)-5 for the calendar year that contains on the annuity starting date or the joint life and last survivor expectancy of the employee and the employee's designated beneficiary, determined using the designated beneficiary as of the annuity starting date and using their ages as of their birthdays in the calendar year that the contains the annuity starting date. See A-10 for the rule for annuity payments with an annuity starting date before the required beginning date.

(b) *Life expectancy rule.* (1) If annuity distributions commence after the death of the employee under the life expectancy rule (under section 401(a)(9)(iii) or (iv)), the period certain for any distributions commencing after death cannot exceed the applicable distribution period determined under A-5(b) of §1.401(a)(9)-5 for the distribution calendar year that contains the annuity starting date.

(2) If the annuity starting date is in a calendar year before the first distribution calendar year, the period certain may not exceed the life expectancy of the designated beneficiary using the beneficiary's age in the year that contains the annuity starting date.

Q-4. May distributions be made from an annuity contract which is purchased from an insurance company?

A-4. Yes. Distributions may be made from an annuity contract which is purchased with the employee's benefit by the plan from an insurance company and which makes payments that satisfy the provisions of this section. In the case of an annuity contract purchased from an insurance company, there is also an exception to the nonincreasing requirement in A-1(a) of this section for an increase to provide a cash refund upon the employee's death equal to the excess of the amount of the premiums paid for the contract over the prior distributions under the contract. If the payments actually made under the annuity contract do not meet the requirements of section 401(a)(9), the plan fails to satisfy section 401(a)(9).

Q-5. In the case of annuity distributions under a defined benefit plan, how must additional benefits which accrue after the employee's required beginning date be distributed in order to satisfy section 401(a)(9)?

A.-5. (a) In the case of annuity distributions under a defined benefit plan, if any additional benefits accrue after the employee's required beginning date, distribution of such amount as a separate identifiable component must commence in accordance with A-1 of this section beginning with the first payment interval ending in the calendar year immediately following the calendar year in which such amount accrues.

(b) A plan will not fail to satisfy section 401(a)(9) merely because there is an administrative delay in the commencement of the distribution of the separate identifiable component, provided that the actual payment of such amount commences as soon as practicable but not later than by the end of the first calendar year following the calendar year in which the additional benefit accrues, and that the total amount paid during such first calendar year is not less than the total amount that was required to be paid during that year under A-5(a) of this section.

Q-6. If a portion of an employee's benefit is not vested as of the employee's required beginning date, how is the determination of the required minimum distribution affected?

A-6 In the case of annuity distributions from a defined benefit plan, if any portion of the employee's benefit is not vested as of December 31 of a distribution calendar year (or as of the employee's required beginning date in the case of the employee's first distribution calendar year), the portion which is not vested as of such date will be treated as not having accrued for purposes of determining the required minimum distribution for that distribution calendar year. When an additional portion of the employee's benefit becomes vested, such portion will be treated as an additional accrual. See A-5 of this section for the rules for distributing benefits which accrue under a defined benefit plan after the employee's required beginning date.

Q-7. If an employee retires after the calendar year in which the employee attains age 70 ½, for what period must the employee's accrued benefit under a defined benefit plan be actuarially increased?

A-7. (a) *Actuarial increase starting date.* If an employee (other than a 5-percent owner) retires after the calendar year in which in the employee attains age 70 ½, in order to satisfy section 401(a)(9)(C)(iii), the employee's accrued benefit under a defined benefit plan must be actuarially increased to take into account any period after age 70 ½ in which the employee was not receiving any benefits under the plan. The actuarial increase required to satisfy section 401(a)(9)(C)(iii) must be provided for the period starting on the April 1 following the calendar year in which the employee attains age 70 ½.

(b) *Actuarial increase ending date.* The period for which the actuarial increase must be provided ends on the date on which benefits commence after retirement in an amount sufficient to satisfy section 401(a)(9).

(c) *Nonapplication to plan providing same required beginning date for all employees.* If as permitted under A-2(e) of §1.401(a)(9)-2, a plan provides that the required beginning date for purposes of section 401(a)(9) for all employees is April 1 of the calendar year following the calendar year in which the employee attained age 70 ½ (regardless of whether the employee is a 5-percent owner) and the plan makes distributions in an amount sufficient to satisfy section 401(a)(9) using that required beginning date, no actuarial increase is required under section 401(a)(9)(C)(iii).

(d) *Nonapplication to defined contribution plans.* The actuarial increase required under this A-7 does not apply to defined contribution plans.

(e) *Nonapplication to governmental and church plans.* The actuarial increase required under this A-7 does not apply to a governmental plan (within the meaning of section 414(d)) or a church plan. For purposes of this paragraph, the term *church plan* means a plan maintained by a church for church employees, and the term *church* means any church (as defined in section 3121(w)(3)(A)) or qualified church-controlled organization (as defined in section 3121(w)(3)(B)).

Q-8. What amount of actuarial increase is required under section 401(a)(9)(C)(iii)?

A-8. In order to satisfy section 401(a)(9)(C)(iii), the retirement benefits payable with respect to an employee as of the end of the period for actuarial increases (described in A-7 of this section) must be no less than: the actuarial equivalent of the employee's retirement benefits that would have been payable as of the date the actuarial increase must commence under A-7(a) of this section if benefits had commenced on that date; plus the actuarial equivalent of any additional benefits accrued after that date; reduced by the actuarial equivalent of any distributions made with respect to the employee's retirement benefits after that date. Actuarial equivalence is determined using the plan's assumptions for determining actuarial equivalence for purposes of satisfying section 411.

Q-9. How does the actuarial increase required under section 401(a)(9)(C)(iii) relate to the actuarial increase required under section 411?

A-9. In order for any of an employee's accrued benefit to be nonforfeitable as required under section 411, a defined benefit plan must make an actuarial adjustment to an accrued benefit the payment of which is deferred past normal retirement age. The only exception to this rule is that generally no actuarial adjustment is required to reflect the period during which a benefit is suspended as permitted under section 203(a)(3)(B) of the Employee Retirement Income Security Act of 1974 (ERISA). The actuarial increase required under section 401(a)(9) for the period described in A-7 of this section is generally the same as, and not in addition to, the actuarial increase required for the same period under section 411 to reflect any delay in the payment of retirement benefits after normal retirement age. However, unlike the actuarial increase required under section 411, the actuarial increase required under section 401(a)(9)(C) must be provided even during the period during which an employee's benefit has been suspended in accordance with ERISA section 203(a)(3)(B).

Q-10 What rule applies if distributions commence to an employee on a date before the employee's required beginning date over a period permitted under section 401(a)(9)(A)(ii) and the distribution form is an annuity under which distributions are made in accordance with the provisions of A-1 (and if applicable A-4) of this section?

A-10. (a) *General rule.* If distributions irrevocably (except for acceleration) commence to an employee on a date before the employee's required beginning date over a period permitted under section 401(a)(9)(A)(ii) and the distribution form is an annuity under which distributions are made in accordance with the provisions of A-1 (and, if applicable, A-4) of this section, the annuity starting date will be treated as the required beginning date for purposes of applying the rules of this section and §1.401(a)(9)-3. Thus, for example, the designated beneficiary distributions will be determined as of the annuity starting date. Similarly, if the employee dies after the annuity starting date but before the annuity starting date determined under A-2 of §1.401(a)(9)-2, after the employee's death, the remaining portion of the employee's interest must continue to be distributed in accordance with this section over the remaining period over which distributions commenced (single or joint lives and, if applicable, period certain). The rules in §1.401(a)(9)-3 and section 401(a)(9)(B)(ii) or (iii) and (iv) do not apply.

(b) *Period certain.* If as of the employee's birthday in the year that contains the annuity starting date, the age of the employee is under 70, the following rule applies in applying the rule in paragraph (a)(2) of A-3 of this section. The applicable distribution period for the employee (determined in accordance with the table in A-4(a)(2) of §1.401(a)(9)-5) is 26.2 plus the difference between 70 and the age of the employee as of the employee's birthday in the year that contains the annuity starting date.

Q-11. What rule applies if distributions commence irrevocably (except for acceleration) to the surviving spouse of an employee over a period permitted under section 401(a)(9)(B)(iii)(II) before the date on which distributions are required to commence and the distribution form is an annuity under which distributions are made as of the date distributions commence in accordance with the provisions of A-1 (and if applicable A-4) of this section,

A-11. If distributions commence irrevocably (except for acceleration) to the surviving spouse of an employee over a period permitted under section 401(a)(9)(B)(iii)(II) before the date on which distributions are required to commence and the distribution form is an annuity under which distributions are made as of the date distributions commence in accordance with the provisions of A-1 (and if applicable A-4) of this section, distributions will be considered to have begun on the actual commencement date for purposes of section 401(a)(9)(B)(iv)(II). Consequently, in such case, A-5 of § 1.401(a)(9)-3 and section 401(a)(9)(B)(ii) and (iii) will not apply upon the death of the surviving spouse as though the surviving spouse were the employee. Instead, the annuity distributions must continue to be made, in accordance with the provisions of A-1 (and if applicable A-4) of this section over the remaining period over which distributions commenced (single life and, if applicable, period certain).

§ 1.401(a)(9)-7 Rollovers and Transfers.

Q-1. If an amount is distributed by one plan (distributing plan) and is rolled over to another plan, is the benefit or the required minimum distribution under the distributing plan affected by the rollover?

A-1. No. If an amount is distributed by one plan and is rolled over to another plan, the amount distributed is still treated as a distribution by the distributing plan for purposes of section 401(a)(9), notwithstanding the rollover.

Q-2. Q. If an amount is distributed by one plan (distributing plan) and is rolled over to another plan (receiving plan), how are the benefit and the required minimum distribution under the receiving plan affected?

A-2. If an amount is distributed by one plan (distributing plan) and is rolled over to another plan (receiving plan), the benefit of the employee under the receiving plan is increased by the amount rolled over. However, the distribution has no impact on the required minimum distribution to be made by the receiving plan for the calendar year in which the rollover is received. But, if a required minimum distribution is required to be made by the receiving plan for the following calendar year, the rollover amount must be considered to be part of the employee's benefit under the receiving plan. Consequently, for purposes of determining any required minimum distribution for the calendar year immediately following the calendar year in which the amount rolled over is received by the receiving plan, in the case in which the amount rolled over is received after the last valuation date in the calendar year under the receiving plan, the benefit of the employee as of such valuation date, adjusted in accordance with A-3 of § 1.401(a)(9)-5, will be increased by the rollover amount valued as of the date of receipt. For purposes of calculating the benefit under the receiving plan pursuant to the preceding sentence, if the amount rolled over is received by the receiving plan in a different calendar year from the calendar year in which it is distributed by the distributing plan, the amount rolled over is deemed to have been received by the receiving plan in the calendar year in which it was distributed by the distributing plan.

Q-3. In the case of a transfer of an amount of an employee's benefit from one plan (transferor plan) to another plan (transferee plan), are there any special rules for satisfying the required minimum distribution requirement or determining the employee's benefit under the transferor plan?

A-3. (a) In the case of a transfer of an amount of an employee's benefit from one plan to another, the transfer is not treated as a distribution by the transferor plan for purposes of section 401(a)(9). Instead, the benefit of the employee under the transferor plan is decreased by the amount transferred. However, if any portion of an employee's benefit is transferred in a distribution calendar year with respect to that employee, in order to satisfy section 401(a)(9), the transferor plan must determine the amount of the required minimum distribution with respect to that employee for the calendar year of the transfer using the employee's benefit under the transferor plan before the transfer. Additionally, if any portion of an employee's benefit is transferred in the employee's second distribution calendar year but on or before the employee's required beginning date, in order to satisfy section 401(a)(9), the transferor plan must determine the amount of the required minimum distribution requirement for the employee's first distribution calendar year based on the employee's benefit under the transferor plan before the transfer. The transferor plan may satisfy the required minimum distribution requirement for the calendar year of the transfer (and the prior year if applicable) by segregating the amount which must be distributed from the employee's benefit and not transferring that amount. Such amount may be retained by the transferor plan and distributed on or before the date required.

(b) For purposes of determining any required minimum distribution for the calendar year immediately following the calendar year in which the transfer occurs, in the case of a transfer after the last valuation date for the calendar year of the transfer under the transferor plan, the benefit of the employee as of such valuation date, adjusted in accordance with A-3 of § 1.401(a)(9)-5, will be decreased by the amount transferred, valued as of the date of the transfer.

Q-4. If an amount of an employee's benefit is transferred from one plan (transferor plan) to another plan (transferee plan), how are the

benefit and the required minimum distribution under the transferee plan affected?

A-4. In the case of a transfer from one plan (transferor plan) to another (transferee plan), the general rule is that the benefit of the employee under the transferee plan is increased by the amount transferred. The transfer has no impact on the required minimum distribution to be made by the transferee plan in the calendar year in which the transfer is received. However, if a required minimum distribution is required from the transferee plan for the following calendar year, the transferred amount must be considered to be part of the employee's benefit under the transferee plan. Consequently, for purposes of determining any required minimum distribution for the calendar year immediately following the calendar year in which the transfer occurs, in the case of a transfer after the last valuation date of the transferee plan in the transfer calendar year, the benefit of the employee under the receiving plan valued as of such valuation date, adjusted in accordance with A-3 of § 1.401(a)(9)-5, will be increased by the amount transferred valued as of the date of the transfer.

Q-5. How are a spinoff, merger or consolidation (as defined in § 1.414(l)-1) treated for purposes of determining an employee's benefit and required minimum distribution under section 401(a)(9)?

A-5. For purposes of determining an employee's benefit and required minimum distribution under section 401(a)(9), a spinoff, a merger, or a consolidation (as defined in § 1.414(l)-1) will be treated as a transfer of the benefits of the employees involved. Consequently, the benefit and required minimum distribution of each employee involved under the transferor and transferee plans will be determined in accordance with A-3 and A-4 of this section.

§ 1.401(a)(9)-8 Special rules.

Q-1. What distribution rules apply if an employee is a participant in more than one plan?

A-1. If an employee is a participant in more than one plan, the plans in which the employee participates are not permitted to be aggregated for purposes of testing whether the distribution requirements of section 401(a)(9) are met. The distribution of the benefit of the employee under each plan must separately meet the requirements of section 401(a)(9). For this purpose, a plan described in section 414(k) is treated as two separate plans, a defined contribution plan to the extent benefits are based on an individual account and a defined benefit plan with respect to the remaining benefits.

Q-2. If an employee's benefit under a plan is divided into separate accounts (or segregated shares in the case of a defined benefit plan), do the distribution rules in section 401(a)(9) and these regulations apply separately to each separate account (or segregated share)?

A-2. (a) Except as otherwise provided in paragraphs (b) and (c) of this A-2, if an employee's account under a defined contribution plan plan is divided into separate accounts (or if an employee's benefit under a defined benefit plan is divided into segregated shares in the case of a defined benefit plan) under the plan, the separate accounts (or segregated shares) will be aggregated for purposes of satisfying the rules in section 401(a)(9). Thus, except as otherwise provided in paragraphs (b) and (c) of this A-2, all separate accounts, including a separate account for nondeductible employee contributions (under section 72(d)(2)) or for qualified voluntary employee contributions (as defined in section 219(e)), will be aggregated for purposes of section 401(a)(9).

(b) If, for lifetime distributions, as of an employee's required beginning date (or the beginning of any distribution calendar year beginning after the employee's required beginning date), or in the case of distributions under section 401(a)(9)(B)(ii) or (iii) and (iv), as of the end of the year following the year containing the employee's (or spouse's, where applicable) date of death, the beneficiaries with respect to a separate account (or segregated share in the case of a defined benefit plan) under the plan differ from the beneficiaries with respect to the other separate accounts (or segregate shares) of the employee under the plan, such separate account (or segregated share) under the plan need not be aggregated with other separate accounts (or segregated shares) under the plan in order to determine whether the distributions from such separate account (or segregated share) under the plan satisfy section 401(a)(9). Instead, the rules in section 401(a)(9) may separately apply to such separate account (or segregated share) under the plan. For example, if, in the case of a distribution described in section 401(a)(9)(B)(iii) and (iv), the only beneficiary of a separate account (or segregated share) under the plan is the employee's surviving spouse, and beneficiaries other than the surviving spouse are designated with respect to the other separate accounts of the employee, distribution of the spouse's separate account (or segregated share) under the plan need not commence until the date determined under the first sentence in A-3(b) of §1.401(a)(9)-3, even if distribution of the other separate accounts (or segregated shares) under the plan must commence at an earlier date. In the case of a distribution after the death of an employee to which section 401(a)(9)(B)(i) does not apply, distribution from a separate account (or segregated share) of an employee may be made over a beneficiary's life expectancy in accordance with section 401(a)(9)(B)(iii) and (iv) even through distributions from other separate accounts (or segregated shares) under the plan with different beneficiaries are being made in accordance with the five-year rule in section 401(a)(9)(B)(ii).

(c) A portion of an employee's account balance under a defined contribution plan is permitted to be used to purchase an annuity contract with a remaining amount maintained in the separate account. In that case, the separate account under the plan must be distributed in accordance with §1.401(a)(9)-5 in order to satisfy section 401(a)(9) and the annuity payments under the annuity contract must satisfy §1.401(a)(9)-6 in order to satisfy section 401(a)(9).

Q-3. What is a separate account or segregated share for purposes of section 401(a)(9)?

A-3. (a) For purposes of section 401(a)(9), a separate account in an individual account is a portion of an employee's benefit determined by an acceptable separate accounting including allocating investment gains and losses, and contributions and forfeitures, on a pro rata basis in a reasonable and consistent matter between such portion and any other benefits. Further, the amounts of each such portion of the benefit will be separately determined for purposes of determining the amount of the required minimum distribution in accordance with §1.401(a)(9)-5.

(b) A benefit in a defined benefit plan is separated into segregated shares if it consists of separate identifiable components which may be separately distributed.

Q-4. Must a distribution that is required by section 401(a)(9) to be made by the required beginning date to an employee or that is required by section 401(a)(9)(B)(iii) and (iv) to be made by the required time to a designated beneficiary who is a surviving spouse be made notwithstanding the failure of the employee, or spouse where applicable, to consent to a distribution while a benefit is immediately distributable?

A-4. Yes. Section 411(a)(11) and section 417(e) (see §§1.411(a)(11)-1(c)(2) and 1.417(e)-1(c)) require employee and spousal consent to certain distributions of plan benefits while such benefits are immediately distributable. If an employee's normal retirement age is later than the required beginning date for the commencement of distributions under section 401(a)(9) and, therefore, benefits are still immediately distributable, the plan must, nevertheless, distribute plan benefits to the participant (or where applicable, to the spouse) in a manner that satisfies the requirements of section 401(a)(9). Section 401(a)(9) must be satisfied even though the participant (or spouse, where applicable) fails to consent to the distribution. In such a case, the plan may distribute in the form of a qualified joint and survivor annuity (QJSA) or in the form of a qualified preretirement survivor annuity (QPSA) and the consent requirements of sections 411(a)(11) and 417(e) are deemed to be satisfied if the plan has made reasonable efforts to obtain consent from the participant (or spouse if applicable) and if the distribution otherwise meets the requirements of section 417. If, because of section 401(a)(11)(B), the plan is not required to distribute in the form of a QJSA to a participant or a QPSA to a surviving spouse, the plan may distribute the required minimum distribution amount required at the time required to satisfy section 401(a)(9) and the consent requirements of sections 411(a)(11) and 417(e) are deemed to be satisfied if the plan has made reasonable efforts to obtain consent from the participant (or spouse if applicable) and if the distribution otherwise meets the requirements of section 417.

Q-5. Who is an employee's spouse or surviving spouse for purposes of section 401(a)(9)?

A-5. Except as otherwise provided in A-6(a) (in the case of distributions of a portion of an employee's benefit payable to a former spouse of an employee pursuant to a qualified domestic relations order), for purposes of section 401(a)(9), an individual is a spouse or surviving spouse of an employee if such individual is treated as the employee's spouse under applicable state law. In the case of distributions after the death of an employee, for purposes of determining whether, under the life expectancy rule in section 401(a)(9)(B)(iii) and (iv), the provisions of section 401(a)(9)(B)(iv) apply, the spouse of the employee is determined as of the date of death of the employee.

Q-6. In order to satisfy section 401(a)(9), are there any special rules which apply to the distribution of all or a portion of an employee's benefit payable to an alternate payee pursuant to a qualified domestic relations order as defined in section 414(p) (QDRO)?

A-6. (a) A former spouse to whom all or a portion of the employee's benefit is payable pursuant to a QDRO will be treated as a spouse (including a surviving spouse) of the employee for purposes of section 401(a)(9), including the minimum distribution incidental benefit requirement, regardless of whether the QDRO specifically provides that the former spouse is treated as the spouse for purposes of sections 401(a)(11) and 417.

(b)(1) If a QDRO provides that an employee's benefit is to be divided and a portion is to be allocated to an alternate payee, such portion will be treated as a separate account (or segregated share) which separately must satisfy the requirements of section 401(a)(9) and may not be aggregated with other separate accounts (or segregated shares) of the employee for purposes of satisfying section 401(a)(9). Except as otherwise provided in paragraph (b)(2) of this A-6, distribution of such separate account allocated to an alternate payee pursuant to a QDRO must be made in accordance with section 401(a)(9). For example, in general, distribution of such account will satisfy section 401(a)(9)(A) if required minimum distributions from such account during the employee's lifetime begin not later than the employee's required beginning date and the required minimum distribution is determined in accordance with §1.401(a)(9)-5 for each distribution calendar year using an applicable distribution period determined under A-4 of §1.401(a)(9)-5 using the age of the employee in the distribution calendar year for purposes of using the table in A-4(a)(2) of §1.401(a)(9)-5 if applicable or ages of the employee and spousal alternate payee if their joint life expectancy is longer than the distribution period using that table. The determination of whether distribution from such account after the death of the employee to the alternate payee will be made in accordance with section 401(a)(9)(B)(i) or section 401(a)(9)(B)(ii) or (iii) and (iv) will depend on whether distributions have begun as determined under A-5 or §1.401(a)(9)-2 (which provides, in general, that distributions are not treated as having begun until the employee's required beginning date even though payments may actually have begun before that date). For example, if the alternate payee dies before the employee and distribution of the separate account allocated to the alternate payee pursuant to the QDRO is to be made to the alternate payee's beneficiary, such beneficiary may be treated as a designated beneficiary for purposes of determining the required minimum distribution required from such account after the death of the employee if the beneficiary of the alternate payee is an individual and if such beneficiary is a beneficiary under the plan or specified in or in the plan. Specification in or pursuant to the QDRO will also be treated as specification to the plan.

(2) Distribution of the separate account allocated to an alternate payee pursuant to a QDRO satisfy the requirements of section 401(a)(9)(A)(ii) if such account is to be distributed, beginning not later than the employee's required beginning date, over the life of the alternate payee (or over a period not extending beyond the life expectancy of the alternative payee). Also, if the plan permits the employee to elect whether distribution upon the death of the employee will be made in accordance with the five-year rule in section 401(a)(9)(B)(ii) or the life expectancy rule in section 401(a)(9)(B)(iii) and (iv) pursuant to A-4(c) of §1.401(a)(9)-3, such election is to be made only by the alternate payee for purposes of distributing the separate account allocated to the alternate payee pursuant to the QDRO. If the alternate payee dies after distribution of the separate account allocated to the alternate payee pursuant to a QDRO has begun (determined under A-5 of §1.401(a)(9)-2) but before the employee dies, distribution of the remaining portion of that portion of the benefit allocated to the alternate payee must be made in accordance with the rules in §1.401(a)(9)-5 or §1.401(a)(9)-6 for distributions during the life of the employee. Only after the death of the employee is the amount of the required minimum distribution determined in accordance with the rules that apply after the death of the employee.

(c) If a QDRO does not provide that an employee's benefit is to be divided but provides that a portion of an employee's benefit (otherwise payable to the employee) is to be paid to an alternate payee, such portion will not be treated as a separate account (or segregated share) of the employee. Instead, such portion will be aggregated with any amount distributed to the employee and will be treated as having been distributed to the employee for purposes of determining whether the required minimum distribution requirement has been satisfied with respect to that employee.

Q-7. Will a plan fail to satisfy section 401(a)(9) where it is not legally permitted to distribute to an alternate payee all or a portion of an employee's benefit payable to an alternate payee pursuant to a QDRO within the period specified in section 414(p)(7)?

A-7. A plan will not fail to satisfy section 401(a)(9) merely because it fails to distribute a required amount during the period in which the issue of whether a domestic relations order is a QDRO is being determined pursuant to section 414(p)(7), provided that the period does not extend beyond the 18-month period described in section 414(p)(7)(E). To the extent that a distribution otherwise required under section 401(a)(9) is not made during this period, this amount and any additional amount accrued during this period will be treated as though it is not vested during the period and any distributions with respect to such amounts must be made under the relevant rules for nonvested benefits described in either A-8 of §1.401(a)(9)-5 or A-6 of §1.401(a)(9)-6.

Q-8. Will a plan fail to satisfy section 401(a)(9) where an individual's distribution from the plan is less than the amount otherwise required to satisfy section 401(a)(9) under §1.401(a)(9)-5 or §1.401(a)(9)-6 because distributions were being paid under an annuity contract issued by a life insurance company in state insurer delinquency proceedings and have been reduced or suspended by reasons of such state proceedings?

A-8. A plan will not fail to satisfy section 401(a)(9) merely because an individual's distribution from the plan is less than the amount otherwise required to satisfy section 401(a)(9) under §1.401(a)(9)-5 or §1.401(a)(9)-6 because distributions were being paid under an annuity contract issued by a life insurance company in state insurer delinquency proceedings and have been reduced or suspended by reasons of such state proceedings. To the extent that a distribution otherwise required under section 401(a)(9) is not made during the state insurer delinquency proceedings, this amount and any additional amount accrued during this period will be treated as though it is not vested during the period and any distributions with respect to such amounts must be made under the relevant rules for nonvested benefits described in either A-8 of §1.401(a)(9)-5 or A-6 of §1.401(a)(9)-6.

Q-9. Will a plan fail to qualify as a pension plan within the meaning of section 401(a) solely because the plan permits distributions to commence to an employee on or after April 1 of the calendar year following the calendar year in which the employee attains age 70 ½ even though the employee has not retired or attained the normal retirement age under the plan as of the date on which such distributions commence?

A-9. No. A plan will not fail to qualify as a pension plan within the meaning of section 401(a) solely because the plan permits distributions to commence to an employee on or after April 1 of the calendar year following the calendar year in which the employee attains age 70 ½ even though the employee has not retired or attained the normal retirement age under the plan as of the date on which such distributions commence. This rule applies without regard to whether or not the employee is a 5-percent owner with respect to the plan year ending in the calendar year in which distributions commence.

Q-10. Is the distribution of an annuity contract a distribution for purposes of section 401(a)(9)?

A-10. No. The distribution of an annuity contract is not a distribution for purposes of section 401(a)(9).

Q-11. Will a payment by a plan after the death of an employee fail to be treated as a distribution for purposes of section 401(a)(9) solely because it is made to an estate or a trust?

A-11. A payment by a plan after the death of an employee will not fail to be treated as a distribution for purposes of section 401(a)(9) solely because it is made to an estate or a trust. As a result, the estate or trust which receives a payment from a plan after the death of an employee need not distribute the amount of such payment to the beneficiaries of the estate or trust in accordance with section 401(a)(9)(B). However, pursuant to A-3 of §1.401(a)(9)-4, distribution to the estate must satisfy the five-year rule in section 401(a)(9)(B)(iii) if the distribution to the employee had not begun (as defined in A-6 of §1.401(a)(9)-2) as of the employee's date of death, and pursuant to A-3 of §1.401(a)(9)-4, an estate may not be a designated beneficiary. See A-5 and A-6 of §1.401(a)(9)-4 for provisions under which beneficiaries of a trust with respect to the trust's interest in an employee's benefit are treated as having been designated as beneficiaries of the employee under the plan.

Q-12. Will a plan fail to satisfy section 411 if the plan is amended to eliminate benefit options that do not satisfy section 401(a)(9)?

A-12. Nothing in section 401(a)(9) permits a plan to eliminate for all participants a benefit option that could not otherwise be eliminated pursuant to section 411(d)(6). However, a plan must provide that, notwithstanding any other plan provisions, it will not distribute benefits under any option that does not satisfy section 401(a)(9). See A-3 of §1.401(a)(9)-1. Thus, the plan, notwithstanding section 411(d)(6), must prevent participants from electing benefit options that do not satisfy section 401(a)(9).

¶ 20,260C

Q-13. Is a plan disqualified merely because it pays benefits under a designation made before January 1, 1984, in accordance with section 242(b)(2) of the Tax Equity and Fiscal Responsibility Act (TEFRA)?

A-13. No. Even though the distribution requirements added by TEFRA were retroactively repealed by the Tax Reform Act of 1984 (TRA of 1984), the transitional election rule in section 242(b) was preserved. Satisfaction of the spousal consent requirements of section 4l7(a) and (e) (added by the Retirement Equity Act of 1984) will not be considered a revocation of the pre-1984 designation. However, sections 401(a)(11) and 417 must be satisfied with respect to any distribution subject to those sections. The election provided in section 242(b) of TEFRA is hereafter referred to as a section 242(b)(2) election.

Q-14. In the case in which an amount is transferred from one plan (transferor plan) to another plan (transferee plan), may the transferee plan distribute the amount transferred in accordance with a section 242(b)(2) election made under either the transferor plan or under the transferee plan?

A-14. (a) In the case in which an amount is transferred from one plan to another plan, the amount transferred may be distributed in accordance with a section 242(b)(2) election made under the transferor plan if the employee did not elect to have the amount transferred and if the amount transferred is separately accounted for by the transferee plan. However, only the benefit attributable to the amount transferred, plus earnings thereon, may be distributed in accordance with the section 242(b)(2) election made under the transferor plan. If the employee elected to have the amount transferred, the transfer will be treated as a distribution and rollover of the amount transferred for purposes of this section.

(b) In the case in which an amount is transferred from one plan to another plan, the amount transferred may not be distributed in accordance with a section 242(b)(2) election made under the transferee plan. If a section 242(b)(2) election was made under the transferee plan, the amount transferred must be separately accounted for. If the amount transferred is not separately accounted for under the transferee plan, the section 242(b)(2) election under the transferee plan is revoked and section 401(a)(9) will apply to subsequent distributions by the transferee plan.

(c) A merger, spinoff, or consolidation, as defined in §1.414(l)-1(b), will be treated as a transfer for purposes of the section 242(b)(2) election.

Q-15. If an amount is distributed by one plan (distributing plan) and rolled over into another plan (receiving plan), may the receiving plan distribute the amount rolled over in accordance with a section 242(b)(2) election made under either the distributing plan or the receiving plan?

A-15. No. If an amount is distributed by one plan and rolled over into another plan, the receiving plan must distribute the amount rolled over in accordance with section 401(a)(9) whether or not the employee made a section 242(b)(2) election under the distributing plan. Further, if the amount rolled over was not distributed in accordance with the election, the election under the distributing plan is revoked and section 401(a)(9) will apply to all subsequent distributions by the distributing plan. Finally, if the employee made a section 242(b)(2) election under the receiving plan and such election is still in effect, the amount rolled over must be separately accounted for under the receiving plan and distributed in accordance with section 401(a)(9). If amounts rolled over are not separately accounted for, any section 242(b)(2) election under the receiving plan is revoked and section 401(a)(9) will apply to subsequent distributions by the receiving plan.

Q-16. May a section 242(b)(2) election be revoked after the date by which distributions are required to commence in order to satisfy section 401(a)(9) and this section of the regulations?

A-16. Yes. A section 242(b)(2) election may be revoked after the date by which distributions are required to commence in order to satisfy section 401(a)(9) and this section of the regulations. However, if the section 242(b)(2) election is revoked after the date by which distributions are required to commence in order to satisfy section 401(a)(9) and this section of the regulations and the total amount of the distributions which would have been required to be made prior to the date of the revocation in order to satisfy section 401(a)(9), but for the section 242(b)(2) election, have not been made, the trust must distribute by the end of the calendar year following the calendar year in which the revocation occurs the total amount not yet distributed which was required to have been distributed to satisfy the requirements of section 401(a)(9) and continue distributions in accordance with such requirements.

Par. 4. Section 1.403(b)-2 is added to read as follows:

§ 1.403(b)-2 Required minimum distributions from annuity contracts purchased, or custodial accounts or retirement income accounts established, by a section 501(c)(3) organization or a public school.

Q-1. Are section 403(b) contracts subject to the distribution rules provided in section 401(a)(9)?

A-1. (a) Yes. Section 403(b) contracts are subject to the distribution rules provided in section 401(a)(9). For purposes of this section the term *section 403(b) contract* means an annuity contract described in section 403(b)(1), custodial account described in section 403(b)(7), or a retirement income account described in section 403(b)(9).

(b) For purposes of applying the distribution rules in section 401(a)(9), section 403(b) contracts will be treated as individual retirement annuities described in section 408(b) and individual retirement accounts described in section 408(a) (IRAs). Consequently, except as otherwise provided in paragraph (c), the distribution rules in section 401(a)(9) will be applied to section 403(b) contracts in accordance with the provisions in § 1.408-8.

(c)(1) The required beginning date for purposes of section 403(b)(9) is April 1, of the calendar year following the later of the calendar year in which the employee attains 70 ½ or the calendar year in which the employee retires from employment with the employer maintaining the plan. The concept of 5-percent owner has no application in the case of employees of employers described in section 403(b)(1)(A).

(2) The rule in A-5 of § 1.408-8 does not apply to section 403(b) contracts. Thus, the surviving spouse of an employee is not permitted to treat a section 403(b) contract of which the spouse is the sole beneficiary as the spouse's own section 403(b) contract.

Q-2. To what benefits under section 403(b) contracts, do the distribution rules provided in section 401(a)(9) apply?

A-2. (a) The distribution rules provided in section 401(a)(9) apply to all benefits under section 403(b) contracts accruing after December 31, 1986 (post-'86 account balance). The distribution rules provided in section 401(a)(9) do not apply to the balance of the account balance under the section 403(b) contract valued as of December 31, 1986, exclusive of subsequent earnings (pre-'87 account balance). Consequently, the post-'86 account balance includes earnings after December 31, 1986 on contributions made before January 1, 1987, in addition to the contributions made after December 31, 1986 and earnings thereon. The issuer or custodian of the section 403(b) contract must keep records that enable it to identify the pre'87 account balance and subsequent changes as set forth in paragraph (b) of this A-2 and provide such information upon request to the relevant employee or beneficiaries with respect to the contract. If the issuer does not keep such records, the entire account balance will be treated as subject to section 401(a)(9).

(b) In applying the distribution rules in section 401(a)(9), only the post-'86 account balance is used to calculate the required minimum distribution required for a calendar year. The amount of any distribution required to satisfy the required minimum distribution requirement for a calendar year will be treated as being paid from the post-'86 account balance. Any amount distributed in a calendar year in excess of the required minimum distribution requirement for a calendar year will be treated as paid from the pre-'87 account balance. The pre-'87 account balance for the next calendar year will be permanently reduced by the deemed distributions from the account.

(c) The pre-'86 account balance and the post-'87 account balance have no relevance for purposes of determining the amount includible in income under section 72.

Q-3. Must the value of the account balance under a section 403(b) contract as of December 31, 1986 be distributed in accordance with the minimum distribution incidental benefit requirement?

A-3. Distributions of the entire account balance of a section 403(b) contract, including the value of the account balance under the contract or account as of December 31, 1986, must satisfy the minimum distribution incidental benefit requirement. However, distributions attributable to the the value of the account balance under the contract or account as of December 31, 1986 is treated as satisfying the minimum distribution incidental benefit requirement if the such distributions satisfy the rules in effect as July 27, 1987, interpreting 1.401-1(b)(1)(i)

Q-4. Is the required minimum distribution from one section 403(b) contract of an employee permitted to be distributed from another section 403(b) contract in order to satisfy section 401(a)(9)?

A-4. Yes. The required minimum distribution must be separately determined for each section 403(b) contract of an employee. However, such amounts may then be totaled and the total distribution taken from any one or more of the individual section 403(b) contracts. However,

under this rule, only amounts in section 403(b) contracts that an individual holds as an employee may be aggregated. Amounts in section 403(b) contracts that an individual holds as a beneficiary of the same decedent may be aggregated, but such amounts may not be aggregated with amounts held in section 403(b) contracts that the individual holds as the employee or as the beneficiary of another decedent. Distributions from section 403(b) contracts or accounts will not satisfy the distribution requirements from IRAs, nor will distributions from IRAs satisfy the distribution requirements from section 403(b) contracts or accounts.

Par. 5. Section § 1.408-8 is added to read as follows:

§ 1.408-8 Distribution requirements for individual retirement plans.

The following questions and answers relate to the distribution rules for IRAs provided in sections 408(a)(6) and 408(b)(3).

Q-1. Are individual retirement plans (IRAs) subject to the distribution rules provided in section 401(a)(9) and §§ 1.401(a)(9)-1 through 1.401(a)(9)-8 for qualified plans?

A-1. (a) Yes. Except as otherwise provided in this section, IRAs are subject to the required minimum distribution rules provided in section 401(a)(9) and §§ 1.401(a)(9)-1 through 1.401(a)(9)-8 for qualified plans. For example, whether the five year rule or the life expectancy rule applies to distribution after death occurring before the IRA owner's required beginning date will be determined in accordance with § 1.401(a)(9)-3, the rules of § 1.401(a)(9)-4 apply for purposes of determining an IRA owner's designated beneficiary, the amount of the required minimum distribution required for each calendar year from an individual account will be determined in accordance with § 1.401(a)(9)-5, and whether annuity payments from an individual retirement annuity satisfy section 401(a)(9) will be determined under § 1.401(a)(9)-6. For this purpose the term *IRA* means an individual retirement account or annuity described in section 408(a) or (b).

(b) For purposes of applying the required minimum distribution rules in §§ 1.401(a)(9)-1 through 1.401(a)(9)-8 for qualified plans, the IRA trustee, custodian, or issuer is treated as the plan administrator, and the IRA owner is substituted for the employee

Q-2. Are employer contributions under a simplified employee pension (defined in section 408(k)) or a SIMPLE IRA (defined in section 408(p)) treated as contributions to an IRA?

A-2. Yes. IRAs that receive employer contributions under a simplified employee pension (defined in section 408(k)) or a SIMPLE plan (defined in section 408(p)) are treated as IRAs for purposes of section 401(a) and are, therefore, subject to the distribution rules in this section.

Q-3. In the case of distributions from an IRA, what does the term *required beginning date* mean?

A-3. In the case of distributions from an IRA, the term *required beginning date* means April 1 of the calendar year following the calendar year in which the individual attains age 70 ½.

Q-4. When is the amount of a distribution from a IRA not eligible for rollover because the amount is a required minimum distribution?

A-4. The amount of a distribution that is a required minimum distribution from an IRA and thus not eligible for rollover is determined in the same manner as provided in Q&A-7 of § 1.402(c)-2 for distributions from qualified plans. For example, if a required minimum distribution is required for a calendar year, the amounts distributed during a calendar year from an IRA are treated as required minimum distributions under section 401(a)(9) to the extent that the total required minimum distribution for the year under section 401(a)(9) for that IRA has not been satisfied. This requirement may be satisfied by a distribution from the IRA or, as permitted under A-8 of this section, from another IRA.

Q-5. May an individual's surviving spouse elect to treat such spouse's entire interest as a beneficiary in an individual's IRA upon the death of the individual (or the remaining part of such interest if distribution to the spouse has commenced) as the spouse's own account?

A-5. (a) The surviving spouse of an individual may elect in the manner described in paragraph (b) of this A-5 to treat the spouse's entire interest as a beneficiary in an individual's IRA (or the remaining part of such interest if distribution thereof has commenced to the spouse) as the spouse's own IRA. This election is permitted to be made at any time after the distribution of the required minimum amount for the account for the calendar year containing the individual's date of death. In order to make this election, the spouse must be the sole beneficiary of the IRA and have an unlimited right to withdrawal amounts from the IRA. This requirement is not satisfied if a trust is named as beneficiary of the IRA even if the spouse is the sole beneficiary of the trust. If the surviving spouse makes such an election, the surviving spouse's interest in the IRA would then be subject to the distribution requirements of section 401(a)(9)(A) applicable to the spouse as the IRA owner rather than those of section 401(a)(9)(B) applicable to the surviving spouse as the decedent IRA owner's beneficiary. Thus, the required minimum distribution for the year of the election and each subsequent year would be determined under section 401(a)(9)(A) with the spouse as IRA owner and not section 401(a)(9)(B).

(b) The election described in paragraph (a) of this A-5 is made by the surviving spouse redesignating the account as the account in the name of the surviving spouse as IRA owner rather than as beneficiary. Alternatively, a surviving spouse eligible to make the election is deemed to have made the election if, at any time, either of the following occurs:

(1) Any required amounts in the account (including any amounts that have been rolled over or transferred, in accordance with the requirements of section 408(d)(3)(A)(i), into an individual retirement account or individual retirement annuity for the benefit of such surviving spouse) have not been distributed within the appropriate time period applicable to the surviving spouse as beneficiary under section 401(a)(9)(B); or

(2) Any additional amounts are contributed to the account (or to the account or annuity to which the surviving spouse has rolled such amounts over, as described in (1) above) which are subject, or deemed to be subject, to the distribution requirements of section 401(a)(9)(A).

(c) The result of an election described in paragraph (b) of this A-5 is that the surviving spouse shall then be considered the IRA owner for whose benefit the trust is maintained for all purposes under the Code (e.g. section 72(t)).

Q-6. How is the benefit determined for purposes of calculating the required minimum distribution from an IRA?

A-6. For purposes of determining the required minimum distribution required to be made from an IRA in any calendar year, the account balance of the IRA as of the December 31 of the calendar year immediately preceding the calendar year for which distributions are being made will be substituted in A-3 of § 1.401(a)(9)-5 for the account of the employee. The account balance as of December 31 of such calendar year is the value of the IRA upon close of business on such December 31. However, for purposes of determining the required minimum distribution for the second distribution calendar year for an individual, the account balance as of December 31 of such calendar year must be reduced by any distribution (as described in A-3(c)(2) of § 1.401(a)(9)-5) made to satisfy the required minimum distribution requirements for the individual's first distribution calendar year after such date.

Q-7. What rules apply in the case of a rollover to an IRA of an amount distributed by a qualified plan or another IRA?

A-7. If the surviving spouse of an employee rolls over a distribution from a qualified plan, such surviving spouse may elect to treat the IRA as the spouse's own IRA in accordance with the provisions in A-5 of this section. In the event of any other rollover to an IRA of an amount distributed by a qualified plan or another IRA, the rules in § 1.401(a)(9)-3 will apply for purposes of determining the account balance for the receiving IRA and the required minimum distribution from the receiving IRA. However, because the value of the account balance is determined as of December 31 of the year preceding the year for which the required minimum distribution is being determined and not as of a valuation date in the preceding year, the account balance of the receiving IRA need not be adjusted for the amount received as provided in A-2 of § 1.401(a)(9)-7 in order to determine the required minimum distribution for the calendar year following the calendar year in which the amount rolled over is received, unless the amount received is deemed to have been received in the immediately preceding year, pursuant to A-2 of § 1.401(a)(9)-7. In that case, for purposes of determining the required minimum distribution for the calendar year in which such amount is actually received, the account balance of the receiving IRA as of December 31 of the preceding year must be adjusted by the amount received in accordance with A-2 of § 1.401(a)(9)-7.

Q-8. What rules apply in the case of a transfer from one IRA to another?

A-8. In the case of a transfer from one IRA to another IRA, the rules in A-3 or A-4 of § 1.401(a)(9)-7 will apply for purposes of determining the account balance of, and the required minimum distribution from, the IRAs involved. Thus, the transferor IRA must distribute in the year

of the transfer any amount required determined without regard to the transfer. For purposes of determining the account balance of the transferee IRA and the transferor IRA, the account balance need not be adjusted for the amount transferred as provided in A-4(a) of § 1.401(a)(9)-7 in order to calculate the required minimum distribution for the calendar year following the calendar year of the transfer, because the account balance is determined as of December 31 of the calendar year immediately preceding the calendar year for which the required minimum distribution is being determined.

Q-9. Is the required minimum distribution from one IRA of an owner permitted to distributed from another IRA in order to satisfy section 401(a)(9).

A-9. Yes. The required minimum distribution must be calculated separately for each IRA. However, such amounts may then be totaled and the total distribution taken from any one or more of the individual IRAs. However, under this rule, only amounts in IRAs that an individual holds as the IRA owner may be aggregated. Amounts in IRAs that an individual holds as a beneficiary of the same decedent may be aggregated, but such amounts may not be aggregated with amounts held in IRAs that the individual holds as the IRA owner or as the beneficiary of another decedent. Distributions from section 403(b) contracts or accounts will not satisfy the distribution requirements from IRAs, nor will distributions from IRAs satisfy the distribution requirements from section 403(b) contracts or accounts. Distributions from Roth IRAs (defined in section 408A) will not satisfy the distribution requirements applicable to IRAs or section 403(b) accounts or contracts and distributions from IRAs or section 403(b) contracts or accounts will not satisfy the distribution requirements from Roth IRAs.

Q-10. Is the trustee of an IRA required to report the amount that is required to be distributed from that IRA?

A-10. Yes. The trustee of an IRA is required to report to the Internal Revenue Service and to the IRA owner the amount required to be distributed from the IRA for each calendar year at the time and in the manner prescribed in the instructions to the applicable Federal tax forms, as well as any additional information as required by such forms or such instructions.

PART 54—PENSION EXCISE TAXES

Par. 6. The authority citation for part 54 is amended by adding the following citation to read as follows:

Authority: 26 U.S.C. 7805 * * *

§ 54.4974-2 is also issued under 26 U.S.C. 4974.

Par. 7. Section after § 54.4974-2 is added to read as follows:

§ 54.4974-2 Excise tax on accumulations in qualified retirement plans.

Q-1. Is any tax imposed on a payee under any qualified retirement plan or any eligible deferred compensation plan (as defined in section 457(b)) to whom an amount is required to be distributed for a taxable year if the amount distributed during the taxable year is less than the required minimum distribution?

A-1. Yes. If the amount distributed to a payee under any qualified retirement plan or any eligible deferred compensation plan (as defined in section 457(b)) for a calendar year is less than the required minimum distribution for such year, an excise tax is imposed on such payee under section 4974 for the taxable year beginning with or within the calendar year during which the amount is required to be distributed. The tax is equal to 50 percent of the amount by which such required minimum distribution exceeds the actual amount distributed during the calendar year. Section 4974 provides that this tax shall be paid by the payee. For purposes of section 4974, the term *required minimum distribution* means the required minimum distribution amount required to be distributed pursuant to section 401(a)(9), 403(b)(10), 408(a)(6), 408(b)(3), or 457(d)(2), as the case may be, and the regulations thereunder. Except as otherwise provided in Q&A-6, the required minimum distribution for a calendar year is the required minimum distribution amount required to be distributed during the calendar year. Q&A-6 provides a special rule for amounts required to be distributed by an employee's (or individual's) required beginning date.

Q-2. For purposes of section 4974, what is a qualified retirement plan?

A-2. For purposes of section 4974, each of the following is a qualified retirement plan -

(a) A plan described in section 401(a) which includes a trust exempt from tax under section 501(a);

(b) An annuity plan described in section 403(a);

(c) An annuity contract, custodial account, or retirement income account described in section 403(b);

(d) An individual retirement account described in section 408(a);

(e) An individual retirement annuity described in section 408(b); or

(f) Any other plan, contract, account, or annuity that, at any time, has been treated as a plan, account, or annuity described in (a) through (e) of this A-2, whether or not such plan, contract, account, or annuity currently satisfies the applicable requirements for such treatment.

Q-3. If a payee's interest under a qualified retirement plan is in the form of an individual account, how is the required minimum distribution for a given calendar year determined for purposes of section 4974?

A-3. (a) *General rule*. If a payee's interest under a qualified retirement plan is in the form of an individual account and distribution of such account is not being made under an annuity contract purchased in accordance with A-4 of § 1.401(a)(9)-6, the amount of the required minimum distribution for any calendar year for purposes of section 4974 is the required minimum distribution amount required to be distributed for such calendar year in order to satisfy the required minimum distribution requirements in § 1.401(a)(9)-5 as provided in the following (whichever is applicable) -

(1) Section 401(a)(9) and §§ 1.401(a)(9)-1 through 1.401(a)(9)-8 in the case of a plan described in section 401(a) which includes a trust exempt under section 501(a) or an annuity plan described in section 403(a));

(2) Section 403(b)(10) and § 1.403(b)-2 (in the case of an annuity contract, custodial account, or retirement income account described in section 403(b)); or

(3) Section 408(a)(6) or (b)(3) and § 1.408-8 (in the case of an individual retirement account or annuity described in section 408(a) or (b)).

(b) *Default provisions*. Unless otherwise provided under the qualified retirement plan (or, if applicable, the governing instrument of the qualified retirement plan), the default provisions in A-4(a) of § 1.401(a)(9)-3 apply in determining the required minimum distribution for purposes of section 4974.

(c) *Five year rule*. If the five-year rule in section 401(a)(9)(B)(ii) applies to the distribution to a payee, no amount is required to be distributed for any calendar year to satisfy the applicable enumerated section in paragraph (a) of this A-3 until the calendar year which contains the date five years after the date of the employee's death. For the calendar year which contains the date five years after the employee's death, the required minimum distribution amount required to be distributed to satisfy the applicable enumerated section is the payee's entire remaining interest in the qualified retirement plan.

Q-4. If a payee's interest in a qualified retirement plan is being distributed in the form of an annuity, how is the amount of the required minimum distribution determined for purposes of section 4974?

A-4. If a payee's interest in a qualified retirement plan is being distributed in the form of an annuity (either directly from the plan, in the case of a defined benefit plan, or under an annuity contract purchased from an insurance company), the amount of the required minimum distribution for purposes of section 4974 will be determined as follows:

(a) *Permissible annuity distribution option*. A permissible annuity distribution option is an annuity contract (or, in the case of annuity distributions from a defined benefit plan, a distribution option) which specifically provides for distributions which, if made as provided, would for every calendar year equal or exceed the required minimum distribution amount required to be distributed to satisfy the applicable section enumerated in paragraph (a) of A-2 of this section for every calendar year. If the annuity contract (or, in the case of annuity distributions from a defined benefit plan, a distribution option) under which distributions to the payee are being made is a permissible annuity distribution option, the required minimum distribution for a given calendar year will equal the amount which the annuity contract (or distribution option) provides is to be distributed for that calendar year.

(b) *Impermissible annuity distribution option*. An impermissible annuity distribution option is an annuity contract (or, in the case of annuity distributions from a defined benefit plan, a distribution option) under which distributions to the payee are being made that specifically provides for distributions which, if made as provided, would for any calendar year be less than the required minimum distribution amount required to be distributed to satisfy the applicable section enumerated in paragraph (a) of A-2 of this section. If the annuity contract (or, in the case of annuity distributions from a defined benefit plan, the distribu-

tion option) under which distributions to the payee are being made is an impermissible annuity distribution option, the required minimum distribution for each calendar year will be determined as follows:

(1) If the qualified retirement plan under which distributions are being made is a defined benefit plan, the required minimum distribution amount required to be distributed each year will be the amount which would have been distributed under the plan if the distribution option under which distributions to the payee were being made was the following permissible annuity distribution option:

(i) In the case of distributions commencing before the death of the employee, if there is a designated beneficiary under the impermissible annuity distribution option for purposes of section 401(a)(9), the permissible annuity distribution option is the joint and survivor annuity option under the plan for the lives of the employee and the designated beneficiary which provides for the greatest level amount payable to the employee determined on an annual basis. If the plan does not provide such an option or there is no designated beneficiary under the impermissible distribution option for purposes of section 401(a)(9), the permissible annuity distribution option is the life annuity option under the plan payable for the life of the employee in level amounts with no survivor benefit.

(ii) In the case of distributions commencing after the death of the employee, if there is a designated beneficiary under the impermissible annuity distribution option for purposes of section 401(a)(9), the permissible annuity distribution option is the life annuity option under the plan payable for the life of the designated beneficiary in level amounts. If there is no designated beneficiary, the five-year rule in section 401(a)(9)(B)(ii) applies. See paragraph (b)(3) of this A-4. The determination of whether or not there is a designated beneficiary and the determination of which designated beneficiary's life is to be used in the case of multiple beneficiaries will be made in accordance with § 1.401(a)(9)-4 and A-7 of § 1.401(a)(9)-5. If the defined benefit plan does not provide for distribution in the form of the applicable permissible distribution option, the required minimum distribution for each calendar year will be an amount as determined by the Commissioner.

(2) If the qualified retirement plan under which distributions are being made is a defined contribution plan and the impermissible annuity distribution option is an annuity contract purchased from an insurance company, the required minimum distribution amount required to be distributed each year will be the amount which would have been distributed in the form of an annuity contract under the permissible annuity distribution option under the plan determined in accordance with paragraph (b)(1) of this A-4 for defined benefit plans. If the defined contribution plan does not provide the applicable permissible annuity distribution option, the required minimum distribution for each calendar year will be the amount which would have been distributed under an annuity described below in paragraph (b)(2)(i) or (ii) of this A-4 purchased with the employee's or individual's account used to purchase the annuity contract which is the impermissible annuity distribution option.

(i) In the case of distributions commencing before the death of the employee, if there is a designated beneficiary under the impermissible annuity distribution option for purposes of section 401(a)(9), the annuity is a joint and survivor annuity for the lives of the employee and the designated beneficiary which provides level annual payments and which would have been a permissible annuity distribution option. However, the amount of the periodic payment which would have been payable to the survivor will be the applicable percentage under the table in A-2(b) of § 1.401(a)(9)-6 of the amount of the periodic payment which would have been payable to the employee or individual. If there is no designated beneficiary under the impermissible distribution option for purposes of section 401(a)(9), the annuity is a life annuity for the life of the employee with no survivor benefit which provides level annual payments and which would have been a permissible annuity distribution option.

(ii) In the case of a distribution commencing after the death of the employee, if there is a designated beneficiary under the impermissible annuity distribution option for purposes of section 401(a)(9), the annuity option is a life annuity for the life of the designated beneficiary which provides level annual payments and which would have been permissible annuity distribution option. If there is no designated beneficiary, the five year rule in section 401(a)(9)(B)(ii) applies. See paragraph (b)(3) of this A-4.

The amount of the payments under the annuity contract will be determined using the interest rate and actuarial tables prescribed under section 7520 determined using the date determined under A-3 of 1.401(a)(9)-3 when distributions are required to commence and using the age of the beneficiary as of the beneficiary's birthday in the calendar year that contains that date. The determination of whether or not there is a designated beneficiary and the determination of which designated beneficiary's life is to be used in the case of multiple beneficiaries will be made in accordance with § 1.401(a)(9)-3 and A-7 of § 1.401(a)(9)-5.

(3) If the five-year rule in section 401(a)(9)(B)(ii) applies to the distribution to the payee under the contract (or distribution option), no amount is required to be distributed to satisfy the applicable enumerated section in paragraph (a) of this A-4 until the calendar year which contains the date five years after the date of the employee's death. For the calendar year which contains the date five years after the employee's death, the required minimum distribution amount required to be distributed to satisfy the applicable enumerated section is the payee's entire remaining interest in the annuity contract (or under the plan in the case of distributions from a defined benefit plan).

Q-5. If there is any remaining benefit with respect to an employee (or IRA owner) after any calendar year in which the entire remaining benefit is required to be distributed under section, what is the amount of the required minimum distribution for each calendar year subsequent to such calendar year?

A-5. If there is any remaining benefit with respect to an employee (or IRA owner) after the calendar year in which the entire remaining benefit is required to be distributed, the required minimum distribution for each calendar year subsequent to such calendar year is the entire remaining benefit.

Q-6 If a payee has an interest under an eligible deferred compensation plan (as defined in section 457(b)), how is the required minimum distribution for a given taxable year of the payee determined for purposes of section 4974?

A-6. If a payee has an interest under an eligible deferred compensation plan (as defined in section 457(b)), the required minimum distribution for a given taxable year of the payee determined for purposes of section 4974 is determined under section 457(d).

Q-7. With respect to which calendar year is the excise tax under section 4974 imposed in the case in which the amount not distributed is an amount required to be distributed by April 1 of a calendar year (by the employee's or individual's required beginning date)?

A-7. In the case in which the amount not paid is an amount required to be paid by April 1 of a calendar year, such amount is a required minimum distribution for the previous calendar year, i.e., for the employee's or the individual's first distribution calendar year. However, the excise tax under section 4974 is imposed for the calendar year containing the last day by which the amount is required to be distributed, i.e., the calendar year containing the employee's or individual's required beginning date, even though the preceding calendar year is the calendar year for which the amount is required to be distributed. Pursuant to A-2 of § 1.401(a)(9)-5, amounts distributed in the employee's or individual's first distribution calendar year will reduce the amount required to be distributed in the next calendar year by the employee's or individual's required beginning date. There is also a required minimum distribution for the calendar year which contains the employee's required beginning date. Such distribution is also required to be made during the calendar year which contains the employee's required beginning date.

Q-8. Are there any circumstances when the excise tax under section 4974 for a taxable year may be waived?

A-8. (a) *Reasonable cause.* The tax under section 4974(a) may be waived if the payee described in section 4974(a) establishes to the satisfaction of the Commissioner the following -

(1) The shortfall described in section 4974(a) in the amount distributed in any taxable year was due to reasonable error; and

(2) Reasonable steps are being taken to remedy the shortfall.

(b) *Automatic Waiver.* The tax under section 4974 will be automatically waived, unless the Commissioner determines otherwise, if -

(1) The payee described in section 4974(a) is an individual who is the sole beneficiary and whose required minimum distribution amount for a calendar year is determined under the life expectancy rule described in § 1.401(a)(9)-3 A-3 in the case of an employee's death before the employee's required beginning date; and

(2) The employee's or individual's entire benefit to which that beneficiary is entitled is distributed by the end of the fifth calendar year following the calendar year that contains the employee's date of death.

Robert E. Wenzel

Deputy Commissioner of Internal Revenue

¶ 20,260D

[Reserved.]Formerly reproduced here were proposed Circular 230 regulations.

¶ 20,260E

IRS proposed regulations: Catch-up contributions: Elective deferrals: Economic Growth and Tax Relief Reconciliation Act of 2001 (EGTRRA).—The IRS has issued proposed regulations that contain guidance for retirement plans that provide their participants age 50 or older the opportunity to make additional elective deferrals, known as catch-up contributions, pursuant to Code Sec. 414(v), as added by EGTRRA. The proposed regulations impact 401(k) plans, SIMPLE IRA plans, simplified employee pensions, 403(b) tax-sheltered annuity plans, and 457 governmental plans.

The proposed regulations, which were published in the *Federal Register* on October 23, 2001 (66 FR 53555), were previously reproduced below.

Final regulations were published in the *Federal Register* on July 8, 2003 (68 FR 40510), and are found at ¶ 23,208, ¶ 11,755-5 and ¶ 12,364N. The final regulations are applicable to contributions in taxable years beginning on or after January 1, 2004. Taxpayers are permitted to rely on the final regulations and the proposed regulations for taxable years beginning prior to January 1, 2004.

¶ 20,260F

IRS proposed regulation (withdrawn): Incentive stock options (ISOs): Employee stock purchase plans (ESPPs): Federal Insurance Contributions Act (FICA): Federal Unemployment Tax Act (FUTA): Income tax withholding.—The IRS issued, then later withdrew, proposed regulations relating to Incentive Stock Options (ISOs) described in Code Sec. 422(b) and options granted under an Employee Stock Purchase Plan (ESSP) described in Code Sec. 423(b). The proposals, which would have affected employers granting such options and employees exercising such options, provided guidance concerning the application of the Federal Insurance Contributions Act (FICA) and Federal Unemployment Tax Act (FUTA), and the Collection of Income Tax at Source rules for statutory stock options. The IRS also issued two related notices, IRS Notice 2001-72 (CCH PENSION PLAN GUIDE ¶ 17,122Q) and IRS Notice 2001-73 (CCH PENSION PLAN GUIDE ¶ 17,122R) that set forth proposed rules regarding an employer's income tax withholding and reporting obligations upon the sale or disposition of stock acquired pursuant to the exercise of a statutory option and the application of FICA and FUTA to statutory stock options.

The proposed regulations, and the withdrawal of the proposed regulations, were published in the *Federal Register* on November 14, 2001 (66 FR 57023), and July 1, 2005 (70 FR 38057), respectively.

¶ 20,260G

Proposed regulations: Golden parachute payments.—Reproduced below is the text of proposed regulations on golden parachute payments relating to exempt parachute payments and IRS Code Sec. 280G, disqualified individuals, changes in corporate ownership or control, and reasonable compensation. The proposed regulations apply to any payments that are contingent on a change in ownership or control occurring on or after January 1, 2004. Taxpayers may rely on these regulations until the effective date of the final regulations. Alternatively, taxpayers may rely on the 1989 proposed regulations (¶ 20,178) for any payment contingent on a change in ownership or control that occurs prior to January 1, 2004.

The proposed regulations were published in the *Federal Register* on February 20, 2002 (67 FR 7630). The regulations were corrected in the *Federal Register* on June 21, 2002 (67 FR 42210). Final regulations were published in the Federal Register on August 4, 2003 (68 FR 45745). The preamble to the final regulations is at ¶ 23,213. The final regulations are at ¶ 11,358Q.

DEPARTMENT OF THE TREASURY

Internal Revenue Service

26 CFR Part 1

[REG-209114-90]

RIN: 1545-AH49

Golden Parachute Payments

AGENCY: Internal Revenue Service (IRS), Treasury.

ACTION: Notice of proposed rulemaking and notice of public hearing.

SUMMARY: This document contains proposed regulations relating to golden parachute payments to provide guidance to taxpayers who must comply with section 280G. Proposed regulations under section 280G were previously published in the **Federal Register** on May 5, 1989 (the 1989 proposed regulations). These proposed regulations are proposed to apply to any payments that are contingent on a change in ownership or control occurring on or after January 1, 2004. Taxpayers may rely on these proposed regulations until the effective date of the final regulations. Alternatively, taxpayers may rely on the 1989 proposed regulations for any payment contingent on a change in ownership or control that occurs prior to January 1, 2004. [Corrected by IRS on 6/21/02, 67 FR 42210].

DATES: Written or electronic comments must be received by June 5, 2002. Requests to speak and outlines of topics to be discussed at the public hearing scheduled for June 26, 2002, must be received by June 5, 2002.

ADDRESSES: Send submissions to CC:ITA:RU (REG-209114-90), room 5226, Internal Revenue Service, POB 7604, Ben Franklin Station, Washington, DC 20044. Submissions may be hand delivered Monday through Friday between the hours of 8 a.m. and 5 p.m. to: CC:ITA:RU (REG-209114-90), Courier's Desk, Internal Revenue Service, 1111 Constitution Avenue, NW, Washington, DC or sent electronically, via the IRS Internet site *www.irs.gov/regs*. The public hearing will be held in the IRS Auditorium, Internal Revenue Building, 1111 Constitution Avenue, NW, Washington, DC.

FOR FURTHER INFORMATION CONTACT: Concerning the regulations, Erinn Madden at (202) 622-6060 (not at toll-free number). To be placed on the attendance list for the hearing, please contact LaNita M. Vandyke at (202) 622-7180. [Corrected by IRS on 6/21/02, 67 FR 42210].

SUPPLEMENTARY INFORMATION:

Background

This document contains proposed amendments to 26 CFR part 1 under section 280G of the Internal Revenue Code (Code). Sections 280G and 4999 of the Code were added to the Code by sec. 67 of the Deficit Reduction Act, Public Law 98-369 (98 Stat. 585). Section 280G was amended by sec. 1804(j) of the Tax Reform Act of 1986, Public Law 99-514 (100 Stat. 2807), sec. 1018(d) of the Technical and Miscellaneous Revenue Act of 1988, Public Law 100-647 (102 Stat. 3581) and sec. 1421 of the Small Business Job Protection Act of 1996, Public Law 104-188 (110 Stat. 1755).

Section 280G denies a deduction to a corporation for any excess parachute payment. Section 4999 imposes a 20-percent excise tax on the recipient of any excess parachute payment. Related provisions include section 275(a)(6), which denies the recipient a deduction for the section 4999 excise tax, and section 3121(v)(2)(A), which relates to the Federal Insurance Contributions Act. Proposed regulations (PS-217-84) under section 280G were previously published in the **Federal Register** at 54 FR 19390 on May 5, 1989 and corrected in 54 FR 25879 (June 20, 1989) (the 1989 proposed regulations). [Corrected by IRS on 6/21/02, 67 FR 42210].

Explanation Of Provisions

Overview

Section 280G denies a deduction to a corporation for any excess parachute payment. Section 4999 imposes a 20-percent excise tax on the recipient of any excess parachute payment. The disallowance of the deduction under section 280G is not contingent on the imposition of the excise tax under section 4999, and the imposition of the excise tax under section 4999 is not contingent on the disallowance of the deduction under section 280G. For example, an individual may be subject to the 20-percent excise tax under section 4999 even though the payor is a foreign corporation not subject to United States income tax.

Section 280G(b)(2)(A) defines a *parachute payment* as any payment that meets all of the following four conditions: (a) the payment is in the nature of compensation; (b) the payment is, to, or for the benefit of, a disqualified individual; (c) the payment is contingent on a change in the ownership of a corporation, the effective control of a corporation, or the ownership of a substantial portion of the assets of a corporation (a change in ownership or control); and (d) the payment has (together with other payments described in (a), (b), and (c) of this paragraph with respect to the same individual) an aggregate present value of at least 3 times the individual's base amount. Section 280G(b)(2)(B) provides that the term *parachute payment* also includes any payment in the nature of compensation to, or for the benefit of, a disqualified individual if the payment is pursuant to an agreement that violates any generally enforced securities laws or regulations (securities violation parachute payment).

Section 280G(b)(1) defines the term *excess parachute payment* as an amount equal to the excess of any parachute payment over the portion of the disqualified individual's base amount that is allocated to such payment. For this purpose, the portion of the base amount allocated to a parachute payment is the amount that bears the same ratio to the base amount as the present value of the parachute payment bears to the aggregate present value of all such payments to the same disqualified individual.

Generally, excess parachute payments may be reduced by certain amounts of reasonable compensation. Section 280G(b)(4)(B) provides that, except in the case of securities violation parachute payments, the amount of an excess parachute payment is reduced by any portion of the payment that the taxpayer establishes by clear and convincing evidence is reasonable compensation for personal services actually rendered by the disqualified individual before the date of change in ownership or control. Such reasonable compensation is first offset against the portion of the base amount allocated to the payment.

The 1989 proposed regulations provided guidance regarding the application of section 280G to corporations and individuals. Although many aspects of the 1989 proposed regulations were well-received, the IRS has received numerous comments requesting modification and clarification of the 1989 proposed regulations. In response, these proposed regulations clarify and revise, as described below, the 1989 proposed regulations. Many aspects of the 1989 proposed regulations are preserved, and these proposed regulations retain the same organizational structure as the 1989 proposed regulations. Major modifications to the 1989 proposed regulations are described below.

Disqualified Individuals

A payment constitutes a parachute payment only if the payment is made to (or for the benefit of) a disqualified individual. Section 280G(c) defines the term *disqualified individual* to include any individual who (a) is an employee or independent contractor who performs personal services for a corporation, and (b) is an officer, shareholder, or highly-compensated individual.

The determination of whether an individual is a disqualified individual under these proposed regulations is substantially the same as under the 1989 proposed regulations, with three significant changes. First, Q/A-17 of the 1989 proposed regulations provides a *de minimis* rule for purposes of identifying which shareholders of a corporation are disqualified individuals. Under the 1989 proposed regulations, an individual is a shareholder for purposes of section 280G if the individual, at any time during the disqualified individual determination period, owns stock of a corporation with a fair market value exceeding the lesser of $1 million or 1 percent of the total fair market value of the outstanding shares of all classes of the corporation's stock. Since the issuance of the 1989 proposed regulations, it has become apparent that this rule may include individuals who do not possess significant influence over the corporation. Therefore, under Q/A-17 of these proposed regulations, the $1 million test is eliminated. Under these proposed regulations, an individual is a shareholder only if, during the disqualified individual determination period, the individual owns stock of a corporation with a fair market value that exceeds 1 percent of the total fair market value of the outstanding shares of all classes of the corporation's stock. The constructive ownership rules of section 318(a) continue to apply for purposes of determining the amount of stock owned by the individual. Under these rules, for example, to determine the amount of stock owned by an individual, the stock underlying vested stock options is considered constructively owned by that individual. [Corrected by IRS on 6/21/02, 67 FR 42210].

Second, these proposed regulations modify the annualized compensation method for determining who is a highly-compensated individual under Q/A-19. Under the 1989 proposed regulations, no individual whose annualized compensation during the disqualified individual determination period is less than $75,000 is treated as a highly-compensated individual, even if the individual otherwise satisfies the definition of a highly-compensated individual. Q/A-19 is modified to provide that an individual must have annualized compensation equal to at least the amount described in section 414(q)(1)(B)(i). This amount for 2002 is $90,000 and is adjusted periodically for cost-of-living increases. This modification both updates the amount provided in the 1989 proposed regulations and provides a mechanism to update this amount periodically without further amendment of these regulations.

Finally, these proposed regulations change the disqualified individual determination period under Q/A-20. Under the 1989 proposed regulations, the disqualified individual determination period is the portion of the year of the corporation ending on the date of the change in ownership or control and the immediately preceding twelve months (with an option to use the calendar year or the corporation's fiscal year). Q/A-20 of these proposed regulations is modified to change this period to the twelve months prior to and ending on the date of the change in ownership or control of the corporation. Under this rule, the disqualified individual determination period is the same length for any change in ownership or control and is not affected by the date of the change in ownership or control.

Payment in the Nature of Compensation

A payment may be a parachute payment only if it is a payment in the nature of compensation. All payments, in whatever form, are payments in the nature of compensation if the payments arise out of the employment relationship or are associated with the performance of services. In Q/A-11, these proposed regulations clarify that payments in the nature of compensation include cash, the right to receive cash, or a transfer of property.

Q/A-13 of the 1989 proposed regulations provides that the transfer of a nonstatutory option is treated as a payment in the nature of compensation (even if the option does not have a readily ascertainable fair market value within the meaning of § 1.83-7(b)). The 1989 proposed regulations reserve the issue of the treatment of statutory options (i.e., options to which section 421 applies). These proposed regulations revise Q/A-13 to address the treatment of statutory stock options to provide that nonstatutory stock options and statutory stock options are treated the same. Because both the transfer of a statutory option and the transfer of a nonstatutory stock option are payments in the nature of compensation, there is no basis for distinguishing between these two types of options for purposes of section 280G.

In addition, these proposed regulations revise Q/A-13 with respect to the valuation of both statutory and nonstatutory stock options. Under the 1989 proposed regulations, the value of an option with an ascertainable fair market value is determined under all the facts and circumstances, including the difference between the option's exercise price and the value of the property at the time of vesting, the probability of an increase or decrease in the value of such property, and the length of the option exercise period.

Since the issuance of the 1989 proposed regulations, commentators have indicated that Q/A-13 does not provide sufficient guidance about the determination of the value of a stock option. In particular, commentators question whether the intrinsic value of the option (the difference between the exercise price and the value of the property, or spread) determined at the time of the change in ownership or control, or a value determined under a valuation model such as Black-Scholes, should be used for purposes of section 280G. Using the factors listed in the 1989 proposed regulations results in a value different from the value obtained from using only the difference between the exercise price and the value of the property. Commentators have also noted that valuation methods other than spread are often complicated and difficult to apply in some circumstances, particularly when the stock underlying the option is not publicly traded.

These proposed regulations continue to provide for the use of the factors described in the 1989 proposed regulations. To provide further guidance on acceptable and administrable methods for valuing stock options, these proposed regulations delegate authority to the Commissioner to provide methods for valuation of stock options through published guidance. Rev. Proc. 2002-13, 2002-8 I.R.B. (February 25, 2002) published in conjunction with these proposed regulations, provides several valuation methods. One of the methods permitted under this revenue procedure is a simplified safe harbor approach modeled after the Black-Scholes valuation method. The safe harbor allows a corporation to establish a value for stock options based on spread at the time of the change in ownership or control, the remaining term of the option, and a basic assumption regarding the volatility of the underlying stock. Other factors relevant to the Black-Scholes valuation model, including a risk-free rate of return and dividend yield, are addressed in the table contained in the revenue procedure. The safe harbor valuation method provided in the revenue procedure may be used without regard to whether the underlying stock is publicly traded.

Contingent on Change

To be a parachute payment, a payment in the nature of compensation to a disqualified individual must be contingent on a change in ownership or control. Q/A-22 of the 1989 proposed regulations provides guidance on when a payment is contingent on a change in ownership or control. Generally, a payment is treated as contingent on a change in ownership or control if the payment would not in fact have been made had no change in ownership or control occurred. A payment generally is treated as one which would not in fact have been made in the absence of a change in ownership or control unless it is substantially certain, at the time of the change, that the payment would have been made whether or not the change in ownership or control occurred.

These proposed regulations clarify in Q/A-22 that a payment is contingent on a change in ownership or control if the payment would not have been made absent the change in ownership or control, even if the payment is also contingent on a second event, such as termination of employment within a period following the change in ownership or control. In addition, as under the 1989 proposed regulations, a payment generally is treated as contingent on a change in ownership or control if (a) the payment is contingent on an event that is closely associated with such a change, (b) a change in ownership or control actually occurs, and (c) the event is materially related to the change in ownership or control. The fact that a payment that is contingent on an event closely associated with a change in ownership or control is also conditioned on the occurrence of a second event does not affect the determination that the payment is contingent on a change in ownership or control as the result of the occurrence of the first event.

Under Q/A-24 of the 1989 proposed regulations, the entire amount of a payment is generally treated as contingent on a change in ownership or control. These proposed regulations clarify that the general rule of Q/A-24(a) (and not the special rules in either Q/A-24(b) or (c), discussed below) applies to the payment of amounts due under an employment agreement on a termination of employment or change in ownership or control that, without regard to the change, would have been paid for the performance of services after the termination of employment or change in ownership or control, as applicable. Also, the general rules of Q/A-24(a) apply to the accelerated payment of an amount that is otherwise payable only on the attainment of a performance goal or contingent on an event or condition other than the continued performance of services for a specified period of time. In situations governed by Q/A-24(a), the determination of whether a portion of the payment is reasonable compensation for services rendered before, on, or after the change in ownership or control is determined under Q/As-38 through 44. With respect to amounts due under an employment agreement, however, in most situations, a reduction for reasonable compensation for services rendered before the change in ownership or control is inappropriate, given the general expectation that an individual is not under-compensated for services rendered before a change in ownership or control. See Conf. Rep. No. 98-861, at 852 (1984).

Q/A-24(b) and (c) provide an objective method for determining the portion of a payment that is treated as contingent on a change in ownership or control for certain types of payments. These rules are not appropriate in situations such as the acceleration of salary payments under an employment agreement, when the periodic nature of the payments for services means that there is no issue in determining the amount of the payment that is accelerated, or in situations where a payment is conditioned on achievement of a performance goal or other event.

As under the 1989 proposed regulations, these proposed regulations provide that a payment is treated as contingent on a change in ownership or control if the change accelerates the time at which the payment is made or accelerates the vesting of a payment. Q/A-24(b) and (c) provide rules for determining the portion of such payment that is treated as contingent on the change in ownership or control. These proposed regulations clarify when Q/A-24(b) and (c) apply to a contingent payment.

These proposed regulations clarify that Q/A-24(b) applies if a payment is vested, without regard to the change in ownership or control, and is treated as contingent on a change in ownership or control because the change accelerates the time the payment is made. For example, if an individual has a vested right to a payment at normal retirement age under a nonqualified deferred compensation plan, but instead that payment is made immediately following a change in ownership or control, Q/A-24(b) applies to determine the portion, if any, of the payment that is treated as contingent on the change in ownership or control.

These regulations clarify that Q/A-24(c) applies to a payment that becomes vested as a result of a change in ownership or control to the extent that (i) without regard to the change, the payment was contingent only on the performance of services for the corporation for a specified period of time and (ii) the payment is attributable, at least in part, to the performance of services before the date the payment is made or becomes certain to be made. For example, if an individual will receive a bonus if employed at the end of a 3-year period, but the bonus is paid immediately on the date of the change of control, Q/A-24(c) applies to determine the portion of the payment that is treated as contingent on the change in ownership or control.

Q/A-24(b) provides that, when a payment is accelerated, the portion of the payment that is contingent on the change is the amount by which the accelerated payment exceeds the present value of the payment absent acceleration. Q/A-24(b) further provides that if the amount of a payment without acceleration is not reasonably ascertainable, and the acceleration does not significantly increase the value of the payment, then the present value of the payment absent the acceleration is equal to the amount of the accelerated payment. As a result, the value of the accelerated payment is equal to the value of the payment absent acceleration and no portion of the payment is treated as contingent on a change in control. If the value of a payment absent acceleration is not reasonably ascertainable and the acceleration significantly increases the value of the payment, the future value of the payment is equal to the amount of the accelerated payment. When the future value (as opposed to the present value) of the payment is deemed to be the amount of the accelerated payment, then there is an excess and, therefore, a portion of the payment is treated as contingent on the change.

Q/A-24(c) provides that the portion of the payment treated as contingent on the change when both vesting and payment are accelerated is the lesser of (1) the payment or (2) the amount determined under Q/A-24(b) plus an additional amount to reflect the lapse of the obligation to perform additional services. Q/A-24(c) provides that for purposes of determining the amount under paragraph (b), the acceleration of the vesting of a stock option or the lapse of a restriction on restricted stock is considered to increase significantly the value of the payment.

Because Q/A-24(b) and (c) operate to provide an objective basis for determining the portion of a payment that is earned as of the date of a change in ownership or control, and therefore, not contingent on a change in ownership or control, these proposed regulations clarify that the rules in Q/As-38 through 44 (which provide rules related to reasonable compensation for services rendered), are inapplicable if the special rules in Q/A-24(b) or (c) apply to a payment.

Change in Ownership or Control

These proposed regulations follow the same approach as the 1989 proposed regulations for determining when a change in ownership or control occurs. However, these proposed regulations clarify that, for purposes of determining whether two or more persons acting as a group are considered to own more than 50 percent of the total fair market value or total voting power of the stock of a corporation on the date of a merger, acquisition, or similar transaction involving that corporation, a person who owns stock in both corporations involved in the transaction is treated as acting as a group with respect to the other shareholders in a corporation only to the extent of such person's ownership of stock in that corporation prior to the transaction, and not with respect to his or her ownership in the other corporation. For example, assume individual A owns stock in both corporations X and Y when corporation X acquires stock in Y in exchange for X stock. In determining whether corporation Y has undergone a change in ownership or control, individual A is considered to be acting as a group with other shareholders in corporation Y only to the extent of A's holdings

in corporation Y prior to the transaction, and not with respect to A's ownership in X. In determining whether Corporation X has undergone a change in ownership or control, individual A is considered to be acting as a group with other shareholders in Corporation X only to the extent of individual A's holdings in Corporation X prior to the transaction, and not with respect to individual A's ownership interest in Corporation Y. This rule applies without regard to the type of shareholder involved (i.e., whether the shareholder is an individual or an institutional shareholder, such as a corporation, mutual fund, or trust).

Comments are requested with respect to whether the change in ownership or control rules in these proposed regulations should be further revised. Comments are also requested with respect to whether additional guidance is necessary regarding the application of the change in ownership or control provisions, and these proposed regulations in general, in the context of specific business situations such as bankruptcy.

Shareholder Approval Requirements

Section 280G specifically exempts from the definition of the term *parachute payment* several types of payments that would otherwise constitute parachute payments. Deductions for payments exempt from the definition of *parachute payment* are not disallowed by section 280G, and such exempt payments are not subject to the 20-percent excise tax of section 4999. In addition, such exempt payments are not taken into account in applying the 3-times-base-amount test of section 280G(b)(2)(A)(ii).

The most significant revisions made by these proposed regulations with respect to exempt payments are clarifications to the shareholder approval requirements which must be met for payments with respect to a corporation in which no stock is readily tradeable on an established securities market or otherwise immediately before the change in ownership or control.

Section 280G(b)(5)(B) provides that the shareholder approval requirements are met if two conditions are satisfied. First, the payment is approved by a vote of the persons who owned, immediately before the change in ownership or control, more than 75% of the voting power of all outstanding stock of the corporation. Second, there is adequate disclosure to shareholders of all material facts concerning all payments which (but for this rule) would be parachute payments with respect to a disqualified individual. Since the issuance of the 1989 proposed regulations, commentators have indicated that the 1989 proposed regulations do not fully explain how the shareholder approval requirements operate or accurately reflect business practices connected with a change in ownership or control.

The proposed regulations clarify the process of obtaining shareholder approval within the structure provided by section 280G(b)(5)(B). Under this section, a shareholder approval vote is valid only if (1) it is a vote of more than 75% of the shareholders entitled to vote based on ownership in the corporation immediately before the change in ownership or control, and (2) disclosure is made with respect to all payments that would otherwise be parachute payments for an individual.

The first step in obtaining shareholder approval is to identify the shareholders entitled to vote. Q/A-7 is revised to clarify that stock held by a disqualified individual (or by certain entity shareholders) is not entitled to vote with respect to a payment to be made to any disqualified individual and that this stock is disregarded in determining whether the more than 75% approval requirement has been met. Once the stock entitled to vote is determined, more than 75% of the voting power of such stock must approve the payment. Q/A-7 also includes a rule of administrative convenience providing that a vote to approve the payment does not fail to be a vote of the shareholders who own stock immediately before the change in ownership or control if eligibility to vote is based on the shareholders of record at the time of any vote taken in connection with a transaction or event giving rise to the change in ownership or control within the three-month period ending on the date of the change in ownership or control. This rule only applies if the disclosure requirements are also met.

These proposed regulations further clarify that not all parachute payments must be subject to a shareholder vote to satisfy the shareholder approval requirements with respect to a payment. It is permissible for only a portion of the payments that would otherwise be made to a disqualified individual to be subject to vote. For example, assume that a disqualified individual with a base amount of $150,000 would receive payments that (but for the exemption for a corporation with no readily tradeable stock) would be parachute payments including (i) a bonus payment of $200,000, (ii) vesting in stock options with a fair market value of $500,000, $200,000 of which is contingent on the change in ownership or control, and (iii) severance payments of $100,000. In this situation, assuming all of the payments are disclosed, the corporation may submit to the shareholders for approval (1) all of the payments, (2) any one of the three payments, or (3) $50,001 of any one of the payments (e.g., options with a value of $50,001). The issue submitted to a shareholder vote must be whether the payment will be made to the disqualified individual, not whether the corporation will be able to deduct the payment. In addition, the vote must be a separate vote of the shareholders. Therefore, the merger, acquisition, or other transaction cannot be conditioned on the shareholders' approval of the payment.

These proposed regulations also clarify that the shareholder approval requirements are met by a single vote on all payments submitted to the vote, including payments to more than one disqualified individual (assuming the disclosure requirements, described below, are also met).

The shareholder approval requirements also require adequate disclosure of all material facts concerning the amount of all parachute payments. For this purpose, the proposed regulations clarify that the amount of all parachute payments to be made to each disqualified individual, and not just the amount of the payments subject to vote, is a material fact. These proposed regulations also clarify that shareholders should be provided with basic information about the type of payments involved (e.g., vesting of stock options or severance payments). This disclosure of information must be made to all shareholders entitled to vote, not just to shareholders with 75% of the voting power entitled to vote.

Reasonable Compensation

The determination of whether amounts are reasonable compensation is relevant for two purposes. First, an excess parachute payment is reduced by any portion of the payment that constitutes reasonable compensation for services actually rendered before a change in ownership or control. Second, amounts that are reasonable compensation for services to be rendered after a change in ownership or control are exempt from the definition of parachute payment. In both situations, reasonable compensation for services must be demonstrated by clear and convincing evidence.

These proposed regulations clarify two issues with respect to reasonable compensation for services performed after a change in ownership or control. The proposed regulations clarify that clear and convincing evidence that a payment is reasonable compensation for services rendered after a change in ownership or control exists if the individual's annual compensation after the change in ownership or control (apart from normal increases) is not significantly greater then the individual's annual compensation before the change in ownership or control, provided that the individual's duties and responsibilities are substantially the same after the change in ownership or control as they were before the change in ownership or control. If the individual's duties and responsibilities have changed, then the clear and convincing evidence must demonstrate that the individual's annual compensation after the change in ownership or control is not significantly greater than the compensation customarily paid by the employer, or by comparable employers, to persons performing comparable services.

Payments to an individual under an agreement that requires the individual to refrain from providing services (such as under a covenant not to compete) may also constitute reasonable compensation for services to be rendered on or after the date of the change in ownership or control. Under Q/A-42 of these proposed regulations, an agreement is treated as an agreement to refrain from services (rather than an agreement for severance pay) if it is demonstrated with clear and convincing evidence that the agreement substantially constrains the individual's ability to perform services and there is a reasonable likelihood that the agreement will be enforced against the individual. If, under the facts and circumstances, the agreement does not satisfy these criteria, the payments under the agreement are instead treated as severance payments under Q/A-44. If the agreement does satisfy these criteria, then the agreement is treated as an agreement for the performance of services, and the payment are exempt from the definition of *parachute payment* to the extent the payments are shown to be reasonable compensation under Q/A-42(a)(2). [Corrected by IRS on 6/21/02, 67 FR 42210].

Application to Tax-Exempt Organizations

Commentators have asked whether a payment with respect to a tax-exempt entity is exempt from the definition of the term *parachute payment*. These proposed regulations clarify that a payment with respect to a tax-exempt entity that would otherwise constitute a parachute payment is exempt from the definition of the term *parachute payment* if the following two conditions are satisfied.

First, the payment must be made by a corporation undergoing a change in ownership or control that is a *tax-exempt organization*, as defined in these proposed regulations. A *tax-exempt organization* is defined as any organization described in section 501(c) that is subject to an express statutory prohibition against inurement of net earnings to the benefit of any private shareholder or individual, an organization described in subsections 501(c)(1) or 501(c)(21), any religious or apostolic organization described in section 501(d), or any qualified tuition program described in section 529.

Second, the organization must meet the definition of *tax-exempt organization*, as defined in these regulations, both immediately before and immediately after the change in ownership or control. If this second condition is not met, a payment made by a *tax-exempt organization* is not exempt from the definition of *parachute payment*.

As noted above, the term *tax-exempt organizations* includes organizations that are described in section 501(c) that already are subject to express statutory rules that prohibit the inurement of the net earnings of such organizations to the benefit of "any private shareholder or individual." Organizations described in the following subsections of 501(c) are *tax-exempt organizations* under application of this rule: 501(c)(3) (including any organization described in subsections 501(e), (f), or (k)), 501(c)(4), 501(c)(6), 501(c)(9), 501(c)(11), 501(c)(13) (but only with respect to those organizations subject to the express anti-inurement provision), 501(c)(19), and 501(c)(26). In light of the existing restrictions on these organizations, the Service and the Treasury Department believe the additional protections of section 280G are unnecessary. In addition, the term *tax-exempt organization* in the proposed regulations includes federal instrumentalities organized under Act of Congress (described in section 501(c)(1)), black lung trusts (described in section 501(c)(21)), certain religious and apostolic organizations (described in section 501(d)) and qualified tuition programs (described in section 529). The Service and the Treasury Department recognize that it may be appropriate to exempt payments made by other types of tax-exempt organizations. Comments are requested on whether any additional categories of organizations should be included in the definition of *tax-exempt organization* for purposes of section 280G.

Definition of Corporation

Under the 1989 proposed regulations, *corporation* is defined by reference to section 7701(a)(3) of the Code. These proposed regulations clarify that the term *corporation*, for purposes of section 280G and the regulations thereunder, includes any entity described in § 301.7701-2(b) such as, for example, a real estate investment trust under section 856(a), a corporation that has mutual or cooperative (rather than stock) ownership, such as a mutual insurance company, a mutual savings bank, or a cooperative bank (as defined in section 7701(a)(32)), and a foreign corporation (as defined in section 7701(a)(5)).

Accordingly, the term *corporation* also includes any entity described in § 301.7701-3(c)(1)(v)(A). That regulation provides, in general, that an entity that claims to be, or is determined to be, an entity that is exempt from taxation under section 501(a) is treated as an association for purposes of the Code. Because the definition of *corporation* includes an association, any entity described in § 301.7701-3(c)(1)(v)(A) is a corporation for purposes of sections 7701 and 280G.

Determination of Excess Parachute Payments

Once all parachute payments are identified, the determination of what portion, if any, of each parachute payment is an excess parachute payment is made. This determination is based on the aggregate present value of all parachute payments. These proposed regulations modify the method described in Q/A-33 of the 1989 proposed regulations for determining the present value of a payment contingent on an uncertain future event or condition. Under Q/A-33 of these proposed regulations, if there is at least a 50-percent probability that the payment will be made, the entire present value of a contingent payment should be included for purposes of determining if there are excess parachute payments. If there is less than a 50-percent probability, then the present value of the contingent payment is not included. Once it is certain whether or not the payment will be made, the 3-times-base amount test in Q/A-30 is reapplied if the initial determination as to whether to include the payment was incorrect. If the inclusion or exclusion of the payment for purposes of Q/A-30 at the time of the change in ownership or control was correct, there is no need to reapply the 3-times-base-amount test. In addition, if it is reasonably estimated that there is a less than 50-percent probability that the payment will be made and the payment is not included in the 3-times-base-amount test, but the payment is later made, the 3-times-base-amount test is not reapplied if the test without regard to the contingent payment resulted in a determination that the individual received (or would receive) excess parachute payments and no base amount is allocated to the contingent payment.

Finally, Q/A-31 provides guidance on determining the present value of an obligation to provide health care over a period of years. Under these proposed regulations, the determination of the present value of this obligation should be calculated in accordance with generally accepted accounting principles. For purposes of Q/A-31, it is permissible for the obligation to provide health care to be measured by projecting the cost of premiums for purchased health care insurance, even if no health care insurance is actually purchased. If the obligation to provide health care is made in coordination with a health care plan that the corporation makes available to a group, then the premiums used for this purpose may be group premiums. This method only applies for purposes of determining present value. Premiums for health care insurance can be used for purposes of determining a corporation's loss of deduction or the excise tax obligation for a disqualified individual only to the extent such premiums are actually paid for health care insurance used to satisfy the corporation's obligation to provide health care.

Timing of the Payment of Tax under Section 4999

In general, the excise tax under section 4999 is due at the time that the payment is considered made under Q/A-11 through 13. Q/A-11(b) of these proposed regulations clarifies that, except as provided in Q/A-12 or 13, a payment is considered made in the taxable year that it is includible in the disqualified individual's gross income, or for benefits excludible from income, in the year the benefit is received. Q/A-11(c) of these proposed regulations permits a disqualified individual, for purposes of section 4999, to treat certain payments as made in the year of the change in ownership or control (or the first year for which a payment contingent on a change in ownership or control is certain to be made), even though the payment is not yet includible in income (or otherwise received). This treatment is not available, however, for a payment if the present value is not reasonably ascertainable within the meaning of section 3121(v) and § 31.3121(v)2-(e)(4) or for a payment related to health benefits or coverage. These proposed regulations indicate in Q/A-11(c) that the Commissioner may provide through published guidance that Q/A-11(c) is or is not available with respect to other types of payments. [Corrected by IRS on 6/21/02, 67 FR 42210].

According to Q/A-11(c) of these proposed regulations, the payment of the excise tax under section 4999 must be made based on the amount calculated for purposes of determining excess parachute payments. Therefore, to the extent that the determination of whether there is an excess parachute payment is based on an incorrect valuation of the payment, the excise tax payment under this provision is also incorrect.

Proposed Effective Date

These regulations are proposed to apply to any payments that are contingent on a change in ownership or control that occurs on or after January 1, 2004. Taxpayers may rely on these proposed regulations until the effective date of the final regulations. Alternatively, taxpayers may rely on the 1989 proposed regulations for any payment contingent on a change in ownership or control that occurs prior to January 1, 2004. [Corrected by IRS on 6/21/02, 67 FR 42210].

Special Analyses

It has been determined that this notice of proposed rulemaking is not a significant regulatory action as defined in Executive Order 12866. Therefore, a regulatory assessment is not required. It has also been determined that section 553(b) of the Administrative Procedure Act (5

U.S.C. chapter 5) does not apply to these regulations, and, because the regulations do not impose a collection of information on small entities, the Regulatory Flexibility Act (5 U.S.C. chapter 6) does not apply. Pursuant to section 7805(f), this notice of proposed rulemaking will be submitted to the Chief Counsel for Advocacy of the Small Business Administration for comment on its impact on small business.

Comments And Public Hearing

Before these proposed regulations are adopted as final regulations, consideration will be given to any written or electronic comments (a signed original and eight (8) copies) that are submitted timely to the IRS. All comments will be available for public inspection and copying.

A public hearing has been scheduled for June 26, 2002, beginning at 10 a.m. in the IRS Auditorium of the Internal Revenue Building, 1111 Constitution Avenue, NW, Washington, DC. All visitors must present photo identification to enter the building. Because of access restrictions, visitors will not be admitted beyond the immediate entrance area more than 15 minutes before the hearing starts. For information about having your name placed on the building access list to attend the hearing, see the "FOR FURTHER INFORMATION CONTACT" section of this preamble.

The rules of 26 CFR 601.601(a)(3) apply to the hearing. Persons who wish to present oral comments at the hearing must submit written comments and an outline of the topics to be discussed and the time to be devoted to each topic (signed original and eight (8) copies) by June 5, 2002. A period of 10 minutes will be allotted to each person for making comments. An agenda showing the schedule of speakers will be prepared after the deadline for receiving outlines has passed. Copies of the agenda will be available free of charge at the hearing.

Drafting Information

The principal author of these proposed regulations is Erinn Madden, Office of the Division Counsel/Associate Chief Counsel (Tax Exempt and Government Entities). However, other personnel from the IRS and Treasury Department participated in their development.

List Of Subjects In 26 Cfr Part 1

Income taxes, Reporting and recordkeeping requirements.

Proposed Amendments To The Regulations

The proposed amendments to 26 CFR part 1 are as follows:

PART I—INCOME TAX; TAXABLE YEARS BEGINNING AFTER DECEMBER 31, 1986.

Paragraph 1. The authority citation for part 1 is amended by adding the following entry in numerical order to read in part as follows:

Authority: 26 U.S.C. 7805 ***

Section 1.280G-1 also issued under 26 U.S.C. 280G(b) and (e). ***

Par. 2. Section § 1.280G-1 is added to read as follows:

§ 1.280G-1 Golden parachute payments.

The following questions and answers relate to the treatment of golden parachute payments under section 280G of the Internal Revenue Code of 1986, as added by section 67 of the Tax Reform Act of 1984 (Public Law No. 98-369; 98 Stat. 585) and amended by section 1804(j) of the Tax Reform Act of 1986 (Public Law No. 99-514; 100 Stat. 2807), section 1018(d)(6)-(8) of the Technical and Miscellaneous Revenue Act of 1988 (Public Law No. 100-647; 102 Stat. 3581), and section 1421 of the Small Business Job Protection Act of 1996 (Public Law No. 104-188, 110 Stat. 1755). The following is a table of contents for this section:

Overview

Q-1: What is the effect of Internal Revenue Code section 280G?

A-1: (a) Section 280G disallows a deduction for any excess parachute payment paid or accrued. For rules relating to the imposition of a nondeductible 20-percent excise tax on the recipient of any excess parachute payment, see Internal Revenue Code sections 4999, 275(a)(6), and 3121(v)(2)(A).

(b) The disallowance of a deduction under section 280G is not contingent on the imposition of the excise tax under section 4999. The imposition of the excise tax under section 4999 is not contingent on the disallowance of a deduction under section 280G. Thus, for example, because the imposition of the excise tax under section 4999 is not contingent on the disallowance of a deduction under section 280G, a payee may be subject to the 20-percent excise tax under section 4999 even though the disallowance of the deduction for the excess parachute payment may not directly affect the federal taxable income of the payor.

Q-2: What is a parachute payment for purposes of section 280G?

A-2: (a) The term *parachute payment* means any payment (other than an exempt payment described in Q/A-5) that—

(1) Is in the nature of compensation;

(2) Is made or is to be made to (or for the benefit of) a disqualified individual;

(3) Is contingent on a change—

(i) In the ownership of a corporation;

(ii) In the effective control of a corporation; or

(iii) In the ownership of a substantial portion of the assets of a corporation; and

(4) Has (together with other payments described in paragraphs (a)(1), (2), and (3) of this A-2 with respect to the same disqualified individual) an aggregate present value of at least 3 times the individual's base amount.

(b) Hereinafter, a change referred to in paragraph (a)(3) of this A-2 is referred to as a change in ownership or control. For a discussion of the application of paragraph (a)(1), see Q/A-11 through Q/A-14; paragraph (a)(2), Q/A-15 through Q/A-21; paragraph (a)(3), Q/A-22 through Q/A-29; and paragraph (a)(4), Q/A-30 through Q/A-36.

(c) The term *parachute payment* also includes any payment in the nature of compensation to (or for the benefit of) a disqualified individual that is pursuant to an agreement that violates a generally enforced securities law or regulation. This type of parachute payment is referred to in this section as a securities violation parachute payment. See Q/A-37 for the definition and treatment of securities violation parachute payments.

Q-3: What is an excess parachute payment for purposes of section 280G?

A-3: The term *excess parachute payment* means an amount equal to the excess of any parachute payment over the portion of the base amount allocated to such payment. Subject to certain exceptions and limitations, an excess parachute payment is reduced by any portion of the payment which the taxpayer establishes by clear and convincing evidence is reasonable compensation for personal services actually rendered by the disqualified individual before the date of the change in ownership or control. For a discussion of the nonreduction of a securities violation parachute payment by reasonable compensation, see Q/A-37. For a discussion of the computation of excess parachute payments and their reduction by reasonable compensation, see Q/A-38 through Q/A-44.

Q-4: What is the effective date of section 280G and this section?

A-4: In general, section 280G applies to payments under agreements entered into or renewed after June 14, 1984. Section 280G also applies to certain payments under agreements entered into on or before June 14, 1984, and amended or supplemented in significant relevant respect after that date. This section applies to any payment contingent on a change in ownership or control which occurs on or after January 1, 2004. For a discussion of the application of the effective date, see Q/A-47 and Q/A-48.

Exempt Payments

Q-5: Are some types of payments exempt from the definition of the term *parachute payment*?

A-5: (a) Yes, the following five types of payments are exempt from the definition of *parachute payment*—

(1) Payments with respect to a small business corporation (described in Q/A-6 of this section);

(2) Certain payments with respect to a corporation no stock in which is readily tradeable on an established securities market (or otherwise) (described in Q/A-6 of this section);

(3) Payments to or from a qualified plan (described in Q/A-8 of this section);

(4) Certain payments made by a corporation undergoing a change in ownership or control that is described in any of the following sections of the Internal Revenue Code: section 501(c) (but only if such organization is subject to an express statutory prohibition against inurement of net earnings to the benefit of any private shareholder or individual, or if the organization is described in section 501(c)(1) or section 501(c)(21)), section 501(d), or section 529, collectively referred to as *tax-exempt organizations* (described in Q/A-6 of this section); and

(5) Certain payments of reasonable compensation for services to be rendered on or after the change in ownership or control (described in Q/A-9 of this section).

(b) Deductions for payments exempt from the definition of *parachute payment* are not disallowed by section 280G, and such exempt payments are not subject to the 20-percent excise tax of section 4999. In addition, such exempt payments are not taken into account in applying the 3-times-base-amount test of Q/A-30 of this section.

Q-6: Which payments with respect to a corporation referred to in paragraph (a)(1), (a)(2), or (a)(4) of Q/A-5 of this section are exempt from the definition of *parachute payment*?

A-6: (a) The term *parachute payment* does not include—

(1) Any payment to a disqualified individual with respect to a corporation which (immediately before the change in ownership or control) was a small business corporation (as defined in section 1361(b) but without regard to section 1361(b)(1)(C) thereof),

(2) Any payment to a disqualified individual with respect to a corporation (other than a small business corporation described in paragraph (a)(1) of this A-6) if—

(i) Immediately before the change in ownership or control, no stock in such corporation was readily tradeable on an established securities market or otherwise; and

(ii) The shareholder approval requirements described in Q/A-7 of this section are met with respect to such payment; or

(3) Any payment to a disqualified individual made by a corporation which is a tax-exempt organization (as defined in paragraph (a)(4) of Q/A-5 of this section), but only if the corporation meets the definition of a tax-exempt organization both immediately before and immediately after the change in ownership or control.

(b) For purposes of paragraph (a)(1) of this A-6, the members of an affiliated group are not treated as one corporation.

(c) The requirements of paragraph (a)(2)(i) of this A-6 are not met if a substantial portion of the assets of a corporation undergoing a change in ownership or control consists (directly or indirectly) of stock in another entity (or any ownership interest in such entity) and stock of such entity (or any ownership interest in such entity) is readily tradeable on an established securities market or otherwise. For this purpose, such stock constitutes a substantial portion of the assets of an entity if the total fair market value of the stock is equal to or exceeds one third of the total gross fair market value of all of the assets of the entity. If a corporation is a member of an affiliated group (which group is treated as one corporation under A-46 of this section), the requirements of paragraph (a)(2)(i) of this A-6 are not met if any stock in any member of such group is readily tradeable on an established securities market or otherwise.

(d) For purposes of paragraph (a)(2)(i) of this A-6, the term *stock* does not include stock described in section 1504(a)(4) if the payment does not adversely affect the redemption and liquidation rights of any shareholder owning such stock.

(e) For purposes of paragraph (a)(2)(i) of this A-6, stock is treated as readily tradeable if it is regularly quoted by brokers or dealers making a market in such stock.

(f) For purposes of paragraph (a)(2)(i) of this A-6, the term *established securities market* means an established securities market as defined in § 1.897-1(m).

(g) The following examples illustrate the application of this exemption:

Example 1. A small business corporation (within the meaning of paragraph (a)(1) of this A-6) operates two businesses. The corporation sells the assets of one of its businesses, and these assets represent a substantial portion of the assets of the corporation. Because of the sale, the corporation terminates its employment relationship with persons employed in the business the assets of which are sold. Several of these employees are highly-compensated individuals to whom the owners of the corporation make severance payments in excess of 3 times each employee's base amount. Since the corporation is a small business corporation immediately before the change in ownership or control, the payments are not parachute payments.

Example 2. Assume the same facts as in *Example 1*, except that the corporation is not a small business corporation within the meaning of paragraph (a)(1) of this A-6. If no stock in the corporation is readily tradeable on an established securities market (or otherwise) immediately before the change in ownership or control and the shareholder approval requirements described in Q/A-7 of this section are met, the payments are not parachute payments.

Example 3. Stock of Corporation S is wholly owned by Corporation P, stock in which is readily tradeable on an established securities market. The Corporation S stock equals or exceeds one third of the total gross fair market value of Corporation P, and thus, represents a substantial portion of the assets of Corporation P. Corporation S makes severance payments to several of its highly-compensated individuals that are parachute payments under section 280G and Q/A-2 of this section. Because stock in Corporation P is readily tradeable on an established securities market, the payments are not exempt from the definition of *parachute payments* under this A-6.

Example 4. A is a corporation described in section 501(c)(3), and accordingly, its net earnings are prohibited from inuring to the benefit of any private shareholder or individual. A transfers substantially all of its assets to another corporation resulting in a change in ownership or control. Contingent on the change in ownership or control, A makes a payment that, but for the potential application of the exemption described in A-5(a)(4), would constitute a *parachute payment*. However, one or more aspects of the transaction that constitutes the change in ownership or control causes A to fail to be described in section 501(c)(3). Accordingly, A fails to meet the definition of a *tax-exempt organization* both immediately before and immediately after the change in ownership or control, as required by this A-6. As a result, the payment made by A that was contingent on the change in ownership or control is not exempt from the definition of *parachute payment* under this A-6. [Corrected by IRS on 6/21/02, 67 FR 42210].

Example 5. B is a corporation described in section 501(c)(15). B does not meet the definition of a *tax-exempt organization* because section 501(c)(15) does not expressly prohibit inurement of B's net earnings to the benefit of any private shareholder or individual. Accordingly, if B has a change in ownership or control and makes a payment that would otherwise meet the definition of a *parachute payment*, such payment is not exempt from the definition of the term *parachute payment* for purposes of this A-6. [Corrected by IRS on 6/21/02, 67 FR 42210].

Q-7: How are the shareholder approval requirements referred to in paragraph (a)(2)(ii) of Q/A-6 of this section met?

A-7: (a) *General rule.* The shareholder approval requirements referred to in paragraph (a)(2)(ii) of Q/A-6 of this section are met with respect to any payment if—

(1) Such payment was approved by more than 75 percent of the voting power of all outstanding stock of the corporation entitled to vote (as described in this A-7) immediately before the change in ownership or control; and

(2) There was adequate disclosure to all persons entitled to vote (as described in this A-7) of all material facts concerning all material payments which (but for Q/A-6 of this section) would be parachute payments with respect to a disqualified individual.

(b) *Voting requirements*—(1) *General rule.* The vote described in paragraph (a)(1) of this A-7 must determine the right of the disqualified individual to receive the payment, or, in the case of a payment made before the vote, the right of the disqualified individual to retain the payment. For purposes of this A-7, the vote can be on less than the full amount of the payment(s) to be made. The total payment(s) submitted for shareholder approval must be separately approved by the shareholders. Shareholder approval can be a single vote on all payments submitted to vote, including payments to more than one disqualified individual. The requirements of this paragraph (b)(1) are not satisfied if approval of the change in ownership or control is contingent on the approval of any payment that would be a parachute payment but for Q/A-6 of this section to a disqualified individual. [Corrected by IRS on 6/21/02, 67 FR 42210].

(2) *Special rule for vote within 3 months before change.* A vote to approve the payment does not fail to be a vote of the outstanding stock of the corporation entitled to vote immediately before the change in ownership or control merely because the determination of the shareholders entitled to vote on the payment is based on the shareholders of record at the time of any shareholder vote taken in connection with a transaction or event giving rise to such change in ownership or control and within the three-month period ending on date of the change in ownership or control, provided the disclosure requirements described in paragraph (c) of this A-7 are met.

(3) *Entity shareholder.* Approval of a payment by any shareholder that is not an individual (an entity shareholder) generally must be made by the person authorized by the entity shareholder to approve the payment. However, if a substantial portion of the assets of an entity shareholder consists (directly or indirectly) of stock in the corporation undergoing the change in ownership or control, approval of the payment by that entity shareholder must be made by a separate vote of the persons who hold, immediately before the change in ownership or control, more than 75 percent of the voting power of the entity shareholder. The preceding sentence does not apply if the value of the stock of the corporation owned, directly or indirectly, by or for the entity shareholder does not exceed 1 percent of the total value of the outstanding stock of the corporation. Where approval of a payment by an entity shareholder must be made by a separate vote of the owners of the entity shareholder, the normal voting rights of the entity shareholder determine which owners shall vote. For purposes of this A-7, stock represents a substantial portion of the assets of an entity shareholder if the total fair market value of the stock held by the entity shareholder in the corporation undergoing the change in ownership or control is equal to or exceeds one third of the total fair market value of all of the assets of the entity shareholder.

(4) *Attribution of stock ownership.* In determining the persons who comprise the "more than 75 percent" group referred to in paragraph (a)(1) or (b)(3) of this A-7, stock is not counted as outstanding stock if the stock is actually owned or constructively owned under section 318(a) by or for a disqualified individual who receives (or is to receive) payments that would be parachute payments if the shareholder approval requirements described in paragraph (a) of this A-7 were not met. Likewise, stock is not counted as outstanding stock if the owner is considered under section 318(a) to own any part of the stock owned directly or indirectly by or for a disqualified individual described in the preceding sentence. In addition, if a partner authorized by a partnership to approve a payment is a disqualified individual with respect to the corporation undergoing a change in ownership or control, none of the stock held by the partnership is considered outstanding stock. However, if all persons who hold voting power in the corporation are disqualified individuals or related persons described in either of the two preceding sentences, then stock owned by such persons is counted as outstanding stock.

(5) *Disqualified individuals.* To satisfy the approval requirements of paragraph (a) of this A-7, the vote of a disqualified individual who receives (or is to receive) a payment that would be a parachute payment if the shareholder approval requirements described in paragraph (a) of this A-7 were not met is not considered in determining whether the more than 75 percent vote has been obtained for purposes of any vote under paragraph (a) of this A-7. However, if all persons who hold voting power in the corporation are disqualified individuals or related persons, then votes by such persons are considered in determining whether the more than 75% vote has been obtained.

(c) *Adequate disclosure.* To be adequate disclosure for purposes of paragraph (a)(2) of this A-7, disclosure must be full and truthful disclosure of the material facts and such additional information as is necessary to make the disclosure not materially misleading at the time the disclosure was made. Disclosure of such information must be made to every shareholder of the corporation entitled to vote under this A-7. For each disqualified individual, material facts that must be disclosed include the total amount of the payments that would be parachute payments if the shareholder approval requirements described in paragraph (a) of this A-7 were not met and a brief description of each payment (*e.g.,* accelerated vesting of options, bonus, or salary). An omitted fact is considered a material fact if there is a substantial likelihood that a reasonable shareholder would consider it important.

(d) *Corporation without shareholders.* If a corporation does not have shareholders, the exemption described in Q/A-6(a)(2) of this section and the shareholder approval requirements described in this A-7 do not apply. For purposes of this paragraph (d), a shareholder does not include a member in an association, joint stock company, or insurance company.

(e) *Examples.* The following examples illustrate the application of this A-7:

Example 1. Corporation S has two shareholders—Corporation P, which owns 76 percent of the stock of Corporation S, and A, a disqualified individual. No stock of Corporation P or S is readily tradeable on an established securities market (or otherwise). Stock of Corporation S equals or exceeds one third of the assets of Corporation P, and thus, represents a substantial portion of the assets of Corporation P. All of the stock of Corporation S is sold to Corporation M. Contingent on the change in ownership of Corporation S, severance payments are made to the officers of Corporation S in excess of 3 times each officer's base amount. If the payments are approved by a separate vote of the persons who hold, immediately before the sale, more than 75 percent of the voting power of the outstanding stock of Corporation P and the disclosure rules of paragraph (a)(2) of this A-7 are complied with, the shareholder approval requirements of this A-7 are met, and the payments are exempt from the definition of *parachute payment* pursuant to A-6 of this section.

Example 2. Corporation M is wholly owned by Partnership P. No interest in either M or P is readily tradeable on an established securities market (or otherwise). Stock of Corporation M equals or exceeds one third of the assets of Partnership P, and thus, represents a substantial portion of the assets of Partnership P. Corporation M undergoes a change in ownership or control. Partnership P has one general partner and 200 limited partners. None of the limited partners are entitled to vote on issues involving the management of the partnership investments. If the payments that would be parachute payments if the shareholder approval requirements of this A-7 are not met are approved by the general partner and the disclosure rules of paragraph (a)(2) of this A-7 are complied with, the shareholder approval requirements of this A-7 are met, and the payments are exempt from the definition of *parachute payment* pursuant to A-6 of this section.

Example 3. Corporation A has several shareholders including X and Y, who are disqualified individuals with respect to Corporation A. No stock of Corporation A is readily tradeable on an established securities market (or otherwise). Corporation A undergoes a change in ownership or control. Contingent on the change, severance payments are payable to X and Y that are in excess of 3 times each individual's base amount. To determine whether the approval requirements of paragraph (a)(1) of this A-7 are satisfied regarding the payments to X and Y, the stock of X and Y is not considered outstanding, and X and Y are not eligible to vote.

Example 4. Assume the same facts as in *Example 3* except that after adequate disclosure (within the meaning of paragraph (a)(2) of this A-7) to all shareholders entitled to vote, 60 percent of the shareholders who are entitled to vote approve the payments to X and Y. Because more than 75 percent of the shareholders did not approve the payments to X and Y, the shareholder approval requirements of paragraph (a)(1) of this A-7 are not satisfied, and the payments are not made to X and Y.

Example 5. Assume the same facts as in *Example 3* except that disclosure of all the material facts regarding the payments to X and Y is made to two of Corporation A's shareholders, who collectively own 80 percent of Corporation A's stock entitled to vote and approve the payment. Assume further that no disclosure of the material facts regarding the payments to X and Y is made to other Corporation A shareholders who are entitled to vote within the meaning of this A-7. Because disclosure regarding the payments to X and Y is not made to all of Corporation A's shareholders who were entitled to vote, the disclosure requirements of paragraph (a)(2) of this A-7 are not met, and the payments are not exempt from the definition of *parachute payment* pursuant to Q/A-6.

Example 6. Corporation C has three shareholders—Partnership, which owns 20 percent of the stock of Corporation C; A, an individual who owns 60 percent of the stock of Corporation C; and B, an individual who owns 20 percent of Corporation C. Stock of Corporation C does not represent a substantial portion of the assets of Partnership. No interest in either Partnership or Corporation C is readily tradeable on an established securities market (or otherwise). P, a one-third partner in Partnership, is a disqualified individual with respect to Corporation C. Corporation C undergoes a change in ownership or control. Contingent on the change, a severance payment is payable to P in excess of 3 times P's base amount. To determine the persons who comprise the "more than 75 percent group" referred to in paragraph (a)(1) of this A-7 who must approve the payment to P, one third of the stock held by Partnership is not considered outstanding stock. If, however, P is the person authorized by Partnership to approve the payment, none of the shares of Partnership are considered outstanding stock.

Example 7. X, an employee of Corporation E, is a disqualified individual with respect to Corporation E. No stock in Corporation E is readily tradeable on an established securities market (or otherwise). X, Y, and Z are all employees and disqualified individuals with respect to Corporation E. Each individual has a base amount of $100,000. Corporation E undergoes a change in ownership or control. Contingent on the change, a severance payment of $400,000 is payable to X; $600,000 is payable to Y; and $1,000,000 is payable to Z. Corporation E provides a ballot to each Corporation E shareholder entitled to vote under paragraph (a)(1) of this A-7 listing and describing the payments of $400,000 to X; $600,000 to Y; and $1,000,000 to Z. Next to each name and corresponding amount on the ballot, Corporation E requests approval (with a "yes" and "no" box) of each total payment to be made to each individual and states that if the payment is not approved the payment will not be made. Adequate disclosure, within the meaning of this A-7 is made to each shareholder entitled to vote under this A-7. More than 75 percent of the Corporation E shareholders who are entitled to vote under paragraph (a)(1) of this A-7, approve each payment to each individual. The shareholder approval requirements of this A-7 are met, and the payments are exempt from the definition of *parachute payment* pursuant to A-6 of this section. [Corrected by IRS on 6/21/02, 67 FR 42210].

Example 8. Assume the same facts as in *Example 7* except that the ballot does not request approval of each total payment to each individual separately. Instead, the ballot states that $2,000,000 in payments will be made to X, Y, and Z and requests approval of all of the $2,000,000 payments. Assuming the nature and amount of all the payments to X, Y, and Z are separately described to the shareholders entitled to vote under this A-7, the shareholder approval requirements of paragraph (a)(1) of this A-7 are met, and the payments are exempt from the definition of *parachute payment* pursuant to A-6 of this section. [Corrected by IRS on 6/21/02, 67 FR 42210].

Example 9. B, an employee of Corporation X, is a disqualified individual with respect to Corporation X. Stock of Corporation X is not readily tradeable on an established securities market (or otherwise). Corporation X undergoes a change in ownership or control. B's base amount is $205,000. Under B's employment agreement with Corporation X, in the event of a change in ownership or control, B's stock options will vest and B will receive a severance and bonus payment. Contingent on the change, B's stock options immediately vest with a fair market value of $500,000, $200,000 of which is contingent on the change, and B will receive a $200,000 bonus payment and a $400,000 severance payment. Corporation X distributes a ballot to every shareholder of Corporation X who immediately before the change is entitled to vote. The ballot lists the following payments to be made to B: the contingent payment of $200,000 attributable to options, a $200,000 bonus payment, and a $400,000 severance payment. The ballot requests shareholder approval of the $200,000 bonus payment to B and states that whether or not the $200,000 bonus payment is approved, B will receive $200,000 attributable to options and a $400,000 severance payment. More than 75 percent of the shareholders entitled to vote approve the $200,000 bonus payment to B. The shareholder approval requirements of this A-7 are met, and the $200,000 payment is exempt from the definition of *parachute payment* pursuant to A-6 of this section.

Q-8: Which payments under a qualified plan are exempt from the definition of *parachute payment?*

A-8: The term *parachute payment* does not include any payment to or from—

(a) A plan described in section 401(a) which includes a trust exempt from tax under section 501(a);

(b) An annuity plan described in section 403(a);

(c) A simplified employee pension (as defined in section 408(k)); or

(d) A simple retirement account (as defined in section 408(p)).

Q-9: Which payments of reasonable compensation are exempt from the definition of *parachute payment?*

A-9: Except in the case of securities violation parachute payments, the term *parachute payment* does not include any payment (or portion thereof) which the taxpayer establishes by clear and convincing evidence is reasonable compensation for personal services to be rendered by the disqualified individual on or after the date of the change in ownership or control. See Q/A-37 of this section for the definition and treatment of securities violation parachute payments. See Q/A-38 through Q/A-44 of this section for rules on determining amounts of reasonable compensation.

Payor of Parachute Payments

Q-10: Who may be the payor of parachute payments?

A-10: Parachute payments within the meaning of Q/A-2 of this section may be paid, directly or indirectly, by—(a) The corporation referred to in paragraph (a)(3) of Q/A-2 of this section, (b) A person acquiring ownership or effective control of that corporation or ownership of a substantial portion of that corporation's assets, or (c) Any person whose relationship to such corporation or other person is such as to require attribution of stock ownership between the parties under section 318(a).

Payments in the Nature of Compensation

Q-11: What types of payments are in the nature of compensation?

A-11: (a) *General rule.* For purposes of this section, all payments—in whatever form—are payments in the nature of compensation if they arise out of an employment relationship or are associated with the performance of services. For this purpose, the performance of services includes holding oneself out as available to perform services and refraining from performing services (such as under a covenant not to compete or similar arrangement). Payments in the nature of compensation include (but are not limited to) wages and salary, bonuses, severance pay, fringe benefits, and pension benefits and other deferred compensation (including any amount characterized by the parties as interest thereon). A payment in the nature of compensation also includes cash when paid, the value of the right to receive cash, or a transfer of property. However, payments in the nature of compensation do not include attorney's fees or court costs paid or incurred in connection with the payment of any amount described in paragraphs (a)(1), (2), and (3) of Q/A-2 of this section or a reasonable rate of interest accrued on any amount during the period the parties contest whether a payment will be made.

(b) *When payment is considered to be made.* Except as otherwise provided in A-11 through Q/A-13 of this section, a payment in the nature of compensation is considered made (and is subject to the excise tax under section 4999) in the taxable year in which it is includible in the disqualified individual's gross income or, in the case of fringe benefits and other benefits excludible from income, in the taxable year the benefits are received.

(c) *Pre-payment rule.* Notwithstanding the general rule described in paragraph (b) of this A-11, for purposes of section 4999, a disqualified individual is permitted to treat a payment as received in the year of the change in ownership or control or, if later, the first year in which the payment (or payments) is certain to be made without regard to the year in which the payment (or payments) is includible in income (or otherwise received). The payment of the excise tax for purposes of section 4999 must be based on the amount calculated for purposes of determining any excess parachute payments. However, a disqualified individual may not apply this paragraph (c) of this A-11 to a payment to be made in cash if the present value of the payment would be considered not reasonably ascertainable under section 3121(v) and §31.3121(v)2-1(e)(4) of this chapter, or a payment related to health benefits or coverage. The Commissioner is permitted to provide that this paragraph (c) is or is not available for certain types of payments. [Corrected by IRS on 6/21/02, 67 FR 42210].

(d) *Transfers of property.* Transfers of property are treated as payments for purposes of this A-11. See Q/A-12 of this section for rules on determining when such payments are considered made and the amount of such payments. See Q/A-13 of this section for special rules on transfers of statutory and nonstatutory stock options.

Q-12: If a property transfer to a disqualified individual is a payment in the nature of compensation, when is the payment considered made (or to be made), and how is the amount of the payment determined?

A-12: (a) Except as provided in this A-12 and Q/A-13 of this section, a transfer of property is considered a payment made (or to be made) in the taxable year in which the property transferred is includible in the gross income of the disqualified individual under section 83 and the regulations thereunder. Thus, in general, such a payment is considered made (or to be made) when the property is transferred (as defined in

§ 1.83-3(a)) to the disqualified individual and becomes substantially vested (as defined in § 1.83-3(b) and (j)) in such individual. In such case, the amount of the payment is determined under section 83 and the regulations thereunder. Thus, in general, the amount of the payment is equal to the excess of the fair market value of the transferred property (determined without regard to any lapse restriction, as defined in § 1.83-3(i)) at the time that the property becomes substantially vested, over the amount (if any) paid for the property.

(b) An election made by a disqualified individual under section 83(b) with respect to transferred property will not apply for purposes of this A-12. Thus, even if such an election is made with respect to a property transfer that is a payment in the nature of compensation, the payment is generally considered made (or to be made) when the property is transferred to and becomes substantially vested in such individual.

(c) See Q/A-13 of this section for rules on applying this A-12 to transfers of stock options.

(d) The following example illustrates the principles of this A-12:

Example. On January 1, 2006, Corporation M gives to A, a disqualified individual, a bonus of 100 shares of Corporation M stock in connection with the performance of services to Corporation M. Under the terms of the bonus arrangement A is obligated to return the Corporation M stock to Corporation M unless the earnings of Corporation M double by January 1, 2009, or there is a change in ownership or control of Corporation M before that date. A's rights in the stock are treated as substantially nonvested (within the meaning of § 1.83-3(b)) during that period because A's rights in the stock are subject to a substantial risk of forfeiture (within the meaning of § 1.83-3(c)) and are nontransferable (within the meaning of § 1.83-3(d)). On January 1, 2008, a change in ownership or control of Corporation M occurs. On that day, the fair market value of the Corporation M stock is $250 per share. Because A's rights in the Corporation M stock become substantially vested (within the meaning of § 1.83-3(b)) on that day, the payment is considered made on that day, and the amount of the payment for purposes of this section is equal to $25,000 (100×$250). See Q/A-38 through 41 for rules relating to the reduction of the excess parachute payment by the portion of the payment which is established to be reasonable compensation for personal services actually rendered before the date of a change in ownership or control.

Q-13: How are transfers of statutory and nonstatutory stock options treated?

A-13: (a) For purposes of this section, an option (including an option to which section 421 applies) is treated as property that is transferred not later than the time at which the option becomes substantially vested (whether or not the option has a readily ascertainable fair market value as defined in § 1.83-7(b)). Thus, for purposes of this section, the vesting of such an option is treated as a payment in the nature of compensation. The value of an option at the time the option vests is determined under all the facts and circumstances in the particular case. Factors relevant to such a determination include, but are not limited to: the difference between the option's exercise price and the value of the property subject to the option at the time of vesting; the probability of the value of such property increasing or decreasing; and the length of the period during which the option can be exercised. Valuation may be determined by any method prescribed by the Commissioner in published guidance for purposes of this A-13. See Q/A-33 of this section for the treatment of options the granting or vesting of which is contingent on a change in ownership or control and that do not have an ascertainable fair market value at the time of granting or vesting. [Corrected by IRS on 6/21/02, 67 FR 42210].

(b) Any money or other property transferred to the disqualified individual on the exercise, or as consideration on the sale or other disposition, of an option described in paragraph (a) of this A-13 after the time such option vests is not treated as a payment in the nature of compensation to the disqualified individual under Q/A-11 of this section. Nonetheless, the amount of the otherwise allowable deduction under section 162 or 212 with respect to such transfer is reduced by the amount of the payment described in paragraph (a) of this A-13 treated as an excess parachute payment.

Q-14: Are payments in the nature of compensation reduced by consideration paid by the disqualified individual?

A-14: Yes, to the extent not otherwise taken into account under Q/A-12 and Q/A-13 of this section, the amount of any payment in the nature of compensation is reduced by the amount of any money or the fair market value of any property (owned by the disqualified individual without restriction) that is (or will be) transferred by the disqualified individual in exchange for the payment. For purposes of the preceding sentence, the fair market value of property is determined as of the date the property is transferred by the disqualified individual.

Disqualified Individuals

Q-15: Who is a disqualified individual?

A-15: (a) For purposes of this section, an individual is a disqualified individual with respect to a corporation if, at any time during the *disqualified individual determination period* (as defined in Q/A-20 of this section), the individual is an employee or independent contractor of the corporation and is, with respect to the corporation—

(1) A shareholder (but see Q/A-17 of this section);

(2) An officer (see Q/A-18 of this section); or

(3) A highly-compensated individual (see Q/A-19 of this section).

(b) A director is a disqualified individual with respect to a corporation if, at any time during the *disqualified individual determination period* (as defined in Q/A-20 of this section), the director is an employee or independent contractor and is, with respect to the corporation, either a shareholder (see Q/A-17 of this section) or a highly-compensated individual (see Q/A-19 of this section).

Q-16: Is a personal service corporation treated as an individual?

A-16: (a) Yes. For purposes of this section, a personal service corporation (as defined in section 269A(b)(1)), or a noncorporate entity that would be a personal service corporation if it were a corporation, is treated as an individual.

(b) The following example illustrates the principles of this A-16:

Example. Corporation N, a personal service corporation (as defined in section 269A(b)(1)), has a single individual as its sole shareholder and employee. Corporation N performs personal services for Corporation M. The compensation paid to Corporation N by Corporation M puts Corporation N within the group of the highly-compensated individuals of Corporation M as determined under A-19 of this section. Thus, Corporation N is treated as a highly-compensated individual with respect to Corporation M.

Q-17: Are all shareholders of a corporation considered shareholders for purposes of paragraph (a)(1) and (b) of Q/A-15 of this section? [Corrected by IRS on 6/21/02, 67 FR 42210].

A-17: (a) No, only an individual who owns stock of a corporation with a fair market value that exceeds 1 percent of the fair market value of the outstanding shares of all classes of the corporation's stock is treated as a disqualified individual with respect to the corporation by reason of stock ownership. An individual who owns a lesser amount of stock may, however, be a disqualified individual with respect to the corporation if such individual is an officer or highly-compensated individual with respect to the corporation. For purposes of determining the amount of stock owned by an individual, the constructive ownership rules of section 318(a) apply.

(b) The following examples illustrates the principles of this A-17:

Example 1. E, an employee of Corporation A, received options under Corporation A's Stock Option Plan. E's stock options vest three years after the date of grant. E is not an officer or highly compensated individual during the disqualified individual determination period and does not own any other Corporation A stock. Two years after the options are granted to E, all of Corporation A's stock is acquired by Corporation B. Under Corporation A's Stock Option Plan, E's options are converted to Corporation B options and the vesting schedule remains the same. To determine whether E is a disqualified individual based on E's stock ownership, the stock underlying the unvested options held by E on the date of the change in ownership or control is not considered constructively owned by E under section 318(a). Because E does not own, or constructively own, Corporation A stock with a fair market value exceeding 1 percent of the total fair market value of all of the outstanding shares of all classes of Corporation A and E is not an officer or highly-compensated individual during the disqualified individual determination period, E is not a disqualified individual within the meaning of A-15 of this section with respect to Corporation A.

Example 2. Assume the same facts as in *Example 1* except that Corporation A's Stock Option Plan provides that all unvested options will vest immediately on a change in ownership or control. To determine whether E is a disqualified individual based on E's stock ownership, the stock underlying the options that vest on the change in ownership or control is considered constructively owned by E under section 318(a). If the stock constructively held by E exceeds 1 percent of the total fair market value of all of the outstanding shares of all classes of Corporation A stock, E is a disqualified individual within the meaning of this A-15 of this section with respect to Corporation A.

Example 3. Assume the same facts as in *Example 1* except that E received nonstatutory stock options that are exercisable for stock subject to a substantial risk of forfeiture under section 83. Assume further that under Corporation A's Stock Option Plan, the nonstatutory options will vest on a change in ownership or control. To determine whether E is a disqualified individual based on E's stock ownership, the stock underlying the options that vest on the change in ownership or control is not considered constructively owned by E under section 318(a) because the options are exercisable for stock subject to a substantial risk of forfeiture within the meaning of section 83. Because E does not own, or constructively own, Corporation A stock with a fair market value exceeding 1 percent of the total fair market value of all of the outstanding shares of all classes of Corporation A stock and E is not an officer or highly compensated individual during the disqualified individual determination period, E is not a disqualified individual within the meaning of A-15 of this section with respect to Corporation A.

Q-18: Who is an officer?

A-18: (a) For purposes of this section, whether an individual is an officer with respect to a corporation is determined on the basis of all the facts and circumstances in the particular case (such as the source of the individual's authority, the term for which the individual is elected or appointed, and the nature and extent of the individual's duties). Generally, the term *officer* means an administrative executive who is in regular and continued service. The term *officer* implies continuity of service and excludes those employed for a special and single transaction. An individual who merely has the title of officer but not the authority of an officer is not considered an officer for purposes of this section. Similarly, an individual who does not have the title of officer but has the authority of an officer is considered an officer for purposes of this section.

(b) An individual who is an officer with respect to any member of an affiliated group that is treated as one corporation pursuant to Q/A-46 of this section is treated as an officer of such one corporation.

(c) No more than 50 employees (or, if less, the greater of 3 employees, or 10 percent of the employees (rounded up to the nearest integer)) of the corporation (in the case of an affiliated group treated as one corporation, each member of the affiliated group) are treated as disqualified individuals with respect to a corporation by reason of being an officer of the corporation. For purposes of the preceding sentence, the number of employees of the corporation is the greatest number of employees the corporation has during the disqualified individual determination period (as defined in Q/A-20 of this section). The number of employees is determined with regard to the rules in Q/A-19(c). If the number of officers of the corporation exceeds the number of employees who may be treated as officers under the first sentence of this paragraph (c), then the employees who are treated as officers for purposes of this section are the highest paid 50 employees (or, if less, the greater of 3 employees, or 10 percent of the employees (rounded up to the nearest integer)) of the corporation when ranked on the basis of compensation (as determined under Q/A-21 of this section) paid during the disqualified individual determination period.

Q-19: Who is a highly-compensated individual?

A-19: (a) For purposes of this section, a highly-compensated individual with respect to a corporation is any individual who is, or would be if the individual were an employee, a member of the group consisting of the lesser of the highest paid 1 percent of the employees of the corporation (rounded up to the nearest integer), or the highest paid 250 employees of the corporation, when ranked on the basis of compensation (as determined under Q/A-21 of this section) earned during the disqualified individual determination period (as defined in Q/A-20 of this section). For purposes of the preceding sentence, the number of employees of the corporation is the greatest number of employees the corporation has during the disqualified individual determination period (as defined in Q/A-20 of this section). However, no individual whose annualized compensation during the disqualified individual determination period is less than the amount described in section 414(q)(1)(B)(i) for the year in which the change in ownership or control occurs will be treated as a highly-compensated individual. [Corrected by IRS on 6/21/02, 67 FR 42210].

(b) An individual who is not an employee of the corporation is not treated as a highly-compensated individual with respect to the corporation on account of compensation received for performing services (such as brokerage, legal, or investment banking services) in connection with a change in ownership or control of the corporation, if the services are performed in the ordinary course of the individual's trade or business and the individual performs similar services for a significant number of clients unrelated to the corporation.

(c) In determining the total number of employees of a corporation for purposes of this A-19, employees are not counted if they normally work less than 17 1/2 hours per week (as defined in section 414(q)(5)(B) and the regulations thereunder) or if they normally work

during not more than 6 months during any year (as defined in section 414(q)(5)(C) and the regulations thereunder). However, an employee who is not counted for purposes of the preceding sentence may still be a highly-compensated individual.

Q-20: What is the disqualified individual determination period?

A-20: The disqualified individual determination period is the twelve-month period prior to and ending on the date of the change in ownership or control of the corporation.

Q-21: How is *compensation* defined for purposes of determining who is a disqualified individual?

A-21: (a) For purposes of determining who is a disqualified individual, the term *compensation* is the compensation which was earned by the individual for services performed for the corporation with respect to which the change in ownership or control occurs (changed corporation), for a predecessor entity, or for a related entity. Such compensation is determined without regard to sections 125, 132(f)(4), 402(e)(3), and 402(h)(1)(B). Thus, for example, compensation includes elective or salary reduction contributions to a cafeteria plan, cash or deferred arrangement or tax-sheltered annuity and amounts credited under a nonqualified deferred compensation plan.

(b) For purposes of this A-21, a predecessor entity is any entity which, as a result of a merger, consolidation, purchase or acquisition of property or stock, corporate separation, or other similar business transaction transfers some or all of its employees to the changed corporation or to a related entity or to a predecessor entity of the changed corporation. The term *related entity* include—

(1) All members of a controlled group of corporations (as defined in section 414(b)) that includes the changed corporation or a predecessor entity;

(2) All trades or business (whether or not incorporated) that are under common control (as defined in section 414(c)) if such group includes the changed corporation or a predecessor entity;

(3) All members of an affiliated service group (as defined in section 414(m)) that includes the changed corporation or a predecessor entity; and

(4) Any other entities required to be aggregated with the changed corporation or a predecessor entity pursuant to section 414(o) and the regulations thereunder (except leasing organizations as defined in section 414(n)).

(c) For purposes of Q/A-18 and Q/A-19 of this section, compensation that was contingent on the change in ownership or control and that was payable in the year of the change is not treated as compensation.

Contingent on Change in Ownership or Control

Q-22: When is a payment contingent on a change in ownership or control?

A-22: (a) In general, a payment is treated as contingent on a change in ownership or control if the payment would not, in fact, have been made had no change in ownership or control occurred, even if the payment is also conditioned on the occurrence of another event. A payment generally is treated as one which would not, in fact, have been made in the absence of a change in ownership or control unless it is substantially certain, at the time of the change, that the payment would have been made whether or not the change occurred. (But see Q/A-23 of this section regarding payments under agreements entered into after a change in ownership or control.) A payment that becomes vested as a result of a change in ownership or control is not treated as a payment which was substantially certain to have been made whether or not the change occurred. For purposes of this A-22, *vested* means the payment is substantially vested within the meaning of § 1.83-3(b) and (j) or the right to the payment is not otherwise subject to a substantial risk of forfeiture.

(b)(1) For purposes of paragraph (a), a payment is treated as contingent on a change in ownership or control if—

(i) The payment is contingent on an event that is closely associated with a change in ownership or control;

(ii) A change in ownership or control actually occurs; and

(iii) The event is materially related to the change in ownership or control.

(2) For purposes of paragraph (b)(1)(i) of this A-22, a payment is treated as contingent on an event that is closely associated with a change in ownership or control unless it is substantially certain, at the time of the event, that the payment would have been made whether or not the event occurred. An event is considered closely associated with

a change in ownership or control if the event is of a type often preliminary or subsequent to, or otherwise closely associated with, a change in ownership or control. For example, the following events are considered closely associated with a change in the ownership or control of a corporation: The onset of a tender offer with respect to the corporation; a substantial increase in the market price of the corporation's stock that occurs within a short period (but only if such increase occurs prior to a change in ownership or control); the cessation of the listing of the corporation's stock on an established securities market; the acquisition of more than 5 percent of the corporation's stock by a person (or more than one person acting as a group) not in control of the corporation; the voluntary or involuntary termination of the disqualified individual's employment; a significant reduction in the disqualified individual's job responsibilities; and a change in ownership or control as defined in the disqualified individual's employment agreement (or elsewhere) that does not meet the definition of a change in ownership or control described in Q/A-27, 28, or 29 of this section. Whether other events are treated as closely associated with a change in ownership or control is based on all the facts and circumstances of the particular case.

(3) For purposes of determining whether an event (as described in paragraph (b)(2) of this A-22) is materially related to a change in ownership or control, the event is presumed to be materially related to a change in ownership or control if such event occurs within the period beginning one year before and ending one year after the date of change in ownership or control. If such event occurs outside of the period beginning one year before and ending one year after the date of change in ownership or control, the event is presumed not materially related to the change in ownership or control. A payment does not fail to be contingent on a change in ownership or control merely because it is also contingent on the occurrence of a second event (without regard to whether the second event is closely associated with or materially related to a change in ownership or control). Similarly, a payment that is treated as contingent on a change because it is contingent on a closely associated event does not fail to be treated as contingent on a change in ownership or control merely because it is also contingent on the occurrence of a second event (without regard to whether the second event is closely associated with or materially related to a change in ownership or control).

(c) A payment that would in fact have been made had no change in ownership or control occurred is treated as contingent on a change in ownership or control if the change in ownership or control (or the occurrence of an event that is closely associated with and materially related to a change in ownership or control within the meaning of paragraph (b)(1) of this A-22), accelerates the time at which the payment is made. Thus, for example, if a change in ownership or control accelerates the time of payment of deferred compensation that is vested without regard to the change in ownership or control, the payment may be treated as contingent on the change. See Q/A-24 of this section regarding the portion of a payment that is so treated. See also Q/A-8 of this section regarding the exemption for certain payments under qualified plans and Q/A-40 of this section regarding the treatment of a payment as reasonable compensation. [Corrected by IRS on 6/21/02, 67 FR 42210].

(d) A payment is treated as contingent on a change in ownership or control even if the employment or independent contractor relationship of the disqualified individual is not terminated (voluntarily or involuntarily) as a result of the change.

(e) The following examples illustrate the principles of this A-22:

Example 1. A corporation grants a stock appreciation right to a disqualified individual, A, more than one year before a change in ownership or control. After the stock appreciation right vests and becomes exercisable, a change in ownership or control of the corporation occurs, and A exercises the right. Assuming neither the granting nor the vesting of the stock appreciation right is contingent on a change in ownership or control, the payment made on exercise is not contingent on the change in ownership or control.

Example 2. A contract between a corporation and B, a disqualified individual, provides that a payment will be made to B if the corporation undergoes a change in ownership or control and B's employment with the corporation is terminated at any time over the succeeding 5 years. Eighteen months later, a change in the ownership of the corporation occurs. Two years after the change in ownership, B's employment is terminated and the payment is made to B. Because it was not substantially certain that the corporation would have made the payment to B on B's termination of employment if there had not been a change in ownership, the payment is treated as contingent on the change in ownership under paragraph (a) of this A-22. This is true even though

B's termination of employment is presumed not to be, and in fact may not be, materially related to the change in ownership or control.

Example 3. A contract between a corporation and C, a disqualified individual, provides that a payment will be made to C if C's employment is terminated at any time over the succeeding 3 years (without regard to whether or not there is a change in ownership or control). Eighteen months after the contract is entered into, a change in the ownership of the corporation occurs. Six months after the change in ownership, C's employment is terminated and the payment is made to C. Termination of employment is considered an event closely associated with a change in ownership or control. Because the termination occurred within one year after the date of the change in ownership, the termination of C's employment is presumed to be materially related to the change in ownership under paragraph (b)(3) of this A-22. If this presumption is not successfully rebutted, the payment will be treated as contingent on the change in ownership under paragraph (b) of this A-22.

Example 4. A contract between a corporation and a disqualified individual, D, provides that a payment will be made to D upon the onset of a tender offer for shares of the corporation's stock. A tender offer is made on December 1, 2008, and the payment is made to D. Although the tender offer is unsuccessful, it leads to a negotiated merger with another entity on June 1, 2009, which results in a change in the ownership of the corporation. It was not substantially certain, at the time of the onset of the tender offer, that the payment would have been made had no tender offer taken place. The onset of a tender offer is considered closely associated with a change in ownership or control. Because the tender offer occurred within one year before the date of the change in ownership of the corporation, the onset of the tender offer is presumed to be materially related to the change in ownership. If this presumption is not rebutted, the payment will be treated as contingent on the change in ownership. If no change in ownership or control had occurred, the payment would not be treated as contingent on a change in ownership or control; however, the payment still could be a parachute payment under Q/A-37 of this section if the contract violated a generally enforced securities law or regulation.

Example 5. A contract between a corporation and a disqualified individual, E, provides that a payment will be made to E if the corporation's level of product sales or profits reaches a specified level. At the time the contract was entered into, the parties had no reason to believe that such an increase in the corporation's level of product sales or profits would be preliminary or subsequent to, or otherwise closely associated with, a change in ownership or control of the corporation. Eighteen months later, a change in the ownership of the corporation occurs and within one year after the date of the change, the corporation's level of product sales or profits reaches the specified level. Under these facts and circumstances (and in the absence of contradictory evidence), the increase in product sales or profits of the corporation is not an event closely associated with the change in ownership or control of the corporation. Accordingly, even if the increase is materially related to the change, the payment will not be treated as contingent on a change in ownership or control.

Q-23: May a payment be treated as contingent on a change in ownership or control if the payment is made under an agreement entered into after the change?

A-23: (a) No, payments are not treated as contingent on a change in ownership or control if they are made (or to be made) pursuant to an agreement entered into after the change (a post-change agreement). For this purpose, an agreement that is executed after a change in ownership or control pursuant to a legally enforceable agreement that was entered into before the change is considered to have been entered into before the change. (See Q/A-9 of this section regarding the exemption for reasonable compensation for services rendered on or after a change in ownership or control.) If an individual has a right to receive a parachute payment under an agreement entered into prior to a change in ownership or control (pre-change agreement) and gives up that right as bargained-for consideration for benefits under a post-change agreement, the agreement is treated as a post-change agreement only to the extent the value of the payments under the agreement exceed the value of the payments under the pre-change agreement. To the extent payments under the agreement have the same value as the parachute payments under the pre-change agreement, such payments retain their character as parachute payments subject to this section.

(b) The following examples illustrate the principles of this A-23:

Example 1. Assume that a disqualified individual is an employee of a corporation. A change in ownership or control of the corporation occurs, and thereafter the individual enters into an employment agreement with the acquiring company. Because the agreement is entered into after the change in ownership or control occurs, payments to be made under the agreement are not treated as contingent on the change.

Example 2. Assume the same facts as in *Example 1,* except that the agreement between the disqualified individual and the acquiring company is executed after the change in ownership or control, pursuant to a legally enforceable agreement entered into before the change. Payments to be made under the agreement may be treated as contingent on the change in ownership or control pursuant to Q/A-22 of this section. However, see Q/A-9 of this section regarding the exemption from the definition of parachute payment for certain amounts of reasonable compensation.

Example 3. Assume the same facts as in *Example 1* except that prior to the change in ownership or control, the individual and corporation enter into an agreement under which the individual will receive parachute payments in the event of a change in ownership or control of the corporation. After the change, the individual agrees to give up the right to parachute payments under the pre-change agreement in exchange for compensation under a new agreement with the acquiring corporation. Because the individual gave up the right to parachute payments under the pre-change agreement in exchange for other payments under the post-change agreement, payments in an amount equal to the parachute payments under the pre-change agreement are treated as contingent on the change in ownership or control under this A-23. Because the post-change agreement was entered into after the change, payments in excess of this amount are not treated as parachute payments.

Q-24: If a payment is treated as contingent on a change in ownership or control, is the full amount of the payment so treated?

A-24: (a) (1) *General rule.* Yes, if the payment is a transfer of property, the amount of the payment is determined under Q/A-12 or Q/A-13 of this section. For all other payments, the amount of the payment is determined under Q/A-11 of this section. However, in certain circumstances, described in paragraphs (b) and (c) of this A-24, only a portion of the payment is treated as contingent on the change. Paragraph (b) of this A-24 applies to a payment that is vested, without regard to the change in ownership or control, and is treated as contingent on the change in ownership or control because the change accelerates the time at which the payment is made. Paragraph (c) of this A-24 applies to a payment that becomes vested as a result of the change in ownership or control if, without regard to the change in ownership or control, the payment was contingent only on the continued performance of services for the corporation for a specified period of time and if the payment is attributable, at least in part, to services performed before the date the payment becomes vested. For purposes of this A-24, for the definition of vested see Q/A-22(a).

(2) *Reduction by reasonable compensation.* The amount of a payment under paragraph (a)(1) of this A-24 is reduced by any portion of such payment that the taxpayer establishes by clear and convincing evidence is reasonable compensation for personal services rendered by the disqualified individual on or after the date of the change of control. See Q/A-9 and Q/A-38 through 44 of this section for rules concerning reasonable compensation. The portion of an amount treated as contingent under paragraph (b) or (c) of this A-24 may not be reduced by reasonable compensation.

(b) *Vested payments.* This paragraph (b) applies if a payment is vested, without regard to the change in ownership or control, and is treated as contingent on the change in ownership or control because the change accelerates the time at which the payment is made. In such case, the portion of the payment, if any, that is treated as contingent on the change in ownership or control is the amount by which the amount of the accelerated payment exceeds the present value of the payment absent the acceleration. If the value of such a payment absent the acceleration is not reasonably ascertainable, and the acceleration of the payment does not significantly increase the present value of the payment absent the acceleration, the present value of the payment absent the acceleration is treated as equal to the amount of the accelerated payment. If the value of the payment absent the acceleration is not reasonably ascertainable, but the acceleration significantly increases the present value of the payment, the future value of such payment is treated as equal to the amount of the accelerated payment. For rules on determining present value, see paragraph (e) of this A-24, Q/A-32, and Q/A-33 of this section.

(c) (1) *Nonvested payments.* This paragraph (c) applies to a payment that becomes vested as a result of the change in ownership or control to the extent that—

(i) Without regard to the change in ownership or control, the payment was contingent only on the continued performance of services for the corporation for a specified period of time; and

(ii) The payment is attributable, at least in part, to the performance of services before the date the payment is made or becomes certain to be made.

(2) The portion of the payment subject to paragraph (c) of this A-24 that is treated as contingent on the change in ownership or control is the lesser of—

(i) The amount of the accelerated payment; or

(ii) The amount described in paragraph (b) of this A-24, plus an amount, as determined in paragraph (c)(4) of this A-24, to reflect the lapse of the obligation to continue to perform services.

(3) For purposes of this paragraph (c) of this A-24, the acceleration of the vesting of a stock option or the lapse of a restriction on restricted stock is considered to significantly increase the value of a payment.

(4) The amount reflecting the lapse of the obligation to continue to perform services (described in paragraph (c)(2)(ii) of this A-24) is 1 percent of the amount of the accelerated payment multiplied by the number of full months between the date that the individual's right to receive the payment is vested and the date that, absent the acceleration, the payment would have been vested. This paragraph (c)(4) applies to the accelerated vesting of a payment in the nature of compensation even if the time at which the payment is made is not accelerated.

(d) *Application of this A-24 to certain payments.*—(1) *Benefits under a nonqualified deferred compensation plan.* In the case of a payment of benefits under a nonqualified deferred compensation plan, paragraph (b) of this A-24 applies to the extent benefits under the plan are vested without regard to the change in ownership or control. Paragraph (c) of this A-24 applies to the extent benefits under the plan become vested as a result of the change in ownership or control and are attributable, at least in part, to the performance of services prior to vesting. Any other payment of benefits under a nonqualified deferred compensation plan is a payment in the nature of compensation subject to the general rule of paragraph (a) of this A-24 and the rules in Q/A-11 of this section.

(2) *Employment agreements.* The general rule of paragraph (a) of this A-24 applies to the payment of amounts due under an employment agreement on a termination of employment or a change in ownership or control that otherwise would be attributable to the performance of services (or refraining from the performance of services) during any period that begins after the date of termination of employment or change in ownership or control, as applicable. For purposes of this paragraph (d)(2) of this A-24, an employment agreement means an agreement between an employee or independent contractor and employer or service recipient which describes, among other things, the amount of compensation or remuneration payable to the employee or independent contractor. See Q/A-42(b) and 44 of this section for the treatment of the remaining amounts of salary under an employment agreement.

(3) *Vesting due to an event other than services.* Neither paragraph (b) nor (c) of this A-24 applies to a payment if (without regard to the change in ownership or control) vesting of the payment depends on an event other than the performance of services, such as the attainment of a performance goal, and the event does not occur prior to the change in ownership or control. In such circumstances, the full amount of the accelerated payment is treated as contingent on the change in ownership or control under paragraph (a) of this A-24. However, see Q/A-39 of this section for rules relating to the reduction of the excess parachute payment by the portion of the payment which is established to be reasonable compensation for personal services actually rendered before the date of a change in ownership or control.

(e) *Present value.* For purposes of this A-24, the present value of a payment is determined as of the date on which the accelerated payment is made.

(f) *Examples.* The following examples illustrate the principles of this A-24:

Example 1. (i) Corporation maintains a qualified plan and a nonqualified supplemental retirement plan (SERP) for its executives. Benefits under the SERP are not paid to participants until retirement. E, a disqualified individual with respect to Corporation, has a vested account balance of $500,000 under the SERP. A change in ownership or control of Corporation occurs. The SERP provides that in the event of a change in ownership or control, all vested accounts will be paid to SERP participants.

(ii) Because E was vested in $500,000 of benefits under the SERP prior to the change in ownership or control and the change merely accelerated the time at which the payment was made to E, only a portion of the payment, as determined under paragraph (b) of this A-24, is treated as contingent on the change. Thus, the portion of the payment that is treated as contingent on the change is the amount by which the amount of the accelerated payment ($500,000) exceeds the present value of the payment absent the acceleration.

(iii) Assume that instead of having a vested account balance of $500,000 on the date of the change in ownership or control, E will vest in his account balance of $500,000 in 2 years if E continues to perform services for the next 2 years. Assume further that the SERP provides that all unvested SERP benefits vest immediately on a change in ownership or control and are paid to the participants. Because the vesting of the SERP payment, without regard to the change, depends only on the performance of services for a specified period of time and the payment is attributable, in part, to the performance of services before the change in ownership or control, only a portion of the $500,000 payment, as determined under paragraph (c) of this A-24, is treated as contingent on the change. The portion of the payment that is treated as contingent on the change is the lesser of the amount of the accelerated payment or the amount by which the accelerated payment exceeds the present value of the payment absent the acceleration, plus an amount to reflect the lapse of the obligation to continue to perform services.

(iv) Assume further that under the SERP E's vested account balance of $500,000 will be paid to E on the change in ownership or control and an additional $70,000 will be credited to E's account. Because the $500,000 was vested without regard to the change in owner ship or control, paragraph (b) of this A-24 applies to the $500,000 payment. Because the $70,000 is not vested, without regard to the change, and is not attributable to the performance of services prior to the change, the entire $70,000 payment is contingent on the change in ownership or control under paragraph (a) of this A-24.

Example 2. As a result of a change in the effective control of a corporation, a disqualified individual with respect to the corporation, D, receives accelerated payment of D's vested account balance in a non-qualified deferred compensation account plan. Actual interest and other earnings on the plan assets are credited to each account as earned before distribution: Investment of the plan assets is not restricted in such a manner as would prevent the earning of a market rate of return on the plan assets. The date on which D would have received D's vested account balance absent the change in ownership or control is uncertain, and the rate of earnings on the plan assets is not fixed. Thus, the amount of the payment absent the acceleration is not reasonably ascertainable. Under these facts, acceleration of the payment does not significantly increase the present value of the payment absent the acceleration, and the present value of the payment absent the acceleration is treated as equal to the amount of the accelerated payment. Accordingly, no portion of the payment is treated as contingent on the change.

Example 3. (i) On January 15, 2006, a corporation and a disqualified individual, F, enter into a contract providing for a retention bonus of $500,000 to be paid to F on January 15, 2011. The payment of the bonus will be forfeited by F if F does not remain employed by the corporation for the entire 5-year period. However, the contract provides that the full amount of the payment will be made immediately on a change in ownership or control of the corporation during the 5-year period. On January 15, 2009, a change in ownership or control of the corporation occurs and the full amount of the payment ($500,000) is made on that date to F. Under these facts, the payment of $500,000 was contingent only on F's performance of services for a specified period and is attributable, in part, to the performance of services before the change in ownership or control. Therefore, only a portion of the payment is treated as contingent on the change. The portion of the payment that is treated as contingent on the change is the amount by which the amount of the accelerated payment (*i.e.*, $500,000, the amount paid to the individual because of the change in ownership) exceeds the present value of the payment that was expected to have been made absent the acceleration (*i.e.*, $406,838, the present value on January 15, 2009, of a $500,000 payment on January 15, 2011), plus $115,000 (1% × 23 months × $500,000) which is the amount reflecting the lapse of the obligation to continue to perform services. Accordingly, the amount of the payment treated as contingent on the change in ownership or control is $208,162, the sum of $93,162 ($500,000 − $406,838) + $115,000). This result is not changed if F actually remains employed until the end of the 5-year period.

(ii) Assume that the contract provides that the retention bonus will vest on a change in ownership or control, but will not be paid until January 15, 2011 (the original date in the contract). Because the payment of $500,000 was contingent only on F's performance of services for a specified period and is attributable, in part, to the perform-ance of services before the change in ownership or control, only a portion of the $500,000 payment is treated as contingent on the change. Because there is no accelerated payment, the portion of the payment

treated as contingent on the change is an amount reflecting the lapse of the obligation to continue to perform services which is $115,000 (1% × 23 months × $500,000).

Example 4. (i) On January 15, 2006, a corporation gives to a disquali-fied individual, in connection with her performance of services to the corporation, a bonus of 1,000 shares of the corporation's stock. Under the terms of the bonus arrangement, the individual is obligated to return the stock to the corporation if she terminates her employment for any reason prior to January 15, 2011. However, if there is a change in the ownership or effective control of the corporation prior to January 15, 2011, she ceases to be obligated to return the stock. The individ-ual's rights in the stock are treated as substantially nonvested (within the meaning of § 1.83-3(b) and (j)) during that period. On January 15, 2008, a change in the ownership of the corporation occurs. On that day, the fair market value of the stock is $500,000.

(ii) Under these facts, the payment was contingent only on perform-ance of services for a specified period and is attributable, in part, to the performance of services before the change in ownership or control. Thus, only a portion of the payment is treated as contingent on the change in ownership or control. The portion of the payment that is treated as contingent on the change is the amount by which the present value of the accelerated payment on January 15, 2009 ($500,000), exceeds the present value of the payment that was ex-pected to have been made on January 15, 2011, plus an amount reflecting the lapse of the obligation to continue to perform services. At the time of the change, it cannot be reasonably ascertained what the value of the stock would have been on January 15, 2011. The accelera-tion of the lapse of a restriction on stock is treated as significantly increasing the value of the payment. Therefore, the value of such stock on January 15, 2011, is deemed to be $500,000, the amount of the accelerated payment. The present value on January 15, 2009, of a $500,000 payment to be made on January 15, 2011, is $406,838. Thus, the portion of the payment treated as contingent on the change is $208,162, the sum of $93,162 ($500,000 − $406,838), plus $115,000 [1% × 23 months × $500,000], the amount reflecting the lapse of the obliga-tion to continue to perform services. [Corrected by IRS on 6/21/02, 67 FR 42210].

Example 5. (i) On January 15, 2006, a corporation grants to a disquali-fied individual nonqualified stock options to purchase 30,000 shares of the corporation's stock. The options do not have a readily ascertainable fair market value at the time of grant. The options will be forfeited by the individual if he fails to perform personal services for the corpora-tion until January 15, 2009. The options will, however, vest in the individual at an earlier date if there is a change in ownership or control of the corporation. On January 16, 2008, a change in the ownership of the corporation occurs and the options become vested in the individual. On January 16, 2008, the options have an ascertainable fair market value of $600,000.

(ii) The payment of the options to purchase 30,000 shares was contingent only on performance of services for the corporation until January 15, 2009, and is attributable, in part, to the performance of services before the change in ownership or control. Therefore, only a portion of the payment is treated as contingent on the change. The portion of the payment that is treated as contingent on the change is the amount by which the accelerated payment on January 16, 2008 ($600,000) exceeds the present value on January 16, 2008, of the payment that was expected to have been made on January 15, 2009, absent the acceleration, plus an amount reflecting the lapse of the obligation to continue to perform services. At the time of the change, it cannot be reasonably ascertained what the value of the options would have been on January 15, 2009. The acceleration of vesting in the options is treated as significantly increasing the value of the payment. Therefore, the value of such options on January 15, 2009, is deemed to be $600,000, the amount of the accelerated payment. The present value on January 16, 2008 of a $600,000 payment to be made on January 15, 2009, is $549,964.13. Thus, the portion of the payment treated as contingent on the change is $116,035.87, the sum of $50,035.87 ($600,000 − $549,964.13), plus an amount reflecting the lapse of the obligation to continue to perform services which is $66,000 (1% × 11 months × $600,000).

Example 6. (i) The facts are the same as in *Example 5*, except that the options become vested periodically (absent a change in ownership of control), with one-third of the options vesting on January 15, 2007, 2008, and 2009, respectively. Thus, options to purchase 20,000 shares vest independently of the January 16, 2008, change in ownership and the options to purchase the remaining 10,000 shares vest as a result of the change.

(ii) The payment of the options to purchase 10,000 shares was contingent only on performance of services for the corporation until

January 15, 2009, and is attributable, in part, to the performance of services before the change in ownership or control. Therefore, only a portion of the payment is treated as contingent on the change. The portion of the payment that is treated as contingent on the change is the amount by which the accelerated payment on January 16, 2008 ($200,000) exceeds the present value on January 16, 2008, of the payment that was expected to have been made on January 15, 2009, absent the acceleration, plus an amount reflecting the lapse of the obligation to perform services. At the time of the change, it cannot be reasonably ascertained what the value of the options would have been on January 15, 2009. The acceleration of vesting in the options is treated as significantly increasing the value of the payment. Therefore, the value of such options on January 15, 2009, is deemed to be $200,000, the amount of the accelerated payment. The present value on January 16, 2008, of a $200,000 payment to be made on January 15, 2009, is $183,328.38. Thus, the portion of the payment treated as contingent on the change is $38,671.62, the sum of $16,671.62 ($200,000 − $183,328.38), plus an amount reflecting the lapse of the obligation to continue to perform services which is $22,000 (1% × 11 months × $200,000).

Example 7. Assume the same facts as in *Example 5*, except that the option agreement provides that the options will vest either on the corporation's level of profits reaching a specified level, or if earlier, on the date on which there is a change in ownership or control of the corporation. The corporation's level of profits do not reach the specified level prior to January 16, 2008. In such case, the full amount of the payment, $600,000, is treated as contingent on the change because it was not contingent only on performance of services for the corporation for a specified period. See Q/A-39 of this section for rules relating to the reduction of the excess parachute payment by the portion of the payment which is established to be reasonable compensation for personal services actually rendered before the date of a change in ownership or control.

Example 8. On January 1, 2002, E, a disqualified individual with respect to Corporation X, enters into an employment agreement with Corporation X under which E will be paid wages of $200,000 each year during the 5-year employment agreement. The employment agreement provides that if a change in ownership or control of Corporation X occurs, E will be paid the present value of the remaining salary under the employment agreement. On January 1, 2003, a change in ownership or control of Corporation X occurs, E is terminated, and E receives a payment of the present value of $200,000 for each of the 4 years remaining under the employment agreement. Because the payment represents future salary under an employment agreement (i.e., amounts otherwise attributable to the performance of services for periods that begin after the termination of employment), the general rule of paragraph (a) of this A-24 applies to the payment. See Q/A-42(c) and 44 of this section for the treatment of the remaining payments under an employment agreement.

Presumption That Payment Is Contingent on Change

Q-25: Is there a presumption that certain payments are contingent on a change in ownership or control?

A-25: Yes, for purposes of this section, any payment is presumed to be contingent on such change unless the contrary is established by clear and convincing evidence if the payment is made pursuant to—

(a) An agreement entered into within one year before the date of a change in ownership or control; or

(b) An amendment that modifies a previous agreement in any significant respect, if the amendment is made within one year before the date of a change in ownership or control. In the case of an amendment described in paragraph (b) of this A-25, only the portion of any payment that exceeds the amount of such payment that would have been made in the absence of the amendment is presumed, by reason of the amendment, to be contingent on the change in ownership or control.

Q-26: How may the presumption described in Q/A-25 of this section be rebutted?

A-26: (a) To rebut the presumption described in Q/A-25 of this section, the taxpayer must establish by clear and convincing evidence that the payment is not contingent on the change in ownership or control. Whether the payment is contingent on such change is determined on the basis of all the facts and circumstances of the particular case. Factors relevant to such a determination include, but are not limited to the content of the agreement or amendment and the circumstances surrounding the execution of the agreement or amendment, such as whether it was entered into at a time when a takeover attempt had commenced and the degree of likelihood that a change in ownership or control would actually occur. However, even if the presumption is rebutted with respect to an agreement, some or all of the payments

under the agreement may still be contingent on the change in ownership or control pursuant to Q/A-22 of this section.

(b) In the case of an agreement described in paragraph (a) of Q/A-25 of this section, clear and convincing evidence that the agreement is one of the three following types will generally rebut the presumption that payments under the agreement are contingent on the change in ownership or control—

(1) A *nondiscriminatory employee plan or program* as defined in paragraph (c) of this A-26;

(2) A contract between a corporation and an individual that replaces a prior contract entered into by the same parties more than one year before the change in ownership or control, if the new contract does not provide for increased payments (apart from normal increases attributable to increased responsibilities or cost of living adjustments), accelerate the payment of amounts due at a future time, or modify (to the individual's benefit) the terms or conditions under which payments will be made; or

(3) A contract between a corporation and an individual who did not perform services for the corporation prior to the one year period before the change in ownership or control occurs, if the contract does not provide for payments that are significantly different in amount, timing, terms, or conditions from those provided under contracts entered into by the corporation (other than contracts that themselves were entered into within one year before the change in ownership or control and in contemplation of the change) with individuals performing comparable services.

(c) For purposes of this section, the term *nondiscriminatory employee plan or program* means: a group term life insurance plan that meets the requirements of section 79(d); a self insured medical reimbursement plan that meets the requirements of section 105(h); a cafeteria plan (within the meaning of section 125); an educational assistance program (within the meaning of section 127); a dependent care assistance program (within the meaning of section 129); a no-additional-cost service (within the meaning of section 132(b)) qualified employee discount (within the meaning of section 132(c)) qualified retirement planning services under section 132(m); and an adoption assistance program (within the meaning of section 137). Payments under certain other plans are exempt from the definition of *parachute payment* under Q/A-8 of this section. [Corrected by IRS on 6/21/02, 67 FR 42210].

(d) The following examples illustrate the application of the presumption:

Example 1. A corporation and a disqualified individual who is an employee of the corporation enter into an employment contract. The contract replaces a prior contract entered into by the same parties more than one year before the change and the new contract does not provide for any increased payments other than a cost of living adjustment, does not accelerate the payment of amounts due at a future time, and does not modify (to the individual's benefit) the terms or conditions under which payments will be made. Clear and convincing evidence of these facts rebuts the presumption described in A-25 of this section. However, payments under the contract still may be contingent on the change in ownership or control pursuant to Q/A-22 of this section.

Example 2. Assume the same facts as in *Example 1*, except that the contract is entered into after a tender offer for the corporation's stock had commenced and it was likely that a change in ownership would occur and the contract provides for a substantial bonus payment to the individual upon his signing the contract. The individual has performed services for the corporation for many years, but previous employment contracts between the corporation and the individual did not provide for a similar signing bonus. One month after the contract is entered into, a change in the ownership of the corporation occurs. All payments under the contract are presumed to be contingent on the change in ownership even though the bonus payment would have been legally required even if no change had occurred. Clear and convincing evidence of these facts rebuts the presumption described in A-25 of this section with respect to all of the payments under the contract with the exception of the bonus payment (which is treated as contingent on the change). However, payments other than the bonus under the contract still may be contingent on the change in ownership or control pursuant to Q/A-22 of this section.

Example 3. A corporation and a disqualified individual, who is an employee of the corporation, enter into an employment contract within one year of a change in ownership of the corporation. Under the contract, in the event of a change in ownership or control and subsequent termination of employment, certain payments will be made to the individual. A change in ownership occurs, but the individual is not terminated until 2 years after the change. If clear and convincing evidence does not rebut the presumption described in A-25 of this section, because the payment is made pursuant to an agreement entered into within one year of the date of the change in ownership, the payment is presumed contingent on the change under A-25 of this section. This is true even though A's termination of employment is presumed not to be materially related to the change in ownership or control under Q/A-22 of this section.

Change in Ownership or Control

Q-27: When does a change in the ownership of a corporation occur?

A-27: (a) For purposes of this section, a change in the ownership or control of a corporation occurs on the date that any one person, or more than one person acting as a group, acquires ownership of stock of the corporation that, together with stock held by such person or group, owns more than 50 percent of the total fair market value or total voting power of the stock of such corporation. However, if any one person, or more than one person acting as a group, is considered to own more than 50 percent of the total fair market value or total voting power of the stock of a corporation, the acquisition of additional stock by the same person or persons is not considered to cause a change in the ownership of the corporation (or to cause a change in the effective control of the corporation (within the meaning of Q/A-28 of this section)). An increase in the percentage of stock owned by any one person, or persons acting as a group, as a result of a transaction in which the corporation acquires its stock in exchange for property will be treated as an acquisition of stock for purposes of this section.

(b) For purposes of paragraph (a) of this A-27, persons will not be considered to be acting as a group merely because they happen to purchase or own stock of the same corporation at the same time, or as a result of the same public offering. However, persons will be considered to be acting as a group if they are owners of an entity that enters into a merger, consolidation, purchase or acquisition of stock, or similar business transaction with the corporation. If a person, including an entity shareholder, owns stock in both entities that enter into a merger, consolidation, purchase or acquisition of stock, or similar transaction, such shareholder is considered to be acting as a group with other shareholders in an entity only to the extent of his ownership in that entity prior to the transaction giving rise to the change and not with respect to his ownership interest in the other entity.

(c) For purposes of this A-27, section 318(a) applies to determine stock ownership.

(d) The following examples illustrate the principles of this A-27:

Example 1. Corporation M has owned stock with a fair market value equal to 19 percent of the value of the stock of Corporation N (an otherwise unrelated corporation) for many years prior to 2006. Corporation M acquires additional stock with a fair market value equal to 15 percent of the value of the stock of Corporation N on January 1, 2006, and an additional 18 percent on February 21, 2007. As of February 21, 2007, Corporation M has acquired stock with a fair market value greater than 50 percent of the value of the stock of Corporation N. Thus, a change in the ownership of Corporation N is considered to occur on February 21, 2007 (assuming that Corporation M did not have effective control of Corporation N immediately prior to the acquisition on that date).

Example 2. All of the corporation's stock is owned by the founders of the corporation. The board of directors of the corporation decides to offer shares of the corporation to the public. After the public offering, the founders of the corporation own a total of 40 percent of the corporation's stock, and members of the public own 60 percent. If no one person (or more than one person acting as a group) owns more than 50 percent of the corporation's stock (by value or voting power) after the public offering, there is no change in the ownership of the corporation.

Example 3. Corporation P merges into Corporation O (a previously unrelated corporation). In the merger, the shareholders of Corporation P receive Corporation O stock in exchange for their Corporation P stock. Immediately after the merger, the former shareholders of Corporation P own stock with a fair market value equal to 60 percent of the value of the stock of Corporation O, and the former shareholders of Corporation O own stock with a fair market value equal to 40 percent of the value of the stock of Corporation O. The former shareholders of Corporation P will be treated as acting as a group in their acquisition of Corporation O stock. Thus, a change in the ownership of Corporation O occurs on the date of the merger.

Example 4. Assume the same facts as in *Example 3* except that immediately after the change, the former shareholders of Corporation P own stock with a fair market value of 51 percent of the value of Corporation O stock and the former shareholders of Corporation O

own stock with a fair market value equal to 49 percent of the value of Corporation O stock. Assume further that prior to the merger several Corporation O shareholders also owned Corporation P stock (overlapping shareholders) exchanged for O stock with a fair market value of 5 percent of the value of Corporation O stock. The overlapping shareholders consist of Mutual Company A Growth Fund, which prior to the transaction owns P stock that is exchanged for 3 percent of the value of Coroporation O stock, Mutual Company A Income Fund, which prior to the transaction owns P stock that is exchanged for 1 percent of the value of Corporation O stock, and B individual who prior to the transaction owns P stock that is exchanged for 1 percent of the value of Corporation O stock. Growth Fund and Income Fund are treated as separate shareholders with respect to their ownership interests in Corporation O and Corporation P. The overlapping shareholders are not treated as acting as a group with the Corporation P shareholders with respect to the Corporation O stock each overlapping shareholder held before the transaction. Instead, the overlapping shareholders are treated as acting as a group separately with respect to Corporation O and Corporation P. Because the former shareholders of Corporation O are treated as acting as a group with respect to other Corporation O shareholders only to the extent of their ownership interest in Corporation O and not with respect to their ownership interest in Corporation P, a change in the ownership of Corporation O occurs on the date of the merger. [Corrected by IRS on 6/21/02, 67 FR 42210].

Example 5. A, an individual, owns stock with a fair market value equal to 20 percent of the value of the stock of Corporation Q. On January 1, 2007, Corporation Q acquires in a redemption for cash all of the stock held by shareholders other than A. Thus, A is left as the sole shareholder of Corporation O. A change in ownership of Corporation O is considered to occur on January 1, 2007 (assuming that A did not have effective control of Corporation Q immediately prior to the redemption).

Example 6. Assume the same facts as in *Example 5*, except that A owns stock with a fair market value equal to 51 percent of the value of all the stock of Corporation Q immediately prior to the redemption. There is no change in the ownership of Corporation Q as a result of the redemption.

Q-28: When does a change in the effective control of a corporation occur?

A-28: (a) For purposes of this section, a change in the effective control of a corporation is presumed to occur on the date that either—

(1) Any one person, or more than one person acting as a group, acquires (or has acquired during the 12-month period ending on the date of the most recent acquisition by such person or persons) ownership of stock of the corporation possessing 20 percent or more of the total voting power of the stock of such corporation; or

(2) A majority of members of the corporation's board of directors is replaced during any 12-month period by directors whose appointment or election is not endorsed by a majority of the members of the corporation's board of directors prior to the date of the appointment or election.

(b) The presumption of paragraph (a) of this A-28 may be rebutted by establishing that such acquisition or acquisitions of the corporation's stock, or such replacement of the majority of the members of the corporation's board of directors, does not transfer the power to control (directly or indirectly) the management and policies of the corporation from any one person (or more than one person acting as a group) to another person (or group). For purposes of this section, in the absence of an event described in paragraph (a)(1) or (2) of this A-28, a change in the effective control of a corporation is presumed not to have occurred.

(c) If any one person, or more than one person acting as a group, is considered to effectively control a corporation (within the meaning of this A-28), the acquisition of additional control of the corporation by the same person or persons is not considered to cause a change in the effective control of the corporation (or to cause a change in the ownership of the corporation within the meaning of Q/A-27 of this section).

(d) For purposes of this A-28, persons will not be considered to be acting as a group merely because they happen to purchase or own stock of the same corporation at the same time, or as a result of the same public offering. However, persons will be considered to be acting as a group if they are owners of an entity that enters into a merger, consolidation, purchase or acquisition of stock, or similar business transaction with the corporation. If a person, including an entity shareholder, owns stock in both entities that enter into a merger, consolidation, purchase or acquisition of stock, or similar transaction, such shareholder is considered to be acting as a group with other shareholders in an entity only to the extent of his ownership in that entity prior to the transaction giving rise to the change and not with respect to his ownership interest in the other entity.

(e) Section 318(a) applies to determine stock ownership for purposes of this A-28.

(f) The following examples illustrate the principles of this A-28:

Example 1. Shareholder A acquired the following percentages of the voting stock of Corporation M (an otherwise unrelated corporation) on the following dates: 16 percent on January 1, 2005; 10 percent on January 10, 2006; 8 percent on February 10, 2006; 11 percent on March 1, 2007; and 8 percent on March 10, 2007. Thus, on March 10, 2007, A owns a total of 53 percent of M's voting stock. Because A did not acquire 20 percent or more of M's voting stock during any 12-month period, there is no presumption of a change in effective control pursuant to paragraph (a)(1) of this A-28. In addition, under these facts there is a presumption that no change in the effective control of Corporation M occurred. If this presumption is not rebutted (and thus no change in effective control of Corporation M is treated as occurring prior to March 10, 2007), a change in the ownership of Corporation M is treated as having occurred on March 10, 2007 (pursuant to Q/A-27 of this section) because A had acquired more than 50 percent of Corporation M's voting stock as of that date.

Example 2. A minority group of shareholders of a corporation opposes the practices and policies of the corporation's current board of directors. A proxy contest ensues. The minority group presents its own slate of candidates for the board at the next annual meeting of the corporation's shareholders, and candidates of the minority group are elected to replace a majority of the current members of the board. A change in the effective control of the corporation is presumed to have occurred on the date the election of the new board of directors becomes effective.

Q-29: When does a change in the ownership of a substantial portion of a corporation's assets occur?

A-29: (a) For purposes of this section, a change in the ownership of a substantial portion of a corporation's assets occurs on the date that any one person, or more than one person acting as a group, acquires (or has acquired during the 12-month period ending on the date of the most recent acquisition by such person or persons) assets from the corporation that have a total gross fair market value equal to or more than one third of the total gross fair market value of all of the assets of the corporation immediately prior to such acquisition or acquisitions.

(b) A transfer of assets by a corporation is not treated as a change in the ownership of such assets if the assets are transferred to—

(1) A shareholder of the corporation (immediately before the asset transfer) in exchange for or with respect to its stock;

(2) An entity, 50 percent or more of the total value or voting power of which is owned, directly or indirectly, by the corporation;

(3) A person, or more than one person acting as a group, that owns, directly or indirectly, 50 percent or more of the total value or voting power of all the outstanding stock of the corporation; or

(4) An entity, at least 50 percent of the total value or voting power is owned, directly or indirectly, by a person described in paragraph (b)(3) of this A-29.

(c) For purposes of paragraph (b) and except as otherwise provided, a person's status is determined immediately after the transfer of the assets. For example, a transfer of assets pursuant to a complete liquidation of a corporation, a redemption of a shareholder's interest, or a transfer to a majority-owned subsidiary of the corporation is not treated as a change in the ownership of the assets of the transferor corporation.

(d) For purposes of this A-29, persons will not be considered to be acting as a group merely because they happen to purchase or own stock of the same corporation at the same time, or as a result of the same public offering. However, persons will be considered to be acting as a group if they are owners of an entity that enters into a merger, consolidation, purchase or acquisition of stock, or similar business transaction with the corporation. If a person, including an entity shareholder, owns stock in both entities that enter into a merger, consolidation, purchase or acquisition of stock, or similar transaction, such shareholder is considered to be acting as a group with other shareholders in an entity only to the extent of his ownership in that entity prior to the transaction giving rise to the change and not with respect to his ownership interest in the other entity.

(e) For purposes of this A-29, section 318(a) applies in determining stock ownership.

(f) The following examples illustrate the principles of this A-29:

Example 1. Corporation M acquires assets having a gross fair market value of $500,000 from Corporation N (an unrelated corporation) on January 1, 2006. The total gross fair market value of Corporation N's assets immediately prior to the acquisition was $3 million. Since the value of the assets acquired by Corporation M is less than one-third of the fair market value of Corporation N's total assets immediately prior to the acquisition, the acquisition does not represent a change in the ownership of a substantial portion of Corporation N's assets.

Example 2. Assume the same facts as in *Example 1.* Also assume that on November 1, 2006, Corporation M acquires from Corporation N additional assets having a fair market value of $700,000. Thus, Corporation M has acquired from Corporation N assets worth a total of $1.2 million during the 12-month period ending on November 1, 2006. Since $1.2 million is more than one-third of the total gross fair market value of all of Corporation N's assets immediately prior to the earlier of these acquisitions ($3 million), a change in the ownership of a substantial portion of Corporation N's assets is considered to have occurred on November 1, 2006.

Example 3. All of the assets of Corporation P are transferred to Corporation O (an unrelated corporation). In exchange, the shareholders of Corporation P receive Corporation O stock. Immediately after the transfer, the former shareholders of Corporation P own 60 percent of the fair market value of the outstanding stock of Corporation O and the former shareholders of Corporation O own 40 percent of the fair market value of the outstanding stock of Corporation O. Because Corporation O is an entity more than 50 percent of the fair market value of the outstanding stock of which is owned by the former shareholders of Corporation P (based on ownership of Corporation P prior the change), the transfer of assets is not treated as a change in ownership of a substantial portion of the assets of Corporation P. However, a change in the ownership (within the meaning of Q/A-27) of Corporation O occurs.

Three-Times-Base-Amount Test for Parachute Payments

Q-30: Are all payments that are in the nature of compensation, are made to a disqualified individual, and are contingent on a change in ownership or control, parachute payments?

A-30: (a) No, to determine whether such payments are parachute payments, they must be tested against the individual's *base amount* (as defined in Q/A-34 of this section). To do this, the aggregate present value of all payments in the nature of compensation that are made or to be made to (or for the benefit of) the same disqualified individual and are contingent on the change in ownership or control must be determined. If this aggregate present value equals or exceeds the amount equal to 3 times the individual's base amount, the payments are parachute payments. If this aggregate present value is less than the amount equal to 3 times the individual's base amount, no portion of the payment is a parachute payment. See Q/A-31, Q/A-32, and Q/A-33 of this section for rules on determining present value. Parachute payments that are securities violation parachute payments are not included in the foregoing computation if they are not contingent on a change in ownership or control. See Q/A-37 of this section for the definition and treatment of securities violation parachute payments.

(b) The following examples illustrate the principles of this A-30:

Example 1. A is a disqualified individual with respect to Corporation M. A's base amount is $100,000. Payments in the nature of compensation that are contingent on a change in the ownership of Corporation M totaling $400,000 are made to A on the date of the change. The payments are parachute payments since they have an aggregate present value at least equal to 3 times A's base amount of $100,000 (3 × $100,000 = $300,000).

Example 2. Assume the same facts as in *Example 1*, except that the payments contingent on the change in the ownership of Corporation M total $290,000. Since the payments do not have an aggregate present value at least equal to 3 times A's base amount, no portion of the payments is a parachute payment.

Q-31: As of what date is the present value of a payment determined?

A-31: (a) Except as provided in this section, the present value of a payment is determined as of the date on which the change in ownership or control occurs, or, if a payment is made prior to such date, the date on which the payment is made.

(b)(1) For purposes of determining whether a payment is a parachute payment, if a payment in the nature of compensation is the right to receive payments in a year (or years) subsequent to the year of the change in ownership or control, the value of the payment is the present value of such payment (or payments) calculated in accordance with Q/A-32 of this section and based on reasonable actuarial assumptions.

(2) If the payment in the nature of compensation is an obligation to provide health care, then for purposes of this A-31 and for applying the 3-times-base-amount test under Q/A-30 of this section, the present value of such obligation should be calculated in accordance with generally accepted accounting principles. For purposes of Q/A-30 and this A-31, the obligation to provide health care is permitted to be measured by projecting the cost of premiums for purchased health care insurance, even if no health care insurance is actually purchased. If the obligation to provide health care is made in coordination with a health care plan that the corporation makes available to a group, then the premiums used for this purpose may be group premiums.

Q-32: What discount rate is to be used to determine present value?

A-32: For purposes of this section, present value generally is determined by using a discount rate equal to 120 percent of the applicable Federal rate (determined under section 1274(d) and the regulations thereunder) compounded semiannually. The applicable Federal rate to be used for this purpose is the Federal rate that is in effect on the date as of which the present value is determined. See Q/A-24 and 31 of this section. However, for any payment, the corporation and the disqualified individual may elect to use the applicable Federal rate that is in effect on the date that the contract which provides for the payment is entered into, if such election is made in the contract. [Corrected by IRS on 6/21/02, 67 FR 42210].

Q-33: If the present value of a payment to be made in the future is contingent on an uncertain future event or condition, how is the present value of the payment determined?

A-33: (a) In certain cases, it may be necessary to apply the 3-times-base-amount test of Q/A-30 of this section or to allocate a portion of the base amount to a payment described in paragraphs (a)(1), (2), and (3) of Q/A-2 of this section at a time when the aggregate present value of all such payments cannot be determined with certainty because the time, amount, or right to receive one or more such payments is contingent on the occurrence of an uncertain future event or condition. For example, a disqualified individual's right to receive a payment may be contingent on the involuntary termination of such individual's employment with the corporation. In such a case, it must be reasonably estimated whether the payment will be made. If it is reasonably estimated that there is a 50-percent or greater probability that the payment will be made, the full amount of the payment is considered for purposes of the 3-times-base-amount test and the allocation of the base amount. Conversely, if it is reasonably estimated that there is a less than 50-percent probability that the payment will be made, the payment is not considered for either purpose.

(b) If the estimate made under paragraph (a) of this A-33 is later determined to be incorrect, the 3-times-base-amount test described in Q/A-30 of this section must be reapplied (and the portion of the base amount allocated to previous payments must be reallocated (if necessary) to such payments) to reflect the actual time and amount of the payment. Whenever the 3-times-base-amount test is applied (or whenever the base amount is allocated), the aggregate present value of the payments received or to be received by the disqualified individual is redetermined as of the date described in A-31 of this section, using the discount rate described in A-32 of this section. This redetermination may affect the amount of any excess parachute payment for a prior taxable year. Alternatively, if, based on the application of the 3-times-base-amount test without regard to the payment described in paragraph (a) of this A-33, a disqualified individual is determined to have an excess parachute payment or payments, then the 3-times-base-amount test does not have to be reapplied when a payment described in paragraph (a) of this A-33 is made (or becomes certain to be made) if no base amount is allocated to such payment.

(c) The following examples illustrate the principles of this A-33:

Example 1. A, a disqualified individual with respect to Corporation M, has a base amount of $100,000. Under A's employment agreement with Corporation M, A is entitled to receive a payment in the nature of compensation in the amount of $250,000 contingent on a change in ownership or control of Corporation M. In addition, the agreement provides that if A's employment is terminated within 1 year after the change in ownership or control, A will receive an additional payment in the nature of compensation in the amount of $150,000, payable 1 year after the date of the change in ownership or control. A change in ownership or control of Corporation M occurs and A receives the first payment of $250,000. Corporation M reasonably estimates that there is a 50-percent probability that, as a result of the change, A's employment will be terminated within 1 year of the date of the change. For purposes of applying the 3-times-base-amount test (and if the first payment is

determined to be a parachute payment, for purposes of allocating a portion of A's base amount to that payment), because M reasonably estimates that there is a 50-percent or greater probability that, as a result of the change, A's employment will be terminated within 1 year of the date of the change, Corporation M must assume that the $150,000 payment will be made to A as a result of the change in ownership or control. The present value of the additional payment is determined under Q/A-31 and Q/A-32 of this section.

Example 2. Assume the same facts as in *Example 1* except that Corporation M reasonably estimates that there is a less than 50-percent probability that, as a result of the change, A's employment will be terminated within 1 year of the date of the change. For purposes of applying the 3-times-base-amount test, because Corporation M reasonably estimates that there is a less than 50-percent probability that, as a result of the change, A's employment will be terminated within 1 year of the date of the change, Corporation M must assume that the $150,000 payment will not be made to A as a result of the change in ownership or control.

Example 3. B, a disqualified individual with respect to Corporation P, has a base amount of $200,000. Under B's employment agreement with Corporation P, if there is a change in ownership or control of Corporation P, B will receive a severance payment of $600,000 and a bonus payment of $400,000. In addition, the agreement provides that if B's employment is terminated within 1 year after the change, B will receive an additional payment in the nature of compensation of $500,000. A change in ownership or control of Corporation P occurs, and B receives the $600,000 and $400,000 payments. At the time of the change in ownership or control, Corporation P reasonably estimates that there is a less than 50-percent probability that B's employment will be terminated within 1 year of the change. For purposes of applying the 3-times-base-amount test, because Corporation P reasonably estimates that there is a less than 50-percent probability that B's employment will be terminated within 1 year of the date of the change, Corporation P assumes that the $500,000 payment will not be made to B. Eleven months after the change in ownership or control, B's employment is terminated, and the $500,000 payment is made to B. Because B was determined to have excess parachute payments without regard to the $500,000 payment, the 3-times-base-amount test is not reapplied and the base amount is not reallocated to include the $500,000 payment. The entire $500,000 payment is treated as an excess parachute payment.

Q-34: What is the base amount?

A-34: (a) The base amount of a disqualified individual is the average annual compensation for services performed for the corporation with respect to which the change in ownership or control occurs (or for a predecessor entity or a related entity) which was includible in the gross income of such individual for taxable years in the base period (including amounts that were excluded under section 911), or which would have been includible in such gross income if such person had been a United States citizen or resident. See Q/A-35 of this section for the definition of base period and for examples of base amount computations.

(b) If the base period of a disqualified individual includes a short taxable year or less than all of a taxable year, compensation for such short or incomplete taxable year must be annualized before determining the average annual compensation for the base period. In annualizing compensation, the frequency with which payments are expected to be made over an annual period must be taken into account. Thus, any amount of compensation for such a short or incomplete taxable year that represents a payment that will not be made more often than once per year is not annualized.

(c) Because the base amount includes only compensation that is includible in gross income, the base amount does not include certain items that constitute parachute payments. For example, payments in the form of excludible fringe benefits are not included in the base amount but may be treated as parachute payments.

(d) The base amount includes the amount of compensation included in income under section 83(b) during the base period.

(e) The following example illustrates the principles of this A-34:

Example. A disqualified individual, D, receives an annual salary of $500,000 per year during the 5-year base period. D defers $100,000 of D's salary each year under the corporation's nonqualified deferred compensation plan. D's base amount is $400,000 ($400,000 × (5/5)).

Q-35: What is the base period?

A-35: (a) The base period of a disqualified individual is the most recent 5 taxable years of the individual ending before the date of the change in ownership or control. For this purpose, the date of the change in ownership or control is the date the corporation experiences one of the events described in Q/A-27, Q/A-28, or Q/A-29 of this section. However, if the disqualified individual was not an employee or independent contractor of the corporation with respect to which the change in ownership or control occurs (or a predecessor entity or a related entity as defined in Q/A-21 of this section) for this entire 5-year period, the individual's base period is the portion of such 5-year period during which the individual performed personal services for the corporation or predecessor entity or related entity.

(b) The following examples illustrate the principles of Q/A-34 of this section and this Q/A-35:

Example 1. A disqualified individual, D, was employed by a corporation for 2 years and 4 months preceding the taxable year in which a change in ownership or control of the corporation occurs. D's includible compensation income from the corporation was $30,000 for the 4-month period, $120,000 for the first full year, and $150,000 for the second full year. D's base amount is $120,000, ((3 × $30,000) + $120,000 + $150,000)/3.

Example 2. Assume the same facts as in *Example 1*, except that D also received a $60,000 signing bonus when D's employment with the corporation commenced at the beginning of the 4-month period. D's base amount is $140,000, (($60,000 + (3 × $30,000)) + $120,000 + $150,000)/3. Since the bonus will not be paid more often than once per year, the amount of the bonus is not increased in annualizing D's compensation for the 4-month period.

Q-36: How is the base amount determined in the case of a disqualified individual who did not perform services for the corporation (or a predecessor entity or a related entity as defined in Q/A-21 of this section), prior to the individual's taxable year in which the change in ownership or control occurs?

A-36: (a) In such a case, the individual's base amount is the annualized compensation for services performed for the corporation (or a predecessor entity or related entity) which—

(1) Was includible in the individual's gross income for that portion, prior to such change, of the individual's taxable year in which the change occurred (including amounts that were excluded under section 911), or would have been includible in such gross income if such person had been a United States citizen or resident;

(2) Was not contingent on the change in ownership or control; and

(3) Was not a securities violation parachute payment.

(b) The following examples illustrate the principles of this A-36:

Example 1. On January 1, 2006, A, an individual whose taxable year is the calendar year, enters into a 4-year employment contract with Corporation M as an officer of the corporation. A has not previously performed services for Corporation M (or any predecessor entity or related entity as defined in Q/A-21 of this section). Under the employment contract, A is to receive an annual salary of $120,000 for each of the 4 years that he remains employed by Corporation M with any remaining unpaid balance to be paid immediately in the event that A's employment is terminated without cause. On July 1, 2006, after A has received compensation of $60,000, a change in the ownership of Corporation M occurs. Because of the change, A's employment is terminated without cause, and he receives a payment of $420,000. It is established by clear and convincing evidence that the $60,000 in compensation is not contingent on the change in ownership or control, but the presumption that the $420,000 payment is contingent on the change is not rebutted. Thus, the payment of $420,000 is treated as contingent on the change in ownership of Corporation M. In this case, A's base amount is $120,000 (2 × $60,000). Since the present value of the payment which is contingent on the change in ownership of Corporation M ($420,000) is more than 3 times A's base amount of $120,000 (3 × $120,000 = $360,000), the payment is a parachute payment.

Example 2. Assume the same facts as in *Example 1*, except that A also receives a signing bonus of $50,000 from Corporation M on January 1, 2006. It is established by clear and convincing evidence that the bonus is not contingent on the change in ownership. When the change in ownership occurs on July 1, 2006, A has received compensation of $110,000 (the $50,000 bonus plus $60,000 in salary). In this case, A's base amount is $170,000 [$50,000 + (2 × $60,000)]. Since the $50,000 bonus will not be paid more than once per year, the amount of the bonus is not increased in annualizing A's compensation. The present value of the potential parachute payment ($420,000) is less than 3 times A's base amount of $170,000 (3 × $170,000 = $510,000), and therefore no portion of the payment is a parachute payment.

Securities Violation Parachute Payments

Q-37: Must a payment be contingent on a change in ownership or control in order to be a parachute payment?

A-37: (a) No, the term *parachute payment* also includes any payment (other than a payment exempted under Q/A-6 or Q/A-8 of this section) that is in the nature of compensation and is to (or for the benefit of) a disqualified individual, if such payment is a securities violation payment. A securities violation payment is a payment made or to be made—

(1) Pursuant to an agreement that violates any generally enforced Federal or State securities laws or regulations; and

(2) In connection with a potential or actual change in ownership or control.

(b) A violation is not taken into account under paragraph (a)(1) of this A-37 if it is merely technical in character or is not materially prejudicial to shareholders or potential shareholders. Moreover, a violation will be presumed not to exist unless the existence of the violation has been determined or admitted in a civil or criminal action (or an administrative action by a regulatory body charged with enforcing the particular securities law or regulation) which has been resolved by adjudication or consent. Parachute payments described in this A-37 are referred to in this section as securities violation payments.

(c) Securities violation parachute payments that are not contingent on a change in ownership or control within the meaning of Q/A-22 of this section are not taken into account in applying the 3-times-base-amount test of Q/A-30 of this section. Such payments are considered parachute payments regardless of whether such test is met with respect to the disqualified individual (and are included in allocating base amount under Q/A-38 of this section). Moreover, the amount of a securities violation parachute payment treated as an excess parachute payment shall not be reduced by the portion of such payment that is reasonable compensation for personal services actually rendered before the date of a change in ownership or control if such payment is not contingent on such change. Likewise, the amount of a securities violation parachute payment includes the portion of such payment that is reasonable compensation for personal services to be rendered on or after the date of a change in ownership or control if such payment is not contingent on such change.

(d) The rules in paragraph (b) of this A-37 also apply to securities violation parachute payments that are contingent on a change in ownership or control if the application of these rules results in greater total excess parachute payments with respect to the disqualified individual than would result if the payments were treated simply as payments contingent on a change in ownership or control (and hence were taken into account in applying the 3-times-base-amount test and were reduced by, or did not include, any applicable amount of reasonable compensation).

(e) The following examples illustrate the principles of this A-37:

Example 1. A, a disqualified individual with respect to Corporation M, receives two payments in the nature of compensation that are contingent on a change in the ownership or control of Corporation M. The present value of the first payment is equal to A's base amount and is not a securities violation parachute payment. The present value of the second payment is equal to 1.5 times A's base amount and is a securities violation parachute payment. Neither payment includes any reasonable compensation. If the second payment is treated simply as a payment contingent on a change in ownership or control, the amount of A's total excess parachute payments is zero because the aggregate present value of the payments does not equal or exceed 3 times A's base amount. If the second payment is treated as a securities violation parachute payment subject to the rules of paragraph (b) of this A-37, the amount of A's total excess parachute payments is 0.5 times A's base amount. Thus, the second payment is treated as a securities violation parachute payment.

Example 2. Assume the same facts as in *Example 1*, except that the present value of the first payment is equal to 2 times A's base amount. If the second payment is treated simply as a payment contingent on a change in ownership or control, the total present value of the payments is 3.5 times A's base amount, and the amount of A's total excess parachute payments is 2.5 times A's base amount. If the second payment is treated as a securities violation parachute payment, the amount of A's total excess parachute payments is 0.5 times A's base amount. Thus, the second payment is treated simply as a payment contingent on a change in ownership or control.

Example 3. B, a disqualified individual with respect to Corporation N, receives two payments in the nature of compensation that are contingent on a change in the control of Corporation N. The present value of the first payment is equal to 4 times B's base amount and is a securities violation parachute payment. The present value of the second payment is equal to 2 times B's base amount and is not a securities violation parachute payment. B establishes by clear and convincing evidence that the entire amount of the first payment is reasonable compensation for personal services to be rendered after the change in ownership or control. If the first payment is treated simply as a payment contingent on a change in ownership or control, it is exempt from the definition of *parachute payment* pursuant to Q/A-9 of this section. Thus, the amount of B's total excess parachute payment is zero because the present value of the second payment does not equal or exceed three times B's base amount. However, if the first payment is treated as a securities violation parachute payment, the amount of B's total excess parachute payments is 3 times B's base amount. Thus, the first payment is treated as a securities violation parachute payment.

Example 4. Assume the same facts as in *Example 3*, except that B does not receive the second payment and B establishes by clear and convincing evidence that the first payment is reasonable compensation for services actually rendered before the change in the control of Corporation N. If the payment is treated simply as a payment contingent on a change in ownership or control, the amount of B's excess parachute payment is zero because the amount treated as an excess parachute payment is reduced by the amount that B establishes as reasonable compensation. However, if the payment is treated as a securities violation parachute payment, the amount of B's excess parachute payment is 3 times B's base amount. Thus, the payment is treated as a securities violation parachute payment.

Computation and Reduction of Excess Parachute Payments

Q-38: How is the amount of an excess parachute payment computed?

A-38: (a) The amount of an excess parachute payment is the excess of the amount of any parachute payment over the portion of the disqualified individual's base amount that is allocated to such payment. For this purpose, the portion of the base amount allocated to any parachute payment is the amount that bears the same ratio to the base amount as the present value of such parachute payment bears to the aggregate present value of all parachute payments made or to be made to (or for the benefit of) the same disqualified individual. Thus, the portion of the base amount allocated to any parachute payment is determined by multiplying the base amount by a fraction, the numerator of which is the present value of such parachute payment and the denominator of which is the aggregate present value of all such payments. See Q/A-31, Q/A-32, and Q/A-33 of this section for rules on determining present value and Q/A-34 of this section for the definition of *base amount.*

(b) The following example illustrates this principles of this A-38:

Example. An individual with a base amount of $100,000 is entitled to receive two parachute payments, one of $200,000 and the other of $400,000. The $200,000 payment is made at the time of the change in ownership or control, and the $400,000 payment is to be made at a future date. The present value of the $400,000 payment is $300,000 on the date of the change in ownership or control. The portions of the base amount allocated to these payments are $40,000 (($200,000/$500,000) × $100,000) and $60,000 (($300,000/$500,000) × $100,000), respectively. Thus, the amount of the first excess parachute payment is $160,000 ($200,000 – $40,000) and that of the second is $340,000 ($400,000 – $60,000).

Q-39: May the amount of an excess parachute payment be reduced by reasonable compensation for personal services actually rendered before the change in ownership or control?

A-39: (a) Generally, yes, except that in the case of payments treated as securities violation parachute payments or when the portion of a payment that is treated as contingent on the change in ownership or control is determined under paragraph (b) or (c) of Q/A-24 of this section, the amount of an excess parachute payment is reduced by any portion of the payment that the taxpayer establishes by clear and convincing evidence is reasonable compensation for personal services actually rendered by the disqualified individual before the date of the change in ownership or control. Services reasonably compensated for by payments that are not parachute payments (for example, because the payments are not contingent on a change in ownership or control and are not securities violation parachute payments, or because the payments are exempt from the definition of parachute payment under Q/A-6 through Q/A-9 of this section) are not taken into account for this purpose. The portion of any parachute payment that is established as reasonable compensation is first reduced by the portion of the disqualified individual's base amount that is allocated to such parachute payment; any remaining portion of the parachute payment established as reasonable compensation then reduces the excess parachute payment.

(b) The following examples illustrate the principles of this A-39:

Example 1. Assume that a parachute payment of $600,000 is made to a disqualified individual, and the portion of the individual's base amount that is allocated to the parachute payment is $100,000. Also assume that $300,000 of the $600,000 parachute payment is established as reasonable compensation for personal services actually rendered by the disqualified individual before the date of the change in ownership or control. Before the reasonable compensation is taken into account, the amount of the excess parachute payment is $500,000 ($600,000 – $100,000). In reducing the excess parachute payment by reasonable compensation, the portion of the parachute payment that is established as reasonable compensation ($300,000) is first reduced by the portion of the disqualified individual's base amount that is allocated to the parachute payment ($100,000), and the remainder ($200,000) then reduces the excess parachute payment. Thus, in this case, the excess parachute payment of $500,000 is reduced by $200,000 of reasonable compensation.

Example 2. Assume the same facts as in *Example 1*, except that the full amount of the $600,000 parachute payment is established as reasonable compensation. In this case, the excess parachute payment of $500,000 is reduced to zero by $500,000 of reasonable compensation. As a result, no portion of any deduction for the payment is disallowed by section 280G, and no portion of the payment is subject to the 20-percent excise tax of section 4999.

Determination of Reasonable Compensation

Q-40: How is it determined whether payments are reasonable compensation?

A-40: (a) In general, whether payments are reasonable compensation for personal services actually rendered, or to be rendered, by the disqualified individual is determined on the basis of all the facts and circumstances of the particular case. Factors relevant to such a determination include, but are not limited to, the following—

(1) The nature of the services rendered or to be rendered;

(2) The individual's historic compensation for performing such services; and

(3) The compensation of individuals performing comparable services in situations where the compensation is not contingent on a change in ownership or control.

(b) For purposes of section 280G, reasonable compensation for personal services includes reasonable compensation for holding oneself out as available to perform services and refraining from performing services (such as under a covenant not to compete).

Q-41: Is any particular type of evidence generally considered clear and convincing evidence of reasonable compensation for personal services?

A-41: Yes, a showing that payments are made under a nondiscriminatory employee plan or program (as defined in Q/A-26 of this section) generally is considered to be clear and convincing evidence that the payments are reasonable compensation. This is true whether the personal services for which the payments are made are actually rendered before, or to be rendered on or after, the date of the change in ownership or control. Q/A-46 of this section (relating to the treatment of an affiliated group as one corporation) does not apply for purposes of this A-41. No determination of reasonable compensation is needed for payments under qualified plans to be exempt from the definition of *parachute payment* under Q/A-8 of this section.

Q-42: Is any particular type of evidence generally considered clear and convincing evidence of reasonable compensation for personal services to be rendered on or after the date of a change in ownership or control?

A-42: (a) Yes, if payments are made or to be made to (or on behalf of) a disqualified individual for personal services to be rendered on or after the date of a change in ownership or control, a showing of the following generally is considered to be clear and convincing evidence that the payments are reasonable compensation for services to be rendered on or after the date of the change in ownership or control—

(1) The payments were made or are to be made only for the period the individual actually performs such personal services; and

(2) If the individual's duties and responsibilities are substantially the same after the change in ownership or control, the individual's annual compensation for such services is not significantly greater than such individual's annual compensation prior to the change in ownership or control, apart from normal increases attributable to increased responsibilities or cost of living adjustments. If the scope of the individual's duties and responsibilities are not substantially the same, the annual

compensation after the change is not significantly greater than the annual compensation customarily paid by the employer or by comparable employers to persons performing comparable services. However, except as provided in paragraph (b) of this A-42, such clear and convincing evidence will not exist if the individual does not, in fact, perform the services contemplated in exchange for the compensation.

(b) Generally, an agreement under which the disqualified individual must refrain from performing services (such as a covenant not to compete) is an agreement for the performance of personal services for purposes of this A-42 to the extent that it is demonstrated by clear and convincing evidence that the agreement substantially constrains the individual's ability to perform services and there is a reasonable likelihood that the agreement will be enforced against the individual. In the absence of clear and convincing evidence, payments under the agreement are treated as severance payments under Q/A-44 of this section.

(c) If the employment of a disqualified individual is involuntarily terminated before the end of a contract term and the individual is paid damages for breach of contract, a showing of the following factors generally is considered clear and convincing evidence that the payment is reasonable compensation for personal services to be rendered on or after the date of change in ownership or control—

(1) The contract was not entered into, amended, or renewed in contemplation of the change in ownership or control;

(2) The compensation the individual would have received under the contract would have qualified as reasonable compensation under section 162;

(3) The damages do not exceed the present value (determined as of the date of receipt) of the compensation the individual would have received under the contract if the individual had continued to perform services for the employer until the end of the contract term;

(4) The damages are received because an offer to provide personal services was made by the disqualified individual but was rejected by the employer; and

(5) The damages are reduced by mitigation. Mitigation will be treated as occurring when such damages are reduced (or any payment of such damages is returned) to the extent of the disqualified individual's earned income (within the meaning of section 911(d)(2)(A)) during the remainder of the period in which the contract would have been in effect. See Q/A-44 of this section for rules regarding damages for a failure to make severance payments.

(c) The following examples illustrate the principles of this A-42:

Example 1. A, a disqualified individual, has a three-year employment contract with Corporation M, a publicly traded corporation. Under this contract, A is to receive a salary for $100,000 for the first year of the contract and, for each succeeding year, an annual salary that is 10 percent higher than the prior year's salary. During the third year of the contract, Corporation N acquires all the stock of Corporation M. Prior to the change in ownership, Corporation N arranges to retain A's services by entering into an employment contract with A that is essentially the same as A's contract with Corporation M. Under the new contract, Corporation N is to fulfill Corporation M's obligations for the third year of the old contract, and, for each of the succeeding years, pay A an annual salary that is 10 percent higher than A's prior year's salary. Amounts are payable under the new contract only for the portion of the contract term during which A remains employed by Corporation N. A showing of the facts described above (and in the absence of contradictory evidence) is regarded as clear and convincing evidence that all payments under the new contract are reasonable compensation for personal services to be rendered on or after the date of the change in ownership. Therefore, the payments under this agreement are exempt from the definition of *parachute payment* pursuant to Q/A-9 of this section.

Example 2. Assume the same facts as in *Example 1* except that A does not perform the services described in the new contract, but receives payment under the new contract. Because services were not rendered after the change, the payments under this contract are not exempt from the definition of *parachute payment* pursuant to Q/A-9 of this section.

Example 3. Assume the same facts as in *Example 1* except that under the new contract A agrees to perform consulting services to Corporation N, when and if Corporation N requires A's services. Assume further that when Corporation N does not require A's services, the contract provides that A must not perform services for any other competing company. Corporation N previously enforced similar contracts against former employees of Corporation N. Because A is substantially constrained under this contract and Corporation N is

reasonably likely to enforce the contract against A, the agreement is an agreement for the performance of services under paragraph (b) of this A-42. Assuming the requirements of paragraph (a) of this A-42 are met and there is clear and convincing evidence that all payments under the new contract are reasonable compensation for personal services to be rendered on or after the date of the change in ownership, the payments under this contract are exempt from the definition of *parachute payment* pursuant to Q/A-9 of this section. [Corrected by IRS on 6/21/02, 67 FR 42210].

Example 4. Assume the same facts as in *Example 1*, except that the employment contract with Corporation N does not provide that amounts are payable under the contract only for the portion of the term for which A remains employed by Corporation N. Shortly after the change in ownership, and despite A's request to remain employed by Corporation N, A's employment with Corporation N is involuntarily terminated. Shortly thereafter, A obtains employment with Corporation O. A commences a civil action against Corporation N, alleging breach of the employment contract. In settlement of the litigation, A receives an amount equal to the present value of the compensation A would have received under the contract with Corporation N, reduced by the amount of compensation A otherwise receives from Corporation O during the period that the contract would have been in effect. A showing of the facts described above (and in the absence of contradictory evidence) is regarded as clear and convincing evidence that the amount A receives as damages is reasonable compensation for personal services to be rendered on or after the date of the change in ownership. Therefore, the amount received by A is exempt from the definition of *parachute payment* pursuant to Q/A-9 of this section.

Q-43: Is any particular type of payment generally considered reasonable compensation for personal services actually rendered before the date of a change in ownership or control?

A-43: (a) Yes, payments of compensation earned before the date of a change in ownership or control generally are considered reasonable compensation for personal services actually rendered before the date of a change in ownership or control if they qualify as reasonable compensation under section 162.

Q-44: May severance payments be treated as reasonable compensation?

A-44: (a) No, severance payments are not treated as reasonable compensation for personal services actually rendered before, or to be rendered on or after, the date of a change in ownership or control. Moreover, any damages paid for a failure to make severance payments are not treated as reasonable compensation for personal services actually rendered before, or to be rendered on or after, the date of such change. For purposes of this section, the term *severance payment* means any payment that is made to (or for the benefit of) a disqualified individual on account of the termination of such individual's employment prior to the end of a contract term, but does not include any payment that otherwise would be made to (or for the benefit of) such individual on the termination of such individual's employment, whenever occurring.

(b) The following example illustrates the principles of this A-44:

Example. A, a disqualified individual, has a three-year employment contract with Corporation X. Under the contract, A will receive a salary of $200,000 for the first year of the contract, and for each succeeding year, an annual salary that is $100,000 higher than the previous year. In the event of A's termination of employment following a change in ownership or control, the contract provides that A will receive the remaining salary due under the employment contract. At the beginning of the second year of the contract, Corporation Y acquires all of the stock of Corporation X, A's employment is terminated, and A receives $700,000 ($300,000 for the second year of the contract plus $400,000 for the third year of the employment contract) representing the remaining salary due under the employment contract. Because the $700,000 payment is treated as a severance payment, it is not reasonable compensation for personal services on or after the date of the change in ownership or control. Thus, the full amount of the $700,000 is a parachute payment.

Miscellaneous Rules

Q-45: How is the term *corporation* defined?

A-45: For purposes of this section, the term *corporation* has the meaning prescribed by section 7701(a)(3) and §301.7701-2(b). For example, a *corporation*, for purposes of this section, includes a publicly traded partnership treated as a corporation under section 7704(a); an entity described in §301.7701-3(c)(1)(v)(A) of this chapter; a real estate investment trust under section 856(a); a corporation that has mutual or cooperative (rather than stock) ownership, such as a mutual insurance company, a mutual savings bank, or a cooperative bank (as defined in section 7701(a)(32)), and a foreign corporation as defined under section 7701(a)(5).

Q-46: How is an affiliated group treated?

A-46: For purposes of this section, and except as otherwise provided in this section, all members of the same affiliated group (as defined in section 1504, determined without regard to section 1504(b)) are treated as one corporation. Rules affected by this treatment of an affiliated group include (but are not limited to) rules relating to exempt payments of certain corporations (Q/A-6, Q/A-7 of this section (except as provided therein)), payor of parachute payments (Q/A-10 of this section), disqualified individuals (Q/A-15 through Q/A-21 of this section (except as provided therein)), rebuttal of the presumption that payments are contingent on a change (Q/A-26 of this section (except as provide therein)), change in ownership or control (Q/A-27, 28, and 29 of this section), and reasonable compensation (Q/A-42, 43, and 44 of this section).

Effective Date

Q-47: What is the general effective date of section 280G?

A-47: (a) Generally, section 280G applies to payments under agreements entered into or renewed after June 14, 1984. Any agreement that is entered into before June 15, 1984, and is renewed after June 14, 1984, is treated as a new contract entered into on the day the renewal takes effect.

(b) For purposes of paragraph (a) of this A-47, a contract that is terminable or cancellable unconditionally at will by either party to the contract without the consent of the other, or by both parties to the contract, is treated as a new contract entered into on the date any such termination or cancellation, if made, would be effective. However, a contract is not treated as so terminable or cancellable if it can be terminated or cancelled only by terminating the employment relationship or independent contractor relationship of the disqualified individual.

(c) Section 280G applies to payments under a contract entered into on or before June 14, 1984, if the contract is amended or supplemented after June 14, 1984, in significant relevant respect. For this purpose, a *supplement* to a contract is defined as a new contract entered into after June 14, 1984, that affects the trigger, amount, or time of receipt of a payment under an existing contract.

(d)(1) Except as otherwise provided in paragraph (e) of this A-47, a contract is considered to be amended or supplemented in significant relevant respect if provisions for payments contingent on a change in ownership or control (parachute provisions), or provisions in the nature of parachute provisions, are added to the contract, or are amended or supplemented to provide significant additional benefits to the disqualified individual. Thus, for example, a contract generally is treated as amended or supplemented in significant relevant respect if it is amended or supplemented—

(i) To add or modify, to the disqualified individual's benefit, a change in ownership or control trigger;

(ii) To increase amounts payable that are contingent on a change in ownership or control (or, where payment is to be made under a formula, to modify the formula to the disqualified individual's advantage); or

(iii) To accelerate, in the event of a change in ownership or control, the payment of amounts otherwise payable at a later date.

(2) For purposes of paragraph (a) of this A-47, a payment is not treated as being accelerated in the event of a change in ownership or control if the acceleration does not increase the present value of the payment.

(e) A contract entered into on or before June 14, 1984, is not treated as amended or supplemented in significant relevant respect merely by reason of normal adjustments in the terms of employment relationship or independent contractor relationship of the disqualified individual. Whether an adjustment in the terms of such a relationship is considered normal for this purpose depends on all of the facts and circumstances of the particular case. Relevant factors include, but are not limited to, the following—

(1) The length of time between the adjustment and the change in ownership or control;

(2) The extent to which the corporation, at the time of the adjustment, viewed itself as a likely takeover candidate;

(3) A comparison of the adjustment with historical practices of the corporation;

(4) The extent of overlap between the group receiving the benefits of the adjustment and those members of that group who are the beneficiaries of pre-June 15, 1984, parachute contracts; and

(5) The size of the adjustment, both in absolute terms and in comparison with the benefits provided to other members of the group receiving the benefits of the adjustment.

Q-48: What is the effective date of this section?

A-48: This section applies to any payments that are contingent on a change in ownership or control that occurs on or after January 1, 2004. Taxpayers can rely on these rules after February 20, 2002, for the treatment of any parachute payment. [Corrected by IRS on 6/21/02, 67 FR 42210].

Robert E. Wenzel

Deputy Commissioner of Internal Revenue.

CERTIFIED COPY

DALE D. GOODE

¶ 20,260H

IRS proposed regulations: Defined benefit plans: Required minimum distributions: Code Sec. 403(b) annuity contracts: Individual retirement accounts (IRAs).—The IRS has issued proposed regulations by cross-reference to temporary regulations that contain guidance concerning required minimum distribution requirements for defined benefit plans, IRAs, and Code Sec. 403(b) annuity contracts purchased with an employee's accounts balance under a defined contribution plan. Comments and requests for a public hearing must be received by the IRS by July 16, 2002.

The proposed regulations, which were published in the *Federal Register* on April 17, 2002 (67 FR 18834), are reproduced below.

DEPARTMENT OF TREASURY

Internal Revenue Service

26 CFR Part 1

[REG-108697-02]

RIN 1545-BA60

Required Distributions from Retirement Plans

AGENCY: Internal Revenue Service (IRS), Treasury.

ACTION: Notice of proposed rulemaking by cross-reference to temporary regulations.

SUMMARY: In the Rules and Regulations section of this issue of the **Federal Register,** the IRS is issuing temporary regulations that provide guidance concerning required minimum distributions for defined benefit plans and annuity contracts providing benefits under qualified plans, individual retirement plans, and section 403(b) contracts. The regulations will provide the public with guidance necessary to comply with the law and will affect administrators of, participants in, and

beneficiaries of qualified plans; institutions that sponsor and individuals who administer individual retirement plans, individuals who use individual retirement plans for retirement income, and beneficiaries of individual retirement plans; and employees for whom amounts are contributed to section 403(b) annuity contracts, custodial accounts, or retirement income accounts and beneficiaries of such contracts and accounts. The text of those temporary regulations also serves as the text of these proposed regulations.

DATES: Written or electronic comments must be received by July 16, 2002.

ADDRESSES: Send submissions to: CC:ITA:RU (REG-108697-02), room 5226, Internal Revenue Service, POB 7604, Ben Franklin Station, Washington, DC 20044. Submissions may be hand delivered Monday through Friday between the hours of 8 a.m. and 5 p.m. to: CC:ITA:RU (REG-108697-02), Courier's Desk, Internal Revenue Service, 1111 Constitution Avenue, NW., Washington, DC. Alternatively, taxpayers may submit comments electronically directly to the IRS Internet site at http://www.irs.gov/regs.

FOR FURTHER INFORMATION CONTACT: Cathy Vohs at 622-6090

SUPPLEMENTARY INFORMATION:

Background

Final and Temporary regulations in the Rules and Regulations portion of this issue of the **Federal Register** amend the Income Tax Regulations (26 CFR part 1) relating to section 401(a)(9). The temporary regulations (§ 1.401(a)(9)-6T) contain rules relating to minimum distribution requirements for defined benefit plans and annuity contracts purchased with an employee's account balance under a defined contribution plan. The text of those temporary regulations also serves as the text of these proposed regulations. The preamble to the temporary regulations explains the temporary regulations.

Special Analyses

It has been determined that this notice of proposed rulemaking is not a significant regulatory action as defined in Executive Order 12866. Therefore, a regulatory assessment is not required. It also has been determined that section 553(b) of the Administrative Procedure Act (5 U.S.C. chapter 5) does not apply to these regulations. Because § 1.401(a)(9)-6 imposes no new collection of information on small entities, a Regulatory Flexibility Analysis under the Regulatory Flexibility Act (5 U.S.C. chapter 6) is not required. Pursuant to section 7805(f) of the Internal Revenue Code, this notice of proposed rulemaking will be submitted to the Chief Counsel for Advocacy of the Small Business Administration for comment on its impact on small business.

Comments and Requests for a Public Hearing

Before these proposed regulations are adopted as final regulations, consideration will be given to any written comments (a signed original and eight (8) copies) that are submitted timely to the IRS. All comments will be available for public inspection and copying.

A public hearing may be scheduled if requested in writing by a person that timely submits written comments. If a public hearing is scheduled, notice of the date, time, and place for the hearing will be published in the **Federal Register.**

Drafting Information

The principal authors of these regulations are Marjorie Hoffman and Cathy A. Vohs of the Office of the Division Counsel/Associate Chief Counsel (Tax Exempt and Government Entities). However, other personnel from the IRS and Treasury participated in their development.

List of Subjects 26 CFR Part 1

Income taxes, Reporting and recordkeeping requirements.

Proposed Amendments to the Regulations

Accordingly, 26 CFR part 1 is proposed to be amended as follows:

PART 1—INCOME TAXES

Paragraph 1. The authority citation for part 1 is amended by an entry in numerical order to read in part as follows:

Authority: 26 U.S.C. 7805 ***

§ 1.401(a)(9)-6 is also issued under 26 U.S.C. 401(a)(9). ***

Par. 2. Section 1.401(a)(9)-6 is added to read as follows

§ 1.401(a)(9)-6 Required minimum distributions from defined benefit plans

[The text of proposed § 1.401(a)(9)-6 is the same as the text of § 1.401(a)(9)-6T published elsewhere in this issue of the **Federal Register**].

Deputy Commissioner of Internal Revenue.

Robert E. Wenzel

CERTIFIED COPY

JACKIE TURNER

¶ 20,260I

IRS proposed regulations: Notice requirements: Early retirement benefits: Benefit accrual rates: Plan amendments.—The IRS has issued proposed regulations that contain guidance on notice requirements required to be given by plan administrators to adversely affected plan participants when plan amendments significantly reduce either early retirement benefits or the rate of future benefit accruals or when the amendments eliminate early retirement benefits or retirement-type subsidies.

The proposed regulations, which were published in the *Federal Register* on April 23, 2002 (67 FR 19713), were removed on April 9, 2003 by T.D. 9052 (68 FR 17277) and replaced by Reg. Sec. 54.4980F-1 at ¶ 24,507 and ¶ 13,648W-87.

¶ 20,260J

IRS proposed regulations: Withdrawal of proposed regulations: Stock or securities distribution: Corporate acquisition: Recognition of gain.—The IRS has issued proposed regulations by cross-reference to temporary regulations that relate to recognition of gains or losses on distributions of stock or securities of controlled corporations in connection with acquisitions. Comments and requests for a public hearing must be received by the IRS by July 25, 2002.

The proposed regulations, which were published in the *Federal Register* on April 26, 2002 (67 FR 20711), are reproduced below.

DEPARTMENT OF THE TREASURY

Internal Revenue Service

26 CFR Part 1

[REG-163892-01]

RIN 1545-AY42

Guidance under Section 355(e); Recognition of Gain on Certain Distributions of Stock or Securities in Connection with an Acquisition.

AGENCY: Internal Revenue Service (IRS), Treasury.

ACTION: Withdrawal of notice of proposed rulemaking; and notice of proposed rulemaking by cross-reference to temporary regulations.

SUMMARY: This document withdraws the notice of proposed rulemaking published in the **Federal Register** on January 2, 2001. In the Rules and Regulations section of this issue of the **Federal Register,** the IRS is issuing temporary regulations relating to recognition of gain on certain distributions of stock or securities of a controlled corporation in connection with an acquisition. The text of those regulations also serves as the text of these proposed regulations.

DATES: Written and electronic comments and requests for a public hearing must be received by [*INSERT DATE 90 DAYS AFTER PUBLICATION OF THIS DOCUMENT IN THE FEDERAL REGISTER*].

ADDRESSES: Send submissions to: CC:ITA:RU (REG-163892-01), room 5226, Internal Revenue Service, POB 7604, Ben Franklin Station, Washington, DC 20044. Submissions may be hand delivered Monday through Friday between the hours of 8 a.m. and 5 p.m. to: CC:ITA:RU (REG-163892-01), Courier's Desk, Internal Revenue Service, 1111 Constitution Avenue, NW, Washington, DC. Alternatively, taxpayers may submit electronic comments directly to the IRS Internet site at *www.irs.gov/regs.*

FOR FURTHER INFORMATION CONTACT: Concerning the proposed regulations, Amber R. Cook at (202) 622-7530; concerning submissions, Treena Garrett, (202) 622-7180 (not toll-free numbers).

SUPPLEMENTARY INFORMATION:

Background and Explanation of Provisions

On January 2, 2001, the IRS and Treasury published in the **Federal Register** (66 FR 66) a notice of proposed rulemaking (REG-107566-00) under section 355(e) of the Internal Revenue Code of 1986. Those proposed regulations are withdrawn.

Temporary regulations in the Rules and Regulations section of this issue of the **Federal Register** amend the Income Tax Regulations (26 CFR part 1) relating to section 355(e). The temporary regulations provide rules relating to recognition of gain on certain distributions of stock or securities of a controlled corporation in connection with an acquisition. The text of those regulations also serves as the text of these proposed regulations. The preamble to the temporary regulations explains the amendments.

Special Analysis

It has been determined that this notice of proposed rulemaking is not a significant regulatory action as defined in Executive Order 12866. Therefore, a regulatory assessment is not required. It has also been determined that section 553(b) of the Administrative Procedure Act (5 U.S.C. chapter 5) does not apply to these regulations, and, because these regulations do not impose a collection of information on small entities, the Regulatory Flexibility Act (5 U.S.C. chapter 6) does not apply. Pursuant to section 7805(f) of the Internal Revenue Code, this notice of proposed rulemaking will be submitted to the Chief Counsel for Advocacy of the Small Business Administration for comment on its impact.

Comments and Requests for a Public Hearing

Before these proposed regulations are adopted as final regulations, consideration will be given to any written comments (a signed original and eight (8) copies) and electronic comments that are submitted timely to the IRS. The IRS and Treasury Department specifically request comments on the clarity of the proposed rules and how they may be made easier to understand. All comments will be available for public inspection and copying. A public hearing will be scheduled if requested in writing by any person that timely submits written comments. If a public hearing is scheduled, notice of the date, time, and place for the public hearing will be published in the **Federal Register.**

Drafting Information

The principal author of these regulations is Amber R. Cook, Office of Associate Chief Counsel (Corporate). Other personnel from the IRS and Treasury Department, however, participated in their development.

List of Subjects in 26 CFR Part 1

Income taxes, Reporting and recordkeeping requirements.

Withdrawal of Proposed Amendments to the Regulations and Proposed Amendments to the Regulations

Accordingly, under the authority of 26 U.S.C. 7805 and 26 U.S.C. 355(e)(5), the notice of proposed rulemaking (REG-107566-00) that was published in the **Federal Register** on Tuesday, January 2, 2001, (66 FR 66) is withdrawn. In addition, 26 CFR part 1 is proposed to be amended as follows:

PART 1—INCOME TAXES

Paragraph 1. The authority citation for part 1 is amended by adding an entry in numerical order to read in part as follows:

Authority: 26 U.S.C. 7805 ***

Section 1.355-7 also issued under 26 U.S.C. 355(e)(5). ***

Par. 2. Section 1.355-0 is amended by revising the introductory text and adding an entry for § 1.355-7 to read as follows:

§ *1.355-0 Table of contents.*

In order to facilitate the use of §§ 1.355-1 through 1.355-7, this section lists the major paragraphs in those sections as follows:

*****

§ *1.355-7 Recognition of gain on certain distributions of stock or securities in connection with an acquisition.*

(a) In general.

(b) Plan.

(1) In general.

(2) Certain post-distribution acquisitions.

(3) Plan factors.

(4) Non-plan factors.

(c) Operating rules.

(1) Internal discussions and discussions with outside advisors evidence of business purpose.

(2) Takeover defense.

(3) Effect of distribution on trading in stock.

(4) Consequences of section 355(e) disregarded for certain purposes.

(5) Multiple acquisitions.

(d) Safe harbors.

(1) Safe Harbor I.

(2) Safe Harbor II.

(3) Safe Harbor III.

(4) Safe Harbor IV.

(5) Safe Harbor V.

(i) In general.

(ii) Special rules.

(6) Safe Harbor VI.

(i) In general.

(ii) Special rule.

(7) Safe Harbor VII.

(i) In general.

(ii) Special rule.

(e) Stock acquired by exercise of options, warrants, convertible obligations, and other similar interests.

(1) Treatment of options.

(i) General rule.

(ii) Agreement, understanding, or arrangement to write an option.

(iii) Substantial negotiations related to options.

(2) Instruments treated as options.

(3) Instruments generally not treated as options.

(i) Escrow, pledge, or other security agreements.

(ii) Compensatory options.

(iii) Options exercisable only upon death, disability, mental incompetency, or separation from service.

(iv) Rights of first refusal.

(v) Other enumerated instruments.

(f) Multiple controlled corporations.

(g) Valuation.

(h) Definitions.

(1) Agreement, understanding, arrangement, or substantial negotiations.

(2) Controlled corporation.

(3) Controlling shareholder.

(4) Coordinating group.

(5) Discussions.

(6) Established market.

(7) Five-percent shareholder.

(8) Similar acquisition.

(9) Ten-percent shareholder.

(i) [Reserved]

(j) Examples.

(k) Effective date.

Par. 3. Section 1.355-7 is added to read as follows:

§ *1.355-7 Recognition of gain on certain distributions of stock or securities in connection with an acquisition.*

[The text of proposed § 1.355-7 is the same as the text of § 1.355-7T published elsewhere in this issue of the **Federal Register**].

Deputy Commissioner of Internal Revenue.

Robert E. Wenzel

CERTIFIED COPY

¶ 20,260K

IRS proposed regulations: Code Sec. 457 plans: Deferred compensation: Legislative changes.—The IRS has issued proposed regulations that contain guidance for deferred compensation plans maintained by state and local governments pertaining to legislative changes made by the Tax Reform Act of 1986, the Small Business Job Protection Act of 1996, the Taxpayer Relief Act of 1997, the Economic Growth and Tax Relief Reconciliation Act of 2001, and the Job Creation and Worker Assistance Act of 2002. The proposed regulations also make technical changes and clarify existing final regulations.

The proposed regulations, which were published in the *Federal Register* on May 8, 2002 (67 FR 30826), were finalized by T.D. 9075 (68 FR 41230, July 11, 2003). The preamble to the final regulations is reproduced at ¶ 23,209. The final regulations appear at ¶ 13,154 , ¶ 13,154A , ¶ 13,154B , ¶ 13,154C , ¶ 13,154C-1 , ¶ 13,154C-2 , ¶ 13,154C-3 , ¶ 13,154C-4 , ¶ 13,154C-5 , ¶ 13,154C-6 , ¶ 13,154C-7 , and ¶ 13,154C-8 .

¶ 20,260L

IRS proposed regulations: Modified guaranteed contracts: Interest rates: Temporary guaranty period.—The IRS has issued proposed regulations that define the appropriate interest rate to be used when determining tax reserves and required interest for certain modified guaranteed contracts. The subject matter of the proposed regulations was previously covered in Notice 97-32 (¶ 17,112N), which set forth the appropriate interest rate to be used during the temporary guarantee period of modified guarantee contracts.

A portion of the proposed regulations, which were published in the *Federal Register* (67 FR 38214, June 3, 2002), were previously reproduced at this paragraph.

The final regulations were published in the *Federal Register* on May 7, 2003 (68 FR 24349). The regulations are reproduced at ¶ 13,313A and ¶ 13,313B. The preamble to the regulations is found at ¶ 23,205.

¶ 20,260M

Split-dollar life insurance: Tax treatment: Economic benefit regime: Loan regime.—The IRS has issued guidance in the form of proposed regulations that provide two mutually exclusive regimes for taxing split-dollar life insurance arrangements: the economic benefit regime, which governs taxation of endorsement arrangements, and the loan regime, under which an employer's premium payments are treated as loans to the employee. The proposed regulations apply only to split-dollar life insurance arrangements entered into after final regulations are published in the *Federal Register.*

Portions of the proposed regulations, which were published in the *Federal Register* on July 9, 2002 (67 FR 45414), were reproduced below. Final regulations were published in the Federal Register on September 17, 2003 (68 FR 54336). The preamble to the final regulations is at ¶ 23,214. The final regulations are at ¶ 11,172 , ¶ 11,177, ¶ 11,241, ¶ 11,243, ¶ 11,246, ¶ 13,485R, and ¶ 13,959O.

¶ 20,260N

IRS proposed regulations: Welfare benefit plans: 10-or-more employer plans: Funding limitations.—The IRS has issued proposed regulations clarifying when a welfare benefit plan is part of a 10-or-more employer plan, which would make it exempt from Code Sec. 419 and Code Sec. 419A deduction limits that generally apply to welfare benefit plans. Under Code Sec. 419A(f)(6), a plan is a 10-or-more employer plan if more than one employer contributes to it, no employer is normally required to contribute more than 10% of the total contributions made under the plan by all employers, and the plan does not maintain experience-rating arrangements with respect to individual employers. The proposed regulations provide guidance both for verifying that the Code Sec. 419A(f)(6) requirements have been met, as well as for identifying characteristics that indicate when a plan is not a 10-or-more employer plan.

The proposed regulations, which were published in the *Federal Register* on July 11, 2002 (67 FR 45933), were previously reproduced at this paragraph.

The final regulations were published in the *Federal Register* on July 17, 2003 (68 FR 42254) and are reproduced at ¶ 12,960. The preamble to the regulations is found at ¶ 23,211.

¶ 20,260O

Proposed regulations: Individual retirement accounts: Returned contributions: Recharacterized contributions.—The IRS has issued proposed regulations that provide a new method to be used for calculating the net income attributable to IRA contributions that are distributed as returned or recharacterized contributions. The proposed regulations adopt the method set out in Notice 2000-39 (CCH PENSION PLAN GUIDE ¶ 17,118X).

The proposed regulations were published in the Federal Register on July 23, 2002 at 67 FR 48067. Final regulations, which were published in the Federal Register on May 5, 2003, at 68 FR 23586, are reproduced at ¶ 12,056, ¶ 12,063, and ¶ 12,097A-5. The preamble is reproduced at ¶ 23,204.

¶ 20,260P

Qualified joint and survivor annuities (QJSAs): Qualified preretirement survivor annuities (QPSAs): Qualification requirements: Disclosure: Value of benefits.—The IRS has issued proposed regulations in response to concerns that participants who are eligible for both subsidized annuity distributions and unsubsidized single-sum distributions may be receiving notices that do not adequately explain the value of the subsidy that is foregone if the single-sum distribution is elected. The proposed regulations consolidate the content requirements applicable to explanations for QJSAs and QPSAs and specify rules for disclosing the relative values of optional forms of benefit as part of the QJSA explanation.

The proposed regulations, which were published in the *Federal Register* on October 7, 2002 (67 FR 62417), were previously reproduced at this paragraph. The final regulations were published in the *Federal Register* on December 17, 2003 (68 FR 70141) and are reproduced at ¶ 12,551. The preamble to the regulations is found at ¶ 23,215.

DEPARTMENT OF THE TREASURY

Internal Revenue Service

26 CFR Part 1

[REG-124667-02]

RIN 1545-BA78

Disclosure of Relative Values of Optional Forms of Benefit

AGENCY: Internal Revenue Service (IRS), Treasury.

ACTION: Notice of proposed rulemaking and notice of public hearing.

SUMMARY: This document contains proposed regulations that would consolidate the content requirements applicable to explanations of qualified joint and survivor annuities and qualified preretirement survivor annuities payable under certain retirement plans, and would specify requirements for disclosing the relative value of optional forms of benefit that are payable from certain retirement plans in lieu of a qualified joint and survivor annuity. These regulations would affect retirement plan sponsors and administrators, and participants in and beneficiaries of retirement plans. This document also provides notice of a public hearing on these proposed regulations.

DATES: Written comments, requests to speak and outlines of oral comments to be discussed at the public hearing scheduled for January 14, 2003, at 10 a.m., must be received by January 2, 2003.

ADDRESSES: Send submissions to: CC:ITA:RU (REG-124667-02), room 5226, Internal Revenue Service, POB 7604, Ben Franklin Station, Washington, DC 20044. In the alternative, submissions may be hand delivered to: CC:ITA:RU (REG-124667-02), room 5226, Internal Revenue Service, 1111 Constitution Avenue NW., Washington, DC. Alternatively, taxpayers may submit comments electronically via the Internet by submitting comments directly to the IRS Internet site at: *www.irs.gov/regs*. The public hearing will be held in room 4718 of the Internal Revenue Building, 1111 Constitution Avenue NW., Washington, DC.

FOR FURTHER INFORMATION CONTACT:

Concerning the regulations, Linda S. F. Marshall, 202-622-6090; concerning submissions and the hearing, and/or to be placed on the building access list to attend the hearing, Guy Traynor, 202-622-7180 (not toll-free numbers).

SUPPLEMENTARY INFORMATION:

Paperwork Reduction Act

The collections of information contained in this notice of proposed rulemaking have been submitted to the Office of Management and Budget for review in accordance with the Paperwork Reduction Act of 1995 (44 U.S.C. 3507(d)). Comments on the collections of information should be sent to the Office of Management and Budget, Attn: Desk Officer for the Department of the Treasury, Office of Information and Regulatory Affairs, Washington, DC 20503, with copies to the Internal Revenue Service, Attn: IRS Reports Clearance Officer, W:CAR:MP:FP:S Washington, DC 20224. Comments on the collections of information should be received by December 6, 2002. Comments are specifically requested concerning:

Whether the proposed collections of information are necessary for the proper performance of the functions of the IRS, including whether the information will have practical utility;

The accuracy of the estimated burden associated with the proposed collection of information (see below);

How the quality, utility, and clarity of the information to be collected may be enhanced;

How the burden of complying with the proposed collection of information may be minimized, including through the application of automated collection techniques or other forms of information technology; and

Estimates of capital or start-up costs and costs of operation, maintenance, and purchase of services to provide information.

The collections of information in this proposed regulation are in § 1.417(a)(3)-1. This information is required by the IRS to comply with the requirements of section 417(a)(3) regarding explanations that must be provided to participants in a qualified plan prior to a waiver of a qualified joint and survivor annuity (QJSA) or a qualified preretirement survivor annuity (QPSA). This information will be used by participants and spouses of participants to determine whether to waive a QJSA or

QPSA, and by the IRS to confirm that the plan complies with applicable qualification requirements to avoid adverse tax consequences. The collections of information are mandatory. The respondents are non-profit institutions.

Estimated total annual reporting burden: 375,000 hours.

The estimated annual burden per respondent varies from .01 to .99 hours, depending on individual circumstances, with an estimated average of .5 hours.

Estimated number of respondents: 750,000.

The estimated annual frequency of responses: On occasion.

An agency may not conduct or sponsor, and a person is not required to respond to, a collection of information unless it displays a valid control number assigned by the Office of Management and Budget.

Books or records relating to a collection of information must be retained as long as their contents may become material in the administration of any internal revenue law. Generally, tax returns and tax return information are confidential, as required by 26 U.S.C. 6103.

Background

This document contains proposed amendments to 26 CFR part 1 under section 417(a)(3) of the Internal Revenue Code of 1986 (Code).

A qualified retirement plan to which section 401(a)(11) applies must pay a vested participant's retirement benefit under the plan in the form of a qualified joint and survivor annuity (QJSA), except as provided in section 417. Section 401(a)(11) applies to defined benefit plans, money purchase pension plans, and certain other defined contribution plans. A QJSA is defined in section 417(b) as an annuity for the life of the participant with a survivor annuity for the life of the spouse (if the participant is married) that is not less than 50 percent of (and is not greater than 100 percent of) the amount of the annuity that is payable during the joint lives of the participant and the spouse. Under section 417(b)(2), a QJSA for a married participant generally must be the actuarial equivalent of the single life annuity benefit payable for the life of the participant. However, a plan is permitted to subsidize the QJSA for a married participant. If the plan fully subsidizes the QJSA for a married participant so that failure to waive the QJSA would not result in reduced payments over the life of the participant compared to the single life annuity benefit, then the plan need not provide an election to waive the QJSA. *See* section 417(a)(5).

For a married participant, the QJSA must be at least as valuable as any other optional form of benefit payable under the plan at the same time. *See* § 1.401(a)-20, Q&A-16. Further, the antiforfeiture rules of section 411(a) prohibit a participant's benefit under a defined benefit plan from being satisfied through payment that is actuarially less valuable than the value of the participant's accrued benefit expressed in the form of an annual benefit commencing at normal retirement age. These determinations must be made using reasonable actuarial assumptions. However, *see* § 1.417(e)-1(d) for actuarial assumptions required for use in certain present value calculations.

If a plan provides a subsidy for one optional form of benefit (*i.e.*, the payments under an optional form of benefit have an actuarial present value that is greater than the actuarial present value of the accrued benefit), there is no requirement to extend a similar subsidy (or any subsidy) to every other optional form of benefit. Thus, for example, a participant might be entitled to receive a single-sum distribution upon early retirement that does not reflect any early retirement subsidy in lieu of a QJSA that reflects a substantial early retirement subsidy. As a further example, a participant might be entitled to receive a single-sum distribution at normal retirement age in lieu of a QJSA that is subsidized as described in section 417(a)(5).

Section 417(a) provides rules under which a participant (with spousal consent) may waive payment of the participant's benefit in the form of a QJSA. Section 417(a)(3) provides that a plan must provide to each participant, within a reasonable period before the annuity starting date (and consistent with such regulations as the Secretary may prescribe) a written explanation of the terms and conditions of the QJSA, the participant's right to make, and the effect of, an election to waive the QJSA form of benefit, the rights of the participant's spouse, and the right to revoke (and the effect of the revocation of) an election to waive the QJSA form of benefit.

Section 205 of the Employee Retirement Income Security Act of 1974 (ERISA), Public Law 93-406 (88 Stat. 829) as subsequently amended, provides parallel rules to the rules of sections 401(a)(11) and 417 of the Internal Revenue Code. In particular, section 205(a)(3) of ERISA provides a parallel rule to section 417(a)(3) of the Code. Treasury regulations issued under section 417(a)(3) of the Code apply as well for purposes of section 205(a)(3) of ERISA.

Regulations governing the requirements for waiver of a QJSA were published in the **Federal Register** on August 19, 1988 (TD 8219; 53 FR 31837). Section 1.401(a)-20, Q&A-36, provides rules for the explanation that must be provided under section 417(a)(3) as a prerequisite to waiver of a QJSA. Section 1.401(a)-20, Q&A-36, requires that such a written explanation must contain a general description of the eligibility conditions and other material features of the optional forms of benefit and sufficient additional information to explain the relative values of the optional forms of benefit available under the plan (*e.g.*, the extent to which optional forms are subsidized relative to the normal form of benefit or the interest rates used to calculate the optional forms). In addition, § 1.401(a)-20, Q&A-36, provides that the written explanation must comply with the requirements set forth in § 1.401(a)-11(c)(3). Section 1.401(a)-11(c)(3) was issued prior to the enactment of section 417, and provides rules relating to written explanations that were required prior to a participant's election of a preretirement survivor annuity or election to waive a joint and survivor annuity. Section 1.401(a)-11(c)(3)(i)(C) provides that such a written explanation must contain a general explanation of the relative financial effect of these elections on a participant's annuity.

In addition, under section 411 and § 1.411(a)-11(c), so long as a benefit is immediately distributable (within the meaning of § 1.411(a)-11(c)(4)), a participant must be informed of his or her right to defer that distribution. This requirement is independent of the section 417 requirements addressed in these proposed regulations.

Concerns have been expressed that, in certain cases, the information provided to participants under section 417(a)(3) regarding the available distribution forms does not adequately enable them to compare those distribution forms without professional advice. In particular, participants who are eligible for both subsidized annuity distributions and unsubsidized single-sum distributions may be receiving notices that do not adequately explain the value of the subsidy that is foregone if the single-sum distribution is elected. In such a case, merely disclosing the amount of the single-sum distribution and the amount of annuity payments may not adequately enable those participants to make an informed comparison of the relative values of those distribution forms, even if the interest rate used to derive the single sum is disclosed. Furthermore, questions have been raised as to how the relative values of optional forms of benefit are required to be expressed under current regulations. Accordingly, these proposed regulations are being issued to propose disclosure requirements that would enable participants to compare the relative values of the available distribution forms using more readily understandable information.

Explanation of Provisions

The proposed regulations would consolidate the content requirements applicable to explanations of QJSAs and QPSAs under section 417(a)(3), and would specify rules for disclosing the relative value of optional forms of benefit as part of the QJSA explanation. Similar to the requirements in the current regulations, the required explanation must contain, with respect to each of the optional forms of benefit presently available to the participant, a description of the optional form of benefit, a description of the eligibility conditions for the optional form of benefit, a description of the financial effect of electing the optional form of benefit, a description of the relative value of the optional form of benefit, and a description of any other material features of the optional form of benefit. Further, as under the current regulations, the QJSA explanation would be permitted to be made either by providing the participant with information specific to the participant, or by providing the participant with generally applicable information and offering the participant the opportunity to request additional information specifically applicable to the participant with respect to any optional forms of benefit available to the participant. The proposed regulations would clarify that a defined contribution plan is not required to provide a description of the relative values of optional forms of benefit compared to the value of the QJSA.

The proposed regulations would provide additional guidance regarding the required description of the relative values of optional forms of benefit compared to the value of the QJSA and the content of the required disclosure of relative values. Under the proposed regulations, the description of the relative value of an optional form of benefit compared to the value of the QJSA must be expressed in a manner that provides a meaningful comparison of the relative economic values of the two forms of benefit without the participant having to make calculations using interest or mortality assumptions. In order to make this comparison, the benefit under one or both optional forms of benefit must be converted, taking into account the time value of money and life expectancies, so that both are expressed in the same form. The proposed regulations give several examples of techniques that may be used for this comparison: expressing the actuarial present value of the optional form of benefit as a percentage or factor of the actuarial present value of the QJSA; stating the amount of an annuity payable at the same time and under the same conditions as the QJSA that is the actuarial equivalent of the optional form of benefit; or stating the actuarial present value of both the QJSA and the optional form of benefit. For purposes of providing a description of the relative value of an optional form of benefit compared to the value of the QJSA (and also for purposes of comparing the financial effect of the distribution forms available to a participant), a plan would be permitted to provide reasonable estimates (*e.g.*, estimates based on data as of an earlier date than the annuity starting date or an estimate of the spouse's age). If estimates are used, the participant has a right to a more precise calculation upon request.

Since disclosing the relative value of every optional form of benefit regardless of the degree of subsidy may be too burdensome, and may provide participants with information that appears more precise than is warranted based on the inexact nature of the actuarial assumptions used, the proposed regulations would provide some ways to simplify this disclosure of relative values of optional forms of benefit. One way in which this disclosure would be simplified is through a banding rule under which two or more optional forms of benefit that have approximately the same value could be grouped for purposes of disclosing relative value. Under these proposed regulations, two or more optional forms of benefit would be treated as having approximately the same value if those optional forms of benefit vary in relative value in comparison to the value of the QJSA by 5 percentage points or less when the relative value comparison is made by expressing the actuarial present value of each of those optional forms of benefit as a percentage of the actuarial present value of the QJSA. For such a group of optional forms of benefit, the requirement relating to disclosing the relative value of each optional form of benefit compared to the value of the QJSA could be satisfied by disclosing the relative value of any one of the optional forms in the group compared to the value of the QJSA, and disclosing that the other optional forms of benefit in the group are of approximately the same value. If a single-sum distribution is included in such a group of optional forms of benefit, the single-sum distribution must be the distribution form that is used for purposes of this comparison. The relative value of all optional forms of benefit that have an actuarial present value that is at least 95% of the actuarial present value of the QJSA may be described by stating that those optional forms of benefit are of approximately equal value to the value of the QJSA. Thus, these rules would permit a plan that provides no subsidized forms of benefit to state the comparison of relative values simply by stating that all distribution forms are approximately equal in value to the QJSA.

Another way in which this disclosure may be simplified is through the use of representative values: if, under the banding rule, two or more optional forms of benefit are grouped, a representative relative value for all of the grouped options could be used as the approximate relative value for all of the grouped options, in lieu of using the relative value of one of the optional forms of benefit in the group. For this purpose, a representative relative value is any relative value that is not less than the relative value of the member of the group of optional forms of benefit with the lowest relative value and is not greater than the relative value of the member of that group with the highest relative value when measured on a consistent basis. For example, if three optional forms have relative values of 87.5%, 89%, and 91% of the value of the QJSA, all three optional forms can be treated as having a relative value of approximately 90% of the value of the QJSA.

The proposed regulations would also permit the disclosure of the financial effect and relative value of optional forms of benefit to be made in the form of generally applicable information rather than information specific to the participant, provided that information specific to the participant regarding the optional form of benefit must be furnished at the participant's request. Thus, under the proposed regulations, in lieu of providing a QJSA explanation that describes each optional form that is presently available to the participant, the generalized QJSA explanation need only reflect the generally available optional forms of benefits, along with a reference to where a participant can obtain the information for any other optional forms of benefits (such as optional forms from prior benefit structures for limited groups of employees) that are presently available to the participant.

With respect to the generally available optional forms of benefits, in lieu of providing a statement of financial effect and relative value comparison that is specific to the participant, the generalized QJSA explanation is permitted to include a chart or other comparable device showing a series of examples of financial effects and relative value comparisons for hypothetical participants. The examples in the chart should reflect a representative range of ages for the hypothetical participants and use reasonable assumptions for the age of the hypothetical participant's spouse and any other variable that affects the financial effect, or relative value, of the optional form of benefit. The chart must be accompanied by a general statement describing the effect of significant variations between the assumed ages or other variables on the financial effect of electing the optional form of benefit and the comparison of the relative value of the optional form of benefit to the value of the QJSA. A generalized QJSA explanation that includes this chart must also include the amount payable to the participant under the normal form of benefit, either at normal retirement age, or payable immediately. In addition, this chart must be accompanied by a statement that includes an offer to provide, upon the participant's request, a statement of financial effect along with a comparison of relative values that is specific to the participant for one or more presently available optional forms of benefit, and a description of how a participant may obtain this additional information. Thus, with respect to those optional forms of benefit for which additional information is requested, the participant must receive a QJSA explanation specific to the participant that is based on the participant's actual age and benefit.

The proposed regulations would provide rules governing the actuarial assumptions to be used in comparing the value of an optional form of benefit to the QJSA. If an optional form of benefit is subject to the requirements of section 417(e)(3) and § 1.417(e)-1(d) (*e.g.*, a single-sum distribution), any comparison of the value of the optional form of benefit to the value of the QJSA must be made using the applicable mortality table and the applicable interest rate as defined in § 1.417(e)-1(d)(2) and (3) (or, at the option of the plan, another reasonable interest rate and reasonable mortality table used under the plan to calculate the amount payable under the optional form of benefit). All other optional forms of benefit payable to the participant must be compared with the QJSA using a single set of interest rates and mortality tables that are reasonable and that are applied uniformly for this purpose with respect to all such other optional forms payable to the participant. The uniform interest and mortality assumptions should be used regardless of whether those assumptions are actually used to determine the amount of benefit payments under any particular optional form.

The proposed regulations would also require disclosure of information to help a participant understand the significance of a disclosure of the relative value of an optional form of benefit. Under the proposed regulations, the notice would be required to provide an explanation of the concept of relative value. Specifically, the notice would be required to explain that the relative value comparison is intended to allow the participant to compare the total value of distributions paid in different forms, that the relative value comparison is made by converting the value of the optional forms of benefit currently available to a common form (such as the QJSA or single-sum distribution), and that this conversion uses interest and life expectancy assumptions.

Under the proposed regulations, a required numerical comparison of the value of the optional form of benefit to the value of the QJSA under the plan generally would be required to disclose the interest rate that is used to develop a required numerical comparison. However, if all optional forms of benefit are permitted to be treated as having approximately the same value after application of the banding rule described above, then the plan would not be required to disclose the interest rate used to develop a required numerical comparison to the QJSA for optional form of benefit that is not subject to the requirements of section 417(e)(3). In addition, the proposed regulations would require the plan to provide a general statement that all numerical comparisons of relative value provided are based on average life expectancies, and that the relative value of payments ultimately made under an annuity optional form of benefit will depend on actual longevity.

Under the proposed regulations, both the QPSA explanation and the QJSA explanation must be written in a manner calculated to be understood by the average participant. A plan may wish to provide additional information beyond the minimum information that would be required under these proposed regulations, in order to help an employee to evaluate the form of benefit that would be most desirable under the employee's individual circumstances. For example, the plan may wish to add further explanation of the effects of ill health or other factors influencing expected longevity on the desirability of electing annuity forms of distribution.

The proposed regulations contain rules regarding the method for providing the QJSA explanation and the QPSA explanation. Under the proposed regulations, these explanations must be written explanations. First class mail to the last known address of the party is an acceptable delivery method for a section 417(a)(3) explanation. Likewise, hand delivery is acceptable. However, the posting of the explanation is not considered provision of the section 417(a)(3) explanation.

These proposed regulations do not address the extent to which the QJSA explanation or the QPSA explanation can be provided through electronic media. The IRS and the Treasury Department are considering the extent to which the QJSA explanation and the QPSA explanation, as well as other notices under the various Internal Revenue Code requirements relating to qualified retirement plans, can be provided electronically, taking into account the effect of the Electronic Signatures in Global and National Commerce Act (ESIGN), Public Law 106-229, 114 Stat. 464 (2000). The IRS and the Treasury Department anticipate issuing proposed regulations regarding these issues, and invite comments on these issues.

Proposed Effective Date

The regulations are proposed to be applicable to QJSA explanations with respect to distributions with annuity starting dates on or after January 1, 2004, and to QPSA explanations provided on or after January 1, 2004.

Special Analyses

It has been determined that this notice of proposed rulemaking is not a significant regulatory action as defined in Executive Order 12866. Therefore, a regulatory assessment is not required. It is hereby certified that the collection of information in these regulations will not have a significant economic impact on a substantial number of small entities. This certification is based upon the fact that qualified retirement plans of small businesses typically commence distribution of benefits to few, if any, plan participants in any given year and, similarly, only offer elections to waive a QPSA to few, if any, participants in any given year. Thus, the collection of information in these regulations will only have a minimal economic impact on most small entities. Therefore, an analysis under the Regulatory Flexibility Act (5 U.S.C. chapter 6) is not required. Pursuant to section 7805(f) of the Code, this notice of proposed rulemaking will be submitted to the Chief Counsel for Advocacy of the Small Business Administration for comment on its impact on small business.

Comments and Public Hearing

Before these proposed regulations are adopted as final regulations, consideration will be given to written comments (preferably a signed original and eight (8) copies) that are submitted timely to the IRS. Alternatively, taxpayers may submit comments electronically to the IRS Internet site at *http://www.irs.gov/regs*. All comments will be available for public inspection and copying. The IRS and Treasury request comments on the clarity of the proposed rules and how they may be made easier to understand or to implement.

A public hearing has been scheduled for January 14, 2002, at 10 a.m. in room 4718 of the Internal Revenue Building, 1111 Constitution Avenue NW., Washington, DC. All visitors must present photo identification to enter the building. Because of access restrictions, visitors will not be admitted beyond the immediate entrance area more than 30 minutes before the hearing starts at the Constitution Avenue entrance. For information about having your name placed on the building access list to attend the hearing, see the **FOR FURTHER INFORMATION CONTACT** section of this preamble.

The rules of 26 CFR 601.601(a)(3) apply to the hearing. Persons who wish to present oral comments at the hearing must submit written comments and an outline of the topics to be discussed and the time to be devoted to each topic (signed original and eight (8) copies) by January 2, 2002. A period of 10 minutes will be allotted to each person for making comments. An agenda showing the scheduling of the speakers will be prepared after the deadline for receiving outlines has passed. Copies of the agenda will be available free of charge at the hearing.

Drafting Information

The principal author of these proposed regulations is Linda S. F. Marshall of the Office of the Division Counsel/Associate Chief Counsel (Tax Exempt and Government Entities). However, other personnel from the IRS and Treasury participated in their development.

List of Subjects in 26 CFR Part 1

Income taxes, Reporting and recordkeeping requirements.

Proposed Amendments to the Regulations

Accordingly, 26 CFR part 1 is proposed to be amended as follows:

PART 1—INCOME TAX; TAXABLE YEARS BEGINNING AFTER DECEMBER 31, 1986

Paragraph 1. The authority citation for part 1 continues to read in part as follows:

Authority: 26 U.S.C. 7805 * * *

Par. 2. Paragraph (c)(3) of § 1.401(a)-11 is revised to read as follows:

§ 1.401(a)-11 Qualified joint and survivor annuities.

* * *

(c) * * *

(3) *Information to be provided by plan.* For rules regarding the information required to be provided with respect to the election to waive a QJSA or a QPSA, see § 1.417(a)(3)-1.

* * *

Par. 3. A-36 of § 1.401(a)-20 is revised to read as follows:

§ 1.401(a)-20 Requirements of qualified joint and survivor annuity and qualified preretirement survivor annuity.

* * *

A-36. For rules regarding the explanation of QPSAs and QJSAs required under section 417(a)(3), see § 1.417(a)(3)-1.

* * *

Par. 4. Section 1.417(a)(3)-1 is added to read as follows:

§ 1.417(a)(3)-1 Required explanation of qualified joint and survivor annuity and qualified preretirement survivor annuity.

(a) *Written explanation requirement*—(1) *General rule.* A plan meets the survivor annuity requirements of section 401(a)(11) only if the plan meets the requirements of section 417(a)(3) and this section regarding the written explanation required to be provided a participant with respect to a QJSA or a QPSA. A written explanation required to be provided to a participant with respect to either a QJSA or a QPSA under section 417(a)(3) and this section is referred to in this section as a section 417(a)(3) explanation. See § 1.401(a)-20, Q&A-37, for exceptions to the written explanation requirement in the case of a fully subsidized QPSA or QJSA, and § 1.401(a)-20, Q&A-38, for the definition of a fully subsidized QPSA or QJSA.

(2) *Time for providing section 417(a)(3) explanation*—(i) *QJSA explanation.* See § 1.417(e)-1(b)(3)(ii) for rules governing the timing of the QJSA explanation.

(ii) *QPSA explanation.* See § 1.401(a)-20, Q&A-35, for rules governing the timing of the QPSA explanation.

(3) *Required method for providing section 417(a)(3) explanation.* A section 417(a)(3) explanation must be a written explanation. First class mail to the last known address of the participant is an acceptable delivery method for a section 417(a)(3) explanation. Likewise, hand delivery is acceptable. However, the posting of the explanation is not considered provision of the section 417(a)(3) explanation.

(4) *Understandability.* A section 417(a)(3) explanation must be written in a manner calculated to be understood by the average participant.

(b) *Required content of section 417(a)(3) explanation*—(1) *Content of QPSA explanation.* The QPSA explanation must contain a general description of the QPSA, the circumstances under which it will be paid if elected, the availability of the election of the QPSA, and, except as provided in paragraph (d)(3) of this section, a description of the financial effect of the election of the QPSA on the participant's benefits (*i.e.*, an estimate of the reduction to the participant's estimated normal retirement benefit that would result from an election of the QPSA).

(2) *Content of QJSA explanation.* The QJSA explanation must satisfy either paragraph (c) or paragraph (d) of this section. Under paragraph (c) of this section, the QJSA explanation must contain certain specific information relating to the benefits available under the plan to the particular participant. Alternatively, under paragraph (d) of this section, the QJSA explanation can contain generally applicable information in lieu of specific participant information, provided that the participant has the right to request additional information regarding the participant's benefits under the plan.

(c) *Participant-specific information required to be provided*—(1) *In general.* A QJSA explanation satisfies this paragraph (c) if it provides the following information with respect to each of the optional forms of benefit presently available to the participant—

(i) A description of the optional form of benefit;

(ii) A description of the eligibility conditions for the optional form of benefit;

(iii) A description of the financial effect of electing the optional form of benefit (*i.e.*, the amount payable under the form of benefit);

(iv) In the case of a defined benefit plan, a description of the relative value of the optional form of benefit compared to the value of the QJSA, in the manner described in paragraph (c)(2) of this section; and

(v) A description of any other material features of the optional form of benefit.

(2) *Requirement for numerical comparison of relative values*—(i) *In general.* The description of the relative value of an optional form of benefit compared to the value of the QJSA under paragraph (c)(1)(iv) of this section must be expressed to the participant in a manner that provides a meaningful comparison of the relative economic values of the two forms of benefit without the participant having to make calculations using interest or mortality assumptions. Thus, in performing the calculations necessary to make this comparison, the benefits under one or both optional forms of benefit must be converted, taking into account the time value of money and life expectancies, so that the values of both optional forms of benefit are expressed in the same form. For example, such a comparison may be expressed to the participant using any of the following techniques—

(A) Expressing the actuarial present value of the optional form of benefit as a percentage or factor of the actuarial present value of the QJSA;

(B) Stating the amount of the annuity that is the actuarial equivalent of the optional form of benefit and that is payable at the same time and under the same conditions as the QJSA; or

(C) Stating the actuarial present value of both the optional form of benefit and the QJSA.

(ii) *Simplified presentations permitted*—(A) *Grouping of certain optional forms.* Two or more optional forms of benefit that have approximately the same value may be grouped for purposes of a required numerical comparison described in this paragraph (c)(2). For this purpose, two or more optional forms of benefit have approximately the same value if those optional forms of benefit vary in relative value in comparison to the value of the QJSA by 5 percentage points or less when the relative value comparison is made by expressing the actuarial present value of each of those optional forms of benefit as a percentage of the actuarial present value of the QJSA. For such a group of optional forms of benefit, the requirement relating to disclosing the relative value of each optional form of benefit compared to the value of the QJSA can be satisfied by disclosing the relative value of any one of the optional forms in the group compared to the value of the QJSA, and disclosing that the other optional forms of benefit in the group are of approximately the same value. If a single-sum distribution is included in such a group of optional forms of benefit, the single-sum distribution must be the distribution form that is used for purposes of this comparison. In addition, the relative value of all optional forms of benefit that have an actuarial present value that is at least 95% of the actuarial present value of the QJSA is permitted to be described by stating that those optional forms of benefit are approximately equal in value to the QJSA, or that all of those forms of benefit and the QJSA are approximately equal in value.

(B) *Representative relative value for grouped optional forms.* If, in accordance with paragraph (c)(2)(ii)(A) of this section, two or more optional forms of benefits are grouped, the relative values for all of the optional forms of benefit in the group can be stated using a representative relative value as the approximate relative value for the entire group. For this purpose, a representative relative value is any relative value that is not less than the relative value of the member of the group of optional forms of benefit with the lowest relative value and is not greater than the relative value of the member of that group with the highest relative value when measured on a consistent basis. For example, if three optional forms have relative values of 87.5%, 89%, and 91% of the value of the QJSA, all three optional forms can be treated as having a relative value of approximately 90% of the value of the QJSA. As required under paragraph (c)(2)(ii)(A) of this section, if a single-sum distribution is included in the group of optional forms of benefit, the 90% relative factor of the value of the QJSA must be disclosed as the approximate relative value of the single sum, and the other forms can be described as having the same approximate value as the single sum.

(iii) *Actuarial assumptions used to determine relative values.* For the purpose of providing a numerical comparison of the value of an optional form of benefit to the value of the immediately commencing QJSA, the following rules apply—

(A) If an optional form of benefit is subject to the requirements of section 417(e)(3) and § 1.417(e)-1(d), any comparison of the value of the optional form of benefit to the value of the QJSA must be made using the applicable mortality table and the applicable interest rate as defined in § 1.417(e)-1(d)(2) and (3) (or, at the option of the plan, another reasonable interest rate and reasonable mortality table used under the plan to calculate the amount payable under the optional form of benefit); and

(iv) *Required disclosure of assumptions*—(A) *Explanation of concept of relative value.* The notice must provide an explanation of the concept of relative value, communicating that the relative value comparison is intended to allow the participant to compare the total value of distributions paid in different forms, that the relative value comparison is made by converting the value of the optional forms of benefit presently available to a common form (such as the QJSA or a single-sum distribution), and that this conversion uses interest and life expectancy assumptions. The explanation of relative value must include a general statement that all comparisons provided are based on average life expectancies, and that the relative value of payments ultimately made under an annuity optional form of benefit will depend on actual longevity.

(B) *Disclosure of interest assumptions.* A required numerical comparison of the value of the optional form of benefit to the value of the QJSA under the plan is required to disclose the interest rate that is used to develop the comparison. If all optional forms of benefit are permitted to be grouped under paragraph (c)(2)(ii)(A) of this section, then the requirement of this paragraph (c)(2)(iv)(B) does not apply for any optional form of benefit not subject to the requirements of section 417(e)(3) and § 1.417(e)-1(d)(3).

(3) *Permitted estimates of financial effect and relative value*—(i) *General rule.* For purposes of providing a description of the financial effect of the distribution forms available to a participant as required under paragraph (c)(1)(iii) of this section, and for purposes of providing a description of the relative value of an optional form of benefit compared to the value of the QJSA for a participant as required under paragraph (c)(1)(iv) of this section, the plan is permitted to provide reasonable estimates (*e.g.,* estimates based on data as of an earlier date than the annuity starting date, a reasonable assumption for the age of the participant's spouse, or, in the case of a defined contribution plan, reasonable estimates of amounts that would be payable under a purchased annuity contract), including reasonable estimates of the applicable interest rate under section 417(e)(3).

(ii) *Right to more precise calculation.* If a QJSA notice uses a reasonable estimate under paragraph (c)(3)(i) of this section, the QJSA explanation must identify the estimate and explain that the plan will, upon the request of the participant, provide a more precise calculation and the plan must provide the participant with a more precise calculation if so requested. Thus, for example, if a plan provides an estimate of the amount of the QJSA that is based on a reasonable assumption concerning the age of the participant's spouse, the participant can request a calculation that takes into account the actual age of the spouse, as provided by the participant.

(iii) *Revision of prior information.* If a more precise calculation described in paragraph (c)(3)(ii) of this section materially changes the relative value of an optional form compared to the value of the QJSA, the revised relative value of that optional form must be disclosed, regardless of whether the financial effect of selecting the optional form is affected by the more precise calculation.

(4) *Special rules for disclosure of financial effect for defined contribution plans.* For a written explanation provided by a defined contribution plan, a description of financial effect required by paragraph (c)(1)(iii) of this section with respect to an annuity form of benefit must include a statement that the annuity will be provided by purchasing an annuity contract from an insurance company with the participant's account balance under the plan. If the description of the financial effect of the optional form of benefit is provided using estimates rather than by assuring that an insurer is able to provide the amount disclosed to the participant, the written explanation must also disclose this fact.

(d) *Substitution of generally applicable information for participant information in the section 417(a)(3) explanation*—(1) *Forms of benefit available.* In lieu of providing the information required under paragraphs (c)(1)(i) through (v) of this section for each optional form of benefit presently available to the participant as described in paragraph (c) of this section, the QJSA explanation may contain the information required under paragraphs (c)(1)(i) through (v) of this section for the QJSA and each other optional form of benefit generally available under the plan, along with a reference to where a participant may readily obtain the information required under paragraphs (c)(1)(i) through (v) of this section for any other optional forms of benefit that are presently available to the participant.

(2) *Financial effect and comparison of relative values*—(i) *General rule.* In lieu of providing a statement of the financial effect of electing an optional form of benefit as required under paragraph (c)(1)(iii) of this section, or a comparison of relative values as required under paragraph (c)(1)(iv) of this section, based on the actual age and benefit of the participant, the QJSA explanation is permitted to include a chart (or other comparable device) showing the financial effect and relative value of optional forms of benefit in a series of examples specifying the amount of the optional form of benefit payable to a hypothetical participant at a representative range of ages and the comparison of relative

values at those same representative ages. Each example in this chart must show the financial effect of electing the optional form of benefit pursuant to the rules of paragraph (c)(1)(iii) of this section, and a comparison of the relative value of the optional form of benefit to the value of the QJSA pursuant to the rules of paragraph (c)(2) of this section, using reasonable assumptions for the age of the hypothetical participant's spouse and any other variables that affect the financial effect, or relative value, of the optional form of benefit. The requirement to show the financial effect of electing an optional form can be satisfied through the use of other methods (*e.g.,* expressing the amount of the optional form as a percentage or a factor of the amount payable under the normal form of benefit), provided that the method provides sufficient information so that a participant can determine the amount of benefits payable in the optional form. The chart or other comparable device must be accompanied by the disclosures described in paragraph (c)(2)(iv) of this section explaining the concept of relative value and disclosing certain interest assumptions. In addition, the chart or other comparable device must be accompanied by a general statement describing the effect of significant variations between the assumed ages or other variables on the financial effect of electing the optional form of benefit and the comparison of the relative value of the optional form of benefit to the value of the QJSA.

(ii) *Actual benefit must be disclosed.* The generalized notice described in this paragraph (d)(2) will satisfy the requirements of paragraph (b)(2) of this section only if the notice includes either the amount payable to the participant under the normal form of benefit or the amount payable to the participant under the normal form of benefit adjusted for immediate commencement. For this purpose, the normal form of benefit is the form under which payments due to the participant under the plan are expressed under the plan, prior to adjustments for form of benefit. For example, assuming that a plan's benefit accrual formula is expressed as a straight life annuity, the generalized notice must provide the amount of either the straight life annuity commencing at normal retirement age or the straight life annuity commencing immediately.

(iii) *Ability to request additional information* The generalized notice described in this paragraph (d)(2) must be accompanied by a statement that includes an offer to provide, upon the participant's request, a statement of financial effect and a comparison of relative values that is specific to the participant for any presently available optional form of benefit, and a description of how a participant may obtain this additional information.

(3) *Financial effect of QPSA election.* In lieu of providing a specific description of the financial effect of the QPSA election, the QPSA explanation may provide a general description of the financial effect of the election. Thus, for example, the description can be in the form of a chart showing the reduction to a hypothetical participant's normal retirement benefit at a representative range of participant ages as a result of the QPSA election (using a reasonable assumption for the age of the hypothetical participant's spouse relative to the age of the hypothetical participant). In addition, this chart must be accompanied by a statement that includes an offer to provide, upon the participant's request, an estimate of the reduction to the participant's estimated normal retirement benefit, and a description of how a participant may obtain this additional information.

(4) *Additional information required to be furnished at the participant's request*—(i) *Explanation of QJSA.* If, as permitted under paragraphs (d)(1) and (2) of this section, the content of a QJSA explanation does not include all the items described in paragraph (c) of this section, then, upon a timely request from the participant for any of the information required under paragraphs (c)(1)(i) through (v) of this section for one or more presently available optional forms (including a request for all optional forms presently available to the participant), the plan must furnish the information required under paragraphs (c)(1)(i) through (v) of this section with respect to those optional forms. Thus, with respect to those optional forms of benefit, the participant must receive a QJSA explanation specific to the participant that is based on the participant's actual age and benefit. In addition, the plan must comply with paragraph (c)(3)(iii) of this section.

(ii) *Explanation of QPSA.* If, as permitted under paragraph (d)(3) of this section, the content of a QPSA explanation does not include all the items described in paragraph (b)(1) of this section, then, upon a timely request from the participant for an estimate of the reduction to the participant's estimated normal retirement benefit that would result from a QPSA election, the plan must furnish such an estimate.

(e) *Examples.* The following examples illustrate the application of this section. Solely for purposes of these examples, the applicable interest rate that applies to any distribution that is subject to the rules of section 417(e)(3) is assumed to be 512%, and the applicable mortality table under section 417(e)(3) and § 1.417(e)-1(d)(2) is assumed to be the table that applies as of January 1, 2003. In addition, solely for purposes of these examples, assume that a plan which determines actuarial equivalence using 6% interest and the applicable mortality table under section 417(e)(3) and § 1.417(e)-1(d)(2) that applies as of January 1, 1995, is using reasonable actuarial assumptions. The examples are as follows:

Example 1. (i) Participant M participates in Plan A, a qualified defined benefit plan. Under Plan A, the QJSA is a joint and 100% survivor annuity, which is actuarially equivalent to the single life annuity determined using 6% interest and the section 417(e)(3) applicable mortality table that applies as of January 1, 1995. On January 1, 2004, M will terminate employment at age 55. When M terminates employment, M will be eligible to elect an unreduced early retirement benefit, payable as either a life annuity or the QJSA. M will also be eligible to elect a single-sum distribution equal to the actuarial present value of the single life annuity payable at normal retirement age (age 65), determined using the applicable mortality table and the applicable interest rate under section 417(e)(3).

(ii) Participant M is provided with a QJSA explanation that describes the single life annuity, the QJSA, and single-sum distribution option under the plan, and any eligibility conditions associated with these options. The explanation indicates that, if Participant M commenced benefits at age 55 and had a spouse age 55, the monthly benefit under an immediately commencing single life annuity is $3,000, the monthly benefit under the QJSA is estimated to be 89.96% of the monthly benefit under the immediately commencing single life annuity or $2,699, and the single sum is estimated to be 74.7645 times the monthly benefit under the immediately commencing single life annuity or $224,293.

(iii) The QJSA explanation indicates that the single life annuity and the QJSA are of approximately the same value, but that the single-sum option is equivalent in value to a QJSA of $1,215. (This amount is 45% of the value of the QJSA at age 55 ($1,215 divided by 89.96% of $3,000 equals 45%).) The explanation states that the relative value comparison converts the value of the single life annuity and the single-sum options to the value of each if paid in the form of the QJSA and that this conversion uses interest and life expectancy assumptions. The explanation specifies that the calculations relating to the single-sum distribution were prepared using 5.5% interest and average life expectancy, that the other calculations were prepared using a 6% interest rate and that the relative value of actual annuity payments for an individual can vary

depending on how long the individual and spouse live. The explanation notes that the calculation of the QJSA assumed that the spouse was age 55, that the amount of the QJSA will depend on the actual age of the spouse (for example, annuity payments will be significantly lower if the spouse is significantly younger than the participant), and that the amount of the single-sum payment will depend on the interest rates that apply when the participant actually takes a distribution. The explanation also includes an offer to provide a more precise calculation to the participant taking into account the spouse's actual age.

(iv) Participant M requests a more precise calculation of the financial effect of choosing a QJSA, taking into the actual age of Participant M's spouse. Based on the fact that M's spouse is age 50, Plan A determines that the monthly payments under the QJSA are 87.62% of the monthly payments under the single life annuity, or $2,628.60 per month, and provides this information to M. Plan A is not required to provide an updated calculation of the relative value of the single sum because the value of single sum continues to be 45% of the value of the QJSA.

Example 2. (i) The facts are the same as in *Example 1*, except that under Plan A, the single-sum distribution is determined as the actuarial present value of the immediately commencing single life annuity. In addition, Plan A provides a joint and 75% survivor annuity that is reduced from the single life annuity and that is the QJSA under Plan A. For purposes of determining the amount of the QJSA, the reduction is only half of the reduction that would normally apply under the actuarial assumptions specified in Plan A for determining actuarial equivalence of optional forms.

(ii) In lieu of providing information specific to Participant M in the QJSA notice as set forth in paragraph (c) of this section, Plan A satisfies the QJSA explanation requirement in accordance with paragraph (d)(2) of this section by providing M with a statement that M's monthly benefit under an immediately commencing single life annuity (which is the normal form of benefit under Plan A, adjusted for immediate commencement) is $3,000, along with the following chart showing the financial effect and the relative value of the optional forms of benefit compared to the QJSA for a hypothetical participant with a $1,000 benefit and a spouse who is three years younger than the participant. For each optional form generally available under the plan, the chart shows the financial effect and the relative value, using the grouping rules of paragraph (c)(2)(ii) of this section. Separate charts are provided for ages 55, 60, and 65.

AGE 55 COMMENCEMENT

Optional form	Amount of distribution per $1,000 of immediate single life annuity	Relative value
Life Annuity	$1,000 per month	Approximately the same value as the OJSA.
QJSA (joint and 75% survivor annuity)	$956 per month	n/a.
Joint and 100% survivor annuity	$886 per month	Approximately the same value as the QJSA.
Lump sum	$165,959	Approximately the same value as the QJSA.

AGE 60 COMMENCEMENT

Optional form	Amount of distribution per $1,000 of immediate single life annuity	Relative value
Life Annuity	$1,000 per month	Approximately 94% of the value of the QJSA.
QJSA (joint and 75% survivor annuity)	$945 per month	n/a.
Joint and 100% survivor annuity	$859 per month	Approximately 94% of the value of the QJSA.
Lump sum	$151,691	Approximately the same value as the QJSA.

AGE 65 COMMENCEMENT

Optional form	Amount of distribution per $1,000 of immediate single life annuity	Relative value
Life Annuity	$1,000 per month	Approximately 93% of the value of the QJSA.
QJSA (joint and 75% survivor annuity)	$932 per month	n/a.
Joint and 100% survivor annuity	$828 per month	Approximately 93% of the value of the QJSA.
Lump sum	$135,759	Approximately 93% of the value of the QJSA.

(iii) The chart disclosing the financial effect and relative value of the optional forms specifies that the calculations were prepared assuming that the spouse is three years younger than the participant, that the calculations relating to the single-sum distribution were prepared using 5.5% interest and average life expectancy, that the other calculations were prepared using a 6% interest rate, and that the relative value of actual payments for an individual can vary depending on how long the individual and spouse live. The explanation states that the relative value

comparison converts the QJSA, the single life annuity, the joint and 100% survivor annuity, and the single-sum options to an equivalent present value and that this conversion uses interest and life expectancy assumptions. The explanation notes that the calculation of the QJSA depends on the actual age of the spouse (for example, annuity payments will be significantly lower if the spouse is significantly younger than the participant), and that the amount of the single-sum payment will depend on the interest rates that apply when the participant actually takes a distribution. The explanation also includes an offer to provide a calculation specific to the participant upon request.

(iv) Participant M requests information regarding the amounts payable under the QJSA, the joint and 100% survivor annuity, and the single sum.

(v) Based on the information about the age of Participant M's spouse, Plan A determines that M's QJSA is $2,856.30 per month, the joint and 100% survivor annuity is $2,628.60 per month, and the single sum is $497,876. The actuarial present value of the QJSA (determined using the 5.5% interest and the section 417(e)(3) applicable mortality table, the actuarial assumptions required under section 417) is $525,091. Accordingly, the value of the single-sum distribution available to M at January 1, 2004, is 94.8% of the actuarial present value of the QJSA. In addition, the actuarial present value of the life annuity and the 100% joint and survivor annuity are 95.0% of the actuarial present value of the QJSA.

(vi) Plan A provides M with a QJSA explanation that incorporates these more precise calculations of the financial effect and relative value of the optional forms for which M requested information.

(f) *Effective date.* This section applies to QJSA explanations provided with respect to distributions with annuity starting dates on or after January 1, 2004, and to QPSA explanations provided on or after January 1, 2004.

§ *1.417(e)-1 [Amended]*

Par. 5. In § 1.417(e)-1, paragraph (b)(2) is amended by removing the language "§ 1.401(a)-20 Q&A-36" and adding "§ 1.417(a)(3)-1" in its place.

Robert E. Wenzel

Deputy Commissioner of Internal Revenue.

¶ 20,260Q

IRS proposed regulations: Travel expenses: Business expenses: Expense substantiation.—The IRS has issued proposed amendments to regulations under Code Sec. 62, relating to substantiation requirements for reimbursement of business travel expenses, to allow them to conform to cross-referenced regulations under Code Sec. 274. Comments from the public are requested.

The proposed amendments to regulations, were published in the *Federal Register* on November 12, 2002 (67 FR 68539).

IRS final regulations 1.62-2 and 1.274-5, temporary regulation 1.274-5T, and the preamble to the regulations appear at ¶ 11,182, ¶ 11,357B, ¶ 11,357G and ¶ 23,206 respectively. The final and temporary regulations were published in the *Federal Register* on July 1, 2003 (68 FR 39011).

¶ 20,260R

IRS proposed regulations: brokers: information reporting: taxable stock transactions.—The IRS has issued proposed regulations by cross-reference to temporary regulations that contain guidance concerning information reporting requirements for brokers with respect to changes in control and recapitalizations. Comments must be received by February 18, 2003. Topics to be covered at the public hearing (to be held on March 5, 2003), must be received by February 12, 2003.

The proposed regulations were published in the Federal Register on November 18, 2002 (67 FR 69496). They were withdrawn (68 FR 75182, December 30, 2003) upon the publication of revised temporary regulations in the Federal Register on December 30, 2003 (68 FR 75119). The preamble to the revised temporary regulations appears at ¶ 23,216. Portions of the temporary regulations are reproduced at ¶ 13,688D.

¶ 20,260S

IRS proposed regulations: Age discrimination requirements: Cash balance conversions.—The IRS has issued proposed regulations regarding the age discrimination requirements applicable to certain retirement plans, under which accruals and allocations cannot be ceased or reduced because of the attainment of any age. Until this regulation is finalized, the IRS will not process technical advice on the effect of cash balance conversions on the plan's qualified status. Comments must be received by March 13, 2003 for the public hearing to be held on April 10, 2003.

The proposed regulations, which were published in the Federal Register on December 11, 2002 (67 FR 76123), are reproduced below. Proposed Reg. Sec. 1.401(a)(4) was withdrawn by the IRS, as set forth in IRS Announcement 2003-22 (CCH Pension Plan Guide ¶ 17,097S-15).

Note: The proposed regulations were withdrawn by Announcement 2004-57 (see CCH Pension Plan Guide ¶ 17,097S-45).

¶ 20,260T

IRS proposed regulations: Split-dollar life insurance: Tax-free compensation.—The IRS has issued proposed regulations supplementing previous guidance in proposed regulations (see CCH Pension Plan Guide ¶ 20,260M) on the valuation of certain equity split-dollar life insurance arrangements, designed to prevent companies from using such arrangements to provide tax-free compensation to executives. The IRS is requesting comments on the clarity of the proposed regulations. Comments must be received by July 8, 2003 for the public hearing to be held on July 29, 2003.

The proposed regulations, which were published in the *Federal Register* on May 9, 2003 (68 FR 24898), were reproduced below. Final regulations were published in the Federal Register on September 17, 2003 (68 FR 54336). The preamble to the final regulations is at ¶ 23,214. The final regulations are at ¶ 11,177 and ¶ 11,246.

20,260U

IRS proposed regulations: Deemed IRAs: Qualified plans: 401(k) plans: Treatment of assets.—The IRS has issued proposed regulations containing guidance for employers that wish to adopt deemed IRAs under their employee benefit plans. Qualified employer plans, such as 401(k) plans and deemed IRAs are to be treated as separate entities subject to separate rules applicable to qualified plans and IRAs.

The proposed regulations, which were published in the *Federal Register* on May 20, 2003 (68 FR 27493), were previously reproduced at this paragraph.

The final and temporary regulations, which were published in the *Federal Register* on July 22, 2004 (69 FR 43735), are reproduced at ¶ 12,054 (IRS Reg. Sec. 1.408-2), ¶ 12,054A (IRS Reg. Sec. 1.408-2T) and ¶ 12,070(IRS Reg. Sec. 1.408(q)-1).The preamble to the regulations is found at ¶ 23,219.

¶20,260Q

¶ 20,260V

IRS proposed regulations: Method of accounting: Uniform capitalization rules: Adjustment periods.—The IRS has proposed amendments to the change of accounting method regulations under the Code Sec. 263A uniform capitalization rules, so that they conform to general IRS guidance on changes of accounting method. The amendments would allow those changing their accounting method to take any adjustment under Code Sec. 481(a) over the same number of taxable years as is provided under general guidance. Comments on the proposed amendments must be received by July 11, 2003 for the public hearing to be held on August 13, 2003.

The proposed amendment to regulations, published in the Federal Register on May 12, 2003 (68 FR 25310), is reproduced below.

DEPARTMENT OF THE TREASURY

Internal Revenue Service

26 CFR Part 1

[REG-142605-02]

RIN 1545-BB47

Administration Simplification of Section 481(a) Adjustment Periods in Various Regulations

AGENCY: Internal Revenue Service (IRS), Treasury.

ACTION: Notice of proposed rulemaking and notice of public hearing.

SUMMARY: This document contains proposed amendments to regulations under sections 263A and 448 of the Internal Revenue Code. The amendments apply to taxpayers changing a method of accounting under the regulations and are necessary to conform the rules governing those changes to the rules provided in general guidance issued by the IRS for changing a method of accounting. Specifically, the amendments will allow taxpayers changing their method of accounting under the regulations to take any adjustment under section 481(a) resulting from the change into account over the same number of taxable years that is provided in the general guidance.

DATES: Written or electronic comments must be received by July 11, 2003. Requests to speak (with outlines of oral comments to be discussed) at the public hearing scheduled for August 13, 2003, at 10 a.m. must be received by July 23, 2003.

ADDRESSES: Send submissions to: CC:PA:RU (REG-142605-02), room 5226, Internal Revenue Service, POB 7604 Ben Franklin Station, Washington, DC 20044. Submissions of comments may also be hand-delivered Monday through Friday between the hours of 8 a.m. and 5 p.m. to: CC:PA:RU (REG-142605-02), Courier's Desk, Internal Revenue Service, 1111 Constitution Avenue, NW., Washington, DC. Alternatively, taxpayers may submit comments electronically via the Internet direct to the IRS Internet site at http://www.irs.gov/regs. The public hearing will be held in the Internal Revenue Building, 1111 Constitution Avenue, NW., Washington, DC.

FOR FURTHER INFORMATION CONTACT: Concerning the regulations, Christian Wood, 202-622-4930. Concerning the hearing, contact Sonya Cruse, 202-622-7180 (not toll-free numbers).

SUPPLEMENTARY INFORMATION:

Background

This document contains proposed amendments to 26 CFR part 1 under sections 263A and 448. These amendments pertain to the period for taking into account the adjustment required under section 481 to prevent duplications or omissions of amounts resulting from a change in method of accounting under section 263A or 448.

Section 263A (the uniform capitalization rules) generally requires the capitalization of direct costs and indirect costs properly allocable to real property and tangible personal property produced by a taxpayer. Section 263A also requires the capitalization of direct costs and indirect costs properly allocable to real property and personal property acquired by a taxpayer for resale.

Section 448(a) generally prohibits the use of the cash receipts and disbursements method of accounting by C corporations, partnerships with a C corporation partner, and tax shelters. Section 448(b), however, provides exceptions to this general rule in the case of farming businesses, qualified personal service corporations, and entities with gross receipts of not more than $ 5,000,000.

Section 446(e) generally provides that a taxpayer that changes the method of accounting on the basis of which it regularly computes its income in keeping its books must, before computing its taxable income under the new method, secure the consent of the Secretary.

Section 481(a) generally provides that a taxpayer must take into account those adjustments that are determined to be necessary solely by reason of a change in method of accounting in order to prevent amounts from being duplicated or omitted. Sections 481(c) and 1.446-1(e)(3)(ii) and 1.481-4 provide that the adjustment required by

section 481(a) shall be taken into account in determining taxable income in the manner and subject to the conditions agreed to by the Commissioner and the taxpayer.

Rev. Proc. 97-27, 1997-1 C.B. 680 (as modified and amplified by Rev. Proc. 2002-19, 2002-13 I.R.B. 696, and modified by Rev. Proc. 2002-54, 2002-35 I.R.B. 432), provides procedures under which taxpayers may apply for the advance consent of the Commissioner to change a method of accounting. Rev. Proc. 2002-9, 2002-3 I.R.B. 327 (as modified and amplified by Rev. Proc. 2002-19, amplified, clarified, and modified by Rev. Proc. 2002-54, and modified and clarified by Announcement 2002-17, 2002-8 I.R.B. 561), provides procedures under which taxpayers may apply for automatic consent of the Commissioner to change a method of accounting. Under both revenue procedures, as modified, adjustments under section 481(a) are taken into account entirely in the year of change (in the case of a net negative adjustment) and over 4 taxable years (in the case of a net positive adjustment), subject to certain exceptions.

Explanation of Provisions

Regulations under sections 263A and 448 currently provide rules for certain changes in method of accounting under those sections, including the number of taxable years over which an adjustment required under section 481(a) to effect the change is to be taken into account. The adjustment periods provided in the regulations may differ from the general 4-year (net positive adjustment) and 1 year (net negative adjustment) adjustment period rule provided in Rev. Proc. 97-27 and Rev. Proc. 2002-9, as modified. In certain cases, the difference creates a disincentive for certain taxpayers to change their method of accounting in the taxable year required by the regulations under section 263A or 448, as applicable.

The IRS and Treasury Department believe it is appropriate to amend the regulations under sections 263A and 448 to provide that the section 481(a) adjustment period for accounting method changes under those regulations be determined under the applicable administrative procedures issued by the Commissioner (namely, Rev. Proc. 97-27 and Rev. Proc. 2002-9, as modified, or successors). As a result of the amendment, the section 481(a) adjustment period for these changes generally will be 4 years for a net positive adjustment and 1 year for a net negative adjustment, unless otherwise provided in the regulations (see e.g., Sec. 1.448-(g)(2)(ii) and (g)(3)(iii) (providing rules for extended or accelerated adjustment periods in certain cases)) or the applicable revenue procedure (see e.g., section 7.03 of Rev. Proc. 97-27 and section 5.04(3) of Rev. Proc. 2002-9 (providing rules for accelerated adjustment periods in certain cases)). The IRS and Treasury Department believe that amending the regulations in this manner will eliminate the disincentive that currently exists and provide flexibility in the event that any future changes are made to the general section 481(a) adjustment periods.

The IRS and Treasury Department further believe it is appropriate to remove the special adjustment period rule for cooperatives in Sec. 1.448-1(g)(3)(ii), thus directing cooperatives to the rules in Rev. Proc. 97-27 or Rev. Proc. 2002-9, as modified, or successors. Currently, Rev. Proc. 97-27 (section 7.03(2)) and Rev. Proc. 2002-9 (section 5.04(3)(b)) provide that the section 481(a) adjustment period in the case of a cooperative (within the meaning of section 1381(a)) generally is 1 year, whether the net adjustment is positive or negative. The IRS and Treasury Department continue to believe that a 1 year adjustment period is appropriate in the case of accounting method changes by cooperatives. See Rev. Rul. 79-45, 1979-1 C.B. 284.

The IRS and Treasury Department contemplate issuing separate guidance on accounting method changes under section 381. Comments are requested on issues to be addressed in such guidance, including (1) whether the section 481(a) adjustment should be taken into account by the acquired corporation immediately prior to the transaction or the acquiring corporation immediately after the transaction; (2) whether the general section 481(a) adjustment periods of Rev. Proc. 97-27 and Rev. Proc. 2002-9, as modified, or successors, should apply to accounting method changes under section 381; (3) the method for computing the section 481(a) adjustment; (4) whether accounting method changes under section 381 should be requested by filing a Form 3115 or by requesting a private letter ruling; and (5) any other procedural or technical issues (e.g., filing deadlines, audit protection).

Proposed Effective Date

The proposed regulations are applicable to taxable years ending on or after the date these regulations are published as final regulations. However, taxpayers may rely on the proposed regulations for taxable years ending on or after May 12, 2003, by filing a Form 3115, Application for Change of Accounting Method, in the time and manner provided in the regulations (in the case of a change in method of accounting under section 448) or applicable administrative procedure (in the case of a change in method of accounting under section 263A) for such a taxable year that reflects a section 481(a) adjustment period that is consistent with the proposed regulations.

Special Analyses

It has been determined that this notice of proposed rulemaking is not a significant regulatory action as defined in EO 12866. Therefore, a regulatory assessment is not required. It also has been determined that section 553(b) of the Administrative Procedure Act (5 U.S.C. chapter 5) and because this proposed rule does not impose a collection of information on small entities, the provisions of the Regulatory Flexibility Act (5 U.S.C. chapter 6) do not apply. Pursuant to section 7805(f) of the Internal Revenue Code, this notice of proposed rulemaking will be submitted to the Chief Counsel for Advocacy of the Small Business Administration for comment on its impact on small business.

Comments and Public Hearing

Before these proposed regulations are adopted as final regulations, consideration will be given to any written (a signed original and eight (8) copies) or electronic comments that are submitted timely to the IRS. The IRS and Treasury Department request comments on the clarity of the proposed rules and how they can be made easier to understand. All comments will be available for public inspection and copying.

A public hearing has been scheduled for August 13, 2003 beginning at 10 a.m. in the Internal Revenue Building, 1111 Constitution Avenue, NW., Washington, DC. Due to building security procedures, visitors must enter at the Constitution Avenue entrance. In addition, all visitors must present photo identification to enter the building. Because of access restrictions, visitors will not be admitted beyond the immediate entrance area more than 30 minutes before the hearing starts. For information about having your name placed on the building access list to attend the hearing, see the FOR FURTHER INFORMATION CONTACT section of this preamble.

The rules of 26 CFR 601.601(a)(3) apply to the hearing. Persons who wish to present oral comments at the hearing must submit electronic or written comments and an outline of the topics to be discussed and the time to be devoted to each topic (signed original and eight (8) copies) by July 11, 2003.

A period of 10 minutes will be allotted to each person for making comments. An agenda showing the scheduling of the speakers will be prepared after the deadline for receiving outlines has passed. Copies of the agenda will be available free of charge at the hearing.

Drafting Information

The principal authors of these proposed regulations are Christian T. Wood and Grant Anderson of the Office of Associate Chief Counsel (Income Tax and Accounting). However, other personnel from the IRS and Treasury Department participated in their development.

List of Subjects in 26 CFR Part 1

Income taxes, Reporting and record keeping requirements.

Proposed Amendments to the Regulations

Accordingly, 26 CFR part 1 is proposed to be amended as follows:

PART 1—INCOME TAXES

Paragraph 1. The authority citation for part 1 continues to read in part as follows:

Authority: 26 U.S.C. 7805 * * *

Par. 2. In Sec. 1.263A-7, paragraph (b)(2)(ii) is revised to read as follows:

§ 1.263A-7 *Changing a method of accounting under section 263A.*

* * * * *

(b) * * *

(2) * * *

(ii) *Adjustment required by section 481(a).* In the case of any taxpayer required or permitted to change its method of accounting for any taxable year under section 263A and the regulations thereunder, the change will be treated as initiated by the taxpayer for purposes of the adjustment required by section 481(a). The taxpayer must take the net section 481(a) adjustment into account over the section 481(a) adjustment period as determined under the applicable administrative procedures issued under Sec. 1.446-1(e)(3)(ii) for obtaining the Commissioner's consent to a change in accounting method (e.g., Revenue Procedures 97-27 and 2002-9, or successors). This paragraph is effective for taxable years ending on or after the date these regulations are published as final regulations in the Federal Register. However, taxpayers may rely on this paragraph for taxable years ending on or after May 12, 2003, by filing, under the applicable administrative procedure, a Form 3115, Application for Change in Accounting Method, for such a taxable year that reflects a section 481(a) adjustment period that is consistent with this paragraph.

* * * * *

¶ 20,260W

IRS proposed regulations: Incentive stock options: Employee stock purchase plans: Statutory stock options.—The IRS issued proposed regulations that provide guidance and clarification regarding the transfer of stock pursuant to the exercise of incentive stock options and the exercise of options granted pursuant to an employee stock purchase plan (statutory options). The proposed regulations were meant to provide a comprehensive set of rules governing stock options, and provide additional guidance concerning circumstances in which stockholder approval is required.

The proposed regulations were published in the Federal Register on June 9, 2003 (68 FR 34344).

Final regulations were published in the Federal Register on August 3, 2004 (69 FR 46401). The preamble is at ¶ 23,220. The regulations are at ¶ 13,107, ¶ 13,108, ¶ 13,124A, ¶ 13,124B, ¶ 13,125, ¶ 13,125A, 13,125B, ¶ 13,131, ¶ 13,132, ¶ 13,151, and ¶ 13,671A. For statutory options granted on or before June 9, 2003, taxpayers may rely on the 1984 proposed regulations (¶ 20,150E), the 2003 regulations, or the 2004 final regulations until the earlier of January 1, 2006, or the first regularly scheduled stockholders meeting of the granting corporation occurring six months after August 3, 2004. For statutory options granted after June 9, 2003 and before the earlier of January 1, 2006, or the first regularly scheduled stockholders meeting of the granting corporation occurring six months after August 3, 2004, taxpayers may rely on either the proposed regulations or the final regulations.

¶ 20,260X

IRS proposed regulations: Compensatory stock options: Nonstatutory stock options: Listed transactions: Related parties: Federal income taxes: Federal employment taxes.—The IRS has issued proposed regulations containing a comment request on final and temporary regulations that are designed to halt arrangements involving the transfer of compensatory stock options by executives to related parties in an attempt to avoid federal taxes. Comments must be received by September 30, 2003.

The proposed regulations, which were published in the *Federal Register* on July 2, 2003 (68 FR 39498) and corrected on September 4, 2003 (68 FR 52544), are reproduced below.

DEPARTMENT OF THE TREASURY   Internal Revenue Service

¶20,260W

26 CFR Part 1

[REG-116914-03]

RIN 1545-BC06

Transfers of Compensatory Options

AGENCY: Internal Revenue Service (IRS), Treasury.

ACTION: Notice of proposed rulemaking by cross-reference to temporary regulations.

SUMMARY: In the Rules and Regulations section of this issue of the **Federal Register**, the IRS is issuing temporary regulations relating to the sale or other disposition of compensatory nonstatutory stock options to related persons. The text of those regulations also serves as the text of these proposed regulations.

DATES: Written or electronic comments and requests for a public hearing must be received by September 30, 2003.

ADDRESSES: Send submissions to: CC:PA:RU (REG-116914-03), room 5226, Internal Revenue Service, POB 7604, Ben Franklin Station, Washington, DC., 20044. Submissions may be hand delivered Monday through Friday between the hours of 8 a.m. and 4 p.m. to: CC:PA:RU (REG-116914-03), Courier's Desk, Internal Revenue Service, 1111 Constitution Ave., NW., Washington, DC. Alternatively, taxpayers may submit electronic comments directly to the IRS Internet site at www.irs.gov/regs.

FOR FURTHER INFORMATION CONTACT: Concerning the temporary regulations, Stephen Tackney (202) 622-6030; concerning submissions of comments and/or requests for a hearing, Guy Traynor, (202) 622-7180 (not toll-free numbers).

SUPPLEMENTARY INFORMATION:

Background and Explanation of Provisions

Temporary regulations in the Rules and Regulations section of this issue of the **Federal Register** amend 26 CFR part 1. The regulations provide that a sale or other disposition of a nonstatutory stock option to a related person will not be treated as a transaction that closes the application of section 83 with respect to the option. The text of the temporary regulations also serves as the text of these proposed regulations. The preamble to the temporary regulations explains the temporary regulations and these proposed regulations.

Special Analyses

It has been determined that these proposed regulations are not a significant regulatory action as defined in Executive order 12866. Therefore, a regulatory assessment is not required. It also has been determined that section 533(b) of the Administrative Procedures Act (5 U.S.C. chapter 5) does not apply to these regulations, and because these regulations do not impose a collection of information on small entities, the Regulatory Flexibility Act (5 U.S.C. chapter 6) does not apply. Pursuant to section 7805(f) of the Internal Revenue Code, these regulations are being submitted to the Chief Counsel for Advocacy of the Small Business Administration for comment on their impact on small business. [Corrected by IRS on 9/4/03 by 68 FR 52544.]

Comments and Requests for a Public Hearing

Before these proposed regulations are adopted as final regulations, consideration will be given to any written comments (a signed original and eight (8) copies) or electronic comments that are submitted timely to the IRS. The IRS and Treasury Department request comments on the clarity of the proposed rules and how they can be made easier to understand. The IRS and Treasury Department specifically request comments on the clarity and efficacy of the proposed definition of a related person. All comments will be available for public inspection and copying. A public hearing may be scheduled if requested by any person that timely submits written comments. If a public hearing is scheduled, notice of the date, time, and place for the public hearing will be published in the **Federal Register**.

Drafting Information

The principal author of these proposed regulations is Stephen Tackney of the Office of Division Counsel/Associate Chief Counsel (Tax Exempt and Government Entities). However, other personnel from the IRS and Treasury Department participated in their development.

List of Subjects in 26 CFR Part 1

Income taxes, Reporting and recordkeeping requirements.

Adoption of Amendments to the Regulations

Accordingly, 26 CFR part 1 is proposed to be amended as follows:

PART 1—INCOME TAXES

Paragraph 1. The authority citation for part 1 continues to read as follows:

Authority: 26 U.S.C. 7805 ***

Par. 2. Section 1.83-7 is amended as follows:

1. Paragraph (a) is amended by adding a sentence at the end.

2. Paragraphs (a)(1) and (a)(2) are added.

3. Paragraph (d) is added.

The additions read as follows:

(a) [The text of proposed §1.83-7(a) is the same as the text of §1.83-7T(a) published elsewhere in this issue of the **Federal Register**].

*****

(d) *Effective dates*. This section is applicable to sales or other dispositions of options on or after the publication of final regulations in the **Federal Register**. For dates on or after July 2, 2003, see §1.83-7T(d).

Deputy Commissioner of Internal Revenue.

Robert E. Wenzel,

DALE D. GOODE

CERTIFIED COPY

¶ 20,260Y

IRS proposed regulations: Distributions: Defined contribution plans: Elimination of optional forms of benefit: Anti-cutback rule.—The IRS has issued proposed regulations that would modify the circumstances under which the elimination of certain forms of defined contribution plan distributions is permitted.

The proposed regulations, which were published in the *Federal Register* on July 8, 2003 (68 FR 40581) and amended September 19, 2003 (68 FR 54876), are reproduced below.

DEPARTMENT OF THE TREASURY

Internal Revenue Service

26 CFR Part 1

[REG-112039-03]

RIN 1545-BC35

Elimination of Forms of Distribution in Defined Contribution Plans

AGENCY: Internal Revenue Service (IRS), Treasury.

ACTION: Notice of proposed rulemaking.

SUMMARY: This document contains proposed regulations that would modify the circumstances under which certain forms of distribution previously available are permitted to be eliminated from qualified defined contribution plans. These proposed regulations affect qualified retirement plan sponsors, administrators, and participants. [Amended September 19, 2003, 68 FR 54876.]

DATES: Written and electronic comments and requests for a public hearing must be received by October 6, 2003.

ADDRESSES: Send submissions to: CC:PA:RU (REG-112039-03), room 5226, Internal Revenue Service, POB 7604, Ben Franklin Station, Washington, DC 20044. Submissions may be hand delivered Monday through Friday between the hours of 8 a.m. and 5 p.m. to: CC:PA:RU (REG-112039-03), Courier's Desk, Internal Revenue Service, 1111 Constitution Avenue NW., Washington, DC. Alternatively, taxpayers may submit comments electronically directly to the IRS Internet site at: www.irs.gov/regs.

FOR FURTHER INFORMATION CONTACT: Concerning the regulations, Vernon S. Carter, 202-622-6060 (not a toll-free number); concerning submissions or hearing requests, Guy Traynor, 202-622-7180 (not a toll-free number).

SUPPLEMENTARY INFORMATION:

Explanation of Provisions

This document contains proposed amendments to 26 CFR part 1 under section 411(d)(6) of the Internal Revenue Code of 1986 (Code) as amended by the Economic Growth and Tax Relief Reconciliation Act of 2001 (EGTRRA) (115 Stat. 117). Section 411(d)(6)(A) of the Code generally provides that a plan will not be treated as satisfying the requirements of section 411 if the accrued benefit of a participant is decreased by a plan amendment. Section 411(d)(6)(B) prior to amendment by EGTRRA provided that an amendment is treated as reducing an accrued benefit if, with respect to benefits accrued before the amendment is adopted, the amendment has the effect of either eliminating or reducing an early retirement benefit or a retirement-type subsidy, or, except as provided by regulations, eliminating an optional form of benefit.

The IRS published TD 8900 in the **Federal Register** on September 6, 2000 (65 FR 53901). TD 8900, which amended § 1.411(d)-4 of the Income Tax Regulations, added paragraph (e) of Q&A-2 to provide for additional circumstances under which a defined contribution plan can be amended to eliminate or restrict a participant's right to receive payment of accrued benefits under certain optional forms of benefit.

Section 1.411(d)-4, Q&A-2(e)(1) provides that a defined contribution plan may be amended to eliminate or restrict a participant's right to receive payment of accrued benefits under a particular optional form of benefit without violating the section 411(d)(6) anti-cutback rules if, once the plan amendment takes effect for a participant, the alternative forms of payment that remain available to the participant include payment in a single-sum distribution form that is "otherwise identical" to the eliminated or restricted optional form of benefit. The amendment cannot apply to a participant for any distribution with an annuity starting date before the earlier of the 90th day after the participant receives a summary that reflects the plan amendment and that satisfies Department of Labor's requirements for a summary of material modifications under 29 CFR 2520.104b-3, or the first day of the second plan year following the plan year in which the amendment is adopted.Section § 1.411(d)-4, Q&A-2(e)(2) provides that a single-sum distribution form is "otherwise identical" to the optional form of benefit that is being eliminated or restricted only if it is identical in all respects (or would be identical except that it provides greater rights to the participant), except for the timing of payments after commencement. A single-sum distribution form is not "otherwise identical" to a specified installment form of benefit if the single-sum form:

is not available for distribution on any date on which the installment form could have commenced;

is not available in the same medium as the installment form; or

imposes any additional condition of eligibility.

Further, an otherwise identical distribution form need not retain any rights or features of the eliminated or restricted optional form of benefit to the extent those rights or features would not be protected from elimination under the anti-cutback rules. The single-sum distribution form would not, however, be disqualified from being an otherwise identical distribution form if the single-sum form provides greater rights to participants than did the eliminated or restricted optional form of benefits.

Section 645(a)(1) of EGTRRA revised section 411(d)(6) in a manner that is similar to § 1.411(d)-4, Q&A-2(e), but without the advance notice condition. Section 411(d)(6)(E) of the Code provides that, except to the extent provided in regulations, a defined contribution plan is not treated as reducing a participant's accrued benefit where a plan amendment eliminates a form of distribution previously available under the plan if a single-sum distribution is available to the participant at the same time as the form of distribution eliminated by the amendment, and the single-sum distribution is based on the same or greater portion of the participant's account as the form of distribution eliminated by the amendment.

To reflect the addition of section 411(d)(6)(E) by EGTRRA, these proposed regulations would amend § 1.411(d)-4, Q&A-2(e). Under these amendments, the regulations would retain the rules under which a defined contribution plan may be amended to eliminate or restrict a participant's right to receive payment of accrued benefits under a particular optional form of benefit without violating the section 411(d)(6) anti-cutback rules if, once the plan amendment takes effect for a participant, the alternative forms of payment that remain available to the participant include payment in a single-sum distribution. However, these proposed regulations would remove the 90-day notice condition previously applicable to these plan amendments.[1]

Under section 101 of Reorganization Plan No. 4 of 1978 (43 FR 47713), the Secretary of the Treasury has interpretive jurisdiction over the subject matter addressed in these regulations for purposes of the Employee Retirement Income Security Act of 1974 (ERISA), as well as the Code. Section 204(g)(2) of ERISA, as amended by EGTRRA, provides a parallel rule to section 411(d)(6)(E) of the Code that applies under Title I of ERISA, and authorizes the Secretary of the Treasury to provide exception to this parallel ERISA requirement. Therefore, these regulations apply for purposes of the parallel requirements of sections 204(g)(2) of ERISA, as well as for section 411(d)(6)(E) of the Code.

Effective Date and Applicability Date

The proposed regulations are proposed to apply on the date of publication of final regulations in the **Federal Register**.

Special Analyses

It has been determined that this Treasury decision is not a significant regulatory action as defined in Executive Order 12866. Therefore, a regulatory assessment is not required. It also has been determined that section 553(b) of the Administrative Procedure Act (5 U.S.C. chapter 5) does not apply to these regulations, and because the regulation does not impose a collection of information on small entities, the Regulatory Flexibility Act (5 U.S.C. chapter 6) does not apply. Pursuant to section 7805(f) of the Code, this notice of proposed rulemaking will be submitted to the Chief Counsel for Advocacy of the Small Business Administration for comment on its impact on small business.

Drafting Information

The principal author of these regulations is Vernon S. Carter of the Office of the Division Counsel/Associate Chief Counsel (Tax Exempt and Government Entities). However, other personnel from the IRS and Treasury participated in their development.

List of Subjects in 26 CFR Parts 1

Income taxes, Reporting and recordkeeping requirements.

Amendments to the Regulations

Accordingly, 26 CFR part 1 is proposed to be amended as follows:

Paragraph 1. The authority citation for part 1 is amended to read in part as follows:

Authority: 26 U.S.C. 7805 * * *

Section 1.411(d)-4, Q&A-2(e) also issued under 26 U.S.C. 411(d)(6)(E). * * *

Par. 2. Section 1.411(d)-4, Q&A-2(e) is revised to read as follows:

§ 1.411(d)-4 Section 411(d)(6) protected benefits.

* * * * *

A-2: * * *

(e) *Permitted plan amendments affecting alternative forms of payment under defined contribution plans*—(1) *General rule.* A defined contribution plan does not violate the requirements of section 411(d)(6) merely because the plan is amended to eliminate or restrict the ability of a participant to receive payment of accrued benefits under a particular optional form of benefit if, after the plan amendment is effective with respect to the participant, the alternative forms of payment available to the participant include payment in a single-sum distribution form that is otherwise identical to the optional form of benefit that is being eliminated or restricted.

(2) *Otherwise identical single-sum distribution.* For purposes of this paragraph (e), a single-sum distribution form is otherwise identical to an optional form of benefit that is eliminated or restricted pursuant to paragraph (e)(1) of this Q&A-2 only if the single-sum distribution form is identical in all respects to the eliminated or restricted optional form of benefit (or would be identical except that it provides greater rights to the participant) except with respect to the timing of payments after commencement. For example, a single-sum distribution form is not

---

[1] The Department of Labor has advised Treasury and the IRS that it should be noted that plans covered by Title I of ERISA will continue to be subject to the requirement under Title I that plan amendments be described in a timely summary of material modifications (SMM) or a revised summary plan description (SPD) to be distributed to plan participants and beneficiaries in accordance with applicable Department of Labor disclosure rules (see 29 CFR 2520.104b-3).

otherwise identical to a specified installment form of benefit if the single-sum distribution form is not available for distribution on the date on which the installment form would have been available for commencement, is not available in the same medium of distribution as the installment form, or imposes any condition of eligibility that did not apply to the installment form. However, an otherwise identical distribution form need not retain rights or features of the optional form of benefit that is eliminated or restricted to the extent that those rights or features would not be protected from elimination or restriction under section 411(d)(6) or this section.

(3) *Example.* The following example illustrates the application of this paragraph (e):

Example. (i) P is a participant in Plan M, a qualified profit-sharing plan with a calendar plan year that is invested in mutual funds. The distribution forms available to P under Plan M include a distribution of P's vested account balance under Plan M in the form of distribution of various annuity contract forms (including a single life annuity and a joint and survivor annuity). The annuity payments under the annuity contract forms begin as of the first day of the month following P's severance from employment (or as of the first day of any subsequent month, subject to the requirements of section 401(a)(9)). P has not previously elected payment of benefits in the form of a life annuity, and Plan M is not a direct or indirect transferee of any plan that is a defined benefit plan or a defined contribution plan that is subject to section 412.

Distributions on the death of a participant are made in accordance with plan provisions that comply with section 401(a)(11)(B)(iii)(I). On May 2, 2004, Plan M is amended so that, after the amendment is effective, P is no longer entitled to any distribution in the form of the distribution of an annuity contract. However, after the amendment is effective, P is entitled to receive a single-sum cash distribution of P's vested account balance under Plan M payable as of the first day of the month following P's severance from employment (or as of the first day of any subsequent month, subject to the requirements of section 401(a)(9)). The amendment does not apply to P if P elects to have annuity payments begin before July 1, 2004.

(ii) Plan M does not violate the requirements of section 411(d)(6) (or section 401(a)(11)) merely because, as of July 1, 2004, the plan amendment has eliminated P's option to receive a distribution in any of the various annuity contract forms previously available.

(4) *Effective date.* This paragraph (e) is applicable on the date of publication of final regulations in the **Federal Register**.

*****

Robert R. Wenzel,

Deputy Commissioner for Services and Enforcement.

DALE D. GOODE

CERTIFIED COPY

¶ 20,260Z

IRS proposed regulations: Sale of stock: ESOPs: Statement of purchase: Notarization.—The IRS has proposed amendments to temporary regulations which would affect taxpayers making an election to defer the recognition of gain under Code Sec. 1042 on the sale of stock to an employee stock ownership plan (ESOP). The proposed amendments provide guidance on the notarization requirements of the temporary regulations for statements of purchase.

The proposed regulations, which were published in the *Federal Register* on July 10, 2003 (68 FR 41087), are reproduced below.

DEPARTMENT OF THE TREASURY

Internal Revenue Service

26 CFR Part 1

[REG-121122-03]

RIN 1545-BC11

Notarized Statements of Purchase Under Section 1042

AGENCY: Internal Revenue Service (IRS), Treasury.

ACTION: Notice of proposed rulemaking.

SUMMARY: This document contains proposed amendments to the temporary regulations relating to notarized statements of purchase under section 1042 of the Internal Revenue Code of 1986. The proposed regulations would affect taxpayers making an election to defer the recognition of gain under section 1042 on the sale of stock to an employee stock ownership plan. The proposed regulations provide guidance on the notarization requirements of the temporary regulations.

DATES: Written and electronic comments and requests for a public hearing must be received by October 8, 2003.

ADDRESSES: Send submissions to: CC:PA:RU (REG-121122-03), room 5226, Internal Revenue Service, POB 7604, Ben Franklin Station, Washington, DC 20044. Submissions may be hand delivered Monday through Friday between the hours of 8 a.m. and 4 p.m. to: CC:PA:RU (REG-121122-03), Courier's Desk, Internal Revenue Service, 1111 Constitution Avenue, NW., Washington, DC. Alternatively, taxpayers may submit comments electronically directly to the IRS Internet site at *www.irs.gov/regs*.

FOR FURTHER INFORMATION CONTACT: Concerning the regulations, John T. Ricotta at (202) 622-6060 (not a toll-free number); concerning submissions or hearing requests, Sonya Cruse, (202) 622-7180 (not a toll-free number).

SUPPLEMENTARY INFORMATION:

Background

This document contains proposed amendments to the requirement of § 1.1042-1T, A-3(b) of the Temporary Income Tax regulations that a statement of purchase for qualified replacement property be notarized within 30 days of the date of purchase of the property (30-day notarization requirement).

The temporary regulations under section 1042 were published in TD 8073 on February 4, 1986 (EE-63-84) (51 FR 4312) as part of a package of temporary regulations addressing effective dates and other issues under the Tax Reform Act of 1984. The text of the temporary regulations also served as a notice of proposed rulemaking (EE-96-85) (51 FR 4391). A public hearing was held on June 26, 1986, concerning the proposed regulations.

Explanation of Provisions

Overview

Section 1042(a) provides that a taxpayer or executor may elect in certain cases not to recognize long-term capital gain on the sale of *qualified securities* to an employee stock ownership plan (ESOP) (as defined in section 4975(e)(7)) or eligible worker owned cooperative (as defined in section 1042(c)(2)) if the taxpayer purchases *qualified replacement property* (as defined in section 1042(c)(4)) within the replacement period of section 1042(c)(3) and the requirements of section 1042(b) and § 1.1042-1T of the Temporary Income Tax Regulations are satisfied.

Section 1042(c)(1) provides that the term *qualified securities* means employer securities (as defined in section 409(l)) which are issued by a domestic C corporation that has no stock outstanding that is readily tradable on an established securities market and which were not received by the taxpayer in a distribution from a plan described in section 401(a) or in a transfer pursuant to an option or other right to acquire stock to which section 83, 422, or 423 applied.

A sale of *qualified securities* meets the requirements of section 1042(b) if: (1) the qualified securities are sold to an ESOP (as defined in section 4975(e)(7)), or an eligible worker owned cooperative; (2) the plan or cooperative owns (after application of section 318(a)(4)), immediately after the sale, at least 30 percent of (a) each class of outstanding stock of the corporation (other than stock described in section 1504(a)(4)) which issued the securities or (b) the total value of all outstanding stock of the corporation (other than stock described in section 1504(a)(4)); (3) the taxpayer files with the Secretary a verified written statement of the employer whose employees are covered by the ESOP or an authorized officer of the cooperative consenting to the application of sections 4978 and 4979A (which provide for excise taxes on certain dispositions or allocations of securities acquired in a sale to which section 1042 applies) with respect to such employer or cooperative; and (4) the taxpayer's holding period with respect to the qualified securities is at least three years (determined as of the time of the sale).

The taxpayer must purchase *qualified replacement property* within the *replacement period*, which is defined in section 1042(c)(3) as the period which begins three months before the date on which the sale of qualified securities occurs and ends 12 months after the date of such sale.

Section 1042(c)(4)(A) defines *qualified replacement property* as any security issued by a domestic operating corporation which did not, for the taxable year preceding the taxable year in which such security was purchased, have passive investment income (as defined in section 1362(d)(3)(C)) in excess of 25 percent of the gross receipts of such corporation for such preceding taxable year, and is not the corporation which issued the qualified securities which such security is replacing or a member of the same controlled group of corporations (within the meaning of section 1563(a)(1)) as such corporation.

Section 1042(c)(4)(B) defines an *operating corporation* as a corporation more than 50 percent of the assets of which, at the time the security was purchased or before the close of the replacement period, were used in the active conduct of a trade or business.

Section 1.1042-1T A-3(a) of the Temporary Income Tax Regulations states that the election is to be made in a *statement of election* attached to the taxpayer's income tax return filed on or before the due date (including extensions of time) for the taxable year in which the sale occurs.

Section 1.1042-1T A-3(b) states that the *statement of election* must provide that the taxpayer elects to treat the sale of securities as a sale of qualified securities under section 1042(a) and must contain the following information: (1) A description of the qualified securities sold, including the type and number of shares; (2) The date of the sale of the qualified securities; (3) The adjusted basis of the qualified securities; (4) The amount realized upon the sale of the qualified securities; (5) The identity of the ESOP or eligible worker-owned cooperative to which the qualified securities were sold; and (6) If the sale was part of a single interrelated transaction under a prearranged agreement between taxpayers involving other sales of qualified securities, the names and taxpayer identification numbers of the other taxpayers under the agreement and the number of shares sold by the other taxpayers.

Section 1.1042-1T, A-3(b) further provides that, if the taxpayer has purchased qualified replacement property at the time of the election, the taxpayer must attach as part of the statement of election a *statement of purchase* describing the qualified replacement property, the date of the purchase, and the cost of the property, and declaring such property to be qualified replacement property with respect to the sale of qualified securities.

The statement of purchase must be notarized no later than 30 days after the purchase. The purpose of the statement of purchase is to identify qualified replacement property with respect to a sale of qualified securities. The qualified replacement property will have its cost basis reduced under section 1042(d) to reflect the gain on the sale of qualified securities that is being deferred by the taxpayer. Upon subsequent disposition of the qualified replacement property by the taxpayer, the deferred gain will be recognized by the taxpayer under section 1042(e). Under section 1042(f), the filing of the statement of purchase of qualified replacement property (or a statement of the taxpayer's intention not to purchase replacement property) will begin the statutory period for assessment of any deficiency with respect to gain arising from the sale of the qualified securities. The purpose of the 30-day notarization requirement is to provide a contemporaneous identification of replacement property.

However, the 30-day notarization requirement leads to frequent mistakes by taxpayers and their advisors. Taxpayers are often unaware of this requirement and become aware of it only when they prepare their tax returns for the year of sale to the ESOP. By this time, the 30-day period is typically past because purchases of replacement property may have been made up to one year before. A number of private letter rulings have been issued granting relief to taxpayers in these situations as long as the statements were notarized shortly after the taxpayer became aware of the requirement and it was represented that the property listed was the only replacement property purchased for this sale.

A number of commentators on the temporary and proposed regulations criticized this requirement as without statutory authority, a trap for the unwary, and inconsistent with the definition of the qualified replacement period in section 1042(c)(3).

Proposed Amendment to the Regulations

In order to facilitate taxpayer compliance with the temporary regulations concerning identification of qualified replacement property through notarization of the statements of purchase, the proposed amendment to the temporary regulations would modify § 1.1042-1T, A-3(b) to provide that the notarization requirements for the *statement of purchase* are satisfied if the taxpayer's statement of purchase is notarized not later than the time the taxpayer files the income tax return for the taxable year in which the sale of qualified securities occurred in any case in which any qualified replacement property was purchased by such time and during the qualified replacement period. If qualified replacement property was purchased after such filing date and during the qualified replacement period, the statement of purchase must be notarized not later than the time the taxpayer's income tax return is filed for the taxable year following the year for which the election under section 1042(a) was made.

Proposed Effective Date

The proposed amendments to the temporary regulations would apply to taxable years of sellers ending on or after the date of publication of the Treasury decision adopting these amendments as final regulations in the **Federal Register**. However, taxpayers may rely upon these proposed regulations for guidance with respect to all open taxable years pending the issuance of final regulations. If, and to the extent, future guidance is more restrictive than the guidance in these proposed regulations, the future guidance will be applied without retroactive effect.

Special Analyses

It has been determined that this notice of proposed rulemaking is not a significant regulatory action as defined in Executive Order 12866. Therefore, a regulatory assessment is not required. It also has been determined that section 553(b) of the Administrative Procedure Act (5 U.S.C. chapter 5) does not apply to these regulations, and because these regulations do not impose a collection of information on small entities, the Regulatory Flexibility Act (5 U.S.C. chapter 6) does not apply. Pursuant to section 7805(f) of the Internal Revenue Code, these proposed regulations will be submitted to the Chief Counsel for Advocacy of the Small Business Administration for comment on its impact on small business.

Comments and Public Hearing

Before these proposed regulations are adopted as final regulations, consideration will be given to any written (a signed original and 8 copies) or electronic comments that are submitted timely to the IRS. The IRS and Treasury Department request comments on the clarity of the proposed rules and how they can be made easier to understand. All comments will be available for public inspection and copying. A public hearing will be scheduled if requested in writing by any person that timely submits written comments. If a public hearing is scheduled, notice of the date, time, and place for the public hearing will be published in the **Federal Register**.

Drafting Information

The principal author of these regulations is John T. Ricotta of the Office of the Division Counsel/Associate Chief Counsel (Tax Exempt and Government Entities). However, other personnel from The IRS and Treasury participated in their development.

List of Subjects in 26 CFR Part 1

Income taxes, Reporting and recordkeeping requirements.

Proposed Amendments to The Regulations

Accordingly, 26 CFR part 1 is proposed to be amended as follows:

PART 1—INCOME TAXES

Paragraph 1. The authority citation for part 1 continues to read in part as follows:

Authority: 26 U.S.C. 7805 ***

Par. 2. In § 1.1042-1T, A-3, in the undercgnated paragraph following paragraph (a)(6), the penultimate sentence is removed and three sentences added in its place to read as follows:

§ 1.1042-1T Questions and Answers relating to the sales of stock to employee stock ownership plans or certain cooperatives (temporary).

*****

Q-3. ***

A-3. ***

(a) ***

(6) ***

*** Such statement of purchase must be notarized not later than the time the taxpayer files the income tax return for the taxable year in which the sale of qualified securities occurred in any case in which any qualified replacement property was purchased by such time and during the qualified replacement period. If qualified replacement property is purchased after such filing date but during the qualified replacement period, the statement of purchase must be notarized not later than the time the taxpayer's income tax return is filed for the taxable year following the year for which the election under section 1042(a) was made. The previous two sentences apply to taxable years of sellers ending on or after the date final regulations are published in the Federal Register. ***

*****

Robert E. Wenzel,

Deputy Commissioner for Services and Enforcement

DALE D. GOODE

CERTIFIED COPY

¶ 20,261

IRS proposed regulations: 401(k) plans: Plan administration: Qualified nonelective contributions (QNECs): Non-highly compensated employees (NHCEs).—The IRS has issued proposed regulations implementing modifications that would: prohibit prefunding of elective contributions and matching contributions, eliminate mandatory disaggregation of ESOP and 401(k) portions of a plan for purposes of ADP and ACP testing, and severely restrict the use of "bottom-up" QNECs that enable employers to pass the ADP test by making targeted QNECs to a small group of short-service NHCEs.

The proposed regulations, which were published in the *Federal Register* on July 17, 2003 (68 FR 42476), were previously reproduced below. The final regulations were issued on December 29, 2004 by T.D. 9169 (69 FR 78143). The preamble to the final regulations appears at ¶ 23,224.

¶ 20,261A

IRS proposed regulations: Tax shelters: S corporations: Employee stock ownership plans (ESOPs): Disqualified persons: Nonallocation years: Synthetic equity.—The IRS has issued proposed regulations aimed at abuses by S corporation owners that use the tax exemption on S corporation stock held by ESOPs for inappropriate tax deferral or avoidance. In general, an ESOP holding employer securities consisting of S corporation stock must provide that no portion of plan assets attributable to, or allocable in lieu of, such employer securities may, during a nonallocation year, accrue for the benefit of any disqualified persons. The proposed regulations reflect the text of temporary regulations at ¶ 23,215, which contain guidance on the definition of "disqualified persons" and "synthetic equity," as well as how to determine whether a plan year is a nonallocation year.

The proposed regulations, which were published in the *Federal Register* on July 21, 2003 (68 FR 43058), are reproduced below. Subsequently, temporary and proposed regulations were published in the *Federal Register* on December 17, 2004 (69 FR 75455 and 69 FR 75492, respectively). The preambles are found at ¶ 23,223 (temporary) and ¶ 20,261I (proposed).

DEPARTMENT OF TREASURY

Internal Revenue Service (IRS)

26 CFR Parts 1

[REG-129709-03]

RIN 1545-BC34

Prohibited Allocations of Securities in an S Corporation

AGENCY: Internal Revenue Service (IRS), Treasury.

ACTION: Notice of proposed rulemaking by cross-reference to temporary regulations and notice of public hearing.

SUMMARY: In the Rules and Regulations section of this issue of the **Federal Register**, the IRS is issuing temporary regulations that provide guidance on identifying disqualified persons and determining whether a plan year is a nonallocation year under section 409(p) and on the definition of synthetic equity under section 409(p)(5). These proposed regulations would generally affect plan sponsors of, and participants in, ESOPs holding stock of Subchapter S corporations. The text of those temporary regulations also serves as the text of these proposed regulations. This document also provides notice of a public hearing on these proposed regulations.

DATES: Written or electronic comments must be received by October 20, 2003.

Requests to speak (with outlines of oral comments to be discussed) at the public hearing scheduled for November 20, 2003, at 10 a.m. must be received by October 30, 2003.

ADDRESSES: Send submissions to: CC:PA:RU (REG-129709-03), room 5226, Internal Revenue Service, POB 7604, Ben Franklin Station, Washington, DC 20044. Submissions may be hand delivered Monday through Friday between the hours of 8 a.m. and 4 p.m. to: CC:PA:RU (REG-129709-03), Courier's Desk, Internal Revenue Service, 1111 Constitution Avenue, NW., Washington, DC. Alternatively, taxpayers may submit comments electronically directly to the IRS Internet site at *www.irs.gov/regs*. The public hearing will be held in room 6718.

FOR FURTHER INFORMATION CONTACT: Concerning the proposed regulations, John Ricotta at 622-6060; concerning submissions of comments, Guy Traynor, (202) 622-7180 (not toll-free numbers).

SUPPLEMENTARY INFORMATION:

Background

Temporary regulations in the Rules and Regulations portion of this issue of the **Federal Register** amend the Income Tax Regulations (26 CFR part 1) relating to section 409(p). The temporary regulations contain rules relating to the identification of disqualified persons and determination whether a plan year is a nonallocation year under section 409(p) and the definition of synthetic equity under section 409(p)(5). The text of those temporary regulations also serves as the text of these proposed regulations. The preamble to the temporary regulations explains the temporary regulations.

Special Analyses

It has been determined that this notice of proposed rulemaking is not a significant regulatory action as defined in Executive Order 12866. Therefore, a regulatory assessment is not required. It also has been determined that section 553(b) of the Administrative Procedure Act (5 U.S.C. chapter 5) does not apply to these regulations. Because § 1.409(p)-1 imposes no new collection of information on small entities, a Regulatory Flexibility Analysis under the Regulatory Flexibility Act (5 U.S.C. chapter 6) is not required. Pursuant to section 7805(f) of the Internal Revenue Code, this notice of proposed rulemaking will be submitted to the Chief Counsel for Advocacy of the Small Business Administration for comment on its impact on small business.

Comments and Requests for a Public Hearing

Before these proposed regulations are adopted as final regulations, consideration will be given to any written comments (a signed original and eight (8) copies) that are submitted timely to the IRS. All comments will be available for public inspection and copying.

Comments are requested with respect to issues raised by S corporation ESOPs established by March 14, 2001, that will need to comply with the requirements of section 409(p) beginning in 2005. For these ESOPs, the inclusion of deferred compensation as synthetic equity can be avoided by distributing such deferred compensation before 2005. Some employers may prefer other transition approaches. For example, a preferable transition approach may be to spin off and terminate the portion of a plan benefitting disqualified persons. Comments are requested on whether guidance is needed to address these possible transition approaches.

Comments are also requested on issues that are reserved in the regulations with respect to whether certain interests in an S corporation should be treated as synthetic equity, including the extent to which rights to acquire assets of the S corporation or another person are established for reasonable business purposes and should not be treated as synthetic equity. While comments can be filed as late as October 20, 2003, commentators are encouraged to file comments as early as possible because the IRS and Treasury intend to move forward to address these issues as early as 2003.

Commentators may also wish to comment on section 409(p)-related issues that are not directly raised in the proposed regulations. For example, commentators may wish to comment on the extent to which administrative guidance may be needed on an interim basis to deal with specific structures used to avoid or evade the purpose of section 409(p).

A public hearing has been scheduled for November 20, 2003, at 10 a.m. in room 6718 of the Internal Revenue Building, 1111 Constitution Avenue NW., Washington, DC. All visitors must present photo identification to enter the building. Because of access restrictions, visitors will not be admitted beyond the immediate entrance area more than 30 minutes before the hearing starts at the Constitution Avenue entrance. For information about having your name placed on the building access list to attend the hearing, see the "FOR FURTHER INFORMATION CONTACT" section of this preamble.

The rules of 26 CFR 601.601(a)(3) apply to the hearing. Persons who wish to present oral comments at the hearing must submit written comments and an outline of the topics to be discussed and the time to be devoted to each topic (signed original and eight (8) copies) by October 30, 2003. A period of 10 minutes will be allotted to each person for making comments. An agenda showing the scheduling of the speakers will be prepared after the deadline for receiving outlines has passed. Copies of the agenda will be available free of charge at the hearing.

Drafting Information

The principal author of these regulations is John Ricotta of the Office of the Division Counsel/Associate Chief Counsel (Tax Exempt and Government Entities). However, other personnel from the IRS and Treasury participated in their development.

List of Subjects 26 CFR Part 1

Income taxes, Reporting and recordkeeping requirements.

Proposed Amendments to the Regulations

Accordingly, 26 CFR part 1 is proposed to be amended as follows:

PART 1—INCOME TAXES

Paragraph 1. The authority citation for part 1 is amended by an entry in numerical order to read in part as follows:

Authority: 26 U.S.C. 7805 ***

Section 1.409(p)-1 also issued under 26 U.S.C. 409(p)(7)(A). ***

Par. 2. Section 1.409(p)-1 is added to read as follows:

§ 1.409(p)-1 Prohibited allocation of securities in an S corporation.

[The text of proposed § 1.409(p)-1 is the same as the text of § 1.409(p)-1T published elsewhere in this issue of the **Federal Register**].

Robert E. Wenzel,

Deputy Commissioner for Services and Enforcement.

DALE D. GOODE

CERTIFIED COPY

¶ 20,261B

IRS: Fair market value: Taxation on distributee income: Life insurance contracts.—Reproduced below were the text of a proposed rule which clarified that property distributions must be included in a distributee's income at fair market value even where existing regulations provide merely for the inclusion of the entire cash value. Therefore, where a qualified plan distributes a life insurance contract, retirement income contract, endowment contract, or other contract providing life insurance protection, the fair market value of such a contract is generally included in the distributee's income, as opposed to only the entire cash value of the contract. All rights under the contracts, including supplemental agreements, must be considered in determining fair market value.

The proposed regulation was published in the *Federal Register* on February 17, 2004 (69 FR 7384). Final regulations, which were published in the *Federal Register* on August 29, 2005 (70 FR 50967) are reproduced at ¶ 11,231, ¶ 11,243, and ¶ 11,751. The preamble appears at ¶ 23,230.

[¶ 20,261C Reserved.]

¶ 20,261D

IRS: Minimum coverage requirements: Tax-exempt organizations: Nondiscrimination testing.—The IRS has issued proposed regulations, pursuant to which employees of Code Sec. 501(c)(3) tax-exempt organizations may be excluded from the nondiscrimination test applied to determine whether the Code Sec. 401(k) plan of the organization complies with the minimum coverage requirements. The proposed rules, which would retroactively apply to post-1996 plan years and may be relied upon prior to the issuance of final rules, will effectively allow a tax-exempt organization to continue to maintain a Code Sec. 403(b) and a Code Sec. 401(k) plan without having to provide coverage for employees under both plans. This proposed regulation was published in the *Federal Register* on March 16, 2004 (69 FR 12291).

Code Sec. 401(k), Code Sec. 403(b) and Code Sec. 501(c)(3).

DEPARTMENT OF THE TREASURY

Internal Revenue Service

26 CFR Part 1

[REG-149752-03]

RIN 1545-BC87

Exclusion of Employees of 501(c)(3) Organizations in 401(k) and 401(m) Plans

AGENCY: Internal Revenue Service (IRS), Treasury.

ACTION: Notice of proposed rulemaking.

SUMMARY: This document contains proposed amendments to the regulations under section 410(b) of the Internal Revenue Code. The proposed amendments permit, in certain circumstances, employees of a tax-exempt organization described in section 501(c)(3) to be excluded for the purpose of testing whether a section 401(k) plan (or a section 401(m) plan that is provided under the same general arrangement as the section 401(k) plan of the employer) meets the require-

ments for minimum coverage specified in section 410(b). These regulations will affect tax-exempt employers described in section 501(c)(3), retirement plans sponsored by these employers, and participants in these plans.

DATES: Written or electronic comments and requests for a public hearing must be received by June 14, 2004.

ADDRESSES: Send submissions to: CC:PA:LPD:PR (REG-149752-03), room 5203, Internal Revenue Service, POB 7604, Ben Franklin Station, Washington, DC 20044. Submissions may be hand-delivered Monday through Friday between the hours of 8 a.m. and 4 p.m. to CC:PA:LPD:PR (REG-149752-03), Courier's Desk, Internal Revenue Service, 1111 Constitution Avenue NW., Washington, DC. Alternatively, taxpayers may submit comments electronically via the Internet directly to the IRS Internet site at http://www.irs.gov/regs.

FOR FURTHER INFORMATION CONTACT: Concerning the regulations, R. Lisa Mojiri-Azad, 202-622-6060, or Stacey Grundman, 202-622-6090; concerning submissions and delivery of comments, Treena Garrett, 202-622-7180 (not toll-free numbers).

SUPPLEMENTARY INFORMATION:

Background

This document contains proposed amendments to the Income Tax Regulations (26 CFR Part 1) under section 410(b) of the Internal Revenue Code of 1986 (Code). The amendments implement a directive by Congress, contained in section 664 of the Economic Growth and Tax Relief Reconciliation Act of 2001 (Public Law 107-16, 115 Stat. 38) (EGTRRA), to amend Sec. 1.410(b)-6(g) of the regulations.

Prior to the enactment of the Small Business Job Protection Act of 1996 (Pub. L. 104-188, 110 Stat. 1755) (SBJPA), both governmental and tax-exempt entities generally were subject to the section 410(b) coverage requirements and precluded from maintaining section 401(k) plans pursuant to section 401(k)(4)(B). To prevent the section 401(k)(4)(B) prohibition from causing a plan to fail section 410(b), the existing regulations provide that employees of either governmental or tax-exempt entities who are precluded from being eligible employees under a section 401(k) plan by reason of section 401(k)(4)(B) may be treated as excludable in applying the minimum coverage rules to a section 401(k) plan or a section 401(m) plan that is provided under the same general arrangement as the section 401(k) plan, if more than 95 percent of the employees of the employer who are not precluded from being eligible employees by section 401(k)(4)(B) benefit under the plan for the plan year. Although tax-exempt organizations described in section 501(c)(3) were precluded by section 401(k)(4)(B) from maintaining a section 401(k) plan, they were permitted to allow their employees to make salary reduction contributions to a plan or contract that satisfies section 403(b) (a section 403(b) plan).

Section 1426(a) of SBJPA amended section 401(k)(4)(B) to allow nongovernmental tax-exempt organizations (including organizations exempt under section 501(c)(3)) to maintain section 401(k) plans. Thus, a section 501(c)(3) tax-exempt organization can now maintain a section 401(k) plan, a section 403(b) plan, or both. In light of this provision of SBJPA, section 664 of EGTRRA directed the Secretary of the Treasury to modify the regulations under section 410(b) to provide that employees of a tax-exempt organization described in section 501(c)(3) who are eligible to make salary reduction contributions under a section 403(b) plan may be treated as excludable employees for the purpose of testing whether a section 401(k) plan or a section 401(m) plan that is provided under the same general arrangement as the section 401(k) plan meets the minimum coverage requirements contained in section 410(b) if (1) no employee of the organization is eligible to participate in the section 401(k) or section 401(m) plan and (2) at least 95 percent of the employees of the employer who are not employees of the organization are eligible to participate in the section 401(k) or section 401(m) plan.

The change recognizes that many tax-exempt organizations maintained section 403(b) plans prior to the enactment of SBJPA and is needed to allow the continued maintenance of section 403(b) plans by these organizations without requiring the same employees to be covered under a section 401(k) plan and the section 403(b) plan. The change will help an employer that maintains both a section 401(k) plan and a section 403(b) plan to satisfy the section 410(b) coverage requirements without the employer having to provide dual coverage for employees.

Explanation of Provisions

These regulations provide that employees of a tax-exempt organization described in section 501(c)(3) who are eligible to make salary reduction contributions under a section 403(b) plan may be treated as excludable employees for the purpose of testing whether a section 401(k) plan or a section 401(m) plan that is provided under the same general arrangement as the section 401(k) plan meets the minimum coverage requirements contained in section 410(b) if (1) no employee of the tax-exempt organization is eligible to participate in the section 401(k) or section 401(m) plan and (2) at least 95 percent of the employees of the employer who are not employees of the tax-exempt organization are eligible to participate in the section 401(k) or section 401(m) plan.

The proposed regulations do not include any changes to the treatment of governmental plans under the current regulations. Unless grandfathered, State and local governmental entities continue to be precluded from maintaining section 401(k) plans pursuant to section 401(k)(4)(B). However, as a result of section 1505(a)(1) of the Taxpayer Relief Act of 1997 (Public Law 105-34, 111 Stat. 788), which added section 401(a)(5)(G) to the Code, governmental plans (within the meaning of section 414(d)) maintained by a State or local government or political subdivision thereof (or agency or instrumentality thereof) are not subject to the minimum coverage requirements contained in section 410(b). Consequently, the IRS and Treasury request comments on whether it would be appropriate to modify the special rule for governmental plans contained in Sec. 1.410(b)-6(g) to reflect the addition of section 401(a)(5)(G) (including whether there continues to be a need for this special rule with respect to governmental plans).

Effective Date

As directed by Congress in section 664 of EGTRRA, the amendments to Sec. 1.410(b)-6(g) are proposed to be effective for plan years beginning after December 31, 1996. Taxpayers may rely on these proposed regulations for guidance pending the issuance of final regulations. If, and to the extent, future guidance is more restrictive than the guidance in these proposed regulations, the future guidance will be applied without retroactive effect.

Special Analyses

It has been determined that this notice of proposed rulemaking is not a significant regulatory action as defined in Executive Order 12866. Therefore, a regulatory assessment is not required. It also has been determined that section 553(b) of the Administrative Procedure Act (5 U.S.C. chapter 5) does not apply to these regulations, and, because the regulation does not impose a collection of information on small entities, the Regulatory Flexibility Act (5 U.S.C. chapter 6) does not apply. Pursuant to section 7805(f) of the Code, this notice of proposed rulemaking will be submitted to the Chief Counsel for Advocacy of the Small Business Administration for comment on its impact on small business.

Comments and Requests for a Public Hearing

Before these proposed regulations are adopted as final regulations, consideration will be given to any written (a signed original and 8 copies) or electronic comments that are submitted timely to the IRS. The IRS and Treasury request comments on the clarity of the proposed rules and how they can be made easier to understand. All comments will be available for public inspection and copying. A public hearing will be scheduled if requested in writing by any person that timely submits written comments. If a public hearing is scheduled, notice of the date, time, and place for the public hearing will be published in the Federal Register.

Drafting Information

The principal authors of these proposed regulations are R. Lisa Mojiri-Azad and Stacey Grundman of the Office of the Division Counsel/Associate Chief Counsel (Tax Exempt and Government Entities). However, other personnel from the IRS and Treasury participated in the development of these regulations.

List of Subjects in 26 CFR Part 1

Income taxes, Reporting and recordkeeping requirements.

Proposed Amendments to the Regulations

Accordingly, 26 CFR part 1 is proposed to be amended as follows:

PART 1—INCOME TAXES

Paragraph 1. The authority citation for part 1 is amended by removing the entry for Sec. Sec. 1.410(b)-2 through 1.410(b)-10 and adding entries in numerical order to read, in part, as follows:

Authority: 26 U.S.C. 7805. * * *

Section 1.410(b)-2 also issued under 26 U.S.C. 410(b)(6).

Section 1.410(b)-3 also issued under 26 U.S.C. 410(b)(6).

Section 1.410(b)-4 also issued under 26 U.S.C. 410(b)(6).

Section 1.410(b)-5 also issued under 26 U.S.C. 410(b)(6).

Section 1.410(b)-6 also issued under 26 U.S.C. 410(b)(6) and section 664 of the Economic Growth and Tax Relief Reconciliation Act of 2001 (Public Law 107-16, 115 Stat. 38).

Section 1.410(b)-7 also issued under 26 U.S.C. 410(b)(6).

Section 1.410(b)-8 also issued under 26 U.S.C. 410(b)(6).

Section 1.410(b)-9 also issued under 26 U.S.C. 410(b)(6).

Section 1.410(b)-10 also issued under 26 U.S.C. 410(b)(6). * * *

Par. 2. Section 1.410(b)-0, table of contents, the entry for 1.410(b)-6 is amended by:

1. Revising the paragraph heading for 1.410(b)-6(g).

2. Adding paragraph headings for 1.410(b)-6(g)(1) and (g)(2).

The revision and additions read as follows:

§ 1.410(b)-0. Table of contents.

* * *

§ *1.410(b)-6 Excludable employees.*

* * *

(g) Employees of certain governmental or tax-exempt entities.

(1) Employees of governmental entities.

(2) Employees of tax-exempt entities.

* * *

Par. 3. In Sec. 1.410(b)-6, paragraph (g) is revised to read as follows:

§ *1.410(b)-6. Excludable employees.*

* * *

(g) *Employees of certain governmental or tax-exempt entities.* For purposes of testing either a section 401(k) plan or a section 401(m) plan that is provided under the same general arrangement as a section 401(k) plan, an employer may treat as excludable those employees described in paragraphs (g)(1) and (2) of this section.

(1) *Employees of governmental entities.* Employees of governmental entities who are precluded from being eligible employees under a

section 401(k) plan by reason of section 401(k)(4)(B)(ii) may be treated as excludable employees if more than 95 percent of the employees of the employer who are not precluded from being eligible employees by section 401(k)(4)(B)(ii) benefit under the plan for the plan year.

(2) *Employees of tax-exempt entities.* Employees of a tax-exempt organization described in section 501(c)(3) who are eligible to make salary reduction contributions under a section 403(b) plan may be treated as excludable employees if —

(i) No employee of the organization is eligible to participate in the section 401(k) or section 401(m) plan; and

(ii) At least 95 percent of the employees of the employer who are not employees of the organization are eligible to participate in the section 401(k) or section 401(m) plan.

* * *

Mark E. Mathews,

Deputy Commissioner for Services and Enforcement.

[FR Doc. 04-5903 Filed 3-15-04; 8:45 am]

BILLING CODE 4830-01-P

¶ 20,261E

IRS proposed regulations: Minimum vesting rules: Elimination of optional forms of benefit: Notice of amendment reducing benefit accrual.—The Treasury and IRS have issued proposed regulations that would allow employers maintaining qualified plans to adopt amendments that eliminate early retirement benefits, retirement-type subsidies, and optional forms of benefit that create significant burdens or complexities for the plan and its participants, as long as the amendments do not adversely affect the rights of any participants in more than a de minimis manner. The proposed rules would generally authorize the elimination of "redundant" optional forms of benefit, or, alternatively, the elimination of optional forms of benefit that fall outside a list of "core" optional forms of benefit. However, generally an employer would not be allowed to eliminate lump-sum payment options. The proposed rules, which may not be relied upon until finalized, would further: define the conditions under which an early retirement benefit or retirement-type subsidy may be eliminated, clarify the notice requirements applicable when a plan amendment significantly reduces future benefits, and explain when a plant-shutdown benefit or other contingent event benefit is a retirement-type subsidy or an unprotected ancillary benefit.

The proposed regulations, which were published in the Federal Register on March 24, 2004 (69 FR 13769), were finalized on August 12, 2005 by T.D. 9219 (70 FR 47109). The preamble to the final regs appears at ¶ 23,228.

¶ 20,261F

IRS proposed regulations: Deemed IRAs: Qualified nonbank trustees.—The IRS has issued proposed regulations, by cross-reference to temporary regulations at IRS Reg. Sec. 1.408–2T (¶ 12,054A), relating to qualification of governmental units as qualified nonbank trustees for deemed IRAs under section Code Sec. 408(q). Comments must be received by October 20, 2004.

The proposed regulations, which were published in the *Federal Register* on July 22, 2004 (69 FR 43786), were finalized on June 18, 2007 by T.D. 9331 (72 FR 33387). The preamble to the final regulations appears at ¶ 23,248.

¶ 20,261G

IRS proposed regulations: Phased retirement: Distributions: Pro rata approach.—Reproduced below is the text of a proposed rule in which the IRS would permit retirement plans to distribute a portion of a participant's benefits on a pro rata basis depending upon the extent to which the participant has reduced his or her work hours. The number of hours worked would have to be reduced by 20% or more, and the phased retirement program would not be available to participants that have not reached age 59 ½. Additionally, participants in the phased retirement program would be entitled to participant in their retirement plans in generally the same manner they would be participating if they were maintaining a full-time work schedule.

The proposed regulation was published in the *Federal Register* on November 10, 2004 (69 FR 65108) and corrected on December 28, 2004.

DEPARTMENT OF TREASURY

Internal Revenue Service

26 CFR Part 1

[REG-114726-04]

RIN 1545-BD23

Distributions from a Pension Plan under a Phased Retirement Program

AGENCY: Internal Revenue Service (IRS), Treasury.

ACTION: Notice of proposed rulemaking.

SUMMARY: This notice of proposed rulemaking contains proposed amendments to the Income Tax Regulations under section 401(a) of the Internal Revenue Code. These proposed regulations provide rules permitting distributions to be made from a pension plan under a phased retirement program and set forth requirements for a bona fide

phased retirement program. The proposed regulations will provide the public with guidance regarding distributions from qualified pension plans and will affect administrators of, and participants in, such plans.

DATES: Written or electronic comments and requests for a public hearing must be received by February 8, 2005.

ADDRESSES: Send submissions to: CC:PA:LPD:PR (REG-114726-04), room 5203, Internal Revenue Service, PO Box 7604, Ben Franklin Station, Washington, DC 20044. Submissions may be hand-delivered Monday through Friday between the hours of 8 a.m. and 4 p.m. to CC:PA:LPD:PR (REG-114726-04), Courier's Desk, Internal Revenue Service, 1111 Constitution Avenue, NW., Washington, DC, or sent electronically, via the IRS Internet site at *www.irs.gov/regs* or via the Federal eRulemaking Portal at *www.regulations.gov* (indicate IRS and REG-114726-04).

FOR FURTHER INFORMATION CONTACT: Concerning the regulations, Cathy A. Vohs, 202-622-6090; concerning submissions and requests for a public hearing, contact Sonya Cruse, 202-622-7180 (not toll-free numbers).

¶20,261E

SUPPLEMENTARY INFORMATION:

Background

As people are living longer, healthier lives, there is a greater risk that individuals may outlive their retirement savings. In addition, employers have expressed interest in encouraging older, more experienced workers to stay in the workforce. One approach that some employers have implemented is to offer employees the opportunity for phased retirement."

While there is no single approach to phased retirement, these arrangements generally provide employees who are at or near eligibility for retirement with the opportunity for a reduced schedule or workload, thereby providing a smoother transition from full-time employment to retirement. These arrangements permit the employer to retain the services of an experienced employee and provide the employee with the opportunity to continue active employment at a level that also allows greater flexibility and time away from work.

During such a transition arrangement, employees may wish to supplement their part-time income with a portion of their retirement savings. However, phased retirement can also increase the risk of outliving retirement savings for employees who begin drawing upon their retirement savings before normal retirement age. Even though the annuity distribution options offered by defined benefit plans preclude outliving benefits, early distribution of a portion of the employee's benefit will reduce the benefits available after full retirement. On the other hand, phased retirement also can provide employees additional time to save for retirement because employees continue working while they are able to do so, and can accrue additional benefits and reduce or forgo early spending of their retirement savings.

In light of this background, Treasury and the IRS issued Notice 2002-43 in the Cumulative Bulletin (2002-27 C.B. 38 (July 8, 2002)), in which comments were requested regarding phased retirement. Notice 2002-43 specifically requested comments on a wide variety of issues, including the following:

- Under what circumstances, if any, would permitting distributions from a defined benefit plan before an employee attains normal retirement age be consistent with the requirement that a defined benefit plan be established and maintained primarily for purposes of providing benefits after retirement, such as the extent to which an employee has actually reduced his or her workload?

- If there are such circumstances, how should any early retirement subsidy be treated?

Comments Received

Sixteen written comments were formally submitted in response to Notice 2002-43. These comments are in addition to the substantial number of articles and other published materials addressing phased retirement.[1]

While some of the comments expressed concerns over the potential for both dissipation of retirement funds and violation of age discrimination laws, commentators generally responded favorably to the proposal to provide guidance on facilitating phased retirement arrangements. These commentators noted that permitting pension distributions during phased retirement would be attractive to both employers and employees. Commentators also indicated that any guidance issued should provide that establishment of phased retirement arrangements be optional on the part of the employer and that participation in any such arrangement be voluntary on the part of the employee.

Most of the comments recommended that eligibility to participate in a phased retirement program be limited to employees who are eligible for immediately commencing retirement benefits under the plan (including those eligible for early retirement benefits). Other comments recommended that retirement benefits be permitted to start at a specific age or combination of age and service; however, they noted that current legislative constraints, notably the section 72(t) 10 percent additional income tax on early distributions, may limit the desirability of this option.

Some commentators advocated that any phased retirement arrangement should be cost neutral and not create additional funding obligations for employers. Others recommended that any early retirement subsidy available to an employee upon full retirement continue to be available if the employee participates in phased retirement. For example, one such commentator recommended not only that any early retirement subsidy be available upon phased retirement, but also that the subsidy so paid not be permitted to be applied to reduce the remainder of the benefit that is earned by the employee, particularly if the employee continues working past normal retirement age.

The comments were divided over what constituted phased retirement. Several recommended that phased retirement benefits be limited to cases in which there is a reduction in hours worked. Others recommended that a reduction in hours not be required and that a transition to a less stressful job also be considered phased retirement or that the full retirement benefit be payable after the attainment of a specified age or years of service without regard to any change in work.

The commentators who recommended that phased retirement benefits be limited to cases in which there is a reduction in hours worked generally recommended that the phased retirement benefits payable be proportionate to the reduction in work, based on a "dual status" approach. Under this dual status approach, an employee who reduces his or her work schedule to, for example, 80 percent of full-time would be considered to be 20 percent retired and thus entitled to 20 percent of his or her retirement benefit. The employee would continue to accrue additional benefits based on the actual hours he or she continues to work.

Several of the commentators discussed the implications of phased retirement benefits for purposes of the nondiscrimination rules of section 401(a)(4) and the anti-cutback rules of section 411(d)(6). Many of the comments said that phased retirement arrangements must be flexible and that it would be important for employers to be able to adopt a phased retirement arrangement on a temporary (even experimental) basis.

Many commentators expressed concern over the effect that a reduction in hours and the corresponding reduction in compensation would have on the final average pay of an individual for purposes of the benefit calculation when the employee fully retires. These comments generally requested guidance on this issue, including clarification as to whether an employee's final average pay is permitted to decline as a result of the employee's reduction in hours pursuant to participation in a phased retirement arrangement.

Explanation of Provisions

Overview

The proposed regulations would amend § 1.401(a)-1(b) and add § 1.401(a)-3 in order to permit a pro rata share of an employee's accrued benefit to be paid under a bona fide phased retirement program. The pro rata share is based on the extent to which the employee has reduced hours under the program. Under this pro rata approach, an employee maintains a dual status (i.e., partially retired and partially in service) during the phased retirement period. This pro rata or dual status approach to phased retirement was one of the approaches recommended by commentators.

While all approaches suggested by commentators were considered, the pro rata approach is the most consistent with the requirement that benefits be maintained primarily for retirement. Other approaches, such as permitting benefits to be fully available if an employee works reduced hours as part of phased retirement or permitting distributions of the entire accrued benefit to be paid as of a specified age prior to normal retirement age, are fundamentally inconsistent with the § 1.401(a)-1(b) principle that benefits be paid only after retirement. In addition, although a number of commentators suggested that guidance address the practice of terminating an employee with a prearranged rehiring of the employee (or similar sham transactions), the proposed regulations do not address this topic because it involves additional issues outside the scope of this project.

Rules Relating to Phased Retirement

Under the proposed regulations, a plan would be permitted to pay a pro rata portion of the employee's benefits under a bona fide phased retirement program before attainment of normal retirement age. The proposed regulations define a bona fide phased retirement program as a written, employer-adopted program pursuant to which employees may reduce the number of hours they customarily work beginning on

---

[1] See, for example, Pension & Welfare Benefits Administration, U.S. Department of Labor, "Report on Working Group on Phased Retirement to the Advisory Council on Employee Welfare & Pension Benefit Plans," 2000; Forman, Jonathan Barry, "How Federal Pension Laws Influence Individual Work and Retirement Decisions," 54 Tax Law. 143 (2000); Littler Mendelson, "Employers Consider 'Phased Retirement' to Retain Employees," Maryland Employment Law Letter, Vol 10, Issue 6 (April, 2000); Geisel, Jerry,

"Rethinking Phased Retirement; IRS Call for Comment May Signal Pension Law Changes," Business Insurance (June 24, 2002); Flahaven, Brian, "Please Don't Go! Why Phased Retirement May Make Sense For Your Government," 18 Gov't Finance Review 24 (Oct. 1, 2002); NPR, Morning Edition, "Older Workers Turn to 'Phased' Retirement," (May 18, 2004) at *www.npr.org/features/feature.php?wfld=1900465*

or after a retirement date specified under the program and receive phased retirement benefits. Payment of phased retirement benefits is permitted only if the program meets certain conditions, including that employee participation is voluntary and the employee and employer expect the employee to reduce, by 20 percent or more, the number of hours the employee works during the phased retirement period.

Consistent with the pro rata approach discussed above, the maximum amount that is permitted to be paid is limited to the portion of the employee's accrued benefit equal to the product of the employee's total accrued benefit on the date the employee commences phased retirement (or any earlier date selected by the plan for administrative ease) and the employee's reduction in work. The reduction in work is based on the employee's work schedule fraction, which is the ratio of the hours that the employee is reasonably expected to work during the phased retirement period to the hours that would be worked if the employee were full-time. Based in part on commentators' concerns regarding early retirement subsidies, the proposed regulations generally require that all early retirement benefits, retirement-type subsidies, and optional forms of benefit that would be available upon full retirement be available with respect to the phased retirement accrued benefit. However, the proposed regulations would not permit payment to be made in the form of a single-sum distribution (or other eligible rollover distribution) in order to prevent the premature distribution of retirement benefits. The phased retirement benefit is an optional form of benefit protected by section 411(d)(6) and the election of a phased retirement benefit is subject to the provisions of section 417, including the required explanation of the qualified joint and survivor annuity.

Some comments suggested that phased retirement be limited to employees who have attained an age or service (or combination thereof) that is customary for retirement, e.g., where the employer has reasonably determined in good faith that participants who cease employment with the employer after that age or service combination are typically not expected to continue to perform further services of a generally comparable nature elsewhere in the workforce. Such a retirement age might be considerably lower than age 65 in certain occupations (such as police or firefighters). As discussed further below (under the heading *Application to Plans Other Than Qualified Pension Plans*), the Treasury and IRS have concluded that they do not have the authority to permit payments to begin from a section 401(k) plan under a bona fide phased retirement program before the employee attains age 59 ½ or has a severance from employment.[2] Further, section 72(t)(3)(B) provides an additional income tax on early distributions if annuity distributions are made before the earlier of age 59 ½ or separation from service. Accordingly, in lieu of a customary retirement age, the proposed regulations adopt a rule that is consistent with section 401(k) and section 72(t)(3)(B), under which phased retirement benefits may not be paid before an employee attains age 59 ½.

Additional Accruals During Phased Retirement

The regulations provide that, during the phased retirement period, in addition to being entitled to the phased retirement benefit, the employee must be entitled to participate in the plan in the same manner as if the employee were still maintaining a full-time work schedule (including calculation of average earnings) and must be entitled to the same benefits (including early retirement benefits, retirement-type subsidies, and optional forms of benefits) upon full retirement as a similarly situated employee who has not elected phased retirement, except that the years of service credited under the plan for any plan year during the phased retirement period is multiplied by the ratio of the employee's actual hours of service during the year to the employee's full-time work schedule, or by the ratio of the employee's compensation to the compensation that would be paid for full-time work. Thus, for example, under a plan with a 1,000 hours of service requirement to accrue a benefit, an employee participating in a phased retirement program will accrue proportionate additional benefits, even if the employee works fewer than 1,000 hours of service.

The requirement that full-time compensation be imputed, with a proportionate reduction based on an employee's actual service, is intended to ensure that a participant is not disadvantaged by reason of choosing phased retirement. This rule precludes the need for extensive disclosure requirements, e.g., disclosure to alert participants to rights that may be lost as a result of participating in a phased retirement program. To be consistent with the requirement to use full-time compensation, the proposed regulations require an employee who was a highly compensated employee before commencing phased retirement to be treated as a highly compensated employee during phased retirement. See also § 1.414(q)-1T, A-4 & A-5.

Under the proposed regulations, the employee's final retirement benefit is comprised of the phased retirement benefit and the balance of the employee's accrued benefit under the plan (i.e., the excess of the total plan formula benefit over the portion of the accrued benefit paid as a phased retirement benefit). Upon full retirement, the phased retirement benefit can continue unchanged or the plan is permitted to offer a new election with respect to that benefit.

This bifurcation is consistent with commentators' recommendation that an employee who is in a phased retirement program has a dual status, under which the employee is treated as retired to the extent of the reduction in hours and is treated as working to the extent of the employee's continued work with the employer. This approach also ensures that a phased retirement program offers an early retirement subsidy to the extent the employee has reduced his or her hours, and that the remainder of the employee's benefit rights is not adversely affected by participation in the phased retirement program.

Testing and Adjustment of Payments

Subject to certain exceptions, the proposed regulations require periodic testing to ensure that employees in phased retirement are in fact working at the reduced schedule, as expected. Thus, unless an exception applies, a plan must provide for an annual comparison between the number of hours actually worked by an employee during a testing period and the number of hours the employee was reasonably expected to work. If the actual hours worked during the testing period are materially greater than the expected number of hours, then the employee's phased retirement benefit must be reduced prospectively. For this purpose, the employee's hours worked are materially greater than the employee's work schedule if they exceed either 133 ⅓ percent of the work schedule or 90 percent of the hours that the employee would work under a full-time schedule.

This annual comparison is not required after the employee is within 3 months of attaining normal retirement age or if the amount of compensation paid to the employee by the employer during the phased retirement testing period does not exceed the compensation that would be paid to the employee if he or she had worked full time multiplied by the employee's work schedule fraction. Further, no comparison is required during the first year of an employee's phased retirement or if the employee has entered into an agreement with the employer that the employee will retire within 2 years.

In the event that the employer and employee agree to increase prospectively the hours that the employee will work, then the employee's phased retirement benefit must be adjusted based on a new work schedule. The date of the agreement to increase the employee's hours is treated as a comparison date for testing purposes.

In calculating the employee's benefit at full retirement, if an employee's phased retirement benefits have been reduced during phased retirement, the employee's accrued benefit under the plan is offset by an amount that is actuarially equivalent to the additional payments made before the reduction. The potential for this offset, like other material features of the phased retirement optional form of benefit, must be disclosed as part of the QJSA explanation as required under § 1.401(a)-20, Q&A-36, and § 1.417(a)(3)-1(c)(1)(v) and (d)(1).

If the employee's phased retirement benefit is less than the maximum amount permitted or the employee's work schedule is further reduced at a later date, the proposed regulations allow a plan to provide one or more additional phased retirement benefits to the employee. The additional phased retirement benefit, commencing at a later annuity starting date, provides flexibility to reflect future reductions in the employee's work hours.

Provisions Relating to Payment After Normal Retirement Age

The proposed regulations clarify that a pension plan (i.e., a defined benefit plan or money purchase pension plan) is permitted to pay benefits upon an employee's attainment of normal retirement age. However, normal retirement age cannot be set so low as to be a subterfuge to avoid the requirements of section 401(a), and, accordingly, normal retirement age cannot be earlier than the earliest age that is reasonably representative of a typical retirement age for the covered workforce.[3]

---

[2] Cf., *Edwards v. Commissioner*, T.C. Memo. 1989-409, *aff'd*, 906 F.2d 114 (4th Cir. 1990).

[3] While a low normal retirement age may have a significant cost effect on a traditional defined benefit plan, this effect is not as significant for defined contribution plans or for hybrid defined benefit plans.

Application to Plans Other Than Qualified Pension Plans

The regulations that limit distributions that are modified by these proposed regulations only apply to pension plans (i.e., defined benefit or money purchase pension plans). Other types of plans may be subject to less restrictive rules regarding in-service distributions, including amounts held in or attributable to: (1) qualified profit sharing and stock bonus plans to the extent not attributable to elective deferrals under section 401(k); (2) insurance annuities under section 403(b)(1), and retirement income accounts under section 403(b)(9), to the extent not attributable to elective deferrals; (3) custodial accounts under section 403(b)(7) to the extent not attributable to elective deferrals; and (4) elective deferrals under section 401(k) or 403(b). In general, these types of plans are permitted to provide for distributions after attainment of age 59 ½, without regard to whether the employee has retired or had a severance from employment. Accordingly, they may either provide for the same phased retirement rules that are proposed in these regulations or may provide for other partial or full in-service distributions to be available after attainment of age 59 ½. However, eligible governmental plans under section 457(b) are not generally permitted to provide for payments to be made before the earlier of severance from employment or attainment of age 70 ½. See generally § 1.457-6.

Other Issues

The proposed regulations also authorize the Commissioner to issue additional rules in guidance of general applicability regarding the coordination of partial retirement under a phased retirement program and the plan qualification rules under section 401(a).

These proposed regulations do not address all of the issues that commentators raised in response to Notice 2002-43. Thus, as noted above, the proposed regulations do not address when a full retirement occurs and specifically do not endorse a prearranged termination and rehire as constituting a full retirement. Further, the proposed regulations only address certain tax issues. For example, although commentators pointed out that the continued availability of health coverage would be an important feature for employees in deciding whether to participate in phased retirement, the proposed regulations do not include any rules relating to health coverage. Similarly, the proposed regulations do not address any potential age discrimination issues, other than through the requirement that participation in a bona fide phased retirement program be voluntary.

Proposed Effective Date

The rules in these regulations are proposed to apply to plan years beginning on or after the date of publication of the Treasury decision adopting these rules as final regulations in the **Federal Register**. These proposed regulations cannot be relied on before they are adopted as final regulations.

Special Analyses

It has been determined that this notice of proposed rulemaking is not a significant regulatory action as defined in Executive Order 12866. Therefore, a regulatory assessment is not required. It also has been determined that section 553(b) of the Administrative Procedure Act (5 U.S.C. chapter 5) does not apply to these proposed regulations, and, because these regulations do not impose a collection of information on small entities, the Regulatory Flexibility Act (5 U.S.C. chapter 6) does not apply. Pursuant to section 7805(f) of the Internal Revenue Code, this notice of proposed rulemaking will be submitted to the Chief Counsel for Advocacy of the Small Business Administration for comment on its impact on small business.

Comments and Requests for a Public Hearing

Before these proposed regulations are adopted as final regulations, consideration will be given to any written comments (a signed original and eight (8) copies) or electronic comments that are submitted timely to the IRS. All comments will be available for public inspection and copying.

Comments are specifically requested on the following issues:

- Should eligibility to participate in a phased retirement program be extended to employees that reduce their workload using a standard, other than counting hours, to identify the reduction, and, if so, are there administrable methods for measuring the reduction?

- The proposed regulations require periodic testing of the hours an employee actually works during phased retirement, and if the hours are materially greater than the employee's phased retirement work schedule, the phased retirement benefit must be adjusted. As discussed above (under the heading *Testing*), there are a number of exceptions to this requirement. Are there other, less

complex alternatives that also would ensure that phased retirement benefits correspond to the employee's reduction in hours?

- The proposed regulations require an offset for the actuarial value of additional payments made before a reduction in phased retirement benefits. Should the regulations permit this offset to be calculated without regard to any early retirement subsidy and, if so, how should a subsidy be quantified?

- The proposed regulations clarify that the right to receive a phased retirement benefit as a partial payment is a separate optional form of benefit for purposes of section 411(d)(6) and, thus, is a benefit, right, or feature for purposes of the special nondiscrimination rules at § 1.401(a)(4)-4. Comments are requested on whether there are facts and circumstances under which the age and service conditions for a particular employer's phased retirement program should be disregarded in applying § 1.401(a)(4)-4 (even if the program may only be in place for a temporary period), or under which the rules at § 1.401(a)(4)-4 should otherwise be modified with respect to phased retirement.

- Should any special rules be adopted to coordinate the rules regarding distributions and continued accruals during phased retirement with a plan's provisions regarding employment after normal retirement age, such as suspension of benefits?

A public hearing may be scheduled if requested in writing by a person that timely submits written comments. If a public hearing is scheduled, notice of the date, time and place for the hearing will be published in the **Federal Register**.

Drafting Information

The principal author of these proposed regulations is Cathy A. Vohs of the Office of the Division Counsel/Associate Chief Counsel (Tax Exempt and Government Entities). However, other personnel from the IRS and Treasury participated in their development.

List of Subjects 26 CFR Part 1

Income taxes, Reporting and recordkeeping requirements.

Proposed Amendments to the Regulations

Accordingly, 26 CFR part 1 is proposed to be amended as follows:

PART 1—INCOME TAXES

Paragraph 1. The authority citation for part 1 is amended by adding entries in numerical order to read in part as follows:

Authority: 26 U.S.C. 7805 * * *

Section 1.401(a)-1 also issued under 26 U.S.C. 401.

Section 1.401(a)-3 also issued under 26 U.S.C. 401.

Par. 2. In § 1.401(a)-1, paragraph (b)(1)(i) is amended by adding text before the period at the end of the current sentence and a new second sentence, and paragraph (b)(1)(iv) to read as follows:

§ 1.401(a)-1 Post-ERISA qualified plans and qualified trusts; in general.

* * * * *

(b) * * *

(1) * * *

(i) * * * or attainment of normal retirement age. However, normal retirement age cannot be set so low as to be a subterfuge to avoid the requirements of section 401(a), and, accordingly, normal retirement age cannot be earlier than the earliest age that is reasonably representative of a typical retirement age for the covered workforce.

* * * * *

(iv) Benefits may not be distributed prior to normal retirement age solely due to a reduction in hours. However, notwithstanding anything provided elsewhere in paragraph (b) of this section (including the pre-ERISA rules under § 1.401-1), an employee may be treated as partially retired for purposes of paragraph (b)(1)(i) of this section to the extent provided under § 1.401(a)-3 relating to a bona fide phased retirement program. * * * * *

Par. 3. Section 1.401(a)-3 is added to read as follows:

§ 1.401(a)-3 Benefits during phased retirement.

(a) *Introduction* —(1) *General rule.* Under section 401(a), a qualified pension plan may provide for the distribution of phased retirement benefits in accordance with the limitations of this paragraph (a) to the extent that an employee is partially retired under a bona fide phased retirement program, as defined in paragraph (c) of this section, provided the requirements set forth in paragraphs (d) and (e) of this section are satisfied.

(2) *Limitation on benefits paid during phased retirement period —(i) Benefits limited to pro rata retirement benefit.* The phased retirement benefits paid during the phased retirement period cannot exceed the phased retirement accrued benefit payable in the optional form of benefit applicable at the annuity starting date for the employee's phased retirement benefit.

(ii) *Availability of early retirement subsidies, etc.* Except as provided in paragraph (a) (2) (iii) of this section, all early retirement benefits, retirement-type subsidies, and optional forms of benefit available upon full retirement must be available with respect to the portion of an employee's phased retirement accrued benefit that is payable as a phased retirement benefit.

(iii) *Limitation on optional forms of payment.* Phased retirement benefits may not be paid in the form of a single sum or other form that constitutes an eligible rollover distribution under section 402(c) (4).

(3) *Limited to full-time employees who are otherwise eligible to commence benefits.* Phased retirement benefits are only permitted to be made available to an employee who, prior to the phased retirement period, normally maintains a full-time work schedule and who would otherwise be eligible to commence retirement benefits immediately if he or she were to fully retire.

(4) *Authority of Commissioner to adopt other rules.* The Commissioner, in revenue rulings, notices, or other guidance published in the Internal Revenue Bulletin (see § 601.601(d) (2) (ii) (*b*) of this chapter), may adopt additional rules regarding the coordination of partial retirement under a phased retirement program and the qualification rules of section 401(a).

(b) *Definitions —(1) In general.* The definitions set forth in this paragraph (b) apply for purposes of this section.

(2) *Phased retirement program.* The term *phased retirement program* means a written, employer-adopted program pursuant to which employees may reduce the number of hours they customarily work beginning on or after a date specified under the program and commence phased retirement benefits during the phased retirement period, as provided under the plan.

(3) *Phased retirement period.* The term *phased retirement period* means the period of time that the employee and employer reasonably expect the employee to work reduced hours under the phased retirement program.

(4) *Phased retirement accrued benefit.* The term *phased retirement accrued benefit* means the portion of the employee's accrued benefit equal to the product of the employee's total accrued benefit on the annuity starting date for the employee's phased retirement benefit, and one minus the employee's work schedule fraction.

(5) *Phased retirement benefit.* The term *phased retirement benefit* means the benefit paid to an employee upon the employee's partial retirement under a phased retirement program, based on some or all of the employee's phased retirement accrued benefit, and payable in the optional form of benefit applicable at the annuity starting date.

(6) *Work schedule.* With respect to an employee, the term *work schedule* means the number of hours the employee is reasonably expected to work annually during the phased retirement period (determined in accordance with paragraph (c) (4) of this section).

(7) *Full-time work schedule.* With respect to an employee, the term *full-time work schedule* means the number of hours the employee would normally work during a year if the employee were to work on a full-time basis, determined in a reasonable and consistent manner.

(8) *Work schedule fraction.* With respect to an employee, the term *work schedule fraction* means a fraction, the numerator of which is the employee's work schedule and the denominator of which is the employee's full-time work schedule.

(c) *Bona fide phased retirement program —(1) Definition generally.* The term *bona fide phased retirement program* means a phased retirement program that satisfies paragraphs (c) (2) through (5) of this section.

(2) *Limitation to individuals who have attained age 59 ½.* A bona fide phased retirement program must be limited to employees who have attained age 59 ½. A plan is permitted to impose additional requirements for eligibility to participate in a bona fide phased retirement program, such as limiting eligibility to either employees who have satisfied additional age or service conditions (or combination thereof)

specified in the program or employees whose benefit may not be distributed without consent under section 411(a) (11).

(3) *Participation must be voluntary.* An employee's participation in a bona fide phased retirement program must be voluntary.

(4) *Reduction in hours requirement.* An employee who participates in a bona fide phased retirement program must reasonably be expected (by both the employer and employee) to reduce, by 20 percent or more, the number of hours the employee customarily works. This requirement is satisfied if the employer and employee enter into an agreement, in good faith, under which they agree that the employee will reduce, by 20 percent or more, the number of hours the employee works during the phased retirement period.

(5) *Limited to employees who are not key-employee owners.* Phased retirement benefits are not permitted to be made available to a key employee who is described in section 416(i) (1) (A) (ii) or (iii).

(d) *Conditions for commencement of phased retirement benefit —(1) Imputed accruals based on full-time schedule —(i) General rule.* During the phased retirement period, in addition to being entitled to payment of the phased retirement benefit, the employee must be entitled to participate in the plan in the same manner as if the employee still maintained a full-time work schedule (including calculation of average earnings, imputation of compensation in accordance with § 1.414(s)-1(f), and imputation of service in accordance with the service-crediting rules under § 1.401(a) (4)-11(d)), and must be entitled to the same benefits (including early retirement benefits, retirement-type subsidies, and optional forms of benefits) upon full retirement as a similarly situated employee who has not elected phased retirement, except that the years of service credited under the plan for any plan year during the phased retirement period is determined under paragraph (d) (1) (ii) or (iii) of this section, whichever is applicable.

(ii) *Method for crediting years of service for full plan years.* The years of service credited under the plan for any full plan year during the phased retirement period is multiplied by an adjustment ratio that is equal to the ratio of the employee's actual hours worked during that year to the number of hours that would be worked by the employee during that year under a full-time work schedule. Alternatively, on a reasonable and consistent basis, the adjustment ratio may be based on the ratio of an employee's actual compensation during the year to the compensation that would be paid to the employee during the year if he or she had maintained a full-time work schedule.

(iii) *Method for crediting years of service for partial plan years.* In the case of a plan year only a portion of which is during a phased retirement period for an employee, the method described in paragraphs (d) (1) (i) and (ii) of this section is applied with respect to that portion of the plan year. Thus, for example, if an employee works full time until October 1 of a calendar plan year and works one-third time from October 1 through December 31 of the year, then the employee is credited with 10 months for that year (9 months plus ⅓ of 3 months).

(2) *Ancillary benefits during phased retirement period —(i) Death benefits.* If an employee dies while receiving phased retirement benefits, death benefits are allocated between the phased retirement benefit and the benefit that would be payable upon subsequent full retirement. See also § 1.401(a)-20, A-9. Thus, if an employee dies after the annuity starting date for the phased retirement benefit, death benefits are paid with respect to the phased retirement benefit in accordance with the optional form elected for that benefit, and death benefits are paid with respect to the remainder of the employee's benefit in accordance with the plan's provisions regarding death during employment.

(ii) *Other ancillary benefits.* To the extent provided under the terms of the plan, ancillary benefits, other than death benefits described in paragraph (d) (2) (i) of this section, are permitted to be provided during the phased retirement period.

(3) *Calculation of benefit at full retirement —(i) In general.* Upon full retirement following partial retirement under a phased retirement program, the employee's total accrued benefit under the plan (including the employee's accruals during the phased retirement period, determined in accordance with paragraph (d) (1) of this section) is offset by the portion of the employee's phased retirement accrued benefit that is being distributed as a phased retirement benefit at the time of full retirement.

(ii) *Adjustment for prior payments.* If, before full retirement, the employee's phased retirement benefit has been reduced under paragraph (d) (4) of this section, then the employee's accrued benefit under the plan is also offset upon full retirement by an amount that is actuarially equivalent to the phased retirement benefit payments that have been made during the phased retirement period that were not made with respect to the portion of the phased retirement accrued benefit that is applied as an offset under paragraph (d)(3)(i) of this section at the time of full retirement.

(iii) *Election of optional form with respect to net benefit.* Upon full retirement, an employee is entitled to elect, in accordance with section 417, an optional form of benefit with respect to the net accrued benefit determined under paragraph (d)(3)(i) and (ii) of this section.

(iv) *New election permitted for phased retirement benefit.* A plan is permitted to provide that, upon full retirement, an employee may elect, in accordance with section 417 and without regard to paragraph (a)(2)(iii) of this section, a new optional form of benefit with respect to the portion of the phased retirement accrued benefit that is being distributed as a phased retirement benefit. Any such new optional form of benefit is calculated at the time of full retirement as the actuarial equivalent of the future phased retirement benefits (without offset for the phased retirement benefits previously paid).

(4) *Prospective reduction in phased retirement benefit if hours are materially greater than expected* —(i) *General rule.* Except as otherwise provided in this paragraph (d)(4), a plan must compare annually the number of hours actually worked by an employee during the phased retirement testing period and the number of hours the employee was reasonably expected to work during the testing period for purposes of calculating the work schedule fraction. For this purpose, the phased retirement testing period is the 12 months preceding the comparison date (or such longer period permitted under paragraph (d)(4)(iv) of this section, or any shorter period that applies if there is a comparison date as a result of an agreed increase under paragraph (d)(4)(vi) of this section). In the event that the actual hours worked (determined on an annual basis) during the phased retirement testing period exceeds the work schedule, then, except as provided in paragraph (d)(4)(ii) or (v) of this section, the employee's phased retirement benefit must be reduced in accordance with the method provided in paragraph (d)(4)(iii) of this section, effective as of an adjustment date specified in the plan that is not more than 3 months later than the comparison date.

(ii) *Permitted variance in hours.* A plan is not required to reduce the phased retirement benefit unless the hours worked during the phased retirement testing period are materially greater than the hours that would be expected to be worked under the work schedule. For this purpose, the employee's hours worked (determined on annual basis) are materially greater than the employee's work schedule if either—

(A) The employee's hours worked (determined on an annual basis) are more than 133 ⅓ percent of the employee's work schedule; or

(B) The employee's hours worked (determined on an annual basis) exceed 90 percent of the full-time work schedule.

(iii) *Adjustment method.* If a phased retirement benefit must be reduced under paragraph (d)(4) of this section, a new (i.e., reduced) phased retirement benefit must be calculated as provided in this paragraph (d)(4)(iii). First, an adjusted work schedule is determined. The adjusted work schedule is an annual schedule based on the number of hours the employee actually worked during the phased retirement testing period. The adjusted work schedule is applied to the employee's accrued benefit that was used to calculate the prior phased retirement benefit. This results in a new phased retirement accrued benefit for purposes of paragraph (b)(4) of this section. Second, a new phased retirement benefit is determined, based on the new phased retirement accrued benefit and payable in the same optional form of benefit (i.e., using the same annuity starting date and the same early retirement factor and other actuarial adjustments) as the prior phased retirement benefit. If an employee is receiving more than one phased retirement benefit (as permitted under paragraph (e)(2) of this section) and a reduction is required under paragraph (d)(4) of this section, then the reduction is applied first to the most recently commencing phased retirement benefit (and then, if necessary, to the next most recent phased retirement benefit, etc.).

(iv) *Comparison date for phased retirement testing period.* The comparison date is any date chosen by the employer on a reasonable and consistent basis and specified in the plan, such as the last day of the plan year, December 31, or the anniversary of the annuity starting date for the employee's phased retirement benefit. As an alternative to testing the hours worked during the 12 months preceding the comparison date, the plan may, on a reasonable and consistent basis, provide that the comparison of actual hours worked to the work schedule be based on a cumulative period that exceeds 12 months beginning with either the annuity starting date for the employee's phased retirement benefit or any later date specified in the plan.

(v) *Exceptions to comparison requirement* —(A) *In general.* The comparison of hours described in paragraph (d)(4) of this section is not required in the situations set forth in this paragraph (d)(4)(v).

(B) *Employees recently commencing phased retirement.* No comparison is required for an employee who commenced phased retirement benefits within the 12-month period preceding the comparison date.

(C) *Employees with short phased retirement periods.* No comparison is required during the first 2 years of an employee's phased retirement period if—

(1) The employee has entered into an agreement with the employer under which the employee's phased retirement period will not exceed 2 years and the employee will fully retire at the end of such period; and

(2) The employee fully retires after a phased retirement period not in excess of 2 years.

(D) *Employees with proportional pay reduction.* No comparison is required for any phased retirement testing period if the amount of compensation paid to the employee during that period does not exceed the compensation that would be paid to the employee if he or she had maintained a full-time work schedule multiplied by the work schedule fraction.

(E) *Employees at or after normal retirement age.* No comparison is required for any phased retirement testing period ending within 3 months before the employee's normal retirement age or any time thereafter.

(vi) *Agreement to increase hours* —(A) *General rule.* In the event that the employer and the employee agree to increase prospectively the hours under the employee's work schedule prior to normal retirement age, then, notwithstanding the exceptions provided in paragraphs (d)(4)(v)(B) through (D) of this section, the plan must treat the effective date of the agreement to increase the employee's hours as a comparison date for purposes of paragraph (d)(4)(iv) of this section. For purposes of this paragraph (d)(4)(vi), with respect to an employee, the term *new work schedule* means the greater of the actual number of hours the employee worked (determined on an annual basis) during the prior phased retirement testing period or the annual number of hours the employee reasonably expects to work under the new agreement.

(B) *Required adjustments.* If the employee's hours under the new work schedule are materially greater (within the meaning of paragraph (d)(4)(ii) of this section) than the hours the employee would be expected to work (based on the employee's prior work schedule), the employer is required to reduce the employee's phased retirement benefit, effective as of the date of the increase, based on the new work schedule. In this case, the employee's new work schedule is used for future comparisons under paragraph (d)(4) of this section.

(C) *Permitted adjustments.* If the employee's hours under the new work schedule are not materially greater (within the meaning of paragraph (d)(4)(ii) of this section) than the hours the employee would be expected to work (based on the employee's prior work schedule), the employer is permitted, but not required, to reduce the employee's phased retirement benefit, effective as of the date of the increase, based on the new work schedule. If the benefit is so reduced, the employee's new work schedule is used for future comparisons under paragraph (d)(4) of this section. If the employee's phased retirement benefit is not so reduced, future comparisons are determined using the employee's prior work schedule.

(e) *Other rules* —(1) *Highly compensated employees.* An employee who partially retires under a phased retirement program and who was a highly compensated employee, as defined in section 414(q), immediately before the partial retirement is considered to be a highly compensated employee during the phased retirement period, without regard to the compensation actually paid to the employee during the phased retirement period.

(2) *Multiple phased retirement benefits permitted* —(i) *In general.* A plan is permitted to provide one or more additional phased retirement benefits prospectively to an employee who is receiving a phased retirement benefit if the conditions set forth in paragraph (e)(2)(ii) of this section are satisfied. At the later annuity starting date for the additional phased retirement benefit, the additional phased retirement benefits may not exceed the amount permitted to be paid based on the excess of—

(A) The employee's phased retirement accrued benefit at the later annuity starting date, over

(B) The portion of the employee's phased retirement accrued benefit at the earlier annuity starting date that is being distributed as a phased retirement benefit.

(ii) *Conditions.* The additional phased retirement benefit described in paragraph (e)(2)(i) of this section may be provided only if—

(A) The prior phased retirement benefit was not based on the employee's entire phased retirement accrued benefit at the annuity starting date for the prior phased retirement benefit, or

(B) The employee's work schedule at the later annuity starting date is less than the employee's work schedule that was used to calculate the prior phased retirement benefit.

(3) *Application of section 411(d)(6)*. In accordance with § 1.411(d)-4, A-1(b)(1), the right to receive a partial distribution of an employee's accrued benefit as a phased retirement benefit is treated as an optional form of payment that is separate from the right to receive a full distribution of the accrued benefit upon full retirement.

(4) *Application of nondiscrimination rules*. The right to receive a phased retirement benefit is a benefit, right, or feature that is subject to § 1.401(a)(4)-4.

(f) *Examples*. The following examples illustrate the application of this section:

Example 1. (i) *Employer's Plans*. Plan X (as in effect prior to amendment to reflect the phased retirement program described below) is a defined benefit plan maintained by Employer M. Plan X provides an accrued benefit of 1.5 % of the average of an employee's highest three years of pay (based on the highest 36 consecutive months of pay), times years of service (with 1,000 hours of service required for a year of service), payable as a life annuity beginning at age 65. Plan X permits employees to elect to commence actuarially reduced distributions at any time after the later of termination of employment or attainment of age 50, except that if an employee retires after age 55 and completion of 20 years of service, the applicable reduction is only 3 % per year for the years between ages 65 and 62 and 6 % per year for the years between ages 62 to 55. Plan X permits employees to select, with spousal consent, a single life annuity, a joint and contingent annuity with the employee having the right to select any beneficiary and a continuation percentage of 50 %, 75 %, or 100 %, or a 10-year certain and life annuity.

(ii) *Phased Retirement Program*. Employer M adopts a voluntary phased retirement program that will only be available for employees who retire during the two-year period from February 1, 2006 to January 31, 2008. The program will not be available to employees who are not entitled to an immediate pension or who are 1 percent owners. Employer M has determined that employees typically begin to retire after attainment of age 55 with at least 15 years of service. Accordingly, to increase retention of certain employees, the program will provide that employees in certain specified work positions who have reached age 59 ½ and completed 15 years of service may elect phased retirement. The program permits phased retirement to be implemented through a reduction of 25 %, 50 %, or 75 % in the number of hours expected to be worked for up to 5 years following phased retirement (other reduced schedules may be elected with the approval of M), with the employee's compensation during the phased retirement period to be based on what a similar full-time employee would be paid, reduced by the applicable percentage reduction in hours expected to be worked. In order to participate in the program, the employee and the employer must enter into an agreement under which the employee will reduce his or her hours accordingly. The agreement also provides that the employee's compensation during phased retirement will be reduced by that same percentage. The program is announced to employees in the fall of 2005.

(iii) *Plan Provisions Regarding Phased Retirement Benefit*. (A) Plan X is amended, prior to February 1, 2006, to provide that an employee who elects phased retirement under M's phased retirement program is permitted to commence benefits with respect to a portion of his or her accrued retirement benefit (the employee's phased retirement accrued benefit), based on the applicable percentage reduction in hours expected to be worked. For example, for a 25 % reduction in hours, the employee is entitled to commence benefits with respect to 25 % of his or her accrued benefit. Plan X permits an employee who commences phased retirement to elect, with spousal consent, from any of the optional forms provided under the plan.

(B) During the phased retirement period, the employee will continue to accrue benefits (without regard to the plan's 1,000 hour requirement), with his or her pay for purposes of calculating benefits under Plan X increased by the ratio of 100 percent to the percentage of full-time pay that will be paid during phased retirement and with the employee's service credit to be equal to the product of the same percentage times the service credit that would apply if the employee were working full time. Upon the employee's subsequent full retirement, his or her total accrued benefit will be based on the resulting highest three years of pay and total years of service, offset by the phased retirement accrued benefit. The retirement benefit payable upon subsequent full retirement is in addition to the phased retirement

benefit. Plan X does not provide for a new election with respect to the phased retirement benefit.

(C) In the case of death during the phased retirement period, the employee will be treated as a former employee to the extent of his or her phased retirement benefit and as an active employee to the extent of the retirement benefit that would be due upon full retirement.

(D) Because the terms of the phased retirement program provide that the employee's compensation during phased retirement will be reduced by that same percentage as applies to calculate phased retirement benefits, Plan X does not have provisions requiring annual testing of hours actually worked.

(iv) *Application to a Specific Employee* —(A) *Phased retirement benefit*. Employee E is age 59 ½ with 20 years of credited service. Employee E's compensation is $90,000, and E's highest three years of pay is $85,000. Employee E elects phased retirement on April 1, 2006 and elects to reduce hours by 50 % beginning on July 1, 2006. Thus, E's annuity starting date for the phased retirement benefit is July 1, 2006. Employee E's total accrued benefit as of July 1, 2006 as a single life annuity payable at normal retirement age is equal to $25,500 per year (1.5 % times $85,000 times 20 years of service). Thus, Employee E's phased retirement accrued benefit as of July 1, 2006 as a single life annuity payable at normal retirement age is equal to $12,750 per year ($25,500 times 1 minus E's work schedule fraction of 50 %). Accordingly, Employee E's phased retirement benefit payable as a straight life annuity commencing on July 1, 2006 is equal to $9,690 per year ($12,750 per year times 76 % (100 % minus the applicable reduction for early retirement equal to 3 % for 3 years and 6 % for an additional 2 ½ years)). Employee E elects a joint and 50 % survivor annuity, with E's spouse as the contingent annuitant. Under Plan X, the actuarial factor for this form of benefit is 90 %, so E's benefit is $8,721 per year.

(B) *Death during phased retirement*. If Employee E were to die on or after July 1, 2006 and before subsequent full retirement, E's spouse would be entitled to a 50 % survivor annuity based on the joint and 50 % survivor annuity being paid to E, plus a qualified preretirement survivor annuity that complies with section 417 with respect to the additional amount that would be paid to E if he or she had fully retired on the date of E's death.

(C) *Subsequent full retirement benefit*. Three years later, Employee E fully retires from Employer M. Throughout this period, E's compensation has been 50 % of the compensation that would have been paid to E if he or she were working full time. Consequently, no adjustment in E's phased retirement benefit is required. E's highest consecutive 36 months of compensation would be $95,000 if E had not elected phased retirement and E has been credited with 1 ½ years of service credit for the 3 years of phased retirement (.50 times 3 years). Accordingly, prior to offset for E's phased retirement accrued benefit, E's total accrued benefit as of July 1, 2009 as a single life annuity commencing at normal retirement age is equal to $30,637.50 per year ($95,000 times 1.5 % times 21.5 years of service), and after the offset for E's phased retirement accrued benefit, E's retirement benefit as a single life annuity commencing at normal retirement age is equal to $17,887.50 ($30,637.50 minus $12,750). Thus, the amount of E's additional early retirement benefit payable as a straight life annuity at age 62 ½ is equal to $16,545.94 per year ($17,887.50 per year times 92.5 % (100 % minus 3 % for 2 ½ years)). Employee E elects, with spousal consent, a 10-year certain and life annuity that applies to the remainder of E's accrued benefit. This annuity is in addition to the previously elected joint and 50 % survivor annuity payable as E's phased retirement benefit.

Example 2. (i) *Same Plan and Phased Retirement Program, Except Annual Testing Required*. The facts with respect to the Plan X and M's phased retirement program are the same as in *Example 1*, except that the program does not provide that the employee's compensation during phased retirement will be reduced by that same percentage as is applied to calculate phased retirement benefits, but instead the compensation depends on the number of hours worked by the employee. Plan X provides for annual testing on a calendar year basis and for an employee's phased retirement benefit to be reduced proportionately if the hours worked exceed a threshold, under provisions which reflect the variance permitted paragraph (d)(4)(ii) of this section.

(ii) *Employee Has Small Increase in Hours*. The facts with respect to Employee E are the same as in *Example 1*, except that E's full time work schedule would result in 2,000 hours worked annually, E's work schedule fraction is 50 %, and E works 500 hours from July 1, 2006 through December 31, 2006, 1,000 hours in 2007, 1,200 hours in 2008, and 600 hours from January 1, 2009 through E's full retirement on June 30, 2009.

(iii) *Application of Testing Rules*. No comparison of hours is required for the partial testing period that occurs in 2006. For 2007, no reduction is required in E's phased retirement benefit as a result of the hours worked by E during 2007 because the hours did not exceed E's work schedule (50 % of 2,000). For 2008, although the hours worked by E exceeded E's work schedule, no reduction is required because the hours worked in 2008 were not materially greater than E's work schedule (1,200 is not more than the variance permitted under paragraph (d)(4)(ii) of this section, which is 133 ⅓ percent of 1,000). E's total accrued benefit upon E's retirement on July 1, 2009 would be based on 21.65 years of service to reflect the actual hours worked from July 1, 2006 through June 30, 2009.

Example 3. (i) *Same Plan and Phased Retirement Program, Except Material Increase in Hours.* The facts with respect to the Plan X and M's phased retirement program are the same as in *Example 2*, except E works 1,400 hours in 2008 and 700 hours in the first half of 2009.

(ii) *Application of Testing Rules.* No comparison of hours is required for the partial testing period that occurs in 2006. For 2007, no reduction is required in E's phased retirement benefit as a result of the hours worked by E during 2007 because the hours did not exceed 50 % of 2,000. However, the hours worked by E during 2008 exceed 133 ⅓ percent of E's work schedule (50 % of 2,000), so that the phased retirement benefit paid to E during 2009 must be reduced. The reduction is effective March 1, 2009. The new phased retirement benefit of $5,232.60 is based on 30 % of the participant's accrued benefit as of July 1, 2006, payable as a joint and 50 % survivor annuity commencing on that date (30 % times $25,500 times the early retirement factor of 76 % times the joint and 50 % factor of 90 %). This is equivalent to reducing the previously elected joint and 50 % survivor annuity payable with respect to E by 40 % (400 "excess" hours divided by the 1,000 hour expected reduction). When E retires fully on July 1, 2009, E's total accrued benefit as of July 1, 2009 as a single life annuity commencing at normal retirement age is $31,065 per year ($95,000 times 1.5 % times 21.8 years of service). This accrued benefit is offset by (A) E's phased retirement accrued benefit (which is $7,650 (600 divided by 2,000 times

$25,500)) plus (B) the actuarial equivalent of 40 % of the payments that were made to E from January 1, 2008 through February 28, 2009.

Example 4. (i) *Same Plan and Phased Retirement Program, Except Employer and Employee Agree to Decrease Hours.* The facts with respect to the Plan X and M's phased retirement program are the same as in *Example 2*, except before 2008, E enters into an agreement with M to decrease E's number of hours worked from 50 % of full time to 25 % of full time. E works 500 hours in 2008 and 250 hours in 2009.

(ii) *Application of Multiple Benefit Rule.* Under paragraph (e)(2) of this section, Plan M may provide for an additional phased retirement benefit to be offered to E for 2008. The maximum increase would be for the phased retirement benefit paid to E during 2009 to be increased based on a phased retirement accrued benefit equal to 75 % of E's accrued benefit (1,500 divided by 2,000). Thus, the amount being paid to E would be increased, effective January 1, 2008, based on the excess of 75 % of E's total accrued benefit on December 31, 2007, over E's original phased retirement accrued benefit of $12,750. Employee E would have the right to elect, with spousal consent, any annuity form offered under Plan X (with the actuarial adjustment for time of commencement and form of payment to be based on the age of E and any contingent beneficiary (and E's service, if applicable) on June 1, 2008), which would be in addition to the previously elected joint and 50 % survivor annuity payable as E's original phased retirement benefit. When E retires fully on July 1, 2009, Employee E's total accrued benefit as of July 1, 2009 would be offset by (A) E's original phased retirement accrued benefit plus (B) the phased retirement accrued benefit for which additional phased retirement benefits were payable beginning in 2008.

(g) *Effective date.* The rules of this section apply to plan years beginning on or after the date of publication of the Treasury decision adopting these rules as final regulations in the **Federal Register**.

Mark E. Matthews,

Deputy Commissioner for Services and Enforcement.

¶ 20,261H

IRS proposed regulations: 403(b) retirement annuity contracts: Tax-sheltered annuities: Public school employees: 501(c)(3) tax-exempt organizations.—The IRS has issued proposed regulations relating to retirement annuity contracts under Code Sec. 403(b), generally available to public school employees and Code Sec. 501(c)(3) tax-exempt organizations. According to the IRS, the proposed regulations are the first comprehensive guidance on Code Sec. 403(b) arrangements in over 40 years. The proposed regulations would generally apply to tax years after 2005. Comments must be received by February 14, 2005.

The proposed regulations were published in the *Federal Register* on November 16, 2004 (69 FR 67075) and corrected on December 21, 2004 (69 FR 76422). The final regulations were issued on July 26, 2007 (72 FR 41127). The final regulations preamble, with links to the final regulations, appears at ¶ 23,251.

¶ 20,261I

IRS proposed regulations: Tax shelters: S corporations : Employee stock ownership plans (ESOPs): Disqualified persons: Nonallocation years: Synthetic equity.—The IRS has issued proposed regulations aimed at curbing abuses by S corporation owners that use the tax exemption on S corporation stock held by ESOPs for inappropriate tax deferral or avoidance. In general, an ESOP holding employer securities consisting of S corporation stock must provide that no portion of plan assets attributable to, or allocable in lieu of, such employer securities may, during a nonallocation year, accrue for the benefit of any disqualified persons. The text of the temporary regulations also serves as the text of the proposed regulations. The preamble to the temporary regulations appears at ¶ 23,223.

The proposed regulations, which were published in the *Federal Register* on December 17, 2004 (69 FR 75492) and corrected on February 4, 2005 (70 FR 5948), are reproduced below.

[4830-01-p]

DEPARTMENT OF THE TREASURY

Internal Revenue Service

26 CFR Part 1

[REG-129709-03]

RIN 1545-BC34

Prohibited Allocations of Securities in an S Corporation

AGENCY: Internal Revenue Service (IRS), Treasury.

ACTION: Notice of proposed rulemaking by cross-reference to temporary regulations and notice of public hearing.

SUMMARY: In the Rules and Regulations section of this issue of the **Federal Register,** the IRS is issuing temporary regulations that provide guidance on the definition and effects of a prohibited allocation under section 409(p), identification of disqualified persons and determination of a nonallocation year, calculation of synthetic equity under section 409(p)(5), and standards for determining whether a transaction is an avoidance or evasion of section 409(p). These proposed regula-

tions would generally affect plan sponsors of, and participants in, ESOPs holding stock of Subchapter S corporations. The text of those temporary regulations also serves as the text of these proposed regulations. This document also provides notice of a public hearing on these proposed regulations.

DATES: Written or electronic comments must be received by March 17, 2005. Requests to speak (with outlines of oral comments to be discussed) at the public hearing scheduled for April 20, 2005, at 10 a.m. must be received by March 30, 2005.

ADDRESSES: Send submissions to: CC:PA:LPD:PR (REG-129709-03), room 5203, Internal Revenue Service, POB 7604, Ben Franklin Station, Washington, DC 20044. Submissions may be hand delivered Monday through Friday between the hours of 8 a.m. and 4 p.m. to: CC:PA:LPD:PR (REG-129709-03), Courier's Desk, Internal Revenue Service, 1111 Constitution Avenue, N.W., Washington, DC. Alternatively, taxpayers may submit comments electronically via the IRS Internet site at *www.irs.gov/regs* or the Federal eRulemaking Portal at *www.regulations.gov* (indicate IRS and REG-129709-03).

FOR FURTHER INFORMATION CONTACT: Concerning the proposed regulations, John Ricotta at 622-6060; concerning submissions of comments, contact Guy Traynor at 202-622-7180 (not toll-free numbers).

SUPPLEMENTARY INFORMATION:

Background

Temporary regulations in the Rules and Regulations portion of this issue of the **Federal Register** amend the Income Tax Regulations (26 CFR part 1) relating to section 409(p). The temporary regulations contain rules relating to the definition and effects of a prohibited allocation under section 409(p), identification of disqualified persons and determination of a nonallocation year, calculation of synthetic equity under section 409(p)(5), and standards for determining whether a transaction is an avoidance or evasion of section 409(p). The text of those temporary regulations also serves as the text of these proposed regulations. The preamble to the temporary regulations explains the temporary regulations.

Special Analyses

It has been determined that this notice of proposed rulemaking is not a significant regulatory action as defined in Executive Order 12866. Therefore, a regulatory assessment is not required. It also has been determined that section 553(b) of the Administrative Procedure Act (5 U.S.C. chapter 5) does not apply to these regulations. Because § 1.409(p)-1 imposes no new collection of information on small entities, a Regulatory Flexibility Analysis under the Regulatory Flexibility Act (5 U.S.C. chapter 6) is not required. Pursuant to section 7805(f) of the Internal Revenue Code, this notice of proposed rulemaking will be submitted to the Chief Counsel for Advocacy of the Small Business Administration for comment on its impact on small business.

Comments and Requests for a Public Hearing

Before these proposed regulations are adopted as final regulations, consideration will be given to any written (a signed original and 8 copies) or electronic comments that are submitted timely to the IRS. All comments will be available for public inspection and copying.

A public hearing has been scheduled for April 20, 2005, at 10 a.m. in the IRS Auditorium, Internal Revenue Building, 1111 Constitution Avenue NW., Washington, DC. All visitors must present photo identification to enter the building. Because of access restrictions, visitors will not be admitted beyond the immediate entrance area more than 30 minutes before the hearing starts at the Constitution Avenue entrance. For information about having your name placed on the building access list to attend the hearing, see the "FOR FURTHER INFORMATION CONTACT" section of this preamble.

The rules of 26 CFR 601.601(a)(3) apply to the hearing. Persons who wish to present oral comments at the hearing must submit written comments and an outline of the topics to be discussed and the time to be devoted to each topic (signed original and eight (8) copies) by March 30, 2005. A period of 10 minutes will be allotted to each person for making comments. An agenda showing the scheduling of the speakers will be prepared after the deadline for receiving outlines has passed. Copies of the agenda will be available free of charge at the hearing.

Drafting Information

The principal author of these regulations is John Ricotta of the Office of the Division Counsel/Associate Chief Counsel (Tax Exempt and Government Entities). However, other personnel from the IRS and Treasury participated in their development.

List of Subjects in 26 CFR Part 1

Income taxes, Reporting and recordkeeping requirements.

Proposed Amendments to the Regulations

Accordingly, 26 CFR part 1 is proposed to be amended as follows: PART 1—INCOME TAXES

Paragraph 1. The authority citation for part 1 is amended by adding an entry in numerical order to read, in part, as follows:

Authority: 26 U.S.C. 7805 * * *

Section 1.409(p)-1 also issued under 26 U.S.C. 409(p)(7)(A). * * *

Par. 2. Section 1.409(p)-1 is added to read as follows:

§ 1.409(p)-1 Prohibited allocations of securities in an S corporation.

[The text of proposed § 1.409(p)-1 is the same as the text of § 1.409(p)-1T published elsewhere in this issue of the **Federal Register**].

Mark E. Matthews,

Deputy Commissioner for Services and Enforcement.

CERTIFIED COPY

DALE GOODE

¶ 20,261J

IRS proposed regulations: Health plans: HIPAA: Family and Medical Leave Act: Tolling of time periods: Creditable coverage.—The IRS has issued proposed regulations relating to the interaction between the Health Insurance Portability and Accountability Act (HIPAA) and the Family and Medical Leave Act (FMLA). Under the proposed regulations, the beginning of the period that is used for determining whether a significant break in coverage has occurred (generally 63 days) is tolled in cases in which a certificate of creditable coverage is not provided on or before the day coverage ceases. In those cases, the significant break-in-coverage period is tolled until a certificate is provided but not beyond 44 days after the coverage ceases. These rules are being jointly issued with the Employee Benefits Security Administration (EBSA). Comments must be received by March 30, 2005.

The proposed regulations, which were published in the *Federal Register* on December 30, 2004 (69 FR 78799), are reproduced below.

DEPARTMENT OF THE TREASURY

Internal Revenue Service

26 CFR Part 54

[REG-130370-04]

RIN 1545-BD51

Notice of Proposed Rulemaking for Health Coverage Portability: Tolling Certain Time Periods and Interaction With the Family and Medical Leave Act Under HIPAA Titles I and IV

AGENCIES: Internal Revenue Service, Department of the Treasury; Employee Benefits Security Administration, Department of Labor; Centers for Medicare & Medicaid Services, Department of Health and Human Services.

ACTION: Notice of proposed rulemaking and request for comments.

SUMMARY: These proposed rules would clarify certain portability requirements for group health plans and issuers of health insurance coverage offered in connection with a group health plan. These rules propose to implement changes made to the Internal Revenue Code, the Employee Retirement Income Security Act, and the Public Health Service Act enacted as part of the Health Insurance Portability and Accountability Act of 1996.

DATES: Written comments on this notice of proposed rulemaking are invited and must be received by the Departments on or before March 30, 2005.

ADDRESSES: Written comments should be submitted with a signed original and three copies (except for electronic submissions) to any of the addresses specified below. Any comment that is submitted to any Department will be shared with the other Departments.

Comments to the IRS can be addressed to: CC:PA:LPD:PR (REG-130370-04), Room 5203, Internal Revenue Service, POB 7604, Ben Franklin Station, Washington, DC 20044.

In the alternative, comments may be hand-delivered between the hours of 8 a.m. and 4 p.m. to: CC:PA:LPD:PR (REG-130370-04), Courier's Desk, Internal Revenue Service, 1111 Constitution Avenue, NW., Washington, DC 20224.

Alternatively, comments may be transmitted electronically via the IRS or via the Federal eRulemaking Portal at *www.regulations.gov* (IRS-REG-130370-04).

Comments to the Department of Labor can be addressed to: U.S. Department of Labor, Employee Benefits Security Administration, 200 Constitution Avenue NW., Room C-5331, Washington, DC 20210, *Attention:* Proposed Portability Requirements.

Alternatively, comments may be hand-delivered between the hours of 9 a.m. and 5 p.m. to the same address. Comments may also be transmitted by e-mail to: *e-ohpsca.ebsa@dol.gov.*

Comments to HHS can be submitted as described below: In commenting, please refer to file code CMS-2158-P. Because of staff and resource limitations, we cannot accept comments by facsimile (FAX) transmission.

You may submit comments in one of three ways (no duplicates, please):

1. *Electronically.* You may submit electronic comments on specific issues in this regulation to *http://www.cms.hhs.gov/regulations/ecomments.* (Attachments should be in Microsoft Word, WordPerfect, or Excel; however, we prefer Microsoft Word.)

2. *By mail.* You may mail written comments (one original and two copies) to the following address ONLY:

Centers for Medicare & Medicaid Services, Department of Health and Human Services, Attention: CMS-2158-P, P.O. Box 8017, Baltimore, MD 21244-8010.

Please allow sufficient time for mailed comments to be received before the close of the comment period.

3. *By hand or courier.* If you prefer, you may deliver (by hand or courier) your written comments (one original and two copies) before the close of the comment period to one of the following addresses. If you intend to deliver your comments to the Baltimore address, please call telephone number (410) 786-7195 in advance to schedule your arrival with one of our staff members. Room 445-G, Hubert H. Humphrey Building, 200 Independence Avenue, SW., Washington, DC 20201; or 7500 Security Boulevard, Baltimore, MD 21244-1850.

(Because access to the interior of the HHH Building is not readily available to persons without Federal Government identification, commenters are encouraged to leave their comments in the CMS drop slots located in the main lobby of the building. A stamp-in clock is available for persons wishing to retain a proof of filing by stamping in and retaining an extra copy of the comments being filed.)

Comments mailed to the addresses indicated as appropriate for hand or courier delivery may be delayed and received after the comment period.

Submission of comments on paperwork requirements. You may submit comments on this document's paperwork requirements by mailing your comments to the addresses provided at the end of the "Collection of Information Requirements" section in this document.

All submissions to the IRS will be open to public inspection and copying in room 1621, 1111 Constitution Avenue, NW., Washington, DC from 9 a.m. to 4 p.m.

All submissions to the Department of Labor will be open to public inspection and copying in the Public Disclosure Room, Employee Benefits Security Administration, U.S. Department of Labor, Room N-1513, 200 Constitution Avenue, NW., Washington, DC from 8:30 a.m. to 4:30 p.m.

All submissions timely submitted to HHS will be available for public inspection as they are received, generally beginning approximately three weeks after publication of a document, at the headquarters for the Centers for Medicare & Medicaid Services, 7500 Security Boulevard, Baltimore, MD 21244, Monday through Friday of each week from 8:30 a.m. to 4:00 p.m. To schedule an appointment to view public comments, phone 410-786-7195.

FOR FURTHER INFORMATION CONTACT:

Dave Mlawsky, Centers for Medicare & Medicaid Services (CMS), Department of Health and Human Services, at 1-877-267-2323 ext. 61565; Amy Turner, Employee Benefits Security Administration, Department of Labor, at (202) 693-8335; or Russ Weinheimer, Internal Revenue Service, Department of the Treasury, at (202) 622-6080.

SUPPLEMENTARY INFORMATION:

Customer Service Information

To assist consumers and the regulated community, the Departments have issued questions and answers concerning HIPAA. Individuals interested in obtaining copies of Department of Labor publications concerning changes in health care law may call a toll free number, 1-866-444-EBSA (3272), or access the publications on-line at *www.dol.gov/ebsa,* the Department of Labor's Web site. These regulations as well as other information on the new health care laws are also available on the Department of Labor's interactive web pages, Health *E* laws. In addition, CMS's publication entitled "Protecting Your Health

Insurance Coverage" is available by calling 1-800-633-4227 or on the Department of Health and Human Services' Web site (www.cms.hhs.gov/hipaa1), which includes the interactive webpages, HIPAA Online. Copies of the HIPAA regulations, as well as notices and press releases related to HIPAA and other health care laws, are also available at the above-referenced Web sites.

Background

The Health Insurance Portability and Accountability Act of 1996 (HIPAA), Public Law 104-191, was enacted on August 21, 1996. HIPAA amended the Internal Revenue Code of 1986 (Code), the Employee Retirement Income Security Act of 1974 (ERISA), and the Public Health Service Act (PHS Act) to provide for, among other things, improved portability and continuity of health coverage. Interim final regulations implementing the HIPAA provisions were first made available to the public on April 1, 1997 (published in the **Federal Register** on April 8, 1997, 62 FR 16894) (April 1997 interim rules). On December 29, 1997, the Departments published a clarification of the April 1997 interim rules as they relate to excepted benefits. On October 25, 1999, the Departments published a notice in the **Federal Register** (64 FR 57520) soliciting additional comments on the portability requirements based on the experience of plans and issuers operating under the April 1997 interim rules.

After consideration of all the comments received on the portability provisions, the Departments are publishing final regulations elsewhere in this issue of the **Federal Register**. These proposed rules address additional and discrete issues for which the Departments are soliciting further comment before promulgating final regulations.

Overview of the Proposed Regulations

1. Rules Relating to Creditable Coverage—26 CFR 54.9801-4, 29 CFR 2590.701-4, 45 CFR 146.113

Tolling of the 63-Day Break-in-Coverage Rule

These proposed rules would modify the 63-day break-in-coverage rules with one significant substantive change. Under the proposed rules, the beginning of the period that is used for determining whether a significant break in coverage has occurred (generally 63 days) is tolled in cases in which a certificate of creditable coverage is not provided on or before the day coverage ceases. In those cases, the significant-break-in-coverage period is tolled until a certificate is provided but not beyond 44 days after the coverage ceases.

The Departments have fashioned this tolling rule (and a similar tolling rule for the 30-day period for requesting special enrollment) in an effort to address the inequity of individuals' losing coverage without being aware that the coverage has ended while minimizing the burdens on subsequent plans and issuers that are not responsible for providing the missing or untimely certificates. Numerous situations have come to the attention of the Departments in which an individual's health coverage is terminated but in which the individual does not learn of the termination of coverage until well after it occurs. The statute generally requires that a certificate of creditable coverage be provided at the time an individual ceases to be covered under a plan. The statute, the April 1997 interim rules, and the final regulations (published elsewhere in this issue of the **Federal Register**) all permit a plan or issuer to provide the certificate at a later date if it is provided at a time consistent with notices required under a COBRA continuation provision. The statute also directs the Secretaries to establish rules to prevent a plan or issuer's failure to provide a certificate timely from adversely affecting the individual's subsequent coverage. If a plan or issuer chooses to provide a certificate later than the date an individual loses coverage, as the regulations permit in certain circumstances, these proposed rules provide that an individual should not suffer from this rule of convenience for the plan or issuer. However, to prevent the abuse that might result from an open-ended tolling rule, an outside limit of 44 days is placed on this relief. This reflects the fact that, in most cases, plans and issuers are required to provide certificates within 44 days (although some plans and issuers may be required to provide certificates sooner than 44 days after coverage ceases and some entities are not required to provide certificates at all). The Departments have adopted this uniform limit on the tolling rule for purposes of consistency. New examples have been added to illustrate the tolling rule.

2. Evidence of Creditable Coverage—26 CFR 54.9801-5, 29 CFR 2590.701-5, 45 CFR 146.115

Information in Certificate and Model Certificate

These proposed rules would modify the required elements for the educational statement in certificates of creditable coverage to require a disclosure about the Family and Medical Leave Act. Use of the first model certificate below by group health plans and group health insurance issuers, or use of the appropriate model certificate that appears in the preamble to the related final regulations published elsewhere in this issue of the **Federal Register**, will satisfy the requirements of paragraph (a)(3)(ii) in this section of the final regulations. Similarly, for purposes of complying with those final regulations, State Medicaid programs may use the second version below, or may use the appropriate model certificate that appears in the preamble to those final regula-

tions. Thus, until this proposed regulation is published as a final regulation, entities may use either the model certificates published below, or those published elsewhere in this issue of the **Federal Register**. For entities that choose not to use the model certificates below until this proposed regulation is published as a final regulation, we welcome comments as to the applicability date for using them.

BILLING CODE 4830-01-P

CERTIFICATE OF GROUP HEALTH PLAN COVERAGE

1. Date of this certificate: _____

2. Name of group health plan: _____
_____

3. Name of participant: _____

4. Identification number of participant: _____

5 Name of individuals to whom this certificate
applies: _____
_____

6. Name, address, and telephone number of
plan administrator or issuer responsible
for providing this certificate:_____
_____
_____

7. For further information, call: _____

8. If the individual(s) identified in line 5 has (have)
at least 18 months of creditable coverage
(disregarding periods of coverage before
a 63-day break), check here and skip lines 9 and
10: ___

9. Date waiting period or affiliation period
(if any) began: _____

10. Date coverage began: _____

11. Date coverage ended (or if coverage has not
ended, enter "continuing"): _____

[Note: separate certificates will be furnished if information is not identical for the participant and each beneficiary.]

Statement of HIPAA Portability Rights

IMPORTANT — KEEP THIS CERTIFICATE. This certificate is evidence of your coverage under this plan.
Under a federal law known as HIPAA, you may need evidence of your coverage to reduce a preexisting condition
exclusion period under another plan, to help you get special enrollment in another plan, or to get certain types of
individual health coverage even if you have health problems.

Preexisting condition exclusions. Some group health plans restrict coverage for medical conditions present before
an individual's enrollment. These restrictions are known as "preexisting condition exclusions." A preexisting
condition exclusion can apply only to conditions for which medical advice, diagnosis, care, or treatment was
recommended or received within the 6 months before your "enrollment date." Your enrollment date is your first day
of coverage under the plan, or, if there is a waiting period, the first day of your waiting period (typically, your first
day of work). In addition, a preexisting condition exclusion cannot last for more than 12 months after your
enrollment date (18 months if you are a late enrollee). Finally, a preexisting condition exclusion cannot apply to
pregnancy and cannot apply to a child who is enrolled in health coverage within 30 days after birth, adoption, or
placement for adoption.

If a plan imposes a preexisting condition exclusion, the length of the exclusion must be reduced by the amount of
your prior creditable coverage. Most health coverage is creditable coverage, including group health plan coverage,
COBRA continuation coverage, coverage under an individual health policy, Medicare, Medicaid, State Children's
Health Insurance Program (SCHIP), and coverage through high-risk pools and the Peace Corps. Not all forms of
creditable coverage are required to provide certificates like this one. If you do not receive a certificate for past
coverage, talk to your new plan administrator.

You can add up any creditable coverage you have, including the coverage shown on this certificate. However, if at
any time you went for 63 days or more without any coverage (called a break in coverage) a plan may not have to
count the coverage you had before the break.

➔   Therefore, once your coverage ends, you should try to obtain alternative coverage as soon as possible to avoid a
63-day break. You may use this certificate as evidence of your creditable coverage to reduce the length of any
preexisting condition exclusion if you enroll in another plan.

Right to get special enrollment in another plan. Under HIPAA, if you lose your group health plan coverage, you may be able to get into another group health plan for which you are eligible (such as a spouse's plan), even if the plan generally does not accept late enrollees, if you request enrollment within 30 days. (Additional special enrollment rights are triggered by marriage, birth, adoption, and placement for adoption.)

➔   Therefore, once your coverage ends, if you are eligible for coverage in another plan (such as a spouse's plan), you should request special enrollment as soon as possible.

Prohibition against discrimination based on a health factor. Under HIPAA, a group health plan may not keep you (or your dependents) out of the plan based on anything related to your health. Also, a group health plan may no charge you (or your dependents) more for coverage, based on health, than the amount charged a similarly situated individual.

Right to individual health coverage. Under HIPAA, if you are an "eligible individual," you have a right to buy certain individual health policies (or in some states, to buy coverage through a high-risk pool) without a preexisting condition exclusion. To be an eligible individual, you must meet the following requirements:

- You have had coverage for at least 18 months without a break in coverage of 63 days or more;
- Your most recent coverage was under a group health plan (which can be shown by this certificate);
- Your group coverage was not terminated because of fraud or nonpayment of premiums;
- You are not eligible for COBRA continuation coverage or you have exhausted your COBRA benefits (or continuation coverage under a similar state provision); and
- You are not eligible for another group health plan, Medicare, or Medicaid, and do not have any other health insurance coverage.

The right to buy individual coverage is the same whether you are laid off, fired, or quit your job.

➔   Therefore, if you are interested in obtaining individual coverage and you meet the other criteria to be an eligible individual, you should apply for this coverage as soon as possible to avoid losing your eligible individual status due to a 63-day break.

Special information for people on FMLA leave. If you are taking leave under the Family and Medical Leave Act (FMLA) and you drop health coverage during your leave, any days without health coverage while on FMLA leave will not count towards a 63-day break in coverage. In addition, if you do not return from leave, the 30-day period to request special enrollment in another plan will not start before your FMLA leave ends.

➔   Therefore, when you apply for other health coverage, you should tell your plan administrator or health insurer about any prior FMLA leave.

State flexibility. This certificate describes minimum HIPAA protections under federal law. States may require insurers and HMOs to provide additional protections to individuals in that state.

For more information. If you have questions about your HIPAA rights, you may contact your state insurance department or the U.S. Department of Labor, Employee Benefits Security Administration (EBSA) toll-free at 1-866-444-3272 (for free HIPAA publications ask for publications concerning changes in health care laws). You may also contact the CMS publication hotline at 1-800-633-4227 (ask for "Protecting Your Health Insurance Coverage"). These publications and other useful information are also available on the Internet at: http://www.dol.gov/ebsa, the DOL's interactive web pages - Health Elaws, or http://www.cms.hhs.gov/hipaa1.

CERTIFICATE OF MEDICAID COVERAGE

1. Date of this certificate: _____

2. Name of state Medicaid program:
_____

3. Name of recipient: _____

4. Identification number of recipient:
_____

5. Name of individuals to whom this certificate applies: _____
_____

6. Name, address, and telephone number of state Medicaid agency responsible for providing this certificate: _____
_____
_____

7. For further information call: _____

8. If the individual(s) identified in line 5 has (have) at least 18 months of creditable coverage (disregarding periods of coverage before a 63-day break), check here and skip line 9. ____

9. Date coverage began: _____

10. Date coverage ended (or if coverage has not ended, enter "continuing"): _____

[Note: separate certificates will be furnished if information is not identical for the recipient and each dependent.]

Statement of HIPAA Portability Rights

IMPORTANT — KEEP THIS CERTIFICATE. This certificate is evidence of your coverage under this state Medicaid program. Under a federal law known as HIPAA, you may need evidence of your coverage to reduce a preexisting condition exclusion period under a group health plan, to help you get special enrollment in a group health plan, or to get certain types of individual health coverage even if you have health problems.

Preexisting condition exclusions. Some group health plans restrict coverage for medical conditions present before an individual's enrollment. These restrictions are known as "preexisting condition exclusions." A preexisting condition exclusion can apply only to conditions for which medical advice, diagnosis, care, or treatment was recommended or received within the 6 months before your "enrollment date." Your enrollment date is your first day of coverage under the plan, or, if there is a waiting period, the first day of your waiting period (typically, your first day of work). In addition, a preexisting condition exclusion cannot last for more than 12 months after your enrollment date (18 months if you are a late enrollee). Finally, a preexisting condition exclusion cannot apply to pregnancy and cannot apply to a child who is enrolled in health coverage within 30 days after birth, adoption, or placement for adoption.

If a plan imposes a preexisting condition exclusion, the length of the exclusion must be reduced by the amount of your prior creditable coverage. Most health coverage is creditable coverage, including group health plan coverage, COBRA continuation coverage, coverage under an individual health policy, Medicare, Medicaid, State Children's Health Insurance Program (SCHIP), and coverage through high-risk pools and the Peace Corps. Not all forms of creditable coverage are required to provide certificates like this one. If you do not receive a certificate for past coverage, talk to your new plan administrator.

You can add up any creditable coverage you have, including the coverage shown on this certificate. However, if at any time you went for 63 days or more without any coverage (called a break in coverage) a plan may not have to count the coverage you had before the break.

➔ Therefore, once your coverage ends, you should try to obtain alternative coverage as soon as possible to avoid a 63-day break. You may use this certificate as evidence of your creditable coverage to reduce the length of any preexisting condition exclusion if you enroll in a group health plan.

Right to get special enrollment in another plan. Under HIPAA, if you lose your group health plan coverage, you may be able to get into another group health plan for which you are eligible (such as a spouse's plan), even if the plan generally does not accept late enrollees, if you request enrollment within 30 days. (Additional special enrollment rights are triggered by marriage, birth, adoption, and placement for adoption.)

➔ Therefore, once your coverage in a group health plan ends, if you are eligible for coverage in another plan (such as a spouse's plan), you should request special enrollment as soon as possible.

Prohibition against discrimination based on a health factor. Under HIPAA, a group health plan may not keep you (or your dependents) out of the plan based on anything related to your health. Also, a group health plan may not charge you (or your dependents) more for coverage, based on health, than the amount charged a similarly situated individual.

Right to individual health coverage. Under HIPAA, if you are an "eligible individual," you have a right to buy certain individual health policies (or in some states, to buy coverage through a high-risk pool) without a preexisting condition exclusion. To be an eligible individual, you must meet the following requirements:

- You have had coverage for at least 18 months without a break in coverage of 63 days or more;
- Your most recent coverage was under a group health plan;
- Your group coverage was not terminated because of fraud or nonpayment of premiums;
- You are not eligible for COBRA continuation coverage or you have exhausted your COBRA benefits (or continuation coverage under a similar state provision); and
- You are not eligible for another group health plan, Medicare, or Medicaid, and do not have any other health insurance coverage.

The right to buy individual coverage is the same whether you are laid off, fired, or quit your job.

➔ Therefore, if you are interested in obtaining individual coverage and you meet the other criteria to be an eligible individual, you should apply for this coverage as soon as possible to avoid losing your eligible individual status due to a 63-day break.

Special information for people on FMLA leave. If you are taking leave under the Family and Medical Leave Act (FMLA) and you drop health coverage during your leave, any days without health coverage while on FMLA leave will not count towards a 63-day break in coverage. In addition, if you do not return from leave, the 30-day period to request special enrollment in another plan will not start before your FMLA leave ends.

➔ Therefore, when you apply for other health coverage, you should tell your plan administrator or health insurer about any prior FMLA leave.

State flexibility. This certificate describes minimum HIPAA protections under federal law. States may require insurers and HMOs to provide additional protections to individuals in that state.

For more information. If you have questions about your HIPAA rights, you may contact your state insurance department or the U.S. Department of Labor, Employee Benefits Security Administration (EBSA) toll-free at 1-866-444-3272 (for free HIPAA publications ask for publications concerning changes in health care laws). You may also contact the CMS publication hotline at 1-800-633-4227 (ask for "Protecting Your Health Insurance Coverage"). These publications and other useful information are also available on the Internet at: http://www.dol.gov/ebsa or http://www.cms.hhs.gov/hipaa1.

BILLING CODE 4830-01-C

¶20,261J

3. Special Enrollment Periods—26 CFR 54.9801-6, 29 CFR 2590.701-6, 45 CFR 146.117

Tolling of the Special Enrollment Period

Under HIPAA, the April 1997 interim rules, and the final regulations, an individual wishing to special enroll following a loss of coverage is generally required to request enrollment not later than 30 days after the loss of eligibility, termination of employer contributions, or exhaustion of COBRA continuation coverage. For individuals whose coverage ceases and a certificate of creditable coverage is not provided on or before the date coverage ceases, this regulation provides for proposed tolling rules similar to those described above for determining a significant break. That is, the special enrollment period terminates at the end of the 30-day period that begins on the first day after the earlier of the date that a certificate of creditable coverage is provided or the date 44 days after coverage ceases.

Modification of Special Enrollment Procedures and When Coverage Begins Under Special Enrollment

The April 1997 interim rules did not establish procedures for processing requests for special enrollment beyond affirming the statutory requirement that requests be made not later than 30 days after the event giving rise to the special enrollment right and providing that the same requirements could be imposed on special enrollees that were imposed on other enrollees (*e.g.*, that the request be made in writing). Some examples in the April 1997 interim rules could be read to suggest that plans and issuers could require individuals requesting special enrollment to file completed applications for health coverage by the end of the special enrollment period.

It has been brought to the Departments' attention that some plans and issuers were imposing application requirements that could not reasonably be completed within the special enrollment period (for example, requiring the social security number of a newborn within 30 days of the birth), effectively denying individuals their right to special enroll their dependents. In this regard, the statute merely requires an employee to request special enrollment, or an individual to seek to enroll, during the special enrollment period. These proposed regulations preserve individuals' access to special enrollment by clarifying that during the special enrollment period individuals are only required to make an oral or written request for special enrollment.

The proposed regulations provide further that after a timely request, the plan or issuer may require the individual to complete all enrollment materials within a reasonable time after the end of the special enrollment period. However, the enrollment procedure may only require information required from individuals who enroll when first eligible and information about the event giving rise to the special enrollment right. While a plan can impose a deadline for submitting the completed enrollment materials, the deadline must be extended for information that an individual making reasonable efforts cannot obtain within that deadline.

Thus, even where a plan requires social security numbers from individuals who enroll when first eligible, the plan must provide an extended deadline for receiving the social security number in the case of a newborn. In no event could a plan deny special enrollment for newborns because an employee could not provide a social security number for the newborn within the special enrollment period.

As regards the effective date of coverage for special enrollments, the proposed rules generally follow the statute, the April 1997 interim final rules, and the final regulations being published elsewhere in this issue of the **Federal Register.** However clarifications of the effective date of coverage are added to conform to the clarification of the special enrollment procedures. Where the special enrollment right results from a loss of eligibility for coverage or marriage, coverage generally must begin no later than the first day of the first calendar month after the date the plan or issuer receives the request for special enrollment. However, if the plan or issuer requires completion of additional enrollment materials, coverage must begin no later than the first day of the first calendar month after the plan or issuer receives enrollment materials that are substantially complete.

Where the special enrollment right results from a birth, coverage must begin on the date of birth. In the case of adoption or placement for adoption, coverage must begin no later than the date of such adoption or placement for adoption. If a plan or issuer requires completion of additional enrollment materials, the plan or issuer must provide benefits once the plan or issuer receives substantially complete enrollment materials. However, the benefits provided at that time must be retroactive to the date of birth, adoption, or placement for adoption.

The Departments welcome comments on these aspects of the proposed rule.

4. Interaction With the Family and Medical Leave Act—26 CFR 54.9801-7, 29 CFR 701-8, 45 CFR 146.120

The proposed rules address how the HIPAA portability requirements apply in situations where a person is on leave under the Family and Medical Leave Act of 1993 (FMLA). A general principle of FMLA is that an employee returning from leave under FMLA should generally be in the same position the employee was in before taking leave. At issue is how to reconcile that principle of FMLA with the HIPAA rights and requirements that are triggered by an individual ending coverage under a group health plan. These proposed regulations provide specific rules that clarify how HIPAA and FMLA interact when the coverage of an employee or an employee's dependent ends in connection with an employee taking leave under FMLA.

With respect to the rules concerning a significant break in coverage, if an employee takes FMLA leave and does not continue group health coverage for any part of the leave, the period of FMLA leave without coverage is not taken into account in determining whether a significant break in coverage has occurred for the employee or any dependents. To the extent an individual needs to demonstrate that coverage ceased in connection with FMLA leave (which would toll any significant break with respect to another plan or issuer), these regulations provide that a plan or issuer must take into account all information that it obtains about an employee's FMLA leave. Further, if an individual attests to the period of FMLA leave and the individual cooperates with a plan's or issuer's efforts to verify the individual's FMLA leave, the plan or issuer must treat the individual as having been on FMLA leave for the period attested to for purposes of determining if the individual had a significant break in coverage. Nonetheless, a plan or issuer is not prevented from modifying its initial determination of FMLA leave if it determines that the individual did not have the claimed FMLA leave, provided that the plan or issuer follows procedures for reconsideration similar to those set forth in the final rules governing determinations of creditable coverage.

The question has arisen whether it would be appropriate to waive the general requirement to provide automatic certificates of creditable coverage in the case of an individual who declines coverage when electing FMLA leave if the individual will be reinstated at the end of FMLA leave. At the time an employee elects FMLA leave, the employer (as well as the employee) may not know if the employee will later return from FMLA leave and elect to be reinstated. Requiring plans and issuers to provide certificates when individuals cease health coverage in connection with FMLA leave may result in some certificates being issued when individuals ceasing coverage will not need the certificates as evidence of coverage (because of later reinstatement). However, automatic issuance likely imposes less burden because the plan or issuer does not need to determine whether a certificate is required. Moreover, automatic issuance eliminates the need for remedial measures if an individual expected to be reinstated in fact is not later reinstated. Thus, these proposed regulations clarify there is no exception to the general rule requiring automatic certificates when coverage ends and provide that if an individual covered under a group health plan takes FMLA leave and ceases coverage under the plan, an automatic certificate must be provided.

With respect to the special enrollment rules, an individual (or a dependent of the individual) who is covered under a group health plan and who takes FMLA leave has a loss of eligibility that results in a special enrollment period if the individual's group health coverage is terminated at any time during FMLA leave and the individual does not return to work for the employer at the end of FMLA leave. This special enrollment period begins when the period of FMLA leave ends. Moreover, the rules that delay the start of the special enrollment period until the receipt of a certificate of creditable coverage continue to operate.

5. Special Rules—Excepted Plans and Excepted Benefits—26 CFR 54.9831-1, 29 CFR 2590.732, 45 CFR 146.145

Determination of Number of Plans

Various provisions in Chapter 100 of the Code, Part 7 of Subtitle B of Title I of ERISA, and Title XXVII of the PHS Act apply when an individual commences coverage or terminates coverage under a group health plan. For example, a certificate of creditable coverage must be provided when an individual ceases to be covered under a group health plan. Under the April 1997 interim rules, it was not always clear whether an individual changing benefit elections among those offered by an employer or employee organization was merely switching between benefit packages under a single plan or was switching from one plan to another. These proposed regulations add rules to remove this uncertainty.

Under these proposed regulations, all medical care benefits made available by an employer or employee organization (including a board of trustees of a multiemployer trust) are generally considered to constitute one group health plan (the default rule). However, the employer or employee organization can establish more than one group health plan if it is clear from the instruments governing the arrangements to provide medical care benefits that the benefits are being provided under separate plans and if the arrangements are operated pursuant to the instruments as separate plans. A multiemployer plan and a nonmultiemployer plan are always separate plans. Under an anti-abuse rule, separate plans are aggregated to the extent necessary to prevent the evasion of any legal requirement.

These rules provide plan sponsors great flexibility while minimizing the burden of making decisions about how many plans to maintain. For example, many employers may wish to minimize the number of certificates of creditable coverage required to be furnished to continuing employees. Under the default rule, because all health benefits provided by an employer are considered a single group health plan, there is no need to furnish a certificate of creditable coverage when an employee merely switches coverage among the options made available by the employer. This need would arise only if the employer designated separate benefit packages as separate plans in the plan documents and only if the benefit packages were also operated pursuant to the plan documents as separate plans.

The anti-abuse rule limits the flexibility of these rules to prevent evasions. For example, a plan sponsor might design an arrangement under which the participation of each of many employees in the arrangement would be considered a separate plan. On the face of it, such an arrangement might appear to satisfy the requirement for a plan being exempt from the requirements of Chapter 100 of the Code, Part 7 of ERISA, and Title XXVII of the PHS Act because on the first day of the plan year each plan would have fewer than two participants who are current employees. This would give the impression that the plans would not have to comply with the prohibitions against discriminating based on one or more health factors, with the restrictions on preexisting condition exclusions, nor with any of the other requirements of Chapter 100 of the Code, Part 7 of ERISA, and Title XXVII of the PHS Act. The anti-abuse rule would require the aggregation of plans under such an arrangement to the extent necessary to make the plans subject to the requirements of Chapter 100 of the Code, Part 7 of ERISA, and Title XXVII of the PHS Act. The anti-abuse rule would apply in similar fashion to prevent the evasion of any other law that applies to group health plans or to the parties administering them or providing benefits under them.

Counting the Average Number of Employees

These proposed regulations add rules for counting the average number of employees employed by an employer during a year.[1] Various rules in Chapter 100 of the Code, Part 7 of ERISA, and Title XXVII of the PHS Act require the determination of such an average number, including the Mental Health Parity Act provisions, the guaranteed access provisions under the PHS Act for small employers, and the exemption from the excise tax under the Code for certain small employers.

Under these proposed regulations, the average number of employees employed by an employer is determined by using a full-time equivalents method. Each full-time employee employed for the entire previous calendar year counts as one employee. Full-time employees employed less than the entire previous calendar year and part-time employees are counted by totaling their employment hours in the previous calendar year (but not to exceed 40 hours for any week) and dividing that number by the annual full-time hours under the employer's general employment practices (but not exceeding 40 hours per week). Any resulting fraction is disregarded. For example, if these calculations produce a result of 50.9, the average number of employees is considered to be 50. If an employer existed for less than the entire previous calendar year (including not being in existence at all), then the determination of the average number of employees is made by estimating the average number of employees that it is reasonably expected that the employer will employ on business days in the current calendar year. For a multiemployer plan, the number of employees employed by the employer with the most employees is attributed to each employer with at least one employee participating in the plan.

Economic Impact and Paperwork Burden

Summary—Department of Labor and Department of Health and Human Services

HIPAA's group market portability provisions, which limit the scope and application of preexisting condition exclusions and establish special enrollment rights, provide a minimum standard of protection designed to increase access to health coverage. The Departments crafted these proposed regulations to secure these protections under certain special circumstances, consistent with the intent of Congress, and to do so in a manner that is economically efficient. The Departments are unable to quantify the regulations' economic benefits and costs, but believe that their benefits will justify their costs.

HIPAA's primary economic effects ensue directly from its statutory provisions. HIPAA's statutory group market portability provisions extend coverage to certain individuals and preexisting conditions not otherwise covered. This extension of coverage entails both benefits and costs. Individuals enjoying expanded coverage will realize benefits, sometimes including improvements in health and relief from so-called "job lock." The costs of HIPAA's portability provisions generally include the cost of extending coverage, as well as certain attendant administrative costs. The Departments believe that the benefits of HIPAA are concentrated in a relatively small population, while the costs are distributed broadly across group plan enrollees. The economic effects of HIPAA's statutory portability provisions are discussed in detail in the preamble to the final regulation under the "Effects of the Statute" of the "Basis for Assessment of Economic Impact" section, published elsewhere in this issue of the **Federal Register**.

By clarifying and securing HIPAA's statutory portability protections, these proposed regulations will help ensure that HIPAA rights are fully realized. The result is likely to be a small increase at the margin in the economic effects of HIPAA's statutory portability provisions.

These proposed regulations are intended to secure and implement HIPAA's group market portability and special enrollment provisions under certain special circumstances. The regulations will secure HIPAA's portability rights for individuals who are not timely notified that their coverage has ended and for individuals whose coverage ends in connection with the taking of leave that is guaranteed under FMLA. The regulations also will clarify and thereby secure individuals' special enrollment rights under HIPAA, and clarify the methodologies to be used by employers to determine the number of plans offered and the average number of individuals employed during a given year.

Additional economic benefits derive from the regulations' clarifications of HIPAA requirements. The regulations will reduce uncertainty and costly disputes between employees, employers and issuers, and promote confidence among employees in health benefits' value, thereby promoting labor market efficiency and fostering the establishment and continuation by employers of group health plans.

Benefits under these regulations will be concentrated among a small number of affected individuals while costs will be spread thinly across group plan enrollees.

Affected individuals will generally include those who would have lost access to coverage for needed medical care after being denied HIPAA portability and/or special enrollment rights due to time spent without coverage prior to receiving a certificate or while on FMLA-guaranteed leave. The benefits of these regulations for any particular affected individual may be significant. As noted above and under "Effects of the Statute" in the "Basis for Assessment of Economic Impact" section of the preamble to the final regulation, published elsewhere in this issue of the **Federal Register**, access to coverage for needed medical care is important to individuals' health and productivity. However, the number of affected individuals, and therefore the aggregate cost of extended access to coverage under these regulations, is expected to be small, for several reasons. First, these regulations extend HIPAA rights only in instances where individuals are not timely notified that their coverage has ended or their coverage ends in connection with the taking of FMLA-guaranteed leave. Second, the period over which this regulation extends rights will often be short, insofar as certificates are often provided promptly after coverage ends and many family leave periods are far shorter than the guaranteed 12 weeks. Third, it is generally in individuals' interest to minimize periods of uninsurance. Individuals are likely to exercise their portability and special enrollment rights as soon as possible after coverage ends, which will often be before any extension of such rights under these regulations becomes effective. Fourth, only a portion of individuals who enroll in health plans in circum-

---

[1] The rules for determining the average number of employees employed by an employer during a year are not used for counting the number employed by the employer on a given day, such as the first day of a plan year.

stances where these regulations alone guarantee their special enrollment or portability rights would otherwise have been denied such rights. Fifth, only a small minority of individuals who avoid a significant break in coverage as a direct result of these regulations would otherwise have lost coverage for needed medical care. (The affected minority would be those who suffer from preexisting conditions, join health plans that exclude coverage for such conditions, and require treatment of such conditions during the exclusion periods.)

Affected individuals may also include some who would have been denied special enrollment rights if plans or issuers failed to recognize their requests for special enrollment or imposed unreasonable deadlines or requirements for completion of enrollment materials.

As noted above, the Departments expect that these regulations will increase at the margin the economic effects of HIPAA's statutory portability provisions. For the reasons stated immediately above, the Departments believe that these increases will be small on aggregate, adding only a small increment to the costs attributable to HIPAA's statutory portability provisions, which themselves amount to a small fraction of one percent of health plan expenditures. Additionally, as with the cost of HIPAA's statutory portability provisions, the majority of these costs will be borne by group plan enrollees. The Departments expect these regulations to have little or no perceptible negative impact on employers' propensity to offer health benefit plans or on the generosity of those plans. In sum, the Departments expect that the benefits of these regulations, which can be very large for a particular affected individual, will justify their costs. The basis for the Departments' conclusions is detailed below.

The Departments solicit comments on their conclusions and their basis for them, and empirical data or other information that would support a fuller or more accurate analysis.

Executive Order 12866—Department of Labor and Department of Health and Human Services

Under Executive Order 12866 (58 FR 551735, Oct. 4, 1993), the Departments must determine whether a regulatory action is "significant" and therefore subject to the requirements of the Executive Order and subject to review by the Office of Management and Budget (OMB). Under section 3(f), the order defines a "significant regulatory action" as an action that is likely to result in a rule: (1) Having an annual effect on the economy of $100 million or more, or adversely and materially affecting a sector of the economy, productivity, competition, jobs, the environment, public health or safety, or state, local or tribal governments or communities (also referred to as "economically significant"); (2) creating serious inconsistency or otherwise interfering with an action taken or planned by another agency; (3) materially altering the budgetary impacts of entitlement grants, user fees, or loan programs or the rights and obligations of recipients thereof; or (4) raising novel legal or policy issues arising out of legal mandates, the President's priorities, or the principles set forth in the Executive Order.

Pursuant to the terms of the Executive Order, the Departments have determined that this action raises novel policy issues arising out of legal mandates. Therefore, this notice is "significant" and subject to OMB review under Section 3(f)(4) of the Executive Order. Consistent with the Executive Order, the Departments have assessed the costs and benefits of this regulatory action. The Departments' assessment, and the analysis underlying that assessment, is detailed below. The Departments performed a comprehensive, unified analysis to estimate the costs and benefits attributable to the regulations for purposes of compliance with Executive Order 12866, the Regulatory Flexibility Act, and the Paperwork Reduction Act.

Statement of Need for Proposed Action

These proposed regulations clarify and interpret the HIPAA portability provisions under Section 701 of the Employee Retirement Income Security Act of 1974 (ERISA), Section 2701 of the Public Health Service Act, and Section 9801 of the Internal Revenue Code of 1986. The regulations are needed to secure and implement HIPAA's portability rights for individuals who are not timely notified that their coverage has ended and for individuals whose coverage ends in connection with the taking of leave that is guaranteed under FMLA, and to clarify and secure individuals' special enrollment rights under HIPAA.

Economic Effects

As noted above, HIPAA's primary economic effects ensue directly from its statutory provisions. HIPAA's statutory group market portability provisions extend coverage to certain individuals and preexisting conditions not otherwise covered. This extension of coverage entails both benefits and costs. The economic effects of HIPAA's statutory portability provisions is summarized above and discussed in detail under the "Basis for Assessment of Economic Impact" section of the preamble to the final regulation, published elsewhere in this issue of the **Federal Register**.

Also as noted above, by clarifying and securing HIPAA's statutory portability protections, these regulations will help ensure that HIPAA rights are fully realized. The result is likely to be a small increase at the margin in the economic effects of HIPAA's statutory portability provisions. The benefits of these regulations will be concentrated among a small number of affected individuals, while their costs will be spread thinly across plans and issuers. The regulations also will reduce uncertainty about health benefits' scope and value, thereby promoting employee health benefit coverage and labor market efficiency. The Departments believe that the regulations' benefits will justify their cost. The Departments assessment of the expected economic effects of the regulation are summarized above and discussed in detail below.

Regulatory Flexibility Act—The Department of Labor and Department of Health and Human Services

The Regulatory Flexibility Act (5 U.S.C. 601 *et seq.*) (RFA), imposes certain requirements with respect to Federal rules that are subject to the notice and comment requirements of section 553(b) of the Administrative Procedure Act (5 U.S.C. 551 *et seq.*) and which are likely to have a significant economic impact on a substantial number of small entities. Section 603 of the RFA stipulates that an agency, unless it certifies that a proposed rule will not have a significant economic impact on a substantial number of small entities, must present an initial regulatory flexibility analysis at the time of publication of the notice of proposed rulemaking that describes the impact of the rule on small entities and seeks public comment on such impact. Small entities include small businesses, organizations, and governmental jurisdictions.

For purposes of analysis under the RFA, the Departments consider a small entity to be an employee benefit plan with fewer than 100 participants. The basis for this definition is found in section 104(a)(2) of ERISA, which permits the Secretary of Labor to prescribe simplified annual reports for pension plans which cover fewer than 100 participants. Under section 104(a)(3), the Secretary may also provide for simplified annual reporting and disclosure if the statutory requirements of part 1 of Title I of ERISA would otherwise be inappropriate for welfare benefit plans. Pursuant to the authority of section 104(a)(3), the Department of Labor has previously issued at 29 CFR 2520.104-20, 2520.104-21, 2520.104-41, 2520.104-46 and 2520.104b-10 certain simplified reporting provisions and limited exemptions from reporting and disclosure requirements for small plans, including unfunded or insured welfare plans covering fewer than 100 participants and which satisfy certain other requirements.

Further, while some small plans are maintained by large employers, most are maintained by small employers. Both small and large plans may enlist small third party service providers to perform administrative functions, but it is generally understood that third party service providers transfer their costs to their plan clients in the form of fees. Thus, the Departments believe that assessing the impact of this rule on small plans is an appropriate substitute for evaluating the effect on small entities. The definition of small entity considered appropriate for this purpose differs, however, from a definition of small business based on size standards promulgated by the Small Business Administration (SBA) (13 CFR 121.201) pursuant to the Small Business Act (5 U.S.C. 631 *et seq.*). The Department of Labor solicited comments on the use of this standard for evaluating the effects of the proposal on small entities. No comments were received with respect to the standard. Therefore, a summary of the initial regulatory flexibility analysis based on the 100 participant size standard is presented below.

The economic effects of HIPAA's statutory provisions on small plans are discussed extensively under the "Regulatory Flexibility Act—Department of Labor and Department of Health and Human Services" section of the preamble to the final regulation, published elsewhere in this issue of the **Federal Register**.

By clarifying and securing HIPAA's statutory portability protections, these regulations will help ensure that these benefits are fully realized. The result is likely to be a small increase in the economic effects of HIPAA's statutory provisions. The Departments were unable to estimate the amount of this increase. However, the direct financial value of coverage extensions pursuant to HIPAA's statutory portability provisions are estimated to be approximately $180 million for small plans, or a small fraction of one percent of total small plan expenditures.[2]

The regulations also will reduce uncertainty about health benefits' scope and value, thereby promoting employee health benefit coverage, including coverage under small plans, and labor market efficiency.

The benefits of these regulations will be concentrated among a small number of affected small group plan enrollees, while their costs will be spread thinly across small group plans enrollees. The benefits of these regulations for any particular affected individual, which may include improved health and productivity, may be significant. However, as previously noted, the number of affected individuals, and therefore the aggregate cost of these regulations, is expected to be small. The Departments believe that the benefits to affected individuals of the application of these regulations to small plans justify the cost to small plans of such application. The basis for the Departments' conclusions is detailed below.

The Departments generally expect the impact of the regulations on any particular small plan to be small. A very large majority of small plans are fully insured, so the cost will fall nominally on issuers rather than from plans. Issuers are expected to pass this cost back to plans and enrollees, but will spread much of it across a large number of plans, thereby minimizing the impact on any particular plan. However, it is possible that small plans that self-insure, or fully insured small plans whose premiums are tied closely to their particular claims experience, might bear all or most of the cost associated with extensions of coverage attributable directly to these regulations. The Departments have no way to quantify the incidence or magnitude of such costs, and solicit comments on such incidence and magnitude, and on whether these regulations would have a significant impact on a substantial number of small plans.

Special Analyses—Department of the Treasury

Notwithstanding the determinations of the Departments of Labor and of Health and Human Services, for purposes of the Department of the Treasury this notice of proposed rulemaking is not a significant regulatory action. Because this notice of proposed rulemaking does not impose a collection of information on small entities and is not subject to section 553(b) of the Administrative Procedure Act (5 U.S.C. chapter 5), the Regulatory Flexibility Act (5 U.S.C. chapter 6) does not apply pursuant to 5 U.S.C. 603(a), which exempts from the Regulatory Flexibility Act's requirements certain rules involving the internal revenue laws. Pursuant to section 7805(f) of the Internal Revenue Code, this notice of proposed rulemaking will be submitted to the Chief Counsel for Advocacy of the Small Business Administration for comment on its impact on small business.

Paperwork Reduction Act

Department of Labor

These proposed regulations include three separate collections of information as that term is defined in the Paperwork Reduction Act of 1995 (PRA 95), 44 U.S.C. 3502(3): the Notice of Enrollment Rights, Notice of Preexisting Condition Exclusion, and Certificate of Creditable Coverage. Each of these disclosures is currently approved by the Office of Management and Budget (OMB) through October 31, 2006 in accordance with PRA 95 under control numbers 1210-0101, 1210-0102, and 1210-0103.

Department of the Treasury

These proposed regulations include a collection of information as that term is defined in PRA 95: the Notice of Enrollment Rights, Notice of Preexisting Condition Exclusion, and Certificate of Creditable Coverage. Each of these disclosures is currently approved by OMB under control number 1545-1537.

Department of Health and Human Services

These proposed regulations include three separate collections of information as that term is defined in PRA 95: the Notice of Enrollment Rights, Notice of Preexisting Condition Exclusion, and Certificate of Creditable Coverage. Each of these disclosures is currently approved

by OMB through June 30, 2006 in accordance with PRA 95 under control number 0938-0702.

Small Business Regulatory Enforcement Fairness Act

The rule being issued here is subject to the provisions of the Small Business Regulatory Enforcement Fairness Act of 1996 (5 U.S.C. 801 *et seq.*) and, if finalized, will be transmitted to Congress and the Comptroller General for review. The rule is not a "major rule" as that term is defined in 5 U.S.C. 804, because it is not likely to result in (1) an annual effect on the economy of $100 million or more; (2) a major increase in costs or prices for consumers, individual industries, or federal, state, or local government agencies, or geographic regions; or (3) significant adverse effects on competition, employment, investment, productivity, innovation, or on the ability of United States-based enterprises to compete with foreign-based enterprises in domestic or export markets.

Unfunded Mandates Reform Act

Section 202 of the Unfunded Mandates Reform Act of 1995 requires that agencies assess anticipated costs and benefits before issuing any rule that may result in an expenditure in any 1 year by state, local, or tribal governments, in the aggregate, or by the private sector, of $100 million. These proposed regulations have no such mandated consequential effect on state, local, or tribal governments, or on the private sector.

Federalism Statement Under Executive Order 13132—Department of Labor and Department of Health and Human Services

Executive Order 13132 outlines fundamental principles of federalism. It requires adherence to specific criteria by federal agencies in formulating and implementing policies that have "substantial direct effects" on the States, the relationship between the national government and States, or on the distribution of power and responsibilities among the various levels of government. Federal agencies promulgating regulations that have these federalism implications must consult with State and local officials, and describe the extent of their consultation and the nature of the concerns of State and local officials in the preamble to the regulation.

In the Departments' view, these proposed regulations have federalism implications because they may have substantial direct effects on the States, the relationship between the national government and States, or on the distribution of power and responsibilities among the various levels of government. However, in the Departments' view, the federalism implications of these proposed regulations are substantially mitigated because, with respect to health insurance issuers, the vast majority of States have enacted laws which meet or exceed the federal HIPAA portability standards.

In general, through section 514, ERISA supersedes State laws to the extent that they relate to any covered employee benefit plan, and preserves State laws that regulate insurance, banking or securities. While ERISA prohibits States from regulating a plan as an insurance or investment company or bank, HIPAA added a new section to ERISA (as well as to the PHS Act) narrowly preempting State requirements for issuers of group health insurance coverage. Specifically, with respect to seven provisions of the HIPAA portability rules, states may impose stricter obligations on health insurance issuers.[3] Moreover, with respect to other requirements for health insurance issuers, states may continue to apply state law requirements except to the extent that such requirements prevent the application of HIPAA's portability, access, and renewability provisions.

In enacting these new preemption provisions, Congress intended to preempt State insurance requirements only to the extent that they prevent the application of the basic protections set forth in HIPAA. HIPAA's conference report states that the conferees intended the narrowest preemption of State laws with regard to health insurance issuers. H.R. Conf. Rep. No. 736, 104th Cong. 2d Session 205 (1996). State insurance laws that are more stringent than the federal requirements are unlikely to "prevent the application of" the HIPAA portability provisions, and be preempted. Accordingly, States have significant latitude to impose requirements on health insurance insurers that are more restrictive than the federal law.

---

[2] Computer runs using Medical Expenditure Survey Household Component (MEPS-HC) and the Robert Wood Johnson Employer Health Benefits Survey determined that the share of covered private-sector job leavers at small firms average 35 percent of all covered private sector job leavers. From this, we inferred that the financial burden borne by small plans is approximately 35 percent of the total expenditures by private-sector group health plans which was estimated to be $515 million.

[3] States may shorten the six-month look-back period prior to the enrollment date; shorten the 12-month and 18-month maximum preexisting condition exclusion periods;

increase the 63-day significant break in coverage period; increase the 30-day period for newborns, adopted children, and children placed for adoption to enroll in the plan with no preexisting condition exclusion; further limit the circumstances in which a preexisting condition exclusion may be applied (beyond the federal exceptions for certain newborns, adopted children, children placed for adoption, pregnancy, and genetic information in the absence of a diagnosis); require additional special enrollment periods; and reduce the HMO affiliation period to less than 2 months (3 months for late enrollees).

Guidance conveying this interpretation of HIPAA's preemption provisions was published in the **Federal Register** on April 8, 1997, 62 FR 16904. These proposed regulations clarify and implement the statute's minimum standards and do not significantly reduce the discretion given the States by the statute. Moreover, the Departments understand that the vast majority of States have requirements that meet or exceed the minimum requirements of the HIPAA portability provisions.

HIPAA provides that the States may enforce the provisions of HIPAA as they pertain to issuers, but that the Secretary of Health and Human Services must enforce any provisions that a State fails to substantially enforce. To date, CMS enforces the HIPAA portability provisions in only one State in accordance with that State's specific request to do so. When exercising its responsibility to enforce the provisions of HIPAA, CMS works cooperatively with the State for the purpose of addressing the State's concerns and avoiding conflicts with the exercise of State authority. CMS has developed procedures to implement its enforcement responsibilities, and to afford the States the maximum opportunity to enforce HIPAA's requirements in the first instance. CMS's procedures address the handling of reports that States may not be enforcing HIPAA's requirements, and the mechanism for allocating responsibility between the States and CMS. In compliance with Executive Order 13132's requirement that agencies examine closely any policies that may have federalism implications or limit the policymaking discretion of the States, the Department of Labor and CMS have engaged in numerous efforts to consult and work cooperatively with affected State and local officials.

For example, the Departments sought and received input from State insurance regulators and the National Association of Insurance Commissioners (NAIC). The NAIC is a non-profit corporation established by the insurance commissioners of the 50 States, the District of Columbia, and the four U.S. territories. In most States the Insurance Commissioner is appointed by the Governor, in approximately 14 States, the insurance commissioner is an elected official. Among other activities, it provides a forum for the development of uniform policy when uniformity is appropriate. Its members meet, discuss and offer solutions to mutual problems. The NAIC sponsors quarterly meetings to provide a forum for the exchange of ideas and in-depth consideration of insurance issues by regulators, industry representatives and consumers. CMS and the Department of Labor staff have consistently attended these quarterly meetings to listen to the concerns of the State Insurance Departments regarding HIPAA portability issues. In addition to the general discussions, committee meetings, and task groups, the NAIC sponsors the standing CMS/DOL meeting on HIPAA issues for members during the quarterly conferences. This meeting provides CMS and the Department of Labor with the opportunity to provide updates on regulations, bulletins, enforcement actions, and outreach efforts regarding HIPAA.

The Departments received written comments on the interim regulation from the NAIC and from ten States. In general, these comments raised technical issues that the Departments considered in conjunction with similar issues raised by other commenters. In a letter sent before issuance of the interim regulation, the NAIC expressed concerns that the Departments interpret the new preemption provisions of HIPAA narrowly so as to give the States flexibility to impose more stringent requirements. As discussed above, the Departments address this concern in the preamble to the interim regulation.

In addition, the Departments specifically consulted with the NAIC in developing these proposed regulations. Through the NAIC, the Departments sought and received the input of State insurance departments regarding certain insurance industry definitions, enrollment procedures and standard coverage terms. This input is generally reflected in the discussion of comments received and changes made in Section B— Overview of the Regulations of the preamble to the final regulations published elsewhere in this issue of the **Federal Register**.

The Departments have also cooperated with the States in several ongoing outreach initiatives, through which information on HIPAA is shared among federal regulators, State regulators and the regulated community. In particular, the Department of Labor has established a Health Benefits Education Campaign with more than 70 partners, including CMS, NAIC and many business and consumer groups. CMS has sponsored conferences with the States—the Consumer Outreach and Advocacy conferences in March 1999 and June 2000, and the Implementation and Enforcement of HIPAA National State-Federal Conferences in August 1999, 2000, 2001, 2002, and 2003. Furthermore, both the Department of Labor and CMS Web sites offer links to important State web sites and other resources, facilitating coordination between the State and federal regulators and the regulated community.

Throughout the process of developing these regulations, to the extent feasible within the specific preemption provisions of HIPAA, the Departments have attempted to balance the States' interests in regulating health insurance issuers, and the Congress' intent to provide uniform minimum protections to consumers in every State. By doing so, it is the Departments' view that they have complied with the requirements of Executive Order 13132.

Pursuant to the requirements set forth in Section 8(a) of Executive Order 13132, and by the signatures affixed to proposed final regulations, the Departments certify that the Employee Benefits Security Administration and the Centers for Medicare & Medicaid Services have complied with the requirements of Executive Order 13132 for the attached proposed regulation, Notice of Proposed Rulemaking for Health Coverage Portability: Tolling and Certain Time Periods and Interaction with the Family and Medical Leave Act under HIPAA Titles I & IV (RIN 1210-AA54 and RIN 0938-AL88), in a meaningful and timely manner.

Basis for Assessment of Economic Impact—Department of Labor and Department of Health and Human Services

As noted above, the primary economic effects of HIPAA's portability provisions ensue directly from the statute. The Department's assessment of the economic effects of HIPAA's statutory portability provisions and the basis for the assessment is presented in detail under the "Basis for Assessment of Economic Impact" section of the preamble to the final regulation, published elsewhere in this issue of the **Federal Register**. By clarifying and securing HIPAA's statutory portability protections, these regulations will help ensure that HIPAA rights are fully realized. The result is likely to be a small increase in the economic effects of HIPAA's statutory portability provisions.

Additional economic benefits derive from the regulations' clarifications of HIPAA's portability requirements. The regulations provide clarity through both their provisions and their examples of how those provisions apply in various circumstances. By clarifying employees' rights and plan sponsors' obligations under HIPAA's portability provisions, the regulations will reduce uncertainty and costly disputes over these rights and obligations. They will promote employers' and employees' common understanding of the value of group health plan benefits and confidence in the security and predictability of those benefits, thereby improving labor market efficiency and fostering the establishment and continuation of group health plans by employers.[4]

These proposed regulations are intended to secure and implement HIPAA's group market portability provisions under certain special circumstances. The regulations will secure HIPAA's portability rights for individuals who are not timely notified that their coverage has ended and for individuals whose coverage ends in connection with the taking of leave that is guaranteed under FMLA. The regulations also will clarify and thereby secure individuals' special enrollment rights under HIPAA, and clarify the methodologies to be used by employers to determine the number of plans offered and the average number of individuals employed during a given year.

The benefits of these regulations will be concentrated among a small number of affected individuals.

Affected individuals will generally include those who would have lost access to coverage for needed medical care after forfeiting HIPAA portability and/or special enrollment rights due to time spent without

---

[4] The voluntary nature of the employment-based health benefit system in conjunction with the open and dynamic character of labor markets make explicit as well as implicit negotiations on compensation a key determinant of the prevalence of employee benefits coverage. It is likely that 80% to 100% of the cost of employee benefits is borne by workers through reduced wages (see for example Jonathan Gruber and Alan B. Krueger, "The Incidence of Mandated Employer-Provided Insurance: Lessons from Workers Compensation Insurance," in, David Bradford, ed., *Tax Policy and Economy*, pp:111-143 (Cambridge, MA: MIT Press, 1991); Jonathan Gruber, "The Incidence of Mandated Maternity Benefits," *American Economic Review*, Vol. 84 no. 3 (June 1994), pp. 622-641; Lawrence H. Summers, "Some Simple Economics of Mandated Benefits," *American Economic Review*, Vol. 79, No. 2 (May 1989), pp:177-183; Louise Sheiner, "Health Care Costs, Wages, and Aging," Federal Reserve Board of Governors working paper, April 1999; Mark Pauly and Brad Herring, *Pooling Health Insurance Risks* (Washington, DC: AEI Press, 1999), Gail A. Jensen and Michael A. Morrisey, "Endogenous Fringe Benefits, Compensating Wage Differentials and Older Workers," *International Journal of Health Care Finance and Economics* Vol 1, No. 3-4 (forthcoming), and Edward Montgomery, Kathryn Shaw, and Mary Ellen Benedict, "Pensions and Wages: An Hedonic Price Theory Approach," *International Economic Review*, Vol. 33 No. 1 (Feb. 1992.), pp:111-128.) The prevalence of benefits is therefore largely dependent on the efficacy of this exchange. If workers perceive that there is the potential for inappropriate denial of benefits they will discount their value to adjust for this risk. This discount drives a wedge in the compensation negotiation, limiting its efficiency. With workers unwilling to bear the full cost of the benefit, fewer benefits will be provided. The extent to which workers perceive a federal regulation supported by enforcement authority to improve the security and quality of benefits, the differential between the employers costs and workers willingness to accept wage offsets is minimized.

coverage prior to receiving a certificate or while on FMLA-guaranteed leave. Affected individuals may also include some who would have been denied special enrollment rights if plans or issuers failed to recognize their requests for special enrollment or imposed unreasonable deadlines or requirements for completion of enrollment materials. The benefits of these regulations for any particular affected individual may be large. As noted above, access to coverage for needed medical care is important to individuals' health and productivity. However, the number of affected individuals, and therefore the aggregate cost of extended access to coverage under these regulations, is expected to be small, for several reasons.

First, these regulations extend HIPAA rights only in instances where individuals do not receive certificates immediately when coverage ends or their coverage ends in connection with the taking of FMLA-guaranteed leave. The Departments know of no source of data on the timeliness with which certificates are typically provided. The final regulations that accompany these proposed regulations permit plans to provide certificates with COBRA notices, up to 44 days after coverage ends. Plans, however, often do have the option of providing certificates immediately when coverage ends or even in advance, for example as part of exit packages given to terminating employees or in mailings to covered dependents in advance of birthdays that will end their eligibility for coverage. With respect to FMLA-protected leave, data provided in a 1996 report to Congress suggests that the number of employees who lose coverage in connection with FMLA-protected leave is likely to be small. The report notes that over an 18-month period just 1.2 percent of surveyed employees took what they reported to be FMLA leave. A similar survey of employers found that 3.6 percent of employees took such leave. Nearly all of those taking leave continued their health coverage. (This is not surprising, given that FMLA requires covered employers to extend eligibility for health insurance to employees on FMLA-protected leave on the same terms that applied when the employees were not on leave.) Just 9 percent of leave-takers reported that they lost some kind of employee benefit, with one-third of these reporting that they lost health insurance.[5] Putting these numbers together and converting to an annual basis, in a given year between 0.02 percent and 0.07 percent of employees, or well under one in one thousand, might lose health coverage in connection with FMLA-protected leave. Many of these will ultimately exercise their right to be reinstated in the job from which they took leave and to exercise their FMLA-guaranteed right to resume their previous health coverage. Therefore, the number of employees who will lose coverage and then, later and at the conclusion of FMLA-protected leave, enjoy extended portability rights under HIPAA as a result of these regulations, is likely to be very small.

Second, the period over which this regulation extends rights will often be short, insofar as certificates are often provided promptly after coverage ends and many family leave periods are far shorter than the guaranteed 12 weeks. As noted above, plans generally are required to provide certificates no later than 44 days after coverage ends and may provide them sooner. According to the aforementioned report to Congress on FMLA-protected leave, 41 percent of employees taking FMLA-protected leave did so for less than 8 days. Fifty-eight percent were on leave for less than 15 days, and two-thirds were on leave for less than 29 days. (FMLA protects leaves of up to 12 weeks, or 84 days.)

Third, it is generally in individuals' interest to minimize periods of uninsurance. Individuals are likely to exercise their portability and special enrollment rights as soon as possible after coverage ends, which will often be before any extension of such rights under these regulations becomes effective. Over one 36-month period prior to HIPAA, 71 percent of Americans had continuous coverage—that is, incurred not even a single, one-month break in coverage. Just 4 percent were uninsured for the entire period. About one-half of observed spells without insurance lasted less than 5 months. As noted above, few employees taking FMLA-protected leave had a lapse in health coverage.

Fourth, only a portion of individuals who enroll in health plans in circumstances where these regulations alone guarantee their special enrollment or portability rights would otherwise have been denied such rights. HIPAA special enrollment and portability requirements, both as specified under the final regulations and as modified under these proposed regulations, are minimum standards. Plans are free to provide additional enrollment opportunities.

Fifth, only a small minority of individuals who avoid a significant break in coverage solely as a direct result of these regulations would otherwise have lost coverage for needed medical care. The affected minority would be those who suffer from preexisting conditions, join health plans that exclude coverage for such conditions, and require treatment of such conditions during the exclusion periods. GAO estimated that HIPAA could ensure continued coverage for up to 25 million Americans.[6] More recent estimates suggest that the number of individual policy holders and their dependents which could be helped by HIPAA's portability provisions are more in the 14 million range.[7] As noted above, however, the number of workers and dependents actually gaining coverage for a preexisting condition due to credit for prior coverage following a job change under HIPAA will be smaller than this. Both GAO's and our estimates of people who could benefit include all job changers with prior coverage and their dependents, irrespective of whether their new employer offers a plan, whether their new plan imposed a preexisting condition exclusion period, and whether they actually suffer from a preexisting condition. Accounting for these narrower criteria, CBO estimated that, at any point in time, about 100,000 individuals would have a preexisting condition exclusion reduced for prior creditable coverage. An additional 45,000 would gain added coverage in the individual market. The CBO estimate demonstrates that the number of individuals actually gaining coverage for needed medical services will be a small fraction of all those whose right to such coverage HIPAA's portability provisions guarantee. Accordingly, the Departments expect that the number gaining coverage for needed services as a direct result of these regulations will be a small fraction of the already small number whose right to such coverage these regulations would establish.

The Departments attempted to estimate the number of individuals who might avoid a break in coverage because of the provision of these proposed regulations that tolls the break until the individual receives a certification but not more than 44 days. The Departments examined coverage patterns evident in the Survey of Income and Program Participation (SIPP), a longitudinal household survey that tracks transitions in coverage. SIPP interviews households once every four months. The Departments estimate that, in a given year, about 7 million individuals have breaks in coverage lasting 4 months or less. The survey data suffer from so-called "seam bias"—respondents tend to report that status as unchanged over 4-month increments. Of the 7 million reporting breaks of 4 months or less, 6.5 million report breaks of exactly 4 months. This finding is consistent with the more general finding that breaks of 4 months or less are far more common than longer breaks. It seems likely that the 7 million breaks of 4 months or less actually included proportionate or disproportionately large shares of breaks of 1 or 2 months. Assuming the breaks are actually distributed evenly by length between 1 day and 4 months, then about one-half of the breaks, or 3.5 million breaks, would have lasted less than 63 days and therefore would not have constituted breaks for purposes of HIPAA's portability protections even without reference to the provision of this proposed regulation that tolls the break until the individual receives a certification but not more than 44 days. Approximately three-fourths of the remaining breaks or about 2.6 million breaks, would have lasted between 1 and 44 additional days and thereby potentially have been tolled until the individuals received their certifications but not more than 44 days. Thus 2.6 million provides a reasonable upper bound on the number of individuals who might avoid a break in coverage in a given year because of this tolling provision. It is not known what fraction of these would subsequently join group health plans that include preexisting condition exclusions while suffering from and requiring additional care for preexisting conditions. Comparing GAO's (20 million or more) and our (14 million) estimates of the number of individuals who could potentially benefit from HIPAA's portability protections (individuals with prior creditable coverage who join new health plans in a given year) with the CBO estimate of the number who might actually have added group coverage for needed care (100,000) produces a ratio of about 1 percent. If this proportion holds for group health plan enrollees who avoid breaks because of this tolling provision, then an upper bound of about 26,000 individuals annually might gain coverage for needed care under the proposed regulation's provision treating coverage under such programs as creditable coverage.

[5] Commission on Family and Medical Leave and U.S. Department of Labor, *A Workable Balance: Report to Congress on Family and Medical Leave Policies*, transmitted April 30, 1996.

[6] U.S. General Accounting Office, Report HEHS-95-257, "Health Insurance Portability: Reform Could Ensure Continued Coverage for up to 25 Million Americans," September 1995.

[7] We calculated these estimates using internal runs off the MEPS-HC. These runs gave the number of total job changers, total job changers that had employer-sponsored insurance (ESI), and whether this coverage had been for less than 12 months or not. Estimates for dependents were based off the ratio of policy-holders to total dependents from the March 2003 Current Population Survey (March CPS). It should be noted, however, that the EBSA estimate of 14 million does not include estimate of individuals no longer eligible for COBRA continuation coverage or individuals facing job lock, while the GAO numbers do.

The Departments considered whether certain individuals whose HIPAA portability rights these proposed regulations would extend may be disproportionately likely to be in (or have dependents who are in) poor health. Specifically, individuals taking FMLA-protected leave, especially those who elect not to be reinstated in their prior jobs following FMLA-protected leave, may be so likely. On the other hand, individuals in such circumstances are also particularly unlikely to allow their health insurance from their prior job to lapse while they are on leave. Accordingly, most such individuals' special enrollment periods and countable breaks in coverage (if any) would probably have begun at the conclusion of the FMLA-protected leave even in absence of these proposed regulations. The Departments are therefore uncertain whether individuals who would exercise HIPAA portability rights extended solely by these regulations would be more costly to insure than others exercising HIPAA portability rights, and solicit comments on this question.

Affected individuals may also include some who would have been denied special enrollment rights if plans or issuers failed to recognize their requests for special enrollment or imposed unreasonable deadlines or requirements for completion of enrollment materials.

As noted above, the Departments expect that these regulations will result in a small increase in the economic effects of HIPAA's statutory provisions. For the reasons stated immediately above, the Departments believe that this increase will be small on aggregate, adding only a small increment to the cost attributable to HIPAA's statutory portability provisions, which themselves amount to a small fraction of one percent of health plan expenditures. Thus the increase will be negligible relative to typical year-to-year increases in premiums charged by issuers, which can amount to several percentage points or more. Therefore, the Departments expect these regulations to have little or no perceptible negative impact on employers' propensity to offer health benefit plans or on the generosity of those plans. In sum, the Departments expect that the benefits of these regulations, which can be very large for a particular affected individual, will justify their costs.

List of Subjects

26 CFR Part 54

Excise taxes, Health care, Health insurance, Pensions, Reporting and recordkeeping requirements.

29 CFR Part 2590

Continuation coverage, Disclosure, Employee benefit plans, Group health plans, Health care, Health insurance, Medical child support, Reporting and recordkeeping requirements.

45 CFR Part 146

Health care, Health insurance, Reporting and recordkeeping requirements, and State regulation of health insurance.

Proposed Amendments to the Regulations

Internal Revenue Service

26 CFR Chapter I

Accordingly, 26 CFR part 54 is proposed to be amended as follows:

PART 54—PENSION EXCISE TAXES

Paragraph 1. The authority citation for part 54 is amended by:

a. Revising the entries for §§ 54.9801-4 and 54.9801-6.

b. Adding an entry in numerical order for § 54.9801-7.

The addition and revisions read as follows:

Authority: 26 U.S.C. 7805. * * *

Section 54.9801-4 also issued under 26 U.S.C. 9801(e)(3) and 9833.* * *

Section 54.9801-6 also issued under 26 U.S.C. 9801(e)(3) and 9833.

Section 54.9801-7 also issued under 26 U.S.C. 9833.* * *

§ 54.9801-1 [Amended]

Par. 2. Section 54.9801-1 is amended in paragraph (a)(1) by removing the language "54.9801-6" and adding "54.9801-7" in its place.

§ 54.9801-2 [Amended]

Par. 3. Section 54.9801-2 is amended in the first sentence by removing the language "54.9801-6" and adding "54.9801-7" in its place.

Par. 4. Section 54.9801-4 is amended by:

a. Revising paragraphs (b)(2)(iii) and (b)(2)(iv).

b. Adding *Examples 4* and *6* in paragraph (b)(2)(v).

The revisions and additions read as follows:

§ 54.9801-4 Rules relating to creditable coverage.

* * * * *

(b) *Standard method.* * * *

(2) *Counting creditable coverage.* * * *

(iii) *Significant break in coverage defined.* A *significant break in coverage* means a period of 63 consecutive days during each of which an individual does not have any creditable coverage, except that periods described in paragraph (b)(2)(iv) of this section are not taken into account in determining a significant break in coverage. (See section 731(b)(2)(iii) of ERISA and section 2723(b)(2)(iii) of the PHS Act, which exclude from preemption state insurance laws that require a break of more than 63 days before an individual has a significant break in coverage for purposes of state law.)

(iv) *Periods that toll a significant break.* Days in a waiting period and days in an affiliation period are not taken into account in determining whether a significant break in coverage has occurred. In addition, for an individual who elects COBRA continuation coverage during the second election period provided under the Trade Act of 2002, the days between the date the individual lost group health plan coverage and the first day of the second COBRA election period are not taken into account in determining whether a significant break in coverage has occurred. Moreover, in the case of an individual whose coverage ceases, if a certificate of creditable coverage with respect to that cessation is not provided on or before the date coverage ceases, then the period that begins on the first date that an individual has no creditable coverage and that continues through the earlier of the following two dates is not taken into account in determining whether a significant break in coverage has occurred:

(A) The date that a certificate of creditable coverage with respect to that cessation is provided; or

(B) The date 44 days after coverage ceases.

(v) Examples. * * *

Example 4. (i) *Facts.* Individual *B* terminates coverage under a group health plan, and a certificate of creditable coverage is provided 10 days later. *B* begins employment with Employer *R* and begins enrollment in *R*'s plan 60 days after the certificate is provided.

(ii) *Conclusion.* In this *Example 4,* even though *B* had no coverage for 69 days, the 10 days before the certificate of creditable coverage is provided are not taken into account in determining a significant break in coverage. Therefore, *B*'s break in coverage is only 59 days and is not a significant break in coverage. Accordingly, *B*'s prior coverage must be counted by *R*'s plan.

* * * * *

Example 6. (i) *Facts.* Employer *V* sponsors a group health plan. Under the terms of the plan, the only benefits provided are those provided under an insurance policy. Individual *D* works for *V* and has creditable coverage under *V*'s plan. *V* fails to pay the issuer the premiums for the coverage period beginning March 1. Consistent with applicable state law, the issuer terminates the policy so that the last day of coverage is April 30. *V* goes out of business on July 31. On August 15 *D* begins employment with Employer *W* and enrolls in *W*'s group health plan. *W*'s plan imposes a 12-month preexisting condition exclusion on all enrollees. *D* never receives a certificate of creditable coverage for coverage under *V*'s plan.

(ii) *Conclusion.* In this *Example 6,* the period from May 1 (the first day without coverage) through June 13 (the date 44 days after coverage under *V*'s plan ceases) is not taken into account in determining a 63-day break in coverage. This is because, in cases in which a certificate of creditable coverage is not provided by the date coverage is lost, the break begins on the date the certificate is provided, or the date 44 days after coverage ceases, if earlier. Therefore, even though *D*'s actual period without coverage was 106 days (May 1 through August 14), because the period from May 1 through June 13 is not taken into account, *D*'s break in coverage is only 62 days (June 14 through August 14). Thus, *D* has not experienced a significant break in coverage, and *D*'s prior coverage must be counted by *W*'s plan.

* * * * *

Par. 5. Section 54.9801-5 is amended by:

a. Redesignating paragraphs (a)(3)(ii)(H)(*5*) and (*6*) as paragraphs (a)(3)(ii)(H)(*6*) and (*7*), respectively.

b. Adding a new paragraph (a)(3)(ii)(H)(*5*).

The addition reads as follows:

§ 54.9801-5 Evidence of creditable coverage.

(a) *Certificate of creditable coverage.* * * *

(3) *Form and content of certificate.* * * *

(ii) *Required information.* * * *

(H) * * *

(5) The interaction with the Family and Medical Leave Act;

* * * * *

Par. 6. Section 54.9801-6 is amended by:

a. Revising paragraph (a)(1).

b. Revising paragraph (a)(4).

c. Revising paragraph (b)(1).

d. Revising paragraph (b)(3).

e. Revising *Example* 2 in paragraph (b)(4).

f. Adding *Examples 3, 4,* and *5* in paragraph (b)(4).

The additions and revisions read as follows:

§ 54.9801-6 Special enrollment periods.

(a) *Special enrollment for certain individuals who lose coverage*—(1) *In general.* A group health plan is required to permit current employees and dependents (as defined in § 54.9801-2) who are described in paragraph (a)(2) of this section to enroll for coverage under the terms of the plan if the conditions in paragraph (a)(3) of this section are satisfied. Paragraph (a)(4) of this section describes procedures that a plan may require an employee to follow and describes the date by which coverage must begin. The special enrollment rights under this paragraph (a) apply without regard to the dates on which an individual would otherwise be able to enroll under the plan. (See section 701(f)(1) of ERISA and section 2701(f)(1) of the PHS Act, under which this obligation is also imposed on a health insurance issuer offering group health insurance coverage.)

* * * * *

(4) *Applying for special enrollment and effective date of coverage*—(i) *Request.* A plan must allow an employee a period of at least 30 days after an event described in paragraph (a)(3) of this section (loss of eligibility for coverage, termination of employer contributions, or exhaustion of COBRA continuation coverage) to request enrollment (for the employee or the employee's dependent). For this purpose, any written or oral request made to any of the following constitutes a request for enrollment —

(A) The plan administrator;

(B) An issuer offering health insurance coverage under the plan;

(C) A person who customarily handles claims for the plan (such as a third party administrator); or

(D) Any other designated representative.

(ii) *Tolling of period for requesting special enrollment.* (A) In the case of an individual whose coverage ceases, if a certificate of creditable coverage with respect to that cessation is not provided on or before the date coverage ceases, then the period for requesting special enrollment described in paragraph (a)(4)(i) of this section does not end until 30 days after the earlier of —

(1) The date that a certificate of creditable coverage with respect to that cessation is provided; or

(2) The date 44 days after coverage ceases.

(B) For purposes of this paragraph (a)(4), if an individual's coverage ceases due to the operation of a lifetime limit on all benefits, coverage is considered to cease on the earliest date that a claim is denied due to the operation of the lifetime limit. (Nonetheless, the date of a loss of eligibility for coverage is determined under the rules of paragraph (a)(3) of this section, which provides that a loss of eligibility occurs when a claim that would meet or exceed a lifetime limit on all benefits is incurred, not when it is denied.)

(C) The rules of this paragraph (a)(4)(ii) are illustrated by the following examples:

Example 1. (i) *Facts.* Employer *V* provides group health coverage through a policy provided by Issuer *M.* Individual *D* works for *V* and is covered under *V*'s plan. *V* fails to pay *M* the premiums for the coverage period beginning March 1. Consistent with applicable state law, *M* terminates the policy so that the last day of coverage is April 30. On May 15, *M* provides *D* with a certificate of creditable coverage with respect to *D*'s cessation of coverage under *V*'s plan.

(ii) *Conclusion.* In this *Example 1,* the period to request special enrollment ends no earlier than June 14 (which is 30 days after May 15, the day a certificate of creditable coverage is provided with respect to *D*).

Example 2. (i) *Facts.* Same facts as *Example 1,* except *D* is never provided with a certificate of creditable coverage.

(ii) *Conclusion.* In this *Example 2,* the period to request special enrollment ends no earlier than July 13. (July 13 is 74 days after April 30, the date coverage ceases. That is, July 13 is 30 days after the end of the 44-day maximum tolling period.)

Example 3. (i) *Facts.* Individual *E* works for Employer *W* and has coverage under *W*'s plan. *W*'s plan has a lifetime limit of $1 million on all benefits under the plan. On September 13, *E* incurs a claim that would exceed the plan's lifetime limit. On September 28, *W* denies the claim due to the operation of the lifetime limit and a certificate of creditable coverage is provided on October 3. *E* is otherwise eligible to enroll in the group health plan of the employer of *E*'s spouse.

(ii) *Conclusion.* In this *Example 3,* the period to request special enrollment in the plan of the employer of *E*'s spouse ends no earlier than November 2 (30 days after the date the certificate is provided) and begins not later than September 13, the date *E* lost eligibility for coverage.

(iii) *Reasonable procedures for special enrollment.* After an individual has requested enrollment under paragraph (a)(4)(i) of this section, a plan may require the individual to complete enrollment materials within a reasonable time after the end of the 30-day period described in paragraph (a)(4)(i) of this section. In these enrollment materials, the plan may require the individual only to provide information required of individuals who enroll when first eligible and information about the event giving rise to the special enrollment right. A plan may establish a deadline for receiving completed enrollment materials, but such a deadline must be extended for information that an individual making reasonable efforts does not obtain by that deadline.

(iv) *Date coverage must begin.* If the plan requires completion of additional enrollment materials in accordance with paragraph (a)(4)(iii) of this section, coverage must begin no later than the first day of the first calendar month beginning after the date the plan receives enrollment materials that are substantially complete. If the plan does not require completion of additional enrollment materials, coverage must begin no later than the first day of the first calendar month beginning after the date the plan receives the request for special enrollment under paragraph (a)(4)(i) of this section.

(b) *Special enrollment with respect to certain dependent beneficiaries*—(1) *In general.* A group health plan that makes coverage available with respect to dependents is required to permit individuals described in paragraph (b)(2) of this section to be enrolled for coverage in a benefit package under the terms of the plan. Paragraph (b)(3) of this section describes procedures that a plan may require an individual to follow and describes the date by which coverage must begin. The special enrollment rights under this paragraph (b) apply without regard to the dates on which an individual would otherwise be able to enroll under the plan. (See 29 CFR 2590.701-6(b) and 45 CFR 146.117(b), under which this obligation is also imposed on a health insurance issuer offering group health insurance coverage.)

* * * * *

(3) *Applying for special enrollment and effective date of coverage*—(i) *Request.* A plan must allow an individual a period of at least 30 days after the date of the marriage, birth, adoption, or placement for adoption (or, if dependent coverage is not generally made available at the time of the marriage, birth, adoption, or placement for adoption, a period of at least 30 days after the date the plan makes dependent coverage generally available) to request enrollment (for the individual or the individual's dependent). For this purpose, any written or oral request made to any of the following constitutes a request for enrollment—

(A) The plan administrator;

(B) An issuer offering health insurance coverage under the plan;

(C) A person who customarily handles claims for the plan (such as a third party administrator); or

(D) Any other designated representative.

(ii) *Reasonable procedures for special enrollment.* After an individual has requested enrollment under paragraph (b)(3)(i) of this section, a plan may require the individual to complete enrollment materials within a reasonable time after the end of the 30-day period described in paragraph (b)(3)(i) of this section. In these enrollment materials, the plan may require the individual only to provide information required of individuals who enroll when first eligible and information about the event giving rise to the special enrollment right. A plan may establish a deadline for receiving completed enrollment materials, but such a deadline must be extended for information that an individual making reasonable efforts does not obtain by that deadline.

(iii) *Date coverage must begin*—(A) *Marriage.* In the case of marriage, if the plan requires completion of additional enrollment materials in accordance with paragraph (b)(3)(ii) of this section, coverage must begin no later than the first day of the first calendar month beginning after the date the plan receives enrollment materials that are substantially complete. If the plan does not require such additional enrollment materials, coverage must begin no later than the first day of the first calendar month beginning after the date the plan receives the request for special enrollment under paragraph (b)(3)(i) of this section.

(B) *Birth, adoption, or placement for adoption.* Coverage must begin in the case of a dependent's birth on the date of birth and in the case of a dependent's adoption or placement for adoption no later than the date of such adoption or placement for adoption (or, if dependent coverage is not made generally available at the time of the birth, adoption, or placement for adoption, the date the plan makes dependent coverage available). If the plan requires completion of additional enrollment materials in accordance with paragraph (b)(3)(ii) of this section, the plan must provide benefits (including benefits retroactively to the date of birth, adoption, or placement for adoption) once the plan receives enrollment materials that are substantially complete.

(4) *Examples.* * * *

Example 2. (i) *Facts.* Individual *D* works for Employer *X*. *X* maintains a group health plan with two benefit packages—an HMO option and an indemnity option. Self-only and family coverage are available under both options. *D* enrolls for self-only coverage in the HMO option. Then, a child, *E*, is placed for adoption with *D*. Within 30 days of the placement of *E* for adoption, *D* requests enrollment for *D* and *E* under the plan's indemnity option and submits completed enrollment materials timely.

(ii) *Conclusion.* In this *Example 2*, *D* and *E* satisfy the conditions for special enrollment under paragraphs (b)(2)(v) and (b)(3) of this section. Therefore, the plan must allow *D* and *E* to enroll in the indemnity coverage, effective as of the date of the placement for adoption.

Example 3. (i) *Facts.* Same facts as *Example 1*. On March 17 (two days after the birth of *C*), *A* telephones the plan administrator and requests special enrollment of *A*, *B*, and *C*. The plan administrator sends *A* an enrollment form. Under the terms of the plan, enrollment is denied unless a completed form is submitted within 30 days of the event giving rise to the special enrollment right (in this case, *C*'s birth).

(ii) *Conclusion.* In this *Example 3*, the plan does not satisfy paragraph (b)(3) of this section. The plan may require only that *A* request enrollment during the 30-day period after *C*'s birth. *A* did so by telephoning the plan administrator. The plan may not condition special enrollment on filing additional enrollment materials during the 30-day period. To comply with paragraph (b)(3) of this section, the plan must allow *A* a reasonable time after the end of the 30-day period to submit any additional enrollment materials. Once these enrollment materials are received, the plan must allow whatever coverage is chosen to begin on March 15, the date of *C*'s birth.

Example 4. (i) *Facts.* Same facts as *Example 3*, except that *A* telephones the plan administrator to request enrollment on April 13 (29 days after *C*'s birth). Also, under the terms of the plan, the deadline for submitting the enrollment form is 14 days after the end of the 30-day period for requesting special enrollment (thus, in this case, April 28, which is 44 days after *C*'s birth). The form requests the same information for *A*, *B*, and *C* (name, date of birth, and place of birth) as well as a copy of *C*'s birth certificate. *A* fills out the enrollment form and delivers it to the plan administrator on April 28. At that time *A* does not have a birth certificate for *C* but applies on that day for one from the appropriate government office. *A* receives the birth certificate on June 1 and furnishes a copy of the birth certificate to the plan administrator shortly thereafter.

(ii) *Conclusion.* In this *Example 4*, *A*, *B*, and *C* are entitled to special enrollment under the plan even though *A* did not satisfy the plan's requirement of providing a copy of *C*'s birth certificate by the plan's 14-day deadline. While a plan may establish such a deadline, the plan must extend the deadline for information that an individual making reasonable efforts does not obtain by that deadline. *A* delivered the enrollment form to the plan administrator by the deadline and made reasonable efforts to furnish the birth certificate that the plan requires.

Example 5. (i) *Facts.* Same facts as *Example 4*. On May 3 (after *A* has delivered the enrollment form to the plan administrator but before *A* provides the birth certificate) *A* submits claims for all medical expenses incurred for *B* and *C* from the date of *C*'s birth.

(ii) *Conclusion.* In this *Example 5*, the plan must pay all of the claims submitted by *A*. Because the plan requires that individuals seeking special enrollment complete additional enrollment materials, it is required to provide benefits once it receives enrollment materials that are substantially complete. The form that *A* submitted on April 28 was substantially complete. Because *C*'s birth is the event giving rise to the special enrollment right, on April 28 *A*, *B*, and *C* become entitled to benefits under the plan retroactive to the date of *C*'s birth.

* * * * *

Par. 7. A new § 54.9801-7 is added to read as follows:

§ 54.9801-7 Interaction with the Family and Medical Leave Act.

(a) *In general.* The rules of §§ 54.9801-1 through 54.9801-6 apply with respect to an individual on leave under the Family and Medical Leave Act of 1993 (29 U.S.C. 2601) (FMLA), and apply with respect to a dependent of such an individual, except to the extent otherwise provided in this section.

(b) *Tolling of significant break in coverage during FMLA leave.* In the case of an individual (or a dependent of the individual) who is covered under a group health plan, if the individual takes FMLA leave and does not continue group health coverage for any period of FMLA leave, that period is not taken into account in determining whether a significant break in coverage has occurred under § 54.9801-4(b)(2)(iii).

(c) *Application of certification provisions*—(1) *Timing of issuance of certificate*—(i) In the case of an individual (or a dependent of the individual) who is covered under a group health plan, if the individual takes FMLA leave and the individual's group health coverage is terminated during FMLA leave, an automatic certificate must be provided in accordance with the timing rules set forth in § 54.9801-5(a)(2)(ii)(B) (which generally require plans to provide certificates within a reasonable time after coverage ceases).

(ii) In the case of an individual (or a dependent of the individual) who is covered under a group health plan, if the individual takes FMLA leave and continues group health coverage for the period of FMLA leave, but then ceases coverage under the plan at the end of FMLA leave, an automatic certificate must be provided in accordance with the timing rules set forth in § 54.9801-5(a)(2)(ii)(A) (which generally require plans to provide a certificate no later than the time a notice is required to be furnished for a qualifying event under a COBRA continuation provision).

(2) *Demonstrating FMLA leave.* (i) A plan is required to take into account all information about FMLA leave that it obtains or that is presented on behalf of an individual. A plan must treat the individual as having been on FMLA leave for a period if —

(A) The individual attests to the period of FMLA leave; and

(B) The individual cooperates with the plan's efforts to verify the individual's FMLA leave.

(ii) Nothing in this section prevents a plan from modifying its initial determination of FMLA leave if it determines that the individual did not have the claimed FMLA leave, provided that the plan follows procedures for reconsideration similar to those set forth in § 54.9801-3(f).

(d) *Relationship to loss of eligibility special enrollment rules.* In the case of an individual (or a dependent of the individual) who is covered under a group health plan and who takes FMLA leave, a loss of eligibility for coverage under § 54.9801-6(a) occurs when the period of FMLA leave ends if—

(1) The individual's group health coverage is terminated at any time during FMLA leave; and

(2) The individual does not return to work for the employer at the end of FMLA leave.

Par. 8. Section 54.9831-1 is amended by:

a. Adding paragraph (a)(2).

b. Revising paragraph (b).

c. Revising paragraph (c)(1).

d. By adding paragraph (e).

The additions and revisions read as follows:

§ 54.9831-1 Special rules relating to group health plans.

(a) *Group health plan.* * * *

(2) *Determination of number of plans.* The number of group health plans that an employer or employee organization (including for this purpose a joint board of trustees of a multiemployer trust affiliated with one or more multiemployer plans) maintains is determined under the rules of this paragraph (a)(2).

(i) Except as provided in paragraph (a)(2)(ii) or (iii) of this section, health care benefits provided by a corporation, partnership, or other entity or trade or business, or by an employee organization, constitute one group health plan, unless—

(A) It is clear from the instruments governing the arrangement or arrangements to provide health care benefits that the benefits are being provided under separate plans; and

(B) The arrangement or arrangements are operated pursuant to such instruments as separate plans.

(ii) A multiemployer plan and a nonmultiemployer plan are always separate plans.

(iii) If a principal purpose of establishing separate plans is to evade any requirement of law, then the separate plans will be considered a single plan to the extent necessary to prevent the evasion.

(b) *General exception for certain small group health plans.* The requirements of §§ 54.9801-1 through 54.9801-7, 54.9802-1, 54.9802-2, 54.9811-1T, 54.9812-1T, and 54.9833-1 do not apply to any group health plan for any plan year if, on the first day of the plan year, the plan has fewer than two participants who are current employees.

(c) *Excepted benefits—(1) In general.* The requirements of §§ 54.9801-1 through 54.9801-7, 54.9802-1, 54.9802-2, 54.9811-1T, 54.9812-1T, and 54.9833-1 do not apply to any group health plan in relation to its provision of the benefits described in paragraph (c)(2), (3), (4), or (5) of this section (or any combination of these benefits).

* * * * *

(e) *Determining the average number of employees—(1) Scope.* Whenever the application of a rule in this part depends upon the average number of employees employed by an employer, the determination of that number is made in accordance with the rules of this paragraph (e).

(2) *Full-time equivalents.* The average number of employees is determined by calculating the average number of full-time equivalents on business days during the preceding calendar year.

(3) *Methodology.* For the preceding calendar year, the average number of full-time equivalents is determined by—

(i) Determining the number of employees who were employed full-time by the employer throughout the entire calendar year;

(ii) Totaling all employment hours (not to exceed 40 hours per week) for each part-time employee, and for each full-time employee who was not employed full-time with the employer throughout the entire calendar year;

(iii) Dividing the total determined under paragraph (e)(3)(ii) of this section by a figure that represents the annual full-time hours under the employer's general employment practices, such as 2,080 hours (although for this purpose not more than 40 hours per week may be used); and

(iv) Adding the quotient determined under paragraph (e)(3)(iii) of this section to the number determined under paragraph (e)(3)(i).

(4) *Rounding.* For purposes of paragraph (e)(3)(iv) of this section, all fractions are disregarded. For instance, a figure of 50.9 is deemed to be 50.

(5) *Employers not in existence in the preceding year.* In the case of an employer that was in existence for less than the entire preceding calendar year (including an employer that was not in existence at all), a determination of the average number of employees that the employer employs is based on the average number of employees that it is reasonably expected the employer will employ on business days in the current calendar year.

(6) *Scope of the term "employer."* For purposes of this paragraph (e), employer includes any predecessor of the employer. In addition, all persons treated as a single employer under section 414(b), (c), (m), or (o) are treated as one employer.

(7) *Special rule for multiemployer plans.* (i) With respect to the application of a rule in this part to a multiemployer plan (as defined in section 3(37) of ERISA), each employer with at least one employee participating in the plan is considered to employ the same average number of employees. That number is the highest number that results by applying the rules of paragraphs (e)(1) through (6) of this section separately to each of the employers.

(ii) The rules of this paragraph (e)(7) are illustrated by the following example:

Example. (i) *Facts.* Twenty five employers have at least one employee who participates in Multiemployer Plan *M.* Among these 25 employers, Employer *K* has 51 employees, determined under the rules of paragraphs (e)(1) through (6) of this section. Each of the other 24 employers has fewer than 50 employees.

(ii) *Conclusion.* With respect to the application of a rule in this part to *M,* each of the 25 employers is considered to employ 51 employees.

Mark E. Matthews,

Deputy Commissioner for Services and Enforcement, Internal Revenue Service.

¶ 20,261K

IRS proposed regulations: Tax exempt organizations: Form 990: Magnetic media.—The IRS has issued temporary and proposed regulations requiring certain large corporations and tax-exempt organizations to electronically file their income tax or annual information returns beginning in 2006, for the 2005 tax year. In particular, tax-exempt organizations with total assets of $100 million or more will be required to file the tax year 2005 Forms 990 electronically. In 2007, tax-exempt organizations with total assets of $10 million or more for tax year 2006 will be required to file Form 900 electronically. The text of the temporary regulations also serves as the text of the proposed regulations. The temporary regulations, which were published in the *Federal Register* on January 12, 2005 (70 FR 2012), are reproduced in part at ¶ 13,663 (IRS Reg. Sec. 301.6033-4T). The preamble to the temporary regulations is reproduced at ¶ 23,226.

The text of the proposed regulations, which were published in the *Federal Register* on January 12, 2005 (70 FR 2075), are reproduced below.

DEPARTMENT OF THE TREASURY

Internal Revenue Service (IRS)

26 CFR Parts 1 and 301

[REG-130671-04]

RIN 1545-BD65

Returns Required on Magnetic Media

AGENCY: Internal Revenue Service (IRS), Treasury.

ACTION: Notice of proposed rulemaking by cross-reference to temporary regulations and notice of public hearing.

SUMMARY: In the Rules and Regulations section of this issue of the **Federal Register**, the IRS is issuing temporary regulations relating to the requirements for filing corporate income tax returns, S corporation returns, and returns of organizations required under section 6033 on magnetic media under section 6011(e) of the Internal Revenue Code

(Code). The text of those regulations also serves as the text of these proposed regulations. This document also provides notice of a public hearing on these proposed regulations.

DATES: Written or electronic comments must be received by February 26, 2005. Requests to speak (with outlines of topics to be discussed) at the public hearing scheduled for March 16, 2005, must be received by February 26, 2005.

ADDRESSES: Send submissions to: CC:PA:LPD:PR (REG-130671-04), Room 5203, Internal Revenue Service, POB 7604, Ben Franklin Station, Washington, DC 20044. Submissions may be hand delivered Monday through Friday between the hours of 8 a.m. and 4 p.m. to: CC:PA:LPD:PR (REG-130671-04), Courier's Desk, Internal Revenue Service, 1111 Constitution Avenue, NW., Washington, DC. Alternatively, taxpayers may submit comments electronically via the IRS internet website at *www.irs.gov/regs*, or via the Federal eRulemaking Portal, *www.regulations.gov* (IRS-REG-130671-04). The public hearing will be held in the auditorium of the Internal Revenue Building, 1111 Constitution Avenue, NW., Washington, DC 20224.

FOR FURTHER INFORMATION CONTACT: Concerning the proposed regulations, Michael E. Hara, (202) 622-4910 concerning submissions of comments, the hearing, and/or to be placed on the building access list to attend the hearing, Robin Jones at (202) 622-7180 (not toll-free numbers).

SUPPLEMENTARY INFORMATION:

Background

Temporary regulations in the Rules and Regulations section of this issue of the **Federal Register** amend the Regulations on Procedure and Administration (26 CFR part 301) relating to the filing of corporate income tax returns, S corporation returns, and returns of organizations required under section 6033 on magnetic media under section 6011(e). The temporary regulations require corporations and certain organizations to file their Form 1120, "U.S. Corporation Income Tax Return," Form 1120S, "U.S. Income Tax Return for an S Corporation," Form 990, "Return of Organization Exempt From Income Tax," and Form 990-PF, "Return of Private Foundation or Section 4947(a)(1) Trust Treated as a Private Foundation," electronically if they are required to file at least 250 returns during the calendar year ending with or within their taxable year. The text of those regulations also serves as the text of these proposed regulations. The preamble to the temporary regulations explains the amendments.

Special Analyses

It has been determined that these proposed regulations are not a significant regulatory action as defined in Executive Order 12866. Therefore, a regulatory assessment is not required. It also has been determined that section 553(b) of the Administrative Procedure Act (5 U.S.C. chapter 5) does not apply to these regulations. Because these regulations do not impose a collection of information on small entities, the Regulatory Flexibility Act (5 U.S.C. chapter 6) does not apply. The IRS and Treasury Department note that these regulations only prescribe the method of filing returns that are already required to be filed. Further, these regulations are consistent with the requirements imposed by statute.

Section 6011(e)(2)(A) provides that, in prescribing regulations providing standards for determining which returns must be filed on magnetic media or in other machine-readable form, the Secretary shall not require any person to file returns on magnetic media unless the person is required to file at least 250 returns during the calendar year. Consistent with the statutory provision, these regulations do not require Forms 1120, Forms 1120S, Forms 990, or Forms 990-PF to be filed electronically unless 250 or more returns are required to be filed.

Further, if a taxpayer's operations are computerized, reporting in accordance with the regulations should be less costly than filing on paper. If the taxpayer's operations are not computerized, the incremental cost of filing Forms 1120, Forms 1120S, Forms 990, and Forms 990-PF electronically should be minimal in most cases because of the availability of computer service bureaus. In addition, the proposed regulations provide that the IRS may waive the electronic filing requirements upon a showing of hardship.

Pursuant to section 7805(f) of the Code, these proposed regulations will be submitted to the Chief Counsel for Advocacy of the Small Business Administration for comment on their impact on small business.

Comments and Public Hearing

Before these proposed regulations are adopted as final regulations, consideration will be given to any written (a signed original and eight (8) copies) or electronic comments that are submitted timely to the IRS. The IRS and Treasury Department request comments on the clarity of the proposed regulations and how they can be made easier to understand. The IRS and Treasury Department also request comments on the procedures and criteria for hardship waivers from the electronic filing requirements. The IRS and Treasury Department also request comments on the accuracy of the certification that the regulations in this document will not have a significant economic impact on a substantial number of small entities. All comments will be available for public inspection and copying.

A public hearing has been scheduled for March 16, 2005 at 10 a.m. in the auditorium of the Internal Revenue Building, 1111 Constitution Avenue, NW., Washington, DC. Due to building security procedures, visitors must enter at the Constitution Avenue entrance. In addition, all visitors must present photo identification to enter the building. Because of access restrictions, visitors will not be admitted beyond the immediate entrance area more than 30 minutes before the hearing starts. For information about having your name placed on the building access list

to attend the hearing, see the "FOR FURTHER INFORMATION CONTACT" section of this preamble.

The rules of 26 CFR 601.601(a)(3) apply to the hearing. Persons who wish to present oral comments at the hearing must submit comments and an outline of the topics to be discussed and the time to be devoted to each topic by February 26, 2005

A period of 10 minutes will be allotted to each person for making comments. An agenda showing the scheduling of the speakers will be prepared after the deadline for receiving outlines has passed. Copies of the agenda will be available free of charge at the hearing.

Drafting Information

The principal author of these proposed regulations is Michael E. Hara, Office of the Assistant Chief Counsel (Procedure and Administration).

List of Subjects

26 CFR Part 1

Income taxes, Reporting and recordkeeping requirements.

26 CFR Part 301

Employment taxes, Estate taxes, Excise taxes, Gift taxes, Income taxes, Penalties, Reporting and recordkeeping requirements.

Proposed Amendments to the Regulations

Accordingly, 26 CFR parts 1 and 301 are proposed to be amended as follows:

PART 1—INCOME TAXES

Paragraph 1. The authority citation for part 1 continues to read, in part, as follows:

Authority: 26 U.S.C. 7805 * * *

Par. 2. Section 1.6011-5 is added to read as follows:

§ 1.6011-5 Required use of magnetic media for corporate income tax returns.

[The text of proposed § 1.6011-5 is the same as the text of § 1.6011-5T published elsewhere in this issue of the **Federal Register**].

Par.3. Section 1.6033-4 is added to read as follows:

§ 1.6033-4 Required use of magnetic media for returns by organizations required to file returns under section 6033.

[The text of proposed § 1.6033-4 is the same as the text of § 1.6033-4T published elsewhere in this issue of the **Federal Register**].

Par. 4. Section 1.6037-2 is added to read as follows:

§ 1.6037-2 Required use of magnetic media for income tax returns of electing small business corporations.

[The text of proposed § 1.6037-2 is the same as the text of § 1.6037-2T published elsewhere in this issue of the **Federal Register**].

PART 301—PROCEDURE AND ADMINISTRATION

Par. 5. The authority citation for part 301 is amended by adding entries, in numerical order, to read as follows:

Authority: 26 U.S.C. 7805 * * *

Section 301.6011-5 also issued under 26 U.S.C. 6011. * * *

Section 301.6033-4 also issued under 26 U.S.C. 6033. * * *

Section 301.6037-2 also issued under 26 U.S.C. 6037. * * *

Par. 6. Section 301.6011-5 is added to read as follows:

§ 301.6011-5 Required use of magnetic media for corporate income tax returns.

[The text of proposed § 301.6011-5 is the same as the text of § 301.6011-5T published elsewhere in this issue of the **Federal Register**].

Par. 7. Section 301.6033-4 is added to read as follows:

§ 301.6033-4 Required use of magnetic media for returns by organizations required to file returns under section 6033.

[The text of proposed § 301.6033-4 is the same as the text of § 3011.6033-4T published elsewhere in this issue of the **Federal Register**].

Par. 8. Section 301.6037-2 is added to read as follows:

§ 301.6037-2 Required use of magnetic media for returns of electing small business corporation.

[The text of proposed § 301.6037-2 is the same as the text of § 301.6037-2T published elsewhere in this issue of the **Federal Register**].

Deputy Commissioner for Services and Enforcement.

Mark E. Matthews

CERTIFIED COPY

Guy R. Traynor

¶ 20,261L

IRS proposed regulations: QJSAs: Benefit disclosures: Relative values: Optional forms of benefit.—The IRS has issued proposed regulations that would revise final regulations concerning the disclosure of relative values of optional forms of benefit that were issued on December 17, 2003 (see preamble to the final regulations at ¶ 23,215). The effective date of the regulations had previously been extended to October 1, 2004 by Announcement 2004-58 (see ¶ 17,097S-46). The effective date of the final regulations has been extended to apply to the annuity starting dates of qualified joint and survivor annuities (QJSAs) beginning on or after February 1, 2006, unless the actuarial present value of an optional form of benefit is less than the actuarial present value of the QJSA. In that case, the extension is not applicable and the final rules, effective October 1, 2004, must be applied. In the interim, plans that conform to the 2003 final regulations may rely on them, as well as the proposed rules. Otherwise, plans must comply with the 1988 regulations. Regs adopted or amended by T.D. 8219 (53 FR 31837) on August 19, 1988 that are still in effect are ¶ 11,719, ¶ 11,719B, ¶ 11,720F, ¶ 11,755-2, ¶ 12,162A, ¶ 12,162B, ¶ 12,219D, ¶ 12,231, ¶ 12,233, ¶ 12,234, and ¶ 12,556.

The proposed regulations, which were published in the *Federal Register* on January 28, 2005 (70 FR 4058), were adopted, with modifications, and published in the *Federal Register* on March 24, 2006 (71 FR 14798). The preamble to the final regulations is reproduced at ¶ 23,233, and the final regulations appear at ¶ 11,720F and ¶ 12,551.

¶ 20,261M

IRS proposed regulations: Roth 401(k) plans: Special rules.—The IRS has issued proposed regulations that provide guidance on the requirements for Roth 401(k) plans. The proposed rules would amend IRS Reg. § 1.401(k)-1(f) to provide a definition of designated Roth contributions and special rules relating to such contributions. The proposed rules would take effect for plan years beginning on or after January 1, 2006.

The proposed regulations, which were published in the *Federal Register* on March 2, 2005 (70 FR 10062), were previously reproduced below.

The final regulations, which were published in the *Federal Register* on January 3, 2006 (71 FR 6), are reproduced at ¶ 11,731F (IRS Reg. Sec. 1.401(k)-0), ¶ 11,731G (IRS Reg. Sec. 1.401(k)-1(f)), ¶ 11,731H (IRS Reg. Sec. 1.401(k)-2), ¶ 11,731L (IRS Reg. Sec. 1.401(k)-6), ¶ 11,732C (IRS Reg. Sec. 1.401(m)-0), ¶ 11,732H (IRS Reg. Sec. 1.401(m)-2) and ¶ 11,732K (IRS Reg. Sec. 1.401(m)-5). The preamble to the regulations is found at ¶ 23,232.

¶ 20,261N

IRS proposed regulations: Defined benefit plans: Defined contribution plans: Benefit and contribution limits.—The IRS has issued proposed regulations that provide guidance on the Code Sec. 415 limits on benefits and contributions under qualified retirement plans. The proposed rules, which consolidate past guidance on changes in the law since Code Sec. 415 regulations were last published in 1981, provide additional information that answers many outstanding questions for plan sponsors and administrators. Among other things, the regulations address the application of the defined benefit limits when an employee receives multiple benefit streams beginning at different ages and the treatment of compensation paid after an individual terminates employment. Under the proposed rules, National Guard and Reserve members would be permitted to continue to contribute to their employer's retirement plan while on active duty. With certain exceptions, the proposed rules would take effect for limitation years beginning on or after January 1, 2007.

The proposed regulations, which were published in the *Federal Register* on May 31, 2005 (70 FR 31213), are reproduced below.

The final regulations, which were published on April 5, 2007 (72 FR 16878), are generally applicable to limiation years beginning on or after July 1, 2007. The final regulations are reproduced at ¶ 11,715, ¶ 11,716, ¶ 11,720Y-5, ¶ 11,720W-14, ¶ 11,731G, ¶ 11,753-10, ¶ 12,364K, ¶ 12,422, ¶ 12,423, ¶ 12,424, ¶ 12,425, ¶ 12,426, ¶ 12,427, ¶ 12,429, ¶ 12,430, ¶ 12,433, ¶ 12,503, ¶ 13,154C, ¶ 13,154C-1, ¶ 13,154C-2, and ¶ 13,154C-6. The preamble to the final regulations appears at ¶ 23,244.

DEPARTMENT OF THE TREASURY

Internal Revenue Service

26 CFR Parts 1 and 11

[REG-130241-04]

RIN 1545-BD52

Limitations on Benefits and Contributions Under Qualified Plans

AGENCY: Internal Revenue Service (IRS), Treasury.

ACTION: Notice of proposed rulemaking and notice of public hearing.

SUMMARY: This document contains proposed amendments to the regulations under section 415 of the Internal Revenue Code regarding limitations on benefits and contributions under qualified plans. The proposed amendments would provide comprehensive guidance regarding the limitations of section 415, including updates to the regulations for numerous statutory changes since regulations were last published under section 415. The proposed amendments would also make conforming changes to regulations under sections 401(a)(9), 401(k), 403(b), and 457, and would make other minor corrective changes to regulations under section 457. These regulations will affect administrators of, participants in, and beneficiaries of qualified employer plans

and certain other retirement plans. This document also provides notice of a public hearing on these proposed regulations.

DATES: Written or electronic comments must be received by July 25, 2005. Requests to speak and outlines of topics to be discussed at the public hearing scheduled for August 17, 2005, at 10 a.m., must be received by July 27, 2005.

ADDRESSES: Send submissions to: CC:PA:LPD:PR (REG-130241-04), room 5203, Internal Revenue Service, POB 7604, Ben Franklin Station, Washington, DC 20044. Submissions may be hand-delivered Monday through Friday between the hours of 8 a.m. and 4 p.m. to: CC:PA:LPD:PR (REG-130241-04), Courier's Desk, Internal Revenue Service, 1111 Constitution Avenue, NW., Washington D.C. Alternatively, taxpayers may submit comments electronically directly to the IRS Internet site at *www.irs.gov/regs*. The public hearing will be held in the Auditorium, Internal Revenue Building, 1111 Constitution Avenue, NW., Washington, D.C.

FOR FURTHER INFORMATION CONTACT: Concerning the regulations, Vernon S. Carter at (202) 622-6060 or Linda S. F. Marshall at (202) 622-6090; concerning submissions and the hearing and/or to be placed on the building access list to attend the hearing, Richard A. Hurst at (202) 622-7180 (not toll-free numbers).

SUPPLEMENTARY INFORMATION:

¶20,261L

Background

This document contains proposed amendments to the Income Tax Regulations (26 CFR Parts 1 and 11) under section 415 of the Internal Revenue Code (Code) relating to limitations on benefits and contributions under qualified plans. In addition, this document contains conforming amendments to the Income Tax Regulations under sections 401(a)(9), 401(k), 403(b), and 457 of the Code, as well as minor corrective changes to the regulations under section 457.

Section 415 was added to the Internal Revenue Code by the Employee Retirement Income Security Act of 1974 (ERISA), and has been amended many times since. Section 415 provides a series of limits on benefits under qualified defined benefit plans and contributions and other additions under qualified defined contribution plans. See also section 401(a)(16). Pursuant to section 415(a)(2), the limitations of section 415 also apply to section 403(b) annuity contracts and to simplified employee pensions described in section 408(k) (SEPs). In addition, the limitations of section 415 for defined contribution plans apply to contributions allocated to any individual medical account that is part of a pension or annuity plan established pursuant to section 401(h) and to amounts attributable to medical benefits allocated to an account established for a key employee pursuant to section 419A(d)(1).

Section 404(j) provides generally that, in computing the amount of any deduction for contributions under a qualified plan, benefits and annual additions in excess of the applicable limitations under section 415 are not taken into account. In addition, in computing the applicable limits on deductions for contributions to a defined benefit plan, and in computing the full funding limitation, an adjustment under section 415(d)(1) is not taken into account for any year before the year for which that adjustment first takes effect.

The definition of compensation that is used for purposes of section 415 is also used for a number of other purposes under the Internal Revenue Code. Under section 219(b)(3), contributions on behalf of an employee to a plan described in section 501(c)(18) are limited to 25% of compensation as defined in section 415(c)(3). Section 404(a)(12) provides that, for various specified purposes in determining deductible limits under section 404, the term *compensation* includes amounts treated as *participant's compensation* under section 415(c)(3)(C) or (D). Pursuant to section 409(b)(2), for purposes of determining whether employer securities are allocated proportionately to compensation in accordance with the rules of section 409(b)(1), the amount of compensation paid to a participant for any period is the amount of such participant's compensation (within the meaning of section 415(c)(3)) for such period. Under section 414(q)(3), for purposes of determining whether an employee is a highly compensated employee within the meaning of section 414(q), the term *compensation* has the meaning given such term by section 415(c)(3). Section 414(s), which defines the term *compensation* for purposes of certain qualification requirements, generally provides that the term *compensation* has the meaning given such term by section 415(c)(3). Under section 416(c)(2), allocations to participants who are non-key employees under a top-heavy plan that is a defined contribution plan are required to be at least 3% of the participant's compensation (within the meaning of section 415(c)(3)). Pursuant to section 457(e)(5), the term *includible compensation*, which is used in limiting the amount that can be deferred for a participant under an eligible deferred compensation plan as defined in section 457(b), has the same meaning as the term *participant's compensation* under section 415(c)(3).

Comprehensive regulations regarding section 415 were last issued in 1981. See TD 7748, published in the **Federal Register** on January 7, 1981 (46 FR 1687). Since then, changes to section 415 have been made in the Economic Recovery Tax Act of 1981, Public Law 97-34 (95 Stat. 320) (ERTA), the Tax Equity and Fiscal Responsibility Act of 1982, Public Law 97-248 (96 Stat. 623) (TEFRA), the Deficit Reduction Act of 1984, Public Law 98-369 (98 Stat. 494) (DEFRA), the Tax Reform Act of 1986, Public Law 99-514 (100 Stat. 2481) (TRA '86), the Technical and Miscellaneous Revenue Act of 1988, Public Law 100-647 (102 Stat. 3342) (TAMRA), the Uruguay Round Agreements Act of 1994, Public Law 103-465 (108 Stat. 4809) (GATT), the Small Business Job Protection Act of 1996, Public Law 104-188 (110 Stat. 1755) (SBJPA), the Community Renewal Tax Relief Act of 2000, Public Law 106-554 (114 Stat. 2763), the Economic Growth and Tax Relief Reconciliation Act of 2001, Public Law 107-16 (115 Stat. 38) (EGTRRA), the Job Creation and Worker Assistance Act of 2002, Public Law 107-147 (116 Stat. 21) (JCWAA), the Pension Funding Equity Act of 2004, Public Law 108-218 (118 Stat. 596) (PFEA), and the Working Families Tax Relief Act of 2004, Public Law 108-311 (118 Stat. 1166).

Although two minor changes to the regulations were made after 1981, most of the statutory changes made since that time are not reflected in the regulations, but in IRS notices, revenue rulings, and other guidance of general applicability, as follows:

• Notice 82-13 (1982-1 C.B. 360) provides guidance on deductible employee contributions (including guidance under section 415) to reflect the addition of provisions relating to deductible employee contributions in ERTA.

• Notice 83-10 (1983-1 C.B. 536) provides guidance on the changes to section 415 made by TEFRA. The TEFRA changes were extensive, and included reductions of the dollar limits on annual benefits under a defined benefit plan and annual additions under a defined contribution plan, changes to the age and form adjustments made in the application of the limits under a defined benefit plan, and rules regarding the deductibility of contributions with respect to benefits that exceed the applicable limitations of section 415.

• Notice 87-21 (1987-1 C.B. 458) provides guidance on the changes to section 415 made by TRA '86. The TRA '86 changes modified the rules for the indexing of the dollar limit on annual additions under a defined contribution plan, the treatment of employee contributions as annual additions, and the rules for age adjustments under defined benefit plans, and added a phase-in of the section 415(b)(1)(A) dollar limitation over 10 years of participation, as well as rules permitting the limitations of section 415 to be incorporated by reference under the terms of a plan.

• Rev. Rul. 95-6 (1995-1 C.B. 80) and Rev. Rul. 2001-62 (2001-2 C.B. 632) (superseding Rev. Rul. 95-6) provide mortality tables to be used to make certain form adjustments to benefits under a defined benefit plan for purposes of applying the limitations of section 415, pursuant to the requirement to use a specified mortality table added by GATT.

• Rev. Rul. 95-29 (1995-1 C.B. 81) and Rev. Rul. 98-1 (1998-1 C.B. 249) (modifying and superseding Rev. Rul. 95-29) provide guidance regarding certain form and age adjustments under a defined benefit plan pursuant to changes made by GATT (as modified under SBJPA), including transition rules relating to those adjustments.

• Notice 99-44 (1999-2 C.B. 326) provides guidance regarding the repeal under SBJPA of the limitation on the combination of a defined benefit plan and a defined contribution plan under former section 415(e).

• Notice 2001-37 (2001-1 C.B. 1340) provides guidance regarding the inclusion of salary reduction amounts for qualified transportation fringe benefits in the definition of compensation for purposes of section 415, as provided under the Community Renewal Tax Relief Act of 2000.

• Rev. Rul. 2001-51 (2001-2 C.B. 427) provides guidance relating to the increases in the limitations of section 415 for both defined benefit and defined contribution plans, which were enacted as part of EGTRRA.

• Notice 2002-2 (2002-1 C.B. 285) provides guidance regarding the treatment of reinvested ESOP dividends under section 415(c), to reflect changes made by SBJPA.

• Rev. Rul. 2002-27 (2002-1 C.B. 925) provides guidance pursuant to which a definition of compensation can be used for purposes of applying the limitations of section 415 even if that definition treats certain specified amounts that may not be available to an employee in cash as subject to section 125 (and therefore included in compensation).

• Rev. Rul. 2002-45 (2002-2 C.B. 116) provides guidance regarding the treatment of certain payments to defined contribution plans to restore losses resulting from actions by a fiduciary for which there is a reasonable risk of liability for breach of a fiduciary duty (including the treatment of those payments under section 415).

• Notice 2004-78 (2004-48 I.R.B. 879) provides guidance regarding the actuarial assumptions that must be used for distributions with annuity starting dates occurring during plan years beginning in 2004 and 2005, to determine whether an amount payable under a defined benefit plan in a form that is subject to the minimum present value requirements of section 417(e)(3) satisfies the requirements of section 415. This guidance reflects changes made in PFEA.

These guidance items are reflected in the proposed regulations with some modifications. In addition, the proposed regulations reflect other statutory changes not previously addressed by guidance, and include some other changes and clarifications to the existing final regulations. Treasury and the IRS believe that a single restatement of the section 415 rules serves the interests of plan sponsors, third-party administrators, plan participants, and plan beneficiaries. To the extent practicable, this preamble identifies and explains substantive changes from the existing final regulations or existing guidance.

Explanation of Provisions

Overview

A. *Reflection of statutory changes*

These proposed regulations reflect the numerous statutory changes to section 415 and related provisions that have been made since 1981. Some of the statutory changes reflected in the proposed regulations are as follows:

•The current statutory limitations under section 415(b)(1)(A) and 415(c)(1) applicable for defined benefit and defined contribution plans, respectively, as most recently amended by EGTRRA.

•Changes to the rules for age adjustments to the applicable limitations under defined benefit plans, under which the dollar limitation is adjusted for commencement before age 62 or after age 65.

•Changes to the rules for benefit adjustments under defined benefit plans. The proposed regulations also specify the parameters under which a benefit payable in a form other than a straight life annuity is adjusted in order to determine the actuarially equivalent annual benefit that is subject to the limitations of section 415(b).

•The phase-in of the dollar limitation under section 415(b)(1)(A) over 10 years of participation, as added by TRA '86.

•The addition of the section 401(a)(17) limitation on compensation that is permitted to be taken into account in determining plan benefits, as added by TRA '86, and the interaction of this requirement with the limitations under section 415.

•Exceptions to the compensation-based limitation under section 415(b)(1)(B) for governmental plans, multiemployer plans, and certain other collectively bargained plans.

•Changes to the aggregation rules under section 415(f) under which multiemployer plans are not aggregated with single-employer plans for purposes of applying the compensation-based limitation of section 415(b)(1)(B) to a single-employer plan.

•The repeal under SBJPA of the section 415(e) limitation on the combination of a defined benefit plan and a defined contribution plan.

•The changes to section 415(c) that were made in conjunction with the repeal under EGTRRA of the exclusion allowance under section 403(b)(2).

•The current rounding and base period rules for annual cost-of-living adjustments pursuant to section 415(d), as most recently amended in EGTRRA and the Working Families Tax Relief Act of 2004.

•Changes to section 415(c) under which certain types of arrangements are no longer subject to the limitations of section 415(c) (e.g., individual retirement accounts other than SEPs) and other types of arrangements have become subject to the limitations of section 415(c) (e.g., certain individual medical accounts).

•The inclusion in compensation (for purposes of section 415) of certain salary reduction amounts not included in gross income.

B. *Other significant changes*

The proposed regulations contain new rules for determining the annual benefit under a defined benefit plan where there has been more than one annuity starting date (e.g., where benefits under a plan are aggregated with benefits under another plan under which distributions previously commenced). These rules would resolve the numerous issues that have arisen in determining the annual benefit under a plan where the application of the section 415(b) limitations must take into account prior distributions as well as currently commencing distributions.

The proposed regulations also provide specific rules regarding when amounts received following severance from employment are considered compensation for purposes of section 415, and when such amounts are permitted to be deferred pursuant to section 401(k), section 403(b), or section 457(b). These rules would resolve issues that have arisen with respect to payments made after the end of employment. The proposed regulations generally provide that amounts received following severance from employment are not considered to be compensation for purposes of section 415, but provide exceptions for certain payments made within 2 ½ months following severance from

employment. These exceptions apply to payments (such as regular compensation, and payments for overtime, commissions, and bonuses) that would have been payable if employment had not terminated, and to payments with respect to leave that would have been available for use if employment had not terminated. This notice of proposed rulemaking includes corresponding changes to the regulations under sections 401(k), 403(b), and 457 that would provide that amounts receivable following severance from employment can only be deferred if those amounts meet these conditions. The rule pursuant to which compensation received after severance from employment is not considered compensation for purposes of section 415 generally does not apply to payments to an individual in qualified military service.

§ *1.415(a)-1: General rules*

Section 1.415(a)-1 of these proposed regulations sets forth general rules relating to limitations under section 415 and provides an overview of the remaining regulations, including cross-references to special rules that apply to section 403(b) annuities, multiemployer plans, and governmental plans. In addition, this section provides rules for a plan's incorporation by reference of the rules of section 415 pursuant to section 1106(h) of TRA '86 (including detailed guidelines regarding incorporation by reference of the annual cost-of-living adjustments to the statutory limits and the application of default rules), rules for plans maintained by more than one employer, and rules that apply in other special situations.

§ *1.415(b)-1: Limitations applicable to defined benefit plans*

Section 1.415(b)-1 of these proposed regulations sets forth rules for applying the limitations on benefits under a defined benefit plan. Under these limitations, the annual benefit must not be greater than the lesser of $160,000 (as adjusted pursuant to section 415(d)) or 100% of the participant's average compensation for the participant's high 3 consecutive years. A retirement benefit payable in a form other than a straight life annuity is adjusted to an actuarially equivalent straight life annuity to determine the annual benefit payable under that form of distribution. In addition, the dollar limitation under section 415(b)(1)(A) is actuarially adjusted for benefit payments that commence before age 62 or after age 65. The proposed regulations clarify that, in addition to applying to benefits payable to participants and beneficiaries, the limitations of section 415(b) apply to accrued benefits and benefits payable from an annuity contract distributed to a participant. Thus, the limitations of section 415(b) apply to a participant's entire accrued benefit, regardless of whether the benefit is vested. Where a participant's accrued benefit is computed pursuant to the fractional rule of section 411(b)(1)(C), the limitations of section 415(b) apply to the accrued benefit as of the end of the limitation year and, for ages prior to normal retirement age, are not required to be applied to the projected annual benefit commencing at normal retirement age from which the accrued benefit is computed. In addition, the proposed regulations provide a number of other updates, clarifications, and other changes to the existing regulations, as described below.

A. *Actuarial assumptions used to convert benefit to a straight life annuity*

The proposed regulations provide rules under which a retirement benefit payable in any form other than a straight life annuity is converted to the straight life annuity that is actuarially equivalent to that other form to determine the annual benefit (which is used to demonstrate compliance with section 415) with respect to that form of distribution. These rules reflect statutory changes that specify the actuarial assumptions that are to be used for these equivalency calculations (including, for plan years beginning in 2004 and 2005, the use of a 5.5% interest rate for benefits that are subject to the present value rules of section 417(e)(3),[1] as set forth in PFEA, as well as published guidance that has been issued since 1981. In addition to setting forth rules for adjusting forms of benefit other than straight life annuities, the proposed regulations would permit the IRS to issue published guidance setting forth simplified methods for making these adjustments.

Under the proposed regulations, the annual benefit is determined as the greater of the actuarially equivalent straight life annuity determined under the plan's actuarial assumptions or the actuarially equivalent straight life annuity determined under actuarial assumptions specified by statute. This methodology implements the policy reflected in section 415(b)(2)(E), under which the plan's determination that a straight life annuity is actuarially equivalent to a particular optional form of benefit is overridden only when the optional form of benefit is more valuable

---

[1] Section 417(e)(3) provides minimum present value requirements for certain forms of benefit payable from a defined benefit plan under which payments cannot be less than the amount calculated using a specified interest rate and a specified mortality table. For forms of benefit that are subject to the minimum present value rules of section 417(e)(3), the

limitations of section 415(b) apply to limit the amount of a distribution even if those limitations result in a lower distribution than would otherwise be required under the rules of section 417(e)(3). See § 1.417(e)-1(d)(1).

than the corresponding straight life annuity when compared using statutorily specified actuarial assumptions.

The rules in the proposed regulations under which a retirement benefit payable in any form other than a straight life annuity is converted to a straight life annuity to determine the annual benefit with respect to that form of distribution generally follow the rules set forth in Rev. Rul. 98-1. However, the calculation of the actuarially equivalent straight life annuity determined using the plan's assumptions for actuarial equivalence has been simplified for a form of benefit that is not subject to the minimum present value rules of section 417(e)(3). Under the simplified calculation, instead of determining the actuarial assumptions used under the plan and applying those assumptions to convert an optional form of benefit to an actuarially equivalent straight life annuity, the regulations use the straight life annuity, if any, that is payable at the same age under the plan. This straight life annuity is then compared to the straight life annuity that is the actuarial equivalent of the optional form of benefit, determined using the standardized assumptions, and the larger of the two straight life annuities is used for purposes of demonstrating compliance with section 415. This simplification has not been extended to forms of benefit that are subject to the minimum present value rules of section 417(e), however, because under the plan those forms of benefit may be determined as the actuarial equivalent of the deferred annuity, rather than as the actuarial equivalent of the immediate straight life annuity.

B. Inclusion of social security supplements in annual benefit

The proposed regulations clarify that a social security supplement is included in determining the annual benefit. Under section 415(b)(2)(B), the annual benefit does not include ancillary benefits that are not directly related to retirement benefits. However, because a social security supplement is payable upon retirement as a form of retirement income, it is a retirement benefit. Thus, a social security supplement is included in determining the annual benefit without regard to whether it is an ancillary benefit or a QSUPP within the meaning of § 1.401(a)(4)-12.

C. Determination of high 3 average compensation

The proposed regulations would make two changes that would have a significant effect on the determination of a participant's average compensation for the participant's high 3 consecutive years. Consistent with the provisions of section 415(b)(3), the proposed regulations would restrict compensation used for this purpose to compensation earned in periods during which the participant was an active participant in the plan. In addition, the proposed regulations under § 1.415(c)-2 would clarify the interaction of the requirements of section 401(a)(17) and the definition of compensation that must be used for purposes of determining a participant's average compensation for the participant's high 3 consecutive years. Because a plan may not base benefit accruals on compensation in excess of the limitation under section 401(a)(17), a plan's definition of compensation used for purposes of applying the limitations of section 415 is not permitted to reflect compensation in excess of the limitation under section 401(a)(17). Thus, for example, where a participant commences receiving benefits in 2005 at age 75 (so that the adjusted dollar limitation could be as high as $379,783), and the participant had compensation in excess of the applicable section 401(a)(17) limit for 2002, 2003, and 2004, the participant's benefit under the plan is limited by the average compensation for his highest three years as limited by section 401(a)(17) (i.e., $201,667, or the average of $200,000, $200,000, and $205,000).

The proposed regulations set forth rules for computing the limitation of section 415(b)(1)(B) of 100% of the participant's compensation for the period of the participant's high 3 years of service for a participant who is employed with the employer while an active participant for less than 3 consecutive calendar years. For such a participant, the period of a participant's high 3 years of service is the actual number of consecutive years of employment (including fractions of years) while an active participant in the plan. In such a case, the limitation of section 415(b)(1)(B) of 100% of the participant's compensation for the period of the participant's high 3 years of service is computed by averaging the participant's compensation during the participant's longest consecutive period of employment while a plan participant over the actual period of service (including fractions of years, but not less than one year).

D. Treatment of benefits paid partially in the form of a QJSA

Under section 415(b)(2)(B), the portion of any joint and survivor annuity that constitutes a qualified joint and survivor annuity (QJSA) as defined in section 417(b) is not taken into account in determining the annual benefit for purposes of applying the limitations of section 415(b). The proposed regulations would clarify how this exception from the limitations of section 415 for the survivor annuity portion of a

QJSA applies to benefits paid partially in the form of a QJSA and partially in some other form. Under this clarification, the rule excluding the survivor portion of a QJSA from the annual benefit applies to the survivor annuity payments under the portion of a benefit that is paid in the form of a QJSA, even if another portion of the benefit is paid in some other form.

E. Dollar limitation applicable to early or late commencement

The determination of the age-adjusted dollar limitation under the proposed regulations reflects the rules enacted in EGTRRA. As provided in Q&A-3 of Rev. Rul. 2001-51, this determination generally follows the same steps and procedures as those used in Rev. Rul. 98-1, except that such determination takes into account the increased defined benefit dollar limitation enacted by EGTRRA and that the adjustments for early or late commencement are no longer based on social security retirement age. Applying rules that are similar to those that are used for determining actuarial equivalence among forms of benefits, the proposed regulations generally use the plan's determinations for actuarial equivalence of early or late retirement benefits, but override those determinations where the use of the specified statutory assumptions results in a lower limit.

The proposed regulations adopt rules for mortality adjustments used in computing the dollar limitation on a participant's annual benefit for distributions commencing before age 62 or after age 65. Under these rules, to the extent that a forfeiture does not occur upon the participant's death, no adjustment is made to reflect the probability of the participant's death during the relevant time period, and to the extent a forfeiture occurs upon the participant's death, an adjustment must be applied to reflect the probability of the participant's death during the relevant time period. These rules generally are consistent with the guidance provided in Notice 83-10.

The proposed regulations would also provide a simplified method for applying this rule. Under this simplified method, a plan is permitted to treat no forfeiture as occurring upon a participant's death if the plan does not charge participants for providing a qualified preretirement survivor annuity, but only if the plan applies this treatment for adjustments that apply both before age 62 and after age 65.

F. Nonapplication of adjustment to dollar limitation for early commencement with respect to police department and fire department employees

Consistent with section 415(b)(2)(G) and (H), the proposed regulations would provide that the early retirement reduction does not apply to certain participants in plans of state and local government units who are employees of a police department or fire department, or former members of the Armed Forces of the United States. This rule applies to any participant in a plan maintained by a state or political subdivision of a state who is credited, for benefit accrual purposes, with at least 15 years of service as either (1) a full-time employee of any police department or fire department of the state or political subdivision that provides police protection, firefighting services, or emergency medical services, or (2) a member of the Armed Forces of the United States. The proposed regulations would clarify that the application of this rule depends on whether the employer is a police department or fire department of the state or political subdivision, rather than on the job classification of the individual participant.

G. Application of $10,000 exception

Pursuant to section 415(b)(4), the benefits payable with respect to a participant satisfy the limitations of section 415(b) if the retirement benefits payable with respect to such a participant under the plan and all other defined benefit plans of the employer do not exceed $10,000 for the plan year or for any prior plan year, and the employer has not at any time maintained a defined contribution plan in which the participant participated. The proposed regulations would clarify that the section 415(b)(4) alternative $10,000 limitation is applied to actual distributions made during each year. Thus, a distribution for a limitation year that exceeds $10,000 is not within the section 415(b)(4) alternative limitation (and therefore will not be excepted from the otherwise applicable limits of section 415(b)), even if the distribution is a single-sum distribution that is the actuarial equivalent of an accrued benefit with annual payments that are less than $10,000.

H. Exclusion of annual benefit attributable to mandatory employee contributions from annual benefit

The proposed regulations would retain the rules under existing final regulations that the annual benefit does not include the annual benefit attributable to mandatory employee contributions. For this purpose, the term "mandatory employee contributions" means amounts contributed to the plan by the employee that are required as a condition of employment, as a condition of participation in the plan, or as a condition of obtaining benefits (or additional benefits) under the plan attributable to employer contributions. See section 411(c)(2)(C). Employee contributions to a defined benefit plan that are not maintained in a separate account as described in section 414(k) constitute mandatory employee contributions (even if section 411 does not apply to the plan) because, depending upon the investment performance of plan assets, employer contributions may be needed to pay a portion of the participant's benefit that is conditioned upon these employee contributions. The rules covering mandatory employee contributions do not extend to voluntary contributions because voluntary employee contributions (plus earnings thereon) are treated as a separate defined contribution plan rather than as part of a defined benefit plan.

The proposed regulations would retain the rule under the existing regulations that the annual benefit attributable to mandatory employee contributions is determined using the factors described in section 411(c)(2)(B) and the regulations thereunder, regardless of whether section 411 applies to the plan. The proposed regulations also would clarify that the following are not treated as employee contributions: (1) contributions that are picked up by a governmental employer as provided under section 414(h)(2), (2) repayment of any loan made to a participant from the plan, and (3) repayment of any amount that was previously distributed.

I. Exclusion of annual benefit attributable to rollover contributions from annual benefit

The proposed regulations would clarify that the annual benefit does not include the annual benefit attributable to rollover contributions made to a defined benefit plan (i.e., rollover contributions that are not maintained in a separate account that is treated as a separate defined contribution plan under section 414(k)). In such a case, the annual benefit attributable to rollover contributions is determined by applying the rules of section 411(c) treating the rollover contributions as employee contributions (regardless of whether section 411 applies to the plan). This will occur, for example, if a distribution is rolled over from a defined contribution plan to a defined benefit plan to provide an annuity distribution. Thus, in the case of rollover contributions from a defined contribution plan to a defined benefit plan to provide an annuity distribution, the annual benefit attributable to those rollover contributions for purposes of section 415 is determined by applying the rules of section 411(c), regardless of the assumptions used to compute the annuity distribution under the plan. Accordingly, in such a case, if the plan uses more favorable factors than those specified in section 411(c) to determine the amount of annuity payments arising from a rollover contribution, the annual benefit under the plan would reflect the excess of those annuity payments over the amounts that would be payable using the factors specified in section 411(c)(3).

Rollover contributions to an account that is treated as a separate defined contribution plan under section 414(k) do not give rise to an annual benefit because the separate account is not treated as a defined benefit plan under section 415(b). Furthermore, under the rules relating to defined contribution plans, these rollover contributions to a separate account are excluded from the definition of annual additions to a defined contribution plan.

J. Treatment of benefits transferred among plans

The proposed regulations would modify the rules of the existing final regulations for determining the amount of transferred benefits that are excluded from the annual benefit under a defined benefit plan in the event of a transfer from another defined benefit plan. These modifications are designed to ensure that transferred benefits are not counted twice by the same employer toward the limitations of section 415(b) and, similarly, to prevent the circumvention of the limitations of section 415(b) through benefit transfers to plans of unrelated employers. Under the proposed regulations, if the transferee plan's benefits are required to be taken into account pursuant to section 415(f) and § 1.415(f)-1 in determining whether the transferor plan satisfies the limitations of section 415(b), then the transferred benefits are included in determining the annual benefit under the transferee plan and are disregarded in determining the annual benefit under the transferor plan. Accordingly, in such a case, the annual benefit under each plan is determined taking into account the actual benefits provided under that plan after the transfer.

In contrast, if the transferee plan's benefits are not required to be taken into account pursuant to section 415(f) and § 1.415(f)-1 in determining whether the transferor plan satisfies the limitations of section 415(b), then the assets associated with those transferred liabilities (other than surplus assets) are treated by the transferor plan as distributed as a single-sum distribution. This will occur, for example, if the employer sponsoring the transferor plan is a predecessor employer

with respect to the participant whose benefits are transferred to the transferee plan, where the transferee plan's benefits are not required to be taken into account pursuant to section 415(f) and § 1.415(f)-1 in determining whether the transferor plan satisfies the limitations of section 415(b). Although such a transfer is treated as a distribution in computing the annual benefit under the transferor plan, no corresponding adjustment to the annual benefit under the transferee plan is made to reflect the fact that some of the benefits provided under the transferee plan are attributable to the transfer. Thus, the actual benefit provided under the transferee plan is used to determine the annual benefit under the transferee plan even though the transferred amount is included as a distribution in determining the annual benefit under the transferor plan. In most such cases, however, a participant whose benefits have been transferred would accrue no additional benefit under the transferor plan that would be required to be tested under the that plan (in combination with the transferred benefits).

K. 10-year phase-in of limitations based on years of participation and years of service

The proposed regulations would provide rules for applying the 10-year phase-in of the dollar limitation based on years of participation in the plan, as added by TRA '86, and would modify the rules set forth in final regulations for applying the 10-year phase-in of the compensation limit based on years of service. The proposed regulations follow the guidance set forth in Notice 87-21 for determining years of participation, and apply analogous rules for determining years of service for this purpose.

§ 1.415(b)-2: Multiple annuity starting dates

Section 1.415(b)-2 of the proposed regulations sets forth rules that apply in computing the annual benefit under one or more defined benefit plans in the case of multiple annuity starting dates (i.e., in cases in which a participant has received one or more distributions in limitation years prior to an increase in the accrued benefit occurring during the current limitation year or prior to the annuity starting date for a distribution that commences during the current limitation year). These rules apply, for example, where benefit distributions to a participant have previously commenced under a plan that is aggregated with a plan from which the participant receives current accruals, or where a new distribution election is effective during the current limitation year with respect to a distribution that commenced in a prior limitation year. These rules also apply where benefit payments are increased as a result of plan terms applying a cost-of-living adjustment pursuant to an adjustment of the dollar limit of section 415(b)(1)(A) made pursuant to section 415(d), if the plan does not provide for application of the safe harbor methodology set forth in the proposed regulations for determining the adjusted amount of the benefit.

In the case of multiple annuity starting dates, the annual benefit that is subject to the limits of section 415(b) and § 1.415(b)-1(a) is equal to the sum of (1) the annual benefit determined with respect to any accrued benefit with respect to which distribution has not yet commenced as of the current determination date, computed pursuant to the rules of § 1.415(b)-1, (2) the annual benefit determined with respect to any distribution with an annuity starting date that occurs within the current limitation year and on or before the current determination date, computed pursuant to the rules of § 1.415(b)-1, (3) the annual benefit determined with respect to the remaining amounts payable under any distribution with an annuity starting date that occurred during a prior limitation year, computed pursuant to the rules of § 1.415(b)-1, and (4) the annual benefit attributable to prior distributions. For this purpose, the current determination date is the last day of period for which an increase in the participant's benefit accrues if an increase in the participant's accrued benefit occurs during the limitation year, and if there is no such increase, the current determination date is the annuity starting date for the distribution that commences during the limitation year. The annual benefit determined using this formula is tested for compliance with section 415(b) as of the current determination date, applying the dollar limitation (which is adjusted under section 415(d) to the current determination date and is also adjusted for the participant's age as of the current determination date) and the compensation limitation applicable as of that date (which is adjusted under section 415(d) to the current determination date but is not adjusted based on the participant's age).

Under the proposed regulations, the annual benefit attributable to prior distributions is determined by adjusting the amounts of prior distributions to an actuarially equivalent straight life annuity commencing at the current determination date. The proposed regulations apply rules that are analogous to the rules for adjusting other benefits to determine the amount of the actuarially equivalent straight life annuity for purposes of determining the annual benefit attributable to prior distributions. Under these rules, the amount and time of prior distributions made to the participant is taken into account, and the prior distributions are adjusted to the actuarially equivalent straight life annuity commencing at the current determination date using interest and mortality assumptions that apply generally for purposes of applying the limitations of section 415(b) to a benefit in a form other than a straight life annuity. For this purpose, the actuarially equivalent straight life annuity commencing at the current determination date must reflect an actuarial increase to the present value of payments to reflect that the participant has survived during the interim period.

The actuarial assumptions used to calculate the annual benefit attributable to a prior distribution are determined as of the current determination date, and are based on the form of the prior distribution. For a prior distribution to which section 417(e)(3) did not apply, the annual benefit attributable to the prior distribution is the greater of the annual amount of a straight life annuity commencing at the current determination date that is the actuarial equivalent of that prior distribution, computed using the actuarial factors specified under the plan that provides for the current distribution or current accrual that are used to determine offsets, if any, for prior distributions, or the annual amount of a straight life annuity commencing at the current determination date that is the actuarial equivalent of that prior distribution, computed using the currently applicable statutory actuarial factors under section 415(b)(2)(E)(i) and (v). Similarly, for a prior distribution to which section 417(e)(3) applied, the annual benefit attributable to the prior distribution is the greater of the annual amount of a straight life annuity commencing at the current determination date that is the actuarial equivalent of that prior distribution, computed using the actuarial factors specified under the plan that provides for the current distribution or current accrual that are used to determine offsets, if any, for prior distributions, or the annual amount of a straight life annuity commencing at the current determination date that is the actuarial equivalent of that prior distribution, computed using the currently applicable statutory actuarial factors under section 415(b)(2)(E)(ii) and (v).

Apart from determining the actuarial factors applicable to calculating the annual benefit attributable to prior distributions, the form of the prior distribution does not otherwise affect the determination of the annual benefit attributable to prior distributions. Thus, for example, if a participant has received $50,000 per year for the past four years, the determination of the annual benefit attributable to prior distributions will be the same if those distributions are part of a 10-year certain and life annuity or are part of a straight life annuity because both of those distribution forms are subject to the same actuarial factors for determining the annual benefit attributable to prior distributions. In either case, the determination of the annual benefit attributable to prior distributions will be determined by applying the interest and mortality assumptions used under the plan to determine offsets, if any, for prior distributions to determine a straight life annuity that is actuarially equivalent to the four prior payments of $50,000, applying the statutory actuarial assumptions to determine a straight life annuity that is actuarially equivalent to the four prior payments of $50,000, and then taking the greater of the two straight life annuity amounts. Determining the annual benefit attributable to prior distributions on the basis of the amount of distributions made rather than on the form of those distributions (or on the basis of the accrued benefit that underlies those distributions) is designed to simplify the application of the multiple annuity starting date rules.

The proposed regulations provide that a prior distribution is not reflected in the annual benefit attributable to prior distributions to the extent the prior distribution has been repaid to the plan with interest (because the amounts attributable to such a prior distribution are reflected in the annual benefit in other ways). Thus, a prior distribution that has been entirely repaid to the plan (with interest) does not give rise to an annual benefit attributable to prior distributions. Similarly, if a prior distribution was made, and a repayment was subsequently made that was less than the amount of the prior distribution (including reasonable interest), the annual benefit attributable to prior distributions is determined by multiplying the annual benefit attributable to the prior distribution by one minus a fraction, the numerator of which is the amount of the repayment and the denominator of which is the amount of the prior distribution plus reasonable interest.

The proposed regulations provide an additional requirement that applies where a stream of annuity payments is modified by a new distribution election. This additional requirement is also imposed in § 1.401(a)(9)-6, Q&A-13(c)(3). Under this additional requirement, which is intended to limit the extent to which benefits can increase as a result of a change in market interest rates, if a stream of annuity payments is modified by a new distribution election, the payments under the annuity that are paid before the modification plus the modified payments must satisfy the requirements of § 1.415(b)-1 determined

as of the original annuity starting date, using the interest rates and mortality table applicable to such date. Following the issuance of the regulations under section 401(a)(9), commentators suggested that the rule should be modified to permit a plan to reflect cost-of-living adjustments under section 415(d) that occur between the original annuity starting date and the date of modification in applying the additional test. These proposed regulations adopt this suggestion, and provide that a plan will not fail to satisfy the additional requirement merely because payments reflect cost-of-living adjustments pursuant to section 415(d) for payments no earlier than the time those adjustments are effective and in amounts no greater than amounts determined under § 1.415(d)-1(a)(5). In addition, the proposed regulations include an amendment to § 1.401(a)(9)-6, Q&A-13(c)(3), to reflect this change.

§ 1.415(c)-1: Limitations applicable to defined contribution plans

Section 1.415(c)-1 of these proposed regulations sets forth rules that apply to limitations on annual additions under a defined contribution plan. Under these limitations, annual additions must not be greater than the lesser of $40,000 (as adjusted pursuant to section 415(d)) or 100% of the participant's compensation for the limitation year. The term "annual additions" generally means the sum for any year of employer contributions, employee contributions, and forfeitures. In addition to applying to qualified defined contribution plans, the limitations on defined contribution plans apply to section 403(b) annuity contracts, simplified employee pensions described in section 408(k), mandatory employee contributions to qualified defined benefit plans, and contributions to certain medical accounts.

The proposed regulations reflect a number of statutory changes to section 415(c) that were made after the issuance of existing final regulations. Among these changes are the revised limitation amounts under section 415(c), the revised rules applicable to employee stock ownership plans, and the rules applying the limitations of section 415(c) to certain medical benefit plans. The proposed regulations also would make some other changes to existing regulations, as discussed below.

If annual additions under an annuity contract that otherwise satisfies the requirements of section 403(b) exceed the limitations of section 415(c), then the portion of the contract that includes that excess annual addition fails to be a section 403(b) annuity contract (and instead is a contract to which section 403(c) applies), and the remaining portion of the contract is a section 403(b) annuity contract. As under regulations recently proposed under section 403(b) (69 FR 67075, November 16, 2004), the proposed regulations include a provision under which the status of the remaining portion of the contract as a section 403(b) contract is not retained unless, for the year of the excess and each year thereafter, the issuer of the contract maintains separate accounts for each such portion. In addition, consistent with the change to section 403(b)(1) made in JCWAA, the proposed regulations provide that the limitations under section 415(c) apply to any section 403(b) annuity contract, regardless of whether the contract satisfies the requirements of section 414(i) to be a defined contribution plan. Thus, the limitations under section 415(c) apply to a section 403(b) annuity contract even if the limitations of section 415(b) also apply to the contract (i.e., if the contract is a church plan that is covered by the grandfather rule of section 251(e)(5) of TEFRA).

The proposed regulations clarify that the IRS will treat a sale or exchange by the employee or the employer that transfers assets to a plan where the consideration paid by the plan is less than the fair market value of the assets transferred to the plan as giving rise to an annual addition in the amount of the difference between the value of the assets transferred and the consideration.

Consistent with Rev. Rul. 2002-45, the proposed regulations provide that a restorative payment that is allocated to a participant's account does not give rise to an annual addition for any limitation year. For this purpose, restorative payments are payments made to restore losses to a plan resulting from actions by a fiduciary for which there is reasonable risk of liability for breach of a fiduciary duty under Title I of ERISA, where plan participants who are similarly situated are treated similarly with respect to the payments. Generally, payments to a defined contribution plan are restorative payments only if the payments are made in order to restore some or all of the plan's losses due to an action (or a failure to act) that creates a reasonable risk of liability for such a breach of fiduciary duty. The proposed regulations provide that, in addition to payments to a plan made pursuant to Department of Labor order or court-approved settlement to restore losses to a qualified defined contribution plan on account of the breach of fiduciary duty, restorative payments include payments made pursuant to the Department of Labor's Voluntary Fiduciary Correction Program to restore losses to a qualified defined contribution plan on account of the breach of fiduciary duty. However, payments made to a plan to make up for losses due merely to market fluctuations and other payments that are not made on account of a reasonable risk of liability for breach of a fiduciary duty under Title I of ERISA are contributions that give rise to annual additions and are not restorative payments.

The proposed regulations would retain the rule for taxable employers under existing regulations that the deadline for making a contribution to the plan that is credited to a participant's account for a limitation year for purposes of section 415(c). Under this rule, employer contributions are not treated as credited to a participant's account for a particular limitation year unless the contributions are actually made to the plan no later than 30 days after the end of the period described in section 404(a)(6) applicable to the taxable year with or within which the particular limitation year ends. The proposed regulations would modify the corresponding rule for tax-exempt employers. Under the proposed regulations, the deadline for a tax-exempt employer to make a contribution to the plan that is credited to a participant's account for a limitation year for purposes of section 415(c) is the 15th day of the tenth calendar month following the close of the taxable year with or within which the particular limitation year ends. This date corresponds to the due date for Form 5500 (with extensions) in cases in which the taxable year coincides with the plan year, and generally corresponds to the contribution due date for taxable employers who request filing extensions. The deadline for contributions for tax-exempt employers under the proposed regulations would be an extension from the earlier deadline now applicable under existing regulations (i.e., the 15th day of the sixth calendar month following the close of the taxable year with or within which the particular limitation year ends). The extent to which elective contributions constitute plan assets for purposes of the prohibited transaction provisions of section 4975 and Title I of ERISA is determined in accordance with regulations and rulings issued by the Department of Labor. See 29 CFR 2510.3-102.

The proposed regulations clarify the operation of the special increased limitation applicable to church plans under section 415(c)(7). Under this rule, notwithstanding the generally applicable limitations, annual additions for a section 403(b) annuity contract for a year with respect to an individual who is a church employee are treated as not exceeding the limitation of section 415(c) if such annual additions for the year are not in excess of $10,000. However, the total amount of additions with respect to any participant that are permitted to be taken into account for purposes of this rule for all years may not exceed $40,000. In addition, for any individual who is a church employee performing any services for the church outside the United States, additions for a section 403(b) annuity contract for any year are not treated as exceeding the limitations of section 415(c) if those annual additions for the year do not exceed the greater of $3,000 or the employee's includible compensation. The proposed regulations would clarify that the $40,000 cumulative total only applies to excesses over what would have been permitted to be contributed without regard to this special rule, and clarifies the interaction between the generally applicable church employee rule and the rule for church employees performing services outside the United States. In addition, the proposed regulations would clarify that the special rule that applies to services for a church performed abroad applies to the employee's includible compensation only with respect to services for the church outside the United States.

The correction mechanism in current § 1.415-6(b)(6) for handling excess annual additions is not included in the proposed regulations. It is anticipated that this correction mechanism will be included in the Employee Plans Compliance Resolution System (see Rev. Proc. 2003-44 (2003-1 C.B. 1051)) in the future.

The proposed regulations generally would retain the rules under existing regulations providing that a contribution to reduce accumulated funding deficiencies or a contribution made pursuant to a funding waiver relates to the limitation year of the initial funding obligation. However, the proposed regulations would provide that any interest paid by the employer with respect to such a contribution that is in excess of a reasonable amount is taken into account as an annual addition for the limitation year when the contribution is made (in contrast to existing regulations, which require interest in excess of a reasonable amount to be taken into account as an annual addition for the limitation year for which the contribution was originally required). Rev. Rul. 78-223 (1978-1 C.B. 125) provides a method for determining contributions required to amortize waived contributions under a defined contribution plan. The application of any of the methods described in Rev. Rul. 78-223 will result in reasonable interest payments for purposes of applying the rules of section 415 (provided that, if a fixed interest rate in excess of 5% is used to amortize waived contributions, the interest rate is reasonable). Thus, for example, the actual yield method (under which the adjusted account balance is increased or decreased periodi-

cally at the actual rate of investment return experienced by the plan for such period) can be used for this purpose.

§ 1.415(c)-2: Definition of compensation

Section 1.415(c)-2 of these proposed regulations defines the term *compensation*, which is defined in section 415(c)(3) and used for purposes of applying the limitations of section 415 as well as for various other purposes specified under the Internal Revenue Code. The proposed regulations reflect a number of statutory changes to section 415(c)(3) that were made after the issuance of existing final regulations. Among these changes are the inclusion in compensation of certain deemed amounts for disabled participants and nontaxable elective amounts for deferrals under sections 401(k), 403(b), and 457, cafeteria plan elections under section 125, and qualified transportation fringe elections under section 132(f)(4). In addition to these changes, the proposed regulations would make some other changes to existing regulations, as discussed below.

The proposed regulations provide specific guidelines regarding when amounts received following severance from employment are considered compensation for purposes of section 415. The following are types of post-severance payments that are not excluded from compensation because of timing if they are paid within 2 ½ months following severance from employment: (1) payments that, absent a severance from employment, would have been paid to the employee while the employee continued in employment with the employer and are regular compensation for services during the employee's regular working hours, compensation for services outside the employee's regular working hours (such as overtime or shift differential), commissions, bonuses, or other similar compensation; and (2) payments for accrued bona fide sick, vacation, or other leave, but only if the employee would have been able to use the leave if employment had continued. Under the proposed regulations, the rule generally excluding payments after severance from employment from compensation does not apply to payments to an individual who does not currently perform services for the employer by reason of qualified military service (as that term is used in section 414(u)(1)) to the extent those payments do not exceed the amounts the individual would have received if the individual had continued to perform services for the employer rather than entering qualified military service. This notice of proposed rulemaking also contain corresponding proposed amendments to the regulations under sections 401(k), 403(b), and 457 that would provide that amounts received following severance from employment can be deferred only if they are considered compensation under the rules of section 415.

§ 1.415(d)-1: Cost-of-living adjustments

Section 1.415(d)-1 of these proposed regulations sets forth rules that apply to cost-of-living adjustments to the various limitations of section 415 pursuant to section 415(d). Section 415(d) provides for the dollar and compensation limitations on annual benefits and the dollar limitation on annual additions to be adjusted annually for increases in the cost of living based on adjustment procedures similar to the procedures used to adjust social security benefit amounts. These adjustments also apply for other purposes as specified in the Internal Revenue Code. The proposed regulations specify the manner in which these adjustments are determined each year, and reflect statutory changes to the adjustment methodology made after the 1981 regulations were issued. In addition, the proposed regulations make several other changes to existing final regulations, as discussed below.

The proposed regulations would specify the circumstances under which an adjusted limit is permitted to be applied to participants who have previously commenced receiving benefits under a defined benefit plan. Under the proposed regulations, the adjusted dollar limitation is applicable to current employees who are participants in a defined benefit plan and to former employees who have retired or otherwise terminated their service under the plan and have a nonforfeitable right to accrued benefits, regardless of whether they have actually begun to receive such benefits. A plan is permitted to provide that the annual increase applies for a participant who has previously commenced receiving benefits only to the extent that benefits have not been paid. Thus, for example, a plan cannot provide that this annual increase applies to a participant who has previously received the entire plan benefit in a single-sum distribution. However, a plan is permitted to provide for an increase in benefits to a participant who accrues additional benefits under the plan that could have been accrued without regard to the adjustment of the dollar limitation (including benefits that accrue as a result of a plan amendment) on or after the effective date of the adjusted limitation.

The proposed regulations provide for a safe harbor under which the annual benefit will satisfy the limitations of section 415(b) for the current limitation year following an adjustment to benefit payments that is made to reflect the cost-of-living adjustment made pursuant to section 415(d). If such adjustments are made in accordance with this safe harbor, the multiple annuity starting date rules of §1.415(b)-2 do not apply on account of such adjustments. Under this safe harbor, if a participant has received one or more distributions under an annuity stream that satisfies the requirements of section 415(b) before the adjustment, the plan's benefits will satisfy the limitations of section 415(b) if the amounts payable to the employee for the limitation year and subsequent limitation years are not greater than the amounts that would otherwise be payable under the annuity stream without regard to the adjustment, multiplied by a fraction. The numerator of this fraction is the limitation under section 415(b) (i.e., the lesser of the applicable dollar limitation under section 415(b)(1)(A), as adjusted for age at commencement, and the applicable compensation-based limitation under section 415(b)(1)(B)) in effect for the distribution following the adjustment, and the denominator of this fraction is such limitation under section 415(b) in effect for the distribution immediately before the adjustment.

§ 1.415(f)-1: Combining and aggregating plans

Section 1.415(f)-1 of these proposed regulations sets forth rules for combining and aggregating plans pursuant to section 415(f). Under section 415(f) and these proposed regulations, for purposes of applying the limitations of section 415(b) and (c), all defined benefit plans of an employer are treated as one defined benefit plan, and all defined contribution plans of an employer are treated as one defined contribution plan. The controlled group rules of section 414(b) and (c) (as modified by section 415(h)), the affiliated service group rules of section 414(m), and the leased employee rules of section 415(n) apply for purposes of determining whether a plan that is maintained by an entity other than the employer is considered maintained by the employer for purposes of applying the aggregation rules of section 415(f).

The proposed regulations would also make various changes and clarifications to the existing regulations. The proposed regulations would clarify that an employer's plan must be aggregated with all plans maintained by a predecessor employer (see section 414(a)), regardless of whether any such plan is assumed by the employer. Pursuant to section 414(a)(1), the proposed regulations would provide that, for purposes of section 415, a former employer is a predecessor employer with respect to a participant in a plan maintained by an employer if the employer maintains a plan under which the participant had accrued a benefit while performing services for the former employer, but only if that benefit is provided under the plan maintained by the employer. In addition, the proposed regulations would provide pursuant to section 414(a)(2) that, with respect to an employer of a participant, a former entity that antedates the employer is a predecessor employer with respect to the participant if, under the facts and circumstances, the employer constitutes a continuation of all or a portion of the trade or business of the former entity. This will occur, for example, where formation of the employer constitutes a mere formal or technical change in the employment relationship and continuity otherwise exists in the substance and administration of the business operations of the former entity and the employer. See *Lear Eye Clinic, Ltd. v. Commissioner*, 106 T.C. 418, 425-429 (1996).

The proposed regulations provide rules for aggregating participation and service for purposes of the 10-year phase-in of the limitations on defined benefit plans. Under these rules, years of participation in all aggregated plans and years of service for employers maintaining all aggregated plans are counted for purposes of applying the 10-year phase-in rules.

The proposed regulations clarify the aggregation rules that apply to section 403(b) annuity contracts, other plans of the employer, and plans of related employers, in light of changes made in EGTRRA. Generally a section 403(b) annuity contract is not aggregated with plans that are maintained by the participant's employer because the section 403(b) annuity contract is deemed maintained by the participant and not the employer for purposes of section 415. However, if a participant on whose behalf a section 403(b) annuity contract is purchased is in control of any employer for a limitation year, the annuity contract for the benefit of the participant is treated as a defined contribution plan maintained by both the controlled employer and the participant for that limitation year and accordingly, the section 403(b) annuity contract is aggregated with all other defined contribution plans maintained by the employer. Accordingly, the employer that contributes to the section 403(b) annuity contract must obtain information from participants regarding employers controlled by those participants and plans maintained by those controlled employers to monitor compliance with applicable limitations to comply with applicable reporting and withholding obligations. In addition to applying the rules under existing final regulations for purposes of determining control for purposes

of section 415(f), the proposed regulations would apply the rules under proposed §1.414(c)-5 (regarding aggregation rules for tax-exempt employers), as published in the **Federal Register** on November 16, 2004 (69 FR 67075).

The proposed regulations also provide that a multiemployer plan, as defined in section 414(f), is not aggregated with other multiemployer plans for purposes of determining any section 415 limitation. In addition, a multiemployer plan will not be aggregated with non-multiemployer plans for purposes of applying the 100% of compensation benefit limit to non-multiemployer plans under section 415(b)(1)(B). In general, under the proposed regulations, benefits of all employers are taken into account in applying the limitations of section 415 to a multiemployer plan. However, a multiemployer plan is permitted to provide that, where a participating employer maintains both a plan which is not a multiemployer plan and a multiemployer plan, only the benefits provided by the employer under the multiemployer plan are aggregated with the benefits under the non-multiemployer plan.

§ 1.415(g)-1: Disqualification of plans and trusts

Section 1.415(g)-1 of these proposed regulations sets forth rules regarding disqualification of plans and trusts, including plans and trusts that are aggregated pursuant to §1.415(f)-1. In large part, proposed §1.415(g)-1 replicates the rules of §1.415-9 of the existing final regulations regarding ordering rules for disqualifying plans and trusts that are aggregated for purposes of compliance with section 415. In addition, the proposed regulations provide rules for disqualification where an individual medical account (as described in section 415(l)) and a post-retirement medical benefits account for key employees (as described in section 419A(d)) is combined with a qualified defined contribution plan for purposes of applying section 415(c). If the combined plan exceeds those limitations for a particular limitation year, the qualified defined contribution plan (rather than the medical account) is disqualified for the limitation year.

§ 1.415(i)-1: Limitation year

Section 1.415(j)-1 of these proposed regulations sets forth rules regarding limitation years that are used as the period for demonstrating compliance with section 415. In addition to setting forth general rules that generally correspond to rules under existing regulations, the proposed regulations provide specific guidelines with respect to overlapping limitation years for aggregated plans. These rules reflect the guidance provided in Rev. Rul. 79-5 (1979-1 C.B. 165). Where defined contribution plans with different limitations years are aggregated, the rules of section 415(c) must be applied with respect to each limitation year of each such plan. For each such limitation year, the requirements of section 415(c) are applied to annual additions that are made for that time period with respect to the participant under all aggregated plans. Similarly, where defined benefit plans with different limitations years are aggregated, the rules of section 415(c) must be applied with respect to each limitation year of each such plan. Thus, for example, the dollar limitation of section 415(b)(1)(A) applicable to the limitation year for each plan must be applied to annual benefits under all aggregated plans to determine whether the plan satisfies the requirements of section 415(b).

Sections 415(m) and 415(n)

These proposed regulations do not contain provisions relating to section 415(m) (regarding treatment of qualified governmental excess benefit arrangements) and section 415(n) (regarding the purchase of permissive service credit from a governmental defined benefit plan). Comments are requested regarding the need for regulations or other guidance on issues arising under these statutory provisions.

Other changes: section 457 regulations

These proposed regulations also include revisions to the regulations under section 457 that are in addition to the revisions to reflect the treatment of compensation paid after severance from employment. The additional revisions do not include any substantive changes, but would merely make clarifications, including corrections in an example illustrating the section 457 catch-up rules and a correction in the rules relating to unforeseeable emergencies to reflect recent revisions in the definition of a dependent (made under the Working Families Tax Relief Act of 2004, which modified the definition of the term *dependent* under section 152).

Proposed Effective Dates

The regulations under section 415 are proposed to apply to limitation years beginning on or after January 1, 2007. Except as described below, until these regulations are issued as final regulations, the existing regulations remain in effect (to the extent not modified by statutory changes). A defined benefit plan that was adopted and effective before May 31, 2005 will be considered to satisfy the limitations of section 415(b) for a participant with respect to benefits accrued or payable under the plan as of the effective date of final regulations implementing these proposed regulations pursuant to plan provisions adopted and in effect on May 31, 2005, but only if such plan provisions meet the requirements of statutory provisions, regulations, and other published guidance in effect on May 31, 2005. Thus, plans that were in compliance with the rules of section 415 as in effect prior to the finalization of these regulations will not be disqualified based on benefits that arise pursuant to plan provisions that were adopted and in effect on May 31, 2005 and that accrue prior to the effective date of final regulations implementing these proposed regulations, even if those benefits no longer comply with the requirements of section 415 as set forth under those final regulations. However, such a plan will not be permitted to provide for the accrual of additional benefits for a participant on or after the effective date of final regulations implementing these proposed regulations unless such additional benefits, together with the participant's other accrued benefits, comply with those new final regulations.

Reliance on Compensation Timing Rules and Changes to Regulations Under Sections 401(a)(9) and 457

Pending issuance of final regulations, taxpayers may rely on the modifications in these proposed regulations contained in § 1.401(k)-1(e)(8), § 1.415(c)-2(e), and § 1.457-4(d) regarding post-severance compensation payments and other compensation timing rules, § 1.401(a)(9)-6 regarding certain changes in form of payment, and §§ 1.457-5, -6, and -10 providing corrective and clarifying changes. Pursuant to this reliance, taxpayers may apply the proposed amendments described in this paragraph for periods prior to the effective date of final regulations.

Sunset of EGTRRA Changes

The proposed regulations do not provide rules for the application of the EGTRRA sunset provision (section 901 of EGTRRA), under which the provisions of EGTRRA do not apply to taxable, plan, or limitation years beginning after December 31, 2010. Unless the EGTRRA sunset provision is repealed before it becomes effective, additional guidance will be needed to clarify its application.

Special Analyses

It has been determined that this notice of proposed rulemaking is not a significant regulatory action as defined in Executive Order 12866. Therefore, a regulatory assessment is not required. It has also been determined that section 553(b) of the Administrative Procedure Act (5 U.S.C. chapter 5) does not apply to these regulations, and, because the regulations do not impose a collection of information on small entities, the Regulatory Flexibility Act (5 U.S.C. chapter 6) does not apply. Pursuant to section 7805(f) of the Code, this notice of proposed rulemaking will be submitted to the Chief Counsel for Advocacy of the Small Business Administration for comment on its impact on small business.

Comments and Public Hearing

Before these proposed regulations are adopted as final regulations, consideration will be given to any written (a signed original and eight (8) copies) or electronic comments that are submitted timely to the IRS. The IRS and Treasury Department specifically request comments on the clarity of the proposed regulations and how they may be made easier to understand. All comments will be available for public inspection and copying.

A public hearing has been scheduled for August 17, 2005 at 10 a.m. in the auditorium, Internal Revenue Building, 1111 Constitution Avenue, NW., Washington, DC. Due to building security procedures, visitors must use the main building entrance on Constitution Avenue. In addition, all visitors must present photo identification to enter the building. Because of access restrictions, visitors will not be admitted beyond the immediate entrance area more than 30 minutes before the hearing starts. For more information about having your name placed on the list to attend the hearing, see the "FOR FURTHER INFORMATION CONTACT" section of this preamble.

The rules of 26 CFR 601.601(a)(3) apply to the hearing. Persons who wish to present oral comments at the hearing must submit written (signed original and eight (8) copies) or electronic comments and an outline of the topics to be discussed and the time to be devoted to each topic by July 27, 2005. A period of 10 minutes will be allotted to each person for making comments. An agenda showing the scheduling of the speakers will be prepared after the deadline for receiving outlines has passed. Copies of the agenda will be available free of charge at the hearing.

Drafting Information

The principal authors of these regulations are Vernon S. Carter and Linda S. F. Marshall, Office of Division Counsel/Associate Chief Counsel (Tax Exempt and Government Entities). However, other personnel from the IRS and Treasury participated in the development of these regulations.

List of Subjects

26 CFR Part 1

Income taxes, Reporting and recordkeeping requirements.

26 CFR Part 11

Income taxes, Reporting and recordkeeping requirements.

Proposed Amendments to the Regulations

Accordingly, 26 CFR parts 1 and 11 are proposed to be amended as follows:

PART 1 — INCOME TAXES

Paragraph 1. The authority citation for part 1 continues to read, in part, as follows:

Authority: 26 U.S.C. 7805 * * *

* * * * *

Par. 2. Section 1.401(a)(9)-6, Q&A-13(c)(3) is revised to read as follows:

§ 1.401(a)(9)-6 Required minimum distributions for defined benefit plans and annuity contracts.

A-13. * * * * *

(c) * * *

(3) In accordance with § 1.415(b)-2(c), after taking into account the modification, the payments under the annuity that are paid before the modification plus the modified payments must satisfy the requirements of § 1.415(b)-1 determined as of the original annuity starting date, using the interest rates and mortality table applicable to such date, except that, for this purpose, payments will not fail to satisfy the requirements of § 1.415(b)-1 determined as of the original annuity starting date merely because the payments are adjusted to reflect cost-of-living adjustments pursuant to section 415(d) that are determined in accordance with § 1.415(d)-1(a)(5); and

* * * * *

Par. 3. Section 1.401(k)-1 is amended by adding paragraph (e)(8) to read as follows:

§ 1.401(k)-1 Certain cash or deferred arrangements.

* * * * *

(e) * * *

(8) Section 415 compensation required. A cash or deferred arrangement satisfies this paragraph (e) only if cash or deferred elections can only be made with respect to amounts that are compensation within the meaning of section 415(c)(3) and § 1.415(c)-2. Thus, for example, the arrangement is not a qualified cash or deferred arrangement if an eligible employee who is not in qualified military service (as that term is defined in section 414(u)) can make a cash or deferred election with respect to an amount paid after severance from employment, unless the amount is paid within 2 ½ months following the eligible employee's severance from employment and is described in § 1.415(c)-2(e)(3)(ii).

Par. 4. Section 1.403(b)-3 as proposed to be revised on November 16, 2004 (69 FR 67086), is further proposed to the amended by adding text to paragraph (b)(4)(ii) to read as follows:

§ 1.403(b)-3 Exclusion for contributions to purchase section 403(b) contracts.

(b) * * *

(4) * * *

(ii) Exceptions. The exclusion from gross income provided by section 403(b) applies to contributions made for former employees with respect to compensation described in § 1.415(c)-2(e)(3)(ii) (relating to certain compensation paid within 2 ½ months following severance from employment), compensation described in § 1.415(c)-2(g)(4) (relating to compensation paid to participants who are permanently and totally disabled), and compensation relating to qualified military service under section 414(u).

* * * * *

§ 1.415-1 thru § 1.415-10 [Removed]

Par. 5. Sections 1.415-1 through 1.415-10 are removed.

Par. 6. Section 1.415(a)-1 is added to read as follows:

§ 1.415(a)-1 General rules with respect to limitations on benefits and contributions under qualified plans.

(a) *Trusts.* Under sections 415 and 401(a)(16), a trust that forms part of a pension, profit-sharing, or stock bonus plan will not be qualified under section 401(a) if any of the following conditions exists—

(1) In the case of a defined benefit plan, the annual benefit with respect to any participant for any limitation year exceeds the limitations of section 415(b) and § 1.415(b)-1 (taking into account the rules of § 1.415(b)-2);

(2) In the case of a defined contribution plan, the annual additions credited with respect to any participant for any limitation year exceed the limitations of section 415(c) and § 1.415(c)-1; or

(3) The trust has been disqualified under section 415(g) and § 1.415(g)-1 for any year.

(b) *Certain annuities and accounts*—(1) *In general.* Under section 415, an employee annuity plan described in section 403(a), an annuity contract described in section 403(b), or a simplified employee pension described in section 408(k) will not be considered to be described in the otherwise applicable section if any of the following conditions exists—

(i) The annual benefit under a defined benefit plan with respect to any participant for any limitation year exceeds the limitations of section 415(b) and § 1.415(b)-1 (taking into account the rules of § 1.415(b)-2);

(ii) The contributions and other additions credited under a defined contribution plan with respect to any participant for any limitation year exceed the limitations of section 415(c) and § 1.415(c)-1; or

(iii) The employee annuity plan, annuity contract, or simplified employee pension has been disqualified under section 415(g) and § 1.415(g)-1 for any year.

(2) *Special rule for section 403(b) annuity contracts*—(i) *In general.* If the contributions and other additions under an annuity contract that otherwise satisfies the requirements of section 403(b) with respect to any participant for any limitation year exceed the limitations of section 415(c) and § 1.415(c)-1, then the portion of the contract that includes such excess annual addition fails to be a section 403(b) contract (and instead is a contract to which section 403(c) applies), and the remaining portion of the contract is a section 403(b) contract. The status of the remaining portion of the contract as a section 403(b) contract is not retained unless, for the year of the excess and each year thereafter, the issuer of the contract maintains separate accounts for each such portion. See also § 1.403(b)-3(c)(3).

(ii) *Defined benefit plans.* If the annual benefit under an annuity contract that otherwise satisfies the requirements of section 403(b) and that is a defined benefit plan with respect to any participant for any limitation year exceeds the limitations of section 415(b) and § 1.415(b)-1 (taking into account the rules of § 1.415(b)-2), then the portion of the contract that includes such excess annual benefit fails to be a section 403(b) annuity contract (and instead is a contract to which section 403(c) applies), and the remaining portion of the contract is a section 403(b) annuity contract. The status of the remaining portion of the contract as a section 403(b) annuity contract is not retained unless, for the year of the excess and each year thereafter, the issuer of the contract maintains separate accounts for each such portion.

(3) *Section 403(b) annuity contract.* For purposes of section 415 and regulations thereunder, the term *section 403(b) annuity contract* includes arrangements that are treated as annuity contracts for purposes of section 403(b). For example, such term includes custodial accounts described in section 403(b)(7) and retirement income accounts described in section 403(b)(9).

(c) *Regulations*—(1) *In general.* This section provides general rules regarding the application of section 415. For further rules regarding the application of section 415, see—

(i) Section 1.415(b)-1 (for general rules regarding the limit applicable to defined benefit plans);

(ii) Section 1.415(b)-2 (for special rules for defined benefit plans where a participant has multiple annuity starting dates);

(iii) Section 1.415(c)-1 (for general rules regarding the limit applicable to defined contribution plans);

(iv) Section 1.415(c)-2 (for rules regarding the definition of compensation for purposes of section 415);

(v) Section 1.415(d)-1 (for rules regarding cost-of-living adjustments to the various limits of section 415);

(vi) Section 1.415(f)-1 (for rules for aggregating plans for purposes of section 415);

(vii) Section 1.415(g)-1 (for rules regarding disqualification of plans that fail to satisfy the requirements of section 415); and

(viii) Section 1.415(j)-1 (for rules regarding limitation years).

(2) *Cross references to additional rules for section 403(b) annuity contracts.* For additional rules relating to section 403(b) annuity contracts, see—

(i) Section 1.415(c)-2(g)(1) and (3) (relating to the definition of compensation for such annuity contracts);

(ii) Section 1.415(f)-1(g) (relating to rules for such annuity contracts for purposes of combining plans);

(iii) Section 1.415(g)-1(b)(3)(iv)(C) (regarding disqualification of section 403(b) annuity contract aggregated with a qualified defined contribution plan if the combined plans exceed the limitations of section 415(c));

(iv) Section 1.415(g)-1(e) (relating to the plan year for such annuity contracts); and

(v) Section 1.415(j)-1(e) (relating to the limitation year for such annuity contracts).

(3) *Cross references to additional rules for governmental plans.* For additional rules relating to governmental plans, see—

(i) Section 1.415(b)-1(a)(6)(i) (providing an exception from the compensation-based limit of section 415(b)(1)(B) for governmental plans);

(ii) Section 1.415(b)-1(a)(7)(ii) (regarding a special limitation for governmental plans making an election during 1990);

(iii) Section 1.415(b)-1(b)(4) (regarding qualified governmental excess benefit arrangements);

(iv) Section 1.415(b)-1(d)(3) and (4) (regarding age adjustments to the dollar limit of section 415(b)(1)(A) in the case of employees of police departments and fire departments and former members of the United States Armed Forces, and in the case of survivor and disability benefits);

(v) Section 1.415(b)-1(g)(3) (regarding adjustments to applicable limitations for years of participation, and adjustments to applicable limitations for years of service for survivor and disability benefits); and

(vi) Section 1.415(c)-1(b)(3)(iii) (regarding amounts not treated as annual additions).

(4) *Cross references to additional rules for multiemployer plans.* For additional rules relating to multiemployer plans, see—

(i) Paragraph (e) of this section (regarding benefits or contributions taken into account where a plan is maintained by more than one employer);

(ii) Section 1.415(b)-1(a)(6)(ii) (providing an exception from the compensation-based limit for multiemployer plans);

(iii) Section 1.415(b)-1(f)(3) (regarding the application of the minimum $10,000 limitation on benefits in the case of a multiemployer plan);

(iv) Section 1.415(f)-1(h) (providing special rules for aggregating multiemployer plans with other plans); and

(v) Section 1.415(g)-1(b)(3)(ii) (regarding plan disqualification rules where a multiemployer plan is aggregated with a plan that is not a multiemployer plan and the combined plans exceed the limitations of section 415).

(d) *Plan provisions*—(1) *In general.* Although no specific plan provision is required under section 415 in order for a plan to establish or maintain its qualification, the plan provisions must preclude the possibility that any accrual, distribution, or annual addition will exceed the limitations of section 415. For example, a plan may include provisions that automatically freeze or reduce the rate of benefit accrual (in the case of a defined benefit plan) or the annual addition (in the case of a defined contribution plan) to a level necessary to prevent the limitations from being exceeded with respect to any participant. For rules relating to this type of plan provision and the definitely determinable benefit requirement for pension plans, see § 1.401(a)-1(b)(1).

(2) *Special rule for profit-sharing and stock bonus plans.* A provision of a profit-sharing or stock bonus plan that automatically freezes or reduces the amount of annual additions to ensure that the limitations of section 415 will not be exceeded must comply with the requirement set forth in § 1.401-1(b)(1)(ii) or (iii) (as applicable) that such plans provide a definite predetermined formula for allocating the contributions made to the plan among the participants. If the operation of a provision that automatically freezes or reduces the amount of annual additions to ensure that the limitations of section 415 are not exceeded does not involve discretionary action on the part of the employer, the definite predetermined allocation formula requirement is not violated by the provision. If the operation of such a provision involves discretionary action on the part of the employer, the definite predetermined allocation formula requirement is violated. For example, if two profit-sharing plans of one employer otherwise provide for aggregate contributions which may exceed the limits of section 415(c), the plan provisions must specify (without involving employer discretion) under which plan contributions and allocations will be reduced to prevent an excess annual addition and how the reduction will occur.

(3) *Incorporation by reference*—(i) *In general.* A plan is permitted to incorporate by reference the limitations of section 415, and will not fail to meet the definitely determinable benefit requirement or the definite predetermined allocation formula requirement, whichever applies to the plan, merely because it incorporates the limits of section 415 by reference.

(ii) *Section 415 can be applied in more than one manner, but a statutory or regulatory default rule exists.* Where a provision of section 415 is permitted to be applied in more than one manner but is to be applied in a specified manner in the absence of contrary plan provisions (i.e., a default rule exists), if a plan incorporates the limitations of section 415 by reference with respect to that provision of section 415 and does not specifically vary from the default rule, then the default rule applies. With respect to a provision of section 415 for which a default rule exists, if the limitations of section 415 are to be applied in a manner other than using the default rule, the plan must specify the manner in which the limitation is to be applied in addition to generally incorporating the limitations of section 415 by reference. For example, if a plan generally incorporates the limitations of section 415 by reference and does not restrict the accrued benefits to which the amendments to section 415(b)(2)(E) made by GATT apply (as permitted by Q&A-12 of Rev. Rul. 98-1 (1998-1 C.B. 249) (see § 601.601(d) of this chapter), which reflects the amendments to section 767 of GATT made by section 1449 of SBJPA), then the amendments to section 415(b)(2)(E) made by GATT apply to all benefits under the plan.

(iii) *Section 415 can be applied in more than one manner with no statutory or regulatory default.* If a limitation of section 415 may be applied in more than one manner, and there is no governing principle pursuant to which that limitation is applied in the absence of contrary plan provisions, then the plan must specify the manner in which the limitation is to be applied in addition to generally incorporating the limitations of section 415 by reference. For example, if an employer maintains two profit-sharing plans, and if any participant participates in more than one such plan, then both plans must specify (in a consistent manner) under which of the employer's two profit-sharing plans annual additions must be reduced if aggregate annual additions would otherwise exceed the limitations of section 415(c)).

(iv) *Former requirements.* A plan cannot incorporate by reference formerly applicable requirements of section 415 that are no longer in force (such as the limits of former section 415(e)).

(v) *Cost-of-living adjustments*—(A) *In general.* A plan is permitted to incorporate by reference the annual adjustments to the limitations of section 415 that are made pursuant to section 415(d). See § 1.415(d)-1 for additional rules relating to cost-of-living adjustments under section 415(d).

(B) *Cost-of-living adjustments not included in accrued benefit until effective.* Notwithstanding that a plan incorporates the increases to the applicable limits under section 415(d) by reference, the accrued benefit of a participant for purposes of section 411 and the annual benefit payable to a participant for purposes of § 1.415(b)-1(a)(1) are not permitted to reflect increases pursuant to the annual increase under section 415(d) of the dollar limitation described in section 415(b)(1)(A) or the compensation limit described in section 415(b)(1)(B) for any period before the annual increase becomes effective. A plan amendment does not violate the requirements of section 411(d)(6) merely because it eliminates the incorporation by reference of the increases under section 415(d) with respect to increases that have not yet occurred. Pursuant to § 1.415(d)-1(a)(3), the increase in each limit that is adjusted pursuant to section 415(d) is effective as of January 1 of each calendar year, and applies with respect to limitation years ending

with or within that calendar year. Thus, where an increase in the dollar limitation under section 415(b)(1)(A) results in an increase to the participant's accrued benefit, the increase to the accrued benefit is permitted to occur as of a date no earlier than January 1 of the calendar year for which the increase in the dollar limitation is effective.

(C) *Application of increase in defined benefit dollar limit to participants who have commenced receiving benefits.* The annual increase under section 415(d) of the dollar limitation described in section 415(b)(1)(A) does not apply in limitation years beginning after the annuity starting date to a participant who has previously commenced receiving benefits unless the plan specifies that this annual increase applies to such a participant. Similarly, the annual increase under section 415(d) of the compensation-based limitation described in section 415(b)(1)(B) does not apply in limitation years beginning after the annuity starting date to a participant who has previously commenced receiving benefits unless the plan specifies that this annual increase applies to such a participant.

(D) *Treatment of cost-of-living adjustments for funding purposes.* In general, the annual increase under section 415(d) of the dollar limitation described in section 415(b)(1)(A) and the compensation limitation described in section 415(b)(1)(B) is treated as a plan amendment for purposes of applying sections 404 and 412, regardless of whether the plan is amended to reflect the increase or the plan reflects the increase automatically through operation of plan provisions. However, where a plan reflects the annual increase under section 415(d) of the dollar limitation described in section 415(b)(1)(A) or the compensation limitation described in section 415(b)(1)(B) automatically through operation of plan provisions, the funding method for the plan is permitted to provide for this annual increase to be treated as an experience loss for purposes of applying sections 404 and 412.

(e) *Rules for plans maintained by more than one employer.* Except as provided in § 1.415(f)-1(h)(2)(i) (regarding aggregation of multiemployer plans with plans other than multiemployer plans), for purposes of applying the limitations of section 415 with respect to a participant in a plan maintained by more than one employer, benefits and contributions attributable to such participant from all of the employers maintaining the plan must be taken into account. Furthermore, in applying the limitations of section 415 with respect to such a participant, the total compensation received by the participant from all of the employers maintaining the plan is permitted to be taken into account under any such plan if the plan so provides.

(f) *Special rules*—(1) *Affiliated employers.* Pursuant to section 414(b) and § 1.414(b)-1, all employees of all corporations that are members of a controlled group of corporations (within the meaning of section 1563(a), as modified by section 1563(f)(5), and determined without regard to section 1563(a)(4) and (e)(3)(C)) are treated as employed by a single employer for purposes of section 415. Similarly, pursuant to section 414(c) and §§ 1.414(c)-1 through 1.414(c)-6, all employees of trades or businesses that are under common control are treated as employed by a single employer. Thus, any defined benefit plan or defined contribution plan maintained by any member of a controlled group of corporations (within the meaning of section 414(b)) or by any trade or business (whether or not incorporated) under common control (within the meaning of section 414(c)) is deemed maintained by all such members or such trades or businesses. Pursuant to section 415(h), for purposes of section 415, sections 414(b) and 414(c) are applied by using the phrase "more than 50 percent" instead of the phrase "at least 80 percent" each place the latter phrase appears in section 1563(a)(1), in § 1.414(c)-2, and in § 1.414(c)-5.

(2) *Affiliated service groups.* Any defined benefit plan or defined contribution plan maintained by any member of an affiliated service group (within the meaning of section 414(m)) is deemed maintained by all members of that affiliated service group.

(3) *Leased employees*—(i) *In general.* Pursuant to section 414(n), except as provided in paragraph (f)(3)(ii) of this section, with respect to any person (referred to as the recipient) for whom a leased employee (within the meaning of section 414(n)(2)) performs services, the leased employee is treated as an employee of the recipient, but contributions or benefits provided by the leasing organization that are attributable to services performed for the recipient are treated as provided under a plan maintained by the recipient.

(ii) *Exception for leased employees covered by safe harbor plans.* Pursuant to section 414(n)(5), the rule of paragraph (f)(3)(i) of this section does not apply to a leased employee with respect to services performed for a recipient if—

(A) The leased employee is covered by a plan that is maintained by the leasing organization and that meets the requirements of section 414(n)(5)(B); and

(B) Leased employees (determined without regard to this paragraph (f)(3)(ii)) do not constitute more than 20% of the recipient's nonhighly compensated workforce.

(4) *Permissive service credit under governmental plans.* See section 415(n) for rules regarding the application of the limitations of sections 415(b) and (c) where an employee makes contributions (including a transfer described in section 403(b)(13) or section 457(e)(17)) to a defined benefit governmental plan to purchase permissive service credit under the plan.

(5) *Qualified domestic relations orders.* A benefit provided to an alternate payee (as defined in section 414(p)(8)) of a participant pursuant to a qualified domestic relations order (as defined in section 414(p)(1)(A)) is treated as if it were provided to the participant for purposes of applying the limitations of section 415.

(6) *Effect on other requirements.* Except as provided in § 1.417(e)-1(d)(1), the application of section 415 does not relieve a plan from the obligation to satisfy other applicable qualification requirements. Accordingly, the terms of the plan must provide for the plan to satisfy section 415 as well as all other applicable requirements. For example, if a defined benefit plan has a normal retirement age of 62, and if a participant's benefit remains unchanged between the ages of 62 and 65 because of the application of the section 415(b)(1)(A) dollar limit, the plan satisfies the requirements of section 411 only if the plan either commences distribution of the participant's benefit at normal retirement age (without regard to severance from employment) or provides for a suspension of benefits at normal retirement age that satisfies the requirements of section 411(a)(3)(B) and 29 CFR 2530.203-3. Similarly, if the increase to a participant's benefit under a defined benefit plan in a year after the participant has attained normal retirement age is less than the actuarial increase to the participant's previously accrued benefit because of the application of the section 415(b)(1)(B) compensation limitation (which is not adjusted for commencement after age 65), the plan satisfies the requirements of section 411 only if the plan either commences distribution of the participant's benefit at normal retirement age (without regard to severance from employment) or provides for a suspension of benefits at normal retirement age that satisfies the requirements of section 411(a)(3)(B) and 29 CFR 2530.203-3.

(g) *Effective date*—(1) *General rule.* Except as otherwise provided, §§ 1.415(a)-1, 1.415(b)-1, 1.415(b)-2, 1.415(c)-1, 1.415(c)-2, 1.415(d)-1, 1.415(f)-1, 1.415(g)-1, and 1.415(j)-1 apply to limitation years beginning on or after January 1, 2007.

(2) *Option to apply regulations earlier.* A plan that was adopted and in effect before January 1, 2007, is permitted to apply the provisions of §§ 1.415(a)-1, 1.415(b)-1, 1.415(b)-2, 1.415(c)-1, 1.415(c)-2, 1.415(d)-1, 1.415(f)-1, 1.415(g)-1, and 1.415(j)-1 to limitation years beginning after the date final regulations are published in the **Federal Register**.

(3) *Grandfather rule for preexisting benefits.* A defined benefit plan that was adopted and effective before May 31, 2005 is considered to satisfy the limitations of section 415(b) for a participant with respect to benefits accrued or payable under the plan as of the effective date of final regulations under §§ 1.415(a)-1, 1.415(b)-1, 1.415(b)-2, 1.415(c)-1, 1.415(c)-2, 1.415(d)-1, 1.415(f)-1, 1.415(g)-1, and 1.415(j)-1 (as provided under paragraph (g)(1) and (2) of this section) pursuant to plan provisions that were adopted and in effect on May 31, 2005, but only if such plan provisions meet the requirements of statutory provisions, regulations, and other published guidance in effect on May 31, 2005.

(4) *Sunset of EGTRRA amendments.* Sections 1.415(a)-1, 1.415(b)-1, 1.415(b)-2, 1.415(c)-1, 1.415(c)-2, 1.415(d)-1, 1.415(f)-1, 1.415(g)-1, and 1.415(j)-1 do not address the application of section 901 of the Economic Growth and Tax Relief Reconciliation Act of 2001, Public Law 107-16, 115 Stat. 38 (under which the amendments made by that Act do not apply to limitation years beginning after December 31, 2010).

Par. 7. Section 1.415(b)-1 is added to read as follows:

§ 1.415(b)-1 Limitations for defined benefit plans.

(a) *General rules*—(1) *Maximum limitations.* Except as otherwise provided under this section, a defined benefit plan fails to satisfy the requirements of section 415(a) for a limitation year if, during the limitation year, either the annual benefit (as defined in paragraph (b)(1)(i) of this section) accrued by a participant or the annual benefit payable to a participant at any time under the plan exceeds the lesser of—

(i) $160,000 (as adjusted pursuant to section 415(d), § 1.415(d)-1(a), and this section); or

(ii) 100% of the participant's average compensation for the period of the participant's high 3 years of service (as adjusted pursuant to section 415(d), § 1.415(d)-1(a), and this section).

(2) *Defined benefit plan.* For purposes of section 415 and regulations thereunder, a defined benefit plan is any plan, contract, or account to which section 415 applies pursuant to § 1.415(a)-1(a) or (b) (or any portion thereof) that is not a defined contribution plan within the meaning of § 1.415(c)-1(a)(2). In addition, a section 403(b) contract that is not described in section 414(i) is treated as a defined benefit plan for purposes of section 415 and regulations thereunder.

(3) *Plan provisions.* As required in § 1.415(a)-1(d)(1), in order to satisfy the limitations on benefits under this section, the plan provisions (including the provisions of any annuity) must preclude the possibility that any annual benefit exceeding these limitations will be accrued, distributed, or otherwise payable in any optional form of benefit (including the normal form of benefit) at any time (from the plan, from an annuity contract that will make distributions to the participant on behalf of the plan, or from an annuity contract that has been distributed under the plan). Thus, for example, a plan will fail to satisfy the limitations of this section if the plan does not contain terms that preclude the possibility that any annual benefit exceeding these limitations will be accrued or payable in any optional form of benefit (including the normal form of benefit) at any time, even though no participant has actually accrued a benefit in excess of these limitations.

(4) *Adjustments to dollar limitation for commencement before age 62 or after age 65.* The age-adjusted section 415(b)(1)(A) dollar limit computed pursuant to paragraph (d) or (e) of this section is used in place of the dollar limitation described in section 415(b)(1)(A) and paragraph (a)(1)(i) of this section in the case of a benefit with an annuity starting date that occurs before the participant attains age 62 or after the participant attains age 65.

(5) *Period of high 3 years of service*—(i) *In general.* For purposes of applying the limitation on benefits described in this section, the period of a participant's high 3 years of service is the period of 3 consecutive calendar years during which the employee was an active participant in the plan and had the greatest aggregate compensation (as defined in § 1.415(c)-2) from the employer. For purposes of this paragraph (a)(5), in determining a participant's high 3 years of service, the plan may use any 12-month period to determine a year of service instead of the calendar year, provided that it is uniformly and consistently applied in a manner that is specified under the terms of the plan. As provided under § 1.415(c)-2(f), because a plan may not base benefit accruals (in the case of a defined benefit plan) on compensation in excess of the limitation under section 401(a)(17), a plan's definition of compensation for a limitation year that is used for purposes of applying the limitations of section 415 is not permitted to reflect compensation for a plan year that is in excess of the limitation under section 401(a)(17) that applies to that plan year.

(ii) *Short periods of service.* For those employees who are employed with the employer while an active participant for less than 3 consecutive calendar years, the period of a participant's high 3 years of service is the actual number of consecutive years of employment (including fractions of years) while an active participant in the plan. In such a case, the limitation of section 415(b)(1)(B) of 100% of the participant's compensation for the period of the participant's high 3 years of service is computed by dividing the participant's compensation during the participant's longest consecutive period of employment while a plan participant by the number of years in that period (including fractions of years, but not less than one year).

(iii) *Examples*: The following examples illustrate the rules of this paragraph (a)(5):

Example 1. (i) Plan A, which was established on January 1, 2004, covers Participant M, who was hired on January 1, 2000. The limitation year for Plan A is the calendar year. Participant M's compensation (as defined in § 1.415(c)-2) from the employer maintaining the plan is $120,000 for 2000, $120,000 for 2001, $120,000 for 2002, $120,000 for 2003, $100,000 for 2004, $100,000 for 2005, $100,000 for 2006, and $80,000 for 2007. Plan A does not specify a period other than the calendar year for determining the period of a participant's high 3 years of service while a plan participant.

(ii) As of the end of the 2004 limitation year, the period of M's highest 3 consecutive years of service while a plan participant (or fewer, if applicable) runs from January 1, 2004, through December 31, 2004. As of the end of the 2005 limitation year, the period of M's highest 3 consecutive years of service while a plan participant (or fewer, if applicable) runs from January 1, 2004, through December 31, 2005. As of the end of the 2006 limitation year and the 2007 limitation year, the period of M's highest 3 consecutive years of service while a plan participant (or fewer, if applicable) runs from January 1, 2004, through December 31, 2006. For all of those periods, M's average compensation is $100,000. Thus, the limitation under section 415(b)(1)(B) for 2004 through 2007 is applied using $100,000 as M's average compensation for the period of M's high 3 consecutive years of service while a plan participant (or fewer, if applicable).

Example 2. (i) Participant P has participated in Plan A, maintained by Employer M, for more than 10 years. P's average compensation for P's high 3 years while a participant in Plan A (determined before the application of section 401(a)(17)) is $220,000. On January 1, 2007, P commences receiving benefits from Plan A at the age of 75, 10 years after attaining P's normal retirement age under Plan A. Distributions to P under Plan A are actuarially adjusted to reflect commencement 10 years after normal retirement age using a 5% interest rate and the applicable mortality table under section 417(e)(3) that applies as of January 1, 2003. The limitation year and the plan year for Plan A are the calendar year.

(ii) Pursuant to § 1.415(c)-2(f) and section 401(a)(17), Plan A is not permitted to provide for a definition of compensation that includes compensation for a plan year that is in excess of the limitation under section 401(a)(17) that applies to that plan year. Accordingly, the limitation under section 415(b)(1)(B) based on P's average compensation for P's high three consecutive years must not reflect compensation for any plan year that is in excess of the limitation under section 401(a)(17) that applies to that plan year. Thus, for example, if the limitation under section 401(a)(17) for plan years beginning in 2004, 2005, and 2006 is $205,000, and if P had compensation in excess of $205,000 in each of those years, then the limitation under section 415(b)(1)(B) based on P's average compensation for P's high three consecutive years is $205,000.

(6) *Exceptions from compensation limit.* The limit under paragraph (a)(1)(ii) of this section (i.e., 100% of the participant's average compensation for his high 3 years of service) does not apply to—

(i) A governmental plan (as defined in section 414(d));

(ii) A multiemployer plan (as defined in section 414(f)); or

(iii) A collectively bargained plan that is described in section 415(b)(7).

(7) *Special rules*—(i) *Total benefits not in excess of $10,000.* See section 415(b)(4) and paragraph (f) of this section for an exception from the limits of section 415(b)(1) and paragraph (a)(1) of this section with respect to retirement benefits that do not exceed $10,000 for the limitation year.

(ii) *Governmental plans electing during 1990.* For a special limitation applicable to certain governmental plans electing the application of this rule during the first plan year beginning after December 31, 1989, see section 415(b)(10).

(b) *Annual benefit*—(1) *In general*—(i) *Definition of annual benefit.* For purposes of this section and § 1.415(b)-2, the term *annual benefit* means a benefit that is payable annually in the form of a straight life annuity. With respect to a benefit payable in a form other than a straight life annuity, the annual benefit is determined as the straight life annuity that is actuarially equivalent to the benefit payable in such other form, determined under the rules of paragraph (c) of this section.

(ii) *Rules for determination of annual benefit.* The annual benefit does not include the annual benefit attributable to either employee contributions or rollover contributions (as described in sections 401(a)(31), 402(c)(1), 403(a)(4), 403(b)(8), and 408(d)(3), and 457(e)(16)), determined pursuant to the rules of paragraph (b)(2) of this section. The treatment of transferred benefits is determined under the rules of paragraph (b)(3) of this section. Paragraph (b)(4) of this section discusses the treatment of qualified governmental excess benefit arrangements.

(iii) *Determination of annual benefit in the case of multiple annuity starting dates.* See § 1.415(b)-2 for rules regarding the determination of the annual benefit from one or more plans in cases in which a participant has received one or more distributions in limitation years prior to an increase in the accrued benefit occurring during the current limitation year or prior to the annuity starting date for a distribution that commences during the current limitation year. The rules of § 1.415(b)-2 apply, for example, to multiple annuity starting dates that result from the commencement of an additional distribution and to multiple annuity starting dates that result from a new distribution election with respect to a distribution that commenced in a prior limitation year. For purposes of § 1.415(b)-2, the determination of whether a new annuity starting date has occurred is made without regard to the rule of § 1.401(a)-20, Q&A-10(d) (under which the commencement of certain distributions may not give rise to a new annuity starting date).

(2) *Determination of annual benefit attributable to employee contributions and rollover contributions*—(i) *In general.* If employee contributions (other than contributions described in paragraph (b)(2)(ii) of this section) or rollover contributions are made to the plan, the annual benefit attributable to these contributions is determined as provided in this paragraph (b)(2).

(ii) *Certain employee contributions disregarded.* For purposes of this paragraph (b)(2), the following are not treated as employee contributions—

(A) Contributions that are picked up by a governmental employer as provided under section 414(h)(2);

(B) Repayment of any loan made to a participant from the plan;

(C) Repayment of a previously distributed amount as described in section 411(a)(7)(B) in accordance with section 411(a)(7)(C); and

(D) Repayment of a withdrawal of employee contributions as provided under section 411(a)(3)(D).

(iii) *Annual benefit attributable to mandatory employee contributions.* In the case of mandatory employee contributions as defined in section 411(c)(2)(C) and § 1.411(c)-1(c)(4) (or contributions that would be mandatory employee contributions if section 411 applied to the plan), the annual benefit attributable to those contributions is determined by applying the factors applicable to mandatory employee contributions as described in section 411(c)(2)(B) and (C) and the regulations thereunder to those contributions to determine the amount of a straight life annuity commencing at the annuity starting date, regardless of whether section 411 applies to that plan. See § 1.415(c)-1(a)(2)(ii)(B) and (b)(3) for rules regarding treatment of mandatory employee contributions to a defined benefit plan as annual additions under a defined contribution plan.

(iv) *Voluntary employee contributions.* If voluntary employee contributions are made to the plan, the portion of the plan to which voluntary employee contributions are made is treated as a defined contribution plan pursuant to section 414(k) and, accordingly, is a defined contribution plan pursuant to § 1.415(c)-1(a)(2)(i). Accordingly, the portion of a plan to which voluntary employee contributions are made is not a defined benefit plan within the meaning of paragraph (a)(2) of this section and is not taken into account in determining the annual benefit under the portion of the plan that is a defined benefit plan.

(v) *Annual benefit attributable to rollover contributions.* The annual benefit attributable to rollover contributions from another qualified plan (for example, a contribution received pursuant to a direct rollover under section 401(a)(31)) is determined in the same manner as the annual benefit attributable to mandatory employee contributions if the plan provides for a benefit derived from the rollover contribution (other than a benefit derived from a separate account to be maintained with respect to the rollover contribution and actual earnings and losses thereon). Thus, in the case of rollover contributions from a defined contribution plan to a defined benefit plan to provide an annuity distribution, the annual benefit attributable to those rollover contributions for purposes of section 415 is determined by applying the rules of section 411(c), regardless of the assumptions used to compute the annuity distribution under the plan. Accordingly, in such a case, if the plan uses more favorable factors than those specified in section 411(c) to determine the amount of annuity payments arising from rollover contributions, the annual benefit under the plan would reflect the excess of those annuity payments over the amounts that would be payable using the factors specified in section 411(c)(3). See § 1.415(c)-1(b)(3)(i) for rules excluding rollover contributions maintained in a separate account that is treated as a defined contribution plan pursuant to section 414(k) from annual additions to a defined contribution plan.

(3) *Treatment of transferred benefits*—(i) *In general*—(A) *Transferor plan and transferee plan aggregated.* For the limitation year that includes the date of a transfer between defined benefit plans, if the transferee plan's benefits are required to be taken into account pursuant to section 415(f) and § 1.415(f)-1 in determining whether the transferor plan satisfies the limitations of section 415(b) for that limitation year, then the transferred benefits are included in determining the annual benefit under the transferee plan and are disregarded in determining the annual benefit under the transferor plan. This will occur, for example, if the employer sponsoring the transferor plan and the employer sponsoring the transferee plan are in the same controlled group within the meaning of section 414(b). Similarly, with respect to a transfer between defined benefit plans that occurred in a previous limitation year, if the transferee plan's benefits are required to be taken into account pursuant to section 415(f) and § 1.415(f)-1 in determining whether the transferor plan satisfies the limitations of section 415(b), then the transferred benefits are included in determining the annual

benefit under the transferee plan and are disregarded in determining the annual benefit under the transferor plan for the current limitation year. Accordingly, if the transferee plan's benefits are required to be taken into account pursuant to section 415(f) and § 1.415(f)-1 in determining whether the transferor plan satisfies the limitations of section 415(b) for the limitation year with respect to a transfer occurring in the current limitation year or a prior limitation year, no adjustment is made to the benefits actually provided under either plan for purposes of determining the annual benefit under the plans as aggregated.

(B) *Transferor plan and transferee plan not aggregated.* When there has been a transfer of liabilities from one qualified plan to another, the benefits associated with those transferred liabilities are treated by the transferor plan as distributed as a singlesum distribution in an amount determined under paragraph (b)(3)(ii) of this section if the transferee plan's benefits are not required to be taken into account pursuant to section 415(f) and § 1.415(f)-1 in determining whether the transferor plan satisfies the limitations of section 415(b). Although such a transfer is treated as a distribution in computing the annual benefit under the transferor plan, no adjustment is made to reflect the transfer for purposes of determining the annual benefit under the transferee plan. This will occur, for example, if the employer sponsoring the transferor plan is a predecessor employer with respect to the participant whose benefits are transferred to the transferee plan, where the transferee plan's benefits are not required to be taken into account pursuant to section 415(f) and § 1.415(f)-1 in determining whether the transferor plan satisfies the limitations of section 415(b).

(ii) *Amount of deemed distribution on account of transfer of benefits*— (A) *In general.* Where there has been a transfer of liabilities from one qualified defined benefit plan to another, the amount of the single-sum distribution that is deemed distributed from the transferor plan pursuant to paragraph (b)(3)(i)(B) of this section is the amount of the assets transferred (other than surplus assets transferred). Thus, where the fair market value of assets transferred from another defined benefit plan in connection with the transfer of liabilities equals or exceeds the actuarial present value of liabilities transferred, the annual benefit attributable to the liabilities transferred is determined taking into account the entire amount of liabilities transferred as a single-sum distribution.

(B) *Amount of assets transferred.* Where assets are transferred with respect to more than one participant, the assets transferred with respect to each participant (other than surplus assets transferred) are determined as the actuarial present value of the straight life annuity that is actuarially equivalent to the amount the participant would receive if the plan terminated immediately before the transfer (if the plan had then terminated) under the rules of section 414(I) or Subtitle E of Title IV of ERISA, whichever applies to the transferor plan. If neither the rules of section 414(I) nor the rules of Subtitle E of Title IV of ERISA apply to the plan, then the assets transferred with respect to each participant are determined as the actuarial present value of the straight life annuity that is actuarially equivalent to the amount the participant would receive if the plan terminated immediately before the transfer, determined by allocating the assets, to the extent possible, so that employees who are not officers, shareholders, or highly compensated employees receive from the plan at least the same proportion of the present value of their accrued benefits (whether or not nonforfeitable) as employees who are officers, shareholders, or highly compensated employees.

(iii) *Transfer of immediately distributable amount.* Where an immediately distributable amount is transferred from either a defined contribution plan or a defined benefit plan to a defined benefit plan (see § 1.411(d)-4, Q&A-3(c) regarding certain elective transfers of immediately distributable benefits), the annual benefit attributable to the benefits transferred is determined pursuant to the rules of paragraph (b)(2)(v) of this section regarding rollover contributions.

(4) *Treatment of qualified governmental excess benefit arrangements.* Pursuant to section 415(m), in determining whether a governmental plan (as defined in section 414(d)) meets the requirements of this section and § 1.415(b)-2, the annual benefit does not include benefits provided under a qualified governmental excess benefit arrangement, as defined in section 415(m)(3).

(c) *Adjustment to form of benefit for forms other than a straight life annuity*—(1) *In general.* This paragraph (c) provides rules for adjusting a form of benefit other than a straight life annuity to an actuarially equivalent straight life annuity beginning at the same time for purposes of determining the annual benefit described in paragraph (b) of this section. Examples of benefits that are not in the form of a straight life annuity include an annuity with a post-retirement death benefit and an annuity providing for a guaranteed number of payments. Paragraph (c)(2) of this section describes how to adjust a form of benefit to which

section 417(e)(3) does not apply. Paragraph (c)(3) of this section describes how to adjust a form of benefit to which section 417(e)(3) applies. Paragraph (c)(4) of this section describes benefit forms for which no adjustment is required. Paragraph (c)(5) of this section sets forth examples illustrating the application of this paragraph (c). The Commissioner may, in revenue rulings, notices, or other guidance published in the Internal Revenue Bulletin set forth simplified methods for adjusting a form of benefit other than a straight life annuity to an actuarially equivalent straight life annuity beginning at the same time for purposes of determining the annual benefit described in paragraph (b) of this section. See § 601.601(d) of this chapter.

(2) *Benefits to which section 417(e)(3) does not apply.* For a benefit to which section 417(e)(3) does not apply, the actuarially equivalent straight life annuity benefit is the greater of—

(i) The annual amount of the straight life annuity (if any) payable to the participant under the plan commencing at the same annuity starting date as the form of benefit payable to the participant; or

(ii) The annual amount of the straight life annuity commencing at the annuity starting date that has the same actuarial present value as the particular form of benefit payable, computed using a 5% interest assumption and the applicable mortality table described in § 1.417(e)-1(d)(2) for that annuity starting date.

(3) *Benefits to which section 417(e)(3) applies*—(i) *In general.* Except as provided in paragraph (c)(3)(ii) of this section, for a benefit to which section 417(e) applies, the actuarially equivalent straight life annuity benefit is the greater of—

(A) The annual amount of the straight life annuity commencing at the annuity starting date that has the same actuarial present value as the particular form of benefit payable, computed using the interest rate and mortality table, or tabular factor, specified in the plan for actuarial equivalence; or

(B) The annual amount of the straight life annuity commencing at the annuity starting date that has the same actuarial present value as the particular form of benefit payable, computed using the applicable interest rate for the distribution under § 1.417(d)-1(d)(3) and the applicable mortality table for the distribution under § 1.417(e)-1(d)(2).

(ii) *Special rule for 2004 and 2005.* For distributions to which section 417(e) applies and which have annuity starting dates beginning in 2004 or 2005, except as provided in section 101(d)(3) of the Pension Funding Equity Act of 2004 (118 Stat. 596), the actuarially equivalent straight life annuity benefit is the greater of—

(A) The annual amount of the straight life annuity commencing at the annuity starting date that has the same actuarial present value as the particular form of benefit payable, computed using the interest rate and mortality table, or tabular factor, specified in the plan for actuarial equivalence; or

(B) The annual amount of the straight life annuity commencing at the annuity starting date that has the same actuarial present value as the particular form of benefit payable, computed using a 5.5% interest assumption and the applicable mortality table for the distribution under § 1.417(e)-1(d)(2).

(4) *Certain benefit forms for which no adjustment is required*—(i) *In general.* For purposes of the adjustments described in this paragraph (c), the following benefits are not taken into account—

(A) Survivor benefits payable to a surviving spouse under a qualified joint and survivor annuity (as defined in section 417(b)) to the extent that such benefits would not be payable if the participant's benefit were not paid in the form of a qualified joint and survivor annuity; and

(B) Ancillary benefits that are not directly related to retirement benefits, such as preretirement disability benefits not in excess of the qualified disability benefit, preretirement incidental death benefits (including a qualified preretirement survivor annuity), and post-retirement medical benefits.

(ii) *Rules of application*—(A) *Social security supplements.* Although a social security supplement described in section 411(a)(9) and § 1.411(a)-7(c)(4) may be an ancillary benefit, it is included in determining the annual benefit because it is payable upon retirement and therefore is directly related to retirement income benefits.

(B) *QJSAs combined with other distributions.* If benefits are paid partly in the form of a qualified joint and survivor annuity and partly in some other form (such as a single-sum distribution), the rule of paragraph (c)(4)(i)(A) of this section (under which survivor benefits are not included in determining the annual benefit) applies to the survivor annuity payments under the portion of the benefit that is paid in the form of a QJSA.

(5) *Examples.* The following examples illustrate the provisions of this paragraph (c). For purposes of these examples, except as otherwise stated, actuarial equivalence under the plan is determined using a 5% interest assumption and the mortality table that applies under section 417(e)(3) as of January 1, 2003. It is assumed for purposes of these examples that the interest rate that applies under section 417(e)(3) for relevant time periods is 5.25% and that the mortality table that applies under section 417(e)(3) for relevant time periods is the mortality table that applies under section 417(e)(3) as of January 1, 2003. In addition, it is assumed that all participants discussed in these examples have at least ten years of service with the employer and at least ten years of participation in the plan at issue, and that all payments other than a payment of a single sum are made monthly, on the first day of each calendar month. The examples are as follows:

Example 1. (i) Plan A provides a single-sum distribution determined as the actuarial present value of the straight life annuity payable at the actual retirement date. Plan A provides that a participant's single sum is determined as the greater of the present value using 5% interest and the applicable mortality table under section 417(e)(3) as of January 1, 2003, and the present value using the applicable interest rate and the applicable mortality table under section 417(e). In accordance with §1.417(e)-1(d)(1), Plan A also provides that the single sum is not less than the actuarial present value of the accrued benefit payable at normal retirement age, determined using the applicable interest rate and the applicable mortality table. Participant M retires at age 65 with a formula benefit of $152,619 and elects to receive a distribution in the form of a single sum. Under the plan formula, and before the application of section 415 under the plan, the amount of the single sum is $1,800,002 (which is based on the 5% interest rate and applicable mortality table as of January 1, 2003, since that is greater than the amount that would have been determined using the 5.25% interest rate and the applicable mortality table).

(ii) For purposes of this section, the annual benefit is the greater of the annual amount of the actuarially equivalent straight life annuity commencing at the same age (determined using the plan's actuarial factors), and the annual amount of the actuarially equivalent straight life annuity commencing at the same age (determined using the applicable interest rate and applicable mortality table). Based on the factors used in the plan to determine the actuarially equivalent lump sum (in this case, an interest rate of 5% and the applicable mortality table as of January 1, 2003), $1,800,002 payable as a single sum is actuarially equivalent to an immediate straight life annuity at age 65 of $152,619. Based on the applicable interest rate and the applicable mortality table, $1,800,002 payable as a single sum is actuarially equivalent to an immediate straight life annuity at age 65 of $155,853. With respect to the single-sum distribution, M's annual benefit is equal to the greater of the two resulting amounts ($152,619 and $155,853), or $155,853.

Example 2. (i) The facts are the same as in *Example 1*, except that Participant M elects to receive his benefit in the form of a 10-year certain and life annuity. Applying the plan's actuarial equivalence factors determined using 5% interest and the applicable mortality table as of January 1, 2003, the benefit payable in this form is $146,100.

(ii) For purposes of this section, the annual benefit is the greater of the annual amount of the plan's straight life annuity commencing at the same age or the annual amount of the actuarially equivalent straight life annuity commencing at the same age, determined using a 5% interest rate and the applicable mortality table. In this case, the straight life annuity payable under the plan commencing at the same age is $152,619. Because the plan's factors for actuarial equivalence in this case are the same standardized actuarial factors required to be applied to determine the actuarially equivalent straight life annuity, the actuarially equivalent straight life annuity using the required standardized factors is also $152,619. With respect to the 10-year certain and life annuity distribution, M's annual benefit is equal to the greater of the two resulting amounts ($152,619 and $152,619), or $152,619.

Example 3. (i) The facts are the same as in *Example 1*. Participant N retires at age 62 with a formula benefit, after application of the plan's early retirement factors, of $100,000 and a Social Security supplement of $10,000 per year payable until age 65. N chooses to receive the accrued benefit in the form of a straight life annuity. The Plan has no provisions under which the actuarial value of the Social Security supplement can be paid as a level annuity for life.

(ii) Because the plan does not provide for a straight life annuity beginning at age 62, the annual benefit for purposes of this section is the annual amount of the straight life annuity commencing at age 62 that is actuarially equivalent to the distribution stream of $110,000 for three years and $100,000 thereafter, where actuarial equivalence is determined using a 5% interest rate and the applicable mortality table. In this case, the actuarially equivalent straight life annuity is $102,180.

Accordingly, with respect to this distribution stream, N's annual benefit is equal to $102,180.

Example 4. (i) Plan B is a defined benefit plan that provides a benefit equal to 100% of a participant's compensation for the participant's high 3 years of service while a participant, payable as a straight life annuity. For a married participant who does not elect another form of benefit, the benefit is payable in the form of a joint and 100% survivor annuity benefit that is reduced from the straight life annuity and is a QJSA within the meaning of section 417. For purposes of determining the amount of this QJSA, the plan provides that the reduction is only half of the reduction that would normally apply under the actuarial assumptions specified in the plan for determining actuarial equivalence of optional forms. The plan also provides that a married participant can elect to receive the plan benefits as a straight life annuity, or in the form of a single sum distribution that is the actuarial equivalent of the joint and 100% survivor annuity. Participant O elects, with spousal consent, a single-sum distribution.

(ii) The special rule that disregards the value of the survivor portion of a QJSA set forth in paragraph (c)(4)(i) of this section only applies to a benefit that is payable in the form of a qualified joint and survivor annuity. Any other form of benefit must be adjusted to a straight life annuity in accordance with paragraph (c)(1) of this section. Accordingly, because the benefit payable under the plan in the form of a single-sum distribution is the actuarial equivalent of a straight life annuity that is greater than 100% of a participant's compensation for his high 3 years, the limitation of section 415(b)(1)(B) has been exceeded.

Example 5. (i) Plan C is a defined benefit plan that provides an option to receive the benefit in the form of a joint and 100% survivor annuity with a 10-year certain feature, where the survivor beneficiary is the participant's spouse.

(ii) For a participant at age 65, the annual benefit with respect to the joint and 100% survivor annuity with a 10-year certain feature is determined as the greater of the annual amount of the straight life annuity payable to the participant under the plan at age 65 (if any), or the annual amount of the straight life annuity commencing at age 65 that has the same actuarial present value as the joint and 100% survivor annuity with a 10 year certain feature (but excluding the survivor annuity payments pursuant to paragraph (c)(4)(i)(A) of this section), computing using a 5% interest assumption and the applicable mortality table described in §1.417(e)-1(d)(2) for that annuity starting date. This latter amount is equal to the product of the annual payments under this optional form of benefit and the factor that provides for actuarial equivalence between a straight life annuity and a 10-year certain and life annuity (with no annuity for the survivor) computed using a 5% interest rate and the applicable mortality table.

Example 6. (i) Plan D is a defined benefit plan with a normal retirement age of 65. The normal retirement benefit under Plan D (and the only life annuity available under Plan D) is a life annuity with a fixed increase of 2% per year. The increase applies to the benefit provided in the prior year and is thus compounded. The plan provides that the benefit is limited to the lesser of 84% of the participant's average compensation for the participant's high 3 consecutive years of service while a plan participant or 84% of the section 415(b)(1)(A) dollar limit (which is assumed to be $170,000). Participant P's retires at age 65, at which time P's average compensation for P's high 3 consecutive years of service is $165,000. Accordingly, P commences receiving benefits in the form of a life annuity of $138,600 with a fixed increase of 2% per year.

(ii) Because Plan D does not provide for a straight life annuity, P's annual benefit for purposes of section 415(b) is the annual amount of the straight life annuity, commencing at age 65, that is actuarially equivalent to the distribution stream of $138,600 with a fixed increase of 2% per year, where actuarial equivalence is determined using a 5% interest rate and the applicable mortality table. In order to satisfy the requirements of section 415 and this section, this annual benefit must not exceed 100% of average compensation for the participant's high 3 consecutive years, or $165,000. Using a 5% interest rate and the section 417(e)(3) mortality table, the actuarially equivalent straight life annuity is $165,453, which exceeds $165,000. Accordingly, the plan fails to satisfy the compensation-based limitation of section 415(b)(1)(B).

Example 7. (i) Plan E provides a benefit at age 65 of a straight life annuity equal to the lesser of 90% of the participant's average compensation for the participant's highest 3 consecutive years while a plan participant and $148,500. Upon retirement at age 65, the optional forms of benefit available to a participant include payment of a QJSA with annual payments equal to 50% of the annual payments under the straight life annuity, along with a single-sum distribution that is actuarially equivalent (determined as the greater of the single sum calculated using a 5% interest assumption and the section 417(e)(3) mortality table in effect on January 1, 2003, and the single sum calculated using the section 417(e)(3) interest rate and the section 417(e)(3) mortality table) to 50% of the annual payments under the straight life annuity. Participant Q retires at age 65. Q's average compensation for Q's highest 3 consecutive years is $100,000. Q elects to receive a distribution in the optional form of benefit described above, under which the annual payments under the QJSA are $45,000 and the single-sum distribution is equal to $530,734. Q's spouse is 3 years younger than Q.

(ii) Q's annual benefit under Plan E is determined as the sum of the annual benefit attributable to the QJSA portion of the distribution and the annual benefit attributable to the single-sum portion of the distribution.

(iii) Because survivor benefits are not taken into account in determining the annual benefit attributable to the QJSA portion of the distribution, the annual benefit attributable to the QJSA portion of the distribution is determined as if that distribution were a straight life annuity of $45,000 per year commencing at age 65. Thus, no form adjustment is needed to determine the annual benefit attributable to the QJSA portion of the distribution, and the annual benefit attributable to the QJSA portion of the benefit is $45,000.

(iv) The annual benefit attributable to the single sum portion of the distribution is determined as the greater of the annual amount of the actuarially equivalent straight life annuity commencing at the same age (determined using the plan's actuarial factors), and the annual amount of the actuarially equivalent straight life annuity commencing at the same age (determined using the applicable interest rate and applicable mortality table). With respect to the single-sum distribution, the annual amount of the actuarially equivalent straight life annuity commencing at the same age determined using the plan's actuarial factors is equal to $45,954, and the actuarially equivalent straight life annuity commencing at the same age determined using the applicable interest rate and the applicable mortality table is equal to $45,954. Thus, the annual benefit attributable to the single sum portion of the benefit is $45,954.

(v) Q's annual benefit under the optional form of benefit is equal to the sum of the annual benefit attributable to the QJSA portion of the distribution and the annual benefit attributable to the single sum portion of the distribution, or $90,954. Because Q's average compensation for Q's highest 3 consecutive years is $100,000, the distribution satisfies the compensation limit of section 415(b)(1)(B).

Example 8. (i) R is a participant in a defined benefit plan maintained by A's employer. Under the terms of the plan, R must make contributions to the plan in a stated amount to accrue benefits derived from employer contributions.

(ii) R's contributions are mandatory employee contributions within the meaning of section 411(c)(2)(C) and, thus, the annual benefit attributable to these contributions does not have to be taken into account for purposes of testing the annual benefit derived from employer contributions against the applicable limitation on benefits. However, these contributions are treated as contributions to a defined contribution plan maintained by R's employer for purposes of section 415(c). See § 1.415(c)-1(a)(2)(ii)(B). Accordingly, with respect to the current limitation year, the limitation on benefits (as described in paragraph (a)(1) of this section) is applicable to the annual benefit attributable to employer contributions to the defined benefit plan, and the limitation on contributions and other additions (as described in § 1.415(c)-1) is applicable to the portion of the plan treated as a defined contribution plan, which consists of R's mandatory contributions. These same limitations would also apply if, instead of providing for mandatory employee contributions, the plan permitted voluntary employee contributions, because the portion of the plan attributable to voluntary employee contributions and earnings thereon is treated as a defined contribution plan maintained by the employer pursuant to section 414(k), and thus is not subject to the limitations of section 415(b).

(d) *Adjustment to section 415(b)(1)(A) dollar limit for commencement before age 62*—(1) *General rule.* For a distribution with an annuity starting date that occurs before the participant attains the age of 62, the age-adjusted section 415(b)(1)(A) dollar limit is determined as the lesser of—

(i) The section 415(b)(1)(A) dollar limit (as adjusted pursuant to section 415(d) and § 1.415(d)-1(a) for the limitation year) multiplied by the ratio of the annual amount of the immediately commencing straight life annuity under the plan (if any) to the annual amount of the straight life annuity under the plan commencing at age 62, if any (with both annual amounts determined without applying the rules of section 415); or

(ii) The annual amount of a straight life annuity commencing at the annuity starting date that has the same actuarial present value as a deferred straight life annuity commencing at age 62, where annual payments under the straight life annuity commencing at age 62 are equal to the dollar limitation of section 415(b)(1)(A), and where the actuarially equivalent straight life annuity is computed using a 5% interest rate and the applicable mortality table under § 1.417(e)-1(d)(2) that is effective for that annuity starting date.

(2) *Mortality adjustments*—(i) *In general.* For purposes of determining the amount described in paragraph (d)(1)(ii) of this section, to the extent that a forfeiture does not occur upon the participant's death, no adjustment is made to reflect the probability of the participant's death between the annuity starting date and the participant's attainment of age 62. To the extent that a forfeiture occurs upon the participant's death, an adjustment must be made to reflect the probability of the participant's death between the annuity starting date and the participant's attainment of age 62.

(ii) *No forfeiture deemed to occur where QPSA payable.* For purposes of paragraphs (d)(2)(i) and (e)(2)(i) of this section, a plan is permitted to treat no forfeiture as occurring upon a participant's death if the plan does not charge participants for providing a qualified preretirement survivor annuity (as defined in section 417(c)) on the participant's death, but only if the plan applies this treatment both for adjustments before age 62 and adjustments after age 65. Thus, in such a case, the plan is permitted to provide that, in computing the adjusted dollar limitation under section 415(b)(1)(A), no adjustment is made to reflect the probability of a participant's death between the annuity starting date and the participant's attainment of age 62 or between the age of 65 and the annuity starting date.

(3) *Exception for certain participants of certain governmental plans.* Pursuant to section 415(b)(2)(G) and (H), no age adjustment is made to the dollar limit for commencement before age 62 for any qualified participant. For this purpose, a qualified participant is a participant in a defined benefit plan that is maintained by a state or local government with respect to whom the service taken into account in determining the amount of the benefit under the defined benefit plan includes at least 15 years of service of the participant—

(i) As a full-time employee of any police department or fire department that is organized and operated by the state or political subdivision maintaining such defined benefit plan to provide police protection, firefighting services, or emergency medical services for any area within the jurisdiction of such state or political subdivision; or

(ii) As a member of the Armed Forces of the United States.

(4) *Exception for survivor and disability benefits under governmental plans.* Pursuant to section 415(b)(2)(I), no age adjustment is made to the dollar limit for commencement before age 62 for a distribution from a governmental plan (as defined in section 414(d)) on account of the participant's becoming disabled by reason of personal injuries or sickness, or as a result of the death of the participant.

(5) *Special rule for commercial airline pilots.* Pursuant to section 415(b)(9), no age adjustment is made to the dollar limit for early commencement after age 60 for a participant if—

(i) The participant is a commercial airline pilot;

(ii) The participant separates from service after attaining age 60; and

(iii) As of the time of the participant's retirement, regulations prescribed by the Federal Aviation Administration require an individual to separate from service as a commercial airline pilot after attaining any age occurring on or after age 60 and before age 62.

(6) *Examples.* The following examples illustrate the application of this paragraph (d). For purposes of these examples, it is assumed that the dollar limitation under section 415(b)(1)(A) for all relevant years is $180,000, that the normal form of benefit under the plan is a straight life annuity payable beginning at age 65, and that all payments other than a payment of a single sum are made monthly, on the first day of each calendar month. The examples are as follows:

Example 1. (i) Plan A provides that early retirement benefits are determined by reducing the accrued benefit by 4% for each year that the early retirement age is less than age 65. Participant M retires at age 60 after 30 years of service with a benefit (prior to the application of section 415) in the form of a straight life annuity of $100,000 payable at age 65, and is permitted to elect to commence benefits at any time between M's retirement and M's attainment of age 65. For example, M can elect to commence benefits at age 60 in the amount of $80,000, can wait until age 62 and commence benefits in the amount of $88,000, or can wait until age 65 and commence benefits in the amount of $100,000. Plan A provides a QPSA to all married participants without charge. Plan A provides (consistent with paragraph (d)(2)(ii) of this section) that, for purposes of adjusting the dollar limitation under section

415(b)(1)(A) for commencement before age 62 or after age 65, no forfeiture is treated as occurring upon a participant's death before retirement and, therefore, in computing the adjusted dollar limitation under section 415(b)(1)(A), no adjustment is made to reflect the probability of a participant's death between the annuity starting date and the participant's attainment of age 62 or between the age of 65 and the annuity starting date.

(ii) The age-adjusted section 415(b)(1)(A) dollar limit that applies for commencement of M's benefit at age 60 is the lesser of the section 415(b)(1)(A) dollar limit multiplied by the ratio of the annuity payable at age 60 to the annuity payable at age 62, or the straight life annuity payable at age 60 that is actuarially equivalent, using 5% interest and the applicable mortality table, to the deferred annuity payable at age 62. In this case, the age-adjusted section 415(b)(1)(A) dollar limit at age 60 is $156,229 (the lesser of $163,636 ($180,000* $80,000/$88,000) and $156,229 (the straight life annuity at age 60 that is actuarially equivalent to a deferred annuity of $180,000 commencing at age 62, determined using 5% interest and the applicable mortality table, without a mortality decrement for the period between 60 and 62)).

Example 2. (i) The facts are the same as in *Example 1*, except the plan provides that, if a participant has 30 or more years of service, no reduction applies for benefits commencing at age 62 and later.

(ii) The age-adjusted section 415(b)(1)(A) dollar limit that applies for commencement of M's benefit at age 60 is the lesser of the section 415(b)(1)(A) dollar limit multiplied by the ratio of the annuity payable at age 60 to the annuity payable at age 62, or the straight life annuity payable at age 60 that is actuarially equivalent, using 5% interest and the applicable mortality table, to the deferred annuity payable at age 62. In this case, because M has 30 years of service and would be eligible for the unreduced early retirement benefit at age 62, the age-adjusted section 415(b)(1)(A) dollar limit at age 60 is $144,000 (the lesser of $144,000 ($180,000* $80,000/$100,000) and $156,229 (the straight life annuity at age 60 that is actuarially equivalent to a deferred annuity of $180,000 commencing at age 62, determined using 5% interest and the applicable mortality table).

Example 3. (i) Participant O is a full-time civilian employee of the State of X Police Department who performs clerical services. O is a participant in the defined benefit plan that is maintained by the State of X with respect to whom the years of service taken into account in determining the amount of the benefit under the plan includes 15 years of service working for the State of X Police Department.

(ii) For a distribution with an annuity starting date that occurs before O attains the age of 62, there is no age adjustment to the section 415(b)(1)(A) dollar limit.

Example 4. (i) Participant R is a full-time employee of the Emergency Medical Service Department of County Y (which is not a part of a police or fire department) who performs services as a driver of an ambulance. R is a participant in the defined benefit plan that is maintained by County Y with respect to whom the years of service taken into account in determining the amount of the benefit under the plan includes 15 years of service working for County Y. R does not have service credit for time in Armed Forces of the United States.

(ii) The age adjustments to the limitations of section 415(b)(1)(A) pursuant to section 415(b)(2)(C) and (D) will apply if R commences receiving a distribution at an age to which either of those adjustments applies.

Example 5. (i) The facts are the same as in *Example 1* except that Participant M chooses to receive benefits in the form of a 10-year certain and life annuity under which payments are 97% of the periodic payments that would be made under the immediately commencing straight life annuity. Annual payments to M are 97% of $80,000, or $77,600. As in *Example 1*, the age-adjusted section 415(b)(1)(A) dollar limit at age 60 is $156,229.

· (ii) For purposes of this section, the annual benefit is the greater of the annual amount of the plan's straight life annuity commencing at the same age or the annual amount of the actuarially equivalent straight life annuity commencing at the same age, determined using a 5% interest rate and the applicable mortality table. In this case, the straight life annuity payable under the plan commencing at the same age is $80,000. The annual amount of the actuarially equivalent straight life annuity determined by applying the required standardized factors (i.e., a 5% interest assumption and the applicable mortality under section 417(e)(3)) is $79,416. With respect to the 10-year certain and life annuity commencing at age 62, M's annual benefit is equal to the greater of the two resulting amounts ($80,000 and $79,416), or $80,000.

(e) *Adjustment to section 415(b)(1)(A) dollar limit for commencement after age 65*—(1) *General rule.* For a distribution with an annuity

starting date that occurs after the participant attains the age of 65, the age-adjusted section 415(b)(1)(A) dollar limit is determined as the lesser of—

(i) The section 415(b)(1)(A) dollar limit (as adjusted pursuant to section 415(d) and § 1.415(d)-1 for the limitation year) multiplied by the ratio of the annual amount of the immediately commencing straight life annuity under the plan (if any) to the annual amount of the straight life annuity that would be payable under the plan to a hypothetical participant who is 65 years old and has the same accrued benefit (i.e., with no actuarial increases for commencement after age 65) as the participant receiving the distribution (with both annual amounts determined without applying the rules of section 415); or

(ii) The annual amount of a straight life annuity commencing at the annuity starting date that has the same actuarial present value as a straight life annuity commencing at age 65, where annual payments under the straight life annuity commencing at age 65 are equal to the dollar limitation of section 415(b)(1)(A), and where actuarially equivalent straight life annuity is computed using a 5% interest rate and the applicable mortality table under § 1.417(e)-1(d)(2) that is effective for that annuity starting date.

(2) *Mortality adjustments*—(i) *In general.* For purposes of determining the amount described in paragraph (e)(1)(ii) of this section, to the extent that a forfeiture does not occur upon the participant's death, no adjustment is made to reflect the probability of the participant's death between the participant's attainment of age 65 and the annuity starting date. To the extent that a forfeiture occurs upon the participant's death, an adjustment must be made to reflect the probability of the participant's death between the participant's attainment of age 65 and the annuity starting date.

(ii) *No forfeiture deemed to occur where QPSA payable.* See paragraph (d)(2)(ii) of this section for a rule deeming no forfeiture to occur if the plan does not charge participants for providing a qualified preretirement survivor annuity on the participant's death.

(3) *Example.* The following example illustrates the application of this paragraph (e):

Example. (i) Plan A provides that monthly benefits payable upon commencement after normal retirement age (which is age 65) are increased by 0.5% for each month of delay in commencement after attainment of normal retirement age. Plan A provides a QPSA to all married participants without charge. Plan A provides (consistent with paragraph (d)(2)(ii) of this section) that, for purposes of adjusting the dollar limitation under section 415(b)(1)(A) for commencement before age 62 or after age 65, no adjustment is made to reflect the probability of a participant's death between the annuity starting date and the participant's attainment of age 62 or between the age of 65 and the annuity starting date. The normal form of benefit under Plan A is a straight life annuity commencing at age 65. Participant M retires at age 70 on January 1, 2007, after 30 years of service with a benefit (prior to the application of section 415) that is payable monthly in the form of a straight life annuity of $195,000, which reflects the actuarial increase of 30% applied to the accrued benefit of $150,000.

(ii) The age-adjusted section 415(b)(1)(A) dollar limit at age 70 is the lesser of the section 415(b)(1)(A) dollar limit multiplied by the ratio of the annuity payable at age 70 to the annuity that would be payable at age 65 based on the same accrued benefit (both determined before the application of section 415), or the straight life annuity payable at age 70 that is actuarially equivalent, using 5% interest and the applicable mortality table, to the straight life annuity payable at age 65. In this case, the age-adjusted section 415(b)(1)(A) dollar limit at age 70 is $234,000 (the lesser of $234,000 ($180,000* $195,000/$150,000) and $264,109 (the straight life annuity at age 70 that is actuarially equivalent to an annuity of $180,000 commencing at age 65, determined using 5% interest and the applicable mortality table, without a mortality decrement for the period between 65 and 70)).

(f) *Total annual payments not in excess of $10,000*—(1) *In general.* Pursuant to section 415(b)(4), the annual benefit (without regard to the age at which benefits commence) payable with respect to a participant under any defined benefit plan is not considered to exceed the limitations on benefits described in section 415(b)(1) and in paragraph (a)(1) of this section if—

(i) The benefits (other than benefits not taken into account in the computation of the annual benefit under the rules of paragraph (b) or (c) of this section) payable with respect to the participant under the plan and all other defined benefit plans of the employer do not in the aggregate exceed $10,000 (as adjusted under paragraph (g)) for the limitation year, or for any prior limitation year; and

(ii) The employer (or a predecessor employer) has not at any time, either before or after the effective date of section 415, maintained a defined contribution plan in which the participant participated.

(2) *Computation of benefits for purposes of applying the $10,000 amount.* For purposes of paragraph (f)(1)(i) of this section, the benefits (other than benefits not taken into account in the computation of the annual benefit under the rules of paragraph (b) or (c) of this section) payable with respect to the participant under a plan for a limitation year reflect all amounts payable under the plan for the limitation year, and are not adjusted for form of benefit or commencement date.

(3) *Special rule with respect to participants in multiemployer plans.* The special $10,000 exception set forth in paragraph (f)(1) of this section is applicable to a participant in a multiemployer plan described in section 414(f) without regard to whether that participant ever participated in one or more other plans maintained by an employer who also maintains the multiemployer plan, provided that none of such other plans were maintained as a result of collective bargaining involving the same employee representative as the multiemployer plan.

(4) *Special rule with respect to employee contributions.* For purposes of paragraph (f)(1)(ii) of this section, mandatory employee contributions under a defined benefit plan are not considered a separate defined contribution plan maintained by the employer. Thus, a contributory defined benefit plan may utilize the special dollar limitation provided for in this paragraph (f). Similarly, for purposes of this paragraph (f), an individual medical account under section 401(h) or an account for postretirement medical benefits established pursuant to section 419A(d)(1) is not considered a separate defined contribution plan maintained by the employer.

(5) *Examples.* The application of this paragraph (f) may be illustrated by the following examples. For purposes of these examples, it is assumed that each participant has 10 years of participation in the plan and service with the employer. The examples are as follows:

Example 1. (i) B is a participant in a defined benefit plan maintained by X Corporation, which provides for a benefit payable in the form of a straight life annuity beginning at age 65. B's average compensation for B's high 3 consecutive years of service while a participant in the plan is $6,000. The plan does not provide for employee contributions, and at no time has B been a participant in a defined contribution plan maintained by X. With respect to the current limitation year, B's benefit under the plan (before the application of section 415) is $9,500.

(ii) Because annual payments under B's benefit do not exceed $10,000, and because B has at no time participated in a defined contribution plan maintained by X, the benefits payable under the plan are not considered to exceed the limitation on benefits otherwise applicable to B ($6,000).

(iii) This result would remain the same even if, under the terms of the plan, B's normal retirement age were age 60, or if the plan provided for employee contributions.

Example 2. (i) The facts are the same as in *Example 1*, except that the plan provides for a benefit payable in the form of a life annuity with a 10-year certain feature with annual payments of $9,500. Assume that, after the adjustment described in paragraph (c) of this section, B's actuarially equivalent straight life annuity (which is the annual benefit used for demonstrating compliance with section 415) for the current limitation year is $10,400.

(ii) For purposes of applying the special rule provided in this paragraph for total benefits not in excess of $10,000, there is no adjustment required if the retirement benefit payable under the plan is not in the form of a straight life annuity. Therefore, because B's retirement benefit does not exceed $10,000, B may receive the full $9,500 benefit without the otherwise applicable benefit limitations of this section being exceeded.

Example 3. (i) The facts are the same as in *Example 1*, except that the plan provides for a benefit payable in the form of a single sum and that the amount of the single sum that is the actuarial equivalent of the straight life annuity payable to B (i.e., $9,500 annually), determined in accordance with the rules of section 417(e)(3) and §1.417(e)-1(d) is $95,000.

(ii) Because the amount payable to B for the limitation year would exceed $10,000, the rule of this paragraph (f) does not provide an exception from the generally applicable limits of section 415(b)(1) for the single-sum distribution. Thus, the otherwise applicable limits apply to the single-sum distribution, and a single-sum distribution of $95,000 would not satisfy the requirements of section 415(b). Limiting the single-sum distribution to $60,000 (the present value of the annuity that complies with the compensation-based limitation of section 415(b)(1)(B)) in order to satisfy section 415 would be an impermissible

forfeiture under the requirements of section 411(a). Accordingly, the plan should not provide for a single-sum distribution in these circumstances.

(g) *Special rule for participation or service of less than 10 years*—(1) *Proration of dollar limit based on years of participation*—(i) *In general.* Pursuant to section 415(b)(5)(A), where a participant has less than 10 years of participation in the plan, the dollar limit described in paragraph (a)(1)(i) of this section (as adjusted pursuant to section 415(d), §1.415(d)-1, and paragraphs (d) and (e) of this section) is to be reduced by multiplying the otherwise applicable limitation by a fraction—

(A) The numerator of which is the number of years of participation in the plan (or 1, if greater); and

(B) The denominator of which is 10.

(ii) *Years of participation.* The following rules apply for purposes of determining a participant's years of participation for purposes of this paragraph (g)(1)—

(A) A participant is credited with a year of participation (computed to fractional parts of a year) for each accrual computation period for which the participant is credited with at least the number of hours of service (or period of service if the elapsed time method is used for benefit accrual purposes) required under the terms of the plan in order to accrue a benefit for the accrual computation period, and the participant is included as a plan participant under the eligibility provisions of the plan for at least one day of the accrual computation period. If these two conditions are met, the portion of a year of participation credited to the participant is equal to the amount of benefit accrual service credited to the participant for such accrual computation period. For example, if under the terms of a plan, a participant receives 1/10 of a year of benefit accrual service for an accrual computation period for each 200 hours of service, and the participant is credited with 1,000 hours of service for the period, the participant is credited with 1/2 a year of participation for purposes of section 415(b)(5)(A).

(B) A participant who is permanently and totally disabled within the meaning of section 415(c)(3)(C)(i) for an accrual computation period is credited with a year of participation with respect to that period for purposes of section 415(b)(5)(A).

(C) For a participant to receive a year of participation (or part thereof) for an accrual computation period for purposes of section 415(b)(5)(A), the plan must be established no later than the last day of such accrual computation period.

(D) No more than one year of participation may be credited for any 12-month period for purposes of section 415(b)(5)(A).

(2) *Proration of compensation limit and special rule for total annual payments less than $10,000 based on years of service*—(i) *In general.* Pursuant to section 415(b)(5)(B), where a participant has less than 10 years of service with the employer, the compensation limit described in paragraph (a)(1)(ii) of this section and the $10,000 amount under the special rule for small annual payments under paragraph (f) of this section are reduced by multiplying the otherwise applicable limitation by a fraction—

(A) The numerator of which is the number of years of service with the employer (or 1, if greater); and

(B) The denominator of which is 10.

(ii) *Years of service*—(A) *In general.* For purposes of applying this paragraph (g)(2), the term *year of service* is to be determined on a reasonable and consistent basis. A plan is considered to be determining years of service on a reasonable and consistent basis for this purpose if, subject to the limits of paragraph (g)(2)(ii)(B) of this section, a participant is credited with a year of service (computed to fractional parts of a year) for each accrual computation period for which the participant is credited with at least the number of hours of service (or period of service if the elapsed time method is used for benefit accrual purposes) required under the terms of the plan in order to accrue a benefit for the accrual computation period.

(B) *Rules of application.* No more than one year of service may be credited for any 12-month period for purposes of section 415(b)(5)(B). In addition, only the participant's service with the employer or a predecessor employer (as defined in §1.415(f)-1(c)) may be taken into account in determining the participant's years of service for this purpose.

(C) *Period of disability.* Notwithstanding the rules of paragraph (g)(2)(ii)(B) of this section, a plan is permitted to provide that a participant who is permanently and totally disabled within the meaning of section 415(c)(3)(C)(i) for an accrual computation period is credited with a year of service with respect to that period for purposes of section 415(b)(5)(B).

(3) *Exception for survivor and disability benefits under governmental plans.* The requirements of this paragraph (g) (regarding participation or service of less than 10 years) do not apply to a distribution from a governmental plan on account of the participant's becoming disabled by reason of personal injuries or sickness, or as a result of the death of the participant.

(4) *Examples.* The provision of this paragraph (g) may be illustrated by the following examples:

Example 1. (i) C begins employment with Employer A on January 1, 2005, at the age of 58. Employer A maintains only a noncontributory defined benefit plan which provides for a straight life annuity beginning at age 65 and uses the calendar year for the limitation and plan year. Employer A has never maintained a defined contribution plan. C becomes a participant in Employer A's plan on January 1, 2006, and works through December 31, 2011, when C is age 65. C begins to receive benefits under the plan in 2012. C's average compensation for C's high 3 consecutive years of service is $40,000. Furthermore, under the terms of Employer A's plan, for purposes of computing C's nonforfeitable percentage in C's accrued benefit derived from employer contributions, C has only 7 years of service with Employer A (2005-2011).

(ii) Because C has only 7 years of service with Employer A at the time he begins to receive benefits under the plan, the maximum permissible annual benefit payable with respect to C is $28,000 ($40,000 multiplied by 7/10).

Example 2. (i) The facts are the same as in *Example 1*, except that C's average compensation for his high 3 years is $8,000.

(ii) Because C has only 7 years of service with Employer A at the time he begins to receive benefits, the maximum benefit payable with respect to C would be reduced to $5,600 ($8,000 multiplied by 7/10). However, the special rule for total benefits not in excess of $10,000, provided in paragraph (f) of this section, is applicable in this case. Accordingly, C may receive an annual benefit of $7,000 ($10,000 multiplied by 7/10) without the benefit limitations of this section being exceeded.

Example 3. (i) Employer B maintains a defined benefit plan. Benefits under the plan are computed based on months of service rather than years of service. Accordingly, for purposes of applying the reduction based on years of service less than 10 to the limitations under section 415(b), the otherwise applicable limitation is multiplied by a fraction, the numerator of which is the number of completed months of service with the employer (but not less than 12 months), and the denominator of which is 120. The plan further provides that months of service are computed in the same manner for this purpose as for purposes of computing plan benefits.

(ii) The manner in which the plan applies the reduction based on years of service less than 10 to the limitations under section 415(b) is consistent with the requirements of this paragraph (g).

Example 4. (i) G begins employment with Employer D on January 1, 2003, at the age of 58. Employer D maintains only a noncontributory defined benefit plan which provides for a straight life annuity beginning at age 65 and uses the calendar year for the limitation and plan year. Employer D has never maintained a defined contribution plan. G becomes a participant in Employer D's plan on January 1, 2004, and works through December 31, 2009, when G is age 65. G performs sufficient service to be credited with a year of service under the plan for each year during 2003 through 2009 (although G is not credited with a year of service for 2003 because G is not yet a plan participant). G begins to receive benefits under the plan during 2010. The plan's accrual computation period is the plan year. The plan provides that, for purposes of applying the rules of section 415(b)(5)(B), a participant is credited with a year of service (computed to fractional parts of a year) for each plan year for which the participant is credited with sufficient service to accrue a benefit for the plan year. G's average compensation for G's high 3 years of service is $200,000. It is assumed for purposes of this example that the dollar limitation of section 415(b)(1)(A) for limitation years ending in 2010 is $180,000.

(ii) G has 7 years of service and 6 years of participation in the plan at the time G begins to receive benefits under the plan. Accordingly, the limitation under section 415(b)(1)(B) based on G's average compensation for G's high 3 years of service that applies pursuant to the adjustment required under section 415(b)(5)(B) is $140,000 ($200,000 multiplied by 7/10), and the dollar limitation under section 415(b)(1)(A) that applies to G pursuant to the adjustment required under section 415(b)(5)(A) is $108,000 ($180,000 multiplied by 6/10).

(h) *RPA '94 transition rules.* For special rules affecting the actuarial adjustment for form of benefit under paragraph (c) of this section and the adjustment to the dollar limit for early or late commencement under paragraphs (d) and (e) of this section for certain plans adopted and in effect before December 8, 1994, see section 767(d)(3)(A) of the Retirement Protection Act of 1994, as amended by section 1449(a) of the Small Business Job Protection Act of 1996. The Commissioner may provide guidance regarding these special rules in revenue rulings, notices, and other guidance published in the Internal Revenue Bulletin. See § 601.601(d) of this chapter.

Par. 8. Section 1.415(b)-2 is added to read as follows:

§ 1.415(b)-2 Multiple annuity starting dates.

(a) *Determination of annual benefit where distributions have occurred before the current determination date—*(1) *In general.* This section provides rules for determining the annual benefit of a participant for purposes of applying the limitations of section 415(b) and § 1.415(b)-1 in cases in which a participant has received one or more distributions in limitation years prior to an increase in the accrued benefit occurring during the current limitation year or prior to the annuity starting date for a distribution that commences during the current limitation year. This section applies, for example, where benefit distributions to a participant have previously commenced under a plan that is aggregated for purposes of section 415 with a plan from which the participant receives current accruals, or where a new distribution election is effective during the current limitation year with respect to a distribution that commenced in a prior limitation year. This section also applies where benefit payments are increased as a result of plan terms applying a cost-of-living adjustment pursuant to an increase of the dollar limit of section 415(b)(1)(A), if the plan does not provide for application of the rules of § 1.415(d)-1(a)(5) to determine the adjusted amount of the benefit. Paragraph (b) of this section provides rules for computing the annual benefit in the case of multiple annuity starting dates as described in this paragraph (a)(1). Paragraph (c) of this section provides an additional rule for multiple annuity starting dates that occur when a stream of annuity payments is modified by a new distribution election. Paragraph (d) of this section provides examples to illustrate the rules of this section.

(2) *Annuity starting date.* For purposes of this section, the determination of whether a new annuity starting date has occurred is made pursuant to the rules of § 1.401(a)-20, Q&A-10, but without regard to the rule of § 1.401(a)-20, Q&A-10(d) (under which the commencement of certain distributions may not give rise to a new annuity starting date).

(3) *Annual benefit—*(i) *In general.* Where a participant has received one or more distributions before a current accrual or before the annuity starting date for a currently payable distribution, except as provided in paragraph (a)(3)(iii) of this section (regarding mandatory employee contributions and rollover contributions), the annual benefit that is subject to the limits of section 415(b) and § 1.415(b)-1(a) is equal to the sum of—

(A) The annual benefit determined with respect to any accrued benefit with respect to which distribution has not yet commenced as of the current determination date, computed pursuant to the rules of § 1.415(b)-1(b) and (c);

(B) The annual benefit determined with respect to any distribution with an annuity starting date that occurs within the current limitation year and on or before the current determination date, computed pursuant to the rules of § 1.415(b)-1(b) and (c);

(C) The annual benefit determined with respect to the remaining amounts payable under any distribution with an annuity starting date that occurred during a prior limitation year, computed pursuant to the rules of § 1.415(b)-1(b) and (c) (subject to paragraph (a)(3)(ii) of this section); and

(D) The annual benefit attributable to prior distributions (computed pursuant to the rules of paragraph (b) of this section).

(ii) *Determining actuarial equivalence with respect to remaining amounts payable.* For purposes of computing the annual benefit determined with respect to the remaining amounts payable under any distribution with an annuity starting date that occurred during a prior limitation year under paragraph (a)(3)(i)(C) of this section, § 1.415(b)-1(c)(2) is applied by substituting for the amount described in § 1.415(b)-1(c)(2)(i) the annual amount of a straight life annuity commencing at the annuity starting date that has the same actuarial present value as the particular form of benefit payable, computed using the interest rate and mortality table, or tabular factor, specified in the plan for actuarial equivalence for the particular form of benefit payable.

(iii) *Mandatory employee contributions and rollover contributions.* If mandatory employee contributions or rollover contributions have been made to the plan with respect to a distribution that commenced before the current determination date, the annual benefit is determined by applying the rules of paragraph (a)(3)(i)(C) and (D) of this section and then subtracting the annual benefit attributable to mandatory employee contributions computed pursuant to § 1.415(b)-1(b)(2)(iii) and the annual benefit attributable to rollover contributions computed pursuant to § 1.415(b)-1(b)(2)(v), with both amounts computed as of the annuity starting date for the distribution.

(iv) *Repayments of prior distributions*—(A) *Total repayments.* A prior distribution that has been repaid to the plan with interest does not give rise to an annual benefit attributable to prior distributions for purposes of paragraph (a)(3)(i)(D) of this section (because amounts attributable to those repayments are reflected instead in amounts included in the annual benefit pursuant to paragraphs (a)(3)(i)(A), (B), and (C) of this section).

(B) *Partial repayments.* If a prior distribution was made, and a repayment was subsequently made that was less than the amount of the prior distribution (including reasonable interest), the annual benefit attributable to prior distributions is determined by multiplying the annual benefit attributable to the prior distribution (computed assuming that no repayment occurred) by one minus a fraction, the numerator of which is the amount of the repayment and the denominator of which is the amount of the prior distribution plus reasonable interest.

(b) *Annual benefit attributable to prior distributions*—(1) *In general*— (i) *Adjustment to actuarially equivalent straight life annuity*—(A) *Method of adjustment.* To compute the annual benefit attributable to a prior distribution, the prior distribution is adjusted to an actuarially equivalent straight life annuity commencing at the current determination date in accordance with the rules of paragraph (b)(2) of this section (for a prior distribution to which section 417(e)(3) did not apply) or paragraph (b)(3) of this section (for a prior distribution to which section 417(e)(3) applied).

(B) *Current determination date.* The current determination date is the last day of period for which an increase in the participant's benefit accrues if an increase in the participant's accrued benefit occurs during the limitation year. If there is no such increase, the current determination date is the annuity starting date for the distribution that commences during the limitation year.

(ii) *Rules of application*—(A) *Amount of distribution taken into account.* In applying the rules of paragraphs (b)(2) and (3) of this section to compute the annual benefit attributable to a prior distribution, only the actual amount received as a prior distribution (without regard to either the form of benefits paid, or the form or amount of remaining payments under the prior distribution) is taken into account. Thus, for example, in determining the annual benefit attributable to a prior distribution of $100,000 per year over the past four years, paragraph (b)(2) of this section will apply if the distribution was part of a 10-year certain and life annuity, and paragraph (b)(3) of this section will apply if the distribution was part of installment payments over 10 years. However, in both instances, the amounts taken into account in determining the annual benefit attributable to the prior distribution are the four $100,000 payments already made, without regard to remaining payments.

(B) *Application of mortality adjustments*—(1) *Application of mortality adjustments when standardized assumptions are used.* Under the rules of paragraphs (b)(2)(ii), (b)(3)(i)(B), and (b)(3)(ii)(B) of this section (under which standardized actuarial assumptions are applied), a prior distribution is adjusted to an actuarially equivalent straight life annuity commencing at the current determination date using the specified interest and mortality assumptions to convert the payment stream to an actuarially equivalent straight life annuity commencing at the current determination date. For this purpose, the actuarially equivalent straight life annuity commencing at the current determination date must reflect an actuarial increase to the present value of payments to reflect that the participant has survived during the interim period.

(2) *Application of mortality adjustments when the plan's assumptions for computing offsets are used.* Under the rules of paragraphs (b)(2)(i), (b)(3)(i)(A), and (b)(3)(ii)(A) of this section (under which the plan's assumptions for computing offsets for prior distributions are applied), the actuarially equivalent straight life annuity must reflect mortality adjustment in the same manner as those mortality adjustments are reflected in computing offsets for prior distributions.

(2) *Prior distributions to which section 417(e)(3) did not apply.* For a prior distribution to which section 417(e)(3) did not apply, the actuarially equivalent straight life annuity commencing at the current determination date is the greater of—

(i) The annual amount of a straight life annuity commencing at the current determination date that is the actuarial equivalent of that prior distribution, computed using the interest rate and mortality table specified under the plan that provides for the current distribution or current accrual that are used to determine offsets, if any, for prior distributions; and

(ii) The annual amount of a straight life annuity commencing at the current determination date that is the actuarial equivalent of that prior distribution, computed using a 5% interest assumption and the applicable mortality table described in § 1.417(e)-1(d)(2) that would apply to a distribution to which section 417(e) applies with an annuity starting date of the current determination date.

(3) *Prior distributions to which section 417(e)(3) applied*—(i) *In general.* For a prior distribution to which section 417(e)(3) applied, the actuarially equivalent straight life annuity commencing at the current determination date is the greater of—

(A) The annual amount of a straight life annuity commencing at the current determination date that is the actuarial equivalent of that prior distribution, computed using the interest rate and mortality table specified under the plan that provides for the current distribution or current accrual that are used to determine offsets, if any, for prior distributions; and

(B) The annual amount of a straight life annuity commencing at the current determination date that is the actuarial equivalent of that prior distribution, computed using the applicable interest rate under § 1.417(e)-1(d)(3) and the applicable mortality table under § 1.417(e)-1(d)(2) that would apply to a distribution with an annuity starting date of the current determination date.

(ii) *Special rule for 2004 and 2005.* For a prior distribution to which section 417(e)(3) applied, and for current determination dates or current accruals in 2004 and 2005, except as provided in section 101(d)(3) of the Pension Funding Equity Act of 2004, the actuarially equivalent straight life annuity commencing at the current determination date is the greater of—

(A) The annual amount of a straight life annuity commencing at the current determination date that is the actuarial equivalent of that prior distribution, computed using the interest rate and mortality table specified under the plan that provides for the current distribution or current accrual that are used to determine offsets, if any, for prior distributions; and

(B) The annual amount of a straight life annuity commencing at the current determination date that is the actuarial equivalent of that prior distribution, computed using a 5.5% interest assumption and the applicable mortality table under § 1.417(e)-1(d)(2) that would apply to a distribution with an annuity starting date of the current determination date.

(4) *Benefit forms for which no adjustment is required.* The annual benefit attributable to prior distributions is computed disregarding the portion of prior distributions described in § 1.415(b)-1(c)(4) (regarding benefits for which no adjustment is required). Thus, for example, the annual benefit attributable to prior distributions is computed disregarding the payment of preretirement disability benefits not in excess of the qualified disability benefit.

(c) *Change in distribution form*—(1) *In general.* If a stream of annuity payments is modified by a new distribution election, the requirements of this section are applied treating the modification as a new annuity starting date. In addition, in such a case, the requirements of paragraph (c)(2) of this section must be satisfied.

(2) *Test total annuity stream as of original annuity starting date.* If a stream of annuity payments is modified by a new distribution election, the payments under the annuity that are paid before the modification plus the modified payments must satisfy the requirements of § 1.415(b)-1 determined as of the original annuity starting date, using the interest rates and mortality table applicable to such date. A plan will not fail to satisfy the requirements of this paragraph (c)(2) merely because payments reflect cost-of-living adjustments pursuant to section 415(d) determined in accordance with § 1.415(d)-1(a)(5).

(d) *Examples.* The following examples illustrate the application of this section. For purposes of these examples, except as otherwise stated, actuarial equivalence under the plan (including for purposes of determining offsets for prior distributions and for purposes of determining the amount of annuity distributions commencing after normal retirement age) is determined using a 6% interest assumption and the mortality table that applies under section 417(e)(3) as of January 1, 2003, and all payments other than a payment of a single sum are made monthly, on the first day of each calendar month. It is assumed for purposes of these examples that the interest rate that applies under section 417(e)(3) for relevant time periods is 5.25% and that the mortality table that applies under section 417(e)(3) for relevant time periods is the mortality table that applies under section 417(e)(3) as of January 1, 2003. In addition, it is assumed that all participants discussed in these examples have at least ten years of service with the employer and at least ten years of participation in the plan at issue, and that the dollar limitation of section 415(b)(1)(A) as adjusted pursuant to section 415(d) for 2008 is equal to $180,000. It is further assumed that the product of the annual adjustment factors that apply in adjusting the compensation limitation of section 415(b)(1)(B) for 2005, 2006, 2007, and 2008 is 1.1. The examples are as follows:

Example 1. (i) Employer A previously maintained Plan D, a qualified defined benefit plan. Upon the termination of Plan D on January 1, 1997, Participant M received a single-sum distribution of $537,055 at the age of 54. As of January 1, 2008, Participant M has participated in Plan E (another defined benefit plan maintained by Employer A) for more than 10 years. On January 1, 2008, M retires at the age of 65 and receives a distribution from Plan E.

(ii) Pursuant to section 415(f) and §1.415(f)-1, distributions to M from Plan D and Plan E are aggregated for purposes of applying section 415(b). Pursuant to paragraph (a)(3) of this section, M's annual benefit that is subject to the limits of section 415(b) and §1.415(b)-1(a) is equal to the sum of the annual benefit determined with respect to the distribution commencing on January 1, 2008, and the annual benefit attributable to prior distributions (computed pursuant to the rules of paragraph (b) of this section).

(iii) M's annual benefit attributable to prior distributions is computed by adjusting the single-sum distribution made in 1995 to an actuarially equivalent straight life annuity commencing on January 1, 2008, in accordance with the rules set forth in paragraph (b)(3) of this section. Pursuant to those rules, that actuarially equivalent straight life annuity is computed using either the plan's actuarial assumptions for applying offsets for prior distributions (here, a 6% interest rate and the mortality table that applies under section 417(e)(3) as of January 1, 2003), or the applicable interest rate and the applicable mortality table under section 417(e)(3), both determined as of January 1, 2008, whichever set of actuarial assumptions produces the greater actuarially equivalent annuity. The actuarially equivalent straight life annuity computed using the plan's assumptions used for computing offsets is $100,027 per year, and the actuarially equivalent straight life annuity computed using the applicable interest rate and the applicable mortality table as of January 1, 2008, is $87,035 per year. Thus, M's annual benefit attributable to prior distributions is $100,027.

(iv) To comply with the limitations of section 415, M's annual benefit determined with respect to the distribution commencing on January 1, 2008, must be no greater than the otherwise applicable limit on the annual benefit (i.e., the lesser of $180,000 or 100% of M's average compensation for the period of the participant's high 3 years of service) minus $100,027. Thus, for example, to comply with the dollar limitation of section 415(b)(1)(A), M's annual benefit determined with respect to the distribution commencing on January 1, 2008, must be no greater than $79,973.

Example 2. (i) Employer B maintains Plan F, a qualified defined benefit plan. On January 1, 2002, at the age of 59, Participant N separated from service and commenced receiving a benefit of $80,000 per year for ten years from Plan F. As of January 1, 2008, Plan F is amended to increase N's accrued benefit. N is offered a new QJSA election with respect to the new accrual.

(ii) Pursuant to paragraph (a)(3) of this section, as of January 1, 2008, N's annual benefit that is subject to the limits of section 415(b) and §1.415(b)-1(a) is equal to the sum of the annual benefit determined with respect to remaining amounts payable under the distribution that commenced on January 1, 2002, the annual benefit determined with respect to the accrued benefit with respect to which distribution has not yet commenced, and the annual benefit attributable to prior distributions (computed pursuant to the rules of paragraph (b) of this section).

(iii) N's annual benefit determined with respect to the remaining four annual payments of $80,000 is determined pursuant to §1.415(b)-1(c)(3) as the greater of the annual amount of a straight life annuity commencing at the annuity starting date that has the same actuarial present value as the particular form of benefit payable, computed using the interest rate and mortality table, or tabular factor, specified in the plan for actuarial equivalence for the particular form of benefit payable, or the annual amount of a straight life annuity commencing at the annuity starting date that has the same actuarial present value as the particular form of benefit payable, computed using the applicable interest rate and the applicable mortality table under section 417(e)(3). Using the plan's factors for actuarial equivalence, the actuari-

ally equivalent straight life annuity is $26,334, and using the section 417(e)(3) factors for actuarial equivalence, the actuarially equivalent straight life annuity is $25,109. Accordingly, N's annual benefit determined with respect to the remaining four annual payments of $80,000 is equal to $26,334.

(iv) N's annual benefit attributable to prior distributions is computed by adjusting the six annual payments of $80,000 per year already made before January 1, 2008, to an actuarially equivalent straight life annuity commencing on January 1, 2008, in accordance with the rules set forth in paragraph (b)(3) of this section. Pursuant to those rules, that actuarially equivalent straight life annuity is computed using either the plan's actuarial assumptions for applying offsets for prior distributions (here, a 6% interest rate and the mortality table that applies under section 417(e)(3) as of January 1, 2003), or the applicable interest rate and the applicable mortality table under section 417(e)(3), both determined as of January 1, 2008, whichever set of actuarial assumptions produces the greater actuarially equivalent annuity. The actuarially equivalent straight life annuity computed using the plan's assumptions used for computing offsets is $54,494 per year, and the actuarially equivalent straight life annuity computed using the applicable interest rate and the applicable mortality table as of January 1, 2006, is $50,103 per year. Thus, N's annual benefit attributable to prior distributions is $54,494.

(v) To comply with the limitations of section 415, N's annual benefit determined with respect to the accrued benefit with respect to which distribution has not yet commenced must be no greater than the otherwise applicable limit on the annual benefit (i.e., the lesser of $180,000 or 100% of N's average compensation for period of N's high 3 years of service) minus $80,828 (the $26,334 annual benefit attributable to the remaining payments under the existing form of distribution, plus the $54,494 annual benefit attributable to prior distributions). Thus, for example, to comply with the dollar limitation of section 415(b)(1)(A), N's annual benefit determined with respect to the accrued benefit with respect to which distribution has not yet commenced must be no greater than $99,172.

Example 3. (i) The facts are the same as in *Example 2*, except that, instead of receiving a benefit of $80,000 per year for ten years from Plan F, N receives annual payments of $80,000 under a 10-year certain and life annuity from Plan F.

(ii) Pursuant to paragraph (a)(3) of this section, as of January 1, 2008, N's annual benefit that is subject to the limits of section 415(b) and §1.415(b)-1(a) is equal to the sum of the annual benefit determined with respect to remaining amounts payable under the distribution that commenced on January 1, 2002, the annual benefit determined with respect to the accrued benefit with respect to which distribution has not yet commenced, and the annual benefit attributable to prior distributions (computed pursuant to the rules of paragraph (b) of this section).

(iii) N's annual benefit determined with respect to the remaining portion of the existing annuity (i.e., a four-year certain and life annuity) is determined pursuant to §1.415(b)-1(c)(2) as the greater of the annual amount of a straight life annuity commencing at the annuity starting date that has the same actuarial present value as the particular form of benefit payable, computed using the interest rate and mortality table, or tabular factor, specified in the plan for actuarial equivalence for the particular form of benefit payable, or the annual amount of a straight life annuity commencing at the annuity starting date that has the same actuarial present value as the particular form of benefit payable, computed using an interest rate of 5% and the applicable mortality table under section 417(e)(3). Using the plan's factors for actuarial equivalence, the actuarially equivalent straight life annuity is $80,608, and using the statutory factors for actuarial equivalence, the actuarially equivalent straight life annuity is $80,577. Accordingly, N's annual benefit determined with respect to the remaining 4-year certain and life annuity is equal to $80,608.

(iv) N's annual benefit attributable to prior distributions is computed by adjusting the six annual payments of $80,000 per year already made before January 1, 2008, to an actuarially equivalent straight life annuity commencing on January 1, 2008, in accordance with the rules set forth in paragraph (b)(3) of this section. Pursuant to those rules, that actuarially equivalent straight life annuity is computed using either the plan's actuarial assumptions for applying offsets for prior distributions (here, a 6% interest rate and the mortality table that applies under section 417(e)(3) as of January 1, 2003), or the applicable interest rate and the applicable mortality table under section 417(e)(3), both determined as of January 1, 2008, whichever set of actuarial assumptions produces the greater actuarially equivalent annuity. The actuarially equivalent straight life annuity computed using the plan's assumptions used for computing offsets is $54,494 per year, and the actuarially equivalent straight life annuity computed using the applicable interest rate and the applicable mortality table as of January 1, 2008, is $48,689 per year. Thus, N's annual benefit attributable to prior distributions is $54,494.

(v) To comply with the limitations of section 415, N's annual benefit determined with respect to the accrued benefit with respect to which distribution has not yet commenced must be no greater than the otherwise applicable limit on the annual benefit (i.e., the lesser of $180,000 or 100% of N's average compensation for the highest 3 years) minus $135,102 (the $80,608 annual benefit attributable to the remaining payments under the existing form of distribution, plus the $54,494 annual benefit attributable to prior distributions). Thus, for example, to comply with the dollar limitation of section 415(b)(1)(A), N's annual benefit determined with respect to the accrued benefit with respect to which distribution has not yet commenced must be no greater than $44,898.

Example 4. (i) Participant P retired on January 1, 2004, at age 65, with average compensation for the period of P's high 3 years service of $190,000. P commenced receiving a straight life annuity of $165,000 from Plan E as of January 1, 2004. Plan E adjusts benefit payments to reflect increases in the applicable limitations of section 415(b) in accordance with the safe harbor methodology set forth in § 1.415(d)-1(a)(5). As of January 1, 2005, pursuant to an adjustment under section 415(d) that applies to P's benefit payments under the terms of the plan, annual payments to P from Plan E are adjusted to $170,000, and as of January 1, 2007, pursuant to another such adjustment (under which the section 415(b)(1)(A) dollar limit is assumed to increase to $175,000 for 2007), annual payments to P from Plan E are adjusted to $175,000. On December 1, 2007, P elected to change the form of the remainder of the benefit payable to P under Plan E to a single-sum distribution payable as of January 1, 2008. P receives a single-sum distribution of $1,769,157 on January 1, 2008. It is assumed for purposes of this example that the section 417(e)(3) interest rate that applies to a distribution from Plan E as of January 1, 2004, is 5.25%, and that the section 417(e)(3) interest rate that applies to a distribution from Plan E as of January 1, 2008, is 6%. The normal form of benefit under Plan E is a straight life annuity. Plan E provides a QPSA to all married participants without charge. Plan E provides that, for purposes of adjusting the dollar limitation under section 415(b)(1)(A) for commencement before age 62 or after age 65, no adjustment is made to reflect the probability of a participant's death between the annuity starting date and the participant's attainment of age 62 or between the participant's attainment of age 65 and the annuity starting date. Under Plan E, benefits commencing after the age of 65 are actuarially adjusted to reflect the later commencement date using the plan's generally applicable assumptions for actuarial equivalence.

(ii) To comply with the limitations of section 415 for the 2008 limitation year, Plan E must satisfy two requirements. First, under paragraph (c)(1) of this section, Plan E must limit payments to P so that the sum of the annual benefit attributable to the currently commencing distribution plus the annual benefit attributable to prior distributions is within the limitations of section 415(b) that apply to a benefit commencing at the annuity starting date for the distribution that commences in 2008. Second, under paragraph (c)(2) of this section, the payments under the annuity that are paid before January 1, 2008, plus the single-sum distribution made on January 1, 2008, must satisfy the requirements of § 1.415(b)-1 determined as of January 1, 2004, using the interest rates and mortality table applicable as of January 1, 2004. Pursuant to paragraph (c)(2) of this section, Plan E does not fail to satisfy this latter requirement if payments reflect cost-of-living adjustments pursuant to section 415(d) for payments no earlier than the time those adjustments are effective and in amounts no greater than amounts determined under § 1.415(d)-1(a)(5).

(iii) To satisfy the second requirement described in paragraph (ii) of this *Example 4*, the payments under the annuity that are paid before January 1, 2008 (i.e., $165,000 during 2004, $170,000 during 2005, $170,000 during 2006, and $175,000 during 2007), plus the single-sum distribution of $1,769,157 made on January 1, 2008, must satisfy the requirements of § 1.415(b)-1 determined as of January 1, 2004, using the interest rates and mortality table applicable as of January 1, 2004. As of January 1, 2004, the actuarially equivalent straight life annuity with respect to those payments is $176,698 using the applicable interest rate (assumed to be 5.25%) and the applicable mortality table for that date. As of January 1, 2004, the actuarially equivalent straight life annuity with respect to those payments is $170,239 using the plan's actuarial assumptions (a 6% interest rate and the applicable mortality table as of January 1, 2003). The annual benefit attributable to those payments is the greater of the two amounts, or $176,698. This amount exceeds the applicable dollar limitation as of January 1, 2004 (i.e., $165,000). Accordingly, without application of the special rule for cost-

of-living adjustments, Plan E would fail to satisfy this second requirement.

(iv) Pursuant to the special rule for cost-of-living adjustments under paragraph (c)(2) of this section, Plan E does not fail to satisfy the second requirement described in paragraph (ii) of this *Example 4* if payments reflect cost-of-living adjustments pursuant to section 415(d) for payments no earlier than the time those adjustments are effective and in amounts no greater than amounts determined under § 1.415(d)-1(a)(5). Accordingly, the payment stream that must satisfy the requirements of § 1.415(b)-1 determined as of January 1, 2004, using the interest rates and mortality table applicable as of January 1, 2004, is the payment stream consisting of $165,000 paid each year during 2004 through 2007, and $1,621,727 ($1,769,157 multiplied by 165,000/180,000) paid on January 1, 2008. As of January 1, 2004, the actuarially equivalent straight life annuity with respect to those payments is $158,930 using the applicable interest rate (assumed to be 5.25%) and the applicable mortality table for that date. As of January 1, 2004, the actuarially equivalent straight life annuity with respect to those payments is $165,000 using the plan's actuarial assumptions (a 6% interest rate and the applicable mortality table as of January 1, 2003). The annual benefit attributable to those payments is the greater of the two amounts, or $165,000, which satisfies the applicable limitations as of January 1, 2004. Accordingly, Plan E satisfies the second requirement described in paragraph (ii) of this *Example 4* using the special rule for cost-of-living adjustments under paragraph (c)(2) of this section.

(v) For purposes of determining compliance with the first requirement described in paragraph (ii) of this *Example 4*, P's annual benefit attributable to prior distributions is computed by adjusting the annual payments already received ($165,000 for 2004, $170,000 for 2005, $170,000 for 2006, and $175,000 for 2007) already made before January 1, 2008, to an actuarially equivalent straight life annuity commencing on January 1, 2008, in accordance with the rules set forth in paragraph (b)(3) of this section. Pursuant to those rules, that actuarially equivalent straight life annuity is computed using either the plan's actuarial assumptions for applying offsets for prior distributions (here, a 6% interest rate and the mortality table that applies under section 417(e)(3) as of January 1, 2003), or an interest rate of 5% and the applicable mortality table under section 417(e)(3), both determined as of January 1, 2008, whichever set of actuarial assumptions produces the greater actuarially equivalent annuity. The actuarially equivalent straight life annuity computed using the plan's assumptions used for computing offsets is $80,453 per year, and the actuarially equivalent straight life annuity computed using a 5% interest rate and the applicable mortality table as of January 1, 2008, is $75,046 per year. Thus, P's annual benefit attributable to prior distributions is $80,453.

(vi) P's annual benefit attributable to the single-sum distribution made on January 1, 2008, is determined as the greater of the annual amount of the actuarially equivalent straight life annuity commencing at the same age (determined using the plan's actuarial factors), and the annual amount of the actuarially equivalent straight life annuity commencing at the same age (determined using the applicable interest rate and applicable mortality table). Based on the factors used in the plan to determine the actuarially equivalent lump sum (in this case, an interest rate of 6% and the applicable mortality table as of January 1, 2003), $1,769,157 payable as a single sum at age 69 is actuarially equivalent to an immediate straight life annuity at age 69 of $180,000. Based on the applicable interest rate and the applicable mortality table, $1,769,157 payable as a single sum at age 69 is actuarially equivalent to an immediate straight life annuity at age 69 of $170,451. With respect to the single-sum distribution, P's annual benefit is equal to the greater of the two resulting amounts, or $180,000.

(vii) To satisfy the first requirement described in paragraph (ii) of this *Example 4*, P's annual benefit attributable to prior distributions plus P's annual benefit attributable to the single-sum distribution, determined as of January 1, 2008, must not exceed the applicable limitations. The sum of those annual benefits is $260,453. The age-adjusted dollar limitation as of January 1, 2008, is determined as the lesser of the section 415(b)(1)(A) dollar limit multiplied by the ratio of the annuity payable at age 69 to the annuity that would be payable at age 65 based on the same accrued benefit (both determined before the application of section 415), or the straight life annuity payable at age 69 that is actuarially equivalent, using 5% interest and the applicable mortality table, to the straight life annuity payable at age 65. In this case, the age-adjusted section 415(b)(1)(A) dollar limit at age 69 is $244,013, which is the lesser of 265,320 (the straight life annuity at age 69 that is actuarially equivalent to an annuity of $180,000 commencing at age 65, determined using the plan's interest rate of 6% and the applicable mortality table that applies as of January 1, 2003, without a mortality decrement for the period between 65 and 69) and $244,013 (the straight life annuity at age 69 that is actuarially equivalent to an annuity of $180,000 commencing at age 65, determined using 5% interest and the applicable mortality table, without a mortality decrement for the period between 65 and 69)). The compensation-based limitation of section 415(b)(1)(B) for P in 2008 is $209,000 ($190,000 multiplied by the product of the annual adjustment factors for 2005 through 2008, or 1.1). Accordingly, the limitation under section 415(b) for P as of January 1, 2008, is $209,000 (the lesser of the dollar limitation and the compensation limitation as of that date).

(viii) Because the sum of P's annual benefit attributable to prior distributions plus P's annual benefit attributable to the single-sum distribution ($260,453) exceeds the limitation under section 415(b) determined as of January 1, 2008 ($209,000), the plan fails to satisfy the requirements of section 415(b). In addition, if the plan limits the amount of the single-sum distribution in order to satisfy the requirements of section 415(b) in this case, there may be a forfeiture of a participant's accrued benefit in violation of section 411(a) in some cases where a participant converts annuity payments to a single-sum distribution.

Par. 9. Section 1.415(c)-1 is added to read as follows:

§ 1.415(c)-1 Limitations for defined contribution plans.

(a) *General rules*—(1) *Maximum limitations.* Under section 415(c) and this section, to satisfy the provisions of section 415(a) for any limitation year, except as provided by paragraph (a)(3) of this section, the annual additions (as defined in paragraph (b) of this section) credited to the account of a participant in a defined contribution plan for the limitation year must not exceed the lesser of—

(i) $40,000 (adjusted pursuant to section 415(d) and § 1.415(d)-1(b)); or

(ii) 100% of the participant's compensation (as defined in § 1.415(c)-2) for the limitation year.

(2) *Defined contribution plan*—(i) *Definition.* For purposes of section 415 and regulations thereunder, a *defined contribution plan* means a defined contribution plan within the meaning of section 414(i) (including the portion of a plan treated as a defined contribution plan under the rules of section 414(k)) that is—

(A) A plan described in section 401(a) which includes a trust which is exempt from tax under section 501(a);

(B) An annuity plan described in section 403(a); or

(C) A simplified employee pension described in section 408(k).

(ii) *Additional plans treated as defined contribution plans*—(A) *In general.* Contributions to the types of arrangements described in paragraphs (a)(2)(ii)(B) through (D) of this section are treated as contributions to defined contribution plans for purposes of section 415 and regulations thereunder.

(B) *Employee contributions to a defined benefit plan.* Mandatory employee contributions to a defined benefit plan are treated as contributions to a defined contribution plan. For this purpose, contributions that are picked up by the employer as described in section 414(h)(2) are not considered employee contributions.

(C) *Individual medical accounts under section 401(h).* Pursuant to section 415(l)(1), contributions allocated to any individual medical account which is part of a pension or annuity plan established pursuant to section 401(h) are treated as contributions to a defined contribution plan.

(D) *Post-retirement medical accounts for key employees.* Pursuant to section 419A(d)(2), amounts attributable to medical benefits allocated to an account established for a key employee (i.e., any employee who, at any time during the plan year or any preceding plan year, is or was a key employee as defined in section 416(i)) pursuant to section 419A(d)(1) are treated as contributions to a defined contribution plan.

(iii) *Section 403(b) annuity contracts.* Annual additions under an annuity contract described in section 403(b) are treated as annual additions under a defined contribution plan for purposes of this section.

(3) *Alternative contribution limitations*—(i) *Church plans.* For alternative contribution limitations relating to church plans, see paragraph (d) of this section.

(ii) *Special rules for medical benefits.* For alternative contribution limitations relating to certain medical benefits, see paragraph (e) of this section.

(iii) *Employee stock ownership plans.* For additional rules relating to employee stock ownership plans, see paragraph (f) of this section.

(b) *Annual additions*—(1) *In general*—(i) *General definition.* The term *annual addition* means, for purposes of this section, the sum, credited to a participant's account for any limitation year, of—

(A) Employer contributions;

(B) Employee contributions; and

(C) Forfeitures.

(ii) *Certain excess amounts treated as annual additions.* Contributions do not fail to be annual additions merely because they are excess contributions (as described in section 401(k)(8)(B)) or excess aggregate contributions (as described in section 401(m)(6)(B)), or merely because excess contributions or excess aggregate contributions are corrected through distribution.

(iii) *Direct transfers between defined contribution plans.* The direct transfer of funds or employee contributions from one defined contribution plan to another defined contribution plan does not give rise to an annual addition.

(iv) *Reinvested ESOP dividends.* The reinvestment of dividends on employer securities under an employee stock ownership plan pursuant to section 404(k)(2)(A)(iii)(II) does not give rise to an annual addition.

(2) *Employer contributions*—(i) *Amounts treated as annual additions.* For purposes of paragraph (b)(1)(i)(A) of this section, the term *annual additions* includes employer contributions credited to the participant's account for the limitation year and other allocations described in paragraph (b)(4) of this section that are made during the limitation year. See paragraph (b)(6) of this section for timing rules applicable to annual additions with respect to employer contributions.

(ii) *Amounts not treated as annual additions*—(A) *Certain restorations of accrued benefits.* The restoration of an employee's accrued benefits by the employer in accordance with section 411(a)(3)(D) or section 411(a)(7)(C) or resulting from the repayment of cashouts under a governmental plan (as described in section 415(k)(3)) is not considered an annual addition for the limitation year in which the restoration occurs. (See § 1.411(a)-7(d)(6)(iii)(B).)

(B) *Catch-up contributions.* Catch-up contributions made in accordance with section 414(v) and § 1.414(v)-1 do not give rise to annual additions.

(C) *Restorative payments.* A restorative payment that is allocated to a participant's account does not give rise to an annual addition for any limitation year. For this purpose, restorative payments are payments made to restore losses to a plan resulting from actions by a fiduciary for which there is reasonable risk of liability for breach of a fiduciary duty under Title I of ERISA, where plan participants who are similarly situated are treated similarly with respect to the payments. Generally, payments to a defined contribution plan are restorative payments only if the payments are made in order to restore some or all of the plan's losses due to an action (or a failure to act) that creates a reasonable risk of liability for such a breach of fiduciary duty (other than a breach of fiduciary duty arising from failure to remit contributions to the plan). This includes payments to a plan made pursuant to a Department of Labor order, the Department of Labor's Voluntary Fiduciary Correction Program, or a court-approved settlement, to restore losses to a qualified defined contribution plan on account of the breach of fiduciary duty (other than a breach of fiduciary duty arising from failure to remit contributions to the plan). However, payments made to a plan to make up for losses due merely to market fluctuations and other payments that are not made on account of a reasonable risk of liability for breach of a fiduciary duty under Title I of ERISA are contributions that give rise to annual additions and are not restorative payments.

(D) *Excess deferrals.* Excess deferrals that are distributed in accordance with § 1.402(g)-1(e)(2) or (3) do not give rise to annual additions.

(3) *Employee contributions.* For purposes of paragraph (b)(1)(i)(B) of this section, the term *annual additions* includes mandatory employee contributions (as defined in section 411(c)(2)(C) and the regulations thereunder) as well as voluntary employee contributions. The term "annual additions" does not include—

(i) Rollover contributions (as described in sections 401(a)(31), 402(c)(1), 403(a)(4), 403(b)(8), 408(d)(3), and 457(e)(16)).

(ii) Repayments of loans made to a participant from the plan;

(iii) Repayments of amounts described in section 411(a)(7)(B) (in accordance with section 411(a)(7)(C)) and section 411(a)(3)(D) (see § 1.411(a)-7(d)(6)(iii)(B)) or repayment of contributions to a governmental plan as described in section 415(k)(3); or

(iv) Employee contributions to a qualified cost of living arrangement within the meaning of section 415(k)(2)(B).

(4) *Transactions with plan.* The Commissioner may in an appropriate case, considering all of the facts and circumstances, treat transactions between the plan and the employer, transactions between the plan and the employee, or certain allocations to participants' accounts as giving rise to annual additions. Further, the Commissioner will treat a sale or exchange by the employee or the employer that transfers assets to a plan where the consideration paid by the plan is less than the fair market value of the assets transferred to the plan as giving rise to an annual addition in the amount of the difference between the value of the assets transferred and the consideration. A transaction described in this paragraph (b)(4) may constitute a prohibited transaction with the meaning of section 4975(c)(1).

(5) *Contributions other than cash.* For purposes of this paragraph (b), a contribution by the employer or employee of property rather than cash is considered to be a contribution in an amount equal to the fair market value of the property on the date the contribution is made. For this purpose, the fair market value is the price at which the property would change hands between a willing buyer and a willing seller, neither being under any compulsion to buy or to sell and both having reasonable knowledge of relevant facts. In addition, the contribution described in this paragraph (b)(5) may constitute a prohibited transaction within the meaning of section 4975(c)(1).

(6) *Timing rules*—(i) *In general*—(A) *Date of allocation.* For purposes of this paragraph (b), an annual addition is credited to the account of a participant for a particular limitation year if it is allocated to the participant's account under the terms of the plan as of any date within that limitation year. However, if the allocation is dependent upon participation in the plan as of any date subsequent to the date as of which it is allocated, it is considered allocated only at the end of the period of participation upon which the allocation is conditioned.

(B) *Date of employer contributions.* For purposes of this paragraph (b), employer contributions are not treated as credited to a participant's account for a particular limitation year unless the contributions are actually made to the plan no later than 30 days after the end of the period described in section 404(a)(6) applicable to the taxable year with or within which the particular limitation year ends. If, however, contributions are made by an employer exempt from Federal income tax (including a governmental employer), the contributions must be made to the plan no later than the 15th day of the tenth calendar month following the close of the taxable year with or within which the particular limitation year ends. If contributions are made to a plan after the end of the period during which contributions can be made and treated as credited to a participant's account for a particular limitation year, allocations attributable to those contributions are treated as credited to the participant's account for the limitation year during which those contributions are made.

(C) *Date of employee contributions.* For purposes of this paragraph (b), employee contributions, whether voluntary or mandatory, are not treated as credited to a participant's account for a particular limitation year unless the contributions are actually made to the plan no later than 30 days after the close of that limitation year.

(D) *Date for forfeitures.* A forfeiture is treated as an annual addition for the limitation year that contains the date as of which it is allocated to a participant's account as a forfeiture.

(E) *Treatment of elective contributions as plan assets.* The extent to which elective contributions constitute plan assets for purposes of the prohibited transaction provisions of section 4975 and Title I of the Employee Retirement Income Security Act of 1974 (88 Stat. 829), Public Law 93-406 (ERISA), is determined in accordance with regulations and rulings issued by the Department of Labor. See 29 CFR 2510.3-102.

(ii) *Special timing rules*—(A) *Corrective contributions.* For purposes of this section, if, in a particular limitation year, an employer allocates an amount to a participant's account because of an erroneous forfeiture in a prior limitation year, or because of an erroneous failure to allocate amounts in a prior limitation year, the allocation will not be considered an annual addition with respect to the participant for that particular limitation year, but will be considered an annual addition for the prior limitation year to which it relates. An example of a situation in which an employer contribution might occur under the circumstances described in the preceding sentence is a retroactive crediting of service for an employee under 29 CFR 2530.200b-2(a)(3) in accordance with an award of back pay. For purposes of this paragraph (b)(6)(ii), if the amount so contributed in the particular limitation year takes into account actual investment gains attributable to the period subsequent to the year to which the contribution relates, the portion of the total contribution that consists of such gains is not considered as an annual addition for any limitation year.

(B) *Contributions for accumulated funding deficiencies and previously waived contributions*—(1) *Accumulated funding deficiency.* In the case of a defined contribution plan to which the rules of section 412 apply, a contribution made to reduce an accumulated funding deficiency will be treated as if it were timely made for purposes of determining the limitation year in which the annual additions arising from the contribution are made, but only if the contribution is allocated to those participants who would have received an annual addition if the contribution had been timely made.

(2) *Previously waived contributions.* In the case of a defined contribution plan to which the rules of section 412 apply and for which there has been a waiver of the minimum funding standard in a prior limitation year in accordance with section 412(d), that portion of an employer contribution in a subsequent limitation year which, if not for the waiver, would have otherwise been required in the prior limitation year under section 412(a) will be treated as if it were timely made (without regard to the funding waiver) for purposes of determining the limitation year in which the annual additions arising from the contribution are made, but only if the contribution is allocated to those participants who would have received an annual addition if the contribution had been timely made (without regard to the funding waiver).

(3) *Interest.* For purposes of determining the amount of the annual addition under paragraphs (b)(6)(ii)(B)(1) and (2), a reasonable amount of interest paid by the employer is disregarded. However, any interest paid by the employer that is in excess of a reasonable amount, as determined by the Commissioner, is taken into account as an annual addition for the limitation year during which the contribution is made.

(C) *Simplified employee pensions (SEPs).* For purposes of this paragraph (b), amounts contributed to a simplified employee pension described in section 408(k) are treated as allocated to the individual's account as of the last day of the limitation year ending with or within the taxable year for which the contribution is made.

(D) *Treatment of certain contributions made pursuant to veterans' reemployment rights.* If, in a particular limitation year, an employer contributes an amount to an employee's account with respect to a prior limitation year and such contribution is required by reason of such employee's rights under chapter 43 of title 38, United States Code, resulting from qualified military service, as specified in section 414(u)(1), then such contribution is not considered an annual addition with respect to the employee for that particular limitation year in which the contribution is made, but, in accordance with section 414(u)(1)(B), is considered an annual addition for the limitation year to which the contribution relates.

(c) *Examples.* The following examples illustrate the rules of paragraphs (a) and (b) of this section:

Example 1. (i) P is a participant in a qualified profit-sharing plan maintained by his employer, ABC Corporation. The limitation year for the plan is the calendar year. P's compensation (as defined in § 1.415(c)-2) for the current limitation year is $30,000.

(ii) Because the compensation limitation described in section 415(c)(1)(B) applicable to P for the current limitation year is lower than the dollar limitation described in section 415(c)(1)(A), the maximum annual addition which can be allocated to P's account for the current limitation year is $30,000 (100% of $30,000).

Example 2. (i) Assume the same facts as in *Example 1*, except that P's compensation for the current limitation year is $140,000.

(ii) The maximum amount of annual additions that may be allocated to P's account in the current limitation year is the lesser of $140,000 (100% of P's compensation) or the dollar limitation of section 415(c)(1)(A) as in effect as of January 1 of the calendar year in which the current limitation year ends. If, for example, the dollar limitation of section 415(c)(1)(A) in effect as of January 1 of the calendar year in which the current limitation year ends is $44,000, then the maximum annual addition that can be allocated to P's account for the current limitation year is $44,000.

Example 3. (i) Employer N maintains a qualified profit-sharing plan that uses the calendar year as its plan year and its limitation year. N's taxable year is a fiscal year beginning June 1 and ending May 31. Under the terms of the profit-sharing plan maintained by N, employer contributions are made to the plan two months after the close of N's taxable year and are allocated as of the last day of the plan year ending within the taxable year (and are not conditioned on future participation). Thus, employer contributions for the 2007 calendar year limitation year are made on July 31, 2008 (the date that is two months after the close of N's taxable year ending May 31, 2008) and are allocated as of December 31, 2007.

(ii) Because the employer contributions are actually made to the plan no later than 30 days after the end of the period described in section 404(a)(6) with respect to N's taxable year ending May 31, 2008, the contributions will be considered annual additions for the 2007 calendar year limitation year.

Example 4. (i) Assume the same facts as in *Example 3,* except that the plan year for the profit-sharing plan maintained by N is the 12-month period beginning on February 1 and ending on January 31. The limitation year continues to be the calendar year. Under the terms of the plan, an employer contribution which is made to the plan on July 31, 2008, is allocated to participants' accounts as of January 31, 2008.

(ii) Because the last day of the plan year is in the 2008 calendar year limitation year, and because, under the terms of the plan, employer

Limitation year	Compensation
2007	$30,000
2008	$32,000
2009	$34,000
2010	$36,000

(ii) Participant A makes no voluntary employee contributions during limitation years 2007, 2008, and 2009. On October 1, 2010, participant A makes a voluntary employee contribution of $13,200 (10% of A's aggregate compensation for limitation years 2007, 2008, 2009, and 2010 of $132,000). Under the terms of the plan, $3,000 of this 2010 contribution is allocated to A's account as of limitation year 2007; $3,200 is allocated to A's account of limitation year 2008; $3,400 is allocated to A's account as of limitation year 2009, and $3,600 is allocated to A's account as of limitation year 2010.

(iii) Under the rule set forth in paragraph (c)(6)(ii)(C) of this section, employee contributions will not be considered credited to a participant's account for a particular limitation year for section 415 purposes unless the contributions are actually made to the plan no later than 30 days after the close of that limitation year. Thus, A's voluntary employee contribution of $13,200 made on October 1, 2010 would be considered as credited to A's account only for the 2010 calendar year limitation year, notwithstanding the plan provisions.

(d) *Special rules relating to church plans*—(1) *Alternative contribution limitation*—(i) *In general.* Pursuant to section 415(c)(7)(A), notwithstanding the general rule of paragraph (a)(1) of this section, additions for a section 403(b) annuity contract for a year with respect to a participant who is an employee of a church or a convention or association of churches, including an organization described in section 414(e)(3)(B)(ii), when expressed as an annual addition to such participant's account, are treated as not exceeding the limitation of paragraph (a)(1) of this section if such annual additions for the year are not in excess of $10,000.

(ii) *$40,000 aggregate limitation.* The total amount of annual additions with respect to any participant that are treated as not exceeding the limitation of paragraph (a)(1) of this section (taking into account the rule of paragraph (d)(3) of this section) pursuant to the rule of paragraph (d)(1)(i) of this section even though those annual additions would otherwise exceed that limitation cannot exceed $40,000. Thus, the aggregate of amounts for all limitation years that would exceed the limitation of this section but for this paragraph (d)(1) is limited to $40,000.

(2) *Years of service taken into account for duly ordained, commissioned, or licensed ministers or lay employees.* For purposes of this paragraph (d)—

(i) All years of service by an individual as an employee of a church, or a convention or association of churches, including an organization described in section 414(e)(3)(B)(ii), are considered as years of service for one employer; and

(ii) All amounts contributed for annuity contracts by each such church (or convention or association of churches) during such years for the employee are considered to have been contributed by one employer.

(3) *Foreign missionaries.* Pursuant to section 415(c)(7)(C), in the case of any individual described in paragraph (d)(1) of this section performing any services for the church outside the United States during the limitation year, additions for an annuity contract under section 403(b) for any year are not treated as exceeding the limitation of paragraph (a)(1) of this section if such annual additions for the year do not exceed the greater of $3,000 or the employee's includible

contributions are allocated to participants' accounts as of the last day of the plan year, the contributions are considered annual additions for the 2008 calendar year limitation year.

Example 5. (i) XYZ Corporation maintains a profit-sharing plan to which a participant may make voluntary employee contributions for any year not to exceed 10% of the participant's compensation for the year. The plan permits a participant to make retroactive make-up contributions for any year for which the participant contributed less than 10% of compensation. XYZ uses the calendar year as the plan year and the limitation year. Under the terms of the plan, voluntary employee contributions are credited to a participant's account for a particular limitation year if such contributions are allocated to the participant's account as of any date within that limitation year. Participant A's compensation is as follows—

compensation with respect to services for the church performed outside the United States during the limitation year.

(4) *Church, convention or association of churches.* For purposes of this paragraph (d), the terms *church* and *convention or association of churches* have the same meaning as when used in section 414(e).

(5) *Examples.* The following examples illustrate the rules of this paragraph (d).

Example 1. (i) E is an employee of ABC Church earning $7,000 during each calendar year. E participates in a section 403(b) annuity contract maintained by ABC Church beginning in 2007. The limitation year for the plan coincides with the calendar year. ABC Church contributes $10,000 to be allocated to E's account under the plan for 2007.

(ii) Under paragraph (d)(1) of this section, this allocation is treated as not violating the limits established in paragraph (a)(1) of this section because it does not exceed $10,000. Moreover, since an annual addition of $10,000 would otherwise exceed the limitation of paragraph (a)(1) of this section by $3,000, $3,000 is counted toward the aggregate limitation specified in paragraph (d)(1)(ii) of this section for 2007. Accordingly, ABC Church may make such allocations for 13 years (e.g., for 2007 through 2019) without exceeding the aggregate limitation of $40,000 specified in paragraph (d) of this section. For the fourteenth year, ABC Church could allocate only $8,000 to E's account (i.e., the $7,000 limitation computed under paragraph (a)(1)(ii) of this section, plus the remaining $1,000 of the $40,000 aggregate limitation under paragraph (d)(1)(ii) of this section on annual additions in excess of the limits under paragraph (a)(1) of this section).

Example 2. (i) F is an employee of XYZ Church. F earns $2,000 during each calendar year for services he provides to XYZ Church, all of which are performed outside the United States during each calendar year. F participates in a section 403(b) annuity contract maintained by ABC Church beginning in 2007. The limitation year for the plan coincides with the calendar year. ABC Church contributes $10,000 to be allocated to F's account under the plan for 2007.

(ii) Under paragraph (d)(1) of this section, this allocation is treated as not violating the limits established in paragraph (a)(1) of this section because it does not exceed $10,000. Moreover, since an annual addition of $10,000 would otherwise exceed the limitation of paragraph (a)(1) of this section by $7,000 (i.e., the excess of $10,000 over the greater of the $2,000 compensation limitation under section 415(c)(1)(B) or the $3,000 section 415(c)(7)(C) amount), XYZ Church may make such allocations for 5 years (e.g., for 2006 through 2010) without exceeding the aggregate limitation of $40,000 specified in paragraph (d) of this section. In 2012, XYZ church may contribute $8,000 to be allocated to F's account under the plan (i.e., the $3,000 limitation computed under paragraph (d)(3) of this section, plus the remaining $5,000 of the $40,000 aggregate limitation under paragraph (d)(1)(ii) of this section on annual additions in excess of the limits under paragraph (a)(1) of this section). For years after 2012, pursuant to paragraph (d)(3) of this section, XYZ Church could allocate $3,000 per year to F's account.

(e) *Special rules for medical benefits.* The limit under paragraph (a)(1)(ii) of this section (i.e., 100% of the participant's compensation for the limitation year) does not apply to—

(1) An individual medical account (as defined in section 415(l)); or

(2) A post-retirement medical benefits account for key employees (as defined in section 419A(d)(1)).

(f) *Special rules for employee stock ownership plans*—(1) *In general.* Special rules apply to employee stock ownership plans, as provided in paragraphs (f)(2) through (f)(4) of this section.

(2) *Determination of annual additions for leveraged ESOP*—(i) *In general.* Except as provided in this paragraph (f), in the case of an employee stock ownership plan to which an exempt loan as described in § 54.4975-7(b) has been made, the amount of employer contributions that is considered an annual addition for the limitation year is calculated with respect to employer contributions of both principal and interest used to repay that exempt loan for the limitation year.

(ii) *Employer stock that has decreased in value.* A plan may provide that, in lieu of computing annual additions in accordance with paragraph (f)(2)(i) of this section, annual additions with respect to a loan repayment described in paragraph (f)(2)(i) of this section are determined as the fair market value of shares released from the suspense account on account of the repayment and allocated to participants for the limitation year if that amount is less than the amount determined in accordance with paragraph (f)(2)(i) of this section.

(3) *Exclusions from annual additions for certain ESOPs that allocate to a broad range of participants*—(i) *General rule.* Pursuant to section 415(c)(6), in the case of an employee stock ownership plan (as described in section 4975(e)(7)) that meets the requirements of paragraph (f)(3)(ii) of this section for a limitation year, the limitations imposed by this section do not apply to—

(A) Forfeitures of employer securities (within the meaning of section 409(l)) under such an employee stock ownership plan if such securities were acquired with the proceeds of a loan (as described in section 404(a)(9)(A)); or

(B) Employer contributions to such an employee stock ownership plan which are deductible under section 404(a)(9)(B) and charged against the participant's account.

(ii) *Employee stock ownership plans to which the special exclusion applies.* An employee stock ownership plan meets the requirements of this paragraph (f)(3)(ii) for a limitation year if no more than one-third of the employer contributions for the limitation year that are deductible under section 404(a)(9) are allocated to highly compensated employees (within the meaning of section 414(q)).

(4) *Gratuitous transfers under section 664(g)(1).* The amount of any qualified gratuitous transfer (as defined in section 664(g)(1)) allocated to a participant for any limitation year is not taken into account in determining whether any other annual addition exceeds the limitations imposed by this section, but only if the amount of the qualified gratuitous transfer does not exceed the limitations imposed by section 415.

Par. 10. Section 1.415(c)-2 is added to read as follows:

§ 1.415(c)-2 Compensation.

(a) *General definition.* Except as otherwise provided in this section, compensation from the employer within the meaning of section 415(c)(3), which is applied for purposes of section 415 and regulations thereunder, means all items of remuneration described in paragraph (b) of this section, but excludes the items of remuneration described in paragraph (c) of this section. Paragraph (d) of this section provides safe harbor definitions of compensation that are permitted to be provided in a plan in lieu of the generally applicable definition of compensation. Paragraph (e) of this section provides timing rules relating to compensation. Paragraph (f) of this section provides rules regarding the application of the rules of section 401(a)(17) to the definition of compensation for purposes of section 415. Paragraph (g) of this section provides special rules relating to the determination of compensation, including rules for determining compensation for a section 403(b) annuity contract, rules for determining the compensation of employees of controlled groups or affiliated service groups, rules for disabled employees, rules relating to foreign compensation, rules regarding deemed section 125 compensation, and rules for employees in qualified military service.

(b) *Items includible as compensation.* For purposes of applying the limitations of section 415, except as otherwise provided in this section, the term *compensation* means remuneration for services of the following types—

(1) The employee's wages, salaries, fees for professional services, and other amounts received (without regard to whether or not an amount is paid in cash) for personal services actually rendered in the course of employment with the employer maintaining the plan, to the extent that the amounts are includible in gross income (or to the extent amounts deferred at the election of the employee would be includible

in gross income but for the rules of section 402(e)(3), 402(h)(1)(B), 402(k), 125(a), 132(f)(4), or 457(b)). These amounts include, but are not limited to, commissions paid to salespersons, compensation for services on the basis of a percentage of profits, commissions on insurance premiums, tips, bonuses, fringe benefits, and reimbursements or other expense allowances under a nonaccountable plan as described in § 1.62-2(c).

(2) In the case of an employee who is an employee within the meaning of section 401(c)(1) and the regulations thereunder, the employee's earned income (as described in section 401(c)(2) and the regulations thereunder), plus amounts deferred at the election of the employee that would be includible in gross income but for the rules of section 402(e)(3), 402(h)(1)(B), 402(k), or 457(b).

(3) Amounts described in section 104(a)(3), 105(a), or 105(h), but only to the extent that these amounts are includible in the gross income of the employee.

(4) Amounts paid or reimbursed by the employer for moving expenses incurred by an employee, but only to the extent that at the time of the payment it is reasonable to believe that these amounts are not deductible by the employee under section 217.

(5) The value of a nonqualified option granted to an employee by the employer, but only to the extent that the value of the option is includible in the gross income of the employee for the taxable year in which granted.

(6) The amount includible in the gross income of an employee upon making the election described in section 83(b).

(c) *Items not includible as compensation.* The term *compensation* does not include—

(1) Contributions (other than elective contributions described in section 402(e)(3), section 408(k)(6), section 408(p)(2)(A)(i), or section 457(b)) made by the employer to a plan of deferred compensation (including a simplified employee pension described in section 408(k) or a simple retirement account described in section 408(p), and whether or not qualified) to the extent that the contributions are not includible in the gross income of the employee for the taxable year in which contributed. Additionally, any distributions from a plan of deferred compensation (whether or not qualified) are not considered as compensation for section 415 purposes, regardless of whether such amounts are includible in the gross income of the employee when distributed. However, if the plan so provides, any amounts received by an employee pursuant to an unfunded nonqualified plan are permitted to be considered as compensation for section 415 purposes in the year the amounts are actually received.

(2) Amounts realized from the exercise of a nonqualified option, or when restricted stock or other property held by an employee either becomes freely transferable or is no longer subject to a substantial risk of forfeiture (see section 83 and the regulations thereunder).

(3) Amounts realized from the sale, exchange, or other disposition of stock acquired under a qualified stock option.

(4) Other amounts that receive special tax benefits, such as premiums for group-term life insurance (but only to the extent that the premiums are not includible in the gross income of the employee and are not salary reduction amounts that are described in section 125).

(5) Other items of remuneration that are similar to any of the items listed in paragraphs (c)(1) through (c)(4) of this section.

(d) *Safe harbor rules with respect to plan's definition of compensation*— (1) *In general.* Paragraphs (d)(2) through (4) of this section contain safe harbor definitions of compensation that are automatically considered to satisfy section 415(c)(3) if specified in the plan. The Commissioner may, in revenue rulings, notices, and other guidance of general applicability published in the Internal Revenue Bulletin (see § 601.601(d) of this chapter), provide additional definitions of compensation that are treated as satisfying section 415(c)(3).

(2) *Simplified compensation.* The safe harbor definition of compensation under this paragraph (d)(2) includes only those items specified in paragraph (b)(1) or (2) of this section and excludes all those items listed in paragraph (c) of this section.

(3) *Section 3401(a) wages.* The safe harbor definition of compensation under this paragraph (d)(3) includes wages within the meaning of section 3401(a) (for purposes of income tax withholding at the source), plus amounts deferred at the election of the employee that would be included in wages if not deferred pursuant to the rules of section 402(e)(3), 402(h)(1)(B), 402(k), or 457(b). However, any rules that limit the remuneration included in wages based on the nature or location of the employment or the services performed (such as the

exception for agricultural labor in section 3401(a)(2)) are disregarded for this purpose.

(4) *Information required to be reported under sections 6041, 6051 and 6052.* The safe harbor definition of compensation under this paragraph (d)(4) includes amounts that are compensation under the safe harbor definition of paragraph (d)(3) of this section, plus all other payments of compensation to an employee by his employer (in the course of the employer's trade or business) for which the employer is required to furnish the employee a written statement under sections 6041(d), 6051(a)(3), and 6052. See §§ 1.6041-1(a), 1.6041-2(a)(1), 1.6052-1, and 1.6052-2, and also see § 31.6051-1(a)(1)(i)(C) of this chapter. This safe harbor definition of compensation may be modified to exclude amounts paid or reimbursed by the employer for moving expenses incurred by an employee, but only to the extent that, at the time of the payment, it is reasonable to believe that these amounts are deductible by the employee under section 217.

(e) *Timing rules*—(1) *In general*—(i) *Payment during the limitation year.* Except as otherwise provided in this paragraph (e), in order to be taken into account for a limitation year, compensation within the meaning of section 415(c)(3) must be actually paid or made available to an employee (or, if earlier, includible in the gross income of the employee) within the limitation year. For this purpose, compensation is treated as paid on a date if it is actually paid on that date or it would have been paid on that date but for an election under section 401(k), 403(b), 408(k), 408(p)(2)(A)(i), 457(b), 132(f), or 125.

(ii) *Payment prior to severance from employment.* In order to be taken into account for a limitation year, compensation within the meaning of section 415(c)(3) must be paid or treated as paid to the employee (in accordance with the rules of paragraph (e)(1)(i) of this section) prior to severance from employment (within the meaning of section 401(k)(2)(B)(i)(l)) with the employer maintaining the plan

(2) *Certain de minimis timing differences.* Notwithstanding the provisions of paragraph (e)(1) of this section, a plan may provide that compensation for a limitation year includes amounts earned during that limitation year but not paid during that limitation year solely because of the timing of pay periods and pay dates if—

(i) These amounts are paid during the first few weeks of the next limitation year;

(ii) The amounts are included on a uniform and consistent basis with respect to all similarly situated employees; and

(iii) No compensation is included in more than one limitation year.

(3) *Compensation paid after severance from employment*—(i) *In general.* Any compensation described in paragraph (e)(3)(ii) of this section that is paid within 2 ½ months after an employee's severance from employment does not fail to be compensation (within the meaning of section 415(c)(3)) pursuant to the rule of paragraph (e)(1)(ii) of this section merely because it is paid after the employee's severance from employment.

(ii) *Certain payments made within 2 ½ months after severance from employment.* The following are types of post-severance payments that are not excluded from compensation because of timing if they are paid within 2 ½ months following severance from employment—

(A) Payments that, absent a severance from employment, would have been paid to the employee while the employee continued in employment with the employer and are regular compensation for services during the employee's regular working hours, compensation for services outside the employee's regular working hours (such as overtime or shift differential), commissions, bonuses, or other similar compensation; and

(B) Payments for accrued bona fide sick, vacation, or other leave, but only if the employee would have been able to use the leave if employment had continued.

(iii) *Other post-severance payments are not compensation.* Any payment that is not described in paragraph (e)(3)(ii) of this section is not considered compensation if paid after severance from employment, even if it is paid within 2 ½ months following severance from employment. Thus, for example, compensation does not include amounts paid after severance from employment that are severance pay, unfunded nonqualified deferred compensation, or parachute payments within the meaning of section 280G(b)(2).

(4) *Certain military service.* The rule of paragraph (e)(1)(ii) of this section does not apply to payments to an individual who does not currently perform services for the employer by reason of qualified military service (as that term is used in section 414(u)(1)) to the extent those payments do not exceed the amounts the individual would have received if the individual had continued to perform services for the employer rather than entering qualified military service.

(f) *Interaction with section 401(a)(17).* Because a plan may not base allocations (in the case of a defined contribution plan) or benefit accruals (in the case of a defined benefit plan) on compensation in excess of the limitation under section 401(a)(17), a plan's definition of compensation for a limitation year that is used for purposes of applying the limitations of section 415 is not permitted to reflect compensation for a plan year that is in excess of the limitation under section 401(a)(17) that applies to that plan year.

(g) *Special rules*—(1) *Compensation for section 403(b) annuity contract.* In the case of an annuity contract described in section 403(b), the term *participant's compensation* means the participant's includible compensation determined under section 403(b)(3) and § 1.403(b)-2(a)(11). Accordingly, the rules for determining a participant's compensation pursuant to section 415(c)(3) (other than section 415(c)(3)(E)) and this section do not apply to a section 403(b) annuity contract.

(2) *Employees of controlled groups of corporations, etc.* In the case of an employee of two or more corporations which are members of a controlled group of corporations (as defined in section 414(b) as modified by section 415(h)), the term "compensation" for such employee includes compensation from all employers that are members of the group, regardless of whether the employee's particular employer has a qualified plan. This special rule is also applicable to an employee of two or more trades or businesses (whether or not incorporated) that are under common control (as defined in section 414(c) as modified by section 415(h)), to an employee of two or more members of an affiliated service group as defined in section 414(m), and to an employee of two or more members of any group of employers who must be aggregated and treated as one employer pursuant to section 414(o).

(3) *Aggregation of section 403(b) annuity with qualified plan of controlled employer.* If a section 403(b) annuity contract is combined or aggregated with a qualified plan of a controlled employer in accordance with § 1.415(f)-1(f)(2), then, in applying the limitations of section 415(c) in connection with the combining of the section 403(b) annuity with a qualified plan, the total compensation from both employers is permitted to be taken into account.

(4) *Permanent and total disability of defined contribution plan participant*—(i) *In general.* Pursuant to section 415(c)(3)(C), if the conditions set forth in paragraph (g)(4)(ii) of this section are satisfied, then, in the case of a participant in any defined contribution plan who is permanently and totally disabled (as defined in section 22(e)(3)), the *participant's compensation* means the compensation the participant would have received for the year if the participant was paid at the rate of compensation paid immediately before becoming permanently and totally disabled, if such compensation is greater than the participant's compensation determined without regard to this paragraph (g)(4).

(ii) *Conditions for deemed disability compensation.* The rule of paragraph (g)(4)(i) of this section applies only if the following conditions are satisfied:

(A) Either the participant is not a highly compensated employee (as defined in section 414(q)) immediately before becoming disabled, or the plan provides for the continuation of contributions on behalf of all participants who are permanently and totally disabled for a fixed or determinable period;

(B) The plan provides that the rule of this paragraph (g)(4) (treating certain amounts as compensation for a disabled participant) applies with respect to the participant; and

(C) Contributions made with respect to amounts treated as compensation under this paragraph (g)(4) are nonforfeitable when made.

(5) *Foreign compensation.* Compensation described in paragraphs (b)(1) and (2) of this section includes foreign earned income (as defined in section 911(b)), whether or not excludable from gross income under section 911. Compensation described in paragraph (b)(1) of this section is to be determined without regard to the exclusions from gross income in sections 931 and 933. Similar principles are to be applied with respect to income subject to sections 931 and 933 in determining compensation described in paragraph (b)(2) of this section.

(6) *Deemed section 125 compensation*—(i) *General rule.* A plan is permitted to provide that deemed section 125 compensation (as defined in paragraph (g)(6)(ii) of this section) is compensation within the meaning of section 415(c)(3), provided that the plan applies this rule uniformly to all employees with respect to whom amounts subject to section 125 are included in compensation.

(ii) *Definition of deemed section 125 compensation.* Deemed section 125 compensation is an amount that is excludable from the income of the participant under section 106 that is not available to the participant in cash in lieu of group health coverage under a section 125 arrangement solely because that participant is not able to certify that the participant has other health coverage. Under this definition, amounts are deemed section 125 compensation only if the employer does not otherwise request or collect information regarding the participant's other health coverage as part of the enrollment process for the health plan.

(7) *Employees in qualified military service.* See section 414(u)(7) for special rules regarding compensation of employees who are in qualified military service within the meaning of section 414(u)(5).

Par. 11. Section 1.415(d)-1 is added to read as follows:

§ *1.415(d)-1 Cost of living adjustments.*

(a) *Defined benefit plans*—(1) *Dollar limitation*—(i) *Determination of adjusted limit.* Under section 415(d)(1)(A), the dollar limitation described in section 415(b)(1)(A) applicable to defined benefit plans is adjusted annually to take into account increases in the cost of living. The adjustment of the dollar limitation is made by multiplying the adjustment factor for the year, as described in paragraph (a)(1)(ii)(A) of this section, by $160,000, and rounding the result in accordance with paragraph (a)(1)(iii) of this section. The adjusted dollar limitation is prescribed by the Commissioner and published in the Internal Revenue Bulletin. See § 601.601(d) of this chapter.

(ii) *Determination of adjustment factor*—(A) *Adjustment factor.* The adjustment factor for a calendar year is equal to a fraction, the numerator of which is the value of the applicable index for the calendar quarter ending September 30 of the preceding calendar year, and the denominator of which is the value of such index for the base period. The applicable index is determined consistent with the procedures used to adjust benefit amounts under section 215(i)(2)(A) of the Social Security Act, Public Law 92-336 (86 Stat. 406), as amended. If, however, the value of that fraction is less than one for a calendar year, then the adjustment factor for the calendar year is equal to one.

(B) *Base period.* For the purpose of adjusting the dollar limitation pursuant to paragraph (a)(1)(ii)(A) of this section, the base period is the calendar quarter beginning July 1, 2001.

(iii) *Rounding.* Any increase in the $160,000 amount specified in section 415(b)(1)(A) which is not a multiple of $5,000 is rounded to the next lowest multiple of $5,000.

(2) *Average compensation for high 3 years of service limitation*—(i) *Determination of adjusted limit.* Under section 415(d)(1)(B), with regard to participants who have separated from service with a nonforfeitable right to an accrued benefit, the compensation limitation described in section 415(b)(1)(B) is adjusted annually to take into account increases in the cost of living. For any limitation year beginning after the separation occurs, the adjustment of the compensation limitation is made by multiplying the annual adjustment factor (as defined in paragraph (a)(2)(ii) of this section) by the compensation limitation applicable to the participant in the prior limitation year. The annual adjustment factor is prescribed by the Commissioner and published in the Internal Revenue Bulletin. See § 601.601(d) of this chapter.

(ii) *Annual adjustment factor.* The annual adjustment factor for a calendar year is equal to a fraction, the numerator of which is the value of the applicable index for the calendar quarter ending September 30 of the preceding calendar year, and the denominator of which is the value of such index for the calendar quarter ending September 30 of the calendar year prior to that calendar year. The applicable index is determined consistent with the procedures used to adjust benefit amounts under section 215(i)(2)(A) of the Social Security Act. If the value of the fraction described in the first sentence of this paragraph (a)(2)(ii) is less than one for a calendar year, then the adjustment factor for the calendar year is equal to one. In such a case, the annual adjustment factor for future calendar years will be determined in accordance with revenue rulings, notices, or other published guidance prescribed by the Commissioner and published in the Internal Revenue Bulletin. See § 601.601(d) of this chapter.

(3) *Effective date of adjustment.* The adjusted dollar limitation applicable to defined benefit plans is effective as of January 1 of each calendar year and applies with respect to limitation years ending with or within that calendar year. Benefit payments and accrued benefits for a limitation year cannot exceed the currently applicable dollar limitation (as in effect before the January 1 adjustment) prior to January 1.

(4) *Application of adjusted figure*—(i) *In general.* If the dollar limitation of section 415(b)(1)(A) or the compensation limitation of section

415(b)(1)(B) is adjusted pursuant to section 415(d) for a limitation year, the adjustment is applied as provided in this paragraph (a)(4).

(ii) *Application of adjusted limitations to benefits that have not commenced.* An adjustment to the dollar limitation of section 415(b)(1)(A) applies to any distribution of accrued benefits that did not commence before the beginning of the limitation year for which the adjustment is effective. Annual adjustments to the compensation limit of section 415(b)(1)(B) as described in paragraph (a)(2) of this section are made for all limitation years that begin after the participant's severance from employment, and apply to distributions that commence after the effective dates of such adjustments. However, no adjustment to the compensation limit of section 415(b)(1)(B) is made for any limitation year that begins on or before the date of the participant's severance from employment with the employer maintaining the plan.

(iii) *Application of adjusted dollar limitation to benefits that have commenced.* With respect to a distribution of accrued benefits that commenced before the beginning of the limitation year, a plan is permitted to apply the adjusted limitations to that distribution, but only to the extent that benefits have not been paid. Thus, for example, a plan cannot provide that the adjusted dollar limitation applies to a participant who has previously received the entire plan benefit in a single-sum distribution. However, a plan can provide for an increase in benefits to a participant who accrues additional benefits under the plan that could have been accrued without regard to the adjustment of the dollar limitation (including benefits that accrue as a result of a plan amendment) on or after the effective date of the adjusted limitation.

(iv) *Manner of adjustment for benefits that have commenced.* If a plan adjusts benefits to reflect increases in the applicable limitations pursuant to section 415(d) for a limitation year after the limitation year during which payment of the benefit commenced using the safe harbor methodology described in paragraph (a)(5) of this section, the distribution will be treated as continuing to satisfy the requirements of section 415(b). If a plan adjusts benefits to reflect increases in the applicable limitations pursuant to section 415(d) for a limitation year after the limitation year during which payment of the benefit commenced in a manner other than the manner described in paragraph (a)(5) of this section, the plan must satisfy the requirements of § 1.415(b)-2, treating the commencement of the additional benefit as the commencement of a new distribution that gives rise to a new annuity starting date.

(5) *Safe harbor for adjustments to benefit payments resulting from cost-of-living adjustments.* An adjustment to a distribution that is made on account of an increase in the applicable limits pursuant to section 415(d) is made using the safe harbor methodology of this paragraph (a)(5) if—

(i) The participant has received one or more distributions that satisfy the requirements of section 415(b) before the date the increase to the applicable limits is effective;

(ii) The adjusted distribution is solely as a result of the application of the increase to the applicable limits pursuant to section 415(d); and

(iii) The amount payable to the employee for the limitation year and subsequent limitation years is not greater than the amounts that would otherwise be payable without regard to the adjustment, multiplied by a fraction, the numerator of which is the limitation under section 415(b) (i.e., the lesser of the applicable dollar limitation under section 415(b)(1)(A), as adjusted for age at commencement, and the applicable compensation-based limitation under section 415(b)(1)(B)) in effect for the distribution following the section 415(d) increase, and the denominator of which is such limitation under section 415(b) in effect for the distribution immediately before the increase.

(6) *Examples.* The following examples illustrate the application of this paragraph (a):

Example 1. (i) X is a participant in a qualified defined benefit plan maintained by X's employer. The plan has a calendar year limitation year. Under the terms of the plan, X is entitled to a benefit consisting of a straight life annuity equal to 100% of X's average compensation for the period of X's high 3 years of service, adjusted as of January 1 of each calendar year for increases in the consumer price index. The plan provides that the annual increases in both the dollar limit of section 415(b)(1)(A) and the compensation limit under section 415(b)(1)(B) pursuant to section 415(d) apply to participants who have commenced receiving benefits under the plan at the earliest time at which that increase is permitted to become effective. X's average compensation for X's high 3 years is $50,000. X separates from the service of his employer on October 3, 2006, at age 65 with a nonforfeitable right to the accrued benefit after more than 10 years of service with the employer and more than 10 years of participation in the plan. X begins to receive annual benefit payments (payable monthly) of $50,000, commencing on November 1, 2006. It is assumed for purposes of this

Example 1 that the dollar limitation for 2006 (as adjusted pursuant to section 415(d)) is $170,000, that the dollar limitation for 2007 (as adjusted pursuant to section 415(d)) is $175,000, and that the annual adjustment factor for adjusting the limitation of section 415(b)·(1)(B) for 2007 is 1.0220.

(ii) For the limitation year beginning January 1, 2007, the dollar limit applicable to X under section 415(b)(1)(A) is $175,000, and the compensation limit applicable to X under section 415(b)(1)(B) is $51,100 ($50,000 multiplied by the annual adjustment factor of 1.0220). Accordingly, the adjustment to X's benefit satisfies the safe harbor for cost-of-living adjustments under paragraph (a)(5) of this section if, after the adjustment, X's benefit payable in 2007 is no greater than $50,000 multiplied by $51,100 (X's section 415(b) limitation for 2006)/$50,000 (X's section 415(b) limitation for 2007).

Example 2. (i) The facts are the same as in Example 1 except that X's average compensation for the period of X's high 3 consecutive years of service is $200,000. Consequently, X's annual benefit payments commencing on November 1, 2006, are limited to $170,000.

(ii) For the limitation year beginning January 1, 2007, the dollar limit applicable to X under section 415(b)(1)(A) is $175,000, and the compensation limit applicable to X under section 415(b)(1)(B) is $204,400 ($200,000 multiplied by the annual adjustment factor of 1.0220). Accordingly, the adjustment to X's benefit satisfies the safe harbor for cost-of-living adjustments under paragraph (a)(5) of this section if, after the adjustment, X's benefit payable in 2007 is no greater than $170,000 multiplied by $175,000 (X's section 415(b) limitation for 2006)/$170,000 (X's section 415(b) limitation for 2007).

(b) *Defined contribution plans*—(1) *In general.* Under section 415(d)(1)(C), the dollar limitation described in section 415(c)(1)(A) is adjusted annually to take into account increases in the cost of living. The adjusted dollar limitation is prescribed by the Commissioner and published in the Internal Revenue Bulletin. See § 601.601(d) of this chapter.

(2) *Determination of adjusted limit*—(i) *Base period.* The base period taken into account for purposes of adjusting the dollar limitation pursuant to paragraph (b)(2)(ii) of this section is the calendar quarter beginning July 1, 2001.

(ii) *Method of adjustment*—(A) *In general.* The dollar limitation is adjusted with respect to a calendar year based on the increase in the applicable index for the calendar quarter ending September 30 of the preceding calendar year over such index for the base period. Adjustment procedures similar to the procedures used to adjust benefit amounts under section 215(i)(2)(A) of the Social Security Act will be used.

(B) *Rounding.* Any increase in the $40,000 amount specified in section 415(c)(1)(A) which is not a multiple of $1,000 shall be rounded to the next lowest multiple of $1,000.

(iii) *Effective date of adjustment.* The adjusted dollar limitation applicable to defined contribution plans is effective as of January 1 of each calendar year and applies with respect to limitation years ending with or within that calendar year. Annual additions for a limitation year cannot exceed the currently applicable dollar limitation (as in effect before the January 1 adjustment) prior to January 1. However, after a January 1 adjustment is made, annual additions for the entire limitation year are permitted to reflect the dollar limitation as adjusted on January 1.

(c) *Application of rounding rules to other cost-of-living adjustments.* Pursuant to section 415(d)(4)(A), the $5,000 rounding methodology of paragraph (a)(1)(iii) of this section is used for purposes of any provision of chapter 1 of subtitle A of the Internal Revenue Code that provides for adjustments in accordance with section 415(d), except to the extent provided by that provision. Thus, the $5,000 rounding methodology of paragraph (a)(1)(iii) of this section is used for purposes of—

(1) Determining the level of compensation specified in section 414(q)(1)(B) that is used to determine whether an employee is a highly compensated employee;

(2) Calculating the amounts used pursuant to section 409(o)(1)(C) to determine the maximum period over which distributions from an employee stock ownership plan may be made without participant consent; and

(3) Determining the levels of compensation specified in § 1.61-21(f)(5)(i) and (iii) used in determining whether an employee is a control employee of a nongovernmental employer for purposes of the commuting valuation rule of § 1.61-21(f).

(d) *Implementation of cost-of-living adjustments.* A plan is permitted to be amended to reflect any of the adjustments described in this section at any time after those limitations become applicable. Alternatively, a plan is permitted to incorporate any of the adjustments described in this section by reference in accordance with the rules of § 1.415(a)-1(d)(3)(v). Because the accrued benefit of a participant can reflect increases in the applicable limitations only after those increases become effective, a pattern of repeated plan amendments increasing annual benefits to reflect the increases in the section 415(b) limitations pursuant to section 415(d) does not result in any protection under section 411(d)(6) for future increases to reflect increases in the section 415(b) limitations pursuant to § 1.411(d)-4, Q&A-1(c)(1). Thus, a plan does not violate the requirements of section 411(d)(6) merely because the plan has been amended annually for a number of years to increase annual benefits to reflect the increases in the section 415(b) limitations pursuant to section 415(d) and subsequently is not amended to reflect later increases in the section 415(b) limitations.

Par. 12. Section 1.415(f)-1 is added to read as follows:

§ 1.415(f)-1 Combining and aggregating plans.

(a) *In general.* Under section 415(f) and this section, except as provided in paragraph (g) of this section (regarding multiemployer plans), for purposes of applying the limitations of section 415(b) and (c) applicable to a participant for a particular limitation year—

(1) All defined benefit plans (without regard to whether a plan has been terminated) ever maintained by the employer (or a predecessor employer within the meaning of paragraph (c) of this section) under which the participant has ever accrued a benefit are treated as one defined benefit plan,

(2) All defined contribution plans (without regard to whether a plan has been terminated) ever maintained by the employer (or a predecessor employer within the meaning of paragraph (c) of this section) under which the participant receives annual additions are treated as one defined contribution plan; and

(3) All section 403(b) annuity contracts purchased by an employer (including plans purchased through salary reduction contributions) for the participant are treated as one section 403(b) annuity contract.

(b) *Affiliated employers, affiliated service groups, and leased employees.* See § 1.415(a)-1(f)(1) and (2) for rules regarding aggregation of employers in the case of affiliated employers and affiliated service groups. See § 1.415(a)-1(f)(3) for rules regarding the treatment of leased employees.

(c) *Predecessor employer.* For purposes of section 415 and the regulations thereunder, a former employer is a predecessor employer with respect to a participant in a plan maintained by an employer if the employer maintains a plan under which the participant had accrued a benefit while performing services for the former employer, but only if that benefit is provided under the plan maintained by the employer. In addition, with respect to an employer of a participant, a former entity that antedates the employer is a predecessor employer with respect to the participant if, under the facts and circumstances, the employer constitutes a continuation of all or a portion of the trade or business of the former entity. This will occur, for example, where formation of the employer constitutes a mere formal or technical change in the employment relationship and continuity otherwise exists in the substance and administration of the business operations of the former entity and the employer.

(d) *Annual compensation taken into account where employer maintains more than one defined benefit plan*—(1) *Determination of high 3 years of compensation.* If two or more defined benefit plans are aggregated under section 415(f) and this section for a particular limitation year, in applying the defined benefit compensation limitation (as described in section 415(b)(1)(B)) to the annual benefit of a participant under the aggregated plans, the participant's average compensation for the participant's high 3 years of service is determined in accordance with § 1.415(c)-2(g)(2), and includes compensation for all years in which the participant was an active participant in any of the aggregated plans.

(2) *Requirement of independent satisfaction of compensation limit.* If two or more defined benefit plans are aggregated under section 415(f) and this section for a particular limitation year, then, pursuant to section 415(f)(1)(B), each such plan must also satisfy the compensation limit of section 415(b)(1)(B) on a separate basis, determining each participant's average compensation for the participant's high 3 years of service using only compensation with respect to periods of active participation in that separate plan.

(e) *Years of participation and service taken into account where employer maintains more than one defined benefit plan at different times*—

(1) *Determination of years of participation.* If two or more defined benefit plans are aggregated under section 415(f) and this section for a particular limitation year, in applying the reduction for participation of less than ten years (as described in section 415(b)(5)(A)) to the dollar limitation under section 415(b)(1)(A), time periods that are counted as years of participation under any of the plans are counted in computing the limitation of the combined plans under this section.

(2) *Determination of years of service.* If two or more defined benefit plans are aggregated under section 415(f) and this section for a particular limitation year, in applying the reduction for service of less than ten years (as described in section 415(b)(5)(B)) to the compensation limitation under section 415(b)(1)(B), time periods that are counted as years of service under any of the plans are counted in computing the limitation of the combined plans under this section.

(f) *Previously unaggregated plans*—(1) *In general.* This paragraph (f) provides rules for those situations in which two or more existing plans, which previously were not required to be aggregated pursuant to section 415(f) and this section, are aggregated during a particular limitation year and, as a result, the limitations of section 415(b) or (c) are exceeded for that limitation year. Paragraph (f)(2) of this section provides rules for defined contribution plans that are first required to be aggregated pursuant to section 415(f) and this section in a plan year. Paragraph (f)(3) of this section provides rules for defined benefit plans that are first required to be aggregated pursuant to section 415(f) and this section, and for defined benefit plans under which a participant's benefit is frozen following aggregation.

(2) *Defined contribution plans.* Two or more defined contribution plans that are not required to be aggregated pursuant to section 415(f) and this section as of the first day of a limitation year do not fail to satisfy the requirements of section 415 with respect to a participant for the limitation year merely because they are aggregated later in that limitation year, provided that no annual additions are credited to the participant's account after the date on which the plans are required to be aggregated.

(3) *Defined benefit plans*—(i) *First year of aggregation.* Two or more defined benefit plans that are not required to be aggregated pursuant to section 415(f) and this section as of the first day of a limitation year do not fail to satisfy the requirements of section 415 for the limitation year merely because they are aggregated later in that limitation year, provided that no plan amendments increasing benefits with respect to the participant under either plan are made after the occurrence of the event causing the plan to be aggregated.

(ii) *All years of aggregation in which accrued benefits are frozen.* Two or more defined benefit plans that are required to be aggregated pursuant to section 415(f) and this section during a limitation year subsequent to the limitation year during which the plans were first aggregated do not fail to satisfy the requirements of section 415 with respect to a participant for the limitation year merely because they are aggregated if there have been no increases in the participant's accrued benefit derived from employer contributions (including increases as a result of increased compensation or service) under any of the plans within the period during which the plans have been aggregated.

(g) *Section 403(b) annuity contracts*—(1) *In general.* In the case of a section 403(b) annuity contract, except as provided in paragraph (g)(2) of this section, the participant on whose behalf the annuity contract is purchased is considered for purposes of section 415 to have exclusive control of the annuity contract. Accordingly, except as provided in paragraph (g)(2) of this section, the participant, and not the participant's employer who purchased the section 403(b) annuity contract, is deemed to maintain the annuity contract, and such a section 403(b) annuity contract is not aggregated with a qualified plan that is maintained by the participant's employer.

(2) *Special rules under which the employer is deemed to maintain the annuity contract*—(i) *In general.* Where a participant on whose behalf a section 403(b) annuity contract is purchased is in control of any employer for a limitation year as defined in paragraph (g)(2)(ii) of this section (regardless of whether the employer controlled by the participant is the employer maintaining the section 403(b) annuity contract), the annuity contract for the benefit of the participant is treated as a defined contribution plan maintained by both the controlled employer and the participant for that limitation year. Accordingly, where a participant on whose behalf a section 403(b) annuity contract is purchased is in control of any employer for a limitation year, the section 403(b) annuity contract is aggregated with all other defined contribution plans maintained by that employer. In addition, in such a case, the section 403(b) annuity contract is aggregated with all other defined contribution plans maintained by the employee or any other employer that is controlled by the employee. Thus, for example, if a doctor is employed

by a non-profit hospital to which section 501(c)(3) applies and which provides him with a section 403(b) annuity contract, and the doctor also maintains a private practice as a shareholder owning more than 50% of a professional corporation, then any qualified defined contribution plan of the professional corporation must be combined with the section 403(b) annuity contract for purposes of applying the limitations of section 415(c) and § 1.415(c)-1. For purposes of this paragraph (g)(2), it is immaterial whether the section 403(b) annuity contract is purchased as a result of a salary reduction agreement between the employer and the participant.

(ii) *Definition of control.* For purposes of paragraph (g)(2)(i) of this section, a participant is in control of an employer for a limitation year if, pursuant to paragraph (b) of this section, a plan maintained by that employer would have to be aggregated with a plan maintained by an employer that is 100% owned by the participant. Thus, for example, if a participant owns 60% of the common stock of a corporation, the participant is considered to be in control of that employer for purposes of applying paragraph (g)(2)(i) of this section.

(3) *Aggregation of section 403(b) annuity with qualified plan of controlled employer.* If a section 403(b) annuity contract is combined or aggregated with a qualified plan of a controlled employer in accordance with paragraph (g)(2) of this section, the plans must satisfy the limitations of section 415(c) both separately and in combination. In applying separately the limitations of section 415 to the qualified plan and to the section 403(b) annuity, compensation from the controlled employer may not be aggregated with compensation from the employer purchasing the section 403(b) annuity (i.e., without regard to § 1.415(c)-2(g)(3)).

(h) *Multiemployer plans*—(1) *Multiemployer plan combined with another multiemployer plan.* Pursuant to section 415(f)(3)(B), multiemployer plans, as defined in section 414(f), are not aggregated with other multiemployer plans for purposes of applying the limits of section 415.

(2) *Multiemployer plan combined with other plan*—(i) *Aggregation only for benefits provided by the employer.* Notwithstanding the rule of § 1.415(a)-1(e), a multiemployer plan is permitted to provide that only the benefits under that multiemployer plan that are provided by an employer are aggregated with benefits under plans maintained by that employer that are not multiemployer plans. If the multiemployer plan so provides then, where an employer maintains both a plan which is not a multiemployer plan and a multiemployer plan, only the benefits under the multiemployer plan that are provided by the employer are aggregated with benefits under the employer's plans other than multiemployer plans (in lieu of including benefits provided by all employers under the multiemployer plan pursuant to the generally applicable rule of § 1.415(a)-1(e)).

(ii) *Nonapplication of aggregation for purposes of applying section 415(b)(1)(B) compensation limit.* Pursuant to section 415(f)(3)(A), a multiemployer plan is not combined or aggregated with any other plan that is not a multiemployer plan for purposes of applying the compensation limit of section 415(b)(1)(B) and § 1.415(b)-1(a)(1)(ii).

(i) [Reserved.]

(j) *Special rules for combining certain plans, etc.* If a plan, annuity contract or arrangement is subject to a special limitation in addition to, or instead of, the regular limitations described in section 415(b) or (c), and is combined under this section with a plan which is subject only to the regular section 415(b) or (c) limitations, the following rules apply—

(1) Each plan, annuity contract or arrangement which is subject to a special limitation must meet its own applicable limitation and each plan subject to the regular limitations of section 415 must meet its applicable limitation.

(2) The combined limitation is the larger of the applicable limitations.

(k) *Examples.* The following examples illustrate the rules of this section:

Example 1. (i) M is an employee of ABC Corporation and XYZ Corporation. ABC maintains a qualified defined benefit plan and a qualified defined contribution plan in which M participates and XYZ maintains a qualified defined benefit plan and a qualified defined contribution plan in which M participates. ABC Corporation owns 60% of XYZ Corporation.

(ii) ABC Corporation and XYZ Corporation are members of a controlled group of corporations within the meaning of section 414(b) as modified by section 415(h). Because ABC Corporation and XYZ Corporation are members of a controlled group of corporations within the meaning of section 414(b) as modified by section 415(h), M is treated as being employed by a single employer.

(iii) The sum of M's annual benefit under the defined benefit plan maintained by ABC and M's annual benefit under the defined benefit plan maintained by XYZ is not permitted to exceed the limitations of section 415(b) and § 1.415(b)-1; and the sum of the annual additions to M's account under the defined contribution plans maintained by ABC and XYZ may not exceed the limitations of section 415(c) and § 1.415-(c)-1. For purposes of satisfying the requirements of section 415 on this aggregated basis, M's compensation from both ABC and XYZ is taken into account and years of service and participation under either defined benefit plan are used.

(iv) M's annual benefit under the defined benefit plan maintained by ABC and M's annual benefit under the defined benefit plan maintained by XYZ also must be within the limitations of section 415(b) and § 1.415(b)-1, determined without regard to the aggregation of employers (i.e., by taking into account only compensation and years of service and participation for the respective employers).

Example 2. (i) N is employed by a hospital which purchases an annuity contract described in section 403(b) on N's behalf for the current limitation year. N is in control of the hospital within the meaning of section 414(b) or (c), as modified by section 415(h). The hospital also maintains a qualified defined contribution plan during the current limitation year in which N participates.

(ii) Under section 415(k)(4), the hospital, as well as N, is considered to maintain the annuity contract. Accordingly, the sum of the annual additions under the qualified defined contribution plan and the annuity contract must satisfy the limitations of section 415(c) and § 1.415(c)-1.

Example 3. (i) The facts are the same as in *Example 2*, except that instead of being in control of the hospital, N is the 100% owner of a professional corporation P, which maintains a qualified defined contribution plan in which N participates.

(ii) Under section 415(k)(4), the hospital, as well as N, is considered to maintain the annuity contract. Accordingly, the sum of the annual additions under the qualified defined contribution plan maintained by professional corporation P and the annuity contract must satisfy the limitations of section 415(c) and § 1.415(c)-1. See § 1.415(g)-1(c)(2) for an example of the treatment of a contribution to an annuity contract that exceeds the limits of section 415(c) by reason of the aggregation required by this section.

Example 4. (i) J is an employee of two corporations, N and M, each of which has employed J for more than 10 years. N and M are not required to be aggregated pursuant to section 415(f) and this section. Each corporation has a qualified defined benefit plan in which J has participated for more than 10 years. Each plan provides a benefit which is equal to 75% of a participant's average compensation for his high 3 years of service and is payable in the form of a straight life annuity beginning at age 65. J's average compensation (within the meaning of § 1.415(c)-2) for his high three years of service from each corporation is $160,000. Each plan uses the calendar year for the limitation and plan year. In July 2007, N Corporation becomes a wholly owned subsidiary of M Corporation.

(ii) As a result of the acquisition of N Corporation by M Corporation, J is treated as being employed by a single employer under section 414(b). Therefore, because section 415(f)(1)(A) requires that all defined benefit plans of an employer be treated as one defined benefit plan, the two plans must be aggregated for purposes of applying the limitations of section 415. However, under paragraph (f)(3)(i) of this section, since the plans were not aggregated as of the first day of the 2007 limitation year (January 1, 2007), they will not be considered aggregated until the limitation year beginning January 1, 2008.)

(iii) As a result of such aggregation, J becomes entitled to a combined benefit which is equal to $240,000, which is in excess of the section 415(b) dollar limitation for 2005 of $170,000. However, under paragraph (f)(3)(ii) of this section, the limitations of section 415(b) and § 1.415(b)-1 applicable to J may be exceeded in this situation without plan disqualification so long as J's accrued benefit derived from employer contributions is not increased (i.e., does not increase on account of increased compensation, service, or other accruals) during the period within which the limitations are being exceeded.

Example 5. (i) A, age 30, owns all of the stock of X Corporation and also owns 10% of the stock of Z Corporation. F, A's father, directly owns 75% of the stock of Z Corporation. Both corporations have qualified defined contribution plans in which A participates and both plans use the calendar year for the limitation and plan year. A's compensation (within the meaning of § 1.415(c)-2) for 2007 is $20,000 from Z Corporation and $150,000 from X Corporation. During the period January 1, 2007 through June 30, 2007, annual additions of $20,000 are credited to A's account under the plan of Z Corporation, while annual additions of $40,000 are credited to A's account under the plan of X Corporation. In

both instances, the amount of annual additions represent the maximum allowable under section 415(c) and § 1.415(c)-1. On July 15, 2007, F dies, and A inherits all of F's stock in Z in 2007.

(ii) As of July 15 th 2007, A is considered to be in control of X and Z Corporations, and the two plans must be aggregated for purposes of applying the limitations of section 415. However, even though A's total annual additions for 2007 are $60,000, the limitations of section 415(c) and § 1.415(c)-1 are not violated for 2007, provided no annual additions are credited to A's accounts after July 15, 2007 (the date that A is first in control of Z).

Example 6. (i) P is a key employee of employer XYZ who participates in a qualified defined contribution plan with (Plan X) a calendar year limitation year. P is also provided post-retirement medical benefits, and XYZ has taken into account a reserve for those benefits under section 419A(c)(2). In 2007, P's compensation is $30,000 and P's annual additions under Plan X are $5,000. Pursuant to section 419A(d), a separate account is maintained for P and that account is credited with an allocation of $32,000 for 2007.

(ii) Under paragraph (j)(1) of this section, Plan X and the individual medical account must separately satisfy the requirements of section 415(c), taking into account any special limit applicable to that arrangement. In this case, the contributions to Plan X separately satisfy the limitations of section 415(c). The individual medical account is not subject to the 100% of compensation limit of section 415(c), so the contributions to that account satisfy the limitations of section 415(c).

(iii) The sum of the annual additions under Plan X and the amounts contributed to the separate account on P's behalf must satisfy the requirements of section 415(c). Under paragraph (j)(2) of this section, the limit applicable to the combined plan is equal to the greater of the limits applicable to the separate plan. In this case, the limit applicable to the medical account is $40,000 (which is greater than the limit of $30,000 applicable to the qualified plan), so the limit that applies to the aggregated plan is $40,000 and the aggregated plans satisfy the requirements of section 415.

Par. 13. Section 1.415(g)-1 is added to read as follows:

§ 1.415(g)-1 Disqualification of plans and trusts.

(a) *Disqualification of plans*—(1) *In general.* Under section 415(g) and this section, with respect to a particular limitation year, a plan (and the trust forming part of the plan) is disqualified in accordance with the rules provided in paragraph (b) of this section, if the conditions described in paragraph (a)(2) or (a)(3) of this section apply. For purposes of this paragraph (a), the determination of whether a plan or a combination of plans exceeds the limitations imposed by section 415 for a particular limitation year is, except as otherwise provided, made by taking into account the aggregation of plan rules provided in sections 415(f) and § 1.414(f)-1.

(2) *Defined contribution plans.* A plan is disqualified in accordance with the rules provided in paragraph (b) of this section if annual additions (as defined in § 1.415(c)-1(b)) with respect to the account of any participant in a defined contribution plan maintained by the employer exceed the limitations of section 415(c) and § 1.415(c)-1.

(3) *Defined benefit plans.* A plan is disqualified in accordance with the rules provided in paragraph (b) of this section if the annual benefit (as defined in § 1.415(b)-1(b)(1), taking into account the rules of § 1.415(b)-2) of a participant in a defined benefit plan maintained by the employer exceeds the limitations of section 415(b) and § 1.415(b)-1.

(b) *Rules for disqualification of plans and trusts*—(1) *In general.* If any plan (including a trust which forms part of such plan) is disqualified for a particular limitation year under the rules set forth in this paragraph (b), then the disqualification is effective as of the first day of the first plan year containing any portion of the particular limitation year.

(2) *Single plan.* In the case of a single qualified defined benefit plan (determined without regard to section 415(f) and § 1.415(f)-1) maintained by the employer that provides an annual benefit (as defined in § 1.415(b)-1(b)(1), taking into account the rules of § 1.415(b)-2) in excess of the limitations of section 415(b) and § 1.415(b)-1 for any particular limitation year, such plan is disqualified in that limitation year. Similarly, if the employer only maintains a single defined contribution plan (determined without regard to section 415(f) and § 1.415(f)-1) under which annual additions (as defined in § 1.415(c)-1(b)) allocated to the account of any participant exceed the limitations of section 415(c) and § 1.415(c)-1 for any particular limitation year, such plan is also disqualified in that limitation year.

(3) *Multiple plans*—(i) *In general.* If the limitations of section 415(b) and § 1.415(b)-1 (taking into account the rules of § 1.415(b)-2), or section 415(c) and § 1.415(c)-1 are exceeded for a particular limitation

year with respect to any participant solely because of the application of the aggregation rules of section 415(f)(1) and §1.415(f)-1 or section 414(b) or (c), as modified by section 415(h), then one or more of the plans is disqualified in accordance with the ordering rules set forth in paragraphs (b)(3)(ii) of this section, applied in accordance with the rules of application set forth in paragraph (b)(3)(iii) of this section, subject to the special rules set forth in paragraph (b)(3)(iv) of this section, until, without regard to annual benefits or annual additions under the disqualified plan or plans, the remaining plans satisfy the applicable limitations of section 415.

(ii) *Ordering rules*—(A) *Disqualification of ongoing plans other than multiemployer plans.* If there are two or more plans that have not been terminated at any time including the last day of the particular limitation year, and if one or more of those plans is a multiemployer plan described in section 414(f), then one or more of the plans (as needed to satisfy the limitations of section 415) that has not been terminated and is not a multiemployer plan is disqualified in that limitation year. For purposes of the preceding sentence, the determination of whether a plan is a multiemployer plan described in section 414(f) is made as of the last day of the particular limitation year.

(B) *Disqualification of ongoing multiemployer plans.* If, after the application of paragraph (b)(3)(ii)(A) of this section, there are two or more plans and one or more of the plans has been terminated at any time including the last day of the particular limitation year, then one or more of the plans (as needed to satisfy the applicable limitations of section 415) that has not been so terminated (regardless of whether the plan is a multiemployer plan described in section 414(f)) is disqualified in that limitation year.

(iii) *Rules of application*—(A) *Employer elects which plan is disqualified.* If there are two or more plans of an employer within a group of plans one or more of which is to be disqualified pursuant to paragraph (b)(3)(ii)(A) or (B) of this section, then the employer may elect, in a manner determined by the Commissioner, which plan or plans are disqualified. If those two or more plans are involved because of the application of section 414(b) or (c), as modified by section 415(h), the employers of the controlled group may elect, in a manner determined by the Commissioner, which plan or plans are disqualified. However, the election described in the preceding sentence is not effective unless made by all of the employers within the controlled group.

(B) *Commissioner determines which plan is disqualified.* If the election described in paragraph (b)(3)(iii)(A) of this section is not made with respect to the two plans described in paragraph (b)(3)(iii)(A) of this section, then the Commissioner, taking into account all of the facts and circumstances, has the discretion to determine the plan that is disqualified in the particular limitation year. In making this determination, some of the factors that will be taken into account include, but are not limited to, the number of participants in each plan, the amount of benefits provided on an overall basis by each plan, and the extent to which benefits are distributed or retained in each plan.

(iv) *Special rules*—(A) *Simplified employee pensions (SEPs).* If there are two or more plans one or more of which is to be disqualified pursuant to paragraph (b)(3)(ii)(A) or (B) of this section, and if one of the plans is a simplified employee pension (as defined in section 408(k)), then the simplified employee pension is not disqualified until all of the other plans have been disqualified. However, if one of the plans has been terminated, then the simplified employee pension is disqualified before the terminated plan. For purposes of this paragraph (b)(3)(iv)(A), the disqualification of a simplified employee pension means that the simplified employee pension is no longer described under section 408(k).

(B) *Combining medical accounts with defined contribution plans.* In the event that combining a medical account described in §1.415(c)-1(a)(2)(ii)(C) or (D) and a defined contribution plan other than such a medical account causes the limitations of section 415(c) and §1.415(c)-1 applicable to a participant to be exceeded for a particular limitation year, the defined contribution plan other than the medical account is disqualified for the limitation year.

(C) *Combining section 403(b) annuity contract and qualified defined contribution plan*—(*1*) *In general.* In the event that combining a section 403(b) annuity contract and a qualified defined contribution plan under the provisions of section 415(f)(1)(B) causes the limitations of section 415(c) and §1.415(c)-1 applicable to a participant under the combined defined contribution plans to be exceeded for a particular limitation year, the excess of the contributions to the annuity contract plus the annual additions to the plan over such limitations is treated as a disqualified contribution to the annuity contract and therefore includable in the gross income of the participant for the taxable year with or within which that limitation year ends. See §1.415(a)-1(b)(2) and §1.403(b)-3(b)(2) for rules regarding the treatment of a contribution to

a section 403(b) annuity contract that exceeds the limitations of section 415.

(*2*) *Example.* The following example illustrates the application of this paragraph (b)(3)(iv)(C). It is assumed for purposes of this example that the dollar limitation under section 415(c)(1)(A) that applies for all relevant limitation years is $42,000. The example is as follows:

Example. (i) N is employed by a hospital which purchases an annuity contract described in section 403(b) on N's behalf for the current limitation year. N is also the 100 % owner of a professional corporation P that maintains a qualified defined contribution plan during the current limitation year in which N participates. (The facts of this example are the same as in *Example 3* of §1.415(f)-1(k)). N's compensation (within the meaning of §1.415(c)-2) from the hospital for the current limitation year is $150,000. For the current limitation year, the hospital contributes $ 30,000 for the section 403(b) annuity contract on N's behalf, which is within the limitations applicable to N under the annuity contract (i.e., $42,000)). Professional corporation P also contributes $30,000 to the qualified defined contribution plan on N's behalf for the current limitation year (which represents the only annual additions allocated to N's account under the plan for such year), which is within the $42,000 limitation of section 415(c)(1) applicable to N under the plan.

(ii) Under section 415(k)(4), the hospital, as well as N, is considered to maintain the annuity contract. Accordingly, the sum of the annual additions under the qualified defined contribution plan maintained by professional corporation P and the annuity contract must satisfy the limitations of section 415(c) and §1.415(c)-1.

(iii) Because the total combined contributions ($60,000) exceed the section 415(c) limitation applicable to N under the plan ($42,000), under the special rules contained in this paragraph (b)(3)(iv)(C), $20,000 of the $30,000 contributed to the section 403(b) annuity contract is considered a disqualified contribution and therefore currently includable in N's gross income. The contract continues to be a section 403(b) annuity contract only if, for the current limitation year and all years thereafter, the issuer of the contract maintains separate accounts for each portion attributable to such disqualified contributions. See §§1.415(a)-1(b)(2) and 1.403(b)-3(c)(3).

(c) *Plan year for certain annuity contracts and individual retirement plans.* For purposes of this section, unless the plan under which the annuity contract or individual retirement plan is provided specifies that a different twelve-month period is considered to be the plan year—

(1) An annuity contract described in section 403(b) is considered to have a plan year coinciding with the taxable year of the individual on whose behalf the contract has been purchased; and

(2) A simplified employee pension described in section 408(k) is considered to have a plan year coinciding with the year under the plan that is used pursuant to section 408(k)(7)(C).

Par. 14. Section 1.415(j)-1 is added to read as follows:

§ 1.415(j)-1 Limitation year.

(a) *In general.* Unless the terms of a plan provide otherwise, the limitation year, with respect to any qualified plan maintained by the employer, is the calendar year.

(b) *Alternative limitation year election.* The terms of a plan may provide for the use of any other consecutive twelve month period as the limitation year. This includes a fiscal year with an annual period varying from 52 to 53 weeks, so long as the fiscal year satisfies the requirements of section 441(f). A plan may only provide for one limitation year regardless of the number or identity of the employers maintaining the plan.

(c) *Multiple limitation years*—(1) *In general.* Where an employer maintains more than one qualified plan, those plans may provide for different limitation years. The rule described in this paragraph (c) also applies to a controlled group of employers (within the meaning of section 414(b) or (c), as modified by section 415(h)). If the plans of an employer (or a controlled group of employers whose plans are aggregated) have different limitation years, section 415 is applied in accordance with the rule of paragraphs (c)(2) and (3) of this section.

(2) *Testing rule for defined contribution plans.* If a participant is credited with annual additions in only one defined contribution plan, in determining whether the requirements of section 415(c) are satisfied, only the limitation year applicable to that plan is considered. However, if a participant is credited with annual additions in more than one defined contribution plan, each such plan satisfies the requirements of section 415(c) only if the limitations of section 415(c) are satisfied with respect to amounts that are annual additions for the limitation year with respect to the participant under the plan, plus amounts credited to the

participant's account under all other plans required to be aggregated with the plan pursuant to section 415(f) and § 1.415(f)-1 that would have been considered annual additions for the limitation year under the plan if they had been credited under the plan rather than an aggregated plan.

(3) *Testing rule for defined benefit plans.* If a participant accrues a benefit or receives a distribution under only one defined benefit plan, in determining whether the requirements of section 415(b) are satisfied, only the limitation year applicable to that plan is considered. However, if a participant accrues a benefit or receives a distribution under more than one defined benefit plan, a plan satisfies the requirements of section 415(b) only if the annual benefit under all plans required to be aggregated pursuant to section 415(f) and § 1.415(f)-1 for the limitation year of that plan with respect to the participant satisfy the applicable limitations of section 415(b). Thus, for example, the dollar limitation of section 415(b)(1)(A) applicable to the limitation year for each plan must be applied to annual benefits under all aggregated plans to determine whether the plan satisfies the requirements of section 415(b).

(d) *Change of limitation year*—(1) *In general.* Once established, the limitation year may be changed only by amending the plan. Any change in the limitation year must be a change to a twelve-month period commencing with any day within the current limitation year. For purposes of this section, the limitations of section 415 are to be applied in the normal manner to the new limitation year.

(2) *Application to short limitation period.* Where there is a change of limitation year, the limitations of section 415 are to be separately applied to a "limitation period" which begins with the first day of the current limitation year and which ends on the day before the first day of the first limitation year for which the change is effective. In the case of a defined contribution plan, the dollar limitation with respect to this limitation period is determined by multiplying the applicable dollar limitation for the calendar year in which the limitation period ends by a fraction, the numerator of which is the number of months (including any fractional parts of a month) in the limitation period, and the denominator of which is 12.

(e) *Limitation year for individuals on whose behalf section 403(b) annuity contracts have been purchased.* The limitation year of an individual on whose behalf a section 403(b) annuity contract has been purchased by an employer is determined in the following manner.

(1) If the individual is not in control (within the meaning of § 1.415(f)-1(g)(2)(ii)) of any employer, the limitation year is the calendar year. However, the individual may elect to change the limitation year to another twelve-month period. To do this, the individual must attach a statement to his or her income tax return filed for the taxable year in which the change is made. Any change in the limitation year must comply with the rules set forth in paragraph (d) of this section.

(2) If the individual is in control (within the meaning of § 1.415(f)-1(g)(2)(ii)) of an employer, the limitation year is to be the limitation year of that employer.

(f) *Limitation year for individuals on whose behalf individual retirement plans are maintained.* The limitation year of an individual on whose behalf an individual retirement plan (within the meaning of section 7701(a)(37)) is maintained shall be determined in the manner described in paragraph (e) of this section.

(g) *Examples.* The following examples illustrate the application of this section:

Example 1. (i) Participant M is employed by both Employer A and Employer B, each of which maintains a qualified defined contribution plan. M participates in both of these plans. The limitation year for Employer A's plan is January 1 through December 31, and the limitation year for Employer B's plan is April 1 through March 31. Employer A and Employer B are both corporations, and Corporation X owns 100% of the stock of Employer A and Employer B.

(ii) The two plans in which M participates are required under section 415(f) to be aggregated for purposes of applying the limitations of section 415(c) to annual additions made with respect to M. Thus, for example, for the limitation year of Employer A's plan that begins January 1, 2008, annual additions with respect to M that are subject to the limitations of section 415(c) include both amounts that are annual additions with respect to M under Employer A's plan for the period beginning January 1, 2008, and ending December 31, 2008, and amounts contributed to Employer B's plan with respect to M that would have been considered annual additions for the period beginning January 1, 2008, and ending December 31, 2008, under Employer A's plan if those amounts had instead been contributed to Employer A's plan.

Example 2. In 2007, an employer with a qualified defined contribution plan using the calendar year as the limitation year elects to change the limitation year to a period beginning July 1 and ending June 30. Because of this change, the plan must satisfy the limitations of section 415(c) for the limitation period beginning January 1, 2007, and ending June 30, 2007. In applying the limitations of section 415(c) to this limitation period, the amount of compensation taken into account may only include compensation for this period. Furthermore, the dollar limitation for this period is the otherwise applicable dollar limitation for calendar year 2007, multiplied by 6/12.

Par. 15. Section 1.457-4 is amended by revising paragraph (d) to read as follows:

§ 1.457-4 Annual deferrals, deferral limitations, and deferral agreement under eligible plans.

* * * * *

(d) *Deferrals after severance from employment, including sick, vacation, and back pay under an eligible plan*—(1) In general. An eligible plan may provide that a participant who has not had a severance from employment may elect to defer accumulated sick pay, accumulated vacation pay, and back pay under an eligible plan if the requirements of section 457(b) are satisfied. For example, the plan must provide, in accordance with paragraph (b) of this section, that these amounts may be deferred for any calendar month only if an agreement providing for the deferral is entered into before the beginning of the month in which the amounts would otherwise be paid or made available and the participant is an employee on the date the amounts would otherwise be paid or made available. For purposes of section 457, compensation that would otherwise be paid for a payroll period that begins before severance from employment is treated as an amount that would otherwise be paid or made available before an employee has a severance from employment. In addition, deferrals may be made for former employees with respect to compensation described in § 1.415(c)-2(e)(3)(ii) (relating to certain compensation paid within 2 ½ months following severance from employment), compensation described in § 1.415(c)-2(g)(4) (relating to compensation paid to participants who are permanently and totally disabled), and compensation relating to qualified military service under section 414(u).

(2) *Examples.* The provisions of this paragraph (d) are illustrated by the following examples:

Example 1. (i) *Facts.* Participant G, who is age 62 in 2006, is an employee who participates in an eligible plan providing a normal retirement age of 65 and a bona fide sick leave and vacation pay program of the eligible employer. Under the terms of G's employer's eligible plan and the sick leave and vacation pay program, G is permitted make a one-time election to contribute amounts representing accumulated sick pay to the eligible plan. G has a severance from employment on January 12, 2007, at which time G's accumulated sick and vacation pay that is payable on March 15, 2007 total $12,000. G elects, on February 4, 2007, to have the $12,000 of accumulated sick and vacation pay contributed to the eligible plan.

(ii) *Conclusion.* Under the terms of the eligible plan and the sick and vacation pay program, G may elect before March 1, 2007 to defer the accumulated sick and vacation pay because the agreement providing for the deferral is entered into before the beginning of the month in which the amount is currently available and the amount is bona fide accumulated sick and vacation pay that would otherwise be payable within 2 ½ months after G has a severance from employment, as described in § 1.415(c)-2(e)(3)(ii). Thus, under this section and § 1.415(c)-2(e)(3)(ii), the $12,000 is included in G's includible compensation for purposes of determining G's includible compensation in 2007.

Example 2. (i) *Facts.* Same facts as in *Example 1*, except that G's severance from employment is on December 1, 2006, G's $12,000 of accumulated sick and vacation pay is payable on February 15, 2007 (which is within 2 ½ months after G's severance from employment), and G's election to defer the accumulated sick and vacation pay is made before February 1, 2007.

(ii) *Conclusion.* Under this section and § 1.415(c)-2(e)(3)(ii), the $12,000 is included in G's includible compensation for purposes of determining G's includible compensation in 2007.

Example 3. (i) *Facts.* Employer X maintains an eligible plan and a vacation leave plan. Under the terms of the vacation leave plan, employees generally accrue three weeks of vacation per year. Up to one week's unused vacation may be carried over from one year to the next, so that in any single year an employee may have a maximum of four weeks vacation time. At the beginning of each calendar year, under the terms of the eligible plan (which constitutes an agreement providing for the deferral), the value of any unused vacation time from the prior year in excess of one week is automatically contributed to the eligible plan, to the extent of the employee's maximum deferral limitations. Amounts in excess of the maximum deferral limitations are forfeited.

(ii) *Conclusion.* The value of the unused vacation pay contributed to X's eligible plan pursuant to the terms of the plan and the terms of the vacation leave plan is treated as an annual deferral to the eligible plan for January of the calendar year. No amounts contributed to the eligible plan will be considered made available to a participant in X's eligible plan.

* * * * *

Par. 16. Section 1.457-5 is amended by revising *Example 2* of paragraph (d) to read as follows:

§ *1.457-5 Individual limitation for combined annual deferrals under multiple eligible plans.*

* * * * *

(d) *Examples.* * * *

Example (2). (i) *Facts.* Participant E, who will turn 63 on April 1, 2006, participates in four eligible plans during 2006 Plan W which is an eligible governmental plan; and Plans X, Y, and Z which are each eligible plans of three different tax-exempt entities. For 2006, the limitation that applies to Participant E under all four plans under § 1.457-4 (c) (1) (i) (A) is $15,000. For 2006, the additional age 50 catch-up limitation that applies to Participant E under Plan W under § 1.457-4 (c) (2) is $5,000. Further, for 2006, different limitations under § 1.457-4 (c) (3) and (c) (3) (ii) (B) apply to Participant E under each of these plans, as follows: under Plan W, the underutilized limitation under § 1.457-4 (c) (3) (ii) (B) is $7,000; under Plan X, the underutilized limitation under § 1.457-4 (c) (3) (ii) (B) is $2,000; under Plan Y, the underutilized limitation under § 1.457-4 (c) (3) (ii) (B) is $8,000; and under Plan Z, § 1.457-4 (c) (3) is not applicable since normal retirement age is age 62 under Plan Z. Participant E's includible compensation is in each case in excess of any applicable deferral.

(ii) *Conclusion.* For purposes of applying this section to Participant E for 2006, Participant E could elect to defer $23,000 under Plan Y, which is the maximum deferral limitation under § 1.457-4 (c) (1) through (3), and to defer no amount under Plans W, X, and Z. The $23,000 maximum amount is equal to the sum of $15,000 plus $8,000, which is the catch-up amount applicable to Participant E under Plan Y and which is the largest catch-up amount applicable to Participant E under any of the four plans for 2006. Alternatively, Participant E could instead elect to defer the following combination of amounts: an aggregate total of $15,000 to Plans X, Y, and Z, if no contribution is made to Plan W; an aggregate total of $20,000 to any of the four plans, assuming at least $5,000 is contributed to Plan W; or $22,000 to Plan W and none to any of the other three plans.

(iii) If the underutilized amount under Plans W, X, and Y for 2006 were in each case zero (because E had always contributed the maximum amount or E was a new participant) or an amount not in excess of $5,000, the maximum exclusion under this section would be $20,000 for Participant E for 2006 ($15,000 plus the $5,000 age 50 catch-up amount), which Participant E could contribute to any of the plans assuming at least $5,000 is contributed to Plan W.

Par. 17. Section 1.457-6 is amended by revising paragraphs (a) and (c) to read as follows:

§ *1.457-6 Timing of distributions under eligible plans.*

(a) *In general.* Except as provided in paragraph (c) of this section (relating to distributions on account of an unforeseeable emergency), paragraph (e) of this section (relating to distributions of small accounts), § 1.457-10(a) (relating to plan terminations), or § 1.457-10(c) (relating to domestic relations orders), amounts deferred under an eligible plan may not be paid to a participant or beneficiary before the participant has a severance from employment with the eligible employer or when the participant attains age 70 ½, if earlier. For rules relating to loans, see paragraph (f) of this section. This section does not apply to distributions of excess amounts under § 1.457-4(e). However, except to the extent set forth by the Commissioner in revenue rulings, notices, and other guidance published in the Internal Revenue Bulletin, this section applies to amounts held in a separate account for eligible rollover distributions maintained by an eligible governmental plan as described in § 1.457-10(e) (2).

* * * * *

(c) *Rules applicable to distributions for unforeseeable emergencies—*(1) *In general.* An eligible plan may permit a distribution to a participant or beneficiary faced with an unforeseeable emergency. The distribution must satisfy the requirements of paragraph (c) (2) of this section.

(2) *Requirements—*(i) *Unforeseeable emergency defined.* An unforeseeable emergency must be defined in the plan as a severe financial hardship of the participant or beneficiary resulting from an illness or accident of the participant or beneficiary, the participant's or beneficiary's spouse, or the participant's or beneficiary's dependent (as defined in section 152, and, for taxable years beginning on or after January 1, 2005, without regard to section 152(b)(1), (b)(2), and (d)(1)(B)); loss of the participant's or beneficiary's property due to casualty (including the need to rebuild a home following damage to a home not otherwise covered by homeowner's insurance, e.g., as a result of a natural disaster); or other similar extraordinary and unforeseeable circumstances arising as a result of events beyond the control of the participant or the beneficiary. For example, the imminent foreclosure of or eviction from the participant's or beneficiary's primary residence may constitute an unforeseeable emergency. In addition, the need to pay for medical expenses, including non-refundable deductibles, as well as for the cost of prescription drug medication, may constitute an unforeseeable emergency. Finally, the need to pay for the funeral expenses of a spouse or a dependent (as defined in section 152, and, for taxable years beginning on or after January 1, 2005, without regard to section 152(b)(1), (b)(2), and (d)(1)(B)) may also constitute an unforeseeable emergency. Except as otherwise specifically provided in this paragraph (c)(2)(i), the purchase of a home and the payment of college tuition are not unforeseeable emergencies under this paragraph (c)(2)(i).

(ii) *Unforeseeable emergency distribution standard.* Whether a participant or beneficiary is faced with an unforeseeable emergency permitting a distribution under this paragraph (c) is to be determined based on the relevant facts and circumstances of each case, but, in any case, a distribution on account of unforeseeable emergency may not be made to the extent that such emergency is or may be relieved through reimbursement or compensation from insurance or otherwise, by liquidation of the participant's assets, to the extent the liquidation of such assets would not itself cause severe financial hardship, or by cessation of deferrals under the plan.

(iii) *Distribution necessary to satisfy emergency need.* Distributions because of an unforeseeable emergency must be limited to the amount reasonably necessary to satisfy the emergency need (which may include any amounts necessary to pay any federal, state, or local income taxes or penalties reasonably anticipated to result from the distribution).

* * * * *

Par. 18. Section 1.457-10 is amended by revising paragraph (b) (8) to read as follows:

§ *1.457-10 Miscellaneous provisions.*

* * * * *

(b) *Plan-to-plan transfers.* * * *

(8) *Purchase of permissive service credit by plan-to-plan transfers from an eligible governmental plan to a qualified plan—*(i) *General rule.* An eligible governmental plan of a State may provide for the transfer of amounts deferred by a participant or beneficiary to a defined benefit governmental plan (as defined in section 414(d)), and no amount shall be includible in gross income by reason of the transfer, if the conditions in paragraph (b) (8) (ii) of this section are met. A transfer under this paragraph (b) (8) is not treated as a distribution for purposes of § 1.457-6. Therefore, such a transfer may be made before severance from employment.

(ii) *Conditions for plan-to-plan transfers from an eligible governmental plan to a qualified plan.* A transfer may be made under this paragraph (b) (8) only if the transfer is either—

(A) For the purchase of permissive service credit (as defined in section 415(n) (3) (A)) under the receiving defined benefit governmental plan; or

(B) A repayment to which section 415 does not apply by reason of section 415(k) (3).

(iii) *Example.* The provisions of this paragraph (b) (8) are illustrated by the following example:

Example. (i) *Facts.* Plan X is an eligible governmental plan maintained by County Y for its employees. Plan X provides for distributions only in the event of death, an unforeseeable emergency, or severance from employment with County Y (including retirement from County Y). Plan S is a qualified defined benefit plan maintained by State T for its employees. County Y is within State T. Employee A is an employee of County Y and is a participant in Plan X. Employee A previously was an employee of State T and is still entitled to benefits under Plan S. Plan S includes provisions allowing participants in certain plans, including Plan X, to transfer assets to Plan S for the purchase of service credit under Plan S and does not permit the amount transferred to exceed the amount necessary to fund the benefit resulting from the service credit. Although not required to do so, Plan X allows Employee A to transfer assets to Plan S to provide a service benefit under Plan S.

(ii) *Conclusion.* The transfer is permitted under this paragraph (b)(8).

PART 11—EMPLOYEE RETIREMENT INCOME SECURITY ACT OF 1974

Par. 19. The authority citation for part 11 is amended to read, in part, as follows:

Authority: 26 U.S.C. 7805. * * *

* * * * *

Part 11.415(c)(4)-1 [Removed]

Par. 20. Section 11.415(c)(4)-1 is removed.

Mark E. Matthews,

Deputy Commissioner for Services and Enforcement.

CERTIFIED COPY

DALE D. GOODE

¶ 20,261O

IRS proposed regulations: Participants: Beneficiaries: Electronic media: Notices: Elections: Consents.—The Treasury and IRS have issued proposed regulations setting forth rules regarding the use of electronic media to provide notices to plan participants and beneficiaries or to transmit elections or consents relating to employee benefit arrangements. The proposed rules cannot be relied on prior to their issuance as final regulations.

The proposed regulations, issued on July 14, 2005 (70 FR 40675), were previously reproduced below. The final regulations were issued on October 20, 2006 (71 FR 61877). The preamble to the final regulations appears at ¶ 23,239, which contains cross-references to the final regulations.

¶ 20,261P

IRS proposed regulations: Elimination of optional forms of benefit: Minimum vesting rules: *Central Laborers' Pension Fund v. Heinz:* Notice of amendment reducing benefit accrual.— The Treasury and IRS have issued proposed regulations regarding the timing of permissible changes in optional forms of benefits after the Supreme Court's decision in *Central Laborers' Pension Fund v. Heinz.* The proposed regulations address the interaction between the anti-cutback rules of Code Sec. 411(d)(6) and the nonforfeitability requirements of Code Sec. 411(a), which provides that an employee's right to an accrued benefit derived from employer contributions must become nonforfeitable within a specified period of service. In addition, the proposed rules provide a utilization test under which certain plan amendments with a de minimis effect on participants would be permitted to eliminate or reduce early retirement benefits, retirement-type subsidies, or optional forms of benefit, if certain conditions are met. The utilization test also is used to determine whether a plan may be amended to eliminate all of the optional forms of benefit within a generalized optional form without having to satisfy the de minimis requirements of Reg. § 1.411(d)-3(e) (revised in final regulations issued concurrently at 70 FR 47109, August 12, 2005) (see preamble to final regulations at ¶ 23,228).

The proposed regulations, which were published in the *Federal Register* on August 12, 2005 (70 FR 47155), and technically corrected on September 13, 2005 (70 FR 53973), were previously reproduced below. Final regulations addressing two reserved topics that were the subject of these proposed regs were finalized by T.D. 9280 on August 8, 2006 (71 FR 45379). The preamble to the final regulations is reproduced at ¶ 23,237.

¶ 20,261Q

IRS proposed regulations: Roth IRAs: Conversion of annuity: Valuation.—The Treasury and IRS issued temporary and proposed regulations regarding the valuation of an annuity converted from a traditional IRA to a Roth IRA. The preamble to the temporary regulations, issued concurrently, is located at ¶ 23,229.

The proposed regulations, which were published in the *Federal Register* on August 22, 2005 (70 FR 48924), were previously reproduced below. The regulations were finalized by T.D. 9418 on July 29, 2008 (73 FR 43860). The preamble to the final regulations appears at ¶ 23,255.

¶ 20,261R

IRS proposed regulations: Employee stock ownership plans (ESOPs): Redemption of securities: Dividends paid deduction.— The IRS has released proposed regulations regarding dividends paid deductions of corporations maintaining employee stock ownership plans (ESOPs). The regs address issues that have arisen under the application of stock reacquisition expenses under Code Sec. 162(k) and deductions for dividends paid on employer securities under Code Sec. 404(k). The proposed regulations address which corporation is entitled to the deduction under Code Sec. 404(k) when stock held in an ESOP is redeemed and the applicable employer securities are not securities of the corporation or corporations that maintain the plan. Secondly, the regulations address whether payments in redemption of stock held by an ESOP are deductible.

The proposed regulations, which were published in the *Federal Register* on August 25, 2005 (70 FR 49897), are reproduced below.

DEPARTMENT OF THE TREASURY

Internal Revenue Service

26 CFR Part 1

[REG-133578-05]

RIN 1545-BE74

Dividends Paid Deduction for Stock Held in Employee Stock Ownership Plan

AGENCY: Internal Revenue Service (IRS), Treasury.

ACTION: Notice of proposed rulemaking.

¶20,261O

SUMMARY: This document contains proposed regulations under sections 162(k) and 404(k) of the Internal Revenue Code (Code) relating to employee stock ownership plans (ESOPs). The regulations provide guidance concerning which corporation is entitled to the deduction for applicable dividends under section 404(k). These regulations also clarify that a payment in redemption of employer securities held by an ESOP is not deductible. These regulations will affect administrators of, employers maintaining, participants in, and beneficiaries of ESOPs. In addition, they will affect corporations that make distributions in redemption of stock held in an ESOP.

DATES: Written or electronic comments and requests for a public hearing must be received by November 23, 2005.

ADDRESSES: Send submissions to: CC:PA:LPD:PR (REG-133578-05), room 5203, Internal Revenue Service, POB 7604, Ben Franklin Station, Washington, DC 20044. Submissions may be hand-delivered Monday through Friday between the hours of 8 a.m. and 4 p.m. to: CC:PA:LPD:PR (REG-133578-05), Courier's Desk, Internal Revenue Service, 1111 Constitution Avenue, NW., Washington D.C. Alternatively, taxpayers may submit comments electronically directly to the IRS Internet site at *www.irs.gov/regs*, or via the Federal eRulemaking Portal at *www.regulations.gov* (IRS-REG-133578-05).

FOR FURTHER INFORMATION CONTACT: Concerning the regulations, John T. Ricotta at (202) 622-6060 with respect to section 404(k) or Martin Huck at (202) 622-7750 with respect to section 162(k); concerning submission of comments or to request a public hearing, Robin Jones at (202) 622-7180 (not toll-free numbers).

SUPPLEMENTARY INFORMATION:

Background and Explanation of Provisions

This document contains proposed regulations under sections 162(k) and 404(k) of the Internal Revenue Code (Code). These regulations address two issues that have arisen in the application of these sections. The first issue arises in a case in which the applicable employer securities held in an employee stock ownership plan (ESOP) are not securities of the corporation or corporations that maintain the plan. The issue is which corporation is entitled to the deduction under section 404(k) for certain dividends paid with respect to the stock held in the ESOP. The second issue is whether payments in redemption of stock held by an ESOP are deductible.

Code and Regulations

Section 404(a) provides that contributions paid by an employer to or under a stock bonus, pension, profit sharing, or annuity plan are deductible under section 404(a), if they would be otherwise deductible, within the limitations of that section. Section 404(k)(1) provides that, in the case of a C corporation, there is allowed as a deduction for a taxable year the amount of any applicable dividend paid in cash by such corporation during the taxable year with respect to applicable employer securities held by an ESOP. The deduction under section 404(k) is in addition to the deductions allowed under section 404(a).

Section 4975(e)(7) provides, in relevant part, that an ESOP is a defined contribution plan that is a stock bonus plan qualified under section 401(a) and designed to invest primarily in qualifying employer securities. Section 4975(e)(8) states that the term *qualifying employer security* means any employer security within the meaning of section 409(l). Section 409(l) generally provides that the term *employer security* means common stock issued by the employer (or a corporation that is a member of the same controlled group) that is readily tradable on an established securities market, if the corporation (or a member of the controlled group) has common stock that is readily tradable on an established securities market. Section 409(l)(4)(A) provides that, for purposes of section 409(l), the term *controlled group of corporations* has the meaning given to that term by section 1563(a) (determined without regard to subsections (a)(4) and (e)(3)(C) of section 1563). Section 409(l)(4)(B) provides that, for purposes of section 409(l)(4)(A), if a common parent owns directly stock possessing at least 50 percent of the voting power of all classes of stock and at least 50 percent of each class of nonvoting stock in a first tier subsidiary, such subsidiary (and all corporations below it in the chain which would meet the 80 percent test of section 1563(a) if the first tier subsidiary were the common parent) are treated as includible corporations.

Section 404(k)(2), for taxable years beginning on or after January 1, 2002, generally provides that the term *applicable dividend* means any dividend which, in accordance with the plan provisions — (i) is paid in cash to the participants in the plan or their beneficiaries, (ii) is paid to the plan and is distributed in cash to participants in the plan or their beneficiaries not later than 90 days after the close of the plan year in which paid, (iii) is, at the election of such participants or their beneficiaries — (I) payable as provided in clause (i) or (ii), or (II) paid to the plan and reinvested in qualifying employer securities, or (iv) is used to make payments on a loan described in section 404(a)(9), the proceeds of which were used to acquire the employer securities (whether or not allocated to participants) with respect to which the dividend is paid. Under section 404(k)(4), the deduction is allowable in the taxable year of the corporation in which the dividend is paid or distributed to a participant or beneficiary.

Prior to 2002, section 404(k)(5)(A) provided that the Secretary may disallow the deduction under section 404(k) for any dividend if the Secretary determines that such dividend constitutes, in substance, an evasion of taxation. Section 662(b) of the Economic Growth and Tax Relief Reconciliation Act of 2001 (115 Stat. 38, 2001) amended section 404(k)(5)(A) to provide that the Secretary may disallow a deduction under section 404(k) for any dividend the Secretary determines constitutes, in substance, an avoidance or evasion of taxation. The amendment is effective for tax years after December 31, 2001.

Section 162(k)(1) generally provides that no deduction otherwise allowable under chapter 1 of the Code is allowed for any amount paid or incurred by a corporation in connection with the reacquisition of its stock or the stock of any related person (as defined in section 465(b)(3)(C)). The legislative history of section 162(k) states that the phrase "in connection with" is "intended to be construed broadly." H.R. Conf. Rep. No. 99-841, at 168 (1986).

Corporation Entitled to Section 404(k) Deduction

An ESOP may benefit employees of more than one corporation. In addition, an ESOP may be maintained by a corporation other than the payor of a dividend. In these cases, the issue arises as to which entity is entitled to the deduction provided under section 404(k). Assume, for example, that a publicly traded corporation owns all of the stock of a subsidiary. The subsidiary operates a trade or business with employees in the U.S. and maintains an ESOP that holds stock of its parent for its employees. If the parent distributes a dividend with respect to its stock held in the ESOP maintained by the subsidiary, questions have arisen as to whether the parent or subsidiary is entitled to the deduction under section 404(k). This question arises in cases in which the parent and subsidiary file a consolidated return as well as in cases in which the parent and subsidiary do not file a consolidated return.

The IRS and Treasury Department believe that the statutory language of section 404(k) clearly provides that only the payor of the applicable dividend is entitled to the deduction under section 404(k), regardless of whether the employees of multiple corporations benefit under the ESOP and regardless of whether another member of the controlled group maintains the ESOP. Therefore, in the example above, the parent, not the subsidiary, is entitled to the deduction under section 404(k).

Treatment of Payments Made to Reacquire Stock

Some corporations have claimed deductions under section 404(k) for payments in redemption of stock held by an ESOP that are used to make benefit distributions to participants or beneficiaries, including distributions of a participant's account balance upon severance from employment. These taxpayers have argued that the payments in redemption qualify as dividends under sections 301 and 316 and, therefore, are deductible under section 404(k).

In Rev. Rul. 2001-6 (2001-1 C.B. 491), the IRS concluded that section 162(k) bars a deduction for payments made in redemption of stock from an ESOP. This conclusion was based on the fact that section 162(k)(1) disallows a deduction for payments paid in connection with the reacquisition of an issuer's stock and that the redemption payments are such payments. The IRS also concluded that such payments were not applicable dividends under section 404(k)(1). The IRS reasoned that allowing a deduction for redemption amounts would vitiate important rights and protections for recipients of ESOP distributions, including the right to reduce taxes by utilizing the return of basis provisions under section 72, the right to make rollovers of ESOP distributions received upon separation from service, and the protection against involuntary cash-outs. Finally, the IRS stated that a deduction under section 404(k)(1) for such amounts would constitute, in substance, an evasion of tax.

In *Boise Cascade Corporation v. United States*, 329 F.3d 751 (9th Cir. 2003), the Court of Appeals for the Ninth Circuit held that payments made by a corporation to redeem its stock held by its ESOP were deductible as dividends paid under section 404(k), and that the deduction was not precluded by section 162(k). The court reasoned that the distribution by the ESOP of the redemption proceeds to the participants was a transaction separate from the redemption transaction. Therefore, the court concluded that the distribution did not constitute a payment *in connection with* the corporation's reacquisition of its stock, and section 162(k) did not bar the deduction of such payments.

For the reasons stated in Rev. Rul. 2001-6, the IRS and Treasury Department continue to believe that allowing a deduction for amounts paid to reacquire stock is inconsistent with the intent of, and policies underlying, section 404. In addition, the IRS and Treasury Department believe that allowing such a deduction would constitute, in substance, an avoidance or evasion of taxation within the meaning of section 404(k)(5)(A) because it would allow a corporation to claim two deductions for the same economic cost: once for the value of the stock originally contributed to the ESOP and again for the amount paid to redeem the same stock. See *Charles Ilfeld Co. v. Hernandez*, 292 U.S. 62 (1934). Moreover, despite the Ninth Circuit's conclusion in *Boise*

Cascade, the IRS and Treasury Department continue to believe that, even if a payment in redemption of stock held by an ESOP were to qualify as an applicable dividend, section 162(k) would disallow a deduction for that amount because such payment would be in connection with the reacquisition of the corporation's stock.

This notice of proposed rulemaking, therefore, includes proposed regulations under section 404(k) that confirm that payments made to reacquire stock held by an ESOP are not deductible under section 404(k) because such payments do not constitute applicable dividends under section 404(k)(2) and a deduction for such payments would constitute, in substance, an avoidance or evasion of taxation within the meaning of section 404(k)(5). It also includes proposed regulations under section 162(k) that provide that section 162(k), subject to certain exceptions, disallows any deduction for amounts paid or incurred by a corporation in connection with the reacquisition of its stock or the stock of any related person (as defined in section 465(b)(3)(C)). The proposed regulations also provide that amounts paid or incurred in connection with the reacquisition of stock include amounts paid by a corporation to reacquire its stock from an ESOP that are then distributed by the ESOP to its participants (or their beneficiaries) or otherwise used in a manner described in section 404(k)(2)(A).

Proposed Effective Date

These regulations are proposed to be effective on the date of issuance of final regulations. However, before these regulations become effective, the IRS will continue to assert in any matter in controversy outside of the Ninth Circuit that sections 162(k) and 404(k) disallow a deduction for payments to reacquire employer securities held by an ESOP. See Chief Counsel Notice 2004-038 (October 1, 2004) available at *www.irs.gov/foia* through the *electronic reading room*.

Special Analyses

It has been determined that this notice of proposed rulemaking is not a significant regulatory action as defined in Executive Order 12866. Therefore, a regulatory assessment is not required. It has also been determined that section 553(b) of the Administrative Procedure Act (5 U.S.C. chapter 5) does not apply to these regulations, and, because the regulations do not impose a collection of information on small entities, the Regulatory Flexibility Act (5 U.S.C. chapter 6) does not apply. Pursuant to section 7805(f) of the Code, this notice of proposed rulemaking will be submitted to the Chief Counsel for Advocacy of the Small Business Administration for comment on its impact on small business.

Comments and Public Hearing

Before these proposed regulations are adopted as final regulations, consideration will be given to any written (a signed original and eight (8) copies) or electronic comments that are submitted timely to the IRS. The IRS and Treasury Department specifically request comments on the clarity of the proposed regulations and how they may be made easier to understand. All comments will be available for public inspection and copying. A public hearing will be scheduled if requested in writing by any person that timely submits written comments. If a public hearing is scheduled, notice of the date, time, and place for the public hearing will be published in the **Federal Register**.

Drafting Information

The principal authors of these regulations are John T. Ricotta, Office of Division Counsel/Associate Chief Counsel (Tax Exempt and Government Entities) and Martin Huck of Office of Associate Chief Counsel (Corporate). However, other personnel from the IRS and Treasury participated in the development of these regulations.

List of Subjects in 26 CFR Part 1

Income taxes, Reporting and recordkeeping requirements.

Proposed Amendments to the Regulations

Accordingly, 26 CFR part 1 is proposed to be amended as follows:

PART 1—INCOME TAXES

Paragraph 1. The authority citation for part 1 is amended to read, in part, as follows:

Authority: 26 U.S.C. 7805 * * *

Section 1.162(k)-1 is also issued under 26 U.S.C. 162(k) * * *

Section 1.404(k)-3 is also issued under 26 U.S.C. 162(k) and 404(k)(5)(A) * * *

Par. 2. Section 1.162(k)-1 is added to read as follows:

§ 1.162(k)-1 Disallowance of deduction for reacquisition payments.

(a) *In general.* Except as provided in paragraph (b) of this section, no deduction otherwise allowable is allowed under Chapter 1 of the Internal Revenue Code for any amount paid or incurred by a corporation in connection with the reacquisition of its stock or the stock of any related person (as defined in section 465(b)(3)(C)). Amounts paid or incurred in connection with the reacquisition of stock include amounts paid by a corporation to reacquire its stock from an ESOP that are used in a manner described in section 404(k)(2)(A). See § 1.404(k)-3.

(b) *Exceptions.* Paragraph (a) of this section does not apply to any—

(i) Deduction allowable under section 163 (relating to interest);

(ii) Deduction for amounts that are properly allocable to indebtedness and amortized over the term of such indebtedness;

(iii) Deduction for dividends paid (within the meaning of section 561); or

(iv) Amount paid or incurred in connection with the redemption of any stock in a regulated investment company that issues only stock which is redeemable upon the demand of the shareholder.

(c) *Effective date.* This section applies with respect to amounts paid or incurred on or after the date these regulations are published as final regulations in the **Federal Register**.

Par. 3. Section 1.404(k)-2 is added to read as follows:

§ 1.404(k)-2 Dividends paid by corporation not maintaining ESOP.

Q-1: What corporation is entitled to the deduction provided under section 404(k) for applicable dividends paid on applicable employer securities of a C corporation held by an ESOP if the ESOP benefits employees of more than one corporation or if the corporation paying the dividend is not the corporation maintaining the plan?

A-1: (a) *In general.* Under section 404(k), only the corporation paying the dividend is entitled to the deduction with respect to applicable employer securities held by an ESOP. Thus, no deduction is permitted to a corporation maintaining the ESOP if that corporation does not pay the dividend.

(b) *Example.* (i) *Facts.* S is a U.S. corporation that is wholly owned by P, an entity organized under the laws of Country A that is classified as a corporation for Federal income tax purposes. P is not engaged in a U.S. trade or business. P has a single class of common stock that is listed on a stock exchange in a foreign country. In addition, these shares are listed on the New York Stock Exchange, in the form of American Depositary Shares, and are actively traded through American Depositary Receipts (ADRs) meeting the requirements of section 409(l). S maintains an ESOP for its employees. The ESOP holds ADRs of P on Date X and receives a dividend with respect to those employer securities. The dividends received by the ESOP constitute applicable dividends as described in section 404(k)(2).

(ii) *Conclusion.* P, as the payor of the dividend, is entitled to a deduction under section 404(k) with respect to the dividends, although as a foreign corporation P does not obtain a U.S. tax benefit from the deduction. No corporation other than the corporation paying the dividend is entitled to the deduction under section 404(k). Thus, because S did not pay the dividends, S is not entitled to a deduction under section 404(k). The answer would be the same if P is a U.S. C corporation.

Q-2: What is the effective date of this section?

A-2: This section applies with respect to dividends paid on or after the date these regulations are published as final regulations in the **Federal Register**.

Par. 4. Section 1.404(k)-3 is added to read as follows:

§ 1.404(k)-3 Disallowance of deduction for reacquisition payments.

Q-1: Are payments to reacquire stock held by an ESOP applicable dividends that are deductible under section 404(k)(1)?

A-1: (a) Payments to reacquire stock held by an ESOP, including reacquisition payments that are used to make benefit distributions to participants or beneficiaries, are not deductible under section 404(k) because—

(1) Those payments do not constitute *applicable dividends* under section 404(k)(2); and

(2) The treatment of those payments as applicable dividends would constitute, in substance, an avoidance or evasion on taxation within the meaning of section 404(k)(5).

(b) See § 1.162(k)-1 concerning the disallowance of deductions for amounts paid or incurred by a corporation in connection with the reacquisition of its stock from an ESOP.

Q-2: What is the effective date of this section?

A-2: This section applies with respect to payments to reacquire stock that are made on or after the date these regulations are published as final regulations in the **Federal Register.**

Mark E. Matthews,

Deputy Commissioner for Services and Enforcement.

CERTIFIED COPY

Guy R. Traynor

¶ 20,261S

IRS proposed regulations: Health Savings Accounts (HSAs): Comparability rules.— The Treasury and IRS have issued proposed regulations involving the comparability rules for employer Health Savings Account (HSA) contributions. The proposed regulations generally follow guidance on the comparability rules previously issued by the IRS, including IRS Notice 2004-2 (see ¶ 17,127U) and IRS Notice 2004-50 (see ¶ 17,129F-5), but also provide additional clarification regarding a few HSA comparability issues not previously addressed. Although the proposed regulations apply to employer contributions made on or after the date the regulations are finalized, taxpayers may rely on the proposed rules pending the issuance of final regulations.

The proposed regulations, which were published in the *Federal Register* on August 26, 2005 (70 FR 50233), including technical corrections issued December 8, 2005 (70 FR 72953) were reproduced below. The regulations were finalized on July 31, 2006 by T.D. 9277 (71 FR 43056). The preamble to the final regs appears at ¶ 23,236.

¶ 20,261T

IRS proposed regulations: Deferred compensation: Nonqualified plans: Code Sec. 457 plans: Deferral elections.— The Treasury Department and IRS have issued proposed regulations on deferred compensation under section 409A. Section 409A governs plans and arrangements that provide nonqualified deferred compensation to employees, directors or other service providers. These regulations implement provisions established by the American Jobs Creation Act (AJCA) (P.L. 108-357). The proposed regulations identify which plans and arrangements are covered under Code Sec. 409A, outline operational requirements for deferral elections, and permissible timing for deferred compensation payments made under the rules. They also provide guidance regarding coverage of state and local government and tax plans that fail to qualify as Code Sec. 457(b) plans.

The proposed regulations, which were published in the *Federal Register* on October 4, 2005 (70 FR 57930), were reproduced below. The proposed regulations were corrected on December 19, 2005 by 70 FR 75090, on December 27, 2005 by 70 FR 76502, on January 17, 2006 by 71 FR 2496, and on February 6, 2006 by IRS Announcement 2006-11, I.R.B. 2006-6. The regulations were finalized on April 17, 2007 by T.D. 9321 (72 FR 19234). The final regulations are reproduced at ¶ 12,147A, ¶ 12,147B, ¶ 12,147C, ¶ 12,147D, ¶ 12,147E, ¶ 12,147F, and ¶ 12,147G. The preamble to the final regulations appears at ¶ 23,247.

¶ 20,261U

IRS proposed regulations: Form 5500: Information returns: Extension of time to file.— The IRS has issued final, temporary and proposed regulations regarding the forms necessary to request filing extensions for information returns, the Form 5500 series, as well as other forms. The preamble to the final and temporary regulations, issued concurrently, is located at ¶ 23,231.

The proposed regulations, which were published in the *Federal Register* on November 7, 2005 (70 FR 67397), were reproduced in relevant part below. The regulations were finalized on July 1, 2008 by T.D. 9407 (73 FR 37362). The final regulations are reproduced at ¶ 13,755D and ¶ 13,755L.

¶ 20,261V

IRS proposed regulations: Defined benefit plans: Funding requirements: Current liability: Mortality tables.— The IRS has released proposed regulations that include mortality tables to be used in determining current liability. The tables are used by certain defined benefit pension plans to determine current liability under Code Sec. 412(l)(7). Code Sec. 412(l) generally imposes additional funding requirements for certain plans having unfunded current liability. (Code Sec. 412 corresponds to ERISA § 302.)

The proposed regulations, which were published in the *Federal Register* on December 2, 2005 (70 FR 72260), are reproduced below.

DEPARTMENT OF THE TREASURY

Internal Revenue Service

26 CFR Part 1

[REG-124988-05]

RIN 1545-BE72

Updated Mortality Tables for Determining Current Liability

AGENCY: Internal Revenue Service (IRS), Treasury

ACTION: Notice of proposed rulemaking and notice of public hearing.

SUMMARY: This document contains proposed regulations under section 412(l)(7)(C)(ii) of the Internal Revenue Code (Code) and section 302(d)(7)(C)(ii) of the Employee Retirement Income Security Act of 1974 (ERISA) (Public Law 93-406, 88 Stat. 829). These regulations provide the public with guidance regarding mortality tables to be used in determining current liability under section 412(l)(7) of the Code and section 302(d)(7) of ERISA. These regulations affect plan sponsors and administrators, and participants in and beneficiaries of, certain retirement plans.

DATES: Written or electronic comments and requests to speak and outlines of topics to be discussed at the public hearing scheduled for April 19, 2006, at 10 a.m., must be received by March 29, 2006.

ADDRESSES: Send submissions to: CC:PA:LPD:PR (REG-124988-05), room 5226, Internal Revenue Service, POB 7604, Ben Franklin Station, Washington, DC 20044. Submissions may be hand-delivered Monday through Friday between the hours of 8 a.m. and 4 p.m. to: CC:PA:LPD:PR (REG-124988-05), Courier(s Desk, Internal Revenue Service, 1111 Constitution Avenue, NW., Washington, DC. Alternatively, taxpayers may submit comments electronically directly to the IRS Internet site at *www.irs.gov/regs*. The public hearing will be held in the Auditorium, Internal Revenue Building, 1111 Constitution Avenue, NW., Washington, DC.

FOR FURTHER INFORMATION CONTACT: Concerning the regulations, Bruce Perlin or Linda Marshall at (202) 622-6090 (not a toll-free number); concerning submissions and the hearing and/or to be placed on the building access list to attend the hearing, Treena Garrett at (202) 622-7180 (not toll-free numbers).

SUPPLEMENTARY INFORMATION:

Background

Section 412 of the Internal Revenue Code provides minimum funding requirements with respect to certain defined benefit pension plans.[1] Section 412(l) provides additional funding requirements for certain of these plans, based in part on a plan's unfunded current liability, as defined in section 412(l)(8).

Pursuant to section 412(c)(6), if the otherwise applicable minimum funding requirement exceeds the plan's full funding limitation (defined in section 412(c)(7) as the excess of a specified measure of plan liability over the plan assets), then the minimum funding for the year is reduced by that excess. Under section 412(c)(7)(E), the full funding limitation cannot be less than the excess of 90% of the plan's current liability (including the expected increase in current liability due to benefits accruing during the plan year) over the value of the plan's assets. For this purpose, the term *current liability* generally has the same meaning given that term under section 412(l)(7).

Section 412(l)(7)(C)(ii) provides that, for purposes of determining current liability in plan years beginning on or after January 1, 1995, the mortality table used is the table prescribed by the Secretary. Under section 412(l)(7)(C)(ii)(I), the initial mortality table used in determining current liability under section 412(l)(7) must be based on the prevailing commissioners' standard table (described in section 807(d)(5)(A)) used to determine reserves for group annuity contracts issued on January 1, 1993. For purposes of section 807(d)(5), Rev. Rul. 92-19 (1992-1 C.B. 227) specifies the prevailing commissioners' standard table used to determine reserves for group annuity contracts issued on January 1, 1993, as the 1983 Group Annuity Mortality Table (1983 GAM). Accordingly, Rev. Rul. 95-28 (1995-1 C.B. 74) sets forth two gender-specific mortality tables — based on 1983 GAM — for purposes of determining current liability for participants who are not entitled to disability benefits.[2]

Section 412(l)(7)(C)(iii)(I) specifies that the Secretary is to establish different mortality tables to be used to determine current liability for individuals who are entitled to benefits under the plan on account of disability. One such set of tables is to apply to individuals whose disabilities occur in plan years beginning before January 1, 1995, and a second set of tables for individuals whose disabilities occur in plan years beginning on or after such date. Under section 412(l)(7)(C)(iii)(II), the separate tables for disabilities that occur in plan years beginning after December 31, 1994 apply only with respect to individuals who are disabled within the meaning of title II of the Social Security Act and the regulations thereunder. Rev. Rul. 96-7 (1996-1 C.B. 59) sets forth the mortality tables established under section 412(l)(7)(C)(iii).

Under section 412(l)(7)(C)(ii)(III), the Secretary of the Treasury is required to periodically (at least every 5 years) review any tables in effect under that subsection and, to the extent necessary, by regulation update the tables to reflect the actual experience of pension plans and projected trends in such experience. Section 412(l)(7)(C)(ii)(II) provides that the updated tables are to take into account the results of available independent studies of mortality of individuals covered by pension plans. Pursuant to section 412(l)(7)(C)(ii)(II), any new mortality tables prescribed by regulation can be effective no earlier than the first plan year beginning after December 31, 1999. Under section 412(l)(10), increases in current liability arising from the adoption of such a new mortality table generally are required to be amortized over a 10-year period.

In order to facilitate the review of the applicable mortality tables pursuant to section 412(l)(7)(C)(ii)(III), Rev. Rul. 95-28 requested comments concerning the mortality table to be used for determining current liability for plan years beginning after December 31, 1999, and information on existing or upcoming independent studies of mortality of individuals covered by pension plans. In Announcement 2000-7 (2000-1 C.B. 586), the IRS and the Treasury Department also requested comments regarding mortality tables to be used for determining current liability for plan years beginning after December 31, 1999, but indicated that it was anticipated that in no event would there be any change in the mortality tables for plan years beginning before January 1, 2001.

Notice 2003-62 (2003-2 C.B. 576) was issued as part of the periodic review by the IRS and the Treasury Department of the mortality tables used in determining current liability under section 412(l)(7). At the time the Notice 2003-62 was issued, the IRS and the Treasury Department were aware of two reviews of mortality experience for retirement plan participants undertaken by the Retirement Plans Experience Committee of the Society of Actuaries (the UP-94 Study and the RP-2000 Mortality Tables Report),[3] and commentators were invited to submit any other independent studies of pension plan mortality experience. Notice 2003-62 also requested the submission of studies regarding projected trends in mortality experience. With respect to projecting mortality improvements, the IRS and the Treasury Department requested comments regarding the advantages and disadvantages of reflecting these trends on an ongoing basis through the use of generational, modified generational, or sequentially static mortality tables.

In addition, Notice 2003-62 requested comments on whether certain risk factors should be taken into account in predicting an individual's mortality. Comments were requested as to the extent that separate mortality tables should be prescribed that take into account these factors, with particular attention paid to the administrative issues in applying such distinctions. In this regard, comments were specifically requested as to how it would be determined which category an individual fits into, the extent to which an individual, once categorized, remains in that same category, the classification of individuals for whom adequate information is unavailable, whether distinctions are applicable to beneficiaries, and the extent to which distinctions may overlap or work at cross purposes. Some examples of factors that were listed in Notice 2003-62 are the following: gender, tobacco use, job classification, annuity size, and income. Comments were also requested as to whether classification systems, if permitted, should be mandatory or optional. A number of comments were submitted regarding the issues identified in Notice 2003-62.

The IRS and the Treasury Department have reviewed the mortality tables that are used for purposes of determining current liability for participants and beneficiaries (other than disabled participants). The existing mortality table for determining current liability (1983 GAM) was compared to independent studies of mortality of individuals covered by pension plans, after reflecting projected trends for mortality improvement through 2007. The comparison indicates that the 1983 GAM is no longer appropriate for determining current liability. For example, comparing the RP-2000 Combined Healthy Mortality Table for males projected to 2007 (when this proposed regulation would take effect) with the 1983 GAM shows that a current mortality table reflects a 52% decrease in the number of expected deaths at age 50, a 26% decrease at 65, and an 19% decrease at age 80. Comparing annuity values derived under these updated mortality rates with annuity values determined under the 1983 GAM shows an increase in present value of 12% for a 35-year-old male with a deferred annuity payable at age 65, a 5% increase for a 55-year-old male with an immediate annuity, and a 7% increase for a 75-year-old male with an immediate annuity (all calculated at a 6% interest rate). Female mortality rates also changed, although with a different pattern. For females, the number of expected deaths decreased by 10% at age 50, but increased by 33% at age 65 and increased by 2% at age 80.[4] Comparing annuity values derived under these updated mortality rates with annuity values determined under the 1983 GAM shows a decrease in present value of 3% for a 35-year-old female with a deferred annuity payable at age 65, a 2% decrease for a 55-year-old female with an immediate annuity, and a 2% decrease for a

---

[1] Section 302 of ERISA sets forth funding rules that are parallel to those in section 412 of the Code. Under section 101 of Reorganization Plan No. 4 of 1978 (43 FR 47713) and section 302 of ERISA, the Secretary of the Treasury has interpretive jurisdiction over the subject matter addressed in these proposed regulations for purposes of ERISA, as well as the Code. Thus, these proposed Treasury regulations issued under section 412 of the Code apply as well for purposes of section 302 of ERISA.

[2] Section 417(e)(3)(A)(ii)(I) requires the present value of certain distributions to be determined using a table prescribed by the Secretary based on the prevailing commissioners' standard table (described in section 807(d)(5)(A)) used to determine reserves for group annuity contracts issued on the date as of which present value is being determined. Thus, in contrast to the mortality table initially prescribed for determining current liability under section 412(l)(7)(C)(ii)(I), the mortality table used to determine present value under section 417(e)(3)(A)(ii)(I) is not fixed as of a specified date but, rather, must be updated when the prevailing commissioners' standard table changes. Rev. Rul. 95-6 (1995-1 C.B. 80) set forth tables under section 417(e)(3)(A)(ii)(I) based on 1983 GAM, which was the prevailing commissioners' standard table at that time. The 1994 Group Annuity Reserving Table became the prevailing commissioners' standard table under section 807(d)(5)(A) for annuities issued on or after January 1, 1999. See Rev. Rul. 2001-38 (2001-2 C.B. 124). Accordingly, Rev. Rul. 2001-62 (2001-2 C.B. 632) required plans to adopt a new mortality table (based on the 1994 Group Annuity Reserving Table) for calculating the minimum present value of distributions pursuant to section 417(e).

[3] The UP-94 Study, prepared by the UP-94 Task Force of the Society of Actuaries, was published in the Transactions of the Society of Actuaries, Vol. XLVII (1995), p. 819. The RP-2000 Mortality Table Report was released in July, 2000. Society of Actuaries, RP-2000 Mortality Tables Report, at *http://www.soa.org/ccm/content/research-publications/experience-studies-tools/the-rp-2000-mortality-tables/*.

[4] The developers of the 1983 GAM table acknowledged that the number of female lives used to develop the table had been relatively small and they recommended an age setback to the male table be used rather than a separate female table. See Development of the 1983 Group Annuity Mortality Table, Transaction of the Society of Actuaries, Vol. XXXV (1983), pp. 859, 883-84.

75-year-old female with an immediate annuity (all calculated at a 6% interest rate).

Based on this review of the 1983 GAM compared to more recent mortality experience, the IRS and Treasury Department have determined that updated mortality tables should be used to determine current liability for participants and beneficiaries (other than disabled participants).[5]

Explanation of Provisions

The proposed regulations would set forth the methodology the IRS and Treasury would use to establish mortality tables to be used under section 412(l)(7)(C)(ii) to determine current liability for participants and beneficiaries (other than disabled participants). The mortality tables that would apply for the 2007 plan year are set forth in the proposed regulations. The mortality tables that would be used for subsequent plan years would be published in the Internal Revenue Bulletin. Comments are requested regarding whether it would be desirable to publish a series of tables for each of a number of years (such as five years) along with final regulations, with tables for subsequent years to be published in the Internal Revenue Bulletin.

These new mortality tables would be based on the tables contained in the RP-2000 Mortality Tables Report. Commentators generally recommended that the RP-2000 mortality tables be the basis for the mortality tables used under section 412(l)(7)(C)(ii) (although one commentator urged that large employers be permitted to use mortality tables tailored to their actual mortality experience). The IRS and the Treasury Department have reviewed the RP-2000 mortality tables and the accompanying report published by the Society of Actuaries, and have determined that the RP-2000 mortality tables form the best available basis for predicting mortality of pension plan participants and beneficiaries (other than disabled participants) based on pension plan experience and expected trends. Accordingly, the proposed regulations would change the mortality tables used to determine current liability from tables based on 1983 GAM to updated tables based on the RP-2000 mortality tables. As under the currently applicable mortality tables, the mortality tables set forth in these proposed regulations are gender-distinct because of significant differences between expected male mortality and expected female mortality.

The proposed regulations would provide for separate sets of tables for annuitants and nonannuitants. This distinction has been made because the RP-2000 Mortality Tables Report indicates that these two groups have significantly different mortality experience. This is particularly true at typical ages for early retirees, where the number of health-induced early retirements results in a population that has higher mortality rates than the population of currently employed individuals. Under the proposed regulations, the annuitant mortality table would be applied to determine the present value of benefits for each annuitant. The annuitant mortality table is also used for each nonannuitant (i.e., an active employee or a terminated vested participant) for the period after which the nonannuitant is projected to commence receiving benefits, while the nonannuitant mortality table is applied for the period before the nonannuitant is projected to commence receiving benefits. Thus, for example, with respect to a 45-year-old active participant who is projected to commence receiving an annuity at age 55, current liability would be determined using the nonannuitant mortality table for the period before the participant attains age 55 (i.e., so that the probability of an active male participant living from age 45 to the age of 55 using the mortality table that would apply in 2007 is 98.59%) and the annuitant mortality table after the participant attains age 55. Similarly, if a 45-year-old terminated vested participant is projected to commence an annuity at age 65, current liability would be determined using the nonannuitant mortality table for the period before the participant attains age 65 and the annuitant mortality table for ages 65 and above.

The mortality tables that would be established pursuant to this regulation would be based on mortality improvements through the year of the actuarial valuation and would reflect the impact of further expected improvements in mortality. Commentators generally stated that the projection of mortality improvement is desirable because it reflects expected mortality more accurately than using mortality tables that do not reflect such projection. The IRS and Treasury agree with these comments, and believe that failing to project mortality improvement in determining current liability would tend to leave plans underfunded. The regulations would specify the projection factors that are to be used to calculate expected mortality improvement. These projection factors are from Mortality Projection Scale AA, which was also recommended for use in the UP-94 Study and RP-2000 Mortality

Tables Report. The mortality tables for annuitants are generally based on a future projection period of 7 years, and the mortality tables for nonannuitants are generally based on a future projection period of 15 years. These projection periods were selected as the expected average duration of liabilities and are consistent with projection periods suggested by commentators.

The RP-2000 Mortality Tables Report did not develop mortality rates for annuitants younger than 50 years of age or for nonannuitants older than 70 years of age. The mortality tables for annuitants use the values that apply for the nonannuitant mortality tables at younger ages, with a smoothed transition to the annuitant mortality tables by age 50. Similarly, the mortality tables for both male and female nonannuitants use the values that apply for the annuitant mortality tables at older ages (i.e., ages above 70), with a smoothed transition to the nonannuitant mortality tables by age 70.

The mortality tables for annuitants applicable for the 2007 plan year would use the values that apply for the nonannuitant mortality tables at ages 40 and younger for males and at ages 44 and younger for females with a smoothed transition to the annuitant mortality tables between the ages of 41 and 49 for males and between 45 and 49 for females. Similarly, the mortality tables for both male and female nonannuitants applicable for the 2007 plan year use the values that apply for the annuitant mortality tables at ages 80 and older, with a smoothed transition to the nonannuitant mortality tables between the ages of 71 and 79.

The proposed regulations would provide an option for smaller plans (i.e., plans where the total of active and inactive participants is less than 500) to use a single blended table for all healthy participants — in lieu of the separate tables for annuitants and nonannuitants — in order to simplify the actuarial valuation for these plans. This blended table would be constructed from the separate nonannuitant and annuitant tables using the nonannuitant/annuitant weighting factors published in the RP-2000 Mortality Tables Report. However, because the RP-2000 Mortality Tables Report does not provide weighting factors before age 50 or after age 70, the IRS and the Treasury Department would extend the table of weighting factors for ages 41 through 50 (ages 45-50 for females) and for ages 70 through 79 in order to develop the blended table.

The proposed regulations do not provide for the use of generational mortality tables to compute a plan's current liability. Although commentators generally stated that the use of generational mortality tables provides a more accurate prediction of participant mortality, they urged against requiring the use of generational mortality tables, arguing that many actuarial valuation systems are not currently capable of using a generational approach to mortality improvement. However, several commentators requested that the use of generational mortality tables be permitted on an optional basis. The IRS and the Treasury Department agree that the use of generational mortality tables would be preferable, but believe that the approach taken in the proposed regulations (i.e., projecting liabilities for annuitants and nonannuitants to average expected duration) is appropriate because it reasonably approximates the use of generational tables without being overly complex to apply. In light of several comments requesting that the use of generational tables be optional, the IRS and the Treasury Department are considering adopting such a rule and request comments regarding any issues that might arise in implementing an optional use of a generational table. In addition, comments are requested regarding how much lead time would be appropriate if generational mortality tables were to be required in the future.

The RP-2000 mortality tables and the accompanying report analyze differences in expected mortality based on a number of factors, including job classification, annuity size, employment status (i.e., active or retired), and industry. The IRS and the Treasury Department have considered whether separate mortality tables should be provided based on any of these distinctions, or on other distinctions cited in Notice 2003-62, such as tobacco use or income level. The IRS and the Treasury Department have concluded that it is inappropriate to apply distinctions other than the annuitant and nonannuitant distinction described above. In general, these other distinctions were not made because of the complexity involved in the process. For example, no distinction was made for tobacco use because of the difficulty in obtaining, maintaining, and documenting accurate data on the extent of tobacco use.

Although several commentators recommended that separate mortality tables apply to plans that are determined to be "white collar" or "blue collar" in nature, the IRS and Treasury have not adopted this

---

[5] The IRS and Treasury are in the process of reviewing recent mortality experience and expected trends for disabled participants to determine whether updated mortality tables under section 412(l)(7)(C)(iii) are needed.

recommendation because of serious administrability concerns. Commentators recognized that it may be difficult to identify whether a specific individual falls into the category of blue collar or white collar (especially if an individual has shifted job classifications during his or her career), and suggested that the classification be based on whether the plan is primarily composed of blue collar employees or white collar employees or whether a plan covers a mixed population of blue collar and white collar employees. While the plan-wide classification may avoid the difficulties of categorizing those individuals who are hard to classify as either blue collar or white collar, it would create additional problems if a plan shifted between these categories.

More importantly, the RP-2000 Mortality Tables Report indicates that plans that are primarily blue collar in nature, but that provide large annuities, tend to have significantly better mortality experience than the average mortality for individuals in the RP-2000 Mortality Tables Report. As a result, classifying such a plan as blue collar and allowing the plan to use a weaker mortality table will lead to systematic underfunding of the plan.[6] Other concerns weighing against the use of separate tables for blue collar and white collar plans include the risk of anti-selection by plans in the absence of mandatory adjustments and the lack of research showing the extent to which any mortality differences attributable to blue collar or white collar status extend to beneficiaries of the plan.

As noted above, the mortality experience is significantly different for annuitants and nonannuitants. While the use of separate mortality rates for these groups of individuals will likely entail changes in programming of actuarial software, the IRS and Treasury believe that the improvement in accuracy resulting from the the the use of separate mortality tables for annuitants and nonannuitants more than offsets the added complexity. Furthermore, the annutant/nonannuitant distinction does not have the same difficult administrative issues as separate tables based on collar type, annuity size, or tobacco. This is because it is usually a straightforward process to categorize an individual as an annuitant or a nonannuitant, and once an indvidual is categorized as an annuitant, the individual's status usually does not change again.

Proposed Effective Date

These regulations are proposed to apply to plan years beginning on or after January 1, 2007.

Special Analyses

It has been determined that this notice of proposed rulemaking is not a significant regulatory action as defined in Executive Order 12866. Therefore, a regulatory assessment is not required. It is hereby certified that these regulations will not have a significant economic impact on a substantial number of small entities. This certification is based upon the fact that these regulations provide for special rules to simplify the application of these regulations by actuaries who provide services for small entities. Therefore, a Regulatory Flexibility Analysis under the Regulatory Flexibility Act (5 U.S.C. chapter 6) is not required. Pursuant to section 7805(f) of the Code, this notice of proposed rulemaking will be submitted to the Chief Counsel for Advocacy of the Small Business Administration for comment on its impact on small business.

Comments and Public Hearing

Before these proposed regulations are adopted as final regulations, consideration will be given to any written (a signed original and eight (8) copies) or electronic comments that are submitted timely to the IRS. The IRS and Treasury Department specifically request comments on the clarity of the proposed regulations and how they may be made easier to understand. All comments will be available for public inspection and copying.

A public hearing has been scheduled for April 19, 2006, at 10 a.m. in the auditorium, Internal Revenue Building, 1111 Constitution Avenue, NW., Washington, DC. Due to building security procedures, visitors must use the main building entrance on Constitution Avenue. In addition, all visitors must present photo identification to enter the building. Because of access restrictions, visitors will not be admitted beyond the immediate entrance area more than 30 minutes before the hearing starts. For more information about having your name placed on the list to attend the hearing, see the "FOR FURTHER INFORMATION CONTACT" section of this preamble.

The rules of 26 CFR 601.601(a)(3) apply to the hearing. Persons who wish to present oral comments at the hearing must submit written (signed original and eight (8) copies) or electronic comments and an outline of the topics to be discussed and the time to be devoted to each topic by March 29, 2006. A period of 10 minutes will be allotted to each person for making comments. An agenda showing the scheduling of the speakers will be prepared after the deadline for receiving outlines has passed. Copies of the agenda will be available free of charge at the hearing.

Drafting Information

The principal authors of these regulations are Bruce Perlin and Linda S. F. Marshall, Office of Division Counsel/Associate Chief Counsel (Tax Exempt and Government Entities). However, other personnel from the IRS and Treasury participated in the development of these regulations.

List of Subjects in 26 CFR Part 1

Income taxes, Reporting and recordkeeping requirements.

Amendments to the Regulations

Accordingly, 26 CFR part 1 is proposed to be amended as follows:

PART 1—INCOME TAXES

Paragraph 1. The authority citation for part 1 continues to read, in part, as follows:

Authority: 26 U.S.C. 7805 * * *

Par. 2. Section 1.412(l)(7)-1 is added to read as follows:

§ 1.412(l)(7)-1 Mortality tables used to determine current liability.

(a) *General rules.* This section sets forth the basis used to generate mortality tables to be used in connection with computations under section 412(l)(7)(C)(ii) for determining current liability for participants and beneficiaries (other than disabled participants). The mortality tables, which reflect the probability of death at each age, that are to be used for plan years beginning during 2007, are provided in paragraph (e) of this section. The mortality tables to be used for later plan years are to be provided in guidance published in the Internal Revenue Bulletin. See § 601.601(d) of this chapter.

(b) *Use of the tables—(1) Separate tables for annuitants and nonannuitants.* Separate tables are provided for use by annuitants and nonannuitants. The annuitant mortality table is applied to determine the present value of benefits for each annuitant, and to each nonannuitant for the period after which the nonannuitant is projected to commence receiving benefits. For purposes of this section, an annuitant means a plan participant who is currently receiving benefits and a nonannuitant means a plan participant who is not currently receiving benefits (e.g., an active employee or a terminated vested participant). A participant whose benefit has partially commenced is treated as an annuitant with respect to the portion of the benefit which has commenced and a nonannuitant with respect to the balance of the benefit. The nonannuitant mortality table is applied to each nonannuitant for the period before the nonannuitant is projected to commence receiving benefits. Thus, for example, with respect to a 45-year-old active participant who is projected to commence receiving an annuity at age 55, current liability would be determined using the nonannuitant mortality table for the period before the participant attains age 55 (i.e., so that the probability of an active male participant living from age 45 to the age of 55 for the table that applies in plan years beginning in 2007 is 98.59%) and the annuitant mortality table for the period ages 55 and above. Similarly, if a 45-year-old terminated vested participant is projected to commence an annuity at age 65, current liability would be determined using the nonannuitant mortality table for the period before the participant attains age 65 and the annuitant mortality table for ages 65 and above.

(2) *Small plan tables.* As an alternative to the separate tables specified for annuitants and nonannuitants, a small plan can use a combined table that applies the same mortality rates to both annuitants and nonannuitants. For this purpose, a small plan is defined as a plan with fewer than 500 participants (including both active and inactive participants).

(c) *Construction of the tables—(1) Source of basic data.* The mortality tables are based on the separate mortality tables for employees and healthy annuitants under the RP-2000 Mortality Tables Report (http://www.soa.org/ccm/content/research-publications/experience-studies-

---

[6] Although some commentators suggested addressing this problem by treating some highly compensated union employees as if they were white collar workers, the developers of the RP-2000 Mortality Tables Report (and the researchers they hired to apply a multivariate analysis of the data) were unable to find a practical model to apply the combined effect of collar and annuity amount on mortality.

tools/the-rp-2000-mortality-tables/), as set forth in paragraph (d) of this section.

(2) *Projected mortality improvements.* The mortality rates under the basic mortality tables are projected to improve using Projection Scale AA, as set forth in paragraph (d) of this section. The annuitant mortality rates for a plan year are based on applying the improvement factors from 2000 until 7 years after the plan year. The nonannuitant mortality rates for a plan year are based on applying the improvement factors from 2000 until 15 years after the plan year. The projection scale is applied using the following equation: Projected mortality rate = base mortality rate * [(1 - projection factor) (number of years projected)].

(3) *Treatment of young annutants and older nonannuitants.* The mortality tables for annuitants use the values that apply for the nonannuitant mortality tables at younger ages, with a smoothed transition to the annuitant mortality tables by age 50. Similarly, the mortality tables for both male and female nonannuitants use the values that apply for the annuitant mortality tables at older ages (i.e., ages above 70), with a smoothed transition to the nonannuitant mortality tables by age 70.

(4) *Construction of the combined table for small plans.* The combined table for small plans is constructed from the separate nonannuitant and annuitant tables using the nonannuitant weighting factors as set forth in paragraph (d) of this section. The weighting factors are applied to develop this table using the following equation: Combined mortality rate = [non-annuitant rate * (1- weighting factor)] + [annuitant rate * weighting factor].

(d) *Tables.* As set forth in paragraph (c) of this section, the following values are used to develop the mortality tables that are used for determining current liability under section 412(l)(7)(C)(ii) and this section.

Age	MALE Non-Annuitant Table (Year 2000)	MALE Annuitant Table (Year 2000)	MALE Projection Scale AA [7]	MALE Weighting factors for small plans [8]	FEMALE Non-Annuitant Table (Year 2000)	FEMALE Annuitant Table (Year 2000)	FEMALE Projection Scale AA	FEMALE Weighting factors for small plans
1	0.000637	-	0.020	-	0.000571	-	0.020	-
2	0.000430	-	0.020	-	0.000372	-	0.020	-
3	0.000357	-	0.020	-	0.000278	-	0.020	-
4	0.000278	-	0.020	-	0.000208	-	0.020	-
5	0.000255	-	0.020	-	0.000188	-	0.020	-
6	0.000244	-	0.020	-	0.000176	-	0.020	-
7	0.000234	-	0.020	-	0.000165	-	0.020	-
8	0.000216	-	0.020	-	0.000147	-	0.020	-
9	0.000209	-	0.020	-	0.000140	-	0.020	-
10	0.000212	-	0.020	-	0.000141	-	0.020	-
11	0.000219	-	0.020	-	0.000143	-	0.020	-
12	0.000228	-	0.020	-	0.000148	-	0.020	-
13	0.000240	-	0.020	-	0.000155	-	0.020	-
14	0.000254	-	0.019	-	0.000162	-	0.018	-
15	0.000269	-	0.019	-	0.000170	-	0.016	-
16	0.000284	-	0.019	-	0.000177	-	0.015	-
17	0.000301	-	0.019	-	0.000184	-	0.014	-
18	0.000316	-	0.019	-	0.000188	-	0.014	-
19	0.000331	-	0.019	-	0.000190	-	0.015	-
20	0.000345	-	0.019	-	0.000191	-	0.016	-
21	0.000357	-	0.018	-	0.000192	-	0.017	-
22	0.000366	-	0.017	-	0.000194	-	0.017	-
23	0.000373	-	0.015	-	0.000197	-	0.016	-
24	0.000376	-	0.013	-	0.000201	-	0.015	-
25	0.000376	-	0.010	-	0.000207	-	0.014	-
26	0.000378	-	0.006	-	0.000214	-	0.012	-
27	0.000382	-	0.005	-	0.000223	-	0.012	-
28	0.000393	-	0.005	-	0.000235	-	0.012	-
29	0.000412	-	0.005	-	0.000248	-	0.012	-
30	0.000444	-	0.005	-	0.000264	-	0.010	-
31	0.000499	-	0.005	-	0.000307	-	0.008	-
32	0.000562	-	0.005	-	0.000350	-	0.008	-
33	0.000631	-	0.005	-	0.000394	-	0.009	-
34	0.000702	-	0.005	-	0.000435	-	0.010	-
35	0.000773	-	0.005	-	0.000475	-	0.011	-
36	0.000841	-	0.005	-	0.000514	-	0.012	-
37	0.000904	-	0.005	-	0.000554	-	0.013	-
38	0.000964	-	0.006	-	0.000598	-	0.014	-
39	0.001021	-	0.007	-	0.000648	-	0.015	-
40	0.001079	-	0.008	-	0.000706	-	0.015	-
41	0.001142	-	0.009	0.0045	0.000774	-	0.015	-
42	0.001215	-	0.010	0.0091	0.000852	-	0.015	-
43	0.001299	-	0.011	0.0136	0.000937	-	0.015	-
44	0.001397	-	0.012	0.0181	0.001029	-	0.015	-
45	0.001508	-	0.013	0.0226	0.001124	-	0.016	0.0084
46	0.001616	-	0.014	0.0272	0.001223	-	0.017	0.0167
47	0.001734	-	0.015	0.0317	0.001326	-	0.018	0.0251
48	0.001860	-	0.016	0.0362	0.001434	-	0.018	0.0335
49	0.001995	-	0.017	0.0407	0.001550	-	0.018	0.0419
50	0.002138	0.005347	0.018	0.0453	0.001676	0.002344	0.017	0.0502
51	0.002288	0.005528	0.019	0.0498	0.001814	0.002459	0.016	0.0586
52	0.002448	0.005644	0.020	0.0686	0.001967	0.002647	0.014	0.0744
53	0.002621	0.005722	0.020	0.0953	0.002135	0.002895	0.012	0.0947
54	0.002812	0.005797	0.020	0.1288	0.002321	0.003190	0.010	0.1189
55	0.003029	0.005905	0.019	0.2066	0.002526	0.003531	0.008	0.1897
56	0.003306	0.006124	0.018	0.3173	0.002756	0.003925	0.006	0.2857
57	0.003628	0.006444	0.017	0.3780	0.003010	0.004385	0.005	0.3403

Age	MALE Non-Annuitant Table (Year 2000)	MALE Annuitant Table (Year 2000)	MALE Projection Scale AA [7]	MALE Weighting factors for small plans [8]	FEMALE Non-Annuitant Table (Year 2000)	FEMALE Annuitant Table (Year 2000)	FEMALE Projection Scale AA	FEMALE Weighting factors for small plans
58	0.003997	0.006895	0.016	0.4401	0.003291	0.004921	0.005	0.3878
59	0.004414	0.007485	0.016	0.4986	0.003599	0.005531	0.005	0.4360
60	0.004878	0.008196	0.016	0.5633	0.003931	0.006200	0.005	0.4954
61	0.005382	0.009001	0.015	0.6338	0.004285	0.006919	0.005	0.5805
62	0.005918	0.009915	0.015	0.7103	0.004656	0.007689	0.005	0.6598
63	0.006472	0.010951	0.014	0.7902	0.005039	0.008509	0.005	0.7520
64	0.007028	0.012117	0.014	0.8355	0.005429	0.009395	0.005	0.8043
65	0.007573	0.013419	0.014	0.8832	0.005821	0.010364	0.005	0.8552
66	0.008099	0.014868	0.013	0.9321	0.006207	0.011413	0.005	0.9118
67	0.008598	0.016460	0.013	0.9510	0.006583	0.012540	0.005	0.9367
68	0.009069	0.018200	0.014	0.9639	0.006945	0.013771	0.005	0.9523
69	0.009510	0.020105	0.014	0.9714	0.007289	0.015153	0.005	0.9627
70	0.009922	0.022206	0.015	0.9740	0.007613	0.016742	0.005	0.9661
71	-	0.024570	0.015	0.9766	-	0.018579	0.006	0.9695
72	-	0.027281	0.015	0.9792	-	0.020665	0.006	0.9729
73	-	0.030387	0.015	0.9818	-	0.022970	0.007	0.9763
74	-	0.033900	0.015	0.9844	-	0.025458	0.007	0.9797
75	-	0.037834	0.014	0.9870	-	0.028106	0.008	0.9830
76	-	0.042169	0.014	0.9896	-	0.030966	0.008	0.9864
77	-	0.046906	0.013	0.9922	-	0.034105	0.007	0.9898
78	-	0.052123	0.012	0.9948	-	0.037595	0.007	0.9932
79	-	0.057927	0.011	0.9974	-	0.041506	0.007	0.9966
80	-	0.064368	0.010	1.0000	-	0.045879	0.007	1.0000
81	-	0.072041	0.009	1.0000	-	0.050780	0.007	1.0000
82	-	0.080486	0.008	1.0000	-	0.056294	0.007	1.0000
83	-	0.089718	0.008	1.0000	-	0.062506	0.007	1.0000
84	-	0.099779	0.007	1.0000	-	0.069517	0.007	1.0000
85	-	0.110757	0.007	1.0000	-	0.077446	0.006	1.0000
86	-	0.122797	0.007	1.0000	-	0.086376	0.005	1.0000
87	-	0.136043	0.006	1.0000	-	0.096337	0.004	1.0000
88	-	0.150590	0.005	1.0000	-	0.107303	0.004	1.0000
89	-	0.166420	0.005	1.0000	-	0.119154	0.003	1.0000
90	-	0.183408	0.004	1.0000	-	0.131682	0.003	1.0000
91	-	0.199769	0.004	1.0000	-	0.144604	0.003	1.0000
92	-	0.216605	0.003	1.0000	-	0.157618	0.003	1.0000
93	-	0.233662	0.003	1.0000	-	0.170433	0.002	1.0000
94	-	0.250693	0.003	1.0000	-	0.182799	0.002	1.0000
95	-	0.267491	0.002	1.0000	-	0.194509	0.002	1.0000
96	-	0.283905	0.002	1.0000	-	0.205379	0.002	1.0000
97	-	0.299852	0.002	1.0000	-	0.215240	0.001	1.0000
98	-	0.315296	0.001	1.0000	-	0.223947	0.001	1.0000
99	-	0.330207	0.001	1.0000	-	0.231387	0.001	1.0000
100	-	0.344556	0.001	1.0000	-	0.237467	0.001	1.0000
101	-	0.358628	0.000	1.0000	-	0.244834	0.000	1.0000
102	-	0.371685	0.000	1.0000	-	0.254498	0.000	1.0000
103	-	0.383040	0.000	1.0000	-	0.266044	0.000	1.0000
104	-	0.392003	0.000	1.0000	-	0.279055	0.000	1.0000
105	-	0.397886	0.000	1.0000	-	0.293116	0.000	1.0000
106	-	0.400000	0.000	1.0000	-	0.307811	0.000	1.0000
107	-	0.400000	0.000	1.0000	-	0.322725	0.000	1.0000
108	-	0.400000	0.000	1.0000	-	0.337441	0.000	1.0000
109	-	0.400000	0.000	1.0000	-	0.351544	0.000	1.0000
110	-	0.400000	0.000	1.0000	-	0.364617	0.000	1.0000
111	-	0.400000	0.000	1.0000	-	0.376246	0.000	1.0000
112	-	0.400000	0.000	1.0000	-	0.386015	0.000	1.0000
113	-	0.400000	0.000	1.0000	-	0.393507	0.000	1.0000
114	-	0.400000	0.000	1.0000	-	0.398308	0.000	1.0000
115	-	0.400000	0.000	1.0000	-	0.400000	0.000	1.0000
116	-	0.400000	0.000	1.0000	-	0.400000	0.000	1.0000
117	-	0.400000	0.000	1.0000	-	0.400000	0.000	1.0000
118	-	0.400000	0.000	1.0000	-	0.400000	0.000	1.0000
119	-	0.400000	0.000	1.0000	-	0.400000	0.000	1.0000
120	-	1.000000	0.000	1.0000	-	1.000000	0.000	1.0000

(e) *Tables for plan years beginning during 2007*. The following tables are to be used for determining current liability under section 412 (l) (7) (C) (ii) for plan years beginning during 2007.

Age	MALE Non-Annuitant Table	MALE Annuitant Table	MALE Optional Combined Table for Small Plans	FEMALE Non-Annuitant Table	FEMALE Annuitant Table	FEMALE Optional Combined Table for Small Plans
1	0.000408	0.000408	0.000408	0.000366	0.000366	0.000366
2	0.000276	0.000276	0.000276	0.000239	0.000239	0.000239
3	0.000229	0.000229	0.000229	0.000178	0.000178	0.000178
4	0.000178	0.000178	0.000178	0.000133	0.000133	0.000133
5	0.000163	0.000163	0.000163	0.000121	0.000121	0.000121
6	0.000156	0.000156	0.000156	0.000113	0.000113	0.000113
7	0.000150	0.000150	0.000150	0.000106	0.000106	0.000106
8	0.000138	0.000138	0.000138	0.000094	0.000094	0.000094
9	0.000134	0.000134	0.000134	0.000090	0.000090	0.000090
10	0.000136	0.000136	0.000136	0.000090	0.000090	0.000090
11	0.000140	0.000140	0.000140	0.000092	0.000092	0.000092
12	0.000146	0.000146	0.000146	0.000095	0.000095	0.000095
13	0.000154	0.000154	0.000154	0.000099	0.000099	0.000099
14	0.000167	0.000167	0.000167	0.000109	0.000109	0.000109
15	0.000176	0.000176	0.000176	0.000119	0.000119	0.000119
16	0.000186	0.000186	0.000186	0.000127	0.000127	0.000127
17	0.000197	0.000197	0.000197	0.000135	0.000135	0.000135
18	0.000207	0.000207	0.000207	0.000138	0.000138	0.000138
19	0.000217	0.000217	0.000217	0.000136	0.000136	0.000136
20	0.000226	0.000226	0.000226	0.000134	0.000134	0.000134
21	0.000239	0.000239	0.000239	0.000132	0.000132	0.000132
22	0.000251	0.000251	0.000251	0.000133	0.000133	0.000133
23	0.000267	0.000267	0.000267	0.000138	0.000138	0.000138
24	0.000282	0.000282	0.000282	0.000144	0.000144	0.000144
25	0.000301	0.000301	0.000301	0.000152	0.000152	0.000152
26	0.000331	0.000331	0.000331	0.000164	0.000164	0.000164
27	0.000342	0.000342	0.000342	0.000171	0.000171	0.000171
28	0.000352	0.000352	0.000352	0.000180	0.000180	0.000180
29	0.000369	0.000369	0.000369	0.000190	0.000190	0.000190
30	0.000398	0.000398	0.000398	0.000212	0.000212	0.000212
31	0.000447	0.000447	0.000447	0.000257	0.000257	0.000257
32	0.000503	0.000503	0.000503	0.000293	0.000293	0.000293
33	0.000565	0.000565	0.000565	0.000323	0.000323	0.000323
34	0.000629	0.000629	0.000629	0.000349	0.000349	0.000349
35	0.000692	0.000692	0.000692	0.000372	0.000372	0.000372
36	0.000753	0.000753	0.000753	0.000394	0.000394	0.000394
37	0.000810	0.000810	0.000810	0.000415	0.000415	0.000415
38	0.000844	0.000844	0.000844	0.000439	0.000439	0.000439
39	0.000875	0.000875	0.000875	0.000465	0.000465	0.000465
40	0.000904	0.000904	0.000904	0.000506	0.000506	0.000506
41	0.000936	0.000963	0.000936	0.000555	0.000555	0.000555
42	0.000974	0.001081	0.000975	0.000611	0.000611	0.000611
43	0.001018	0.001258	0.001021	0.000672	0.000672	0.000672
44	0.001071	0.001493	0.001079	0.000738	0.000738	0.000738
45	0.001131	0.001788	0.001146	0.000788	0.000791	0.000788
46	0.001185	0.002142	0.001211	0.000839	0.000896	0.000840
47	0.001244	0.002554	0.001286	0.000889	0.001054	0.000893
48	0.001304	0.003026	0.001366	0.000962	0.001265	0.000972
49	0.001368	0.003557	0.001457	0.001039	0.001528	0.001059
50	0.001434	0.004146	0.001557	0.001149	0.001844	0.001184
51	0.001500	0.004226	0.001636	0.001272	0.001962	0.001312
52	0.001570	0.004254	0.001754	0.001442	0.002173	0.001496
53	0.001681	0.004312	0.001932	0.001637	0.002445	0.001714
54	0.001803	0.004369	0.002134	0.001861	0.002771	0.001969
55	0.001986	0.004514	0.002508	0.002117	0.003155	0.002314
56	0.002217	0.004749	0.003020	0.002414	0.003608	0.002755
57	0.002488	0.005069	0.003464	0.002696	0.004088	0.003170
58	0.002803	0.005501	0.003990	0.002947	0.004588	0.003583
59	0.003095	0.005972	0.004529	0.003223	0.005156	0.004066
60	0.003421	0.006539	0.005177	0.003521	0.005780	0.004640
61	0.003860	0.007284	0.006030	0.003838	0.006450	0.005354
62	0.004244	0.008024	0.006929	0.004170	0.007168	0.006148
63	0.004746	0.008989	0.008099	0.004513	0.007932	0.007084
64	0.005154	0.009947	0.009159	0.004862	0.008758	0.007996
65	0.005553	0.011015	0.010377	0.005213	0.009662	0.009018
66	0.006073	0.012379	0.011951	0.005559	0.010640	0.010192
67	0.006447	0.013705	0.013349	0.005896	0.011690	0.011323
68	0.006650	0.014940	0.014641	0.006220	0.012838	0.012522
69	0.006974	0.016504	0.016231	0.006528	0.014126	0.013843
70	0.007115	0.017971	0.017689	0.006818	0.015607	0.015309

Age	MALE Non-Annuitant Table	MALE Annuitant Table	MALE Optional Combined Table for Small Plans	FEMALE Non-Annuitant Table	FEMALE Annuitant Table	FEMALE Optional Combined Table for Small Plans
71	0.008002	0.019884	0.019606	0.007450	0.017078	0.016784
72	0.009777	0.022078	0.021822	0.008714	0.018995	0.018716
73	0.012439	0.024592	0.024371	0.010610	0.020819	0.020577
74	0.015988	0.027435	0.027256	0.013139	0.023074	0.022872
75	0.020425	0.031057	0.030919	0.016299	0.025117	0.024967
76	0.025749	0.034615	0.034523	0.020092	0.027673	0.027570
77	0.031961	0.039054	0.038999	0.024516	0.030911	0.030846
78	0.039059	0.044018	0.043992	0.029573	0.034074	0.034043
79	0.047046	0.049617	0.049610	0.035261	0.037618	0.037610
80	0.055919	0.055919	0.055919	0.041582	0.041582	0.041582
81	0.063476	0.063476	0.063476	0.046024	0.046024	0.046024
82	0.071926	0.071926	0.071926	0.051021	0.051021	0.051021
83	0.080176	0.080176	0.080176	0.056651	0.056651	0.056651
84	0.090433	0.090433	0.090433	0.063006	0.063006	0.063006
85	0.100383	0.100383	0.100383	0.071188	0.071188	0.071188
86	0.111295	0.111295	0.111295	0.080522	0.080522	0.080522
87	0.125051	0.125051	0.125051	0.091080	0.091080	0.091080
88	0.140385	0.140385	0.140385	0.101448	0.101448	0.101448
89	0.155142	0.155142	0.155142	0.114246	0.114246	0.114246
90	0.173400	0.173400	0.173400	0.126258	0.126258	0.126258
91	0.188868	0.188868	0.188868	0.138648	0.138648	0.138648
92	0.207683	0.207683	0.207683	0.151126	0.151126	0.151126
93	0.224037	0.224037	0.224037	0.165722	0.165722	0.165722
94	0.240367	0.240367	0.240367	0.177747	0.177747	0.177747
95	0.260098	0.260098	0.260098	0.189133	0.189133	0.189133
96	0.276058	0.276058	0.276058	0.199703	0.199703	0.199703
97	0.291564	0.291564	0.291564	0.212246	0.212246	0.212246
98	0.310910	0.310910	0.310910	0.220832	0.220832	0.220832
99	0.325614	0.325614	0.325614	0.228169	0.228169	0.228169
100	0.339763	0.339763	0.339763	0.234164	0.234164	0.234164
101	0.358628	0.358628	0.358628	0.244834	0.244834	0.244834
102	0.371685	0.371685	0.371685	0.254498	0.254498	0.254498
103	0.383040	0.383040	0.383040	0.266044	0.266044	0.266044
104	0.392003	0.392003	0.392003	0.279055	0.279055	0.279055
105	0.397886	0.397886	0.397886	0.293116	0.293116	0.293116
106	0.400000	0.400000	0.400000	0.307811	0.307811	0.307811
107	0.400000	0.400000	0.400000	0.322725	0.322725	0.322725
108	0.400000	0.400000	0.400000	0.337441	0.337441	0.337441
109	0.400000	0.400000	0.400000	0.351544	0.351544	0.351544
110	0.400000	0.400000	0.400000	0.364617	0.364617	0.364617
111	0.400000	0.400000	0.400000	0.376246	0.376246	0.376246
112	0.400000	0.400000	0.400000	0.386015	0.386015	0.386015
113	0.400000	0.400000	0.400000	0.393507	0.393507	0.393507
114	0.400000	0.400000	0.400000	0.398308	0.398308	0.398308
115	0.400000	0.400000	0.400000	0.400000	0.400000	0.400000
116	0.400000	0.400000	0.400000	0.400000	0.400000	0.400000
117	0.400000	0.400000	0.400000	0.400000	0.400000	0.400000
118	0.400000	0.400000	0.400000	0.400000	0.400000	0.400000
119	0.400000	0.400000	0.400000	0.400000	0.400000	0.400000
120	1.000000	1.000000	1.000000	1.000000	1.000000	1.000000

(f) *Effective date.* The mortality tables described in this section apply for plan years beginning on or after January 1, 2007.

Mark E. Matthews

Deputy Commissioner for Services and Enforcement.

¶ 20,261W

IRS proposed regulations: 401(k) plans: Designated Roth contributions: Participant loans: Hardship distributions.— The IRS has released proposed Roth 401(k) regulations addressing issues not addressed in recently released final Roth 401(k) regulations (see ¶ 23,232), including rules for taxation of distributions, rollovers between such plans and to Roth IRAs, and excess deferrals.

The proposed regulations, published in the *Federal Register* on January 26, 2006 (71 FR 4320), were previously reproduced below. The final regulations were issued on April 30, 2007 (72 FR 21103). The preamble to the final regulations appears at ¶ 23,246, which contains cross-references to the final egulations.

¶ 20,261X

IRS proposed regulations: Exemptions: Definitions: Dependents: Divorce or separation.— The IRS has issued proposed regulations under Code Sec. 152 to clarify which parent may claim a child as a dependent in cases of divorce, legal separation or when the parents of the child live apart at all times during the last six months of the calendar year. A state court order or decree does not operate to allocate the federal dependency exemption between parents. The regulations are proposed to apply to tax years beginning after the date the regulations are published as final regulations in the Federal Register.

The proposed regulations, which were published in the Federal Register on May 2, 2007 (72 FR 24192-24196), were formerly reproduced below. The final regs. which were published in the Federal Register on July 2, 2008, are reproduced at ¶ 11,295A, ¶ 11,295B, ¶ 11,295C, and ¶ 11,295D.

¶ 20,261Y

IRS proposed regulations: Defined benefit plans: Funding requirements: Present value: Mortality tables: Multiemployer plans.— The IRS has released proposed regulations to establish the methodology used to determine present value or make any calculation under Code Sec. 430, added to the Code by the Pension Protection Act of 2006 (P.L. 109-280). The proposed rules include mortality tables that would apply to the determination of current liability for multiemployer plans pursuant to Code Sec. 431(c)(6)(D)(iv)(II).)

The proposed regulations were published in the Federal Register on May 29, 2007 (72 FR 29456). Official corrections were made on July 20, 2007 (72 FR 39770). The proposed regulations were previously reproduced below. The final regulations were adopted with minor modifications on July 31, 2008 (73 FR 44632). The preamble to the final regulations is reproduced at ¶ 23,256; the regulations appear at ¶ 13,151L-20, ¶ 13,151L-22, and ¶ 13,151M-15.

¶ 20,261Z

IRS: Health savings accounts (HSAs): Accelerated contributions: Comparable contributions.—The IRS has detailed for employers how they can comply with the comparable contribution requirements for HSAs, when an employee has not established an HSA by December 31st or has not notified the employer that he or she has established an HSA. The following proposed regulation also addresses the acceleration of employer contributions for the calendar year for employees who have incurred qualified medical expenses exceeding the employer's cumulative HSA contributions at the time the expenses were incurred.

The proposed regulation, issued on June 1, 2007 (72 FR 30501), was previously reproduced below. Official corrections were made on June 29, 2007 (72 FR 35672) and on July 17, 2007 (72 FR 39139).

The final regulation was published in the *Federal Register* on April 17, 2008 (73 FR 20794) and is reproduced at ¶ 13,648W-104. The Preamble to the regulation is at ¶ 23,254.

¶ 20,262

IRS proposed regulations: Tax-exempt entities: Excise taxes: Disclosure: Return filing .—The IRS has released proposed regulations which provide guidance under Code Sec. 4965 regarding entity-level and manager-level excise taxes with respect to prohibited tax shelter transactions to which tax-exempt entities are parties; guidance under Code Sec. 6033(a)(2) and Code Sec. 6011(g) regarding certain disclosure obligations with respect to such transactions; and guidance under Code Sec. 6011 and Code Sec. 6071 regarding the requirement of a return and time for filing with respect to Code Sec. 4965 taxes. The proposed regulations cross-reference final and temporary regulations (see ¶ 23,249 and ¶ 23,250).

The proposed regulations, which were published in the Federal Register on July 6, 2007 (72 FR 36927), were previously reproduced below. The final regulations were published in the Federal Register on July 6, 2010 (75 FR 38700). The preamble to the final regulations is at ¶ 23,274. The final regulations are at ¶ 13,663W, ¶ 13,663W-10, ¶ 13,598B, ¶ 13,598C, ¶ 13,598D, ¶ 13,598E, ¶ 13,598F, ¶ 13,598G, ¶ 13,598H, ¶ 13,598I, ¶ 13,598J, ¶ 13,649A, ¶ 13,649B, and ¶ 13,649N.

¶ 20,262A

IRS: Variable annuities: Permitted investors Diversification requirements.—The IRS has proposed changes to the regulations concerning diversification requirements of Code Sec. 817(h). The amendments would expand the list of permitted investors in Reg. § 1.817-5(f)(3) to include trustees of pension or retirement plans established and maintained outside the United States primarily for the benefit of individuals substantially all of whom are nonresident aliens.

The proposed regulation was published in the Federal Register on July 31, 2007 (72 FR 41651) and was previously reproduced below. The final regulation was issued March 7, 2008 (73 FR 12263). The preamble to the final regulation appears at ¶ 23,253, and the final regulation appears at ¶ 13,312B.

¶ 20,262B

IRS proposed regulations: Cafeteria plans: Eligibility: Benefit elections: Expense reimbursement.—The IRS has released proposed cafeteria plan regulations that incorporate legislative changes since previous proposed regulations were drafted and clarify prior rules under Code Sec. 125. The regulations also consolidate and withdraw five prior proposed regulations under Code Sec. 125.

The proposed regulations, which were published in the Federal Register on August 6, 2007 (72 FR 43938), are reproduced below. IRS made a correction to the regulations on September 21, 2007 (72 FR 53977).

[4830-01-p]

DEPARTMENT OF THE TREASURY

Internal Revenue Service

26 CFR Part 1

[REG-142695-05]

RIN 1545-BF00

Employee Benefits - Cafeteria Plans

AGENCY: Internal Revenue Service (IRS), Treasury.

ACTION: Withdrawal of prior notices of proposed rulemaking, notice of proposed rulemaking and notice of public hearing.

SUMMARY: This document contains new proposed regulations providing guidance on cafeteria plans. This document also withdraws the notices of proposed rulemaking relating to cafeteria plans under section 125 that were published on May 7, 1984, December 31, 1984, March 7, 1989, November 7, 1997 and March 23, 2000. In general, these proposed regulations would affect employers that sponsor a cafeteria plan, employees that participate in a cafeteria plan, and third-party cafeteria plan administrators.

DATES: Written or electronic comments must be received by November 5, 2007 . Outlines of topics to be discussed at the hearing scheduled for November 15, 2007, at 10 a.m., must be received by October 25, 2007.

ADDRESSES: Send submissions to: CC:PA:LPD:PR (REG-142695-05), room 5203, Internal Revenue Service, P.O. Box 7604, Ben Franklin

Station, Washington, DC 20044. Submissions may be hand delivered Monday through Friday between the hours of 8 a.m. and 4 p.m. to CC:PA:LPD:PR (REG-142695-05), Courier's Desk, Internal Revenue Service, 1111 Constitution Avenue, NW., Washington, DC or sent electronically via the Federal eRulemaking Portal at *www.regulations.gov* (IRS REG-142695-05). The public hearing will be held at the IRS Auditorium, Internal Revenue Building, 1111 Constitution Avenue, NW, Washington, DC.

FOR FURTHER INFORMATION CONTACT: Concerning the proposed regulations, Mireille T. Khoury at (202) 622-6080; concerning submissions of comments, the hearing, and/or to be placed on the building access list to attend the hearing, Oluwafunmilayo Taylor of the Publications and Regulations Branch at (202) 622-7180 (not toll-free numbers).

SUPPLEMENTARY INFORMATION

Paperwork Reduction Act

The collections of information contained in this notice of proposed rulemaking have been submitted to the Office of Management and Budget for review in accordance with the Paperwork Reduction Act of 1995 (44 U.S.C. 3507(d)). Comments on the collections of information should be sent to the **Office of Management and Budget** , Attn: Desk Officer for the Department of Treasury, Office of Information and Regulatory Affairs, Washington, DC 20503, with copies to the **Internal Revenue Service** , Attn: IRS Reports Clearance Officer, SE:W:CAR:MP:T:T:SP, Washington, DC 20224. Comments on the collections of information should be received by October 5, 2007. Comments are specifically requested concerning:

Whether the proposed collections of information is necessary for the proper performance of the functions of the Internal Revenue Service, including whether the information will have practical utility;

The accuracy of the estimated burden associated with the proposed collection of information;

How the quality, utility, and clarity of the information to be collected may be enhanced;

How the burden of complying with the proposed collections of information may be minimized, including through the application of automatic collection techniques or other forms of information technology; and

Estimates of the capital or start-up costs and costs of operation, maintenance, and purchase of service to provide information.

The collection of information in this proposed regulation is in § 1.125-2 (cafeteria plan elections); § 1.125-6(b)-(g) (substantiation of expenses), and § 1.125-7 (cafeteria plan nondiscrimination rules). This information is required to file employment tax returns and Forms W-2. The collection of information is voluntary to obtain a benefit. The likely respondents are Federal, state or local governments, business or other for-profit institutions, nonprofit institutions, and small businesses or organizations.

Estimated total annual reporting burden: 34,000,000 hours.

Estimated average annual burden per respondent: 5 hours.

Estimated annual frequency of responses: once.

An agency may not conduct or sponsor, and a person is not required to respond to, a collection of information unless it displays a valid control number assigned by the Office of Management and Budget.

Books or records relating to a collection of information must be retained as long as their contents may become material in the administration of any internal revenue law. Generally, tax returns and tax return information are confidential, as required by 26 U.S.C. 6103.

Background

This document contains proposed Income Tax Regulations (26 CFR Part 1) under section 125 of the Internal Revenue Code (Code). On May 7, 1984, December 31, 1984, March 7, 1989, November 7, 1997, and March 23, 2000, the IRS and Treasury Department published proposed amendments to 26 CFR Part 1 under section 125 in the **Federal Register** (49 FR 19321, 49 FR 50733, 54 FR 9460, 62 FR 60196 and 65 FR 15587). These 1984, 1989, 1997 and 2000 proposed regulations are hereby withdrawn. Also, the temporary regulations under section 125 that were published on February 4, 1986 in the **Federal Register** (51 FR 4318) are being withdrawn in a separate document. The new proposed regulations that are published in this document replace those proposed regulations.

Explanation of Provisions

Overview

The new proposed regulations are organized as follows: general rules on qualified and nonqualified benefits in cafeteria plans (new proposed § 1.125-1), general rules on elections (new proposed § 1.125-2), general rules on flexible spending arrangements (new proposed § 1.125-5), general rules on substantiation of expenses for qualified benefits (new proposed § 1.125-6) and nondiscrimination rules (new proposed § 1.125-7). The new proposed regulations, new Proposed §§ 1.125-1, 1.125-2, 1.125-5, 1.125-6 and § 1.125-7, consolidate and restate Proposed § 1.125-1 (1984, 1997, 2000), § 1.125-2 (1989, 1997, 2000) and § 1.125-2T (1986). Unless otherwise indicated, references to "new proposed regulations" or "these proposed regulations" mean the proposed section 125 regulations being published in this document.

The new proposed regulations reflect changes in tax law since the prior regulations were proposed, including: the change in the definition of dependent (section 152) and the addition of the following as qualified benefits: adoption assistance (section 137), additional deferred compensation benefits described in section 125(d)(1)(B), (C) and (D), Health Savings Accounts (HSAs) (sections 223, 125(d)(2)(D) and 4980G), and qualified HSA distributions from health FSAs (section 106(e)). Other changes include the prohibition against long-term care insurance and long-term care services (section 125(f)) and the addition of the key employee concentration test in section 125(b)(2).

The prior proposed regulations, §§ 1.125-1 and 1.125-2, provide the basic framework and requirements for cafeteria plans and elections under cafeteria plans. The prior proposed regulations also outlined the most significant rules for benefits under a health flexible spending arrangement (health FSA) offered by a cafeteria plan - the requirement that the maximum reimbursement be available at all times during the coverage period (the uniform coverage rule), the requirement of a 12-month period of coverage, the requirement that the health FSA only reimburse medical expenses, the requirement that all medical expenses be substantiated by a third party before reimbursement, the requirement that expenses be incurred during the period of coverage, and the prohibition against deferral of compensation (including the use-or-lose rule). The prior proposed regulations also provided guidelines for dependent care FSAs, and the application of section 125 to paid vacation days offered under a cafeteria plan. These remain substantially unchanged in the new proposed regulations, with certain clarifications. Finally, the prior proposed regulations included a number of Q & As addressing transitional issues relating to the enactment of section 125, as well as the application of the now-repealed section 89 (special nondiscrimination rules with respect to certain employee benefit plans). These provisions are omitted from the new proposed regulations.

I. *New Proposed § 1.125-1--Qualified and nonqualified benefits in cafeteria plans Section 125 exclusive noninclusion rule*

Section 125 provides that, except in the case of certain discriminatory benefits, no amount shall be included in the gross income of a participant in a cafeteria plan (as defined in section 125(d)) solely because, under the plan, the participant may choose among the benefits of the plan. The new proposed regulations clarify and amplify the general rule in the prior proposed regulations that section 125 is the exclusive means by which an employer can offer employees a choice between taxable and nontaxable benefits without the choice itself resulting in inclusion in gross income by the employees. When employees may elect between taxable and nontaxable benefits, this election results in gross income to employees, unless a specific Internal Revenue Code (Code) section (such as section 125) intervenes to prevent gross income inclusion. Thus, except for an election made through a cafeteria plan that satisfies section 125 or another specific Code section (such as section 132(f)(4)), any opportunity to elect among taxable and nontaxable benefits results in inclusion of the taxable benefit regardless of what benefit is elected and when the election is made. This interpretation of section 125 is consistent with the legislative history of section 125. The legislative history begins with the interim ERISA rules for cafeteria plans:

> Under ... ERISA, an employer contribution made before January 1, 1977, to a cafeteria plan in existence on June 27, 1974, is required to be included in an employees' gross income only to the extent that the employee actually elects taxable benefits. In the case of a plan not in existence on June 27, 1974, the employer contribution is required to be included in an employee's gross income to the extent the employee could have elected taxable benefits. S. Rep. No. 1263, 95\th/ Cong., 2d Sess. 74 (1978), reprinted in 1978 U.S.C.C.A.N. 6837; H. R. Rep. No. 1445, 95\th/ Cong., 2d Sess. 63 (1978); H.R. Conf. Rep. No. 1800, 95\th/ Cong., 2d Sess. 206 (1978).

The legislative history also provides:

[G]enerally, employer contributions under a written cafeteria plan which permits employees to elect between taxable and nontaxable benefits are excluded from the gross income of an employee to the extent that nontaxable benefits are elected. S. Rep. No. 1263, 95\th/ Cong., 2d Sess. 75 (1978), reprinted in 1978 U.S.C.C.A.N. 6838; H. R. Rep. No. 1445, 95\th/ Cong., 2d Sess. 63 (1978). See also H.R. Conf. Rep. No. 1800, 95\th/ Cong., 2d Sess. 206 (1978).

The legislative history to the 1984 amendments to section 125 continues:

The cafeteria plan rules of the Code provide that a participant in a nondiscriminatory cafeteria plan will not be treated as having received a taxable benefit offered under the plan solely because the participant has the opportunity, before the benefit becomes available, to choose among the taxable and nontaxable benefits under the plan. H.R. Conf. Rep. No. 861, 98\th/ Cong., 2d Sess. 1173 (1984), reprinted in 1984 U.S.C.C.A.N. 1861. See also H.R. Conf. Rep. No. 736, 104\th/ Cong., 2d Sess. 295, reprinted in 1996 U.S.C.C.A.N. 2108.

The new proposed regulations provide that unless a plan satisfies the requirements of section 125 and the regulations, the plan is not a cafeteria plan. Reasons that a plan would fail to satisfy the section 125 requirements include: offering nonqualified benefits; not offering an election between at least one permitted taxable benefit and at least one qualified benefit; deferring compensation; failing to comply with the uniform coverage rule or use-or-lose rule; allowing employees to revoke elections or make new elections during a plan year, except as provided in §1.125-4; failing to comply with substantiation requirements; paying or reimbursing expenses incurred for qualified benefits before the effective date of the cafeteria plan or before a period of coverage; allocating experience gains (forfeitures) other than as expressly allowed in the new proposed regulations; and failing to comply with grace period rules.

Definition of a cafeteria plan

The new proposed regulations provide that a cafeteria plan is a separate written plan that complies with the requirements of section 125 and the regulations, that is maintained by an employer for employees and that is operated in compliance with the requirements of section 125 and the regulations. Participants in a cafeteria plan must be permitted to choose among at least one permitted taxable benefit (for example, cash, including salary reduction) and at least one qualified benefit. A plan offering only elections among nontaxable benefits is not a cafeteria plan. Also, a plan offering only elections among taxable benefits is not a cafeteria plan. See Rev. Rul. 2002-27, Situation 2 (2002-1 CB 925), see §601.601(d)(2)(ii)(b). Finally, a cafeteria plan must not provide for deferral of compensation, except as specifically permitted in section 125(d)(2)(B), (C), or (D).

Written plan

Section 125(d)(1) requires that a cafeteria plan be in writing. The cafeteria plan must be operated in accordance with the written plan terms. The new proposed regulations require that the written plan specifically describe all benefits, set forth the rules for eligibility to participate and the procedure for making elections, provide that all elections are irrevocable (except to the extend that the plan includes the optional change in status rules in §1.125-4), and state how employer contributions may be made under the plan (for example, salary reduction or nonelective employer contributions), the maximum amount of elective contributions, and the plan year. If the plan includes a flexible spending arrangement (FSA), the written plan must include provisions complying with the uniform coverage rule and the use-or-lose rule. Because section 125(d)(1)(A) states that a cafeteria plan is a written plan under which "all participants are employees," the new proposed regulations require that the written cafeteria plan specify that only employees may participate in the cafeteria plan. The new proposed regulations also require that all provisions of the written plan apply uniformly to all participants.

Individuals who may participate in a cafeteria plan

All participants in a cafeteria plan must be employees. See section 125(d)(1)(A). These proposed regulations provide that employees include common law employees, leased employees described in section 414(n), and full-time life insurance salesmen (as defined in section 7701(a)(20)). These proposed regulations further provide that former employees (including laid-off employees and retired employees) may participate in a plan, but a plan may not be maintained predominantly for former employees. See Rev. Rul. 82-196 (1982-2 CB 53); Rev. Rul. 85-121 (1985-2 CB 57), see §601.601(d)(2)(ii)(b). All employees who are treated as employed by a single employer under section 414(b), (c)

or (m) are treated as employed by a single employer for purposes of section 125. See section 125(g)(4). A participant's spouse or dependents may receive benefits through a cafeteria plan although they cannot participate in the cafeteria plan.

Self-employed individuals are not treated as employees for purposes of section 125. Accordingly, the new proposed regulations make clear that sole proprietors, partners, and directors of corporations are not employees and may not participate in a cafeteria plan. In addition, the new proposed regulations clarify that 2-percent shareholders of an S corporation are not employees for purposes of section 125. The new proposed regulations provide rules for dual status individuals and individuals moving between employee and non-employee status. A self-employed individual may, however, sponsor a cafeteria plan for his or her employees.

Election between taxable and nontaxable benefits

The new proposed regulations require that a cafeteria plan offer employees an election among only permitted taxable benefits (including cash) and qualified nontaxable benefits. See section 125(d)(1)(B). For purposes of section 125, cash means cash from current compensation (including salary reduction), payment for annual leave, sick leave, or other paid time off, severance pay, property, and certain after-tax employee contributions. Distributions from qualified retirement plans are not cash or taxable benefits for purposes of section 125. See Rev. Rul. 2003-62 (2003-1 CB 1034) (distributions to former employees from a qualified employees' trust, applied to pay health insurance premiums, are includible in former employees' gross income under section 402), see §601.601(d)(2)(ii)(b).

Qualified benefits

In general, in order for a benefit to be a qualified benefit for purposes of section 125, the benefit must be excludible from employees' gross income under a specific provision of the Code and must not defer compensation, except as specifically allowed in section 125(d)(2)(B), (C) or (D). Examples of qualified benefits include the following: group-term life insurance on the life of an employee (section 79); employer-provided accident and health plans, including health flexible spending arrangements, and accidental death and dismemberment policies (sections 106 and 105(b)); a dependent care assistance program (section 129); an adoption assistance program (section 137); contributions to a section 401(k) plan; contributions to certain plans maintained by educational organizations, and contributions to HSAs. Section 125(f), (d)(2)(B), (C), (D). See Notice 97-9 (1997-2 CB 35) (adoption assistance), see §601.601(d)(2)(ii)(b); Notice 2004-2, Q & A-33 (2004-1 CB 269) (HSAs), see §601.601(d)(2)(ii)(b). A cafeteria plan may also offer long-term and short-term disability coverage as a qualified benefit (see section 106). However, see paragraph (q) in §1.125-1 for nonqualified benefits.

Group-term life insurance

An employer may provide group-term life insurance through a combination of methods. Generally, under section 79(a), the cost of $50,000 or less of group-term life insurance on the life of an employee provided under a policy (or policies) carried directly or indirectly by an employer is excludible from the employee's gross income. (Special rules apply to key employees if the group-term life insurance plan does not satisfy the nondiscrimination rules in section 79(d)). However, if the group-term life insurance provided to an employee by an employer or employers exceeds $50,000 (taking into account all coverage provided both through a cafeteria plan and outside a cafeteria plan), the cost of coverage exceeding coverage of $50,000 is includible in the employee's gross income. For this purpose, the cost of group-term life insurance is shown in §1.79-3(d)(2), Table I (Table I). The Table I cost of the excess group-term life insurance (minus all after-tax contributions by the employee for group-term life insurance coverage) is includible in each covered employee's gross income. The new proposed regulations provide that the cost of group-term life insurance on the life of an employee, that either is less than or equal to the amount excludible from gross income under section 79(a) or provides coverage in excess of that amount, but not combined with any permanent benefit, is a qualified benefit that may be offered in a cafeteria plan. The new proposed regulations also provide that the entire amount of salary reduction and employer flex-credits for group-term life insurance coverage on the life of an employee is excludible from an employee's gross income.

The rule in the new proposed regulations differs from Notice 89-110 (1989-2 CB 447), see §601.601(d)(2)(ii)(b). Notice 89-110 provides that an employee includes in gross income the greater of the Table I cost of group-term life insurance coverage exceeding $50,000 or the employee's salary reduction and employer flex-credits for excess group-term life insurance coverage. The new proposed regulations provide instead that the employee includes in gross income the Table I cost of the excess coverage (minus all after-tax contributions by the employee for group-term life insurance coverage) and that the entire amount of salary reduction and employer flex-credits for group-term life insurance coverage on the life of the employee is excludible from the employee's gross income. As noted in this preamble, taxpayers may rely on the new proposed regulations for guidance pending the issuance of final regulations.

Employer-provided accident and health plan

Coverage under an employer-provided accident and health plan that satisfies the requirements of section 105(b) may be provided as a qualified benefit through a cafeteria plan and is excludible from employees' gross income. Section 106; § 1.106-1. The nondiscrimination rules under section 105(h) apply to self-insured medical reimbursement arrangements (including health FSAs).

The new proposed regulations specifically permit a cafeteria plan (but not a health FSA) to pay or reimburse substantiated individual accident and health insurance premiums. See Rev. Rul. 61-146 (1961-2 CB 25), see § 601.601(d)(2)(ii)(b). In addition, a cafeteria plan may provide for payment of COBRA premiums for an employee.

For employer-provided accident and health plans and medical reimbursement plans, the definition of dependents is the definition in section 105(b) as amended by the Working Families Tax Relief Act of 2004 (WFTRA), Public Law 108-311, section 207(9) (118 Stat. 1166) (that is, a dependent as defined in section 152, determined without regard to section 152(b)(1), (b)(2), or (d)(1)(B)). See Notice 2004-79 (2004-2 CB 898), see § 601.601(d)(2)(ii)(b). For purposes of the exclusion from employees' gross income for accident and health plans and for medical reimbursement under sections 105(b) and 106, the spouse or dependent of a former employee (including a retired employee or a laid-off employee) or of a deceased employee is treated as a spouse or dependent. See Rev. Rul. 82-196 (1982-2 CB 53); Rev. Rul. 85-121 (1985-2 CB 57), see § 601.601(d)(2)(ii)(b).

Dependent care assistance programs and adoption assistance programs

If the requirements of section 129 are satisfied, up to $5,000 of employer-provided assistance for amounts paid or incurred by employees for dependent care is excludible from employees' gross income. The new proposed regulations outline the general requirements for providing dependent care assistance programs and adoption assistance programs under section 137 through a cafeteria plan. See Notice 97-9, section II (1997-2 CB 35), see § 601.601(d)(2)(ii)(b).

Cafeteria plan year

The new proposed regulations require that a cafeteria plan year must be 12 consecutive months and must be set out in the written cafeteria plan. A short plan year (or a change in plan year resulting in a short plan year) is permitted only for a valid business purpose. A change in plan year resulting in a short plan year, for other than a valid business purpose, is disregarded. If a principal purpose of a change in plan year is to circumvent the rules of section 125, the change in plan year is ineffective.

No deferral of compensation

Qualified benefits must be current benefits. In general, a cafeteria plan may not offer benefits that defer compensation or operate to defer compensation. Section 125(d)(2)(A). In general, benefits may not be carried over to a later plan year or used in one plan year to purchase benefits to be provided in a later plan year. For example, life insurance with a cash value build-up or group-term life insurance with a permanent benefit (within the meaning of § 1.79-0) defers the receipt of compensation and thus is not a qualified benefit.

The new proposed regulations clarify whether certain benefits and plan administration practices defer compensation. For example, the regulations permit an accident and health insurance policy to provide certain benefit features that apply for more than one plan year, such as reasonable lifetime limits on benefits, level premiums, premium waiver during disability, guaranteed renewability of coverage, coverage for specified accidental injury or specific diseases, and the payment of a fixed amount per day for hospitalization. But these insurance policies must not provide an investment fund or cash value to pay premiums, and no part of the premium may be held in a separate account for any beneficiary. The new proposed regulations also provide that the following benefits and practices do not defer compensation: a long-term disability policy paying benefits over more than one plan year; reasonable premium rebates or policy dividends; certain two-year lock-in vision

and dental policies; certain advance payments for orthodontia; salary reduction contributions in the last month of a plan year used to pay accident and health insurance premiums for the first month of the following plan year; reimbursement of section 213(d) expenses for durable medical equipment; and allocation of experience gains (forfeitures) among participants.

Paid time off

Under the prior proposed regulations, permitted taxable benefits included various forms of paid leave. Since the prior proposed regulations were issued, many employers have recharacterized and combined vacation days, sick leave and personal days into a single category of "paid time off." The new proposed regulations use the term "paid time off" to refer to vacation days and other types of paid leave. The new proposed regulations contain the same ordering rule for elective and nonelective paid time off as set forth in Prop. § 1.125-1, Q & A-7 (1984). A plan offering an election solely between paid time off and taxable benefits is not a cafeteria plan.

Grace period

The new proposed regulations allow a written cafeteria plan to provide an optional grace period immediately following the end of each plan year, extending the period for incurring expenses for qualified benefits. A grace period may apply to one or more qualified benefits (for example, health FSA or dependent care assistance program) but in no event does it apply to paid time off or contributions to section 401(k) plans. Unused benefits or contributions for one qualified benefit may only be used to reimburse expenses incurred during the grace period for that same qualified benefit. The amount of unused benefits and contributions available during the grace period may be limited by the employer. A grace period may extend to the fifteenth day of the third month after the end of the plan year (but may be for a shorter period). Benefits or contributions not used as of the end of the grace period are forfeited under the use-or-lose rule. The grace period applies to all employees who are participants (including through COBRA), as of the last day of the plan year. Grace period rules must apply uniformly to all participants. The grace period rules in these proposed regulations are based on Notice 2005-42 (2005-1 CB 1204), modified in Notice 2007-22 (2007-10 IRB 670), see § 601.601(d)(2)(ii)(b), amplified in Notice 2005-86 (2005-2 CB 1075), amplified in Notice 2007-22 (2007-10 IRB 670), see § 601.601(d)(2)(ii)(b). For eligibility to contribute to a Health Savings Account (HSA) during a grace period, see Notice 2005-86 (2005-2 CB 1075), see § 601.601(d)(2)(ii)(b). For Form W-2 reporting for unused dependent care assistance used for expenses incurred during a grace period, see Notice 2005-61 (2005-2 CB 607), see § 601.601(d)(2)(ii)(b).

Contributions to section 401(k) plans through a cafeteria plan

A cafeteria plan may include contributions to a section 401(k) plan. Section 125(d)(2)(B). The new proposed regulations clarify the interactions between section 125 and section 401(k). Contributions to a section 401(k) plan expressed as a percentage of compensation are permitted. Pursuant to § 1.401(k)-1(a)(3)(ii), elective contributions to a section 401(k) plan may be made through automatic enrollment (that is, when the employee does not affirmatively elect cash, the employee's compensation is reduced by a fixed percentage, which is contributed to a section 401(k) plan).

Nonqualified benefits

A cafeteria plan must not offer any of the following benefits: scholarships (section 117); employer-provided meals and lodging (section 119); educational assistance (section 127); fringe benefits (section 132); long-term care insurance. See section 125(f). Long-term care services are nonqualified benefits, H.R. Conf. Rep. No. 736, 104\th/ Cong., 2d Sess. 296, reprinted in 1996 U.S.C.C.A.N. 2109. (An HSA funded through a cafeteria plan may, however, be used to pay premiums for long-term care insurance or for long-term care services.) The new proposed regulations clarify that contributions to Archer Medical Savings Accounts (sections 220, 106(b)), group term life insurance for an employee's spouse, child or dependent, and elective deferrals to section 403(b) plans are also nonqualified benefits. A plan offering any nonqualified benefit is not a cafeteria plan. A cafeteria plan may not offer a health FSA that provides for the carryover of unused benefits. See Notice 2002-45, Part I (2002-2 CB 93); Rev. Rul. 2002-41 (2002-2 CB 75), see § 601.601(d)(2)(ii)(b). [Corrected on 9/21/07 (72 FR 53977).]

After-tax employee contributions

The new proposed regulations allow a cafeteria plan to offer after-tax employee contributions for qualified benefits or paid time off. A cafeteria plan may only offer the taxable benefits specifically permitted in the new proposed regulations. Nonqualified benefits may not be offered through a cafeteria plan, even if paid with after-tax employee contributions.

Employer contributions through salary reduction

Employees electing a qualified benefit through salary reduction are electing to forego salary and instead to receive a benefit which is excludible from gross income because it is provided by employer contributions. Section 125 provides that the employee is treated as receiving the qualified benefit from the employer in lieu of the taxable benefit. A cafeteria plan may also impose reasonable fees to administer the cafeteria plan which may be paid through salary reduction. A cafeteria plan is not required to allow employees to pay for any qualified benefit with after-tax employee contributions.

II. *New Prop. § 1.125-2 - Elections in cafeteria plans*

Making, revoking and changing elections

Generally, a cafeteria plan must require employees to elect annually between taxable benefits and qualified benefits. Elections must be made before the earlier of the first day of the period of coverage or when benefits are first currently available. The determination of whether a taxable benefit is currently available does not depend on whether it has been constructively received by the employee for purposes of section 451. Annual elections generally must be irrevocable and may not be changed during the plan year. However, § 1.125-4 permits a cafeteria plan to provide for changes in elections based on certain changes in status. An employer that wishes to permit such changes in elections must incorporate the rules in § 1.125-4 in its written cafeteria plan. These proposed regulations omit the rule in Q & A-6(b) in Prop. § 1.125-2 (1989) (cessation of required contributions), because the change in status rules in § 1.125-4 superseded this provision of the 1989 proposed regulations.

If HSA contributions are made through salary reduction under a cafeteria plan, employees may prospectively elect, revoke or change salary reduction elections for HSA contributions at any time during the plan year with respect to salary that has not become currently available at the time of the election.

A cafeteria plan is permitted to include an automatic election for new employees or current employees. Rev. Rul. 2002-27 (2002-1 CB 925), see § 601.601(d)(2)(ii)(b). A new rule also permits a cafeteria plan to provide an optional election for new employees between cash and qualified benefits. New employees avoid gross income inclusion if they make an election within 30 days after the date of hire even if benefits provided pursuant to the election relate back to the date of hire. However, salary reduction amounts used to pay for such an election must be from compensation not yet currently available on the date of the election. Also, this special election rule for new employees does not apply to any employee who terminates employment and is rehired within 30 days after terminating employment (or who returns to employment following an unpaid leave of absence of less than 30 days).

New elections and revocations or changes in elections can be made electronically. The safe harbor for electronic elections in § 1.401(a)-21 is available. Only an employee can make an election or revoke or change his or her election. An employee's spouse or dependent may not make an election under a cafeteria plan and may not revoke or change an employee's election.

III. *New Prop. § 1.125-5-Flexible spending arrangements*

Overview

In general, a flexible spending arrangement (FSA) is a benefit designed to reimburse employees for expenses incurred for certain qualified benefits, up to a maximum amount not substantially in excess of the salary reduction and employer flex-credits allocated for the benefit. The maximum amount of reimbursement reasonably available must be less than five times the value of the coverage. Employer flex-credits are non-elective employer contributions that an employer makes available for every employee eligible to participate in the cafeteria plan, to be used at the employee's election only for one or more qualified benefits (but not as cash or other taxable benefits). The three types of FSAs are dependent care assistance, adoption assistance and medical care reimbursements (health FSA).

Uniform coverage rule

The new proposed regulations retain the rule that the maximum amount of reimbursement from a health FSA must be available at all times during the period of coverage (properly reduced as of any particular time for prior reimbursements). The uniform coverage rule does not apply to FSAs for dependent care assistance or adoption assistance.

Use-or-lose rule

An FSA must satisfy all the requirements of section 125, including the prohibition against deferring compensation. In general, as discussed under "No deferral of compensation", in order to satisfy this requirement of section 125, all benefits and contributions must be used by the end of the plan year (or grace period, if applicable), or are forfeited. The new proposed regulations continue the use-or-lose rule.

Period of coverage

The required period of coverage for all FSAs continues to be twelve months, with an exception for short plan years that satisfy the conditions in the new proposed regulations. The period of coverage and the plan year need not be the same. The beginning and end of a period of coverage is clarified. The new proposed regulations also clarify that FSAs for different qualified benefits need not have the same coverage period. See also "Grace period", discussed in this preamble. The new proposed regulations also continue to provide that expenses are incurred when services are provided. Expenses incurred before or after the period of coverage may not be reimbursed.

Health FSA

A health FSA may only reimburse certain substantiated section 213(d) medical care expenses incurred by the employee, or by the employee's spouse or dependents. A health FSA may be limited to a subset of permitted section 213(d) medical expenses (for example, a health FSA is permitted to exclude reimbursement of over-the-counter drugs described in Rev. Rul. 2003-102 (2003-2 CB 559), see § 601.601(d)(2)(ii)(b)). Similarly, a health FSA may be an HSA-compatible limited-purpose health FSA or post-deductible health FSA. Rev. Rul. 2004-45 (2004-1 CB 971), see § 601.601(d)(2)(ii)(b), amplified, Notice 2005-86 (2005-2 CB 1075). A health FSA may not reimburse premiums for accident and health insurance or long-term care insurance. See section 125(f).

A health FSA must satisfy all requirements of section 105(b), §§ 1.105-1 and 1.105-2. The section 105(h) nondiscrimination rules apply to health FSAs. All medical expenses must be substantiated before expenses are reimbursed. See *Incurring and reimbursing expenses for qualified* benefits, discussed in this preamble. The new proposed regulations also clarify when medical expenses are incurred.[1] A cafeteria plan may limit enrollment in a health FSA to those employees who participate in the employer's accident and health plan.

Qualified HSA distributions

Section 106(e), enacted in section 302 of the Health Opportunity Patient Empowerment Act of 2006, Public Law 109-432 (120 Stat. 2922 (2006)) allows "qualified HSA distributions" from health FSAs to HSAs. Section 106(e) applies to distributions between December 20, 2006 and December 31, 2011. The proposed regulations incorporate the rules on qualified HSA distributions set forth in Notice 2007-22 (2007-10 IRB 670). See § 601.601(d)(2)(ii)(b).

Dependent care assistance after termination

A new optional rule permits an employer to reimburse a terminated employee's qualified dependent care expenses incurred after termination through a dependent care FSA, if all section 129 requirements are otherwise satisfied.

Experience gains

If an employee fails to use all contributions and benefits for a plan year before the end of the plan year (and the grace period, if applicable), those unused contributions and benefits are forfeited under the use-or-lose rule. Unused amounts are also known as experience gains. The new proposed regulations retain the forfeiture allocation rules in the 1989 proposed regulations, and clarify that the employer sponsoring the cafeteria plan may retain forfeitures, use forfeitures to defray

---

[1] See Rev. Rul. 2005-55 (2005-2 CB 284) and Rev. Rul. 2005-24 (2005-1 CB 892), see § 601.601(d)(2)(ii)(b) (section 105(b) exclusion only applicable to reimbursements for medical expenses incurred by employee, or by the employee's spouse or dependents); Rev. Rul. 2003-3 (2002-1 CB 316) (purported reimbursements to employees of health insurance premiums not paid by employees and therefore impermissible); Rev. Rul. 2002-80 (2002-2 CB 925), see § 601.601(d)(2)(ii)(b) (so-called advance reimbursements and purported loans are impermissible); Rev. Rul. 2003-43 (2003-1 CB 935), see § 601.601(d)(2)(ii)(b); Notice 2006-69 (2006-31 IRB 107) (substantiation requirements for debit cards), amplified in Notice 2007-2 (2007-2 IRB 254), see § 601.601(d)(2)(ii)(b).

expenses of administering the plan or allocate forfeitures among employees contributing through salary reduction on a reasonable and uniform basis.

FSA Administrative rules

Salary reduction contributions may be made at whatever interval the employer selects, including ratably over the plan year based on the employer's payroll periods or in equal installments at other regular intervals (for example, quarterly installments). These rules must apply uniformly to all participants.

IV. New Prop. § 1.125-6-Substantiation of expenses for all cafeteria plans Incurring and reimbursing expenses for qualified benefits

The new proposed regulations provide that only expenses for qualified benefits incurred after the later of the effective date or the adoption date of the cafeteria plan are permitted to be reimbursed under the cafeteria plan. Similarly, if a plan amendment adds a new qualified benefit, only expenses incurred after the later of the effective date or the adoption date are eligible for reimbursement.[2] This rule applies to all qualified benefits. Similarly, a cafeteria plan may pay or reimburse only expenses for qualified benefits incurred during a participant's period of coverage.

Substantiation and reimbursement of expenses for qualified benefits

The new proposed regulations provide, after an employee incurs an expense for a qualified benefit during the coverage period, the expense must first be substantiated before the expense may be paid or reimbursed. All expenses must be substantiated (substantiating only a limited number of total claims, or not substantiating claims below a certain dollar amount does not satisfy the requirements in the new proposed regulations). See § 1.105-2; Rul. 2003-80; Rev. Rul. 2003-43 (2002-1 CB 935), see § 601.601(d)(2)(ii)(b); Notice 2006-69 (2006-31 IRB 107), Notice 2007-2 (2007-2 IRB 254). FSAs for dependent care assistance and adoption assistance must follow the substantiation procedures applicable to health FSAs.

Debit cards

The new proposed regulations incorporate previously issued guidance on substantiating, paying and reimbursing expenses for section 213(d) medical care incurred at a medical care provider when payment is made with a debit card. Rev. Rul. 2003-43 (2003-1 CB 935), amplified, Notice 2006-69 (2006-31 IRB 107), Notice 2007-2 (2007-2 IRB 254); Rev. Proc. 98-25 (1998-1 CB 689), see § 601.601(d)(2)(ii)(b). Among the permissible substantiation methods are copayment matches, recurring expenses, and real-time substantiation. The new proposed regulations also allow point-of-sale substantiation through matching inventory information with a list of section 213(d) medical expenses. The employer is responsible for ensuring that the inventory information approval system complies with the new regulations and with the recordkeeping requirements in section 6001. Rev. Rul. 2003-43 (2003-1 CB 935), amplified, Notice 2006-69 (2006-31 IRB 107), Notice 2007-2 (2007-2 IRB 254); Rev. Proc. 98-25 (1998-1 CB 689), see § 601.601(d)(2)(ii)(b). The new proposed regulations also provide rules under which an FSA may pay or reimburse dependent care expenses using debit cards.

Pursuant to prior guidance (in Notice 2006-69 (2006-31 IRB 107), amplified, Notice 2007-2 (2007-2 IRB 254)), for plan years beginning after December 31, 2006, the recordkeeping requirements described in paragraph (f) in § 1.125-6 apply (that is, responsibility of employers relying on the inventory information approval system for health FSA debit cards to ensure that the system complies with the new proposed recordkeeping requirements, including Rev. Proc. 98-25 (1998-1 CB 689), Notice 2006-69 (2006-31 IRB 107), amplified, Notice 2007-2 (2007-2 IRB 254). For health FSA debit card transactions occurring on or before December 31, 2007, all supermarkets, grocery stores, discount stores and wholesale clubs that do not have a medical care merchant category code (as described in Rev. Rul. 2003-43 (2003-2 CB 935) are nevertheless deemed to be an "other medical provider" as described in Rev. Rul. 2003-43. (For a list of merchant category codes, see Rev. Proc. 2004-43 (2004-2 CB 124).) During this time period, mail-order vendors and web-based vendors that sell prescription drugs are also deemed to be an "other medical provider" as described in Rev. Rul. 2003-43. After December 31, 2008, health FSA debit cards may not be used at stores with the Drug Stores and Pharmacies merchant category code unless (1) the store participates in the inventory information

approval system described in Notice 2006-69, or (2) on a store location by store location basis, 90 percent of the store's gross receipts during the prior taxable year consisted of items which qualify as expenses for medical care under section 213(d) (including nonprescription medications described in Rev. Rul. 2003-102 (2003-2 CB 559)). Notice 2006-69 (2006-31 IRB 107), amplified, Notice 2007-2 (2007-2 IRB 254).

V. New Prop. § 1.125-7-Nondiscrimination rules

Discriminatory benefits provided to highly compensated participants and individuals and key employees are included in these employees' gross income. See section 125(b), (c). The new proposed regulations reflect changes in tax law since Prop. § 1.125-1, Q & A-9 through 13 and 19 were proposed in 1984, including the key employee concentration test, statutory nontaxable benefits (enacted in the Deficit Reduction Act of 1984 (DEFRA), Public Law 98-369, section 531(b), (98 Stat. 881(1984)), and the change in definition of dependent in WFTRA.

The new proposed regulations provide additional guidance on the cafeteria plan nondiscrimination rules, including definitions of key terms, guidance on the eligibility test and the contributions and benefits tests, descriptions of employees allowed to be excluded from testing and a safe harbor nondiscrimination test for premium-only-plans.

Specifically, the new proposed regulations define several key terms, including highly compensated individual or participant (consistent with the section 414(q) definition of highly compensated employee), officer, five percent shareholder, key employee and compensation. The new proposed regulations also provide guidance on the nondiscrimination as to eligibility requirement by incorporating some of the rules under section 410(b) (specifically the rules under § 1.410(b)-4(b) and (c) dealing with reasonable classification, the safe harbor percentage test and the unsafe harbor percentage component of the facts and circumstances test).

The new proposed regulations also provide additional guidance on the contributions and benefits test and, unlike the prior proposed regulations, the new proposed regulations provide an objective test to determine when the actual election of benefits is discriminatory. Specifically, the new proposed regulations provide that a cafeteria plan must give each similarly situated participant a uniform opportunity to elect qualified benefits, and that highly compensated participants must not actually disproportionately elect qualified benefits. Finally, the new rules provide guidance on the safe harbor for cafeteria plans providing health benefits and create a safe harbor for premium-only-plans that satisfy certain requirements.

The example in Prop. § 1.125-1, Q & A-11 (1984) is deleted because it concerns a qualified legal services plan, which is no longer a qualified benefit.

Other issues

These proposed regulations provide guidance under section 125 (26 U.S.C. 125). Other statutes may impose additional requirements (for example, the Employee Retirement Income Security Act of 1974 (ERISA) (29 U.S.C. 1000), the Health Insurance Portability and Accountability Act of 1996 (HIPAA), (sections 9801-9803); and the continuation coverage requirements under the Consolidated Omnibus Budget Reconciliation Act of 1985 (COBRA) (section 4980B).

Proposed Effective Date

With the exceptions noted in the "Effect on other documents" section of this preamble and under the "Debit cards" section of the preamble, it is proposed that these regulations apply for plan years beginning on or after January 1, 2009. Taxpayers may rely on these regulations for guidance pending the issuance of final regulations. Prior published guidance on qualified benefits under sections 79, 105, 106, 129, 137 and 223 that is affected by these proposed regulations remains applicable through the effective date of the final regulations (except as modified in "Effect on other documents" section of this preamble).

Effect on Other Documents

Notice 89-110 (1989-2 CB 447), see § 601.601(d)(2)(ii)(b), states that where group-term life insurance provided to an employee by an employer exceeds $50,000, the employee includes in gross income the greater of the cost of group-term life insurance shown in § 1.79-3(d)(2), Table I (Table I) on the excess coverage or the employee's salary reduction and employer flex-credits for excess coverage. Notice 89-110

---

[2] See *American Family Mut. Ins. Co. v. United States*, 815 F. Supp. 1206 (W.D. Wis. 1992); *Wollenberg v. United States*, 75 F. Supp.2d 1032 (D. Neb. 1999); Rev. Rul. 2002-58 (2002-2 CB 541), see § 601.601(d)(2)(ii)(b); Notice 97-9, section II (adoption assistance)

is modified, effective as of the date the proposed regulations are published in the **Federal Register**.

Published guidance under § 105(b) states that if any person has the right to receive cash or any other taxable or nontaxable benefit under a health FSA other than the reimbursement of section 213(d) medical expenses of the employee, employee's spouse or employee's dependents, then all distributions made from the arrangement are included in the employee's gross income, even amounts paid to reimburse medical care. See Rev. Rul. 2006-36 (2006-36 IRB 353); Rev. Rul. 2005-24 (2005-1 CB 892); Rev. Rul. 2003-102 (2003-2 CB 559); Notice 2002-45 (2002-2 CB 93); Rev. Rul. 2002-41 (2002-2 CB 75); Rev. Rul. 69-141 (1969-1 CB 48). New section 106(e) provides that a health FSA will not fail to satisfy the requirements of sections 105 or 106 merely because the plan provides for a qualified HSA distribution. Amounts rolled into an HSA may be used for purposes other than reimbursing the section 213(d) medical expenses of the employee, spouse or dependents. Accordingly, Rev. Rul. 2006-36, Rev. Rul. 2005-24, Rev. Rul. 2003-102, Notice 2002-45, Rev. Rul. 2002-41, and Rev. Rul. 69-141 are modified with respect to qualified HSA distributions described in section 106(e). See Notice 2007-22 (2007-10 IRB 670), see § 601.601(d)(2)(ii)(*b*).

Special Analyses

It has been determined that this notice of proposed rulemaking is not a significant regulatory action as defined in Executive Order 12866. Therefore, a regulatory assessment is not required. It also has been determined that section 553(b) of the Administrative Procedure Act (5 U.S.C. chapter 5) does not apply to this regulation. It is hereby certified that the collection of information in this regulation will not have a significant economic impact on a substantial number of small entities. This certification is based on the fact that the regulations will only minimally increase the burdens on small entities. The requirements under these regulations relating to maintaining a section 125 cafeteria plan are a minimal additional burden independent of the burdens encompassed under existing rules for underlying employee benefit plans, which exist whether or not the benefits are provided through a cafeteria plan. In addition, most small entities that will maintain cafeteria plans already use a third-party plan administrator to administer the cafeteria plan. The collection of information required in these regulations, which is required to comply with the existing substantiation requirements of sections 105, 106, 129 and 125, and the recordkeeping requirements of section 6001, will only minimally increase the third-party administrator's burden with respect to the cafeteria plan. Therefore, an analysis under the Regulatory Flexibility Act (5 U.S.C. chapter 6) is not required. Pursuant to section 7805(f) of the Internal Revenue Code, this proposed regulation has been submitted to the Chief Counsel for Advocacy of the Small Business Administration for comment on its impact on small business.

Comments and Public Hearing

Before these proposed regulations are adopted as final regulations, consideration will be given to any written comments (a signed original and eight (8) copies) or electronic comments that are submitted timely to the IRS. The IRS and Treasury Department specifically request comments on the clarity of the proposed rules and how they can be made easier to understand. In addition, comments are requested on the following issues:

1. Whether, consistent with section 125 of the Internal Revenue Code, multiple employers (other than members of a controlled group described in section 125(g)(4)) may sponsor a single cafeteria plan;

2. Whether salary reduction contributions may be based on employees' tips and how that would work;

3. For cafeteria plans adopting the change in status rules in § 1.125-4, when a participant has a change in status and changes his or her salary reduction amount, how should the participant's uniform coverage amount be computed after the change in status.

All comments will be available for public inspection and copying.

A public hearing has been scheduled for November 15, 2007, beginning at 10 a.m. in the Auditorium, Internal Revenue Service, 1111 Constitution Avenue, NW., Washington, DC. Due to building security procedures, visitors must enter at the Constitution Avenue entrance. In addition, all visitors must present photo identification to enter the building. Because of access restrictions, visitors will not be admitted beyond the immediate entrance area more than 30 minutes before the hearing starts. For information about having your name placed on the building access list to attend the hearing, see the "FOR FURTHER INFORMATION CONTACT" section of this preamble.

The rules of 26 CFR 601.601(a)(3) apply to the hearing. Persons who wish to present oral comments at the hearing must submit written or electronic comments and an outline of the topics to be discussed and the amount of time to be devoted to each topic (a signed original and eight (8) copies) by October 25, 2007. A period of 10 minutes will be allotted to each person for making comments. An agenda showing the scheduling of the speakers will be prepared after the deadline for receiving outlines has passed. Copies of the agenda will be available free of charge at the hearing.

Drafting Information

The principal author of these proposed regulations is Mireille T. Khoury, Office of Division Counsel/Associate Chief Counsel (Tax Exempt and Government Entities), Internal Revenue Service. However, personnel from other offices of the IRS and Treasury Department participated in their development.

List of Subjects in 26 CFR Part 1

Income taxes, reporting and recordkeeping requirements.

Withdrawal of Proposed Regulations

Accordingly, under the authority of 26 U.S.C. 7805, the notice of proposed rulemaking (EE-16-79) that was published in the **Federal Register** on Monday, May 7, 1984 (49 FR 19321), and Monday, December 31, 1984 (49 FR 50733), the notice of proposed rulemaking (EE-130-86) that was published in the **Federal Register** on Tuesday, March 7, 1989 (54 FR 9460), and Friday, November 7, 1997 (62 FR 60196) and the notice of proposed rulemaking (REG-117162-99) that was published in the **Federal Register** on Thursday, March 23, 2000 (65 FR 15587) are withdrawn.

Proposed Amendment to the Regulations

Accordingly, 26 CFR Part 1 is proposed to be amended as follows:

PART 1—INCOME TAXES

Paragraph 1. The authority citation for part 1 continues to read, in part, as follows:

Authority: 26 U.S.C. 7805 * * *

Par. 2. Sections 1.125-0, 1.125-1 and 1.125-2 are added to read as follows:

§ 1.125-0 Table of contents.

This section lists captions contained in §§ 1.125-1, 1.125-2, 1.125-5, 1.125-6 and § 1.125-7.

§ 1.125-1 Cafeteria plans; general rules.

(a) Definitions.

(b) General rules.

(c) Written plan requirements.

(d) Plan year requirements.

(e) Grace period.

(f) Run-out period.

(g) Employee for purpose of Section 125.

(h) After-tax employee contributions.

(i) Prohibited taxable benefits.

(j) Coordination with other rules.

(k) Group-term life insurance.

(l) COBRA premiums.

(m) Payment or reimbursement of employees' individual accident and health insurance premiums.

(n) Section 105 rules for accident and health plan offered through a cafeteria plan.

(o) Prohibition against deferred compensation.

(p) Benefits relating to more than one year.

(q) Nonqualified benefits.

(r) Employer contributions to a cafeteria plan.

(s) Effective/applicability date.

§ 1.125-2 Cafeteria plans; elections.

(a) Rules relating to making elections and revoking elections.

(b) Automatic elections.

(c) Election rules for salary reduction contributions to HSAs.

(d) Optional election for new employees.

(e) Effective/applicability date.

§ 1.125-5 Flexible spending arrangements.

(a) Definition of flexible spending arrangement.

(b) Flex-credits allowed.

(c) Use-or-lose rule.

(d) Uniform coverage rules applicable to health FSAs.

(e) Required period of coverage for a health FSA, dependent care FSA and adoption assistance FSA.

(f) Coverage on a month-by-month or expense-by-expense basis prohibited.

(g) FSA administrative practices.

(h) Qualified benefits permitted to be offered through a FSA.

(i) Section 129 rules for dependent care assistance program offered through a cafeteria plan.

(j) Section 137 rules for adoption assistance program offered through a cafeteria plan.

(k) FSAs and the rules governing the tax-favored treatment of employer-provided health benefits.

(l) Section 105(h) requirements.

(m) HSA-compatible FSAs- limited-purpose health FSAs and post-deductible health FSAs.

(n) Qualified HSA distributions.

(o) FSA experience gains or forfeitures.

(p) Effective/applicability date.

§ 1.125-6 Substantiation of expenses for all cafeteria plans.

(a) Cafeteria plan payments and reimbursements.

(b) Rules for claims substantiation for cafeteria plans.

(c) Debit cards - overview.

(d) Mandatory rules for all debit cards usable to pay or reimburse medical expenses.

(e) Substantiation of expenses incurred at medical care providers and certain other stores with Drug Stores and Pharmacies merchant category code.

(f) Inventory information approval system.

(g) Debit cards used to pay or reimburse dependent care assistance.

(h) Effective/applicability date.

§ 1.125-7 Cafeteria plan nondiscrimination rules.

(a) Definitions.

(b) Nondiscrimination as to eligibility.

(c) Nondiscrimination as to contributions and benefits.

(d) Key employees.

(e) Section 125(g)(2) safe harbor for cafeteria plans providing health benefits.

(f) Safe harbor test for premium-only-plans.

(g) Permissive disaggregation for nondiscrimination testing.

(h) Optional aggregation of plans for nondiscrimination testing.

(i) Employees of certain controlled groups.

(j) Time to perform nondiscrimination testing.

(k) Discrimination in actual operation prohibited.

(l) Anti-abuse rule.

(m) Tax treatment of benefits in a cafeteria plan.

(n) Employer contributions to employees' Health Savings Accounts.

(o) Effective/applicability date.

§ 1.125-1 Cafeteria plans; general rules.

(a) *Definitions.* The definitions set forth in this paragraph (a) apply for purposes of section 125 and the regulations.

(1) The term *cafeteria plan* means a separate written plan that complies with the requirements of section 125 and the regulations, that is maintained by an employer for the benefit of its employees and that is operated in compliance with the requirements of section 125 and the regulations. All participants in a cafeteria plan must be employees. A cafeteria plan must offer at least one permitted taxable benefit (as defined in paragraph (a)(2) of this section) and at least one qualified benefit (as defined in paragraph (a)(3) of this section). A cafeteria plan must not provide for deferral of compensation (except as specifically permitted in paragraph (o) of this section).

(2) The term *permitted taxable benefit* means cash and certain other taxable benefits treated as cash for purposes of section 125. For purposes of section 125, *cash* means cash compensation (including salary reduction), payments for annual leave, sick leave, or other paid time off and severance pay. A distribution from a trust described in section 401(a) is not cash for purposes of section 125. *Other taxable benefits treated as cash* for purposes of section 125 are:

(i) Property;

(ii) Benefits attributable to employer contributions that are currently taxable to the employee upon receipt by the employee; and

(iii) Benefits purchased with after-tax employee contributions, as described in paragraph (h) of this section.

(3) *Qualified benefit.* Except as otherwise provided in section 125(f) and paragraph (q) of this section, the term *qualified benefit* means any benefit attributable to employer contributions to the extent that such benefit is not currently taxable to the employee by reason of an express provision of the Internal Revenue Code (Code) and which does not defer compensation (except as provided in paragraph (o) of this section). The following benefits are qualified benefits that may be offered under a cafeteria plan and are excludible from employees' gross income when provided in accordance with the applicable provisions of the Code—

(A) Group-term life insurance on the life of an employee in an amount that is less than or equal to the $50,000 excludible from gross income under section 79(a), but not combined with any permanent benefit within the meaning of § 1.79-0;

(B) An accident and health plan excludible from gross income under section 105 or 106, including self-insured medical reimbursement plans (such as health FSAs described in § 1.125-5);

(C) Premiums for COBRA continuation coverage (if excludible under section 106) under the accident and health plan of the employer sponsoring the cafeteria plan or premiums for COBRA continuation coverage of an employee of the employer sponsoring the cafeteria plan under an accident and health plan sponsored by a different employer;

(D) An accidental death and dismemberment insurance policy (section 106);

(E) Long-term or short-term disability coverage (section 106);

(F) Dependent care assistance program (section 129);

(G) Adoption assistance (section 137);

(H) A qualified cash or deferred arrangement that is part of a profit-sharing plan or stock bonus plan, as described in paragraph (o)(3) of this section (section 401(k));

(I) Certain plans maintained by educational organizations (section 125(d)(2)(C) and paragraph (o)(3)(iii) of this section); and

(J) Contributions to Health Savings Accounts (HSAs) (sections 223 and 125(d)(2)(D)).

(4) *Dependent.* The term *dependent* generally means a dependent as defined in section 152. However, the definition of dependent is modified to conform with the underlying Code section for the qualified benefit. For example, for purposes of a benefit under section 105, the term dependent means a dependent as defined in section 152, determined without regard to section 152(b)(1), (b)(2) or (d)(1)(B).

(5) *Premium-only-plan.* A *premium-only-plan* is a cafeteria plan that offers as its sole benefit an election between cash (for example, salary) and payment of the employee share of the employer-provided accident and health insurance premium (excludible from the employee's gross income under section 106).

(b) *General rules* —(1) *Cafeteria plans.* Section 125 is the exclusive means by which an employer can offer employees an election between taxable and nontaxable benefits without the election itself resulting in inclusion in gross income by the employees. Section 125 provides that cash (including certain taxable benefits) offered to an employee through a nondiscriminatory cafeteria plan is not includible in the employee's gross income merely because the employee has the opportunity to choose among cash and qualified benefits (within the meaning of section 125(e)) through the cafeteria plan. Section 125(a), (d)(1). However, if a plan offering an employee an election between taxable benefits (including cash) and nontaxable qualified benefits does not meet the section 125 requirements, the election between taxable and nontaxable benefits results in gross income to the employee, regardless of what benefit is elected and when the election is made. An employee who has an election among nontaxable benefits and taxable benefits (including cash) that is not through a cafeteria plan that satisfies section 125 must include in gross income the value of the taxable benefit with the greatest value that the employee could have elected to receive, even if the employee elects to receive only the nontaxable benefits offered. The amount of the taxable benefit is includible in the employee's income in the year in which the employee would have actually received the taxable benefit if the employee had elected such benefit. This is the result even if the employee's election between the nontaxable benefits and taxable benefits is made prior to the year in which the employee would actually have received the taxable benefits. See paragraph (q) in § 1.125-1 for nonqualified benefits.

(2) *Nondiscrimination rules for qualified benefits.* Accident and health plan coverage, group-term life insurance coverage, and benefits under a dependent care assistance program or adoption assistance program do not fail to be qualified benefits under a cafeteria plan merely because they are includible in gross income because of applicable nondiscrimination requirements (for example, sections 79(d), 105(h),129(d), 137(c)(2)). See also §§ 1.105-11(k) and 1.125-7.

(3) *Examples.* The following examples illustrate the rules of paragraph (b)(1) of this section.

Example 1. Distributions from qualified pension plan used for health insurance premiums. (i) Employer A maintains a qualified section 401(a) retirement plan for employees. Employer A also provides accident and health insurance (as described in section 106) for employees and former employees, their spouses and dependents. The health insurance premiums are partially paid through a cafeteria plan. None of Employer A's employees are public safety officers. Employer A's health plan allows former employees to elect to have distributions from the qualified retirement plan applied to pay for the health insurance premiums through the cafeteria plan.

(ii) Amounts distributed from the qualified retirement plan which the former employees elect to have applied to pay health insurance premiums through the cafeteria plan are includible in their gross income. The same result occurs if distributions from the qualified retirement plan are applied directly to reimburse section 213(d) medical care expenses incurred by a former employee or his or her spouse or dependents. These distributions are includible in their income, and are not cash for purposes of section 125. The plan is not a cafeteria plan with respect to former employees.

Example 2. Severance pay used to pay COBRA premiums. Employer B maintains a cafeteria plan, which offers employees an election between cash and employer-provided accident and health insurance (excludible from employees' gross income under section 106). Employer B pays terminating employees severance pay. The cafeteria plan also allows a terminating employee to elect between receiving severance pay and using the severance pay to pay the COBRA premiums for the accident and health insurance. These provisions in the cafeteria plan are consistent with the requirements in section 125.

(4) *Election by participants.* (i) *In general.* A cafeteria plan must offer participants the opportunity to elect between at least one permitted taxable benefit and at least one qualified benefit. For example, if employees are given the opportunity to elect only among two or more nontaxable benefits, the plan is not a cafeteria plan. Similarly, a plan that only offers the election among salary, permitted taxable benefits, paid time off or other taxable benefits is not a cafeteria plan. See section 125(a), (d). See § 1.125-2 for rules on elections.

(ii) *Premium-only-plan.* A cafeteria plan may be a premium-only-plan.

(iii) *Examples.* The following examples illustrate the rules of paragraph (b)(4)(i) of this section.

Example 1. No election. Employer C covers all its employees under its accident and health plan (excludible from employees' gross income under section 106). Coverage is mandatory (that is, employees have no election between cash and the Employer C's accident and health plan). This plan is not a cafeteria plan, because the plan offers employees no election between taxable and nontaxable benefits. The accident and health coverage is excludible from employees' gross income

Example 2. Election between cash and at least one qualified benefit. Employer D offers its employees a plan with an election between cash and an employer-provided accident and health plan (excludible from employees' gross income under section 106). If the plan also satisfies all the other requirements of section 125, the plan is a cafeteria plan because it offers an election between at least one taxable benefit and at least one nontaxable qualified benefit.

Example 3. Election between employer flex-credits and qualified benefits. Employer E offers its employees an election between an employer flex-credit (as defined in paragraph (b) in § 1.125-5) and qualified benefits. If an employee does not elect to apply the entire employer flex-credit to qualified benefits, the employee will receive no cash or other taxable benefit for the unused employer flex-credit. The plan is not a cafeteria plan because it does not offer an election between at least one taxable benefit and at least one nontaxable qualified benefit.

Example 4. No election between cash and qualified benefits for certain employees. (i) Employer F maintains a calendar year plan offering employer-provided accident and health insurance coverage which includes employee-only and family coverage options.

(ii) The plan provides for an automatic enrollment process when a new employee is hired, or during the annual election period under the plan: only employees who certify that they have other health coverage are permitted to elect to receive cash. Employees who cannot certify are covered by the accident and health insurance on a mandatory basis. Employer F does not otherwise request or collect information from employees regarding other health coverage as part of the enrollment process. If the employee has a spouse or child, the employee can elect between cash and family coverage.

(iii) When an employee is hired, the employee receives a notice explaining the plan's automatic enrollment process. The notice includes the salary reduction amounts for employee-only coverage and family coverage, procedures for certifying whether the employee has other health coverage, elections for family coverage, information on the time by which a certification or election must be made, and the period for which a certification or election will be effective. The notice is also given to each current employee before the beginning of each plan year, (except that the notice for a current employee includes a description of the employee's existing coverage, if any).

(iv) For a new employee, an election to receive cash or to have family coverage is effective if made when the employee is hired. For a current employee, an election is effective if made prior to the start of each calendar year or under any other circumstances permitted under § 1.125-4. An election for any prior year carries over to the next succeeding plan year unless changed. Certification that the employee has other health coverage must be made annually.

(v) Contributions used to purchase employer-provided accident and health coverage under section 125 are not includible in an employee's gross income if the employee can elect cash. Section 125 does not apply to the employee-only coverage of an employee who cannot certify that he or she has other health coverage and, therefore, does not have the ability to elect cash in lieu of health coverage.

(5) *No deferred compensation.* Except as provided in paragraph (o) of this section, in order for a plan to be a cafeteria plan, the qualified benefits and the permitted taxable benefits offered through the cafeteria plan must not defer compensation. For example, a cafeteria plan may not provide for retirement health benefits for current employees beyond the current plan year or group-term life insurance with a permanent benefit, as defined under § 1.79-0.

(c) *Written plan requirements* —(1) *General rule.* A cafeteria plan must contain in writing the information described in this paragraph (c), and depending on the qualified benefits offered in the plan, may also be required to contain additional information described in paragraphs (c)(2) and (c)(3) of this section. The cafeteria plan must be adopted and effective on or before the first day of the cafeteria plan year to which it relates. The terms of the plan must apply uniformly to all participants. The cafeteria plan document may be comprised of multiple documents. The written cafeteria plan must contain all of the following information—

(i) A specific description of each of the benefits available through the plan, including the periods during which the benefits are provided (the periods of coverage);

(ii) The plan's rules governing participation , and specifically requiring that all participants in the plan be employees;

(iii) The procedures governing employees' elections under the plan, including the period when elections may be made, the periods with respect to which elections are effective, and providing that elections are irrevocable, except to the extent that the optional change in status rules in § 1.125-4 are included in the cafeteria plan;

(iv) The manner in which employer contributions may be made under the plan, (for example, through an employee's salary reduction election or by nonelective employer contributions (that is, flex-credits, as defined in paragraph (b) in § 1.125-5) or both);

(v) The maximum amount of employer contributions available to any employee through the plan, by stating:

(A) The maximum amount of elective contributions (i.e., salary reduction) available to any employee through the plan, expressed as a maximum dollar amount or a maximum percentage of compensation or the method for determining the maximum dollar amount; and

(B) For contributions to section 401(k) plans, the maximum amount of elective contributions available to any employee through the plan, expressed as a maximum dollar amount or maximum percentage of compensation that may be contributed as elective contributions through the plan by employees .

(vi) The plan year of the cafeteria plan;

(vii) If the plan offers paid time off, the required ordering rule for use of nonelective and elective paid time off in paragraph (o)(4) of this section;

(viii) If the plan includes flexible spending arrangements (as defined in § 1.125-5(a)), the plan's provisions complying with any additional requirements for those FSAs (for example, the uniform coverage rule and the use-or-lose rules in paragraphs (d) and (c) in § 1.125-5);

(ix) If the plan includes a grace period, the plan's provisions complying with paragraph (e) of this section; and

(x) If the plan includes distributions from a health FSA to employees' HSAs, the plan's provisions complying with paragraph (n) in § 1.125-5.

(2) *Additional requirements under sections 105(h), 129, and 137.* A written plan is required for self-insured medical reimbursement plans (§ 1.105-11(b)(1)(i)), dependent care assistance programs (section 129(d)(1)), and adoption assistance (section 137(c)). Any of these plans or programs offered through a cafeteria plan that satisfies the written plan requirement in this paragraph (c) for the benefits under these plans and programs also satisfies the written plan requirements in § 1.105-11(b)(1)(i), section 129(d)(1), and section 137(c) (whichever is applicable). Alternatively, a self-insured medical reimbursement plan, a dependent care assistance program, or an adoption assistance program is permitted to satisfy the requirements in § 1.105-11(b)(1)(i), section 129(d)(1), or section 137(c) (whichever is applicable) through a separate written plan, and not as part of the written cafeteria plan.

(3) *Additional requirements under section 401(k).* See § 1.401(k)-1(e)(7) for additional requirements that must be satisfied in the written plan if the plan offers deferrals into a section 401(k) plan.

(4) *Cross-reference allowed.* In describing the benefits available through the cafeteria plan, the written cafeteria plan need not be self-contained. For example, the written cafeteria plan may incorporate by reference benefits offered through other *separate written plans*, such as a section 401(k) plan, or coverage under a dependent care assistance program (section 129), without describing in full the benefits established through these other plans. But, for example, if the cafeteria plan offers different maximum levels of coverage for dependent care assistance programs, the descriptions in the separate written plan must specify the available maximums.

(5) *Amendments to cafeteria plan.* Any amendment to the cafeteria plan must be in writing. A cafeteria plan is permitted to be amended at any time during a plan year. However, the amendment is only permitted to be effective for periods after the later of the adoption date or effective date of the amendment. For an amendment adding a new benefit, the cafeteria plan must pay or reimburse only those expenses for new benefits incurred after the later of the amendment's adoption date or effective date.

(6) *Failure to satisfy written plan requirements.* If there is no written cafeteria plan, or if the written plan fails to satisfy any of the requirements in this paragraph (c) (including cross-referenced requirements), the plan is not a cafeteria plan and an employee's election between taxable and nontaxable benefits results in gross income to the employee.

(7) *Operational failure* —(i) *In general.* If the cafeteria plan fails to operate according to its written plan or otherwise fails to operate in compliance with section 125 and the regulations, the plan is not a cafeteria plan and employees' elections between taxable and nontaxable benefits result in gross income to the employees.

(ii) *Failure to operate according to written cafeteria plan or section 125.* Examples of failures resulting in section 125 not applying to a plan include the following—

(A) Paying or reimbursing expenses for qualified benefits incurred before the later of the adoption date or effective date of the cafeteria plan, before the beginning of a period of coverage or before the later of the date of adoption or effective date of a plan amendment adding a new benefit;

(B) Offering benefits other than permitted taxable benefits and qualified benefits;

(C) Operating to defer compensation (except as permitted in paragraph (o) of this section);

(D) Failing to comply with the uniform coverage rule in paragraph (d) in § 1.125-5;

(E) Failing to comply with the use-or-lose rule in paragraph (c) in § 1.125-5;

(F) Allowing employees to revoke elections or make new elections, except as provided in § 1.125-4 and paragraph (a) in § 1.125-2;

(G) Failing to comply with the substantiation requirements of § 1.125-6;

(H) Paying or reimbursing expenses in an FSA other than expenses expressly permitted in paragraph (h) in § 1.125-5;

(I) Allocating experience gains other than as expressly permitted in paragraph (o) in § 1.125-5;

(J) Failing to comply with the grace period rules in paragraph (e) of this section; or

(K) Failing to comply with the qualified HSA distribution rules in paragraph (n) in § 1.125-5.

(d) *Plan year requirements* —(1) *Twelve consecutive months.* The plan year must be specified in the cafeteria plan. The plan year of a cafeteria plan must be twelve consecutive months, unless a short plan year is allowed under this paragraph (d). A plan year is permitted to begin on any day of any calendar month and must end on the preceding day in the immediately following year (for example, a plan year that begins on October 15, 2007, must end on October 14, 2008). A calendar year plan year is a period of twelve consecutive months beginning on January 1 and ending on December 31 of the same calendar year. A plan year specified in the cafeteria plan is effective for the first plan year of a cafeteria plan and for all subsequent plan years, unless changed as provided in paragraph (d)(2) of this section.

(2) *Changing plan year.* The plan year is permitted to be changed only for a valid business purpose. A change in the plan year is not permitted if a principal purpose of the change in plan year is to circumvent the rules of section 125 or these regulations. If a change in plan year does not satisfy this subparagraph, the attempt to change the plan year is ineffective and the plan year of the cafeteria plan remains the same.

(3) *Short plan year.* A short plan year of less than twelve consecutive months is permitted for a valid business purpose.

(4) *Examples.* The following examples illustrate the rules in paragraph (d) of this section:

Example 1. Employer with calendar year. Employer G, with a calendar taxable year, first establishes a cafeteria plan effective July 1, 2009. The cafeteria plan specifies a calendar plan year. The first cafeteria plan year is the period beginning on July 1, 2009, and ending on December 31, 2009. Employer G has a business purpose for a short first cafeteria plan year.

Example 2. Employer changes insurance carrier. Employer H establishes a cafeteria plan effective January 1, 2009, with a calendar year plan year. The cafeteria plan offers an accident and health plan through Insurer X. In March 2010, Employer H contracts to provide accident and health insurance through another insurance company, Y. Y's accident and health insurance is offered on a July 1-June 30 benefit year. Effective July 1, 2010, Employer H amends the plan to change to a July 1-June 30 plan year. Employer H has a business purpose for changing the cafeteria plan year and for the short plan year ending June 30, 2010.

(5) *Significance of plan year.* The plan year generally is the coverage period for benefits provided through the cafeteria plan to which annual elections for these benefits apply. Benefits elected pursuant to the employee's election for a plan year generally may not be carried forward to subsequent plan years. However, see the grace period rule in paragraph (e) of this section.

(e) *Grace period* —(1) *In general.* A cafeteria plan may, at the employer's option, include a grace period of up to the fifteenth day of the third month immediately following the end of each plan year. If a cafeteria plan provides for a grace period, an employee who has unused benefits or contributions relating to a qualified benefit (for example, health flexible spending arrangement (health FSA) or dependent care assistance) from the immediately preceding plan year, and who incurs expenses for that same qualified benefit during the grace period, may be paid or reimbursed for those expenses from the unused benefits or contributions as if the expenses had been incurred in the immediately preceding plan year. A grace period is available for all qualified benefits described in paragraph (a)(3) of this section, except that the grace period does not apply to paid time off and elective contributions under a section 401(k) plan. The effect of the grace period is that the employee may have as long as 14 months and 15 days (that is, the 12 months in the current cafeteria plan year plus the grace period) to use the benefits or contributions for a plan year before those amounts are *forfeited* under the *use-or-lose* rule in paragraph (c) in §1.125-5. If the grace period is added to a cafeteria plan through an amendment, all requirements in paragraph (c) of this section must be satisfied.

(2) *Grace period optional features.* A grace period provision may contain any or all of the following—

(i) The grace period may apply to some qualified benefits described in paragraph (a)(3) of this section, but not to others;

(ii) The grace period provision may limit the amount of unused benefits or contributions available during the grace period. The limit must be uniform and apply to all participants. However, the limit must not be based on a percentage of the amount of the unused benefits or contributions remaining at the end of the immediately prior plan year;

(iii) The last day of the grace period may be sooner than the fifteenth day of the third month immediately following the end of the plan year (that is, the grace period may be shorter than two and one half months);

(iv) The grace period provision is permitted to treat expenses for qualified benefits incurred during the grace period either as expenses incurred during the immediately preceding plan year or as expenses incurred during the current plan year (for example, the plan may first apply the unused contributions or benefits from the immediately preceding year to pay or reimburse grace period expenses and then, when the unused contributions and benefits from the prior year are exhausted, the grace period expenses may be paid from current year contributions and benefits.); and

(v) The grace period provision may permit the employer to defer the allocation of expenses described in paragraph (e)(2)(iv) of this section until after the end of the grace period.

(3) *Grace period requirements.* A grace period must satisfy the requirements in paragraph (c) of this section and all of the following requirements:

(i) The grace period provisions in the cafeteria plan (including optional provisions in paragraph (e)(2) of this section) must apply uniformly to all participants in the cafeteria plan, determined as of the last day of the plan year. Participants in the cafeteria plan through COBRA and participants who were participants as of the last day of the plan year but terminate during the grace period are participants for purposes of the grace period. See §54.4980B-2, Q&A-8 of this chapter;

(ii) The grace period provision in the cafeteria plan must state that unused benefits or contributions relating to a particular qualified benefit may only be used to pay or reimburse expenses incurred with respect to the same qualified benefit. For example, unused amounts elected to pay or reimburse medical expenses in a health FSA may not be used to pay or reimburse dependent care expenses incurred during the grace period; and

(iii) The grace period provision in the cafeteria plan must state that to the extent any unused benefits or contributions from the immediately preceding plan year exceed the expenses for the qualified benefit incurred during the grace period, those remaining unused benefits or contributions may not be carried forward to any subsequent period (including any subsequent plan year), cannot be cashed-out and must be forfeited under the use-or-lose rule. See paragraph (c) in §1.125-5

(4) *Examples.* The following examples illustrate the rules in this paragraph (e).

Example 1. Expenses incurred during grace period and immediately following plan year. (i) Employer I's calendar year cafeteria plan includes a grace period allowing all participants to apply unused benefits or contributions remaining at the end of the plan year to qualified benefits incurred during the grace period immediately following that plan year. The grace period for the plan year ending December 31, 2009, ends on March 15, 2010.

(ii) Employee X timely elected salary reduction of $1,000 for a health FSA for the plan year ending December 31, 2009. As of December 31, 2009, X has $200 remaining unused in his health FSA. X timely elected

salary reduction for a health FSA of $1,500 for the plan year ending December 31, 2010.

(iii) During the grace period from January 1 through March 15, 2010, X incurs $300 of unreimbursed medical expenses (as defined in section 213(d)). The unused $200 from the plan year ending December 31, 2009, is applied to pay or reimburse $200 of X's $300 of medical expenses incurred during the grace period. Therefore, as of March 16, 2010, X has no unused benefits or contributions remaining for the plan year ending December 31, 2009.

(iv) The remaining $100 of medical expenses incurred between January 1 and March 15, 2010, is paid or reimbursed from X's health FSA for the plan year ending December 31, 2010. As of March 16, 2010, X has $1,400 remaining in the health FSA for the plan year ending December 31, 2010.

Example 2. Unused benefits exceed expenses incurred during grace period. Same facts as *Example 1*, except that X incurs $150 of section 213(d) medical expenses during the grace period (January 1 through March 15, 2010). As of March 16, 2010, X has $50 of unused benefits or contributions remaining for the plan year ending December 31, 2009. The unused $50 cannot be cashed-out, converted to any other taxable or nontaxable benefit, or used in any other plan year (including the plan year ending December 31, 2009). The unused $50 is subject to the use-or-lose rule in paragraph (c) in §1.125-5 and is forfeited. As of March 16, 2010, X has the entire $1,500 elected in the health FSA for the plan year ending December 31, 2010.

Example 3. Terminated participants. (i) Employer J's cafeteria plan includes a grace period allowing all participants to apply unused benefits or contributions remaining at the end of the plan year to qualified benefits incurred during the grace period immediately following that plan year. For the plan year ending on December 31, 2009, the grace period ends March 15, 2010.

(ii) Employees A, B, C, and D each timely elected $1,200 salary reduction for a health FSA for the plan year ending December 31, 2009. Employees A and B terminated employment on September 15, 2009. Each has $500 of unused benefits or contributions in the health FSA.

(iii) Employee A elected COBRA for the health FSA. Employee A is a participant in the cafeteria plan as of December 31, 2009, the last day of the 2009 plan year. Employee A has $500 of unused benefits or contributions available during the grace period for the 2009 plan year (ending March 15, 2010).

(iv) Employee B did not elect COBRA for the health FSA. Employee B is not a participant in the cafeteria plan as of December 31, 2009. The grace period does not apply to Employee B.

(v) Employee C has $500 of unused benefits in his health FSA as of December 31, 2009, and terminated employment on January 15, 2010. Employee C is a participant in the cafeteria plan as of December 31, 2009 and has $500 of unused benefits or contributions available during the grace period ending March 15, 2010, even though he terminated employment on January 15, 2010.

(vi) Employee D continues to work for Employer H throughout 2009 and 2010, also has $500 of unused benefits or contributions in his health FSA as of December 31, 2009, but made no health FSA election for 2010. Employee D is a participant in the cafeteria plan as of December 31, 2009 and has $500 of unused benefits or contributions available during the grace period ending March 15, 2010, even though he is not a participant in a health FSA for the 2010 plan year.

(f) *Run-out period.* A cafeteria plan is permitted to contain a run-out period as designated by the employer. A run-out period is a period after the end of the plan year (or grace period) during which a participant can submit a claim for reimbursement for a qualified benefit incurred during the plan year (or grace period). Thus, a plan is also permitted to provide a deadline on or after the end of the plan year (or grace period) for submitting a claim for reimbursement for the plan year. Any run-out period must be provided on a uniform and consistent basis with respect to all participants.

(g) *Employee for purposes of section 125*—(1) *Current employees, former employees.* The term employee includes any current or former employee (including any laid-off employee or retired employee) of the employer. See paragraph (g)(3) of this section concerning limits on participation by former employees. Specifically, the term *employee* includes the following—

(i) Common law employee;

(ii) Leased employee described in section 414(n);

(iii) Full-time life insurance salesman (as defined in section 7701(a)(20)); and

(iv) A current employee or former employee described in paragraphs (g)(1)(i) through (iii) of this section.

(2) *Self-employed individual not an employee.* (i) *In general.* The term *employee* does not include a self-employed individual or a 2-percent shareholder of an S corporation, as defined in paragraph (g)(2)(ii) of this subsection. For example, a sole proprietor, a partner in a partnership, or a director solely serving on a corporation's board of directors (and not otherwise providing services to the corporation as an employee) is not an employee for purposes of section 125, and thus is not permitted to participate in a cafeteria plan. However, a sole proprietor may sponsor a cafeteria plan covering the sole proprietor's employees (but not the sole proprietor). Similarly, a partnership or S corporation may sponsor a cafeteria plan covering employees (but not a partner or 2-percent shareholder of an S corporation).

(ii) *Two percent shareholder of an S corporation.* A 2-percent shareholder of an S corporation has the meaning set forth in section 1372(b).

(iii) *Certain dual status individuals.* If an individual is an employee of an employer and also provides services to that employer as an independent contractor or director (for example, an individual is both a director and an employee of a C corp), the individual is eligible to participate in that employer's cafeteria plan solely in his or her capacity as an employee. This rule does not apply to partners or to 2-percent shareholders of an S corporation.

(iv) *Examples.* The following examples illustrate the rules in paragraphs (g)(2)(ii) and (g)(2)(iii) of this section:

Example 1. Two-percent shareholders of an S corporation. (i) Employer K, an S corporation, maintains a cafeteria plan for its employees (other than 2-percent shareholders of an S corporation). Employer K's taxable year and the plan year are the calendar year. On January 1, 2009, individual Z owns 5 percent of the outstanding stock in Employer K. Y, who owns no stock in Employer K, is married to Z. Y and Z are employees of Employer K. Z is a 2-percent shareholder in Employer K (as defined in section 1372(b)). Y is also a 2-percent shareholder in Employer K by operation of the attribution rules in section 318(a)(1)(A)(i).

(ii) On July 15, 2009, Z sells all his stock in Employer K to an unrelated third party, and ceases to be a 2-percent shareholder. Y and Z continue to work as employees of Employer K during the entire 2009 calendar year. Y and Z are ineligible to participate in Employer K's cafeteria plan for the 2009 plan year.

Example 2. Director and employee. T is an employee and also a director of Employer L, a C corp that sponsors a cafeteria plan. The cafeteria plan allows only employees of Employer L to participate in the cafeteria plan. T's annual compensation as an employee is $50,000; T is also paid $3,000 annually in director's fees. T makes a timely election to salary reduce $5,000 from his employee compensation for dependent care benefits. T makes no election with respect to his compensation as a director. T may participate in the cafeteria plan in his capacity as an employee of Employer L.

(3) *Limits on participation by former employees.* Although former employees are treated as employees, a cafeteria plan may not be established or maintained predominantly for the benefit of former employees of the employer. Such a plan is not a cafeteria plan.

(4) *No participation by the spouse or dependent of an employee.* (i) *Benefits allowed to participant's spouse or dependents but not participation.* The spouse or dependents of employees may not be participants in a cafeteria plan unless they are also employees. However, a cafeteria plan may provide benefits to spouses and dependents of participants. For example, although an employee's spouse may benefit from the employee's election of accident and health insurance coverage or of coverage through a dependent care assistance program, the spouse may not participate in a cafeteria plan (that is, the spouse may not be given the opportunity to elect or purchase benefits offered by the plan).

(ii) *Certain elections after employee's death.* An employee's spouse is not a participant in a cafeteria plan merely because the spouse has the right, upon the death of the employee, to elect among various settlement options or to elect among permissible distribution options with respect to the deceased employee's benefits through a section 401(k) plan, Health Savings Account, or certain group-term life insurance offered through the cafeteria plan. See §54.4980B-2, Q & A 8 and §54.4980B-4, Q & A-1 of this chapter on COBRA rights of a participant's spouse or dependents.

(5) *Employees of certain controlled groups.* All employees who are treated as employed by a single employer under section 414(b), (c), (m), or (o) are treated as employed by a single employer for purposes of section 125. Section 125(g)(4); section 414(t).

¶ 20,262B

(h) *After-tax employee contributions* —(1) *Certain after-tax employee contributions treated as cash.* In addition to the cash benefits described in paragraph (a)(2) of this section, in general, a benefit is treated as cash for purposes of section 125 if the benefit does not defer compensation (except as provided in paragraph (o) of this section) and an employee who receives the benefit purchases such benefit with after-tax employee contributions or is treated, for all purposes under the Code (including, for example, reporting and withholding purposes), as receiving, at the time that the benefit is received, cash compensation equal to the full value of the benefit at that time and then purchasing the benefit with after-tax employee contributions. Thus, for example, long-term disability coverage is treated as cash for purposes of section 125 if the cafeteria plan provides that an employee may purchase the coverage through the cafeteria plan with after-tax employee contributions or provides that the employee receiving such coverage is treated as having received cash compensation equal to the value of the coverage and then as having purchased the coverage with after-tax employee contributions. Also, for example, a cafeteria plan may offer employees the opportunity to purchase, with after-tax employee contributions, group-term life insurance on the life of an employee (providing no permanent benefits), an accident and health plan, or a dependent care assistance program.

(2) *Accident and health coverage purchased for someone other than the employee's spouse or dependents with after-tax employee contributions.* If the requirements of section 106 are satisfied, employer-provided accident and health coverage for an employee and his or her spouse or dependents is excludible from the employee's gross income. The fair market value of coverage for any other individual, provided with respect to the employee, is includible in the employee's gross income. §1.106-1; §1.61-21(a)(4), and §1.61-21(b)(1). A cafeteria plan is permitted to allow employees to elect accident and health coverage for an individual who is not the spouse or dependent of the employee as a taxable benefit.

(3) *Example.* The following example illustrates the rules of this paragraph (h):

Example. Accident and health plan coverage for individuals who are not a spouse or dependent of an employee. (i) Employee C participates in Employer M's cafeteria plan. Employee C timely elects salary reduction for employer-provided accident and health coverage for himself and for accident and health coverage for his former spouse. C's former spouse is not C's dependent. A former spouse is not a spouse as defined in section 152.

(ii) The fair market value of the coverage for the former spouse is $1,000. Employee C has $1,000 includible in gross income for the accident and health coverage of his former spouse, because the section 106 exclusion applies only to employer-provided accident and health coverage for the employee or the employee's spouse or dependents.

(iii) No payments or reimbursements received under the accident and health coverage result in gross income to Employee C or to the former spouse. The result is the same if the $1,000 for coverage of C's former spouse is paid from C's after-tax income outside the cafeteria plan.

(i) *Prohibited taxable benefits.* Any taxable benefit not described in paragraph (a)(2) of this section and not treated as cash for purposes of section 125 in paragraph (h) of this section is not permitted to be included in a cafeteria plan. A plan that offers taxable benefits other than the taxable benefits described in paragraph (a)(2) and (h) of this section is not a cafeteria plan.

(j) *Coordination with other rules* —(1) *In general.* If a benefit is excludible from an employee's gross income when provided separately, the benefit is excludible from gross income when provided through a cafeteria plan. Thus, a qualified benefit is excludible from gross income if both the rules under section 125 and the specific rules providing for the exclusion of the benefit from gross income are satisfied. For example, if the nondiscrimination rules for specific qualified benefits (for example, sections 79(d), 105(h), 129(d)(2), 137(c)(2)) are not satisfied, those qualified benefits are includible in gross income. Thus, if $50,000 in group-term life insurance is offered through a cafeteria plan, the nondiscrimination rules in section 79(d) must be satisfied in order to exclude the coverage from gross income.

(2) *Section 125 nondiscrimination rules.* Qualified benefits are includible in the gross income of highly compensated participants or key employees if the nondiscrimination rules of section 125 are not satisfied. See §1.125-7.

(3) *Taxable benefits.* If a benefit that is includible in gross income when offered separately is offered through a cafeteria plan, the benefit continues to be includible in gross income.

(k) *Group-term life insurance* —(1) *In general.* In addition to offering up to $50,000 in group-term life insurance coverage excludible under section 79(a), a cafeteria plan may offer coverage in excess of that amount. The cost of coverage in excess of $50,000 in group-term life insurance coverage provided under a policy or policies carried directly or indirectly by one or more employers (taking into account all coverage provided both through a cafeteria plan and outside a cafeteria plan) is includible in an employee's gross income. Group-term life insurance combined with permanent benefits, within the meaning of § 1.79-0, is a prohibited benefit in a cafeteria plan.

(2) *Determining cost of insurance includible in employee's gross income.* (i) *In general.* If the aggregate group-term life insurance coverage on the life of the employee (under policies carried directly or indirectly by the employer) exceeds $50,000, all or a portion of the insurance is provided through a cafeteria plan, and the group-term life insurance is provided through a plan that meets the nondiscrimination rules of section 79(d), the amount includible in an employee's gross income is determined under paragraphs (k)(2)(i)(A) through (C) of this section. For each employee—

(A) The entire amount of salary reduction and employer flex-credits through a cafeteria plan for group-term life insurance coverage on the life of the employee is excludible from the employee's gross income, regardless of the amount of employer-provided group-term life insurance on the employee's life (that is, whether or not the coverage provided to the employee both through the cafeteria plan and outside the cafeteria plan exceeds $50,000);

(B) The cost of the group-term life insurance in excess of $50,000 of coverage is includible in the employee's gross income. The amount includible in the employee's income is determined using the rules of § 1.79-3 and Table I (*Uniform Premiums for $1,000 of Group-Term Life Insurance Protection*). See subparagraph (C) of this paragraph (k)(2)(i) for determining the amount paid by the employee for purposes of reducing the Table I amount includible in income under § 1.79-3.

(C) In determining the amount paid by the employee toward the purchase of the group-term life insurance for purposes of § 1.79-3, only an employee's after-tax contributions are treated as an amount paid by the employee.

(ii) *Examples.* The rules in this paragraph (k) are illustrated by the following examples, in which the group-term life insurance coverage satisfies the nondiscrimination rules in section 79(d), provides no permanent benefits, is for a 12-month period, is the only group-term life insurance coverage provided under a policy carried directly or indirectly by the employer, and applies Table I (*Uniform Premiums for $1,000 of Group-Term Life Insurance Protection) effective July 1, 1999:*

Example 1. Excess group-term life insurance coverage provided through salary reduction in a cafeteria plan. (i) Employer N provides group-term life insurance coverage to its employees only through its cafeteria plan. Employer N's cafeteria plan allows employees to elect salary reduction for group-term life insurance. Employee B, age 42, elected salary reduction of $200 for $150,000 of group-term life insurance. None of the group-term life insurance is paid through after-tax employee contributions.

(ii) B's $200 of salary reduction for group-term life insurance is excludible from B's gross income under paragraph (k)(2)(i)(A).

(iii) B has a total of $150,000 of group-term life insurance. The group-term life insurance in excess of the dollar limitation of section 79 is $100,000 (150,000 - 50,000).

(iv) The Table I cost is $120 for $100,000 of group-term life insurance for an individual between ages 40 to 44. The Table I cost of $120 is reduced by zero (because B paid no portion of the group-term life insurance with after-tax employee contributions), under paragraphs (k)(2)(i)(A)-(B) of this section.

(v) The amount includible in B's gross income for the $100,000 of excess group-term life insurance is $120.

Example 2. Excess group-term life insurance coverage provided through salary reduction in a cafeteria plan where employee purchases a portion of group-term life insurance coverage with after-tax contributions. (i) Same facts as *Example 1,* except that B elected salary reduction of $100 and makes an after-tax contribution of $100 toward the purchase of group-term life insurance coverage.

(ii) B's $100 of salary reduction for group-term life insurance is excludible from B's gross income, under paragraph (k)(2)(i)(A) of this section.

(iii) B has a total of $150,000 of group-term life insurance. The group-term life insurance in excess of the dollar limitation of section 79 is $100,000 (150,000 - 50,000).

(iv) The Table I cost is $120 for $100,000 of group-term life insurance for an individual between ages 40 to 44, under (k)(2)(i)(B). The Table I cost of $120 is reduced by $100 (because B paid $100 for the group-term life insurance with after-tax employee contributions), under paragraphs (k)(2)(i)(B) and (k)(2)(i)(C) of this section.

(v) The amount includible in B's gross income for the $100,000 of excess group-term life insurance coverage is $20.

Example 3. Excess group-term life insurance coverage provided through salary reduction in a cafeteria plan and outside a cafeteria plan. (i) Same facts as *Example 1* except that Employer N also provides (at no cost to employees) group-term life insurance coverage equal to each employee's annual salary. Employee B's annual salary is $150,000. B has $150,000 of group-term life insurance directly from Employer N, and also $150,000 coverage through Employer N's cafeteria plan.

(ii) B's $200 of salary reduction for group-term life insurance is excludible from B's gross income, under paragraph (k)(2)(i)(A) of this section.

(iii) B has a total of $300,000 of group-term life insurance. The group-term life insurance in excess of the dollar limitation of section 79 is $250,000 (300,000 - 50,000).

(iv) The Table I cost is $300 for $250,000 of group-term life insurance for an individual between ages 40 to 44. The Table I cost of $300 is reduced by zero (because B paid no portion of the group-term life insurance with after-tax employee contributions), under paragraphs (k)(2)(i)(B) and (k)(2)(i)(C) of this section.

(v) The amount includible in B's gross income for the $250,000 of excess group-term life insurance is $300.

Example 4. Excess group-term life insurance coverage provided through salary reduction in a cafeteria plan and outside a cafeteria plan. (i) Same facts as *Example 3* except that Employee C's annual salary is $30,000. C has $30,000 of group-term life insurance coverage provided directly from Employer N, and elects an additional $30,000 of coverage for $40 through Employer N's cafeteria plan. C is 42 years old.

(ii) C's $40 of salary reduction for group-term life insurance is excludible from C's gross income, under paragraph (k)(2)(i)(A) of this section.

(iii) C has a total of $60,000 of group-term life insurance. The group-term life insurance in excess of the dollar limitation of section 79 is $10,000 (60,000 - 50,000).

(iv) The Table I cost is $12 for $10,000 of group-term life insurance for an individual between ages 40 to 44. The Table I cost of $12 is reduced by zero (because C paid no portion of the group-term life insurance with after-tax employee contributions), under paragraphs (k)(2)(i)(B) and (k)(2)(i)(C) of this section.

(v) The amount includible in C's gross income for the $10,000 of excess group-term life insurance coverage is $12.

(l) *COBRA premiums* —(1) *Paying COBRA premiums through a cafeteria plan.* Under § 1.125-4(c)(3)(iv), COBRA premiums for an employer-provided group health plan are qualified benefits if:

(i) The premiums are excludible from an employee's income under section 106; or

(ii) The premiums are for the accident and health plan of the employer sponsoring the cafeteria plan, even if the fair market value of the premiums is includible in an employee's gross income. See also paragraph (e)(2) in § 1.125-5 and § 54.4980B-2, Q & A-8 of this chapter for COBRA rules for health FSAs.

(2) *Example.* The following example illustrates the rules of this paragraph (l):

Example. COBRA premiums. (i) Employer O maintains a cafeteria plan for full-time employees, offering an election between cash and employer-provided accident and health insurance and other qualified benefits. Employees A, B, and C participate in the cafeteria plan. On July 1, 2009, Employee A has a qualifying event (as defined in § 54.4980B-4 of this chapter).

(ii) Employee A was a full-time employee and became a part-time employee and for that reason, is no longer covered by Employer O's accident and health plan. Under § 1.125-4(f)(3)(ii), Employee A changes her election to salary reduce to pay her COBRA premiums.

(iii) Employee B previously worked for another employer, quit and elected COBRA. Employee B begins work for Employer O on July 1, 2009, and becomes eligible to participate in Employer O's cafeteria plan on July 1, 2009, but will not be eligible to participate in Employer O's accident and health plan until October 1, 2009. Employee B elects to salary reduce to pay COBRA premiums for coverage under the accident and health plan sponsored by B's former employer.

(iv) Employee C and C's spouse are covered by Employer O's accident and health plan until July 1, 2009, when C's divorce from her spouse became final. C continues to be covered by the accident and health plan. On July 1, 2009, C requests to pay COBRA premiums for her former spouse (who is not C's dependent (as defined in section 152)) with after-tax employee contributions.

(v) Salary reduction elections for COBRA premiums for Employees A and B are qualified benefits for purposes of section 125 and are excludible from the gross income of Employees A and B. Employer O allows A and B to salary reduce for these COBRA premiums.

(vi) Employer O allows C to pay for COBRA premiums for C's former spouse, with after-tax employee contributions because although accident and health coverage for C's former spouse is permitted in a cafeteria plan, the premiums are includible in C's gross income.

(vii) The operation of Employer O's cafeteria plan satisfies the requirements of this paragraph (l).

(m) *Payment or reimbursement of employees' individual accident and health insurance premiums* —(1) *In general.* The payment or reimbursement of employees' substantiated individual health insurance premiums is excludible from employees' gross income under section 106 and is a qualified benefit for purposes of section 125.

(2) *Example.* The following example illustrates the rule of this paragraph (m):

Example. Payment or reimbursement of premiums. (i) Employer P's cafeteria plan offers the following benefits for employees who are covered by an individual health insurance policy. The employee substantiates the expenses for the premiums for the policy (as required in paragraph (b)(2) in § 1.125-6) before any payments or reimbursements to the employee for premiums are made. The payments or reimbursements are made in the following ways:

(ii) The cafeteria plan reimburses each employee directly for the amount of the employee's substantiated health insurance premium;

(iii) The cafeteria plan issues the employee a check payable to the health insurance company for the amount of the employee's health insurance premium, which the employee is obligated to tender to the insurance company;

(iv) The cafeteria plan issues a check in the same manner as (iii), except that the check is payable jointly to the employee and the insurance company; or

(v) Under these circumstances, the individual health insurance policies are accident and health plans as defined in § 1.106-1. This benefit is a qualified benefit under section 125.

(n) *Section 105 rules for accident and health plan offered through a cafeteria plan* —(1) *General rule.* In order for an accident and health plan to be a qualified benefit that is excludible from gross income if elected through a cafeteria plan, the cafeteria plan must satisfy section 125 and the accident and health plan must satisfy section 105(b) and (h).

(2) *Section 105(b) requirements in general.* Section 105(b) provides an exclusion from gross income for amounts paid to an employee from an employer-funded accident and health plan specifically to reimburse the employee for certain expenses for medical care (as defined in section 213(d)) incurred by the employee or the employee's spouse or dependents during the period for which the benefit is provided to the employee (that is, when the employee is covered by the accident and health plan).

(o) *Prohibition against deferred compensation* —(1) *In general.* Any plan that offers a benefit that defers compensation (except as provided in this paragraph (o)) is not a cafeteria plan. See section 125(d)(2)(A). A plan that permits employees to carry over unused elective contributions, after-tax contributions, or plan benefits from one plan year to another (except as provided in paragraphs (e), (o)(3) and (4) and (p) of this section) defers compensation. This is the case regardless of how the contributions or benefits are used by the employee in the subsequent plan year (for example, whether they are automatically or electively converted into another taxable or nontaxable benefit in the subsequent plan year or used to provide additional benefits of the same type). Similarly, a cafeteria plan also defers compensation if the plan permits employees to use contributions for one plan year to purchase a benefit that will be provided in a subsequent plan year (for example, life, health or disability if these benefits have a savings or investment feature, such as whole life insurance). See also Q & A-5 in § 1.125-3, prohibiting deferring compensation from one cafeteria plan year to a subsequent cafeteria plan year. See paragraph (e) of this section for

grace period rules. A plan does not defer compensation merely because it allocates experience gains (or forfeitures) among participants in compliance with paragraph (o) in § 1.125-5.

(2) *Effect if a plan includes a benefit that defers the receipt of compensation or a plan operates to defer compensation.* If a plan violates paragraph (o)(1) of this section, the availability of an election between taxable and nontaxable benefits under such a plan results in gross income to the employees.

(3) *Cash or deferred arrangements that may be offered in a cafeteria plan.* (i) *In general.* A cafeteria plan may offer the benefits set forth in this paragraph (o)(3), even though these benefits defer compensation.

(ii) *Elective contributions to a section 401(k) plan.* A cafeteria plan may permit a covered employee to elect to have the employer, on behalf of the employee, pay amounts as contributions to a trust that is part of a profit-sharing or stock bonus plan or rural cooperative plan (within the meaning of section 401(k)(7)), which includes a qualified cash or deferred arrangement (as defined in section 401(k)(2)). In addition, after-tax employee contributions under a qualified plan subject to section 401(m) are permitted through a cafeteria plan. The right to make such contributions does not cause a plan to fail to be a cafeteria plan merely because, under the qualified plan, employer matching contributions (as defined in section 401(m)(4)(A)) are made with respect to elective or after-tax employee contributions.

(iii) *Additional permitted deferred compensation arrangements.* A plan maintained by an educational organization described in section 170(b)(1)(A)(ii) to the extent of amounts which a covered employee may elect to have the employer pay as contributions for post-retirement group life insurance is permitted through a cafeteria plan, if—

(A) All contributions for such insurance must be made before retirement; and

(B) Such life insurance does not have a cash surrender value at any time. (iv) *Contributions to HSAs.* Contributions to covered employees' HSAs as defined in section 223 (but not contributions to Archer MSAs).

(4) *Paid time off.* (i) *In general.* A cafeteria plan is permitted to include elective paid time off (that is, vacation days, sick days or personal days) as a permitted taxable benefit through the plan by permitting employees to receive more paid time off than the employer otherwise provides to the employees on a nonelective basis, but only if the inclusion of elective paid time off through the plan does not operate to permit the deferral of compensation. In addition, a plan that only offers the choice of cash or paid time off is not a cafeteria plan and is not subject to the rules of section 125. In order to avoid deferral of compensation, the cafeteria plan must preclude any employee from using the paid time off or receiving cash, in a subsequent plan year, for any portion of such paid time off remaining unused as of the end of the plan year. (See paragraph (o)(4)(iii) of this section for the deadline to cash out unused elective paid time off.) For example, a plan that offers employees the opportunity to purchase paid time off (or to receive cash or other benefits through the plan in lieu of paid time off) is not a cafeteria plan if employees who purchase the paid time off for a plan year are allowed to use any unused paid time off in a subsequent plan year. This is the case even though the plan does not permit the employee to convert, in any subsequent plan year, the unused paid time off into any other benefit.

(ii) *Ordering of elective and nonelective paid time off.* In determining whether a plan providing paid time off operates to permit the deferral of compensation, a cafeteria plan must provide that employees are deemed to use paid time off in the following order:

(A) *Nonelective paid time off.* Nonelective paid time off (that is, paid time off with respect to which the employee has no election) is used first;

(B) *Elective paid time off.* Elective paid time off is used after all nonelective paid time off is used.

(iii) *Cashing out or forfeiture of unused elective paid time off, in general.* The cafeteria plan must provide that all unused elective paid time off (determined as of the last day of the plan year) must either be paid in cash (within the time specified in this paragraph (o)(4)) or be forfeited. This provision must apply uniformly to all participants in the cafeteria plan.

(A) *Cash out of unused elective paid time off.* A plan does not operate to permit the deferral of compensation merely because the plan provides that an employee who has not used all elective paid time off for a plan year receives in cash the value of such unused paid time off. The employee must receive the cash on or before the last day of the cafeteria plan's plan year to which the elective contributions used to purchase the unused elective paid time off relate.

(B) *Forfeiture of unused elective paid time off.* If the cafeteria plan provides for forfeiture of unused elective paid time off, the forfeiture must be effective on the last day of the plan year to which the elective contributions relate.

(iv) *No grace period for paid time off.* The grace period described in paragraph (e) of this section does not apply to paid time off.

(v) *Examples.* The following examples illustrate the rules of this paragraph (o)(4):

Example 1. Plan cashes out unused elective paid time off on or before the last day of the plan year. (i) Employer Q provides employees with two weeks of paid time off for each calendar year. Employer Q's human resources policy (that is, outside the cafeteria plan), permits employees to carry over one nonelective week of paid time off to the next year. Employer Q maintains a calendar year cafeteria plan that permits the employee to purchase, with elective contributions, an additional week of paid time off.

(ii) For the 2009 plan year, Employee A (with a calendar tax year), timely elects to purchase one additional week of paid time off. During 2009, Employee A uses only two weeks of paid time off. Employee A is deemed to have used two weeks of nonelective paid time off and zero weeks of elective paid time off.

(iii) Pursuant to the cafeteria plan, the plan pays Employee A the value of the unused elective paid time off week in cash on December 31, 2009. Employer Q includes this amount on the 2009 Form W-2 for Employee A. This amount is included in Employee A's gross income in 2009. The cafeteria plan's terms and operations do not violate the prohibition against deferring compensation.

Example 2. Unused nonelective paid time off carried over to next plan year. (i) Same facts as *Example 1*, except that Employee A uses only one week of paid time off during the year. Pursuant to the cafeteria plan, Employee A is deemed to have used one nonelective week, and having retained one nonelective week and one elective week of paid time off. Employee A receives in cash the value of the unused elective paid time off on December 31, 2009. Employer Q includes this amount on the 2009 Form W-2 for Employee A. Employee A must report this amount as gross income in 2009.

(ii) Pursuant to Employer Q's human resources policy, Employee A is permitted to carry over the one nonelective week of paid time off to the next year. Nonelective paid time off is not part of the cafeteria plan (that is, neither Employer Q nor the cafeteria plan permit employees to exchange nonelective paid time off for other benefits).

(iii) The cafeteria plan's terms and operations do not violate the prohibition against deferring compensation.

Example 3. Forfeiture of unused elective paid time off. Same facts as *Example 2*, except that pursuant to the cafeteria plan, Employee A forfeits the remaining one week of elective paid time off. The cafeteria plan's terms and operations do not violate the prohibition against deferring compensation.

Example 4. Unused elective paid time off carried over to next plan year. Same facts as *Example 1*, except that Employee A uses only two weeks of paid time off during the 2009 plan year, and, under the terms of the cafeteria plan, Employee A is treated as having used the two nonelective weeks and as having retained the one elective week. The one remaining week (that is, the elective week) is carried over to the next plan year (or the value thereof used for any other purpose in the next plan year). The plan operates to permit deferring compensation and is not a cafeteria plan.

Example 5. Paid time off exchanged for accident and health insurance premiums. Employer R provides employees with four weeks of paid time off for a year. Employer R's calendar year cafeteria plan permits employees to exchange up to one week of paid time off to pay the employee's share of accident and health insurance premiums. For the 2009 plan year, Employee B (with a calendar tax year), timely elects to exchange one week of paid time off (valued at $769) to pay accident and health insurance premiums for 2009. The $769 is excludible from Employee B's gross income under section 106. The cafeteria plan's terms and operations do not violate the prohibition against deferring compensation.

(p) *Benefits relating to more than one year* —(1) *Benefits in an accident and health insurance policy relating to more than one year.* Consistent with section 125(d), an accident and health insurance policy may include certain benefits, as set forth in this paragraph (p)(1), without violating the prohibition against deferred compensation.

(i) *Permitted benefits.* The following features or benefits of insurance policies do not defer compensation—

(A) Credit toward the deductible for unreimbursed covered expenses incurred in prior periods;

(B) Reasonable lifetime maximum limit on benefits;

(C) Level premiums;

(D) Premium waiver during disability;

(E) Guaranteed policy renewability of coverage, without further evidence of insurability (but not guaranty of the amount of premium upon renewal);

(F) Coverage for a specified accidental injury;

(G) Coverage for a specified disease or illness, including payments at initial diagnosis of the specified disease or illness, and progressive payments of a set amount per month following the initial diagnosis (sometimes referred to as progressive diagnosis payments); and

(H) Payment of a fixed amount per day (or other period) of hospitalization.

(ii) *Requirements of permitted benefits.* All benefits described in paragraph (p)(1)(i) of this section must in addition satisfy all of the following requirements—

(A) No part of any benefit is used in one plan year to purchase a benefit in a subsequent plan year;

(B) The policies remain in force only so long as premiums are timely paid on a current basis, and, irrespective of the amount of premiums paid in prior plan years, if the current premiums are not paid, all coverage for new diseases or illnesses lapses. See paragraph (p)(1)(i)(D), allowing premium waiver during disability;

(C) There is no investment fund or cash value to rely upon for payment of premiums; and

(D) No part of any premium is held in a separate account for any participant or beneficiary, or otherwise segregated from the assets of the insurance company.

(2) *Benefits under a long-term disability policy relating to more than one year.* A long-term disability policy paying disability benefits over more than one year does not violate the prohibition against deferring compensation.

(3) *Reasonable premium rebates or policy dividends.* Reasonable premium rebates or policy dividends paid with respect to benefits provided through a cafeteria plan do not constitute impermissible deferred compensation if such rebates or dividends are paid before the close of the 12-month period immediately following the cafeteria plan year to which such rebates and dividends relate.

(4) *Mandatory two-year election for vision or dental insurance.* When a cafeteria plan offers vision or dental insurance that requires a mandatory two-year coverage period, but not longer (sometimes referred to as a "two-year lock-in"), the mandatory two-year coverage period does not result in deferred compensation in violation of section 125(d)(2), provided both of the following requirements are satisfied—

(i) The premiums for each plan year are paid no less frequently than annually; and

(ii) In no event does a cafeteria plan use salary reduction or flex-credits relating to the first year of a two-year election to apply to vision or dental insurance for the second year of the two-year election.

(5) *Using salary reduction amounts from one plan year to pay accident and health insurance premiums for the first month of the immediately following plan year.*

(i) *In general.* Salary reduction amounts from the last month of one plan year of a cafeteria plan may be applied to pay accident and health insurance premiums for insurance during the first month of the immediately following plan year, if done on a uniform and consistent basis with respect to all participants (based on the usual payroll interval for each group of participants).

(ii) *Example.* The following example illustrates the rules in this paragraph (p)(5):

Example. Salary reduction payments in December of calendar plan year to pay accident and health insurance premiums for January. Employer S maintains a calendar year cafeteria plan. The cafeteria plan offers employees a salary reduction election for accident and health insurance. The plan provides that employees' salary reduction amounts for the last pay period in December are applied to pay accident and health insurance premiums for the immediately following January. All employees are paid bi-weekly. For the plan year ending December 31, 2009, Employee C elects salary reduction of $3,250 for accident and health coverage. For the last pay period in December 2009, $125 (3,250/26) is applied to the accident and health insurance premium for January 2010. This plan provision does not violate the prohibition against deferring compensation.

(q) *Nonqualified benefits* —(1) *In general.* The following benefits are nonqualified benefits that are not permitted to be offered in a cafeteria plan—

(i) Scholarships described in section 117;

(ii) Employer-provided meals and lodging described in section 119;

(iii) Educational assistance described in section 127;

(iv) Fringe benefits described in section 132;

(v) Long-term care insurance, or any product which is advertised, marketed or offered as long-term care insurance;

(vi) Long-term care services (but see paragraph (q)(3) of this section);

(vii) Group-term life insurance on the life of any individual other than an employee (whether includible or excludible from the employee's gross income);

(viii) Health reimbursement arrangements (HRAs) that provide reimbursements up to a maximum dollar amount for a coverage period and that all or any unused amount at the end of a coverage period is carried forward to increase the maximum reimbursement amount in subsequent coverage periods;

(ix) Contributions to Archer MSAs (section 220); and

(x) Elective deferrals to a section 403(b) plan.

(2) *Nonqualified benefits not permitted in a cafeteria plan.* The benefits described in this paragraph (q) are not qualified benefits or taxable benefits or cash for purposes of section 125 and thus may not be offered in a cafeteria plan regardless of whether any such benefit is purchased with after-tax employee contributions or on any other basis. A plan that offers a nonqualified benefit is not a cafeteria plan. Employees' elections between taxable and nontaxable benefits through such plan result in gross income to the participants for any benefit elected. See section 125(f). See paragraph (q)(3) of this section for special rule on long-term care insurance purchased through an HSA.

(3) *Long-term care insurance or services purchased through an HSA.* Although long-term care insurance is not a qualified benefit and may not be offered in a cafeteria plan, a cafeteria plan is permitted to offer an HSA as a qualified benefit, and funds from the HSA may be used to pay eligible long-term care premiums on a qualified long-term care insurance contract or for qualified long-term care services.

(r) *Employer contributions to a cafeteria plan* —(1) *Salary reduction-in general.* The term *employer contributions* means amounts that are not currently available (after taking section 125 into account) to the employee but are specified in the cafeteria plan as amounts that an employee may use for the purpose of electing benefits through the plan. A plan may provide that employer contributions may be made, in whole or in part, pursuant to employees' elections to reduce their compensation or to forgo increases in compensation and to have such amounts contributed, as employer contributions, by the employer on their behalf. See also § 1.125-5 (flexible spending arrangements). Also, a cafeteria plan is permitted to require employees to elect to pay the employees' share of any qualified benefit through salary reduction and not with after-tax employee contributions. A cafeteria plan is also permitted to pay reasonable cafeteria plan administrative fees through salary reduction amounts, and these salary reduction amounts are excludible from an employee's gross income.

(2) *Salary reduction as employer contribution.* Salary reduction contributions are employer contributions. An employee's salary reduction election is an election to receive a contribution by the employer in lieu of salary or other compensation that is not currently available to the employee as of the effective date of the election and that does not subsequently become currently available to the employee.

(3) *Employer flex-credits.* A cafeteria plan may also provide that the employer contributions will or may be made on behalf of employees equal to (or up to) specified amounts (or specified percentages of compensation) and that such nonelective contributions are available to employees for the election of benefits through the plan.

(4) *Elective contributions to a section 401(k) plan.* See § 1.401(k)-1 for general rules relating to contributions to section 401(k) plans.

(s) *Effective/applicability date.* It is proposed that these regulations apply on and after plan years beginning on or after January 1, 2009, except that the rule in paragraph (k)(2)(i)(B) of this section is effective as of the date the proposed regulations are published in the **Federal Register**.

§ 1.125-2 Cafeteria plans; elections.

(a) *Rules relating to making and revoking elections* —(1) *Elections in general.* A plan is not a cafeteria plan unless the plan provides in writing that employees are permitted to make elections among the permitted taxable benefits and qualified benefits offered through the plan for the plan year (and grace period, if applicable). All elections must be irrevocable by the date described in paragraph (a)(2) of this section except as provided in paragraph (a)(4) of this section. An election is not irrevocable if, after the earlier of the dates specified in paragraph (a)(2) of this section, employees have the right to revoke their elections of qualified benefits and instead receive the taxable benefits for such period, without regard to whether the employees actually revoke their elections.

(2) *Timing of elections.* In order for employees to exclude qualified benefits from employees' gross income, benefit elections in a cafeteria plan must be made before the earlier of—

(i) The date when taxable benefits are currently available; or

(ii) The first day of the plan year (or other coverage period).

(3) *Benefit currently available to an employee-in general.* Cash or another taxable benefit is currently available to the employee if it has been paid to the employee or if the employee is able currently to receive the cash or other taxable benefit at the employee's discretion. However, cash or another taxable benefit is not currently available to an employee if there is a significant limitation or restriction on the employee's right to receive the benefit currently. Similarly, a benefit is not currently available as of a date if the employee may under no circumstances receive the benefit before a particular time in the future. The determination of whether a benefit is currently available to an employee does not depend on whether it has been constructively received by the employee for purposes of section 451.

(4) *Exceptions to rule on making and revoking elections.* If a cafeteria plan incorporates the change in status rules in § 1.125-4, to the extent provided in those rules, an employee who experiences a change in status (as defined in § 1.125-4) is permitted to revoke an existing election and to make a new election with respect to the remaining portion of the period of coverage, but only with respect to cash or other taxable benefits that are not yet currently available. See paragraph (c)(1) of this section for a special rule for changing elections prospectively for HSA contributions and paragraph (r)(4) in § 1.125-1 for section 401(k) elections. Also, only an employee of the employer sponsoring a cafeteria plan is allowed to make, revoke or change elections in the employer's cafeteria plan. The employee's spouse, dependent or any other individual other than the employee may not make, revoke or change elections under the plan.

(5) *Elections not required on written paper documents.* A cafeteria plan does not fail to meet the requirements of section 125 merely because it permits employees to use electronic media for such transactions. The safe harbor in § 1.401(a)-21 applies to electronic elections, revocations and changes in elections under section 125.

(6) *Examples.* The following examples illustrate the rules in this paragraph (a):

Example 1. Election not revocable during plan year. Employer A's cafeteria plan offers each employee the opportunity to elect, for a plan year, between $5,000 cash for the plan year and a dependent care assistance program of up to $5,000 of dependent care expenses incurred by the employee during the plan year. The cafeteria plan requires employees to elect between these benefits before the beginning of the plan year. After the year has commenced, employees are prohibited from revoking their elections. The cafeteria plan allows revocation of elections based on changes in status (as described in § 1.125-4). Employees who elected the dependent care assistance program do not include the $5,000 cash in gross income. The cafeteria plan satisfies the requirements in this paragraph (a).

Example 2. Election revocable during plan year. Same facts as *Example 1* except that Employer A's cafeteria plan allows employees to revoke their elections for dependent care assistance at any time during the plan year and receive the unused amount of dependent care assistance as cash. The cafeteria plan fails to satisfy the requirements in this paragraph (a), and is not a cafeteria plan. All employees are treated as having received the $5,000 in cash even if they do not revoke their elections. The same result occurs even though the cash is not payable until the end of the plan year.

(b) *Automatic elections* —(1) *In general.* For new employees or current employees who fail to timely elect between permitted taxable benefits and qualified benefits, a cafeteria plan is permitted, but is not required, to provide default elections for one or more qualified benefits (for example, an election made for any prior year is deemed to be continued for every succeeding plan year, unless changed).

(2) *Example.* The following example illustrates the rules in this paragraph (b):

Example. Automatic elections for accident and health insurance. (i) Employer B maintains a calendar year cafeteria plan. The cafeteria plan offers accident and health insurance with an option for employee-only or family coverage. All employees are eligible to participate in the cafeteria plan immediately upon hire.

(ii) The cafeteria plan provides for an automatic enrollment process: each new employee and each current employee is automatically enrolled in employee-only coverage under the accident and health insurance plan, and the employee's salary is reduced to pay the employee's share of the accident and health insurance premium, unless the employee affirmatively elects cash. Alternatively, if the employee has a spouse or child, the employee can elect family coverage.

(iii) When an employee is hired, the employee receives a notice explaining the automatic enrollment process and the employee's right to decline coverage and have no salary reduction. The notice includes the salary reduction amounts for employee-only coverage and family coverage, procedures for exercising the right to decline coverage, information on the time by which an election must be made, and the period for which an election is effective. The notice is also given to each current employee before the beginning of each subsequent plan year, except that the notice for a current employee includes a description of the employee's existing coverage, if any.

(iv) For a new employee, an election to receive cash or to have family coverage rather than employee-only coverage is effective if made when the employee is hired. For a current employee, an election is effective if made prior to the start of each calendar year or under any other circumstances permitted under § 1.125-4. An election made for any prior year is deemed to be continued for every succeeding plan year, unless changed.

(v) Contributions used to purchase accident and health insurance through a cafeteria plan are not includible in the gross income of the employee solely because the plan provides for automatic enrollment as a default election whereby the employee's salary is reduced each year to pay for a portion of the accident and health insurance through the plan (unless the employee affirmatively elects cash).

(c) *Election rules for salary reduction contributions to HSAs* —(1) *Prospective elections and changes in salary reduction elections allowed.* Contributions may be made to an HSA through a cafeteria plan. A cafeteria plan offering HSA contributions through salary reduction may permit employees to make prospective salary reduction elections or change or revoke salary reduction elections for HSA contributions (for example, to increase or decrease salary reduction elections for HSA contributions) at any time during the plan year, effective before salary becomes currently available. If a cafeteria plan offers HSA contributions as a qualified benefit, the plan must—

(i) Specifically describe the HSA contribution benefit;

(ii) Allow a participant to prospectively change his or her salary reduction election for HSA contributions on a monthly basis (or more frequently); and

(iii) Allow a participant who becomes ineligible to make HSA contributions to prospectively revoke his or her salary reduction election for HSA contributions.

(2) *Example.* The following example illustrates the rules in this paragraph (c):

Example. Prospective HSA salary reduction elections. (i) A cafeteria plan with a calendar plan year allows employees to make salary reduction elections for HSA contributions through the plan. The cafeteria plan permits employees to prospectively make, change or revoke salary contribution elections for HSA contributions, limited to one election, change or revocation per month.

(ii) Employee M participates in the cafeteria plan. Before salary becomes currently available to M, M makes the following elections. On January 2, 2009, M elects to contribute $100 for each pay period to an HSA, effective January 3, 2009. On March 15, 2009, M elects to reduce the HSA contribution to $35 per pay period, effective April 1, 2009. On May 1, 2009, M elects to discontinue all HSA contributions, effective May 15, 2009. The cafeteria plan implements all of Employee M's elections,

(iii) The cafeteria plan's operation is consistent with the section 125 election, change and revocation rules for HSA contributions.

(d) *Optional election for new employees.* A cafeteria plan may provide new employees 30 days after their hire date to make elections between cash and qualified benefits. The election is effective as of the employee's hire date. However, salary reduction amounts used to pay for such an election must be from compensation not yet currently available on the date of the election. The written cafeteria plan must provide that any employee who terminates employment and is rehired within 30 days after terminating employment (or who returns to employment following an unpaid leave of absence of less than 30 days) is not a new employee eligible for the election in this paragraph (d).

(e) *Effective/applicability date.* It is proposed that these regulations apply on and after plan years beginning on or after January 1, 2009.

Par. 3. Sections 1.125-5, 1.125-6 and 1.125-7 are added to read as follows:

§ 1.125-5 Flexible spending arrangements.

(a) *Definition of flexible spending arrangement* —(1) *In general.* An FSA generally is a benefit program that provides employees with coverage which reimburses specified, incurred expenses (subject to reimbursement maximums and any other reasonable conditions). An expense for qualified benefits must not be reimbursed from the FSA unless it is incurred during a period of coverage. See paragraph (e) of this section. After an expense for a qualified benefit has been incurred, the expense must first be substantiated before the expense is reimbursed. See paragraphs (a) through (f) in § 1.125-6.

(2) *Maximum amount of reimbursement.* The maximum amount of reimbursement that is reasonably available to an employee for a period of coverage must not be substantially in excess of the total salary reduction and employer flex-credit for such participant's coverage. A maximum amount of reimbursement is not substantially in excess of the total salary reduction and employer flex-credit if such maximum amount is less than 500 percent of the combined salary reduction and employer flex-credit. A single FSA may provide participants with different levels of coverage and maximum amounts of reimbursement. See paragraph (r) in § 1.125-1 and paragraphs (b) and (d) in this section for the definition of salary reduction, employer flex-credit, and uniform coverage rule.

(b) *Flex-credits allowed* —(1) *In general.* An FSA in a cafeteria plan must include an election between cash or taxable benefits (including salary reduction) and one or more qualified benefits, and may include, in addition, "employer flex-credits." For this purpose, flex-credits are non-elective employer contributions that the employer makes for every employee eligible to participate in the employer's cafeteria plan, to be used at the employee's election only for one or more qualified benefits (but not as cash or a taxable benefit). See § 1.125-1 for definitions of qualified benefits, cash and taxable benefits.

(2) *Example.* The following example illustrates the rules in this paragraph (b):

Example. Flex-credit. Contribution to health FSA for employees electing employer-provided accident and health plan. Employer A maintains a cafeteria plan offering employees an election between cash or taxable benefits and premiums for employer-provided accident and health insurance or coverage through an HMO. The plan also provides an employer contribution of $200 to the health FSA of every employee who elects accident and health insurance or HMO coverage. In addition, these employees may elect to reduce their salary to make additional contributions to their health FSAs. The benefits offered in this cafeteria plan are consistent with the requirements of section 125 and this paragraph (b).

(c) *Use-or-lose rule* —(1) *In general.* An FSA may not defer compensation. No contribution or benefit from an FSA may be carried over to any subsequent plan year or period of coverage. See paragraph (k)(3) in this section for specific exceptions. Unused benefits or contributions remaining at the end of the plan year (or at the end of a grace period, if applicable) are forfeited.

(2) *Example.* The following example illustrates the rules in this paragraph (c):

Example. Use-or-lose rule. (i) Employer B maintains a calendar year cafeteria plan, offering an election between cash and a health FSA. The cafeteria plan has no grace period.

(ii) Employee A plans to have eye surgery in 2009. For the 2009 plan year, Employee A timely elects salary reduction of $3,000 for a health FSA. During the 2009 plan year, Employee A learns that she cannot have eye surgery performed, but incurs other section 213(d) medical expenses totaling $1,200. As of December 31, 2009, she has $1,800 of unused benefits and contributions in the health FSA. Consistent with the rules in this paragraph (c), she forfeits $1,800.

(d) *Uniform coverage rules applicable to health FSAs* —(1) *Uniform coverage throughout coverage period- in general*. The maximum amount of reimbursement from a health FSA must be available at all times during the period of coverage (properly reduced as of any particular time for prior reimbursements for the same period of coverage). Thus, the maximum amount of reimbursement at any particular time during the period of coverage cannot relate to the amount that has been contributed to the FSA at any particular time prior to the end of the plan year. Similarly, the payment schedule for the required amount for coverage under a health FSA may not be based on the rate or amount of covered claims incurred during the coverage period. Employees' salary reduction payments must not be accelerated based on employees' incurred claims and reimbursements.

(2) *Reimbursement available at all times*. Reimbursement is deemed to be available at all times if it is paid at least monthly or when the total amount of the claims to be submitted is at least a specified, reasonable minimum amount (for example, $50).

(3) *Terminated participants*. When an employee ceases to be a participant, the cafeteria plan must pay the former participant any amount the former participant previously paid for coverage or benefits to the extent the previously paid amount relates to the period from the date the employee ceases to be a participant through the end of that plan year. See paragraph (e)(2) in this section for COBRA elections for health FSAs.

(4) *Example*. The following example illustrates the rules in this paragraph (d):

Example. Uniform coverage. (i) Employer C maintains a calendar year cafeteria plan, offering an election between cash and a health FSA. The cafeteria plan prohibits accelerating employees' salary reduction payments based on employees' incurred claims and reimbursements.

(ii) For the 2009 plan year, Employee N timely elects salary reduction of $3,000 for a health FSA. Employee N pays the $3,000 salary reduction amount through salary reduction of $250 per month throughout the coverage period. Employee N is eligible to receive the maximum amount of reimbursement of $3,000 at all times throughout the coverage period (reduced by prior reimbursements).

(iii) N incurs $2,500 of section 213(d) medical expenses in January, 2009. The full $2,500 is reimbursed although Employee N has made only one salary reduction payment of $250. N incurs $500 in medical expenses in February, 2009. The remaining $500 of the $3,000 is reimbursed. After Employee N submits a claim for reimbursement and substantiates the medical expenses, the cafeteria plan reimburses N for the $2,500 and $500 medical expenses. Employer C's cafeteria plan satisfies the uniform coverage rule.

(5) *No uniform coverage rule for FSAs for dependent care assistance or adoption assistance*. The uniform coverage rule applies only to health FSAs and does not apply to FSAs for dependent care assistance or adoption assistance. See paragraphs (i) and (j) of this section for the rules for FSAs for dependent care assistance and adoption assistance.

(e) *Required period of coverage for a health FSA, dependent care FSA and adoption assistance FSA* —(1) *Twelve-month period of coverage—in general*. An FSA's period of coverage must be 12 months. However, in the case of a short plan year, the period of coverage is the entire short plan year. See paragraph (d) in §1.125-1 for rules on plan years and changing plan years.

(2) *COBRA elections for health FSAs*. For the application of the health care continuation rules of section 4980B of the Code to health FSAs, see Q & A-2 in §54.4980B-2 of this chapter.

(3) *Separate period of coverage permitted for each qualified benefit offered through FSA*. Dependent care assistance, adoption assistance, and a health FSA are each permitted to have a separate period of coverage, which may be different from the plan year of the cafeteria plan.

(f) *Coverage on a month-by-month or expense-by-expense basis prohibited*. In order for reimbursements from an accident and health plan to qualify for the section 105(b) exclusion, an employer-funded accident and health plan offered through a cafeteria plan may not operate in a manner that enables employees to purchase the accident and health plan coverage only for periods when employees expect to incur medical care expenses. Thus, for example, if a cafeteria plan permits employees to receive accident and health plan coverage on a month-by-month or an expense-by-expense basis, reimbursements from the accident and health plan fail to qualify for the section 105(b) exclusion. If, however, the period of coverage under an accident and health plan offered through a cafeteria plan is twelve months and the cafeteria plan does not permit an employee to elect specific amounts of coverage, reimbursement, or salary reduction for less than twelve months, the cafete-

ria plan does not operate to enable participants to purchase coverage only for periods during which medical care will be incurred. See §1.125-4 and paragraph (a) in §1.125-2 regarding the revocation of elections during a period of coverage on account of changes in family status.

(g) *FSA administrative practices* —(1) *Limiting health FSA enrollment to employees who participate in the employer's accident and health plan*. At the employer's option, a cafeteria plan is permitted to provide that only those employees who participate in one or more specified employer-provided accident and health plans may participate in a health FSA. See §1.125-7 for nondiscrimination rules.

(2) *Interval for employees' salary reduction contributions*. The cafeteria plan is permitted to specify any interval for employees' salary reduction contributions. The interval specified in the plan must be uniform for all participants.

(h) *Qualified benefits permitted to be offered through an FSA*. Dependent care assistance (section 129), adoption assistance (section 137) and a medical reimbursement arrangement (section 105(b)) are permitted to be offered through an FSA in a cafeteria plan.

(i) *Section 129 rules for dependent care assistance program offered through a cafeteria plan* —(1) *General rule*. In order for dependent care assistance to be a qualified benefit that is excludible from gross income if elected through a cafeteria plan, the cafeteria plan must satisfy section 125 and the dependent care assistance must satisfy section 129.

(2) *Dependent care assistance in general*. Section 129(a) provides an employee with an exclusion from gross income both for an employer-funded dependent care assistance program and for amounts paid or incurred by the employer for dependent care assistance provided to the employee, if the amounts are paid or incurred through a dependent care assistance program. See paragraph (a)(4) in §1.125-6 on when dependent care expenses are incurred.

(3) *Reimbursement exclusively for dependent care assistance*. A dependent care assistance program may not provide reimbursements other than for dependent care expenses; in particular, if an employee has dependent care expenses less than the amount specified by salary reduction, the plan may not provide other taxable or nontaxable benefits for any portion of the specified amount not used for the reimbursement of dependent care expenses. Thus, if an employee has elected coverage under the dependent care assistance program and the period of coverage has commenced, the employee must not have the right to receive amounts from the program other than as reimbursements for dependent care expenses. This is the case regardless of whether coverage under the program is purchased with contributions made at the employer's discretion, at the employee's discretion, or pursuant to a collective bargaining agreement. Arrangements formally outside of the cafeteria plan providing for the adjustment of an employee's compensation or an employee's receipt of any other benefits on the basis of the assistance or reimbursements received by the employee are considered in determining whether a dependent care benefit is a dependent care assistance program under section 129.

(j) *Section 137 rules for adoption assistance program offered through a cafeteria plan* —(1) *General rule*. In order for adoption assistance to be a qualified benefit that is excludible from gross income if elected through a cafeteria plan, the cafeteria plan must satisfy section 125 and the adoption assistance must satisfy section 137.

(2) *Adoption assistance in general*. Section 137(a) provides an employee with an exclusion from gross income for amounts paid or expenses incurred by the employer for qualified adoption expenses in connection with an employee's adoption of a child, if the amounts are paid or incurred through an adoption assistance program. Certain limits on amount of expenses and employee's income apply.

(3) *Reimbursement exclusively for adoption assistance*. Rules and requirements similar to the rules and requirements in paragraph (i)(3) of this section for dependent care assistance apply to adoption assistance.

(k) *FSAs and the rules governing the tax-favored treatment of employer-provided health benefits* —(1) *Medical expenses*. Health plans that are flexible spending arrangements, as defined in paragraph (a)(1) of this section, must conform to the generally applicable rules under sections 105 and 106 in order for the coverage and reimbursements under such plans to qualify for tax-favored treatment under such sections. Thus, health FSAs must qualify as accident and health plans. See paragraph (n) in §1.125-1. A health FSA is only permitted to reimburse medical expenses as defined in section 213(d). Thus, for example, a health FSA is not permitted to reimburse dependent care expenses.

(2) *Limiting payment or reimbursement to certain section 213(d) medical expenses*. A health FSA is permitted to limit payment or reimbursement to only certain section 213(d) medical expenses (except

health insurance, long-term care services or insurance). See paragraph (q) in §1.125-1. For example, a health FSA in a cafeteria plan is permitted to provide in the written plan that the plan reimburses all section 213(d) medical expenses allowed to be paid or reimbursed under a cafeteria plan except over-the-counter drugs.

(3) *Application of prohibition against deferred compensation to medical expenses.* (i) *Certain advance payments for orthodontia permitted.* A cafeteria plan is permitted, but is not required to, reimburse employees for orthodontia services before the services are provided but only to the extent that the employee has actually made the payments in advance of the orthodontia services in order to receive the services. These orthodontia services are deemed to be incurred when the employee makes the advance payment. Reimbursing advance payments does not violate the prohibition against deferring compensation.

(ii) *Example.* The following example illustrates the rules in paragraph (k)(3):

Example. Advance payment to orthodontist. Employer D sponsors a calendar year cafeteria plan which offers a health FSA. Employee K elects to salary reduce $3,000 for a health FSA for the 2009 plan year. Employee K's dependent requires orthodontic treatment. K's accident and health insurance does not cover orthodontia. The orthodontist, following the normal practice, charges $3,000, all due in 2009, for treatment, to begin in 2009 and end in 2010. K pays the $3,000 in 2009. In 2009, Employer D's cafeteria plan may reimburse $3,000 to K, without violating the prohibition against deferring compensation in section 125(d)(2).

(iii) *Reimbursements for durable medical equipment.* A health FSA in a cafeteria plan that reimburses employees for equipment (described in section 213(d)) with a useful life extending beyond the period of coverage during which the expense is incurred does not provide deferred compensation. For example, a health FSA is permitted to reimburse the cost of a wheelchair for an employee.

(4) *No reimbursement of premiums for accident and health insurance or long-term care insurance or services.* A health FSA is not permitted to treat employees' premium payments for other health coverage as reimbursable expenses. Thus, for example, a health FSA is not permitted to reimburse employees for payments for other health plan coverage, including premiums for COBRA coverage, accidental death and dismemberment insurance, long-term disability or short-term disability insurance or for health coverage under a plan maintained by the employer of the employee or the employer of the employee's spouse or dependent. Also, a health FSA is not permitted to reimburse expenses for long-term care insurance premiums or for long-term care services for the employee or employee's spouse or dependent. See paragraph (q) in §1.125-1 for nonqualified benefits

(l) *Section 105(h) requirements.* Section 105(h) applies to health FSAs. Section 105(h) provides that the exclusion provided by section 105(b) is not available with respect to certain amounts received by a highly compensated individual (as defined in section 105(h)(5)) from a discriminatory self-insured medical reimbursement plan, which includes health FSAs. See §1.105-11. For purposes of section 105(h), coverage by a self-insured accident and health plan offered through a cafeteria plan is an optional benefit (even if only one level and type of coverage is offered) and, for purposes of the optional benefit rule in §1.105-11(c)(3)(i), employer contributions are treated as employee contributions to the extent that taxable benefits are offered by the plan.

(m) *HSA-compatible FSAs-limited-purpose health FSAs and post-deductible health FSAs* —(1) *In general.* Limited-purpose health FSAs and *post-deductible health FSAs* which satisfy all the requirements of section 125 are permitted to be offered through a cafeteria plan.

(2) *HSA-compatible FSAs.* Section 223(a) allows a deduction for certain contributions to a "Health Savings Account" (HSA) (as defined in section 223(d)). An *eligible individual* (as defined in section 223(c)(1)) may contribute to an HSA. An eligible individual must be covered under a "high deductible health plan" (HDHP) and not, while covered under an HDHP, under any health plan which is not an HDHP. A general purpose health FSA is not an HDHP and an individual covered by a general purpose health FSA is not eligible to contribute to an HSA. However, an individual covered by an HDHP (and who otherwise satisfies section 223(c)(1)) does not fail to be an eligible individual merely because the individual is also covered by a limited-purpose health FSA or post-deductible health FSA (as defined in this paragraph (m)) or a combination of a limited-purpose health FSA and a post-deductible health FSA.

(3) *Limited-purpose health FSA.* A limited-purpose health FSA is a health FSA described in the cafeteria plan that only pays or reimburses permitted coverage benefits (as defined in section 223(c)(2)(C)), such

as vision care, dental care or preventive care (as defined for purposes of section 223(c)(2)(C)). See paragraph (k) in this section.

(4) *Post-deductible health FSA* —(i) *In general.* A post-deductible health FSA is a health FSA described in the cafeteria plan that only pays or reimburses medical expenses (as defined in section 213(d)) for preventive care or medical expenses incurred after the minimum annual HDHP deductible under section 223(c)(2)(A)(i) is satisfied. See paragraph (k) in this section. No medical expenses incurred before the annual HDHP deductible is satisfied may be reimbursed by a post-deductible FSA, regardless of whether the HDHP covers the expense or whether the deductible is later satisfied. For example, even if chiropractic care is not covered under the HDHP, expenses for chiropractic care incurred before the HDHP deductible is satisfied are not reimbursable at any time by a post-deductible health FSA.

(ii) *HDHP and health FSA deductibles.* The deductible for a post-deductible health FSA need not be the same amount as the deductible for the HDHP, but in no event may the post-deductible health FSA or other coverage provide benefits before the minimum annual HDHP deductible under section 223(c)(2)(A)(i) is satisfied (other than benefits permitted under a limited-purpose health FSA). In addition, although the deductibles of the HDHP and the other coverage may be satisfied independently by separate expenses, no benefits may be paid before the minimum annual deductible under section 223(c)(2)(A)(i) has been satisfied. An individual covered by a post-deductible health FSA (if otherwise an eligible individual) is an eligible individual for the purpose of contributing to the HSA.

(5) *Combination of limited-purpose health FSA and post-deductible health FSA.* An FSA is a combination of a limited-purpose health FSA and post-deductible health FSA if each of the benefits and reimbursements provided under the FSA are permitted under either a limited-purpose health FSA or post-deductible health FSA. For example, before the HDHP deductible is satisfied, a combination limited-purpose and post-deductible health FSA may reimburse only preventive, vision or dental expenses. A combination limited-purpose and post-deductible health FSA may also reimburse any medical expense that may otherwise be paid by an FSA (that is, no insurance premiums or long-term care benefits) that is incurred after the HDHP deductible is satisfied.

(6) *Substantiation.* The substantiation rules in this section apply to limited-purpose health FSAs and to post-deductible health FSAs. In addition to providing third-party substantiation of medical expenses, a participant in a post-deductible health FSA must provide information from an independent third party that the HDHP deductible has been satisfied. A participant in a limited-purpose health FSA must provide information from an independent third-party that the medical expenses are for vision care, dental care or preventive care.

(7) *Plan amendments.* See paragraph (c) in §1.125-1 on the required effective date for amendments adopting or changing limited-purpose, post-deductible or combination limited-purpose and post-deductible health FSAs.

(n) *Qualified HSA distributions* —(1) *In general.* A health FSA in a cafeteria plan is permitted to offer employees the right to elect qualified HSA distributions described in section 106(e). No qualified HSA distribution may be made in a plan year unless the employer amends the health FSA written plan with respect to all employees, effective by the last day of the plan year, to allow a qualified HSA distribution satisfying all the requirements in this paragraph (n). See also section 106(e)(5)(B). In addition, a distribution with respect to an employee is not a qualified HSA distribution unless all of the following the requirements are satisfied—

(i) No qualified HSA distribution has been previously made on behalf of the employee from this health FSA;

(ii) The employee elects to have the employer make a qualified HSA distribution from the health FSA to the HSA of the employee;

(iii) The distribution does not exceed the lesser of the balance of the health FSA on- -

(A) September 21, 2006; or

(B) The date of the distribution;

(iv) For purposes of this paragraph (n)(1), balances as of any date are determined on a cash basis, without taking into account expenses incurred but not reimbursed as of a date, and applying the uniform coverage rule in paragraph (d) in this section;

(v) The distribution is made no later than December 31, 2011; and

(vi) The employer makes the distribution directly to the trustee of the employee's HSA.

(2) *Taxation of qualified HSA distributions.* A qualified HSA distribution from the health FSA covering the participant to his or her HSA is a rollover to the HSA (as defined in section 223(f)(5)) and thus is generally not includible in gross income. However, if the participant is not an eligible individual (as defined in section 223(c)(1)) at any time during a testing period following the qualified HSA distribution, the amount of the distribution is includible in the participant's gross income and he or she is also subject to an additional 10 percent tax (with certain exceptions). Section 106(e)(3).

(3) *No effect on health FSA elections, coverage, use-or-lose rule.* A qualified HSA distribution does not alter an employee's irrevocable election under paragraph (a) of §1.125-2, or constitute a change in status under §1.125-4(a). If a qualified HSA distribution is made to an employee's HSA, even if the balance in a health FSA is reduced to zero, the employee's health FSA coverage continues to the end of the plan year. Unused benefits and contributions remaining at the end of a plan year (or at the end of a grace period, if applicable) must be forfeited.

(o) *FSA experience gains or forfeitures* —(1) *Experience gains in general.* An FSA experience gain (sometimes referred to as forfeitures in the use-or-lose rule in paragraph (c) in this section) with respect to a plan year (plus any grace period following the end of a plan year described in paragraph (e) in §1.125-1), equals the amount of the employer contributions, including salary reduction contributions, and after-tax employee contributions to the FSA minus the FSA's total claims reimbursements for the year . Experience gains (or forfeitures) may be—

(i) Retained by the employer maintaining the cafeteria plan; or

(ii) If not retained by the employer, may be used only in one or more of the following ways—

(A) To reduce required salary reduction amounts for the immediately following plan year, on a reasonable and uniform basis, as described in paragraph (o)(2) of this section;

(B) Returned to the employees on a reasonable and uniform basis, as described in paragraph (o)(2) of this section; or

(C) To defray expenses to administer the cafeteria plan .

(2) *Allocating experience gains among employees on reasonable and uniform basis.* If not retained by the employer or used to defray expenses of administering the plan, the experience gains must be allocated among employees on a reasonable and uniform basis. It is permissible to allocate these amounts based on the different coverage levels of employees under the FSA. Experience gains allocated in compliance with this paragraph (o) are not a deferral of the receipt of compensation. However, in no case may the experience gains be allocated among employees based (directly or indirectly) on their individual claims experience. Experience gains may not be used as contributions directly or indirectly to any deferred compensation benefit plan.

(3) *Example.* The following example illustrates the rules in this paragraph (o):

Example . *Allocating experience gains* . (i) Employer L maintains a cafeteria plan for its 1,200 employees, who may elect one of several different annual coverage levels under a health FSA in $100 increments from $500 to $2,000.

(ii) For the 2009 plan year, 1,000 employees elect levels of coverage under the health FSA. For the 2009 plan year, the health FSA has an experience gain of $5,000.

(iii) The $5,000 may be allocated to all participants for the plan year on a per capita basis weighted to reflect the participants' elected levels of coverage.

(iv) Alternatively, the $5,000 may be used to reduce the required salary reduction amount under the health FSA for all 2009 participants (for example, a $500 health FSA for the next year is priced at $480) or to reimburse claims incurred above the elective limit in 2010 as long as such reimbursements are made on a reasonable and uniform level.

(p) *Effective/applicability date.* It is proposed that these regulations apply on and after plan years beginning on or after January 1, 2009.

§1.125-6 Substantiation of expenses for all cafeteria plans.

(a) *Cafeteria plan payments and reimbursements* —(1) *In general.* A cafeteria plan may pay or reimburse only those substantiated expenses for qualified benefits incurred on or after the later of the effective date of the cafeteria plan and the date the employee is enrolled in the plan. This requirement applies to all qualified benefits offered through the cafeteria plan. See paragraph (b) of this section for substantiation rules.

(2) *Expenses incurred.* (i) *Employees' medical expenses must be incurred during the period of coverage.* In order for reimbursements to be excludible from gross income under section 105(b), the medical expenses reimbursed by an accident and health plan elected through a cafeteria plan must be incurred during the period when the participant is covered by the accident and health plan. A participant's period of coverage includes COBRA coverage. See §54.4980B-2 of this chapter. Medical expenses incurred before the later of the effective date of the plan and the date the employee is enrolled in the plan are not incurred during the period for which the employee is covered by the plan. However, the actual reimbursement of covered medical care expenses may be made after the applicable period of coverage.

(ii) *When medical expenses are incurred.* For purposes of this rule, medical expenses are incurred when the employee (or the employee's spouse or dependents) is provided with the medical care that gives rise to the medical expenses, and not when the employee is formally billed, charged for, or pays for the medical care.

(iii) *Example.* The following example illustrates the rules in this paragraph (a)(2):

Example. Medical expenses incurred after termination. (i) Employer E maintains a cafeteria plan with a calendar year plan year. The cafeteria plan provides that participation terminates when an individual ceases to be an employee of Employer E, unless the former employee elects to continue to participate in the health FSA under the COBRA rules in §54.4980B- 2 of this chapter. Employee G timely elects to salary reduce $1,200 to participate in a health FSA for the 2009 plan year. As of June 30, 2009, Employee G has contributed $600 toward the health FSA, but incurred no medical expenses. On June 30, 2009, Employee G terminates employment and does not continue participation under COBRA. On July 15, 2009, G incurs a section 213(d) medical expense of $500.

(ii) Under the rules in paragraph (a)(2) of this section, the cafeteria plan is prohibited from reimbursing any portion of the $500 medical expense because, at the time the medical expense is incurred, G is not a participant in the cafeteria plan.

(3) *Section 105(b) requirements for reimbursement of medical expenses through a cafeteria plan.* (i) *In general.* In order for medical care reimbursements paid to an employee through a cafeteria plan to be excludible under section 105(b), the reimbursements must be paid pursuant to an employer-funded *accident and health plan,* as defined in section 105(e) and §§1.105-2 and 1.105-5.

(ii) *Reimbursement exclusively for section 213(d) medical expenses.* A cafeteria plan benefit through which an employee receives reimbursements of medical expenses is excludable under section 105(b) only if reimbursements from the plan are made specifically to reimburse the employee for medical expenses (as defined in section 213(d)) incurred by the employee or the employee's spouse or dependents during the period of coverage. Amounts paid to an employee as reimbursement are not paid specifically to reimburse the employee for medical expenses if the plan provides that the employee is entitled, or operates in a manner that entitles the employee, to receive the amounts, in the form of cash (for example, routine payment of salary) or any other taxable or nontaxable benefit irrespective of whether the employee (or the employee's spouse or dependents) incurs medical expenses during the period of coverage. This rule applies even if the employee will not receive such amounts until the end or after the end of the period. A plan under which employees (or their spouses and dependents) will receive reimbursement for medical expenses up to a specified amount and, if they incur no medical expenses, will receive cash or any other benefit in lieu of the reimbursements is not a benefit qualifying for the exclusion under sections 106 and 105(b). See §1.105-2. This is the case without regard to whether the benefit was purchased with contributions made at the employer's discretion, at the employee's discretion (for example, by salary reduction election), or pursuant to a collective bargaining agreement.

(iii) *Other arrangements.* Arrangements formally outside of the cafeteria plan that adjust an employee's compensation or an employee's receipt of any other benefits on the basis of the expenses incurred or reimbursements the employee receives are considered in determining whether the reimbursements are through a plan eligible for the exclusions under sections 106 and 105(b).

(4) *Reimbursements of dependent care expenses.* (i) *Dependent care expenses must be incurred.* In order to satisfy section 129, dependent care expenses may not be reimbursed before the expenses are incurred. For purposes of this rule, dependent care expenses are incurred when the care is provided and not when the employee is formally billed, charged for, or pays for the dependent care.

(ii) *Dependent care provided during the period of coverage.* In order for dependent care assistance to be provided through a dependent care assistance program eligible for the section 129 exclusion, the care must be provided to or on behalf of the employee during the period for which the employee is covered by the program. For example, if for a plan year, an employee elects a dependent care assistance program providing for reimbursement of dependent care expenses, only reimbursements for dependent care expenses incurred during that plan year are provided from a dependent care assistance program within the scope of section 129. Also, for purposes of this rule, expenses incurred before the later of the program's effective date and the date the employee is enrolled in the program are not incurred during the period when the employee is covered by the program. Similarly, if the dependent care assistance program furnishes the dependent care in-kind (for example, through an employer-maintained child care facility), only dependent care provided during the plan year of coverage is provided through a dependent care assistance program within the meaning of section 129. See also § 1.125-5 for FSA rules.

(iii) *Period of coverage.* In order for dependent care assistance through a cafeteria plan to be provided through a dependent care assistance program eligible for the section 129 exclusion, the plan may not operate in a manner that enables employees to purchase dependent care assistance only for periods during which the employees expect to receive dependent care assistance. If the period of coverage for a dependent care assistance program offered through a cafeteria plan is twelve months (or, in the case of a short plan year, at least equal to the short plan year) and the plan does not permit an employee to elect specific amounts of coverage, reimbursement, or salary reduction for less than twelve months, the plan is deemed not to operate to enable employees to purchase coverage only for periods when dependent care assistance will be received. See paragraph (a) in § 1.125-2 and § 1.125-4 regarding the revocation of elections during the period of coverage on account of changes in family status. See paragraph (e) in this section for required period of coverage for dependent care assistance.

(iv) *Examples.* The following examples illustrate the rules in paragraphs (a)(4)(i)-(iii) of this section:

Example 1. Initial non-refundable fee for child care. (i) Employer F maintains a calendar year cafeteria plan, offering employees an election between cash and qualified benefits, including dependent care assistance. Employee M has a one-year old dependent child. Employee M timely elected $5,000 of dependent care assistance for 2009. During the entire 2009 plan year, Employee M satisfies all the requirements in section 129 for dependent care assistance.

(ii) On February 1, 2009, Employee M pays an initial non-refundable fee of $500 to a licensed child care center (unrelated to Employer F or to Employee M), to reserve a space at the child care center for M's child. The child care center's monthly charges for child care are $1,200. When the child care center first begins to care for M's child, the $500 non-refundable fee is applied toward the first month's charges for child care.

(iii) On March 1, 2009, the child care center begins caring for Employee M's child, and continues to care for the child through December 31, 2009. On March 1, 2009, M pays the child care center $700 (the balance of the $1,200 in charges for child care to be provided in March 2009). On April 1, 2009, M pays the child care center $1,200 for the child care to be provided in April 2009.

(iv) Dependent care expenses are incurred when the services are provided. For dependent care services provided in March 2009, the $500 nonrefundable fee paid on February 1, 2009, and the $700 paid on March 1, 2009 may be reimbursed on or after the later of the date when substantiated or April 1, 2009. For dependent care services provided in April 2009, the $1,200 paid on April 1, 2009 may be reimbursed on or after the later of the date when substantiated or May 1, 2009.

Example 2. Non-refundable fee forfeited. Same facts as *Example 1,* except that the child care center never cared for M's child (who was instead cared for at Employer F's onsite child care facility). Because the child care center never provided child care services to Employee M's child, the $500 non-refundable fee is not reimbursable.

(v) *Optional spend-down provision.* At the employer's option, the written cafeteria plan may provide that dependent care expenses incurred after the date an employee ceases participation in the cafeteria plan (for example, after termination) and through the last day of that plan year (or grace period immediately after that plan year) may be reimbursed from unused benefits, if all of the requirements of section 129 are satisfied.

(vi) *Example.* The following example illustrates the rules in paragraph (a)(4)(v) of this section:

Example. Terminated employee's post-termination dependent care expenses. (i) For calendar year 2009, Employee X elects $5,000 salary reduction for dependent care assistance through Employer G's cafeteria plan. X works for Employer G from January 1 through June 30, 2009, when X terminates employment. As of June 30, 2009, X had paid $2,500 in salary reduction and had incurred and was reimbursed for $2,000 of dependent care expenses.

(ii) X does not work again until October 1, 2009, when X begins work for Employer H. X was employed by Employer H from October 1, 2009 through December 31, 2009. During this period, X also incurred $500 of dependent care expenses. During all the periods of employment in 2009, X satisfied all requirements in section 129 for excluding payments for dependent care assistance from gross income.

(iii) Employer G's cafeteria plan allows terminated employees to "spend down" unused salary reduction amounts for dependent care assistance, if all requirements of section 129 are satisfied. After X's claim for $500 of dependent care expenses is substantiated, Employer G's cafeteria plan reimburses X for $500 (the remaining balance) of dependent care expenses incurred during X's employment for Employer H between October 1, 2009 and December 31, 2009. Employer G's cafeteria plan and operation are consistent with section 125.

(b) *Rules for claims substantiation for cafeteria plans* —(1) *Substantiation required before reimbursing expenses for qualified benefits.* This paragraph (b) sets forth the substantiation requirements that a cafeteria plan must satisfy before paying or reimbursing any expense for a qualified benefit.

(2) *All claims must be substantiated.* As a precondition of payment or reimbursement of expenses for qualified benefits, a cafeteria plan must require substantiation in accordance with this section. Substantiating only a percentage of claims, or substantiating only claims above a certain dollar amount, fails to comply with the substantiation requirements in § 1.125-1 and this section.

(3) *Substantiation by independent third-party.* (i) *In general.* All expenses must be substantiated by information from a third-party that is independent of the employee and the employee's spouse and dependents. The independent third-party must provide information describing the service or product, the date of the service or sale, and the amount. Self-substantiation or self-certification of an expense by an employee does not satisfy the substantiation requirements of this paragraph (b). The specific requirements in sections 105(b), 129, and 137 must also be satisfied as a condition of reimbursing expenses for qualified benefits. For example, a health FSA does not satisfy the requirements of section 105(b) if it reimburses employees for expenses where the employees only submit information describing medical expenses, the amount of the expenses and the date of the expenses but fail to provide a statement from an independent third-party (either automatically or subsequent to the transaction) verifying the expenses. Under § 1.105-2, all amounts paid under a plan that permits self-substantiation or self-certification are includible in gross income, including amounts reimbursed for medical expenses, whether or not substantiated. See paragraph (m) in § 1.125-5 for additional substantiation rules for limited-purpose and post-deductible health FSAs.

(ii) *Rules for substantiation of health FSA claims using an explanation of benefits provided by an insurance company.* (A) *Written statement from an independent third-party.* If the employer is provided with information from an independent third-party (such as an " *explanation of benefits* " (*EOB*) from an insurance company) indicating the date of the section 213(d) medical care and the employee's responsibility for payment for that medical care (that is, coinsurance payments and amounts below the plan's deductible), and the employee certifies that any expense paid through the health FSA has not been reimbursed and that the employee will not seek reimbursement from any other plan covering health benefits, the claim is fully substantiated without the need for submission of a receipt by the employee or further review.

(B) *Example.* The following example illustrates the rules in this paragraph (b)(3):

Example. Explanation of benefits. (i) During the plan year ending December 31, 2009, Employee Q is a participant in the health FSA sponsored by Employer J and is enrolled in Employer J's accident and health plan.

(ii) On March 1, 2009, Q visits a physician's office for medical care as defined in section 213(d). The charge for the physician's services is $150. Under the plan, Q is responsible for 20 percent of the charge for the physician's services (that is, $30). Q has sufficient FSA coverage for the $30 claim.

(iii) Employer J has coordinated with the accident and health plan so that Employer J or its agent automatically receives an EOB from the plan indicating that Q is responsible for payment of 20 percent of the $150 charged by the physician. Because Employer J has received a statement from an independent third-party that Q has incurred a medical expense, the date the expense was incurred, and the amount of the expense, the claim is substantiated without the need for J to submit additional information regarding the expense. Employer J's FSA reimburses Q the $30 medical expense without requiring Q to submit a receipt or a statement from the physician. The substantiation rules in paragraph (b) in this section are satisfied.

(4) *Advance reimbursement of expenses for qualified benefits prohibited.* Reimbursing expenses before the expense has been incurred or before the expense is substantiated fails to satisfy the substantiation requirements in § 1.105-2, § 1.125-1 and this section.

(5) *Purported loan from employer to employee.* In determining whether, under all the facts and circumstances, employees are being reimbursed for unsubstantiated claims, special scrutiny will be given to other arrangements such as employer-to-employee loans based on actual or projected employee claims.

(6) *Debit cards.* For purposes of this section, a *debit card* is a debit card, credit card, or stored value card. See also paragraphs (c) through (g) of this section for additional rules on payments or reimbursements made through debit cards.

(c) *Debit cards-overview* —(1) *Mandatory rules for all debit cards usable to pay or reimburse medical expenses.* Paragraph (d) of this section sets forth the mandatory procedures for debit cards to substantiate section 213(d) medical expenses. These rules apply to all debit cards used to pay or reimburse medical expenses. Paragraph (e) of this section sets forth additional substantiation rules that may be used for medical expenses incurred at medical care providers and certain stores with the Drug Stores and Pharmacies merchant category code. Paragraph (f) in this section sets forth the requirements for an inventory information approval system which must be used to substantiate medical expenses incurred at merchants or service providers that are not medical care providers or certain stores with the Drug Stores and Pharmacies merchant category code and that may be used for medical expenses incurred at all merchants.

(2) *Debit cards used for dependent care assistance.* Paragraph (g) of this section sets forth additional rules for debit cards usable for reimbursing dependent care expenses.

(3) *Additional guidance.* The Commissioner may prescribe additional guidance of general applicability, published in the Internal Revenue Bulletin (see § 601.601(d)(2)(ii)(*b*) of this chapter), to provide additional rules for debit cards.

(d) *Mandatory rules for all debit cards usable to pay or reimburse medical expenses.* A health FSA paying or reimbursing section 213(d) medical expenses through a debit card must satisfy all of the following requirements—

(1) Before any employee participating in a health FSA receives the debit card, the employee agrees in writing that he or she will only use the card to pay for medical expenses (as defined in section 213(d)) of the employee or his or her spouse or dependents, that he or she will not use the debit card for any medical expense that has already been reimbursed, that he or she will not seek reimbursement under any other health plan for any expense paid for with a debit card, and that he or she will acquire and retain sufficient documentation (including invoices and receipts) for any expense paid with the debit card.

(2) The debit card includes a statement providing that the agreements described in paragraph (d)(1) of this section are reaffirmed each time the employee uses the card.

(3) The amount available through the debit card equals the amount elected by the employee for the health FSA for the cafeteria plan year, and is reduced by amounts paid or reimbursed for section 213(d) medical expenses incurred during the plan year.

(4) The debit card is automatically cancelled when the employee ceases to participate in the health FSA.

(5) The employer limits use of the debit card to—

(i) Physicians, dentists, vision care offices, hospitals, other medical care providers (as identified by the merchant category code);

(ii) Stores with the merchant category code for Drugstores and Pharmacies if, on a location by location basis, 90 percent of the store's gross receipts during the prior taxable year consisted of items which qualify as expenses for medical care described in section 213(d); and

(iii) Stores that have implemented the inventory information approval system under paragraph (f).

(6) The employer substantiates claims based on payments to medical care providers and stores described in paragraphs (d)(5)(i) and (ii) of

this section in accordance with either paragraph (e) or paragraph (f) of this section.

(7) The employer follows all of the following correction procedures for any improper payments using the debit card—

(i) Until the amount of the improper payment is recovered, the debit card must be de-activated and the employee must request payments or reimbursements of medical expenses from the health FSA through other methods (for example, by submitting receipts or invoices from a merchant or service provider showing the employee incurred a section 213(d) medical expense);

(ii) The employer demands that the employee repay the cafeteria plan an amount equal to the improper payment;

(iii) If, after the demand for repayment of improper payment (as described in paragraph (d)(7)(ii) of this section), the employee fails to repay the amount of the improper charge, the employer withholds the amount of the improper charge from the employee's pay or other compensation, to the full extent allowed by applicable law;

(iv) If any portion of the improper payment remains outstanding after attempts to recover the amount (as described in paragraph (d)(7)(ii) and (iii) of this section), the employer applies a claims substitution or offset to resolve improper payments, such as a reimbursement for a later substantiated expense claim is reduced by the amount of the improper payment. So, for example, if an employee has received an improper payment of $200 and subsequently submits a substantiated claim for $250 incurred during the same coverage period, a reimbursement for $50 is made; and

(v) If, after applying all the procedures described in paragraph (d)(7)(ii) through (iv) of this section, the employee remains indebted to the employer for improper payments, the employer, consistent with its business practice, treats the improper payment as it would any other business indebtedness.

(e) *Substantiation of expenses incurred at medical care providers and certain other stores with Drug Stores and Pharmacies merchant category code* —(1) *In general.* A health FSA paying or reimbursing section 213(d) medical expenses through a debit card is permitted to comply with the substantiation provisions of this paragraph (e), instead of complying with the provisions of paragraph (f), for medical expenses incurred at providers described in paragraph (e)(2) of this section.

(2) *Medical care providers and certain other stores with Drug Stores and Pharmacies merchant category code.* Medical expenses may be substantiated using the methods described in paragraph (e)(3) of this section if incurred at physicians, pharmacies, dentists, vision care offices, hospitals, other medical care providers (as identified by the merchant category code) and at stores with the Drug Stores and Pharmacies merchant category code, if, on a store location-by-location basis, 90 percent of the store's gross receipts during the prior taxable year consisted of items which qualify as expenses for medical care described in section 213(d).

(3) *Claims substantiation for copayment matches, certain recurring medical expenses and real-time substantiation.* If all of the requirements in this paragraph (e)(3) are satisfied, copayment matches, certain recurring medical expenses and medical expenses substantiated in real-time are substantiated without the need for submission of receipts or further review.

(i) *Matching copayments-multiples of five or fewer.* If an employer's accident or health plan covering the employee (or the employee's spouse or dependents) has copayments in specific dollar amounts, and the dollar amount of the transaction at a medical care provider equals an exact multiple of not more than five times the dollar amount of the copayment for the specific service (for example, pharmacy benefit copayment, copayment for a physician's office visit) under the accident or health plan covering the specific employee-cardholder, then the charge is fully substantiated without the need for submission of a receipt or further review.

(A) *Tiered copayments.* If a health plan has multiple copayments for the same benefit, (for example, tiered copayments for a pharmacy benefit), exact matches of multiples or combinations of up to five copayments are similarly fully substantiated without the need for submission of a receipt or further review.

(B) *Copayment match must be exact multiple.* If the dollar amount of the transaction is not an exact multiple of the copayment (or an exact match of a multiple or combination of different copayments for a benefit in the case of multiple copayments), the transaction must be treated as conditional pending confirmation of the charge, even if the amount is less than five times the copayment.

(C) *No match for multiple of six or more times copayment.* If the dollar amount of the transaction at a medical care provider equals a multiple of six or more times the dollar amount of the copayment for the specific service, the transaction must be treated as conditional pending confirmation of the charge by the submission of additional third-party information. See paragraph (d) of this section. In the case of a plan with multiple copayments for the same benefit, if the dollar amount of the transaction exceeds five times the maximum copayment for the benefit, the transaction must also be treated as conditional pending confirmation of the charge by the submission of additional third-party information. In these cases, the employer must require that additional third-party information, such as merchant or service provider receipts, be submitted for review and substantiation, and the third-party information must satisfy the requirements in paragraph (b)(3) of this section.

(D) *Independent verification of copayment required.* The copayment schedule required under the accident or health plan must be independently verified by the employer. Statements or other representations by the employee are not sufficient. Self-substantiation or self-certification of an employee's copayment in connection with copayment matching procedures through debit cards or otherwise does not constitute substantiation. If a plan's copayment matching system relies on an employee to provide a copayment amount without verification of the amount, claims have not been substantiated, and all amounts paid from the plan are included in gross income, including amounts paid for medical care whether or not substantiated. See paragraph (b) in this section.

(4) *Certain recurring medical expenses.* Automatic payment or reimbursement satisfies the substantiation rules in this paragraph (e) for payment of recurring expenses that match expenses previously approved as to amount, medical care provider and time period (for example, for an employee who refills a prescription drug on a regular basis at the same provider and in the same amount). The payment is substantiated without the need for submission of a receipt or further review.

(5) *Real-time substantiation.* If a third party that is independent of the employee and the employee's spouse and dependents (for example, medical care provider, merchant, or pharmacy benefit manager) provides, at the time and point of sale, information to verify to the employer (including electronically by email, the internet, intranet or telephone) that the charge is for a section 213(d) medical expense, the expense is substantiated without the need for further review.

(6) *Substantiation requirements for all other medical expenses paid or reimbursed through a health FSA debit card.* All other charges to the debit card (other than substantiated copayments, recurring medical expenses or real-time substantiation, or charges substantiated through the inventory information approval system described in paragraph (f) of this section) must be treated as conditional, pending substantiation of the charge through additional independent third-party information describing the goods or services, the date of the service or sale and the amount of the transaction. All such debit card payments must be substantiated, regardless of the amount of the payment.

(f) *Inventory information approval system* —(1) *In general.* An inventory information approval system that complies with this paragraph (f) may be used to substantiate payments made using a debit card, including payments at merchants and service providers that are not described in paragraph (e)(2) of this section. Debit card transactions using this system are fully substantiated without the need for submission of a receipt by the employee or further review.

(2) *Operation of inventory information approval system.* An inventory information approval system must operate in the manner described in this paragraph (f)(2).

(i) When an employee uses the card, the payment card processor's or participating merchant's system collects information about the items purchased using the inventory control information (for example, *stock keeping units* (SKUs)). The system compares the inventory control information for the items purchased against a list of items, the purchase of which qualifies as expenses for medical care under section 213(d) (including nonprescription medications).

(ii) The section 213(d) medical expenses are totaled and the merchant's or payment card processor's system approves the use of the card only for the amount of the section 213(d) medical expenses eligible for coverage under the health FSA (taking into consideration the uniform coverage rule in paragraph (d) of § 1.125-5);

(iii) If the transaction is only partially approved, the employee is required to tender additional amounts, resulting in a split-tender transaction. For example, if, after matching inventory information, it is determined that all items purchased are section 213(d) medical expenses, the entire transaction is approved, subject to the coverage limitations of the health FSA;

(iv) If, after matching inventory information, it is determined that only some of the items purchased are section 213(d) medical expenses, the transaction is approved only as to the section 213(d) medical expenses. In this case, the merchant or service-provider must request additional payment from the employee for the items that do not satisfy the definition of medical care under section 213(d);

(v) The merchant or service-provider must also request additional payment from the employee if the employee does not have sufficient health FSA coverage to purchase the section 213(d) medical items;

(vi) Any attempt to use the card at non-participating merchants or service-providers must fail.

(3) *Employer's responsibility for ensuring inventory information approval system's compliance with § 1.105-2, § 1.125-1, § 1.125-6 and recordkeeping requirements.* An employer that uses the inventory information approval system must ensure that the inventory information approval system complies with the requirements in §§ 1.105-2, 1.125-1, and § 1.125-6 for substantiating, paying or reimbursing section 213(d) medical expenses and with the recordkeeping requirements in section 6001.

(g) *Debit cards used to pay or reimburse dependent care assistance* — (1) *In general.* An employer may use a debit card to provide benefits under its dependent care assistance program (including a dependent care assistance FSA). However, dependent care expenses may not be reimbursed before the expenses are incurred. See paragraph (a)(4) in this section. Thus, if a dependent care provider requires payment before the dependent care services are provided, the expenses cannot be reimbursed at the time of payment through use of a debit card or otherwise.

(2) *Reimbursing dependent care assistance through a debit card.* An employer offering a dependent care assistance FSA may adopt the following method to provide reimbursements for dependent care expenses through a debit card—

(i) At the beginning of the plan year or upon enrollment in the dependent care assistance program, the employee pays initial expenses to the dependent care provider and substantiates the initial expenses by submitting to the employer or plan administrator a statement from the dependent care provider substantiating the dates and amounts for the services provided.

(ii) After the employer or plan administrator receives the substantiation (but not before the date the services are provided as indicated by the statement provided by the dependent care provider), the plan makes available through the debit card an amount equal to the lesser of—

(A) The previously incurred and substantiated expense; or

(B) The employee's total salary reduction amount to date.

(iii) The card may be used to pay for subsequently incurred dependent care expenses.

(iv) The amount available through the card may be increased in the amount of any additional dependent care expenses only after the additional expenses have been incurred.

(3) *Substantiating recurring dependent care expenses.* Card transactions that collect information matching expenses previously substantiated and approved as to dependent care provider and time period may be treated as substantiated without further review if the transaction is for an amount equal to or less than the previously substantiated expenses. Similarly, dependent care expenses previously substantiated and approved through nonelectronic methods may also be treated as substantiated without further review. In both cases, if there is an increase in previously substantiated amounts or a change in the dependent care provider, the employee must submit a statement or receipt from the dependent care provider substantiating the claimed expenses before amounts relating to the increased amounts or new providers may be added to the card.

(4) *Example.* The following example illustrates the rules in this paragraph (g):

Example. Recurring dependent care expenses. (i) Employer K sponsors a dependent care assistance FSA through its cafeteria plan. Salary reduction amounts for participating employees are made on a weekly payroll basis, which are available for dependent care coverage on a weekly basis. As a result, the amount of available dependent care coverage equals the employee's salary reduction amount minus claims previously paid from the plan. Employer K has adopted a payment card program for its dependent care FSA.

(ii) For the plan year ending December 31, 2009, Employee F is a participant in the dependent care FSA and elected $5,000 of dependent care coverage. Employer K reduces F's salary by $96.15 on a weekly basis to pay for coverage under the dependent care FSA.

(iii) At the beginning of the 2009 plan year, F is issued a debit card with a balance of zero. F's childcare provider, ABC Daycare Center, requires a $250 advance payment at the beginning of the week for dependent care services that will be provided during the week. The dependent care services provided for F by ABC qualify for reimbursement under section 129. However, because as of the beginning of the plan year, no services have yet been provided, F cannot be reimbursed for any of the amounts until the end of the first week of the plan year (that is, the week ending January 5, 2009), after the services have been provided.

(iv) F submits a claim for reimbursement that includes a statement from ABC with a description of the services, the amount of the services, and the dates of the services. Employer K increases the balance of F's payment card to $96.15 after the services have been provided (i.e., the lesser of F's salary reduction to date or the incurred dependent care expenses). F uses the card to pay ABC $96.15 on the first day of the next week (January 8, 2009) and pays ABC the remaining balance due for that week ($153.85) by check.

(v) To the extent that this card transaction and each subsequent transaction is with ABC and is for an amount equal to or less than the previously substantiated amount, the charges are fully substantiated without the need for the submission by F of a statement from the provider or further review by the employer. However, the subsequent amount is not made available on the card until the end of the week when the services have been provided. Employer K's dependent care debit card satisfies the substantiation requirements of this paragraph (g).

(h) *Effective/applicability date.* It is proposed that these regulations apply on and after plan years beginning on or after January 1, 2009. However, the effective dates for the previously issued guidance on debit cards, which is incorporated in this section, remain applicable.

§ 1.125-7 Cafeteria plan nondiscrimination rules

(a) *Definitions* —(1) *In general.* The definitions set forth in this paragraph (a) apply for purposes of section 125(b), (c), (e) and (g) and this section.

(2) *Compensation.* The term *compensation* means compensation as defined in section 415(c)(3).

(3) *Highly compensated individual.* (i) *In general.* The term *highly compensated individual* means an individual who is—

(A) An officer;

(B) A five percent shareholder (as defined in paragraph (a)(8) of this section); or

(C) Highly compensated.

(ii) *Spouse or dependent.* A spouse or a dependent of any highly compensated individual described in (a)(3)(i) of this section is a highly compensated individual. Section 125(e).

(4) *Highly compensated participant.* The term *highly compensated participant* means a highly compensated individual who is eligible to participate in the cafeteria plan.

(5) *Nonhighly compensated individual.* The term *nonhighly compensated individual* means an individual who is not a highly compensated individual.

(6) *Nonhighly compensated participant.* The term *nonhighly compensated participant* means a participant who is not a highly compensated participant.

(7) *Officer.* The term officer means any individual or participant who for the preceding plan year (or the current plan year in the case of the first year of employment) was an officer. Whether an individual is an *officer* is determined based on all the facts and circumstances, including the source of the individual's authority, the term for which he or she is elected or appointed, and the nature and extent of his or her duties. Generally, the term officer means an administrative executive who is in regular and continued service. The term officer implies continuity of service and excludes individuals performing services in connection with a special and single transaction. An individual who merely has the title of an officer but not the authority of an officer, is not an officer. Similarly, an individual without the title of an officer but who has the authority of an officer is an officer. Sole proprietorships, partnerships, associations, trusts and labor organizations also may have officers. See §§ 301.7701-1 through -3

(8) *Five percent shareholder.* A *five percent shareholder* is an individual who in either the preceding plan year or current plan year owns more than five percent of the voting power or value of all classes of stock of the employer, determined without attribution.

(9) *Highly compensated.* The term *highly compensated* means any individual or participant who for the preceding plan year (or the current plan year in the case of the first year of employment) had compensation from the employer in excess of the compensation amount specified in section 414(q)(1)(B), and, if elected by the employer, was also in the top-paid group of employees (determined by reference to section 414(q)(3)) for such preceding plan year (or for the current plan year in the case of the first year of employment).

(10) *Key employee.* A *key employee* is a participant who is a key employee within the meaning of section 416(i)(1) at any time during the preceding plan year. A key employee covered by a collective bargaining agreement is a key employee.

(11) *Collectively bargained plan.* A *collectively bargained plan* is a plan or the portion of a plan maintained under an agreement which is a collective bargaining agreement between employee representatives and one or more employers, if there is evidence that cafeteria plan benefits were the subject of good faith bargaining between such employee representatives and such employer or employers.

(12) *Year of employment.* For purposes of section 125(g)(3)(B)(i), a *year of employment* is determined by reference to the elapsed time method of crediting service. See § 1.410(a)-7.

(13) *Premium-only-plan.* A premium-only-plan is described in paragraph (a)(5) in § 1.125-1.

(14) *Statutory nontaxable benefits. Statutory nontaxable benefits* are qualified benefits that are excluded from gross income (for example, an employer-provided accident and health plan excludible under section 106 or a dependent care assistance program excludible under section 129). Statutory nontaxable benefits also include group-term life insurance on the life of an employee includible in the employee's gross income solely because the coverage exceeds the limit in section 79(a).

(15) *Total benefits. Total benefits* are qualified benefits and permitted taxable benefits.

(b) *Nondiscrimination as to eligibility* —(1) *In general.* A cafeteria plan must not discriminate in favor of highly compensated individuals as to eligibility to participate for that plan year. A cafeteria plan does not discriminate in favor of highly compensated individuals if the plan benefits a group of employees who qualify under a reasonable classification established by the employer, as defined in § 1.410(b)-4(b), and the group of employees included in the classification satisfies the safe harbor percentage test or the unsafe harbor percentage component of the facts and circumstances test in § 1.410(b)-4(c). (In applying the § 1.410(b)-4 test, substitute highly compensated individual for highly compensated employee and substitute nonhighly compensated individual for nonhighly compensated employee).

(2) *Deadline for participation in cafeteria plan.* Any employee who has completed three years of employment (and who satisfies any conditions for participation in the cafeteria plan that are not related to completion of a requisite length of employment) must be permitted to elect to participate in the cafeteria plan no later than the first day of the first plan year beginning after the date the employee completed three years of employment (unless the employee separates from service before the first day of that plan year).

(3) *The safe harbor percentage test.* (i) *In general.* For purposes of the safe harbor percentage test and the unsafe harbor percentage component of the facts and circumstances test, if the cafeteria plan provides that only employees who have completed three years of employment are permitted to participate in the plan, employees who have not completed three years of employment may be excluded from consideration. However, if the cafeteria plan provides that employees are allowed to participate before completing three years of employment, all employees with less than three years of employment must be included in applying the safe harbor percentage test and the unsafe harbor percentage component of the facts and circumstances test. See paragraph (g) of this section for a permissive disaggregation rule.

(ii) *Employees excluded from consideration.* In addition, for purposes of the safe harbor percentage test and the unsafe harbor percentage component of the facts and circumstances test, the following employees are excluded from consideration—

(A) Employees (except key employees) covered by a collectively bargained plan as defined in paragraph (a)(11) of this section;

(B) Employees who are nonresident aliens and receive no earned income (within the meaning of section 911(d)(2)) from the employer which constitutes income from sources within the United States (within the meaning of section 861(a)(3)); and

(C) Employees participating in the cafeteria plan under a COBRA continuation provision.

(iv) *Examples.* The following examples illustrate the rules in paragraph (b) of this section:

Example 1. Same qualified benefit for same salary reduction amount. Employer A has one employer-provided accident and health insurance plan. The cost to participants electing the accident and health plan is $10,000 per year for single coverage. All employees have the same opportunity to salary reduce $10,000 for accident and health plan. The cafeteria plan satisfies the eligibility test.

Example 2. Same qualified benefit for unequal salary reduction amounts. Same facts as *Example 1* except the cafeteria plan offers nonhighly compensated employees the election to salary reduce $10,000 to pay premiums for single coverage. The cafeteria plan provides an $8,000 employer flex-credit to highly compensated employees to pay a portion of the premium, and provides an election to them to salary reduce $2,000 to pay the balance of the premium. The cafeteria plan fails the eligibility test.

Example 3. Accident and health plans of unequal value. Employer B's cafeteria plan offers two employer-provided accident and health insurance plans: Plan X, available only to highly compensated participants, is a low-deductible plan. Plan Y, available only to nonhighly compensated participants, is a high deductible plan (as defined in section 223(c)(2)). The annual premium for single coverage under Plan X is $15,000 per year, and $8,000 per year for Plan Y. Employer B's cafeteria plan provides that highly compensated participants may elect salary reduction of $15,000 for coverage under Plan X, and that nonhighly compensated participants may elect salary reduction of $8,000 for coverage under Plan Y. The cafeteria plan fails the eligibility test.

Example 4. Accident and health plans of unequal value for unequal salary reduction amounts. Same facts as *Example 3*, except that the amount of salary reduction for highly compensated participants to elect Plan X is $8,000. The cafeteria plan fails the eligibility test.

(c) *Nondiscrimination as to contributions and benefits* —(1) *In general.* A cafeteria plan must not discriminate in favor of highly compensated participants as to contributions and benefits for a plan year.

(2) *Benefit availability and benefit election.* A cafeteria plan does not discriminate with respect to contributions and benefits if either qualified benefits and total benefits, or employer contributions allocable to statutory nontaxable benefits and employer contributions allocable to total benefits, do not discriminate in favor of highly compensated participants. A cafeteria plan must satisfy this paragraph (c) with respect to both benefit availability and benefit utilization. Thus, a plan must give each similarly situated participant a uniform opportunity to elect qualified benefits, and the actual election of qualified benefits through the plan must not be disproportionate by highly compensated participants (while other participants elect permitted taxable benefits). Qualified benefits are disproportionately elected by highly compensated participants if the aggregate qualified benefits elected by highly compensated participants, measured as a percentage of the aggregate compensation of highly compensated participants, exceed the aggregate qualified benefits elected by nonhighly compensated participants measured as a percentage of the aggregate compensation of nonhighly compensated participants. A plan must also give each similarly situated participant a uniform election with respect to employer contributions, and the actual election with respect to employer contributions for qualified benefits through the plan must not be disproportionate by highly compensated participants (while other participants elect to receive employer contributions as permitted taxable benefits). Employer contributions are disproportionately utilized by highly compensated participants if the aggregate contributions utilized by highly compensated participants, measured as a percentage of the aggregate compensation of highly compensated participants, exceed the aggregate contributions utilized by nonhighly compensated participants measured as a percentage of the aggregate compensation of nonhighly compensated participants.

(3) *Example.* The following example illustrates the rules in paragraph (c) of this section:

Example. Contributions and benefits test. Employer C's cafeteria plan satisfies the eligibility test in paragraph (b) of this section. Highly compensated participants in the cafeteria plan elect aggregate qualified benefits equaling 5 percent of aggregate compensation; nonhighly compensated participants elect aggregate qualified benefits equaling 10 percent of aggregate compensation. Employer C's cafeteria plan passes the contribution and benefits test.

(d) *Key employees* —(1) *In general.* If for any plan year, the statutory nontaxable benefits provided to key employees exceed 25 percent of the aggregate of statutory nontaxable benefits provided for all employees through the cafeteria plan, each key employee includes in gross income an amount equaling the maximum taxable benefits that he or she could have elected for the plan year. However, see safe harbor for premium-only-plans in paragraph (f) of this section.

(2) *Example.* The following example illustrates the rules in paragraph (d) of this section:

Example. (i) *Key employee concentration test.* Employer D's cafeteria plan offers all employees an election between taxable benefits and qualified benefits. The cafeteria plan satisfies the eligibility test in paragraph (b) of this section. Employer D has two key employees and four nonhighly compensated employees. The key employees each elect $2,000 of qualified benefits. Each nonhighly compensated employee also elects $2,000 of qualified benefits. The qualified benefits are statutory nontaxable benefits.

(ii) Key employees receive $4,000 of statutory nontaxable benefits and nonhighly compensated employees receive $8,000 of statutory nontaxable benefits, for a total of $12,000. Key employees receive 33 percent of statutory nontaxable benefits (4,000/12,000). Because the cafeteria plan provides more than 25 percent of the aggregate of statutory nontaxable benefits to key employees, the plan fails the key employee concentration test.

(e) *Safe harbor for cafeteria plans providing health benefits* —(1) *In general.* A cafeteria plan that provides health benefits is not treated as discriminatory as to benefits and contributions if:

(i) Contributions under the plan on behalf of each participant include an amount which equals 100 percent of the cost of the health benefit coverage under the plan of the majority of the highly compensated participants similarly situated, or equals or exceeds 75 percent of the cost of the health benefit coverage of the participant (similarly situated) having the highest cost health benefit coverage under the plan, and

(ii) Contributions or benefits under the plan in excess of those described in paragraph (e)(1)(i) of this section bear a uniform relationship to compensation.

(2) *Similarly situated.* In determining which participants are similarly situated, reasonable differences in plan benefits may be taken into account (for example, variations in plan benefits offered to employees working in different geographical locations or to employees with family coverage versus employee-only coverage).

(3) *Health benefits.* Health benefits for purposes of this rule are limited to major medical coverage and exclude dental coverage and health FSAs.

(4) *Example.* The following example illustrates the rules in paragraph (e) of this section:

Example. (i) All 10 of Employer E's employees are eligible to elect between permitted taxable benefits and salary reduction of $8,000 per plan year for self-only coverage in the major medical health plan provided by Employer E. All 10 employees elect $8,000 salary reduction for the major medical plan.

(ii) The cafeteria plan satisfies the section 125(g)(2) safe harbor for cafeteria plans providing health benefits.

(f) *Safe harbor test for premium-only-plans* —(1) *In general.* A premium-only-plan (as defined in paragraph (a)(13) of this section) is deemed to satisfy the nondiscrimination rules in section 125(c) and this section for a plan year if, for that plan year, the plan satisfies the safe harbor percentage test for eligibility in paragraph (b)(3) of this section.

(2) *Example.* The following example illustrates the rules in paragraph (f) of this section:

Example. Premium-only-plan. (i) Employer F's cafeteria plan is a premium-only-plan (as defined in paragraph (a)(13) of this section). The written cafeteria plan offers one employer-provided accident and health plan and offers all employees the election to salary reduce same amount or same percentage of the premium for self-only or family coverage. All key employees and all highly compensated employees elect salary reduction for the accident and health plan, but only 20 percent of nonhighly compensated employees elect the accident and health plan.

(ii) The premium-only-plan satisfies the nondiscrimination rules in section 125(b) and (c) and this section.

(g) *Permissive disaggregation for nondiscrimination testing* —(1) *General rule.* If a cafeteria plan benefits employees who have not completed three years of employment, the cafeteria plan is permitted to test for nondiscrimination under this section as if the plan were two separate plans—

(i) One plan benefiting the employees who completed one day of employment but less than three years of employment; and

(ii) Another plan benefiting the employees who have completed three years of employment.

(2) *Disaggregated plans tested separately for eligibility test and contributions and benefits test.* If a cafeteria plan is disaggregated into two separate plans for purposes of nondiscrimination testing, the two separate plans must be tested separately for both the nondiscrimination as to eligibility test in paragraph (b) of this section and the nondiscrimination as to contributions and benefits test in paragraph (c) of this section.

(h) *Optional aggregation of plans for nondiscrimination testing.* An employer who sponsors more than one cafeteria plan is permitted to aggregate two or more of the cafeteria plans for purposes of nondiscrimination testing. If two or more cafeteria plans are aggregated into a combined plan for this purpose, the combined plan must satisfy the nondiscrimination as to eligibility test in paragraph (b) of this section and the nondiscrimination as to contributions and benefits test in paragraph (c) of this section, as though the combined plan were a single plan. Thus, for example, in order to satisfy the benefit availability and benefit election requirements in paragraph (c)(2) of this section, the combined plan must give each similarly situated participant a uniform opportunity to elect qualified benefits and the actual election of qualified benefits by highly compensated participants must not be disproportionate. However, if a principal purpose of the aggregation is to manipulate the nondiscrimination testing requirements or to otherwise discriminate in favor of highly compensated individuals or participants, the plans will not be permitted to be aggregated for nondiscrimination testing.

(i) *Employees of certain controlled groups.* All employees who are treated as employed by a single employer under section 414(b), (c), (m), or (o) are treated as employed by a single employer for purposes of section 125. Section 125(g)(4); section 414(t).

(j) *Time to perform nondiscrimination testing* —(1) *In general.* Nondiscrimination testing must be performed as of the last day of the plan year, taking into account all non-excludable employees (or former employees) who were employees on any day during the plan year.

(2) The following example illustrates the rules in paragraph (j) of this section:

Example. When to perform discrimination testing. (i) Employer H employs three employees and maintains a calendar year cafeteria plan. During the 2009 plan year, Employee J was an employee the entire calendar year, Employee K was an employee from May 1, through August 31, 2009, and Employee L worked from January 1, 2009 to April 15, 2009, when he retired.

(ii) Nondiscrimination testing for the 2009 plan year must be performed on December 31, 2009, taking into account employees J, K, and L's compensation in the preceding year.

(k) *Discrimination in actual operation prohibited.* In addition to not discriminating as to either benefit availability or benefit utilization, a cafeteria plan must not discriminate in favor of highly compensated participants in actual operation. For example, a plan may be discriminatory in actual operation if the duration of the plan (or of a particular nontaxable benefit offered through the plan) is for a period during which only highly compensated participants utilize the plan (or the benefit). See also the key employee concentration test in section 125(b)(2).

(l) *Anti-abuse rule* —(1) *Interpretation.* The provisions of this section must be interpreted in a reasonable manner consistent with the purpose of preventing discrimination in favor of highly compensated individuals, highly compensated participants and key employees.

(2) *Change in plan testing procedures.* A plan will not be treated as satisfying the requirements of this section if there are repeated changes to plan testing procedures or plan provisions that have the effect of manipulating the nondiscrimination testing requirements of this section, if a principal purpose of the changes was to achieve this result.

(m) *Tax treatment of benefits in a cafeteria plan* —(1) *Nondiscriminatory cafeteria plan.* A participant in a nondiscriminatory cafeteria plan (including a highly compensated participant or key employee) who elects qualified benefits is not treated as having received taxable benefits offered through the plan, and thus the qualified benefits elected by the employee are not includible in the employee's gross income merely because of the availability of taxable benefits. But see paragraph (j) in § 1.125-1 on nondiscrimination rules for sections 79(d), 105(h), 129(d), and 137(c)(2), and limitations on exclusion.

(2) *Discriminatory cafeteria plan.* A highly compensated participant or key employee participating in a discriminatory cafeteria plan must include in gross income (in the participant's taxable year within which ends the plan year with respect to which an election was or could have been made) the value of the taxable benefit with the greatest value that the employee could have elected to receive, even if the employee elects to receive only the nontaxable benefits offered.

(n) *Employer contributions to employees' Health Savings Accounts.* If an employer contributes to employees' Health Savings Accounts (HSAs) through a cafeteria plan (as defined in § 54.4980G-5 of this chapter) those contributions are subject to the to the nondiscrimination rules in section 125 and this section and are not subject to the comparability rules in section 4980G. See §§ 54.4980G-0 through 54.4980G-5 of this chapter.

(o) *Effective/applicability date.* It is proposed that these regulations apply on and after plan years beginning on or after January 1, 2009.

Deputy Commissioner for Services and Enforcement.

Kevin M. Brown

¶ 20,262C

IRS proposed regulations: Qualified plans: Medical or accident insurance: Tax treatment.—The IRS has released proposed regulations concerning the tax treatment of payments made by qualified plans for medical or accident insurance under Code Sec. 402(a). Also included are conforming amendments under Code Secs. 72, 105, 106, 401, 402(c), 403(a) and 403(b).

The proposed regulations, which were published in the Federal Register on August 20, 2007 (72 FR 46421), are reproduced below. The regulations were corrected on September 26, 2007 (72 FR 54614). The regulations were finalized on May 12, 2014 (79 FR 26838). The preamble to the final regulations is at ¶ 23,300. The final regulations are at ¶ 11,205, ¶ 11,274, ¶ 11,276, ¶ 11,281, ¶ 11,701, ¶ 11,751, ¶ 11,753-10, ¶ 11,801, and ¶ 11,803-14.

DEPARTMENT OF THE TREASURY

Internal Revenue Service

26 CFR Part 1

[REG-148393-06]

RIN 1545-BG12

Medical and Accident Insurance Benefits under Qualified Plans

AGENCY: Internal Revenue Service (IRS), Treasury.

ACTION: Notice of proposed rulemaking and notice of public hearing.

SUMMARY: This document contains proposed regulations under section 402(a) of the Internal Revenue Code (Code) regarding the tax treatment of payments by qualified plans for medical or accident insurance. These regulations would affect administrators of, participants in, and beneficiaries of qualified retirement plans. This document also provides notice of a public hearing on these proposed regulations.

DATES: Written or electronic comments must be received by November 19, 2007. Outlines of topics to be discussed at the public hearing scheduled for December 6, 2007, at 10 a.m., must be received by November 15, 2007.

ADDRESSES: Send submissions to: CC:PA:LPD:PR (REG-148393-06), room 5203, Internal Revenue Service, PO Box 7604, Ben Franklin Station, Washington, DC 20044. Submissions may be hand-delivered Monday through Friday between the hours of 8 a.m. and 4 p.m. to CC:PA:LPD:PR (REG-148393-06), Courier's Desk, Internal Revenue Service, 1111 Constitution Avenue, NW, Washington, DC, or send electronically via the Federal eRulemaking Portal at http://www.regulations.gov (IRS REG-148393-06). The public hearing will be held in the IRS Auditorium, Internal Revenue Service, 1111 Constitution Avenue, NW., Washington, DC.

FOR FURTHER INFORMATION CONTACT: Concerning the proposed regulations, Pamela R. Kinard (202) 622-6060; concerning submissions of comments, the hearing, and/or to be placed on the building access list to attend the hearing, Kelly Banks, (202) 622-7180 (not toll-free numbers).

SUPPLEMENTARY INFORMATION:

Background

This document contains proposed amendments to 26 CFR part 1 under section 402(a) of the Code, as well as conforming amendments under sections 72, 105, 106, 401, 402(c), 403(a), and 403(b).

Section 104(a)(3) provides, in general, that gross income does not include amounts received through accident or health insurance (or through an arrangement having the effect of accident or health insurance) for personal injuries or sickness. This exclusion does not apply to amounts attributable to (and not in excess of) deductions allowed under section 213 for any prior taxable year, or to other amounts received by an employee to the extent such amounts either are attributable to contributions by the employer that were not includible in the gross income of the employee or are paid by the employer.

Section 105(a) provides that, except as otherwise provided, amounts received by an employee through accident or health insurance for personal injuries or sickness are included in gross income to the extent such amounts (1) are attributable to contributions by the employer which were not includible in the gross income of the employee or (2) are paid by the employer.

Section 105(b) generally provides that, except in the case of amounts attributable to deductions allowed under section 213 for any prior taxable year, gross income does not include amounts referred to in section 105(a) if such amounts are paid, directly or indirectly, to the taxpayer to reimburse the taxpayer for expenses incurred by the taxpayer for the medical care of the taxpayer and his or her spouse or dependents.

Section 106 provides that the gross income of an employee does not include employer-provided coverage under an accident or health plan. Section 1.106-1 provides that the gross income of an employee does not include contributions that the employer makes to an accident or health plan for compensation (through insurance or a separate trust or fund) for personal injuries or sickness to the employee or the employee's spouse or dependents.

Section 7702B(a)(1) provides that, for purposes of the Code, a qualified long-term care insurance contract is treated as an accident and health insurance contract.

Section 213 generally allows a deduction for expenses paid during the taxable year, not compensated for by insurance or otherwise, for medical care of the taxpayer, his or her spouse, and dependents, to the extent that the expenses exceed 7.5 percent of the taxpayer's adjusted gross income. Section 213(d)(1) provides that the term "medical care" includes amounts paid for insurance covering medical care (including eligible long-term care premiums with respect to qualified long-term care insurance contracts).

Section 401(a) sets forth requirements for a trust forming part of a pension, profit-sharing, or stock bonus plan to be qualified under section 401(a).

Section 401(h) provides that a pension or annuity plan may provide for the payment of benefits for sickness, accident, hospitalization, and medical expenses of retired employees, their spouses and their dependents only if certain enumerated conditions are met. Those conditions include: (1) The aggregate actual contributions for medical benefits (when added to actual contributions for life insurance protection under the plan) may not exceed 25 percent of the total actual contributions to the plan (other than contributions to fund past service credits) after the date on which the account is established; (2) a separate account must be established and maintained for such benefits; (3) the employer's contributions to the separate account must be reasonable and ascertainable; (4) it must be impossible, at any time prior to the satisfaction of all liabilities under the plan to provide such benefits, for any part of the corpus or income of such separate account to be (within the taxable year or thereafter) used for, or diverted to, any purpose other than the providing of such benefits; (5) any amount remaining after satisfaction of all liabilities must, under the terms of the plan, be returned to the employer; and (6) special limitations for the accounts of key employees must be satisfied.

Section 402(a) provides, in general, that any amount actually distributed by a qualified plan is taxable under section 72 in the taxable year in which distributed.

Section 72(a) provides that, except as otherwise provided, gross income includes any amount received as an annuity (whether for a period certain or during one or more lives) under an annuity, endowment, or life insurance contract. Sections 72(d) and (e) provide rules for determining the portion of any distribution that is not includable in gross income as a recovery of a participant's investment in the contract (generally the amount of the unrecovered after-tax employee contributions) under a qualified employer retirement plan.

Section 402(l), added by section 845(a) of the Pension Protection Act of 2006, Public Law 109-280 (120 Stat. 780) (PPA '06), provides a limited exclusion from gross income for distributions from an eligible retirement plan used to pay health or long-term care insurance premiums of an eligible retired public safety officer to the extent that the aggregate amount of the distributions for the taxable year is not in excess of the qualified health insurance premiums of the retired public safety officer and his or her spouse or dependents. The total amount excluded from gross income pursuant to section 402(l) shall not exceed $3,000.

Section 1.72-15 provides rules relating to the tax treatment of amounts paid from an employer-established plan to which section 72 applies and which provides for distributions of accident or health benefits. With respect to benefits that are attributable to employer contributions, § 1.72-15(d) provides that any amount received as an accident or health benefit is includible in gross income, except to the extent excludable from gross income under section 105(b) (relating to reimbursements of medical care expenses as defined in section 213(d)).1 Section 1.72-15(e) provides that the taxability of benefits that are not accident or health benefits is determined under section 72 without regard to any exclusion under section 104 or 105.

Section 1.401-1(b)(1)(i) provides that a plan is not a pension plan within the meaning of section 401(a) if it provides for the payment of benefits not customarily included in a pension plan such as layoff benefits or benefits for sickness, accident, hospitalization, or medical expenses (except for medical benefits described in section 401(h)). See § 1.401(a)-1(b)(1)(ii).

Section 1.401-1(b)(1)(ii) provides that a profit-sharing plan within the meaning of section 401(a) is primarily a plan of deferred compensation, but that amounts allocated to the account of a participant may be used to provide incidental life or accident or health insurance for the participant and the participant's family. Section 1.401-1(b)(1)(iii) provides that a stock bonus plan is a plan established and maintained by the employer to provide benefits similar to those of a profit-sharing plan.

Rev. Rul. 61-164 (1961-2 CB 99), see § 601.601(d)(2) of this chapter, holds that a profit-sharing plan does not violate the incidental benefit rule in § 1.401-1(b)(1)(ii) merely because, in accordance with the terms of the plan, each participant's account under the plan is charged with the cost of health insurance for the participant under group hospitalization insurance for the employer's employees, provided that the total amount used for life or accident or health insurance for the employee and the employee's family is incidental. The ruling concludes that such insurance is treated as incidental if the amount expended does not exceed 25 percent of the funds allocated to a participant's account that have not been accumulated for the period prescribed by the plan for the deferment of distributions. The ruling also concludes that the use of profit-sharing plan funds to pay for medical insurance for a participant and his or her beneficiary is a distribution within the meaning of section 402.

Rev. Rul. 73-501 (1973-2 CB 127), see § 601.601(d)(2) of this chapter, applies the incidental benefit rule to the purchase of life insurance by a profit-sharing plan. The ruling states that "[u]nder a qualified profit-sharing plan, the use of trust funds to pay the cost of life, accident, or health insurance for an employee is a distribution within the purview of section 402 of the Code."

Rev. Rul. 2003-62 (2003-1 CB 1034), see § 601.601(d)(2) of this chapter, concludes that amounts distributed from a qualified retirement plan that the distributee elects to have applied to pay health insurance premiums under a cafeteria plan are includible in the distributee's gross income. The ruling also holds that the same conclusion applies where amounts distributed from the plan are applied directly to reimburse medical care expenses incurred by a participant.

Rev. Rul. 2005-55 (2005-2 CB 284), see § 601.601(d)(2) pf this chapter, holds that a profit-sharing plan that provides a sub-account which permits distributions only for the purpose of reimbursing the participant for substantiated medical expenses imposes conditions on the entitlement of the participant to amounts held in the sub-account and, as a result of the conditions, does not meet the nonforfeitability requirements of section 411.

Explanation of Provisions

The proposed regulations would clarify that a payment from a qualified plan for an accident or health insurance premium generally constitutes a distribution under section 402(a) that is taxable to the distributee under section 72 in the taxable year in which the premium is paid. The taxable amount generally equals the amount of the premium charged against the participant's benefits under the plan. If a defined contribution plan pays these premiums from a current year contribution or forfeiture that has not been allocated to a participant's account, then the amount of the premium for each participant will be treated as first being allocated to the participant and then charged against the participant's benefits under the plan, so that the amount of the distribution is the same as determined under the preceding sentence.

These regulations would also provide that a distribution for the payment of the premiums by a qualified plan generally is not excluded from gross income under section 104, 105, or 106, but such distribution would constitute an amount paid for accident or health insurance under section 213. Furthermore, to the extent that the payment of premiums for accident or health insurance has been treated as a distribution from a qualified plan, amounts received through the accident or health insurance for personal injuries or sickness are excludable from gross income under section 104(a)(3) and are not treated as distributions from the plan.

A related issue is whether the purchase of accident and health insurance can be treated as if the trust merely purchased an investment under which an insurer's payments for medical expenses are made to the trust and then treated as a return on that investment. The proposed regulations would clarify that payments from accident or health insurance for medical expenses that are made to the trust (rather than made to the medical service provider or the participant as reimbursement for covered expenses) are treated as having been made to the participant and then contributed by the participant to the plan. Comments are requested on whether there should be limited exceptions to this general rule (such as an exception for a provision that has the effect of a waiver of premium in the case of disability).

The proposed regulations would not alter the incidental benefit rule of § 1.401-1(b)(1)(ii) (which provides that a profit-sharing plan may provide incidental life or accident or health insurance for the participant and the participant's family) nor would they alter the tax treatment of the payment of life insurance. For the tax treatment of payments for life insurance, see section 72(m)(3) and § 1.72-16.

The general rule that accident and health insurance premiums are taxable distributions would not apply to amounts held under a medical account that satisfies all the requirements of section 401(h). Accident or health insurance purchased through a section 401(h) account does not constitute a taxable distribution. See § 1.72-15(h), providing that employer contributions to provide medical benefits in a section 401(h) account under a qualified plan or annuity are not includible in the gross income of the employee on whose behalf contributions were made.2 The result is the same if the section 401(h) account is funded with a transfer from a qualified pension plan in accordance with section 420. Similarly, section 402(l), as added by PPA '06, permits an exclusion from gross income, up to $3,000 annually, for distributions paid directly to an insurer to purchase accident or health insurance or qualified long-term care insurance for an eligible retired public safety officer and his or her spouse or dependents. The existence of narrow exceptions for retiree medical benefits under section 401(h) and for distributions for the payment of premiums on behalf of eligible retired public safety officers under section 402(l) is consistent with a general rule for inclusion in gross income of the payments of premiums for accident and health insurance. [Corrected by IRS on 9/26/07 (72 FR 54614).]

Section 402(a) provides that amounts actually distributed from a qualified plan are generally taxable to the distributee in the year of the distribution. There is no general exception in section 402 for a distribution in the form of accident or health insurance.3 Moreover, Congress has carefully prescribed and strictly limited the ability to pre-fund accident and health insurance benefits on a tax-favored basis. The rules specifically prescribed by Congress relating to the pre-funding of future health benefits on a tax-favored basis include the rules in section 223 (providing contribution limits and distribution rules for health savings accounts (HSAs)); sections 419 and 419A (limiting employer deductions for contributions to welfare benefit funds); section 501(c)(9) (providing requirements for tax-exempt Voluntary Employee Beneficiary Associations (VEBAs)); section 512 (providing for the taxation of a VEBA's unrelated business income); and by sections 401(h) and 420 (governing retiree health benefits provided through a separate health benefits account that is part of a pension or annuity plan). Therefore,

because Congress specifically prescribed these limited provisions for favorable tax-treatment, a broad exclusion permitting tax-favored treatment of any distribution used to pay accident or health insurance premiums would be inconsistent with this intentional statutory scheme.

In addition, the existence of the incidental benefit rule in § 1.401-1(b)(1)(ii) is not an indication that distributions used to provide incidental life or accident or health insurance benefits are eligible for tax-favorable treatment because the incidental benefit rule relates solely to the qualification of a profit-sharing plan, not to the tax treatment of amounts used to provide medical or accident insurance benefits under such plan.

The proposed regulations also contain conforming amendments to the Income Tax Regulations under sections 72, 105, 106, 401, and 402(c). These conforming amendments would remove obsolete provisions, as well as cite to the rules in these proposed regulations for determining the tax treatment of the payment of premiums for accident and health insurance from a qualified plan. Conforming amendments under sections 403(a) and 403(b) would also add a cross-reference to the regulations under section 403(a) and section 403(b) that would apply the rules in these proposed regulations to those arrangements. In addition, the proposed regulations would revise the first sentence of § 1.106-1 in order to update the definition of dependent in light of section 207 of the Working Families Tax Relief Act of 2004, Public Law 108-311 (118 Stat. 1166) and Notice 2004-79 (2004-2 CB 898), see § 601.601(d)(2). The proposed regulations would also amend § 1.402(c)-2, Q&A-4 to add distributions of premiums for accident or health insurance under § 1.402(a)-1(e)(1) to the list of items that are not eligible rollover contributions. Finally, these proposed regulations would also include a cross-reference to section 402(l), as added by PPA '06. For additional guidance on section 402(l), see Notice 2007-7 (2007-5 IRB 395), see § 601.601(d)(2). [Corrected by IRS on 9/26/07 (72 FR 54614).]

Proposed Effective Date

It is expected that the regulations will apply for calendar years after the publication of final regulations in the Federal Register. However, no inference should be drawn that the payment of premiums from a qualified plan does not constitute a taxable distribution if made prior to the effective date of these regulations.

Special Analyses

It has been determined that this notice of proposed rulemaking is not a significant regulatory action as defined in Executive Order 12866. Therefore, a regulatory assessment is not required. It also has been determined that section 553(b) of the Administrative Procedure Act (5 U.S.C. chapter 5) does not apply to these regulations, and because these regulations do not impose a collection of information on small entities, the Regulatory Flexibility Act (5 U.S.C. chapter 6) does not apply. Pursuant to section 7805(f) of the Code, this proposed regulation has been submitted to the Chief Counsel for Advocacy of the Small Business Administration for comment on its impact on small business.

Comments and Public Hearing

Before these proposed regulations are adopted as final regulations, consideration will be given to any written (a signed original and eight (8) copies) or electronic comments that are submitted timely to the IRS. The Treasury Department and the IRS request comments on the clarity of the proposed rules and how they may be made easier to understand. All comments will be available for public inspection and copying.

A public hearing has been scheduled for December 6, 2007, beginning at 10 a.m. in the Auditorium, Internal Revenue Service, 1111 Constitution Avenue, NW., Washington, DC. Due to building security procedures, visitors must enter at the Constitution Avenue entrance. In addition, all visitors must present photo identification to enter the building. Because of access restrictions, visitors will not be admitted beyond the immediate entrance area more than 30 minutes before the hearing starts. For information about having your name placed on the building access list to attend the hearing, see the FOR FURTHER INFORMATION CONTACT section of this preamble.

The rules of 26 CFR 601.601(a)(3) apply to the hearing. Persons who wish to present oral comments at the hearing must submit written or electronic comments by November 19, 2007 and an outline of the topics to be discussed and the amount of time to be devoted to each topic (a signed original and eight (8) copies) by November 15, 2007. A period of 10 minutes will be allotted to each person for making comments. An agenda showing the scheduling of the speakers will be prepared after the deadline for receiving outlines has passed. Copies of the agenda will be available free of charge at the hearing.

Drafting Information

The principal authors of these regulations are Pamela R. Kinard and Michael P. Brewer, Office of Division Counsel/Associate Chief Counsel (Tax Exempt and Government Entities). However, other personnel from the IRS and the Treasury Department participated in their development.

List of Subjects in 26 CFR Part 1

Income taxes, Reporting and recordkeeping requirements.

Proposed Amendments to the Regulations

Accordingly, 26 CFR part 1 is proposed to be amended as follows:

PART—INCOME TAXES

Paragraph 1. The authority citation for part 1 continues to read in part as follows:

Authority: 26 U.S.C. 7805 * * *

Par. 2. Section 1.72-15 is amended by:

1. Revising paragraphs (d), (h), and (i).

2. Removing and reserving paragraph (f).

The revisions read as follows:

§ 1.72-15 Applicability of section 72 to accident or health plans.

* * * * *

(d) Accident or health benefits attributable to employer contributions. Any amounts received as accident or health benefits and not attributable to contributions of the employee are includible in gross income except to the extent that such amounts are excludable from gross income under section 105(b) or (c) and the regulations thereunder. See § 1.402(a)-1(e) for rules relating to the use of a qualified plan under section 401(a) to pay premiums for accident or health insurance.

* * * * *

(h) Medical benefits for retired employees, etc. See § 1.402(a)-1(e)(2) for rules relating to the payment of medical benefits described in section 401(h) under a qualified pension or annuity plan.

(i) Special rules—(1) In general. For purposes of section 72(b) and (d), and this section, the taxpayer shall maintain such records as are necessary to substantiate the amount treated as an investment in the taxpayer's annuity contract.

(2) Delegation to Commissioner. The Commissioner may prescribe a form and instructions with respect to the taxpayer's past and current treatment of amounts received under section 72 or 105, and the taxpayer's computation, or recomputation, of the taxpayer's investment in his or her annuity contract. This form may be required to be filed with the taxpayer's returns for years in which such amounts are excluded under section 72 or 105.

§ 1.105-4 [Removed]

Par. 3. Section 1.105-4 is removed.

§ 1.105-6 [Removed]

Par. 4. Section 1.105-6 is removed.

Par. 5. Section 1.106-1 is amended by revising the first sentence and adding a new sentence at the end of the paragraph to read as follows:

§ 1.106-1 Contributions by employer to accident and health plans.

The gross income of an employee does not include the contributions which the employer makes to an accident or health plan for compensation (through insurance or otherwise) to the employee for personal injuries or sickness incurred by the employee, the employee's spouse, or the employee's dependents (as defined in section 152 determined without regard to section 152(b)(1), (b)(2), or (d)(1)(B)).

* * *

For the treatment of the payment of premiums for accident or health insurance from a qualified trust under section 401(a), see § § 1.72-15 and 1.402(a)-1(e).

Par. 6. Section 1.401-1 is amended by adding a new sentence at the end of paragraph (b)(1)(ii) to read as follows:

§ 1.401-1 Qualified pension, profit-sharing, and stock bonus plans.

* * * * *

(b) * * * (1)(i) * * *

(ii) * * * See § § 1.72-15, 1.72-16, and 1.402(a)-1(e) for rules regarding the tax treatment of incidental life or accident or health insurance.

* * * * *

Par. 7. Section 1.402(a)-1 is amended by removing the last two sentences of paragraph (a)(1)(ii) and adding a new sentence in their place and by adding a new paragraph (e) to read as follows:

§ 1.402(a)-1 Taxability of beneficiary under a trust which meets the requirements of section 401(a).

(a) * * * (1) (i) * * *

(ii) * * * Paragraph (e) of this section provides rules relating to use of a qualified pension, annuity, profit-sharing, or stock bonus plan to provide accident or health benefits or coverage otherwise described in section 104, 105, or 106. [Corrected by IRS on 9/26/07 (72 FR 54614).]

* * * * *

(e) Medical, accident, etc. benefits paid from a qualified pension, annuity, profit-sharing, or stock bonus plan—(1) Payment of premiums—(i) General rule. The payment of premiums from a qualified trust for accident or health insurance, including a qualified long-term care insurance contract under section 7702B, constitutes a distribution under section 402(a) to the participant against whose benefit the premium is charged. The amount of the distribution equals the amount of the premium charged against the participant's benefits under the plan. If a defined contribution plan pays these premiums from a current year contribution or forfeiture that has not been allocated to a participant's account, then the amount of the premium for each participant will be treated as first being allocated to the participant and then charged against the participant's benefits under the plan, so that the amount of the distribution is treated in the same manner as determined under the preceding sentence. Except as described in paragraphs (e)(2) and (3) of this section, a distribution described in this paragraph (e)(1) is not excludable from gross income. [Corrected by IRS on 9/26/07 (72 FR 54614).]

(ii) Treatment of amounts received through accident or health insurance. To the extent that the premium for accident or health insurance constitutes a distribution under this paragraph (e)(1), amounts received through accident or health insurance are neither attributable to contributions by the employer which are not includible in the gross income of the employee nor are such amounts paid by the employer. Accordingly, amounts received through the accident or health insurance for personal injuries or sickness are excludable from gross income under section 104(a)(3) and are not treated as distributions from the plan. If amounts received through accident or health insurance are paid to the plan instead of the employee, these amounts are treated as having been paid to the employee and then contributed by the employee to the plan (and these amounts must satisfy the qualification requirements applicable to employee contributions).

(2) Medical benefits for retired employees provided under an account described in section 401(h). The payment of medical benefits described in section 401(h) under a pension or annuity plan is treated in the same manner as a payment of accident or health benefits attributable to employer contributions, or employer-provided coverage under an accident or health plan. See § 1.401-14(a) for the definition of medical benefits described in section 401(h). Accordingly, amounts applied for the payment of accident or health benefits, or for the payment of accident or health coverage, from a section 401(h) account are not includible in the gross income of the participant on whose behalf such contributions are made to the extent they are excludible from gross income under section 104, 105, or 106.

(3) Distributions to eligible retired public safety officers. See section 402(1) for a limited exclusion from gross income for distributions used to pay for certain accident or health premiums (including premiums for qualified long-term care insurance contracts). This limited exclusion applies to eligible retired public safety officers, as defined in section 402(1)(4)(B).

(4) Effect of making a distribution of insurance premiums on qualification. See § 1.401-1(b)(1) for rules concerning the types and amount of medical coverage and benefits that are permitted to be provided under a plan that is part of a trust described in section 401(a). For example, § 1.401-1(b)(1)(ii) provides that a profit-sharing plan is primarily a plan of deferred compensation, but the amounts allocated to the account of a participant may be used to provide incidental accident or health insurance for the participant and the participant's family. See also, section 401(k)(2)(B) for certain restrictions on the distribution of elective contributions.

(5) Application of this paragraph (e). This paragraph (e) applies to the payment of premiums charged against the benefits of a beneficiary or

an alternate payee in the same manner as the payment of premiums charged against the account of a participant.

(6) Example. The provisions of this paragraph (e) are illustrated by the following example:

Example. (i) Facts. Employer sponsors a profit-sharing plan qualified under section 401(a). The plan provides solely for non-elective employer profit-sharing contributions. The plan's trustee enters into a contract with a third-party insurance carrier to provide health insurance for certain plan participants. The insurance policy provides for the payment of medical expenses incurred by those participants. The plan limits the amounts used to provide medical benefits with respect to a participant to 25 percent of the funds held in the participant's account. The trustee makes monthly payments of $1,000 to pay the premiums due for Participant A's health insurance. The trustee also reduces Participant A's account balance by $1,000 at the time of each premium payment. In June of a year, Participant A is admitted to the hospital for covered medical care, and in July of the same year, the health insurer pays the hospital $5,000 for the medical care provided to Participant A in June.

(ii) Conclusion. Under paragraph (e)(1) of this section, each of the trustee's payments of $1,000 constitutes a distribution under section 402(a) to Participant A on the date of each payment. To the extent provided under section 213, the amount of these distributions constitutes payments for medical care. The $5,000 payment to the hospital is excludable from Participant A's gross income under section 104(a)(3) and is not treated as a distribution from the plan. [Corrected by IRS on 9/26/07 (72 FR 54614).]

Par. 8. Section 1.402(c)-2 is amended by redesignating paragraph A-4(h) as paragraph A-4(i) and adding a new paragraph A-4(h) to read as follows:

§ 1.402(c)-2 Eligible rollover contributions; questions and answers.

* * * * *

A-4: * * *

(h) Distributions of premiums for accident or health insurance under § 1.402(a)-1(e).

* * * * *

Par. 9. Section 1.403(a)-1 is amended by revising paragraph (g) to read as follows:

§ 1.403(a)-1 Taxability of beneficiary under a qualified annuity plan.

* * * * *

(g) The rules of § 1.402(a)-1(e) apply for purposes of determining the treatment of amounts paid to provide accident and health insurance benefits.

Par. 10. Section 1.403(b)-6 is amended by adding a sentence following the first sentence of paragraph (g) to read as follows:

§ 1.403(b)-6 Timing of distributions and benefits.

* * * * * (g) Death benefits and other incidental benefits. * * * The rules of § 1.402(a)-1(e) apply for purposes of determining when incidental benefits are treated as distributed and included in gross income. See § § 1.72-15 and 1.72-16. * * *

* * * * *

Linda E. Stiff,

Acting Deputy Commissioner for Services and Enforcement.

g) Death benefits and other incidental benefits. * * * The rules of § 1.402(a)-1(e) apply for purposes of determining when incidental benefits are treated as distributed and included in gross income. See § § 1.72-15 and 1.72-16. * * *

* * * * *

Linda E. Stiff,

Acting Deputy Commissioner for Services and Enforcement.

1 Section 1.72-15(d) also refers to benefits excludible under section 105(c) (relating to certain payments unrelated to absence from work) or 105(d), which was repealed in 1983 (and which related to certain disability payments).

2 See also H.R. Rep. No. 2317, 87th Cong., 2nd Sess. at 4 (1962), stating that no part of the contributions paid by the employer to a section 401(h) account will be taxed currently to the employee.

3 See, for example, the Joint Committee on Taxation's Technical Explanation, Technical Explanation of H.R. 4, the "Pension Protection Act of 2006" as passed by the House on July 28, 2006, and Considered by the Senate on August 3, 2006 (JCX-38-06), August 3, 2006, 109th Cong., 2nd Sess. 244 (2006), relating to the exception under section 402(1), which states that, under present law, distributions from a qualified plan are generally included in gross income (subject to exceptions for investment in the contract and qualified distributions from a designated Roth account).

¶ 20,262D

IRS proposed regulations: Underfunded plans: Benefit restrictions.—The IRS has issued proposed regulations on benefit restrictions for underfunded single-employer defined benefit pension plans, pursuant to new rules in the Pension Protection Act of 2006 (PPA). The proposed regulations would apply to plan years beginning after December 31, 2007.

The proposed regulations, which were published in the Federal Register on August 31, 2007 (72 FR 50544), are reproduced below. Technical corrections were made on November 9, 2007 (72 FR 63528) and November 16, 2007 (72 FR 64708). The regulations were finalized on October 15, 2009 (74 FR 53003). The preamble to the final regulations is at ¶ 23,264. The final regulations are at 13,151L-12, 13,151O-5, and 13,151O-6.

DEPARTMENT OF THE TREASURY

Internal Revenue Service

26 CFR Part 1

[REG-113891-07]

RIN 1545-BG72

Benefit Restrictions for Underfunded Pension Plans

AGENCY: Internal Revenue Service (IRS), Treasury.

ACTION: Notice of proposed rulemaking.

SUMMARY: This document contains proposed regulations providing guidance regarding the use of certain funding balances maintained for defined benefit pension plans and regarding benefit restrictions for certain underfunded defined benefit pension plans. The proposed regulations reflect changes made by the Pension Protection Act of 2006. These regulations affect sponsors, administrators, participants, and beneficiaries of single employer defined benefit pension plans.

DATES: Written or electronic comments and requests for a public hearing must be received by November 28, 2007.

ADDRESSES: Send submissions to: CC:PA:LPD:PR (REG-113891-07), room 5203, Internal Revenue Service, P.O. Box 7604, Ben Franklin Station, Washington, DC 20044. Submissions may be hand-delivered

Monday through Friday between the hours of 8 a.m. to 4 p.m. to CC:PA:LPD:PR (REG-113891-07), Courier's Desk, Internal Revenue Service, 1111 Constitution Avenue, NW., Washington, DC., or sent electronically via the Federal eRulemaking Portal at *www.regulations.gov* (IRS REG-113891-07).

FOR FURTHER INFORMATION CONTACT: Lauson C. Green or Linda S.F. Marshall at (202) 622-6090; concerning submissions and requests for a public hearing, contact Kelly Banks at (202) 622-7180 (not toll-free numbers).

SUPPLEMENTARY INFORMATION:

Paperwork Reduction Act

The collections of information contained in this notice of proposed rulemaking have been submitted to the Office of Management and Budget for review in accordance with the Paperwork Reduction Act of 1995 (44 U.S.C. 3507(d)). Comments on the collections of information should be sent to the Office of Management and Budget, Attn: Desk Officer for the Department of the Treasury, Office of Information and Regulatory Affairs, Washington, DC 20503, with copies to the Internal Revenue Service, Attn: IRS Reports Clearance Officer, SE:W:CAR:MP:T:T:SP, Washington, DC 20224. Comments on the collection of information should be received by October 29, 2007. Comments are specifically requested concerning:

Whether the proposed collection of information is necessary for the proper performance of the functions of the Internal Revenue Service, including whether the information will have practical utility;

The accuracy of the estimated burden associated with the proposed collection of information;

How the quality, utility, and clarity of the information to be collected may be enhanced;

How the burden of complying with the proposed collections of information may be minimized, including through the application of automated collection techniques or other forms of information technology; and

Estimates of capital or start-up costs and costs of operation, maintenance, and purchase of service to provide information.

The collection of information in this proposed regulation is in § 1.430(f)-1(f) and §§ 1.436-1(f) and 1.436-1(h). This information is required in order for a qualified defined benefit plan's enrolled actuary to provide a timely certification of the plan's AFTAP for each plan year to avoid certain benefit restrictions. In addition, these proposed regulations provide for several written elections to be made by the plan sponsor upon occasion. This information is voluntary to obtain a benefit. The likely respondents are qualified retirement plan sponsors and enrolled actuaries.

Estimated total annual reporting burden: 60,000 hours.

Estimated average annual burden hours per respondent: 0.75 hours.

Estimated number of respondents: 80,000.

Estimated annual frequency of responses: occasional.

An agency may not conduct or sponsor, and a person is not required to respond to, a collection of information unless it displays a valid control number assigned by the Office of Management and Budget.

Books or records relating to a collection of information must be retained as long as their contents may become material in the administration of any internal revenue law. Generally, tax returns and tax return information are confidential, as required by 26 U.S.C. 6103.

Background

This document contains proposed Income Tax Regulations (26 CFR part 1) under sections 430(f) and 436, as added to the Code by the Pension Protection Act of 2006 (PPA '06), Public Law 109-280, 120 Stat. 780.

Section 412 contains minimum funding rules that generally apply to defined benefit plans.[1] The minimum funding rules that apply specifically to single employer defined benefit plans (including multiple employer plans within the meaning of section 413(c)) are set forth in new section 430.

Section 430 generally provides that the minimum required contribution for a year is the sum of the target normal cost for the year and the shortfall and waiver amortization charges. Under section 430(f)(3), certain funding balances referred to as the prefunding balance and the funding standard carryover balance are permitted to be used to reduce the otherwise applicable minimum required contribution for a plan year in certain situations. Under section 430(f)(7), the funding standard carryover balance is based on the funding standard account credit balance as determined under section 412 for a plan as of the last day of the last plan year beginning in 2007. Under section 430(f)(6), the prefunding balance represents the accumulation of the contributions that an employer makes for a plan year that exceed the minimum required contribution for the year. Thus, an employer that makes additional contributions for a plan year is permitted in certain circumstances to use those excess contributions in order to satisfy the minimum funding requirement in a subsequent plan year.

The treatment of these balances under section 430 reflects congressional concern with the treatment of a funding standard account credit balance under the section 412 rules in effect prior to PPA '06. Accordingly, section 430(f)(3) sets forth new limits on the ability of a poorly funded plan to use the prefunding balance and the funding standard carryover balance for a plan year. In addition, section 430(f)(4) requires that the prefunding balance and the funding standard carryover balance be subtracted from the value of plan assets for certain purposes

(including the determination of the plan's funding target attainment percentage (FTAP), as defined under section 430(d)(2)) and section 430(f)(8) requires that the prefunding balance and the funding standard carryover balance be adjusted for actual investment return on the plan assets. In order to give employers the opportunity to minimize the impact of the requirement to subtract the prefunding balance and funding standard carryover balance from the plan assets, section 430(f)(5) permits an employer to elect to reduce the balances.

Section 401(a)(29) requires that a defined benefit plan (other than a multiemployer plan) satisfy the requirements of section 436. Section 436 sets forth a series of limitations on the accrual and payment of benefits under an underfunded plan. Under section 436(g), these limitations (other than the limitations on accelerated benefit payments under section 436(d)) do not apply to a plan for the first 5 plan years of the plan, taking into account any predecessor plan.

Section 436(b) sets forth a limitation on plan shutdown and other unpredictable contingent event benefits in situations where the plan's adjusted funding target attainment percentage (AFTAP) for the plan year is less than 60 percent or would be less than 60 percent taking into account the occurrence of the event. For this purpose, an "unpredictable contingent event benefit" means any benefit payable solely by reason of (1) a plant shutdown (or a similar event) or (2) an event other than attainment of age, performance of service, receipt or derivation of compensation, or the occurrence of death or disability. Under section 436(b)(2), the limitation does not apply for a plan year if the plan sponsor makes a specified contribution (in addition to any minimum required contribution). If the AFTAP for a plan year is less than 60 percent, then the specified contribution is equal to the amount of the increase in the plan's funding target for the plan year attributable to the occurrence of the event. If the AFTAP for a plan year is 60 percent or more but would be less than 60 percent taking into account the occurrence of the event, then the specified contribution is the amount sufficient to result in an AFTAP of 60 percent taking into account the occurrence of the event.

Under section 436(c), a plan amendment that has the effect of increasing the liabilities of the plan by reason of any increase in benefits (including changes in vesting) may not take effect if the plan's AFTAP for the plan year is less than 80 percent or would be less than 80 percent taking into account the amendment. Under section 436(c)(2), the limitation does not apply for a plan year if the plan sponsor makes a specified contribution (in addition to any minimum required contribution). If the plan's AFTAP for the plan year is less than 80 percent, then the specified contribution is equal to the amount of the increase in the plan's funding target for the plan year attributable to the amendment. If the plan's AFTAP for the plan year is 80 percent or more but would be less than 80 percent taking into account the amendment, then the specified contribution is the amount sufficient to result in an AFTAP of 80 percent taking into account the amendment. In addition, under section 436(c)(3), the limitation does not apply to an amendment that provides for a benefit increase under a formula not based on compensation, but only if the rate of increase does not exceed the contemporaneous rate of increase in average wages of the participants covered by the amendment.

Under section 436(d), a plan is required to set forth certain limitations on accelerated benefit distributions. If the plan's AFTAP for a plan year is less than 60 percent, the plan must not make any prohibited payments after the valuation date for the plan year. If the plan's AFTAP for a plan year is at least 60 percent but is less than 80 percent, the plan must not pay any prohibited payment to the extent the payment exceeds the lesser of (1) 50 percent of the amount otherwise payable under the plan and (2) the present value of the maximum PBGC guarantee with respect to a participant. In addition, if the plan sponsor is in bankruptcy proceedings, the plan may not pay any prohibited payment unless the plan's enrolled actuary certifies that the AFTAP of the plan is at least 100 percent. However, section 436(d) does not apply to a plan for a plan year if the terms of the plan provide for no benefit accruals with respect to any participant for the period beginning on September 1, 2005, and extending throughout the plan year.

Under section 436(d)(5), a "prohibited payment" is (1) any payment, in excess of the monthly amount paid under a single life annuity (plus any social security supplements that are provided under the plan), to a participant or beneficiary, (2) any payment for the purchase of an irrevocable commitment from an insurer to pay benefits (an annuity

---

[1] Section 302 of the Employee Retirement Income Security Act of 1974, as amended (ERISA), sets forth funding rules that are parallel to those in section 412 of the Code, section 303 of ERISA sets forth additional funding rules for defined benefit plans (other than multiemployer plans) that are parallel to those in section 430 of the Code, and section 206(g) of ERISA sets forth funding-based limitations for defined benefit plans (other than multiemployer plans) that are parallel to those in section 436 of the Code. Under section

101 of Reorganization Plan No. 4 of 1978 (43 FR 47713) and section 302 of ERISA, the Secretary of the Treasury has interpretive jurisdiction over the subject matter addressed in these proposed regulations for purposes of ERISA, as well as the Code. Thus, these proposed Treasury regulations issued under sections 430(f) and 436 of the Code apply as well for purposes of ERISA sections 303(f) and 206(g), respectively.

contract), or (3) any other payment specified by the Secretary by regulations.

Under section 436(e), a plan is required to provide that if the plan's AFTAP is less than 60 percent for a plan year, all future benefit accruals under the plan must cease as of the valuation date for the plan year. Under section 436(e)(2), the limitation ceases to apply with respect to any plan year, effective as of the first day of the plan year, if the plan sponsor makes a contribution (in addition to any minimum required contribution for the plan year) equal to the amount sufficient to result in an AFTAP of 60 percent.

Section 436(f) sets forth a series of rules under which the limitations of section 436 will not apply to a plan. Under section 436(f)(1), an employer is permitted to provide security to the plan (in the form of a surety bond, cash, or other forms satisfactory to the Treasury Department and the parties involved) that is treated as an asset of the plan for purposes of determining the plan's AFTAP. Under section 436(f)(2), if an employer uses the option in section 436(b)(2), 436(c)(2), or 436(e)(2) to make the specified contribution that would avoid a limitation under section 436, the specified contribution must be an actual contribution and the employer may not use a prefunding balance or funding standard carryover balance in lieu of making the specified contribution. In addition, a contribution to avoid a benefit limitation is disregarded in determining whether the minimum required contribution under section 430 has been made and in determining the plan's prefunding balance.

Section 436(f)(3) describes certain situations in which an employer is deemed to have made the election in section 430(f)(5) to reduce the plan's funding standard carryover balance or prefunding balance. Such an election has the effect of increasing the plan's FTAP (because the result of the election is a higher asset value used to determine the FTAP) and could lead to the plan not being subject to a benefit limitation under section 436. In particular, if the limitation under section 436(d) would otherwise apply to a plan, the plan sponsor is treated as having made an election (a deemed election) to reduce any prefunding balance or funding standard carryover balance by the amount necessary to prevent the benefit limitation from applying. A comparable rule applies to the other benefit limitations under sections 436(b), 436(c), and 436(e), but only in the case of a plan maintained pursuant to a collective bargaining agreement. In either case, this deeming rule applies only if the prefunding balance and funding standard carryover balances are large enough to avoid the application of a section 436 limitation.

Section 436(h) sets forth a series of presumptions that apply during the portion of the plan year that is before the plan's enrolled actuary has certified the plan's AFTAP for the year. Under section 436(h)(1), if a plan was subject to a limitation under section 436(b), 436(c), 436(d), or 436(e) for the plan year preceding the current plan year, the plan's AFTAP for the current year is presumed to be the same as for the preceding year until the plan's enrolled actuary certifies the plan's AFTAP for the current year. Under section 436(h)(3), if any of these limitations did not apply to the plan for the preceding year, but the plan's AFTAP for the preceding year was within 10 percentage points of the limitation's threshold, the plan's AFTAP is presumed to be reduced by 10 percentage points as of the first day of the 4th month of the current plan year, unless the plan's enrolled actuary has certified the plan's AFTAP for the current year by that day (and that day is deemed to be the plan's valuation date for purposes of applying the benefit limitations). If the plan's enrolled actuary has not certified the plan's AFTAP by the first day of the 10th month of the current plan year, section 436(h)(2) provides that the plan's AFTAP is conclusively presumed to be less than 60 percent as of that day (and that day is deemed to be the valuation date for purposes of applying the benefit limitations).

Under section 436(i), unless the plan provides otherwise, if a limitation on prohibited payments or future benefit accruals under section 436(d) or (e) ceases to apply to a plan, all such payments and benefit accruals resume, effective as of the day following the close of the limitation period.

Section 436(j) provides definitions that are used under section 436, including the plan's AFTAP. In general, the plan's AFTAP is based on the plan's FTAP for the plan year. However, the plan's AFTAP is determined by adding the aggregate amount of purchases of annuities for employees other than highly compensated employees (within the meaning of section 414(q)) made by the plan during the two preceding plan years to the numerator and the denominator of the fraction used to determine the FTAP.

In addition, section 436(j)(3) provides a special rule which applies to certain well-funded plans under which the plan's FTAP for purposes of section 436 (and hence the plan's AFTAP) is determined by using the plan's assets without reduction for the prefunding balance and the funding standard carryover balance. Section 436(j)(3)(B) sets forth a transition rule for determining eligibility for this special rule.

Section 436(k) provides that, for plan years that begin in 2008, the determination of the plan's FTAP for the preceding year is to be made pursuant to guidance issued by the Secretary.

Explanation of Provisions

I. *Section 430(f) — Effect of Prefunding Balance and Funding Standard Carryover Balance.*

A. *Overview.*

1. *In general.*

The proposed regulations would be the second in a series of proposed regulations under new section 430.[2] These regulations would provide guidance on the application of section 430(f), relating to the establishment and maintenance of a funding standard carryover balance and a prefunding balance for purposes of sections 430 and 436. The Treasury Department and the IRS intend to issue additional proposed regulations relating to other portions of the rules under section 430 later in 2007.

2. *Multiple employer plans.*

The proposed regulations under section 430(f) apply to plans subject to section 412 that are maintained by one employer or a controlled group of employers and to multiple employer plans within the meaning of section 413(c). In the case of a multiple employer plan to which section 413(c)(4)(A) applies, the rules under the proposed regulations would be applied separately for each employer under the plan, as if each employer maintained a separate plan. Thus, each employer under such a multiple employer plan may have a separate funding standard carryover balance and a prefunding balance for the plan. In the case of a multiple employer plan to which section 413(c)(4)(A) does not apply (that is, a plan described in section 413(c)(4)(B) that has not made the election for section 413(c)(4)(A) to apply), the proposed regulations under section 430(f) would apply as if all participants in the plan were employed by a single employer.

B. *Establishment of prefunding balance and funding standard carryover balance.*

The proposed regulations would provide that an employer is permitted to establish a prefunding balance for a plan that represents the accumulation of contributions made for plan years beginning on or after the effective date of section 430 with respect to the plan (the first effective plan year) that are in excess of the minimum required contributions (determined without regard to the prefunding balance and funding standard carryover balance) for those plan years. Specifically, for the first effective plan year of a plan, the prefunding balance is initialized at zero dollars and an employer is permitted to elect to add some or all of the excess contributions made to a plan for each plan year to the prefunding balance as of the first day of the next plan year. For this purpose, the excess contributions are generally determined as the amount by which the employer contributions to the plan for the plan year exceed the minimum required contribution for the plan year, with appropriate adjustments for interest determined at the effective interest rate under section 430(h)(2)(A). However, the proposed regulations would provide that any contribution that is made to avoid the application of a benefit limitation under section 436 is not taken into account in determining the amount of excess contributions.

The proposed regulations would also provide that the minimum required contribution for purposes of determining the amount of excess contributions for the year is determined without regard to any offset of the minimum required contribution for the year as a result of the use of the prefunding or funding standard carryover balances. Accordingly, an employer would not be permitted to add to the prefunding balance any amount of contributions that are "excess" by reason of an offset of the minimum required contribution for the year through the use of the prefunding balance or funding standard carryover balance. This prohibition precludes an employer from avoiding

---

[2] Proposed regulation §§ 1.430(h)(3)-1 and 1.430(h)(3)-2, relating to the mortality tables used to determine liabilities under section 430(h)(3), were issued May 29, 2007 (REG-143601-06, 72 FR 29456).

the requirement to adjust the prefunding balance and funding standard carryover balance by the actual rate of return on plan assets in the situation where the plan assets have experienced a loss (or a rate of return that is lower than the effective interest rate that is used for interest adjustments with respect to minimum required contributions for the plan year).

The proposed regulations would provide that the funding standard carryover balance is initialized as the balance in the funding standard account as of the last day of the last plan year before section 430 applies to a plan (the pre-effective plan year). This is generally the last plan year beginning in 2007, but could be a later year in the case of a plan to which a delayed effective date applies under the rules of sections 104 through 106 of PPA '06.

C. *Maintenance of prefunding balance and funding standard carryover balance.*

The proposed regulations would provide that a plan's prefunding balance and funding standard carryover balance as of the beginning of a plan year are adjusted to reflect the actual rate of return on plan assets for the plan year. This calculation of the actual rate of return on plan assets for the plan year is determined on the basis of fair market value and must take into account the amount and timing of all contributions, distributions, and other plan payments made during the year. The adjustment for investment return is applied to the prefunding balance and funding standard carryover balance after any reductions to those balances as described under the following two headings in this preamble. In addition, the proposed regulations would provide special rules in the case of a plan with a valuation date that is not the first day of the plan year.

D. *Use of prefunding balance and funding standard carryover balance to offset minimum funding requirements for a year.*

The proposed regulations would provide that the employer may elect to use some or all of the prefunding balance or funding standard carryover balance to offset the otherwise applicable minimum required contribution for a plan year, provided that the plan met a funding percentage threshold for the preceding plan year. Specifically, an employer is permitted to make such an election only if the plan's prior year funding ratio was at least 80 percent. For this purpose, the plan's prior year funding ratio generally is a fraction (expressed as a percentage), the numerator of which is the value of plan assets on the valuation date for the preceding plan year, reduced by the amount of any prefunding balance (but not the amount of any funding standard carryover balance), and the denominator of which is the funding target of the plan for the preceding plan year (determined without regard to the at-risk rules of section 430(i)(1)).

The proposed regulations would provide a transition rule to determine a plan's prior year funding ratio for the first effective plan year. Under this transition rule, the current liability for the plan for the pre-effective plan year is substituted for the funding target of the plan for that plan year. In addition, the transition rule provides that the value of plan assets is determined under section 412(c)(2) as in effect for that pre-effective plan year, except that the value of plan assets must be limited so that it is not less than 90 percent and not more than 110 percent of the fair market value of plan assets.

The proposed regulations would reflect the rule in section 430(f)(3)(B) that requires the plan sponsor to have reduced the funding standard carryover balance in full (either by using the funding standard carryover balance to offset the minimum required contribution for a year or through a voluntary reduction under section 430(f)(5)) before the prefunding balance is permitted to be used to offset a current year minimum funding requirement.

E. *Subtraction from plan assets and employer election to reduce balances.*

The proposed regulations would reflect the rules under section 430(f)(4) which provide that the prefunding balance and funding standard carryover balance are subtracted from the plan assets for certain purposes. These include the determination of the FTAP, which is also relevant for purposes of applying the benefit limitations of section 436.

In accordance with section 430(f)(4)(A), the proposed regulations would provide that the amount of the prefunding balance is subtracted from the value of plan assets for purposes of determining whether a plan is exempt from the requirement to establish a new shortfall amortization base under section 430(c)(5) only if an election to use the prefunding balance to offset the minimum required contribution is made for the plan year. In addition, pursuant to section 430(f)(4)(B)(ii), the proposed regulations would provide that the prefunding balance and funding standard carryover balance are not subtracted from plan assets for purposes of determining the funding shortfall under section

430(c)(4) to the extent that there is a binding written agreement with the Pension Benefit Guaranty Corporation (PBGC) which provides that all or a portion of those balances cannot be used to offset the minimum required contribution for a plan year. For this purpose, an agreement with the PBGC is taken into account with respect to a plan year only if the agreement was executed prior to the valuation date for the plan year.

In addition, section 436(j) sets forth an exception from the requirement to subtract the plan's prefunding balance and funding standard carryover balance from the value of plan assets in determining a plan's FTAP for purposes of the benefit limitation rules of section 436 provided that the plan's FTAP would meet certain standards if it were calculated without subtracting the balances from plan assets.

Section 430(f)(5) provides that an employer may elect to reduce the amount of the prefunding balance and the funding standard carryover balance. This will have the effect of increasing the plan assets for various purposes. For example, the increase in plan assets will increase the FTAP, which may allow the plan to avoid the application of section 436 limitations. The proposed regulations would reflect the rule in section 430(f)(5)(B) that requires the employer to reduce the funding standard carryover balance in full (either by using the funding standard carryover balance to offset the minimum required contribution for a year or through a voluntary reduction under section 430(f)(5)) before any reduction is permitted for the prefunding balance.

F. *Elections under section 430(f).*

The proposed regulations would provide that an election under section 430(f) is made by the plan sponsor by providing written notification of the election to the plan's enrolled actuary and the plan administrator, must be irrevocable when made, and must satisfy certain timing rules. The written notification must set forth the relevant details of the election, including the specific amounts involved in the election with respect to the prefunding balance and funding standard carryover balance. An election under section 430(f) generally must be made on or before the due date (with extensions) for the filing of the plan's Form 5500 "Annual Return/Report of Employee Benefit Plan" for the plan year to which the election relates (or, in the case of a plan not required to file a Form 5500 for the plan year, on or before the last day of the seventh month after the end of the plan year to which the election relates). For this purpose, an election to add to the prefunding balance relates to the plan year for which excess contributions were made. However, the proposed regulations would require any section 430(f)(5) election to reduce a portion of the prefunding balance or funding standard carryover balance for a plan year to be made by the end of the plan year to which the election relates. For example, in the case of a calendar year plan required to file Form 5500, an election to add to the prefunding balance as of the first day of the 2010 plan year (in an amount not in excess of the 2009 interest-adjusted excess contributions), must be made no later than the due date for filing the 2009 Form 5500 (with extensions), while an election to reduce the prefunding balance as of the first day of the 2010 plan year must be made by the end of the 2010 plan year. In both cases, the election would be reported on the 2010 Form 5500 (Schedule SB) that would be filed in 2011.

The proposed regulations would provide that, for purposes of elections under section 430(f), any reference in the proposed regulations to the plan sponsor generally means the employer or employers responsible for making contributions to the plan. However, in the case of elections under section 430(f) for multiple employer plans to which section 413(c)(4)(A) does not apply, any reference in the proposed regulations to the plan sponsor means the plan administrator within the meaning of section 414(g).

II. *Section 436 — Limits on Benefits and Benefit Accruals Under Single Employer Defined Benefit Plans.*

A. *Overview and general rules.*

1. *In general.*

The proposed regulations would set forth the rules that a defined benefit pension plan that is subject to section 412 and that is not a multiemployer plan must satisfy in order to comply with the requirement in section 401(a)(29) that the plan meet the requirements of section 436. This requirement is a qualification requirement. A plan satisfies the requirements of section 436 only if the plan meets the requirements of these regulations.

2. *New plans.*

In accordance with section 436(g), the proposed regulations would provide that the limitations described in sections 436(b), 436(c), and 436(e) do not apply to a plan for the first five plan years of the plan. For purposes of applying this new plan rule, plan years under a plan are aggregated with plan years under a predecessor plan. Thus, the only benefit limitation that could apply under a plan that is not a successor plan during the first five years of its existence is the section 436(d) limitation applicable to accelerated benefit payments (such as single sum distributions).

3. *Multiple employer plans.*

The proposed regulations under section 436 apply to plans maintained by one employer (including a controlled group of employers) and to multiple employer plans (within the meaning of section 413(c)). In the case of a multiple employer plan to which section 413(c)(4)(A) applies, the rules under the proposed regulations would be applied separately for each employer under the plan, as if each employer maintained a separate plan. Thus, the benefit limitations under section 436 could apply differently to employees of different employers under such a multiple employer plan. In the case of a multiple employer plan to which section 413(c)(4)(A) does not apply (that is, a plan described in section 413(c)(4)(B) that has not made the election for section 413(c)(4)(A) to apply), the proposed regulations under section 436 would apply as if all participants in the plan were employed by a single employer.

4. *Treatment of plan as of close of prohibited or cessation period.*

The proposed regulations would provide that, if a limitation on accelerated benefit payments under section 436(d) (such as single sum distributions) applies to a plan as of a section 436 measurement date, but that limit subsequently ceases to apply to the plan as of a later section 436 measurement date, then the limitation does not apply to benefits with annuity starting dates that are on or after that later section 436 measurement date. In addition, the proposed regulations would provide that, if a limitation on benefit accruals under section 436(e) applies to a plan, unless the plan provides otherwise, benefit accruals under the plan will resume effective as of the section 436 measurement date as of which benefit accruals are no longer restricted.

With respect to a participant who had an annuity starting date within a period during which the accelerated benefit payment limitation rules of section 436(d) applied to the plan, once the limitation ceases to apply, the participant's benefits will continue to be paid in the form previously elected unless the plan permits the participant to be offered a new election which would modify the prior election. The proposed regulations would permit a plan to provide that the participant will be offered the opportunity to have a new election under which the form of benefit previously elected may be modified, subject to applicable qualification requirements, and that new election will constitute a new annuity starting date for purposes of section 417. Similarly, a plan is permitted to be amended to provide that any benefit accruals that were limited under the rules of section 436(e) will be credited under the plan once the limitation no longer applies, subject to applicable qualification requirements. If a plan provides for the restoration of benefit accruals for the period of the limitation under preexisting plan terms, the plan is treated as having adopted an amendment that has the effect of increasing liabilities under the plan if the period of the limitation exceeded 12 months. Whether a plan is amended or is treated as having been amended as described above, the amendment or pre-existing plan provision is subject to the limitations of section 436(c).[3]

In addition, the proposed regulations would provide that a plan is permitted to be amended to provide that any unpredictable contingent event benefits that were limited under the rules of section 436(b) will be paid or reinstated when the limitation no longer applies, subject to applicable qualification requirements. Any such amendment is subject to the limitations of section 436(c). A plan is not permitted to provide for restoration of any such unpredictable contingent event benefits without an amendment that complies with section 436(c).

5. *Deemed election to reduce prefunding and funding standard carryover balances.*

The proposed regulations would provide that, if a limitation on accelerated benefit payments under section 436(d) would otherwise apply to a plan, the plan sponsor is treated as having made an election under section 430(f) to reduce the prefunding balance or funding standard carryover balance by such amount as is necessary for the AFTAP to be at or above the applicable threshold (60, 80, or 100 percent, as the case may be) in order for the benefit limitation not to

apply to the plan. In such a case, the plan sponsor is treated as having made that election on the section 436 measurement date as of which the benefit limitation would otherwise apply. This deemed election applies if the plan provides for accelerated distributions that would be limited in a plan year, regardless of whether a plan participant is eligible or elects to receive such a distribution during the plan year (but does not apply if the plan does not provide for any accelerated distributions that are subject to the benefit limitation). However, the deemed reduction applies with respect to this limitation only if the prefunding and funding standard carryover balances to be reduced are large enough to avoid the application of the limitation. Thus, no reduction of prefunding and funding standard carryover balances is required if the limitation would still apply for a year even if those balances were reduced to zero.

In addition, the proposed regulations would provide that, in the case of a plan maintained pursuant to one or more collective bargaining agreements between an employee representative and one or more employers in which a benefit limitation under section 436(b), 436(c), or 436(e) would otherwise apply to the plan, the employer is treated for purposes of section 436 as having made an election under section 430(f) to reduce the prefunding balance or funding standard carryover balance by such amount as is necessary for the AFTAP to be at or above the applicable threshold for the benefit limitation not to apply to the plan, taking into account the unpredictable contingent event benefits or plan amendment, as applicable. The proposed regulations would provide that, in the case of a plan with respect to which collective bargaining agreements apply to some, but not all, of the plan participants, the plan is considered a collectively bargained plan for purposes of this provision if at least 25 percent of the participants in the plan are members of the collective bargaining units for whom the benefit levels under the plan are specified under the collective bargaining agreements. As in the case of the deemed reduction in funding balances for the accelerated benefit distributions under section 436(d), the deemed reduction applies only if the prefunding and funding standard carryover balances to be reduced are large enough to avoid the application of the limitation under section 436(b), 436(c), or 436(e), as applicable.

If the mandatory reduction of funding balances applies to a plan, the employer is treated as having made that election on the date as of which the applicable benefit restriction would otherwise apply. In addition, the proposed regulations would provide that, if a plan (whether or not collectively bargained) is presumed to have an AFTAP of less than 60 percent under the section 436(h) presumption rules, then the plan is treated as if the plan's funding standard carryover balance and prefunding balance are insufficient to increase the plan's AFTAP to the threshold percentage.

6. *Section 436 measurement date.*

The "section 436 measurement date" is a defined term under the proposed regulations that is used to describe the date that stops or starts the application of the limitations of sections 436(d) and 436(e) and is also used for calculations with respect to applying the limitations of sections 436(b) and 436(c). The regulations would provide that the date of the enrolled actuary's certification of the AFTAP for the plan year is a section 436 measurement date if it occurs within the first nine months of the plan year. If the date of an enrolled actuary's certification of the AFTAP is between the first day of the 10th month of a plan year and the last day of that plan year, that date is not a section 436 measurement date for purposes of the limitations of section 436(d) or 436(e) because, in that case, the plan's AFTAP is presumed to be under 60 percent (however, receipt of the enrolled actuary's certification during that period impacts the plan's presumed "carryover" AFTAP for the following year). The proposed regulations would provide that a section 436 measurement date occurs where there is a change in the plan's AFTAP under the presumption rules of section 436(h). In addition, the proposed regulations would provide a series of rules in cases where the enrolled actuary's certification of the AFTAP for a plan year is made after the end of the plan year, as described below under the heading "Presumed underfunding for purposes of benefit limitations."

B. *Limitation on plant shutdown and other unpredictable contingent event benefits.*

In accordance with section 436(b), the proposed regulations would provide that a plan that provides for any unpredictable contingent event benefit[4] must provide that the benefit will not be paid to a plan participant during a plan year if the AFTAP for the plan year is less

---

[3] The PBGC has informed the IRS and the Treasury Department that it expects similarly to treat such an automatic restoration of missed benefit accruals as a plan amendment.

[4] See also Notice 2007-14, 2007-7 IRB 501, (see § 601.601(d)(2) of this chapter) requesting comments on the types of benefits that are permitted to be provided in a qualified defined benefit plan, including benefits payable in the event of a plant shutdown or similar event.

than 60 percent (or is 60 percent or more but would be less than 60 percent if the benefits attributable to the unpredictable contingent event were taken into account in determining the AFTAP). However, this prohibition on payment of unpredictable contingent event benefits no longer applies for a plan year, effective as of the first day of the plan year, if the employer makes the contribution specified in section 436(b)(2), as described in paragraph II. F in this preamble.

For this purpose, the proposed regulations would provide that an "unpredictable contingent event benefit" means any benefit or increase in benefits to the extent the benefit or increase would not be payable but for the occurrence of an unpredictable contingent event, and an "unpredictable contingent event" means a plant shutdown (whether full or partial) or similar event, or an event other than the attainment of any age, performance of any service, receipt or derivation of any compensation, or the occurrence of death or disability. Thus, for example, if a plan provides for an unreduced early retirement benefit upon the occurrence of an event other than the attainment of any age, performance of any service, receipt or derivation of any compensation, or the occurrence of death or disability, then that unreduced early retirement benefit is an unpredictable contingent event benefit to the extent of any portion of the benefit that would not be payable but for the occurrence of the event, even if the remainder of the benefit is payable without regard to the occurrence of the event. Similarly, an unpredictable contingent event benefit under the proposed regulations includes a benefit payable upon the presence of circumstances specified in the plan (other than the attainment of any age, performance of any service, receipt or derivation of any compensation, or the occurrence of death or disability), so that a plan that provides those benefits upon a participant's severance from employment in those circumstances, but not upon a severance from employment that does not involve those circumstances, is providing an unpredictable contingent event benefit.

Unpredictable contingent event benefits attributable to a plant shutdown or other unpredictable contingent event that occurred within a period during which no limitation under section 436(b) applied to the plan are not affected by the limitation as it applies in a subsequent period. For example, if a plant shutdown occurs in 2010 and a plan's funded status is such that its shutdown benefits are not subject to the limitation for that plan year, benefits paid pursuant to that shutdown are permitted to be paid in a later plan year even if the plan's AFTAP for the subsequent year is less than 60 percent. Conversely, if a plant shutdown occurs in 2010 and a plan's funded status is such that its shutdown benefits are subject to the limitation under section 436(b) for that plan year and cannot be paid, those shutdown benefits related to the 2010 plant shutdown are not permitted to be paid in a later year even if the plan's AFTAP for the later year is at or above the 60 percent threshold for the section 436(b) limitation (subject to the rules permitting plan amendments to reinstate previously restricted benefits, including unpredictable contingent event benefits, as described in paragraph II.A.4 of this preamble).

C. *Limitations on plan amendments increasing liability for benefits.*

In accordance with section 436(c), the proposed regulations would provide that a plan satisfies the limitation on plan amendments increasing liability for benefits only if the plan provides that no amendment to the plan that has the effect of increasing liabilities of the plan by reason of increases in benefits, establishment of new benefits, changing the rate of benefit accrual, or changing the rate at which benefits become nonforfeitable is permitted to take effect if the AFTAP for the plan year is less than 80 percent (or is 80 percent or more but would be less than 80 percent if the benefits attributable to the amendment were taken into account in determining the AFTAP). However, this prohibition on plan amendments no longer applies for a plan year if the employer makes the contribution specified in section 436(c)(2), as described in paragraph II. F of this preamble.

In accordance with section 436(c)(3), the limitation on amendments increasing liabilities does not apply to any amendment that provides for an increase in benefits under a formula that is not based on a participant's compensation, but only if the rate of increase in benefits does not exceed the contemporaneous rate of increase in average wages of participants covered by the amendment. The proposed regulations would provide that the determination of the rate of increase in average wages is made by taking into consideration the net increase in average wages during the period beginning with the effective date of the most recent benefit increase applicable to all of those participants who are covered by the current amendment and ending on the effective date of the current amendment. If the participants covered by an amendment include both currently employed participants and terminated participants (who will have no increase or decrease in wages for this purpose after severance from employment), all covered participants must be included in determining the increase in average wages of the partici-

pants covered by the amendment. Alternatively, the employer could adopt two amendments — one that increases benefits for currently employed participants and another one that increases benefits for the terminated participants. In that case, this exception from application of the section 436(c) limitation generally would apply to the amendment that increases benefits for currently employed participants (based solely on the wages of those current employees), but the amendment that applies only to terminated participants (who received no increase in wages from the employer during the period over which the increase in average wages is determined) would not be eligible for the exception.

In addition, the proposed regulations would provide that, to the extent that any amendment results in (or is made pursuant to) a mandatory increase in the vesting of benefits under the Code or ERISA (such as vesting rate increases pursuant to statute and plan termination amendments under section 411(d)(3)), that amendment does not constitute an amendment that changes the rate at which benefits become nonforfeitable for purposes of section 436(c).

D. *Limitations on accelerated benefit distributions.*

1. *Funding percentage less than 60 percent.*

In accordance with section 436(d)(1), under the proposed regulations, a plan must provide that, if the plan's AFTAP for a plan year is less than 60 percent, the plan will not pay any prohibited payment with an annuity starting date that is on or after the applicable section 436 measurement date. However, if a participant requests such a prohibited distribution, the plan must permit the participant to elect another form of benefit available under the plan or to defer payment to a later date to the extent permitted under applicable qualification requirements. Similar rules apply in any case in which a beneficiary is entitled to a prohibited payment (for example, where a qualified pre-retirement survivor annuity is offered in an alternative single sum payment).

2. *Bankruptcy.*

In accordance with section 436(d)(2), under the proposed regulations, a plan must provide that the plan will not pay any prohibited payment with an annuity starting date that is during any period during a plan year in which the plan sponsor is a debtor in a case under title 11, United States Code, or similar Federal or State law, until the date on which the enrolled actuary of the plan certifies that the plan's AFTAP is not less than 100 percent.

3. *Limited payment if percentage at least 60 percent but less than 80 percent.*

In accordance with section 436(d)(3), under the proposed regulations, a plan must provide that, in any case in which the plan's AFTAP for a plan year is 60 percent or more but is less than 80 percent, a participant is permitted to elect a prohibited payment only if the present value of the portion of the payment that is greater than the amount of the monthly straight life annuity under the plan (and any social security supplement, if applicable) does not exceed 50 percent of the present value of the participant's benefits (or if less, 100 percent of the present value of the maximum guarantee with respect to the participant under section 4022 of ERISA). For this purpose, present value is determined using the rules of section 417(e) except that, if the plan provides a single sum distribution that is larger than the present value of the benefit determined using the rules of section 417(e), then that larger benefit is substituted for the present value of the participant's benefits before applying the 50 percent factor. Similar rules apply in any case in which a beneficiary is entitled to a prohibited payment.

If an optional form of benefit that is otherwise available under the terms of the plan is not available as of the annuity starting date because it is a prohibited payment that cannot be paid under the preceding paragraph, then the plan must provide a participant who elects such an optional form with the option either to defer payment to a later date (to the extent permitted under applicable qualification requirements) or to bifurcate the benefit into unrestricted and restricted portions. If the participant elects to bifurcate the benefit, the plan must permit the participant to elect, with respect to the unrestricted portion, any optional form of benefit otherwise available under the plan with respect to the participant's entire benefit (whether or not the optional form of benefit with respect to the unrestricted portion is a prohibited payment). The unrestricted portion of the benefit is the lesser of (i) 50 percent of the benefit and (ii) the benefit that has a present value that does not exceed 100 percent of the present value of the maximum PBGC guarantee with respect to the participant under section 4022 of ERISA. If the participant elects payment of the unrestricted portion of the benefit in the form of a prohibited payment, then the plan must permit the participant to elect payment of the restricted portion in any optional form of benefit under the plan that would have been permitted with respect to the participant's entire benefit other than a prohibited payment. A plan is also permitted (but not required) to offer optional forms of benefit that are solely available during the period section 436(d)(3) applies to the plan, such as an optional form of benefit that provides for the current payment of the unrestricted portion of the benefit, with a delayed commencement for the restricted portion of the benefit, subject to other applicable qualification requirements.

A participant who receives a prohibited payment (or a series of prohibited payments under a single optional form of benefit) under the rule permitting certain prohibited payments cannot receive any additional payment that would be a prohibited payment until there is a plan year for which none of the limitations on accelerated distributions under section 436(d) apply. Benefits provided to a participant and any beneficiary are aggregated for purposes of determining the limited distribution under section 436(d)(3). The proposed regulations would also reflect the rules of section 436(d)(3)(B)(ii), which describes how this limited distribution is allocated among the beneficiaries of a participant.

4. Exception for certain frozen plans.

In accordance with section 436(d)(4), the limitations under section 436(d) will not apply to a plan for any plan year if the terms of the plan, as in effect for the period beginning on September 1, 2005, provided for no benefit accruals with respect to any participants. However, if such a plan provides for any benefit accruals during a plan year, this exception will cease to apply for the plan as of the date those accruals start.

5. Prohibited payment.

In accordance with section 436(d)(5), the proposed regulations would provide that the term "prohibited payment" means:

(i) Any payment for a month that is in excess of the monthly amount paid under a single life annuity (plus any social security supplements described in the last sentence of section 411(a)(9)), to a participant or beneficiary whose annuity starting date (as defined in section 417(f)(2)) occurs during any period that a limitation on accelerated benefit payments is in effect;

(ii) Any payment for the purchase of an irrevocable commitment from an insurer to pay benefits; and

(iii) Any other payment that is identified as a prohibited payment by the Commissioner in revenue rulings and procedures, notices and other guidance published in the Internal Revenue Bulletin (see § 601.601(d)(2) of this chapter).

In addition, for purposes of applying the limitations on accelerated benefit payments under the requirements of section 436(d), the term *annuity starting date* means, as applicable—

(a) The first day of the first period for which an amount is payable as an annuity as described in section 417(f)(2)(A)(i);

(b) In the case of a benefit not payable in the form of an annuity, the first day on which all events have occurred (including the participant's election, the participant's severance from employment if the participant is below normal retirement age, and, if applicable, the participant's survival to the date as of which payment is made) which entitle the participant to such benefit as described in section 417(f)(2)(A)(ii);

(c) In the case of an amount payable under a retroactive annuity starting date, the benefit commencement date; and

(d) The date of any payment for the purchase of an irrevocable commitment from an insurer to pay benefits under the plan.

E. Limitation on benefit accruals.

In accordance with section 436(e), under the proposed regulations, a plan must provide that, in any case in which the plan's AFTAP for a plan year is less than 60 percent, benefit accruals under the plan will cease as of the applicable section 436 measurement date. If a plan must cease benefit accruals under this limitation, then the plan is also not permitted to be amended in a manner that would increase the liabilities of the plan by reason of an increase in benefits or establishment of new benefits. This rule applies regardless of whether an amendment would otherwise be permissible under section 436(c)(3) (involving certain amendments to increase benefits under a formula not based on a participant's compensation). This prohibition on additional benefit accruals will no longer apply for a plan year if the plan sponsor makes the contribution specified in section 436(e)(2), as described in paragraph II. F of this preamble.

F. Rules relating to contributions required to avoid benefit limitations.

The proposed regulations provide rules regarding contributions by the plan sponsor to avoid benefit limitations under section 436. An employer sponsoring a plan that would otherwise be subject to the limitations of section 436 can avoid the application of those limits through one of four different techniques: 1) reducing the funding standard carryover balance and prefunding balance; 2) making additional contributions for a prior plan year that are not added to the prefunding balance; 3) making the specific contributions described in sections 436(b)(2), 436(c)(2), and 436(e)(2); and 4) providing security, as described in section 436(f)(1).

As noted in this preamble, under the first of the techniques, if a plan sponsor elects to reduce the plan's funding standard carryover balance or the prefunding balance, this will have the effect of increasing the plan assets that are taken into account in determining the plan's FTAP and AFTAP and, thereby, will raise the AFTAP to a level so that the benefit limitations may no longer apply to the plan. Alternatively, if the deadline for making prior year contributions has not passed, the plan sponsor could utilize the second technique — making additional contributions for the prior plan year. If these additional contributions are not added to the prefunding balance, then the additional contributions will also have the effect of increasing the plan's FTAP and AFTAP.

The third and fourth techniques for avoiding the application of the benefit limitations of section 436 are described in § 1.436-1(f) of the proposed regulations. Under the third technique, the plan sponsor makes additional contributions that are specifically designated at the time the contribution is used to avoid the application of a limitation under section 436(b), 436(c), or 436(e). The proposed regulations would provide for this designation to be provided to the plan's enrolled actuary and plan administrator in writing. Furthermore, the designation must be irrevocable, except as described below. If the contributions are made on a date other than the valuation date for the plan year, the contributions must be adjusted for interest (using the plan's effective interest rate, except as provided in the proposed regulations). These contributions are separate from any minimum required contributions required by section 430, and no prefunding balance or funding standard carryover balance under section 430(f) may be used as a contribution to avoid a section 436 benefit limitation. A plan sponsor that makes such a current year contribution will nonetheless fail to satisfy the minimum funding requirements if it does not make the minimum required contribution under section 430 for the year. In addition, as noted above, these contributions are not taken into account in determining whether a plan sponsor is making excess contributions for purposes of adding to the plan's prefunding balance.

The fourth technique for a plan sponsor to avoid the application of the benefit limitations of section 436 is for the plan sponsor to provide security. In such a case, the AFTAP for the plan year is determined by treating as an asset of the plan any security provided by a plan sponsor by the valuation date for the plan year in a form meeting certain specified requirements. However, this security is not taken into account for any other purpose, including section 430. The only security permitted to be provided by a plan sponsor for this purpose is (i) a bond issued by a corporate surety company that is an acceptable surety for purposes of section 412 of ERISA, or (ii) cash or United States obligations that mature in three years or less that are held in escrow by a bank or insurance company. The regulations would reflect sections 436(f)(1)(C) and (D) in specifying when the security is to be contributed to the plan and when it may be released. If the security is turned over to the plan, then that amount is treated as an employer contribution when it is turned over to the plan. The proposed regulations would provide that any such security turned over to the plan pursuant to the enforcement mechanism cannot be treated as a contribution to avoid or terminate the application of a section 436 benefit limitation under section 436(b)(2), 436(c)(2), or 436(e)(2).

G. Presumed underfunding for purposes of benefit limitations.

The proposed regulations reflect the rules of section 436(h), which sets forth a series of presumptions that are used to apply the section 436 benefit limitations in situations where the plan's enrolled actuary has not yet issued a certification of the plan's AFTAP for the plan year. In addition, the proposed regulations also set forth rules for the application of the limitations prior to and during the period those presumptions apply to a plan, and describe the interaction of those presumptions with plan operations after the plan's enrolled actuary has issued a certification of the plan's AFTAP for the plan year. These rules are designed to encourage plans to obtain certifications in a timely manner, with a particular emphasis with respect to plans that have a greater likelihood of having a new section 436 benefit limitation apply because they had an AFTAP for the prior plan year that was near a threshold for a benefit limitation to apply.

The proposed regulations would provide that, in any case in which a plan was subject to a benefit limitation on the last day of the prior plan year, the first day of the plan year is a section 436 measurement date and the AFTAP of the plan for the current plan year is presumed to be equal to the preceding year's certified AFTAP until the plan's enrolled actuary certifies the AFTAP of the plan for the current plan year. Because no plan could be subject to a benefit limitation for a plan year that precedes the plan year that begins in 2008, the section 436(h)(1) presumption generally will not apply to any plan before the first plan year beginning in 2009.

In accordance with section 436(h)(3), the proposed regulations would provide that, if the enrolled actuary of the plan has not certified the AFTAP of the plan for the current plan year by the first day of the 4th month of the plan year and the AFTAP for the preceding year was certified to be at least 60 percent but less than 70 percent or at least 80 percent but less than 90 percent (or, if that preceding plan year is the pre-effective plan year, was certified to be less than 90 percent), then the first day of the 4th month of the current plan year is a section 436 measurement date, and the AFTAP of the plan is presumed to be equal to 10 percentage points less than the AFTAP of the plan for the preceding plan year. This presumption will apply until the earlier of the date the enrolled actuary certifies the AFTAP for the plan year or the first day of the 10th month of the plan year.

In accordance with section 436(h)(2), the proposed regulations would provide that, in any case in which no certification of the specific AFTAP for the current plan year is made before the first day of the 10th month of such year, that date is a section 436 measurement date and, as of that date, the plan's AFTAP is conclusively presumed to be less than 60 percent. In such a case, the presumed AFTAP of under 60 percent for the current plan year will continue to apply under the rules of section 436(h)(1) for the next plan year, until such time as the enrolled actuary certifies the AFTAP for either the current plan year or the next plan year.

The proposed regulations would provide rules that apply the section 436(h) presumptions for the plan year in cases in which the enrolled actuary's certification for the prior plan year is made on or after the first day of the 10th month of that prior plan year. If the date of the enrolled actuary's certification of the specific AFTAP for a plan year occurs on or after the date the conclusive presumption applies but on or before the last day of the plan year, the proposed regulations would provide that the certified percentage is disregarded for that plan year but is used for purposes of the presumption rule of section 436(h)(1) starting with the beginning of the following plan year (rather than continuing to apply the less-than-60 percent presumption that applied before the first day of that following plan year). If the date of the enrolled actuary's certification of the specific AFTAP for a plan year occurs after the end of the plan year but prior to the first day of the 4th month in the following plan year, the proposed regulations would provide that the certification date is treated as a section 436 measurement date for that following plan year and that, starting on that date, the plan's AFTAP is presumed to be the certified AFTAP for the prior year (rather than continuing to apply the less-than-60 percent presumption that applied before the certification). If the date of the enrolled actuary's certification of the specific AFTAP for a plan year occurs after the first day of the 4th month in the following plan year but before the first day of the 10th month, the proposed regulations would provide that the certification date also is a section 436 measurement date for that following plan year, and the plan's AFTAP for that following year beginning on that date is presumed to be the certified AFTAP for the prior year (rather than continuing to apply the less-than-60 percent presumption that applied before the certification). However, in such a case, if a 10 percentage point reduction in the AFTAP would have applied on the first day of the 4th month of that following plan year if the AFTAP for the prior plan year had been certified before that day, then the same 10 percentage point reduction applies on the date of the certification. These presumption rules based on the prior year AFTAP do not apply once a certification of the following year's AFTAP is issued by the plan's enrolled actuary.

The enrolled actuary's certification of the AFTAP for a plan year must be made in writing, must be provided to the plan administrator, and must certify the plan's AFTAP for the plan year. As an alternative to certifying a specific number for the plan's AFTAP, the regulations would provide that the enrolled actuary is permitted to certify during the first nine months of a plan year that the plan's AFTAP for that year is within a percentage "range" that is either (i) 60 percent or higher, but less than 80 percent, (ii) 80 percent or higher, or (iii) 100 percent or higher. The proposed regulations would provide that such a "range" certification ends the application of the presumptions provided that the enrolled actuary follows up with a certification of the specific AFTAP before the first day of the 10th month of that year and that the certified specific AFTAP is within the range of the earlier certification.

If this "range" certification alternative is followed, the plan is treated as having a certified AFTAP at the smallest value within the applicable range. Thus, for example, if the enrolled actuary certified that the AFTAP was more than 60 percent but less than 80 percent, then the plan is treated as having an AFTAP of 60 percent for purposes of applying the limitations of section 436(b) until the earlier of the date of the specific AFTAP certification or the first day of the 10th month of the plan year. In such a case, if the plan has an unpredictable contingent event or a plan amendment that increases liability for benefits, unpredictable contingent event benefits cannot be paid and the plan amendment cannot take effect unless the plan sponsor makes a contribution described in section 436(b)(2) or 436(c)(2), as applicable. If the plan sponsor makes a contribution under section 436(b)(2) or section 436(c)(2), the proposed regulations would provide that the contribution is recharacterized as a regular employer contribution that is taken into account under section 430 for the current plan year to the extent it is determined that the contribution was not needed to avoid the application of the benefit limit, based on the subsequent calculation of the specific AFTAP.

The proposed regulations would specify that the enrolled actuary is generally not permitted to certify the AFTAP based on a value of assets that includes contributions receivable for the prior year that have not actually been made as of the date of the certification. However, this rule would not apply to certifications that are made for plan years beginning before January 1, 2009. Thus, for a certification with respect to 2008, the enrolled actuary is permitted to take in account contributions for 2007 that are reasonably expected but have not yet been made by the plan sponsor at the time of the certification. However, if the plan sponsor does not make those contributions, the enrolled actuary's certification will be incorrect, which will result in a failure to satisfy section 401(a)(29) and section 436 if the difference constitutes a material change.

If the enrolled actuary for the plan provides a certification of the AFTAP for the plan year (including a range certification) and that certified percentage is superseded by a subsequent determination of the AFTAP for that plan year, that later percentage must be applied and a determination must be made whether the change in the applicable percentage is a material change or an immaterial change. For this purpose, the proposed regulations would specify that there is a material change if plan operations with respect to benefits that are addressed by section 436, taking into account any actual contributions and elections under section 430(f) made by the plan sponsor based on the prior certified percentage, would have been different based on the subsequent determination of the plan's AFTAP for the plan year. Thus, for example, if after the actuary certifies the plan's AFTAP for a plan year, the plan sponsor elects to add excess contributions for the prior plan year to the plan's prefunding balance, this would have the effect of reducing the plan's AFTAP, and such a change could be a material change.

The proposed regulations would specify that an immaterial change is a change in an AFTAP that is not a material change. In addition, the proposed regulations would provide that if the difference between the AFTAP for a plan year and the later revised determination of that percentage is the result of additional contributions for the preceding year that are made by the plan sponsor after the date of the enrolled actuary's certification or results from the plan sponsor's election to reduce the prefunding or funding standard carryover balance after the date of the certification, such change is always treated as an immaterial change (regardless of whether it would otherwise affect the application of the section 436 benefit limitations).

In the case of a material change where the plan was operated in accordance with the prior certification of the AFTAP for the plan year, the plan will not have satisfied the requirements of section 401(a)(29) and section 436. In the case of a material change where the plan was operated in accordance with the subsequent certification of the AFTAP during the period of time the prior certification applied, the plan will not have been operated in accordance with its terms. In addition, in the case of a material change, the rules requiring application of a presumed AFTAP under section 436(h) continue to apply from and after the date of the prior certification until the date of the subsequent certification. In the case of an immaterial change, the revised percentage applies prospectively but it does not change the inapplicability of the presumptions under section 436(h) for the plan year prior to the date of the subsequent certification.

H. *Coordination between presumptions and determination of AFTAP.*

1. *Periods during which a presumption applies to the plan.*

A plan must provide that, for any period during which a presumption under section 436(h) applies to the plan, the limitations applicable under sections 436(b), 436(c), 436(d), and 436(e) apply to the plan as if the actual AFTAP for the year were the presumed AFTAP. During that period, the rules relating to the deemed election to reduce the funding standard carryover balance and the prefunding balance must be applied based on the presumed percentage with respect to the applicable limitations. Thus, a plan's prefunding balance and funding standard carryover balance must be reduced if the reduction would be sufficient to avoid the applicable limitation. The proposed regulations provide rules for determining the amount of the reduction in balances.

If the presumed AFTAP for the plan year changes during the year because of application of the presumption in section 436(h)(3), the rules regarding the deemed election to reduce funding balances must be reapplied based on the new presumed AFTAP. This reapplication of the deemed election may require an additional reduction in funding balances if the amount of the reduction in funding balances that is necessary to reach the applicable threshold to avoid the application of the limitation under section 436(d) or 436(e) is greater than the amount that was initially reduced.

2. *Periods prior to certification where no presumption applies.*

If no presumptions under section 436(h) apply to a plan for a period and the plan's enrolled actuary has not yet issued the certification of the plan's AFTAP for the plan year, the plan is not permitted to limit the payment of unpredictable contingent event benefits or the accrual of benefits based on an expectation that the limitations under section 436(d) or 436(e) will apply to the plan once the enrolled actuary's certification of the AFTAP is issued. In addition, the proposed regulations would provide that, if no presumptions under section 436(h) apply to a plan during a period and the plan's enrolled actuary has not yet issued a certification of the plan's AFTAP for the plan year, the limitations under sections 436(b) and 436(c) that apply to unpredictable contingent event benefits and certain plan amendments, respectively, during that period must be applied following the special rules described below in paragraph H.3. of this preamble. Thus, if after application of those rules the plan would be treated as having an AFTAP below the applicable threshold under section 436(b) or 436(c), the limitation will apply unless the plan sponsor makes a contribution to avoid application of the applicable benefit limitations described in section 436(b)(2) or 436(c)(2). In such case, following the certification of the AFTAP for the current plan year by the plan's enrolled actuary, the proposed regulations would provide that those contributions are recharacterized as employer contributions under section 430 for the current plan year to the extent they exceed the amount necessary to avoid application of the applicable limitation under section 436(b) or 436(c) based on the certified percentage.

3. *Periods prior to certification — special rules for unpredictable contingent event benefits and plan amendments that increase liability.*

The proposed regulations would provide that, during the pre-certification period, the rules relating to the deemed election to reduce the funding standard carryover balance and the prefunding balance must be applied based on the plan's presumed AFTAP. The proposed regulations would provide rules for determining the amount of the reduction in those balances that would apply in such a situation and provide that, in making such determination, the presumed adjusted funding target is increased to take into account the benefits attributable to the unpredictable contingent event or the plan amendment described in section 436(b) and 436(c), respectively. For this purpose, if no presumption applies under the rules of section 436(h) (for example, because the plan's actual AFTAP for the prior year was certified to be at least 80 percent), then that prior year's actual AFTAP is substituted for the presumed AFTAP for the plan year in determining the presumed adjusted funding target. In the case of a plan that is not a collectively bargained plan with a funding standard carryover balance or a prefunding balance, the deemed election rules do not apply for purposes of sections 436(b) and 436(c), and the plan sponsor is permitted (but not required) to reduce those balances in order to increase the adjusted plan assets that are compared to the presumed AFTAP.

If, after application of such funding balance reductions and the other calculations set forth in the proposed regulations, the plan's AFTAP (taking into account the additional benefits) is less than the applicable threshold under section 436(b) or 436(c), as applicable, then the plan is not permitted to provide any benefits attributable to the unpredictable contingent event or plan amendment unless the plan sponsor makes a contribution that would allow payment of unpredictable contingent event benefits or would permit a plan amendment increasing benefit liabilities to go into effect under the rules of section 436(b)(2) or 436(c)(2).

If, after application of such funding balance reductions, the plan's AFTAP (taking into account the additional benefits) is greater than or equal to the applicable threshold under section 436(b) or 436(c), as applicable, then the plan is not permitted to limit the payment of unpredictable contingent event benefits under section 436(b) or to restrict a plan amendment increasing liability for benefits from taking effect under section 436(c) based on an expectation that those limitations will apply to the plan once the enrolled actuary's certification is issued.

4. *Limitations based on AFTAP.*

The proposed regulations would provide that, on and after the date the enrolled actuary for the plan issues a certification of the AFTAP for the current plan year, the plan must apply that certified percentage (however, if the certification is issued on or after the first day of the 10th month of the current plan year but before the first day of the following plan year, the certified percentage applies under the presumption rules beginning on the first day of that following plan year). For example, the plan sponsor must apply the certified AFTAP for a plan year to an unpredictable contingent event that occurs or a plan amendment that is effective on or after the date of the enrolled actuary's certification during the plan year. Thus, the plan administrator must determine if the AFTAP is at or above the applicable threshold, taking into account the increase in the funding target that would be attributable to the unpredictable contingent event or plan amendment if the unpredictable contingent event benefits or the increase in liability attributable to the plan amendment were taken into account.

After the AFTAP for a plan year is certified by the plan's enrolled actuary, with respect to the application of limitations under sections 436(d) and 436(e) (accelerated benefit payments and benefit accruals, respectively) for the plan year, the deemed election to reduce funding balances must be reapplied based on the actual funding target for the year (provided the certification is issued by the first day of the 10th month). This reapplication of the deemed election may require an additional reduction in funding balances if the amount of the reduction in funding balances that is necessary to reach the applicable threshold to avoid the application of those limitations is greater than the amount of a prior reduction for the plan year. The proposed regulations would also reflect section 436(d)(2), which provides that no prohibited payments under section 436(d)(5) are permitted to be paid by a plan during any period in which the plan sponsor is a debtor in a case under title 11, United States Code, or any similar Federal or State law, if the plan's enrolled actuary has not yet certified the plan's AFTAP for the plan year to be at least 100 percent. Thus, the presumptions do not apply for purposes of section 436(d)(2).

The proposed regulations would provide that the enrolled actuary's certification of the AFTAP does not affect the application of the limitation under section 436(d) for participants with annuity starting dates before the certification. Similarly, the enrolled actuary's certification for the plan year does not affect the application of the limitation under section 436(e) of this section prior to the date of that certification.

With respect to the impact of the enrolled actuary's certification of the AFTAP for a plan year on periods prior to the certification, the proposed regulations would provide that the certification does not affect the application of limitations under sections 436(b) and 436(c) for periods prior to the date the certification is issued, regardless of the extent to which the certified percentage varies from the presumed percentage. Notwithstanding the foregoing, in the case of a plan that, for a plan year, did not provide benefits attributable to an unpredictable contingent event or plan amendment based on the preceding year's certified AFTAP (and where sufficient contributions under section 436(b)(2) or 436(c)(2) were not made), the plan must provide any benefits that were not so provided if those benefits would be permitted under the rules of section 436 based on the certified AFTAP, taking into account the increase in the funding target that would be attributable to the unpredictable contingent event benefits or increase in liability due to the plan amendment.

A special rule applies if a plan is providing benefits with respect to one or more unpredictable contingent events occurring within the plan year or amendments taking effect within the plan year. In such a case, the restrictions on unpredictable contingent event benefits and plan amendments are applied with respect to a subsequent unpredictable contingent event or amendment by treating the increase in the funding target attributable to the subsequent event or amendment as if it included the increases in the funding target attributable to all such earlier events or amendments.

I. Determination of funding target attainment percentage.

For purposes of section 436, the *funding target* means the funding target under section 430(d) or section 430(i), as applicable to the plan for a plan year.

For purposes of section 436, the *funding target attainment percentage* (FTAP) for any plan year is the fraction (expressed as a percentage), the numerator of which is the value of net plan assets, and the denominator of which is the plan's funding target (determined without regard to the at-risk rules under section 430(i) even in the case of a plan that is in at-risk status). For this purpose, pursuant to section 430(f)(4), the value of net plan assets for the plan year is generally determined by subtracting the plan's funding standard carryover balance and prefunding balance (if any) for the plan year from the value of plan assets.

The *adjusted funding target attainment percentage* (AFTAP) for any plan year is the fraction (expressed as a percentage), the numerator of which is the adjusted plan assets and the denominator of which is the adjusted funding target. The adjusted plan assets equals the net plan assets, increased by the aggregate amount of purchases of annuities for employees other than highly compensated employees (as defined in section 414(q)) which were made by the plan during the preceding 2 plan years. The proposed regulations would provide that the adjusted funding target equals the funding target for the plan year (determined without regard to the at-risk rules under section 430(i)), increased by the aggregate amount of purchases of annuities for employees other than highly compensated employees (as defined in section 414(q)) which were made by the plan during the preceding 2 plan years.

If the FTAP for a plan year, determined without regard to the section 430(f)(4) subtraction of the funding standard carryover balance and the prefunding balance from the value of plan assets, would be 100 percent or more, then, for purposes of section 436 (but not section 430(d)), the value of net plan assets used in the determination of the FTAP and the AFTAP is determined without regard to any subtraction of funding balances under section 430(f)(4). The proposed regulations would reflect the transition rule of section 436(j)(3)(B) under which a plan is permitted to phase up to 100 percent for purposes of the preceding sentence.

The proposed regulations would also provide that, in the case of the first plan year beginning in 2008, the FTAP for the preceding plan year is determined as a fraction (expressed as a percentage), the numerator of which is the value of net plan assets, and the denominator of which is the plan's current liability determined pursuant to section 412(l)(7) on the valuation date for the last plan year that begins before 2008 (the 2007 plan year). For this purpose, the value of plan assets is determined under section 412(c)(2) as in effect for the 2007 plan year, except that the value of plan assets prior to subtraction of the plan's funding standard account credit balance described below can neither be less than 90 percent of the fair market value of plan assets nor greater than 110 percent of the fair market value of plan assets on the valuation date for that plan year. If a plan has a funding standard account credit balance as of the valuation date for the 2007 plan year, that balance must be subtracted from the asset value described above as of that date unless the value of plan assets is greater than or equal to 90 percent of the plan's current liability determined under section 412(l)(7) on the valuation date for the 2007 plan year.

In the case of the first plan year beginning in 2008, for purposes of determining the AFTAP for the 2007 plan year, the proposed regulations provide that the adjusted funding target is equal to the current liability determined pursuant to section 412(l)(7) on the valuation date for the 2007 plan year, increased by the aggregate amount of purchases of annuities for employees other than highly compensated employees (as defined in section 414(q)) which were made by the plan during the preceding 2 plan years. In any case in which the plan's enrolled actuary has not issued a certification of the AFTAP of the plan for the 2007 plan year using this rule, the AFTAP of the plan for the first plan year beginning in 2008 is presumed to be less than 60 percent until the AFTAP of the plan for the 2007 plan year has been certified or the AFTAP of the plan for the first plan year beginning in 2008 has been certified. This rule applies for purposes of sections 436(b) and 436(c) at the beginning of the first plan year beginning in 2008 and applies for purposes of sections 436(d) and 436(e) as of the first day of the 4th month of the first plan year beginning in 2008. The special rules

permitting range certifications for plan years beginning after 2007 do not apply to the 2007 plan year.

However, if the employer makes an election to reduce some or all of the funding standard carryover balance as of the first day of the first plan year beginning in 2008 in accordance with proposed § 1.430(f)-1(e), then the present value (determined as of the valuation date for the prior year using the valuation interest rate for that prior year) of the amount so reduced is not treated as part of the funding standard account credit balance when that balance is subtracted from the value of net plan assets. Thus, an employer's election to reduce the funding standard carryover balance in 2008 will have the effect of reducing the amount that must be subtracted from the assets in determining the 2007 AFTAP for purposes of applying the presumptions under section 436(h)(3) as of the first day of the 4th month of the plan year beginning in 2008.

Proposed Legislation

As of the date of issuance of these proposed regulations, bills have been introduced in the House of Representatives and the Senate that would exclude mandatory cash-out distributions under section 411(a)(11) from application of the accelerated payments limitation under section 436(d) and that would provide the Treasury Department with authority to address application of the presumptions under section 436(h) to plans that have valuation dates that are later than the first day of the plan year.[5] Proposed § 1.436-1(d)(6) and § 1.436-1(h)(5), respectively, are reserved in order to accommodate such changes.

Section 1107 of PPA '06 and Code Section 411(d)(6)

Under section 1107 of PPA '06, a plan sponsor is permitted to delay adopting a plan amendment pursuant to statutory provisions under PPA '06 (or pursuant to any regulation issued under PPA '06) until the last day of the first plan year beginning on or after January 1, 2009 (January 1, 2011 in the case of governmental plans). As described in Rev. Proc. 2007-44, 2007-28 IRB 54, this amendment deadline applies to both interim and discretionary amendments that are made pursuant to PPA '06 statutory provisions or any regulation issued under PPA '06. See § 601.601(d)(2) of this chapter. If section 1107 of PPA '06 applies to an amendment of a plan, section 1107 provides that the plan does not fail to meet the requirements of section 411(d)(6) by reason of such amendment, except as provided by the Secretary of the Treasury.[6] For example, section 411(d)(6) relief would be available for plan amendments that would prohibit single sum or other accelerated distributions if the plan's AFTAP was less than 60 percent, in accordance with section 436(d) and § 1.436-1(d) of the proposed regulations. Plan sponsors should note that the IRS and the Treasury Department are reviewing whether sample plan amendments should be issued with respect to section 436 and the § 1.436-1 regulations.

ERISA notice to participants and beneficiaries

Under section 101(j) of ERISA, as amended by PPA '06, the plan administrator of a single employer plan is required to provide a written notice to participants and beneficiaries within 30 days after:

- The date the plan has become subject to a restriction described in the ERISA provisions that are parallel to paragraphs (b) and (d) of Code section 436;

- In the case of a plan that is subject to the ERISA provisions that are parallel to paragraph (e) of Code section 436, the valuation date for the plan year for which the plan's AFTAP is less than 60 percent (or, if earlier, the date the AFTAP is presumed to be less than 60 percent under the ERISA provisions that parallel the presumption rules in paragraph (h) of Code section 436); and

- At such other time as may be determined by the Secretary of the Treasury.

The notice is required to be provided in writing, except that the notice may be in electronic or other form to the extent that such form is reasonably accessible to the recipient.

Effective/Applicability Dates

1. Section 1.430(f)-1.

In general, these regulations under section 430(f) are proposed to apply to plan years beginning on or after January 1, 2008. However, in

---

[5] H.R. 3361 (August 3, 2007) and S. 1974 (August 2, 2007), at sections 2(c)(1)(C), 2(c)(2)(C), 2(c)(1)(F), and 2(c)(2)(F).

[6] Except to the extent permitted under section 411(d)(6) and the § 1.411(d)-4 regulations, or under a statutory provision such as section 1107 of PPA '06, section 411(d)(6) prohibits a plan amendment that decreases a participant's accrued benefits or that has the effect of eliminating or reducing an early retirement benefit or retirement-type subsidy, or eliminating an optional form of benefit, with respect to benefits attributable to service before the amendment. However, an amendment that eliminates or decreases benefits that have not yet accrued does not violate section 411(d)(6), provided the amendment is adopted and effective before the benefits accrue.

the case of a plan for which the effective date of section 430 is delayed in accordance with sections 104 through 106 of the Pension Protection Act of 2006, Public Law 109-280, 120 Stat. 780, the regulations under section 430(f) are proposed to apply to plan years beginning on or after the effective date of section 430 with respect to the plan. Unlike section 436, section 430 and the regulations under section 430(f) do not include a delayed effective date for collectively bargained plans.

2. *Section 1.436-1.*

In general, the regulations under section 436 are proposed to apply to plan years beginning on or after January 1, 2008. However, in the case of a plan for which the effective date of section 436 is delayed in accordance with sections 104 through 106 of the Pension Protection Act of 2006, Public Law 109-280, 120 Stat. 780, the regulations under section 436 are proposed to apply to plan years beginning on or after the effective date of section 436 with respect to the plan. In addition, in the case of a collectively bargained plan maintained pursuant to one or more collective bargaining agreements between employee representatives and one or more employers ratified before January 1, 2008, the regulations under section 436 would not apply to plan years beginning before the earlier of: (1) the later of the date on which the last collective bargaining agreement relating to the plan terminates (determined without regard to any extension thereof agreed to after August 17, 2006), or the first day of the first plan year to which the proposed regulations under section 436 would otherwise apply, or (2) January 1, 2010. For this purpose, any plan amendment made pursuant to a collective bargaining agreement relating to the plan which amends the plan solely to conform to any requirement under the proposed regulations would not be treated as a termination of the collective bargaining agreement. The determination of whether a plan is a collectively bargained plan is the same as described above in paragraph II.A.5 of this preamble with respect to a plan sponsor's deemed election to reduce funding balances.

3. *Reliance on proposed regulations.*

For periods following the issuance of these proposed regulations and before final regulations are issued, these proposed regulations may be relied upon for plan qualification purposes, provided that such reliance is on a consistent and reasonable basis.

4. *Effect on plans subject to section 402 of PPA '06.*

The IRS and the Treasury Department are reviewing the applicability of section 436 and the funding balance rules of section 430(f) to plans that have made elections under section 402 of PPA '06 (taking into account the amendments to section 402 of PPA '06 by section 6615 of the U.S. Troop Readiness, Veterans' Care, Katrina Recovery, and Iraq Accountability-Appropriations Act, 2007 (Public Law 110-28)) and any special rules for such plans will be addressed in future guidance.

Special Analyses

It has been determined that this notice of proposed rulemaking is not a significant regulatory action as defined in Executive Order 12866. Therefore, a regulatory assessment is not required. It has also been determined that section 553(b) of the Administrative Procedure Act (5 U.S.C. chapter 5) does not apply to these regulations. It is hereby certified that the collection of information imposed by these proposed regulations will not have a significant economic impact on a substantial number of small entities. Accordingly, a regulatory flexibility analysis is not required. The estimated burden imposed by the collection of information contained in these proposed regulations is 0.75 hours per respondent. Moreover, most of this burden is attributable to the requirement for a qualified defined benefit plan's enrolled actuary to provide a timely certification of the plan's AFTAP for each plan year to avoid certain benefit restrictions, which is imposed by section 436(h) of the Code. In addition, these proposed regulations provide for several written elections to be made by the plan sponsor upon occasion; these written elections will require minimal time to prepare. Pursuant to section 7805(f) of the Code, these regulations have been submitted to the Chief Counsel for Advocacy of the Small Business Administration for comment on its impact on small business.

Comments and Requests for a Public Hearing

Before these proposed regulations are adopted as final regulations, consideration will be given to any written (one signed and eight (8) copies) or electronic comments that are submitted timely to the IRS. The IRS and Treasury Department specifically request comments on the clarity of the proposed regulations and how they may be made easier to understand. All comments will be available for public inspection and copying. A public hearing will be scheduled if requested in writing by any person who timely submits written comments. If a

public hearing is scheduled, notice of the date, time, and place of the public hearing will be published in the Federal Register.

Drafting Information

The principal authors of these regulations are Lauson C. Green and Linda S.F. Marshall, Office of Division Counsel/Associate Chief Counsel (Tax Exempt and Government Entities). However, other personnel from the IRS and the Treasury Department participated in the development of these regulations.

List of Subjects in 26 CFR Part 1

Income taxes, Reporting and recordkeeping requirements.

Proposed Amendments to the Regulations

Accordingly, 26 CFR part 1 is proposed to be amended as follows: PART 1—INCOME TAXES

Paragraph 1. The authority citation for part 1 continues to read in part as follows:

Authority: 26 U.S.C. 7805 * * *

Par. 2. Section 1.430(f)-1 is added to read as follows:

§ 1.430(f)-1 *Effect of prefunding balance and funding standard carryover balance.*

(a) *In general*—(1) *Overview.* This section provides rules relating to the application of prefunding balances and funding standard carryover balances under section 430(f). Section 430 and this section apply to single employer defined benefit plans (including multiple employer plans) that are subject to section 412, but do not apply to multiemployer plans (as defined in section 414(f)). Paragraph (b) of this section sets forth rules regarding a plan sponsor's election to maintain a funding standard carryover balance or a prefunding balance. Paragraph (c) of this section provides rules under which those balances must be subtracted from plan assets. Paragraph (d) of this section describes a plan sponsor's election to use those balances to offset the minimum required contribution. Paragraph (e) of this section describes a plan sponsor's election to reduce those balances (which will affect the determination of the value of plan assets for purposes of sections 430 and 436). Paragraph (f) of this section sets forth rules regarding elections under this section. Paragraph (g) of this section contains examples. Paragraph (h) of this section contains effective/applicability dates and transitional provisions.

(2) *Special rules for multiple employer plans.* In the case of a multiple employer plan to which section 413(c)(4)(A) applies, the rules of this section are applied separately for each employer under the plan, as if each employer maintained a separate plan. Thus, each employer under such a multiple employer plan may have a separate funding standard carryover balance and a prefunding balance for the plan. In the case of a multiple employer plan to which section 413(c)(4)(A) does not apply (that is, a plan described in section 413(c)(4)(B) that has not made the election for section 413(c)(4)(A) to apply), the rules of this section are applied as if all participants in the plan were employed by a single employer.

(b) *Election to maintain balances*—(1) *Prefunding balance*—(i) *In general.* A plan sponsor is permitted to maintain a prefunding balance for a plan. A prefunding balance maintained for a plan consists of a beginning balance of zero, increased by the amount of excess contributions to the extent the employer elects to do so as described in paragraph (b)(1)(ii) of this section, and decreased to the extent provided in paragraph (b)(1)(iii) of this section. The prefunding balance is adjusted further for investment return and interest as provided in paragraphs (b)(3) and (b)(4) of this section.

(ii) *Increases*—(A) *In general.* If the plan sponsor of a plan elects to add to the plan's prefunding balance, as of the first day of each plan year following the first effective plan year for the plan, the prefunding balance is increased by the amount so elected by the plan sponsor for the plan year. The amount added to the prefunding balance cannot exceed the interest-adjusted excess contributions for the preceding plan year determined under paragraph (b)(1)(ii)(B) of this section.

(B) *Interest-adjusted excess contribution.* For purposes of this paragraph (b)(1)(ii), the interest-adjusted excess contribution for the preceding plan year is the amount, increased with interest in accordance with the rules of paragraph (b)(1)(iv)(A) of this section, of the excess, if any, of—

(*1*) The present value of the employer contributions (other than contributions to avoid or terminate benefit limitations described in § 1.436-1(f)(2)) to the plan for the preceding plan year determined under the rules of paragraph (b)(1)(iv)(B) of this section); over

(*2*) The minimum required contribution for the preceding plan year (determined without regard to any election to offset the minimum required contribution under paragraph (d) of this section for the preceding plan year).

(iii) *Decreases*. The prefunding balance of a plan is decreased (but not below zero) by the sum of—

(A) As of the first day of each plan year after the first effective plan year for the plan, any amount of the prefunding balance that was used under paragraph (d) of this section to offset the minimum required contribution of the plan for the preceding plan year; and

(B) As of the first day of each plan year, any reduction in the prefunding balance under paragraph (e) of this section for the plan year.

(iv) *Adjustments for interest*—(A) *Adjustment of excess contribution*. The amount of the excess contribution for the preceding year (as determined under paragraph (b)(1)(ii)(B) of this section) is increased for interest accruing for the period between the valuation date for the preceding plan year and the first day of the current year. For this purpose, interest is determined by using the plan's effective interest rate under section 430(h)(2)(A) for the preceding plan year.

(B) *Determination of present value*. The present value of the contributions described in paragraph (b)(1)(ii)(B)(*1*) of this section is determined as of the valuation date for the preceding plan year, using the plan's effective interest rate under section 430(h)(2)(A) for the preceding plan year.

(2) *Funding standard carryover balance*—(i) *In general*. A funding standard carryover balance is only permitted to be maintained by a plan that had a positive balance in the funding standard account under section 412(b) as of the end of the pre-effective plan year for the plan. The funding standard carryover balance as of the beginning of the first effective plan year for the plan is the positive balance in the funding standard account under section 412(b) as of the end of the pre-effective plan year for the plan, decreased to the extent provided in paragraph (b)(2)(ii) of this section and adjusted further for investment return and interest as provided in paragraphs (b)(3) and (b)(4) of this section.

(ii) *Decreases*. The funding standard carryover balance of a plan is decreased (but not below zero) by the sum of—

(A) As of the first day of each plan year after the first effective plan year for the plan, any amount of the funding standard carryover balance that was used under paragraph (d) of this section to offset the minimum required contribution of the plan for the preceding plan year; and

(B) As of the first day of each plan year, any reduction in the funding standard carryover balance under paragraph (e) of this section for the plan year.

(3) *Adjustments for investment experience*. In determining a plan's prefunding balance under paragraph (b)(1) of this section or a plan's funding standard carryover balance under paragraph (b)(2) of this section as of the first day of a plan year, the balance must be adjusted to reflect the actual rate of return on plan assets for the preceding plan year. This adjustment is applied to the balance after subtracting amounts used to offset the minimum required contribution for the preceding plan year pursuant to paragraph (d) of this section and after any reduction of balances for that preceding plan year under paragraph (e) of this section. For this purpose, the actual rate of return on plan assets for the preceding plan year is determined on the basis of fair market value and must take into account the amount and timing of all contributions, distributions, and other plan payments made during that period.

(4) *Valuation date other than the first day of the plan year*—(i) *In general*. If a plan's valuation date is not the first day of the plan year, solely for purposes of applying paragraphs (c), (d), and (e) of this section, the plan's prefunding balance and funding standard carryover balance (if any) determined under this paragraph (b) are increased to the valuation date using the plan's effective interest rate under section 430(h)(2)(A) for the plan year.

(ii) *Special rule for adjustments for investment experience*. For purposes of applying the rules regarding the adjustments for investment experience in paragraph (b)(3) of this section, in the case of a plan with a valuation date that is not the first day of the plan year, the amount of the funding balances that must be subtracted from plan assets under paragraph (d) of this section (because they are used to offset the minimum required contribution for the plan year) must be adjusted to the first day of the plan year using the effective interest rate under section 430(h)(2)(A) for that year.

(c) *Effect of balances on plan assets*—(1) *In general*. In the case of any plan with a prefunding balance or a funding standard carryover balance, the amount of those balances must be subtracted from the value of plan assets for purposes of sections 430 and 436, except as provided in paragraphs (c)(2), (c)(3), and (c)(4) of this section.

(2) *Subtraction of balances in determining new shortfall amortization base*—(i) *Prefunding balance*. For purposes of determining whether a plan is exempt from the requirement to establish a new shortfall amortization base under section 430(c)(5), the amount of the prefunding balance is subtracted from the value of plan assets only if an election under paragraph (d) of this section to use the prefunding balance to offset the minimum required contribution is made for the plan year.

(ii) *Funding standard carryover balance*. For purposes of determining whether a plan is exempt from the requirement to establish a new shortfall amortization base under section 430(c)(5), the funding standard carryover balance is not subtracted from the value of plan assets regardless of whether any portion of either the funding standard carryover balance or the prefunding balance is used to offset the minimum required contribution for the plan year under paragraph (d) of this section.

(3) *Special rule for certain binding agreements with PBGC*. If there is in effect for a plan year a binding written agreement with the Pension Benefit Guaranty Corporation (PBGC) which provides that all or a portion of the prefunding balance or funding standard carryover balance (or both balances) is not available to offset the minimum required contribution for a plan year, that specified amount is not subtracted from the value of plan assets for purposes of determining the funding shortfall under section 430(c)(4). For example, if a PBGC agreement provides that $5 million of a plan's balances is unavailable to offset the minimum required contribution for a plan year, the sum of the plan's prefunding balance and funding standard carryover balance is $20 million, and the plan's assets are $100 million, the value of plan assets for purposes of determining the funding shortfall under section 430(c)(4) is reduced by $15 million ($20 million less $5 million) to $85 million. For purposes of this paragraph (c)(3), an agreement with the PBGC is taken into account with respect to a plan year only if the agreement was executed prior to the valuation date for the plan year.

(4) *Exception for section 436(j) and (k) special adjustment rules*. See section 436(j) and (k) and §1.436-1(j)(2)(ii) and (iii) for exceptions from the requirement to subtract the prefunding and funding standard carryover balances from plan assets in determining a plan's funding target attainment percentage for purposes of section 436.

(d) *Election to apply balances against minimum required contribution*—(1) *In general*. Subject to the limitations provided in paragraphs (d)(2) and (d)(3) of this section, in the case of any plan year in which the plan sponsor elects to use all or a portion of the prefunding balance or the funding standard carryover balance to offset the minimum required contribution for the current plan year, the minimum required contribution for the plan year (determined after taking into account any waiver under section 412(c)) is offset as of the valuation date for the plan year by the amount so used.

(2) *Requirement to use funding standard carryover balance before prefunding balance*. To the extent that a plan has a funding standard carryover balance greater than zero, no amount of the plan's prefunding balance may be used to offset the minimum required contribution. Thus, a plan's funding standard carryover balance must be exhausted before the plan's prefunding balance may be applied under paragraph (d)(1) of this section to offset the minimum required contribution.

(3) *Limitation for underfunded plans*. An election to apply a funding standard carryover balance or a prefunding balance under paragraph (d)(1) of this section is not available for a plan year if the plan's prior year funding ratio is less than 80 percent. For purposes of this paragraph (d)(3), except as provided in paragraph (h)(5) of this section, the plan's prior year funding ratio is the fraction (expressed as a percentage)—

(i) The numerator of which is the value of plan assets on the valuation date for the preceding plan year, reduced by the amount of any prefunding balance (but not the amount of any funding standard carryover balance); and

(ii) The denominator of which is the funding target of the plan for the preceding plan year (determined without regard to section 430(i)(1)).

(e) *Election to reduce balances*—(1) *In general*. A plan sponsor may make an election for a plan year to reduce any portion of a plan's prefunding balance and funding standard carryover balance under this paragraph (e). If such an election is made, the amount of those balances that must be subtracted from plan assets pursuant to paragraph (c)(1) of this section will be smaller and, accordingly, the plan assets taken into account for purposes of sections 430 and 436 will be larger. Thus, this election to reduce a plan's prefunding balance and funding standard carryover balance is taken into account in the determination of plan assets for the plan year and applies for all purposes under sections 430 and 436, including for purposes of determining the plan's prior year funding ratio under paragraph (d)(3) of this section for the following plan year. See also section 436(f)(3) and § 1.436-1(a)(5) for a rule under which the plan sponsor is deemed to make the election described in this paragraph (e).

(2) *Coordination between prefunding balance and funding standard carryover balance.* To the extent that a plan has a funding standard carryover balance greater than zero, no election under paragraph (e)(1) of this section is permitted to be made that reduces the plan's prefunding balance. Thus, a plan must exhaust its funding standard carryover balance before it is permitted to make an election under paragraph (e)(1) of this section with respect to its prefunding balance.

(f) *Elections*—(1) *Method of making elections.* Any election under this section by the plan sponsor must be made by providing written notification of the election to the plan's enrolled actuary and the plan administrator. The written notification must set forth the relevant details of the election, including the specific amounts involved in the election with respect to the prefunding balance and funding standard carryover balance.

(2) *Timing of elections*—(i) *General rule.* Except as provided in paragraph (f)(2)(ii) of this section, any election under this section must be made on or before the due date (with extensions) for the filing of the plan's Form 5500 "Annual Return/Report of Employee Benefit Plan" for the plan year to which the election relates (or, in the case of a plan not required to file a Form 5500 for the plan year, on or before the last day of the seventh month after the end of the plan year to which the election relates). For this purpose, an election to add to the prefunding balance relates to the plan year for which excess contributions were made. For example, in the case of a plan required to file a Form 5500, an election to add to the prefunding balance as of the first day of the 2010 plan year (in an amount not in excess of the 2009 interest-adjusted excess contributions under the rules of paragraph (b)(1)(ii) of this section) must be made no later than the due date for filing the 2009 Form 5500 even though the election is reported on the 2010 Form 5500 (Schedule SB).

(ii) *Election to reduce balances.* Any election under paragraph (e) of this section to reduce the prefunding balance or funding standard carryover balance for a plan year (for example, in order to avoid a benefit restriction under section 436) must be made by the end of the plan year to which the election relates.

(3) *Irrevocability of elections.* A plan sponsor's election under this section with respect to the plan's funding standard carryover balance or prefunding balance is irrevocable (and must be unconditional).

(4) *Plan sponsor*—(i) *In general.* For purposes of the elections described in this section, except as provided in paragraph (f)(4)(ii) of this section, any reference to the plan sponsor means the employer or employers responsible for making contributions to or under the plan.

(ii) *Certain multiple employer plans.* For purposes of the elections described in this section, in the case of plans that are multiple employer plans to which section 413(c)(4)(A) does not apply, any reference to the plan sponsor means the plan administrator within the meaning of section 414(g).

(g) *Examples.* The following examples illustrate the application of this section:

Example 1. (i) Plan P is a defined benefit plan with a plan year that is the calendar year and a valuation date of January 1. The funding standard carryover balance of Plan P is $25,000 as of the beginning of the 2008 plan year. The sponsor of Plan P, Sponsor S, does not elect in 2008, pursuant to paragraph (e)(1) of this section, to reduce any portion of the funding standard carryover balance prior to the determination of the value of plan assets. The actual rate of return on plan P's assets in 2008 is 2%. The effective interest rate in 2008 for Plan P is 6%. The minimum required contribution for Plan P under section 430 for 2008 is $100,000. The prior year funding ratio for Plan P for 2008, as determined under paragraph (h)(5) of this section, is not less than 80%.

(ii) Sponsor S makes a contribution to Plan P of $150,000 on December 1, 2008, for the 2008 plan year and makes no other contributions for the 2008 plan year. Because this contribution was made on a date other than the valuation date for the 2008 plan year, the contribution must be adjusted to reflect interest that would otherwise have accrued between the valuation date and the date of the contribution, at the effective rate

of interest for the 2008 plan year. The amount of the contribution after adjustment is $142,198, determined as $150,000 discounted for 11 months of compound interest at an effective annual interest rate of 6%.

(iii) The excess of employer contributions for 2008 over the minimum required contribution for 2008, as of the valuation date, is $42,198 ($142,198 less $100,000). Accordingly, the increase in Plan P's prefunding balance as of January 1, 2009, cannot exceed $44,730 (which is the excess contribution of $42,198 adjusted for 12 months of interest at an effective interest rate of 6%).

(iv) Furthermore, if Sponsor S does not elect to apply any portion of the funding standard carryover balance toward the minimum contribution in 2008, the funding standard carryover balance as of January 1, 2009, is $25,500 (which is the funding standard balance as of January 1, 2008, adjusted for investment experience at an effective interest rate of 2%).

Example 2. (i) The facts are the same as in *Example 1* except that the contribution of $150,000 is made on February 1, 2009, for the 2008 plan year.

(ii) The amount of the contribution after adjustment is $140,824, which is determined as $150,000 discounted for 13 months of interest at an effective interest rate of 6%. Accordingly, the increase in Plan P's prefunding balance as of January 1, 2009, cannot exceed $43,273 (which is the excess contribution of $40,824 adjusted for 12 months of interest at an effective interest rate of 6%).

Example 3. (i) The facts are the same as in *Example 1* except that Sponsor S contributes $85,000 to Plan P on January 1, 2008, for the 2008 plan year and makes no other contributions to Plan P for the 2008 plan year. In addition, Sponsor S elects to use $15,000 of the funding standard carryover balance to offset P's minimum required contribution in 2008, pursuant to paragraph (d)(1) of this section.

(ii) With respect to the 2009 plan year, the adjustment for investment experience under paragraph (b)(3) of this section for the funding standard carryover balance for the preceding plan year is $200, determined as the actual rate of return on plan assets for 2008 as applied to the 2008 funding standard carryover balance after reduction for the amount of that balance used under paragraph (d)(1) of this section (that is, $25,000 less $15,000, multiplied by the actual rate of return of 2%).

(iii) The funding standard carryover balance, as of January 1, 2009, is $10,200, determined as the 2008 funding standard carryover balance less the amount used to offset the 2008 minimum required contribution, adjusted for investment experience during the 2008 year ($25,000 less $15,000 plus $200).

Example 4. (i) The facts are the same as in *Example 3* except that Sponsor S contributes $90,000 (instead of $85,000) to Plan P on January 1, 2008, for the 2008 plan year.

(ii) Notwithstanding the fact that the amount that Sponsor S contributed to Plan P exceeds the minimum required contribution ($85,000) after it has been offset as a result of the use of the funding standard carryover balance, the maximum amount that Sponsor S may add to the prefunding balance as of January 1, 2009, is $0. This is because the maximum amount that may be added to the prefunding balance is the excess of $90,000 over $100,000. See paragraphs (b)(1)(ii)(A) and (B) of this section.

Example 5. (i) Plan Q is a defined benefit plan with a plan year that is the calendar year and a valuation date of July 1. The funding standard carryover balance of Plan Q is $50,000 as of January 1, 2009, the beginning of the 2009 plan year. The prefunding balance of Plan Q as of the beginning of the 2009 plan year is $0. The actual rate of return on Plan Q's assets in 2009 is 10%. The effective interest rate for Plan Q for 2009 is 5%. The funding ratio for Plan Q in 2008 is 85%, as determined under paragraph (d)(3) of this section. Thus, the prior year funding ratio for 2009 is not less than 80%.

(ii) Pursuant to paragraph (b)(4) of this section, the funding standard carryover balance is increased to $51,235 as of July 1, 2009 (that is, an increase to reflect 6 months of interest at an effective interest rate of 5%). Sponsor T does not elect in 2009 to reduce any portion of the funding standard carryover balance pursuant to paragraph (e) of this section. The funding standard carryover balance ($51,235) is subtracted from the value of plan assets, as of July 1, 2009, prior to the determination of the minimum funding contribution and, accordingly, $51,235 is the maximum amount that may applied against the minimum required contribution.

(iii) The minimum required contribution for Plan Q for 2009 is $200,000. Sponsor T makes a contribution to Plan Q of $190,000 on July 1, 2009, for the 2009 plan year, and makes no other contributions for the 2009 plan year. Sponsor T elects to use $10,000 of the funding standard carryover balance to offset Plan Q's minimum required contribution in 2009. Accordingly, the value of the funding standard carryover balance as of July 1, 2009, prior to adjustment for investment experience, is $41,235 (that is, $51,235 less $10,000).

(iv) The value of the funding standard carryover balance as of January 1, 2010, is determined by first discounting the value as of July 1, 2009, after amounts have been used to offset the minimum required contribution, to January 1, 2009, at the effective interest rate and then crediting this so determined amount with a full year's investment experience at a rate equal to the actual rate of return. Thus, the July 1, 2009, value of $41,235 is discounted for 6 months of interest, at an effective interest rate of 5%, to obtain a January 1, 2009, value of $40,241. Accordingly, the value of the funding standard carryover balance as of January 1, 2010, is $44,265 (that is, $40,241 increased with one year's investment return at a rate of 10%).

(h) *Effective/applicablility date and transition rules*—(1) *General effective/applicability date.* Except as provided in paragraph (h)(2) of this section, this section applies to plan years beginning on or after January 1, 2008.

(2) *Plans with delayed effective date.* In the case of a plan for which the effective date of section 430 is delayed in accordance with sections 104 through 106 of the Pension Protection Act of 2006, Public Law 109-280, 120 Stat. 780, this section applies to plan years beginning on or after the effective date of section 430 with respect to the plan.

(3) *First effective plan year.* For purposes of this section, the first effective plan year for a plan is the first plan year to which this section applies under paragraph (h)(1) or (h)(2) of this section.

(4) *Pre-effective plan year.* For purposes of this section, the pre-effective plan year for a plan is the last plan year beginning before the first effective date applicable under paragraph (h)(1) or (h)(2) of this section. Thus, except for plans with a delayed effective date under paragraph (h)(2) of this section, the pre-effective plan year for a plan is the last plan year beginning before January 1, 2008.

(5) *Special lookback rule for pre-effective plan year's funding ratio*—(i) *Plan assets.* For purposes of determining a plan's prior year funding ratio pursuant to paragraph (d)(3) of this section for the first effective plan year, the value of plan assets on the valuation date of the preceding plan year is determined under section 412(c)(2) as in effect for that pre-effective plan year, except that—

(A) If the value of plan assets is less than 90 percent of the fair market value of plan assets for the pre-effective plan year on that date, for this purpose such value is considered to be 90 percent of the fair market value; and

(B) If the value of plan assets is greater than 110 percent of the fair market value of plan assets on the valuation date for the pre-effective plan year on that date, for this purpose such value is considered to be 110 percent of the fair market value.

(ii) *Funding target.* For purposes of determining a plan's prior year funding ratio pursuant to paragraph (d)(3) of this section for the first effective plan year, the funding target of the plan for the preceding plan year is equal to the plan's current liability under section 412(l)(7) on the valuation date for the plan's pre-effective plan year.

Par. 3. Section 1.436-1 is added to read as follows:

§ 1.436-1 Limits on benefits and benefit accruals under single employer defined benefit plans.

(a) *General rules*—(1) *Qualification requirement.* Section 401(a)(29) provides that a defined benefit pension plan that is subject to section 412 and that is not a multiemployer plan (within the meaning of section 414(f)) is a qualified plan only if it satisfies the requirements of section 436. This section provides rules relating to funding-based limitations on certain benefits under section 436, and the requirements of section 436 are satisfied only if the plan meets the requirements of this section beginning with the plan's first effective plan year. This section applies to single employer defined benefit plans (including multiple employer plans), but does not apply to multiemployer plans.

(2) *Organization of the regulation.* Paragraph (b) of this section describes a limitation on shutdown benefits and other unpredictable contingent event benefits. Paragraph (c) of this section describes limitations on plan amendments increasing liabilities. Paragraph (d) of this section describes limitations on accelerated benefit payments. Paragraph (e) of this section describes limitations on benefit accruals. Paragraph (f) of this section provides rules relating to methods to avoid benefit limitations. Paragraph (g) of this section provides rules for the operation of the plan in relation to benefit limitations under section 436. Paragraph (h) of this section describes related presumptions regarding

underfunding that apply for purposes of the benefit limitations under section 436. Paragraph (j) of this section contains definitions. Paragraph (k) of this section contains effective/applicability date provisions.

(3) *Special rules for certain plans*—(i) *New plans.* The limitations described in paragraphs (b), (c), and (e) of this section do not apply to a plan for the first 5 plan years of the plan. For purposes of applying this rule, plan years of a plan are aggregated with plan years of a predecessor plan in accordance with section 414(a) or § 1.415(f)-1(c).

(ii) *Multiple employer plans.* In the case of a multiple employer plan to which section 413(c)(4)(A) applies, this section applies separately with respect to each employer under the plan, as if each employer maintained a separate plan. Thus, the benefit limitations under section 436 and this section could apply differently to participants who are employees of different employers under such a multiple employer plan. In the case of a multiple employer plan to which section 413(c)(4)(A) does not apply (that is, a plan described in section 413(c)(4)(B) that has not made the election for section 413(c)(4)(A) to apply), this section applies as if all participants in the plan were employed by a single employer.

(4) *Treatment of plan as of close of prohibited or cessation period*—(i) *Resumption of benefit payments and accruals*—(A) *Resumption of accelerated payments.* If a limitation on accelerated benefit payments under paragraph (d) of this section applied to a plan as of a section 436 measurement date, but that limit no longer applies to the plan as of a later section 436 measurement date, then the prohibition on paying accelerated benefits under the plan does not apply to benefits with annuity starting dates that are on or after that later section 436 measurement date. Any amendment to eliminate the payment of accelerated benefit payments for periods in which they are not restricted under section 436 is subject to the rules of section 411(d)(6).

(B) *Resumption of benefit accruals.* Unless the plan provides otherwise, benefit accruals under the plan resume effective as of the section 436 measurement date on which benefit accruals are no longer restricted under paragraph (e) of this section.

(ii) *Missed benefit payments and accruals*—(A) *Option to amend plan to restore benefits.* A plan is permitted to be amended to provide participants who had an annuity starting date within a period during which the rules of paragraph (d) of this section applied to the plan with the opportunity to have a new election under which the form of benefit previously elected may be modified, subject to applicable qualification requirements. A participant who makes such a new election is treated as having a new annuity starting date under section 417. Similarly, a plan is permitted to be amended to provide that any benefit accruals which were limited under the rules of paragraph (e) of this section are credited under the plan when the limitation no longer applies, subject to applicable qualification requirements. Any such plan amendment with respect to a new annuity starting date or crediting of benefit accruals is subject to the requirements of section 436(c) and paragraph (c) of this section.

(B) *Automatic plan provisions to restore benefits.* A plan is permitted to provide that participants who had an annuity starting date within a period during which the rules of paragraph (d) of this section applied to the plan are automatically provided with the opportunity to have a new annuity starting date (which would constitute a new annuity starting date under section 417) under which the form of benefit previously elected may be modified, subject to applicable qualification requirements, once the rules of paragraph (d) of this section cease to apply. In addition, a plan is permitted to provide for the automatic restoration of benefit accruals that had been limited under section 436(e) as of the section 436 measurement date that the limitation ceases to apply, as described in paragraph (a)(4)(ii)(A) of this section. However, if a plan provides for the automatic restoration of those benefit accruals and the period of the limitation exceeds 12 months, the plan will be treated as having adopted, effective as of the section 436 measurement date on which the limitation ceases to apply, a plan amendment that has the effect of increasing liabilities under the plan. Such an amendment is subject to the limitations of paragraph (c) of this section.

(iii) *Shutdown and other unpredictable contingent event benefits*—(A) *In general.* If any unpredictable contingent event benefits under paragraph (b) of this section are limited with respect to an unpredictable contingent event, that limitation applies to all such benefits that otherwise would have been paid to any plan participant with respect to that unpredictable contingent event.

(B) *Benefits not paid.* Notwithstanding paragraph (a)(4)(iii)(A) of this section, a plan is permitted to be amended to provide that any unpredictable contingent event benefits that were limited under the rules of paragraph (b) of this section will be paid or reinstated as of the section 436 measurement date on which the limitation no longer applies, subject to applicable qualification requirements. Such a plan amendment is subject to the requirements of section 436(c) and paragraph (c) of this section. A plan is not permitted to provide for restoration of any such unpredictable contingent event benefits without an amendment that complies with section 436(c).

(iv) *Example*. The following example illustrates the application of this paragraph (a)(4):

Example. (i) Plan T is a non-collectively bargained defined benefit plan with a plan year that is the calendar year and a valuation date of January 1. As of January 1, 2011, Plan T does not have a funding standard carryover balance or a prefunding balance. Plan T's sponsor is not in bankruptcy. Beginning January 1, 2011, Plan T is subject to the restriction on accelerated benefit distributions under paragraph (d)(3) of this section based on a presumed adjusted funding target attainment percentage (AFTAP) of 75%, and can therefore only pay a portion (generally 50%) of the accelerated benefit distributions otherwise payable to participants who commence benefit payments while the restriction is in effect.

(ii) U is a participant in Plan T. Participant U retires on February 1, 2011, and elects to receive benefits in the form of a single sum. However, because U elected a form of payment that is a prohibited payment that is not permitted to be paid under paragraph (d)(3)(i) of this section, U elects in accordance with paragraph (d)(3)(ii) of this section to receive 50% of his benefit in a single sum and the remainder as an immediately commencing straight life annuity.

(iii) On March 1, 2011, the enrolled actuary for the Plan certifies that the AFTAP for 2011 is 80%. Accordingly, beginning March 1, 2011, Plan T is no longer subject to the restriction under paragraph (d)(3) of this section.

(iv) Effective March 1, 2011, Plan T is amended to provide that a participant whose benefits were restricted under paragraph (d)(3) of this section may elect within a specified period on or after March 1, 2011, a new annuity starting date and receive the remainder of his or her pension benefits in an accelerated form of payment. Plan T's enrolled actuary determines that the AFTAP, taking into account the amendment, is still 80%. The amendment is permitted to take effect because Plan T has an AFTAP of 80% taking into account the amendment, and is therefore neither subject to the restriction on plan amendments in paragraph (c) of this section nor the restrictions on accelerated benefit payments under paragraphs (d)(1) and (d)(3) of this section. Accordingly, Participant U may elect, subject to otherwise applicable qualification rules, including spousal consent, to receive the remainder of his benefits in the form of a single sum on or after March 1, 2011.

(5) *Deemed election to reduce funding balances*—(i) *Limitations on accelerated benefit payments*. If a benefit limitation under paragraph (d) of this section would (but for this paragraph (a)(5)) apply to a plan, the employer is treated as having made an election under section 430(f) to reduce the prefunding balance or funding standard carryover balance by such amount as is necessary for the adjusted funding target attainment percentage to be at or above the applicable threshold (60, 80, or 100 percent, as the case may be) in order for the benefit limitation not to apply to the plan. In such a case, the employer is treated as having made that election on the section 436 measurement date as of which the benefit limitation would otherwise apply (without regard to whether a participant is eligible for or requests a payment that is a prohibited payment described in paragraph (d)(5) of this section).

(ii) *Other limitations for collectively bargained plans*—(A) *General rule*. In the case of a collectively bargained plan to which a benefit limitation under paragraph (b), (c), or (e) of this section would (but for this paragraph (a)(5)) apply, the employer is treated as having made an election under section 430(f) to reduce the prefunding balance or funding standard carryover balance by such amount as is necessary for the adjusted funding target attainment percentage to be at or above the applicable threshold in order for the benefit limitation not to apply to the plan, taking into account the unpredictable contingent event benefits or plan amendment, as applicable. In such a case, the employer is treated as having made that election on the date as of which the applicable benefit limitation would otherwise apply.

(B) *Treatment of plans with both collectively bargained and non-collectively bargained employees*. In the case of a plan with respect to which collective bargaining agreements apply to some, but not all, of the plan participants, the plan is considered a collectively bargained plan for purposes of this paragraph (a)(5)(ii) if at least 25 percent of the participants in the plan are members of collective bargaining units for which the benefit levels under the plan are specified under a collective bargaining agreement.

(iii) *Exception for insufficient funding balances*—(A) *In general*. Paragraphs (a)(5)(i) and (a)(5)(ii) of this section apply with respect to a benefit limitation for any plan year only if the application of those paragraphs would result in the corresponding benefit limitation not applying for such plan year. Thus, if the plan's prefunding and funding standard carryover balances were reduced to zero and the resulting increase in plan assets taken into account would still not increase the plan's adjusted funding target attainment percentage enough to reach the threshold percentage applicable to the benefit limitation, the deemed election to reduce those balances pursuant to paragraph (a)(5)(i) or (a)(5)(ii) of this section does not apply.

(B) *Presumed adjusted funding target attainment percentage less than 60 percent*. If a plan is presumed to have an adjusted funding target attainment percentage of less than 60 percent under paragraph (h)(3) of this section, then the plan is treated as if the funding standard carryover balance and the prefunding balance are insufficient to increase the adjusted funding target attainment percentage to the threshold percentage of 60 percent. Accordingly, paragraphs (a)(5)(i) and (a)(5)(ii) of this section do not apply to such a plan.

(iv) *Example*. The following example illustrates the application of this paragraph (a)(5):

Example. (i) Plan W is a collectively bargained, single-employer defined benefit plan sponsored by Sponsor X, with a plan year that is the calendar year and a valuation date of January 1. Sponsor X is not in bankruptcy.

(ii) The enrolled actuary for Plan W issues a certification on March 1, 2010, that the 2010 AFTAP is 81%. Sponsor X adopts an amendment on March 25, 2010, to increase benefits under a formula based on participant compensation, with an effective date of May 1, 2010. (Because the formula is based on compensation, the exception in paragraph (c)(3) of this section for increases with respect to a formula not based on compensation does not apply.) The plan's enrolled actuary determines that the plan's AFTAP for 2010 would be 75% if the benefits attributable to the plan amendment were taken into account. This percentage is below the 80% threshold for the plan amendment limitation under paragraph (c) of this section.

(iii) Because the AFTAP would be below the 80% threshold if the benefits attributable to the plan amendment were taken into account, Sponsor X is deemed to have made an election under paragraph (a)(5)(ii) of this section to reduce Plan W's prefunding balance and funding standard carryover balance by the amount necessary for the AFTAP to reach the 80% threshold (reflecting the increase in funding target attributable to the plan amendment) in order for the limitation under paragraph (c) of this section not to apply.

(iv) In this case, provided the reduction in funding balances is sufficient for the limitation not to apply, the plan amendment will go into effect on its effective date (May 1). See paragraph (f) of this section for other methods to avoid benefit limitations (where, for example, the amount necessary for a benefit limitation not to apply for a plan year exceeds the aggregate funding balances).

(b) *Limitation on shutdown benefits and other unpredictable contingent event benefits*—(1) *In general*. A plan that contains an unpredictable contingent event benefit satisfies section 436(b) and this section only if it provides that the benefit will not be paid to a plan participant during a plan year if the adjusted funding target attainment percentage for the plan year—

(i) Is less than 60 percent; or

(ii) Is 60 percent or more, but would be less than 60 percent if the benefits attributable to the unpredictable contingent event were taken into account in determining the adjusted funding target attainment percentage.

(2) *Exemption*—(i) *In general*. The prohibition on payment of unpredictable contingent event benefits under paragraph (b)(1) of this section ceases to apply with respect to a plan year, effective as of the first day of the plan year, upon payment by the plan sponsor of the contribution described in paragraph (f)(2) of this section.

(ii) *Prior unpredictable contingent event*. Unpredictable contingent event benefits attributable to an unpredictable contingent event that occurred within a period during which no limitation under this paragraph (b) applied to the plan are not affected by the limitation described in this paragraph (b) as it applies in a subsequent period. For example, if a plant shutdown occurs in 2010 and the plan's funded status is such that shutdown benefits related to that shutdown are not subject to the limitation described in this paragraph (b) for that calendar plan year, this paragraph (b) will not apply to restrict payment of those shutdown benefits even if another shutdown occurs in 2012 that results in shutdown benefits related to that later shutdown being restricted under this paragraph (b) (where the plan's adjusted funding target attainment percentage for 2012 is less than 60 percent taking into account the liability attributable to those shutdown benefits).

(3) *Unpredictable contingent event.* For purposes of this section, an *unpredictable contingent event benefit* means any benefit or increase in benefits to the extent the benefit or increase would not be payable but for the occurrence of an unpredictable contingent event. For this purpose, an *unpredictable contingent event* means a plant shutdown (whether full or partial) or similar event, or an event other than the attainment of any age, performance of any service, receipt or derivation of any compensation, or the occurrence of death or disability. Thus, for example, if a plan provides for an unreduced early retirement benefit upon the occurrence of an event other than the attainment of any age, performance of any service, receipt or derivation of any compensation, or the occurrence of death or disability, then that unreduced early retirement benefit is an unpredictable contingent event benefit to the extent of any portion of the benefit that would not be payable but for the occurrence of the event, even if the remainder of the benefit is payable without regard to the occurrence of the event. Similarly, if a plan includes a benefit payable upon the presence of circumstances specified in the plan (other than the attainment of any age, performance of any service, receipt or derivation of any compensation, or the occurrence of death or disability), but not upon a severance from employment that does not include those circumstances, the plan is providing an unpredictable contingent event benefit.

(c) *Limitations on plan amendments increasing liability for benefits—* (1) *In general.* Except as provided in this paragraph (c), a plan satisfies section 436(c) and this section only if the plan provides that no amendment to the plan that has the effect of increasing liabilities of the plan by reason of increases in benefits, establishment of new benefits, changing the rate of benefit accrual, or changing the rate at which benefits become nonforfeitable takes effect if the adjusted funding target attainment percentage for the plan year is—

(i) Less than 80 percent; or

(ii) Is 80 percent or more, but would be less than 80 percent if the benefits attributable to the amendment were taken into account in determining the adjusted funding target attainment percentage.

(2) *Exemption.* The limitations on plan amendments in paragraph (c)(1) of this section cease to apply and the amendment is permitted to take effect as of the later of the first day of the plan year or the effective date of the amendment upon payment by the plan sponsor of the contribution described in paragraph (f)(2) of this section.

(3) *Exception for certain benefit increases—* (i) *In general.* The limitation on plan amendments under paragraph (c)(1) of this section does not apply to any amendment that provides for an increase in benefits under a formula that is not based on a participant's compensation, but only if the rate of increase in benefits does not exceed the contemporaneous rate of increase in average wages of participants covered by the amendment. The determination of the rate of increase in average wages is made by taking into consideration the net increase in average wages from the period of time beginning with the effective date of the most recent benefit increase applicable to all of those participants who are covered by the current amendment and ending on the effective date of the current amendment.

(ii) *Application to terminated participants.* If an amendment applies to both currently employed and terminated participants, all such participants must be included in determining the increase in average wages of the participants covered by the amendment. For this purpose, terminated participants are treated as having no increase or decrease in wages for the period after severance from employment.

(iii) *Separate amendments for different plan populations.* In lieu of a single amendment that applies to both currently employed participants and terminated participants as described in paragraph (c)(3)(ii) of this section, the employer could adopt two amendments — one that increases benefits for currently employed participants and another one that increases benefits for terminated participants. In that case, the two amendments are considered separately in determining the increase in average wages, and the exception in this paragraph (c)(3) from application of the section 436(c) limitation would apply separately to each amendment (so that an amendment providing for increases in benefits for currently employed participants could go into effect, but an amendment providing for increases in benefits for terminated participants who received no increase in wages from the employer during the period over which the increase in average wages is determined could not go into effect).

(4) *Exception for statutorily required vesting.* To the extent that any amendment results in (or is made pursuant to) a mandatory increase in the vesting of benefits under the Code or ERISA (such as vesting rate increases pursuant to statute, plan termination amendments under section 411(d)(3), and amendments that lead to vesting increases required by top heavy rules under section 416), that amendment does not constitute an amendment that changes the rate at which benefits become nonforfeitable for purposes of section 436(c) and this paragraph (c).

(d) *Limitations on accelerated benefit payments—* (1) *Funding percentage less than 60 percent—* (i) *In general.* A plan satisfies the requirements of section 436(d)(1) and this paragraph (d)(1) only if the plan provides that, if the plan's adjusted funding target attainment percentage for a plan year is less than 60 percent, the plan will not pay any prohibited payment with an annuity starting date on or after the applicable section 436 measurement date.

(ii) *Request for prohibited distribution.* If a participant or beneficiary requests a distribution that is prohibited under paragraph (d)(1)(i) of this section, the plan must permit the participant or beneficiary to elect another form of benefit available under the plan or to defer payment to a later date to the extent permitted under applicable qualification requirements.

(2) *Bankruptcy.* A plan satisfies the requirements of section 436(d)(2) and this paragraph (d)(2) only if the plan provides that the plan will not pay any prohibited payment with an annuity starting date that is during any period in which the plan sponsor is a debtor in a case under title 11, United States Code, or similar Federal or State law, except for payments made with an annuity starting date within a plan year that is on or after the date on which the enrolled actuary of the plan certifies that the plan's adjusted funding target attainment percentage for that plan year is not less than 100 percent. The rules of paragraph (d)(1)(ii) of this section apply if payments are prohibited under this paragraph (d)(2).

(3) *Limited payment if percentage at least 60 percent but less than 80 percent—* (i) *In general.* A plan satisfies the requirements of section 436(d)(3) and this paragraph (d)(3) only if the plan provides that, in any case in which the plan's adjusted funding target attainment percentage for a plan year is 60 percent or more but is less than 80 percent, a participant or beneficiary is permitted to elect the payment of a benefit with an annuity starting date on or after the applicable section 436 measurement date in the form of a prohibited payment only if the present value, determined in accordance with section 417(e)(3), of the portion of the payment that is greater than the amount of the straight life annuity under the plan (as described in paragraph (d)(5)(i)(A) of this section) does not exceed the lesser of—

(A) 50 percent of the present value of the benefits, determined in accordance with section 417(e)(3) (or, if greater, 50 percent of the amount of any single sum that would be payable without regard to this paragraph (d)); or

(B) 100 percent of the PBGC guarantee amount described in paragraph (d)(3)(iv) of this section.

(ii) *Bifurcation if optional form unavailable—* (A) *General rule.* If an optional form of benefit that is otherwise available under the terms of the plan is not available as of the annuity starting date because of the application of paragraph (d)(3)(i) of this section, then the plan must provide a participant or beneficiary who elects such an optional form with the option either to defer payment to a later date (to the extent permitted under applicable qualification requirements) or to bifurcate the benefit into unrestricted and restricted portions. If the participant or beneficiary elects to bifurcate the benefit, the plan must permit the participant or beneficiary to elect, with respect to the unrestricted portion, any optional form of benefit otherwise available under the plan with respect to the participant's or beneficiary's entire benefit (whether or not the optional form of benefit with respect to the unrestricted portion is a prohibited payment). In such a case, if the participant or beneficiary elects payment of the unrestricted portion of the benefit described in paragraph (d)(3)(ii)(B) of this section in the form of a prohibited payment, the plan must permit the participant or beneficiary to elect payment of the restricted portion described in paragraph (d)(3)(ii)(C) of this section in any optional form of benefit under the plan that is not a prohibited payment and that would have been permitted with respect to the participant's or beneficiary's entire benefit. A plan is also permitted to offer optional forms of benefit that are solely available during the period this paragraph (d)(3) applies to the plan, such as an optional form of benefit that provides for the current payment of the unrestricted portion of the benefit, with a delayed commencement for the restricted portion of the benefit, subject to other applicable qualification requirements.

(B) *Unrestricted portion of the benefit.* The unrestricted portion of the benefit is the lesser of—

(*1*) 50 percent of the benefit; and

(*2*) The portion of the benefit that has a present value equal to the PBGC guarantee amount described in paragraph (d)(3)(iv) of this section.

(C) *Restricted portion of the benefit*. The restricted portion of the benefit is the portion of the benefit that is not described in paragraph (d)(3)(ii)(B) of this section.

(iii) *One-time application*—(A) *In general*. A plan satisfies the requirements of this paragraph (d) only if the plan provides that, in the case of a participant who receives a prohibited payment (or series of prohibited payments under a single optional form of benefit) pursuant to paragraph (d)(3)(i) or (ii) of this section, the participant cannot thereafter receive any additional prohibited payment during any period of consecutive plan years to which the limitations under either this paragraph (d)(3), paragraph (d)(1) of this section, or paragraph (d)(2) of this section apply.

(B) *Treatment of beneficiaries*. For purposes of this paragraph (d)(3), benefits provided to a participant and any beneficiary (including an alternate payee, as defined in section 414(p)(8)) are aggregated. If the accrued benefit of a participant is allocated to such an alternate payee and one or more other persons, the unrestricted amount under paragraphs (d)(3)(i) and (d)(3)(ii) of this section is allocated among such persons in the same manner as the accrued benefit is allocated, unless a qualified domestic relations order (as defined in section 414(p)(1)(A)) with respect to the participant or the alternate payee provides otherwise.

(iv) *Present value of PBGC maximum benefit guarantee*. The amount described in this paragraph (d)(3)(iv) is, with respect to a participant, the present value (determined under guidance prescribed by the Pension Benefit Guaranty Corporation, using the interest and mortality assumptions under section 417(e)) of the maximum benefit guarantee under section 4022 of the Employee Retirement Income Security Act of 1974, as amended.

(v) *Examples*. The following examples illustrate the application of this paragraph (d)(3):

Example 1. (i) Plan A is subject to the restriction on accelerated benefit distributions under paragraph (d)(3) of this section for the 2010 plan year, and can therefore only pay a portion of the accelerated benefit payments otherwise payable to participants whose annuity starting date occurs while the restriction applies.

(ii) Participant P is not married, and retires at age 65 during 2010, while the restriction under paragraph (d)(3) of this section applies to Plan A. P's accrued benefit is $10,000 per month, payable commencing at age 65 as a straight life annuity. Plan A provides for an optional single sum payment (subject to the restrictions under section 436) equal to the present value of the participant's accrued benefit using actuarial assumptions under section 417(e). P's single sum payment, determined without regard to this paragraph (d), is calculated to be $1,416,000, payable at age 65.

(iii) The PBGC guaranteed monthly benefit for a straight life annuity payable at age 65 in 2010 (for purposes of this example) is $4,500. The present value of the PBGC guaranteed benefit using actuarial assumptions under section 417(e) is $637,200.

(iv) Because Participant P retires during a period when the restriction in paragraph (d)(3) of this section applies to Plan A, only a portion of the benefit can be paid in the form of a single sum. P elects a single sum payment. Because a single sum payment is a prohibited payment, a determination must be made whether the payment can be paid under paragraph (d)(3)(i) of this section. In this case, because the portion of Participant P's benefit that is greater than a straight life annuity exceeds the lesser of 50% of the benefit otherwise payable, or the present value of the PBGC guaranteed benefit, it cannot be paid under paragraph (d)(3)(i) of this section. Accordingly, the maximum single sum that Participant P can receive is $637,200 (that is, the lesser of 50% of $1,416,000 or $637,200).

(v) Pursuant to paragraph (d)(3)(ii) of this section, the plan must offer P the option to bifurcate the benefit into restricted and unrestricted portions. The unrestricted portion is a monthly straight life annuity of $4,500, which can be paid in a single sum of $637,200. If P elects to receive the unrestricted portion of the benefit in the form of a single sum, then, with respect to the $5,500 restricted portion, the plan must permit P to elect any form of benefit that would otherwise be permitted with respect to the full $10,000 that is not a prohibited payment. Alternatively, the plan could permit P to elect to defer commencement of the restricted portion, subject to applicable qualification rules.

Example 2. (i) The facts are the same as in *Example 1*. In addition, Plan A provides an optional form of payment (subject to any benefit restrictions under section 436) that consists of a partial payment equal to the total return of employee contributions to the plan accumulated with interest, with an annuity payment for the remainder of the participant's benefit.

(ii) Participant Q is not married, and retires at age 65 during 2010, while Plan A is subject to the restriction under paragraph (d)(3) of this section. Participant Q has an accrued benefit equal to a straight life annuity of $3,000 per month. Under the optional form described in paragraph (i) of this *Example 2*, Q may elect a partial payment of $99,120 (representing the return of employee contributions accumulated with interest) plus a straight life annuity of $2,300 per month. The present value of Participant Q's accrued benefit, using actuarial assumptions under section 417(e), is $424,800. The present value of the PBGC guarantee payable at age 65 in the form of a straight life annuity is determined to be $637,200 for the purposes of this *Example 2*.

(iii) Under the bifurcation approach of paragraph (d)(3)(ii) of this section, Q can receive the partial single sum payment available under the terms of Plan A as long as the amount of the single sum does not exceed the unrestricted portion of the benefit under paragraph (d)(3)(ii)(B) of this section. The unrestricted portion of Q's benefit is the lesser of 50% of the benefit otherwise payable, or the present value of the PBGC guaranteed benefit. Accordingly, the maximum single sum that Q can receive is $212,400 (that is, the lesser of 50% of $424,800, or $637,200).

(iv) Because the present value of the portion of Q's benefit that is greater than the straight life annuity ($99,120) is less than the lesser of 50% of the present value of benefits (50% of $424,800) and $637,200 (100% of the PBGC guaranteed benefit), the optional form described in paragraph (i) of this *Example 2* is permitted to be paid under paragraph (d)(3)(i) of this section.

(4) *Exception for cessation of benefit accruals*. This paragraph (d) does not apply to a plan for a plan year if the terms of the plan, as in effect for the period beginning on September 1, 2005, provided for no benefit accruals with respect to any participants. If a plan that is described in this paragraph (d)(4) provides for benefit accruals during any time after September 1, 2005, this paragraph (d)(4) ceases to apply for the plan as of the date any benefits accrue under the plan.

(5) *Prohibited payment*—(i) *In general*. For purpose of this paragraph (d), the term *prohibited payment* means—

(A) Any payment for a month that is in excess of the monthly amount paid under a straight life annuity (plus any social security supplements described in the last sentence of section 411(a)(9)) to a participant or beneficiary whose annuity starting date occurs during any period that a limitation under this paragraph (d) is in effect;

(B) Any payment for the purchase of an irrevocable commitment from an insurer to pay benefits; and

(C) Any other payment that is identified as a prohibited payment by the Commissioner in revenue rulings and procedures, notices and other guidance published in the Internal Revenue Bulletin (see §601.601(d)(2) of this chapter).

(ii) *Annuity starting date*. Solely for purposes of applying the limitations on accelerated benefit payments under this paragraph (d), the term *annuity starting date* means, as applicable—

(A) The first day of the first period for which an amount is payable as an annuity as described in section 417(f)(2)(A)(i);

(B) In the case of a benefit not payable in the form of an annuity, the first day on which all events have occurred (including the participant's election, the participant's severance from employment if the participant is below normal retirement age, and, if applicable, the participant's survival to the date as of which payment is made) which entitle the participant to such benefit as described in section 417(f)(2)(A)(ii);

(C) In the case of an amount payable under a retroactive annuity starting date, the benefit commencement date; and

(D) The date of any payment for the purchase of an irrevocable commitment from an insurer to pay benefits under plan.

(6) *Involuntary distributions under section 411(a)(11)*. [Reserved].

(e) *Limitation on benefit accruals for plans with severe funding shortfalls*—(1) *In general*. A plan satisfies the requirements of section 436(e) and this paragraph (e) only if it provides that, in any case in which the plan's adjusted funding target attainment percentage for a plan year is less than 60 percent, benefit accruals under the plan will cease as of the applicable section 436 measurement date. If a plan is required to cease benefit accruals under this paragraph (e), then the plan is not permitted to be amended in a manner that would increase the liabilities of the plan by reason of an increase in benefits or establishment of new benefits. The preceding sentence applies regardless of whether an amendment would otherwise be permissible under paragraph (c)(3) of this section.

(2) *Exemption.* The prohibition on additional benefit accruals under a plan described in paragraph (e)(1) of this section ceases to apply with respect to any plan year, effective as of the first day of the plan year, upon payment by the plan sponsor of the contribution described in paragraph (f)(2) of this section.

(f) *Methods to avoid benefit limitations*—(1) *In general.* This paragraph (f) sets forth rules relating to employer contributions and other methods to avoid the application of section 436 limitations under a plan for a plan year. In general, there are four methods a plan sponsor may utilize to avoid or terminate one or more of the benefit limitations under this section for a plan year. Two of these methods (where the plan sponsor elects to reduce the prefunding balance or funding standard carryover balance and where the plan sponsor makes additional contributions under section 430 for the prior plan year within the time period provided by section 430(j)(1) which are not added to the prefunding balance) involve increasing the amount of plan assets which are taken into account in determining the adjusted funding target attainment percentage. The other two methods (making a contribution that is specifically designated as a current year contribution to avoid application of a benefit limitation under paragraph (b), (c), or (e) of this section, and providing security under section 436(f)(1)) are described in paragraphs (f)(2) and (f)(3) of this section, respectively.

(2) *Current year contributions to avoid or terminate benefit limitations*—(i) *General rules*—(A) *Amount of contribution*—(1) *In general.* This paragraph (f)(2) sets forth rules regarding contributions to avoid the application of section 436 limitations under a plan for a plan year that apply to unpredictable contingent event benefits, plan amendments that increase liabilities for benefits, and benefit accruals.

(2) *Interest adjustment.* Any contribution made by a plan sponsor pursuant to this paragraph (f)(2) on a date other than the valuation date for the plan year must be adjusted with interest at the plan's effective interest rate under section 430(h)(2)(A) for the plan year. If the plan's effective interest rate for the plan year has not been determined at the time of the contribution, then this interest adjustment must be made using the highest of the three segment rates as applicable for the plan year under section 430(h)(2)(C). In such a case, if the effective interest rate for the year under section 430(h)(2)(A) is subsequently determined to be less than that highest rate, the excess is recharacterized as a section 430 contribution for the current plan year.

(B) *Prefunding balance or funding standard carryover balance may not be used.* No prefunding balance or funding standard carryover balance under section 430(f) may be used as a contribution described in this paragraph (f)(2). However, a plan sponsor is permitted to elect to reduce the funding standard carryover balance or the prefunding balance in order to increase the adjusted funding target attainment percentage for a plan year. See paragraph (a)(5) of this section for a rule mandating such a reduction in certain situations.

(ii) *Section 436 contributions separate from minimum required contributions*—(A) *In general.* The contributions described in this paragraph (f)(2) are contributions described in section 436(b)(2), (c)(2), and (e)(2), and are separate from any minimum required contributions under section 430. Thus, if a plan sponsor makes a contribution described in this paragraph (f)(2) for a plan year but does not make the minimum required contribution for the plan year, the plan will fail to satisfy the minimum funding requirements under section 430 for the plan year. In addition, a contribution described in this paragraph (f)(2) is disregarded in determining the prefunding balance under section 430(f)(6) and § 1.430(f)-1(b)(1)(i).

(B) *Designation requirement.* Any contribution made by a plan sponsor pursuant to this paragraph (f)(2) must be designated as such at the time the contribution is used to avoid or terminate the limitations under this paragraph (f)(2) and, except as specifically provided in paragraph (g) or (h) of this section, cannot subsequently be recharacterized with respect to any plan year as a contribution to satisfy a minimum required contribution obligation, or otherwise. The designation must be made in accordance with the rules and procedures that otherwise apply to elections under § 1.430(f)-1(f) with respect to funding balances.

(iii) *Contribution for unpredictable contingent event benefits.* In the case of a contribution to avoid the application of the limitation on benefits attributable to an unpredictable contingent event under section 436(b)—

(A) If the adjusted funding target attainment percentage for the plan year determined without taking into account the liability attributable to the unpredictable contingent event benefits is less than 60 percent, then the amount of the contribution under section 436(b)(2) is equal to

the amount of the increase in the funding target of the plan for the plan year if the benefits attributable to the unpredictable contingent event were included in the determination of the funding target.

(B) If the adjusted funding target attainment percentage for the plan year determined without taking into account the liability attributable to the unpredictable contingent event benefits is 60 percent or more, then the amount of the contribution under section 436(b)(2) is the amount that would be sufficient to result in an adjusted funding target attainment percentage for the plan year of 60 percent if—

(1) The benefits attributable to the unpredictable contingent event were included in the determination of the funding target; and

(2) The contribution were included as part of the assets of the plan.

(iv) *Contribution for plan amendments increasing liability for benefits.* In the case of a contribution to avoid the application of the limitation on benefits attributable to a plan amendment under Section 436(c)—

(A) If the adjusted funding target attainment percentage for the plan year determined without taking into account the liability attributable to the plan amendment is less than 80 percent, then the amount of the contribution under section 436(c)(2) is equal to the amount of the increase in the funding target of the plan for the plan year if the liabilities attributable to the amendment were included in the determination of the funding target.

(B) If the adjusted funding target attainment percentage for the plan year determined without taking into account the liability attributable to the plan amendment is 80 percent or more, then the amount of the contribution under section 436(c)(2) is the amount that would be sufficient to result in an adjusted funding target attainment percentage for the plan year of 80 percent if—

(1) The liabilities attributable to the plan amendment were included in the determination of the funding target; and

(2) The contribution were included as part of the assets of the plan.

(v) *Contribution required for continued benefit accruals.* In the case of a contribution to avoid the application of the limitation on accruals under section 436(e), the amount of the contribution under section 436(e)(2) is equal to the amount sufficient to result in an adjusted funding target attainment percentage for the plan year of 60 percent if the contribution were included as part of the assets of the plan.

(3) *Security to increase adjusted funding target attainment percentage*—(i) *In general.* For purposes of avoiding benefit limitations under section 436, a plan sponsor may provide security in the form described in paragraph (f)(3)(ii) of this section. In such a case, the adjusted funding target attainment percentage for the plan year is determined by treating as an asset of the plan any security provided by a plan sponsor by the valuation date for the plan year in a form meeting the requirements of paragraph (f)(3)(ii) of this section. However, this security is not taken into account as a plan asset for any other purpose, including section 430.

(ii) *Form of security.* The forms of security permitted under paragraph (f)(3)(i) of this section are limited to—

(A) A bond issued by a corporate surety company that is an acceptable surety for purposes of section 412 of ERISA; or

(B) Cash, or United States obligations which mature in 3 years or less, held in escrow by a bank or an insurance company.

(iii) *Enforcement.* Any form of security provided under paragraph (f)(3)(i) of this section must provide—

(A) That it will be paid to the plan upon the earliest of—

(1) The plan termination date as defined in section 4048 of ERISA;

(2) If there is a failure to make a payment of the minimum required contribution for any plan year beginning after the security is provided, the due date for the payment under section 430(j)(1) or 430(j)(3); or

(3) If the plan's adjusted funding target attainment percentage is less than 60 percent (without regard to any security provided under this paragraph (f)(3)) for a consecutive period of 7 years, the valuation date for the last year in the 7-year period; and

(B) That the plan administrator must notify the surety, bank, or insurance company that issued or holds the security of any event described in paragraph (f)(3)(iii)(A) of this section within 10 days of its occurrence.

(iv) *Release of security.* The form of security is permitted to provide that it will be released (and any amounts thereunder will be refunded together with any interest accrued thereon) as provided in the agreement governing the escrow, but such release is not permitted until the plan's enrolled actuary has certified that the plan's adjusted funding target attainment percentage for a plan year is at least 90 percent (without regard to any security provided under this paragraph (f)(3)).

(v) *Contribution of security to plan.* Any amount of security provided under this paragraph (f)(3) that is subsequently turned over to the plan (whether pursuant to the enforcement mechanism of paragraph (f)(3)(iii) of this section or after its release under paragraph (f)(3)(iv) of this section) is treated as a contribution by the plan sponsor under section 430 when contributed and, if turned over pursuant to paragraph (f)(3)(iii) of this section, is not a contribution under paragraph (f)(2) of this section.

(4) *Examples.* The following examples illustrate the application of this paragraph (f):

Example 1. (i) Plan Z is a non-collectively bargained defined benefit plan with a plan year that is the calendar year and a valuation date of January 1. Plan Z's sponsor is not in bankruptcy and did not purchase any annuities in 2009 or 2010. As of January 1, 2011, Plan Z does not have a funding standard carryover balance or a prefunding balance. As of that date, Plan Z has plan assets (and adjusted plan assets) of $2,000,000 and a funding target (and an adjusted funding target) of $2,550,000. On March 1, 2011, the enrolled actuary for the plan certifies that the AFTAP as of January 1, 2011, is 78.43%. The effective rate of interest for Plan Z for the 2011 plan year is 5.5%.

(ii) On May 1, 2011, the plan sponsor amends Plan Z to increase benefits. The enrolled actuary for the plan determines that the present value, as of January 1, 2011, of the increase in the funding target due to this amendment is $400,000. Because the AFTAP prior to the plan amendment is less than 80%, Plan Z is subject to the restriction on plan amendments in paragraph (c) of this section, and the amendment cannot take effect unless the employer utilizes one of the methods described in paragraph (f) of this section to avoid benefit limitations.

(iii) In order for this amendment to be permitted to become effective, the plan sponsor makes a contribution described in paragraph (f)(2) of this section. Because the AFTAP prior to the amendment was less than 80%, the provisions of paragraph (f)(2)(iv)(A) of this section apply. The amount of the contribution as of January 1, 2011, needed to avoid the restriction on plan amendments under paragraph (c) of this section is equal to the amount of the increase in funding target attributable to the amendment, or $400,000. Under the provisions of paragraph (f)(2)(iv)(A) of this section, this contribution is required even though, if the contribution were included as part of the plan assets and the liability attributable to the plan amendment were included in the funding target, the AFTAP would be 81.36% (because the adjusted plan assets would have been $2,400,000 and the adjusted funding target would have been $2,950,000 (that is, adjusted plan assets of $2,000,000 plus the contribution of $400,000 as of January 1, 2011; divided by the adjusted funding target of $2,550,000 increased to reflect the additional $400,000 in the funding target attributable to the plan amendment)).

(iv) However, because the contribution is not paid until May 1, 2011, the necessary contribution amount must be adjusted to reflect interest that would otherwise have accrued between the valuation date and the date of the contribution, at Plan Z's effective rate of interest for the 2011 plan year. The amount of the required contribution after adjustment is $407,203, determined as $400,000 increased for 4 months of compound interest at an effective annual interest rate of 5.5%.

(v) A contribution of $407,203 is made on May 1, 2011, and is designated as a contribution under paragraph (f)(2) of this section. Accordingly, the contribution is not applied toward minimum funding requirements under section 430, and is not eligible for inclusion in the prefunding balance under § 1.430(f)-1(b)(1). Since this contribution meets the requirements of paragraph (f)(2) of this section, the plan amendment can take effect.

Example 2. (i) The facts are the same as in *Example 1*, except that the plan is in at-risk status under section 430(i). The funding target determined under section 430(i) is $2,600,000, and the funding target determined without regard to section 430(i) is $2,550,000.

(ii) On May 1, 2011, the plan sponsor amends Plan Z to increase benefits. The plan's enrolled actuary determines that the present value as of January 1, 2011 of the increase in the funding target due to the amendment (taking into account the at-risk status of the plan) is $440,000. Because the AFTAP prior to the plan amendment is less than 80%, Plan Z is subject to the restriction on plan amendments in paragraph (c) of this section, and the amendment cannot take effect unless the employer utilizes one of the methods described in paragraph (f) of this section to avoid benefit limitations.

(iii) In order for this amendment to be permitted to become effective, the plan sponsor makes a contribution described in paragraph (f)(2) of this section. Because the AFTAP prior to the amendment was less than 80%, the provisions of paragraph (f)(2)(iv)(A) of this section apply. The amount of the contribution as of January 1, 2011, needed to avoid the restriction on plan amendments under paragraph (c) of this section is equal to the amount of the increase in funding target attributable to the amendment, or $440,000. Under the provisions of paragraph (f)(2)(iv)(A) of this section, this contribution is required even though, if the contribution were included as part of the plan assets and the liability attributable to the plan amendment were included in the funding target, the AFTAP would exceed 80%.

(iv) However, because the contribution is not paid until May 1, 2011, the necessary contribution amount must be adjusted to reflect interest that would otherwise have accrued between the valuation date and the date of the contribution, at Plan Z's effective rate of interest for the 2011 plan year. The amount of the required contribution after adjustment is $447,923, determined as $440,000 increased for 4 months of compound interest at an effective annual interest rate of 5.5%.

(v) A contribution of $447,923 is made on May 1, 2011, and is designated as a contribution under paragraph (f)(2) of this section. Accordingly, the contribution is not applied toward minimum funding requirements under section 430, and is not eligible for inclusion in the prefunding balance under § 1.430(f)-1(b)(1). Since this contribution meets the requirements of paragraph (f)(2) of this section, the plan amendment can take effect.

Example 3. (i) The facts are the same as in *Example 1*, except that the enrolled actuary for the plan does not issue the certification of the 2011 AFTAP until September 1, 2011. Prior to October 1, 2010, the enrolled actuary had certified the 2010 AFTAP to be 82%. The highest of the three segment rates applicable to the 2011 plan year under section 430(h)(2)(C) is 6%.

(ii) Because the enrolled actuary has not certified the actual AFTAP as of January 1, 2011, and the amendment is scheduled to take effect after April 1, 2011, the rules of paragraph (h)(2)(ii) of this section apply. Accordingly, the AFTAP for 2011 (prior to reflecting the effect of the amendment) is presumed to be 10 percentage points lower than the 2010 AFTAP, or 72%. Because this presumed AFTAP is less than 80%, the restriction on plan amendments in paragraph (c) of this section applies, and the plan amendment cannot take effect.

(iii) In order to allow the plan amendment to take effect, the plan sponsor decides to make a contribution under paragraph (f)(2) of this section on May 1, 2011. Because the presumed AFTAP was less than 80% prior to reflecting the plan amendment, the rules of paragraph (f)(2)(iv)(A) of this section apply, and the amount of the contribution under section 436(c)(2) is the amount of the increase in the funding target for the year if the plan amendment were included in the determination of the funding target. Accordingly, an additional contribution of $400,000 is required as of January 1, 2011, to avoid the restriction on plan amendments under paragraph (c) of this section.

(iv) However, since the contribution is not made until May 1, 2011, the amount of the required contribution must be adjusted to reflect interest that would have accrued between the valuation date and the date of the contribution. Since the effective interest rate has not yet been determined, the interest adjustment is based on the highest of the three segment rates applicable for the 2011 plan year under section 430(h)(2)(C), or 6%. The amount of the required contribution after adjustment is $407,845, determined as $400,000 increased for 4 months of compound interest at the highest segment interest rate for 2011, or 6%.

(v) Once the plan's effective interest rate has been determined, if that rate for the year is less than 6%, the amount of excess interest previously contributed is recharacterized as a section 430 contribution for the current plan year.

(g) *Rules of operation for periods prior to and after certification*—(1) *In general.* Section 436(h) and paragraph (h) of this section set forth a series of presumptions that apply before the enrolled actuary for a plan issues a certification of the plan's adjusted funding target attainment percentage for a plan year. This paragraph (g) sets forth rules for the application of limitations under sections 436(b), 436(c), 436(d), and 436(e) prior to and during the period those presumptions apply to a plan, and describes the interaction of those presumptions with plan operations after the plan's enrolled actuary has issued a certification of the plan's adjusted funding target attainment percentage for the plan year. Paragraph (g)(2) of this section sets forth rules that apply to periods during which a presumption under section 436(h) applies. Paragraph (g)(3) of this section sets forth rules that apply to periods during which no presumptions under section 436(h) apply but which are prior to the enrolled actuary's certification of the plan's adjusted funding target attainment percentage for the plan year. Paragraph (g)(4) of this section sets forth rules that apply after the enrolled actuary's certification of the plan's adjusted funding target attainment percentage for a plan year. Paragraph (g)(5) of this section sets forth additional rules that apply prior to the enrolled actuary's certification of the adjusted funding target attainment percentage for a plan year with respect to the limitations on unpredictable contingent event benefits and plan amendments that increase liabilities under paragraphs (b) and (c) of this section, respectively. Paragraph (g)(6) of this section sets forth rules for multiple unpredictable contingent events and amendments during a plan year. Paragraph (g)(7) of this section sets forth examples of the application of this paragraph (g).

(2) *Periods prior to certification during which a presumption applies*— (i) *Plan must follow presumptions.* A plan must provide that, for any period during which paragraph (h)(1), (2), or (3) of this section applies to the plan, the limitations applicable under paragraphs (b), (c), (d), and (e) of this section apply to the plan as if the actual adjusted funding target attainment percentage for the year were the presumed adjusted funding target attainment percentage determined under the rules of paragraph (h) of this section.

(ii) *Determination of amount of reduction in balances*—(A) *Valuation date adjustment.* During the period described in this paragraph (g)(2), the rules of paragraph (a)(5) of this section (relating to the deemed election to reduce the funding standard carryover balance and the prefunding balance) must be applied based on the presumed percentage with respect to the limitations under paragraphs (b), (c), (d), and (e) of this section. In order to determine the amount of the reduction in those balances that would apply in such a situation, a presumed adjusted funding target must be established, which is then compared to the interim value of adjusted plan assets as of the valuation date for the current plan year. For this purpose, the interim value of adjusted plan assets is equal to the value of adjusted plan assets as of the valuation date, determined without regard to future contributions, future elections to add to the prefunding balance for the prior year, and future elections (including deemed elections under paragraph (a)(5) of this section) to reduce the prefunding and funding standard carryover balances for the current plan year, and the presumed adjusted funding target is equal to the interim value of adjusted plan assets for the plan year divided by the presumed adjusted funding target attainment percentage.

(B) *Change in presumed percentage in 4th month.* If the presumed adjusted funding target attainment percentage for the plan year changes during the year because of application of the presumption in paragraph (h)(2) of this section, the rules regarding the deemed election to reduce funding balances described in paragraph (a)(5) of this section must be reapplied based on the new presumed adjusted funding target attainment percentage. This will typically occur on the first day of the 4th month of a plan year, but could happen later if the enrolled actuary's certification of the adjusted funding target attainment percentage for a plan year occurs after the first day of the 4th month of the following plan year. In order to perform this reapplication, a new adjusted funding target must be determined based on the new presumed adjusted funding target attainment percentage and must be compared to an updated interim value of adjusted plan assets. For this purpose, the new presumed adjusted funding target is redetermined based on the new presumed adjusted funding target attainment percentage, and is compared to the adjusted plan assets updated to take into account the plan sponsor's contributions made for the prior plan year and section 430(f) elections with respect to the plan's prefunding and funding standard carryover balances since the earlier determination of the interim plan assets. This reapplication of the deemed election may require an additional reduction in funding balances if the amount of the reduction in funding balances that is necessary to reach the applicable threshold to avoid the application of the limitation under paragraph (d) or (e) of this section is greater than the amount that was initially reduced. Prior reductions of funding balances continue to apply in accordance with the rules of paragraph (g)(4)(i)(C) of this section.

(iii) *Bankruptcy of plan sponsor.* Pursuant to section 436(d)(2), during any period in which the plan sponsor of a plan is a debtor in a case under title 11, United States Code, or any similar Federal or State law (as described in paragraph (d)(2) of this section), if the plan's enrolled actuary has not yet certified the plan's adjusted funding target attainment percentage for the plan year to be at least 100 percent, no prohibited payments within the meaning of paragraph (d)(5) of this section may be paid. Thus, the presumption rules of paragraph (h) of this section do not apply for purposes of section 436(d)(2) and this paragraph (g)(2)(iii).

(iv) *Application to unpredictable contingent events and plan amendments.* For purposes of applying the limitations under paragraphs (b) and (c) of this section during the period described in this paragraph (g)(2), the presumed adjusted funding target under paragraph (g)(2)(ii) of this section is adjusted to reflect the increase in the

funding target that would be attributable to the unpredictable contingent event or the plan amendment if the unpredictable contingent event benefits or the increase in liability attributable to the plan amendment were taken into account. See paragraph (g)(5)(i) of this section for related rules regarding funding balances that apply in the case of unpredictable contingent event benefits or plan amendments increasing benefit liabilities.

(3) *Periods prior to certification during which no presumption applies*—(i) *Accelerated benefit payments and benefit accruals.* If no presumptions under section 436(h) apply to a plan during a period and the plan's enrolled actuary has not yet issued the certification of the plan's actual adjusted funding target attainment percentage for the plan year, the plan is not permitted to limit the payment of accelerated benefits under paragraph (d) of this section or the accrual of benefits under paragraph (e) of this section based on an expectation that those paragraphs will apply to the plan once an actuarial certification is issued. However, see paragraph (g)(2)(iii) of this section for a restriction on prohibited payments during any period in which the plan sponsor of a plan is a debtor in a case under title 11, United States Code, or any similar Federal or State law.

(ii) *Unpredictable contingent event benefits and plan amendments increasing benefit liability*—(A) *In general.* If no presumptions under section 436(h) apply to a plan during a period and the plan's enrolled actuary has not yet issued a certification of the plan's adjusted funding target attainment percentage for the plan year, the limitations on unpredictable contingent event benefits under paragraph (b) of this section or plan amendments increasing benefit liability under paragraph (c) of this section during that period must be applied following the rules of paragraph (g)(5) of this section, based on the preceding year's certified adjusted funding target attainment percentage. Thus, if after application of those rules the plan would be treated as having an adjusted funding target attainment percentage below the applicable threshold under paragraph (b) or (c) of this section (taking into account the increase in the funding target attributable to the unpredictable contingent event benefits or the increase in liability attributable to the plan amendment), the unpredictable contingent event benefits are not permitted to be paid, and the plan amendment is not permitted to go into effect, unless the contribution described in paragraph (g)(5)(ii) of this section is made.

(B) *Recharacterization of contributions to avoid benefit limitations.* If, pursuant to paragraph (g)(3)(ii)(A) of this section, the plan sponsor makes contributions described in paragraph (g)(5)(ii) of this section to avoid application of the applicable benefit limitations, then, after the certification of the adjusted funding target attainment percentage for the current plan year is issued by the plan's enrolled actuary, those contributions are recharacterized as employer contributions under section 430 for the current plan year to the extent they exceed the amount necessary to avoid application of the applicable limitation under paragraph (b) or (c) of this section based on the certified percentage.

(4) *Periods after certification of adjusted funding target attainment percentage*—(i) *Plan must follow certified percentage*—(A) *In general.* The rules of paragraphs (g)(2) and (g)(3) of this section no longer apply for a plan year on and after the date the enrolled actuary for the plan issues a certification of the adjusted funding target attainment percentage of the plan for the current plan year, provided that the certification is issued before the first day of the 10th month of the plan year. Thus, for example, the plan must provide that paragraph (d) of this section applies for distributions with annuity starting dates on and after the date of that certification using the certified adjusted funding target attainment percentage of the plan for the plan year. Similarly, the plan must provide that any prohibition on accruals under paragraph (e) of this section as a result of the enrolled actuary's certification that the adjusted funding target attainment percentage of the plan for the plan year is less than 60 percent is effective as of the date of the certification and that any prohibition on accruals ceases to be effective on the date the enrolled actuary issues a certification that the adjusted funding target attainment percentage of the plan for the plan year is at least 60 percent. In addition, in the case of a plan that has been issued a certification of the plan's adjusted funding target attainment percentage for a plan year by the plan's enrolled actuary, the plan sponsor must comply with the requirements of paragraphs (b) and (c) of this section for an unpredictable contingent event that occurs or a plan amendment that is effective on or after the date of the enrolled actuary's certification. Thus, the plan administrator must determine if the adjusted funding target attainment percentage is at or above the applicable threshold, taking into account the increase in the funding target that would be attributable to the unpredictable contingent event or plan amendment if the unpredictable contingent event benefits or the increase in liability attributable to the plan amendment were taken into account.

(B) *Application of rule for deemed election to reduce funding balances.* After the adjusted funding target attainment percentage for a plan year is certified by the plan's enrolled actuary, the deemed election to reduce funding balances under paragraph (a)(5) of this section must be reapplied based on the actual funding target for the year (provided the certification is issued before the first day of the 10th month of the plan year). This reapplication of the deemed election may require an additional reduction in funding balances if the amount of the reduction in funding balances that is necessary to reach the applicable threshold to avoid the application of the limitations under paragraph (d) or (e) of this section is greater than the amount that was reduced under paragraph (g)(2) or (g)(3) of this section.

(C) *Prior reductions continue to apply.* If the amount of the reduction in funding balances that is necessary to reach the applicable threshold to avoid the application of the benefit limitation is less than the amount that was reduced under paragraph (g)(2) or (g)(3) of this section, then the prior reduction continues to apply. Similarly, if the amount of the reduction in funding balances that is necessary to reach the applicable threshold to avoid the application of the corresponding benefit limitation exceeds the amount of the funding balances, then the prior reduction continues to apply and no further reduction under paragraph (a)(5) of this section is provided.

(ii) *Applicability to prior periods*—(A) *In general.* Except as provided in paragraph (g)(4)(ii)(B) of this section, the enrolled actuary's certification of the adjusted funding target attainment percentage for the plan for the plan year does not affect the application of the limitation under paragraph (b) of this section with respect to unpredictable contingent events that occur during the periods to which paragraphs (g)(2) and (g)(3) of this section apply. Except as provided in paragraph (g)(4)(ii)(B) of this section, the enrolled actuary's certification of the adjusted funding target attainment percentage for the plan for the plan year does not affect the application of the limitation under paragraph (c) of this section to a plan amendment that increases liability for benefits where the amendment is first effective during the periods to which paragraphs (g)(2) and (g)(3) apply. The enrolled actuary's certification of the adjusted funding target attainment percentage for the plan for the plan year does not affect the application of the limitation under paragraph (d) of this section for distributions with annuity starting dates before the certification. Similarly, the enrolled actuary's certification of the adjusted funding target attainment percentage for the plan for the plan year does not affect the application of the limitation under paragraph (e) of this section prior to the date of that certification. See paragraph (a)(4) of this section for rules relating to the period of time after benefits cease to be limited.

(B) *Special rule for unpredictable contingent event benefits and plan amendments that increase liability.* If a plan does not pay benefits attributable to an unpredictable contingent event or plan amendment because of the application of paragraph (g)(5)(ii) of this section, the plan must provide for benefits that were not previously paid (or accrued) if such benefits would be permitted under the rules of section 436 based on the certified actual adjusted funding target attainment percentage, taking into account the increase in the funding target that would be attributable to the unpredictable contingent event benefits or increase in liability due to the plan amendment.

(5) *Additional rules regarding limitations on unpredictable contingent event benefits and certain plan amendments based on presumed adjusted funding target prior to certification*—(i) *Reduction in funding balances*—(A) *Mandatory reduction for collectively bargained plans.* During the period described in paragraph (g)(2) or (g)(3) of this section, the rules of paragraph (a)(5) of this section (relating to the deemed election to reduce the funding standard carryover balance and the prefunding balance) must be applied based on the presumed percentage. In order to determine the amount of the reduction in those balances that would apply to a collectively bargained plan during that period with respect to an unpredictable contingent event or a plan amendment that increases liability for benefits, the rules of paragraph (g)(2)(ii) of this section are applied, except that the presumed adjusted funding target is increased to take into account the benefits attributable to the unpredictable contingent event or the plan amendment. For this purpose, if no presumption applies under the rules of paragraph (h) of this section (for example, because the plan's actual adjusted funding target attainment percentage for the prior year was certified to be at least 80 percent), then that prior year's actual adjusted funding target attainment percentage is substituted for the presumed adjusted funding target attainment percentage for the plan year in determining the presumed adjusted funding target.

(B) *Optional reduction for plans that are not collectively bargained plans.* A plan sponsor of a plan that is not a collectively bargained plan (and, thus, is not required to reduce the funding standard account carryover balance and the prefunding balance under the rules of para-

graph (a)(5) of this section) is permitted to reduce those balances in order to increase the interim value of adjusted plan assets (as defined in paragraph (g)(2)(ii)(A) of this section) that is compared to the presumed adjusted funding target determined under this paragraph (g)(5)(i).

(ii) *Plans funded below the threshold.* If, after application of paragraph (g)(5)(i) of this section, the ratio of the interim value of adjusted plan assets (as defined in paragraph (g)(2)(ii)(A) of this section) to the presumed adjusted funding target determined under that paragraph is less than the applicable threshold under section 436(b) or 436(c), as applicable, then the plan is not permitted to provide any benefits attributable to the unpredictable contingent event or plan amendment unless the plan sponsor makes a contribution that would allow payment of unpredictable contingent event benefits or would permit a plan amendment increasing benefit liabilities to go into effect under the rules of paragraph (b)(2) or (c)(2) of this section.

(iii) *Plans funded at or above the threshold.* If, after application of paragraph (g)(5)(i) of this section, the ratio of the interim value of adjusted plan assets (as defined in paragraph (g)(2)(ii)(A) of this section) to the presumed adjusted funding target is greater than or equal to the applicable threshold under section 436(b) or 436(c), as applicable, then the plan is not permitted to limit the payment of unpredictable contingent event benefits described in paragraph (b) of this section nor is the plan permitted to restrict a plan amendment increasing benefit liability described in paragraph (c) of this section from becoming effective based on an expectation that the limitations under paragraph (b) or (c) of this section will apply to the plan once an actuarial certification is received.

(6) *Application to multiple events and amendments.* For purposes of this paragraph (g), if a plan is providing benefits with respect to one or more unpredictable contingent events occurring within the plan year or amendments taking effect within the plan year, then paragraphs (b) and (c) of this section are applied with respect to a subsequent unpredictable contingent event or amendment by treating the increase in the funding target attributable to the subsequent event or amendment as if it included the increases in the funding target attributable to all such earlier events or amendments.

(7) *Examples.* The following examples illustrate the application of this paragraph (g). Unless otherwise indicated, these examples are based on the following facts: each plan has a plan year that is the calendar year and a valuation date of January 1; the first effective plan year is 2008; the plan sponsor is not in bankruptcy; and no annuity purchases have been made from the plan. No plan is in at-risk status for the years discussed in the examples.

Example 1. (i) As of January 1, 2011, Plan A has assets of $3,300,000 and a prefunding balance of $300,000. Plan A has no funding standard carryover balance. Beginning on January 1, 2011, Plan A's AFTAP for 2011 is presumed to be 75%, under the rules of paragraph (h) of this section and based on the certified AFTAP for 2010.

(ii) Based on Plan A's presumed AFTAP of 75%, Plan A would be subject to the restriction on prohibited payments in paragraph (d)(3) of this section as of January 1, 2011. However, under the provisions of paragraph (a)(5) of this section, if the prefunding balance is large enough, Plan A's sponsor is deemed to elect to reduce the prefunding balance to the extent needed to avoid this restriction.

(iii) The amount needed to avoid the restriction in paragraph (d)(3) of this section is determined by comparing the presumed adjusted funding target for Plan A with the interim value of adjusted plan assets as of the valuation date. The interim value of plan assets for Plan A is $3,000,000 (that is, the asset value of $3,300,000 reduced by the prefunding balance of $300,000). The presumed adjusted funding target for Plan A is the interim value of the adjusted plan assets divided by the presumed AFTAP, or $4,000,000 (that is, $3,000,000 divided by 75%).

(iv) In order to avoid the restriction on prohibited payments in paragraph (d)(3) of this section, Plan A's presumed AFTAP must be increased to 80%. This requires an increase in Plan A's adjusted plan assets of $200,000 (that is, 80% of the presumed adjusted funding target of $4,000,000, minus the interim value of the adjusted plan assets of $3,000,000). Plan A's prefunding balance as of January 1, 2011, is reduced by $200,000 under the deemed election provisions of paragraph (a)(5) of this section. Accordingly, Plan A's prefunding balance is $100,000 (that is, $300,000 minus $200,000) and the interim value of adjusted plan assets is increased to $3,200,000 (that is, $3,300,000 minus the reduced prefunding balance of $100,000). Plan A must pay the full amount of the accelerated benefit distributions elected by participants with an annuity starting date of January 1, 2011, or later.

Example 2. [Reserved.]

Example 3. (i) The facts are the same as in *Example 1.* On July 1, 2011, the enrolled actuary for Plan A calculates the actual adjusted funding target as $3,700,000 as of January 1, 2011. Therefore, the 2011 AFTAP would have been 81.08% without reducing the prefunding balance (that is, plan assets of $3,300,000 minus the prefunding balance of $300,000, divided by the adjusted funding target of $3,700,000), and Plan A would not have been subject to the restrictions under paragraph (d)(3) of this section.

(ii) However, paragraph (g)(4)(i)(C) of this section requires that any prior reductions in the prefunding or funding standard carryover balances continue to apply, and so Plan A's prefunding balance remains at the reduced amount of $100,000 as of January 1, 2011. The enrolled actuary certifies that the 2011 AFTAP is 86.49% (that is, plan assets of $3,300,000 reduced by the prefunding balance of $100,000, divided by the adjusted funding target of $3,700,000).

Example 4. (i) Plan B is a collectively bargained plan with assets of $2,500,000 and a prefunding balance of $150,000 as of January 1, 2011. Plan B has no funding standard carryover balance. Beginning on January 1, 2011, Plan B's AFTAP for 2011 is presumed to be 83% under the rules of paragraph (g)(3) of this section and based on the certified AFTAP for 2010.

(ii) On January 10, 2011, Plan B's sponsor amends the plan to increase benefits effective on February 1, 2011. The amendment would increase Plan B's funding target by $350,000. Under the rules of paragraph (g)(5) of this section, the presumed adjusted funding target is calculated, and then the presumed adjusted funding target is increased to take into account the benefits attributable to the plan amendment.

(iii) Plan B's interim value of adjusted plan assets as of the valuation date is $2,350,000 (that is, $2,500,000 minus the prefunding balance of $150,000). Prior to reflecting the amendment, Plan B's presumed adjusted funding target as of January 1, 2011, is $2,831,325, which is equal to the interim value of adjusted plan assets as of the valuation date of $2,350,000, divided by the presumed AFTAP of 83%. Increasing Plan B's presumed adjusted funding target by $350,000 to reflect the amendment results in a presumed adjusted funding target of $3,181,325 and a presumed AFTAP of 73.87% (that is, the interim value of adjusted plan assets as of the valuation date of $2,350,000 divided by the presumed adjusted funding target of $3,181,325).

(iv) Because Plan B's presumed AFTAP was over 80% prior to taking the amendment into account but less than 80% when the amendment is reflected, section 436(c) and paragraph (c) of this section prohibit the plan amendment from taking effect unless the adjusted plan assets are increased so that the presumed AFTAP (reflecting the increase due to the amendment) is increased to 80%. This would require an additional amount of $195,060 (that is, 80% of the presumed adjusted funding target of $3,181,325 less the interim value of adjusted plan assets of $2,350,000).

(v) Plan B's prefunding balance of $150,000 is not large enough for Plan B to avoid the restriction on plan amendments, and therefore the deemed election to reduce the prefunding balance under paragraph (a)(5) of this section does not apply and the amendment cannot take effect.

Example 5. (i) The facts are the same as in *Example 4,* except that Plan B's sponsor decides to make a contribution on February 1, 2011, to avoid the benefit limitation as provided in paragraph (f)(2) of this section. Pursuant to paragraph (f)(2)(i)(A)(*2*) of this section, Plan B's effective rate of interest for 2011 is treated as 5.25%.

(ii) The amount of the contribution as of January 1, 2011, needed to avoid the restriction on plan amendments under paragraph (c) of this section is $195,060. However, because the contribution is not paid until February 1, 2011, the necessary contribution amount must be adjusted to reflect interest that would otherwise have accrued between the valuation date and the date of the contribution, at Plan B's effective rate of interest for the 2011 plan year. The amount of the required contribution after adjustment is $195,894, determined as $195,060 increased for one month of compound interest at an effective annual interest rate of 5.25%.

(iii) As of April 1, 2011, the enrolled actuary for the plan has not certified the 2011 AFTAP. Therefore, beginning April 1, 2011, Plan A's presumed AFTAP is presumed to be 73%, 10 percentage points lower than the 2010 AFTAP, in accordance with paragraph (h)(2) of this section. However, paragraph (g)(2)(ii)(B) of this section does not require reapplication of the deemed election if necessary to avoid the application of benefit restrictions under paragraph (c) of this section. Therefore, since the effective date of the plan amendment occurred prior to April 1, 2011, no additional reduction in the prefunding balance

is required and no additional contribution is required for the plan amendment to remain in effect.

(iv) On July 1, 2011, the enrolled actuary for the plan calculates the actual adjusted funding target, prior to taking the plan amendment into account, as $2,700,000 and certifies the actual AFTAP for 2011 (prior to taking the amendment into account) as 87.04% (that is, adjusted assets of $2,350,000 divided by the adjusted funding target of $2,700,000). Reflecting the $350,000 increase in funding target due to the plan amendment would increase the adjusted funding target to $3,050,000 and would decrease Plan B's AFTAP to 77.05%.

(v) Based on the certified AFTAP, the amount necessary to avoid the benefit restriction under paragraph (c) of this section is $90,000 (that is, 80% of the adjusted funding target reflecting the plan amendment (or $3,050,000), minus the adjusted value of plan assets of $2,350,000). This amount must be adjusted for interest between the valuation date and the date the contribution was made using the effective interest rate for Plan B. Therefore, the amount required on the payment date of February 1, 2011, is $90,385 (that is, $90,000 adjusted for compound interest for one month at Plan B's effective interest rate of 5.25% per year).

(vi) Under paragraph (g)(3)(ii)(B) of this section, the contribution made under paragraph (g)(5)(ii) of this section is recharacterized as an employer contribution under section 430 to the extent that it exceeds the amount necessary to avoid application of the restriction on plan amendments under paragraph (c) of this section. Therefore, $105,509 (that is, the $195,894 actual contribution paid on February 1, 2011, minus the $90,385 required contribution based on the actual certified AFTAP) is recharacterized as an employer contribution under section 430 for the 2011 plan year. As such, it may be applied toward the minimum required contribution for 2011, or the plan sponsor can elect to credit the contribution to Plan B's prefunding balance to the extent that the contributions for the 2011 plan year exceed the minimum required contribution.

Example 6. (i) The facts are the same as in *Example 5,* except that on July 1, 2011, the enrolled actuary for Plan B calculates the actual adjusted funding target (before reflecting the plan amendment) as $3,000,000 and certifies the actual AFTAP as 78.33% prior to reflecting the plan amendment (that is, adjusted plan assets of $2,350,000 divided by the actual adjusted funding target of $3,000,000). Based on the provisions of paragraph (c) of this section, because the AFTAP prior to reflecting the amendment is less than 80%, the contribution required to avoid the restriction on plan amendments would have been the amount equal to the increase in funding target due to the plan amendment, or $350,000.

(ii) However, according to paragraph (g)(4)(ii)(A) of this section, the enrolled actuary's certification of the 2011 AFTAP does not affect the application of the limitation under paragraph (c) of this section regardless of the extent to which the certified percentage varies from the presumed percentage, because the amendment to Plan B was effective prior to the date of the certification. Therefore, it is not necessary for Plan B's sponsor to contribute an additional amount in order for the plan amendment to remain in effect.

(h) *Presumed underfunding for purposes of benefit limitations*—(1) *Presumption of continued underfunding*—(i) *In general.* This paragraph (h)(1) applies to a plan for which a limitation under paragraph (b), (c), (d), or (e) of this section applied to the plan on the last day of the plan year preceding the current plan year. If this paragraph (h)(1) applies to a plan, the first day of the plan year is a section 436 measurement date and the presumed adjusted funding target attainment percentage for the plan is the percentage under paragraph (h)(1)(ii) or (iii) of this section, whichever applies to the plan, beginning on that first day until it is changed under this paragraph (h).

(ii) *Rule where preceding year certification issued during preceding year.* In any case in which the plan's enrolled actuary has issued a certification under paragraph (h)(4) of this section of the adjusted funding target attainment percentage for the plan year preceding the current year before the first day of the current year, the adjusted funding target attainment percentage of the plan for the current plan year is presumed to be equal to the preceding year's actual adjusted funding target attainment percentage until the plan's enrolled actuary issues a certification of the adjusted funding target attainment percentage of the plan for the current plan year under paragraph (h)(4) of this section or until changed under paragraph (h)(2) or (h)(3) of this section.

(iii) *No certification for preceding year issued during preceding year*—(A) *Deemed percentage under 60 percent.* In any case in which the plan's enrolled actuary has not issued a certification under paragraph (h)(4) of this section of the adjusted funding target attainment percentage of the plan for the plan year preceding the current year during that prior plan year, the adjusted funding target attainment percentage of the plan for the current plan year is presumed to be less than 60 percent until changed under paragraph (h)(1)(iii)(B) or (h)(2)(iii) of this section or where the plan's enrolled actuary issues the certification of the adjusted funding target attainment percentage for the current year under paragraph (h)(4) of this section.

(B) *Enrolled actuary's certification in first 3 months of following year.* In any case in which the plan's enrolled actuary has issued the certification under paragraph (h)(4) of this section of the adjusted funding target attainment percentage of the plan for the plan year preceding the current year on or after the first day of the current year but before the first day of the 4th month of that year, the date of that prior year certification is a new section 436 measurement date for the plan year. In such a case, until it is changed by a certification of the current year's adjusted funding target attainment percentage under paragraph (h)(4) of this section or otherwise changed under paragraph (h)(2) or (h)(3) of this section, the presumed percentage for the current year beginning on the date of certification is equal to the certified percentage for the preceding year.

(2) *Presumption of underfunding after first day of 4th month for nearly underfunded plans*—(i) *In general.* This paragraph (h)(2) applies to a plan for which the actual adjusted funding target attainment percentage for the plan year preceding the current plan year was certified for that prior plan year to be at least 60 percent but less than 70 percent, or was certified for that prior plan year to be at least 80 percent but less than 90 percent (or, if that prior plan year is the pre-effective plan year, was certified to be less than 90 percent), and where the enrolled actuary for the plan has not issued a certification of the adjusted funding target attainment percentage for the plan year by the first day of the 4th month of the plan year. If this paragraph (h)(2) applies to a plan, the presumed adjusted funding target attainment percentage for the plan is the percentage under paragraph (h)(2)(ii) or (iii) of this section, as applicable.

(ii) *Presumed adjusted funding target attainment percentage.* If this paragraph (h)(2) applies to a plan, and the date of the enrolled actuary's certification under paragraph (h)(4) of this section for the plan year preceding the current year occurred before the first day of the 4th month of the current plan year, then, commencing on the first day of the 4th month of the current plan year and continuing until the earlier of the date the enrolled actuary issues a certification under paragraph (h)(4) of this section of the adjusted funding target attainment percentage for the plan year or the first day of the 10th month of the plan year as described in paragraph (h)(3) of this section—

(A) The adjusted funding target attainment percentage of the plan as of the valuation date for the plan year is presumed to be equal to 10 percentage points less than the actual adjusted funding target attainment percentage of the plan for the preceding plan year; and

(B) The first day of the 4th month of the plan year is treated as a section 436 measurement date.

(iii) *Certification for prior year.* If this paragraph (h)(2) applies to a plan, and the date of the enrolled actuary's certification under paragraph (h)(4) of this section of the actual adjusted funding target attainment percentage for the plan year preceding the current year occurs on or after the first day of the 4th month of the current plan year, then, commencing on the date of that prior year certification and continuing until the earlier of the date the enrolled actuary issues a certification under paragraph (h)(4) of this section of the adjusted funding target attainment percentage for the plan year or the first day of the 10th month of the plan year as described in paragraph (h)(3) of this section—

(A) The adjusted funding target attainment percentage of the plan as of the valuation date for the plan year is presumed to be equal to 10 percentage points less than the actual adjusted funding target attainment percentage of the plan for the preceding plan year; and

(B) The date of the prior year certification is treated as a section 436 measurement date.

(3) *Presumption of underfunding on and after first day of 10th month*—(i) *Section 436 measurement date.* In any case in which no certification of the specific adjusted funding target attainment percentage for the current plan year under paragraph (h)(4) of this section is made with respect to the plan before the first day of the 10th month of the plan year, that first day is treated as a section 436 measurement date.

(ii) *Presumed percentage under 60 percent.* In any case in which no certification of the specific adjusted funding target attainment percentage for the current plan year under paragraph (h)(4) of this section is made with respect to the plan before the first day of the 10th month of the plan year, the plan's adjusted funding target attainment percentage

is presumed to be less than 60 percent beginning on that date and continuing through the remainder of the plan year.

(4) *Certification of adjusted funding target attainment percentage*—(i) *Rules generally applicable to certifications*—(A) *In general.* The enrolled actuary's certification referred to in this section must be made in writing, must be provided to the plan administrator, and, except as provided in paragraph (h)(4)(ii) of this section, must certify the plan's adjusted funding target attainment percentage for the plan year (including setting forth the aggregate amount of annuity purchases taken into account under paragraph (j)(3)(ii) of this section).

(B) *Determination of plan assets.* For purposes of making any determination of the adjusted funding target attainment percentage under this section, the determination is not permitted to take into account assets that have not been contributed to the plan by the certification date. For example, the enrolled actuary's certification of the adjusted funding target attainment percentage for a plan year cannot take into account contributions that are expected to be made after the certification date. Notwithstanding the foregoing, for plan years beginning before January 1, 2009, the enrolled actuary's certification of the adjusted funding target attainment percentage is permitted to take into account employer contributions for the prior plan year that are reasonably expected to be made for that prior plan year but have not been contributed by the date of the enrolled actuary's certification. See paragraph (h)(4)(iii) of this section for rules relating to changes in the certified percentage.

(ii) *Special rules for certification within range*—(A) *In general.* Under this paragraph (h)(4)(ii), the plan's enrolled actuary is permitted to certify during the first nine months of a plan year that the plan's adjusted funding target attainment percentage for that plan year either is 60 percent or higher (but is less than 80 percent), is 80 percent or higher, or is 100 percent or higher. If the enrolled actuary has issued such a range certification for a plan year and the enrolled actuary subsequently issues a certification of the specific adjusted funding target attainment percentage for the plan before the first day of the 10th month of that plan year, the certification of the specific adjusted funding target attainment percentage is treated as a change in the applicable percentage to which paragraph (h)(4)(iii) of this section applies. If a the enrolled actuary has issued a range certification for a plan year but no specific certification of the adjusted funding target attainment percentage of the plan for the plan year is issued by the plan's enrolled actuary before the first day of the 10th month of that plan year, then the rules of paragraph (h)(3) of this section apply and the change in the applicable percentage to under 60 percent on that date is treated as a change in the applicable percentage which is subject to the rules of paragraph (h)(4)(iii) of this section.

(B) *Effect of range certification*—(*1*) *Before certification of specific percentage.* If a plan's enrolled actuary issues a range certification pursuant to this paragraph (h)(4)(ii), then, for all purposes under this section (for example, applying the limitations of sections 436(b) and (c), making contributions described in sections 436(b)(2), 436(c)(2), and 436(e)(2), and the mandatory reduction of funding balances under paragraph (a)(5) of this section), the plan is treated as having a certified percentage at the smallest value within the applicable range.

(*2*) *On and after certification of specific percentage.* Once the certification of the specific adjusted funding target attainment percentage is issued by the plan's enrolled actuary (before the first day of the 10th month of the plan year), that certified percentage applies for all purposes of this section on and after the date of that certification. If the plan sponsor made section 436 contributions to avoid application of a benefit limitation during the period a range certification was in effect, those section 436 contributions will be recharacterized as employer contributions under section 430 to the extent the contributions exceed the amount necessary to avoid application of a limitation based on the specific adjusted funding target attainment percentage as certified by the plan's enrolled actuary before the first day of the 10th month of the plan year.

(iii) *Change of certified percentage*—(A) *Application of new percentage.* If the enrolled actuary for the plan provides a certification of the adjusted funding target attainment percentage of the plan for the plan year under this paragraph (h)(4) (including a range certification) and that certified percentage is superseded by a subsequent determination of the adjusted funding target attainment percentage for that plan year, that later percentage must be applied.

(B) *Determination of materiality*—(*1*) *In general.* With respect to the effect of that subsequent determination of the adjusted funding target attainment percentage on the plan for the period during which the plan's operation was based on the prior percentage, a determination must be made whether the change in the applicable percentage is a material change or an immaterial change.

(*2*) *Definition of material change.* For this purpose, there is a material change in a plan's certified adjusted funding target attainment percentage if plan operations with respect to benefits that are addressed by section 436, taking into account any actual contributions and elections under section 430(f) made by the plan sponsor based on the prior certified percentage, would have been different based on the subsequent determination of the plan's adjusted funding target attainment percentage for the plan year. However, if the difference between the adjusted funding target attainment percentage for a plan year and the later revised determination of that percentage is the result of additional contributions for the preceding year that are made by the plan sponsor after the date of the enrolled actuary's certification or results from the plan sponsor's election to reduce the prefunding balance or funding standard carryover balance after the date of the certification, such change is not treated as a material change.

(*3*) *Definition of immaterial change.* An immaterial change is any change in an adjusted funding target attainment percentage for a plan year that is not a material change.

(C) *Effect of change in percentage*—(*1*) *Material change.* In the case of a material change where the plan was operated in accordance with the prior certification of the adjusted funding target attainment percentage for the plan year, the plan will not have satisfied the requirements of section 401(a)(29) and section 436. In the case of a material change where the plan was operated in accordance with the subsequent certification of the adjusted funding target attainment percentage during the period of time the prior certification applied, the plan will not have been operated in accordance with its terms. In addition, in the case of a material change, the rules requiring application of a presumed adjusted funding target attainment percentage under paragraphs (h)(1) through (h)(3) of this section continue to apply from and after the date of the prior certification until the date of the subsequent certification.

(*2*) *Effect of immaterial change.* If the enrolled actuary for a plan provides a certification of the adjusted funding target attainment percentage of the plan for the plan year under this paragraph (h)(4) and that certified percentage is superseded by a subsequent determination of the adjusted funding target attainment percentage for that plan year that does not result in a material change under paragraph (h)(4)(iii)(B) of this section, the revised percentage does not change the inapplicability of the presumptions under paragraphs (h)(1), (2), and (3) of this section prior to the date of the later certification.

(5) *Application to plan with valuation date after first day of plan year.* [Reserved].

(6) *Examples of application of paragraphs (h)(1), (h)(2), and (h)(3) of this section.* The following examples illustrate the application of paragraphs (h)(1), (h)(2), and (h)(3) of this section. Unless otherwise indicated, the examples in this section are based on the information in this paragraph. Each plan is a non-collectively bargained defined benefit plan with a plan year that is the calendar year and a valuation date of January 1. The first effective plan year is 2008. The plan does not have a funding standard carryover balance or a prefunding balance as of any of the dates mentioned, and the plan sponsor does not elect to utilize any of the methods in paragraph (f) of this section to avoid applicable benefit restrictions. No range certification under paragraph (h)(4) of this section has been issued. The plan sponsor is not in bankruptcy.

Example 1. (i) On July 15, 2010, the adjusted funding target attainment percentage ("AFTAP") for Plan T is certified to be 65%. Based on this AFTAP, Plan T is subject to the restriction on prohibited payments in paragraph (d)(3) of this section for the remainder of 2010.

(ii) Beginning January 1, 2011, Plan T's AFTAP for 2011 is presumed to be equal to the AFTAP for 2010, or 65%, under the provisions of paragraph (h)(1)(ii) of this section. Accordingly, the restriction on accelerated benefit distributions in paragraph (d)(3) of this section continues to apply.

(iii) On March 1, 2011, the enrolled actuary for the plan certifies that the actual AFTAP for 2011 is 80%. Therefore, beginning March 1, 2011, Plan T is no longer subject to the restriction under paragraph (d)(3) of this section, and so Plan T resumes paying the full amount of any accelerated benefit distributions elected by participants with an annuity starting date of March 1, 2011, or later.

Example 2. (i) The facts are the same as in *Example 1,* except that the enrolled actuary for the plan does not certify the AFTAP for 2011 until June 1, 2011. Accordingly, Plan T's AFTAP for 2011 is presumed to be equal to the AFTAP for 2010 of 65% from January 1, 2011, through March 31, 2011, and Plan T is subject to the restriction on accelerated benefit distributions under paragraph (d)(3) of this section during this period.

(ii) Beginning April 1, 2011, the provisions of paragraph (h)(2)(ii) of this section apply because the enrolled actuary for the plan still has not certified the actual AFTAP as of January 1, 2011. Under the provisions of paragraph (h)(2)(ii) of this section, the AFTAP for Plan T is presumed to be 10 percentage points lower, or 55%, beginning April 1, 2011. Accordingly, Plan T is now subject to the restriction in paragraph (d)(1) of this section, and so cannot pay any accelerated benefit distributions otherwise payable to plan participants who have annuity starting dates on or after April 1, 2011.

(iii) On June 1, 2011, the enrolled actuary for the plan certifies that the AFTAP for 2011 for Plan T is 66%. Accordingly, Plan T is no longer subject to the restriction under paragraph (d)(1) of this section, but it is subject to the restriction under paragraph (d)(3) of this section.

(iv) Since Plan T is no longer subject to the restriction on payment of accelerated benefit distributions under paragraph (d)(1) of this section, Plan T must resume paying the accelerated benefit distributions, as restricted under paragraph (d)(3) of this section, for participants who elect benefits in accelerated forms of payment and who have an annuity starting date of June 1, 2011, or later.

Example 3. (i) The facts are the same as in *Example 1,* except that the enrolled actuary for the plan does not certify the 2011 AFTAP until November 15, 2011. Beginning October 1, 2011, Plan T is conclusively presumed to have an AFTAP of less than 60%, in accordance with the provisions of paragraph (h)(3) of this section. Accordingly, Plan T is subject to the restriction in paragraph (d)(1) of this section, and cannot pay any accelerated benefit distributions to participants whose annuity starting date occurs on or after October 1, 2011.

(ii) On November 15, 2011, the enrolled actuary for the plan certifies that the AFTAP for 2011 is 72%. However, because the certification occurred after October 1, 2011, the certification does not constitute a new section 436 measurement date, and Plan T continues to be subject to the restrictions on accelerated benefit distributions and benefit accruals under paragraphs (d)(1) and (e) of this section.

(iii) Beginning January 1, 2012, the 2012 AFTAP for Plan T is presumed to be equal to the 2011 AFTAP of 72%. Because the presumed 2012 AFTAP is between 70% and 80% and, therefore, paragraph (h)(2) of this section (which provides for a 10 percentage point reduction in a plan's AFTAP in certain cases) will not apply, the presumed AFTAP will remain at 72% until the plan's enrolled actuary certifies the AFTAP for 2012 or until paragraph (h)(3) of this section applies on the first day of the 10th month of the plan year. Because the presumed AFTAP is 72%, Plan T is no longer subject to the restrictions on accelerated benefit distributions under paragraph (d)(1) of this section, and Plan T must resume paying accelerated benefit distributions, as restricted under paragraph (d)(3) of this section, that are elected by participants with annuity starting dates on or after January 1, 2012. Similarly, Plan T is no longer subject to the restriction on benefit accruals under paragraph (e) of this section, and benefit accruals resume under Plan T beginning January 1, 2012, unless Plan T provides otherwise.

Example 4. (i) The facts are the same as in *Example 3,* except that the enrolled actuary for the plan does not issue a certification of the AFTAP for 2011 for Plan T until February 1, 2012.

(ii) Beginning on January 1, 2012, the presumptions in paragraph (h)(1)(iii) of this section apply for the 2012 plan year. Because the enrolled actuary for the plan has not certified the AFTAP for 2011, the presumed AFTAP as of October 1, 2011, continues to apply for the period beginning January 1, 2012. Therefore, the AFTAP as of January 1, 2012, is presumed to be less than 60%, and Plan T continues to be subject to the restriction on accelerated benefit distributions in paragraph (d)(1) of this section and the restriction on benefit accruals under paragraph (e) of this section.

(iii) On February 1, 2012, the enrolled actuary for the plan certifies that the AFTAP for 2011 for Plan T is 65%. Because the enrolled actuary for the plan has not issued a certification of the AFTAP for 2012, the provisions of paragraph (h)(1)(iii)(B) of this section apply. Accordingly, the certification date for the 2011 AFTAP (February 1, 2012) is a section 436 measurement date and 65% is the presumed AFTAP for 2012 beginning on that date.

(iv) Because the presumed AFTAP is over 60% but less than 80%, the full restriction on accelerated benefit distributions under paragraph (d)(1) of this section no longer applies; however the partial restriction on accelerated benefit distributions under paragraph (d)(3) of this section applies beginning on February 1, 2012. Therefore, Plan T must pay a portion of accelerated benefit distributions elected by participants with annuity starting dates on or after February 1, 2012. Furthermore, based on the presumed AFTAP of 65%, the restriction on benefit accruals under paragraph (e) of this section no longer applies, and unless Plan T provides otherwise, benefit accruals will resume as of February 1, 2012.

Example 5. (i) The facts are the same as in *Example 3*, except that the enrolled actuary for the plan does not issue a certification of the actual AFTAP for Plan T as of January 1, 2011, until May 1, 2012.

(ii) Beginning on January 1, 2012, the presumptions in paragraph (h)(1)(iii) of this section apply for the 2012 plan year. Because the enrolled actuary for the plan has not certified the actual AFTAP as of January 1, 2011, the presumed AFTAP as of October 1, 2011, continues to apply for the period beginning January 1, 2012. Therefore, the AFTAP as of January 1, 2012, is presumed to be less than 60%, and Plan T continues to be subject to the restriction on accelerated benefit distributions in paragraph (d)(1) of this section and the restriction on benefit accruals under paragraph (e) of this section.

(iii) Since the enrolled actuary for the plan has not issued a certification of the actual AFTAP as of January 1, 2011, the rules of paragraph (h)(1)(iii) of this section apply beginning April 1, 2012, and the AFTAP is presumed to remain less than 60%. Plan T continues to be subject to the restriction on accelerated benefit distributions and benefit accruals under paragraphs (d)(1) and (e) of this section.

(iv) On May 1, 2012, the enrolled actuary for the plan certifies that the actual AFTAP for 2011 for Plan T is 65%. Because the enrolled actuary for the plan has not issued a certification of the actual AFTAP as of January 1, 2012, the provisions of paragraph (h)(2)(iii) of this section apply. Accordingly, on May 1, 2012, the 2012 AFTAP is presumed to be 10 percentage points less than the 2011 AFTAP, or 55%, so that the restrictions under paragraphs (d) and (e) of this section continue to apply.

Example 6. (i) The enrolled actuary for Plan V certifies the plan's AFTAP for 2010 to be 69%. Based on this AFTAP, Plan V is subject to the restriction in paragraph (d)(3) of this section, and can only pay a portion (generally 50%) of accelerated benefit distributions otherwise due to plan participants who commence benefits while the restriction is in effect. The enrolled actuary for the plan does not issue a certification of the AFTAP for 2011 until June 1, 2011.

(ii) Beginning January 1, 2011, Plan V's 2011 AFTAP is presumed to be equal to the 2010 AFTAP, or 69%, under the provisions of paragraph (h)(1)(ii) of this section. Accordingly, the restriction on accelerated benefit distributions in paragraph (d)(3) of this section continues to apply from January 1, 2011, through March 31, 2011, and Plan T may only pay a portion of accelerated benefit distributions otherwise due to participants who commence benefit payments during this period.

(iii) Beginning April 1, 2011, the provisions of paragraph (h)(2)(ii) of this section apply. Under those provisions, the AFTAP beginning April 1, 2011, is presumed to be 10 percentage points lower than the presumed 2011 AFTAP, or 59%. Because Plan V's presumed AFTAP for 2011 is less than 60%, the restriction on the payment of accelerated benefit distributions under paragraph (d)(1) of this section and the restriction on benefit accruals under paragraph (e) of this section apply. Accordingly, Plan V cannot pay any accelerated benefit distributions to participants with an annuity starting date on or after April 1, 2011, and benefit accruals cease as of March 31, 2011.

(iv) On June 1, 2011, Plan V's enrolled actuary certifies that the plan's AFTAP for 2011 is 71%. Therefore, the restrictions on accelerated benefit distributions and benefit accruals in paragraphs (d)(1) and (e) of this section no longer apply, but the partial restriction on benefit payments in paragraph (d)(3) of this section does apply. Accordingly, Plan V begins paying a portion of the accelerated benefit distributions elected by participants with an annuity starting date on or after June 1, 2011, and benefit accruals previously restricted under paragraph (e) of this section resume effective June 1, 2011, unless Plan V provides otherwise.

(v) Participants who were not able to elect an accelerated form of payment during the period from April 1, 2011, through May 31, 2011, would be able to elect a new annuity starting date with a partial distribution of accelerated benefits effective June 1, 2011, if Plan V contained a preexisting provision permitting such an election after the restriction in paragraph (d)(1) of this section no longer applies. This is permitted because, under paragraph (a)(4)(ii)(A) of this section, a preexisting provision of this type is not considered a plan amendment and is therefore not subject to the plan amendment restriction in paragraph (c) of this section even though Plan V's AFTAP for 2011 is less than 80%.

(vi) Benefit accruals for the period beginning April 1, 2011, through May 31, 2011, would be automatically restored if Plan V contained a preexisting provision to retroactively restore benefit accruals restricted under paragraph (e) of this section after the restriction no longer

applies. This is permitted because under paragraph (a)(4)(ii)(A) of this section, a preexisting provision of this type is not considered to be a plan amendment and is therefore not subject to the plan amendment restriction in paragraph (c) of this section even though Plan V's AFTAP for 2011 is less than 80%, because the period of the restriction did not exceed 12 months.

(7) *Examples of application of paragraph (h)(4) of this section.* The following examples illustrate the application of paragraph (h)(4) of this section:

Example 1. (i) Plan Y is a non-collectively bargained defined benefit plan with a plan year that is the calendar year and a valuation date of January 1. Plan Y does not have a funding standard carryover balance or a prefunding balance. Plan Y's sponsor is not in bankruptcy. In June of 2010, the actual AFTAP for 2010 for Plan Y is certified as 65%. On the last day of the 2010 plan year, Plan Y is subject to the restrictions in paragraph (d)(3) of this section.

(ii) The enrolled actuary for the plan issues a range certification on March 21, 2011, certifying that the AFTAP for 2011 is at least 60% and less than 80%. Because the certification was issued before the first day of the 4th month of the plan year, the 10 percentage point reduction in the presumed AFTAP under paragraph (h)(2) of this section does not apply. In addition, because the enrolled actuary for the plan has certified that the AFTAP is within this range, Plan Y is not subject to the full restriction on accelerated benefit payments in paragraph (d)(1) of this section or the restriction on benefit accruals under paragraph (e) of this section.

(iii) On August 1, 2011, the enrolled actuary for the plan certifies that the actual AFTAP as of January 1, 2011, is 75.86%. This AFTAP falls within the previously certified range. Thus, the change is immaterial under paragraph (h)(4)(iii) of this section and the new certification does not change the applicability or inapplicability of the restrictions in this section.

Example 2. (i) The facts are the same as in *Example 1*, except that the plan sponsor makes an additional contribution for the 2010 plan year on September 1, 2011, that is not added to the prefunding balance. Reflecting this contribution, the enrolled actuary for the plan issues a revised certification stating that the AFTAP for 2011 is 81%, and Plan Y is no longer subject to the restriction on accelerated benefit payments under paragraph (d)(3) of this section on that date.

(ii) Although the revised certification changes the applicability of the restriction under paragraph (d)(3) of this section, the change not a material change under paragraph (h)(4)(iii)(B)(*2*) of this section because it changed only because of additional contributions for the preceding year made by the plan sponsor after the date of the enrolled actuary's initial certification.

(i) [Reserved].

(j) *Definitions.* For purposes of this section—

(1) *Funding target.* For purposes of section 436, the *funding target* means the funding target under section 430(d) or 430(i), as applicable to the plan for the plan year.

(2) *Funding target attainment percentage*—(i) *In general.* For purposes of section 436, the *funding target attainment percentage* for any plan year is the fraction (expressed as a percentage), the numerator of which is the value of net plan assets for the plan year, and the denominator of which is the plan's funding target for the plan year (but determined without regard to the at-risk rules under section 430(i) even in the case of a plan that is in at-risk status). For this purpose, pursuant to section 430(f)(4), the value of net plan assets for the plan year is generally determined by subtracting the plan's funding standard carryover balance and prefunding balance (if any) for the plan year from the value of plan assets. A plan with a value of net plan assets for a plan year of zero is treated as having a funding target attainment percentage of zero, regardless of the amount of the plan's funding target.

(ii) *Application to plans that are fully funded without regard to subtraction of funding balances from plan assets*—(A) *In general.* If the funding target attainment percentage for a plan year, determined without regard to the section 430(f)(4) subtraction of the funding standard carryover balance and the prefunding balance from the value of plan assets, would be 100 percent or more, then, solely for purposes of section 436 and this section (but not section 430(d)), the value of net plan assets used in the determination of the funding target attainment percentage described in this paragraph (j)(2) (and the adjusted funding target attainment percentage described in paragraph (j)(3) of this section) is determined without regard to any subtraction of funding balances under section 430(f)(4).

(B) *Transition rule.* Paragraph (j)(2)(ii)(A) of this section is applied to plan years beginning after 2007 and before 2011 by substituting for

In the case of a plan year beginning in calendar year:	The applicable percentage is:
2008	92
2009	94
2010	96

(C) *Limitation.* Paragraph (j)(2)(ii)(B) of this section does not apply with respect to any plan year after 2008 unless the funding target attainment percentage (determined without regard to the section 430(f)(4) subtraction of the funding standard carryover balance and the prefunding balance from the value of plan assets) of the plan for each preceding plan year (after 2007) was not less than the applicable percentage with respect to such preceding plan year determined under paragraph (j)(2)(ii)(B) of this section.

(iii) *Special rules for first effective plan year*—(A) *In general.* In the case of the plan's first effective plan year, the funding target attainment percentage under section 436 for the plan's pre-effective plan year is determined as the fraction (expressed as a percentage), the numerator of which is the net plan assets determined under paragraph (j)(2)(iii)(B) of this section, and the denominator of which is the plan's current liability determined pursuant to section 412(l)(7) on the valuation date for the plan's pre-effective plan year.

(B) *General determination of value of net plan assets*—(*1*) *In general.* The value of net plan assets for purposes of this paragraph (j)(2)(iii) is determined under section 412(c)(2) as in effect for the plan's pre-effective plan year, except that the value of plan assets prior to subtracting the plan's funding standard account credit balance described in paragraph (j)(2)(iii)(B)(*2*) of this section can neither be less than 90 percent of the fair market value of plan assets nor greater than 110 percent of the fair market value of plan assets on the valuation date for that plan year.

(*2*) *Subtraction of credit balance.* If a plan has a funding standard account credit balance as of the valuation date for the plan's pre-effective plan year, that balance is subtracted from the net asset value described in paragraph (j)(2)(iii)(B)(*1*) of this section as of that valuation date. However, the subtraction does not apply if the value of plan assets determined in paragraph (j)(2)(iii)(B)(*1*) of this section is greater than or equal to 90 percent of the plan's current liability as of the valuation date for the plan determined under paragraph (j)(2)(iii)(A) of this section.

(*3*) *Effect of funding standard carryover balance reduction for first effective plan year.* Notwithstanding paragraph (j)(2)(iii)(B)(*2*) of this section, if, for the first effective plan year, the employer has made an election to reduce some or all of the funding standard carryover balance as of the first day of that year in accordance with §1.430(f)-1(e), then the present value (determined as of the valuation date for the pre-effective plan year using the valuation interest rate for that pre-effective plan year) of the amount so reduced is not treated as part of the funding standard account credit balance when that balance is subtracted from the asset value under paragraph (j)(2)(iii)(B)(*2*) of this section.

(3) *Adjusted funding target attainment percentage*—(i) *In general.* The *adjusted funding target attainment percentage* for any plan year is the fraction (expressed as a percentage), the numerator of which is the adjusted plan assets described in paragraph (j)(3)(ii) of this section and the denominator of which is the adjusted funding target described in paragraph (j)(3)(iii) of this section.

(ii) *Adjusted plan assets.* The adjusted plan assets equals the net plan assets (determined under paragraph (j)(2) of this section), increased by the aggregate amount of purchases of annuities for employees other than highly compensated employees (as defined in section 414(q)) which were made by the plan during the preceding 2 plan years.

(iii) *Adjusted funding target*—(A) *In general.* The adjusted funding target equals the funding target for the plan year (determined in accordance with paragraph (j)(1) of this section but without regard to the at-risk rules under section 430(i)), increased by the aggregate amount of purchases of annuities for employees other than highly compensated employees (as defined in section 414(q)) which were made by the plan during the preceding 2 plan years.

(B) *Special rule for first effective plan year.* In the case of the plan's first effective plan year, for purposes of determining the adjusted funding target attainment percentage for the pre-effective plan year, the adjusted funding target is equal to the current liability determined pursuant to section 412(l)(7) as of the plan's valuation date for the pre-effective plan year, increased by the aggregate amount of purchases of annuities for employees other than highly compensated employees (as

defined in section 414(q)) which were made by the plan during the preceding 2 plan years.

(iv) *Special rule where current liability not certified for pre-effective plan year.* In any case in which the plan's enrolled actuary has not issued a certification under paragraph (h)(4)(i) of this section of the adjusted funding target attainment percentage of the plan for the pre-effective plan year, the adjusted funding target attainment percentage of the plan for the first effective plan year is presumed to be less than 60 percent until the adjusted funding target attainment percentage of the plan for the pre-effective plan year has been certified. The preceding sentence applies for purposes of paragraphs (b) and (c) of this section at the beginning of the first effective plan year and applies for purposes of paragraphs (d) and (e) of this section as of the first day of the 4th month of the first effective plan year. See paragraph (h) of this section for rules that apply after the adjusted funding target attainment percentage for the plan has been certified for either the pre-effective plan year or the first effective plan year.

(4) *Section 436 measurement date.* The section 436 measurement date is the date that is used to stop or start the application of the limitations of sections 436(d) and 436(e), and is also used for calculations with respect to applying the limitations of paragraphs (b) and (c) of this section. See paragraph (h) of this section regarding section 436 measurement dates that result from application of the presumptions under that paragraph (h) of this section.

(5) *Examples.* The following examples illustrate the application of this paragraph (j):

Example 1. (i) Plan S is a non-collectively bargained defined benefit plan with a plan year that is the calendar year and a valuation date of January 1. The first effective plan year is 2008.

(ii) As of January 1, 2008, Plan S has a value of plan assets (equal to the market value of assets) of $2,100,000 and a funding standard carryover balance of $200,000. During 2006, assets from Plan S were used to purchase a total of $100,000 in annuities for employees other than highly compensated employees. No annuities were purchased during 2007. On May 1, 2008, the enrolled actuary for the plan determines that the funding target as of January 1, 2008, is $2,500,000.

(iii) The adjusted value of assets for Plan S as of January 1, 2008, is $2,000,000 (that is, plan assets of $2,100,000 plus annuity purchases of $100,000 minus the funding standard carryover balance of $200,000). The adjusted funding target is $2,600,000 (that is, the funding target of $2,500,000, increased by the annuity purchases of $100,000).

(iv) Based on the above adjusted plan assets and adjusted funding target, the AFTAP as of January 1, 2008, would be 76.92%. Since the AFTAP is less than 80% but is at least 60%, Plan S is subject to the restrictions in paragraph (d)(3) of this section.

Example 2. (i) The facts are the same as in *Example 1*, except that it is reasonable to expect that the plan sponsor will make a contribution of $80,000 to Plan S for the 2007 plan year by September 15, 2008. This amount is in excess of the minimum required contribution for 2007. The plan sponsor elects to reduce the funding standard carryover balance by $80,000.

(ii) Because it is reasonable to expect that the $80,000 will be contributed by the plan sponsor, that amount is taken into account when the enrolled actuary certifies the 2008 AFTAP under the special rule in paragraph (h)(4)(i)(B) of this section for plan years beginning before 2009. Accordingly, the enrolled actuary for the plan certifies the 2008 AFTAP as 80% (that is, adjusted plan assets of $2,080,000, reflecting the $80,000 in contributions receivable, divided by the adjusted funding target of $2,600,000).

(iii) The ability to take contributions into account before they are actually paid to the plan is available only for plan years beginning before 2009. Furthermore, if the employer does not actually make the contribution and the difference between the incorrect certification and the corrected AFTAP constitutes a material change, the plan will have violated section 401(a)(29) or will not have been operated in accordance with its terms.

Example 3. (i) Plan R is a defined benefit plan with a plan year that is the calendar year and a valuation date of January 1. The first effective plan year for Plan R is 2008. The valuation interest rate for the 2007 plan year for Plan R is 7%. The fair market value of assets of Plan R as of January 1, 2007, is $1,000,000. The actuarial value of assets of Plan R as of January 1, 2007, is $1,200,000. The current liability of Plan R as of January 1, 2007, is $1,500,000. The funding standard account credit balance as of January 1, 2007, is $80,000. The funding standard carry-over balance of Plan R is $50,000 as of the beginning of the 2008 plan year. The sponsor of Plan R, Sponsor T, elects in 2008 to reduce the funding standard carryover balance in accordance with § 1.430(f)-1 by $45,000.

(ii) Pursuant to paragraph (j)(2)(iii)(B)(*1*) of this section, the asset value used to determine the funding target attainment percentage (FTAP) for the 2007 plan year is limited to 110% of the fair market value of assets on January 1, 2007, or $1,100,000 (110% of $1,000,000).

(iii) Pursuant to paragraph (j)(2)(iii)(B)(*2*) of this section, the funding standard account credit balance as of January 1, 2007, is subtracted from the asset value used to determine the FTAP for the 2007 plan year. However, pursuant to paragraph (j)(2)(iii)(B)(*3*) of this section, the present value of the amount by which Sponsor T elected to reduce the funding standard carryover balance in 2008 is not subtracted.

(iv) The present value, determined at an interest rate of 7%, of the $45,000 reduction in the funding standard account carryover balance elected by Sponsor T in 2008 is $42,056. Thus, $42,056 is not subtracted from the 2007 plan year asset value. Accordingly, the funding standard account credit balance that is subtracted from the 2007 plan year asset value is $37,944 (that is, $80,000 less $42,056).

(v) Thus, the asset value that is used to determine the FTAP for the 2007 plan year is $1,100,000 less $37,944, or $1,062,056. Accordingly, for purposes of this section, the FTAP for the 2007 plan year for Plan R is 70.8% (that is, $1,062,056 divided by $1,500,000).

(k) *Effective/applicability dates*—(1) *In general.* In general, this section applies to plan years beginning on or after January 1, 2008.

(2) *Plans with delayed effective/applicability date.* In the case of a plan for which the effective date of section 436 is delayed in accordance with sections 104 through 106 of the Pension Protection Act of 2006, Public Law 109-280, 120 Stat. 780, this section applies to plan years beginning on or after the effective date of section 436 with respect to the plan.

(3) *Collective bargaining exception*—(i) *In general.* In the case of a collectively bargained plan that is maintained pursuant to one or more collective bargaining agreements between employee representatives and one or more employers ratified before January 1, 2008, this section does not apply to plan years beginning before the earlier of—

(A) The date described in paragraph (k)(3)(ii) of this section; or

(B) January 1, 2010.

(ii) *Termination of collective bargaining agreement.* The date described in this paragraph (k)(3)(ii) is the later of—

(A) The date on which the last collective bargaining agreement relating to the plan terminates (determined in accordance with paragraph (k)(3)(iii) of this section and without regard to any extension thereof agreed to after August 17, 2006); or

(B) The first day of the first plan year to which this section would (but for this paragraph (k)(3)) apply.

(iii) *Treatment of certain plan amendments.* Any plan amendment made pursuant to a collective bargaining agreement relating to the plan which amends the plan solely to conform to any requirement added by section 436 is not treated as a termination of the collective bargaining agreement.

(iv) *Treatment of plans with both collectively bargained and non-collectively bargained employees.* In the case of a plan with respect to which a collective bargaining agreement applies to some, but not all, of the plan participants, the plan is considered a collectively bargained plan for purposes of this paragraph (k)(3) if it is considered a collectively bargained plan under the rules of paragraph (a)(5)(ii)(B) of this section.

(4) *First effective plan year.* For purposes of this section, the first effective plan year for a plan is the first plan year to which this section applies under paragraph (k)(1), (k)(2), or (k)(3) of this section.

(5) *Pre-effective plan year.* For purposes of this section, the pre-effective plan year for a plan is the last plan year beginning before the effective date applicable under paragraph (k)(1), (k)(2), or (k)(3) of this section. Thus, except for plans with a delayed effective date under paragraph (k)(2) or (k)(3) of this section, the pre-effective plan year for a plan is the last plan year beginning before January 1, 2008.

Kevin M. Brown

Deputy Commissioner for Services and Enforcement

¶ 20,262E

IRS proposed regulations: Qualified automatic contribution arrangements: 401k: 403(b): 457(b).—The IRS has released proposed regulations that will allow sponsors of 401(k), 403(b), and 457(b) plans greater flexibility in implementing qualified automatic contribution arrangements. The proposed rules permit variations in the elective deferral percentage and provide for a deemed timing rule that will allow for satisfaction of the annual notice requirement.

The regulations are proposed to be effective for plan years beginning on or after January 1, 2008, but may be relied upon pending issuance of the final rules.

The proposed regulations, which were published in the Federal Register on November 8, 2007 (72 FR 63144), are reproduced below. The final regulations were issued on February 24, 2009 (74 FR 8200). The preamble to the final regulations appears at ¶ 23,260, which contains cross references to the final regulations.

DEPARTMENT OF THE TREASURY

Internal Revenue Service

26 CFR Part 1

[REG-133300-07]

RIN-1545-BG80

Automatic Contribution Arrangements

AGENCY: Internal Revenue Service (IRS), Treasury.

ACTION: Notice of proposed rulemaking.

SUMMARY: This document contains proposed regulations under sections 401(k), 401(m), 402(c), 411(a), 414(w), and 4979(f) of the Internal Revenue Code relating to automatic contribution arrangements. These proposed regulations will affect administrators of, employers maintaining, participants in, and beneficiaries of eligible plans that include an automatic contribution arrangement under section 401(k)(13), 401(m)(12), or 414(w).

DATES: Written or electronic comments and requests for a public hearing must be received by February 6, 2008.

ADDRESSES: Send submissions to CC:PA:LPD:PR (REG-133300-07), room 5203, Internal Revenue Service, PO Box 7604, Ben Franklin Station, Washington DC 20044. Submissions may be hand-delivered Monday through Friday between the hours of 8 a.m. and 4 p.m. to CC:PA:LPD:PR (REG-133300-07), Courier's Desk, Internal Revenue Service, 1111 Constitution Avenue, NW., Washington, DC 20224 or sent electronically via the Federal erulemaking Portal at www.regulations.gov (IRS REG-133300-07).

FOR FURTHER INFORMATION CONTACT: Concerning the regulations, R. Lisa Mojiri-Azad, Dana Barry or William D. Gibbs at (202) 622-6060; concerning the submission of comments or to request a public hearing, Richard.A.Hurst@irscounsel.treas.gov, (202) 622-7180 (not toll-free numbers).

SUPPLEMENTARY INFORMATION:

Paperwork Reduction Act

The collection of information contained in this notice of proposed rulemaking has been submitted to the Office of Management and Budget for review in accordance with the Paperwork Reduction Act of 1995 (44 U.S.C. 3507(d)). Comments on the collection of information should be sent to the Office of Management and Budget, Attn: Desk Officer for the Department of the Treasury, Office of Information and Regulatory Affairs, Washington, DC 20503, with copies to the Internal Revenue Service, Attn: IRS Reports Clearance Officer, SE:W:CAR:MP:T:T:SP; Washington, DC 20224. Comments on the collection of information should be received by January 7, 2008. Comments are specifically requested concerning:

Whether the proposed collection of information is necessary for the proper performance of the functions of the Internal Revenue Service, including whether the information will have practical utility;

The accuracy of the estimated burden associated with the proposed collection of information;

How the quality, utility, and clarity of the information to be collected may be enhanced;

How the burden of complying with the proposed collections of information may be minimized, including through the application of automated collection techniques or other forms of information technology; and

Estimates of capital or start-up costs and costs of operation, maintenance, and purchase of service to provide information.

The collection of information in these proposed regulations is in §§ 1.401(k)-3 and 1.414(w)-1. The collection of information in § 1.401(k)-3 is required to comply with the statutory notice requirements of sections 401(k)(13) and 401(m)(12), and is expected to be included in the notices currently provided to employees that inform them of their rights and benefits under the plan. The collection of information under § 1.414(w)-1 is required to comply with the statutory notice requirements of section 414(w), and is expected to be included in the notices currently provided to employees that inform them of their rights and benefits under the plan. The likely recordkeepers are businesses or other for-profit institutions, nonprofit institutions, organizations, and state or local governments.

Estimated total average annual recordkeeping burden: 30,000 hours.

Estimated average annual burden hours per recordkeeper: 1 hour.

Estimated number of recordkeepers: 30,000.

An agency may not conduct or sponsor, and a person is not required to respond to, a collection of information unless it displays a valid control number assigned by the Office of Management and Budget.

Books or records relating to a collection of information must be retained as long as their contents may become material in the administration of any internal revenue law. Generally, tax returns and tax return information are confidential, as required by 26 U.S.C. 6103.

Background

This document contains proposed amendments to regulations under sections 401(k), 401(m), 402(c), 411(a), and 4979 of the Internal Revenue Code (Code) and new proposed regulations under section 414(w) in order to reflect the provisions of section 902 of the Pension Protection Act of 2006, Public Law 109-280 (PPA '06). Section 902 of PPA '06 added sections 401(k)(13), 401(m)(12), and 414(w) to the Code to facilitate automatic contribution arrangements (sometimes referred to as automatic enrollment) in qualified cash or deferred arrangements under section 401(k), as well as in similar arrangements under sections 403(b) and 457(b). An automatic contribution arrangement is a cash or deferred arrangement that provides that, in the absence of an affirmative election by an eligible employee, a default election applies under which the employee is treated as having made an election to have a specified contribution made on his or her behalf under the plan. These regulations would also amend the comprehensive regulations under sections 401(k) and 401(m) (published in 2004) and regulations under section 4979 to reflect other changes made by section 902 of PPA '06.

Section 401(k)(1) provides that a profit-sharing, stock bonus, pre-ERISA money purchase or rural cooperative plan will not fail to qualify under section 401(a) merely because it contains a qualified cash or deferred arrangement. Section 1.401(k)-1(a)(2) defines a cash or deferred arrangement (CODA) as an arrangement under which an eligible employee may make a cash or deferred election with respect to contributions to, or accruals or other benefits under, a plan that is intended to satisfy the requirements of section 401(a). Section 1.401(k)-1(a)(3) defines a cash or deferred election as any direct or indirect election (or modification of an earlier election) by an employee to have the employer either: (1) Provide an amount to the employee in the form of cash (or some other taxable benefit) that is not currently available; or (2) contribute an amount to a trust, or provide an accrual or other benefit, under a plan deferring the receipt of compensation. For purposes of determining whether an election is a cash or deferred election, § 1.401(k)-1(a)(3) provides that it is irrelevant whether the default that applies in the absence of an affirmative election is cash (or some other taxable benefit) or a contribution, an accrual, or other benefit under a plan deferring the receipt of compensation. Contributions that are made pursuant to a cash or deferred election under a qualified CODA are commonly referred to as elective contributions.

In order for a CODA to be a qualified CODA, it must satisfy a number of other requirements. First, pursuant to section 401(k)(2)(A), the amount that each eligible employee under the arrangement may defer as an elective contribution must be available to the employee in cash. Section 1.401(k)-1(e)(2) provides that, in order for a CODA to satisfy this requirement, the arrangement must provide each eligible employee with an effective opportunity to make (or change) a cash or deferred election at least once during each plan year.

Section 401(k)(2)(B) provides that a qualified CODA must provide that elective contributions may only be distributed after certain events, including hardship and severance from employment. Similar distribution restrictions apply under sections 403(b)(7) and 403(b)(11). Section 457(d)(1)(A) includes distribution restrictions for eligible governmental deferred compensation plans.

Section 401(k)(3)(A)(ii) applies a special nondiscrimination test to the elective contributions of highly compensated employees, within the meaning of section 414(q) (HCEs). Under this test, called the actual deferral percentage (ADP) test, the average percentage of compensation deferred for HCEs is compared annually to the average percentage of compensation deferred for nonhighly compensated employees (NHCEs) eligible under the plan, and if certain limits are exceeded by the HCEs, corrective action must be taken. Pursuant to section 401(k)(8), one method of correction is distribution to HCEs of excess contributions made on their behalf.

Section 401(m) provides a parallel test for matching contributions and employee after-tax contributions under a defined contribution plan, called the actual contribution percentage (ACP) test. Similarly, pursuant to section 401(m)(6), one method of correction of the ACP test is distribution to HCEs of excess aggregate contributions made on their behalf.

Sections 401(k)(12) and 401(m)(11) provide a design-based safe harbor under which a CODA and any associated matching contributions are treated as satisfying the ADP and ACP tests if the arrangement meets certain contribution and notice requirements. Sections 1.401(k)-3 and 1.401(m)-3 provide guidance on the requirements for this design-based safe harbor.

Sections 401(k)(13) and 401(m)(12), added by PPA '06 and effective for plan years beginning on or after January 1, 2008, provide an alternative design-based safe harbor for a CODA that provides for automatic contributions at a specified level of contributions and meets certain contribution, notice, and other requirements. A CODA that satisfies these requirements, referred to as a qualified automatic contribution arrangement (QACA), is treated as satisfying the ADP and ACP tests.

Section 414(w), added to the Code by section 902(d)(1) of PPA '06 and effective for plan years beginning on or after January 1, 2008, further facilitates automatic enrollment by providing limited relief from the distribution restrictions under sections 401(k)(2)(B), 403(b)(7), 403(b)(11), or 457(d)(1)(A) for an eligible automatic contribution arrangement (EACA).

Sections 414(w)(1) and 414(w)(2) provide that an applicable employer plan that contains an EACA is permitted to allow employees to elect to receive a distribution equal to the amount of elective contributions (and attributable earnings) made with respect to the employee beginning with the first payroll period to which the eligible automatic contribution arrangement applies to the employee and ending with the effective date of the election. The election must be made within 90 days after the date of the first elective contribution with respect to the employee under the arrangement. Sections 414(w)(1)(A) and 414(w)(1)(B) provide that the amount of the distribution is includible in gross income for the taxable year in which the distribution is made, but is not subject to the additional income tax under section 72(t).

Section 414(w)(3) defines an EACA as an arrangement under which: (1) a participant may elect to have the employer make payments as contributions under the plan on behalf of the participant, or to the participant directly in cash, (2) the participant is treated as having elected to have the employer make such contributions in an amount equal to a uniform percentage of compensation provided under the plan until the participant specifically elects not to have such contributions made (or specifically elects to have such contributions made at a different percentage), (3) in the absence of an investment election by the participant, such contributions are invested in accordance with regulations prescribed by the Secretary of Labor under section 404(c)(5) of the Employee Retirement Income Security Act of 1974 (ERISA), and (4) participants are provided a notice that satisfies the requirements of section 414(w)(4).

Section 414(w)(4) requires that, within a reasonable period before each plan year, each employee to whom the arrangement applies for such year receive written notice of the employee's rights and obligations under the arrangement which is sufficiently accurate and comprehensive to apprise the employee of such rights and obligations. Section

414(w)(4)(A)(ii) requires that the notice be written in a manner calculated to be understood by the average employee to whom the arrangement applies. Section 414(w)(4)(B) provides that the notice must explain: (1) The employee's rights under the arrangement to elect not to have elective contributions made on the employee's behalf or to elect to have contributions made at a different percentage; and (2) how contributions made under the automatic contribution arrangement will be invested in the absence of any investment decision by the employee. In addition, the employee must be given a reasonable period of time after receipt of the notice and before the first elective contribution is made to make an election with respect to contributions. In many respects, the notice under section 414(w)(4) is the same as the notice required under section 401(k)(13) for a qualified automatic contribution arrangement.

Section 414(w)(5) defines an applicable employer plan as an employee's trust described in section 401(a) that is exempt from tax under section 501(a), a plan described in section 403(b), or a section 457(b) eligible governmental plan.

Section 414(w)(6) provides that a withdrawal described in section 414(w)(1) is not to be taken into account for purposes of the ADP test.

Section 411(a)(3)(G), as amended by section 902(d)(2) of PPA '06, provides that a matching contribution shall not be treated as forfeitable merely because the matching contribution is forfeitable if it relates to a contribution that is withdrawn under an automatic contribution arrangement that satisfies the requirements of section 414(w).

Section 4979 provides an excise tax on excess contributions (within the meaning of section 401(k)(8)(B)) and excess aggregate contributions (within the meaning of section 401(m)(6)(B)) not distributed within 21/2 months after the close of the plan year for which the contributions are made. Section 902 of PPA '06 amended section 4979 to lengthen this 21/2 month correction period for excess contributions and excess aggregate contributions under an EACA to 6 months. Thus, in the case of an EACA, the section 4979 excise tax does not apply to any excess contributions or excess aggregate contributions which, together with income allocable to the contributions, are distributed or forfeited (if forfeitable) within six months after the close of the plan year.

Section 902 of PPA '06 amended section 4979(f)(2) to provide that any distributions of excess contributions and excess aggregate contributions are includible in the employee's gross income for the taxable year in which distributed. However, pursuant to sections 401(k)(8)(D) and 401(m)(7)(A), the distributions are not subject to the additional income tax under section 72(t). Section 902 of PPA '06 also amended sections 401(k)(8), 401(m)(6), and 4979(f)(1) to eliminate the requirement that excess contributions or excess aggregate contributions (whether or not under an EACA) include income allocable to the period after the end of the plan year (gap period income).

Section 624 of PPA '06 amended section 404(c) of ERISA to provide that a participant in an individual account plan meeting the notice requirements of section 404(c)(5)(B) of ERISA is treated as exercising control over the assets in the account which, in the absence of an investment election by the participant, are invested in accordance with regulations prescribed by the Secretary of Labor. The specific timing and content requirements for the notice required under section 404(c)(5)(B) of ERISA are generally the same as under section 414(w)(4), but the Department of Labor (DOL) has interpretative jurisdiction for that notice.

Section 902 of PPA '06 also amended section 514 of ERISA to preempt any State law which would directly or indirectly prohibit or restrict the inclusion in any plan of an automatic contribution arrangement. The Secretary of Labor is authorized to prescribe regulations which would establish minimum standards that such an arrangement would be required to satisfy in order for this preemption to apply to such an arrangement. The definition of an automatic contribution arrangement under section 514 of ERISA is generally the same as the definition of an EACA under section 414(w)(3), (including the requirement that automatic contributions under the arrangement must be invested in accordance with regulations prescribed by the Secretary of Labor under section 404(c)(5) of ERISA), but the definition does not include a notice requirement. However, section 514(e)(3) of ERISA requires a notice to be provided to each participant to whom the arrangement applies. As in the case for the notice under section 404(c)(5)(B) of ERISA, the specific timing and content requirements under section 514(e)(3) of ERISA are generally the same as the notice requirements under section 414(w)(4), but the interpretative jurisdiction for that notice is also with the DOL.

¶20,262E

Explanation of Provisions

1. Qualified Automatic Contribution Arrangement under Section 401(k)(13)

The proposed regulations would amend §§1.401(k)-3 and 1.401(m)-3 to reflect the provisions of sections 401(k)(13) and 401(m)(12) for a QACA, the new design-based safe harbor for satisfying the ADP and ACP tests. To the extent that the requirements to be a QACA are the same as those for the safe harbor described in sections 401(k)(12) and 401(m)(11), these proposed regulations would apply the existing rules currently in §§1.401(k)-3 and 1.401(m)-3 to a QACA. Thus, for example, because §1.401(k)-3(e) applies to a QACA, except to the extent otherwise provided in section 1107 of PPA '06 or §1.401(k)-3(f) or §1.401(k)-3(g), the plan provision implementing the QACA for an existing qualified CODA would be required to be adopted before the first day of the plan year and remain in effect for an entire 12-month plan year. Similarly under §1.401(k)-3(c)(6), a plan would be permitted to limit the amount of elective contributions that may be made by an eligible employee under the QACA, provided that each NHCE who is an eligible employee generally is permitted to make elective contributions in an amount that is at least sufficient to receive the maximum amount of matching contributions available under the plan for the plan year, and the employee is permitted to elect any lesser amount of elective contributions.

In order to be a QACA, the plan must provide a specified schedule of automatic contributions (called qualified percentages) for each eligible employee beginning with an initial minimum qualified percentage of 3 percent of compensation. This minimum qualified percentage begins when the employee first participates in the automatic contribution arrangement that is intended to be a QACA and ends on the last day of the following plan year. Thus, this initial period for a participant could last as long as two full plan years. After this initial period, the minimum qualified percentage increases by 1 percent for each of the next three plan years. Thus, the minimum qualified percentage for the plan year after the initial period is 4 percent. This minimum qualified percentage increases to 5 percent for the next plan year, and then is 6 percent for all plan years thereafter. These are merely minimum qualified percentages. Thus, a QACA can provide for higher percentages. For example, a QACA could provide for a qualified percentage in the initial period of 4 percent of compensation. If a plan did so, it could also provide a 4 percent qualified percentage for the plan year after the initial period (the statutory minimum percentage for that plan year), 5 percent in the next plan year and 6 percent thereafter. However, the qualified percentage can at no time exceed 10 percent of compensation.

Under section 401(k)(13)(C)(iii), the qualified percentage must be applied uniformly to all eligible employees. The proposed regulations would provide that a plan does not fail this requirement merely because the percentage varies for the following reasons: (1) The percentage varies based on the number of years an eligible employee has participated in the automatic contribution arrangement intended to be a QACA; (2) the rate of elective contributions under a cash or deferred election that is in effect on the effective date of the default percentage under the QACA is not reduced; or (3) the amount of elective contributions is limited so as not to exceed the limits of sections 401(a)(17), 402(g) (determined with or without catch-up contributions described in section 402(g)(1)(C) or section 402(g)(7)) or 415. Further, the proposed regulations would provide that a cash or deferred arrangement does not fail to satisfy the uniformity requirement merely because an employee is not automatically enrolled during a period that the employee is not permitted to make elective contributions because of the requirement to suspend elective contributions for a 6-month period following a hardship distribution. In the case of an employee whose elective contributions have been suspended (for example, because of a hardship distribution), the plan must provide that the employee will, at the end of the suspension period, resume elective contributions at the level (percentage) that would apply if the suspension had not occurred.

Reflecting section 401(k)(13)(C)(ii), the proposed regulations provide that the default election ceases to apply to any eligible employee if the employee makes an affirmative election that remains in effect to not have any elective contributions made on his or her behalf or to have elective contributions made in a specified amount or percentage of compensation on his or her behalf. Thus, an employee can make an affirmative election to contribute at a certain level and have that election apply for all subsequent plan years. Similarly, an employee can make an affirmative election to have no elective contributions made on his or her behalf. This latter election is not the same as the election to withdraw prior elective contributions under section 414(w).

The proposed regulations also reflect section 401(k)(13)(C)(iv), which provides an exception from the default election for eligible employees who were eligible to participate in the CODA (or a predecessor CODA) immediately before the effective date of the QACA and who have an election in effect on that effective date. The proposed regulations would provide that an election in effect means an affirmative election that remains in effect to have the employer make elective contributions on his or her behalf (in a specified amount or percentage of compensation) or to not have the employer make elective contributions on his or her behalf. Generally, this would require that the employee have completed an election form and chosen an amount or percentage (including zero) of his compensation to be deferred.

The proposed regulations reflect the matching or nonelective contribution requirement of section 401(k)(13)(D). As with the safe harbor in section 401(k)(12), section 401(k)(13) provides a choice for an employer between satisfying a matching contribution requirement or a nonelective contribution requirement. However, while the QACA requires the same level of employer nonelective contributions as under section 401(k)(12), the matching contribution requirement for a QACA allows for a lower level of matching contributions. Specifically, a QACA using the matching contribution alternative need only provide for matching contributions on behalf of each eligible NHCE equal to 100 percent of the employee's elective contributions that do not exceed one percent of compensation and 50 percent of the employee's elective contributions that exceed one percent but do not exceed six percent of compensation. In addition, a QACA allows a slower schedule of vesting for both matching and nonelective safe harbor contributions than the safe harbor in section 401(k)(12). All QACA safe harbor contributions must be fully vested after 2 years of vesting service (within the meaning of section 411(a)), rather than immediately as required by section 401(k)(12). In addition, the proposed regulations would apply the same distribution restrictions that apply to safe harbor contributions and nonelective contributions under section 401(k)(12) to QACA safe harbor contributions.

Each eligible employee under a QACA must receive a safe harbor notice within a reasonable period before each plan year. The proposed regulations reflect the requirement that this notice must provide the information required under section 401(k)(12). The regulations also reflect the additional timing and content requirements described in section 401(k)(13)(E)(i). Thus, the notice must also explain: (1) The employee's right under the arrangement to elect not to have elective contributions made on the employee's behalf or to elect to have contributions made in a different amount or percentage of compensation; and (2) how contributions made under the automatic contribution arrangement will be invested in the absence of any investment decision by the employee (including, in the case of an arrangement under which the employee may elect among two or more investment options, how contributions made under the automatic contribution arrangement will be invested in the absence of an investment election by the employee). These additional requirements cannot be satisfied by reference to the plan's summary plan description. Further, the proposed regulations would provide that in order to satisfy section 401(k)(13)(E)(ii)(III), under the QACA, the employee must be given a reasonable period of time after receipt of the notice and before the first elective contribution is to be made to make an election with respect to contributions and investments.

The proposed regulations interpret the requirement under section 401(k)(13)(E)(i) to provide a notice within a reasonable period before each plan year by applying the rules of § 1.401(k)-3(d)(3). Thus, the proposed regulations would provide that the general determination of whether the timing requirement is satisfied is based on all of the relevant facts and circumstances, and the deemed timing rule of § 1.401(k)-3(d)(3)(ii) applies. Under this deemed timing rule, the timing requirement is satisfied if at least 30 days (and no more than 90 days) before the beginning of each plan year, the notice is given to each eligible employee for the plan year. The proposed regulations would also provide that in the case of an employee who does not receive the notice within the period described in the previous sentence because the employee becomes eligible after the 90th day before the beginning of the plan year, the timing requirement is deemed to be satisfied if the notice is provided no more than 90 days before the employee becomes eligible (and no later than the date the employee becomes eligible). Thus, for example, the preceding sentence would apply to all eligible employees for the first plan year under a newly established plan that provides for elective contributions, and to the first plan year in which an employee becomes eligible under an existing plan that provides for elective contributions. In the case of a plan with immediate eligibility when an employee is hired, this deemed timing rule would be satisfied if the employee is provided the notice on the first day of employment.

2. Eligible Automatic Contribution Arrangement under Section 414(w)

In order to further facilitate automatic enrollment, section 414(w) provides limited relief from the distribution restrictions under sections 401(k)(2), 403(b)(7), 403(b)(11), and 457(d) (as well as certain other relief provisions) for an applicable plan (that is, a section 401(k) plan, a section 403(b) plan, or a section 457(b) eligible governmental plan) with an EACA. Specifically, section 414(w)(2) provides that, under an applicable employer plan with an EACA, an employee can be permitted to elect to receive a distribution equal to the amount of default elective contributions (and attributable earnings) made with respect to the first payroll period to which the EACA applies to the employee and any succeeding payroll periods beginning before the effective date of the election.

An employer is permitted, but not required, to include the section 414(w)(2) permissible withdrawal provision in an applicable employer plan, and an employer who does offer this option is not required to make it available to all employees eligible under the EACA. Thus, for example, an employer might choose to make the withdrawal option available only to employees for whom no elective contributions have been made under the CODA (or a predecessor CODA) before the EACA is effective. However, under a section 401(k) plan or a section 403(b) plan, the employer may not condition the right to take the withdrawal on the employee making an election to have no future elective contributions made on the employee's behalf because such a condition would violate the contingent benefit rule under section 401(k)(4)(A) or the universal availability requirement under section 403(b)(12)(A)(ii). Nonetheless, the employer could provide in the withdrawal election form a default election under which elective contributions would cease unless the employee makes an affirmative election.

Under section 414(w)(2)(B), the election to withdraw the contributions that were made under an EACA must be made within 90 days of the "first elective contribution with respect to the employee under the arrangement." The proposed regulations would define the arrangement for this purpose as the EACA so that the withdrawal option could apply to employees previously eligible under the CODA (including a CODA that is an automatic contribution arrangement but was not an EACA). Because section 414(w) only applies to plan years beginning on or after January 1, 2008, an automatic contribution arrangement can only become an EACA on or after that date. Accordingly, a withdrawal election under section 414(w) can only apply to elective contributions made after that date. The proposed regulations would provide that the 90-day window for making the withdrawal election begins on the date on which the compensation that is subject to the cash or deferred election would otherwise have been included in gross income. In addition, the proposed regulations would provide that the effective date of the election must be no later than the last day of the payroll period that begins after the date of the election.

The proposed regulations would provide that the distribution is generally the account balance attributable to the default elective contributions, adjusted for gains and losses. The distribution may be reduced by any generally applicable fees. However, the proposed regulations provide that the plan may not charge a different fee for this distribution than would apply to other distributions. Also, if the default elective contributions are not maintained in a separate account, the amount of the allocable gains and losses will be determined under rules similar to those provided under § 1.401(k)-2(b)(2)(iv) for the distribution of excess contributions.

The amount withdrawn under section 414(w) is includible in gross income in the year in which it is distributed, except amounts that are distributions of designated Roth contributions are not included in an employee's gross income a second time. The proposed regulations would require that this amount be reported on Form 1099-R, Distributions From Pensions, Annuities, Retirement or Profit-Sharing Plans, IRAs, Insurance Contracts, etc. However, the amount is not subject to the additional income tax under section 72(t). Finally, the proposed regulations would amend § 1.402(c)-2 to include these withdrawals in the list of distributions that are not eligible for rollover.

Any employer matching contribution with respect to the default elective contribution distributed pursuant to section 414(w) must be forfeited. The forfeited matching contribution is not a mistaken contribution or other erroneous contribution, and, thus, it cannot be returned to the employer (or be distributed to the employee as is permitted for an excess aggregate contribution). The proposed regulations would provide that the forfeited contribution must remain in the plan and be treated in the same manner under the plan terms as any other forfeiture under the plan.

Under section 414(w)(3)(B), an EACA must provide that the default elective contribution is a uniform percentage of compensation. The proposed regulations would provide that the permitted differences in contribution rates provided in these proposed regulations under section 401(k)(13) for a QACA also apply to an EACA.

Another requirement to be an EACA under section 414(w)(3)(C) is that automatic contributions are invested in accordance with regulations prescribed by the Secretary of Labor under section 404(c)(5) of ERISA. These proposed regulations would provide that this requirement only applies if the plan is otherwise subject to Title I of ERISA. Thus, for example, this provision would not apply to a governmental plan (within the meaning of section 414(d)).

The proposed regulations reflect the section 414(w) notice requirement under which notice must be provided to each employee to whom the EACA applies within a "reasonable period" before each plan year, but provide that, if an employee becomes eligible in a given year, notice must be given within a "reasonable period" before the employee becomes eligible. The proposed regulations provide a deemed timing requirement that is generally the same as the deemed timing rule in § 1.401(k)-3(d)(3)(ii).

3. Coordinated Notices

As noted in this preamble, PPA '06 provides for several notices relating to automatic contribution arrangements that have similar content and timing requirements, including the notices required by sections 404(c)(5)(B) and 514(e)(3) of ERISA. The IRS, in coordination with DOL, anticipates that a single document can satisfy all of these notice requirements, so long as it has all of the requisite information for plan participants and satisfies the timing requirements for each of those notices.

4. Other Provisions of Section 902 of PPA '06

The proposed regulations also reflect the amendments to section 4979 made by section 902 of PPA '06. First, the proposed regulations reflect the substitution of 6 months for 21/2 months as the time period under section 4979(f) by which excess contributions or excess aggregate contributions with respect to an EACA must be distributed to avoid the excise tax under section 4979(a). Further, the proposed regulations reflect the elimination of the requirement that distributions of excess contributions or excess aggregate contributions (whether or not under an EACA) include attributable earnings for the period after the end of the plan year (gap period income). The proposed regulations also reflect the change in the tax treatment of a distribution of excess contributions or excess aggregate contributions (whether or not under an EACA) under which the distribution of excess contributions or excess aggregate contributions (including earnings) is includible in the participant's gross income for the year of the distribution (without regard to the amount of the distribution). The proposed regulations would also amend §§ 1.401(k)-2 and 1.401(m)-2 to reflect these provisions in the correction rules for the ADP and ACP tests. All of these changes are proposed to be effective January 1, 2008 and will impact corrective distributions made in 2009.

In addition, the proposed regulations would amend §§ 1.401(k)-2 and 1.401(m)-2 to reflect the provisions of section 414(w)(6) that default elective contributions distributed under section 414(w) are not taken into account in the ADP test. They are also not permitted to be taken into account in the ACP test. The proposed regulations under section 401(m) have added a conforming change for other elective contributions that are not taken into account in the ADP test. The proposed regulations would also amend § 1.411(a)-4(b)(7) to reflect the amendment to section 411(a)(3)(G) made by PPA '06 section 902(d)(2).

Effective Date

Sections 401(k)(13), 401(m)(12), and 414(w), and the amended provisions of sections 411(a)(3)(G) and 4979(f), are effective for plan years beginning on or after January 1, 2008. These regulations are proposed to be effective for plan years beginning on or after January 1, 2008. Taxpayers may rely on these proposed regulations for guidance pending the issuance of final regulations. If, and to the extent, the final regulations are more restrictive than the guidance in these proposed regulations, those provisions of the final regulations will be applied without retroactive effect.

Special Analyses

It has been determined that this notice of proposed rulemaking is not a significant regulatory action as defined in Executive Order 12866. Therefore, a regulatory assessment is not required. It has been determined that 5 U.S.C. 533(b) of the Administrative Procedure Act (5 U.S.C. chapter 5) does not apply to these regulations. It is hereby certified that the collection of information in these proposed regulations will not have a significant economic impact on a substantial number of small entities. This certification is based on the fact that most small entities that maintain plans that will be eligible for the safe

harbor provisions of sections 401(k) and 401(m) or the distribution relief provisions of section 414(w) currently provide a similar notice with which this notice can be combined. Therefore, an analysis under the Regulatory Flexibility Act (5 U.S.C. chapter 6) is not required. Pursuant to section 7805(f) of the Internal Revenue Code, these regulations have been submitted to the Chief Counsel for Advocacy of the Small Business Administration for comments on its impact on small business.

Comments and Requests for Public Hearing

Before these proposed regulations are adopted as final regulations, consideration will be given to any written (one signed and eight (8) copies) or electronic comments that are submitted timely to the IRS. The IRS and Treasury Department specifically request comments on the clarity of the proposed rules and how they can be made easier to understand. All comments will be available for public inspection and copying. A public hearing will be scheduled if requested in writing by any person who timely submits written comments. If a public hearing is scheduled, notice of the date, time, and place of the public hearing will be published in the Federal Register.

Drafting Information

The principal authors of these regulations are Dana Barry, William Gibbs, and Lisa Mojiri-Azad, Office of Division Counsel/Associate Chief Counsel (Tax Exempt and Government Entities). However, other personnel from the IRS and Treasury Department participated in the development of these regulations.

List of Subjects in 26 CFR Part 1

Income taxes, Reporting and recordkeeping requirements.

Proposed Amendments to the Regulations

Accordingly, 26 CFR part 1 is proposed to be amended as follows:

PART 1—INCOME TAXES

Paragraph 1. The authority citation for part 1 is amended to read as follows:

Authority: 26 U.S.C. 7805 * * *

Section 1.401(k)-3 is also issued under 26 U.S.C. 401(k)(13)

Par. 2. Section 1.401(k)-0 is amended by:

1. Amending the entry for § 1.401(k)-2 by adding entries for §§ 1.401(k)-2(a)(5)(vi) and 1.401(k)-2(b)(2)(iv)(D).

2. Revising the entries for §§ 1.401(k)-2(b)(2)(vi)(A) and 1.401(k)-2(b)(2)(vi)(B).

3. Adding an entry for § 1.401(k)-2(b)(5)(iii).

4. Revising the entries for §§ 1.401(k)-3(a)(1), 1.401(k)-3(a)(2) and 1.401(k)-3(a)(3).

5. Adding entries for §§ 1.401(k)-3(i), 1.401(k)-3(j) through (j)(2)(iii).

6. Adding entries for § 1.401(k)-3(k) through (k)(4)(iii).

The additions and revisions read as follows:

§ 1.401(k)-0 Table of Contents.

* * * * *

§ 1.401(k)-2 ADP test.

(a) * * *

(5) * * *

(vi) Default elective contributions pursuant to section 414(w).

* * * * *

(b) * * *

(2) * * *

(iv) * * *

(A) * * *

(D) Plan years before 2008.

* * * * *

(vi) * * *

(A) Corrective distributions for plan years beginning on or after January 1, 2008.

(B) Corrective distributions for plan years beginning before January 1, 2008.

* * * * *

(5) * * *

(iii) Special rule for eligible automatic contribution arrangements.

* * * * *

§ 1.401(k)-3 Safe harbor requirements.

(a) * * *

(1) Section 401(k)(12) safe harbor.

(2) Section 401(k)(13) safe harbor.

(3) Requirements applicable to safe harbor contributions.

* * * * *

(i) Reserved.

(j) Qualified automatic contribution arrangement.

(1) Automatic contribution requirement.

(i) In general.

(ii) Automatic contribution arrangement.

(iii) Exception for certain current employees.

(2) Qualified percentage.

(i) In general.

(ii) Minimum percentage requirements.

(A) Initial-year requirement.

(B) Second-year requirement.

(C) Third-year requirement.

(D) Later years requirement.

(iii) Exception to uniform percentage requirement.

(k) Modifications to contribution requirements and notice requirements for automatic contribution safe harbor.

(1) In general.

(2) Lower matching requirement.

(3) Modified nonforfeiture requirement.

(4) Additional notice requirements.

(i) In general.

(ii) Additional information.

(iii) Timing requirements.

Par. 3. Section 1.401(k)-1 is amended by:

1. Revising paragraph (b)(1)(ii)(C) and adding new paragraph (b)(1)(ii)(D).

2. Revising paragraph (e)(7) by adding a new sentence after the fifth sentence.

The additions and revisions to read as follows:

§ 1.401(k)-1 Certain cash or deferred arrangements.

* * * * *

(b) * * * (1) * * * (ii) * * *

(C) The ADP safe harbor provisions of section 401(k)(13) described in § 1.401(k)-3; or

(D) The SIMPLE 401(k) provisions of section 401(k)(11) described in § 1.401(k)-4.

* * * * *

(e) * * *

(7) Plan provision requirement. * * * In addition, a plan that uses the safe harbor method of section 401(k)(13), as described in paragraph (b)(1)(ii)(C) of this section, must specify the default percentages that apply for the plan year, and whether the safe harbor contribution will be the nonelective safe harbor contribution or the matching safe harbor contribution and is not permitted to provide that ADP testing will be used if the requirements for the safe harbor are not satisfied. * * *

* * * * *

Par. 4. Section 1.401(k)-2 is amended by:

1. Adding paragraph (a)(5)(vi).

2. Revising paragraphs (b)(2)(iv)(A) and (b)(2)(iv)(D).

3. Removing paragraph (b)(2)(iv)(E).

4. Revising paragraph (b)(2)(vi)(A).

5. Adding a new first sentence to paragraph (b)(2)(vi)(B).

6. Removing and reserving Example (3), Example (4), and Example (5) from § 1.401(k)-2(b)(2)(viii).

7. Revising paragraph (b)(4)(iii) and adding paragraph (b)(5)(iii).

The additions and revisions to read as follows:

§ 1.401(k)-2 ADP test.

(a) * * *

(5) * * *

(vi) Default elective contributions pursuant to section 414(w). Default elective contributions made under an eligible automatic contribution arrangement (within the meaning of § 1.414(w)-1(b) that are distributed pursuant to § 1.414(w)-1(c) for plan years beginning on or after January 1, 2008, are not taken into account under paragraph (a)(4) of this section for the plan year for which the contributions are made, or for any other plan year.

(b) * * *

(2) * * *

(iv) Income allocable to excess contributions— (A) General rule. For plan years beginning on or after January 1, 2008, the income allocable to excess contributions is equal to the allocable gain or loss through the end of the plan year. See paragraph (b)(2)(iv)(D) of this section for rules that apply to plan years beginning before January 1, 2008.

* * * * *

(D) Plan years before 2008. For plan years beginning before January 1, 2008, the income allocable to excess contributions is determined under § 1.401(k)-2(b)(2)(iv) (as it appeared in the April 1, 2007, edition of 26 CFR part 1).

* * * * *

(vi) Tax treatment of corrective distributions— (A) Corrective distributions for plan years beginning on or after January 1, 2008. Except as provided in this paragraph (b)(2)(vi), for plan years beginning on or after January 1, 2008, a corrective distribution of excess contributions (and allocable income) is includible in the employee's gross income for the employee's taxable year in which distributed. In addition, the corrective distribution is not subject to the early distribution tax of section 72(t). See also paragraph (b)(5) of this section for additional rules relating to the employer excise tax on amounts distributed more than 21/2 months (6 months in the case of a plan that includes an eligible automatic contribution arrangement within the meaning of section 414(w)) after the end of the plan year. See also § 1.402(c)-2, A-4 for restrictions on rolling over distributions that are excess contributions.

(B) Corrective distributions for plan years beginning before January 1, 2008. The tax treatment of corrective distributions for plan years beginning before January 1, 2008, is determined under § 1.401(k)-2(b)(2)(vi) (as it appeared in the April 1, 2007, edition of 26 CFR Part 1). * * *

* * * * *

(4) * * *

(iii) Permitted forfeiture of QMAC. Pursuant to section 401(k)(8)(E), a qualified matching contribution is not treated as forfeitable under § 1.401(k)-1(c) merely because under the plan it is forfeited in accordance with paragraph (b)(4)(ii) of this section or § 1.414(w)-1(d)(2).

* * * * *

(5) * * *

(iii) Special rule for eligible automatic contribution arrangements. In the case of a plan that includes an eligible automatic contribution arrangement within the meaning of section 414(w), 6 months is substituted for 21/2 months in paragraph (b)(5)(i) of this section.

* * * * *

Par. 5. Section 1.401(k)-3 is amended by:

1. Revising paragraph (a).

2. Revising the first sentence of paragraph (e)(1).

3. Revising the last sentence of paragraph (h)(2).

4. Revising the first sentence of paragraph (h)(3).

5. Reserving paragraph (i) and adding paragraphs (j), and (k).

The additions and revisions to read as follows:

§ 1.401(k)-3 Safe harbor requirements.

(a) ADP test safe harbor—(1) Section 401(k)(12) safe harbor. A cash or deferred arrangement satisfies the ADP safe harbor provision of section 401(k)(12) for a plan year if the arrangement satisfies the safe harbor contribution requirement of paragraph (b) or (c) of this section for the plan year, the notice requirement of paragraph (d) of this section, the plan year requirements of paragraph (e) of this section, and the additional rules of paragraphs (f), (g), and (h) of this section, as applicable.

(2) Section 401(k)(13) safe harbor. For plan years beginning on or after January 1, 2008, a cash or deferred arrangement satisfies the ADP safe harbor provision of section 401(k)(13) for a plan year if the arrangement is described in paragraph (j) of this section and satisfies the safe harbor contribution requirement of paragraph (k) of this section for the plan year, the notice requirement of paragraph (d) of this section (modified to include the information set forth in paragraph (k)(4) of this section), the plan year requirements of paragraph (e) of this section, and the additional rules of paragraphs (f), (g), and (h) of this section, as applicable. A cash or deferred arrangement that satisfies the requirements of this paragraph is referred to as a qualified automatic contribution arrangement.

(3) Requirements applicable to safe harbor contributions. Pursuant to section 401(k)(12)(E)(ii) and section 401(k)(13)(D)(iv), the safe harbor contribution requirement of paragraph (b), (c), or (k) of this section must be satisfied without regard to section 401(1). The contributions made under paragraph (b) or (c) of this section (and the corresponding contributions under paragraph (k) of this section) are referred to as safe harbor nonelective contributions and safe harbor matching contributions, respectively.

* * * * *

(e) * * * (1) General rule. Except as provided in this paragraph (e) or in paragraph (f) of this section, a plan will fail to satisfy the requirements of sections 401(k)(12), 401(k)(13), and this section unless plan provisions that satisfy the rules of this section are adopted before the first day of the plan year and remain in effect for an entire 12-month plan year. * * *

* * * * *

(h) * * *

(2) Use of safe harbor nonelective contributions to satisfy other discrimination tests. * * * However, pursuant to section 401(k)(12)(E)(ii) and section 401(k)(13)(D)(iv), to the extent they are needed to satisfy the safe harbor contribution requirement of paragraph (b) of this section, safe harbor nonelective contributions may not be taken into account under any plan for purposes of section 401(1) (including the imputation of permitted disparity under § 1.401(a)(4)-7).

(3) Early participation rules. Section 401(k)(3)(F) and § 1.401(k)-2(a)(1)(iii)(A), which provide an alternative nondiscrimination rule for certain plans that provide for early participation, do not apply for purposes of section 401(k)(12), section 401(k)(13), and this section. * * *

* * * * *

(i) [RESERVED].

(j) Qualified automatic contribution arrangement— (1) Automatic contribution requirement—(i) In general. A cash or deferred arrangement is described in this paragraph (j) if it is an automatic contribution arrangement described in paragraph (j)(1)(ii) of this section where the default election under that arrangement is a contribution equal to the qualified percentage described in paragraph (j)(2) of this section multiplied by the eligible employee's compensation from which elective contributions are permitted to be made under the cash or deferred arrangement.

(ii) Automatic contribution arrangement. An automatic contribution arrangement is a cash or deferred arrangement within the meaning of § 1.401(k)-1(a)(2) that provides that in the absence of an eligible employee's affirmative election, a default applies under which the employee is treated as having made an election to have a specified contribution made on his or her behalf under the plan. The default election ceases to apply with respect to an eligible employee if the employee makes an affirmative election (that remains in effect) to—

(A) Have elective contributions made in a different amount on his or her behalf (in a specified amount or percentage of compensation); or

(B) Not have any elective contributions made on his or her behalf.

(iii) Exception for certain current employees. An automatic contribution arrangement will not fail to be a qualified automatic contribution arrangement merely because the default election provided under para-

graph (j)(1)(i) of this section is not applied to an employee who was an eligible employee under the cash or deferred arrangement (or a predecessor arrangement) immediately prior to the effective date of the qualified automatic contribution arrangement and on that effective date had an affirmative election in effect (that remains in effect) to—

(A) Have elective contributions made on his or her behalf (in a specified amount or percentage of compensation); or

(B) Not have elective contributions made on his or her behalf.

(2) Qualified percentage—(i) In general. A percentage is a qualified percentage only if it—

(A) Is uniform for all employees (except to the extent provided in paragraph (j)(2)(iii) of this section);

(B) Does not exceed 10 percent; and

(C) Satisfies the minimum percentage requirements of paragraph (j)(2)(ii) of this section.

(ii) Minimum percentage requirements—(A) Initial-period requirement. The minimum percentage requirement of this paragraph (j)(2)(ii)(A) is satisfied only if the percentage that applies for the period that begins when the employee first participates in the automatic contribution arrangement that is a qualified automatic contribution arrangement and ends on the last day of the following plan year is at least 3 percent.

(B) Second-year requirement. The minimum percentage requirement of this paragraph (j)(2)(ii)(B) is satisfied only if the percentage that applies for the plan year immediately following the last day described in paragraph (j)(2)(ii)(A) of this section is at least 4 percent.

(C) Third-year requirement. The minimum percentage requirement of this paragraph (j)(2)(ii)(C) is satisfied only if the percentage that applies for the plan year immediately following the plan year described in paragraph (j)(2)(ii)(B) of this section is at least 5 percent.

(D) Later years requirement. A percentage satisfies the minimum percentage requirement of this paragraph (j)(2)(ii)(D) only if the percentage that applies for all plan years following the plan year described in paragraph (j)(2)(ii)(C) of this section is at least 6 percent.

(iii) Exception to uniform percentage requirement. A plan does not fail to satisfy the uniform percentage requirement of paragraph (j)(2)(i)(A) of this section merely because—

(A) The percentage varies based on the number of years an eligible employee has participated in the automatic contribution arrangement intended to be a qualified automatic contribution arrangement;

(B) The rate of elective contributions under a cash or deferred election that is in effect immediately prior to the effective date of the default percentage under the qualified automatic contribution arrangement is not reduced;

(C) The rate of elective contributions is limited so as not to exceed the limits of sections 401(a)(17), 402(g) (determined with or without catch-up contributions described in section 402(g)(1)(C) or 402(g)(7)), and 415; or

(D) The default election provided under paragraph (j)(1)(i) of this section is not applied during the period an employee is not permitted to make elective contributions in order for the plan to satisfy the requirements of § 1.401(k)-1(d)(3)(iv)(E)(2).

(k) Modifications to contribution requirements and notice requirements for automatic contribution safe harbor—(1) In general. A cash or deferred arrangement satisfies the contribution requirements of this paragraph (k) only if it satisfies the contribution requirements of either paragraph (b) or (c) of this section, as modified by the rules of paragraphs (k)(2) and (k)(3) of this section. In addition, a cash or deferred arrangement described in paragraph (j) of this section satisfies the notice requirement of section 401(k)(13)(E) only if the notice satisfies the additional requirements of paragraph (k)(4) of this section.

(2) Lower matching requirement. In applying the requirement of paragraph (c) of this section, in the case of a cash or deferred arrangement described in paragraph (j) of this section, the basic matching formula is modified so that each eligible NHCE must receive the sum of—

(i) 100 percent of the employee's elective contributions that do not exceed 1 percent of the employee's safe harbor compensation; and

(ii) 50 percent of the employee's elective contributions that exceed 1 percent of the employee's safe harbor compensation but that do not exceed 6 percent of the employee's safe harbor compensation.

(3) Modified nonforfeiture requirement. A cash or deferred arrangement described in paragraph (j) of this section will not fail to satisfy the requirements of paragraph (b) or (c) of this section, as applicable,

merely because the safe harbor contributions are not qualified nonelective contributions or qualified matching contributions provided that—

(i) The contributions are subject to the withdrawal restrictions set forth in § 1.401(k)-1(d); and

(ii) Any employee who has completed 2 years of service (within the meaning of section 411(a)) has a nonforfeitable right to the account balance attributable to the safe harbor contributions.

(4) Additional notice requirements—(i) In general. A notice satisfies the requirements of this paragraph (k)(4) only if it includes the additional information described in paragraph (k)(4)(ii) of this section and satisfies the timing requirements of paragraph (k)(4)(iii) of this section.

(ii) Additional information. A notice satisfies the additional information requirement of this paragraph (k)(4)(ii) only if it explains—

(A) The level of elective contributions which will be made on the employee's behalf if the employee does not make an affirmative election;

(B) The employee's right under the automatic contribution arrangement to elect not to have elective contributions made on the employee's behalf (or to elect to have such contributions made in a different amount or percentage of compensation); and

(C) How contributions under the automatic contribution arrangement will be invested (including, in the case of an arrangement under which the employee may elect among 2 or more investment options, how contributions made under the automatic contribution arrangement will be invested in the absence of an investment election by the employee).

(iii) Timing requirements. A notice satisfies the timing requirements of this paragraph (k)(4)(iii) only if it is provided sufficiently early so that the employee has a reasonable period of time after receipt of the notice and before the first elective contribution is made under the arrangement to make the elections described under paragraph (k)(4)(ii)(B) and (C) of this section.

* * * * *

Par. 6. Section 1.401(k)-6 is amended by revising the last sentence in the definition of "Qualified matching contributions (QMACs)" to read as follows:

§ 1.401(k)-6 Definitions.

* * * * *

Qualified matching contributions (QMACs). * * * See also § 1.401(k)-2(b)(4)(iii) for a rule providing that a matching contribution does not fail to qualify as a QMAC solely because it is forfeitable under section 411(a)(3)(G) as a result of being a matching contribution with respect to an excess deferral, excess contribution, excess aggregate contribution, or it is forfeitable under § 1.414(w)-1(d)(2).

* * * * *

Par. 7. Section 1.401(m)-0 is amended to read as follows:

Adding an entry for § 1.401(m)-2(b)(4)(iii).

§ 1.401(m)-0 Table of Contents.

* * * * *

§ 1.401(m)-2 ACP Test.

* * * * *

(b) * * *

(2) * * *

(iv) * * *

(A) * * *

(D) Plan years before 2008.

* * * * *

(4) * * *

(iii) Special rule for eligible automatic contribution arrangements.

* * * * *

Par. 8. Section 1.401(m)-1 is amended by:

1. Revising paragraph (b)(1)(iii) and adding paragraph (b)(1)(iv).

2. Revising the last sentence of paragraph (b)(4)(iii)(B).

3. Revising the fifth sentence of paragraph (c)(2).

The additions and revisions to read as follows:

§ 1.401(m)-1 Employee contributions and matching contributions.

* * * * *

(b) * * *

(1) * * *

(iii) The ACP safe harbor provisions of section 401(m)(12) described in § 1.401(m)-3; or

(iv) The SIMPLE 401(k) provisions of sections 401(k)(11) and 401(m)(10) described in § 1.401(k)-4.

* * * * *

(b) * * *

(4) * * *

(iii) * * *

(B) Arrangements with inconsistent ACP testing methods. * * * Similarly, an employer may not aggregate a plan (within the meaning of § 1.410(b)-7) that is using the ACP safe harbor provisions of section 401(m)(11) or 401(m)(12) and another plan that is using the ACP test of section 401(m)(2).

* * * * *

(c) * * *

(2) Plan provision requirement. * * * Similarly, a plan that uses the safe harbor method of section 401(m)(11) or 401(m)(12), as described in paragraphs (b)(1)(ii) and (b)(1)(iii) of this section, must specify the default percentages that apply for the plan year and whether the safe harbor contribution will be the nonelective safe harbor contribution or the matching safe harbor contribution and is not permitted to provide that ACP testing will be used if the requirements for the safe harbor are not satisfied. * * *

* * * * *

Par. 9. Section 1.401(m)-2 is amended by:

1. Revising the first and second sentences of paragraph (a)(5)(iv).

2. Revising paragraph (a)(5)(v).

3. Adding a new sentence to the end of paragraph (a)(6)(ii).

4. Revising paragraphs (b)(2)(iv)(A) and (b)(2)(iv)(D).

5. Removing paragraph (b)(2)(iv)(E).

6. Revising paragraph (b)(2)(vi)(A).

7. Adding a new sentence to the beginning of paragraph (b)(2)(vi)(B).

8. Adding paragraph (b)(4)(iii).

The additions and revisions to read as follows:

§ 1.401(m)-2 ACP test.

(a) * * * * *

(5) * * * * *

(iv) Matching contributions taken into account. A plan that satisfies the ACP safe harbor requirements of section 401(m)(11) or 401(m)(12) for a plan year but nonetheless must satisfy the requirements of this section because it provides for employee contributions for such plan year is permitted to apply this section disregarding all matching contributions with respect to all eligible employees. In addition, a plan that satisfies the ADP safe harbor requirements of § 1.401(k)-3 for a plan year using qualified matching contributions but does not satisfy the ACP safe harbor requirements of section 401(m)(11) or 401(m)(12) for such plan year is permitted to apply this section by excluding matching contributions with respect to all eligible employees that do not exceed 4 percent (3.5 percent in the case of a plan that satisfies the ADP safe harbor under section 401(k)(13)) of each employee's compensation. * * *

(v) Treatment of forfeited matching contributions. A matching contribution that is forfeited because the contribution to which it relates is treated as an excess contribution, excess deferral, excess aggregate contribution, or a default elective contribution that is distributed under section 414(w), is not taken into account for purposes of this section.

* * * * *

(6) * * * * *

(ii) Elective contributions taken into account under the ACP test. * * * In addition, for plan years ending on or after November 8, 2007, elective contributions which are not permitted to be taken into account for the ADP test for the plan year under § 1.401(k)-2(a)(5)(ii), (iii), (v), or (vi) are not permitted to be taken into account for the ACP test.

¶ 20,262E

* * * * *

(b) * * * * *

(2) * * * * *

(iv) Income allocable to excess aggregate contributions—(A) General rule. For plan years beginning on or after January 1, 2008, the income allocable to excess aggregate contributions is equal to the allocable gain or loss through the end of the plan year. See paragraph (b)(2)(iv)(D) of this section for rules that apply to plan years beginning before January 1, 2008.

* * * * *

(D) Plan years before 2008. For plan years beginning before January 1, 2008, the income allocable to excess aggregate contributions is determined under § 1.401(m)-2(b)(2)(iv) (as it appeared in the April 1, 2007, edition of 26 CFR part 1).

* * * * *

(vi) Tax treatment of corrective distributions—(A) Corrective distributions for plan years beginning on or after January 1, 2008. Except as otherwise provided in this paragraph (b)(2)(vi), for plan years beginning on or after January 1, 2008, a corrective distribution of excess aggregate contributions (and allocable income) is includible in the employee's gross income in the taxable year of the employee in which distributed. The portion of the distribution that is treated as an investment in the contract and is therefore not subject to tax under section 72 is determined without regard to any plan contributions other than those distributed as excess aggregate contributions. Regardless of when the corrective distribution is made, it is not subject to the early distribution tax of section 72(t). See paragraph (b)(4) of this section for additional rules relating to the employer excise tax on amounts distributed more than 2 1/2 months (6 months in the case of a plan that includes an eligible automatic contribution arrangement within the meaning of section 414(w)) after the end of the plan year. See also § 1.402(c)-2, A-4 prohibiting rollover of distributions that are excess aggregate contributions.

(B) Corrective distributions for plan years beginning before January 1, 2008. The tax treatment of corrective distributions for plan years beginning before January 1, 2008, is determined under § 1.401(m)-2(b)(2)(vi) (as it appeared in the April 1, 2007, edition of 26 CFR Part 1). * * *

(4) * * *

(iii) Special rule for eligible automatic contribution arrangements. In the case of a plan that includes an eligible automatic contribution arrangement (within the meaning of section 414(w)), 6 months is substituted for 2 1/2 months in paragraph (b)(4)(i) of this section.

* * * * *

Par. 10. Section 1.401(m)-3 is amended by:

1. Revising paragraph (a).

2. Revising the first sentences of paragraphs (f)(1) and (j)(3).

The additions and revisions to read as follows:

§ 1.401(m)-3 Safe harbor requirements.

(a) ACP test safe harbor—(1) Section 401(m)(11) safe harbor. Matching contributions under a plan satisfy the ACP safe harbor provisions of section 401(m)(11) for a plan year if the plan satisfies the safe harbor contribution requirement of paragraph (b) or (c) of this section for the plan year, the limitations on matching contributions of paragraph (d) of this section, the notice requirement of paragraph (e) of this section, the plan year requirements of paragraph (f) of this section, and the additional rules of paragraphs (g), (h) and (j) of this section, as applicable.

(2) Section 401(m)(12) safe harbor. For a plan year beginning on or after January 1, 2008, matching contributions under a plan satisfy the ACP safe harbor provisions of section 401(m)(12) for a plan year if the matching contributions are made with respect to a qualified automatic contribution arrangement described in paragraph § 1.401(k)-3(j) that satisfies the safe harbor requirements of § 1.401(k)-3, the limitations on matching contributions of paragraph (d) of this section, the notice requirement of paragraph (e) of this section, the plan year requirements of paragraph (f) of this section, and the additional rules of paragraphs (g), (h) and (j) of this section, as applicable.

(3) Requirements applicable to safe harbor contributions. Pursuant to sections 401(k)(12)(E)(ii) and 401(k)(13)(D)(iv), the safe harbor contribution requirement of paragraph (b) or (c) of this section, and § 1.401(k)-3(k) must be satisfied without regard to section 401(l). The contributions made under paragraphs (b) and (c) of this section, and

§ 1.401(k)-3(k) are referred to as safe harbor nonelective contributions and safe harbor matching contributions.

* * * * *

(f) Plan year requirement—(1) General rule. Except as provided in this paragraph (f) or in paragraph (g) of this section, a plan will fail to satisfy the requirements of section 401(m)(11), section 401(m)(12), and this section unless plan provisions that satisfy the rules of this section are adopted before the first day of that plan year and remain in effect for an entire 12-month plan year. * * *

* * * * *

(j) * * *

(3) Early participation rules. Section 401(m)(5)(C) and § 1.401(m)-2(a)(1)(iii)(A), which provide an alternative nondiscrimination rule for certain plans that provide for early participation, do not apply for purposes of section 401(m)(11), section 401(m)(12), and this section. * * *

* * * * *

Par. 11. Section 1.402(c)-2, A-4 is amended by redesignating paragraph (i) as (j) and adding a new paragraph (i) to read as follows:

§ 1.402(c)-2 Eligible rollover distributions, questions and answers.

* * * * *

A-4 * * *

(i) A distribution that is a permissible withdrawal from an eligible automatic contribution arrangement within the meaning of section 414(w).

* * * * *

Par. 12. Section 1.411(a)-4 is amended by revising paragraph (b)(7) to read as follows:

§ 1.411(a)-4 Forfeitures, suspensions, etc.

* * * * *

(b) * * *

(7) Certain matching contributions. A matching contribution (within the meaning of section 401(m)(4)(A) and § 1.401(m)-1(a)(2)) is not treated as forfeitable even if under the plan it may be forfeited under § 1.401(m)-2(b)(1) because the contribution to which it relates is treated as an excess contribution (within the meaning of § 1.401(k)-2(b)(2)(ii) and 1.401(k)-6), excess deferral (within the meaning of § 1.402(g)-1(e)(1)(iii)), excess aggregate contribution (within the meaning of § 1.401(m)-5), or default elective contributions (within the meaning of § 1.414(w)-1(e)) that are withdrawn in accordance with the requirements of § 1.414(w)-1(c).

Par. 13. Section 1.414(w)-1 is added to read as follows:

§ 1.414(w)-1 Permissible Withdrawals from Eligible Automatic Contribution Arrangements.

(a) Overview. Section 414(w) provides rules under which certain employees are permitted to elect to make a withdrawal from an eligible automatic contribution arrangement. This section sets forth the rules applicable to permissible withdrawals from an eligible automatic contribution arrangement within the meaning of section 414(w). Paragraph (b) of this section defines an eligible automatic contribution arrangement. Paragraph (c) of this section describes a permissible withdrawal and addresses which employees are eligible to elect a withdrawal, the timing of the withdrawal election, and the amount of the withdrawal. Paragraph (d) of this section describes the tax and other consequences of the withdrawal. Paragraph (e) of this section includes the definitions applicable to this section.

(b) Eligible automatic contribution arrangement—(1) In general. An eligible automatic contribution arrangement is an automatic contribution arrangement under an applicable employer plan that, for the plan year, satisfies the uniformity requirement under paragraph (b)(2) of this section, the notice requirement under paragraph (b)(3) of this section, and the default investment requirement under (b)(4) of this section.

(2) Uniformity requirement. An eligible automatic contribution arrangement must provide that the default elective contribution is a uniform percentage of compensation. An arrangement does not violate the uniformity requirement of this paragraph (b)(2) merely because the percentage varies in a manner that is permitted under § 1.401(k)-3(j)(2)(iii), except that the rules of §§ 1.401(k)-3(j)(2)(iii)(A) and 1.401(k)-3(j)(2)(iii)(B) are applied without regard to whether the

arrangement is intended to be a qualified automatic contribution arrangement.

(3) Notice requirement—(i) General rule. The notice requirement of this paragraph (b)(3) is satisfied for a plan year if each eligible employee is given notice of the employee's rights and obligations under the arrangement. The notice must be sufficiently accurate and comprehensive to apprise the employee of such rights and obligations, and be written in a manner calculated to be understood by the average employee to whom the arrangement applies. The notice must be in writing, however, see § 1.401(a)-21 for rules permitting the use of electronic media to provide applicable notices.

(ii) Content requirement. The notice must include the provisions found in § 1.401(k)-3(d)(2)(ii) to the extent those provisions apply to the arrangement. A notice is not considered sufficiently accurate and comprehensive unless the notice accurately describes—

(A) The level of elective contributions which will be made on the employee's behalf if the employee does not make an affirmative election;

(B) The employee's rights to elect not to have default elective contributions made to the plan on his or her behalf or to have a different percentage of compensation or amount of elective contributions made to the plan on his or her behalf;

(C) How contributions made under the arrangement will be invested in the absence of any investment election by the employee; and

(D) The employee's rights to make a permissible withdrawal, if applicable, and the procedures to elect such a withdrawal.

(iii) Timing—(A) General rule. The timing requirement of this paragraph (b)(3)(iii) is satisfied if the notice is provided within a reasonable period before the beginning of each plan year (or, in the year an employee becomes an eligible employee, within a reasonable period before the employee becomes an eligible employee). In addition, a notice satisfies the timing requirements of paragraph (b)(3) of this section only if it is provided sufficiently early so that the employee has a reasonable period of time after receipt of the notice and before the first elective contribution is made under the arrangement to make the election described under paragraph (b)(ii)(A) of this section.

(B) Deemed satisfaction of timing requirement. The timing requirement of this paragraph (b)(3)(iii) is satisfied if at least 30 days (and no more than 90 days) before the beginning of each plan year, the notice is given to each eligible employee for the plan year. In the case of an employee who does not receive the notice within the period described in the previous sentence because the employee becomes an eligible employee after the 90th day before the beginning of the plan year, the timing requirement is deemed to be satisfied if the notice is provided no more than 90 days before the employee becomes an eligible employee (and no later than the date the employee becomes an eligible employee).

(4) Default investment requirement. To the extent the plan is subject to Title I of ERISA, default elective contributions under an eligible automatic contribution arrangement must be invested in accordance with regulations prescribed by the Secretary of Labor under section 404(c)(5) of ERISA.

(c) Permissible withdrawal—(1) In general. If the plan provides, any employee who has default elective contributions made under the eligible automatic contribution arrangement may elect to make a withdrawal of such contributions (and earnings attributable thereto) in accordance with the requirements of this paragraph (c). An applicable employer plan that includes an eligible automatic contribution arrangement will not fail to satisfy the prohibition on in-service withdrawals under sections 401(k)(2)(B), 403(b)(7), 403(b)(11), or 457(d)(1) merely because it permits withdrawals that satisfy the timing requirement of paragraph (c)(2) of this section and the amount requirement of paragraph (c)(3) of this section.

(2) Timing. The election to withdraw default elective contributions must be made no later than 90 days after the date of the first default elective contribution under the eligible automatic contribution arrangement. The date of the first default elective contribution is the date that the compensation that is subject to the cash or deferred election would otherwise have been included in gross income. The effective date of an election described in this paragraph (c)(2) cannot be later than the last day of the payroll period that begins after the date the election is made.

(3) Amount of distributions—(i) In general. A distribution satisfies the requirement of this paragraph (c)(3) if the distribution is equal to the amount of default elective contributions made under the eligible automatic contribution arrangement through the effective date of the election described in paragraph (c)(2) of this section (adjusted for allocable gains and losses to the date of distribution). If default elective contributions are separately accounted for in the participant's account, the amount of the distribution will be the total amount in that account. However, if default elective contributions are not separately accounted for under the plan, the amount of the allocable gains and losses will be determined under rules similar to those provided under § 1.401(k)-2(b)(2)(iv) for the distribution of excess contributions.

(ii) Fees. The distribution amount as determined under this paragraph (c)(3) may be reduced by any generally applicable fees. However, the plan may not charge a different fee for a distribution under section 414(w) than applies to other distributions.

(d) Consequences of the withdrawal—(1) Income tax consequences—(i) Year of inclusion. The amount of the withdrawal is includible in the eligible employee's gross income for the taxable year in which the distribution is made. However, the portion of the distribution consisting of designated Roth contributions is not included in an employee's gross income a second time. The portion of the withdrawal that is treated as an investment in the contract is determined without regard to any plan contributions other than those distributed as withdrawal default elective contributions.

(ii) No additional tax on early distributions from qualified retirement plans. The withdrawal is not subject to the additional tax under section 72(t).

(iii) Reporting. The amount of the withdrawal is reported on Form 1099-R, Distributions From Pensions, Annuities, Retirement or Profit-Sharing Plans, IRAs, Insurance Contracts, etc., as described in the applicable instructions.

(2) Forfeiture of matching contributions. In the case of any withdrawal made under paragraph (c) of this section, employer matching contributions with respect to the amount withdrawn must be forfeited.

(3) Consent rules. A withdrawal made under paragraph (c) of this section may be made without regard to any notice or consent otherwise required under section 401(a)(11) or 417.

(e) Definitions. Unless indicated otherwise, the following definitions apply for purposes of section 414(w) and this section.

(1) Applicable employer plan. An applicable employer plan means a plan that—

(i) Is qualified under section 401(a);

(ii) Satisfies the requirements of section 403(b); or

(iii) Is a section 457(b) eligible governmental plan described in § 1.457-2(f).

(2) Automatic contribution arrangement. An automatic contribution arrangement means an arrangement that provides for a cash or deferred election that provides that in the absence of an eligible employee's affirmative election, a default election applies under which the employee is treated as having elected to have default elective contributions made on his or her behalf under the plan. This default election ceases to apply with respect to an employee if the employee makes an affirmative election (that remains in effect) to—

(i) Not have any default elective contributions made on his or her behalf; or

(ii) Have default elective contributions made in a different amount or percentage of compensation.

(3) Default elective contributions. Default elective contributions means contributions made at a specified level or amount under an automatic contribution arrangement that are—

(i) Contributions described in section 402(g)(3)(A) or 402(g)(3)(C); or

(ii) Contributions made pursuant to a cash or deferred election within the meaning of section 457(b)(4) where the contributions are under a section 457(b) eligible governmental plan.

(4) Eligible employee. An eligible employee means an employee who is eligible to make a cash or deferred election under the plan.

(f) Effective date. Section 414(w) and this section apply to plan years beginning on or after January 1, 2008.

* * * * *

PART 54—EXCISE TAXES. PENSIONS, REPORTING AND RECORDKEEPING REQUIREMENTS

Par. 14. The authority citation for part 54 continues to read in part as follows:

Authority: 26 U.S.C. 7805 * * *

Par. 15. Section 54.4979-1(c)(1) is amended by:

Revising the first and second sentences of paragraph (c)(1) to read as follows:

§ 54.4979-1 Excise tax on certain excess contributions and excess aggregate contributions.

* * * * *

(c) No tax when excess distributed within 2 1/2 months of close of year or additional employer contributions made—(1) General rule. No tax is imposed under this section on any excess contribution or excess aggregate contribution, as the case may be, to the extent the contribution (together with any income allocable thereto) is corrected before the close of the first 2 1/2 months of the following plan year (6 months in the case of a plan that includes an eligible automatic contribution arrangement within the meaning of section 414(w)). Qualified nonelective contributions and qualified matching contributions taken into account under § 1.401(k)-2(a)(6) of this Chapter or qualified nonelective contributions or elective contributions taken into account under § 1.401(m)-2(a)(6) of this Chapter for a plan year may permit a plan to avoid excess contributions or excess aggregate contributions, respectively, even if made after the close of the 2 1/2 month period (6 months in the case of a plan that includes an eligible automatic contribution arrangement within the meaning of section 414(w)). * * *

* * * * *

Linda E. Stiff,

Deputy Commissioner for Services and Enforcement.

¶ 20,262F

IRS: Hybrid plans: Cash balance plans: Pension Protection Act of 2006.— The IRS has issued proposed regulations providing guidance on hybrid plans, including cash balance plans, under Code Secs. 411(a)(13) and 411(b)(5), as amended by the Pension Protection Act of 2006 (P.L. 109-280). The proposed regulations incorporate transitional guidance provided under Notice 2007-6 (¶ 17,135Q), as well as additional guidance, taking into account comments received in response to Notice 2007-6.

The proposed regulations were published in the Federal Register on December 28, 2007 (72 FR 73680) and corrected on April 15, 2008 (73 FR 20367), and on April 25, 2008 (73 FR 22300).

Final regulations on hybrid plans were published on October 19, 2010 (75 FR 64123). The preamble to the final regulations is at ¶ 23,277. The final regulations are at ¶ 12,220 and ¶ 12,224. Additional proposed regulations on hybrid plans were also published on October 19, 2010 (75 FR 64197).

DEPARTMENT OF THE TREASURY

Internal Revenue Service

26 CFR Part 1

[REG-104946-07]

RIN 1545-BG36

Hybrid Retirement Plans

AGENCY: Internal Revenue Service (IRS), Treasury.

ACTION: Notice of proposed rulemaking.

SUMMARY: This document contains proposed regulations providing guidance relating to sections 411(a)(13) and 411(b)(5) of the Internal Revenue Code (Code) concerning certain hybrid defined benefit plans. These regulations provide guidance on changes made by the Pension Protection Act of 2006. These regulations affect sponsors, administrators, participants, and beneficiaries of hybrid defined benefit plans.

DATES: Written or electronic comments and requests for a public hearing must be received by March 27, 2008.

ADDRESSES: Send submissions to: CC:PA:LPD:PR (REG-104946-07), Room 5203, Internal Revenue Service, PO Box 7604, Ben Franklin Station, Washington, DC 20044. Submissions may be hand-delivered Monday through Friday between the hours of 8 a.m. and 4 p.m. to: CC:PA:LPD:PR (REG-104946-07), Courier's Desk, Internal Revenue Service, 1111 Constitution Avenue, NW., Washington, DC, or sent electronically via the Federal eRulemaking Portal at http://www.regulations.gov (IRS REG-104946-07).

FOR FURTHER INFORMATION CONTACT: Concerning the regulations, Lauson C. Green or Linda S. F. Marshall at (202) 622-6090; concerning submissions of comments or to request a public hearing, Funmi Taylor at (202) 622-7180 (not toll-free numbers).

SUPPLEMENTARY INFORMATION:

Background

This document contains amendments to the Income Tax Regulations (26 CFR part 1) under sections 411(a)(13) and 411(b)(5) of the Code. Generally, a defined benefit pension plan must satisfy the minimum vesting standards of section 411(a) and the accrual requirements of section 411(b) in order to be qualified under section 401(a) of the Code. Sections 411(a)(13) and 411(b)(5), which were added to the Code by section 701(b) of the Pension Protection Act of 2006, Public Law 109-280, 120 Stat. 780 (PPA '06), modify the minimum vesting standards of section 411(a) and the accrual requirements of section 411(b).

Section 411(a)(13)(A) provides that an applicable defined benefit plan (which is defined in section 411(a)(13)(C)) is not treated as failing to meet either (i) The requirements of section 411(a)(2) (subject to a special vesting rule in section 411(a)(13)(B) with respect to benefits derived from employer contributions) or (ii) The requirements of section 411(c) or 417(e) with respect to contributions other than employee contributions, merely because the present value of the accrued benefit (or any portion thereof) of any participant is, under the terms of the plan, equal to the amount expressed as the balance in a hypothetical account or as an accumulated percentage of the participant's final average compensation. Section 411(a)(13)(B) requires an applicable defined benefit plan to provide that an employee who has completed at least 3 years of service has a nonforfeitable right to 100 percent of the employee's accrued benefit derived from employer contributions.

Under section 411(a)(13)(C)(i), a plan is an applicable defined benefit plan if the plan is a defined benefit plan under which the accrued benefit (or any portion thereof) of a participant is calculated as the balance of a hypothetical account maintained for the participant or as an accumulated percentage of the participant's final average compensation. Under section 411(a)(13)(C)(ii), the Secretary of the Treasury is to issue regulations which include in the definition of an applicable defined benefit plan any defined benefit plan (or portion of such a plan) which has an effect similar to a plan described in section 411(a)(13)(C)(i).

Section 411(b)(1)(H)(i) provides that a defined benefit plan fails to comply with section 411(b) if, under the plan, an employee's benefit accrual is ceased, or the employee's rate of benefit accrual is reduced, because of the attainment of any age. Section 411(b)(5), which was added to the Code by section 701(b)(1) of PPA '06, provides additional rules related to section 411(b)(1)(H)(i). Section 411(b)(5)(A) generally provides that a plan is not treated as failing to meet the requirements of section 411(b)(1)(H)(i) if a participant's accrued benefit, as determined as of any date under the terms of the plan, would be equal to or greater than that of any similarly situated younger individual who is or could be a participant. Section 411(b)(5)(G) provides that, for purposes of section 411(b)(5), any reference to the accrued benefit of a participant shall be a reference to the participant's benefit accrued to date. For purposes of section 411(b)(5)(A), section 411(b)(5)(A)(iv) provides that the accrued benefit may, under the terms of the plan, be expressed as an annuity payable at normal retirement age, the balance of a hypothetical account, or the current value of the accumulated percentage of the employee's final average compensation.

Section 411(b)(5)(B) imposes several requirements on an applicable defined benefit plan as a condition of the plan satisfying section 411(b)(1)(H). Section 411(b)(5)(B)(i) provides that such a plan is treated as failing to meet the requirements of section 411(b)(1)(H) if the terms of the plan provide for an interest credit (or an equivalent amount) for any plan year at a rate that is greater than a market rate of return. Under section 411(b)(5)(B)(i)(I), a plan is not treated as having an above-market rate merely because the plan provides for a reasonable minimum guaranteed rate of return or for a rate of return that is equal to the greater of a fixed or variable rate of return. Section 411(b)(5)(B)(i)(II) provides that an interest credit (or an equivalent amount) of less than zero can in no event result in the hypothetical account balance or similar amount being less than the aggregate amount of contributions credited to the account. Section

411(b)(5)(B)(i)(III) specifies that the Secretary of the Treasury may provide by regulation for rules governing the calculation of a market rate of return for purposes of section 411(b)(5)(B)(i)(I) and for permissible methods of crediting interest to the account (including fixed or variable interest rates) resulting in effective rates of return meeting the requirements of section 411(b)(5)(B)(i)(I).

Section 411(b)(5)(B)(ii), (iii), and (iv) contain minimum benefit rules that apply if, after June 29, 2005, an applicable plan amendment is adopted. Section 411(b)(5)(B)(v)(I) defines an applicable plan amendment as an amendment to a defined benefit plan which has the effect of converting the plan to an applicable defined benefit plan. Under section 411(b)(5)(B)(ii), if, after June 29, 2005, an applicable plan amendment is adopted, the plan is treated as failing to meet the requirements of section 411(b)(1)(H) unless the requirements of section 411(b)(5)(B)(iii) are met with respect to each individual who was a participant in the plan immediately before the adoption of the amendment. Section 411(b)(5)(B)(iii) specifies that, subject to section 411(b)(5)(B)(iv), the requirements of section 411(b)(5)(B)(iii) are met with respect to any participant if the accrued benefit of the participant under the terms of the plan as in effect after the amendment is not less than the sum of: (I) The participant's accrued benefit for years of service before the effective date of the amendment, determined under the terms of the plan as in effect before the amendment; plus (II) The participant's accrued benefit for years of service after the effective date of the amendment, determined under the terms of the plan as in effect after the amendment. Section 411(b)(5)(B)(iv) provides that, for purposes of section 411(b)(5)(B)(iii)(I), the plan must credit the participant's account or similar amount with the amount of any early retirement benefit or retirement-type subsidy for the plan year in which the participant retires if, as of such time, the participant has met the age, years of service, and other requirements under the plan for entitlement to such benefit or subsidy.

Section 411(b)(5)(B)(v) sets forth certain provisions related to an applicable plan amendment. Section 411(b)(5)(B)(v)(II) provides that if the benefits under two or more defined benefit plans of an employer are coordinated in such a manner as to have the effect of adoption of an applicable plan amendment, the plan sponsor is treated as having adopted an applicable plan amendment as of the date the coordination begins. Section 411(b)(5)(B)(v)(III) directs the Secretary of the Treasury to issue regulations to prevent the avoidance of the purposes of section 411(b)(5)(B) through the use of two or more plan amendments rather than through a single plan amendment.

Section 411(b)(5)(B)(vi) provides a special rule for converting a variable interest crediting rate to a fixed rate for purposes of determining plan benefits in the case of a terminating applicable defined benefit plan.

Section 411(b)(5)(C) provides that a plan is not treated as failing to meet the requirements of section 411(b)(1)(H)(i) solely because the plan provides offsets against benefits under the plan to the extent the offsets are allowable in applying the requirements of section 401(a). Section 411(b)(5)(D) provides that a plan is not treated as failing to meet the requirements of section 411(b)(1)(H) solely because the plan provides a disparity in contributions or benefits with respect to which the requirements of section 401(l) (relating to permitted disparity for Social Security benefits and related matters) are met.

Section 411(b)(5)(E) provides that a plan is not treated as failing to meet the requirements of section 411(b)(1)(H) solely because the plan provides for indexing of accrued benefits under the plan. Under section 411(b)(5)(E)(iii), indexing means the periodic adjustment of the accrued benefit by means of the application of a recognized investment index or methodology. Section 411(b)(5)(E)(ii) requires that, except in the case of a variable annuity, the indexing not result in a smaller benefit than the accrued benefit determined without regard to the indexing.

Section 701(a) of PPA '06 added provisions to the Employee Retirement Income Security Act of 1974, Public Law 93-406 (88 Stat. 829) (ERISA), that are parallel to the above-described sections of the Code that were added by section 701(b) of PPA '06. The guidance provided in these proposed regulations with respect to the Code would also apply for purposes of the parallel amendments to ERISA made by section 701(a) of PPA '06.[1]

Section 701(c) of PPA '06 added provisions to the Age Discrimination in Employment Act of 1967, Public Law 90-202 (81 Stat. 602) (ADEA), that are parallel to section 411(b)(5) of the Code. Executive Order 12067 requires all Federal departments and agencies to advise and offer to consult with the Equal Employment Opportunity Commission (EEOC) during the development of any proposed rules, regulations, policies, procedures or orders concerning equal employment opportunity. The IRS and the Treasury Department have consulted with the EEOC prior to the issuance of these proposed regulations.

Section 701(d) of PPA '06 provides that nothing in the amendments made by section 701 should be construed to create an inference concerning the treatment of applicable defined benefit plans or conversions of plans into applicable defined benefit plans under section 411(b)(1)(H), or concerning the determination of whether an applicable defined benefit plan fails to meet the requirements of section 411(a)(2), 411(c), or 417(e) as in effect before such amendments solely because the present value of the accrued benefit (or any portion thereof) of any participant is, under the terms of the plan, equal to the amount expressed as the balance in a hypothetical account or as an accumulated percentage of the participant's final average compensation.

Section 701(e) of PPA '06 sets forth the effective date provisions with respect to amendments made by section 701 of PPA '06. Section 701(e)(1) specifies that the amendments made by section 701 generally apply to periods beginning on or after June 29, 2005. Thus, the age discrimination safe harbors under section 411(b)(5)(A) and section 411(b)(5)(E) are effective for periods beginning on or after June 29, 2005. Section 701(e)(2) provides that the special present value rules of section 411(a)(13)(A) are effective for distributions made after August 17, 2006.

Under section 701(e)(3) of PPA '06, in the case of a plan in existence on June 29, 2005, the 3-year vesting rule under section 411(a)(13)(B) and the market rate of return limitation under section 411(b)(5)(B)(i) are generally effective for years beginning after December 31, 2007. In the case of a plan not in existence on June 29, 2005, those sections are effective for periods beginning on or after June 29, 2005. Section 701(e)(4) of PPA '06 contains special effective date provisions for collectively bargained plans that modify these effective dates.

Under section 701(e)(5) of PPA '06, sections 411(b)(5)(B)(ii), (iii), and (iv) apply to a conversion amendment that is adopted after, and takes effect after, June 29, 2005.

Section 702 of PPA '06 provides for regulations to be prescribed by August 16, 2007, addressing the application of rules set forth in section 701 of PPA '06 where the conversion of a defined benefit pension plan into an applicable defined benefit plan is made with respect to a group of employees who become employees by reason of a merger, acquisition, or similar transaction.

Proposed regulations (EE-184-86) under sections 411(b)(1)(H) and 411(b)(2) were published by the Treasury Department and the IRS in the Federal Register on April 11, 1988 (53 FR 11876), as part of a package of regulations that also included proposed regulations under sections 410(a), 411(a)(2), 411(a)(8), and 411(c) (relating to the maximum age for participation, vesting, normal retirement age, and actuarial adjustments after normal retirement age, respectively).[2]

Notice 96-8 (1996-1 CB 359), see § 601.601(d)(2)(ii)(b) of this chapter, described the application of sections 411 and 417(e) to a single sum distribution under a cash balance plan where interest credits under the plan are frontloaded (that is, where future interest credits to an employee's hypothetical account balance are not conditioned upon future service and thus accrue at the same time that the benefits attributable to a hypothetical allocation to the account accrue). Under the analysis set forth in Notice 96-8, in order to comply with sections 411(a) and 417(e) in calculating the amount of a single sum distribution under a cash balance plan, the balance of an employee's hypothetical account must be projected to normal retirement age and converted to an annuity under the terms of the plan, and then the employee must be paid at least the present value of the projected annuity, determined in accordance with section 417(e). Under that analysis, where a cash balance plan provides frontloaded interest credits using an interest rate that is higher than the section 417(e) applicable interest rate, payment of a single sum distribution equal to the current hypothetical account

---

[1] Under section 101 of Reorganization Plan No. 4 of 1978 (43 FR 47713), the Secretary of the Treasury has interpretive jurisdiction over the subject matter addressed by these proposed regulations for purposes of ERISA, as well as the Code.

[2] On December 11, 2002, the Treasury Department and the IRS issued proposed regulations regarding the age discrimination requirements of section 411(b)(1)(H) that specifically addressed cash balance plans as part of a package of regulations that also addressed section 401(a)(4) nondiscrimination cross-testing rules applicable to cash balance plans (67 FR 76123). The 2002 proposed regulations were intended to replace the 1988 proposed regulations. In Ann. 2003-22 (2003-1 CB 847), see § 601.601(d)(2)(ii)(b) of this chapter, the Treasury Department and the IRS announced the withdrawal of the 2002 proposed regulations under section 401(a)(4), and in Ann. 2004-57 (2004-2 CB 15), see § 601.601(d)(2)(ii)(b) of this chapter, the Treasury Department and the IRS announced the withdrawal of the 2002 proposed regulations relating to age discrimination.

balance as a complete distribution of the employee's accrued benefit may result in a violation of section 417(e) or a forfeiture in violation of section 411(a). In addition, Notice 96-8 proposed a safe harbor which provided that, if frontloaded interest credits are provided under a plan at a rate no greater than the sum of identified standard indices and associated margins, no violation of section 411(a) or 417(e) would result if the employee's entire accrued benefit is distributed in the form of a single sum distribution equal to the employee's hypothetical account balance, provided the plan uses appropriate annuity conversion factors. Since the issuance of Notice 96-8, four federal appellate courts have followed the analysis set out in the Notice: Esden v. Bank of Boston, 229 F.3d 154 (2d Cir. 2000), cert. dismissed, 531 U.S. 1061 (2001); West v. AK Steel Corp. Ret. Accumulation Pension Plan, 484 F.3d 395 (6th Cir. 2007), reh'g and reh'g en banc denied, No. 06-3442, 2007 U.S. App. LEXIS 20447 (6th Cir. Aug. 8, 2007); Berger v. Xerox Corp. Ret. Income Guarantee Plan, 338 F.3d 755 (7th Cir. 2003), reh'g and reh'g en banc denied, No. 02-3674, 2003 U.S. App. LEXIS 19374 (7th Cir. Sept. 15, 2003); Lyons v. Georgia-Pacific Salaried Employees Ret. Plan, 221 F.3d 1235 (11th Cir. 2000), cert. denied, 532 U.S. 967 (2001).

Notice 2007-6, 2007-3 IRB 272 (January 16, 2007), see § 601.601(d)(2)(ii)(b) of this chapter, provides transitional guidance with respect to certain requirements of sections 411(a)(13) and 411(b)(5) and section 701(b) of PPA '06. Notice 2007-6 includes certain special definitions, including: accumulated benefit, which is defined as a participant's benefit accrued to date under a plan; lump sum-based plan, which is defined as a defined benefit plan under the terms of which the accumulated benefit of a participant is expressed as the balance of a hypothetical account maintained for the participant or as the current value of the accumulated percentage of the participant's final average compensation; and statutory hybrid plan, which is a lump sum-based plan or a plan which has an effect similar to a lump sum-based plan. Notice 2007-6 provides guidance on a number of issues, including a rule under which a plan that provides for indexed benefits described in section 411(b)(5)(E) is a statutory hybrid plan (because it has an effect similar to a lump sum-based plan), unless the plan either solely provides for post-retirement adjustment of the amounts payable to a participant or is a variable annuity plan under which the assumed interest rate used to determine adjustments is at least 5 percent. The Notice provides a safe harbor for applying the rules set forth in section 701 of PPA '06 where the conversion of a defined benefit pension plan into an applicable defined benefit plan is made with respect to a group of employees who become employees by reason of a merger, acquisition, or similar transaction. This transitional guidance, along with other guidance provided in Part III of Notice 2007-6, applies pending the issuance of further guidance and, thus, will cease to apply when these regulations are finalized and become effective.

Explanation of Provisions

Overview

In general, these proposed regulations would incorporate the transitional guidance provided under Notice 2007-6. However, the proposed regulations would utilize new terminology (such as statutory hybrid benefit formula and lump sum-based benefit formula) to take into account situations where plans provide more than one benefit formula. These proposed regulations would also provide additional guidance with respect to sections 411(a)(13) and 411(b)(5), taking into account comments received in response to Notice 2007-6.

Section 411(a)(13): Special vesting rules for applicable defined benefit plans and applicable definitions

The proposed regulations would reflect new section 411(a)(13)(A) by providing that an applicable defined benefit plan does not violate the requirements of section 411(a)(2), or the requirements of section 411(c) or 417(e), with respect to a participant's accrued benefit derived from employer contributions, merely because the plan determines the present value of benefits determined under a lump sum-based benefit formula as the amount of the hypothetical account maintained for the participant or as the current value of the accumulated percentage of the participant's final average compensation under that formula. However, section 411(a)(13) does not alter the definition of an accrued benefit under section 411(a)(7)(A) (which generally defines a participant's accrued benefit as the annual benefit commencing at normal retirement age), nor does it alter the definition of a normal retirement benefit under section 411(a)(9) (which generally defines a participant's normal retirement benefit as the benefit under the plan commencing at normal retirement age).

Section 411(b)(5)(G) provides that, for purposes of section 411(b)(5), any reference to the accrued benefit means the benefit accrued to date. The proposed regulations refer to this as the accumulated benefit, which is distinct from the participant's accrued benefit under section 411(a)(7) (an annuity beginning at normal retirement age that is actuarially equivalent to the participant's accumulated benefit).

The regulations define a lump sum-based benefit formula as a benefit formula used to determine all or any part of a participant's accumulated benefit under which the benefit provided under the formula is expressed as the balance of a hypothetical account maintained for the participant or as the current value of the accumulated percentage of the participant's final average compensation. Under the proposed regulations, whether a benefit formula is a lump sum-based benefit formula would be determined based on how the accumulated benefit of a participant is expressed under the terms of the plan, and would not depend on whether the plan provides an optional form of benefit in the form of a single sum payment. Similarly, a formula would not fail to be a lump sum-based benefit formula merely because the plan's terms state that the accrued benefit is an annuity at normal retirement age that is actuarially equivalent to a hypothetical account balance. In addition, the regulations would provide that a participant is not treated as having a lump sum-based benefit formula merely because the participant is entitled to a benefit under a defined benefit plan that is not less than the benefit properly attributable to after-tax employee contributions.

Section 411(a)(13)(A) applies only with respect to a benefit provided under a lump sum-based benefit formula. Accordingly, if the present value rules of section 417(e) apply to a form of benefit under a plan and the plan provides benefits under a benefit formula that is not a lump sum-based benefit formula (including, for example, a plan that provides for indexing as described in section 411(b)(5)(E)), then the plan must set forth a methodology to determine the projected benefit under that formula at normal retirement age for purposes of applying the rules of section 417(e), as described in the "Analysis" section of Notice 96-8.

The proposed regulations use the term statutory hybrid benefit formula to describe the portion of a defined benefit plan that is an applicable defined benefit plan described in section 411(a)(13)(C)(i) or the portion of the plan that has a similar effect. Specifically, the proposed regulations would define a statutory hybrid benefit formula as a benefit formula that is either a lump sum-based benefit formula or a formula that has an effect similar to a lump sum-based benefit formula. For this purpose, under the proposed regulations, a benefit formula under a defined benefit plan has an effect similar to a lump sum-based benefit formula if the formula provides that a participant's accrued benefit payable at normal retirement age (or at benefit commencement, if later) is expressed as a benefit that includes periodic adjustments (including a formula that provides for indexed benefits described in section 411(b)(5)(E)) that are reasonably expected to result in a smaller annual benefit at normal retirement age (or at commencement of benefits, if later) for the participant, when compared to a similarly situated, younger individual who is or could be a participant in the plan. Thus, a benefit formula under a plan has an effect similar to a lump sum-based benefit formula if the right to future adjustments accrues at the same time as the benefit that is subject to the adjustments. (Corrected by IRS on April 25, 2008 (73 FR 22300)).

The proposed regulations would set forth certain additional rules that are used in determining whether a benefit formula has an effect similar to a lump sum-based benefit formula. For example, the proposed regulations provide that a benefit formula that does not include periodic adjustments is treated as a formula with an effect similar to a lump sum-based benefit formula if the formula is otherwise described in the preceding paragraph and the adjustments are provided pursuant to a pattern of repeated plan amendments. See § 1.411(d)-4, A-1(c)(1). The proposed regulations would provide that, for purposes of determining whether a benefit formula has an effect similar to a lump sum-based benefit formula, indexing that applies to adjust benefits after the annuity starting date (for example, cost-of-living increases) is disregarded. In addition, the proposed regulations would provide that a benefit formula under a defined benefit plan that provides for a benefit properly attributable to after-tax employee contributions does not have an effect similar to a lump sum-based benefit formula. The proposed regulations would also provide that adjustments under a variable annuity do not have an effect similar to a lump sum-based benefit formula if the assumed interest rate used to determine the adjustments is at least 5 percent. Such an annuity does not have an effect similar to a lump sum-based benefit formula even if post-annuity starting date adjustments are made using a specified assumed interest rate that is less than 5 percent.

Pursuant to new section 411(a)(13)(B), the proposed regulations would provide that, in the case of a participant whose accrued benefit (or any portion thereof) under a defined benefit plan is determined under a statutory hybrid benefit formula, the plan is not treated as meeting the requirements of section 411(a)(2) unless the plan provides that the participant has a nonforfeitable right to 100 percent of the participant's accrued benefit if the participant has 3 or more years of service. This requirement would apply on a participant-by-participant basis and would apply to the participant's entire benefit (not just the portion of the participant's benefit that is determined under a statutory hybrid benefit formula). Furthermore, if the participant is entitled to the greater of two benefits under a plan, one of which is a benefit calculated under a statutory hybrid benefit formula, the proposed regulations would provide that the 3-year vesting requirement applies to that participant even if the participant's benefit under the statutory hybrid benefit formula is ultimately smaller than under the other formula. The proposed regulations do not address how the 3-year vesting requirement applies in the case of floor-offset arrangements.[3] See the discussion in this preamble under the heading "Comments and Requests for Public Hearing."

Section 411(b)(5): Safe harbor for age discrimination, conversion protection, and market rate of return limitation

A. Safe harbor for age discrimination

The proposed regulations under new section 411(b)(5)(A) would provide that a plan is not treated as failing to meet the requirements of section 411(b)(1)(H)(i) with respect to certain benefit formulas if, as determined as of any date, a participant's accumulated benefit expressed under one of those formulas would not be less than any similarly situated, younger participant's accumulated benefit expressed under the same formula. A plan that does not satisfy this test is required to satisfy the general nondiscrimination test of section 411(b)(1)(H)(i).

Under the proposed regulations, the safe harbor standard for satisfying section 411(b)(5)(A) would be available only where a participant's accumulated benefit under the terms of the plan is expressed as an annuity payable at normal retirement age (or current age, if later), the balance of a hypothetical account, or the current value of the accumulated percentage of the employee's final average compensation. For this purpose, if the accumulated benefit of a participant is expressed as an annuity payable at normal retirement age (or current age, if later) under the plan terms, then the comparison of benefits is made using such an annuity. If the accumulated benefit of a participant is expressed under the plan terms as the balance of a hypothetical account or the current value of an accumulated percentage of the participant's final average compensation, then the comparison of benefits is made using the balance of a hypothetical account or the current value of the accumulated percentage of the participant's final average compensation, respectively.

The proposed regulations would require a comparison of the accumulated benefit of each possible participant in the plan to the accumulated benefit of each other similarly situated, younger individual who is or could be a participant in the plan. For this purpose, the proposed regulations would provide that an individual is similarly situated to another individual if the individual is identical to that other individual in every respect that is relevant in determining a participant's benefit under the plan (including but not limited to period of service, compensation, position, date of hire, work history, and any other respect) except for age.[4] In determining whether an individual is similarly situated to another individual, any characteristic that is relevant for determining benefits under the plan and that is based directly or indirectly on age is disregarded. For example, if a particular benefit formula applies to a participant on account of the participant's age, an individual to whom the benefit formula does not apply and who is identical to a participant in all respects other than age is similarly situated to the participant. By contrast, an individual is not similarly situated to a participant if a different benefit formula applies to the individual and the application of the different formula is based neither directly nor indirectly on age.

The comparison of accumulated benefits is made without regard to any subsidized portion of any early retirement benefit that is included in a participant's accumulated benefit. For this purpose, the subsidized portion of an early retirement benefit is the retirement-type subsidy within the meaning of § 1.411(d)-3(g)(6) that is contingent on a participant's severance from employment and commencement of benefits before normal retirement age.

In addition, the comparison of accumulated benefits generally must be made using the same form of benefit. Thus, the safe harbor is not available for comparing the accumulated benefit of a participant ex-

pressed as an annuity at normal retirement age with the accumulated benefit of a similarly situated, younger participant expressed as a hypothetical account balance. Nevertheless, the proposed regulations would permit a plan that provides the sum of benefits that are expressed in two or more different forms of benefit to satisfy the safe harbor if the plan would separately satisfy the safe harbor for each separate form of benefit. Similarly, the proposed regulations would permit a plan that provides the greater of benefits that are expressed in two or more different forms of benefit to satisfy the safe harbor if the plan would separately satisfy the safe harbor for each separate form of benefit. For this purpose, a similarly situated, younger participant is treated as having an accumulated benefit of zero with respect to a benefit formula that does not apply to the participant. Thus, the safe harbor would be available if an older participant is entitled to benefits under more than one type of benefit formula, even if not all of those types of benefit formulas are available to every similarly situated participant who is younger.

The proposed regulations would reflect new section 411(b)(5)(C), which provides that a plan is not treated as failing to meet the requirements of section 411(b)(1)(H) solely because the plan provides offsets of benefits under the plan to the extent such offsets are allowable in applying the requirements under section 401 and the applicable requirements of the Employee Retirement Income Security Act of 1974, Public Law 93-406 (88 Stat. 829) (ERISA) and the Age Discrimination in Employment Act of 1967, Public Law 90-202 (81 Stat. 602) (ADEA). The proposed regulations incorporate the provisions of section 411(b)(5)(D) (relating to permitted disparity under section 401(1)) without providing additional guidance.

The proposed regulations would reflect new section 411(b)(5)(E), which provides for the disregard of certain indexing of benefits for purposes of the age discrimination rules of section 411(b)(1)(H). The proposed regulations limit the disregard of indexing to formulas under defined benefit plans other than lump sum-based formulas. In addition, the proposed regulations limit the disregard of indexing to situations in which the extent of the indexing for a participant would not be less than the indexing applicable to a similarly situated, younger participant. Thus, the disregard of indexing is only available if the indexing is neither terminated nor reduced on account of the attainment of any age.

Section 411(b)(5)(E) requires that the indexing methodology be a recognized methodology. The proposed regulations would treat only the following indexing methodologies as recognized for this purpose: indexing using an eligible cost-of-living index as described in § 1.401(a)(9)-6, A-14(b); indexing using the rate of return on the aggregate assets of the plan; and indexing using the rate of return on the annuity contract for the employee issued by an insurance company licensed under the laws of a State.

Under the proposed regulations, the section 411(b)(5)(E)(ii) protection against loss ("no-loss") requirement for an indexed plan (which provides that the indexing not result in a smaller accrued benefit) would be implemented by applying the "preservation of capital" rule of section 411(b)(5)(B)(i)(II) to indexed plans. (The preservation of capital rule is discussed in this preamble paragraph heading "C. Market rate of return limitation.") For this purpose, the exemption from the application of the no-loss rule for variable annuities would be limited to situations in which the variable annuity adjustment is based on the rate of return on the aggregate assets of the plan or the annuity contract. Thus, the exemption from the application of the no-loss rule would not apply if the variable annuity adjustment is based on the rate of return of a portion of the assets of the plan. In addition, this exemption would also apply for purposes of the preservation of capital requirement that applies to statutory hybrid plans. (Corrected by IRS on April 25, 2008 (73 FR 22300)).

B. Conversion protection

The regulations would provide guidance on the new conversion protections under section 411(b)(5)(B)(ii), (iii), and (iv). Under the proposed regulations, a participant whose benefits are affected by a conversion amendment which occurred after June 29, 2005, must generally be provided with a benefit after the conversion that is at least equal to the sum of the benefits accrued through the date of the conversion and benefits earned after the conversion, with no permitted interaction between these two portions. This would assure participants that there will be no "wear-away" as a result of a conversion, both with respect to

---

[3] See Rev. Rul. 76-259 (1976-2 CB 111), see § 601.601(d)(2)(ii)(b) of this chapter, for certain standards applicable to floor-offset arrangements.

[4] For example, if a plan provides for an election extended to all participants that affects a participant's accumulated benefit, then someone who makes such an election is similarly situated to a participant who makes such an election, and someone who does not make an election is similarly situated to a participant who does not make such an election.

the participant's accrued benefits and any early retirement subsidy to which the participant is entitled based on the pre-conversion benefits.

The proposed regulations would provide an alternative mechanism under which the plan provides for the establishment of an opening hypothetical account balance as part of the conversion and keeps separate track of (1) The opening hypothetical account balance and interest credits attributable thereto, and (2) The post-conversion hypothetical contributions and interest credits attributable thereto. Under this alternative, the plan must provide that, when a participant commences benefits, the plan will determine whether the benefit attributable to the opening hypothetical account payable in the particular optional form of benefit selected is greater than or equal to the benefit accrued under the plan prior to the date of conversion and payable in the same generalized optional form of benefit (within the meaning of § 1.411(d)-3(g)(8)) at the same annuity starting date. For example, if a participant elects a straight life annuity payable at age 60, the plan must determine if the straight life annuity payable at age 60 that is attributable to the opening hypothetical account balance is greater than or equal to the straight life annuity payable at age 60 based on service prior to the conversion and determined under the terms of the pre-conversion plan. If the benefit attributable to the opening hypothetical account balance is greater, then the plan must provide that such benefit is paid in lieu of the pre-conversion benefit together with the benefit attributable to post-conversion contribution credits. If the benefit attributable to the opening hypothetical account balance is less, then the plan must provide that such benefit will be increased sufficiently to provide the pre-conversion benefit. In such a case, the participant must also be entitled to the benefit attributable to post-conversion contribution credits.

The proposed regulations would provide that, if an optional form of benefit is available on the annuity starting date with respect to the benefit attributable to the opening hypothetical account balance or opening accumulated percentage, but no optional form within the same generalized optional form of benefit was available at that annuity starting date under the terms of a plan as in effect immediately prior to the effective date of the conversion amendment, then the comparison must still be made by assuming that the pre-conversion plan had such an optional form of benefit. For example, if the pre-conversion plan did not provide for a single sum distribution option, the alternative would require that any single sum distribution option that is attributable to the opening hypothetical account balance be greater than or equal to the present value of the pre-conversion benefit, where present value is determined in accordance with section 417(e).

The IRS and the Treasury Department are seeking comments on another alternative means of satisfying the conversion requirements that would involve establishing an opening hypothetical account balance, but in limited situations would not require the subsequent comparison. Any such alternative would be permitted only if it were designed to provide adequate protection to participants in plans that adopt conversion amendments. For example, such an alternative might be limited to situations in which the participant elects a single sum distribution, and where the pre-conversion plan either did not provide a single sum option or had a single sum option that was based on the benefit payable at normal retirement age (rather than the benefit payable at early retirement age). In those situations, the alternative might provide that the comparison is not necessary if (1) The opening hypothetical account balance is equal to the present value of the pre-conversion benefit determined in accordance with section 417(e), (2) The interest credits on the opening hypothetical account balance are reasonably expected to be no lower than the interest rate used to determine the opening hypothetical account balance, and (3) Either the plan provides a death benefit equal to the hypothetical account balance or no pre-retirement mortality decrement is applied in establishing the opening hypothetical account balance. Such an alternative could result in a single sum distribution attributable to the pre-conversion benefit that is lower, or higher, than the present value of the pre-conversion benefit, depending on whether the actual interest credits applicable to the opening hypothetical account balance during the interim are lower, or higher, than the interest rate used in determining the opening hypothetical account balance and whether the applicable interest rate and applicable mortality table under section 417(e)(3) have changed in the interim.

The proposed regulations also would provide guidance on what constitutes a conversion amendment under section 411(b)(5)(B)(v). Under the proposed regulations, whether an amendment is a conversion amendment is determined on a participant-by-participant basis. The proposed regulations would provide that an amendment (or amendments) is a conversion amendment with respect to a participant if it meets two criteria: (1) The amendment reduces or eliminates the benefits that, but for the amendment, the participant would have ac-

crued after the effective date of the amendment under a benefit formula that is not a statutory hybrid benefit formula and under which the participant was accruing benefits prior to the amendment, and (2) After the effective date of the amendment, all or a portion of the participant's benefit accruals under the plan are determined under a statutory hybrid benefit formula.

The proposed regulations would provide that only amendments that reduce or eliminate accrued benefits described in section 411(a)(7), or retirement-type subsidies described in section 411(d)(6)(B)(i), that would otherwise accrue as a result of future service are treated as amendments that reduce or eliminate the participant's benefits that would have accrued after the effective date of the amendment under a benefit formula that is not a statutory hybrid benefit formula. Under the proposed regulations, a plan is treated as having been amended for this purpose if, under the terms of the plan, a change in the conditions of a participant's employment results in a reduction or elimination of the benefits that the participant would have accrued in the future under a benefit formula that is not a statutory hybrid benefit formula (for example, a job transfer from an operating division covered by a non-statutory hybrid defined benefit plan to an operating division that is covered by a cash balance formula). However, in the absence of coordination between the formulas, the special requirements for conversion amendments typically will be satisfied automatically.

The proposed regulations would provide rules prohibiting the avoidance of the conversion protections through the use of multiple plans or multiple employers. Under the proposed regulations, an employer is treated as having adopted a conversion amendment if the employer adopts an amendment under which a participant's benefits under a plan that is not a statutory hybrid plan are coordinated with a separate plan that is a statutory hybrid plan, such as through a reduction (offset) of the benefit under the plan that is not a statutory hybrid plan. In addition, if an employee's employer changes as a result of a merger, acquisition, or other transaction described in § 1.410(b)-2(f), then the two employers would be treated as a single employer for this purpose. Thus, for example, in an acquisition, if the buyer adopts an amendment to its statutory hybrid plan under which a participant's benefits under the seller's plan (that is not a statutory hybrid plan) are coordinated with benefits under the buyer's plan, such as through a reduction (offset) of the buyer's plan benefits, the seller and buyer would be treated as a single employer and as having adopted a conversion amendment. However, if there is no coordination between the plans, there is no conversion amendment.

The proposed regulations would provide that a conversion amendment also includes multiple amendments that result in a conversion amendment, even if the amendments would not be conversion amendments individually. Under the proposed regulations, if an amendment to provide a benefit under a statutory hybrid benefit formula is adopted within 3 years after adoption of an amendment to reduce non-statutory hybrid benefit formula benefits, then those amendments would be consolidated in determining whether a conversion amendment has been adopted. In the case of an amendment to provide a benefit under a statutory hybrid benefit formula that is adopted more than 3 years after adoption of an amendment to reduce non-statutory hybrid benefit formula benefits, there would be a presumption that the amendments are not consolidated unless the facts and circumstances indicate that adoption of an amendment to provide a statutory hybrid benefit formula was intended at the time of the reduction in the non-statutory hybrid benefit formula.

The proposed regulations would provide that the effective date of a conversion amendment is, with respect to a participant, the date as of which the reduction occurs of the benefits that the participant would have accrued after the effective date of the amendment under a benefit formula that is not a statutory hybrid benefit formula. In accordance with section 411(d)(6), the proposed regulations would provide that the date of a reduction of those benefits cannot be earlier than the date of adoption of the conversion amendment.

C. Market rate of return limitation

The proposed regulations would reflect the rule in section 411(b)(5)(B)(i)(I) under which a statutory hybrid plan is treated as failing to satisfy section 411(b)(1)(H) if it provides an interest crediting rate that is in excess of a market rate of return. The proposed regulations would define an interest crediting rate as the rate by which a participant's benefit is increased under the ongoing terms of a plan to the extent the amount of the increase is not conditioned on current service, regardless of how the amount of that increase is calculated. Thus, whether the amount is an interest credit for this purpose is determined without regard to whether the amount is calculated by reference to a rate of interest, a rate of return, an index, or otherwise.

The proposed regulations would require a plan to specify the timing for determining the plan's interest crediting rate that will apply for each plan year (or portion of a plan year) using one of two permitted methods — either pursuant to a daily interest crediting rate based on permissible interest crediting rates specified in the proposed regulations, or pursuant to a specified lookback month and stability period. For this purpose, the plan's lookback month and stability period must satisfy the rules for selecting the lookback month and stability period under § 1.417(e)-1(d)(4). However, the stability period and lookback month need not be the same as those used under the plan for purposes of section 417(e)(3).

In addition, the proposed regulations would require a plan to specify the periodic (at least annual) frequency at which interest credits are made under the plan. If, under a plan, interest is credited more frequently than annually (for example, monthly or quarterly), then the interest credit for that period must be a pro rata portion of the annual interest credit. Thus, for example, in the case of a plan the terms of which provide for interest to be credited at an interest crediting rate that would be permitted under the proposed regulations, if the plan provides for monthly interest credits and if the interest rate for a plan year has a value of 6 percent, then the accumulated benefits at the beginning of each month would be increased by 0.5 percent per month during the plan year. The proposed regulations would provide that interest credits are not treated as creating an effective rate of return in excess of a market rate of return merely because an otherwise permissible interest crediting rate is compounded more frequently than annually.

The proposed regulations would provide that an interest crediting rate for a plan year is not in excess of a market rate of return if it is based on specified indices. As in Notice 2007-6, these include the safe harbor rates described in Notice 96-8, the interest rates on 30-Year Treasury securities, and the rate of interest on long-term investment grade corporate bonds (as described in section 412(b)(5)(B)(ii)(II) prior to amendment by PPA '06 for plan years beginning before January 1, 2008, and the third-segment bond rate used under section 430 for subsequent plan years). For this purpose, the third-segment bond rate is permitted to be determined with or without regard to the transition rules of section 430(h)(2)(G).

These rates would be required to change on at least an annual basis.[5] These rates are market yields to maturity on outstanding bonds and do not reflect the change in the market value of an outstanding bond as a result of future changes in the interest rate environment or in a bond issuer's risk profile.[6] As noted in the preceding paragraph, the proposed rules generally are similar to those described in Notice 2007-6 but do not provide guidance on a number of issues related to market rate of return. It is expected that these issues will be addressed in the first part of 2008.

The proposed regulations would reflect the preservation of capital rule in section 411(b)(5)(B)(i)(II) that requires a statutory hybrid plan to provide that interest credits will not result in a hypothetical account balance (or similar amount) being less than the aggregate amount of the hypothetical allocations. Under the proposed regulations, this requirement would be applied at the participant's annuity starting date. In addition, the proposed regulations would provide that the combination of this preservation of capital protection with a rate of return which otherwise satisfies the market rate of return limitation will not result in an effective interest crediting rate that is in excess of a market rate of return.

While the second sentence of section 411(b)(5)(B)(i)(I) provides that a statutory hybrid plan is not treated as having an above-market rate merely because the plan provides for a reasonable minimum guaranteed rate of return or for a rate of return that is equal to the greater of a fixed or variable rate of return, these proposed regulations do not provide guidance for these alternatives. Moreover, the presence of a preservation of capital requirement indicates that Congress considered that a rate of return that could be negative in some years (such as a rate of return on an equity portfolio) could be permissible. However, as discussed in the following paragraphs, the Treasury Department and the IRS have concerns that the use of a minimum guaranteed rate of return or the use of the greater of a fixed and a variable rate could result in effective interest crediting rates that are above market rates of return and are soliciting comments on how to avoid that result.

Some commentators have suggested that it should be acceptable for a plan to adopt a fixed interest crediting rate that would apply without regard to changes in the interest rate environment. This is particularly important where the plan provides for hypothetical contributions that increase with age or service and the plan needs a minimum interest crediting rate in order to satisfy the accrual rules of section 411(b). While this issue is reserved under these proposed regulations, the approach suggested by commentators could be accomplished in two different ways. Under one possibility, the regulations might set forth a specific interest crediting rate (such as 4 percent or 5 percent) that a plan may be permitted to use. Under an alternative approach, the regulations might set forth a permitted methodology under which a plan would be permitted to establish a fixed interest crediting rate based on the then-applicable level of a permissible rate, such as the 3rd segment rate. For example, if the 3rd segment rate were 5.5 percent at the time the fixed rate is established under the plan, then under the alternative approach the plan might be permitted to fix the interest crediting rate at 5.5 percent. Comments are requested on these alternatives. In particular, comments are requested as to rules that the regulations could set forth that would avoid the potential for the fixed rate to be established at a time when interest rates are unusually high, such as occurred in the early 1980s.

With respect to the option for a plan to use an interest crediting rate that is the greater of a fixed or variable interest rate, the Treasury Department and the IRS believe that the interaction between the two interest rates must be taken into account in determining whether the effective interest crediting rate under a plan which provides an interest crediting rate that is equal to the greater of a fixed or variable interest rate is above a market rate of return. Whether a statutory hybrid plan that is providing interest credits based on the greater of a fixed or variable interest rate effectively provides an interest crediting rate that exceeds a market rate of return depends on a number of factors, including how high the fixed interest rate is, how frequently the "greater of" determination is applied, and the volatility of the variable interest rate.

As noted earlier, the proposed regulations would provide that including the preservation of capital rule does not cause the plan's effective interest crediting rate to be in excess of a market rate of return. This rule reflects the fact that the minimum rate under the preservation of capital rule is an interest rate of 0 percent which is applied on a one-time basis at the annuity starting date, and is premised on the expectation that the variable rate would rarely be negative for extended periods of time (so that the inclusion of the capital preservation rule should not significantly increase the effective rate of return under the plan). If the variable rate is the rate of interest on bonds that would be permitted under the proposed regulations, then that expectation is easily met.

By contrast, if the variable interest rate is the rate of return on an equity investment, the expectation that the capital preservation rule does not significantly increase the effective interest crediting rate is only applicable if the equity investment is a well-diversified portfolio. This is because a well-diversified portfolio should have sufficiently limited volatility so that the inclusion of the preservation of capital rule should not significantly increase the effective rate of return resulting from interest credits that are based on that portfolio. Accordingly, if the regulations were to permit the use of an interest crediting rate based on an asset portfolio as an interest credit, the regulations might limit the choice of portfolio to the actual plan assets (relying on the fiduciary rules to ensure that the portfolio is adequately diversified). Of course, any such regulations would only permit the use of an interest crediting rate based on an asset portfolio if the use of such a rate is prospective and is selected before the period during which the rate is determined.

Comments are requested on what other asset portfolios have sufficiently constrained volatility that they should be permitted to form the basis of a market rate of return for interest crediting under a statutory hybrid plan and whether it is appropriate to base an interest crediting rate on the value of an index. For example, are the assets under a regulated investment company (RIC) described in section 851 sufficiently diversified such that a statutory hybrid plan will not be treated as providing an effective interest crediting rate in excess of a market rate of return where it credits interest based on the rate of return on the RIC and also provides for the preservation of capital (as required for a statutory hybrid plan under section 411(b)(5)(B)(i)(II))? Similarly, if a statutory hybrid plan credits interest based on the rate of return on an equity index that is not a narrow-based equity index (as defined under section 3(a)(55) of the Securities Exchange Act of 1934) and which also provides for the preservation of capital, is the plan

---

[5] The requirement that an interest crediting rate change not less frequently than annually is intended to distinguish these rates from fixed rates, which are discussed later in this preamble. See also § 31.3121(v)(2)-1(d)(2)(i)(C)(2) of the Employment Tax Regulations, which permits a rate to be fixed for up to 5 years.

[6] Because this interest rate does not reflect the change in the market value of an outstanding bond when an issuer becomes higher risk or the bond goes into default, the bonds have been limited to investment grade bonds in the top three quality levels where the risk of default is small.

providing an interest crediting rate that is not in excess of a market rate of return?

If the determination of the greater of a fixed interest crediting rate and a variable interest crediting rate is made more frequently than required to comply with the capital preservation rule, the added frequency is more likely to result in an effective interest crediting rate that is in excess of a market rate of return. For example, if a statutory hybrid plan were to credit interest each day based on the greater of the actual rate of return on the plan assets for that day or 0 percent, the effective interest crediting rate would be far in excess of a market rate of return.

The Treasury Department and the IRS are considering providing that a plan will not have an effective interest crediting rate in excess of a market rate of return merely because it provides annual interest credits based on the greater of a reasonable fixed rate (such as 3 percent or 4 percent) and one of the rates of interest set forth in the proposed regulations. However, if a statutory hybrid plan were to provide interest credits based on the greater of a fixed rate (including a fixed rate of 0 percent) and the rate of return on plan assets or the value of an equity-based index, determined on an annual basis, then the effective interest crediting rate would typically be in excess of a market interest rate. Comments are requested on what types of reductions to the variable rate would be appropriate in order to ensure that the effective interest crediting rate under these situations does not exceed a market rate of return. In addition, comments are requested on whether regulations should establish reductions in these situations where the determination of whether the fixed or variable interest crediting rate is greater is made more frequently than annually.

Pending issuance of guidance addressing this issue, plan sponsors should be cautious in adopting interest crediting rates other than those explicitly permitted in these proposed regulations. If such a rate were adopted, and it did not satisfy the requirement not to be in excess of a market rate of return under rules provided in future guidance, the rate would have to be reduced in order to satisfy the requirement.

The proposed regulations would provide that, to the extent that interest credits (or equivalent amounts) have accrued under the terms of a statutory hybrid plan, section 411(d)(6) is violated by a plan amendment that changes the interest crediting rate if the revised rate under any circumstances could result in a lower rate of return after the applicable amendment date of the plan amendment. An exception is provided that would permit certain changes in a plan's interest crediting rate without violating section 411(d)(6). Under this exception, the proposed regulations would permit an amendment to change the plan's interest crediting rate for future periods from the safe harbor market rates of interest (for example, rates based on eligible cost-of-living indices, or rates based on Treasury bonds with the margins specified in the proposed regulations) to the rate of interest on long-term investment grade corporate bonds. Such a change would not constitute a reduction in accrued benefits in violation of section 411(d)(6) because it is expected that the change would result in a reduction only in rare and unusual circumstances, and the change would be permitted only if the amendment is effective not less than 30 days after adoption and, on the effective date of the amendment, the new interest crediting rate is not less than the interest crediting rate that would have applied in the absence of the amendment. In addition, the IRS and the Treasury Department may provide additional guidance regarding changes to the ongoing interest crediting rate under a plan that would or would not constitute a reduction of accrued benefits in violation of section 411(d)(6).

Pension Equity Plans (PEPs)

These proposed regulations do not include any rules specifically relating to plans that are often referred to as pension equity plans, or PEPs (other than defining a participant's accumulated benefit under a PEP as the accumulated percentage of final average compensation). Notice 2007-6 requested comments on the application of qualification requirements other than sections 411(b)(1)(H) and 417(e) to such plans, including the treatment of interest credited with respect to terminated vested participants. See §601.601(d)(2)(ii)(b) of this chapter. The IRS and the Treasury Department have received a number of comments pursuant to this request. These comments indicate that, apart from determining the accumulated benefit as a percentage of final average compensation, this design often provides explicit or implicit interest credits by determining the normal retirement benefit to be: (1) The accumulated percentage of final average compensation divided by a deferred annuity factor (thus implicitly providing interest and mortality credits for deferred benefits); or (2) The lesser of (a) the current single sum benefit projected to normal retirement age and using an interest rate set forth in the plan or (b) the projected single sum benefit based on projected service to normal retirement age (taking into account the plan's formula for the accumulated percentage of final average compensation without salary increases), with the lesser of these two amounts converted to an annuity. The right to future interest credits under these designs is earned at the same time as the related percentage of final average compensation; however, the comments indicated that the interest typically commences only after active participation ceases.

The IRS and the Treasury Department will continue to evaluate comments received regarding PEPs and are focusing on the following questions in situations where the interest credit is credited only after active participation ceases:

* Are these designs properly treated as plans under which the accrued benefit is expressed "as an accumulated percentage of the participant's final average compensation" within the meaning of section 411(a)(13)(A)? After the date on which interest credits commence, should these designs be treated as plans under which the accrued benefit is expressed "as the balance of a hypothetical account" within the meaning of section 411(a)(13)(A)?

* Do any of the designs in (1) or (2) of the preceding paragraph provide for a lower rate of accrual for additional years of service (because no interest is credited if service is continued)? See section 411(b)(1)(G). Alternatively, can this issue be avoided by treating the annual rate at which the normal retirement benefit accrues as declining with each additional year of service?

* How should the backloading rules of section 411(b)(1)(A)-(C) apply to these designs and do they raise issues on which comments were requested in Notice 2007-14 (2007-7 IRB 501)? See §601.601(d)(2)(ii)(b) of this chapter.

Section 1107 of PPA '06 and Code Section 411(d)(6)

Under section 1107 of PPA '06, a plan sponsor is permitted to delay adopting a plan amendment pursuant to statutory provisions under PPA '06 (or pursuant to any regulation issued under PPA '06) until the last day of the first plan year beginning on or after January 1, 2009 (January 1, 2011 in the case of governmental plans). As described in Rev. Proc. 2007-44 (2007-28 IRB 54), this amendment deadline applies to both interim and discretionary amendments that are made pursuant to PPA '06 statutory provisions or any regulation issued under PPA '06. See §601.601(d)(2)(ii)(b) of this chapter. If section 1107 of PPA '06 applies to an amendment of a plan, section 1107 provides that the plan does not fail to meet the requirements of section 411(d)(6) by reason of such amendment, except as provided by the Secretary of the Treasury.[7]

The IRS and the Treasury Department are considering whether relief from section 411(d)(6) should be provided for particular amendments that would be made pursuant to section 701 of PPA '06 or these proposed regulations. In the following provisions of this section of the preamble, the IRS and the Treasury Department have set forth a description of amendments that are and are not entitled to section 411(d)(6) relief. Comments are requested on whether section 411(d)(6) relief is or is not appropriate for any additional amendments related to section 701 of PPA '06 or these proposed regulations.

Until further guidance is provided by the IRS and the Treasury Department, section 411(d)(6) relief is not available for the following amendments that are described in section 1107 of PPA '06:

* A conversion amendment where the effective date of the reduction in benefits that a participant, but for the amendment, would have accrued under a benefit formula that is not a statutory hybrid benefit formula is earlier than the date of adoption of the reduction amendment.

* An amendment that reduces a participant's hypothetical account balance or accumulated percentage of final average compensation below the amount on the date the amendment is adopted.

* An amendment to change the interest crediting rate from one of the rates specified in Notice 96-8 using a margin that is less than or equal to the maximum margin for that rate to the same or another rate specified in Notice 96-8 with an associated margin where the excess (if any) of the maximum margin under the second rate over the margin used for that second rate exceeds the excess (if any) of the maximum margin under the first rate over the margin used for that first rate.

---

[7] Except to the extent permitted under section 411(d)(6) and §§1.411(d)-3 and 1.411(d)-4, or under a statutory provision such as section 1107 of PPA '06, section 411(d)(6) prohibits a plan amendment that decreases a participant's accrued benefits or that has the effect of eliminating or reducing an early retirement benefit or retirement-type subsidy, or eliminating an optional form of benefit, with respect to benefits attributable to service before the amendment. However, an amendment that eliminates or decreases benefits that have not yet accrued does not violate section 411(d)(6), provided that the amendment is adopted and effective before the benefits accrue.

Until further guidance is provided by the IRS and the Treasury Department, section 411(d)(6) relief is available for the following amendments that are described in section 1107 of PPA '06: (Corrected by IRS on April 25, 2008 (73 FR 22300)).

* As provided in Notice 2007-6, in the case of a plan that provides for a single sum distribution to a participant that exceeds the participant's hypothetical account balance or accumulated percentage of final average compensation, the plan may be amended to eliminate the excess for distributions made after August 17, 2006. See § 601.601(d)(2)(ii)(b) of this chapter.

* An amendment to change the interest crediting rate from one of the rates specified in Notice 96-8 using a margin that is less than or equal to the maximum margin for that rate to one of the other rates specified in Notice 96-8 with an associated margin where the excess (if any) of the maximum margin under the second rate over the margin used for that second rate does not exceed the excess (if any) of the maximum margin under the first rate over the margin used for that first rate.

These rules under section 1107 of PPA '06 will be reflected in future guidance on the market rate of return rules under section 411(b)(5)(B)(i). The IRS and the Treasury Department expect that section 411(d)(6) relief under section 1107 of PPA '06 will be available in the case of an amendment pursuant to that future guidance to change a plan's interest crediting rate (including credits on pre-August 18, 2006 accruals) from an interest rate that is above a market rate of return to an interest rate that constitutes a market rate of return, provided that any retroactive change in the crediting rate does not apply for periods before the date that section 411(b)(5)(B)(i) first applies to the plan. In addition, to the extent permitted under future guidance, the IRS and the Treasury Department expect that section 411(d)(6) relief under section 1107 of PPA '06 will be available in the case of an amendment to change the plan's interest crediting rate to a rate that is expected to be higher than the plan's current rate (such as an amendment to change to an equity-based rate of return).

Effective/Applicability Dates

Pursuant to section 701(e)(1) of PPA '06, the amendments made by section 701 of PPA '06 are generally effective for periods beginning on or after June 29, 2005. However, sections 701(e)(2) through 701(e)(5) of PPA '06 set forth a number of special effective/applicability date rules that are described earlier in the Background section of the preamble of these proposed regulations.

These proposed regulations reflect the statutory effective dates set forth in section 701(e) of PPA '06. Thus, the proposed regulations would reflect that section 411(a)(13)(A) applies to distributions made after August 17, 2006. In addition, the proposed regulations would reflect that, in the case of a plan that is in existence on June 29, 2005, section 411(a)(13)(B) applies to plan years beginning on or after January 1, 2008. At the date of issuance of these proposed regulations, bills have been introduced in the House of Representatives and the Senate which provide that (1) section 411(a)(13)(B) only applies to a participant who performs at least one hour of service on or after the effective date of section 411(a)(13)(B) with respect to the plan, and (2) in the case of a plan other than a plan described in section 701(e)(3) or 701(e)(4) of PPA '06, section 411(a)(13)(B) applies to years ending on or after June 29, 2005.[8] Proposed § 1.411(a)(13)-1(e)(1)(iii)(A)(2) and § 1.411(a)(13)-1(e)(1)(iii)(B)(2) have been reserved in order to accommodate these changes.

These regulations are proposed to be effective for plan years beginning on or after January 1, 2009 (or, if later, the date that applies to certain collectively bargained plans pursuant to section 701(e)(4) of PPA '06). For periods after the statutory effective date and before the regulatory effective date set forth in the preceding sentence, a plan must comply with sections 411(a)(13) and 411(b)(5). During these periods, a plan is permitted to rely on the provisions set forth in the proposed regulations for purposes of satisfying the requirements of sections 411(a)(13) and 411(b)(5).

These regulations should not be construed to create any inference concerning the applicable law prior to the effective dates of sections 411(a)(13) and 411(b)(5). See also section 701(d) of PPA '06.

Special Analyses

It has been determined that these proposed regulations are not a significant regulatory action as defined in Executive Order 12866. Therefore, a regulatory assessment is not required. It also has been determined that section 553(b) of the Administrative Procedure Act (5 U.S.C. chapter 5) does not apply to these regulations, and because the regulation does not impose a collection of information on small entities, the Regulatory Flexibility Act (5 U.S.C. chapter 6) does not apply. Pursuant to section 7805(f) of the Code, these regulations will be submitted to the Chief Counsel for Advocacy of the Small Business Administration for comment on its impact on small business.

Comments and Requests for Public Hearing

Before these proposed regulations are adopted as final regulations, consideration will be given to any written (one signed and eight (8) copies) or electronic comments that are submitted timely to the IRS.

The IRS and the Treasury Department specifically request comments on the clarity of the proposed regulations and how they may be made easier to understand.

In addition to the comments requested under the "Conversion protection" and "Market rate of return limitation" headings of this preamble (and in Part V of Notice 2007-6), comments are also requested on issues not addressed in these proposed regulations, including:

* The application of the 3-year vesting requirement in section 411(a)(13)(B) to a plan that is not a statutory hybrid plan when the plan is part of a floor-offset arrangement with a plan that includes a lump sum-based benefit formula.

* Whether guidance should be issued under section 411(b)(5) as to whether a characteristic is indirectly on account of age.

* Whether the age discrimination safe harbor in section 411(b)(5)(A) should be available in the case of any plan that does not express a participant's accumulated benefit as either an annuity payable at normal retirement age (or current age, if later), the balance of a hypothetical account, or the current value of the accumulated percentage of a participant's final average compensation.

All comments will be available for public inspection and copying. A public hearing will be scheduled if requested in writing by any person who timely submits written comments. If a public hearing is scheduled, notice of the date, time, and place of the public hearing will be published in the Federal Register.

Drafting Information

The principal authors of these regulations are Lauson C. Green and Linda S. F. Marshall, Office of Division Counsel/Associate Chief Counsel (Tax Exempt and Government Entities). However, other personnel from the IRS and the Treasury Department participated in the development of these regulations.

List of Subjects in 26 CFR Part 1

Income taxes, Reporting and recordkeeping requirements.

Proposed Amendments to the Regulations

Accordingly, 26 CFR part 1 is proposed to be amended as follows:

PART 1—INCOME TAXES

Paragraph 1. The authority citation for part 1 is amended by adding entries as follows:

Authority: 26 U.S.C. 7805 * * *

Section 1.411(a)(13)-1 also issued under 26 U.S.C. 411(a)(13).

Section 1.411(b)(5)-1 also issued under 26 U.S.C. 411(b)(5). * * *

Par. 2. Section 1.411(a)(13)-1 is added to read as follows:

§ 1.411(a)(13)-1 Statutory hybrid plans.

(a) In general. This section sets forth certain rules that apply to statutory hybrid plans under section 411(a)(13). Paragraph (b) of this section describes special rules for certain statutory hybrid plans that determine benefits under a lump sum-based benefit formula. Paragraph (c) of this section describes the vesting requirement for statutory hybrid plans. Paragraphs (d) and (e) of this section contain definitions and effective/applicability dates, respectively.

(b) Calculation of benefit by reference to hypothetical account balance or accumulated percentage. Pursuant to section 411(a)(13)(A), a statutory hybrid plan that determines any portion of a participant's benefits under a lump sum-based benefit formula is not treated as failing to meet the requirements of section 411(a)(2), or the requirements of section 411(c) or 417(e) with respect to the participant's accrued benefit derived from employer contributions, solely because, with respect to benefits determined under that formula, the present value of those benefits is, under the terms of the plan, equal to the balance of the hypothetical account maintained for the participant or to the cur-

---

[8] H.R. 3361 (Aug. 3, 2007) and S. 1974 (Aug. 2, 2007), at section 8(3)(B)(iv).

rent value of the accumulated percentage of the participant's final average compensation under that formula.

(c) Three-year vesting requirement—(1) In general. Pursuant to section 411(a)(13)(B), if any portion of the participant's accrued benefit under a defined benefit plan is determined under a statutory hybrid benefit formula, the plan is not treated as meeting the requirements of section 411(a)(2) unless the plan provides that the participant has a nonforfeitable right to 100 percent of the participant's accrued benefit if the participant has 3 or more years of service. Thus, this 3-year vesting requirement applies with respect to the entire accrued benefit of a participant under a defined benefit plan even if only a portion of the participant's accrued benefit under the plan is determined under a statutory hybrid benefit formula. Similarly, if the participant's accrued benefit under a defined benefit plan is, under the plan's terms, the larger of two (or more) benefit amounts, where each amount is determined under a different benefit formula (including a benefit determined pursuant to an offset among formulas within the plan) and at least one of those formulas is a statutory hybrid benefit formula, the participant's entire accrued benefit under the defined benefit plan is subject to the 3-year vesting rule of section 411(a)(13)(B) and this paragraph (c). The rule described in the preceding sentence applies even if the larger benefit is ultimately the benefit determined under a formula that is not a statutory hybrid benefit formula.

(2) Floor-offset arrangements involving a statutory hybrid plan. [Reserved]

(3) Examples. The provisions of this paragraph (c) are illustrated by the following examples:

Example 1. Employer M sponsors Plan X, pursuant to which each participant's accrued benefit is equal to the sum of the benefit provided under two benefit formulas. The first benefit formula is a statutory hybrid benefit formula, and the second formula is not. Because a portion of each participant's accrued benefit provided under Plan X is determined under a statutory hybrid benefit formula, the 3-year vesting requirement described in paragraph (c)(1) of this section applies to each participant's entire accrued benefit provided under Plan X.

Example 2. The facts are the same as in Example 1, except that the benefit formulas described in Example 1 only apply to participants for service performed in Division A of Employer M and a different benefit formula applies to participants for service performed in Division B of Employer M. Pursuant to the terms of Plan X, the accrued benefit of a participant attributable to service performed in Division B is equal to the benefit provided by a benefit formula that is not a statutory hybrid benefit formula. Therefore, the 3-year vesting requirement described in paragraph (c)(1) of this section does not apply to a participant with an accrued benefit under Plan X if the participant's benefit is solely attributable to service performed in Division B.

(d) Definitions—(1) In general. The definitions in this paragraph (d) apply for purposes of this section.

(2) Lump sum-based benefit formula. The term lump sum-based benefit formula means a lump sum-based benefit formula as defined in § 1.411(b)(5)-1(e)(3).

(3) Statutory hybrid benefit formula—(i) In general. A statutory hybrid benefit formula means a benefit formula that is either a lump sum-based benefit formula or a formula that is not a lump sum-based benefit formula but that has an effect similar to a lump sum-based benefit formula.

(ii) Effect similar to a lump sum-based benefit formula. Except as provided in paragraph (d)(3)(iii) of this section, a benefit formula under a defined benefit plan that is not a lump sum-based benefit formula has an effect similar to a lump sum-based benefit formula if the formula provides that a participant's accumulated benefit (within the meaning of § 1.411(b)(5)-1(e)(2)) payable at normal retirement age (or benefit commencement, if later) is expressed as a benefit that includes the right to periodic adjustments (including a formula that provides for indexed adjustments under § 1.411(b)(5)-1(b)(2)) that are reasonably expected to result in a smaller annual benefit at normal retirement age (or benefit commencement, if later) for the participant than for a similarly situated, younger individual (within the meaning of § 1.411(b)(5)-1(b)(5)) who is or could be a participant in the plan. A benefit formula that does not include periodic adjustments is treated as a formula with an effect similar to a lump sum-based benefit formula if the formula is otherwise described in the preceding sentence and the adjustments are provided pursuant to a pattern of repeated plan amendments. See § 1.411(d)-4, A-1(c)(1). (Corrected by IRS on April 25, 2008 (73 FR 22300)).

(iii) Exceptions—(A) Post-retirement benefit adjustments. Post-annuity starting date adjustments of the amounts payable to a participant (such as cost-of-living increases) are disregarded in determining whether a benefit formula under a defined benefit plan has an effect similar to a lump sum-based benefit formula.

(B) Certain variable annuity benefit formulas. If the assumed interest rate used for purposes of the adjustment of amounts payable to a participant under a variable annuity benefit formula is at least 5 percent, then the adjustments under the variable annuity benefit formula are not treated as being reasonably expected to result in a smaller annual benefit at normal retirement age (or benefit commencement, if later) for the participant than for a similarly situated, younger individual (within the meaning of § 1.411(b)(5)-1(b)(5)) who is or could be a participant in the plan, and thus such a variable annuity benefit formula does not have an effect similar to a lump sum-based benefit formula. (Corrected by IRS on April 25, 2008 (73 FR 22300)).

(C) Contributory plans. A benefit formula under a defined benefit plan that provides for a benefit equal to the benefit properly attributable to after-tax employee contributions does not have an effect similar to a lump sum-based benefit formula. See section 411(c)(2) for rules for determining benefits attributable to after-tax employee contributions.

(4) Variable annuity benefit formula. A variable annuity benefit formula means any benefit formula under a defined benefit plan which provides that the amount payable is periodically adjusted by reference to the difference between the rate of return of plan assets (or specified market indices) and a specified assumed interest rate.

(e) Effective/applicability date—(1) Statutory effective/applicability date—(i) In general. Except as provided in paragraphs (e)(1)(ii) and (e)(1)(iii) of this section, section 411(a)(13) applies for periods beginning on or after June 29, 2005.

(ii) Calculation of benefits. Section 411(a)(13)(A) applies to distributions made after August 17, 2006.

(iii) Vesting—(A) Plans in existence on June 29, 2005—(1) General rule. In the case of a plan that is in existence on June 29, 2005 (regardless of whether the plan is a statutory hybrid plan on that date), section 411(a)(13)(B) applies to plan years beginning on or after January 1, 2008.

(2) Hour of service required. [Reserved]

(3) Exception for plan sponsor election. See § 1.411(b)(5)-1(f)(1)(iii)(A)(2) for a special election for early application of section 411(a)(13)(B).

(B) Plans not in existence on June 29, 2005—(1) In general. In the case of a plan not in existence on June 29, 2005, section 411(a)(13)(B) applies for periods beginning on or after June 29, 2005.

(2) Hour of service required. [Reserved]

(C) Collectively bargained plans. Notwithstanding paragraphs (e)(1)(iii)(A) and (B) of this section, in the case of a collectively bargained plan maintained pursuant to one or more collective bargaining agreements between employee representatives and one or more employers ratified on or before August 17, 2006, the requirements of section 411(a)(13)(B) do not apply for plan years beginning before the earlier of—

(1) The later of—

(i) The date on which the last of those collective bargaining agreements terminates (determined without regard to any extension thereof on or after August 17, 2006), or

(ii) January 1, 2008; or

(2) January 1, 2010.

(D) Treatment of plans with both collectively bargained and non-collectively bargained employees. In the case of a plan where a collective bargaining agreement applies to some, but not all, of the plan participants, the plan is considered a collectively bargained plan for purposes of paragraph (e)(1)(iii)(C) of this section if at least 25 percent of the participants in the plan are members of collective bargaining units for which the benefit levels under the plan are specified under a collective bargaining agreement.

(2) Effective/applicability date of regulations. This section applies for plan years beginning on or after January 1, 2009 (or, if later, the date applicable under paragraph (e)(1)(iii)(C) of this section). For the periods after the statutory effective date set forth in paragraph (e)(1) of this section and before the regulatory effective date set forth in the preceding sentence, a plan must comply with section 411(a)(13). During these periods, a plan is permitted to rely on the provisions of this section for purposes of satisfying the requirements of section 411(a)(13).

Par. 3. Section 1.411(b)(5)-1 is added to read as follows:

§ 1.411(b)(5)-1 Reduction in rate of benefit accrual under a defined benefit plan.

(a) In general. This section sets forth certain rules related to reduction in the rate of benefit accrual under a defined benefit plan. Paragraph (b) of this section describes certain plan design-based safe harbors (including statutory hybrid plans) that are deemed to satisfy the age discrimination rules under section 411(b)(1)(H). Paragraph (c) of this section describes rules relating to statutory hybrid plan conversion amendments. Paragraph (d) of this section describes rules restricting interest credits (or equivalent amounts) under a statutory hybrid plan to a market rate of return. Paragraphs (e) and (f) of this section contain definitions and effective/applicability dates, respectively.

(b) Safe harbors for certain plan designs—(1) Accumulated benefit testing—(i) In general. Pursuant to section 411(b)(5)(A), and subject to paragraph (b)(1)(ii) of this section, a plan is not treated as failing to meet the requirements of section 411(b)(1)(H)(i) if, as of any date, the accumulated benefit of a participant would not be less than the accumulated benefit of any similarly situated, younger participant. This test requires a comparison of the accumulated benefit of each individual who is or could be a participant in the plan with the accumulated benefit of each other similarly situated, younger individual who is or could be a participant in the plan. See paragraph (b)(5) of this section for rules regarding whether each younger individual who is or could be a participant is similarly situated to a participant. The comparison described in this paragraph (b)(1)(i) is based on—

(A) The annuity payable at normal retirement age (or current age, if later) if the accumulated benefit of the participant under the terms of the plan is expressed as an annuity payable at normal retirement age (or current age, if later);

(B) The balance of a hypothetical account if the accumulated benefit of the participant under the terms of the plan is expressed as a hypothetical account balance; or

(C) The current value of an accumulated percentage of the participant's final average compensation if the accumulated benefit of the participant under the terms of the plan is expressed as an accumulated percentage of final average compensation.

(ii) Benefit formulas for comparison—(A) In general. The safe harbor provided by section 411(b)(5)(A) and paragraph (b)(1)(i) of this section does not apply to a plan if the accumulated benefit of a participant under the plan is not described in paragraph (b)(1)(i)(A), (B), or (C) of this section. In addition, except as provided in paragraph (b)(1)(ii)(B) of this section, that safe harbor also does not apply to a plan if the comparison required under paragraph (b)(1)(i) of this section involves comparing accumulated benefits that are described in different subparagraphs of paragraph (b)(1)(i) of this section. Thus, for example, if a plan provides an accumulated benefit that is expressed under the terms of the plan as an annuity payable at normal retirement age as described in paragraph (b)(1)(i)(A) of this section for participants who are age 55 or over, and the plan provides an accumulated benefit that is expressed as the balance of a hypothetical account as described in paragraph (b)(1)(i)(B) of this section for participants who are younger than age 55, the safe harbor described in section 411(b)(5)(A) and paragraph (b)(1)(i) of this section does not apply to the plan.

(B) Greater-of and sum-of benefit formulas. If a plan provides that a participant's accumulated benefit is equal to the sum of accumulated benefits that are described in different subparagraphs of paragraph (b)(1)(i) of this section, then the plan is deemed to satisfy paragraph (b)(1)(i) of this section if the plan satisfies the comparison described in paragraph (b)(1)(i) of this section separately for each of the different accumulated benefits. Similarly, if a plan provides that a participant's accumulated benefit is equal to the greater of accumulated benefits that are described in different subparagraphs of paragraph (b)(1)(i) of this section, then the plan is deemed to satisfy paragraph (b)(1)(i) of this section if the plan satisfies the comparison described in paragraph (b)(1)(i) of this section separately for each of the different accumulated benefits. For purposes of this paragraph (b)(1)(ii)(B), a similarly situated, younger participant is treated as having an accumulated benefit of zero under a benefit formula if the benefit formula does not apply to the participant.

(iii) Disregard of certain subsidized benefits. For purposes of paragraph (b)(1)(i) of this section, any subsidized portion of any early retirement benefit that is included in a participant's accumulated benefit is disregarded. For this purpose, the subsidized portion of an early retirement benefit is the retirement-type subsidy within the meaning of § 1.411(d)-3(g)(6) that is contingent on a participant's severance from employment and commencement of benefits before normal retirement age.

(2) Indexed benefits—(i) In general. Except as provided in paragraph (b)(2)(iv) of this section, pursuant to section 411(b)(5)(E) and this paragraph (b)(2)(i), a defined benefit plan is not treated as failing to meet the requirements of section 411(b)(1)(H) solely because a benefit formula under the plan (other than a lump sum-based benefit formula) provides for the periodic adjustment of accrued benefits under the plan, but only if the adjustment is by means of the application of a recognized investment index or methodology described in paragraph (b)(2)(ii) of this section and the plan satisfies paragraph (b)(2)(iii) of this section. A statutory hybrid plan that is not treated as failing to satisfy section 411(b)(1)(H) pursuant to the preceding sentence must nevertheless satisfy the qualification requirements otherwise applicable to statutory hybrid plans, including the requirements of § 1.411(a)(13)-1(c) (relating to minimum vesting standards), paragraph (c) of this section (relating to plan conversion amendments), and paragraph (d) of this section (relating to market rates of return).

(ii) Recognized investment index or methodology. An adjustment is made pursuant to a recognized investment index or methodology if it is made pursuant to—

(A) An eligible cost-of-living index as described in § 1.401(a)(9)-6, A-14(b);

(B) The rate of return on the aggregate assets of the plan; or

(C) The rate of return on the annuity contract for the employee issued by an insurance company licensed under the laws of a State.

(iii) Similarly situated participant test. A plan satisfies this paragraph (b)(2)(iii) if the aggregate periodic adjustments of each participant's accrued benefit under the plan (determined as a percentage of the unadjusted accrued benefit) would not be less than the aggregate periodic adjustments of any similarly situated, younger participant. This test requires a comparison of the aggregate periodic adjustments of each individual who is or could be a participant in the plan for any specified period with the aggregate periodic adjustments of each other similarly situated, younger individual who is or could be a participant in the plan for the same period. See paragraph (b)(5) of this section for rules regarding whether each younger individual who is or could be a participant is similarly situated to a participant.

(iv) Protection against loss—(A) In general. Paragraph (b)(2)(i) of this section does not apply unless the plan satisfies section 411(b)(5)(E)(ii) and paragraph (d)(2)(ii) of this section (relating to preservation of capital).

(B) Exception for variable annuity benefit formulas. The requirement to satisfy 411(b)(5)(E)(ii) and paragraph (d)(2)(ii) of this section does not apply in the case of a benefit provided under a variable annuity benefit formula, but only if the adjustments under the variable annuity benefit formula are based on the rate of return on the aggregate assets of the plan or the rate of return on the annuity contract for the employee issued by an insurance company licensed under the laws of a State.

(3) Certain offsets permitted. A plan is not treated as failing to meet the requirements of section 411(b)(1)(H) solely because the plan provides offsets against benefits under the plan to the extent the offsets are allowable in applying the requirements of section 401(a) and the applicable requirements of the Employee Retirement Income Security Act of 1974, Public Law 93-406 (88 Stat. 829), and the Age Discrimination in Employment Act of 1967, Public Law 90-202 (81 Stat. 602).

(4) Permitted disparities in plan contributions or benefits. A plan is not treated as failing to meet the requirements of section 411(b)(1)(H) solely because the plan provides a disparity in contributions or benefits with respect to which the requirements of section 401(1) are met.

(5) Definition of similarly situated. For purposes of paragraphs (b)(1) and (b)(2) of this section, an individual is similarly situated to another individual if the individual is identical to that other individual in every respect that is relevant in determining a participant's benefit under the plan (including period of service, compensation, position, date of hire, work history, and any other respect) except for age. In determining whether an individual is similarly situated to another individual, any characteristic that is relevant for determining benefits under the plan and that is based directly or indirectly on age is disregarded. For example, if a particular benefit formula applies to a participant on account of the participant's age, an individual to whom the benefit formula does not apply and who is identical to the participant in all other respects is similarly situated to the participant. By contrast, an individual is not similarly situated to a participant if a different benefit formula applies to the individual and the application of the different formula is not based directly or indirectly on age.

(c) Special rules for plan conversion amendments—(1) In general. Pursuant to section 411(b)(5)(B)(ii), (iii), and (iv), if there is a conversion amendment within the meaning of paragraph (c)(4) of this section with respect to a defined benefit plan, then the plan is treated as failing to meet the requirements of section 411(b)(1)(H) unless the plan, after the amendment, satisfies the requirements of paragraph (c)(2) of this section.

(2) Separate calculation of post-conversion benefit—(i) In general. A statutory hybrid plan satisfies the requirements of this paragraph (c)(2) if the plan provides that, in the case of an individual who was a participant in the plan immediately before the date of adoption of the conversion amendment, the participant's benefit at any subsequent annuity starting date is not less than the sum of:

(A) The participant's section 411(d)(6) protected benefit (as defined in § 1.411(d)-3(g)(14)) with respect to service before the effective date of the conversion amendment, determined under the terms of the plan as in effect immediately before the effective date of the amendment; and

(B) The participant's section 411(d)(6) protected benefit with respect to service on and after the effective date of the conversion amendment, determined under the terms of the plan as in effect after the effective date of the amendment.

(ii) Rules of application. For purposes of this paragraph (c)(2), except as provided in paragraph (c)(3) of this section, the benefits under paragraph (c)(2)(i)(A) and (B) of this section must each be determined in the same manner as if they were provided under separate plans that are independent of each other (for example, without any benefit offsets), and, except to the extent permitted under § 1.411(d)-3 or § 1.411(d)-4 (or other applicable law), each optional form of payment provided under the terms of the plan with respect to a participant's section 411(d)(6) protected benefit as in effect before the amendment must be available thereafter to the extent of the plan's benefits for service prior to the effective date of the amendment.

(3) Establishment of opening hypothetical account balance—(i) In general. Provided that the requirements of paragraph (c)(3)(ii) of this section are satisfied, a statutory hybrid plan under which an opening hypothetical account balance or opening accumulated percentage of the participant's final average compensation is established as of the effective date of the conversion amendment does not fail to satisfy the requirements of paragraph (c)(2) of this section merely because benefits attributable to that opening hypothetical account balance or opening accumulated percentage (that is, benefits that are not described in paragraph (c)(2)(i)(B) of this section) are substituted for benefits described in paragraph (c)(2)(i)(A) of this section.

(ii) Comparison of benefits—(A) Testing requirement. For any optional form of benefit payable at an annuity starting date where there was an optional form of benefit within the same generalized optional form of benefits (within the meaning 1.411(d)-3(g)(8)) that would have been available to the participant at that annuity starting date under the terms of the plan as in effect immediately before the effective date of the conversion amendment, the requirements of this paragraph (c)(3)(ii) are satisfied only if the plan provides that the amount of the benefit under that optional form of benefit available to the participant under the lump sum-based benefit formula that is attributable to the opening hypothetical account balance or opening accumulated percentage as described in paragraph (c)(3)(i) of this section, determined under the terms of the plan as of the annuity starting date (including actuarial conversion factors), is not less than the benefit under that optional form of benefit described in paragraph (c)(2)(i)(A) of this section. To satisfy this requirement, if the benefit under an optional form attributable to the opening hypothetical account balance or opening accumulated percentage is less than the benefit described in paragraph (c)(2)(i)(A) of this section, then the benefit attributable to the opening hypothetical account balance or opening accumulated percentage must be increased to the extent necessary to provide the minimum benefit described in this paragraph (c)(3)(ii)(A). Thus, if a plan is using the option under this paragraph (c)(3) to satisfy paragraph (c)(2) of this section with respect to a participant, the participant must receive a benefit equal to not less than the sum of:

(1) The greater of the benefit attributable to the opening hypothetical account balance as described in this paragraph (c)(3)(ii) and the benefit described in paragraph (c)(2)(i)(A) of this section, and

(2) The benefit described in paragraph (c)(2)(i)(B) of this section. (Corrected by IRS on April 25, 2008 (73 FR 22300)).

(B) Special rule for post-conversion optional forms of benefit. If an optional form of benefit is available on the annuity starting date with respect to the benefit attributable to the opening hypothetical account balance or opening accumulated percentage, but no optional form within the same generalized optional form of benefit (within the meaning of § 1.411(d)-3(g)(8)) was available at that annuity starting date under the terms of a plan as in effect immediately prior to the effective

date of the conversion amendment, then, for purposes of this paragraph (c)(3)(ii), the plan is treated as if such an optional form of benefit were available immediately prior to the effective date of the conversion amendment. In that event, paragraph (c)(3)(ii)(A) of this section must be applied by taking into account the optional form of benefit that is treated as if it were available on the annuity starting date under the terms of the plan as in effect immediately prior to the effective date of the conversion amendment. Thus, for example, if a single sum optional form of payment is not available under the plan terms applicable to the accrued benefit described in paragraph (c)(2)(i)(A) of this section, but a single sum form of payment is available with respect to the benefit attributable to the opening hypothetical account balance or opening accumulated percentage as of the annuity starting date, then, for purposes of paragraph (c)(3)(ii)(A) of this section, the plan is treated as if a single sum (to which section 417(e)(3) applies) were available under the terms of the plan as in effect immediately prior to the effective date of the conversion amendment.

(4) Conversion amendment—(i) In general. An amendment is a conversion amendment that is subject to the requirements of this paragraph (c) with respect to a participant if—

(A) The amendment reduces or eliminates the benefits that, but for the amendment, the participant would have accrued after the effective date of the amendment under a benefit formula that is not a statutory hybrid benefit formula (and under which the participant was accruing benefits prior to the amendment); and

(B) After the effective date of the amendment, all or a portion of the participant's benefit accruals under the plan are determined under a statutory hybrid benefit formula.

(ii) Rules of application—(A) In general. Paragraphs (c)(4)(iii), (iv), and (v) of this section describe special rules that treat certain arrangements as conversion amendments. The rules described in those paragraphs apply both separately and in combination. Thus, for example, in an acquisition described in § 1.410(b)-2(f), if the buyer adopts an amendment under which a participant's benefits under the seller's plan that is not a statutory hybrid plan are coordinated with a separate plan of the buyer that is a statutory hybrid plan, such as through an offset of the participant's benefit under the buyer's plan by the participant's benefit under the seller's plan, the seller and buyer are treated as a single employer under paragraph (c)(4)(iv) of this section and they are treated as having adopted a conversion amendment under paragraph (c)(4)(iii) of this section. However, pursuant to paragraph (c)(4)(iii) of this section, if there is no coordination between the two plans, there is no conversion amendment.

(B) Covered amendments. Only amendments that eliminate or reduce accrued benefits described in section 411(a)(7), or a retirement-type subsidy described in section 411(d)(6)(B)(i), that would otherwise accrue as a result of future service are treated as amendments described in paragraph (c)(4)(i)(A) of this section.

(C) Operation of plan terms treated as covered amendment. If, under the terms of a plan, a change in the conditions of a participant's employment results in a reduction of the participant's benefits that would have accrued in the future under a benefit formula that is not a statutory hybrid benefit formula, the plan is treated for purposes of this paragraph (c)(4) as if such plan terms constitute an amendment that reduces the participant's benefits that would have accrued after the effective date of the change under a benefit formula that is not a statutory hybrid benefit formula. Thus, for example, if a participant transfers from an operating division that is covered by a non-statutory hybrid benefit formula to an operating division that is covered by a statutory hybrid benefit formula, there has been a conversion amendment as of the date of the transfer.

(iii) Multiple plans. An employer is treated as having adopted a conversion amendment if the employer adopts an amendment under which a participant's benefits under a plan that is not a statutory hybrid plan are coordinated with a separate plan that is a statutory hybrid plan, such as through a reduction (offset) of the benefit under the plan that is not a statutory hybrid plan.

(iv) Multiple employers. If the employer of an employee changes as a result of a transaction described in § 1.410(b)-2(f), then the two employers are treated as a single employer for purposes of this paragraph (c)(4).

(v) Multiple amendments—(A) In general—(1) General rule. For purposes of this paragraph (c)(4), a conversion amendment includes multiple amendments that result in a conversion amendment even if the amendments are not conversion amendments individually. For example, an employer is treated as having adopted a conversion amendment if the employer first adopts an amendment described in paragraph (c)(4)(i)(A) of this section and, at a later date, adopts an amendment that adds a benefit under a statutory hybrid benefit formula as described in paragraph (c)(4)(i)(B) of this section, if they are consolidated under paragraph (c)(4)(v)(A)(2) of this section. (Corrected April 15, 2008 (73 FR 20367).

(2) Delay between plan amendments. In the case of an amendment to provide a benefit under a statutory hybrid benefit formula that is adopted within three years after adoption of an amendment to reduce non-statutory hybrid benefit formula benefits, those amendments are consolidated in determining whether a conversion amendment has been adopted. Thus, the later adoption of the statutory hybrid benefit formula will cause the earlier amendment to be treated as a conversion amendment. In the case of an amendment to provide a benefit under a statutory hybrid benefit formula that is adopted more than three years after adoption of an amendment to reduce benefits under a non-statutory hybrid benefit formula, there is a presumption that the amendments are not consolidated unless the facts and circumstances indicate that adoption of the amendment to provide a benefit under a statutory hybrid benefit formula was intended at the time of reduction in the non-statutory hybrid benefit formula.

(B) Multiple conversion amendments. If an employer adopts multiple amendments reducing benefits described in paragraph (c)(4)(i)(A) of this section, each amendment is treated as a separate conversion amendment, provided that paragraph (c)(4)(i)(B) of this section is applicable at the time of the amendment (taking into account the rules of this paragraph (c)(4)).

(vi) Effective date of a conversion amendment. The effective date of a conversion amendment is, with respect to a participant, the date as of which the reduction of the participant's benefits described in paragraph (c)(4)(i)(A) of this section occurs. In accordance with section 411(d)(6), the date of a reduction of those benefits cannot be earlier than the date of adoption of the conversion amendment.

(5) Examples. The following examples illustrate the application of paragraph (c) of this section:

Example 1. (i) Facts where plan does not establish opening hypothetical account balance for participants and participant elects life annuity at normal retirement age. Employer N sponsors Plan E, a defined benefit plan that provides an accumulated benefit, payable as a straight life annuity commencing at age 65 (which is Plan E's normal retirement age), based on a percentage of highest average compensation times the participant's years of service. Plan E permits any participant who has had a severance from employment to elect payment in the following optional forms of benefit (with spousal consent if applicable), with any payment not made in a straight life annuity converted to an equivalent form based on reasonable actuarial assumptions: a straight life annuity; and a 50 percent, 75 percent, or 100 percent joint and survivor annuity. The payment of benefits may commence at any time after attainment of age 55, with an actuarial reduction if the commencement is before normal retirement age. In addition, the plan offers a single sum payment after attainment of age 55 equal to the present value of the normal retirement benefit using the applicable interest rate and mortality table under section 417(e)(3) in effect under the terms of the plan on the annuity starting date.

(ii) Facts relating to the conversion amendment. On January 1, 2010, Plan E is amended to eliminate future accruals under the highest average compensation benefit formula and to base future benefit accruals on a hypothetical account balance. For service on or after January 1, 2010, each participant's hypothetical account balance is credited monthly with a pay credit equal to a specified percentage of the participant's compensation during the month and also with interest based on the third segment rate described in section 430(h)(2)(C)(iii). With respect to benefits under the hypothetical account balance attributable to service on and after January 1, 2010, a participant is permitted to elect (with spousal consent if applicable) payment in the same generalized optional forms of benefit (even though different actuarial factors apply) as under the terms of the plan in effect before January 1, 2010, and also as a single sum distribution. The plan provides for the benefits attributable to service before January 1, 2010, to be determined under the terms of the plan as in effect immediately before the effective date of the amendment, and the benefits attributable to service on and after January 1, 2010 to be determined separately, under the terms of the plan as in effect after the effective date of the amendment, with neither benefit offsetting the other in any manner. Thus, each participant's benefits are equal to the sum of the benefits attributable to service before January 1, 2010 (to be determined under the terms of the plan as in effect immediately before the effective date of the amendment), plus the benefits attributable to the participant's hypothetical account balance. (Corrected by IRS on April 25, 2008 (73 FR 22300)).

(iii) Facts relating to an affected participant. Participant A is age 62 on January 1, 2010 and, on December 31, 2009, A's benefit for years of service before January 1, 2010, payable as a straight life annuity commencing at A's normal retirement age (age 65) which is January 1, 2013, is $1,000 per month. Participant A has a severance from employment on January 1, 2013, and, on January 1, 2013, the hypothetical account balance, with pay credits and interest from January 1, 2010, to January 1, 2013, has become $11,000. Using the conversion factors under the plan as amended on January 1, 2013, that balance is equivalent to a straight life annuity of $100 per month commencing on January 1, 2013. This benefit is in addition to the benefit attributable to service before January 1, 2010. Participant A elects (with spousal consent) a straight life annuity of $1,100 per month commencing January 1, 2013.

(iv) Conclusion. Participant A's benefit satisfies the requirements of paragraph (c)(3)(ii)(A) of this section because Participant A's benefit is not less than the sum of Participant A's section 411(d)(6) protected benefit (as defined in §1.411(d)-3(g)(14)) with respect to service before the effective date of the conversion amendment, determined under the terms of the plan as in effect immediately before the effective date of the amendment, and Participant A's section 411(d)(6) protected benefit with respect to service on and after the effective date of the conversion amendment, determined under the terms of the plan as in effect after the effective date of the amendment.

Example 2. (i) Facts involving plan's establishment of opening hypothetical account balance and payment of pre-conversion accumulated benefit in life annuity at normal retirement age. The facts in this Example 2 are the same as the facts under paragraph (i) of Example 1.

(ii) Facts relating to the conversion amendment. On January 1, 2010, Plan E is amended to eliminate future accruals under the highest average compensation benefit formula and to base future benefit accruals on a hypothetical account balance. An opening hypothetical account balance is established for each participant, and, under the plan's terms, that balance is equal to the present value of the participant's accumulated benefit on December 31, 2009 (payable as a straight life annuity at normal retirement age or immediately, if later), using the applicable interest rate and applicable mortality table under section 417(e)(3) on January 1, 2010. Under Plan E, the account based on this opening hypothetical account balance is maintained as a separate account from the account for accruals on or after January 1, 2010. The hypothetical account balance maintained for each participant for accruals on or after January 1, 2010, is credited monthly with a pay credit equal to a specified percentage of the participant's compensation during the month. A participant's hypothetical account balance (including both of the separate accounts) is credited monthly with interest based on the third segment rate described in section 430(h)(2)(C)(iii).

(iii) Facts relating to optional forms of benefit. Following severance from employment and attainment of age 55, a participant is permitted to elect (with spousal consent if applicable) payment in the same generalized optional forms of benefit as under the plan in effect prior to January 1, 2010, with the amount payable calculated based on the hypothetical account balance on the annuity starting date and the applicable interest rate and applicable mortality table on the annuity starting date. The single sum distribution is equal to the hypothetical account balance. (Corrected by IRS on April 25, 2008 (73 FR 22300)).

(iv) Facts relating to conversion protection. The plan provides that, as of a participant's annuity starting date, the plan will determine whether the benefit attributable to the opening hypothetical account payable in the particular optional form of benefit selected is greater than or equal to the benefit accrued under the plan through the date of conversion and payable in the same generalized optional form of benefit with the same annuity starting date. If the benefit attributable to the opening hypothetical account balance is greater, the plan provides that such benefit is paid in lieu of the pre-conversion benefit, together with the benefit attributable to post-conversion contribution credits. If the benefit attributable to the opening hypothetical account balance is less, the plan provides that such benefit is increased sufficiently to provide the pre-conversion benefit, together with the benefit attributable to post-conversion contribution credits.

(v) Facts relating to an affected participant. On January 1, 2010, the opening hypothetical account balance established for Participant A is $80,000, which is the present value of Participant A's straight life annuity of $1,000 per month commencing on January 1, 2013, using the applicable interest rate and applicable mortality table under section 417(e)(3) in effect on January 1, 2010. On January 1, 2010, the applicable interest rate for Participant A is equivalent to a level rate of 5.5 percent. Thereafter, Participant A's hypothetical account balance for subsequent accruals is credited monthly with a pay credit equal to a specified percentage of the participant's compensation during the month. In addition, Participant A's hypothetical account balance (including both of the separate accounts) is credited monthly with interest based on the third segment rate described in section 430(h)(2)(C)(iii). (Corrected by IRS on April 25, 2008 (73 FR 22300)).

(vi) Facts relating to calculation of the participant's benefit. Participant A has a severance from employment on January 1, 2013 at age 65, and elects (with spousal consent) a straight life annuity commencing January 1, 2013. On January 1, 2013, the opening hypothetical account balance, with interest credits from January 1, 2010, to January 1, 2013, has become $95,000, which, using the conversion factors under the plan on January 1, 2013, is equivalent to a straight life annuity of $1,005 per month commencing on January 1, 2013 (which is greater than the $1,000 a month payable at age 65 under the terms of the plan in effect before January 1, 2010). This benefit is in addition to the benefit determined using the hypothetical account balance for service after January 1, 2010.

(vii) Conclusion. The benefit satisfies the requirements of paragraph (c)(3)(ii)(A) of this section with respect to Participant A because A's benefit is not less than the sum of (A) the greater of Participant A's benefits attributable to the opening hypothetical account balance and A's section 411(d)(6) protected benefit (as defined in §1.411(d)-3(g)(14)) with respect to service before the effective date of the conversion amendment, determined under the terms of the plan as in effect immediately before the effective date of the amendment, and (B) Participant A's section 411(d)(6) protected benefit with respect to service on and after the effective date of the conversion amendment, determined under the terms of the plan as in effect after the effective date of the amendment.

Example 3. (i) Facts involving a subsequent decrease in interest rates. The facts are the same as in Example 2, except that, because of a decrease in bond rates after January 1, 2010, and before January 1, 2013, the rate of interest credited in that period averages less than 5.5 percent, and, on January 1, 2013, the effective applicable interest rate under section 417(e)(3) under the plan's terms is 4.7 percent. As a result, Participant A's opening hypothetical account balance plus attributable interest credits has increased to only $87,000 on January 1, 2013, and, using the conversion factors under the plan on January 1, 2013, is equivalent to a straight life annuity commencing on January 1, 2013, of $775 per month. Under the terms of Plan E, the benefit attributable to A's opening account balance is increased so that A's straight life annuity commencing on January 1, 2013, is $1,000 per month. This benefit is in addition to the benefit attributable to the hypothetical account balance for service after January 1, 2010.

(ii) Conclusion. The benefit satisfies the requirements of paragraph (c)(3)(ii)(A) of this section with respect to Participant A because A's benefit is not less than the sum of (A) the greater of A's benefits attributable to the opening hypothetical account balance and A's section 411(d)(6) protected benefit (as defined in §1.411(d)-3(g)(14)) with respect to service before the effective date of the conversion amendment, determined under the terms of the plan as in effect immediately before the effective date of the amendment, and (B) A's section 411(d)(6) protected benefit with respect to service on and after the effective date of the conversion amendment, determined under the terms of the plan as in effect after the effective date of the amendment.

Example 4. (i) Facts involving payment of a subsidized early retirement benefit. The facts are the same as in Example 2, except that under the terms of Plan E on December 31, 2009, a participant who retires before age 65 and after age 55 with 30 years of service has only a 3 percent per year actuarial reduction. Participant A has a severance from employment on January 1, 2011, when A is age 63 and has 30 years of service. On January 1, 2011, A's opening hypothetical account balance, with interest from January 1, 2010, to January 1, 2011, has become $86,000, which, using the conversion factors under the plan (as amended) on January 1, 2011, is equivalent to a straight life annuity commencing on January 1, 2011, of $850 per month.

(ii) Facts relating to calculation of the participant's benefit. Under the terms of Plan E on December 31, 2009, Participant A is entitled to a straight life annuity commencing on January 1, 2011, equal to at least $940 per month ($1,000 reduced by 3 percent for each of the 2 years that A's benefits commence before normal retirement age). Under the terms of Plan E, the benefit attributable to A's opening account balance is increased so that A is entitled to a straight life annuity of $940 per month commencing on January 1, 2013. This benefit is in addition to the benefit determined using the hypothetical account balance for service after January 1, 2010.

(iii) Conclusion. The benefit satisfies the requirements of paragraph (c)(3)(ii)(A) of this section with respect to Participant A because A's benefit is not less than the sum of (A) the greater of Participant A's benefits attributable to the opening hypothetical account balance (in-

creased by attributable interest credits) and A's section 411(d)(6) protected benefit (as defined in §1.411(d)-3(g)(14)) with respect to service before the effective date of the conversion amendment, determined under the terms of the plan as in effect immediately before the effective date of the amendment, and (B) Participant A's section 411(d)(6) protected benefit with respect to service on and after the effective date of the conversion amendment, determined under the terms of the plan as in effect after the effective date of the amendment.

Example 5. (i) Facts involving addition of a single sum payment option. The facts are the same as in Example 2, except that, before January 1, 2010, Plan E did not offer payment in a single sum distribution for amounts in excess of $5,000. Plan E, as amended on January 1, 2010, offers payment in any of the available annuity distribution forms commencing at any time following severance from employment as were provided under Plan E before January 1, 2010. In addition, Plan E, as amended on January 1, 2010, offers payment in the form of a single sum attributable to service before January 1, 2010, which is the greater of the opening hypothetical account balance (increased by attributable interest credits) or a single sum distribution of the straight life annuity payable at age 65 using the same actuarial factors as are used for mandatory cashouts for amounts equal to $5,000 or less under the terms of the plan on December 31, 2009. Participant B is age 40 on January 1, 2010, and B's opening hypothetical account balance (increased by attributable interest credits) is $33,000 (which is the present value, using the conversion factors under the plan (as amended) on January 1, 2010, of Participant B's straight life annuity of $1,000 per month commencing at January 1, 2035, which is when B will be age 65). Participant B has a severance from employment on January 1, 2013, and elects (with spousal consent) an immediate single sum distribution. Participant B's opening hypothetical account balance (increased by attributable interest) on January 1, 2013, is $45,000. The present value, on January 1, 2013, of Participant B's benefit of $1,000 per month, commencing immediately using the actuarial factors for mandatory cashouts under the terms of the plan on December 31, 2009, would result in a single sum payment of $44,750. Participant B is paid a single sum distribution equal to the sum of $45,000 plus an amount equal to B's January 1, 2013, hypothetical account balance for benefit accruals for service after January 1, 2010.

(ii) Conclusion. Because, under Plan E, Participant B is entitled to the sum of (A) The greater of the $45,000 opening hypothetical account balance (increased by attributable interest credits) and $44,750 (present value of the benefit with respect to service prior to January 1, 2010, using the actuarial factors for mandatory cashout distributions under the terms of the plan on December 31, 2009), plus (B) An amount equal to B's hypothetical account balance for benefit accruals for service after January 1, 2010, the benefit satisfies the requirements of paragraph (c)(3)(ii)(A) of this section with respect to Participant B. If Participant B's hypothetical account balance under Plan E was instead less than $44,750 on January 1, 2013, Participant B would be entitled to a single sum payment equal to the sum of $44,750 and an amount equal to B's hypothetical account balance for benefit accruals for service after January 1, 2010.

Example 6. (i) Facts involving addition of new annuity optional form of benefit. The facts are the same as in Example 2, except that, after December 31, 2009, and before January 1, 2013, Plan E is amended to offer payment in a 5-, 10-, or 15-year term certain and life annuity, using the same actuarial assumptions that apply for other optional forms of distribution. When Participant A has a severance from employment on January 1, 2013, A elects (with spousal consent) a 5-year term certain and life annuity commencing immediately equal to $935 per month. Application of the same actuarial assumptions to Participant A's benefit of $1,000 per month (under Plan E as in effect on December 31, 2009), commencing immediately on January 1, 2013, would result in a 5-year term certain and life annuity commencing immediately equal to $955 per month. Under the terms of Plan E, the benefit attributable to A's opening account balance is increased so that, using the conversion factors under the plan (as amended) on January 1, 2013, A's opening hypothetical account balance (increased by attributable interest credits) produces a 5-year term certain and life annuity commencing immediately equal to $955 per month commencing on January 1, 2013. This benefit is in addition to the benefit determined using the January 1, 2013, hypothetical account balance for service after January 1, 2010.

(ii) Conclusion. This benefit satisfies the requirements of paragraph (c)(3)(ii)(A) of this section with respect to Participant A.

Example 7. (i) Facts involving addition of distribution option before age 55. The facts are the same as in Example 5, except that Participant B (age 43) elects (with spousal consent) a straight life annuity. Under Plan E, the straight life annuity attributable to Participant B's opening hypothetical account balance at age 43 is $221 per month. Application of the same actuarial assumptions to Participant B's benefit of $1,000 per month (under Plan E as in effect on December 31, 2009), commencing immediately on January 1, 2013, would result in a straight life annuity at age 43 equal to $219 per month.

(ii) Conclusion. Because, under its terms, Plan E provides that Participant B is entitled to an amount not less than the present value (using the same actuarial assumptions as apply on January 1, 2013, in converting the $45,000 hypothetical account balance attributable to the opening hypothetical account balance to the $221 straight life annuity) of Participant B's straight life annuity of $1,000 per month commencing at January 1, 2035, and the $221 straight life annuity is in addition to the benefit accruals for service after January 1, 2010, payment of the $221 monthly annuity would satisfy the requirements of paragraph (c)(3)(ii)(A) of this section with respect to Participant B.

(d) Market rate of return—(1) In general—(i) Basic test. Subject to paragraph (d)(3) of this section, a statutory hybrid plan satisfies the requirements of section 411(b)(1)(H) and this paragraph (d) only if, for any plan year, the interest crediting rate under the terms of the plan is no greater than a market rate of return.

(ii) Definition of interest crediting rate and interest credit. For purposes of this paragraph (d), a plan's interest crediting rate means the rate by which a participant's benefit is increased under the ongoing terms of the plan to the extent the amount of the increase is not conditioned on current service, regardless of how the amount of that increase is calculated. The amount of such an increase is an interest credit. Thus, whether the amount is an interest credit for this purpose is determined without regard to whether the amount is calculated by reference to a rate of interest, a rate of return, an index, or otherwise.

(iii) Single rates. Except as is otherwise provided in this paragraph (d)(1), an interest crediting rate is not in excess of a market rate of return only if the plan provides an interest credit for the year at a rate that is equal to one of the following rates that is specified in the terms of the plan:

(A) The interest rate on long-term investment grade corporate bonds (as described in paragraph (d)(4) of this section);

(B) An interest rate that is deemed to be not in excess of a market rate of return under paragraph (d)(5) of this section; or

(C) An interest rate that is described in paragraph (d)(6) of this section.

(iv) Timing rules—(A) In general. A plan must specify the timing for determining the plan's interest crediting rate that will apply for each plan year (or portion of a plan year) using either of the methods described in paragraph (d)(1)(iv)(B) of this section and must specify the frequency of interest crediting under the plan pursuant to paragraph (d)(1)(iv)(C) of this section.

(B) Methods to determine interest crediting rate. A plan is permitted to provide daily interest credits using a daily interest crediting rate based on the permitted rates specified in paragraph (d)(1)(iii) of this section. Alternatively, a plan is permitted to provide an interest credit for a stability period that is based on the interest crediting rate for a specified lookback month with respect to that stability period. The stability period and lookback month must satisfy the rules for selecting the stability period and lookback month under §1.417(e)-1(d)(4). (However, the interest rates can be any of the rates in paragraph (d)(1)(iii) of this section and the stability period and lookback month need not be the same as those used under the plan for purposes of section 417(e)(3).)

(C) Frequency of interest crediting. Interest credits under a plan must be made on an annual or more frequent periodic basis. If a plan provides for the crediting of interest more frequently than annually (for example, monthly or quarterly), then the interest credit for that period must be a pro rata portion of the annual interest credit. Thus, for example, if a plan's terms provide for interest to be credited monthly and for the interest crediting rate to be equal to the interest rate on long-term investment grade corporate bonds (as described in paragraph (d)(4) of this section), and that interest rate for a plan year is 6 percent, the accumulated benefits at the beginning of each month would be increased by 0.5 percent per month during the plan year. Interest credits under the terms of a plan are not treated as creating an effective rate of return that is in excess of a market rate of return merely because an otherwise permissible interest crediting rate is compounded more frequently than annually.

(v) Lesser rates. An interest crediting rate is not in excess of a market rate of return if the plan provides an interest crediting rate that, under all circumstances, is always less than one of the rates described in paragraph (d)(1)(iii) of this section.

(vi) Greater-of rates. If a statutory hybrid plan provides for an interest credit that is equal to the interest credits determined under the greater of 2 or more different interest crediting rates, the effective interest crediting rate is not in excess of a market rate of return only if each of the different rates satisfies the requirements of paragraph (d)(1)(ii) of this section and the additional requirements of paragraph (d)(7) of this section are satisfied.

(2) Preservation of capital requirement—(i) In general. A statutory hybrid plan is treated as failing to meet the requirements of section 411(b)(1)(H) if the requirements of paragraph (d)(2)(ii) of this section are not satisfied.

(ii) Preservation of capital defined—(A) In general. The requirements of this paragraph (d)(2)(ii) are satisfied if the plan provides that, as of the participant's annuity starting date, the participant's benefit under the plan is no less than the benefit determined as of that date based on the sum of the hypothetical contributions credited under the plan (or the accumulated percentage of the participant's final average compensation, or the participant's accrued benefits determined without regard to any indexing under section 411(b)(5)(E), as applicable).

(B) Hypothetical contributions defined. For purposes of this paragraph (d)(2)(ii), a hypothetical contribution is any amount credited under a statutory hybrid plan other than an interest credit (as defined in paragraph (d)(1)(ii) of this section). Thus, if an opening hypothetical account balance or opening accumulated percentage of the participant's final average compensation is established pursuant to paragraph (c)(3) of this section, that opening hypothetical account balance or opening accumulated percentage as of the date established is treated as a hypothetical contribution and, thus, is taken into account for purposes of the preservation of capital requirement of this paragraph (d)(2)(ii).

(3) Plan termination—(i) In general. Except as provided in paragraph (d)(3)(ii) of this section, a statutory hybrid plan is treated as meeting the requirements of paragraph (d)(1) of this section only if the terms of the plan provide that, upon termination of the plan, a participant's benefit as of the termination is determined using the interest rate and mortality table otherwise applicable for determining that benefit under the plan (without regard to termination of the plan).

(ii) Variable interest rates. A statutory hybrid plan is treated as meeting the requirements of paragraph (d)(1) of this section only if the terms of the plan provide that, upon termination of the plan, any interest rate used to determine a participant's benefits under the plan (including any interest crediting rate and any interest rate used to determine annuity benefits) that is a variable rate is determined as the average of the rates of interest used under the plan for that purpose during the 5-year period ending on the termination date.

(4) Long-term investment grade corporate bonds. For purposes of this paragraph (d), the rate of interest on long-term investment grade corporate bonds means the third segment rate described in section 430(h)(2)(C)(iii) (determined with or without regard to the transition rules of section 430(h)(2)(G)), provided that such rate floats on a periodic basis not less frequently than annually. However, for plan years beginning prior to January 1, 2008, the rate of interest on long-term investment grade corporate bonds means the rate described in section 412(b)(5)(B)(ii)(II) prior to amendment by the Pension Protection Act of 2006, Public Law 109-280 (120 Stat. 780) (PPA '06).

(5) Safe harbor rates of interest—(i) Rates based on Treasury bonds with margins. An interest crediting rate is deemed to be not in excess of a market rate of return if the rate is adjusted at least annually and is equal to the sum of any of the following rates of interest for Treasury bonds and the associated margin for that interest rate:

Treasury bond interest rates	Associated Margin
The discount rate on 3-month Treasury Bills	175 basis points
The discount rate on 12-month or shorter Treasury Bills	150 basis points
The yield on 1-year Treasury Constant Maturities	100 basis points
The yield on 3-year or shorter Treasury bonds	50 basis points
The yield on 7-year or shorter Treasury bonds	25 basis points
The yield on 30-year or shorter Treasury bonds	

0 basis points

(ii) Eligible cost-of-living indices. An interest crediting rate is deemed to be not in excess of a market rate of return if the rate is adjusted no less frequently than annually and is equal to the rate of increase with respect to an eligible cost-of-living index described in § 1.401(a)(9)-6, A-14(b), except that for purposes of this paragraph (d)(5)(ii), the eligible cost-of-living index described in § 1.401(a)(9)-6, A-14(b)(2), is increased by 300 basis points.

(iii) Additional safe harbors. The Commissioner may, in guidance of general applicability, specify additional interest crediting rates that are deemed to be not in excess of a market rate of return. See § 601.601(d)(2)(ii)(b) of this chapter.

(6) Other interest rates—(i) Reasonable minimum guaranteed rate of return. [Reserved]

(ii) Equity-based rates. [Reserved]

(7) Combinations of rates of return—(i) In general. If a plan provides an interest crediting rate that is equal to the interest credits determined under the greater of 2 or more different interest crediting rates where each of the different rates satisfies the requirements of paragraph (d)(1)(iii) of this section, then the interest credits provided by the plan satisfy this paragraph (d)(7) only if one or more of the different interest crediting rates under the plan are adjusted as provided in paragraphs (d)(7)(iii) or (d)(7)(iv) of this section in order to provide that the effective interest crediting rate resulting from the use of the greater of 2 or more rates does not exceed a market rate of return. This paragraph (d)(7) provides the exclusive rules that may be used for this purpose and, therefore, a plan does not satisfy the requirements of this paragraph (d) if the plan provides for interest credits determined using the greater of 2 or more interest crediting rates and that combination of interest crediting rates is not specifically permitted by this paragraph (d)(7).

(ii) Coordination with preservation of capital rule. No adjustment under this paragraph (d)(7) is required merely because the plan satisfies the requirements of paragraph (d)(2) of this section.

(iii) Combination of fixed and variable interest rates. [Reserved]

(iv) Other combinations. [Reserved]

(8) Section 411(d)(6)—(i) General rule. Except as provided in this paragraph (d)(8), to the extent that benefits have accrued under the terms of a statutory hybrid plan that entitle the participant to future interest credits, an amendment to the plan to change the interest crediting rate for such interest credits violates section 411(d)(6) if the revised rate under any circumstances could result in a lower interest crediting rate as of any date after the applicable amendment date of the amendment (within the meaning of § 1.411(d)-3(g)(4)) changing the interest crediting rate. For additional rules, see § 1.411(d)-3(a)(1).

(ii) Adoption of long-term investment grade corporate bond rate or safe harbor rate. An amendment to a statutory hybrid plan to change the interest crediting rate for future periods from an interest crediting rate described in paragraph (d)(5) of this section to the interest crediting rate described in paragraph (d)(4) of this section does not constitute a decrease of an accrued benefit and, therefore, does not violate section 411(d)(6). However, an amendment described in this paragraph (d)(8)(ii) cannot be effective less than 30 days after adoption and, on the effective date of the amendment, the new interest crediting rate cannot be less than the interest crediting rate that would have applied in the absence of the amendment.

(iii) Other changes not treated as prohibited reduction of accrued benefit. [Reserved].

(e) Definitions—(1) In general. The definitions in this paragraph (e) apply for purposes of this section.

(2) Accumulated benefit. A participant's accumulated benefit at any date means the participant's benefit, as expressed under the terms of the plan, accrued to that date. For this purpose, the accumulated benefit of a participant may be expressed under the terms of the plan as either the balance of a hypothetical account or the current value of an accumulated percentage of the participant's final average compensation, even if the plan defines the participant's accrued benefit as an annuity beginning at normal retirement age that is actuarially equivalent to that balance or value.

(3) Lump sum-based benefit formula—(i) In general. A lump sum-based benefit formula means a benefit formula used to determine all or any part of a participant's accumulated benefit under a defined benefit plan under which the benefit provided under the formula is expressed as the balance of a hypothetical account maintained for the participant or as the current value of the accumulated percentage of the partici-

pant's final average compensation. Whether a benefit formula is a lump sum-based benefit formula is determined based on how the accumulated benefit of a participant is expressed under the terms of the plan, and does not depend on whether the plan provides an optional form of benefit in the form of a single sum payment.

(ii) Exception for contributory plans. A participant is not treated as having a lump sum-based benefit formula merely because the participant is entitled to a benefit under a defined benefit plan that is equal to the greater of the otherwise applicable benefit formula and the benefit properly attributable to after-tax employee contributions.

(4) Statutory hybrid benefit formula. A statutory hybrid benefit formula means a statutory hybrid benefit formula as defined in § 1.411(a)(13)-1(d)(3).

(5) Statutory hybrid plan. A statutory hybrid plan means a defined benefit plan that contains a statutory hybrid benefit formula.

(6) Variable annuity benefit formula. A variable annuity benefit formula means a variable annuity benefit formula as defined in § 1.411(a)(13)-1(d)(4).

(f) Effective/applicability date—(1) Statutory effective/applicability dates—(i) In general. Except as provided in paragraph (f)(1)(iii) of this section, section 411(b)(5) applies for periods beginning on or after June 29, 2005.

(ii) Conversion amendments. The requirements of section 411(b)(5)(B)(ii), (iii), and (iv) apply to a conversion amendment (as defined in paragraph (c)(4) of this section) that is adopted after, and takes effect after, June 29, 2005.

(iii) Market rate of return—(A) Plans in existence on June 29, 2005—(1) In general. In the case of a plan that is in existence on June 29, 2005 (regardless of whether the plan is a statutory hybrid plan on that date), section 411(b)(5)(B)(i) only applies to plan years beginning on or after January 1, 2008. (Corrected April 15, 2008 (73 FR 20367).

(2) Exception for plan sponsor election. Notwithstanding paragraph (f)(1)(iii)(A)(1) of this section, a plan sponsor of a plan that is in existence on June 29, 2005 (regardless of whether the plan is a statutory hybrid plan on that date) may elect to have the requirements of section 411(a)(13)(B) and section 411(b)(5)(B)(i) apply for any period after June 29, 2005, and before the first plan year beginning after December 31, 2007. In accordance with section 1107 of the PPA '06, an employer is permitted to adopt an amendment to make this election as late as the last day of the first plan year that begins on or after January 1, 2009 (January 1, 2011, in the case of a governmental plan as defined in section 414(d)) if the plan operates in accordance with the election.

(B) Plans not in existence on June 29, 2005. In the case of a plan not in existence on June 29, 2005, section 411(b)(5)(B)(i) applies to the plan on and after the later of June 29, 2005, and the date the plan becomes a statutory hybrid plan.

(2) Effective/applicability date of regulations. This section applies for plan years beginning on or after January 1, 2009 (or, if later, the date applicable under paragraph (f)(3) of this section). For the periods after the statutory effective date set forth in paragraph (f)(1) or (f)(3) of this section and before the regulatory effective date set forth in the preceding sentence, a plan must comply with section 411(b)(5). During these periods, a plan is permitted to rely on the provisions of this section for purposes of satisfying the requirements of section 411(b)(5).

(3) Collectively bargained plans—(i) In general. Notwithstanding paragraph (f)(1)(iii) of this section, in the case of a collectively bargained plan maintained pursuant to one or more collective bargaining agreements between employee representatives and one or more employers ratified on or before August 17, 2006, the requirements of section 411(b)(5)(B)(i) do not apply to plan years beginning before the earlier of—

(A) The later of—

(1) The date on which the last of those collective bargaining agreements terminates (determined without regard to any extension thereof on or after August 17, 2006), or

(2) January 1, 2008; or

(B) January 1, 2010.

(ii) Treatment of plans with both collectively bargained and non-collectively bargained employees. In the case of a plan where a collective bargaining agreement applies to some, but not all, of the plan participants, the plan is considered a collectively bargained plan for purposes of paragraph (f)(3)(i) of this section if at least 25 percent of the participants in the plan are members of collective bargaining units for which the benefit levels under the plan are specified under the collective bargaining agreement.

Linda E. Stiff,

Deputy Commissioner for Services and Enforcement.

¶ 20,262G

IRS: Funding rules: Pension assets and liabilities: Pension Protection Act of 2006.— The IRS has issued proposed regulations that provide employers sponsoring single-employer defined benefit plans with guidance regarding the measurement of pension assets and liabilities under the new funding rules enacted under the Pension Protection Act of 2006 (P.L. 109-280). The proposed regulations are designed to assist plan sponsors in determining the contribution requirements that apply to their defined benefit plans for the first year that the new funding rules apply. The proposed regulations would be effective for plan years beginning on or after January 1, 2009. However, plan sponsors can rely on the proposed regulations for purposes of satisfying the requirements of Code Sec. 430 for plan years beginning in 2008.

The proposed regulations were published in the Federal Register on December 31, 2007 (72 FR 74215). The regulations were finalized on October 15, 2009 (74 FR 53003). The preamble to the final regulations is at ¶ 23,264. The final regulations are at ¶ 13,151L-8, ¶ 13,151L-14, ¶ 13,151L-19, and ¶ 13,151L-30.

[4830-01-p]

DEPARTMENT OF THE TREASURY

Internal Revenue Service

26 CFR Part 1

[REG-139236-07]

RIN 1545-BH07

Measurement of Assets and Liabilities for Pension Funding Purposes

AGENCY: Internal Revenue Service (IRS), Treasury.

ACTION: Notice of proposed rulemaking.

SUMMARY: This document contains proposed regulations providing guidance on the determination of plan assets and benefit liabilities for purposes of the funding requirements that apply to single employer defined benefit plans. These regulations affect sponsors, administrators, participants, and beneficiaries of single employer defined benefit plans.

DATES: Written or electronic comments and requests for a public hearing must be received by March 31, 2008.

ADDRESSES: Send submissions to: CC:PA:LPD:PR (REG-139236-07), room 5203, Internal Revenue Service, PO Box 7604, Ben Franklin Station, Washington, DC 20044. Submissions may be hand-delivered Monday through Friday between the hours of 8 a.m. and 4 p.m. to CC:PA:LPD:PR (REG-139236-07), Courier's Desk, Internal Revenue Service, 1111 Constitution Avenue NW., Washington, DC, or sent electronically via the Federal eRulemaking Portal at *www.regulations.gov* (IRS-REG-139236-07).

FOR FURTHER INFORMATION CONTACT: Concerning the regulations, Lauson C. Green or Linda S. F. Marshall at (202) 622-6090; concerning submissions and requests for a public hearing, Richard A. Hurst at *Richard.A.Hurst@ irscounsel.treas.gov* or at (202) 622-7180 (not toll-free numbers).

SUPPLEMENTARY INFORMATION:

Paperwork Reduction Act

The collections of information contained in this notice of proposed rulemaking have been submitted to the Office of Management and Budget for review in accordance with the Paperwork Reduction Act of 1995 (44 U.S.C. 3507(d)). Comments on the collections of information should be sent to the **Office of Management and Budget**, Attn: Desk Officer for the Department of the Treasury, Office of Information and Regulatory Affairs, Washington, DC 20503, with copies to the **Internal Revenue Service**, Attn: IRS Reports Clearance Officer, SE:W:CAR:MP:T:T:SP, Washington, DC 20224. Comments on the collection of information should be received by February 29, 2008. Comments are specifically requested concerning:

Whether the proposed collection of information is necessary for the proper performance of the functions of the Internal Revenue Service, including whether the information will have practical utility;

The accuracy of the estimated burden associated with the proposed collection of information;

How the quality, utility, and clarity of the information to be collected may be enhanced;

How the burden of complying with the proposed collections of information may be minimized, including through the application of automated collection techniques or other forms of information technology; and

Estimates of capital or start-up costs and costs of operation, maintenance, and purchase of service to provide information.

The collection of information in this proposed regulation is in § 1.430(h)(2)-1(e). This information is required in order for a plan sponsor to make an election to use an alternative interest rate for purposes of determining a plan's funding obligations under § 1.430(h)(2)-1. This information is required to obtain or retain benefits. The likely respondents are qualified retirement plan sponsors.

Estimated total annual reporting burden: 54,000 hours.

Estimated average annual burden hours per respondent: 0.75 hours.

Estimated number of respondents: 72,000.

Estimated annual frequency of responses: occasional.

An agency may not conduct or sponsor, and a person is not required to respond to, a collection of information unless it displays a valid control number assigned by the Office of Management and Budget.

Books or records relating to a collection of information must be retained as long as their contents may become material in the administration of any internal revenue law. Generally, tax returns and tax return information are confidential, as required by 26 U.S.C. 6103.

Background

This document contains proposed Income Tax Regulations (26 CFR part 1) under sections 430(d), 430(g), 430(h)(2), and 430(i), as added to the Internal Revenue Code (Code) by the Pension Protection Act of 2006 (PPA '06), Public Law 109-280 (120 Stat. 780).

Section 412 provides minimum funding requirements that generally apply for pension plans (including both defined benefit plans and money purchase pension plans). PPA '06 makes extensive changes to those minimum funding requirements that generally apply for plan years beginning on or after January 1, 2008. Section 430, which was added by PPA '06, specifies the minimum funding requirements that apply to single employer defined benefit pension plans (including multiple employer plans) pursuant to section 412.[1]

Section 430(a) defines the minimum required contribution for a single employer plan as the sum of the plan's target normal cost and the shortfall and waiver amortization charges for the plan year. Under section 430(b), a plan's target normal cost for a plan year is the present value of all benefits expected to accrue or be earned under the plan during the plan year. For this purpose, section 430(b) provides that an increase in any benefit attributable to services performed in a preceding plan year by reason of a compensation increase during the current plan year is treated as having accrued during the current plan year.

One of the amortization charges used in determining the minimum required contribution, the shortfall amortization charge, is determined based on the difference between the plan's funding target and the value of plan assets. Under section 430(d), except as provided in section 430(i)(1) (regarding plans in at-risk status), a plan's "funding target" for a plan year is the present value of all benefits accrued or earned under the plan as of the beginning of the plan year.

---

[1] Section 302 of the Employee Retirement Income Security Act of 1974, as amended (ERISA), sets forth funding rules that are parallel to those in section 412 of the Internal Revenue Code (Code), and section 303 of ERISA sets forth additional funding rules for single employer plans that are parallel to those in section 430 of the Code. Under section 101 of Reorganization Plan No. 4 of 1978 (43 FR 47713) and section 302 of ERISA, the Secretary of the Treasury has interpretive jurisdiction over the subject matter addressed in these proposed regulations for purposes of ERISA, as well as the Code. Thus, these proposed Treasury regulations issued under section 430 of the Code apply as well for purposes of section 303 of ERISA.

Section 430(g)(1) provides that all determinations made with respect to minimum required contributions for a plan year (such as the value of plan assets and liabilities) must be made as of the plan's valuation date. Section 430(g)(2) provides that, other than for plans with 100 or fewer participants (determined as provided in section 430(g)(2)(B) and (C)), the valuation date for a plan year must be the first day of the plan year. Under section 430(g)(3), the value of plan assets is generally the fair market value of those assets. However, the value of plan assets may be determined on the basis of the averaging of fair market values, but only if the averaging method is permitted under regulations and satisfies certain other requirements.

Under section 430(g)(4), if a required contribution for a preceding plan year is made after the valuation date for the current plan year, the contribution is taken into account in determining the value of plan assets for the current plan year. For 2009 and future plan years, only the present value (determined as of the valuation date for the current plan year, using the plan's effective interest rate for the preceding plan year) of the contributions made for the preceding plan year is taken into account. If any contributions for the current plan year are made before the valuation date (which could only occur for a small plan with a valuation date that is not the first day of the plan year), plan assets as of the valuation date must exclude (1) those contributions, and (2) interest on those contributions (determined at the plan's effective interest rate for the plan year) for the period between the date of the contribution and the valuation date. Under section 430(h)(2)(A), a plan's effective interest rate for a plan year is defined as the single interest rate that, if used to determine the present value of the benefits taken into account in determining the plan's funding target for the plan year, would result in an amount equal to the plan's funding target determined for the plan year under section 430(d).

Under section 430(h)(1), the determination of any present value or other computation under section 430 is to be made on the basis of actuarial assumptions and methods each of which is reasonable (taking into account the experience of the plan and reasonable expectations) and which, in combination, offer the actuary's best estimate of anticipated experience under the plan.

Section 430(h)(2) specifies the interest rates that must be used in determining a plan's target normal cost and funding target. Under the provision, present value is determined using three interest rates (segment rates), each of which applies to benefit payments expected to be paid during a certain period. The first segment rate applies to benefits reasonably determined to be payable during the 5-year period beginning on the first day of the plan year. The second segment rate applies to benefits reasonably determined to be payable during the 15-year period following the initial 5-year period. The third segment rate applies to benefits reasonably determined to be payable after the end of that 15-year period.

Each segment rate is a single interest rate determined monthly by the Treasury Department on the basis of a corporate bond yield curve. The corporate bond yield curve used for this purpose is to be prescribed monthly by the Treasury Department and is to reflect the average, for the 24-month period ending with the preceding month, of yields on investment grade corporate bonds with varying maturities that are in the top three quality levels available. Under section 430(h)(2)(F), the Secretary of the Treasury is directed to publish each month the corporate bond yield curve and each of the segment rates for the month. In addition, the Secretary is directed to publish a description of the methodology used to determine the yield curve and segment rates to enable plans to make reasonable projections regarding the yield curve and segment rates for future months, based on a plan's projection of future interest rates.

Section 430(h)(2)(G) provides a transition rule for plan years beginning in 2008 and 2009 (other than for plans where the first plan year begins on or after January 1, 2008). Under this transition rule, the interest rates to be used in the valuation are based on a blend of the segment rates and the long-term corporate bond rates used for plan years prior to the effective date of PPA '06. Under section 430(h)(2)(G)(iv), a plan sponsor may elect to have this transition rule not apply. In addition, solely for purposes of determining minimum required contributions under section 430, in lieu of using the segment rates, an employer may elect under section 430(h)(2)(D)(ii) to use interest rates on a yield curve based on the yields on investment grade corporate bonds within the top three quality levels without regard to the 24-month averaging described above.

Section 430(i) requires the application of special assumptions in determining the funding target and target normal cost of a plan in at-risk status. Under section 430(i)(4), a plan is in at-risk status for a year if, for the preceding year: (1) the plan's funding target attainment percentage, determined without regard to the at-risk assumptions, was less than 80 percent (with a transition rule discussed below), and (2) the plan's funding target attainment percentage, determined using the at-risk assumptions (without regard to whether the plan was in at-risk status for the preceding year), was less than 70 percent. Under a transition rule applicable for plan years beginning in 2008, 2009, and 2010, the following percentages apply instead of 80 percent in the first part of the test for determining at-risk status: 65 percent for 2008, 70 percent for 2009, and 75 percent for 2010. In the case of plan years beginning in 2008, the plan's funding target attainment percentage for the preceding plan year is to be determined under rules provided by the Treasury Department.

Under section 430(i)(6), the at-risk rules do not apply if a plan had 500 or fewer participants on each day during the preceding plan year. For this purpose, all defined benefit pension plans (other than multiemployer plans) maintained by the same employer (or a predecessor employer), or by any member of the employer's controlled group, are treated as a single plan.

If a plan is in at-risk status, the plan's funding target and normal cost are determined (under section 430(i)(1) and (2)) using special actuarial assumptions. Under these assumptions, all employees who are not otherwise assumed to retire as of the valuation date, but who will be eligible to elect to commence benefits in the current and 10 succeeding plan years, are assumed to retire at the earliest retirement date under the plan, but not before the end of the current plan year. All employees are assumed to elect the form of retirement benefit available under the plan at that assumed retirement age that results in the highest present value.

The funding target of a plan in at-risk status for a plan year is generally the sum of: (1) the present value of all benefits accrued or earned as of the beginning of the plan year, and (2) in the case of a plan that has been in at-risk status for at least 2 of the 4 preceding plan years, a loading factor. That loading factor is equal to the sum of: (1) $700 multiplied by the number of participants in the plan, plus (2) 4% of the funding target determined without regard to the loading factor. The target normal cost of a plan in at-risk status for a plan year is generally the sum of: (1) the present value of benefits expected to accrue or be earned under the plan during the plan year, determined using the special assumptions described above, and (2) in the case of a plan that has been in at-risk status for at least 2 of the 4 preceding plans years, a loading factor of 4% of the target normal cost determined without regard to the loading factor. If a plan has been in at-risk status for fewer than 5 consecutive plan years, a phase-in rule applies to the determination of the "funding target" and "target normal cost" under section 430(i)(5).

Explanation of Provisions

I. Overview

These proposed regulations are the third in a series of proposed regulations under new section 430.[2] These proposed regulations would provide guidance on the determination of assets and liabilities for purposes of applying the new funding rules of section 430. The Treasury Department and the IRS intend to issue additional proposed regulations relating to other portions of the rules under section 430 (including sections 430(a), (c), and (j)) in the first part of 2008. It is expected that those regulations will be effective for plan years beginning on or after January 1, 2009.

II. Section 1.430(d)-1 Determination of Funding Target and Target Normal Cost

Section 1.430(d)-1 would provide rules for determining the funding target and the target normal cost of a plan that is not in at-risk status (within the meaning of section 430(i)). The proposed regulations would provide that the funding target is the present value of all benefits that have been accrued or earned under the plan as of the first day of the plan year, and that the target normal cost for the plan year is the present value of all benefits that accrue or are earned (or that are expected to accrue or to be earned) under the plan during the plan year. Thus, if the actuarial valuation date for the plan year is not the first day of the plan year, the target normal cost will include the benefits actually earned during the year through the valuation date for

---

[2] Proposed regulation §§ 1.430(h)(3)-1 and 1.430(h)(3)-2, relating to the mortality tables used to determine liabilities under section 430(h)(3), were issued May 29, 2007 (REG-143601-06, 72 FR 29456), and proposed regulation § 1.430(f)-1, relating to prefunding and funding standard carryover balances under section 430(f), was issued August 31, 2007 (REG-113891-07, 72 FR 50544).

the plan year plus a projection of benefits that will be earned through the rest of the plan year.

In order to determine the funding target and target normal cost, the future benefits to be paid from the plan must be allocated among prior plan years (in which case they will be taken into account in determining the funding target for the current year), the current plan year (in which case they will be taken into account in determining the target normal cost of the plan for the plan year), and future years. If the amount of a benefit that is expected to be paid is a function of the accrued benefit at the time the benefit is expected to be paid, then the amount taken into account in the funding target is determined by applying that function to the accrued benefit as of the beginning of the plan year and the amount of the benefit taken into account in the target normal cost is determined by applying that function to the increase in the accrued benefit for the plan year. If the amount of a benefit that is expected to be paid is not a function of the accrued benefit at the time the benefit is expected to be paid (for example, certain ancillary benefits), but is a function of the participant's service at that time, then the amount taken into account for purposes of determining the funding target for a plan year is based on a participant's service as of the first day of the plan year and the amount of the benefit that is taken into account in the target normal cost is the increase in that benefit for the plan year based on the additional year of service. If the amount of a benefit that is expected to be paid is neither a function of the accrued benefit at the time the benefit is expected to be paid nor a function of the participant's service at that time, then the portion of the benefit taken into account for purposes of determining the funding target for a plan year is based on the proportion of a participant's service as of the first day of the plan year relative to the service the participant will have when the participant meets the age and service eligibility requirement for the benefit, and the portion of the benefit that is taken into account in the target normal cost is the increase in the proportional benefit for the plan year.

The proposed regulations would provide that the determination of the funding target and the target normal cost for a plan year is not permitted to take into account any limitations or anticipated limitations under section 436. Also, the proposed regulations would provide that plan administrative expenses paid (or expected to be paid) from plan assets for a plan year are not taken into account in determining a plan's target normal cost and funding target for that plan year. With respect to benefits provided by insurance, the proposed regulations would provide that, in general, a plan must reflect the liability for benefits that are funded through insurance contracts held by the plan in the plan's funding target and target normal cost, and must include the value of the corresponding insurance contracts in plan assets. However, an alternative rule is provided in the case of benefits that are funded through certain insurance contracts purchased from an insurance company licensed under the laws of a State. Under this rule, a plan is permitted to exclude benefits provided under such contracts from the plan's funding target and target normal cost and to exclude the corresponding insurance contracts from plan assets, but only to the extent that a participant's or beneficiary's right to receive those benefits is an irrevocable contractual right based on premiums paid to the insurance company prior to the valuation date under the insurance contracts.

The proposed regulations would provide that, except as provided in section 412(d)(2), the funding target and target normal cost are determined based on the plan terms that are adopted no later than the valuation date for the plan year and become effective during that plan year. Thus, the rules of Revenue Ruling 77-2 (1977-1 CB 120) would no longer apply. See §601.601(d)(2) of this chapter. For example, if an amendment that increases plan liabilities is adopted on or before the plan's valuation date and is effective during the plan year that includes the valuation date, the full increase in liability with respect to the amendment is taken into account as of that year's valuation date. However, with respect to the pre-PPA counterpart to section 412(d)(2) (section 412(c)(8) as in effect prior to amendments made by PPA '06), Rev. Rul. 79-325 (1979-2 CB 190) provides that section 412(c)(8) applies to plan amendments made during the plan year (as well as to plan amendments made within 2 ½ months after the end of the plan year), and this same rule applies under the identical statutory provisions of section 412(d)(2). See §601.601(d)(2) of this chapter. Thus, if an amendment that increases plan liabilities is adopted after the valuation date for a plan year but the amendment is effective during that plan year, the full increase in liability will be taken into account as of the valuation date for that plan year if a section 412(d)(2) election is made, and none of the increase in liability will be taken into account as of the valuation date for that plan year if no section 412(d)(2) election is made. Regardless of whether a section 412(d)(2) election is made, the rules of section 436(c) must be applied in determining whether the amendment is permitted to take effect during the plan year. Section 430 does not contain a corresponding provision to former section

412(c)(12) under which the provisions of a collective bargaining agreement are taken into account for funding purposes before the corresponding plan amendments have been made.

The proposed regulations would require all currently employed plan participants, formerly employed plan participants (including retirees and terminated vested participants), and other individuals currently entitled to benefits under the plan to be included in the valuation. Unlike §1.412(c)(3)-1(c)(3)(ii), the proposed regulations would not permit exclusion from the valuation of those plan participants who could have been excluded from participation in the plan under the rules of section 410(a). However, the proposed regulations would continue to apply the rules of §1.412(c)(3)-1(c)(3)(iii) (relating to the exclusion of terminated employees who do not have a vested benefit under the plan but whose service might be taken into account in future years upon rehire) and the rules of §1.412(c)(3)-1(d)(2) (under which the future participation in the plan of current employees who are not yet participants is permitted to be anticipated).

Section 1.430(d)-1 of the proposed regulations would cross-reference other regulations for the details of the statutorily specified interest rates, mortality tables, and actuarial assumptions that apply to plans in at-risk status. With respect to the actuarial assumptions that are not specified by statute or regulations, the proposed regulations would require that the actuarial assumptions used to determine present value satisfy the section 430(h)(1) requirements to be individually reasonable (taking into account the experience of the plan and reasonable expectations) and, in combination, offer the plan's enrolled actuary's best estimate of anticipated experience under the plan.

The proposed regulations would provide that, once the actuarial assumptions for a plan year are established, they are not permitted to be changed for that plan year (unless the Commissioner determines that the assumptions are unreasonable). Similarly, the proposed regulations would provide that, once the funding method for a plan year is established, it is not permitted to be changed for that plan year (unless the Commissioner determines that the use of the funding method for the plan year is impermissible).

In general, the actuarial assumptions and funding method used by a plan for a plan year are required to be established not later than the due date (with extensions) for the filing of Form 5500, "Annual Return/ Report of Employee Benefit Plan," for that plan year (or not later than the last day of the seventh month after the end of the plan year in the case of a plan not required to file Form 5500). The proposed regulations would provide that the filing of the first actuarial report (Schedule SB) under section 6059 for a plan year that reflects the use of actuarial assumptions and a funding method is treated as the establishment of those assumptions and the funding method for that plan year.

In accordance with section 430(h)(4), the proposed regulations would provide that the plan's actuarial valuation must take into account the probability that future benefits will be paid in optional forms of benefit under the plan, including single sum distributions, determined on the basis of the plan's experience and other relevant assumptions. In addition, the plan's enrolled actuary must take into account any difference in the present value of those future benefit payments that results from the use of actuarial assumptions in determining benefit payments in any such optional forms of benefit that are different from those prescribed by section 430(h).

In the case of a distribution that is subject to section 417(e)(3) and that is determined using the applicable interest rate and applicable mortality table under section 417(e)(3), the proposed regulations would provide that the computation of the present value of that distribution will be treated as having taken into account any difference in present value that results from the use of actuarial assumptions that are different from those prescribed by section 430(h) only if the present value of the distribution is determined by valuing the annuity that corresponds to the distribution using special actuarial assumptions. Under these special assumptions, for the period beginning with the annuity starting date, the current applicable mortality table under section 417(e)(3) is substituted for the mortality table under section 430(h)(3) that would otherwise apply. In addition, under these special actuarial assumptions, the valuation interest rates under section 430(h)(2) are used for all periods (as opposed to the interest rates under section 417(e)(3) which the plan uses to determine the amount of the benefit).

The proposed regulations provide two elective adjustments to this methodology for valuing distributions subject to section 417(e)(3). First, in determining the present value of such a distribution, if a plan uses the generational mortality tables under §1.430(h)(3)-1(a)(4) or under §1.430(h)(3)-2, the plan would be permitted to use a 50-50 male-female blend of the annuitant mortality rates under the §1.430(h)(3)-1(a)(4) generational mortality tables in lieu of the applicable mortality table under section 417(e)(3) that would apply to a distribution with an annuity starting date occurring on the valuation date. Second, a plan would be permitted to make adjustments to reflect differences between the phase-in of the section 430(h)(2) segment rates under section 430(h)(2)(G) and the adjustments to the segment rates under section 417(e)(3)(D)(iii).

In the case of a distribution that is subject to section 417(e)(3) but that is determined as the greater of the benefit determined using the applicable interest rate and the applicable mortality table under section 417(e)(3) and the benefit determined using some basis other than the section 417(e)(3) assumptions, the proposed regulations would provide that the computation of present value must take into account the extent to which the present value of the distribution is greater than the present value determined using the applicable interest rate and applicable mortality table.

In the case of an applicable defined benefit plan described in section 411(a)(13)(C) (such as a cash balance plan), the proposed regulations would provide that, if the distribution is determined under the rules of section 411(a)(13)(A), the amount of the future distribution must be determined by projecting the future interest credits or equivalent amounts under the plan's interest crediting rules to the expected date of payment using reasonable actuarial assumptions. Thus, the present value of a future distribution is not necessarily the current amount of a participant's hypothetical account balance.

The proposed regulations would provide that any reasonable technique can be used to determine the present value of the benefits expected to be paid during a plan year, based on the interest rates and mortality assumptions applicable for the plan year. For example, the present value of a monthly retirement annuity payable at the beginning of each month can be determined using the standard actuarial approximation that reflects $13/24$ths of the discounted expected payments for the year as of the beginning of the year and $11/24$ths of the discounted expected payments for the year as of the end of the year, or by assuming that the payment is made in the middle of the year.

The proposed regulations would also reflect the provisions of section 430(h)(5), requiring approval of the Commissioner for large changes in actuarial assumptions. In general, this rule applies where the application of the changes in actuarial assumptions results in a decrease in the plan's funding shortfall for the current plan year (disregarding the effect on the plan's funding shortfall resulting from changes in interest and mortality assumptions) that exceeds $50,000,000, or that exceeds $5,000,000 and that is 5 percent or more of the funding target of the plan before the change. Thus, for example, if a plan leaves at-risk status and consequently makes changes to its actuarial assumptions (including a return to previously used assumptions) that result in a reduction in the funding shortfall that exceeds $50,000,000, that change in actuarial assumptions would require approval of the Commissioner. In determining whether aggregate unfunded vested benefits exceed $50,000,000, the proposed regulations would provide that multiemployer plans and plans with no unfunded vested benefits are disregarded. In addition, the proposed regulations would provide that the aggregate unfunded vested benefits used to determine premiums for the current plan year (as determined under section 4006(a)(3)(E)(iii) of ERISA) are used for purposes of calculating whether unfunded vested benefits exceed $50,000,000.

III. *Section 1.430(g)-1 Valuation Date and Value of Plan Assets*

Section 1.430(g)-1 would provide rules for a plan's valuation date and the value of plan assets.[3] Under the proposed regulations, except in the case of a small plan, a plan's valuation date is the first day of the plan year. For this purpose, a small plan is defined as a plan sponsored by an employer that had 100 or fewer participants in defined benefit plans (other than multiemployer plans as defined in section 414(f)) sponsored by the employer or members of the employer's controlled group, including active and inactive participants and all other individuals entitled to future benefits. A small plan is permitted to have a valuation date other than the first day of a plan year. The selection of a valuation date by a small plan is part of the plan's funding method and, thus, is permitted to be changed only with the Commissioner's consent. If a plan that was using a valuation date that was not the first day of the plan year is no longer eligible to use that date because the plan is no longer a small plan, the required change of the valuation date to the first day of the plan year is treated as automatically approved and no prior approval of the Commissioner is necessary.

The proposed regulations would provide that plan assets must be valued either at their fair market value on the valuation date or at the "average" value of assets on the valuation date. Under this average value, the value of plan assets is set equal to the average of the fair market value of assets on the valuation date and the adjusted fair market value of assets determined for one or more earlier determination dates. The proposed regulations would provide that the period of time between the valuation date and each of the earlier determination dates must be equal (with a period that is not more than 12 months), and the earliest of these determination dates cannot be earlier than the last day of the 25th month before the valuation date of the plan year. In a typical situation, the earlier determination dates will be the two immediately preceding valuation dates. The proposed regulations would provide that this average of fair market values is increased for contributions included in the plan's asset balance on the current valuation date that were not included in the plan's asset balance on an earlier determination date, and reduced for benefits and administrative expenses paid from plan assets during the same period.[4] After these adjustments, as well as the adjustments described in the following two paragraphs, the resulting average value must be constrained so that it falls between 90 and 110 percent of the fair market value of plan assets.

The proposed regulations would implement the rules of section 430(g)(4) relating to the treatment of contributions for a prior plan year that are made after the valuation date for the current plan year. These rules work in conjunction with the rules of section 430(j)(2) in order to keep employers and plans neutral regarding the timing of contributions that are paid after the end of the plan year. Under section 430(j)(2), the amount of the contribution must be adjusted for interest at the effective interest rate under section 430(h)(2) in order to take into account the delay in contributions (including the period after the end of the year). For this purpose, section 430(g)(4) requires that only the present value of a prior year contribution paid after the valuation date be included in plan assets, so that the value of plan assets for the next plan year is not inflated by reflecting a delayed contribution at full value. This effectively means that the present value of the contribution is the same from the perspective of the employer and the plan, regardless of when it is made. Because the requirement to adjust contributions for delayed payment after the end of the plan year is first effective for plan years beginning in 2008 (except for certain plans with a delayed effective date), the corresponding requirement to include only the present value of a prior year contribution paid after the valuation date is not effective until the second plan year for which section 430 applies to the plan. Thus, this corresponding requirement will become effective in plan years beginning in 2009, except with respect to plans for which the effective date of section 430 is delayed.

The proposed regulations would specify the treatment of current year contributions that are made before the valuation date (which could only occur for small plans with valuation dates other than the first day of the plan year). These contributions, adjusted for interest at the effective interest rate under section 430(h)(2) for the plan year, must be subtracted from plan assets in determining the actuarial value of plan assets. This is similar to the pre-PPA '06 requirement to subtract these contributions from plan assets after adjustment using the plan's valuation interest rate.

The proposed regulations would incorporate the provisions of section 430(l) (involving qualified transfers to health benefit accounts under section 420).

IV. *Section 1.430(h)(2)-1 Interest Rates*

Section 1.430(h)(2)-1 would specify the interest rates that are to be used to determine present value and to make other calculations under section 430. These rates are generally based on the 24-month moving averages of 3 separate segment rates for the month that includes the valuation date (the applicable month). The first segment rate, which is based on the portion of the corporate bond yield curve over the period from 0 to 5 years, applies for purposes of discounting benefits that are expected to be paid during the 5-year period beginning on the valuation date for a plan year. The second segment rate, which is based on the portion of the corporate bond yield curve over the period between 5 and 20 years, applies for purposes of discounting benefit payments that are expected to be paid at least 5 years after the valuation date, but before 20 years. The third segment rate applies to benefit payments that are expected to be paid at least 20 years after the valuation date. Thus, for example, if a series of monthly payments is assumed to be made beginning on the valuation date, the second segment rate will

---

[3] The value of plan assets under these proposed regulations is referred to in Schedule SB of Form 5500 as "actuarial assets."

[4] Note that this average of fair market values is different from the calculation of average value under §1.412(c)(2)-1(b)(7). For example, the adjusted value described in the pro-

posed regulations does not include interest and dividends on plan assets attributable to the period between the earlier determination date and the valuation date in determining the adjusted fair market value of assets.

apply to the 61st such payment and the third segment rate will apply beginning with the 241st such payment.[5] Except in the case of a new plan, a transition rule applies for 2008 and 2009 under which these segment rates are blended with the long-term corporate bond rate that applies under pre-PPA law.

The monthly corporate bond yield curve is, with respect to any month, a yield curve that is prescribed by the Commissioner for that month based on yields for that month on investment grade corporate bonds with varying maturities that are in the top three quality levels available. Notice 2007-81 (2007-44 IRB 899) provides guidance on the monthly corporate bond yield curve and related interest rates used to make certain computations related to the funding requirements that apply to single employer defined benefit plans under section 430(h)(2), including a description of the methodology for determining the monthly corporate bond yield curve. See §601.601(d)(2) of this chapter.

The proposed regulations would reflect the special interest rate for determining a plan's funding target in the case of airlines that make the 10-year amortization election described in section 402(a)(2) of PPA '06, in accordance with section 6615 of the U.S. Troop Readiness, Veterans' Care, Katrina Recovery, and Iraq Accountability Appropriations Act, 2007, Public Law 110-28 (121 Stat. 112). The special interest rate does not apply for other purposes such as the determination of the plan's target normal cost.

The proposed regulations describe several elections a plan sponsor is permitted to make in order to use an alternative interest rate rather than the segment rates. These elections are made by providing written notification of the election to the plan's enrolled actuary. Such an election is part of the plan's funding method and, accordingly, may only be adopted or changed with the consent of the Commissioner. Under one such election, a plan sponsor that is using segment rates may elect the use of an alternative month as the applicable month, provided that the alternative month is one of the 4 months that precede the month that includes the valuation date for the plan year. Under another such election, the plan sponsor may elect not to apply the transition rule under which the segment rates are blended with the 30-year Treasury rate for 2008 and 2009. Under the third such election, for purposes of determining the minimum required contribution under section 430 (including the determination of shortfall amortization installments, waiver amortization installments, and the present value of those installments), the plan sponsor may elect to use interest rates under the monthly corporate bond yield curve—which is a set of spot rates for the month preceding the valuation date rather than a 24-month moving average for that month or an alternative applicable month—in lieu of the segment rates. The amount of the funding target calculated in accordance with any of these elections applies for all purposes, including determining the adjusted funding target attainment percentage under section 436 and the applicable limitations under section 404. In the case of the first plan year to which section 430 applies to a plan (the first plan year beginning in 2008 other than for a plan with a delayed section 430 effective date), any of these elections are treated as having been approved by the Commissioner and do not require the Commissioner's specific prior approval.

In the case of a plan sponsor that has elected to use interest rates under the monthly corporate bond yield curve, if with respect to a decrement the benefit is only expected to be paid for one-half of a year (because the decrement was assumed to occur in the middle of the year), the proposed regulations would provide that the interest rate for that year can be determined as if the benefit were being paid for the entire year.

Under the proposed regulations, the effective interest rate determined under section 430(h)(2)(A) is the single interest rate that, if used to determine the present value of the benefits taken into account in determining the plan's funding target for a plan year, would result in an amount equal to the plan's funding target determined for the plan year under section 430(d) as described in §1.430(d)-1(b)(2) (without regard to calculations for plans in at-risk status under section 430(i)). The effective interest rate is used to adjust plan contributions made on a date other than the valuation date.

Under the proposed regulations, the interest rates used to determine the amount of shortfall amortization installments and waiver amortization installments are determined based on the dates those installments are assumed to be paid, using the same timing rules that apply for purposes of determining the target normal cost. Thus, for a plan that uses the segment rates, the first segment rate applies to the five

shortfall amortization installments assumed to be paid during the first five years beginning on the valuation date for the plan year, and the second segment rate applies to the two shortfall amortization installments that are assumed to be paid after that period.

V. *Section 1.430(i)-1 Plans in At-risk Status*

The proposed regulations would provide rules and assumptions for determining the funding target and making other computations for certain defined benefit plans that are referred to as plans in "at-risk" status due to their significantly underfunded status. These rules apply to single employer defined benefit plans (including multiple employer plans) but do not apply to multiemployer plans. The at-risk rules do not apply to small plans. For this purpose, a small plan is defined as a plan sponsored by an employer that had 500 or fewer participants (including both active and inactive participants) in defined benefit plans (other than multiemployer plans) sponsored by the employer or any member of the employer's controlled group on each day during the preceding plan year.

In general, the proposed regulations would provide that a plan is in at-risk status for a plan year if the funding target attainment percentage (FTAP) for the preceding plan year is less than 80% (65%, 70%, and 75%, for plan years beginning in 2008, 2009, and 2010, respectively),[6] and the at-risk FTAP for the preceding plan year is less than 70 percent. For this purpose, the proposed regulations would provide that a plan's FTAP for a plan year is a fraction (expressed as a percentage) determined as: (i) the value of plan assets for the plan year after subtraction of the prefunding balance and the funding standard carryover balance under section 430(f)(4)(B)), divided by (ii) the funding target of the plan for the plan year (determined without regard to section 430(i) and these proposed regulations). The proposed regulations would provide that the at-risk FTAP of a plan for a plan year is determined similarly except that the denominator is the at-risk funding target of the plan for the plan year (but determined without regard to the loading factor discussed in the following paragraph). The proposed regulations would provide that, in the case of a newly established plan, this FTAP and at-risk FTAP determination are assumed to be 100% for years before the plan exists.

In general, in accordance with section 430(i)(1), the proposed regulations would provide that the at-risk funding target and the at-risk target normal cost of the plan for the plan year are generally determined in the same manner as for plans not in at-risk status but using special actuarial assumptions. In addition, the at-risk funding target and the at-risk target normal cost are increased to take into account a loading factor. In any case, the at-risk funding target and the at-risk target normal cost of a plan for a plan year cannot be less than the plan's funding target and target normal cost determined without regard to the at-risk rules. This minimum value is determined on a plan-wide (rather than a participant-by-participant) basis.

The actuarial assumptions used to determine a plan's at-risk funding target for a plan year are the actuarial assumptions that are applied under section 430, with certain modifications as set forth in the proposed regulations. Under these special actuarial assumptions, if an employee would be eligible to commence an immediate distribution upon termination of employment by the end of the plan year that begins 10 years after the end of the current plan year (that is, the end of the 11th plan year beginning with the current plan year), that employee is assumed to terminate and commence an immediate distribution at the earliest retirement date under the plan, or, if later, at the end of the current plan year. (However, the proposed regulations would provide that this special assumption does not apply to the extent the employee is otherwise assumed to retire during the current plan year. Thus, for example, if generally applicable retirement assumptions would provide for a 25% probability that an employee will retire during the current plan year, the special retirement age assumption would require the plan to assume a 75% probability that the employee will retire at the end of the plan year.) For this purpose, the proposed regulations would define the earliest retirement age under the plan as the earliest age at which a participant could terminate employment and receive an immediate distribution. In addition, the special actuarial assumptions in the proposed regulations would provide that all employees are assumed to elect the optional form of benefit available under the plan at the assumed retirement age that would result in the highest present value of benefits.

If a plan that is in at-risk status for the plan year has been in at-risk status for a consecutive period of fewer than 5 plan years, the plan's funding target for the plan year is determined as a blend of the funding

---

[5] The same interest rate timing rules apply for purposes of determining present values for purposes of section 417(e)(3).

[6] This phase-in of the 80% rule applies solely for plan years beginning in 2008 through 2010 and is not adjusted for plans described in §1.430(i)-1(f)(2) for which the effective date of section 430 is delayed.

target determined as if the plan were not in at-risk status and the funding target determined as if the plan had been in at-risk status for each of the previous 5 plan years. For this purpose, the funding target determined as if the plan had been in at-risk status for each of the previous 5 plan years is determined without applying the loading factor if the plan has not been in at-risk status for two of the last four plan years. The increase in the funding target to reflect the at-risk rules is phased in over 5 years at 20% per year. The proposed regulations provide similar rules for determining the at-risk target normal cost of a plan that has been in at-risk status for fewer than 5 consecutive plan years.

For purposes of applying the rules under section 430(i), the proposed regulations set forth rules for making certain calculations with respect to the first plan year to which section 430 applies to the plan. These rules are generally the same as the rules that apply for that plan year for purposes of section 436.

There is no special rule for determining the at-risk funding target for the plan year preceding the plan year section 430 first applies to the plan. This is because, for a plan to which section 430 applies beginning in 2008, if the plan's FTAP for the preceding plan year was less than the 65% needed to be in at-risk status (pursuant to the transition rule described in section 430(i)(4)(B)), then the at-risk FTAP would necessarily be below the 70% needed for the plan to be in at-risk status (because the at-risk funding target cannot be less than the funding target for a plan that is not in at-risk status). However, plans for which the effective date of section 430 is delayed will have to determine the at-risk funding target for the plan year that precedes the plan year for which section 430 is first effective with respect to the plan.

Effective/Applicability Dates

Section 430 generally applies to plan years beginning on or after January 1, 2008. These regulations are proposed to apply to plan years beginning on or after January 1, 2009. However, in the case of a plan for which the effective date of section 430 is delayed in accordance with sections 104 through 106 of the Pension Protection Act of 2006, Public Law 109-280 (120 Stat. 780), the regulations are proposed to apply to plan years beginning on or after the date section 430 applies with respect to the plan. For plan years beginning in 2008, plans are permitted to rely on the provisions set forth in these proposed regulations for purposes of satisfying the requirements of section 430.

Under the proposed regulations, any change in a plan's funding method that is made for the first plan year section 430 applies to the plan and that is not inconsistent with the requirements of section 430 would be treated as having been approved by the Commissioner and would not require the Commissioner's specific prior approval. In addition, the Commissioner's specific prior approval is not required with respect to any actuarial assumptions that are adopted for the first plan year for which section 430 applies to the plan and that are not inconsistent with the requirements of section 430. Future guidance will cover procedures for obtaining the Commissioner's approval for changes in funding method and may provide for additional circumstances in which automatic approval is granted.

Special Analyses

It has been determined that this notice of proposed rulemaking is not a significant regulatory action as defined in Executive Order 12866. Therefore, a regulatory assessment is not required. It has also been determined that section 553(b) of the Administrative Procedure Act (5 U.S.C. chapter 5) does not apply to these regulations. It is hereby certified that the collection of information imposed by these proposed regulations will not have a significant economic impact on a substantial number of small entities. Accordingly, a regulatory flexibility analysis is not required. The estimated burden imposed by the collection of information contained in these proposed regulations is 0.75 hours per respondent. Moreover, this burden is attributable to the flexibility given under the applicable statutory requirements under which a plan sponsor may make any of several elections related to the interest rate used for minimum funding purposes. The written elections under these proposed regulations are made by the plan sponsor upon occasion and will require minimal time to prepare. Pursuant to section 7805(f) of the Code, these regulations have been submitted to the Chief Counsel for Advocacy of the Small Business Administration for comment on its impact on small business.

Comments and Requests for Public Hearing

Before these proposed regulations are adopted as final regulations, consideration will be given to any written (a signed original and eight (8) copies) or electronic comments that are submitted timely to the IRS. The IRS and the Treasury Department specifically request comments on the clarity of the proposed regulations and how they may be made easier to understand. All comments will be available for public inspection and copying. A public hearing will be scheduled if requested in writing by any person that timely submits written comments. If a public hearing is scheduled, notice of the date, time, and place for the public hearing will be published in the **Federal Register**.

Drafting Information

The principal authors of these regulations are Lauson C. Green and Linda S. F. Marshall, Office of Division Counsel/Associate Chief Counsel (Tax Exempt and Government Entities). However, other personnel from the IRS and the Treasury Department participated in the development of these regulations.

List of Subjects in 26 CFR Part 1

Income taxes, Reporting and recordkeeping requirements.

Proposed Amendments to the Regulations

Accordingly, 26 CFR part 1 is proposed to be amended as follows:

PART 1—INCOME TAXES

Paragraph 1. The authority citation for part 1 continues to read, in part, as follows:

Authority: 26 U.S.C. 7805 ***

Par. 2. Section 1.430(d)-1 is added to read as follows:

§ 1.430(d)-1 Determination of target normal cost and funding target.

(a) *In general* —(1) *Overview.* This section sets forth rules for determining a plan's target normal cost and funding target under sections 430(b) and 430(d), including guidance relating to the application of actuarial assumptions described in sections 430(h)(1) and 430(h)(4). Section 430 and this section apply to single employer defined benefit plans (including multiple employer plans as defined in section 413(c)) that are subject to section 412 but do not apply to multiemployer plans (as defined in section 414(f)). For further guidance on actuarial assumptions, see § 1.430(h)(2)-1 (relating to interest rates) and §§ 1.430(h)(3)-1 and 1.430(h)(3)-2 (relating to mortality tables). See also § 1.430(i)-1 for the determination of the funding target and target normal cost for a plan that is in at-risk status.

(2) *Organization of regulation.* Paragraph (b) of this section sets forth definitions of target normal cost and funding target. Paragraph (c) of this section provides rules regarding which benefits are taken into account in determining a plan's target normal cost and funding target. Paragraph (d) of this section sets forth the rules regarding the plan provisions that are taken into account in making these determinations, and paragraph (e) of this section provides rules on which plan participants are taken into account for this purpose. Paragraph (f) of this section provides rules relating to the actuarial assumptions and the plan's funding method that are used to determine present values. Paragraph (g) of this section contains effective/applicability dates and transition rules.

(3) *Special rules for multiple employer plans.* In the case of a multiple employer plan to which section 413(c)(4)(A) applies, the rules of section 430 and this section are applied separately for each employer under the plan, as if each employer maintained a separate plan. Thus, the plan's funding target and target normal cost are computed separately for each employer under such a multiple employer plan. In the case of a multiple employer plan to which section 413(c)(4)(A) does not apply (that is, a plan described in section 413(c)(4)(B) that has not made the election for section 413(c)(4)(A) to apply), the rules of section 430 and this section are applied as if all participants in the plan were employed by a single employer.

(b) *Definition of target normal cost, funding target, and funding target attainment percentage* —(1) *Target normal cost* —(i) *In general.* For a plan that is not in at-risk status under section 430(i) for the plan year, the target normal cost of the plan for the plan year is the present value of all benefits that have accrued or have been earned (or that are expected to accrue or to be earned) under the plan during the plan year. See § 1.430(i)-1(d) and (e)(2) for the determination of target normal cost for a plan that is in at-risk status.

(ii) *Benefits accruing for a plan year.* The benefits that have been accrued or have been earned (or that are expected to accrue or to be earned) under a plan during a plan year include any increase in benefits during the plan year that is a result of any actual or projected increase in compensation during the current plan year, even if that increase in benefits is with respect to benefits attributable to services performed in a preceding plan year.

(2) *Funding target.* For a plan that is not in at-risk status under section 430(i) for the plan year, the funding target of the plan for the

plan year is the present value of all benefits that have been accrued or earned under the plan as of the first day of the plan year. See § 1.430(i)-1(c) and (e)(1) for the determination of the funding target for a plan that is in at-risk status.

(3) *Funding target attainment percentage.* See § 1.430(i)-1(b)(3) and § 1.436-1(j)(2) for rules relating to the determination of the funding target attainment percentage under section 430(d)(2).

(c) *Benefits taken into account* —(1) *In general* —(i) *Basic rule.* The benefits taken into account in determining the funding target and target normal cost under paragraph (b) of this section are all benefits earned or accrued under the plan, including retirement-type and ancillary benefits.

(ii) *Allocation of benefits* —(A) *Benefits that are based on accrued benefits.* If the amount of a benefit that is expected to be paid is a function of the accrued benefit at the time the benefit is expected to be paid, then the amount of the benefit that is taken into account in the funding target is determined by applying that function to the accrued benefit as of the beginning of the plan year and the amount of the benefit that is taken into account in the target normal cost is determined by applying that function to the increase in the accrued benefit for the plan year. For example, a benefit that is assumed to be payable at a particular early retirement age in the amount of 90% of the accrued benefit is taken into account in the funding target in the amount of 90% of the accrued benefit as of the beginning of the plan year, and that benefit is taken into account in the target normal cost in the amount of 90% of the increase in the accrued benefit for the plan year.

(B) *Benefits that are based on service.* If the amount of a benefit that is expected to be paid is not a function of the accrued benefit at the time the benefit is expected to be paid, but is a function of the participant's service at that time, then the portion of the benefit taken into account for purposes of determining the funding target for a plan year is determined by applying that function to the participant's service as of the first day of the plan year and the amount of the benefit that is taken into account in the target normal cost is the increase in that benefit for the plan year based on the additional year of service. For example, if a plan provides a post-retirement death benefit of $500 per year of service, then the funding target is determined based on a death benefit of $500 multiplied by a participant's service at the beginning of the year and the target normal cost is based on the additional $500 in death benefits earned for one more year of service.

(C) *Other benefits.* If the amount of a benefit that is expected to be paid is neither a function of the accrued benefit at the time the benefit is expected to be paid as described in paragraph (c)(1)(ii)(A) of this section nor a function of the participant's service at that time as described in paragraph (c)(1)(ii)(B) of this section, then the portion of the benefit taken into account for purposes of determining the funding target for a plan year is based on the proportion of a participant's service as of the first day of the plan year relative to the service the participant will have when the participant meets the age and service eligibility requirements for the benefit, and the portion of the benefit that is taken into account in the target normal cost is the increase in the proportional benefit for the plan year. For example, if a plan provides a Social Security supplement for a participant who retires after 30 years of service that is equal to a participant's Social Security benefit, the funding target is determined based on the participant's Social Security benefit as of the beginning of the plan year multiplied by a fraction, the numerator of which is the participant's service as of the first day of the plan year and the denominator of which is 30 years. In such a case, the target normal cost is based on the increase in the proportional benefit taking into account one additional year of service and any changes in the participant's Social Security benefit.

(iii) *Application of section 436 limitations to funding target and target normal cost determination.* The determination of the funding target and target normal cost of a plan for a plan year is not permitted to take into account any limitations or anticipated limitations under section 436.

(2) *Payment of expenses from plan assets.* Plan administrative expenses paid (or expected to be paid) from plan assets for a plan year are not taken into account in the determination of a plan's target normal cost and funding target for that plan year.

(3) *Benefits provided by insurance.* A plan generally is required to reflect in the plan's funding target and target normal cost the liability for benefits that are funded through insurance contracts held by the plan, and to include in plan assets the value of the corresponding insurance contracts. Alternatively, in the case of benefits that are funded through insurance contracts purchased from an insurance company licensed under the laws of a State, the plan is permitted to exclude benefits provided under such contracts from the plan's funding target and target normal cost and to exclude the corresponding insurance contracts from plan assets, but only to the extent that a participant's or beneficiary's right to receive those benefits is an irrevocable contractual right, based on premiums paid to the insurance company prior to the valuation date under the insurance contracts. Thus, for example, in the case of a retired participant receiving benefits from an annuity contract in pay status under which no premiums are required on or after the valuation date, a plan is permitted to exclude the benefits provided by the contract from the plan's funding target and target normal cost, provided that the value of the contract is also excluded from plan assets. Similarly, in the case of an active or deferred vested participant whose benefits are funded by a life insurance or annuity contract under which further premiums are required on or after the valuation date, a plan is permitted to exclude the benefits, if any, that would be paid from the contract if no further premiums were to be paid (for example, if the contract were to go on reduced paid-up status) from the plan's funding target and target normal cost, provided that the value of the contract is excluded from plan assets. A plan's treatment of benefits funded through insurance contracts pursuant to this paragraph (c)(3) is part of the plan's funding method. Accordingly, that treatment can be changed only with the consent of the Commissioner.

(d) *Plan provisions taken into account.* Except as provided in section 412(d)(2), the determination of a plan's funding target and target normal cost for a plan year is based on plan provisions that are adopted no later than the valuation date for the plan year and that become effective during that plan year. Section 412(d)(2) applies for purposes of determining whether a plan amendment is treated as having been adopted on the first day of the plan year (including a plan amendment adopted within months after the close of the plan year).

(e) *Plan population taken into account* —(1) *In general.* In making any determination of the funding target or target normal cost under paragraph (b) of this section, the plan population is determined as of the valuation date. The plan population must include three classes of individuals—

(i) Participants currently employed in the service of the employer;

(ii) Participants who are retired under the plan or who are otherwise no longer employed in the service of the employer; and

(iii) All other individuals currently entitled to benefits under the plan.

(2) *Special exclusion for "rule of parity" cases.* Certain individuals may be excluded from the class of individuals described in paragraph (e)(1)(ii) of this section. The excludable individuals are those former participants who, prior to the valuation date for the plan year, have terminated service with the employer without vested benefits and whose service might be taken into account in future years because the 'rule of parity' of section 411(a)(6)(D) does not permit that service to be disregarded. However, if the plan's experience as to separated employees returning to service has been such that the exclusion described in this paragraph (e)(2) would be unreasonable, the exclusion would no longer apply.

(3) *Anticipated future participants.* In making any determination of the funding target or target normal cost under paragraph (b) of this section, the actuarial assumptions and funding method used for the plan must not anticipate the affiliation with the plan of future participants not employed in the service of the employer on the plan valuation date. However, any such determination may anticipate the affiliation with the plan of current employees who have not yet satisfied the participation (age and service) requirements of the plan as of the valuation date.

(f) *Actuarial assumptions and funding method used in determination of present value* —(1) *Establishment of actuarial assumptions and funding method* —(i) *General rules* —(A) *Assumptions and method cannot be changed for a plan year once established.* The determination of any present value or other computation under section 430 must be made on the basis of actuarial assumptions and a funding method. Actuarial assumptions established for a plan year in accordance with paragraph (f)(1)(ii) of this section cannot subsequently be changed for that plan year unless the Commissioner determines that the assumptions that were used are unreasonable. Similarly, a funding method established for a plan year in accordance with paragraph (f)(1)(ii) of this section cannot subsequently be changed for that plan year unless the Commissioner determines that the use of that funding method for that plan year is impermissible.

(B) *Scope of funding method.* A plan's funding method includes not only the overall funding method used by the plan but also each specific method of computation used in applying the overall method. However, the choice of which actuarial assumptions are appropriate to the overall method or to the specific method of computation is not a part of the funding method.

(ii) *Timing rule for establishing actuarial assumptions and funding method.* The actuarial assumptions and the funding method used by a plan for a plan year must be established not later than the due date (with extensions) for the filing of Form 5500, "Annual Return/Report of Employee Benefit Plan," for that plan year (or the last day of the 7th month after the end of the plan year in the case of a plan not required to file Form 5500). The filing of the first actuarial report (Schedule SB) for a plan year under section 6059 that reflects the use of actuarial assumptions and a funding method is treated as the establishment of those assumptions and the funding method for that plan year.

(2) *Interest and mortality rates.* Section 430(h)(2) and § 1.430(h)(2)-1 set forth the interest rates, and section 430(h)(3) and §§ 1.430(h)(3)-1 and 1.430(h)(3)-2 set forth the mortality tables, that must be used for purposes of determining any present value under this section.

(3) *Other assumptions.* In the case of actuarial assumptions other than those specified in sections 430(h)(2), 430(h)(3), and 430(i), each of those actuarial assumptions must be reasonable (taking into account the experience of the plan and reasonable expectations), and the actuarial assumptions, in combination, must offer the plan's enrolled actuary's best estimate of anticipated experience under the plan. See paragraph (f)(4)(iii) of this section for special rules for determining the present value of a single sum and similar distributions.

(4) *Probability of benefit payments in single sum or other optional forms* —(i) *In general.* This paragraph (f)(4) provides rules relating to the probability that benefit payments will be paid as single sums or other optional forms under a plan and the impact of that probability on the determination of the present value of those benefit payments under section 430.

(ii) *General rules of application.* Any determination of present value or any other computation under this section must take into account—

(A) The probability that future benefit payments under the plan will be made in the form of optional forms of benefits provided under the plan (including single sum distributions), determined on the basis of the plan's experience and other related assumptions; and

(B) Any difference in the present value of future benefit payments that results from the use of actuarial assumptions in determining benefit payments in any such optional form of benefits that are different from those prescribed by section 430(h).

(iii) *Single sum and similar distributions* —(A) *Distributions using section 417(e) assumptions.* In the case of a distribution that is subject to section 417(e)(3) and that is determined using the applicable interest rate and applicable mortality table under section 417(e)(3), for purposes of applying paragraph (f)(4)(ii) of this section, the computation of the present value of that distribution will be treated as having taken into account any difference in present value that results from the use of actuarial assumptions that are different from those prescribed by section 430(h) (as required under paragraph (f)(4)(ii)(B) of this section) if the present value of the distribution is determined in accordance with paragraph (f)(4)(iii)(B) of this section.

(B) *Substitution of annuity form* —(1) *In general.* Except as otherwise provided in this paragraph (f)(4)(iii)(B), the present value of a distribution is determined in accordance with this paragraph (f)(4)(iii)(B) if it is determined by valuing the annuity that corresponds to the distribution using special actuarial assumptions. Under these special assumptions, for the period beginning with the annuity starting date, the current applicable mortality table under section 417(e)(3) that would apply to a distribution with an annuity starting date occurring on the valuation date is substituted for the mortality table under section 430(h)(3) that would otherwise be used. In addition, under these special assumptions, the valuation interest rates under section 430(h)(2) are used for this purpose for all periods (as opposed to the interest rates under section 417(e)(3) which the plan uses to determine the amount of the benefit).

(2) *Optional application of generational mortality.* In determining the present value of a distribution under this paragraph (f)(4)(iii)(B), if a plan uses the generational mortality tables under § 1.430(h)(3)-1(a)(4) or § 1.430(h)(3)-2, the plan is permitted to use a 50-50 male-female blend of the annuitant mortality rates under the § 1.430(h)(3)-1(a)(4) generational mortality tables in lieu of the applicable mortality table under section 417(e)(3) that would apply to a distribution with an annuity starting date occurring on the valuation date.

(3) *Optional phase-in of section 417(e)(3) segment interest rates.* In determining the present value of a distribution under this paragraph (f)(4)(iii)(B), a plan is permitted to make adjustments to reflect differences between the phase-in of the section 430(h)(2) segment rates under section 430(h)(2)(G) and the adjustments to the segment rates under section 417(e)(3)(D)(iii).

(C) *Distributions subject to section 417(e)(3) using other assumptions.* In the case of a distribution that is subject to section 417(e)(3) but that is determined as the greater of the benefit determined using the applicable interest rate and the applicable mortality table under section 417(e)(3) and the benefit determined using some basis other than the section 417(e)(3) assumptions, for purposes of applying paragraph (f)(4)(ii)(B) of this section, the computation of present value must take into account the extent to which the present value of the distribution is greater than the present value determined using the rules of paragraph (f)(4)(iii)(B) of this section.

(D) *Distributions subject to section 411(a)(13).* In the case of an applicable defined benefit plan described in section 411(a)(13)(C), if the distribution is determined under the rules of section 411(a)(13)(A), the amount of the future distribution must be determined by projecting the future interest credits or equivalent amounts under the plan's interest crediting rules to the expected date of payment using reasonable actuarial assumptions.

(5) *Reasonable techniques permitted.* Any reasonable technique can be used to determine the present value of the benefits expected to be paid during a plan year, based on the interest rates and mortality assumptions applicable for the plan year. For example, the present value of a monthly retirement annuity payable at the beginning of each month can be determined—

(i) Using the standard actuarial approximation that reflects 13/24ths of the discounted expected payments for the year as of the beginning of the year and 11/24ths of the discounted expected payments for the year as of the end of the year; or

(ii) By assuming that the payment is made in the middle of the year.

(6) *Approval of significant changes in actuarial assumptions for large plans* —(i) *In general.* A large plan as described in paragraph (f)(6)(ii) of this section cannot change any actuarial assumption used to determine the plan's funding target for a plan year without the approval of the Commissioner if the change in assumptions results in a decrease in the plan's funding shortfall (within the meaning of section 430(c)(4)) for the current plan year (disregarding the effect on the plan's funding shortfall resulting from changes in interest and mortality assumptions) that exceeds $50,000,000, or that exceeds $5,000,000 and is 5 percent or more of the funding target of the plan before such change.

(ii) *Affected plans.* A plan is a large plan as described in this paragraph (f)(6)(ii) if—

(A) The plan is a defined benefit plan (other than a multiemployer plan) to which Title IV of the Employee Retirement Income Security Act of 1974 (ERISA) applies; and

(B) The aggregate unfunded vested benefits used to determine premiums for the plan year (as determined under section 4006(a)(3)(E)(iii) of ERISA) of the plan and all other plans maintained by the contributing sponsors (as defined in section 4001(a)(13) of ERISA) and members of such sponsors' controlled groups (as defined in section 4001(a)(14) of ERISA) which are covered by Title IV (disregarding multiemployer plans and disregarding plans with no unfunded vested benefits) exceed $50,000,000.

(7) *Examples.* The following examples illustrate the rules of this section. Unless otherwise indicated, these examples are based on the following assumptions: the normal retirement age is 65, the plan is subject to section 430 starting in 2008, the plan year is the calendar year, and the valuation date is January 1. The examples read as follows:

Example 1. (i) Plan P provides an accrued benefit equal to 1.0% of a participant's highest 3-year average compensation for each year of service. Plan P provides that an early retirement benefit can be received at age 60 equal to the participant's accrued benefit reduced by 0.5% per month for early commencement. On January 1, 2008, Participant A is age 60 and has 12 years of past service. Participant A's compensation for the years 2005 through 2007 was $47,000, $50,000, and $52,000, respectively. Participant A's rate of compensation at December 31, 2007, is $54,000 and A's rate of compensation for 2008 is assumed not to increase at any point during 2008.

(ii) Participant A's annual accrued benefit as of January 1, 2008, is $5,960 [0.01 ×12× ($47,000+$50,000+$52,000)/3]. Participant A's expected benefit accrual for 2008 is $800 [0.01×13× ($50,000+$52,000+$54,000)/3−$5,960].

(iii) The early retirement benefit, with respect to the decrement at age 60, that is taken into account when determining the 2008 funding target is $4,172 [$5,960 accrued benefit× (1−0.005×60 months)]. The annual accrual of the early retirement benefit, with respect to the decrement at age 60, that is taken into account when determining the

2008 target normal cost is $560 [$800 annual accrual×(1-0.005×60 months)].

(iv) The early retirement benefit, with respect to the decrement at age 61, that is taken into account when determining the 2008 funding target is $4,529.60 [$5,960 accrued benefit×(1-0.005×48 months)]. The annual accrual of the early retirement benefit, with respect to the decrement at age 61, that is taken into account when determining the 2008 target normal cost is $608 [$800 annual accrual×(1-0.005×48 months)].

Example 2. (i) The facts are the same as in *Example 1.* In addition, the plan offers a $500 temporary monthly supplement to participants who complete 15 years of service and retire from active employment after attaining age 60. The temporary supplement is available for retirements occurring at ages 60 and 61, and is payable until the participant turns age 62. In addition, the supplement is limited so that it does not exceed the participant's social security benefit payable at age 62. On January 1, 2008, Participant B is age 55 and has 20 years of past service, and Participant C is age 60 and has 14 years of past service. For Participants B and C, the projected social security benefit is greater than $500 per month.

(ii) For Participant B, the allocable portion of the annual temporary supplement that is taken into account when determining the funding target for 2008 is $4,800, which applies for the decrement at age 60 until age 62 [($500×12 months)×20 years of past service / 25 years of service at eligibility for the supplement]. This same dollar amount will apply for the assumed decrement at age 60 or age 61, but the period of time the amount will be paid is different for those two decrements.

(iii) For Participant C, the allocable portion of the annual temporary supplement that is taken into account when determining the funding target for 2008 is $5,600, which is payable for the decrement at age 61 until age 62 [($500×12 months)×14 years of past service / 15 years of service at eligibility for the supplement].

Example 3. (i) The facts are the same as in *Example 1.* In addition, the plan provides a disability benefit to participants who become disabled after completing 15 years of service. The disability benefit is payable at normal retirement age. For purposes of calculating the disability benefit, service continues to accrue until normal retirement age (unless recovery or retirement occurs earlier). Further, compensation is deemed to continue to normal retirement age at the same rate as when the disability began.

(ii) Participant A will be eligible for the disability benefit at age 63 when he will have 15 years of service. Participant A's projected annual disability benefit at normal retirement age is $9,180 (that is, 1% of highest 3-year average compensation of $54,000 multiplied by 17 years of deemed service at normal retirement age).

(iii) The allocable portion of the disability benefit that is taken into account when determining the 2008 funding target with respect to the disability decrements occurring at age 63 and later is $7,344 [$9,180× (12 years of past service / 15 years of service at eligibility for disability benefits)].

(iv) The disability benefit accrual that is taken into account when determining the 2008 target normal cost with respect to the disability decrements occurring at age 63 and later is $612 [$9,180×(1 year of deemed service / 15 years of service at eligibility for disability benefits)].

Example 4. (i) Retiree D, a participant in Plan P, is a male age 72 and is receiving a $100 monthly straight life annuity. The 2008 actuarial valuation is performed using the segment rates applicable for September 2007 (determined without regard to the transitional rule of section 430(h)(2)(G)), and the 2008 annuitant and nonannuitant (male and female) mortality tables (published in § 1.430(h)(3)-1).

(ii) The present value of Retiree D's straight life annuity on the valuation date is $10,624. This is equal to the sum of: $5,005, which is the present value of payments expected to be made during the first 5 years, using the first segment interest rate of 5.26%; $5,431, which is the present value of payments expected to be made during the next 15 years, using the second segment interest rate of 5.82%; and $188, which is the present value of payments expected to be made after 20 years, using the third segment interest rate of 6.38%.

Example 5. (i) The facts are same as in *Example 4,* except Plan P does not provide for early retirement benefits or single sum distributions. The actuary assumes that no participants terminate employment prior to age 50 (other than by death), there is a 5% probability of withdrawal at age 50, and that those participants who do withdraw

receive a deferred annuity starting at age 65. Participant E is a male age 46 on January 1, 2008, and has an annual accrued benefit of $23,000 beginning at age 65.

(ii) After taking into account the 5% probability of withdrawal, the funding target associated with Participant E's assumed age 50 withdrawal benefit in the 2008 actuarial valuation is $3,573.69. This is equal to the sum of: $363.55, which is the present value of payments expected to be made during the year the participant turns age 65 (the 20th year after the valuation date), using the second segment interest rate of 5.82%; and $3,210.14, which is the present value of payments expected to be made after the 20th year, using the third segment interest rate of 6.38%.

Example 6. (i) The facts are the same as in *Example 5,* except the plan offers a single sum distribution payable at normal retirement age (age 65) determined based on the applicable interest rate and the applicable mortality table under section 417(e)(3). The actuary assumes that 70% of the participants will elect a single sum upon retirement and the remaining 30% will elect a straight life annuity.

(ii) After taking into account the 5% probability of withdrawal, the portion of the 2008 funding target that is attributable to Participant E's assumed single sum payment, deferred to age 65, is $2,564.86. This is calculated in the same manner as the present value of annuity payments, except that the 2008 applicable mortality rates are substituted for the 2008 male annuitant mortality rates. This portion of the 2008 funding target is equal to the sum of: $254.63, which is the present value of annuity payments expected to be made between age 65 and 66 (during the 20th year after the valuation date), using the second segment interest rate of 5.82%; and $2,310.23, which is the present value of annuity payments expected to be made after the 20th year following the valuation date, using the third segment interest rate of 6.38%. These present value amounts reflect the 2008 male nonannuitant mortality rates prior to the assumed commencement of benefits at age 65, the 100% probability of retiring at age 65, and the 70% probability that E will elect a single sum distribution.

(iii) After taking into account the 5% probability of withdrawal, the portion of the 2008 funding target that is attributable to Participant E's assumed straight life annuity, deferred to age 65, is equal to 30% of the result obtained in *Example 5.*

Example 7. (i) The facts are the same as in *Example 6,* except the plan offers an immediate single sum upon withdrawal at age 50 determined based on the applicable interest rate and the applicable mortality table under section 417(e)(3). The actuary assumes that 70% of the participants will elect to receive a single sum distribution upon withdrawal.

(ii) After taking into account the 5% probability of withdrawal, the portion of the 2008 funding target that is attributable to Participant E's assumed single sum payment is $2,523.03. This is calculated in the same manner as the present value of annuity payments, except that the 2008 applicable mortality rates are substituted for the 2008 male annuitant and nonannuitant mortality rates after the annuity starting date. This portion of the 2008 funding target is equal to the sum of: $250.48, which is the present value of annuity payments expected to be made between age 65 and 66 (during the 20th year after the valuation date), using the second segment interest rate at an interest rate of 5.82%; and $2,272.55, which is the present value of annuity payments expected to be made after the 20th year following the valuation date, using the third segment interest rate of 6.38%. These present value amounts reflect the 2008 male nonannuitant mortality rates prior to the assumed single sum distribution age of 50, and the 70% probability that E will elect a single sum distribution.

Example 8. (i) The facts are the same as in *Example 5,* except that the plan sponsor elects under section 430(h)(2)(D)(ii) to use the monthly corporate bond yield curve instead of segment rates. The enrolled actuary assumes payments are made monthly throughout the year and uses the interest rate from the middle of the monthly corporate bond yield curve because this mid-year yield rate most closely matches the average timing of benefits paid. Solely for purposes of this example, assume that the monthly yield curve derived from the August 2007 data is applicable (even though the plan would actually have to use the yield curve derived from the December 2007 data).

(ii) After taking into account the 5% probability of withdrawal, the funding target associated with Participant E's assumed age 50 withdrawal benefit in the 2008 actuarial valuation is $3,359.69. This reflects the sum of each year's expected payments, discounted at the yield rates described in paragraph (i) of this *Example 8,* as shown below:

Age	Discount period		Yield rate	Present value
65	19.5		6.47%	$322.75
66	20.5		6.49%	298.51
67	21.5		6.51%	275.62
68 and over	Varies		Varies	2,462.81
Total				$3,359.69

Example 9. (i) Plan F is a cash balance plan that permits an immediate payment of a single sum equal to the participant's hypothetical account balance upon termination of employment. Plan terms provide that the hypothetical account is credited with interest at the 3rd segment rate. In the 2008 actuarial valuation, the enrolled actuary assumes that the hypothetical account balances will increase with annual interest credits of 5.0% until the participant commences receiving his or her benefit, that all participants will retire on the first day of the plan year in which they attain age 65 (that is, no participant will terminate employment prior to age 65 other than by death), and that 100% of participants will elect a single sum upon retirement. The 2008 actuarial valuation is performed using the 24-month average segment rates applicable for September 2007 (determined without regard to the transitional rule of section 430(h)(2)(G)), and the separate annuitant and non-annuitant mortality tables under § 1.430(h)(3)-1 for 2008 for periods prior to commencement of benefits (however, the annuitant mortality table is never used because the only assumed payment is a single sum). No mortality table is required for the period after commencement of benefits because the single sum payment is equal to the account balance. Participant F is a male age 61 on January 1, 2008, and has a hypothetical account balance equal to $150,000 on that date.

(ii) Participant F's hypothetical account balance projected to January 1, 2012 (the plan year in which F attains age 65) is $182,326 based on the assumed annual interest crediting rate of 5%. The 2008 funding target attributable to Participant F's benefit at age 65 is $145,905, which is calculated by discounting the projected hypothetical account balance of $182,326 using the first segment rate of 5.26% and the male non-annuitant mortality rates.

(iii) In contrast, if the enrolled actuary assumes that the hypothetical account balances increase with annual interest credits of 6.0%, the 2008 funding target attributable to Participant F's benefit at age 65 is $151,544 calculated by discounting the projected hypothetical account balance of $189,372 using the first segment rate of 5.26% and the male non-annuitant mortality rates.

(g) *Effective/applicability dates and transition rules* —(1) *In general.* Section 430 generally applies to plan years beginning on or after January 1, 2008. In general, this section applies to plan years beginning on or after January 1, 2009. For plan years beginning in 2008, plans are permitted to rely on the provisions set forth in this section for purposes of satisfying the requirements of section 430.

(2) *Plans with delayed effective date.* In the case of a plan for which the effective date of section 430 is delayed in accordance with sections 104 through 106 of the Pension Protection Act of 2006, Public Law 109-280 (120 Stat. 780), this section applies to plan years beginning on or after the date section 430 applies with respect to the plan.

(3) *Approval for changes in funding method.* Any change in a plan's funding method that is made for the first plan year for which section 430 applies to the plan and that is not inconsistent with the requirements of section 430 is treated as having been approved by the Commissioner and does not require the Commissioner's specific prior approval.

(4) *Approval for changes in actuarial assumptions.* The Commissioner's specific prior approval is not required with respect to any actuarial assumptions that are adopted for the first plan year for which section 430 applies to the plan and that are not inconsistent with the requirements of section 430.

Par. 3 Section 1.430(g)-1 is added to read as follows:

§ 1.430(g)-1 Valuation date and valuation of plan assets.

(a) *In general* —(1) *Overview.* This section provides rules relating to a plan's valuation date and the valuation of a plan's assets for a plan year under section 430(g). Section 430 and this section apply to single employer defined benefit plans (including multiple employer plans as defined in section 413(c)) that are subject to the rules of section 412, but do not apply to multiemployer plans (as defined in section 414(f)). Paragraph (b) of this section describes valuation date rules. Paragraph (c) of this section describes rules regarding the determination of the asset value for purposes of a plan's actuarial valuation. Paragraph (d) of this section contains rules for taking employer contributions into account in the determination of the value of plan assets. Paragraph (e) of

this section contains an example. Paragraph (f) of this section sets forth effective/applicability dates and transition rules.

(2) *Special rules for multiple employer plans.* In the case of a multiple employer plan to which section 413(c)(4)(A) applies, the rules of section 430 and this section are applied separately for each employer under the plan as if each employer maintained a separate plan. Thus, in such a case, the value of plan assets is determined separately for each employer under the plan. In the case of a multiple employer plan to which section 413(c)(4)(A) does not apply (that is, a plan described in section 413(c)(4)(B) that has not made the election for section 413(c)(4)(A) to apply), the rules of section 430 and this section are applied as if all participants in the plan were employed by a single employer.

(b) *Valuation date* —(1) *In general.* The determination of the funding target, target normal cost, and asset value of a plan for a plan year is made as of the valuation date of the plan for that plan year. Except as provided in paragraph (b)(2) of this section, the valuation date of a plan for any plan year is the first day of the plan year.

(2) *Exception for small plans* —(i) *In general.* If, on each day during the preceding plan year, a plan had 100 or fewer participants (including active and inactive participants and all other individuals entitled to future benefits), the plan may designate any day during the plan year as its valuation date for that plan year and succeeding plan years. For purposes of this paragraph (b)(2)(i), all defined benefit plans (other than multiemployer plans as defined in section 414(f)) maintained by an employer are treated as one plan, but only participants with respect to that employer or that employer's controlled group members are taken into account.

(ii) *Employer determination.* For purposes of this paragraph (b)(2), the employer includes all members of the employer's controlled group determined pursuant to sections 414(b), (c), (m), and (o).

(iii) *Application of exception in first plan year.* In the case of the first plan year of any plan, the exception for small plans under paragraph (b)(2)(i) of this section is applied by taking into account the number of participants that the plan is reasonably expected to have on each day during the first plan year.

(iv) *Valuation date is part of funding method.* The selection of a plan's valuation date is part of the plan's funding method and, accordingly, may only be changed with the consent of the Commissioner. The change of a plan's valuation date that is required by section 430 is treated as having been approved by the Commissioner and does not require the Commissioner's prior specific approval.

(c) *Determination of asset value* —(1) *In general* —(i) *General use of fair market value.* Except as provided in this paragraph (c), the value of plan assets for purposes of section 430 is equal to the fair market value of plan assets on the valuation date. Prior year contributions made after the valuation date and current year contributions made before the valuation date are taken into account to the extent provided in paragraph (d) of this section.

(ii) *Fair market value.* The fair market value of an asset is determined as the price at which the asset would change hands between a willing buyer and a willing seller, neither being under any compulsion to buy or sell and both having reasonable knowledge of relevant facts. The Commissioner may, in guidance of general applicability, issue guidance on the valuation of insurance contracts. See § 601.601(d)(2) of this chapter.

(2) *Averaging of fair market values* —(i) *In general.* Subject to the plan asset corridor rules of paragraph (c)(2)(iii) of this section, a plan is permitted to determine the value of plan assets on the valuation date as the average of the fair market value of assets on the valuation date and the adjusted fair market value of assets determined for one or more earlier determination dates using the method described in this paragraph (c)(2). The period of time between the valuation date and each of the earlier determination dates must be equal and that period of time cannot exceed 12 months. In addition, the earliest such determination date cannot be earlier than the last day of the 25th month before the valuation date of the plan year. In a typical situation, the earlier determination dates will be the two immediately preceding valuation dates. The method of determining the value of assets is part of the

plan's funding method and, accordingly, may only be changed with the consent of the Commissioner.

(ii) *Adjusted fair market value.* The adjusted fair market value of plan assets for a prior determination date is the fair market value of plan assets on that date, increased for contributions included in the plan's asset balance on the current valuation date that were not included in the plan's asset balance on the earlier determination date, and reduced for benefits and administrative expenses paid from plan assets during the same period.

(iii) *Restriction to 90-110 percent corridor* —(A) *Asset value less than 90 percent of fair market value.* If the value of plan assets determined under paragraph (c) (2) (i) of this section is less than 90 percent of the fair market value of plan assets on the valuation date, then the value of plan assets under this paragraph (c) (2) is equal to 90 percent of the fair market value of plan assets.

(B) *Asset value greater than 110 percent of fair market value.* If the value of plan assets determined under paragraph (c) (2) (i) of this section is greater than 110 percent of the fair market value of plan assets on the valuation date, then the value of plan assets under this paragraph (c) (2) is equal to 110 percent of the fair market value of plan assets.

(3) *Qualified transfers to health benefit accounts.* In the case of a qualified transfer (as defined in section 420), any assets so transferred are not treated as plan assets for purposes of section 430 and this section.

(d) *Accounting for contribution receipts* —(1) *Prior year contributions* —(i) *In general.* For purposes of determining the value of plan assets under paragraph (c) of this section, if an employer makes a contribution to the plan after the valuation date for the plan year, and the contribution is for a preceding plan year, then the present value of the contribution determined as of that valuation date is taken into account as an asset of the plan as of the valuation date. For this purpose, the present value is determined using the effective interest rate under section 430(h) (2) (A) for the preceding plan year.

(ii) *Special rule for plan years beginning before plan's first effective plan year.* Notwithstanding paragraph (d) (1) (i) of this section, in the case of a plan's first effective plan year, if the plan sponsor makes a contribution to the plan after the valuation date for the first effective plan year and that contribution is for a preceding plan year, then the contribution is taken into account as a plan asset under paragraph (d) (1) (i) of this section without applying any present value discount.

(2) *Current year contributions made before valuation date.* For purposes of determining the value of plan assets under paragraph (c) of this section, if an employer makes a contribution for a plan year before that year's valuation date, that contribution (and any interest on the contribution for the period between the contribution date and the valuation date, determined using the effective interest rate under section 430(h) (2) (A) for the plan year) must be subtracted from plan assets in determining the value of plan assets as of the valuation date.

(e) *Example.* The following example illustrates the application of this section:

Example. (i) *Facts.* All assets of Plan F are invested in a trust fund, the plan year is the calendar year, and the valuation date is January 1. The actuarial value is determined by averaging fair market value over the valuation date and the preceding two valuation dates. For each plan year, all contributions for the plan year are made during that plan year. An actuarial valuation is performed as of January 1, 2019. The fair market value of assets, the plan contributions, the benefit payments, and other relevant items for 2017 through 2019 are as follows:

	2017	2018	2019
Fair market value: Jan. 1	$196,500	$238,000	$228,000
Contributions	$ 62,000	$ 66,000	
Benefit payments	$ (24,000)	$ (25,000)	
Expenses	$ (7,000)	$ (7,500)	
Interest and dividends	$ 7,500	$ 7,000	
Net realized gains (losses)	$ 6,000	$ (8,500)	
Balancing item	$ (3,000)	$ (42,000)	
Fair market value: Dec. 31	$238,000	$228,000	

(ii) *Computation of average value.* The average value as of January 1, 2019, is computed as follows:

Adjusted values	2017	2018	2019
Fair market value: January 1	$ 196,500	$238,000	$ 228,000
Net adjustments:			
Contributions	$ 128,000	$ 66,000	
Benefits Paid	$ (49,000)	$ (25,000)	
Expenses Paid	$ (14,500)	$ (7,500)	
Total	$ 261,000	$ 271,500	$ 228,000

Average value as of January 1, 2019 equals:
$261,000 + $271,500 + $228,000 ÷ 3 = $253,500

(iii) *Conclusion.* Having determined an average value as of January 1, 2019 equal to $253,500, Plan F must confirm that this value satisfies the 90-110 percent corridor rules under paragraph (c) (2) (iii) of this section. Because 110% of $228,000 equals $250,800, the value of Plan F's assets under paragraph (c) (2) of this section must be limited to $250,800 (rather than $253,500) for this purpose. This valuation method meets the requirements of this section.

(f) *Effective/applicability dates and transition rules* —(1) *In general.* Section 430 generally applies to plan years beginning on or after January 1, 2008. In general, this section applies to plan years beginning on or after January 1, 2009. For plan years beginning in 2008, plans are permitted to rely on the provisions set forth in this section for purposes of satisfying the requirements of section 430.

(2) *Plans with delayed effective date.* In the case of a plan for which the effective date of section 430 is delayed in accordance with sections 104 through 106 of the Pension Protection Act of 2006, Public Law 109-280 (120 Stat. 780), this section applies to plan years beginning on or after the date section 430 applies with respect to the plan.

(3) *First effective plan year.* For purposes of this section, the first effective plan year for a plan is the first plan year to which section 430 applies to the plan.

(4) *Approval for changes in the valuation date and valuation method for first effective plan year.* Any change in a plan's valuation date or asset valuation method that is made for the first effective plan year and that is not inconsistent with the requirements of section 430 is treated as having been approved by the Commissioner and does not require the Commissioner's specific prior approval.

Par. 4 Section 1.430(h) (2)-1 is added to read as follows:

§ 1.430(h) (2)-1 Interest rates used to determine present value.

(a) *In general* —(1) *Overview.* This section provides rules relating to the interest rates to be applied for a plan year under section 430(h) (2). Section 430(h) (2) and this section apply to single employer defined benefit plans (including multiple employer plans as defined in section 413(c)) that are subject to section 412 but do not apply to multiemployer plans (as defined in section 414(f)). Paragraph (b) of this section describes how the segment interest rates are used for a plan year. Paragraph (c) of this section describes those segment rates. Paragraph (d) of this section describes the monthly corporate bond yield curve that is used to develop the segment rates. Paragraph (e) of this section describes certain elections that are permitted to be made under this section. Paragraph (f) of this section describes other rules related to interest rates. Paragraph (g) contains effective/applicability dates and transition rules.

(2) *Special rules for multiple employer plans.* In the case of a multiple employer plan to which section 413(c)(4)(A) applies, the rules of section 430 and this section are applied separately for each employer under the plan as if each employer maintained a separate plan. Thus, each employer under such a multiple employer plan may make elections with respect to the interest rate rules under this section that are independent of the elections of other employers under the plan. In the case of a multiple employer plan to which section 413(c)(4)(A) does not apply (that is, a plan described in section 413(c)(4)(B) that has not made the election for section 413(c)(4)(A) to apply), the rules of section 430 and this section are applied as if all participants in the plan were employed by a single employer.

(b) *Interest rates for determining plan liabilities* —(1) *In general.* For purposes of determining the target normal cost and the funding target for any plan year, the interest rates used in determining the present value of the benefits that are included in the target normal cost and the funding target for the plan are determined as set forth in this paragraph (b).

(2) *Benefits payable within 5 years.* In the case of benefits expected to be payable during the 5-year period beginning on the valuation date for the plan year, the interest rate used in determining the present value of the benefits that are included in the target normal cost and the funding target for the plan is the first segment rate with respect to the applicable month, as described in paragraph (c)(2)(i) of this section.

(3) *Benefits payable after 5 years and within 20 years.* In the case of benefits expected to be payable during the 15-year period beginning after the end of the period described in paragraph (b)(2) of this section, the interest rate used in determining the present value of the benefits that are included in the target normal cost and the funding target for the plan is the second segment rate with respect to the applicable month, as described in paragraph (c)(2)(ii) of this section.

(4) *Benefits payable after 20 years.* In the case of benefits expected to be payable after the period described in paragraph (b)(3) of this section, the interest rate used in determining the present value of the benefits that are included in the target normal cost and the funding target for the plan is the third segment rate with respect to the applicable month, as described in paragraph (c)(2)(iii) of this section.

(5) *Applicable month.* Except as provided in paragraph (e) of this section, the term "applicable month" for purposes of this paragraph (b) means the month that includes the valuation date of the plan for the plan year.

(6) *Special rule for certain airlines* —(i) *In general.* Pursuant to section 6615 of the U.S. Troop Readiness, Veterans' Care, Katrina Recovery, and Iraq Accountability Appropriations Act, 2007, Public Law 110-28 (121 Stat. 112), for a plan sponsor that makes the election described in section 402(a)(2) of the Pension Protection Act of 2006 (PPA '06), Public Law 109-280 (120 Stat. 780), the interest rate required to be used to determine the plan's funding target for each of the 10 years under that election is 8.25 percent (rather than the segment rates otherwise described in this paragraph (b)).

(ii) *Special interest rate not applicable for other purposes.* The special interest rate described in paragraph (b)(6)(i) of this section does not apply for other purposes such as the determination of the plan's target normal cost.

(c) *Segment rates* —(1) *Overview.* This paragraph (c) sets forth rules for determining the first, second, and third segment rates for purposes of paragraph (b) of this section. The first, second, and third segment rates are set forth in revenue rulings, notices, or other guidance published in the Internal Revenue Bulletin. See §601.601(d)(2) of this chapter. See paragraph (g)(3) of this section for a transition rule under which the definition of the segment rates is modified for plan years beginning in 2008 and 2009.

(2) *Definition of segment rates* —(i) *First segment rate.* For purposes of this section, except as provided under the transition rule of paragraph (g)(3) of this section, the "first segment rate" is, with respect to any month, the single rate of interest determined by the Commissioner on the basis of the average of the monthly corporate bond yield curves (described in paragraph (d) of this section) for the 24-month period ending with the month preceding that month, taking into account only the first 5 years of each of those yield curves.

(ii) *Second segment rate.* For purposes of this section, except as provided under the transition rule of paragraph (g)(3) of this section, the "second segment rate" is, with respect to any month, the single rate of interest determined by the Commissioner on the basis of the average of the monthly corporate bond yield curves (described in para-

graph (d) of this section) for the 24-month period ending with the month preceding that month, taking into account only the portion of each of those yield curves corresponding to the 15-year period that follows the end of the 5-year period described in paragraph (c)(2)(i) of this section.

(iii) *Third segment rate.* For purposes of this section, except as provided under the transition rule of paragraph (g)(3) of this section, the "third segment rate" is, with respect to any month, the single rate of interest determined by the Commissioner on the basis of the average of the monthly corporate bond yield curves (described in paragraph (d) of this section) for the 24-month period ending with the month preceding that month, taking into account only the portion of each of those yield curves corresponding to the 40-year period that follows the end of the 15-year period described in paragraph (c)(2)(ii) of this section.

(d) *Monthly corporate bond yield curve* —(1) *In general.* For purposes of this section, the "monthly corporate bond yield curve" is, with respect to any month, a yield curve that is prescribed by the Commissioner for that month based on yields for that month on investment grade corporate bonds with varying maturities that are in the top three quality levels available.

(2) *Determination and publication of yield curve.* A description of the methodology for determining the monthly corporate bond yield curve is provided in guidance issued by the Commissioner that is published in the Internal Revenue Bulletin. The yield curve for a month will be set forth in revenue rulings, notices, or other guidance published in the Internal Revenue Bulletin. See §601.601(d)(2) of this chapter.

(e) *Elections* —(1) *In general.* This paragraph (e) describes elections that a plan sponsor can make to use alternative interest rates under this section. Any election under this section must be made by providing written notification of the election to the plan's enrolled actuary. Any election in this paragraph (e) is part of the plan's funding method and, accordingly, may only be adopted or changed with the consent of the Commissioner.

(2) *Elections for alternative date.* A plan sponsor that is using segment rates as provided under paragraph (b) of this section may elect the use of an alternative month as the applicable month for purposes of paragraph (b)(5) of this section, provided that the alternative month is one of the 4 months that precede the month that includes the valuation date of the plan for the plan year.

(3) *Election not to apply transition rule.* The plan sponsor may elect not to apply the transition rule in paragraph (g)(3) of this section.

(4) *Election to use full yield curve* —(i) *In general.* For purposes of determining the minimum required contribution under section 430, the plan sponsor may elect to use interest rates under the monthly corporate bond yield curve described in paragraph (d) of this section for the month preceding the month that includes the valuation date in lieu of the segment rates determined under paragraph (c) of this section. These purposes include determining the installments and present values described in paragraph (f)(2) of this section. In order to address the timing of benefit payments during a year, reasonable approximations are permitted to be used to value benefit payments that are expected to be made during a plan year.

(ii) *Reasonable techniques permitted.* In the case of a plan sponsor using the monthly corporate bond yield curve under this paragraph (e)(4), if with respect to a decrement the benefit is only expected to be paid for one-half of a year (because the decrement was assumed to occur in the middle of the year), the interest rate for that year can be determined as if the benefit were being paid for the entire year. See §1.430(d)-1(f)(5) for additional reasonable techniques that can be used in determining present value.

(5) *Plan sponsor.* For purposes of the elections described in this section, any reference to the plan sponsor generally means the employer or employers responsible for making contributions to or under the plan. In the case of plans that are multiple employer plans to which section 413(c)(4)(A) does not apply, any reference to the plan sponsor means the plan administrator within the meaning of section 414(g).

(f) *Interest rates used for other purposes* —(1) *Effective interest rate.* The effective interest rate determined under section 430(h)(2)(A) is the single interest rate that, if used to determine the present value of the benefits that are taken into account in determining the plan's funding target for a plan year, would result in an amount equal to the plan's funding target determined for the plan year under section 430(d) as described in §1.430(d)-1(b)(2) (without regard to calculations for plans in at-risk status under section 430(i)).

(2) *Interest rates used for determining shortfall amortization installments and waiver amortization installments.* The interest rates used to

determine the amount of shortfall amortization installments and waiver amortization installments and the present value of those installments are determined based on the dates those installments are assumed to be paid, using the same timing rules that apply in determining target normal cost as described in paragraph (b) of this section. Thus, for a plan that uses the segment rates described in paragraph (c) of this section, the first segment rate applies to installments assumed to be paid during the first five plan years beginning on the valuation date for the plan year, and the second segment rate applies to installments assumed to be paid during the subsequent 15-year period. For purposes of this paragraph (f)(2), the shortfall amortization installments for a plan year are assumed to be paid on the valuation date for that plan year. Thus, for example, for a plan that uses the segment rates described in paragraph (c) of this section, the shortfall amortization installment for the fifth plan year following the current plan year (the sixth installment) is assumed to be paid on the valuation date for that year so that such shortfall amortization installment will be determined using the second segment rate.

(g) *Effective/applicability dates and transition rules* —(1) *In general.* Section 430 generally applies to plan years beginning on or after January 1, 2008. In general, this section applies to plan years beginning on or after January 1, 2009. For plan years beginning in 2008, plans are permitted to rely on the provisions set forth in this section for purposes of satisfying the requirements of section 430.

(2) *Plans with delayed effective date.* In the case of a plan for which the effective date of section 430 is delayed in accordance with sections 104 through 106 of PPA '06, this section applies to plan years beginning on or after the date section 430 applies with respect to the plan.

(3) *Transition rule* —(i) *In general.* Notwithstanding the general rules for determination of segment rates under paragraph (c)(2) of this section, for plan years beginning in 2008 or 2009, the first, second, or third segment rate for a plan with respect to any month is equal to the sum of—

(A) The product of that rate for that month determined without regard to this paragraph (g)(3), multiplied by the applicable percentage; and

(B) The product of the weighted average interest rate determined under the rules of section 412(b)(5)(B)(ii)(II) (as that provision was in effect for plan years beginning in 2007), multiplied by a percentage equal to 100 percent minus the applicable percentage.

(ii) *Applicable percentage.* For purposes of this paragraph (g)(3), the applicable percentage is 33 ⅓ percent for plan years beginning in 2008 and 66 ⅔ percent for plan years beginning in 2009.

(iii) *New plans ineligible.* The transition rule of this paragraph (g)(3) does not apply to a plan if the first plan year of the plan begins on or after January 1, 2008.

(4) *Approval to make elections in first effective plan year.* In the case of the first plan year to which section 430 applies to a plan, the plan sponsor's elections described in paragraph (e) of this section are treated as having been approved by the Commissioner and do not require the Commissioner's specific prior approval.

Par. 5 Section 1.430(i)-1 is added to read as follows:

§ *1.430(i)-1 Special rules for plans in at-risk status.*

(a) *In general* —(1) *Overview.* This section provides special rules related to determining the funding target and making other computations for certain defined benefit plans that are in at-risk status for the plan year. Section 430(i) and this section apply to single employer defined benefit plans (including multiple employer plans) but do not apply to multiemployer plans (as defined in section 414(f)). Paragraph (b) of this section describes rules for determining whether a plan is in at-risk status for a plan year, including the determination of a plan's funding target attainment percentage and at-risk funding target attainment percentage. Paragraph (c) of this section describes the funding target for a plan in at-risk status. Paragraph (d) of this section describes the target normal cost for a plan in at-risk status. Paragraph (e) of this section describes rules regarding how the funding target and target normal cost are determined for a plan that has been in at-risk status for fewer than 5 consecutive years. Paragraph (f) of this section sets forth effective/applicability dates and transition rules.

(2) *Special rules for multiple employer plans.* In the case of a multiple employer plan to which section 413(c)(4)(A) applies, the rules of section 430 and this section are applied separately for each employer under the plan, as if each employer maintained a separate plan. Thus, for example, at-risk status is determined separately for each employer under such a multiple employer plan. In the case of a multiple employer plan to which section 413(c)(4)(A) does not apply (that is, a plan

described in section 413(c)(4)(B) that has not made the election for section 413(c)(4)(A) to apply), the rules of section 430 and this section are applied as if all participants in the plan were employed by a single employer.

(b) *Determination of at-risk status of a plan* —(1) *General rule.* Except as otherwise provided in this section, a plan is in at-risk status for a plan year if—

(i) The funding target attainment percentage for the preceding plan year (determined under paragraph (b)(3) of this section) is less than 80 percent; and

(ii) The at-risk funding target attainment percentage for the preceding plan year (determined under paragraph (b)(4) of this section) is less than 70 percent.

(2) *Small plan exception.* If, on each day during the preceding plan year, a plan had 500 or fewer participants (including both active and inactive participants), the plan is not treated as in at-risk status for the plan year. For purposes of this paragraph (b)(2), all defined benefit plans (other than multiemployer plans as defined in section 414(f)) maintained by an employer (or any member of the employer's controlled group) are treated as one plan, but only participants with respect to that employer or member are taken into account. For this purpose, the rules of section 412(d)(3) and § 1.430(g)-1(b)(2)(ii) apply.

(3) *Funding target attainment percentage.* The funding target attainment percentage of a plan for a plan year is a fraction (expressed as a percentage)—

(i) The numerator of which is the value of plan assets for the plan year after subtraction of the prefunding balance and the funding standard carryover balance under section 430(f)(4)(B)); and

(ii) The denominator of which is the funding target of the plan for the plan year (determined without regard to section 430(i) and this section).

(4) *At-risk funding target attainment percentage.* The at-risk funding target attainment percentage of a plan for a plan year is a fraction (expressed as a percentage)—

(i) The numerator of which is the value of plan assets for the plan year after subtraction of the prefunding balance and the funding standard carryover balance under section 430(f)(4)(B); and

(ii) The denominator of which is the at-risk funding target of the plan for the plan year (determined under paragraph (c) of this section, but without regard to the loading factor imposed under paragraph (c)(2)(ii) of this section).

(5) *Special rules* —(i) *Special rule for new plans.* In the case of a newly established plan, the funding target attainment percentage under paragraph (b)(3) of this section and the at-risk funding target attainment percentage under paragraph (b)(4) of this section are assumed to be 100 percent for years before the plan exists. Except as otherwise provided in paragraph (b)(5)(ii) of this section, a plan that has a predecessor plan in accordance with section 414(a) or § 1.415(f)-1(c) is not a newly established plan under this rule.

(ii) *Special rules for mergers, acquisitions, and spinoffs.* [Reserved]

(6) *Special rule for determining at-risk status of plans of specified automobile manufacturers.* See section 430(i)(4)(C) for special rules for determining the at-risk status of plans of specified automobile and automobile parts manufacturers.

(c) *Funding target for plans in at-risk status* —(1) *In general.* If the plan has been in at-risk status for 5 consecutive years, including the current plan year, then the funding target for the plan is the at-risk funding target determined under paragraph (c)(2) of this section. See paragraph (e) of this section for the determination of the funding target where the plan is in at-risk status for the plan year but was not in at-risk status for one or more of the 4 preceding plan years.

(2) *At risk funding target* —(i) *Use of modified actuarial assumptions.* Except as provided in this paragraph (c)(2), the at-risk funding target of the plan for the plan year is equal to the present value of all benefits accrued or earned under the plan as of the beginning of the plan year, as determined in accordance with § 1.430(d)-1 but using the additional actuarial assumptions described in paragraph (c)(3) of this section.

(ii) *Funding target includes load.* The at-risk funding target is increased by the sum of—

(A) $700 multiplied by the number of participants in the plan (including active participants, inactive participants, and beneficiaries); plus

(B) Four percent of the funding target (determined under § 1.430(d)-1(b)(2) as if the plan was not in at-risk status) of the plan for the plan year.

(iii) *Minimum amount.* Notwithstanding any otherwise applicable provisions of this section, the at-risk funding target of a plan for a plan year is not less than the plan's funding target for the plan year determined without regard to this section.

(3) *Additional actuarial assumptions* —(i) *In general.* The actuarial assumptions used to determine a plan's at-risk funding target for a plan year are the actuarial assumptions that are applied under section 430, with the modifications described in this paragraph (c)(3).

(ii) *Special retirement age assumption* —(A) *Employees eligible to retire and collect benefits within 11 years.* Subject to paragraph (c)(3)(ii)(B) of this section, if an employee would be eligible to commence an immediate distribution by the end of the plan year that begins 10 years after the end of the current plan year (that is, the end of the 11th plan year beginning with the current plan year), that employee is assumed to commence an immediate distribution at the earliest retirement date under the plan, or, if later, at the end of the current plan year. The rule of this paragraph (c)(3)(ii)(A) does not affect the application of plan assumptions regarding an employee's termination of employment prior to the employee's earliest retirement date.

(B) *Employees otherwise assumed to retire immediately.* The special retirement age assumption of paragraph (c)(3)(ii)(A) of this section does not apply to an employee to the extent the employee is otherwise assumed to retire during the current plan year. Thus, for example, if generally applicable retirement assumptions would provide for a 25% probability that an employee will retire during the current plan year, the special retirement age assumption of paragraph (c)(3)(ii)(A) of this section will require the plan to assume a 75% probability that the employee will retire at the end of the plan year.

(C) *Definition of earliest retirement date.* For purposes of paragraph (c)(3)(ii) of this section, a plan's earliest retirement date is the earliest date on which a participant can commence receiving an immediate distribution. See § 1.401(a)-20, Q&A-17(b).

(iii) *Requirement to assume most valuable benefit.* An employee who is assumed to retire at a date determined under paragraph (c)(3)(ii) of this section is assumed to elect the optional form of benefit available under the plan at that date that would result in the highest present value of benefits. The plan's actuary is permitted to use reasonable assumptions in determining the optional form of benefit under the plan that would result in the highest present value of benefits for this purpose.

(d) *Target normal cost of plans in at-risk status* —(1) *General rule.* If the plan has been in at-risk status for 5 consecutive years, including the current plan year, then the target normal cost for the plan is the at-risk target normal cost determined under paragraph (d)(2) of this section. See paragraph (e) of this section for the determination of the target normal cost where the plan is in at-risk status for the plan year but was not in at-risk status for one or more of the 4 preceding plan years.

(2) *At-risk target normal cost* —(i) *Use of modified actuarial assumptions.* Except as provided in this paragraph (d)(2), the at-risk target normal cost of a plan for the plan year is equal to the present value of all benefits expected to be accrued or earned under the plan during the plan year, as determined in accordance with § 1.430(d)-1 but using the additional actuarial assumptions described in paragraph (c)(3) of this section.

(ii) *Loading factor.* The at-risk target normal cost is increased by a loading factor equal to 4 percent of the target normal cost determined without regard to section 430(i) and this section.

(iii) *Minimum amount.* The at-risk target normal cost of a plan for a plan year is not less than the plan's target normal cost determined without regard to section 430(i) and this section.

(e) *Transition between applicable funding targets and applicable target normal costs* —(1) *Funding target.* If a plan that is in at-risk status for the plan year has been in at-risk status for a consecutive period of fewer than 5 plan years, the plan's funding target for the plan year is determined as the sum of—

(i) The funding target determined without regard to this section; plus

(ii) The phase-in percentage for the plan year multiplied by the excess of—

(A) The at-risk funding target determined under paragraph (c)(2) of this section (determined taking into account paragraph (e)(4) of this section); over

(B) The funding target determined without regard to this section.

(2) *Target normal cost.* If a plan that is in at-risk status for the plan year has been in at-risk status for a consecutive period of fewer than 5 plan years, the plan's target normal cost for the plan year is determined as the sum of—

(i) The target normal cost determined without regard to section 430(i) and this section; plus—

(ii) The phase-in percentage for the plan year multiplied by the excess of—

(A) The at-risk target normal cost determined under paragraph (d)(2) of this section (determined taking into account paragraph (e)(4) of this section); over

(B) The target normal cost determined without regard to section 430(i) and this section.

(3) *Phase-in percentage.* For purposes of this paragraph (e), the phase-in percentage is 20 percent multiplied by the number of consecutive plan years that the plan has been in at-risk status (including the current plan year).

(4) *Transition funding target and target normal cost determined without load.* Notwithstanding paragraph (c)(2)(ii) of this section, if a plan has not been in at-risk status for 2 of the last 4 plan years, the plan's at-risk funding target that is used for purposes of paragraph (e)(1)(ii)(A) (to calculate the plan's funding target where the plan has been in at-risk status for fewer than 5 plan years) is determined without regard to the load set forth in paragraph (c)(2)(ii) of this section. Similarly, if a plan has not been in at-risk status for 2 of the last 4 plan years, the plan's at-risk target normal cost that is used for purposes of paragraph (e)(2)(ii)(A) (to calculate the plan's target normal cost where the plan has been in at-risk status for fewer than 5 plan years) is determined without regard to the load set forth in paragraph (d)(2)(ii) of this section.

(f) *Effective/applicability dates and transition rules* —(1) *In general.* Section 430 generally applies to plan years beginning on or after January 1, 2008. In general, this section applies to plan years beginning on or after January 1, 2009. For plan years beginning in 2008, plans are permitted to rely on the provisions set forth in this section for purposes of satisfying the requirements of section 430.

(2) *Plans with delayed effective date.* In the case of a plan for which the effective date of section 430 is delayed in accordance with sections 104 through 106 of the Pension Protection Act of 2006, Public Law 109-280 (120 Stat. 780), this section applies to plan years beginning on or after the date section 430 applies with respect to the plan.

(3) *First effective plan year.* For purposes of this section, the first effective plan year for a plan is the first plan year to which section 430 applies.

(4) *Pre-effective plan year.* For purposes of this section, the pre-effective plan year for a plan is the last plan year beginning before the first day of the first effective plan year. Thus, except for plans with a delayed effective date under paragraph (f)(2) of this section, the pre-effective plan year for a plan is the last plan year beginning before January 1, 2008.

(5) *Transition rule for determining funding target attainment percentage for the plan's pre-effective date plan year* —(i) *In general.* In the case of the plan's first effective plan year, the funding target attainment percentage for the plan's pre-effective plan year is determined as the fraction (expressed as a percentage), the numerator of which is the plan assets determined under paragraph (f)(5)(ii) of this section, and the denominator of which is the plan's current liability determined pursuant to section 412(l)(7) on the valuation date for the plan's pre-effective plan year.

(ii) *General determination of value of net plan assets* —(A) *In general.* The value of net plan assets for purposes of this paragraph (f)(5)(ii) is determined under section 412(c)(2) as in effect for the plan's pre-effective plan year, except that the value of plan assets prior to subtracting the plan's funding standard account credit balance described in paragraph (f)(5)(ii)(B) of this section can neither be less than 90 percent of the fair market value of plan assets nor greater than 110 percent of the fair market value of plan assets on the valuation date for that plan year. If the value of plan assets determined under this paragraph (f)(5)(ii) is less than 90 percent of the fair market value of plan assets on the valuation date, then the value of plan assets under this paragraph (f)(5)(ii) is equal to 90 percent of the fair market value of plan assets. If the value of plan assets determined under this paragraph (f)(5)(ii) is greater than 110 percent of the fair market value of plan assets on the valuation date, then the value of plan assets under this paragraph (f)(5)(ii) is equal to 110 percent of the fair market value of plan assets.

(B) *Subtraction of credit balance.* If a plan has a funding standard account credit balance as of the valuation date for the plan's pre-effective plan year, that balance is subtracted from the net asset value described in paragraph (f)(5)(ii)(A) of this section as of that valuation date.

(C) *Effect of funding standard carryover balance reduction for first effective plan year.* Notwithstanding paragraph (f)(5)(ii)(B) of this section, if, for the first effective plan year, the employer has made an election to reduce some or all of the funding standard carryover balance as of the first day of that year in accordance with § 1.430(f)-1(e), then the present value (determined as of the valuation date for the pre-effective plan year using the valuation interest rate for that pre-effective plan year) of the amount so reduced is not treated as

part of the funding standard account credit balance when that balance is subtracted from the asset value under paragraph (f)(5)(ii)(B) of this section.

(6) *Transition rule for determining at-risk status.* In the case of plan years beginning in 2008, 2009, and 2010, paragraph (b)(1)(i) of this section is applied by substituting the following percentages for '80 percent'—

(i) 65 percent in the case of 2008;

(ii) 70 percent in the case of 2009; and

(iii) 75 percent in the case of 2010.

Linda E. Stiff, Deputy Commissioner for Services and Enforcement

---

¶ 20,262H

IRS proposed regulations: Defined contribution plans: Employer securities: Diversification requirements.— The IRS has proposed regulations under Code Sec. 401(a)(35) concerning diversification requirements for certain defined contribution plans that use publicly traded employer securities. The proposed regs incorporate much of the guidance under IRS Notice 2006-107 (CCH PENSION PLAN GUIDE ¶ 17,135E), with some clarifications and extensions.

The regulations are proposed to be effective for plan years beginning on or after January 1, 2009, but may be relied on before final regulations go into effect.

The proposed regulations were published in the Federal Register on January 3, 2008 (73 FR 421). Final Regulations were issued as T.D. 9484 on May 19, 2010 (75 FR 27927). The final regulations are reproduced at ¶ 11,720Z-75. The preamble to the final regulations is at ¶ 23,270.

DEPARTMENT OF THE TREASURY

Internal Revenue Service

26 CFR Part 1

[REG-136701-07]

RIN1545-BH04

Diversification Requirements for Certain Defined Contribution Plans

AGENCY: Internal Revenue Service (IRS), Treasury.

ACTION: Notice of proposed rulemaking.

SUMMARY: This document contains proposed regulations under section 401(a)(35) of the Internal Revenue Code (Code) relating to diversification requirements for certain defined contribution plans and to publicly traded employer securities. These regulations will affect administrators of, employers maintaining, participants in, and beneficiaries of defined contribution plans that are invested in employer securities.

DATES: Written or electronic comments and requests for a public hearing must be received by April 2, 2008.

ADDRESSES: Send submissions to: CC:PA:LPD:PR (Reg-136701-07), room 5203, Internal Revenue Service, PO Box 7604, Ben Franklin Station, Washington DC 20044. Submissions may be hand-delivered Monday through Friday between the hours of 8 a.m. and 4 p.m. to: CC:PA:LPD:PR (Reg-136701-07), Courier's Desk, Internal Revenue Service, 1111 Constitution Avenue, NW., Washington, DC, or sent electronically via the Federal eRulemaking Portal at http://www.regulations.gov (IRS REG-136701-07).

FOR FURTHER INFORMATION CONTACT: Concerning the regulations, R. Lisa Mojiri-Azad or Dana Barry at (202) 622-6060; concerning submission of comments or to request a public hearing, Kelly Banks at (202) 622-7180 (not toll-free numbers).

SUPPLEMENTARY INFORMATION:

Background

This document contains proposed regulations under section 401(a)(35) of the Code, which was added by section 901 of the Pension Protection Act of 2006, Public Law 109-280, 120 Stat. 780 (PPA '06).[1]

Section 401(a)(35)(A) provides that a trust which is part of an applicable defined contribution plan is not a qualified trust under section 401(a) unless the plan satisfies the diversification requirements of sections 401(a)(35)(B), (C), and (D). Under section 401(a)(35)(B),

each individual must have the right to direct the plan to divest employer securities allocated to the individual's account that are attributable to employee contributions or elective deferrals and to reinvest an equivalent amount in other investment options meeting the requirements of section 401(a)(35)(D).[2]

Under section 401(a)(35)(C), each individual who is a participant who has completed at least three years of service, a beneficiary of a participant who has completed at least three years of service, or a beneficiary of a deceased participant must be permitted to elect to direct the plan to divest employer securities allocated to the individual's account and to reinvest an equivalent amount in other investment options meeting the requirements of section 401(a)(35)(D).

Section 401(a)(35)(D)(i) requires an applicable defined contribution plan to offer individuals not less than three investment options, other than employer securities, to which the individuals may direct the proceeds from the divestment of employer securities, each of which is diversified and has materially different risk and return characteristics.

Under section 401(a)(35)(D)(ii)(I), a plan does not fail to meet the requirements of section 401(a)(35)(D) if it allows individuals to divest employer securities and reinvest the proceeds at periodic, reasonable opportunities occurring no less frequently than quarterly.

Under section 401(a)(35)(D)(ii)(II), a plan is not permitted to impose restrictions or conditions with respect to the investment of employer securities that are not imposed on the investment of other assets of the plan. However, this rule does not apply to restrictions or conditions imposed to comply with securities laws. The Secretary is authorized to issue regulations providing additional exceptions to the requirements of section 401(a)(35)(D)(ii)(II).

An applicable defined contribution plan under section 401(a)(35) is a defined contribution plan that holds any publicly traded employer securities. A publicly traded employer security is defined as an employer security under section 407(d)(1) of the Employee Retirement Income Security Act of 1974, Public Law 93-406, 88 Stat. 829 (ERISA) which is readily tradable on an established securities market. Section 401(a)(35)(F)(i) provides that a plan that does not hold publicly traded employer securities is nevertheless treated as holding publicly traded employer securities if any employer corporation or any member of a controlled group of corporations which includes the employer (determined by applying section 1563(a), except substituting 50 percent for 80 percent) has issued a class of stock that is a publicly traded employer security. However, section 401(a)(35)(F) does not apply to a plan if no employer corporation, or parent corporation (as defined in section 424(e)) of an employer corporation, has issued any publicly

---

[1] Section 901 of PPA '06 also added a parallel provision at section 204(j) of the Employee Retirement Income Security Act of 1974, Public Law 93-406, 88 Stat. 829 (ERISA). Under section 101 of Reorganization Plan No. 4 of 1978 (43 FR 47713), the Secretary of Treasury has interpretative jurisdiction over the subject matter addressed in these proposed regulations for purposes of section 204(j) of ERISA. Thus, the guidance provided in these proposed regulations with respect to section 401(a)(35) of the Code also applies for purposes of section 204(j) of ERISA.

[2] Section 401(a)(28) provides certain diversification rights to participants in an employee stock ownership plan within the meaning of section 4975(e)(7) (ESOP). Section 401(a)(28)(B) also generally requires that the plan offer at least three alternative investment options. Section 401(a)(28)(B) permits a plan to satisfy these diversification requirements by distributing, within 90 days after the period during which the election may be made, the portion of the participant's account that is subject to section 401(a)(28)(B). Section 401(a)(28)(B) was amended by section 901(a)(2)(A) of PPA '06 not to apply to a plan to which section 401(a)(35) applies.

traded employer security and no employer or parent corporation has issued any special class of stock which grants particular rights to, or bears particular risks for, the holder or issuer with respect to any corporation described in section 401(a)(35)(F)(i) which has issued any publicly traded employer security.

Section 401(a)(35)(E) provides that section 401(a)(35) does not apply to an employee stock ownership plan within the meaning of section 4975(e)(7) (ESOP) that holds no contributions (or earnings thereunder) that are subject to section 401(k) or (m) (generally relating to elective deferrals and matching and employee after-tax contributions) and the ESOP is a separate plan for purposes of section 414(1) with respect to any other defined benefit plan or defined contribution plan maintained by the same employer or employers. Section 401(a)(35)(E) further provides that section 401(a)(35) does not apply to one-participant retirement plans.

Section 401(a)(35) is generally effective for plan years beginning after December 31, 2006. Section 401(a)(35)(H) generally provides a three year phase-in rule with respect to an individual's right to direct the divestment of employer securities attributable to employer contributions, except with respect to certain participants who have attained age 55. Section 901(c)(2) of PPA '06 includes a special rule for a plan maintained pursuant to one or more collective bargaining agreements between employee representatives and one or more employers that was ratified on or before August 17, 2006. Under this rule, section 401(a)(35) is not effective until plan years beginning after the earlier of (1) the later of (a) December 31, 2007 or (b) the date on which the last of such collective bargaining agreements terminates (determined without regard to any extension thereof after August 17, 2006) or (2) December 31, 2008.

Notice 2006-107 (2006-2 CB 1114 (December 18, 2006)) (see § 601.601(d)(2)(ii)(b) of this chapter), includes guidance and transitional rules with respect to the diversification requirements of section 401(a)(35).[3] Notice 2006-107 provides that a plan (and an investment option described in section 401(a)(35)(D)(i)) is not treated as holding employer securities to which section 401(a)(35) applies with respect to any securities held through either an investment company registered under the Investment Company Act of 1940 or a similar pooled investment vehicle that is regulated and subject to periodic examination by a State or Federal agency and with respect to which investment in securities is made both in accordance with the stated investment objectives of the investment vehicle and independent of the employer and any affiliate thereof, but only if the holdings of the investment company or similar investment vehicle are diversified so as to minimize the risk of large losses. Notice 2006-107 also provides that investment options satisfy the requirement that investment options be diversified and have materially different risk and return characteristics under section 401(a)(35)(D)(i) if the investment options satisfy the requirements of section 2550.404c-1(b)(3) of the Department of Labor regulations.

Notice 2006-107 further provides that, for purposes of section 401(a)(35), the date on which a participant completes three years of service occurs immediately after the end of the third vesting computation period provided for under the plan that constitutes the completion of a third year of service under section 411(a)(5). For a plan using the elapsed time method of crediting service for vesting purposes (or a plan that provides for immediate vesting without using a vesting computation period or elapsed time method of determining vesting), the date on which a participant completes three years of service is the third anniversary of the participant's date of hire.

Notice 2006-107 includes special rules regarding restrictions or conditions with respect to employer securities under section 401(a)(35)(D)(ii)(II). An impermissible restriction or condition is either a restriction on an individual's right to divest an investment in employer securities that is not imposed on an investment that is not in employer securities or a benefit that is conditioned on an investment in employer securities. Examples of restrictions or conditions that are prohibited by section 401(a)(35)(D)(ii)(II) under Notice 2006-107 include: (1) A plan allows an individual the right to divest employer securities on a quarterly basis but permits divestiture of another investment on a more frequent basis; (2) a plan provides that a participant who divests his or her account of employer securities receives less favorable treatment (such as a lower rate of matching contributions) than a participant whose account remains invested in employer securities; and (3) a plan that provides if a participant divests his or her account balance with respect to investment in a class of employer securities, the participant is not permitted for a period of time to

reinvest in that class of securities where that restriction is not imposed on other investments. Notice 2006-107 also provided examples of restrictions or conditions that are not prohibited by section 401(a)(35)(D)(ii)(II): (1) A provision that limits the extent to which an individual's account balance can be invested in employer securities; (2) a provision under which an employer securities fund is closed; (3) a restriction imposed by reason of application of securities laws or a restriction that is reasonably designed to ensure compliance with such laws; (4) an imposition of fees on other investment options under the plan but not on investments in employer securities; and (5) a plan restriction on the availability of otherwise applicable diversification rights under the plan for up to 90 days following an initial public offering of the employer's stock.

Notice 2006-107 provides certain transition rules. For example, for the period prior to January 1, 2008, a plan does not impose a restriction or condition prohibited by section 401(a)(35)(D)(ii)(II) merely because the plan, as in effect on December 18, 2006, (1) does not impose an otherwise applicable restriction on a stable value fund or (2) allows individuals the right to divest employer securities on a periodic basis (at least quarterly), but permits divestiture of another investment on a more frequent basis, provided that the other investment is not a generally available investment.

Explanation of Provisions

Overview

The proposed regulations would provide guidance with respect to the requirements of section 401(a)(35) that incorporates much of the guidance provided under Notice 2006-107. The regulations would clarify the scope of the rule in section 401(a)(35)(D)(ii)(II) that generally prohibits restrictions and conditions on investment in employer securities, but would specifically permit certain restrictions and conditions on such investment that are consistent with the statute, and would also define when employer securities are publicly traded on an established securities market under section 401(a)(35)(D).

Basic Diversification Rights

The proposed regulations incorporate the guidance on the basic diversification rights of section 401(a)(35) that is contained in Notice 2006-107. Thus, if an applicable defined contribution plan holds employee contributions (including rollover contributions) or elective deferrals with respect to an individual that are invested in employer securities, the plan must provide that the individual is given the opportunity to divest the employer securities and reinvest an equivalent amount in another investment. These rights must be provided to each participant, to each alternate payee who has an account under the plan, and to each beneficiary of a deceased participant.

If employer contributions (other than elective deferrals) are invested in employer securities under the plan, the divestment right must be provided to each participant who has completed at least three years of service, to each alternate payee who has an account under the plan with respect to a participant who has at least three years of service, and to each beneficiary of a deceased participant (regardless of whether the participant had completed at least three years of service). For this purpose, the regulations would provide that a participant has completed three years of service on the last day of the vesting computation period as determined under the plan that constitutes the completion of the third year of service (or the third anniversary of hire for a plan that either uses the elapsed time method or that does not define the vesting computation period because the plan provides for full and immediate vesting).

The regulations would require a plan to provide individuals who have section 401(a)(35) diversification rights the opportunity to divest the employer securities and reinvest an equivalent amount in another investment at least quarterly. The individuals must be permitted to select among no less than three investment options, each of which is diversified and has materially different risk and return characteristics. For this purpose, investment options that constitute a broad range of investment alternatives within the meaning of Department of Labor Regulations section 2550.404c-1(b)(3) are treated as being diversified and having materially different risk and return characteristics.

Plans subject to section 401(a)(35)

Under the proposed regulations, a defined contribution plan which holds publicly-traded employer securities (referred to as an applicable defined contribution plan) is subject to the diversification requirements

---

[3] Notice 2006-107 also includes guidance regarding the related notice requirements of section 101(m) of ERISA, including a model notice.

of section 401(a)(35), unless it is exempted under section 401(a)(35)(E) as a stand-alone ESOP or as a one-participant retirement plan. For this purpose, an employer security is defined by reference to section 407(d)(1) of ERISA.

Under section 401(a)(35)(G)(v), an employer security is a publicly traded employer security if it is readily tradable on an established securities market. The regulations would provide separate rules for securities traded on domestic securities exchanges and foreign securities exchanges.

If a security is traded on a securities exchange that is registered under section 6 of the Securities Exchange Act of 1934, then the security would be deemed to be readily tradable on an established securities market. This definition is consistent with the definition of publicly traded found in §54.4975-7(b)(1)(iv), but deletes the reference to a system sponsored by the National Association of Securities Dealers (NASDAQ) registered under section 15A(b) of the Act (15 U.S.C. 78o) because NASDAQ is now registered as a securities exchange under section 6 of the Securities Exchange Act of 1934. Thus, if a security is not traded on a national securities exchange that is registered under section 6 of the Securities Exchange Act of 1934, then the security would not be publicly traded for purposes of section 401(a)(35), (unless it is traded on a foreign securities exchange and has a "ready market" as described in the next paragraph). This would apply to U.S. securities that are only traded on the "Over-The-Counter Bulletin Board" and the "pink sheets."

Under the proposed regulations, if a security is not listed on a securities exchange that is registered under section 6 of the Securities Exchange Act of 1934, but is traded on a foreign national securities exchange that is officially recognized, sanctioned, or supervised by a governmental authority, then under the proposed regulations, the security would be traded on an established securities market. The proposed regulations would provide that such a security is readily tradable if the security is deemed by the Securities and Exchange Commission (SEC) as having a "ready market" under SEC Rule 15c3-1 (17 CFR 240.15c3-1).[4]

The proposed regulations would reflect section 401(a)(35)(F), which, subject to certain exceptions, treats a plan holding employer securities that are not publicly traded as nonetheless subject to the rules of section 401(a)(35) if any employer sponsoring the plan, or any member of the controlled group of corporations (determined by applying section 1563(a), except substituting 50 percent for 80 percent) has issued a class of stock which is publicly traded (as defined above).

Section 401(a)(35)(E)(ii) provides that an ESOP that is a separate plan holding no contributions that are subject to section 401(k) or section 401(m) is not an applicable defined contribution plan. (As noted earlier in this preamble, such a plan is subject to the diversification requirements of section 401(a)(28)(B).) The proposed regulations would clarify that a plan does not lose this exemption merely because it receives rollover contributions of amounts from another plan that are held in a separate account, even if those amounts were attributable to contributions that were subject to section 401(k) or 401(m) in the other plan. In addition, the proposed regulations would reflect the exemption for one-participant retirement plans under section 401(a)(35)(E)(iv).

Notice 2006-107 provides that employer securities held by an investment company registered under the Investment Company Act of 1940 or similar pooled investment vehicle are not treated as being held by the plan. Some comments on Notice 2006-107 had recommended a broader rule, under which a commingled fund that holds employer securities and other securities would not be treated as holding employer securities that are subject to the section 401(a)(35) diversification requirement. The proposed regulations would not adopt this broad exemption from the diversification rules.

The proposed regulations, however, clarify the types of pooled investment vehicles that are exempt from the diversification requirements. Under the proposed regulations, in order to be exempt from the diversification requirements, the pooled investment vehicle must be a common or collective trust fund or pooled investment fund maintained by a bank or trust company supervised by a State or Federal agency, a pooled investment fund of an insurance company that is qualified to do business in a State, or an investment fund designated by the Commissioner in revenue rulings, notices, or other guidance published in the Internal Revenue Bulletin. As under Notice 2006-107, the regulations would include the requirement that in order to be exempt from the diversification requirements the pooled investment fund that holds the employer securities must have stated investment objectives and the

investment must be independent of the employer and any affiliate thereof. The proposed regulations would add a percentage limitation rule to ensure that the investment in the employer securities through a pooled fund is not an attempt to evade the rules of section 401(a)(35). Under this rule, if the employer securities held by such fund is more than 10 percent of the total value of all of the fund's investment, then the fund is not considered to be independent of the employer.

Prohibition on restrictions or conditions

The proposed regulations would provide that the section 401(a)(35)(D)(ii)(II) prohibition on restrictions or conditions with respect to the investment of employer securities which are not imposed on the investment of other assets of the plans applies to a direct or indirect restriction on an individual's rights to divest an investment in employer securities that is not imposed on an investment that is not employer securities as well as a direct or indirect benefit that is conditioned on investment in employer securities. However, like Notice 2006-107, the regulations would not apply this prohibition to restrictions that are imposed by reason of the application of securities laws and in certain other situations described below.

Like Notice 2006-107, the proposed regulations would allow a plan to impose a restriction on divestiture that is reasonably designed to comply with securities law, even if the restriction is broader than the minimum restriction needed to comply with securities laws. The proposed regulations incorporate the example of such a restriction from Notice 2006-107. This is merely an example and broader restrictions on divestiture are permitted, provided they are reasonably designed to comply with securities law. For example, in some smaller entities a broad restriction allowing divestiture to occur only once a quarter might be a restriction that is reasonably designed to comply with securities law.

Notice 2006-107 includes a rule that permits a plan to restrict the otherwise applicable diversification rights under section 401(a)(35) for a period of up to 90 days following an initial public offering of the employer's stock. The proposed regulations would extend this rule to apply to the first 90 days after the plan becomes an applicable defined contribution plan. This could happen, for example, when some other entity in the controlled group first issues stock which is publicly traded or when a stand-alone ESOP first provides for contributions that are subject to section 401(k) or section 401(m).

Notice 2006-107 permits a plan to impose a restriction on an investment in employer securities that is not imposed on a stable value fund. The proposed regulations extend this rule to a fund that is similar to a stable value fund. Specifically, the proposed regulations would provide that in the case of a plan that has several investment funds, including a fund invested in employer securities, a fund which is a stable value or similar fund, and other funds which are not invested in employer securities, the plan does not impose a restriction prohibited under section 401(a)(35)(D)(ii)(II) merely because the plan permits transfers to be made into the stable value or similar fund more frequently than into the fund invested in employer securities (assuming the plan does not impose a restriction on transfers to or from the employer securities fund that it does not impose with respect to the other funds).

While the proposed regulations would generally prohibit indirect restrictions on an individual's exercise of diversification rights (such as a plan provision that limits the right of an individual who diversifies out of employer securities by providing that such a participant is not permitted to reinvest in employer securities for a period of time), the rules would permit certain indirect restrictions, as well as certain indirect benefits that are conditioned on investment in employer securities. Under the proposed regulations, a plan would be permitted to limit the extent to which an individual's account balance can be invested in employer securities. For example, a plan would not be treated as imposing a restriction that violates section 401(a)(35)(D)(ii)(II) merely because the plan prohibits a participant from investing additional amounts in employer securities if more than 10 percent of that participant's account balance is (or would be after the change) invested in employer securities. In addition, an applicable defined contribution plan does not violate a prohibition against reinvestment in employer securities if the plan has terminated any further investment in employer securities.

The proposed regulations would provide that a plan is not providing an indirect benefit that is conditioned on investment in employer securities merely because the plan imposes fees on other investment options that are not imposed on the investment in employer securities. In addition, a plan is not providing a restriction on the right to divest an

---

[4] Under the current SEC rules, a security is deemed to have a ready market if it is included on the FTSE Group (FTSE) World Index.

investment in employer securities merely because the plan imposes a reasonable fee for the divestment of employer securities.

The proposed regulations would permit a restriction on the frequency of investment elections that was not in Notice 2006-107. Under this rule, a plan would be permitted to impose reasonable restrictions on the timing and number of investment elections that an individual can make to invest in employer securities, provided that the restrictions are designed to limit short-term trading in the employer securities. For example, a fund could limit the purchase of employer securities if there has been a sale within a short period of time, such as 7 days. The regulations, however, would not permit a plan to limit an individual's right to divest employer securities.

Proposed Effective Date

Section 401(a)(35) is applicable to plan years beginning on or after January 1, 2007, subject to certain deferred effective dates and transition rules. The proposed regulations would provide guidance on these effective dates and transition rules. In particular, the regulations would provide that a plan is eligible for the deferred effective date applicable to collectively bargained plans only if at least 25 percent of the participants in the plan are members of collective bargaining units for which the contributions under the plan are specified under a collective bargaining agreement.

The regulations under section 401(a)(35) are proposed to be effective for plan years beginning on or after January 1, 2009. Until the regulations go into effect, Notice 2006-107 will continue to apply. For this purpose, the transitional relief provided for the period prior to January 1, 2008, in paragraph 4 of Section III.D. of Notice 2006-107 will continue to apply after 2007 until the regulations go into effect.[5] In addition, plans are also permitted to apply the proposed regulations for plan years before the regulations go into effect.

Special Analyses

It has been determined that this notice of proposed rulemaking is not a significant regulatory action as defined in Executive Order 12866. Therefore, a regulatory assessment is not required. It also has been determined that section 553(b) of the Administrative Procedure Act (5 U.S.C. chapter 5) does not apply to these regulations, and, because § 1.401(a)(35)-1 would not impose a collection of information on small entities, the Regulatory Flexibility Act (5 U.S.C. chapter 6) does not apply. Pursuant to section 7805(f) of the Code, this notice of proposed rulemaking will be submitted to the Chief Counsel for Advocacy of the Small Business Administration for comment on its impact on small business.

Comments and Requests for Public Hearing

Before these proposed regulations are adopted as final regulations, consideration will be given to any written (one signed and eight (8) copies) or electronic comments that are submitted timely to the IRS. The IRS and the Treasury Department specifically request comments on the clarity of the proposed regulations and how they can be made easier to understand.

In particular, the IRS and Treasury Department request comments on whether the determination of when an employer security is readily tradable on an established securities market under these proposed regulations should also be applied for purposes of determining whether an employer security is readily tradable on an established securities market in applying other provisions relating to qualified plans, given that the same words used in interrelated provisions of the Code are presumed to have the same meaning. These interrelated provisions include section 401(a)(28)(C) (requiring the use of an independent appraiser for valuation of employer securities that are not readily tradable on an established securities market), section 409(h)(1)(B) (relating to put options for employer securities that are not readily tradable on an established market), the definition of employer securities under section 409(1)(1) (including regulations under section 4975), and the special rules under section 1042 (providing nonrecognition treatment for certain sales to an ESOP).

All comments will be available for public inspection and copying. A public hearing will be scheduled if requested in writing by any person who timely submits written comments. If a public hearing is scheduled, notice of the date, time, and place of the public hearing will be published in the Federal Register.

Drafting Information

The principal authors of these regulations are Dana A. Barry and Lisa Mojiri-Azad, Office of Division Counsel/Associate Chief Counsel (Tax Exempt and Government Entities). However, other personnel from the IRS and the Treasury participated in the development of these regulations.

List of Subjects in 26 CFR Part 1

Income taxes, reporting and recordkeeping requirements.

Proposed Amendments to the Regulations

Accordingly, 26 CFR part 1 is proposed to be amended as follows:

PART 1—INCOME TAXES

Paragraph 1. The authority citation for part 1 is amended by adding an entry in numerical order to read as follows:

Authority: 26 U.S.C. 7805 * * *

Section 1.401(a)(35)-1 is also issued under 26 U.S.C. 401(a)(35). * * *

Par. 2. Section 1.401(a)(35)-1 is added to read as follows:

§ 1.401(a)(35)-1 Diversification Requirements for Certain Defined Contribution Plans.

(a) General rule—(1) Diversification requirements. Section 401(a)(35) imposes diversification requirements on applicable defined contribution plans. A trust that is part of an applicable defined contribution plan is not a qualified trust under section 401(a) unless the plan—

(i) Satisfies the diversification election requirements for elective deferrals and employee contributions set forth in paragraph (b) of this section;

(ii) Satisfies the diversification election requirements for employer nonelective contributions set forth in paragraph (c) of this section;

(iii) Satisfies the investment option requirement set forth in paragraph (d) of this section; and

(iv) Does not apply any restrictions or conditions on investments in employer securities that violate the requirements of paragraph (e) of this section.

(2) Definitions, effective dates, and transition rules. The definitions of applicable defined contribution plan, employer security, parent corporation, and publicly traded are set forth in paragraph (f) of this section. Effective/applicability dates and transition rules are set forth in paragraph (g) of this section.

(b) Diversification requirements for elective deferrals and employee contributions invested in employer securities—(1) General rule. With respect to any individual described in paragraph (b)(2) of this section, if any portion of the individual's account under an applicable defined contribution plan attributable to elective deferrals (as described in section 402(g)(3)(A)), after-tax employee contributions, or rollover contributions is invested in employer securities, then the plan satisfies the requirements of this paragraph (b) if the individual may elect to divest those employer securities and reinvest an equivalent amount in other investment options. The plan may limit the time for divestment and reinvestment to periodic, reasonable opportunities occurring no less frequently than quarterly.

(2) Applicable individual with respect to elective deferrals and employee contributions. An individual is described in this paragraph (b)(2) if the individual is—

(i) A participant;

(ii) An alternate payee who has an account under the plan; or

(iii) A beneficiary of a deceased participant.

(c) Diversification requirements for employer nonelective contributions invested in employer securities—(1) General rule. With respect to any individual described in paragraph (c)(2) of this section, if a portion of the individual's account under an applicable defined contribution plan attributable to employer nonelective contributions, other than elective deferrals, is invested in employer securities, then the plan satisfies the requirements of this paragraph (c) if the individual may elect to divest those employer securities and reinvest an equivalent amount in other investment options. The plan may limit the time for divestment and reinvestment to periodic, reasonable opportunities occurring no less frequently than quarterly.

---

[5] The Treasury and IRS are issuing a notice to reflect this extension. The notice is expected to be published as Notice 2008-7 in the 2008-3 issue of the IRB on January 22, 2008, (see § 601.601(d)(2)(ii)(b) of this chapter).

(2) Applicable individual with respect to employer nonelective contributions. An individual is described in this paragraph (c)(2) if the individual is—

(i) A participant who has completed at least three years of service;

(ii) An alternate payee who has an account under the plan with respect to a participant who has completed at least three years of service; or

(iii) A beneficiary of a deceased participant.

(3) Completion of 3 years of service. For purposes of paragraph (c)(2) of this section, a participant completes three years of service on the last day of the vesting computation period provided for under the plan that constitutes the completion of the third year of service under section 411(a)(5). However, for a plan that uses the elapsed time method of crediting service for vesting purposes (or a plan that provides for immediate vesting without using a vesting computation period or the elapsed time method of determining vesting), a participant completes three years of service on the day immediately preceding the third anniversary of the participant's date of hire.

(d) Investment option. An applicable defined contribution plan must offer not less than three investment options, other than employer securities, to which an individual who has the right to divest under paragraph (b)(1) or (c)(1) of this section may direct the proceeds from the divestment of employer securities. Each of the three investment options must be diversified and have materially different risk and return characteristics. For this purpose, investment options that constitute a broad range of investment alternatives within the meaning of Department of Labor Regulation section 2550.404c-1(b)(3) are treated as being diversified and having materially different risk and return characteristics.

(e) Restrictions or conditions on investments in employer securities— (1) Impermissible restrictions or conditions—(i) General rule. Except as provided in paragraph (e)(2) of this section, an applicable defined contribution plan violates the requirements of this paragraph (e) if the plan imposes restrictions or conditions with respect to the investment of employer securities that are not imposed on the investment of other assets of the plan. A restriction or condition with respect to employer securities means—

(A) A restriction on an individual's right to divest an investment in employer securities that is not imposed on an investment that is not employer securities; and

(B) A benefit that is conditioned on investment in employer securities.

(ii) Indirect restrictions or conditions. Except as provided in paragraph (e)(3) of this section, a plan violates the requirements of this paragraph (e) if the plan imposes a restriction or condition in paragraph (e)(1)(i)(A) or (B) of this section either directly or indirectly. For example, a plan imposes an indirect restriction on an individual's right to divest an investment in employer securities if the plan provides that a participant who divests his or her account balance with respect to investment in employer securities is not permitted for a period of time thereafter to reinvest in employer securities.

(2) Permitted restrictions or conditions—(i) In general. An applicable defined contribution plan does not violate the requirements of this paragraph (e) merely because it imposes a restriction or a condition set forth in paragraph (e)(2)(ii) or (e)(2)(iii) of this section.

(ii) Securities laws. A plan is permitted to impose a restriction or condition on the divestiture of employer securities that is either required in order to ensure compliance with applicable securities laws or is reasonably designed to ensure compliance with applicable securities laws. For example, it is permissible for a plan to limit divestiture rights for participants who are subject to section 16(b) of the Securities Exchange Act of 1934 to a reasonable period (such as 3 to 12 days) following publication of the employer's quarterly earnings statements because it is reasonably designed to ensure compliance with Rule 10b-5 of the Securities and Exchange Commission.

(iii) Deferred application of the diversification requirements. An applicable defined contribution plan is permitted to restrict the application of the diversification requirements of section 401(a)(35) and this section for up to 90 days after the plan becomes an applicable defined contribution plan (for example, the date on which the employer securities held under the plan become publicly traded).

(3) Permitted indirect restrictions or conditions—(i) In general. An applicable defined contribution plan does not violate the requirements of this paragraph (e) merely because it imposes an indirect restriction or condition set forth in paragraphs (e)(3)(ii) through (e)(3)(v) of this section.

(ii) Limitation on investment in employer securities. The plan is permitted to limit the extent to which an individual's account balance can be invested in employer securities, provided the limitation applies without regard to a prior exercise of rights to divest employer securities. For example, a plan does not impose a restriction that violates this paragraph (e) merely because the plan prohibits a participant from investing additional amounts in employer securities if more than 10 percent of that participant's account balance is invested in employer securities.

(iii) Trading frequency. A plan is permitted to impose reasonable restrictions on the timing and number of investment elections that an individual can make to invest in employer securities, provided that the restrictions are designed to limit short-term trading in the employer securities. For example, a plan could provide that a participant may not elect to invest in employer securities if the employee has elected to divest employer securities within a short period of time, such as seven days.

(iv) Frozen funds. A plan is permitted to prohibit any further investment in employer securities.

(v) Fees. The plan has not provided an indirect benefit that is conditioned on investment in employer securities merely because the plan imposes fees on other investment options that are not imposed on the investment in employer securities. In addition, the plan has not provided a restriction on the right to divest an investment in employer securities merely because the plan imposes a reasonable fee for the divestment of employer securities.

(vi) Transfers to stable value fund. In the case of a plan that has several investment funds, including one or more funds invested in employer securities, a fund which is a stable value or similar fund, and other funds which are not invested in employer securities, the plan does not impose a restriction prohibited under this paragraph (e) merely because the plan permits transfers to be made into the stable value or similar fund more frequently than other funds (including funds invested in employer securities).

(f) Definitions—(1) Application of definitions. This paragraph (f) contains definitions that are applicable for purposes of this section.

(2) Applicable defined contribution plan—(i) General rule. Except as provided in this paragraph (f)(2), an applicable defined contribution plan means any defined contribution plan which holds employer securities that are publicly traded. See paragraph (f)(2)(iv) of this section for a special rule that treats certain plans that hold employer securities that are not publicly traded as applicable defined contribution plans and paragraph (f)(3)(ii) of this section for a special rule that treats certain plans as not holding publicly traded employer securities for purposes of this section.

(ii) Exception for certain ESOPs. An employee stock ownership plan (ESOP), as defined in section 4975(e)(7), is not an applicable defined contribution plan if the plan is a separate plan for purposes of section 414(1) with respect to any other defined benefit plan or defined contribution plan maintained by the same employer or employers and holds no contributions (or earnings thereunder) that are (or were ever) subject to section 401(k) or 401(m). Thus, an employee stock ownership plan is an applicable defined contribution plan if that ESOP is a portion of a larger plan (whether or not that larger plan includes contributions that are subject to section 401(k) or 401(m)). For purposes of this paragraph (f)(2)(ii), a plan is not considered to hold amounts ever subject to section 401(k) or 401(m) merely because the plan holds amounts attributable to rollover amounts in a separate account that were previously subject to section 401(k) or 401(m).

(iii) Exception for one-participant plans. A one-participant plan, as defined in section 401(a)(35)(E)(iv), is not an applicable defined contribution plan.

(iv) Certain defined contribution plans treated as holding publicly traded employer securities—(A) General rule. A defined contribution plan holding employer securities that are not publicly traded is treated as an applicable defined contribution plan if any employer maintaining the plan or any member of a controlled group of corporations that includes such employer has issued a class of stock which is publicly traded. For purposes of this paragraph (f)(2)(iv), a controlled group of corporation has the meaning given such term by section 1563(a), except that "50 percent" is substituted for "80 percent" each place it appears.

(B) Exception for certain plans. Paragraph (f)(2)(iv)(A) of this section does not apply to a plan if—

(1) No employer maintaining the plan (or a parent corporation with respect to such employer) has issued stock that is publicly traded; and

(2) No employer maintaining the plan (or parent corporation with respect to such employer) has issued any special class of stock which grants to the holder or issuer particular rights, or bears particular risks

¶20,262H

for the holder or issuer, with respect to any employer maintaining the plan (or any member of a controlled group of corporations that includes such employer) which has issued any stock that is publicly traded.

(3) Employer security—(i) General rule. Employer security has the meaning given such term by section 407(d)(1) of the Employee Retirement Income Security Act of 1974, as amended.

(ii) Certain defined contribution plans or investment funds not treated as holding employer securities—(A) Exception for certain flow-through investments. Subject to paragraph (f)(3)(ii)(B) and (C) of this section, a plan (and an investment option described in paragraph (d) of this section) is not treated as holding employer securities for purposes of this section to the extent the employer securities are held indirectly through—

(1) An investment company registered under the Investment Company Act of 1940;

(2) A common or collective trust fund or pooled investment fund maintained by a bank or trust company supervised by a State or a Federal agency;

(3) A pooled investment fund of an insurance company that is qualified to do business in a State; or

(4) Any other investment fund designated by the Commissioner in revenue rulings, notices, or other guidance published in the Internal Revenue Bulletin.

(B) Investment must be independent. The exception set forth in paragraph (f)(3)(ii)(A) of this section applies only if the investment in the employer securities are held in a fund under which—

(1) There are stated investment objectives of the fund; and

(2) The investment is independent of the employer and any affiliate thereof.

(C) Percentage limitation rule. For purposes of paragraph (f)(3)(ii)(B)(2) of this section, an investment in employer securities in a fund is considered to be independent of the employer and any affiliate thereof only if the aggregate value of the employer securities held in the fund is not in excess of 10 percent of the total value of all of the fund's investments.

(4) Parent corporation. Parent corporation has the meaning given such term by section 424(e).

(5) Publicly traded—(i) In general. A security is publicly traded if it is readily tradable on an established securities market.

(ii) Established securities market. For purposes of this paragraph (f)(5), a security is traded on an established securities market if—

(A) The security is traded on a national securities exchange that is registered under section 6 of the Securities and Exchange Act of 1934 (15 U.S.C. 78f); or

(B) The security is traded on a foreign national securities exchange that is officially recognized, sanctioned, or supervised by a governmental authority.

(iii) Readily tradable. For purposes of this paragraph (f)(5), except as provided by the Commissioner in revenue rulings, notices, or other guidance published in the Internal Revenue Bulletin, a security is readily tradable if—

(A) The security is traded on a securities exchange that is described in paragraph (f)(5)(ii)(A) of this section; or

(B) The security is traded on a securities exchange that is described in paragraph (f)(5)(ii)(B) of this section and the security is deemed by the Securities and Exchange Commission (SEC) as having a "ready market" under SEC Rule 15c3-1 (17 CFR 240.15c3-1).

(g) Effective date and transition rules—(1) Statutory effective date—(i) General rule. Except as otherwise provided in this paragraph (g), section 401(a)(35) is effective for plan years beginning after December 31, 2006.

(ii) Collectively bargained plans—(A) Delayed effective date. In the case of a plan maintained pursuant to one or more collective bargaining agreements between employee representatives and one or more employers ratified on or before August 17, 2006, section 401(a)(35) is effective for plan years beginning after the earlier of (1) the later of—

(i) December 31, 2007; or

(ii) the date on which the last such collective bargaining agreement terminates (determined without regard to any extension thereof); or

(2) December 31, 2008.

(B) Definition of collectively bargained plans. For purposes of this paragraph (g)(1)(ii), in the case of a plan for which one or more collective bargaining agreements apply to some, but not all, of the plan participants, the plan is considered a collectively bargained plan if at least 25 percent of the participants in the plan are members of collective bargaining units for which the contributions under the plan are specified under a collective bargaining agreement.

(iii) Special rule for certain employer securities held in an ESOP. Section 901(c)(3)(A) and (B) of the Pension Protection Act of 2006, Public Law 109-280, 120 Stat. 780 (PPA '06), provides a special effective date for an employee stock ownership plan that holds a class of preferred stock with a guaranteed minimum value, as described in that section.

(2) Statutory transition rules—(i) General rule. Pursuant to section 401(a)(35)(H), in the case of the portion of an account to which paragraph (c) of this section applies and that consists of employer securities acquired in a plan year beginning before January 1, 2007, the requirements of paragraph (c) of this section only apply to the applicable percentage of such securities.

(ii) Applicable percentage—(A) Phase-in percentage. For purposes of this paragraph (g)(2), the applicable percentage is determined as follows—

Plan year to which paragraph (c) of this section applies:

The applicable percentage is:

1st	33
2nd	66
3rd and following	100

(B) Special rule. For a plan described in paragraph (g)(1)(iii) of this section for which the special effective date under section 901(c)(3) of PPA '06 applies, the applicable percentage under this paragraph (g)(2)(ii) is determined without regard to the delayed effective date in section 901(c)(3)(A) and (B) of PPA '06.

(iii) Nonapplication for participants age 55 with three years of service. Paragraph (g)(2)(i) of this section does not apply to an individual who is a participant who attained age 55 and had completed at least three years of service (as defined in paragraph (c)(3) of this section) before the first day of the first plan year beginning after December 31, 2005.

(iv) Separate application by class of securities. This paragraph (g)(2) applies separately with respect to each class of securities.

(3) Regulatory effective date. This section is effective for plan years beginning on or after January 1, 2009.

Linda E. Stiff,

Deputy Commissioner for Services and Enforcement.

¶ 20,2621

IRS: Multiemployer plans: Defined benefit plans: Underfunded plans: Endangered or critical status: Pension Protection Act of 2006.—The IRS has issued proposed regulations under the Pension Protection Act of 2006 (PPA; 109-280) to implement Code Sec. 432 for multiemployer defined benefit (DB) plans that are in endangered or critical underfunded status. ERISA §305 is parallel to Code Sec. 432. The Secretary of the Treasury has interpretive jurisdiction over the subject matter addressed in these proposed regulations for purposes of ERISA, as well as the Code. The Treasury Department regulations issued under Code Sec. 432. therefore, apply for purposes of ERISA §305 as well.

The proposed regulations were published in the Federal Register on March 18, 2008 (73 FR 14417), and corrected on April 10, 2008 (73 FR 19451).

DEPARTMENT OF THE TREASURY

Internal Revenue Service

26 CFR Part 1

[REG-151135-07]

RIN 1545-BH39

Multiemployer Plan Funding Guidance

AGENCY: Internal Revenue Service (IRS), Treasury

ACTION: Notice of proposed rulemaking.

SUMMARY: This document contains proposed regulations under section 432 of the Internal Revenue Code (Code). These proposed regulations provide additional rules for certain multiemployer defined benefit plans that are in effect on July 16, 2006. These proposed regulations affect sponsors and administrators of, and participants in multiemployer plans that are in either endangered or critical status. These regulations are necessary to implement the new rules set forth in section 432 that are effective for plan years beginning after 2007. The proposed regulations reflect changes made by the Pension Protection Act of 2006.

DATES: Written or electronic comments and requests for public hearing must be received by *[INSERT DATE 90 DAYS AFTER PUBLICATION OF THIS DOCUMENT IN THE FEDERAL REGISTER].*

ADDRESSES: Send submissions to: CC:PA:LPD:PR (REG-151135-07), room 5203, Internal Revenue Service, PO Box 7604, Ben Franklin Station, Washington, DC 20044. Submissions may be hand-delivered Monday through Friday between the hours of 8 a.m. and 4 p.m. to CC:PA:LPD:PR (REG-151135-07), Courier's Desk, Internal Revenue Service, 1111 Constitution Avenue, NW, Washington, DC 20224, or sent electronically via the Federal eRulemaking Portal at *www.regulations.gov* (IRS REG-151135-07).

FOR FURTHER INFORMATION CONTACT: Concerning the regulations, Bruce Perlin, (202) 622-6090; concerning submissions and requests for a public hearing, *Richard.A.Hurst@irscounsel.treas.gov* or at (202) 622-7180 (not toll-free numbers).

SUPPLEMENTARY INFORMATION:

Paperwork Reduction Act

The collection of information contained in this notice of proposed rulemaking have been submitted to the Office of Management and Budget for review in accordance with the Paperwork Reduction Act of 1995 (44 U.S.C. 3507(d). Comments on the collection of information should be sent to the **Office of Management and Budget,** Attn: Desk Officer for the Department of the Treasury, Office of Information and Regulatory Affairs, Washington, DC 20503, with copies to the **Internal Revenue Service,** Attn: IRS Reports Clearance Officer, SE:CAR:MP:T:T:SP, Washington, DC 20224. Comments on the collection of information should be received by *June 16, 2008.*

Comments are specifically requested concerning:

Whether the proposed collection of information is necessary for the proper performance of the functions of the Internal Revenue Service, including whether the information will have practical utility;

The accuracy of the estimated burden associated with the collection of information;

How the quality, utility, and clarity of the information to be collected may be enhanced;

How the burden of complying with the collection of information may be minimized, including through the application of automated collection techniques or other forms of information technology; and

Estimates of capital or start-up costs and costs of operation, maintenance, and purchase of service to provide information.

The collection of information in this regulation is in § 1.432(b)-1(d) and (e). This information is required in order for a qualified multiemployer defined benefit plan's enrolled actuary to provide a timely certification of the plan's funding status. In addition, if it is certified that a plan is or will be in critical or endangered status, the plan sponsor is required to notify the Department of Labor, the Pension Benefit Guaranty Corporation, the bargaining parties, participants, and beneficiaries

of the status designation. For plans in critical status, the plan sponsor is required to include in the notice an explanation of the possibility that adjustable benefits may be reduced at a later date and that certain benefits are restricted as of the date the notice is sent. The annual certification by the enrolled actuary for the plan will be used to provide an accurate determination and certification of the plan's funded status and to provide notice to the required parties of the status designation. The collection of information is mandatory. The likely respondents are multiemployer plan sponsors and enrolled actuaries.

Estimated total annual reporting burden: 1,200 hours.

Estimated average annual burden hours per respondent: 0.75 hours.

Estimated number of respondents: 1,600.

Estimated annual frequency of responses: occasional.

An agency may not conduct or sponsor, and a person is not required to respond to, a collection of information unless it displays a valid control number assigned by the Office of Management and Budget.

Books or records relating to a collection of information must be retained as long as their contents may become material in the administration of any internal revenue law. Generally, tax returns and tax return information are confidential, as required by 26 U.S.C. 6103.

Background

This document contains proposed Income Tax Regulations (26 CFR part 1) under section 432, as added to the Internal Revenue Code by the Pension Protection Act of 2006 (PPA '06), Public Law 109-280, 120 Stat 780.

Section 412 contains minimum funding rules that generally apply to pension plans. Section 431 sets forth the funding rules that apply specifically to multiemployer defined benefit plans. Section 432 sets forth additional rules that apply to multiemployer plans in effect on July 16, 2006, that are in endangered or critical status[1].

Section 432 generally provides for a determination by the enrolled actuary for a multiemployer plan as to whether the plan is in endangered status or in critical status for a plan year. In the first year that the actuary certifies that the plan is in endangered status, section 432(a)(1) requires that the plan sponsor adopt a funding improvement plan. The funding improvement plan must meet the requirements of section 432(c) and the plan must apply the rules of section 432(d) during the period that begins when the plan is certified to be in endangered status and ends when the plan is no longer in that status. In the first year that the actuary certifies that the plan is in critical status, section 432(a)(2) requires that the plan sponsor adopt a rehabilitation plan. The rehabilitation plan must meet the requirements of section 432(e) and the plan must apply the rules of section 432(f) during the period that begins when the plan is certified to be in critical status and ends when the plan is no longer in that status. In addition, section 432(f)(2) requires that the plan suspend certain actions as described more fully in this preamble.

Section 432(b)(3)(A) requires an actuarial certification of whether or not a multiemployer plan is in endangered status, and whether or not a multiemployer plan is or will be in critical status, for each plan year. This certification must be completed by the 90th day of the plan year and must be provided to the Secretary of the Treasury and to the plan sponsor. If the certification is with respect to a plan year that is within the plan's funding improvement period or rehabilitation period arising from a prior certification of endangered or critical status, the actuary must also certify whether or not the plan is making scheduled progress in meeting the requirements of its funding improvement or rehabilitation plan. Failure of the plan's actuary to certify the status of the plan is treated as a failure to file the annual report under section 502(c)(2) of the Employee Retirement Income Security Act of 1974 (ERISA). Thus, a penalty of up to $1,100 per day applies.

Under section 432(b)(1), a multiemployer plan is in endangered status if the plan is not in critical status and, as of the beginning of the plan year, (1) the plan's funded percentage for the plan year is less than 80 percent, or (2) the plan has an accumulated funding deficiency for the plan year or is projected to have an accumulated funding deficiency in any of the six succeeding plan years (taking into account amortization extensions under section 431(d)). Under section 432(i), a plan's funded percentage is the percentage determined by dividing the value of the plan's assets by the accrued liability of the plan.

---

[1] Section 302 and section 304 of the Employee Retirement Income Security Act of 1974, as amended (ERISA) sets forth funding rules that are parallel to those in section 412 and section 431 of the Code. Section 305 of ERISA sets forth additional rules for multiemployer plans that are parallel to those in section 432 of the Code. Under section 101 of Reorganization Plan No. 4 of 1978 (43 FR 47713) and section 302 of ERISA, the Secretary of the

Treasury has interpretive jurisdiction over the subject matter addressed in these proposed regulations for purposes of ERISA, as well as the Code. Thus, these Treasury Department regulations issued under section 432 of the Code apply as well for purposes of ERISA section 305.

Under section 432(b)(2), a multiemployer plan is in critical status for a plan year if it meets any of four specified tests. Under section 432(b)(2)(A), a plan is in critical status if, as of the beginning of the plan year: (1) the funded percentage of the plan is less than 65 percent and (2) the sum of (A) the market value of plan assets, plus (B) the present value of reasonably anticipated employer contributions for the current plan year and each of the six succeeding plan years is less than the present value of all nonforfeitable benefits projected to be payable under the plan during the current plan year and each of the six succeeding plan years (plus administrative expenses). For this purpose, employer contributions are determined assuming that the terms of all collective bargaining agreements pursuant to which the plan is maintained for the current plan year continue in effect for succeeding plan years.

Under section 432(b)(2)(B), a plan is in critical status if the plan has an accumulated funding deficiency for the current plan year or is projected to have an accumulated funding deficiency for any of the three succeeding plan years. For purposes of this test, the determination of accumulated funding deficiency is made not taking into account any amortization extension under section 431(d). In addition, if a plan has a funded percentage of 65 percent or less, the three-year period for projecting whether the plan will have an accumulated funding deficiency is extended to four years.

Under section 432(b)(2)(C), a plan is in critical status for the plan year if (1) the plan's normal cost for the current plan year, plus interest for the current plan year on the amount of unfunded benefit liabilities under the plan as of the last day of the preceding year, exceeds the present value of the reasonably anticipated employer and employee contributions for the current plan year, (2) the present value of nonforfeitable benefits of inactive participants is greater than the present value of nonforfeitable benefits of active participants, and (3) the plan has an accumulated funding deficiency for the current plan year, or is projected to have an accumulated funding deficiency for any of the four succeeding plan years (not taking into account amortization period extensions under section 431(d)).

Under section 432(b)(2)(D), a plan is in critical status for a plan year if the sum of (A) the market value of plan assets, and (B) the present value of the reasonably anticipated employer contributions for the current plan year and each of the four succeeding plan years is less than the present value of all benefits projected to be payable under the plan during the current plan year and each of the four succeeding plan years (plus administrative expenses). For this purpose, employer contributions are determined assuming that the terms of all collective bargaining agreements pursuant to which the plan is maintained for the current plan year continue in effect for succeeding plan years.

In making the determinations and projections applicable under the endangered and critical status rules, the plan actuary must make projections for the current and succeeding plan years of the current value of the assets of the plan and the present value of all liabilities to participants and beneficiaries under the plan for the current plan year as of the beginning of such year. The actuary's projections must be based on reasonable actuarial estimates, assumptions, and methods that offer the actuary's best estimate of anticipated experience under the plan. An exception to this rule applies in the case of projected industry activity. Any projection of activity in the industry or industries covered by the plan, including future covered employment and contribution levels, must be based on information provided by the plan sponsor, and the plan sponsor must act reasonably and in good faith. The projected present value of liabilities as of the beginning of the year must be based on either the most recent actuarial statement required with respect to the most recently filed annual report or the actuarial valuation for the preceding plan year.

Under section 432(b)(3)(B)(ii), any actuarial projection of plan assets must assume (1) reasonably anticipated employer contributions for the current and succeeding plan years, assuming that the terms of one or more collective bargaining agreements pursuant to which the plan is maintained for the current plan year continue in effect for the succeeding plan years, or (2) that employer contributions for the most recent plan year will continue indefinitely, but only if the plan actuary determines that there have been no significant demographic changes that would make continued application of such terms unreasonable.

The first year that an actuary certifies that a plan is in endangered or critical status establishes a timetable for a number of actions. Under section 432(b)(3)(D), within 30 days after the date of certification, the plan sponsor must notify the participants and beneficiaries, the bargaining parties, the PBGC and the Secretary of Labor of the plan's endangered or critical status. If it is certified that a plan is or will be in critical status, the plan sponsor must include in the notice an explanation of the possibility that (1) adjustable benefits (as defined in section

432(e)(8)) may be reduced and (2) such reductions may apply to participants and beneficiaries whose benefit commencement date is on or after the date such notice is provided for the first plan year in which the plan is in critical status.

If a plan is certified to be in critical status, the plan must take certain actions after notifying the plan participants of the critical status. Specifically, section 432(f)(2) restricts the payment of benefits that are in excess of a single life annuity (plus any social security supplement) effective on the date the notice is sent. Section 432(f)(2)(B) provides that this restriction does not apply to amounts that may be immediately distributed without the consent of the employee under section 411(a)(11) and to any makeup payment in the case of a retroactive annuity starting date or a similar payment of benefits owed with respect to a prior period. In addition, the plan sponsor must refrain from making any payment for the purchase of an irrevocable commitment from an insurer to pay benefits.

Sections 432(c)(1) and 432(e)(1) provide that in the first year that a plan is certified to be in endangered or critical status, the plan sponsor must adopt a funding improvement plan (in the case of a plan that is in endangered status) or a rehabilitation plan (in the case of a plan that is in critical status). The deadline for adoption of the funding improvement plan or rehabilitation plan is 240 days after the deadline for the certification. Accordingly, if the actuarial certification is made after the 90-day deadline, the amount of time for adopting the funding improvement plan or rehabilitation plan is shortened.

Section 432(c)(3) defines a funding improvement plan as a plan which consists of the actions, including options or a range of options, to be proposed to the bargaining parties, formulated to provide, based on reasonably anticipated experience and reasonable actuarial assumptions, for the attainment by the plan of certain requirements. Those requirements are based on a statutorily specified improvement in the plan's funding percentage from the percentage that applied on the first day of the funding improvement period. The first day of the funding improvement period is defined in section 432(c)(4) as the first day of the first plan year beginning after the earlier of (1) the second anniversary of the date of the adoption of the funding improvement plan or (2) the expiration of the collective bargaining agreements in effect on the due date for the actuarial certification of endangered status for the initial endangered year and covering, as of such due date, at least 75 percent of the active participants in such multiemployer plan.

Section 432(d)(1) sets forth rules that apply after the certification of endangered status and before the first day of the funding improvement period. After the adoption of the funding improvement plan, section 432(d)(2) prohibits any amendments that are inconsistent with the funding improvement plan. In addition, section 432(d)(2) provides special rules for acceptance of collective bargaining agreements and plan amendments that increase benefits.

A rehabilitation plan is a plan which consists of the actions, including options or a range of options, to be proposed to the bargaining parties, formulated to provide, based on reasonably anticipated experience and reasonable actuarial assumptions, for the attainment by the plan of certain requirements. Generally, the rehabilitation plan should enable the plan to emerge from critical status by the end of a 10-year period that begins after the earlier of (1) the second anniversary of the date of the adoption of the rehabilitation plan or (2) the expiration of the collective bargaining agreements in effect on the due date for the actuarial certification of critical status for the initial critical year and covering, as of such due date, at least 75 percent of the active participants in such multiemployer plan. For this purpose a plan emerges from critical status when the plan actuary certifies that the plan is not projected to have an accumulated funding deficiency for the plan year or any of the nine succeeding plan years, without regard to the use of the shortfall method and taking into account amortization period extensions under section 431(d). As an alternative, if the plan sponsor determines that, based on reasonable actuarial assumptions and upon exhaustion of all reasonable measures, the plan cannot reasonably be expected to emerge from critical status by the end of the 10-year period, the requirements for a rehabilitation plan are that the plan include reasonable measures to emerge from critical status at a later time or to forestall possible insolvency (within the meaning of section 4245 of ERISA).

Section 432(e)(8) allows a rehabilitation plan for a plan that is in critical status to provide for a reduction of certain "adjustable" benefits that would otherwise be protected by section 411(d)(6). These adjustable benefits include early retirement benefits and retirement-type subsidies within the meaning of section 411(d)(6)(B)(i). Under section 432(e)(8)(A)(ii), no reduction will apply to a participant whose benefit commencement date is before the date the notice under section 432(b)(3)(D) for the initial critical year is provided. Under section

432(e)(8)(B), except with respect to certain benefit increases described in 432(e)(8)(A)(iv)(III), a plan is not permitted to reduce the level of a participant's accrued benefit payable at normal retirement age. Furthermore, section 432(e)(8)(C) prohibits any reduction until 30 days after plan participants and beneficiaries, employers and employee organizations are notified of the reduction.

In years after the initial critical year or initial endangered year, sections 432(c)(6) and 432(e)(3)(B) provide that the plan sponsor must annually update the funding improvement or rehabilitation plan. This includes updating the schedule of contribution rates. Updates are required to be filed with the plan's annual report.

Section 432(f)(4) sets forth rules that apply after the certification of critical status and before the first day of the rehabilitation period. After the adoption of the rehabilitation plan, section 432(f)(1) prohibits any amendments that are inconsistent with the rehabilitation plan.

Section 432(h) provides rules for the treatment of employees who participate in the plan even though they are not covered by a collective bargaining agreement.

Section 432(i) provides a number of definitions that apply for purposes of section 432. For example, under section 432(i)(8), the actuary's determination with respect to a plan's normal cost, actuarial accrued liability, and improvements in a plan's funded percentage must be based on the unit credit funding method (whether or not that method is used for the plan's actuarial valuation).

Section 432 is effective for plan years beginning on or after January 1, 2008. Section 212(e)(2) of PPA '06 provides a special rule permitting a plan to provide the notice described in section 432(b)(3)(D) on an early basis. Specifically, if the plan actuary certifies that the plan is reasonably expected to be in critical status for the first plan year beginning after 2007, the plan is permitted to provide the notice described in section 432(b)(3)(D) at any time between the enactment of PPA '06 and the date the notice is otherwise required to be provided.

Explanation of Provisions

Overview

These regulations provide guidance with respect to certain of the provisions of section 432. Specifically, these regulations provide guidance regarding the determination of when a plan is in endangered status or critical status and the associated notices. These regulations do not provide guidance with respect to all issues relating to a multiemployer plan that is in endangered or critical status. For example, no guidance is provided on the parameters for the adoption of a funding improvement plan or rehabilitation plan. Guidance with respect to additional issues will be included in a second set of regulations that are expected to be issued this year.

§ 1.432(a)-1 General rules relating to section 432

Section 1.432(a)-1 provides general rules relating to section 432, including definitions of certain terms used for purposes of section 432 and the special rules that apply to participants in multiemployer plans who are not participating pursuant to a collective bargaining agreement. (Corrected by FR Doc. 2008-7558, 04/10/2008).

The regulations provide that effective on the date that a notice of critical status for the initial critical year is sent to the plan participants, the plan must not pay any benefit in excess of the monthly amount paid under a single life annuity (plus any social security supplement) and is not permitted to purchase an irrevocable commitment from an insurer to pay benefits. The restriction does not apply to the small-dollar cashouts allowed under section 411(a)(11) nor to the make-up payments under a retroactive annuity starting date.

The regulations provide that if the notice described in section 432(b)(3)(D) has been sent and the restrictions provided under section 432(f)(2) have been applied, and it is later determined that the restrictions should not have been applied, then the plan must correct any benefit payments that were restricted in error. The regulations provide two examples of situations requiring this correction, each of which involves an actuary certifying that the plan is reasonably expected to be in critical status for the first plan year beginning after 2007, followed by an early notification of critical status that is made to employees under the rules of section 212(e)(2) of PPA '06. In one example of a plan taking actions that require correction, the plan restricts benefits before the first plan year beginning after 2007 (the effective date of section 432). In the second such example, the plan is not in critical status for the first plan year beginning after 2007 (even though the enrolled actuary for the plan had certified that it is reasonably expected that the plan will be in critical status with respect to that year).

The regulations incorporate a number of definitions listed in section 432(i) along with other definitions that are located in sections 432(c) and (e). The regulations do not include the broad provision under section 432(i)(8) to use the unit credit funding method for purposes of the plan's "normal cost, actuarial accrued liability, and improvements in a plan's funded percentage." Instead, consistent with the intended scope of section 432(i)(8), the regulations require the use of this funding method solely for purposes of determining a plan's funded percentage and the section 432(b)(2)(C)(i) comparison of contributions with the sum of the plan's normal cost and interest on the amount of unfunded liability. Thus, the determination of whether a plan is projected to have an accumulated funding deficiency in the determination of a plan's status under section 432 is based on the plan's actual funding method, rather than the unit credit funding method. The regulations substitute the term "initial endangered year" for the statutory term "initial determination year."

In addition, the regulations provide guidance for plans that change their status in subsequent years. For example, a plan that is in critical status may emerge from that status and later reenter critical status. In such a circumstance, the year of reentry into critical status is treated as the initial critical year. Similarly, a plan that is in endangered status may have a status change and at a later date reenter endangered status. In such a circumstance, the year of reentry into endangered status is treated as the initial endangered year.

§ 1.432(b)-1 Determination of status and adoption of a plan

The regulations provide rules for the determination of whether a plan is in endangered status or critical status within the meaning of section 432(b)(1) and (2). These rules reflect the different ways a plan can be in endangered status under section 432(b)(1)(A) or (B) and in critical status under section 432(b)(2)(A), (B), (C), or (D). The regulations also provide that a plan is in critical status for a plan year if it was in critical status in the immediately preceding year and the plan does not meet the emergence from critical status rule of section 432(e)(4)(B). Thus, a plan that was in critical status for the prior year will remain in critical status if the enrolled actuary for the plan certifies that the plan is projected to have an accumulated funding deficiency for the plan year or any of the 9 succeeding plan years, without regard to the use of the shortfall funding method, but taking into account any extensions of the amortization periods under section 431(d).

The regulations provide limited guidance on the actuarial projections that are used for purposes of the certification of status by the enrolled actuary for the plan. The projections must generally be based on reasonable actuarial assumptions and methods that, as under section 431(c)(3), offer the actuary's best estimate of anticipated experience under the plan. The actuarial projection of future contributions and assets must assume either that the terms of the one or more collective bargaining agreements pursuant to which the plan is maintained for the current plan year continue in effect for succeeding plan years, or that the dollar amount of employer contributions for the most recent plan year will continue indefinitely. If the actuarial projections assume the continued maintenance of the collective bargaining agreements, the plan sponsor must provide a projection of activity in the industry, including future covered employment, to the plan actuary, and the actuary is permitted to rely on those projections. In making these projections, the plan sponsor must act reasonably and in good faith. The alternative assumption that the dollar amount of contributions remains unchanged into the future is only available if the enrolled actuary for the plan determines there have been no significant demographic changes that would make such assumption unreasonable. In addition, the regulations provide that the alternative assumption is not available for purposes of determining whether the plan is in critical status under the tests in section 432(b)(2)(A) and (D).

The projected present value of liabilities as of the beginning of such year is determined based on the most recent information reported on the most recent of either the actuarial statement required under section 103(d) of ERISA that has been filed with respect to the most recent year, or the actuarial valuation for the preceding plan year.

The regulations provide that, for purposes of section 432, if the plan received an extension of any amortization period under section 412(e), the extension is treated the same as an extension under section 431(d). Thus, such an extension is taken into account in determining endangered status under section 432(b)(1)(B) and emergence from critical status under section 432(e)(4)(B). In contrast, such an extension is not taken into account in determining whether a plan has or will have an accumulated funding deficiency for purposes of determining critical status under section 432(b)(2)(B) and (C).

The regulations describe the content of the annual certification required under section 432(b)(3) that must be sent to the plan sponsor and the IRS. The annual certification must be provided regardless of whether the plan is in endangered or critical status. If the plan is certified to be in endangered or critical status, then the certification must identify the plan, the plan sponsor, and the enrolled actuary who signs the certification; provide contact information for the plan sponsor and actuary; state whether or not the plan is in endangered or critical status for the plan year; and, if the certification is for a year other than the initial endangered year or the initial critical year, whether the plan is making the scheduled progress described in the plan's funding improvement plan or rehabilitation plan. The regulations also provide an IRS address to which the certification is to be mailed.

The regulations also provide that the content of the annual certification and the IRS address to which it is mailed may be added to or modified in guidance of general applicability to be published in the Internal Revenue Bulletin. Such additional information may include, for instance, which endangered status or critical status standard(s) applies to the plan; supporting information for the classification; a description of the actuarial assumptions used in making the certification; and a projection of the plan's funded percentage for future years. The guidance may also require additional supporting information for certifications made prior to the issuance of the guidance.

The regulations provide guidance on the notice required under section 432(b)(3)(D).[2] In particular the regulations require that, in the case of a plan that is in critical status and which provides for benefits that would be restricted under section 432(f)(2), the notice for the initial critical year must tell participants about the restriction. A plan sponsor that sends the model notice provided by the Secretary of Labor pursuant to section 432(b)(3)(D)(iii) satisfies this requirement.

If a section 432(b)(3)(D) notice for such a plan was sent prior to the deadline in that section and the notice did not contain the disclosure regarding the immediate restriction on benefits under section 432(f)(2), then the regulations provide that the notice does not satisfy the requirements for notice under section 432(b)(3)(D). Accordingly, the restrictions under section 432(f)(2) do not apply as a result of the issuance of such a notice and the plan will not be treated as having issued the notice for purposes of the section 432(e)(8)(A)(ii) restriction on reducing adjustable benefits for participants whose benefit commencement dates are prior to the issuance of that notice. However, if additional notice that includes all of the information required under the regulations is provided prior to the required date for notice for the initial critical year under section 432(b)(3)(D) (that is, 30 days after the certification for the plan year), then the notice requirements of section 432(b)(3)(D) are satisfied as of the date of the later notice. In such a case, if the earlier notice contained the information described in section 432(b)(3)(D)(ii), then the date of that earlier notice will apply for purposes of the section 432(e)(8)(A)(ii) restriction.

The regulations reflect the rules of section 212(e)(2) of PPA under which a plan sponsor is permitted to send an early notice to plan participants. This early notice, which applies solely to the first plan year beginning after 2007, is only available if the plan actuary certifies to the plan sponsor that the plan is reasonably expected to be in critical status for that initial plan year. This preliminary certification that the plan is reasonably expected to be in critical status is different from the annual certification that the plan actuary must make; accordingly, the plan actuary must still certify whether the plan is in critical or endangered status (or in neither critical nor endangered status) for that plan year by the normal 90-day deadline for the certification.

Proposed legislation

As of the date of the issuance of these proposed regulations, bills have been introduced in the House of Representatives and the Senate that would exclude from the section 432(f)(2) limitation on accelerated benefits a distribution with an annuity starting date that is before the date that the notice under section 432(b)(3)(D) is provided.[3] Section 1.432(a)-1(a)(3)(iii)(C) has been reserved in order to accommodate any enacted changes.

Effective/Applicability Dates

These regulations apply to plan years ending after **March 18, 2008,** but only with respect to plan years that begin on or after January 1, 2008. These regulations do not address the sunset provision provided by PPA '06 section 221(c).

Special Analyses

It has been determined that this notice of proposed rulemaking is not a significant regulatory action as defined in Executive Order 12866. Therefore, a regulatory assessment is not required. It has also been determined that section 553(b) of the Administrative Procedure Act (5 U.S.C. chapter 5) does not apply to these regulations. It is hereby certified that the collection of information imposed by these proposed regulations will not have a significant economic impact on a substantial number of small entities. Accordingly, a regulatory flexibility analysis is not required. The estimated burden imposed by the collection of information contained in these proposed regulations is 0.75 hours per respondent. Moreover, most of this burden is attributable to the requirement for a qualified multiemployer defined benefit plan's enrolled actuary to provide a timely certification of the plan's funding status. In addition, if a plan is certified that it is or will be in critical or endangered status, the plan sponsor is required to notify the Department of Labor, the Pension Benefit Guaranty Corporation, the bargaining parties, participants, and beneficiaries of the status designation. For plans in critical status, the plan sponsor is required to include an explanation of the possibility that adjustable benefits may be reduced and that certain benefits are restricted as of the date the notice is sent. Pursuant to section 7805(f) of the Internal Revenue Code, this regulations has been submitted to the Chief Counsel for Advocacy of the Small Business Administration for comment on its impact on small business.

Comments and Requests for a Public Hearing

Before these proposed regulations are adopted as final regulations, consideration will be given to any written (one signed and eight (8) copies) or electronic comments that are submitted timely to the IRS. The IRS and the Treasury Department request comments on the clarity of the proposed rules and how they may be made easier to understand. All comments will be available for public inspection and copying. A public hearing will be scheduled if requested in writing by any person who timely submits written comments. If a public hearing is scheduled, notice of the date, time, and place of the public hearing will be published in the **Federal Register.**

Drafting Information

The principal author of this regulation is Bruce Perlin, Office of Division Counsel/Associate Chief Counsel (Tax Exempt and Government Entities). However, other personnel from the IRS and the Treasury Department participated in their development.

List of Subjects in 29 CFR Part 1

Income taxes, Reporting and recordkeeping requirements.

Proposed Amendments to the Regulations

Accordingly, 26 CFR part 1 is proposed to be amended as follows:

PART 1—INCOME TAXES

Paragraph 1. The authority citation for part 1 continues to read in part as follows:

Authority: 26 U.S.C. 7805 * * *

Par. 2. Section 1.432(a)-1 is added to read as follows:

§ 1.432(a)-1 General rules relating to section 432.

(a) *In general*—(1) *Overview.* This section provides rules relating to multiemployer plans (within the meaning of section 414(f)) that are in endangered status or critical status under section 432. Section 432 and this section only apply to multiemployer plans that are in effect on July 16, 2006. Paragraph (b) of this section sets forth definitions of terms that apply for purposes of section 432. Paragraph (c) of this section sets forth special rules for plans described in section 404(c) and for the treatment of nonbargained participation.

(2) *Plans in endangered status*—(i) *Plan sponsor must adopt funding improvement plan.* If a plan is in endangered status, the plan sponsor must adopt and implement a funding improvement plan that satisfies the requirements of section 432(c).

(ii) *Restrictions applicable to plans in endangered status.* If a plan is in endangered status, the plan and plan sponsor must satisfy the requirements of section 432(d)(1) during the funding plan adoption period specified in section 432(c)(8).

---

[2] Under section 432(b)(3)(D)(ii), the Secretary of Labor is to prescribe a model notice that a multiemployer plan may use to satisfy this notice requirement.

[3] See H.R. 3361 (August 3, 2007) and S. 1974 (August 2, 2007) at sections 3(b)(1)(E) and 3(b)(2)(E)(ii). However, S. 1974, as amended and passed by the Senate on December 19, 2007, did not include this provision.

(iii) *Restrictions applicable after the adoption of funding improvement plan.* In the case of a plan that is in endangered status after adoption of the funding improvement plan, the plan and the plan sponsor must satisfy the requirements of section 432(d)(2) until the end of the funding improvement period.

(3) *Plans in critical status*—(i) *Plan sponsor must adopt rehabilitation plan.* If a plan is in critical status, the plan sponsor must adopt and implement a rehabilitation plan that satisfies the requirements of section 432(e).

(ii) *Restrictions applicable to plans in critical status.* If a plan is in critical status, the plan and the plan sponsor must satisfy the requirements of section 432(f)(4) during the rehabilitation plan adoption period as defined in section 432(e)(5). The plan must also apply the restrictions on single sum and other accelerated benefits set forth in paragraph (a)(3)(iii) of this section.

(iii) *Restrictions on single sums and other accelerated benefits*—(A) *In general.* A plan in critical status is required to provide that, effective on the date the notice of certification of the plan's critical status for the initial critical year under §1.432(b)-1(e) is sent, no payment in excess of the monthly amount payable under a single life annuity (plus any social security supplements described in the last sentence of section 411(a)(9)), and no payment for the purchase of an irrevocable commitment from an insurer to pay benefits, may be made except as provided in section 432(f)(2). A plan amendment that provides for these restrictions does not violate section 411(d)(6).

(B) *Exceptions.* Pursuant to section 432(f)(2)(B), the restrictions under this paragraph (a)(3)(iii) do not apply to a benefit which under section 411(a)(11) may be immediately distributed without the consent of the participant or to any makeup payment in the case of a retroactive annuity starting date or any similar payment of benefits owed with respect to a prior period.

(C) [Reserved.]

(D) *Correction of erroneous restrictions.* If the notice described in §1.432(b)-1(e) has been sent and the restrictions provided under this paragraph (a)(3)(iii) have been applied, and it is later determined that the restrictions should not have been applied, then the plan must correct any benefit payments that were restricted in error. Thus, for example, if pursuant to section 212(e)(2) of the Pension Protection Act of 2006, Public Law 109-280, 120 Stat. 780 the enrolled actuary for the plan certified that it was reasonably expected that the plan would be in critical status with respect to the first plan year beginning after 2007, and the notice described in §1.432(b)-1(e)(3)(i) was sent, but the plan is not later certified to be in critical status for that plan year, then the plan must correct any benefit payments that were restricted after the notice was sent. Similarly, if the enrolled actuary for the plan certified that it was reasonably expected that the plan would be in critical status with respect to the first plan year beginning after 2007, and the notice described in §1.432(b)-1(e)(3)(i) was sent before the first day of that plan year, the restriction on benefits under section 432(f)(2) first applies beginning on the first day of the first plan year beginning after 2007. If the plan restricts benefits before that date, then the plan must correct any improperly restricted benefits.

(iv) *Restrictions applicable after the adoption of rehabilitation plan.* In the case of a plan that is in critical status after the adoption of the rehabilitation plan, the plan and the plan sponsor must satisfy the requirements of section 432(f)(1) until the end of the rehabilitation period.

(b) *Definitions.* The following definitions apply for purposes of section 432 and the regulations:

(1) *Accumulated funding deficiency.* The term accumulated funding deficiency has the same meaning as the term accumulated funding deficiency under section 431(a).

(2) *Active participant.* The term active participant means a participant who is in covered service under the plan.

(3) *Bargaining party.* Except as provided in paragraph (c)(1) of this section, the term bargaining party means an employer who has an obligation to contribute under the plan and an employee organization which, for purposes of collective bargaining, represents plan participants employed by an employer which has an obligation to contribute under the plan.

(4) *Benefit commencement date.* The term benefit commencement date means the annuity starting date (or in the case of a retroactive annuity starting date, the date on which benefit payments begin).

(5) *Critical status.* A multiemployer plan is in critical status if the plan meets one of the tests set forth in §1.432(b)-1(c).

(6) *Endangered status.* A plan is in endangered status if the plan meets one of the tests set forth in §1.432(b)-1(b).

(7) *Funded percentage.* The term funded percentage means a fraction (expressed as a percentage) the numerator of which is the actuarial value of the plan's assets as determined under section 431(c)(2) and the denominator of which is the accrued liability of the plan, determined using the actuarial assumptions described in section 431(c)(3) and the unit credit funding method.

(8) *Funding improvement period for endangered or seriously endangered plans.* The term funding improvement period means the period that begins on the first day of the first plan year beginning after the earlier of the second anniversary of the date of the adoption of the funding improvement plan, or the expiration of the collective bargaining agreements that are in effect on the due date for the actuarial certification of endangered status for the initial endangered year and which cover, as of such due date, at least 75 percent of the active participants in the plan. The funding improvement period ends on the last day of the 10th year (15 years for seriously endangered plans, except as provided in section 432(c)(5)) after it begins or, if earlier, the date of the change in status described in section 432(c)(4)(C).

(9) *Funding plan adoption period.* The term funding plan adoption period means the period that begins on the date of the actuarial certification for the initial endangered year and ends on the day before the first day of the funding improvement period.

(10) *Inactive participant.* The term inactive participant means —

(i) A participant who is not an active participant,

(ii) A beneficiary under the plan, or

(iii) An alternate payee under the plan.

(11) *Initial critical year.* The term initial critical year means the first year for which the enrolled actuary for the plan has certified that the plan is or will be in critical status. If a plan is in critical status in one year, emerges from critical status in a subsequent year and then returns to critical status, the year of reentry into critical status is treated as the initial critical year with respect to subsequent years.

(12) *Initial endangered year.* The term initial endangered year means the first year for which the enrolled actuary for the plan has certified that the plan is in endangered status. If a plan is in endangered status in one year, changes from endangered status in a subsequent year and then returns to endangered status, the year of reentry into endangered status is treated as the initial endangered year with respect to subsequent years.

(13) *Nonbargained participant.* The term nonbargained participant means a participant in the plan whose participation is other than pursuant to a collective bargaining agreement within the meaning of section 7701(a)(46). A participant will not be treated as a nonbargained participant merely because the participant is no longer covered by the collective bargaining agreement solely as a result of retirement or severance from employment.

(14) *Obligation to contribute.* The term obligation to contribute means an obligation to contribute arising under one or more collective bargaining (or related) agreements or as a result of a duty under applicable labor-management relations law.

(15) *Plan sponsor.* Except as provided in paragraph (c)(1) of this section, the term plan sponsor means the association, committee, joint board of trustees, or other similar group of representatives of the parties who establish or maintain the plan.

(16) *Rehabilitation period.* The term rehabilitation period means the period that begins on the first day of the first plan year beginning after the earlier of the second anniversary of the date of the adoption of the rehabilitation plan, or the expiration of the collective bargaining agreements that are in effect on the due date for the actuarial certification of critical status for the initial critical year and which cover, as of such due date, at least 75 percent of the active participants in the plan. The rehabilitation period ends on the last day of the 10th year after it begins or, if earlier, the plan year preceding the plan year in which the plan has emerged from critical status as described in section 432(e)(4)(B).

(17) *Rehabilitation plan adoption period.* The term rehabilitation plan adoption period means the period that begins on the date of the actuarial certification for the initial critical year and ends on the day before the first day of the rehabilitation period.

(18) *Seriously endangered status.* A plan is in seriously endangered status if the plan is in endangered status and is described in both §1.432(b)-1(b)(2) and (3).

(c) *Special rules*—(1) *Plan described in section 404(c).* In the case of a plan described in section 404(c), or a continuation of such a plan, the association of employers that is the employer settlor of the plan is treated as a bargaining party and is treated as the plan sponsor for purposes of section 432.

(2) *Plans covering both bargained and nonbargained participants.* In the case of an employer that contributes to a plan with respect to both employees who are covered by one or more collective bargaining agreements and employees who are nonbargained participants, if the plan is in endangered status or critical status, benefits of and contributions for the nonbargained participants (including surcharges on those contributions) are determined as if those nonbargained participants were covered under the employer's collective bargaining agreement in effect when the plan entered endangered or critical status that is the first to expire.

(3) *Plans covering nonbargained participants only.* In the case of an employer that contributes to a multiemployer plan only with respect to employees who are not covered by a collective bargaining agreement, section 432 and the regulations thereunder are applied as if the employer were the bargaining party, and its participation agreement with the plan were a collective bargaining agreement with a term ending on the first day of the plan year beginning after the employer is provided the schedules described in sections 432(c) and (e).

(d) *Effective/applicability date.* These regulations apply to plan years ending after **June 18, 2008,** but only with respect to plan years that begin on or after January 1, 2008.

Par. 3. Section 1.432(b)-1 is added to read as follows:

§ *1.432(b)-1 Determination of status and adoption of a plan.*

(a) *In general.* This section provides rules relating to multiemployer plans (within the meaning of section 414(f)) that are in endangered status or critical status under section 432. Section 432 and this section only apply to multiemployer plans that are in effect on July 16, 2006. Paragraph (b) of this section sets forth the factors for determining whether a plan is in endangered status. Paragraph (c) of this section sets forth the factors for determining whether a plan is in critical status. Paragraph (d) sets forth the requirements for the annual certification by the plan's enrolled actuary. Paragraph (e) of this section describes the notice to employees that is required for plans that are in endangered or critical status.

(b) *Determination of endangered status*—(1) *In general.* A plan is in endangered status for a plan year if, as determined by the enrolled actuary for the plan, the plan is not in critical status for the plan year and if, as of the beginning of the plan year, the plan is described either in paragraph (b)(2) of this section or paragraph (b)(3) of this section. The enrolled actuary's determination of whether a plan is in endangered status is made under the rules of paragraph (d)(5) of this section.

(2) *Endangered status based on funding percentage.* A plan is described in this paragraph (b)(2) for a plan year if the plan's funded percentage for such plan year is less than 80 percent.

(3) *Endangered status based on projection of funding deficiency.* A plan is described in this paragraph (b)(3) for a plan year if the plan has an accumulated funding deficiency for such plan year (or is projected to have such an accumulated funding deficiency for any of the 6 succeeding plan years), taking into account any extension of amortization periods under section 431(d).

(c) *Critical Status*—(1) *In general.* A multiemployer plan is in critical status for a plan year if, as determined by the enrolled actuary for the plan, the plan is described in one or more of paragraphs (c)(2) through (c)(6) of this section as of the beginning of the plan year. The enrolled actuary's determination of critical status must be made in accordance with the rules of paragraph (d)(5) of this section. Notwithstanding paragraph (d)(5)(iii) of this section, for purposes of applying the critical status tests described in paragraphs (c)(2) and (c)(5) of this section, the actuary must assume that the terms of all collective bargaining agreements pursuant to which the plan is maintained for the current plan year continue in effect for succeeding plan years.

(2) *Critical status based on 6-year projection of benefit payments.* A plan is described in this paragraph (c)(2) if the funded percentage of the plan is less than 65 percent, and the present value of all nonforfeitable benefits projected to be payable under the plan during the current plan year and each of the 6 succeeding plan years (plus administrative expenses for such plan years) is greater than the sum of—

(i) The fair market value of plan assets, plus

(ii) The present value of the reasonably anticipated employer contributions for the current plan year and the 6 succeeding plan years.

(3) *Critical status based on short term funding deficiency.* A plan is described in this paragraph (c)(3) if—

(i) The plan has an accumulated funding deficiency for the current plan year, not taking into account any extension of amortization periods under section 431(d), or

(ii) The plan is projected to have an accumulated funding deficiency for any of the 3 succeeding plan years (4 succeeding plan years if the funded percentage of the plan is 65 percent or less), not taking into account any extension of amortization periods under section 431(d).

(4) *Critical status based on contributions less than normal cost plus interest.* A plan is described in this paragraph (c)(4) if—

(i) The present value of the reasonably anticipated employer and employee contributions for the current plan year is less than the sum of—

(A) The plan's normal cost (determined under the unit credit funding method), and

(B) Interest (determined at the rate used for determining costs under the plan) on the excess if any of—

(*1*) The accrued liability of the plan (determined using the actuarial assumptions described in section 431(c)(3) and the unit credit funding method) over

(*2*) The actuarial value of assets determined under section 431(c)(2),

(ii) The present value, as of the beginning of the current plan year, of nonforfeitable benefits of inactive participants is greater than the present value of nonforfeitable benefits of active participants, and

(iii) The plan has an accumulated funding deficiency for the current plan year (or is projected to have such a deficiency for any of the 4 succeeding plan years), not taking into account any extension of amortization periods under section 431(d).

(5) *Critical status based on 4-year projection of benefit payments.* A plan is described in this paragraph (c)(5) if the present value of all benefits projected to be payable under the plan during the current plan year or any of the 4 succeeding plan years (plus administrative expenses for such plan years) is greater than the sum of—

(i) The fair market value of plan assets, plus

(ii) The present value of the reasonably anticipated employer contributions for the current plan year and each of the 4 succeeding plan years.

(6) *Critical status based on failure to meet emergence criteria.* A plan is described in this paragraph (c)(6) if—

(i) The plan was in critical status for the immediately preceding plan year, and

(ii) The enrolled actuary for the plan has certified that the plan is projected to have an accumulated funding deficiency for the plan year or any of the 9 succeeding plan years, without regard to the use of the shortfall funding method but taking into account any extensions of the amortization periods under section 431(d).

(d) *Annual certification by the plan's enrolled actuary*—(1) *In general.* Not later than the 90th day of each plan year of a multiemployer plan, the enrolled actuary for the plan must certify to the Secretary of the Treasury and to the plan sponsor—

(i) Whether or not the plan is in endangered status for such plan year;

(ii) Whether or not the plan is or will be in critical status for such plan year, and

(iii) In the case of a plan which is in a funding improvement or rehabilitation period, whether or not the plan is making the scheduled progress in meeting the requirements of its funding improvement or rehabilitation plan.

(2) *Transmittal of certification*—(i) *Transmittal to the plan sponsor.* The certification of plan status described in paragraph (d)(1) must be submitted to the plan sponsor at the address stated by the plan sponsor on their Annual Report (Form 5500) or such other address as the plan sponsor may designate in writing for receipt of this certification.

(ii) *Transmittal to the Secretary of the Treasury.* Except as provided in guidance of general applicability to be published in the Internal Revenue Bulletin, the annual certification of plan status described in paragraph (d)(1) must be transmitted to the Secretary of the Treasury by mailing the certification to:

Internal Revenue Service

Employee Plans Compliance Unit

Group 7602 (SE:TEGE:EP)

Room 1700 - 17th Floor

230 S. Dearborn Street

Chicago, IL 60604

(3) *Content of annual certification*—(i) *In general.* The annual certification must contain the information described in this paragraph (d)(3). The Secretary may add to or otherwise modify the requirements in this paragraph (d)(3) in guidance of general applicability to be published in the Internal Revenue Bulletin.

(ii) *Plan identification.* The annual certification must include the name of the plan; the plan number; the name, address, and telephone number of the plan sponsor; and the plan year for which the certification is being made.

(iii) *Enrolled actuary identification.* The annual certification must include the name, address and telephone number of the enrolled actuary signing the certification; the actuary's enrollment identification number; the actuary's signature, and the date of the signature.

(iv) *Information on plan status.* The annual certification must state whether the plan is in endangered status (which includes seriously endangered status); critical status, or neither endangered nor critical status.

(v) *Information on scheduled progress.* If the annual certification is made with respect to a plan year that is within the plan's funding improvement period or rehabilitation period arising from a prior certification of endangered or critical status, the actuary must also certify whether or not the plan is making scheduled progress in meeting the requirements of its funding improvement or rehabilitation plan.

(4) *Penalty for failure to secure timely actuarial certification.* A failure of a plan's actuary to certify the plan's status under this paragraph (d) by the date specified in paragraph (d)(1) of this section is treated as a failure or refusal by the plan administrator to file the annual report required to be filed with the Secretary of Labor under section 101(b)(4) of the Employee Retirement Income Security Act of 1974.

(5) *Actuarial projections of assets and liabilities*—(i) *In general.* In making the determinations and projections under section 432(b) and this section, the enrolled actuary for the plan must make projections required for the current and succeeding plan years of the current value of the assets of the plan and the present value of all liabilities to participants and beneficiaries under the plan for the current plan year as of the beginning of such year. These projections must be based on reasonable actuarial estimates, assumptions, and methods in accordance with section 431(c)(3) and that offer the actuary's best estimate of anticipated experience under the plan. Notwithstanding the previous sentence, the actuary is permitted to rely on the plan sponsor's projection of activity in the industry provided under paragraph (d)(5)(iii) of this section. The projected present value of liabilities as of the beginning of such year must be determined based on the most recent information reported on the most recent of either—

(A) The actuarial statement required under section 103(d) of the Employee Retirement Income Security Act of 1974 that has been filed with respect to the most recent year, or

(B) The actuarial valuation for the preceding plan year.

(ii) *Determinations of future contributions.* Any actuarial projection of plan assets shall assume either—

(A) Reasonably anticipated employer contributions for the current and succeeding plan years, assuming that the terms of the one or more collective bargaining agreements pursuant to which the plan is maintained for the current plan year continue in effect for succeeding plan years, or

(B) That employer contributions for the most recent plan year will continue indefinitely, but only if the enrolled actuary for the plan determines there have been no significant demographic changes that would make such assumption unreasonable.

(iii) *Projected industry activity.* The plan sponsor shall provide any necessary projection of activity in the industry, including future covered employment, to the plan actuary. For this purpose, the plan sponsor must act reasonably and in good faith.

(6) *Treatment of amortization extensions under section 412(e).* For purposes of section 432, if the plan received an extension of any amortization period under section 412(e), the extension is treated the same as an extension under section 431(d). Thus, such an extension is not taken into account in determining whether a plan has or will have an accumulated funding deficiency under paragraph (c)(3) and (c)(4) of this section, but it is taken into account in determining whether a plan has or will have an accumulated funding deficiency under paragraph (b)(3) of this section.

(e) *Notice of endangered or critical status*—(1) *In general.* In any case in which the enrolled actuary for the plan certifies that a multiemployer plan is or will be in endangered or critical status for a plan year, the plan sponsor must, not later than 30 days after the date of the certification, provide notification of the endangered or critical status to the participants and beneficiaries, the bargaining parties, the Pension Benefit Guaranty Corporation, and the Secretary of Labor.

(2) *Plans in critical status.* If it is certified that a multiemployer plan is or will be in critical status for a plan year, the plan sponsor must include in the notice an explanation of the possibility that adjustable benefits (as defined in section 432(e)(8)) may be reduced, and such reductions may apply to participants and beneficiaries whose benefit commencement date is on or after the date such notice is provided for the first plan year in which the plan is in critical status. If the plan provides benefits that are restricted under section 432(f)(2), the notice must also include an explanation that the plan cannot pay single sums and similar benefits described in section 432(f)(2) that are greater than the monthly amount due under a single life annuity. A plan sponsor that sends the model notice issued by the Secretary of Labor pursuant to section 432(b)(3)(D)(iii) satisfies this requirement.

(3) *Transition rules*—(i) *Early notice permitted.* If, after August 17, 2006, the enrolled actuary for the plan certifies that a plan is reasonably expected to be in critical status with respect to the first plan year beginning after 2007, then the notice described in this paragraph (e) may be provided before the date the actuary certifies the plan is in critical status for that plan year. The ability to provide early notice does not extend the otherwise applicable deadline for providing the notice under paragraph (e)(1) of this section.

(ii) *Reformation of prior notice.* If notice has been provided prior to the date required under paragraph (e)(1) of this section, but the notice did not include all of the information described in paragraph (e)(2) of this section, then that notice will not satisfy the requirements for notice under section 432(b)(3)(D). Accordingly, the restrictions under section 432(f)(2) will not apply as a result of the issuance of such a notice. However, if prior to the date notice is required to be provided under paragraph (e)(1) of this section additional notice is provided that includes all of the information required under paragraph (e)(2) of this section, then the notice requirements of section 432(b)(3)(D) are satisfied as of the date of that additional notice and the restrictions of section 432(f)(2) will apply beginning on that date. In such a case, the date of the earlier notice will still apply for purposes of section 432(e)(8)(A)(ii) provided that the earlier notice included all of the information required under section 432(b)(3)(D)(ii).

(f) *Effective applicability.* These regulations apply to plan years ending after **June 18, 2008,** but only with respect to plan years that begin on or after January 1, 2008.

Deputy Commissioner for Services and Enforcement.

Linda E. Stiff

¶ 20,262J

IRS: Notice requirements: Benefit accruals: Plan amendments.—The IRS has issued proposed regulations which would amend the requirements for providing notice to certain affected persons when a plan significantly reduces benefit accruals. The proposed regulations set forth timing rules for ERISA §204(h) notices for plan amendments which are permitted to be effective before the applicable amendment date, and reflect other changes to notice requirements made by the Pension Protection Act of 2006 (PPA; P.L. 109–280).

The proposed regulations were published in the Federal Register on March 21, 2008 (73 FR 15101). The regulations were finalized on November 24, 2009 (74 FR 61270). The preamble to the final regulations is at ¶ 23,267. The final regulations are at ¶ 12,231 and ¶ 13,648W-87.

¶ 20,262K

IRS proposed regulations: Minimum required contribution.—The IRS has issued proposed regulations under Code Sec. 430 which provide guidance on the minimum contribution rules applicable to single employer defined benefit plans.

The proposed regulations, which were published in the Federal Register on April 15, 2008 (73 FR 20203), are reproduced below.The regulations were finalized on September 9, 2015 (80 FR 54373). The preamble to the final regulations is at ¶ 23,318. The final regulations are at ¶ 13,151L-2, ¶ 13,151L-12, ¶ 13,151L-19, ¶ 13,151L-32, ¶ 13,151O-6, and ¶ 13,600I.

[4830-01-p]

DEPARTMENT OF THE TREASURY

Internal Revenue Service

26 CFR Parts 1 and 54

[REG-108508-08]

RIN 1545-BH71

Determination of Minimum Required Pension Contributions

AGENCY: Internal Revenue Service (IRS), Treasury.

ACTION: Notice of proposed rulemaking and notice of public hearing.

SUMMARY: This document contains proposed regulations providing guidance on the determination of minimum required contributions for purposes of the funding rules that apply to single employer defined benefit plans. These regulations would affect sponsors, administrators, participants, and beneficiaries of single employer defined benefit plans. This document also provides a notice of a public hearing on these proposed regulations.

DATES: Written or electronic comments must be received by July 14, 2008. Outlines of topics to be discussed at the public hearing scheduled for August 4, 2008, at 10 a.m. must be received by July 15, 2008.

ADDRESSES: Send submissions to: CC:PA:LPD:PR (REG-108508-08), room 5203, Internal Revenue Service, PO Box 7604, Ben Franklin Station, Washington, DC 20044. Submissions may be hand-delivered Monday through Friday between the hours of 8 a.m. and 4 p.m. to CC:PA:LPD:PR (REG-108508-08), Courier's Desk, Internal Revenue Service, 1111 Constitution Avenue NW., Washington, DC, or sent electronically via the Federal eRulemaking Portal at www.regulations.gov (IRS-REG-108508-08). The public hearing will be held in the IRS Auditorium, Internal Revenue Building, 1111 Constitution Avenue, NW.,Washington, DC.

FOR FURTHER INFORMATION CONTACT: Concerning the regulations, Lauson C. Green or Linda S. F. Marshall at (202) 622-6090; concerning submissions of comments, the hearing, and/or being placed on the building access list to attend the hearing, Richard A. Hurst, at Richard.A.Hurst@irscounsel.treas.gov or (202) 622-7180 (not toll-free numbers).

SUPPLEMENTARY INFORMATION:

Background

This document contains proposed Income Tax Regulations (26 CFR part 1) under sections 430(a), 430(c), 430(e), and 430(j), as added to the Internal Revenue Code (Code) by the Pension Protection Act of 2006 (PPA '06), Public Law 109-280 (120 Stat. 780). In addition, this document contains proposed Excise Tax Regulations (26 CFR part 54) under section 4971.

Section 412 provides minimum funding requirements that generally apply for pension plans (including both defined benefit pension plans and money purchase pension plans). PPA '06 makes extensive changes to those minimum funding requirements that generally apply for plan years beginning on or after January 1, 2008. Section 430, which was added by PPA '06, specifies the minimum funding requirements that apply to single employer defined benefit pension plans (including multiple employer plans) pursuant to section 412.[1]

Section 430(a) provides that a plan's minimum required contribution for a plan year is determined under one of two rules, depending on whether the value of plan assets is less than, or is equal to or greater than, the plan's funding target. If the value of plan assets is less than the funding target, the minimum required contribution is the sum of: (1) target normal cost; (2) any shortfall amortization charge; and (3) any waiver amortization charge. If the value of plan assets equals or exceeds the funding target, the minimum required contribution is the

plan's target normal cost, reduced (but not below zero) by the excess of the value of plan assets over the plan's funding target. For purposes of section 430(a), the value of plan assets is determined after reduction for certain funding balances as provided under section 430(f)(4)(B).

Section 430(c) provides that a shortfall amortization charge is the total (not less than zero) of the shortfall amortization installments for the plan year with respect to any shortfall amortization base established for that plan year and the 6 preceding plan years. Section 430(c)(2)(A) provides that the shortfall amortization installments with respect to a shortfall amortization base established for a plan year are the amounts necessary to amortize the shortfall amortization base in level annual installments over the 7-plan-year period beginning with that plan year.

Section 430(c)(3) provides that a shortfall amortization base is determined for a plan year based on the plan's funding shortfall for the plan year. Under section 430(c)(4), the funding shortfall is the amount (if any) by which the plan's funding target for the year exceeds the value of the plan's assets (as reduced by the funding standard carryover balance and prefunding balance under section 430(f)(4)(B)). The shortfall amortization base for a plan year is the plan's funding shortfall, minus the present value (determined using the interest rates under section 430(h)(2)) of the total of the shortfall amortization installments and waiver amortization installments that have been determined for the plan year and any succeeding plan year with respect to any shortfall amortization bases and waiver amortization bases for preceding plan years.

Under section 430(c)(5), a shortfall amortization base is not established for a plan year if the value of a plan's assets is at least equal to the plan's funding target for the plan year. For this purpose, the prefunding balance is subtracted from the value of plan assets, but only if an election to use that prefunding balance to offset the minimum required contribution is in effect for the plan year. A transition rule applies for plan years beginning after 2007 and before 2011 under which only a specified percentage of the plan's funding target is taken into account for purposes of section 430(c)(5). The transition rule does not apply to a plan that is not in effect for 2007 or to a plan that is subject to the pre-PPA '06 deficit reduction contribution rules for 2007 (that is, a plan covering more than 100 participants and with a funded current liability below the applicable threshold).

Under section 430(e), the waiver amortization charge for a plan year is the total of the waiver amortization installments for the plan year with respect to any waiver amortization bases for the 5 preceding plan years. Under section 430(e)(2), the waiver amortization installments with respect to a waiver amortization base established for a plan year are the amounts necessary to amortize the waiver amortization base in level annual installments over the 5-plan-year period beginning with the succeeding plan year. Under section 430(e)(4), the waiver amortization base for a plan year is the amount of the waived funding deficiency (if any) for that plan year.

If a plan's funding shortfall for a plan year is zero (that is, the value of the plan's assets, reduced by the funding standard carryover balance and prefunding balance to the extent provided under section 430(f)(4)(B), is at least equal to the plan's funding target for the year), any shortfall amortization bases and waiver amortization bases for preceding plan years (and any associated shortfall amortization installments and waiver amortization installments) are eliminated. Under section 430(j), as under pre-PPA '06 law, the due date for the payment of a minimum required contribution for a plan year is generally 8½ months after the end of the plan year. Any payment made on a date other than the valuation date for the plan year must be adjusted for interest accruing at the plan's effective interest rate under section 430(h)(2)(A) for the plan year for the period between the valuation date and the payment date. Pursuant to section 430(g)(2), the valuation date for a plan year must be the first day of the plan year except in the case of a small plan described in section 430(g)(2)(B).

Under section 430(j)(3)(A), quarterly contributions must be made during a plan year if the plan had a funding shortfall for the preceding

---

[1] Section 302 of the Employee Retirement Income Security Act of 1974, as amended (ERISA), sets forth funding rules that are parallel to those in Code section 412, and section 303 of ERISA sets forth additional funding rules for single employer plans that are parallel to those in section 430 of the Code. Under section 101 of Reorganization Plan No. 4 of 1978

(43 FR 47713) and section 302 of ERISA, the Secretary of the Treasury has interpretive jurisdiction over the subject matter addressed in these proposed regulations for purposes of ERISA, as well as the Code. Thus, these proposed Treasury regulations issued under section 430 of the Code would apply as well for purposes of section 303 of ERISA.

plan year. Each quarterly installment is 25% of the required annual payment. The required annual payment is equal to the lesser of 90% of the minimum required contribution under section 430 for the plan year or 100% of the minimum required contribution under section 430 (determined without regard to any waiver under section 412) for the preceding plan year. If a quarterly installment is not made, the interest charge that applies for the period of underpayment is determined using the plan's effective interest rate plus 5 percentage points. The requirements regarding quarterly contributions are similar to the requirements that formerly applied under section 412(m) as in effect before amendments made by PPA '06.

Under section 430(j)(4), a plan sponsor of a plan that is subject to the quarterly contribution requirements for a plan year (other than a small plan described in section 430(g)(2)(B)) must make additional quarterly contributions in order to ensure that a minimum level of liquid assets is available to pay benefits as of the end of each quarter. Generally, this required minimum level of liquid assets is the amount of liquid assets needed to pay for three years of benefits, and an additional quarterly contribution (made in liquid assets) is due if the plan has insufficient liquid assets to meet this minimum level. A plan sponsor that fails to satisfy this liquidity requirement is treated as failing to make the required quarterly contribution and, pursuant to section 206(e) of ERISA, is required to cease making certain types of accelerated payments that are described in section 401(a)(32)(B) of the Code. Pursuant to section 430(j)(4)(C), the portion of an installment that is treated as not made because of the liquidity requirement continues to be treated as unpaid until the close of the quarter that contains the due date for the contribution. These liquidity requirements are substantially similar to the requirements that formerly applied under section 412(m)(5), as in effect before amendments made by PPA '06.

Section 402 of PPA '06 provides a series of special funding rules for a plan maintained by a commercial passenger airline (or by an employer whose principal business is providing catering services to a commercial passenger airline) if such an employer has made an election provided under that section. If an eligible employer has made the election described in section 402(a)(1) of PPA '06 (which is only available for a frozen plan), the calculation of the minimum required contribution for the plan is determined using a special 17-plan-year amortization period and an interest rate of 8.85%. If an eligible employer has made the election described in section 402(a)(2) of PPA '06 (which can be made without regard to whether the plan is frozen), calculation of the minimum required contribution for the plan is determined using a special 10-plan-year amortization period for the initial shortfall amortization base (that is, the shortfall amortization base for the first plan year for which section 430 applies to the plan) and, pursuant to the amendment to section 402 of PPA '06 made by section 6615 of the U.S. Troop Readiness, Veterans' Care, Katrina Recovery, and Iraq Accountability Appropriations Act, 2007, Public Law 110-28 (121 Stat. 112), an interest rate of 8.25% is used to determine the funding target for each of those 10 plan years.

Section 4971(a) provides an excise tax on a failure to meet applicable minimum funding requirements. In the case of a single employer plan, the tax is 10% of the aggregate unpaid minimum required contributions for all plan years remaining unpaid as of the end of any plan year ending with or within a taxable year. In the case of a multiemployer plan, the tax is 5% of the accumulated funding deficiency as of the end of any plan year ending with or within the taxable year. Section 4971(b) provides an additional excise tax that applies where the applicable minimum funding requirements remain unsatisfied for a specified period. Section 4971(c) provides definitions that apply for purposes of section 4971, including a definition of unpaid minimum required contribution (which is based on the new section 430 rules for determining the minimum required contribution for a year). Section 4971(f) imposes a tax of 10% of the amount of the liquidity shortfall for a quarter that is not paid by the due date for the installment for that quarter.

Regulations under section 4971 were issued on May 1, 1986 (TD 8084). In addition, proposed regulations regarding section 4971 were issued on the same date. Guidance regarding quarterly contribution requirements under former section 412(m) was issued in Notice 89-52 (1989-1 C.B. 692), and guidance regarding the liquidity requirements under former section 412(m)(5) was issued in Rev. Rul. 95-31 (1995-1 C.B. 76). See § 601.601(d)(2).

Explanation of Provisions

I. *Overview*

These proposed regulations are the fourth in a series of proposed regulations under new section 430.[2] These proposed regulations would provide guidance regarding the minimum contribution rules that apply to sponsors of single employer defined benefit plans under section 430. In addition, this document includes proposed regulations under section 4971, reflecting changes to the excise tax rules under PPA '06.

II. *Section 1.430(a)-1 Determination of Minimum Required Contribution*

Section 1.430(a)-1 would provide rules for determining the minimum required contribution for a single employer defined benefit plan (including a multiple employer plan under section 413(c)) for a plan year under section 430(a). The determination of the amount of the minimum required contribution for a plan year depends on whether the value of plan assets, as reduced to reflect certain funding balances pursuant to section 430(f)(4)(B) (but not below zero), equals or exceeds the plan's funding target for the plan year. If this value of plan assets is less than the funding target for the plan year, the minimum required contribution for that plan year is equal to the sum of the plan's target normal cost for the plan year plus any applicable shortfall amortization installments and waiver amortization installments. If this value of plan assets equals or exceeds the funding target for the plan year, the minimum required contribution for that plan year is equal to the target normal cost of the plan for the plan year reduced (but not below zero) by any such excess.

The proposed regulations provide that the shortfall amortization installments with respect to a shortfall amortization base established for a plan year are the annual amounts necessary to amortize that shortfall amortization base in level annual installments over the 7-year period beginning with that plan year. As provided in proposed § 1.430(h)(2)-1(f)(2), these installments are determined assuming that the installments are paid on the valuation date for each plan year and using the interest rates applicable under section 430(h)(2)(C) or (D). The shortfall amortization installments are determined using the interest rates that apply for the plan year for which the shortfall amortization base is established and are not redetermined in subsequent plan years to reflect changes in interest rates under section 430(h)(2) for those subsequent plan years.[3]

Under the proposed regulations, if the value of plan assets (reduced by the prefunding balance if the prefunding balance is used to offset the minimum required contribution for the plan year as provided under § 1.430(f)-1(c), but not below zero) is equal to or greater than the funding target for the plan year, then no shortfall amortization base is established for that plan year. If this value of plan assets is less than the funding target for the plan year, a shortfall amortization base is established for the plan year. In such a case, the shortfall amortization base (which can be either positive or negative) is equal to the funding shortfall of the plan for the plan year, minus the sum of the present values of any remaining shortfall amortization installments and waiver amortization installments (determined in accordance with § 1.430(h)(2)-1(f)(2) using the interest rates that apply for the current plan year). For this purpose, the funding shortfall of a plan for any plan year is the excess (if any) of the funding target of the plan for the plan year, over the value of plan assets for the plan year (as reduced to reflect the subtraction of the funding standard carryover balance and prefunding balance to the extent provided under § 1.430(f)-1(c)).

The proposed regulations reflect the transition rule under section 430(c)(5)(B) under which only a specified portion of the funding target is taken into account in determining whether a shortfall amortization base is established for plan years beginning before January 1, 2011. This transition rule does not apply with respect to any plan year beginning after 2008 if a shortfall amortization base was required to be established for any preceding year, nor does it apply to a plan that was not in effect for a plan year beginning in 2007 or to a plan that was subject to section 412(l) for the last plan year before section 430 applies to the plan (the pre-effective plan year), determined after the application of section 412(l)(6) and (9). The proposed regulations would not provide for any adjustment to the applicable percentages under this transition rule for a plan for which the effective date of section 430 is delayed under sections 104 through 106 of PPA '06.

---

[2] Proposed §§ 1.430(h)(3)-1 and 1.430(h)(3)-2, relating to the mortality tables used to determine liabilities under section 430(h)(3), were issued May 29, 2007 (REG-143601-06, 72 FR 29456), proposed § 1.430(f)-1, relating to prefunding and funding standard carryover balances under section 430(f), was issued August 31, 2007 (REG-113891-07, 72 FR 50544), and proposed §§ 1.430(d)-1, 1.430(g)-1, 1.430(h)(2)-1, and 1.430(i)-1, relating to measurement of plan assets and liabilities for pension funding purposes, were issued December 31, 2007 (REG-139236-07, 72 FR 74215).

[3] The proposed regulations reflect the alternative amortization periods and interest rates that apply to a commercial passenger airline (or other eligible employer) that has made an election under section 402 of PPA '06.

Under the proposed regulations, the waiver amortization installments with respect to a waiver amortization base established for a plan year are the annual amounts necessary to amortize that waiver amortization base in level annual installments over the 5-year period beginning with the following plan year. As provided in proposed § 1.430(h)(2)-1(f)(2), these installments are determined assuming that the installments are paid on the valuation date for each plan year and using the interest rates applicable under section 430(h)(2). Thus, if the plan is using segment rates, the installments are determined by applying the first segment rate to the first four installments and the second segment rate to the fifth (and final) installment. The waiver amortization installments established with respect to a waiver amortization base are determined using the interest rates that apply for the plan year for which the waiver is granted (even though the first installment with respect to the waiver amortization base is not due until the subsequent plan year) and are not redetermined in subsequent plan years to reflect changes in interest rates under section 430(h)(2) for those subsequent plan years. A waiver amortization base is established for each plan year for which a waiver of the minimum funding standard has been granted, and the amount of that waiver amortization base is equal to the amount of the minimum required contribution waived (or the waived funding deficiency) for the plan year.

In the case of a plan that received a funding waiver under section 412 for a plan year for which section 430 was not yet effective with respect to the plan, the proposed regulations provide that the waiver is treated as giving rise to a waiver amortization base, and the amortization charges with respect to that funding waiver are treated as waiver amortization installments. With respect to such a preexisting funding waiver, the amount of the annual waiver amortization installment is equal to the amortization charge with respect to that waiver determined using the interest rate or rates that applied for the pre-effective plan year. Thus, for a plan that received a waiver in the past, the plan sponsor would have to contribute the amounts needed to amortize that waiver over the original schedule as previously established.

In accordance with section 430(c)(6), the proposed regulations provide that, in any case in which the funding shortfall of a plan for a plan year is zero, the shortfall amortization bases for all preceding plan years (and all shortfall amortization installments determined with respect to those shortfall amortization bases) are reduced to zero, and the waiver amortization bases for all preceding plan years (and all waiver amortization installments determined with respect to such bases) are reduced to zero.

The proposed regulations would provide rules for determining the amount of a minimum required contribution for a short plan year. Under the proposed regulations, the amortization installments are prorated for a short plan year. The proposed regulations would not provide for any proration of the target normal cost. Instead, the determination of target normal cost would reflect actual accruals that accrue or are expected to accrue during the plan year.[4] The proposed regulations also provide rules for the treatment of installments in subsequent plan years to take into account the proration of these installments for short plan years and any change in valuation date.

III. Section 1.430(j)-1 Payment of Minimum Required Contributions

The proposed regulations under section 430(j) would provide rules related to the payment of minimum required contributions, including the payment of quarterly contributions and liquidity requirements. The proposed regulations provide that any payment of the minimum required contribution under section 430 for a plan year that is made on a date other than the valuation date for that plan year is adjusted for interest accruing for the period between the valuation date and the payment date, at the effective interest rate for the plan for that plan year determined pursuant to § 1.430(h)(2)-1(f)(1). The direction of the adjustment depends on whether the contribution is paid before or after the valuation date for the plan year. If the contribution is paid after the valuation date for the plan year, the contribution is discounted to the valuation date using the plan's effective interest rate. By contrast, if the contribution is paid before the valuation date for the plan year (which could only occur in the case of a small plan described in section 430(g)(2)(B)), the contribution is increased for interest at that same interest rate.

Under the proposed regulations, a payment of the minimum required contribution under section 430 for a plan year can be made no earlier than the first day of the plan year. The deadline for any payment of any minimum required contribution for a plan year is 8 1/2 months after the close of the plan year. If a minimum required contribution is not paid by this deadline, an excise tax applies under section 4971.

The proposed regulations would provide rules for accelerated quarterly contributions for underfunded plans. These rules are similar to the rules provided under Notice 89-52; however, these rules have been updated to reflect statutory changes. These statutory changes include changes regarding which plans are subject to the quarterly contribution requirements as well as the interest rates applicable to missed quarterly contributions.

Under the proposed regulations, in any case in which the plan has a funding shortfall for the preceding plan year, the employer maintaining the plan must make the required quarterly installments.[5] The amount of each required quarterly installment is equal to 25% of the required annual payment. For this purpose, the required annual payment is equal to the lesser of 90% of the minimum required contribution under section 430(a) for the plan year, or 100% of the minimum required contribution under section 430(a) (determined without regard to any funding waiver under section 412) for the preceding plan year. These minimum required contributions are determined under section 430 as of the valuation date for each year and have no adjustment for interest.[6] The proposed regulations provide that, for purposes of determining the required annual payment, the minimum required contribution for a plan year is determined without regard to use of the prefunding balance or funding standard carryover balance in the current year or any prior year.

Pursuant to section 430(j)(3)(C), the proposed regulations would provide that the due dates for the four required quarterly installments with respect to a full plan year are as follows: the first installment is due on the 15th day of the 4th plan month, the second installment is due on the 15th day of the 7th plan month, the third installment is due on the 15th day of the 10th plan month, and the fourth installment is due on the 15th day following the close of the plan year. In the case of a short plan year, the proposed regulations would provide rules for determining the amount of the required annual payment, the number and due dates of installments, and the amount of those installments. The proposed regulations also provide rules for determining the plan month in the case of a plan year that does not begin on the first day of a calendar month.

The proposed regulations would provide that, if the employer fails to pay the full amount of a required installment, then the rate of interest used to adjust the amount of the contribution with respect to the underpayment of the required installment for the period of time that begins on the due date for the required installment and that ends on the date of payment is equal to the effective interest rate for the plan for that plan year determined pursuant to § 1.430(h)(2)-1(f)(1) plus 5 percentage points. This increased interest rate applies only to installments that are due after the valuation date for the plan year because section 430(j)(3) refers to interest being charged on late quarterly contributions. The amount of the underpayment is equal to the excess of the required installment over the amount (if any) of the installment contributed to or under the plan on or before the due date for the installment. For this purpose, the proposed regulations contain an ordering rule under which contributions are to be credited against unpaid required installments in the order in which those installments were required to be paid.

As was the case in Notice 89-52, the proposed regulations would provide that a plan sponsor generally can use a plan's funding balances to satisfy quarterly contribution requirements. However, this rule is subject to the new limitation on the use of funding balances by underfunded plans pursuant to section 430(f)(3)(C). An eligible plan sponsor's election to use the plan's prefunding balance and funding standard carryover balance under section 430(f) satisfies the obligation to make an installment on the date of the election, to the extent of the amount elected, as adjusted with interest at the plan's effective interest rate under section 430(h)(2)(A) for the plan year from the valuation date through the due date of the installment. Comments are requested regarding whether rules should be provided under which a plan spon-

---

[4] See 29 CFR § 2530.204-2(e) for rules relating to changes in accrual computation periods.

[5] These proposed regulations do not provide rules for determining whether a plan has a funding shortfall for the 2007 plan year for purposes of determining whether the plan must make required quarterly installments for the 2008 plan year. Nonetheless, plans must make this determination on a reasonable basis. See the discussion in this preamble under the heading "Proposed Legislation" for a rule that the IRS and the Treasury Department are considering for this purpose.

[6] In determining required installments for the plan year that begins in 2008, the minimum required contribution for the 2007 plan year under section 412 is used as the minimum required contribution for the preceding plan year. This amount, which does not reflect either use of the credit balance or the granting of any funding waiver, is adjusted with interest to the end of the 2007 plan year at the plan's valuation interest rate for the 2007 plan year.

sor is deemed to make an election to use a funding balance to the extent it is available to avoid a failure to make any required quarterly installment or under which a plan sponsor can make a single election that will apply to all future quarterly installments until revoked.

A plan sponsor that uses the plan's prefunding balance or funding standard carryover balance toward satisfaction of the plan's quarterly contribution requirement before the plan's effective interest rate for the plan year has been determined should assume, in order to ensure that the quarterly contribution requirements are satisfied, that the effective interest rate is equal to the lowest of the three segment rates (generally the first segment rate) to adjust the elected amount. Plan sponsors should also note that, pursuant to proposed § 1.430(f)-1(b)(1)(ii)(B), the amount of the funding balance that is used to satisfy the quarterly contribution requirements cannot later be added back to the prefunding balance (because only contributions in excess of the minimum funding requirement, determined without regard to the offset under section 430(f)(3), are eligible to be added to the prefunding balance).

The proposed regulations would provide rules for the liquidity requirements that generally apply to plans for which quarterly contributions are required. Under the proposed regulations, a plan subject to the requirement to make quarterly contributions (other than a small plan described in section 430(g)(2)(B)) is treated as failing to pay the full amount of the required installment for a quarter to the extent that the value of the liquid assets paid after the close of that quarter and on or before the due date for the installment is less than the liquidity shortfall for that quarter. Thus, in order to satisfy the quarterly contribution requirement for a quarter, liquid assets in the amount of the liquidity shortfall must be contributed after the close of that quarter and on or before the due date for the installment.[7] The use of funding balances or the contribution of illiquid assets cannot remedy a liquidity shortfall.

The rules under the proposed regulations relating to the liquidity requirements are similar to the rules provided under Rev. Rul. 95-31; however, these rules have been updated to reflect statutory changes. For example, the definition of liquid assets under the proposed regulations is the same as the definition of liquid assets under Rev. Rul. 95-31. Unlike Rev. Rul. 95-31, the proposed regulations measure satisfaction of a liquidity shortfall by reference to contributions made after the close of the quarter and by the due date for the installment while including contributions made during the plan quarter in plan assets. Although this appears to be a change from the rules of Rev. Rul. 95-31, the two formulations are mathematically identical.

The proposed regulations provide that, for purposes of applying the additional 5 percentage point interest adjustment in the case of a quarterly contribution that is not fully paid, the liquidity increment for the quarter (the portion of the quarterly installment that is due solely by reason of the liquidity requirements) continues to be treated as unpaid until the close of the quarter in which the due date for that installment occurs, regardless of when it is contributed. However, for purposes of adjusting the contribution to the valuation date at the effective interest rate, the adjustment is made from the actual contribution date (rather than from the close of the quarter). In addition, the proposed regulations provide an ordering rule under which, if a contribution for a quarter is less than the total amount needed to satisfy the quarterly contribution requirement taking into account the liquidity requirement, then the contribution is first attributed toward satisfying the quarterly contribution requirement determined without regard to the liquidity requirement.

Under the proposed regulations, if the amount of any required installment is increased because of the liquidity shortfall rules, that increase cannot exceed the amount that, when added to prior required installments determined under section 430(j) for the plan year, would increase the funding target attainment percentage of the plan for the plan year (taking into account the expected increase in funding target due to benefits accruing or earned during the plan year) to 100%.

The proposed regulations would provide that the rules under section 430(j) generally apply to a plan maintained by a commercial passenger airline (or other eligible employer) that has made an election under section 402(a)(1) or 402(a)(2) of PPA '06 in the same manner as they apply to any other plan subject to section 430. However, in the case of a plan with respect to which the election under section 402(a)(1) of PPA '06 has been made, the determination of the funding shortfall for a plan year is made by reference to the unfunded liability under section 402(e)(3)(A) of PPA '06. In addition, the effective interest rate for a plan with respect to which the election under section 402(a)(1) of PPA '06 has been made is deemed to be 8.85%. Pursuant to proposed § 1.430(h)(2)-1(f)(1), the effective interest rate for a plan with respect to which the election under section 402(a)(2) of PPA '06 has been made will be 8.25% for the 10-year period during which the election applies to the plan.

IV. *Section 54.4971(c)-1 Taxes on Failure to Meet Minimum Funding Standards*

These proposed regulations set forth the definitions that apply for purposes of applying the rules of section 4971 that were modified by PPA '06.

The proposed regulations define the term *accumulated funding deficiency* (which is only relevant for a multiemployer plan) as having the meaning given to that term by section 431. A multiemployer plan's accumulated funding deficiency for a plan year takes into account all charges and credits to the funding standard account under section 412 for plan years before the first plan year for which section 431 applies to the plan.

The proposed regulations define the term *unpaid minimum required contribution*, with respect to any plan year, as any minimum required contribution under section 430 for the plan year that is not paid on or before the due date for the plan year under section 430(j)(1). The proposed regulations provide that a plan's accumulated funding deficiency under section 412 for the pre-effective plan year is treated as an unpaid minimum required contribution for that plan year until correction is made. Unlike the determination of accumulated funding deficiency which applied under section 412 prior to PPA '06, the total unpaid minimum required contributions is not adjusted with interest. However, as described in the following paragraph, correction of an unpaid minimum required contribution does require a contribution that includes an adjustment for interest.

The proposed regulations define the term *correct* as it applies to the accumulated funding deficiency and the unpaid minimum required contribution of a plan. With respect to an accumulated funding deficiency under a multiemployer plan, the proposed regulations set forth rules that are the same as the rules set forth in proposed § 54.4971-2(a). Under the proposed regulations, the correction of an unpaid minimum required contribution under a single employer plan for a plan year requires the contribution, to or under the plan, of the amount that, when discounted to the valuation date for the plan year for which the unpaid minimum required contribution is due at the appropriate rate of interest, equals or exceeds the unpaid minimum required contribution. For this purpose, the appropriate rate of interest is the plan's effective interest rate for the plan year for which the unpaid minimum required contribution is due except to the extent that the payments are subject to additional interest as provided under section 430(j)(3) or (4). With respect to an unpaid minimum required contribution, the proposed regulations provide an ordering rule under which a contribution is attributable first to the earliest plan year of any unpaid minimum required contribution for which correction has not yet been made. With respect to an accumulated funding deficiency under section 412 for the pre-effective plan year that is treated as an unpaid minimum required contribution, the proposed regulations provide that correction requires the contribution, to or under the plan, of the amount of that accumulated funding deficiency adjusted with interest from the end of the preeffective plan year to the date of the contribution at the plan's valuation interest rate for the pre-effective plan year.

The IRS and the Treasury Department intend to issue further guidance in the future on the application of section 4971, including special rules applicable to multiemployer plans that are in critical or endangered status under section 432.

Proposed Legislation

As of the date of the issuance of these proposed regulations, bills have been passed in the House of Representatives and the Senate that would provide for technical corrections to PPA '06.[8] These bills would amend section 430(j)(3)(A) to authorize the Treasury Department to provide rules for determining the funding shortfall for purposes of the pre-effective plan year and would add section 430(j)(3)(E)(iii) to authorize the Treasury Department to provide special rules for the treatment of quarterly contributions in the case of a plan with a valuation date other than the first day of the plan year. These bills would also specify an effective date for the PPA '06 amendments to section 4971.

---

[7] In this context, see Department of Labor Interpretive Bulletin 94-3 (29 CFR 2509.94-3), which sets forth the Department's view that, in the absence of an applicable exemption, a contribution by an employer to a defined benefit plan in a form other than cash constitutes a prohibited transaction under section 406 of ERISA and section 4975 of the Code.

[8] See H.R. 3361 as passed by the House of Representatives on March 13, 2008 and S. 1974 as passed by the Senate on December 19, 2007.

These proposed regulations have reserved §1.430(j)-1(c)(6) and §1.430(j)-1(g)(5)(ii) in order to accommodate any enacted changes to section 430(j). If legislation similar to that in the proposed technical corrections is enacted, the IRS and the Treasury Department are considering including the following provisions in final regulations. First, the funding shortfall for the pre-effective plan year would be determined as the excess (if any) of the plan's current liability determined pursuant to section 412(l)(7) on the valuation date for the plan's pre-effective plan year, over the net plan assets for the pre-effective plan year as determined under §1.430(i)-1(f)(5)(ii). Second, if a quarterly installment is due before the valuation date for the plan year, the minimum required contribution for the plan year would be increased by an additional amount if that quarterly installment is not paid by the due date. This additional amount would be determined by applying interest at an annual rate of 5% to the underpayment of the required installment for the period of time between the due date for the required installment and the earlier of the date of payment or the valuation date.

Effective/Applicability Dates of Regulations

Section 430 generally applies to plan years beginning on or after January 1, 2008. The proposed regulations under section 430 are proposed to apply generally to plan years beginning on or after January 1, 2009. When the regulations are finalized, plans will be permitted to apply them for plan years beginning in 2008. In addition, for plan years beginning in 2008, plans are permitted to rely on the proposed regulations for purposes of satisfying the requirements of section 430. In the case of a plan for which the effective date of section 430 is delayed in accordance with sections 104 through 106 of PPA '06, the regulations are proposed to apply to plan years beginning on or after the date section 430 first applies with respect to the plan.

The amendments made to section 4971 by section 114 of PPA '06 do not have a specific effective date. The regulations provide that the amendments to section 4971 generally apply at the same time as the amendments to section 430 (or section 431, as applicable) apply to the plan. Thus, the regulations provide that the amendments to section 4971 generally apply to taxable years beginning on or after January 1, 2008, but only with respect to plan years for which section 430 (or section 431) applies to the plan that end with or within any such taxable year. In the case of a plan to which a delayed effective date applies pursuant to sections 104 through 106 of PPA '06, the regulations provide that the amendments made to section 4971 apply to the same taxable years, but only with respect to plan years for which section 430 applies to the plan. The regulations under section 4971 generally are proposed to apply at the same time the statutory changes to section 4971 under PPA '06 become effective but would not apply to taxable years ending before April 15, 2008. Thus, for example, the regulations under section 4971 would not apply to a short taxable year beginning January 1, 2008, and ending February 29, 2008.

Special Analyses

It has been determined that this notice of proposed rulemaking is not a significant regulatory action as defined in Executive Order 12866. Therefore, a regulatory assessment is not required. It has also been determined that section 553(b) of the Administrative Procedure Act (5 U.S.C. chapter 5) does not apply to these regulations and, because the proposed regulations do not impose a collection of information on small entities, a regulatory flexibility analysis is not required. Pursuant to section 7805(f) of the Code, these regulations have been submitted to the Chief Counsel for Advocacy of the Small Business Administration for comment on its impact on small business.

Comments and Public Hearing

Before these proposed regulations are adopted as final regulations, consideration will be given to any written (a signed original and eight (8) copies) or electronic comments that are submitted timely to the IRS. The IRS and the Treasury Department specifically request comments on the clarity of the proposed regulations and how they may be made easier to understand. All comments will be available for public inspection and copying.

A public hearing has been scheduled for August 4, 2008, beginning at 10 a.m. in the Auditorium, Internal Revenue Service, 1111 Constitution Avenue, NW., Washington, DC. Due to building security procedures, visitors must enter at the Constitution Avenue entrance. In addition, all visitors must present photo identification to enter the building. Because of access restrictions, visitors will not be admitted beyond the immediate entrance area more than 30 minutes before the hearing starts. For information about having your name placed on the building access list to attend the hearing, see the **FOR FURTHER INFORMATION CONTACT** section of this preamble.

The rules of 26 CFR 601.601(a)(3) apply to the hearing. Persons who wish to present oral comments at the hearing must submit written or electronic comments by July 15, 2008, and an outline of topics to be discussed and the amount of time to be devoted to each topic (a signed original and eight (8) copies) by July 15, 2008. A period of 10 minutes will be allotted to each person for making comments. An agenda showing the scheduling of the speakers will be prepared after the deadline for receiving outlines has passed. Copies of the agenda will be available free of charge at the hearing.

Drafting Information

The principal authors of these regulations are Lauson C. Green and Linda S. F. Marshall, Office of Division Counsel/Associate Chief Counsel (Tax Exempt and Government Entities). However, other personnel from the IRS and the Treasury Department participated in the development of these regulations.

List of Subjects

26 CFR Part 1

Income taxes, Reporting and recordkeeping requirements.

26 CFR Part 54

Excise taxes, Insurance, Reporting and recordkeeping requirements.

Proposed Amendments to the Regulations

Accordingly, 26 CFR part 1 is proposed to be amended as follows:

PART 1—INCOME TAXES

Paragraph 1. The authority citation for part 1 continues to read in part as follows:

Authority: 26 U.S.C. 7805 * * *

Par. 2. Section 1.430(a)-1 is added to read as follows:

§ 1.430(a)-1 Determination of minimum required contribution.

(a) *In general*—(1) *Overview.* This section sets forth rules for determining a plan's minimum required contribution for a plan year under section 430(a). Section 430 and this section apply to single employer defined benefit plans (including multiple employer plans as defined in section 413(c) that are subject to section 412 but do not apply to multiemployer plans (as defined in section 414(f)). Paragraph (b) of this section defines a plan's minimum required contribution for a plan year. Paragraph (c) of this section provides rules for determining shortfall amortization installments. Paragraph (d) of this section provides rules for determining waiver amortization installments. Paragraph (e) of this section provides for early deemed amortization of shortfall and waiver amortization bases for fully funded plans. Paragraph (f) of this section provides definitions that apply for purposes of this section. Paragraph (g) of this section provides examples that illustrate the application of this section. Paragraph (h) of this section provides effective/applicability dates and transition rules.

(2) *Special rules for multiple employer plans.* In the case of a multiple employer plan to which section 413(c)(4)(A) applies, the rules of section 430 and this section are applied separately for each employer under the plan, as if each employer maintained a separate plan. Thus, the minimum required contribution is computed separately for each employer under such a multiple employer plan. In the case of a multiple employer plan to which section 413(c)(4)(A) does not apply (that is, a plan described in section 413(c)(4)(B) that has not made the election for section 413(c)(4)(A) to apply), the rules of section 430 and this section are applied as if all participants in the plan were employed by a single employer.

(b) *Definition of minimum required contribution*—(1) *In general.* In the case of a defined benefit plan that is not a multiemployer plan (within the meaning of section 414(f)), except as offset under section 430(f) and §1.430(f)-1, the minimum required contribution for a plan year is determined as the applicable amount determined under paragraph (b)(2) of this section or paragraph (b)(3) of this section, reduced by the amount of any funding waiver under section 412(c) that is granted for the plan year. See paragraph (b)(4) of this section for special rules for a plan maintained by a commercial passenger airline (or other eligible employer) for which an election under section 402 of the Pension Protection Act of 2006, Public Law 109-280 (120 Stat. 780) (PPA '06), has been made, and see section 430(j) and §1.430(j)-1 for rules regarding the required interest adjustment for a contribution that is paid on a date other than the valuation date for the plan year.

(2) *Plan assets less than funding target*—(i) *General rule.* For any plan year in which the value of plan assets of the plan (as reduced to reflect

the subtraction of certain funding balances as provided under § 1.430(f)-1(c), but not below zero) is less than the funding target of the plan for the plan year, the minimum required contribution for that plan year is equal to the sum of—

(A) The target normal cost of the plan for the plan year;

(B) The total (not less than zero) of the shortfall amortization installments determined with respect to the shortfall amortization bases for the plan year and each of the 6 preceding plan years as described in paragraph (c) of this section; and

(C) The total of the waiver amortization installments determined with respect to the waiver amortization bases for each of the 5 preceding plan years as described in paragraph (d) of this section.

(ii) *Special rule for short plan years*—(A) *Proration of amortization installments.* In determining the minimum required contribution in the case of a plan year that is shorter than 12 months (and is not a 52-week plan year of a plan that uses a 52-53 week plan year), the shortfall amortization installments and waiver amortization installments that are taken into account under paragraphs (b)(2)(i)(B) and (C) of this section are determined by multiplying the amount of those installments that would be taken into account for a 12-month plan year by a fraction, the numerator of which is the duration of the short plan year and the denominator of which is 1 year.

(B) *Effect on subsequent years.* In plan years after the short plan year, installments with respect to a shortfall amortization base (or waiver amortization base) continue to be taken into account under paragraphs (b)(2)(i)(B) and (C) of this section until the total amount of those installments, as originally determined to be paid over 7 years (or 5 years in the case of waiver amortization installments), has been taken into account. Thus, for example, in the case of a plan that has a short plan year, an additional partial installment will be taken into account under paragraphs (b)(2)(i)(B) and (C) of this section during the plan year after the end of the original amortization period in an amount determined so that the total of the amortization installments (including the prorated installment payable for the short plan year and the additional partial installment) is equal to the total amount of the amortization installments as originally determined. Similarly, in the case of a plan that has a short plan year, the total number of plan years required to take into account the full amount of installments will exceed 7 plan years (or 5 plan years in the case of waiver amortization installments), and, accordingly, the number of preceding plan years taken into account in paragraphs (b)(2)(i)(B) and (C) of this section is correspondingly increased so that the total amount of the amortization installments as originally determined is taken into account. In addition, for plan years beginning after the close of the short plan year, the shortfall amortization installments and waiver amortization installments that are taken into account under paragraphs (b)(2)(i)(B) and (C) of this section are assumed to be paid on the valuation date for the new plan year (rather than on the valuation date for the short plan year and preceding plan years).

(3) *Plan assets equal or exceed funding target.* For any plan year in which the value of plan assets (as reduced to reflect the subtraction of certain funding balances as provided under § 1.430(f)-1(c), but not below zero) equals or exceeds the funding target of the plan for the plan year, the minimum required contribution for that plan year is equal to the target normal cost of the plan for the plan year reduced (but not below zero) by that excess.

(4) *Special rules for commercial passenger airlines*—(i) *In general.* This paragraph (b)(4) provides special rules for a plan maintained by a commercial passenger airline (or an employer whose principal business is providing catering services to a commercial passenger airline) for which an election under section 402 of PPA '06 has been made.

(ii) *Frozen plans*—(A) *Determinations during 17-year amortization period.* If an election described in section 402(a)(1) of PPA '06 applies for the plan year with respect to an eligible plan described in section 402(c)(1) of PPA '06, then the plan's minimum required contribution for purposes of section 430 of the Code for the plan year is equal to the amount necessary to amortize (at an interest rate of 8.85 percent) the unfunded liability of the plan in equal installments over the remaining amortization period. For this purpose, the unfunded liability means the excess of the accrued liability under the plan determined using the unit credit funding method and an interest rate of 8.85 percent over the fair market value of assets, and the remaining amortization period is the 17-plan-year period beginning with the first plan year for which the election was made, reduced by 1 year for each plan year after the first plan year for which the election was made. In addition, the section 430(f)(3) election to apply funding balances against the minimum required contribution does not apply to a plan to which the election described in section 402(a)(1) of PPA '06 applies for the plan year.

(B) *Determinations following 17-year amortization period.* If an election described in section 402(a)(1) of PPA '06 applied to the plan for any preceding plan year but does not apply for the current plan year, then the plan's minimum required contribution for purposes of section 430 of the Code for the plan year is determined without regard to that election. For the first plan year for which that election no longer applies to the plan, any prefunding balance or funding standard carryover balance is reduced to zero.

(iii) *Other plans of commercial passenger airlines.* If an election described in section 402(a)(2) of PPA '06 has been made for an eligible plan described in section 402(c)(1) of PPA '06, then the minimum required contribution for purposes of section 430 is determined under generally applicable rules, except that the shortfall amortization base for the first plan year for which section 430 applies to the plan is amortized over 10 years (rather than over 7 years as provided in paragraph (c)(1) of this section) in accordance with § 1.430(h)(2)-1(e) and (f) using the interest rates that apply for the first plan year for which section 430 applies to the plan. In such a case, the shortfall amortization installments with respect to the shortfall amortization base for that plan year will continue to be included in determining the minimum required contribution for 10 years rather than 7 years. See also § 1.430(h)(2)-1(b)(6) for a special rule for determining the funding target in the case of a plan for which an election under section 402(a)(2) of PPA '06 has been made.

(c) *Shortfall amortization installments*—(1) *In general.* For purposes of this section, the shortfall amortization installments with respect to a shortfall amortization base established for a plan year are the annual amounts necessary to amortize that shortfall amortization base in level annual installments over the 7-year period beginning with that plan year. See § 1.430(h)(2)-1(e) and (f) for rules regarding interest rates used for determining shortfall amortization installments and the date within each plan year on which the installments are assumed to be paid. The shortfall amortization installments are determined using the interest rates that apply for the plan year for which the shortfall amortization base is established and are not redetermined in subsequent plan years to reflect changes in interest rates under section 430(h)(2) for those subsequent plan years.

(2) *Shortfall amortization base*—(i) *In general.* For purposes of this section, unless the value of plan assets (as reduced to reflect the subtraction of certain funding balances as provided under § 1.430(f)-1(c)(2), but not below zero) is equal to or greater than the funding target of the plan for the plan year, a shortfall amortization base is established for the plan year equal to—

(A) The funding shortfall of the plan for the plan year; minus

(B) The amount attributable to future installments determined under paragraph (c)(2)(ii) of this section.

(ii) *Amount attributable to future installments.* The amount attributable to future installments is equal to the sum of the present values (determined in accordance with § 1.430(h)(2)-1(e) and (f) using the interest rates that apply for the current plan year) of—

(A) The shortfall amortization installments that have been determined for the plan year and any succeeding plan year with respect to the shortfall amortization bases of the plan for any plan year preceding the plan year; and

(B) The waiver amortization installments that have been determined for the plan year and any succeeding plan year with respect to the waiver amortization bases of the plan for any plan year preceding the plan year.

(iii) *Transition rule.* See paragraph (h)(4) of this section for a transition rule under which only a portion of the funding target is taken into account in determining whether a shortfall amortization base is established under this paragraph (c)(2).

(d) *Waiver amortization installments*—(1) *In general.* For purposes of this section, the waiver amortization installments with respect to a waiver amortization base established for a plan year are the annual amounts necessary to amortize that waiver amortization base in level annual installments over the 5-year period beginning with the following plan year. See § 1.430(h)(2)-1(e) and (f) for rules regarding interest rates used for determining waiver amortization installments and the date within each plan year on which the installments are assumed to be paid. The waiver amortization installments established with respect to a waiver amortization base are determined using the interest rates that apply for the plan year for which the waiver is granted (even though the first installment with respect to the waiver amortization base is not due until the subsequent plan year) and are not redetermined in subsequent plan years to reflect changes in interest rates under section 430(h)(2) for those subsequent plan years.

(2) *Waiver amortization base*—(i) *In general.* For purposes of this section, a waiver amortization base is established for each plan year for which a waiver of the minimum funding standard has been granted in accordance with section 412(c). The amount of the waiver amortization base is equal to the amount of the minimum required contribution waived (or the waived funding deficiency) for the plan year.

(ii) *Transition rule.* See paragraph (h)(3) of this section for the treatment of funding waivers granted for plan years beginning before 2008.

(e) *Early deemed amortization upon attainment of funding target.* In any case in which the funding shortfall of a plan for a plan year is zero—

(1) The shortfall amortization bases for all preceding plan years (and all shortfall amortization installments determined with respect to those shortfall amortization bases) are reduced to zero; and

(2) The waiver amortization bases for all preceding plan years (and all waiver amortization installments determined with respect to such bases) are reduced to zero.

(f) *Definitions*—(1) *In general.* The definitions set forth in this paragraph (f) apply for purposes of this section.

(2) *Funding shortfall.* The term *funding shortfall* means the excess (if any) of—

(i) The funding target of the plan for a plan year; over

(ii) The value of plan assets for the plan year (as reduced to reflect the subtraction of the funding standard carryover balance and prefunding balance to the extent provided under § 1.430(f)-1(c), but not below zero).

(3) *Funding target.* The term *funding target* means the plan's funding target for a plan year determined under § 1.430(d)-1(b)(2), § 1.430(i)-1(c), or § 1.430(i)-1(e)(1), whichever applies to the plan for the plan year.

(4) *Target normal cost.* The term *target normal cost* means the plan's target normal cost for a plan year determined under § 1.430(d)-1(b)(1), § 1.430(i)-1(d), or § 1.430(i)-1(e)(2), whichever applies to the plan for the plan year.

(g) *Examples.* The following examples illustrate the rules of this section. Unless otherwise indicated, these examples are based on the following assumptions: the plan is subject to section 430 starting in 2008; the plan year is the calendar year; the valuation date is January 1; and the plan's funding standard carryover balance is $0.

Example 1. (i) Plan A has a funding target of $2,500,000 and assets totaling $1,800,000 as of January 1, 2008. The 2008 actuarial valuation is performed using the 24-month average segment rates applicable for September 2007 (determined without regard to the transitional rule of section 430(h)(2)(G)).

(ii) A $700,000 shortfall amortization base is established for 2008, which is equal to the $2,500,000 funding target less $1,800,000 of assets.

(iii) With respect to this shortfall amortization base of $700,000, there is a shortfall amortization installment of $116,852 (which is equal to the $700,000 shortfall amortization base amortized over 7 years) for each year from 2008 through 2014. The amount of this shortfall amortization installment is determined by discounting the first five installments using the first segment interest rate of 5.26%, and by discounting the sixth and seventh installments using the second segment rate of 5.82%.

Example 2. (i) The facts are the same as in *Example 1,* except that the plan was granted a funding waiver of $300,000 in 2006, as of December 31, 2006. The valuation interest rate for the January 1, 2007, actuarial valuation is 8.50% (which exceeds 150% of the applicable federal midterm rate).

(ii) The waiver amortization installment for the plan year beginning January 1, 2007, is $70,166, which is equal to the $300,000 funding waiver base amortized over 5 years at the valuation interest rate of 8.50%.

(iii) As of January 1, 2008, the present value of the remaining waiver amortization installments is $260,318, which is determined by discounting the remaining four waiver amortization installments of $70,166 to January 1, 2008, using the first segment rate of 5.26%. See paragraph (h)(3) of this section.

(iv) A $439,682 shortfall amortization base is established for 2008, which is equal to the $2,500,000 funding target, less $1,800,000 of assets, less $260,318 (which is the present value of the remaining waiver amortization installments).

(v) With respect to this shortfall amortization base of $439,682, there is a shortfall amortization installment of $73,397 (which is equal to the $439,682 shortfall amortization base amortized over 7 years) for each year from 2008 through 2014.

Example 3. (i) The facts are the same as in *Example 2.* Plan A has a $100,000 target normal cost for the 2008 plan year and was granted a funding waiver for 2008 to the largest extent permitted under section 412(c).

(ii) The minimum required contribution is $243,563 as of January 1, 2008. This is equal to the $100,000 target normal cost, plus the $70,166 waiver amortization installment from the 2006 waiver, plus the $73,397 January 1, 2008, shortfall amortization installment.

(iii) In accordance with section 412(c)(1)(C), the portion of the minimum required contribution attributable to the amortization of the 2006 funding waiver cannot be waived. Therefore, the maximum amount of the January 1, 2008, minimum required contribution that can be waived is $173,397.

(iv) In accordance with paragraph (d) of this section, a waiver amortization base of $173,397 is established as of January 1, 2008, to be amortized over 5 years beginning with the 2009 plan year. Although the waiver amortization installments for the 2008 funding waiver are not included in the minimum required contribution until 2009, the amount of those installments is determined based on the interest rates used for the 2008 plan year.

(v) The waiver amortization installments are calculated using the first segment interest rate of 5.26% for the first four installments (calculated as of January 1, 2009, through January 1, 2012) and the second segment interest rate of 5.82% for the final installment payable as of January 1, 2013. Accordingly, the waiver amortization installments that are payable beginning January 1, 2009, are $40,530 each.

Example 4. (i) The facts are the same as in *Example 3.* As of January 1, 2009, Plan A has a funding target of $2,750,000 and assets totaling $1,900,000. The 2009 actuarial valuation is performed using the 24-month average segment rates applicable for September 2008 (determined without regard to the transitional rule of section 430(h)(2)(G)). For the 2009 plan year, the first segment rate is equal to 5.50%, the second segment rate is equal to 6.00%, and the third segment rate is equal to 6.50%.

(ii) As of January 1, 2009, the present value of the remaining three waiver amortization installments with respect to the 2006 waiver is $199,715, which is determined using the first segment rate of 5.50%.

(iii) As of January 1, 2009, the present value of the remaining five waiver amortization installments with respect to the 2008 waiver is $182,594, which is determined using the first segment rate of 5.50%.

(iv) As of January 1, 2009, the present value of the remaining six shortfall amortization installments with respect to the 2008 shortfall amortization base is $385,511, which is determined using the first segment rate of 5.50% for the first five installments and the second segment rate of 6.00% for the sixth installment.

(v) A shortfall amortization base of $82,180 is established for 2009, which is equal to the $2,750,000 funding target, less $1,900,000 of assets, less $199,715 (the present value of the remaining waiver amortization installments with respect to the 2006 waiver), less $182,594 (the present value of the remaining waiver amortization installments with respect to the 2008 waiver), less $385,511 (the present value of the remaining installments with respect to the 2008 shortfall amortization base).

(vi) With respect to this shortfall amortization base of $82,180, there is a shortfall amortization installment of $13,795 (which is equal to the $82,180 shortfall amortization base amortized over 7 years) for each year from 2009 through 2015.

Example 5. (i) The facts are the same as in *Example 4,* except that Plan A has assets totaling $2,000,000 as of January 1, 2009. Plan A has a target normal cost of $110,000 as of January 1, 2009.

(ii) A shortfall amortization base of -$17,820 is established for 2009, which is equal to the $2,750,000 funding target, less $2,000,000 of assets, less $199,715 (the present value of the remaining installments with respect to the 2006 waiver), less $182,594 (the present value of the remaining installments with respect to the 2008 waiver), less $385,511 (the present value of the remaining installments with respect to the 2008 shortfall amortization base).

(iii) The shortfall amortization installment for the 2009 shortfall amortization base is -$2,991, which is equal to the -$17,820 shortfall amortization base amortized over 7 years. The first five shortfall amortization installments are discounted using the first segment rate of 5.50%

and the sixth and seventh shortfall amortization installments are discounted using the second segment rate of 6.00%.

(iv) The minimum required contribution for the 2009 plan year is $291,102. This is equal to the target normal cost of $110,000 plus the shortfall amortization charge of $70,406 (that is, $73,397 minus $2,991) plus the waiver amortization charge of $110,696 (that is, $70,166 plus $40,530).

Example 6. (i) The facts are the same as in *Example 5*, except that Plan A has assets totaling $2,800,000 as of January 1, 2009.

(ii) Because the assets of $2,800,000 exceed the funding target of $2,750,000 as of January 1, 2009, no new shortfall amortization base is established under paragraph (c)(2) of this section.

(iii) Furthermore, under paragraph (e) of this section, all shortfall amortization bases and waiver amortization bases (and all shortfall amortization installments and waiver amortization installments associated with those bases) are reduced to zero as of January 1, 2009.

(iv) The minimum required contribution for the 2009 plan year is $60,000, which is equal to the $110,000 target normal cost less the excess of the assets over the funding target ($2,800,000 minus $2,750,000).

Example 7. (i) The actuarial valuation for Plan B as of January 1, 2008, based on a 12-month plan year, determines a target normal cost of $110,000 and a shortfall amortization installment for 2008 of $185,000. The plan year for Plan B is changed to April 1 through March 31, effective April 1, 2008, resulting in a short plan year beginning January 1, 2008, and ending March 31, 2008.

(ii) The target normal cost for the short plan year is redetermined in order to reflect the fact that there is a short plan year. An actuarial valuation shows that the target normal cost is $25,000 for the short plan year based on the accruals for that short plan year (determined in accordance with 29 CFR § 2530.204-2(e)).

(iii) In accordance with paragraph (b)(2)(ii)(A) of this section, the shortfall amortization base is prorated to reflect the three months covered by the short plan year. Accordingly, the shortfall amortization installment for the short plan year is $46,250 (that is, $185,000 multiplied by 3/12).

(iv) The total minimum required contribution for the short plan year (without offset for any carryover balance as of January 1, 2008) is $71,250 (that is, the sum of the target normal cost of $25,000 plus the shortfall amortization installment of $46,250).

Example 8. (i) The facts are the same as in *Example 7*. The first segment rate for the plan year beginning April 1, 2008, is 5.30%, and the second segment rate is 5.80%.

(ii) The present value of the remaining shortfall amortization installments with respect to the January 1, 2008, shortfall amortization base is equal to $1,074,937. This is determined by discounting the remaining installments (6 full-year installments due April 1, 2008 through April 1, 2013, and a final 9-month installment due April 1, 2014) using the first segment rate of 5.30% for the first five installments and the second segment rate of 5.80% for the remaining installments.

(h) *Effective/applicability dates and transition rules*—(1) *In general.* Section 430 generally applies to plan years beginning on or after January 1, 2008. In general, this section applies to plan years beginning on or after January 1, 2009. However, plans are permitted to apply this section in determining the minimum required contribution for plan years beginning in 2008.

(2) *Plans with delayed effective date.* In the case of a plan for which the effective date of section 430 is delayed in accordance with sections 104 through 106 of PPA '06, this section applies to plan years beginning on or after the date section 430 first applies with respect to the plan.

(3) *Treatment of pre-2008 funding waivers.* In the case of a plan that has received a funding waiver under section 412 for a plan year for which section 430 was not yet effective with respect to the plan, the waiver is treated as giving rise to a waiver amortization base and the amortization charges with respect to that funding waiver are treated as waiver amortization installments as described in paragraph (d) of this section. With respect to such a preexisting funding waiver, the amount of the waiver amortization installment is equal to the amortization charge with respect to that waiver determined using the interest rate or rates that applied for the pre-effective plan year.

(4) *Transition rule for determining whether shortfall amortization base is established*—(i) *In general.* Except as provided in paragraphs (h)(4)(iii) and (iv) of this section, in the case of plan years beginning after 2007 and before 2011, only the applicable percentage of the funding target is taken into account in determining whether a shortfall amortization base is established for the plan year under paragraph (c)(2) of this section.

(ii) *Applicable percentage.* For purposes of paragraph (h)(4)(i) of this section, the applicable percentage is determined in accordance with the following table:

Calendar year in which the plan year begins	Applicable percentage
2008	92
2009	94
2010	96

(iii) *Transition rule not available if funding falls below applicable percentage.* The transition rule of paragraph (h)(4)(i) of this section does not apply with respect to any plan year beginning after 2008 if a shortfall amortization base was required to be established under paragraph (c)(2) of this section for any preceding year.

(iv) *Transition rule not available for new plans or deficit reduction plans.* The transition rule of paragraph (h)(4)(i) of this section does not apply to a plan—

(A) That was not in effect for a plan year beginning in 2007; or

(B) That was subject to section 412(l) for the pre-effective plan year, determined after the application of sections 412(l)(6) and (9) (regardless of whether the deficit reduction contribution for the pre-effective plan year was equal to zero).

(v) *Pre-effective plan year.* For purposes of this section, the pre-effective plan year for a plan is the last plan year beginning before section 430 applies to the plan. Thus, except for plans with a delayed effective date under paragraph (h)(2) of this section, the pre-effective plan year for a plan is the last plan year beginning before January 1, 2008.

Par. 3. Section 1.430(j)-1 is added to read as follows:

§ 1.430(j)-1 *Payment of minimum required contributions.*

(a) *In general*—(1) *Overview.* This section provides rules related to the payment of minimum required contributions, including the payment of quarterly contributions. Section 430(j) and this section apply to single employer defined benefit plans (including multiple employer plans as defined in section 413(c)) but do not apply to multiemployer plans (as defined in section 414(f)). Paragraph (b) of this section describes the general timing requirement for minimum required contributions. Paragraph (c) of this section describes the accelerated quarterly contribution schedule for plans with a funding shortfall in the preceding plan year. Paragraph (d) of this section provides rules regarding liquidity requirements. Paragraph (e) of this section provides definitions. Paragraph (f) of this section provides examples that illustrate the rules of this section. Paragraph (g) of this section sets forth effective/applicability dates and transition rules.

(2) *Special rules for multiple employer plans.* In the case of a multiple employer plan to which section 413(c)(4)(A) applies, the rules of section 430 and this section are applied separately for each employer under the plan, as if each employer maintained a separate plan. Thus, for example, required quarterly contributions are determined separately for each employer under such a multiple employer plan. In the case of a multiple employer plan to which section 413(c)(4)(A) does not apply (that is, a plan described in section 413(c)(4)(B) that has not made the election for section 413(c)(4)(A) to apply), the rules of section 430 and this section are applied as if all participants in the plan were employed by a single employer.

(3) *Applicability of section 430(j) to plans of commercial passenger airlines*—(i) *In general.* Except as otherwise provided in this section, the rules of section 430(j) and this section apply to a plan for which an election described in section 402 of the Pension Protection Act of 2006, Public Law 109-280 (120 Stat. 780) (PPA '06), has been made in the same manner as those rules apply to any other plan subject to section 430.

(ii) *Special rules for plans for which election was made pursuant to section 402(a)(1) of PPA '06.* For purposes of applying the rules of section 430(j) and this section to a plan with respect to which the election under section 402(a)(1) of PPA '06 has been made, the effective interest rate for the plan is deemed to be 8.85% during the period for which the election applies. In addition, see paragraph (e)(4)(ii) of this section for a special determination of the funding shortfall for a plan for which the election in section 402(a)(1) of PPA '06 has been made.

(b) *General timing requirement for minimum required contributions—* (1) *Earliest date for contributions.* A payment of the minimum required contribution under section 430 for a plan year can be made no earlier than the first day of the plan year.

(2) *Deadline for contributions.* The deadline for any payment of any minimum required contribution for a plan year is 8 1/2 months after the close of the plan year. See section 4971 and the regulations thereunder regarding an excise tax that applies with respect to minimum required contributions not paid by this deadline. See also section 430(k) of the Code and section 101(d) of the Employee Retirement Income Security Act of 1974 (ERISA), 29 U.S.C. 1021(d), for additional rules that apply in the case of a failure to pay minimum required contributions by this deadline.

(3) *Adjustment for interest.* Any payment of the minimum required contribution under section 430 for a plan year that is made on a date other than the valuation date for that plan year is adjusted for interest accruing for the period between the valuation date and the payment date, at the effective interest rate for the plan for that plan year determined pursuant to § 1.430(h)(2)-1(f)(1). The direction of the adjustment depends on whether the contribution is paid before or after the valuation date for the plan year. If the contribution is paid after the valuation date for the plan year, the contribution is discounted to the valuation date using the plan's effective interest rate. By contrast, if the contribution is paid before the valuation date for the plan year (which could only occur in the case of a small plan described in section 430(g)(2)(B)), the contribution is increased for interest using the plan's effective interest rate.

(c) *Accelerated quarterly contribution schedule for underfunded plans—*(1) *In general—*(i) *Plan subject to quarterly contribution requirement.* In any case in which the plan has a funding shortfall for the preceding plan year, the employer maintaining the plan shall make the required installments described in paragraph (c)(3) of this section by the due dates described in paragraph (c)(4) of this section.

(ii) *Satisfaction of installments through use of funding balances.* In the case of a plan that is subject to the quarterly contribution requirement under this paragraph (c), if the plan sponsor makes an election to use the plan's prefunding balance or funding standard carryover balance under section 430(f), then the plan sponsor is treated as satisfying the obligation to make a required installment under paragraph (c)(1)(i) of this section on the date of the election to the extent of the amount elected, as adjusted with interest. This interest adjustment is made at the plan's effective interest rate under section 430(h)(2)(A) for the plan year from the valuation date through the due date of the installment.

(iii) *Consequences of failure to make quarterly contribution—*(A) *Interest adjustment.* If the full amount of a required installment is not paid by

the due date for that installment, then an increased rate of interest applies in adjusting the payment to the valuation date. This increased rate of interest is equal to the rate otherwise used under paragraph (b) of this section plus 5 percentage points, and applies with respect to the underpayment of the required installment (determined pursuant to paragraph (c)(2) of this section) for the period of time that begins on the due date for the required installment and that ends on the date on which payment is made.

(B) *Application to required installments due before the valuation date.* The modified interest rate described in paragraph (c)(1)(iii)(A) of this section only applies to a required installment that is due on or after the valuation date for the plan year. See paragraph (c)(6) of this section for rules that apply to required installments that are due before the valuation date for the plan year.

(C) *Additional consequences.* See section 430(k) of the Code and section 101(d) of ERISA for examples of additional consequences of failure to make quarterly contributions.

(2) *Determination of underpayment—*(i) *Underpayment for a quarter.* For purposes of this section, the amount of the underpayment with respect to a required installment for a quarter is equal to the excess of—

(A) The required installment; over

(B) The amount (if any) of the installment contributed to or under the plan on or before the due date for the installment.

(ii) *Order of crediting contributions.* For purposes of this section, contributions are first credited against the earliest unpaid required installments.

(3) *Amount of required installment—*(i) *In general.* For purposes of this section, the amount of any required installment is equal to 25% of the required annual payment described in paragraph (c)(3)(ii) of this section.

(ii) *Required annual payment.* The required annual payment is equal to the lesser of—

(A) 90% of the minimum required contribution under section 430 for the plan year; or

(B) 100% of the minimum required contribution under section 430 (determined without regard to any funding waiver under section 412) for the preceding plan year.

(iii) *Treatment of funding balances.* For purposes of paragraph (c)(3)(ii) of this section, the minimum required contribution for a plan year is determined without regard to the use of the prefunding balance or funding standard carryover balance in the current year or any prior year. However, see paragraph (c)(1)(ii) of this section regarding a plan sponsor's election to use the plan's prefunding balance or funding standard carryover balance in the current year for the payment of quarterly installments.

(4) *Due dates for installments.* For purposes of this section, there is a required installment for each quarter of the plan year. The due dates for the four required quarterly installments with respect to a full plan year are set forth in the following table:

Installment	Due date
First quarter's installment	15 th day of 4th plan month
Second quarter's installment	15 th day of 7th plan month
Third quarter's installment	15 th day of 10th plan month
Fourth quarter's installment	15 th day after the close of the plan year

(5) *Special rules for short plan years—*(i) *In general.* In the case of a short plan year, the rules of this paragraph (c) are modified as provided in this paragraph (c)(5).

(ii) *Current plan year is short plan year—*(A) *Amount of required annual payment.* In determining the required annual payment pursuant to paragraph (c)(3)(ii) of this section for a short plan year, the amount otherwise determined under paragraph (c)(3)(ii)(B) (based on the prior year's minimum required contribution) is multiplied by a fraction, the numerator of which is the duration of the short plan year and the denominator of which is 1 year.

(B) *Number and due dates of installments.* If the plan has a short plan year, then an installment is due 15 days after the close of that short plan year. In addition, an installment is required for each due date determined under paragraph (c)(4) of this section that falls within the

short plan year. Thus, for example, if the short plan year ends before the 15th day of the 4th plan month of the plan year, there will be only one installment for that short plan year, and that installment will be due on the 15th day after the close of the short plan year.

(C) *Amount of installments.* The amount of each installment required to be paid for the short plan year is equal to the required annual payment determined pursuant to paragraph (c)(3)(ii) of this section (as modified by paragraph (c)(5)(ii)(A) of this section) divided by the number of installments determined pursuant to paragraph (c)(5)(ii)(B) of this section.

(iii) *Prior plan year is short plan year.* If the prior plan year is a short plan year, then the rule of paragraph (c)(3)(ii)(B) regarding the use of 100% of the prior year's minimum required contribution in determining the required annual payment does not apply. Accordingly, in such a case, the required annual payment is equal to 90% of the minimum required contribution under section 430 for the current plan year.

(6) *Special rule for plans with valuation dates after the first day of the plan year.* [Reserved]

(d) *Liquidity requirement in connection with quarterly contributions*—(1) *In general*—(i) *Requirement to make additional quarterly contributions.* Except as provided in paragraphs (d)(1)(ii) and (iii) of this section, if a plan is subject to the requirement to make quarterly contributions under paragraph (c) of this section, then the plan is treated as failing to pay the full amount of a required installment for a quarter to the extent that the value of the liquid assets contributed after the close of that quarter and on or before the due date for the installment is less than the liquidity shortfall for that quarter.

(ii) *Limitation on increase.* The amount by which any required installment is increased by reason of paragraph (d)(1)(i) of this section cannot exceed the amount that, when added to prior required installments for the plan year, would increase the funding target attainment percentage of the plan for the plan year (taking into account the expected increase in the funding target due to benefits accruing or earned during the plan year) to 100%.

(iii) *Small plan exception.* The liquidity requirement of this paragraph (d) does not apply to a small plan that is described in § 1.430(g)-1(b)(2).

(2) *Period of underpayment*—(i) *General rule.* For purposes of applying the additional 5 percentage point interest adjustment pursuant to paragraph (c)(1)(iii) of this section, the liquidity increment with respect to a quarter as described in paragraph (d)(2)(ii) of this section continues to be treated as unpaid until the close of the quarter in which the due date for that installment occurs without regard to when that portion is paid. However, for purposes of adjusting the contribution to the valuation date at the effective interest rate under paragraph (b)(3) of this section, the adjustment is made from the contribution date (rather than the close of the quarter).

(ii) *Liquidity increment.* For purposes of this paragraph (d), the liquidity increment with respect to a quarter is the portion of the required installment for that quarter that is treated as not paid solely by reason of paragraph (d)(1)(i) of this section.

(iii) *Ordering rule.* If the employer makes a contribution for a quarter that, after application of paragraph (c)(2)(ii) of this section, is less than the total amount needed to satisfy the requirements of paragraph (c) of this section as increased by this paragraph (d) for a quarter, then the contribution is first attributed toward satisfying the requirements of paragraph (c) of this section (without regard to this paragraph (d)) and then to the liquidity increment.

(3) *Consequences of failure to pay liquidity shortfall.* See section 4971(f) for an excise tax on the failure to pay a liquidity shortfall. See also section 206(e) of ERISA.

(e) *Definitions*—(1) *In general.* The definitions set forth in this paragraph (e) apply for purposes of this section.

(2) *Adjusted disbursements.* The term *adjusted disbursements* means disbursements from the plan reduced by the product of—

(i) The plan's funding target attainment percentage determined under section 430(d)(2) for the plan year; and

(ii) The sum of the purchases of annuities and payments of single sums.

(3) *Disbursements from the plan.* The term *disbursements from the plan* means all disbursements from the trust, including purchases of annuities, payments of single sums and other benefits, and administrative expenses.

(4) *Funding shortfall*—(i) *In general.* The term *funding shortfall* means the excess (if any) of—

(A) The funding target of the plan for a plan year; over

(B) The value of plan assets for the plan year (as reduced to reflect the subtraction of certain funding balances as provided under § 1.430(f)-1(c), but not below zero).

(ii) *Special rule for plans of commercial passenger airlines.* In the case of a plan year for which an election described in section 402(a)(1) of PPA '06 is in effect, the term *funding shortfall* means the unfunded liability for that plan year determined under § 1.430(a)-1(b)(4)(ii).

(iii) *Special rule for first effective plan year.* See paragraph (g)(5)(ii) of this section for a calculation of the funding shortfall for the plan's pre-effective plan year.

(iv) *Special rule for plan spinoffs and mergers.* [Reserved]

(5) *Liquid assets*—(i) *In general.* The term *liquid assets* means cash, marketable securities, and other assets described in this paragraph (e)(5)(i). For this purpose, marketable securities include financial instruments such as stocks and other equity interests, evidences of indebtedness (including certificates of deposit), options, futures contracts, and other derivatives, for which there is a liquid financial market, and other interests in entities (such as partnerships, trusts, or regulated investment companies) for which there is a liquid financial market. For purposes of the preceding sentence, a liquid financial market is an established financial market described in § 1.1092(d)-1(b) (other than an interbank market or an interdealer market described in § 1.1092(d)-1(b)(1)(v) and (vi), respectively). Any security that is issued or guaranteed by the government of the United States or an agency or instrumentality thereof for which there is an established financial market described in § 1.1092(d)-1(b) is a marketable security. Finally, any financial instrument or other interest in an entity that, under its terms, contains a right by which the instrument or other interest may immediately be redeemed, exchanged, or converted into cash or a marketable security, is a marketable security, provided there are no restrictions on the exercise of that right.

(ii) *Insurance and annuity contracts.* Other assets that are treated as liquid assets of a plan are insurance, annuity, or other contracts issued by an insurance company that is licensed to do business under the laws of any State, but only if the insurance, annuity, or other contract—

(A) Would be treated as a marketable security under paragraph (e)(5)(i) of this section if it were a financial instrument;

(B) Provides for substantially equal monthly disbursements to the extent provided in paragraph (e)(5)(iii) of this section; or

(C) Is benefit responsive within the meaning of paragraph (e)(5)(iv) of this section.

(iii) *Insurance and annuity contracts providing for substantially equal periodic payments.* If the contract provides for substantially equal monthly disbursements (for example, an annuity contract in pay status), the only portion of the contract that may be treated as liquid assets for a quarter is the amount equal to 36 times the monthly disbursement (in the month containing the last day of the quarter) which is available under the terms of the contract, provided there are no restrictions (within the meaning of paragraph (e)(5)(v) of this section) on the disbursements.

(iv) *Benefit responsive insurance and annuity contracts.* A contract is considered benefit responsive if, under applicable law and contractual provisions, the plan has the right to receive disbursements from the contract in order to pay plan benefits for any participant in the plan, without restrictions (within the meaning of paragraph (e)(5)(v) of this section).

(v) *Restrictions.* For purposes of paragraphs (e)(5)(iii) and (iv) of this section, a restriction on a redemption, exchange or conversion right, or a restriction on a disbursement, may result not only from applicable law or contractual provisions, but also from rehabilitation, conservatorship, receivership, insolvency, bankruptcy or similar proceedings.

(6) *Liquidity shortfall*—(i) *In general.* The term *liquidity shortfall* means, with respect to any required installment, an amount equal to the excess (as of the last day of the quarter for which that installment is made) of—

(A) The base amount with respect to the quarter, over

(B) The value (as of the last day of the quarter) of the plan's liquid assets.

(ii) *Base amount*—(A) *In general.* For purposes of this paragraph (e)(6)(ii), the term *base amount* means, with respect to any quarter, an amount equal to 3 times the sum of the adjusted disbursements from the plan for the 12 months ending on the last day of such quarter.

(B) *Special rule.* If the generally applicable base amount for a quarter determined under paragraph (e)(6)(ii)(A) of this section exceeds an amount equal to 2 times the sum of the adjusted disbursements from the plan for the 36 months ending on the last day of the quarter and the enrolled actuary for the plan certifies to the satisfaction of the Commissioner that such excess is the result of nonrecurring circumstances, the base amount with respect to that quarter is determined without regard to amounts related to those nonrecurring circumstances.

(7) *Plan month*—(i) *Plan year begins on the first day of a calendar month.* For a plan year that begins with the first day of a calendar month, the term *plan month* means any calendar month that begins during the plan year.

(ii) *Plan year begins on a date other than the first day of a calendar month.* For a plan year that begins on a date other than the first day of a calendar month, the first day of each *plan month* is the day of the calendar month that corresponds to the day of the calendar month that is the first day of the plan year. Thus, for example, if the first day of a plan year is January 15, then a plan month starts on the 15th of each calendar month. However, if a calendar month does not contain a day that corresponds to the day of the calendar month which is the first day of the plan year (for example, if a calendar month has only 30 days and the first day of the plan year is the 31st day of a calendar month), then the first day of the plan month that begins during that calendar month is the last day of that calendar month.

(8) *Quarter.* The term *quarter* means, with respect to any required installment, the 3-plan-month period preceding the plan month in which the due date for that installment occurs.

(9) *Short plan year.* The term *short plan year* means a plan year that is shorter than 12 months (and is not a 52-week plan year of a plan that uses a 52-53 week plan year).

(f) *Examples.* The following examples illustrate the rules of this section.

Example 1. (i) Plan A has a calendar year plan year and a January 1 valuation date. Plan A has a funding standard carryover balance of $15,000 as of January 1, 2008, and the plan's funding ratio for 2007 (determined using the transition rule in §1.430(f)-1(h)(5)) was over 80%. The minimum required contribution for Plan A (prior to any offset for the carryover balance) is $100,000 for 2008 and is $125,000 for 2009. The effective interest rate for the 2009 plan year is 5.90%. Plan A is subject to the quarterly contribution requirements for 2008.

(ii) The required annual payment for 2009 is equal to the lesser of (a) 100% of the 2008 minimum required contribution ($100,000) or (b) 90% of the 2009 minimum required contribution (90% of $125,000, or $112,500). Therefore, each required quarterly installment for 2009 is 25% of $100,000, or $25,000.

(iii) Installments of $25,000 each are due by April 15, 2009, July 15, 2009, October 15, 2009, and January 15, 2010. The final contribution for the 2009 plan year is due by September 15, 2010. The amount of this contribution is equal to $125,000, less the contributions made prior to that date, with all contributions adjusted to the valuation date using the effective interest rate for the 2009 plan year. If the plan sponsor makes each required quarterly installment on the date due, the remaining amount due is determined as follows:

(A) The contribution paid April 15, 2009, is adjusted by discounting the contribution amount for 3 ½ months at the effective interest rate ($25,000 ÷ $1.0590^{(3.5/12)}$ = $24,585).

(B) The contribution paid July 15, 2009, is discounted for 6 ½ months at the effective interest rate ($25,000 ÷ $1.0590^{(6.5/12)}$ = $24,236).

(C) The contribution paid October 15, 2009, is discounted for 9 ½ months at the effective interest rate ($25,000 ÷ $1.0590^{(9.5/12)}$ = $23,891).

(D) The contribution paid January 15, 2010, is discounted for 12 ½ months at the effective interest rate ($25,000 ÷ $1.0590^{(12.5/12)}$ = $23,551).

(E) The sum of the above contributions for the 2009 plan year paid through January 15, 2010, adjusted for interest to the valuation date, is $96,263. The remaining amount due for the 2009 plan year is $125,000 minus $96,263, or $28,737, as of January 1, 2009.

(iv) If the final contribution is made on September 15, 2010, the remaining amount due must be increased for interest at the plan's effective interest rate for the 20 ½ months between January 1, 2009, and September 15, 2010 (so that when it is discounted with interest for those 20 ½ months the resulting amount will equal $28,737). Therefore, the remaining contribution made on September 15, 2010, is $28,737 × $1.0590^{(20.5/12)}$ = $31,694.

Example 2. (i) The facts are the same as in *Example 1*, except that the plan sponsor elects to use the $15,000 carryover balance as of January 1, 2008, to offset the minimum required contribution for the 2008 plan year. The plan sponsor makes a contribution on January 1, 2008, of $85,000, which satisfies the minimum contribution requirement for 2008.

(ii) The required quarterly installment for 2009 is unaffected by the plan sponsor's election to offset the minimum required contribution by the carryover balance for 2008. Therefore, the required annual payment is $100,000 (determined as the lesser of (a) 100% of $100,000 or (b) 90% of $125,000) and the amount of each required quarterly installment for 2009 is 25% of the required annual payment, or $25,000.

Example 3. (i) The facts are the same as in *Example 1*. Plan A's funding standard carryover balance has increased to $17,000 as of

January 1, 2009, based on the actual rate of return of plan assets for the 2008 plan year. Plan A's funding ratio for 2008 (determined under §1.430(f)-1(d)(3)) is over 80%. On April 13, 2009, the plan sponsor elects to use the entire amount of the carryover balance to offset the minimum required contribution for 2009.

(ii) The plan sponsor's election to use the carryover balance to offset the minimum required contribution is treated as satisfying the requirement to make a required installment to the extent of the amount elected, adjusted with interest. This adjustment is made at the plan's effective interest rate for the 2009 plan year, and applies for the period between January 1, 2009, and April 15, 2009. Therefore, the $17,000 carryover balance as of January 1, 2009, offsets $17,000 × $1.0590(3.5/12)$ or $17,287 of the $25,000 quarterly contribution installment due April 15, 2009, and the remaining contribution due on April 15, 2009, is $25,000 minus $17,287, or $7,713.

(iii) The interest adjustments in paragraph (ii) of this *Example 3* are based on the effective interest rate even if that rate is not determined by the time that the quarterly contribution is due. If the plan's effective interest rate for the plan year has not been determined at the time that the quarterly contribution is due, the actual amount of the required installment satisfied by the use of the carryover balance is determined after the effective interest rate is determined. If the extent to which the carryover balance satisfies the installment requirement is overestimated and the result is the full amount of the required quarterly installment is not paid by the due date, the plan is subject to the consequences for late or unpaid quarterly contributions as described in paragraph (c)(1)(iii) of this section.

Example 4. (i) The facts are the same as in *Example 3*. The plan sponsor makes a contribution of $7,713 (which is equal to the remaining portion of the first required quarterly installment) on April 15, 2009. For the 2009 plan year, the plan sponsor makes another contribution of $200,000 on June 30, 2009. No further contributions are made for the 2009 plan year.

(ii) The contributions made for the 2009 plan year are adjusted to the valuation date using the plan's effective interest rate for the 2009 plan year. The contribution paid April 15, 2009, is discounted for the 3 ½ months between January 1, 2009, and the date of payment, using the effective interest rate of 5.90% ($7,713 / $1.0590^{(3.5/12)}$ = $7,585). The contribution paid June 30, 2009, is discounted for 6 months using the effective interest rate ($200,000 / $1.0590^{(6/12)}$ = $194,349), for a total interest-adjusted contribution of $201,934.

(iii) The minimum required contribution for 2009 (prior to any offset for the carryover balance) is $125,000 and, under §1.430(f)-1(b)(1)(ii)(B), this amount is used to determine the interest-adjusted excess contribution. Accordingly, the interestadjusted excess contribution for 2009 is $201,934 minus $125,000, or $76,934, increased for interest to January 1, 2010, using the effective interest rate for 2009 of 5.90%. Thus, the interest-adjusted excess contribution as of January 1, 2010, is $76,934 multiplied by 1.059, or $81,473. All or a portion of this amount may be credited to the prefunding balance at the election of the plan sponsor.

Example 5. (i) The facts are the same as in *Example 3*. The plan sponsor pays the required quarterly installment of $7,713 on April 15, 2009, and installments of $25,000 each on July 15, 2009, and October 15, 2009. However, only $10,000 of the installment due on January 15, 2010, is paid. No additional contributions are made until the final contribution for the plan year of $55,000 is paid on September 15, 2010.

(ii) The 2009 Schedule SB shows that the contributions for the plan year exceed the minimum required contribution. This is determined by comparing the minimum required contribution of $108,000 ($125,000 offset by $17,000 for the amount of carryover balance used) and the interest-adjusted contributions made for the 2009 plan year, developed as shown below:

(A) The contribution paid April 15, 2009, is adjusted by discounting the contribution amount for 3 ½ months at the effective interest rate ($7,713 ÷ $1.0590^{(3.5/12)}$ = $7,585).

(B) The contribution paid July 15, 2009, is discounted for 6 ½ months at the effective interest rate ($25,000 ÷ $1.0590^{(6.5/12)}$ = $24,236).

(C) The contribution paid October 15, 2009, is discounted for 9 ½ months at the effective interest rate ($25,000 ÷ $1.0590^{(9.5/12)}$ = $23,891).

(D) The contribution paid January 15, 2010, is discounted for 12 ½ months at the effective interest rate ($10,000 ÷ $1.0590^{(12.5/12)}$ = $9,420).

(E) Pursuant to paragraph (c)(1)(iii)(A) of this section, the adjustment for interest on the $15,000 underpayment of the quarterly installment due January 15, 2010, is increased by 5 percentage points for the 8-month period of underpayment (January 15, 2010, through September 15, 2010). Accordingly, $15,000 of the contribution paid on September 15, 2010, is discounted using a rate of 10.90% for 8 months and at the 5.90% effective interest rate for the remaining 12 ½ months between the quarterly contribution due date of January 15, 2010, and the valuation date of January 1, 2009. This portion of the September 15, 2010, contribution results in an adjusted amount of $13,189 as of January 1, 2009 ($15,000 ÷ 1.1090 $^{(8/12)}$ ÷ 1.0590 $^{(12.5/12)}$).

(F) The remaining $40,000 of the contribution paid on September 15, 2010, is discounted using the effective interest rate of 5.90% for the 20 ½-month period between the date of payment and the valuation date. This portion of the payment is therefore adjusted to $36,268 as of the valuation date (that is, $40,000 ÷ 1.0590 $^{(20.5/12)}$).

(G) The sum of the above contributions for the 2009 plan year paid through January 15, 2010, adjusted for interest to the valuation date, is $114,589. This is greater than the minimum required contribution for the 2009 plan year of $108,000.

Example 6. (i) The facts are the same as in *Example 5*, except that the plan sponsor does not make a contribution on September 15, 2010. Another contribution is not made until December 15, 2010.

(ii) The 2009 Schedule SB shows an unpaid minimum required contribution of $42,868 as of January 1, 2009. This is equal to the difference between the minimum required contribution of $108,000 ($125,000 offset by $17,000 for the amount of carryover balance used) and $65,132 (the interest-adjusted contributions made for the 2009 plan year before the 8 ½ month deadline, as illustrated in paragraphs (ii)(A) through (ii)(D) of *Example 5*).

Example 7. (i) The facts are the same as in *Example 1*, except that the plan year is changed to an August 1 - July 31 plan year effective August 1, 2009. This results in a short plan year beginning January 1, 2009, and ending July 31, 2009. The minimum required contribution for the 7-month period covered by the plan year is calculated as $72,917 in accordance with § 1.430(a)-1(b)(2)(ii).

(ii) As provided in paragraph (c)(5) of this section, a required installment is due 15 days after the close of the short plan year (August 15, 2009), and required installments are also due on the regularly scheduled due dates for quarterly installments that occur within the short plan year (April 15, 2009, and July 15, 2009).

(iii) The required installments are determined based on the lesser of (a) 90% of the minimum required contribution for the short plan year ending July 31, 2009 (90% of $72,917, or $65,625) or (b) 7/12 of 100% of the 2008 minimum required contribution ($100,000 × 7/12, or $58,333). The required installments are thus based on $58,333 since that is the smaller amount.

(iv) The amount of each required installment is determined by dividing the amount determined in paragraph (iii) of this *Example 7* by the number of required installments for the short plan year. This calculation results in required installments of $19,444 each (that is, $58,333 divided by 3 installments).

(v) The deadline for the remaining payment is 8 ½ months after the end of the short plan year, or April 15, 2010. If the plan sponsor pays the minimum required amount at each installment date, does not elect to offset any amounts by any carryover or prefunding balance, and makes a final payment on April 15, 2010, then the remaining payment is $17,429, determined as follows:

(A) The contribution paid April 15, 2009, is adjusted by discounting the contribution amount for 3 ½ months at the effective interest rate ($19,444 ÷ 1.0590 $^{(3.5/12)}$ = $19,122).

(B) The contribution paid July 15, 2009, is discounted for 6 ½ months at the effective interest rate ($19,444 ÷ 1.0590 $^{(6.5/12)}$ = $18,850).

(C) The contribution paid August 15, 2009, is discounted for 7 ½ months at the effective interest rate ($19,444 ÷ 1.0590 $^{(7.5/12)}$ = $18,760).

(D) The sum of the above contributions for the 2009 plan year paid through August 15, 2009, adjusted for interest to the valuation date, is $56,732. The remaining amount paid April 15, 2010, for the 2009 plan year is ($72,917 - $56,732) x 1.059 $^{(15.5/12)}$ = $17,429.

Example 8. (i) Plan B has an August 10 to August 9 plan year. Quarterly installments are required for the plan year that begins August 10, 2009.

(ii) For the plan year that begins on August 10, 2009, a plan month begins on the 10th day of each calendar month. Accordingly, the due dates for the required installments for that plan year are November 24,

2009, February 24, 2010, May 24, 2010, and August 24, 2010. The deadline for the final contribution for the plan year is April 24, 2011.

Example 9. (i) Plan C has a calendar-year plan year and is not a small plan described in section 430(g)(2)(B). Plan C is subject to the requirement to pay quarterly contributions under paragraph (c) of this section for the 2009 plan year. The valuation date for Plan C is January 1, and Plan C's funding target attainment percentage ("FTAP") is 85% as of January 1, 2009. Before taking the liquidity requirement of paragraph (d) of this section into account, quarterly contributions are required for the 2009 plan year in the amount of $50,000 each. During the 12-month period ending March 31, 2009, periodic annuity payments of $350,000 and lump sum payments of $200,000 were made by Plan C. None of these payments were due to nonrecurring circumstances. In addition, administrative expenses of $100,000 were paid from the plan trust. The market value of Plan C's assets is $1,500,000 as of March 31, 2008, of which $1,300,000 is in liquid assets. The amount needed to increase the plan's FTAP (including the expected increase in the funding target due to benefits accruing or earned during the plan year) to 100% is $500,000.

(ii) The amount of the adjusted disbursements from Plan C for the 12-month period ending March 31, 2009, is calculated as the sum of the annuity benefits, lump sum payments, and administrative expenses paid during the 12-month period, reduced by the product of the lump sum payments and the plan's FTAP. This results in adjusted disbursements for the period of $480,000 (that is, $350,000 plus $200,000 plus $100,000, reduced by 85% of $200,000 in lump sum payments).

(iii) The base amount is calculated in accordance with paragraph (e)(6)(ii) of this section as three times the adjusted disbursements determined in paragraph (ii) of this *Example 9*, or $1,440,000.

(iv) The liquidity shortfall is the difference between the base amount of $1,440,000 determined in paragraph (iii) of this *Example 9* and the $1,300,000 in liquid assets as of March 31, 2008, or $140,000. The quarterly contribution due on April 15, 2009, is therefore $140,000, since this amount is larger than the $50,000 quarterly contribution requirement otherwise applicable but less than the $500,000 needed to increase the plan's FTAP (including the expected increase in the funding target due to benefits accruing or earned during the plan year) to 100%. The liquidity increment is $90,000.

(v) Note that any contributions made through March 31, 2009, are included in Plan C's assets as of March 31, 2009, and would therefore not be applied toward satisfying the liquidity shortfall contribution requirement due April 15, 2009. Similarly, any funding standard carryover balance or prefunding balance as of January 1, 2009, cannot be applied to offset the liquidity shortfall contribution requirement. Only contributions made in cash or other liquid assets made after March 31, 2009, and by April 15, 2009, can be used to timely satisfy this requirement.

Example 10. (i) The facts are the same as in *Example 9*. The plan sponsor makes a contribution of $30,000 on April 15, 2009, and makes an additional contribution of $110,000 on April 30, 2009. The effective interest rate for Plan C for the 2009 plan year is 5.90%.

(ii) The contribution paid on April 15, 2009, is applied first to the portion of the quarterly contribution that is required under paragraph (c) of this section (that is, the portion not attributable to the liquidity shortfall contribution). This results in an underpayment of this portion of the quarterly contribution due April 15, 2009, of $20,000 (that is, $50,000 minus $30,000). In accordance with paragraph (c)(1)(iii)(A) of this section, the interest rate used to adjust this portion of the late quarterly contribution is increased by 5 percentage points for the ½-month period of underpayment. Accordingly, $20,000 of the April 15, 2009, contribution is adjusted to the January 1, 2009, valuation date using an interest rate of 10.90% for the ½ month between the April 15, 2009, due date and the April 30, 2009, payment date, and by 5.90% for the 3 ½-month period between January 1, 2009, and the April 15, 2009, due date. This portion results in an interest-adjusted contribution of $19,584 as of January 1, 2009 ($20,000 ÷ 1.1090 $^{(0.5/12)}$ ÷ 1.059 $^{(3.5/12)}$).

(iii) Under paragraph (d)(2) of this section, the interest rate used to adjust the portion of the underpayment attributable to the liquidity shortfall contribution is increased by 5 percentage points, and the contribution is treated as unpaid until the close of the quarter in which the due date occurs. Therefore, even though the full amount of the liquidity shortfall was paid by April 30, 2009, the increase in the interest rate is applied as if the late liquidity shortfall contribution was not made until June 30, 2009, 2 ½ months after the contribution was due.

(iv) However, in accordance with paragraph (d)(2) of this section, each payment is discounted for interest based on the date of the actual payment, despite the fact that the 5-percentage-point increase in the interest rate is calculated as if the payment was not made until the end of the quarter. Therefore, the portion of the underpayment due to the liquidity increment ($140,000 minus the $50,000 quarterly contribution requirement otherwise required, or $90,000) is adjusted for interest for the 4-month period between the January 1, 2009, valuation date and the April 30, 2009, date of payment. An interest rate of 10.90% is used for 2 ½ months (corresponding to the period between the April 15, 2009, due date and June 30, 2009, the end of the quarter in which the payment was due), and Plan C's effective interest rate for the 2009 plan year (5.90%) is used for the remaining 1 ½ months. Therefore, the portion of the April 30, 2009, contribution attributable to the liquidity increment is adjusted to $87,452 as of January 1, 2009 ($90,000 ÷ $1.1090 (2.5/12) ÷ 1.0590 (1.5/12)).

Example 11. (i) The facts are the same as in *Example 10*, except that the plan sponsor does not make the second contribution of $110,000 until July 15, 2009.

(ii) The July 15, 2009, contribution is adjusted for interest for a total of 6 ½ months for the period between January 1, 2009, and the payment date of July 15, 2009. In accordance with paragraph (d)(2) of this section, the 5-percentage-point increase in the interest rate used to adjust the portion of the contribution attributable to the unpaid liquidity shortfall contribution is applied as if the contribution was made at the end of the quarter in which the payment was due. Therefore, the interest adjustment for the $90,000 attributable to the late liquidity shortfall contribution uses an interest rate of 10.90% for the 2 ½ -month period corresponding to the period between the April 15, 2009, due date and June 30, 2009, the end of the quarter in which the payment was due, and the effective interest rate of 5.90% for the remaining 4 months.

(iii) The liquidity shortfall is recalculated as of June 30, 2009, and the larger of the resulting amount or the $50,000 quarterly contribution otherwise applicable is due on July 15, 2009. This amount is required to be paid in addition to the unpaid liquidity shortfall contribution due April 15, 2009. Note that the amount of liquid assets as of June 30, 2009 is smaller than it would have been had the April 15, 2009, liquidity shortfall payment been made. Therefore, the fact that the April 15, 2009, liquidity shortfall payment was not made before June 30, 2009, means that the plan sponsor is required to contribute more than the amount needed to increase the liquid assets to the base amount as of June 30, 2009. However, in accordance with paragraph (d)(1)(ii) of this section, the total amount of the required installments (including those due but not paid) is limited so that it is no larger than the amount that would increase the plan's FTAP (taking into account the expected increase in the funding target due to benefits accruing or earned during the plan year) to 100%.

Example 12. (i) Plan D, which is a small plan described in section 430(g)(2)(B), has a calendar year plan year and a valuation date of December 31. The quarterly required installments for the 2009 plan year are $30,000 each and each of the required installments is paid on the due date. The effective interest rate for Plan D for the 2009 plan year is 5.90%.

(ii) The total contributions made for the plan year and before the valuation date, adjusted with interest to the valuation date, equal $92,402. This is developed as shown below:

(A) The contribution paid April 15, 2009, is adjusted by increasing the contribution amount for 8 ½ months at the effective interest rate ($30,000 × 1.0590 (8.5/12) = $31,243).

(B) The contribution paid July 15, 2009, is increased for 5 ½ months at the effective interest rate ($30,000 × 1.0590 (5.5/12) = $30,799).

(C) The contribution paid October 15, 2009, is increased for 2 ½ months at the effective interest rate ($30,000 × 1.0590 (2.5/12) = $30,360).

(iii) Pursuant to §1.430(g)-1(d)(2), the interest-adjusted value of the contributions for the 2009 plan year that are made before the valuation date is subtracted from the December 31, 2009, plan assets in determining the value of plan assets for the December 31, 2009 actuarial valuation.

(g) *Effective/applicability dates and transition rules*—(1) *In general.* Section 430 generally applies to plan years beginning on or after January 1, 2008. In general, this section applies to plan years beginning on or after January 1, 2009. However, plans are permitted to apply this section in applying the rules of section 430(j) for plan years beginning in 2008.

(2) *Plans with delayed effective date.* In the case of a plan for which the effective date of section 430 is delayed in accordance with sections 104 through 106 of PPA '06, this section applies to plan years beginning on or after the first day of the first effective plan year.

(3) *First effective plan year.* For purposes of this section, the first effective plan year for a plan is the first plan year for which section 430 applies to the plan.

(4) *Pre-effective plan year.* For purposes of this section, the pre-effective plan year for a plan is the last plan year before the first effective plan year. Thus, except for plans with a delayed effective date under paragraph (g)(2) of this section, the preeffective plan year for a plan is the last plan year beginning before January 1, 2008.

(5) *Special rules relating to first effective plan year*—(i) *Determination of minimum required contribution for pre-effective plan year.* In the case of the plan's first effective plan year, the minimum required contribution for the preceding plan year for purposes of paragraph (c)(3)(ii)(B) of this section is equal to the minimum required contribution under section 412 for the pre-effective plan year (determined without regard to any funding waiver under section 412), which is determined as of the last day of the pre-effective plan year and is determined without regard to the use of the plan's credit balance.

(ii) *Determination of funding shortfall for pre-effective plan year.* [Reserved]

PART 54—PENSION EXCISE TAXES

Par. 4. The authority citation for part 54 continues to read in part as follows:

Authority: 26 U.S.C. 7805 * * *

Par. 5. Section 54.4971(c)-1 is added to read as follows:

§54.4971(c)-1 Taxes on failure to meet minimum funding standards; definitions

(a) *In general.* This section sets forth definitions that apply for purposes of applying the rules of section 4971.

(b) *Accumulated funding deficiency.* With respect to a multiemployer plan, the term *accumulated funding deficiency* has the meaning given to that term by section 431. A plan's accumulated funding deficiency for a plan year takes into account all charges and credits to the funding standard account under section 412 for plan years before the first plan year for which section 431 applies to the plan.

(c) *Unpaid minimum required contribution*—(1) *In general.* The term *unpaid minimum required contribution* means, with respect to any plan year, any minimum required contribution under section 430 for the plan year that is not paid on or before the due date for the plan year under section 430(j)(1).

(2) *Accumulated funding deficiency for pre-effective plan year.* For purposes of this section, a plan's accumulated funding deficiency under section 412 for the preeffective plan year is treated as an unpaid minimum required contribution for that plan year until correction is made under the rules of paragraph (d)(2) of this section.

(d) *Correct*—(1) *Accumulated funding deficiency.* The term correct means, with respect to an accumulated funding deficiency for a plan year, the contribution, to or under the plan, of the amount necessary to reduce the accumulated funding deficiency as of the end of that plan year to zero. To reduce the deficiency to zero, the contribution must include interest at the plan's valuation interest rate for the period between the end of that plan year and the date of the contribution.

(2) *Unpaid minimum required contribution*—(i) *Interest adjustments*—(A) *General rule.* The term *correct* means, with respect to an unpaid minimum required contribution for a plan year, the contribution, to or under the plan, of an amount that, when discounted to the valuation date for the plan year for which the unpaid minimum required contribution is due at the appropriate rate of interest, equals or exceeds the unpaid minimum required contribution. For this purpose, the appropriate rate of interest is the plan's effective interest rate for the plan year for which the unpaid minimum required contribution is due except to the extent that the payments are subject to additional interest as provided under section 430(j)(3) or (4).

(B) *Pre-PPA accumulated funding deficiency.* The term *correct* means, with respect to the accumulated funding deficiency under section 412 for the pre-effective plan year that is described in paragraph (c)(2) of this section, the contribution, to or under the plan, of the amount of that accumulated funding deficiency increased with interest from the end of the pre-effective plan year to the date of the contribution at the plan's valuation interest rate for the pre-effective plan year.

(ii) *Ordering rule.* For purposes of section 4971 and this section, a contribution is attributable first to the earliest plan year of any unpaid minimum required contribution for which correction has not yet been made.

(3) *Corrective action of certain retroactive plan amendments.* Certain retroactive plan amendments that meet the requirements of section 412(d)(2) may reduce the minimum required contribution for a plan year, which would reduce the accumulated funding deficiency or the amount of the unpaid minimum required contribution for a plan year.

(e) *Taxable period.* The term *taxable period* has the same meaning given that term under § 54.4971-1(e).

(f) *Examples.* The following examples illustrate the rules of this section.

Example 1. (i) Plan A, a single employer defined benefit plan, has a calendar year plan year and a January 1 valuation date. The sponsor of Plan A has a calendar taxable year. Plan A has no funding shortfall as of the end of 2008, and Plan A has no unpaid minimum required contributions for 2008 or any earlier plan year. The minimum required contribution for the 2009 plan year is $250,000. The plan sponsor makes one contribution for 2009 on July 1, 2009, in the amount of $200,000, and the sponsor does not make an election to use the prefunding balance or funding standard carryover balance to offset the minimum required contribution for 2009. The effective interest rate for Plan A for the 2009 plan year is 5.90%.

(ii) The interest-adjusted contribution for 2009 is $200,000 divided by 1.0590 $^{(6/12)}$, or $194,349, as of January 1, 2009. The unpaid minimum required contribution for the 2009 plan year is $250,000 minus $194,349, or $55,651. The excise tax due under section 4971(a) is 10% of the unpaid minimum required contribution, or $5,565.

Example 2. (i) The facts are the same as in *Example 1.* The plan sponsor makes a contribution of $175,000 on December 31, 2010.

(ii) Under the ordering rule in paragraph (d)(2)(ii) of this section, the contribution made on December 31, 2010, is applied first to correct the unpaid minimum required contribution for 2009. The portion of the contribution paid December 31, 2010, that is required to eliminate the unpaid minimum required contribution for 2009 (taking into account the 2009 effective interest rate for the 24 months between January 1, 2009, and the payment date of December 31, 2010), is $55,651 multiplied by 1.059(24/12) or $62,412. The remaining payment of $112,588 ($175,000 minus $62,412) is applied to the contribution required for the 2010 plan year.

Example 3. (i) Plan B, a single employer defined benefit plan, has a calendar plan year. The sponsor of Plan B has a calendar taxable year. Plan B has an accumulated funding deficiency of $100,000 as of December 31, 2007, including additional interest due to late quarterly contributions during 2007. The valuation interest rate for the 2007 plan year is 7.5%.

(ii) In accordance with paragraph (c)(2) of this section, the accumulated funding deficiency under section 412 as of December 31, 2007, is considered an unpaid minimum required contribution until it is corrected. Pursuant to paragraph (d)(2)(i)(B) of this section, the amount needed to correct that accumulated funding deficiency is $100,000 plus interest at the valuation interest rate of 7.5% for the period between December 31, 2007, and the date of payment of the contribution.

(iii) The funding shortfall as of January 1, 2008, is calculated as the difference between the funding target and the value of assets as of that date. The assets are not adjusted by the amount of the accumulated funding deficiency; the fact that the contribution was not made for the 2007 plan year means that the January 1, 2008, funding shortfall is larger than it would have been otherwise.

Example 4. (i) The facts are the same as in *Example 3.* The minimum required contribution for the 2008 plan year is $125,000, but the plan sponsor does not make any required contributions for 2008.

(ii) The total unpaid minimum required contribution as of December 31, 2008, is the sum of the $100,000 accumulated funding deficiency under section 412 from 2007 and the $125,000 unpaid minimum required contribution for 2008, or $225,000. The section 4971(a) excise tax applies to the aggregate unpaid minimum required contributions for all plan years that remain unpaid as of the end of 2008. In this case, there is an unpaid minimum required contribution of $100,000 for the 2007 plan year and an unpaid minimum required contribution of $125,000 for the 2008 plan year. The section 4971(a) excise tax is 10% of the aggregate of those unpaid amounts, or $22,500.

Example 5. (i) The facts are the same as in *Example 4,* except that the plan sponsor makes a contribution of $150,000 on December 31, 2008. No additional contributions are paid through September 15, 2009. Quarterly contributions of $25,000 each are due April 15, 2008, July 15, 2008, October 15, 2008, and January 15, 2009. Plan B's effective interest rate for the 2008 plan year is 5.75%.

(ii) In accordance with paragraph (c)(2) of this section, the accumulated funding deficiency under section 412 as of December 31, 2007, is treated as an unpaid minimum required contribution until it is corrected.

(iii) The December 31, 2008, contribution is first applied to the 2007 accumulated funding deficiency under section 412 that is treated as an unpaid minimum required contribution. Accordingly, the amount needed to correct the 2007 unpaid minimum required contribution ($100,000 multiplied by 1.075, or $107,500) is applied to eliminate this unpaid minimum required contribution for the 2007 plan year.

(iv) The remaining December 31, 2008, contribution ($150,000 minus $107,500, or $42,500) is then applied to the 2008 minimum required contribution. This amount is first allocated to the quarterly contribution due April 15, 2008. In accordance with § 1.430(j)-1(c)(1)(iii)(A), the adjustment for interest on late quarterly contributions is increased by 5 percentage points for the period of underpayment. Therefore, $25,000 of the remaining December 31, 2008, contribution is discounted using an interest rate of 10.75% for the 8 ½-month period between the payment date of December 31, 2008 and the quarterly contribution due date of April 15, 2008, and at the 5.75% effective interest rate for the 3 ½ months between April 15, 2008, and January 1, 2008. This portion of the December 31, 2008, contribution results in an adjusted amount of $22,880 (that is, $25,000 ÷ 1.1075 $^{(8.5/12)}$ ÷ 1.0575 $^{(3.5/12)}$) as of January 1, 2008.

(v) The remaining December 31, 2008, contribution is then applied to the quarterly contribution due July 15, 2008. The balance of the December 31, 2008, contribution ($150,000 minus $107,500 minus $25,000, or $17,500) is paid after the due date for the second required quarterly installment. Accordingly, the remaining $17,500 contribution is adjusted using an interest rate of 10.75% for the 5 ½-month period between the payment date of December 31, 2008 and the quarterly contribution due date of July 15, 2008, and at the 5.75% effective interest rate for the 6 ½ months between July 15, 2008, and January 1, 2008. This portion of the December 31, 2008, contribution results in an adjusted amount of $16,202 (that is, $17,500 ÷ 1.1075 $^{(5.5/12)}$ ÷ 1.0575 $^{(6.5/12)}$) as of January 1, 2008.

(vi) The remaining unpaid minimum required contribution for 2008 is $125,000 minus the interest-adjusted amounts of $22,880 and $16,202 applied towards the 2008 minimum required contribution as determined in paragraphs (iv) and (v) of this *Example 5.* This results in an unpaid minimum required contribution of $85,918 for 2008. The section 4971(a) excise tax is 10% of the unpaid minimum required contribution, or $8,592.

Example 6. (i) Plan C, a single employer defined benefit plan, has a calendar year plan year and a January 1 valuation date, and has no funding standard carryover balance or prefunding balance as of January 1, 2008. Plan C's sponsor has a calendar year taxable year. The minimum required contributions for Plan C are $100,000 for the 2008 plan year, $110,000 for the 2009 plan year, $125,000 for the 2010 plan year, and $135,000 for the 2011 plan year. No contributions for these plan years are made until September 15, 2012, at which time the plan sponsor contributes $273,000 (which is exactly enough to correct the unpaid minimum required contributions for the 2008 and 2009 plan years).

(ii) The excise tax under section 4971(a) is 10% of the aggregate unpaid minimum required contributions for all plan years remaining unpaid as of the end of any plan year ending within the 2008 taxable year. Accordingly, the excise tax for the 2008 taxable year is $10,000 (that is, 10% of $100,000). The excise tax for the 2009 taxable year is $21,000 (that is, 10% of the sum of $100,000 and $110,000) and the excise tax for the 2010 taxable year is $33,500 (that is, 10% of the sum of $100,000, $110,000, and $125,000).

(iii) The contribution made on September 15, 2012, is applied to correct the unpaid minimum required contributions for the 2008 and 2009 plan years by the deadline for making contributions for the 2011 plan year. Therefore, the excise tax under section 4971(a) for the 2011 taxable year is based only on the remaining unpaid minimum required contributions for the 2010 and 2011 plan years, or $26,000 (that is, 10% of the sum of $125,000 and $135,000).

(iv) The plan sponsor may also be required to pay an excise tax of 100% under section 4971(b), if the unpaid minimum required contributions are not corrected by the end of the taxable period.

(g) *Effective/applicability dates and transition rules—*(1) *Statutory effective date—*(i) *In general.* In general, the amendments made to section 4971 by section 114 of the Pension Protection Act of 2006, Public Law 109-280, 120 Stat. 780 (PPA '06), apply to taxable years beginning on or after January 1, 2008, but only with respect to plan years that end with or within any such taxable year.

(ii) *Plans with delayed PPA '06 effective dates.* In the case of a plan for which the effective date of section 430 is delayed in accordance with sections 104 through 106 of PPA '06, the amendments made to section 4971 by section 114 of PPA '06 apply to taxable years beginning on or after January 1, 2008, but only with respect to plan years beginning on or after the date section 430 first applies with respect to the plan.

(2) *Effective date of regulations.* This section is effective for taxable years beginning on and after the statutory effective date described in paragraph (g)(1) of this section, but in no event does this section apply to taxable years ending before April 15, 2008.

(3) *Pre-effective plan year.* For purposes of this section, the pre-effective plan year for a plan is the last plan year beginning before section 430 applies to the plan. Thus, except for plans with a delayed effective date under paragraph (g)(1)(ii) of this section, the pre-effective plan year for a plan is the last plan year beginning before January 1, 2008.

Linda E. Stiff

Deputy Commissioner for Services and Enforcement

¶ 20,262L

IRS: Defined benefit plans: Accrual rules: Code Sec. 411(b)(1)(B).—The IRS has issued a proposed rule that extends the defined benefit (DB) plan accrual rules of Code Sec. 411(b) for plans with two or more benefit accrual formulas for plan years beginning in 2009. The proposed regulation provides a limited exception to the existing requirement under Reg. § 1.411(b)-1(a)(1) to aggregate the accrued benefits under all formulas in order to determine whether or not the accrued benefits for participants under the plan satisfy one of the alternative methods in Code Sec. 411(b)(1)(A)—(C). Under the proposed exception, certain plans that determine a participant's benefits as the greatest of the benefits determined under two or more separate formulas would be permitted to demonstrate satisfaction of the 133 1/3 percent rule of Code Sec. 411(b)(1)(B) by demonstrating that each separate formula satisfies the 133 1/3 percent rule of Code Sec. 411(b)(1)(B). The proposed rule extends the application of Rev. Rul. 2008-7. (See CCH Pension Plan Guide 19,948Z-220.)

The proposed regulation was published in the Federal Register on June 18, 2008 (73 FR 34665).

DEPARTMENT OF THE TREASURY

Internal Revenue Service

26 CFR Part 1

[REG-100464-08]

RIN 1545-BH50

Accrual rules for defined benefit plans

AGENCY: Internal Revenue Service (IRS), Treasury.

ACTION: Notice of proposed rulemaking and notice of public hearing.

SUMMARY: This document contains proposed regulations providing guidance on the application of the accrual rule for defined benefit plans under section 411(b)(1)(B) of the Internal Revenue Code (Code) in cases where plan benefits are determined on the basis of the greatest of two or more separate formulas. These regulations would affect sponsors, administrators, participants, and beneficiaries of defined benefit plans. This document also provides a notice of a public hearing on these proposed regulations.

DATES: Written or electronic comments must be received by *September 16, 2008*. Outlines of topics to be discussed at the public hearing scheduled for October 15, 2008, at 10 a.m. must be received by September 24, 2008. ADDRESSES: Send submissions to: CC:PA:LPD:PR (REG 100464-08), room 5203, Internal Revenue Service, PO Box 7604, Ben Franklin Station, Washington, DC 20044. Submissions may be hand-delivered Monday through Friday between the hours of 8 a.m. and 4 p.m. to CC:PA:LPD:PR (REG 100464-08), Courier's Desk, Internal Revenue Service, 1111 Constitution Avenue NW., Washington, DC., or sent electronically via the Federal eRulemaking Portal at www.regulations.gov (IRS REG-100464-08). The public hearing will be held in the IRS Auditorium, Internal Revenue Building, 1111 Constitution Avenue NW., Washington, DC.

FOR FURTHER INFORMATION CONTACT: Concerning the regulations, Lauson C. Green or Linda S. F. Marshall at (202) 622-6090; concerning submissions of comments, the hearing, and/or being placed on the building access list to attend the hearing, Richard A. Hurst at Richard.A.Hurst@irscounsel.treas.gov or at (202) 622-7180 (not toll-free numbers).

SUPPLEMENTARY INFORMATION:

Background

This document contains proposed Income Tax Regulations (26 CFR part 1) under section 411(b) of the Code.[1]

Section 401(a)(7) provides that a trust is not a qualified trust under section 401 unless the plan of which such trust is a part satisfies the requirements of section 411 (relating to minimum vesting standards).

Section 411(a) requires a qualified plan to provide that an employee's right to the normal retirement benefit is nonforfeitable upon attainment of normal retirement age and that an employee's right to his or her accrued benefit is nonforfeitable upon completion of the specified number of years of service under one of the vesting schedules set forth in section 411(a)(2). Section 411(a)(7)(A)(i) defines a participant's accrued benefit under a defined benefit plan as the employee's accrued benefit determined under the plan, expressed in the form of an annual benefit commencing at normal retirement age, subject to an exception in section 411(c)(3) under which the accrued benefit is the actuarial equivalent of the annual benefit commencing at normal retirement age in the case of a plan that does not express the accrued benefit as an annual benefit commencing at normal retirement age.

Section 411(a) also requires that a defined benefit plan satisfy the requirements of section 411(b)(1). Section 411(b)(1) provides that a defined benefit plan must satisfy one of the three accrual rules of section 411(b)(1)(A), (B), and (C) with respect to benefits accruing under the plan. The three accrual rules are the 3 percent method of section 411(b)(1)(A), the 133 ⅓ ⅓ ⅓ ⅓ percent rule of section 411(b)(1)(B), and the fractional rule of section 411(b)(1)(C).

Section 411(b)(1)(A) provides that a defined benefit plan satisfies the requirements of the 3 percent method if, under the plan, the accrued benefit payable upon the participant's separation from service is not less than (A) 3 percent of the normal retirement benefit to which the participant would be entitled if the participant commenced participation at the earliest possible entry age under the plan and served continuously until the earlier of age 65 or the normal retirement age under the plan, multiplied by (B) the number of years (not in excess of 33 ⅓ years) of his or her participation in the plan. Section 411(b)(1)(A) provides that, in the case of a plan providing retirement benefits based on compensation during any period, the normal retirement benefit to which a participant would be entitled is determined as if the participant continued to earn annually the average rate of compensation during consecutive years of service, not in excess of 10, for which his or her compensation was highest. Section 411(b)(1)(A) also provides that Social Security benefits and all other relevant factors used to compute benefits are treated as remaining constant as of the current plan year for all years after the current year.

Section 411(b)(1)(B) provides that a defined benefit plan satisfies the requirements of the 133 ⅓ percent rule for a particular plan year if, under the plan, the accrued benefit payable at the normal retirement age is equal to the normal retirement benefit, and the annual rate at which any individual who is or could be a participant can accrue the retirement benefits payable at normal retirement age under the plan for any later plan year is not more than 133 ⅓ percent of the annual rate at which the individual can accrue benefits for any plan year beginning on or after such particular plan year and before such later plan year.

For purposes of applying the 133 ⅓ percent rule, section 411(b)(1)(B)(i) provides that any amendment to the plan which is in effect for the current year is treated as in effect for all other plan years.

---

[1] Section 204(b) of the Employee Retirement Income Security Act of 1974, Public Law 93-406 (88 Stat. 829), as amended (ERISA), sets forth rules that are parallel to those in section 411(b) of the Code. Under section 101 of Reorganization Plan No. 4 of 1978 (43 FR 47713), the Secretary of the Treasury has interpretive jurisdiction over the subject matter addressed in these proposed regulations for purposes of ERISA, as well as the Code. Thus, these proposed Treasury regulations issued under section 411(b)(1)(B) of the Code would apply as well for purposes of section 204(b)(1)(B) of ERISA.

Section 411(b)(1)(B)(ii) provides that any change in an accrual rate which does not apply to any individual who is or could be a participant in the current plan year is disregarded. Section 411(b)(1)(B)(iii) provides that the fact that benefits under the plan may be payable to certain participants before normal retirement age is disregarded. Section 411(b)(1)(B)(iv) provides that Social Security benefits and all other relevant factors used to compute benefits are treated as remaining constant as of the current plan year for all years after the current year.

Section 411(b)(1)(C) provides that a defined benefit plan satisfies the fractional rule if the accrued benefit to which any participant is entitled upon his or her separation from service is not less than a fraction of the annual benefit commencing at normal retirement age to which the participant would be entitled under the plan as in effect on the date of separation if the participant continued to earn annually until normal retirement age the same rate of compensation upon which the normal retirement benefit would be computed under the plan, determined as if the participant had attained normal retirement age on the date on which any such determination is made (but taking into account no more than 10 years of service immediately preceding separation from service). This fraction, which cannot exceed 1, has a numerator that is the total number of the participant's years of participation in the plan (as of the date of separation from service) and a denominator that is the total number of years the participant would have participated in the plan if the participant separated from service at normal retirement age. Section 411(b)(1)(C) also provides that Social Security benefits and all other relevant factors used to compute benefits are treated as remaining constant as of the current plan year for all years after the current year.

Section 1.411(a)-7(a)(1) of the Income Tax Regulations provides that, for purposes of section 411 and the regulations under section 411, the accrued benefit of a participant under a defined benefit plan is either (A) the accrued benefit determined under the plan if the plan provides for an accrued benefit in the form of an annual benefit commencing at normal retirement age, or (B) an annual benefit commencing at normal retirement age which is the actuarial equivalent (determined under section 411(c)(3) and §1.411(c)-1)) of the accrued benefit under the plan if the plan does not provide for an accrued benefit in the form of an annual benefit commencing at normal retirement age.

Section 1.411(b)-1(a)(1) provides that a defined benefit plan is not a qualified plan unless the method provided by the plan for determining accrued benefits satisfies at least one of the alternative methods in §1.411(b)-1(b) for determining accrued benefits with respect to all active participants under the plan. The three alternative methods are the 3 percent method, the 133 ⅓ percent rule, and the fractional rule. A defined benefit plan may provide that accrued benefits for participants are determined under more than one plan formula. Section 1.411(b)-1(a)(1) provides that, in such a case, the accrued benefits under all such formulas must be aggregated in order to determine whether or not the accrued benefits under the plan for participants satisfy one of these methods. Under §1.411(b)-1(a)(1), a plan may satisfy different methods with respect to different classifications of employees, or separately satisfy one method with respect to the accrued benefits for each such classification, provided that such classifications are not so structured as to evade the accrued benefit requirements of section 411(b) and §1.411(b)-1.

Section 1.411(b)-1(b)(2)(i) provides that a defined benefit plan satisfies the 133 ⅓ percent rule for a particular plan year if (A) under the plan the accrued benefit payable at the normal retirement age (determined under the plan) is equal to the normal retirement benefit (determined under the plan), and (B) the annual rate at which any individual who is or could be a participant can accrue the retirement benefits payable at normal retirement age under the plan for any later plan year cannot be more than 133 ⅓ percent of the annual rate at which the participant can accrue benefits for any plan year beginning on or after such particular plan year and before such later plan year.

Section 1.411(b)-1(b)(2)(ii)(A) through (D) sets forth a series of rules that correspond to the rules of section 411(b)(1)(B)(i) through (iv). For example, §1.411(b)-1(b)(2)(ii)(A) sets forth a special plan amendment rule for purposes of satisfying the 133 ⅓ percent rule that corresponds to section 411(b)(1)(B)(i). Under that rule, any amendment to a plan that is in effect for the current year is treated as if it were in effect for all other plan years.

Section 1.411(b)-1(b)(2)(ii)(E) provides that a plan is not treated as failing to satisfy the requirements of §1.411(b)-1(b)(2) for a plan year merely because no benefits under the plan accrue to a participant who continues service with the employer after the participant has attained normal retirement age.[2] Section 1.411(b)-1(b)(2)(ii)(F) provides that a plan does not satisfy the requirements of §1.411(b)-1(b)(2) if the base for the computation of retirement benefits changes solely by reason of an increase in the number of years of participation.

Rev. Rul. 2008-7 (2008-7 IRB 419), see §601.601(d)(2)(ii)(b), describes the application of the accrual rules of section 411(b)(1)(A) through (C) and the regulations under section 411(b)(1)(A) through (C) to a defined benefit plan that was amended to change the plan's benefit formula from a traditional formula based on highest average compensation to a new lump sum-based benefit formula. Under the terms of the plan described in the revenue ruling, for an employee who was employed on the day before the change, a hypothetical account was established equal to the actuarial present value of the employee's accrued benefit as of that date, and that account was also to be credited with subsequent pay credits and interest credits. Under transition rules set forth in the plan, the accrued benefit of certain participants is the greater of the accrued benefit provided by the hypothetical account balance at the age 65 normal retirement age and the accrued benefit determined under the traditional formula as in effect on the day before the change, but taking into account post-amendment compensation and service for a limited number of years.

Revenue Ruling 2008-7 describes how the accrued benefits of different participant groups satisfy, or fail to satisfy, the accrual rules under section 411(b)(1)(A) through (C), taking into account the requirement in §1.411(a)(1) that a plan that determines a participant's accrued benefits under more than one formula must aggregate the accrued benefits under all of those formulas in order to determine whether or not the accrued benefits under the plan satisfy one of the alternative methods under section 411(b)(1)(A) through (C). However, Revenue Ruling 2008-7 explains that, in the case of a plan amendment that replaces the benefit formula under the plan for all periods after the amendment, pursuant to section 411(b)(1)(B)(i) and §1.411(b)-1(b)(2)(ii)(A), the rule that would otherwise require aggregation of the multiple formulas does not apply. Under section 411(b)(1)(B)(i) and §1.411(b)-1(b)(2)(ii)(A), any amendment to the plan which is in effect for the current plan year is treated as if it were in effect for all other plan years (including past and future plan years).

Revenue Ruling 2008-7 illustrates the application of this rule with respect to participants who only accrue benefits under the new formula (who in the ruling are referred to as participants who are not "grandfathered"). For these participants, the plan amendment completely ceases accruals under a traditional pension benefit formula that provides an annuity at normal retirement age based on service and average pay and, for all periods after the amendment, provides for the greater of the section 411(d)(6) protected benefit under the pre-amendment formula and the benefit under a new post-amendment lump sum-based benefit formula. In such a case, as stated in Revenue Ruling 2008-7, the section 411(d)(6) protected benefit under the pre-amendment formula is not aggregated with the post-amendment formula, but rather is entirely disregarded, for purposes of applying the 133 ⅓ percent rule because the new formula is treated under section 411(b)(1)(B)(i) and §1.411(b)-1(b)(2)(ii)(A) as having been in effect for all plan years. This analysis was reflected in *Register v. PNC Fin. Servs. Group, Inc.*, 477 F.3d 56 (3d Cir. 2007).

In addition to satisfying the requirements of section 411(b)(1)(B), a defined benefit plan must also satisfy the age discrimination rules of section 411(b)(1)(H), taking into account section 411(b)(5), as added to the Code by the Pension Protection Act of 2006, Public Law 109-280 (120 Stat. 780) (PPA '06). In the case of a conversion of a plan to a statutory hybrid plan pursuant to an amendment that is adopted after June 29, 2005 (a "post-PPA conversion plan"), the conversion amendment must satisfy the rule of section 411(b)(5)(B)(iii) that prohibits wearaway of benefits upon conversion. In the case of a plan converted to a statutory hybrid plan pursuant to an amendment that is adopted on or before June 29, 2005 (a "pre-PPA conversion plan"), as provided in Notice 2007-6, the IRS will not consider and will not issue determination letters with respect to whether such a pre-PPA conversion plan satisfies the requirements of section 411(b)(1)(H) (as in effect prior to the addition of section 411(b)(5) by PPA '06), including the effect of any wearaway. Thus, although wearaway upon conversion is expressly prohibited with respect to post-PPA conversion plans pursuant to section 411(b)(5), the IRS will not address and will not issue determination letters with respect to whether a conversion that results in wearaway

---

[2] However, section 411(b)(1)(H), which was added to the Code after the issuance of §1.411(b)-1, generally requires the continued accrual of benefits after attainment of normal retirement age.

with respect to a pre-PPA conversion plan violates the age discrimination rules of section 411(b)(1)(H). See § 601.601(d)(2)(ii)(*b*).

Revenue Ruling 2008-7 provides a different analysis as to whether a plan with wearaway fails to satisfy the accrual rules of section 411(b)(1)(B) when the preamendment formula continues in place after the amendment for a group of participants. In such a case, where an amendment has gone into effect but continues the prior formula for some period of time with respect to one or more participants, the application of the rule in section 411(b)(1)(B)(i) and § 1.411(b)-1(b)(2)(ii)(A) does not result in a disregard of the prior plan formula (which remains in effect after the amendment). Instead, the 133 ⅓ percent rule must be applied with respect to those participants based on the combined effect of the two ongoing formulas.[3]

Revenue Ruling 2008-7 provides relief from disqualification under the Internal Revenue Code (under the authority of section 7805(b)) for a limited class of plans under which a group of employees specified under the plan receives a benefit equal to the greatest of the benefits provided under two or more formulas (an applicable "greater-of" benefit), provided that each such formula standing alone would satisfy an accrual rule of section 411(b)(1)(A), (B), or (C) for the years involved. Under the relief set forth in Rev. Rul. 2008-7, for plan years beginning before January 1, 2009, the IRS will not treat a plan eligible for the relief as failing to satisfy the accrual rules of section 411(b)(1)(A), (B), and (C) solely because the plan provides an applicable "greater-of" benefit, where the separate formulas, standing alone, would satisfy an accrual rule of section 411(b)(1)(A), (B), and (C).

Explanation of Provisions

The fact pattern described in Revenue Ruling 2008-7 has occurred in a number of situations over the past few years. Employers sponsoring these plans have suggested that their plans should satisfy the accrual rules of section 411(b)(1)(A), (B), and (C), contending that any technical violation of the accrual rules is directly because the participant has higher frontloaded accruals under one formula when compared to the other formula that will ultimately provide the larger benefit under the plan. While the relief under section 7805(b) that is provided under Revenue Ruling 2008-7 addresses the situation for past years, the relief does not apply for the parallel accrual rules of section 204(b)(1)(A), (B) and (C) of ERISA and only applies to plan years beginning before January 1, 2009.

The proposed regulations would provide a limited exception to the existing requirement under § 1.411(b)-1(a)(1) to aggregate the accrued benefits under all formulas in order to determine whether or not the accrued benefits under the plan for participants satisfy one of the alternative methods under section 411(b)(1)(A) through (C). Under this limited exception, certain plans that determine a participant's benefits as the greatest of the benefits determined under two or more separate formulas would be permitted to demonstrate satisfaction of the 133 ⅓ percent rule of section 411(b)(1)(B) by demonstrating that each separate formula satisfies the 133 ⅓ percent rule of section 411(b)(1)(B).[4]

A plan would be eligible for this exception only if each of the separate formulas uses a different basis for determining benefits. For example, a plan would be eligible for this special rule if it provides a benefit equal to the greater of the benefits under two formulas, one of which determines benefits on the basis of highest average compensation and the other of which determines benefits on the basis of career average compensation. As another example, a traditional defined benefit plan which determined benefits based on highest average compensation that is amended to add a cash balance formula (as in the facts of Rev. Rul. 2008-7) would be eligible for this exception where, in order to provide a better transition for longer service active participants, the plan provides that a group of participants is entitled to the greater of the benefit provided by the hypothetical account balance and the benefit determined under the continuing traditional formula. In each of the above two examples, each separate formula under the plan uses a different basis for determining benefits and, therefore, both of those plans would be eligible to utilize this exception. Accordingly, both plans would be permitted to demonstrate satisfaction of the 133 ⅓ percent rule of section 411(b)(1)(B) by demonstrating that each separate formula under the plan satisfies the 133 ⅓ percent rule of section 411(b)(1)(B).

The utility of this exception can be seen from the following example of a plan that provides a benefit equal to the greater of two formulas. One formula provides a benefit of 1 percent of average compensation for the 3 consecutive years of service with the highest such average multiplied by the number of years of service at normal retirement age (not in excess of 25 years of service), and the other formula provides a benefit that is the accumulation of 1.5 percent of compensation for each year of service. Under the existing final regulations, the 133 ⅓ percent rule of section 411(b)(1)(B) is applied by reference to the annual rate of accrual for each year from the year of the test through normal retirement age. If the participant's accrued benefit currently is determined using the 1 percent formula (because the high-3 average compensation is significantly higher than the effective career average compensation that is used under the 1.5 percent formula), but the participant's normal retirement benefit will ultimately be determined using the 1.5 percent formula if service continues to normal retirement age (because the 25-year service cap will apply to the 1 percent formula, but not the 1.5 percent formula), then the annual rate of accrual will have to be determined for testing purposes on a consistent basis for each year, either using each year's compensation or high-3 average compensation. Thus, in order to test the plan under the 133 ⅓ percent rule, the existing final regulations would require that either the accruals under the 1 percent formula be expressed in terms of a single year's pay or the accruals under the 1.5 percent formula be expressed in terms of high-3 average compensation. In either case, the annual rates of accrual would differ from the stated rates under the plan formulas. In addition, the annual rates of accrual for the accumulation formula when those rates are expressed in terms of high-3 average compensation could be negative in some cases. In contrast, using the exception set forth in the proposed regulation would enable the plan to be tested using the annual rates of accrual expressed in the plan formulas.

The proposed regulations would also provide an extension of this exception in the case of a plan that provides benefits based on the greatest of three or more benefit formulas. In such a case, the plan would be eligible for a modified version of the formula-by-formula testing under the proposed regulations. Under this modification, the accrued benefits determined under all benefit formulas that have the same basis are first aggregated and then those aggregated formulas are treated as a single formula for purposes of applying the separate testing rule under the proposed regulations.

Eligibility for separate testing under the proposed regulations would be constrained by an anti-abuse rule. The proposed regulations would provide that a plan is not eligible for separate testing if the Commissioner determines that the plan's use of separate formulas with different bases is structured to evade the general requirement to aggregate formulas under § 1.411(b)-1(a)(1) (for example, if the differences between the bases of the separate formulas are minor).

Proposed Effective/Applicability Date

These regulations are proposed to be effective for plan years beginning on or after January 1, 2009.

Special Analyses

It has been determined that this notice of proposed rulemaking is not a significant regulatory action as defined in Executive Order 12866. Therefore, a regulatory assessment is not required. It also has been determined that section 553(b) of the Administrative Procedure Act (5 U.S.C. chapter 5) does not apply to these regulations, and because the regulations do not impose a collection of information on small entities, the Regulatory Flexibility Act (5 U.S.C. chapter 6) does not apply. Pursuant to section 7805(f) of the Code, this regulation has been submitted to the Chief Counsel for Advocacy of the Small Business Administration for comment on its impact on small business.

Comments and Public Hearing

Before these proposed regulations are adopted as final regulations, consideration will be given to any written (a signed original and eight (8) copies) or electronic comments that are submitted timely to the IRS. The IRS and the Treasury Department specifically request comments on the clarity of the proposed regulations and how they may be made easier to understand. All comments will be available for public inspection and copying.

---

[3] Two federal courts have taken a position contrary to this interpretation of section 411(b)(1)(B)(i) and § 1.411(b)-1(b)(2)(ii)(A) as set forth in Revenue Ruling 2008-7. See *Tomlinson v. El Paso Corp.*, 2008 WL 762456 (D. Colo. Mar. 19, 2008); *Wheeler v. Pension Value Plan for Employees of Boeing Corp.*, 2007 WL 2608875 (S.D. Ill. Sept. 6, 2007).

[4] These proposed regulations would only apply for purposes of the 133 ⅓ percent rule of section 411(b)(1)(B) (and the parallel rule of section 204(b)(1)(B) of ERISA). Neither Rev. Rul. 2008-7 nor these proposed regulations are relevant to (and thus they do not affect) the application of the age discrimination rules of section 411(b)(1)(H) (or the parallel age discrimination rules of section 204(b)(1)(H) of ERISA).

Under these proposed regulations, a plan eligible for the separate testing option would not violate the accrual rules merely because the plan provides higher frontloaded accruals under one formula when compared to the other formula that will ultimately provide the larger benefit under the plan. Some commentators have suggested a broader rule that would modify the regulations to provide that a plan does not violate the accrual rules where the plan provides a pattern of accruals that affords higher benefits in earlier years (that is, benefit accruals are frontloaded) relative to a pattern of accruals that satisfies the accrual rules. The 3 percent method of section 411(b)(1)(A) and the fractional rule of section 411(b)(1)(C) automatically achieve this result because they are cumulative tests that test on the basis of the total accrued benefit compared to the projected normal retirement benefit. By contrast, the 133 ⅓ percent rule is based on a comparison of the "annual rate at which any individual who is or could be a participant can accrue the retirement benefits payable at normal retirement age" for a later plan year with the annual rate for an earlier plan year. The existing final regulations include an example (§ 1.411(b)-1(b)(2)(iii), Example (3)) that demonstrates how a plan fails the 133 ⅓ percent rule where it provides accruals in earlier years that are frontloaded relative to accruals that apply in later years. The proposed regulations do not include a provision under the 133 ⅓ percent rule that recognizes prior frontloading of benefits. However, commentators who would suggest such a provision under the 133 ⅓ percent rule should describe how that provision would fit within the statutory language of section 411(b)(1)(B), including the application of section 411(b)(1)(B)(i) (which requires that an amendment to the plan that is in effect for the current year be treated as in effect for all other plan years).

A public hearing has been scheduled for October 15, 2008, beginning at 10 a.m. in the Auditorium, Internal Revenue Service, 1111 Constitution Avenue, NW., Washington, DC. Due to building security procedures, visitors must enter at the Constitution Avenue entrance. In addition, all visitors must present photo identification to enter the building. Because of access restrictions, visitors will not be admitted beyond the immediate entrance area more than 30 minutes before the hearing starts. For information about having your name placed on the building access list to attend the hearing, see the **FOR FURTHER INFORMATION CONTACT** section of this preamble.

The rules of 26 CFR 601.601(a)(3) apply to the hearing. Persons who wish to present oral comments at the hearing must submit written or electronic comments by ***September 16, 2008,*** and an outline of topics to be discussed and the amount of time to be devoted to each topic (a signed original and eight (8) copies) by September 24, 2008. A period of 10 minutes will be allotted to each person for making comments. An agenda showing the scheduling of the speakers will be prepared after the deadline for receiving outlines has passed. Copies of the agenda will be available free of charge at the hearing.

Drafting Information

The principal authors of these regulations are Lauson C. Green and Linda S. F. Marshall, Office of Division Counsel/Associate Chief Counsel (Tax Exempt and Government Entities). However, other personnel from the IRS and the Treasury Department participated in the development of these regulations.

List of Subjects in 26 CFR Part 1

Income taxes, Reporting and recordkeeping requirements.

Proposed Amendments to the Regulations

Accordingly, 26 CFR part 1 is proposed to be amended as follows:

PART 1—INCOME TAXES

Paragraph 1. The authority citation for part 1 continues to read in part as follows:

Authority: 26 U.S.C. 7805 * * *

Par. 2. Section 1.411(b)-1 is amended by adding new paragraph (b)(2)(ii)(G) to read as follows:

§ 1.411(b)-1 Accrued benefit requirements.

* * * * *

(b) * * *

(2) * * *

(ii) * * *

(G) *Special rule for multiple formulas —(1) In general.* Notwithstanding paragraph (a)(1) of this section, a plan that determines a participant's accrued benefit as the greatest of the benefits determined under two or more separate formulas is permitted, to the extent provided under this paragraph (b)(2)(ii)(G), to demonstrate satisfaction of section 411(b)(1)(B) and this paragraph (b) by demonstrating that each separate formula satisfies the requirements of section 411(b)(1)(B) and this paragraph (b).

(2) *Separate bases requirement.* A plan is eligible for separate testing under this paragraph (b)(2)(ii)(G) if each of the separate formulas uses a different basis for determining benefits. For example, a plan is eligible for this special rule if it provides an accrued benefit equal to the greater of the benefits under two formulas, one of which determines accrued benefits on the basis of highest average compensation and the other of which determines accrued benefits on the basis of career average compensation. As another example, a defined benefit plan that bases benefits on highest average compensation and that is amended to add a statutory hybrid benefit formula (as defined in § 1.411(a)(13)-1(d)(3)) that provides for pay credits to be made based on each year's compensation is eligible for this separate testing exception if the plan provides that one or more participants are entitled to the greater of the benefit determined under the statutory hybrid benefit formula and the benefit determined under the original formula.

(3) *Plans with three or more formulas.* If a plan determines a participant's benefits as the greatest of the benefits determined under three or more separate formulas, but two or more of the formulas use the same basis for determining benefits, then the plan may nonetheless apply paragraphs (b)(2)(ii)(G)(1) and (2) of this section by aggregating all benefit formulas that have the same basis and treating those aggregated formulas as a single formula for purposes of paragraphs (b)(2)(ii)(G)(1) and (2) of this section.

(4) *Anti-abuse rule.* A plan is not eligible for separate testing under this paragraph (b)(2)(ii)(G) if the Commissioner determines that the plan's use of separate formulas with different bases is structured to evade the requirement to aggregate formulas under paragraph (a)(1) of this section (for example, if the differences between the bases of the separate formulas are minor).

(5) *Effective/applicability date.* This paragraph (b)(2)(ii)(G) is applicable for plan years beginning on or after January 1, 2009.

Steven T. Miller

Acting Deputy Commissioner for Services and Enforcement

¶ 20,262M

IRS: Required minimum distribution rules: Governmental plans: Code Sec. 401(a)(9).—The IRS has issued a proposed rule permitting governmental plans to comply with the required minimum distribution rules under Code Sec. 401(a)(9) by using a "reasonable good faith interpretation" of the statute. Under the Pension Protection Act of 2006 (P.L. 109-280; PPA), the Secretary of the Treasury was instructed to issue such regulations under which, a governmental plan shall be treated as having complied with Code Sec. 401(a)(9) if the plan complied with a "reasonable good faith interpretation" of section 401(a)(9).

The proposed regulations were published in the Federal Register on July 10, 2008 (73 FR 39630). The regulations were finalized on September 8, 2009 (74 FR 45993). The preamble to the final regulations is at ¶ 23,261. The final regulations are at ¶ 11,720Y-1, ¶ 11,720Y-6, and ¶ 11,803-14.

¶ 20,262N

IRS proposed regulations: Health Savings Accounts (HSAs): Employer comparable contributions.—The IRS has issued proposed regulations on employer comparable contributions to Health Savings Accounts (HSAs) which, among other provisions, permit larger employer contributions to the HSAs of nonhighly compensated employees than their contributions for highly compensated employees' HSAs.

The proposed regulations, which were published in the Federal Register on July 16, 2008 (73 FR 40793), were reproduced below. The regulations were finalized on September 8, 2009 (74 FR 45994). The preamble to the final regulations is at ¶ 23,262. The final regulations are at ¶ 13,648W-5, ¶ 13,648W-7, ¶ 13,648W-55, ¶ 13,648W-101, ¶ 13,648W-103, ¶ 13,648W-104, ¶ 13,648W-106, ¶ 13,648W-107, and ¶ 13,649C.

¶ 20,262O

IRS proposed regulations: Stock Options.—The IRS has issued proposed regulations which will require additional information in returns to the IRS and information statements to employees when a transfer of stock is made in connection with the exercise of an option through an employee stock purchase plan or through an incentive stock option program.

The proposed regulations, which were published in the Federal Register on July 16, 2008 (73 FR 40999), and corrected on August 14, 2008 (73 FR 47563), are reproduced below. The regulations were finalized on November 17, 2009 (74 FR 59087). The preamble to the final regulations is at ¶ 23,266. The final regulations are at ¶ 13,671A and ¶ 13,672.

¶ 20,262P

IRS proposed regulations: Tax deadline postponement: Disasters: Terrorism: Military action.—The IRS has issued proposed regulations, amending existing regulations under Code Sec. 7508A, to clarify rules relating to the postponement of certain tax-related acts by reason of a Presidentially declared disaster or terroristic or military action.

The proposed regulations, which were published in the Federal Register on July 15, 2008 (73 FR 40471), are reproduced below. The regulations were finalized on January 15, 2009 (74 FR 2370). The final regulations are at ¶ 13,919M.

¶ 20,262Q

IRS proposed regulations: Statutory options: Employee stock purchase plans.— The IRS has issued proposed regulations, amending existing regulations under Code Sec. 423, which affect those who participate in the transfer of stock pursuant to the exercise of options granted under an employee stock purchase plan.

The proposed regulations would apply to any option issued under an employee stock purchase plan that is granted on or after January 1, 2010. Pending issuance of final regulations, taxpayers may rely upon the proposed regulations for options issued under an employee stock purchase plan granted after July 29, 2008, the date these proposed regulations were published in the *Federal Register* (73 FR 43875). The proposed regulations are reproduced below.

The regulations were finalized on November 17, 2009 (74 FR 59074). The preamble is at ¶ 23,265. The final regulations are at ¶ 13,107, ¶ 13,124B, ¶ 13,125B, ¶ 13,131, ¶ 13,132, and ¶ 13,151.

¶ 20,262R

IRS proposed regulations: Distributions.—The IRS has issued proposed regulations which provide that the notice required under Code Sec. 411(a)(11) to be provided to a participant of his right to defer receipt of an immediately distributable benefit, if any, must also describe the consequences of failing to defer receipt of the distribution.

The proposed regulations, which were published in the Federal Register on October 9, 2008 (73 FR 59575), are reproduced below.

[4830-01-p]

DEPARTMENT OF THE TREASURY

Internal Revenue Service

26 CFR Part 1

[REG-107318-08]

Notice to Participants of Consequences of Failing to Defer Receipt of Qualified Retirement Plan Distributions; Expansion of Applicable Election Period and Period for Notices

RIN 1545-BH75

AGENCY: Internal Revenue Service (IRS), Treasury.

ACTION: Notice of Proposed Rulemaking and notice of public hearing.

SUMMARY: This document contains proposed regulations under sections 402(f), 411(a)(11), and 417 of the Internal Revenue Code (Code). The proposed regulations would provide that the notice required under section 411(a)(11) to be provided to a participant of his or her right, if any, to defer receipt of an immediately distributable benefit must also describe the consequences of failing to defer receipt of the distribution. The proposed regulations would also provide that the applicable election period for waiving the qualified joint and survivor annuity form of benefit under section 417 is the 180-day period ending on the annuity starting date, and that a notice required to be provided under section 402(f), section 411(a)(11), or section 417 may be provided to a participant as much as 180 days before the annuity starting date (or, for a notice under section 402(f), the distribution date). These regulations would affect administrators of, employers maintaining, participants in, and beneficiaries of tax-favored retirement plans.

DATES: Written or electronic comments and requests to speak at the public hearing must be received by *[INSERT DATE 90 DAYS AFTER PUBLICATION OF THIS DOCUMENT IN THE FEDERAL REGISTER]*.

ADDRESSES: Send submissions to: CC:PA:LPD:PR (REG-107318-08), room 5203, Internal Revenue Service, PO Box 7604, Ben Franklin Station, Washington D.C. 20044. Submissions may be hand-delivered Monday through Friday between the hours of 8 a.m. and 4 p.m. to: CC:PA:LPD:PR (REG-107318-08), Courier's Desk, Internal Revenue Service, 1111 Constitution Avenue, N.W., Washington, D.C., or sent electronically via the Federal eRulemaking Portal at *http://www.regulations.gov* (IRS REG-107318-08).

FOR FURTHER INFORMATION CONTACT: Concerning the regulations, Michael P. Brewer at (202) 622-6090; concerning submission of comments or to request to speak at the public hearing, Funmi Taylor at (202) 622-7180 (not toll-free numbers).

SUPPLEMENTARY INFORMATION:

Paperwork Reduction Act

The collection of information contained in this notice of proposed rulemaking has been submitted to the Office of Management and Budget for review in accordance with the Paperwork Reduction Act of 1995 (44 U.S.C. 3507(d)). Comments on the collection of information should be sent to the **Office of Management and Budget**, Attn: Desk Officer for the Department of the Treasury, Office of Information and Regulatory Affairs, Washington, DC 20503, with copies to the **Internal Revenue Service**, Attn: IRS Reports Clearance Officer, SE:W:CAR:MP:T:T:SP; Washington, DC 20224. Comments on the collection of information should be received by *[INSERT DATE 60 DAYS AFTER PUBLICATION OF THIS DOCUMENT IN THE FEDERAL REGISTER]*. Comments are specifically requested concerning:

Whether the proposed collection of information is necessary for the proper performance of the functions of the Internal Revenue Service, including whether the information will have practical utility;

The accuracy of the estimated burden associated with the proposed collection of information;

How the quality, utility, and clarity of the information to be collected may be enhanced;

How the burden of complying with the proposed collections of information may be minimized, including through the application of automated collection techniques or other forms of information technology; and

Estimates of capital or start-up costs and costs of operation, maintenance, and purchase of service to provide information.

The collection of information in these proposed regulations is in § 1.411(a)-11(c)(2) of the Income Tax Regulations. This collection of information is required to comply with the statutory notice requirements of section 411(a), and is expected to be included in the notices currently provided to employees that inform them of their rights and benefits under the plan. The likely recordkeepers are businesses or other for-profit institutions and nonprofit institutions and organizations.

Estimated total annual recordkeeping burden: 100,000 hours.

Estimated average annual burden hours per recordkeeper: 1 hour.

Estimated number of recordkeepers: 100,000.

An agency may not conduct or sponsor, and a person is not required to respond to, a collection of information unless it displays a valid control number assigned by the Office of Management and Budget.

Books or records relating to a collection of information must be retained as long as their contents may become material in the administration of any internal revenue law. Generally, tax returns and tax return information are confidential, as required by 26 U.S.C. 6103.

Background

A. Notice of Consequences of Failing to Defer

Section 411(a)(11)(A) provides that, if the present value of any nonforfeitable accrued benefit exceeds $5,000, a qualified plan must provide that such benefit may not be immediately distributed without the consent of the participant. Similarly, section 203(e) of the Employee Retirement Income Security Act of 1974, as amended (ERISA), provides that if the present value of any nonforfeitable accrued benefit with respect to a participant in a plan exceeds $5,000, the benefit may not be immediately distributed without the consent of the participant.

Section 1102(b)(1) of the Pension Protection Act of 2006 (PPA '06), 109 Public Law 280, 120 Stat. 780, instructs the Secretary of the Treasury to modify the regulations under section 411(a)(11) of the Code "to provide that the description of a participant's right, if any, to defer receipt of a distribution shall also describe the consequences of failing to defer such receipt." Section 1102(b)(2)(A) of PPA '06 provides that the modifications required by section 1102(b)(1) of PPA '06 shall apply to years beginning after December 31, 2006. Section 1102(b)(2)(B) of PPA '06, however, states that a plan shall not be treated as failing to meet the requirements of section 411(a)(11) with respect to any description of the consequences of failing to defer provided "within 90 days after the Secretary of the Treasury issues the modifications required by [section 1102(b)(1) of PPA '06]if the plan administrator makes a reasonable attempt to comply with such requirements."

Section 1.411(a)-11(c)(2)(i) states that, in order for a plan to obtain valid consent under section 411(a)(11), "so long as a benefit is immediately distributable, a participant must be informed of the right, if any, to defer receipt of the distribution." Section 1.411(a)-11(c)(4) states that a distribution is immediately distributable prior to the later of the time a participant has attained normal retirement age or age 62.

Q&A-32 of Notice 2007-7, 2007-5 I.R.B. 395, provides that a plan administrator is required to revise the notice required under section 411 to reflect the modifications made by section 1102(b) of PPA '06 for notices provided in plan years beginning after December 31, 2006. Notice 2007-7 further provides that, pursuant to section 1102(b)(2)(B) of PPA '06, a plan will not be treated as failing to meet the new requirements of section 1102(b) of PPA '06 if the plan administrator makes a reasonable attempt to comply with the new requirements with respect to a notice that is provided prior to the 90th day after the issuance of regulations reflecting the modifications required by such section 1102(b) of PPA '06. See § 601.601(b)(2)(ii)(b).

Q&A-33 of Notice 2007-7 includes a safe harbor that would be considered a reasonable attempt to comply with the requirement in section 1102(b)(1) of PPA '06 that a description of a participant's right to defer receipt of a distribution include a description of the consequences of failing to defer. In particular, Q&A-33 provides that a description that is written in a manner reasonably calculated to be understood by the average participant and that includes the following

information is a reasonable attempt to comply with the requirements of section 1102(b)(2)(B) of PPA '06: (a) in the case of a defined benefit plan, a description of how much larger benefits will be if the commencement of distributions is deferred; (b) in the case of a defined contribution plan, a description indicating the investment options available under the plan (including fees) that will be available if distributions are deferred; and (c) the portion of the summary plan description that contains any special rules that might materially affect a participant's decision to defer. For purposes of clause (a), a plan administrator can use a description that includes the financial effect of deferring distributions, as described in § 1.417(a)(3)-1(d)(2)(i), based solely on the normal form of benefit.

Q&A-31 of Notice 2007-7 provides that the provisions of section 1102 apply to plan years that begin after December 31, 2006. Q&A-31 explains that this means that the new rules relating to the content of the notices apply only to notices issued in those plan years, without regard to the annuity starting date for the distributions.

B. Expansion of Applicable Election Period

Section 401(a)(11)(A)(i) provides that, except as provided in section 417, a plan that is qualified under section 401(a) must provide the accrued benefit payable to a vested participant who does not die before the annuity starting date in the form of a qualified joint and survivor annuity.

Section 417(a)(1)(A) provides that, in general, a plan satisfies section 401(a)(11) only if each participant may elect at any time during the "applicable election period" to waive the qualified joint and survivor annuity form of benefit (and to revoke the waiver), and certain other requirements are satisfied. Before PPA '06, section 417(a)(6)(A) provided that the "applicable election period" for a participant to waive the qualified joint and survivor annuity form of distribution was the 90-day period ending on the annuity starting date.

Section 1102(a)(1)(A) of PPA '06 amended section 417(a)(6)(A) by changing the 90-day "applicable election period" for electing a distribution subject to the qualified joint and survivor annuity (QJSA) rules of sections 401(a)(11) and 417 in a form other than a QJSA to a 180-day applicable election period. Section 1102(a)(2)(A) of PPA '06 made a parallel amendment to section 205(c)(7)(A) of ERISA by striking "90-day" and inserting "180-day".

Sections 1102(a)(1)(B) and 1102(a)(2)(B) of PPA '06 provide that the Secretary of the Treasury shall modify the regulations relating to section 417 of the Code and section 205 of ERISA by substituting "180 days" for "90 days" each place it appears.

Section 1102(a)(3) of PPA '06 provides that the amendments to the applicable election period apply to years beginning after December 31, 2006.

C. Expansion of Period for Notices

Section 417(a)(3)(A) of the Code and section 205(c)(3)(A) of ERISA provide that a plan must provide to each participant, "within a reasonable period of time before the annuity starting date" and consistent with such regulations as the Secretary of the Treasury may prescribe, a written explanation that describes the terms and conditions of the qualified joint and survivor annuity and certain other information. Similarly, section 402(f)(1) provides that a plan administrator must, "within a reasonable period of time" before making an eligible rollover distribution, provide to recipients an explanation of certain tax consequences of the distribution.

Section 1102(a)(1)(B) of PPA '06 provides that the Secretary of the Treasury shall modify the regulations under sections 402(f), 411(a)(11), and 417 by substituting "180 days" for "90 days" each place it appears in § § 1.402(f)-1, 1.411(a)-11(c), and 1.417(e)-1(b). Similarly, section 1102(a)(2)(B) of PPA '06 provides that the Secretary of the Treasury shall modify the regulations relating to sections 203(e) and 205 of ERISA by substituting "180 days" for "90 days" each place it appears.

Section 1102(a)(3) provides that the amendments to the notice periods apply to years beginning after December 31, 2006. Q&A-31 of Notice 2007-7 explains that the 180-day period for distributing notices applies to notices distributed in a plan year that begins after December 31, 2006.

D. Requirements under ERISA

ERISA section 203(e) is the parallel provision to section 411(a)(11) of the Code and ERISA section 205 is the ERISA parallel to section 417 of the Code. Pursuant to section 101 of Reorganization Plan No. 4 of 1978, 29 U.S.C. 1001nt (the Reorganization Plan), the Secretary of the Treasury generally has authority to issue regulations under parts 2 and 3 of subtitle B of title I of ERISA, including sections 203(e) and 205 of ERISA. Thus, the changes required by section 1102 of PPA '06 would apply as well for purposes of ERISA sections 203(e) and 205.

Explanation of Provisions

A. Notice of Consequences of Failing to Defer

These proposed regulations would provide that the notice required by section 411(a)(11) advising a participant of the right, if any, to defer receipt of a distribution must also inform the participant of the consequences of failing to defer such receipt. The proposed regulations would also provide guidance on the relevant information that must be provided to a participant in order to satisfy the requirement that the participant be notified of the consequences of failing to defer.

Specifically, these proposed regulations would require that the participant be provided a description of specified federal tax implications of failing to defer and, in the case of a defined benefit plan, a statement of the amount payable to the participant under the normal form of benefit both upon immediate commencement and when the benefit is no longer immediately distributable (that is, the later of age 62 or attainment of normal retirement age). Section 1.417(a)(3)-1(c)(2)(ii) permits a plan to provide participants with a QJSA explanation, which does not vary based on the participant's marital status, of the relative value of optional forms of benefit compared to the value of a QJSA. These proposed regulations would permit the statement of the amount payable to not be based on the participant's marital status, to the extent the plan is permitted under §1.417(a)(3)-1(c)(2)(ii) to use a QJSA explanation that does not vary based on whether the participant is married or unmarried.

The proposed regulations would also require the information in the notice to include, in the case of a defined contribution plan, a statement that some currently available investment options in the plan may not be generally available on similar terms outside the plan and contact information for obtaining additional information on the general availability outside the plan of currently available investment options in the plan. In addition, the proposed regulations would require the notice to include, in the case of a defined contribution plan, a statement that fees and expenses (including administrative or investment-related fees) outside the plan may be different from fees and expenses that apply to the participant's account and contact information for obtaining information on such fees.

The proposed regulations also include an additional category of information that must be provided relating to any provisions of the plan (and provisions of any accident or health plan maintained by the employer) that could reasonably be expected to materially affect a participant's decision whether to defer receipt of the distribution. Thus, for example, the proposed regulations would require a description of the eligibility requirements for retiree health benefits if such benefits are limited to participants who have an undistributed benefit under the employer's retirement plan.

In general, the proposed regulations would also provide that the required information regarding the consequences of a participant's failing to defer receipt of a distribution must appear together. However, the proposed regulations would permit a cross-reference to where the required information may be found in notices or other information provided or made available to the participant, as long as the notice of consequences of failing to defer includes a statement of how the referenced information may be obtained without charge and explains why the referenced information is relevant to a decision whether to defer.

B. Expansion of Applicable Election Period and Period for Notices

Consistent with sections 1102(a)(1)(A) and (1)(B) and 1102(a)(2)(A) and (2)(B) of PPA '06, the proposed regulations would both (1) expand the definition of applicable election period to up to 180 days, and (2) expand the time period for notices issued under sections 402(f), 411(a)(11), and 417 to allow the notices to be issued up to 180 days prior to the annuity starting date (or, in the case of a notice under section 402(f), the date of distribution). Specifically, the proposed regulations would substitute "180 days" for "90 days" and "180-day" for "90-day" each place those terms appear in §1.401(a)-13(g)(4)(ii), §1.401(a)-20, A-3(b)(1), A-4, A-10(a), A-16, and A-24(a)(1), §1.402(f)-1, §1.411(a)-11(c), and §1.417(e)-1(b).

Pursuant to section 101 of the Reorganization Plan, the Secretary of Treasury has the authority to issue regulations under ERISA sections 203(e) and 205. Thus, these proposed regulations that apply to sections 402(f), 411(a)(11), and 417 of the Code would apply as well for purposes of sections 203(e) and 205 of ERISA.

Proposed Effective/Applicability Date

These regulations are proposed to become effective for notices provided (and election periods beginning) on or after the first day of the first plan year beginning on or after January 1, 2010. However, in no event will the regulations become effective for notices provided (and election periods beginning) earlier than the first day of the first plan year beginning 90 days after publication of final regulations in the **Federal Register**.

With respect to the regulations relating to the notice of consequences of failing to defer the receipt of distributions, until these regulations become effective, a plan will be treated as complying if: (1) the plan complies either with these proposed regulations or with Q&A-32 and Q&A-33 in Notice 2007-7; or (2) if the plan administrator makes a reasonable attempt to comply with the requirement that the description of a participant's right, if any, to defer receipt of a distribution shall also describe the consequences of failing to defer such receipt.

With respect to the proposed regulations relating to the expanded applicable election period and the expanded period for notices, plans may rely on these proposed regulations for notices provided (and election periods beginning) during the period beginning on the first day of the first plan year beginning on or after January 1, 2007 and ending on the effective date of final regulations.

Special Analyses

It has been determined that this notice of proposed rulemaking is not a significant regulatory action as defined in Executive Order 12866. Therefore, a regulatory assessment is not required. It also has been determined that section 553(b) of the Administrative Procedure Act (5 U.S.C. chapter 5) does not apply to these regulations.

It is hereby certified that the collection of information contained in this regulation will not have a significant economic impact on a substantial number of small entities. This certification is based on several factors, including that the regulation merely provides guidance to implement a statutorily-required notice, and that the incremental burden in the regulation would be minimal because it only requires including additional information in notices already provided by all of the affected entities. Accordingly, a Regulatory Flexibility Analysis under the Regulatory Flexibility Act (5 U.S.C. chapter 6) is not required. Pursuant to section 7805(f) of the Code, this notice of proposed rulemaking will be submitted to the Chief Counsel for Advocacy of the Small Business Administration for comment on its impact on small business.

Comments and Public Hearing

Before these proposed regulations are adopted as final regulations, consideration will be given to any written (one signed and eight (8) copies) or electronic comments that are submitted timely to the IRS. All comments will be available for public inspection and copying.

A public hearing has been scheduled for Friday, February 20, 2009, at 10 a.m. in the IRS Auditorium, Internal Revenue Building, 1111 Constitution Avenue, N.W., Washington, DC. Due to building security procedures, visitors must enter at the Constitution Avenue entrance. In addition, all visitors must present photo identification to enter the building. Because of access restrictions, visitors will not be admitted beyond the immediate entrance area more than 30 minutes before the hearing starts. For information about having your name placed on the building access list to attend the hearing, see the FOR FURTHER INFORMATION CONTACT section of this preamble.

Persons who wish to present oral comments at the hearing must submit written or electronic comments by *[INSERT DATE 90 DAYS AFTER THIS DOCUMENT IS PUBLISHED IN THE FEDERAL REGISTER]* and submit an outline of the topics to be discussed and the amount of time to be devoted to each topic (a signed original and eight (8) copies) by January 16, 2009. A period of 10 minutes will be allotted to each person for making comments.

An agenda showing the scheduling of the speakers will be prepared after the deadline for receiving outlines has passed. Copies of the agenda will be available free of charge at the hearing.

Drafting Information

The principal author of these regulations is Michael P. Brewer, Office of Division Counsel/Associate Chief Counsel (Tax Exempt and Government Entities). However, other personnel from the Office of Chief Counsel, IRS, and the Department of Treasury participated in the development of these regulations.

¶20,262R

Proposed Amendments to the Regulations

Accordingly, 26 CFR part 1 is proposed to be amended as follows:

Part 1—INCOME TAXES

Paragraph 1. The authority citation for part 1 continues to read as follows:

Authority: 26 U.S.C. 7805 ***

§ 1.401(a)-13; § 1.401(a)-20; § 1.402(f)-1; § 1.411(a)-11; § 1.417(e)-1 [Amended]

Par. 2. For each entry listed in the "Location" column, remove the language in the "Remove" column and add the language in the "Add" column in its place.

Location	Remove	Add
1.401(a)-13(g)(4)(ii), first sentence	90 days	180 days
1.401(a)-20, A-4, third sentence	90 days	180 days
1.401(a)-20, A-10(a), fifth and sixth sentences	90 days	180 days
1.401(a)-20, A-16, sixth sentence	90 days	180 days
1.401(a)-20, A-24(a)(1), fifth sentence	90 days	180 days
1.402(f)-1, A-2(a), first sentence	90 days	180 days
1.411(a)-11(c)(2)(ii)	90 days	180 days
1.411(a)-11(c)(2)(iii)(A), first sentence	90 days	180 days
1.417(e)-1(b)(3)(i)	90 days	180 days
1.417(e)-1(b)(3)(ii), first sentence	90 days	180 days
1.417(e)-1 (b)(3)(iii)	90 days	180 days
1.417(e)-1 (b)(3)(vi), second sentence	90 days	180 days
1.417(e)-1(b)(3)(vii)	90 days	180 days
1.417(e)-1(b)(3)(vii)	90-day	180-day

§ 1.411(a)-11 [Amended]

Par. 3. Section 1.411(a)-11 is amended as follows:

1. The second sentence of paragraph (c)(2)(i) is revised.

2. The second sentence of paragraph (c)(2)(iii)(B)(3) is revised.

3. Paragraphs (c)(2)(vi) and (h) are added.

The additions and revisions read as follows:

§ 1.411(a)-11 Restriction and valuation of distributions.

*****

(c) ***

(2) *Consent* —(i) *** In addition, so long as a benefit is immediately distributable, a participant must be informed of the right, if any, to defer receipt of the distribution and of the consequences of failing to defer such receipt. ***

*****

(iii) ***

(B) ***

(*3*) *** The summary described in paragraph (c)(2)(iii)(B)(*2*) of this section must advise the participant of the right, if any, to defer receipt of the distribution and of the consequences of failing to defer such receipt, must set forth a summary of the distribution options under the plan, must refer the participant to the most recent version of the notice (and, in the case of a notice provided in any document containing information in addition to the notice, must identify that document and must provide a reasonable indication of where the notice may be found in that document, such as by index reference or by section heading), and must advise the participant that, upon request, a copy of the notice will be provided without charge.

*****

(vi) *Consequences of failing to defer* –(A) A notice under this paragraph (c)(2) that is required to describe the consequences of failing to defer receipt of a distribution until it is no longer immediately distributable must, to the extent applicable under the plan and in a manner designed to be easily understood, provide the participant with the information set out in paragraphs (c)(2)(vi)(A)(*1*) through (*5*) of this section and explain why it is relevant to a decision whether to defer.

(*1*) A description of the following federal tax implications of failing to defer: differences in the timing of inclusion in taxable income of an immediately commencing distribution that is not rolled over (or not eligible to be rolled over) and a distribution that is deferred until it is no longer immediately distributable (including, as applicable, differences in the taxation of distributions of designated Roth contributions within the meaning of section 402A); application of the 10% additional tax on certain distributions before age 59 ½ under section 72(t); and, in the case of a defined contribution plan, loss of the opportunity upon immediate commencement for future tax-favored treatment of earnings if the distribution is not rolled over (or not eligible to be rolled over) to an eligible retirement plan described in section 402(c)(8)(B).

(*2*) In the case of a defined benefit plan, a statement of the amount payable to the participant under the normal form of benefit both upon immediate commencement and upon commencement when the benefit is no longer immediately distributable (assuming no future benefit accruals). The statement need not vary based on the participant's marital status if the plan is permitted, pursuant to § 1.417(a)(3)-1(c)(2)(ii), to provide a QJSA explanation that does not vary based on the participant's marital status.

(*3*) In the case of a defined contribution plan, a statement that some currently available investment options in the plan may not be generally available on similar terms outside the plan and contact information for obtaining additional information on the general availability outside the plan of currently available investment options in the plan.

(*4*) In the case of a defined contribution plan, a statement that fees and expenses (including administrative or investment-related fees) outside the plan may be different from fees and expenses that apply to the participant's account and contact information for obtaining additional information on the fees and expenses that apply to the participant's account.

(*5*) An explanation of any provisions of the plan (and provisions of an accident or health plan maintained by the employer) that could reasonably be expected to materially affect a participant's decision whether to defer receipt of the distribution. Such provisions would include, for example: plan terms under which a participant who fails to defer may lose eligibility for retiree health coverage or eligibility for early retirement subsidies or social security supplements; plan terms under which the benefit of a rehired participant who failed to defer may be adversely affected by the decision not to defer; and, in the case of a defined contribution plan, plan terms under which undistributed benefits that otherwise are nonforfeitable become forfeitable upon the participant's death.

(B) *Location of information; incorporation by reference.* In general, the information required to be provided in a notice under this paragraph (c)(2)(vi) must appear together (for example, in a list of consequences of failing to defer). However, the notice will not be treated as failing to satisfy the requirements of this paragraph (c)(2)(vi) merely because the notice includes a cross-reference to where the required information may be found in notices or other information provided or made available to the participant, as long as the notice of consequences of failing to defer includes a statement of how the referenced information may be obtained without charge and explains why the referenced information is relevant to a decision whether to defer.

*****

(h) *Consequences of Failing to Defer Effective/Applicability Date.* The provisions in paragraph (c) of this section that describe the requirement to notify participants of the consequences of failing to defer are effective for notices provided on or after the first day of the first plan year beginning on or after January 1, 2010.

/s/ Linda E. Stiff

Deputy Commissioner for Services and Enforcement

[FR Doc. 2008-23918 Field 10/08/2008 at 8:45 am; Publication Date: 10/09/2008]

¶ 20,262S

IRS proposed regulations: 409A compliance failure: Income inclusion: Tax consequences.—The IRS has issued proposed regulations on the calculation of amounts includible in income under Code Sec. 409A(a), and the calculation of the additional taxes applicable to such income in the event of a plan compliance failure. The regulations are proposed to be generally applicable for taxable years beginning on or after the issuance of final regulations.

The proposed regulations, which were published in the Federal Register on December 8, 2008 (73 FR 74380), are reproduced below. The IRS issued proposed regulations in June 2016 that withdraw IRS Proposed Reg. §1.409A-4(a)(1)(ii)(B) reproduced below and replace it with a new Proposed Reg. §1.409A-4(a)(1)(ii)(B). See ¶ 20,264L.

DEPARTMENT OF THE TREASURY

Internal Revenue Service

26 CFR Part 1

[REG-148326-05]

RIN 1545-BF50

Further Guidance on the Application of Section 409A to Nonqualified Deferred Compensation Plans

AGENCY: Internal Revenue Service (IRS), Treasury.

ACTION: Notice of proposed rulemaking and notice of public hearing.

SUMMARY: This document contains proposed regulations on the calculation of amounts includible in income under section 409A(a) and the additional taxes imposed by such section with respect to service providers participating in certain nonqualified deferred compensation plans. The regulations would affect such service providers and the service recipients for whom the service providers provide services. This document also provides a notice of public hearing on these proposed regulations.

DATES: Written or electronic comments must be received by [*IN-SERT DATE 90 DAYS AFTER PUBLICATION OF THIS DOCUMENT IN THE FEDERAL REGISTER*].

Outlines of topics to be discussed at the public hearing scheduled for April 2, 2009, must be received by March 9, 2009.

ADDRESSES: Send submissions to: CC:PA:LPD:PR (REG-148326-05), room 5203, Internal Revenue Service, PO Box 7604, Ben Franklin Station, Washington, DC 20044. Submissions may be hand-delivered Monday through Friday between the hours of 8 a.m. and 4 p.m. to CC:PA:LPD:PR (REG-148326-05), Courier's Desk, Internal Revenue Service, 1111 Constitution Avenue, NW., Washington, DC or sent electronically, via the Federal eRulemaking Portal at *www. Regulations.gov* (IRS REG-148326-05). The public hearing will be held in the auditorium, Internal Revenue Building, 1111 Constitution Avenue, NW., Washington, DC.

FOR FURTHER INFORMATION CONTACT: Concerning the proposed regulations, Stephen Tackney, at (202) 927-9639; concerning submissions of comments, the hearing, and/or to be placed on the building access list to attend the hearing, Funmi Taylor at (202) 622-3628 not toll-free numbers). [Corrected 2/18/09 by 74 FR 7575]

SUPPLEMENTARY INFORMATION:

Background

Section 409A was added to the Internal Revenue Code (Code) by section 885 of the American Jobs Creation Act of 2004, Public Law 108-357 (118 Stat. 1418). Section 409A generally provides that if certain requirements are not met at any time during a taxable year, amounts deferred under a nonqualified deferred compensation plan for that year and all previous taxable years are currently includible in gross income to the extent not subject to a substantial risk of forfeiture and not previously included in gross income. Section 409A also includes rules applicable to certain trusts or similar arrangements associated with nonqualified deferred compensation.

On December 20, 2004, the IRS issued Notice 2005-1 (2005-2 CB 274), setting forth initial guidance on the application of section 409A, and providing transition guidance in accordance with the terms of the statute. On April 10, 2007, the Treasury Department and the IRS issued final regulations under section 409A. (72 FR 19234, April 17, 2007). The final regulations are applicable for taxable years beginning after December 31, 2008. See Notice 2007-86 (2007-46 IRB 990). Notice 2005-1 and the final regulations do not address the calculation of the amount includible in income under section 409A if a plan fails to meet the requirements of section 409A and the calculation of the additional taxes applicable to such income. On November 30, 2006, the Treasury Department and the IRS issued Notice 2006-100 (2006-51 IRB 1109) providing interim guidance for taxable years beginning in 2005 and 2006 on the calculation of the amount includible in income if the

requirements of section 409A were not met, and requesting comments on these issues for use in formulating future guidance. On October 23, 2007, the Treasury Department and the IRS issued Notice 2007-89 (2007-46 IRB 998) providing similar interim guidance for taxable years beginning in 2007. See § 601.601(d)(2)(ii)(*b*).

Commentators submitted a number of comments addressing the topics covered by these proposed regulations in response to Notice 2005-1, Notice 2006-100, Notice 2007-89, and the regulations, all of which were considered by the Treasury Department and the IRS in formulating these proposed regulations.

Explanation of Provisions

I. *Scope of Proposed Regulations*

These proposed regulations address the calculation of amounts includible in income under section 409A(a), and related issues including the calculation of the additional taxes applicable to such income. Section 409A(a) generally provides that amounts deferred under a nonqualified deferred compensation plan in all years are includible in income unless certain requirements are met. The requirements under section 409A(a) generally relate to the time and form of payment of amounts deferred under the plan, including the establishment of the time and form of payment through initial deferral elections and restrictions on the ability to change the time and form of payment through subsequent deferral elections or the acceleration of payment schedules. As provided in the regulations previously issued under section 409A, a nonqualified deferred compensation plan must comply with the requirements of section 409A(a) both in form and in operation.

Taxpayers may also be required to include amounts in income under section 409A(b). Section 409A(b) generally applies to a transfer of assets to a trust or similar arrangement, or to a restriction of assets, for purposes of paying nonqualified deferred compensation, if such trust or assets are located outside the United States, if such assets are transferred during a restricted period with respect to a single-employer defined benefit plan sponsored by the service recipient, or if such assets are restricted to the provision of benefits under a nonqualified deferred compensation plan in connection with a change in the service recipient's financial health. These proposed regulations do not address the application of section 409A(b), including the calculation of amounts includible in income if the requirements of section 409A(b) are not met. For guidance on the calculation of such amounts for taxable years beginning on or before January 1, 2007, including the application of the Federal income tax withholding requirements, see Notice 2007-89. The Treasury Department and the IRS anticipate issuing further interim guidance for later taxable years on the calculation of the amount includible in income under section 409A(b) and the application of the Federal income tax withholding requirements to such an amount.

II. *Effect of a Failure to Comply with Section 409A(a) on Amounts Deferred in Subsequent Years*

Commentators asked how section 409A(a) applies if a plan fails to comply with section 409A(a) during a taxable year and the service provider continues to have amounts deferred under the plan in subsequent years during which the plan otherwise complies with section 409A(a) both in form and in operation. The statutory language may be construed to provide that a failure is treated as continuing during taxable years beyond the year in which the initial failure occurred, if the failure continues to affect amounts deferred under the plan. For example, if an amount has been improperly deferred under the plan, the statutory language could be construed to provide that the plan fails to comply with section 409A(a) during all taxable years during which the improperly deferred amounts remain deferred. However, this position could cause harsh results and would add administrative complexity. For example, a service provider could be required to include in income, and pay additional taxes on, amounts deferred over a number of taxable years even if the sole failure to comply with section 409A(a) occurred many years earlier. In addition, even if there were no failure in the current year, to determine a taxpayer's liability for income taxes with respect to nonqualified deferred compensation for a particular year, the taxpayer and the IRS would need to examine the plan's form and operation for every year in which the service provider had an amount deferred under the plan to determine if there was a failure to comply with section 409A(a) during any of those years.

For these reasons, the proposed regulations do not adopt this interpretation and instead generally would apply the adverse tax consequences that result from a failure to comply with section 409A(a) only with respect to amounts deferred under a plan in the year in which such noncompliance occurs and all previous taxable years, to the extent such amounts are not subject to a substantial risk of forfeiture and have not previously been included in income. Therefore, under the proposed regulations, a failure to meet the requirements of section 409A(a) during a service provider's taxable year generally would not affect the taxation of amounts deferred under the plan for a subsequent taxable year during which the plan complies with section 409A(a) in form and in operation with respect to all amounts deferred under the plan. This would apply even though the amount deferred under the plan as of the end of such subsequent taxable year includes amounts deferred in earlier years during which the plan failed to comply with section 409A(a) (including, for example, amounts deferred pursuant to an untimely deferral election in the earlier year), as long as there was no failure under the plan in a later year. Because there would be no continuing or permanent failure with respect to a plan that fails to comply with section 409A(a) during an earlier year, each taxable year would be analyzed independently to determine if there was a failure. As a result, assessment of tax liabilities due to a plan's failure to comply with the requirements of section 409A(a) in a closed year would be time-barred. But, if a service provider fails to properly include amounts in income under section 409A(a) for a taxable year during which there was a failure to comply with section 409A(a), and assessment of taxes with respect to such year becomes barred by the statute of limitations, then the taxpayer's duty of consistency would prevent the service provider from claiming a tax benefit in a later year with respect to such amount (such as, for example, by claiming any type of "basis" or "investment in the contract" in the year the service recipient paid such amount to the service provider pursuant to the plan's terms).

Under the general rule in the proposed regulations, if all of a taxpayer's deferred amounts under a plan are nonvested and the taxpayer makes an impermissible deferral election or accelerates the time of payment with respect to some or all of the nonvested deferred amount, the nonvested deferred amount generally would not be includible in income under section 409A(a) in the year of the impermissible change in time and form of payment (although if there were vested amounts deferred under the plan, such amounts would be includible in income under section 409A(a)). In the subsequent taxable year in which the service provider becomes vested in the deferred amount, the plan might comply with section 409A(a) in form and in operation, so that under the general rule no income inclusion would be required and no additional taxes would be due for that year as a result of the late deferral election or acceleration of payment. In proposing to adopt this interpretation of the statute, the Treasury Department and the IRS do not intend to create an opportunity for taxpayers who ignore the requirements of section 409A(a) with respect to nonvested amounts to avoid the payment of taxes that would otherwise be due as a result of such a failure to comply. To ensure that this rule does not become a means for taxpayers to disregard the requirements of the statute, the proposed regulations would disregard a substantial risk of forfeiture for purposes of determining the amount includible in income under section 409A[1] with respect to certain nonvested deferred amounts, if the facts and circumstances indicate that the service recipient has a pattern or practice of permitting such impermissible changes in the time and form of payment with respect to nonvested deferred amounts (regardless of whether such changes also apply to vested deferred amounts). If such a pattern or practice exists, an amount deferred under a plan that is otherwise subject to a substantial risk of forfeiture is not treated as subject to a substantial risk of forfeiture if an impermissible change in the time and form of payment (including an impermissible initial deferral election) applies to the amount deferred or if the facts and circumstances indicate that the amount deferred would be affected by such pattern or practice.

III. *Calculation of the Amount Deferred under a Plan for the Taxable Year in which the Plan Fails to Meet the Requirements of Section 409A(a) and all Preceding Taxable Years*

A. *In general*

Section 409A(a)(1)(A) generally provides that if at any time during a taxable year a nonqualified deferred compensation plan fails to meet the requirements of section 409A(a)(2) (payments), section 409A(a)(3) (the acceleration of payments), or section 409A(a)(4) (deferral elections), or is not operated in accordance with such requirements, all compensation deferred under the plan for the taxable year and all preceding taxable years is includible in gross income for the taxable year to the extent not subject to a substantial risk of forfeiture and not previously included in gross income. Accordingly, to calculate the amount includible in income upon a failure to meet the requirements of section 409A(a), the first step is to determine the total amount deferred under the plan for the service provider's taxable year and all preceding taxable years. The second step is to calculate the portion of the total amount deferred for the taxable year, if any, that is either subject to a substantial risk of forfeiture (nonvested) or has been included in income in a previous taxable year. The last step is to subtract the amount determined in step two from the amount determined in step one. The excess of the amount determined in step one over the amount determined in step two is the amount includible in income and subject to additional income taxes for the year as a result of the plan's failure to comply with section 409A(a). Sections III.B through III.D of this preamble explain how the proposed regulations would address the first step in the process of determining the amount includible in income under section 409A, calculating the total amount deferred for the taxable year.

B. *Total amount deferred*

1. In General

In general, under the proposed regulations, the amount deferred under a plan[2] for a taxable year and all preceding taxable years would be referred to as the total amount deferred for a taxable year and would be determined as of the last day of the taxable year. Therefore, for calendar year taxpayers, such as most individuals, the relevant calculation date would be December 31. Determining the total amount deferred for the taxable year as of the last day of the taxable year during which a plan fails to comply with section 409A(a) would allow taxpayers to avoid the administrative burden of tracking amounts deferred under a plan on a daily basis, because adjustments would not be made to reflect notional earnings or losses or other fluctuations in the amount payable under the plan as they occur during the taxable year, but would be applied only on a net basis as of the last day of the taxable year. For example, if a service provider has a calendar year taxable year, and if the service provider's account balance under a plan is $105,000 as of July 1, but is only $100,000 as of December 31 of the same year, due solely to deemed investment losses (with no payments made under the plan during the year), the total amount deferred under the plan for that taxable year would be $100,000.

Similarly, the total amount deferred for a taxable year would not necessarily be the greatest total amount deferred for any previous year, even if no amount has been paid under the plan. For example, if a service provider has a calendar year taxable year, and if the service provider's account balance under a plan as of December 31, 2010 is $105,000, as of December 31, 2011 is $100,000, and as of December 31, 2012 is $95,000, and if those decreases are due solely to deemed investment losses (and no payments were made under the plan in 2011 or 2012), then the total amount deferred for 2011 would be $100,000 and the total amount deferred for 2012 would be $95,000.

2. Treatment of Payments

If a service recipient pays an amount deferred under a plan during a taxable year, the amount remaining to be paid to (or on behalf of) the service provider under the plan as of the last day of the taxable year will have been reduced as a result of such payment. To reasonably reflect the effect of payments made during a taxable year, the proposed regulations provide that the sum of all payments of amounts deferred under a plan during a taxable year, including all payments that are substitutes for an amount deferred, would be added to the amounts deferred outstanding as of the last day of the taxable year (determined in accordance with the regulations) to calculate the total amount deferred for such taxable year. To lower the administrative burden of the calculation, the proposed regulations provide that the addition of such payments to the total amount deferred for the taxable year would not be increased by any interest or other amount to reflect the time value of money. The total amount deferred for a taxable year would include all payments, regardless of whether the service recipient made some or all of the payments in accordance with the requirements of section 409A(a). For example, if during a taxable year an employee receives a single sum payment of the entire amount deferred under a plan, the

---

[1] Under section 409A(e)(5), the Treasury Department and the IRS have the authority to disregard a substantial risk of forfeiture where necessary to carry out the purposes of section 409A.

[2] For this purpose, the term plan refers to a plan as defined under § 1.409A-1(c), including any applicable plan aggregation rules.

employee would have a total amount deferred under the plan for the taxable year equal to the amount paid.

3. Treatment of Deemed Losses

Because the total amount deferred would be determined as of the last day of the taxable year, losses that occur during a taxable year (due to losses on deemed investments, actuarial losses, and other similar reductions in the amount payable under a plan) generally would be netted with any gains that occur during the same taxable year (due to deemed investment or actuarial gains, additional deferrals, or other additions to the amount payable under the plan). To that extent, deemed investment losses, actuarial losses, or other similar reductions could offset deemed investment or actuarial gains, additional deferrals, or other increases in the amount deferred under the plan for purposes of determining the total amount deferred for the taxable year. This would apply regardless of whether a deemed loss occurs before or after the date of any specific failure to comply with section 409A(a). For example, assume a service provider begins a taxable year with a $10,000 balance under an account balance plan. During the year, the service provider has an additional deferral to the plan of $5,000 and incurs net deemed investment losses of $2,000. No payments are made pursuant to the plan during the year, the employee has no vested legally binding right to further deferrals to the plan, and there are no other changes to the account balance. The total amount deferred for the taxable year would equal the $13,000 account balance ($10,000 + $5,000 - $2,000) as of the last day of the taxable year.

4. Treatment of Rights to Deemed Earnings on Amounts Deferred

Under section 409A(d)(5), income (whether actual or notional) attributable to deferred compensation constitutes deferred compensation for purposes of section 409A. See § 1.409A-1(b)(2). For example, if a service provider must include a deferred amount in income because an account balance plan in which the service provider participates fails to satisfy the requirements of section 409A(a), notional earnings credited with respect to such amount constitute deferred compensation and are subject to section 409A. If the plan also fails to comply with the requirements of section 409A(a) during a subsequent taxable year, the notional earnings must be included in income and are subject to the additional taxes under section 409A(a), notwithstanding that the "principal" amount of deferred compensation has already been included in income under section 409A(a) for a previous year.

In this respect, the treatment of earnings on nonqualified deferred compensation for purposes of section 409A is significantly different from the treatment of such earnings for purposes of section 3121(v)(2) (application of Federal Insurance Contributions Act (FICA) tax to nonqualified deferred compensation). As a result, notional earnings ordinarily are deferred compensation that is subject to section 409A even if such earnings would not constitute wages for purposes of the FICA tax when paid to the service provider because of the special timing rule under section 3121(v)(2) and § 31.3121(v)(2)-1(a)(2). Accordingly, the proposed regulations provide that earnings that are credited with respect to deferred compensation during a taxable year or that were credited in previous taxable years, and earnings with respect to deferred compensation that are paid during such taxable year, must be included in determining the total amount deferred for the taxable year.

5. Total Amount Deferred for a Taxable Year Relates to the Entire Taxable Year, Regardless of Date or Period of Failure

Section 409A(a)(1)(A)(i) states that if at any time during a taxable year a nonqualified deferred compensation plan fails to meet the requirements of section 409A(a), all compensation deferred under the plan for the taxable year and all preceding years shall be includible in gross income for the taxable year to the extent not subject to a substantial risk of forfeiture (vested) and not previously included in gross income. The statutory reference to the deferred compensation required to be included in income under section 409A(a) does not distinguish between amounts deferred in a taxable year before a failure to meet the requirements of section 409A(a), and amounts deferred in the same taxable year after such failure. Accordingly, under the proposed regulations the total amount deferred under a plan for a taxable year would refer to the total amount deferred as of the last day of the taxable year, regardless of the date upon which a failure occurs. For example, if a plan is amended during a service provider's taxable year to add a provision that fails to meet the requirements of section 409A(a), the total amount deferred as of the last day of the taxable year would be includible in income under section 409A(a). This would include all payments under the plan during the taxable year, including payments made before the amendment (regardless of whether such payments are made in accordance with the requirements of section 409A(a)). Similarly, if the plan in operation fails to meet the require-

ments of section 409A(a) during the taxable year, the total amount deferred for the taxable year would include all payments under the plan during the taxable year, including payments made before and after the date the failure occurred.

The proposed regulations provide that amounts deferred under a plan during a taxable year in which a failure occurs must be included in income under section 409A(a) even if such deferrals occur after the failure and are otherwise made in compliance with section 409A(a). For example, salary deferrals for periods during a taxable year after an impermissible accelerated payment under the same plan during the same taxable year would be required to be included in the total amount deferred for the taxable year and included in income under section 409A(a), regardless of whether the salary deferrals are made in accordance with an otherwise compliant deferral election.

6. Treatment of Short-Term Deferrals

Under § 1.409A-1(b)(4), an arrangement may not provide for deferred compensation if the amount is payable, and is paid, during a limited period of time following the later of the date the service provider obtains a legally binding right to the payment or the date such right is no longer subject to a substantial risk of forfeiture (generally referred to as the applicable 2 1/2 month period). Whether an amount will be treated as a short-term deferral or as deferred compensation may not be determinable as of the last day of the service provider's taxable year, because it may depend upon whether the amount is paid on or before the end of the applicable 2 1/2 month period. For purposes of calculating the total amount deferred for a taxable year, the proposed regulations provide that the right to a payment that, under the terms of the arrangement and the facts and circumstances as of the last day of the taxable year, may or may not be a short-term deferral, is not included in the total amount deferred. In addition, even if such amount is not paid by the end of the applicable 2 1/2 month period so that the amount would be deferred compensation, the amount would not be includible in the total amount deferred until the service provider's taxable year in which the applicable 2 1/2 month period expired. For example, assume that as of December 31, 2010, an employee whose taxable year is the calendar year is entitled to an annual bonus that is scheduled to be paid on March 15, 2011, and that the bonus would qualify as a shortterm deferral if paid on or before the end of the applicable 2 1/2 month period, which ends on March 15, 2011. The bonus would not be included in the total amount deferred for 2010. This would be true regardless of whether the bonus is paid on or before March 15, 2011. However, the bonus would be includible in the total amount deferred for 2011 if the bonus is not paid on or before March 15, 2011.

C. *Calculation of total amount deferred - general principles*

1. General Rule

Generally, the proposed regulations provide that the total amount deferred under a plan for a taxable year is the present value as of the close of the last day of a service provider's taxable year of all amounts payable to the service provider under the plan, plus amounts paid to the service provider during the taxable year. For this purpose, present value generally would mean the value as of the close of the last day of the service provider's relevant taxable year of the amount or series of amounts due thereafter, where each such amount is multiplied by the probability that the condition or conditions on which payment of the amount is contingent would be satisfied (subject to special treatment for certain contingencies), discounted according to an assumed rate of interest to reflect the time value of money. A discount for the probability that the service provider will die before commencement of payments under the plan would be permitted to the extent that the payments would be forfeited upon the service provider's death. The proposed regulations provide that the present value cannot be discounted for the probability that payments will not be made (or will be reduced) because of the unfunded status of the plan, the risk associated with any deemed investment of amounts deferred under the plan, the risk that the service recipient or another party will be unwilling or unable to pay amounts deferred under the plan when due, the possibility of future plan amendments, the possibility of a future change in the law, or similar risks or contingencies. The proposed regulations further provide that restrictions on payment that will or may lapse with the passage of time, such as a temporary risk of forfeiture that is not a substantial risk of forfeiture, are not taken into account in determining present value. However, any potential additional deferrals contingent upon a bona fide requirement that the service provider perform services after the taxable year, such as potential salary deferrals, service credits or additions due to increases in compensation, would not be taken into account in determining the total amount deferred for the taxable year.

For purposes of calculating the present value of the benefit, the proposed regulations require the use of reasonable actuarial assumptions and methods. Whether assumptions and methods are reasonable for this purpose would be determined as of each date the benefit is valued for purposes of determining the total amount deferred.

The proposed regulations also provide certain rules relating to the crediting of earnings, generally providing that the schedule for crediting earnings will be respected if the earnings are credited at least once a year. In general, if the rules with respect to the crediting of earnings are met, any additional earnings that would be credited after the end of the taxable year only if the service provider continued performing services after the end of the year would not be includible in the total amount deferred for the year. If the right to earnings is based on an unreasonably high interest rate, the proposed regulations generally would characterize the unreasonable portion of earnings as a current right to additional deferred compensation. In addition, if earnings are based on a rate of return that does not qualify as a predetermined actual investment or a reasonable interest rate, the proposed regulations provide that the general calculation rules as applied to formula amounts would apply.

The proposed regulations provide other general rules that address issues such as plan terms under which amounts may be payable when a triggering event occurs, rather than on a fixed date, or plan terms under which the amount payable is determined in accordance with a formula, rather than being set at a fixed amount. In addition, the proposed regulations provide specific rules under which the total amounts deferred under certain types of nonqualified deferred compensation plans would be determined. The rules applicable to specific types of plans would apply in conjunction with the general rules. As a result, under the proposed regulations, an amount of deferred compensation may be includible in income under section 409A(a) even if the same amount would not yet be includible in wages under section 3121(v)(2).

2. Rules Regarding Alternative Times and Forms of Payment

To calculate the total amount deferred under a nonqualified deferred compensation plan, it is necessary to determine the time and form of payment pursuant to which the amount will be paid. Under the proposed regulations, if an amount deferred under a plan could be payable pursuant to more than one time and form of payment under the plan, the amount would be treated as payable in the available time and form of payment that has the highest present value. For this purpose, a time and form of payment generally would be an available time and form of payment to the extent a deferred amount under the plan could be payable pursuant to such time and form of payment under the plan's terms, provided that if there is a bona fide requirement that the service provider continue to perform services after the end of the taxable year to be eligible for the time and form of payment, the time and form of payment would not be treated as available. If an alternative time and form of payment is available only at the service recipient's discretion, the time and form of payment would not be treated as available unless the service provider has a legally binding right under the principles of § 1.409A-1(b)(1) to any additional value that would be generated by the service recipient's exercise of such discretion. If a service provider has begun receiving payments of an amount deferred under a plan and neither the service provider nor the service recipient can change the time and form of payment of such deferred amount without the other party's approval, then no other time and form of payment under the plan would be treated as available if such approval requirement has substantive significance.

In certain instances, a service provider will be eligible for an alternative time and form of payment only if the service provider has a certain status as of a future date. For example, a time and form of payment may be available only if the service provider is married at the time the payment commences. The proposed regulations generally provide that for purposes of determining whether the service provider will meet the eligibility requirements so that an alternative time and form of payment is available, the service provider is assumed to continue in the service provider's status as of the last day of the taxable year. However, if the eligibility requirement is not bona fide and does not serve a bona fide business purpose, the eligibility requirement would be disregarded and the service provider would be treated as eligible for the alternative time and form of payment. For this purpose, an eligibility condition based upon the service provider's marital status, parental status, or status as a U.S. citizen or lawful permanent resident would be presumed to be bona fide and to serve a bona fide business purpose.

If the calculation of the present value of the amount payable to a service provider under a plan requires assumptions relating to the timing of the payment because the payment date is, or could be, a triggering event rather than a specified date, the proposed regulations

specify certain assumptions that must be applied to make such calculation. First, the possibility that a particular payment trigger would occur generally would not be taken into account if the right to the payment would be subject to a substantial risk of forfeiture if that payment trigger were the only specified payment trigger. For example, if an amount is payable upon the earlier of the attainment of a specified age or an involuntary separation from service (as defined in the § 1.409A-1(n)), the present value of the amount payable upon involuntary separation from service would not be taken into account if the payment would be subject to a substantial risk of forfeiture if that were the only payment trigger. However, if multiple triggers with respect to the same payment would, applied individually, constitute substantial risks of forfeiture, such triggers would not be disregarded under this rule unless all such triggers, applied in the aggregate, would also constitute a substantial risk of forfeiture. Second, the possibility that an unforeseeable emergency, as defined in § 1.409A-3(i)(3), would occur and result in a payment also would not be taken into account for purposes of calculating the amount deferred.

If an amount is payable upon a service provider's death, it generally would not be necessary to make assumptions concerning when the service provider would die because any additional value due to the amount becoming payable upon the service provider's death generally would be treated as an amount payable under a death benefit plan, and amounts payable under a death benefit plan are not deferred compensation for purposes of section 409A(a). Similarly, such assumptions generally would not be necessary for an amount payable upon a service provider's disability, because any additional value due to the amount becoming payable upon the service provider's disability generally would be payable under a disability plan, and amounts payable under a disability plan are not deferred compensation for purposes of section 409A. See § 1.409A-1(a)(5).

In other cases where it is necessary to make assumptions concerning when a payment trigger would occur to determine the amount deferred under a plan, taxpayers generally would be required to assume that the payment trigger would occur at the earliest possible time that the conditions under which the amount would become payable reasonably could occur, based on the facts and circumstances as of the last day of the taxable year. However, the proposed regulations provide a special rule for amounts payable due to the service provider's separation from service, termination of employment, or other event requiring the service provider's reduction or cessation of services for the service recipient. In such a case, the total amount deferred would be calculated as if the service provider had met the required reduction or cessation of services as of the close of the last day of the service provider's taxable year for which such calculation was being made. These rules would apply regardless of whether the payment trigger has or has not occurred as of any future date upon which the amount deferred for a prior taxable year was being determined.

The Treasury Department and the IRS recognize that for some service providers, the earliest possible time that a payment trigger reasonably could occur will not be the most likely time the trigger will occur. Similarly, the Treasury Department and the IRS recognize that for many service providers, the assumption that the service provider ceases providing services as of the end of the taxable year may not be realistic. The Treasury Department and the IRS request comments on alternative standards that could be utilized for these payment triggers.

An alternative approach might presume a date upon which the service provider will separate from service such as, for example, 100 months after the last day of the service provider's taxable year for which the amount deferred is being calculated. Cf. § 1.280G-1 Q&A 24(c)(4). Such a standard, however, would not reflect the value of additional deferred compensation that would be paid only if the service provider separates from service before the end of the 100-month period, such as an early retirement subsidy or a window benefit, unless special rules were developed to address such situations. Another issue that arises is whether such a standard should apply if the service provider is likely to retire during the next 100 months, such as if a service provider has attained a certain age, number of years of service, or level of financial independence. However, the Treasury Department and the IRS are concerned whether an approach involving the application of individualized standards to determine the probability that a particular service provider will separate from service will be administrable in practice.

3. Treatment of Rights to Formula Amounts

Once the date that a payment will occur has been fixed (either as a specified date under the plan's terms or through application of the rules in the proposed regulations), it is necessary to quantify the amount of the payment to which the service provider will be entitled to calculate the total amount deferred under a nonqualified deferred compensation plan. However, certain plans may define the amount payable by a formula or other method that is based on factors that may vary in future years. In general, if, at the end of the service provider's taxable year, the amount to be paid in a future year is a formula amount, the proposed regulations provide that the amount payable in the future year for purposes of calculating the total amount deferred must be determined using reasonable assumptions.

A deferred amount generally would be a formula amount subject to the reasonable assumptions standard if calculating the payment amount is dependent upon factors that are not determinable after taking into consideration all of the assumptions and other calculation rules provided in the proposed regulations. For example, a future payment equal to one percent of a corporation's net profits over five calendar years generally would be a formula amount until the last day of the fifth year, because the corporation's net profits over the five calendar years could not be determined by applying the assumptions and rules set out in the proposed regulations until the end of the fifth calendar year.

A deferred amount would not be a formula amount at the end of the taxable year merely because the information necessary to determine the amount is not readily available, if such information exists at the end of such taxable year. For example, if a deferred amount is based upon the service recipient's profits for its taxable year that coincides with the service provider's taxable year, the amount would be considered a non-formula amount at the end of the taxable year because the information necessary to determine the service recipient's profits exists, although such information may not be immediately accessible.

The right to have a deferred amount credited with reasonable earnings that may vary, for example because the earnings are based on the value of a deemed investment, would not affect whether the right to the underlying deferred amount is a formula amount. In addition, the amount of earnings to which the service provider has become entitled at the end of a particular taxable year would not be treated as a formula amount, regardless of whether such earnings could subsequently be reduced by future losses. For example, assume a service provider has a $10,000 account under an account balance plan, to be paid out in three years subject to earnings based on a mutual fund designed to replicate the performance of the S&P 500 index. At the end of Year 1, the account balance is $10,500. For Year 1, the service provider would have a total amount deferred equal to $10,500, notwithstanding that the amount could be reduced by future losses based on losses in the mutual fund.

D. Calculation of total amounts deferred - specific types of plans

1. Account Balance Plans

Under the proposed regulations, the amount deferred under an account balance plan for a taxable year generally equals the aggregate balance of all accounts under the plan as of the close of the last day of the taxable year, plus any amounts paid from such plan during the taxable year, so long as the aggregate account balance is determined using not more than a reasonable interest rate or the return on a predetermined actual investment. This rule would apply regardless of whether the applicable interest rate used to determine the earnings was higher or lower than the applicable Federal rate (AFR) under section 1274(d), provided that the interest rate was no more than a reasonable rate of interest. For a description of the proposed rules on how to calculate the total amount deferred if the right to earnings is based on an unreasonably high interest rate, see section III.C.1 of this preamble.

2. Nonaccount Balance Plans

Under the proposed regulations, the total amount deferred for a taxable year under a nonaccount balance plan generally is calculated under the general calculation rule. See section III.C of this preamble. For example, if a service provider has the right to be paid on a specified future date a fixed amount that is not credited with earnings, the total amount deferred for a year generally would be the present value as of the last day of the service provider's taxable year of the amount to which the service provider has a right to be paid in the future year (assuming no payments were made under the plan during the year). Increases in the present value of the payment in subsequent years due to the passage of time would be treated as earnings in the years in which such increases occur. For example, a right to a payment of $10,000 in Year 3 may have a present value in Year 1 equal to $8,900, and a present value in Year 2 equal to $9,434, so that the total amount deferred in Year 1 would be $8,900, the total amount deferred in Year 2 would be $9,434, and the total amount deferred in Year 3 would be $10,000 (assuming no payments were made during any year except Year 3). Any potential additional service credits or increases in com-

pensation after the end of the taxable year for which the calculation is being made would not be taken into account in determining the total amount deferred for the taxable year.

3. Stock Rights

In general, the proposed regulations provide that the total amount deferred under an outstanding stock right is the amount of money and the fair market value of the property that the service provider would receive by exercising the right on the last day of the taxable year, reduced by the amount (if any) the service provider must pay to exercise the right and any amount the service provider paid for the right, which is commonly referred to as the spread. Accordingly, for an outstanding stock option, the total amount deferred generally would equal the underlying stock's fair market value on the last day of the taxable year, less the sum of the exercise price and any amount paid for the stock option. For an outstanding stock appreciation right, the total amount deferred generally would equal the underlying stock's fair market value on the last day of the taxable year, less the sum of the exercise price and any amount paid for the stock appreciation right. For this purpose, the stock's fair market value would be determined applying the principles set forth in § 1.409A-1(b)(5).

The Treasury Department and the IRS recognize that the spread generally is less than the fair market value of the stock right, which is used for purposes of determining the amount taxable under other Code provisions such as section 83 (if a stock option has a readily ascertainable fair market value), section 4999, and section 457(f). However, because these types of stock rights typically will fail to comply with section 409A(a) in multiple years, a taxpayer who holds such a stock right generally will be required to include amounts in income under section 409A in more than one taxable year. Therefore, the Treasury Department and the IRS believe that it is more appropriate to use the spread for purposes of applying section 409A(a) to stock rights.

4. Separation Pay Arrangements

A deferred amount that is payable only upon an involuntary separation from service generally will be treated as subject to a substantial risk of forfeiture until the service provider involuntarily separates from service. Accordingly, under the proposed regulations the amount of deferred compensation generally would not be required to be calculated until the service provider has involuntarily separated from service. In addition, if the amount were payable upon either an involuntary separation from service or some other trigger, such as a fixed date, the possibility of payment upon an involuntary separation from service generally would be ignored for purposes of determining the total amount deferred under the arrangement. See section III.C.2 of this preamble. Once an involuntary separation from service has occurred, the amount deferred under the plan would be determined using the rules that would apply to the schedule of payments if the right to payment were not contingent upon an involuntary separation from service. For example, if the amounts payable are installment payments and the remaining installment payments include interest credited at a reasonable rate, the total amount deferred under the plan would be determined under the rules governing account balance plans. If more than one type of deferred compensation arrangement were provided under the separation pay agreement, the amount deferred under each arrangement would be determined using the rules applicable to that type of arrangement. The total amount deferred for the taxable year would be the sum of all of the amounts deferred under the various arrangements constituting the plan.

5. Reimbursement Arrangements

The proposed regulations provide a method of calculating the amount deferred under a reimbursement arrangement, including an arrangement where the benefit is provided as an in-kind benefit from the service recipient or the service recipient will pay directly the third-party provider of the goods or services to the service provider. For example, the amount deferred under an arrangement providing a specified number of hours of financial planning services after a service provider's separation from service would be determined using the rules applicable to reimbursement arrangements, regardless of whether the service recipient reimburses the service provider for the service provider's expenses in purchasing such services, provides the financial planning services directly to the service provider, or pays a third-party financial planner to provide such services. The rules for reimbursement arrangements would apply to all such types of arrangements, including arrangements that would not be disaggregated from a nonaccount balance plan under § 1.409A-1(c)(2)(i)(E) because the amounts subject to reimbursement exceed the applicable limits.

The proposed calculation rules provide that if a service provider has a right to reimbursements but only up to a specified maximum amount, it is presumed that the taxpayer will incur the maximum amount of expenses eligible for reimbursement, at the earliest possible time such expenses may be incurred and payable at the earliest possible time the amount may be reimbursed under the plan's terms. The service provider could rebut the presumption if the service provider demonstrates by clear and convincing evidence that it is unreasonable to assume that the service provider would expend (or would have expended) the maximum amount of expenses eligible for reimbursement. For example, if a service provider is entitled to the reimbursement of country club dues the service provider incurs in the next taxable year, not to exceed $30,000, if the service provider can demonstrate that the most expensive country club within reasonable geographic proximity of the service provider's residence and work location will cost $20,000 per year, and that the service provider's level of compensation and financial resources make it unreasonable to assume that the service provider would travel periodically to the locales of other, more expensive country clubs, the service provider can calculate the amount deferred based upon the $20,000 being eligible for reimbursement. The presumption of maximum utilization of expenses eligible for reimbursement generally would not apply if the expenses subject to reimbursement are medical expenses.

If a right to reimbursement is not subject to a maximum amount, the taxpayer would be treated as having deferred a formula amount, provided that the taxpayer would be required to calculate the amount based on the maximum amount that reasonably could be expended and reimbursed. The amount would be considered a nonformula amount as soon as the taxpayer incurs the expense that is subject to reimbursement, in an amount equal to the reimbursement to which the taxpayer is entitled. For example, a right to the reimbursement of half of the expenses the service provider incurs to purchase a boat without any limitation with respect to the cost would be treated as a deferral of a formula amount, until such time as the service provider purchases the boat.

6. Split-Dollar Life Insurance Arrangements

The amount deferred under a split-dollar life insurance arrangement would be determined based upon the amount that would be required to be included in income in a future year under the applicable split-dollar life insurance rules. Determination of the amount includible in income would depend upon the Federal tax regime and guidance applicable to such arrangement. If the split-dollar life insurance arrangement is not subject to § 1.61-22 or § 1.7872-15 due to application of the effective date provisions under § 1.61-22(j), the amount payable would be determined by reference to Notice 2002-8 (2002-1 CB 398) and any other applicable guidance. If the split-dollar life insurance arrangement is subject to § 1.61-22 or § 1.7872-15, the amount payable would be determined by reference to such regulations, based upon the type of arrangement. For this purpose, the amount includible in income generally would be determined by applying the split-dollar life insurance rules to the arrangement in conjunction with the general rules providing assumptions on payment dates of deferred amounts. However, in the case of an arrangement subject to § 1.7872-15, to the extent the rules regarding time and form of payment and other payment assumptions under these proposed regulations conflict with the provisions of § 1.7872-15, the provisions of § 1.7872-15 would apply instead of the conflicting rules under these proposed regulations. As provided in Notice 2007-34 (2007-17 IRB 996), the portion of the benefit provided under the split-dollar life insurance arrangement consisting of the cost of current life insurance protection is not treated as deferred compensation for this purpose. See § 601.601(d)(2)(ii)(b).

7. Foreign Arrangements

Although certain foreign arrangements are a separate category under the plan aggregation rules (§ 1.409A-1(c)(2)(i)(G)), the amounts deferred under such arrangements would be determined using the same rules that would apply if the arrangements were not foreign arrangements. For example, the total amount deferred by a United States citizen participating in a salary deferral arrangement in France that meets the requirements of § 1.409A-1(c)(2)(i)(G), but that otherwise would constitute an elective account balance plan under § 1.409A-1(c)(2)(i)(A), would be determined using the rules applicable to account balance plans.

8. Other Plans

The calculation of the total amount deferred under a plan that does not fall into any of the enunciated categories (and accordingly is treated as a separate plan under § 1.409A-1(c)(2)(i)(I)), would be determined by applying the general calculation rules.

E. *Calculation of amounts includible in income.*

This section III.E of the preamble addresses the second step in determining the amount includible in income under section 409A for a taxable year - the determination of the portion of the total amount deferred for a taxable year that was either subject to a substantial risk of forfeiture or had previously been included in income. That portion of the total amount deferred for the taxable year would not be includible in income under section 409A.

1. Determination of the Portion of the Total Amount Deferred for a Taxable Year that is Subject to a Substantial Risk of Forfeiture

In general, the proposed regulations provide that the portion of the total amount deferred for a taxable year that is subject to a substantial risk of forfeiture (nonvested) is determined as of the last day of the service provider's taxable year. Accordingly, all amounts that vest during the taxable year in which a failure occurs would be treated as vested for purposes of section 409A(a), regardless of whether the vesting event occurs before or after the failure to meet the requirements of section 409A(a). For example, if a plan fails to comply with section 409A(a) due to an operational failure on July 1 of a taxable year, and the substantial risk of forfeiture applicable to an amount deferred under the plan lapses as of October 1 of the same taxable year, that amount would be treated as a vested amount for purposes of determining the amount includible in income for the taxable year.

2. Determination of the Portion of the Total Amount Deferred for a Taxable Year that has been Previously Included in Income

For a deferred amount to be treated as previously included in income, the proposed regulations would require that the service provider actually and properly have included the amount in income in accordance with a provision of the Internal Revenue Code. This would include amounts reflected on an original or amended return filed before expiration of the applicable statute of limitations on assessment and amounts included in income as part of an audit or closing agreement process. In addition, a deferred amount would be treated as an amount previously included in income only until the amount is paid. Accordingly, if a deferred amount is paid in the same taxable year in which an amount is included in income under section 409A, or all or a portion of an amount previously included in income is allocable to a payment made under the plan (see section VI.A of this preamble), in subsequent taxable years that amount would not be treated as an amount previously included in income. For example, if an employee includes $100,000 in income under section 409A(a), and $10,000 of the amount includible in income consists of a payment under the plan during the taxable year, only $90,000 would remain to be treated as a deferred amount previously included in income. Similarly, if in the next year the employee receives a payment, to the extent any or all of that $90,000 amount previously included in income is allocated to that payment so that all or a portion of the payment is not includible in gross income, the amount allocated would no longer be treated as an amount previously included in income.

F. *Treatment of failures continuing during more than one taxable year*

A plan term that fails to meet the requirements of section 409A(a) may be retained in the plan over multiple taxable years. In addition, operational failures may occur in multiple years. This section III.F of the preamble discusses how section 409A(a) applies in such cases.

Each of the service provider's taxable years would be analyzed independently to determine if amounts were includible in income under section 409A(a). See section II of this preamble. Thus, for any taxable year during which a failure occurs, all amounts deferred under the plan would be includible in income unless the amount has previously been included in income or is subject to a substantial risk of forfeiture. Generally, this means that a service provider who includes in income under section 409A(a) all amounts deferred under a plan for a taxable year would not be relieved of the requirement to include amounts in income for an earlier taxable year in which a failure also occurred. It would undermine the statutory purpose to allow a service provider to include an amount in income under section 409A(a) (or otherwise) on a current basis with respect to a failure that occurred in a prior taxable year and thereby eliminate the taxes owed for the earlier year, especially if intervening payments of deferred amounts have reduced the total amount deferred as of the end of such current year. In addition, this rule generally would prohibit a service provider from selecting from among several previous taxable years the most favorable year in which to include income. However, if an amount was actually and properly included in income under section 409A(a) in a previous year, the amount would be treated as an amount previously in income for purposes of all subsequent years. Accordingly, this rule would never make the same amount includible in income twice under section 409A(a).

For example, assume an employee participates in a nonqualified deferred compensation plan and defers $10,000 each year, credited annually with interest at 5 percent (assumed to be reasonable for purposes of this example), and receives no payments under the plan. The employee's total amount deferred would be $10,500 for Year 1, $21,525 for Year 2, and $33,101 for Year 3. If the nonqualified deferred compensation plan fails to meet the requirements of section 409A(a) in each year, the employee would be required to include $10,500 in income under section 409A(a) for Year 1, $11,025 in income for Year 2, and $11,576 in income for Year 3. If the employee includes $33,101 in income under section 409A(a) for Year 3, the employee would not have properly reported income for Year 1 and Year 2. However, an amount included in income for Year 3 would be treated as previously included in income for purposes of any further failures in subsequent years. In addition, if the employee subsequently properly includes amounts in income for Year 1 and Year 2 on amended returns, the employee could claim a refund of the tax paid on the excess amounts included in income for Year 3. Similar consequences apply to the employer. If the employer fails to report and withhold on amounts includible in income under section 409A(a) in Year 1 and Year 2, the employer could not avoid liability for the failure to withhold in Year 1 and Year 2 by reporting the full amount and withholding in Year 3.

Because each taxable year would be analyzed independently, the IRS could elect to audit and assess with respect to a single taxable year, and require inclusion of all amounts deferred under the plan through that taxable year (even if failures also occurred in prior taxable years). Under those circumstances, the taxpayer could simply include amounts in income under section 409A(a) for that taxable year. However, before expiration of the applicable statute of limitations, the taxpayer could amend returns for previous taxable years and include in income amounts required to be included under section 409A(a), lowering the amount includible in income under section 409A(a) for the audited taxable year because, for purposes of that taxable year, those amounts would have been included in income in previous years. For example, an audit of Year 3 in the example above could result in an adjustment requiring $33,101 to be included in income under section 409A(a). However, before expiration of the applicable statute of limitations, the employee could amend the employee's Year 1 and Year 2 Federal tax returns to include $10,500 in income under section 409A(a) for Year 1, and $11,025 in income under section 409A(a) for Year 2, and accordingly include only $11,576 in income under section 409A(a) for Year 3. However, the employee would be required to pay the additional section 409A(a) taxes for Year 1 and Year 2, including the premium interest tax. In addition, if amounts deferred under the plan had been paid in Year 1 or Year 2, the employee would be required to include those additional amounts in income under section 409A(a) for the year paid (meaning, if the payment had been included in income for the year in which it was paid, the employee would be required to amend the previously filed tax returns to pay the additional section 409A(a) taxes on such income).

IV. *Application of Additional 20 Percent Tax*

Section 409A(a)(1)(B)(i)(II) provides that if compensation is required to be included in gross income under section 409A(a)(1)(A) for a taxable year, the income tax imposed is increased by an amount equal to 20 percent of the compensation that is required to be included in gross income. This amount is an additional income tax, subject to the rules governing the assessment, collection, and payment of income tax, and is not an excise tax.

V. *Application of Premium Interest Tax*

A. *In general*

Section 409A(a)(1)(B)(i)(I) provides that if compensation is required to be included in gross income under section 409A(a)(1)(A) for a taxable year, the income tax imposed is increased by an amount equal to the amount of interest determined under section 409A(a)(1)(B)(ii). This amount is an additional income tax, subject to the rules governing assessment, collection, and payment of income tax, and is not an excise tax or interest on an underpayment. Section 409A(a)(1)(B)(ii) provides that this premium interest tax is determined as the amount of interest at the underpayment rate (established under section 6621) plus one percentage point on the underpayments that would have occurred had the deferred compensation been includible in gross income for the taxable year in which first deferred or, if later, the first taxable year in which such deferred compensation is not subject to a substantial risk of forfeiture (vested). Thus, section 409A(a)(1)(B) requires that the premium interest tax be applied to hypothetical underpayments where the hypothetical underpayments are determined by first allocating the

amounts deferred under the plan required to be included in income under section 409A(a) to the initial year (or years) the amount was deferred or vested, then determining the hypothetical underpayment that would have resulted had such amounts been includible in income at that time, and then determining the interest that would be due upon that hypothetical underpayment based upon a premium interest rate equal to the underpayment rate plus one percentage point.

B. *Amounts to which the premium interest tax applies*

Section 409A(a)(1)(B)(ii) provides for an additional tax based upon the interest that would be applied to the resulting underpayments of tax if the deferred compensation includible in income under section 409A(a) had been includible in income in previous years. Because the total amount deferred for the taxable year in which a failure occurs (the current year) may be less than the amounts deferred under the same plan in a previous year due to payments or deemed investment or other losses in the previous year, so that a portion of the amount deferred in the previous year would not be includible in income under section 409A(a) for the current year, commentators have asked what amounts deferred under the plan must be taken into account in determining the premium interest tax. Section 409A(a)(1)(B)(i) refers first to the compensation required to be included in gross income under section 409A(a)(1)(A). Accordingly, under the proposed regulations the amount required to be included in income under section 409A(a) for the taxable year is the only deferred amount required to be allocated to previous taxable years for purposes of determining the premium interest tax under section 409A(a)(1)(B)(i)(I).

For example, assume an employee who participates in a plan has a total amount deferred in Year 1 of $100,000 and a total amount deferred in Year 2 of $80,000 due to deemed investment losses in Year 2. If the plan fails to meet the requirements of section 409A(a) in Year 2 (and not Year 1), the employee is required to include $80,000 in income under section 409A(a). In calculating the premium interest tax, the employee must allocate only the $80,000 required to be included in income under section 409A(a) to the year or years the amount was first deferred or vested, even though additional amounts were deferred under the plan in previous taxable years.

C. *Identification of initial years of deferral for includible amounts*

1. Identification of Amounts Deferred in a Particular Taxable Year - General Principles

To calculate the premium underpayment interest tax, the taxable year or years during which the amount required to be included in income was first deferred or first vested must be determined. The proposed regulations provide that the amount deferred during a particular taxable year generally is the excess (if any) of the vested total amount deferred for that taxable year over the vested total amount deferred for the immediately preceding taxable year. For example, if a service provider first participated in a plan in the taxable year 2010 and has a vested total amount deferred under the plan for 2010 of $10,000, a vested total amount deferred for 2011 of $15,000, and a vested total amount deferred for 2012 of $25,000, then the service provider would be treated as having first deferred $10,000 during 2010, $5,000 during 2011, and $10,000 during 2012.

2. Identification of Initial Years of Deferral - Treatment of Amounts Previously Included in Income, Payments, and Investment Losses

The general rule would apply in cases where during previous taxable years there have been no payments under the plan, no net deemed investment or other losses, and no amounts otherwise included in income. If a service provider has received a payment, incurred net deemed losses, or included an amount in income, the general rule would need to be modified. For example, assume that the vested total amount deferred for Year 1 is $100,000, for Year 2 is $200,000 (including a $50,000 payment), and for Year 3 is $250,000. If there is a failure to meet the requirements of section 409A(a) in Year 3, the service provider would be required to include $250,000 in income. The service provider would also need to determine the year or years during which the $250,000 was first deferred and vested for purposes of calculating the premium interest tax. The issue then arises whether the $50,000 payment in Year 2 was a payment of an amount first deferred and vested in Year 1 or Year 2. If the $50,000 payment is treated as a payment of an amount first deferred and vested in Year 1, then only $50,000 of the $100,000 deferred in Year 1 would remain to be treated as part of the $250,000 includible in income in Year 3. In contrast, if the $50,000 payment is treated as a payment of an amount first deferred in Year 2, then the entire $100,000 deferred in Year 1 would remain to be treated as part of the $250,000. Similar issues arise with respect to the treatment of deemed investment losses and amounts previously included in income.

Under the calculation method set forth in the proposed regulations, payments, deemed investment or other losses, and amounts included in income during taxable years before the year in which the failure occurs, generally are attributed to amounts deferred and vested in the earliest year or years in which there are amounts deferred. The proposed calculation method generally achieves this result by reducing the amount deferred for each year preceding the payment or deemed investment or other loss, and treating only the remaining deferred amounts as the source of the outstanding deferrals and payments includible in income under section 409A for the year in which the failure occurs. This proposed rule generally should result in the lowest possible amount of premium interest tax, because deferred amounts includible in income under section 409A would be treated as first deferred and vested in the latest possible years, resulting in less premium interest on the hypothetical underpayments.

D. *Calculation of the hypothetical underpayment*

The hypothetical underpayment would be calculated as if the amount were paid to the service provider as a cash payment of compensation during the taxable year. Further, the hypothetical underpayment would be calculated based on the taxpayer's taxable income, credits, filing status, and other tax information for the year, based on the original return the taxpayer filed for such year, as adjusted as a result of any examination for such year or any amended return the taxpayer filed for such year that was accepted by the IRS. The hypothetical underpayment would reflect the effect that such additional compensation would have had on the amount of Federal income tax owed by the taxpayer for such year, including the continued availability of any deductions taken, and the use of any carryovers such as carryover losses. For purposes of calculating a hypothetical underpayment in a subsequent year (whether or not a portion of the deferred amount was first deferred and vested in the subsequent year), any changes to the taxpayer's Federal income tax liability for the subsequent year that would have occurred if the portion of the deferred amount that was first deferred and vested during the previous taxable year had been included in the taxpayer's income for the previous year would be taken into account. For example, if in calculating the hypothetical underpayment for one year, an additional amount of unused charitable contribution deductions is absorbed, the use of the additional charitable contributions would be reflected in determining the hypothetical underpayment for a subsequent year (meaning that the same portion of the charitable contribution could not be deducted twice in determining the hypothetical underpayments for more than one year).

Calculation of the premium interest tax would take into account only the consequences the additional income would have had on the Federal income tax due based on items of income and deduction, credits, filing status and similar information existing as of the end of the taxable year at issue. Other potential effects of the additional compensation payment on service provider or service recipient actions or elections would not be taken into account, including how such additional compensation could have affected participation in an employee benefit plan or other arrangement. For example, the impact such additional compensation would have had on contributions to a qualified plan, even if the additional compensation would have affected the amount the service provider would have been permitted or required to contribute, would be disregarded.

E. *Potential safe harbor calculation methods*

The Treasury Department and the IRS recognize that calculation of the premium underpayment interest tax may be cumbersome, potentially involving the recalculation of several years' tax returns. In response, the Treasury Department and the IRS are considering whether safe harbor calculation methods could be devised that would reduce the calculation burden but still result in an appropriate amount of tax applicable to the amount includible in income under section 409A(a). Specifically, the Treasury Department and the IRS request comments on calculation methods that would more easily identify the taxable year or years during which an amount includible in income under section 409A(a) was first deferred and vested, and that would more easily determine the hypothetical underpayments applicable to such year or years. Comments should consider both how the safe harbor method would be applied by taxpayers, and the extent to which such methods could be applied by the IRS in the examination context.

VI. *Treatment of Payments, Forfeitures, or Permanent Losses of Deferred Amounts in Taxable Years after the Amount is Included in Income under Section 409A(a)*

A. *Payments of deferred compensation in taxable years after the inclusion of such amounts in income under section 409A(a)*

Section 409A(c) provides that any amount included in gross income under section 409A is not required to be included in gross income under any other provision of the Code or any other rule of law later than the time provided in section 409A. Accordingly, if a service provider includes an amount in income under section 409A, the proposed regulations provide for a type of deemed "basis" or "investment in the contract" such that the amount would not be required to be included in income again (for example, when the amount was actually paid). For this purpose, the amount previously included in income would be treated as the inclusion in income of an amount deferred under the plan, but would not be allocated to any specific amount deferred under the plan. Accordingly, if an amount under the plan would be includible in income if section 409A were disregarded (for example, because an amount is paid under the plan), the amount previously included in income would be immediately applied to the amount paid under the plan such that the amount paid would not be required to be included in gross income a second time.

For example, assume that in Year 1 an employee defers $10,000 under a salary deferral elective account balance plan and is required to include that amount in income under section 409A. Assume that in Year 2 the employee defers $15,000 under the same salary deferral elective account balance plan, and an additional $5,000 under a bonus deferral elective account balance plan, both of which are compliant with section 409A. Assume that in Year 3 the employee receives a payment of $5,000 under the bonus deferral elective account balance plan. Because the payment would be treated for purposes of section 409A as made from a single elective account balance plan in which the employee participated, and because the employee has already included $10,000 in income under section 409A due to participation in the plan, the employee would apply $5,000 of the $10,000 that was previously included in income to the $5,000 payment and not include the $5,000 payment in gross income in Year 3 (or any subsequent year). The remaining amount previously included in income would be $5,000.

The employee could not elect the extent to which the amount previously included in income would be applied in this context. Rather, the amount previously included in income would be required to be applied immediately to the extent an amount deferred under the same plan would otherwise become includible in income under a Code section other than section 409A. The inclusion of any amount in income and the resulting amount previously included in income for subsequent years would not affect the potential for earnings related to such amounts to be subject to section 409A or to be required to be included in income under section 409A.

B. *Permanent forfeiture or loss of a deferred amount previously included in income under section 409A(a)*

The application of section 409A(a) may require inclusion in income of amounts that the service provider ultimately never receives. This result may occur under four different circumstances. First, because a nonqualified deferred compensation plan generally involves an unfunded, unsecured promise of a service recipient to pay compensation in a future year, the funds to pay the deferred amount may not be available in the future year. For example, the service recipient may be insolvent, bankrupt or have ceased to exist at the time the payment is due.

Second, some amounts of deferred compensation may be included in income under section 409A(a) if the amounts are subject to a risk of forfeiture, but the risk of forfeiture does not qualify as a substantial risk of forfeiture. For example, a deferred amount payable only if the service provider does not compete with the service recipient for a defined period is not subject to a substantial risk of forfeiture. However, if the service provider actually competes with the service recipient, the service provider may forfeit the right to the amount.

Third, the deferred amount may be subject to deemed investment losses. If losses occur after the deferred amount has been included in income under section 409A(a), the amount paid to the service provider may be less than the amount included in income.

Fourth, in the case of a formula amount, the calculation of the deferred amount may result in the inclusion in income under section 409A(a) of an amount that is greater than the amount ultimately paid. For example, if a service provider receives a right to a certain percentage of the service recipient's profits payable at separation from service, and determines that the total amount deferred under the plan is

$100,000, once the profits are calculated the service provider may be entitled to a lesser amount.

1. Effect on Service Provider

The proposed regulations provide that a service provider who is required to include an amount in income under section 409A(a) with respect to a deferred amount under a nonqualified deferred compensation plan is entitled to a deduction at the time the service provider's legally binding right to all deferred compensation under the plan (including all arrangements treated as a single plan under the aggregation rules) is permanently forfeited under the plan's terms, or the right to such compensation is otherwise permanently lost. The available deduction would equal the excess of the amount included in income under section 409A(a) in a previous year over any amount actually or constructively received by the service provider. A right to an amount would not be treated as permanently lost merely because the deferred amount had decreased, for example due to deemed investment losses, if the service provider retains a right to an amount deferred under the plan. In addition, a right to an amount would not be treated as permanently forfeited or otherwise lost if the obligation to make such payment is substituted for another deferred amount or obligation to make a payment in a future year. However, the right to an amount would be treated as permanently lost if the right to the payment of the amount becomes wholly worthless. A service provider would not be entitled to a deduction with respect to an amount previously included in income under section 409A(a) if the service provider retains a right to any amount deferred under all arrangements treated as a single plan under § 1.409A-1(c)(2). However, if the entire deferred amount payable under the plan has been paid out and the service recipient has no remaining liability to the service provider under the plan, any remaining unpaid deferred amount that had previously been included in income would be treated as permanently lost.

For example, if at the end of Year 1 an employee has an account balance of $100,000 which is required to be included in income under section 409A, and at the end of Year 2 an employee has an account balance of $90,000 due to notional investment losses, the employee would not be entitled to a deduction for Year 2. However, if in Year 3 the entire account balance of $95,000 is paid to the employee, so there no longer are any amounts deferred under the plan (determined after applying applicable aggregation rules) and nothing remains to be paid to the employee, the employee would be entitled to a $5,000 deduction for Year 3.

In the case of a service provider that is an employee, the available deduction generally would be treated as a miscellaneous itemized deduction, subject to the deduction limitations applicable to such expenses. Section 1341 would not be applicable to such deduction because inclusion of an amount in income as a result of noncompliance with section 409A(a) would not constitute receipt of an amount to which it appeared that the taxpayer had an unrestricted right in the taxable year of inclusion. In the first circumstance listed above, a service provider that does not receive payment of deferred compensation because of the bankruptcy or insolvency of the service recipient retains the legal right to the income even though the income is not collectible. In each of the three other circumstances in which such a deduction becomes available, the deferred compensation is not paid because of an event that occurred after the taxable year in which the amount deferred was included in income under section 409A, rather than from the absence of a right to the deferred compensation in the year in which it was includible in gross income. Finally, certain of such circumstances, such as the actual amount received differing from the amount included in income because the amount deferred was a formula amount, result from the inherent uncertainties in valuing rights to such amounts, rather than from a lack of a claim of right to income.

2. Effect on Service Recipient

If a service provider is entitled to a deduction with respect to a deferred amount included in income under section 409A(a) that is subsequently permanently forfeited or otherwise lost, to the extent the service recipient has benefited from a deduction or increased the basis of an asset because the deferred amount was included in the service provider's gross income, or such inclusion by the service provider has otherwise reduced or could otherwise reduce the service recipient's gross income, the service recipient may be required to recognize income under the tax benefit rule and section 111, or make other appropriate adjustments to reflect that the deferred amount included in income by the service provider under section 409A(a) has been permanently forfeited or otherwise lost, and thus will not be paid by the service recipient.

VII. *Service Provider Income Inclusion and Additional Taxes and Service Recipient Reporting and Withholding Obligations*

A. *Service provider income inclusion*

The Treasury Department and the IRS anticipate issuing interim guidance during 2008 addressing the extent to which taxpayers may rely on the proposed regulations with respect to the calculation of the amounts includible in income under section 409A(a) and the calculation of the additional taxes under section 409A(a). The interim guidance is also expected to address the calculation of the amounts includible in income and additional taxes under section 409A(b) and service recipient reporting and withholding obligations with respect to amounts includible in income under section 409A(a) or (b) for taxable years beginning before the final regulations become applicable. The Treasury Department and the IRS anticipate that such interim guidance will provide that taxpayers may rely upon the proposed regulations in their entirety (but that taxpayers may not rely on part, but not all, of the proposed regulations).

B. *Annual deferral reporting*

Section 885(b) of the Act amended sections 6041 and 6051 to require that an employer or payer report all deferrals for the year under a nonqualified deferred compensation plan on a Form W-2, "Wage and Tax Statement" or a Form 1099-MISC, "Miscellaneous Income", regardless of whether such deferred compensation is includible in gross income under section 409A(a) (annual deferral reporting). Notice 2007-89 permanently waives this requirement for 2007 Forms W-2 and Forms 1099. Notice 2006-100 permanently waives this requirement for 2005 and 2006 Forms W-2 and Forms 1099. The Treasury Department and the IRS anticipate that this reporting will be implemented beginning with the first taxable year for which these proposed regulations are finalized and effective. The Treasury Department and the IRS further anticipate that the annual deferral reporting rules will be based upon the principles set forth in these regulations as finalized, except that taxpayers will not be required to report deferred amounts that are not reasonably ascertainable (as defined in § 31.3121(v)(2)-1(e)(4)(i)(B)) until such amounts become reasonably ascertainable. The Treasury Department and the IRS anticipate that the deferred amounts required to be reported will reflect earnings on the amounts deferred in previous years, if the amount of such earnings is reasonably ascertainable, because section 409A specifically treats earnings on deferred amounts as additional deferred amounts. The Treasury Department and the IRS request comments on the potential application of the standards set forth in these regulations to this reporting requirement, including suggestions for possible adaptations or modifications that may decrease the administrative burden of compliance while maintaining the integrity of the information reported.

C. *Income inclusion reporting and income tax withholding*

Section 885(b) of the Act also amended section 3401(a) to provide that the term "wages" includes any amount includible in the gross income of an employee under section 409A, and amended section 6041 to require that a payer report amounts includible in gross income under section 409A that are not treated as wages under section 3401(a) (income inclusion reporting). Notice 2005-1 provides that an employer should report amounts includible in gross income under section 409A and in wages under section 3401(a) in box 1 of Form W-2 as wages paid to the employee during the year and subject to income tax withholding, and that the employer should also report such amounts in box 12 of Form W-2 using code Z. Notice 2005-1 also provides that a payer should report amounts includible in gross income under section 409A and not treated as wages under section 3401(a) as nonemployee compensation in box 7 of Form 1099-MISC, and should also report such amounts in box 15b of Form 1099-MISC. Notice 2006-100 provided guidance on income inclusion reporting for the 2005 and 2006 Forms W-2 and Forms 1099. Notice 2007-89 provided guidance on income inclusion reporting for the 2007 Forms W-2 and Forms 1099. The Treasury Department and the IRS anticipate issuing further interim guidance during 2008 on income inclusion reporting for 2008 Forms W-2 and Forms 1099 for taxable years beginning before the final regulations become applicable. The Treasury Department and the IRS anticipate that such interim guidance will provide that taxpayers may rely upon the proposed regulations in their entirety (but that taxpayers may not rely on part, but not all, of the proposed regulations).

Amounts includible in an employee's income under section 409A also are treated as wages for purposes of section 3401. Notice 2007-89 provides guidance on a service recipient's income tax withholding obligations for 2007. The Treasury Department and the IRS anticipate issuing further interim guidance during 2008 on a service recipient's income tax withholding obligations for calendar years beginning before the final regulations become applicable. The Treasury Department and the IRS anticipate that such interim guidance will provide that taxpayers may rely upon the proposed regulations in their entirety (but that taxpayers may not rely on part, but not all, of the proposed regulations).

Proposed Effective Date

These regulations are proposed to be generally applicable for taxable years beginning on or after the issuance of final regulations. Before the applicability date of the final regulations, taxpayers may rely on these proposed regulations only to the extent provided in further guidance.

Special Analyses

It has been determined that this notice of proposed rulemaking is not a significant regulatory action as defined in Executive Order 12866. Therefore, a regulatory assessment is not required. It has also been determined that section 553(b) of the Administrative Procedure Act (5 U.S.C. chapter 5) does not apply to these regulations, and because the regulation does not impose a collection of information on small entities, the Regulatory Flexibility Act (5 U.S.C. chapter 6) does not apply. Pursuant to section 7805(f) of the Code, this notice of proposed rulemaking will be submitted to the Chief Counsel for Advocacy of the Small Business Administration for comment on its impact on small business.

Comments and Public Hearing

Before these proposed regulations are adopted as final regulations, consideration will be given to any written (a signed original and eight (8) copies) or electronic comments that are submitted timely to the IRS. The IRS and Treasury Department request comments on the clarity of the proposed rules and how they can be made easier to understand. All comments will be available for public inspection and copying.

A public hearing has been scheduled for April 2, 2009 at 10:00 a.m., in the auditorium. Due to building security procedures, visitors must enter at the Constitution Avenue entrance. In addition, all visitors must present photo identification to enter the building. Because of access restrictions, visitors will not be admitted beyond the immediate entrance area more than 30 minutes before the hearing starts. For information about having your name placed on the building access list to attend the hearing, see the "FOR FURTHER INFORMATION CONTACT" section of this preamble.

The rules of 26 CFR 601.601(a)(3) apply to the hearing. Persons who wish to present oral comments at the hearing must submit written or electronic comments and an outline of the topics to be discussed and the time to be devoted to each topic (a signed original and eight (8) copies) by March 9, 2009. A period of 10 minutes will be allotted to each person for making comments. An agenda showing the scheduling of the speakers will be prepared after the deadline for receiving outlines has passed. Copies of the agenda will be available free of charge at the hearing.

Drafting Information

The principal author of these regulations is Stephen Tackney of the Office of Division Counsel/Associate Chief Counsel (Tax Exempt and Government Entities). However, other personnel from the IRS and the Treasury Department participated in their development.

List of Subjects 26 CFR Part 1

Income taxes, Reporting and recordkeeping requirements

Proposed Amendments to the Regulations

Accordingly, 26 CFR part 1 is proposed to be amended as follows:

Part 1—INCOME TAXES

Paragraph 1. The authority citation for part 1 continues to read in part as follows:

Authority: 26 U.S.C. 7805 * * *

Par. 2. Section 1.409A-0 is amended by adding entries for § 1.409A-4 to read as follows:

§ 1.409A-0 Table of contents.

* * * * *

§ 1.409A-4 Calculation of amount includible in income and additional income taxes.

(a) Amount includible in income due to failure to meet the requirements of section 409A(a).

(1) In general.

(i) Calculation formula.

(ii) Each taxable year analyzed independently.

(A) In general.

(B) Treatment of certain deferred amounts otherwise subject to a substantial risk of forfeiture.

(iii) Examples.

(2) Identification of the portion of the total amount deferred for a taxable year that is subject to a substantial risk of forfeiture.

(i) In general.

(ii) Example.

(3) Identification of amount previously included in income.

(i) In general.

(ii) Examples.

(b) The total amount deferred under a plan for a taxable year.

(1) Application of general rules and specific rules for specific types of plans.

(2) General definition of total amount deferred.

(i) General calculation rules.

(ii) Actuarial assumptions and methods

(A) Requirement of reasonable actuarial assumptions and methods.

(B) Use of an unreasonable actuarial assumption or method.

(iii) Crediting of earnings and losses.

(iv) Application of the general calculation rules to formula amounts.

(A) In general.

(B) Examples.

(v) Treatment of payment restrictions.

(vi) Treatment of alternative times and forms of a future payment.

(A) In general.

(B) Effect of status of service provider on available times and forms of payment.

(vii) Treatment of payment triggers based upon events.

(A) In general.

(B) Certain payment triggers disregarded.

(viii) Treatment of amounts that may qualify as short-term deferrals.

(ix) Examples.

(3) Account balance plans.

(i) In general.

(ii) Unreasonable rate of return.

(A) Application

(B) Unreasonably high interest rate.

(C) Other rates of return.

(4) Reimbursement and in-kind benefit arrangements.

(5) Split-dollar life insurance arrangements.

(6) Stock rights.

(7) Anti-abuse provision.

(c) Additional 20 percent tax under section 409A(a)(1)(B)(i)(II).

(d) Premium interest tax under section 409A(a)(1)(B)(i)(I).

(1) In general.

(2) Identification of taxable year deferred amount was first deferred or vested.

(i) Method of identification.

(ii) Examples.

(3) Calculation of hypothetical underpayment for the taxable year during which a deferred amount was first deferred and vested.

(i) Calculation method.

(ii) Examples.

(4) Calculation of hypothetical premium underpayment interest.

(i) Calculation method.

(ii) Examples.

(e) Amounts includible in income under section 409A(b) [Reserved]

(f) Application of amounts included in income under section 409A to payments of amounts deferred.

(1) In general.

(2) Application of the plan aggregation rules.

(3) Examples.

(g) Forfeiture or other permanent loss of right to deferred compensation.

(1) Availability of deduction to the service provider.

(2) Application of the plan aggregation rules.

(3) Examples.

(h) Effective/applicability date.

* * * * *

Par. 3. Section 1.409A-4 is added to read as follows:

§ *1.409A-4 Calculation of amount includible in income and additional income taxes.*

(a) *Amount includible in income due to failure to meet the requirements of section 409A(a)*—(1) *In general*—(i) *Calculation formula.* The amount includible in income for a service provider's taxable year due to a failure to meet the requirements of section 409A(a) with respect to a plan is the excess (if any) of—

(A) The service provider's total amount deferred under the plan for the taxable year, including the amount of any payments of amounts deferred under the plan to (or on behalf of) the service provider during such taxable year; over

(B) The portion of such amount, if any, that is either subject to a substantial risk of forfeiture (as defined in § 1.409A-1(d) and applying paragraph (a)(1)(ii)(B) of this section) or has been previously included in income (as defined in § 1.409A-4(a)(3)).

(ii) *Each taxable year analyzed independently*—(A) *In general.* An amount is includible in income under section 409A(a) for a taxable year only if a plan fails to meet the requirements of section 409A(a) during such taxable year. Whether an amount is includible in income for a taxable year due to a failure to meet the requirements of section 409A(a) during such taxable year is determined independently of whether such amounts are also includible in income due to a failure to meet the requirements of section 409A(a) in a previous or subsequent taxable year. Accordingly, an amount may be includible in income for a taxable year during which a plan fails to meet the requirements of section 409A(a), even if the same amount was includible in income in a previous taxable year, except to the extent provided in § 1.409A-4(a)(3) (identification of amount previously included in income).

(B) *Treatment of certain deferred amounts otherwise subject to a substantial risk of forfeiture.* For purposes of determining the amount includible in income under section 409A(a) and paragraph (a)(1)(i) of this section, if the facts and circumstances indicate that a service recipient has a pattern or practice of permitting impermissible changes in the time and form of payment with respect to nonvested deferred amounts under one or more plans, an amount deferred under a plan that is otherwise subject to a substantial risk of forfeiture is not treated as subject to a substantial risk of forfeiture if an impermissible change in the time and form of payment (including an impermissible initial deferral election) applies to the amount deferred or if the facts and circumstances indicate that the amount deferred would be affected by such pattern or practice.

(iii) *Examples.* The following examples illustrate the provisions of this paragraph (a)(1). For each of the examples, Employee A is an individual taxpayer with a calendar year taxable year. Employee A has a total amount deferred under a nonqualified deferred compensation plan of $0 in 2010, $100,000 in 2011, and $250,000 in 2012. No payments are made under the plan. The plan under which the amounts are deferred fails to meet the requirements of section 409A(a) during 2011 and 2012. The examples read as follows:

Example 1. With respect to Employee A, at no time is any deferred amount subject to a substantial risk of forfeiture. Employee A has $100,000 includible in income under section 409A(a) for 2011, because no portion of the total deferred amount for 2011 is subject to a substantial risk of forfeiture or has previously been included in income. If that $100,000 is included in income for 2011, Employee A has $150,000 includible in income under section 409A(a) for 2012 because for the

taxable year 2012 the $100,000 is previously included in income (see paragraphs (a)(1)(i)(B) and (a)(3) of this section). If that $100,000 is not included in income for 2011, Employee A has $250,000 includible in income under section 409A(a) for 2012. Employee A does not avoid the requirement to include $100,000 in income under section 409A(a) for 2011 by including $250,000 in income under section 409A(a) for 2012.

Example 2. The same facts as *Example 1*, except that, with respect to Employee A, the statute of limitations on assessments has expired for 2011, but has not expired for 2012. Employee A has $250,000 includible in income under section 409A(a) for 2012, because no portion of the total deferred amount for 2012 is subject to a substantial risk of forfeiture or has previously been included in income.

(2) *Identification of the portion of the total amount deferred for a taxable year that is subject to a substantial risk of forfeiture*—(i) *In general.* The portion of the total amount deferred for a taxable year that is subject to a substantial risk of forfeiture (as defined in § 1.409A-1(d)) is determined as of the last day of the service provider's taxable year. Accordingly, an amount may be includible in income under section 409A(a) for a taxable year even if such amount is subject to a substantial risk of forfeiture during the taxable year if the substantial risk of forfeiture lapses during such taxable year, including if the substantial risk of forfeiture lapses after the date the nonqualified deferred compensation plan under which the amount is deferred first fails to meet the requirements of section 409A(a).

(ii) *Example.* The following example illustrates the provisions of this paragraph (a)(2): Employee B is an individual taxpayer with a calendar year taxable year. Employee B has a total amount deferred under a nonqualified deferred compensation plan of $0 for 2010, $100,000 for 2011, and $250,000 for 2012. No payments are made under the plan. Under the terms of the plan, if Employee B voluntarily separates from service before July 1, 2012, Employee B will forfeit 50 percent of the Employee B's total amount deferred under the plan. If Employee B voluntarily separates from service after June 30, 2012 but before July 1, 2013, Employee B will forfeit 20 percent of the total amount deferred under the plan. If Employee B voluntarily separates from service after June 30, 2013, Employee B will not forfeit any amount deferred under the plan. As of December 31, 2011, 50 percent of the total amount deferred under the plan ($50,000) is subject to a substantial risk of forfeiture, and the remaining amount deferred under the plan ($50,000) is not subject to a substantial risk of forfeiture. As of December 31, 2012, 20 percent of the total amount deferred under the plan ($50,000) is subject to a substantial risk of forfeiture, and the remaining amount deferred under the plan ($200,000) is not subject to a substantial risk of forfeiture. At all times the terms of the plan meet the requirements of section 409A(a) and the applicable regulations, and through May 31, 2012, the plan is operated in a manner that complies with the terms of the plan. On June 1, 2012, the plan is operated in a manner that fails to meet the requirements of section 409A(a). For purposes of determining the amount includible in income under section 409A(a), except as provided in paragraph (a)(1)(ii)(B) of this section, the portion of the total amount deferred for 2012 that is subject to a substantial risk of forfeiture is $50,000 (20 percent of $250,000).

(3) *Identification of amount previously included in income*—(i) *In general.* For purposes of this section, an amount is previously included in income only if the service provider has included the amount in income under an applicable provision of the Internal Revenue Code for a previous taxable year. An amount is treated as included in income for a taxable year only to the extent that the amount was properly includible in income and the service provider actually included the amount in income (including on an original or amended return or as a result of an IRS examination or a final decision of a court of competent jurisdiction). For future taxable years, the amount previously included in income is reduced to reflect any amount that was paid during the taxable year for which the amount was included in income, any amount allocated to a payment made under the plan under paragraph (f) of this section, and any amount deductible under paragraph (g) of this section.

(ii) *Examples.* The following examples illustrate the provisions of this paragraph (a)(3). For all of the examples, Employee C is an individual taxpayer with a calendar year taxable year. Employee C has a total amount deferred under a nonqualified deferred compensation plan of $0 in 2010, $100,000 in 2011, and $250,000 in 2012. With respect to Employee C, the statute of limitations on assessments has not expired for 2011 or 2012. Except as otherwise explicitly provided in the following examples, Employee C has not included in income for 2011 on any original or amended tax return any amount deferred under the plan, none of the $250,000 total amount deferred for 2012 has previously been included in income, no payments are made under the plan, and at no time is any deferred amount subject to a substantial risk of forfeiture. The plan under which the amounts are deferred fails to meet the requirements of section 409A(a) during 2011 and 2012. The examples read as follows:

Example 1. After filing an original Federal income tax return for 2011 that did not include any amount in income under section 409A(a), on April 1, 2013, Employee C files an amended Federal income tax return for 2011 and properly includes $100,000 in income under section 409A(a) for 2011. For purposes of determining the amount includible in income under section 409A(a) for 2012, $100,000 of the $250,000 total amount deferred for 2012 has previously been included in income with respect to the plan. For 2012, Employee C includes in income $150,000 under section 409A(a) on Employee C's original Federal income tax return. As of January 1, 2013, the amount that Employee C has previously included in income under section 409A(a) with respect to the plan is $250,000.

Example 2. The facts are the same as in *Example 1*, except that Employee C receives a $10,000 payment in 2011 so that the total amount deferred for 2012 is $240,000. For purposes of determining the amount includible in income under section 409A(a) for 2012, the $100,000 amount previously included in income is reduced by the $10,000 payment so that $90,000 of the $240,000 total amount deferred for 2012 has previously been included in income. For 2012, Employee C includes in income $150,000 under section 409A(a) on Employee C's original Federal income tax return. As of January 1, 2013, the amount that Employee C has previously included in income under section 409A(a) with respect to the plan is $240,000.

Example 3. The facts are the same as in *Example 2.* Due to deemed investment losses during 2013, Employee C has an $80,000 total amount deferred under the plan for 2013. On December 31, 2013, Employee C's total amount deferred ($80,000) is paid to Employee C as a single sum payment. Pursuant to paragraph (f) of this section, $80,000 of the $240,000 amount previously included in income is allocated to the $80,000 payment so that none of the $80,000 is includible in income. In addition, pursuant to paragraph (g) of this section, Employee C is entitled to deduct $160,000 for 2013 equal to the remaining amount previously included in income the right to which is permanently lost. Because the entire $240,000 amount previously included in income has been allocated to a payment under paragraph (f) of this section or was deductible under paragraph (g) of this section, no portion of such amount is treated as previously included in income for 2014 or any subsequent taxable year. As of January 1, 2014, the amount that Employee C has previously included in income under section 409A(a) with respect to the plan is $0.

(b) *The total amount deferred under a plan for a taxable year*—(1) *Application of general rules and specific rules for specific types of plans.* Paragraph (b)(2) of this section provides general rules governing the determination of the total amount deferred under a plan for a taxable year, including the treatment of plans providing for alternative times and forms of payment and plans providing for certain payments the amount of which is determined by a formula that includes one or more variables dependent upon future events (formula amounts). Paragraphs (b)(3) through (b)(6) of this section provide specific rules governing the determination of the total amount deferred under certain types of plans. Except as otherwise provided, any applicable rules of paragraphs (b)(3) through (b)(6) of this section are applied in conjunction with the general rules provided in paragraph (b)(2) of this section.

(2) *General definition of total amount deferred*—(i) *General calculation rules.* Except as otherwise provided, the total amount deferred for a taxable year equals the present value of the future payments to which the service provider has a legally binding right under the plan as of the last day of the taxable year, plus the amount of any payments of amounts deferred under the plan to (or on behalf of) the service provider during such taxable year. For purposes of this section, present value means the value, as of a specified date, of an amount or series of amounts due thereafter, determined in accordance with the rules and assumptions of this paragraph (b)(2), as applicable, where each amount is multiplied by the probability that the condition or conditions on which payment of the amount is contingent will be satisfied, also determined in accordance with the rules and assumptions set forth in this paragraph (b)(2), as applicable, discounted according to an assumed rate of interest to reflect the time value of money. For this purpose, a discount for the probability that an employee will die before commencement of benefit payments is permitted, but only to the extent that benefits will be forfeited upon death. In addition, the present value cannot be discounted for the probability that payments will not be made (or will be reduced) because of the unfunded status of the plan, the risk associated with any deemed or actual investment of amounts deferred under the plan, the risk that the service recipient, the trustee, or another party will be unwilling or unable to pay, the possibility of future plan amendments, the possibility of a future change in the law, or similar risks or contingencies. If the amount payable under a plan or

the value of a benefit under a plan is expressed in a currency other than the U.S. dollar, the total amount deferred is translated from foreign currency into U.S. dollars at the spot exchange rate on the last day of the service provider's taxable year. No adjustment is made to the total amount deferred to reflect the risk that the currency in which the amount payable or the value of the benefit is expressed may in the future increase or decrease in value with respect to the U.S. dollar or any other currency.

(ii) *Actuarial assumptions and methods*—(A) *Requirement of reasonable actuarial assumptions and methods.* For purposes of this section, the present value must be determined as of the last day of the service provider's taxable year using actuarial assumptions and methods that are reasonable as of that date, including an interest rate for purposes of discounting for present value that is reasonable as of that date.

(B) *Use of an unreasonable actuarial assumption or method.* If any actuarial assumption or method used to determine the total amount deferred for a taxable year under a plan is not reasonable, as determined by the Commissioner, then the total amount deferred is determined by the application of the AFR and, if applicable, the applicable mortality table under section 417(e)(3)(A)(ii)(I) (the 417(e) mortality table), both determined as of the last month of the taxable year for which the amount deferred is being determined. For purposes of this section, *AFR* means the appropriate applicable Federal rate (as defined pursuant to section 1274(d)) based on annual compounding, for the last month of the taxable year for which the amount includible in income is being determined. The period for which excess interest will be credited, beginning with the last day of the taxable year and ending with the date the excess interest will no longer be credited (determined in accordance with the payment timing assumptions set forth in paragraph (b)(2)(vi) and (vii) of this section) is used to determine the appropriate AFR (short-term, mid-term, or long-term).

(iii) *Crediting of earnings and losses.* The earnings and losses credited under a plan as of the last day of the service provider's taxable year pursuant to the plan are given effect only to the extent the plan's terms reasonably reflect the value of the service provider's rights under the plan. For example, a plan's method of determining the amount of such earnings or losses generally will be respected for purposes of determining the total amount deferred for the taxable year, provided that the earnings and losses are credited at least once per taxable year. If earnings and losses are not credited at least annually, the total amount deferred is calculated as if the earnings or losses were credited as of the last day of the taxable year. In addition, any change in the schedule for crediting earnings during the taxable year for which the total amount deferred is calculated that would reduce the earnings credited for a taxable year in which an amount is required to be included in income under section 409A(a) is disregarded for such taxable year. For example, if a plan is amended during a taxable year that is a calendar year to change the date for crediting earnings from December 31 to July 1 of that year and the plan fails to meet the requirements of section 409A(a) during that year, the amendment is disregarded for purposes of determining the total amount deferred for the year and December 31 is treated as the date for crediting earnings and losses. If no further changes are made to the plan with respect to the crediting of earnings and losses, for subsequent taxable years, July 1 is treated as the date for crediting earnings and losses.

(iv) *Application of the general calculation rules to formula amounts*—(A) *In general.* With respect to a right to a payment to which this paragraph applies, the amount payable for purposes of determining the total amount deferred for the taxable year must be determined based on all of the facts and circumstances existing as of the close of the last day of the taxable year. Such determination must reflect reasonable, good faith assumptions with respect to any contingencies as to the amount of the payment, both with respect to each contingency and with respect to all contingencies in the aggregate. An assumption based on the facts and circumstances as of the close of the last day of a taxable year may be reasonable even if the facts and circumstances change in a subsequent year so that if the amount payable were determined for such subsequent year, the amount payable would be a greater (or lesser) amount. In such a case, the increase (or decrease) due to the change in the facts and circumstances is treated as earnings (or losses). This paragraph (b)(2)(iv) applies to the extent that the amount payable in a future taxable year is a formula amount to the extent that the amount payable in a future taxable year is dependent upon factors that, after applying the assumptions and other rules set out in this section, are not determinable as of the end of the taxable year for which the total amount deferred is being calculated, so that the amount payable may not readily be determined as of the end of such taxable year under the other provisions of this section. If a portion of a deferred amount is determinable under the other rules of this paragraph (b)(2), the determination of the amount deferred with respect to such portion must be determined under the rules applicable to amounts that are not formula amounts, and only the balance of the deferred amount is determined under this paragraph.

(B) *Examples.* The following examples illustrate the provisions of this paragraph (b)(2)(iv):

Example 1. On January 1, 2020, a service provider receives a legally binding right to a payment of one percent of the service recipient's net profits for the calendar years 2020, 2021, and 2022, payable on the later of January 1, 2024 or the service provider's separation from service. The amount payable is a formula amount and this paragraph (b)(2)(iv) applies.

Example 2. On January 1, 2020, a service provider receives a legally binding right to a payment of the greater of one percent of the service recipient's net profits for the calendar years 2020, 2021, and 2022 or $10,000, payable on the later of January 1, 2024 or the service provider's separation from service. The portion of the amount payable that is a $10,000 payment, payable at the later of January 1, 2024 or the service provider's separation from service, is not a formula amount. The portion of the amount payable that is the excess, if any, of one percent of the service recipient's net profits for the calendar years 2020, 2021, and 2022 over $10,000 is a formula amount and this paragraph (b)(2)(iv) applies.

Example 3. On January 1, 2020, a service provider receives a legally binding right to payment equal to the value of 10,000 shares of service recipient stock, payable on the later of January 1, 2024 or the service provider's separation from service. Because the amount payable may increase or decrease only due to a change in value of a predetermined actual investment (10,000 shares of service recipient stock), the amount payable is not treated as a formula amount and this paragraph (b)(2)(iv) does not apply.

(v) *Treatment of payment restrictions.* Except as specifically provided, a restriction on the payment of all or part of a deferred amount that will or may lapse under the terms of the plan, including a risk of forfeiture that is not a substantial risk of forfeiture as defined in § 1.409A-1(d) or is disregarded under § 1.409A-4(a)(1)(ii)(B), is ignored for purposes of determining the total amount deferred under the plan. Accordingly, in calculating the total amount deferred, there is no reduction to account for a risk that the amount may be forfeited if the risk of forfeiture is not a substantial risk of forfeiture. For example, if an amount deferred is subject to forfeiture under a noncompetition provision applicable for a prescribed period, the forfeiture provision is disregarded for purposes of determining the total amount deferred for the taxable year.

(vi) *Treatment of alternative times and forms of a future payment*—(A) *In general.* For purposes of determining the total amount deferred for a taxable year, if payment of a deferred amount may be made at alternative times or in alternative forms, each amount deferred under the plan is treated as payable at the time and under the form of payment for which the present value is highest. A time and form of payment is available to the extent a deferred amount under the plan may be payable in such time and form of payment under the plan's terms. If the service recipient has commenced payment of a deferred amount in a time and form of payment under the plan, or the service provider or service recipient has elected a time and form of payment under the plan, and under the plan's terms neither party can change such time and form of payment without the consent of the other party (and such consent requirement has substantive significance), the time and form of payment elected or the time and form of payment in which payments have commenced is treated as the sole available time and form of payment for such amount. If an alternative time and form of payment is available only at the service recipient's discretion, the time and form of payment is not available unless the service provider has a legally binding right under the principles of § 1.409A-1(b)(1) to any additional value that would be generated by the service recipient's exercise of such discretion. For purposes of determining the value of each available time and form of payment, the assumptions and methods described in this paragraph (b)(2)(vi) are applied, and then the value of each available time and form of payment is determined in accordance with the other applicable rules provided in paragraph (b) of this section.

(B) *Effect of status of service provider on available times and forms of payment.* For purposes of determining whether a time and form of payment is available, if eligibility for a time and form of payment depends upon the service provider's status as of a future date, the service provider is assumed to continue in the service provider's status as of the last day of the taxable year. However, if the eligibility requirement is not bona fide and does not serve a bona fide business purpose, the eligibility requirement will be disregarded and the service provider will be treated as eligible for the alternative time and form of payment. For this purpose, an eligibility condition based upon the service provider's marital status (including status as a registered do-

mestic partner or similar requirement), parental status, or status as a U.S. citizen or lawful permanent resident under section 7701(b)(6) is presumed to be bona fide and serve a bona fide business purpose. Notwithstanding the foregoing, if eligibility for a certain time or form of payment includes a bona fide requirement that the service provider provide additional services after the end of the taxable year, the time and form of payment is not treated as an available time and form of payment. The rules of this paragraph (b)(2)(vi)(B) apply regardless of whether the service provider's status changes during a subsequent taxable year.

(vii) *Treatment of payment triggers based upon events*—(A) *In general.* For purposes of determining the total amount deferred for a taxable year, if a payment trigger has occurred on or before the last day of the taxable year, a deferred amount payable upon such trigger is treated as payable at the time the payment is scheduled to be made under the terms of the plan. If the payment trigger has not occurred on or before the last day of the taxable year, the trigger is treated as occurring on the earliest possible date the trigger reasonably could occur based on the facts and circumstances as of the last day of the taxable year, and the deferred amount is treated as payable based upon the schedule of payments that would be triggered by such occurrence. Notwithstanding the foregoing, if the payment trigger requires a separation from service, a termination of employment, or other similar reduction or cessation of services, the service provider is treated as meeting such requirement as of the last day of the taxable year. For purposes of determining the earliest date the payment trigger reasonably could occur, whether the payment trigger actually occurs in a subsequent taxable year is disregarded. For purposes of this paragraph (b)(2)(vii), a payment trigger means an event (not including the mere passage of time) upon which an amount may become payable. Generally if an amount would be payable in a different time and form of payment depending upon some characteristic of an event, each type of event upon which an amount would become payable is treated as a separate payment trigger. For example, if an amount would be payable as a single sum payment if one subsidiary corporation of a service recipient that consists of multiple corporations is sold, but as an installment payment if another subsidiary corporation of the same service recipient is sold, then the sale of the one subsidiary corporation is treated as a separate payment trigger from the sale of the other subsidiary corporation.

(B) *Certain payment triggers disregarded.* The possibility that the following payment triggers will occur in the future is disregarded for purposes of determining the total amount deferred (but not for purposes of determining whether the plan otherwise complies with the requirements of section 409A(a)):

(*1*) A payment trigger that, if the trigger were the sole trigger determining when the amount would become payable, would cause the amount to be subject to a substantial risk of forfeiture, provided that if there is more than one payment trigger applicable to an amount that otherwise would be disregarded under this paragraph (b)(2)(vii)(B)(*1*), none of such payment triggers will be disregarded unless all such payment triggers, if applied in combination as the only payment triggers, would also cause the amount to be subject to a substantial risk of forfeiture.

(*2*) An unforeseeable emergency (as defined in § 1.409A-3(i)(3)).

(viii) *Treatment of amounts that may qualify as short-term deferrals.* For purposes of calculating the total amount deferred for a taxable year, the right to a payment that, under the terms of the arrangement and the facts and circumstances as of the last day of the taxable year, may be a short-term deferral as defined under § 1.409A-1(b)(4), is not included in the total amount deferred. In addition, even if such amount is not paid by the end of the applicable 2 ½ month period so that the amount is deferred compensation, the amount is not includible in the total amount deferred until the service provider's taxable year in which the applicable 2 ½ month period expires.

(ix) *Examples.* The following examples illustrate the provisions of paragraphs (b)(2)(vi) through (viii) of this section. For all of the examples, the service provider is an individual taxpayer who is an employee of the service recipient, the service provider has a calendar year taxable year, and the total amount deferred is being calculated for the taxable year ending December 31, 2010. In each case, the service provider is not entitled to earnings on the amount deferred. The examples read as follows:

Example 1. Employee D, who is employed by Employer Z, is entitled to commence receiving payments at age 65. The plan provides that Employee D will receive a single sum payment, except that, after Employee D attains age 62 but before Employee D attains age 64 (whether or not Employee D is then employed by Employer Z), Employee D can elect to receive payments as a single life annuity. Employee D is age 54 as of December 31, 2010. For purposes of determining the available times and forms of payment, Employee D is assumed to survive to age 62 and be eligible to elect a single life annuity. Accordingly, for purposes of determining the total amount deferred for 2010, the amount is treated as payable as either a single sum payment or a single life annuity, whichever is more valuable.

Example 2. Employee E is entitled to a single life annuity commencing on January 1, 2020 if Employee E is not married as of January 1, 2020. Employee E is entitled to either a single life annuity or a subsidized joint and survivor annuity commencing on January 1, 2020 if Employee E is married as of January 1, 2020. Employee E is not married as of December 31, 2010. For purposes of determining the total amount deferred for 2010, Employee E is assumed to remain unmarried indefinitely, so that the subsidized joint and survivor annuity is not an available form of payment. Accordingly, for purposes of determining the total amount deferred for 2010, the amount is treated as payable as a single life annuity commencing January 1, 2020.

Example 3. Employee F is entitled to a series of three payments of $1,000 due on January 1, 2020, January 1, 2021, and January 1, 2022. Under the plan's terms, Employer X has the discretion to accelerate one or more of the payments, provided that no payment may be made before January 1, 2020. Because there is no reduction in the amount payable if a payment is accelerated, an accelerated payment is more valuable than a payment made in accordance with the three-year schedule of payments. If Employee F does not have a legally binding right to a single sum payment on January 1, 2020 (or any other form of accelerated payment), then an accelerated payment is not an available time and form of payment and, for purposes of determining the total amount deferred for 2010, the amount is treated as payable as a series of three payments of $1,000 on January 1, 2020, January 1, 2021, and January 1, 2022.

Example 4. The facts are the same as in *Example 3*, except that Employer X has no discretion to accelerate one or more of the payments. Rather, Employee F has the right to accelerate one or more of the payments provided that a payment may not be paid at any date before the later of January 1, 2020 or the date 12 months after the date of such election. As of December 31, 2010, the earliest date upon which Employee F may elect to have a payment made is January 1, 2020. Because there is no reduction in the amount payable if a payment is accelerated, the earliest possible date of payment is the most valuable time and form of payment. Accordingly, for purposes of determining the total amount deferred for 2010, the amount is treated as payable as a single sum payment of $3,000 on January 1, 2020.

Example 5. Employee G is entitled to a single sum payment upon separation from service if Employee G separates from service before January 1, 2020 and a single life annuity if Employee G separates from service after December 31, 2019. As of December 31, 2010, Employee G has not separated from service. Under paragraph (b)(2)(vi)(A) of this section, the total amount deferred is determined based upon the amount that would be payable if Employee G separated from service on December 31, 2010. Accordingly, the single life annuity is not treated as an available time and form of payment, so that the amount is treated as payable as a single sum payment upon separation from service.

Example 6. Employee H is entitled to a single sum payment of deferred compensation upon the earlier of January 1, 2020 or an unforeseeable emergency. Because the payment upon an unforeseeable emergency is disregarded, for purposes of determining the total amount deferred, the deferred amount is treated as payable only on January 1, 2020.

Example 7. Employee I is entitled to a single sum payment of deferred compensation upon the earlier of January 1, 2020 or Employee I's involuntary separation from service. Under the facts and circumstances existing at the time the right to the payment was granted, if the deferred amount had been payable only upon Employee I's involuntary separation from service, the amount would have been subject to a substantial risk of forfeiture. Under paragraph (b)(2)(iv)(B) of this section, the right to a payment upon the Employee I's involuntary separation from service is disregarded, and the amount is treated as payable only on January 1, 2020.

Example 8. Employee J is entitled to a single sum payment of deferred compensation upon the earlier of January 1, 2020 or Employee J's separation from service. As of December 31, 2010, Employee J has not separated from service. Under paragraph (b)(2)(vi)(A) of this section, the total amount deferred is determined based upon the amount that would be payable if Employee J separated from service on December 31, 2010 and therefore had the right to receive the payment on December 31, 2010. The total amount deferred for 2010 is the greater of the amount that would be payable on December 31, 2010 or

the present value of the amount that would be payable on January 1, 2020.

Example 9. Employee K is entitled to a single sum payment of deferred compensation upon the earlier of January 1, 2020 or the first day of the third month following Employee K's separation from service. As of December 31, 2010, Employee K has not separated from service. Under paragraph (b)(2)(vi)(A) of this section, the total amount deferred is determined based upon the amount that would be payable if Employee K separated from service on December 31, 2010, and therefore had a right to a payment on March 1, 2011. The total amount deferred for 2010 is the greater of the present value as of December 31, 2010 of the amount that would be payable on March 1, 2011 or the present value as of December 31, 2010 of the amount that would be payable on January 1, 2020.

Example 10. Employee L is entitled to a single sum payment of deferred compensation upon the earlier of January 1, 2020 or a separation from service that occurs on or before July 1, 2010. As of December 31, 2010, Employee L has not separated from service. For purposes of determining the total amount deferred, the right to be paid upon a separation from service on or before July 1, 2010 is ignored because it is no longer a possible payment trigger, and the amount is treated as payable only on January 1, 2020.

Example 11. Employee M is entitled to a single sum payment of deferred compensation upon the earliest of the date Employee M dies, Employee M attains age 65, or a child of Employee M becomes a full-time student at an accredited college or university (whether or not Employee M continues to be employed on such date). As of December 31, 2010, Employee M has a 10-year old child who is in the fifth grade. For purposes of determining the total amount deferred, the earliest time that the payment reasonably could be due upon Employee M's child entering a college or university is August 1, 2018. Thus, the total amount deferred for 2010 is the more valuable of the amount that would be payable on the Employee M's 65th birthday and the amount that would be payable on August 1, 2018. Because any additional value that would be payable upon Employee M's death is a death benefit excluded from the definition of deferred compensation under section 409A(d)(1)(B) and §1.409A-1(a)(5), that additional value, if any, is not required to be calculated.

(3) *Account balance plans*—(i) *In general.* For purposes of this section, if benefits are provided under a nonqualified deferred compensation plan that is described in §1.409A-1(c)(2)(i)(A) or (B) (an account balance plan), the present value of the amount payable equals the amount credited to the service provider's account as of the last day of the taxable year, including both the principal amount credited to the account, and any earnings or losses attributable to the principal amounts credited to the account through the last day of the taxable year. For purposes of this section, earnings or losses means any increase or decrease in the amount credited to a service provider's account that is attributable to amounts previously credited to the service provider's account, regardless of whether the plan denominates that increase or decrease as earnings or losses. For rules related to the crediting of earnings, see paragraph (b)(2)(iii) of this section. For rules relating to earnings based on an unreasonable interest rate or a rate of return based on an investment other than a single predetermined actual investment or a single reasonable interest rate, see paragraph (b)(3)(ii) of this section.

(ii) *Unreasonable rate of return*—(A) *Application.* This paragraph (b)(3)(ii) applies to an account balance plan under which the amount of earnings or losses credited is not based on either a predetermined actual investment, within the meaning of §31.3121(v)(2)-1(d)(2)(i)(B) of this chapter, or a rate of interest that is not higher than a reasonable rate of interest, within the meaning of §31.3121(v)(2)-1(d)(2)(i)(C) of this chapter, as determined by the Commissioner.

(B) *Unreasonably high interest rate.* If the earnings or losses to be credited under a plan are based on an unreasonably high rate of interest, the amount deferred under the plan is equal to the present value as of the end of the taxable year (using a reasonable interest rate) of the amount that will be credited to the service recipient's account using the unreasonably high rate for the entire period for which the unreasonably high interest will be credited under the plan, beginning with the last day of such taxable year and ending with the date the unreasonably high interest will no longer be credited (determined in accordance with the payment timing assumptions set forth in paragraph (b)(2)(vi) and (vii) of this section). If the service recipient fails to use a reasonable interest rate to determine the amount includible in income, AFR will be used. For purposes of this section, *AFR* means the appropriate applicable Federal rate (as defined pursuant to section 1274(d)) based on annual compounding, for the last month of the taxable year for which the amount includible in income is being determined. The period described in the first sentence of this paragraph (b)(3)(ii)(B) is used to determine the appropriate AFR (short-term, mid-term, or long-term). For purposes of this paragraph (b)(3)(ii)(B), an unreasonably high interest rate includes a fixed interest rate that exceeds an interest rate that is reasonable, within the meaning of § 31.3121(v)(2)-1(d)(2)(i)(C) of this chapter.

(C) *Other rates of return.* If the amount of earnings or losses credited is based on a rate of return that is not an unreasonably high interest rate, within the meaning of paragraph (b)(3)(ii)(B) of this section, but is also not a predetermined actual investment, within the meaning of § 31.3121(v)(2)-1(d)(2)(i)(B) of this chapter or a rate of interest that is no more than a reasonable rate of interest, within the meaning of § 31.3121(v)(2)-1(d)(2)(i)(C) of this chapter, the amount payable is a formula amount.

(4) *Reimbursement and in-kind benefit arrangements.* For purposes of this section, if benefits for a service provider are provided under a nonqualified deferred compensation plan described in § 1.409A-1(c)(2)(i)(E) (a reimbursement arrangement), or under a nonqualified deferred compensation plan that would be described in § 1.409A-1(c)(2)(i)(E) except that the amounts, separately or in the aggregate, constitute a substantial portion of either the overall compensation earned by the service provider for performing services for the service recipient or the overall compensation received due to a separation from service, the arrangement is treated as providing for a formula amount to the extent that the expenses to be reimbursed are not explicitly identified to be a specific amount. Notwithstanding the foregoing, if the expenses eligible for reimbursement are limited, it is presumed that the limit reflects the reasonable amount of eligible expenses that the service provider will incur at the earliest possible date during the time period to which the limit applies, and for which the service provider will request reimbursement at the earliest possible date that the service provider may request reimbursement. This presumption may be rebutted only by demonstrating by clear and convincing evidence that it is unreasonable to assume that a service provider would incur such amount of expenses during the applicable time period. This presumption is not applicable to any reimbursement arrangement to which § 1.409A-3(i)(1)(iv)(B) applies (certain medical reimbursement arrangements). In addition, this paragraph (b)(4) also applies to an arrangement providing a service provider a right to in-kind benefits from the service recipient, or a payment by the service recipient directly to the person providing the goods or services to the service provider.

(5) *Split-dollar life insurance arrangements.* For purposes of this section, if benefits for a service provider are provided under a nonqualified deferred compensation plan described in § 1.409A-1(c)(2)(i)(F) (a split-dollar life insurance arrangement), the amount of the future payment to which the service provider is entitled is treated as the amount that would be includible in income under § 1.61-22 or § 1.7872-15 (as applicable) or, if those regulations are not applicable, the amount that would be includible in income under any other applicable guidance. For this purpose, the payment timing assumptions set forth in paragraph (b)(2)(vi) and (vii) of this section generally apply. However, in the case of an arrangement subject to § 1.7872-15, to the extent the assumptions set forth in paragraph (b)(2)(vi) and (vii) of this section conflict with the provisions of § 1.7872-15, the provisions of § 1.7872-15 apply, and the conflicting assumptions set forth in paragraph (b)(2)(vi) and (vii) of this section do not apply. In either case, for purposes of determining the total amount deferred under the plan for the taxable year, the benefits under the split-dollar life insurance arrangement are included only to the extent that the right to such benefits constitutes a right to deferred compensation under § 1.409A-1(b).

(6) *Stock rights.* If a stock right has not been exercised during the service recipient's taxable year, and remains outstanding as of the last day of the service provider's taxable year for which the total amount deferred is being calculated, the total amount deferred under the stock right for such taxable year is the excess of the fair market value of the underlying stock on the last day of the service provider's taxable year (determined in accordance with § 1.409A-1(b)(5)(iv)) over the sum of the stock right's exercise price plus any amount paid for the stock right. If a stock right has been exercised during the service provider's taxable year, the payment amount for purposes of calculating the total amount deferred for the taxable year under the stock right is the excess of the fair market value of the underlying stock (as determined in accordance with § 1.409A-1(b)(5)(iv)) on the date of exercise over the sum of the exercise price of the stock right and any amount paid for the stock right.

(7) *Anti-abuse provision.* The Commissioner may disregard all or part of the rules of paragraphs (b)(2) through (b)(6) of this section or all or part of the plan's terms if the Commissioner determines based on all of the facts and circumstances that the plan terms have been established to eliminate or minimize the total amount deferred under the plan determined in accordance with the rules of paragraphs (b)(2) through (b)(6) of this section and if the rules of paragraphs (b)(2) through (b)(6) of this section were applied or such plan terms were given effect, the total amount deferred would not reasonably reflect the present value of the right. For example, if a plan provides that a deferred amount is payable upon a separation from service but also contains a provision that the amount will be forfeited upon a separation from service occurring on the last day of the service provider's taxable year (so that the application of paragraph (b)(2)(vii)(A) of this section treating the service provider as separating from service on the last day of the taxable year for purposes of determining the timing of the payment in calculating the total amount deferred would result in a zero amount deferred), the latter provision will be disregarded.

(c) *Additional 20 percent tax under section 409A(a)(1)(B)(i)(II).* With respect to an amount required to be included in income under section 409A(a) for a taxable year, the amount is subject to an additional income tax equal to 20 percent of the amount required to be included in income under section 409A(a).

(d) *Premium interest tax under section 409A(a)(1)(B)(i)(I)*—(1) *In general.* With respect to an amount required to be included in income under section 409A(a) for a taxable year, the amount is subject to an additional income tax equal to the amount of interest at the underpayment rate plus one percentage point on the underpayments that would have occurred had the deferred compensation been includible in the service provider's gross income for the taxable year in which first deferred or, if later, the first taxable year in which such deferred compensation is not subject to a substantial risk of forfeiture. The amount required to be allocated to determine the additional tax described in this paragraph (d) is the amount required to be included in income under section 409A(a) for the taxable year, regardless of whether additional amounts were deferred under the plan in previous years.

(2) *Identification of taxable year deferred amount was first deferred or vested*—(i) *Method of identification.* The following method is applied for purposes of determining the taxable year or years in which an amount required to be included in income under section 409A(a) was first deferred and not subject to a substantial risk of forfeiture.

(A) For each taxable year preceding the taxable year for which the deferred amount is includible in income (the current taxable year) in which the service provider had an amount deferred under the plan that was not subject to a substantial risk of forfeiture (vested), ending with the later of the first taxable year in which the service provider had no vested amount deferred or the first taxable year beginning after December 31, 2004, calculate the vested total amount deferred for such year. For each year, include any deferred amount that was previously included in income under paragraph (a)(3) of this section but has not been paid, but exclude any amount paid to (or on behalf of) the service provider during such taxable year.

(B) Identify any payments made under the plan to (or on behalf of) the service provider for each taxable year identified in paragraph (d)(2)(i)(A) of this section.

(C) Identify any deemed net investment losses or other net decreases in the amount deferred (other than as a result of a payment) applicable to amounts that are vested for the current taxable year and each preceding taxable year identified in paragraph (d)(2)(i)(A) of this section.

(D) Starting with the first taxable year during which there was a payment identified under paragraph (d)(2)(i)(B) of this section or a loss identified under paragraph (d)(2)(i)(C) of this section (or both), subtract the total payments and loss for such taxable year from the amount determined under paragraph (d)(2)(i)(A) of this section for the earliest taxable year before such year in which there is such an amount, and from the amount determined under paragraph (d)(2)(i)(A) of this section for each subsequent taxable year ending before the taxable year in which the payment was made or the loss incurred. Do not reduce any taxable year-end balance below zero.

(E) Repeat this process for each subsequent taxable year during which there was a payment identified under paragraph (d)(2)(i)(B) of this section or a loss identified under paragraph (d)(2)(i)(C) of this section (or both).

(F) For each taxable year identified in paragraph (d)(2)(i)(A) of this section, determine the excess (if any) of the remaining amount deferred for the taxable year over the remaining amount deferred for the previous taxable year. Treat the amount deferred in taxable years beginning before January 1, 2005 as zero.

(G) Determine how much of the total amount deferred for the current taxable year was previously included in income in accordance with paragraph (a)(3) of this section.

(H) Subtract the amount determined in paragraph (d)(2)(i)(G) of this section from the excess amount determined in paragraph (d)(2)(i)(F) of this section for the earliest taxable year in which there is any such excess amount, but do not reduce the balance below zero. If the amount determined in paragraph (d)(2)(i)(G) of this section exceeds the amount determined in paragraph (d)(2)(i)(F) of this section for that earliest taxable year, subtract the excess from the amount determined in paragraph (d)(2)(i)(F) of this section for the next succeeding taxable year, but do not reduce the balance below zero. Repeat this process until the excess has been reduced to zero. The balance remaining with respect to each taxable year identified in paragraph (d)(2)(i)(A) of this section is the portion of the amount includible in income under section 409A(a) in the current taxable year that was first deferred and vested in that taxable year.

	Year 1
Opening Total Amount	0
Bonus Deferral	100
Net Gains (Losses)	10
Payments	0
Closing Total Amount	110

(i) The amount required to be included in income under section 409A is 770. To calculate the premium interest tax, the 770 must be allocated to the year or years in which the amount was first deferred and vested.

Year 1	Year 2
110	275

(iii) *Step B.* Identification of any payments for each year other than Year 4.

Year 1	Year 2
0	0

(iv) *Step C.* Identification of any other decreases attributable to vested amounts.

Year 1	Year 2
0	0

(v) *Steps D and E.* Subtraction of payments and decreases from amounts deferred.

Year 1	Year 2
110	275
-0	-0
110	275

(vi) *Step F.* Subtraction of previous year total from each year's total.

Year 1	Year 2
110	275
-0	-110
110	165

(vii) Because no amount was previously included in income, Step G does not apply. Accordingly, the 770 is allocated such that 110 is treated as first deferred and vested in Year 1, 165 in Year 2, 220 in Year 3. The remainder (275) is treated as first deferred in Year 4, but is not

	Year 1
Opening Total Amount	0
Bonus Deferral	100
Net Gains (Losses)	10
Payments	0
Closing Total Amount	110

(ii) *Examples.* The following examples illustrate the provisions of paragraph (d)(2) of this section. In all of the following examples, the service provider is an individual taxpayer with a calendar year taxable year who elects to defer a portion of the bonus that would otherwise be payable to the service provider in each of Year 1 through Year 4. All amounts deferred are deferred under the same plan, and no amount deferred under the plan is ever subject to a substantial risk of forfeiture. The plan does not fail to meet the requirements of section 409A(a) in any year prior to Year 4, and no amounts deferred under the plan are otherwise includible in income until Year 4, except for payments actually made to the service provider. The service provider had no amount deferred under the plan prior to Year 1. The plan fails to meet the requirements of section 409A(a) in Year 4. The examples read as follows:

Example 1.

	Year 2	Year 3	Year 4
Opening Total Amount	110	275	495
Bonus Deferral	150	200	250
Net Gains (Losses)	15	20	25
Payments	0	0	0
Closing Total Amount	275	495	770

(ii) *Step A.* Identification of vested total amount deferred excluding payments and including deferred amounts previously included in income.

Year 3
495

Year 3
0

Year 3	Year 4
0	0

Year 3
495
-0
495

Year 3
495
-275
220

required to be allocated for purposes of the premium interest tax because there is no hypothetical underpayment for such year.

Example 2.

	Year 2	Year 3	Year 4
Opening Total Amount	110	235	365
Bonus Deferral	150	200	250
Net Gains (Losses)	(25)	(30)	25
Payments	0	(40)	(50)
Closing Total Amount	235	365	590

(i) The amount that is includible in income under section 409A(a) for Year 4 is the closing total amount (590), plus the amounts paid during Year 4 that were includible in income (50) or 640. To calculate the premium interest tax, the 640 must be allocated to the year or years in which the amount was first deferred and vested.

Year 1	Year 2
110	235

(iii) *Step B*. Identification of any payments for each year other than Year 4

Year 1	Year 2
0	0

(iv) *Step C*. Identification of any other decreases attributable to vested amounts

Year 1	Year 2	Year 3	Year 4
0	(25)	(30)	0

(v) *Steps D and E*. Subtraction of payments and decreases from amounts deferred

Year 1	Year 2	Year 3
110	235	365
-25(Year 2)	-40(Year 3)	
-40(Year 3)	-30(Year 3)	
-30(Year 3)		
15	165	365

(vi) *Step F*. Subtraction of previous year total from each year's total.

Year 1	Year 2	Year 3
15	165	365
-0	-15	-165
15	150	200

(vii) Because no amount was previously included in income, Step G does not apply. Accordingly, the 640 is allocated such that 15 is treated as first deferred and vested in Year 1, 150 in Year 2, and 200 in Year 3. The remaining amount includible in income under section 409A for Year 4 (275) is treated as first deferred in Year 4, but is not required to be allocated for purposes of the premium interest tax because there is no hypothetical underpayment for Year 4.

Year 1	Year 2	Year 3
15	150	200
-15	-110	-0
0	40	200

(iii) Accordingly, for purposes of calculating the premium interest tax, the 125 previously included in income is allocated so that of the 515 includible in income under section 409A(a), 0 is treated as first deferred and vested in Year 1, 40 in Year 2, and 200 in Year 3.

(3) *Calculation of hypothetical underpayment for the taxable year during which a deferred amount was first deferred and vested*—(i) *Calculation method*. The hypothetical underpayment for a taxable year is determined by treating as an additional cash payment of compensation to the service provider for such taxable year, the amount determined pursuant to paragraph (d)(2) of this section to be the portion of the amount includible in income under section 409A(a) that was first deferred and vested during such taxable year. The hypothetical underpayment is calculated based on the service provider's taxable income, credits, filing status, and other tax information for the year, based on the service provider's original return filed for such year, as adjusted by any examination for such year or any amended return the service provider filed for such year that was accepted by the Commissioner. The hypothetical underpayment must reflect the effect that such additional compensation would have had on the service provider's Federal income tax liability for such year, including the continued availability of any deductions taken, and the use of any carryovers such as carryover losses. For purposes of calculating a hypothetical underpayment in a subsequent year (whether or not a portion of the amount includible in income under section 409A(a) was first deferred and vested in the subsequent year), any changes to the service provider's Federal income tax liability for the subsequent year that would have occurred if the portion of the amount that was first deferred and vested during the previous taxable year had been included in the

(ii) *Step A*. Identification of vested total amount deferred excluding payments and including deferred amounts previously included in income.

Year 3
365

Year 3
(40)

Example 3. (i) The facts are the same as in *Example 2* except 125 was previously included in income under paragraph (a)(3) of this section. Accordingly, of the 590 closing total amount for Year 4 plus the 50 payment during Year 4, or 640, only 515 (640 - 125) must be included in income under section 409A(a). To calculate the premium interest tax, the 125 must be allocated to the year or years in which such amount was first deferred.

(ii) *Step G*. Allocation of amounts previously included in income.

Year 3
200
-0
200

service provider's income for the previous year must be taken into account. Assumptions not based on the service provider's taxable income, credits, filing status, and other tax information for the year, based on the service provider's original return for such year, as adjusted by any examination for such year or any amended return the service provider filed for such year that was accepted by the Commissioner, may not be applied. For example, the service provider may not assume that some of the additional compensation would have been deferred under the terms of a qualified plan. If the service provider's Federal income tax liability for the taxable year in which an amount required to be included in income under section 409A(a) was first deferred and vested is adjusted (for example, by an amended return or IRS examination), and the adjustment affects the amount of the hypothetical underpayment, the service provider must recalculate the hypothetical underpayment and adjust the amount of premium interest tax due with respect to such inclusion in income under section 409A(a), as appropriate.

(ii) *Examples*. The following examples illustrate the provisions of paragraph (d)(3)(i) of this section. In all of the following examples, Employee N is an individual taxpayer with a calendar year taxable year. For the year 2020, Employee N has a total amount deferred of $100,000 which is includible in income under section 409A(a). For purposes of determining the premium interest tax, assume that $30,000 was first deferred and vested in 2018, $35,000 was first deferred and vested in 2019, and $35,000 was first deferred and vested in 2020. The first year that Employee N had a vested deferred amount under the plan was 2018. The examples read as follows:

Example 1. For the taxable years 2018 and 2019, Employee N has no carryover losses or other items a change in which could affect the adjusted gross income for a subsequent taxable year. Employee N determines the hypothetical underpayment for 2018 by assuming an additional cash compensation payment of $30,000 for 2018, and determining the hypothetical underpayment of Federal income tax that would result. Employee N determines the hypothetical underpayment for 2019 by assuming an additional cash compensation payment of $35,000 in 2019, and determining the hypothetical underpayment of Federal income tax for 2019 that would result. There is no hypothetical underpayment with respect to hypothetical income in 2020 because the tax payment would not have been due until 2021. Therefore, Employee N is not required to determine a hypothetical underpayment for 2020.

Example 2. The facts are the same as in *Example 1*, except that in 2018, Employee N had an excess charitable contribution the deduction of which was not permitted under section 170(b), and which was carried over to subsequent taxable years under section 170(d). For purposes of determining the hypothetical underpayment for 2018, Employee N uses the charitable contribution deduction that otherwise would have been available if the $30,000 compensation payment had actually been made. Employee N must then calculate the hypothetical underpayment for all subsequent years in a manner that eliminates the portion of any carryovers of excess contributions under section 170(d) related to the charitable contribution in 2018 that would not have been available in such subsequent years as a result of having been deducted in 2018.

Example 3. The facts are the same as in *Example 2*, except that in 2021 the IRS examines Employee N's 2018 return and determines that Employee N had $20,000 in unreported income for that year. In addition to paying the tax deficiency owed for 2018, Employee N must redetermine the hypothetical underpayment for 2018 and recalculate the premium interest tax owed for 2020.

(4) *Calculation of hypothetical premium underpayment interest*—(i) *Calculation method.* The amount of hypothetical premium underpayment interest is determined for any taxable year by applying the applicable rate of interest under section 6621 plus one percentage point to determine the underpayment interest under section 6601 that would be due for such underpayment as of the last day of the taxable year for which the amount deferred is includible in income under section 409A(a). The amount of additional income tax under paragraph (d)(2) of this section with respect to an amount required to be included in income under section 409A(a) is the sum of all of the hypothetical premium underpayment interest for all years in which there was determined a hypothetical underpayment.

(ii) *Examples.* The following examples illustrate the provisions of this paragraph (d)(4). In each of these examples, the service provider is an individual taxpayer with a calendar year taxable year. At all times the total amount deferred under the nonqualified deferred compensation plan is not subject to a substantial risk of forfeiture. The examples read as follows:

Example 1. Employee O has a total amount deferred under a nonqualified deferred compensation plan for 2010 of $100,000. The entire deferred amount was first deferred in 2006. For purposes of calculating the hypothetical premium underpayment interest tax, Employee O first must determine the hypothetical underpayment for taxable years 2006 through 2009 under the rules of paragraph (d)(3) of this section. Then Employee O must determine the underpayment interest under section 6601 that would have accrued, calculated using the applicable underpayment interest rate under section 6621 increased by one percentage point, applied through December 31, 2010. That amount is the premium interest tax that is due for 2010.

Example 2. Employee P has a total amount deferred under a nonqualified deferred compensation plan for 2010 of $100,000. $60,000 of that deferred amount was first deferred in 2006. $30,000 of that amount was first deferred in 2008. $10,000 of that amount was first deferred in 2010. For purposes of calculating the hypothetical premium underpayment interest tax, Employee P first must determine the hypothetical underpayment for taxable years 2006 through 2009 under the rules of paragraph (d)(3) of this section applying $60,000 of hypothetical additional compensation for 2006, and applying $30,000 of hypothetical additional compensation for 2008. The $10,000 of hypothetical additional compensation in 2010 would not result in a hypothetical underpayment because the Federal income tax applicable to that hypothetical additional compensation would not yet be due. Second, Employee P must determine the underpayment interest under section 6601 that would have accrued, calculated using the applicable underpayment interest rate under section 6621 increased by one percentage point, applied through December 31, 2010, for both the hypothetical underpayment occurring in 2006 and the hypothetical

underpayment occurring in 2008. The sum of those two amounts is the premium interest tax that is due for 2010.

(e) *Amounts includible in income under section 409A(b)* [Reserved].

(f) *Application of amounts included in income under section 409A to payments of amounts deferred*—(1) *In general.* Section 409A(c) provides that any amount included in gross income under section 409A is not required to be included in gross income under any other provision of this chapter or any other rule of law later than the time provided in this section. An amount included in income under section 409A that has neither been paid in the taxable year the amount was included in income under section 409A nor served as the basis for a deduction under paragraph (g) of this section is allocated to the first payment of an amount deferred under the plan in any year subsequent to the year the amount was included in income under section 409A. To the extent the amount included in income under section 409A exceeds such payment, the excess is allocated to the next payment of an amount deferred under the plan. This process is repeated until the entire amount included in income under section 409A has been paid or the service provider has become entitled to a deduction under paragraph (g) of this section.

(2) *Application of the plan aggregation rules.* The plan aggregation rules of § 1.409A-1(c)(2) apply to the allocation of amounts previously included in income under section 409A to payments made under the plan. Accordingly, references to an amount deferred under a plan, or a payment of an amount deferred under a plan, refer to an amount deferred or a payment made under all arrangements in which a service provider participates that together are treated as a single plan under § 1.409A-1(c)(2).

(3) *Examples.* The following examples illustrate the provisions of this section. In each of these examples, the service provider is an individual taxpayer with a calendar year taxable year. Each service provider has a total amount deferred under a nonqualified deferred compensation plan of $0 for 2010, a total amount deferred under the plan of $100,000 for 2011, a total amount deferred under the plan of $250,000 for 2012, and a total amount deferred under the plan of $400,000 for 2013. At all times the total amount deferred under the plan is not subject to a substantial risk of forfeiture. During 2011, the plan fails to comply with section 409A(a) and each service provider includes $100,000 in income under section 409A. Except as otherwise provided in the following examples, the service provider does not receive any payments of amounts deferred under the plan. The examples read as follows:

Example 1. During 2012, Employee Q receives a $10,000 payment under the plan. During 2013, Employee Q receives a $150,000 payment under the plan. For 2012, $10,000 of the $100,000 included in income under section 409A(a) is allocated under paragraph (f)(1) of this section to the $10,000 payment, so that no amount is includible in gross income as a result of such payment and Employee Q retains $90,000 of amounts previously included in income under the plan to allocate to future plan payments. For 2013, the remaining $90,000 included in income under section 409A(a) is allocated to the $150,000 payment, so that only $60,000 is includible in income as a result of such payment.

Example 2. During 2012, Employee R receives a $10,000 payment under the plan. During 2014, Employee R receives a $50,000 payment, equaling the entire amount deferred under the plan. For 2012, $10,000 of the $100,000 previously included in income is allocated pursuant to paragraph (f)(1) of this section to the $10,000 payment, so that no amount is includible in gross income as a result of such payment. For 2014, $50,000 of the $90,000 remaining amount previously included in income is allocated pursuant to paragraph (f)(1) of this section to the $50,000 payment, so that no amount is includible in gross income as a result of such payment. Provided that the requirements of paragraph (g) of this section are otherwise met, Employee R is entitled to a deduction for 2014 equal to the remaining amount ($40,000) that was previously included in income under section 409A(a) that has not been allocated to a payment under the plan.

(g) *Forfeiture or other permanent loss of right to deferred compensation*—(1) *Availability of deduction to the service provider.* If a service provider has included a deferred amount in income under section 409A, but has not actually received payment of such deferred amount or otherwise allocated the amount included in income under paragraph (f) of this section, the service provider is entitled to a deduction for the taxable year in which the right to that amount of deferred compensation is permanently forfeited under the plan's terms or the right to the payment of the amount is otherwise permanently lost. The deduction to which the service provider is entitled equals the deferred amount included in income under section 409A in a previous year, less any portion of such deferred amount previously included in income under section 409A that was allocated under paragraph (f) of this section to amounts paid under the plan, including any deferred amount paid in the year the right to any remaining deferred compensation is permanently forfeited or otherwise lost. For this purpose, a mere diminution in the deferred amount under the plan due to deemed investment loss, actuarial reduction, or other decrease in the amount deferred is not treated as a permanent forfeiture or loss of the right if the service provider retains the right to an amount deferred under the plan (whether or not such right is subject to a substantial risk of forfeiture as defined in § 1.409A-1(d)). In addition, a deferred amount is not treated as permanently forfeited or otherwise lost if the obligation to make the payment of such deferred amount is substituted for another deferred amount or obligation to make a payment in a future year. However, a deferred amount is treated as permanently lost if the service provider's right to receive the payment of the deferred amount becomes wholly worthless during the taxable year. Whether the right to the payment of a deferred amount has become wholly worthless is determined based on all the facts and circumstances existing as of the last day of the relevant service provider taxable year.

(2) *Application of the plan aggregation rules.* For purposes of determining whether the right to a deferred amount is permanently forfeited or otherwise lost, the plan aggregation rules of § 1.409A-1(c) apply. Accordingly, if the right to an identified deferred amount under a plan is permanently forfeited or otherwise lost, but an additional amount remains deferred under the plan, the service provider is not entitled to a deduction.

(3) *Examples.* The following examples illustrate the provisions of this paragraph (g). In each example, the service provider is an individual taxpayer who has a calendar year taxable year and the service recipient does not experience bankruptcy at any time or otherwise discharge any obligation to make a payment of a deferred amount, except as expressly provided in the example. The examples read as follows:

Example 1. For 2010, Employee S has a total amount deferred under an elective account balance plan of $1,000,000. The plan fails to meet the requirements of section 409A(a) during 2010 and Employee S includes $1,000,000 in income under section 409A(a) for the year 2010. In 2011, Employee S experiences investment losses but no payments before July 1, 2011, such that Employee S's account balance under the plan is $500,000. On July 1, 2011, Employee S separates from service and receives a $500,000 payment equal to the entire amount deferred under the plan, and retains no other right to deferred compensation

under the plan (including all arrangements aggregated with the arrangement under which the payment was made). For 2011, Employee S is entitled to deduct $500,000 (which is the amount Employee S previously included in income under section 409A(a) ($1,000,000) less the amount actually received by Employee S ($500,000)).

Example 2. For 2010, Employee T has a total amount deferred under an elective account balance plan of $1,000,000. The plan fails to meet the requirements of section 409A(a) for 2010 and Employee T includes $1,000,000 in income under section 409A(a) for 2010. For 2011, Employee T has a total amount deferred under the plan of $500,000, due solely to the deemed investment losses attributable to Employee T's account balance (with no payments being made during 2011). Because Employee T retains the right to an amount deferred under the plan, Employee T is not entitled to a deduction for 2011 as a result of the deemed investment losses.

Example 3. For 2010, Employee U has a total amount deferred under an elective account balance plan of $1,000,000. The elective account balance plan consists of one arrangement providing for salary deferrals with an amount deferred for 2010 of $600,000, and another arrangement providing for bonus deferrals with an amount deferred for 2010 of $400,000. The plan fails to meet the requirements of section 409A(a) during 2010 and Employee U includes $1,000,000 in income under section 409A(a) for 2010. On July 1, 2011, Employee U's account balance attributable to the salary deferral arrangement is $500,000, the reduction of which is due solely to deemed investment losses in 2011 and not any payments. On July 1, 2011, Employee U is paid the $500,000 equaling the entire account balance attributable to the salary deferral arrangement. On December 31, 2011, Employee U has an account balance attributable to the bonus deferral arrangement equal to $300,000. Because Employee U retains an amount deferred under the elective account balance plan, Employee U is not entitled to a deduction for 2011 as a result of the deemed investment losses.

(h) *Effective/applicability date.* The rules of this section apply to taxable years ending on or after the date of publication of the Treasury decision adopting these rules as final regulation in the **Federal Register**.

Linda E. Stiff,

Deputy Commissioner for Services and Enforcement.

¶ 20,262T

IRS: 401(k) plans: 403(b) plans: Nondiscrimination: Design-based safe harbors: Qualified automatic contribution arrangements: Substantial business hardship: Reduction or suspension of nonelective contributions.—The IRS has issued proposed regulations that would allow an employer sponsoring a 401(k) or 403(b) design-based safe harbor plan, including a qualified automatic contribution arrangement under Code Sec. 413, to reduce or suspend safe harbor nonelective contributions when the employer incurs a substantial business hardship during the plan year. The proposed rules would provide an employer an alternative to the option of terminating the employer's safe harbor plan in such a situation. The reduction or suspension of safe harbor nonelective contributions would be allowed under rules generally comparable to the provision relating to the reduction or suspension of safe harbor matching contributions. The proposed regulations may be relied on for guidance pending issuance of final regulations.

The proposed regulations , which were published in the Federal Register on May 18, 2009 (74 FR 23134), were reproduced below. The final regulations are at ¶ 11,731F, ¶ 11,731I, ¶ 11,732C, and ¶ 11,732I.

¶ 20,262U

IRS: Paul Wellstone and Pete Domenici Mental Health Parity and Addiction Equity Act of 2008: Group health plans: Coverage.—The IRS has issued proposed regulations implementing the Paul Wellstone and Pete Domenici Mental Health Parity and Addiction Equity Act of 2008, which requires parity between mental health or substance use disorder benefits and medical/surgical benefits concerning financial requirements and treatment limitations under group health plans and health insurance coverage offered by a group health plan. In addition, the IRS issued temporary regulations, the preamble of which is at ¶ 23,268. The text of the temporary regulations at ¶ 13,968U-11 (Reg. Sec. 54.9812-1T) serve as the text of the proposed regulations (Reg. Sec. 54.9812-1). The IRS also is withdrawing proposed regulations relating to mental health parity requirements for group health plans issued on December 22, 1997 (¶ 20,228).

The proposed regulation was published in the Federal Register on February 2, 2010 (75 FR 5452). Final regulations were issued on November 13, 2013 (78 FR 68239). The preamble to the final regulations is at ¶ 23,292. The final regulations are at ¶ 13,968U-12.

¶ 20,262V

IRS: Hybrid plans: Cash balance plans: Pension Protection Act of 2006.—The IRS has issued proposed regulations that provide guidance on hybrid defined benefit plans, such as cash balance plans, reflecting changes made by the Pension Protection Act of 2006 (P.L. 109-280), as amended by the Worker, Retiree, and Employer Recovery Act of 2008 (P.L. 110-458). The proposed regulations address certain issues under Code Sec. 411(a)(13) and Code Sec. 411(b)(5) that are not addressed in the final regulations issued on October 19, 2010 (see ¶ 23,277). In addition, guidance is provided for hybrid plans that adjust benefits using a variable rate. Written or electronic comments on the proposed regulations must be received by January 12, 2011.

The proposed regulations were published in the Federal Register on October 19, 2010 (75 FR 64197), and corrected on December 28, 2010 by 75 FR 81543. The regulations were finalized on September 19, 2014 (79 FR 56442). The preamble to the final regulations is at ¶ 23,306. The final regulations are at ¶ 12,220, ¶ 12,223, and ¶ 12,224.

DEPARTMENT OF THE TREASURY

Internal Revenue Service

26 CFR Part 1

[REG-132554-08]

RIN 1545-BI16

Additional Rules Regarding Hybrid Retirement Plans

AGENCY: Internal Revenue Service (IRS), Treasury.

ACTION: Notice of proposed rulemaking and notice of public hearing.

SUMMARY: This document contains proposed regulations providing guidance relating to certain provisions of the Internal Revenue Code (Code) that apply to hybrid defined benefit pension plans. These regulations would provide guidance on changes made by the Pension Protection Act of 2006, as amended by the Worker, Retiree, and Employer Recovery Act of 2008. These regulations would affect sponsors, administrators, participants, and beneficiaries of hybrid defined benefit pension plans. This document also provides a notice of a public hearing on these proposed regulations.

DATES: Written or electronic comments must be received by Wednesday, January 12, 2011. Outlines of topics to be discussed at the public hearing scheduled for Wednesday, January 26, 2011, at 10 a.m. must be received by Friday, January 14, 2011.

ADDRESSES: Send submissions to: CC:PA:LPD:PR (REG-132554-08), Room 5203, Internal Revenue Service, PO Box 7604, Ben Franklin Station, Washington, DC 20044. Submissions may be hand-delivered Monday through Friday between the hours of 8 a.m. and 4 p.m. to: CC:PA:LPD:PR (REG-132554-08), Courier's Desk, Internal Revenue Service, 1111 Constitution Avenue, NW., Washington, DC, or sent electronically, via the Federal eRulemaking Portal at *http:// www.regulations.gov* (IRS REG-132554-08). The public hearing will be held in the IRS Auditorium, Internal Revenue Building, 1111 Constitution Avenue, NW., Washington, DC. FOR FURTHER INFORMATION CONTACT: Concerning the regulations, Neil S. Sandhu, Lauson C. Green, or Linda S. F. Marshall at (202) 622-6090; concerning submissions of comments, the hearing, and/or being placed on the building access list to attend the hearing, Regina Johnson, at (202) 622-7180 (not toll-free numbers).

SUPPLEMENTARY INFORMATION:

Background

This document contains proposed amendments to the Income Tax Regulations (26 CFR part 1) under sections 411(a)(13), 411(b)(1), and 411(b)(5) of the Code. Generally, a defined benefit pension plan must satisfy the minimum vesting standards of section 411(a) and the accrual requirements of section 411(b) in order to be qualified under section 401(a) of the Code. Sections 411(a)(13) and 411(b)(5), which modify the minimum vesting standards of section 411(a) and the accrual requirements of section 411(b), were added to the Code by section 701(b) of the Pension Protection Act of 2006, Public Law 109-280 (120 Stat. 780 (2006)) (PPA '06). Sections 411(a)(13) and 411(b)(5), as well as certain effective date provisions related to these sections, were subsequently amended by the Worker, Retiree, and Employer Recovery Act of 2008, Public Law 110-458 (122 Stat. 5092 (2008)) (WRERA '08).

Section 411(a)(13)(A) provides that an applicable defined benefit plan (which is defined in section 411(a)(13)(C)) is not treated as failing to meet either (i) the requirements of section 411(a)(2) (subject to a special vesting rule in section 411(a)(13)(B) with respect to benefits derived from employer contributions) or (ii) the requirements of section 411(a)(11), 411(c), or 417(e), with respect to accrued benefits derived from employer contributions, merely because the present value of the accrued benefit (or any portion thereof) of any participant is, under the terms of the plan, equal to the amount expressed as the balance of a hypothetical account or as an accumulated percentage of the participant's final average compensation. Section 411(a)(13)(B) requires an applicable defined benefit plan to provide that an employee who has completed at least 3 years of service has a nonforfeitable right to 100 percent of the employee's accrued benefit derived from employer contributions.

Under section 411(a)(13)(C)(i), an applicable defined benefit plan is defined as a defined benefit plan under which the accrued benefit (or any portion thereof) of a participant is calculated as the balance of a hypothetical account maintained for the participant or as an accumulated percentage of the participant's final average compensation. Under section 411(a)(13)(C)(ii), the Secretary of the Treasury is to issue regulations which include in the definition of an applicable defined benefit plan any defined benefit plan (or portion of such a plan) which has an effect similar to a plan described in section 411(a)(13)(C)(i).

Section 411(a) requires that a defined benefit plan satisfy the requirements of section 411(b)(1). Section 411(b)(1) provides that a defined benefit plan must satisfy one of the three accrual rules of section 411(b)(1)(A), (B), and (C) with respect to benefits accruing under the plan. The three accrual rules are the 3 percent method of section 411(b)(1)(A), the 133. percent rule of section 411(b)(1)(B), and the fractional rule of section 411(b)(1)(C).

Section 411(b)(1)(B) provides that a defined benefit plan satisfies the requirements of the 133. percent rule for a particular plan year if, under the plan, the accrued benefit payable at the normal retirement age is equal to the normal retirement benefit, and the annual rate at which any individual who is or could be a participant can accrue the retirement benefits payable at normal retirement age under the plan for any later plan year is not more than 133. percent of the annual rate at which the individual can accrue benefits for any plan year beginning on or after such particular plan year and before such later plan year.

For purposes of applying the 133. percent rule, section 411(b)(1)(B)(i) provides that any amendment to the plan which is in effect for the current year is treated as in effect for all other plan years. Section 411(b)(1)(B)(ii) provides that any change in an accrual rate which does not apply to any individual who is or could be a participant in the current plan year is disregarded. Section 411(b)(1)(B)(iii) provides that the fact that benefits under the plan may be payable to certain participants before normal retirement age is disregarded. Section 411(b)(1)(B)(iv) provides that social security benefits and all other relevant factors used to compute benefits are treated as remaining constant as of the current plan year for all years after the current year.

Section 411(b)(1)(H)(i) provides that a defined benefit plan fails to comply with section 411(b) if, under the plan, an employee's benefit accrual is ceased, or the rate of an employee's benefit accrual is reduced, because of the attainment of any age.

Section 411(b)(5), which was added to the Code by section 701(b)(1) of PPA '06, provides additional rules related to section 411(b)(1)(H)(i). Section 411(b)(5)(A) generally provides that a plan is not treated as failing to meet the requirements of section 411(b)(1)(H)(i) if a participant's accrued benefit, as determined as of any date under the terms of the plan, would be equal to or greater than that of any similarly situated, younger individual who is or could be a participant. For this purpose, section 411(b)(5)(A)(iv) provides that the accrued benefit may, under the terms of the plan, be expressed as an annuity payable at normal retirement age, the balance of a hypothetical account, or the current value of the accumulated percentage of the employee's final average compensation. Section 411(b)(5)(G) provides that, for purposes of section 411(b)(5), any reference to the accrued benefit of a participant refers to the participant's benefit accrued to date.

Section 411(b)(5)(B) imposes certain requirements on an applicable defined benefit plan in order for the plan to satisfy section 411(b)(1)(H). Section 411(b)(5)(B)(i) provides that such a plan is treated as failing to meet the requirements of section 411(b)(1)(H) if the terms of the plan provide for an interest credit (or an equivalent amount) for any plan year at a rate that is greater than a market rate of return. Under section 411(b)(5)(B)(i)(I), a plan is not treated as having an above-market rate merely because the plan provides for a reasonable minimum guaranteed rate of return or for a rate of return that is equal to the greater of a fixed or variable rate of return. Section 411(b)(5)(B)(i)(II) provides that an applicable defined benefit plan is treated as failing to meet the requirements of section 411(b)(1)(H) unless the plan provides that an interest credit (or an equivalent amount) of less than zero can in no event result in the account balance or similar amount being less than the aggregate amount of contributions credited to the account. Section 411(b)(5)(B)(i)(III) authorizes the Secretary of the Treasury to provide by regulation for rules governing the calculation of a market rate of return for purposes of section 411(b)(5)(B)(i)(I) and for permissible methods of crediting interest to the account (including fixed or variable interest rates) resulting in effective rates of return meeting the requirements of section 411(b)(5)(B)(i)(I).

Sections 411(b)(5)(B)(ii), 411(b)(5)(B)(iii), and 411(b)(5)(B)(iv) contain additional requirements that apply if, after June 29, 2005, an applicable plan amendment is adopted. Section 411(b)(5)(B)(v)(I) defines an applicable plan amendment as an amendment to a defined benefit plan which has the effect of converting the plan to an applicable defined benefit plan. Under section 411(b)(5)(B)(ii), if, after June 29, 2005, an applicable plan amendment is adopted, the plan is treated as failing to meet the requirements of section 411(b)(1)(H) unless the requirements of section 411(b)(5)(B)(iii) are met with respect to each individual who was a participant in the plan immediately before the adoption of the amendment. Section 411(b)(5)(B)(iii) specifies that, subject to section 411(b)(5)(B)(iv), the requirements of section 411(b)(5)(B)(iii) are met with respect to any participant if the accrued benefit of the participant under the terms of the plan as in effect after the amendment is not less than the sum of: (I) the participant's accrued benefit for years of service before the effective date of the amendment, determined under the terms of the plan as in effect before the amendment; plus (II) the participant's accrued benefit for years of service after the effective date of the amendment, determined under the terms of the plan as in effect after the amendment. Section 411(b)(5)(B)(iv) provides that, for purposes of section 411(b)(5)(B)(iii)(I), the plan must credit the participant's account or similar amount with the amount of any early retirement benefit or retirement-type subsidy for the plan year in which the participant retires if, as of such time, the participant has met the age, years of service, and other requirements under the plan for entitlement to such benefit or subsidy.

Section 411(b)(5)(B)(v) sets forth certain provisions related to an applicable plan amendment. Section 411(b)(5)(B)(v)(II) provides that if the benefits under two or more defined benefit plans of an employer are coordinated in such a manner as to have the effect of adoption of an applicable plan amendment, the plan sponsor is treated as having adopted an applicable plan amendment as of the date the coordination begins. Section 411(b)(5)(B)(v)(III) directs the Secretary of the Treasury to issue regulations to prevent the avoidance of the purposes of section 411(b)(5)(B) through the use of two or more plan amendments rather than a single amendment.

Section 411(b)(5)(B)(vi) provides special rules for determining benefits upon termination of an applicable defined benefit plan. Under section 411(b)(5)(B)(vi)(I), an applicable defined benefit plan is not treated as satisfying the requirements of section 411(b)(5)(B)(i) (regarding permissible interest crediting rates) unless the plan provides that, upon plan termination, if the interest crediting rate under the plan is a variable rate, the rate of interest used to determine accrued benefits under the plan is equal to the average of the rates of interest used under the plan during the 5-year period ending on the termination date. In addition, under section 411(b)(5)(B)(vi)(II), the plan must provide that, upon plan termination, the interest rate and mortality table used to determine the amount of any benefit under the plan payable in the form of an annuity payable at normal retirement age is the rate and table specified under the plan for this purpose as of the termination date, except that if the interest rate is a variable rate, the rate used is the average of the rates used under the plan during the 5-year period ending on the termination date.

Section 411(b)(5)(C) provides that a plan is not treated as failing to meet the requirements of section 411(b)(1)(H)(i) solely because the plan provides offsets against benefits under the plan to the extent the offsets are otherwise allowable in applying the requirements of section 401(a). Section 411(b)(5)(D) provides that a plan is not treated as failing to meet the requirements of section 411(b)(1)(H) solely because the plan provides a disparity in contributions or benefits with respect to which the requirements of section 401(l) (relating to permitted disparity for Social Security benefits and related matters) are met.

Section 411(b)(5)(E) provides that a plan is not treated as failing to meet the requirements of section 411(b)(1)(H) solely because the plan provides for indexing of accrued benefits under the plan. Under section 411(b)(5)(E)(iii), indexing means the periodic adjustment of the accrued benefit by means of the application of a recognized investment index or methodology. Section 411(b)(5)(E)(ii) requires that, except in the case of a variable annuity, the indexing not result in a smaller benefit than the accrued benefit determined without regard to the indexing.

Section 701(a) of PPA '06 added provisions to the Employee Retirement Income Security Act of 1974, Public Law 93-406 (88 Stat. 829 (1974)) (ERISA), that are parallel to sections 411(a)(13) and 411(b)(5) of the Code. The guidance provided in these regulations with respect to sections 411(a)(13) and 411(b)(5) of the Code would also apply for purposes of the parallel amendments to ERISA made by section 701(a) of PPA '06, and the guidance provided in these regulations with respect to section 411(b)(1) of the Code would also apply for purposes of section 204(b)(1) of ERISA.[1]

Section 701(c) of PPA '06 added provisions to the Age Discrimination in Employment Act of 1967, Public Law 90-202 (81 Stat. 602 (1967)), that are parallel to section 411(b)(5) of the Code. Executive Order 12067 requires all Federal departments and agencies to advise and offer to consult with the Equal Employment Opportunity Commission (EEOC) during the development of any proposed rules, regulations, policies, procedures, or orders concerning equal employment opportunity. The Treasury Department and the IRS have consulted with the EEOC prior to the issuance of these regulations.

Section 701(d) of PPA '06 provides that nothing in the amendments made by section 701 should be construed to create an inference concerning the treatment of applicable defined benefit plans or conversions of plans into applicable defined benefit plans under section 411(b)(1)(H), or concerning the determination of whether an applicable defined benefit plan fails to meet the requirements of section 411(a)(2), 411(c), or 417(e), as in effect before such amendments, solely because the present value of the accrued benefit (or any portion thereof) of any participant is, under the terms of the plan, equal to the amount expressed as the balance of a hypothetical account or as an accumulated percentage of the participant's final average compensation.

Section 701(e) of PPA '06 sets forth the effective date provisions with respect to amendments made by section 701 of PPA '06. Section 701(e)(1) specifies that the amendments made by section 701 generally apply to periods beginning on or after June 29, 2005. Thus, the age discrimination safe harbors under section 411(b)(5)(A) and section 411(b)(5)(E) are effective for periods beginning on or after June 29, 2005. Section 701(e)(2) provides that the special present value rules of section 411(a)(13)(A) are effective for distributions made after August 17, 2006 (the date PPA '06 was enacted).

Under section 701(e) of PPA '06, the 3-year vesting rule under section 411(a)(13)(B) is generally effective for years beginning after December 31, 2007, for a plan in existence on June 29, 2005, while, pursuant to the amendments made by section 107(c) of WRERA '08, the rule is generally effective for plan years ending on or after June 29, 2005, for a plan not in existence on June 29, 2005. The market rate of return limitation under section 411(b)(5)(B)(i) is generally effective for years beginning after December 31, 2007, for a plan in existence on June 29, 2005, while the limitation is generally effective for periods beginning on or after June 29, 2005, for a plan not in existence on June 29, 2005. Section 701(e)(4) of PPA '06 contains special effective date provisions for collectively bargained plans that modify these effective dates.

Under section 701(e)(5) of PPA '06, as amended by WRERA '08, sections 411(b)(5)(B)(ii), (iii), and (iv) apply to a conversion amendment that is adopted on or after, and takes effect on or after, June 29, 2005.

Under section 701(e)(6) of PPA '06, as added by WRERA '08, the 3-year vesting rule under section 411(a)(13)(B) does not apply to a participant who does not have an hour of service after the date the 3-year vesting rule would otherwise be effective.

Section 702 of PPA '06 provides for regulations to be prescribed by August 16, 2007, addressing the application of rules set forth in section 701 of PPA '06 where the conversion of a defined benefit pension plan into an applicable defined benefit plan is made with respect to a group of employees who become employees by reason of a merger, acquisition, or similar transaction.

Under section 1107 of PPA '06, a plan sponsor is permitted to delay adopting a plan amendment pursuant to statutory provisions under PPA '06 (or pursuant to any regulation issued under PPA '06) until the last day of the first plan year beginning on or after January 1, 2009 (January 1, 2011, in the case of governmental plans). As described in Rev. Proc. 2007-44 (2007-28 IRB 54), this amendment deadline applies to both interim and discretionary amendments that are made pursuant to PPA '06 statutory provisions or any regulation issued under PPA '06. See § 601.601(d)(2)(ii)(*b*).

Section 1107 of PPA '06 also permits certain amendments to reduce or eliminate section 411(d)(6) protected benefits. Except to the extent permitted under section 1107 of PPA '06 (or under another statutory provision, including section 411(d)(6) and §§ 1.411(d)-3 and 1.411(d)-4), section 411(d)(6) prohibits a plan amendment that decreases a participant's accrued benefits or that has the effect of eliminating or reducing an early retirement benefit or retirement-type subsidy, or eliminating an optional form of benefit, with respect to benefits attributable to service before the amendment. However, an amendment that eliminates or decreases benefits that have not yet accrued does not violate section 411(d)(6), provided that the amendment is adopted and effective before the benefits accrue. If section 1107 of PPA '06 applies to an amendment of a plan, section 1107 provides

---

[1] Under section 101 of Reorganization Plan No. 4 of 1978 (43 FR 47713), the Secretary of the Treasury has interpretive jurisdiction over the subject matter addressed by these regulations for purposes of ERISA, as well as the Code.

that the plan does not fail to meet the requirements of section 411(d)(6) by reason of such amendment, except as provided by the Secretary of the Treasury.

Section 1.411(b)-1(a)(1) of the Treasury Regulations provides that a defined benefit plan is not a qualified plan unless the method provided by the plan for determining accrued benefits satisfies at least one of the alternative methods in §1.411(b)-1(b) for determining accrued benefits with respect to all active participants under the plan. Section 1.411(b)-1(b)(2)(i) provides that a defined benefit plan satisfies the 133. percent rule of section 411(b)(1)(B) for a particular plan year if (A) under the plan the accrued benefit payable at the normal retirement age (determined under the plan) is equal to the normal retirement benefit (determined under the plan), and (B) the annual rate at which any individual who is or could be a participant can accrue the retirement benefits payable at normal retirement age under the plan for any later plan year cannot be more than 133. percent of the annual rate at which the participant can accrue benefits for any plan year beginning on or after such particular plan year and before such later plan year. Section 1.411(b)-1(b)(2)(ii)(A) through (D) sets forth a series of rules that correspond to the rules of section 411(b)(1)(B)(i) through (iv). Section 1.411(b)-1(b)(2)(ii)(D) provides that, for purposes of the 133. percent rule, for any plan year, social security benefits and all relevant factors used to compute benefits, e.g., consumer price index, are treated as remaining constant as of the beginning of the current plan year for all subsequent plan years.

Proposed regulations (EE-184-86) under sections 411(b)(1)(H) and 411(b)(2) were published by the Treasury Department and the IRS in the **Federal Register** on April 11, 1988 (53 FR 11876), as part of a package of regulations that also included proposed regulations under sections 410(a), 411(a)(2), 411(a)(8), and 411(c) (relating to the maximum age for participation, vesting, normal retirement age, and actuarial adjustments after normal retirement age, respectively).[2]

Notice 96-8 (1996-1 CB 359), see §601.601(d)(2)(ii)(b), described the application of sections 411 and 417(e)(3) to a single-sum distribution under a cash balance plan where interest credits under the plan are frontloaded (that is, where future interest credits to an employee's hypothetical account balance are not conditioned upon future service and thus accrue at the same time that the benefits attributable to a hypothetical allocation to the account accrue). Under the analysis set forth in Notice 96-8, in order to comply with sections 411(a) and 417(e)(3) in calculating the amount of a single-sum distribution under a cash balance plan, the balance of an employee's hypothetical account must be projected to normal retirement age and converted to an annuity under the terms of the plan, and then the employee must be paid at least the present value of the projected annuity, determined in accordance with section 417(e). Under that analysis, where a cash balance plan provides frontloaded interest credits using an interest rate that is higher than the section 417(e) applicable interest rate, payment of a single-sum distribution equal to the current hypothetical account balance as a complete distribution of the employee's accrued benefit may result in a violation of the minimum present value requirements of section 417(e) or a forfeiture in violation of section 411(a). In addition, Notice 96-8 proposed a safe harbor which provided that, if frontloaded interest credits are provided under a plan at a rate no greater than the sum of identified standard indices and associated margins, no violation of section 411(a) or 417(e) would result if the employee's entire accrued benefit were to be distributed in the form of a single-sum distribution equal to the employee's hypothetical account balance, provided the plan uses appropriate annuity conversion factors. Since the issuance of Notice 96-8, four Federal appellate courts have followed the analysis set out in the Notice: *Esden v. Bank of Boston*, 229 F.3d 154 (2d Cir. 2000), *cert. dismissed*, 531 U.S. 1061 (2001); *West v. AK Steel Corp. Ret. Accumulation Pension Plan*, 484 F.3d 395 (6th Cir. 2007), *cert. denied*, 129 S. Ct. 895 (2009); *Berger v. Xerox Corp. Ret. Income Guarantee Plan*, 338 F.3d 755 (7th Cir. 2003), *reh'g and reh'g en banc denied*, No. 02-3674, 2003 U.S. App. LEXIS 19374 (7th Cir. Sept. 15, 2003); *Lyons v. Georgia-Pacific Salaried Employees Ret. Plan*, 221 F.3d 1235 (11th Cir. 2000), *cert. denied*, 532 U.S. 967 (2001).

Notice 2007-6 (2007-1 CB 272), see §601.601(d)(2)(ii)(b), provides transitional guidance with respect to certain requirements of sections 411(a)(13) and 411(b)(5) and section 701(b) of PPA '06. Notice 2007-6 includes certain special definitions, including: accumulated benefit,

which is defined as a participant's benefit accrued to date under a plan; lump sum-based plan, which is defined as a defined benefit plan under the terms of which the accumulated benefit of a participant is expressed as the balance of a hypothetical account maintained for the participant or as the current value of the accumulated percentage of the participant's final average compensation; and statutory hybrid plan, which is defined as a lump sum-based plan or a plan which has an effect similar to a lump sum-based plan. Notice 2007-6 provides guidance on a number of issues, including a rule under which a plan that provides for indexed benefits described in section 411(b)(5)(E) is a statutory hybrid plan (because it has an effect similar to a lump sum-based plan), unless the plan either solely provides for post-retirement adjustment of the amounts payable to a participant or is a variable annuity plan under which the assumed interest rate used to determine adjustments is at least 5 percent. Notice 2007-6 provides a safe harbor for applying the rules set forth in section 701 of PPA '06 where the conversion of a defined benefit pension plan into an applicable defined benefit plan is made with respect to a group of employees who become employees by reason of a merger, acquisition, or similar transaction. This transitional guidance, along with the other guidance provided in Part III of Notice 2007-6, applies pending the issuance of further guidance and, thus, does not apply for periods to which the 2010 final regulations (as described later in this preamble) apply.

Proposed regulations (REG-104946-07) under sections 411(a)(13) and 411(b)(5) (2007 proposed regulations) were published by the Treasury Department and the IRS in the **Federal Register** on December 28, 2007 (72 FR 73680). The Treasury Department and the IRS received written comments on the 2007 proposed regulations and a public hearing was held on June 6, 2008.

Proposed regulations (REG-100464-08) under section 411(b)(1)(B) (2008 proposed backloading regulations) were published by the Treasury Department and the IRS in the **Federal Register** on June 18, 2008 (73 FR 34665). The 2008 proposed backloading regulations would provide guidance on the application of the accrual rule for defined benefit plans under section 411(b)(1)(B) in cases where plan benefits are determined on the basis of the greatest of two or more separate formulas. The Treasury Department and the IRS received written comments on the 2008 proposed backloading regulations and a public hearing was held on October 15, 2008.

Announcement 2009-82 (2009-48 IRB 720) and Notice 2009-97 (2009-52 IRB 972) announced certain expected relief with respect to the requirements of section 411(b)(5). In particular, Announcement 2009-82 stated that the rules in the regulations specifying permissible market rates of return are not expected to go into effect before the first plan year that begins on or after January 1, 2011. In addition, Notice 2009-97 stated that, once final regulations under sections 411(a)(13) and 411(b)(5) are issued, it is expected that relief from the requirements of section 411(d)(6) will be granted for a plan amendment that eliminates or reduces a section 411(d)(6) protected benefit, provided that the amendment is adopted by the last day of the first plan year that begins on or after January 1, 2010, and the elimination or reduction is made only to the extent necessary to enable the plan to meet the requirements of section 411(b)(5).[3] Notice 2009-97 also extended the deadline for amending cash balance and other applicable defined benefit plans, within the meaning of section 411(a)(13)(C), to meet the requirements of section 411(a)(13) (other than section 411(a)(13)(A)) and section 411(b)(5), relating to vesting and other special rules applicable to these plans. Under Notice 2009-97, the deadline for these amendments is the last day of the first plan year that begins on or after January 1, 2010.

Final regulations (2010 final regulations) under sections 411(a)(13) and 411(b)(5) are being issued at the same time as these proposed regulations. The 2010 final regulations adopt most of the provisions of the 2007 proposed regulations, with certain modifications, and also reserve a number of sections relating to issues that are not addressed in those final regulations. These reserved issues relate to the scope of relief provided under section 411(a)(13)(A), a potential alternative method of satisfying the conversion protection requirements, additional rules with respect to the market rate of return requirement, and the application of the special plan termination rules. These proposed regulations generally address these issues, as well as an issue under section 411(b)(1).

---

[2] On December 11, 2002, the Treasury Department and the IRS issued proposed regulations regarding the age discrimination requirements of section 411(b)(1)(H) that specifically addressed cash balance plans as part of a package of regulations that also addressed section 401(a)(4) nondiscrimination crosstesting rules applicable to cash balance plans (67 FR 76123). The 2002 proposed regulations were intended to replace the 1988 proposed regulations. In Ann. 2003-22 (2003-1 CB 847), see §601.601(d)(2)(ii)(b), the

Treasury Department and the IRS announced the withdrawal of the 2002 proposed regulations under section 401(a)(4), and in Ann. 2004-57 (2004-2 CB 15), see §601.601(d)(2)(ii)(b), the Treasury Department and the IRS announced the withdrawal of the 2002 proposed regulations relating to age discrimination.

[3] However, see footnote 6 in Section IV.C of this preamble.

Explanation of Provisions

Overview

In general, these proposed regulations would provide guidance with respect to certain issues under sections 411(a)(13) and 411(b)(5) that are not addressed in the 2010 final regulations, as well as an issue under section 411(b)(1) for hybrid defined benefit plans that adjust benefits using a variable rate.

I. Section 411(a)(13): Scope of relief of section 411(a)(13)(A)

A. The 2010 final regulations

The 2010 final regulations define a lump sum-based benefit formula as a benefit formula used to determine all or any part of a participant's accumulated benefit under which the accumulated benefit provided under the formula is expressed as the current balance of a hypothetical account maintained for the participant or as the current value of an accumulated percentage of the participant's final average compensation. The 2010 final regulations provide that the relief of section 411(a)(13)(A) applies to the benefits determined under a lump sum-based benefit formula.

B. Limitations on the relief of section 411(a)(13)(A)

The proposed regulations would provide that the relief of section 411(a)(13)(A) does not apply with respect to the benefits determined under a lump sum-based benefit formula unless certain requirements are satisfied. In particular, the proposed regulations would provide that the relief does not apply unless, at all times on or before normal retirement age, the then-current hypothetical account balance or the thencurrent accumulated percentage of the participant's final average compensation is not less than the present value, determined using reasonable actuarial assumptions, of the portion of the participant's accrued benefit that is determined under the lump sum-based benefit formula. However, the plan would be deemed to satisfy this requirement for periods before normal retirement age if, upon attainment of normal retirement age, the then-current balance of the hypothetical account or the then-current value of the accumulated percentage of the participant's final average compensation is actuarially equivalent (using reasonable actuarial assumptions) to the portion of the participant's accrued benefit that is determined under the lump sum-based benefit formula. Thus, for periods before normal retirement age, a statutory hybrid plan with a lump sum-based benefit formula that meets the requirements of the preceding sentence need not project interest credits to normal retirement age and discount the resulting accrued benefit back in order to apply the relief of section 411(a)(13)(A) with respect to the benefit determined under the lump sum-based benefit formula.

In addition, the proposed regulations would provide that the relief of section 411(a)(13)(A) does not apply unless, as of each annuity starting date after normal retirement age, the then-current balance of the hypothetical account or the then-current value of the accumulated percentage of the participant's final average compensation satisfies the requirements of section 411(a)(2) or would satisfy those requirements but for the fact that the plan suspends benefits in accordance with section 411(a)(3)(B). Thus, for example, a plan that expresses the accumulated benefit as the balance of a hypothetical account and that does not comply with the suspension of benefit rules may have difficulty obtaining the relief of section 411(a)(13)(A) if, after normal retirement age, the plan credits interest at such a low rate that the adjustments provided by the interest credits, together with any principal credits, are insufficient to provide any required actuarial increases.

The proposed regulations would also provide that the relief of section 411(a)(13)(A) does not apply unless the balance of the hypothetical account or the accumulated percentage of the participant's final average compensation may not be reduced except as a result of one of the specified reasons set forth in the regulations. Under the proposed regulations, reductions would only be permissible as a result of: (1) benefit payments, (2) qualified domestic relations orders under section 414(p), (3) forfeitures that are permitted under section 411(a) (such as charges for providing a qualified preretirement survivor annuity), (4) amendments that are permitted under section 411(d)(6), and (5) adjustments resulting from the application of interest credits (under the rules of §1.411(b)(5)-1) that are negative for a period, for plans that express the accumulated benefit as the balance of a hypothetical account.

C. Application of section 411(a)(13)(A) to distributions other than single sums

The proposed regulations would provide that the relief under section 411(a)(13)(A) (with respect to the requirements of sections 411(a)(2),

411(c), and 417(e)) extends to certain other forms of benefit under a lump sum-based benefit formula, in addition to a single-sum payment of the entire benefit. In particular, the proposed regulations would clarify that the relief provided under section 411(a)(13)(A) extends to an optional form of benefit that is currently payable with respect to a lump sum-based benefit formula if, under the terms of the plan, the optional form of benefit is determined as of the annuity starting date as the actuarial equivalent, determined using reasonable actuarial assumptions, of the then-current balance of the hypothetical account or the then-current value of an accumulated percentage of the participant's final average compensation.

In addition, the proposed regulations would create a special rule that provides that the relief under section 411(a)(13)(A) also extends to an optional form of benefit that is not subject to the minimum present value requirements of section 417(e) and that is currently payable with respect to a lump sum-based benefit formula if, under the terms of the plan, this optional form of benefit is determined as of the annuity starting date as the actuarial equivalent (using reasonable actuarial assumptions) of the optional form of benefit that: (1) commences as of the same annuity starting date; (2) is payable in the same generalized optional form (within the meaning of §1.411(d)-3(g)(8)) as the accrued benefit; and (3) is the actuarial equivalent (using reasonable actuarial assumptions) of the then-current balance of the hypothetical account maintained for the participant or the then-current value of an accumulated percentage of the participant's final average compensation. This special rule would facilitate the payment of an immediate annuity, such as a joint and survivor annuity or life annuity with period certain, that is calculated as the actuarial equivalent of the form of payment of the accrued benefit under the plan, such as an immediately payable straight life annuity.

Finally, the proposed regulations would provide that the relief under section 411(a)(13)(A) applies on a proportionate basis to a payment of a portion of the benefit under a lump sum-based benefit formula that is not paid in the form of an annuity, such as a payment of a specified dollar amount or percentage of the then-current balance of a hypothetical account maintained for the participant or then-current value of an accumulated percentage of the participant's final average compensation. Thus, for example, if a plan that expresses the participant's entire accumulated benefit as the balance of a hypothetical account distributes 40 percent of the participant's then-current hypothetical account balance, the plan is treated as satisfying the requirements of section 411(a) and the minimum present value rules of section 417(e) with respect to 40 percent of the participant's then-current accrued benefit.

D. Application of section 411(a)(13)(A) to plans with multiple formulas

The proposed regulations would clarify that the relief provided under section 411(a)(13)(A) does not apply to any portion of the participant's benefit that is determined under a formula that is not a lump sum-based benefit formula. Thus, for example, where the participant's accrued benefit equals the greater of the benefit under a hypothetical account formula and the benefit under a traditional defined benefit formula, a single-sum payment of the participant's entire benefit must equal the greater of the then-current balance of the hypothetical account and the present value, determined in accordance with section 417(e), of the benefit under the traditional defined benefit formula. On the other hand, where the plan provides an accrued benefit equal to the sum of the benefit under a hypothetical account formula plus the excess of the benefit under a traditional defined benefit formula over the benefit under the hypothetical account formula, a single-sum payment of the participant's entire benefit must equal the then-current balance of the hypothetical account plus the excess of the present value, determined in accordance with section 417(e), of the benefit under the traditional defined benefit formula over the present value, determined in accordance with section 417(e), of the benefit under the hypothetical account formula. See the request for comments under the heading " **Comments and Public Hearing**" on the issue of determining the present value of a benefit determined, in part, based on the benefit under a lump sum-based benefit formula.

E. Application of section 411(a)(13)(A) to pension equity plans

The preamble to the 2007 proposed regulations asked for comments on plan formulas that calculate benefits as the current value of an accumulated percentage of the participant's final average compensation (often referred to as "pension equity plans" or "PEPs"). Commenters indicated that some of these plans never credit interest, directly or indirectly, some explicitly credit interest after cessation of PEP accruals, and some do not credit interest explicitly but provide for specific amounts to be payable after cessation of PEP accruals (both immediately and at future dates) based on actuarial equivalence using specified actuarial factors applied upon cessation of PEP accruals.

The 2010 final regulations clarify that a formula is expressed as the balance of a hypothetical account maintained for the participant if it is expressed as a current single-sum dollar amount. Thus, a PEP formula that credits interest after cessation of PEP accruals is considered a formula that is expressed as the balance of a hypothetical account after cessation of PEP accruals. As a result, such a formula is a lump sumbased benefit formula that is subject to the rules of section 411(a)(13)(A) set forth earlier in this preamble, as those rules are applied to PEP formulas during the period of PEP accruals and as those rules are applied to hypothetical account balance formulas after cessation of PEP accruals.

Under these proposed regulations, any other PEP formula (including those that do not credit interest, directly or indirectly, and those that offer actuarially equivalent forms of payment using specified actuarial factors applied after cessation of PEP accruals) would also be subject to the rules of section 411(a)(13)(A), as explained earlier in this preamble. Thus, for example, a PEP that does not explicitly credit interest but, instead, calculates the annuity benefit commencing at future ages as the actuarial equivalent of the PEP value as of cessation of PEP accruals would be eligible for the relief of section 411(a)(13)(A) with respect to the PEP value as of every period before cessation of PEP accruals. In addition, since the accrued benefit is calculated as an annuity commencing at normal retirement age that is actuarially equivalent to the PEP value as of cessation of PEP accruals, the relief described above that applies to annuities that are calculated as the actuarial equivalent of the then-current PEP value would not apply.

II. *Section 411(b)(1): Special rule with respect to statutory hybrid plans*

Under the regulations with respect to the 133. percent rule of section 411(b)(1)(B), for any plan year, social security benefits and all relevant factors used to compute benefits, e.g., consumer price index, are treated as remaining constant as of the beginning of the current plan year for all subsequent plan years. A number of commenters on both the 2007 proposed regulations and the 2008 proposed backloading regulations expressed concern that this rule might effectively preclude statutory hybrid plans from using an interest crediting rate that is a variable rate that could potentially be negative in a year, such as an equity-based rate. This is because, if a plan treated an interest crediting rate that was negative as remaining constant in all future years for purposes of the backloading test of section 411(b)(1)(B), a principal credit (such as a pay credit) that accrues in a later year would result in a greater benefit accrual than an otherwise identical principal credit that accrues in an earlier year because the principal credit that accrues later is credited with negative interest credits for fewer years. Thus, these commenters were concerned that a plan that uses a variable rate could fail the backloading rules of section 411(b)(1) even where both the pay crediting and interest crediting formulas do not vary over time.

In response to these comments, the proposed regulations contain a special rule regarding the application of the 133. percent rule of section 411(b)(1)(B) to a statutory hybrid plan that adjusts benefits using a variable interest crediting rate that can potentially be negative in any given year. Under this proposed rule, a plan that determines any portion of the participant's accrued benefit pursuant to a statutory hybrid benefit formula (as defined in § 1.411(a)(13)-1(d)(4)) that utilizes an interest crediting rate described in § 1.411(b)(5)-1(d) that is a variable rate that was less than zero for the prior plan year would not be treated as failing to satisfy the requirements of the 133. percent rule for the current plan year merely because the section 411(b)(1)(B) backloading calculation is performed assuming that the variable rate is zero for the current plan year and all future plan years.

III. *Section 411(b)(5): Special conversion protection rule and additional rules with respect to the market rate of return limitation*

A. *Comparison at effective date of conversion amendment*

In accordance with the requirements of section 411(b)(5)(B)(ii), the 2010 final regulations provide that a participant whose benefits are affected by a conversion amendment generally must be provided with a benefit after the conversion that is at least equal to the sum of benefits accrued through the date of conversion and benefits earned after the conversion, with no permitted interaction between the two portions. The 2010 final regulations provide for an alternative method of satisfying the conversion protection requirements where an opening hypothetical account balance or opening accumulated percentage of the participant's final average compensation is established at the time of the conversion and the plan provides for separate calculation of (1) the benefit attributable to the opening hypothetical account balance (including interest credits attributable thereto) or attributable to the opening accumulated percentage of the participant's final average compensation and (2) the benefit attributable to postconversion service under the post-conversion benefit formula. Under this alternative, the

plan must provide that, when a participant commences benefits, the participant's benefit will be increased if the benefit attributable to the opening hypothetical account or opening accumulated percentage that is payable in the particular optional form of benefit selected is less than the benefit accrued under the plan prior to the date of conversion and that was payable in the same generalized optional form of benefit (within the meaning of §1.411(d)-3(g)(8)) at the same annuity starting date.

The preamble to the 2007 proposed regulations requested comments on another alternative method of satisfying the conversion protection requirements that would not require this comparison at the annuity starting date. In response to favorable comments related to this alternative, these proposed regulations would provide that certain plans may satisfy the conversion protection requirements of sections 411(b)(5)(B)(ii), 411(b)(5)(B)(iii), and 411(b)(5)(B)(iv) by establishing an opening hypothetical account balance without a subsequent comparison of benefits at the annuity starting date. While testing at the annuity starting date would not be required under this method, a number of requirements like those described in the preamble to the 2007 proposed regulations would need to be satisfied in order to ensure that the hypothetical account balance used to replicate the pre-conversion benefit (the opening hypothetical account balance and interest credits on that account balance) is reasonably expected in most, but not necessarily all, cases to provide a benefit at least as large as the pre-conversion benefit for all periods after the conversion amendment.

This alternative method would be limited to situations where an opening hypothetical account balance is established and would not be available where an opening accumulated percentage of the participant's final average compensation is established because these plans would be unable to reliably replicate the preconversion benefit. This is because the value of the opening accumulated percentage would only increase as a result of unpredictable increases in compensation for periods after the conversion amendment until cessation of PEP accruals, rather than by application of an annual interest crediting rate.

This alternative would only be available where the participant elects to receive payment in the form of a single-sum distribution equal to the sum of the then-current balance of the hypothetical account used to replicate the pre-conversion benefit and the benefit attributable to post-conversion service under the post-conversion benefit formula. Because of the limited availability of this alternative, plans will still need to separately keep track of the pre-conversion benefit in order to satisfy the conversion protection requirements for all forms of distribution other than a single-sum distribution. See the related request for comments in this preamble under the heading "**Comments and Public Hearing.**"

Under this alternative, in order to satisfy the requirements of section 411(d)(6), the participant's benefit after the effective date of the conversion amendment must not be less than the participant's section 411(d)(6) protected benefit (as defined in §1.411(d)-3(g)(14)) with respect to service before the effective date of the conversion amendment (determined under the terms of the plan as in effect immediately before the effective date of the amendment). Also, the plan, as in effect immediately before the effective date of the conversion amendment, either must not have provided a singlesum payment option (for benefits that cannot be immediately distributed under section 411(a)(11)) or must have provided a single-sum payment option that was based solely on the present value of the benefit payable at normal retirement age (or at date of benefit commencement, if later) and which was not based on the present value of the benefit payable commencing at any date prior to normal retirement age. This condition ensures that the hypothetical account balance used to replicate the pre-conversion benefit does not result in a single-sum distribution that is less than would have been available under an early retirement subsidy under the pre-conversion formula.

Under this alternative method of satisfying the conversion protection requirements, the opening hypothetical account balance must be established in accordance with the rules under which this opening balance is not less than the present value, determined in accordance with section 417(e), of the accrued benefit immediately prior to the effective date of the conversion amendment. In addition, under this alternative, the interest crediting rate under the plan as of the effective date of the conversion amendment must be either the rate of interest on long-term investment grade corporate bonds (the third segment rate) or one of several specified safe harbor rates. Also, as of that date, the value of the index used to determine the interest crediting rate under the plan must be at least as great for every participant or beneficiary as the interest rate that was used to determine the opening hypothetical account balance. This requirement is satisfied, for example, if each participant's opening hypothetical account balance is determined using the applicable interest rate and applicable mortality table under section 417(e)(3), the interest crediting rate under the plan is the third segment rate, and, at the effective date of the conversion amendment, the third segment rate is the highest of the three segment rates. If, subsequent to the effective date of the conversion amendment, the interest crediting rate changes (whether by plan amendment or otherwise) with respect to a participant who was a participant at the time of the effective date of the conversion amendment from an interest crediting rate that is either the rate of interest on long-term investment grade corporate bonds or one of the specified safe harbor rates to a different interest crediting rate that is not in all cases at least as great as the prior interest crediting rate under the plan, then the new interest crediting rate does not apply to the existing hypothetical account balance as of the effective date of the change in interest crediting rates (or, if the plan created a subaccount consisting of the opening hypothetical account balance and interest credits on that subaccount, then the new interest crediting rate does not apply to the subaccount).

Finally, either the plan must provide a death benefit after the effective date of the conversion amendment which has a present value that is at all times at least equal to the then-current balance of the hypothetical account used to replicate the preconversion benefit or the plan must not have applied a pre-retirement mortality decrement in establishing the opening hypothetical account balance.

B. *Market rate of return*

The 2010 final regulations provide that a plan that credits interest must specify how the plan determines interest credits and must specify how and when interest credits are credited. In addition, the 2010 final regulations contain certain specific rules regarding the method and timing of interest credits, including a requirement that interest be credited at least annually.

The proposed regulations include a rule that would provide that a plan is not treated as failing to meet the interest crediting requirements merely because the plan does not provide for interest credits on amounts distributed prior to the end of the interest crediting period. Thus, if a plan credits interest at periodic intervals, the plan would not be required to credit interest on amounts that were distributed between the dates on which interest under the plan is credited to the account balance.

Furthermore, the proposed regulations include a rule that would allow plans to credit interest taking into account increases or decreases to the participant's accumulated benefit that occur during the period. In particular, the rule would provide that a plan is not treated as failing to meet the market rate of return limitations merely because the plan calculates increases or decreases to the participant's accumulated benefit by applying a rate of interest or rate of return (including a rate of increase or decrease under an index) to the participant's adjusted accumulated benefit (or portion thereof) for the period. For this purpose, the participant's adjusted accumulated benefit equals the participant's accumulated benefit as of the beginning of the period, adjusted for debits and credits (other than interest credits) made to the accumulated benefit prior to the end of the interest crediting period, with appropriate weighting for those debits and credits based on their timing within the period. For plans that calculate increases or decreases to the participant's accumulated benefit by applying a rate of interest or rate of return to the participant's adjusted accumulated benefit (or portion thereof) for the period, interest credits include these increases and decreases, to the extent provided under the terms of the plan at the beginning of the period and to the extent not conditioned on current service and not made on account of imputed service, and the interest crediting rate with respect to a participant equals the total amount of interest credits for the period divided by the participant's adjusted accumulated benefit for the period.

The proposed regulations would provide that the preservation of capital requirement is applied only at an annuity starting date on which a distribution of the participant's entire benefit as of that date under the plan's statutory hybrid benefit formula commences. The proposed regulations would also provide special rules to ensure that prior distributions are taken into account in determining the guarantee provided by the preservation of capital requirement with respect to a current distribution to which the rule applies.

These proposed regulations would broaden the list of permitted interest crediting rates from those permitted under the 2010 final regulations. A number of commenters on the 2007 proposed regulations requested that the rate of return on plan assets be treated as a market rate of return for all types of statutory hybrid plans, and not just indexed plans. In response to these comments, the proposed regulations would permit the use of the rate of return on plan assets as a market rate of return for statutory hybrid plans generally if the plan's assets are diversified so as to minimize the volatility of returns. Like the

2010 final regulations, the proposed regulations would provide that this requirement that plan assets be diversified so as to minimize the volatility of returns does not require greater diversification than is required under section 404(a)(1)(C) of Title I of the Employee Retirement Income Security Act of 1974, Public Law 93-406 (88 Stat. 829 (1974)) with respect to defined benefit pension plans.

The preamble to the 2007 proposed regulations asked for comments about the possibility of allowing an interest credit to be determined by reference to a rate of return on a regulated investment company (RIC) described in section 851. The preamble focused on whether such an investment has sufficiently constrained volatility that the existence of the capital preservation rule would not result in an above market rate of return. In response to comments received on the 2007 proposed regulations, these proposed regulations would provide that an interest crediting rate is not in excess of a market rate of return if it is equal to the rate of return on a RIC, as defined in section 851, that is reasonably expected to be not significantly more volatile than the broad United States equities market or a similarly broad international equities market. For example, a RIC that has most of its assets invested in securities of issuers (including other RICs) concentrated in an industry sector or a country other than the United States, that uses leverage, or that has significant investment in derivative financial products, for the purpose of achieving returns that amplify the returns of an unleveraged investment, generally would not meet this requirement. Thus, a RIC that has most of its investments concentrated in the semiconductor industry or that uses leverage in order to provide a rate of return that is twice the rate of return on the Standard & Poor's 500 index (S&P 500) would not meet this requirement. On the other hand, a RIC whose investments track the rate of return on the S&P 500, a broad-based "small-cap" index (such as the Russell 2000 index), or a broad-based international equities index would meet this requirement. The requirement that the RIC's investments not be concentrated in an industry sector or a specific international country is intended to limit the volatility of the returns, as well as the risk inherent in non-diversified investments. Similarly, the requirement that the RIC not provide leveraged returns is intended both to ensure that rates provided by the RIC do not exceed an unleveraged market rate as well as to limit the volatility of the returns provided. Subject to these requirements, the proposed rule is intended to provide plan sponsors with greater flexibility in choosing an equity-based rate than would be provided if the regulations were to list particular equity-based rates that satisfy the market rate of return requirement.

The preamble to the 2007 proposed regulations requested comments as to how to implement a rule that provides that interest credits are determined under the greater of two or more interest crediting rates without violating the market rate of return limitation. In response to such comments, these proposed regulations would provide that in certain limited circumstances a plan can provide interest credits based on the greater of two or more interest crediting rates without exceeding a market rate of return.

The Treasury Department and the IRS have modeled the historical distribution of rates of interest on long-term investment grade corporate bonds and have determined that those rates have only infrequently been lower than 4 percent and, when lower, were generally lower by small amounts and for limited durations. Therefore, the increase in the effective rate of return resulting from adding an annual 4 percent floor to one of these bond rates has historically been small enough that the effective rate of return is not in excess of a market rate of return. As a result, the proposed rules would provide that it is permissible for a plan to utilize an annual floor of 4 percent in conjunction with a permissible bond rate. Specifically, the proposed regulations would provide that a plan does not provide an interest crediting rate that is in excess of a market rate of return merely because the plan provides that the interest crediting rate for an interest crediting period equals the greater of the rate of interest on long-term investment grade corporate bonds (or one of the safe harbor rates that, under the regulations, are deemed not to be in excess of that rate) and an annual interest rate of 4 percent.

This rule permitting a plan to utilize an annual floor of 4 percent in conjunction with a permissible bond-based rate would also permit plans that credit interest more frequently than annually using a permissible bond-based rate to also utilize a periodic floor that is a pro rata portion of an annual 4 percent floor. Thus, plans that credit interest more frequently than annually could provide an effective annual floor that is greater than 4 percent, both due to the effect of compounding because the floor would be applied more frequently than annually and because the floor would be applied in any period that the bond-based rate was below the floor, even if the annual rate exceeded 4 percent for the plan year. However, given the nature of bond-based rates, including the serial correlation of rates from one period to the next, as well as the fact that 4 percent is not expected to exceed a permissible bond-based rate except infrequently, by small amounts, and for limited durations, in most instances a periodic floor that is based on a 4 percent annual floor will not provide a floor that is significantly different than an annual floor of 4 percent.

In contrast, because of the volatility of equity-based rates, adding an annual floor to an equity-based rate often provides a cumulative rate of return that far exceeds the rate of return provided by the equity-based rate without such floor. It should also be noted that commenters on the 2007 proposed regulations generally did not request that such an annual floor be permitted (perhaps in recognition that a minimum guaranteed annual return when applied to equity-based rates could have a significant impact on funding). Accordingly, the proposed regulations would not allow the use of an annual floor in conjunction with the rate of return on plan assets or on a permissible RIC.

On the other hand, if, instead of applying a floor on each year's rate of return, a cumulative floor is applied to an equity-based rate, the effective rate of return is not necessarily substantially greater than the rate of return provided without the floor. Specifically, the Treasury Department and the IRS have determined that, based on the modeling of long-term historical returns, a 3 percent floor that applies cumulatively (in the aggregate from the date of each principal credit until the annuity starting date, without a floor on the rate of return provided in any interim period) could be combined with any permissible rate (including a permissible equity-based rate), without increasing the effective rate of return to such an extent that the effective rate of return would be in excess of a market rate of return. As a result, the proposed rule would provide that a plan that determines interest credits using any particular interest crediting rate that satisfies the market rate of return limitation does not provide an effective interest crediting rate in excess of a market rate of return merely because the plan provides that the participant's benefit, as of the participant's annuity starting date, is equal to the greater of the benefit determined using the interest crediting rate and the benefit determined as if the plan had used a fixed annual interest crediting rate equal to 3 percent (or a rate not in excess of 3 percent) for principal credits in all years. This rule in the proposed regulations that allows for plans to utilize a cumulative floor of up to 3 percent would also allow plans some additional flexibility in design. Thus, for example, a plan that utilizes annual ceilings in conjunction with a permissible rate could also provide a cumulative floor of up to 3 percent.

Similar to the rules with respect to application of the preservation of capital requirement, the proposed regulations would provide that the determination of the guarantee provided by any cumulative floor with respect to the participant's benefit is made only at an annuity starting date on which a distribution of the participant's entire benefit as of that date under the plan's statutory hybrid benefit formula commences. The proposed regulations would also provide special rules to ensure that prior distributions are taken into account in determining whether the guarantee exceeds the benefit otherwise provided under the plan.

In addition to permitting certain fixed floors to be applied to variable rates, the proposed regulations would also permit a standalone fixed rate of interest to be used for interest crediting purposes. While the statutory language at section 411(b)(5)(B)(i)(I) does not explicitly reference a fixed interest crediting rate, the reference to "a reasonable minimum guaranteed rate of return" and the reference to "the greater of a fixed or variable rate of return" necessarily mean that some fixed rate must also be permissible. Further, the statutory language at section 411(b)(5)(B)(i)(III) specifically authorizes the Treasury Department to issue regulations permitting a fixed rate of interest under the rules relating to a market rate of return. However, reconciling a fixed interest crediting rate with the statutory requirement that an interest crediting rate " *for any plan year* shall be at a rate which is not greater than a market rate of return" [emphasis added] presents unique challenges because, by definition, fixed rates do not adjust with the market. As a result, the use of any fixed rate will result in an interest crediting rate that is above a then-current market rate of interest during any period in which the current market rate falls below the fixed rate.

In light of this fact, the Treasury Department and the IRS believe that, in order to satisfy the market rate of return requirement, any fixed interest crediting rate allowed under the rules must not be expected to exceed future market rates of interest, except infrequently, by small amounts, and for limited durations. Based on the historical modeling described above, the Treasury Department and the IRS have determined that a 5 percent fixed rate satisfies these criteria and that any higher fixed rate would result in an effective rate of return that is in excess of a market rate of return.

Specifically, the proposed rules would provide that an annual interest crediting rate of a fixed 5 percent is a safe harbor rate deemed to be not

in excess of the rate of interest on long-term investment grade corporate bonds. As a result, an interest crediting rate of a fixed 5 percent would satisfy the market rate of return limitation. In addition, the special section 411(d)(6) rule set forth in the 2010 final regulations with respect to certain changes in interest crediting rates would apply to an interest crediting rate of a fixed 5 percent and, as a result, a plan amendment that changes the interest crediting rate under the plan to the third segment rate from a fixed 5 percent is deemed to satisfy the requirements of section 411(d)(6), provided certain requirements are met.

The 2010 final regulations provide that §§1.411(b)(5)-1(d)(1)(iii), 1.411(b)(5)-1(d)(1)(vi), and 1.411(b)(5)-1(d)(6), which provide that the regulations set forth the exclusive list of interest crediting rates and combinations of interest crediting rates that satisfy the market rate of return requirement under section 411(b)(5), apply to plan years that begin on or after January 1, 2012. For plan years that begin before January 1, 2012, statutory hybrid plans may utilize a rate that is permissible under the 2010 final regulations or these proposed regulations for purposes of satisfying the statutory market rate of return requirement.

C. *Plan termination*

The proposed regulations would provide guidance with respect to the application of the rules of section 411(b)(5)(B)(vi), which require special plan provisions relating to interest crediting rates and annuity conversion rates that apply when the plan is terminated. Under the proposed regulations, a statutory hybrid plan is treated as meeting the market rate of return requirements only if the terms of the plan satisfy the rules in the regulations relating to section 411(b)(5)(B)(vi). Title IV of ERISA also imposes special rules that apply when a single employer pension plan is terminated (including special rules relating to plan amendments). See regulations of the Pension Benefit Guaranty Corporation for additional rules that apply when a pension plan is terminated.

These proposed regulations reflect the statutory requirement that a plan provide that, if the interest crediting rate used to determine a participant's accumulated benefit (or a portion thereof) varied (that is, was not a constant fixed rate) during the 5-year period ending on the plan termination date, then the interest crediting rate used to determine the participant's accumulated benefit under the plan after the date of plan termination is equal to the average of the rates used under the plan during the 5-year period ending on the plan termination date. If the interest crediting rate used to determine a participant's accumulated benefit (or a portion thereof) was instead a single fixed rate for all periods during the 5-year period ending on the plan termination date, then the interest crediting rate used to determine the participant's accumulated benefit after the date of plan termination would be equal to that fixed rate.

Under this rule, the interest crediting rate used after plan termination would be based on the average of the rates that applied under the plan during the 5-year period preceding plan termination, without regard to whether this average rate exceeds thencurrent market rates of return (but, in determining the average rate, a rate would only be taken into account to the extent that the rate did not exceed a market rate of return when the rate actually applied). For purposes of this calculation, the proposed regulations would provide that, subject to certain other rules described in this preamble, the average of the rates used under the plan during the 5-year period ending on the termination date is determined with respect to a participant as the arithmetic average, expressed as an annual rate, of the applicable interest crediting rates that applied in the 5-year period. In determining this average, each interest crediting period for which the interest crediting date is within the 5-year period ending on the plan termination date would be taken into account, with interest crediting rates for periods that are less than a year in length adjusted and weighted proportionally. However, under this rule, if a period begins on or before the date that is 5 years before the termination date and ends within the 5-year period ending on the plan termination date, the period would be weighted as though the entire period were within the 5-year period ending on the plan termination date.

Section 411(b)(5)(B)(vi) does not explicitly provide rules with respect to plans that determine interest credits based on equity-based rates of return that may involve potential losses. Since the trailing 5-year average of an equity-based rate of return may have little, if any, correlation to the actual future equity-based rate of return, the Treasury Department and the IRS do not believe it is appropriate to provide that the trailing 5-year average of such rate of return be used to determine benefits after plan termination. In such cases, the Treasury Department and the IRS believe that it is appropriate to apply a bond-based rule instead. Thus, the proposed regulations would provide that, with respect to an interest crediting rate used to determine a participant's accumulated benefit for an interest crediting period during the 5-year period ending on the termination date that is not a fixed interest rate or a bond-based rate of interest (or is based on a variable rate that is not permissible under the regulations), the terms of the plan must provide that, for purposes of determining the average upon plan termination, the interest crediting rate for the interest crediting period is deemed to be equal to the third segment rate for the last calendar month ending before the beginning of the interest crediting period, as adjusted for any actual applicable floors and ceilings that applied to the rate of return in the period, but without regard to any reductions that applied to the rate of return in the period. Thus, for example, if the actual interest crediting rate in an interest crediting period was equal to the rate of return on plan assets, but not greater than 5 percent, then for purposes of determining the plan's average interest crediting rate, the interest crediting rate for that interest crediting period would be deemed to equal to the lesser of the applicable third segment rate for the period and 5 percent. However, if the actual interest crediting rate in an interest crediting period was equal to the rate of return on plan assets minus 200 basis points, then for purposes of determining the plan's average interest crediting rate, the interest crediting rate for that interest crediting period would be deemed to equal the third segment rate (not the third segment rate minus 200 basis points). See the request for comments in this preamble under the heading "**Comments and Public Hearing**" regarding the application of floors, ceilings, and reductions for purposes of the plan termination provisions when the third segment rate is substituted for an equity-based rate.

As provided in section 411(b)(5)(B)(i), the regulations require that the terms of the plan also provide that the interest rate and mortality table (including tabular adjustment factors) used on and after plan termination for purposes of determining the amount of any benefit under the plan payable in the form of an annuity (commencing at or after normal retirement age) be based on the interest rate and mortality table specified under the plan for that purpose as of the termination date, except that if the interest rate is a variable rate, the interest rate is instead based on the rules described in the preceding paragraphs of this preamble using a 5-year average.

A number of special rules apply for purposes of determining the interest crediting rate that applies after plan termination. In particular, for purposes of determining the average rate during the five-year period ending on plan termination, the interest crediting rate that applied for each interest crediting period is generally the ongoing interest crediting rate that was specified under the plan in that period, without regard to any section 411(d)(6) protected benefit using an old interest crediting rate. However, if, at the end of the last interest crediting period prior to plan termination, the participant's accumulated benefit is based on a section 411(d)(6) protected benefit that results from a prior amendment to change the rate of interest crediting applicable under the plan, then, for purposes of determining the average rate, the pre-amendment interest crediting rate is treated as having applied for each interest crediting period after the date of the interest crediting rate change. In addition, the proposed regulations would provide that if the plan determines a participant's interest credits in any interest crediting period by applying different rates to different predetermined portions of the accumulated benefit as permissible under the regulations, then the participant's interest crediting rate for the interest crediting period is assumed for purposes of the plan termination provisions to be the weighted average of the fixed interest rates, determined under the plan termination rules, that apply to each portion of the accumulated benefit.

Furthermore, to reduce the administrative burden and to determine the average rate for each participant based on 5 years of interest crediting data, if the plan provided for interest credits for any interest crediting period in which, pursuant to the terms of the plan, the individual was not eligible to receive interest credits (because the individual was not a participant or beneficiary in the relevant interest crediting period or otherwise), then, for purposes of determining the interest crediting rate that applies after plan termination, the individual is treated as though the individual received interest credits in that period using the interest crediting rate that applied in that period under the terms of the plan to determine the benefit of a similarly situated participant or beneficiary who was eligible to receive interest credits. However, if, under the terms of the plan, the individual was not eligible to receive any interest credits during the entire 5-year period ending on the plan termination date, then the rules fixing the interest crediting rate do not apply to determine the individual's benefit after plan termination.

The proposed regulations include examples to illustrate the application of these plan termination rules, including how these rules would apply where a plan bases its interest crediting rate on a weighted average of more than one rate, how these rules would apply where the plan's ongoing interest crediting rate is an equity-based rate of return, and how these rules would apply to a participant whose benefits are determined where the plan had switched interest crediting rates in the past and where the interest credit prior to termination was determined by applying the old rate to the benefit attributable to principal credits before the applicable amendment date.

D. *Special rule with respect to changes in interest crediting rates where plan provides section 411(d)(6) protection*

An inherent tension exists between the requirement not to reduce a participant's accrued benefit and the requirement that an interest crediting rate not be in excess of a market rate of return that makes changes in interest crediting rates difficult to implement for statutory hybrid plans in many circumstances. This is because, in order to satisfy section 411(d)(6), a participant's benefit can never be less than the pre-amendment benefit increased for periods after the amendment using the pre-amendment interest crediting rate, thereby effectively requiring a minimum interest crediting rate. In light of this tension, the proposed regulations would create a special market rate of return rule that applies in the case of an amendment to change the plan's interest crediting rate.

In particular, the proposed rule would provide that, in the case of an amendment to change a plan's interest crediting rate for periods after the applicable amendment date from one interest crediting rate (the old rate) that is not in excess of a market rate of return to another interest crediting rate (the new rate) that is not in excess of a market rate of return, the plan's effective interest crediting rate is not in excess of a market rate of return merely because the plan provides for the benefit of any participant who is benefiting under the plan on the applicable amendment date to never be less than what it would be if the old rate had continued but without taking into account any principal credits after the applicable amendment date. A pattern of repeated plan amendments each of which provides for a prospective change in the plan's interest crediting rate with respect to the benefit as of the applicable amendment date will be treated as resulting in the ongoing plan terms providing that the interest crediting rate equals the greater of each of the interest crediting rates, so that the special rule in the preceding sentence would not apply. See § 1.411(d)-4, A-1(c)(1). Thus, in such cases the plan will be treated as providing a rate of return that is in excess of a market rate of return, unless the resulting greater-of rate satisfies the market rate of return rules.

E. *Special rule with respect to interest crediting rate after normal retirement age*

In coordination with the rules under section 411(a)(13)(A) (as described in section I of this preamble) that apply with respect to the benefit determined as of each annuity starting date after normal retirement age, the proposed regulations would provide that a statutory hybrid plan is not treated as providing an effective interest crediting rate that is in excess of a market rate of return merely because the plan provides that the participant's benefit, as of each annuity starting date after normal retirement age, is equal to the greater of the benefit determined using an interest crediting rate that is not otherwise in excess of a market rate of return and the benefit that satisfies the requirements of section 411(a)(2). Thus, for example, a cash balance plan would not be treated as providing an effective interest crediting rate in excess of a market rate of return merely because the plan credits interest after normal retirement age at a rate that is sufficient to provide any required actuarial increases.

IV. *Changes in interest crediting rates and Code section 411(d)(6)*

A. *Background*

An amendment to change a plan's interest crediting rate that only applies with respect to benefits that have not yet accrued (such as where the plan establishes a second hypothetical account balance for future principal credits to which a different interest crediting rate is applied) would not result in a reduction in accrued benefits attributable to service before the applicable amendment date and, therefore, such a change would not violate section 411(d)(6).[4] However, except to the extent permitted under section 1107 of PPA '06 or as otherwise described in section IV of this preamble, an amendment to change a plan's future interest crediting rate with respect to benefits that have

---

[4] However, see section 204(h) of ERISA and section 4980F of the Code for notice requirements relating to amendments that provide for a significant reduction in the rate of future benefit accrual.

already accrued (in other words, with respect to an existing account balance) must satisfy section 411(d)(6) if the change could result in interest credits that are smaller as of any date after the applicable amendment date than the interest credits that would be credited without regard to the amendment.[5]

B. *Special section 411(d)(6) rule with respect to changes in future interest crediting rates*

Under the 2010 final regulations, a plan is not treated as providing smaller interest credits after the applicable amendment date merely because the amendment changes the plan's future interest crediting rate with respect to benefits that have already accrued to the rate of interest on long-term investment grade corporate bonds (the third segment rate under section 430(h)(2)(C)(iii)) from one of the other bond-based safe harbor rates permitted under the 2010 final regulations (for example, a rate based on Treasury bonds with any of the margins specified in the regulations or an eligible cost-of-living index). However, the change is permitted only if: (1) the effective date of the amendment is at least 30 days after adoption, (2) the new interest crediting rate only applies to interest to be credited after the effective date of the amendment, and (3) on the effective date of the amendment, the new interest crediting rate is not lower than the interest crediting rate that would have applied in the absence of the amendment.

C. *Changes that would otherwise violate section 411(d)(6) but that are made to the extent necessary to satisfy section 411(b)(5)*

After these proposed regulations under sections 411(a)(13) and 411(b)(5) are issued as final regulations, it is expected that relief from the requirements of section 411(d)(6) will be granted for a plan amendment that eliminates or reduces a section 411(d)(6) protected benefit, provided that the amendment is adopted before those final regulations apply to the plan, and the elimination or reduction is made only to the extent necessary to enable the plan to meet the requirements of section 411(b)(5).[6] It is expected that this section 411(d)(6) relief will be available in the case of an amendment that reduces the future interest crediting rate with respect to benefits that have already accrued from a rate that is in excess of a market rate of return under the final market rate of return rules to the extent necessary to constitute a permissible rate under the final market rate of return rules. However, it is expected that this relief would not permit a plan with an interest crediting rate within the list of permitted rates under the final market rate of return rules to change to another permitted rate because the change would not be necessary to enable the plan to satisfy the requirements of section 411(b)(5). Similarly, it is expected that this relief would not permit a plan with an interest crediting rate that is impermissible under the final market rate of return rules to change to a permissible rate using less than the maximum permitted margin for that rate because the reduction would be more than necessary to enable the plan to satisfy the requirements of section 411(b)(5). For purposes of the preceding sentence, a rate without an associated margin is treated as having a maximum permitted margin of zero. See the request for comments, under the heading "**Comments and Public Hearing**" in this preamble, regarding limitations on the scope of this anticipated relief under § 1.411(d)-4, A-2(b)(2)(i) because the relief must be limited to amendments that change a plan's interest crediting rate only to the extent necessary to enable the plan to satisfy the requirements of section 411(b)(5).

Proposed Effective/Applicability Dates

The specific rules that would be implemented under the proposed regulations generally would apply to plan years that begin on or after January 1, 2012. However, as stated in the preamble to the 2010 final regulations, a plan is permitted to rely on the provisions of these proposed regulations, as well as the 2010 final regulations, the 2007 proposed regulations, and Notice 2007-6, for purposes of satisfying the requirements of sections 411(a)(13) and 411(b)(5) for periods before the regulatory effective date.

Special Analyses

It has been determined that these proposed regulations are not a significant regulatory action as defined in Executive Order 12866. Therefore, a regulatory assessment is not required. It also has been determined that section 553(b) of the Administrative Procedure Act (5 U.S.C. chapter 5) does not apply to these regulations, and because the regulation does not impose a collection of information on small entities, the Regulatory Flexibility Act (5 U.S.C. chapter 6) does not apply. Pursuant to section 7805(f) of the Code, these regulations have been submitted to the Chief Counsel for Advocacy of the Small Business Administration for comment on its impact on small business.

Comments and Public Hearing

Before these proposed regulations are adopted as final regulations, consideration will be given to any written (a signed original and eight (8) copies) or electronic comments that are submitted timely to the IRS. The Treasury Department and the IRS specifically request comments on the clarity of the proposed regulations and how they may be made easier to understand.

In addition to comments on issues addressed in these proposed regulations, the Treasury Department and the IRS specifically request comments on the following issues:

- Should a defined benefit plan that expresses a participant's accumulated benefit as a current single-sum dollar amount and that does not provide for interest credits be excluded from the definition of a statutory hybrid plan?

- In the case of a statutory hybrid plan that credits interest using an interest crediting rate equal to the rate of return on a RIC, how does section 411(d)(6) apply if the underlying RIC subsequently ceases to exist?

- The proposed regulations permit certain fixed interest crediting rates (a fixed 5 percent rate for any year, the greater of 4 percent or certain bond-based indices for any year, and a cumulative minimum 3 percent annual rate). Comments regarding these specific proposed rules should take into account how any general legal standard for a market rate of return would be applied in different economic circumstances with variable interest rate markets, as well as the related ability that would generally be available under these proposed regulations at § 1.411(b)(5)-1(e)(3)(iii) for the plan sponsor to change the crediting rate on an existing hypothetical account balance for active participants from one interest crediting rate to another, including the risk that whatever fixed rate is permitted might allow a plan's interest credits to exceed market rates of interest either frequently, by an amount that might be large, or for an extended duration. Commenters recommending any additional types of rates of return than those in these proposed regulations should justify how those rates meet a market rate of return, taking into account the minimum guarantee rules.

- Should a statutory hybrid plan be able to offer participants a menu of hypothetical investment options (including a life-cycle investment option, whereby participants are automatically transitioned incrementally at certain ages from a blended rate that is more heavily equity-weighted to a rate that is more heavily bond-weighted) and, if so, what plan qualification issues (i.e., forfeiture, section 411(d)(6), market rate of return, and other section 411(b)(5) issues) arise under such a plan design? In particular, do the following events raise issues: (1) a participant elects to switch from one investment option to another; (2) a bond index or RIC underlying one of the investment options ceases to exist; (3) the plan is amended to eliminate an investment option; (4) a participant elects to switch from an investment option with a cumulative minimum to an investment option without a cumulative minimum (or vice versa); or (5) the plan is terminated and, pursuant to the special rules that apply upon plan termination, the interest crediting rate that applies to determine a participant's benefit after plan termination must be fixed?

- How does a statutory hybrid plan that provides benefits under a statutory hybrid benefit formula other than a lump sum-based benefit formula (such as a plan that provides for indexing as described in section 411(b)(5)(E)) — a plan to which section 411(a)(13)(A) does not apply — ensure compliance with the minimum present value rules of section 417(e)?

- How does a statutory hybrid plan determine the section 417(e) minimum present value of the participant's benefit where a portion of the benefit is determined based partly on the benefit under a lump sum-based benefit formula, although that portion is not determined under a lump sum-based benefit formula? For example, where a portion of the accrued benefit is equal to the excess of the benefit under a

---

[5] Except to the extent permitted under section 411(d)(6) and §§ 1.411(d)-3 and 1.411(d)-4, another Code provision, or another statutory provision such as section 1107 of PPA '06, section 411(d)(6) prohibits a plan amendment that decreases a participant's accrued benefits or that has the effect of eliminating or reducing an early retirement benefit or retirement-type subsidy, or eliminating an optional form of benefit, with respect to benefits attributable to service before the amendment.

[6] Announcement 2009-82 and Notice 2009-97 stated that the IRS and the Treasury Department expected to provide such relief. While Notice 2009-97 indicated the relief would only apply if the amendment is adopted by the last day of the first plan year that begins on or after January 1, 2010, this preamble supersedes that applicability date to provide that it is expected that this relief would apply if the amendment is adopted before final regulations that finalize these proposed regulations apply to the plan.

traditional defined benefit formula over the benefit under a hypothetical account formula, how is the present value of that portion of the accrued benefit determined?

• Should the proposed alternative method of satisfying the conversion protection requirements that does not require a comparison of benefits at the annuity starting date be broadened to apply to forms of distribution other than a single-sum distribution? If this rule should be broadened, what rules would ensure that the benefit attributable to the opening hypothetical account balance is not less than the benefit available under the same generalized optional form under the pre-conversion formula (which may include subsidized early retirement benefits and other retirement-type subsidies) consistent with the goal of having a simplified alternative?

• How does a statutory hybrid plan that uses a variable interest crediting rate that may potentially be negative satisfy the fractional rule of section 411(b)(1)(C) if the 133. percent rule of section 411(b)(1)(B) is not satisfied?

• For purposes of the plan termination rules, should a floor, ceiling, or reduction that applied to an equity-based rate in an interest crediting period be treated as applying in the same manner to the third segment rate or is it appropriate for such an adjustment to be disregarded or otherwise modified for purposes of such rules?

• Under the relief to be provided pursuant to §1.411(d)-4, A-2(b)(2)(i), which authorizes amendments that reduce a section 411(d)(6) protected benefit only to the extent necessary to satisfy the requirements of section 411(b)(5), should a statutory hybrid plan with an interest crediting rate that is impermissible under the final market rate of return rules be permitted to be amended to change the future interest crediting rate with respect to benefits that have already accrued to any permissible rate using the maximum permitted margin for that rate or should that be dependent upon the reasons that the pre-amendment rate exceeded a market rate of return? Thus, for example, should a plan with an impermissible bond-based rate (without a fixed component) be permitted to switch to any permissible rate, bond-based or otherwise, using the maximum permitted margin for that rate? Should a plan with an impermissibly high standalone fixed rate be permitted to switch to the maximum rate of any type, should it be permitted to switch to the maximum permitted bond-based rate with the maximum permitted floor for that rate (the third segment rate with a fixed 4 percent floor), or must it switch to the maximum permitted standalone fixed rate (a fixed rate of 5 percent)? Should a plan with a permissible bond-based rate but with an impermissibly high fixed floor be permitted to switch to the maximum rate of any type, should it be permitted to retain the pre-amendment bond-based rate while reducing the floor to the maximum permitted floor for that rate (a fixed 4 percent floor), should it be permitted to switch to the maximum permitted standalone fixed rate (a fixed rate of 5 percent), or must it switch to the maximum permitted bond-based rate with the maximum permitted floor for that rate (the third segment rate with a fixed 4 percent floor)?

All comments will be available for public inspection and copying. A public hearing has been scheduled for Wednesday, January 26, 2011, beginning at 10 a.m. in the Auditorium, Internal Revenue Service, 1111 Constitution Avenue, NW., Washington, DC. Due to building security procedures, visitors must enter at the Constitution Avenue entrance. In addition, all visitors must present photo identification to enter the building. Because of access restrictions, visitors will not be admitted beyond the immediate entrance area more than 30 minutes before the hearing starts. For information about having your name placed on the building access list to attend the hearing, see the " **FOR FURTHER INFORMATION CONTACT**" section of this preamble.

The rules of 26 CFR 601.601(a)(3) apply to the hearing. Persons who wish to present oral comments at the hearing must submit written or electronic comments by Wednesday, January 12, 2011, and an outline of topics to be discussed and the amount of time to be devoted to each topic (a signed original and eight (8) copies) by Friday, January 14, 2011. A period of 10 minutes will be allotted to each person for making comments. An agenda showing the scheduling of the speakers will be prepared after the deadline for receiving outlines has passed. Copies of the agenda will be available free of charge at the hearing.

Drafting Information

The principal authors of these regulations are Neil S. Sandhu, Lauson C. Green, and Linda S. F. Marshall, Office of Division Counsel/Associate Chief Counsel (Tax Exempt and Government Entities). However, other personnel from the IRS and the Treasury Department participated in the development of these regulations.

List of Subjects in 26 CFR Part 1

Income taxes, Reporting and recordkeeping requirements.

Proposed Amendments to the Regulations

Accordingly, 26 CFR part 1 is proposed to be amended as follows:

PART 1—INCOME TAXES

Paragraph 1. The authority citation for part 1 continues to read in part as follows:

Authority: 26 U.S.C. 7805 * * *

Par. 2. Section 1.411(a)(13)-1 is amended by revising paragraphs (b)(2), (b)(3), (b)(4), and (e)(2)(ii) to read as follows:

§ 1.411(a)(13)-1 Statutory hybrid plans.

* * * * *

(b) * * *

(2) *Requirements that lump sum-based benefit formula must satisfy to obtain relief*—(i) *In general.* The relief of paragraph (b)(1) of this section does not apply with respect to benefits determined under a lump sum-based benefit formula unless the requirements of paragraphs (b)(2)(ii) through (iv) of this section are satisfied.

(ii) *Benefit on or before normal retirement age.* A plan satisfies this paragraph (b)(2)(ii) only if, at all times on or before normal retirement age, the then-current balance of the hypothetical account or the then-current value of the accumulated percentage of the participant's final average compensation is not less than the present value, determined using reasonable actuarial assumptions, of the portion of the participant's accrued benefit that is determined under the lump sum-based benefit formula. However, a plan is deemed to satisfy the requirement in the preceding sentence for periods before normal retirement age if, upon attainment of normal retirement age, the then-current balance of the hypothetical account or the then-current value of the accumulated percentage of the participant's final average compensation is actuarially equivalent (using reasonable actuarial assumptions) to the portion of the participant's accrued benefit that is determined under the lump sum-based benefit formula.

(iii) *Benefit after normal retirement age.* A plan satisfies this paragraph (b)(2)(iii) only if, as of each annuity starting date after normal retirement age, the then-current balance of the hypothetical account or the then-current value of the accumulated percentage of the participant's final average compensation—

(A) Satisfies the requirements of section 411(a)(2); or

(B) Would satisfy the requirements of section 411(a)(2) but for the fact that the plan suspends benefits in accordance with section 411(a)(3)(B).

(iv) *Reductions limited.* A plan satisfies this paragraph (b)(2)(iv) only if the balance of the hypothetical account or accumulated percentage of the participant's final average compensation may not be reduced except as a result of—

(A) Benefit payments under paragraph (b)(3) of this section;

(B) Qualified domestic relations orders under section 414(p);

(C) Forfeitures that are permitted under section 411(a) (such as charges for providing a qualified preretirement survivor annuity);

(D) Amendments that are permitted under section 411(d)(6); or

(E) Adjustments resulting from the application of interest credits (under the rules of §1.411(b)(5)-1) that are negative for a period, for plans that express the accumulated benefit as the balance of a hypothetical account.

(3) *Alternative forms of distribution under a lump sum-based benefit formula*—(i) *Payment of current account balance or current value.* The relief of paragraph (b)(1) of this section applies with respect to a single-sum payment equal to the then-current balance of a hypothetical account maintained for the participant or the then-current value of an accumulated percentage of the participant's final average compensation.

(ii) *Payment of benefits that are actuarially equivalent to current account balance or current value.* With respect to the benefits under a lump sum-based benefit formula, the relief of paragraph (b)(1) of this section applies to an optional form of benefit that is determined as of the annuity starting date as the actuarial equivalent, using reasonable actuarial assumptions, of the then-current balance of a hypothetical account maintained for the participant or the then-current value of an accumulated percentage of the participant's final average compensation.

(iii) *Payment of benefits based on immediate annuity.* With respect to the benefits under a lump sum-based benefit formula, the relief of paragraph (b)(1) of this section applies to an optional form of benefit that is not subject to the minimum present value requirements of section 417(e) and that is determined under the plan as of the annuity starting date as the actuarial equivalent (using reasonable actuarial assumptions) of the optional form of benefit that—

(A) Commences as of the same annuity starting date;

(B) Is payable in the same generalized optional form (within the meaning of §1.411(d)-3(g)(8)) as the accrued benefit; and

(C) Is the actuarial equivalent (using reasonable actuarial assumptions) of the then-current balance of a hypothetical account maintained for the participant or the then-current value of an accumulated percentage of the participant's final average compensation.

(iv) *Payment of portion of current account balance or current value.* The relief of paragraph (b)(1) of this section applies on a proportionate basis to a payment of a portion of the benefit under a lump sum-based benefit formula that is not paid in a form otherwise described in this paragraph (b)(3), such as a payment of a specified dollar amount or percentage of the then-current balance of a hypothetical account maintained for the participant or then-current value of an accumulated percentage of the participant's final average compensation. Thus, for example, if a plan that expresses the participant's entire accumulated benefit as the balance of a hypothetical account distributes 40 percent of the participant's then-current hypothetical account balance in a single payment, the plan is treated as satisfying the requirements of section 411(a) and the minimum present value rules of section 417(e) with respect to 40 percent of the participant's then-current accrued benefit. See paragraph (b)(3)(ii) or (iii) of this section for relief applicable with respect to a distribution with respect to the remainder (60 percent) of the participant's accumulated benefit.

(v) *Conditions for applicability.* This paragraph (b)(3) applies to a payment of benefits under a lump sum-based benefit formula only if the requirements of paragraph (b)(2) of this section are also satisfied.

(4) *Rules of application.* The relief of paragraph (b)(1) of this section applies only to the portion of the participant's benefit that is determined under a lump sum-based benefit formula and does not apply to any portion of the participant's benefit that is determined under a formula that is not a lump sum-based benefit formula. Thus, the following rules apply:

(i) *Greater-of formulas.* Where the participant's accrued benefit equals the greater of the benefit under a lump sum-based benefit formula and the benefit under another formula, a single-sum payment of the participant's entire benefit must equal the greater of the then-current accumulated benefit under the lump sum-based benefit formula and the present value, determined in accordance with section 417(e), of the benefit under the other formula. Applying this rule where the non-lump sum-based benefit formula provides a benefit equal to a pro rata portion of the benefit determined by projecting a future hypothetical account balance (including future principal credits), a single-sum payment of the participant's entire benefit must equal the greater of the then-current balance of the hypothetical account and the present value, determined in accordance with section 417(e), of the pro-rata benefit determined by projecting the future hypothetical account balance.

(ii) *"Sum-of" formulas.* Where the accrued benefit equals the sum of the benefit under a lump sum-based benefit formula plus the excess of the benefit under another formula over the benefit under the lump sum-based benefit formula, a single-sum payment of the participant's entire benefit must equal the then-current accumulated benefit under the lump sum-based benefit formula plus the excess of the present value, determined in accordance with section 417(e), of the benefit under the other formula over the present value, determined in accordance with section 417(e), of the benefit under the lump sum-based benefit formula.

* * * * *

(e) * * *

(2) * * *

(ii) *Special effective date.* Paragraphs (b)(2), (b)(3), and (b)(4) of this section apply to plan years that begin on or after January 1, 2012.

* * * * *

Par. 3. Section 1.411(b)-1 is amended by adding paragraph (b)(2)(ii)(G) and (b)(2)(ii)(H) to read as follows:

§ *1.411(b)-1 Accrued benefit requirements.*

* * * * *

(b) * * *

(2) * * *

(ii) * * *

(G) Special rule for multiple formulas. [Reserved]

(H) *Variable interest crediting rate under a statutory hybrid benefit formula.* For plan years that begin on or after January 1, 2012, a plan that determines any portion of the participant's accrued benefit pursuant to a statutory hybrid benefit formula (as defined in §1.411(a)(13)-1(d)(4)) that utilizes an interest crediting rate described in §1.411(b)(5)-1(d) that is a variable rate that was less than zero for the prior plan year is not treated as failing to satisfy the requirements of paragraph (b)(2) of this section for the current plan year merely because the plan assumes for purposes of paragraph (b)(2) of this section that the variable rate is zero for the current plan year and all future plan years.

* * * * *

Par. 4. Section 1.411(b)(5)-1 is amended by:

1. Revising paragraph (c)(3)(iii).

2. Adding *Example 8* to paragraph (c)(5).

3. Revising paragraphs (d)(1)(iv)(D), (d)(2)(ii), (d)(4)(iv), (d)(5)(ii), (d)(5)(iv), (d)(6)(ii), (d)(6)(iii), (e)(2), (e)(3)(iii), (e)(4), and (f)(2)(i)(B).

The revisions and addition read as follows:

§ *1.411(b)(5)-1 Reduction in rate of benefit accrual under a defined benefit plan.*

* * * * *

(c) * * *

(3) * * *

(iii) *Comparison of benefits at effective date of conversion amendment—* (A) *In general.* A plan satisfies the requirements of this paragraph (c)(3)(iii) with respect to a participant only if an opening hypothetical account balance is established to replicate the pre-conversion benefit and the requirements of paragraphs (c)(3)(iii)(B) through (c)(3)(iii)(G) of this section are each satisfied.

(B) *Single-sum payment.* At the annuity starting date, the participant elects to receive payment in the form of a single-sum distribution equal to the sum of the thencurrent balance of the hypothetical account used to replicate the pre-conversion benefit and the benefit attributable to post-conversion service under the post-conversion benefit formula.

(C) *Not less than pre-conversion benefit.* In accordance with section 411(d)(6), the aggregate benefit payable at the annuity starting date after the effective date of the conversion amendment is not less than the benefit described in paragraph (c)(2)(i)(A) of this section.

(D) *Form of pre-conversion benefit.* The plan, as in effect immediately prior to the effective date of the conversion amendment, either did not provide a single-sum payment option (for benefits that cannot be immediately distributed under section 411(a)(11)) or provided a single-sum payment option that was based solely on the present value of the benefit payable at normal retirement age (or at date of benefit commencement, if later), and which was not based on the present value of the benefit payable commencing at any date prior to normal retirement age.

(E) *Minimum opening account balance.* The plan provides for the opening hypothetical account balance under paragraph (c)(3)(i) of this section to be established in accordance with rules under which the amount of this opening balance will not be less than the present value, determined in accordance with section 417(e), of the participant's accrued benefit under the plan immediately prior to the effective date of the conversion amendment.

(F) *Interest credits—(1) Requirement as of effective date of conversion amendment.* As of the effective date of the conversion amendment, the interest crediting rate under the plan is an interest crediting rate described in paragraph (d)(3) or (d)(4) of this section. In addition, as of that date, the value of the index used to determine the interest crediting rate under the plan is at least as great for every participant or beneficiary as the interest rate that was used pursuant to paragraph (c)(3)(iii)(E) of this section to determine the opening hypothetical account balance. This requirement is satisfied, for example, if each participant's opening hypothetical account balance is determined using the applicable interest rate and applicable mortality table under section 417(e)(3), the interest crediting rate under the plan is the third segment rate, and, at the effective date of the conversion amendment, the third segment rate is the highest of the three segment rates.

(*2) Requirement for later interest crediting rate changes.* If, subsequent to the effective date of the conversion amendment, the interest crediting rate changes (whether by plan amendment or otherwise) with respect to a participant who was a participant at the time of the effective date of the conversion amendment from a particular interest crediting rate described in paragraph (d)(3) or (d)(4) of this section to a different interest crediting rate that is not in all cases at least as great as the prior interest crediting rate under the plan, then the new interest crediting rate does not apply to the existing hypothetical account balance as of the effective date of the change in interest crediting rates (or, if the plan created a subaccount consisting of the opening hypothetical account balance and interest credits on that subaccount, then the new interest crediting rate does not apply to the subaccount).

(G) *Death benefits.* The plan either—

(*1*) Provides a death benefit after the effective date of the conversion amendment which has a present value that is at all times at least equal to the then-current balance of the hypothetical account used to replicate the pre-conversion benefit; or

(*2*) Applied no pre-retirement mortality decrement in establishing the opening hypothetical account balance under paragraph (c)(3)(iii)(E) of this section.

* * * * *

(c) * * *

(5) * * *

Example 8. (i) *Facts where plan establishes opening hypothetical account balance under paragraph (c)(3)(iii) of this section.* Employer O sponsors Plan F, a defined benefit plan that provides an accumulated benefit, payable as a straight life annuity commencing at age 65 (which is Plan F's normal retirement age), based on a percentage of highest average compensation times the participant's years of service. Plan F permits any participant who has had a severance from employment to elect payment in the following optional forms of benefit (with spousal consent if applicable), with any payment not made in a straight life annuity converted to an equivalent form based on reasonable actuarial assumptions: a straight life annuity; and a 50 percent, 75 percent, or 100 percent joint and survivor annuity. The payment of benefits may commence at any time after attainment of age 55, with an actuarial reduction if the commencement is before normal retirement age. In addition, the plan offers a singlesum payment after attainment of age 55 equal to the present value of the normal retirement benefit using the applicable interest rate and mortality table under section 417(e)(3) in effect under the terms of the plan on the annuity starting date. (These facts are the same as those in paragraph (i) of *Example 1.*)

(ii) *Facts relating to the conversion amendment and establishment of opening balance.* On January 1, 2012, Plan F is amended to eliminate future accruals under the highest average compensation benefit formula and to base future benefit accruals on a hypothetical account balance. As of January 1, 2012, the plan establishes an opening hypothetical account balance for each individual who was a participant in the plan on December 31, 2011, equal to the present value of the participant's accumulated benefits, payable as a straight life annuity commencing at age 65, based on the actuarial assumptions then applicable under section 417(e)(3). New participants begin with a hypothetical account balance of zero on their date of participation. For service on or after January 1, 2012, each participant's hypothetical account balance is credited monthly with a pay credit equal to a specified percentage of the participant's compensation during the month and also with interest based on the third segment rate described in section 430(h)(2)(C)(iii). With respect to benefits under the hypothetical account balance, a participant is permitted to elect (with spousal consent) payment in the same generalized optional forms of benefit (even though different actuarial factors apply) as under the terms of the plan in effect before January 1, 2012, and also as a single-sum distribution. The plan provides that in no event will the benefit payable be less than the benefits attributable to service before January 1, 2012, to be determined under the terms of the plan as in effect immediately before the effective date of the amendment. In the event of death prior to the annuity starting date, the plan provides a death benefit equal to the hypothetical account balance (and allows a surviving spouse to elect payment in the form of an actuarially equivalent life annuity).

(iii) *Conclusion.* Plan F satisfies the requirements of paragraph (c)(3)(iii) of this section for participants who elect to receive payment in the form of a single-sum distribution equal to the hypothetical account balance in accordance with the requirements of paragraph (c)(3)(iii)(B) of this section for the following reasons. First, Plan F satisfies the requirements of paragraph (c)(3)(iii)(C) of this section because the benefit payable can never be less than the pre-conversion benefit, in accordance with the requirements of section 411(d)(6). Second, Plan F satisfies the requirements of paragraph (c)(3)(iii)(D) of

this section because prior to conversion it provided for a single-sum payment option that was based solely on the present value of the benefit payable at normal retirement age. Third, Plan F satisfies the requirements of paragraph (c)(3)(iii)(E) of this section because the amount of the opening balance is not less than the present value of the participant's accrued benefit under the plan immediately prior to the effective date of the conversion amendment, as determined in accordance with section 417(e). Fourth, Plan F satisfies the requirements of paragraph (c)(3)(iii)(F) of this section because it provides for interest credits that are described in paragraph (d)(3) of this section on the opening balance and the interest credits are reasonably expected to be no lower than the interest rate used to determine the opening balance. This is the case because interest is credited at least annually after the effective date of the conversion amendment and the interest rate used to establish the opening balance (which is based on the first, second, and third segment rates described in section 430(h)(2)(C) referenced under section 417(e)(3)) is not greater than the interest rate applicable under the third segment rate described in section 430(h)(2)(C)(iii) which the plan uses to determine interest for all future periods after the effective date of the conversion amendment. Fifth, Plan F satisfies the requirements of paragraph (c)(3)(iii)(G) of this section because it provides a death benefit after the effective date of the conversion amendment which has a present value that is at all times at least equal to the hypothetical account balance at the date of death.

* * * * *

(d) * * *

(1) * * *

(iv) * * *

(D) *Debits and credits during the interest crediting period.* A plan is not treated as failing to meet the requirements of this paragraph (d) merely because the plan does not provide for interest credits on amounts distributed prior to the end of the interest crediting period. Furthermore, a plan is not treated as failing to meet the requirements of this paragraph (d) merely because the plan calculates increases or decreases to the participant's accumulated benefit by applying a rate of interest or rate of return (including a rate of increase or decrease under an index) to the participant's adjusted accumulated benefit (or portion thereof) for the period. For this purpose, the participant's adjusted accumulated benefit equals the participant's accumulated benefit as of the beginning of the period, adjusted for debits and credits (other than interest credits) made to the accumulated benefit prior to the end of the interest crediting period, with appropriate weighting for those debits and credits based on their timing within the period. For plans that calculate increases or decreases to the participant's accumulated benefit by applying a rate of interest or rate of return to the participant's adjusted accumulated benefit (or portion thereof) for the period, interest credits include these increases and decreases, to the extent provided under the terms of the plan at the beginning of the period and to the extent not conditioned on current service and not made on account of imputed service (as defined in § 1.401(a)(4)-11(d)(3)(ii)(B)), and the interest crediting rate with respect to a participant equals the total amount of interest credits for the period divided by the participant's adjusted accumulated benefit for the period.

* * * * *

(2) * * *

(ii) *Application to multiple annuity starting dates*—(A) *In general.* Paragraph (d)(2)(i) of this section applies only at an annuity starting date, within the meaning of § 1.401(a)-20, A-10(b), on which a distribution of the participant's entire benefit under the plan's statutory hybrid benefit formula as of that date commences. For a participant who has more than one annuity starting date, paragraph (d)(2)(ii)(B) of this section provides rules for the application of paragraph (d)(2)(i) of this section, taking into account prior distributions. If the comparison under paragraph (d)(2)(ii)(B) of this section results in the sum of principal credits exceeding the sum of the amounts described in paragraphs (d)(2)(ii)(B)(1) through (d)(2)(ii)(B)(3) of this section, then the participant's benefit to be distributed at the current annuity starting date is increased by an amount equal to the excess.

(B) *Comparison to reflect prior distributions.* For a participant who has more than one annuity starting date, the sum of all principal credits credited to the participant under the plan, as of the current annuity starting date, is compared to the sum of—

(*1*) The participant's benefit as of the current annuity starting date;

(*2*) The amount of the offset to the participant's benefit under the statutory hybrid benefit formula that is attributable to any prior distribution of the participant's benefit under that formula; and

(3) The amount of any increase to the participant's benefit as a result of the application of paragraph (d)(2)(i) of this section to a prior distribution.

* * * * *

(4) * * *

(iv) *Fixed rate of interest.* An annual interest crediting rate equal to a fixed 5 percent is deemed to be not in excess of the interest rate described in paragraph (d)(3) of this section.

* * * * *

(5) * * *

(ii) *Actual rate of return on plan assets.* An interest crediting rate equal to the actual rate of return on the aggregate assets of the plan, including both positive returns and negative returns, is not in excess of a market rate of return if the plan's assets are diversified so as to minimize the volatility of returns. This requirement that plan assets be diversified so as to minimize the volatility of returns does not require greater diversification than is required under section 404(a)(1)(C) of Title I of the Employee Retirement Income Security Act of 1974, Public Law 93-406 (88 Stat. 829 (1974)) with respect to defined benefit pension plans.

* * * * *

(iv) *Rate of return on certain RICs.* An interest crediting rate is not in excess of a market rate of return if it is equal to the rate of return on a regulated investment company (RIC), as defined in section 851, that is reasonably expected to be not significantly more volatile than the broad United States equities market or a similarly broad international equities market. For example, a RIC that has most of its assets invested in securities of issuers (including other RICs) concentrated in an industry sector or a country other than the United States, that uses leverage, or that has significant investment in derivative financial products, for the purpose of achieving returns that amplify the returns of an unleveraged investment, generally would not meet this requirement. Thus, a RIC that has most of its investments concentrated in the semiconductor industry or that uses leverage in order to provide a rate of return that is twice the rate of return on the Standard & Poor's 500 index (S&P 500) would not meet this requirement. On the other hand, a RIC whose investments track the rate of return on the S&P 500, a broad-based "small-cap" index (such as the Russell 2000 index), or a broad-based international equities index would meet this requirement.

* * * * *

(6) * * *

(ii) *Annual or more frequent floor applied to bond-based rates.* An interest crediting rate under a plan does not fail to be described in paragraph (d)(3) or (d)(4) of this section for an interest crediting period merely because the plan provides that the interest crediting rate for that interest crediting period equals the greater of—

(A) An interest crediting rate described in paragraph (d)(3) or (d)(4) of this section; and

(B) An annual interest rate of 4 percent (or a pro rata portion of an annual interest rate of 4 percent for plans that provide interest credits more frequently than annually).

(iii) *Cumulative floor applied to equity-based or bond-based rates*—(A) *In general.* A plan that determines interest credits under a statutory hybrid benefit formula using a particular interest crediting rate described in paragraph (d)(3), (d)(4), or (d)(5) of this section (or an interest crediting rate that can never be in excess of a particular interest crediting rate described in paragraph (d)(3), (d)(4), or (d)(5) of this section) does not provide an effective interest crediting rate in excess of a market rate of return merely because the plan provides that the participant's benefit under the statutory hybrid benefit formula determined as of the participant's annuity starting date is equal to the greater of—

(1) The benefit determined using the interest crediting rate; and

(2) The benefit determined as if the plan had used a fixed annual interest crediting rate equal to 3 percent (or a lower rate) for all principal credits that are made during the guarantee period (minimum guarantee amount).

(B) *Guarantee period defined.* The guarantee period is the prospective period that begins on the date on which the cumulative floor described in this paragraph (d)(6)(iii) begins to apply to the participant's benefit and which ends on the date on which that cumulative floor ceases to apply to the participant's benefit.

(C) *Application to multiple annuity starting dates.* The determination under paragraph (d)(6)(iii)(A) of this section is made only at an annuity starting date, within the meaning of §1.401(a)-20, A-10(b), on which a distribution of the participant's entire benefit under the plan's statutory hybrid benefit formula as of that date commences. For a participant who has more than one annuity starting date, paragraph (d)(6)(iii)(D) of this section provides rules for the application of paragraph (d)(6)(iii)(A) of this section, taking into account any prior distributions. If the comparison under paragraph (d)(6)(iii)(D) of this section results in the minimum guarantee amount exceeding the sum of the amounts described in paragraphs (d)(6)(iii)(D)(1) through (d)(6)(iii)(D)(3) of this section, then the participant's benefit to be distributed at the current annuity starting date is increased by an amount equal to the excess.

(D) *Comparison to reflect prior distributions.* For a participant who has more than one annuity starting date, the minimum guarantee amount (described in paragraph (d)(6)(iii)(A)(2) of this section), as of the current annuity starting date, is compared to the sum of—

(1) The participant's benefit, as of the current annuity starting date, to which a minimum guaranteed rate described in paragraph (d)(6)(iii)(A)(2) of this section applies;

(2) The amount of the offset to the participant's benefit under the statutory hybrid benefit formula that is attributable to any prior distribution of the participant's benefit under that formula and to which a minimum guaranteed rate described in paragraph (d)(6)(iii)(A)(2) of this section applied, together with interest at that minimum guaranteed rate annually from the prior annuity starting date to the current annuity starting date; and

(3) The amount of any increase to the participant's benefit as a result of the application of paragraph (d)(6)(iii)(A) of this section to any prior distribution, together with interest annually at the minimum guaranteed rate that applied to the prior distribution from the prior annuity starting date to the current annuity starting date.

(E) *Application to portion of participant's benefit.* A cumulative floor described in this paragraph (d)(6)(iii) may be applied to a portion of a participant's benefit, provided the requirements of this paragraph (d)(6)(iii) are satisfied with respect to that portion of the benefit. If a cumulative floor described in this paragraph (d)(6)(iii) applies to a portion of a participant's benefit, only the principal credits that are attributable to that portion of the participant's benefit are taken into account in determining the amount of the guarantee described in paragraph (d)(6)(iii)(A)(2) of this section.

* * * * *

(e) * * *

(2) *Plan termination*—(i) *In general*—(A) *Interest crediting rates.* If the interest crediting rate used to determine a participant's accumulated benefit (or a portion thereof) has been a variable rate during the interest crediting periods in the 5-year period ending on the plan termination date (including any case in which the rate was not the same fixed rate during all such periods), then a statutory hybrid plan is treated as meeting the requirements of section 411(b)(5)(B)(i) and paragraph (d)(1) of this section only if the terms of the plan satisfy the requirements of paragraph (e)(2)(ii) of this section. See regulations of the Pension Benefit Guaranty Corporation for additional rules that apply when a pension plan is terminated.

(B) *Annuity conversion factors.* A statutory hybrid plan is treated as meeting the requirements of section 411(b)(5)(B)(i) and paragraph (d)(1) of this section only if the terms of the plan provide that the interest rate and mortality table (including tabular adjustment factors) used on and after plan termination for purposes of determining the amount of any benefit under the plan payable in the form of an annuity commencing at or after normal retirement age are the interest rate and mortality table specified under the plan for that purpose as of the termination date, except that if the interest rate is a variable rate (as described in paragraph (e)(2)(i) of this section), then the interest rate for that purpose is determined pursuant to the rules of paragraph (e)(2)(ii) of this section.

(ii) *Interest crediting rates that are variable*—(A) *General rule.* Subject to the other rules in this paragraph (e)(2), a plan satisfies this paragraph (e)(2)(ii) only if the terms of the plan provide that, on the plan termination date, if the interest crediting rate used to determine a participant's accumulated benefit has been a variable rate as described in paragraph (e)(2)(i) of this section, then the interest crediting rate used to determine the participant's accumulated benefit under the plan after the date of plan termination is equal to the average of the interest crediting rates used under the plan during the 5-year period ending on the plan termination date. For this purpose, an interest crediting rate is used under the plan if the rate applied under the terms of the plan during an interest crediting period for which the interest crediting date is within the 5-year period ending on the plan termination date and the average is determined as the arithmetic average of the rates used, with each rate adjusted to reflect the length of the interest crediting period and the average rate expressed as an annual rate.

(B) *Variable interest crediting rates that are based on interest rates.* With respect to an interest crediting rate that was a variable interest rate described in paragraph (d)(3) or (d)(4) of this section (taking into account the rules of paragraph (d)(6)(ii) of this section), a variable interest rate that can never be in excess of a rate described in paragraph (d)(3) or (d)(4) of this section, or a fixed interest rate that has not been the same rate during the entire 5-year period ending on the plan termination date, the actual interest rate that applied under the plan for the interest crediting period is used for purposes of determining the average interest crediting rate. For this purpose, the rate that applied for the interest crediting period takes into account minimums, maximums, and other reductions that applied in the period, other than cumulative floors under paragraph (d)(6)(iii) of this section.

(C) *Variable interest crediting rates that are other rates of return.* With respect to any interest crediting rate not described in paragraph (e)(2)(ii)(B) of this section (that is, a variable rate described in paragraph (d)(5) of this section), the interest crediting rate that applied for the interest crediting period for purposes of determining the average interest crediting rate is deemed to be equal to the third segment rate under section 430(h)(2)(C)(iii) for the last calendar month ending before the beginning of the interest crediting period, as adjusted to account for any minimums or maximums that applied in the period (other than cumulative floors under paragraph (d)(6)(iii) of this section), but without regard to other reductions that applied in the period. Thus, for example, if the actual interest crediting rate in an interest crediting period was equal to the rate of return on plan assets, but not greater than 5 percent, then for purposes of determining the plan's average interest crediting rate, the interest crediting rate for that interest crediting period would be deemed to equal the lesser of the applicable third segment rate for the period and 5 percent. However, if the actual interest crediting rate in an interest crediting period was equal to the rate of return on plan assets minus 200 basis points, then for purposes of determining the plan's average interest crediting rate, the interest crediting rate for that interest crediting period would be deemed to equal the third segment rate.

(iii) *Rules of application*—(A) *Section 411(d)(6) protected benefits.* In general, for purposes of determining the average interest crediting rate under paragraph (e)(2)(ii) of this section, the interest crediting rate that applied for each interest crediting period is the ongoing interest crediting rate that was specified under the plan in that period, without regard to any section 411(d)(6) protected benefit using an interest crediting rate that applied under the plan prior to amendment. However, if, at the end of the last interest crediting period prior to plan termination, the participant's accumulated benefit is based on a section 411(d)(6) protected benefit that results from a prior amendment to change the interest crediting rate applicable under the plan, then, for purposes of determining the average interest crediting rate under paragraph (e)(2)(ii) of this section, the pre-amendment interest crediting rate is treated as having applied for each interest crediting period after the date of the interest crediting rate change. [Corrected by 75 FR 81543, 12/28/10.]

(B) *Weighted averages.* If the plan determines the interest credit in any interest crediting period by applying different rates to different predetermined portions of the accumulated benefit under paragraph (d)(1)(vii) of this section, then, for purposes of determining the average interest crediting rate under paragraph (e)(2)(ii) of this section, the interest crediting rate that applied for the interest crediting period is the weighted average of the relevant interest rates that apply, under the rules of paragraph (e)(2)(ii) of this section, to each portion of the accumulated benefit.

(C) *Participants with less than five years of interest credits upon plan termination.* If the plan provided for interest credits for any interest crediting period in which, pursuant to the terms of the plan, the individual was not eligible to receive interest credits (because the individual was not a participant or beneficiary in the relevant interest crediting period or otherwise), then, for purposes of determining the individual's average interest crediting rate under paragraph (e)(2)(ii) of this section, the individual is treated as though the individual received interest credits in that period using the interest crediting rate that applied in that period under the terms of the plan to a similarly situated participant or beneficiary who was eligible to receive interest credits. However, if, under the terms of the plan, the individual was not eligible to receive any interest credits during the entire 5-year period ending on the plan termination date, then the rules under paragraph (e)(2)(ii) do not apply to determine the individual's benefit after plan termination.

(iv) *Examples.* The following examples illustrate the rules of this paragraph (e)(2). In each case, it is assumed that the plan is terminated in a standard termination.

Example 1. (i) *Facts.* Plan A is a defined benefit plan with a calendar plan year that expresses each participant's accumulated benefit in the form of a hypothetical account balance to which principal credits are made at the end of each calendar quarter and to which interest is credited at the end of each calendar quarter based on the balance at the beginning of the quarter. Interest credits under Plan A are based on a rate of interest fixed at the beginning of each plan year equal to the third segment rate for the preceding December, except that the plan used the rate of interest on 30-year Treasury bonds (instead of the third segment rate) for plan years before 2012. The plan is terminated on March 3, 2016. The third segment rate credited under Plan A from January 1, 2012, through December 31, 2015, is assumed to be: 6 percent annually for each of the four quarters in 2015 (1.5 percent quarterly); 6.5 percent annually for each of the four quarters in 2014 (1.625 percent quarterly); 6 percent annually for each of the four quarters in 2013 (1.5 percent quarterly); and 5.5 percent annually for each of the four quarters in 2012 (1.375 percent quarterly). The rate of interest on 30-year Treasury bonds credited under Plan A for each of the four quarters in 2011 is assumed to be 4.4 percent annually (1.1 percent quarterly).

(ii) *Conclusion.* Pursuant to paragraph (e)(2)(ii)(B) of this section, the interest crediting rate used to determine accrued benefits under the plan on and after the date of plan termination is 5.68 percent. This is determined by calculating the average quarterly rate of 1.42 percent (the sum of 1.5 percent times 4, 1.625 times 4, 1.5 times 4, 1.375 times 4, and 1.1 percent times 4, divided by the 20 quarters that end in the 5-year period from March 4, 2011 to March 3, 2016) and multiplying such rate by 4 to determine the average annual rate.

Example 2. (i) *Facts.* The facts are the same as *Example 1*, except that Participant B commenced participation in Plan A on April 17, 2013.

(ii) *Conclusion.* Pursuant to paragraph (e)(2)(iii)(C) of this section, the interest crediting rate used to determine Participant B's accrued benefits under Plan A on and after the date of plan termination is 5.68 percent, which is the same rate that would have applied to Participant B if Participant B had participated in the plan during the 5-year period preceding the date of plan termination, as described in *Example 1*.

Example 3. (i) *Facts.* Plan C is a defined benefit plan with a calendar plan year that expresses each participant's accumulated benefit in the form of a hypothetical account balance to which principal credits are made at the end of each calendar year and to which interest is credited at the end of each calendar year based on the balance at the end of the preceding year. The plan is terminated on January 27, 2014. The plan's interest crediting rate for each calendar year during the entire 5-year period ending on the plan termination date is equal to (A) 50 percent of the greater of the rate of interest on 3-month Treasury Bills for the preceding December and an annual rate of 4 percent, plus (B) 50 percent of the rate of return on plan assets. The rate of interest on 3-month Treasury Bills credited under Plan C is assumed to be: 3.4 percent for 2013; 4 percent for 2012; 4.5 percent for 2011; 3.5 percent for 2010; and 4.2 percent for 2009. Each of these rates applied under Plan C for interest credited during this period for purposes of the interest credits described in clause (A) of this paragraph (i), except that the 4 percent minimum rate applied for 2013 and 2010. For purposes of the interest credits described in clause (B) of this paragraph (i), the rate of interest on the third segment rate in the prior years (based on the rate for the preceding December) is assumed to be: 6 percent for 2013; 6.5 percent for 2012; 6 percent for 2011; 5.5 percent for 2010; and 6 percent for 2009.

(ii) *Conclusion.* Pursuant to paragraph (e)(2)(ii) of this section, the interest crediting rate used to determine accrued benefits under the plan on and after the date of plan termination is 5.07 percent. This number is equal to the sum of 50 percent of 4.14 percent (which is the sum of 4 percent, 4 percent, 4.5 percent, 4 percent, and 4.2 percent, divided by 5), and 50 percent of 6 percent (which is the average third segment rate for the 5 interest crediting periods ending within the 5-year period).

Example 4. (i) *Facts.* The facts are the same as in *Example 3*, except that the plan had credited interest before January 1, 2012, using the rate of return on a RIC and was amended effective January 1, 2012, to base interest credits for all plan years after 2011 on the interest rate formula described in *Example 3*(i). In order to comply with section 411(d)(6), the plan provides that, for each participant or beneficiary who was a participant on December 31, 2011, the benefits at any date are based on either the ongoing hypothetical account balance on that date (which is based on the December 31, 2011 balance, with interest credited thereafter at the rate described in the first sentence of *Exam-*

ple 3(i) and taking principal credits after 2011 into account) or a special hypothetical account balance (the pre-2012 balance) on that date, whichever balance is greater. For each participant, the pre-2012 balance is a hypothetical account balance equal to the participant's December 31, 2011, balance, with interest credited thereafter at the RIC rate of return, but with no principal credits after 2011. There are 10 participants for whom his or her pre-2012 balance exceeded his or her ongoing hypothetical account balance at the end of 2013.

(ii) *Conclusion.* Since Plan C credited interest prior to 2012 using the rate of return on a RIC (a rate not described in paragraph (d)(3) or (d)(4) of this section), for purposes of determining the average interest crediting rate upon plan termination, the interest crediting rate used to determine accrued benefits under Plan C for all participants during those periods (for the calendar years 2009, 2010, and 2011) is deemed to be equal to the third segment rate for the preceding December. In addition, since the pre-2012 balances exceeded the ongoing hypothetical account balance for 10 participants in the last interest crediting period prior to plan termination, for purposes of determining the average interest crediting rate upon plan termination, the interest crediting rate used to determine accrued benefits under Plan C for 2012 and 2013 for those participants is deemed to be equal to the third segment rate for the month of December preceding 2012 and the month of December preceding 2013, respectively. For all other participants, for purposes of determining the average interest crediting rate upon plan termination, the interest crediting rate used to determine accrued benefits under Plan C for 2012 and 2013 is based on the ongoing interest crediting rate (the formula described in *Example 3*).

(3) * * *

(iii) *Coordination of section 411(d)(6) and market rate of return limitation*—(A) *In general.* An amendment to a statutory hybrid plan that preserves a section 411(d)(6) protected benefit is subject to the rules under paragraph (d) of this section relating to market rate of return. However, in the case of an amendment to change a plan's interest crediting rate for periods after the applicable amendment date from one interest crediting rate (the old rate) that satisfies the requirements of paragraph (d) of this section to another interest crediting rate (the new rate) that satisfies the requirements of paragraph (d) of this section, the plan's effective interest crediting rate is not in excess of a market rate of return for purposes of paragraph (d) of this section

merely because the plan provides for the benefit of any participant who is benefiting under the plan (within the meaning of § 1.410(b)-3(a)) on the applicable amendment date to never be less than what it would be if the old rate had continued but without taking into account any principal credits (as defined in paragraph (d)(1)(ii)(D) of this section) after the applicable amendment date.

(B) *Multiple amendments.* A pattern of repeated plan amendments each of which provides for a prospective change in the plan's interest crediting rate with respect to the benefit as of the applicable amendment date will be treated as resulting in the ongoing plan terms providing that the interest crediting rate equals the greater of each of the interest crediting rates, so that the rule in paragraph (e)(3)(iii)(A) of this section would not apply. See § 1.411(d)-4, A-1(c)(1).

(4) *Actuarial increases after normal retirement age.* A statutory hybrid plan is not treated as providing an effective interest crediting rate that is in excess of a market rate of return for purposes of paragraph (d) of this section merely because the plan provides that the participant's benefit, as of each annuity starting date after normal retirement age, is equal to the greater of—

(i) The benefit determined using an interest crediting rate that is not in excess of a market rate of return under paragraph (d) of this section; and

(ii) The benefit that satisfies the requirements of section 411(a)(2).

* * * * *

(f) * * *

(2) * * *

(i) * * *

(B) *Special effective date.* Paragraphs (c)(3)(iii), (d)(1)(iii), (d)(1)(iv)(D), (d)(1)(vi), (d)(2)(ii), (d)(4)(iv), (d)(5)(iv), (d)(6), (e)(2), (e)(3)(iii), and (e)(4) of this section apply to plan years that begin on or after January 1, 2012.

* * * * *

Steven T. Miller

Deputy Commissioner for Services and Enforcement.

¶ 20,262W

IRS: Employee remuneration in excess of $1 million: Deduction limits: Stock options: Stock appreciation rights.—The IRS has issued proposed regulations relating to the deduction limitation for certain employee remuneration in excess of $1,000,000 under Code Sec. 162(m). The proposed regulations clarify that qualified performance-based compensation attributable to stock options and stock appreciation rights must specify the maximum number of shares with respect to which options or rights may be granted to each individual employee during a specified period. A related clarification provides that the requirement for compensation is satisfied where the maximum number of shares for which grants may be made to each individual employee during a specified period and the exercise price of those options is disclosed to the shareholders of the corporation. The proposed regulations also clarify the application of the transition rule for taxpayers that are not publicly held corporations and then become publicly held corporations. Written or electronic comments must be received by September 22, 2011.

The proposed regulations were published in the Federal Register on June 24, 2011 (76 FR 37034). They were corrected on September 7, 2011 (76 FR 55321). The regulations were finalized on March 31, 2015 (80 FR 16970). The preamble to the final regulations is at ¶ 23,311. The final regulations are at ¶ 11,307.

¶ 20,262X

IRS: Affordable Insurance Exchanges: Health insurance coverage: Health insurance premium tax credit.—The IRS has issued proposed regulations relating to the health insurance premium tax credit enacted by the Patient Protection and Affordable Care Act (P.L. 111-148). The proposed regulations provide guidance to individuals who enroll in qualified health plans through affordable insurance exchanges (AIEs) and claim the premium tax credit, and to AIEs that make qualified health plans available to individuals and employers. These regulations are proposed to apply for taxable years ending after December 31, 2013.

The proposed regulation was published in the Federal Register on August 17, 2011 (76 FR 50931). The final regulations were issued on May 23, 2012 (77 FR 30377). The preamble to the final regulations is at ¶ 24,284. The final regulations are at ¶ 11,112F-1, ¶ 11,112F-2, ¶ 11,112F-3, ¶ 11,112F-4, ¶ 11,112F-5, ¶ 11,112F-6, and ¶ 13,649E-15.

DEPARTMENT OF THE TREASURY

Internal Revenue Service

26 CFR Part 1

[REG-131491-10]

RIN 1545-BJ82

Health Insurance Premium Tax Credit

AGENCY: Internal Revenue Service (IRS), Treasury.

ACTION: Notice of proposed rulemaking and notice of public hearing.

SUMMARY: This document contains proposed regulations relating to the health insurance premium tax credit enacted by the Patient Protection and Affordable Care Act and the Health Care and Education Reconciliation Act of 2010, as amended by the Medicare and Medicaid Extenders Act of 2010, the Comprehensive 1099 Taxpayer Protection and Repayment of Exchange Subsidy Overpayments Act of 2011, and the Department of Defense and Full-Year Continuing Appropriations Act, 2011. These proposed regulations provide guidance to individuals who enroll in qualified health plans through Affordable Insurance Exchanges and claim the premium tax credit, and to Exchanges that make qualified health plans available to individuals and employers. This document also provides notice of a public hearing on these proposed regulations.

DATES: Written (including electronic) comments must be received by October 31, 2011. Outlines of topics to be discussed at the public hearing scheduled for November 17, 2011, at 10 a.m. must be received by November 10, 2011.

ADDRESSES: Send submissions to: CC:PA:LPD:PR (REG-131491-10), Room 5203, Internal Revenue Service, PO Box 7604, Ben Franklin Station, Washington, DC 20044. Submissions may be hand-delivered Monday through Friday between the hours of 8 a.m. and 4 p.m. to CC:PA:LPD:PR (REG-131491-10), Courier's Desk, Internal Revenue Service, 1111 Constitution Avenue, NW., Washington, DC, or sent electronically via the Federal eRulemaking Portal at *http://www.regulations.gov* (IRS REG-131491-10). The public hearing will be held in the IRS Auditorium, Internal Revenue Building, 1111 Constitution Avenue, NW., Washington, DC.

FOR FURTHER INFORMATION CONTACT: Concerning the proposed regulations, Shareen S. Pflanz, (202) 622-4920, or Frank W. Dunham III, (202) 622-4960; concerning the submission of comments, the public hearing, and to be placed on the building access list to attend the public hearing, Funmi Taylor, (202) 622-7180 (not toll-free calls).

SUPPLEMENTARY INFORMATION:

Paperwork Reduction Act

The collection of information contained in this notice of proposed rulemaking has been submitted to the Office of Management and Budget in accordance with the Paperwork Reduction Act of 1995 (44 U.S.C. 3507(d)). Comments on the collection of information should be sent to the Office of Management and Budget, *Attn:* Desk Officer for the Department of the Treasury, Office of Information and Regulatory Affairs, Washington, DC 20503, with copies to the Internal Revenue Service, Attn: IRS Reports Clearance Officer, SE:W:CAR:MP:T:T:SP, Washington, DC 20224. Comments on the collection of information should be received by October 17, 2011. Comments are specifically requested concerning:

Whether the proposed collection of information is necessary for the proper performance of the functions of the IRS, including whether the information will have practical utility;

How the quality, utility, and clarity of the information to be collected may be enhanced;

How the burden of complying with the proposed collection of information may be minimized, including through the application of automated collection techniques or other forms of information technology; and

Estimates of capital or start-up costs and costs of operation, maintenance, and purchase of services to provide information.

The collection of information in these proposed regulations is in § 1.36B-5. The collection of information is necessary to properly reconcile the amount of the premium tax credit with advance credit payments made under section 1412 of the Patient Protection and Affordable Care Act (42 U.S.C. 18082). The collection of information is required to comply with the provisions of section 36B(f)(3) of the Internal Revenue Code (Code). The likely respondents are Affordable Insurance Exchanges established under section 1311 or 1321 of the Patient Protection and Affordable Care Act (42 U.S.C. 13031 or 42 U.S.C. 18041).

The burden for the collection of information contained in proposed regulation § 1.36B-5 will be reflected in the burden on a form that the IRS will create to request the information in the proposed regulation.

An agency may not conduct or sponsor, and a person is not required to respond to, a collection of information unless it displays a valid control number assigned by the Office of Management and Budget.

Background

Beginning in 2014, under the Patient Protection and Affordable Care Act, Public Law 111-148 (124 Stat. 119 (2010)), and the Health Care and Education Reconciliation Act of 2010, Public Law 111-152 (124 Stat. 1029 (2010)) (collectively, the Affordable Care Act), individuals and small businesses will be able to purchase private health insurance through State-based competitive marketplaces called Affordable Insurance Exchanges (Exchanges). Exchanges will offer Americans competition and choice. Insurance companies will compete for business on a level playing field, driving down costs. Consumers will have a choice of health plans to fit their needs and Exchanges will give individuals and

small businesses the same purchasing power as big businesses. The Departments of Health and Human Services and Treasury are working in close coordination to release guidance related to Exchanges, in several phases. The first in this series was a Request for Comment relating to Exchanges, published in the **Federal Register** on August 3, 2010 (75 FR 45584). Second, Initial Guidance to States on Exchanges was issued on November 18, 2010. Third, proposed regulations on the application, review, and reporting process for waivers for State innovation was published in the **Federal Register** on March 14, 2011 (76 FR 13553). Fourth, two proposed regulations were published in the **Federal Register** on July 15, 2011 (76 FR 41866 and 76 FR 41930) to implement components of the Exchange and health insurance premium stabilization policies in the Affordable Care Act. Fifth, three proposed regulations, including this one, are being published in the **Federal Register** on August 17, 2011 to provide guidance on the eligibility determination process related to enrollment in a qualified health plan or insurance affordability program; on Medicaid, the Children's Health Insurance Program (CHIP), and other State health coverage programs; and these proposed regulations on the premium tax credit.

Section 1401 of the Affordable Care Act amended the Code to add section 36B, allowing a refundable premium tax credit to help individuals and families afford health insurance coverage. Section 36B was subsequently amended by the Medicare and Medicaid Extenders Act of 2010, Public Law 111-309 (124 Stat. 3285 (2010)); the Comprehensive 1099 Taxpayer Protection and Repayment of Exchange Subsidy Overpayments Act of 2011, Public Law 112-9 (125 Stat. 36 (2011)); and the Department of Defense and Full-Year Continuing Appropriations Act, 2011, Public Law 112-10 (125 Stat. 38 (2011)). The section 36B credit is designed to make a qualified health plan affordable by reducing a taxpayer's out-of-pocket premium cost.

Under section 1411 of the Affordable Care Act (42 U.S.C. 18081), an Exchange makes an advance determination of credit eligibility for individuals enrolling in coverage through the Exchange and seeking financial assistance. Using information available at the time of enrollment, the Exchange determines (1) whether the individual meets the income and other requirements for advance credit payments, and (2) the amount of the advance payments. Advance payments are made monthly under section 1412 of the Affordable Care Act (42 U.S.C. 18082) to the issuer of the qualified health plan in which the individual enrolls.

Eligibility

To be eligible for a premium tax credit, an individual must be an applicable taxpayer. Under section 36B(c)(1), an applicable taxpayer is a taxpayer (1) With household income for the taxable year between 100 percent and 400 percent of the federal poverty line (FPL) for the taxpayer's family size, (2) who may not be claimed as a dependent by another taxpayer, and (3) who files a joint return if married.

Section 36B(c)(1)(B) provides that a taxpayer who is an alien lawfully present in the United States, whose household income is 100 percent of the FPL or less, and who is not eligible for Medicaid, nonetheless is treated as an applicable taxpayer. Under section 36B(e)(2), an individual is lawfully present if the individual is, and is reasonably expected to be for the entire period of enrollment for which the credit is claimed, a U.S. citizen or national or an alien lawfully present in the United States.

Under section 36B(d)(1), a taxpayer's family consists of the individuals for whom the taxpayer claims a personal exemption deduction under section 151 for the taxable year. Taxpayers may claim a personal exemption deduction for themselves, a spouse, and each of their dependents. Section 152 provides that a taxpayer's dependent may be a qualifying child or qualifying relative, including an unrelated individual who lives with the taxpayer. Family size is equal to the number of individuals in the taxpayer's family.

Section 36B(d)(2) defines household income as the modified adjusted gross income of all individuals included in family size who are required to file an income tax return. Modified adjusted gross income means adjusted gross income (within the meaning of section 62) increased by amounts excluded from gross income under section 911 and tax-exempt interest a taxpayer receives or accrues during the taxable year.

Under section 36B(b)(1), a taxpayer's premium assistance credit amount is the sum of the premium assistance amounts for all coverage months in the taxable year for individuals in the taxpayer's family. Section 36B(c)(2)(A) provides that a coverage month is any month for which the taxpayer or any family member is covered by a qualified health plan enrolled in through an Exchange and the premium is paid by the taxpayer or through an advance credit payment.

Under section 36B(c)(2)(B), a coverage month for an individual does not include a month in which the individual is eligible for minimum essential coverage, as defined in section 5000A(f), other than coverage offered in the individual market. Minimum essential coverage may be government-sponsored coverage such as Medicare, Medicaid, CHIP, TRICARE, and veterans' health care under Title 38 U.S.C. Certain employer-sponsored plans also may be minimum essential coverage. In general, under section 36B(c)(2)(C), an individual is eligible for employer-sponsored minimum essential coverage only if the employee's share of the premiums is affordable and the coverage provides minimum value. However, under section 36B(c)(2)(C)(iii), an individual is treated as eligible for employer-sponsored minimum essential coverage if the individual actually enrolls in an eligible employer-sponsored plan, even if the coverage does not meet the affordability and minimum value requirements.

Under section 5000A(f)(1)(E), the Department of Health and Human Services, in coordination with the Treasury Department, may designate other health benefits coverage as minimum essential coverage. Regulations under section 5000A are expected to provide additional guidance on minimum essential coverage.

Credit Computation

Section 36B(b)(1) provides that the premium assistance credit amount is the sum of the premium assistance amounts for all coverage months in the taxable year for individuals in the taxpayer's family. The premium assistance amount for a coverage month is the lesser of (1) the premiums for the month for one or more qualified health plans that cover a taxpayer or family member, or (2) the excess of the adjusted monthly premium for the second lowest cost silver plan (as described in section 1302(d)(1)(B) of the Affordable Care Act (42 U.S.C. 18022(d)(1)(B))) (the benchmark plan) that applies to the taxpayer over 1.12 of the product of the taxpayer's household income and the applicable percentage for the taxable year. The adjusted monthly premium, in general, is the premium an insurer would charge for the plan adjusted only for the ages of the covered individuals.

Therefore, the monthly premium assistance amount is the lesser of the premium for the qualified health plan in which a taxpayer or family member enrolls, or the excess of the premium for the benchmark plan over the applicable percentage of the taxpayer's household income. In general, this percentage of the taxpayer's household income represents the amount of the taxpayer's required out-of-pocket contribution to the premium cost if the taxpayer purchases the benchmark plan. The remainder of the premium for the benchmark plan is the premium assistance amount.

A taxpayer's applicable percentage increases as the taxpayer's household income as a percentage of the FPL (FPL percentage) for the taxpayer's family size increases. For 2014, the applicable percentage is 2 percent for taxpayers with household income up to 133 percent of the FPL and increases from 3 percent to 9.5 percent for taxpayers with household incomes between 133 percent and 400 percent of the FPL. The applicable percentages may be adjusted after 2014.

Taxpayers must pay the difference between the premium assistance amount and the premium for the plan they choose. The amount of a taxpayer's credit is limited to the amount of actual premiums for the taxable year.

Individuals not lawfully present are not eligible to enroll in a qualified health plan through an Exchange. Accordingly, section 36B(e)(1)(A) provides that, for a household with at least one individual not lawfully present, the portion (if any) of the premium attributable to that individual is not included in determining the taxpayer's credit. Section 36B(e)(1)(B) provides that the family size for computing the FPL percentage for a family with at least one unlawfully present individual is determined by excluding the unlawfully present individual. Household income for computing the FPL percentage and determining the applicable percentage is the product of the taxpayer's household income (determined without regard to section 36B(e)) and a fraction, the numerator of which is the FPL for the taxpayer's family size excluding individuals who are not lawfully present, and the denominator of which is the FPL for the taxpayer's family size including individuals who are not lawfully present.

Reconciliation

A taxpayer must reconcile the actual credit for the taxable year computed on the taxpayer's tax return with the amount of advance payments. If a taxpayer's credit amount exceeds the amount of the taxpayer's advance payments for the taxable year, the taxpayer may receive the excess as an income tax refund. If a taxpayer's advance payments exceed the taxpayer's credit amount, the taxpayer owes the excess as an additional income tax liability. However, section 36B(f)(2)(B) places a graduated set of caps on the additional tax liability for taxpayers with household income under 400 percent of the FPL. The repayment limitation amounts range from $600 to $2,500 (one-half that amount for single taxpayers) depending on FPL, and are adjusted to reflect changes in the cost of living beginning in 2015.

Section 36B(g) directs the Secretary of the Treasury to issue regulations that provide for coordinating the premium tax credit with the program for advance payments and for reconciling the credit and advance payments when the taxpayer's filing status changes during the taxable year.

Information Reporting

Section 36B(f)(3) directs an Exchange to report to the IRS and taxpayers certain information relating to health plans provided through the Exchange, including the amount of any advance credit payments.

Explanation of Provisions

1. Eligibility for the Premium Tax Credit

The proposed regulations provide that a taxpayer is eligible for the credit for a taxable year if the taxpayer is an applicable taxpayer and the taxpayer or a member of the taxpayer's family (1) is enrolled in one or more qualified health plans through an Exchange established under section 1311 or 1321 of the Affordable Care Act (42 U.S.C. 13031 or 42 U.S.C. 18041) and (2) is not eligible for minimum essential coverage other than coverage in the individual market.

a. Applicable Taxpayer

i. Lawfully Present Aliens

In general, to be an applicable taxpayer, a taxpayer must have household income that is at least 100 percent but not more than 400 percent of the FPL. Under section 36B(c)(1)(B), a lawfully present alien with household income under 100 percent of the FPL and not eligible for Medicaid is treated as having household income of 100 percent of the FPL for purposes of qualifying as an applicable taxpayer. The proposed regulations provide that premium assistance amounts for these taxpayers are computed based on actual household income. The proposed regulations define lawfully present by reference to 45 CFR 152.2, which determines lawful presence for purposes of the Pre-Existing Condition Insurance Plan Program.

ii. Taxpayers With Household Income Under 100 Percent of the FPL

The proposed regulations clarify the treatment of a taxpayer who receives advance credit payments but has household income below 100 percent of the FPL for the taxable year.

Taxpayers with household incomes below 100 percent of the FPL (other than lawfully present aliens) are not eligible for the premium tax credit because they are eligible to receive assistance through Medicaid. However, an Exchange may approve a taxpayer for advance credit payments based on projecting a level of household income for the taxable year that makes the taxpayer ineligible for Medicaid. If, contrary to that projection, the taxpayer's actual household income for the taxable year is under 100 percent of the FPL (for example, because the taxpayer experiences a change in circumstances, such as a job loss, during the year), the taxpayer would not be an applicable taxpayer, and would not be eligible for the credit under the general rule. Accordingly, the proposed regulations provide a special rule treating a taxpayer with household income below 100 percent of the FPL as an applicable taxpayer if, when a taxpayer enrolls in a qualified health plan, an Exchange projects that household income for the taxpayer will be between 100 and 400 percent of the FPL for the taxable year and approves advance credit payments. Premium assistance amounts for these taxpayers also are computed based on actual household income and not a deemed household income that equals 100 percent of the FPL.

iii. Individuals Who Are Incarcerated or Not Lawfully Present

Under section 1312(f) of the Affordable Care Act, individuals who are incarcerated (other than pending disposition of charges) or not lawfully present in the United States may not enroll in a qualified health plan through an Exchange. However, these individuals may have family members who are eligible for Exchange coverage. Accordingly, the proposed regulations provide that an individual who is not lawfully present in the United States or is incarcerated, although not eligible to enroll in a qualified health plan, may be an applicable taxpayer if a family member is eligible to and does enroll in a qualified health plan.

b. Minimum Essential Coverage

i. Government-Sponsored Coverage

Under the proposed regulations, an individual generally is eligible for government-sponsored minimum essential coverage for any month that the individual meets the requirements for coverage under a government-sponsored program described in section 5000A(f)(1)(A). However, for purposes of the premium tax credit, an individual is eligible for minimum essential coverage under a veterans' health care program only if the individual is enrolled in a veteran's health care program identified as minimum essential coverage in regulations issued under section 5000A. The Commissioner may define eligibility for specific government-sponsored programs further in published guidance of general applicability, see § 601.601(d)(2) of this chapter. For example, it is expected that future guidance will provide that a person is eligible for Medicaid on the basis of being blind or disabled or needing long-term care services only when a State Medicaid agency or the Social Security Administration, as appropriate, determines that the individual is blind or disabled or requires long-term care services.

In general, an individual is treated as eligible for a government-sponsored program on the first day of the first full month in which the individual may receive benefits. Thus, taxpayers would not lose eligibility for the credit for a month in which the taxpayer or a family member is technically eligible for a government program but cannot yet receive benefits due to, for example, the need for administrative processing. However, an individual who fails to complete the requirements to obtain coverage available under a government-sponsored program (other than coverage under the veteran's health care program) reasonably promptly is treated as eligible for the coverage on the first day of the second calendar month following the event that establishes eligibility (such as reaching age 65 for Medicare).

An individual receiving advance credit payments may apply and be approved for government-sponsored minimum essential coverage such as Medicaid that, after approval, is effective retroactively (overlapping some advance payment coverage months). The proposed regulations provide that an individual in this situation is treated as eligible for minimum essential coverage no sooner than the first day of the first calendar month after the approval.

Comments are requested on whether rules should provide additional flexibility if operational challenges prevent timely transition from coverage under a qualified health plan to coverage under a government-sponsored program.

A taxpayer whom an Exchange has determined to be ineligible for Medicaid, CHIP, or a similar program at the time of enrollment may end up with household income for the taxable year within the eligibility criteria for these programs. Therefore, the proposed regulations provide that an individual is treated as not eligible for Medicaid, CHIP, or a similar program for the months of coverage under a qualified health plan if an Exchange determines that the individual is not eligible when the individual enrolls. If the individual subsequently enrolls in Medicaid, CHIP, or a similar program, however, the full months of enrollment in the government-sponsored coverage are not coverage months.

ii. Employer-Sponsored Coverage

A. In General

Section 5000A(f)(1)(B) provides that minimum essential coverage includes coverage under an eligible employer-sponsored plan. Under section 5000A(f)(2), an eligible employer-sponsored plan is a group health plan or group health insurance coverage offered by an employer to an employee that is a governmental plan (within the meaning of section 2791(d)(8) of the Public Health Service Act (42 U.S.C. 300gg-91(d)(8))), any other plan or coverage offered in the small or large group market, or a grandfathered plan offered in the group market. Regulations under section 5000A are expected to provide that an employer-sponsored plan will not fail to be minimum essential coverage solely because it is a plan to reimburse employees for medical care for which reimbursement is not provided under a policy of accident and health insurance (a self-insured plan).

Continuation coverage required under federal law or required under a state law that provides comparable continuation coverage is eligible employer-sponsored coverage. The proposed regulations provide a special rule that an individual eligible to enroll in continuation coverage

is eligible for minimum essential coverage only if the individual enrolls in the coverage.

The proposed regulations provide that an individual generally is eligible for minimum essential coverage through an eligible employer-sponsored plan for a month during a plan year if the individual had the opportunity to enroll in the plan, even if the enrollment period has since closed. Thus, once an individual fails to enroll in eligible employer-sponsored coverage during an employer-sponsored plan's enrollment period after having had the opportunity to do so (assuming the coverage is affordable and provides minimum value), the months during the plan year are not coverage months for the individual, notwithstanding that the individual is precluded from later enrolling in the employer-sponsored coverage for those months because the enrollment period has expired.

Under section 36B(c)(2)(C), an individual generally is eligible for employer-sponsored minimum essential coverage only if the employee's share of the premiums is affordable and the coverage provides minimum value. An individual is treated as eligible for minimum essential coverage through an eligible employer-sponsored plan, however, if the individual actually enrolls in the coverage, including coverage that does not meet the requirements for affordability and minimum value.

B. Affordability of Employer-Sponsored Coverage

Section 36B(c)(2)(C)(i) prescribes the standards for determining whether employer-sponsored coverage is affordable for an employee as well as for other individuals. In the case of an employee, under section 36B(c)(2)(C)(i), an employer-sponsored plan is not affordable if "the employee's required contribution (within the meaning of section 5000A(e)(1)(B)) with respect to the plan exceeds 9.5 percent of the applicable taxpayer's household income" for the taxable year. This percentage may be adjusted after 2014.[1]

In the case of an individual other than an employee, section 36B(c)(2)(C)(i) provides that "this clause shall also apply to an individual who is eligible to enroll in the plan by reason of a relationship the individual bears to the employee." The cross-referenced section 5000A(e)(1)(B) defines the term "required contribution" for this purpose as "the portion of the annual premium which would be paid by the individual * * * for self-only coverage."

Thus, the statutory language specifies that for both employees and others (such as spouses or dependents) who are eligible to enroll in employer-sponsored coverage by reason of their relationship to an employee (related individuals), the coverage is unaffordable if the required contribution for "self-only" coverage (as opposed to family coverage or other coverage applicable to multiple individuals) exceeds 9.5 percent of household income. See Joint Committee on Taxation, General Explanation of Tax Legislation Enacted in the 111th Congress, JCS-2-11 (March 2011) at 265 (stating that, for purposes of the premium tax credit provisions of the Act, "[u]naffordable is defined as coverage with a premium required to be paid by the employee that is more than 9.5 percent of the employee's household income, based on the self-only coverage").

Consistent with these statutory provisions, the proposed regulations provide that an employer-sponsored plan also is affordable for a related individual for purposes of section 36B if the employee's required contribution for self-only coverage under the plan does not exceed 9.5 percent of the applicable taxpayer's household income for the taxable year, even if the employee's required contribution for the family coverage does exceed 9.5 percent of the applicable taxpayer's household income for the year.

Although the affordability test for related individuals for purposes of the premium tax credit is based on the cost of self-only coverage, future proposed regulations under section 5000A are expected to provide that the affordability test for purposes of applying the individual responsibility requirement to related individuals is based on the employee's required contribution for employer-sponsored family coverage. Section 5000A addresses affordability for employees in section 5000A(e)(1)(B) and, separately, for related individuals in section 5000A(e)(1)(C).

C. Employee Affordability Safe Harbor

The proposed regulations provide an employee safe harbor for individuals who were offered eligible employer-sponsored coverage that ultimately proves to be affordable based on household income for the taxable year but who declined the offer because, at the time of enroll-

---

[1] In addition, the statute provides for the Comptroller General, within 5 years of enactment, to conduct a study, including legislative recommendations, on the affordability of coverage, including whether the percentage of household income specified in section 36B(c)(2)(C) "is the appropriate level for determining whether employer-provided coverage is affordable for an employee and whether such level may be lowered without significantly increasing the costs to the Federal Government and reducing employer-provided coverage." See section 1401(c)(1) of the Affordable Care Act.

ment in a qualified health plan, the Exchange determined that the employer coverage would be unaffordable. Under the safe harbor, an eligible employer-sponsored plan is treated as unaffordable for an entire plan year. Thus, for the months during the plan year (which may coincide or overlap with the taxable year) a taxpayer will not lose credit eligibility because, as a result of changes during the taxable year, the employer coverage would have been affordable based on the household income for that taxable year. The taxpayer may, however, lose credit eligibility for other reasons, for example if the taxpayer's household income for the taxable year exceeds 400 percent of the FPL. Regulations under section 4980H are expected to provide that an employer is not subject to a penalty merely because an employee receives a premium tax credit under this employee safe harbor if the employer offered to its employees affordable coverage that otherwise meets the requirements of section 4980H.

D. Affordability Safe Harbor for Employers

In general, an applicable large employer (as defined in section 4980H(c)(2)) that offers health coverage to its full-time employees and their dependents is subject to the assessable payment under section 4980H(b) if at least one full-time employee is certified to receive a premium tax credit or cost-sharing reduction because the employer-sponsored coverage either does not provide minimum value or is unaffordable to the employee.

Employers have commented that they will not know their employees' actual household income. As a result, even if an employer intends to offer affordable coverage to all full-time employees, one or more full-time employees may be certified to receive the premium tax credit, and the employer may be subject to the assessable payment under 4980H(b). Future proposed regulations under section 4980H are expected to provide an affordability safe harbor for employers. Under this anticipated safe harbor, an employer that meets certain requirements, including offering its full-time employees (and their dependents) the opportunity to enroll in eligible employer-sponsored coverage, will not be subject to an assessable payment under section 4980H(b) with respect to an employee who receives a premium tax credit or cost-sharing reduction for a taxable year if the employee portion of the self-only premium for the employer's lowest cost plan that provides minimum value does not exceed 9.5 percent of the employee's current W-2 wages from the employer.

Giving employers the ability to base their affordability calculations on their employees' wages (which employers know) instead of employees' household income (which employers generally do not know) is intended to provide a more workable and predictable method of facilitating affordable employer-sponsored coverage for the benefit of both employers and employees. Notwithstanding this safe harbor, employees' eligibility for a premium tax credit would continue to be based on affordability of employer-sponsored coverage relative to employees' household income. Accordingly, some employees—among the small percentage of employees whose household income is less than their wages from the employer—would receive a premium tax credit without resulting in an assessable payment by their employer. The Treasury Department and the IRS intend to issue a request for comments on this affordability safe harbor for employers.

E. Minimum Value

Section 36B(c)(2)(C)(ii) provides that an eligible employer-sponsored plan generally provides minimum value if the plan's share of the total allowed costs of benefits provided under the plan is at least 60 percent of those costs. Under section 1302(d)(2) of the Affordable Care Act (42 U.S.C. 18022(d)(2)), regulations to be issued by the Secretary of Health and Human Services will apply in determining the percentage of "the total allowed costs of benefits" provided under a group health plan or health insurance coverage that are covered by that plan or coverage. The regulations under section 1302(d)(2) are expected to be proposed later this year and to reflect the fact that employer-sponsored group health plans and health insurance coverage in the large group market are not required to provide each of the essential health benefits or each of the 10 categories of benefits described in section 1302(b)(1) of the Affordable Care Act. It is also anticipated that the regulations will seek to further the objective of preserving the existing system of employer-sponsored coverage, but without permitting the statutory employer responsibility standards to be avoided. We also are contemplating whether to provide appropriate transition relief with respect to the minimum value requirement for employers currently offering health care coverage.

2. Computing the Premium Tax Credit

A taxpayer's credit is the sum of the premium assistance amounts for each coverage month in the taxable year. A premium assistance amount is computed for each coverage month during the taxable year based on several factors: household income, family size, applicable percentage, benchmark plan premium, and actual plan premium. A month during which no one in the taxpayer's family is enrolled in a qualified health plan through an Exchange is not a coverage month. A month is a coverage month only if the taxpayer pays the premium for coverage or receives the benefit of an advance payment. The premium assistance amount for a month that is not a coverage month is zero. Household income is determined on an annual basis and is prorated for each month to determine the monthly premium assistance amount. The applicable percentage is the same for each month because it is derived from annual household income and family size. A taxpayer's benchmark plan premium may change during the year if, for example, there are changes in the members of the household covered through the Exchange or the taxpayer moves to a new State with different plan rates.

a. Premiums Paid on Behalf of the Taxpayer

The proposed regulations provide that, in determining whether a month is a coverage month, premiums that another person pays for the coverage of the taxpayer or a family member are treated as paid by the taxpayer.

b. Applicable Benchmark Plan

Under section 36B(b)(2), the monthly premium for the applicable second lowest cost silver plan offered through an Exchange is the benchmark for computing a taxpayer's monthly premium assistance amount. To determine the amount of premium tax credit, a taxpayer must compute the difference between the premium for this plan and the applicable percentage of the taxpayer's household income, regardless of the qualified health plan the taxpayer purchases.

i. Multiple Categories of Coverage Offered on an Exchange

Section 36B(b)(3)(B)(ii) identifies only self-only and family as the categories of coverage for the benchmark plan. However, qualified health plans may offer other categories of coverage based on family composition, such as children only, two adults, or one adult plus children. See proposed 45 CFR 156.255(b). Thus, the proposed regulations define family coverage as any health insurance that covers more than one individual.

Under the proposed regulations, the "applicable" benchmark plan for a taxpayer is determined by finding the second lowest cost plan at the silver level that would cover those family members actually enrolled in a qualified health plan, not eligible for minimum essential coverage other than coverage in the individual market, not incarcerated, and lawfully present in the United States (the coverage family). Thus, the applicable benchmark plan is the self-only category of coverage for a taxpayer who files as single with no dependents, a taxpayer who purchases self-only coverage, and a taxpayer whose family includes only one individual who is not eligible for minimum essential coverage or one lawfully present individual (thus excluding from the credit computation the portion of the premium attributable to an individual not lawfully present, as required by section 36B(e)(1)(A)). If an Exchange offers more categories of coverage than self-only and family, the applicable benchmark plan is the coverage category that applies to the members of the taxpayer's coverage family.

ii. Families Who Purchase More Than One Qualified Health Plan

Section 36B determines family size by reference to individuals for whom the taxpayer claims a personal exemption, and family coverage under some qualified health plans may not extend to certain tax dependents (for example, a niece). We note that the Department of Health and Human Services has requested comments in its proposed regulations on Exchanges on whether qualified health plans offered on an Exchange should be required to cover all members of the family if they live in the same Exchange service area. Pending the issuance of additional guidance on this issue by Health and Human Services, the proposed regulations provide that, if the applicable benchmark plan does not cover a taxpayer's full family, the applicable benchmark plan premium for these families is the sum of the premiums for the benchmark plans that cover the taxpayer's family (for example, for an uncle and two adult dependent nieces, a self-only benchmark plan for the uncle and a two-adult or family plan for the nieces). The applicable benchmark plan is similarly modified for taxpayers with family members residing in different rating areas (also known as Exchange service areas, see proposed 45 CFR155.20). However, the IRS and Treasury Department are considering other approaches for determining the applicable benchmark plan in these cases. For example, the applicable benchmark plan for these families could be the benchmark plan that would apply to the family composition (such as one adult plus children) if one plan covered all members of the taxpayer's family. Alternatively, the applicable benchmark plan premium could be the lesser of (1) the premium for a combination of plans that cover the taxpayer's entire family, or (2) the premium for a single plan that covers the taxpayer's entire family and is more expensive than the second lowest cost silver plan. Comments are requested on these and other possible approaches.

iii. One Qualified Health Plan Covering More Than One Family

If a single qualified health plan covers more than one taxpayer's family (for example a plan that covers adult children under age 26 who are not tax dependents), the allowable section 36B credit is computed for each applicable taxpayer covered by the plan. An individual applicable percentage is determined for each taxpayer based on the taxpayer's household income and family size, and the separate applicable benchmark plan. The premiums for the qualified health plan the taxpayers purchase are allocated to each taxpayer in proportion to the premiums for each taxpayer's benchmark plan to determine whether the premiums paid are less than the benchmark premium minus the taxpayer's applicable percentage of household income.

iv. Applicable Benchmark Plan That Terminates or Closes to Enrollment

A qualified health plan that is the second lowest cost silver plan for a particular category of coverage, or the lowest cost silver plan in that category, may close to enrollment or terminate during the taxable year. The proposed regulations clarify that an applicable benchmark plan is a plan offered through the Exchange when a taxpayer or family member enrolls in a qualified health plan. Unless the taxpayer or a family member is enrolled in the applicable benchmark plan, a plan does not cease to be the applicable benchmark plan solely because the plan or the lowest cost silver plan terminates or closes to further enrollment during the taxable year.

c. Pediatric Dental Coverage

Section 36B(b)(3)(E) provides that, for purposes of determining the amount of any monthly premium, if an individual enrolls in both a qualified health plan and a plan providing dental coverage as described in section 1311(d)(2)(B)(ii) of the Affordable Care Act (42 U.S.C. 13031(d)(2)(B)(ii)), the portion of the premium for the dental plan that is properly allocable to pediatric dental benefits that are essential health benefits is treated as a premium payable for the individual's qualified health plan. Thus, the portion of the premium for the separate pediatric dental coverage is added to the premium for the benchmark plan in computing the credit. Comments are requested on methods of determining the amount of the premium properly allocable to pediatric dental benefits.

3. Reconciling the Credit and Advance Credit Payments

The proposed regulations describe the requirements for reconciling advance payments of the credit with the actual credit amount and determining the amount of any resulting additional credit or additional income tax liability. The proposed regulations explain that the credit is computed by using the household income and family size for the taxable year, but premium assistance amounts for different coverage months may be based on different applicable benchmark plans if, for example, the taxpayer's family composition changes during the taxable year.

a. Changes in Filing Status

Section 36B(g)(2) directs the Secretary to provide regulations specifying how to reconcile advance payments with the actual credit when the taxpayer's filing status on the return claiming the credit differs from the filing status used to determine advance payments of the credit. Filing status may be any of the following: single, married filing jointly, married filing separately, head of household, or surviving spouse.

i. Computing the Credit When Taxpayer's Marital Status Changes

The proposed regulations provide that, for a taxpayer who has a change in marital status during the taxable year, the credit generally is computed according to the same rules that apply to other taxpayers, using the applicable benchmark plan or plans that apply to the taxpayer's marital status as of the first day of each month. However, the proposed regulations include special rules for computing the credit for taxpayers who divorce during the taxable year. Comments are requested on special rules for taxpayers who marry during the taxable year and for married taxpayers who face challenges in being able to file a joint return.

ii. Taxpayers Who Divorce During the Taxable Year

The proposed regulations provide that, for purposes of reconciliation, taxpayers who for some months during a taxable year were married (within the meaning of section 7703) and were covered by the same qualified health plan but are no longer married on the last day of the taxable year, may agree to allocate between themselves, in the same proportion, the premiums for the benchmark plan, premiums paid and advance credit payments made during the marriage. If the taxpayers do not agree on an allocation, the taxpayers must allocate 50 percent of these amounts to each taxpayer. If only one of the formerly married taxpayers was enrolled in the plan, 100 percent of the benchmark premiums, premiums for the plan that taxpayer purchases, and advance payments are allocated to that taxpayer.

iii. Taxpayers Who Marry During the Taxable Year

For individuals who marry during a taxable year and receive advance credit payments during the time before they are married, the general rules for credit computation and reconciliation could lead to the individuals facing additional tax upon reconciliation, even if the Exchange accurately determines each individual's separate income for the year at the time of enrollment. This may occur, for example, in situations in which the combination of two individuals' household incomes and families results in the combined family having a higher FPL percentage than either of the component families would have had if the individuals had not married, and therefore having a higher applicable percentage or being ineligible for a credit. Comments are requested on rules providing relief to certain individuals who would owe additional tax because they marry during a taxable year when one or both individuals receive advance credit payments prior to marriage. Comments are requested on how the premium assistance credit amount should be computed in this circumstance, including how household income (which is required to be determined on an annual basis) and dependents for the taxable year would be taken into account in the credit computation.

iv. Married Taxpayers Filing Separately

Married taxpayers who file their returns as married filing separately are not applicable taxpayers and generally are ineligible for the premium tax credit for any month during the taxable year. The proposed regulations provide that taxpayers who receive advance credit payments and file their tax returns as married filing separately must allocate 50 percent of any advance credit payments to each spouse for purposes of determining their excess advance payment amounts as part of the reconciliation process. Although the taxpayers owe additional tax for the entire amount of the advance credit payments, the section 36B(f)(2)(B) repayment limitation applies to each taxpayer whose household income is below 400 percent of the federal poverty line based on the household income and family size reported on the return.

Some taxpayers who are married at the time they enroll in a qualified health plan and begin to receive advance credit payments may not be able to file a joint return for the coverage year. For example, in situations involving domestic abuse, when a divorce is pending but not yet final, or when one spouse is incarcerated, filing a joint return may not be possible or prudent. Comments are requested on rules to provide relief for those married taxpayers who have received advance credit payments but face challenges in being able to file a joint return. Comments are requested in particular on whether rules should take into account whether (1) The spouses have filed jointly for the preceding taxable year, (2) the spouses attested to an expectation to file jointly for purposes of receiving the advance credit payments, and (3) the spouses should be allowed relief of this type for more than one year.

Comments are requested on other rules for reconciling the credit with advance payments for taxpayers whose filing status changes during the taxable year.

b. Requirement To File a Return

The proposed regulations require every taxpayer receiving advance credit payments to file an income tax return on or before the fifteenth day of the fourth month following the close of the taxable year. The requirement to file a return applies whether or not a taxpayer is otherwise required to file a return under section 6012 or claims a premium tax credit for the taxable year. Under section 6081, the Commissioner may grant a reasonable extension of time for filing any income tax return.

Effective/Applicability Date

These regulations are proposed to apply for taxable years ending after December 31, 2013.

Special Analyses

It has been determined that this notice of proposed rulemaking is not a significant regulatory action as defined in Executive Order 12866, as supplemented by Executive Order 13563. Therefore, a regulatory assessment is not required. It has also been determined that section 553(b) of the Administrative Procedure Act (5 U.S.C. chapter 5) does not apply to these regulations, and, because the regulations do not impose a collection of information requirement on small entities, the Regulatory Flexibility Act (5 U.S.C. chapter 6) does not apply. Pursuant to section 7805(f) of the Code, this notice of proposed rulemaking has been submitted to the Chief Counsel for Advocacy of the Small Business Administration for comment on its impact on small business.

Comments and Public Hearing

Before these proposed regulations are adopted as final regulations, consideration will be given to any written comments (either electronic or a signed paper original and eight (8) copies) that are submitted timely to the IRS. The IRS and Treasury Department request comments on the clarity of the proposed rules and how they can be made easier to understand. All comments will be available for public inspection and copying.

A public hearing has been scheduled for November 17, 2011, at 10 a.m., in the auditorium, Internal Revenue Building, 1111 Constitution Avenue, NW., Washington, DC. Due to building security procedures, visitors must enter at the Constitution Avenue entrance. All visitors must present photo identification to enter the building. Because of access restrictions, visitors will not be admitted beyond the immediate entrance more than 30 minutes before the hearing starts. For information about having your name placed on the building access list to attend the hearing, see the **FOR FURTHER INFORMATION CONTACT** section of this preamble.

The rules of 26 CFR 601.601(a)(3) apply to the hearing. Persons who wish to present oral comments at the hearing must submit written comments (electronic or a signed paper original and eight (8) copies) and an outline of topics to be discussed and the time devoted to each topic by November 10, 2011. A period of 10 minutes will be allotted to each person for making comments.

An agenda showing the scheduling of the speakers will be prepared after the deadline for receiving outlines has passed. Copies of the agenda will be available free of charge at the hearing.

Drafting Information

The principal authors of these proposed regulations are Shareen S. Pflanz, Frank W. Dunham III, and Stephen J. Toomey of the Office of Associate Chief Counsel (Income Tax and Accounting). However, other personnel from the IRS and the Treasury Department participated in the development of the regulations.

List of Subjects in 26 CFR Part 1

Income taxes, Reporting and recordkeeping requirements.

Proposed Amendments to the Regulations

Accordingly, 26 CFR part 1 is proposed to be amended as follows:

PART 1—INCOME TAXES

Paragraph 1. The authority citation for part 1 is amended by adding entries in numerical order to read in part as follows:

Authority: 26 U.S.C. 7805 * * *

Section 1.36B-4 also issued under 26 U.S.C. 36B(g).

Par. 2. Sections 1.36B-0, 1.36B-1, 1.36B-2, 1.36B-3, 1.36B-4, and 1.36B-5 are added to read as follows:

§ 1.36B-0 Table of contents.

This section lists the captions contained in §§ 1.36B-1 through 1.36B-5.

§ 1.36B-1 Premium tax credit definitions.

(a) In general.

(b) Affordable Care Act.

(c) Qualified health plan.

(d) Family and family size.

(e) Household income.

(1) In general.

(2) Modified adjusted gross income.

(f) Dependent.

(g) Lawfully present.

(h) Federal poverty line.

(i) Reserved.

(j) Advance credit payment.

(k) Exchange.

(l) Self-only coverage.

(m) Family coverage.

(n) Rating area.

(o) Effective/applicability date.

§ 1.36B-2 Eligibility for premium tax credit.

(a) In general.

(b) Applicable taxpayer.

(1) In general.

(2) Married taxpayers must file joint return.

(3) Dependents.

(4) Individuals not lawfully present or incarcerated.

(5) Individuals lawfully present.

(6) Special rule for taxpayers with household income below 100 percent of the federal poverty line for the taxable year.

(7) Computation of premium assistance amounts for taxpayers with household income below 100 percent of the federal poverty line.

(c) Minimum essential coverage.

(1) In general.

(2) Government-sponsored minimum essential coverage.

(i) In general.

(ii) Special rule for coverage under the veteran's health care program under chapter 17 or 18 of Title 38, U.S.C.

(iii) Time of eligibility.

(A) In general.

(B) Retroactive effect of eligibility determination.

(iv) Determination of Medicaid or Children's Health Insurance Program (CHIP) ineligibility.

(v) Examples.

(3) Employer-sponsored minimum essential coverage.

(i) In general.

(ii) Plan year.

(iii) Eligibility for coverage months during a plan year.

(A) In general.

(B) Example.

(iv) Special rule for continuation coverage.

(v) Affordable coverage.

(A) In general.

(1) Affordability.

(2) Employee safe harbor.

(B) Required contribution percentage.

(C) Examples.

(vi) Minimum value.

(vii) Enrollment in eligible employer-sponsored plan.

(A) In general.

(B) Example.

§ 1.36B-3 Computing the premium assistance credit amount.

(a) In general.

(b) Definitions.

(c) Coverage month.

(1) In general.

(2) Premiums paid for the taxpayer.

(3) Examples.

(d) Premium assistance amount.

(e) Adjusted monthly premium.

(f) Applicable benchmark plan.

(1) In general.

(2) Family coverage.

(3) Second lowest cost silver plan not covering the taxpayer's family.

(4) Benchmark plan terminates or closes to enrollment.

(5) Examples.

(g) Applicable percentage.

(1) In general.

(2) Applicable percentage table.

(3) Examples.

(h) Plan covering more than one family.

(1) In general.

(2) Example.

(i) Reserved.

(j) Additional benefits.

(1) In general.

(2) Method of allocation.

(k) Pediatric dental coverage.

(1) In general.

(2) Method of allocation.

(l) Families including individuals not lawfully present.

(1) In general.

(2) Revised household income computation.

(i) Statutory method.

(ii) Comparable method.

§ 1.36B-4 Reconciling the premium tax credit with advance credit payments.

(a) Reconciliation.

(1) In general.

(2) Credit computation.

(3) Limitation on additional tax.

(i) In general.

(ii) Additional tax limitation table.

(4) Examples.

(b) Changes in filing status.

(1) In general.

(2) Taxpayers not married to each other at the end of the taxable year.

(3) Married taxpayers filing separate returns.

(4) Examples.

§ 1.36B-5 Information reporting by Exchanges.

(a) Information required to be reported.

(b) Time and manner of reporting.

§ 1.36B-1 Premium tax credit definitions.

(a) *In general.* Section 36B allows a refundable premium tax credit for taxable years ending after December 31, 2013. The definitions in this section apply to this section and §§ 1.36B-2 through 1.36B-5.

(b) *Affordable Care Act.* The term *Affordable Care Act* refers to the Patient Protection and Affordable Care Act, Public Law 111-148 (124 Stat. 119 (2010)), and the Health Care and Education Reconciliation Act of 2010, Public Law 111-152 (124 Stat. 1029 (2010)), as amended by the Medicare and Medicaid Extenders Act of 2010, Public Law 111-309 (124 Stat. 3285 (2010)), the Comprehensive 1099 Taxpayer Protection and Repayment of Exchange Subsidy Overpayments Act of 2011, Public Law 112-9 (125 Stat. 36 (2011)), and the Department of Defense and

Full-Year Continuing Appropriations Act, 2011, Public Law 112-10 (125 Stat. 38 (2011)).

(c) *Qualified health plan.* The term *qualified health plan* has the same meaning as in section 1301(a) of the Affordable Care Act (42 U.S.C. 18021(a)) but does not include a catastrophic plan described in section 1302(e) of the Affordable Care Act (42 U.S.C. 18022(e)).

(d) *Family and family size.* A taxpayer's family means the individuals for whom a taxpayer properly claims a deduction for a personal exemption under section 151 for the taxable year. Family size means the number of individuals in the family. Family and family size include an individual who is exempt from the requirement to maintain minimum essential coverage under section 5000A.

(e) *Household income*—(1) *In general.* Household income means the sum of—

(i) A taxpayer's modified adjusted gross income; plus

(ii) The aggregate modified adjusted gross income of all other individuals who—

(A) Are included in the taxpayer's family under paragraph (d) of this section; and

(B) Are required to file an income tax return for the taxable year (determined without regard to the exception under section (1)(g)(7) to the requirement to file a return).

(2) *Modified adjusted gross income.* Modified adjusted gross income means adjusted gross income (within the meaning of section 62) increased by amounts excluded from gross income under section 911 and tax-exempt interest the taxpayer receives or accrues during the taxable year.

(f) *Dependent.* Dependent has the same meaning as in section 152.

(g) *Lawfully present.* Lawfully present has the same meaning as in 45 CFR 152.2.

(h) *Federal poverty line.* The federal poverty line means the most recently published poverty guidelines (updated periodically in the **Federal Register** by the Secretary of Health and Human Services under the authority of 42 U.S.C. 9902(2)) as of the first day of the regular enrollment period for coverage by a qualified health plan offered through an Exchange for a calendar year. Thus, the federal poverty line for computing the premium tax credit for a taxable year is the federal poverty line in effect on the first day of the initial or annual open enrollment period preceding that taxable year. See 45 CFR 155.410.

(i) [Reserved]

(j) *Advance credit payment.* Advance credit payment means an advance payment of the premium tax credit as provided in section 1412 of the Affordable Care Act (42 U.S.C. 18082).

(k) *Exchange.* Exchange has the same meaning as in 45 CFR 155.20.

(l) *Self-only coverage.* Self-only coverage means health insurance that covers one individual.

(m) *Family coverage.* Family coverage means health insurance that covers more than one individual.

(n) *Rating area.* Rating area means an Exchange service area, as described in 45 CFR 155.20.

(o) *Effective/applicability date.* This section and §§ 1.36B-2 through 1.36B-5 apply for taxable years ending after December 31, 2013.

§ 1.36B-2 Eligibility for premium tax credit.

(a) *In general.* An applicable taxpayer (within the meaning of paragraph (b) of this section) is allowed a premium assistance amount only for any month that the applicable taxpayer, or the applicable taxpayer's spouse or dependent—

(1) Is enrolled in one or more qualified health plans through an Exchange; and

(2) Is not eligible for minimum essential coverage (within the meaning of paragraph (c) of this section) other than coverage described in section 5000A(f)(1)(C) (relating to coverage in the individual market).

(b) *Applicable taxpayer*—(1) *In general.* Except as otherwise provided in this paragraph (b), an applicable taxpayer is a taxpayer whose household income is at least 100 percent but not more than 400 percent of the federal poverty line for the taxpayer's family size for the taxable year.

(2) *Married taxpayers must file joint return.* A taxpayer who is married (within the meaning of section 7703) at the close of the taxable

year is an applicable taxpayer only if the taxpayer and the taxpayer's spouse file a joint return for the taxable year.

(3) *Dependents.* An individual is not an applicable taxpayer if another taxpayer may claim a deduction under section 151 for the individual for a taxable year beginning in the calendar year in which the individual's taxable year begins.

(4) *Individuals not lawfully present or incarcerated.* An individual who is not lawfully present in the United States or is incarcerated (other than incarceration pending disposition of charges) may not be covered by a qualified health plan through an Exchange. However, the individual may be an applicable taxpayer if a family member is eligible to enroll in a qualified health plan. See sections 1312(f)(1)(B) and 1312(f)(3) of the Affordable Care Act (42 U.S.C. 18032(f)(1)(B) and (f)(3)) and § 1.36B-3(b)(2).

(5) *Individuals lawfully present.* If a taxpayer's household income is less than 100 percent of the federal poverty line for the taxpayer's family size and the taxpayer or a member of the taxpayer's family is an alien lawfully present in the United States, the taxpayer is treated as an applicable taxpayer if—

(i) The taxpayer or family member is not eligible for the Medicaid program; and

(ii) The taxpayer would be an applicable taxpayer if the taxpayer's household income for the taxable year was between 100 and 400 percent of the federal poverty line for the taxpayer's family size.

(6) *Special rule for taxpayers with household income below 100 percent of the federal poverty line for the taxable year.* A taxpayer (other than a taxpayer described in paragraph (b)(5) of this section) whose household income for a taxable year is less than 100 percent of the federal poverty line for the taxpayer's family size is treated as an applicable taxpayer if—

(i) The taxpayer or a family member enrolls in a qualified health plan through an Exchange;

(ii) An Exchange estimates at the time of enrollment that the taxpayer's household income will be between 100 and 400 percent of the federal poverty line for the taxable year;

(iii) Advance credit payments are authorized and paid for one or more months during the taxable year; and

(iv) The taxpayer would be an applicable taxpayer if the taxpayer's household income for the taxable year was between 100 and 400 percent of the federal poverty line for the taxpayer's family size.

(7) *Computation of premium assistance amounts for taxpayers with household income below 100 percent of the federal poverty line.* If a taxpayer is treated as an applicable taxpayer under paragraph (b)(5) or (b)(6) of this section, the taxpayer's actual household income for the taxable year is used to compute the premium assistance amounts under § 1.36B-3(d).

(c) *Minimum essential coverage*—(1) *In general.* Minimum essential coverage is defined in section 5000A(f) and regulations issued under that section. As described in section 5000A(f), government-sponsored programs, eligible employer-sponsored plans, grandfathered health plans, and certain other health benefits coverage are minimum essential coverage.

(2) *Government-sponsored minimum essential coverage*—(i) *In general.* Except as provided in paragraph (c)(2)(ii) of this section, for purposes of section 36B, an individual is eligible for government-sponsored minimum essential coverage if the individual meets the criteria for coverage under a government-sponsored program described in section 5000A(f)(1)(A). The Commissioner may define eligibility for specific government-sponsored programs further in published guidance of general applicability, see § 601.601(d)(2) of this chapter.

(ii) *Special rule for coverage under the veteran's health care program under chapter 17 or 18 of Title 38, U.S.C.* An individual is eligible for minimum essential coverage under the veteran's health care program authorized under chapter 17 or 18 of Title 38, U.S.C., only if the individual is enrolled in a veteran's health care program identified as minimum essential coverage in regulations issued under section 5000A.

(iii) *Time of eligibility*—(A) *In general.* An individual generally is treated as eligible for a government-sponsored program on the first day of the first full month in which the individual may receive benefits under the program. However, an individual who fails to complete the requirements necessary to receive benefits available under a government-sponsored program (other than a veteran's health care program) reasonably promptly is treated as eligible for government-sponsored

minimum essential coverage as of the first day of the second calendar month following the event that establishes eligibility under paragraph (c)(2)(i) of this section.

(B) *Retroactive effect of eligibility determination.* If an individual receiving advance credit payments is determined to be eligible for government-sponsored minimum essential coverage that is effective retroactively (such as Medicaid), the individual is treated as eligible for minimum essential coverage under that program no earlier than the first day of the first calendar month beginning after the approval.

(iv) *Determination of Medicaid or Children's Health Insurance Program (CHIP) ineligibility.* An individual is treated as not eligible for Medicaid, CHIP, or a similar program for a period of coverage under a qualified health plan if an Exchange determines that the individual is not eligible for the program when the individual enrolls in the qualified health plan.

(v) *Examples.* The following examples illustrate the provisions of this paragraph (c)(2).

Example 1. Delay in coverage effectiveness. On April 10, Taxpayer D applies for coverage under a government-sponsored health care program. D's application is approved on July 12 but her coverage is not effective until September 1. Under paragraph (c)(2)(iii)(A) of this section, D is eligible for government-sponsored minimum essential coverage on September 1.

Example 2. Time of eligibility. Taxpayer E turns 65 on June 3 and becomes eligible for Medicare. Under section 5000A(f)(1)(A), Medicare is minimum essential coverage. However, E must enroll in Medicare to receive benefits. E enrolls in Medicare on June 11 and may receive benefits immediately. Under paragraph (c)(2)(iii)(A) of this section, E is eligible for government-sponsored minimum essential coverage on July 1, the first day of the first full month that E may receive benefits under the program.

Example 3. Time of eligibility, individual fails to complete necessary requirements. The facts are the same as in *Example 2,* except that E fails to enroll in the Medicare coverage. E is treated as eligible for government-sponsored minimum essential coverage under paragraph (c)(2)(iii)(A) of this section as of August 1, the first day of the second month following the event that establishes eligibility (E turning 65).

Example 4. Retroactive effect of eligibility. On April 10, 2015, Taxpayer G applies for coverage under the Medicaid program. G's application is approved on May 15, 2015, and her Medicaid coverage is effective as of April 1, 2015. Under paragraph (c)(2)(iii)(B) of this section, G is eligible for government-sponsored minimum essential coverage on June 1, 2015, the first day of the first calendar month after approval.

Example 5. Determination of Medicaid ineligibility. In November 2014, Taxpayer H applies to the Exchange to enroll in a qualified health plan and for advance credit payments for 2015. The Exchange estimates that H's household income will be 140 percent of the federal poverty line for H's family size and determines that H is not eligible for Medicaid. The Exchange authorizes advance credit payments for H for 2015. H experiences a loss of household income in June 2015 but does not return to the Exchange in 2015 to apply for Medicaid benefits or report his change in income. H's household income for 2015 is 130 percent of the federal poverty line (within the Medicaid income threshold). Under paragraph (c)(2)(iv) of this section, H is treated as not eligible for Medicaid for 2015.

Example 6. Mid-year Medicaid eligibility redetermination. The facts are the same as in *Example 5,* except that H returns to the Exchange in July 2015 and the Exchange determines H is eligible for Medicaid. The Exchange discontinues H's advance credit payments effective August 1. Under paragraphs (c)(2)(iii)(B) and (c)(2)(iv) of this section, H is treated as not eligible for Medicaid for the coverage months when H is covered by a qualified health plan. H is eligible for government-sponsored minimum essential coverage for the coverage months after H is approved for Medicaid, August through December 2015.

(3) *Employer-sponsored minimum essential coverage*—(i) *In general.* For purposes of section 36B, an employee who may enroll in an eligible employer-sponsored plan (as defined in section 5000A(f)(2)) and an individual who may enroll in the plan because of a relationship to the employee (a related individual) are eligible for minimum essential coverage under the plan for any month only if the plan is affordable and provides minimum value. Government-sponsored programs described in section 5000A(f)(1)(A) are not eligible employer-sponsored plans.

(ii) *Plan year.* For purposes of this paragraph (c)(3), a plan year is an eligible employer-sponsored plan's regular 12-month coverage period (or the remainder of a 12-month coverage period for a new employee or an individual who enrolls during a special enrollment period).

(iii) *Eligibility for coverage months during a plan year*—(A) *In general.* An employee or related individual may be eligible for minimum essential coverage under an eligible employer-sponsored plan for a coverage month during a plan year if the employee or related individual could have enrolled in the plan for that month during an open or special enrollment period.

(B) *Example.* The following example illustrates the provisions of this paragraph (c)(3)(iii).

Example. (i) Taxpayer B is an employee of Employer X. X offers its employees a health insurance plan that has a plan year (within the meaning of paragraph (c)(3)(ii) of this section) from October 1 through September 30. Employees may enroll during an open season from August 1 to September 15. B does not enroll in X's plan for the plan year October 1, 2014, to September 30, 2015. In November 2014 B enrolls in a qualified health plan through an Exchange for calendar year 2015.

(ii) B could have enrolled in X's plan during the August 1 to September 15 enrollment period. Therefore, unless X's plan is not affordable for B or does not provide minimum value, B is eligible for minimum essential coverage for the months that B is enrolled in the qualified health plan during X's plan year (January through September 2015).

(iv) *Special rule for continuation coverage.* An individual who may enroll in continuation coverage required under federal law or a state law that provides comparable continuation coverage is eligible for minimum essential coverage only if the individual enrolls in the coverage.

(v) *Affordable coverage*—(A) *In general*—(*1*) *Affordability.* Except as provided in paragraph (c)(3)(v)(A)(*2*) of this section, an eligible employer-sponsored plan is affordable for an employee or a related individual if the portion of the annual premium the employee must pay, whether by salary reduction or otherwise (required contribution), for self-only coverage for the taxable year does not exceed the required contribution percentage (as defined in paragraph (c)(3)(v)(B) of this section) of the applicable taxpayer's household income for the taxable year.

(*2*) *Employee safe harbor.* An employer-sponsored plan is treated as not affordable for an employee or a related individual for a plan year if, when the employee or a related individual enrolls in a qualified health plan for a period coinciding with the plan year (in whole or in part), an Exchange determines that the eligible employer-sponsored plan is not affordable.

(B) *Required contribution percentage.* The required contribution percentage is 9.5 percent. The percentage may be adjusted in published guidance of general applicability, see § 601.601(d)(2) of this chapter, for taxable years beginning after December 31, 2014, to reflect rates of premium growth relative to growth in income and, for taxable years beginning after December 31, 2018, to reflect rates of premium growth relative to growth in the consumer price index.

(C) *Examples.* The following examples illustrate the provisions of this paragraph (c)(3)(v). Unless stated otherwise, in each example the taxpayer is single and has no dependents, the employer's plan is an eligible employer-sponsored plan and provides minimum value, the employee is not eligible for other minimum essential coverage, and the taxpayer, related individual, and employer-sponsored plan have a calendar taxable year.

Example 1. Basic determination of affordability. In 2014 Taxpayer C has household income of $47,000. C is an employee of Employer X, which offers its employees a health insurance plan that requires C to contribute $3,450 for self-only coverage for 2014 (7.3 percent of C's household income). Because C's required contribution for self-only coverage does not exceed 9.5 percent of household income, under paragraph (c)(3)(v)(A)(*1*) of this section, X's plan is affordable for C, and C is eligible for minimum essential coverage for all months in 2014.

Example 2. Basic determination of affordability for a related individual. The facts are the same as in *Example 1,* except that C is married to J and X's plan requires C to contribute $5,300 for coverage for C and J for 2014 (11.3 percent of C's household income). Because C's required contribution for self-only coverage ($3,450) does not exceed 9.5 percent of household income, under paragraph (c)(3)(v)(A)(*1*) of this section, X's plan is affordable for C and J, and C and J are eligible for minimum essential coverage for all months in 2014.

Example 3. Determination of unaffordability at enrollment. (i) Taxpayer D is an employee of Employer X. In November 2013 the Exchange in D's rating area projects that D's 2014 household income will be $37,000. It also verifies that D's required contribution for self-only coverage under X's health insurance plan will be $3,700 (10 percent of household income). Consequently, the Exchange determines that X's

plan is unaffordable. D enrolls in a qualified health plan and not in X's plan. In December 2014, X pays D a $2,500 bonus. Thus, D's actual 2014 household income is $39,500 and D's required contribution for coverage under X's plan is 9.4 percent of household income.

(ii) Based on D's actual 2014 household income, D's required contribution does not exceed 9.5 percent of household income and X's health plan is affordable for D. However, when D enrolled in a qualified health plan for 2014, the Exchange determined that X's plan was not affordable for D for 2014. Consequently, under paragraph (c)(3)(v)(A)(*2*) of this section, X's plan is treated as not affordable for D and D is treated as not eligible for minimum essential coverage for 2014.

Example 4. Determination of unaffordability for plan year. The facts are the same as in *Example 3,* except that X's employee health insurance plan year is September 1 to August 31. The Exchange in D's rating area determines in August 2014 that X's plan is unaffordable for D based on D's projected household income for 2014. D enrolls in a qualified health plan as of September 1, 2014. Under paragraph (c)(3)(v)(A)(*2*) of this section, X's plan is treated as not affordable for D and D is treated as not eligible for minimum essential coverage under X's plan for the coverage months September to December 2014 and January through August 2015.

Example 5. Determination of unaffordability for part of plan year. (i) Taxpayer E is an employee of Employer X beginning in May 2015. X's employee health insurance plan year is September 1 to August 31. E's required contribution for self-only coverage for May through August is $150 per month ($1,800 for the full plan year). The Exchange in E's rating area determines E's household income for purposes of eligibility for advance credit payments as $18,000. E's actual household income for the 2015 taxable year is $20,000.

(ii) Whether coverage under X's plan is affordable for E is determined for the remainder of X's plan year (May through August). E's required contribution for a full plan year ($1,800) exceeds 9.5 percent of E's household income (1,800/18,000 = 10 percent). Therefore, the Exchange determines that X's coverage is unaffordable for May through August. Although E's actual household income for 2015 is $20,000 (and E's required contribution of $1,800 does not exceed 9.5 percent of E's household income), under paragraph (c)(3)(v)(A)(*2*) of this section, X's plan is treated as unaffordable for E for the part of the plan year May through August 2015. Consequently, E is not eligible for minimum essential coverage under X's plan for the period May through August 2015.

Example 6. Affordability determined for part of a taxable year (part-year period). (i) Taxpayer F is an employee of Employer X. X's employee health insurance plan year is September 1 to August 31. F's required contribution for self-only coverage for the period September 2014 through August 2015 is $150 per month or $1,800 for the plan year. F does not ask the Exchange in his rating area to determine whether X's coverage is affordable for F. F does not enroll in X's plan during X's open season but enrolls in a qualified health plan for September through December 2014. F's household income in 2014 is $18,000.

(ii) Because F is a calendar year taxpayer and Employer X's plan is not a calendar year plan, F must determine the affordability of X's coverage for the part-year period in 2014 (September-December). F determines the affordability of X's plan for the September through December 2014 period by comparing the annual premiums ($1,800) to F's 2014 household income. F's required contribution of $1,800 is 10 percent of F's 2014 household income. Because F's required contribution exceeds 9.5 percent of F's 2014 household income, X's plan is not affordable for F for the part-year period September through December 2014 and F is not eligible for minimum essential coverage under X's plan for that period.

(iii) F enrolls in Exchange coverage for 2015 and does not ask the Exchange to determine whether X's coverage is affordable. F's 2015 household income is $20,000.

(iv) F must determine if X's plan is affordable for the part-year period January 2015 through August 2015. F's annual required contribution ($1,800) is 9 percent of F's 2015 household income. Because F's required contribution does not exceed 9.5 percent of F's 2015 household income, X's plan is affordable for F for the part-year period January through August 2015 and F is eligible for minimum essential coverage for that period.

Example 7. Coverage unaffordable at year end. Taxpayer G is employed by Employer X. In November 2014 the Exchange in G's rating area determines that G is eligible for affordable employer-sponsored coverage for 2015. G nonetheless enrolls in a qualified health plan for 2015 but does not receive advance credit payments. G's 2015 household income is less than expected and G's required contribution for employer-sponsored coverage for 2015 exceeds 9.5 percent of G's actual 2015 household income. Under paragraph (c)(3)(v)(A)(*1*) of this section, G is not eligible for minimum essential coverage for 2015 and, if otherwise eligible, G may claim a premium tax credit.

(vi) *Minimum value.* An eligible employer-sponsored plan provides minimum value only if the plan's share of the total allowed costs of benefits provided under the plan (as determined under regulations issued by the Secretary of Health and Human Services under section 1302(d)(2) of the Affordable Care Act (42 U.S.C. 18022(d)(2))) is at least 60 percent.

(vii) *Enrollment in eligible employer-sponsored plan—(A)* *In general.* The requirements of affordability and minimum value do not apply if an individual enrolls in an eligible employer-sponsored plan.

(B) *Example.* The following example illustrates the provisions of this paragraph (c)(3)(vii).

Example. Taxpayer H is employed by Employer X in 2014. H's required contribution for employer coverage exceeds 9.5 percent of H's 2014 household income. H enrolls in X's plan for 2014. Under paragraph (c)(3)(vii) of this section, H is eligible for minimum essential coverage for 2014 because H is enrolled in an eligible employer-sponsored plan for 2014.

§ 1.36B-3 Computing the premium assistance credit amount.

(a) *In general.* A taxpayer's premium assistance credit amount for a taxable year is the sum of the premium assistance amounts determined under paragraph (d) of this section for all coverage months for individuals in the taxpayer's family.

(b) *Definitions.* For purposes of this section—

(1) The cost of a qualified health plan is the premium the plan charges; and

(2) The term *coverage family* refers to members of the taxpayer's family who are not eligible for minimum essential coverage (other than coverage in the individual market), are lawfully present in the United States, and are not incarcerated (except pending disposition of charges).

(c) *Coverage month—(1) In general.* A month is a coverage month for an individual if, as of the first day of the month—

(i) The individual is covered by a qualified health plan enrolled in through an Exchange;

(ii) The individual's premiums for coverage under the plan are paid by the taxpayer or by an advance credit payment; and

(iii) The individual is not eligible for minimum essential coverage (within the meaning of § 1.36B-2(c)) other than coverage described in section 5000A(f)(1)(C) (relating to coverage in the individual market).

(2) *Premiums paid for the taxpayer.* Premiums another person pays for coverage of the taxpayer, taxpayer's spouse, or dependent are treated as paid by the taxpayer.

(3) *Examples.* The following examples illustrate the provisions of this paragraph (c). In each example, unless stated otherwise, the individuals are not eligible for minimum essential coverage other than coverage in the individual market and the taxpayer is an applicable taxpayer.

Example 1. (i) Taxpayer M is single with no dependents. In December 2013 M enrolls in a qualified health plan for 2014 and the Exchange approves advance credit payments. On May 15, 2014, M enlists in the U.S. Army and is eligible immediately for government-sponsored minimum essential coverage.

(ii) Under paragraph (c)(1) of this section, January through May 2014 are coverage months for M. June through December 2014 are not coverage months because M is eligible for minimum essential coverage for those months. Thus, under paragraph (a) of this section, M's premium assistance credit amount for 2014 is the sum of the premium assistance amounts for the months January through May.

Example 2. (i) Taxpayer N has one dependent, S. S is eligible for government-sponsored minimum essential coverage. N is not eligible for minimum essential coverage. N enrolls in a qualified health plan for 2014 and the Exchange approves advance credit payments. On August 1, 2014, S loses eligibility for minimum essential coverage. N cancels the qualified health plan that covers only N and enrolls in a qualified health plan that covers N and S for August through December 2014.

(ii) Under paragraph (c)(1) of this section, January through December of 2014 are coverage months for N and August through December are coverage months for N and S. N's premium assistance credit amount for 2014 is the sum of the premium assistance amounts for these coverage months.

Example 3. (i) O and P are the divorced parents of T. Under the divorce agreement between O and P, T resides with P and P claims T as a dependent. However, O must pay premiums for health insurance for T. P enrolls T in a qualified health plan for 2014. O pays the premiums to the insurance company.

(ii) Because P claims T as a dependent, P (and not O) may claim a premium tax credit for coverage for T. See § 1.36B-2(a). Under paragraph (c)(2) of this section, the premiums that O pays for coverage for T are treated as paid by P. Thus, the months when T is covered by a qualified health plan are coverage months under paragraph (c)(1) of this section in computing P's premium tax credit under paragraph (a) of this section.

(d) *Premium assistance amount.* The premium assistance amount for a coverage month is the lesser of—

(1) The premiums for the month for one or more qualified health plans in which a taxpayer or a member of the taxpayer's family enrolls; or

(2) The excess of the adjusted monthly premium for the applicable benchmark plan over 1.12 of the product of a taxpayer's household income and the applicable percentage for the taxable year.

(e) *Adjusted monthly premium.* The adjusted monthly premium is the premium an insurer would charge for the applicable benchmark plan to cover all members of the taxpayer's coverage family, adjusted only for the age of each member of the coverage family as allowed under section 2701 of the Public Health Service Act (42 U.S.C. 300gg).

(f) *Applicable benchmark plan—(1) In general.* Except as otherwise provided in this paragraph (f), the applicable benchmark plan for a coverage month is the second lowest cost silver plan (as described in section 1302(d)(1)(B) of the Affordable Care Act (42 U.S.C. 18022(d)(1)(B))) offered at the time a taxpayer or family member enrolls in a qualified health plan through the Exchange in the rating area where the taxpayer resides for—

(i) Self-only coverage for a taxpayer—

(A) Who computes tax under section 1(c) (unmarried individuals other than surviving spouses and heads of household) and is not allowed a deduction under section 151 for a dependent for the taxable year;

(B) Who purchases only self-only coverage for one individual; or

(C) Whose coverage family includes only one individual; and

(ii) Family coverage for all other taxpayers.

(2) *Family coverage.* If an Exchange offers categories of family coverage (for example, two adults, one adult with children, two or more adults with children, or children only), the applicable benchmark plan for family coverage is the coverage category that applies to the members of the taxpayer's coverage family who enroll in a qualified health plan (such as a plan covering two adults if the members of taxpayer's coverage family are two adults).

(3) *Second lowest cost silver plan not covering the taxpayer's family.* If the applicable benchmark plan determined under paragraphs (f)(1) and (f)(2) of this section does not cover all members of a taxpayer's coverage family (for example, because family members reside in different rating areas), the premium for the applicable benchmark plan is the sum of the premiums for the applicable benchmark plans determined under paragraphs (f)(1) and (f)(2) of this section that cover the components of the taxpayer's coverage family.

(4) *Benchmark plan terminates or closes to enrollment.* A qualified health plan that is the applicable benchmark plan under this paragraph (f) for a taxpayer does not cease to be the applicable benchmark plan solely because the plan or a lower cost plan terminates or closes to enrollment during the taxable year.

(5) *Examples.* The following examples illustrate the rules of this paragraph (f). In each example, unless otherwise stated, the taxpayer is eligible to receive a premium tax credit.

Example 1. Single taxpayer with no dependents. Taxpayer V is single and resides with his 24-year-old daughter but may not claim her as a dependent. Taxpayer V purchases family coverage for himself and his daughter. The exchange in V's rating area offers only self-only and family coverage categories. Under paragraph (f)(1)(i)(A) of this section, V's applicable benchmark plan is the second lowest cost silver self-only plan. But see paragraph (h) of this section for computing the credit when multiple taxpayers are covered by one qualified health plan.

Example 2. Single taxpayer with one dependent, two coverage categories. The facts are the same as in *Example 1,* except that V also resides with his teenage son and claims him as a dependent. V purchases family coverage for himself, his son, and his daughter. Under paragraph (f)(1)(ii) of this section, V's applicable benchmark plan is the second lowest cost silver family plan.

Example 3. Single taxpayer with one dependent, multiple coverage categories. The facts are the same as in *Example 2,* except that the Exchange where V resides offers a category of coverage for one adult and children. Under paragraphs (f)(1)(ii) and (f)(2) of this section, V's applicable benchmark plan is the second lowest cost silver plan for one adult plus children.

Example 4. Single taxpayer with one dependent, multiple coverage categories. The facts are the same as in *Example 2,* except that the Exchange where V resides offers a category of coverage for one adult and one child in addition to coverage for one adult and children. Under paragraphs (f)(1)(ii) and (f)(2) of this section, V's applicable benchmark plan is the second lowest cost silver plan for one adult and one child.

Example 5. Applicable benchmark plan unrelated to coverage purchased. Taxpayers W and X, who are married, reside with X's two teenage daughters, whom they claim as dependents. The Exchange where W and X reside offers a category of coverage for one adult plus children. W and X purchase self-only coverage for W and one adult plus children coverage for X and X's daughters. Under paragraph (f)(1)(ii) of this section, W's and X's applicable benchmark plan is the second lowest cost silver family plan.

Example 6. Minimum essential coverage for some coverage months. Taxpayer Y claims his daughter as a dependent. Y and his daughter enroll in a qualified health plan for 2014. The exchange in Y's rating area offers only self-only and family coverage categories. Y, but not his daughter, is eligible for government-sponsored minimum essential coverage for September to December 2014. Thus, under paragraph (c)(1)(iii) of this section, January through December are coverage months for Y's daughter and January through August are coverage months for Y. Because, under paragraphs (d) and

(f)(1) of this section, the premium assistance amount for a coverage month is computed based on the applicable benchmark plan for that coverage month, Y's applicable benchmark plan for January through August is the second lowest cost silver family plan under paragraph (f)(1)(ii) of this section. Under paragraph (f)(1)(i)(C) of this section, Y's applicable benchmark plan for September through December is the second lowest cost silver self-only plan.

Example 7. Family member eligible for minimum essential coverage for the taxable year. The facts are the same as in *Example 6,* except that Y is not eligible for government-sponsored minimum essential coverage for any months and Y's daughter is eligible for government-sponsored minimum essential coverage for the entire year. Under paragraph (f)(1)(i)(C) of this section, Y's applicable benchmark plan is the second lowest cost silver self-only plan.

Example 8. Family required to buy multiple plans to obtain coverage. (i) Taxpayers X and Z are married and live in different Exchange rating areas. X and Z have one child, M, whom they claim as a dependent and who resides with X. X and M enroll in a qualified health plan covering one adult plus children through the Exchange in X's rating area, and Z enrolls in a qualified health plan providing self-only coverage through the Exchange in Z's rating area.

(ii) Under paragraph (f)(3) of this section, the premium for the applicable benchmark plan for computing X's and Z's premium assistance credit amount is the sum of the premium for the second lowest cost silver one adult plus children plan offered through the Exchange in X's rating area and the premium for the second lowest cost silver self-only plan offered through the Exchange in Z's rating area.

Example 9. Benchmark plan closes to new enrollees during the year. Taxpayers X, Y, and Z each have coverage families consisting of two adults. In the rating area where X, Y, and Z reside, Plan 2 is the second lowest cost silver plan and Plan 3 is the third lowest cost silver plan covering two adults offered through the Exchange. The X and Y families each enroll in a qualified health plan that is not the applicable benchmark plan in November during the regular open enrollment period. Plan 2 closes to new enrollees the following June. Thus, on July 1, Plan 3 is the second lowest cost silver plan available to new enrollees through the Exchange. The Z family enrolls in a qualified health plan in July. Under paragraphs (f)(1), (f)(2), and (f)(4) of this section, the applicable benchmark plan is Plan 2 for X and Y for all coverage months during the year. The applicable benchmark plan for Z is Plan 3, because Plan 2 is not offered through the Exchange when the Z family enrolls.

Example 10. Benchmark plan terminates for all enrollees during the year. The facts are the same as in *Example 9,* except that Plan 2 terminates for all enrollees on June 30. Under paragraphs (f)(1), (f)(2), and (f)(4) of this section, Plan 2 is the applicable benchmark plan for X and Y for all coverage months during the year and Plan 3 is the applicable benchmark plan for Z.

(g) *Applicable percentage*—(1) *In general.* The applicable percentage multiplied by a taxpayer's household income determines the taxpayer's required share of premiums for the benchmark plan. This amount is subtracted from the adjusted monthly premium for the applicable benchmark plan when computing the premium assistance amount. The applicable percentage is computed by first determining the percentage that the taxpayer's household income bears to the federal poverty line for the taxpayer's family size. The resulting federal poverty line percentage is then compared to the income categories described in the table in paragraph (g)(2) of this section (or successor tables). An applicable percentage within an income category increases on a sliding scale in a linear manner and is rounded to the nearest one-hundredth of one percent. The applicable percentages in the table may be adjusted in published guidance of general applicability, see § 601.601(d)(2) of this chapter, for taxable years beginning after December 31, 2014, to reflect rates of premium growth relative to growth in income and, for taxable years beginning after December 31, 2018, to reflect rates of premium growth relative to growth in the consumer price index.

(2) *Applicable percentage table.*

Household income percentage of federal poverty line	Initial percentage	Final percentage
Less than 133%	2.00	2.00
At least 133% but less than 150%	3.00	4.00
At least 150% but less than 200%	4.00	6.30
At least 200% but less than 250%	6.30	8.05
At least 250% but less than 300%	8.05	9.50
At least 300% but less than 400%	9.50	9.50

(3) *Examples.* The following examples illustrate the rules of this paragraph (g).

Example 1. A's household income is 275 percent of the federal poverty line for A's family size for that taxable year. In the table in paragraph (g)(2) of this section, the initial percentage for a taxpayer with household income of 250 to 300 percent of the federal poverty line is 8.05 and the final percentage is 9.5. A's federal poverty line percentage of 275 percent is halfway between 250 percent and 300 percent. Thus, rounded to the nearest one-hundredth of one percent, A's applicable percentage is 8.78, which is halfway between the initial percentage of 8.05 and the final percentage of 9.5.

Example 2. (i) B's household income is 210 percent of the federal poverty line for B's family size. In the table in paragraph (g)(2) of this section, the initial percentage for a taxpayer with household income of 200 to 250 percent of the federal poverty line is 6.3 and the final percentage is 8.05. B's applicable percentage is 6.65, computed as follows:

(ii) Determine the excess of B's FPL percentage (210) over the initial household income percentage in B's range (200), which is 10. Determine the difference between the initial household income percentage in the taxpayer's range (200) and the ending household income percentage in the taxpayer's range (250), which is 50. Divide the first amount by the second amount:

$210 - 200 = 10$

$250 - 200 = 50$

$10/50 = .20.$

(iii) Compute the difference between the initial premium percentage (6.3) and the second premium percentage (8.05) in the taxpayer's range; $8.05 - 6.3 = 1.75.$

(iv) Multiply the amount in the first calculation (.20) by the amount in the second calculation (1.75) and add the product (.35) to the initial premium percentage in B's range (6.3), resulting in B's applicable percentage of 6.65:

.20 × 1.75 = .35

6.3 + .35 = 6.65.

(h) *Plan covering more than one family*—(1) *In general.* If a single qualified health plan covers more than one family, each applicable taxpayer covered by the plan may claim a premium tax credit, if otherwise allowable. Each taxpayer computes the credit using that taxpayer's applicable percentage, household income, and the benchmark plan that applies to the taxpayer under paragraph (f) of this section. In determining whether the amount computed under paragraph (d)(1) of this section (the premiums for the qualified health plan in which the taxpayer enrolls) is less than the amount computed under paragraph (d)(2) of this section (the benchmark plan premium minus the product of household income and the applicable percentage), the premiums paid are allocated to each taxpayer in proportion to the premiums for each taxpayer's benchmark plan.

(2) *Example.* The following example illustrates the rules of this paragraph (h).

Example. (i) Taxpayers A and B enroll in a single qualified health plan. B is A's 25-year-old child who is not A's dependent. B has no dependents. The plan covers A, B, and A's two children who are A's dependents. The premium for the plan in which A and B enroll is $15,000. The premium for the second lowest cost silver family plan is $12,000 and the premium for the second lowest cost silver self-only plan is $6,000. A and B are applicable taxpayers and otherwise eligible to claim the premium tax credit.

(ii) Under paragraph (h)(1) of this section, both A and B may claim premium tax credits. A computes her credit using her household income, a family size of three, and a benchmark plan premium of $12,000. B computes his credit using his household income, a family size of one, and a benchmark plan premium of $6,000.

(iii) In determining whether the amount in paragraph (d)(1) of this section (the premiums for the qualified health plan A and B purchase) is less than the amount in paragraph (d)(2) of this section (the benchmark plan premium minus the product of household income and the applicable percentage), the $15,000 premiums paid are allocated to A and B in proportion to the premiums for their applicable benchmark plans. Thus, the portion of the premium allocated to A is $10,000 ($15,000 × $12,000/$18,000) and the portion allocated to B is $5,000 ($15,000 × $6,000/$18,000).

(i) [Reserved]

(j) *Additional benefits*—(1) *In general.* If a qualified health plan offers benefits in addition to the essential health benefits a qualified health plan must provide under section 1302 of the Affordable Care Act (42 U.S.C. 18022), or a State requires a qualified health plan to cover benefits in addition to these essential health benefits, the portion of the premium for the plan properly allocable to the additional benefits is excluded from the monthly premiums under paragraph (d)(1) or (d)(2) of this section.

(2) *Method of allocation.* The portion of the premium properly allocable to additional benefits is determined under regulations issued by the Secretary of Health and Human Services. See section 36B(b)(3)(D).

(k) *Pediatric dental coverage*—(1) *In general.* For purposes of determining the amount of the monthly premium a taxpayer pays for coverage under paragraph (d)(1) of this section, if an individual enrolls in both a qualified health plan and a plan described in section 1311(d)(2)(B)(ii) of the Affordable Care Act (42 U.S.C.

13031(d)(2)(B)(ii)) (Affordable Care Act dental plan), the portion of the premium for the Affordable Care Act dental plan that is properly allocable to pediatric dental benefits that are essential benefits required to be provided by a qualified health plan is treated as a premium payable for the individual's qualified health plan.

(2) *Method of allocation.* [Reserved]

(l) *Families including individuals not lawfully present*—(1) *In general.* If one or more individuals for whom a taxpayer is allowed a deduction under section 151 are not lawfully present (within the meaning of § 1.36B-1(g)), the percentage a taxpayer's household income bears to the federal poverty line for the taxpayer's family size for purposes of determining the applicable percentage under paragraph (g) of this section is determined by excluding individuals who are not lawfully present from family size and by determining household income in accordance with paragraph (l)(2) of this section.

(2) *Revised household income computation*—(i) *Statutory method.* For purposes of paragraph (l)(1) of this section, household income is equal to the product of the taxpayer's household income (determined without regard to this paragraph (l)(2)) and a fraction—

(A) The numerator of which is the federal poverty line for the taxpayer's family size determined by excluding individuals who are not lawfully present; and

(B) The denominator of which is the federal poverty line for the taxpayer's family size determined by including individuals who are not lawfully present.

(ii) *Comparable method.* [Reserved]

§ 1.36B-4 Reconciling the premium tax credit with advance credit payments.

(a) *Reconciliation*—(1) *In general.* The amount of credit allowed under section 36B and this section is reconciled with advance credit payments on a taxpayer's income tax return for a taxable year. A taxpayer whose premium tax credit for the taxable year exceeds the taxpayer's advance credit payments may receive the excess as an income tax refund. A taxpayer whose advance credit payments for the taxable year exceed the taxpayer's premium tax credit owes the excess as an additional income tax liability.

(2) *Credit computation.* The premium assistance credit amount is computed on the taxpayer's return using the taxpayer's household income and family size for the taxable year. Thus, the taxpayer's contribution amount (household income for the taxable year times the applicable percentage) is determined using the taxpayer's household income and family size at the end of the taxable year. If the applicable benchmark plan changes during the taxable year, the taxpayer may be required to use a different applicable benchmark plan to determine the premium assistance amounts for the coverage months.

(3) *Limitation on additional tax*—(i) *In general.* The additional tax imposed under paragraph (a)(1) of this section on a taxpayer whose household income is less than 400 percent of the federal poverty line is limited to the amounts provided in the table in paragraph

(a)(3)(ii) of this section (or successor tables). For taxable years beginning after December 31, 2014, the limitation amounts may be adjusted in published guidance of general applicability, see § 601.601(d)(2) of this chapter, to reflect changes in the consumer price index.

(ii) *Additional tax limitation table.*

Household income percentage of federal poverty line	Limitation amount for taxpayers whose tax is determined under section 1(c)	Limitation amount for all other taxpayers
Less than 200%	$300	$600
At least 200% but less than 300%	750	1,500
At least 300% but less than 400%	1,250	2,500

(4) *Examples.* The rules of this paragraph (a) are illustrated by the following examples. Unless otherwise stated, in each example the taxpayer is allowed a premium tax credit, has a calendar taxable year, and files an income tax return for the taxable year.

Example 1. Household income increases. (i) Taxpayer A is single and has no dependents. The Exchange in A's rating area projects A's 2014 household income to be $27,225 (250 percent of the federal poverty line for a family of one, applicable percentage 8.05). A enrolls in a qualified health plan. The annual premium for the applicable benchmark plan is $5,200. A's advance credit payments are $3,008 (benchmark plan premium of $5,200 less contribution amount of $2,192 (projected household income of $27,225 ×.0805) = $3,008).

(ii) A's household income for 2014 is $32,800, which is 301 percent of the federal poverty line for a family of one (applicable percentage 9.5). Consequently, A's premium tax credit for 2014 is $2,084 (benchmark plan premium of $5,200 less contribution amount of $3,116 (household income of $32,800 ? .095). Because A's advance credit payments for 2014 are $3,008 and A's 2014 credit is $2,084, A has excess advance payments of $924. Under paragraph (a)(1) of this section, A's tax liability for 2014 is increased by $924.

Example 2. Household income decreases. The facts are the same as in *Example 1,* except that A's actual household income for 2014 is $21,780 (200 percent of the federal poverty line for a family of one, applicable percentage 6.3). Consequently, A's premium tax credit for 2014 is

$3,828 ($5,200 benchmark plan premium less contribution amount of $1,372 (household income of $21,780 ×.063)). Because A's advance credit payments for 2014 are $3,008, A is allowed an additional credit of $820 ($3,828 less $3,008).

Example 3. Family size decreases.

(i) Taxpayers B and C are married and have two children (ages 17 and 20) whom they claim as their dependents in 2013. The Exchange in their rating area projects their 2014 household income to be $61,460 (275 percent of the federal poverty line for a family of four, applicable percentage 8.78). B and C enroll in a qualified health plan for 2014 that covers the four family members. The annual premium for the applicable benchmark plan is $14,100. B and C's advance credit payments for 2014 are $8,704 (benchmark plan premium of $14,100 less contribution amount of $5,396 (projected household income of $61,460 ×.0878)).

(ii) In 2014 B and C do not claim their 20-year old child as their dependent. Consequently, B and C's family size for 2014 is three and their household income is 332 percent of the federal poverty line for a family of three (applicable percentage 9.5). Their premium tax credit for 2014 is $8,261 ($14,100 benchmark plan premium less $5,839 contribution amount (household income of $61,460 ×.095)). Because B and C's advance credit payments for 2014 are $8,704 and their 2014 credit is $8,261, B and C have excess advance payments of $443. Under paragraph (a)(1) of this section, B and C's tax liability for 2014 is increased by $443. Because B and C's household income is below 400 percent of the federal poverty line, if B and C's excess advance payments exceeded $2,500, under the limitation of paragraph (a)(3) of this section, B and C's additional tax liability would be limited to that amount.

Example 4. Repayment limitation does not apply. (i) Taxpayer D is single and has no dependents. The Exchange in D's rating area approves advance credit payments for D based on 2014 household income of $38,115 (350 percent of the federal poverty line for a family of one, applicable percentage 9.5). D enrolls in a qualified health plan. The annual premium for the applicable benchmark plan is $5,200. D's advance credit payments are $1,579 (benchmark plan premium of $5,200 less contribution amount of $3,621 (projected household income of $38,115 ×.095) = $3,621).

(ii) D's actual household income for 2014 is $43,778, which is 402 percent of the federal poverty line for a family of one. D is not an applicable taxpayer and may not claim a premium tax credit. Additionally, the repayment limitation of paragraph (a)(3) of this section does not apply. Consequently, D has excess advance payments of $1,579 (the total amount of the advance credit payments in 2014). Under paragraph (a)(1) of this section, D's tax liability for 2014 is increased by $1,579.

Example 5. Coverage for less than a full taxable year. (i) Taxpayer F is single and has no dependents. In November 2013 the Exchange in F's rating area projects F's 2014 household income to be $27,225 (250 percent of the federal poverty line for a family of one, applicable percentage 8.05). F enrolls in a qualified health plan. The annual premium for the applicable benchmark plan is $5,200. F's monthly advance credit payment is $251 (benchmark plan premium of $5,200

less contribution amount of $2,192 (projected household income of $27,225 ×.0805) = $3,008; $3,008/12 = $251).

(ii) F begins a new job in August 2014 and is eligible for employer-sponsored minimum essential coverage for the period September through December 2014. F discontinues her Exchange coverage effective November 1, 2014. F's household income for 2014 is $28,000 (257 percent of the federal poverty line for a family size of one, applicable percentage 8.25).

(iii) Under § 1.36B-3(a), F's premium assistance credit amount is the sum of the premium assistance amounts for the coverage months. Under § 1.36B-3(c)(1)(iii), a month in which an individual is eligible for minimum essential coverage other than coverage in the individual market is not a coverage month. Because F is eligible for employer-sponsored minimum essential coverage as of September 1, only the months January through August of 2014 are coverage months.

(iv) If F had 12 coverage months in 2014, F's premium tax credit would be $2,890 (benchmark plan premium of $5,200 less contribution amount of $2,310 (household income of $28,000 ×.0825)). Because F has only eight coverage months in 2014, F's credit is $1,927 ($2,890/12 ×8). Because F does not discontinue her Exchange coverage until November 1, 2014, F's advance credit payments for 2014 are $2,510 ($251 ×10). Consequently, F has excess advance payments of $583 ($2,510 less $1,927) and F's tax liability for 2014 is increased by $583 under paragraph (a)(1) of this section.

Example 6. Changes in coverage months and applicable benchmark plan. (i) Taxpayer E claims one dependent, F. E is eligible for government-sponsored minimum essential coverage. E enrolls F in a qualified health plan for 2014. The Exchange in E's rating area projects E's 2014 household income to be $29,420 (200 percent of the federal poverty line for a family of two, applicable percentage 6.3). The annual premium for E's applicable benchmark plan is $5,200. E's monthly advance credit payment is $279 (benchmark plan premium of $5,200 less contribution amount of $1,853 (projected household income of $29,420 ×.063) = $3,347; $3,347/12 = $279).

(ii) On August 1, 2014, E loses her eligibility for government-sponsored minimum essential coverage. E cancels the qualified health plan that covers F and enrolls in a qualified health plan that covers E and F for August through December 2014. The annual premium for the applicable benchmark plan is $10,000. The Exchange computes E's monthly advance credit payments for the period September through December as $679 (benchmark plan premium of $10,000 less contribution amount of $1,853 (projected household income of $29,420 ×.063) = $8,147; $8,147/12 = $679). E's household income for 2014 is $28,000 (190 percent of the federal poverty line, applicable percentage 5.84).

(iii) Under § 1.36B-3(c)(1), January through July of 2014 are coverage months for F and August through December are coverage months for E and F. Under paragraph (a)(2) of this section, E must compute her premium tax credit using the premium for the applicable benchmark plan for each coverage month. E's premium assistance credit amount for 2014 is the sum of the premium assistance amounts for all coverage months. E reconciles her premium tax credit with advance credit payments as follows:

Advance credit payments (Jan. to July)	$1,953
Advance credit payments (Aug. to Dec.)	3,395
Total advance credit payments	**5,348**
Benchmark plan premium (Jan. to July)	3,033
Benchmark plan premium (Aug. to Dec.)	4,167
Total benchmark plan premium	**7,200**
Contribution amount (taxable year household income × applicable percentage)	1,635
Credit (total benchmark plan premium less required contribution, assuming not more than premium paid)	5,565

(iv) E's advance credit payments for 2014 are $5,348. E's premium tax credit is $5,565. Thus, E is allowed an additional credit of $217.

Example 7. Part-year coverage and changes in coverage months and applicable benchmark plan. (i) The facts are the same as in *Example 7,* except that both E and F are eligible for government-sponsored mini-

mum essential coverage for January and February 2014, and E enrolls F in a qualified health plan beginning in March 2014.

(ii) E reconciles her premium tax credit with advance credit payments as follows:

Advance credit payments (March to July)	$1,395
Advance credit payments (Aug. to Dec.)	3,395
Total advance credit payments	**4,790**
Benchmark plan premium (March to July)	2,167
Benchmark plan premium (Aug. to Dec.)	4,166
Total benchmark plan premium	**6,333**

Contribution amount for 10 coverage months (taxable year household income × applicable percentage × 10/12) 1,363
Credit (total benchmark plan premium less required contribution, assuming not more than premium paid) 4,970

(iii) E's advance credit payments for 2014 are $4,790. E's premium tax credit is $4,970. Thus, E is allowed an additional credit of $180.

(b) *Changes in filing status*—(1) *In general.* A taxpayer whose marital status changes during the taxable year computes the premium tax credit by using the applicable benchmark plan or plans for the taxpayer's marital status as of the first day of each coverage month. The taxpayer's contribution amount (household income for the taxable year times the applicable percentage) is determined using the taxpayer's household income and family size at the end of the taxable year.

(2) *Taxpayers not married to each other at the end of the taxable year.* Taxpayers who are married (within the meaning of section 7703) to each other during a taxable year but are not married to each other on the last day of the taxable year, and who are enrolled in the same qualified health plan at any time during the taxable year, must allocate the premium for the applicable benchmark plan, the premium for the plan in which the taxpayers enroll, and the advance credit payments for the period the taxpayers are married during the taxable year. The taxpayers may allocate these items to each former spouse in any proportion but must allocate all items in the same proportion. If the taxpayers cannot agree on an allocation, 50 percent of the premium for the applicable benchmark plan, the premiums for the plan in which the taxpayers enroll, and the advance credit payments for the period are allocated to each taxpayer. If a plan covers only one of these taxpayers for any period during a taxable year, the amounts for that period are allocated entirely to that taxpayer.

(3) *Married taxpayers filing separate tax returns.* The premium tax credit is allowed to married taxpayers only if they file joint returns. See § 1.36B-2(b)(2). Married taxpayers who receive advance credit payments and file their income tax returns as married filing separately have received excess advance payments. The taxpayers must allocate the advance credit payments to each taxpayer equally for purposes of determining their excess advance payment amounts under paragraph (a)(1) of this section. The repayment limitation described in paragraph (a)(3) of this section applies to each taxpayer based on the household income and family size reported on that taxpayer's return.

(4) *Examples.* The following examples illustrate the provisions of this paragraph (b). In each example, unless otherwise indicated, each taxpayer uses a calendar taxable year and no individuals are eligible for minimum essential coverage other than coverage in the individual market.

Example 1. Taxpayers marry during the taxable year. (i) P is a single taxpayer with no dependents. In 2013 the Exchange in the rating area where P resides determines that P's 2014 household income will be $40,000 (367 percent of the federal poverty line, applicable percentage 9.5). P enrolls in a qualified health plan. The premium for the applicable benchmark plan is $5,200. The Exchange approves advance credit payments of $117 per month, computed as follows: $5,200 benchmark plan premium minus contribution amount of $3,800 ($40,000 ? .095) equals $1,400 (total advance credit); $1,400/12 = $117.

(ii) Q is a single taxpayer with two dependents. In 2013 the Exchange in the rating area where Q resides determines that Q's 2014 household income will be $35,000 (189 percent of the federal poverty line, applicable percentage 5.79). Q enrolls in a qualified health plan. The premium for the applicable benchmark plan is $14,100. The Exchange approves advance credit payments of $1,006 per month, computed as follows: $14,100 benchmark plan premium minus contribution amount of $2,027 ($35,000 ? .0579) equals $12,073 (total advance credit); $12,073/12 = $1,006.

(iii) P and Q marry on June 17, 2014, and enroll in one qualified health plan covering four family members, beginning July 1, 2014. The premium for the applicable benchmark plan is $14,100. Based on household income of $75,000 and a family size of four (336 percent of the federal poverty line, applicable percentage 9.5), the Exchange approves advance credit payments of $581 per month, computed as follows: $14,100 benchmark plan premium minus contribution amount of $7,125 ($75,000 ×.095) equals $6,975 (total advance credit); $6,975/12 = $581.

(iv) P and Q file a joint return for 2014 and report $75,000 in household income and a family size of four. Under paragraph (b)(1) of this section, P and Q compute their credit at reconciliation using the premiums for the applicable benchmark plans that apply for the months married and the months not married, and their contribution amount based on their federal poverty line percentage at the end of the taxable year. P and Q reconcile their premium tax credit with advance credit payments as follows:

Advance payments for P (Jan. to June)	$700
Advance payments for Q (Jan. to June)	6,036
Advance payments for P and Q (July to Dec.)	3,486
Total advance payments	10,222
Benchmark plan premium for P (Jan. to June)	2,600
Benchmark plan premium for Q (Jan. to June)	7,050
Benchmark plan premium for P and Q (July to Dec.)	7,050
Total benchmark plan premium	16,700
Contribution amount (taxable year household income × applicable percentage)	7,125
Credit (total benchmark plan premium less required contribution, assuming not more than premium paid)	9,575
Additional tax	647

(v) P's and Q's tax liability for 2014 is increased by $647 under paragraph (a)(1) of this section.

Example 2. Taxpayers divorce during the taxable year, 50 percent allocation. (i) Taxpayers R and S are married and have two dependents. In 2013 the Exchange in the rating area where the family resides determines that their 2014 household income will be $76,000 (340 percent of the federal poverty line for a family of 4, applicable percentage 9.5). R and S enroll in a qualified health plan for 2014. The premium for the applicable benchmark plan is $14,100. The Exchange approves advance credit payments of $573 per month, computed as follows: $14,100 benchmark plan premium minus R and S's contribution amount of $7,220 ($76,000 ×.095) equals $6,880 (total advance credit); $6,880/12 = $573.

(ii) R and S divorce on June 17, 2014, and obtain separate qualified health plans beginning July 1, 2014. R enrolls based on household income of $60,000 and a family size of three (324 percent of the federal poverty line, applicable percentage 9.5). The premium for the applicable benchmark plan is $14,100. The Exchange approves advance credit payments of $700 per month, computed as follows: $14,100 benchmark plan premium minus R's contribution amount of $5,700 ($60,000 ×.095) equals $8,400 (total advance credit); $8,400/12 = $700.

(iii) S enrolls based on household income of $16,000 and a family size of one (147 percent of the federal poverty line, applicable percent-age 3.82). The premium for the applicable benchmark plan is $5,200. The Exchange approves advance credit payments of $382 per month, computed as follows: $5,200 benchmark plan premium minus S's contribution amount of $611 ($16,000 × .0382) equals $4,589 (total advance credit); $4,589/12 = $382. R and S do not agree on an allocation of the premium for the applicable benchmark plan, the premiums for the plan in which they enroll, and the advance credit payments for the period they were married in the taxable year.

(iv) Under paragraph (b)(1) of this section, R and S each compute their credit at reconciliation using the premiums for the applicable benchmark plans that apply to them for the months married and the months not married, and contribution amount based on their federal poverty line percentages at the end of the taxable year. Under paragraph (b)(2) of this section, because R and S do not agree on an allocation, R and S must equally allocate the benchmark plan premium ($7,050) and the advance credit payments ($3,440) for the six-month period January through June 2014 when they are married and enrolled in the same qualified health plan. Thus, R and S each are allocated $3,525 of the benchmark plan premium ($7,050/2) and $1,720 of the advance credit payments ($3,440/2) for January through June.

(v) R reports on his 2014 tax return $60,000 in household income and family size of three. S reports on her 2014 tax return $16,000 in household income and family size of one. R and S reconcile their premium tax credit with advance credit payments as follows:

	R	S
Allocated advance payments (Jan. to June)	$1,720	$1,720
Actual advance payments (July to Dec.)	4,200	2,292
Total advance payments	5,920	4,012
Allocated benchmark plan premium (Jan. to June)	3,525	3,525
Actual benchmark plan premium (July to Dec.)	7,050	2,600
Total benchmark plan premium	10,575	6,125
Contribution amount (taxable year household income × applicable percentage)	5,700	611
Credit (total benchmark plan premium less required contribution, assuming not more than premium paid)	4,875	5,514
Additional credit		1,502
Additional tax	1,045	

(vi) Under paragraph (a)(1) of this section, on their tax returns R's tax liability is increased by $1,045 and S is allowed $1,502 as additional credit.

Example 3. Taxpayers divorce during the taxable year, allocation in proportion to household income. (i) The facts are the same as in *Example 2*, except that R and S decide to allocate the benchmark plan premium ($7,050) and the advance credit payments ($3,440) for January through June 2014 in proportion to their household incomes (79 percent and 21 percent). Thus, R is allocated $5,570 of the benchmark plan premiums ($7,050 ×.79) and $2,718 of the advance credit payments ($3,440 ×.79), and S is allocated $1,480 of the benchmark plan premiums ($7,050 × .21) and $722 of the advance credit payments ($3,440 ×.21). R and S reconcile their premium tax credit with advance credit payments as follows:

	R	S
Allocated advance payments (Jan. to June)	$2,718	$722
Actual advance payments (July to Dec.)	4,200	2,292
Total advance payments	6,918	3,014
Allocated benchmark plan premium (Jan. to June)	5,570	1,480
Actual benchmark plan premium (July to Dec.)	7,050	2,600
Total benchmark plan premium	12,620	4,080
Contribution amount (taxable year household income ×applicable percentage)	5,700	611
Credit (total benchmark plan premium less required contribution, assuming not more than premium paid)	6,920	3,469
Additional credit	2	455

(ii) Under paragraph (a)(1) of this section, on their tax returns R is allowed an additional credit of $2 and S is allowed an additional credit of $455.

Example 4. Married taxpayers filing separate tax returns. (i) Taxpayers T and U are married and have two dependents. In 2013, the Exchange in the rating area where the family resides determines that their 2014 household income will be $76,000 (340 percent of the federal poverty line for a family of 4, applicable percentage 9.5). T and U enroll in a qualified health plan for 2014. The premium for the applicable benchmark plan is $14,100. The Exchange approves advance credit payments of $573 per month, computed as follows: $14,100 benchmark plan premium minus T and U's contribution amount of $7,220 ($76,000 × .095) equals $6,880 (total advance credit); $6,880/12 = $573.

(ii) T and U file income tax returns for 2014 using a married filing separately filing status. T reports household income of $60,000 and a family size of three (324 percent of the federal poverty line). U reports household income of $16,000 and a family size of one (147 percent of the federal poverty line).

(iii) Because T and U are married but do not file a joint return for 2014, T and U are not applicable taxpayers and are not allowed a premium tax credit for 2014. See § 1.36B-2(b)(2). Under paragraph (b)(3) of this section, half of the advance credit payments ($6,880/2 = $3,440) is allocated to T and half is allocated to U for purposes of determining their excess advance payments. The repayment limitation described in paragraph (a)(3) of this section applies to T and U based on the household income and family size reported on each return. Consequently, T's tax liability for 2014 is increased by $2,500 and U's tax liability for 2014 is increased by $600.

§ 1.36B-5 Information reporting by Exchanges.

(a) *Information required to be reported.* An Exchange must report to the IRS and a taxpayer the following information for a qualified health plan the taxpayer enrolls in through the Exchange—

(1) The premium and category of coverage (such as self-only) for the applicable benchmark plans used to compute advance credit payments and the period coverage was in effect;

(2) The total premium for the coverage without reduction for advance credit payments or cost sharing;

(3) The aggregate amounts of any advance credit payments or cost sharing reductions;

(4) The name, address and taxpayer identification number (TIN) of the primary insured and the name and TIN of each other individual covered under the policy;

(5) All information provided to the Exchange at enrollment or during the taxable year, including any change in circumstances, necessary to determine eligibility for and the amount of the premium tax credit;

(6) All information necessary to determine whether a taxpayer has received excess advance payments; and

(7) Any other information required in published guidance of general applicability, see § 601.601(d)(2) of this chapter.

(b) *Time and manner of reporting.* The Commissioner may provide rules in published guidance of general applicability, see § 601.601(d)(2) of this chapter, for the time and manner of reporting under this section.

Par. 3. Section 1.6011-8 is added to read as follows:

§ 1.6011-8 Requirement of income tax return for taxpayers who claim the premium tax credit under section 36B.

(a) *Requirement of return.* A taxpayer who receives advance payments of the premium tax credit under section 36B must file an income tax return for that taxable year on or before the fifteenth day of the fourth month following the close of the taxable year.

(b) *Effective/applicability date.* This section applies for taxable years ending after December 31, 2013.

Par. 4. In § 1.6012-1, paragraph (a)(2)(viii) is added to read as follows:

§ 1.6012-1 Individuals required to make returns of income.

(a) * * *

(2) * * *

(viii) For rules relating to returns required of taxpayers who receive advance payments of the premium tax credit under section 36B, see § 1.6011-8(a).

* * * * *

Steven T. Miller,
Deputy Commissioner for Services and Enforcement.

[FR Doc. 2011-20728 Filed 8-12-11; 8:45 am]

BILLING CODE 4830-01-P

¶ 20,262Y

IRS regulations : Employee Benefits Security Administration (EBSA): Group health plans: Health insurance coverage: Summary of benefits and coverage: Uniform glossary: Disclosure requirements.—The IRS, EBSA, and Department of Health and Human Services have issued proposed regulations that implement disclosure requirements under the Patient Protection and Affordable Care Act (PPACA) concerning the provision of a summary of benefits and coverage and a uniform glossary for group health plans and health insurance coverage in the group and individual markets. The disclosures are intended to help plans and individuals better understand their health coverage and other coverage options.

The proposed regulations, which were reproduced below, were published in the Federal Register on August 22, 2011 (76 FR 52442). The Agencies have also issued templates, instructions, and sample language for making disclosures of the summary of benefits and coverage, and a uniform glossary. The templates, instructions, sample language, and the uniform glossary, which are also reproduced below, were published in the Federal Register August 22, 2011 (76 FR 52475).

The regulations were finalized on February 14, 2012 (77 FR 8668). The preamble to the final regulations is at ¶ 23,282. The final regulations are at ¶ 13,968V-20RR. As to the templates, instructions, sample language, and uniform glossary, the Agencies issued a separate document, Guidance for Compliance and Notice of Availability of Templates, Instructions, and Related Materials, explaining where to find the materials (77 FR 8706, February 14, 2012).

¶ 20,262Z

IRS: Advance notice of proposed rulemaking : Governmental plans.—The IRS has issued an advance notice of proposed rulemaking, which includes draft proposed regulations relating to the determination of whether a plan is a "governmental plan" within the meaning of Code Sec. 414(d). Comments are invited from the public. Written or electronic comments must be received by February 6, 2012.

The advance notice of proposed rulemaking, which is reproduced below, was published in the Federal Register on November 8, 2011 (76 FR 69172). Official corrections were published in the Federal Register on December 8, 2011 (76 FR 76633).

DEPARTMENT OF THE TREASURY

Internal Revenue Service

26 CFR Part 1

[REG-157714-06]

RIN 1545-BG43

Determination of Governmental Plan Status

AGENCY: Internal Revenue Service (IRS), Department of the Treasury.

ACTION: Advance notice of proposed rulemaking.

SUMMARY: The Treasury Department and IRS anticipate issuing regulations under section 414(d) of the Internal Revenue Code (Code) to define the term "governmental plan." This document describes the rules that the Treasury Department and IRS are considering proposing relating to the determination of whether a plan is a governmental plan within the meaning of section 414(d) and contains an appendix that includes a draft notice of proposed rulemaking on which the Treasury Department and IRS invite comments from the public. This document applies to sponsors of, and participants and beneficiaries in, employee benefit plans that are determined to be governmental plans.

DATES: Written or electronic comments must be received by February 6, 2012.

ADDRESSES: Send submissions relating to the section 414(d) draft general regulations to: CC:PA:LPD:PR (REG-157714-06), room 5203, Internal Revenue Service, PO Box 7604, Ben Franklin Station, Washington DC, 20044. Submissions may be hand delivered Monday through Friday, between the hours of 8 a.m. and 4 p.m. to CC:PA:LPD:PR (REG-157714-06), Courier's Desk, Internal Revenue Service, 1111 Constitution Avenue, NW., Washington, DC.

Alternately, taxpayers may submit comments relating to the section 414(d) draft general regulations electronically via the Federal eRulemaking Portal at *www.regulations.gov* (IRS-REG-157714-06).

FOR FURTHER INFORMATION CONTACT: Concerning the ANPRM, Pamela R. Kinard, at (202) 622-6060; concerning submission of comments, Richard A. Hurst, at *Richard.A.Hurst@irscounsel.treas.gov* or at (202) 622-7180 (not toll-free numbers).

SUPPLEMENTARY INFORMATION:

Background

This document describes rules that the Treasury Department and IRS are considering proposing and contains a draft notice of proposed rulemaking (in the Appendix to this ANPRM) under section 414(d) of the Internal Revenue Code (Code). Under the draft notice of proposed rulemaking (in the Appendix to this ANPRM), the rules would provide general guidance relating to the determination of whether a retirement plan is a governmental plan within the meaning of section 414(d) (section 414(d) draft general regulations). The principles described in this ANPRM could also apply for purposes of certain parallel terms in sections 403(b) and 457 of the Code.

Section 414(d) of the Code provides that the term "governmental plan" generally means a plan established and maintained for its employees by the Government of the United States, by the government of any State or political subdivision thereof, or by any agency or instrumentality of any of the foregoing. See sections 3(32) and 4021(b)(2) of the Employee Retirement Income Security Act of 1974 (ERISA) for definitions of the term "governmental plan," which govern respectively for purposes of title I and title IV of ERISA[1].

The term "governmental plan" also includes any plan to which the Railroad Retirement Act of 1935 or 1937 (49 Stat. 967, as amended by 50 Stat. 307) applies and which is financed by contributions required under that Act and any plan of an international organization which is exempt from taxation by reason of the International Organizations Immunities Act (59 Stat. 669). See section 414(d)(2) of the Code.

Section 414(d) was amended by the Pension Protection Act of 2006, Public Law 109-280 (120 Stat. 780) (PPA '06) to include certain plans of Indian tribal governments and related entities.[2] Section 906(a)(1) of PPA '06 provides that the term "governmental plan" includes a plan which is established and maintained by an Indian tribal government (as defined in section 7701(a)(40)), a subdivision of an Indian tribal government (determined in accordance with section 7871(d)), or an agency or instrumentality of either (ITG), and all the participants of which are employees of such entity substantially all of whose services as such an employee are in the performance of essential governmental functions but not in the performance of commercial activities (whether or not an essential governmental function).

Neither section 414(d) of the Code, section 3(32) of ERISA, nor section 4021(b)(2) of ERISA define key terms relating to governmental plans, including the terms "established and maintained," "political subdivision," "agency," and "instrumentality." Currently, there are no regulations interpreting section 414(d). Revenue Ruling 89-49 (1989-1 CB 117), see § 601.601(d)(2), sets forth a facts and circumstances analysis

---

[1] The three definitions of the term "governmental plan" are essentially the same. The only difference is that, in defining the term "governmental plan," section 3(32) of ERISA uses the phrase "established or maintained," whereas section 414(d) of the Code and section 4021(b) of ERISA use the term "established and maintained."

[2] Section 906(a) of PPA '06 made similar amendments to sections 3(32) and 4021(b)(2) of ERISA.

for determining whether a retirement plan is a governmental plan within the meaning of section 414(d).[3] This analysis is used by the IRS in issuing letter rulings.

Governmental plans are subject to different rules than retirement plans of nongovernmental employers. Governmental plans are excluded from the provisions of titles I and IV of ERISA. In addition, governmental plans receive special treatment under the Code. These plans are exempt from certain qualification requirements and they are deemed to satisfy certain other qualification requirements under certain conditions. As a result, the principal qualification requirements for a tax-qualified governmental plan[4] are that the plan—

- Be established and maintained by the employer for the exclusive benefit of the employer's employees or their beneficiaries;
- Provide definitely determinable benefits;
- Be operated pursuant to its terms;
- Satisfy the direct rollover rules of section 401(a)(31);
- Satisfy the section 401(a)(17) limitation on compensation;
- Comply with the statutory minimum required distribution rules under section 401(a)(9);
- Satisfy the pre-ERISA vesting requirements under section 411(e)(2);[5]
- Satisfy the section 415 limitations on benefits, as applicable to governmental plans; and
- Satisfy the prohibited transaction rules in section 503.

State and local governments, political subdivisions thereof, and agencies or instrumentalities thereof are generally not permitted to offer cash or deferred arrangements under section 401(k). However, an ITG is permitted to offer a cash or deferred arrangement under section 401(k).

For further background, see the "Background" section of the preamble in the section 414(d) draft general regulations in the Appendix to this ANPRM under the headings, "Exclusion of Governmental Plans from ERISA," "Exemption of Governmental Plans from Certain Qualified Plan Rules," and "Exemption of Governmental Plans from Other Employee Benefit Rules Relating to Retirement Plans."

Over the past several years, the IRS has been coordinating with the Department of Labor (DOL) and Pension Benefit Guaranty Corporation (PBGC) (the "Agencies") on governmental plan determinations. Although the anticipated proposed regulations would only be applicable for purposes of section 414(d), the DOL and PBGC were consulted when drafting this proposal. DOL and PBGC agreed that it would be advantageous for the Agencies and the regulated community for there to be coordinated criteria for determining whether a plan is a governmental plan within the meaning of section 414(d) of the Code, section 3(32) of ERISA, and section 4021(b)(2) of ERISA. See the "Background" section of the preamble in the section 414(d) draft general regulations in the Appendix to this ANPRM under the heading, "Interagency Coordination on Governmental Plan Determinations."

The Treasury Department and the IRS have determined to seek public comment on the draft proposed regulations in the Appendix to this ANPRM in advance of issuing a notice of proposed rulemaking. In light of the interaction of the governmental plan definitions in the Code and ERISA, a copy of the comments will be forwarded to DOL and PBGC.

Explanation of Provisions

Attached to the Appendix to this ANPRM is a draft notice of proposed rulemaking. The draft regulations include proposed rules, a preamble, and a request for comments. The Treasury Department and IRS invite the public to comment on the rules that the Treasury Department and IRS are considering proposing, which would generally define the term "governmental plan" within the meaning of section 414(d), as well as other key related terms, including "State," "political subdivision of a State," and "agency or instrumentality of a State or political subdivision of a State."

In determining whether an entity is an agency or instrumentality of the United States or an agency or instrumentality of a State or political subdivision of a State, the anticipated guidance would provide a facts and circumstances analysis. The factors used in these analyses are drawn from the factors historically used in governmental plan determinations, including Rev. Ruls. 57-128 and 89-49. The anticipated guidance would provide several examples illustrating the application of the facts and circumstances tests. See the "Explanation of Provisions" section in the section 414(d) draft general regulations in the Appendix to this ANPRM under the headings, "Definitions of the United States and agency or instrumentality of the United States" and "Definition of agency or instrumentality of a State or a political subdivision of a State." See § 601.601(d)(2).

The anticipated proposed regulations would include numerous factors for determining whether an entity is an agency or instrumentality of a State or a political subdivision of a State. The section 414(d) draft proposed regulations in the Appendix to this ANPRM would categorize these factors into major factors and other factors. The section 414(d) draft general regulations would also request comments from the public on whether the final regulations should eliminate the distinction between main and other factors. In addition, the section 414(d) draft general regulations would request comments on the ordering and application of main and other factors; for example, whether, as an alternative to the ranking of major factors and other factors, the regulations could provide a safe harbor standard focusing on control and fiscal responsibility under which the entity would be treated as an agency or instrumentality of a State or a political subdivision of a State. For further explanation of the safe harbor standard, see the "Comments and Public Hearing" section in the preamble of the section 414(d) draft general regulations, which is located in the Appendix to this ANPRM.

The anticipated proposed regulations do not address the special rules that apply in determining whether a plan of an Indian tribal government is a governmental plan within the meaning of section 414(d). That topic would be reserved in the proposed regulations and is addressed in an ANPRM (REG-133223-08) that is being published elsewhere in this issue of the **Federal Register**.

The anticipated proposed regulations would provide rules for determining whether a governmental entity has established and maintained a plan for purposes of section 414(d). The anticipated proposed regulations might provide that a plan is established and maintained for the employees of a governmental entity if: (1) the plan is established and maintained by an employer within the meaning of § 1.401-1(a)(2), (2) the employer is a governmental entity, and (3) the only participants covered by the plan are employees of that governmental entity. The anticipated proposed regulations might also provide rules covering circumstances involving a change in status of an entity (that is, when a private entity becomes a governmental entity or when a governmental entity becomes a private entity) due to an acquisition or asset transfer. See the "Explanation of Provisions" section in the section 414(d) draft general regulations in the Appendix to this ANPRM under the heading, "Requirements for establishing and maintaining a section 414(d) governmental plan."

Recognizing that the guidance might affect numerous governmental plan participants and their beneficiaries, the anticipated proposed regulations request comments on transition rules, including transitional relief for governmental plans that permitted participation of a small number of former employees in their plans. See the "Comments and Public Hearing" section in the preamble of the section 414(d) draft general regulations that is located in the Appendix to this ANPRM.

Request for Comments

Before the notice of proposed rulemaking is issued, consideration will be given to any written comments that are submitted timely (preferably a signed original and eight (8) copies) to the IRS. All comments will be available for public inspection and copying. Copies of the comments will be provided to the DOL and PBGC.

The IRS and Department of Treasury plan to schedule a public hearing on the ANPRM. That hearing will be scheduled and announced at a later date. In addition to a public hearing, the Treasury Department and IRS anticipate scheduling "Town Hall" meetings in order to obtain comments from the public on the section 414(d) draft general regulations. It is expected that these "Town Hall" meetings will take place in different locations across the country. Participants will be encouraged

---

[3] See also Rev. Rul. 57-128 (1957-1 CB 311), see § 601.601(d)(2), which provides guidance on determining when an entity is a governmental instrumentality for purposes of the exemption from employment taxes under section 3121(b)(7) and 3306(c)(7).

[4] A special rule applies to contributory plans of certain governmental entities. Section 414(h)(2) provides that, for a qualified plan established by a State government or political subdivision thereof, or by any agency or instrumentality of the foregoing, where the

contributions of the governmental employer are designated as employee contributions under section 414(h)(1) but the governmental employer picks up the contributions, the contributions picked up will be treated as employer contributions.

[5] Section 411(e)(2) states that a plan described in section 411(e)(1) is treated as meeting the requirements of section 411 if the plan meets the vesting requirements resulting from the application of section 401(a)(4) and (a)(7) as in effect on September 1, 1974.

to pre-register for the meetings. Information relating to these "Town Hall" meetings, including dates, times, locations, registration, and the procedures for submitting written and oral comments, will be available on the IRS website relating to governmental plans at *http:// www.irs.gov/retirement/article/0,,id=181779,00.html* .

Drafting Information

The principal author of this advance notice of proposed rulemaking is Pamela R. Kinard, Office of the Chief Counsel (Tax-exempt and Government Entities), however, other personnel from the IRS and Treasury Department participated in its development.

Steven T. Miller,

Deputy Commissioner for Services and Enforcement.

APPENDIX

The following is draft language for a notice of proposed rulemaking that would set forth rules relating to the determination of whether a plan is a governmental plan within the meaning of section 414(d). The IRS and Treasury release this draft language in order to solicit comments from the governmental plans community:

Background

This document contains proposed regulations under section 414(d) of the Internal Revenue Code (Code). These regulations, when finalized, would provide guidance relating to the determination of whether a retirement plan is a governmental plan within the meaning of section 414(d). The definition of a governmental plan under section 414(d) applies for purposes of Part I of Subchapter D of Chapter 1 of Subtitle A (Income Taxes) of the Code (sections 401 through 420) and certain other Code provisions that refer to section 414(d) (such as sections 72(t)(10), 501(c)(25)(C), 4975(g)(2), 4980B(d)(2), 9831(a)(1), and 9832(d)(1)). It is expected that the principles set forth in these regulations would generally also apply for purposes of sections 403(b) and 457.

Statutory Definition of Governmental Plan

Both the Code and the Employee Retirement Income Security Act of 1974 (ERISA) define the term "governmental plan." Section 414(d) of the Code provides that the term "governmental plan" generally means a plan established and maintained for its employees by the Government of the United States, by the government of any State or political subdivision thereof, or by any agency or instrumentality of any of the foregoing. See sections 3(32) and 4021(b)(2) of ERISA for parallel definitions of the term *governmental plan*, discussed under the heading, "Exclusion of Governmental Plans from ERISA."

The term "governmental plan" also includes any plan to which the Railroad Retirement Act of 1935 or 1937 (49 Stat. 967, as amended by 50 Stat. 307) applies and which is financed by contributions required under that Act and any plan of an international organization which is exempt from taxation by reason of the International Organizations Immunities Act, Public Law 79-291 (59 Stat. 669). Section 414(d) was amended by the Pension Protection Act of 2006, Public Law 109-280 (120 Stat. 780) (PPA '06) to include certain plans of Indian tribal governments.[6] See Notice 2006-89 (2006-43 IRB 772), see § 601.601(d)(2), for guidance relating to plans established and maintained by Indian tribal governments.[7] These proposed regulations do not provide any guidance concerning the special provisions in section 414(d) relating to the Railroad Retirement Act of 1935 or 1937, the International Organizations Immunities Act, or Indian tribal governments.

Application of Section 414(d)

These proposed regulations are only applicable for purposes of section 414(d), and not for any other purpose under the Code.[8] However, the section 414(d) definition of "governmental plan" applies for other sections of the Code, including:

- Section 72(t)(10)(A) (exception to the early withdrawal tax for certain distributions from a defined benefit governmental plan);

- Section 457(e)(17) (special rules for: (1) direct trustee-to-trustee transfers from a section 457 deferred compensation plan to a section 414(d) governmental plan in order to purchase permissive service credit under section 414(n)(3)(A) or (2) the repayments of cashouts under governmental plans);

- Section 501(c)(25)(C)(ii) (exempting section 414(d) governmental plans from taxation);

- Section 503(a)(1) (applying the prohibited transaction rules in section 503 to governmental plans as defined in section 4975(g)(2))

- Section 818(a)(6)(A) (defining the term "pension plan contract");

- Section 1400Q(d)(2)(A)(ii) (special timing rule for section 414(d) governmental plans to make certain conforming amendments);

- Section 4972(d)(1)(B) (exempting section 414(d) governmental plans from the excise tax on nondeductible contributions to a qualified employer plan);

- Section 4975(g)(2) (exempting section 414(d) governmental plans from the prohibited transaction rules of section 4975);

- Section 4980(c)(1)(B) (exempting section 414(d) governmental plans from the tax on the reversion of qualified plan assets to an employer under section 4980);

- Section 4980B(d)(2) (exempting section 414(d) governmental plans from the COBRA requirements under section 4980B);

- Section 4980F(f)(2) (exempting section 414(d) governmental plans from the requirement to provide a notice required under section 204(h) of ERISA);

- Section 6057(c)(2) (providing rules relating to the voluntary submission of annual registration statements by section 414(d) governmental plans); and,

- Sections 9831(a)(1) and 9832(d)(2) (exempting section 414(d) governmental plans from the group health plan requirements).

The definitions and rules also apply for purposes of section 101(h)(1)(A) (special rule exempting governmental plan survivor benefits attributable to service of a public safety officer killed in the line of duty).

Currently, there are no regulations interpreting section 414(d). Neither section 414(d) of the Code nor ERISA defines key terms relating to governmental plans, including the terms "established and maintained," "political subdivision," "agency," and "instrumentality."

Executive Order 13132

Executive Order 13132 requires that Federal departments and agencies engage in consultation procedures in certain circumstances where regulations are issued which have a substantial direct effect on States. While these regulations when issued as final regulations would not have such a substantial direct effect, the IRS and Treasury Department have followed similar procedures, including issuance not only of these proposed regulations, but also an advance notice of these regulations which was published (date to be provided) in the **Federal Register**.

Judicial Determinations of Governmental Entity Status

Historically, courts have used the test in *NLRB v. Natural Gas Utility District of Hawkins County, Tennessee*, 402 U.S. 600 (1971), in determining whether an entity is an agency or instrumentality of a State or a political subdivision of a State. In *Hawkins County*, the Supreme Court interpreted the term "political subdivision" for purposes of 29 U.S.C. 152(2) (section 2(2) of the National Labor Relations Act (NLRA), as amended by the Labor-Management Relations Act).[9] Although the Supreme Court in *Hawkins County* analyzed whether the employer at issue was a political subdivision for purposes of the NLRA, courts use the same analysis for determining whether an entity is an agency or

---

[6] Section 906(a)(1) of PPA '06 provides that the term "governmental plan" includes a plan which is established and maintained by an Indian tribal government (as defined in section 7701(a)(40)), a subdivision of an Indian tribal government (determined in accordance with section 7871(d)), or an agency or instrumentality of either, and all the participants of which are employees of such entity substantially all of whose services as such an employee are in the performance of essential governmental functions but not in the performance of commercial activities (whether or not an essential government function). Section 906(a) of PPA '06 made similar amendments to sections 3(32) and 4021(b) of ERISA.

[7] See also Notice 2007-67 (2007-35 IRB 467), see § 601.601(d)(2) (extending transitional relief for plans of Indian tribal governments to comply with the requirements of section 906 of PPA '06).

[8] However, as indicated earlier, it is expected that the principles set forth in these regulations would also be taken into account for purposes of sections 403(b) and 457.

[9] 29 U.S.C. 152(2) provides that the term "employer" includes any person acting as an agent of an employer, directly or indirectly, but shall not include the United States or any wholly owned Government corporation, or any Federal Reserve Bank, or any State or political subdivision thereof, or any person subject to the Railway Labor Act, as amended from time to time, or any labor organization (other than when acting as an employer), or anyone acting in the capacity of officer or agent of such labor organization.

instrumentality of a State or a political subdivision of a State for purposes of ERISA.[10] The two-prong test in *Hawkins County* analyzes whether the entity has been "(1) created directly by the state, so as to constitute departments or administrative arms of the government, or (2) administered by individuals who are responsible to public officials or to the general electorate." *Hawkins County*, 402 U.S. at 604-05. In addition to this two-prong test, the Supreme Court also analyzed other factors, including: whether the utility had broad powers to accomplish its public purpose; whether the utility's property and revenue were exempt from state and local taxes (as well as whether its bonds were tax-exempt); whether the utility had the power of eminent domain; whether the utility was required to maintain public records; whether the utility's commissioners were appointed by an elected county judge; and whether the commissioners could be removed by the State of Tennessee pursuant to State procedures for removal of public officials. Many of these factors are similar to the factors used in determining whether an entity is an agency or instrumentality of a State or a political subdivision of a State under these proposed regulations.

In determining whether an entity is an agency or instrumentality of the United States, courts either apply a facts and circumstances analysis or look to the relationship between the entity and its employees. In *Alley v. Resolution Trust Corporation*, 984 F.2d 1201 (D.C.Cir. 1993), in analyzing whether the Federal Asset Disposition Association (FADA), a savings and loan association established by the Federal Home Loan Bank Board, was a Federal instrumentality for governmental plan purposes, the court focused on the employment relationship between the entity and its employees.[11] In looking at the employer-employee relationship, the *Alley* court concluded that FADA functioned more like a private enterprise than a governmental agency in the area of its employment relations. "Measured by the terms and conditions of their employment, FADA personnel far more closely resembled private sector employees than they did government workers. Like employees of 'ordinary' Federally chartered S&Ls, FADA's employees were outside the civil service system, and were not subject to the personnel rules or restrictions on salaries and benefits imposed generally on Federal employees."[12]

However, in *Berini v. Federal Reserve Bank of St. Louis, Eighth District*, 420 F.Supp.2d 1021 (E.D. Mo. 2005), the court reviewed administrative and judicial authority in determining whether an entity is a Federal agency or instrumentality and applied a multi-factor test in determining whether the employee benefit plans maintained by the Federal Reserve System are governmental plans within the meaning of section 3(32) of ERISA. The *Berini* test was based on the six factors in Rev. Rul. 57-128 (1957-1 CB 311), see § 601.601(d)(2), which was also the test applied by the court in *Rose v. Long Island Railroad Pension Plan*, 828 F.2d 910, 918 (2nd Cir. 1987), *cert. denied*, 485 U.S. 936 (1988). Factors weighed by the *Berini* court included that the Federal reserve banks were established directly by Congressional legislation to perform an important governmental function (to increase control of the nation's currency and banking system), the banks exist only by an enabling statute, they possess only the powers granted by the legislation, the private interests involved do not have the typical interests of an owner, and the banks are controlled by the Federal Reserve Board of Governors, which is a governmental agency.[13]

Agency Guidance Regarding Governmental Entity Status

Revenue Ruling 57-128 provides guidance on when an entity is a governmental instrumentality for purposes of the exemption from employment taxes under sections 3121(b)(7) and 3306(c)(7). The revenue ruling lists the following factors to be considered in determining whether an organization is an instrumentality of one or more States or political subdivisions thereof: (1) whether the organization is used for a governmental purpose and performs a governmental function; (2) whether performance of its function is on behalf of one or more States or political subdivisions; (3) whether there are any private interests involved, or whether the States or political subdivisions involved have the powers and interests of an owner; (4) whether control and supervision of the organization is vested in public authority or authorities; (5) whether express or implied statutory authority or other authority is

necessary for the creation and/or use of such an instrumentality, and whether such authority exists; and (6) the degree of the organization's financial autonomy and the source of its operating expenses.

Revenue Ruling 89-49 (1989-1 CB 117), see § 601.601(d)(2), provides guidance for determining whether a retirement plan maintained by an organization is a governmental plan within the meaning of section 414(d). The revenue ruling lists several factors for determining whether a sponsoring organization is an agency or instrumentality of the United States or any State or political subdivision thereof. While the factors in Rev. Rul. 89-49 are similar to the factors listed in Rev. Rul. 57-128, Rev. Rul. 89-49 focuses more on the degree of control that the Federal or State government has over the organization's everyday operations. Other factors considered include: whether there is specific legislation creating the organization; the source of funds for the organization; the manner in which the organization's trustees or operating board are selected; and whether the applicable government unit considers the employees of the organization to be employees of the applicable government unit. Rev. Rul. 89-49 provides that satisfaction of one or all of the factors is not necessarily determinative of whether an organization is a governmental entity. See § 601.601(d)(2)(ii)(b).

In Rev. Rul. 89-49, citizens of a municipality organized a volunteer fire company. The company was incorporated under its State laws as a nonprofit corporation, and the company was managed under the exclusive control of a board of trustees elected by the volunteer firefighters. Area municipalities, including the municipality that created the company, entered into contracts with the company to receive fire protection services. Under the contracts, it was agreed that the operations of the volunteer fire company would be under the exclusive control of the board of trustees. While the municipalities made payments for fire protection services to the volunteer fire company pursuant to these contracts, the municipalities did not contribute to the company's retirement plan, and the employees of the company were not considered employees of the State or any of the participating municipalities. The ruling concludes that the retirement plan established and maintained by the volunteer fire company is not a governmental plan within the meaning of section 414(d) because the degree of control that the participating municipalities exert over the volunteer fire company is minimal.

Exclusion of Governmental Plans from ERISA

Section 4(b)(1) of ERISA provides that title I of ERISA does not apply to an employee benefit plan that is a governmental plan as defined in section 3(32) of ERISA. Section 3(32) of ERISA generally provides that the term "governmental plan" means a plan established or maintained for its employees by the Government of the United States, by the government of any State or political subdivision thereof, or by any agency or instrumentality of any of the foregoing.[14] The ERISA section 3(32) definition of a governmental plan also includes any plan to which the Railroad Retirement Act of 1935 or 1937 applies, and which is financed by contributions required under that Act and any plan of an international organization which is exempt from taxation under the provisions of the International Organizations Immunities Act. Section 906 of PPA '06 amended section 3(32) of ERISA to include in the definition of governmental plan a plan which is established and maintained by an Indian tribal government (as defined in section 7701(a)(40)), a subdivision of an Indian tribal government (determined in accordance with section 7871(d)), or an agency or instrumentality of either. Under this definition, all of the participants of which are employees of such entity substantially all of whose services as such an employee are in the performance of essential governmental functions but not in the performance of commercial activities (whether or not an essential government function).

Section 4021(b)(2) of ERISA provides that title IV of ERISA does not apply to any plan established and maintained for its employees by the Government of the United States, by the government of any State or political subdivision thereof, or by any agency or instrumentality of any of the foregoing, or to which the Railroad Retirement Act of 1935 or 1937 applies and which is financed by contributions required under

---

[10] "The NLRB guidelines are a useful aid in interpreting ERISA's governmental exemption, because ERISA, like the National Labor Relations Act, 'represent[s] an effort to strike an appropriate balance between the interests of employers and labor organizations.'" *Rose v. Long Island Railroad Pension Plan*, 828 F.2d 910, 916 (2nd Cir. 1987), *cert. denied*, 485 U.S. 936 (1988) (quoting H.R. Rep. No. 533, reprinted in 1974 USCCAN at 4647). *See also, Shannon v. Shannon*, 965 F.2d 542, 547 (7th Cir. 1992), *cert. denied*, 506 U.S. 1028 (1992) (stating that the proper test for determining whether an entity is an agency or instrumentality of a State or political subdivision for purposes of ERISA is the *Hawkins* test), *Koval v. Washington County Redevelopment Authority*, 574 F.3d 238, 242 (3rd Cir. 2009) (stating that the *Hawkins* test is the most fitting analysis for determining whether an entity is a political subdivision), and *Brooks v. Chicago Housing Authority*, No. 89-C-9304, 1990 WL 103572 at 1, 1990 U.S. Dist. LEXIS 8233 at 3 (N.D. Ill. July 5, 1990) (applying the *Hawkins* test).

[11] "We focus our attention . . . on what should be the core concern for ERISA purposes—the nature of an entity's relationship to and governance of its employees." *Alley v. Resolution Trust Corporation*, 984 F.2d at 1206, n. 11.

[12] *Alley v. Resolution Trust Corporation*, 984 F.2d at 1206.

[13] *Berini v. Federal Reserve Bank of St. Louis*, 420 F.Supp.2d at 1026-29.

[14] In defining the term "governmental plan," section 3(32) of ERISA uses the phrase "established or maintained," whereas section 414(d) of the Code and section 4021(b) of ERISA use the term "established and maintained." For further discussion, see the Explanation of Provisions section of the preamble under the heading, "Requirements for establishing and maintaining a section 414(d) governmental plan."

that Act. Similar to section 3(32) of ERISA, section 4021(b) of ERISA was amended by section 906 of PPA '06 to include certain plans of Indian tribal governments in the definition of governmental plan for purposes of section 4021(b) of ERISA.

Neither the DOL nor the PBGC has issued regulations interpreting the terms of sections 3(32) and 4021(b) of ERISA. Both agencies have, however, provided guidance for specific entities in the form of administrative determinations, and advisory opinions or other opinion letters. The IRS, the Department of Labor (DOL), and the Pension Benefit Guaranty Corporation (PBGC) have generally applied a facts and circumstances approach in providing governmental plan determinations.[15] For example, the IRS issues private letter rulings relating to governmental plan status using a facts and circumstances analysis.

Exemption of Governmental Plans from Certain Qualified Plan Rules

Governmental plans under Code section 414(d) are exempt from certain qualification requirements and are deemed to satisfy certain other qualification requirements under certain conditions. For example, the nondiscrimination and minimum participation rules do not apply to governmental plans. Section 1505 of the Taxpayer Relief Act of 1997, Public Law 105-34 (111 Stat. 788, 1063) (TRA '97), amended sections 401(a)(5)(G) and 401(a)(26)(G) of the Code to provide that the minimum participation standards and nondiscrimination requirements of section 410 and the additional participation requirements under section 401(a)(26)(G) do not apply to State or local governmental plans.[16] Section 1505 of TRA '97 also amended section 401(k)(3)(G) of the Code to provide that certain State and local governmental plans are treated as meeting the requirements of the average deferral percentage test of section 401(k)(3) and the average contribution percentage test of section 401(m)(2).[17]

Section 861 of PPA '06 exempts all governmental plans (as defined in section 414(d)) from the nondiscrimination and minimum participation requirements of sections 401(a)(5)(G) and 401(a)(26)(G) of the Code, as well as the nondiscrimination and participation requirements applicable to qualified cash or deferred arrangements under section 401(k)(3)(G) of the Code.

In addition to the nondiscrimination requirements, the Code provides other exemptions for governmental plans:

- Section 401(a)(10)(B)(iii), which provides that the top heavy requirements of section 416 do not apply to a governmental plan.
- Section 410(c)(1)(A), which provides that the minimum participation provisions of section 410 do not apply to a governmental plan.
- Section 411(e), which provides that a governmental plan is treated as satisfying the requirements of section 411 if the plan meets the pre-ERISA vesting requirements.
- Section 412(e)(2)(C), which provides that the minimum funding standards of section 412 do not apply to a governmental plan.
- Section 417, which provides rules relating to qualified joint and survivor annuities and qualified preretirement survivor annuities.

Section 415 also provides a number of special rules for governmental plans. The special rules include section 415(b)(11) (the 100 percent of a participant's average high 3 compensation limitation does not apply), section 415(b)(2)(C) (the reduced limitation to the annual benefit payable beginning before age 62 and the reduction in the dollar limitation to the annual benefit payable for participation or services of less than 10 years do not apply to disability or survivor benefits received from a governmental plan), section 415(m) (benefits provided under a qualified governmental excess benefit arrangement are not taken into account in determining the section 415 benefit limitations under a section 414(d) governmental plan), and section 415(n) (permissive service credit).[18]

As a result, the principal qualification requirements for a tax-qualified governmental plan[19] are the requirements that the plan —

- Be established and maintained by the employer for the exclusive benefit of the employer's employees or their beneficiaries,
- Provide definitely determinable benefits,
- Satisfy the direct rollover rules of sections 401(a)(31) and 402(f),
- Be operated pursuant to its terms,
- Satisfy the section 401(a)(17) limitation on compensation,
- Comply with the statutory minimum required distribution rules under section 401(a)(9),
- Satisfy the pre-ERISA vesting requirements under section 411(e)(2),
- Satisfy the section 415 limitations on benefits, as applicable to governmental plans, and
- Satisfy the prohibited transaction rules in section 503.

State and local governments, political subdivisions thereof, and agencies or instrumentalities thereof are generally not permitted to offer cash or deferred arrangements under section 401(k). Instead, they can offer a somewhat similar elective contribution program through an eligible governmental section 457(b) plan to which section 457(g) applies. In addition, section 403(b) includes special rules for plans covering public school teachers, including rules under which, in conjunction with an eligible governmental section 457(b) plan, the maximum dollar amount of the elective contribution for a public school teacher is in effect double the maximum for other public or private employees.

Exemption of Governmental Plans from Other Employee Benefit Rules Relating to Retirement Plans

The Code and regulations also provide that plans of governmental entities are treated differently than plans of non-governmental entities with respect to certain requirements for section 403(b) plans and eligible section 457(b) plans, including:

- Section 403(b)(1)(A)(ii), which provides that the exclusion allowance under section 403(b)(1) applies to employees who perform services for a public school of a State, a political subdivision of a State, or an agency or instrumentality of any one or more of the foregoing.
- Section 403(b)(12)(C), which provides that the nondiscrimination requirements of section 403(b)(12) (other than the compensation limitations of section 401(a)(17)) do not apply to a State or local governmental plan within the meaning of section 414(d).
- Section 457(f)(2)(E), under which section 457(f) (relating to nonqualified deferred compensation) does not apply to a qualified governmental excess benefit arrangement under section 415(m).
- Section 457(e)(1)(B), which includes as an eligible employer a State, political subdivision, or agency or instrumentality thereof and any taxexempt organization other than a governmental unit.
- Section 457(g), which provides that a deferred compensation plan maintained by a State, political subdivision of a State, or any agency or instrumentality thereof is not treated as an eligible section 457(b) plan unless the assets and income of the plan are held in trust for the exclusive benefit of plan participants and beneficiaries.
- Section 402(c)(8)(B)(v), which provides that an eligible section 457(b) governmental plan is an eligible retirement plan for purposes of the rollover rules under section 402(c), so that payments from an eligible section 457(b) governmental plan can be rolled over to another eligible retirement plan, such as a qualified plan or an IRA, and payments from an eligible retirement plan can be rolled over into an eligible section 457(b) governmental plan.[20] An

---

[15] The DOL issues advisory opinions. The PBGC issues administrative determinations and opinion letters. The IRS issues letter rulings relating to section 414(d) governmental plans. For this purpose, a letter ruling is a written statement issued to a taxpayer by the IRS that interprets and applies tax laws or any nontax laws applicable to employee benefit plans to the taxpayer's specific set of facts. *See* section 3.02 of Rev. Proc. 2011-4 (2011-1 IRB 123, 127), see § 601.601(d)(2).

[16] In addition, section 1505(a)(3) of TRA '97 amended section 410(c)(2) to provide that all governmental plans within the meaning of section 414(d) are treated as satisfying the nondiscrimination requirements of section 410.

[17] A State or local government, political subdivision, or agency or instrumentality thereof, is not permitted to establish and maintain a section 401(k) plan. See section 401(k)(4)(B)(ii). There is an exception for a grandfathered section 401(k) plan, which is generally a plan established by a governmental unit (a State or local government or political subdivision thereof) before May 7, 1986. See § 1.401(k)-1(e)(4).

[18] See also Notice 89-23 (1989-1 CB 654), and Notice 96-64 (1996-2 CB 229), see § 601.601(d)(2), for guidance relating to the nondiscrimination rules that apply to qualified plans maintained by governments.

[19] A special rule applies to contributory plans of certain governmental entities. Section 414(h)(2) provides that, for a qualified plan established by a State government or political subdivision thereof, or by any agency or instrumentality of the foregoing, where the contributions of the governmental employer are designated as employee contributions under section 414(h)(1) but the governmental employer picks up the contributions, the contributions picked up will be treated as employer contributions.

[20] Section 402(c)(8)(B) defines an eligible retirement plan as an individual retirement account under section 408(a), an individual retirement annuity under section 408(b), a qualified plan, a section 403(a) annuity, a section 403(b) plan, and an eligible section 457(b) governmental plan.

eligible section 457(b) plan of a nongovernmental tax-exempt entity is not eligible for this rollover treatment.

Legislative History of ERISA

The legislative history of ERISA and its predecessor bills indicate that there were two reasons for the governmental plan exemption: (1) federalism concerns; and (2) the taxing power of State and local governments was thought to offer sufficient protection for participants in public plans.[21] In a summary of ERISA's predecessor bill, Senator Lloyd Bentsen commented that "State and local governments must be allowed to make their own determination of the best method to protect the pension rights of municipal and state employees. These are questions of state and local sovereignty and the Federal Government should not interfere."[22]

While Congress was concerned about pension protection for public as well as private employees, governmental plans have been excluded from many of the qualification requirements because, in addition to federalism concerns, Congress believed that "the ability of governmental bodies to fulfill their obligations to employees through their taxing powers is an adequate substitute for termination insurance."[23] As a result, ERISA includes exclusions for governmental plans under titles I and IV of ERISA and an exemption for governmental plans from most of the qualification requirements under the Code that were added under title II of ERISA (as described in this preamble under the heading, "Exemption of Governmental Plans from Certain Qualified Plan Rules").

Interagency Coordination on Governmental Plan Determinations

Historically, the IRS, DOL, and PBGC (the Agencies) have informally conferred prior to making determinations on governmental plan status in individual cases. In Notice 2005-58 (2005-2 CB 295), see § 601.601(d)(2), the Treasury Department and the IRS stated their intention of publishing guidance regarding governmental plans under section 414(d). The Agencies have become increasingly concerned with the growing number of requests for governmental plan determinations from plan sponsors whose relationships to States or political subdivisions thereof are increasingly remote and whose arguments for concluding that their plans are governmental plans raise novel issues. The use of differing approaches by the courts and the Agencies has resulted in uncertainty as entities with organizational, regulatory, and contractual connections with States or political subdivisions of States try to ascertain which statutory and regulatory requirements apply to their retirement plans. These proposed regulations are intended to address this issue by establishing coordinated criteria for determining whether a plan is a governmental plan within the meaning of section 414(d) of the Code. Although these proposed regulations are only applicable for purposes of section 414(d), the DOL and the PBGC were consulted in developing this proposal. The DOL and the PBGC agreed that it would be advantageous for the Agencies and other affected parties to have coordinated criteria for determining whether a plan is a governmental plan within the meaning of section 414(d) of the Code, section 3(32) of title I of ERISA, and section 4021(b) of title IV of ERISA. In that regard, comments are requested on any issues arising from these proposed regulations in light of the interaction of the governmental plan definition in the Code with the governmental plan definitions in section 3(32) of title I of ERISA and section 4021(b) of title IV of ERISA. Copies of the comments on these regulations will be forwarded to the DOL and the PBGC.

Explanation of Provisions

I. Overview

A. *In general.*

These proposed regulations would generally define the term "governmental plan" within the meaning of section 414(d) of the Code. These proposed regulations would also define other key terms relating to the general definition of "governmental plan," including the definitions of "State," "political subdivision of a State," and "agency or instrumentality of a State or political subdivision of a State." While

these terms are commonly used in other Code sections, the definitions in these proposed regulations are only applicable for purposes of section 414(d), and not for any other purpose under the Code. For example, the definition of the term "instrumentality" under these proposed regulations may be different for other purposes under the Code.

As stated, the regulations under section 414(d) would only define the term "agency or instrumentality of the United States" and "agency or instrumentality of a State or political subdivision of a State" for purposes of determining whether a plan is a governmental plan under section 414(d). Thus, the rules in these proposed regulations would not apply for purposes of defining the term "instrumentality," under any other provisions of the Code.

In addition, these regulations do not address certain issues relating to governmental entities, including when an entity is so closely related to a State that it constitutes an "integral part" of a State.[24] The criteria for treating an entity as an "integral part" of a State will be the subject of a separate guidance project. Such guidance defining "integral part" may include stricter criteria than would apply under these proposed regulations for determining whether an entity is an agency or instrumentality of a State.

B. *Definition of governmental plan.*

These proposed regulations reflect the statutory definition of the term "governmental plan" as a plan established and maintained for its employees by the Government of the United States, by the government of any State or political subdivision thereof, or by any agency or instrumentality of the foregoing. Within this definition, there are several key terms relating to governmental plans, the definitions of which are set forth in these proposed regulations. As mentioned in the "Background" section of this preamble, section 414(d) also includes special rules relating to the Railroad Retirement Act of 1935 or 1937, the International Organizations Immunities Act, and plans of Indian tribal governments. These proposed regulations do not address the term "governmental plan" as it relates to the special provisions in section 414(d) relating to the Railroad Retirement Act of 1935 or 1937, or the International Organizations Immunities Act. The special rules for Indian tribal governments are reserved in these proposed regulations and are in a separate notice of proposed rulemaking, which is being published elsewhere in the Rules and Regulations portion of this issue in the **Federal Register**.

C. *Definitions of the United States and agency or instrumentality of the United States.*

These proposed regulations would define the term "United States," for purposes of the governmental plan definition under section 414(d), as having the same meaning set forth in section 7701(a)(9). Section 7701(a)(9) provides that the term "United States," when used in a geographical sense, includes only the States and the District of Columbia.

Whether an entity is an "agency or instrumentality of the United States" is determined based on the specific purpose for which the designation is sought and is decided by determining if Congress intended the entity to be treated as a Federal entity for the specific purpose.[25] The proposed regulations would define the term "agency or instrumentality of the United States" as an entity that satisfies the facts and circumstances test as set forth in these regulations. The facts and circumstances test, similar to the factors weighed by the *Berini* court, focuses on the "degree to which the entity is connected with the . . . federal government."[26] The factors in this test are a compilation of various different tests used for governmental plan determinations, including factors in the *Berini* and *Rose* cases, as well as Rev. Ruls. 57-128 and 89-49. The facts and circumstances test is similar to that proposed for agencies and instrumentalities of a State or political subdivision thereof, (which is described in this preamble under the heading, "Definition of agency or instrumentality of a State or political subdivision of a State") but modified to reflect that this definition does not implicate the federalism concerns present in making determinations relating to agencies and instrumentalities of a State or political subdivision thereof.

---

[21] ERISA included a directive for the Committee on Education and Labor and the Committee on Ways and Means of the House of Representatives and the Committees on Finance and on Labor and Public Welfare of the Senate to study pension retirement plans sponsored by Federal, State, and local governments and analyze: (1) the adequacy of existing levels of participation, vesting and financing arrangements; (2) existing fiduciary standards; and (3) the necessity for Federal legislation and standards with respect to such plans. See Staff of House Comm. On Education and Labor, 95 th Cong., 2d Sess., *Pension Task Force Report on Public Employee Retirement Systems* (Comm. Print 1978).

[22] Staff of the Senate Comm. on Labor and Public Welfare, 94 th Cong., Legislative History of the Employee Retirement Income Security Act of 1974, Vol. I 220 (Comm. Print 1976).

[23] S. Rep. No. 93-383, at 81 (1973). See also H.R. Rep. No. 93-807, at 164-5 (1974).

[24] Over the years, the IRS has extended the income tax exemption it provides to states and political subdivisions to entities it regards as their "integral parts." *See* Rev. Rul. 87-2, 1987-1 C.B. 18; *see also* Treas. Reg. § 301.7701-1(a)(3).

[25] See *Berini v. Federal Reserve Bank of St. Louis*, 420 F.Supp.2d at 1025.

[26] *Id.*

The proposed regulations provide that, in making a determination of whether an entity is an "agency or instrumentality of the United States," the factors to be considered include whether:

- The entity performs or assists in the performance of a governmental function.

- There are no private interests involved, or the Government of the United States has all of the powers and interests of an owner. In determining whether an entity that holds stock has a private interest, stock will not be considered a private interest if the stock of the corporation is not acquired for investment purposes or for purposes of control.[27]

- The control and supervision of the entity is vested in the Government of the United States. Control must be more than the government's extensive Federal regulation of an industry.

- The entity is exempt from Federal, State, and local tax by an Act of Congress.

- The entity is created by the United States Government pursuant to a specific enabling statute that prescribes the purposes, powers, and manner in which the entity is to be established and operated.

- The entity receives financial assistance from the Government of the United States. However, an entity is not a governmental entity merely because it receives funds from the Government of the United States under a contract to provide a governmental service.

- The entity is determined to be an agency or instrumentality of the United States by a Federal court.

- Other governmental entities recognize and rely on the entity as an arm of the Government of the United States.

- The entity's employees are treated in the same manner as Federal employees for purposes other than providing employee benefits (for example, the entity's employees are granted civil service protection).

These proposed regulations also provide an example, illustrating the application of the facts and circumstances test to a particular entity — a Federal credit union. As announced in previous guidance, one purpose of these regulations is to address whether a Federal credit union is a governmental entity for purposes of determining whether the Federal credit union can maintain an eligible nonqualified deferred compensation plan. Notice 2005-58 addresses certain income tax issues with respect to nonqualified deferred compensation plans maintained by Federal credit unions, including whether a Federal credit union can maintain an eligible nonqualified deferred compensation plan described in section 457(b). Under Notice 2005-58, a plan in effect on August 15, 2005, that is maintained by a Federal credit union and that is intended to be an eligible nonqualified deferred compensation plan of a nongovernmental taxexempt employer would not fail to be an eligible plan under section 457(b) solely because the employer is a Federal credit union, provided that certain conditions are satisfied (including the condition that the plan of the Federal credit union not have claimed to be a governmental plan for purposes of section 414(d) of the Code and section 3(32) of ERISA). The rule in Notice 2005-58 only applies pending the issuance of future guidance regarding section 414(d). See § 601.601(d)(2)(ii)(b). Accordingly, upon adoption of these regulations as final regulations, the special treatment provided in Notice 2005-58 for Federal credit unions will no longer apply. However, after issuance of these regulations as final regulations, a Federal credit union can be an eligible employer within the meaning of section 457(e)(1)(B) on the basis that Federal credit unions are non-governmental tax-exempt organizations.

D. *Definitions of State and political subdivision of a State.*

The proposed regulations define the term "State" as any State of the United States and the District of Columbia. This definition, which is based on the definition of "State" in section 7701(a)(10), is different from the definition of "State" under section 3(10) of ERISA, which defines, in relevant part, the term "State" as any State of the United

States, the District of Columbia, Puerto Rico, the Virgin Islands, America Samoa, Guam, and Wake Island.

The term "political subdivision of a State" is defined in these proposed regulations as a regional, territorial, or local authority, such as a county or municipality (including a municipal corporation), that is created or recognized by State statute to exercise sovereign powers.[28] Examples of sovereign powers include the power of taxation, the power of eminent domain, and the police power. The definition of "political subdivision of a State" also provides that the governing officers of the authority must be appointed by State officials or publicly elected.

The term "political subdivision of a State" has been used for purposes other than section 414(d), including the NLRA and section 103.[29] The definition in these proposed regulations of the term "political subdivision of a State" applies only for purposes of section 414(d), and not for any other purposes under the Code or any other statute, including whether an entity is treated as a political subdivision for purposes of the NLRA or section 103 of the Code.

E. *Definition of agency or instrumentality of a State or a political subdivision of a State.*

These proposed regulations would provide guidance on determining whether an entity is an "agency or instrumentality of a State or a political subdivision of a State." These regulations would provide that the determination is based on a facts and circumstances test. The proposed regulations provide that numerous factors have been applied by the IRS in determining whether an entity is an agency or instrumentality of a State or a political subdivision of a State. Satisfaction of one or more of the factors is not necessarily determinative of whether an organization is a governmental entity. One factor that is not weighed by the IRS is the way the entity refers to itself. For example, the mere fact that an entity is called the "Educational Service Agency of City A" would not be a factor in determining whether the entity is an agency or instrumentality of City A.

Major factors for determining whether an entity is an agency or instrumentality of a State or political subdivision of a State are whether:

- The entity's governing board or body is controlled by a State or political subdivision.

- The members of the governing board or body are publicly nominated and elected.

- The entity's employees are treated in the same manner as employees of the State (or political subdivision thereof) for purposes other than providing employee benefits (for example, the entity's employees are granted civil service protection).

- A State (or political subdivision thereof) has fiscal responsibility for the general debts and other liabilities of the entity (including funding responsibility for the employee benefits under the entity's plans).

- In the case of an entity that is not a political subdivision, the entity is delegated, pursuant to a statute of a State or political subdivision, the authority to exercise sovereign powers of the State or political subdivision (such as, the power of taxation, the power of eminent domain, and the police power).

It is expected that, in applying the factor relating to whether the entity's governing board or body is controlled by a State or political subdivision, the control cannot be a mere legal possibility. Examples of situations in which the control factor might be a mere legal possibility are cases in which there are a number of tiers of intervening corporations between the entity and the State, and cases in which the legal power to control is shared among so many governing entities that none of them can be said to be responsible in the event of a failure to exercise control. In addition, since these two factors are interrelated, an entity that would satisfy the control factor would not be expected to satisfy the factor relating to whether members of the governing board or body are publicly elected or nominated. Alternatively, an entity that would satisfy the factor relating to whether members of the governing

---

[27] The Department of Treasury and the IRS recognize that an entity may hold stock for purposes other than investment and control. For example, the federal reserve banks are required to hold stock in the Federal Reserve Bank of its district because ownership is a condition of being a member in the Federal Reserve System. Unlike stock in a private corporation, this stock is not acquired for investment purposes or for purposes of control. See *Berini v. Federal Reserve Bank of St. Louis*, 420 F. Supp.2d at 1024, citing *Lee Const. Co., Inc. v. Federal Reserve Bank of Richmond*, 558 F.Supp. 165, 177 n.17 (D.Mich. 1982), citing 4 F. Solomon, W. Schlicting, T. Rice & J. Cooper, *Banking Law*, § 77.02, at 77-6 to 77-7 (1982).

[28] For certain purposes, the effect of an entity being determined to be a political subdivision of a State may be similar to the entity being determined to be an agency or

instrumentality of a State or political subdivision and for other purposes the effects may be different. Examples in which it is relevant whether an entity is a political subdivision in contrast to an agency or instrumentality of a State or political subdivision include the exclusion provided under section 402(l), the excise tax under section 4965, and the exception to the 10 percent additional tax under section 72(t)(10).

[29] Two court cases that have analyzed whether an entity is a "political subdivision of a State" for purposes of section 103 of the Code are *Commissioner of Internal Revenue v. Shamberg's Estate*, 144 F.2d 998 (2nd Cir. 1944), *cert. denied*, 323 U.S. 792 (1945), and *Commissioner of Internal Revenue v. White's Estate*, 144 F.2d 1019 (2nd Cir. 1944), *cert. denied*, 323 U.S. 792 (1945).

board or body are publicly elected or nominated would not be expected to satisfy the control factor.

Other factors for determining whether an entity is an agency or instrumentality of a State or political subdivision of a State are whether:

- The entity is created by a State government or political subdivision pursuant to a specific enabling statute that prescribes the purposes and powers of the entity, and the manner in which the entity is to be established and operated.

- The entity is directly funded through tax revenues or other public sources.

- The entity is treated as a governmental entity for Federal employment tax or income tax purposes (for example, whether the entity has the authority to issue tax-exempt bonds under section 103(a) of the Code) or under other Federal laws.

- The entity's operations are controlled by a State or political subdivision.

- The entity is determined to be an agency or instrumentality of a State or political subdivision thereof for purposes of State law. For example, the entity is subject to open meetings laws or the requirement to maintain public records that apply only to governmental entities, or the State attorney general represents the entity in court under a State statute that only permits representation of State entities.

- The entity is determined to be an agency or instrumentality of a State or political subdivision thereof by a State or Federal court for purposes other than section 414(d).

There are two additional factors to be considered. First, if a party other than a State (or political subdivision, agency, or instrumentality thereof) has an ownership interest, or other similar interests, in the entity, this factor would indicate that the entity is not an agency or instrumentality of a State or political subdivision thereof (however, an entity would not necessarily be considered an agency or instrumentality of a State or political subdivision thereof merely because there is no private ownership in the entity or the entity serves a governmental purpose). Second, if an entity does not serve a governmental purpose, this factor would indicate that it is not an agency or instrumentality of a State (or political subdivision thereof).

The proposed regulations include a variety of examples to illustrate whether an entity is an agency or instrumentality of a State or political subdivision thereof. Many of these examples are drawn from prior judicial opinions, as well as the Agencies' determinations.[30] Within the description of particular factors, there are some examples that illustrate whether a particular factor is satisfied. However, the mere satisfaction of a particular factor is not conclusive in determining whether an entity is an agency or instrumentality within the meaning of these regulations.

F. Requirements for establishing and maintaining a section 414(d) governmental plan.

The proposed regulations would provide that a plan is established and maintained for the employees of a governmental entity if the following requirements are satisfied: (1) the plan is established and maintained by an employer within the meaning of § 1.401-1(a)(2) of the Income Tax Regulations;[31] (2) the employer is a governmental entity; and (3) the only participants covered by the plan are employees of the governmental entity. For purposes of determining whether employees covered by a plan are employees of a governmental entity, employee representatives described in section 413(b)(8) (including individuals who are employed by the plan) would be treated as employees of the plan sponsor.[32]

The proposed regulations would provide rules for changes in status of an entity from a private entity to a governmental entity and from a governmental entity to a private entity. As mentioned in the "Background" section of this preamble, the qualification requirements for a private qualified plan differ substantially from those of a governmental qualified plan. The issue of whether a plan of a private employer that later becomes a governmental entity can be a governmental plan raises a question regarding the interaction among the three definitions of the term "governmental plan" in ERISA. Section 414(d) of the Code defines the term "governmental plan" as "a plan established and maintained by the Government of the United States, by the government of any State or political subdivision thereof, or by any agency or instrumentality of the foregoing." In title IV of ERISA, section 4021(b)(2) provides that any plan "established and maintained for its employees by the Government of the United States, by the government of any State or political subdivision thereof, or by any agency or instrumentality of the foregoing" is exempt from coverage by ERISA. In title I of ERISA, section 3(32) defines a governmental plan as "a plan established or maintained by the Government of the United States, by the government of any State or political subdivision thereof, or by any agency or instrumentality of the foregoing." While the definitions in title II of ERISA (Code) and title IV of ERISA (PBGC provisions) use the language "established *and* maintained" by a governmental employer, the title I definition uses the language "established *or* maintained."

This difference in statutory language was addressed in *Rose v. Long Island Railroad Pension Plan*, 828 F.2d 910 (2nd Cir. 1987), *cert. denied*, 485 U.S. 936 (1988). In *Rose*, the State of New York, through the Metropolitan Transportation Authority (MTA), acquired the Long Island Railroad Company in 1966 (LIRR). The LIRR had originally been chartered as a private stock corporation. As part of the acquisition, the State also assumed sponsorship of the Long Island Railroad Pension Plan (LIRR Pension Plan). After ERISA was enacted in 1974, the widow of a participant who died in 1976 in the LIRR Pension Plan sued the plan under title I of ERISA after being denied survivorship benefits. The *Rose* court concluded that the LIRR Pension Plan was a governmental plan within the meaning of section 3(32) of ERISA because the LIRR was an agency or instrumentality of a political subdivision, the MTA.

The *Rose* court took the position that if a private entity is acquired by a governmental entity which becomes the plan sponsor, the plan can be established by the governmental entity and, thus, be a governmental plan. The court interpreted the "established or maintained" language in section 3(32) literally, but also noted the discrepancy between the "established *or* maintained" language in ERISA section 3(32) and the "established *and* maintained" language in Code section 414(d) and ERISA section 4021(b)(2) (emphasis added). Despite this difference in the three statutory definitions, Congress intended all three definitions to be interpreted in a similar manner. The *Rose* court reasoned that:

> "If a plan is required to have been both established and maintained by a governmental entity in order to qualify for exemption, then a plan which was established by a private entity but subsequently taken over by a governmental body would continue to be subject to ERISA. This outcome conflicts with the federalism-based concerns which led Congress to exempt governmental plans in the first place." *Rose v. Long Island Railroad Pension Plan*, 828 F.2d at 920.

The *Rose* court stated that courts have interpreted the word "and" as meaning "or" if such interpretation would reflect the legislative intent of the statute.[33] The *Rose* court noted that its conclusion was consistent with the approach taken by the PBGC in a similar matter involving an entity's change to governmental status prior to the enactment of ERISA where the PBGC stated that it would not impose the "established" requirement when doing so would frustrate the congressional intent of section 4021(b)(2) of ERISA.[34]

The *Rose* court also noted that the LIRR Pension Plan had been rewritten and substantially funded by the State since its acquisition of the LIRR in 1966, and stated that it would have reached the same conclusion regarding the plan's governmental status even if the definition under section 3(32) of ERISA used the phrase "established and maintained."

> "In any event, even if we agreed with Rose that the correct interpretation of [section 3(32) of ERISA] was established and maintained, we would still not conclude that the LIRR Plan was covered by ERISA, because the Plan was in fact established and maintained by the LIRR."

Rose v. Long Island Railroad Pension Plan, 828 F.2d at 920. *See also Roy v. Teachers Insurance and Annuity Association*, 878 F.2d 47 (2nd Cir. 1989).

The court concluded that a broad reading of the term "established"—whereby a plan not previously established under ERISA may become a plan established under ERISA without the preexisting one

---

[30] *See, for example, Brock v. Chicago Zoological Society*, 820 F.2d 909 (7th Cir. 1987) and *NLRB v. Parents & Friends of the Specialized Living Center*, 879 F.2d 1442 (7th Cir. 1989).

[31] Section 1.401-1(a)(2) generally provides that a qualified pension, profit-sharing, or stock bonus plan is a definite written program and arrangement which is communicated to the employees and which is established and maintained by an employer.

[32] See § 1.413-1(i)(1) for rules for when an employee is an employee representative.

[33] *See Rose v. Long Island Railroad Pension Plan*, 828 F.2d at 919.

[34] The *Rose* court said that: "We find the PBGC's approach to be a sensible one; the status of the entity which currently maintains a particular pension plan bears more relation to Congress' goals in enacting ERISA and its various exemptions, than does the status of the entity which established the plan." *Rose v. Long Island Railroad Pension Plan*, 828 F.2d at 920. See PBGC Opinion Letter 75-44 (December 9, 1975).

having been formally "terminated"—is more consistent with the legislative intent behind the governmental plan exemption.[35]

For reasons similar to those presented by the *Rose* court, but consistent with the "established and maintained" language in section 414(d), the proposed regulations would set forth rules for employers changing status from private to governmental that are consistent with the legislative intent of the exemption of governmental plans. The proposed regulations would provide that if an employer becomes a governmental entity or a governmental entity becomes the employer under the plan (for example, in connection with an asset transfer), the plan will be treated as a governmental plan established by a governmental employer on the date of the change (including all of the plan's assets and liabilities attributable to service before and after the date of the change). Thus, in such a case, under the proposed regulations, the plan would have to comply with all the requirements for a private plan up to the date of the change and then comply with the requirements for a governmental plan after the date of the change. These same rules would also apply if a portion of a private plan was spun off to a plan maintained by a governmental employer: that portion of the plan would cease to be subject to Code rules applicable to nongovernmental employers, and instead would become part of a governmental plan, while the remaining portion of the private plan that was not spun off would continue to be subject to the protection and other rules applicable to private plans. These rules would provide standards for determining when the Code protections and other rules for a private plan cease to apply (and when the substantially different rules for a governmental plan begin to apply).

In the case of a change in status from a private plan to a governmental plan, comments are requested on whether, and if so how, these regulations should address rights and obligations that accrued prior to the conversion to a governmental plan, including the responsibility of the former private plan sponsor (or former private plan) for benefits that accrued prior to the conversion. Any comments that address the potential impact of the proposed regulation's approach on rights and responsibilities under title I and title IV of ERISA will be forwarded to the DOL and the PBGC.

Similarly, the regulations would provide that if a governmental employer ceases to be a governmental entity, the plan will be treated as being established by a private employer thereafter (including all of the plan's assets and liabilities attributable to service before and after the date of the change). Such a change would occur either where the employer entity ceases to be a governmental entity (such as a spin-off of a corporation) or where the employees become employees of a different entity (such as in an asset transfer). Thus, for example, the entity in either case would no longer satisfy the requirement that the employer be a governmental entity. If such a change occurs, the plan must comply with the requirements for a governmental plan up to the change and then comply with all the requirements for a private plan for periods after the date of the change. (See also the related discussion under the heading, "Comments and Public Hearing.")

In the case of a formerly governmental plan becoming a private plan, the plan and plan sponsor may secure certain advantages, such as PBGC coverage or ERISA preemption, not available to governmental plans and governmental sponsors. However, nothing in these proposed income tax regulations should be construed to mean that, with respect to a transaction such as an asset sale, in which assets and liabilities of a governmental plan are transferred to a private plan, the assumption of benefit liabilities accrued prior to the transfer to the private plan relieves the former governmental employer (or former governmental plan) from responsibility for those benefits.

As previously stated, the proposed regulations would provide that if a governmental employer ceases to be a governmental entity, the plan will be treated as being established by a private employer on the date of the change. The proposed regulations would provide an exception to this general rule when there is a change in status from a governmental entity to a private entity under certain circumstances. Specifically, if a governmental plan ceases to be maintained by a governmental employer, the plan will nevertheless be treated as continuing to be a governmental plan if the benefits held under the governmental plan are frozen and a governmental entity assumes responsibility for the plan. While the frozen plan would continue to be treated as a governmental plan, the plan would be permitted (but not required) to provide partici-

pating employees with credit for service with the new employer for purposes of vesting, final pay adjustments, entitlements to benefits such as early retirement benefits, and similar service credit other than benefit accrual credit.

Further, certain types of plans are limited under the Code to specific types of employers, including limitations that apply differently depending on whether or not the employer is or is not a governmental entity. These limitations on employer eligibility raise special problems for cases in which an entity becomes or ceases to be a governmental employer. For example, because a qualified cash or deferred arrangement under section 401(k) generally cannot be maintained by a State or local government or political subdivision, or any agency or instrumentality thereof, such a plan maintained by a private employer cannot be continued if the employer later becomes part of a State. Other special problems arise if a governmental employer that is not a tax-exempt organization under section 501(c)(3) and that is not a public school attempts to become a sponsoring employer of a section 403(b) plan of a tax-exempt organization under section 501(c)(3). Likewise, a State entity cannot maintain an unfunded section 457(b) plan of a tax-exempt organization described in section 457(e)(1)(B). These proposed regulations would not alter rules relating to the eligibility of an employer to establish or maintain a particular type of retirement plan. An employer that is considering a change in its status should evaluate whether it is eligible to sponsor any plan that it assumes, taking into account the employer eligibility rules. Therefore, sponsors should not assume from these proposed regulations that a change of sponsorship from a private to governmental employer, or vice versa, will not result in any adverse tax consequences. As emphasized elsewhere in this preamble, the proposed regulations would provide that the established and maintained rules apply only for purposes of section 414(d).

Proposed Effective Date

It is expected that these proposed regulations would not be applicable earlier than for plan years beginning after the date of the publication of the Treasury decision adopting these rules as final regulations in the **Federal Register**. Generally, amendment of a State or local retirement plan requires enactment of State legislation. The Department of Treasury and IRS intends to take into consideration the time required to complete the State legislative process when determining an effective date for these regulations.

Special Analyses

It has been determined that this notice of proposed rulemaking is not a significant regulatory action as defined in Executive Order 12866. Therefore, a regulatory assessment is not required. It has also been determined that section 553(b) of the Administrative Procedure Act (5 U.S.C. chapter 5) does not apply to these regulations. In addition, because no collection of information is imposed on small entities, the provisions of the Regulatory Flexibility Act (5 U.S.C. chapter 6) do not apply, and therefore, a Regulatory Flexibility Analysis is not required. Pursuant to section 7805(f) of the Code, this notice of proposed rulemaking will be submitted to the Small Business Administration for comment on its impact on small business.

Comments and Public Hearing

Before these proposed regulations are adopted as final regulations, consideration will be given to any written comments (a signed original and eight (8) copies) or electronic comments that are submitted timely to the IRS. The Treasury Department and the IRS specifically request comments on the clarity of the proposed rules and how they can be made easier to understand. All comments will be available for public inspection and copying.

These proposed regulations would provide that a determination of whether an entity is an agency or instrumentality of a State or a political subdivision thereof is based on a facts and circumstances analysis. Under the proposed regulations, the factors to be applied would be ranked into main factors and other factors.[36] Comments are requested on whether the final regulations should eliminate the distinction between main and other factors. Comments are also requested on the ordering and the application of the main and other factors; for example, whether the final regulations should provide a list of factors with a safe harbor standard under which, if an entity satisfies identified factors, the

---

[35] *But see Hightower v. Texas Hospital Association*, 65 F.3d 443, 448 (5th Cir. 1995), in which the Fifth Circuit held that if the plan was "established or maintained" for its employees by a governmental employer, the plan was exempt from coverage under title I of ERISA, even if it was not exempt from coverage under the title IV "established and maintained" test. The Court of Appeals held that the difference in statutory language between "established or maintained" and "established and maintained" had to be given some meaning, and held that for a plan to be a governmental plan under ERISA section

4021(b)(2), the plan had to be both established *and* maintained by the government. *Id.* at 450-51. The court did not discuss what, if any, actions would be sufficient for an employer assuming sponsorship of an existing plan to be treated as having "established" the plan.

[36] For a list of the factors, see discussion under the heading *Definition of Agency or Instrumentality of a State or a Political Subdivision of a State* in the Explanation of Provisions of this preamble.

entity will be treated as an agency or instrumentality of a State or political subdivision thereof, for purposes of section 414(d). Comments are also requested on whether the distinction between main and other factors should be retained, in addition to providing a safe harbor standard.

The factors identified in this bright line test might be whether: (1) a majority of the entity's governing board or body are either controlled by a State or political subdivision thereof or elected through periodic, publicly held elections (with the nominees elected by the voters); and (2) a State or political subdivision thereof has the fiscal responsibility for the general debts and other liabilities of the entity, including the entity's employee benefit plans. This standard might be available only if the entity was created by a State government or political subdivision pursuant to a specific enabling statute that prescribes the purposes, powers, and manner in which the entity is to be established and operated.

Apart from the special rules relating to plan coverage for employees of a labor union or plan under section 413(b)(8), these proposed regulations do not include special rules addressing existing practices under which a small number of private employees participate in a plan that would otherwise constitute a governmental plan under section 414(d). Comments are requested on whether an exception should be provided in such cases. Parameters that could be taken into account for such a special rule include the following: (1) whether the private employees were previously employees of the sponsoring governmental entity; (2) whether the private employees were previously participants in the governmental plan; (3) whether the number or percentage of such former employees who participate in the governmental plan is de minimis (and, if so, what constitutes a de minimis number or percentage); (4) whether the coverage is pursuant to pre-existing plan provisions; (5) whether the private employer performs a governmental function and has been officially designated as a State entity for plan participation purposes; and (6) whether the employer is ineligible to sponsor the particular type of governmental plan (for example, whether a private employer is a taxexempt organization under section 501(c)(3) that can sponsor a section 403(b) plan, and whether the private employer sponsors or has sponsored plans that cannot be sponsored by a State governmental entity, such as a cash or deferred arrangement under section 401(k) or an unfunded section 457(b) plan of a tax-exempt entity (described in section 457(e)(1)(B)).

If any special rule for such circumstances were to be included in the final regulation, there would be a number of related issues. These issues would include how to address the status of such a plan as a governmental multiple employer plan. Other issues might include how section 414(h) governmental pick-up plans should be treated, differences resulting from the application of federal employment taxes to a private employer participating in a governmental multiple employer plan, the application of the minimum funding rules with respect to a private employer participating in a governmental multiple employer plan, how the prohibited transaction rules of section 4975 would apply with respect to a private employer participating in a governmental multiple employer plan, how the special benefit limitation rules of section 415 would apply to private plan participants in the governmental plan; and what treatment should apply where the plan was previously a funded section 457(b) plan of a State or local government.

If the final regulations do not provide any special rule for cases in which a governmental plan continues to cover private employees who were formerly governmental employees, it is expected that a reasonable transition period following publication of the final regulations will be provided. Comments are requested on what transitional relief should be provided to a governmental plan that covers private employees who were formerly governmental employees and continue to participate in the plan that would otherwise constitute a governmental plan under section 414(d) (such as the governmental plan spinning off a portion of the assets and liabilities of the plan with respect to the former employees as a separate non-governmental plan). Comments are also requested on whether this method of correction might also be appropriate in situations such as described in *Example 5* in paragraph (k)(4) of the proposed regulations.

The final regulations may also provide transitional relief for entities that previously operated as if they were governmental entities eligible to participate or sponsor governmental plans but later were determined to be private entities under the regulations. Comments are requested on what transitional relief should be provided to an entity that is later determined to be a private entity. The Treasury Department and the IRS anticipate that there will be a reasonable transition period following the final regulations for a plan to revise its arrangements in order to avoid the adverse tax consequences of failing to comply with all the requirements of a private retirement plan.

A public hearing has been scheduled for (date to be provided when proposed regulations are published), beginning at 10 a.m. in the Auditorium, Internal Revenue Building, 1111 Constitution Avenue, NW., Washington DC. Due to building security procedures, visitors must enter at the main entrance located at 1111 Constitution Avenue, NW. In addition, all visitors must present photo identification to enter the building. Because of access restrictions, visitors will not be admitted beyond the immediate entrance area more than 30 minutes before the hearing starts. For information about having your name placed on the building access list to attend the hearing, see the "FOR FURTHER INFORMATION CONTACT" portion of this preamble.

The rules of 26 CFR 601.601(a)(3) apply to the hearing. Persons who wish to present oral comments must submit written or electronic comments and an outline of the topics to be discussed and time to be devoted to each topic (signed original and eight (8) copies) by (date to be provided when proposed regulations are published). A period of 10 minutes will be allotted to each person for making comments. An agenda showing the scheduling of the speakers will be prepared after the deadline for receiving comments has passed. Copies of the agenda will be available free of charge at the hearing.

Drafting Information

The principal author of these proposed regulations is Pamela R. Kinard, Office of Division Counsel/Associate Chief Counsel (Tax Exempt and Government Entities), Internal Revenue Service. However, personnel from other offices of the IRS and Treasury participated in their development.

List of Subjects in 26 CFR Part 1

Income taxes, Reporting and recordkeeping requirements.

Proposed Amendments to the Regulations

Accordingly, 26 CFR part 1 is proposed to be amended as follows:

PART 1—INCOME TAXES

Paragraph 1. The authority citation for part 1 continues to read in part as follows:

Authority: 26 U.S.C. 7805 * * *

Par.2. Section 1.414(d)-1 is added to read as follows:

§ 1.414(d)-1 Definition of governmental plan.

(a) *Definition of governmental plan*—(1) *In general.* In accordance with section 414(d), for purposes of part I of subchapter D of chapter 1 of the Internal Revenue Code and the regulations, the term *governmental plan* means a plan established and maintained for its employees by the Government of the United States, by the government of any State or political subdivision thereof, or by any agency or instrumentality of the foregoing, as determined pursuant to the requirements of this section. The definitions set forth in this section only apply for purposes of section 414(d) and this section.

(2) *Definition for plans subject to certain statutes.* For purposes of part I of subchapter D of chapter 1 of the Internal Revenue Code and the regulations, the term "governmental plan" also includes any plan to which the Railroad Retirement Act of 1935 or 1937 applies and which is financed by contributions required under that Act and any plan of an international organization which is exempt from taxation by reason of the International Organizations Immunities Act (59 Stat. 669).

(3) *Definition for certain plans of Indian tribal governments.* For purposes of part I of subchapter D of chapter 1 of the Internal Revenue Code and the regulations, the term "governmental plan" also includes a plan which is established and maintained by an Indian tribal government (as defined in section 7701(a)(40)), a subdivision of an Indian tribal government (determined in accordance with section 7871(d)), or an agency or instrumentality of either, and all of the participants of which are employees of such entity substantially all of whose services as such an employee are in the performance of essential governmental functions but not in the performance of commercial activities (whether or not an essential governmental function).

(b) *Definition of United States.* The term *United States* has the meaning set forth in section 7701(a)(9).

(c) *Definition of agency or instrumentality of the United States*—(1) *Agency or instrumentality of the United States.* For purposes of the definition of "governmental plan" in paragraph (a)(3) of this section, the term *agency or instrumentality of the United States* means an entity that satisfies the facts and circumstances test in paragraph (c)(2) of this section.

(2) *Facts and circumstances test.* Whether an entity is an agency or instrumentality of the United States is based on facts and circumstances. In making this determination, the facts to be considered include the following:

(i) The entity performs or assists in the performance of a governmental function.

(ii) There are no private interests involved, or the Government of the United States has all of the powers and interests of an owner. In determining whether an entity that holds stock has a private interest, stock will not be considered a private interest if the stock of the corporation is not acquired for investment purposes or for purposes of control.

(iii) The control and supervision of the entity is vested in the Government of the United States. Control must be more than the government's extensive Federal regulation of an industry.

(iv) The entity is exempt from Federal, State, and Local tax by an Act of Congress.

(v) The entity is created by the United States Government pursuant to a specific enabling statute that prescribes the purposes, powers, and manner in which the entity is to be established and operated.

(vi) The entity receives financial assistance from the Government of the United States. However, an entity is not a governmental entity merely because it receives funds from the Government of the United States under a contract to provide a governmental service.

(vii) The entity is determined to be an agency or instrumentality of the United States by a Federal court.

(viii) Other governmental entities recognize and rely on the entity as an arm of the Government of the United States.

(ix) The entity's employees are treated in the same manner as Federal employees for purposes other than providing employee benefits (for example, the entity's employees are granted civil service protection).

(3) *Example.* The following example illustrates the application of this paragraph (c):

Example. (i) *Facts.* Entity A is a Federal credit union, which is created pursuant to the Federal Credit Union Act, and is a tax-exempt organization under section 501(c)(1)(A)(i). Membership in the Federal credit union is not open to the general public but to individuals who share a common bond, current or former employees of specified employers. Entity A is member-owned and is controlled by a board of directors that is elected by its membership. Entity A, along with other Federal credit unions, is subject to regulation by the National Credit Union Administration (NCUA), which is a Federal agency that charters and regulates Federal credit unions.

(ii) *Conclusion.* Based on the facts and circumstances and the factors in paragraph (c)(2) of this section, Entity A is not an agency or instrumentality of the United States because its board of directors is elected by its own members and the directors are not responsible to the United States, except to the limited extent set forth in the Federal Credit Union Act and regulated by the NCUA. Thus, Entity A is not a governmental entity within the meaning of paragraph (c) of this section.

(d) *Definition of State.* The term *State* means any State of the United States and the District of Columbia.

(e) *Definition of political subdivision of a State.* The term *political subdivision of a State* means—

(1) A regional, territorial, or local authority, such as a county or municipality (such as, a municipal corporation), that is created or recognized by State statute to exercise sovereign powers (which generally means the power of taxation, the power of eminent domain, and the police power); and

(2) The governing officers either are appointed by State officials or publicly elected.

(f) *Definition of agency or instrumentality of a State or political subdivision of a State*—(1) *Agency or instrumentality of a State or political subdivision of a State.* The term *agency or instrumentality of a State or political subdivision of a State* means an entity that satisfies the facts and circumstances test in paragraph (f)(2) of this section.

(2) *Facts and circumstances test*—(i) *Factors to be considered.* In making the determination of whether an entity is an agency or instrumentality of a State or political subdivision of a State, the main factors to be considered are—

(A) The entity's governing board or body is controlled by a State (or political subdivision thereof). For example, an entity's governing board or body is controlled by a State (or political subdivision thereof) if the public officials of the State (or political subdivision thereof) have the power to appoint, and to remove and replace, a majority of the entity's governing board or body. This factor is not satisfied if the power to control is materially restricted (for example, if any board member of the entity can be replaced only with an individual chosen from a list of designees selected by the other members of the governing board or body);

(B) The members of the governing board or body are publicly nominated and elected;

(C) A State (or political subdivision thereof) has fiscal responsibility for the general debts and other liabilities of the entity, including responsibility for the funding of benefits under the entity's employee benefit plans;

(D) The entity's employees are treated in the same manner as employees of the State (or political subdivision thereof) for purposes other than providing employee benefits (for example, the entity's employees are granted civil service protection); and

(E) In the case of an entity that is not a political subdivision, the entity is delegated the authority to exercise sovereign powers (which generally means the power of taxation, the power of eminent domain, and police powers) of the State (or political subdivision thereof) and the delegation of authority is pursuant to a statute of a State (or political subdivision thereof).

(ii) *Other factors to be considered.* In making the determination of whether an entity is an agency or instrumentality of a State or a political subdivision of a State, other factors include—

(A) The entity's operations are controlled by a State (or political subdivision thereof);

(B) The entity is directly funded through tax revenues or other public sources. However, this factor is not satisfied if an entity that is not otherwise an agency or instrumentality is paid from public funds under a contract to provide a governmental service or is funded through grants by the State or Federal government;

(C) The entity is created by a State government or political subdivision of a State pursuant to a specific enabling statute that prescribes the purposes, powers, and manners in which the entity is to be established and operated. However, a nonprofit corporation that is incorporated under a State's general corporation laws is not created under a specific enabling statute;

(D) The entity is treated as a governmental entity for Federal employment tax or income tax purposes (such as, the authority to issue tax-exempt bonds under section 103(a)) or under other Federal laws;

(E) The entity is determined to be an agency or instrumentality of a State (or political subdivision thereof) for purposes of State laws. For example, the entity is subject to open meetings laws or the requirement to maintain public records that apply only to governmental entities, or the State attorney general represents the entity in court under a State statute that only permits representation of State entities;

(F) The entity is determined to be an agency or instrumentality of a State (or political subdivision thereof) by a State or Federal court;

(G) A State (or political subdivision thereof) has the ownership interest in the entity and no private interests are involved; and

(H) The entity serves a governmental purpose.

(3) *Examples.* The following examples illustrate the application of this paragraph (f). In each of these examples, unless otherwise stated, only facts that are relevant to the examples are included and it is assumed that no party other than a State or political subdivision thereof has an ownership interest in the entity and that the entity serves a governmental purpose. The examples are as follows:

Example 1. (i) *Facts.* Entity C is a utility company located in County B of State A. Entity C is created pursuant to a State A statute by a petition of 25 private citizens who are landowners, and approved by an order of a judge in County B. Entity C is administered by a board of commissioners named in the original petition, with vacancies to be filled by the incumbents, but with State A having the right to remove a board member for malfeasance. Entity C has the power of eminent domain. In addition, the records of Entity C are public records.

(ii) *Conclusion.* Based on the facts and circumstances, Entity C is not an agency or instrumentality of County B within the meaning of paragraph (f) of this section because it does not satisfy the control factors described in paragraphs (f)(2)(i)(A) and (ii)(A) of this section because Entity C is under the control of a self-perpetuating board of directors and because State A or its officials do not exercise control over the directors.

Example 2. (i) *Facts.* The facts are the same as in Example 1, except that Entity C is administered by a board of commissioners which is appointed by the Governor of State A and is subject to removal proceedings by the Governor of State A, the County B prosecutor, or the general public in County B. Vacancies on Entity C's district board are filled by popular election or by appointment of the Governor of State A. Entity C has the power of eminent domain. In addition, the records of Entity C are public records.

(ii) *Conclusion.* Based on the facts and circumstances, Entity C is an agency or instrumentality of County B within the meaning of paragraph (f) of this section.

Example 3. (i) *Facts.* Entity K is a non-profit corporation that operates a zoo in County J. Entity K is organized under the laws of State L. Although Entity K was not created by State law, the legislature of State L authorized the State's forest districts to contract with zoological societies for the creation, operation, and maintenance of zoological parks. County J entered into a contract with Entity K, giving Entity K exclusive control and management authority over the zoo in County J. Entity K, through government contracts, receives over half of its revenues from taxes raised by County J. The remaining revenues are from admission and parking fees, concessions, souvenirs, and private donations. County J maintains a significant amount of control over the budget of Entity K, including overseeing the expenditures of nontax revenues generated by Entity K. The zoo is located on land owned by County J, and vehicles used at the zoo are owned by County J and licensed as municipal vehicles. Entity K is managed by a 35-member board of trustees. Only one member of the board of trustees is a public official. Of the 240 members of Entity K who elect the board of trustees, only 4 members are County J public officials. In addition, County J has no direct role in Entity K's operation and maintenance of the zoo. Employees of Entity K are not treated in the same manner as public employees and, thus, are not covered under the civil service rules, pension plan, or workers' compensation funds of County J or State L.

(ii) *Conclusion.* Based on the facts and circumstances, Entity K is not an agency or instrumentality of County J or State L within the meaning of paragraph (f) of this section. Although Entity K is partly funded by County J, it receives those funds under a contract to provide governmental service and very few members of both the board of trustees and the governing members of Entity K are public officials.

Example 4. (i) *Facts.* Entity P is a non-profit corporation that operates a 24-hour intermediate care facility for mentally challenged adults located in State O. Entity P is licensed and regulated by State O. While not created by statute, Entity P's facility was built pursuant to statutory directives. Entity P is managed by a 9-member board of directors, which consists of parents of the patients at the facility and other volunteers. The directors are elected by Entity P's corporate members. State O has no authority to appoint or remove directors. The facility is managed by an executive director who is hired by the board without State approval. Pursuant to regulations, State O mandates certain personnel requirements, including staffing levels and minimum qualification requirements for staff members at the facility. However, Entity P is responsible for hiring, firing, and other disciplinary decisions. State O prescribes an hourly mean wage for the employees of Entity P, which limits the total amount that Entity P can pay its employees. In addition, State O imposes a ceiling on fringe benefits available to employees of Entity P, but Entity P is responsible for allocating the funds to pay for the fringe benefits.

(ii) *Conclusion.* Based on the facts and circumstances, Entity P is not an agency or instrumentality of State O within the meaning of paragraph (f) of this section. Although Entity P is directly funded by State O, it receives those funds under a contract to provide services to State O. Entity P does not satisfy the control factors described in paragraphs (f)(2)(i)(A) and (ii)(A) of this section because Entity P is controlled by directors who are chosen by Entity P's corporate members. While State O has some oversight control over Entity P's employees, through certification requirements and the imposition of limitations on pay and fringe benefits, Entity P has control over most employment decisions, as well as setting policies for holidays, vacations, insurance, and retirement benefits.

Example 5. (i) *Facts relating to University U.* University U was created by the legislature of State A and is an agency or instrumentality of State A under this paragraph (f). The board of trustees of University U appoints the president of University U. The president of University U appoints the chancellor of the medical school of University U. The chancellor of the medical school is also a vice-president of University U. The chancellor of the medical school appoints the various chairs of the clinical departments of the medical school.

(ii) *Facts relating to the corporate structure of Employer M.* The chairs of the clinical departments of the medical school have incorporated a separate entity, Employer M, under State A's not-for-profit law. Employer M is an integrated group practice for managing the clinical practice activities of the medical school faculty and was established in order to advance the purposes of the medical educational program and related activities of the medical school of University U. Under the by-laws of Employer M, any physician employee of Employer M must be a faculty member of the medical school (and if any physician employee of Employer M leaves the faculty of the medical school, his or her employment with Employer M terminates automatically).

(iii) *Facts relating to the control of Employer M.* Employer M is governed by a board of trustees consisting of the chancellor of the medical school, the clinical department chairs, and full-time faculty members appointed by two-thirds of the clinical department chairs. Performance of services as an employee of Employer M is a condition of employment for all full-time faculty members of the medical school. The faculty members are employees of University U and, in the capacity of their employment at University U, participate in the State A public employees' pension plan. Employer M also employs administrative and non-faculty employees who are not treated in the same manner as employees of State A (or University U). Employer M charges patients for the services provided by Employer M, and a portion of the fees collected are paid to University U. The compensation levels for employees of Employer M are set by faculty members who serve on the board of trustees of Employer M. The compensation paid to faculty members by Employer M is a substantial portion of the total compensation paid to them by University U and Employer M. Audited financial records of Employer M are submitted annually to the president of University U.

(iv) *Conclusion.* Employer M does not satisfy any of the factors listed in paragraphs (f)(2)(i)(B) through (E) of this section (that is, its trustees are not publicly nominated and elected, State A has no fiscal responsibility for Employer M, administrative and non-faculty employees of Employer M are not treated in the same manner as employees of State A, and Employer M has no sovereign powers). Employer M also does not satisfy any of the additional factors listed in paragraphs (f)(2)(ii)(B) through (G) of this section, but does satisfy the governmental purpose factor in paragraph (f)(2)(ii)(H) of this section. With respect to the control factors in paragraphs (f)(2)(i)(A) and (ii)(A) of this section, while all of Employer M's trustees are employees of University U, the majority of the board of trustees is not controlled by University U but by clinical department chairs and full-time faculty members of University U. Their service on the board of trustees of Employer M is in their capacity as representatives of Employer M, not as representatives of University U or State A. Accordingly, based on the facts and circumstances, including the lack of involvement of University U in overseeing the conduct of the board of trustees and the operations of Employer M beyond review of its audited financials, Employer M is not an agency or instrumentality of State A within the meaning of paragraph (f) of this section.

Example 6. (i) *Facts.* Entity W, a private foundation, provides public assistance to the indigent elderly in a residence hall built on land privately donated to Entity W, located in City V. City V contracts with Entity W to provide elder care to residents of City V. Over the years, City V has regularly budgeted for services provided by Entity W to its residents, including maintenance and upkeep of its facilities, and salaries of employees. In 1970, Entity W and City V together incorporated a non-profit organization, Entity X, called "City V Eldercare Residence," through which Entity W would provide its services to the residents of City V. Under Entity X's bylaws, Entity X is governed by a board of directors, six of whom are appointed by the Mayor of City V, and six of whom are appointed by Entity W. Entity X's employees are considered employees of Entity X and are not treated in the same manner as municipal employees of City V.

(ii) *Conclusion.* Although City V is a political subdivision of a State within the meaning of paragraph (e)(1) of this section, Entity X is not an agency or instrumentality of City V within the meaning of paragraph (f) of this section. While Entity X satisfies the governmental purpose factor described in paragraph (f)(2)(ii)(H) of this section, it does not satisfy any other factor, including the control factors described in paragraphs (f)(2)(i)(A) and (ii)(A) of this section or the employee factor described in paragraph (f)(2)(i)(D) of this section (because a majority of the board is not appointed by City V and Entity X's employees are not treated in the same manner as employees of City V).

Example 7. (i) *Facts.* Five States created Commission D as a body corporate of each compacting State and territory. Commission D was created to provide services to the States on issues relating to higher education. Each governor of the five States appoints three persons to the governing board of Commission D, which is subject to the joint control of the five States. Commission D submits yearly reports and budgets to the governors of each of the five States. Commission D's operating costs are apportioned equally among the States. The IRS determined in a ruling that Commission D was exempt from gross income under section 115. The IRS also determined that Commission D was an instrumentality of each of the five States for employment tax purposes.

(ii) *Conclusion.* Based on the facts and circumstances, Commission D is an agency or instrumentality of each of the five States within the meaning of paragraph (f) of this section.

Example 8. (i) *Facts.* Entity S, incorporated under the laws of State T as a nonprofit corporation, operates a hospital in City R. City R leases the hospital and its entire operation to Entity S. The lease between City R and Entity S requires Entity S to transfer its assets and liabilities back to the City upon expiration of the lease. City R created the first board of directors for the hospital, but it does not have the power to remove or replace any board member. Only one of the 13 board members of Entity S is a public official, an *ex officio* voting member. In addition, the board of directors is not elected by the general public of City R. To fund a subsequent expansion of the hospital facility, City R issued tax-exempt bonds. Entity S does not have the authority to issue tax-exempt bonds. Entity S does not exercise any sovereign powers. Employees of Entity S are not treated in the same manner as employees of City R. For example, Entity S and City R maintain separate payrolls, health insurance plans, and pension plans.

(ii) *Conclusion.* Based on the facts and circumstances, Entity S is not an agency or instrumentality of City R within the meaning of paragraph (f) of this section. Although City R had the power of the initial appointment of the board members, it cannot subsequently appoint or remove any directors of Entity S, therefore, Entity S does not satisfy the control factor described in paragraph (f)(2)(i)(A) of this section.

(g) *Special rules for plans of Indian tribal governments.* [Reserved].

(h) *Special rules for plans subject to the Railroad Retirement Act of 1935 or 1937.* [Reserved].

(i) [Reserved].

(j) *Special rules for plans subject to the International Organizations Immunities Act.* [Reserved].

(k) *Established and maintained*—(1) *In general.* For purposes of applying this section (and not for any other purpose) with respect to a governmental entity (which is an entity defined in paragraph (b), (c), (d), (e), or (f) of this section), a plan is established and maintained for the employees of a governmental entity if—

(i) The plan is established and maintained for employees by an employer, within the meaning of § 1.401-1(a)(2);

(ii) The employer is a governmental entity; and

(iii) The participants covered by the plan are employees of that governmental entity.

(2) *Changes in status*—(i) *Ceasing to be a private entity.* If an employer becomes a governmental entity (for example, as a result of a stock acquisition) or a governmental entity becomes the employer under the plan (for example, in connection with an asset transfer), the plan (including all of the plan's assets and liabilities attributable to service before and after the date of the change) will be treated, for purposes of paragraph (k)(1)(i) of this section, as being established by that governmental entity on the date of that change.

(ii) *Ceasing to be a governmental entity*—(A) *General rule.* Except as provided in paragraph (k)(2)(ii)(B) of this section, if an employer that is a governmental entity ceases to be a governmental entity (for example, as a result of a stock acquisition) or a private entity becomes the employer under the plan (for example, in connection with an asset transfer), the plan (including all of the plan's assets and liabilities attributable to service before and after the date of the change) is treated, for purposes of paragraph (k)(1)(ii) of this section, as being established by the non-governmental employer on the date of that change.

(B) *Exception.* If a plan is established and maintained for the employees of a governmental entity in accordance with paragraph (k)(1) of this section (without regard to this paragraph (k)(2)(ii)) and, at a subsequent date, the employer ceases to be a governmental entity (for example, as a result of an assets transfer), the plan is treated as continuing to be a governmental plan if—

(*1*) A governmental entity continues to be the plan sponsor after the change (for example, a governmental entity assumes the plan on or before the date on which the private entity becomes the employer (including becoming responsible for the employer obligations with respect to the payment of benefits under the plan)); and

(*2*) Benefits under the plan are frozen (with, if provided under the plan, participating employees to receive credit for service with the new employer for purposes of vesting, final pay adjustments, entitlement to benefits such as early retirement benefits, and similar service credit other than benefit accrual credit).

(C) *Governmental liability for spun-off benefits.* In the case of a transaction such as an asset sale in which assets and liabilities of a governmental plan are transferred to a private plan, the private employer would be responsible for satisfying the minimum funding standards of section 412 (including with respect to benefits attributable to service performed before the date of the change). However, nothing in this paragraph (k)(2)(ii) should be construed to mean that, with respect to such a transaction, the assumption of benefit liabilities accrued prior to the transfer to the private plan would relieve the former governmental employer (or former governmental plan) from responsibilities for those benefits.

(3) *Plan coverage for employees of a labor union or plan.* For purposes of paragraph (k)(1)(iii) of this section, employees of employee representatives described in section 413(b)(8) (including employees of a plan) are treated as employees of the plan sponsor. See § 1.413-1(i).

(4) *Examples.* The following examples illustrate the application of this paragraph (k):

Example 1. (i) *Facts.* Employer C, a non-profit corporation whose principal place of business is located in City F, is not a governmental entity. Plan B, a retirement plan, is established and maintained by Employer C. In a stock acquisition, City F acquires all the shares of stock of Employer C and, as a result, Employer C becomes a governmental entity.

(ii) *Conclusion.* After the acquisition, Plan B is established and maintained by a governmental entity. In addition, the employees covered by Plan B are employees of a governmental entity. Thus, Plan B, including the assets and liabilities attributable to benefits accrued in Plan B prior to the date of the acquisition, is a governmental plan within the meaning of section 414(d) and this section.

Example 2. (i) *Facts.* Employer G is a hospital that is an agency or instrumentality of State A. Plan J, a retirement plan, is established and maintained by Employer G. Plan J satisfies the requirements of this paragraph (k) and is a governmental plan within the meaning of section 414(d). The assets of Employer G are transferred to a non-profit corporation, Employer M, which is not a governmental entity. All employees of Employer G become employees of Employer M. As part of the transaction, Employer M assumes Plan J, with respect to benefits accrued for service both before and after the transaction.

(ii) *Conclusion.* Plan J is no longer maintained by a governmental entity. In addition, the employees covered by Plan J are no longer employees of a governmental entity. Therefore, Plan J no longer constitutes a governmental plan within the meaning of section 414(d) and this section. In order for Plan J to continue to be a qualified plan, Plan J must satisfy the qualification requirements relating to non-governmental plans, including with respect to the assets and liabilities attributable to benefits accrued in Plan J prior to the date of the sale. The same conclusion would apply if the transfer were a stock transaction.

Example 3. (i) *Facts.* Same facts as in *Example 2*, except that, on the date of the sale, Employer G freezes Plan J, so that participants in Plan J are no longer accruing benefits under the plan and all accrued benefits are limited to service before the sale. In addition, on the date of the acquisition, State A assumes Plan J, including responsibility for the payment of benefits previously accrued to participants in Plan J.

(ii) *Conclusion.* In accordance with paragraph (k)(2)(ii)(B) of this section, Plan J continues to be a governmental plan within the meaning of section 414(d) and this section.

Example 4. (i) *Facts.* Pursuant to a State statute, State L permits local towns and villages to establish recreational facility authorities to build and promote recreational activities. Under Statute K, unincorporated Townships M, N, and O (which are political subdivisions of State L, within the meaning of paragraph (d) of this section) jointly establish a recreational facility authority, Authority R. Financing for Authority F is through local taxes and fees. Authority R operates under a three-person board of directors, one each appointed by townships M, N, and O. Authority R built and operates a skating rink, Facility S, which is located in Township O, but is open to the residents of Townships M, N, and O. Facility S is wholly owned and controlled by Townships M, N, and O. Township O maintains Pension Plan P for its seven employees, which is a governmental plan under section 414(d). Township O amends its plan to permit the three employees of Facility S to participate. The employees of Facility S are not employees of Township O and are not employees of a labor union described in section 413(b)(8).

(ii) *Conclusion.* The governmental plan status of Pension Plan P is not affected by the participation of Facility S's employees because Facility S is a governmental entity within the meaning of section 414(d) and this section.

Example 5. (i) *Facts.* Same facts as *Example 4*, except that Township O amends Plan P to permit participation by 10 employees of candy and soft drink Vendor T, a supplier for Facility S. Vendor T is not a governmental entity.

(ii) *Conclusion.* Plan P is no longer a governmental plan within the meaning of section 414(d) because it provides benefits to employees of a non-governmental employer, Vendor T.

(l) *Employee.* For purposes of this section, the term *employee* means a common law employee of the employer (and the rules in section 401(c) do not apply).

¶ 20,263

IRS: Advance notice of proposed rulemaking: Governmental plans: Indian tribal governments.—The IRS has issued an advance notice of proposed rulemaking, which contains draft proposed regulations relating to the determination of whether a plan of an Indian tribal government is a "governmental plan" within the meaning of Code Sec. 414(d). Comments are invited from the public. Written or electronic comments must be received by February 6, 2012.

The advance notice of proposed rulemaking, which is reproduced below, was published in the Federal Register on November 8, 2011 (76 FR 69188). Official corrections were published in the Federal Register on December 8, 2011 (76 FR 76633).

DEPARTMENT OF THE TREASURY

Internal Revenue Service

26 CFR Part 1

[REG-133223-08]

RIN 1545-BI19

Indian Tribal Governmental Plans

AGENCY: Internal Revenue Service (IRS), Department of the Treasury.

ACTION: Advance notice of proposed rulemaking.

SUMMARY: The Treasury Department and IRS anticipate issuing regulations under section 414(d) of the Internal Revenue Code (Code) to define the term "governmental plan." This document describes the rules the Treasury Department and IRS are considering proposing relating to the determination of whether a plan of an Indian tribal government is a governmental plan within the meaning of section 414(d) and contains an appendix that includes a draft notice of proposed rulemaking on which the Treasury Department and IRS invite comments from the public. This document applies to sponsors of, and participants and beneficiaries in, employee benefit plans of Indian tribal governments.

DATES: Written or electronic comments must be received by February 6, 2012.

ADDRESSES: Send submissions relating to the section 414(d) draft ITG regulations to: CC:PA:LPD:PR (REG-133223-08), room 5203, Internal Revenue Service, PO Box 7604, Ben Franklin Station, Washington DC, 20044. Submissions may be hand delivered Monday through Friday, between the hours of 8 a.m. and 4 p.m. to CC:PA:LPD:PR (REG-133223-08), Courier's Desk, Internal Revenue Service, 1111 Constitution Avenue, NW., Washington, DC.

Alternately, taxpayers may submit comments relating to the section 414(d) draft ITG regulations located in the Appendix to this ANPRM electronically via the Federal eRulemaking Portal at *www.regulations.gov* (IRS-REG-133223-08).

FOR FURTHER INFORMATION CONTACT:

Concerning the ANPRM, Pamela R. Kinard, at (202) 622-6060; concerning submission of comments, Richard Hurst, at (202) 622-7180 (not toll-free numbers).

SUPPLEMENTARY INFORMATION:

Background

This document describes rules that the Treasury Department and IRS are considering proposing and contains a draft notice of proposed rulemaking (in the Appendix to this ANPRM) under section 414(d) of the Internal Revenue Code (Code). Under the draft notice of proposed rulemaking (in the Appendix to this ANPRM), the rules would provide guidance relating to the determination of whether a plan of an Indian tribal government, a subdivision of an Indian tribal government, or an agency or instrumentality of either (ITG) is a governmental plan within the meaning of section 414(d) of the Code (section 414(d) draft ITG regulations).

Section 414(d) of the Code provides that the term "governmental plan" generally means a plan established and maintained for its employees by the Government of the United States, by the government of any State or political subdivision thereof, or by any agency or instrumentality of any of the foregoing. See sections 3(32) and 4021(b)(2) of the Employee Retirement Income Security Act of 1974 (ERISA) for definitions of the term "governmental plan," which govern respectively for purposes of title I and title IV of ERISA[1].

The term "governmental plan" also includes any plan to which the Railroad Retirement Act of 1935 or 1937 (49 Stat. 967, as amended by 50 Stat. 307) applies and which is financed by contributions required under that Act and any plan of an international organization which is exempt from taxation by reason of the International Organizations Immunities Act (59 Stat. 669). See section 414(d)(2) of the Code.

Section 414(d) was amended by the Pension Protection Act of 2006, Public Law 109-280 (120 Stat. 780) (PPA '06) to include certain plans of Indian tribal governments and related entities.[2] Section 906(a)(1) of PPA '06 provides that the term "governmental plan" includes a plan which is established and maintained by an Indian tribal government (as defined in section 7701(a)(40)), a subdivision of an Indian tribal government (determined in accordance with section 7871(d)), or an agency or instrumentality of either (ITG), and all the participants of which are employees of such entity substantially all of whose services as such an employee are in the performance of essential governmental functions but not in the performance of commercial activities (whether or not an essential governmental function).

Neither section 414(d) of the Code, section 3(32) of ERISA, nor section 4021(b)(2) of ERISA define key terms relating to governmental plans, including the terms "established and maintained," "political subdivision," "agency," and "instrumentality." Currently, there are no regulations interpreting section 414(d). Revenue Ruling 89-49 (1989-1 CB 117), see § 601.601(d)(2), sets forth a facts and circumstances analysis for determining whether a retirement plan is a governmental plan within the meaning of section 414(d).[3] This analysis is used by the IRS in issuing letter rulings. In connection with this advanced notice of proposed rulemaking, an advance notice of proposed rulemaking is also being issued with respect to the general definition of a governmental plan (REG-157714-06 that is being published elsewhere in this issue of the **Federal Register**).

Governmental plans are subject to different rules than retirement plans of nongovernmental employers. Governmental plans are excluded from the provisions of titles I and IV of ERISA. In addition, governmental plans receive special treatment under the Code. These plans are exempt from certain qualification requirements and they are deemed to satisfy certain other qualification requirements under certain conditions. As a result, the principal qualification requirements for a tax-qualified governmental plan[4] are that the plan—

---

[1] The three definitions of the term "governmental plan" are essentially the same. The only difference is that, in defining the term "governmental plan," section 3(32) of ERISA uses the phrase "established or maintained," whereas section 414(d) of the Code and section 4021(b) of ERISA use the term "established and maintained."

[2] Section 906(a) of PPA '06 made similar amendments to sections 3(32) and 4021(b)(2) of ERISA.

[3] See also Rev. Rul. 57-128 (1957-1 CB 311), see § 601.601(d)(2), which provides guidance on determining when an entity is a governmental instrumentality for purposes of the exemption from employment taxes under section 3121(b)(7) and 3306(c)(7).

[4] A special rule applies to contributory plans of certain governmental entities. Section 414(h)(2) provides that, for a qualified plan established by a State government or political subdivision thereof, or by any agency or instrumentality of the foregoing, where the

- Be established and maintained by the employer for the exclusive benefit of the employer's employees or their beneficiaries;

- Provide definitely determinable benefits;

- Be operated pursuant to its terms;

- Satisfy the direct rollover rules of section 401(a)(31);

- Satisfy the section 401(a)(17) limitation on compensation;

- Comply with the statutory minimum required distribution rules under section 401(a)(9);

- Satisfy the pre-ERISA vesting requirements under section 411(e)(2);[5]

- Satisfy the section 415 limitations on benefits, as applicable to governmental plans; and

- Satisfy the prohibited transaction rules in section 503.

State and local governments, political subdivisions thereof, and agencies or instrumentalities thereof are generally not permitted to offer cash or deferred arrangements under section 401(k). However, an ITG is permitted to offer a cash or deferred arrangement under section 401(k).

Notice 2006-89 (2006-2 CB 772) and Notice 2007-67 (2007-35 IRB 465), see § 601.601(d)(2), summarize the changes made by section 906(a)(1) of PPA '06 and provide transitional relief to ITGs under a reasonable and good faith standard to comply with such changes. The notices provide that until such guidance is issued, a plan established and maintained by an ITG for its employees is treated as satisfying the requirements of section 906(a)(1) of PPA '06 to be a governmental plan under section 414(d) of the Code if it complies with those requirements based on a reasonable and good faith interpretation of section 414(d). For further background, see the "Background" section of the preamble of the section 414(d) draft ITG regulations in the Appendix to this ANPRM under the headings, "Notices Issued by the IRS Relating to ITG Retirement Plans under PPA '06."

The Treasury Department and the IRS participated in a series of telephone listening meetings with the ITG community following the passage of PPA '06. The attached draft notice of proposed rulemaking in the Appendix to this ANPRM takes into account comments provided through a number of informative and cooperative comments received in response to Notices 2006-89 and 2007-67 and open and direct consultations with the Indian tribal community. Those comments received from Notices 2006-89 and 2007-67 and during the consultations were considered in drafting the proposed rulemaking.

The Treasury Department and the IRS have determined to seek public comment and consult with ITGs on the draft proposed regulations in advance of issuing a notice of proposed rulemaking. In light of the interaction of the governmental plan definitions in the Code and ERISA, a copy of the comments will be forwarded to DOL and PBGC.

Explanation of Provisions

Attached to the Appendix to this ANPRM is a draft notice of proposed rulemaking. These draft regulations include proposed rules, a preamble, and a request for comments. The Treasury Department and IRS invite the public to comment on the rules that ehe Treasury Department and IRS are considering proposing, which would set forth special rules relating to retirement plans of ITGs.

Section 414(d) Draft ITG regulations

A plan established and maintained by an ITG is a governmental plan under section 414(d), as amended by section 906 of PPA '06, only if all of its participants are employees substantially all of whose services are in the performance of essential governmental functions (but not in the performance of commercial activities whether or not an essential governmental function). Therefore, the rules under the section 414(d) draft general regulations (in the Appendix to the ANPRM that is being published elsewhere in this issue of the **Federal Register**) would apply to ITG governmental plans, as well as the special rules under the attached section 414(d) draft ITG regulations. The anticipated proposed regulations would use the broader concepts of governmental activity and commercial activity, instead of the terms essential governmental function and commercial activity. See the "Explanation of Provisions" section in the section 414(d) draft ITG regulations in the Appendix to this ANPRM under the heading, "Determination of Governmental and Commercial Activities."

Under the section 414(d) draft ITG regulations (in the Appendix to this ANPRM), whether a plan of an ITG is a governmental plan or a nongovernmental plan within the meaning of section 414(d) would be based, in part, on: (1) a determination of which activities are commercial activities and (2) a determination of whether employees of the ITG covered by the plan are employees who perform substantial services in commercial activities of the ITG (and are thus commercial employees).

The anticipated proposed regulations would provide that certain specific activities are deemed to be governmental or commercial for purposes of section 414(d). Under the anticipated proposed regulations, commercial activities would be operations involving a hotel, casino, service station, convenience store, or marina. These activities are examples that were identified as commercial activities in Notices 2006-89 and 2007- 67, as well as in the Joint Committee on Taxation Technical Explanation to section 906 of PPA '06. The section 414(d) draft ITG regulations in the Appendix to this ANPRM would provide that governmental activities include activities related to the building and maintenance of public roads, sidewalks, and buildings, activities related to public work projects (such as schools and government buildings), and activities that are subject to a treaty or special rules that pertain to trust land ownership and use. See § 601.601(d)(2).

In addition to listing certain specified activities, the anticipated proposed regulations would provide a facts and circumstances test for determining whether an activity is a governmental or commercial activity. See the "Explanation of Provisions" section in the section 414(d) draft ITG regulations in the Appendix to this ANPRM under the heading, "Governmental and Commercial Activities." The anticipated proposed regulations would also provide examples illustrating the application of the facts and circumstances tests to particular activities.

The anticipated proposed regulations would also provide rules for determining whether employees covered by an ITG plan are employees who perform substantial services in activities that are governmental. For this purpose, the determination of whether an employee's services are for governmental or commercial activities would generally be based on the employee's assigned duties and responsibilities. See the "Explanation of Provisions" section in the section 414(d) draft ITG regulations in the Appendix to this ANPRM under the headings, "Determination of Governmental ITG Employees" and "Determination of Commercial ITG Employees."

The anticipated proposed regulations do not address the broader issue of whether a retirement plan is a governmental plan within the meaning of section 414(d). That topic is addressed in the advance notice of proposed rulemaking relating generally to the definition of governmental plan that is being published elsewhere in this issue of the **Federal Register**.

Request for Comments

Before a notice of proposed rulemaking is issued, consideration will be given to any written comments that are submitted timely (preferably a signed original and eight (8) copies) to the IRS. All comments will be available for public inspection and copying. Copies of the comments will be provided to the DOL and PBGC.

Comments are also requested on whether, as an alternative to issuing proposed regulations, the Department of Treasury and IRS should publish a notice that reflects some or all of the rules in the draft proposed regulations and that also modifies the rule in Notice 2007-67 concerning when a mixed ITG is required to be amended to be two different plans, one for governmental employees and another for commercial employees. If so, the notice would include a significant transitional period for compliance similar to the transition period that would be expected to apply for regulations (such as not being effective until plan years that begin at least 18 months after publication of the notice). The Department of Treasury and IRS invite comments on whether this method of guidance would be preferable to the issuance of regulations.

The IRS and Department of Treasury plan to schedule a public hearing on the ANPRM. That hearing will be scheduled and announced at a later date. In addition to a public hearing, the Treasury Department and IRS anticipate scheduling consultation listening meetings in order to obtain comments from tribal governments on the section 414(d) draft ITG regulations. It is expected that these meetings will take place in different locations across the country. Participants will be encouraged to pre-register for the meetings. Information relating to these meetings, including dates, times, locations, registration, and the procedures for submitting written and oral comments, will be available on

---

(Footnote Continued)

contributions of the governmental employer are designated as employee contributions under section 414(h)(1) but the governmental employer picks up the contributions, the contributions picked up will be treated as employer contributions.

[5] Section 411(e)(2) states that a plan described in section 411(e)(1) is treated as meeting the requirements of section 411 if the plan meets the vesting requirements resulting from the application of section 401(a)(4) and (a)(7) as in effect on September 1, 1974.

the IRS website relating to governmental plans at *http://www.irs.gov/retirement/article/0,,id=181779,00.html.*

EO 13175, Consultation and Coordination with Indian Tribal Governments In the Appendix to this ANPRM is a draft notice of proposed rulemaking. These draft regulations include proposed rules, a preamble, and a request for comments. The Treasury Department and the IRS invite the public to comment on the rules under consideration, which would set forth special rules relating to retirement plans of ITGs. This solicitation of comments is in furtherance of the objective of Executive Order 13175 under which Treasury consults with tribal officials in the development of Federal policies that may have tribal implications. The IRS and Treasury Department will consult with Indian tribes through the normal comment process in the **Federal Register**, issuing this advance notice of public rulemaking, and reaching out to Indian tribes through a series of consultation listening meetings.

Drafting Information

The principal author of this advance notice of proposed rulemaking is Pamela R. Kinard, Office of the Chief Counsel (Tax-exempt and Government Entities), however, other personnel from the IRS and Treasury Department participated in its development.

Steven T. Miller,

Deputy Commissioner for Services and Enforcement.

APPENDIX

The following is draft language for a notice of proposed rulemaking that would set forth rules relating to the determination of whether a plan of an Indian tribal government is a governmental plan within the meaning of section 414(d). The IRS and Treasury release this draft language in order to solicit comments from the governmental plans community:

Background

This document contains proposed regulations under section 414(d) of the Internal Revenue Code (Code). These regulations, when finalized, would provide guidance relating to the determination of whether a plan of an Indian tribal government or other entities related to an Indian tribal government is a governmental plan within the meaning of section 414(d). The definition of a governmental plan under section 414(d) applies for purposes of Part I of Subchapter D of Chapter 1 of Subtitle A (Income Taxes) of the Code (sections 401 through 420) and certain other Code provisions that refer to section 414(d) (such as sections 72(t)(10), 501(c)(25)(C), 4975(g)(2), 4980B(d)(2), 9831(a)(1), and 9832(d)(1) of the Code).

Statutory Definition of Governmental Plan

Both the Code and the Employee Retirement Income Security Act of 1974 (ERISA) define the term "governmental pension." Prior to the Pension Protection Act of 2006, Public Law 109-280 (120 Stat. 780) (PPA '06), section 414(d) of the Code provides that the term "governmental plan" means a plan established and maintained for its employees by the Government of the United States, by the government of any State or political subdivision thereof, or by any agency or instrumentality of any of the foregoing. Sections 3(32) and 4021(b)(2) of ERISA have parallel definitions of the term "governmental plan." The term "governmental plan" also includes any plan to which the Railroad Retirement Act of 1935 or 1937 (49 Stat. 967, as amended by 50 Stat. 307) applies and which is financed by contributions required under that Act and any plan of an international organization which is exempt from taxation by reason of the International Organizations Immunities Act Public Law 79-291 (59 Stat. 669).

Section 906 of PPA '06

Section 906(a) of PPA '06 amended section 414(d) of the Code (and the parallel provisions in sections 3(32) and 4021(b)(2) of ERISA) to include in the definition of "governmental plan" certain plans of an Indian tribal government, a subdivision of an Indian tribal government, or an agency or instrumentality thereof. Specifically, under section

906(a)(1) of PPA '06, the term "governmental plan" includes a plan which is established and maintained for its employees by an Indian tribal government (as defined in section 7701(a)(40)), a subdivision of an Indian tribal government (determined in accordance with section 7871(d)), or an agency or instrumentality of either (ITG), and all of the participants of which are employees of such entity substantially all of whose services as such an employee are in the performance of essential governmental functions but not in the performance of commercial activities (whether or not an essential governmental function). Section 906(c) of PPA '06 provides that the amendments made by section 906 of PPA '06 apply to any year beginning on or after the date of enactment, which is August 17, 2006.

In its Technical Explanation[6] to section 906 of PPA '06, the Joint Committee on Taxation refers to an employee substantially all of whose services for an ITG are in the performance of essential governmental services and not in the performance of commercial activities (whether or not such activities are an essential governmental function) as a qualified employee who is eligible to participate in a governmental plan as described in section 414(d). The Technical Explanation states, for example, that a governmental plan includes a plan of an ITG, all of the participants of which are teachers in tribal schools. However, the Technical Explanation also states that a governmental plan does not include a plan covering tribal employees who are employed by a hotel, casino, service station, convenience store, or marina operated by a tribal government.

Exemption of Governmental ITG Plans from Certain Qualified Plan Rules

Governmental plans under Code section 414(d), including governmental ITG plans, receive special treatment with respect to certain qualification rules. Such plans are exempt from certain qualification requirements and are deemed to satisfy certain other qualification requirements under certain conditions. For example, the nondiscrimination and minimum participation rules do not apply to governmental plans.[7] In addition, the Code provides other exemptions for section 414(d) governmental plans:

- Section 401(a)(10)(B)(iii), which provides that the top-heavy requirements of section 416 do not apply to a governmental plan.

- Section 410(c)(1)(A), which provides that the minimum participation provisions of section 410 do not apply to a governmental plan.

- Section 411(e), which provides that a governmental plan is treated as satisfying the requirements of section 411 if the plan meets the pre-ERISA vesting requirements.

- Section 412(e)(2)(C), which provides that the minimum funding standards of section 412 do not apply to a governmental plan.

- Section 417, which provides rules relating to qualified joint and survivor annuities and qualified preretirement survivor annuities .

Section 415 also provides a number of special rules for governmental plans. The special rules include section 415(b)(11) (under which governmental pensions are not limited to 100% of a participant's average high 3 compensation), section 415(b)(2)(I) (the reduced limitation to the annual benefit payable beginning before age 62 and the reduction in the dollar limitation to the annual benefit payable for participation or services of less than 10 years do not apply to disability or survivor benefits received from a governmental plan), section 415(m) (benefits provided under a qualified governmental excess benefit arrangement are not taken into account in determining the section 415 benefit limitations under a section 414(d) governmental plan), and section 415(n) (permissive service credit).

As a result, the principal qualification requirements for a tax-qualified governmental plan[8] are that the plan—

- Be established and maintained by the employer for the exclusive benefit of the employer's employees or their beneficiaries;

- Provide definitely determinable benefits;

- Be operated pursuant to its terms;

- Satisfy the direct rollover rules of sections 401(a)(31) and 402(f);

- Satisfy the section 401(a)(17) limitation on compensation;

---

[6] Joint Committee on Taxation, Technical Explanation of H.R. 4, the "Pension Protection Act of 2006" as passed by the House on July 28, 2006, and considered by the Senate on August 3, 2006 (JCX-38-06), August 3, 2006, 109th Cong., 2nd Sess. 244 (2006).

[7] Section 861 of PPA '06 amended sections 401(a)(5)(G) and 401(a)(26)(G) of the Code to provide that the minimum participation standards and nondiscrimination requirements of section 410 and the additional participation requirements under section 401(a)(26) do not apply to governmental plans within the meaning of section 414(d) of the Code. Section 861 of PPA '06 also exempts governmental plans from the nondiscrimination and participa-

tion requirements applicable to qualified cash or deferred arrangements under section 401(k)(3) of the Code.

[8] A special rule applies to contributory plans of certain governmental entities. Section 414(h)(2) provides that, for a qualified plan established by a State government or political subdivision thereof, or by any agency or instrumentality of the foregoing, where the contributions of the governmental employer are designated as employee contributions under section 414(h)(1) but the governmental employer picks up the contributions, the contributions picked up will be treated as employer contributions.

- Comply with the statutory minimum required distribution rules under section 401(a)(9);
- Satisfy the pre-ERISA vesting requirements under section 411(e)(2);[9]
- Satisfy the section 415 limitations on benefits, as applicable to governmental plans; and
- Satisfy the prohibited transaction rules in section 503.

State and local governments, political subdivisions thereof, and agencies or instrumentalities thereof are generally not permitted to offer cash or deferred arrangements under section 401(k).[10] However, Indian tribal governments and their related entities are permitted to offer cash or deferred arrangements as part of a plan maintained by an ITG.[11]

Rules Treating Indian Tribal Governments as States for Purposes of Issuing Tax-Exempt Bonds

Section 7871 provides special rules for Indian tribal governments. Section 7871(a)(4) provides that an Indian tribal government is to be treated as a State for purposes of section 103, relating to tax-exempt bonds.[12] Section 7871(c)(1) generally provides that section 103(a) applies to an obligation issued by an Indian tribal government only if such obligation is part of an issue substantially all of the proceeds of which are to be used in the exercise of any essential governmental function.

On August 9, 2006, an advance notice of proposed rulemaking under section 7871 was published in the **Federal Register** (71 FR 45474). The ANPRM describes the rules that the Treasury Department and the IRS anticipate proposing on the definition of essential governmental function under section 7871(e). The rules would provide that an activity is considered an essential governmental function that is customarily performed by State and local governments if: (1) there are numerous State and local governments with general taxing powers that have been conducting the activity and financing it with tax-exempt governmental bonds; (2) State and local governments with general taxing powers have been conducting the activity and financing it with tax-exempt governmental bonds for many years; and (3) the activity is not a commercial or industrial activity. The ANPRM provides examples of activities customarily performed by State and local governments, including public works projects such as roads, schools, and government buildings.

Notices Issued by the IRS Relating to ITG Retirement Plans under PPA '06

Notice 2006-89 (2006-2 CB 772) and Notice 2007-67 (2007-35 IRB 467), see § 601.601(d)(2), summarize the changes made by section 906(a)(1) of PPA '06 and provide transitional relief to ITGs under a reasonable and good faith standard to comply with such changes. The notices provide that, until such guidance is issued, a plan established and maintained by an ITG for its employees is treated as satisfying the requirements of section 906(a)(1) of PPA '06 to be a governmental plan under section 414(d) of the Code if it complies with those requirements based on a reasonable and good faith interpretation of section 414(d). The notices further provide that it is not a reasonable and good faith interpretation of section 414(d) for an ITG plan to claim to be a governmental plan within the meaning of section 414(d) if employees participating in the plan perform services for a hotel, casino, service station, convenience store, or marina operated by an ITG.

In Notices 2006-89 and 2007-67, the Treasury Department and IRS announced that regulations would be proposed to provide guidance on section 414(d), including changes made to section 414(d) by section 906 of PPA '06, and to provide transitional relief pending the issuance of these regulations. Comments were requested on issues relating to section 906 of PPA '06, including transitional issues not addressed in the notice.

The transitional relief provided to plans of ITGs under Notices 2006-89 and 2007-67 continues up to the date that is six months after the date that guidance is issued under section 414(d) of the Code, as amended by section 906 of PPA '06 (extended date). For ITG plans that

provide benefits both to employees substantially all of whose work is in essential governmental functions that are not commercial activities (governmental ITG employees) and to employees who perform services substantially in the performance of commercial activities (commercial ITG employees), the Notices provide that the ITG plan will be treated as satisfying the reasonable, good faith standard if certain steps are taken, which include adopting a separate plan covering commercial ITG employees effective as of the beginning of the first plan year beginning on or after August 17, 2006, the enactment of PPA '06. The commercial ITG plan, beginning on the same effective date, must comply with the qualification requirements for plans that are not governmental plans.

These proposed regulations would provide guidance relating to ITG plans under section 414(d). The transitional relief provided under Notices 2006-89 and 2007-67 would end six months after the effective date of the final regulations published in the **Federal Register**.

The transitional relief in Notices 2006-89 and 2007-67 is conditioned on the ITG plans involved not being amended, for periods before the extended date, to reduce benefits unless the reduction does not distinguish between reductions for commercial ITG employees and governmental ITG employees or the reduction for commercial ITG employees is the minimum amount necessary to satisfy any requirement under the Code. If any reduction occurs that does not satisfy these conditions, the transitional relief provided under Notices 2006-89 and 2007-67 ends on the date that the reduction goes into effect.

Executive Order 13175

Executive Order 13175 requires that Federal departments and agencies engage in consultation procedures in certain circumstances where regulations are issued which have substantial direct effects with respect to the Federal government and Indian tribes. While these regulations when issued as final regulations would not have such substantial direct effects, the IRS and Treasury Department have followed similar procedures. Further, the Treasury Department and the IRS participated in a series of telephone listening meetings with the ITG community following the passage of PPA '06 and these proposed regulations also take into account the comments that were provided in response to Notices 2006-89 and 2007-67, including the related open and direct consultations with the Indian tribal community.

Judicial Determinations

The few court cases that discuss section 906 of PPA '06 primarily relate to welfare benefit plans. One reason for the legislative change to section 414(d) of the Code and section 3(32) of ERISA is "to clarify the legal ambiguity regarding the status of employee benefit plans established and maintained by tribal governments."[13] In *Bolssen v. Unum Life Insurance Company of America*, 629 F.Supp. 2d 878 (E.D. Wis. 2009), Mr. Bolssen sued the Unum Life Insurance Company for failing to provide disability insurance benefits. He argued that the case should be remanded to state court because the insurance plan sponsored by his employer, an Indian tribal casino, was a governmental plan within the meaning of section 3(32) of ERISA. In analyzing whether the welfare benefit plan was a governmental plan, the *Bolssen* court looked to another case involving an Indian tribal casino, *San Manuel Indian Bingo & Casino v. NLRB*, 475 F.3d 1306 (D.C. Cir. 2007). In *San Manuel Indian Bingo & Casino*, the court held that the National Labor Relations Act applied to an Indian tribal casino because the operation of the casino was a commercial function. The court reasoned that "it can be argued any activity of a tribal government is by definition 'governmental,' and even more so an activity aimed at raising revenue that will fund governmental functions. Here, though, we use the term 'governmental' in a restrictive sense to distinguish between the traditional acts governments perform and collateral acts that, though perhaps in some way related to the foregoing, lie outside their scope."[14]

The court, in *San Manuel Indian Bingo & Casino*, held that operating a casino is not a traditional act of government, but is commercial in nature.[15] The court in *Bolssen* applied the same reasoning to conclude that disability plan of the casino was not a governmental plan within the meaning of section 3(32) of ERISA.

---

[9] Section 411(e)(2) states that a plan described in section 411(e)(1) is treated as meeting the requirements of section 411 if the plan meets the vesting requirements resulting from the application of section 401(a)(4) and (a)(7) as in effect on September 1, 1974.

[10] Section 401(k)(4)(B)(ii) provides that a cash or deferred arrangement shall not be treated as a qualified cash or deferred arrangement if it is part of a plan maintained by a State or local government or political subdivision thereof, or any or agency or instrumentality thereof.

[11] See section 401(k)(4)(B)(iii). For a general overview of the special rules relating to plans of ITGs, see the Joint Committee on Taxation, *Overview of Federal Tax Provisions Relating to Native American Tribes and Their Members* (JCX 61-08), July 18, 2008.

[12] An Indian tribal government is treated in the same manner as a State for certain specified purposes under the Code, but not for purposes of section 414(d) (or any provision in sections 401 through 424, other than sections 403(b)(1)(A)(ii)).

[13] See *Dobbs v. Anthem Blue Cross & Blue Shield*, 475 F.3d 1176, 1178 (10 th Cir. 2007) (citing 150 Cong. Rec. S9526, 9533), *rev'd in part* 600 F.3d 1275 (2010). See also *Bolssen v. Unum Life Insurance Company of America*, 629 F.Supp. 2d 878, 881 (E.D. Wis. 2009).

[14] *San Manuel Indian Bingo & Casino*, 475 F.3d at 1313.

[15] Id. at 1315.

Explanation of Provisions

These proposed regulations would provide special rules for purposes of the definition of a "governmental plan" under section 414(d) of the Code, as it relates to plans of ITGs. The Treasury Department and IRS also expect to issue separate proposed regulations under section 414(d) to define a governmental plan for purposes other than the special rules applicable to ITGs. However, these proposed regulations relating to ITGs would provide Indian tribal governments with guidance in determining whether an ITG plan is a governmental ITG plan or a commercial ITG plan. As discussed in the background of this preamble, under the heading "Exemption of Governmental ITG Plans from Certain Qualified Plan Rules," governmental plans receive special treatment with respect to certain qualification rules. Thus, the determination of whether an ITG plan is a governmental ITG plan is essential in ensuring compliance with the qualified plan rules because an ITG must be able to ascertain which of its plans are governmental plans under section 414(d) and which of its plans must comply with the requirements for a plan that is not a governmental plan. These proposed regulations take into account comments received in response to Notices 2006-89 and 2007-67 and a number of open and direct consultations with the Indian tribal community. Those comments received from Notices 2006-89 and 2007-67 and during the consultations were considered in drafting these proposed regulations.

Determination of Governmental and Commercial Activities

As discussed earlier in the background section of this preamble, a governmental plan, as it relates to ITGs, may include a plan established and maintained by an ITG, but such a plan is a governmental plan under section 414(d) only if all of its participants are employees substantially all of whose services are in the performance of essential governmental functions (but not in the performance of commercial activities whether or not an essential governmental function). Key to determining whether a plan of an ITG is a governmental plan within the meaning of section 414(d) is the determination of the terms "essential governmental function" and "commercial activity."

These proposed regulations would use the concepts of "governmental activity" and "commercial activity," instead of the terms "essential governmental function" and "commercial activity." The terms "governmental activity" and "commercial activity" would apply only for purposes of the governmental plan rules under section 414(d) and not for any other purpose under the Code, including section 7871. The use of these terms is meant to provide guidance on the requirements of section 414(d) with respect to ITG plans, while maintaining flexibility and without directly impacting future guidance on section 7871.

These proposed regulations would define a governmental ITG plan as any plan that is established and maintained by an Indian tribal government, a subdivision of an Indian tribal government, or an agency or instrumentality of either, and all of its participants are employees substantially all of whose services are in the performance of governmental activities. The regulations would define a commercial ITG plan as a plan covering any ITG employees who perform substantial services in a commercial activity, such as a hotel, casino, service station, convenience store, or marina, which are examples of commercial activities that are listed in the Joint Committee on Taxation Technical Explanation to section 906 of PPA '06.[16] A plan would also be a commercial plan if it covers any individual who is not an employee of an ITG.

Governmental and Commercial Activities

Under the proposed regulations, whether a plan of an ITG is a commercial plan or a governmental plan within the meaning of section 414(d) is based in part on (1) a determination of which activities are commercial activities and (2) a determination of whether employees of the Indian tribal government covered by the plan are employees who perform substantial services in commercial activities (and are thus commercial employees).

Under the first step, the proposed regulations would provide guidance for determining whether an activity operated by an ITG is a governmental activity or a commercial activity for purposes of section 414(d). This is achieved by listing certain specific activities that are deemed to be governmental or commercial for purposes of section 414(d). Specific governmental activities would include the following: (1) activities that are related to public infrastructure, such as the building and maintaining of public roads and buildings; (2) activities that involve providing criminal protection services to the public (such as police and fire departments) or providing civil or public administra-

tive service (such as providing public housing and operating public schools and hospitals, as well as managing the ITG's civil service system); and (3) activities subject to a treaty or special rules that pertain to trust land ownership and use. Under the regulations, operations involving a hotel, casino, service station, convenience store, and marina would be commercial activities. As discussed above, these activities are examples that are identified as commercial activities in Notices 2006-89 and 2007-67, as well as in the Joint Committee on Taxation Technical Explanation to section 906 of PPA '06.

In addition to listing certain specified activities, the proposed regulations would provide a facts and circumstances test for determining whether an activity is a governmental or commercial activity. The proposed regulations provide that, in making a determination of whether an activity is a governmental activity, the factors to be considered include whether—

- The activity provides a public benefit to members of the Indian tribal government (not treating the generation of profits from commercial acts as providing a public benefit); and

- The absence of one or more of the relevant factors listed for a commercial activity as provided in these proposed regulations.

The proposed regulations also provide that, in making a determination of whether an activity is a commercial activity, the factors to be considered include whether—

- The activity is a type of activity that is operated to earn a profit;

- The activity is a type of activity that is typically performed by private businesses; and

- The activity is a type of activity where the customers are substantially from outside of the Indian tribal community, including whether the activity is located or conducted outside of Indian tribal land.

These proposed regulations also provide examples illustrating the application of the facts and circumstances tests to particular activities. Some examples of activities of an Indian tribal government that are commercial might include: (1) operating a bank for a profit, serving tribal and non-tribal customers; (2) operating a trucking business for a profit; and (3) operating a factory producing goods for sale primarily to non-tribal customers. Conversely, examples of activities of an Indian tribal government that are governmental could include: (1) a community swimming pool on tribal land used primarily by tribal members; and (2) the operation of a cultural center and a museum on tribal land.

The proposed regulations would also delegate to the Commissioner of Internal Revenue the authority to publish guidance under section 414(d) that the Commissioner determines to be necessary or appropriate with respect to determining whether a plan of an Indian tribal government is a commercial ITG plan because the tribe's employees are performing services in an activity that the Commissioner determines to be a commercial activity. Any such guidance would be published in the form of revenue rulings, notices, or other guidance published in the Internal Revenue Bulletin (see § 601.601(d)(2)).

Determination of Governmental ITG Employees

These proposed regulations would also provide rules for the second step, namely determining whether employees covered by an ITG plan are employees who perform substantially all of their services in activities that are governmental. For this purpose, the determination of whether an employee's services are for governmental or commercial activities would generally be based on the employee's assigned duties and responsibilities. In making this determination, the rules in these regulations would not require that a plan keep track of the individual hours worked by any employee or that the compensation of any particular employee be traced through the hours worked by that employee. The proposed regulations would provide that an employee whose assigned duties and responsibilities are in the performance of a governmental activity is treated as performing substantially all of his or her services in a governmental activity, and not treated as performing services for a commercial activity, even though the performance of those services for the governmental activity may temporarily involve significant time working in the commercial activity. For example, the chief financial officer (CFO) for an ITG may be expected to spend a substantial amount of time working on the financing for any casino, marina, or hotel to be built on the ITG's tribal lands, but, despite temporarily working in a commercial activity, the proposed regulations

---

[16] Joint Committee on Taxation, *Technical Explanation of H.R. 4, the "Pension Protection Act of 2006" as passed by the House on July 28, 2006, and considered by the Senate on August 3, 2006* (JCX-38-06), August 3, 2006, 109th Cong., 2nd Sess. 244 (2006).

would provide that the CFO is a governmental employee of the ITG all of whose services are in that capacity.

Determination of Commercial ITG Employees

The proposed regulations set forth rules for determining an employee's assigned duties and responsibilities, and thus when his or her services are substantially in the performance of a governmental or commercial activity. The analysis would start with the location of the employee's services in relation to the activity. The regulations provide that if a commercial activity has a specific location that is identifiable and is not associated with a governmental activity, any employee performing services at the location of activity is a commercial employee. One example is a security guard whose work is providing security services at a location which is an Indian tribal casino. In the case of an employee who works at a location other than a location where a commercial activity is being performed, the result would depend on the employee's assigned duties and responsibilities.

Another key part of the analysis is who pays the employee. If an employee is on the payroll of an ITG entity that is engaged in a commercial activity, the employee's assigned duties and responsibilities are treated as being for a commercial activity and, thus, the employee is a commercial ITG employee. For example, if a cashier is on the payroll of a convenience store (which is a commercial activity) owned by an ITG, the cashier is a commercial ITG employee. However, in the case of an employee who is not on a payroll of an ITG that engages in a commercial activity, the result would depend on the employee's assigned duties and responsibilities.

Where an employee neither works at a location where a commercial activity is being performed nor is on the payroll of a commercial entity, the result would depend on the employee's assigned duties and responsibilities, taking into account the facts and circumstances. Thus, for example, a bookkeeper located in a governmental building and paid through the general payroll of the ITG would nevertheless be a commercial employee if the facts and circumstances indicate that his or her assigned duties and responsibilities are to maintain the books and records for a hotel owned and operated by an ITG.

The statutory language in section 414(d) makes it clear that a plan is not a governmental ITG plan if it covers any employee who is a commercial ITG employee. There is no de minimis exception relating to this rule under section 414(d). In light of these circumstances, an ITG may choose to use caution when covering employees in a governmental plan. If, after applying the rules, an ITG plan sponsor is not certain whether an employee is a governmental ITG or commercial ITG employee, the ITG may choose to provide coverage for the employee in its commercial ITG plan in order to ensure the preservation of the status of the governmental ITG plan. Coverage of a governmental employee in a commercial plan would not adversely affect the qualified status of the commercial plan.

Reasonable, Good Faith Interpretation

The proposed regulations provide that, in general, an ITG plan will not be treated as failing to satisfy the assignment of employee rules if the plan complies with those rules under a standard that constitutes a reasonable, good faith interpretation of the statute, taking into account the final regulations and any other published guidance that relates to the application of section 414(d) to ITGs. The reasonable, good faith interpretation standard for the assignment of employees to governmental and commercial plans would only apply if the benefit levels between the separate governmental and commercial plans are uniform. Thus, this reasonable, good faith interpretation standard would not apply if the benefit level for employees under a plan purporting to be a governmental plan is higher than that of the benefit level under a separate plan covering employees who include commercial employees.

Assignment of Shared Employees

Under these rules, there may be cases in which an employee is transferred from one ITG employer to another. An employee may also perform substantially all of his or her services in the performance of a governmental activity and later the employee's assigned duties and responsibilities may change, so that the employee is subsequently performing substantially all of his or her duties in the performance of a commercial activity. In addition, an employee may work two separate and distinct jobs, one in a commercial activity of an ITG and another in a governmental activity of an ITG (for example, an ITG employee who works as a full-time police officer and also works at the front desk in the lobby of a hotel over the weekends). For all of these scenarios, assuming the ITG maintains separate plans for its governmental and commercial employees, the ITG should assign the employee to either plan based on prorating service credits and allocating compensation between the governmental and commercial activities.

Application of the Controlled Group Rules to ITG Plans

These proposed regulations do not address the rules under which, for purposes of sections 401, 408(k), 408(p), 410, 411, 415, and 416, all employees of all corporations that are members of a controlled group of corporations are treated as employed by a single employer for purposes of these controlled group rules. Note that, under current guidance, a reasonable, good faith interpretation standard applies with respect to governments. See Notice 89-23 (1989-1 CB 654) and Notice 96-64 (1996-2 CB 229), see § 601.601(d)(2) of this chapter.

Proposed Effective Date

The proposed regulations would apply to plan years beginning 6 months after publication of these regulations as final regulations. For plan years after the statutory effective date of the PPA '06 amendment of section 414(d) and prior to the effective date of these regulations as final regulations, a plan of an ITG would be treated as a governmental plan for purposes of section 414(d), providing that a reasonable, good faith effort is made to ensure that the plan satisfy the conditions for being a governmental plan under section 414(d), taking into account relevant guidance, including Notices 2006-89 and 2007-67. To the extent that a plan of an Indian tribal government complies with the requirements under either the notices or the proposed regulations, the plan will be treated as making a reasonable, good faith effort to satisfy the requirements of section 414(d).

Special Analyses

It has been determined that this notice of proposed rulemaking is not a significant regulatory action as defined in Executive Order 12866. Therefore, a regulatory assessment is not required. It has also been determined that section 553(b) of the Administrative Procedure Act (5 U.S.C. chapter 5) does not apply to these regulations. In addition, because no collection of information is imposed on small entities, the provisions of the Regulatory Flexibility Act (5 U.S.C. chapter 6) do not apply, and therefore, a Regulatory Flexibility Analysis is not required. Pursuant to section 7805(f) of the Code, this notice of proposed rulemaking will be submitted to the Small Business Administration for comment on its impact on small business.

Comments and Public Hearing

Before these proposed regulations are adopted as final regulations, consideration will be given to any written comments (a signed original and eight (8) copies) or electronic comments that are submitted timely to the IRS. The Treasury Department and the IRS specifically request comments on the clarity of the proposed rules and how they can be made easier to understand. Comments are specifically requested on whether a correction mechanism under the Employee Plans Compliance Resolution System (EPCRS), as set forth in Rev. Proc. 2008-50 (2008-35 IRB 464), see § 601.601(d)(2), might be helpful for cases in which an employee substantially all of whose services are not in the performance of a governmental activity has nevertheless inadvertently become a participant in a plan purporting to be a governmental plan. For example, assuming the various conditions for self correction have been satisfied (see section 4.09 of Rev. Proc. 2008-50, which provides that the failure must be an operational failure which occurred by mistake or oversight, even though the plan had established practices and procedure to ensure qualification, and which is promptly corrected), the plan's assets and liabilities with respect to the employee might be transferred to a similar plan covering commercial employees under which the employee would accrue benefits up to the level that would have applied if he or she had participated in that commercial plan during the period when he or she was a commercial employee. All comments will be available for public inspection and copying.

A public hearing has been scheduled for (date to be provided when proposed regulations are published), beginning at 10 a.m. in the Auditorium, Internal Revenue Building, 1111 Constitution Avenue, NW., Washington DC. Due to building security procedures, visitors must enter at the main entrance, located at 1111 Constitution Avenue, NW. In addition, all visitors must present photo identification to enter the building. Because of access restrictions, visitors will not be admitted beyond the immediate entrance area more than 30 minutes before the hearing starts. For information about having your name placed on the building access list to attend the hearing, see the "FOR FURTHER INFORMATION CONTACT" portion of this preamble.

The rules of 26 CFR 601.601(a)(3) apply to the hearing. Persons who wish to present oral comments must submit written or electronic comments and an outline of the topics to be discussed and time to be devoted to each topic (signed original and eight (8) copies) by (date to be provided when proposed regulations are published). A period of 10 minutes will be allotted to each person for making comments. An agenda showing the scheduling of the speakers will be prepared after the deadline for receiving comments has passed. Copies of the agenda will be available free of charge at the hearing.

Drafting Information

The principal author of these proposed regulations is Pamela R. Kinard, Office of Division Counsel/Associate Chief Counsel (Tax Exempt and Government Entities), Internal Revenue Service. However, personnel from other offices of the IRS and Treasury Department participated in their development.

List of Subjects in 26 CFR Part 1

Income taxes, Reporting and recordkeeping requirements.

Proposed Amendments to the Regulations

Accordingly, 26 CFR part 1 is proposed to be amended as follows:

PART 1—INCOME TAXES

Paragraph 1. The authority citation for part 1 continues to read in part:

Authority: 26 U.S.C. 7805 * * *

Par.2. Section 1.414(d)-1 is amended by adding paragraph (g) to read as follows:

§ 1.414(d)-1 Definition of governmental plan.

* * * * *

(g) *Special rules for plans of Indian tribal governments*—(1) *Definition of governmental plan as it relates to Indian tribal governments.* For purposes of applying paragraph (a)(3) of this section, a governmental plan as it relates to an Indian tribal government is a plan that is established and maintained for its employees by an Indian tribal government, a subdivision of an Indian tribal government, or an agency or instrumentality of either (ITG), provided that the employees covered under the plan provide substantially all of their services in the performance of governmental activities as determined in paragraph (g)(6) of this section.

(2) *Definition of commercial ITG plans.* For purposes of paragraph (g) of this section, the term *commercial ITG plan* means a plan of an ITG that covers any ITG employee who is not a governmental ITG employee under paragraph (g)(8) of this section or that covers any individual who is not an employee of an ITG.

(3) *Definition of an Indian tribal government.* For purposes of this paragraph (g), the term *Indian tribal government* has the meaning set forth in section 7701(a)(40).

(4) *Definition of subdivision of an Indian tribal government.* For purposes of this paragraph (g), the term *subdivision of an Indian tribal government* has the meaning set forth in section 7871(d).

(5) *Definition of agency or instrumentality of an Indian tribal government or subdivision of an Indian tribal government.* For purposes of this paragraph (g, the term *agency or instrumentality of an Indian tribal government or subdivision of an Indian tribal government* means an entity that would be treated as an "agency or instrumentality of a State or political subdivision of a State" under paragraph (f) of this section if the related Indian tribal government or subdivision of an Indian tribal government were treated as a State or political subdivision of a State, respectively.

(6) *Definition of governmental activities*—(i) *In general.* The following activities are governmental activities for purposes of paragraph (g)(1) of this section:

(A) Activities that are related to the building and maintaining of public roads;. public sidewalks, public buildings, and related areas, such as parking lots.

(B) Activities that are related to public sewer and drainage facilities, and related facilities such as a waste-water treatment plant.

(C) Activities relating to public works projects, such as schools and government buildings.

(D) Activities relating to public utilities, such as electricity and other power sources, including the development of newer and emerging technologies.

(E) Activities related to providing criminal protection services, such as police and fire departments, providing civil and public administrative services, such as operating and managing public housing, libraries, judiciary buildings, and administrative buildings, teaching in and managing public schools, managing and providing services at public hospitals and health clinics, operating the government's civil service system, and other related public services.

¶ 20,263

(F) Activities subject to a treaty or special rules that pertain to trust land ownership and use.

(ii) *Facts and circumstances test.* Whether any other activity is a governmental activity for purposes of section 414(d) is based on facts and circumstances. In making this determination, the facts to be considered include the following:

(A) Whether the activity provides a public benefit to members of the Indian tribal government; and

(B) Whether there is the absence of one or more of the relevant factors listed for a commercial activity as provided in paragraph (g)(7) of this section.

(iii) *Examples.* The following examples illustrate the application of this paragraph (g)(6):

Example 1. (i) *Facts.* Indian tribal government C owns and operates a community swimming pool on tribal land. Indian tribal members of Indian tribal government C may use the pool for free. Other local community members pay a fee to use the pool. Due to its location, this pool is used primarily by tribal members of Indian tribal government C.

(ii) *Conclusion.* Based on the facts and circumstances and the factors in paragraph (g)(6)(ii) of this section, the operation of the community swimming pool is a governmental activity of Indian tribal government C because it is a type of activity that is operated on a nonprofit basis and is similar to an activity that other non-tribal local governments operate for their communities. In addition, the pool is located inside tribal land and provides recreational benefits to tribal members.

Example 2. (i) *Facts.* Indian tribal government D owns and operates a cultural center and a museum on tribal land. The purpose of the cultural center and museum is to preserve and showcase items related to the culture of Indian tribal government D, including crafts and artistry. The center contains an exhibit area, a lobby and reception area, a small gift shop, a theater and various activity rooms. A variety of civic functions are held in the activity rooms. The other areas display and sell local handicraft items produced locally by members of Indian tribal government D.

(ii) *Conclusion.* Based on the facts and circumstances and the factors in paragraph (g)(6)(ii) of this section, the operation of the cultural center and museum is a governmental activity of Indian tribal government D even though the majority of its visitors are individuals who are not members of the tribe. Its purpose is to promote and display the culture of Indian tribal government D, which is a type of activity that is generally operated on a nonprofit basis (similar to municipal museums operated by public authorities) and not by private businesses. In addition, the center and museum are located inside tribal land and provide a public benefit by educating the public and preserving and highlighting the culture of the tribe.

(7) *Definition of commercial activities*—(i) *In general.* The following activities are commercial activities for purposes of paragraph (g)(2) of this section:

(A) Activities relating to the operation of a hotel.

(B) Activities relating to the operation of a casino.

(C) Activities relating to the operation of a service station.

(D) Activities relating to the operation of a convenience store.

(E) Activities relating to the operation of a marina.

(ii) *Facts and circumstances test.* Whether any other activity is a commercial activity for purposes of section 414(d) is based on facts and circumstances. In making this determination, the facts to be considered include the following:

(A) Whether the activity is a type of activity that is operated to earn a profit.

(B) Whether the activity is a type of activity that is typically performed by private businesses.

(C) Whether the activity is a type of activity where the customers are substantially from outside of the Indian tribal community, including whether the activity is located or conducted outside of Indian tribal land.

(iii) *Delegation of authority to the Commissioner.* Any activity that the Commissioner of the Internal Revenue Service determines is a commercial activity under section 414(d), in revenue rulings, notices, or other guidance published in the Internal Revenue Bulletin (see § 601.601(d)(2) of this chapter).

(iv) *Examples.* The following examples illustrate the application of this paragraph (g)(7)(ii):

Example 1. (i) *Facts.* Indian tribal government A owns and operates a recreational RV park and campground facility, serving transient non-tribal customers, primarily tourists. Other RV parks and campgrounds in the area operated by non-tribal private entities also attract the same type of customers. Very few, if any, tribal members of Indian tribal government A use this RV park and campground facility. Indian tribal government A charges a fee to customers to use the RV park and campground.

(ii) *Conclusion.* Based on the facts and circumstances and the factors in paragraph (g)(7)(ii) of this section, the operation of the recreational RV park and campground facility is a commercial activity of Indian tribal government A because it is the type of activity that is operated to earn a profit and is the type of activity that is performed by other private businesses. In addition, the facility includes customers who are substantially from outside of the Indian tribal community.

Example 2. (i) *Facts.* Indian tribal government B owns and operates a bank. This bank serves both tribal and non-tribal customers primarily living in the local area (either on or off the tribal land). No distinction is made between the services and fees provided to any customer based on whether or not he or she is a tribal member of Indian tribal government B.

(ii) *Conclusion.* Based on the facts and circumstances and the factors in paragraph (g)(7)(ii) of this section, the operation of a bank is a commercial activity of Indian tribal government B because it is the type of activity that is operated to earn a profit and is the type of activity that is performed by other private businesses.

Example 3. (i) *Facts.* Indian tribal government E entered into a lease with Company X, which is in the trucking business. The lease provides that Indian tribal government E will purchase tractors, trailers and other equipment and lease such equipment to Company X on a long-term basis.

(ii) *Conclusion.* Based on the facts and circumstances and the factors in paragraph (g)(7)(ii) of this section, the leasing transactions relate to a commercial activity of Indian tribal government E because it is the type of activity that is operated to earn a profit and is the type of activity that is performed by other private businesses.

Example 4. (i) *Facts.* Indian tribal government G operates a factory on tribal land that produces goods for sale primarily to non-tribal customers, intended to earn a profit.

(ii) *Conclusion.* Based on the facts and circumstances and the factors in paragraph (g)(7)(ii) of this section, this is a commercial activity of Indian tribal government G because the activity is operated to earn a profit and is the type of activity that is performed by private businesses. In addition, the customers are substantially from outside of the Indian tribal community. The result could be different if the factory produced goods to promote and display the culture of Indian tribal government G, even if non-tribal customers primarily purchase the goods. This could be a governmental activity, depending on the factors.

(8) *Determination of ITG employees*—(i) *Governmental and commercial ITG employees.* This paragraph (g)(8) applies to determine whether an employee is an employee substantially all of whose services are in the performance of a governmental activity of an ITG (a governmental ITG employee), or is instead an employee who renders a significant portion of his or her services in the performance of a commercial activity of an ITG (a commercial ITG employee), for purposes of this paragraph (g). As provided in paragraph (g)(8)(iv) of this section, this determination is based on the employee's assigned duties and responsibilities.

(ii) *Location of the activity.* If a commercial activity (within the meaning of paragraph (g)(7) of this section) of an ITG has a specific location that is readily identifiable and is not associated with a governmental activity, an employee performing substantial services at such a location is treated as having assigned duties and responsibilities for that commercial activity and, thus, the employee is a commercial ITG employee within the meaning of paragraph (g)(8) of this section. For example, a guard who is assigned to provide security services for an Indian tribal government at an Indian tribal casino (which is a commercial activity under paragraph (g)(7)(i)(B) of this section) is a commercial ITG employee within the meaning of paragraph (g)(8) of this section. However, where an employee is not on a payroll of an ITG that engages in a commercial activity, the result would depend on the other rules in this paragraph (g)(8).

(iii) *Payroll records.* If an employee is on the payroll of an ITG entity that is engaged in a commercial activity (within the meaning of paragraph (g)(7) of this section), the employee's assigned duties and responsibilities are being treated as for the commercial activity and,

thus, the employee is a commercial ITG employee. For example, if a cashier is on the payroll of a convenience store (which is a commercial activity under paragraph (g)(7)(i)(D) of this section) owned by an ITG, the cashier is a commercial ITG employee within the meaning of paragraph (g)(8) of this section.

(iv) *Duties and responsibilities.* Subject to the specific rules in paragraph (g)(8)(ii) or (iii) of this section, whether an employee is a governmental or commercial ITG employee within the meaning of this paragraph (g)(8) is based on the employee's assigned duties and responsibilities, taking into account facts and circumstances. Thus, whether an employee is a governmental or commercial ITG employee depends on whether the facts and circumstances indicate that the employee's assigned duties and responsibilities are substantially in the performance of a governmental or commercial activity. Thus, for example, a bookkeeper located in a governmental building and on the payroll of the general ITG government would nevertheless be a commercial employee if the facts and circumstances indicate that his or her assigned duties and responsibilities are to maintain the books and records for the hotel owned and operated by an ITG. However, an employee whose assigned duties and responsibilities are in the performance of a governmental activity, based on all the facts and circumstances, in accordance with the standards set forth in this paragraph (g)(8), is not treated as performing services for a commercial activity, even if the performance of services for the governmental activity may temporarily involve significant time working in a commercial activity in furtherance of the employee's duties and responsibilities for the governmental activity. For example, although, over a six-month period, the chief financial officer (CFO) for an ITG may spend a substantial amount of time working on the financing for a casino to be built on the ITG's tribal lands, the CFO would not be a commercial employee within the meaning of this paragraph (g)(8) because the CFO's duties and responsibilities are for a governmental activity.

(v) *Reasonable, good faith interpretation.* Except as provided in paragraph (g)(8)(ii) and (iii) of this section, an ITG plan will not be treated as failing to satisfy the rules in this paragraph (g)(8) if it complies with those rules under a standard that constitutes a reasonable, good faith interpretation of the statute, taking into account the rules in this paragraph (g) and any other published guidance that relates to the application of section 414(d) to ITGs. However, this paragraph (g)(8)(v) applies with respect to the assignment of employees to governmental and commercial plans only if the benefit levels provided by the separate governmental and commercial plans are uniform. Thus, this paragraph (g)(8)(v) would not apply if the benefit level for employees under a plan purported to be a governmental plan is higher than that provided under a separate plan which covers commercial ITG employees.

(vi) *Examples.* The following examples further illustrate the application of this paragraph (g)(8):

Example 1. (i) *Facts.* Employee A, who is an attorney, works at the Attorney General's office of Indian tribal government B. Employee A's job location is in a government office building on tribal lands. The assigned duties and responsibilities of Employee A are principally to review the operations of marina boat operators to ensure that they comply with tribal rules and regulations as applicable to marina boat operators. Employee A provides some services for the marina, such as speaking at conferences or meetings with marina boat operators. Employee A's area of expertise is contract law.

(ii) *Conclusion.* Based on the facts and circumstances and the factors in paragraph (g)(8)(ii) through (iv) of this section, Employee A is a governmental ITG employee within the meaning of this paragraph (g)(8). Employee A primarily performs services for Indian tribal government B at a government building which is a governmental location and Employee A is on the payroll of Indian tribal government B. In addition, Employee A's assigned duties and responsibilities are primarily to provide government oversight services for Indian tribal government B.

Example 2. (i) *Facts.* Employee C is a police officer providing services for Indian tribal government D. Employee C's job location is the tribal police station located in a government building on tribal lands. The assigned duties and responsibilities of Employee C indicate that Employee C is expected to maintain public order, detect crime, and apprehend offenders on tribal lands of Indian tribal government D. Occasionally, while on patrol, Employee C must go to the casino operated by Indian tribal government D to restore order relating to a disturbance. Employee C's area of expertise is in general law enforcement.

(ii) *Conclusion.* Based on the facts and circumstances and the factors in paragraph (g)(8)(ii) through

(iv) of this section, Employee C is a governmental ITG employee within the meaning of this paragraph (g)(8). Employee C primarily performs services for Indian tribal government D at either a government building or while on patrol, even though Employee C's patrol duties include providing law enforcement services at the casino, which is a commercial activity under paragraph (g)(7)(i)(B) of this section. In addition, the assigned duties and responsibilities of Employee C, as well as Employee C's area of expertise, relate to general law enforcement and do not substantially relate to a commercial activity.

¶ 20,263A

IRS: Defined contribution plans: Tax-sheltered annuities: IRAs: Eligible governmental plans: Longevity annuity contracts.—The IRS has issued proposed regulations relating to the purchase of longevity annuity contracts under defined contribution plans, 403(b) plans, IRAs, and eligible governmental section 457 plans. The proposed regulations are designed to provide guidance necessary to comply with the required minimum distribution rules under Code Sec. 401(a)(9).

The proposed regulations were published in the Federal Register on February 3, 2012 (77 FR 5443). The regulations were finalized on July 2, 2014 (79 FR 37633). The preamble to the final regulations is at ¶ 23,302. The final regulations are at ¶ 11,720Y-5, ¶ 11,720Y-6, ¶ 11,803-14, ¶ 12,060, ¶ 12,097A-6, and ¶ 13,691B.

¶ 20,263B

IRS: Defined benefit plans: Minimum present value requirements.—The IRS has issued proposed regulations providing guidance relating to the minimum present value requirements applicable to certain defined benefit plans. The proposed regulations would change the regulations regarding the minimum present value requirements for defined benefit plan distributions to permit plans to simplify the treatment of certain optional forms of benefit that are paid partly in the form of an annuity and partly in a more accelerated form.

The proposed regulations were published in the Federal Register on February 3, 2012 (77 FR 5454). A correction to the proposed regulations was published on March 9, 2012 (77 FR 14321), applicable February 3, 2012. The regulations were finalized on September 9, 2016 (81 FR 62359). The preamble to the final regulations is at ¶ 23,327. The final regulations are at ¶ 12,556.

¶ 20,263C

IRS: Proposed regulations: Self-insured health plans: Plan sponsors: Fees.—The IRS has issued proposed regulations that implement and provide guidance on the fees imposed by the Patient Protection and Affordable Care Act (PPACA) on issuers of certain health insurance policies and plan sponsors of certain self-insured health plans to fund the Patient-Centered Outcomes Research Trust Fund. Comments are invited on all aspects of the proposed rules. Written or electronic comments must be received by July 16, 2012.

These regulations are proposed to apply to policy and plan years ending on or after October 1, 2012 and before October 1, 2019. The IRS states that issuers and plan sponsors may rely on the proposed regulations for guidance pending issuance of final regulations. The final regulations will be effective as of the date these proposed regulations are published in the Federal Register (i.e., April 17, 2012). If future guidance is more restrictive than these proposed regulations, the future guidance will be applied without retroactive effect.

The proposed regulation, portions of which were reproduced below, was published in the Federal Register on April 17, 2012 (77 FR 22691).

Final regulations (T.D. 9602) were published in the Federal Register on December 6, 2012 (77 FR 72721). The preamble to the final regulations is at ¶ 24,286. The IRS final regulations are reproduced at ¶ 13,578A-1, ¶ 13,578F-1, and ¶ 13,578K-1.

¶ 20,263D

IRS: Proposed regulations: Reporting and disclosure: Return information: Patient Protection and Affordable Care Act: Affordable Insurance Exchanges.—The IRS has issued proposed regulations concerning the disclosure of return information by the IRS under Code Sec. 6103(l)(21), as enacted by the Patient Protection and Affordable Care Act (PPACA; P.L. 111-148). In the proposed regulations, the IRS describes the items of return information that it will disclosure, upon written request, to the Department of Health and Human Services for the purpose of establishing whether an individual is eligible to participate in an Affordable Insurance Exchange, including the determination of the individual's eligibility for advance payments of the premium tax credit under Code Sec. 36B, the reduced cost-sharing under Sec. 1402 of PPACA, and certain state health insurance affordability programs.

The proposed regulation was published in the Federal Register on April 30, 2012 (77 FR 25378). Final regulations were published in the Federal Register on August 14, 2013 (78 FR 49367). The preamble to the final regulations is at ¶ 23,290.

¶ 20,263E

IRS: Proposed regulations: Property transferred in connection with the performance of services: Substantial risk of forfeiture.—The IRS has issued proposed amendments to Reg. § 1.83-3(c), that would clarify the meaning of "substantial risk of forfeiture" where property is transferred in connection with the performance of services. The proposed regulations would apply as of January 1, 2013 and would apply to property transferred on or after that date. However, taxpayers may rely on the proposed rules for property transferred after the date of publication in the Federal Register.

The proposed regulations were published in the Federal Register on May 30, 2012 (77 FR 31783). A correction to the proposed regulations was published on June 18, 2012 (77 FR 36229). Final regulations were published in the Federal Register on February 26, 2014 (79 FR 10663). The preamble to the final regulations is at ¶ 23,296. The IRS final regulations are reproduced at ¶ 11,243.

¶ 20,263F

IRS: Plan amendments: Anti-cutback rules: Bankruptcy of plan sponsor.—The IRS has issued proposed regulations that would provide an additional limited exception to the anti-cutback rules of Code Sec. 411(d)(6) to permit a plan sponsor that is a debtor in a bankruptcy proceeding to amend its single-employer defined benefit plan to eliminate a single-sum distribution option (or other optional form of benefit providing for accelerated payments) under the plan if certain specified conditions are satisfied.

The proposed regulations were published in the Federal Register on June 21, 2012 (77 FR 37349). The regulations were finalized on November 8, 2012 (77 FR 66915). The preamble to the final regulations is at ¶ 24,285. The final regulations are at ¶ 12,233.

¶ 20,263G

IRS: Proposed regulations: Reporting and disclosure: Form 8955-SSA: Filing extension: Form 5500.—The IRS has issued proposed regulations that allow plan administrators that intend to file Form 8955-SSA to request an automatic extension of time to file on Form 5558 without providing a signature. Thus, under these proposed regulations the same rules that apply for requesting an extension of time to file the Form 5500 series would also apply to filing for an extension of time to file Form 8955-SSA. The proposed regulations may be relied upon pending issuance of final regulations.

The proposed regulations were published in the Federal Register on June 21, 2012 (77 FR 37352) and officially corrected on July 19, 2012 (77 FR 42462).

DEPARTMENT OF THE TREASURY

Internal Revenue Service

26 CFR Parts 1 and 301

[REG-153627-08]

RIN-1545-B140

Reporting and Notice Requirements for Deferred Vested Benefits Under Section 6057

AGENCY: Internal Revenue Service (IRS), Treasury

ACTION: Notice of proposed rulemaking.

SUMMARY: This document contains proposed regulations that would provide guidance relating to automatic extensions of time for filing certain employee plan returns by adding the Form 8955-SSA, "Annual Registration Statement Identifying Separated Participants With Deferred Vested Benefits," to the list of forms that are covered by the Income Tax Regulations on automatic extensions. The proposed regulations would also provide guidance on applicable reporting and participant notice rules that require certain plan administrators to file registration statements and provide notices that set forth information for deferred vested participants. These regulations would affect administrators of, employers maintaining, participants in, and beneficiaries of plans that are subject to the reporting and participant notice requirements.

DATES: Comments and requests for a public hearing must be received by September 19, 2012.

ADDRESSES: Send submissions to CC:PA:LPD:PR (REG-153627-08), room 5205, Internal Revenue Service, PO Box 7604, Ben Franklin Station, Washington D.C. 20044. Submissions may be hand-delivered Monday through Friday between the hours of 8 a.m. and 4 p.m. to CC:PA:LPD:PR (REG-153627-08), Courier's Desk, Internal Revenue Service, 1111 Constitution Avenue, N.W., Washington, DC, 20224, or sent electronically via the Federal eRulemaking Portal at *www.regulations.gov* (IRS REG-153627-08).

FOR FURTHER INFORMATION CONTACT: Concerning the proposed regulations, William Gibbs, Sarah Bolen, or Pamela Kinard at (202) 622-6060; concerning the submission of comments or to request a public hearing, Oluwafunmilayo Taylor, (202) 622-7180 (not toll-free numbers).

SUPPLEMENTARY INFORMATION:

Paperwork Reduction Act

The collection of information contained in this notice of proposed rulemaking has been approved by the Office of Management and Budget for review in accordance with the Paperwork Reduction Act of 1995 (44 U.S.C. 3507(d)) under 1545-2187 and 1545-0212. Comments on the collection of information should be sent to the **Office of Management and Budget,** Attn: Desk Officer for the Department of the Treasury, Office of Information and Regulatory Affairs, Washington D.C. 20503, with copies to the **Internal Revenue Service,** Attn: IRS Reports Clearance Officer, SE:CAR:MP:T:T:SP; Washington DC 20224. Comments on the collection of information should be received by August 20, 2012. Comments are specifically requested concerning:

Whether the proposed collection of information is necessary for the proper performance of the functions of the Internal Revenue Service, including whether the information will have practical utility;

The accuracy of the estimated burden associated with the proposed collection of information;

How the quality, utility, and clarity of the information to be collected may be enhanced;

How the burden of complying with the proposed collection of information may be minimized, including through the application of automated collection techniques or other forms of information technology; and

Estimates of capital or start-up costs and costs of operation, maintenance, and purchase of service to provide information.

The collection of information in these proposed regulations is in §§ 301.6057-1 and 1.6081-11. This information is required in order to comply with the reporting and notice requirements of section 6057 and to provide automatic extensions of time for filing certain employee plan returns under section 6081. Information relating to these proposed regulations will be collected through Form 8955-SSA and Form 5558. This information relates to plan participants who separate from service covered under the plan and who are entitled to deferred vested retirement benefits under the plan. Any burden relating to these proposed regulations will be included and reported in the next revisions of Form 8955-SSA and Form 5558, after these proposed regulations are accepted as final.

An agency may not conduct or sponsor, and a person is not required to respond to, a collection of information, unless it displays a valid control number assigned by the Office of Management and Budget.

Books or records relating to a collection of information must be retained as long as their contents may become material in the administration of any internal revenue law. Generally, tax returns and tax return information are confidential, as required by 26 U.S.C. 6103.

Background

Section 6057(a) of the Internal Revenue Code (Code) requires the administrator of a plan that is subject to the vesting standards of section 203 of the Employee Retirement Income Security Act of 1974 (ERISA) to file, within the time prescribed by regulations, a registration statement with the Secretary of the Treasury. The registration statement sets forth certain information relating to the plan, plan participants who separate from service covered by the plan and are entitled to deferred vested retirement benefits, and the nature, amount, and form of deferred vested retirement benefits to which the plan participants are entitled.

Section 6057(b) provides that any plan administrator required to register under section 6057(a) shall, within the time prescribed by regulations, also notify the Secretary of any change in the name of the plan or the name and address of the plan administrator, the termination of the plan, or the merger or consolidation of the plan with any other plan or its division into two or more plans.

Section 6057(c) provides that, to the extent provided in regulations prescribed by the Secretary, the administrator of a plan not subject to the reporting requirements of section 6057(a) (including a governmental plan within the meaning of section 414(d) or a church plan within the meaning of section 414(e)) may at its option file such information as the plan administrator may wish to file with respect to the deferred retirement vested benefit rights of any plan participant separated from service covered by the plan.

Section 6057(d) requires the Secretary to transmit copies of any statements, notifications, reports, or other information obtained by the Secretary under section 6057 to the Commissioner of Social Security.

Section 6057(e) of the Code and section 105(c) of ERISA require each plan administrator that is subject to the reporting requirements of section 6057 to furnish to each deferred vested participant an individual statement setting forth the information required by section 6057(a)(2). The individual statement required by section 6057(e) must also notify each participant of any benefits that are forfeitable if the participant dies before a certain date. The individual statement must be furnished no later than the date for filing the registration statement required under section 6057(a).

Section 6057(f)(1) provides that the Secretary, after consultation with the Commissioner of Social Security, may issue such regulations as may be necessary to carry out the provisions of this section.

Since the enactment of ERISA, the Schedule SSA, a schedule to the Form 5500, "Annual Return/Report of Employee Benefit Plan," has been the form used by plan administrators to comply with the reporting requirements of section 6057. On July 21, 2006, the Department of Labor (DOL) published a final rule in the **Federal Register** (71 FR

41359) requiring electronic filing of the Form 5500 series for plan years beginning after January 1, 2008. On November 16, 2007, the DOL published a final rule in the **Federal Register** (72 FR 64710) postponing the effective date of the electronic filing mandate to apply to plan years beginning on or after January 1, 2009. See 29 CFR § 2520.104a-2.

In order to implement the DOL's mandate for electronic filing of the Form 5500, the IRS-only schedules to the Form 5500, including Schedule SSA, were eliminated from the Form 5500. One result of the elimination of the Schedule SSA is that Form 5500 filings that include Schedule SSA information regarding participants are now subject to rejection (even for late or amended filings for plan years before 2009). The Schedule SSA was replaced by Form 8955-SSA, "Annual Registration Statement Identifying Separated Participants With Deferred Vested Benefits," an IRS-only stand-alone form. Announcement 2011-21 (2011-12 IRB 567), see § 601.601(d)(2), designates Form 8955-SSA as the form to be used to satisfy the reporting requirements of section 6057 for plan years beginning on or after January 1, 2009. Announcement 2011-21 also established an annual due date for the filing of the Form 8955-SSA. In general, if a Form 8955-SSA must be filed for a plan year, it must be filed by the last day of the 7th month following the last day of that plan year (plus extensions).

Section 6081(a) provides that the Secretary may grant a reasonable extension of time for filing any required return, declaration, statement, or other document. Except for certain taxpayers, the extension of time shall not exceed 6 months.

Section 1.6081-1(a) of the Income Tax Regulations provides that the Commissioner is authorized to grant a reasonable extension of time for filing any return, declaration, statement, or other document that relates to any tax imposed under subtitle A of the Code. Under § 1.6081-1(b), the application must be in writing, be signed by the taxpayer or his representative, and set forth the reason for requesting an extension.

Section 1.6081-11 of the regulations provides that a plan administrator or sponsor of an employee benefit plan required to file a Form 5500 will be allowed an automatic extension of the time to file the Form 5500. To receive an automatic extension of time to file, the plan administrator or sponsor must complete a Form 5558, "Application for Extension of Time To File Certain Employee Plan Returns," and file the application with the Internal Revenue Service on or before the date that the Form 5500 series return must be filed.

Form 5558 is used to request an automatic extension of time to file a Form 5500 return or Form 8955-SSA. In accordance with § 1.6081-11 and Form 5558 (including instructions), an application for an extension of time to file a Form 5500 series return need not be signed. However, in accordance with § 1.6081-1, Form 5558 provides that an application for an extension of time to file Form 8955-SSA must be signed.

Explanation of Provisions

After the current version of the Form 5558 was issued, several comments were received that questioned the need for a signature to extend the time for filing Form 8955-SSA, particularly since a signature is not required to extend the time to file a Form 5500 series return. The commentators noted that, like its predecessor, the Schedule SSA, the Form 8955-SSA is generally prepared in conjunction with the preparation of a plan's Form 5500. They also stated that a signature requirement for the Form 8955-SSA is likely to cause confusion and missed deadlines because of the different rule for the Form 5500. Finally, the commentators contended that the signature requirement is burdensome for both filers and the IRS because the requirement complicates the extension request process.

The proposed regulations would amend § 1.6081-11, relating to automatic extensions of time for filing certain employee plan returns, by adding the Form 8955-SSA to the list of forms that are covered by the automatic 2 1/2 month extension that applies by filing Form 5558. This will permit a plan administrator to receive an automatic extension of 2 1/2 months by submitting, on or before the general due date of the Form 8955-SSA, a Form 5558 indicating that an extension is being requested for filing the Form 8955-SSA. Thus, under the proposed regulations, the same rules that apply to request an extension of time to file the Form 5500 series would also apply to request an extension of time to file Form 8955-SSA. In addition, the proposed regulations would amend § 1.6081-11 to provide that a signature would not be required to request an extension of time to file Form 5500 and Form 8955-SSA. It is anticipated that the Form 5558 and instructions will be revised to reflect this change for the Form 8955-SSA.

In addition, pursuant to section 6011(a), these proposed regulations would formally designate the Form 8955-SSA as the form used to satisfy the reporting requirements of section 6057. These proposed regulations would retain the general reporting requirements that applied to the Schedule SSA with certain minor modifications.

As discussed in the background section of this preamble, section 6057(a) requires the plan administrator (within the meaning of section 414(g)) of a plan that is subject to the vesting standards of section 203 of ERISA to file, within the time prescribed by regulations, a registration statement that sets forth certain information on deferred vested participants. Under existing § 301.6057-1(c)(1) of the Procedure and Administration regulations, the plan administrator of an employee benefit plan described in § 301.6057-1(a)(3), or any other employee retirement benefit plan (including a governmental or church plan), may at its option file on the Schedule SSA information relating to the deferred vested retirement benefit of any plan participant who separates at any time from service covered under the plan. These proposed regulations would retain the ability of such plans to report deferred vested information on a voluntary basis but require that the information be submitted to the IRS on Form 8955-SSA. The proposed regulations would also delegate authority to the Commissioner of the Internal Revenue Service to provide special rules under section 6057 (including designating the form used to comply with section 6057) in revenue rulings, notices, or other guidance published in the Internal Revenue Bulletin (see § 601.601(d)(2)(ii)(b) of this chapter). Finally, the proposed regulations would delete certain obsolete transition rules and update cross-references in § § 1.6057-1 and 1.6057-2.

Proposed Effective Date

These regulations are generally proposed to be effective on or after June 21, 2012. Taxpayers may rely on these proposed regulations for guidance pending the issuance of final regulations. If, and to the extent, the final regulations are more restrictive than the guidance in these proposed regulations, those provisions of the final regulations will be applied without retroactive effect.

Special Analyses

It has been determined that this notice of proposed rulemaking is not a significant regulatory action as defined in Executive Order 12866. Therefore, a regulatory assessment is not required. It has been determined that 5 U.S.C. 533(b) of the Administrative Procedure Act (5 U.S.C. chapter 5) does not apply to these regulations. It is hereby certified that the collection of information in these proposed regulations will not have a significant economic impact on a substantial number of small entities. This certification is based on the fact that most small entities that maintain employee retirement income benefit plans use third party administrators to perform their recordkeeping function. Therefore, an analysis under the Regulatory Flexibility Act (5 U.S.C. chapter 6) is not required. Pursuant to section 7805(f) of the Internal Revenue Code, these regulations have been submitted to the Office of Chief Counsel for Advocacy of the Small Business Administration for comments on its impact on small business.

Comments and Requests for Public Hearing

Before these proposed regulations are adopted as final regulations, consideration will be given to any comments that are submitted timely to the IRS as prescribed in this preamble under the "Addresses" heading. The IRS and Treasury Department request comments on all aspects of the proposed rules. All comments are available at *www.regulations.gov* or upon request. A public hearing will be scheduled if requested in writing by any person who timely submits written comments. If a public hearing is scheduled, notice of the date, time, and place of the public hearing will be published in the **Federal Register**.

Drafting Information

The principal authors of these regulations are Sarah R. Bolen and Pamela R. Kinard, Office of Division Counsel/Associate Chief Counsel (Tax Exempt and Government Entities). However, other personnel from the IRS and the Treasury Department participated in the development of these regulations.

List of subjects

26 CFR Part 1

Income taxes, Reporting and recordkeeping requirements.

26 CFR Part 301

Employment taxes, Estate taxes, Gift taxes, Income taxes, Penalties, Reporting and Recordkeeping requirements.

Proposed Amendments to the Regulations

Accordingly, 26 CFR parts 1 and 301 are proposed to be amended as follows:

Part 1—INCOME TAXES

Paragraph 1. The authority citation for part 1 continues to read in part as follows:

Authority: 26 U.S.C. 7805 * * *

Par. 2. Section 1.6081-11 is amended by:

1. Revising paragraph (a).

2. Adding paragraph (b)(3).

3. Revising the paragraph heading of paragraph (d) and adding paragraph (d)(2).

4. Revising the paragraph heading of paragraph (e) and adding paragraph (e)(2).

The revisions and additions read as follows:

§ 1.6081-11 Automatic extension of time for filing certain employee plan returns.

(a) *In general.* An administrator or sponsor of an employee benefit plan required to file a return under the provisions of subpart E of part III of chapter 61 or the regulations under that chapter on Form 5500 (series), "Annual Return/Report of Employee Benefit Plan" or Form 8955-SSA, "Annual Registration Statement Identifying Separated Participants with Deferred Vested Benefits," will be allowed an automatic extension of time to file the return until the 15th day of the third month following the date prescribed for filing the return if the administrator or sponsor files an application under this section in accordance with paragraph (b) of this section.

(b) * * *

(3) A signature is not required for an automatic extension of time to file Form 5500 (series) and Form 8955-SSA.

* * * * *

(d) *Penalties*—(1) *Form 5500.* * * *

(2) *Form 8955-SSA.* See section 6652 for penalties for failure to file a timely and complete Form 8955-SSA.

(e) *Effective/Applicability dates*—(1) *Form 5500.* * * *

(2) *Form 8955-SSA.* This section is applicable for applications for an automatic extension of time to file Form 8955-SSA filed after June 21, 2012.

Part 301—PROCEDURE AND ADMINISTRATION

Par. 3. The authority for part 301 continues to read in part as follows:

Authority: 26 U.S.C. 7508* * *

Par. 4. Section 301.6057-1 is amended by:

1. Revising paragraphs (a)(4) and (a)(5)(ii).

2. Removing paragraph (b)(2)(iii) and redesignating paragraph (b)(2)(iv) as (b)(2)(iii).

3. Revising newly designated paragraph (b)(2)(iii).

4. Revising paragraphs (b)(3)(ii), (b)(3)(iii), (c), (d), (f), and (g).

The revisions read as follows:

§301.6057-1 Employee retirement benefit plans; identification of participant with deferred vested retirement benefit.

(a) * * *

(4) *Filing requirements*—(i) *In general.* Information relating to the deferred vested retirement benefit of a plan participant must be filed on Form 8955-SSA, "Annual Registration Statement Identifying Separated Participants With Deferred Vested Benefits." Form 8955-SSA shall be filed on behalf of an employee retirement benefit plan for each plan year for which information relating to the deferred vested retirement benefit of a plan participant is filed under paragraph (a)(5) or (b)(2) of this section. There shall be reported on Form 8955-SSA the name and Social Security number of the participant, a description of the nature, form and amount of the deferred vested retirement benefit to which the participant is entitled, and such other information as is required by section 6057(a) or Form 8955-SSA and the accompanying instructions. The form of the benefit reported on Form 8955-SSA shall be the normal form of benefit under the plan, or, if the plan administrator (within the meaning of section 414(g)) considers it more appropriate, any other form of benefit.

(ii) *General due date for filing.* The forms prescribed by section 6057(a), including Form 8955-SSA, shall be filed in the manner and at the time as required by the forms and related instructions applicable to the annual period.

(iii) *Delegation of authority to Commissioner.* The Commissioner may provide special rules under section 6057 (including designating the form used to comply with section 6057) in revenue rulings, notices, or other guidance published in the Internal Revenue Bulletin (see § 601.601(d)(2)(ii)(b) of this chapter) that the Commissioner determines to be necessary or appropriate with respect to the filing requirements under section 6057.

(5) * * *

(ii) *Exception.* Nothwithstanding paragraph (a)(5)(i) of this section, no information relating to the deferred vested retirement benefit of a separated participant is required to be filed on Form 8955-SSA if, before the date such Form 8955-SSA is required to be filed (including any extension of time for filing granted pursuant to section 6081), the participant—

(A) Is paid some or all of the deferred vested retirement benefit under the plan;

(B) Returns to service covered under the plan; or

(C) Forfeits all of the deferred vested retirement benefit under the plan.

(b) * * *

(2) * * *

(iii) *Exception.* Notwithstanding paragraph (b)(2)(i) of this section, no information relating to a participant's deferred vested retirement benefit is required to be filed on Form 8955-SSA if, before the date such Form 8955-SSA is required to be filed (including any extension of time for filing granted pursuant to section 6081), the participant—

(A) Is paid some or all of the deferred vested retirement benefit under the plan;

(B) Accrues additional retirement benefits under the plan; or

(C) Forfeits all of the deferred vested retirement benefit under the plan.

(3) * * *

(ii) *Inability to determine correct amount of participant's deferred vested retirement benefit.* The plan administrator must indicate on Form 8955-SSA that the amount of a participant's deferred vested retirement benefit showed therein may be other than that to which the participant is actually entitled if such amount is computed on the basis of plan records that the plan administrator maintains and such records—

(A) Are incomplete with respect to the participant's service covered by the plan (as described in paragraph (b)(3)(i) of this section); or

(B) Fail to account for the participant's service not covered by the plan which is relevant to a determination of the participant's deferred vested retirement benefit under the plan (as described in paragraph (b)(3)(i) of this section).

(iii) *Inability to determine whether participant vested in deferred retirement benefit.* Where, as described in paragraph (b)(3)(i) of this section, information to be reported on Form 8955-SSA is to be based upon records which are incomplete with respect to a participant's service covered by the plan or which fail to take into account relevant service not covered by the plan, the plan administrator may be unable to determine whether or not the participant is vested in any deferred retirement benefit. If, in view of information provided either by the incomplete records or the plan participant, there is a significant likelihood that the plan participant is vested in a deferred retirement benefit under the plan, information relating to the participant must be filed on Form 8955-SSA with the notation that the participant may be entitled to a deferred vested benefit under the plan, but information relating to the amount of the benefit may be omitted. This paragraph (b)(3)(iii) does not apply in a case in which it can be determined from plan records maintained by the plan administrator that the participant is vested in a deferred retirement benefit. Paragraph (b)(3)(ii) of this section, however, may apply in such a case.

(c) *Voluntary filing*—(1) *In general.* The plan administrator of an employee retirement benefit plan described in paragraph (a)(3) of this section, or any other employee retirement benefit plan (including a governmental plan within the meaning of section 414(d) or a church plan within the meaning of section 414(e)), may, at its option, file on Form 8955-SSA information relating to the deferred vested retirement benefit of any plan participant who separates at any time from service covered by the plan.

(2) *Deleting previously filed information.* If, after information relating to the deferred vested retirement benefit of a plan participant is filed on Form 8955-SSA (or a predecessor to Form 8955-SSA), the plan participant is paid some or all of the deferred vested retirement benefit under the plan or forfeits all of the deferred vested retirement benefit under the plan, the plan administrator may, at its option, file on Form 8955-SSA (or such other form as may be provided for this purpose) the name and Social Security number of the plan participant with the notation that information previously filed relating to the participant's deferred vested retirement benefit should be deleted.

(d) *Filing incident to cessation of payment of benefits*—(1) *In general.* No information relating to the deferred vested retirement benefit of a plan participant is required to be filed on Form 8955-SSA if before the date such Form 8955-SSA is required to be filed, some of the deferred vested retirement benefit is paid to the participant, and information relating to a participant's deferred vested retirement benefit which was previously filed on Form 8955-SSA (or a predecessor to Form 8955-SSA) may be deleted if the participant is paid some of the deferred vested retirement benefit. If payment of the deferred vested retirement benefit ceases before all of the benefit to which the participant is entitled is paid to the participant, information relating to the deferred vested retirement benefit to which the participant remains entitled shall be filed on the Form 8955-SSA filed for the plan year following the last plan year within which a portion of the benefit is paid to the participant.

(2) *Exception.* Notwithstanding paragraph (d)(1) of this section, no information relating to the deferred vested retirement benefit to which the participant remains entitled is required to be filed on Form 8955-SSA if, before the date such Form 8955-SSA is required to be filed (including any extension of time for filing granted pursuant to section 6081), the participant—

(i) Returns to service covered by the plan;

(ii) Accrues additional retirement benefits under the plan; or

(iii) Forfeits the benefit under the plan.

* * * * *

(f) *Penalties.* For amounts imposed in the case of failure to file the report of deferred vested retirement benefits required by section 6057(a) and paragraph (a) or (b) of this section, see section 6652(d)(1).

(g) *Effective/applicability date*—(1) *In general.* Except as otherwise provided in this paragraph (g), this section is applicable for filings on or after June 21, 2012.

(2) *Special effective date rules for periods before the general effective date.* Section 301.6057-1 of this chapter, as it appeared in the April 1, 2008 edition of 26 CFR part 301, applies for periods before the general effective date. **§ 301.6057-1 [Amended]**

Par. 5. Section 301.6057-1 is amended by removing the language "schedule SSA" and adding "Form 8955-SSA" in its place.

Par. 6. Section 301.6057-2 is amended by revising paragraph (c) as follows: *§ 301.6057-2 Employee retirement benefit plans; notification of change in plan status.*

* * * * *

(c) *Penalty.* For amounts imposed in the case of failure to file a notification of a change in plan status required by section 6057(b) and this section, see section 6652(d)(2).

* * * * *

Steven T. Miller

Deputy Commissioner for Services and Enforcement

¶ 20,263H

IRS regulations: Employee Benefits Security Administration (EBSA): Group health plans: Health insurance: Wellness programs: Nondiscrimination: Incentives.—The IRS, EBSA, and Department of Health and Human Services have issued proposed regulations, consistent with the Patient Protection and Affordable Care Act (PPACA), concerning nondiscriminatory wellness programs in group health plans. The proposed regulations increase the maximum permissible reward under a health-contingent wellness program offered in connection with a group health plan and any related health insurance coverage from 20% to 30% of the cost of coverage. In addition, the maximum permissible reward would be increased to 50% for wellness programs designed to prevent or reduce tobacco use. Other clarifications regarding the reasonable design of health-contingent wellness programs and the reasonable alternatives they must offer to avoid prohibited discrimination are included in the proposed regulations.

The proposed regulations replace the wellness program provisions of the HIPAA nondiscrimination regulations issued in 2006 (see ¶ 13,968R-3), but they do not modify any other provisions of those regulations. The proposed rules would apply to both grandfathered and non-grandfathered group health plans and group health insurance coverage for plan years beginning on or after January 1, 2014.

The proposed regulations, which are reproduced below, were published in the Federal Register on November 26, 2012 (77 FR 70620). The regulations were finalized on June 3, 2013 (78 FR 33157). The preamble to the final regulations is at ¶ 23,288. The final regulations are at ¶ 13,968R-3 and ¶ 13,968V-20H.

DEPARTMENT OF THE TREASURY

Internal Revenue Service

26 CFR Part 54

[REG-122707-12]

RIN 1545-BL07

DEPARTMENT OF LABOR

Employee Benefits Security

Administration

29 CFR Part 2590

RIN 1210-AB55

DEPARTMENT OF HEALTH AND

HUMAN SERVICES

45 CFR Parts 146 and 147

[CMS-9979-P]

RIN 0938-AR48

Incentives for Nondiscriminatory Wellness Programs in Group Health Plans

AGENCY: Internal Revenue Service, Department of the Treasury; Employee Benefits Security Administration, Department of Labor; Centers for Medicare & Medicaid Services, Department of Health and Human Services.

ACTION: Notice of proposed rulemaking.

SUMMARY: This document proposes amendments to regulations, consistent with the Affordable Care Act, regarding nondiscriminatory wellness programs in group health coverage. Specifically, these proposed regulations would increase the maximum permissible reward under a health-contingent wellness program offered in connection with a group health plan (and any related health insurance coverage) from 20 percent to 30 percent of the cost of coverage. The proposed regulations would further increase the maximum permissible reward to 50 percent for wellness programs designed to prevent or reduce tobacco use. These regulations also include other proposed clarifications regarding the reasonable design of health-contingent wellness programs and the reasonable alternatives they must offer in order to avoid prohibited discrimination.

DATES: Comments are due on or before January 25, 2013.

ADDRESSES: Written comments may be submitted to the Department of Labor as specified below. Any comment that is submitted will be shared with the other Departments and will also be made available to the public. Warning: Do not include any personally identifiable information (such as name, address, or other contact information) or confidential business information that you do not want publicly disclosed. All comments may be posted on the Internet and can be retrieved by most Internet search engines. No deletions, modifications, or redactions will be made to the comments received, as they are public records. Comments may be submitted anonymously.

Comments, identified by "Wellness Programs", may be submitted by one of the following methods:

Federal eRulemaking Portal: http://www.regulations.gov. Follow the instructions for submitting comments.

Mail or Hand Delivery: Office of Health Plan Standards and Compliance Assistance, Employee Benefits Security Administration, Room N-5653, U.S. Department of Labor, 200 Constitution Avenue NW., Washington, DC 20210, *Attention:* Wellness Programs.

Comments received will be posted without change to *www.regulations.gov* and *www.dol.gov/ebsa*, and available for public inspection at the Public Disclosure Room, N-1513, Employee Benefits Security Administration, 200 Constitution Avenue NW., Washington, DC 20210, including any personal information provided.

FOR FURTHER INFORMATION CONTACT: Amy Turner or Beth Baum, Employee Benefits Security Administration, Department of Labor, at (202) 693-8335; Karen Levin, Internal Revenue Service, Department of the Treasury, at (202) 622-6080; or Jacob Ackerman, Centers for Medicare & Medicaid Services, Department of Health and Human Services, at (410) 786-1565.

Customer Service Information: Individuals interested in obtaining information from the Department of Labor concerning employment-based health coverage laws may call the EBSA Toll-Free Hotline at 1-866-444-EBSA (3272) or visit the Department of Labor's Web site (*www.dol.gov/ebsa*). In addition, information from HHS on private health insurance for consumers can be found on the Centers for Medicare & Medicaid Services (CMS) Web site (*www.cciio.cms.gov/*) and information on health reform can be found at *www.HealthCare.gov.* **SUPPLEMENTARY INFORMATION:**

I. Background

A. Introduction

The Patient Protection and Affordable Care Act, Public Law 111-148, was enacted on March 23, 2010; the Health Care and Education Reconciliation Act, Public Law 111-152, was enacted on March 30, 2010 (these are collectively known as the "Affordable Care Act"). The Affordable Care Act reorganizes, amends, and adds to the provisions of part A of title XXVII of the Public Health Service Act (PHS Act) relating to group health plans and health insurance issuers in the group and individual markets. The term "group health plan" includes both insured and self-insured group health plans.[1] The Affordable Care Act adds section 715(a)(1) to the Employee Retirement Income Security Act (ERISA) and section 9815(a)(1) to the Internal Revenue Code (the Code) to incorporate the provisions of part A of title XXVII of the PHS Act into ERISA and the Code, and to make them applicable to group health plans and health insurance issuers providing health insurance coverage in connection with group health plans. The PHS Act sections incorporated by these references are sections 2701 through 2728.

B. Wellness Exception to HIPAA Nondiscrimination Provisions

Prior to the enactment of the Affordable Care Act, Titles I and IV of the Health Insurance Portability and Accountability Act of 1996 (HIPAA), Public Law 104-191, added section 9802 of the Code, section 702 of ERISA, and section 2702 of the PHS Act (HIPAA nondiscrimination and wellness provisions). These provisions generally prohibit group health plans and group health insurance issuers from discriminating against individual participants and beneficiaries in eligibility, benefits, or premiums based on a health factor.[2] An exception to the general rule allows premium discounts or rebates or modification to otherwise applicable cost sharing (including copayments, deductibles or coinsurance) in return for adherence to certain programs of health promotion and disease prevention. The Departments of Labor, Health and Human Services (HHS), and the Treasury (collectively, the Departments) have implemented this exception by allowing benefits (including cost sharing), premiums, or contributions to vary based on

participation in a wellness program if such a program adheres to certain conditions set forth in regulations.

The Departments published joint final regulations on December 13, 2006 at 71 FR 75014 (the 2006 regulations) regarding the HIPAA nondiscrimination and wellness provisions.[3] The 2006 regulations divide wellness programs into two general categories. The first category is programs that either do not require an individual to meet a standard related to a health factor in order to obtain a reward or that do not offer a reward at all ("participatory wellness programs"). Participatory wellness programs comply with the nondiscrimination requirements without having to satisfy any additional standards if participation in the program is made available to all similarly situated individuals.[4] Examples of participatory wellness programs in the 2006 regulations include a fitness center reimbursement program,[5] a diagnostic testing program that does not base any reward on test outcomes, a program that waives cost sharing for prenatal or well-baby visits,[6] a program that reimburses employees for the costs of smoking cessation programs regardless of whether the employee quits smoking, and a program that provides rewards for attending a free health education seminar. There is no limit on the financial incentives for participatory wellness programs.

The second category of wellness programs under the 2006 regulations consists of programs that require individuals to satisfy a standard related to a health factor in order to obtain a reward ("health-contingent wellness programs"). This category includes wellness programs that require an individual to attain or maintain a certain health outcome in order to obtain a reward (such as not smoking, attaining certain results on biometric screenings, or meeting targets for exercise). As outlined in the 2006 regulations,[7] plans and issuers may vary benefits (including cost-sharing mechanisms), premiums, or contributions based on whether an individual has met the standards of a wellness program that meets the requirements of paragraph (f). Paragraph (f)(2) of the 2006 regulations prescribes the following consumer-protection conditions for health-contingent wellness programs:

1. The total reward for such wellness programs offered by a plan sponsor does not exceed 20 percent of the total cost of coverage under the plan.

2. The program is reasonably designed to promote health or prevent disease. For this purpose, it must have a reasonable chance of improving health or preventing disease, not be overly burdensome, not be a subterfuge for discriminating based on a health factor, and not be highly suspect in method.

3. The program gives eligible individuals an opportunity to qualify for the reward at least once per year.

4. The reward is available to all similarly situated individuals. For this purpose, a reasonable alternative standard (or waiver of the otherwise applicable standard) must be made available to any individual for whom it is unreasonably difficult due to a medical condition to satisfy the otherwise applicable standard during that period (or for whom it is medically inadvisable to attempt to satisfy the otherwise applicable standard).

5. In all plan materials describing the terms of the program, the availability of a reasonable alternative standard (or the possibility of waiver of the otherwise applicable standard) is disclosed.

C. Amendments Made by the Affordable Care Act

The Affordable Care Act (section 1201) amended the nondiscrimination and wellness program provisions of the PHS Act (but not of ERISA section 702 or Code section 9802). (Affordable Care Act section 1201 also moved those provisions from PHS Act section 2702 to PHS Act

---

[1] The term "group health plan" is used in title XXVII of the PHS Act, part 7 of ERISA, and chapter 100 of the Code, and is distinct from the term "health plan," as used in other provisions of title I of the Affordable Care Act. The term "health plan" does not include self-insured group health plans.

[2] The HIPAA nondiscrimination provisions set forth eight health status-related factors, which the December 13, 2006 final regulations on nondiscrimination and wellness programs refer to as "health factors." Under HIPAA and the 2006 regulations, the eight health factors are health status, medical condition (including both physical and mental illnesses), claims experience, receipt of health care, medical history, genetic information, evidence of insurability (including conditions arising out of acts of domestic violence), and disability. *See* 66 FR 1379, January 8, 2001.

[3] *See* 26 CFR 54.9802-1; 29 CFR 2590.702; 45 CFR 146.121. Prior to issuance of the final 2006 regulations, the Departments published interim final regulations with request for comment implementing the HIPAA nondiscrimination provisions on April 8, 1997 at 62 FR 16894, followed by proposed regulations regarding wellness programs on January 8, 2001 at 66 FR 1421.

[4] *See* paragraph (f)(1) of the 2006 regulations. *See also* 26 CFR 54.9802-1(d), 29 CFR 2590.702(d), and 45 CFR 146.121(d), which provide that, generally, distinctions among groups of similarly situated participants in a health plan must be based on bona fide

employment-based classifications consistent with the employer's usual business practice. A plan may also distinguish between beneficiaries based on, for example, their relationship to the plan participant (such as spouse or dependent child) or based on the age of dependent children. Distinctions are not permitted to be based on any of the health factors noted earlier.

[5] The Treasury and the IRS note that satisfying the rules for wellness programs does not determine the tax treatment of benefits provided by the wellness program. For example, fitness center fees are generally considered expenses for general good health and thus payment of the fee by the employer is not excluded from income as the reimbursement of a medical expense.

[6] Note that section 2713 of the PHS Act, as added by the Affordable Care Act, and the Departments' interim final regulations at 26 CFR 54.9815-2713T, 29 CFR 2590.715-2713, and 45 CFR 147.130 require non-grandfathered group health plans and health insurance issuers offering non-grandfathered group or individual health insurance coverage to provide benefits for certain preventive health services without the imposition of cost sharing. *See also* 26 CFR 54.9815-1251T, 29 CFR 2590.715-1251, and 45 CFR 147.140 (regarding the definition of grandfathered health plan coverage).

[7] *See* 26 CFR 54.9802-1(b)(2)(ii) and (c)(3); 29 CFR 2590.702(b)(2)(ii) and (c)(3); and 45 CFR 146.121(b)(2)(ii) and (c)(3).

section 2705). As amended by the Affordable Care Act, the nondiscrimination and wellness provisions of PHS Act section 2705 largely reflect the 2006 regulations (except as discussed later in this preamble), and extend the nondiscrimination protections to the individual market.[8] The wellness program exception to the prohibition on discrimination under PHS Act section 2705 applies with respect to group health plans (and any health insurance coverage offered in connection with such plans). Section 2705(l) separately provides for a 10-State wellness program demonstration project in the individual market, to be established not later than July 1, 2014 (as such, this proposed rule does not include wellness program policy for the individual market).

D. Application to Grandfathered Plans

Section 1251 of the Affordable Care Act provides that certain amendments made by the Affordable Care Act generally do not apply to plans or health insurance coverage that are in effect on the date of enactment (and that are not changed in ways specified in implementing regulations),[9] except as specified in section 1251(a)(3) and (4) of the Affordable Care Act. Specifically, section 1251(a)(2) of the Affordable Care Act provides that subtitles A and C of title I of the Affordable Care Act, and the amendments made by such subtitles, "shall not apply" to such grandfathered health plans.

Because the amendments made to the PHS Act in section 1201 of the Affordable Care Act do not apply to grandfathered health plans, the version of PHS Act section 2702 in effect at the time of enactment of the Affordable Care Act (and the 2006 regulations under that section) continues to apply to grandfathered health plans, while the provisions of the new PHS Act section 2705 apply to non-grandfathered health plans for plan years (in the individual market, policy years) beginning on or after January 1, 2014.[10] ERISA section 702 and Code section 9802 continue to govern all group health plans, including grandfathered health plans, and, for plan years beginning on or after January 1, 2014, ERISA section 715(a)(1) and Code section 9815(a)(1) will also apply new PHS Act section 2705 to non-grandfathered health plans.

However, because the Departments believe that the provisions of these proposed regulations would be authorized under either HIPAA or the Affordable Care Act, the Departments are proposing in this rulemaking to apply the same set of standards to both grandfathered and non-grandfathered health plans. As noted, PHS Act section 2705(j) largely adopts the wellness program provisions of the 2006 regulations with some modification and clarification. Consistent with the statutory approach, these proposed regulations would apply the rules of PHS Act section 2705, governing rewards for adherence to certain wellness programs, to grandfathered health plans by regulation under authority in the HIPAA nondiscrimination and wellness provisions as was done in the 2006 regulations. This approach is intended to avoid inconsistency across group health coverage and to provide grandfathered plans the same flexibility to promote health and prevent disease as non-grandfathered plans.

II. Overview of the Proposed Rule

These regulations generally propose standards for group health plans and health insurance issuers offering group health insurance coverage with respect to wellness programs. These proposed regulations would replace the wellness program provisions of paragraph (f) of the 2006 regulations and would apply to both grandfathered and non-grandfathered group health plans and group health insurance coverage for plan years beginning on or after January 1, 2014. These regulations also propose to implement the nondiscrimination provisions made applicable to the individual market by section 1201 of the Affordable Care Act. This rulemaking does not propose to modify provisions of the 2006 regulations other than paragraph (f).

A. Two Categories of Wellness Programs

Consistent with the 2006 regulations and PHS Act section 2705(j), these proposed regulations would continue to divide wellness programs into two categories: "Participatory wellness programs", which are a majority of wellness programs (as noted below) and "health-contingent wellness programs." Participatory wellness programs are programs that are made available to all similarly situated individuals

and that either do not provide a reward or do not include any conditions for obtaining a reward that are based on an individual satisfying a standard that is related to a health factor. Several examples of participatory wellness programs are provided in these proposed regulations, including: (1) A program that reimburses for all or part of the cost of membership in a fitness center; and (2) a program that provides a reward to employees for attending a monthly, no-cost health education seminar. Participatory programs are not required to meet the five requirements applicable to health-contingent wellness programs.

In contrast, health-contingent wellness programs require an individual to satisfy a standard related to a health factor to obtain a reward (or require an individual to do more than a similarly situated individual based on a health factor in order to obtain the same reward). Like the 2006 regulations, these proposed regulations would continue to permit rewards to be in the form of a discount or rebate of a premium or contribution, a waiver of all or part of a cost-sharing mechanism (such as deductibles, copayments, or coinsurance), the absence of a surcharge, the value of a benefit that otherwise would not be provided under the plan, or other financial or nonfinancial incentives or disincentives. Examples of health-contingent wellness programs in these proposed regulations are: (1) A program that imposes a premium surcharge based on tobacco use; and (2) a program that uses a biometric screening or a health risk assessment to identify employees with specified medical conditions or risk factors (such as high cholesterol, high blood pressure, abnormal body mass index, or high glucose level) and provides a reward to employees identified as within a normal or healthy range (or at low risk for certain medical conditions), while requiring employees who are identified as outside the normal or healthy range (or at risk) to take additional steps (such as meeting with a health coach, taking a health or fitness course, adhering to a health improvement action plan, or complying with a health care provider's plan of care) to obtain the same reward. Under paragraphs (b)(2)(ii) and (c)(3) of the 2006 regulations (which remain unchanged),[11] health-contingent wellness programs are permissible only if they comply with the provisions of paragraph (f)(3), which are proposed to be amended in this rulemaking.[12]

The Departments believe that appropriately designed wellness programs have the potential to contribute importantly to promoting health and preventing disease. Even after the issuance of the 2006 regulations and the enactment of the Affordable Care Act wellness provisions, however, stakeholder feedback suggests that there continues to be a degree of confusion regarding the scope of the rules governing wellness programs. The Departments hope that these proposed regulations will help dispel the confusion by reiterating that the five regulatory requirements relating to frequency of opportunity to qualify, size of reward, uniform availability and reasonable alternative standards, reasonable design, and notice of other means of qualifying for the reward (summarized below and contained in paragraph (f)(3) of the proposed regulations) apply only to those wellness programs that meet the definition of "health-contingent" programs. As discussed above, these are wellness programs that both provide a reward and condition the reward on satisfying a standard that is related to a health factor. Many wellness programs (those characterized in these regulations as "participatory wellness programs") do not both provide a reward and condition the reward on satisfying a standard that is related to a health factor. Accordingly, as noted, participatory wellness programs are not required to meet the five enumerated requirements applicable to health-contingent wellness programs, but they are required to be made available to all similarly situated individuals.

B. Requirements for Health-Contingent Wellness Programs

Consistent with the 2006 regulations, these proposed regulations generally would maintain the five requirements for health-contingent wellness programs with one significant modification relating to the size of the reward. In addition, several regulatory provisions have been re-ordered, and clarifications are proposed to address questions and issues raised by stakeholders since the 2006 regulations were issued and to be consistent with the amendments made by the Affordable Care Act, as discussed below.

(1) *Frequency of Opportunity to Qualify.*

---

[8] Section 1201 of the Affordable Care Act also moved the guaranteed availability provisions that were previously codified in PHS Act section 2711 to PHS Act section 2702, and extended those requirements to the individual market.

[9] *See* 26 CFR 54.9815-1251T, 29 CFR 2590.715-1251, and 45 CFR 147.140 (75 FR 34538, June 17, 2010), as amended (75 FR 70114, November 17, 2010). *See also* Q5 of Affordable Care Act Implementation FAQs Part II (October 8, 2010), available at http://www.dol.gov/ebsa/faqs/faq-aca2.html and *http://cciio.cms.gov/resources/factsheets/aca_implementation_faqs2.html.*

[10] *See* 26 CFR 54.9815-1251T(c)(2), 29 CFR 2590.715-1251(c)(2), and 45 CFR 147.140(c)(2), providing that a grandfathered health plan must comply with the require-

ments of the PHS Act, ERISA, and the Code applicable prior to the changes enacted by the Affordable Care Act, to the extent not inconsistent with the rules applicable to a grandfathered health plan (75 FR 34538, June 17, 2010).

[11] 26 CFR 54.9802-1(b)(2)(ii) and (c)(3); 29 CFR 2590.702(b)(2)(ii) and (c)(3); and 45 CFR 146.121(b)(2)(ii) and (c)(3).

[12] Until these proposed regulations are finalized and effective, the provisions of the 2006 regulations, at 26 CFR 54.9802-1(f), 29 CFR 2590.702(f), and 45 CFR 146.121(f) generally remain applicable to group health plans and group health insurance issuers.

These proposed regulations would, consistent with the 2006 regulations and the amendments made by the Affordable Care Act, require health-contingent wellness programs to give individuals eligible for the program the opportunity to qualify for the reward at least once per year. As stated in the preamble to the 2006 regulations, the once-per-year requirement was included as a bright-line standard for determining the minimum frequency that is consistent with a reasonable design for promoting good health or preventing disease.[13]

(2) *Size of Reward.*

Like the 2006 regulations, these proposed regulations would continue to limit the total amount of the reward for health-contingent wellness programs with respect to a plan, whether offered alone or coupled with the reward for other health-contingent wellness programs. Specifically, the total reward offered to an individual under an employer's health-contingent wellness programs could not exceed a specified percentage (referred to as the "applicable percentage" in the proposed regulations) of the total cost of employee-only coverage under the plan, taking into account both employer and employee contributions towards the cost of coverage. If, in addition to employees, any class of dependents (such as spouses, or spouses and dependent children) may participate in the health-contingent wellness program, the reward could not exceed the applicable percentage of the total cost of the coverage in which the employee and any dependents are enrolled (such as family coverage or employee-plus-one coverage).

Some stakeholders have raised questions about health-contingent wellness programs that allow dependents to participate, and what portion of the reward should be attributable to each participating dependent. If a class of dependents may participate in a health-contingent wellness program, some have suggested that there be a maximum reward attributable to the employee's participation in the wellness program, such as an amount that does not exceed the applicable percentage of the cost of employee-only coverage. The proposed regulation being issued contemporaneously by HHS proposes that, to comply with PHS Act section 2701, with respect to family coverage, any premium variation for tobacco use must be applied to the portion of premium attributable to each family member. The Departments invite comments on apportionment of rewards in health-contingent wellness programs (which may involve tobacco use and/or other health factors)—for example, should the reward be prorated if only one family member fails to qualify for it.

The 2006 regulations specify 20 percent as the maximum permissible reward for participation in a health-contingent wellness program. PHS Act section 2705(j)(3)(A), effective for plan years beginning on or after January 1, 2014, increases the maximum reward to 30 percent and authorizes the Departments to increase the maximum reward to as much as 50 percent if the Departments determine that such an increase is appropriate. In these proposed regulations, the increase in the applicable percentage from 20 percent to 30 percent, which is effective for plan years beginning on or after January 1, 2014, conforms to the new PHS Act section 2705(j)(3)(A). In addition, the Departments have determined that an increase of an additional 20 percentage points (to 50 percent) for health-contingent wellness programs designed to prevent or reduce tobacco use is warranted to conform to the new PHS Act section 2701, to avoid inconsistency across group health coverage, whether insured or self-insured, or offered in the small group or large group market, and to provide grandfathered plans the same flexibility to promote health and prevent disease as non-grandfathered plans.

Specifically, PHS Act section 2701, the "fair health insurance premium" provision, sets forth the factors that issuers may use to vary premium rates in the individual or small group market.[14] PHS Act section 2701(a)(1)(A)(iv) provides that issuers in the individual and small group markets cannot vary rates for tobacco use by more than a ratio of 1.5 to 1 (that is, allowing up to a 50 percent premium surcharge for tobacco use).

Contemporaneously with the publication of these proposed wellness program regulations, HHS is publishing a proposed regulation that would implement PHS Act section 2701. HHS proposes that a health insurance issuer in the small group market would be able to implement the tobacco use surcharge under PHS Act section 2701 to employees only in connection with a wellness program meeting the standards of PHS Act section 2705(j) and its implementing regulations. As discussed

in the preamble to the proposed regulation implementing PHS Act section 2701, HHS is proposing in that rule that the definition of "tobacco use" for purposes of section 2701 be consistent with the approach taken with respect to health-contingent wellness programs designed to prevent or reduce tobacco use under section 2705(j). Comments are solicited in the preamble to the proposed rules implementing section 2701 on possible definitions of "tobacco use" that would be applied for purposes of PHS Act sections 2701 and 2705(j).

To coordinate these proposed regulations with the tobacco use rating provisions of PHS Act section 2701, as proposed by HHS, these proposed wellness program regulations would use the new authority in PHS Act section 2705(j)(3)(A) (and, with respect to grandfathered health plans, the preexisting authority in the HIPAA nondiscrimination and wellness provisions) to increase the applicable percentage for determining the size of the reward for participating in a health-contingent wellness program by an additional 20 percentage points (to 50 percent) to the extent that the additional percentage is attributed to tobacco use prevention or reduction. Applying these proposed regulations to all group health plans would provide consistency across markets, giving large, self-insured, and grandfathered employment-based health plans the same added flexibility to promote tobacco-free workforces as small, insured, non-grandfathered health plans.

Examples included in these proposed regulations illustrate how to calculate the applicable percentage. The Departments invite comments on the proposed approach in general and other ideas for coordinating the implementation of the tobacco rating factor under PHS Act section 2701 with the nondiscrimination and wellness program provisions. The Departments also invite comments as to whether additional rules or examples would be helpful to demonstrate compliance with the limitation on the size of the reward when the amount of the reward is variable and is not determinable at the time the reward is established (for example, when the reward is waiver of a copayment for outpatient office visits, the frequency of which will not be predictable for any particular participant or beneficiary under the plan).

(3) *Uniform Availability and Reasonable Alternative Standards.*

A critical element of these proposed regulations is the requirement that the reward under a health-contingent wellness program be available to all similarly situated individuals. To meet this requirement, a "reasonable alternative standard" (or waiver of the otherwise applicable standard) for obtaining the reward must be provided for any individual for whom, for that period, it is either unreasonably difficult due to a medical condition to meet the otherwise applicable standard, or for whom it is medically inadvisable to attempt to satisfy the otherwise applicable standard. That is, the same, full reward must be available to individuals who qualify by satisfying a reasonable alternative standard as is provided to individuals who qualify by satisfying the program's otherwise applicable standard. These proposed regulations would generally reiterate the requirements set forth in the 2006 regulations and codified in PHS Act section 2705(j), and provide several additional clarifications.

First, under these proposed regulations, as under the 2006 regulations, in lieu of providing a reasonable alternative standard, a plan or issuer may always waive the otherwise applicable standard and provide the reward. The plan or issuer may waive the otherwise applicable standard and provide a reward for an entire class of individuals or may do so on an individual-by-individual basis based on the facts and circumstances presented.

Second, these proposed regulations would not require plans and issuers to establish a particular alternative standard in advance of an individual's specific request for one. However, a reasonable alternative standard would have to be provided by the plan or issuer (or the condition for obtaining the reward would be required to be waived) upon an individual's request. In this connection, the Departments note that, as stated in the preamble to the 2006 regulations with respect to tobacco cessation, "overcoming an addiction sometimes requires a cycle of failure and renewed effort."[15] Plans and issuers cannot cease to provide a reasonable alternative standard merely because one was not successful before; they must continue to offer a reasonable alternative standard, whether it is the same standard or a new reasonable alternative standard (such as a new weight-loss class or a new nicotine

---

[13] *See* 71 FR at 75018.

[14] Small group market means the health insurance market under which individuals obtain health insurance coverage (directly or through any arrangement) on behalf of themselves (and their dependents) through a group health plan maintained by a small employer. *See* PHS Act section 2791(e)(5); 45 CFR 144.103. For plan years beginning on or after January 1, 2014, amendments made by the Affordable Care Act provide that the term "small employer" means, in connection with a group health plan with respect to a calendar

year and a plan year, an employer who employed an average of at least 1 but not more than 100 employees on business days during the preceding calendar year and who employs at least 1 employee on the first day of the plan year. *See* PHS Act section 2791(e)(4). In the case of plan years beginning before January 1, 2016, a State may elect to substitute "50 employees" for "100 employees" in its definition of a small employer. *See* section 1304(b)(3) of the Affordable Care Act.

[15] *See* 71 FR 75019.

replacement therapy).[16] All the facts and circumstances would be taken into account in determining whether a plan or issuer has provided a reasonable alternative standard, including but not limited to the following proposed factors:

• If the reasonable alternative standard is completion of an educational program, the plan or issuer must make the educational program available instead of requiring an individual to find such a program unassisted, and may not require an individual to pay for the cost of the program.

• If the reasonable alternative standard is a diet program, the plan or issuer is not required to pay for the cost of food but must pay any membership or participation fee.

• If the reasonable alternative standard is compliance with the recommendations of a medical professional who is an employee or agent of the plan or issuer, and an individual's personal physician states that the medical professional's recommendations are not medically appropriate for that individual, the plan or issuer must provide a reasonable alternative standard that accommodates the recommendations of the individual's physician with regard to medical appropriateness.[17] Plans and issuers may impose standard cost sharing under the plan or coverage for medical items and services furnished in accordance with the physician's recommendations.

The Departments intend that these clarifications with respect to offering reasonable alternative standards will help prevent health-contingent wellness programs that provide little to no support to enrollees to improve individuals' health. In addition, as explained later in this preamble, clarifications are proposed to ensure that a health-contingent wellness program is reasonably designed to improve health and is not a subterfuge for underwriting or reducing benefits based on health status. Comments are invited on these provisions, as well as whether other facts and circumstances should be specifically addressed. For example, the Departments seek comment on whether any additional rules or clarifications are needed with respect to the process for determining a reasonable alternative standard.

Finally, the 2006 regulations provided that it is permissible for a plan or issuer to seek verification, such as a statement from the individual's personal physician, that a health factor makes it unreasonably difficult for the individual to satisfy, or medically inadvisable for the individual to attempt to satisfy, the otherwise applicable standard. The Affordable Care Act amendments codified this provision with one modification: PHS Act section 2705(j)(3)(D)(ii) makes clear that physician verification may be required by a plan or issuer "if reasonable under the circumstances." These proposed regulations clarify that it would not be reasonable for a plan or issuer to seek verification of a claim that is obviously valid based on the nature of the individual's medical condition that is known to the plan or issuer. Plans and issuers are permitted under the proposed regulations to seek verification of claims that require the use of medical judgment to evaluate. The Departments solicit comments on whether additional clarifications would be helpful regarding the reasonableness of physician verification.

(4) Reasonable Design.

Consistent with the 2006 regulations and PHS Act section 2705(j), these proposed regulations would continue to require that health-contingent wellness programs be reasonably designed to promote health or prevent disease, not be overly burdensome, not be a subterfuge for discrimination based on a health factor, and not be highly suspect in the method chosen to promote health or prevent disease. The preamble to the 2006 regulations stated that the "reasonably designed" standard was designed to prevent abuse, but otherwise was "intended to be an easy standard to satisfy * * *. There does not need to be a scientific record that the method promotes wellness to satisfy this standard. The standard is intended to allow experimentation in diverse ways of promoting wellness."[18] The preamble also stated that the Departments did not "want plans and issuers to be constrained by a narrow range of programs * * * but want plans and issuers to feel free to consider innovative programs for motivating individuals to make efforts to improve their health."[19] These proposed regulations would continue to provide plans and issuers flexibility and encourage innovation. Also, as discussed later in this preamble, the regulations include several clarifications to ensure against subterfuge and discrimination. Comments are welcome on whether certain standards, including evidence- or practice-based standards, are needed to ensure that wellness programs are reasonably designed to promote health or prevent disease.

The Departments also welcome comments on best practices guidance regarding evidence- and practice-based strategies in order to increase the likelihood of wellness program success. Resources for employers and plans include the Healthier Worksite Initiative of the Centers for Disease Control and Prevention (CDC) at *http://www.cdc.gov/nccdphp/dnpao/hwi/*.

Under the proposed regulations, the determination of whether a health-contingent wellness program is reasonably designed is based on all the relevant facts and circumstances. To ensure that programs are not a subterfuge for discrimination or underwriting based on health factors such as weight, blood pressure, glucose levels, cholesterol levels, or tobacco use with no or insufficient support to improve individuals' health, the Departments propose that, to the extent a plan's initial standard for obtaining a reward (or a portion of a reward) is based on results of a measurement, test, or screening that is related to a health factor (such as a biometric examination or a health risk assessment), the plan is not reasonably designed unless it makes available to all individuals who do not meet the standard based on the measurement, test, or screening a different, reasonable means of qualifying for the reward. Accordingly, the general approach that was adopted in the 2006 regulations is preserved, which allows plans and issuers to conduct screenings and employ measurement techniques in order to target wellness programs effectively. For example, plans and issuers could target individuals with high cholesterol for participation in cholesterol reduction programs, or individuals who use tobacco for participation in tobacco cessation programs, rather than the entire population of participants and beneficiaries if individuals who do not meet a plan's target biometrics (or similar standards) are provided a different, reasonable means of qualifying for the same reward. The Departments invite comments on this approach, including on ways to ensure that employees will not be subjected to an unreasonable "one-size-fits-all" approach to designing the different means of qualifying for the reward that would fail to take an employee's circumstances into account to the extent that, as a practical matter, they would make it unreasonably difficult for the employee to access those different means of qualifying. Comments also are invited on whether any other consumer protections are needed to ensure that wellness programs are reasonably designed to promote health or prevent disease.

(5) Notice of Other Means of Qualifying for the Reward.

These proposed regulations, consistent with the 2006 regulations and the amendments made by the Affordable Care Act, would require plans and issuers to disclose the availability of other means of qualifying for the reward or the possibility of waiver of the otherwise applicable standard in all plan materials describing the terms of a health-contingent wellness program. If plan materials merely mention that a program is available, without describing its terms, this disclosure is not required. For example, a summary of benefits and coverage (SBC) required under section 2715 of the PHS Act that notes that cost sharing may vary based on participation in a diabetes wellness program, without describing the standards of the program, would not trigger this disclosure.

The 2006 regulations provided sample language that could be used to satisfy this requirement in both the regulatory text and in several examples. However, feedback and experience since the 2006 regulations were published have indicated that the sample language was complicated and confusing to some individuals and may have led fewer individuals to seek a reasonable alternative standard than were eligible. Accordingly, these proposed regulations provide new sample language in the regulatory text and in examples that is intended to be simpler for individuals to understand and to increase the likelihood that those who qualify for a different means of obtaining a reward will contact the plan or issuer to request it. The Departments invite comment on the sample language in both the regulatory text and in the examples.

C. Application to the Individual Health Insurance Market

PHS Act sections 2705(a) and (b), as added by section 1201 of the Affordable Care Act, apply the HIPAA nondiscrimination requirements to health insurance issuers in the individual health insurance market. Accordingly, the HHS proposed regulations include a new § 147.110 which applies the nondiscrimination protections of the 2006 regulations to non-grandfathered, individual health insurance coverage, effective for policy years beginning on or after January 1, 2014. By their terms, the wellness program provisions of PHS Act section 2705(j), however, do not apply to health insurance coverage in the individual market. Accordingly, the wellness program provisions of § 146.121(f) apply only

---

[16] *Id.*

[17] As stated in the preamble to the Departments' regulations on internal claims and appeals and external review processes, adverse benefit determinations based on whether a participant or beneficiary is entitled to a reasonable alternative standard for a reward under

a plan's wellness program are situations in which a claim is considered to involve medical judgment and therefore is eligible for Federal external review. *See* 76 FR 37216.

[18] 71 FR 75018.

[19] 71 FR 75019.

to group health plans and group health insurance coverage, not individual market coverage.

D. Applicability Date

These proposed regulations would apply for plan years (in the individual market, policy years) beginning on or after January 1, 2014, consistent with the statutory effective date of PHS Act section 2705, as well as PHS Act section 2701. Comments are invited on this proposed applicability date.

III. Economic Impact and Paperwork Burden

A. Executive Orders 12866 and 13563— Department of Labor and Department of Health and Human Services

Executive Orders 12866 and 13563 direct agencies to assess all costs and benefits of available regulatory alternatives and, if regulation is necessary, to select regulatory approaches that maximize net benefits (including potential economic, environmental, public health and safety effects; distributive impacts; and equity). Executive Order 13563 emphasizes the importance of quantifying both costs and benefits, reducing costs, harmonizing rules, and promoting flexibility. The Office of Management and Budget (OMB) has determined that this proposed rule is a "significant regulatory action" under section 3(f)(4) of Executive Order 12866, because it raises novel legal or policy issues arising from the President's priorities. Accordingly, the rule has been reviewed by the OMB.

TABLE 1—*Accounting Table*

Benefits	Quantified: Minimal due to low expected use of higher reward limits.
	Qualitative: Benefits include the ability to increase the reward based on a health factor to incentivize individuals to meet a health standard associated with improved health, which could reduce health care costs. Improved standards could reduce the use of wellness programs as a subterfuge for discrimination based on a health factor.
Costs	Quantified: Minimal since employers are expected to create or expand wellness programs only if the expected benefit exceeds the cost as well as due to low expected use of higher reward limits.
	Qualitative: Costs of the rule include clarifications regarding what costs individuals may pay as part of an alternative means of complying with the health standard. To the extent an individual faces an increased cost for not meeting a health standard, the individual would have reduced resources to use for other purposes.
Transfers	Quantified: Minimal due to low expected use of higher reward limits.
	Qualitative: Transfers resulting from the rule include transfers from those who do not meet a health standard to those who do meet the standard or the associated alternative standard.

Based on the Departments' review of the most recent literature and studies regarding wellness programs, the Departments reached the conclusion that the impact of the benefits, costs, and transfers associated with the proposed rules will be minimal. As discussed in this analysis, few health-contingent wellness programs today come close to meeting the 20 percent limit (based on the data, the usual reward percentage ranges from three to 11 percent); therefore, the Departments do not believe that expanding the limit to 30 percent (or 50 percent for programs designed to prevent or reduce tobacco use) will result in significantly higher participation of employers in such programs. The Departments provide a qualitative discussion below and cite the survey data used to substantiate this conclusion. Moreover, most wellness programs appear to be participatory programs that do not require an individual to meet a standard related to a health factor in order to obtain a reward. As stated earlier in this preamble, these participatory wellness programs are not required to meet the five requirements that apply to health-contingent wellness programs, but they are required to be made available to all similarly situated individuals.

Although the Departments believe few plans will expand the reward percentage, the Departments provide a qualitative discussion regarding the sources of benefits, costs, and transfers that could occur if plans were to expand the reward beyond the current maximum of 20 percent. Currently, insufficient broad-based evidence makes it difficult to definitively assess the impact of workplace wellness programs on health outcomes and cost, although, overall, employers largely report that workplace wellness programs in general (participatory programs and health-contingent programs) are delivering on their intended benefit of improving health and reducing costs.

The one source of potential additional cost discussed in the impact analysis is the clarification that plans must provide a reasonable alternative means of satisfying the otherwise applicable standard. The Departments present evidence that currently employers not only allow a reasonable alternative standard, but that most employers already pay for these alternatives. The Departments do not have an estimate of how many plans are not currently paying for alternatives consistent with the clarifications set forth in the proposed regulations, but the number appears to be small. The Departments also employ economic logic to conclude that employers will create or expand their wellness program and provide reasonable alternatives only if the expected benefits exceed the expected costs. Therefore, the Departments believe that the benefits of the proposed rule will justify the costs. The Departments invite comments on these conclusions and request input for improving the analysis, including additional data, surveys, or studies.

B. Background and Need for Regulatory Action—Department of Labor and Department of Health and Human Services

As discussed earlier in this preamble, on December 13, 2006, the Departments issued joint final regulations regarding the HIPAA nondiscrimination and wellness provisions. The 2006 regulations set forth the requirements for wellness programs that provide a reward to individuals who satisfy a standard related to a health factor or provide a reward to individuals to do more than a similarly situated individual based on a health factor. *See* section I.B. of this preamble for a detailed discussion of the HIPAA nondiscrimination and wellness provisions and the 2006 regulations.

PHS Act section 2705 largely reflects the provisions of the 2006 regulations with some modification and clarification. Most notably, it increased the maximum reward that can be provided under a health-contingent wellness program from 20 percent to 30 percent of the total cost of coverage under the plan and authorized the Departments to increase this percentage to as much as 50 percent of the total cost of coverage under the plan, if the Departments determine that such an increase is appropriate. Accordingly, as discussed in section II.B of this preamble, these proposed regulations increase the applicable percentage for the maximum reward from 20 percent to 30 percent, with an additional increase of 20 percentage points (to 50 percent) for health-contingent wellness programs designed to prevent or reduce tobacco use. The additional increase is warranted to conform to PHS Act section 2701, to avoid inconsistency across group health coverage, whether insured or self-insured, or offered in the small group or large group market, and to provide grandfathered plans the same flexibility to promote health and prevent disease as non-grandfathered plans.[20]

C. Regulatory Alternatives—Department of Labor and Department of Health and Human Services

As stated earlier in this preamble, the 2006 regulations prescribed several requirements for health-contingent wellness programs, including a limitation on the maximum reward of 20 percent of the total cost of coverage under the plan.[21] PHS Act section 2705 largely reflects the requirements for wellness programs from the 2006 regulations with some modification and clarification. Most notably, it increased the maximum reward that can be provided under a health-contingent wellness program from 20 percent to 30 percent of the total cost of coverage under the plan and authorized the Departments to increase this percentage to as much as 50 percent, if the Departments determine that such an increase is appropriate.

PHS Act section 2701(a)(1)(A)(iv) provides that issuers in the individual and small group markets cannot vary rates for tobacco use by more than a ratio of 1.5 to 1 (that is, allowing up to a 50 percent rating factor for tobacco use) for non-grandfathered plans. PHS Act section 2701 applies to the individual market and the small group market, but does not apply in the large group market or to self-insured plans. Contemporaneously with the publication of these proposed regulations, HHS is publishing a proposed rule that would provide that an issuer in the small group market would not be able to impose the tobacco rating factor on an individual in the plan under PHS Act section 2701 unless it was imposed as part of a wellness program meeting the standards of PHS Act section 2705(j) and its implementing regulations.

---

[20] For a discussion of PHS Act section 2701 and the HHS proposed regulation being published contemporaneously with these proposed regulations, see section II.B.2. of this preamble.

[21] *See* section I.B, earlier in this preamble.

An important policy goal of the Departments is to provide the large group market and self-insured plans and grandfathered health plans with the same flexibility as non-grandfathered plans in the small group market to promote tobacco-free workforces. The Departments considered several regulatory alternatives to meet this objective, including the following:

(1) *Stacking premium differentials.* One alternative considered was to permit a 50 percent premium differential for tobacco use in the small group market under PHS Act section 2701 without requiring a reasonable alternative standard. Under PHS Act section 2705, an additional 30 percent premium differential would also be permitted if the five criteria for a health-contingent wellness program are met (including the offering of a reasonable alternative standard). Under this option, an 80 percent premium differential would have been allowable in the small group market based on factors related to health status. Large and self-insured plans would have been limited to the 30 percent maximum reward. Allowing such a substantial difference between what was permissible in the small group market and the large group market was not in line with the Departments' policy goal of providing consistency in flexibility for plans.

(2) *Concurrent premium differentials with no reasonable alternative required to be offered for tobacco use.* Another alternative would be to read sections 2701 and 2705 together such that, for non-grandfathered health plans in the small group market, up to a 50 percent premium differential would be permitted based on tobacco use, as authorized under PHS Act section 2701(a)(1)(A)(iv), with no reasonable alternative standard required for the tobacco use program. With respect to non-tobacco-related wellness programs, a reward could be offered only to the extent that a tobacco use wellness program were less than 30 percent of the cost of coverage because the two provisions apply concurrently, and a reward would not be permitted under PHS Act section 2705 if the maximum reward already were exceeded by virtue of PHS Act section 2701. Thus, the 50 percent tobacco surcharge under PHS Act section 2701 would be available only to non-grandfathered, insured, small group plans. The chosen approach is intended to avoid inconsistency and to provide grandfathered plans the same flexibility to promote health and prevent disease as non-grandfathered plans.

D. Current Use of Wellness Programs and Economic Impacts—Department of Labor and Department of Health and Human Services

The current use of wellness programs and economic impacts of these proposed regulations are discussed in this analysis.

Wellness programs[22] have become common among employers in the United States. The 2012 Kaiser/HRET survey indicates that 63 percent of all employers who offered health benefits also offered at least one wellness program.[23] The uptake of wellness programs continues to be more common among large employers. For example, the 2012 Kaiser/HRET survey found that health risk assessments are offered by 38 percent of large employers offering health benefits, but only 18 percent of employers with fewer than 200 workers.

The Kaiser/HRET survey indicates that 29 percent of all firms and 53 percent of large firms offered weight loss programs, while 30 percent and 64 percent, respectively, offered gym memberships or on-site exercise facilities. Meanwhile, 32 percent of all employers and 63 percent of large employers offered smoking cessation resources. Despite widespread availability, actual participation of employees in well-

ness programs remains limited. While no nationally representative data exist, a 2010 non-representative survey suggests that typically less than 20 percent of eligible employees participate in wellness interventions such as smoking cessation.[24]

Currently, insufficient broad-based evidence makes it difficult to definitively assess the impact of workplace wellness on health outcomes and cost. Yet, overall, employers largely report that workplace wellness programs are delivering on their intended benefit of improving health and reducing costs. According to the 2011 Kaiser/HRET survey, 65 percent of respondents that offered wellness programs stated that these programs improved employee health, and 53 percent believed that they reduced costs. Larger firms (defined as those with more than 200 workers in the Kaiser/HRET survey) were significantly more positive, as 74 percent affirmed that workplace wellness programs improved health and 65 percent said that it reduced cost, as opposed to 65 percent and 52 percent, respectively, among smaller firms.[25] Forty percent of respondents to a survey by Buck Consultants indicated that they had measured the impact of their wellness program on the growth trend of their health care costs, and of these, 45 percent reported a reduction in that growth trend. The majority of these employers, 61 percent, reported that the reduction in growth trend of their health care costs was between two and five percentage points per year.[26] There are numerous accounts of the positive impact of workplace wellness programs in many industries, regions, and types of employers. For example, a recent article published by the *Harvard Business Review* cited positive outcomes reported by private-sector employers along several different dimensions, including health care savings, reduced absenteeism, and employee satisfaction.[27]

Several studies that looked at the impact of smoking cessation programs found significantly higher quit rates or less tobacco use.[28] [29] Smoking cessation programs typically offered education and counseling to increase social support.[30] Two studies reported that individuals in the intervention group quit smoking at a rate approximately 10 percentage points higher than those in the control group, and another reported that participants were almost four times as likely as nonparticipants to reduce tobacco use.[31] [32] However, these effects should be interpreted with caution. One study showed significant differences in smoking rates at a one-month follow-up, but showed no significant differences in quit rates at six months, highlighting the importance of long-term follow-up to investigate the sustainability of results.[33]

While employer sponsors generally are satisfied with the results, more than half stated in a recent survey that they do not know their programs' return on investment.[34] The peer-reviewed literature, while predominantly positive, covers only a small proportion of the universe of programs, limiting the generalizability of the reported findings. Evaluating such complex interventions is difficult and poses substantial methodological challenges that can invalidate findings.

Overall, surveys suggest that a relatively small percentage of employers use incentives, dollar or otherwise, for wellness programs, although incentive use is more prevalent among larger employers. Data from the 2011 Kaiser/HRET Survey of Employer Health Benefits indicate that 14 percent of all employers offered cash, gift cards, merchandise, or travel as incentives for wellness program participation. Among large firms (greater than 200 workers), only 27 percent offered these kinds of incentives. Mercer Consulting's 2009 National Survey of Employer-Sponsored Health Plans found similar patterns, estimating that six

---

[22] On behalf of the Departments, RAND researchers did a review of the current literature on this topic. "A Review of the U.S. Workplace Wellness Market" February 2012. The report can be found at *http://www.dol.gov/ebsa/pdf/workplace wellnessmarketreview2012.pdf.*

[23] Kaiser Family Foundation, *Employer Health Benefits: 2011 Annual Survey.* 2011, The Kaiser Family Foundation, Menlo Park, CA; Health Research & Educational Trust, Chicago, IL.

[24] Nyce, S. *Boosting Wellness Participation Without Breaking the Bank.* TowersWatson Insider. July, 2010:1-9.

[25] Kaiser Family Foundation, Employer Health Benefits: 2010 Annual Survey. 2010, The Kaiser Family Foundation, Menlo Park, CA; Health Research & Educational Trust, Chicago, IL.

[26] Buck Consultants, Working Well: A Global Survey of Health Promotion and Workplace Wellness Strategies. 2010, Buck Consultants: San Francisco, CA.

[27] Berry, L., A. Mirabito, and W. Baun, What's the Hard Return on Employee Wellness Programs? Harvard Business Review, 2010. 88(12): p. 104.

[28] Heirich, M. and C.J. Sieck, Worksite cardiovascular wellness programs as a route to substance abuse prevention. J Occup Environ Med, 2000. 42(1): p. 47-56; 40; McMahon, S.D. and L.A. Jason, Social support in a worksite smoking intervention. A test of theoretical models. Behav Modif, 2000. 24(2): p. 184-201; Okechukwu, C.A., et al., MassBuilt: Effectiveness of an apprenticeship site-based smoking cessation intervention for unionized building trades workers. Cancer Causes Control, 2009. 20(6): p. 887-94; Sorensen, G., et al., A comprehensive worksite cancer prevention intervention: Behavior change results from a randomized controlled trial (United States). J Public Health Policy, 2003. 24(1): p. 5-25.

[29] Gold, D.B., D.R. Anderson, and S.A. Serxner, *Impact of a telephone-based intervention on the reduction of health risks.* Am J Health Promot, 2000. 15(2): p. 97-106; Herman, C.W., et al., *Effectiveness of an incentive-based online physical activity intervention on employee health status.* Journal of Occupational and Environmental Medicine, 2006. 48(9): p. 889-895; Ozminkowski, R.J., et al., *The impact of the Citibank, NA, health management program on changes in employee health risks over time.* J Occup Environ Med, 2000. 42(5): p. 502-11.

[30] Heirich, M. and C.J. Sieck, Worksite cardiovascular wellness programs as a route to substance abuse prevention. J Occup Environ Med, 2000. 42(1): p. 47-56; McMahon, S.D. and L.A. Jason, Social support in a worksite smoking intervention. A test of theoretical models. Behav Modif, 2000. 24(2): p. 184-201.

[31] Heirich, M. and C.J. Sieck, Worksite cardiovascular wellness programs as a route to substance abuse prevention. J Occup Environ Med, 2000. 42(1): p. 47-56; Okechukwu, C.A., et al., MassBuilt: Effectiveness of an apprenticeship site-based smoking cessation intervention for unionized building trades workers. Cancer Causes Control, 2009. 20(6): p. 887-94.

[32] In the study, 42% of participants reduced their risk for tobacco use. See Gold, D.B., D.R. Anderson, and S.A. Serxner, Impact of a telephone-based intervention on the reduction of health risks. Am J Health Promot, 2000. 15(2): p. 97-106.

[33] Kechukwu, C.A., et al., MassBuilt: Effectiveness of an apprenticeship site-based smoking cessation intervention for unionized building trades workers. Cancer Causes Control, 2009. 20(6): p. 887-94.

[34] Buck Consultants, Working Well: A Global Survey of Health Promotion and Workplace Wellness Strategies. 2010, Buck Consultants: San Francisco, CA.

percent of all firms and 21 percent of those with 500 or more employees provided financial incentives for participating in at least one program.[35] Employers are also looking to continue to add incentives to their wellness programs, for example 17 percent intend to add a reward or penalty based on tobacco-use status.[36] The use of incentives to promote employee engagement remains poorly understood, so it is not clear how type (e.g., cash or non-cash), direction (reward versus penalty), and strength of incentive are related to employee engagement and outcomes. The Health Enhancement Research Organization and associated organizations also recognized this deficiency and provided seven questions for future research.[37] There are also no data on potential unintended effects, such as discrimination against employees based on their health or health behaviors.

Currently, the most commonly incentivized program appears to be associated with completion of a health risk assessment. According to the 2009 Mercer survey, 10 percent of all firms and 23 percent of large employers that offered a health risk assessment provided an incentive for completing the assessment. For other types of health management programs that the survey assessed, only two to four percent of all employers and 13 to 19 percent of large employers offered incentives.[38] The 2011 Kaiser/HRET survey found that 10 percent of all employers and 42 percent of large firms that offered a health risk assessment provided a financial incentive to employees who completed it.

Incentives are offered in a variety of forms, such as cash, gift cards, merchandise, time off, awards, recognition, raffles or lotteries, reduced health plan premiums and co-pays, and contributions to flexible spending or health savings accounts. As noted previously, the Kaiser/HRET 2011 survey reported that among firms offering health benefits with more than 200 workers, 27 percent offered cash or cash equivalent incentives (including gift cards, merchandise, or travel incentives). In addition, 11 percent of these firms offered lower employee health plan premiums to wellness participants, two percent offered lower deductibles, and 11 percent offered higher health reimbursement account or health savings account contributions. Meanwhile, 13 percent of firms with fewer than 200 workers offered cash or equivalent incentives, and each of the other types of incentives were offered by only two percent or less of firms.

Cash and cash-equivalent incentives remain the most popular incentive for completion of a health risk assessment. The Kaiser/HRET 2011 survey reports that among employers incentivizing completion of a health risk assessment, 41 percent offered cash, gift cards, merchandise or travel, 23 percent allowed workers to pay a smaller proportion of premiums, 12 percent offered lower deductibles, and one percent offered lower coinsurance. Among large employers, 57 percent utilized cash incentives, 34 percent offered smaller premiums, six percent provided lower deductibles, and three percent provided lower coinsurance. Findings from Mercer's 2009 survey suggest similar trends, with five percent of all employers and ten percent of those with 500 or more workers providing cash incentives for completion of a health risk assessment; one percent and two percent, respectively, offering lower cost sharing; and two percent and seven percent, respectively, offering lower premium contributions.[39] Note that in the Mercer survey, the results cited reflect the incentives provided by all firms that offer a health risk assessment, while the Kaiser/HRET results previously mentioned reflect only firms that incentivize completion of a health risk assessment.

Incentives may be triggered by a range of different levels of employee engagement. The simplest incentives are triggered by program enrollment—that is, by merely signing up for a wellness program. At the next level, incentives are triggered by program participation—for instance, attending a class or initiating a program, such as a smoking cessation intervention. Other incentive programs may require completion of a program, whether or not any particular health-related goals are achieved, to earn an incentive. The health-contingent incentive programs require successfully meeting a specific health outcome (or an alternative standard) to trigger an incentive, such as verifiably quitting smoking. There is little representative data indicating the relative prevalence of these different types of triggers. The most common form of outcome-based incentives is reportedly awarded for smoking cessation. The 2010 survey by NBGH and TowersWatson indicated that while 25 percent of responding employers offered a financial incentive for employees to become tobacco-free, only four percent offered financial incentives for maintaining a BMI within target levels, three percent did so for maintaining blood pressure within targets, and three percent for maintaining targeted cholesterol levels.[40]

The value of incentives can vary widely. Estimates from representative surveys of the average value of incentives per year range between $152[41] and $557,[42] or between three and 11 percent of the $5,049 average cost of individual coverage in 2010,[43] among employees who receive them. This suggests that companies typically are not close to reaching the 20 percent of the total cost of coverage threshold set forth in the 2006 regulations. These findings indicate that based on currently available data, increasing the maximum reward for participating in a health-contingent wellness program to 30 percent (and the Departments' decision to propose an additional 20 percentage points for programs designed to prevent or reduce tobacco use) is unlikely to have a significant impact. Additionally, as discussed earlier in this preamble, today most incentive-based wellness programs are associated with completion of a health risk assessment irrespective of the results, and therefore are not subject to the limitation, because such programs are not health-contingent wellness programs.

The Departments lack sufficient information to assess how firms that currently are at the 20 percent limit will respond to the increased limits and welcome public comments regarding this issue. If firms already viewed the current 20 percent reward limit as sufficient, then the Departments would not expect that increasing the limit would provide an incentive for program design changes.

It is possible that the increased wellness program reward limits will incentivize firms without health-contingent wellness programs to establish them. The Departments, however, do not expect a significant number of new programs to be created as a result of this change because firms without health-contingent wellness programs could already have provided rewards up to the 20 percent limit before the enactment of the Affordable Care Act, but did not.

Two critical elements of these proposed regulations are (1) the standard that the reward under a health-contingent wellness program be available to all similarly situated individuals and (2) the standard that a program be reasonably designed to promote health or prevent disease.[44]

As discussed earlier in this preamble, the regulation does not prescribe a particular type of alternative standard that must be provided. Instead, it permits plan sponsors flexibility to provide any reasonable alternative. The Departments expect that plan sponsors will select alternatives that entail the minimum net costs (or, stated differently, the maximum net benefits) that are possible to achieve derive offsetting benefits, such as a higher smoking cessation success rate.

It seems reasonable to presume that the net cost plan sponsors will incur in the provision of alternatives, including transfers as well as new economic costs and benefits, will not exceed the transfer cost of waiving surcharges for all plan participants who qualify for alternatives. The Departments expect that many plan sponsors will find more cost effective ways to satisfy this requirement, should they exercise the option to provide incentives through a health-contingent wellness program and that the true net cost to them will therefore be much smaller than the transfer cost of waiving surcharges for all plan participants who qualify for alternatives. The Departments have no basis for estimating the magnitude of the cost of providing alternative standards or of potential offsetting benefits, however, and therefore solicit comments from the public on this question.

The Departments note that plan sponsors will have strong motivation to identify and provide alternative standards that have positive net economic effects. Plan sponsors will be disinclined to provide alternatives that undermine their overall wellness program and worsen behav-

---

[35] Mercer, National Survey of Employer-Sponsored Health Plans: 2009 Survey Report. 2010, Mercer.

[36] "Employer Survey on Purchasing Value in Health Care," 17th Annual Towers Watson/National Business Group on Health Employer Survey on Purchasing Value in Health Care.

[37] "Guidance for a Reasonably Designed, Employer-Sponsored Wellness Program Using Outcomes-Based Incentives," joint consensus statement of the Health Enhancement Research Organization, American College of Occupational and Environmental Medicine, American Cancer Society and American Cancer Society Cancer Action Network, American Diabetes Association, and American Heart Association.

[38] Mercer, National Survey of Employer-Sponsored Health Plans: 2009 Survey Report. 2010, Mercer.

[39] Mercer, National Survey of Employer-Sponsored Health Plans: 2009 Survey Report. 2010, Mercer.

[40] TowersWatson, Raising the Bar on Health Care: Moving Beyond Incremental Change.

[41] Mercer, *National Survey of Employer-Sponsored Health Plans: 2009 Survey Report.* 2010, Mercer.

[42] Linnan, L., et al., *Results of the 2004 national worksite health promotion survey.* American Journal of Public Health, 2008. 98(8): p. 1503-1509.

[43] Kaiser Family Foundation, *Employer Health Benefits: 2010 Annual Survey.*

[44] *See* section II.B, earlier in this preamble for a more detailed discussion of these requirements.

ioral and health outcomes, or that make financial rewards available absent meaningful efforts by participants to improve their health habits and overall health. Instead plan sponsors will be inclined to provide alternatives that sustain or reinforce plan participants' incentive to improve their health habits and overall health, and/or that help participants make such improvements. It therefore seems likely that gains in economic welfare from this requirement will equal or outweigh losses. The Departments intend that the requirement to provide reasonable alternatives will reduce instances where wellness programs serve only to shift costs to higher risk individuals and increase instances where programs succeed at helping high risk individuals improve their health. The Departments solicit comments on its assumption.

In considering the transfers that might derive from the availability of (and participants' satisfaction with) alternative means of qualifying for the reward, the transfers arising from this requirement may take the form of transfers to participants who satisfy new alternative wellness program standards from plan sponsors, to such participants from other participants, or some combination of these. The existence of a wellness program with a reward contingent on meeting a standard related to a health factor creates a transfer from those who do not meet the standard to those who do meet the standard. Allowing individuals to meet an alternative standard to receive the reward is a transfer to those who use the alternative standard from everyone else in the risk pool.

The reward associated with the wellness program is an incentive to encourage individuals to meet health standards associated with better or improved health, which in turn is associated with lower health care costs. If the rewards are effective, health care costs will be reduced as an individual's health improves. Some of these lower health care costs could translate into lower premiums paid by employers and employees, which could offset some of the transfers. To the extent larger rewards are more effective at improving health and lowering costs, these proposed regulations would produce more benefits than the current regulations.

Rewards also could create costs to individuals and to the extent the new larger rewards create more costs than smaller rewards, these proposed regulations could increase the costs relative to the existing regulations. To the extent an individual does not meet a standard or satisfy an alternative standard, they could face higher costs, for example in the case of a surcharge for smoking they could face up to a 50 percent increase in their premiums.

Based on the foregoing discussion, the Departments expect the benefits, costs, and transfers associated with these proposed regulations to be minimal. However, the Departments are not able to provide aggregate estimates, because they do not have sufficent data to estimate the number of plans that will take advantage of the new limits.

E. Regulatory Flexibility Act—Department of Labor and Department of Health and Human Services

The Regulatory Flexibility Act (5 U.S.C. 601 et seq.) (RFA) applies to most Federal rules that are subject to the notice and comment requirements of section 553(b) of the Administrative Procedure Act (5 U.S.C. 551 et seq.). Unless an agency certifies that such a rule will not have a significant economic impact on a substantial number of small entities, section 603 of the RFA requires the agency to present an initial regulatory flexibility analysis at the time of the publication of the notice of proposed rulemaking describing the impact of the rule on small entities. Small entities include small businesses, organizations and governmental jurisdictions.

For purposes of analysis under the RFA, the Departments propose to continue to consider a small entity to be an employee benefit plan with fewer than 100 participants. The basis of this definition is found in section 104(a)(3) of ERISA, which permits the Secretary of Labor to prescribe simplified annual reports for welfare benefit plans that cover fewer than 100 participants.[45]

Further, while some large employers may have small plans, in general, small employers maintain most small plans. Thus, the Departments believe that assessing the impact of these proposed regulations on small plans is an appropriate substitute for evaluating the effect on small entities.

The definition of small entity considered appropriate for this purpose differs, however, from a definition of small business that is based on size standards promulgated by the Small Business Administration

(SBA) (13 CFR 121.201) pursuant to the Small Business Act (15 U.S.C. 631 et seq.). The Departments therefore request comments on the appropriateness of the size standard used in evaluating the impact of these proposed regulations on small entities. The Departments have consulted with the SBA Office of Advocacy concerning use of this participant count standard for RFA purposes. See 13 CFR 121.902(b)(4).

The Departments expect that these proposed regulations will affect few small plans. While a large number of small plans offer a wellness program, the 2011 Kaiser/HRET survey reported that only 13 percent of employers with fewer than 200 employees had a wellness program that offered cash or cash equivalent incentives (including gift cards, merchandise, or travel incentives).[46] In addition, only two percent of these firms offered lower employee health plan premiums to wellness participants, one percent offered lower deductibles, and one percent offered higher health reimbursement account or health savings account contributions. Therefore, the Departments expect that few small plans will be affected by increasing the rewards threshold from 20 percent to 30 percent (50 percent for programs targeting tobacco use prevention or reduction), because a small percentage of plans have rewards-based wellness programs. Moreover, as discussed in the Economic Impacts section earlier in this preamble, few plans that offer rewards-based wellness programs come close to reaching the 20 percent limit, and most incentive-based wellness programs are associated with completing the health risk assessment irrespective of the results, which are not subject to the limitation.

The Kaiser/HRET survey also reports that about 88 percent of small plans had their wellness programs provided by the health plan provider. Industry experts indicated to the Departments that when wellness programs are offered by the health plan provider, they typically supply alternative education programs and offer them free of charge. This finding indicates that the requirement in the proposed rule for rewards-based wellness programs to provide and pay for a reasonable alternative standard for individuals for whom it is either unreasonably difficult or medically inadvisable to meet the original standard will impose little new costs or transfers to the affected plans.

Based on the foregoing, the Departments herby certify that these proposed regulations will not have a significant economic impact on a substantial number of small entities.

F. Paperwork Reduction Act—Department of Labor and Department of the Treasury

The 2006 final regulations regarding wellness programs did not include an information collection request (ICR). These proposed regulations, like the 2006 final regulations, provide that if a plan's wellness program requires individuals to meet a standard related to a health factor in order to qualify for a reward and if the plan materials describe this standard, the materials must also disclose the availability of other means of qualifying for the reward or the possibility of waiver of the otherwise applicable standard. If plan materials merely mention that a program is available, the disclosure relating to alternatives is not required. These proposed regulations include samples of disclosures that could be used to satisfy this requirement.

In concluding that these proposed regulations did not include an ICR, the Departments reasoned that much of the information required was likely already provided as a result of state and local requirements or the usual business practices of group health plans and group health insurance issuers in connection with the offer and promotion of health care coverage. In addition, the sample disclosures would enable group health plans to make any necessary modifications with minimal effort.

Finally, although the proposed regulations do not include an ICR, the regulations could be interpreted to require a revision to an existing collection of information. Administrators of group health plans covered under Title I of ERISA are generally required to make certain disclosures about the terms of a plan and material changes in terms through a Summary Plan Description (SPD) or Summary of Material Modifications (SMM) pursuant to sections 101(a) and 102(a) of ERISA and related regulations. The ICR related to the SPD and SMM is currently approved by OMB under OMB control number 1210-0039, which is currently scheduled to expire on April 30, 2013. While these materials may in some cases require revisions to comply with the proposed regulations, the associated burden is expected to be negligible, and is already accounted for in the SPD, SMM, and the ICR by a burden estimation methodology, which anticipates ongoing revisions. Based

---

[45] Under ERISA section 104(a)(2), the Secretary may also provide exemptions or simplified reporting and disclosure requirements for pension plans. Pursuant to the authority of ERISA section 104(a)(3), the Department of Labor has previously issued at 29 CFR 2520.104-20, 2520.104-21, 2520.104-41, 2520.104-46, and 2520.104b-10 certain simplified reporting provisions and limited exemptions from reporting and disclosure requirements

for small plans, including unfunded or insured welfare plans, that cover fewer than 100 participants and satisfy certain other requirements.

[46] Kaiser Family Foundation, *Employer Health Benefits: 2011 Annual Survey*. 2011, The Kaiser Family Foundation, Menlo Park, CA; Health Research & Educational Trust, Chicago, IL.

on the foregoing, the Departments do not expect that any change to the existing ICR arising from these proposed regulations will be substantive or material. Accordingly, the Departments have not filed an application for approval of a revision to the existing ICR with OMB in connection with these proposed regulations.

G. Paperwork Reduction Act—Department of Health and Human Services

Under the Paperwork Reduction Act of 1995, the Department is required to provide 60-day notice in the **Federal Register** and solicit public comment before a collection of information requirement is submitted to OMB for review and approval. In order to fairly evaluate whether an information collection should be approved by OMB, section 3506(c)(2)(A) of the Paperwork Reduction Act of 1995 requires the Department to solicit comment on the following issues:

• The need for the information collection and its usefulness in carrying out the proper functions of our agency.

• The accuracy of our estimate of the information collection burden.

• The quality, utility, and clarity of the information to be collected.

• Recommendations to minimize the information collection burden on the affected public, including automated techniques.

Section 146.121(f)(1)(iv) stipulates that the plan or issuer disclose in all plan materials describing the terms of the program the availability of a reasonable alternative standard to qualify for the reward under a wellness program. However, for plan materials that merely mention that a program is available, without describing its terms, the disclosure is not required. The burden associated with this requirement was previously approved under OMB control number 0938-0819. We are not seeking reinstatement of the information collection request under the aforementioned OMB control number, since we believe that much of the information required is likely already provided as a result of state and local requirements or the usual business practices of group health plans and group health insurance issuers in connection with the offer and promotion of health care coverage. In addition, the sample disclosures would enable group health plans to make any necessary modifications with minimal effort.

H. Special Analyses—Department of the Treasury

For purposes of the Department of the Treasury it has been determined that this notice of proposed rulemaking is not a significant regulatory action as defined in Executive Order 12866. Therefore, a regulatory assessment is not required. It has also been determined that section 553(b) of the Administrative Procedure Act (5 U.S.C. chapter 5) does not apply to these proposed regulations, and, because these proposed regulations do not impose a collection of information on small entities, a Regulatory Flexibility Analysis under the Regulatory Flexibility Act (5 U.S.C. chapter 6) is not required. Pursuant to section 7805(f) of the Code, this notice of proposed rulemaking has been submitted to the Small Business Administration for comment on its impact on small business.

I. Congressional Review Act

These proposed regulations are subject to the Congressional Review Act provisions of the Small Business Regulatory Enforcement Fairness Act of 1996 (5 U.S.C. 801 *et seq.*) and, if finalized, will be transmitted to Congress and the Comptroller General for review. These regulations do not constitute a "major rule," as that term is defined in 5 U.S.C. 804 because they are unlikely to result in (1) an annual effect on the economy of $100 million or more; (2) a major increase in costs or prices for consumers, individual industries, or federal, State or local government agencies, or geographic regions; or (3) significant adverse effects on competition, employment, investment, productivity, innovation, or on the ability of United States-based enterprises to compete with foreign-based enterprises in domestic or export markets.

J. Unfunded Mandates Reform Act

For purposes of the Unfunded Mandates Reform Act of 1995 (Pub. L. 104-4), as well as Executive Order 12875, these proposed regulations do not include any federal mandate that may result in expenditures by state, local, or tribal governments, nor does it include mandates which may impose an annual burden of $100 million, adjusted for inflation,[47] or more on the private sector.

K. Federalism Statement—Department of Labor and Department of Health and Human Services

Executive Order 13132 outlines fundamental principles of federalism, and requires the adherence to specific criteria by federal agencies in the process of their formulation and implementation of policies that have "substantial direct effects" on the States, the relationship between the national government and States, or on the distribution of power and responsibilities among the various levels of government. Federal agencies promulgating regulations that have these federalism implications must consult with State and local officials, and describe the extent of their consultation and the nature of the concerns of State and local officials in the preamble to the regulation.

In the Departments' view, these proposed regulations have federalism implications, however, in the Departments' view, the federalism implications of these final regulations are substantially mitigated because, with respect to health insurance issuers, the vast majority of States have enacted laws, which meet or exceed the federal HIPAA standards prohibiting discrimination based on health factors. Therefore, the regulations are not likely to require substantial additional oversight of States by the Department of HHS.

In general, through section 514, ERISA supersedes State laws to the extent that they relate to any covered employee benefit plan, and preserves State laws that regulate insurance, banking, or securities. While ERISA prohibits States from regulating a plan as an insurance or investment company or bank, HIPAA added a new preemption provision to ERISA (as well as to the PHS Act) narrowly preempting State requirements for group health insurance coverage. With respect to the HIPAA nondiscrimination provisions, States may continue to apply State law requirements except to the extent that such requirements prevent the application of the portability, access, and renewability requirements of HIPAA, which include HIPAA's nondiscrimination requirements provisions. HIPAA's Conference Report states that the conferees intended the narrowest preemption of State laws with regard to health insurance issuers (H.R. Conf. Rep. No. 736, 104th Cong. 2d Session 205, 1996). State insurance laws that are more stringent than the federal requirements are unlikely to "prevent the application of" the HIPAA nondiscrimination provisions, and therefore are not preempted. Accordingly, States have significant latitude to impose requirements on health insurance issuers that are more restrictive than the federal law.

Guidance conveying this interpretation was published in the **Federal Register** on April 8, 1997 (62 FR 16904) and on December 30, 2004 (69 FR 78720), and these proposed regulations clarify and implement the statute's minimum standards and do not significantly reduce the discretion given the States by the statute. Moreover, the Departments understand that the vast majority of States have requirements that meet or exceed the minimum requirements of the HIPAA nondiscrimination provisions.

HIPAA provides that the States may enforce the provisions of HIPAA as they pertain to issuers, but that the Secretary of HHS must enforce any provisions that a State chooses not to or fails to substantially enforce. When exercising its responsibility to enforce provisions of HIPAA, HHS works cooperatively with the State for the purpose of addressing the State's concerns and avoiding conflicts with the exercise of State authority.[48] HHS has developed procedures to implement its enforcement responsibilities, and to afford the States the maximum opportunity to enforce HIPAA's requirements in the first instance. In compliance with Executive Order 13132's requirement that agencies examine closely any policies that may have federalism implications or limit the policy making discretion of the States, DOL and HHS have engaged in numerous efforts to consult with and work cooperatively with affected State and local officials.

In conclusion, throughout the process of developing these regulations, to the extent feasible within the specific preemption provisions of HIPAA, the Departments have attempted to balance the States' interests in regulating health plans and health insurance issuers, and the rights of those individuals that Congress intended to protect through the enactment of HIPAA.

IV. Statutory Authority

The Department of the Treasury regulations are proposed to be adopted pursuant to the authority contained in sections 7805 and 9833 of the Code.

The Department of Labor regulations are proposed to be adopted pursuant to the authority contained in 29 U.S.C. 1027, 1059, 1135, 1161-1168, 1169, 1181-1183, 1181 note, 1185, 1185a, 1185b, 1185d, 1191, 1191a, 1191b, and 1191c; sec. 101(g), Public Law 104-191, 110 Stat. 1936; sec. 401(b), Public Law 105-200, 112 Stat. 645 (42 U.S.C. 651

---

[47] In 2012, that threshold level is approximately $139 million.

[48] This authority applies to insurance issued with respect to group health plans generally, including plans covering employees of church organizations. Thus, this discussion of federalism applies to all group health insurance coverage that is subject to the PHS Act, including those church plans that provide coverage through a health insurance issuer (but not to church plans that do not provide coverage through a health insurance issuer).

note); sec. 512(d), Public Law 110-343, 122 Stat. 3881; sec. 1001, 1201, and 1562(e), Public Law 111-148, 124 Stat. 119, as amended by Public Law 111-152, 124 Stat. 1029; Secretary of Labor's Order 3-2010, 75 FR 55354 (September 10, 2010).

The Department of Health and Human Services regulations are proposed to be adopted, with respect to 45 CFR part 146, pursuant to the authority contained in sections 2702 through 2705, 2711 through 2723, 2791, and 2792 of the PHS Act (42 U.S.C. 300gg-1 through 300gg-5, 300gg-11 through 300gg-23, 300gg-91, and 300gg-92) prior to the amendments made by the Affordable Care Act and sections 2701 through 2763, 2791, and 2792 of the Public Health Service Act (42 U.S.C. 300gg through 300gg-63, 300gg-91, and 300gg-92), as amended by the Affordable Care Act; with respect to 45 CFR part 147, pursuant to the authority contained in sections 2701 through 2763, 2791, and 2792 of the PHS Act (42 U.S.C. 300gg through 300gg-63, 300gg-91, and 300gg-92), as amended by the Affordable Care Act.

List of Subjects

26 CFR Part 54

Excise taxes, Health care, Health insurance, Pensions, Reporting and recordkeeping requirements.

29 CFR Part 2590

Continuation coverage, Disclosure, Employee benefit plans, Group health plans, Health care, Health insurance, Medical child support, Reporting and recordkeeping requirements.

45 CFR Parts 146 and 147

Health care, Health insurance, Reporting and recordkeeping requirements, and State regulation of health insurance.

Steven T. Miller,

Deputy Commissioner for Services and Enforcement, Internal Revenue Service.

Signed this 8th day of November, 2012.

Phyllis C. Borzi,

Assistant Secretary, Employee Benefits Security Administration, Department of Labor.

Dated: August 1, 2012.

Marilyn Tavenner,

Acting Administrator, Centers for Medicare & Medicaid Services.

Dated: August 7, 2012.

Kathleen Sebelius,

Secretary, Department of Health and Human Services.

Department of the Treasury

Internal Revenue Service

26 CFR Chapter I

Accordingly, 26 CFR part 54 is proposed to be amended as follows:

PART 54—PENSION EXCISE TAXES

Paragraph 1. The authority citation for Part 54 is amended by adding an entry for § 54.9815-2705 in numerical order to read in part as follows:

Authority: 26 U.S.C. 7805. * * * Section 54.9815-2705 also issued under 26 U.S.C. 9833.

Par. 2. In § 54.9802-1, paragraph (f) is revised to read as follows:

§ 54.9802-1 Prohibiting discrimination against participants and beneficiaries based on a health factor.

* * * * *

(f) *Nondiscriminatory wellness programs—in general.* A wellness program is a program of health promotion or disease prevention. Paragraphs (b)(2)(ii) and (c)(3) of this section provide exceptions to the general prohibitions against discrimination based on a health factor for plan provisions that vary benefits (including cost-sharing mechanisms) or the premium or contribution for similarly situated individuals in connection with a wellness program that satisfies the requirements of this paragraph (f). If a wellness program is a participatory wellness program, as defined in paragraph (f)(1) of this section, that paragraph also makes clear that the wellness program does not violate this section if participation in the program is made available to all similarly situated individuals. If a wellness program is a health-contingent wellness program, as defined in paragraph (f)(2) of this section, the wellness program does not violate this section if the requirements of paragraph

(f)(3) of this section are met. Except where expressly provided otherwise, references in this section to an individual obtaining a reward include both obtaining a reward (such as a premium discount or rebate, a waiver of all or part of a cost-sharing mechanism, an additional benefit, or any financial or other incentive) and avoiding a penalty (such as the absence of a premium surcharge, or other financial or nonfinancial disincentive). References in this section to a plan providing a reward include both providing a reward (such as a premium discount or rebate, a waiver of all or part of a cost-sharing mechanism, an additional benefit, or any financial or other incentive) and imposing a penalty (such as a surcharge or other financial or nonfinancial disincentive).

(1) *Participatory wellness programs defined.* If none of the conditions for obtaining a reward under a wellness program is based on an individual satisfying a standard that is related to a health factor (or if a wellness program does not provide a reward), the wellness program is a participatory wellness program and, if participation in the program is made available to all similarly situated individuals, does not violate this section. Examples of participatory wellness programs are:

(i) A program that reimburses all or part of the cost for membership in a fitness center.

(ii) A diagnostic testing program that provides a reward for participation and does not base any part of the reward on outcomes.

(iii) A program that encourages preventive care through the waiver of the copayment or deductible requirement under a group health plan for the costs of, for example, prenatal care or well-baby visits. (Note that, with respect to non-grandfathered plans, § 54.9815-2713T requires benefits for certain preventive health services without the imposition of cost sharing.) (iv) A program that reimburses employees for the costs of participating, or that otherwise provides a reward for participating, in a smoking cessation program without regard to whether the employee quits smoking.

(v) A program that provides a reward to employees for attending a monthly no-cost health education seminar.

(vi) A program that provides a reward to employees who complete a health risk assessment regarding current health status, without any further action (educational or otherwise) required by the employee with regard to the health issues identified as part of the assessment. (*See also* § 54.9802-3T for rules prohibiting collection of genetic information).

(2) *Health-contingent wellness programs defined.* If any of the conditions for obtaining a reward under a wellness program is based on an individual satisfying a standard that is related to a health factor, the wellness program is a health-contingent wellness program and the program is permissible under this section only if all of the requirements of paragraph (f)(3) of this section are satisfied. Examples of health-contingent wellness programs are:

(i) A program that imposes a premium surcharge based on tobacco use.

(ii) A program that uses a biometric screening or a health risk assessment to identify employees with specified medical conditions or risk factors (such as high cholesterol, high blood pressure, unhealthy body mass index, or high glucose level) and provides a reward to employees identified as within a normal or healthy range for biometrics (or at low risk for certain medical conditions), while requiring employees who are identified as outside the normal or healthy range (or at risk) to take additional steps (such as meeting with a health coach, taking a health or fitness course, adhering to a health improvement action plan, or complying with a health care provider's plan of care) to obtain the same reward.

(3) *Requirements for health-contingent wellness programs.* A health-contingent wellness program does not violate this section if all of the following requirements are satisfied:

(i) *Frequency of opportunity to qualify.* The program must give individuals eligible for the program the opportunity to qualify for the reward under the program at least once per year.

(ii) *Size of reward.* The reward for a health-contingent wellness program, together with the reward for other health-contingent wellness programs with respect to the plan, must not exceed the applicable percentage of the total cost of employee-only coverage under the plan, as defined in this paragraph (f)(3)(ii). However, if, in addition to employees, any class of dependents (such as spouses, or spouses and dependent children) may participate in the wellness program, the reward must not exceed the applicable percentage of the total cost of the coverage in which an employee and any dependents are enrolled. For purposes of this paragraph (f)(3)(ii), the cost of coverage is determined based on the total amount of employer and employee contributions for the benefit package under which the employee is (or the employee and any dependents are) receiving coverage.

(A) *Applicable percentage.* For purposes of this paragraph (f)(3)(ii), the applicable percentage is 30 percent, except that the applicable percentage is increased an additional 20 percentage points (to 50 percent) to the extent that the additional percentage is in connection with a program designed to prevent or reduce tobacco use.

(B) *Examples.* The rules of this paragraph (f)(3)(ii) are illustrated by the following examples:

Example 1. (i) *Facts.* An employer sponsors a group health plan. The annual premium for employee-only coverage is $6,000 (of which the employer pays $4,500 per year and the employee pays $1,500 per year). The plan offers employees a health-contingent wellness program focused on exercise, blood sugar, weight, cholesterol, and blood pressure. The reward for compliance is an annual premium rebate of $600.

(ii) *Conclusion.* In this *Example 1,* the program satisfies the requirements of this paragraph (f)(3)(ii) because the reward for the wellness program, $600, does not exceed 30 percent of the total annual cost of employee-only coverage, $1,800. ($6,000 = 30% = $1,800.)

Example 2. (i) *Facts.* Same facts as *Example 1,* except the wellness program is exclusively a tobacco prevention program. Employees who have used tobacco in the last 12 months and who are not enrolled in the plan's tobacco cessation program are charged a $1,000 premium surcharge (in addition to their employee contribution towards the coverage). (Those who participate in the plan's tobacco cessation program are not assessed the $1,000 surcharge.)

(ii) *Conclusion.* In this *Example 2,* the program satisfies the requirements of this paragraph (f)(3)(ii) because the reward for the wellness program (absence of a $1,000 surcharge), does not exceed 50 percent of the total annual cost of employee-only coverage, $3,000. ($6,000 × 50% = $3,000.)

Example 3. (i) *Facts.* Same facts as *Example 1,* except that, in addition to the $600 reward for compliance with the health-contingent wellness program, the plan also imposes an additional $2,000 tobacco premium surcharge on employees who have used tobacco in the last 12 months and who are not enrolled in the plan's tobacco cessation program. (Those who participate in the plan's tobacco cessation program are not assessed the $2,000 surcharge.)

(ii) *Conclusion.* In this *Example 3,* the program satisfies the requirements of this paragraph (f)(3)(ii) because both: The total of all rewards (including absence of a surcharge for participating in the tobacco program) is $2,600 ($600 + $2,000 = $2,600), which does not exceed 50 percent of the total annual cost of employee-only coverage ($3,000); and, tested separately, the $600 reward for the wellness program unrelated to tobacco use does not exceed 30 percent of the total annual cost of employee-only coverage, $1,800.

Example 4. (i) *Facts.* An employer sponsors a group health plan. The total annual premium for employee-only coverage (including both employer and employee contributions towards the coverage) is $5,000. The plan provides a $250 reward to employees who complete a health risk assessment, without regard to the health issues identified as part of the assessment. The plan also offers a Healthy Heart program, which is a health-contingent wellness program under paragraph (f)(2) of this section, with an opportunity to earn a $1,500 reward.

(ii) *Conclusion.* In this *Example 4,* the plan satisfies the requirements of this paragraph (f)(3)(ii). Even though the total reward for all wellness programs under the plan is $1,750 ($250 + $1,500 = $1,750, which exceeds 30 percent of the cost of the annual premium for employee-only coverage ($5,000 × 30% = $1,500)), only the reward offered for compliance with the health-contingent wellness program ($1,500) is taken into account in determining whether the rules of this paragraph (f)(3)(ii) are met. (The $250 reward is offered in connection with a participatory wellness program and therefore is not taken into account under this paragraph (f)(3)(ii)). The health-contingent wellness program offers a reward that does not exceed 30 percent of the total annual cost of employee-only coverage.

(iii) *Uniform availability and reasonable alternative standards.* The reward under the program must be available to all similarly situated individuals.

(A) Under this paragraph (f)(3)(iii), a reward under a program is not available to all similarly situated individuals for a period unless the program meets both of the following requirements:

(*1*) The program allows a reasonable alternative standard (or waiver of the otherwise applicable standard) for obtaining the reward for any individual for whom, for that period, it is unreasonably difficult due to a medical condition to satisfy the otherwise applicable standard; and

(*2*) The program allows a reasonable alternative standard (or waiver of the otherwise applicable standard) for obtaining the reward for any individual for whom, for that period, it is medically inadvisable to attempt to satisfy the otherwise applicable standard.

(B) While plans are not required to determine a particular alternative standard in advance of an individual's request for one, if an individual is described in either paragraph (f)(3)(iii)(A)(*1*) or (*2*) of this section, a reasonable alternative standard must be furnished by the plan upon the individual's request or the condition for obtaining the reward must be waived. All the facts and circumstances are taken into account in determining whether a plan has furnished a reasonable alternative standard, including but not limited to the following:

(*1*) If the reasonable alternative standard is completion of an educational program, the plan must make the educational program available instead of requiring an individual to find such a program unassisted, and may not require an individual to pay for the cost of the program.

(*2*) If the reasonable alternative standard is a diet program, plans are not required to pay for the cost of food but must pay any membership or participation fee.

(*3*) If the reasonable alternative standard is compliance with the recommendations of a medical professional who is an employee or agent of the plan, and an individual's personal physician states that the plan's recommendations are not medically appropriate for that individual, the plan must provide a reasonable alternative standard that accommodates the recommendations of the individual's personal physician with regard to medical appropriateness. Plans may impose standard cost sharing under the plan or coverage for medical items and services furnished pursuant to the physician's recommendations.

(C) If reasonable under the circumstances, a plan may seek verification, such as a statement from an individual's personal physician, that a health factor makes it unreasonably difficult for the individual to satisfy, or medically inadvisable for the individual to attempt to satisfy, the otherwise applicable standard. It would not be reasonable, for example, for a plan to seek verification of a claim that is obviously valid based on the nature of the individual's medical condition that is known to the plan. However, plans may seek verification in the case of claims for which it is reasonable to determine that medical judgment is required to evaluate the validity of the claim.

(iv) *Reasonable design.* The program must be reasonably designed to promote health or prevent disease. A program satisfies this standard if it has a reasonable chance of improving the health of, or preventing disease in, participating individuals and it is not overly burdensome, is not a subterfuge for discriminating based on a health factor, and is not highly suspect in the method chosen to promote health or prevent disease. This determination is based on all the relevant facts and circumstances. To the extent a plan's initial standard for obtaining a reward (including a portion of a reward) is based on the results of a measurement, test, or screening relating to a health factor (such as a biometric examination or a health risk assessment), the plan must make available to any individual who does not meet the standard based on the measurement, test, or screening a different, reasonable means of qualifying for the reward.

(v) *Notice of availability of other means of qualifying for the reward.* (A) The plan must disclose in all plan materials describing the terms of the program the availability of other means of qualifying for the reward or the possibility of waiver of the otherwise applicable standard. If plan materials merely mention that a program is available, without describing its terms, this disclosure is not required.

(B) The following language, or substantially similar language, can be used to satisfy the notice requirement of this paragraph (f)(3)(v): "Your health plan is committed to helping you achieve your best health status. Rewards for participating in a wellness program are available to all employees. If you think you might be unable to meet a standard for a reward under this wellness program, you might qualify for an opportunity to earn the same reward by different means. Contact us at [insert contact information] and we will work with you to find a wellness program with the same reward that is right for you in light of your health status." Additional sample language is provided in the examples of paragraph (f)(4) of this section.

(4) *Examples.* The rules of paragraphs (f)(3)(iii), (iv), and (v) of this section are illustrated by the following examples:

Example 1. (i) *Facts.* A group health plan provides a reward to individuals who participate in a reasonable specified walking program. If it is unreasonably difficult due to a medical condition for an individual to participate (or if it is medically inadvisable for an individual to participate), the plan will waive the walking program requirement and provide the reward. All materials describing the terms of the walking program disclose the availability of the waiver.

(ii) *Conclusion.* The program satisfies the requirements of paragraph (f)(3)(iii) of this section because the reward under the program is available to all similarly situated individuals because it accommodates individuals who cannot participate in the walking program due to a medical condition (or for whom it would be medically inadvisable to attempt to participate) by providing them the reward even if they do not participate in the walking program (that is, by waiving the condition). The program satisfies the requirements of paragraph (f)(3)(iv) of this section because the walking program is reasonably designed to promote health and prevent disease. Last, the plan complies with the disclosure requirement of paragraph (f)(3)(v) of this section. Thus, the plan satisfies paragraphs (f)(3)(iii), (iv), and (v) of this section.

Example 2. (i) *Facts.* A group health plan offers a reward to individuals who achieve a count under 200 on a cholesterol test. If a participant does not achieve the targeted cholesterol count, the plan will make available a different, reasonable means of qualifying for the reward. In addition, all plan materials describing the terms of the program include the following statement: "Your health plan wants to help you take charge of your health. Rewards are available to all employees who participate in our Cholesterol Awareness Wellness Program. If your cholesterol count is under 200, you will receive the reward. If not, you will still have an opportunity to qualify for the reward. We will work with you to find a Health Smart program that is right for you." Individual *D* is identified as having a cholesterol count above 200. The plan partners *D* with a nurse who makes recommendations regarding diet and exercise, with which it is not unreasonably difficult due to a medical condition of *D* or medically inadvisable for *D* to comply, and which is otherwise reasonably designed, based on all the relevant facts and circumstances. In addition, the plan makes available to all other individuals who do not meet the cholesterol standard a different, reasonable means of qualifying for the reward which is not unreasonably burdensome or impractical. *D* will qualify for the discount if *D* follows the recommendations regardless of whether *D* achieves a cholesterol count that is under 200.

(ii) *Conclusion.* In this *Example 2,* the program satisfies the requirements of paragraphs (f)(3)(iii), (iv), and (v) of this section. The program's initial standard for obtaining a reward is dependent on the results of a cholesterol screening, which is related to a health factor. However, the program is reasonably designed under paragraphs (f)(3)(iii) and (iv) of this section because the plan makes available to all individuals who do not meet the cholesterol standard a different, reasonable means of qualifying for the reward and because the program is otherwise reasonably designed based on all the relevant facts and circumstances. The plan also discloses in all materials describing the terms of the program the opportunity to qualify for the reward through other means. Thus, the program satisfies paragraphs (f)(3)(iii), (iv), and (v) of this section.

Example 3. (i) *Facts.* Same facts as *Example 2,* except that, following diet and exercise, *D* again fails to achieve a cholesterol count that is under 200, and the program requires *D* to visit a doctor and follow any additional recommendations of *D'* s doctor with respect to *D'* s cholesterol. The program permits *D* to select *D'* s own doctor for this purpose. *D* visits *D'* s doctor, who determines *D* should take a prescription medication for cholesterol. In addition, the doctor determines that *D* must be monitored through periodic blood tests to continually reevaluate *D'* s health status. The plan accommodates *D* by making the discount available to *D,* but only if *D* actually follows the advice of *D'* s doctor's regarding medication and blood tests.

(ii) *Conclusion.* In this *Example 3,* the program's requirements to follow up with, and follow the recommendations of, *D'* s doctor do not make the program unreasonable under paragraph (f)(3)(iii) or (iv) of this section. The program continues to satisfy the conditions of paragraph (f)(3)(iii), (iv), and (v) of this section.

Example 4. (i) *Facts.* A group health plan will provide a reward to participants who have a body mass index (BMI) that is 26 or lower, determined shortly before the beginning of the year. Any participant who does not meet the target BMI is given the same discount if the participant complies with an exercise program that consists of walking 150 minutes a week. Any participant for whom it is unreasonably difficult due to a medical condition to comply with this walking program (and any participant for whom it is medically inadvisable to attempt to comply with the walking program) during the year is given the same discount if the individual satisfies an alternative standard that is reasonable taking into consideration the individual's medical situation, is not unreasonably burdensome or impractical to comply with,

and is otherwise reasonably designed based on all the relevant facts and circumstances. All plan materials describing the terms of the wellness program include the following statement: "Fitness is Easy! Start Walking! Your health plan cares about your health. If you are overweight, our Start Walking program will help you lose weight and feel better. We will help you enroll. (** If your doctor says that walking isn't right for you, that's okay too. We will develop a wellness program that is.)" Individual is unable to achieve a BMI that is 26 or lower within the plan's timeframe and is also not reasonably able to comply with the walking program. *E* proposes a program based on the recommendations of *E'* s physician. The plan agrees to make the discount available to *E,* but only if *E* actually follows the physician's recommendations.

(ii) *Conclusion.* In this *Example 4,* the program satisfies the requirements of paragraphs (f)(3)(iii), (iv), and (v) of this section. The program's initial standard for obtaining a reward is dependent on the results of a BMI screening, which is related to a health factor. However, the plan complies with the requirements of paragraph (f)(3)(iv) of this section because it makes available to all individuals who do not satisfy the BMI standard a different reasonable means of qualifying for the reward (a walking program that is not unreasonably burdensome or impractical for individuals to comply with and that is otherwise reasonably designed based on all the relevant facts and circumstances). In addition, the plan complies with the requirements of paragraph (f)(3)(iii) of this section because, if there are individuals for whom it is unreasonably difficult due to a medical condition to comply, or for whom it is medically inadvisable to attempt to comply, with the walking program, the plan provides a reasonable alternative to those individuals. Moreover, the plan satisfies the requirements of paragraph (f)(3)(v) of this section because it discloses, in all materials describing the terms of the program, the availability of other means of qualifying for the reward or the possibility of waiver of the otherwise applicable standard. Thus, the plan satisfies paragraphs (f)(3)(iii), (iv), and (v) of this section.

Example 5. (i) *Facts.* In conjunction with an annual open enrollment period, a group health plan provides a premium differential based on tobacco use, determined using a health risk assessment. The following statement is included in all plan materials describing the tobacco premium differential: "Stop smoking today! We can help! If you are a smoker, we offer a smoking cessation program. If you complete the program, you can avoid this surcharge." The plan accommodates participants who smoke by facilitating their enrollment in a smoking cessation program that requires participation at a time and place that are not unreasonably burdensome or impractical for participants, and that is otherwise reasonably designed based on all the relevant facts and circumstances. The plan pays the cost of the program. Any participant can avoid the surcharge by participating in the program, regardless of whether the participant stops smoking.

(ii) *Conclusion.* In this *Example 5,* the premium differential satisfies the requirements of paragraphs (f)(3)(iii), (iv), and (v) of this section. The program's initial standard for obtaining a reward is dependent on the results of a health risk assessment, which is a screening. However, the plan is reasonably designed under paragraph (f)(3)(iv) because the plan provides a different, reasonable means of qualifying for the reward to all tobacco users. The plan discloses, in all materials describing the terms of the program, the availability of other means of qualifying for the reward. Thus, the plan satisfies paragraphs (f)(3)(iii), (iv), and (v) of this section.

Example 6. (i) *Facts.* Same facts as *Example 5,* except the plan does not facilitate *F'* s enrollment in any program. Instead the plan advises *F* to find a program, pay for it, and provide a certificate of completion to the plan.

(ii) *Conclusion.* In this *Example 6,* the requirement for *F* to find and pay for *F'* s own smoking cessation program means that the alternative program is not reasonable. Accordingly, the plan has not offered a reasonable alternative standard that complies with paragraphs (f)(3)(iii) and (iv) of this section and the premium differential violates paragraph (c) of this section.

* * * * *

Par. 3. Section 54.9815-2705 is added to read as follows:

§ 54.9815-2705 Prohibiting discrimination against participants and beneficiaries based on a health factor.

(a) *In general.* A group health plan and a health insurance issuer offering group health insurance coverage must comply with the requirements of § 54.9802-1. Accordingly, with respect to health insurance issuers offering group health insurance coverage, the issuer is subject to the requirements of § 54.9802-1 to the same extent as a group health plan.

(b) *Applicability date.* This section is applicable to group health plans and health insurance issuers offering group health insurance coverage for plan years beginning on or after January 1, 2014. *See* §54.9815-1251T, which provides that the rules of this section do not apply to grandfathered health plans.

Department of Labor

Employee Benefits Security Administration

29 CFR Chapter XXV

29 CFR Part 2590 is proposed to be amended as follows:

PART 2590—RULES AND REGULATIONS FOR GROUP HEALTH PLANS

1. The authority citation for Part 2590 continues to read as follows:

Authority: 29 U.S.C. 1027, 1059, 1135, 1161-1168, 1169, 1181-1183, 1181 note, 1185, 1185a, 1185b, 1185d, 1191, 1191a, 1191b, and 1191c; sec. 101(g), Pub. L. 104-191, 110 Stat. 1936; sec. 401(b), Pub. L. 105-200, 112 Stat. 645 (42 U.S.C. 651 note); sec. 12(d), Pub. L. 110-343, 122 Stat. 3881; sec. 1001, 1201, and 1562(e), Pub. L. 111-148, 124 Stat. 119, as amended by Pub. L. 111-152, 124 Stat. 1029; Secretary of Labor's Order 3-2010, 75 FR 55354 (September 10, 2010).

Subpart B—Health Coverage Portability, Nondiscrimination, and Renewability

2. Section 2590.702 is amended by revising paragraph (f) to read as follows:

§2590.702 Prohibiting discrimination against participants and beneficiaries based on a health factor.

* * * * *

(f) *Nondiscriminatory wellness programs—in general.* A wellness program is a program of health promotion or disease prevention. Paragraphs (b)(2)(ii) and (c)(3) of this section provide exceptions to the general prohibitions against discrimination based on a health factor for plan provisions that vary benefits (including cost-sharing mechanisms) or the premium or contribution for similarly situated individuals in connection with a wellness program that satisfies the requirements of this paragraph (f). If a wellness program is a participatory wellness program, as defined in paragraph (f)(1) of this section, that paragraph also makes clear that the wellness program does not violate this section if participation in the program is made available to all similarly situated individuals. If a wellness program is a health-contingent wellness program, as defined in paragraph (f)(2) of this section, the wellness program does not violate this section if the requirements of paragraph (f)(3) of this section are met. Except where expressly provided otherwise, references in this section to an individual obtaining a reward include both obtaining a reward (such as a premium discount or rebate, a waiver of all or part of a cost-sharing mechanism, an additional benefit, or any financial or other incentive) and avoiding a penalty (such as the absence of a premium surcharge, or other financial or nonfinancial disincentive). References in this section to a plan providing a reward include both providing a reward (such as a premium discount or rebate, a waiver of all or part of a cost-sharing mechanism, an additional benefit, or any financial or other incentive) and imposing a penalty (such as a surcharge or other financial or nonfinancial disincentive).

(1) *Participatory wellness programs defined.* If none of the conditions for obtaining a reward under a wellness program is based on an individual satisfying a standard that is related to a health factor (or if a wellness program does not provide a reward), the wellness program is a participatory wellness program and, if participation in the program is made available to all similarly situated individuals, does not violate this section. Examples of participatory wellness programs are:

(i) A program that reimburses all or part of the cost for membership in a fitness center.

(ii) A diagnostic testing program that provides a reward for participation and does not base any part of the reward on outcomes.

(iii) A program that encourages preventive care through the waiver of the copayment or deductible requirement under a group health plan for the costs of, for example, prenatal care or well-baby visits. (Note that, with respect to non-grandfathered plans, section 2590.715-2713 of this Part requires benefits for certain preventive health services without the imposition of cost sharing.)

(iv) A program that reimburses employees for the costs of participating, or that otherwise provides a reward for participating, in a smoking cessation program without regard to whether the employee quits smoking.

(v) A program that provides a reward to employees for attending a monthly no-cost health education seminar.

(vi) A program that provides a reward to employees who complete a health risk assessment regarding current health status, without any further action (educational or otherwise) required by the employee with regard to the health issues identified as part of the assessment. (*See also* §2590.702-1 for rules prohibiting collection of genetic information).

(2) *Health-contingent wellness programs defined.* If any of the conditions for obtaining a reward under a wellness program is based on an individual satisfying a standard that is related to a health factor, the wellness program is a health-contingent wellness program and the program is permissible under this section only if all of the requirements of paragraph (f)(3) of this section are satisfied. Examples of health-contingent wellness programs are:

(i) A program that imposes a premium surcharge based on tobacco use.

(ii) A program that uses a biometric screening or a health risk assessment to identify employees with specified medical conditions or risk factors (such as high cholesterol, high blood pressure, unhealthy body mass index, or high glucose level) and provides a reward to employees identified as within a normal or healthy range for biometrics (or at low risk for certain medical conditions), while requiring employees who are identified as outside the normal or healthy range (or at risk) to take additional steps (such as meeting with a health coach, taking a health or fitness course, adhering to a health improvement action plan, or complying with a health care provider's plan of care) to obtain the same reward.

(3) *Requirements for health-contingent wellness programs.* A health-contingent wellness program does not violate this section if all of the following requirements are satisfied:

(i) *Frequency of opportunity to qualify.* The program must give individuals eligible for the program the opportunity to qualify for the reward under the program at least once per year.

(ii) *Size of reward.* The reward for a health-contingent wellness program, together with the reward for other health-contingent wellness programs with respect to the plan, must not exceed the applicable percentage of the total cost of employee-only coverage under the plan, as defined in this paragraph (f)(3)(ii). However, if, in addition to employees, any class of dependents (such as spouses, or spouses and dependent children) may participate in the wellness program, the reward must not exceed the applicable percentage of the total cost of the coverage in which an employee and any dependents are enrolled. For purposes of this paragraph (f)(3)(ii), the cost of coverage is determined based on the total amount of employer and employee contributions for the benefit package under which the employee is (or the employee and any dependents are) receiving coverage.

(A) *Applicable percentage.* For purposes of this paragraph (f)(3)(ii), the applicable percentage is 30 percent, except that the applicable percentage is increased an additional 20 percentage points (to 50 percent) to the extent that the additional percentage is in connection with a program designed to prevent or reduce tobacco use.

(B) *Examples.* The rules of this paragraph (f)(3)(ii) are illustrated by the following examples:

Example 1. (i) *Facts.* An employer sponsors a group health plan. The annual premium for employee-only coverage is $6,000 (of which the employer pays $4,500 per year and the employee pays $1,500 per year). The plan offers employees a health-contingent wellness program focused on exercise, blood sugar, weight, cholesterol, and blood pressure. The reward for compliance is an annual premium rebate of $600.

(ii) *Conclusion.* In this *Example 1,* the program satisfies the requirements of this paragraph (f)(3)(ii) because the reward for the wellness program, $600, does not exceed 30 percent of the total annual cost of employee-only coverage, $1,800. ($6,000 × 30% = $1,800.)

Example 2. (i) *Facts.* Same facts as *Example 1,* except the wellness program is exclusively a tobacco prevention program. Employees who have used tobacco in the last 12 months and who are not enrolled in the plan's tobacco cessation program are charged a $1,000 premium surcharge (in addition to their employee contribution towards the coverage). (Those who participate in the plan's tobacco cessation program are not assessed the $1,000 surcharge.)

(ii) *Conclusion.* In this *Example 2,* the program satisfies the requirements of this paragraph (f)(3)(ii) because the reward for the wellness program (absence of a $1,000 surcharge), does not exceed 50 percent of the total annual cost of employee-only coverage, $3,000. ($6,000 × 50% = $3,000.)

Example 3. (i) *Facts.* Same facts as *Example 1,* except that, in addition to the $600 reward for compliance with the health-contingent wellness program, the plan also imposes an additional $2,000 tobacco premium surcharge on employees who have used tobacco in the last 12 months and who are not enrolled in the plan's tobacco cessation program. (Those who participate in the plan's tobacco cessation program are not assessed the $2,000 surcharge.)

(ii) *Conclusion.* In this *Example 3,* the program satisfies the requirements of this paragraph (f)(3)(ii) because: Both the total of all rewards (including absence of a surcharge for participating in the tobacco program) is $2,600 ($600 + $2,000 = $2,600), which does not exceed 50 percent of the total annual cost of employee-only coverage ($3,000); and, tested separately, the $600 reward for the wellness program unrelated to tobacco use does not exceed 30 percent of the total annual cost of employee-only coverage, $1,800.

Example 4. (i) *Facts.* An employer sponsors a group health plan. The total annual premium for employee-only coverage (including both employer and employee contributions towards the coverage) is $5,000. The plan provides a $250 reward to employees who complete a health risk assessment, without regard to the health issues identified as part of the assessment. The plan also offers a Healthy Heart program, which is a health-contingent wellness program under paragraph (f)(2) of this section, with an opportunity to earn a $1,500 reward.

(ii) *Conclusion.* In this *Example 4,* the plan satisfies the requirements of this paragraph (f)(3)(ii). Even though the total reward for all wellness programs under the plan is $1,750 ($250 + $1,500 = $1,750, which exceeds 30 percent of the cost of the annual premium for employee-only coverage ($5,000 × 30% = $1,500)), only the reward offered for compliance with the health-contingent wellness program ($1,500) is taken into account in determining whether the rules of this paragraph (f)(3)(ii) are met. (The $250 reward is offered in connection with a participatory wellness program and therefore is not taken into account under this paragraph (f)(3)(ii)). The health-contingent wellness program offers a reward that does not exceed 30 percent of the total annual cost of employee-only coverage.

(iii) *Uniform availability and reasonable alternative standards.* The reward under the program must be available to all similarly situated individuals.

(A) Under this paragraph (f)(3)(iii), a reward under a program is not available to all similarly situated individuals for a period unless the program meets both of the following requirements:

(*1*) The program allows a reasonable alternative standard (or waiver of the otherwise applicable standard) for obtaining the reward for any individual for whom, for that period, it is unreasonably difficult due to a medical condition to satisfy the otherwise applicable standard; and

(*2*) The program allows a reasonable alternative standard (or waiver of the otherwise applicable standard) for obtaining the reward for any individual for whom, for that period, it is medically inadvisable to attempt to satisfy the otherwise applicable standard.

(B) While plans and issuers are not required to determine a particular alternative standard in advance of an individual's request for one, if an individual is described in either paragraph (f)(3)(iii)(A)(*1*) or (*2*) of this section, a reasonable alternative standard must be furnished by the plan or issuer upon the individual's request or the condition for obtaining the reward must be waived. All the facts and circumstances are taken into account in determining whether a plan or issuer has furnished a reasonable alternative standard, including but not limited to the following:

(*1*) If the reasonable alternative standard is completion of an educational program, the plan or issuer must make the educational program available instead of requiring an individual to find such a program unassisted, and may not require an individual to pay for the cost of the program.

(*2*) If the reasonable alternative standard is a diet program, plans and issuers are not required to pay for the cost of food but must pay any membership or participation fee.

(*3*) If the reasonable alternative standard is compliance with the recommendations of a medical professional who is an employee or agent of the plan or issuer, and an individual's personal physician states that the plan's recommendations are not medically appropriate for that individual, the plan or issuer must provide a reasonable alternative standard that accommodates the recommendations of the individual's personal physician with regard to medical appropriateness. Plans and issuers may impose standard cost sharing under the plan or coverage for medical items and services furnished pursuant to the physician's recommendations.

(C) If reasonable under the circumstances, a plan or issuer may seek verification, such as a statement from an individual's personal physician, that a health factor makes it unreasonably difficult for the individual to satisfy, or medically inadvisable for the individual to attempt to satisfy, the otherwise applicable standard. It would not be reasonable, for example, for a plan and issuer to seek verification of a claim that is obviously valid based on the nature of the individual's medical condition that is known to the plan or issuer. However, plans and issuers may seek verification in the case of claims for which it is reasonable to determine that medical judgment is required to evaluate the validity of the claim.

(iv) *Reasonable design.* The program must be reasonably designed to promote health or prevent disease. A program satisfies this standard if it has a reasonable chance of improving the health of, or preventing disease in, participating individuals and it is not overly burdensome, is not a subterfuge for discriminating based on a health factor, and is not highly suspect in the method chosen to promote health or prevent disease. This determination is based on all the relevant facts and circumstances. To the extent a plan's initial standard for obtaining a reward (including a portion of a reward) is based on the results of a measurement, test, or screening relating to a health factor (such as a biometric examination or a health risk assessment), the plan must make available to any individual who does not meet the standard based on the measurement, test, or screening a different, reasonable means of qualifying for the reward.

(v) *Notice of availability of other means of qualifying for the reward.* (A) The plan or issuer must disclose in all plan materials describing the terms of the program the availability of other means of qualifying for the reward or the possibility of waiver of the otherwise applicable standard. If plan materials merely mention that a program is available, without describing its terms, this disclosure is not required.

(B) The following language, or substantially similar language, can be used to satisfy the notice requirement of this paragraph (f)(3)(v): "Your health plan is committed to helping you achieve your best health status. Rewards for participating in a wellness program are available to all employees. If you think you might be unable to meet a standard for a reward under this wellness program, you might qualify for an opportunity to earn the same reward by different means. Contact us at [insert contact information] and we will work with you to find a wellness program with the same reward that is right for you in light of your health status." Additional sample language is provided in the examples of paragraph (f)(4) of this section.

(4) *Examples.* The rules of paragraphs (f)(3)(iii), (iv), and (v) of this section are illustrated by the following examples:

Example 1. (i) *Facts.* A group health plan provides a reward to individuals who participate in a reasonable specified walking program. If it is unreasonably difficult due to a medical condition for an individual to participate (or if it is medically inadvisable for an individual to participate), the plan will waive the walking program requirement and provide the reward. All materials describing the terms of the walking program disclose the availability of the waiver.

(ii) *Conclusion.* The program satisfies the requirements of paragraph (f)(3)(iii) of this section because the reward under the program is available to all similarly situated individuals because it accommodates individuals who cannot participate in the walking program due to a medical condition (or for whom it would be medically inadvisable to attempt to participate) by providing them the reward even if they do not participate in the walking program (that is, by waiving the condition). The program satisfies the requirements of paragraph (f)(3)(iv) of this section because the walking program is reasonably designed to promote health and prevent disease. Last, the plan complies with the disclosure requirement of paragraph (f)(3)(v) of this section. Thus, the plan satisfies paragraphs (f)(3)(iii), (iv), and (v) of this section.

Example 2. (i) *Facts.* A group health plan offers a reward to individuals who achieve a count under 200 on a cholesterol test. If a participant does not achieve the targeted cholesterol count, the plan will make available a different, reasonable means of qualifying for the reward. In addition, all plan materials describing the terms of the program include the following statement: "Your health plan wants to help you take charge of your health. Rewards are available to all employees who participate in our Cholesterol Awareness Wellness Program. If your cholesterol count is under 200, you will receive the reward. If not, you will still have an opportunity to qualify for the reward. We will work with you to find a Health Smart program that is right for you." Individual *D* is identified as having a cholesterol count above 200. The plan partners *D* with a nurse who makes recommendations regarding diet and exercise, with which it is not unreasonably difficult due to a medical condition of *D* or medically inadvisable for *D* to comply, and which is otherwise reasonably designed, based on all the relevant facts and circumstances. In addition, the plan makes available to all other individuals who do not meet the cholesterol standard a different, reasonable means of qualifying for the reward which is not unreasonably burdensome or impractical. *D* will qualify for the discount if *D* follows the recommendations regardless of whether *D* achieves a cholesterol count that is under 200.

(ii) *Conclusion.* In this *Example 2,* the program satisfies the requirements of paragraphs (f)(3)(iii), (iv), and (v) of this section. The program's initial standard for obtaining a reward is dependent on the results of a cholesterol screening, which is related to a health factor. However, the program is reasonably designed under paragraphs (f)(3)(iii) and (iv) of this section because the plan makes available to all individuals who do not meet the cholesterol standard a different, reasonable means of qualifying for the reward and because the program is otherwise reasonably designed based on all the relevant facts and circumstances. The plan also discloses in all materials describing the terms of the program the opportunity to qualify for the reward through other means. Thus, the program satisfies paragraphs (f)(3)(iii), (iv), and (v) of this section.

Example 3. (i) *Facts.* Same facts as *Example 2,* except that, following diet and exercise, *D* again fails to achieve a cholesterol count that is under 200, and the program requires *D* to visit a doctor and follow any additional recommendations of *D's* doctor with respect to *D's* cholesterol. The program permits *D* to select *D's* own doctor for this purpose. *D* visits *D's* doctor, who determines *D* should take a prescription medication for cholesterol. In addition, the doctor determines that *D* must be monitored through periodic blood tests to continually reevaluate *D's* health status. The plan accommodates *D* by making the discount available to *D,* but only if *D* actually follows the advice of *D's* doctor's regarding medication and blood tests.

(ii) *Conclusion.* In this *Example 3,* the program's requirements to follow up with, and follow the recommendations of, *D's* doctor do not make the program unreasonable under paragraphs (f)(3)(iii) or (iv) of this section. The program continues to satisfy the conditions of paragraphs (f)(3)(iii), (iv), and (v) of this section.

Example 4. (i) *Facts.* A group health plan will provide a reward to participants who have a body mass index (BMI) that is 26 or lower, determined shortly before the beginning of the year. Any participant who does not meet the target BMI is given the same discount if the participant complies with an exercise program that consists of walking 150 minutes a week. Any participant for whom it is unreasonably difficult due to a medical condition to comply with this walking program (and any participant for whom it is medically inadvisable to attempt to comply with the walking program) during the year is given the same discount if the individual satisfies an alternative standard that is reasonable taking into consideration the individual's medical situation, is not unreasonably burdensome or impractical to comply with, and is otherwise reasonably designed based on all the relevant facts and circumstances. All plan materials describing the terms of the wellness program include the following statement: "Fitness is Easy! Start Walking! Your health plan cares about your health. If you are overweight, our Start Walking program will help you lose weight and feel better. We will help you enroll. (**If your doctor says that walking isn't right for you, that's okay too. We will develop a wellness program that is.)" Individual *E* is unable to achieve a BMI that is 26 or lower within the plan's timeframe and is also not reasonably able to comply with the walking program. *E* proposes a program based on the recommendations of *E's* physician. The plan agrees to make the discount available to *E,* but only if *E* actually follows the physician's recommendations.

(ii) *Conclusion.* In this *Example 4,* the program satisfies the requirements of paragraphs (f)(3)(iii), (iv), and (v) of this section. The program's initial standard for obtaining a reward is dependent on the results of a BMI screening, which is related to a health factor. However, the plan complies with the requirements of paragraph (f)(3)(iv) of this section because it makes available to all individuals who do not satisfy the BMI standard a different reasonable means of qualifying for the reward (a walking program that is not unreasonably burdensome or impractical for individuals to comply with and that is otherwise reasonably designed based on all the relevant facts and circumstances). In addition, the plan complies with the requirements of paragraph (f)(3)(iii) of this section because, if there are individuals for whom it is unreasonably difficult due to a medical condition to comply, or for whom it is medically inadvisable to attempt to comply, with the walking program, the plan provides a reasonable alternative to those individuals. Moreover, the plan satisfies the requirements of paragraph (f)(3)(v) of this section because it discloses, in all materials describing the terms of the program, the availability of other means of qualifying for the reward or the possibility of waiver of the otherwise applicable standard. Thus, the plan satisfies paragraphs (f)(3)(iii), (iv), and (v) of this section.

Example 5. (i) *Facts.* In conjunction with an annual open enrollment period, a group health plan provides a premium differential based on tobacco use, determined using a health risk assessment. The following statement is included in all plan materials describing the tobacco premium differential: "Stop smoking today! We can help! If you are a smoker, we offer a smoking cessation program. If you complete the program, you can avoid this surcharge." The plan accommodates participants who smoke by facilitating their enrollment in a smoking cessation program that requires participation at a time and place that are not unreasonably burdensome or impractical for participants, and that is otherwise reasonably designed based on all the relevant facts and circumstances. The plan pays the cost of the program. Any participant can avoid the surcharge by participating in the program, regardless of whether the participant stops smoking.

(ii) *Conclusion.* In this *Example 5,* the premium differential satisfies the requirements of paragraphs (f)(3)(iii), (iv), and (v) of this section. The program's initial standard for obtaining a reward is dependent on the results of a health risk assessment, which is a screening. However, the plan is reasonably designed under paragraph (f)(3)(iv) because the plan provides a different, reasonable means of qualifying for the reward to all tobacco users. The plan discloses, in all materials describing the terms of the program, the availability of other means of qualifying for the reward. Thus, the plan satisfies paragraphs (f)(3)(iii), (iv), and (v) of this section.

Example 6. (i) *Facts.* Same facts as *Example 5,* except the plan does not facilitate *F's* enrollment in any program. Instead the plan advises *F* to find a program, pay for it, and provide a certificate of completion to the plan.

(ii) *Conclusion.* In this *Example 6,* the requirement for *F* to find and pay for *F's* own smoking cessation program means that the alternative program is not reasonable. Accordingly, the plan has not offered a reasonable alternative standard that complies with paragraphs (f)(3)(iii) and (iv) of this section and the premium differential violates paragraph (c) of this section.

* * * * *

Subpart C—Other Requirements

3. Section 2590.715-2705 is added to read as follows:

§2590.715-2705 Prohibiting discrimination against participants and beneficiaries based on a health factor.

(a) *In general.* A group health plan and a health insurance issuer offering group health insurance coverage must comply with the requirements of § 2590.702.

(b) *Applicability date.* This section is applicable to group health plans and health insurance issuers offering group health insurance coverage for plan years beginning on or after January 1, 2014. *See* § 2590.715-1251, which provides that the rules of this section do not apply to grandfathered health plans.

* * * * *

[FR Doc. 2012-28361 Filed 11-20-12; 11:15 am]

BILLING CODE 4830-01-P; 4510-029-P; 4120-01-P

¶ 20,263I

IRS: Employee health coverage: Applicable large employers: Shared responsibility.—The IRS has released proposed regulations that provide guidance under Code Sec. 4980H with respect to an applicable large employer's shared responsibility for employee health coverage under the Patient Protection and Affordable Care Act (P.L. 111-148; PPACA). Under certain circumstances, an assessable payment is imposed on applicable large employers under Code Sec. 4980H. Code Sec. 4980H is effective for months beginning after December 31, 2013. However, an employer may rely on the proposed regulations for guidance pending the issuance of final regulations or other applicable guidance. Final regulations will be effective as of a date not earlier than the date the final regulations are published in the Federal Register.

The proposed regulations, which are reproduced below, were published in the Federal Register on January 2, 2013 (78 FR 218). The proposed regulations were corrected on March 15, 2013 (78 FR 16445). The regulations were finalized on February 12, 2014 (79 FR 8543). The preamble to the final regulations is at ¶ 23,294. The final regulations are at ¶ 13,648W-142, ¶ 13,648W-143, ¶ 13,648W-144, ¶ 13,648W-145, ¶ 13,648W-146, ¶ 13,648W-147, ¶ 13,648W-148, and ¶ 13,922.

DEPARTMENT OF THE TREASURY

Internal Revenue Service

26 CFR Parts 1, 54 and 301

[REG-138006-12]

RIN 1545-BL33

Shared Responsibility for Employers Regarding Health Coverage

AGENCY: Internal Revenue Service (IRS), Treasury.

ACTION: Notice of proposed rulemaking and notice of public hearing.

SUMMARY: This document contains proposed regulations providing guidance under section 4980H of the Internal Revenue Code (Code) with respect to the shared responsibility for employers regarding employee health coverage. These proposed regulations would affect only employers that meet the definition of "applicable large employer" as described in these proposed regulations. As discussed in section X of this preamble, employers may rely on these proposed regulations for guidance pending the issuance of final regulations or other applicable guidance. This document also provides notice of a public hearing on these proposed regulations.

DATES: Written or electronic comments must be received by March 18, 2013. Outlines of topics to be discussed at the public hearing scheduled for April 23, 2013, at 10:00 am, must be received by April 3, 2013.

ADDRESSES: Send submissions to: CC:PA:LPD:PR (REG-138006-12), Internal Revenue Service, room 5203, POB 7604, Ben Franklin Station, Washington, DC 20044. Submissions may be hand-delivered Monday through Friday between the hours of 8 a.m. and 4 p.m. to CC:PA:LPD:PR (REG-138006-12), Courier's Desk, Internal Revenue Service, 1111 Constitution Avenue, NW., Washington, DC. Alternatively, taxpayers may submit comments electronically via the Federal eRulemaking Portal at *http://www.regulations.gov* (IRS REG-138006-12). The public hearing will be held in the Auditorium, Internal Revenue Building, 1111 Constitution Avenue, NW, Washington, DC.

FOR FURTHER INFORMATION CONTACT: Concerning the proposed regulations, call Kathryn Bjornstad at (202) 927-9639; concerning submissions of comments, the hearing, and/or to be placed on the building access list to attend the hearing, call Oluwafunmilayo Taylor at (202) 622-7180 (not toll-free numbers).

SUPPLEMENTARY INFORMATION:

Background

This document contains proposed Pension Excise Tax Regulations (26 CFR part 54) under section 4980H of the Code. Section 4980H was added to the Code by section 1513 of the Patient Protection and Affordable Care Act, enacted March 23, 2010, Public Law No. 111-148, and amended by section 1003 of the Health Care and Education Reconciliation Act of 2010, enacted March 30, 2010, Public Law No. 111-152, and further amended by the Department of Defense and Full-Year Continuing Appropriations Act, 2011, Public Law 112-10 (125 Stat. 38, (2011)), (collectively, the Affordable Care Act). Section 4980H is effective for months beginning after December 31, 2013.

I. *Section 4980H*

In General

Section 4980H generally provides that an applicable large employer is subject to an assessable payment if either (1) the employer fails to offer to its full-time employees (and their dependents) the opportunity to enroll in minimum essential coverage[1] (MEC) under an eligible employer-sponsored plan and any full-time employee is certified to the employer as having received an applicable premium tax credit or cost-sharing reduction (section 4980H(a) liability), or (2) the employer offers its full-time employees (and their dependents) the opportunity to enroll in MEC under an eligible employer-sponsored plan and one or more full-time employees is certified to the employer as having received an applicable premium tax credit or cost-sharing reduction (section 4980H(b) liability). Generally, section 4980H(b) liability may

arise because, with respect to a full-time employee who has been certified to the employer as having received an applicable premium tax credit or cost-sharing reduction, the employer's coverage is unaffordable within the meaning of section 36B(c)(2)(C)(i) or does not provide minimum value within the meaning of section 36B(c)(2)(C)(ii).[1] As noted, an employer may be liable for an assessable payment under section 4980H(a) or (b) only if one or more full-time employees are certified to the employer as having received an applicable premium tax credit or cost-sharing reduction.

The assessable payment under section 4980H(a) is based on all (excluding the first 30) full-time employees, while the assessable payment under section 4980H(b) is based on the number of full-time employees who are certified to the employer as having received an applicable premium tax credit or cost-sharing reduction with respect to that employee's purchase of health insurance for himself or herself on an Exchange. In contrast, an employee's receipt of a premium tax credit or cost sharing reduction with respect to coverage for a dependent will not result in liability for the employer under section 4980H. Under section 4980H(b), liability is contingent on whether the employer offers minimum essential coverage under an eligible employer-sponsored plan, and whether that coverage is affordable and provides minimum value, as determined by reference to the cost and characteristics of employee-only coverage offered to the employee. Section 4980H(c)(4) provides that a full-time employee with respect to any month is an employee who is employed on average at least 30 hours of service per week. An applicable large employer with respect to a calendar year is defined in section 4980H(c)(2) as an employer that employed an average of at least 50 full-time employees on business days during the preceding calendar year. For purposes of determining whether an employer is an applicable large employer, full-time equivalent employees (FTEs), which are statutorily determined based on the hours of service of employees who are not full-time employees, are taken into account.

II. *Previous Guidance*

The Treasury Department and the IRS have published four notices addressing issues under section 4980H. Each notice, briefly summarized in this section of the preamble, outlined potential approaches to future guidance, and each requested public comments. See Notice 2011-36 (2011-21 IRB 792), Notice 2011-73 (2011-40 IRB 474), Notice 2012-17 (2012-9 IRB 430), and Notice 2012-58 (2012-41 IRB 436). Notice 2012-58 also provided guidance that taxpayers may rely upon for periods specified in the notice. Extensive public comments were submitted in response to each of the four notices. See § 601.601(d)(2).

A. *Notice 2011-36*

Notice 2011-36 addressed the definitions of employer, employee, and hours of service. The notice also specifically described and requested comments on a possible approach that would permit employers to use an optional "look-back/stability period safe harbor" to determine whether ongoing employees (that is, employees other than new employees) are full-time employees for purposes of determining and calculating assessable payments under section 4980H. (In the proposed regulations and the remainder of this preamble, this optional safe harbor method generally is referred to, for convenience, as the "look-back measurement method.") This method may not be used for purposes of determining status as an applicable large employer, which is prescribed by the statute.

Under this method, an employer would determine each ongoing employee's status as a full-time employee by looking back at a defined period of not less than three but not more than 12 consecutive calendar months, as chosen by the employer (the measurement period), to determine whether during that measurement period the employee was employed on average at least 30 hours of service per week. If the employee were determined to be employed on average at least 30 hours of service per week during the measurement period, then the employee would be treated as a full-time employee during a subsequent period (the stability period), regardless of the employee's hours of service during the stability period, so long as he or she remained an employee. For an employee who has been determined to be employed on average at least 30 hours of service per week during the measurement period, the stability period would be a period that followed the

---

[1] See section III of the Background section of the preamble for a discussion of MEC, minimum value and affordability.

measurement period, and the duration of which was at least the greater of six consecutive calendar months or the length of the measurement period. If the employee were employed on average less than 30 hours per week during the measurement period, the employer would be permitted to treat the employee as not a full-time employee during a stability period that followed the measurement period, but the length of the stability period could not exceed the length of the measurement period.

Notice 2011-36 also outlined potential approaches under section 4980H for determining whether an employer is an applicable large employer, including calculating the number of the employer's full-time employees and full-time equivalents, defining employer and employee, and calculating the number of hours of service completed by an employee.

B. *Notice 2011-73*

Notice 2011-73 addressed the requirement that, in order to avoid a potential assessable payment under section 4980H(b), the coverage offered be affordable, generally meaning that the employee portion of the self-only premium for the employer's lowest cost coverage that provides minimum value not exceed 9.5 percent of the employee's household income. Recognizing the inability of employers to ascertain their employees' total household incomes, Notice 2011-73 described a potential safe harbor under which coverage offered by an employer to an employee would be treated as affordable for section 4980H liability purposes if the employee's required contribution for that coverage was no more than 9.5 percent of the employee's wages from the employer reported in Box 1 of the Form W-2 (Form W-2 wages) instead of household income. This potential affordability safe harbor would apply in determining whether an employer is subject to the assessable payment under section 4980H(b), but would not affect an employee's eligibility for a premium tax credit under section 36B.

C. *Notice 2012-17*

Notice 2012-17 stated that the Treasury Department and the IRS intended to incorporate the look-back measurement method described in Notice 2011-36 and the affordability safe harbor described in Notice 2011-73 into upcoming proposed regulations or other guidance.

Notice 2012-17 also described and requested comments on a potential approach for determining the full-time status of a new employee. Under that approach, if, based on the facts and circumstances at the date the employee began providing services to the employer (the start date), a new employee was reasonably expected to be employed an average of 30 hours of service per week on an annual basis and was employed full-time during the first three months of employment, the employer's group health plan would be required to offer the employee coverage as of the end of that period in order to avoid a potential section 4980H assessable payment for periods after the end of that three-month period. In contrast, if, based on the facts and circumstances at the start date, it could not reasonably be determined whether the new employee was expected to be employed on average at least 30 hours of service per week because the employee's hours were variable or otherwise uncertain, employers would be given three months or, in certain cases, six months, without incurring an assessable payment under section 4980H, to determine whether the employee was a full-time employee.

In response to Notice 2012-17, many commenters requested that employers be allowed to use a measurement period of up to 12 months to determine the status of new employees, similar to the potential approach outlined in Notice 2011-36 to determine the status of ongoing employees (although some commenters were not in favor of allowing a measurement period of up to 12 months for new employees).

D. *Notice 2012-58*

Notice 2012-58 provided employers reliance, through at least the end of 2014, on the guidance contained in that notice and on the following approaches described in the prior notices discussed in this section of the preamble: (1) for ongoing employees, an employer will be permitted to use measurement and stability periods of up to 12 months; (2) for new employees who are reasonably expected to be full-time employees, an employer that maintains a group health plan that meets certain requirements will not be subject to an assessable payment under section 4980H for failing to offer coverage to the employee for the initial three months of employment; and (3) for all employees, an employer will not be subject to an assessable payment under section 4980H(b) for failure to offer affordable coverage to an employee if the

coverage offered to that employee was affordable based on the employee's Form W-2 wages and otherwise provided minimum value.

Notice 2012-58 also announced and provided similar reliance on a revised optional look-back measurement method for new employees with variable hours and new seasonal employees that more closely resembled the optional method for ongoing employees described in Notice 2011-36. The expanded method provides employers the option to use a measurement period of up to 12 months to determine whether new variable-hour employees or seasonal employees are full-time employees, without being subject to an assessable payment under section 4980H for this period with respect to those employees. Under this approach, a new employee is a variable hour employee if, based on the facts and circumstances at the employee's start date, it cannot be determined that the employee is reasonably expected to be employed on average at least 30 hours of service per week.

In addition, Notice 2012-58 proposed and provided similar reliance on an option for employers to use specified administrative periods (in conjunction with specified measurement periods) for ongoing employees and certain new employees, and facilitated a transition for new employees from the determination method the employer chose to use for new employees to the determination method the employer chose to use for ongoing employees. Notice 2012-58 provided employers reliance for these options, through at least the end of 2014.

III. *Minimum Essential Coverage, Minimum Value and Affordability*

Under section 4980H, an applicable large employer member[2] may be subject to an assessable payment under section 4980H(a) if the employer fails to offer its full-time employees (and their dependents) the opportunity to enroll in MEC under an eligible employer-sponsored plan. Also, under section 4980H(b), an applicable large employer member may be subject to an assessable payment if its offer of MEC under an eligible employer-sponsored plan is unaffordable (within the meaning of section 36B(c)(2)(C)(i)) or does not provide minimum value (within the meaning of section 36B(c)(2)(C)(ii)). The determinations of MEC, minimum value and affordability are all determined by reference to other statutory provisions, but also all relate to the determination of liability under section 4980H, as described in this section of the preamble.

A. *Minimum Essential Coverage - In general*

MEC is defined in section 5000A(f). Section 5000A(f)(1)(B) provides that MEC includes coverage under an eligible employer-sponsored plan. Under section 5000A(f)(2), an eligible employer-sponsored plan is a group health plan or group health insurance coverage offered by an employer to an employee that is a governmental plan (within the meaning of section 2791(d)(8) of the Public Health Service Act (42 U.S.C. 300gg-91(d)(8))), any other plan or coverage offered in the small or large group market, or a grandfathered plan offered in the group market. Section 5000A(f)(3) provides that MEC does not include health insurance coverage which consists of coverage of excepted benefits described in section 2791(c)(1) of the Public Health Service Act, or sections 2971(c)(2), (3) or (4) of the Public Health Service Act if the benefits are provided under a separate policy, certificate, or contract of insurance. Future regulations under section 5000A are expected to provide further guidance on the definition of MEC and eligible employer-sponsored plans. These regulations under section 5000A are expected to provide that an employer-sponsored plan will not fail to be MEC solely because it is a plan to reimburse employees for medical care for which reimbursement is not provided under a policy of accident and health insurance (a self-insured plan).

B. *Minimum Value - In general*

If the coverage offered by an applicable large employer fails to provide minimum value, an employee may be eligible to receive a premium tax credit. Under section 36B(c)(2)(C)(ii), a plan fails to provide minimum value if the plan's share of the total allowed costs of benefits provided under the plan is less than 60 percent of those costs. Section 1302(d)(2)(C) of the Affordable Care Act sets forth the rules for calculating the percentage of total allowed costs of benefits provided under a group health plan or health insurance plan. Notice 2012-31 (2012-20 IRB 906) requested comments on potential approaches for determining minimum value.

On November 26, 2012, the Department of Health and Human Services (HHS) issued proposed regulations providing guidance on methodologies for determining minimum value (77 FR 70644). Those HHS proposed regulations provide that the percentage of the total

---

[2] For explanation of applicable large employer and applicable large employer member, see section I.A.2. and section III.A. of the preamble. If the applicable large employer consists of only one entity, rather than a controlled group of entities, then the applicable large employer member is the applicable large employer.

allowed cost of benefits will be determined using one of the main methodologies described in those proposed regulations and Notice 2012-31. These methodologies include a minimum value calculator which will be made available by HHS and the IRS. The proposed regulations also provide that minimum value for employer-sponsored self-insured group health plans and insured large group health plans will be determined using a standard population that is based upon large self-insured group health plans. Also, as there is no requirement that employer-sponsored self-insured and insured large group health plans offer all categories of essential health benefits or conform to any of the essential health benefit benchmarks, the proposed regulations describe how to take account of a benefit that an employer offers that is outside the parameters of the minimum value calculator. The Treasury Department and the IRS intend to propose additional guidance under section 36B with respect to minimum value. All comments received in response to Notice 2012-31 are being considered in connection with the development of that guidance.

C. *Affordability - In general*

For purposes of eligibility for the premium tax credit, coverage for an employee under an employer-sponsored plan is affordable if the employee's required contribution (within the meaning of section 5000A(e)(1)(B)) for self-only coverage[3] does not exceed 9.5 percent of the employee's household income for the taxable year. See section 36B(c)(2)(C)(i) and § 1.36B-1(e). Household income for purposes of section 36B is defined as the modified adjusted gross income of the employee and any members of the employee's family (including a spouse and dependents) who are required to file an income tax return. Section 36B(d)(2)(A). Modified adjusted gross income means adjusted gross income (within the meaning of section 62) increased by (1) amounts excluded from gross income under section 911, (2) the amount of any tax-exempt interest a taxpayer receives or accrues during the taxable year, and (3) an amount equal to the portion of the taxpayer's social security benefits (as defined in section 86(d)) which is not included in gross income under section 86 for the taxable year. See section 36B(d)(2)(B) and § 1.36B-1(e)(2).

Explanation of Provisions

The proposed regulations generally incorporate the provisions of Notice 2012-58, as well as many of the provisions of Notices 2011-36, 2011-73, and 2012-17, with some modifications in response to comments. The regulations also propose guidance on additional issues. Employers will be permitted to rely on these proposed regulations to the extent described in the section X of this preamble.

The proposed regulations are organized as follows: definitions (proposed § 54.4980H-1), rules for determining status as an applicable large employer and applicable large employer member (proposed § 54.4980H-2), rules for determining full-time employees (proposed § 54.4980H-3), rules for determining assessable payments under section 4980H(a) (proposed § 54.4980H-4), rules for determining whether an employer is subject to assessable payments under section 4980H(b) (proposed § 54.4980H-5), and rules relating to the administration and assessment of assessable payments under section 4980H (proposed § 54.4980H-6).

I. *Determination of Applicable Large Employer Status*

A. *Identification of Employer and Employees*

1. *In General*

Only applicable large employers may be liable for an assessable payment under section 4980H. Section 4980H(c)(2) defines an applicable large employer with respect to a calendar year as an employer that employed an average of at least 50 full-time employees (taking into account FTEs) on business days during the preceding calendar year. The proposed regulations adopt the position outlined in Notice 2011-36 under which an employee is an individual who is an employee under the common law standard, and an employer is the person that is the employer of an employee under the common law standard. Under the common law standard, an employment relationship exists when the person for whom the services are performed has the right to control and direct the individual who performs the services, not only as to the result to be accomplished by the work but also as to the details and means by which that result is accomplished. Under the common law standard, an employment relationship exists if an employee is subject to the will and control of the employer not only as to what shall be done but how it shall be done. In this connection, it is not necessary that the

employer actually direct or control the manner in which the services are performed; it is sufficient if the employer has the right to do so. See §§ 31.3121(d)-1(c), 31.3231(b)-1(a)(2), 31.3306(i)-1(b), and 31.3401(c)-1(b).

Several commenters responding to Notice 2011-36 asked that the definition of employer in the Fair Labor Standards Act be used instead of the common law employer. However, the term employer, as generally used in the Code, refers to the common law employer. Further, use of the common law standard is consistent with the definition of employer generally applied in Title I of the Affordable Care Act (which includes section 4980H). Specifically, section 1551 of the Affordable Care Act provides that "unless specifically provided otherwise, the definitions contained in section 2791 of the Public Health Service Act (42 USC 300gg-91) shall apply with respect to this title." Section 2791 of the Public Health Service Act provides that the term employer has the meaning given that term in section 3(5) of the Employee Retirement Income Security Act (ERISA) (29 USC 1002(5)), that is, the common law employer. For these reasons, the proposed regulations do not adopt this comment and instead use the common law standard for determining an employee's employer.

As noted in Notice 2011-36, section 414(n), which treats leased employees (as defined in section 414(n)(2)) as employees of the service recipient for various purposes, does not cross-reference section 4980H (and is not cross-referenced by section 4980H) and accordingly does not apply for section 4980H purposes. In addition, for purposes of section 4980H, a sole proprietor, a partner in a partnership, or a 2-percent S corporation shareholder is not an employee; but an individual who provides services as both an employee and a non-employee (such as an individual serving as both an employee and a director) is an employee with respect to his or her hours of service as an employee.

The identification of full-time employees for purposes of determining status as an applicable large employer under section 4980H is, by statute, performed on a look-back basis using data from the prior year, taking into account the hours of service of all employees employed in the prior year (full-time employees and non-full-time employees). Therefore, the look-back measurement method that may be used to identify full-time employees for purposes of determining potential section 4980H(a) or (b) liability does not apply for purposes of determining status as an applicable large employer. Instead, the determination of whether an employer is an applicable large employer for a year is based upon the actual hours of service of employees in the prior year. But see section IX.E. of this preamble for transition relief allowing use of a shorter look-back period in 2013 for purposes of determining applicable large employer status for 2014.

2. *Application of Aggregation Rules*

For purposes of counting the number of full-time and full-time equivalent employees for determining whether an employer is an applicable large employer, section 4980H(c)(2)(C)(i) provides that all entities treated as a single employer under section 414(b), (c), (m), or (o) are treated as a single employer for purposes of section 4980H. Thus, all employees of a controlled group under section 414(b) or (c), or an affiliated service group under section 414(m), are taken into account in determining whether the members of the controlled group or affiliated service group together constitute an applicable large employer.

Section 4980H applies to all common law employers, including an employer that is a government entity (such as Federal, State, local or Indian tribal government entities) and an employer that is an organization described in section 501(c) that is exempt from Federal income tax under section 501(a). The proposed regulations reserve on the application of the section 414(b), (c), (m), and (o) aggregation rules in section 4980H(c)(2)(C)(i) to government entities and churches, or a convention or association of churches (as defined in § 1.170A-9(b)). Until further guidance is issued, government entities, churches, and a convention or association of churches may rely on a reasonable, good faith interpretation of section 414(b), (c), (m), and (o) in determining whether a person or group of persons is an applicable large employer.

Several commenters asked for clarification of whether the aggregation rules used in determining applicable large employer status also applied for purposes of determining liability for, and the amount of, an assessable payment. The proposed regulations clarify that for a calendar year during which an employer is an applicable large employer, the section 4980H standards generally are applied separately to each person that is a member of the controlled group comprising the employer (with each such person referred to as an applicable large employer

---

[3] TD 9590 (77 FR 30377) reserved the rules under section 36B on determining affordability of coverage under an eligible employer-sponsored plan for individuals eligible for coverage because of a relationship to an employee.

member) in determining liability for, and the amount of, any assessable payment. For example, if an applicable large employer is comprised of a parent corporation and 10 wholly owned subsidiary corporations, each of the 11 corporations, regardless of the number of employees, is an applicable large employer member. For a discussion of the related information reporting requirements for applicable large employer members under section 6056, see section VII of this preamble.

3. *Foreign Employers and Foreign Employees*

Some commenters on Notice 2011-36 requested guidance on whether foreign employees working for foreign entities are excluded in determining status as an applicable large employer, and in determining any potential liability under section 4980H. For example, commenters asked whether a large foreign corporation with a small U.S. presence (under 50 employees) would be subject to section 4980H. These proposed regulations generally address these issues through the definition of hours of service, discussed in section II.B.2. of this preamble.

4. *Successor Employers*

Section 4980H(c)(2)(C)(iii) provides that, for purposes of determining applicable large employer status, an employer includes a predecessor employer. The regulations reserve, and therefore do not address, the specific rules for identifying a predecessor employer (or the corresponding successor employer). Rules for identifying successor employers have been developed in the employment tax context for determining when wages paid by a predecessor may be attributed to a successor employer (see §31.3121(a)(1)-1(b)). The Treasury Department and the IRS anticipate that rules similar to this provision may form the basis for the rule on identifying a predecessor or successor employer for purposes of the section 4980H applicable large employer determination, and invite comments on whether these employment tax rules are appropriate and whether any modifications of the rules may be necessary. Until further guidance is issued, taxpayers may rely upon a reasonable, good faith interpretation of the statutory provision on predecessor (and successor) employers for purposes of the applicable large employer determination.

For purposes of assessment and collection, and not for purposes of the applicable large employer determination, State law may provide for liability of a successor employer for a section 4980H assessable payment which has been, or could have been, imposed on a predecessor employer. In that case, the liability could be assessed, paid, and collected from the successor employer in accordance with section 6901.

5. *New Employers*

Section 4980H(c)(2)(C)(ii) and these proposed regulations provide that an employer not in existence during an entire preceding calendar year is an applicable large employer for the current calendar year if it is reasonably expected to employ an average of at least 50 full-time employees (taking into account FTEs) on business days during the current calendar year. One commenter suggested that a new employer be exempted from any potential assessable payment under section 4980H, or alternatively, that the standard should be a minimum period of operations in the preceding calendar year. The proposed regulations do not adopt this suggestion because it is inconsistent with the statutory provision addressing new employers in section 4980H(c)(2)(C)(ii). However, comments are requested on whether the final regulations should adopt any safe harbors or presumptions to assist a new employer in determining whether it is an applicable large employer.

6. *Seasonal Workers*

Section 4980H(c)(2)(B)(ii) provides that if an employer's workforce exceeds 50 full-time employees for 120 days or fewer during a calendar year, and the employees in excess of 50 who were employed during that period of no more than 120 days were seasonal workers, the employer is not an applicable large employer. Notice 2011-36 provided that, for this purpose only, four calendar months would be treated as the equivalent of 120 days. In response to comments, and consistent with Notice 2011-36 , these proposed regulations provide that, solely for purposes of the seasonal worker exception in determining whether an employer is an applicable large employer, an employer may apply either a period of four calendar months (whether or not consecutive) or a period of 120 days (whether or not consecutive). Because the 120-day period referred to in section 4980H(c)(2)(B)(ii) is not part of the definition of the term seasonal worker, an employee would not necessarily be precluded from being treated as a seasonal worker merely because the employee works, for example, on a seasonal basis for five consecutive months. In addition, the 120-day period referred to in section 4980H(c)(2)(B)(ii) is relevant only for applying the seasonal worker exception for determining status as an applicable large employer, and is not relevant for determining whether an employee is a

seasonal employee for purposes of the look-back measurement method (meaning that an employee who provides services for more than 120 days per year may nonetheless qualify as a seasonal employee). See section II.C.2. of this preamble for a discussion of the application of the look-back measurement method to seasonal employees.

For purposes of the definition of an applicable large employer, section 4980H(c)(2)(B)(ii) defines a seasonal worker as a worker who performs labor or services on a seasonal basis, as defined by the Secretary of Labor, including (but not limited to) workers covered by 29 CFR 500.20(s)(1) and retail workers employed exclusively during holiday seasons. This definition of seasonal worker is incorporated in these proposed regulations. The Department of Labor (DOL) regulations at 29 CFR 500.20(s)(1) to which section 4980H(c)(2)(B)(ii) refers, and that interpret the Migrant and Seasonal Agricultural Workers Protection Act, provide that "[l]abor is performed on a seasonal basis where, ordinarily, the employment pertains to or is of the kind exclusively performed at certain seasons or periods of the year and which, from its nature, may not be continuous or carried on throughout the year. A worker who moves from one seasonal activity to another, while employed in agriculture or performing agricultural labor, is employed on a seasonal basis even though he may continue to be employed during a major portion of the year."

After consultation with the DOL, the Treasury Department and the IRS have determined that the term seasonal worker, as incorporated in section 4980H, is not limited to agricultural or retail workers. Until further guidance is issued, employers may apply a reasonable, good faith interpretation of the statutory definition of seasonal worker, including a reasonable good faith interpretation of the standard set forth under the DOL regulations at 29 CFR 500.20(s)(1) and quoted in this paragraph, applied by analogy to workers and employment positions not otherwise covered under those DOL regulations.

Several commenters suggested that seasonal workers not be counted in determining whether an employer is an applicable large employer. However, because section 4980H(c)(2) requires the inclusion of seasonal workers in the applicable large employer determination (and then excludes them only if certain conditions are satisfied), this suggestion is not adopted.

7. *Full-Time Equivalent Employees*

Solely for purposes of determining whether an employer is an applicable large employer for the current calendar year, section 4980H(c)(2)(E) provides that the employer must calculate the number of full-time equivalent employees (FTEs) it employed during the preceding calendar year and count each FTE as one full-time employee for that year. The proposed regulations apply this provision using the calculation method for FTEs that was included in Notice 2011-36. Under that method, all employees (including seasonal workers) who were not full-time employees for any month in the preceding calendar year are included in calculating the employer's FTEs for that month by (1) calculating the aggregate number of hours of service (but not more than 120 hours of service for any employee) for all employees who were not employed on average at least 30 hours of service per week for that month, and (2) dividing the total hours of service in step (1) by 120. This is the number of FTEs for the calendar month.

In determining the number of FTEs for each calendar month, fractions are taken into account. For example, if for a calendar month employees who were not employed on average at least 30 hours of service per week have 1,260 hours of service in the aggregate, there would be 10.5 FTEs for that month. However, after adding the 12 monthly full-time employee and FTE totals, and dividing by 12, all fractions would be disregarded. For example, 49.9 full-time employees (including FTEs) for the preceding calendar year would be rounded down to 49 full-time employees (and thus the employer would not be an applicable large employer in the current calendar year).

Some commenters suggested that the definition of FTE in section 45R be used, or that equivalencies be used, or that employees not averaging at least 30 hours of service per week be counted at fractions of their hours of service. Because section 4980H(c)(2)(E) prescribes specific definitions and steps in computing FTEs, these suggestions have not been adopted.

II. *Identifying Full-Time Employees for Section 4980H Purposes*

A. *General Rule*

Section 4980H(c)(4) provides that, for purposes of section 4980H, a full-time employee is an employee who was employed on average at least 30 hours of service per week. One commenter suggested that the proposed regulations use the term "hours of service" instead of, for example, "hours worked" (a term sometimes used in Notice 2012-58), noting that "hours of service" is the statutory term and includes not only hours when work is performed but also hours for which an employee is paid or entitled to payment even when no work is performed. This suggestion has been adopted. In addition, various commenters responding to Notice 2011-36 suggested that, for purposes of section 4980H, the term "full-time employee" should be defined by reference to a higher threshold, for example 32, 35, or 40 hours of service per week. Because section 4980H(c)(4)(A) defines a full-time employee as an employee employed on average at least 30 hours of service per week, these suggestions have not been adopted.

Pursuant to the approach initially described in Notice 2011-36, these proposed regulations would treat 130 hours of service in a calendar month as the monthly equivalent of 30 hours of service per week ((52 × 30) ÷ 12 = 130). This monthly standard takes into account that the average month consists of more than four weeks. Some commenters argued that the 130 hour monthly standard is not an appropriate proxy for 30 hours per week during certain shorter calendar months. However, the 130 hour monthly standard may also be lower than an average of 30 hours per week during other longer months of the calendar year (for example, the seven calendar months that consist of 31 days) and, therefore, any effect of this approximation will balance out over the calendar year (for example, over a 12-month measurement period, over two successive six-month measurement periods, or over four successive three-month measurement periods). Accordingly, in the interest of administrative simplicity, the proposed regulations retain the 130-hour standard as a monthly equivalent of 30 hours per week.

Several commenters suggested that rather than calculating hours of service on a monthly basis, employers be permitted to determine hours of service on a payroll period basis using successive payroll periods as approximations of calendar months. This approach would be problematic, however, because payroll periods generally are not evenly divisible by the twelve calendar months. For example, treating two successive standard two-week payroll periods as equivalent to a calendar month generally would leave two payroll periods per year unassigned, requiring the arbitrary assignment of those two extra payroll periods to two calendar months.

The Treasury Department and the IRS anticipate that a significant majority of employers will use some form of the optional look-back measurement method described in these proposed regulations to identify full-time employees. Because the measurement periods must extend for at least three months, and may extend for as many as twelve months, the use of payroll periods to approximate months generally will not be necessary. However, for those using payroll periods, an adjustment may be needed at the beginning and end of the measurement period. The proposed regulations address this by permitting adjustments for cases in which the measurement period begins or ends in the middle of a payroll period. See section II.C.1. of this preamble.

B. *Hours of Service Rules*

1. *In General*

Hours of service are used in determining whether an employee is a full-time employee for purposes of section 4980H, and in calculating an employer's FTEs. Section 4980H(c)(4)(B) provides that the "Secretary, in consultation with the Secretary of Labor, shall prescribe regulations, rules, and guidance as may be necessary to determine the hours of service of an employee", including for employees who are not compensated on an hourly basis. Notice 2011-36 suggested rules for determining hours of service for purposes of section 4980H. As required by section 4980H(c)(4)(B), the Treasury Department and the IRS consulted with the DOL about the definition of hours of service in developing the rules described in Notice 2011-36 and these proposed regulations. Consistent with existing DOL regulations and other guidance under the Affordable Care Act (for example, Notice 2010-44 (2010-22 IRB 717)), and with Notice 2011-36, the proposed regulations provide that an employee's hours of service include the following: (1) each hour for which an employee is paid, or entitled to payment, for the performance of duties for the employer; and (2) each hour for which an employee is paid, or entitled to payment by the employer on account of a period of time during which no duties are performed due to vacation, holiday, illness, incapacity (including disability), layoff, jury duty, military duty or leave of absence (29 CFR 2530.200b-2(a)).

Several comments requested that the definition of hours of service exclude all hours of service for paid leave. The proposed regulations do not adopt these suggestions because they are not consistent with the DOL regulations or the general concept of when employees are credited with hours of service. Notice 2011-36 described a potential rule providing that, for any single continuous period during which the employee was paid or entitled to payment but performed no duties, no more than 160 hours of service would be counted as hours of service. A

number of commenters on Notice 2011-36 requested that the 160-hour limit be removed because they viewed it as restrictive, and expressed concern about the potential negative impact on employees who are on longer paid leaves, such as maternity or paternity leave. In response, these proposed regulations remove the 160-hour limit on paid leave, so that all periods of paid leave must be taken into account.

For purposes of calculating an employee's average hours of service under the look-back measurement method, the proposed regulations would limit the number of hours that an employer that is an educational organization is required to take into account in a calendar year with respect to most periods of absence with zero hours of service (as described in section II.C.4 of this preamble). The limit is 501 hours based on a longstanding 501-hour limit that applies in a different but related context under the service crediting rules applicable to retirement plans which are familiar to and administered by many employers.

For purposes of calculating an employee's hours of service, the proposed regulations provide rules for hourly employees and non-hourly employees, generally consistent with the approach outlined in Notice 2011-36. For employees paid on an hourly basis, employers must calculate actual hours of service from records of hours worked and hours for which payment is made or due for vacation, holiday, illness, incapacity (including disability), layoff, jury duty, military duty or leave of absence. For employees not paid on an hourly basis, employers are permitted to calculate the number of hours of service under any of the following three methods: (1) counting actual hours of service (as in the case of employees paid on an hourly basis) from records of hours worked and hours for which payment is made or due for vacation, holiday, illness, incapacity (including disability), layoff, jury duty, military duty or leave of absence; (2) using a days-worked equivalency method whereby the employee is credited with eight hours of service for each day for which the employee would be required to be credited with at least one hour of service under these service crediting rules; or (3) using a weeks-worked equivalency of 40 hours of service per week for each week for which the employee would be required to be credited with at least one hour of service under these service crediting rules. These equivalents are based on DOL regulations (29 CFR 2530.200b-2(a)), modified as described in this preamble and in the proposed regulations.

Although an employer must use one of these three methods for counting hours of service for all non-hourly employees, under these proposed regulations, an employer need not use the same method for all non-hourly employees. Rather, an employer may apply different methods for different classifications of non-hourly employees, so long as the classifications are reasonable and consistently applied. In addition, an employer may change the method of calculating non-hourly employees' hours of service for each calendar year. For example, for all non-hourly employees, an employer may use the actual hours worked method for the calendar year 2014, but may use the days-worked equivalency method for counting hours of service for the calendar year 2015.

However, consistent with Notice 2011-36, these proposed regulations prohibit use of the days-worked or weeks-worked equivalency method if the result would be to substantially understate an employee's hours of service in a manner that would cause that employee not to be treated as a full-time employee. For example, an employer may not use a days-worked equivalency in the case of an employee who generally works three 10-hour days per week, because the equivalency would substantially understate the employee's hours of service as 24 hours of service per week, which would result in the employee being treated as not a full-time employee. Rather, the number of hours of service calculated using the days-worked or weeks-worked equivalency method must reflect generally the hours actually worked and the hours for which payment is made or due.

For purposes of identifying the employee as a full-time employee, all hours of service performed for all entities treated as a single employer under section 414(b), (c), (m), or (o) must be taken into account.

2. *Services Performed Outside Of The United States*

The proposed regulations provide that hours of service do not include hours of service to the extent the compensation for those hours of service constitutes foreign source income, consistent with the rules of Federal taxation for determining whether compensation for services is attributable to services performed within or outside the United States. Thus, hours of service generally do not include hours of service worked outside the United States. This rule applies without regard to the residency or citizenship status of the individual. Therefore, employees working overseas generally will not have hours of service, and will not qualify as full-time employees either for purposes of determining an employer's status as an applicable large employer or for purposes of determining and calculating any potential liability under section 4980H. However, all hours of service for which an individual receives U.S. source income are hours of service for purposes of section 4980H.

3. *Teachers And Other Employees Of Educational Organizations*

Several comments were submitted on behalf of teachers and other employees of schools, colleges, universities, and other educational organizations in response to the look-back measurement method. The comments noted that educational organizations present a special situation compared to other workplaces because they typically function on the basis of an academic year, which involves various extended periods in which the organization is not in session or is engaged in only limited classroom activities. Because the services of many of the employees of these educational organizations follow the academic year, many of the employees, while typically employed for at least 30 hours of service per week during the active portions of the academic year, are precluded from working (or from working normal hours) during periods when the organization is entirely or largely closed. The commenters were concerned that use of a 12-month measurement period for employees who provide services only during the active portions of the academic year could inappropriately result in these employees not being treated as full-time employees. The concern is that employees' average hours of service for the 12-month measurement period would be distorted (and employees therefore would be inappropriately treated as not full-time employees) by averaging in the periods during or outside of the academic year (such as, typically, the summer months) during which teachers and other similarly situated employees of educational organizations may have no hours or only a few hours of required workplace attendance, because the institution is not in session or is engaged in only limited classroom activities. Traditional breaks in the academic or school year such as winter or spring breaks will often be periods of paid leave; in those cases employees will be required to be credited with hours of service under the general hours of service rules under the look-back measurement method. See section II.B.1 of this preamble.

These proposed regulations address these special issues presented by educational institutions by providing an averaging method for employment break periods that generally would result in an employee who works full-time during the active portions of the academic year being treated as a full-time employee for section 4980H. See section II.C.4. of the preamble. Comments are invited on any remaining issues relating to teachers, other educational organization employees, or industries with comparable circumstances.

4. *Employees Compensated On A Commission Basis, Adjunct Faculty, Transportation Employees And Analogous Employment Positions*

One commenter expressed concern the hours of service framework underlying the measurement and stability periods did not reflect the wide variety of workplaces, schedules, and specific work patterns in different industries and sectors of the economy, and that, consequently, the look-back method could be misused to treat employees long considered full-time employees as not full-time employees. A number of commenters requested special rules for employees whose compensation is not based primarily on hours and employees whose active work hours may be subject to safety-related regulatory limits (for example, salespeople compensated on a commission basis or airline pilots whose flying hours are subject to limits). Generally, the commenters suggest determining whether such employees are full-time employees for purposes of section 4980H by using hourly standards that, for the relevant industries or occupations, would be equivalent to the 30-hour and 130-hour standards applicable to other employees. Thus, for example, some commenters noted that educational organizations generally do not track the full hours of service of adjunct faculty, but instead compensate adjunct faculty on the basis of credit hours taught. Some comments suggested that hours of service for adjunct faculty should be determined by crediting three hours of service per week for each course credit taught. Others explained that some educational organizations determine whether an adjunct faculty member will be treated as a full-time employee by comparing the number of course credit hours taught by the adjunct faculty member to the number of credit hours taught by typical non-adjunct faculty members working in the same or a similar discipline who are considered full-time employees. Commenters on behalf of airline pilots noted that the number of hours of service that a pilot is permitted to operate an aircraft is limited under Federal law. The commenters requested that the guidance provide lower hourly standards for pilots that would be treated as equivalent to the 30-hour per week or 130-hour per month standard, or alternatively establish a special rule treating pilots as full-time employees regardless of their hours of service.

The rules for counting hours of service and applying equivalents contained in the proposed regulations should assist in addressing some of the concerns raised in the comments. The Treasury Department and the IRS are continuing to consider, and invite further comment on, how best to determine the full-time status of employees in the circumstances described in the preceding paragraph and in other circumstances that may present similar difficulties in determining hours of service. Further guidance to address potentially common challenges arising in determining hours of service for certain categories of employees may be provided in the final regulations, or through Revenue Procedures, or other forms of subregulatory guidance.

Until further guidance is issued, employers of employees in positions described in the first paragraph of this section II.B.4. of this preamble (and in other positions that raise similar issues with respect to the crediting of hours of service) must use a reasonable method for crediting hours of service that is consistent with the purposes of section 4980H. A method of crediting hours would not be reasonable if it took into account only some of an employee's hours of service with the effect of recharacterizing, as non-fulltime, an employee in a position that traditionally involves more than 30 hours of service per week. For example, it would not be a reasonable method of crediting hours to fail to take into account travel time for a travelling salesperson compensated on a commission basis, or in the case of an instructor, such as an adjunct faculty member, to take into account only classroom or other instruction time and not other hours that are necessary to perform the employee's duties, such as class preparation time.

C. *Look-Back Measurement Method for Determination of Full-Time Employees*

As described in section III.A. of this preamble, the assessable payment under section 4980H(a) and section 4980H(b) is computed for each applicable large employer member. The potential section 4980H(a) liability of an applicable large employer member is determined by reference to the number of full-time employees employed by that member for a given calendar month, and its potential section 4980H(b) liability is determined by reference to the number of full-time employees of that member with respect to whom an applicable premium tax credit or cost-sharing reduction is allowed or paid for a given calendar month. Section 4980H(c)(4)(A) provides that "[t]he term "full-time employee" means, with respect to any month, an employee who is employed on average at least 30 hours of service per week." As explained in Notice 2011-36 and subsequent notices, determining full-time employee status on a monthly basis may cause practical difficulties for employers, employees, and Affordable Insurance Exchanges (Exchanges). For employers, these difficulties include uncertainty and inability to predictably identify which employees are full-time employees to whom coverage must be provided to avoid a potential section 4980H liability. This problem is particularly acute if employees have varying hours or employment schedules (for example, employees whose hours vary from month to month). A month-by-month determination may also result in employees moving in and out of employer coverage (and potentially Exchange coverage) as frequently as monthly. This result would be undesirable from both the employee's and the employer's perspective, and would also create administrative challenges for the Exchanges.

To address these concerns, and to give employers flexible and workable options and greater predictability, Notice 2011-36, Notice 2012-17, and Notice 2012-58 outlined a potential optional look-back measurement method as an alternative to a month-by-month method of determining full-time employee status. See the discussion in the Background section of this preamble. The response to this look-back measurement method generally was favorable. Most commenters supported the general structure of the method, although, some expressed concern that the potential difficulties in identifying full-time employees were overstated, that the look-back measurement method might be manipulated by employers, and that there was a need to prescribe rules that would address special workplace situations to ensure that certain classes of employees would be treated as full-time employees even though their hours might not result in full-time employee treatment under the look-back measurement method described in Notice 2012-58. After considering all of the comments on the notices, the Treasury Department and the IRS have incorporated in the proposed regulations the optional look-back measurement method described and cross-referenced in Notice 2012-58, with modifications as described in this preamble. See §601.601(d)(2).

While the look-back measurement method prescribes minimum standards to facilitate the identification of full-time employees, employers always can treat more employees as eligible for coverage, or otherwise offer coverage more widely, than would be required to avoid an assessable payment under section 4980H, assuming they do so consistent with any other applicable law.

1. *Look-Back Measurement Method for Ongoing Employees*

The proposed regulations define an ongoing employee as, generally, an employee who has been employed by an employer for at least one standard measurement period. For ongoing employees, the proposed regulations, consistent with Notice 2012-58, provide that an applicable large employer member has the option to determine each ongoing employee's full-time status by looking back at a measurement period (a defined time period of not less than three but not more than 12 consecutive months, as chosen by the employer). The measurement period that the employer chooses to apply to ongoing employees is referred to as the standard measurement period. If the employer determines that an employee was employed on average at least 30 hours of service per week during the standard measurement period, then the employer treats the employee as a full-time employee during a subsequent stability period, regardless of the employee's number of hours of service during the stability period, so long as he or she remains an employee. The applicable large employer member, at its option, may also elect to add an administrative period between the measurement period and the stability period as part of this method.

For an employee whom the employer determines to be a full-time employee during the standard measurement period, the stability period would be a period that immediately followed the standard measurement period (and any applicable administrative period), the duration of which would be at least the greater of six consecutive calendar months or the length of the standard measurement period. If the employer determines that the employee did not work full-time during the standard measurement period, the employer would be permitted to treat the employee as not a full-time employee during the immediately following stability period (which may be no longer than the associated standard measurement period).

Generally, the standard measurement period and stability period selected by the applicable large employer member must be uniform for all employees; however, the applicable large employer member may apply different measurement periods, stability periods, and administrative periods for the following categories of employees: (1) each group of collectively bargained employees covered by a separate collective bargaining agreement, (2) collectively bargained and non-collectively bargained employees, (3) salaried employees and hourly employees, and (4) employees whose primary places of employment are in different states. Notice 2012-58 had also included "employees of different entities" as a separate category of employees. However, because section 4980H generally is applied on an applicable large employer member-by-member basis, including the method of identifying full-time employees, there is no need for a distinct category for employees of different entities, as each such member is a separate entity. The applicable large employer member may change its standard measurement period and stability period for subsequent years, but generally may not change the standard measurement period or stability period once the standard measurement period has begun.

Comments have included requests that, in the interest of administrative convenience, the regulations permit employers to adjust the starting and ending dates of their three-to-twelve-month measurement periods in order to avoid splitting employees' regular payroll periods. The proposed regulations accommodate these requests to begin and end measurement periods with the beginning and ending of regular payroll periods if each of the payroll periods is one week, two weeks, or semi-monthly in duration. Pursuant to this accommodation, employers may make certain adjustments at the beginning and end of the measurement period. For example, an employer using the calendar year as a measurement period could exclude the entire payroll period that included January 1 (the beginning of the year) if it included the entire payroll period that included December 31 (the end of that same calendar year), or, alternatively, could exclude the entire payroll period that included December 31 if it included the entire payroll period that included January 1.

Because employers may need time between the end of the standard measurement period and the beginning of the associated stability period to determine which ongoing employees are eligible for coverage, and to notify and enroll employees, the proposed regulations, consistent with Notice 2012-58, allow an applicable large employer member the option of having an administrative period between the end of a measurement period and the start of a stability period. The administrative period may last up to 90 days. However, any administrative period between the standard measurement period and the stability period may neither reduce nor lengthen the measurement period or the stability period. Also, to prevent this administrative period from creating any potential gaps in coverage, it must overlap with the prior stability period, so that, for ongoing employees, during any such administrative period applicable following a standard measurement period, those employees who are enrolled in coverage because of their status as full-time employees based on a prior measurement period will continue to be covered.

2. *New Employees*

These proposed regulations also provide rules for determining the full-time employee status of new employees, including an optional look-back measurement method for certain new employees generally based upon the approach outlined in Notice 2012-58. The methods for new employees vary depending upon whether the new employees are reasonably expected to work full-time (and are not seasonal) or are variable hour employees or seasonal employees.

a. *New Full-time Employees*

The proposed regulations provide that, for an employee who is reasonably expected at his or her start date to be employed on average 30 hours of service per week (and who is not a seasonal employee), an employer that sponsors a group health plan that offers coverage to the employee at or before the conclusion of the employee's initial three calendar months of employment will not be subject to an assessable payment under section 4980H by reason of its failure to offer coverage to the employee for up to the initial three calendar months of employment. This rule continues the approach outlined in Notice 2012-17 and Notice 2012-58.

Notice 2012-58 requested comments on whether the Treasury Department and the IRS should develop additional guidance for determining whether an employee is reasonably expected, as of the employee's start date, to be employed on average at least 30 hours of service per week or whether the employee is a variable hour employee. The commenters suggested that the following factors could be used to determine whether an employee is reasonably expected to be employed on average at least 30 hours of service per week: (1) whether the employee is replacing an employee who is a full-time employee; and (2) whether the hours of service of ongoing employees in the same or comparable positions actually vary. The Treasury Department and the IRS are continuing to consider whether such factors are appropriate or useful and welcome any additional comments on this issue.

b. *Look-Back Measurement Method for New Variable Hour and Seasonal Employees*

If an applicable large employer member uses the look-back measurement method for its ongoing employees, the employer may also use the optional method for new variable hour employees and for seasonal employees. The proposed regulations, consistent with Notice 2012-58, provide that a new employee is a variable hour employee if, based on the facts and circumstances at the start date, it cannot be determined that the employee is reasonably expected to be employed on average at least 30 hours per week. A new employee who is expected to be employed initially at least 30 hours per week may be a variable hour employee if, based on the facts and circumstances at the start date, the period of employment at more than 30 hours per week is reasonably expected to be of limited duration and it cannot be determined that the employee is reasonably expected to be employed on average at least 30 hours per week over the initial measurement period. Effective as of January 1, 2015, and except in the case of seasonal employees, the employer will be required to assume for this purpose that although the employee's hours of service might be expected to vary, the employee will continue to be employed by the employer for the entire initial measurement period; accordingly, the employer will not be permitted to take into account the likelihood that the employee's employment will terminate before the end of the initial measurement period. See section IX.G. of the preamble for transition relief for the effective date of the rule described in the immediately preceding sentence.

Notice 2012-58 provides that, through at least 2014, employers are permitted to use a reasonable, good faith interpretation of the term "seasonal employee" for purposes of this notice. Notice 2012-58 also requested comments on the definition of "seasonal worker" as set forth in section 4980H(c)(2)(B)(ii) for purposes of determining status as an applicable large employer. Specifically, the request for comments asked about the practicability of using different definitions for different purposes (such as for determining status as an applicable large employer versus determining the full-time employee status of a new employee); and whether other, existing legal definitions should be considered in defining a seasonal worker under section 4980H (such as the safe harbor for seasonal employees in the final sentence of § 1.105-11(c)(2)(iii)(C)).

The proposed regulations reserve the definition of seasonal employee, and provide that, as set forth in Notice 2012-58, employers are permitted, through 2014, to use a reasonable, good faith interpretation of the term seasonal employee for purposes of section 4980H. It is not a reasonable good faith interpretation of the term seasonal employee to treat an employee of an educational organization, who works during the active portions of the academic year, as a seasonal employee. The Treasury Department and the IRS contemplate that the final regulations may add to the definition of seasonal employee a specific time limit in the form of a defined period. For example, the limit specified in the current safe harbor for treatment as a seasonal employee under regulations for self-insured medical reimbursement plans (see final sentence of § 1.105-11(c)(2)(iii)(C)) could be adapted to the definition of seasonal employee in the final regulations by prescribing, in the interest of simplicity and clarity, a specific time limit of not more than six months. Comments are requested on this approach, including any necessary modifications for purposes of section 4980H and any alternative approaches that should be considered.

As provided in Notice 2012-58, in general, an employer may use both an initial measurement period of between three and 12 months (the same as allowed for ongoing employees) and an administrative period of up to 90 days for variable hour and seasonal employees. However, the initial measurement period and the administrative period combined may not extend beyond the last day of the first calendar month beginning on or after the one-year anniversary of the employee's start date (totaling, at most, 13 months and a fraction of a month).

If the employer complies with these requirements, no assessable payment under section 4980H will be due with respect to the variable hour or seasonal employee during the initial measurement period or the administrative period. Note that an employee or related individual is not considered eligible for minimum essential coverage under the employer's plan (and therefore may be eligible for a premium tax credit or cost-sharing reduction through an Exchange) during any period when coverage is not offered, including any measurement period or administrative period prior to when coverage takes effect, even if the employer is not subject to an assessable payment for this period.

During the initial measurement period, the employer measures the hours of service for the new employee or seasonal employee and determines whether the employee was employed an average of 30 hours of service per week or more during this period. The stability period for that employee must be the same length as the stability period for ongoing employees. As in the case of a standard measurement period, if an employee is determined to be a full-time employee during the initial measurement period, the stability period must be a period of at least six consecutive calendar months that is no shorter in duration than the initial measurement period and that begins immediately after the initial measurement period (and any associated administrative period).

If a new variable hour or seasonal employee is determined not to be a full-time employee during the initial measurement period, the employer is permitted to treat the employee as not a full-time employee during the stability period that follows the initial measurement period. This stability period must not be more than one month longer than the initial measurement period and, as explained herein, must not exceed the remainder of the standard measurement period (plus any associated administrative period) in which the initial measurement period ends. In these circumstances, allowing a stability period to exceed the initial measurement period by one month is intended to give additional flexibility to employers that wish to use a 12-month stability period for new variable hour and seasonal employees and an administrative period that exceeds one month. To that end, such an employer could use an 11-month initial measurement period (in lieu of the 12-month initial measurement period that would otherwise be required) and still comply with the general rule that the initial measurement period and administrative period combined may not extend beyond the last day of the first calendar month beginning on or after the one-year anniversary of the employee's start date.

For purposes of applying the look-back measurement method, the proposed regulations provide that an employee's start date is the first date for which the employee would be required to be credited with at least one hour of service under the hours of service rules. See section II.B.1. of this preamble for a discussion of those rules. See also section II.C.4. of this preamble for a description of the proposed rules on when an employee who has experienced a period with no hours of service is treated as a newly rehired employee rather than as a continuing employee. As indicated, this rule applies solely for purposes of determining the employee's start date for determining hours of service under section 4980H, and not for determining the beginning of an employment relationship for any other purpose under the Code or other applicable law.

3. Change in Employment Status

The proposed regulations address the treatment of new variable or seasonal employees who have a change in employment status during

the initial measurement period (for example, in the case of a new variable hour employee who is promoted during the initial measurement period to a position in which employees are reasonably expected to be employed on average 30 hours of service per week). The proposed regulations define a change in employment status as a material change in the position of employment or other employment status that, had the employee begun employment in the new position or status, would have resulted in the employee being reasonably expected to be employed on average at least 30 hours of service per week. The proposed regulations provide that a new variable hour or seasonal employee who has a change in employment status during an initial measurement period is treated as a full-time employee under section 4980H as of the first day of the fourth month following the change in employment status or, if earlier and the employee averages more than 30 hours of service per week during the initial measurement period, the first day of the first month following the end of the initial measurement period (including any optional administrative period applicable to the initial measurement period). The change in employment status rule only applies to new variable hour and seasonal employees. A change in employment status for an ongoing employee does not change the employee's status as a full-time employee or non full-time employee during the stability period.

4. Employees Rehired After Termination of Employment or Resuming Service After Other Absence.

An employee might work for the same applicable large employer on and off during different periods. For example, an employee's employment could terminate but the employee could later be rehired by the same employer. Alternatively, even without a termination of employment, there might be a continuous period during which an employee is not credited with any hours of service under the hours of service rules described in these proposed regulations (for example, in the case of a period of unpaid leave of absence). When such an employee is rehired or returns from unpaid leave, this raises the issue of whether the employee may be treated as a new employee. A number of commenters requested clarification regarding how to treat rehired employees, in particular whether employees who are rehired during a measurement period are treated as new hires or whether their prior service must be taken into account in determining their status. In addition, several commenters expressed concern that employers might terminate an employee with an intent to later rehire that employee in order to delay offering health coverage to employees working full-time.

The proposed regulations include rules designed to prevent this type of period without credited hours of service from inappropriately restarting an employee's initial measurement period, or causing the employee to be subject to a new 90-day waiting period for new full-time employees. For example, a variable hour employee terminated near the end of his or her initial measurement period and then rehired shortly thereafter, if treated again as a new variable hour employee, could be left out of coverage for an entire new initial measurement period without resulting in 4980H liability.

Under the proposed regulations, if the period for which no hours of service is credited is at least 26 consecutive weeks, an employer may treat an employee who has an hour of service after that period, for purposes of determining the employee's status as a full-time employee, as having terminated employment and having been rehired as a new employee of the employer. The employer may also choose to apply a rule of parity for periods of less than 26 weeks. Under the rule of parity, an employee may be treated as having terminated employment and having been rehired as a new employee if the period with no credited hours of service (of less than 26 weeks) is at least four weeks long and is longer than the employee's period of employment immediately preceding that period with no credited hours of service (with the length of that previous period determined with application to that period of these rules governing employee rehires or other resumptions of service). For example, under the optional rule of parity if an employee works three weeks for an applicable large employer, terminates employment, and is rehired by that employer ten weeks after terminating employment, that rehired employee is treated as a new employee because the ten-week period with no credited hours of service is longer than the immediately preceding three-week period of employment.

Note that this rule applies solely for purposes of determining the full-time employee status for employers using the look-back measurement method and not for any other purpose under the Code or other applicable law (including for determining status as an applicable large employer and for applying the 90-day waiting period limitation under section 2708 of the Public Health Service Act). [Corrected 3/15/13 (78 FR 16445).]

For an employee who is treated as a continuing employee (as opposed to an employee who is treated as terminated and rehired), the measurement and stability period that would have applied to the employee had the employee not experienced the period of no credited hours of service would continue to apply upon the employee's resumption of service. For example, if the continuing employee returns during a stability period in which the employee is treated as a full-time employee, the employee is treated as a full-time employee upon return and through the end of that stability period. For this purpose, the proposed regulations provide that a continuing employee treated as a full-time employee will be treated as offered coverage upon resumption of services if the employee is offered coverage as of the first day that employee is credited with an hour of service, or, if later, as soon as administratively practicable.

The proposed regulations propose a method for averaging hours when applying the look-back measurement method to measurement periods that include special unpaid leave. This method applies only to an employee treated as a continuing employee upon the resumption of services, and not to an employee treated as terminated and rehired. For this purpose, special unpaid leave refers to a period of unpaid leave subject to the Family and Medical Leave Act of 1993 (FMLA), Public Law 103-3, 20 U.S.C. 2601 et. seq., unpaid leave subject to the Uniformed Services Employment and Reemployment Rights Act of 1994 (USERRA), Public Law 103-353, 38 U.S.C. 4301 et. seq., and unpaid leave on account of jury duty.

Under this proposed averaging method, the employer determines the average hours of service per week for the employee during the measurement period excluding special unpaid leave period and uses that average as the average for the entire measurement period. Alternatively, the employer may choose to treat employees as credited with hours of service for special unpaid leave at a rate equal to the average weekly rate at which the employee was credited with hours of service during the weeks in the measurement period that are not special unpaid leave.

Additional requirements apply to employment break periods for employees of an educational organization (meaning an organization described in § 1.170A-9(c)(1), whether or not described in section 501(c)(3) and exempt under section 501(a), and an educational organization owned, controlled, or operated by a government entity (as defined in § 54.4980H-1(a)(20)). For this purpose, an employment break period is a period of at least four consecutive weeks (disregarding special unpaid leave) during which an employee is not credited with an hour of service. As noted above, educational organizations are different than other workplaces because they typically function on the basis of an academic year, which involves various extended periods in which the organization is not in session or is engaged in only limited classroom activities. The proposed regulations provide that the educational organization must apply one of the methods in the preceding paragraph to employment break periods related to or arising out of non-working weeks or months under the academic calendar. Accordingly, the educational organization must either determine the average hours of service per week for the employee during the measurement period excluding the employment break period and use that average as the average for the entire measurement period, or treat employees as credited with hours of service for the employment break period at a rate equal to the average weekly rate at which the employee was credited with hours of service during the weeks in the measurement period that are not part of an employment break period. However, the educational organization is not required to credit an employee in any calendar year with more than 501 hours of service for any employment break period (although this 501-hour limit does not apply to, or take into account, hours of service required to be credited for special unpaid leave). The rules governing employment break period for educational organizations apply only to an employee treated as a continuing employee upon the resumption of services, and not to an employee treated as terminated and rehired.

The Treasury Department and the IRS are considering whether final regulations should extend the employment break period rules described in the preceding paragraph to all employers (not only educational organizations) and request comments. Any such extension of the rule would not take effect prior to 2015. Comments are invited in particular on how the proposed averaging methods should apply to employment break periods or other periods of absence, how the proposed approach would affect employees and employers, and whether the proposed treatment of employment break periods would be appropriate.

The proposed regulations also contain an anti-abuse rule to address practices that have the effect of circumventing or manipulating the application of the employee rehire rules.

5. New Short-Term Employees

Notice 2012-58 requested comments on the application of section 4980H to employees hired for short-term periods but expected to be employed on average 30 hours of service per week or more for the duration of the short-term employment. Section 4980H would not apply to full-time employees employed for three months or less because, if the applicable large employer member were otherwise offering coverage, the section 4980H assessable payment would not apply to a failure to offer coverage during that period. However, section 4980H issues may arise for short-term employment exceeding three months.

Some comments were received requesting special rules for determining the full-time employee status of short-term employees. The Treasury Department and the IRS have been concerned that the potential for abuse and manipulation of any special rules addressing short-term employees might outweigh the considerations of avoiding churning and inefficiency associated with offering coverage to employees whose employment is anticipated to last, for example, no more than four or five months. Commenters that wish to submit additional comments on whether any special rules would be appropriate with respect to short-term employees, and if so, whether there are any methods that could be used to determine the full-time status of these employees that are consistent with the provisions of section 4980H, are requested to take these concerns into account.

6. New Employees Hired Into High-Turnover Positions

Notice 2012-58 also requested comments on the application of section 4980H to new hires of full-time employees in high-turnover positions. An employer that otherwise offers coverage is not subject to a section 4980H assessable payment with respect to an employee whose employment terminates within three months of the employee's start date. However, some commenters raised concerns that employers with employees working full-time in typically high-turnover positions who, because of the high turnover, have a high probability of not being employed for the entire measurement period (for example, employees, a significant portion of whom are expected to remain employed for more than three months, but not more than six months) will be required to offer coverage for only a relatively brief period of time for a significant portion of the high-turnover employees.

The proposed regulations do not contain special rules for high-turnover positions for several reasons. As noted by comments in response to Notice 2012-58, "high-turnover" is a category that would require a complex definition (for example, how to define classes of employees and how much turnover of employment would be required over what period) and that could be subject to manipulation. In addition, any special treatment that is provided for employees hired into a high-turnover position could provide an incentive for employers to terminate employees to ensure that the position remains a high-turnover position under whatever standard was used to make that determination. Commenters who wish to provide additional comments on this issue are requested to address the concerns identified in this paragraph.

D. Temporary Staffing Agencies

1. Application Of Rules To Temporary Staffing Agencies

The Treasury Department and the IRS recognize that the application of section 4980H may be particularly challenging for temporary staffing agencies because of the distinctive nature of their employees' work schedules. In particular, several commenters discussed the challenges involved in applying the look-back measurement method to employees of temporary staffing agencies. It is anticipated that many new employees of temporary staffing agencies will be variable hour employees under the rules in these proposed regulations because, based on the facts and circumstances, their periods of employment at 30 or more hours per week are reasonably expected to be of limited duration with the potential for significant gaps between assignments, and there is often considerable uncertainty as to the likelihood and duration of assignments and as to whether an individual will accept any given assignment and will continue in it. For instance, as illustrated in Example 12 in § 54.4980H-3(c)(5) of the proposed regulations, if an individual hired by a temporary staffing agency as its common law employee can be expected to be offered one or more assignments with different clients each generally lasting no more than two or three months, and if the agency can expect the clients to have different requests with respect to hours of service (some above and some below 30 hours of service per week) and for there to be gaps of time between assignments during which the employee is not requested to provide services, then the employee generally would be a variable hour employee. For these and other reasons, it often cannot be determined that the employees are reasonably expected to be employed on average at least 30 hours per week over the initial measurement period.

Some commenters have suggested that, in view of the structure of the employment relationship, employees of temporary staffing agencies should be deemed to be variable hour employees, or at least that a presumption of status as a variable hour employee be established in the regulations. While, as noted, the Treasury Department and the IRS agree that many employees of temporary staffing agencies will likely be variable hour employees, we do not anticipate that all employees of a temporary staffing agency are inherently variable hour employees (especially employees on longer-term assignments with predictable requests for hours of service, as may be the case, for example, with particularly high-skilled technical or professional workers). In addition, the Treasury Department and the IRS are concerned that such a conclusion or presumption could lead employers to purport to use temporary staffing agencies (or other staffing agencies that may attempt to fit within such a presumption) in situations in which the employer "client" is the individual's common law employer and the staffing agency is inserted solely in an attempt to avoid application of section 4980H.

For these reasons, comments are invited on whether and, if so, how a special safe harbor or presumption should or could be developed with respect to the variable hour employee classification of the common law employees of temporary staffing agencies that would contain restrictions or safeguards intended to address these concerns while still providing useful guidance for employers and employees in this industry. More generally, further comments are invited on whether special rules for identifying full-time employees or any other issues relating to section 4980H may be necessary in the case of temporary staffing agencies, especially in light of the employment break period rules proposed in these regulations.

For purposes of this discussion, a temporary staffing agency refers only to an entity that is the common law employer of the individual that is providing services to a client of the temporary staffing agency. For an illustration of the facts and circumstances under which a temporary staffing agency (rather than its client) is the individual's common law employer, see Rev. Rul. 70-630 (1970-2 CB 229). In considering any requests for special consideration for temporary staffing agencies or other staffing agencies, the Treasury Department and the IRS will take into account the factual nature of the common law analysis in determining who is the common law employer of the workers providing the services and the potential implications for other Code sections, including employment tax liability provisions, for which the determination of common law employer status is necessary. See § 601.601(d)(2).

2. Separation From Service and Employment Break Period Rules

Commenters have also noted that, because of the intermittent nature of temporary staffing agency assignments, including employees' ability to accept or decline such assignments and the fact that some individuals are on multiple temporary staffing agencies' lists of potential workers, a temporary staffing agency may not be able in all cases to readily determine the date on which the individual separated from service as an employee of the agency. For instance, an individual may remain on an agency's list of potential workers even after the individual has decided (without necessarily informing the agency) not to take any further assignments from that agency. The Treasury Department and the IRS request comments on particular situations involving temporary staffing agencies that these proposed rules fail to address and on whether special consideration may be needed.

3. Anti-Abuse Rules

The Treasury Department and the IRS are aware of various structures being considered under which employers might use temporary staffing agencies (or other staffing agencies) purporting to be the common law employer to evade application of section 4980H. In one structure, the employer (referred to in this section as the "client") would purport to employ its employees for only part of a week, such as 20 hours, and then to hire those same individuals through a temporary staffing agency (or other staffing agency) for the remaining hours of the week, thereby resulting in neither the "client" employer nor the temporary staffing agency or other staffing agency appearing to employ the individual as a full-time employee. In another structure, one temporary staffing agency (or other staffing agency) would purport to employ an individual and supply the individual as a worker to a client for only part of a week, such as 20 hours, while a second temporary staffing agency or other staffing agency would purport to employ the same individual and supply that individual as a worker to the same client for the remainder of the week, thereby resulting in neither the temporary staffing agencies or the other staffing agencies, nor the client, appearing to employ the individual as a full-time employee. The Treasury

Department and the IRS anticipate that only in rare circumstances, if ever, would the "client" under these fact patterns not employ the individual under the common law standard as a full-time employee. Rather, the Treasury Department and the IRS believe that the primary purpose of using such an arrangement would be to avoid the application of section 4980H.

It is anticipated that the final regulations will contain an anti-abuse rule to address the situations described in this section of the preamble. Under that anticipated rule, if an individual performs services as an employee of an employer, and also performs the same or similar services for that employer in the individual's purported employment at a temporary staffing agency or other staffing agency of which the employer is a client, then all the hours of service are attributed to the employer for purposes of applying section 4980H. Similarly, to the extent an individual performs the same or similar services for the same client of two or more temporary staffing agencies or other staffing agencies, it is anticipated that all hours of service for that client are attributed to the client, if the client is the common law employer, or, if not, one of the temporary staffing agencies (or other staffing agencies) that purports to employ the individual with respect to services performed for that client.

III. Compliance with Section 4980H - In General

A. No Aggregation in Determining Liability of An Applicable Large Employer Member

The proposed regulations address the application of section 4980H to an applicable large employer member. As noted in section I.A.2. of this preamble, under section 4980H(c)(2), the determination of applicable large employer status is made on a controlled group basis applying the aggregation rules under section 414(b), (c), (m), and (o). Section 4980H(c)(2)(D) provides that, in calculating the liability under section 4980H(a), the applicable large employer, as determined applying these same aggregation rules, is permitted one reduction of 30 full-time employees, and that the reduction must be allocated ratably among the members of the applicable large employer based on each member's number of full-time employees.

The proposed regulations provide that, although applicable large employer status and the 30-employee reduction is determined on an aggregated basis, the determination of whether an employer is subject to an assessable payment and the amount of any such payment is determined on a member-by-member basis. Therefore, the liability for, and the amount of, any assessable payment under section 4980H is computed and assessed separately for each applicable large employer member, taking into account that member's offer of coverage (or lack thereof) and based on that member's number of full-time employees. For example, if a parent corporation owns 100 percent of all classes of stock of 20 subsidiary corporations, and the controlled group is an applicable large employer, each of the 21 members of this controlled group (the parent corporation plus 20 subsidiary corporations) is considered separately in computing and assessing a section 4980H payment. In addition, each of the 21 group members is liable only for its separate section 4980H assessable payment.

B. Certification Of Payment of Subsidy

Under section 4980H, an applicable large employer member is subject to an assessable payment if at least one full-time employee of that member has been certified to the member under section 1411 of the Affordable Care Act as having enrolled in a qualified health plan with respect to which a premium tax credit is allowed or paid. Section 1411(a) of the Affordable Care Act gives the Secretary of Health and Human Services the authority to determine whether individuals are eligible to enroll in qualified health plans through the Exchange and whether they are eligible for a premium tax credit. It is anticipated that, in upcoming regulations to be proposed under section 1411(a) of the Affordable Care Act, the Department of Health and Human Services (HHS) will establish a process under which employees who have enrolled for a month in a qualified health plan with respect to which an applicable premium tax credit or cost-sharing reduction is allowed or paid with respect to the employee will be certified to the employer and that, pursuant to the proposed regulations, the certification to the employer will consist of methods adopted by the IRS to provide this information to an employer as part of its determination of liability under section 4980H. Existing HHS regulations also provide for a separate process for notification of employers.

IV. Compliance with Section 4980H(a)

A. In General

Section 4980H(a) provides that an applicable large employer is liable for an assessable payment under section 4980H(a) if, for any month, any full-time employee is certified to receive an applicable premium tax credit (section 4980H(c)(3)) or cost-sharing reduction and the applicable large employer fails to offer its full-time employees (and their dependents) the opportunity to enroll in minimum essential coverage (MEC) (as defined in section 5000A(f)) under an eligible employer-sponsored plan. If an employer offers MEC under an eligible employer-sponsored plan to its full-time employees (and their dependents), it will not be subject to the penalty under section 4980H(a), regardless of whether the coverage it offers is affordable to the employees or provides minimum value. For any calendar month, an applicable large employer member may be liable for an assessable payment under section 4980H(a) or under section 4980H(b), but cannot be liable under both section 4980H(a) and section 4980H(b) for the same calendar month.

B. *Offer of Coverage To The Employee And The Employee's Dependents*

Under section 4980H(a), an applicable large employer member is subject to an assessable payment if the member fails to offer its full-time employees (and their dependents) the opportunity to enroll in MEC under an eligible employer-sponsored plan and any full-time employee receives a premium tax credit or cost-sharing reduction. Commenters have asked whether coverage must be offered to the employee's dependents, and if so, to which individuals the term "dependents" refers. Some commenters argued that an offer of dependent coverage is not required under section 4980H because the statutory reference to dependents is in parentheses, and others noted that the liability under section 4980H is triggered only by a full-time employee receiving a premium tax credit (regardless of whether any dependents are eligible for, or receive, a premium tax credit).

The fundamental rules of statutory construction provide that effect must be given, to the extent possible, to every word, clause and sentence. *See* 2A Sutherland Statutory Construction 46:6 (7th ed. 2007). Applying these principles to the words "employees (and their dependents)," the language cannot be construed to mean only employees. To accept the commenters' argument that the statute requires an offer of coverage only to full-time employees would require ignoring the words "and their dependents" in their entirety. Accordingly, the proposed regulations provide that the words "and their dependents" in section 4980H refer to an offer of coverage to dependents.

Section 4980H does not contain a statutory definition of the term dependents for purposes of the references to dependents in section 4980H(a) and (b). The proposed regulations define an employee's *dependents* for purposes of section 4980H as an employee's child (as defined in section 152(f)(1)) who is under 26 years of age. A child attains age 26 on the 26th anniversary of the date the child was born. For example, a child born on April 10, 1986 attained age 26 on April 10, 2012. Employers may rely on employees' representations concerning the identity and ages of the employees' children. The term *dependents*, as defined in these proposed regulations for purposes of section 4980H, does not include any individual other than children as described in this paragraph of the preamble, including an employee's spouse. Thus, an offer of coverage to an employee's spouse is not required for purposes of section 4980H because section 4980H refers only to dependents (and not spouses). This definition of dependents applies only for purposes of section 4980H and does not apply for purposes of any other section of the Code. But see section IX.F. of the preamble for transition relief with respect to the requirement to offer coverage to dependents.

C. *Offer Of Coverage*

1. *In General*

For an employee to be treated as having been offered coverage for a month (or any day in that month), the coverage offered, if accepted, must be applicable for that month (or that day). These regulations clarify that if an applicable large employer member fails to offer coverage to a full-time employee for any day of a calendar month during which the employee was employed by the employer, the employee is treated as not being offered coverage during that entire month. However, in a calendar month when a full-time employee terminates employment, if the employee would have been offered coverage for the entire month if the employee had been employed for the entire month, the employee is treated as having been offered coverage during that month.

Several commenters requested clarification of what an employer would be required to provide to adequately demonstrate that it had offered coverage to an employee. These regulations do not propose any new specific rules for demonstrating that an offer of coverage was made. The otherwise generally applicable substantiation and record-keeping requirements in section 6001 would apply, including Rev. Proc. 98-25 (1998-1 CB 689), (see § 601.601(d)(2)(ii)(b) of this chap-

ter). In addition, the provision of the offer generally could be made electronically. Section 1.401(a)-21 provides a safe harbor method for use of electronic media. See also Notice 99-1 (1999-1 CB 269).

However, these regulations provide that if an employee has not been offered an effective opportunity to accept coverage, the employee will not be treated as having been offered the coverage for purposes of section 4980H. The employee must also have an effective opportunity to decline an offer of coverage that is not minimum value coverage or that is not affordable. Thus, an employer may not render an employee ineligible for a premium tax credit by providing an employee with mandatory coverage (that is, coverage which the employee is not offered an effective opportunity to decline) that does not meet minimum value. For an analogous provision relating to the effective opportunity to participate (or refuse participation) in an employee benefit arrangement, see § 1.401(k)-1(e)(2)(ii).

2. *Offer of Coverage In the Case of Nonpayment or Late Payment of Premiums*

Some commenters noted that in certain instances the employee share of the premium is not collected through withholding from the employee's salary but instead is billed to the employee. This may arise, for example, with respect to tipped employees, and may apply with respect to employees who were full-time employees during a measurement period but who work very few hours during the corresponding stability period. These commenters stated that in some instances employees do not pay their share of the premium on a timely basis and requested guidance on whether the employer would still be required to continue to provide coverage to those employees to avoid potential liability under section 4980H. The proposed regulations provide that, if an employee enrolls in coverage but fails to pay the employee's share of the premium on a timely basis, the employer is not required to provide coverage for the period for which the premium is not timely paid, and that employer is treated as having offered that employee coverage for the remainder of the coverage period (typically the remainder of the plan year) for purposes of section 4980H. The regulations generally adopt the provisions applicable for purposes of payment for COBRA continuation coverage under Q&A-5 of § 54.4980B-8, which generally provides a 30-day grace period for payment and also provides rules with respect to timely payments that are not significantly less than the amount required to be paid and for responding to requests by health care providers for confirmation of coverage during the grace period.

D. *Section 4980H(a) Relief For Failure To Offer Coverage To A Limited Number Of Full-Time Employees*

Section 4980H(a) liability is predicated on an applicable large employer member failing to offer its full-time employees (and their dependents) the opportunity to enroll in minimum essential coverage under an employer-sponsored plan. If section 4980H(a) liability is triggered, the amount of the assessable payment is determined by reference to a member's total number of full-time employees (including full-time employees offered employer-sponsored coverage). The Treasury Department and the IRS contemplate that the assessable payment should not apply in the case of a member that intends to offer coverage to all its full-time employees, but fails to offer coverage with respect to a few full-time employees. Notice 2011-36 initially addressed this issue by indicating that the Treasury Department and the IRS were contemplating providing in the proposed regulations that an employer offering coverage to all, or substantially all, of its full-time employees would not be subject to a section 4980H(a) assessable payment. Commenters generally welcomed the prospect of some flexibility or margin in lieu of an absolute standard that the employer offer coverage to all full-time employees (and their dependents). Many comments supported a "substantially all" standard, but many requested that the regulations prescribe a more definitive rule, specifying a particular percentage of full-time employees and their dependents (with comments suggesting various percentages) who need not be offered coverage for this purpose.

After further study and consideration of the comments, the Treasury Department and the IRS believe that they should exercise their administrative authority to allow recognition of a margin of error consistent with an intent to recognize the possibility of inadvertent errors together with the specificity and administrability of a specific percentage, and therefore have concluded that a clear and definitive 95 percent standard would be an administrable and appropriate interpretation of the statutory provision. Accordingly, the proposed regulations provide that an applicable large employer member will be treated as offering coverage to its full-time employees (and their dependents) for a calendar month if, for that month, it offers coverage to all but five percent or, if greater, five of its full-time employees (provided that an employee is treated as having been offered coverage only if the employer also offered coverage to that employee's dependents). The alternative margin of five full-time employees (and their dependents), if greater than five percent of full-time employees (and their dependents), is designed to accommodate relatively small applicable large employer members because a failure to offer coverage to a handful of full-time employees (and their dependents) might exceed five percent of the applicable large employer member's full-time employees. This relief applies to a failure to offer coverage to the specified number or percentage of employees (and their dependents), regardless of whether the failure to offer was inadvertent.

E. *Application Of The Section 4980H(c)(2)(D) 30-Employee Reduction*

Section 4980H(c)(2)(D)(i) provides that the number of individuals employed by an applicable large employer as full-time employees during any month shall be reduced by 30 solely for purposes of calculating the assessable payment under section 4980H(a) and the overall limit on the liability under section 4980H(b)(2) for any calendar month (which is equal to the product of the applicable payment amount described in section 4980H(c)(1) and the number of individuals employed by the employer as full-time employees during that calendar month). Section 4980H(c)(2)(D)(ii) further provides that in the case of persons treated as a single applicable large employer under the aggregation rules, only one 30-employee reduction is allowed with respect to those persons and the reduction is allocated among them ratably on the basis of the number of full-time employees employed by each. If an applicable large employer has more than 30 applicable large employer members, with some or all of the applicable large employer members receiving a ratable allocation of more than zero but less than one full-time employee, the proposed regulations provide that the applicable large employer member's share of the 30-employee reduction will be rounded up to one full-time employee (which may result in an overall reduction to all members of the applicable large employer of more than 30 employees).

F. *Section 4980H(a) Assessable Payment Amount*

The assessable payment amount under section 4980H(a) equals, with respect to any calendar month, the number of full-time employees of the applicable large employer member (reduced by the allocable share of the 30-employee reduction) multiplied by the section 4980H(a) applicable payment amount. The initial section 4980H(a) applicable payment amount for a calendar month equals 1/12 th of $2,000. For subsequent years, that amount is adjusted for inflation pursuant to section 4980H(c)(5) based upon the premium adjustment percentage (as defined in section 1302(c)(4) of the Affordable Care Act) for the calendar year, rounded down to the next lowest multiple of $10.

V. *Section 4980H(b) Liability*

A. *In General*

If an applicable large employer member offers its full-time employees (and their dependents) the opportunity to enroll in MEC under an eligible employer-sponsored plan but nonetheless one or more full-time employees have been certified for the payment of an applicable premium tax credit or cost-sharing reduction, the employer generally is liable for a section 4980H(b) penalty based on the number of its full-time employees receiving an applicable premium tax credit or cost-sharing reduction. This may occur because (1) the coverage under the plan is unaffordable within the meaning of section 36(B)(c)(2)(C)(i) for the employee (and the employer does not meet the requirements of any of the affordability safe harbors described in section V.B.2. of this preamble), (2) the coverage under the plan does not provide minimum value within the meaning of section 36(B)(c)(2)(C)(ii), or (3) the employer offers coverage to at least 95 percent (or, if greater, five) but less than 100 percent of its full-time employees (and to those employees' dependents) and one or more of those employees who are not offered coverage receive a premium tax credit or cost-sharing reduction. See section IV of the preamble; see also section 36B(c)(2)(C) and § 1.36B-2(c)(3). Regulations under section 36B were published on May 23, 2012 (77 FR 30377), as corrected on July 13, 2012 (77 FR 41270).

B. *Affordable Coverage*

1. *In General*

Generally, section 4980H(b) liability may arise because, with respect to a full-time employee who has been certified to the employer as having received an applicable premium tax credit or cost-sharing reduction, the employer's coverage is unaffordable within the meaning of section 36B(c)(2)(C)(i) or does not provide minimum value within the meaning of section 36B(c)(2)(C)(ii). Therefore, section 4980H(b) effectively creates an affordability test based on section 36B affordability. For purposes of eligibility for the premium tax credit, coverage for an employee under an employer-sponsored plan is affordable if the employee's required contribution (within the meaning of section 5000A(e)(1)(B)) for self-only coverage does not exceed 9.5 percent of the employee's household income for the taxable year. See sections 36B(c)(2)(C)(i) and 36B(d)(2), and section III.C. of the preamble.

As noted in of the Background section of the preamble, Notice 2011-73 (2011-40 IRB 474) outlined a proposed affordability safe harbor (referred to as the Form W-2 safe harbor) in connection with the assessable payment under section 4980H(b) and requested comments on other potential safe harbors. The comments with respect to the proposed safe harbor generally were favorable and some commenters outlined other potential safe harbors they argued could assist employers in their efforts to determine affordability of coverage for purposes of section 4980H. See also Notice 2012-58 regarding reliance on the Form W-2 safe harbor for 2014. In response to the comments, the proposed regulations provide for the Form W-2 safe harbor and two additional safe harbors for determining affordability, as described in section V.B.2. of the preamble.

2. *Affordability Safe Harbors*

The three section 4980H(b) affordability safe harbors, as described in this preamble and incorporated into the proposed regulations, would apply only for purposes of determining whether an employer's coverage satisfies the 9.5 percent affordability test for purposes of the assessable payment under section 4980H(b). The section 4980H(b) safe harbors do not apply for purposes of determining the assessable payment under section 4980H(a). The safe harbors also would not affect an employee's eligibility for a premium tax credit under section 36B, which would continue to be based on the cost of employer-sponsored coverage relative to an employee's household income. Accordingly, in some instances, the effect of the safe harbor could be to treat an employer's offer of coverage to an employee as affordable (based on Form W-2 wages or one of the other affordability safe harbor standards) for purposes of determining whether the employer is subject to an assessable payment under section 4980H(b), while that same offer of coverage could be treated as unaffordable (based on household income) for purposes of determining whether the employee is eligible for a premium tax credit under section 36B.

These safe harbors are all optional. An employer may choose to use one or more of these safe harbors for all its employees or for any reasonable category of employees, provided it does so on a uniform and consistent basis for all employees in a category.

a. *Form W-2 safe harbor*

The proposed regulations provide a safe harbor under which an employer could determine affordability for purposes of section 4980H(b) liability by reference to an employee's wages from that employer. Under this proposed regulation, wages for this purpose would be the total amount of wages as defined in section 3401(a), which is the amount required to be reported in Box 1 of Form W-2, Wage and Tax Statement (referred to in this preamble as Form W-2 wages).

For the proposed Form W-2 wages safe harbor to apply, an employer must meet certain requirements, including: (1) that the employer offers its full-time employees (and their dependents) the opportunity to enroll in minimum essential coverage under an eligible employer-sponsored plan; and (2) that the required employee contribution toward the self-only premium for the employer's lowest cost coverage that provides minimum value (the employee contribution) not exceed 9.5 percent of the employee's Form W-2 wages for that calendar year. For this purpose, an employer may count wages paid to its employees by a third party that are reported on a Form W-2 that reflects the third party's EIN, for example because the Form W-2 was filed by an agent designated under section 3504 of the Code, or because the third party paying the wages was treated as the employer for employment tax purposes under section 3401(d)(1). If the employer satisfies both of these requirements for a particular employee (as well as any other conditions for the safe harbor), the employer will not be subject to an assessable payment under section 4980H(b) with respect to that particular employee, even if that employee receives a premium tax credit or cost sharing reduction because the employee's actual household income was less than the Form W-2 wages and, based on that household income, the coverage offered was not affordable.

Application of this safe harbor is determined after the end of the calendar year and on an employee-by-employee basis, taking into account the employee's Form W-2 wages from the employer and the employee contribution. So, for example, the employer determines whether it met the Form W-2 safe harbor for 2014 for an employee by looking at that employee's 2014 Form W-2 wages (meaning the wages reported on the 2014 Form W-2 that generally is furnished to the employee in January 2015) and comparing 9.5 percent of that amount to the employee's 2014 employee contribution. Although the determination of whether an employer actually satisfied the safe harbor is made after the end of the calendar year, an employer could also use the safe harbor prospectively, at the beginning of the year, to set the employee contribution at a level so that the employee contribution for each employee would not exceed 9.5 percent of that employee's Form W-2 wages for that year (for example, by automatically deducting 9.5 percent, or a lower percentage, from an employee's Form W-2 wages for each pay period). See also the rate of pay affordability safe harbor and the Federal poverty line safe harbor, discussed in section V.B.2. of this preamble.

In response to Notice 2011-73, several commenters noted that Box 1 of the Form W-2 excludes elective deferrals that an employee makes into a section 401(k) plan or section 403(b) plan, and excludes amounts that an employee elects to contribute to a section 125 cafeteria plan through salary reduction (for example, for health insurance premiums,[4] health flexible spending arrangements, dependent care assistance, or health savings accounts). The commenters contended that the measure of an employee's total compensation for purposes of the affordability safe harbor calculation should include the employee's elective deferrals to a retirement savings plan or cafeteria plan. The proposed regulations do not adopt this comment. The determination of whether employer-sponsored coverage is affordable for an employee under section 36B(c)(2)(C)(i) is based on modified adjusted income and does not take into account any elective deferrals to a section 401(k), section 403(b) or cafeteria plan. Given that these amounts are not taken into account in determining the affordability of coverage for purposes of an employee's eligibility for a section 36B credit, it would be inconsistent to allow employers to add back those amounts in determining their liability under section 4980H(b), which is linked to that employee's section 36B credit. However, see the rate of pay affordability safe harbor described in this section V.B.2. of the preamble, which could be used regardless of the amount of an employee's elective deferrals.

Notice 2011-73 also requested comments on how wages and employee contributions would need to be determined for employees employed for less than a full year by an employer (for example, a new employee hired during the calendar year or an employee who terminated employment during the calendar year) or an employee who was not offered coverage for the full year (for example, a new employee hired during the calendar year or an employee who switches positions of employment during the calendar year and so becomes eligible for coverage). Under section 36B, affordability for a part-year period is determined by comparing annual income to an annualized premium. See § 1.36B-2(c)(3)(v)(B). However, using this test to determine liability under section 4980H(b) could, in certain cases, result in penalizing employers that offer coverage that would be affordable based on the wages paid to, and premiums charged to, an employee for a given period. For example, if an employee was employed for six months of a calendar year by an employer, and offered coverage for those six months with an employee premium that did not exceed 9.5 percent of the employee's wages for those six months, and if the employee was not employed by the employer or any other employer for the other six months of the calendar year, the annualized premium may be higher than 9.5 percent of the employee's Form W-2 wages for the year. Commenters on Notice 2011-73 recommended several approaches, including prorating wages and premiums, using a reasonable estimate of Form W-2 wages for the year, and applying the safe harbor on a month-by-month basis.

The proposed regulations address this issue by providing that, for an employee who was not a full-time employee for the entire calendar year, the Form W-2 safe harbor is applied by adjusting the employee's Form W-2 wages to reflect the period when the employee was offered coverage, and then comparing those adjusted wages to the employee share of the premium during that period. Specifically, the amount of the employee's compensation for purposes of the safe harbor is determined by multiplying the wages for the calendar year by a fraction equal to the months for which coverage was offered to the employee over the months the employee was employed. That adjusted wage amount is then compared to the employee share of the premium for the months that coverage was offered to determine whether the Form W-2 safe harbor was satisfied for that period. For example, if the employee worked eight months of a calendar year, during five months of which the employee was offered coverage, and received a Form W-2 reflecting Form W-2 wages of $24,000, the adjusted wages would be

$24,000 multiplied by 5/8 or $15,000. That $15,000 is then treated as the adjusted Form W-2 wages for purposes of determining whether the employee share of the premium for each of the five months of coverage offered was affordable under the section 4980H safe harbor (meaning the employee would be treated for this purpose as earning $3,000 per month during that five-month period).

b. Rate of pay safe harbor

Notice 2011-73 requested comments on other possible safe harbor methods for determining the affordability of employer-sponsored coverage for purposes of section 4980H(b). Several commenters suggested a safe harbor that is based on a rate of pay (either the employer's lowest rate of pay or each employee's individual rate of pay). In response to these comments, the proposed regulations provide a rate of pay safe harbor under which the employer would (1) take the hourly rate of pay for each hourly employee who is eligible to participate in the health plan as of the beginning of the plan year, (2) multiply that rate by 130 hours per month (the benchmark for full-time status for a month under section 4980H), and (3) determine affordability based on the resulting monthly wage amount. Specifically, the employee's monthly contribution amount (for the self-only premium of the employer's lowest cost coverage that provides minimum value) is affordable if it is equal to or lower than 9.5 percent of the computed monthly wages (that is, the employee's applicable hourly rate of pay × 130 hours). For salaried employees, monthly salary would be used instead of hourly salary multiplied by 130. An employer may use this safe harbor only if, with respect to the employees for whom the employer applies the safe harbor, the employer did not reduce the hourly wages of hourly employees or the monthly wages of salaried employees during the year. The rate of pay safe harbor is a design-based safe harbor that should be easy for employers to apply and allows them to prospectively satisfy affordability without the need to analyze every employee's wages and hours.

c. Federal poverty line safe harbor

Some commenters suggested that determinations of affordability should disregard employees whose income would qualify the employee for coverage under Medicaid (and, accordingly, would disqualify the employee from receiving the premium tax credit.) The suggestions reflect that employees who cannot receive a premium tax credit, which are not available by law to individuals with income below 100 percent of the Federal poverty line, cannot trigger 4980H(b) liability.

In response to these suggestions, the proposed regulations provide that an employer may also rely on a design-based safe harbor using the Federal poverty line (FPL) for a single individual. Specifically, for purposes of section 4980H, employer-provided coverage offered to an employee is affordable if the employee's cost for self-only coverage under the plan does not exceed 9.5 percent of the FPL for a single individual. For households with families, the amount that is considered to be below the poverty line is higher, so using the amount for a single individual ensures that the employee contribution for affordable coverage is minimized. In the interest of administrative convenience, employers are permitted to use the most recently published poverty guidelines as of the first day of the plan year of the applicable large employer member's health plan.

C. Section 4980H(b) Assessable Payment Amount

The assessable payment amount under section 4980H(b) equals, for any calendar month, the number of full-time employees of the applicable large employer member who receive an applicable premium tax credit or cost-sharing reduction multiplied by the section 4980H(b) applicable payment amount. The initial section 4980H(b) applicable payment amount for a calendar month equals 1/12 th of $3,000. For subsequent years, that amount is adjusted for inflation pursuant to section 4980H(c)(5) based upon the premium adjustment percentage (as defined in section 1302(c)(4) of the Affordable Care Act) for the calendar year, rounded down to the next lowest multiple of $10. Notwithstanding the foregoing, the assessable payment under section 4980H(b) cannot exceed the amount of the assessable payment that would have been imposed under section 4980H(a) if the applicable large employer member had failed to offer coverage to its full-time employees (and their dependents). Also, for any employee for whom the employer satisfies at least one of the affordability safe harbors described in section V.B.2. of this preamble, the employer is not subject to an assessable payment under section 4980H(b) for that employee if the coverage offered to that employee otherwise satisfies minimum value.

---

[4] As a practical matter, if an employee makes a salary reduction to pay for employer-provided MEC and thus is actually receiving the employer-provided MEC, the employee will not be eligible to receive the section 36B credit for that period. See section 36B(c)(2)(C)((iii).

VI. *Assessment and Payment of Section 4980H Liability*

Each applicable large employer member is liable for its section 4980H assessable payment, and is not liable for the section 4980H assessable payment of any other entity in the controlled group comprising the applicable large employer. With respect to a disregarded entity, as defined in §301.7701-2, the proposed regulations regard the entity for purposes of an assessable payment under section 4980H and for purposes of reporting under section 6056. Therefore, the assessable payment and reporting requirements are imposed on the disregarded entity, and not on the owner of the disregarded entity. See proposed §301.7701-2(c)(2)(v)(A)(5). These rules would also apply to a qualified subchapter S subsidiary. See proposed §1.1361-4(a)(8)(i)(E).

Any assessable payment under section 4980H is payable upon notice and demand and is assessed and collected in the same manner as an assessable penalty under subchapter B of chapter 68 of the Code. Pursuant to regulations to be issued by HHS, the IRS will follow procedures that ensure employers receive certification that one or more employees have received premium tax credits or cost-sharing reductions and are provided an opportunity to respond before the issuance of any notice and demand for payment.

In complying with section 4980H, including relying on a look-back measurement method for determining full-time employees and non full-time employees and safe harbor methods for determining affordability for purposes of section 4980H(b) (as described in sections II and V.B.2. of this preamble), applicable large employer members are responsible for insuring that they comply with the recordkeeping requirements in section 6001, including Rev. Proc. 98-25 (1998-1 CB 689), (see §601.601(d)(2)(ii)(*b*) of this chapter).

Pursuant to section 275(a)(6) regarding the nondeductibility of certain excise taxes, including those under chapter 43, an assessable payment imposed under section 4980H is not deductible.

VII. *Information Reporting Under Section 6056*

Applicable large employer members are required to report certain information on employer-provided health coverage under section 6056. Reporting will begin in 2015 for coverage provided on or after January 1, 2014. Notice 2012-33 (2012-20 IRB 912) requests comments on section 6056 information reporting. The Treasury Department and the IRS intend to publish separate proposed regulations implementing section 6056. For purposes of this reporting requirement, the proposed regulations are expected to apply to each applicable large employer member, as defined for purposes of section 4980H. The proposed regulations are also expected to align most definitions and rules so that, for example, if an employer is treated as offering coverage for a month for purposes of section 4980H, the employer would report the coverage was offered for that month.

VIII. *Public Health Service Act Section 2708 - The 90-Day Maximum Waiting Period*

Public Health Service Act (PHS Act) section 2708 provides that, for plan years beginning on or after January 1, 2014, a group health plan or health insurance issuer offering group health insurance coverage shall not apply any waiting period that exceeds 90 days. PHS Act section 2704(b)(4), ERISA section 701(b)(4), and Code section 9801(b)(4) define a waiting period to be the period that must pass with respect to an individual before the individual is eligible to be covered for benefits under the terms of the plan. PHS Act section 2708 does not require the employer to offer coverage to any particular employee or class of employees, including part-time employees; but merely prevents an otherwise eligible employee (or dependent) from having to wait more than 90 days before coverage becomes effective.

Notice 2012-17 outlined various approaches under consideration with respect to both the 90-day waiting period limitation and the employer shared responsibility provisions under section 4980H,[5] and invited comments on the approaches contained in the notice, including a request for comments on how rules relating to the potential look-back measurement method for determining the full-time status of employees under Code section 4980H should be coordinated with the 90-day waiting period limitation of PHS Act section 2708. Subsequent guidance, under Notice 2012-59, provided temporary guidance on compliance with PHS Act section 2708, and provided that this temporary guidance would remain in effect at least through the end of 2014.[6]

IX. *Transition Rules*

A. *Plans with Fiscal Year Plan Years*

Commenters on behalf of employers sponsoring plans with plan years other than the calendar year (fiscal year plans) addressed two issues in particular. First, these commenters noted that because the terms and conditions of coverage are difficult to change in the middle of a plan year, application of section 4980H to fiscal year plans as of January 1, 2014 would, in many cases, require compliance with section 4980H for the entire fiscal year plan year beginning in 2013 (the 2013 plan year). In addition, these commenters observed that, in order to use the look-back measurement method to determine their employees' status as full-time employees for the 2013 plan year ending in 2014, employers with fiscal year plans would be required to determine the employees' hours of service for periods before the publication of these proposed regulations.

In response to these concerns, transition relief is being provided for applicable large employer members with fiscal year plans. If an applicable large employer member maintains a fiscal year plan as of December 27, 2012, the relief applies with respect to employees of the applicable large employer member (whenever hired) who would be eligible for coverage, as of the first day of the first fiscal year of that plan that begins in 2014 (the 2014 plan year) under the eligibility terms of the plan as in effect on December 27, 2012. If an employee described in the preceding sentence is offered affordable, minimum value coverage no later than the first day of the 2014 plan year, no section 4980H assessable payment will be due with respect to that employee for the period prior to the first day of the 2014 plan year. [Corrected 3/15/13 (78 FR 16445).]

While transition relief is provided with respect to all enrollees (and other eligible employees) in fiscal year plans, further relief is also provided for employers that have a significant percentage of their employees eligible for or covered under one or more fiscal year plans that have the same plan year as of December 27, 2012 and want to offer certain other employees coverage under these plans. Specifically, if an applicable large employer member has at least one-quarter of its employees covered under one or more fiscal year plans that have the same plan year as of December 27, 2012 or offered coverage under those plans to one-third or more of its employees during the most recent open enrollment period before December 27, 2012, no payment under section 4980H will be due for any month prior to the first day of the 2014 plan year of that fiscal year plan with respect to employees who (1) are offered affordable, minimum value coverage no later than the first day of the 2014 plan year of the fiscal year plan, and (2) would not have been eligible for coverage under any group health plan maintained by the applicable large employer member as of December 27, 2012 that has a calendar year plan year. For purposes of this transition relief, an applicable large employer member may determine the percentage of its employees covered under the fiscal year plan or plans as of the end of the most recent enrollment period or any date between October 31, 2012 and December 27, 2012.

Employers using this transition relief will still be subject to the reporting requirements under section 6056 for the entire 2014 calendar year. The concerns described in this section of the preamble with respect to the application of section 4980H do not apply with respect to reporting by a fiscal year plan under section 6056. Because no section 4980H liability will occur whether or not a full-time employee is offered coverage during the portion of the 2013 plan year falling in 2014, the applicable large employer may determine the full-time employees for that period for purposes of the section 6056 reporting requirements after the period has ended, using actual service data rather than the look-back measurement method, and use those determinations for the reporting required at the beginning of 2015 to cover the entire 2014 calendar year. In addition, the identification of whether the coverage offered provides minimum value and the employee portion of the applicable premium should be available to the employer in time to complete the required reporting. Therefore, because this reporting is essential to the administration of the premium tax credit under section 36B, applicable large employers will be required to report this information for the entire 2014 calendar year, even if during some calendar months in 2014 section 4980H liability will not apply due to application of the transition rules for fiscal year plan years.

The Treasury Department and the IRS are developing appropriate transition rules for employees of employers with fiscal year plans to account for the fact that premium tax credits will first become available for the 2014 calendar year.

---

[5] Department of Labor Technical Release 2012-01, IRS Notice 2012-17, and HHS FAQs issued February 9, 2012.

[6] Department of Labor Technical Release 2012-02, IRS Notice 2012-59, and HHS FAQs issued August 31, 2012.

B. *Salary Reduction Elections For Accident And Health Plans Provided Through Cafeteria Plans For Cafeteria Plan Years Beginning in 2013*

Many employers offer health plans to employees through salary reduction under a section 125 cafeteria plan. Generally, cafeteria plan elections must be made before the start of the plan year, and are irrevocable during the plan year. See proposed § 1.125-2. However, the final regulations under § 1.125-4 permit a cafeteria plan to provide for changes in elections in certain circumstances, such as for change in status events. An employer that wishes to permit such changes in elections must incorporate the rules in § 1.125-4 in its written cafeteria plan.

In 2014, employees of an applicable large employer member covered under their employer's health plan through salary reduction under their employer's cafeteria plan may wish to enroll in coverage through an Exchange and discontinue their employer's coverage. However, the availability of health plan coverage through an Exchange beginning in 2014 does not constitute a change in status under § 1.125-4. As a result, employees would not be permitted to change their salary reduction elections for accident and health coverage during the plan year to cease salary reduction under the cafeteria plan and purchase coverage through an Exchange. Conversely, to avoid the individual responsibility payment under section 5000A, employees not covered under their employer's health plan may wish to enroll in the plan beginning after December 31, 2013.

The Treasury Department and the IRS have concluded that it is appropriate to provide transition relief from the election rules in proposed § 1.125-2 with respect to salary reduction elections under a cafeteria plan for an employer-provided accident and health plan with a fiscal year beginning in 2013. This transition relief applies only to the revocation, modification, or commencement of salary reductions for accident and health coverage offered through a cafeteria plan of an employer with a cafeteria fiscal year plan beginning in 2013 (and does not apply to any other qualified benefit offered through a cafeteria plan).

Thus, an applicable large employer member is permitted, at its election, to amend one or more of its written cafeteria plans to permit either or both of the following changes in salary reduction elections:

(1) An employee who elected to salary reduce through the cafeteria plan for accident and health plan coverage with a fiscal plan year beginning in 2013 is allowed to prospectively revoke or change his or her election with respect to the accident and health plan once, during that plan year, without regard to whether the employee experienced a change in status event described in § 1.125-4; and

(2) An employee who failed to make a salary reduction election through his or her employer's cafeteria plan for accident and health plan coverage with a fiscal plan year beginning in 2013 before the deadline in proposed § 1.125-2 for making elections for the cafeteria plan year beginning in 2013 is allowed to make a prospective salary reduction election for accident and health coverage on or after the first day of the 2013 plan year of the cafeteria plan, without regard to whether the employee experienced a change in status event described in § 1.125-4.

An applicable large employer member that wants to permit the change in election rules under this transition relief for fiscal plan years must incorporate these rules in its written cafeteria plan. Pursuant to proposed § 1.125-1(c), a plan may be amended at any time on a prospective basis. Notwithstanding the general rule that amendments to cafeteria plans may only be effective prospectively from the date of the plan amendment, a cafeteria plan may be amended retroactively to implement these transition rules. The retroactive amendment must be made by December 31, 2014, and be effective retroactively to the date of the first day of the 2013 plan year of the cafeteria plan.

C. *Measurement Periods for Stability Periods Starting in 2014*

Section 4980H is effective for months beginning after December 31, 2013. Employers that intend to utilize the look-back measurement method for determining full-time status for 2014 will need to begin their measurement periods in 2013 to have corresponding stability periods for 2014. The Treasury Department and the IRS recognize, however, that employers intending to adopt a 12-month measurement period, and in turn a 12-month stability period, will face time constraints in doing so. Consequently, solely for purposes of stability periods beginning in 2014, employers may adopt a transition measurement period that is shorter than 12 months but that is no less than 6 months long and that begins no later than July 1, 2013 and ends no earlier than 90-days before the first day of the plan year beginning on or after January 1, 2014 (90-days being the maximum permissible administrative period). For example, an employer with a calendar year plan could use a measurement period from April 15, 2013 through October 14,

2013 (six months), followed by an administrative period ending on December 31, 2013. An employer with a plan with a fiscal plan year beginning April 1 that also elected to implement a 90-day administrative period could use a measurement period from July 1, 2013 through December 31, 2013 (six months), followed by an administrative period ending on March 31, 2014. However, an employer with a fiscal plan year beginning on July 1, 2014 must use a measurement period that is longer than 6 months in order to comply with the requirement that the measurement period begin no later than July 1, 2013 and end no earlier than 90 days before the stability period. For example, the employer could have a 10-month measurement period from June 15, 2013 through April 14, 2014, followed by an administrative period from April 15, 2014 through June 30, 2014. This transition relief is solely for the application of a stability period beginning in 2014 through the end of that stability period (including any portion of the stability period falling in 2015).

Note that employers who use a full 12-month measurement period are not required to begin the measurement period by July 1, 2013. For example, an employer with a fiscal plan year beginning on November 1, 2014 could use a 12-month measurement period from September 1, 2013 through August 31, 2014, followed by an administrative period from September 1, 2014 through October 31, 2014.

See section II.C.1. of this preamble for rules on changing measurement periods from year to year.

D. *Applicable Large Employer Members Participating in Multiemployer Plans*

Several comments requested a special rule for employers participating in multiemployer plans in view of such plans' unique operating structures. Multiemployer plans are maintained pursuant to collective bargaining agreements, and have joint boards of trustees representing employees and employers. Each participating employer's relationship with the plan and the employee's participation in the plan differs from the typical single-employer-sponsored arrangement. For example, service at participating employers generally is aggregated to determine an employee's eligibility to participate in the multiemployer plan, even though the participating employers generally are not related. Because many of the collective bargaining agreements governing multiemployer plans provide that contributions be made to the multiemployer fund based on requirements other than hours worked, such as on a days worked, projects completed, or percentage of earnings basis, contributing employers may not be in a position to know how many hours any individual employee worked. This problem is exacerbated by the fact that covered employees often work for multiple employers and it is thus impracticable for any one employer, or the fund, to determine how many hours any individual employee worked. For these reasons, further comments are requested on how section 4980H should apply to employers participating in multiemployer plans.

The transition rule described in this section X.D. applies through 2014 for contributions made by applicable large employers participating in a multiemployer plan. The rule is intended to provide an administratively feasible means for employers that contribute to multiemployer plans to comply with section 4980H. If any assessable payment were due under section 4980H, it would be payable by a participating applicable large employer member and that member would be responsible for identifying its full-time employees for this purpose (which would be based on hours of service for that employer). If the applicable large employer contributes to one or more multiemployer plans and also maintains a single employer plan, the rule applies to each multiemployer plan but not to the single employer plan.

This transition rule applies to an applicable large employer member that is required by a collective bargaining agreement to make contributions, with respect to some or all of its employees, to a multiemployer plan that offers, to individuals who satisfy the plan's eligibility conditions, coverage that is affordable and provides minimum value, and that offers coverage to those individuals' dependents. Under this transition rule, the applicable large employer member will not be treated, with respect to employees for whom the employer is required by the collective bargaining agreement to make contributions to the multiemployer plan, as failing to offer the opportunity to enroll in minimum essential coverage to full-time employees (and their dependents) for purposes of section 4980H(a), and will not be subject to a penalty under section 4980H(b). For purposes of this paragraph, whether the employee is a full-time employee is determined under section 4980H(c)(4), whether coverage is affordable is determined under section 36(c)(2)(C)(i), and whether coverage provides minimum value is determined under section 36B(c)(2)(C)(ii). Notwithstanding this transition relief, any waiting period for coverage under the plan must separately comply with the 90-day limitation on waiting periods in section 2708 of the Public Health Service Act. Further guidance under section 2708 of the Public Health Service Act will address this limitation. In addition to the transition rule provided under this section IX.D, the transition rule under section IX.F of this preamble (relief with respect to offers of coverage to dependents) is applicable to multiemployer plans and employers participating in those plans. [Corrected 3/15/13 (78 FR 16445).]

For purposes of determining whether coverage under the multiemployer plan is affordable, employers participating in the plan may use any of the affordability safe harbors set forth in the proposed regulations (and described in section V.B.2. of this preamble). Coverage under a multiemployer plan will also be considered affordable with respect to a full-time employee if the employee's required contribution, if any, toward self-only health coverage under the plan does not exceed 9.5 percent of the wages reported to the qualified multiemployer plan, which may be determined based on actual wages or an hourly wage rate under the applicable collective bargaining agreement.

E. *Applicable Large Employer Determination for 2014*

Section 4980H(c)(2) defines an applicable large employer with respect to a calendar year as an employer that employed an average of at least 50 full-time employees on business days during the preceding calendar year. For purposes of determining whether an employer is an applicable large employer, full-time equivalents (FTEs), which are determined based on the hours of service of employees who are not full-time employees, are taken into account. For most employers, their status as an applicable large employer will be evident without the need for an actual employee calculation (for example, employers with a number of employees that is well in excess of the 50-employee threshold). However, for some employers (those sufficiently close to the 50-employee threshold), a calculation will be required and will be performed for the first time. The Treasury Department and the IRS have concluded that transition relief is appropriate for those employers because they will be becoming familiar with the applicable large employer determination method and applying it for the first time in 2013. Specifically, transition relief is provided for purposes of the applicable large employer determination for the 2014 calendar year that allows an employer the option to determine its status as an applicable large employer by reference to a period of at least six consecutive calendar months, as chosen by the employer, in the 2013 calendar year (rather than the entire 2013 calendar year). Thus, an employer may determine whether it is an applicable large employer for 2014 by determining whether it employed an average of at least 50 full-time employees on business days during any consecutive six-month period in 2013.

This will allow these employers to choose to use either, or both, a period to prepare to count their employees and a period afterward to ascertain and implement the results of the determination. For example, an employer could use the period from January to February, 2013 to establish its counting method, the period from March through August, 2013 to determine its applicable large employer status and, if it is an applicable large employer, the period from September through December, 2013 to make any needed adjustments to its plan (or to establish a plan) in order to comply with section 4980H.

F. *Coverage for Dependents*

A number of employers currently offer coverage only to their employees, and not to dependents. For these employers, expanding their health plans to add dependent coverage will require substantial revisions to their plans and to their procedures for administration of the plans. To provide employers sufficient time to implement these changes, it is appropriate to provide transition relief with respect to dependent coverage for plan years that begin in 2014. Accordingly, any employer that takes steps during its plan year that begins in 2014 toward satisfying the section 4980H provisions relating to the offering of coverage to full-time employees' dependents will not be liable for any assessable payment under section 4980H solely on account of a failure to offer coverage to the dependents for that plan year.

G. *Variable Hour Employee Definition*

The proposed regulations, consistent with Notice 2012-58, provide that a new employee is a variable hour employee if, based on the facts and circumstances at the start date, it cannot be determined that the employee is reasonably expected to be employed on average at least 30 hours per week. A new employee who is expected to be employed initially at least 30 hours per week may be a variable hour employee if, based on the facts and circumstances at the start date, the period of employment at more than 30 hours per week is reasonably expected to be of limited duration and it cannot be determined that the employee is reasonably expected to be employed on average at least 30 hours per

week over the initial measurement period. Effective as of January 1, 2015, and except in the case of seasonal employees, the employer will be required to assume for this purpose that although the employee's hours of service might be expected to vary, the employee will continue to be employed by the employer for the entire initial measurement period; accordingly, the employer will not be permitted to take into account the likelihood that the employee's employment will terminate before the end of the initial measurement period. The effective date of the rule described in the immediately preceding sentence is delayed until 2015 to provide transition relief because some plan sponsors may have interpreted Notice 2012-58 (which gave reliance for 2014) more broadly. Even with respect to 2014, however, the status of any individual employee as a variable hour employee cannot be based on employer expectations regarding aggregate turnover. Rather there must be objective facts and circumstances specific to the newly hired employee at the start date demonstrating that the individual employee's employment is reasonably expected to be of limited duration within the initial measurement period.

X. *Effective Dates and Reliance*

Section 4980H is effective for months after December 31, 2013.

Employers may rely on these proposed regulations for guidance pending the issuance of final regulations or other guidance. Final regulations will be effective as of a date not earlier than the date the final regulations are published in the **Federal Register**. If and to the extent future guidance is more restrictive than the guidance in these proposed regulations, the future guidance will be applied without retroactive effect and employers will be provided with sufficient time to come into compliance with the final regulations.

Special Analyses

It has been determined that this notice of proposed rulemaking is not a significant regulatory action as defined in Executive Order 12866. Therefore, a regulatory assessment is not required.

It has also been determined that section 553(b) of the Administrative Procedure Act (5 U.S.C. chapter 5) does not apply to this regulation, and because the regulation does not impose a collection of information on small entities, the Regulatory Flexibility Act (5 U.S.C. chapter 6) does not apply.

Pursuant to section 7805(f) of the Code, this notice of proposed rulemaking has been submitted to the Chief Counsel for Advocacy of the Small Business Administration for comment on its impact on small business.

Comments and Public Hearing

Before the proposed regulations are adopted as final regulations, consideration will be given to any written comments (a signed original and eight (8) copies) or electronic comments that are submitted timely to the IRS. The Treasury Department and the IRS request comments on all aspects of the proposed rules. All comments will be available for public inspection and copying.

A public hearing has been scheduled for **April 23, 2013,** beginning at **10:00 am** in the Auditorium, Internal Revenue Building, 1111 Constitution Avenue, NW, Washington, DC. Due to building security procedures, visitors must enter at the Constitution Avenue entrance. In addition, all visitors must present photo identification to enter the building. Because of access restrictions, visitors will not be admitted beyond the immediate entrance area more than 30 minutes before the hearing starts. For information about having your name placed on the building access list to attend the hearing, see the "FOR FURTHER INFORMATION CONTACT" section of this preamble.

The rules of 26 CFR 601.601(a)(3) apply to the hearing. Persons who wish to present oral comments at the hearing must submit electronic or written comments by **March 18, 2013**, and an outline of the topics to be discussed and the time to be devoted to each topic (signed original and eight (8) copies) by **April 3, 2013**. A period of 10 minutes will be allotted to each person for making comments. An agenda showing the scheduling of the speakers will be prepared after the deadline for receiving outlines has passed. Copies of the agenda will be available free of charge at the hearing.

Drafting Information

These proposed regulations were drafted by the Office of Tax Exempt and Government Entities. Other personnel from the Treasury Department and the IRS participated in the development of the regulations.

List of Subjects

26 CFR Part 1

Income taxes, Reporting and recordkeeping requirements.

26 CFR Part 54

Excise taxes, Pensions, Reporting and recordkeeping requirements.

26 CFR Part 301

Employment taxes, Estate taxes, Excise taxes, Gift taxes, Income taxes, Penalties, Reporting and recordkeeping requirements.

Proposed Amendments to the Regulations

Accordingly, 26 CFR parts 1, 54, and 301 are proposed to be amended as follows:

PART 1—INCOME TAXES

Paragraph 1. The authority citation for part 1 continues to read in part as follows:

Authority: 26 U.S.C. 7805 * * *

Par. 2. Section 1.1361-4 is amended as follows:

1. In paragraph (a)(8)(i)(C), the language "and 4412; and" is removed and "and 4412;" is added in its place.

2. In paragraph (a)(8)(i)(D), the language "or 6427." is removed and "or 6427; and " is added in its place.

3. Paragraphs (a)(8)(i)(E) is added.

4. In paragraph (a)(8)(ii), the language "January 1, 2008." is removed and "January 1, 2008, except that paragraph (a)(8)(i)(E) of this section applies for months after December 31, 2013." is added in its place.

The additions read as follows:

§ 1.1361-4 *Effect of QSub election.*

(a) * * *

(8) * * *

(i) * * *

(E) Assessment and collection of an assessable payment imposed by section 4980H and reporting required by section 6056.

* * * * *

PART 54—PENSION EXCISE TAXES

Par. 3. The authority citation for part 54 is amended by adding entries in numerical order to read as follows:

Authority: 26 U.S.C. 7805 * * *

Section 54.4980H-3 is also issued under 26 U.S.C. 4980H(c)(4)(B).

Par. 4. Sections 54.4980H-0, 54.4980H-1, 54.4980H-2, 54.4980H-3, 54.4980H-4, 54.4980H-5, and 54.4980H-6 are added to read as follows:

§ 54.4980H-0 *Table of contents.*

This section lists the table of contents for §§ 54.4980H-1 through 54.4980H-6.

Section 54.4980H-1 Definitions.

(a) Definitions.

(1) Administrative period.

(2) Advance credit payment.

(3) Affordable Care Act.

(4) Applicable large employer.

(5) Applicable large employer member.

(6) Applicable premium tax credit.

(7) Calendar month.

(8) Church, or a convention or association of churches.

(9) Collective bargaining agreement.

(10) Cost sharing reduction.

(11) Dependent.

(12) Eligible employer-sponsored plan.

(13) Employee.

(14) Employer.

(15) Exchange.

(16) Federal poverty line.

(17) Form W-2 wages.

(18) Full-time employee.

(19) Full-time equivalent employee (FTE).

(20) Government entity.

(21) Hour of service.

(22) Initial measurement period.

(23) Minimum essential coverage.

(24) Minimum value.

(25) Month.

(26) New employee.

(27) Ongoing employee.

(28) Period of employment.

(29) Person.

(30) Plan year.

(31) Predecessor employer.

(32) Qualified health plan.

(33) Seasonal employee.

(34) Seasonal worker.

(35) Section 1411 certification.

(36) Section 4980H(a) applicable payment amount.

(37) Section 4980H(b) applicable payment amount.

(38) Self-only coverage.

(39) Stability period.

(40) Standard measurement period.

(41) Start date.

(42) United States.

(43) Variable hour employee.

(44) Week.

(b) Effective/applicability date.

Section 54.4980H-2 Applicable large employer and applicable large employer member.

(a) In general.

(b) Determining applicable large employer status.

(1) In general.

(2) Seasonal worker exception.

(3) Employers not in existence in preceding calendar year.

(4) Special rules for government entities, churches, and conventions and associations of churches.

(c) Full-time equivalent employees (FTEs).

(1) In general.

(2) Calculating the number of FTEs.

(d) Examples.

(e) Effectively/applicability date.

Section 54.4980H-3 Determining full-time employees.

(a) In general.

(b) Hours of service.

(1) Hourly employee calculation.

(2) Non-hourly employee's calculation.

(c) Look-back measurement method.

(1) Ongoing employees.

(2) New non-variable hour and non-seasonal employees.

(3) New variable hour and new seasonal employees.

(4) Transition from new employee to ongoing employee.

(5) Examples.

(d) Change in employment status.

(1) In general.

(2) Examples.

(e) Employee rehires.

(1) Treatment as a new employee.

(2) Employment break period defined.

(3) Special unpaid leave defined.

(4) Averaging method for employment break periods and certain other unpaid leave.

(5) Anti-abuse rule.

(6) Examples.

(f) Nonpayment or late payment of premiums.

(g) Effective/applicability date.

Section 54.4980H-4 Assessable payments under section 4980H(a).

(a) In general.

(b) Offer of coverage.

(c) Partial calendar month.

(d) Allocated reduction of 30 full-time employees.

(e) Example.

(f) Effective/applicability date.

Section 54.4980H-5 Assessable payments under section 4980H(b).

(a) In general.

(b) Offer of coverage.

(c) Partial calendar month.

(d) Applicability to applicable large employer member.

(e) Affordability.

(1) In general.

(2) Affordability safe harbors for section 4980H(b) purposes.

(f) Effective/applicability date.

Section 54.4980H-6 Administration and procedure.

(a) Reserved.

(b) Effective/applicability date.

§ 54.4980H-1 Definitions.

(a) *Definitions.* The definitions in this section apply to this section and §§ 54.4980H-2 through 54.4980H-6.

(1) *Administrative period.* The term *administrative period* is an optional period, selected by an applicable large employer member, of no longer than 90 days beginning immediately following the end of a measurement period and ending immediately before the start of the associated stability period.

(2) *Advance credit payment.* The term *advance credit payment* means an advance payment of the premium tax credit as provided in Affordable Care Act section 1412 (42 U.S.C. 18082).

(3) *Affordable Care Act.* The term *Affordable Care Act* means the Patient Protection and Affordable Care Act, Public Law 111-148 (124 Stat. 119 (2010)), and the Health Care and Education Reconciliation Act of 2010, Public Law 111-152, (124 Stat. 1029 (2010)), as amended by the Medicare and Medicaid Extenders Act of 2010 Public Law 111-309 (124 Stat. 3285 (2010)), the Comprehensive 1099 Taxpayer Protection and Repayment of Exchange Subsidy Overpayments Act of 2011, Public Law 112-9 (125 Stat. 28, (2011)), the Department of Defense and Full-Year Continuing Appropriations Act, 2011, Public Law 112-10 (125 Stat. 38, (2011)), and the 3% Withholding Repeal and Job Creation Act, Public Law 112-56 (125 Stat. 711 (2011)).

(4) *Applicable large employer.* The term *applicable large employer* means, with respect to a calendar year, an employer that employed an average of at least 50 full-time employees (including full-time equivalent employees) on business days during the preceding calendar year. For rules relating to the determination of applicable large employer status, see Reg. § 54.4980H-2. [Corrected 3/15/13 (78 FR 16445).]

(5) *Applicable large employer member.* The term *applicable large employer member* means a person that, together with one or more other persons, is treated as a single employer that is an applicable large employer. For this purpose, if a person, together with one or more other persons, is treated as a single employer that is an applicable large employer on any day of a calendar month, that person is an applicable large employer member for that calendar month. If the applicable large employer comprises one person, that one person is the applicable large employer member. An applicable large employer member does not include a person that is not an employer or only an employer of employees with no hours of service for the calendar year. For rules for government entities, and churches, or conventions or associations of churches, see § 54.4980H-2(b)(4).

(6) *Applicable premium tax credit.* The term *applicable premium tax credit* means any premium tax credit that is allowed or paid under section 36B and any advance payment of such credit.

(7) *Calendar month.* The term *calendar month* means one of the 12 full months named in the calendar, such as January, February, or March.

(8) *Church, or a convention or association of churches.* The term *church, or a convention or association of churches* has the same meaning as provided in § 1.170A-9(b) of this chapter.

(9) *Collective bargaining agreement.* The term *collective bargaining agreement* means an agreement that the Secretary of Labor determines to be a collective bargaining agreement, provided that the health benefits provided under the collective bargaining agreement are the subject of good faith bargaining between employee representatives and one or more employers, and the agreement between employee representatives and one or more employers satisfies section 7701(a)(46).

(10) *Cost-sharing reduction.* The term *cost-sharing reduction* means a cost-sharing reduction and any advance payment of the reduction as defined under section 1402 of the Affordable Care Act.

(11) *Dependent.* The term *dependent* means a child (as defined in section 152(f)(1)) of an employee who has not attained age 26. A child attains age 26 on the 26th anniversary of the date the child was born. Absent knowledge to the contrary, applicable large employer members may rely on an employee's' representation about that employee's children and the ages of those children. Dependent does not include the spouse of an employee.

(12) *Eligible employer-sponsored plan.* The term *eligible employer-sponsored plan* has the same meaning as provided under section 5000A(f)(2) and any applicable guidance thereunder.

(13) *Employee.* The term *employee* means an individual who is an employee under the common-law standard. See § 31.3401(c)-1(b) of this chapter. For purposes of this paragraph, a leased employee (as defined in section 414(n)(2)), a sole proprietor, a partner in a partnership, or a 2-percent S corporation shareholder is not an employee.

(14) *Employer.* The term *employer* means the person that is the employer of an employee under the common-law standard. See § 31.3121(d)-1(c) of this chapter. For purposes of determining whether an employer is an applicable large employer, all persons treated as a single employer under section 414 (b), (c), (m), or (o) are treated as a single employer. Thus, all employees of a controlled group of entities under section 414 (b) or (c), an affiliated service group under section 414 (m), or under section 414(o) are taken into account in determining whether the members of the controlled group or affiliated service group together are an applicable large employer. For purposes of determining applicable large employer status, the term employer also includes a predecessor employer and a successor employer.

(15) *Exchange.* The term *Exchange* means an Exchange as defined in 45 CFR 155.20.

(16) *Federal Poverty Line.* The term *Federal poverty line* means the most recently published poverty guidelines (updated periodically in the **Federal Register** by the Secretary of Health and Human Services under the authority of 42 U.S.C. 9902(2)) as of the first day of the plan year of the applicable large employer member's health plan.

(17) *Form W-2 wages.* The term *Form W-2 wages* with respect to an employee refers to the amount of wages as defined under section 3401(a) for the applicable calendar year (required to be reported in Box 1 of the Form W-2) received from an applicable large employer.

(18) *Full-time employee.* The term *full-time employee* means, with respect to a calendar month, an employee who is employed an average of at least 30 hours of service per week with an employer. For this purpose, 130 hours of service in a calendar month is treated as the monthly equivalent of at least 30 hours of service per week, provided the employer applies this equivalency rule on a reasonable and consistent basis. For rules on the determination of whether an employee is a full-time employee, including the look-back measurement method for

purposes of determining and computing liability under section 4980H (but not for the purpose of determining status as an applicable large employer), see § 54.4980H-3.

(19) *Full-time equivalent employee (FTE)*. The term *full-time equivalent employee*, or *FTE*, means a combination of employees, each of whom individually is not treated as a full-time employee because he or she is not employed on average at least 30 hours of service per week with an employer, who, in combination, are counted as the equivalent of a full-time employee solely for purposes of determining whether the employer is an applicable large employer. For rules on the method for determining the number of an employer's full-time equivalent employees, or FTEs, see § 54.4980H-2(c).

(20) *Government entity*. The term *government entity* means the government of the United States, any State or political subdivision thereof, any Indian tribal government (as defined in section 7701(a)(40)) or subdivision of an Indian tribal government (determined in accordance with section 7871(d)), or any agency or instrumentality of any of the foregoing.

(21) *Hour of service*—(i) *In general*. The term *hour of service* means each hour for which an employee is paid, or entitled to payment, for the performance of duties for the employer; and each hour for which an employee is paid, or entitled to payment by the employer for a period of time during which no duties are performed due to vacation, holiday, illness, incapacity (including disability), layoff, jury duty, military duty or leave of absence (as defined in 29 CFR 2530.200b-2 (a)). For the rules for determining an employee's hour of service, see § 54.4980H-3.

(ii) *Service for other applicable large employer members*. In determining hours of service and status as a full-time employee for all purposes under section 4980H, an hour of service for one applicable large employer member is treated as an hour of service for all other applicable large employer members for all periods during which the applicable large employer members are part of the same group of employers forming an applicable large employer.

(iii) *Service of a nonresident alien individuals and service outside the United States*. Hours of service do not include hours of service to the extent the compensation for those hours of service constitutes income from sources without the United States (within the meaning of section 862(a)(3)).

(22) *Initial measurement period*. The term *initial measurement period* means a time period selected by an applicable large employer member of at least three consecutive calendar months but not more than 12 consecutive calendar months used by the applicable large employer as part of the process of determining whether certain new employees are full-time employees under the look-back measurement method in § 54.4980H-3(c). See § 54.4980H-3(c)(1)(ii) for rules on pay periods including the beginning and end dates of the measurement period.

(23) *Minimum essential coverage*. The term *minimum essential coverage* (or *MEC*) has the same meaning as provided in section 5000A(f) and any regulations or other administrative guidance thereunder.

(24) *Minimum value*. The term *minimum value* has the same meaning as provided in section 36B(c)(2)(C)(ii) and any regulations or other administrative guidance thereunder.

(25) *Month*. The term *month* refers to the period that begins on any date following the first day of a calendar month and that ends on the immediately preceding date in the immediately following calendar month (for example, from February 2 to March 1 or from December 15 to January 14) or that is a calendar month. See § 54.4980H-1(a)(7) for the definition of calendar month.

(26) *New employee*. The term *new employee* means an employee who has been employed by an applicable large employer for less than one complete standard measurement period. For treatment of the employee as a new employee or ongoing employee following a period for which no hours of service are earned, see the employment break period rules at § 54.4980H-3(e).

(27) *Ongoing employee*. The term *ongoing employee* means an employee who has been employed by an applicable large employer member for at least one complete standard measurement period.

(28) *Period of employment*. The term *period of employment* means the period of time beginning on the first date for which an employee is credited with an hour of service for an applicable large employer (including any member of that applicable large employer) and ending on the last date on which the employee is credited with an hour of service for that applicable large employer, both dates inclusive. An employee may have one or more periods of employment with the same applicable large employer.

(29) *Person*. The term *person* has the same meaning as provided in section 7701(a)(1) and the regulations thereunder.

(30) *Plan year*. The plan year must be twelve consecutive months, unless a short plan year of less than twelve consecutive months is permitted for a valid business purpose. A plan year is permitted to begin on any day of a year and must end on the preceding day in the immediately following year (for example, a plan year that begins on October 15, 2014, must end on October 14, 2015). A calendar year plan year is a period of twelve consecutive months beginning on January 1 and ending on December 31 of the same calendar year. Once established, a plan year is effective for the first plan year and for all subsequent plan years, unless changed, provided that such change will only be recognized if made for a valid business purposes. A change in the plan year is not permitted if a principal purpose of the change in plan year is to circumvent the rules of section 4980H or these regulations.

(31) *Predecessor employer*. [Reserved]

(32) *Qualified health plan*. The term *qualified health plan* means a qualified health plan as defined in Affordable Care Act section 1301(a) (42 U.S.C. 18021(a)), but does not include a catastrophic plan described in Affordable Care Act section 1302(e) (42 U.S.C. 18022(e)).

(33) *Seasonal employee*. [Reserved]

(34) *Seasonal worker*. The term *seasonal worker* means a worker who performs labor or services on a seasonal basis as defined by the Secretary of Labor, including (but not limited to) workers covered by 29 CFR 500.20(s)(1), and retail workers employed exclusively during holiday seasons. Employers may apply a reasonable, good faith interpretation of the term "seasonal worker" and a reasonable good faith interpretation of 29 CFR 500.20(s)(1) (including as applied by analogy to workers and employment positions not otherwise covered under 29 CFR 500.20(s)(1)).

(35) *Section 1411 Certification*. The term *Section 1411 Certification* means the certification received as part of the process established by the Secretary of Health and Human Services under which an employee is certified to the employer under section 1411 of the Affordable Care Act as having enrolled for a calendar month in a qualified health plan with respect to which an applicable premium tax credit or cost-sharing reduction is allowed or paid with respect to the employee.

(36) *Section 4980H(a) applicable payment amount*. The term *section 4980H(a) applicable payment amount* means, with respect to any month, 1/12 of $2,000, adjusted for inflation in accordance with section 4980H(c)(5) and any applicable guidance thereunder.

(37) *Section 4980H(b) applicable payment amount*. The term *section 4980H(b) applicable payment amount* means, with respect to any month, 1/12 of $3,000, adjusted for inflation in accordance with section 4980H(c)(5) and any applicable guidance thereunder.

(38) *Self-only coverage*. The term *self-only coverage* means health insurance coverage provided to only one individual, generally the employee.

(39) *Stability period*. The term *stability period* means a time period selected by an applicable large employer member that follows, and is associated with, a standard measurement period or an initial measurement period, and is used by the applicable large employer member as part of the process of determining whether an employee is a full-time employee under the look-back measurement method in § 54.4980H-3(c).

(40) *Standard measurement period*. The term *standard measurement period* means a time period of at least three but not more than 12 consecutive months that an applicable large employer member selects and uses in determining whether an ongoing employee is a full-time employee under the look-back measurement method in § 54.4980H-3(c). See § 54.4980H-3(c)(1)(ii) for rules on payroll periods that include the beginning and end dates of the measurement period.

(41) *Start date*. The term *start date* means the first date on which an employee is required to be credited with an hour of service with an employer. For rules relating to when, following a period for which an employee does not earn an hour of service, that employee may be treated as a new employee with a new start date rather than a continuing employee, see the averaging method for employment break periods at § 54.4980H-3(e).

(42) *United States*. The term *United States* means United States as defined in section 7701(a)(9).

(43) *Variable hour employee*. The term *variable hour employee* means an employee if, based on the facts and circumstances at the employee's start date, the applicable large employer member cannot determine whether the employee is reasonably expected to be employed on

average at least 30 hours of service per week during the initial measurement period because the employee's hours are variable or otherwise uncertain. For this purpose, the applicable large employer member may not take into account the likelihood that the employee may terminate employment with the applicable large employer (including any member of the applicable large employer) before the end of the initial measurement period.

(44) *Week.* The term *week* means any period of seven consecutive calendar days applied consistently by the applicable large employer member.

(b) *Effective/applicability date.* This section is applicable for periods after December 31, 2013.

54.4980H-2 Applicable large employer and applicable large employer member.

(a) *In general.* Section 4980H applies to an applicable large employer and to all of the applicable large employer members that comprise that applicable large employer.

(b) *Determining applicable large employer status*—(1) *In general.* An employer's status as an applicable large employer for a calendar year is determined by taking the sum of the total number of full-time employees (including any seasonal workers) for each calendar month in the preceding calendar year and the total number of FTEs (including any seasonal workers) for each calendar month in the preceding calendar year, and dividing by 12. The result, if not a whole number, is then rounded to the next lowest whole number. If the result of this calculation is less than 50, the employer is not an applicable large employer for the current calendar year. If the result of this calculation is 50 or more, the employer is an applicable large employer for the current calendar year, unless the seasonal worker exception in paragraph (b)(2) of this section applies.

(2) *Seasonal worker exception.* If the sum of an employer's full-time employees and FTEs exceeds 50 for 120 days or less during the preceding calendar year, and the employees in excess of 50 who were employed during that period of no more than 120 days are seasonal workers, the employer is not considered to employ more than 50 full-time employees (including FTEs) and the employer is not an applicable large employer for the current calendar year. For purposes of this paragraph (b)(2) only, four calendar months may be treated as the equivalent of 120 days. The four calendar months and the 120 days are not required to be consecutive.

(3) *Employers not in existence in preceding calendar year.* An employer not in existence throughout the preceding calendar year is an applicable large employer for the current calendar year if it is reasonably expected to employ an average of at least 50 full-time employees (taking into account FTEs) on business days during the current calendar year and it actually employs an average of at least 50 full-time employees (taking into account FTEs) on business days during the calendar year.

(4) *Special rules for government entities, churches, and conventions and associations of churches.* [Reserved]

(c) *Full-time equivalent employees (FTEs)*—(1) *In general.* In determining whether an employer is an applicable large employer, the number of FTEs it employed during the preceding calendar year are taken into account. All employees (including seasonal workers) who were not employed on average at least 30 hours of service per week for a calendar month in the preceding calendar year are included in calculating the employer's FTEs for that calendar month.

(2) *Calculating the number of FTEs.* The number of FTEs for each calendar month in the preceding calendar year is determined by calculating the aggregate number of hours of service for that calendar month for employees who were not full-time employees (but not more than 120 hours of service for any employee) and dividing that number by 120. In determining the number of FTEs for each calendar month, fractions are taken into account.

(d) *Examples.* The following examples illustrate the rules of paragraphs (a) through (c) of this section. In these examples, hours of service are computed following the rules set forth in § 54.4980H-3, and references to years refer to calendar years unless otherwise specified. The Employers in *Examples 2* through *5* are each the sole applicable large employer member of the applicable large employer, as determined under section 414(b), (c), (m) and (o).

Example 1. Applicable large employer/controlled group. (i) *Facts.* For 2015 and 2016, corporation P owns 100 percent of all classes of stock of corporation S and corporation T. P has no employees at any time in 2015. For every calendar month in 2015, S has 40 full-time employees

and T has 60 full-time employees. P, S, and T are a controlled group of corporations under section 414(b).

(ii) *Conclusion.* Because P, S and T have a combined total of 100 full-time employees during 2015, P, S, and T is an applicable large employer for 2016. Each of P, S and T is an applicable large employer member for 2016.

Example 2. Applicable large employer with FTEs. (i) *Facts.* During each calendar month of 2015, Employer L has 20 full-time employees each of whom averages 35 hours of service per week, 40 employees each of whom averages 90 hours of service per month, and no seasonal workers.

(ii) *Conclusion.* Each of the 20 employees who average 35 hours of service per week count as one full-time employee for each month. To determine the number of FTEs for each month, the total hours of service of the employees who are not full-time employees (but not more than 120 hours of service per employee) are aggregated and divided by 120. The result is that the employer has 30 FTEs for each month (40 × 90 = 3,600, and 3,600 ÷ 120 = 30). Because Employer L has 50 full-time employees (the sum of 20 full-time employees and 30 FTEs) during each month in 2015, and because the seasonal worker exception is not applicable, Employer L is an applicable large employer for 2016.

Example 3. Seasonal worker exception. (i) *Facts.* During 2015, Employer N has 40 full-time employees for the entire calendar year, none of whom are seasonal workers. In addition, Employer N also has 80 seasonal full-time workers who work for Employer N from September through December, 2015. Employer N has no FTEs during 2015.

(ii) *Conclusion.* Before applying the seasonal worker exception, Employer N has 40 full-time employees during each of eight calendar months of 2015, and 120 full-time employees during each of four calendar months of 2015, resulting in an average of 66.5 employees for the year (rounded down to 66 full-time employees). However, Employer N's workforce equaled or exceeded 50 full-time employees (counting seasonal workers) for no more than four calendar months (treated as the equivalent of 120 days) in calendar year 2015, and the number of full-time employees would be less than 50 during those months if seasonal workers were disregarded. Accordingly, because after application of the seasonal worker exception in paragraph (b)(2) of this section Employer N is not considered to employ more than 50 full-time employees, Employer N is not an applicable large employer for 2016.

Example 4. Seasonal workers and other FTEs. (i) *Facts.* Same facts as in *Example 3,* except that Employer N has 20 FTEs in August, some of whom are seasonal workers.

(ii) *Conclusion.* The seasonal worker exception in paragraph (b)(2) of this section does not apply if the number of an employer's full-time employees (including seasonal workers) and FTEs equals or exceeds 50 employees for more than 120 days during the calendar year. Because Employer N has at least 50 full-time employees for a period greater than four calendar months (treated as the equivalent of 120 days) during 2015, the exception in paragraph (b)(2) of this section does not apply. Employer N averaged 68 full-time employees in 2015: [(40 × 7) + (60 × 1) + (120 x 4)] ÷ 12 = 68.33, rounded down to 68, and accordingly, Employer N is an applicable large employer for calendar year 2016.

Example 5. New employer. (i) *Facts.* Corporation A is incorporated on January 1, 2015. On January 1, 2015, Corporation A has three employees. However, prior to incorporation, Corporation A's owners purchased a factory intended to open within two months of incorporation and to employ approximately 100 employees. By March 15, 2015, Corporation A has more than 75 full-time employees.

(ii) *Conclusion.* Because Corporation A can reasonably be expected to employ on average at least 50 full-time employees on business days during 2015, and actually employs an average of at least 50 full-time employees on business days during 2015, Corporation A is an applicable large employer (and an applicable large employer member).

(e) *Effective/applicability date.* This section is applicable for periods after December 31, 2013.

§ 54.4980H-3 Determining full-time employees.

(a) *In general.* This section sets forth the rules for determining hours of service and status as a full-time employee for all purposes of section 4980H, provided that the look-back measurement methods for determining status as a full-time employee under paragraph (c) of this section apply solely for purposes of determining and calculating liability under section 4980H(a) and (b) (and not for purposes of determining status as an applicable large employer). See § 54.4980H-1(a)(18) for the definition of full-time employee.

(b) *Hours of service*—(1) *Hourly employees calculation*. For employees paid on an hourly basis, an employer must calculate actual hours of service from records of hours worked and hours for which payment is made or due.

(2) *Non-hourly employees calculation*—(i) *In general*. For employees paid on a non-hourly basis, an employer must calculate hours of service by using one of the following methods:

(A) Using actual hours of service from records of hours worked and hours for which payment is made or due.

(B) Using a days-worked equivalency whereby the employee is credited with eight hours of service for each day for which the employee would be required to be credited with at least one hour of service in accordance with paragraph (b)(1) of this section.

(C) Using a weeks-worked equivalency whereby the employee is credited with 40 hours of service for each week for which the employee would be required to be credited with at least one hour of service in accordance with paragraph (b)(1) of this section.

(ii) *Change in method*. An employer must use one of the three methods in paragraph (b)(2) of this section for calculating the hours of service for non-hourly employees. An employer is not required to use the same method for all non-hourly employees, and may apply different methods for different classifications of non-hourly employees, provided the classifications are reasonable and consistently applied. Similarly, an applicable large employer member is not required to apply the same methods as other applicable large employer members of the same applicable large employer for the same or different classifications of non-hourly employees, provided that in each case the classifications are reasonable and consistently applied by the applicable large employer member.

(iii) *Prohibited use of equivalencies*. The number of hours of service calculated using the days-worked or weeks-worked equivalency must reflect generally the hours actually worked and the hours for which payment is made or due. An employer is not permitted to use the days-worked equivalency or the weeks-worked equivalency if the result is to substantially understate an employee's hours of service in a manner that would cause that employee not to be treated as full-time. For example, an employer may not use a days-worked equivalency in the case of an employee who generally works three 10-hour days per week, because the equivalency would substantially understate the employee's hours of service as 24 hours of service per week, which would result in the employee being treated as not a full-time employee. Rather, the number of hours of service calculated using the days-worked or weeks-worked equivalency method must reflect generally the hours actually worked and the hours for which payment is made or due.

(c) *Look-back measurement method*—(1) *Ongoing employees*—(i) *In general*. Under the look-back measurement method for ongoing employees, an applicable large employer determines each ongoing employee's full-time status by looking back at the standard measurement period. The applicable large employer member determines the months in which the standard measurement period starts and ends, provided that the determination must be made on a uniform and consistent basis for all employees in the same category (see paragraph (c)(1)(v) of this section for a list of permissible categories). For example, if an applicable large employer member chooses a standard measurement period of 12 months, the applicable large employer member could choose to make it the calendar year, a non-calendar plan year, or a different 12-month period, such as one that ends shortly before the start of the plan's annual open enrollment period. If the applicable large employer member determines that an employee was employed on average at least 30 hours per week during the standard measurement period, then the applicable large employer member treats the employee as a full-time employee during a subsequent stability period, regardless of the employee's number of hours of service during the stability period, so long as he or she remains an employee.

(ii) *Use of payroll periods*. For payroll periods that are one week, two weeks, or semi-monthly in duration, an employer is permitted to treat as a measurement period a period that ends on the last day of the payroll period preceding the payroll period that includes the date that would otherwise be the last day of the measurement period, provided that the measurement period begins on the first day of the payroll period that includes the date that would otherwise be the first day of the measurement period. An employer may also treat as a measurement period a period that begins on the first day of the payroll period that follows the payroll period that includes the date that would otherwise be the first day of the measurement period, provided that the

measurement period ends on the last day of the payroll period that includes the date that would otherwise be the last day of the measurement period. For example, an employer using the calendar year as a measurement period could exclude the entire payroll period that included January 1 (the beginning of the year) if it included the entire payroll period that included December 31 (the end of that same year), or, alternatively, could exclude the entire payroll period that included December 31 of a calendar year if it included the entire payroll period that included January 1 of that calendar year.

(iii) *Employee determined to be employed an average of at least 30 hours of service per week*. An employee who was employed on average at least 30 hours of service per week during the standard measurement period must be treated as a full-time employee for a stability period that begins immediately after the standard measurement period and any applicable administrative period. The stability period must be at least six consecutive calendar months but no shorter in duration than the standard measurement period.

(iv) *Employee determined not to be employed on average at least 30 hours of service per week*. If an employee was not employed an average at least 30 hours of service per week during the standard measurement period, the applicable large employer member may treat the employee as not a full-time employee during the stability period that follows, but is not longer than, the standard measurement period. The stability period must begin immediately after the end of the measurement period and any applicable administrative period.

(v) *Permissible employee categories*. Subject to the rules governing the relationship between the length of the measurement period and the stability period, applicable large employer members may use measurement periods and stability periods that differ either in length or in their starting and ending dates for the following categories of employees:

(A) Collectively bargained employees and non-collectively bargained employees.

(B) Each group of collectively bargained employees covered by a separate collective bargaining agreement.

(C) Salaried employees and hourly employees.

(D) Employees whose primary places of employment are in different States.

(vi) *Optional administrative period*. An applicable large employer member may provide for an administrative period that begins immediately after the end of a standard measurement period and that ends immediately before the associated stability period; however, any administrative period between the standard measurement period and the stability period for ongoing employees may neither reduce nor lengthen the measurement period or the stability period. The administrative period following the standard measurement period may last up to 90 days. To prevent this administrative period from creating a gap in coverage, the administrative period must overlap with the prior stability period, so that, during any such administrative period applicable to ongoing employees following a standard measurement period, ongoing employees who are enrolled in coverage because of their status as full-time employees based on a prior measurement period must continue to be covered through the administrative period. Applicable large employer members may use administrative periods that differ in length for the categories of employees identified in paragraph (c)(1)(v) of this section.

(vii) *Change in position of employment or other employment status*. If an ongoing employee's position of employment or other employment status changes before the end of a stability period, the change will not affect the application of the classification of the employee as a full-time employee (or not a full-time employee) for the remaining portion of the stability period. For example, if an ongoing employee in a certain position of employment is not treated as a full-time employee during a stability period because the employee's hours of service during the prior measurement period were insufficient for full-time-employee treatment, and the employee changes position of employment to a position that involves an increased level of hours of service, the treatment of the employee as a non-full time employee during the remainder of the stability period is unaffected. Similarly, if an ongoing employee in a certain position of employment is treated as a full-time employee during a stability period because the employee's hours of service during the prior measurement period were sufficient for full-time-employee treatment, and the employee changes position of employment to a position that involves a lower level of hours of service, the treatment of the employee as a full-time employee during the remainder of the stability period is unaffected.

(viii) *Example*. The following example illustrates the application of paragraph (c)(1) of this section:

(i) *Facts.* Employer W is an applicable large employer member and computes hours of service following the rules in this section. Employer W chooses to use a 12-month stability period that begins January 1 and a 12-month standard measurement period that begins October 15. Consistent with the terms of Employer W's group health plan, only employees classified as full-time employees using the look-back measurement method are eligible for coverage. Employer W chooses to use an administrative period between the end of the standard measurement period (October 14) and the beginning of the stability period (January 1) to determine which employees were employed on average 30 hours of service per week during the measurement period, notify them of their eligibility for the plan for the calendar year beginning on January 1 and of the coverage available under the plan, answer questions and collect materials from employees, and enroll those employees who elect coverage in the plan. Previously-determined full-time employees already enrolled in coverage continue to be offered coverage through the administrative period.

Employee A and Employee B have been employed by Employer W for several years, continuously from their start date. Employee A was employed on average 30 hours of service per week during the standard measurement period that begins October 15, 2015 and ends October 14, 2016 and for all prior standard measurement periods. Employee B also was employed on average 30 hours of service per week for all prior standard measurement periods, but is not a full-time employee during the standard measurement period that begins October 15, 2015 and ends October 14, 2016.

(ii) *Conclusions.* Because Employee A was employed for the entire standard measurement period that begins October 15, 2015 and ends October 14, 2016, Employee A is an ongoing employee with respect to the stability period running from January 1, 2017 through December 31, 2017. Because Employee A was employed on average 30 hours of service per week during that standard measurement period, Employee A is offered coverage for the entire 2017 stability period (including the administrative period from October 15, 2017 through December 31, 2017). Because Employee A was employed on average 30 hours of service per week during the prior standard measurement period, Employee A is offered coverage for the entire 2016 stability period and, if enrolled, would continue such coverage during the administrative period from October 15, 2016 through December 31, 2016.

Because Employee B was employed for the entire standard measurement period that begins October 15, 2015 and ends October 14, 2016, Employee B is also an ongoing employee with respect to the stability period in 2017. Because Employee B did not work full-time during this standard measurement period, Employee B is not required to be offered coverage for the stability period in 2017 (including the administrative period from October 15, 2017 through December 31, 2017). However, because Employee B was employed on average 30 hours of service per week during the prior standard measurement period, Employee B is offered coverage through the end of the 2016 stability period and, if enrolled, would continue such coverage during the administrative period from October 15, 2016 through December 31, 2016. Employer W complies with the standards of paragraph (c)(1) of this section because the measurement and stability periods are no longer than 12 months, the stability period for ongoing employees who work full-time during the standard measurement period is not shorter than the standard measurement period, the stability period for ongoing employees who do not work full-time during the standard measurement period is no longer than the standard measurement period, and the administrative period is no longer than 90 days.

(2) *New non-variable hour and non-seasonal employees.* If an employee is reasonably expected at his or her start date to be a full-time employee (and is not a seasonal employee), an employer that sponsors a group health plan that offers coverage to the employee at or before the conclusion of the employee's initial three full calendar months of employment will not be subject to an assessable payment under section 4980H by reason of its failure to offer coverage to the employee for up to the initial full three calendar months of employment; however, if the employer did not offer coverage to the employee by the end of the employee's initial three full calendar months of employment, the employer may be subject to a section 4980H assessable payment for those months as well as for any subsequent months for which coverage was not offered.

(3) *New variable hour and new seasonal employees*—(i) *In general.* For new variable hour employees and new seasonal employees, applicable large employer members are permitted to determine whether the new employee is a full-time employee using an initial measurement period of between three and 12 months (as selected by the applicable large employer member) that begins on any date between the employee's start date and the first day of the first calendar month following the employee's start date. The applicable large employer member measures the new employee's hours of service during the initial measurement period and determines whether the employee was employed on average at least 30 hours of service per week during this period. The stability period for such employees must be the same length as the stability period for ongoing employees.

(ii) *Employees determined to be employed on average at least 30 hours of service per week.* If a new variable hour employee or new seasonal employee has on average at least 30 hours of service per week during the initial measurement period, the applicable large employer member must treat the employee as a full-time employee during the stability period that begins after the initial measurement period (and any associated administrative period). The stability period must be a period of at least six consecutive calendar months that is no shorter in duration than the initial measurement period.

(iii) *Employees determined not to be employed on average at least 30 hours of service per week.* If a new variable hour employee or new seasonal employee does not have on average at least 30 hours of service per week during the initial measurement period, the applicable large employer member is permitted to treat the employee as not a full-time employee during the stability period that follows the initial measurement period. This stability period for such employees must not be more than one month longer than the initial measurement period and, in accordance with paragraph (c)(4) of this section, must not exceed the remainder of the standard measurement period (plus any associated administrative period) in which the initial measurement period ends.

(4) *Transition from new employee to ongoing employee*—(i) *In general.* Once a new variable hour employee or new seasonal employee has been employed for an entire standard measurement period, the applicable large employer must test the employee for full-time employee status, beginning with that standard measurement period, at the same time and under the same conditions as apply to other ongoing employees. Accordingly, for example, an applicable large employer member with a calendar year standard measurement period that also uses a one-year initial measurement period beginning on the employee's start date would test a new variable hour employee whose start date is February 12 for full-time status first based on the initial measurement period (February 12 through February 11 of the following year) and again based on the calendar year standard measurement period (if the employee continues in employment for that entire standard measurement period) beginning on January 1 of the year after the start date.

(ii) *Employee determined to be employed an average of at least 30 hours of service per week.* An employee who was employed an average of at least 30 hours of service per week during an initial measurement period or standard measurement period must be treated as a full-time employee for the entire associated stability period. This is the case even if the employee was employed an average of at least 30 hours of service per week during the initial measurement period but was not employed an average of at least 30 hours of service per week during the overlapping or immediately following standard measurement period. In that case, the applicable large employer member may treat the employee as not a full-time employee only after the end of the stability period associated with the initial measurement period. Thereafter, the applicable large employer member must determine the employee's status as a full-time employee in the same manner as it determines such status in the case of its other ongoing employees as described in paragraph (c)(1) of this section.

(iii) *Employee determined not to be employed an average of at least 30 hours of service per week.* If the employee was not employed an average of at least 30 hours of service per week during the initial measurement period, but was employed at least 30 hours of service per week during the overlapping or immediately following standard measurement period, the employee must be treated as a full-time employee for the entire stability period that corresponds to that standard measurement period (even if that stability period begins before the end of the stability period associated with the initial measurement period). Thereafter, the applicable large employer member must determine the employee's status as a full-time employee in the same manner as it determines such status in the case of its other ongoing employees as described in paragraph (c)(1) of this section.

(iv) *Permissible differences in measurement or stability periods for different categories of employees.* Subject to the rules governing the relationship between the length of the measurement period and the stability period, applicable large employer members may use measurement periods and stability periods that differ either in length or in their starting and ending dates for the categories of employees identified in paragraph (c)(1)(v) of this section.

(v) *Optional administrative period*—(A) *In general.* Subject to the limits in paragraph (c)(4)(v)(B) of this section, an applicable large employer member is permitted to apply an administrative period in connection with an initial measurement period and before the start of the stability period. This administrative period must not exceed 90 days in total. For this purpose, the administrative period includes all periods between the start date of a new variable hour employee or new seasonal employee and the date the employee is first offered coverage under the applicable large employer member's group health plan, other than the initial measurement period. Thus, for example, if the applicable large employer member begins the initial measurement period on the first day of the first month following a new variable hour or new seasonal employee's start date, the period between the employee's start date and the first day of the next month must be taken into account in applying the 90-day limit on the administrative period. Similarly, if there is a period between the end of the initial measurement period and the date the employee is first offered coverage under the plan, that period must be taken into account in applying the 90-day limit on the administrative period. Applicable large employer members may use administrative periods that differ in length for the categories of employees identified in paragraph (c)(1)(v) of this section.

(B) *Limit on combined length of initial measurement period and administrative period.* In addition to the specific limits on the initial measurement period (which must not exceed 12 months) and the administrative period (which must not exceed 90 days), there is a limit on the combined length of the initial measurement period and the administrative period applicable to a new variable hour employee or new seasonal employee. Specifically, the initial measurement period and administrative period together cannot extend beyond the last day of the first calendar month beginning on or after the first anniversary of the employee's start date. For example, if an applicable large employer member uses a 12-month initial measurement period for a new variable hour employee, and begins that initial measurement period on the first day of the first calendar month following the employee's start date, the period between the end of the initial measurement period and the offer of coverage to a new variable hour employee who works full time during the initial measurement period must not exceed one month.

(5) *Examples.* The following examples illustrate the look-back measurement methods described in paragraphs (c)(2) through (c)(4) of this section. In all of the following examples, the applicable large employer member offers all of its full-time employees (and their dependents) the opportunity to enroll in minimum essential coverage under an eligible employer-sponsored plan. The coverage is affordable within the meaning of section 36B(c)(2)(C)(i) (or is treated as affordable coverage under one of the affordability safe harbors described in §54.4980H-5) and provides minimum value within the meaning of section 36B(c)(2)(C)(ii). In *Example 1* through *Example 8*, the new employee is a new variable hour employee, and the employer has chosen to use a 12-month standard measurement period for ongoing employees starting October 15 and a 12-month stability period associated with that standard measurement period starting January 1. (Thus, during the administrative period from October 15 through December 31 of each calendar year, the employer continues to offer coverage to employees who qualified for coverage for that entire calendar year based upon working on average at least 30 hours per week during the prior standard measurement period.) Also, the employer offers health plan coverage only to full-time employees (and their dependents). In *Example 9* and *Example 10*, the new employee is a new variable hour employee, and the employer uses a six-month standard measurement period, starting each May 15 and November 15, with six-month stability periods associated with those standard measurement periods starting January 1 and July 1.

Example 1 (12-Month Initial Measurement Period Followed by 1+ Partial Month Administrative Period). (i) *Facts.* For new variable hour employees, Employer B uses a 12-month initial measurement period that begins on the start date and applies an administrative period from the end of the initial measurement period through the end of the first calendar month beginning on or after the end of the initial measurement period. Employer B hires Employee Y on May 10, 2015. Employee Y's initial measurement period runs from May 10, 2015, through May 9, 2016. Employee Y has an average of 30 hours of service per week during this initial measurement period. Employer B offers coverage to Employee Y for a stability period that runs from July 1, 2016 through June 30, 2017.

(ii) *Conclusion.* Employee Y has an average of 30 hours of service per week during his initial measurement period and Employer B uses an initial measurement period that does not exceed 12 months; an administrative period totaling not more than 90 days; and a combined initial measurement period and administrative period that does not last beyond the final day of the first calendar month beginning on or after the one-year anniversary of Employee Y's start date. Accordingly, from Employee Y's start date through June 30, 2017, Employer B is not

subject to any payment under section 4980H with respect to Employee Y, because Employer B complies with the standards for the initial measurement period and stability periods for a new variable hour employee. Employer B must test Employee Y again based on the period from October 15, 2015 through October 14, 2016 (Employer B's first standard measurement period that begins after Employee Y's start date).

Example 2 (11-Month Initial Measurement Period Followed by 2 + Partial Month Administrative Period). (i) *Facts.* Same as *Example 1*, except that Employer B uses an 11-month initial measurement period that begins on the start date and applies an administrative period from the end of the initial measurement period until the end of the second calendar month beginning after the end of the initial measurement period. Employer B hires Employee Y on May 10, 2015. Employee Y's initial measurement period runs from May 10, 2015, through April 9, 2016. Employee Y has an average of 30 hours of service per week during this initial measurement period. Employer B offers coverage to Employee Y for a stability period that runs from July 1, 2016 through June 30, 2017.

(ii) *Conclusion.* Same as *Example 1*.

Example 3 (11-Month Initial Measurement Period Preceded by Partial Month Administrative Period and Followed by 2-Month Administrative Period). (i) *Facts.* Same as Example 1, except that Employer B uses an 11-month initial measurement period that begins on the first day of the first calendar month beginning after the start date and applies an administrative period that runs from the end of the initial measurement period through the end of the second calendar month beginning on or after the end of the initial measurement period. Employer B hires Employee Y on May 10, 2015. Employee Y's initial measurement period runs from June 1, 2015, through April 30, 2016. Employee Y has an average of 30 hours of service per week during this initial measurement period. Employer B offers coverage to Employee Y for a stability period that runs from July 1, 2016 through June 30, 2017.

(ii) *Conclusion.* Same as *Example 1*.

Example 4 (12-Month Initial Measurement Period Preceded by Partial Month Administrative Period and Followed by 2-Month Administrative Period). (i) *Facts.* For new variable hour employees, Employer B uses a 12-month initial measurement period that begins on the first day of the first month following the start date and applies an administrative period that runs from the end of the initial measurement period through the end of the second calendar month beginning on or after the end of the initial measurement period. Employer B hires Employee Y on May 10, 2015. Employee Y's initial measurement period runs from June 1, 2015, through May 31, 2016. Employee Y has an average of 30 hours of service per week during this initial measurement period. Employer B offers coverage to Employee Y for a stability period that runs from August 1, 2016 through July 31, 2017.

(ii) *Conclusion.* Employer B does not satisfy the standards for the look-back measurement method in paragraph (c)(4)(v) of this section because the combination of the initial partial month delay, the 12-month initial measurement period, and the two month administrative period means that the coverage offered to Employee Y does not become effective until after the first day of the second calendar month following the first anniversary of Employee Y's start date. Accordingly, Employer B is potentially subject to a payment under section 4980H.

Example 5 (Continuous Full-Time Employee). (i) *Facts.* Same as *Example 1*; in addition, Employer B tests Employee Y again based on Employee Y's hours of service from October 15, 2015 through October 14, 2016 (Employer B's first standard measurement period that begins after Employee Y's start date), determines that Employee Y has an average of 30 hours of service a week during that period, and offers Employee Y coverage for July 1, 2017 through December 31, 2017. (Employee Y already has an offer of coverage for the period of January 1, 2017 through June 30, 2017 because that period is covered by the initial stability period following the initial measurement period, during which Employee Y was determined to be a full-time employee.)

(ii) *Conclusion.* Employer B is not subject to any payment under section 4980H for 2017 with respect to Employee Y.

Example 6 (Initially Full-Time Employee, Becomes Non-Full-Time Employee). (i) *Facts.* Same as *Example 1*; in addition, Employer B tests Employee Y again based on Employee Y's hours of service from October 15, 2015 through October 14, 2016 (Employer B's first standard measurement period that begins after Employee Y's start date), and determines that Employee Y has an average of 28 hours of service a week during that period. Employer B continues to offer coverage to Employee Y through June 30, 2017 (the end of the stability period based on the initial measurement period during which Employee Y was determined to be a full-time employee), but does not offer coverage to Employee Y for the period of July 1, 2017 through December 31, 2017.

(ii) *Conclusion.* Employer B is not subject to any payment under section 4980H for 2016 with respect to Employee Y, provided that it offers coverage to Employee Y from July 1, 2016 through June 30, 2017 (the entire stability period associated with the initial measurement period).

Example 7 (Initially Non-Full-Time Employee). (i) *Facts.* Same as *Example 1*, except that Employee Y has an average of 28 hours of service per week during the period from May 10, 2015 through May 9, 2016 and Employer B does not offer coverage to Employee Y in 2016.

(ii) *Conclusion.* From Employee Y's start date through the end of 2016, Employer B is not subject to any payment under section 4980H, because Employer B complies with the standards for the measurement and stability periods for a new variable hour employee with respect to Employee Y.

Example 8 (Initially Non-Full-Time Employee, Becomes Full-Time Employee). (i) *Facts.* Same as *Example 7*; in addition, Employer B tests Employee Y again based on Employee Y's hours of service from October 15, 2015 through October 14, 2016 (Employer B's first standard measurement period that begins after Employee Y's start date), determines that Employee Y has an average of 30 hours of service per week during this standard measurement period, and offers coverage to Employee Y for 2017.

(ii) *Conclusion.* Employer B is not subject to any payment under section 4980H for 2017 with respect to Employee Y.

Example 9 (Initially Full-Time Employee). (i) *Facts.* For new variable hour employees, Employer C uses a six-month initial measurement period that begins on the start date and applies an administrative period that runs from the end of the initial measurement period through the end of the first full calendar month beginning after the end of the initial measurement period. Employer C hires Employee Z on May 10, 2015. Employee Z's initial measurement period runs from May 10, 2015, through November 9, 2015, during which Employee Z has an average of 30 hours of service per week. Employer C offers coverage to Employee Z for a stability period that runs from January 1, 2016 through June 30, 2016.

(ii) *Conclusion.* Employer C uses an initial measurement period that does not exceed 12 months; an administrative period totaling not more than 90 days; and a combined initial measurement period and administrative period that does not last longer than the final day of the first calendar month beginning on or after the one-year anniversary of Employee Z's start date. From Employee Z's start date through June 30, 2016, Employer C is not subject to any payment under section 4980H, because Employer C complies with the standards for the measurement and stability periods for a new variable hour employee with respect to Employee Z. Employer C must test Employee Z again based on Employee Z's hours of service during the period from November 15, 2015 through May 14, 2016 (Employer C's first standard measurement period that begins after Employee Z's start date).

Example 10 (Initially Full-Time Employee, Becomes Non-Full-Time Employee). (i) *Facts.* Same as *Example 9*; in addition, Employer C tests Employee Z again based on Employee Z's hours of service during the period from November 15, 2015 through May 14, 2016 (Employer C's first standard measurement period that begins after Employee Z's start date), during which period Employee Z has an average of 28 hours of service per week. Employer C continues to offer coverage to Employee Z through June 30, 2016 (the end of the initial stability period based on the initial measurement period during which Employee Z has an average of 30 hours of service per week), but does not offer coverage to Employee Z from July 1, 2016 through December 31, 2016.

(ii) *Conclusion.* Employer C is not subject to any payment under section 4980H with respect to Employee Z for 2016.

Example 11 (Seasonal Employee, 12-Month Initial Measurement Period; 1+ Partial Month Administrative Period). (i) *Facts.* Employer D offers health plan coverage only to full-time employees (and their dependents). Employer D uses a 12-month initial measurement period for new variable hour employees and seasonal employees that begins on the start date and applies an administrative period from the end of the initial measurement period through the end of the first calendar month beginning after the end of the initial measurement period. Employer D hires Employee S, a ski instructor, on November 15, 2015 with an anticipated season during which Employee S will work running through March 15, 2016. Employer D determines that Employee S is a seasonal employee based upon a reasonable good faith interpretation of that term. Employee S's initial measurement period runs from November 15, 2015, through November 14, 2016. Employee S is expected to

have 50 hours of service per week from November 15, 2015 through March 15, 2016, but is not reasonably expected to average 30 hours of service per week for the 12-month initial measurement period.

(ii) *Conclusion.* Employer D cannot determine whether Employee S is reasonably expected to average at least 30 hours of service per week for the 12-month initial measurement period. Accordingly, Employer D may treat Employee S as a variable hour employee during the initial measurement period.

Example 12 (Variable Hour Employee). (i) *Facts.* Employer E is in the trade or business of providing temporary workers to numerous clients that are unrelated to Employer E and to one another. Employer E is the common law employer of the temporary workers based on all of the facts and circumstances. Employer E offers health plan coverage only to full-time employees (including temporary workers who are full-time employees) and their dependents. Employer E uses a 12-month initial measurement period for new variable hour employees and new seasonal employees that begins on the start date and applies an administrative period from the end of the initial measurement period through the end of the first calendar month beginning after the end of the initial measurement period. Employer E hires Employee T on January 1, 2015 and anticipates that it will assign Employee T to provide services for various clients. As of the beginning of the initial measurement period, Employer E reasonably expects that, over the initial measurement period, Employee T is likely to be offered short-term assignments with several different clients, with significant gaps between the assignments and that the assignments will differ in the average hours of service per week (meaning averaging both above and below 30 hours of service per week), all depending on client needs and Employee T's availability. The number of actual assignments that Employee T will be offered, the number that Employee T will accept, the duration of assignments, the length of the gaps between assignments, and whether various assignments will result in Employee T being employed on average at least 30 hours of service per week during the assignment, are all uncertain.

(ii) *Conclusion.* Employer E cannot determine whether Employee T is reasonably expected to average at least 30 hours of service per week for the 12-month initial measurement period. Accordingly, Employer E may treat Employee T as a variable hour employee during the initial measurement period.

Example 13 (Variable Hour Employee). (i) *Facts.* Employee A is hired on an hourly basis by Employer Y to fill in for employees who are absent and to provide additional staffing at peak times. Employer Y expects that Employee A will average 30 hours of service per week or more for A's first few months of employment, while assigned to a specific project, but also reasonably expects that the assignments will be of unpredictable duration, that there will be gaps of unpredictable duration between assignments, that the hours per week required by subsequent assignments will vary, and that A will not necessarily be available for all assignments.

(ii) *Conclusion.* Employer Y cannot determine whether Employee A is reasonably expected to average at least 30 hours of service per week for the initial measurement period. Accordingly, Employer Y may treat Employee A as a variable hour employee.

(d) *Change in employment status*—(1) *In general.* If the position of employment or other employment status of a new variable hour employee or new seasonal employee materially changes before the end of the initial measurement period in such a way that, if the employee had begun employment in the new position or status, the employee would have reasonably been expected to be employed on average at least 30 hours of service per week, the employer is not required to treat the employee as a full-time employee for purposes of determining and calculating any liability under section 4980H until the first day of the fourth month following the change in employment status or, if earlier and the employee averages more than 30 hours of service per week during the initial measurement period, the first day of the first month following the end of the initial measurement period (including any optional administrative period associated with the initial measurement period).

(2) *Example.* The following example illustrates the provisions of paragraph (d)(1) of this section. In the following example, the applicable large employer member offers all of its full-time employees (and their dependents) the opportunity to enroll in minimum essential coverage under an eligible employer-sponsored plan. The coverage is affordable within the meaning of section 36B(c)(2)(C)(i) (or is treated as affordable coverage under one of the affordability safe harbors described in §54.4980H-5) and provides minimum value within the meaning of section 36B(c)(2)(C)(ii).

Example (Change in employment from variable hour employee to non-variable hour employee). (i) *Facts.* For new variable hour employees,

Employer A uses a 12-month initial measurement period that begins on the start date and applies an administrative period from the end of the initial measurement period through the end of the first calendar month beginning on or after the end of the initial measurement period. Employer A hires Employee Z on May 10, 2015. Employer A's initial measurement period runs from May 10, 2015, through May 9, 2016, with the optional administrative period ending June 30, 2016. At Employee Z's May 10, 2015 start date, Employee Z is a variable hour employee. On September 15, 2015, Employer A promotes Employee Z to a position that can reasonably be expected to average at least 30 hours of service per week.

(ii) *Conclusion.* For purposes of determining Employer A's potential liability under section 4980H, Employee Z must be treated as a full-time employee as of January 1, 2016, because that date is the earlier of the first day of the fourth calendar month following the change in position (January 1, 2016) or the first day of the calendar month after the end of the initial measurement period plus the optional administrative period (July 1, 2016).

(e) *Employees rehired after termination of employment or resuming service after other absence*—(1) *Treatment as a new employee after a period of absence.* Solely for purposes of section 4980H, an employee who resumes providing services to (or is otherwise credited with an hour of service for) an applicable large employer after a period during which the employee was not credited with any hours of service may be treated as having terminated employment and having been rehired, and therefore may be treated as a new employee upon the resumption of services only if the employee did not have an hour of service for the applicable large employer for a period of at least 26 consecutive weeks immediately preceding the resumption of services or, if chosen by the applicable large employer, for a shorter period (measured in weeks) of at least four consecutive weeks that exceeds the number of weeks of that employee's period of employment with the applicable large employer immediately preceding the period during which the employee was not credited with any hours of service. For purposes of the preceding sentence, the duration of the period of employment immediately preceding the period during which the employee was not credited with any hours of service is determined after application to that period of employment of the averaging methods described in paragraph (e)(4) of this section, if applicable. An employee treated as a continuing employee retains, upon resumption of services, the status that employee had with respect to the application of any stability period (for example, if the continuing employee returns during a stability period in which the employee is treated as a full-time employee, the employee is treated as a full-time employee upon return and through the end of that stability period). For purpose of the preceding sentence, a continuing employee treated as a full-time employee will be treated as offered coverage upon resumption of services if the employee is offered coverage as of the first day that employee is credited with an hour of service, or, if later, as soon as administratively practicable. This rule set forth in this paragraph (e)(1) applies solely for the purpose of determining whether the employee, upon the resumption of services, is treated as a new employee or as a continuing employee, and does not determine whether the employee is treated as a continuing full-time employee or a terminated employee during the period during which no hours of service are credited.

(2) *Employment break period defined.* An employment break period is a period of at least four consecutive weeks (disregarding special unpaid leave as defined in paragraph (e)(3) of this section) during which an employee of an educational organization is not credited with hours of service for an applicable large employer.

(3) *Definitions*—(i) *Special unpaid leave defined.* For purposes of this paragraph (e), special unpaid leave refers to—

(A) Unpaid leave that is subject to the Family and Medical Leave Act of 1993 (FMLA), Public Law 103-3, 20 U.S.C. 2601 et seq.,

(B) Unpaid leave that is subject to the Uniformed Services Employment and Reemployment Rights Act of 1994 (USERRA), Public Law 103-353, 38 U.S.C. 4301 et seq., or

(C) Unpaid leave on account of jury duty.

(ii) *Educational organization.* For purposes of this paragraph (e), educational organization means an entity described in § 1.170A-9(c)(1) of this chapter, whether or not described in section 501(c)(3) and exempt under section 501(a). Thus, the term educational organization includes taxable entities, tax-exempt entities and government entities.

(4) *Averaging method for special unpaid leave and employment break periods.* For purposes of applying the look-back measurement method described in paragraph (c) of this section to an employee who is not treated as a new employee under paragraph (e)(1) of this section, the employer determines the employee's average hours of service for a measurement period by computing the average after excluding any special unpaid leave (and, in the case of an employer that is an educational organization, also excluding any employment break period) during that measurement period and by using that average as the average for the entire measurement period. Alternatively, for purposes of determining the employee's average hours of service for the measurement period, the employer may choose to treat the employee as credited with hours of service for any periods of special unpaid leave (and, in the case of an employer that is an educational organization, any employment break period) during that measurement period at a rate equal to the average weekly rate at which the employee was credited with hours of service during the weeks in the measurement period that are not part of a period of special unpaid leave (or, in the case of an employer that is an educational organization, an employment break period). Notwithstanding the preceding two sentences, no more than 501 hours of service during employment break periods in a calendar year are required to be excluded (under the first sentence) or credited (under the second sentence) by an educational organization, provided that this 501-hour limit does not apply to hours of service required to be excluded or credited (as the case may be) in respect of special unpaid leave. In applying the preceding sentence, an employer that uses the method described in the first sentence of this paragraph (e)(4) determines the number of hours excluded by multiplying the average weekly rate for the measurement period (determined as in the second sentence of this paragraph (e)(4)) by the number of weeks in the employment break period and periods of special unpaid leave. For purposes of this paragraph (e)(4), in computing the average weekly rate, employers are permitted to use any reasonable method if applied on a consistent basis. In addition, if an employee's average weekly rate under this paragraph (e)(4) is being computed for a measurement period and that measurement period is shorter than six months, the six-month period ending with the close of the measurement period is used to compute the average hours of service.

(5) *Averaging rules for employment break periods for employers other than educational organizations.* [RESERVED]

(6) *Anti-abuse rule.* For purposes of this paragraph (e), any hour of service will be disregarded if the hour of service is credited, or the services giving rise to the crediting of the hour of service are requested or required of the employee, for a purpose of avoiding or undermining the application of the employee rehire rules under paragraph (e)(1) of this section, or the application of the averaging method for employment break periods under paragraph (e)(4) of this section. For example, if an employee of an educational organization would otherwise have a period with no hours of service to which the rules under paragraph (e)(4) of this section would apply, but for the employer's request or requirement that the employee perform one or more than one hour of service for a purpose of avoiding the application of those rules, any such hours of service for the week are disregarded, and the rules under paragraphs (e)(4) of this section will apply.

(7) *Examples.* The following examples illustrate the provisions of paragraph (e) of this section. All employers in these examples are applicable large employer members, each is in a different applicable large employer group, and each computes hours of service under the rules in paragraphs (a) through (e) of this section. None of the periods during which an employee is not credited with an hour of service for an employer involve special unpaid leave (as defined in paragraph (e)(3) of this section) or the employee being credited with hours of service for any applicable large employer member in the same applicable large employer as the employer.

Example 1. (i) *Facts.* As of April 1, 2015, Employee A has been an employee of Employer Z (which is not an educational organization as defined in paragraph (e)(3) of this section) for 10 years. On April 1, 2015, Employee A terminates employment and is not credited with an hour of service until September 1, 2015 when Employer Z rehires Employee A and Employee A continues as an employee through December 31, 2015, which is the close of the measurement period as applied by employer Z.

(ii) *Conclusion.* Because Employee A's period for which he is not credited with any hour of service is not longer than Employee A's prior period of employment and is less than 26 weeks, Employee A is not treated as having terminated employment and been rehired for purposes of determining whether Employee A is treated as a new employee upon resumption of services. Therefore, Employee A's hours of service prior to termination are required to be taken into account for purposes of the measurement period, and, Employee A's period with no hours of service is taken into account as a period of zero hours of service during the measurement period.

Example 2. (i) *Facts.* Same facts as *Example 1*, except that Employee A is rehired on December 1, 2015.

(ii) *Conclusion*. Because the period during which Employee A is not credited with an hour of service for Employer Z, exceeds 26 weeks, Employee A may be treated as having terminated employment on April 1, 2015, and having been rehired as a new employee on December 1, 2015, for purposes of determining Employee A's full-time employee status. Because Employee A is treated as a new employee, Employee A's hours of service prior to termination are not required to be taken into account for purposes of the measurement period, and the period between termination and rehire with no hours of service is not taken into account in the new measurement period that begins after the employee is rehired.

Example 3. (i) *Facts*. Employee B is employed by Employer X, an educational organization as defined in paragraph (e)(3) of this section. Employee B is employed for 38 hours of service per week on average from September 7, 2013 through May 22, 2014, and then does not provide services (and is not otherwise credited with an hour of service) during the summer break when the school is generally not in session except for limited summer classes and activities. Employee B resumes providing services for Employer X on September 5, 2014, when the new school year begins.

(ii) *Conclusion*. Because the period from May 23 through September 4, 2014 (a total of 15 weeks) during which Employee B is not credited with an hour of service does not exceed 26 weeks, and also does not exceed the number of weeks of Employee B's immediately preceding period of employment, Employee B is not treated as having terminated employment on May 23, 2014 and having been rehired on September 5, 2014. Also, for purposes of determining Employee B's average hours per week for the measurement period, Employee B is credited, under the averaging method for employment break periods applicable to educational organizations, as having an average of 38 hours per week for the 15 weeks between May 23 and September 4, 2014, during which Employee B otherwise was credited with no hours of service.

(f) *Nonpayment or late payment of premiums*. An applicable large employer member will not be treated as failing to offer to a full-time employee (and his or her dependents) the opportunity to enroll in minimum essential coverage under an eligible employer-sponsored plan for an employee whose coverage under the plan is terminated during the coverage period solely due to the employee failing to make a timely payment of the employee portion of the premium. This treatment continues only through the end of the coverage period (typically the plan year). For this purpose, the rules in §54.4980B-8, Q&A-5(a), (c), (d) and (e) apply under this section to the payment for coverage with respect to a full-time employee in the same manner that they apply to payment for COBRA continuation coverage under §54.4980B-8.

(g) *Effective/applicability date*. This section is applicable for periods after December 31, 2013.

§54.4980H-4 Assessable payments under section 4980H(a).

(a) *In general*. If an applicable large employer member fails to offer to its full-time employees (and their dependents) the opportunity to enroll in minimum essential coverage under an eligible employer-sponsored plan for any calendar month, and the applicable large employer member has received a Section 1411 Certification with respect to at least one full-time employee, an assessable payment is imposed. For the calendar month, the applicable large employer member will owe an assessable payment equal to the product of the section 4980H(a) applicable payment amount and the number of full-time employees of the applicable large employer member (adjusted in accordance with paragraph (d) of this section). For purposes of this paragraph (a), an applicable large employer member is treated as offering such coverage to its full-time employees (and their dependents) for a calendar month if, for that month, it offers such coverage to all but five percent (or, if greater, five) of its full-time employees (provided that an employee is treated as having been offered coverage only if the employer also offers coverage to that employee's dependents).

(b) *Offer of coverage*. An applicable large employer member will not be treated as having made an offer of coverage to a full-time employee for a plan year if the employee does not have an effective opportunity to elect to enroll (or decline to enroll) in the coverage no less than once during the plan year. Whether an employee has an effective opportunity is determined based on all the relevant facts and circumstances, including adequacy of notice of the availability of the offer of coverage, the period of time during which acceptance of the offer of coverage may be made, and any other conditions on the offer.

(c) *Partial calendar month*. If an applicable large employer member fails to offer coverage to a full-time employee for any day of a calendar month, that employee is treated as not offered coverage during that entire month. However, in a calendar month in which the employment of a full-time employee terminates, if the employee would have been offered coverage for the entire month had the employee been employed for the entire month, the employee is treated as having been offered coverage for that entire month.

(d) *Allocated reduction of 30 full-time employees*. For purposes of the liability calculation under paragraph (a) of this section, an applicable large employer member's number of full-time employees is reduced by that member's allocable share of 30. The applicable large employer member's allocation is equal to 30 allocated ratably among all members of the applicable large employer on the basis of the number of full-time employees employed by each applicable large employer member during the calendar year. If an applicable large employer member's total allocation is a fractional number that is less than one, it will be rounded up to one. This rounding rule may result in the aggregate reduction for the entire group of applicable large employer members exceeding 30.

(e) *Example*. The following example illustrates the provisions of paragraphs (a) and (b) of this section.

Example. (i) *Facts*. Applicable large employer member A and applicable large employer member B are the two members of an applicable large employer. Applicable large employer member A employs 40 full-time employees in each calendar month of 2015. Applicable large employer member B employs 35 full-time employees in each calendar month of 2015. For 2015, the applicable payment amount for a calendar month is $2,000 divided by 12. Applicable large employer member A does not sponsor an eligible employer-sponsored plan for any calendar month of 2015, and receives a Section 1411 Certification for 2015 with respect to at least one of its full-time employees. Applicable large employer member B sponsors an eligible employer-sponsored plan under which all of its full-time employees are eligible for minimum essential coverage.

(ii) *Conclusion*. Pursuant to section 4980H(a) and this section, applicable large employer member A is subject to an assessable payment under section 4980H(a) for 2015 of $48,000, which is equal to 24 × $2,000 (40 full-time employees reduced by 16 (its allocable share of the 30-employee offset ((40/75) × 30 = 16)) and then multiplied by $2,000). Applicable large employer member B is not subject to an assessable payment under section 4980H(a) for 2015.

(f) *Effective/applicability date*. This section is applicable for periods after December 31, 2013.

§54.4980H-5 Assessable payments under section 4980H(b).

(a) *In general*. If an applicable large employer member offers to its full-time employees (and their dependents) the opportunity to enroll in minimum essential coverage under an eligible employer-sponsored plan for any calendar month (including an offer of coverage to all but five percent or less (or, if greater, five or less) of its full-time employees (and their dependents)) and the applicable large employer member has received a Section 1411 Certification with respect to one or more full-time employees of the applicable large employer, then there is imposed on the applicable large employer member an assessable payment equal to the product of the number of full-time employees of the applicable large employer member for which it has received a Section 1411 Certification (minus the number of those employees who are new full-time employees during their first three months of employment, who are new variable hour or new seasonal employees during the months of that employee's initial measurement period (and associated administrative period) under §54.4980H-3(c)(3), or who were offered the opportunity to enroll in minimum essential coverage under an eligible employer-sponsored plan that satisfied minimum value and met one or more of the affordability safe harbors described in paragraph (e) of this section) and the section 4980H(b) applicable payment amount. Notwithstanding the foregoing, the aggregate amount of assessable payment determined under this paragraph (a) with respect to all employees of an applicable large employer for any calendar month may not exceed the product of the section 4980H(a) applicable payment amount and the number of full-time employees of the applicable large employer member during that calendar month (reduced by the applicable large employer member's ratable allocation of the 30 employee reduction under §54.4980H-4(d).

(b) *Offer of coverage*. For purposes of this section, the same rules, with respect to an offer of coverage for purposes of section 4980H(a), apply. See §54.4980H-4(b).

(c) *Partial calendar month*. If an applicable large employer member fails to offer coverage to a full-time employee for any day of a calendar month, that employee is treated as not offered coverage during that entire month. However, in a calendar month in which a full-time employee's employment terminates, if the employee would have been offered coverage if the employee had been employed for the entire month, the employee is treated as having been offered coverage during that month.

(d) *Applicability to applicable large employer member.* The liability for an assessable payment under section 4980H(b) for a calendar month with respect to a full-time employee applies solely to the applicable large employer member that was the employer of that employee for that calendar month, provided that, if the employee was an employee of more than one applicable large employer member during that calendar month, the liability for the assessable payment under section 4980H(b) is allocated among the different members in accordance with the number of hours of service the employee had from each such member for that calendar month. For a calendar month, an applicable large employer member may be liable for an assessable payment under section 4980H(a) or under section 4980H(b), but may not be liable for an assessable payment under both section 4980H(a) and section 4980H(b).

(e) *Affordability*—(1) *In general.* An employee who is offered coverage by an applicable large employer member may be eligible for a premium tax credit or cost reduction if that offer of coverage is not affordable within the meaning of section 36B(c)(2)(C)(i). Under section 36B(c)(2)(C)(i), coverage under an employer-sponsored plan is affordable to a particular employee if the employee's required contribution (within the meaning of section 5000A(e)(1)(B)(i)) to the plan does not exceed 9.5 percent of the employee's household income for the taxable year. For this purpose, section 36B(d)(2)(A) defines the term *household income* to mean the modified adjusted gross income of the employee and any members of the employee's family (which would include any spouse and dependents) who are required to file a federal income tax return. Section 36B(d)(2)(B) and §1.36B-1(e)(2) of this chapter define the term *modified adjusted gross income* for this purpose as adjusted gross income (within the meaning of section 62) increased by—

(i) Amounts excluded from gross income under section 911,

(ii) The amount of any tax-exempt interest a taxpayer receives or accrues during the taxable year, and

(iii) An amount equal to the portion of the taxpayer's social security benefits (as defined in section 86(d)) which is not included in gross income under section 86 for the taxable year.

(2) *Affordability safe harbors for section 4980H(b) purposes.* The following affordability safe harbors apply solely for purposes of section 4980H(b), so that an applicable large employer member that offers minimum essential coverage providing minimum value will not be subject to an assessable payment under section 4980H(b) with respect to any employee receiving the premium tax credit or cost sharing reduction for a period for which the coverage is determined to be affordable under the requirements of an affordability safe harbor. This rule applies even if the applicable large employer member's offer of coverage that meets the requirements of an affordability safe harbor is not affordable for a particular employee under section 36B(c)(2)(C)(i) and a premium tax credit or cost-sharing is allowed or paid with respect to that employee

(i) *Conditions of using an affordability safe harbor.* An applicable large employer member may use one or more of the affordability safe harbors described in paragraph (e)(2) of this section only if the employer offers its full-time employees and their dependents the opportunity to enroll in MEC under an eligible employer-sponsored plan that provides minimum value with respect to the self-only coverage offered to the employee. Use of any of the safe harbors is optional for an applicable large employer, and an applicable large employer member may choose to apply the safe harbors for any reasonable category of employees, provided it does so on a uniform and consistent basis for all employees in a category.

(ii) *Form W-2 safe harbor* -(A) *Full-year offer of coverage.* An employer will not be subject to an assessable payment under section 4980H(b) with respect to a full-time employee if that employee's required contribution for the calendar year for the employer's lowest cost self-only coverage that provides minimum value during the entire calendar year (excluding COBRA or other continuation coverage) does not exceed 9.5 percent of that employee's Form W-2 wages from the employer for the calendar year. Application of this safe harbor is determined after the end of the calendar year and on an employee-by-employee basis, taking into account the Form W-2 wages and the required employee contribution for that year. In addition, to qualify for this safe harbor, the employee's required contribution must remain a consistent amount or percentage of all Form W-2 wages during the calendar year (or for plans with fiscal year plan years, within the portion of each plan year during the calendar year) so that an applicable large employer member is not permitted to make discretionary adjustments to the required employee contribution for a pay period. A periodic contribution that is based on a consistent percentage of all Form W-2 wages may be subject to a dollar limit specified by the employer.

(B) *Adjustment for partial-year offer of coverage.* For an employee not offered coverage for an entire calendar year, the Form W-2 safe harbor is applied by adjusting the Form W-2 wages to reflect the period for which coverage was offered, then determining whether the employee's required contribution for the employer's lowest cost self-only coverage that provides minimum value, totaled for the periods during which coverage was offered, does not exceed 9.5 percent of the adjusted amount of Form W-2 wages. To adjust Form W-2 wages for this purpose, the Form W-2 wages are multiplied by a fraction equal to the number of calendar months for which coverage was offered over the number of calendar months in the employee's period of employment with the employer during the calendar year. For this purpose, if coverage is offered during at least one day during the calendar month, or the employee is employed for at least one day during the calendar month, the entire calendar month is counted in determining the applicable fraction.

(iii) *Rate of pay safe harbor.* An applicable large employer member satisfies the rate of pay safe harbor with respect to an employee for a calendar month if the employee's required contribution for the month for the applicable large employer member's lowest cost self-only coverage that provides minimum value does not exceed 9.5 percent of an amount equal to 130 hours multiplied by the employee's hourly rate of pay as of the first day of the coverage period (generally the first day of the plan year). For salaried employees, monthly salary is used instead of 130 multiplied by the hourly rate of pay, and, solely for purposes of this paragraph (e)(2)(iii), an applicable large employer member may use any reasonable method for converting payroll periods to monthly salary. An applicable large employer member may use this safe harbor only to the extent it does not reduce the hourly wage of hourly employees or the monthly wages of salaried employees during the calendar year (including through the transfer of employment to another applicable large employer member of the same applicable large employer). For this purpose, if coverage is offered during at least one day during the calendar month, the entire calendar month is counted both for purposes of determining the assumed income for the calendar month and for determining the employee's share of the premium for the calendar month.

(iv) *Federal poverty line safe harbor.* An applicable large employer member satisfies the Federal poverty line safe harbor with respect to an employee for a calendar month if the employee's required contribution for the calendar month for the applicable large employer member's lowest cost self-only coverage that provides minimum value does not exceed 9.5 percent of a monthly amount determined as the Federal poverty line for a single individual for the applicable calendar year, divided by 12. For this purpose, if coverage is offered during at least one day during the calendar month, the entire calendar month is counted both for purposes of determining the assumed income for the calendar month and for determining the employee's share of the premium for the calendar month. For this purpose, the applicable Federal poverty line is the Federal poverty line for the State in which the employee is employed.

(v) *Examples.* The following examples illustrate the application of the affordability safe harbors described in paragraph (e)(2) of this section:

Example 1. (Form W-2 wages safe harbor). (i) *Facts.* Employee A is employed by applicable large employer member Z consistently from January 1, 2015 through December 31, 2015. In addition, Z offers Employee A and his dependents minimum essential coverage during that period that meets the minimum value requirements. The employee contribution for self-only coverage is $100 per calendar month, or $1,200 for the calendar year. For 2015, Employee A's Form W-2 wages with respect to employment with Z are $24,000.

(ii) *Conclusion.* Because the employee contribution for 2015 is less than 9.5% of Employee A's Form W-2 wages for 2015, the coverage offered is treated as affordable with respect to Employee A for 2015 ($1,200 is 5% of $24,000).

Example 2. (Form W-2 wages safe harbor). (i) *Facts.* Employee B is employed by applicable large employer member Y from January 1, 2015 through September 30, 2015. In addition, Y offers Employee B and his dependents minimum essential coverage during that period that meets the minimum value requirements. The employee contribution for self-only coverage is $100 per calendar month, or $900 for Employee B's period of employment. For 2015, Employee B's Form W-2 wages with respect to employment with Y are $18,000. For purposes of applying the affordability safe harbor, the Form W-2 wages are multiplied by 9/9 (9 calendar months of coverage offered over 9 months of employment during the calendar year) or 1. Accordingly, affordability is determined by comparing the adjusted Form W-2 wages ($18,000) to the employee contribution for the period for which coverage was offered ($900).

(ii) *Conclusion*. Because the result is less than 9.5% of Employee B's Form W-2 wages for 2015, the coverage offered is treated as affordable with respect to Employee B for 2015 ($900 is 5% of $18,000).

Example 3. (Form W-2 wages safe harbor). (i) *Facts*. Employee C is employed by applicable large employer member X from May 15, 2015 through December 31, 2015. In addition, X offers Employee C and her dependents minimum essential coverage during the period from August 1, 2015 through December 31, 2015 that meets the minimum value requirements. The employee contribution for self-only coverage is $100 per calendar month, or $500 for Employee C's period of employment. For 2015, Employee C's Form W-2 wages with respect to employment with X are $15,000. For purposes of applying the affordability safe harbor, the Form W-2 wages are multiplied by 5/8 (5 calendar months of coverage offered over 8 months of employment during the calendar year). Accordingly, affordability is determined by comparing the adjusted Form W-2 wages ($9,375 or $15,000 × 5/8) to the employer contribution for the period for which coverage was offered ($500).

(ii) *Conclusion*. Because $500 is less than 9.5% of $9,375 (Employee C's adjusted Form W-2 wages for 2015), the coverage offered is treated as affordable with respect to Employee C for 2015 ($500 is 5.33% of $9,375).

Example 4. (Rate of pay safe harbor). (i) *Facts*. Employee D is employed by applicable large employer member W from January 1, 2015 through December 31, 2015. In addition, W offers Employee D and his dependents minimum essential coverage during that period that meets the minimum value requirements. The employee contribution for self-only coverage is $85 per calendar month. Employee D is paid at a rate of $7.25 per hour (the minimum wage in Employer W's jurisdiction), for the entire year 2015. For purposes of applying the affordability safe harbor, W may assume that Employee D earned $942.50 per calendar month (130 hours of service multiplied by $7.25 per hour). Accordingly, affordability is determined by comparing the assumed income per month ($942.50) to the employee contribution per month ($85).

(ii) *Conclusion*. Because $85 is less than 9.5% of Employee D's assumed income, the coverage offered is treated as affordable with respect to Employee D for 2015 ($85 is 9.01% of $942.50).

Example 5. (Rate of pay safe harbor). (i) *Facts*. Employee E is employed by applicable large employer member V from May 15, 2015 through December 31, 2015. In addition, V offers Employee E and her dependents minimum essential coverage from August 1, 2015 through December 31, 2015 that meets the minimum value requirements. The employee contribution for self-only coverage is $100 per calendar month. From May 15, 2015 through October 31, 2015, Employee E is paid at a rate of $10 per hour. From November 1, 2015 through December 31, 2015, Employee E is paid at a rate of $12 per hour. For purposes of applying the affordability safe harbor V may assume that Employee E earned $1,300 per calendar month (130 hours of service multiplied by the lowest hourly rate of pay for the calendar year, or $10). Accordingly, affordability is determined by comparing the assumed income ($1,300 per month) to the employee contribution ($100 per month).

(ii) *Conclusion*. Because $100 is less than 9.5% of Employee E's assumed monthly income, the coverage offered is treated as affordable with respect to Employee E for 2015 ($100 is 7.69% of $1,300).

Example 6. (Federal poverty line safe harbor). (i) *Facts*. Employee F is employed by applicable large employer member W from January 1, 2015 through December 31, 2015. In addition, W offers Employee F and his dependents minimum essential coverage during that period that meets the minimum value requirements. W uses the look-back

measurement method. Under that method as applied by W, Employee F is treated as a full-time employee for the entire calendar year 2015. Employee F is regularly credited with 35 hours of service per week but is credited with only 20 hours of service during the month of March, 2015 and only 15 hours of service during the month of August, 2015. Assume for this purpose that the Federal poverty line for 2015 for an individual is $11,170. With respect to Employee F, W determines the monthly employee contribution for employee single-only coverage for each calendar month of 2015 as an amount equal to 9.5% multiplied by $11,170, which is $1,061.15, and that amount is then divided by 12, and the result is $88.43.

(ii) *Conclusion*. Regardless of Employee F's actual wages for any calendar month, including the months of March, 2015 and August, 2015 when Employee F has lower wages because of significantly lower hours of service, the coverage under the plan is treated as affordable with respect to Employee F.

(f) *Effective/applicability date*. This section is applicable for periods after December 31, 2013.

§ 54.4980H-6 Administration and Procedure

(a) *In general*. [Reserved]

(b) *Effective/applicability date*. This section is applicable for periods after December 31, 2013.

PART 301—PROCEDURE AND ADMINISTRATION

Par. 5. The authority citation for part 301 continues to read in part as follows:

Authority: 26 U.S.C. 7805 * * *

Par. 6. Section 301.7701-2 is amended as follows:

1. In paragraph (c)(2)(v)(A)(3), the language "and 4412; and" is removed and "and 4412;" is added in its place.

2. In paragraph (c)(2)(v)(A)(4), the language "or 6427." is removed and "or 6427; and " is added in its place.

3. Paragraphs (c)(2)(v)(A)(5) and (e)(6)(iii) are added.

The additions read as follows:

§ 301.7701-2 Business entities; definitions.

* * * * *

(c) * * *

(2) * * *

(v) * * *

(A) * * *

(5) Assessment and collection of an assessable payment imposed by section 4980H and reporting required by section 6056.

* * * * *

(e) * * *

(6) * * *

(iii) Paragraph (c)(2)(v)(A)(5) of this section applies for periods after December 31, 2013.

* * * * *

Steven T. Miller

Deputy Commissioner for Services and Enforcement.

IRS: Employee health coverage: Minimum essential coverage: Shared responsibility.—The IRS has issued proposed regulations relating to the requirement to maintain minimum essential coverage under Code Sec. 5000A, enacted by the Patient Protection and Affordable Care Act (P.L. 111-148) and amended by the TRICARE Affirmation Act of 2010 (P.L. 111-159) and P.L. 111-173. The proposed regulations provide guidance on the liability for the shared responsibility payment when a nonexempt individual does not maintain minimum essential coverage. The regulations are proposed to apply for months beginning after December 31, 2013.

The proposed regulations were published in the Federal Register on February 1, 2013 (78 FR 7314). The regulations were corrected March 25, 2013 (78 FR 17900) and March 29, 2013 (78 FR 19155). The regulations were finalized on August 30, 2013 (78 FR 53646). The preamble to the final regulations is at ¶ 23,291. The final regulations are at ¶ 13,648Z-55, ¶ 13,648Z-56, ¶ 13,648Z-57, ¶ 13,648Z-58, ¶ 13,648Z-59, and ¶ 13,648Z-60.

DEPARTMENT OF THE TREASURY

Internal Revenue Service

26 CFR Part 1

[REG-148500-12]

RIN 1545-BL36

Shared Responsibility Payment for Not Maintaining Minimum Essential Coverage

AGENCY: Internal Revenue Service (IRS), Treasury.

ACTION: Notice of proposed rulemaking and notice of public hearing.

SUMMARY: This document contains proposed regulations relating to the requirement to maintain minimum essential coverage enacted by the Patient Protection and Affordable Care Act and the Health Care and Education Reconciliation Act of 2010, as amended by the TRICARE Affirmation Act and Public Law 111-173. These proposed regulations provide guidance on the liability for the shared responsibility payment for not maintaining minimum essential coverage. This document also provides notice of a public hearing on these proposed regulations.

DATES: Comments must be received by May 2, 2013. Outlines of topics to be discussed at the public hearing scheduled for May 29, 2013, at 10 a.m., must be received by May 3, 2013.

ADDRESSES: Send submissions to: CC:PA:LPD:PR (REG-148500-12), Room 5203, Internal Revenue Service, PO Box 7604, Ben Franklin Station, Washington, DC 20044. Submissions may be hand-delivered Monday through Friday between the hours of 8 a.m. and 4 p.m. to CC:PA:LPD:PR (REG-148500-12), Courier's Desk, Internal Revenue Service, 1111 Constitution Avenue NW., Washington, DC, or sent electronically via the Federal eRulemaking Portal at *www.regulations.gov* (IRS REG-148500-12). The public hearing will be held in the IRS Auditorium, Internal Revenue Building, 1111 Constitution Avenue NW., Washington, DC.

FOR FURTHER INFORMATION CONTACT: Concerning the proposed regulations, Sue-Jean Kim or John B. Lovelace, (202) 622-4960; concerning the submission of comments, the public hearing, and to be placed on the building access list to attend the public hearing, Oluwafunmilayo Taylor, (202) 622-7180 (not toll-free numbers).

SUPPLEMENTARY INFORMATION:

Paperwork Reduction Act

The collection of information contained in this notice of proposed rulemaking has been submitted to the Office of Management and Budget in accordance with the Paperwork Reduction Act of 1995 (44 U.S.C. 3507(d)). Comments on the collection of information should be sent to the Office of Management and Budget, Attn: Desk Officer for the Department of the Treasury, Office of Information and Regulatory Affairs, Washington, DC 20503, with copies to the Internal Revenue Service, Attn: IRS Reports Clearance Officer, SE:W:CAR:MP:T:T:SP, Washington, DC 20224.

Comments on the collection of information should be received by April 2, 2013. Comments are specifically requested concerning:

Whether the proposed collection of information is necessary for the proper performance of the functions of the IRS, including whether the information will have practical utility;

The accuracy of the estimated burden associated with the proposed collection of information;

How the quality, utility, and clarity of the information to be collected may be enhanced;

How the burden of complying with the proposed collection of information may be minimized, including through the application of automated collection techniques or other forms of information technology; and

Estimates of capital or start-up costs and costs of operation, maintenance, and purchase of services to provide information.

The collection of information in these proposed regulations is in § 1.5000A-3 and § 1.5000A-4. The collection of information is necessary to determine whether the shared responsibility payment provision applies to a taxpayer and compute any shared responsibility payment imposed on a taxpayer. The likely respondents are individuals required to file Federal income tax returns under section 6012(a)(1) of the Internal Revenue Code (Code).

The burden for the collection of information contained in proposed regulation § 1.5000A-3 and § 1.5000A-4 will be reflected in the burden

on a form that the IRS will create to request the information in the proposed regulation.

An agency may not conduct or sponsor, and a person is not required to respond to, a collection of information unless it displays a valid control number assigned by the Office of Management and Budget.

Background

Under the Patient Protection and Affordable Care Act, Public Law 111-148 (124 Stat. 119 (2010)) and the Health Care and Education Reconciliation Act of 2010, Public Law 111-152 (124 Stat. 1029 (2010)) (collectively, the Affordable Care Act), the Federal government, State governments, insurers, employers, and individuals are entrusted with shared responsibility to reform and improve the availability, quality, and affordability of health insurance coverage in the United States. The Affordable Care Act expands Medicaid eligibility for residents of electing States and increases Federal funding for the expansion. The Affordable Care Act also provides individuals and small businesses the ability to purchase private health insurance through State-based, State Partnership, or Federally facilitated competitive market places called Affordable Insurance Exchanges (Exchanges). Through Exchanges, insurance companies will compete for business on a level playing field and qualified consumers will have a choice of health plans to fit their needs.

In addition, the Affordable Care Act includes various insurance market reforms to increase the ability of individuals to enroll in health insurance coverage regardless of preexisting conditions and to eliminate the ability of insurers to charge higher premium prices based on factors other than age, tobacco use, rating area, or family size. Moreover, the Affordable Care Act builds upon the existing private employer-based health insurance system to ensure continued access to high quality health insurance coverage at low cost.

Finally, to ensure effective and efficient implementation of the insurance market reforms, the Affordable Care Act requires a nonexempt individual to maintain minimum essential coverage or make a shared responsibility payment. Section 1501(b) of the Affordable Care Act added section 5000A to a new chapter 48 of subtitle D (Miscellaneous Excise Taxes) of the Code effective for months beginning after December 31, 2013. Section 5000A was subsequently amended by the TRICARE Affirmation Act of 2010, Public Law 111-159 (124 Stat. 1123) and Public Law 111-173 (124 Stat. 1215).

Shared Responsibility Payment for Not Maintaining Minimum Essential Coverage

Section 5000A provides nonexempt individuals with a choice: maintain minimum essential coverage for themselves and any nonexempt family members or include an additional payment with their Federal income tax return. Section 5000A(a) and section 5000A(b) provide that nonexempt individuals must have minimum essential coverage for each month beginning after December 31, 2013, or make an additional payment (the shared responsibility payment) with their Federal income tax return for the taxable year that includes such month. Under section 5000A(b)(3)(A), a taxpayer is liable for the shared responsibility payment if any nonexempt individual who may be claimed by the taxpayer as a dependent for a taxable year does not have minimum essential coverage in a month included in that taxable year. Married taxpayers filing a joint return for any taxable year are jointly liable for any shared responsibility payment imposed for the year.

Exempt Individuals

Many individuals are exempt from the shared responsibility payment, including some whose religious beliefs conflict with acceptance of the benefits of private or public insurance and those who do not have an affordable health insurance coverage option available. Section 1311(d)(4)(H) of the Affordable Care Act (42 U.S.C. 18031(d)(4)(H)) directs Exchanges to issue to qualified individuals certificates of exemption from the requirement to maintain minimum essential coverage or the shared responsibility payment under section 5000A. Section 1411 of the Affordable Care Act (42 U.S.C. 18081) generally provides procedures for determining an individual's eligibility for various benefits relating to health coverage, including exemptions from the application of section 5000A. The Department of Health and Human Services and the Department of the Treasury are working in close coordination to release regulations and other guidance related to Exchanges.

On March 27, 2012, the Department of Health and Human Services released final regulations related to the establishment of, and the standards applicable to, Exchanges (45 CFR 155.10 and following sections (Exchange regulations)). Section 155.200(b) of the Exchange regulations directs an Exchange to issue exemption certificates in accordance with sections 1311(d)(4)(H) and 1411 of the Affordable

Care Act (42 U.S.C. 18031(d)(4)(H), 18081). The Department of Health and Human Services is publishing proposed regulations detailing the standards by which Exchanges will issue certificates of exemption under section 5000A. Patient Protection and Affordable Care Act; Exchange Functions: Eligibility for Exemptions; Minimum Essential Coverage Provisions (to be codified at 45 CFR 155.600 and following sections).

Section 5000A(d) and (e) describe individuals who are exempt from making the shared responsibility payment even if they do not have minimum essential coverage for a given month. Under section 5000A(d)(2)(A), an individual is exempt for a month for which an Exchange certifies that the individual is a member of a recognized religious sect or a division thereof described in section 1402(g)(1) and is an adherent of established tenets or teachings of that sect or division. Section 1402(g)(1) provides an exemption from self-employment tax for members of a qualified religious sect or division thereof. A qualified religious sect or division thereof described in section 1402(g)(1) is a sect or division thereof that the Commissioner of Social Security finds: (1) has established tenets or teachings by reason of which its members and adherents are conscientiously opposed to acceptance of the benefits of any private or public insurance that makes payments in the event of death, disability, old age, or retirement or makes payments toward the cost of, or provides services for, medical care (including the benefits of any insurance system established by the Social Security Act); (2) maintains, and has maintained for a substantial period of time, a practice whereby its members make provision for its dependent members that is reasonable in view of their general level of living; and (3) has been in existence at all times since December 31, 1950.

Section 5000A(d)(2)(B) provides that an individual is exempt for a month that the individual is a member of a health care sharing ministry. A health care sharing ministry is an organization: (1) which is described in section 501(c)(3) and exempt from tax under section 501(a); (2) members of which share a common set of ethical or religious beliefs and share medical expenses among themselves in accordance with those beliefs, and regardless of the State in which a member resides or is employed; (3) members of which retain membership even after they develop a medical condition; (4) which has itself (or a predecessor of which has) been in existence at all times since December 31, 1999; (5) members of which have continuously and without interruption shared medical expenses since at least December 31, 1999; and (6) which conducts an annual audit performed by an independent certified public accounting firm in accordance with generally accepted accounting principles the report of which is made available to members of the public upon request.

Section 5000A(d)(3) provides that an individual is exempt for a month that the individual is neither a citizen or national of the United States nor an alien lawfully present in the United States.

Section 5000A(d)(4) provides that an individual is exempt for a month that the individual is incarcerated, except for incarceration pending the disposition of charges.

Section 5000A(e)(1) provides that an individual is exempt for a month for which the individual lacks access to affordable minimum essential coverage. For this purpose, an individual lacks access to affordable coverage if the individual's required contribution (determined on an annual basis) for minimum essential coverage exceeds a percentage (8 percent for 2014) of the individual's household income for the most recent taxable year for which the Secretary of Health and Human Services, in consultation with the Secretary, determines information is available.

In general, section 5000A(c)(4)(B) defines a taxpayer's *household income* as the sum of the taxpayer's modified adjusted gross income and the modified adjusted gross income of any other member of a taxpayer's family (that is, individuals for whom the taxpayer properly claims a deduction under section 151 (relating to the personal exemption deduction)) who are required to file a Federal income tax return. Under section 5000A(c)(4)(C), *modified adjusted gross income* means adjusted gross income (within the meaning of section 62) increased by amounts excluded from gross income under section 911 and tax-exempt interest a taxpayer receives or accrues in the taxable year. Unlike section 36B(d)(2)(B), modified adjusted gross income for purposes of section 5000A does not include Social Security benefits that are not includable in gross income. For purposes of determining the affordability of minimum essential coverage under section 5000A(e)(1), the taxpayer's household income is increased by the portion of the required contribution made through a salary reduction arrangement and excluded from gross income.

For purposes of determining household income, a taxpayer's family includes all individuals for whom the taxpayer properly claims a personal exemption deduction under section 151 for the taxable year. *See*

also § 1.36B-1(d). Taxpayers may claim a personal exemption deduction for themselves, a spouse, and each of their dependents. Section 152 provides that a taxpayer's dependent may be a qualifying child or qualifying relative, including an unrelated individual who lives with the taxpayer.

For an employee eligible to purchase coverage under an eligible employer-sponsored plan, the required contribution for purposes of the exemption under section 5000A(e)(1) is the employee's share of the annual premium for self-only coverage. For an individual eligible to purchase coverage under an eligible employer-sponsored plan because the individual is related to an employee, the determination of whether the individual's coverage is affordable is made by reference to the employee's required contribution. For all individuals who are ineligible to purchase coverage under an eligible employer-sponsored plan, the required contribution is the annual premium for the lowest cost bronze plan available on the Exchange where the individual lives reduced by the credit allowable under section 36B for the taxable year (determined as if the individual enrolled in a plan through such Exchange for the entire taxable year).

Section 5000A(e)(2) provides that an individual is exempt for a month included in a calendar year if the individual's household income for the most recent taxable year for which information is available is less than the amount of gross income specified in section 6012(a)(1) for the taxpayer. Section 6012(a)(1) provides, for each filing status, gross income thresholds above which individuals are required to file Federal income tax returns.

As described in this preamble, income-based exemptions under section 5000A(e)(1) and section 5000A(e)(2) rely upon household income for the most recent taxable year that the Secretary of Health and Human Services, after consultation with the Secretary of the Treasury, determines information is available. The Secretary of Health and Human Services, after consultation with the Secretary of the Treasury, determined that the household income for these exemptions that is available and relevant is the household income for the year for which an exemption is being claimed. See section III.A.3.b. of the preamble to Patient Protection and Affordable Care Act; Exchange Functions: Eligibility for Exemptions; Minimum Essential Coverage Provisions (to be codified at 45 CFR 155.600 and following sections, and 45 CFR 156.600 and following sections). The determination by the Secretary of Health and Human Services is reflected in the proposed regulations. [Corrected 3/25/2013 (78 FR 17900).]

Section 5000A(e)(3) provides that an individual is exempt for a month that the individual is a member of an Indian tribe as defined in section 45A(c)(6). Section 45A(c)(6) describes certain Federally recognized Indian tribes (including any qualified Alaska Native village or regional or village corporation). The Federally recognized Indian tribes are listed in Indian Entities Recognized and Eligible to Receive Services from the United States Bureau of Indian Affairs, 75 FR 60810 (Oct. 1, 2010), as supplemented by 75 FR 661124 (Oct. 27, 2010), or its successor.

Under section 5000A(e)(4), an individual is exempt for a month the last day of which occurs in a period when the individual does not have minimum essential coverage for a continuous period of less than three months (a short coverage gap). The length of a gap in coverage is determined without regard to the calendar years in which months in the gap occur. If an individual has more than one short coverage gap in a calendar year, the exemption applies only to the earliest short coverage gap. Section 5000A(e)(4) authorizes the Secretary to issue regulations that provide for collecting the shared responsibility payment in cases where gaps in coverage straddle more than one taxable year.

Section 5000A(e)(5) provides that an individual is exempt for a month that the Exchange determines, in accordance with guidance promulgated by the Secretary of Health and Human Services, the individual suffered a hardship that prevented the individual from obtaining coverage under a qualified health plan. The Department of Health and Human Services is proposing rules on the criteria for application of the hardship exemption. Patient Protection and Affordable Care Act; Exchange Functions: Eligibility for Exemptions; Minimum Essential Coverage (to be codified at 45 CFR 155.605(g)).

Computation of Shared Responsibility Payment

Under section 5000A(c), the amount of the shared responsibility payment for any taxable year is generally the sum of monthly penalty amounts for all months in the taxable year in which any nonexempt individual for whom the taxpayer is liable under section 5000A(b) did not have minimum essential coverage. The shared responsibility payment amount for any taxable year may not exceed an amount equal to the national average premium for bronze-level qualified health plans offered through Exchanges for the applicable family size involved.

The monthly penalty amount for a month is equal to $1/12$ of the greater of the following amounts: (1) the flat dollar amount or (2) the percentage of income. The flat dollar amount is the lesser of the following amounts: (a) the sum of the applicable dollar amounts for all nonexempt individuals without minimum essential coverage for whom the taxpayer is liable or (b) 300 percent of the applicable dollar amount. The applicable dollar amount is $95 for 2014, $325 for 2015, and $695 for 2016, and will be increased for calendar years beginning after 2016 by a cost-of-living adjustment. If a nonexempt individual has not attained the age of 18 as of the beginning of a month, the applicable dollar amount for that individual is one-half of the regular applicable dollar amount. [Corrected 3/25/2013 (78 FR 17900).]

The percentage of income is calculated as the excess of the taxpayer's household income over the taxpayer's Federal income tax return filing threshold under section 6012(a)(1), multiplied by a percentage figure. The percentage figure is 1 percent for taxable years beginning in 2014, 2 percent for taxable years beginning in 2015, and 2.5 percent for taxable years beginning after 2015.

Minimum Essential Coverage

Section 5000A(f) defines *minimum essential coverage* as one of the following: (1) coverage under a specified government sponsored program; (2) coverage under an eligible employer-sponsored plan; (3) coverage under a health plan offered in the individual market within a State; (4) coverage under a grandfathered health plan; and (5) other health benefits coverage that the Secretary of Health and Human Services, in coordination with the Secretary, recognizes for purposes of section 5000A(f). [Corrected 3/25/2013 (78 FR 17900).]

Under section 5000A(f)(1)(A), specified government sponsored programs include the following: (1) the Medicare program under part A of title XVIII of the Social Security Act; (2) the Medicaid program under title XIX of the Social Security Act; (3) the Children's Health Insurance Program (CHIP) under title XXI of the Social Security Act; (4) medical coverage under chapter 55 of title 10, United States Code, including the TRICARE program; (5) veterans health care programs under chapter 17 or 18 of title 38, as determined by the Secretary of Veterans Affairs, in coordination with the Secretary of Health and Human Services and the Secretary of Treasury; (6) a health plan under section 2504(e) of title 22 relating to Peace Corps volunteers; and (7) the Nonappropriated Fund Health Benefits Program of the Department of Defense, established under section 349 of the National Defense Authorization Act for Fiscal Year 1995, Public Law 103-337 (10 U.S.C. 1587 note). [Corrected 3/25/2013 (78 FR 17900).]

Under section 5000A(f)(2), an eligible employer-sponsored plan is, with respect to an employee, a group health plan or group health insurance coverage offered by an employer to the employee that is: (1) a governmental plan, within the meaning of section 2791(d)(8) of the Public Health Service Act, or (2) any other plan or coverage offered in the small or large group market within a State. An eligible employer-sponsored plan also includes a grandfathered health plan offered in a group market.

Under section 1251 of the Affordable Care Act (42 U.S.C. 18011), a grandfathered health plan is a group health plan or health insurance coverage that provided coverage as of the enactment date of the Affordable Care Act (March 23, 2010) or in which an individual was enrolled as of that date. *See also* § 54.9815-1251T(a) (providing guidance regarding grandfathered health plans).

As described in this preamble, the Department of Health and Human Services, in coordination with the Treasury Department, may designate other health benefits coverage as minimum essential coverage. The Department of Health and Human Services is proposing a regulation that provides criteria and a process by which other types of coverage may be designated as minimum essential coverage. Patient Protection and Affordable Care Act; Exchange Functions: Eligibility for Exemptions; Minimum Essential Coverage Provisions (to be codified at 45 CFR 156.600 and following sections).

Under section 5000A(f)(3), health coverage that consists of coverage of certain excepted benefits specified in section 2791(c) of the Public Health Service Act (42 U.S.C. 300gg-91(c)) is not minimum essential coverage. There are four categories of excepted benefits. The first category includes accidental death and dismemberment coverage, disability insurance, general liability insurance, automobile liability insurance, workers' compensation, credit-only insurance (for example, mortgage insurance), and coverage for employer-provided on-site medical clinics. *See* 42 U.S.C. 300gg-91(c)(1). The second category of excepted benefits includes limited-scope dental or vision benefits, long-term care benefits, and benefits provided under certain health flexible spending arrangements. *See* 42 U.S.C. 300gg-91(c)(2). The third category of excepted benefits includes, but only if offered under a policy, certificate, or contract of insurance separate from, and not coordinated with, any group or individual health plan maintained by the same plan sponsor, coverage only for a specified disease or illness (for example, cancer-only policies) or fixed indemnity insurance (for example, a policy that pays a fixed dollar amount, such as $100, per day of hospitalization or illness regardless of the amount of medical expense incurred). *See* 42 U.S.C. 300gg-91(c)(3). The last category of excepted benefits includes, but only if offered under a policy, certificate, or contract of insurance separate from the primary health coverage, Medicare supplemental polices (also known as Medigap or MedSupp insurance), TRICARE supplemental policies, and similar supplemental coverage to coverage under a group health plan. *See* 42 U.S.C. 300gg-91(c)(4).

Under section 5000A(f)(4), an individual is treated as having minimum essential coverage for a month: (1) if the individual is a bona fide resident of a United States possession for the month, or (2) if the month occurs during any period described in section 911(d)(1)(A) or section 911(d)(1)(B) that is applicable to the individual. Section 911(d)(1)(A) is applicable to a citizen of the United States who has a tax home outside the United States and is a bona fide resident of a foreign country or countries during an uninterrupted period that includes an entire taxable year. For example, an individual who resides abroad for an entire calendar year is treated as having minimum essential coverage for each month of that calendar year regardless of whether the individual has health coverage of any type. Section 911(d)(1)(B) is applicable to a U.S. citizen or U.S. resident (within the meaning of section 7701(b)) who has a tax home outside the United States and is present in a foreign country or countries for at least 330 full days during a period of 12 consecutive months. In general, an individual who meets either of the foregoing residency requirements under section 911(d)(1) is treated as a qualified individual for purposes of section 911 and may elect to exclude certain foreign earned income and housing costs from gross income. [Corrected 3/25/2013 (78 FR 17900).]

Administration and Procedure

Under section 5000A(b)(2), an individual liable for the shared responsibility payment under section 5000A must report the payment with the individual's Federal income tax return for the taxable year including the month or months for which the payment is owed.

Under section 5000A(g)(1), the shared responsibility payment is payable upon notice and demand by the Secretary. The shared responsibility payment is generally assessed and collected in the same manner as an assessable penalty under subchapter B of chapter 68 (sections 6671 through 6725). Unlike the assessable penalties, however, the Secretary may not file notice of lien or levy on the taxpayer's property for failing to pay the assessed shared responsibility payment. Further, a taxpayer may not be subject to criminal prosecution or penalty for failing to pay the assessed shared responsibility payment in a timely manner.

Explanation of Provisions

1. Maintenance of Minimum Essential Coverage and Liability for Shared Responsibility Payment

The proposed regulations provide that, for a month, a nonexempt individual must either have minimum essential coverage or pay the shared responsibility payment.

a. Coverage for a Month

The proposed regulations provide that, for any calendar month, an individual is treated as having minimum essential coverage if the individual is enrolled in and entitled to receive benefits under a program or plan that is minimum essential coverage for at least one day during the month.

b. Liability for Shared Responsibility Payment

i. Liability for Dependents

Under section 5000A(b)(3)(A), if an individual with respect to whom the shared responsibility payment is imposed for a month is another individual's dependent (as defined in section 152) for the taxable year including that month, the other individual is liable for the shared responsibility payment for the dependent. The proposed regulations clarify that a taxpayer is liable for the shared responsibility payment imposed with respect to any individual for a month in a taxable year for which the taxpayer may claim a personal exemption deduction for the individual (that is, the dependent) for that taxable year. Whether the taxpayer actually claims the individual as a dependent for the taxable year does not affect the taxpayer's liability for the shared responsibility payment for the individual.

The proposed regulations provide special rules for determining liability for the shared responsibility payment attributable to individuals who are adopted or placed in foster care during a taxable year. If a taxpayer legally adopts a child and is entitled to claim the child as a dependent under section 151 for the taxable year when the adoption occurs, the taxpayer is not liable for a shared responsibility payment attributable to the child for the months before the adoption. Conversely, if a taxpayer who is entitled to claim a child as a dependent under section 151 for the taxable year places the child for adoption during the year, the taxpayer is not liable for a shared responsibility payment attributable to the child for the months after the adoption.

The proposed regulations define *shared responsibility family* to include all individuals for whom a taxpayer (including a spouse, if married filing jointly) is liable for the shared responsibility payment. The proposed regulations clarify that a taxpayer who is an exempt individual remains liable for a shared responsibility payment imposed for a nonexempt dependent who does not have minimum essential coverage.

ii. Joint Liability

Section 5000A(b)(3)(B) provides that, if an individual for whom the shared responsibility payment is imposed for a month files a joint return for the taxable year including that month, the individual and the individual's spouse are jointly liable for the shared responsibility payment. The proposed regulations clarify that whether one spouse is an exempt individual does not affect the joint liability of the two spouses for the shared responsibility payment.

2. Minimum Essential Coverage

a. Government Sponsored Programs

Section 5000A(f)(1)(A) specifies several government sponsored programs as providing minimum essential coverage by referring to the Federal law authorizing a particular program. In most cases, the relevant law describes a single program or a discrete portion of a larger program. For example, section 5000A(f)(1)(A)(i) lists Part A of the Medicare program under title XVIII of the Social Security Act. However, in some cases, the relevant law establishes programs with limited coverage. For instance, some of the programs under title XIX of the Social Security Act do not provide a scope of benefits comparable to the primary Medicaid program under the same title. In addition, the Secretary of Veterans Affairs, in coordination with the Secretaries of Health and Human Services and Treasury, determined that only certain health care programs under chapter 17 or 18 of title 38, United States Code provide comprehensive benefits. The programs with limited coverage are similar to coverage consisting of excepted benefits that is not minimum essential coverage under section 5000A(f)(3). Accordingly, the proposed regulations identify limited benefit programs under title XIX of the Social Security Act that are not minimum essential coverage and specify comprehensive health care programs under chapter 17 or 18 of title 38, United States Code, that are minimum essential coverage.

b. Eligible Employer-Sponsored Plans

i. In General

Section 5000A(f)(2) defines *eligible employer-sponsored plan,* for an employee, as a group health plan or group health insurance coverage offered by an employer to the employee that is either of the following: (1) a governmental plan (within the meaning of section 2791(d)(8) of the Public Health Service Act (PHSA) (42 U.S.C. 300gg-91(d)(8)), or (2) any other plan or coverage offered in the small or large group market within a State. The terms *group health plan* and *group health insurance coverage* are not defined in section 5000A. However, section 5000A(f)(5) provides that any term used in section 5000A that is also used in title I of the Affordable Care Act has the same meaning as when used in that title. [Corrected 3/25/2013 (78 FR 17900).]

Section 1301(b)(3) of the Affordable Care Act (42 U.S.C. 18021(b)(3)) provides that *group health plan* has the same meaning as in section 2791(a) of the PHSA (42 U.S.C. 301gg-91(a)(1)). Section 2791(a) of the PHSA provides that *group health plan* means an employee welfare benefit plan (as defined in section 3(1) of the Employee Retirement Income Security Act of 1974 (ERISA) (29 U.S.C. 1002(1)) to the extent that the plan provides medical care (as defined in section 2791(a)(2) of the PHSA and including items and services paid for as medical care) to employees and their dependents directly or through insurance, reimbursement, or otherwise. Section 3(1) of ERISA defines *employee welfare benefit plan* as any plan, fund, or program established

or maintained by an employer or by an employee organization, or by both, to the extent that the plan, fund, or program is established or maintained for the purpose of providing for its participants or their beneficiaries, through the purchase of insurance or otherwise, various benefits, which may include medical, surgical, or hospital care or benefits.

Group health plans within the meaning of section 1301(b)(3) of the Affordable Care Act (42 U.S.C. 18021(b)(3)) include both insured health plans and self-insured health plans. Accordingly, a self-insured group health plan is an eligible employer-sponsored plan.

ii. Continuation and Retiree Coverage

Employers are required to offer certain former employees continuation coverage under Federal or State law. Many employers offer health benefits coverage to retired employees. Under the PHSA and ERISA, group health plans and employee welfare benefit plans, respectively, include plans offered to former employees. Accordingly, the proposed regulations clarify that coverage provided by an employer to a former employee, including coverage under the Consolidated Omnibus Budget Reconciliation Act of 1985 (COBRA), Public Law 99-272 (100 Stat. 82), and retiree health coverage, qualifies as coverage under an eligible employer-sponsored plan.

c. Other Health Benefits Coverage

Under section 5000A(f)(1)(E), the Secretary of Health and Human Services, in coordination with the Secretary of the Treasury, may designate other health benefits coverage as minimum essential coverage. The Department of Health and Human Services is proposing rules providing standards for determining whether certain other types of health insurance coverage constitute minimum essential coverage and procedures for plan sponsors to follow for a plan to be identified as minimum essential coverage under section 5000A. Patient Protection and Affordable Care Act; Exchange Functions: Eligibility for Exemptions; Minimum Essential Coverage Provisions (to be codified at 45 CFR 156.600 and following sections).

3. Exempt Individuals

a. In General

The term *applicable individual* is used in section 5000A to describe an individual who is subject to the minimum essential coverage provision under section 5000A(a). Section 5000A(d)(2) through section 5000A(d)(4) describe one category of individuals who are not applicable individuals for purposes of section 5000A. Section 5000A(e)(1) through 5000A(e)(5) describe another category of individuals who are exempt from liability for the shared responsibility payment imposed under section 5000A(b). Although the two categories are distinct in the statute, the consequence for individuals described in either category is the same: individuals in both categories are not subject to the shared responsibility payment for not maintaining minimum essential coverage. Accordingly, the proposed regulations refer to all individuals described in section 5000A(d)(2), (d)(3), or (d)(4), or section 5000A(e)(1), (e)(2), (e)(3), (e)(4), or (e)(5), as *exempt individuals.* For a month, a nonexempt individual is any individual who is alive for the entire month and is not an exempt individual for the month.

The proposed regulations provide that, in general, an individual is treated as an exempt individual for a month if the individual is an exempt individual for at least one day in the month. In the case of certain individuals who are nonresident aliens (as defined in section 7701(b)(1)(B)), individuals whose household income falls below the return filing threshold, and individuals who experience short coverage gaps, the proposed regulations provide rules on how to determine whether an individual is exempt for a particular month. An individual is exempt for all months included in a taxable year when the individual is a nonresident alien. In the case of an individual whose household income falls below the return filing threshold for a taxable year, the individual is exempt for all months in the taxable year. In the case of an individual experiencing a coverage gap, the individual is exempt for a month included in the first short coverage gap in a calendar year.

b. Members of Recognized Religious Sects or Divisions

Under section 5000A(d)(2)(A), an individual is exempt for a month that the individual has in effect a religious conscience exemption certification. Only an Exchange may grant a religious conscience exemption certification. Individuals who are members of a recognized religious sect or division thereof described in section 1402(g)(1) and who are adherents of the established tenets or teachings of the sect or division are eligible to receive a religious conscience exemption certification.

c. Exempt Noncitizens

The proposed regulations clarify that an individual who is not a citizen or national of the United States is exempt for a month if the individual is not lawfully present in the United States in that month within the meaning of 45 CFR 155.20 (referring to lawful immigration status within the United States). In addition, an individual who is not a citizen or national of the United States is treated as not lawfully present in the United States for a month in a taxable year if the individual is a nonresident alien as defined in section 7701(b)(1)(B) for that taxable year.

d. Incarcerated Individuals

Section 5000A(d)(4) provides that an individual is exempt for a month for which the individual is incarcerated (other than incarceration pending the disposition of charges). The proposed regulations clarify that an individual confined for at least one day in a jail, prison, or similar penal institution or correctional facility after the disposition of charges is exempt for the month that includes the day.

e. Individuals Who Cannot Afford Coverage

Section 5000A(e)(1)(A) provides that an individual is exempt for a month for which the individual does not have access to affordable minimum essential coverage. For this purpose, an individual does not have access to affordable coverage for a month if the individual's required contribution (determined on an annual basis) for coverage for the month exceeds 8 percent of the taxpayer's household income for the taxable year. Under section 5000A(e)(1)(D), for any plan year beginning after 2014, the 8 percent figure is replaced by the percentage figure that the Secretary of Health and Human Services determines reflects the excess of the rate of premium growth between the preceding calendar year and 2013 over the rate of income growth for the same period.

For purposes of determining affordability of coverage, in accordance with section 5000A(e)(1)(A), the proposed regulations require that the taxpayer's household income be increased by the portion of the required contribution made through a salary reduction arrangement and excluded from gross income. In many cases, information on the excluded amount may not be available to the IRS or to the employee. Comments are requested on practicable ways, if any, in which the required adjustment to household income may be made with the information available under sections 6051, 6055, 6056, or other provisions of the Code.

i. Individuals Eligible for Minimum Essential Coverage Under an Eligible Employer-Sponsored Plan

A. Eligibility for Coverage Under an Eligible Employer-Sponsored Plan

If an individual is eligible for coverage under an eligible employer-sponsored plan, whether as an employee or as an individual related to an employee, the individual's qualification for the lack of affordable coverage exemption is determined solely by reference to the cost of coverage under the eligible employer-sponsored plan. The proposed regulations clarify that an employee or related individual is treated as eligible for coverage under an eligible employer-sponsored plan for each month included in the plan year if the employee or related individual could have enrolled in the plan for that month during an open or special enrollment period.

The proposed regulations also clarify that an employed individual who is eligible for coverage under an eligible employer-sponsored plan offered by the individual's employer is not treated as eligible as a related individual for coverage under a plan offered by the employer of another employed individual. Thus, if two or more members of a family are employed and their respective employers offer self-only and family coverage under eligible employer-sponsored plans, each employed individual determines the affordability of coverage using the premium for the self-only coverage offered by the individual's employer. Neither individual may determine the affordability of coverage using the premium for family coverage offered by the other individual's employer. In these cases, each employed individual's self-only coverage may be treated as affordable, even though the aggregate cost of covering all employed individuals may exceed 8 percent of the family's household income. The Department of Health and Human Services is proposing rules that would permit families in these circumstances to qualify for the hardship exemption described in section 5000A(e)(5). Patient Protection and Affordable Care Act; Exchange Functions: Eligibility for Exemptions; Minimum Essential Coverage Provisions (to be codified at 45 CFR 155.605(g)).

The proposed regulations provide that *employee* includes a former employee. Thus, an individual eligible to enroll in retiree coverage

under a group health plan that is an eligible employer-sponsored plan as defined in section 5000A(f)(2) is treated as eligible to purchase minimum essential coverage under an eligible employer-sponsored plan under the same rules applicable to current employees. The treatment of former employees is consistent with other provisions of the Code, the PHSA, and ERISA that apply to group health plans of employers.

In addition, the proposed regulations provide that an individual eligible to enroll in continuation coverage required under Federal law, such as COBRA, or a comparable State law is eligible to purchase minimum essential coverage under an eligible employer-sponsored plan only if the individual enrolls in the coverage. This treatment of former employees eligible for continuation coverage is consistent with the rules provided in § 1.36B-2(c)(3)(iv).

B. Required Contribution for Employees Eligible for Coverage Under an Employer-Sponsored Plan

Section 5000A(e)(1)(B)(i) provides that, in the case of an employee eligible to purchase minimum essential coverage through an eligible employer-sponsored plan, the required contribution is the portion of the annualized premium that the individual would pay (without regard to whether paid through salary reduction or otherwise) for self-only coverage. The proposed regulations clarify that, for an employee eligible for coverage under an eligible employer-sponsored plan, the required contribution is the portion of the annual premium that the employee would pay for the lowest cost self-only coverage.

C. Required Contribution for a Related Individual Eligible for Coverage Under an Eligible Employer-Sponsored Plan

Section 5000A(e)(1)(C) provides that, in the case of a related individual eligible to purchase minimum essential coverage under an eligible employer-sponsored plan because of the individual's relationship with an employee, the related individual's affordability determination is made by reference to the employee's required contribution. The proposed regulations provide that a related individual is an individual who is eligible for coverage under an eligible employer-sponsored plan because of a relationship to an employee and for whom a personal exemption deduction under section 151 is properly claimed on the employee's Federal income tax return. For example, an employee's spouse is treated as a related individual if the spouse files a joint return with the employee and is eligible for employer-sponsored coverage only under the plan offered to the employee. An individual who is eligible to enroll in an eligible employer-sponsored plan by reason of a relationship to an employee, but who is not claimed as a dependent by the employee, is not treated as a related individual. For purposes of section 5000A, the unclaimed dependent's household income is independently determined.

The proposed regulations clarify that if an employee or related individual is eligible to enroll in an eligible employer-sponsored plan, any eligibility for other coverage (for example, government sponsored minimum essential coverage) is disregarded for purposes of the exemption for lack of affordable coverage.

The proposed regulations further clarify that the required contribution for a related individual's coverage is determined by reference to the premium for the lowest cost coverage under the eligible employer-sponsored plan in which the employee and all related individuals who are included in the employee's family and not otherwise exempt are eligible to enroll. Thus, the required contribution for a spouse and claimed dependents (who are not otherwise exempt) is the premium that the employee would pay for the lowest cost coverage covering the employee, the spouse, and the claimed dependents. The required contribution for self-only coverage under an eligible employer-sponsored plan may cost less than 8 percent of household income, while the required contribution for family coverage under the same employer plan may cost more than 8 percent of household income. In such a case, the employee is not exempt under section 5000A(e)(1), while the employee's spouse and claimed dependents are exempt.

Finally, some individuals who are claimed as dependents by a taxpayer may not be eligible for coverage under the taxpayer's eligible employer-sponsored plan. The affordability of coverage for these individuals is determined in the manner that applies to them individually. Thus, if a taxpayer is not allowed to enroll a niece who is the taxpayer's dependent in the taxpayer's eligible employer-sponsored plan, the required contribution for the niece is not determined by reference to the cost of coverage under the plan. Instead, unless the niece is eligible for coverage under another eligible employer-sponsored plan, her required contribution is determined under the rules applicable to individuals eligible only to purchase coverage in the individual market.

ii. Individuals eligible only to purchase coverage in the individual market

Section 5000A(e)(1)(B)(ii) defines the term *required contribution* for an individual eligible only to purchase coverage in the individual market. The proposed regulations clarify that, for any individual who is not an employee or related individual eligible for minimum essential coverage under an eligible employer-sponsored plan, the required contribution is the premium for the lowest cost bronze plan available in the individual market through the Exchange serving the rating area where the individual resides, reduced by the maximum amount of any premium tax credit that would be allowable if the individual were enrolled in the plan offered through the Exchange.

As explained in this preamble, under the proposed regulations, both the annual premium for the applicable lowest cost bronze plan and the credit allowable under section 36B are determined by reference to coverage for those members of the individual's family who are not otherwise exempt (*nonexempt family*). Consequently, the required contribution is the same for all members of a nonexempt family who are ineligible for coverage under an eligible employer-sponsored plan.

A. Premium for the Lowest Cost Bronze Plan

The proposed regulations provide that the lowest cost bronze plan is the lowest cost bronze-level qualified health plan available in the Exchange serving the rating area that would cover all members of the nonexempt family who are ineligible for coverage under an eligible employer-sponsored plan. Accordingly, the premium for the lowest cost bronze plan is the same for all individuals in a nonexempt family.

The proposed regulations provide special rules for determining the premium for the lowest cost bronze plan if the Exchange does not offer a bronze-level plan that would cover the taxpayer's entire nonexempt family. The proposed regulations provide that, in general, the premium for the lowest cost bronze plan is the sum of the premiums for the lowest cost bronze plans that would, taken together, cover the taxpayer's nonexempt family (for example, for an uncle and two adult dependent nieces, a self-only plan for the uncle and a two-adult or family plan for the nieces). Alternatively, the proposed regulations provide that a taxpayer may elect to use the premium for the lowest cost bronze plan that would apply to a set of individuals that have the same characteristics as the taxpayer's nonexempt family (such as one adult plus children) as if one plan covered all members of the taxpayer's shared responsibility family.

B. Credit Allowable Under Section 36B

In general, a premium tax credit is allowable under section 36B for any coverage month (within the meaning of § 1.36B-3(c)) that occurs in a taxable year in which a taxpayer is an applicable taxpayer (within the meaning of § 1.36B-2(b)). A month is not a coverage month for an individual, and thus no premium tax credit is allowable for the individual's coverage, if the individual is eligible for minimum essential coverage other than coverage offered in the individual market for that month. In general, an applicable taxpayer is a taxpayer whose household income for the taxable year is between 100 percent and 400 percent of the Federal poverty line for the taxpayer's family size.

Section 36B(b)(1) provides that the premium tax credit for any taxable year is the sum of the premium assistance amounts with respect to all coverage months occurring in the taxable year. Under section 36B(b)(2), for any coverage month, the premium assistance amount is the lesser of the following: (1) the monthly premiums for the month for one or more qualified health plans in which the taxpayer or a member of the taxpayer's family (coverage family) is enrolled through the Exchange serving the rating area where they reside or (2) any excess of the adjusted monthly premium for the month for the applicable second lowest cost silver plan for the taxpayer over an amount equal to $1/12$ of the product of the applicable percentage and the taxpayer's household income for the month. Section 36B, therefore, calculates the allowable credit by treating the family as a single, aggregated unit. [Corrected 3/25/2013 (78 FR 17900) and 3/29/2013 (78 FR 19155).]

The proposed regulations take a similar family-unit approach to determine the affordability of Exchange coverage. The proposed regulations provide that, for purposes of section 5000A, each individual in the taxpayer's nonexempt family is treated as having enrolled in a qualified health plan through the appropriate Exchange for purposes of determining the credit allowable under section 36B. Therefore, for each individual, a month is treated as a coverage month if the individual is ineligible for minimum essential coverage other than coverage in the individual market for the month. The proposed regulations further provide that the premium assistance amount for the month is the amount that would be allowable under the rules of section 36B if each

member of the individual's nonexempt family enrolled in a qualified health plan through an Exchange. Accordingly, for a month that an individual included in a nonexempt family is eligible for minimum essential coverage other than coverage in the individual market, the month is not a coverage month for that individual, the individual is not included in the coverage family for purposes of section 36B, and no premium assistance amount is allowable for the coverage attributable to such individual.

f. Household Income Below Return Filing Threshold

Section 5000A(e)(2) provides that an individual is exempt for a month in a calendar year if the individual's household income for the taxable year is less than the amount of gross income specified in section 6012(a)(1) with respect to the taxpayer. The proposed regulations refer to "the amount of gross income specified in section 6012(a)(1) with respect to the taxpayer" (that is, the minimum amount of gross income that triggers the individual's requirement to file a Federal income tax return under that section) as the applicable filing threshold.

The proposed regulations further clarify that, for any individual who is properly claimed as a dependent, the applicable filing threshold is that of the taxpayer who claims the individual as a dependent. Therefore, if a taxpayer is exempt under section 5000A(e)(2), any individual the taxpayer properly claims as a dependent also is exempt. The Treasury Department and the IRS recognize that some taxpayers who do not have sufficient gross income to trigger a return filing requirement nevertheless may have household income that exceeds the return filing threshold. For example, if a taxpayer whose gross income is below the applicable filing threshold files a Federal income tax return in order to claim certain tax benefits (such as the earned income credit or additional child tax credit) and claims a dependent whose gross income triggers a return filing requirement, the household income (which combines the taxpayer's and the dependent's income) may exceed the filing threshold. The Department of Health and Human Services is proposing rules providing that individuals in this circumstance may qualify for a hardship exemption. Patient Protection and Affordable Care Act; Exchange Functions: Eligibility for Exemptions; Minimum Essential Coverage Provisions (to be codified at 45 CFR 155.605(g)). The Treasury Department and the IRS are considering additional methods of accommodating individuals in these circumstances. [Corrected 3/25/2013 (78 FR 17900).]

g. Short Coverage Gap

The proposed regulations clarify that a continuous period without minimum essential coverage is determined by reference to calendar months (for example, January or February) in conjunction with the coverage rule in § 1.5000A-1(b). Therefore, if an individual is enrolled in and entitled to receive benefits under a plan identified as minimum essential coverage for one day in a calendar month, the month is not included in the continuous period when determining the application of the short coverage gap exemption. As a result, the proposed regulations provide that an individual qualifies for the short coverage gap exemption if the continuous period without minimum essential coverage is less than three full calendar months and is the first short coverage gap in the individual's taxable year.

i. Coverage Gap Straddling Multiple Taxable Years

In general, section 5000A(e)(4)(B)(i) provides that the length of a continuous period is determined without regard to the calendar years in which months in the period occur. However, whether an individual had coverage during the last month, or the last two months, of a taxable year affects the determination of whether any gap in coverage that the individual experiences in the first month, or the first and second months, of the following taxable year qualifies as a short coverage gap. Accordingly, if a calendar year taxpayer has a continuous period of 3 months or longer that starts in November or December of one taxable year and ends in the next taxable year, then January and any ensuing months of the second taxable year that are included in the period are ineligible for the short coverage gap exemption.

Section 5000A(e)(4) expressly authorizes the Secretary to prescribe rules for the collection of the shared responsibility payment in cases in which continuous periods include months in more than one taxable year. Each Federal income tax return covers a single taxable year and requires the taxpayer to account for coverage of the taxpayer's shared responsibility family during the months included in that taxable year. To require a taxpayer to take into account months in the following taxable year may delay or impede the taxpayer's ability to file a timely Federal income tax return. Accordingly, to provide taxpayers with certainty when filing their Federal income tax returns, the proposed regulations provide that an individual who lacks minimum essential coverage for a period no longer than the last two months of a taxable year will be deemed to have a short coverage gap exemption for those months if the short coverage gap is the first to occur in that taxable year, without regard to whether the individual is covered during the first months of the following taxable year.

ii. Coordination With Other Exemptions

The proposed regulations clarify that, for purposes of determining whether a short coverage gap applies, an individual is treated as covered under minimum essential coverage for a month in which the individual qualifies for a section 5000A exemption (other than the short coverage gap exemption). Therefore, the short coverage exemption applies to a month in which no other section 5000A exemption applies, and a month in which an individual is otherwise exempt is not taken into account in determining the length of the continuous period without coverage.

h. Claiming Section 5000A Exemptions

The exemptions for members of recognized religious sects or divisions and for individuals who have suffered a hardship are available only to individuals who have been certified as meeting the relevant criteria by the Exchange serving the rating area where the individuals seeking the exemption reside.

In addition, Exchanges will provide, upon request, exemption certifications for members of health care sharing ministries, incarcerated individuals, and members of Indian tribes. If an individual receives an exemption certification from an Exchange, the taxpayer who is responsible for accounting for that individual's coverage must provide information about the certification on the taxpayer's Federal income tax return. Alternatively, a taxpayer may claim any of these exemptions on the taxpayer's Federal income tax return for the taxable year.

Finally, the income-based exemptions for individuals who lack affordable coverage or have household income below the applicable income tax return filing threshold and the exemption for short coverage gaps may be claimed only on the individual's Federal income tax return for the applicable year. Thus, an individual claiming the affordability exemption under section 5000A(e)(1) for part or all of a taxable year will do so on the Federal income tax return that reports the individual's income establishing qualification for the exemption. An individual who has household income below the applicable Federal income tax return filing threshold and files a Federal income tax return may claim the exemption under section 5000A(e)(2) on the return. However, an individual who has household income below the applicable Federal income tax return filing threshold is not required to file a Federal income tax return to claim the exemption under section 5000A(e)(2).

Pursuant to section 6001, taxpayers are required to maintain all records and information substantiating any claim for exemption on the taxpayer's Federal income tax return, regardless of whether the individual was certified by an Exchange as qualifying for an exemption or first claimed the exemption on a Federal income tax return.

4. Computation of Shared Responsibility Payment

Under section 5000A(b)(1) and 5000A(b)(3)(A), a taxpayer is liable for the shared responsibility payment with respect to any nonexempt individual who is included in the taxpayer's shared responsibility family. The maximum annual amount of the shared responsibility payment for a taxpayer is the national average premium for the bronze level plan available through Exchanges that provides coverage for the applicable family size involved. The proposed regulations clarify that the applicable family size involved for purposes of identifying the appropriate bronze level plan includes only the nonexempt members of the taxpayer's shared responsibility family who do not have minimum essential coverage.

Under section 5000A(c), the annual amount of the shared responsibility payment is the lesser of the applicable national average bronze plan premium or the sum of the monthly penalty amounts. The monthly penalty amount may vary month to month because of changes in the composition of the taxpayer's shared responsibility family. To provide a meaningful value with which the sum of the monthly penalty amounts are compared, the proposed regulations provide that the applicable national average bronze plan premium must similarly be determined for each month and then aggregated for comparison with the sum of the monthly penalty amounts.

Consequently, the applicable national average bronze plan premium may vary from month to month during the year to account for changes in the taxpayer's shared responsibility family.

5. Procedure and Administration

a. Inclusion With Federal Income Tax Return

Section 5000A(b)(2) provides that the shared responsibility payment for a month must be included with a taxpayer's Federal income tax return for the taxable year that includes the month. The proposed regulations clarify that the time for assessing the shared responsibility payment is the same time as that prescribed by section 6501 for the taxable year including the month for which the taxpayer is liable for the payment.

b. Assessment and Collection

Section 5000A(g)(1) provides that the shared responsibility payment is payable upon notice and demand by the Secretary and, except as provided in section 5000A(g)(2), is assessed and collected in the same manner as an assessable penalty under subchapter B of chapter 68 of the Code (sections 6671 through 6725). The proposed regulations clarify that the shared responsibility payment is not subject to deficiency procedures of subchapter B of chapter 63 of the Code. In addition, the proposed regulations clarify that interest on the shared responsibility payment accrues in accordance with the rules in section 6601. The proposed regulations further provide that the Secretary may offset any liability for the shared responsibility payment against any overpayment due the taxpayer, in accordance with section 6402(a).

Applicability Date

These regulations are proposed to apply for months beginning after December 31, 2013.

Special Analyses

It has been determined that this notice of proposed rulemaking is not a significant regulatory action as defined in Executive Order 12866, as supplemented by Executive Order 13563. Therefore, a regulatory assessment is not required. It also has been determined that section 553(b) of the Administrative Procedure Act (5 U.S.C. chapter 5) does not apply to the proposed regulations. Pursuant to the Regulatory Flexibility Act (RFA) (5 U.S.C. chapter 6), it is hereby certified that the proposed regulations will not have a significant economic impact on a substantial number of small entities. The applicability of the proposed regulations is limited to individuals, who are not small entities as defined by the RFA (5 U.S.C. 601). Accordingly, the RFA does not apply. Therefore, a regulatory flexibility analysis is not required. Pursuant to section 7805(f) of the Code, the proposed regulations have been submitted to the Chief Counsel for Advocacy of the Small Business Administration for comment on its impact on small business.

Comments and Public Hearing

Before the proposed regulations are adopted as final regulations, consideration will be given to any comments that are submitted timely to the IRS as prescribed in this preamble under the "Addresses" heading. The Treasury Department and the IRS request comments on all aspects of the proposed rules. All comments will be available at *www.regulations.gov* or upon request.

A public hearing has been scheduled for May 29, 2013, beginning at 10:00 a.m., in the Auditorium, Internal Revenue Building, 1111 Constitution Avenue NW., Washington, DC. Due to building security procedures, visitors must enter at the Constitution Avenue entrance. In addition, all visitors must present photo identification to enter the building. Because of access restrictions, visitors will not be admitted beyond the immediate entrance area more than 30 minutes before the hearing starts. For information about having your name placed on the building access list to attend the hearing, see the **FOR FURTHER INFORMATION CONTACT** section of this preamble.

The rules of § 601.601(a)(3) of this chapter apply to the hearing. Persons who wish to present oral comments at the hearing must submit electronic or written comments, and an outline of the topics to be discussed and the time to be devoted to each topic (signed original and eight (8) copies) by May 3, 2013. A period of 10 minutes will be allotted to each person for making comments. An agenda showing the scheduling of the speakers will be prepared after the deadline for receiving outlines has passed. Copies of the agenda will be available free of charge at the hearing.

Drafting Information

The principal authors of the proposed regulations are William L. Candler and Sue-Jean Kim, Office of the Associate Chief Counsel (Income Tax & Accounting). Other personnel from the Treasury Department and the IRS participated in the development of the regulations.

List of Subjects in 26 CFR Part 1

Income taxes, Reporting and recordkeeping requirements.

Proposed Amendments to the Regulations

Accordingly, 26 CFR part 1 is proposed to be amended to read as follows:

PART 1—INCOME TAXES

■ **Paragraph 1.** The authority citation for part 1 is amended by adding an entry in numerical order to read in part as follows:

Authority: 26 U.S.C. 7805* * * Section 1.5000A-4 also issued under 26 U.S.C. 5000A(e)(4).

■ **Par 2.** Sections 1.5000A-0 through 1.5000A-5 are added to read as follows:

§ 1.5000A-0 Table of contents.

This section lists the captions contained in §§ 1.5000A-1 through 1.5000A-5.

(j) Individuals with certain short coverage gaps.

(1) In general.

(2) Short coverage gap.

(i) In general.

(ii) Coordination with other exemptions.

(iii) More than one short coverage gap during calendar year.

(3) Continuous period.

(i) In general.

(ii) Continuous period straddling more than one taxable year.

(4) Examples.

(k) Claiming exemptions from the shared responsibility payment.

(1) Exemptions requiring certification by an Exchange.

(2) Exemptions that may be certified by an Exchange or claimed on a Federal income tax return.

(i) Exemption certified by an Exchange.

(ii) Exemption claimed on a Federal income tax return.

(3) Exemptions that are claimed on Federal income tax returns.

§ 1.5000A-4 Computation of shared responsibility payment.

(a) In general.

(b) Monthly penalty amount.

(1) In general.

(2) Flat dollar amount.

(i) In general.

(ii) Applicable dollar amount.

(iii) Special applicable dollar amount for individuals under age 18.

(iv) Indexing of applicable dollar amount.

(3) Excess income amount.

(i) In general.

(ii) Income percentage.

(c) Monthly national average bronze plan premium.

(d) Examples.

§ 1.5000A-5 Administration and procedure.

(a) In general.

(b) Special rules.

(1) Waiver of criminal penalties.

(2) Limitations on liens and levies.

(3) Authority to offset against overpayment.

(c) Effective/applicability date.

§ 1.5000A-1 Maintenance of minimum essential coverage and liability for the shared responsibility payment.

(a) *In general.* For each month during the taxable year, a nonexempt individual must have minimum essential coverage or pay the shared responsibility payment. For a month, a nonexempt individual is an individual in existence for the entire month who is not an exempt individual described in § 1.5000A-3.

(b) *Coverage under minimum essential coverage*—(1) *In general.* An individual has minimum essential coverage for a month in which the individual is enrolled in and entitled to receive benefits under a program or plan identified as minimum essential coverage in § 1.5000A-2 for at least one day in the month.

(2) *Special rule for United States citizens or residents residing outside the United States or residents of territories.* An individual is treated as having minimum essential coverage for a month—

(i) If the month occurs during any period described in section 911(d)(1)(A) or section 911(d)(1)(B) that is applicable to the individual; or

(ii) If, for the month, the individual is a bona fide resident of a possession of the United States (as determined under section 937(a)).

(c) *Liability for shared responsibility payment*—(1) *In general.* A taxpayer is liable for the shared responsibility payment for a month for which—

(i) The taxpayer is a nonexempt individual without minimum essential coverage; or

(ii) A nonexempt individual for whom the taxpayer is liable under paragraph (c)(2) or (c)(3) of this section does not have minimum essential coverage.

(2) *Liability for dependents*—(i) *In general.* For a month when a nonexempt individual does not have minimum essential coverage, if the nonexempt individual is a dependent (as defined in section 152) of another individual for the other individual's taxable year including that month, the other individual is liable for the shared responsibility payment attributable to the dependent's lack of coverage. An individual is a dependent of a taxpayer for a taxable year if the individual satisfies the definition of dependent under section 152, regardless of whether the taxpayer claims the individual as a dependent on a Federal income tax return for the taxable year. If an individual may be claimed as a dependent by more than one taxpayer in the same calendar year, the taxpayer who properly claims the individual as a dependent for the taxable year is liable for the shared responsibility payment attributable to the individual. If more than one taxpayer may claim an individual as a dependent in the same calendar year but no one claims the individual as a dependent, the taxpayer with priority under the rules of section 152 to claim the individual as a dependent is liable for the shared responsibility payment for the individual.

(ii) *Special rules for dependents adopted or placed in foster care during the taxable year*—(A) *Taxpayers adopting an individual.* If a taxpayer adopts a nonexempt dependent (or accepts a nonexempt dependent who is an eligible foster child as defined in section 152(f)(1)(C)) during the taxable year and is otherwise liable for a nonexempt dependent under paragraph (c)(2)(i) of this section, the taxpayer is liable under paragraph (c)(2)(i) of this section for the nonexempt dependent only for the full months in the taxable year that follow the month in which the adoption or acceptance occurs.

(B) *Taxpayers placing an individual for adoption.* If a taxpayer who is otherwise liable for a nonexempt dependent under paragraph (c)(2)(i) of this section places (or, by operation of law, must place) the nonexempt dependent for adoption or foster care during the taxable year, the taxpayer is liable under paragraph (c)(2)(i) of this section for the nonexempt dependent only for the full months in the taxable year that precede the month in which the adoption or foster care placement occurs.

(C) *Examples.* The following examples illustrate the provisions of this paragraph (c)(2)(ii). In each example the taxpayer's taxable year is a calendar year.

Example 1. Taxpayers adopting a child. (i) E and F, married individuals filing a joint return, initiate proceedings for the legal adoption of a 2-year old child, G, in January 2016. On May 15, 2016, G becomes the adopted child (within the meaning of section 152(f)(1)(B)) of E and F, and resides with them for the remainder of 2016. G meets all requirements under section 152 to be E and F's dependent for 2016. Prior to the adoption, G resides with H, an unmarried individual, with H providing all of G's support. (ii) Under paragraph (c)(2) of this section, E and F are not liable for a shared responsibility payment attributable to G for January through May of 2016, but are liable for a shared responsibility payment attributable to G, if any, for June through December of 2016. H is not liable for a shared responsibility payment attributable to G for any month in 2016, because G is not H's dependent for 2016 under section 152.

Example 2. Taxpayers placing a child for adoption. (i) The facts are the same as *Example 1,* except the legal adoption occurs on August 15, 2016. G meets all requirements under section 152 to be H's dependent for 2016.

(ii) Under paragraph (c)(2) of this section, H is liable for a shared responsibility payment attributable to G, if any, for January through July of 2016, but is not liable for a shared responsibility payment attributable to G for August through December of 2016. E and F are not liable for a shared responsibility payment attributable to G for any month in 2016, because G is not E and F's dependent for 2016 under section 152.

(3) *Liability of individuals filing a joint return.* Married individuals (within the meaning of section 7703) who file a joint return for a taxable year are jointly liable for any shared responsibility payment for a month included in the taxable year.

(d) *Definitions.* The definitions in this paragraph (d) apply to this section and §§ 1.5000A-2 through 1.5000A-5.

(1) *Affordable Care Act. Affordable Care Act* refers to the Patient Protection and Affordable Care Act, Public Law 111-148 (124 Stat. 119

(2010)), and the Health Care and Education Reconciliation Act of 2010, Public Law 111-152 (124 Stat. 1029 (2010)), as amended.

(2) *Qualified health plan. Qualified health plan* has the same meaning as in section 1301(a) of the Affordable Care Act (42 U.S.C. 18021(a)).

(3) *Exchange. Exchange* has the same meaning as in 45 CFR 155.20.

(4) *Rating area. Rating area* has the same meaning as in § 1.36B-1(n). [Corrected 3/25/2013 (78 FR 17900).]

(5) *Shared responsibility family. Shared responsibility family* means, for a month, all nonexempt individuals for whom the taxpayer (and the taxpayer's spouse, if the taxpayer is married and files a joint return with the spouse) is liable for the shared responsibility payment under paragraph (c) of this section.

(6) *Family.* A taxpayer's family means the individuals for whom the taxpayer properly claims a deduction for a personal exemption under section 151 for the taxable year.

(7) *Household income*—(i) *In general. Household income* means the sum of—

(A) A taxpayer's modified adjusted gross income; and

(B) The aggregate modified adjusted gross income of all other individuals who—

(*1*) Are included in the taxpayer's family under paragraph (d)(6) of this section; and

(*2*) Are required to file a Federal income tax return for the taxable year (determined without regard to the exception under section 1(g)(7) to the requirement to file a Federal income tax return).

(ii) *Modified adjusted gross income. Modified adjusted gross income* means adjusted gross income (within the meaning of section 62) increased by—

(A) Amounts excluded from gross income under section 911; and

(B) Tax-exempt interest the taxpayer receives or accrues during the taxable year.

(8) *Self-only coverage. Self-only coverage* means health insurance that covers one individual.

(9) *Family coverage. Family coverage* means health insurance that covers more than one individual.

(10) *Employee. Employee* includes former employees.

(11) *Month. Month* means calendar month.

§ 1.5000A-2 Minimum essential coverage.

(a) *In general. Minimum essential coverage* means coverage under a government sponsored program (described in paragraph (b) of this section), an eligible employer-sponsored plan (described in paragraph (c) of this section), a plan in the individual market (described in paragraph (d) of this section), a grandfathered health plan (described in paragraph (e) of this section), or other health benefits coverage (described in paragraph (f) of this section). Minimum essential coverage does not include coverage described in paragraph (g) of this section. All terms defined in this section apply for purposes of this section and § 1.5000A-1 and §§ 1.5000A-3 through 1.5000A-5.

(b) *Government sponsored program. Government sponsored program* means any of the following:

(1) The Medicare program under part A of title XVIII of the Social Security Act (42 U.S.C. 1395c and following sections);

(2) The Medicaid program under title XIX of the Social Security Act (42 U.S.C. 1396 and following sections) other than—

(i) Optional coverage of family planning services under section 1902(a)(10)(A)(ii)(XXI) of the Social Security Act (42 U.S.C. 1396a(a)(10)(A)(ii)(XXI));

(ii) Optional coverage of tuberculosis-related services under section 1902(a)(10)(A)(ii)(XII) (42 U.S.C. 1396a(a)(10)(A)(ii)(XII));

(iii) Coverage of pregnancy-related services under section 1902(a)(10)(A)(i)(IV) and (a)(10)(A)(ii)(IX) (42 U.S.C. 1396a(a)(10)(A)(i)(IV), (a)(10)(A)(ii)(IX)); or

(iv) Coverage of medical emergency services under 8 U.S.C. 1611(b)(1)(A), as authorized by section 1903(v) of the Social Security Act (42 U.S.C. 1396b(v)).

(3) The Children's Health Insurance Program (CHIP) under title XXI of the Social Security Act (42 U.S.C 1397aa and following sections);

(4) Medical coverage under chapter 55 of title 10, U.S.C., including coverage under the TRICARE program;

(5) The following health care programs under chapter 17 or 18 of title 38, U.S.C.:

(i) The medical benefits package authorized for eligible veterans under 38 U.S.C. 1710 and 38 U.S.C. 1705;

(ii) The Civilian Health and Medical Program of the Department of Veterans Affairs (CHAMPVA) authorized under 38 U.S.C. 1781; and

(iii) The comprehensive health care program authorized under 38 U.S.C. 1803 and 38 U.S.C. 1821 for certain children of Vietnam Veterans and Veterans of covered service in Korea who are suffering from spina bifida.

(6) A health plan under section 2504(e) of title 22, U.S.C. (relating to Peace Corps volunteers); and

(7) The Nonappropriated Fund Health Benefits Program of the Department of Defense, established under section 349 of the National Defense Authorization Act for Fiscal Year 1995 (Public Law No. 103-337; 10 U.S.C. 1587 note). [Corrected 3/25/2013 (78 FR 17900).]

(c) *Eligible employer-sponsored plan*—(1) *In general. Eligible employer-sponsored plan* means, with respect to any employee, a group health plan (whether an insured group health plan or a self-insured group health plan) or group health insurance coverage offered by an employer to the employee that—[Corrected 3/25/2013 (78 FR 17900).]

(i) A governmental plan (within the meaning of section 2791(d)(8) of the Public Health Service Act (42 U.S.C. 300gg-91(d)(8)));

(ii) Any other plan or coverage offered in the small or large group market within a State;

(iii) A grandfathered health plan (within the meaning of paragraph (e) of this section) offered in a group market.

(2) *Group health plan. Group health plan* has the same meaning as in section 2791(a) of the Public Health Service Act (42 U.S.C. 300gg-91(a)(1)).

(3) *Group health insurance coverage. Group health insurance coverage* has the same meaning as in section 2791(b) of the Public Health Service Act (42 U.S.C. 300gg-91(b)).

(4) *Large and small group market. Large group market* and *small group market* have the same meanings as in section 1304(a)(3) of the Affordable Care Act (42 U.S.C. 18024(a)(3)).

(5) *Government sponsored program not treated as eligible employer-sponsored plan.* A government sponsored program described in paragraph (b) of this section is not an eligible employer-sponsored plan.

(d) *Plan in the individual market. Plan in the individual market* means health insurance coverage offered to individuals not in connection with a group health plan, including a qualified health plan offered by an Exchange.

(e) *Grandfathered health plan. Grandfathered health plan* means any group health plan or group health insurance coverage to which section 1251 of the Affordable Care Act (42 U.S.C.18011) applies.

(f) *Other health benefits coverage.* Minimum essential coverage includes any plan or arrangement recognized by the Secretary of Health and Human Services as minimum essential coverage for purposes of section 5000A under 45 CFR 156.600 and following sections.

(g) *Excepted benefits.* Minimum essential coverage does not include any health insurance coverage that consists of excepted benefits that are described in section 2791(c)(1), (c)(2), (c)(3), or (c)(4) of the Public Health Service Act (42 U.S.C. 300gg-91(c)).

§ 1.5000A-3 Exempt individuals.

(a) *Members of recognized religious sects*—(1) *In general.* An individual is an exempt individual for a month that includes a day on which the individual has in effect a religious conscience exemption certification described in paragraph (a)(2) of this section.

(2) *Exemption certification.* A religious conscience exemption certification is issued by an Exchange in accordance with the requirements of section 1311(d)(4)(H) of the Affordable Care Act (42 U.S.C. 18031(d)(4)(H)) and 45 CFR 155.605(c), 45 CFR 155.615(b) and certifies that an individual is—

(i) A member of a recognized religious sect or division thereof that is described in section 1402(g)(1); and

(ii) An adherent of established tenets or teachings of the sect or division as described in that section.

(b) *Member of health care sharing ministries*—(1) *In general.* An individual is an exempt individual for a month that includes a day on which the individual is a member of a health care sharing ministry.

(2) *Health care sharing ministry.* For purposes of this section, *health care sharing ministry* means an organization—

(i) That is described in section 501(c)(3) and is exempt from tax under section 501(a);

(ii) Members of which share a common set of ethical or religious beliefs and share medical expenses among themselves in accordance with those beliefs and without regard to the State in which a member resides or is employed;

(iii) Members of which retain membership even after they develop a medical condition;

(iv) That (or a predecessor of which) has been in existence at all times since December 31, 1999;

(v) Members of which have shared medical expenses continuously and without interruption since at least December 31, 1999; and

(vi) That conducts an annual audit performed by an independent certified public accounting firm in accordance with generally accepted accounting principles and makes the annual audit report available to the public upon request.

(c) *Exempt noncitizens*—(1) *In general.* An individual is an exempt individual for a month that the individual is an exempt noncitizen.

(2) *Exempt noncitizens.* For purposes of this section, an individual is an exempt noncitizen for a month if the individual—

(i) Is not a U.S. citizen or U.S. national for any day during the month; and

(ii) Is either—

(A) A nonresident alien (within the meaning of section 7701(b)(1)(B)) for the taxable year that includes the month; or

(B) An individual who is not lawfully present (within the meaning of 45 CFR 155.20) in the United States on any day in the month.

(d) *Incarcerated individuals*—(1) *In general.* An individual is an exempt individual for a month that includes a day on which the individual is incarcerated.

(2) *Incarcerated.* For purposes of this section, the term *incarcerated* means confined, after the disposition of charges, in a jail, prison, or similar penal institution or correctional facility.

(e) *Individuals with no affordable coverage*—(1) *In general.* An individual is an exempt individual for a month in which the individual lacks affordable coverage. For purposes of this paragraph (e), an individual lacks affordable coverage in a month if the individual's required contribution (determined on an annual basis) for minimum essential coverage for the month exceeds the required contribution percentage (as defined in paragraph (e)(2) of this section) of the individual's household income. For purposes of this paragraph (e), an individual's household income is increased by any amount of the required contribution made through a salary reduction arrangement that is excluded from gross income.

(2) *Required contribution percentage*—(i) *In general.* Except as provided in paragraph (e)(2)(ii) of this section, the required contribution percentage is 8 percent.

(ii) *Indexing.* For plan years beginning in any calendar year after 2014, the required contribution percentage is the percentage determined by the Department of Health and Human Services that reflects the excess of the rate of premium growth between the preceding calendar year and 2013 over the rate of income growth for the period.

(iii) *Plan year.* For purposes of this paragraph (e), *plan year* means the eligible employer-sponsored plan's regular 12-month coverage period (or the remainder of a 12-month coverage period for a new employee or an individual who enrolls during a special enrollment period).

(3) *Individuals eligible for coverage under eligible employer-sponsored plans*—(i) *Eligibility*—(A) *In general.* Except as provided in paragraph (e)(3)(i)(B) of this section, an employee or related individual (as defined in paragraph (e)(3)(ii)(B) of this section) is treated as eligible for coverage under an eligible employer-sponsored plan for a month during a plan year if the employee or related individual could have enrolled in the plan for any day in that month during an open or special enrollment period, regardless of whether the employee or related individual is eligible for any other type of minimum essential coverage. For purposes of this paragraph (e)(3), an employee eligible for coverage under an eligible employer-sponsored plan offered by the employee's employer is not treated as eligible as a related individual for coverage under an eligible employer-sponsored plan (for example, an eligible employer-sponsored plan offered by the employer of the em-

ployee's spouse) for any month included in the plan year of the eligible employer-sponsored plan offered by the employee's employer.

(B) *Special rule for continuation coverage.* An individual who may enroll in continuation coverage required under Federal law or a State law that provides comparable continuation coverage is eligible for coverage under an eligible employer-sponsored plan only if the individual enrolls in the coverage.

(ii) *Required contribution for individuals eligible for coverage under an eligible employer-sponsored plan*— (A) *Employees.* In the case of an employee who is eligible to purchase coverage under an eligible employer-sponsored plan sponsored by the employee's employer, the required contribution is the portion of the annual premium that the employee would pay (whether through salary reduction or otherwise) for the lowest cost self-only coverage. [Corrected 3/25/2013 (78 FR 17900).]

(B) *Individuals related to employees.* In the case of an individual who is eligible for coverage under an eligible employer-sponsored plan because of a relationship to an employee and for whom a personal exemption deduction under section 151 is claimed on the employee's Federal income tax return (related individual), the required contribution is the portion of the annual premium that the employee would pay (whether through salary reduction or otherwise) for the lowest cost family coverage that would cover the employee and all related individuals who are included in the employee's family and are not otherwise exempt under § 1.5000A-3.

(C) *Required contribution for part-year period.* For each individual described in paragraph (e)(3)(ii)(A) or (e)(3)(ii)(B) of this section, affordability under paragraph (e)(3) of this section is determined separately for each employment period that is less than a full calendar year or for the portions of an employer's plan year that fall in different taxable years of the individual. Coverage under an eligible employer-sponsored plan is affordable for a part-year period if the annualized required contribution for self-only coverage (in the case of the employee) or family coverage (in the case of a related individual) under the plan for the part-year period does not exceed the required contribution percentage of the individual's household income for the taxable year. The annualized required contribution is the required contribution determined under paragraph (e)(3)(ii)(A) or (e)(3)(ii)(B) of this section for the part-year period times a fraction, the numerator of which is 12 and the denominator of which is the number of months in the part-year period during the individual's taxable year. Only full calendar months are included in the computation under this paragraph (e)(3)(ii)(C).

(D) *Examples.* The following examples illustrate the application of this paragraph (e)(3). Unless stated otherwise, in each example, each individual's taxable year is a calendar year, the individual is ineligible for any other exemptions described in this section for a month, the rate of premium growth has not exceeded the rate of income growth since 2013, and the individual's employer offers a single plan that uses a calendar plan year and is an eligible employer-sponsored plan as described in § 1.5000A-2(c).

Example 1. Unmarried employee with no dependents. Taxpayer A is an unmarried individual with no dependents. In November 2015, A is eligible to enroll in self-only coverage under a plan offered by A's employer for calendar year 2016. If A enrolls in the coverage, A is required to pay $5,000 of the total annual premium. In 2016, A's household income is $60,000. Under paragraph (e)(3)(ii)(A) of this section, A's required contribution is $5,000, the portion of the annual premium A pays for self-only coverage. Under paragraph (e)(1) of this section, A lacks affordable coverage for 2016 because A's required contribution ($5,000) is greater than 8 percent of A's household income ($4,800).

Example 2. Married employee with dependents. Taxpayers B and C are married and file a joint return for 2016. B and C have two children, D and E. In November 2015, B is eligible to enroll in self-only coverage under a plan offered by B's employer for calendar year 2016 at a cost of $5,000 to B. C, D, and E are eligible to enroll in family coverage under the same plan for 2016 at a cost of $20,000 to B. B, C, D, and E's household income is $90,000. Under paragraph (e)(3)(ii)(A) of this section, B's required contribution is B's share of the cost for self-only coverage, $5,000. Under paragraph (e)(1) of this section, B has affordable coverage for 2016 because B's required contribution ($5,000) does not exceed 8 percent of B's household income ($7,200). Under paragraph (e)(3)(ii)(B) of this section, the required contribution for C, D, and E is B's share of the cost for family coverage, $20,000. Under paragraph (e)(1) of this section, C, D, and E lack affordable coverage for 2016 because their required contribution ($20,000) exceeds 8 percent of their household income ($7,200).

Example 3. Plan year is a fiscal year. (i) Taxpayer F is an unmarried individual with no dependents. In June 2015, F is eligible to enroll in self-only coverage under a plan offered by F's employer for the period July 2015 through June 2016 at a cost to F of $4,750. In June 2016, F is eligible to enroll in self-only coverage under a plan offered by F's employer for the period July 2016 through June 2017 at a cost to F of $5,000. In 2016, F's household income is $60,000.

(ii) Under paragraph (e)(3)(ii)(C) of this section, F's annualized required contribution for the period January 2016 through June 2016 is $4,750 ($2,375 paid for premiums in 2016 × 12/6). Under paragraph (e)(1) of this section, F has affordable coverage for January 2016 through June 2016 because F's annualized required contribution ($4,750) does not exceed 8 percent of F's household income ($4,800).

(iii) Under paragraph (e)(3)(ii)(C) of this section, F's annualized required contribution for the period July 2016 to December 2016 is $5,000 ($2,500 paid for premiums in 2016 x 12/6). Under paragraph (e)(1) of this section, F lacks affordable coverage for July 2016 through December 2016 because F's annualized required contribution ($5,000) exceeds 8 percent of F's household income ($4,800).

Example 4. Eligibility for coverage under an eligible employer-sponsored plan and under government sponsored coverage. Taxpayer G is unmarried and has one child, H. In November 2015, H is eligible to enroll in family coverage under a plan offered by G's employer for 2016. H is also eligible to enroll in the CHIP program for 2016. Under paragraph (e)(3)(i) of this section, H is treated as eligible for coverage under an eligible employer-sponsored plan for each month in 2016, notwithstanding that H is eligible to enroll in government sponsored coverage for the same period.

(4) *Individuals ineligible for coverage under eligible employer-sponsored plans—(i) Eligibility for coverage other than an eligible employer-sponsored plan.* An individual is treated as ineligible for coverage under an eligible employer-sponsored plan for a month that is not described in paragraph (e)(3)(i) of this section.

(ii) *Required contribution for individuals ineligible for coverage under eligible employer-sponsored plans—(A) In general.* In the case of an individual who is ineligible for coverage under an eligible employer-sponsored plan, the required contribution is the premium for the applicable plan, reduced by the maximum amount of any credit allowable under section 36B for the taxable year (determined as if the individual was covered for the entire taxable year by a qualified health plan offered through the Exchange serving the rating area where the individual resides).

(B) *Applicable plan—(1) In general.* Except as provided in paragraph (e)(4)(ii)(B)(2) of this section, *applicable plan* means the single lowest cost bronze plan available in the individual market through the Exchange serving the rating area in which the individual resides (without regard to whether the individual purchased a qualified health plan through the Exchange) that would cover all individuals in the individual's nonexempt family. For purposes of this paragraph (e)(4), an individual's *nonexempt family* means the family (as defined in §1.5000A-1(d)(6)) that includes the individual, excluding any family members who are otherwise exempt under section 1.5000A-3 or are treated as eligible for coverage under an eligible employer-sponsored plan under paragraph (e)(3)(i) of this section. The premium for the applicable plan takes into account rating factors (for example, an individual's age) that an Exchange would use to determine the cost of coverage. [Corrected 3/25/2013 (78 FR 17900).]

(2) *Lowest cost bronze plan does not cover all individuals included in the taxpayer's nonexempt family—(i) In general.* If the Exchange serving the rating area where the individual resides does not offer a single bronze plan that would cover all individuals included in the individual's nonexempt family, the premium for the applicable plan is the sum of the premiums for the lowest cost bronze plans that are offered through the Exchanges serving the rating areas where one or more of the individuals reside and that would, in the aggregate, cover all the individuals in the individual's nonexempt family.

(ii) *Simplified method for applicable plan identification.* In lieu of the premium for the applicable plan determined under paragraph (e)(4)(ii)(B)(2)(i) of this section, a taxpayer may irrevocably elect to use the premium for the lowest cost bronze plan offered by the Exchange serving the rating area where the individual resides that would cover individuals with the characteristics (for example, the individuals' ages) of the individuals in the taxpayer's nonexempt family. For example, if a taxpayer's nonexempt family includes one adult and two children, the taxpayer may elect to use the premium for the lowest cost bronze plan that would cover individuals having the same characteristics as the adult and the two children in the taxpayer's nonexempt

family. A taxpayer makes the election by using the simplified method described in this paragraph (e)(4)(ii)(B)(2)(ii).

(C) *Credit allowable under section 36B.* For purposes of paragraph (e)(4)(ii)(A) of this section, *credit allowable under section 36B* means the maximum amount of the credit that would be allowable to the individual (or to the taxpayer who can properly claim the individual as a dependent) under section 36B if all members of the individual's nonexempt family enrolled in a qualified health plan through the Exchange serving the rating area where the individual resides.

(D) *Required contribution for part-year period.* For each individual described in paragraph (e)(4)(ii)(A) of this section, affordability under paragraph (e)(4) of this section is determined separately for each period described in paragraph (e)(4)(ii)(E) of this section that is less than a 12-month period. Coverage under a plan is affordable for a part-year period if the annualized required contribution for coverage under the plan for the part-year period does not exceed the required contribution percentage of the individual's household income for the taxable year. The annualized required contribution is the required contribution determined under paragraph (e)(4)(ii)(A) of this section for the part-year period times a fraction, the numerator of which is 12 and the denominator of which is the number of months in the part-year period during the individual's taxable year. Only full calendar months are included in the computation under this paragraph (e)(4)(ii)(D).

(iii) *Examples.* The following examples illustrate the provisions of this paragraph (e)(4). Unless stated otherwise, in each example the taxpayer's taxable year is a calendar year, the rate of premium growth has not exceeded the rate of income growth since 2013, and the taxpayer is ineligible for any of the exemptions described in paragraphs (b) through (i) of this section for a month.

Example 1. Unmarried employee with no dependents. (i) Taxpayer G is an unmarried individual with no dependents. G is ineligible to enroll in any minimum essential coverage other than coverage in the individual market for all months in 2016. The annual premium for the lowest cost bronze self-only plan in G's rating area (G's applicable plan) is $5,000. The adjusted annual premium for the second lowest cost silver self-only plan in G's rating area (G's applicable benchmark plan within the meaning of §1.36B-3(f)) is $5,500. In 2016 G's household income is $40,000, which is 358 percent of the Federal poverty line for G's family size for the taxable year.

(ii) Under paragraph (e)(4)(ii)(C) of this section, the credit allowable under section 36B is determined pursuant to section 36B. With household income at 358 percent of the Federal poverty line, G's applicable percentage is 9.5. Because each month in 2016 is a coverage month (within the meaning of §1.36B-3(c)), G's maximum credit allowable under section 36B is the excess of G's premium for the applicable benchmark plan over the product of G's household income and G's applicable percentage ($1,700). Therefore, under paragraph (e)(4)(ii)(A) of this section, G's required contribution is $3,300. Under paragraph (e)(1) of this section, G lacks affordable coverage for 2016 because G's required contribution ($3,300) exceeds 8 percent of G's household income ($3,200).

Example 2. Family. (i) In 2016 Taxpayers M and N are married and file a joint return. M and N have two children, P and Q. M, N, P, and Q are ineligible to enroll in minimum essential coverage other than coverage in the individual market for a month in 2016. The annual premium for M, N, P, and Q's applicable plan is $20,000. The adjusted annual premium for M, N, P, and Q's applicable benchmark plan (within the meaning of §1.36B-3(f)) is $25,000. M and N's household income is $80,000, which is 347 percent of the Federal poverty line for a family size of 4 for the taxable year.

(ii) Under paragraph (e)(4)(ii)(C) of this section, the credit allowable under section 36B is determined pursuant to section 36B. With household income at 347 percent of the Federal poverty line, the applicable percentage is 9.5. Because each month in 2016 is a coverage month (within the meaning of §1.36B-3(c)), the maximum credit allowable under section 36B is the excess of the premium for the applicable benchmark plan over the product of the household income and the applicable percentage ($17,400). Therefore, under paragraph (e)(4)(ii)(A) of this section, the required contribution for M, N, P, and Q is $2,600. Under paragraph (e)(1) of this section, M, N, P, and Q have affordable coverage for 2016 because their required contribution ($2,600) does not exceed 8 percent of their household income ($6,400). [Corrected 3/25/2013 (78 FR 17900).]

Example 3. Family with some members eligible for government sponsored coverage. (i) In 2016 Taxpayers U and V are married and file a joint return. U and V have two children, W and X. U and V are ineligible to enroll in minimum essential coverage other than coverage in the individual market for all months in 2016; however, W and X are eligible for coverage under CHIP for 2016 at an annual cost of $1,000 per child. The annual premium for U, V, W, and X's applicable plan is $20,000. The adjusted annual premium for the second lowest cost silver plan that would cover U and V (the applicable benchmark plan (within the meaning of §1.36B-3(f)) is $12,500. U and V's household income is $50,000, which is 217 percent of the Federal poverty line for a family size of 4 for the taxable year. W and X do not enroll in CHIP coverage.

(ii) Under paragraph (e)(4)(ii)(C) of this section, the credit allowable under section 36B is determined pursuant to section 36B. With household income at 217 percent of the Federal poverty line, the applicable percentage is 6.89. Each month in 2016 is a coverage month (within the meaning of §1.36B-3(c)) for U and V, but no months in 2016 are coverage months for W and X because they are eligible for CHIP coverage. The maximum credit allowable under section 36B is the excess of the premium for the applicable benchmark plan over the product of the household income and the applicable percentage ($9,055). Therefore, under paragraph (e)(4)(ii)(A) of this section, the required contribution is $10,945. Under paragraph (e)(1) of this section, U, V, W, and X lack affordable coverage for 2016 because their required contribution ($10,945) exceeds 8 percent of their household income ($4,000).

Example 4. Family with some members enrolled in government sponsored minimum essential coverage. The facts are the same as *Example 3*, except W and X enroll in CHIP coverage on January 1, 2016. Under paragraph (e)(4)(ii)(B), U, V, W, and X are members of U and V's nonexempt family for 2016. Therefore, the annual premium for the applicable plan is the same as in *Example 3* ($20,000). The maximum credit allowable under section 36B is also the same as in *Example 3* ($9,055). Under paragraph (e)(4)(ii)(A) of this section, the required contribution is $10,945. Under paragraph (e)(1) of this section, U and V lack affordable coverage for 2016 because their required contribution ($10,945) exceeds 8 percent of their household income ($4,000).

Example 5. Simplified method for applicable plan identification. (i) In 2016 Taxpayer Y, a 42-year old unmarried individual, lives with her 17-year old nephew, Z. Y properly claims Z as a dependent for 2016. Neither Y nor Z is eligible for minimum essential coverage other than coverage in the individual market in 2016. The Exchange serving the rating area where Y and Z reside does not offer any plan that would cover them both. For 2016, the annual premium for the lowest cost bronze plan covering Y is $5,000, and the annual premium for the lowest cost bronze plan covering Z is $4,500. The premium for the lowest cost bronze plan that would cover individuals with the characteristics of Y and Z that is offered in the Exchange serving the rating area where Y and Z reside is $10,000.

(ii) Under paragraph (e)(4)(ii)(B), Z is included in Y's nonexempt family. Under paragraph (e)(4)(ii)(B)(*2*)(*i*) of this section, the premium for the applicable plan is the sum of the premiums for the lowest cost bronze plans that would cover Y and Z, or $9,500 ($5,000 + $4,500). Alternatively, under paragraph (e)(4)(ii)(B)(*2*)(*ii*) of this section, Y may irrevocably elect to use the premium for the lowest cost bronze plan that would cover individuals with the characteristics of Y and Z that is offered in the Exchange ($10,000) as the premium for the applicable plan in determining qualification for the exemption described in paragraph (e)(1) of this section.

(f) *Household income below filing threshold*—(1) *In general.* An individual is an exempt individual for any taxable year for which the individual's household income is less than the applicable filing threshold.

(2) *Applicable filing threshold*—(i) *In general.* For purposes of this section, *applicable filing threshold* means the amount of gross income that would trigger an individual's requirement to file a Federal income tax return under section 6012(a)(1).

(ii) *Certain dependents.* The applicable filing threshold for an individual who is properly claimed as a dependent by another taxpayer is equal to the other taxpayer's applicable filing threshold.

(g) *Members of Indian tribes.* An individual is an exempt individual for a month that includes a day on which the individual is a member of an Indian tribe. For purposes of this section, *Indian tribe* means a group or community described in section 45A(c)(6).

(h) *Individuals with hardship exemption certification*—(1) *In general.* An individual is an exempt individual for a month that includes a day on which the individual has in effect a hardship exemption certification described in paragraph (h)(2) of this section.

(2) *Hardship exemption certification.* A hardship exemption certification is issued by an Exchange under section 1311(d)(4)(H) of the Affordable Care Act (42 U.S.C. 18031(d)(4)(H)) and 45 CFR 155.605(g) and 45 CFR 155.615(f) and certifies that an individual has suffered a

hardship (as that term is defined in 45 CFR 166.605(g)) with respect to the capability to obtain minimum essential coverage.

(i) [Reserved]

(j) *Individuals with certain short coverage gaps*—(1) *In general.* An individual is an exempt individual for a month the last day of which is included in a short coverage gap.

(2) *Short coverage gap*—(i) *In general. Short coverage gap* means a continuous period of less than three months in which the individual is not covered under minimum essential coverage. If the individual does not have minimum essential coverage for a continuous period of three or more months, none of the months included in the continuous period is treated as included in a short coverage gap.

(ii) *Coordination with other exemptions.* For purposes of this paragraph (j), an individual is treated as having minimum essential coverage for a month in which an individual is exempt under any of paragraphs (a) through (h) of this section.

(iii) *More than one short coverage gap during calendar year.* If a calendar year includes more than one short coverage gap, the exemption provided by this paragraph (j) only applies to the earliest short coverage gap.

(3) *Continuous period*—(i) *In general.* Except as provided in paragraph (j)(3)(ii) of this section, the number of months included in a continuous period is determined without regard to the calendar years in which months included in that period occur.

(ii) *Continuous period straddling more than one taxable year.* If an individual does not have minimum essential coverage for a continuous period that begins in one taxable year and ends in the next, for purposes of applying this paragraph (j) to the first taxable year, the months in the second taxable year included in the continuous period are disregarded. For purposes of applying this paragraph (j) to the second taxable year, the months in the first taxable year included in the continuous period are taken into account.

(4) *Examples.* The following examples illustrate the provisions of this paragraph (j). Unless stated otherwise, in each example the taxpayer's taxable year is a calendar year and the taxpayer is ineligible for any of the exemptions described in paragraphs (a) through (h) of this section for a month.

Example 1. Short coverage gap. Taxpayer D has minimum essential coverage in 2016 from January 1 through March 2. After March 2, D does not have minimum essential coverage until D enrolls in an eligible employer-sponsored plan effective June 15. Under §1.5000A-1(b), for purposes of section 5000A, D has minimum essential coverage for January, February, March, and June through December. D's continuous period without coverage is 2 months, April and May. April and May constitute a short coverage gap under paragraph (j)(2)(i) of this section.

Example 2. Continuous period of 3 months or more. The facts are the same as in *Example 1*, except D's coverage is not effective until July 1. D's continuous period without coverage is 3 months, April, May, and June. Under paragraph (j)(2)(i) of this section, April, May, and June are not included in a short coverage gap.

Example 3. Short coverage gap following exempt period. Taxpayer E is incarcerated from January 1 through June 2. E enrolls in an eligible employer-sponsored plan effective September 15. Under paragraph (d) of this section, E is exempt for the period January through June. Under paragraph (j)(2)(ii) of this section, E is treated as having minimum essential coverage for this period, and E's continuous period without minimum essential coverage is 2 months, July and August. July and August constitute a short coverage gap under paragraph (j)(2)(i) of this section.

Example 4. Continuous period covering more than one taxable year. Taxpayer F, an unmarried individual with no dependents, has minimum essential coverage for the period January 1 through October 15, 2016. F is without coverage until enrolling in an eligible employer-sponsored plan effective February 15, 2017. F files his Federal income tax return for 2016 on March 10, 2017. Under paragraph (j)(3)(ii) of this section, November and December of 2016 are treated as a short coverage gap. However, November and December of 2016 are included in the continuous period that includes January 2017. The continuous period for 2017 is over 3 months and, therefore, is not a short coverage gap.

Example 5. Enrollment following loss of coverage. The facts are the same as in *Example 4* except F loses coverage on June 15, 2017. F enrolls in a new eligible employer-sponsored plan effective September 15, 2017. The continuous period without minimum essential coverage in July and August of 2017 is two months and, therefore, is a short coverage gap. Because January 2017 was not part of a short coverage gap, the earliest short coverage gap occurring in 2017 is the gap that includes July and August.

Example 6. Multiple coverage gaps. (i) The facts are the same as in *Example 5* except F has minimum essential coverage for November 2016. Under paragraph (j)(3)(ii) of this section, December 2016 is treated as a short coverage gap.

(ii) December 2016 is included in the continuous period that includes January 2017. This continuous period is two months and, therefore, January 2017 is the earliest month in 2017 that is included in a short coverage gap. Under paragraph (j)(2)(iii) of this section, the exemption under this paragraph (j) applies only to January 2017. Thus, the continuous period without minimum essential coverage in July and August of 2017 is not a short coverage gap.

(k) *Claiming exemptions from the shared responsibility payment*—(1) *Exemptions requiring certification by an Exchange.* An individual obtains a religious conscience exemption certification (described in paragraph (a) of this section) or a hardship exemption certification (described in paragraph (h) of this section) from the Exchange serving the rating area where the individual resides. To claim the exemption, the individual includes the information specified in published guidance of general applicability, see § 601.601(d)(2) of this chapter, with the Federal income tax return for the taxable year that includes the months for which the exemption is sought.

(2) *Exemptions that may be certified by an Exchange or claimed on a Federal income tax return*—(i) *Exemption certified by an Exchange.* The exemptions for members of health care sharing ministries (described in paragraph (b) of this section), incarcerated individuals (described in paragraph (d) of this section), and members of Indian tribes (described in paragraph (g) of this section) may be certified in the manner and within the time specified in 45 CFR 155.610. To claim the exemption, an individual includes the information specified in published guidance of general applicability, see § 601.601(d)(2) of this chapter, with the Federal income tax return for the taxable year that includes the months for which the exemption is sought.

(ii) *Exemption claimed on a Federal income tax return.* Alternatively, an individual, or a taxpayer who may claim the individual as a dependent for the taxable year, may claim the exemptions for members of health care sharing ministries (described in paragraph (b) of this section), incarcerated individuals (described in paragraph (d) of this section), and members of Indian tribes (described in paragraph (g) of this section) without certification by an Exchange by including the information specified in published guidance of general applicability, see § 601.601(d)(2) of this chapter, with the Federal income tax return for the taxable year that includes the months for which the exemption is sought.

(3) *Exemptions that are claimed on Federal income tax returns.* The exemptions for individuals who lack affordable coverage (described in paragraph (e) of this section), individuals with household income below the applicable return filing threshold (described in paragraph (f) of this section), and individuals with short coverage gaps (described in paragraph (j) of this section) may be claimed only by including the information specified in published guidance of general applicability, see § 601.601(d)(2) of this chapter, with the Federal income tax return for the taxable year that includes the months for which the exemption is sought. Taxpayers are not required to file Federal income tax returns solely to claim the exemption for individuals with household income below the applicable return filing threshold (described in paragraph (f) of this section).

§ 1.5000A-4 Computation of shared responsibility payment.

(a) *In general.* For each taxable year the shared responsibility payment is the lesser of—

(1) The sum of the monthly penalty amounts for each individual in the shared responsibility family; or

(2) The sum of the monthly national average bronze plan premiums for the shared responsibility family.

(b) *Monthly penalty amount*—(1) *In general. Monthly penalty amount* means, for a month that a nonexempt individual is not covered under minimum essential coverage, 1/12 multiplied by the greater of—

(i) The flat dollar amount; or

(ii) The excess income amount.

(2) *Flat dollar amount*—(i) *In general. Flat dollar amount* means the lesser of—

(A) The sum of the applicable dollar amounts for all individuals included in the taxpayer's shared responsibility family; or

(B) 300 percent of the applicable dollar amount (determined without regard to paragraph (b)(2)(iii) of this section) for the calendar year with or within which the taxable year ends.

(ii) *Applicable dollar amount.* Except as provided in paragraphs (b)(2)(iii) and (b)(2)(iv) of this section, the applicable dollar amount is—

(A) $95 in 2014;

(B) $325 in 2015; or

(C) $695 in 2016.

(iii) *Special applicable dollar amount for individuals under age 18.* If an individual has not attained the age of 18 on the first day of a month, the applicable dollar amount for the individual is equal to one-half of the applicable dollar amount (as expressed in paragraph (b)(2)(ii) of this section) for the calendar year in which the month occurs. For purposes of this paragraph (b)(2)(iii), an individual attains the age of 18 on the anniversary of the date when the individual was born. For example, an individual born on March 1, 1999, attains the age of 18 on March 1, 2017.

(iv) *Indexing of applicable dollar amount.* In any calendar year after 2016, the applicable dollar amount is $695 as increased by the product of $695 and the cost-of-living adjustment determined under section 1(f)(3) for the calendar year. For purposes of this paragraph (b)(2)(iv) of this section, the cost-of-living adjustment is determined by substituting "calendar year 2015" for "calendar year 1992" in section 1(f)(3)(B). If any increase under this paragraph (b)(2)(iv) is not a multiple of $50, the increase is rounded to the next lowest multiple of $50.

(3) *Excess income amount*—(i) *In general. Excess income amount* means the product of—

(A) The excess of the taxpayer's household income over the taxpayer's applicable filing threshold (as defined in § 1.5000A-3(f)(2)); and

(B) The income percentage.

(ii) *Income percentage.* For purposes of this section, *income percentage* means—

(A) 1.0 percent for taxable years beginning in 2013;

(B) 1.0 percent for taxable years beginning in 2014;

(C) 2.0 percent for taxable years beginning in 2015; or

(D) 2.5 percent for taxable years beginning after 2015.

(c) *Monthly national average bronze plan premium. Monthly national average bronze plan premium* means, for a month for which a shared responsibility payment is imposed, 1/12 of the annual national average premium for qualified health plans that have a bronze level of coverage, would provide coverage for the taxpayer's shared responsibility family members who do not have minimum essential coverage for the month, and are offered through Exchanges for plan years beginning in the calendar year with or within which the taxable year ends.

(d) *Examples.* The following examples illustrate the provisions of this section. In each example the taxpayer's taxable year is a calendar year and all members of the taxpayer's shared responsibility family are ineligible for any of the exemptions described in § 1.5000A-3 for a month.

Example 1. Unmarried taxpayer without minimum essential coverage. (i) In 2016 Taxpayer G is an unmarried individual with no dependents. G does not have minimum essential coverage for any month in 2016. G's household income is $120,000. G's applicable filing threshold is $12,000. The annual national average bronze plan premium for G is $5,000.

(ii) For each month in 2016, under paragraph (b)(2)(ii) of this section, G's applicable dollar amount is $695. Under paragraph (b)(2) of this section, G's flat dollar amount is $695 (the lesser of $695 and $2,085 ($695 × 3)). Under paragraph (b)(3) of this section, G's excess income amount is $2,700 (($120,000 - $12,000) × 0.025). Therefore, under paragraph (b)(1) of this section, the monthly penalty amount is $225 (the greater of $58 ($695/12) or $225 ($2,700/12)).

(iii) The sum of the monthly penalty amounts is $2,700 ($225 × 12). The sum of the monthly national average bronze plan premiums is $5,000 ($5,000/12 × 12). Therefore, under paragraph (a) of this section, the shared responsibility payment imposed on G for 2016 is $2,700 (the lesser of $2,700 or $5,000).

Example 2. Part-year coverage. The facts are the same as in *Example 1,* except G has minimum essential coverage for January through June. The sum of the monthly penalty amounts is $1,350 ($225 × 6). The sum of the monthly national average bronze plan premiums is $2,500 ($5,000/12 × 6). Therefore, under paragraph (a) of this section, the shared responsibility payment imposed on G for 2016 is $1,350 (the lesser of $1,350 or $2,500).

Example 3. Family without minimum essential coverage. (i) In 2016, Taxpayers H and J are married and file a joint return. H and J have three children: K, age 21, L, age 15, and M, age 10. No member of the family has minimum essential coverage for any month in 2016. H and J's household income is $120,000. H and J's applicable filing threshold is $24,000. The annual national average bronze plan premium for a family of 5 (2 adults, 3 children) is $20,000.

(ii) For each month in 2016, under paragraphs (b)(2)(ii) and (b)(2)(iii) of this section, the applicable dollar amount is $2,780 (($695 × 3 adults) + (($695/2) × 2 children)). Under paragraph (b)(2)(i) of this section, the flat dollar amount is $2,085 (the lesser of $2,780 and $2,085 ($695 × 3)). Under paragraph (b)(3) of this section, the excess income amount is $2,400 (($120,000 - $24,000) × 0.025). Therefore, under paragraph (b)(1) of this section, the monthly penalty amount is $200 (the greater of $173.75 ($2,085/12) or $200 ($2,400/12)).

(iii) The sum of the monthly penalty amounts is $2,400 ($200 × 12). The sum of the monthly national average bronze plan premiums is $20,000 ($20,000/12 × 12). Therefore, under paragraph (a) of this section, the shared responsibility payment imposed on H and J for 2016 is $2,400 (the lesser of $2,400 or $20,000).

Example 4. Change in shared responsibility family during the year. (i) The facts are the same as in *Example 3,* except J has minimum essential coverage for January through June. The annual national average bronze plan premium for a family of 4 (1 adult, 3 children) is $18,000.

(ii) For the period January through June 2016, under paragraphs (b)(2)(ii) and (b)(2)(iii) of this section the applicable dollar amount is $2,085 (($695 × 2 adults) + (($695/2) × 2 children)). Under paragraph (b)(2)(i) of this section, the flat dollar amount is $2,085 (the lesser of $2,085 or $2,085 ($695 × 3)).

(iii) For the period July through December 2016, the applicable dollar amount is $2,780 (($695 × 3 adults) + (($695/2) × 2 children)). Under paragraph (b)(2) of this section, the flat dollar amount is $2,085 (the lesser of $2,780 or $2,085 ($695 × 3)). Under paragraph (b)(3) of this section, the excess income amount is $2,400 (($120,000 - $24,000) × 0.025). Therefore, under paragraph (b)(1) of this section, for January through June the monthly penalty amount is $200 (the greater of $173.75 ($2,085/12) or $200 ($2,400/12)). The monthly penalty amount for July through December is $200 (the greater of $173.75 ($2,085/12) or $200 ($2,400/12)).

(iv) The sum of the monthly penalty amounts is $2,400 ($200 × 12). The sum of the monthly national average bronze plan premiums is $19,000 ((($18,000/12) × 6) + (($20,000/12) × 6))). Therefore, under paragraph (a) of this section, the shared responsibility payment imposed on H and J for 2016 is $2,400 (the lesser of $2,400 or $19,000).

Example 5. Eighteenth birthday during the year. (i) In 2016 Taxpayers S and T are married and file a joint return. S and T have one child, U, who turns 18 years old on June 28. No member of the family has minimum essential coverage for any month in 2016. S and T's household income is $60,000. S and T's applicable filing threshold is $24,000. The annual national average bronze plan premium for a family of 3 (2 adults, 1 child) is $15,000.

(ii) For the period January through June 2016, under paragraphs (b)(2)(ii) and (b)(2)(iii) of this section, the applicable dollar amount is $1,737.50 (($695 × 2 adults) + ($695/2) × 1 child)). Under paragraph (b)(2) of this section, the flat dollar amount is $1,737.50 (the lesser of $1,737.50 or $2,085 ($695 × 3)).

(iii) For the period July through December 2016, the applicable dollar amount is $2,085 ($695 × 3). Under paragraph (b)(2) of this section, the flat dollar amount is $2,085 (the lesser of $2,085 or $2,085 ($695 × 3)). Under paragraph (b)(3) of this section, the excess income amount is $900 (($60,000 - $24,000) × 0.025). Therefore, under paragraph (b)(1) of this section, for January through June the monthly penalty amount is $144.79 (the greater of $144.79 ($1,737.50/12) or $75 ($900/12)). The monthly penalty amount for July through December is $173.75 (the greater of $173.75 ($2,085/12) or $75 ($900/12)).

(iv) The sum of the monthly penalty amounts is $1,911.24 (($144.79 × 6) + ($173.75 × 6)). The sum of the monthly national average bronze plan premiums is $15,000 ($15,000/12 × 12). Therefore, under paragraph (a) of this section, the shared responsibility payment imposed on H and J for 2016 is $1,911.24 (the lesser of $1,911.24 or $15,000).

§ 1.5000A-5 Administration and procedure.

(a) *In general.* A taxpayer's liability for the shared responsibility payment for a month must be reported on the taxpayer's Federal income tax return for the taxable year that includes the month. The time for assessing the shared responsibility payment is the same as that prescribed by section 6501 for the taxable year to which the Federal income tax return on which the shared responsibility payment is to be reported relates. The shared responsibility payment is payable upon notice and demand by the Secretary, and except as provided in paragraph (b) of this section, is assessed and collected in the same manner as an assessable penalty under subchapter B of chapter 68 of the Internal Revenue Code. Therefore, the shared responsibility payment is not subject to deficiency procedures of subchapter B of chapter 63 of the Internal Revenue Code. Interest on this payment accrues in accordance with the rules in section 6601.

(b) *Special rules.* Notwithstanding any other provision of law—

(1) *Waiver of criminal penalties.* In the case of a failure by a taxpayer to timely pay the shared responsibility payment, the taxpayer is not subject to criminal prosecution or penalty for the failure.

(2) *Limitations on liens and levies.* If a taxpayer fails to pay the shared responsibility payment imposed by this section and §§ 1.5000A-1 through 1.5000A-4, the Secretary will not file notice of lien with respect to any property of the taxpayer, or levy on any such property with respect to such failure.

(3) *Authority to offset against overpayment.* Nothing in this section prohibits the Secretary from offsetting any liability for the shared responsibility payment against any overpayment due the taxpayer, in accordance with section 6402(a).

(c) *Effective/applicability date.* This section and §§ 1.5000A-1 through 1.5000A-4 apply for months beginning after December 31, 2013.

Steven T. Miller,

Deputy Commissioner for Services and Enforcement.

[FR Doc. 2013-02141 Filed 1-30-13; 11:15 am]

BILLING CODE 4830-01-P

¶ 20,263K

IRS: Proposed rules: Employee Benefits Security Administration (EBSA): Group health plans: Preventive health services: Religious employers: Contraceptive services.—The IRS, EBSA, and the Department of Health and Human Services have issued proposed regulations that clarify the definition of religious employer under the Patient Protection and Affordable Care Act's (PPACA's, P.L. 111-148) no-cost sharing contraceptive coverage requirement for non-exempt, non-grandfathered group health plans. In addition, the proposed rules accommodate nonprofit religious organizations that do not qualify as religious employers by providing their enrollees separate contraceptive coverage, with no copayments, but at no cost to the religious organization.

The proposed regulations, portions of which are reproduced below, were published in the Federal Register on February 6, 2013 (78 FR 8456). The regulations were corrected February 28, 2013 (78 FR 13575). The regulations were finalized on July 2, 2013 (78 FR 39869). The preamble to the final regulations is at ¶ 23,289. The final regulations are at ¶ 13,968V-20PA and ¶ 13,968V-20PB.

DEPARTMENT OF THE TREASURY

Internal Revenue Service

26 CFR Part 54

[REG-120391-10] [Corrected 2/28/2013 (78 FR 13575).]

RIN 1545-BJ60

DEPARTMENT OF LABOR

¶20,263K

Employee Benefits Security Administration

29 CFR Part 2590

RIN 1210-AB44

DEPARTMENT OF HEALTH AND HUMAN SERVICES

45 CFR Parts 147, 148, and 156

[CMS-9968-P]

RIN 0938-AR42

Coverage of Certain Preventive Services Under the Affordable Care Act

AGENCY: Internal Revenue Service, Department of the Treasury; Employee Benefits Security Administration, Department of Labor; Centers for Medicare & Medicaid Services, Department of Health and Human Services.

ACTION: Proposed rules.

SUMMARY: This document proposes amendments to rules regarding coverage for certain preventive services under section 2713 of the Public Health Service Act, as added by the Patient Protection and Affordable Care Act, as amended, and incorporated into the Employee Retirement Income Security Act of 1974 and the Internal Revenue Code. Section 2713 of the Public Health Service Act requires coverage without cost sharing of certain preventive health services, including certain contraceptive services, in non-exempt, non-grandfathered group health plans and health insurance coverage. The proposed rules would amend the authorization to exempt group health plans established or maintained by certain religious employers (and group health insurance coverage provided in connection with such plans) with respect to the requirement to cover contraceptive services. The proposed rules would also establish accommodations for group health plans established or maintained by eligible organizations (and group health insurance coverage offered in connection with such plans), including student health insurance coverage arranged by eligible organizations that are religious institutions of higher education. This document also proposes related amendments to regulations concerning excepted benefits and Affordable Insurance Exchanges.

DATES: Comments are due on or before April 8, 2013.

ADDRESSES: In commenting, please refer to file code CMS-9968-P. Because of staff and resource limitations, the Departments cannot accept comments by facsimile (FAX) transmission.

You may submit comments in one of four ways (please choose only one of the ways listed):

1. *Electronically.* You may submit electronic comments to *http://www.regulations.gov.* Follow the "Submit a comment" instructions.

2. *By Regular Mail.* You may mail written comments to the following address only: Centers for Medicare & Medicaid Services, Department of Health and Human Services, Attention: CMS-9968-P, P.O. Box 8013, Baltimore, MD 21244-1850.

Please allow sufficient time for mailed comments to be received before the close of the comment period.

3. *By Express or Overnight Mail.* You may send written comments to the following address only:

Centers for Medicare & Medicaid Services, Department of Health and Human Services, Attention: CMS-9968-P, Mail Stop C4-26-05, 7500 Security Boulevard, Baltimore, MD 21244-1850.

4. *By Hand or Courier.* You may deliver (by hand or courier) your written comments to the following addresses only:

a. For delivery in Washington, DC—Centers for Medicare & Medicaid Services, Department of Health and Human Services, Room 445-G, Hubert H. Humphrey Building, 200 Independence Avenue SW., Washington, DC 20201.

Because access to the interior of the Hubert H. Humphrey Building is not readily available to persons without federal government identification, commenters are encouraged to leave their comments in the Centers for Medicare & Medicaid Services drop slots located in the main lobby of the building. A stamp-in clock is available for persons wishing to retain a proof of filing by stamping in and retaining an extra copy of the comments being filed.

b. For delivery in Baltimore, MD—Centers for Medicare & Medicaid Services, Department of Health and Human Services, 7500 Security Boulevard, Baltimore, MD 21244-1850.

If you intend to deliver your comments to the Baltimore address, call (410) 786-9994 in advance to schedule your arrival with one of our staff members.

Do not mail comments to the addresses indicated as appropriate for hand or courier delivery because they may be delayed and received after the close of the comment period.

For information on viewing public comments, see the beginning of the **SUPPLEMENTARY INFORMATION** section.

FOR FURTHER INFORMATION CONTACT: Jacob Ackerman, Centers for Medicare & Medicaid Services (CMS), Department of Health and Human Services (HHS), at (410) 786-1565. Amy Turner or Beth Baum, Employee Benefits Security Administration (EBSA), Department of Labor, at (202) 693-8335.

Karen Levin, Internal Revenue Service (IRS), Department of the Treasury, at (202) 927-9639.

Customer Service Information: Individuals interested in obtaining information from the Department of Labor concerning employment-based health coverage laws may call the EBSA Toll-Free Hotline at 1-866-444-EBSA (3272) or visit the Department of Labor's Web site (*www.dol.gov/ebsa*). In addition, information from HHS on private health insurance coverage can be found on CMS's Web site (*www.cciio.cms.gov*), and information on health care reform can be found at *www.HealthCare.gov.*

SUPPLEMENTARY INFORMATION:

Inspection of Public Comments: All comments received before the close of the comment period are available for viewing by the public, including any personally identifiable or confidential business information that is included in a comment. The Departments post all comments received before the close of the comment period on the following Web site as soon as possible after they have been received: *www.regulations.gov.* Follow the search instructions on that Web site to view public comments.

Comments received timely will also be available for public inspection as they are received, generally beginning approximately three weeks after publication of a document, at the headquarters of the Centers for Medicare & Medicaid Services, 7500 Security Boulevard, Baltimore, Maryland 21244, Monday through Friday of each week from 8:30 a.m. to 4:00 p.m. To schedule an appointment to view public comments, call (800) 743-3951.

I. Background

The Patient Protection and Affordable Care Act (Pub. L. 111-148) was enacted on March 23, 2010, and amended by the Health Care and Education Reconciliation Act of 2010 (Pub. L. 111-152) on March 30, 2010. These statutes are referred to collectively as the Affordable Care Act. The Affordable Care Act reorganizes, amends, and adds to the provisions of part A of title XXVII of the Public Health Service Act (PHS Act) relating to group health plans and health insurance issuers in the group and individual markets. The Affordable Care Act adds section 715(a)(1) to the Employee Retirement Income Security Act of 1974 (ERISA) and section 9815(a)(1) to the Internal Revenue Code (Code) to incorporate the provisions of part A of title XXVII of the PHS Act into ERISA and the Code, and to make them applicable to group health plans. The PHS Act sections incorporated by these references are sections 2701 through 2728.

Section 2713 of the PHS Act, as added by the Affordable Care Act and incorporated into ERISA and the Code, requires that non-grandfathered group health plans and health insurance issuers offering non-grandfathered group or individual health insurance coverage provide benefits for certain preventive health services without the imposition of cost sharing. These preventive health services include, with respect to women, preventive care and screenings as provided for in comprehensive guidelines supported by the Health Resources and Services Administration (HRSA).

The Departments of Health and Human Services (HHS), Labor, and the Treasury (collectively, the Departments) published interim final rules with a request for comments implementing section 2713 of the PHS Act in the July 19, 2010 **Federal Register** (75 FR 41726) (2010 interim final rules). Among other things, the 2010 interim final rules provide that a plan or issuer must provide coverage, without cost sharing, for certain newly recommended preventive health services starting with the first plan year (or, in the individual market, policy year) that begins on or after the date that is one year after the date on which the recommendation or guideline is issued.[1]

On August 1, 2011, HRSA adopted and released guidelines for women's preventive services based on recommendations of the independent Institute of Medicine, which had undertaken a review of the scientific and medical evidence on women's preventive services (Women's Preventive Services: Required Health Plan Coverage Guidelines, or HRSA Guidelines).[2] As relevant here, the HRSA Guidelines include all Food and Drug Administration (FDA)-approved contraceptive methods, sterilization procedures, and patient education and counseling for all women with reproductive capacity, as prescribed by a health care

---

[1] 26 CFR 54.9815-2713T(b)(1); 29 CFR 2590.715-2713(b)(1); 45 CFR 147.130(b)(1).

[2] The HRSA Guidelines are available at: *http://www.hrsa.gov/womensguidelines.*

provider (collectively, contraceptive services).[3] Accordingly, under section 2713 of the PHS Act and the 2010 interim final rules, non-grandfathered group health plans and health insurance issuers offering non-grandfathered group or individual health insurance coverage are required to provide coverage without cost sharing of women's preventive health services, including contraceptive services, consistent with the HRSA Guidelines in plan years (or, in the individual market, policy years) beginning on or after August 1, 2012, except as discussed later in this section.

Contemporaneous with the issuance of the HRSA Guidelines, the Departments amended the 2010 interim final rules (76 FR 46621) (2011 amended interim final rules). The amendment provided HRSA with the authority to exempt group health plans established or maintained by religious employers (and group health insurance coverage provided in connection with such plans) from the requirement to cover contraceptive services pursuant to the HRSA Guidelines.[4] The 2011 amended interim final rules specified that, for purposes of this exemption, a religious employer is one that: (1) Has the inculcation of religious values as its purpose; (2) primarily employs persons who share its religious tenets; (3) primarily serves persons who share its religious tenets; and (4) is a nonprofit organization described in section 6033(a)(1) and (a)(3)(A)(i) or (iii) of the Code. Section 6033(a)(3)(A)(i) and (iii) of the Code refers to churches, their integrated auxiliaries, and conventions or associations of churches, as well as to the exclusively religious activities of any religious order. HRSA exercised this authority in the HRSA Guidelines such that group health plans established or maintained by these religious employers (and group health insurance coverage provided in connection with such plans) are exempt from the requirement to cover contraceptive services.

On February 10, 2012, the Departments issued final rules that adopted the definition of religious employer in the 2011 amended interim final rules for purposes of the exemption from the requirement to cover contraceptive services (2012 final rules).[5] Contemporaneous with the issuance of the 2012 final rules, HHS, with the agreement of the Departments of Labor and the Treasury, issued guidance establishing a temporary enforcement safe harbor for group health plans established or maintained by certain nonprofit organizations that have religious objections to contraceptive coverage (and any group health insurance coverage provided in connection with such plans).[6]

The guidance provides that, under the temporary enforcement safe harbor, the Departments will not take any enforcement action against an employer, group health plan, or health insurance issuer for failing to cover some or all recommended contraceptive services in a non-grandfathered group health plan (or any group health insurance coverage provided in connection with such a plan) where the plan is established or maintained by an organization meeting all of the following criteria:

• The organization is organized and operates as a nonprofit entity.

• From February 10, 2012, onward, the group health plan established or maintained by the organization has consistently not covered all or the same subset of recommended contraceptive services, consistent with any applicable state law, because of the religious beliefs of the organization.

• The group health plan established or maintained by the organization (or another entity on behalf of the plan, such as a health insurance issuer or third party administrator) provides to participants a notice indicating that some or all contraceptive services will not be covered under the plan for the first plan year beginning on or after August 1, 2012, as set forth in the guidance.

• The organization self-certifies that it satisfies the foregoing three criteria and documents its self-certification, as set forth in the guidance.

The temporary enforcement safe harbor is also available for insured student health insurance coverage arranged by nonprofit institutions of

higher education with religious objections to contraceptive coverage that similarly meet the four criteria.[7]

The temporary enforcement safe harbor is in effect until the first plan year that begins on or after August 1, 2013. The Departments committed to rulemaking during this 1-year safe harbor period to provide women with contraceptive coverage without cost sharing as required by section 2713 of the PHS Act, while protecting certain additional organizations from having to contract, arrange, pay, or refer for any contraceptive coverage to which they object on religious grounds.

The first step toward realizing these policy goals was an advance notice of proposed rulemaking (ANPRM) published on March 21, 2012 (77 FR 16501). The ANPRM presented potential approaches and solicited comments on alternative ways to fulfill the requirements of section 2713 of the PHS Act when health coverage is established or maintained by eligible organizations, or arranged by eligible organizations that are religious institutions of higher education,[8] with religious objections to contraceptive coverage. The 90-day comment period on the ANPRM closed on June 19, 2012.

These proposed rules mark the next step in the process. The proposed rules would make two principal changes to the preventive services coverage rules to provide women contraceptive coverage without cost sharing, while taking into account religious objections to contraceptive services of eligible organizations, including eligible organizations that are religious institutions of higher education, that establish or maintain or arrange health coverage. First, the proposed rules would amend the criteria for the religious employer exemption to ensure that an otherwise exempt employer plan is not disqualified because the employer's purposes extend beyond the inculcation of religious values or because the employer serves or hires people of different religious faiths. Second, the proposed rules would establish accommodations for health coverage established or maintained by eligible organizations, or arranged by eligible organizations that are religious institutions of higher education, with religious objections to contraceptive coverage. The proposed rules also propose related amendments to other rules, consistent with the proposed accommodations. The Departments intend to finalize all such proposed amendments before the end of the temporary enforcement safe harbor.

Comments are welcome on any aspect of the proposed rules, including on how best to provide women with contraceptive coverage without cost sharing as required by section 2713 of the PHS Act, while protecting eligible organizations from having to contract, arrange, pay, or refer for any contraceptive coverage to which they object on religious grounds.

II. Overview of the Public Comments on the Advance Notice of Proposed Rulemaking

The Departments received approximately 200,000 comments in response to the ANPRM. Commenters represented a wide variety of stakeholders, including religious groups; religiously affiliated educational institutions, health care organizations, charities, and associations; civil rights organizations; consumer groups; group health plan sponsors and administrators; third party administrators and other plan service providers; health insurance issuers; law and public policy organizations; states; secular organizations; private citizens; and women's rights and reproductive health advocacy organizations.

Comments addressed both the religious employer exemption and the suggested accommodations, among other issues. Although the Departments do not separately address each comment received, the significant issues raised in the comments are summarized in this section. The Departments considered these comments in developing the policies in these proposed rules.

A. Comments on the Religious Employer Exemption

Some commenters asserted that the definition of religious employer as formulated in the 2012 final rules is too narrow. Some of these commenters expressed concern that the group health plans of a num-

---

[3] This excludes services relating to a man's reproductive capacity, such as vasectomies and condoms.

[4] The 2011 amended interim final rules were issued and effective on August 1, 2011, and published on August 3, 2011.

[5] The 2012 final rules were published on February 15, 2012 (77 FR 8725).

[6] Guidance on the Temporary Enforcement Safe Harbor for Certain Employers, Group Health Plans, and Group Health Insurance Issuers with Respect to the Requirement to Cover Contraceptive Services Without Cost Sharing Under Section 2713 of the Public Health Service Act, Section 715(a)(1) of the Employee Retirement Income Security Act, and Section 9815(a)(1) of the Internal Revenue Code, issued on February 10, 2012, and reissued on August 15, 2012. Available at: *http://cciio.cms.gov/resources/files/prev-services-guidance-08152012.pdf.* The guidance, as reissued on August 15, 2012, clarifies, among

other things, that group health plans that took some action before February 10, 2012, to try, without success, to exclude or limit contraceptive coverage are not precluded from eligibility for the safe harbor.

[7] *See* final rule on student health insurance coverage published by HHS on March 21, 2012 (77 FR 16456 and 16457).

[8] In these proposed rules, any proposed accommodation specific to a religious institution of higher education is intended to accommodate the religious institution of higher education only with respect to its arrangement of student health insurance coverage. With respect to the establishment or maintenance of a group health plan by a religious institution of higher education, the religious institution of higher education is intended to be accommodated the same way as any other religious organization that has established or maintained a group health plan.

ber of religious employers, including houses of worship, do not qualify for the exemption because the employers' purposes extend beyond the inculcation of religious values or because the employers serve or hire people of different religious faiths. Commenters noted that employers may not know the religious beliefs of those they serve or hire, and that employment discrimination laws may prohibit them from inquiring about the religious beliefs of their employees. Other commenters expressed concern that the definition of religious employer is not broad enough to allow them to continue their current exclusion of contraceptive services from coverage under their group health plans and warned that, if the definition of religious employer is not broadened, they could cease to offer health coverage to their employees in order to avoid having to offer coverage to which they object on religious grounds.

Commenters also asserted that federal laws, including the Affordable Care Act, provide for conscience clauses and religious exemptions broader than the religious employer exemption provided for in the 2012 final rules. Other commenters asserted that the narrow scope of the exemption raises concerns under the First Amendment and the Religious Freedom Restoration Act (RFRA). Some commenters asserted that the criteria for the religious employer exemption could result in excessive government entanglement in religion. Several commenters expressed concern that the definition of religious employer sets a precedent for use in other areas of federal and state law. These commenters urged that the definition of religious employer be broadened such that more group health plans may qualify for the exemption.

Other commenters, however, disputed claims that the contraceptive coverage requirement infringes on rights protected by the First Amendment or RFRA, noting that the requirement is neutral and generally applicable. They also explained that the requirement does not substantially burden religious exercise and, in any event, serves compelling governmental interests and is the least restrictive means to achieve those interests.

Some commenters supported the inclusion of contraceptive services in the HRSA Guidelines and urged that the Departments not broaden the religious employer exemption. These commenters asserted that the definition of religious employer is appropriately targeted at houses of worship and argued that making contraceptive coverage available to as many women as possible would enhance access to important preventive health care services and would significantly reduce long-term health care costs and consequences associated with unplanned pregnancies. These commenters asserted that expanding the exemption would undermine the benefits of the law. Some commenters believed that the exemption should be eliminated entirely due to the importance of extending these benefits to as many women as possible.

Several commenters requested clarification as to whether, if employees of multiple employers are covered under a single group health plan, each employer must independently meet the definition of religious employer for the plan to qualify for the exemption.

B. Comments on the Suggested Accommodations for Health Coverage Established or Maintained by Religious Organizations or Arranged by Religious Institutions of Higher Education

Several commenters asserted that the suggested accommodations described in the ANPRM would fail to adequately accommodate religious objections to contraceptive coverage. These commenters emphasized that, in their view, religious organizations would continue to be involved, whether directly or indirectly, in providing coverage for services that they find religiously objectionable. For example, with respect to insured group health plans, these commenters disputed the claim that contraceptive coverage is at least cost neutral and argued that plan sponsors would end up funding the coverage in the form of higher premiums or fees. These commenters generally argued that, in order to provide adequate relief, the Departments would need to rescind the contraceptive coverage requirement in its entirety, provide an exemption for the group health plan of any organization with a religious or moral objection to contraceptive coverage, or provide government funding for provision of contraceptive services.

Other commenters recommended that the Departments expand the suggested accommodations to encompass the group health plans of a broader class of religiously affiliated organizations. Several commenters stated that the rules should accommodate all organizations with a religious or moral objection to contraceptive coverage, whether the organization is religious or secular, or nonprofit or for-profit, among other potential distinctions. These commenters also argued that an accommodation should be available without regard to whether an organization has covered contraceptive services in its group health plan in the past.

Some commenters recommended using criteria in other federal laws, such as the National Labor Relations Act, for determining whether the

group health plan of an organization qualifies for an accommodation. Some commenters suggested accommodating the group health plans of religiously affiliated organizations recognized as tax-exempt under an IRS group ruling.

In contrast, other commenters urged that any accommodation apply only to health coverage established or maintained by a limited class of religiously affiliated organizations or arranged by a limited class of religiously affiliated institutions of higher education. For example, several commenters suggested limiting any accommodation to only health coverage established or maintained by nonprofit organizations owned or controlled by a church, association of churches, or religious order, or arranged by nonprofit institutions of higher education owned or controlled by a religious organization as defined for purposes of Title IX of the Education Amendments of 1972. These commenters also generally argued that health coverage established or maintained by for-profit organizations or arranged by for-profit institutions of higher education, or health coverage established or maintained by organizations, or arranged by institutions of higher education, that object to only some types of contraceptive services, should not qualify for an accommodation.

A number of commenters supported a self-certification process, similar to that used for the temporary enforcement safe harbor, for religious organizations seeking to avail themselves of an accommodation. Some commenters urged that the Departments adopt appropriate oversight and enforcement mechanisms to monitor compliance with the criteria for any accommodation and recommended self-certification as a tool to promote transparency and support compliance and enforcement. Other commenters suggested that the Departments consider any such self-certification to be conclusive to avoid inquiry into a religious organization's character, mission, or practices.

Comments were quite varied regarding the ANPRM's suggested approaches with respect to the provision of contraceptive coverage to participants and beneficiaries enrolled in self-insured group health plans established or maintained by religious organizations with religious objections to such coverage. Many commenters supported the general approach suggested in the ANPRM of ensuring that participants and beneficiaries enrolled in such self-insured plans receive contraceptive coverage without cost sharing. These commenters stated that any accommodation should not create delays in or barriers to contraceptive benefits, and that these benefits should be provided without participants and beneficiaries having to specifically elect such benefits.

Concerns were raised by some commenters about an objecting organization's ability to not administer, facilitate, or otherwise involve itself in the provision of contraceptive coverage to such participants and beneficiaries. Many commenters were concerned about how third party administrators would be able to fund these benefits. They noted that drug rebates, one suggested source of funds, often belong to another entity (such as the plan sponsor and/or the plan participants and beneficiaries), not the third party administrator, and stated that, in their view, costs incurred by third party administrators would ultimately be passed on to plan sponsors and/or plan participants and beneficiaries unless a separate source of funding could be found, such as some form of public funding or stand-alone contraceptive coverage with no premium or cost sharing. Others raised questions about the responsibility for communications regarding contraceptive coverage. Some third party administrators were concerned about becoming surrogate insurers, which might subject them to the application of state insurance laws. At the same time, other commenters believed that, with funding, notice, and adequate claims information, contraceptive coverage could be administered effectively by third party administrators.

III. Provisions of the Proposed Rules

A. Overview

The Departments aim to secure the protections under section 2713 of the PHS Act that are designed to enhance coverage of important preventive services for women without cost sharing while accommodating the religious objections to contraceptive coverage of eligible organizations.

The Departments propose two key changes to the preventive services coverage rules codified in 26 CFR 54.9815-2713T, 29 CFR 2590.715-2713, and 45 CFR 147.130 to meet these goals. First, the proposed rules would amend the criteria for the religious employer exemption to ensure that an otherwise exempt employer plan is not disqualified because the employer's purposes extend beyond the inculcation of religious values or because the employer serves or hires people of different religious faiths. Second, the proposed rules would establish accommodations for health coverage established or maintained by eligible organizations, or arranged by eligible organizations that are religious institutions of higher education, with religious objections to contraceptive coverage.

Amendments to rules concerning excepted benefits and Affordable Insurance Exchanges (Exchanges) are also proposed in connection with the proposed accommodations.

B. Explanation of Terms

In these proposed rules, all references to "contraceptive coverage" are references to coverage of the contraceptive services that are required to be covered without cost sharing in accordance with the HRSA Guidelines (that is, all FDA-approved contraceptive methods, sterilization procedures, and patient education and counseling for all women with reproductive capacity, as prescribed by a health care provider).

All references to "accommodation" are references to an arrangement under which contraceptive coverage is provided without cost sharing to plan participants and beneficiaries (or, in the case of student health insurance coverage, student enrollees and their covered dependents) independent of health coverage established or maintained or arranged by an objecting religious organization, including an objecting religious institution of higher education.

Finally, all references to "religious organization" and "religious institution of higher education" are references to the class of organizations and institutions of higher education that establish or maintain or arrange health coverage that qualifies for an accommodation. These organizations are collectively referred to as "eligible organizations" in these proposed rules.

C. Religious Employer Exemption and Accommodations for Health Coverage Established or Maintained or Arranged by Eligible Organizations

For purposes of organization and clarity, proposed 45 CFR 147.130(a)[9] would provide that the requirement to provide coverage for recommended preventive services without cost sharing is subject to a new 45 CFR 147.131, which would establish standards and processes related to both the religious employer exemption and the accommodations for health coverage established or maintained or arranged by eligible organizations, as discussed in more detail later in this section.

Accordingly, the proposed rules would move to new 45 CFR 147.131[10] the language currently in 45 CFR 147.130(a)(1)(iv)(A) and (B) (incorporated by reference in the rules of the Departments of Labor and the Treasury) that authorizes HRSA to exempt group health plans of religious employers (and group health insurance coverage provided in connection with such plans) from the contraceptive coverage requirement and that defines religious employer for this purpose, and would amend the authorization and definition as discussed later in this section.

1. Religious Employer Exemption

Currently, under the 2012 final rules, a religious employer is one that: (1) Has the inculcation of religious values as its purpose; (2) primarily employs persons who share its religious tenets; (3) primarily serves persons who share its religious tenets; and (4) is a nonprofit organization described in section 6033(a)(1) and 6033(a)(3)(A)(i) or (iii) of the Code. Section 6033(a)(3)(A)(i) and (iii) of the Code refers to churches, their integrated auxiliaries, and conventions or associations of churches, as well as to the exclusively religious activities of any religious order. The Departments explained in the 2011 amended interim final rules that this definition was intended to focus the religious employer exemption on "the unique relationship between a house of worship and its employees in ministerial positions."[11]

Some commenters brought to the Departments' attention that the group health plans of certain religious entities that meet the fourth prong of the definition of religious employer (providing that a religious employer is a nonprofit organization described in section 6033(a)(1) and (a)(3)(A)(i) or (iii) of the Code) may not qualify for the exemption because those entities provide benevolent services to their communities. For example, if a church maintains a soup kitchen that provides free meals to low-income individuals irrespective of their religious faiths, it could fail to satisfy the third prong of the definition of religious employer (providing that a religious employer primarily serves persons who share its religious tenets). The same question could arise if a church runs a parochial school that employs people of different religious faiths.

The Departments agree that the exemption should not exclude group health plans of religious entities that would qualify for the exemption but for the fact that, for example, they provide charitable social services to persons of different religious faiths or employ persons of different religious faiths when running a parochial school. Indeed, this was never the Departments' intention in connection with the 2011 amended interim final rules or the 2012 final rules. Accordingly, in 45 CFR 147.131(a) (and the related rules of the Departments of Labor and the Treasury), the Departments propose to amend the definition of religious employer that was adopted in the 2012 final rules by eliminating the first three prongs of the definition and clarifying the application of the fourth. Under this proposal, an employer that is organized and operates as a nonprofit entity and referred to in section 6033(a)(3)(A)(i) or (iii) of the Code would be considered a religious employer for purposes of the religious employer exemption. For this purpose, an organization that is organized and operates as a nonprofit entity is not limited to any particular form of entity under state law, but may include organizations such as trusts and unincorporated associations, as well as nonprofit, not-for-profit, non-stock, public benefit, and similar types of corporations. However, for this purpose, an organization is not considered to be organized and operated as a nonprofit entity if its assets or income accrue to the benefit of private individuals or shareholders. Under this standard, it is not necessary to determine the federal tax-exempt status of the nonprofit entity in determining whether the religious employer exemption applies. The Departments note that eliminating the first three prongs would avoid any inquiry into an employer's purposes, as well as any inquiry into the religious beliefs of its employees and the religious beliefs of those it serves.

The Departments believe that this proposal would not expand the universe of employer plans that would qualify for the exemption beyond that which was intended in the 2012 final rules. As previously noted, when the Departments first defined religious employer, the primary goal was to exempt the group health plans of houses of worship. Section 6033(a)(3)(A)(i) and (iii) of the Code refers to churches, their integrated auxiliaries, and conventions or associations of churches, as well as to the exclusively religious activities of any religious order. By restricting the exemption primarily to group health plans established or maintained by churches, synagogues, mosques, and other houses of worship, and religious orders, the fourth prong of the current definition of religious employer would alone suffice to meet the goal. By eliminating the first three prongs of the current definition, there no longer would be any question as to whether group health plans of houses of worship that provide educational, charitable, or social services to their communities qualify for the exemption.

The Departments welcome comments on this proposal, including whether it would unduly expand the universe of employer plans that would qualify for the exemption and whether additional or different language is needed to clarify the scope of the exemption.

2. Accommodations for Health Coverage Established or Maintained or Arranged by Eligible Organizations

In proposed 45 CFR 147.131(b) through (e) (and the related rules of the Departments of Labor and the Treasury) and as discussed later in this section, the Departments propose policies relating to the accommodation of certain group health plans and group health insurance coverage with respect to the contraceptive coverage requirement. The Departments propose a comparable accommodation with respect to student health insurance coverage arranged by eligible organizations that are religious institutions of higher education. The Departments believe these proposed accommodations, as opposed to the exemption that is provided to religious employers, are warranted given that participants and beneficiaries in group health plans established or maintained by eligible organizations, as well as student enrollees and their covered dependents in student health insurance coverage arranged by eligible organizations, may be less likely than participants and beneficiaries in group health plans established or maintained by religious employers to share such religious objections of the eligible organizations. The proposed accommodations would provide such plan participants and beneficiaries contraceptive coverage without cost sharing while insulating their employers or institutions of higher education from contracting, arranging, paying, or referring for such coverage.

a. Definition of Eligible Organization

These proposed rules would provide that group health plans established or maintained by eligible organizations with religious objections

---

[9] For simplicity, this preamble refers only to provisions of 45 CFR 147.130. Parallel provisions to 45 CFR 147.130 are contained in 26 CFR 54.9815-2713T and 29 CFR 2590.715-2713.

[10] For simplicity, this preamble refers only to provisions of 45 CFR 147.131. Parallel provisions to 45 CFR 147.131 are contained in 26 CFR 54.9815-2713A and 29 CFR 2590.715-2713A.

[11] 76 FR 46623.

to contraceptive coverage (and group health insurance coverage provided in connection with such plans), and student health insurance coverage arranged by eligible organizations that are religious institutions of higher education with such objections, comply with the requirement to provide coverage for contraceptive services under section 2713 of the PHS Act if the conditions of the accommodation are satisfied.

For purposes of these proposed rules only, the Departments propose to define an eligible organization as an organization that meets all of the following criteria:

• The organization opposes providing coverage for some or all of the contraceptive services required to be covered under section 2713 of the PHS Act on account of religious objections.

• The organization is organized and operates as a nonprofit entity.

• The organization holds itself out as a religious organization.

• The organization self-certifies that it satisfies the first three criteria, as described later in this section.

This proposed definition of eligible organization is intended to allow health coverage established or maintained or arranged by nonprofit religious organizations, including nonprofit religious institutional health care providers, educational institutions, and charities, with religious objections to contraceptive coverage to qualify for an accommodation. For this purpose, an organization that is organized and operated as a nonprofit entity is not limited to any particular form of entity under state law, but may include organizations such as trusts and unincorporated associations, as well as nonprofit, not-for-profit, non-stock, public benefit, and similar types of corporations. However, for this purpose an organization is not considered to be organized and operated as a nonprofit entity if its assets or income accrue to the benefit of private individuals or shareholders.

The Departments believe that the proposed definition of eligible organization would strike an appropriate balance because it would limit any accommodation to nonprofit organizations that hold themselves out as religious. The Departments solicit comments on whether the proposed definition of eligible organization would allow an appropriate universe of nonprofit religious organizations and institutions of higher education establishing or maintaining or arranging health coverage to qualify for an accommodation, including comments on whether it would be too broad or too narrow.

The Departments do not propose that the definition of eligible organization extend to for-profit secular employers. Religious accommodations in related areas of federal law, such as the exemption for religious organizations under Title VII of the Civil Rights Act of 1964, are available to nonprofit religious organizations but not to for-profit secular organizations. Accordingly, the Departments believe it would be appropriate to define eligible organization to include nonprofit religious organizations, but not to include for-profit secular organizations.

b. Self-Certification

Each organization seeking accommodation under the proposed rules would be required to self-certify that it meets the definition of eligible organization, following a self-certification process similar to that under the temporary enforcement safe harbor. The self-certification would also specify the contraceptive services for which the organization will not establish, maintain, administer, or fund coverage. The organization would not be required to submit the self-certification to any of the Departments. The organization would maintain the self-certification (executed by an authorized representative of the organization) in its records for each plan year to which the accommodation applies and make the self-certification available for examination upon request so that regulators, issuers, third party administrators, and plan participants and beneficiaries may verify that an organization has qualified for an accommodation, while avoiding any inquiry into the organization's character, mission, or practices. The Departments intend to specify in guidance the form to be used for the self-certification.

c. Separate Contraceptive Coverage Without Cost Sharing for Plan Participants and Beneficiaries

These proposed rules aim to provide women with contraceptive coverage without cost sharing and to protect eligible organizations from having to contract, arrange, pay, or refer for contraceptive coverage to which they object on religious grounds.

1. Insured Plans

To achieve these goals, under HHS's authority in section 2792 of the PHS Act to promulgate rules "necessary or appropriate" to carry out the provisions of title XXVII of the PHS Act, and the parallel authorities of the Department of Labor in section 734 of ERISA and the Department of the Treasury in section 9833 of the Code, these proposed rules would provide that, in the case of an insured group health plan established or maintained by an eligible organization, the health insurance issuer providing group coverage in connection with the plan would assume sole responsibility, independent of the eligible organization and its plan, for providing contraceptive coverage without cost sharing, premium, fee, or other charge to plan participants and beneficiaries.

The eligible organization would provide the issuer with a copy of its self-certification. If the plan uses a separate issuer for certain coverage, such as prescription drug coverage, the eligible organization may also need to provide a copy of its self-certification to the separate issuer. Nothing more would be required of the eligible organization to qualify for the accommodation.

The proposed rules would direct the issuer receiving the copy of the self-certification to ensure that the coverage for those contraceptive services identified in the self-certification is not included in the group policy, certificate, or contract of insurance; that such coverage is not reflected in the group health insurance premium; and that no fee or other charge in connection with such coverage is imposed on the eligible organization or its plan.

The proposed rules would further direct the issuer receiving the copy of the self-certification to provide contraceptive coverage under individual policies, certificates, or contracts of insurance (hereinafter referred to as individual health insurance policies) for plan participants and beneficiaries without cost sharing, premium, fee, or other charge. The coverage would not be offered by or through a group health plan. (As discussed later in this section, the Departments propose that this type of individual health insurance policy be a new category of excepted benefits.)

The issuer would automatically enroll plan participants and beneficiaries in a separate individual health insurance policy that covers recommended contraceptive services. The Departments envision that the issuer would ensure that contraceptive coverage for plan participants and beneficiaries is effective at the beginning of the plan year of their group health plan, to the extent possible, to prevent a delay or gap in contraceptive coverage. The eligible organization would have no role in contracting, arranging, paying, or referring for this separate contraceptive coverage. Such coverage would be offered at no charge to plan participants and beneficiaries, that is, the issuer would provide benefits for such contraceptive services without the imposition of any cost sharing requirement (such as a copayment, coinsurance, or a deductible), premium, fee, or other charge, consistent with section 2713 of the PHS Act. The requirements of section 2713 of the PHS Act, its implementing regulations, and other applicable federal and state law (as well as their enforcement mechanisms) would continue to apply with respect to such coverage. For example, an issuer providing such coverage could use reasonable medical management techniques consistent with 45 CFR 147.130(a)(4).

The Departments believe that, in the case of insured group health plans, this proposed arrangement would alleviate the need for the eligible organization to contract, arrange, pay, or refer for contraceptive coverage while providing contraceptive coverage to plan participants and beneficiaries at no additional cost. Actuaries, economists, and insurers estimate that providing contraceptive coverage is at least cost neutral, and may result in cost-savings when taking into account all costs and benefits for the insurer.[12] In this instance, contraceptive coverage without cost sharing would be provided to plan participants and beneficiaries through individual health insurance policies, separate from the group policy through which all other coverage would be provided to plan participants and beneficiaries. The Departments believe that issuers generally would find that providing such contraceptive coverage is cost neutral because they would be they would be insuring the same set of individuals under both policies and would experience lower costs from improvements in women's health and fewer childbirths.

The Departments note that a health insurance issuer providing coverage in connection with a plan established or maintained by an eligible organization would be held harmless under the accommodation if a representation by the organization to the issuer that the

[12] Bertko, John, F.S.A., M.A.A.A., Director of Special Initiatives and Pricing, Center for Consumer Information and Insurance Oversight, Centers for Medicare & Medicaid Services, Glied, Sherry, Ph.D., Assistant Secretary for Planning and Evaluation, Department of Health and Human Services (ASPE/HHS), et al., "The Cost of Covering Contraceptives Through Health Insurance," (February 9, 2012), available at: http://aspe.hhs.gov/health/reports/2012/contraceptives/ib.shtml.

organization is an eligible organization on which the issuer relied in good faith were determined later to be incorrect. Conversely, the eligible organization and its plan would be held harmless if the issuer were to fail to comply with the requirement that it provide separate contraceptive coverage for plan participants and beneficiaries at no charge.

The Departments request comments on this proposed arrangement.

2. Self-Insured Plans

The Departments are considering alternative approaches for providing participants and beneficiaries in self-insured group health plans established or maintained by eligible organizations with contraceptive coverage at no additional cost, while protecting the eligible organizations from having to contract, arrange, pay, or refer for such coverage. Under each of these approaches, a health insurance issuer that provides individual health insurance policies for contraceptive coverage for plan participants and beneficiaries at no additional cost would be able to offset the costs of providing such coverage by claiming an adjustment in Federally-facilitated Exchange (FFE) user fees that would reduce the amount of the such fees for the issuer (or an affiliated issuer), as discussed later in this section. The Departments envision that the issuer would ensure that contraceptive coverage for plan participants and beneficiaries is effective at the beginning of the plan year of their group health plans, to the extent possible, to prevent a delay or gap in contraceptive coverage. Under each of these approaches, HHS would assist in identifying issuers offering the separate individual health insurance policies for contraceptive coverage.

Under all approaches, if there is a third party administrator for the self-insured group health plan of the eligible organization, the eligible organization would provide the third party administrator with a copy of its self-certification. If the plan uses a separate third party administrator for certain coverage, such as prescription drug coverage, the eligible organization would also provide a copy of its self-certification to the separate third party administrator if the coverage administered by the separate third party administrator includes coverage of any contraceptive service listed in the self-certification.

Further, under all approaches, a third party administrator receiving a copy of the self-certification would automatically arrange separate individual health insurance policies for contraceptive coverage from an issuer providing such polices, as described above. The issuer providing the coverage (or an affiliated issuer) would receive an additional adjustment in the user fees that otherwise would be charged by an FFE in an amount that would offset a reasonable charge by the third party administrator for performing this service. In turn, the issuer would be required to pass the amount of this additional adjustment in FFE user fees on to the third party administrator as a condition of receiving any FFE user fee adjustment, and would be required to attest to HHS that it has in fact passed the amount of this additional adjustment on to the third party administrator. As a condition of payment of this amount by the issuer, the third party administrator would not be permitted to charge any amount to the eligible organization, its plan, or to plan participants or beneficiaries for performing the service. The Departments note that the issuer could either be affiliated with or be independent of the third party administrator.

The Departments solicit comment on which of the proposed approaches below would best provide participants and beneficiaries in self-insured group health plans established or maintained by eligible organizations with contraceptive coverage at no additional cost, while protecting eligible organizations from having to contract, arrange, pay, or refer for such coverage. The Departments also request comment on whether there are other approaches that should be considered that would achieve the same goals.

Under the first approach, a third party administrator receiving the copy of the self-certification would have an economic incentive to voluntarily arrange for the separate individual health insurance policies for contraceptive coverage for plan participants and beneficiaries because it would be compensated for a reasonable charge for automatically arranging for the contraceptive coverage through payment by the issuer of the contraceptive coverage. Under this approach, in automatically arranging for the contraceptive coverage, the third party administrator would be acting, not as the third party administrator to the self-insured plan of the eligible organization, but rather in its independent capacity apart from its capacity as the agent of the plan. Under this

approach, the self-insured plan of the eligible organization would be treated as complying with the requirement to provide contraceptive coverage based on the third party administrator's receipt of the copy of the self-certification.

Under the second approach, coverage under the plan of the eligible organization would comply with the requirement to provide contraceptive coverage without cost sharing only if the third party administrator administering coverage in connection with the plan automatically arranges for an issuer to assume sole responsibility for providing separate individual health insurance policies offering contraceptive coverage without cost sharing, premium, fee, or other charge to plan participants and beneficiaries, the eligible organization, or its plan. As discussed above, any reasonable administrative costs of the third party administrator in performing this service would be covered through payment by the issuer of the contraceptive coverage. If the third party administrator performs the services, coverage under the plan of the eligible organization would comply with 45 CFR 147.130. While the third party administrator would not be directly responsible for assuring compliance with section 2713 of the PHS Act, the Departments expect that third party administrators would seek to assist eligible organizations such that eligible organizations would be able to avail themselves of the proposed accommodation.

Under the third approach, the third party administrator receiving the copy of the self-certification would be directly responsible for automatically arranging for contraceptive coverage for plan participants and beneficiaries. Specifically, the self-certification would have the effect of designating the third party administrator[13] as the plan administrator under section 3(16) of ERISA solely for the purpose of fulfilling the requirement that the plan provide contraceptive coverage without cost sharing. The third party administrator would satisfy its responsibility to automatically arrange for contraceptive coverage for plan participants and beneficiaries by arranging for an issuer to assume sole responsibility for providing separate individual health insurance policies offering contraceptive coverage without cost sharing, premium, fee, or other charge to plan participants and beneficiaries, the eligible organization, or its plan. The Departments note that there would be no obligation on a third party administrator to enter into or continue a third party administration contract with an eligible organization if the third party administrator were to object to having to carry out this responsibility. Although this approach would place the legal responsibility for assuring compliance with section 2713 of the PHS Act solely on the third party administrator, it would have legal implications under ERISA's reporting, disclosure, claims processing, and fiduciary provisions for both the third party administrator and the eligible organization. The Departments seek comment specifically on potential issues arising under ERISA if the third party administrator were to become the designated plan administrator under section 3(16) of ERISA, and therefore a plan fiduciary, even for the limited purposes contemplated.

The Departments also seek comment on whether there is a need to provide an accommodation for self-insured plans of eligible organizations without third party administrators, and, if so, how best to ensure that participants and beneficiaries in such plans receive separate contraception coverage without cost sharing. No comments were submitted in response to the request in the ANPRM on the extent to which there are such plans without a third party administrator. The Departments continue to believe that there are very few, if any, self-insured plans of eligible organizations in this circumstance.

The Departments solicit comment on these alternative approaches.

3. Notice of Availability of Contraceptive Coverage and Coordination of Benefits

The proposed rules would direct a health insurance issuer providing separate individual health insurance policies for contraceptive coverage at no additional cost to participants and beneficiaries in plans of eligible organizations to provide a written notice to plan participants and beneficiaries regarding the availability of the separate contraceptive coverage. Issuers providing such contraceptive coverage would be responsible for providing the notice of availability of such coverage to participants and beneficiaries in both insured and self-insured group health plans of eligible organizations. The notice would be provided directly to plan participants and beneficiaries by the issuer, separate from but contemporaneous with (to the extent possible) any application materials distributed in connection with enrollment (or re-enrollment) in group coverage established, maintained, or arranged by the eligible

---

[13] To the extent the plan uses more than one third party administrator (for example, one pharmacy benefit manager (PBM) to handle claims administration for prescription drugs and another entity to handle claims for inpatient and outpatient medical/surgical benefits), each third party administrator would become the plan administrator upon receiving the copy of the self-certification with respect to the types of claims that it normally processes

(that is, the PBM would continue to handle claims for prescription drugs and the other entity would continue to handle claims for inpatient and outpatient medical/surgical benefits), and each would do so in accordance with section 2713 of the PHS Act (even if plan terms might otherwise provide differently) as plan administration with an independent funding source.

organization in any plan year to which the accommodation is to apply. As such, this notice generally would be provided annually. To satisfy the proposed notice requirement, issuers could use the model language set forth in the proposed rules or substantially similar language. The Departments request comments on the proposed notice requirement, including ways to improve the proposed model language, the timing and delivery (including electronically) of the notice to plan participants and beneficiaries, and whether this notice requirement could be combined with other existing notice requirements to simplify administration for issuers.

The Departments also seek comment on whether there are efficient ways to limit the benefits provided under the separate individual health insurance policies for contraceptive coverage to match the contraceptive benefits identified in the self-certification or whether the separate individual health insurances policies for contraceptive coverage should simply cover the full set of recommended contraceptive services. One option would be to require coordination of benefits such that the contraceptive coverage is secondary to the coverage provided by the group health plan established or maintained by the eligible organization (and any group health insurance coverage provided in connection with the plan). The Departments solicit comment on this issue.

d. Adjustments of Federally-Facilitated Exchange (FFE) User Fees

To fund contraceptive coverage for participants and beneficiaries in self-insured plans established or maintained by eligible organizations at no cost to plan participants or beneficiaries, HHS proposes that the existing proposed FFE user fee calculation, set forth in the December 7, 2012 proposed rule titled "Patient Protection and Affordable Care Act; HHS Notice of Benefit and Payment Parameters for 2014" (77 FR 73213), take into account that an issuer that offers a qualified health plan (QHP) through an FFE (or an affiliated issuer in a state without an FFE) provides such contraceptive coverage by reducing the amount of the user fee.

Consistent with Office of Management and Budget (OMB) Circular No. A25-R, the proposed revised FFE user fee calculation (which would result in an adjustment of the FFE user fee) would facilitate the proposed accommodation of self-insured plans established or maintained by eligible organizations by ensuring that plan participants and beneficiaries have separate individual health insurance policies for contraceptive coverage at no additional cost such that eligible organizations are not required to administer or fund such coverage. It would thereby support many of the goals of the Affordable Care Act, including improving the health of the population, reducing health care costs, providing access to health coverage, encouraging eligible organizations to continue to offer health coverage, and ensuring access to affordable QHPs via efficiently operated Exchanges. Moreover, as described in the 2012 final rules and the ANPRM, there are significant benefits associated with contraceptive coverage without cost sharing. Such contraceptive coverage significantly furthers the governmental interests in promoting public health and in promoting gender equality.

Under this proposal, the FFE user fee calculation would take into account contraceptive coverage that is provided by an issuer in a state without an FFE so long as the issuer is affiliated with an issuer that offers a QHP through an FFE.[14] The affiliated issuer would not be required to be a QHP issuer. An issuer that provides contraceptive coverage in a state without an FFE could offset the estimated cost of such coverage through an affiliated QHP issuer in a state with an FFE. This would encourage issuers to provide this type of coverage widely, to meet the goal of providing all plan participants and beneficiaries of self-insured plans established or maintained by eligible organizations with separate contraceptive coverage without cost sharing.

HHS proposes that, in order for the FFE user fee calculation to take into account that a QHP issuer (or an affiliated issuer) provides contraceptive coverage, the issuer providing coverage for contraceptive services for the plan participants and beneficiaries of a self-insured plan established or maintained by an eligible organization must provide coverage for all recommended contraceptive services identified in the self-certification of the eligible organization, and do so without cost sharing, premiums, fees, or other costs to the plan participants and beneficiaries. It also must pay the reasonable charge of third party administrators. The contraceptive coverage would be subject to all applicable federal and state laws, including state filing and rate review requirements. HHS seeks comment on ways to streamline the regulatory processes for, and minimize the costs of, obtaining approval of such coverage in all states.

HHS further proposes that, if an issuer provides contraceptive coverage to plan participants and beneficiaries of self-insured plans of eligible organizations at no additional cost, and it, or another issuer in the same issuer group, is required to pay an FFE user fee, an adjustment in the FFE user fee may be sought for the estimated cost of the contraceptive coverage. HHS would use the definition of issuer group proposed at 45 CFR 156.20 for this purpose. That section proposes that issuer group means all entities treated under section 52(a) or (b) of the Code as a member of the same controlled group of corporations as (or under common control with) a health insurance issuer, or issuers affiliated by the common use of a nationally licensed service mark. HHS seeks comment on whether this definition would provide the appropriate amount of flexibility in calculating the FFE user fee to correctly reflect the costs of issuers in states without an FFE, and on the advantages and disadvantages of permitting an adjustment in the FFE user fee with respect to unaffiliated issuers.

Under this proposal, the issuer providing the contraceptive coverage would provide certain information and documentation (jointly with the affiliated QHP issuer if applicable) to HHS. First, monthly data on the number of individuals for whom the contraceptive coverage is being provided would be submitted, along with an attestation that a copy of the self-certification of the eligible organization was provided by the third party administrator that arranged for the coverage for the plan participants and beneficiaries. Second, the issuer(s) would be required to provide an attestation that coverage for all recommended contraceptive services identified in the self-certification of the eligible organization is being provided, and being provided without cost sharing, premiums, fee, or other costs to the plan participants or beneficiaries. The issuer also would attest to HHS that it passed the portion of its adjustment attributable to reasonable charges by third party administrators on to those parties. Third, the issuer(s) would be required to identify the QHP(s) being offered through an FFE with respect to which the FFE user fee adjustment is to be made. In addition, if the issuer providing the contraceptive coverage is not the QHP issuer for which the adjustment in the FFE user fee is being sought, HHS proposes to require an attestation that the issuers are from the same issuer group. Finally, the issuer(s) would be required to submit to HHS an estimate of the cost of the contraceptive coverage, along with data or documentation supporting that estimate. HHS approval of the cost estimate would be required before a QHP issuer could receive an FFE user fee adjustment. HHS solicits comment on whether additional information or attestations should be required of issuers, for example, whether issuers should be required to attest that they provided the required notice of availability of contraceptive coverage to plan participants and beneficiaries.

HHS is considering two approaches to ensuring that the cost estimate reasonably reflects the cost of the contraceptive coverage. One approach would require the issuer(s) to submit to HHS the estimated per capita cost of the contraceptive coverage, as well as an actuarial memorandum prepared by a member of the American Academy of Actuaries in accordance with generally accepted actuarial principles and methodologies validating the estimate. HHS seeks comment on appropriate standards to guide such calculations. Under this approach, HHS expects that, in 2016 and beyond, the estimated cost of providing the contraceptive coverage would be based on the issuer's experience in previous years.

HHS also proposes that the estimate of the cost of the contraceptive coverage could include a reasonable charge for the issuer's administrative costs, including the costs of obtaining regulatory approval of the contraceptive coverage policy in the applicable state as well as a third party administrator's charge. HHS seeks comment on the magnitude of a reasonable administrative charge. HHS recognizes that the contraceptive coverage that issuers would provide under this proposed accommodation could see limited enrollment in a particular state. Given the potentially narrow markets available to the issuers of the contraceptive coverage, the per capita cost of administering this type of coverage may be higher than that for major medical coverage or other excepted benefits. On the other hand, given that a third party administrator would be connecting the plan participants and beneficiaries with the issuer, and there would therefore be reduced marketing costs, the administrative costs could be lessened. HHS seeks comment on the appropriate magnitude of these administrative costs generally, as well as ways of minimizing the administrative costs. In particular, HHS notes the issues associated with reimbursing for fixed costs, including the cost of obtaining regulatory approval for the policy in the applicable state. Fixed administrative costs could be amortized across the expected life of the policy, or could be reimbursed in the first year of

---

[14] For simplicity, the discussion that follows uses the shorthand "contraceptive coverage" to refer to contraceptive coverage for participants and beneficiaries in self-insured plans established or maintained by eligible organizations at no cost to plan participants or beneficiaries.

operation. HHS seeks comment on the appropriate manner of compensating for such costs.

HHS also seeks comment on whether HHS should limit the number of issuers providing the contraceptive coverage in each state with respect to which an FFE user fee adjustment may be made. If HHS were to modify its proposal in this way, HHS would add that an issuer must be willing and have the ability to offer the contraceptive coverage to any participant or beneficiary in a self-insured plan of an eligible organization who resides in the state.

HHS notes that the estimate of the cost of the contraceptive coverage could include a reasonable margin. HHS seeks comment on the magnitude of a reasonable margin, and notes that the proposed HHS Notice of Benefit and Payment Parameters for 2014 proposes a presumed margin of 3 percent within allowable administrative costs for the risk corridors program.

The proposed inclusion of reasonable administrative costs and margin in the estimate of the cost of the contraceptive coverage is intended to ensure that issuers receive reasonable compensation for providing the contraceptive coverage, as they would expect to receive in their other commercial businesses. HHS would review the submission by the issuer(s) to ensure that the cost estimate reflects reasonable assumptions and was calculated in accordance with applicable standards and generally accepted actuarial principles and methodologies. HHS would multiply the estimated per capita cost of the contraceptive coverage by the number of individuals being provided the contraceptive coverage each month in order to determine the magnitude of the FFE user fee adjustment. The amount should also take into account the reasonable administrative charges of third party administrators.

Alternatively, HHS could provide a national per capita estimate for the cost of the contraceptive coverage, which would also include adjustments for reasonable administrative costs and margin. This estimate could then be multiplied by the monthly enrollment in the contraceptive coverage in order to determine the magnitude of the FFE user fee adjustment for each QHP issuer concerned. This latter approach would provide for a more standardized approach, but could result in FFE user fee adjustments that do not fund the entire cost of the contraceptive coverage for some issuers, or that overcompensate other issuers. The former approach, however, would place a greater administrative burden on issuers, and would require a more in-depth review by HHS. HHS seeks comment on these two approaches, as well as alternative approaches for determining the estimated cost of the contraceptive coverage.

In both approaches to establishing an estimated cost of providing the contraceptive coverage described above, HHS seeks comment on the appropriate manner of accounting for a third party administrator's administrative costs of arranging for the contraceptive coverage in the issuer's estimated cost of the contraceptive coverage. For example, a flat administrative fee approved by HHS could be included in that estimated cost—with that flat administrative fee including an appropriate margin for the third party administrator. However, such an approach risks providing over-or under-incentives to the third party administrator for arranging for the contraceptive coverage, if the flat administrative fee is too high or too low. Alternatively, the third party administrator's actual reasonable charge, or actual reasonable administrative costs, for arranging the contraceptive coverage could be included in the estimated cost of the contraceptive coverage. HHS seeks comment on these and other approaches to estimating the third party administrator's administrative costs, and how HHS may ensure that they reflect reasonable administrative costs.

HHS proposes that, if the information described previously is provided and the cost estimate is approved, the FFE user fee will be reduced for the issuer of the identified QHP(s) by the amount of the approved estimate of the cost of the contraceptive coverage (multiplied by enrollment in the coverage for the month). While a highly unlikely occurrence given the relatively small population under consideration, HHS proposes that, if the amount of the adjustment is greater than the amount of the obligation to pay the FFE user fee in a particular month, the issuer of the identified QHP(s) will be provided a credit for the FFE user fee charged in succeeding months in the amount of the excess, consistent with OMB Circular No. A25-R. HHS seeks comment on whether a QHP issuer's FFE user fee should be adjusted for any excess in succeeding months at all; whether, if a QHP issuer's FFE user fee is adjusted for any excess in succeeding months, any time limit should be placed on how much later the adjustment should take place; and alternative methods of compensating an issuer with greater contraceptive coverage costs than its (or its affiliated QHP issuer's) FFE user fees.

HHS also proposes that an issuer providing contraceptive coverage for which the FFE user fee has been adjusted (whether the adjustment was provided to the issuer or an affiliated QHP issuer) must maintain for 10 years and make available to HHS upon request: documentation demonstrating that the contraceptive coverage was provided to participants or beneficiaries in a self-insured plan of an eligible organization, as evidenced by the copy of the self-certification that was provided by the third party administrator that arranged for such coverage; documentation demonstrating that the contraceptive coverage was provided without the imposition of any cost sharing, premium, fee, or other charge; documentation or data supporting the estimate of the cost of the contraceptive coverage; and documentation or data on the actual cost of providing the contraceptive coverage. This record-keeping requirement is consistent with timeframes under the False Claims Act, 31 U.S.C. 3729-3733. HHS is considering mechanisms for ensuring program integrity with respect to the provision of the contraceptive coverage under this proposed accommodation. These mechanisms may include requiring cooperation with audits and investigations, and requiring corrective action. HHS seeks comment on the oversight requirements that should be implemented with respect to the contraceptive coverage under this proposal.

Finally, HHS is proposing that a QHP issuer that is to receive an FFE user fee adjustment as described above prior to January 1, 2014, will be provided a credit in the amount of the adjustment beginning in January 2014. HHS seeks comment on issuers' ability to fund the contraceptive coverage under the proposal between the end of the temporary enforcement safe harbor and December 31, 2013, if HHS is not able to provide the FFE user fee adjustment until January 2014.

The Departments also seek comment on alternative ways to finance separate contraceptive coverage without cost sharing with respect to participants and beneficiaries in self-insured plans of eligible organizations.

e. Treatment of Multiple Employer Group Health Plans

The Departments recognize that, in some instances, several affiliated employers—only some of which are eligible organizations or religious employers—offer health coverage to their employees and their covered dependents through a single group health plan. The Departments considered allowing all employers in such instances to qualify for an accommodation or the religious employer exemption if any single employer met the definition of eligible organization or religious employer. Alternatively, the Departments considered precluding all employers in such instances from qualifying for an accommodation or the religious employer exemption if any single employer failed to meet the definition of eligible organization or religious employer.

The Departments propose to make the accommodation or the religious employer exemption available on an employer-by-employer basis. That is, each employer would have to independently meet the definition of eligible organization or religious employer in order to take advantage of the accommodation or the religious employer exemption with respect to its employees and their covered dependents. Conversely, an employer that did not meet the definition of eligible organization or religious employer could not take advantage of the accommodation or the religious employer exemption with respect to its employees and their covered dependents. This approach would prevent what could be viewed as a potential way for employers that are not eligible for the accommodation or the religious employer exemption to avoid the contraceptive coverage requirement by offering coverage in conjunction with an eligible organization or religious employer through a common plan. The Departments seek comment on this approach, including comments on the extent to which an employer-by-employer approach would pose administrative challenges for plans and issuers, as well as comments on alternative approaches.

f. Student Health Insurance Coverage

Many institutions of higher education administer programs that provide students and their dependents with access to health coverage. Some institutions of higher education sponsor self-insured student health plans, but the vast majority of student health plans are insured, meaning that a health insurance issuer contracts with the institution of higher education to issue a blanket health insurance policy, from which students can buy coverage. Under final rules published by HHS on March 21, 2012, student health insurance coverage is a type of individual health insurance coverage offered to students and their covered dependents under a written agreement between an institution of higher education and an issuer.[15]

Some religiously affiliated colleges and universities object to signing a written agreement for student health insurance coverage that provides benefits for contraceptive services. Such colleges and universities sometimes include funding for student health plans in their student financial aid packages and object to funding student health plans that include coverage for contraceptive services.

The proposed rules would provide for an accommodation for student health insurance coverage arranged by a nonprofit religious institution of higher education with religious objections to contraceptive coverage comparable to the proposed accommodation for group health insurance coverage provided in connection with a group health plan established or maintained by a nonprofit religious organization with religious objections to contraceptive coverage. Accordingly, among other things, upon receiving a copy of the self-certification from an institution of higher education that meets the criteria for being an eligible organization, an issuer offering student health insurance coverage would provide contraceptive coverage, without cost sharing or additional premium, fee, or other charge, directly to student enrollees and their covered dependents, independent of the issuer's written agreement with the institution of higher education to offer the student health plan. The Departments solicit comments on this proposal.

g. Contraceptive-Only Excepted Benefits

In order to implement the proposed accommodations, it would be necessary and appropriate to establish a new contraceptive-only excepted benefits category. Sections 2722(c)(2) and 2763(b) of the PHS Act provide that the requirements of parts A and B of title XXVII of the PHS Act do not apply to any individual health insurance coverage in relation to its provision of excepted benefits described in section 2791(c)(2) of the PHS Act if the benefits are provided under a separate policy, certificate, or contract of insurance. Section 2791(c)(2) of the PHS Act provides that this category of excepted benefits includes limited scope dental or vision benefits, as well as benefits for long-term care, nursing home care, home health care, or community-based care, or any combination thereof. The law authorizes similar limited benefits to be specified in rule as excepted benefits. Additionally, section 2792 of the PHS Act authorizes HHS to promulgate such rules as may be necessary or appropriate to carry out the provisions of title XXVII of the PHS Act. Parallel provisions in section 734 of ERISA and section 9833 of the Code do the same with respect to the Departments of Labor and the Treasury.

Pursuant to the authority in section 2791(c)(2) of the PHS Act (and companion provisions in ERISA and the Code), the proposed rules would provide that benefits for contraceptive services only, when provided under a separate individual market health insurance policy, certificate, or contract of insurance constitute excepted benefits (subject to the conditions discussed later in this section). The Departments propose to establish this new category of excepted benefits to ensure that individual health insurance policies providing contraceptive coverage offered by an issuer pursuant to the proposed accommodations are not subject to certain generally applicable PHS Act and Affordable Care Act requirements, such as guaranteed availability (section 2702 of the PHS Act) given the unique nature of this coverage. Thus, for example, while issuers would offer this coverage to plan participants and beneficiaries in plans established or maintained by eligible organizations, issuers would not be required to make this coverage available to all other individuals in a state. These proposed amendments are reflected in proposed 45 CFR 148.220(b).

Notwithstanding this proposed excepted benefits status, the Departments believe that a core set of basic consumer protection requirements should apply to individual health insurance policies providing contraceptive-only coverage. This core set of consumer protection requirements would be drawn from the broader set of requirements applicable to individual health insurance coverage under the PHS Act. This core set would include the requirements regarding guaranteed renewability of coverage (section 2703 of the PHS Act), the prohibition against lifetime and annual dollar limits on benefits (section 2711 of the PHS Act), the prohibition against rescissions of coverage (section 2712 of the PHS Act), and internal appeals and external review rights (section 2719 of the PHS Act). Accordingly, pursuant to the authority in section 2792 of the PHS Act to promulgate rules that are "necessary or appropriate" to carry out section 2713 of the PHS Act (and companion provisions in ERISA and the Code), the proposed rules would require compliance with these provisions of federal law as a condition of excepted benefits status. The Departments welcome comments on which requirements of the PHS Act, ERISA, and the Code should or should not apply to individual health insurance policies that provide contraceptive-only coverage. We also seek comments on how to simplify the establishment of these products and how best to ensure their availability in all states, including alternatives to excepted benefits in any state without any such product.

D. No Effect on Other Law

The religious employer exemption and accommodations in these proposed rules are intended to have meaning solely with respect to the contraceptive coverage requirement under section 2713 of the PHS Act and the companion provisions of ERISA and the Code. Whether an employer or organization (including an institution of higher education) is designated as "religious" for these purposes is not intended as a judgment about the mission, sincerity, or commitment of the employer or organization (including an institution of higher education), or intended to differentiate among the religious merits, commitment, mission, or public or private standing of religious entities. The use of such designation is limited solely to defining the class of employers or organizations (including institutions of higher education) that would qualify for the religious employer exemption and accommodations under these proposed rules. The definition of religious employer or eligible organization in these proposed rules is not being proposed to apply with respect to, or relied upon for the interpretation of, any other provision of the PHS Act, ERISA, the Code, or any other provision of federal law, nor is it intended to set a precedent for any other purpose. For example, nothing in these proposed rules should be construed as affecting the interpretation of federal or state civil rights statutes, such as Title VII of the Civil Rights Act of 1964 or Title IX of the Education Amendments of 1972.

Furthermore, nothing in these proposed rules would preclude employers or others from expressing their opposition, if any, to the use of contraceptives; require anyone to use contraceptives; or require health care providers to prescribe contraceptives if doing so is against their religious beliefs.

Finally, the provisions of these proposed rules would not prevent states from enacting stronger consumer protections than these minimum standards. Federal health insurance regulation generally establishes a federal floor to ensure that individuals in every state have certain basic protections. State health insurance laws requiring coverage for contraceptive services that provide more access to contraceptive coverage than the federal standards would therefore continue under the proposed rules. The Departments solicit comment on the interaction between state law and these proposed rules.

IV. Economic Impact and Paperwork Burden

A. Executive Orders 12866 and 13563—Department of Health and Human Services and Department of Labor

Executive Orders 12866 and 13563 direct agencies to assess all costs and benefits of available regulatory alternatives and, if regulation is necessary, to select regulatory approaches that maximize net benefits (including potential economic, environmental, and public health and safety effects; distributive impacts; and equity). Executive Order 13563 emphasizes the importance of quantifying both costs and benefits, reducing costs, harmonizing rules, and promoting flexibility.

Section 3(f) of Executive Order 12866 defines a "significant regulatory action" as an action that is likely to result in a rule: (1) Having an annual effect on the economy of $100 million or more in any one year, or adversely and materially affecting a sector of the economy, productivity, competition, jobs, the environment, public health or safety, or state, local, or tribal governments or communities (also referred to as "economically significant"); (2) creating a serious inconsistency or otherwise interfering with an action taken or planned by another agency; (3) materially altering the budgetary impacts of entitlement grants, user fees, or loan programs or the rights and obligations of recipients thereof; or (4) raising novel legal or policy issues arising out of legal mandates, the President's priorities, or the principles set forth in the Executive Order.

A regulatory impact analysis must be prepared for major rules with economically significant effects ($100 million or more in any one year), and an "economically significant" regulatory action is subject to review by the Office of Management and Budget (OMB). The Departments have concluded that these proposed rules are not likely to have eco-

---

[15] Because student health plans are not employment-based, they are not group health plans under federal law. Section 2791(a)(1) of the PHS Act defines "group health plan" as an employee welfare benefit plan as defined in section 3(1) of ERISA to the extent that the plan provides medical care to employees and their dependents directly or through insurance, reimbursement, or otherwise.

nomic impacts of $100 million or more in any one year, and therefore do not meet the definition of "economically significant" under Executive Order 12866.

1. Need for Regulatory Action

As stated earlier in this preamble, the Departments previously issued amended interim final rules authorizing an exemption for group health plans established or maintained by religious employers (and any group health insurance coverage provided in connection with such plans) from certain coverage requirements under section 2713 of the PHS Act (76 FR 46621, August 3, 2011). The amended interim final rules were finalized on February 15, 2012 (77 FR 8725). The Departments are proposing in these proposed rules to amend the definition of religious employer in the HHS rule at 45 CFR 147.130(a)(1)(iv)(B) (incorporated by reference in the rules of the Departments of Labor and the Treasury) by eliminating the first three prongs of the definition of religious employer that was established in the 2012 final rules and clarifying the fourth prong. Under this proposal, an employer that is an organization that is organized and operates as a nonprofit entity and is referred to in section 6033(a)(3)(A)(i) or (iii) of the Code would be considered a religious employer and its group health plan would qualify for the exemption from the requirement to cover contraceptive services. In addition, the proposed rules would establish accommodations for health coverage established or maintained or arranged by eligible organizations, which have religious objections to contraceptive coverage, while providing women contraceptive coverage without cost sharing.

2. Anticipated Effects

The Departments expect that these proposed rules would not result in any additional significant burden on or costs to the affected entities.

B. Special Analyses—Department of the Treasury

For purposes of the Department of the Treasury, it has been determined that this notice of proposed rulemaking is not a significant regulatory action as defined in Executive Order 12866, as amended by Executive Order 13563. Therefore, a regulatory assessment is not required. It has also been determined that section 553(b) of the Administrative Procedure Act (5 U.S.C. chapter 5) does not apply to this proposed rule. It is hereby certified that the collections of information contained in this notice of proposed rulemaking would not have a significant impact on a substantial number of small entities. Accordingly, a regulatory flexibility analysis under the Regulatory Flexibility Act (5 U.S.C. chapter 6) is not required.

The proposed rules would require each organization seeking accommodation under the proposed rules to self-certify that it meets the definition of eligible organization in the proposed rules. Each organization must self-certify that: (1) On account of religious objections, it opposes providing coverage for some or all of the contraceptive items or services that it would otherwise be required to provide; (2) it is organized and operates as a nonprofit entity; and (3) it holds itself out as a religious organization. The self-certification must be executed by an authorized representative of the organization. The organization must maintain the self-certification in its records for each plan year to which the accommodation is to apply and make it available for examination upon request. The proposed rules would also require each eligible organization that establishes or maintains an insured group health plan to provide a copy of its self-certification to the group health insurance issuer. If the group health plan of the eligible organization is self-insured, the proposed rules would direct the eligible organization to provide a copy of its self-certification to the third party administrator.

The Departments intend to specify in guidance the form to be used for the self-certification, similar to the form previously prescribed in guidance for the temporary enforcement safe harbor. The Departments are unable to estimate the number of eligible organizations that would seek an accommodation. The Departments seek comment on the likely number of eligible organizations seeking an accommodation. Of the eligible organizations, some would likely be small entities. It is estimated that each eligible organization would need only approximately 50 minutes of labor (30 minutes of clerical labor at a cost of $30.64 per hour, 10 minutes for a manager at a cost of $55.22 per hour, 5 minutes for legal counsel at a cost of $83.10 per hour, and 5 minutes for a senior executive at a cost of $112.43 per hour) each year to prepare and provide the information in the self-certification. This would not be a significant economic impact. For these reasons, this information collection requirement would not have a significant impact on a substantial number of small entities.

The proposed rules also would require health insurance issuers providing separate contraceptive coverage to provide written notice to plan participants and beneficiaries regarding the availability of the contraceptive coverage. The notice would be provided separate from but contemporaneous with (to the extent possible) any application materials distributed in connection with enrollment (or re-enrollment) in group coverage established, maintained, or arranged by the eligible organization in any plan year to which the accommodation is to apply. The proposed rules contain model language for issuers to use to satisfy the notice requirement. There are 446 issuers in the individual and group markets. It is believed that very few, if any, of them are small entities. Moreover, the cost for preparation and distribution of the notice would not be significant. It is estimated that each issuer would need approximately 1 hour of clerical labor (at $31.64 per hour) and 15 minutes of management review (at $55.22 per hour) to prepare the notices for a total cost of approximately $44. It is estimated that each notice would require $0.46 in postage and $0.05 in materials cost (paper and ink) and the total postage and materials cost for each notice sent via mail would be $0.51. For these reasons, these information collection requirements would not have a significant impact on a substantial number of small entities.

HHS is soliciting public comment on each of these issues for purposes of the following section as well.

Pursuant to section 7805(f) of the Code, this proposed rule has been submitted to the Chief Counsel for Advocacy of the Small Business Administration for comment on its impact on small business.

C. Paperwork Reduction Act—Department of Health and Human Services

Under the Paperwork Reduction Act of 1995, HHS is required to provide 60-day notice in the **Federal Register** and solicit public comment before an information collection requirement (ICR) is submitted to the Office of Management and Budget (OMB) for review and approval. These proposed rules contain proposed ICRs that are subject to review by OMB. A description of these provisions is given in the following paragraphs with an estimate of the annual burden. In order to fairly evaluate whether an ICR should be approved by OMB, section 3506(c)(2)(A) of the Paperwork Reduction Act of 1995 requires that HHS solicit public comment on the following issues:

- The need for the information collection and its usefulness in carrying out the proper functions of HHS.

- The accuracy of our estimate of the information collection burden.

- The quality, utility, and clarity of the information to be collected.

- Recommendations to minimize the information collection burden on the affected public, including automated collection techniques.

HHS is soliciting public comment on each of these issues for the following sections of these proposed rules that contain proposed ICRs. Average labor costs (including fringe benefits) used to estimate the costs are calculated using data available from the Bureau of Labor Statistics.

1. Self-Certification (§§ 147.131(b)(4), 147.131(c)(1), 147.131(c)(2))

Each organization seeking accommodation under the proposed rules would be required to self-certify that it meets the definition of an eligible organization. The self-certification would be executed by an authorized representative of the organization and would also specify the contraceptive services for which the organization will not establish, maintain, administer, or fund coverage. The self-certification would not be submitted to any of the Departments. The form that would be used by organizations for their self-certification would be specified. This form is available for inspection at *http://www.cms.gov/Regulations-and-Guidance/Legislation/PaperworkReductionActof1995/PRA-Listing.html*. The organization would maintain the self-certification in its records for each plan year to which the accommodation is to apply. The eligible organization would need to provide a copy of its self-certification to a health insurance issuer (for insured group health plans or student health insurance coverage) or to a third party administrator (for self-insured group health plans).

HHS does not have an estimate for how many organizations would seek an accommodation. HHS seeks comment on the likely number of organizations seeking an accommodation or the number of participants and beneficiaries in the plans of such organizations. Therefore, the burden for only one eligible organization, as opposed to all eligible organizations in total, is estimated. It is assumed that, for each eligible organization, clerical staff would gather and enter the necessary information, send the self-certification electronically to the issuer or third party administrator, and retain a copy for record-keeping, a manager and legal counsel would review it, and a senior executive would execute it. HHS estimates that an organization would need approximately 50 minutes (30 minutes of clerical labor at a cost of $30.64 per hour, 10 minutes for a manager at a cost of $55.22 per hour, 5 minutes for legal counsel at a cost of $83.10 per hour, and 5 minutes for a senior executive at a cost of $112.43 per hour) to execute the self-certification. Therefore, the total annual burden for preparing and providing the information in the self-certification would be approximately $41 for each eligible organization.

With respect to self-insured plans of eligible organizations, the third party administrator would provide a health insurance issuer a copy of the self-certification of the eligible organization. The third party administrator would be able to provide a copy of the self-certification to the issuer electronically at minimal cost.

2. Notice of Availability of Contraceptive Coverage (§ 147.131(d))

The proposed rules would direct a health insurance issuer providing separate individual contraceptive coverage at no additional cost to participants and beneficiaries in insured plans of eligible organizations (or to student enrollees and covered dependents in student health insurance coverage arranged by eligible organizations) and to participants and beneficiaries in self-insured plans of eligible organizations whose coverage is automatically arranged for them by a third party administrator to provide a written notice to such plan participants and beneficiaries (or to such student enrollees and covered dependents) regarding the separate contraceptive coverage. The notice would be separate from but contemporaneous with (to the extent possible) any application materials distributed in connection with enrollment (or re-enrollment) in group coverage of the eligible organization in any plan year to which the accommodation is to apply and would be provided annually. To satisfy the proposed notice requirement, issuers could use the model language set forth in the proposed rules or substantially similar language.

It is unknown how many issuers provide health insurance coverage in connection with insured plans of eligible organizations or how many third party administrators provide services to self-insured plans of eligible organizations or how many issuers would provide separate individual contraceptive coverage to plan participants and beneficiaries of self-insured plans of eligible organizations. Therefore, the burden for only one issuer, as opposed to all issuers in total, is estimated. It is estimated that each issuer would need approximately 1 hour of clerical labor (at $31.64 per hour) and 15 minutes of management review (at $55.22 per hour) to prepare the notices for a total cost of approximately $44. It is estimated that each notice would require $0.46 in postage and $0.05 in materials cost (paper and ink) and the total postage and materials cost for each notice sent via mail would be $0.51.

3. FFE User Fee Adjustments (§ 156.50(d))

In order for a QHP issuer to be eligible for the proposed FFE user fee adjustment, the proposed rules would provide that the issuer providing the contraceptive coverage would provide certain information and documentation (jointly with the affiliated QHP issuer for which the reduction in the FFE user fee is being sought, if the issuers are not the same) to HHS. First, monthly data on the number of individuals for whom the contraceptive coverage is being provided would be required, along with an attestation that a copy of the self-certification of the eligible organization was provided by the third party administrator that arranged for the coverage for the plan participants and beneficiaries. Second, the issuer would provide an attestation that coverage for all recommended contraceptive services identified in the self-certification of the eligible organization is being provided, and being provided without cost sharing, premiums, fee, or other costs to the plan participants or beneficiaries. The issuer also would attest to HHS that it passed the portion of its adjustment attributable to reasonable charges by third party administrators on to those parties. Third, the issuer(s) would identify the QHP(s) being offered through an FFE with respect to which the FFE user fee reduction is to be applied. In addition, where the issuer providing the contraceptive coverage is not the QHP issuer for which the reduction in the FFE user fee is being sought, an attestation that the issuers are from the same issuer group would be submitted. Finally, the issuer(s) would submit to HHS an estimate of the cost of the contraceptive coverage, along with data or documentation supporting that estimate. HHS approval of the cost estimate would be required before a QHP issuer could receive an FFE user fee adjustment.

Although the number of QHP issuers that would seek an FFE user fee adjustment is unknown at this point, HHS anticipates that a small number of issuer groups would provide such contraceptive coverage nationwide, and that, for purposes of efficiency, those issuer groups would consolidate their applications for FFE user fee adjustments with fewer than 9 issuers of QHPs on FFEs. Collections from fewer than 10 persons are exempt from the Paperwork Reduction Act under 44 U.S.C. 3502(3)(A)(i). Therefore, HHS does not plan to seek OMB approval for this proposed ICR. However, in the event that, by the time of the issuance of the final rules, HHS believes that the number of QHP

issuers that would seek an FFE user fee adjustment would be greater than 9, HHS would seek OMB approval for this proposed ICR.

To obtain copies of the supporting statement and any related forms for the proposed ICRs referenced above, access CMS's web site at *http://www.cms.gov/Regulations-and-Guidance/Legislation/PaperworkReductionActof1995/PRA-Listing.html* or email your request, including your address, phone number, OMB number, and CMS document identifier, to *paperwork@cms.hhs.gov,* or call the Reports Clearance Office at (410) 786-1326.

If you comment on these proposed ICRs, please do either of the following:

1. Submit your comments electronically as specified in the **ADDRESSES** section of these proposed rules; or

2. Submit your comments to the Office of Information and Regulatory Affairs, Office of Management and Budget, Attention: CMS Desk Officer, 9968-P, FAX: (202) 395-5806, or email: *OIRA_submission@omb.eop.gov.*

D. Paperwork Reduction Act—Department of Labor and Department of the Treasury

As noted above, each organization seeking accommodation under the proposed rules would be required to self-certify that it meets the definition of an eligible organization. This proposed requirement, which is the same in all three sets of proposed rules, is set out in proposed 26 CFR 54.9815-2713A(b)(4) and proposed 29 CFR 2590.715-2713A(b)(4). The Departments are soliciting public comments for 60 days concerning this record-keeping requirement. The Departments will submit a copy of these proposed rules to OMB in accordance with 44 U.S.C. 3507(d) for review of the proposed ICRs. The Departments and OMB are particularly interested in comments that:

• Evaluate whether the collection of information is necessary for the proper performance of the functions of the agency, including whether the information will have practical utility;

• Evaluate the accuracy of the agency's estimate of the burden of the collection of information, including the validity of the methodology and assumptions used;

• Enhance the quality, utility, and clarity of the information to be collected; and

• Minimize the burden of the collection of information on those who are to respond, including through the use of appropriate automated, electronic, mechanical, or other technological collection techniques or other forms of information technology, for example, by permitting electronic submission of responses.

Comments should be sent to the Office of Information and Regulatory Affairs, Attention: Desk Officer for the Employee Benefits Security Administration either by Fax to (202) 395-5806 or by email to *oira_submission@omb.eop.gov.* A copy of the proposed ICRs may be obtained by contacting the PRA addressee: G. Christopher Cosby, Office of Policy and Research, Department of Labor, Employee Benefits Security Administration, 200 Constitution Avenue NW., Room N-5718, Washington, DC 20210; telephone: (202) 693-8410; Fax: (202) 219-4745 (please note that these numbers are not toll-free numbers); email: *ebsa.opr@dol.gov.* Proposed ICRs submitted to OMB also are available at *www.reginfo.gov (http://www.reginfo.gov/public/do/PRAMain).*

Consistent with the HHS analysis presented above, the Departments do not have an estimate for how many organizations would seek an accommodation. The Departments seek comment on the likely number of organizations seeking an accommodation and the number of participants and beneficiaries in the plans of such organizations. The Departments rely on the same estimates noted above: 50 minutes per organization to execute the self-certification (*i.e.,* approximately $41 for each eligible organization).

With respect to self-insured plans of eligible organizations, the third party administrator would provide a health insurance issuer a copy of the self-certification of the eligible organization. The third party administrator would be able to provide a copy of the self-certification to the issuer electronically at minimal cost.

The Departments note that persons are not required to respond to, and generally are not subject to any penalty for failing to comply with, an ICR unless the ICR has a valid OMB control number. The paperwork burden estimates are summarized as follows:

Type of Review: New collection.

Agencies: Employee Benefits Security Administration, Department of Labor; Internal Revenue Service, Department of the Treasury.

Title: Self-Certification; Preventive Services Coverage.

OMB Number: XXXX-XXXX; XXXX-XXXX.

Affected Public: Business or other for-profit; not-for-profit institutions.

Total Respondents: Unknown.

Total Responses: Unknown.

Frequency of Response: Once.

Estimated Total Annual Burden Hours: 50 minutes per respondent.

Estimated Total Annual Burden Cost: Unknown.

V. Unfunded Mandates Reform Act

For purposes of the Unfunded Mandates Reform Act of 1995 (Pub. L. 104-4), as well as Executive Order 12875, these proposed rules do not include any proposed federal mandate that may result in expenditures by state, local, or tribal governments, nor does it include any proposed federal mandates that may impose an annual burden of $100 million, adjusted for inflation, or more on the private sector.[16]

VI. Federalism—Department of Health and Human Services and Department of Labor

Executive Order 13132 outlines fundamental principles of federalism, and requires the adherence to specific criteria by federal agencies in the process of their formulation and implementation of policies that have "substantial direct effects" on states, the relationship between the federal government and states, or the distribution of power and responsibilities among the various levels of government. Federal agencies promulgating rules that have these federalism implications must consult with state and local officials, and describe the extent of their consultation and the nature of the concerns of state and local officials in the preamble to the rules.

In the Departments' view, these proposed rules have federalism implications, but the federal implications are substantially mitigated because, with respect to health insurance issuers, 15 states have enacted specific laws, rules, or bulletins that meet or exceed the federal standards requiring coverage of specified preventive services without cost sharing. The remaining states which provide oversight for these federal law requirements are doing so using their general authority to enforce these federal standards. Therefore, the proposed rules are not likely to require substantial additional oversight of states by HHS.

In general, section 514 of ERISA provides that state laws are superseded to the extent that they relate to any covered employee benefit plan, and preserves state laws that regulate insurance, banking, or securities. ERISA also prohibits states from regulating a covered plan as an insurance or investment company or bank. HIPAA added a new preemption provision to ERISA (as well as to the PHS Act) narrowly preempting state requirements for group health insurance coverage. States may continue to apply state law requirements but not to the extent that such requirements prevent the application of the federal requirement that group health insurance coverage provided in connection with group health plans provide coverage for specified preventive services without cost sharing. HIPAA's Conference Report states that the conferees intended the narrowest preemption of state laws with regard to health insurance issuers (H.R. Conf. Rep. No. 104-736, 104th Cong. 2d Session 205, 1996). State insurance laws that are more stringent than the federal requirement are unlikely to "prevent the application of" the preventive services coverage provision, and therefore are not preempted. Accordingly, states have significant latitude to impose requirements on health insurance issuers that are more restrictive than those in federal law.

Guidance conveying this interpretation was published in the **Federal Register** on April 8, 1997 (62 FR 16904), and December 30, 2004 (69 FR 78720), and these proposed rules would clarify and implement the statute's minimum standards and would not significantly reduce the discretion given the states by the statute.

The PHS Act provides that the states may enforce the provisions of title XXVII of the PHS Act as they pertain to issuers, but that the Secretary of HHS will enforce any provisions that a state does not have authority to enforce or that a state has failed to substantially enforce. When exercising its responsibility to enforce provisions of the PHS Act, HHS works cooperatively with the state for the purpose of addressing the state's concerns and avoiding conflicts with the exercise of state authority.[17] HHS has developed procedures to implement its enforcement responsibilities, and to afford states the maximum opportunity to enforce the PHS Act's requirements in the first instance. In compliance with Executive Order 13132's requirement that agencies examine closely any policies that may have federalism implications or limit the policymaking discretion of states, the Departments have engaged in numerous efforts to consult and work cooperatively with affected state and local officials.

In conclusion, throughout the process of developing these proposed rules, to the extent feasible within the specific preemption provisions of ERISA and the PHS Act, the Departments have attempted to balance states' interests in regulating health plans and health insurance issuers, and the rights of those individuals that Congress intended to protect in the PHS Act.

VII. Statutory Authority

The Department of the Treasury regulations are proposed to be adopted pursuant to the authority contained in sections 7805 and 9833 of the Code.

The Department of Labor regulations are proposed to be adopted pursuant to the authority contained in 29 U.S.C. 1002(16), 1027, 1059, 1135, 1161-1168, 1169, 1181-1183, 1181 note, 1185, 1185a, 1185b, 1185d, 1191, 1191a, 1191b, and 1191c; sec. 101(g), Public Law 104-191, 110 Stat. 1936; sec. 401(b), Public Law 105-200, 112 Stat. 645 (42 U.S.C. 651 note); sec. 512(d), Public Law 110-343, 122 Stat. 3881; sec. 1001, 1201, and 1562(e), Public Law 111-148, 124 Stat. 119, as amended by Public Law 111-152, 124 Stat. 1029; Secretary of Labor's Order 3-2010, 75 FR 55354 (September 10, 2010).

The Department of Health and Human Services regulations are proposed to be adopted pursuant to the authority contained in sections 2701 through 2763, 2791, and 2792 of the PHS Act (42 U.S.C. 300gg through 300gg-63, 300gg-91, and 300gg-92), as amended; and Title I of the Affordable Care Act, sections 1301-1304, 1311-1312, 1321-1322, 1324, 1334, 1342-1343, 1401-1402, and 1412, Public Law 111-148, 124 Stat. 119 (42 U.S.C. 18021-18024, 18031-18032, 18041-18042, 18044, 18054, 18061, 18063, 18071, 18082, 26 U.S.C. 36B, and 31 U.S.C. 9701).

List of Subjects

26 CFR Part 54

Excise taxes, Health care, Health insurance, Pensions, Reporting and recordkeeping requirements.

29 CFR Part 2590

Continuation coverage, Disclosure, Employee benefit plans, Group health plans, Health care, Health insurance, Medical child support, Reporting and recordkeeping requirements.

45 CFR Part 147

Health care, Health insurance, Reporting and recordkeeping requirements, and State regulation of health insurance.

45 CFR Part 148

Administrative practice and procedure, Health care, Health insurance, Penalties, and Reporting and recordkeeping requirements.

45 CFR Part 156

Administrative practice and procedure, Advertising, Advisory committees, Brokers, Conflict of interest, Consumer protection, Grant programs—health, Grants administration, Health care, Health insurance, Health maintenance organization (HMO), Health records, Hospitals, American Indian/Alaska Natives, Individuals with disabilities, Loan programs—health, Organization and functions (Government agencies), Medicaid, Public assistance programs, Reporting and recordkeeping requirements, State and local governments, Sunshine Act, Technical assistance, Women, and Youth.

Department of the Treasury

Internal Revenue Service

Accordingly, 26 CFR part 54 is proposed to be amended as follows:

PART 54—PENSION EXCISE TAXES

■ **Paragraph 1.** The authority citation for part 54 continues to read in part as follows:

Authority: 26 U.S.C. 7805. * * *

---

[16] In early 2013, that threshold level is approximately $139 million.

[17] This authority applies to insurance issued with respect to group health plans generally, including plans covering employees of church organizations. Thus, this discussion of federalism applies to all group health insurance coverage that is subject to the PHS Act, including those church plans that provide coverage through a health insurance issuer (but not to church plans that do not provide coverage through a health insurance issuer).

■ **Par. 2.** Section 54.9801-2 is amended by revising the definition of *excepted benefits* as follows:

§ 54.9801-2 Definitions.

* * * * *

Excepted benefits means the benefits described as excepted in § 54.9831(c), or 45 CFR § 148.220 (describing when individual health insurance policies constitute excepted benefits).

* * * * *

■ **Par. 3.** Section 54.9815-2713 is amended by adding paragraph (a)(1) introductory text and revising paragraph (a)(1)(iv) to read as follows:

§ 54.9815-2713 Coverage of preventive health services.

(a) *Services*—(1) *In general.* Beginning at the time described in paragraph (b) of this section and subject to § 54.9815-2713A, a group health plan, or a health insurance issuer offering group health insurance coverage, must provide coverage for all of the following items and services, and may not impose any cost sharing requirement (such as a copayment, coinsurance, or a deductible) with respect to those items and services:

* * * * *

(iv) With respect to women, to the extent not described in paragraph (a)(1)(i) of this section, evidence-informed preventive care and screenings provided for in binding comprehensive health plan coverage guidelines supported by the Health Resources and Services Administration, in accordance with 45 CFR 147.131(a).

* * * * *

■ **Par. 4.** Section 54.9815-2713A is added to read as follows:

§ 54.9815-2713A Accommodations in connection with coverage of preventive health services.

(a) *Eligible organizations.* An eligible organization is an organization that satisfies all of the following requirements:

(1) The organization opposes providing coverage for some or all of any contraceptive services required to be covered under § 54.9815-2713(a)(1)(iv) on account of religious objections.

(2) The organization is organized and operates as a nonprofit entity.

(3) The organization holds itself out as a religious organization.

(4) The organization maintains in its records a self-certification, made in the manner and form specified by the Secretary of Health and Human Services, for each plan year to which the accommodation is to apply, executed by a person authorized to make the certification on behalf of the organization, indicating that the organization satisfies the criteria in paragraphs (a)(1) through (3) of this section, and, specifying those contraceptive services for which the organization will not establish, maintain, administer, or fund coverage, and makes such certification available for examination upon request.

(b) *Contraceptive coverage—self-insured group health plan coverage.* [Reserved.]

(c) *Contraceptive coverage—insured group health plan coverage*—(1) A group health plan established or maintained by an eligible organization and that provides benefits through one or more issuers complies with any requirement under § 54.9815-2713(a)(1)(iv) to provide contraceptive coverage if the eligible organization or plan administrator furnishes each issuer that would otherwise provide coverage for any contraceptive services required to be covered under § 54.9815-2713(a)(1)(iv) with a copy of the self-certification described in paragraph (a)(4) of this section.

(2) A group health insurance issuer that receives a copy of the self-certification described in paragraph (a)(4) of this section with respect to a plan for which the issuer would otherwise provide coverage for any contraceptive services required to be covered under § 54.9815-2713(a)(1)(iv) must automatically provide health insurance coverage for any contraceptive services required to be covered by § 54.9815-2713(a)(1)(iv) and identified in the self-certification, through a separate health insurance policy that is excepted under 45 CFR 148.220(b)(7), for each plan participant and beneficiary. The issuer providing the individual market excepted benefits policy may not impose any cost sharing requirement (such as a copayment, coinsurance, or a deductible) with respect to coverage of those services, or impose any premium, fee, or other charge, or portion thereof, directly or indirectly, on the eligible organization, its group health plan, or plan participants or beneficiaries with respect to coverage of those services.

(d) *Notice of availability of contraceptive coverage.* An issuer providing contraceptive coverage arranged pursuant to paragraph (b) or (c) of this section must provide to plan participants and beneficiaries written notice of the availability of the contraceptive coverage, separate from but contemporaneous with (to the extent possible) application materials distributed in connection with enrollment (or re-enrollment) in group coverage of the eligible organization for any plan year to which this paragraph applies. The following model language, or substantially similar language, may be used to satisfy the notice requirement of this paragraph: "The organization that establishes and maintains, or arranges, your health coverage has certified that your group health plan qualifies for an accommodation with respect to the federal requirement to cover all Food and Drug Administration-approved contraceptive services for women, as prescribed by a health care provider, without cost sharing. This means that your health coverage will not cover the following contraceptive services: [contraceptive services specified in self-certification]. Instead, these contraceptive services will be covered through a separate individual health insurance policy, which is not administered or funded by, or connected in any way to, your health coverage. You and any covered dependents will be enrolled in this separate individual health insurance policy at no additional cost to you. If you have any questions about this notice, contact [contact information for health insurance issuer]."

Department of Labor

Employee Benefits Security Administration

For the reasons stated in the preamble, the Department of Labor proposes to amend 29 CFR part 2590 as follows:

PART 2590—RULES AND REGULATIONS FOR GROUP HEALTH PLANS

■ 1. The authority citation for part 2590 continues to read as follows:

Authority: 29 U.S.C. 1027, 1059, 1135, 1161-1168, 1169, 1181-1183, 1181 note, 1185, 1185a, 1185b, 1185c, 1185d, 1191, 1191a, 1191b, and 1191c; sec. 101(g), Public Law 104-191, 110 Stat. 1936; sec. 401(b), Public Law 105-200, 112 Stat. 645 (42 U.S.C. 651 note); sec. 512(d), Public Law 110-343, 122 Stat. 3881; sec. 1001, 1201, and 1562(e), Public Law 111-148, 124 Stat. 119, as amended by Public Law 111-152, 124 Stat. 1029; Secretary of Labor's Order 3-2010, 75 FR 55354 (September 10, 2010).

■ 2. Section 2590.701-2 is amended by revising the definition of *Excepted benefits* as follows:

§ 2590.701-2 Definitions.

* * * * *

Excepted benefits means the benefits described as excepted in § 2590.732(c), or 45 CFR § 148.220 (describing when individual health insurance policies constitute excepted benefits).

* * * * *

■ 3. Section 2590.715-2713 is amended by revising paragraphs (a)(1) introductory text and (a)(1)(iv) to read as follows:

§ 2590.715-2713 Coverage of preventive health services.

(a) *Services*—(1) *In general.* Beginning at the time described in paragraph (b) of this section and subject to § 2590.715-2713A, a group health plan, or a health insurance issuer offering group health insurance coverage, must provide coverage for all of the following items and services, and may not impose any cost sharing requirement (such as a copayment, coinsurance, or a deductible) with respect to those items and services:

* * * * *

(iv) With respect to women, to the extent not described in paragraph (a)(1)(i) of this section, evidence-informed preventive care and screenings provided for in binding comprehensive health plan coverage guidelines supported by the Health Resources and Services Administration, in accordance with 45 CFR 147.131(a).

* * * * *

■ 4. A new § 2590.715-2713A is added to read as follows:

§ 2590.715-2713A Accommodations in connection with coverage of preventive health services.

(a) *Eligible organizations.* An eligible organization is an organization that satisfies all of the following requirements:

(1) The organization opposes providing coverage for some or all of any contraceptive services required to be covered under § 2590.715-713(a)(1)(iv) on account of religious objections.

(2) The organization is organized and operates as a nonprofit entity.

(3) The organization holds itself out as a religious organization.

(4) The organization maintains in its records a self-certification, made in the manner and form specified by the Secretary of Health and Human Services, for each plan year to which the accommodation is to apply, executed by a person authorized to make the certification on behalf of the organization, indicating that the organization satisfies the criteria in paragraphs (a)(1) through (3) of this section, and, specifying those contraceptive services for which the organization will not establish, maintain, administer, or fund coverage, and makes such certification available for examination upon request.

(b) *Contraceptive coverage—self-insured group health plan coverage.* [Reserved.]

(c) *Contraceptive coverage—insured group health plan coverage.* (1) A group health plan established or maintained by an eligible organization and that provides benefits through one or more issuers complies with any requirement under § 2590.715-2713(a)(1)(iv) to provide contraceptive coverage if the eligible organization or plan administrator furnishes each issuer that would otherwise provide coverage for any contraceptive services required to be covered under § 2590.715-2713(a)(1)(iv) with a copy of the self-certification described in paragraph (a)(4) of this section.

(2) A group health insurance issuer that receives a copy of the self-certification described in paragraph (a)(4) of this section with respect to a plan for which the issuer would otherwise provide coverage for any contraceptive services required to be covered under § 2590.715-2713(a)(1)(iv) must automatically provide health insurance coverage for any contraceptive services required to be covered by § 2590.715-2713(a)(1)(iv) and identified in the self-certification, through a separate health insurance policy that is excepted under 45 CFR 148.220(b)(7), for each plan participant and beneficiary. The issuer providing the individual market excepted benefits policy may not impose any cost sharing requirement (such as a copayment, coinsurance, or a deductible) with respect to coverage of those services, or impose any premium, fee, or other charge, or portion thereof, directly or indirectly, on the eligible organization, its group health plan, or plan participants or beneficiaries with respect to coverage of those services.

(d) *Notice of availability of contraceptive coverage.* An issuer providing contraceptive coverage arranged pursuant to paragraph (b) or (c) of this section must provide to plan participants and beneficiaries written notice of the availability of the contraceptive coverage, separate from but contemporaneous with (to the extent possible) application materials distributed in connection with enrollment (or re-enrollment) in group coverage of the eligible organization for any plan year to which this paragraph applies. The following model language, or substantially similar language, may be used to satisfy the notice requirement of this paragraph: "The organization that establishes and maintains, or arranges, your health coverage has certified that your group health plan qualifies for an accommodation with respect to the federal requirement to cover all Food and Drug Administration-approved contraceptive services for women, as prescribed by a health care provider, without cost sharing. This means that your health coverage will not cover the following contraceptive services: [contraceptive services specified in self-certification]. Instead, these contraceptive services will be covered through a separate individual health insurance policy, which is not administered or funded by, or connected in any way to, your health coverage. You and any covered dependents will be enrolled in this separate individual health insurance policy at no additional cost to you. If you have any questions about this notice, contact [contact information for health insurance issuer]."

* * *

Signed this 30th day of January 2013.

Steven T. Miller,

Deputy Commissioner for Services and Enforcement, Internal Revenue Service.

Signed this 30th day of January 2013.

Phyllis C. Borzi,

Assistant Secretary, Employee Benefits Security Administration, Department of Labor.

* * *

[FR Doc. 2013-02420 Filed 2-1-13; 11:15 am]

BILLING CODE 4830-01; 4510-029; 4120-01; 6325-64-P

¶ 20,263L

IRS: Proposed regulations: Employee Benefits Security Administration (EBSA): Patient Protection and Affordable Care Act (P.L. 111-148, PPACA): Group health plans: Waiting periods.—The IRS, EBSA, and the Department of Health and Human Services have issued proposed regulations that implement the 90-day waiting period limitation under Sec. 2708 of the Public Health Service Act, as added by the PPACA and incorporated into the Code and ERISA. Sec. 2708 provides that a group health plan and a health insurance issuer offering group health insurance coverage may not apply any waiting period that exceeds 90 days. The proposed regulations would also amend regulations to conform PPACA provisions already in effect and provisions that will become effective in 2014.

The proposed regulations would generally apply to plan years beginning on or after January 1, 2014. The Departments note that the August 2012 temporary guidance (see PENSION PLAN GUIDE ¶ 19,966H for the EBSA guidance) provided that group health plans and health insurance issuers could rely on the guidance through at least the end of 2014. The Departments believe that the proposed regulations are consistent with, and no more restrictive than, the August 2012 guidance. Therefore, the Departments will consider compliance with the proposed regulations as compliance with Sec. 2708 at least through the end of 2014.

The proposed regulation was published in the Federal Register on March 21, 2013 (78 FR 17313). The regulations were finalized on February 24, 2014 (79 FR 10295). The preamble to the final regulations is at ¶ 23,295. The final regulations are at ¶ 13,968Q-10, ¶ 13,968Q-12, ¶ 13,968Q-14, ¶ 13,968Q-16, ¶ 13,968Q-18, ¶ 13,968Q-20, ¶ 13,968R-3, ¶ 13,968V-20K, and ¶ 13,968W-10.

DEPARTMENT OF THE TREASURY

Internal Revenue Service

26 CFR Part 54

[REG-122706-12]

RIN 1545-BL50

DEPARTMENT OF LABOR

Employee Benefits Security Administration

29 CFR Part 2590

RIN 1210-AB56

DEPARTMENT OF HEALTH AND HUMAN SERVICES

45 CFR Parts 144, 146, and 147

[CMS-9952-P]

RIN 0938-AR77

Ninety-Day Waiting Period Limitation and Technical Amendments to Certain Health Coverage Requirements Under the Affordable Care Act

AGENCY: Internal Revenue Service, Department of the Treasury; Employee Benefits Security Administration, Department of Labor; Centers for Medicare & Medicaid Services, Department of Health and Human Services.

ACTION: Proposed rules.

SUMMARY: These proposed rules implement the 90-day waiting period limitation under section 2708 of the Public Health Service Act, as added by the Patient Protection and Affordable Care Act (Affordable Care Act), as amended, and incorporated into the Employee Retirement Income Security Act of 1974 and the Internal Revenue Code. They also propose amendments to regulations to conform to Affordable Care Act provisions already in effect as well as those that will become effective beginning 2014. The proposed conforming amendments make changes to existing requirements such as preexisting condition limitations and other portability provisions added by the Health Insurance Portability and Accountability Act of 1996 (HIPAA) and implementing regulations because they have become moot or need amendment due to new market reform protections under the Affordable Care Act.

DATES: Comments are due on or before May 20, 2013.

ADDRESSES: Written comments may be submitted to the Department of Labor as specified below. Any comment that is submitted will be shared with the other Departments and will also be made available to the public. Warning: Do not include any personally identifiable information (such as name, address, or other contact information) or confidential business information that you do not want publicly disclosed. All comments may be posted on the Internet and can be retrieved by most Internet search engines. No deletions, modifications, or redactions will be made to the comments received, as they are public records. Comments may be submitted anonymously.

Comments, identified by "Waiting Periods", may be submitted by one of the following methods:

Federal eRulemaking Portal: http://www.regulations.gov. Follow the instructions for submitting comments.

Mail or Hand Delivery: Office of Health Plan Standards and Compliance Assistance, Employee Benefits Security Administration, Room N-5653, U.S. Department of Labor, 200 Constitution Avenue NW., Washington, DC 20210, *Attention:* Waiting Periods.

Comments received will be posted without change to *www.regulations.gov* and available for public inspection at the Public Disclosure Room, N-1513, Employee Benefits Security Administration, 200 Constitution Avenue NW., Washington, DC 20210, including any personal information provided.

FOR FURTHER INFORMATION CONTACT: Amy Turner or Elizabeth Schumacher, Employee Benefits Security Administration, Depart-

ment of Labor, at (202) 693-8335; Karen Levin or Kathryn Johnson, Internal Revenue Service, Department of the Treasury, at (202) 927-9639; or Cam Moultrie Clemmons, Centers for Medicare & Medicaid Services, Department of Health and Human Services, at (410) 786-1565. *Customer service information:* Individuals interested in obtaining information from the Department of Labor concerning employment-based health coverage laws may call the EBSA Toll-Free Hotline at 1-866-444-EBSA (3272) or visit the Department of Labor's Web site (*www.dol.gov/ebsa*). In addition, information from HHS on private health insurance for consumers can be found on the Centers for Medicare & Medicaid Services (CMS) Web site (*www.cciio.cms.gov/*) and information on health reform can be found at *www.HealthCare.gov.*

SUPPLEMENTARY INFORMATION:

I. Background

The Patient Protection and Affordable Care Act, Public Law 111-148, was enacted on March 23, 2010, and the Health Care and Education Reconciliation Act, Public Law 111-152, was enacted on March 30, 2010. (They are collectively known as the "Affordable Care Act".) The Affordable Care Act reorganizes, amends, and adds to the provisions of part A of title XXVII of the Public Health Service Act (PHS Act) relating to group health plans and health insurance issuers in the group and individual markets. The term "group health plan" includes both insured and self-insured group health plans.[1] The Affordable Care Act adds section 715(a)(1) to the Employee Retirement Income Security Act (ERISA) and section 9815(a)(1) to the Internal Revenue Code (the Code) to incorporate the provisions of part A of title XXVII of the PHS Act into ERISA and the Code, and to make them applicable to group health plans and health insurance issuers providing health insurance coverage in connection with group health plans. The PHS Act sections incorporated by these references are sections 2701 through 2728.

PHS Act section 2708, as added by the Affordable Care Act and incorporated into ERISA and the Code, provides that a group health plan or health insurance issuer offering group health insurance coverage shall not apply any waiting period (as defined in PHS Act section 2704(b)(4)) that exceeds 90 days. PHS Act section 2704(b)(4), ERISA section 701(b)(4), and Code section 9801(b)(4) define a waiting period to be the period that must pass with respect to an individual before the individual is eligible to be covered for benefits under the terms of the plan. In 2004 regulations implementing the Health Insurance Portability and Accountability Act of 1996 (HIPAA) portability provisions (2004 HIPAA regulations), the Departments of Labor, Health and Human Services, and the Treasury (the Departments) defined a waiting period to mean the period that must pass before coverage for an employee or dependent who is otherwise eligible to enroll under the terms of a group health plan can become effective.[2] PHS Act section 2708 applies to both grandfathered and non-grandfathered group health plans and group health insurance coverage for plan years beginning on or after January 1, 2014.

PHS Act section 2708 does not require an employer to offer coverage to any particular employee or class of employees, including part-time employees. PHS Act section 2708 merely prevents an otherwise eligible employee (or dependent) from being required to wait more than 90 days before coverage becomes effective. Furthermore, nothing in the Affordable Care Act penalizes small employers for choosing not to offer coverage, or applicable large employers, as defined in the employer shared responsibility provisions under Code section 4980H, for choosing to limit their offer of coverage to full-time employees (and their dependents), as defined in the employer shared responsibility provisions under Code section 4980H. On February 9, 2012, the Departments issued guidance[3] outlining various approaches under consideration with respect to both the 90-day waiting period limitation and the employer shared responsibility provisions under Code section 4980H (February 2012 guidance). Public comments were invited generally, as well as specifically, regarding how rules relating to the potential look-back/stability period safe harbor method for determining the number of full-time employees under Code section 4980H should be coordinated with the 90-day waiting period limitation.

On August 31, 2012, following their review of the comments on the February 2012 guidance, the Departments provided temporary guidance,[4] to remain in effect at least through the end of 2014, regarding the 90-day waiting period limitation, and described the approach they intended to propose in rulemaking in the future (August 2012 guidance). The August 2012 guidance provides that employers, plans, and

---

[1] The term "group health plan" is used in title XXVII of the PHS Act, part 7 of ERISA, and chapter 100 of the Code, and is distinct from the term "health plan," as used in other provisions of title I of the Affordable Care Act. The term "health plan" does not include self-insured group health plans.

[2] 26 CFR 54.9801-3(a)(3)(iii), 29 CFR 2590.701-3(a)(3)(iii), and 45 CFR 146.111(a)(3)(iii).

[3] Department of Labor Technical Release 2012-01, IRS Notice 2012-17, and HHS FAQs issued February 9, 2012.

[4] Department of Labor Technical Release 2012-02, IRS Notice 2012-59, and HHS FAQs issued August 31, 2012.

issuers may rely on the compliance guidance at least through the end of 2014 and that, for purposes of enforcement by the Departments, compliance with the approach set forth in the August 2012 guidance will be considered compliance with the provisions of PHS Act section 2708 at least through the end of 2014.

In general, the August 2012 guidance provides, among other things, that eligibility conditions based solely on the lapse of a time period are permissible for no more than 90 days. Other conditions for eligibility under the terms of a group health plan are generally permissible under PHS Act section 2708, unless the condition is designed to avoid compliance with the 90-day waiting period limitation. The August 2012 guidance further clarifies that if, under the terms of a plan, an employee may elect coverage that would begin on a date that does not exceed the 90-day waiting period limitation, the 90-day waiting period limitation is considered satisfied and, accordingly, a plan or issuer will not be considered to have violated PHS Act section 2708 solely because employees may take additional time to elect coverage.

The August 2012 guidance also addresses the application of PHS Act section 2708 to variable-hour employees in cases in which a specified number of hours of service per period is a plan eligibility condition. Specifically, the guidance provides that if a group health plan conditions eligibility on an employee regularly working a specified number of hours per period (or working full-time), and it cannot be determined that a newly-hired employee is reasonably expected to regularly work that number of hours per period (or work full-time), the plan may take a reasonable period of time to determine whether the employee meets the plan's eligibility condition, which may include a measurement period that is consistent with the timeframe permitted for such determinations under Code section 4980H.[5] Except in cases in which a waiting period that exceeds 90 days is imposed in addition to a measurement period, the time period for determining whether such an employee meets the plan's eligibility condition will not be considered to be designed to avoid compliance with the 90-day waiting period limitation if coverage is made effective no later than 13 months from the employee's start date, plus if the employee's start date is not the first day of a calendar month, the time remaining until the first day of the next calendar month.

The August 2012 guidance also addresses application of the rules to plans with cumulative hours-of-service requirements. The August 2012 guidance includes an example stating that, if a plan's cumulative hours-of-service requirement is more than 1,200 hours, the Departments would consider the requirement to be designed to avoid compliance with the 90-day waiting period limitation.

After consideration of all of the comments received in response to the February 2012 guidance and in response to the August 2012 guidance, the Departments are proposing these regulations. Public comments on these proposed regulations are invited.

II. Overview of the Proposed Regulations

A. Prohibition on Waiting Periods That Exceed 90 Days

These regulations propose that a group health plan, and a health insurance issuer offering group health insurance coverage, not apply any waiting period that exceeds 90 days. (Neither a plan nor an issuer offering coverage is required to have any waiting period.) If, under the terms of the plan, an employee can elect coverage that becomes effective on a date that does not exceed the 90-day waiting period limitation, the coverage complies with the waiting period rules, and the plan or issuer will not be considered to violate the waiting period rules merely because individuals choose to elect coverage beyond the end of the 90-day waiting period.

In these proposed regulations, the definition of waiting period is the same as that used in the 2004 HIPAA regulations. (However, the definition is proposed to be moved from the section on preexisting condition exclusions to this section. See below for an explanation of other technical and conforming changes proposed to be made to the 2004 HIPAA regulations.) Accordingly, under these proposed regulations, waiting period would continue to be defined as the period that must pass before coverage for an employee or dependent who is otherwise eligible to enroll under the terms of a group health plan can become effective. These proposed regulations would also continue to include the clarification that, if an employee or dependent enrolls as a late enrollee or special enrollee, any period before such late or special enrollment is not a waiting period. The effective date of coverage for

special enrollees continues to be that set forth in the Departments' 2004 HIPAA regulations governing special enrollment.[6]

Paragraph (c) of the proposed regulations sets forth rules governing the relationship between a plan's eligibility criteria and the 90-day waiting period limitation. Specifically, this paragraph provides that being otherwise eligible to enroll in a plan means having met the plan's substantive eligibility conditions (such as being in an eligible job classification or achieving job-related licensure requirements specified in the plan's terms). However, the 90-day waiting period limitation generally does not require the plan sponsor to offer coverage to any particular employee or class of employees (including, for example, part-time employees). Instead, these proposed regulations would prohibit requiring otherwise eligible participants and beneficiaries to wait more than 90 days before coverage is effective.[7]

Under these proposed regulations, eligibility conditions that are based solely on the lapse of a time period would be permissible for no more than 90 days. Other conditions for eligibility under the terms of a group health plan (*i.e.,* those that are not based solely on the lapse of a time period) are generally permissible under PHS Act section 2708 and these proposed regulations unless the condition is designed to avoid compliance with the 90-day waiting period limitation.

These regulations propose an approach when applying waiting periods to variable-hour employees in cases in which a specified number of hours of service per period (such as 30 hours per week or 250 hours per quarter) is a plan eligibility condition. Under these proposed regulations, if a group health plan conditions eligibility on an employee regularly having a specified number of hours of service per period (or working full-time), and it cannot be determined that a newly-hired employee is reasonably expected to regularly work that number of hours per period (or work full-time), the plan may take a reasonable period of time to determine whether the employee meets the plan's eligibility condition, which may include a measurement period of no more than 12 months that begins on any date between the employee's start date and the first day of the first calendar month following the employee's start date. (This is consistent with the timeframe permitted for such determinations under Code section 4980H and its implementing regulations.) Except for cases in which a waiting period that exceeds 90 days is imposed in addition to a measurement period, the time period for determining whether a variable-hour employee meets the plan's hours of service per period eligibility condition will not be considered to be designed to avoid compliance with the 90-day waiting period limitation if coverage is made effective no later than 13 months from the employee's start date, plus if the employee's start date is not the first day of a calendar month, the time remaining until the first day of the next calendar month.

Some commenters requested clarification regarding employees with specific or unique work schedules, and whether they would be treated as variable-hour employees. In this regard, unlike the rules under Code section 4980H, whether an employee has been appropriately classified as part-time, full-time, or variable-hour is of limited application under PHS Act section 2708. That is, conditions for eligibility under the terms of a group health plan are generally permissible under PHS Act section 2708, unless based solely on the lapse of time or designed to avoid compliance with the 90-day waiting period limitation. Accordingly, plan provisions that base eligibility on whether an employee is, for example, meeting certain sales goals or earning a certain level of commission, are generally substantive eligibility provisions that do not trigger the 90-day waiting period limitation. Some plan eligibility provisions, such as whether an employee has a specified number of hours of service per period (such as 30 hours per week or 250 hours per quarter) necessarily require the passage of time in order to determine whether the plan's substantive eligibility provision has been met. These proposed regulations set forth an approach under which such plan provisions will not be considered to be designed to avoid compliance with the 90-day waiting period limitation. However, whether a particular employee is classified appropriately as part-time, full-time, or variable-hour is generally not an issue under PHS Act section 2708, although other provisions of law (such as Code section 4980H, the HIPAA nondiscrimination provisions, and other provisions of ERISA) may be applicable.

Another type of plan eligibility provision addressed in the August 2012 guidance was cumulative hours-of-service requirements, which use more than solely the passage of a time period in determining whether employees are eligible for coverage. Specifically, the August 2012 guidance included an example stating that if a plan's cumulative

---

[5] The August 2012 guidance provides that an employer may use a measurement period that is consistent with Code section 4980H, whether or not it is an applicable large employer subject to Code section 4980H.

[6] 26 CFR 54.9801-6, 29 CFR 2590.701-6, and 45 CFR 146.117.

[7] While a substantive eligibility condition that denies coverage for employees may be permissible under PHS Act section 2708, an applicable large employer's denial of coverage to a full-time employee may, nonetheless, give rise to an assessable payment under section 4980H of the Code and its implementing regulations.

hours-of-service requirement were more than 1,200 hours, the Departments would consider the requirement to be designed to avoid compliance with the 90-day waiting period limitation. Under these proposed regulations, if a group health plan or health insurance issuer conditions eligibility on any employee's (part-time or full-time) having completed a number of cumulative hours of service, the eligibility condition is not considered to be designed to avoid compliance with the 90-day waiting period limitation if the cumulative hours-of-service requirement does not exceed 1,200 hours.[8] Under the proposed rules, the plan's waiting period must begin once the new employee satisfies the plan's cumulative hours-of-service requirement and may not exceed 90 days. Furthermore, this provision is designed to be a one-time eligibility requirement only; these proposed regulations do not permit, for example, re-application of such a requirement to the same individual each year.

In response to the August 2012 guidance, some commenters requested clarification regarding application of the rule to plan provisions that require employees to work sufficient number of hours per measurement period but permit employees, if they do not have a sufficient number of hours, to make a self-payment (or buy-in) equal to the amount which would allow them to have a sufficient number of hours within the measurement period. PHS Act section 2708 and these proposed regulations do not prohibit plan procedures permitting self-payment (or buy-in) to satisfy any otherwise permissible hours-of-service requirement.

Some commenters raised concerns about communication between a plan and issuer regarding the 90-day limitation on waiting periods. Commenters stated that many issuers rely on the plan sponsor for information about an individual's eligibility for coverage and that issuers may not have knowledge of certain plan terms, such as eligibility conditions and waiting periods. These commenters expressed concern that health insurance issuers are required to comply with the requirements of PHS Act section 2708, but must rely on the information plan sponsors and employers report to them regarding eligibility information such as an employee's start date. At the same time, small employers purchasing insurance coverage often rely on their issuers for compliance assistance. Therefore, while the requirements of PHS Act section 2708 and these proposed regulations would be applicable to both the plan and issuer, to the extent coverage under a group health plan is insured by a health insurance issuer, paragraph (f) of the proposed regulations would provide that the issuer can rely on the eligibility information reported to it by an employer (or other plan sponsor) and will not be considered to violate the requirements of these proposed regulations in administering the 90-day waiting period limitation if the issuer requires the plan sponsor to make a representation regarding the terms of any eligibility conditions or waiting periods imposed by the plan sponsor before an individual is eligible to become covered under the terms of the employer's plan (and requires the plan sponsor to update this representation with any changes), and the issuer has no specific knowledge of the imposition of a waiting period that would exceed the permitted 90-day period.

Paragraph (d) of the proposed regulations clarifies the method for counting days when applying a 90-day waiting period. Some commenters stated that it is common practice to have a 90-day waiting period with coverage effective the first day of the month after the 90-day waiting period and requested flexibility for administrative ease. Others requested the Departments to create a *de minimis* exception for the difference between 90 days and 3 months. Under these proposed regulations, due to the clear text of the statute, the waiting period may not extend beyond 90 days and all calendar days are counted beginning on the enrollment date, including weekends and holidays. For a plan with a waiting period, "enrollment date" is defined as the first day of the waiting period.[9] If, with respect to a plan or issuer imposing a 90-day waiting period, the 91st day is a weekend or holiday, the plan or issuer may choose to permit coverage to be effective earlier than the 91st day, for administrative convenience. However, a plan or issuer may not make the effective date of coverage later than the 91st day.

The Departments recognize that multiemployer plans maintained pursuant to collective bargaining agreements have unique operating structures and may include different eligibility conditions based on the participating employer's industry or the employee's occupation. For example, some comments received on the August 2012 guidance gave examples of plan eligibility provisions based on complex formulas for earnings and residuals. As discussed earlier, the Departments view

eligibility provisions that are based on compensation as substantive eligibility provisions that are not designed to avoid compliance with the 90-day waiting period limitation. In addition, hours banks, which are common multiemployer plan provisions that allow workers to bank excess hours from one measurement period and then draw down on them to compensate for any shortage in a succeeding measurement period and prevent lapses in coverage, function as buy-in provisions, which were discussed earlier as permissible. It is the Departments' view that the proposed rules provide flexibility to both multiemployer and single-employer health plans to meet their needs in defining eligibility criteria, while also ensuring that employees are protected from excessive waiting periods. Comments are invited on these proposed rules and on whether any additional examples or provisions are needed to address multiemployer plans.

These proposed regulations generally would apply for plan years beginning on or after January 1, 2014, consistent with the statutory effective date of PHS Act section 2708. The rules would apply to both grandfathered and non-grandfathered group health plans and health insurance issuers offering group health insurance coverage. As with the applicability of the 2004 HIPAA regulations, with respect to individuals who are in a waiting period for coverage before the applicability date, beginning on the first day these rules apply to the plan, any waiting period can no longer apply in a manner that exceeds 90 days. However, as discussed below, the proposed amendment to eliminate the requirement to issue a certificate of creditable coverage is proposed to apply December 31, 2014, so that individuals needing to offset a preexisting condition exclusion under a plan that operates with a plan year beginning later than January 1 would still have access to the certificate for proof of coverage. Comments are invited on these proposed applicability dates.

The August 2012 guidance provided that group health plans and health insurance issuers may rely on the compliance guidance through at least the end of 2014. In the Departments' view, these proposed regulations are consistent with, and no more restrictive on employers than, the August 2012 guidance. Therefore, the Departments will consider compliance with these proposed regulations as compliance with PHS Act section 2708 at least through the end of 2014. (However, for changes outside of PHS Act section 2708 made to existing HIPAA regulations, such as the elimination of the requirement to provide a certificate of creditable coverage, the existing HIPAA regulations continue to apply until amended in new final regulations.) To the extent final regulations or other guidance with respect to the 90-day waiting period limitation is more restrictive on plans and issuers than these proposed regulations, the final regulations or other guidance will not be effective prior to January 1, 2015.

B. Conforming Changes to Existing Regulations

Sections 9801 of the Code and 701 of ERISA, and section 2701 of the PHS Act as originally added by HIPAA included requirements pertaining to the application of preexisting condition exclusions and waiting periods, as well as methods of crediting coverage. Final regulations implementing Code section 9801, ERISA section 701, and PHS Act section 2701 (as originally added by HIPAA) were adopted in 2004. The 2004 HIPAA regulations permit limited exclusions of coverage based on a preexisting condition under certain circumstances. PHS Act section 2704, added by the Affordable Care Act and incorporated into ERISA and the Code, amends the HIPAA requirements relating to preexisting conditions to provide that a group health plan and a health insurance issuer offering group or individual health insurance coverage may not impose any preexisting condition exclusion.[10] PHS Act section 2704 and the interim final regulations implementing that section are generally effective with respect to plan years (in the individual market, policy years) beginning on or after January 1, 2014, but for enrollees who are under 19 years of age, this prohibition became effective for plan years (in the individual market, policy years) beginning on or after September 23, 2010.[11] Therefore, these proposed regulations would amend the 2004 HIPAA regulations implementing Code sections 9801, ERISA section 701, and PHS Act section 2701 (as originally added by HIPAA), to remove provisions superseded by the prohibition on preexisting conditions under PHS Act section 2704 and the implementing regulations. Additionally, these regulations propose to amend examples in 26 CFR Part 54, 29 CFR Part 2590, and 45 CFR Parts 144 and 146 to conform to other changes made by the Affordable Care Act, such as

---

[8] While a cumulative hours-of-service eligibility condition up to 1,200 hours may be permissible under PHS Act section 2708, an applicable large employer's denial of coverage to a full-time employee may, nonetheless, give rise to an assessable payment under section 4980H of the Code and its implementing regulations.

[9] *See* 26 CFR 54.9801-3(a)(3)(i); 29 CFR 2590.701-3(a)(3)(i); and 45 CFR 146(a)(3)(i), which would be moved under these proposed rules to 26 CFR 54.9801-2; 29 CFR 2590.701-2; and 45 CFR 144.103.

[10] Affordable Care Act section 1201 also moved those provisions from PHS Act section 2701 to PHS Act section 2704.

[11] 75 FR 37188 (June 28, 2010).

the elimination of lifetime and annual limits under PHS Act section 2711 and its implementing regulations,[12] as well as the provisions governing dependent coverage of children to age 26 under PHS Act section 2714 and its implementing regulations.[13]

C. Technical Amendment Relating to OPM Multi-State Plan Program and External Review

Section 1334 of the Affordable Care Act creates the Multi-State Plan Program (MSPP) to foster competition in the Affordable Insurance Exchanges (Exchanges) and directs the U.S. Office of Personnel Management (OPM) to contract with private health insurance issuers to offer at least two multi-state plans (MSPs) on each of the Exchanges in the 50 states and the District of Columbia. Under Affordable Care Act section 1334(a)(4), OPM is to administer this program "in a manner similar to the manner in which" it implements the contracting provisions of the Federal Employee Health Benefits Program (FEHBP). OPM has interpreted Affordable Care Act section 1334(a)(4) to require implementation of a uniform, nationally applicable external review process consistent with the requirements of PHS Act section 2719 for MSPs similar to that administered by OPM under FEHBP,[14] to ensure that the MSPP contract is administered consistently throughout all 51 jurisdictions that would be served by an MSP (as FEHBP currently does).

The "level playing field" requirement in section 1324 of the Affordable Care Act provides that "[n]otwithstanding any other provision of law," requirements under State or Federal law in 13 categories (including appeals) "shall not" apply to "health insurance offered by a private health insurance issuer" if the requirement does not apply to MSPs established under the Affordable Care Act. Non-grandfathered health insurance coverage is generally required to comply with PHS Act section 2719 and its implementing regulations regarding internal claims and appeals and external review processes.[15] As a result, MSPP plans must also so comply, or other non-grandfathered insurance coverage would have to be similarly exempted.[16]

PHS Act section 2719 and its implementing regulations provide that group health plans and health insurance issuers must comply with either a State external review process or the Federal external review process. Generally, if a State has an external review process that meets, at a minimum, the consumer protections set forth in the interim final regulations, then the issuer (or a plan) subject to the State process must comply with the State process.[17] For plans and issuers not subject to an existing State external review process (including self-insured plans), a Federal external review process applies.[18] The statute requires the Departments to establish standards, "through guidance," governing a Federal external review process. Among such guidance that has been issued by the Departments, HHS has established a Federal external review process for self-insured nonfederal governmental health plans, as well as for plans and issuers in States that do not meet the minimum consumer protections in the regulations.

In this rule, the Departments propose to clarify that MSPs will be subject to the Federal external review process under PHS section 2719(b)(2) and paragraph (d) of the internal claims and appeals and external review regulations. In doing so, the Departments interpret section 2719(b)(2) to apply to all plans *not subject to a State's external review process* (emphasis added).[19] OPM's final rule on the establishment of the multi-State plan program[20] requires the MSPP external review process to meet the requirements of PHS Act section 2719 and its implementing regulations.

Additionally, the Departments propose to clarify that the scope of the Federal external review process, as described in paragraph (d)(1)(ii) of

the regulations, is the minimum required scope of claims eligible for external review for plans using a Federal external review process, and that Federal external review processes developed in accordance with paragraph (d) may have a scope that exceeds the minimum requirements. For example, OPM stated that the scope of the MSP external review process would allow for appeals of all disputed claims.[21] This clarification would reiterate that the proposed external review process would meet the minimum requirement for the scope of a Federal external review process under the regulations.

III. Economic Impact and Paperwork Burden

A. Executive Order 12866 and 13563—Department of Labor and Department of Health and Human Services

Executive Order 13563 emphasizes the importance of quantifying both costs and benefits, of reducing costs, of harmonizing and streamlining rules, and of promoting flexibility. It also requires federal agencies to develop a plan under which the agencies will periodically review their existing significant regulations to make the agencies' regulatory programs more effective or less burdensome in achieving their regulatory objectives.

Under Executive Order 12866, a regulatory action deemed "significant" is subject to the requirements of the Executive Order and review by the Office of Management and Budget (OMB). Section 3(f) of the Executive Order defines a "significant regulatory action" as an action that is likely to result in a rule (1) having an annual effect on the economy of $100 million or more, or adversely and materially affecting a sector of the economy, productivity, competition, jobs, the environment, public health or safety, or State, local or tribal governments or communities (also referred to as "economically significant"); (2) creating serious inconsistency or otherwise interfering with an action taken or planned by another agency; (3) materially altering the budgetary impacts of entitlement grants, user fees, or loan programs or the rights and obligations of recipients thereof; or (4) raising novel legal or policy issues arising out of legal mandates, the President's priorities, or the principles set forth in the Executive Order.

These proposed regulations are not economically significant within the meaning of section 3(f)(1) of the Executive Order. However, OMB has determined that the actions are significant within the meaning of section 3(f)(4) of the Executive Order. Therefore, OMB has reviewed these proposed regulations, and the Departments have provided the following assessment of their impact.

1. Summary

As stated earlier in this preamble, these proposed regulations would implement PHS Act section 2708, which provides that a group health plan, and a health insurance issuer offering group health insurance coverage, may not apply any waiting period that exceeds 90 days. The proposed regulations define "waiting period" as the period that must pass before coverage for an employee or dependent who is otherwise eligible to enroll under the terms of a group health plan can become effective, which is the same definition used in the 2004 HIPAA regulations. The proposed regulations would generally apply to plan years beginning on or after January 1, 2014, consistent with the statutory effective date of PHS Act section 2708.[22]

The Departments have crafted these proposed regulations to secure the protections intended by Congress in an economically efficient manner. The Departments do not have sufficient data to quantify the regulations' economic cost or benefits; therefore, they have provided a qualitative discussion of their economic impacts and request detailed comment and data that would allow for quantification of the costs,

---

[12] 75 FR 37188 (June 28, 2010).

[13] 75 FR 27122 (May 13, 2010).

[14] OPM published a final rule on establishment of the MSPP on March 11, 2013 at 78 FR 15559.

[15] The interim final regulations relating to internal claims and appeals and external review processes are codified at 26 CFR 54.9815-2719T, 29 CFR 2590.715-2719, and 45 CFR 147.136. These requirements do not apply to grandfathered health plans. The interim final regulations relating to status as a grandfathered health plan are codified at 26 CFR 54.9815-1251T, 29 CFR 2590.715-1251, and 45 CFR 147.140.

[16] The amendments in these proposed regulations only seek to address the differences that exist between the proposed MSPP external review process and the external review requirements for group health plans and health insurance issuers. While MSPP is also required to comply with the requirements related to internal claims and appeals, OPM's proposed process does not differ from the internal claims and appeals requirements for group health plans and health insurance issuers.

[17] More information on the regulatory requirements for State external review processes, including the regulations, Uniform Health Carrier External Review Model Act promulgated

by the National Association of Insurance Commissioners, technical releases, and other guidance, is available at *http://www.dol.gov/ebsa* and *http://cciio.cms.gov.*

[18] More information on the regulatory requirements for the Federal external review process, including the regulations, technical releases, and other guidance, is available at *http://www.dol.gov/ebsa* and *http://cciio.cms.gov.*

[19] We note that this interpretation of section 2719(b)(2) as applicable to MSPs is supported by the fact that Congress directed that the MSPP be implemented by OPM, and OPM is not a state.

[20] See *45 CFR 800.115(k)* and *45 CFR part 800.*

[21] 45 CFR 800.504(a). See also 78 FR 15559, 15582-15584 (March 11, 2013), the Preamble to the Patient Protection and Affordable Care Act; Establishment of the Multi-State Plan Program for the Affordable Insurance Exchanges; Final Rule.

[22] As stated earlier, the Departments' August 2012 guidance provided that group health plans and health insurance issuers may rely on the compliance guidance through at least the end of 2014. In the Departments' view, these proposed regulations are consistent with, and no more restrictive on employers than, the August 2012 guidance. Therefore, the Departments will consider compliance with these proposed regulations as compliance with PHS Act section 2708 at least through the end of 2014.

benefits, and transfers that would be brought about by the proposed rule.

2. Estimated Number of Affected Entities

The Departments estimate that 4.1 million new employees receive group health insurance coverage through private sector employers and 1.0 million new employees receive group health insurance coverage through public sector employers annually.[23] The 2012 Kaiser Family Foundation and Health Research and Education Trust Employer Health Benefits Annual Survey (the "2012 Kaiser Survey") finds that only eight percent of covered workers were subject to waiting periods of four months or more.[24] If eight percent of new employees receiving health care from their employers are subject to a waiting period of four months or more, then 408,000 new employees (5.1 million × 0.08) would be affected by this rule.[25] However, the Departments would note that it is unlikely that the survey defines the term "waiting period" in the same manner as these proposed regulations. For example, waiting period may have been defined by reference to an employee's start date, and it seems unlikely that the 2012 Kaiser Survey would have included the clarifications included in these proposed regulations regarding the measurement period for variable-hour employees or the clarification regarding cumulative hours-of-service requirements.

3. Benefits

Before Congress enacted PHS Act section 2708, federal law did not prescribe any limits on waiting periods for group health insurance coverage.

If employees delay health care treatment until the expiration of a prolonged waiting period, detrimental health effects can result, especially for employees and their dependents requiring higher levels of health care, such as older Americans, pregnant women, young children, and those with chronic conditions. This could lead to lower work productivity and missed school days. Low-wage workers also are vulnerable, because they have less income to spend out-of-pocket to cover medical expenses. The Departments anticipate that these proposed regulations can help reduce these effects, although the overall benefit may be limited because—as discussed in greater detail below—a small fraction of employers are expected to offer earlier health insurance coverage as a result of these proposed regulations.

As discussed earlier in this preamble, these proposed regulations would amend the 2004 HIPAA regulations implementing Code sections 9801, ERISA section 701, and PHS Act section 2701 (as originally added by HIPAA) to remove provisions superseded by the prohibition on preexisting conditions under PHS Act section 2704 and the implementing regulations. These amendments would provide a benefit to plans by reducing the burden associated with complying with the several Paperwork Reduction Act information collections that are associated with the superseded regulations. For a discussion of the affected information collections and the estimated cost and burden hour reduction, please see the Paperwork Reduction Act section, below.

4. Transfers Associated with the Rule

The possible transfers associated with this proposed rule would arise if employers begin to pay their portion of health insurance premiums or contributions sooner than they did before the enactment of PHS Act section 2708 and issuance of these proposed regulations. Recipients of the transfers would be covered employees and their dependents who would, if these proposed regulations are finalized, not be subject to excessive waiting periods during which they must forgo health coverage, purchase COBRA continuation coverage, or obtain an individual health insurance policy—all of which are options that could lead to higher out-of-pocket costs for employees to cover their healthcare expenditures. As discussed above, federal law did not limit the duration of waiting periods in the group health plans market before the enactment of PHS Act section 2708.

The Departments do not believe that this rule, on its own, will cause more than a marginal number of employers to offer coverage earlier to their employees because this provision on its own does not require employers to offer coverage and there is significant flexibility afforded to employers in these proposed regulations to maintain or revise their current group health plan eligibility conditions. For example, paragraph (c)(3)(ii) of the proposed regulations provides that if a group health plan or health insurance issuer conditions eligibility on any

employee's (part-time or full-time) having completed a number of cumulative hours of service, the eligibility condition is not considered to be designed to avoid compliance with the 90-day waiting period limitation if the cumulative hours-of-service requirement does not exceed 1,200 hours. This is intended to provide plan sponsors with flexibility to continue the common practice of utilizing a probationary or trial period to determine whether a new employee will be able to handle the duties and challenges of the job, while providing protections against excessive waiting periods for such employees. Under these proposed regulations, the plan's waiting period must begin once the new employee satisfies the plan's cumulative hours-of-service requirement and may not exceed 90 days.

Therefore, an employee who must meet a cumulative hours-of-service requirement of 1,200 hours could be employed for ten months[26] before their health coverage becomes effective and only employers that had a waiting period longer than ten months before the enactment of PHS Act section 2708 and these proposed regulations would necessarily incur a transfer for additional coverage. Because the 2012 Kaiser Survey reports that just eight percent of covered workers are in plans with waiting periods of four months or more and the overall average waiting period is just 2.3 months, the Departments are confident that such long waiting periods are rare.

B. Paperwork Reduction Act

1. Department of Labor and Department of the Treasury

As stated above, Sections 9801 of the Code and 701 of ERISA, and 2701 of the PHS Act as originally added by Health Insurance Portability and Accountability Act of 1996, included requirements pertaining to the application of preexisting conditions exclusions and waiting periods as well as methods of crediting coverage. The 2004 HIPAA regulations (in effect prior to the effective date of these amendments) permit limited exclusions of coverage based on a preexisting condition under certain circumstances.

PHS Act section 2704, added by the Affordable Care Act and incorporated into ERISA and the Code, amends the 2004 HIPAA regulations relating to preexisting conditions to provide that a group health plan and a health insurance issuer offering group or individual health insurance coverage may not impose any preexisting condition exclusion. PHS Act section 2704 and the interim final regulations implementing that section are generally effective with respect to plan years (in the individual market, policy years) beginning on or after January 1, 2014, but for enrollees who are under 19 years of age, this prohibition became effective for plan years (in the individual market, policy years) beginning on or after September 23, 2010. Therefore, these regulations propose to amend the 2004 HIPAA regulations implementing Code sections 9801, ERISA section 701, and PHS Act section 2701 (as originally added by HIPAA), to remove provisions superseded by the prohibition on preexisting conditions under PHS Act section 2704 and the implementing regulations.

The Departments are proposing to discontinue the following Information Collection Requests (ICRs) that are associated with the superseded regulation: The Notice of Preexisting Condition Exclusion under Group Health Plans, which is approved under OMB Control Number 1210-0102 through January 31, 2016, and Establishing Creditable Coverage under Group Health Plans, which is approved under OMB Control Number 1210-0103 through January 31, 2016.

Additionally, the Departments are proposing to revise Final Regulations for Health Coverage Portability for Group Health Plans and Group Health Insurance Issuers under HIPAA Titles I & IV, which is approved under OMB Control Number 1545-1537 through January 31, 2014, to remove the Health Plans Imposing Pre-existing Condition Notification Requirements, Certification Requirements, and Exclusion Period Notification Information Collections within this ICR because they are associated with the superseded regulation.

Discontinuing and revising these ICRs would result in a total burden reduction of approximately 341,000 hours (5,000 hours attributable to OMB Control Number 1210-0102, 74,000 hours attributable to OMB Control Number 1210-0103, and 262,000 hours attributable to OMB Control Number 1545-1537) and a total cost burden reduction of approximately $32.7 million ($1.1 million attributable to OMB Control Number 1210-0102, $12.4 million attributable to OMB Control Number

---

[23] This estimate is based upon internal Department of Labor calculations derived from the 2009 Medical Expenditure Panel Survey.

[24] *See e.g.*, Kaiser Family Foundation and Health Research and Education Trust, *Employer Health Benefits 2012 Annual Survey* (2012) available at *http://ehbs.kff.org/pdf/2012/8345.pdf*.

[25] Approximately 331,000 private sector employees and 77,000 state and local public sector employees.

[26] 1,200 hours/40 hours per week = 30 weeks; 30 weeks *7 days/week = 210 days; 210 days eligibility requirement + 90 day wait period = 300 days.

1210-0103, and $19.2 million attributable to OMB Control Number 1545-1537).

C. Regulatory Flexibility Act—Department of Labor and Department of Health and Human Services

The Regulatory Flexibility Act (5 U.S.C. 601 et seq.) (RFA) applies to most Federal rules that are subject to the notice and comment requirements of section 553(b) of the Administrative Procedure Act (5 U.S.C. 551 et seq.). Unless an agency certifies that such a rule will not have a significant economic impact on a substantial number of small entities, section 603 of the RFA requires the agency to present an initial regulatory flexibility analysis at the time of the publication of the notice of proposed rulemaking describing the impact of the rule on small entities. Small entities include small businesses, organizations and governmental jurisdictions.

For purposes of analysis under the RFA, the Departments propose to continue to consider a small entity to be an employee benefit plan with fewer than 100 participants. The basis of this definition is found in section 104(a)(3) of ERISA, which permits the Secretary of Labor to prescribe simplified annual reports for welfare benefit plans that cover fewer than 100 participants.[27]

Further, while some large employers may have small plans, in general, small employers maintain most small plans. Thus, the Departments believe that assessing the impact of these proposed regulations on small plans is an appropriate substitute for evaluating the effect on small entities.

The definition of small entity considered appropriate for this purpose differs, however, from a definition of small business that is based on size standards promulgated by the Small Business Administration (SBA) (13 CFR 121.201) pursuant to the Small Business Act (15 U.S.C. 631 et seq.). The Departments therefore request comments on the appropriateness of the size standard used in evaluating the impact of these proposed regulations on small entities.

The Departments carefully considered the likely impact of the rule on small entities in connection with their assessment under Executive Order 12866. The Departments lack data to focus only on the impacts on small business. However, the Departments believe that the proposed rule includes flexibility that would allow small employers to minimize the transfers in health insurance premiums that they would have to pay to employees.

The Departments hereby certify that these proposed regulations will not have a significant economic impact on a substantial number of small entities. Consistent with the policy of the RFA, the Departments encourage the public to submit comments that would allow the Departments to assess the impacts specifically on small plans or suggest alternative rules that accomplish the stated purpose of PHS Act section 2708 and minimize the impact on small entities.

D. Special Analyses—Department of the Treasury

For purposes of the Department of the Treasury, it has been determined that this notice of proposed rulemaking is not a significant regulatory action as defined in Executive Order 12866, as supplemented by Executive Order 13563. Therefore, a regulatory assessment is not required. It has also been determined that section 553(b) of the Administrative Procedure Act (5 U.S.C. chapter 5) does not apply to these proposed regulations, and, because these proposed regulations do not impose a collection of information requirement on small entities, a regulatory flexibility analysis under the Regulatory Flexibility Act (5 U.S.C. chapter 6) is not required. Pursuant to Code section 7805(f), this notice of proposed rulemaking has been submitted to the Small Business Administration for comment on its impact on small business.

E. Congressional Review Act

These proposed regulations are subject to the Congressional Review Act provisions of the Small Business Regulatory Enforcement Fairness Act of 1996 (5 U.S.C. 801 et seq.) and, if finalized, will be transmitted to the Congress and the Comptroller General for review.

F. Unfunded Mandates Reform Act

For purposes of the Unfunded Mandates Reform Act of 1995 (Pub. L. 104-4), as well as Executive Order 12875, these proposed rules do not include any proposed federal mandate that may result in expenditures

by state, local, or tribal governments, or by the private sector, of $100 million or more adjusted for inflation ($141 million in 2013).

G. Federalism Statement—Department of Labor and Department of Health and Human Services

Executive Order 13132 outlines fundamental principles of federalism, and requires the adherence to specific criteria by Federal agencies in the process of their formulation and implementation of policies that have "substantial direct effects" on the States, the relationship between the national government and States, or on the distribution of power and responsibilities among the various levels of government. Federal agencies promulgating regulations that have these federalism implications must consult with State and local officials, and describe the extent of their consultation and the nature of the concerns of State and local officials in the preamble to the regulation.

In the Departments' view, these proposed regulations have federalism implications, because they have direct effects on the States, the relationship between the national government and States, or on the distribution of power and responsibilities among various levels of government. In general, through section 514, ERISA supersedes State laws to the extent that they relate to any covered employee benefit plan, and preserves State laws that regulate insurance, banking, or securities. While ERISA prohibits States from regulating a plan as an insurance or investment company or bank, the preemption provisions of ERISA section 731 and PHS Act section 2724 (implemented in 29 CFR 2590.731(a) and 45 CFR 146.143(a)) apply so that the HIPAA requirements (including those of the Affordable Care Act) are not to be "construed to supersede any provision of State law which establishes, implements, or continues in effect any standard or requirement solely relating to health insurance issuers in connection with group health insurance coverage except to the extent that such standard or requirement prevents the application of a requirement" of a federal standard. The conference report accompanying HIPAA indicates that this is intended to be the "narrowest" preemption of State laws. (See House Conf. Rep. No. 104-736, at 205, reprinted in 1996 U.S. Code Cong. & Admin. News 2018.)

States may continue to apply State law requirements except to the extent that such requirements prevent the application of the Affordable Care Act requirements that are the subject of this rulemaking. State insurance laws that are more stringent than the Federal requirements are unlikely to "prevent the application of" the Affordable Care Act, and be preempted. Accordingly, States have significant latitude to impose requirements on health insurance issuers that are more restrictive than the Federal law.

Guidance conveying this interpretation was published in the **Federal Register** on April 8, 1997 (62 FR 16904), and December 30, 2004 (69 FR 78720), and these proposed rules would clarify and implement the statute's minimum standards and would not significantly reduce the discretion given the states by the statute.

In compliance with the requirement of Executive Order 13132 that agencies examine closely any policies that may have federalism implications or limit the policy making discretion of the States, the Departments have engaged in efforts to consult with and work cooperatively with affected State and local officials, including attending conferences of the National Association of Insurance Commissioners and consulting with State insurance officials on an individual basis.

Throughout the process of developing these proposed regulations, to the extent feasible within the specific preemption provisions of HIPAA as it applies to the Affordable Care Act, the Departments have attempted to balance the States' interests in regulating health insurance issuers, and Congress' intent to provide uniform minimum protections to consumers in every State. By doing so, it is the Departments' view that they have complied with the requirements of Executive Order 13132.

IV. Statutory Authority

The Department of the Treasury regulations are proposed to be adopted pursuant to the authority contained in sections 7805 and 9833 of the Code.

The Department of Labor regulations are proposed to be adopted pursuant to the authority contained in 29 U.S.C. 1027, 1059, 1135, 1161-1168, 1169, 1181-1183, 1181 note, 1185, 1185a, 1185b, 1185d, 1191, 1191a, 1191b, and 1191c; sec. 101(g), Public Law 104-191, 110 Stat.

---

[27] Under ERISA section 104(a)(2), the Secretary may also provide exemptions or simplified reporting and disclosure requirements for pension plans. Pursuant to the authority of ERISA section 104(a)(3), the Department of Labor has previously issued at 29 CFR 2520.104-20, 2520.104-21, 2520.104-41, 2520.104-46, and 2520.104b-10 certain simplified

reporting provisions and limited exemptions from reporting and disclosure requirements for small plans, including unfunded or insured welfare plans, that cover fewer than 100 participants and satisfy certain other requirements.

1936; sec. 401(b), Public Law 105-200, 112 Stat. 645 (42 U.S.C. 651 note); sec. 512(d), Public Law 110-343, 122 Stat. 3881; sec. 1001, 1201, and 1562(e), Public Law 111-148, 124 Stat. 119, as amended by Public Law 111-152, 124 Stat. 1029; Secretary of Labor's Order 3-2010, 75 FR 55354 (September 10, 2010).

List of Subjects

26 CFR Part 54

Excise taxes, Health care, Health insurance, Pensions, Reporting and recordkeeping requirements.

29 CFR Part 2590

Continuation coverage, Disclosure, Employee benefit plans, Group health plans, Health care, Health insurance, Medical child support, Reporting and recordkeeping requirements.

45 CFR Part 144

Health care, Health insurance, Reporting and recordkeeping requirements.

45 CFR Parts 146 and 147

Health care, Health insurance, Reporting and recordkeeping requirements, and State regulation of health insurance.

Signed this 14th day of March, 2013.

Steven T. Miller,

Deputy Commissioner for Services and Enforcement, Internal Revenue Service.

Signed this 14th day of March, 2013.

Phyllis C. Borzi,

Assistant Secretary, Employee Benefits Security Administration, Department of Labor.

Dated: March 13, 2013.

Marilyn Tavenner,

Acting Administrator, Centers for Medicare & Medicaid Services.

Dated: March 14, 2013.

Kathleen Sebelius,

Secretary, Department of Health and Human Services.

DEPARTMENT OF THE TREASURY

Internal Revenue Service

Accordingly, 26 CFR part 54 is proposed to be amended as follows:

PART 54—PENSION EXCISE TAXES

■ **Paragraph 1.** The authority citation for Part 54 is amended by adding an entry for § 54.9815-2708 in numerical order to read in part as follows:

Authority: 26 U.S.C. 7805. * * *

Section 54.9815-2708 is also issued under 26 U.S.C. 9833.

■ **Par. 2.** Section 54.9801-1 is amended by revising paragraph (b) to read as follows:

§ 54.9801-1 Basis and scope.

* * * * *

(b) *Scope.* A group health plan or health insurance issuer offering group health insurance coverage may provide greater rights to participants and beneficiaries than those set forth in the portability and market reform sections of this part 54. This part 54 sets forth minimum requirements for group health plans and group health insurance issuers offering group health insurance coverage concerning certain consumer protections of the Health Insurance Portability and Accountability Act (HIPAA), including special enrollment periods and the prohibition against discrimination based on a health factor, as amended by the Patient Protection and Affordable Care Act (Affordable Care Act). Other consumer protection provisions, including other protections provided by the Affordable Care Act and the Mental Health Parity and Addiction Equity Act are set forth in this part 54.

* * * * *

■ **Par. 3.** Section 54.9801-2 is amended by revising the definitions of "*enrollment date*", "*late enrollment*", and "*waiting period*", and by adding definitions of "*first day of coverage*" and "*late enrollee*" in alphabetical order, to read as follows:

§ 54.9801-2 Definitions.

* * * * *

Enrollment date means the first day of coverage or, if there is a waiting period, the first day of the waiting period. If an individual receiving benefits under a group health plan changes benefit packages, or if the plan changes group health insurance issuers, the individual's enrollment date does not change.

* * * * *

First day of coverage means, in the case of an individual covered for benefits under a group health plan, the first day of coverage under the plan and, in the case of an individual covered by health insurance coverage in the individual market, the first day of coverage under the policy or contract.

* * * * *

Late enrollee means an individual whose enrollment in a plan is a late enrollment.

Late enrollment means enrollment of an individual under a group health plan other than the earliest date on which coverage can become effective for the individual under the terms of the plan, or through special enrollment. (For rules relating to special enrollment, see § 54.9801-6.) If an individual ceases to be eligible for coverage under a plan, and then subsequently becomes eligible for coverage under the plan, only the individual's most recent period of eligibility is taken into account in determining whether the individual is a late enrollee under the plan with respect to the most recent period of coverage. Similar rules apply if an individual again becomes eligible for coverage following a suspension of coverage that applied generally under the plan.

* * * * *

Waiting period means *waiting period* within the meaning of § 54.9815-2708(b).

* * * * *

■ **Par. 4.** Section 54.9801-3 is amended by:

■ A. Removing paragraphs (a)(2), (a)(3), (c), (d), (e) and (f).

■ B. Revising the heading to paragraph (a).

■ C. Removing paragraph (a)(1) introductory text, and redesignating paragraphs (a)(1)(i) and (a)(1)(ii) as paragraphs (a)(1) and (a)(2).

■ D. Amending paragraph (a)(2) by revising paragraph (ii) of Examples 1 and 2, by revising Example 3 and Example 4, and by revising paragraph (ii) of Examples 5, 6, 7 and 8.

■ E. Revising paragraph (b).

The revisions read as follows:

§ 54.9801-3 Limitations on preexisting condition exclusion period.

(a) *Preexisting condition exclusion defined—*

* * * * *

(2) * * *

Example 1. * * *

(ii) *Conclusion.* In this *Example 1,* the exclusion of benefits for any prosthesis if the body part was lost before the effective date of coverage is a preexisting condition exclusion because it operates to exclude benefits for a condition based on the fact that the condition was present before the effective date of coverage under the policy. The exclusion of benefits, therefore, is prohibited.

Example 2. * * *

(ii) *Conclusion.* In this *Example 2,* the plan provision excluding cosmetic surgery benefits for individuals injured before enrolling in the plan is a preexisting condition exclusion because it operates to exclude benefits relating to a condition based on the fact that the condition was present before the effective date of coverage. The plan provision, therefore, is prohibited.

Example 3. (i) *Facts.* A group health plan provides coverage for the treatment of diabetes, generally not subject to any requirement to obtain an approval for a treatment plan. However, if an individual was diagnosed with diabetes before the effective date of coverage under the plan, diabetes coverage is subject to a requirement to obtain approval of a treatment plan in advance.

(ii) *Conclusion.* In this *Example 3*, the requirement to obtain advance approval of a treatment plan is a preexisting condition exclusion because it limits benefits for a condition based on the fact that the condition was present before the effective date of coverage. The plan provision, therefore, is prohibited.

Example 4. (i) *Facts.* A group health plan provides coverage for three infertility treatments. The plan counts against the three-treatment limit benefits provided under prior health coverage.

(ii) *Conclusion.* In this *Example 4,* counting benefits for a specific condition provided under prior health coverage against a treatment limit for that condition is a preexisting condition exclusion because it operates to limit benefits for a condition based on the fact that the condition was present before the effective date of coverage. The plan provision, therefore, is prohibited.

Example 5. * * *

(ii) *Conclusion.* In this *Example 5,* the requirement to be covered under the plan for 12 months to be eligible for pregnancy benefits is a subterfuge for a preexisting condition exclusion because it is designed to exclude benefits for a condition (pregnancy) that arose before the effective date of coverage. The plan provision, therefore, is prohibited.

Example 6. * * *

(ii) *Conclusion.* In this *Example 6,* the exclusion of coverage for treatment of congenital heart conditions is a preexisting condition exclusion because it operates to exclude benefits relating to a condition based on the fact that the condition was present before the effective date of coverage. The plan provision, therefore, is prohibited.

Example 7. * * *

(ii) *Conclusion.* In this *Example 7,* the exclusion of coverage for treatment of cleft palate is not a preexisting condition exclusion because the exclusion applies regardless of when the condition arose relative to the effective date of coverage. The plan provision, therefore, is not prohibited. (But see 45 CFR 147.150, which may require coverage of cleft palate as an essential health benefit for health insurance coverage in the individual or small group market).

Example 8. * * *

(ii) *Conclusion.* In this *Example 8,* the exclusion of coverage for treatment of cleft palate for individuals who have not been covered under the plan from the date of birth operates to exclude benefits in relation to a condition based on the fact that the condition was present before the effective date of coverage. The plan provision, therefore, is prohibited.

* * * * *

(b) *General rules.* See § 54.9815-2704T for rules prohibiting the imposition of a preexisting condition exclusion.

■ **Par. 5.** Section 54.9801-4 is amended by removing paragraphs (a)(3) and (c), and revising paragraph (b) to read as follows:

§ 54.9801-4 Rules relating to creditable coverage.

* * * * *

(b) *Counting creditable coverage rules superseded by prohibition on preexisting condition exclusion.* See § 54.9815-2704T for rules prohibiting the imposition of a preexisting condition exclusion.

■ **Par. 6.** Section 54.9801-5 is revised to read as follows:

§ 54.9801-5 Evidence of creditable coverage.

(a) *In general.* The rules for providing certificates of creditable coverage and demonstrating creditable coverage have been superseded by the prohibition on preexisting condition exclusions. *See* § 54.9815-2704T for rules prohibiting the imposition of a preexisting condition exclusion.

(b) *Applicability.* The amendments made under this section apply beginning December 31, 2014.

■ **Par. 7.** Section 54.9801-6 is amended by removing paragraph (a)(3)(i)(E) and revising paragraphs (a)(3)(i)(C), (a)(3)(i)(D), (a)(4)(i) and (d)(2) to read as follows:

§ 54.9801-6 Special enrollment periods.

* * * * *

(a) * * *

(3) * * *

(i) * * *

(C) In the case of coverage offered through an HMO, or other arrangement, in the group market that does not provide benefits to individuals who no longer reside, live, or work in a service area, loss of coverage because an individual no longer resides, lives, or works in the service area (whether or not within the choice of the individual), and no other benefit package is available to the individual; and

(D) A situation in which a plan no longer offers any benefits to the class of similarly situated individuals (as described in § 54.9802-1(d)) that includes the individual.

* * * * *

(4) * * *

(i) A plan or issuer must allow an employee a period of at least 30 days after an event described in paragraph (a)(3) of this section to request enrollment (for the employee or the employee's dependent).

* * * * *

(d) * * *

(2) Special enrollees must be offered all the benefit packages available to similarly situated individuals who enroll when first eligible. For this purpose, any difference in benefits or cost-sharing requirements for different individuals constitutes a different benefit package. In addition, a special enrollee cannot be required to pay more for coverage than a similarly situated individual who enrolls in the same coverage when first eligible.

* * * * *

■ **Par. 8.** Section 54.9802-1 is amended by:

■ A. Removing paragraph (b)(3) and revising paragraphs (b)(1)(i) and (b)(2)(i)(B).

■ B. Revising Example 1, paragraph (i) of Example 2, paragraph (ii) of Example 4, paragraph (ii) of Example 5, and removing Example 8 in paragraph (b)(2)(i)(D).

■ C. Revising Example 2, and paragraph (i) of Example 5, in paragraph (d)(4).

■ D. Revising paragraph (ii) of Example 2 in paragraph (e)(2)(i)(B).

■ E. Revising Example 1 in paragraph (g)(1)(ii).

The revisions read as follows:

§ 54.9802-1 Prohibiting discrimination against participants and beneficiaries based on a health factor.

* * * * *

(b) * * *

(1) * * *

(i) A group health plan may not establish any rule for eligibility (including continued eligibility) of any individual to enroll for benefits under the terms of the plan that discriminates based on any health factor that relates to that individual or a dependent of that individual. This rule is subject to the provisions of paragraph (b)(2) of this section (explaining how this rule applies to benefits), paragraph (d) of this section (containing rules for establishing groups of similarly situated individuals), paragraph (e) of this section (relating to nonconfinement, actively-at-work, and other service requirements), paragraph (f) of this section (relating to wellness programs), and paragraph (g) of this section (permitting favorable treatment of individuals with adverse health factors).

* * * * *

(2) * * *

(i) * * *

(B) However, benefits provided under a plan must be uniformly available to all similarly situated individuals (as described in paragraph (d) of this section). Likewise, any restriction on a benefit or benefits must apply uniformly to all similarly situated individuals and must not be directed at individual participants or beneficiaries based on any health factor of the participants or beneficiaries (determined based on all the relevant facts and circumstances). Thus, for example, a plan may limit or exclude benefits in relation to a specific disease or condition, limit or exclude benefits for certain types of treatments or drugs, or limit or exclude benefits based on a determination of whether the benefits are experimental or not medically necessary, but only if the benefit limitation or exclusion applies uniformly to all similarly situated individuals and is not directed at individual participants or beneficiaries based on any health factor of the participants or beneficiaries. In addition, a plan may require the satisfaction of a deductible, copayment, coinsurance, or other cost-sharing requirement in order to obtain a benefit if the limit or cost-sharing requirement applies uniformly to all similarly situated individuals and is not directed at individual participants or beneficiaries based on any health factor of the participants or beneficiaries. In the case of a cost-sharing requirement, see also paragraph (b)(2)(ii) of this section, which permits variances in the application of a cost-sharing mechanism made available under a wellness program. (Whether any plan provision or practice with respect to benefits complies with this paragraph (b)(2)(i) does not affect whether the provision or practice is permitted under ERISA, the Affordable Care Act (including the requirements related to essential health benefits), the Americans with Disabilities Act, or any other law, whether State or Federal.)

* * * * *

(D) * * *

Example 1. (i) *Facts.* A group health plan applies a $10,000 annual limit on a specific covered benefit that is not an essential health benefit to each participant or beneficiary covered under the plan. The limit is not directed at individual participants or beneficiaries.

(ii) *Conclusion.* In this *Example 1,* the limit does not violate this paragraph (b)(2)(i) because coverage of the specific, non-essential health benefit up to $10,000 is available uniformly to each participant and beneficiary under the plan and because the limit is applied uniformly to all participants and beneficiaries and is not directed at individual participants or beneficiaries.

Example 2. (i) *Facts.* A group health plan has a $500 deductible on all benefits for participants covered under the plan. Participant *B* files a claim for the treatment of AIDS. At the next corporate board meeting of the plan sponsor, the claim is discussed. Shortly thereafter, the plan is modified to impose a $2,000 deductible on benefits for the treatment of AIDS, effective before the beginning of the next plan year.

* * * * *

Example 4. * * *

(ii) *Conclusion.* In this *Example 4,* the limit does not violate this paragraph (b)(2)(i) because $2,000 of benefits for the treatment of TMJ are available uniformly to all similarly situated individuals and a plan may limit benefits covered in relation to a specific disease or condition if the limit applies uniformly to all similarly situated individuals and is not directed at individual participants or beneficiaries. (However, applying a lifetime limit on TMJ may violate § 54.9815-2711, if TMJ coverage is an essential health benefit. This example does not address whether the plan provision is permissible under any other applicable law, including PHS Act section 2711 or the Americans with Disabilities Act.)

Example 5. * * *

(ii) *Conclusion.* In this *Example 5,* the lower lifetime limit for participants and beneficiaries with a congenital heart defect violates this paragraph (b)(2)(i) because benefits under the plan are not uniformly available to all similarly situated individuals and the plan's lifetime limit on benefits does not apply uniformly to all similarly situated individuals. Additionally, this plan provision is prohibited under § 54.9815-2711 because it imposes a lifetime limit on essential health benefits.

* * * * *

(d) * * *

(4) * * *

Example 2. (i) *Facts.* Under a group health plan, coverage is made available to employees, their spouses, and their children. However, coverage is made available to a child only if the child is under age 26 (or under age 29 if the child is continuously enrolled full-time in an institution of higher learning (full-time students)). There is no evidence to suggest that these classifications are directed at individual participants or beneficiaries.

(ii) *Conclusion.* In this *Example 2,* treating spouses and children differently by imposing an age limitation on children, but not on spouses, is permitted under this paragraph (d). Specifically, the distinction between spouses and children is permitted under paragraph (d)(2) of this section and is not prohibited under paragraph (d)(3) of this section because it is not directed at individual participants or beneficiaries. It is also permissible to treat children who are under age 26 (or full-time students under age 29) as a group of similarly situated individuals separate from those who are age 26 or older (or age 29 or older if they are not full-time students) because the classification is permitted under paragraph (d)(2) of this section and is not directed at individual participants or beneficiaries.

* * * * *

Example 5. (i) *Facts.* An employer sponsors a group health plan that provides the same benefit package to all seven employees of the employer. Six of the seven employees have the same job title and responsibilities, but Employee *G* has a different job title and different responsibilities. After *G* files an expensive claim for benefits under the plan, coverage under the plan is modified so that employees with *G*'s job title receive a different benefit package that includes a higher deductible than in the benefit package made available to the other six employees.

* * * * *

(e) * * *

(2) * * *

(i) * * *

(B) * * *

Example 2. * * *

(ii) *Conclusion.* In this Example 2, the plan violates this paragraph (e)(2) (and thus also paragraph (b) of this section) because the 90-day continuous service requirement is a rule for eligibility based on whether an individual is actively at work. However, the plan would not violate this paragraph (e)(2) or paragraph (b) of this section if, under the plan, an absence due to any health factor is not considered an absence for purposes of measuring 90 days of continuous service. (In addition, any eligibility provision that is time-based must comply with the requirements of PHS Act section 2708 and its implementing regulations.)

* * * * *

(g) * * *

(1) * * *

(ii) * * *

Example 1. (i) *Facts.* An employer sponsors a group health plan that generally is available to employees, spouses of employees, and dependent children until age 26. However, dependent children who are disabled are eligible for coverage beyond age 26.

(ii) *Conclusion.* In this Example 1, the plan provision allowing coverage for disabled dependent children beyond age 26 satisfies this paragraph (g)(1) (and thus does not violate this section).

* * * * *

■ **Par. 9.** Section 54.9815-2708 is added to read as follows:

§ 54.9815-2708 Prohibition on waiting periods that exceed 90 days.

(a) *General rule.* A group health plan, and a health insurance issuer offering group health insurance coverage, must not apply any waiting period that exceeds 90 days, in accordance with the rules of this section. If, under the terms of a plan, an employee can elect coverage that would begin on a date that is not later than the end of the 90-day waiting period, this paragraph (a) is considered satisfied. Accordingly, a plan or issuer in that case will not be considered to have violated this paragraph (a) solely because employees (or other classes of participants) may take additional time (beyond the end of the 90-day waiting period) to elect coverage.

(b) *Waiting period defined.* For purposes of this part, a waiting period is the period that must pass before coverage for an employee or dependent who is otherwise eligible to enroll under the terms of a group health plan can become effective. If an employee or dependent enrolls as a late enrollee (as defined under § 54.9801-2) or special enrollee (as described in § 54.9801-6), any period before such late or special enrollment is not a waiting period.

(c) *Relation to a plan's eligibility criteria*—(1) Except as provided in paragraphs (c)(2) and (c)(3) of this section, being otherwise eligible to enroll under the terms of a group health plan means having met the plan's substantive eligibility conditions (such as, for example, being in an eligible job classification or achieving job-related licensure requirements specified in the plan's terms). Moreover, except as provided in paragraphs (c)(2) and (c)(3) of this section, nothing in this section requires a plan sponsor to offer coverage to any particular employee or class of employees (including, for example, part-time employees). Instead, this section prohibits requiring otherwise eligible participants and beneficiaries to wait more than 90 days before coverage is effective. (While a substantive eligibility condition that denies coverage to employees may be permissible under this section, a failure by an applicable large employer (as defined in section 4980H) to offer coverage to a full-time employee might, for example, nonetheless give rise to an assessable payment under section 4980H and its implementing regulations.)

(2) *Eligibility conditions based solely on the lapse of time.* Eligibility conditions that are based solely on the lapse of a time period are permissible for no more than 90 days.

(3) *Other conditions for eligibility.* Other conditions for eligibility under the terms of a group health plan are generally permissible under PHS Act section 2708, unless the condition is designed to avoid compliance with the 90-day waiting period limitation, determined in accordance with the rules of this paragraph (c)(3).

(i) *Application to variable-hour employees in cases in which a specified number of hours of service per period is a plan eligibility condition.* If a group health plan conditions eligibility on an employee regularly having a specified number of hours of service per period (or working full-time), and it cannot be determined that a newly-hired employee is reasonably expected to regularly work that number of hours per period (or work full-time), the plan may take a reasonable period of time, not to exceed 12 months and beginning on any date between the employee's start day and the first day of the first calendar month following the employee's start date, to determine whether the employee meets the plan's eligibility condition. Except in cases in which a waiting period that exceeds 90 days is imposed in addition to a measurement period, the time period for determining whether such an employee meets the plan's eligibility condition will not be considered to be designed to avoid compliance with the 90-day waiting period limitation if coverage is made effective no later than 13 months from the employee's start date, plus if the employee's start date is not the first day of a calendar month, the time remaining until the first day of the next calendar month.

(ii) *Cumulative service requirements.* If a group health plan or health insurance issuer conditions eligibility on an employee's having completed a number of cumulative hours of service, the eligibility condition is not considered to be designed to avoid compliance with the 90-day waiting period limitation if the cumulative hours-of-service requirement does not exceed 1,200 hours.

(d) *Counting days.* Under this section, all calendar days are counted beginning on the enrollment date (as defined in § 54.9801-2), including weekends and holidays. If, in the case of a plan or issuer imposing a 90-day waiting period, the 91st day is a weekend or holiday, the plan or issuer may choose to permit coverage to become effective earlier than the 91st day, for administrative convenience. Similarly, plans and issuers that do not want to start coverage in the middle of a month (or pay period) may choose to permit coverage to become effective earlier than the 91st day, for administrative convenience. For example, a plan may impose a waiting period of 60 days plus a fraction of a month (or pay period) until the first day of the next month (or pay period). However, a plan or issuer that extends the effective date of coverage beyond the 91st day fails to comply with the 90-day waiting period limitation.

(e) *Examples.* The rules of this section are illustrated by the following examples:

Example 1. (i) *Facts.* A group health plan provides that full-time employees are eligible for coverage under the plan. Employee *A* begins employment as a full-time employee on January 19.

(ii) *Conclusion.* In this *Example 1,* any waiting period for *A* would begin on January 19 and may not exceed 90 days. Coverage under the plan must become effective no later than April 19 (assuming February lasts 28 days).

Example 2. (i) *Facts.* A group health plan provides that only employees with job title *M* are eligible for coverage under the plan. Employee *B* begins employment in job title *L* on January 30.

(ii) *Conclusion.* In this *Example 2, B* is not eligible for coverage under the plan, and the period while *B* is working in job title *L* and therefore not in an eligible class of employees is not part of a waiting period under this section.

Example 3. (i) *Facts.* Same facts as *Example 2,* except that *B* transfers to a new position with job title *M* on April 11.

(ii) *Conclusion.* In this *Example 3, B* becomes eligible for coverage on April 11, but for the waiting period. Any waiting period for *B* begins on April 11 and may not exceed 90 days. Coverage under the plan must become effective no later than July 10.

Example 4. (i) *Facts.* A group health plan provides that only employees who have completed specified training and achieved specified certifications are eligible for coverage under the plan. Employee *C* is hired on May 3 and meets the plan's eligibility criteria on September 22.

(ii) *Conclusion.* In this *Example 4, C* becomes eligible for coverage on September 22, but for the waiting period. Any waiting period for *C* would begin on September 22 and may not exceed 90 days. Coverage under the plan must become effective no later than December 21.

Example 5. (i) *Facts.* A group health plan provides that employees are eligible for coverage after one year of service.

(ii) *Conclusion.* In this *Example 5,* the plan's eligibility condition is based solely on the lapse of time and, therefore, is impermissible under paragraph (c)(2) of this section because it exceeds 90 days.

Example 6. (i) *Facts.* Employer *W*'s group health plan provides for coverage to begin on the first day of the first payroll period on or after the date an employee is hired and completes the applicable enrollment forms. Enrollment forms are distributed on an employee's start date and may be completed within 90 days. Employee *D* is hired and starts on October 31, which is the first day of a pay period. *D* completes the enrollment forms and submits them on the 90th day after *D*'s start date. Coverage is made effective 7 days later, which is the first day of the next pay period.

(ii) *Conclusion.* In this *Example 6,* under the terms of *W*'s plan, coverage may become effective as early as October 31, depending on when *D* completes the applicable enrollment forms. Under the terms of the plan, when coverage becomes effective is dependent solely on the length of time taken by *D* to complete the enrollment materials. Therefore, under the terms of the plan, *D* may elect coverage that would begin on a date that does not exceed the 90-day waiting period limitation, and the plan complies with this section.

Example 7. (i) *Facts.* Under Employer *Y*'s group health plan, only employees who are full-time (defined under the plan as regularly averaging 30 hours of service per week) are eligible for coverage. Employee *E* begins employment for Employer *Y* on November 26 of Year 1. *E*'s hours are reasonably expected to vary, with an opportunity to work between 20 and 45 hours per week, depending on shift availability and *E*'s availability. Therefore, it cannot be determined at *E*'s start date that *E* is reasonably expected to work full-time. Under the terms of the plan, variable-hour employees, such as *E*, are eligible to enroll in the plan if they are determined to be a full-time employee after a measurement period of 12 months that begins on the employee's start date. Coverage is made effective no later than the first day of the first calendar month after the applicable enrollment forms are received. *E*'s 12-month measurement period ends November 25 of Year 2. *E* is determined to be a full-time employee and is notified of *E*'s plan eligibility. If *E* then elects coverage, *E*'s first day of coverage will be January 1 of Year 3.

(ii) *Conclusion.* In this *Example 7,* the measurement period is permissible because it is not considered to be designed to avoid compliance with the 90-day waiting period limitation. The plan may use a reasonable period of time to determine whether a variable-hour employee is a full-time employee, provided the period of time is no longer than 12 months and begins on a date between the employee's start date and the first day of the next calendar month, provided coverage is made effective no later than 13 months from *E*'s start date (plus if the employee's start date is not the first day of a calendar month, the time remaining until the first day of the next calendar month) and provided that, in addition to the measurement period, no more than 90 days elapse prior to the employee's eligibility for coverage.

Example 8. (i) *Facts.* Employee *F* begins working 25 hours per week for Employer *Z* on January 6 and is considered a part-time employee for purposes of *Z*'s group health plan. *Z* sponsors a group health plan that provides coverage to part-time employees after they have completed a cumulative 1,200 hours of service. *F* satisfies the plan's cumulative hours of service condition on December 15.

(ii) *Conclusion.* In this *Example 8,* the cumulative hours of service condition with respect to part-time employees is not considered to be designed to avoid compliance with the 90-day waiting period limitation. Accordingly, coverage for *F* under the plan must begin no later than the 91st day after *F* completes 1,200 hours. (If the plan's cumulative hours-of-service requirement was more than 1,200 hours, the requirement would be considered to be designed to avoid compliance with the 90-day waiting period limitation.)

(f) *Special rule for health insurance issuers.* To the extent coverage under a group health plan is insured by a health insurance issuer, the issuer is permitted to rely on the eligibility information reported to it by the employer (or other plan sponsor) and will not be considered to violate the requirements of this section with respect to its administration of any waiting period, if both of the following conditions are satisfied:

(1) The issuer requires the plan sponsor to make a representation regarding the terms of any eligibility conditions or waiting periods imposed by the plan sponsor before an individual is eligible to become covered under the terms of the employer's plan (and requires the plan sponsor to update this representation with any changes); and

(2) The issuer has no specific knowledge of the imposition of a waiting period that would exceed the permitted 90-day period.

(g) *No effect on other laws.* Compliance with this section is not determinative of compliance with any other provision of State or Federal law (including ERISA, the Code, or other provisions of the Patient Protection and Affordable Care Act). *See e.g.,* § 54.9802-1, which prohibits discrimination in eligibility for coverage based on a health factor, and section 4980H, which generally requires applicable large employers to offer coverage to full-time employees and their dependents or make an assessable payment.

(h) *Applicability date*—(1) *In general.* The provisions of this section apply for plan years beginning on or after January 1, 2014. *See* § 54.9815-1251T providing that the prohibition on waiting periods exceeding 90 days applies to all group health plans and health insurance issuers, including grandfathered health plans.

(2) *Application to individuals in a waiting period prior to the applicability date*—(i) With respect to individuals who are in a waiting period for coverage before the applicability date of this section, beginning on the first day the section applies, the waiting period can no longer apply to the individual if it would exceed 90 days with respect to the individual.

(ii) This paragraph (h)(2) is illustrated by the following example:

Example. (i) *Facts.* A group health plan is a calendar year plan. Prior to January 1, 2014, the plan provides that full-time employees are eligible for coverage after a 6-month waiting period. Employee *A* begins work as a full-time employee on October 1, 2013.

(ii) *Conclusion.* In this *Example 1,* the first day of A's waiting period is October 1, 2013 because that is the first day *A* is otherwise eligible to enroll under the plan's substantive eligibility provisions, but for the waiting period. Beginning January 1, 2014, the plan may not apply a waiting period that exceeds 90 days. Accordingly, *A* must be given the opportunity to elect coverage that begins no later than January 1, 2014 (which is 93 days after *A*'s start date) because otherwise, on January 1, 2014, the plan would be applying a waiting period that exceeds 90 days. The plan is not required to make coverage effective before January 1, 2014 under the rules of this section.

Par. 10. Section 54.9815-2719T is amended by adding a sentence to the end of the introductory text of paragraph (d) and revising paragraph (d)(1)(i) to read as follows:

§ 54.9815-2719T Internal claims and appeals and external review processes.

* * * * *

(d) * * * A Multi State Plan or MSP, as defined by 45 CFR 800.20, must provide an effective Federal external review process in accordance with this paragraph (d).

(1) * * *

(i) *In general.* Subject to the suspension provision in paragraph (d)(1)(ii) of this section and except to the extent provided otherwise by the Secretary in guidance, the Federal external review process established pursuant to this paragraph (d) applies, at a minimum, to any adverse benefit determination or final adverse benefit determination (as defined in paragraphs (a)(2)(i) and (a)(2)(v) of this section), except that a denial, reduction, termination, or a failure to provide payment for a benefit based on a determination that a participant or beneficiary fails to meet the requirements for eligibility under the terms of a group health plan is not eligible for the Federal external review process under this paragraph (d).

* * * * *

Par. 11. Section 54.9831-1 is amended by removing paragraph (b)(2)(i), and redesignating paragraphs (b)(2)(ii) through (b)(2)(viii) as (b)(2)(i) through (b)(2)(vii).

DEPARTMENT OF LABOR

Employee Benefits Security Administration

29 CFR Chapter XXV

For the reasons stated in the preamble, the Department of Labor proposes to amend 29 CFR part 2590 as follows:

PART 2590—RULES AND REGULATIONS FOR GROUP HEALTH PLANS

■ 12. The authority citation for Part 2590 continues to read as follows:

Authority: 29 U.S.C. 1027, 1059, 1135, 1161-1168, 1169, 1181-1183, 1181 note, 1185, 1185a, 1185b, 1185c, 1185d, 1191, 1191a, 1191b, and 1191c; sec. 101(g), Pub. L.104-191, 110 Stat. 1936; sec. 401(b), Pub. L. 105-200, 112 Stat. 645 (42 U.S.C. 651 note); sec. 512(d), Pub. L. 110-343, 122 Stat. 3881; sec. 1001, 1201, and 1562(e), Pub. L. 111-148, 124 Stat. 119, as amended by Pub. L. 111-152, 124 Stat. 1029; Secretary of Labor's Order 3-2010, 75 FR 55354 (September 10, 2010).

■ 13. Section 2590.701-1 is amended by revising paragraph (b) to read as follows:

§ 2590.701-1 Basis and scope.

* * * * *

■ (b) *Scope.* A group health plan or health insurance issuer offering group health insurance coverage may provide greater rights to participants and beneficiaries than those set forth in this Subpart B. This Subpart B sets forth minimum requirements for group health plans and group health insurance issuers offering group health insurance coverage concerning certain consumer protections of the Health Insurance Portability and Accountability Act (HIPAA), including special enrollment periods and the prohibition against discrimination based on a health factor, as amended by the Patient Protection and Affordable Care Act (Affordable Care Act). Other consumer protection provisions, including other protections provided by the Affordable Care Act and the Mental Health Parity and Addiction Equity Act are set forth in Subpart C of this part.

■ 14. Section 2590.701-2 is amended by revising the definitions of "*enrollment date*", "*late enrollment*", and "*waiting period*", and by adding definitions of "*first day of coverage*" and "*late enrollee*" in alphabetical order, to read as follows:

§ 2590.701-2 Definitions.

* * * * *

Enrollment date means the first day of coverage or, if there is a waiting period, the first day of the waiting period. If an individual receiving benefits under a group health plan changes benefit packages, or if the plan changes group health insurance issuers, the individual's enrollment date does not change.

* * * * *

First day of coverage means, in the case of an individual covered for benefits under a group health plan, the first day of coverage under the plan and, in the case of an individual covered by health insurance coverage in the individual market, the first day of coverage under the policy or contract.

* * * * *

Late enrollee means an individual whose enrollment in a plan is a late enrollment.

Late enrollment means enrollment of an individual under a group health plan other than on the earliest date on which coverage can become effective for the individual under the terms of the plan; or through special enrollment. (For rules relating to special enrollment, see § 2590.701-6.) If an individual ceases to be eligible for coverage under a plan, and then subsequently becomes eligible for coverage under the plan, only the individual's most recent period of eligibility is taken into account in determining whether the individual is a late enrollee under the plan with respect to the most recent period of coverage. Similar rules apply if an individual again becomes eligible for coverage following a suspension of coverage that applied generally under the plan.

* * * * *

Waiting period means *waiting period* within the meaning of § 2590.715-2708(b).

■ 15. Section 2590.701-3 is amended by:

■ A. Removing paragraphs (a)(2), (a)(3), (c), (d), (e), and (f).

■ B. Revising the heading to paragraph (a).

■ C. Removing paragraph (a)(1) introductory text, and redesignating paragraphs (a)(1)(i) and (a)(1)(ii) as paragraphs (a)(1) and (a)(2).

■ D. Amending paragraph (a)(2) by revising paragraph (ii) of Examples 1 and 2, by revising Example 3 and Example 4, by revising paragraph (ii) of Examples 5, 6, 7 and 8.

■ E. Revising paragraph (b). The revisions read as follows:

§ 2590.701-3 Limitations on preexisting condition exclusion period.

(a) *Preexisting condition exclusion defined—*

* * * * *

(2) * * *

Example 1. * * *

(ii) *Conclusion.* In this *Example 1,* the exclusion of benefits for any prosthesis if the body part was lost before the effective date of coverage is a preexisting condition exclusion because it operates to exclude benefits for a condition based on the fact that the condition was present before the effective date of coverage under the policy. The exclusion of benefits, therefore, is prohibited.

Example 2. * * *

(ii) *Conclusion.* In this *Example 2,* the plan provision excluding cosmetic surgery benefits for individuals injured before enrolling in the plan is a preexisting condition exclusion because it operates to exclude benefits relating to a condition based on the fact that the condition was present before the effective date of coverage. The plan provision, therefore, is prohibited.

Example 3. (i) *Facts.* A group health plan provides coverage for the treatment of diabetes, generally not subject to any requirement to obtain an approval for a treatment plan. However, if an individual was diagnosed with diabetes before the effective date of coverage under the plan, diabetes coverage is subject to a requirement to obtain approval of a treatment plan in advance.

(ii) *Conclusion.* In this *Example 3,* the requirement to obtain advance approval of a treatment plan is a preexisting condition exclusion because it limits benefits for a condition based on the fact that the condition was present before the effective date of coverage. The plan provision, therefore, is prohibited.

Example 4. (i) *Facts.* A group health plan provides coverage for three infertility treatments. The plan counts against the three-treatment limit benefits provided under prior health coverage.

(ii) *Conclusion.* In this *Example 4,* counting benefits for a specific condition provided under prior health coverage against a treatment limit for that condition is a preexisting condition exclusion because it operates to limit benefits for a condition based on the fact that the condition was present before the effective date of coverage. The plan provision, therefore, is prohibited.

Example 5. * * *

(ii) *Conclusion.* In this *Example 5,* the requirement to be covered under the plan for 12 months to be eligible for pregnancy benefits is a subterfuge for a preexisting condition exclusion because it is designed to exclude benefits for a condition (pregnancy) that arose before the effective date of coverage. The plan provision, therefore, is prohibited.

Example 6. * * *

(ii) *Conclusion.* In this *Example 6,* the exclusion of coverage for treatment of congenital heart conditions is a preexisting condition exclusion because it operates to exclude benefits relating to a condition based on the fact that the condition was present before the effective date of coverage. The plan provision, therefore, is prohibited.

Example 7. * * *

(ii) *Conclusion.* In this *Example 7,* the exclusion of coverage for treatment of cleft palate is not a preexisting condition exclusion because the exclusion applies regardless of when the condition arose relative to the effective date of coverage. The plan provision, therefore, is not prohibited. (But see 45 CFR 147.150, which may require coverage of cleft palate as an essential health benefit for health insurance coverage in the individual or small group market).

Example 8. * * *

(ii) *Conclusion.* In this *Example 8,* the exclusion of coverage for treatment of cleft palate for individuals who have not been covered under the plan from the date of birth operates to exclude benefits in relation to a condition based on the fact that the condition was present before the effective date of coverage. The plan provision, therefore, is prohibited.

* * * * *

(b) *General rules.* See § 2590.715-2704 for rules prohibiting the imposition of a preexisting condition exclusion.

■ 16. Section 2590.701-4 is amended by removing paragraphs (a)(3) and (c), and revising paragraph (b) to read as follows:

§ 2590.701-4 Rules relating to creditable coverage.

* * * * *

(b) *Counting creditable coverage rules superseded by prohibition on preexisting condition exclusion.* See § 2590.715-2704 for rules prohibiting the imposition of a preexisting condition exclusion.

■ 17. Section 2590.701-5 is revised to read as follows:

§ 2590.701-5 Evidence of creditable coverage.

(a) *In general.* The rules for providing certificates of creditable coverage and demonstrating creditable coverage have been superseded by the prohibition on preexisting condition exclusions. *See* § 2590.715-2704 for rules prohibiting the imposition of a preexisting condition exclusion.

(b) *Applicability.* The amendments made under this section apply beginning December 31, 2014.

■ 18. Section 2590.701-6 is amended by removing paragraph (a)(3)(i)(E) and revising paragraphs (a)(3)(i)(C), (a)(3)(i)(D), (a)(4)(i), and (d)(2) to read as follows:

§ 2590.701-6 Special enrollment periods.

* * * * *

(a) * * *

(3) * * *

(i) * * *

(C) In the case of coverage offered through an HMO, or other arrangement, in the group market that does not provide benefits to individuals who no longer reside, live, or work in a service area, loss of coverage because an individual no longer resides, lives, or works in the service area (whether or not within the choice of the individual), and no other benefit package is available to the individual; and

(D) A situation in which a plan no longer offers any benefits to the class of similarly situated individuals (as described in § 2590.702(d)) that includes the individual.

* * * * *

(4) * * *

(i) A plan or issuer must allow an employee a period of at least 30 days after an event described in paragraph (a)(3) of this section to request enrollment (for the employee or the employee's dependent).

* * * * *

(d) * * *

(2) Special enrollees must be offered all the benefit packages available to similarly situated individuals who enroll when first eligible. For this purpose, any difference in benefits or cost-sharing requirements for different individuals constitutes a different benefit package. In addition, a special enrollee cannot be required to pay more for coverage than a similarly situated individual who enrolls in the same coverage when first eligible.

* * * * *

■ 19. Section 2590.701-7 is revised to read as follows:

§ 2590.701-7 HMO affiliation period as an alternative to a preexisting condition exclusion.

The rules for HMO affiliation periods have been superseded by the prohibition on preexisting condition exclusions. *See* § 2590.715-2704 for rules prohibiting the imposition of a preexisting condition exclusion.

■ 20. Section 2590.702 is amended by:

■ A. Removing paragraph (b)(3) and revising paragraphs (b)(1)(i) and (b)(2)(i)(B).

■ B. Revising Example 1, paragraph (i) of Example 2, paragraph (ii) of Example 4, paragraph (ii) of Example 5, and removing Example 8, in paragraph (b)(2)(i)(D).

■ C. Revising Example 2, and paragraph (i) of Example 5, in paragraph (d)(4).

■ D. Revising paragraph (ii) of Example 2 in paragraph (e)(2)(i)(B).

■ E. Revising Example 1 in paragraph (g)(1)(ii).

The revisions read as follows:

§2590.702 Prohibiting discrimination against participants and beneficiaries based on a health factor.

* * * * *

(b) * * *

(1) * * *

(i) A group health plan, and a health insurance issuer offering health insurance coverage in connection with a group health plan, may not establish any rule for eligibility (including continued eligibility) of any individual to enroll for benefits under the terms of the plan or group health insurance coverage that discriminates based on any health factor that relates to that individual or a dependent of that individual. This rule is subject to the provisions of paragraph (b)(2) of this section (explaining how this rule applies to benefits), paragraph (d) of this section (containing rules for establishing groups of similarly situated individuals), paragraph (e) of this section (relating to nonconfinement, actively-at-work, and other service requirements), paragraph (f) of this section (relating to wellness programs), and paragraph (g) of this section (permitting favorable treatment of individuals with adverse health factors).

* * * * *

(2) * * *

(i) * * *

(B) However, benefits provided under a plan must be uniformly available to all similarly situated individuals (as described in paragraph (d) of this section). Likewise, any restriction on a benefit or benefits must apply uniformly to all similarly situated individuals and must not be directed at individual participants or beneficiaries based on any health factor of the participants or beneficiaries (determined based on all the relevant facts and circumstances). Thus, for example, a plan may limit or exclude benefits in relation to a specific disease or condition, limit or exclude benefits for certain types of treatments or drugs, or limit or exclude benefits based on a determination of whether the benefits are experimental or not medically necessary, but only if the benefit limitation or exclusion applies uniformly to all similarly situated individuals and is not directed at individual participants or beneficiaries based on any health factor of the participants or beneficiaries. In addition, a plan or issuer may require the satisfaction of a deductible, copayment, coinsurance, or other cost-sharing requirement in order to obtain a benefit if the limit or cost-sharing requirement applies uniformly to all similarly situated individuals and is not directed at individual participants or beneficiaries based on any health factor of the participants or beneficiaries. In the case of a cost-sharing requirement, see also paragraph (b)(2)(ii) of this section, which permits variances in the application of a cost-sharing mechanism made available under a wellness program. (Whether any plan provision or practice with respect to benefits complies with this paragraph (b)(2)(i) does not affect whether the provision or practice is permitted under ERISA, the Affordable Care Act (including the requirements related to essential health benefits), the Americans with Disabilities Act, or any other law, whether State or Federal.)

* * * * *

(D) * * *

Example 1. (i) *Facts.* A group health plan applies a $10,000 annual limit on a specific covered benefit that is not an essential health benefit to each participant or beneficiary covered under the plan. The limit is not directed at individual participants or beneficiaries.

(ii) *Conclusion.* In this *Example 1,* the limit does not violate this paragraph (b)(2)(i) because coverage of the specific, non-essential health benefit up to $10,000 is available uniformly to each participant and beneficiary under the plan and because the limit is applied uniformly to all participants and beneficiaries and is not directed at individual participants or beneficiaries.

Example 2. (i) *Facts.* A group health plan has a $500 deductible on all benefits for participants covered under the plan. Participant *B* files a claim for the treatment of AIDS. At the next corporate board meeting of the plan sponsor, the claim is discussed. Shortly thereafter, the plan is modified to impose a $2,000 deductible on benefits for the treatment of AIDS, effective before the beginning of the next plan year.

* * * * *

Example 4. * * *

(ii) *Conclusion.* In this *Example 4,* the limit does not violate this paragraph (b)(2)(i) because $2,000 of benefits for the treatment of TMJ are available uniformly to all similarly situated individuals and a plan may limit benefits covered in relation to a specific disease or condition

if the limit applies uniformly to all similarly situated individuals and is not directed at individual participants or beneficiaries. (However, applying a lifetime limit on TMJ may violate §2590.715-2711, if TMJ coverage is an essential health benefit. This example does not address whether the plan provision is permissible under any other applicable law, including PHS Act section 2711 or the Americans with Disabilities Act.)

Example 5. * * *

(ii) *Conclusion.* In this *Example 5,* the lower lifetime limit for participants and beneficiaries with a congenital heart defect violates this paragraph (b)(2)(i) because benefits under the plan are not uniformly available to all similarly situated individuals and the plan's lifetime limit on benefits does not apply uniformly to all similarly situated individuals. Additionally, this plan provision is prohibited under §2590.715-2711 because it imposes a lifetime limit on essential health benefits.

* * * * *

(d) * * *

(4) * * *

Example 2. (i) *Facts.* Under a group health plan, coverage is made available to employees, their spouses, and their children. However, coverage is made available to a child only if the child is under age 26 (or under age 29 if the child is continuously enrolled full-time in an institution of higher learning (full-time students)). There is no evidence to suggest that these classifications are directed at individual participants or beneficiaries.

(ii) *Conclusion.* In this Example 2, treating spouses and children differently by imposing an age limitation on children, but not on spouses, is permitted under this paragraph (d). Specifically, the distinction between spouses and children is permitted under paragraph (d)(2) of this section and is not prohibited under paragraph (d)(3) of this section because it is not directed at individual participants or beneficiaries. It is also permissible to treat children who are under age 26 (or full-time students under age 29) as a group of similarly situated individuals separate from those who are age 26 or older (or age 29 or older if they are not full-time students) because the classification is permitted under paragraph (d)(2) of this section and is not directed at individual participants or beneficiaries.

* * * * *

Example 5. (i) *Facts.* An employer sponsors a group health plan that provides the same benefit package to all seven employees of the employer. Six of the seven employees have the same job title and responsibilities, but Employee *G* has a different job title and different responsibilities. After *G* files an expensive claim for benefits under the plan, coverage under the plan is modified so that employees with *G*'s job title receive a different benefit package that includes a higher deductible than in the benefit package made available to the other six employees.

* * * * *

(e) * * *

(2) * * *

(i) * * *

(B) * * *

Example 2. * * *

(ii) *Conclusion.* In this Example 2, the plan violates this paragraph (e)(2) (and thus also paragraph (b) of this section) because the 90-day continuous service requirement is a rule for eligibility based on whether an individual is actively at work. However, the plan would not violate this paragraph (e)(2) or paragraph (b) of this section if, under the plan, an absence due to any health factor is not considered an absence for purposes of measuring 90 days of continuous service. (In addition, any eligibility provision that is time-based must comply with the requirements of PHS Act section 2708 and its implementing regulations.)

* * * * *

(g) * * *

(1) * * *

(ii) * * *

Example 1. (i) *Facts.* An employer sponsors a group health plan that generally is available to employees, spouses of employees, and dependent children until age 26. However, dependent children who are disabled are eligible for coverage beyond age 26.

1720

(ii) *Conclusion.* In this Example 1, the plan provision allowing coverage for disabled dependent children beyond age 26 satisfies this paragraph (g)(1) (and thus does not violate this section).

* * * * *

21. Section 2590.715-2708 is added to read as follows:

§2590.715-2708 Prohibition on waiting periods that exceed 90 days.

(a) *General rule.* A group health plan, and a health insurance issuer offering group health insurance coverage, must not apply any waiting period that exceeds 90 days, in accordance with the rules of this section. If, under the terms of a plan, an employee can elect coverage that would begin on a date that is not later than the end of the 90-day waiting period, this paragraph (a) is considered satisfied. Accordingly, a plan or issuer in that case will not be considered to have violated this paragraph (a) solely because employees (or other classes of participants) may take additional time (beyond the end of the 90-day waiting period) to elect coverage.

(b) *Waiting period defined.* For purposes of this part, a waiting period is the period that must pass before coverage for an employee or dependent who is otherwise eligible to enroll under the terms of a group health plan can become effective. If an employee or dependent enrolls as a late enrollee (as defined under §2590.701-2) or special enrollee (as described in §2590.701-6), any period before such late or special enrollment is not a waiting period.

(c) *Relation to a plan's eligibility criteria*—(1) Except as provided in paragraphs (c)(2) and (c)(3) of this section, being otherwise eligible to enroll under the terms of a group health plan means having met the plan's substantive eligibility conditions (such as, for example, being in an eligible job classification or achieving job-related licensure requirements specified in the plan's terms). Moreover, except as provided in paragraphs (c)(2) and (c)(3) of this section, nothing in this section requires a plan sponsor to offer coverage to any particular employee or class of employees (including, for example, part-time employees). Instead, this section prohibits requiring otherwise eligible participants and beneficiaries to wait more than 90 days before coverage is effective. (While a substantive eligibility condition that denies coverage to employees may be permissible under this section, a failure by an applicable large employer (as defined in section 4980H of the Code) to offer coverage to a full-time employee might, for example, nonetheless give rise to an assessable payment under Code section 4980H and its implementing regulations.)

(2) *Eligibility conditions based solely on the lapse of time.* Eligibility conditions that are based solely on the lapse of a time period are permissible for no more than 90 days.

(3) *Other conditions for eligibility.* Other conditions for eligibility under the terms of a group health plan are generally permissible under PHS Act section 2708, unless the condition is designed to avoid compliance with the 90-day waiting period limitation, determined in accordance with the rules of this paragraph (c)(3).

(i) *Application to variable-hour employees in cases in which a specified number of hours of service per period is a plan eligibility condition.* If a group health plan conditions eligibility on an employee regularly having a specified number of hours of service per period (or working full-time), and it cannot be determined that a newly-hired employee is reasonably expected to regularly work that number of hours per period (or work full-time), the plan may take a reasonable period of time, not to exceed 12 months and beginning on any date between the employee's start day and the first day of the first calendar month following the employee's start date, to determine whether the employee meets the plan's eligibility condition. Except in cases in which a waiting period that exceeds 90 days is imposed in addition to a measurement period, the time period for determining whether such an employee meets the plan's eligibility condition will not be considered to be designed to avoid compliance with the 90-day waiting period limitation if coverage is made effective no later than 13 months from the employee's start date, plus if the employee's start date is not the first day of a calendar month, the time remaining until the first day of the next calendar month.

(ii) *Cumulative service requirements.* If a group health plan or health insurance issuer conditions eligibility on an employee's having completed a number of cumulative hours of service, the eligibility condition is not considered to be designed to avoid compliance with the 90-day waiting period limitation if the cumulative hours-of-service requirement does not exceed 1,200 hours.

(d) *Counting days.* Under this section, all calendar days are counted beginning on the enrollment date (as defined in §2590.701-2), including weekends and holidays. If, in the case of a plan or issuer imposing a

90-day waiting period, the 91st day is a weekend or holiday, the plan or issuer may choose to permit coverage to become effective earlier than the 91st day, for administrative convenience. Similarly, plans and issuers that do not want to start coverage in the middle of a month (or pay period) may choose to permit coverage to become effective earlier than the 91st day, for administrative convenience. For example, a plan may impose a waiting period of 60 days plus a fraction of a month (or pay period) until the first day of the next month (or pay period). However, a plan or issuer that extends the effective date of coverage beyond the 91st day fails to comply with the 90-day waiting period limitation.

(e) *Examples.* The rules of this section are illustrated by the following examples:

Example 1. (i) *Facts.* A group health plan provides that full-time employees are eligible for coverage under the plan. Employee A begins employment as a full-time employee on January 19.

(ii) *Conclusion.* In this *Example 1,* any waiting period for A would begin on January 19 and may not exceed 90 days. Coverage under the plan must become effective no later than April 19 (assuming February lasts 28 days).

Example 2. (i) *Facts.* A group health plan provides that only employees with job title M are eligible for coverage under the plan. Employee B begins employment in job title L on January 30.

(ii) *Conclusion.* In this *Example 2,* B is not eligible for coverage under the plan, and the period while B is working in job title L and therefore not in an eligible class of employees is not part of a waiting period under this section.

Example 3. (i) *Facts.* Same facts as *Example 2,* except that B transfers to a new position with job title M on April 11.

(ii) *Conclusion.* In this *Example 3,* B becomes eligible for coverage on April 11, but for the waiting period. Any waiting period for B begins on April 11 and may not exceed 90 days. Coverage under the plan must become effective no later than July 10.

Example 4. (i) *Facts.* A group health plan provides that only employees who have completed specified training and achieved specified certifications are eligible for coverage under the plan. Employee C is hired on May 3 and meets the plan's eligibility criteria on September 22.

(ii) *Conclusion.* In this *Example 4,* C becomes eligible for coverage on September 22, but for the waiting period. Any waiting period for C would begin on September 22 and may not exceed 90 days. Coverage under the plan must become effective no later than December 21.

Example 5. (i) *Facts.* A group health plan provides that employees are eligible for coverage after one year of service.

(ii) *Conclusion.* In this *Example 5,* the plan's eligibility condition is based solely on the lapse of time and, therefore, is impermissible under paragraph (c)(2) of this section because it exceeds 90 days.

Example 6. (i) *Facts.* Employer W's group health plan provides for coverage to begin on the first day of the first payroll period on or after the date an employee is hired and completes the applicable enrollment forms. Enrollment forms are distributed on an employee's start date and may be completed within 90 days. Employee D is hired and starts on October 31, which is the first day of a pay period. D completes the enrollment forms and submits them on the 90th day after D's start date. Coverage is made effective 7 days later, which is the first day of the next pay period.

(ii) *Conclusion.* In this *Example 6,* under the terms of W's plan, coverage may become effective as early as October 31, depending on when D completes the applicable enrollment forms. Under the terms of the plan, when coverage becomes effective is dependent solely on the length of time taken by D to complete the enrollment materials. Therefore, under the terms of the plan, D may elect coverage that would begin on a date that does not exceed the 90-day waiting period limitation, and the plan complies with this section.

Example 7. (i) *Facts.* Under Employer Y's group health plan, only employees who are full-time (defined under the plan as regularly averaging 30 hours of service per week) are eligible for coverage. Employee E begins employment for Employer Y on November 26 of Year 1. E's hours are reasonably expected to vary, with an opportunity to work between 20 and 45 hours per week, depending on shift availability and E's availability. Therefore, it cannot be determined at E's start date that E is reasonably expected to work full-time. Under the terms of the plan, variable-hour employees, such as E, are eligible to enroll in the plan if they are determined to be a full-time employee after a measurement period of 12 months that begins on the employee's start date. Coverage is made effective no later than the first day of the first calendar month after the applicable enrollment forms are received. E's

12-month measurement period ends November 25 of Year 2. *E* is determined to be a full-time employee and is notified of *E'* s plan eligibility. If *E* then elects coverage, *E'* s first day of coverage will be January 1 of Year 3.

(ii) *Conclusion.* In this *Example 7,* the measurement period is permissible because it is not considered to be designed to avoid compliance with the 90-day waiting period limitation. The plan may use a reasonable period of time to determine whether a variable-hour employee is a full-time employee, provided the period of time is no longer than 12 months and begins on a date between the employee's start date and the first day of the next calendar month, provided coverage is made effective no later than 13 months from *E'* s start date (plus if the employee's start date is not the first day of a calendar month, the time remaining until the first day of the next calendar month) and provided that, in addition to the measurement period, no more than 90 days elapse prior to the employee's eligibility for coverage.

Example 8. (i) *Facts.* Employee *F* begins working 25 hours per week for Employer *Z* on January 6 and is considered a part-time employee for purposes of *Z'* s group health plan. *Z* sponsors a group health plan that provides coverage to part-time employees after they have completed a cumulative 1,200 hours of service. *F* satisfies the plan's cumulative hours of service condition on December 15.

(ii) *Conclusion.* In this *Example 8,* the cumulative hours of service condition with respect to part-time employees is not considered to be designed to avoid compliance with the 90-day waiting period limitation. Accordingly, coverage for *F* under the plan must begin no later than the 91st day after *F* completes 1,200 hours. (If the plan's cumulative hours-of-service requirement was more than 1,200 hours, the requirement would be considered to be designed to avoid compliance with the 90-day waiting period limitation.)

(f) *Special rule for health insurance issuers.* To the extent coverage under a group health plan is insured by a health insurance issuer, the issuer is permitted to rely on the eligibility information reported to it by the employer (or other plan sponsor) and will not be considered to violate the requirements of this section with respect to its administration of any waiting period, if both of the following conditions are satisfied:

(1) The issuer requires the plan sponsor to make a representation regarding the terms of any eligibility conditions or waiting periods imposed by the plan sponsor before an individual is eligible to become covered under the terms of the employer's plan (and requires the plan sponsor to update this representation with any changes), and

(2) The issuer has no specific knowledge of the imposition of a waiting period that would exceed the permitted 90-day period.

(g) *No effect on other laws.* Compliance with this section is not determinative of compliance with any other provision of State or Federal law (including ERISA, the Code, or other provisions of the Patient Protection and Affordable Care Act). *See e.g.,* § 2590.702, which prohibits discrimination in eligibility for coverage based on a health factor and Code section 4980H, which generally requires applicable large employers to offer coverage to full-time employees and their dependents or make an assessable payment.

(h) *Applicability date*—(1) *In general.* The provisions of this section apply for plan years beginning on or after January 1, 2014. *See* § 2590.715-1251 providing that the prohibition on waiting periods exceeding 90 days applies to all group health plans and health insurance issuers, including grandfathered health plans.

(2) *Application to individuals in a waiting period prior to the applicability date*—(i) With respect to individuals who are in a waiting period for coverage before the applicability date of this section, beginning on the first day the section applies, the waiting period can no longer apply

to the individual if it would exceed 90 days with respect to the individual.

(ii) This paragraph (h) (2) is illustrated by the following example:

Example. (i) *Facts.* A group health plan is a calendar year plan. Prior to January 1, 2014, the plan provides that full-time employees are eligible for coverage after a 6-month waiting period. Employee *A* begins work as a full-time employee on October 1, 2013.

(ii) *Conclusion.* In this *Example 1,* the first day of A's waiting period is October 1, 2013 because that is the first day *A* is otherwise eligible to enroll under the plan's substantive eligibility provisions, but for the waiting period. Beginning January 1, 2014, the plan may not apply a waiting period that exceeds 90 days. Accordingly, *A* must be given the opportunity to elect coverage that begins no later than January 1, 2014 (which is 93 days after *A'* s start date) because otherwise, on January 1, 2014, the plan would be applying a waiting period that exceeds 90 days. The plan is not required to make coverage effective before January 1, 2014 under the rules of this section.

■ 22. Section 2590.715-2719 is amended by adding a sentence to the end of the introductory text of paragraph (d) and revising paragraph (d) (1) (i) to read as follows:

§ 2590.715-2719 Internal claims and appeals and external review processes.

* * * * *

(d) * * * A Multi State Plan or MSP, as defined by 45 CFR 800.20, must provide an effective Federal external review process in accordance with this paragraph (d).

(1) * * *

(i) *In general.* Subject to the suspension provision in paragraph (d) (1) (ii) of this section and except to the extent provided otherwise by the Secretary in guidance, the Federal external review process established pursuant to this paragraph (d) applies, at a minimum, to any adverse benefit determination or final adverse benefit determination (as defined in paragraphs (a) (2) (i) and (a) (2) (v) of this section), except that a denial, reduction, termination, or a failure to provide payment for a benefit based on a determination that a participant or beneficiary fails to meet the requirements for eligibility under the terms of a group health plan is not eligible for the Federal external review process under this paragraph (d).

* * * * *

■ 23. Section 2590.731 is amended by revising paragraph (c) (2) to read as follows:

§ 2590.731 Preemption; State flexibility; construction.

* * * * *

(c) * * *

(2) *Exceptions.* Only in relation to health insurance coverage offered by a health insurance issuer, the provisions of this part do not supersede any provision of State law to the extent that such provision requires special enrollment periods in addition to those required under section 701 (f) of the Act.

* * * * *

■ 24. Section 2590.732 is amended by removing paragraph (b) (2) (i), and redesignating paragraphs (b) (2) (ii) through (b) (2) (ix) as (b) (2) (i) through (b) (2) (viii).

* * * * *

[FR Doc. 2013-06454 Filed 3-18-13; 4:15 pm]

BILLING CODE 4830-01-P; 4510-029-P; 4120-01-P; 6325-64

¶ 20,263M

IRS: Executive compensation: Health insurance providers: Deduction limit: Remuneration in excess of $500,000.—The IRS has released proposed regulations on the application of the $500,000 deduction limitation for remuneration provided by certain health insurance providers under Code Sec. 162(m)(6), which was added to the Code by the Patient Protection and Affordable Care Act (P.L. 111-148). These regulations affect health insurance providers that pay such remuneration. They apply to tax years that begin after December 31, 2012, and end on or after April 2, 2013, and are effective on publication of final regulations in the Federal Register. The proposed regulations may be relied upon until the issuance of the final regulations.

The proposed regulations were published in the Federal Register on April 2, 2013 (78 FR 19950). The regulations were finalized September 23, 2014 (79 FR 56892). The preamble to the final regulations is at ¶ 23,307. The final regulations are at ¶ 11,307G.

April 2, 2013

Part V

Department of the Treasury

Internal Revenue Service

26 CFR Part 1

The $500,000 Deduction Limitation for Remuneration Provided by Certain Health Insurance Providers; Proposed Rule

DEPARTMENT OF THE TREASURY

Internal Revenue Service

26 CFR Part 1

[REG-106796-12]

RIN 1545-BK88

The $500,000 Deduction Limitation for Remuneration Provided by Certain Health Insurance Providers

AGENCY: Internal Revenue Service (IRS), Treasury.

ACTION: Notice of proposed rulemaking.

SUMMARY: This document contains proposed regulations on the application of the $500,000 deduction limitation for remuneration provided by certain health insurance providers under section 162(m)(6) of the Internal Revenue Code (Code). These regulations affect health insurance providers that pay such remuneration.

DATES: Written or electronic comments and requests for a hearing must be received by July 1, 2013.

ADDRESSES: Send submissions to CC:PA:LPD:PR (REG-106796-12), Internal Revenue Service, PO Box 7604, Ben Franklin Station, Washington DC 20044. Submissions may be hand-delivered Monday through Friday between the hours of 8 a.m. and 4 p.m. to CC:PA:LPD:PR (REG-106796-12), Courier's Desk Internal Revenue Service, 1111 Constitution Avenue NW., Washington, DC, or sent electronically via the IRS Internet site via the Federal eRulemaking Portal at *www.regulations.gov* (IRS REG-106796-12).

FOR FURTHER INFORMATION CONTACT:

Concerning these proposed regulations, Ilya Enkishev at (202) 622-6030; concerning the submission of comments or to request a public hearing, Oluwafunmilayo (Funmi) Taylor at (202) 622-7180 (not toll-free numbers).

SUPPLEMENTARY INFORMATION:

Background

This document contains a proposed amendment to 26 CFR part 1 under section 162(m)(6) of the Code. Section 162(m)(6) limits the allowable deduction for remuneration attributable to services provided by applicable individuals to certain health insurance providers that receive premiums from providing health insurance coverage. Section 162(m)(6) was added to the Code by section 9014 of the Patient Protection and Affordable Care Act (ACA) (Pub. L. 111-148, 124 Stat. 119, 868 (2010)).

On December 23, 2010, the Treasury Department and the IRS released Notice 2011-2 (2011-1 CB 260), which provides guidance on certain issues under section 162(m)(6). Specifically, the notice provides guidance on the application of the $500,000 deduction limitation to deferred deduction remuneration that is earned during taxable years beginning after December 31, 2009 and before January 1, 2013 and deductible in a taxable year beginning after December 31, 2012. The notice also provides a *de minimis* exception under which a covered health insurance provider is exempt from the deduction limitation if the health insurance premiums received by it and all other entities with which it must be aggregated under section 162(m)(6) are less than two percent of their combined gross revenues. In addition, the notice provides that remuneration subject to section 162(m)(6) does not include remuneration earned by independent contractors who are not subject to section 409A (meaning generally that the independent contractor provides substantial services to multiple unrelated customers). Finally, the notice provides that premiums under a reinsurance contract are not treated as premiums for providing health insurance coverage for purposes of section 162(m)(6).

Notice 2011-2 requested comments on the following issues:

• Application of the term *covered health insurance provider,* including the *de minimis* exception set forth in the notice and possible alternative *de minimis* exceptions;

• How deferred deduction remuneration should be attributed to a taxable year of an employer;

• Application of the term *covered health insurance provider* in the case of a corporate event such as a merger, acquisition, or reorganization; and

• Application of the deduction limitation to remuneration for services performed for insurers who are captive insurance companies or that provide reinsurance or stop loss insurance.

In drafting these proposed regulations, the Treasury Department and the IRS have considered all comments received, many of which are discussed in this preamble. See § 601.601(d)(2)(ii)(b).

Explanation of Provisions

For taxable years beginning after December 31, 2012, section 162(m)(6) limits to $500,000 the allowable deduction for the aggregate applicable individual remuneration and deferred deduction remuneration attributable to services performed by an applicable individual for a covered health insurance provider in a disqualified taxable year beginning after December 31, 2012 that (but for section 162(m)(6)) is otherwise deductible under chapter 1 of the Code (referred to in this preamble as remuneration that is otherwise deductible). Deferred deduction remuneration attributable to services performed in a disqualified taxable year beginning after December 31, 2009 and before January 1, 2013 that becomes otherwise deductible in taxable years beginning after December 31, 2012 is also subject to the $500,000 deduction limitation, determined as if the deduction limitation applied to disqualified taxable years beginning after December 31, 2009.

Accordingly, if applicable individual remuneration, deferred deduction remuneration, or a combination of applicable individual remuneration and deferred deduction remuneration that is attributable to services performed by an applicable individual for a covered health insurance provider in a disqualified taxable year exceeds $500,000, the amount of the remuneration that exceeds $500,000 is not allowable as a deduction in any taxable year. To the extent that the aggregate applicable individual remuneration and deferred deduction remuneration attributable to services performed by an applicable individual for a covered health insurance provider in a disqualified taxable year is less than $500,000, the remuneration generally may be deducted by the covered health insurance provider in the taxable year or years in which the amount is otherwise deductible.

The following example illustrates the application of the section 162(m)(6) deduction limitation. In Year 1, a covered health insurance provider pays $400,000 in salary (applicable individual remuneration) to an applicable individual and also credits $300,000 to an account for the applicable individual under a nonqualified deferred compensation plan, which is payable in Year 5 (deferred deduction remuneration). The $300,000 credit is fully vested in Year 1 and is attributable to services provided by the applicable individual in that year. In Year 1, the covered health insurance provider may deduct the $400,000 of applicable individual remuneration paid to the applicable individual for services provided during that year because the amount of this payment is less than the $500,000 deduction limit. In Year 5, the covered health insurance provider pays the $300,000 that was credited under the nonqualified deferred compensation plan for services provided by the applicable individual in Year 1. Because the aggregated applicable individual remuneration and deferred deduction remuneration attributable to services performed by the applicable individual in Year 1 exceeds the $500,000 deduction limit by $200,000 ($400,000 + $300,000 = $700,000), the covered health insurance provider can deduct only $100,000 of the $300,000 payment in year 5, and the remaining $200,000 is not deductible by the covered health insurance provider in any year.

I. Covered Health Insurance Provider

A. In General

Section 162(m)(6)(C) provides that a covered health insurance provider is any health insurance issuer described in section 162(m)(6)(C)(i) and certain persons that are treated as a single employer with that health insurance issuer, as described in section 162(m)(6)(C)(ii). These proposed regulations include rules for determining whether a health insurance issuer is a covered health insurance provider for any taxable year and whether a person is treated as a single employer with a health insurance issuer that is a covered health insurance provider for any taxable year. A person may be treated as a covered health insurance provider for one taxable year, but not be treated as a covered health insurance provider for another taxable year, depending on whether that person meets the requirements to be a covered health insurance provider under section 162(m)(6)(C) for a particular taxable year.

B. Health Insurance Issuers

For taxable years beginning after December 31, 2009 and before January 1, 2013, section 162(m)(6)(C)(i)(I) provides that a health insurance issuer (as defined in section 9832(b)(2)) is a covered health insurance provider for a taxable year if that health insurance issuer receives premiums from providing health insurance coverage (as defined in section 9832(b)(1)) during the taxable year. For taxable years beginning after December 31, 2012, section 162(m)(6)(C)(i)(II) provides that a health insurance issuer (as defined in section 9832(b)(2)) is a covered health insurance provider for a taxable year if not less than 25 percent of the gross premiums that the provider receives from providing health insurance coverage (as defined in section 9832(b)(1)) during the taxable year are from minimum essential coverage (as defined in section 5000A(f)).

C. Persons Treated as a Single Employer with a Health Insurance Issuer

Section 162(m)(6)(C)(ii) provides that two or more persons that are treated as a single employer under sections 414(b), (c), (m), or (o) are treated as a single employer for purposes of determining whether a person is a covered health insurance provider, except that in applying section 1563(a) for purposes of these subsections of section 414, sections 1563(a)(2) and (3) (which provide for brother-sister groups and combined groups) are disregarded. Accordingly, these proposed regulations provide that each member of an aggregated group (as described in the final sentence of this paragraph) that includes a health insurance issuer described in section 162(m)(6)(C)(i) at any time during a taxable year is also a covered health insurance provider for purposes of section 162(m)(6), even if the member is not a health insurance issuer and does not provide health insurance coverage. (An exception for certain corporate transactions is provided in the transition rules described in section IX of this preamble.) For this purpose, these proposed regulations define the term *aggregated group* as a health insurance issuer (as defined in section 9832(b)(2)) and all persons that are treated as a single employer with the health insurance issuer under sections 414(b), (c), (m) or (o), disregarding sections 1563(a)(2) and (3) (with respect to controlled groups of corporations) and § 1.414(c)-(2)(c) (with respect to trades or businesses under common control).

For members of an aggregated group that have different taxable years, these proposed regulations provide rules to determine whether a member of an aggregated group that is not a health insurance issuer is a covered health insurance provider for a particular taxable year. Under these rules, the parent entity (as defined in the following paragraph of this preamble) of an aggregated group is a covered health insurance provider for its taxable year with which, or in which, ends the taxable year of the health insurance issuer that is a covered health insurance provider in the aggregated group of which the parent entity is a member. Each other member of an aggregated group is a covered health insurance provider for its taxable year that ends with, or within, the taxable year of the parent entity during which the parent entity is a covered health insurance provider. For purposes of these proposed regulations, the term *parent entity* refers to the common parent of an aggregated group that is a parent-subsidiary controlled group of corporations (within the meaning of section 414(b)) or a parent-subsidiary group of trades or businesses under common control (within the meaning of section 414(c)). With respect to an aggregated group that is an affiliated service group within the meaning of section 414(m) or other group within the meaning of section 414(o), the parent entity is the health insurance issuer in the aggregated group if the aggregated group includes only one health insurance issuer If an aggregated group that is an affiliated service group within the meaning of section 414(m) or other group within the meaning of section 414(o) includes more than one health insurance issuer, the parent entity is any health insurance issuer in the aggregated group that is designated in writing by the other members of the group as the parent entity for purposes of section 162(m)(6), provided that the members of the group treat the health insurance issuer as the parent entity consistently for all taxable years. If the members of an aggregated group that is an affiliated service group or other group fail to designate a parent entity in writing (or fail to apply the designation consistently for all taxable years), the members of the group are deemed to have a parent entity with a taxable year that is the calendar year. A health insurance issuer that has been designated as the parent entity of an aggregated group may leave that group as a result of a merger, disposition, or other corporate transaction; the Treasury Department and the IRS request comments on the circumstances under which a successor parent entity may be designated and any transition rules that may be necessary in this situation.

D. Self-insurers

In response to a request for comments in Notice 2011-2, commenters suggested that an employer that sponsors a self-insured medical reimbursement plan should not be treated as a covered health insurance provider because benefits under this type of plan should not be treated as health insurance coverage for purposes of section 162(m)(6) if the employer assumes the financial risk of providing health benefits to its employees and limits the availability of benefits only to employees (which may include former employees). The Treasury Department and the IRS agree that an employer should not be treated as a covered health insurance provider under these circumstances. Accordingly, these proposed regulations provide that an employer is not a covered health insurance provider solely because it maintains a self-insured medical reimbursement plan. For this purpose, the term *self-insured medical reimbursement plan* means a separate written plan for the benefit of employees (which may include former employees) that provides for reimbursement of employee medical expenses referred to in section 105(b) and that does not provide for reimbursement under an individual or group policy of accident or health insurance issued by a licensed insurance company or under an arrangement in the nature of a prepaid health care plan that is regulated under federal or state law in a manner similar to the regulation of insurance companies. An arrangement described in the prior sentence may include a plan maintained by an employee organization described in section 501(c)(9). A captive insurance company, however, is treated as a covered health insurance provider under these proposed regulations if it is a health insurance issuer that is otherwise described in section 162(m)(6)(C).

E. De Minimis Exception

1. In General

After section 162(m)(6) was enacted, some commenters observed that the aggregation rule in section 162(m)(6)(C)(ii) could result in unintended consequences in situations in which a health insurance issuer's activities and revenue constitute an insignificant portion of the activities and revenue of persons that are treated as a single employer with the health insurance issuer under the aggregation rules. Commenters also suggested that employers that maintain only legacy policies (policies that are no longer sold but for which current policyholders have automatic renewal rights) should not be considered covered health insurance providers because those employers are no longer accepting new policyholders and may find it difficult to transfer the legacy policies for regulatory and other reasons.

In response to these concerns, Notice 2011-2 provides a *de minimis* exception under which a person that would otherwise be a covered health insurance provider under section 162(m)(6)(C)(i)(I) for a taxable year beginning after December 31, 2009 and before January 1, 2013 is not treated as a covered health insurance provider for that taxable year if the premiums received by that person and all other members of its aggregated group from providing health insurance coverage are less than two percent of the gross revenue of that person and all other members of its aggregated group for that taxable year. For taxable years beginning after December 31, 2012, the notice provides that a person that would otherwise be a covered health insurance provider under section 162(m)(6)(C)(i)(II) for a taxable year is not treated as a covered health insurance provider for that taxable year if the premiums received by that person and all other members of its aggregated group from providing health insurance coverage that constitutes minimum essential coverage are less than two percent of the gross revenue of that person and all other members of its aggregated group for that taxable year.

Commenters generally reacted favorably to the *de minimis* exception set forth in Notice 2011-2. One commenter, however, suggested that the *de minimis* exception should be based on compensation instead of revenues. The commenter suggested that a health insurance issuer and the persons that are treated as a single employer with the health insurance issuer under the aggregation rule should not be treated as covered health insurance providers if the compensation paid by the health insurance issuer is less than two percent of the total compensation paid by all members of the aggregated group. The commenter reasoned that comparing compensation rather than gross revenue and premiums would be a better method to measure the importance of the health insurance business to an aggregated group because basing a *de minimis* exception on gross revenue could overemphasize the importance of health insurance activities, which may generate relatively higher revenues but operate on slimmer profit margins. These proposed regulations do not adopt this suggestion. The Treasury Department and the IRS do not agree that comparing compensation paid by the health insurance issuer with the overall compensation paid by the aggregated group would be a better method of measuring the importance of the health insurance business to an aggregated group than comparing premiums with gross revenues. The Treasury Department and the IRS are also concerned that a *de minimis* exception based on compensation would be inadministrable because it would require taxpayers and the IRS to allocate compensation between members of an aggregated group if an individual performs services for more than one member of the aggregated group.

The commenter also suggested that if an individual provides services for a member of an aggregated group, but does not provide any services to the health insurance issuer within the group, then the remuneration for those services should not be subject to the section 162(m)(6) deduction limitation. These proposed regulations do not adopt this suggestion because that rule would be inconsistent with section 162(m)(6)(C)(ii), which treats all members of an aggregated group that includes a health insurance issuer described in section 162(m)(6)(C)(i) as covered health insurance providers subject to the section 162(m)(6) deduction limitation.

One commenter requested that the two-percent threshold for the *de minimis* exception be increased slightly to an unspecified percentage to avoid treating certain aggregated groups of employers that utilize captive insurance companies as covered health insurance providers. Several other commenters, however, requested that the two-percent threshold not be increased because a higher threshold could allow health insurance issuers that sell significant amounts of health insurance coverage to be exempt from the deduction limitation, and thereby provide them with a competitive advantage. After carefully considering these comments, the Treasury Department and the IRS have concluded that the two-percent threshold remains appropriate. Accordingly, these proposed regulations adopt a *de minimis* exception that is substantially similar to the *de minimis* exception set forth in Notice 2011-2.

To accommodate unexpected changes in the revenue sources of an aggregated group and other events that could affect application of the *de minimis* exception, and also to provide a reasonable period for employers that have not previously been treated as covered health insurance providers to adjust their compensation programs, these proposed regulations provide that if a person is not treated as a covered health insurance provider for one or more taxable years solely by reason of the *de minimis* exception, and then fails to meet the requirements for the *de minimis* exception for one or more taxable years, the person will not be treated as a covered health insurance provider for the first taxable year in which it fails to meet the requirements for the *de minimis* exception after previously not being treated as a covered health insurance provider solely by reason of the *de minimis* exception.

2. Application of the De Minimis Exception to Aggregated Groups the Members of Which Have Different Taxable Years

Commenters asked how the *de minimis* exception would apply in situations in which the members of the aggregated group have different taxable years. These proposed regulations provide that the *de minimis* exception applies based on the premiums and gross revenues received for the taxable year of the health insurance issuer and the taxable years of the other members of the aggregated group for which they would otherwise be treated as covered health insurance providers in the absence of the *de minimis* exception. In other words, the *de minimis* exception applies based on the premiums and gross revenues of (i) the health insurance issuer for its taxable year, (ii) the parent entity for its taxable year with which, or in which, ends the taxable year of the health insurance issuer, and (iii) each other member of the aggregated group for its taxable year that ends with, or within, the taxable year of the parent entity.

II. Premiums

A. In General

Section 162(m)(6)(C)(i) provides that a health insurance issuer is a covered health insurance provider for a taxable year only if it receives premiums from providing health insurance coverage (as defined in section 9832(b)(1)). These proposed regulations include rules specifying that amounts received under an indemnity reinsurance contract and amounts that are direct service payments are not treated as premiums from providing health insurance coverage for purposes of section 162(m)(6)(C)(i).

B. Amounts Received Under an Indemnity Reinsurance Contract

Health insurance issuers may reinsure a portion of their risks by entering into an indemnity reinsurance contract with a reinsurer. After Congress enacted section 162(m)(6), commenters suggested that premiums received under an indemnity reinsurance contract should not be treated as premiums from providing health insurance coverage. An indemnity reinsurance contract is a contract between a health insurance issuer and a reinsurer under which a reinsurance claim is payable only after the health insurance issuer has paid an amount for health benefits under its own insurance agreement with the policy holder.

Thus, commenters reasoned, premiums for reinsurance coverage should not be treated as premiums from providing health insurance coverage for purposes of section 162(m)(6). In response to these comments, Notice 2011-2 provides that, solely for purposes of determining whether a taxpayer is a covered health insurance provider, premiums received under an indemnity reinsurance contract are not treated as premiums from providing health insurance coverage.

Consistent with Notice 2011-2, these proposed regulations provide that, solely for purposes of determining whether a person is a covered health insurance provider, premiums received under an indemnity reinsurance contract are not treated as premiums from providing health insurance coverage, provided that under the reinsurance contract (1) the reinsuring company agrees to indemnify the health insurance issuer for all or part of the risk of loss under policies specified in the agreement, and (2) the health insurance issuer retains its liability to, and its contractual relationship with, the individual insured.

C. Direct Service Payments

A health insurance issuer or other person that receives premiums from providing health insurance coverage may enter into an arrangement with a third party to provide, manage, or arrange for the provision of services by physicians, hospitals, or other healthcare providers. In connection with this arrangement, the health insurance issuer or other person that receives premiums from providing health insurance coverage may pay compensation to the third party in the form of capitated, prepaid, periodic, or other payments, and the third party may bear some or all of the risk that the compensation is insufficient to pay the full cost of providing, managing, or arranging for the provision of services by physicians, hospitals, or other healthcare providers as required under the arrangement. In addition, the third party may be subject to healthcare provider, health insurance, licensing, financial solvency, or other regulation under state insurance law. Commenters suggested that compensation payments to these third parties under these types of arrangements should not be treated as premiums from providing health insurance coverage for purposes of section 162(m)(6) because, while the third party bears some risk in connection with providing, managing, or arranging for the provision of healthcare services, a health insurance issuer or other entity that receives premiums from providing health insurance coverage is ultimately responsible for providing health insurance coverage to the insureds. The commenters explained that these risk shifting arrangements are simply methods by which health insurance issuers and other entities that provide health insurance coverage diversify and manage their risk, in a manner similar to reinsurance. The Treasury Department and the IRS agree with this comment. Accordingly, these proposed regulations provide that capitated, prepaid, periodic, or other payments (referred to as direct service payments) made by a health insurance issuer or other person that receives premiums from providing health insurance coverage to a third party as compensation for providing, managing, or arranging for the provision of healthcare services by physicians, hospitals, or other healthcare providers are not treated as premiums for purposes of section 162(m)(6), regardless of whether the third party is subject to healthcare provider, health insurance, licensing, financial solvency, or other similar regulatory requirements under state law.

The Treasury Department and the IRS also understand that certain government entities may make similar capitated, prepaid, or periodic payments to third parties to provide, manage, or arrange for the provision of services by physicians, hospitals, or other healthcare providers and that these third parties may also bear some or all of the risk that the payments are insufficient to pay the full cost of providing, managing, or arranging for the provision of services subject to the arrangement. Under certain circumstances, it may be inappropriate to treat these payments made by government entities as premiums for purposes of section 162(m)(6). However, because these payments are not made by an entity that has received premiums from providing health insurance, it may be difficult to distinguish between payments made to third parties that should be treated as premiums from providing health insurance and payments that should not be treated as premiums from providing health insurance. The Treasury Department and the IRS request comments on when such payments should be treated as premiums from providing health insurance coverage for purposes of section 162(m)(6) and when they should not be treated as premiums for these purposes.

III. Disqualified Taxable Year

Section 162(m)(6)(B) provides that a disqualified taxable year is, with respect to any employer, any taxable year for which the employer is a covered health insurance provider. Consistent with the statutory language, these proposed regulations provide that a disqualified taxable year is, with respect to any person, any taxable year for which that person is a covered health insurance provider.

IV. Applicable Individual

Section 162(m)(6)(F) provides that with respect to a covered health insurance provider for a disqualified taxable year, an applicable individual is any individual (i) who is an officer, director, or employee in such taxable year, or (ii) who provides services for, or on behalf of, the covered health insurance provider during the taxable year. As noted in the Background section of this preamble, Notice 2011-2 provides that the term *applicable individual* for a taxable year does not include an independent contractor with respect to whom a compensation arrangement would not be subject to section 409A pursuant to § 1.409A-1(f)(2). Section 1.409A-1(f)(2) generally provides an exception from section 409A for arrangements that are made with independent contractors that provide substantial services to multiple unrelated service recipients. Commenters suggested that future guidance adopt this rule for purposes of section 162(m)(6).

These proposed regulations adopt this rule. The proposed regulations provide that remuneration for services provided by an independent contractor to a covered health insurance provider will not be subject to the deduction limitation under section 162(m)(6) if each of the following conditions are met. First, the independent contractor is actively engaged in the trade or business of providing services to recipients, other than as an employee or as a member of the board of directors of a corporation (or in a similar position with respect to an entity that is not a corporation). Second, the independent contractor provides significant services (as defined in § 1.409A-1(f)(2)(iii)) to two or more persons to which the independent contractor is not related and that are not related to one another (as defined in § 1.409A-1(f)(2)(ii)). Third, the independent contractor is not related to the covered health insurance provider or any member of its aggregated group, applying the definition of related person contained in § 1.409A-1(f)(2)(ii), except that for purposes of applying the references to sections 267(b) and 707(b)(1), the language "20 percent" is not substituted for "50 percent" in each place "50 percent" appears in sections 267(b) and 707(b)(1).

Commenters also suggested that future guidance clarify that the section 162(m)(6) deduction limitation applies to services provided by individuals that are natural persons and not services provided pursuant to a contract or arrangement with a corporation or partnership. For example, commenters were concerned that remuneration paid to doctors working for practice groups that provide services to a covered health insurance provider would be subject to the deduction limitation under section 162(m)(6). In general, a corporation or a partnership (for federal tax purposes) would not be treated as an applicable individual. However, the Treasury Department and the IRS remain concerned that covered health insurance providers may attempt to avoid the application of the deduction limitation under section 162(m)(6) by encouraging employees and independent contractors who are natural persons to form small or single-member personal service corporations or other similar entities to provide services that are historically provided by natural persons. The Treasury Department and the IRS invite comments regarding how the final regulations might address this potential abuse.

V. Applicable Individual Remuneration

Section 162(m)(6)(D) and these proposed regulations provide that applicable individual remuneration is the aggregate amount that is allowable as a deduction with respect to an applicable individual for a disqualified taxable year (determined without regard to section 162(m)) for remuneration for services performed by that individual (whether or not during the taxable year), except that applicable individual remuneration does not include any amount that is deferred deduction remuneration. Unlike the definition of remuneration in section 162(m)(1), the definition of applicable individual remuneration in section 162(m)(6)(D) includes remuneration that is performance-based compensation, remuneration payable on a commission basis, and remuneration payable under existing binding contracts. Whether remuneration is applicable individual remuneration is determined without regard to when the services for the remuneration are performed. For example, a discretionary bonus first granted and paid to an applicable individual in a disqualified taxable year solely in recognition of services provided in prior years is applicable individual remuneration for the disqualified taxable year even though the bonus does not relate to services provided in the disqualified taxable year. In addition, a grant of restricted stock in a disqualified taxable year for which an applicable individual makes an election under section 83(b) is applicable individual remuneration for the disqualified taxable year of the covered health insurance provider in which the grant of the restricted stock is made.

VI. Deferred Deduction Remuneration

Section 162(m)(6)(E) and these regulations provide that deferred deduction remuneration is remuneration that would be applicable individual remuneration for services that an applicable individual performs during a disqualified taxable year, but for the fact that it is not deductible until a later taxable year (such as generally occurs, for example, with nonqualified deferred compensation). Whether remuneration is deferred deduction remuneration is determined based on when the remuneration is deductible, regardless of when the remuneration is paid. For example, a bonus that is paid within 21.2 months after the end of a covered health insurance provider's taxable year in which an applicable individual first obtains a right to the remuneration is deductible in the covered health insurance provider's taxable year in which the applicable individual obtains the right and, therefore, is applicable individual remuneration, rather than deferred deduction remuneration. See section 404(a)(5); § 1.404(b)-1T Q&A-2.

VII. Attribution of Applicable Individual Remuneration and Deferred Deduction Remuneration to Services Performed in Taxable Years

The $500,000 deduction limitation under section 162(m)(6) applies to the applicable individual remuneration and deferred deduction remuneration that is attributable to services performed by an applicable individual for a covered health insurance provider in a disqualified taxable year. Accordingly, at the time that an amount of applicable individual remuneration or deferred deduction remuneration for an applicable individual becomes otherwise deductible (and not before that time), the remuneration must be attributed to services provided by the applicable individual during a particular taxable year or years of a covered health insurance provider.

In response to a request for comments in Notice 2011-2, some commenters asked that taxpayers be permitted to use any reasonable method to attribute remuneration to taxable years of a covered health insurance provider, as long as the method is applied consistently. Commenters observed that the allocation methods for purposes of section 162(m)(5) set forth in Notice 2008-94 (relating to recipients of payments under the Troubled Asset Relief Program) may not be appropriate for purposes of section 162(m)(6) because the methods in Notice 2008-94 were developed for employers expected to be subject to the deduction limitation under section 162(m)(5) only temporarily, and thus necessarily provided less flexibility than may be appropriate for purposes of section 162(m)(6). Permitting taxpayers to use any reasonable method to attribute remuneration to a taxable year of a covered health insurance provider, however, may lead to results that are inconsistent with section 162(m)(6) and the legislative intent underlying the statute. Accordingly, these proposed regulations provide rules for attributing applicable individual remuneration and deferred deduction remuneration to services performed by an applicable individual during a taxable year or years of a covered health insurance provider. Nonetheless, the Treasury Department and the IRS remain concerned about imposing undue burdens on taxpayers and request comments regarding the ease or difficulty of applying the attribution rules described in these proposed regulations and regarding specific alternatives for attributing applicable individual remuneration and deferred deduction remuneration to services performed during taxable years of a covered health insurance provider that would be less burdensome or otherwise more appropriate.

A. In General

These proposed regulations provide that remuneration is attributable to services performed by an applicable individual in the taxable year of the covered health insurance provider in which the applicable individual obtains a legally binding right to the remuneration, unless the remuneration is attributable to a different taxable year under another provision of these regulations.

In addition, these proposed regulations provide that deferred deduction remuneration is not attributable to a taxable year ending before the later of the date that (i) an applicable individual begins providing services to a covered health insurance provider, or (ii) an applicable individual obtains a legally binding right to the remuneration. If any amount of remuneration that becomes otherwise deductible would be attributable under the rules provided in these proposed regulations to a taxable year ending before the applicable individual begins providing services to a covered health insurance provider or obtains a legally binding right to the remuneration, these proposed regulations provide that this remuneration is attributed to services performed by the applicable individual in the taxable year in which the latter of these two dates occurs.

These proposed regulations further provide that remuneration is not attributable to periods when an applicable individual is not a service provider. Solely for purposes of these proposed regulations, an individual is treated as a service provider for any period during which the individual is an officer, director, or employee of, or providing services for, or on behalf of, a covered health insurance provider or any member of its aggregated group. An amount of remuneration that otherwise would be attributable under the rules set forth in these proposed regulations to a period when an applicable individual is not a service provider must be reattributed to a period during which the applicable individual is a service provider in accordance with the rules set forth in these proposed regulations.[1] Accordingly, for example, compensation such as earnings on an account balance after termination of employment but before payment, or appreciation of a share's fair market value after termination of employment but before the exercise of a stock option or stock appreciation right, must be attributed to the period during which the applicable individual is a service provider.

If an amount of remuneration that becomes otherwise deductible may be attributed to services performed by an applicable individual in two or more taxable years of a covered health insurance provider in accordance with the rules for attributing remuneration set forth in the immediately following sections of this preamble for attributing remuneration under an account balance plan or a nonaccount balance plan, the amount must be attributed first to services performed by the applicable individual in the earliest taxable year to which the amount could be attributed under the applicable attribution rules, and then to the next subsequent taxable year to which the amount could be attributed under those attribution rules, until the entire amount has been attributed to one or more taxable years of the covered health insurance provider.

B. Account Balance Plans

To minimize the administrative burden on taxpayers in applying the remuneration attribution rules for account balance plans (as described in §1.409A-1(c)(2)(i)(A) and (B)), these proposed regulations provide that remuneration for an account balance plan may be attributed to a taxable year based on the increase in the account balance during the taxable year, taking into account adjustments for the amount of any payments from that account during the taxable year. This method of attributing remuneration is referred to in the proposed regulations as the standard attribution method. Under the standard attribution method, the amount of remuneration attributable to services performed in a taxable year of a covered health insurance provider is equal to the excess of the account balance as of the last day of the taxable year, plus any payments made from that account during the taxable year, over the account balance as of the last day of the immediately preceding taxable year. Any net decrease in an account balance during a taxable year (again after adding back payments made under the plan during the taxable year) is treated as a reduction to deferred deduction remuneration for that taxable year and may offset other deferred deduction remuneration (but not applicable individual remuneration) attributable to services performed by the applicable individual in that year. If there is not sufficient other deferred deduction remuneration for that taxable year to offset the entire reduction, the excess may offset deferred deduction remuneration in the first subsequent taxable year or years in which the applicable individual has deferred deduction remuneration to be offset by the loss.

Under the standard attribution method, any increases or decreases in an account balance that occur in taxable years in which an applicable individual is not a service provider must be attributed to taxable years of the covered health insurance provider (i) during which the applicable individual is a service provider, and (ii) on one or more days of which the applicable individual retains an account balance under the plan. The Treasury Department and the IRS request comments on the appropriate method for attributing this remuneration to these taxable years. For taxable years beginning in 2013, and thereafter until the Treasury Department and the IRS issue further guidance prescribing the method for attributing this remuneration to these taxable years, this remuneration may be attributed using any reasonable method to taxable years of the covered health insurance provider (i) during which the applicable individual is a service provider, and (ii) on one or more days of which the applicable individual retains an account balance under the plan. For this purpose, a method is reasonable only if it is consistent with a reasonable, good faith interpretation of section 162(m)(6) and is applied consistently for all remuneration provided by the covered health insurance provider under substantially similar plans or arrangements.

These proposed regulations provide an alternative method for attributing increases and decreases in account balance plans to services performed during a taxable year of a covered health insurance provider. Under the alternative attribution method, earnings and losses on a principal addition (including earnings and losses that occur in taxable years during which an applicable individual is not a service provider) are attributed to the taxable year in which an applicable individual is credited with the principal addition under the plan. For example, if a principal addition is credited to the account balance of an applicable individual for the 2014 taxable year, earnings (or losses) on that principal addition in 2028 are treated as additional deferred deduction remuneration (or reductions to deferred deduction remuneration) for the 2014 taxable year, and not the 2028 taxable year.

After an amount of remuneration has been attributed to a taxable year under a particular attribution method (for example, because a payment has been made and the amount of the payment becomes otherwise deductible), it is administratively difficult for the attribution method to be changed for future years. In addition, the Treasury Department and the IRS are concerned that the ability to change attribution methods may lead to selective use of methods to maximize deductions. Therefore, these proposed regulations provide that a covered health insurance provider must use the method chosen to attribute remuneration under all of its account balance plans consistently for all taxable years. However, the Treasury Department and the IRS understand that there may be valid business reasons for changing attribution methods, such as a merger or acquisition, change in compensation structure, or change in accounting method. Accordingly, the Treasury Department and the IRS request comments on the standards that should be applied to determine whether and when a method may be changed, and how that change would apply if deductions for some portion of the deferred deduction remuneration have already been taken.

C. Nonaccount Balance Plans

These proposed regulations provide that remuneration under a nonaccount balance plan (as described in §1.409A-1(c)(2)(i)(C)) is attributable to services performed by an applicable individual in a taxable year based on the increase (or decrease) in the present value of the applicable individual's benefit under the plan during the taxable year. Under this method, the amount of remuneration attributable to services performed in a taxable year of a covered health insurance provider is equal to the increase (or decrease) in the present value of the future payment or payments due under the plan as of the last day of the taxable year of the covered health insurance provider, increased by any payments made during that year, over (or under) the present value of the future payment or payments as of the last day of the covered health insurance provider's preceding taxable year. For purposes of determining the increase (or decrease) in the present value of a future payment or payments, the rules of §31.3121(v)(2)-1(c)(2) apply. Like losses under account balance plans, losses attributable to any taxable year under a nonaccount balance plan may offset other deferred deduction remuneration attributable to services performed by the applicable individual in that year (or, if there is not sufficient other deferred deduction remuneration for that taxable year to offset the entire reduction, the excess may offset deferred deduction remuneration in the first subsequent taxable year or years in which the applicable individual has deferred deduction remuneration to be offset by the loss).

Any increase (or decrease) in the present value of a future payment or payments under a nonaccount balance plan that occurs in a taxable year when an applicable individual is not a service provider must be attributed to taxable years of the covered health insurance provider during which the applicable individual (i) is a service provider and (ii) has a legally binding right to a future payment or payments under the nonaccount balance plan. The Treasury Department and IRS request comments on the appropriate method for attributing this remuneration to these taxable years. For taxable years beginning in 2013, and thereafter until the Treasury Department and the IRS issue further guidance prescribing the method for attributing this remuneration to these taxable years, this remuneration may be attributed using any reasonable method to taxable years during which the applicable individual (i) is a service provider and (ii) has a legally binding right to the future payment or payments. For this purpose, a method is reasonable only if it is consistent with a reasonable, good faith interpretation of section 162(m)(6) and is applied consistently for all remuneration provided by the covered health insurance provider under substantially similar plans or arrangements.

---

[1] These proposed regulations apply solely for purposes of section 162(m)(6), and therefore have no effect on the determination whether an amount is remuneration attributable to a particular taxable year for employment tax purposes, and thus wages subject to federal employment taxation (including the Federal Insurance Contributions Act, the Federal Unemployment Tax Act, the Railroad Retirement Tax Act, and the Collection of Income Tax at Source on Wages (chapters 21, 22, 23, and 24 of the Code)), or the timing or amount of any applicable federal employment taxation.

D. Equity-Based Remuneration

These proposed regulations provide specific rules for the attribution of equity-based remuneration to services performed in specific taxable years. They provide that remuneration resulting from the exercise of stock options and stock appreciation rights (SARs) generally is attributable, on a daily *pro rata* basis, to services performed by the applicable individual over the period beginning on the date of grant of the stock option or SAR and ending on the date that the stock right is exercised, excluding any days on which an applicable individual is not a service provider.

These proposed regulations further provide that remuneration resulting from the vesting or transfer (or transferability) of restricted stock for which an election under section 83(b) has not been made generally is attributable, on a daily *pro rata* basis, to services performed by the applicable individual over the period beginning on the grant date of the restricted stock and ending on the earliest of the date on which (i) the substantial risk of forfeiture lapses or (ii) the restricted stock is transferred (or becomes transferable), excluding any days on which an applicable individual is not a service provider.

These proposed regulations provide that remuneration resulting from restricted stock units (RSUs) is generally attributable, on a daily *pro rata* basis, to services performed over the period beginning on the date the applicable individual obtains the legally binding right to the RSU and ending on the date the remuneration is paid or made available such that it is includible in gross income, excluding any days on which an applicable individual is not a service provider.

E. Involuntary Separation Pay

These proposed regulations provide that involuntary separation pay is attributable to services performed by an applicable individual during the taxable year of the covered health insurance provider in which the involuntary separation from service occurs. Alternatively, involuntary separation pay may be attributable, on a daily *pro rata* basis, to services performed by the applicable individual beginning on the date that the applicable individual obtains a legally binding right to the involuntary separation pay and ending on the date of the applicable individual's involuntary separation from service with the covered health insurance provider and all members of its aggregated group. Involuntary separation pay to different individuals may be attributed using different methods; however, if involuntary separation payments are made to the same individual over multiple taxable years, all the payments must be attributed using the same method. These regulations define involuntary separation pay as remuneration to which an applicable individual obtains a right to payment solely as a result of an involuntary separation from service. For these purposes, an involuntary separation from service means an involuntary separation from service under § 1.409A-1(n).

F. Substantial Risk of Forfeiture

An applicable individual's right to remuneration may be subject to a substantial risk of forfeiture. In response to Notice 2011-2, commenters suggested that remuneration be attributed to services performed over the period during which amounts are subject to a substantial risk of forfeiture (the vesting period). Consistent with this suggestion, these proposed regulations provide that in the case of remuneration that is subject to a substantial risk of forfeiture and that would otherwise be attributed to taxable years of a covered health insurance provider in accordance with (i) the general rule that attributes remuneration to the taxable year in which an applicable individual obtains a legally binding right to the remuneration, (ii) the attribution rules applicable to account balance plans, or (iii) the attribution rules applicable to nonaccount balance plans, the remuneration is attributed to taxable years of the covered health insurance provider using a two-step process. First, the remuneration is attributed to taxable years of the covered health insurance provider pursuant to the legally-binding-right rule or the rules applicable to account balance or nonaccount balance plans, as applicable. Second, the remuneration that was subject to a substantial risk of forfeiture is reattributed on a daily *pro rata* basis over the period that the remuneration was subject to a substantial risk of forfeiture (in other words, reattributed evenly over the vesting period).

If a vesting period ends on a day other than the last day of the covered health insurance provider's taxable year, the remuneration attributable to that taxable year under the first step of the attribution process is divided between the portion of the taxable year that includes the vesting period and the portion of the taxable year that does not include the vesting period. The amount attributed to the portion of the taxable year that includes the vesting period is equal to the total amount of remuneration that would be attributable to the taxable year under the first step of the attribution process, multiplied by a fraction, the numerator of which is the number of days during the taxable year that the amount is subject to a substantial risk of forfeiture and the denominator of which is the number of days in such taxable year. The remaining amount is attributed to the portion of the taxable year that does not include the vesting period and, therefore, is not reattributed over the vesting period under the second step of the attribution process.

For purposes of these proposed regulations, a substantial risk of forfeiture means a substantial risk of forfeiture under § 1.409A-1(d). If an individual makes an election pursuant to section 83(b), then the remuneration included in the individual's gross income is applicable individual remuneration that is attributed to the year in which the transfer of the property occurs.

VIII. Application of the $500,000 Deduction Limitation

A. In General

The section 162(m)(6) deduction limitation applies to the aggregate applicable individual remuneration and deferred deduction remuneration attributable to services performed by an applicable individual for a covered health insurance provider in a disqualified taxable year. Accordingly, if the applicable individual remuneration and deferred deduction remuneration attributable to services performed by an applicable individual for a covered health insurance provider in a disqualified taxable year exceed $500,000, the amount of the remuneration that exceeds $500,000 is not allowable as a deduction in any taxable year.

B. Timing of Application of the Deduction Limitation

The $500,000 deduction limitation with respect to the applicable individual remuneration and deferred deduction remuneration attributable to services performed by an applicable individual in a disqualified taxable year is applied to that remuneration at the time that the remuneration otherwise becomes deductible. The deduction limitation with respect to an applicable individual for any particular disqualified taxable year is applied first to any applicable individual remuneration attributable to services performed by the applicable individual in that disqualified taxable year. If the amount of the applicable individual remuneration is less than the $500,000 deduction limitation, all of the applicable individual remuneration is deductible by the covered health insurance provider in that disqualified taxable year. To the extent the applicable individual remuneration exceeds the $500,000 deduction limitation, the covered health insurance provider's deduction for the applicable individual remuneration is limited to $500,000, and the amount of the applicable individual remuneration that exceeds $500,000 and, if applicable, any deferred deduction remuneration attributable to services performed by the applicable individual in that disqualified taxable year, cannot be deducted in any taxable year.

When the $500,000 deduction limitation is applied to an amount of applicable individual remuneration attributable to services performed by an applicable individual in a disqualified taxable year, the deduction limitation with respect to that applicable individual for that disqualified taxable year is reduced by the amount of the applicable individual remuneration against which it is applied, but not below zero. If the applicable individual also has an amount of deferred deduction remuneration attributable to services performed in that disqualified taxable year that becomes otherwise deductible in a subsequent taxable year, the deduction limitation, as reduced, is applied to that amount of deferred deduction remuneration in the first taxable year in which it becomes otherwise deductible. If the amount of the deferred deduction remuneration that becomes otherwise deductible is less than the reduced deduction limitation, then the full amount of the deferred deduction remuneration is deductible in that taxable year. To the extent that the amount of the deferred deduction remuneration exceeds the reduced deduction limitation, the covered health insurance provider's deduction for the deferred deduction remuneration is limited to the amount of the reduced deduction limitation and the amount of the deferred deduction remuneration that exceeds the deduction limitation cannot be deducted in any taxable year.

After the deduction limitation with respect to an applicable individual for a disqualified taxable year (the original disqualified taxable year) is applied to an amount of deferred deduction remuneration, the deduction limitation with respect to that applicable individual for the original disqualified taxable year is further reduced by the amount of the deferred deduction remuneration against which it is applied, but not below zero. If the applicable individual has an additional amount of deferred deduction remuneration attributable to services performed in the original disqualified taxable year that becomes otherwise deductible in a subsequent taxable year, the deduction limitation, as further reduced, is applied to that amount of deferred deduction remuneration in the taxable year in which it is otherwise deductible. This process continues for future taxable years in which deferred deduction remuneration attributable to services performed by the applicable individual in the original disqualified taxable year is otherwise deductible. No deduction is allowed for any applicable individual remuneration or deferred deduction remuneration to the extent that remuneration exceeds the deduction limitation in effect at the time it is applied to the remuneration.

C. Application of Deduction Limitation to Payments of Deferred Deduction Remuneration

Any payment of deferred deduction remuneration may include remuneration that is attributable to services performed by an applicable individual in one or more taxable years of a covered health insurance provider under the rules set out in these proposed regulations. For example, remuneration resulting from the vesting of restricted stock that is subject to a substantial risk of forfeiture for three full taxable years of a covered health insurance provider is attributable to services performed in each of the three years during which the restricted stock was subject to a substantial risk of forfeiture. In that case, a separate deduction limitation applies to each portion of the payment that is attributed to services performed in a different disqualified taxable year of the covered health insurance provider. Any portion of the payment that is attributed to a disqualified taxable year will be deductible only to the extent that it does not exceed the deduction limit that applies to the applicable individual for that disqualified taxable year, as that deduction limit may have been previously reduced by the amount of any applicable individual remuneration or deferred deduction remuneration attributable to services performed in that disqualified taxable year that was previously deductible. If payments of deferred deduction remuneration under an account balance plan or a nonaccount balance plan are paid in installments (rather than a single lump-sum), the payments are deemed to be made from the deferred deduction remuneration to which they are attributable under the applicable attribution rules, with payments deemed to be made first with respect to the earliest taxable years to which they could be attributed. The proposed regulations contain numerous examples to illustrate how these rules apply to services performed and compensation payments made over multiple taxable years.

D. Application of the Deduction Limitation to an Aggregated Group

For purposes of applying the section 162(m)(6) deduction limitation, all members of an aggregated group are treated as a single employer. Accordingly, one $500,000 deduction limitation applies to the aggregate applicable individual remuneration and deferred deduction remuneration attributable to services performed by an applicable individual during a disqualified taxable year for any member of the aggregated group. Each time this deduction limitation is applied to an amount of applicable individual remuneration or deferred deduction remuneration otherwise deductible by any member of the aggregated group, the deduction limitation is reduced by the amount of the remuneration against which it is applied, and the reduced deduction limitation is then applied to other remuneration attributable to services performed by the applicable individual in the original disqualified taxable year that is otherwise deductible by any member of the aggregated group, in the manner previously described.

In the case of two or more members of an aggregated group that are otherwise entitled to deduct in any taxable year applicable individual remuneration or deferred deduction remuneration attributable to services performed by an applicable individual in a disqualified taxable year that exceeds the applicable deduction limitation for that disqualified taxable year, the deduction limitation is prorated and allocated to the members of the aggregated group in proportion to the applicable individual remuneration or deferred deduction remuneration that each otherwise would be entitled to deduct in the taxable year (but for section 162(m)(6)).

IX. Corporate Transactions

A corporation or other person may become a covered health insurance provider as a result of a merger, acquisition of assets or stock, disposition, reorganization, consolidation, or separation, or any other transaction (including a purchase or sale of stock or other equity interest) resulting in a change in the composition of its aggregated group (generally referred to in these proposed regulations as a corporate transaction). For example, as a result of the aggregation rules, members of a controlled group of corporations may become covered health insurance providers if a health insurance issuer that is a covered health insurance provider becomes a member of the controlled group. In response to Notice 2011-2, commenters suggested that if a person becomes a covered health insurance provider as a result of a corporate transaction, the person should not be treated as a covered health insurance provider for the taxable year in which the corporate transac-

tion occurs. These proposed regulations adopt this suggestion by providing transition period relief to ease the administrative burden on persons that become covered health insurance providers solely as a result of a corporate transaction. Specifically, these proposed regulations provide that if a person that is not otherwise a covered health insurance provider would become a covered health insurance provider solely as a result of a corporate transaction, the person generally is not treated as a covered health insurance provider for the taxable year in which the transaction occurs (referred to as the transition period). The corporation or other person, however, is treated as a covered health insurance provider for any subsequent taxable year for which it qualifies as a covered health insurance provider under the general rules for determining whether a person is a covered health insurance provider. A person that was a covered health insurance provider immediately before a corporate transaction is not eligible for this transition period relief because the person did not become a covered health insurance provider solely as a result of a corporate transaction.

However, these proposed regulations provide that in certain circumstances the deduction limitation under section 162(m)(6) may apply to a person that is not treated as a covered health insurance provider during the transition period. Specifically, these proposed regulations provide that transition period relief does not extend to remuneration provided to applicable individuals of a health insurance issuer that is a covered health insurance provider (which is not eligible for the transition period because it does not become a covered health insurance provider solely as a result of a corporate transaction) by other members of the acquiring aggregated group that are otherwise eligible for the transition period relief. For example, if a health insurance issuer that is a covered health insurance provider becomes a member of an acquiring aggregated group that is a consolidated group described in § 1.1502-1(h), the other members of which are not treated as covered health insurance providers in the year in which the corporate transaction occurs because of the transition period relief, then any applicable individual remuneration and deferred deduction remuneration attributable to services provided by an applicable individual of the health insurance issuer for the health insurance issuer or for the other members of the acquiring aggregated group during the transition period are subject to the deduction limitation of section 162(m)(6).

These proposed regulations also provide rules for covered health insurance providers that have short taxable years as a result of a corporate transaction. See proposed § 1.162-31(f).

X. Grandfathered Amounts Attributable to Services Performed Before January 1, 2010

The section 162(m)(6) deduction limitation only applies to applicable individual remuneration attributable to services performed by an applicable individual during taxable years beginning after December 31, 2012 and to deferred deduction remuneration attributable to services performed by an applicable individual during taxable years beginning after December 31, 2009. It does not apply to remuneration attributable to services performed during taxable years beginning before January 1, 2010. These proposed regulations provide rules for determining whether remuneration is attributable to services performed in taxable years beginning before January 1, 2010 that are in some ways different from the general attribution rules.

Commenters suggested that deferred deduction remuneration earned or granted in taxable years beginning before January 1, 2010, be attributed to services performed before that time, regardless of whether the remuneration was subject to a substantial risk of forfeiture after that time. Commenters reasoned that Congress did not intend for the deduction limitation to apply to remuneration attributable to taxable years starting before January 1, 2010 (even if such remuneration was not vested as of the first day of the taxable year beginning after December 31, 2009), because Congress enacted section 162(m)(6) to encourage the use of health insurance coverage premiums to lower insurance rates for taxable years beginning after December 31, 2012 (when health insurance issuers would begin to benefit from a substantial increase in new customers). Commenters also asserted that the statute should not apply to arrangements that existed before the statute was enacted because covered health insurance providers could not change those arrangements unilaterally in response to the statute.

In response to these comments, these proposed regulations provide that the section 162(m)(6) deduction limitation does not apply to deferred deduction remuneration attributable to services performed during taxable years beginning before January 1, 2010, regardless of whether the remuneration was subject to a substantial risk of forfeiture after that time. These proposed regulations provide special rules for determining the amount of remuneration attributable to services performed in taxable years beginning before January 1, 2010 with respect to account balance plans, nonaccount balance plans, and equity-based remuneration. For account balance plans and nonaccount balance plans, these proposed regulations provide that amounts are attributed based on the general attribution rules, except that any substantial risk of forfeiture is disregarded. For equity-based compensation, any remuneration resulting from equity-based compensation granted in a taxable year beginning before January 1, 2010, is not subject to the deduction limitation. Earnings on these grandfathered amounts, including earnings accruing in taxable years beginning after December 31, 2009, are also generally treated as remuneration attributable to services performed in taxable years beginning before January 1, 2010.

XI. Transition Rules for Certain Deferred Deduction Remuneration

Section 162(m)(6) applies to deferred deduction remuneration attributable to services performed in a disqualified taxable year beginning after December 31, 2009 that is otherwise deductible in a taxable year beginning after December 31, 2012. As described in section I.B of this preamble, for taxable years beginning before January 1, 2013, a covered health insurance provider is any health insurance issuer (as defined in section 9832(b)(2)) that receives premiums from providing health insurance coverage (as defined in section 9832(b)(1)) (a pre-2013 covered health insurance provider). For taxable years beginning after December 31, 2012, a covered health insurance provider is any health insurance issuer (as defined in section 9832(b)(2)) that receives at least 25 percent of its gross premiums from providing minimum essential coverage (as defined in section 5000A(f)) (a post-2012 covered health insurance provider). Thus, the definition of the term *covered health insurance provider* is narrower for taxable years beginning after December 31, 2012, than it is for taxable years beginning before January 1, 2013.

After the enactment of section 162(m)(6), commenters suggested that if a pre-2013 covered health insurance provider does not qualify as a post-2012 covered health insurance provider, the section 162(m)(6) deduction limitation should not apply to deferred deduction remuneration attributable to services performed during taxable years when the health insurance issuer was a pre-2013 covered health insurance provider. These commenters cited legislative history suggesting that section 162(m)(6) was enacted to encourage health insurance issuers to use premiums from new customers to lower health insurance rates. 155 Cong. Rec. S12,540 (Dec. 6, 2009) (statement of Sen. Lincoln). These commenters reasoned that if a pre-2013 covered health insurance is not also a post-2012 covered health insurance provider, the health insurance issuer is not benefiting from new customers who are paying premiums for minimum essential coverage, and the health insurance issuer should not be subject to the deduction limitation.

In response to these comments, Notice 2011-2 provides that the section 162(m)(6) deduction limitation applies to deferred deduction remuneration attributable to services performed in a taxable year beginning after December 31, 2009 and before January 1, 2013 only if the covered health insurance provider is a pre-2013 covered health insurance provider for the taxable year to which the deferred deduction remuneration is attributable and a post-2012 covered health insurance provider for the taxable year in which that deferred deduction remuneration is otherwise deductible. These proposed regulations adopt this transition rule.

In response to Notice 2011-2, some commenters requested that the transition rule be applied more broadly, so that the section 162(m)(6) deduction limitation would not apply to deferred deduction remuneration for services attributable to taxable years beginning before January 1, 2013 if the employer is not a covered health insurance provider in 2013, regardless of whether the employer is a covered health insurance provider for the year the deferred deduction remuneration becomes otherwise deductible. The Treasury Department and the IRS have concluded that the standard set forth in Notice 2011-2 appropriately limits the transition rule to circumstances in which the deferred deduction remuneration is otherwise deductible in a taxable year for which the covered health insurance provider is not a post-2013 covered health insurance provider, and therefore these proposed regulations do not adopt this suggestion.

Effect on Other Documents

These proposed regulations do not affect the applicability of Notice 2011-2, (2011-1 CB 260). However, upon the effective date of the final regulations, the Treasury Department and the IRS anticipate that Notice 2011-2 will become obsolete for periods after the effective date of the final regulations.

Proposed Effective Date

These proposed regulations are proposed to be effective upon publication in the **Federal Register** of a Treasury decision adopting these rules as final regulations, and applicable to taxable years that begin after December 31, 2012, and end on or after April 2, 2013. Taxpayers may rely on these proposed regulations until the issuance of final regulations. The Treasury Department and the IRS anticipate that the final regulations will be issued before a covered health insurance provider is required to file an income tax return reflecting application of the section 162(m)(6) deduction limitation. However, to the extent the final regulations contain rules more restrictive than the rules contained in these proposed regulations, a covered health insurance provider will be able to rely on these proposed regulations for the purposes of the application of the section 162(m)(6) to its first taxable year beginning after December 31, 2012. Although these regulations will not apply to taxable years beginning after December 31, 2012 and ending before April 2, 2013, taxpayers may rely on these proposed regulations with respect to those taxable years to the same extent as taxpayers may rely with respect to taxable years to which the regulations will apply.

Special Analyses

It has been determined that this notice of proposed rulemaking is not a significant regulatory action as defined in Executive Order 12866. Therefore, a regulatory assessment is not required. It also has been determined that section 553(b) of the Administrative Procedure Act (5 U.S.C. chapter 5) does not apply to these regulations, and because the regulations do not impose a collection of information on small entities, the Regulatory Flexibility Act (5 U.S.C. chapter 6) does not apply. Pursuant to section 7805(f) of the Code, this regulation has been submitted to the Chief Counsel for Advocacy of the Small Business Administration for comment on its impact on small business.

Comments and Requests for Public Hearing

Before these proposed regulations are adopted as final regulations, consideration will be given to any written (a signed original and eight (8) copies) or electronic comments that are timely submitted to the IRS. Treasury and the IRS request comments on all aspects of the proposed rules. All comments will be available for public inspection and copying. A public hearing will be scheduled if requested in writing by any person that timely submits written comments. If a public hearing is scheduled, notice of the date, time, and place for the public hearing will be published in the **Federal Register**.

Drafting Information

The principal author of these proposed regulations is Ilya Enkishev, Office of the Division Counsel/Associate Chief Counsel (Tax Exempt and Government Entities). However, other personnel from Treasury Department and the IRS participated in their development.

List of Subjects in 26 CFR Part 1

Income taxes, Reporting and recordkeeping requirements.

Proposed Amendments to the Regulations

Accordingly, 26 CFR part 1 is proposed to be amended as follows:

PART 1—INCOME TAXES

■ **Paragraph 1.** The authority citation for part 1 continues to read in part as follows:

Authority: 26 U.S.C. 7805.

■ **Par. 2.** Section 1.162-31 is added to read as follows:

§1.162-31 The $500,000 deduction limitation for remuneration provided by certain health insurance providers.

(a) *Scope.* This §1.162-31 provides rules regarding the deduction limitation under section 162(m)(6), which provides that a covered health insurance provider's deduction for applicable individual remuneration and deferred deduction remuneration attributable to services performed by an applicable individual in a disqualified taxable year is limited to $500,000. Paragraph (b) of this section provides definitions of the terms used in this section. Paragraph (c) of this section states the general limitation on deductions under section 162(m)(6). Paragraph (d) of this section provides rules on the attribution of applicable individual remuneration and deferred deduction remuneration to services provided in one or more taxable years of a covered health insurance provider. Paragraph (e) of this section provides rules on the application of the deduction limitation to applicable individual remuneration and deferred deduction remuneration that is otherwise deductible under chapter 1 of the Internal Revenue Code (Code) but for the deduction limitation under section 162(m)(6) (referred to in these regulations as remuneration that is otherwise deductible). Paragraph (f) of this section provides rules for persons participating in certain corporate transactions. Paragraph (g) of this section provides rules on the coordination of section 162(m)(6) with sections 162(m)(1) and 280G. Paragraph (h) of this section provides rules for determining the amount of remuneration that is not subject to the deduction limitation under section 162(m)(6) due to application of the statutory effective date (referred to in these regulations as grandfathered amounts). Paragraph (i) of this section provides transition rules for deferred deduction remuneration that is attributable to services performed in taxable years beginning after December 31, 2009 and before January 1, 2013. Paragraph (j) of this section provides the effective and applicability dates of the rules in this section.

(b) *Definitions*—(1) *Health insurance issuer.* For purposes of this section, a *health insurance issuer* is a health insurance issuer as defined in section 9832(b)(2).

(2) *Aggregated group.* For purposes of this section, an *aggregated group* is a health insurance issuer and each other person that is treated as a single employer with the health insurance issuer at any time during the taxable year of the health insurance issuer under sections 414(b) (controlled groups of corporations), 414(c) (partnerships, proprietorships, etc. under common control), 414(m) (affiliated service groups), or 414(o), except that the rules in section 1563(a)(2) and (a)(3) (with respect to corporations) and the rules in § 1.414(c)-2(c) (with respect to trades or businesses under common control) for brother-sister groups and combined groups are disregarded.

(3) *Parent entity*—(i) *In general.* For purposes of this section, a *parent entity* is either—

(A) The common parent of a parent-subsidiary controlled group of corporations (within the meaning of section 414(b)) or a parent-subsidiary group of trades or businesses under common control (within the meaning of section 414(c)) that includes a health insurance issuer, or

(B) The health insurance issuer in an aggregated group that is an affiliated service group (within the meaning of section 414(m)) or a group described in section 414(o).

(ii) *Certain aggregated groups with multiple health insurance issuers.* If two or more health insurance issuers are members of an aggregated group that is an affiliated service group (within the meaning of section 414(m)) or group described in section 414(o), the parent entity is the health insurance issuer in the aggregated group that is designated in writing by the other members of the group to act as the parent entity, provided the group treats that health insurance issuer as the parent entity consistently for all taxable years. If the members of a group that are required to designate in writing a health insurance issuer to act as a parent entity fail to do so, or if the members of the group fail to treat the health insurance issuer that they have designated as the parent entity consistently as such for all taxable years, the parent entity of the group is deemed to be an entity with a taxable year that is the calendar year (without regard to whether the aggregated group includes an entity with a calendar year taxable year) for all purposes under this section for which a parent entity's taxable year is relevant.

(4) *Covered health insurance provider*—(i) *In general.* For purposes of this section and except as otherwise provided in this paragraph (b)(4), a *covered health insurance provider* is—

(A) A health insurance issuer for any of its taxable years beginning after December 31, 2009 and before January 1, 2013 in which it receives premiums from providing health insurance coverage (as defined in section 9832(b)(1)),

(B) A health insurance issuer for any of its taxable years beginning after December 31, 2012 in which at least 25 percent of the gross premiums it receives from providing health insurance coverage (as defined in section 9832(b)(1)) are from providing minimum essential coverage (as defined in section 5000A(f)),

(C) The parent entity of an aggregated group of which one or more health insurance issuers described in paragraphs (b)(4)(i)(A) or (B) of this section are members for the taxable year of the parent entity with which, or in which, ends the taxable year of any such health insurance issuer, and

(D) Each other member of an aggregated group of which one or more health insurance issuers described in paragraphs (b)(4)(i)(A) or (B) of this section are members for the taxable year of the other member ending with, or within, the parent entity's taxable year.

(ii) *Self-insured plans.* For purposes of this section, a person is not a covered health insurance provider solely because it maintains a self-insured medical reimbursement plan. For this purpose, a self-insured medical reimbursement plan is a separate written plan for the benefit of employees (including former employees) that provides for reimbursement of medical expenses referred to in section 105(b) and does not provide for reimbursement under an individual or group policy of

accident or health insurance issued by a licensed insurance company or under an arrangement in the nature of a prepaid health care plan that is regulated under federal or state law in a manner similar to the regulation of insurance companies, and may include a plan maintained by an employee organization described in section 501(c)(9).

(iii) *De minimis exception*—(A) *In general.* A health insurance issuer and any member of its aggregated group that would otherwise be a covered health insurance provider under paragraph (b)(4)(i) of this section for a taxable year beginning after December 31, 2009 and before January 1, 2013 is not treated as a covered health insurance provider for purposes of this section for that taxable year if the premiums received by the health insurance issuer and any other health insurance issuers in its aggregated group from providing health insurance coverage (as defined in section 9832(b)(1)) are less than two percent of the gross revenues of the health insurance issuer and all other members of its aggregated group for the taxable year that the health insurance issuer and the other members of its aggregated group would otherwise be treated as covered health insurance providers under paragraph (b)(4)(i) of this section. A health insurance issuer and any member of its aggregated group that would otherwise be a covered health insurance provider under paragraph (b)(4)(i) of this section for a taxable year beginning after December 31, 2012 is not treated as a covered health insurance provider under this section for that taxable year if the premiums received by the health insurance issuer and any other health insurance issuers in its aggregated group for providing health insurance coverage (as defined in section 9832(b)(1)) that constitutes minimum essential coverage (as defined in section 5000A(f)) are less than two percent of the gross revenues of the health insurance issuer and all other members of its aggregated group for the taxable year that the health insurance issuer and the other members of its aggregated group would otherwise be treated as covered health insurance providers under paragraph (b)(4)(i) of this section. In determining whether premiums constitute less than two percent of gross revenues, the amount of premiums and gross revenues must be determined in accordance with generally accepted accounting principles.

(B) *One-year grace period.* If a health insurance issuer or a member of an aggregated group is not treated as a covered health insurance provider for a taxable year solely by reason of the *de minimis* exception described in paragraph (b)(4)(iii)(A) of this section, but fails to meet the requirements of the *de minimis* exception described in paragraph (b)(4)(iii)(A) of this section for the immediately following taxable year, that health insurance issuer or member of an aggregated group will not be treated as a covered health insurance provider for that immediately following taxable year.

(C) *Examples.* The following examples illustrate the principles of this paragraph (b)(4). For purposes of these examples, each corporation has a taxable year that is the calendar year, unless the example provides otherwise.

Example 1. (i) Corporations Y and Z are members of an aggregated group under paragraph (b)(2) of this section. Y is a health insurance issuer that is a covered health insurance provider pursuant to paragraph (b)(4)(i)(B) of this section and receives premiums from providing health insurance coverage that is minimum essential coverage during its 2015 taxable year in an amount that is less than two percent of the combined gross revenues of Y and Z for their 2015 taxable years. Z is not a health insurance issuer.

(ii) Y and Z are not treated as covered health insurance providers within the meaning of paragraph (b)(4) of this section for their 2015 taxable years because they meet the requirements of the *de minimis* exception under paragraph (b)(4)(iii)(A) of this section.

Example 2. (i) Corporations V, W, and X are members of an aggregated group under paragraph (b)(2) of this section. V is a health insurance issuer that is a covered health insurance provider pursuant to paragraph (b)(4)(i)(B) of this section, but neither W nor X is a health insurance issuer. W is the parent entity of the aggregated group. V's taxable year ends on December 31, W's taxable year ends on June 30, and X's taxable year ends on September 30. For its taxable year ending December 31, 2016, V receives $3x of premiums from providing minimum essential coverage and has no other revenue. For its taxable year ending June 30, 2017, W has $100x in gross revenue. For its taxable year ending September 30, 2016, X has $60x in gross revenue.

(ii) In the absence of the *de minimis* exception, V (the health insurance issuer) would be a covered health insurance provider for its taxable year ending December 31, 2016. W (the parent entity) would be a covered health insurance provider for its taxable year ending June 30, 2017 (its taxable year with which, or within which, ends the taxable year of the health insurance issuer), and X (the other member of the aggregated group) would be a covered health insurance provider for its taxable year ending on September 30, 2016 (its taxable year ending with, or within, the taxable year of the parent entity). However, the premiums received by V (the health insurance issuer) from providing minimum essential coverage during the taxable year that it would otherwise be treated as a covered health insurance provider under paragraph (b)(4)(i)(B) of this section are less than two percent of the combined gross revenues of V, W, and X for the related taxable years that they would otherwise be treated as covered health insurance providers under paragraph (b)(4)(i) of this section ($3x is less than two percent of $163x). Therefore, the *de minimis* exception of paragraph (b)(4)(iii)(A) of this section applies, and V, W, and X are not treated as covered health insurance providers for these taxable years.

Example 3. (i) The facts are the same as *Example 2,* except that V receives $4x of premiums for providing minimum essential coverage for its taxable year ending June 30, 2016. In addition, the members of the V, W, and X aggregated group were not treated as covered health insurance providers for their taxable years ending December 31, 2015, June 30, 2016, and September 30, 2015, respectively (their immediately preceding taxable years) solely by reason of the *de minimis* exception of paragraph (b)(4)(iii)(A) of this section.

(ii) Although the premiums received by the members of the aggregated group from providing minimum essential coverage are more than two percent of the gross revenues of the aggregated group for the taxable years during which the members would otherwise be treated as covered health insurance providers under paragraph (b)(4)(i) of this section ($4x is greater than two percent of $164x), they were not treated as covered health insurance providers for their immediately preceding taxable years solely by reason of the *de minimis* exception of paragraph (b)(4)(iii)(A) of this section. Therefore, V, W, and X are not treated as covered health insurance providers for their taxable years ending in December 31, 2016, June 30, 2017, and September 30, 2016, respectively, because of the one-year grace period under paragraph (b)(4)(iii)(B) of this section. However, the members of the V, W, and X aggregated group will be covered health insurance providers for their subsequent taxable years if they would otherwise be covered health insurance providers for those taxable years under paragraph (b)(4) of this section.

(5) *Premiums*—(i) For purposes of paragraph (b)(4) of this section, the term *premiums* means amounts received by a health insurance issuer from providing health insurance coverage (as defined in section 9832(b)(1)), except that premiums do not include—

(A) Amounts received under an indemnity reinsurance contract described in paragraph (b)(5)(ii) of this section, or

(B) Direct service payments described in paragraph (b)(5)(iii) of this section.

(ii) *Indemnity reinsurance contract.* For purposes of this paragraph (b)(5), the term *indemnity reinsurance contract* means an agreement between a health insurance issuer and a reinsuring company under which—

(A) The reinsuring company agrees to indemnify the health insurance issuer for all or part of the risk of loss under policies specified in the agreement, and

(B) The health insurance issuer retains its liability to provide health insurance coverage (as defined in section 9832(b)(1)) to, and its contractual relationship with, the insured.

(iii) *Direct service payments.* For purposes of this paragraph (b)(5), the term *direct service payment* means a capitated, prepaid, periodic, or other payment made by a health insurance issuer or another entity that receives premiums from providing health insurance coverage (as defined in section 9832(b)(1)) to another organization as compensation for providing, managing, or arranging for the provision of healthcare services by physicians, hospitals, or other healthcare providers, regardless of whether the organization that receives the compensation is subject to healthcare provider, health insurance, health plan licensing, financial solvency, or other similar regulatory requirements under state insurance law.

(6) *Disqualified taxable year.* For purposes of this section, the term *disqualified taxable year* means, with respect to any person, any taxable year for which the person is a covered health insurance provider.

(7) *Applicable individual*—(i) *In general.* For purposes of this section, except as provided in paragraph (b)(7)(ii) of this section, the term *applicable individual* means, with respect to any covered health insurance provider for any disqualified taxable year, any individual—

(A) Who is an officer, director, or employee in that taxable year, or

(B) Who provides services for or on behalf of the covered health insurance provider during that taxable year.

(ii) *Independent contractors*— Remuneration for services provided by an independent contractor to a covered health insurance provider is subject to the deduction limitation under section 162(m)(6). However, an independent contractor will not be treated as an applicable individual with respect to a covered health insurance provider for a disqualified taxable year if each of the following requirements is satisfied:

(A) The independent contractor is actively engaged in the trade or business of providing services to recipients, other than as an employee or as a member of the board of directors of a corporation (or similar position with respect to an entity that is not a corporation);

(B) The independent contractor provides significant services (as defined in §1.409A-1(f)(2)(iii)) to two or more persons to which the independent contractor is not related and that are not related to one another (as defined in §1.409A-1(f)(2)(ii)); and

(C) The independent contractor is not related to the covered health insurance provider or any member of its aggregated group, applying the definition of related person contained in §1.409A-1(f)(2)(ii), subject to the modification that for purposes of applying the references to sections 267(b) and 707(b)(1), the language "20 percent" is not used instead of "50 percent" each place "50 percent" appears in sections 267(b) and 707(b)(1).

(8) *Service provider.* For purposes of this section, the term *service provider* means, with respect to a covered health insurance provider for any period, an individual who is an officer, director, or employee, or who provides services for, or on behalf of, the covered health insurance provider or any member of its aggregated group.

(9) *Remuneration*—(i) *In general.* For purposes of this section, except as provided in paragraph (b)(9)(ii) of this section, the term *remuneration* has the same meaning as applicable employee remuneration, as defined in section 162(m)(4), but without regard to the exceptions under section 162(m)(4)(B) (remuneration payable on a commission basis), section 162(m)(4)(C) (performance-based compensation), and section 162(m)(4)(D) (existing binding contracts), and the regulations under those sections.

(ii) *Exceptions.* For purposes of this section, remuneration does not include—

(A) A payment made to, or for the benefit of, an applicable individual from or to a trust described in section 401(a) within the meaning of section 3121(a)(5)(A),

(B) A payment made under an annuity plan described in section 403(a) within the meaning of section 3121(a)(5)(B),

(C) A payment made under a simplified employee pension plan described in section 408(k)(1) within the meaning of section 3121(a)(5)(C),

(D) A payment made under an annuity contract described in section 403(b) within the meaning of section 3121(a)(5)(D),

(E) Salary reduction contributions described in section 3121(v)(1), and

(F) Remuneration consisting of any benefit provided to, or on behalf of, an employee if, at the time the benefit is provided, it is reasonable to believe that the employee will be able to exclude the value of the benefit from gross income.

(10) *Applicable individual remuneration.* For purposes of this section, the term *applicable individual remuneration* means, with respect to any applicable individual for any disqualified taxable year, the aggregate amount allowable as a deduction under this chapter for that taxable year (determined without regard to section 162(m)) for remuneration for services performed by that applicable individual (whether or not in that taxable year), except that applicable individual remuneration does not include any deferred deduction remuneration with respect to services performed during any taxable year. Applicable individual remuneration for a disqualified taxable year may include remuneration for services performed in a taxable year before the taxable year in which the deduction for the remuneration is allowable. For example, a discretionary bonus granted and paid to an applicable individual in a disqualified taxable year in recognition of services performed in prior taxable years is applicable individual remuneration for that disqualified taxable year. In addition, a grant of restricted stock in a disqualified taxable year with respect to which an applicable individual makes an election under section 83(b) is applicable individual remuneration for the disqualified taxable year of the covered health insurance provider in which the grant of the restricted stock is made. See paragraphs (d)(1)(iv) and (d)(5)(v) of this section for certain remuneration that is not treated as applicable individual remuneration for purposes of this section.

(11) *Deferred deduction remuneration.* For purposes of this section, the term *deferred deduction remuneration* means remuneration that would be applicable individual remuneration for services performed in a disqualified taxable year but for the fact that the deduction (determined without regard to section 162(m)(6)) for the remuneration is allowable in a subsequent taxable year. Whether remuneration is deferred deduction remuneration is determined without regard to when the remuneration is paid, except to the extent that the timing of the payment affects the taxable year in which the remuneration is otherwise deductible. For example, payments that are otherwise deductible by a covered health insurance provider in an initial taxable year, but are paid to an applicable individual by the 15th day of the third month of the immediately subsequent taxable year of the covered health insurance provider (as described in §1.404(b)-1T, Q&A-2(b)(1)), are applicable individual remuneration for the initial taxable year (and not deferred deduction remuneration) because the deduction for the payments is allowable in the initial taxable year, and not a subsequent taxable year. Except as otherwise provided in paragraph (i) of this section (regarding transition rules for certain deferred deduction remuneration attributable to services performed in taxable years beginning before January 1, 2013), deferred deduction remuneration that is attributable to services performed in a disqualified taxable year of a covered health insurance provider is subject to the section 162(m)(6) deduction limitation even if the taxable year in which the remuneration is otherwise deductible is not a disqualified taxable year. Similarly, deferred deduction remuneration is subject to the section 162(m)(6) deduction limitation regardless of whether an applicable individual is a service provider of the covered health insurance provider in the taxable year in which the deferred deduction remuneration is otherwise deductible. However, remuneration that is attributable to services performed in a taxable year that is not a disqualified taxable year is not deferred deduction remuneration even if the remuneration is otherwise deductible in a disqualified taxable year. See also paragraphs (d)(1)(iv) and (d)(5)(v) of this section for certain remuneration that is not treated as deferred deduction remuneration for purposes of this section.

(12) *Substantial risk of forfeiture.* For purposes of this section, the term *substantial risk of forfeiture* has the same meaning as provided in §1.409A-1(d).

(c) *Deduction Limitation*—(1) *Applicable individual remuneration.* For any disqualified taxable year beginning after December 31, 2012, no deduction is allowed under this chapter for applicable individual remuneration that is attributable to services performed by an applicable individual in that taxable year to the extent that the amount of that remuneration exceeds $500,000.

(2) *Deferred deduction remuneration.* For any taxable year beginning after December 31, 2012, no deduction is allowed under this chapter for deferred deduction remuneration that is attributable to services performed by an applicable individual in any disqualified taxable year beginning after December 31, 2009, to the extent that the amount of such remuneration exceeds $500,000 reduced (but not below zero) by the sum of:

(i) The applicable individual remuneration for that applicable individual for that disqualified taxable year; and

(ii) The portion of the deferred deduction remuneration for those services that was deductible under section 162(m)(6)(A)(ii) and this paragraph (c)(2) in a preceding taxable year, or would have been deductible under section 162(m)(6)(A)(ii) and this paragraph (c)(2) in a preceding taxable year if section 162(m)(6) was effective for taxable years beginning after December 31, 2009 and before January 1, 2013.

(d) *Services to which remuneration is attributable*—(1) *Attribution to a taxable year*—(i) *In general.* The deduction limitation under section 162(m)(6) applies to applicable individual remuneration and deferred deduction remuneration attributable to services performed by an applicable individual in a disqualified taxable year of a covered health insurance provider. When an amount of applicable individual remuneration or deferred deduction remuneration becomes otherwise deductible (and not before that time), that remuneration must be attributed to services performed by an applicable individual in a taxable year of the covered health insurance provider in accordance with the rules of this paragraph (d). After the remuneration has been attributed to services performed by an applicable individual in a taxable year of a covered health insurance provider, the rules of paragraph (e) of this section are then applied to determine whether the deduction with respect to the remuneration is limited by section 162(m)(6).

(ii) *Attribution of deferred deduction remuneration to earliest years first.* If an amount of deferred deduction remuneration that becomes otherwise deductible may be attributed to services performed by an applicable individual in two or more taxable years of a covered health insurance provider in accordance with paragraphs (d)(3) (providing for

the attribution of amounts credited under an account balance plan) or (d)(4) (providing for the attribution of amounts credited under a nonaccount balance plan) of this section, the amount must be attributed first to services performed by the applicable individual in the earliest year to which the amount could be attributable under paragraphs (d)(3) or (4) of this section, as applicable, and then to the next subsequent taxable year or years to which the amount could be attributable under paragraphs (d)(3) or (4) of this section, as applicable, until the entire amount has been attributed to one or more taxable years of the covered health insurance provider.

(iii) *Example.* The following example illustrates the principles of paragraph (d)(1)(ii) of this section.

Example. (i) A is an employee of corporation Z, which has a taxable year that is the calendar year and is a covered health insurance provider for all relevant taxable years. A participates in a nonqualified deferred compensation plan that is an account balance plan maintained by Z. A's account balances under the plan on the last day of all relevant taxable years are as follows: $10,000 for 2014, $13,000 for 2015, $17,000 for 2016, and $24,000 for 2017. A's account balance is fully vested at all times. In accordance with the terms of the plan, Z pays $15,000 to A in 2018 and $9,000 to A in 2019. These amounts are otherwise deductible by Z in the year in which they are paid.

(ii) Because the nonqualified deferred compensation plan is an account balance plan, deferred deduction remuneration provided under the plan is attributable to services provided by A in accordance with paragraph (d)(3)(i) of this section. Z does not use the alternate method of allocating earnings and losses permitted under paragraph (d)(3)(ii) of this section. Accordingly, the deferred deduction remuneration under the plan attributable to services provided by A in a taxable year is generally equal to the increase in the account balance on the last day of each taxable year over the account balance on the last day of the immediately preceding taxable year, increased by the amount of any payments made during the taxable year. The increases in A's account balances are $10,000 for 2014, $3,000 for 2015, $4,000 for 2016, and $7,000 for 2017. Therefore, pursuant to paragraph (d)(1)(ii), Z must attribute $10,000 of the $15,000 payment to services performed by A in 2014, $3,000 of the $15,000 payment to services performed by A in 2015, and $2,000 of the $15,000 payment to services performed by A in 2016 (leaving $2,000 remaining to be attributed to 2016). Similarly, Z must attribute $2,000 of the $9,000 payment to services performed by A in 2016, and the remaining $7,000 of the $9,000 payment to services performed by A in 2017.

(iv) *No attribution to taxable years during which no services are performed or before a legally binding right arises*— (A) *In general.* For purposes of this section, remuneration is not attributable—

(*1*) to a taxable year of a covered health insurance provider ending before the later of the date the applicable individual begins providing services to the covered health insurance provider (or any member of its aggregated group) and the date the applicable individual obtains a legally binding right to the remuneration, or

(*2*) to any other taxable year of a covered health insurance provider during which the applicable individual is not a service provider.

(B) *Attribution of remuneration before commencement of services or legally binding right.* To the extent that remuneration would otherwise be attributed to a taxable year ending before the later of the date the applicable individual begins providing services to the covered health insurance provider (or any member of its aggregated group) and the date the applicable individual obtains a legally binding right to the remuneration in accordance with paragraphs (d)(2) through (d)(8) or paragraph (d)(10) of this section, the remuneration is attributable to services provided in the taxable year in which the latter of these dates occurs. For example, if an applicable individual obtains a contractual right to remuneration in a taxable year of a covered health insurance provider and the remuneration would otherwise be attributable to that taxable year pursuant to paragraph (d)(2) of this section, but the applicable individual does not begin providing services to the covered health insurance provider until the next taxable year, the remuneration is attributable to the taxable year in which the applicable individual begins providing services.

(v) *Attribution to 12-month periods.* To the extent that a covered health insurance provider is required to attribute remuneration on a daily *pro rata* basis under this paragraph (d), it may assume that any 12-month period has 365 days (and so may ignore the extra day in leap years).

(vi) *Remuneration subject to nonlapse restriction or similar formula.* For purposes of this section, if stock or other equity is subject to a nonlapse restriction (as defined in §1.83-3(h)), or if the remuneration payable to an applicable individual is determined under a formula that, if applied to stock or other equity, would be a nonlapse restriction, the amount of the remuneration and the attribution of that remuneration to taxable years must be determined based upon application of the nonlapse restriction or formula. For example, if the earnings or losses on an account under an account balance plan are determined based upon the performance of company stock, the valuation of which is based on a formula that if applied to the stock would be a nonlapse restriction, then that formula must be used consistently for purposes of determining the amount of the remuneration credited to that account balance to taxable years and the attribution of that remuneration to taxable years.

(2) *Legally binding right.* Unless remuneration is attributable to services performed in a different taxable year pursuant to paragraphs (d)(3) through (d)(8) or paragraph (d)(10) of this section, the remuneration is attributable to services performed in the taxable year of a covered health insurance provider in which an applicable individual obtains a legally binding right to the remuneration. An applicable individual does not have a legally binding right to remuneration if the remuneration may be reduced unilaterally or eliminated by the covered health insurance provider or other person after the services creating the right to the remuneration have been performed. However, if the facts and circumstances indicate that the discretion to reduce or eliminate the remuneration is available or exercisable only upon a condition, or the discretion to reduce or eliminate the remuneration lacks substantive significance, the applicable individual will be considered to have a legally binding right to the remuneration. For this purpose, remuneration is not considered to be subject to unilateral reduction or elimination merely because it may be reduced or eliminated by operation of the objective terms of a plan, such as the application of a nondiscretionary, objective provision creating a substantial risk of forfeiture.

(3) *Account balance plans*—(i) *Standard attribution method*—(A) *In general.* Except as provided in paragraphs (d)(3)(i)(B) and (d)(3)(ii) of this section, the increase (or decrease) in the account balance of an applicable individual under a plan described in § 1.409A-1(c)(2)(i)(A) or (B) (an account balance plan) as of the last day of a taxable year of the covered health insurance provider (the measurement date), over (or under) the account balance as of the last day of the immediately preceding taxable year, is attributable to services provided by the applicable individual in the taxable year that includes the measurement date. For purposes of determining the increase (or decrease) in an account balance in any taxable year, the applicable individual's account balance as of the last day of the taxable year that includes the measurement date is increased by any payments made during that taxable year that reduce the account balance. If an account balance plan credits income or earnings based on a method or formula that is neither a predetermined actual investment within the meaning of § 31.3121(v)(2)-1(d)(2)(i)(B) nor a rate of interest that is reasonable within the meaning of § 31.3121(v)(2)-1(d)(2)(i)(B), the excess of the amount that would be credited as income or earnings under the terms of the plan over the amount that would be credited as income or earnings under a reasonable rate of interest (as described in § 31.3121(v)(2)-1(d)(2)(iii)) must be included in the account balance. Increases in the applicable individual's account balance with respect to any taxable year are treated as remuneration attributable to services performed during that taxable year. Decreases in the applicable individual's account balance with respect to any taxable year are treated as reductions to deferred deduction remuneration for that taxable year and may offset other deferred deduction remuneration (but not applicable individual remuneration) attributable to services performed by the applicable individual during that taxable year under any plan or arrangement (or if there is not sufficient deferred deduction remuneration for that taxable year to offset the reduction entirely, the excess may offset deferred deduction remuneration in first subsequent taxable year or years in which the applicable individual has deferred deduction remuneration to be offset by the loss).

(B) *Attribution of increases (or decreases) in an account balance in taxable years during which an applicable individual is not a service provider.* [Reserved].

(ii) *Alternative attribution method*— (A) *Attribution of principal additions*— (*1*) *In general.* Except as provided in paragraph (d)(3)(ii)(A)(*2*), any increase in the account balance of an applicable individual in an account balance plan as of the last day of a taxable year, increased by any payments made during the taxable year, over the account balance as of the last day of the immediately preceding taxable year that is not due to earnings or losses (as described in paragraph (d)(3)(ii)(C) of this section) is treated as a principal addition and is remuneration attributable to services performed during that taxable year.

(*2*) *Attribution of principal additions in taxable years during which an applicable individual is not a service provider.* [Reserved].

(B) *Attribution of earnings or losses.* Earnings or losses on a principal addition (including earnings and losses arising after an applicable individual ceases to be a service provider) are attributable to the services provided by the applicable individual in the same disqualified taxable year of the covered health insurance provider to which the principal addition is attributed in accordance with paragraph (d)(3)(ii)(A) of this section. Earnings are treated as remuneration for the taxable year to which they are attributed, and losses are treated as reductions to deferred deduction remuneration for that taxable year and may offset other deferred deduction remuneration (but not applicable individual remuneration) attributable to services performed by the applicable individual during that taxable year (or if there is not sufficient deferred deduction remuneration to offset the reduction entirely during that taxable year, the first subsequent taxable year or years in which the applicable individual has deferred deduction remuneration to be offset by the loss, if applicable).

(C) *Earnings.* Whether remuneration constitutes earnings on a principal addition is determined under the principles defining income attributable to an amount taken into account under § 31.3121(v)(2)-1(d)(2). Therefore, for an account balance plan (as defined in § 31.3121(v)(2)-1(c)(1)(ii)(A)), earnings on an amount deferred generally include an amount credited on behalf of the applicable individual under the terms of the arrangement that reflects a rate of return that does not exceed either the rate of return on a predetermined actual investment (as defined in § 31.3121(v)(2)-1(d)(2)(i)(B)), or, if the income does not reflect the rate of return on a predetermined actual investment, a reasonable rate of interest. For purposes of this section, the use of an unreasonable rate of return generally will result in the treatment of some or all of the remuneration as a principal addition that is attributable to services provided by an applicable individual in a taxable year of a covered health insurance provider in accordance with paragraph (d)(3)(ii)(A) of this section. For purposes of determining whether an account balance plan has a reasonable rate of return, the rules of § 31.3121(v)(2)-1(d)(2)(iii)(A) apply.

(D) *Consistency requirement.* If a covered health insurance provider applies a method described in either paragraph (d)(3)(i) or paragraph (d)(3)(ii) of this section, the covered health insurance provider must apply that method consistently for all taxable years for all plans of the covered health insurance provider that would be aggregated and treated as a single account balance plan under § 1.409A-1(c)(2) if one hypothetical applicable individual had deferrals of compensation under all of the plans described in this paragraph.

(4) *Nonaccount balance plans*—(i) *In general.* The increase (or decrease) in the present value of the future payment or payments to which an applicable individual has a legally binding right under a plan described in § 1.409A-1(c)(2)(i)(C) (nonaccount balance plan) as of a measurement date (as defined in paragraph (d)(3)(i)), over (or under) the present value of the future payment or payments as of the last day of the immediately preceding taxable year is attributable to services provided by the applicable individual in the taxable year of the covered health insurance provider that includes the measurement date. For purposes of determining the increase (or decrease) in the present value of a future payment or payments under a nonaccount balance plan, the rules of § 31.3121(v)(2)-1(c)(2) apply (including the requirement that reasonable actuarial assumptions and methods be used). For purposes of determining the increase (or decrease) in the present value of a future payment or payments under a nonaccount balance plan attributable to any taxable year, the present value of the future payment or payments as of the last day of the taxable year is increased by the amount of any payments made during that taxable year. Increases in the present value of the future payment or payments to which an applicable individual has a legally binding right under a nonaccount balance plan with respect to any taxable year are treated as remuneration attributable to services performed in that taxable year. Decreases in the present value of the future payment or payments to which an applicable individual has a legally binding right under a nonaccount balance plan with respect to any taxable year are treated as reductions to deferred deduction remuneration for that taxable year and may offset other deferred deduction remuneration (but not applicable individual remuneration) attributable to services performed by the applicable individual during that taxable year under any plan or arrangement (or if there is not sufficient deferred deduction remuneration for that taxable year to offset the reduction entirely, the excess may offset deferred deduction remuneration in the first subsequent taxable year or years in which the applicable individual has deferred deduction remuneration to be offset by the loss).

(ii) *Attribution of increases (or decreases) in the present value of a future payment or payments in taxable years during which an applicable individual is not a service provider.* [Reserved].

(5) *Equity-based remuneration*—(i) *Stock options and stock appreciation rights.* Remuneration resulting from the exercise of a stock option (including an incentive stock option described in section 422 and an option under an employee stock purchase plan described in section 423) or a stock appreciation right (SAR) is attributable to services performed by an applicable individual for a covered health insurance provider, and it must be allocated on a daily *pro rata* basis over the period beginning on the date of grant (within the meaning of § 1.409A-1(b)(5)(vi)(B)) of the stock option or SAR and ending on the date that the stock right is exercised, excluding any days on which the applicable individual is not a service provider.

(ii) *Restricted stock.* Remuneration resulting from the vesting or transfer of restricted stock for which an election under section 83(b) has not been made is attributable on a daily *pro rata* basis to services performed by an applicable individual for a covered health insurance provider over the period, excluding any days on which the applicable individual is not a service provider, beginning on the date the applicable individual obtains a legally binding right to the restricted stock and ending on the earliest of—

(A) the date the substantial risk of forfeiture lapses with respect to the restricted stock, or

(B) the date the restricted stock is transferred by the applicable individual (or becomes transferable as defined in § 1.83-3(d)).

(iii) *Restricted stock units.* Remuneration resulting from a restricted stock unit (RSU) is attributable to services performed by an applicable individual for a covered health insurance provider, and must be allocated on a daily *pro rata* basis, over the period beginning on the date the applicable individual obtains a legally binding right to the RSU and ending on the date the remuneration is paid or made available such that it is includible in gross income, excluding any days on which the applicable individual is not a service provider.

(iv) *Partnership interests and other equity.* The rules provided in this paragraph (d)(5) may be applied by analogy to grants of equity-based compensation in situations in which the compensation is determined by reference to equity in an entity treated as a partnership for federal tax purposes, or where compensation is determined by reference to equity interests in an entity described in § 1.409A-1(b)(5)(iii) (for example, a mutual company).

(6) *Involuntary separation pay.* Involuntary separation pay is attributable to services performed by an applicable individual for a covered health insurance provider in the taxable year in which the involuntary separation from service occurs. Alternatively, the covered health insurance provider may attribute involuntary separation pay to services performed by an applicable individual on a daily *pro rata* basis beginning on the date that the applicable individual obtains a legally binding right to the involuntary separation pay and ending on the date of the involuntary separation from service. Involuntary separation pay to different individuals may be attributed using different methods; however, if involuntary separation payments are made to the same individual over multiple taxable years, all the payments must be attributed using the same method. For purposes of this section, the term *involuntary separation pay* means remuneration to which an applicable individual has a right to payment solely as a result of the individual's involuntary separation from service (within the meaning of § 1.409A-1(n)).

(7) *Reimbursements.* Remuneration that is provided in the form of a reimbursement or benefit provided in-kind (other than cash) is attributable to services performed by an applicable individual in the taxable year of the covered health insurance provider in which the applicable individual makes a payment for which the applicable individual has a right to reimbursement or receives the in-kind benefit, except that remuneration provided in the form of a reimbursement or in-kind benefit during a taxable year of the covered health insurance provider in which an applicable individual is not a service provider is attributable to services provided in the first preceding taxable year of the covered health insurance provider in which the applicable individual is a service provider.

(8) *Split-dollar life insurance.* Remuneration resulting from a split-dollar life insurance arrangement (as defined in § 1.61-22(b)) under which an applicable individual has a legally binding right to economic benefits described in § 1.61-22(d)(2)(ii) (policy cash value to which the non-owner has current access within the meaning of § 1.61-22(d)(4)(ii)) or § 1.61-22(d)(2)(iii) (any other economic benefits provided to the non-owner) is attributable to services performed in the taxable year of the covered health insurance provider in which the legally binding right arises. Split-dollar life insurance arrangements under which payments are treated as split-dollar loans under § 1.7872-15 generally will not give rise to deferred deduction remuneration within the meaning of paragraph (b)(11) of this section, although they may give rise to applicable

individual remuneration. However, in certain situations, this type of arrangement may give rise to deferred deduction remuneration for purposes of section 162(m)(6), for example, if amounts on a split-dollar loan are waived, cancelled, or forgiven.

(9) *Examples.* The following examples illustrate the principles of paragraphs (d)(1) through (8) of this section. For purposes of these examples, each corporation has a taxable year that is the calendar year and is a covered health insurance provider for all relevant taxable years; deferred deduction remuneration is otherwise deductible in the taxable year in which it is paid; and amounts payable under nonaccount balance plans are not forfeitable upon the death of the applicable individual.

Example 1 (Account balance plan with earnings using the standard attribution method). (i) B is an applicable individual of corporation Y for all relevant taxable years. On January 1, 2016, B begins participating in a nonqualified deferred compensation plan of Y that is an account balance plan. Under the terms of the plan, all amounts are fully vested at all times, and Y will pay B's entire account balance on January 1, 2019. Y credits $10,000 to B under the plan annually on January 1 for three years beginning on January 1, 2016. The account earns interest at a fixed rate of five percent per year, compounded annually under the terms of the plan, which solely for purposes of this example, is assumed to be a reasonable rate of interest. Thus, B's account balance is $10,500 ($10,000 + ($10,000 × 5%)) on December 31, 2016; $21,525 ($10,500 + $10,000 + ($20,500 × 5%)) on December 31, 2017; and $33,101 ($21,525 + $10,000 + ($31,525 × 5%)) on December 31, 2018. Y attributes increases and decreases in account balances under the plan using the standard allocation method described in paragraph (d)(3)(i) of this section.

(ii) Under the standard attribution method for account balance plans described in paragraph (d)(3)(i) of this section, any increase in B's account balance as of the last day of Y's taxable year over the account balance as of the last day of the immediately preceding taxable year, increased by any payments made during the taxable year, is remuneration that is attributable to services provided by B in that taxable year. Accordingly, $10,500 of deferred deduction remuneration is attributable to services performed by B in Y's 2016 taxable year (the difference between the $10,500 account balance on December 31, 2016 and the zero account balance on December 31, 2015); $11,025 of deferred deduction remuneration is attributable to services performed in Y's 2017 taxable year (the difference between the $21,525 account balance on December 31, 2017 and the $10,500 account balance on December 31, 2016); and $11,576 of deferred deduction remuneration is attributable services performed in Y's 2018 taxable year (the difference between the $33,101 account balance on December 31, 2018 and the $21,525 account balance on December 31, 2017).

Example 2 (Account balance plan with earnings using the alternate attribution method). (i) The facts are the same as in *Example 1*, except that Y allocates earnings and losses based on the alternative attribution method described in paragraph (d)(3)(ii) of this section.

(ii) Under the alternative attribution method described in paragraph (d)(3)(ii) of this section, each principal addition of $10,000 is attributed to the taxable year of Y as of which the addition is credited, and earnings and losses on each principal addition are attributed to the same taxable year to which the principal addition is attributed. Therefore, $1,576 of earnings are attributable to Y's 2016 taxable year (interest on the 2016 $10,000 principal addition at five percent for three years compounded annually); $1,025 of earnings are attributable to Y's 2017 taxable year (interest on the 2017 $10,000 principal addition at five percent for two years compounded annually); and $500 of earnings are attributable to Y's 2018 taxable year (interest on the 2018 $10,000 principal addition at five percent for one year).

Example 3 (Account balance plan with earnings and losses using the standard attribution method). (i) The facts are the same as in *Example 1,* except that the earnings under the terms of the plan are based on a notional investment in a predetermined actual investment (as defined in § 31.3121(v)(2)-1(e)(2)(i)(B)), which results in B's account balance increasing by five percent in the 2016 taxable year, decreasing by five percent in the 2017 taxable year, and increasing again by five percent in the 2018 taxable year. Therefore, on December 31, 2016, B's account balance is $10,500 ($10,000 + ($10,000 × 5%)); on December 31, 2017, B's account balance is $19,475 ($10,500 + $10,000 − ($20,500 × 5%)); and on December 31, 2018, B's account balance is $30,479 ($19,475 + $10,000 + ($29,475 × 5%)).

(ii) Under the standard attribution method for account balance plans described in paragraph (d)(3)(i) of this section, increases (or decreases) in B's account balance as of the last day of Y's taxable year over (or under) the account balance as of the last day of the immediately preceding taxable year, increased by any payments made during the taxable year, are attributable to services provided by B in that taxable year.

(iii) Accordingly, $10,500 of deferred deduction remuneration is attributable to services performed by B in Y's 2016 taxable year (the difference between the $10,500 account balance on December 31, 2016 and the zero account balance on December 31, 2015); $8,975 of deferred deduction remuneration is attributable to services performed in Y's 2017 taxable year (the difference between the $19,475 account balance on December 31, 2017 and the $10,500 account balance on December 31, 2016); and $11,474 of deferred deduction remuneration is attributable to services performed in Y's 2018 taxable year (the difference between the $30,949 account balance on December 31, 2018 and the $19,475 account balance on December 31, 2017).

Example 4 (Account balance plan with earnings and losses using the alternative attribution method). (i) The facts are the same as in *Example 3,* except that Y attributes earnings and losses based on the method described in paragraph (d)(3)(ii) of this section.

(ii) Under the alternative attribution method for account balance plans described in paragraph (d)(3)(ii) of this section, each $10,000 principal addition is attributed to the taxable year of Y as of which the addition is made, and earnings and losses on each principal addition are attributed to the same taxable year of Y to which the principal addition is attributed. With respect to the $10,000 principal addition to B's account for 2016, the account balance is $10,500 on December 1, 2016 ($500 of earnings), $9,975 on December 31, 2017 ($525 of losses), and $10,474 on December 31, 2018 ($499 of earnings). Accordingly, $474 ($500 − $525 + $499) of net earnings is attributable to Y's 2016 taxable year. With respect to the $10,000 principal addition to B's account for 2017, the account balance is $9,500 on December 31, 2017 ($500 of losses), and $9,975 on December 31, 2018 ($475 of earnings). Accordingly, $25 in net losses are attributable to Y's 2017 taxable year ($500 losses for 2017 and $475 earnings for 2018). Because losses attributable to a taxable year may reduce deferred deduction remuneration attributable to that taxable year (but not applicable individual remuneration), the $25 loss reduces the $10,000 principal addition to B's account in 2017 for purposes of applying the section 162(m)(6) deduction limitation. With respect to the $10,000 principal addition to B's account in 2018, the account balance is $10,500 on December 31, 2018. Therefore, the $500 of earnings is attributable to Y's 2018 taxable year.

Example 5 (Nonaccount balance plan). (i) C is an applicable individual of corporation X for all relevant taxable years. On January 1, 2015, X grants C a vested right to a $100,000 payment on January 1, 2020.

(ii) Under the attribution method for nonaccount balance plans described in paragraph (d)(4) of this section, any increase (or decrease) in the present value of the future payment that C is entitled to receive under the nonaccount balance plan as of the last day of X's taxable year, over (or under) the present value of the future payment as of the last day of the preceding taxable year, increased by any payments made during the taxable year, is attributable to services provided by C in that taxable year. X determines the present value of the payment using an interest rate of five percent for all years, which, solely for purposes of this example, is assumed to be a reasonable actuarial assumption. The present value of $100,000 payable on January 1, 2020, determined using a five percent interest rate, is $82,300 as of December 31, 2015; $86,400 as of December 31, 2016; $90,700 as of December 31, 2017; and $95,200 as of December 31, 2018. Accordingly, $82,300 of deferred deduction remuneration is attributable to services performed by C in X's 2015 taxable year; $4,100 ($86,400 − $82,300) of deferred deduction remuneration is attributable to services performed by C in X's 2016 taxable year; $4,300 ($90,700 − $86,400) of deferred deduction remuneration is attributable to services performed by C in X's 2017 taxable year; $4,500 ($95,200 − $90,700) of deferred deduction remuneration is attributable to services performed by C in X's 2018 taxable year; and $4,800 ($100,000 − $95,200) of remuneration is attributable to services performed by C in X's 2019 taxable year.

Example 6 (Nonaccount balance plan). (i) D is an applicable individual of corporation W for all relevant taxable years. D begins employment with W on January 1, 2016. On December 31, 2020, D obtains the right to a payment from W equal to 10 percent of D's highest annual salary multiplied by D's years of service commencing on January 1 of the year following D's separation from service. In 2020, D has an annual salary of $375,000, which increases by $25,000 on January 1 of each subsequent calendar year. D separates from service with W on December 31, 2023, and W pays $360,000 to D on January 1, 2024. W determines the present value of amounts to be paid under the plan using an interest rate of five percent for all years, which, solely for purposes of this example, is assumed to be a reasonable actuarial assumption.

(ii) Under the attribution method for nonaccount balance plans described in paragraph (d)(4) of this section, the increase (or decrease) in the present value of the future payment to which D is entitled under the nonaccount balance plan as of the last day of W's taxable year, over (or under) the present value of the future payment as of the last day of the preceding taxable year, increased by any payments made during the taxable year, is attributable to services provided by D in that taxable year. W determines the present value of this payment using an interest rate of five percent for all years, which solely for purposes of this example, is assumed to be a reasonable actuarial assumption. As of December 31, 2021, D has the right to a payment of $240,000 on January 1, 2024 ($400,000 × 10% × 6 years of service). The present value as of December 31, 2021 of $240,000 payable on January 1, 2024 is $217,687. Therefore, $217,687 of deferred deduction remuneration is attributable to services performed by D in W's 2021 taxable year.

(iii) As of December 31, 2022, D has the right to a payment of $297,500 on January 1, 2023 ($425,000 × 10% × 7 years of service). The present value as of December 31, 2022 of $297,500 payable on January 1, 2023 is $283,333. Therefore, the deferred deduction remuneration attributable to services performed by D in W's 2022 taxable year is $65,546 ($283,333 − $217,680).

(iv) As of December 31, 2023, D has the right to a payment of $360,000 on January 1, 2024 ($450,000 × 10% × 8 years of service). The present value as of December 31, 2023 of $360,000 payable on January 1, 2024 is $360,000. Therefore, the deferred deduction remuneration attributable to services performed by D in W's 2023 taxable year is $76,767 ($360,000 − $283,333).

Example 7 (Stock option). (i) E is an applicable individual of corporation V for all relevant taxable years. On January 1, 2016, V grants E an option to purchase 100 shares of V common stock at an exercise price of $50 per share (the fair market value of V common stock on the date of grant). On December 31, 2017, E ceases to be a service provider of V or any member of V's aggregated group. On January 1, 2019, E resumes providing services for V and again becomes both a service provider and an applicable individual of V. On December 31, 2020, when the fair market value of V common stock is $196 per share, E exercises the stock option. The remuneration resulting from the stock option exercise is $14,600 (($196 − $50) × 100).

(ii) Pursuant to paragraph (d)(5)(i) of this section, the remuneration resulting from the exercise of a stock option is attributable to services performed by E over the period beginning on the date of grant of the stock option and ending on the date that the stock right is exercised, excluding any days on which E is not a service provider of V. Therefore, the $14,600 is attributed *pro rata* over the 1,460 days from January 1, 2016 to December 31, 2017 and from January 1, 2019 to December 31, 2020 (365 days per year for the 2016, 2017, 2019, and 2020 taxable years), so that $10 ($14,600 divided by 1,460) is attributed to each calendar day in this period, and $3,650 (365 days × $10) of remuneration is attributed to services performed by E in each of V's 2016, 2017, 2019, and 2020 taxable years.

Example 8 (Restricted stock). (i) F is an applicable individual of corporation U for all relevant taxable years. On January 1, 2017, U grants F 100 shares of restricted U common stock. Under the terms of the grant, the shares will be forfeited if F voluntarily terminates employment before December 31, 2019 (so that the shares are subject to a substantial risk of forfeiture through that date) and are nontransferable until the substantial risk of forfeiture lapses. F does not make an election under section 83(b) and continues in employment with U through December 31, 2019, at which time F's rights in the stock become substantially vested within the meaning of § 1.83-3(b) and the fair market value of a share of the stock is $109.50. The deferred deduction remuneration resulting from the vesting of the restricted stock is $10,950 ($109.50 × 100).

(ii) Pursuant to paragraph (d)(5)(ii) of this section, the remuneration resulting from the vesting of restricted stock is attributable to services performed by F on a daily *pro rata* basis over the period, excluding any days on which F is not a service provider of U, beginning on the date F is granted the restricted stock and ending on the earliest of the date the substantial risk of forfeiture lapses or the date the restricted stock is transferred (or becomes transferable as defined in § 1.83-3(d)). Therefore, the $10,950 of remuneration is attributed to services performed by F over the 1,095 days between January 1, 2017 and December 31, 2019 (365 days per year for the 2017, 2018, and 2019 taxable years), so that $10 ($10,950 divided by 1,095) is attributed to each calendar day in this period, and remuneration of $3,650 (365 days × $10) is attributed to services performed by F in each of U's 2017, 2018, and 2019 taxable years.

Example 9 (Restricted stock units (RSUs)). (i) G is an applicable individual of corporation T for all relevant taxable years. On January 1, 2018, T grants G 100 RSUs. Under the terms of the grant, T will pay G an amount on December 31, 2020 equal to the fair market value of 100 shares of T common stock on that date, but only if G continues to provide substantial services to T (so that the RSU is subject to a substantial risk of forfeiture) through December 31, 2020. G remains employed by T through December 31, 2020, at which time the fair market value of a share of the stock is $219, and T pays G $21,900 ($219 × 100).

(ii) Pursuant to paragraph (d)(5)(iii) of this section, remuneration from the payment under the RSUs is attributed on a daily *pro rata* basis to services performed by G over the period beginning on the date the RSUs are granted and ending on the date the remuneration is paid or made available, excluding any days on which G is not a service provider of T. Therefore, the $21,900 in remuneration is attributed over the 1,095 days beginning on January 1, 2018 and ending on December 31, 2020 (365 days per year for the 2018, 2019, and 2020 taxable years), so that $20 ($21,900 divided by 1,095) is attributed to each calendar day in this period, and $7,300 (365 days × $20) is attributed to service performed by G in each of T's 2018, 2019, and 2020 taxable years.

Example 10 (Involuntary separation pay). (i) H is an applicable individual of corporation S. On January 1, 2015, H and S enter into an employment contract providing that S will make two payments of $150,000 each to H if H has an involuntary separation from service. Under the terms of the contract, the first payment is due on January 1 following the involuntary separation from service, and the second payment is due on January 1 of the following year. On December 31, 2016, H has an involuntary separation from service. S pays H $150,000 on January 1, 2017 and $150,000 on January 1, 2018.

(ii) Pursuant to paragraph (d)(6) of this section, involuntary separation pay may be attributed to services performed by H in the taxable year of S in which the involuntary separation from service occurs. Alternatively, involuntary separation pay may be attributed to services performed by H on a daily *pro rata* basis beginning on the date H obtains a right to the involuntary separation pay and ending on the date of the involuntary separation from service. The entire $300,000 amount, including both $150,000 payments, must be attributed using the same method. Therefore, the entire $300,000 amount (comprised of two $150,000 payments) may be attributed to services performed by H in S's 2016 taxable year, which is the taxable year in which the involuntary separation from service occurs. Alternatively, the two $150,000 payments may be attributable to the period beginning on January 1, 2015 and ending December 31, 2016, so that $410.96 ($300,000/(365 × 2)) is attributed to each day of S's 2015 and 2016 taxable years, and $150,000 ($410.96 × 365) is attributed to services performed by H in each of S's 2015 and 2016 taxable years.

Example 11 (Reimbursement after termination of services). (i) I is an applicable individual of corporation R. On January 1, 2018, I enters into an agreement with R under which R will reimburse I's country club dues for two years following I's separation from service. On December 31, 2020, I ceases to be a service provider of R. I pays $50,000 in country club dues on January 1, 2021 and $50,000 on January 2, 2022. Pursuant to the agreement, R reimburses I $50,000 for the country club dues in 2021 and $50,000 in 2022.

(ii) Pursuant to paragraph (d)(7) of this section, remuneration provided in the form of a reimbursement or in-kind benefit after I ceases to be a service provider of R is attributed to services provided by I in R's taxable year in which I ceases to be an officer, director, or employee of R and ceases performing services for, or on behalf of, R. Therefore, $100,000 is attributed to services performed in R's 2020 taxable year.

(10) *Certain deferred deduction remuneration subject to a substantial risk of forfeiture.* If remuneration is attributable in accordance with paragraph (d)(2) (legally binding right), (d)(3) (account balance plan), or (d)(4) (nonaccount balance plan) of this section to services performed in a period that includes two or more taxable years of a covered health insurance provider during which the remuneration is subject to a substantial risk of forfeiture, that remuneration must be attributed using a two-step process. First, the remuneration must be attributed to the taxable years of the covered health insurance provider in accordance with paragraph (d)(2), (3), or (4) of this section, as applicable. Second, the remuneration attributed to the period during which the remuneration is subject to a substantial risk of forfeiture (the vesting period) must be reattributed on a daily *pro rata* basis over that period beginning on the date that the applicable individual obtains a legally binding right to the remuneration and ending on the date that the substantial risk of forfeiture lapses. If a vesting period ends on a day other than the last day of the covered health insurance provider's taxable year, the remuneration attributable to that taxable year under

the first step of the attribution process is divided between the portion of the taxable year that includes the vesting period and the portion of the taxable year that does not include the vesting period. The amount attributed to the portion of the taxable year that includes the vesting period is equal to the total amount of remuneration that would be attributable to the taxable year under the first step of the attribution process, multiplied by a fraction, the numerator of which is the number of days during the taxable year that the amount is subject to a substantial risk of forfeiture and the denominator of which is the number of days in such taxable year. The remaining amount is attributed to the portion of the taxable year that does not include the vesting period and, therefore, is not reattributed under the second step of the attribution process. For purposes of this section, the date on which a substantial risk of forfeiture lapses is the date on which the substantial risk of forfeiture lapses for any reason, including the death, disability, or involuntary termination of employment of the applicable individual, or the discretionary action of a covered health insurance provider or any other person.

(11) *Examples.* The following examples illustrate the principles of paragraph (d)(10) of this section. For purposes of these examples, each corporation has a taxable year that is the calendar year and is a covered health insurance provider for all relevant taxable years; deferred deduction remuneration is otherwise deductible in the taxable year in which it is paid; and amounts payable under nonaccount balance plans are not forfeitable upon the death of the applicable individual.

Example 1 (Account balance plan subject to a substantial risk of forfeiture using the standard attribution method). (i) J is an applicable individual of corporation Q for all relevant taxable years. On January 1, 2016, J begins participating in a nonqualified deferred compensation plan that is an account balance plan. Under the terms of the plan, Q will pay J's account balance on January 1, 2021, but only if J continues to provide substantial services to Q through December 31, 2018 (so that the amount credited to J's account is subject to a substantial risk of forfeiture through that date). Q credits $10,000 to J's account annually for five years on January 1 of each year beginning on January 1, 2016. The account earns interest at a fixed rate of five percent per year, compounded annually, which solely for the purposes of this example, is assumed to be a reasonable rate of interest. Therefore, J's account balance is $10,500 ($10,000 + ($10,000 × 5%)) on December 31, 2016; $21,525 ($10,500 + $10,000 + ($20,500 × 5%)) on December 31, 2017; $33,101 ($21,525 + $10,000 + ($31,525 × 5%)) on December 31, 2018; $45,256 ($33,101 + $10,000 + ($43,101 × 5%)) on December 31, 2019; and $58,019 ($45,256 + $10,000 + ($55,256 × 5%)) on December 31, 2020. Q attributes increases and decreases in account balances under the plan using the standard attribution method described in paragraph (d)(3)(i) of this section.

(ii) Under the standard attribution method for account balance plans described in paragraph (d)(3)(i) of this section, any increases in J's account balance as of the last day of Q's taxable year over the account balance as of the last day of the immediately preceding taxable year, increased by any payments made during the taxable year, is attributable to services provided by J in that taxable year. Accordingly, $10,500 of deferred deduction remuneration is initially attributable to services performed by J in Q's 2016 taxable year (the difference between the $10,500 account balance on December 31, 2016 and the zero account balance on December 31, 2015); $11,025 of deferred deduction remuneration is initially attributable to services performed by J in Q's 2017 taxable year (the difference between the $21,525 account balance on December 31, 2017 and the $10,500 account balance on December 31, 2016); $11,576 of deferred deduction remuneration is initially attributable to services performed by J in Q's 2018 taxable year (the difference between the $33,101 account balance on December 31, 2018 and the $21,525 account balance on December 31, 2017); $12,155 of deferred deduction remuneration is attributable to services performed by J in Q's 2019 taxable year (the difference between the $45,256 account balance on December 31, 2019 and the $33,101 account balance on December 31, 2018); and $12,763 of deferred deduction remuneration is attributable to services performed by J in Q's 2020 taxable year (the difference between the $58,019 account balance on December 31, 2020 and the $45,256 account balance on December 31, 2018).

(iii) Under the attribution method described in paragraph (d)(10) of this section, deferred deduction remuneration that is attributable to services performed in a period that includes two or more taxable years of Q during which the deferred deduction remuneration is subject to a substantial risk of forfeiture must be reattributed on a daily *pro rata* basis over the period beginning on the date that J obtains a legally binding right to the remuneration and ending on the date that the substantial risk of forfeiture lapses. Therefore, $33,101 ($10,500 + $11,025 + $11,576) is reattributed on a daily *pro rata* basis over the period beginning on January 1, 2016, and ending on December 31,

2018, and $11,034 is attributed to each of Q's 2016, 2017, and 2018 taxable years.

Example 2 (Account balance plan subject to a substantial risk of forfeiture using the alternative attribution method). (i) The facts are the same as in *Example 1,* except that Q allocates earnings and losses using the alternative attribution method described in paragraph (d)(3)(ii) of this section.

(ii) Under the alternative attribution method for account balance plans described in paragraph (d)(3)(ii) of this section, earnings and losses on a principal addition are attributed to the same disqualified taxable year of Q to which the principal addition is attributed. Therefore, the amount initially attributable to Q's 2016 taxable year is $12,763 (the $10,000 principal addition in 2016 at five percent interest for five years); the amount initially attributable to Q's 2017 taxable year is $12,155 (the $10,000 principal addition in 2017 at five percent interest for four years); the amount initially attributable to Q's 2018 taxable year is $11,576 (the $10,000 principal addition in 2018 at five percent interest for three years); the amount attributable to Q's 2019 taxable year is $11,025 (the $10,000 principal addition in 2019 at five percent interest for two years), and the amount attributable to Q's 2020 taxable year is $10,500 (the $10,000 principal addition in 2020 at five percent interest for one year).

(iii) Under the attribution method described in paragraph (d)(10) of this section, deferred deduction remuneration that is attributable to two or more taxable years of Q during which the deferred deduction remuneration is subject to a substantial risk of forfeiture must be reattributed on a daily *pro rata* basis to that period beginning on the date that J obtains a legally binding right to the remuneration and ending on the date that the substantial risk of forfeiture lapses. Therefore, $36,494 ($12,763 + $12,155 + $11,576) is reattributed on a daily *pro rata* basis over the period beginning on January 1, 2016, and ending on December 31, 2018, and $12,165 is attributed to each of Q's 2016, 2017, and 2018 taxable years.

Example 3 (Nonaccount balance plan subject to a substantial risk of forfeiture). (i) K is an applicable individual of corporation J for all relevant taxable years. K begins employment with J on January 1, 2016 and begins participating in a nonqualified deferred compensation plan that is a defined benefit plan. Under the terms of the plan, J will pay K an amount equal to ten percent of K's highest annual salary multiplied by K's years of service as of K's separation from service, but only if K remains employed through December 31, 2020 (so that the right to the remuneration is subject to a substantial risk of forfeiture through that date). In 2016, K has annual salary of $275,000, which increases by $25,000 on January 1 of each subsequent calendar year. K has a separation from service from J on December 31, 2025, and J pays $500,000 to K on January 1, 2026 pursuant to the terms of the plan. J determines the present value of amounts to be paid under the plan using an interest rate of five percent for all years, which, solely for purposes of this example, is assumed to be a reasonable actuarial assumption.

(ii) As of December 31, 2016, K has a right to a payment of $27,500 on January 1, 2026 ($275,000 × 10% × 1 years of service). The present value as of December 31, 2021, of a $27,500 payment to be made on January 1, 2026, is $17,727. Therefore, the remuneration initially attributable to services performed by K in J's 2021 taxable year is $17,727 ($17,727–$0).

(iii) As of December 31, 2017, K has a right to a payment of $60,000 on January 1, 2026 ($300,000 × 10% × 2 years of service). The present value as of December 31, 2021, of a $60,000 payment to be made on January 1, 2026, is $40,610. Therefore, the remuneration initially attributable to services performed by K in J's 2021 taxable year is $22,884 ($40,610–$17,727).

(iv) As of December 31, 2018, K has a right to a payment of $97,500 on January 1, 2026 ($325,000 × 10% × 3 years of service). The present value as of December 31, 2021, of a $97,500 payment to be made on January 1, 2026, is $69,291. Therefore, the remuneration initially attributable to services performed by K in J's 2021 taxable year is $28,681 ($69,291–$40,610).

(v) As of December 31, 2019, K has a right to a payment of $140,000 on January 1, 2026 ($350,000 × 10% × 4 years of service). The present value as of December 31, 2021, of a $140,000 payment to be made on January 1, 2026, is $104,470. Therefore, the remuneration initially attributable to services performed by K in J's 2021 taxable year is $35,179 ($104,470–$69,291).

(vi) As of December 31, 2020, K has a right to a payment of $187,500 on January 1, 2026 ($375,000 × 10% × 5 years of service). The present value as of December 31, 2021, of a $187,500 payment to be made on January 1, 2026, is $146,911. Therefore, the remuneration initially

attributable to services performed by K in J's 2021 taxable year is $42,441 ($146,911–$104,470).

(vii) As of December 31, 2021, K has a right to a payment of $240,000 on January 1, 2026 ($400,000 × 10% × 6 years of service). The present value as of December 31, 2021, of a $240,000 payment to be made on January 1, 2026, is $197,449. Therefore, the remuneration attributable to services performed by K in J's 2021 taxable year is $50,537 ($197,449–$146,911).

(viii) As of December 31, 2022, K has a right to a $297,500 payment on January 1, 2026 ($425,000 × 10% × 7 years of service). The present value as of December 31, 2022, of a $297,500 payment to be made on January 1, 2026, is $256,992. Therefore, the remuneration attributable to services performed by K in J's 2022 taxable year is $59,543 ($256,992–$197,449).

(ix) As of December 31, 2023, K has a right to a $360,000 payment on January 1, 2026 ($450,000 × 10% × 8 years of service). The present value as of December 31, 2023 of a $360,000 payment to be made on January 1, 2026 is $326,532. Therefore, the remuneration attributable to services performed by K in J's 2023 taxable year is $69,539 ($326,531–$256,992).

(x) As of December 31, 2024, K has a right to a $427,500 payment on January 1, 2026 ($475,000 × 10% × 9 years of service). The present value as of December 31, 2024 of a $427,500 payment to be made on January 1, 2026 is $407,143. Therefore, the remuneration attributable to services performed by K in J's 2024 taxable year is $80,612 ($407,143–$326,531).

(xi) As of December 31, 2025, K has a right to a $500,000 payment on January 1, 2026 ($500,000 × 10% × 10 years of service). The present value as of December 31, 2025 of a $500,000 payment to be made on January 1, 2026 is $500,000. Therefore, the applicable individual remuneration attributable to services performed by K in J's 2025 taxable year is $92,857 ($500,000–$407,143).

(xii) Under the attribution method described in paragraph (d)(10) of this section, deferred deduction remuneration that is attributable to two or more taxable years of a covered health insurance provider during which the deferred deduction remuneration is subject to a substantial risk of forfeiture must be reattributed on a daily *pro rata* basis to that period beginning on the date that the applicable individual obtains a legally binding right to the remuneration and ending on the date that the substantial risk of forfeiture lapses. Therefore, $146,911 ($17,727 + $22,884 + $28,681 + $35,179 + $42,441) is reattributed on a daily *pro rata* basis over the period beginning on January 1, 2016, and ending on December 31, 2020, and, accordingly, $29,382 (($146,911/(5 × 365)) × 365) is attributed to services performed by K in each of L's 2016, 2017, 2018, 2019, and 2020 taxable years.

(e) *Application of the deduction limitation-*(1) *To aggregate amounts.* The $500,000 deduction limitation is applied to the aggregate amount of applicable individual remuneration and deferred deduction remuneration attributable to services performed by an applicable individual in a disqualified taxable year. The aggregate amount of applicable individual remuneration and deferred deduction remuneration attributable to services performed by an applicable individual in a disqualified taxable year that exceeds the $500,000 deduction limitation is not allowed as a deduction in any taxable year. Therefore, for example, if an applicable individual has $500,000 or more of applicable individual remuneration attributable to services provided to a covered health insurance provider in a disqualified taxable year, the amount of that applicable individual remuneration that exceeds $500,000 is not deductible in any taxable year, and no deferred deduction remuneration attributable to services performed by the applicable individual in that disqualified taxable year is deductible in any taxable year. However, if an applicable individual has applicable individual remuneration for a disqualified taxable year that is less than $500,000 and deferred deduction remuneration attributable to services performed in the same disqualified taxable year that, when combined with the applicable individual remuneration for the year, is greater than $500,000, all of the applicable individual remuneration is deductible in that disqualified taxable year, but the amount of deferred deduction remuneration that is deductible in future taxable years is limited to the excess of $500,000 over the amount of the applicable individual remuneration for that year.

(2) *Order of application and calculation of deduction limitation-*(i) *In general.* The deduction limitation with respect to any applicable individual for any disqualified taxable year is applied to applicable individual remuneration and deferred deduction remuneration attributable to services performed by that applicable individual in that disqualified taxable year at the time that the remuneration becomes otherwise deductible, and each time the deduction limitation is applied to an amount that is otherwise deductible, the deduction limitation is re-

duced (but not below zero) by the amount against which it is applied. Accordingly, the deduction limitation is applied first to an applicable individual's applicable individual remuneration attributable to services performed in a disqualified taxable year and is reduced (but not below zero) by the amount of the applicable individual remuneration against which it is applied. If the applicable individual also has an amount of deferred deduction remuneration attributable to services performed in that disqualified taxable year that becomes otherwise deductible in a subsequent taxable year, the deduction limitation, as reduced, is applied to that amount of deferred deduction remuneration in the first taxable year in which it becomes otherwise deductible. The deduction limitation is then further reduced (but not below zero) by the amount of the deferred deduction remuneration against which it is applied. If the applicable individual has an additional amount of deferred deduction remuneration attributable to services performed in the original disqualified taxable year that becomes otherwise deductible in a subsequent taxable year, the deduction limitation, as further reduced, is applied to that amount of deferred deduction remuneration in the taxable year in which it is otherwise deductible. This process continues for future taxable years in which deferred deduction remuneration attributable to services performed by the applicable individual in the original disqualified taxable year is otherwise deductible. No deduction is allowed in any taxable year for any applicable individual remuneration or deferred deduction remuneration attributable to services performed by an applicable individual in a disqualified taxable year to the extent that it exceeds the deduction limitation (as reduced, if applicable) for that disqualified taxable year at the time the deduction limitation is applied to the remuneration.

(ii) *Application to payments*—(A) *In general.* Any payment of deferred deduction remuneration may include remuneration that is attributable to services performed by an applicable individual in one or more earlier taxable years of a covered health insurance provider pursuant to paragraphs (d)(2) through (d)(8) and paragraph (d)(10) of this section. In that case, a separate deduction limitation applies to each portion of the payment that is attributed to services performed in a different disqualified taxable year. Any portion of a payment that is attributed to a taxable year that is a disqualified taxable year is deductible only to the extent that it does not exceed the deduction limit that applies with respect to the applicable individual for that disqualified taxable year, as reduced by the amount, if any, of applicable individual remuneration and deferred deduction remuneration attributable to services performed in that disqualified taxable year that was deductible in an earlier taxable year.

(B) *Application to series of payments.* Under the rule described in paragraph (d)(1)(ii) of this section, amounts attributable to services performed by an applicable individual pursuant to paragraph (d)(3) or (4) of this section must be attributed to services performed by the applicable individual in the earliest year that the amount could be attributable under paragraph (d)(3) of (4) of this section, as applicable. Any portion of a payment that is attributed to services performed in a taxable year is treated as paid for all purposes under this section, including the calculation of future earnings and the attribution of other remuneration.

(3) *Examples.* The following examples illustrate the rules of paragraphs (e)(1) and (e)(2) of this section. For purposes of these examples, each corporation has a taxable year that is the calendar year and is a covered health insurance provider for all relevant taxable years; deferred deduction remuneration is otherwise deductible in the taxable year in which it is paid, and amounts payable under nonaccount balance plans are not forfeitable upon the death of the applicable individual.

Example 1 (Lump-sum payment of deferred deduction remuneration attributable to a single taxable year).

(i) L is an applicable individual of corporation O. During O's 2015 taxable year, O pays L $550,000 in salary, which is applicable individual remuneration, and grants L a right to $50,000 of deferred deduction remuneration payable upon L's separation from service from O. L has a separation from service in 2020, at which time O pays L the $50,000 of deferred deduction remuneration attributable to services performed by L in O's 2015 taxable year.

(ii) The $500,000 deduction limitation for 2015 is applied first to L's $550,000 of applicable individual remuneration for 2015. Because the $550,000 otherwise deductible by O in 2015 is greater than the deduction limitation, O may deduct only $500,000 of the applicable individual remuneration for 2015, and $50,000 of the $550,000 of applicable individual remuneration is not deductible for any taxable year. The deduction limitation for remuneration attributable to services provided by L in O's 2015 taxable year is then reduced to zero. Because the $50,000 in deferred deduction remuneration attributable to services performed by

L in 2015 exceeds the reduced deduction limitation of zero, that $50,000 is not deductible for any taxable year.

Example 2 (Installment payments of deferred deduction remuneration attributable to a single taxable year). (i) M is an applicable individual of corporation N. During N's 2016 taxable year, N pays M $300,000 in salary, which is applicable individual remuneration, and grants M a right to $220,000 of deferred deduction remuneration payable on a fixed schedule beginning upon M's separation from service. The $220,000 is attributable to services provided by M in N's 2016 taxable year. M has a separation from service in 2020. In 2020, N pays M $400,000 in salary, which is applicable individual remuneration, and also pays M $120,000 of deferred deduction remuneration that is attributable to services performed in N's 2016 taxable year. In 2021, N pays M the remaining $100,000 of deferred deduction remuneration attributable to services performed by M in N's 2016 taxable year.

(ii) The $500,000 deduction limitation for 2016 is applied first to M's $300,000 of applicable individual remuneration for 2016. Because the deduction limitation is greater than the applicable individual remuneration, N may deduct the entire $300,000 of applicable individual remuneration paid in 2016. The $500,000 deduction limitation is then reduced to $200,000 by the amount of the applicable individual remuneration ($500,000-$300,000). The reduced deduction limitation is applied to M's $120,000 of deferred deduction remuneration attributable to services performed by M in N's 2016 taxable year that is paid in 2020. Because the reduced deduction limitation of $200,000 is greater than the $120,000 of deferred deduction remuneration, for N's 2020 taxable year, N may deduct the entire $120,000 of deferred deduction remuneration paid in 2020. The $200,000 deduction limitation is reduced to $80,000 by the $120,000 in deferred deduction remuneration against which it was applied ($200,000-$120,000). The reduced deduction limitation of $80,000 is then applied to the remaining $100,000 payment of deferred deduction remuneration attributable to services performed by M in N's 2016 taxable year. Because the $100,000 in deferred deduction remuneration otherwise deductible by N for 2021 exceeds the reduced deduction limitation of $80,000, N may deduct only $80,000 of the deferred deduction remuneration for the 2021 taxable year, and $20,000 of the $100,000 payment is not deductible by N for any taxable year.

Example 3 (Lump-sum payment attributable to multiple years from an account balance plan using the standard attribution method). (i) N is an applicable individual of corporation M for all relevant taxable years. On January 1, 2013, N begins participating in a nonqualified deferred compensation plan sponsored by M that is an account balance plan. Under the plan, all amounts are fully vested at all times. The balances in N's account (including principal additions and earnings) are $50,000 on December 31, 2013, $100,000 on December 31, 2014, and $200,000 on December 2015. N's applicable individual remuneration from M is $425,000 for 2013, $450,000 for 2014, and $500,000 for 2015. On January 1, 2016, in accordance with the plan terms, M pays $200,000 to N, which is a payment of N's entire account balance under the plan.

(ii) To determine the extent to which M is entitled to a deduction for any portion of the $200,000 payment under the plan, the payment must first be attributed to services performed by N in M's taxable years in accordance with the attribution rules set forth in paragraph (d) of this section. Under the standard attribution method for account balance plans in paragraph (d)(3)(i) of this section, remuneration under an account balance plan is attributed to services performed by N in M's taxable years in an amount equal to the increase (or decrease) in the account balance as of the last day of M's taxable year over the account balance as of the last day of the immediately preceding taxable year, increased by any payments made during that year. Therefore, N's remuneration under the account balance plan is attributed to services performed by N in M's taxable years as follows: $50,000 ($50,000-$0) in 2013, $50,000 ($100,000-$50,000) in 2014, and $100,000 ($200,000-$100,000) in 2015.

(iii) Under the rules in paragraphs (d)(1)(ii) and (e)(2)(ii)(B) of this section, the January 1, 2016 payment of $200,000 is deemed a payment of remuneration attributed to services performed by N in the earliest year that the amount could be attributed under paragraph (d)(3)(i) of this section. M's first taxable year to which any portion of the payment could be attributed is M's 2013 taxable year. Accordingly, $50,000 of the $200,000 payment is attributed to services performed by N in M's 2013 taxable year. M's next earliest taxable year to which any portion of the payment could be attributed is M's 2014 taxable year. Accordingly, $50,000 of the $200,000 payment is attributed to services performed by N in M's 2014 taxable year. M's next earliest disqualified taxable year to which any portion of the payment could be attributed is M's 2015 taxable year. Accordingly, the remaining $100,000 of the $200,000 payment is attributed to services performed by N in M's 2015 taxable year.

(iv) The portion of the deferred deduction remuneration attributed to services performed in a disqualified taxable year under paragraph (d) of this section that exceeds the deduction limitation for that disqualified taxable year, as reduced through the date of payment, is not deductible in any taxable year. For M's 2013 taxable year, the deduction limitation is reduced to $75,000 by the $425,000 of applicable individual remuneration for that year. Because $50,000 does not exceed that reduced deduction limitation, all $50,000 of the deferred deduction remuneration attributed to services performed by N in M's 2013 taxable year is deductible for 2016, the year of payment. The deduction limitation for remuneration attributable to services performed by N that are attributable to 2013 is then reduced to $25,000, and this reduced limitation is applied to any future payment of deferred deduction remuneration attributable to services performed by N in 2013. For M's 2014 taxable year, the deduction limitation is reduced to $50,000 by N's $450,000 of applicable individual remuneration for that year. Because $50,000 does not exceed that reduced deduction limitation, all $50,000 of the deferred deduction remuneration attributed to M's 2014 taxable year is deductible for 2016, the year of payment. The deduction limitation for remuneration attributable to services performed by N in 2014 is then reduced to zero, and this reduced limitation is applied to any future payment of deferred deduction remuneration attributable to services performed by N in 2014. For M's 2015 taxable year, the deduction limitation is reduced to zero during 2015 by N's $500,000 of applicable individual remuneration for that year. Because $100,000 exceeds the reduced limit of zero, the $100,000 of the deferred deduction remuneration attributed to services performed by N in M's 2015 taxable year is not deductible for the year of payment (or any other taxable year). As a result, $100,000 of the $200,000 payment ($50,000 + $50,000 + $0) is deductible by M for M's 2016 taxable year, and the remaining $100,000 is not deductible by M for any taxable year.

Example 4 (Installment payments attributable to multiple taxable years from an account balance plan using the standard attribution method). (i) O is an applicable individual of corporation L for all relevant taxable years. On January 1, 2016, O begins participating in a nonqualified deferred compensation plan sponsored by L that is an account balance plan. Under the plan, all amounts are fully vested at all times. L credits principal additions to O's account each year, and credits earnings based on a predetermined actual investment within the meaning of §31.3121(v)(2)-1(d)(2)(i)(B). The balances in O's account (including principal additions and earnings) are $100,000 on December 31, 2016, $250,000 on December 31, 2017, and $450,000 on December 2018. O's applicable individual remuneration from L is $500,000 for 2016, $300,000 for 2017, and $450,000 for 2018. On January 1, 2019, L pays O $400,000 in accordance with the plan terms. As a result of the payment, O's remaining account balance is $50,000 ($450,000 – $400,000). On December 31, 2019, O's account balance is increased to $200,000 by additional credits made during the year. O's applicable remuneration from L is $200,000 for 2019. On January 1, 2020, L pays O $200,000 in accordance with the plan terms.

(ii) To determine the extent to which L is entitled to a deduction for any portion of either of the payments under the plan, O's payments under the plan must first be attributed to services performed by O in L's taxable years in accordance with the attribution rules set forth in paragraph (d) of this section. Under the standard attribution method for account balance plans described in paragraph (d)(3)(i) of this section, remuneration is attributed to services performed by O in L's taxable years in an amount equal to the increase in O's account balance as of the last day of L's taxable year over the account balance as of the last day of the immediately preceding taxable year, increased by any payments made during that year. Therefore, O's deferred deduction remuneration under the plan is attributed to L's taxable years as follows: $100,000 ($100,000 – $0) in 2016, $150,000 ($250,000 – $100,000) in 2017, $200,000 ($450,000 – $250,000) in 2018, and $150,000 ($200,000 – $450,000 + $400,000) in 2019.

(iii) Under the rules in paragraphs (d)(1)(ii) and (e)(2)(ii)(B) of this section, the January 1, 2019 payment of $400,000 is deemed a payment of remuneration attributed to services performed by O in the earliest taxable year that the amount could be attributed under paragraph (d)(3)(i) of this section. L's first taxable year to which any portion of the payment could be attributed is L's 2016 taxable year. Accordingly, $100,000 of the $400,000 payment is attributed to services performed by O in L's 2016 taxable year. L's next earliest taxable year to which any portion of the payment could be attributed is L's 2017 taxable year. Accordingly, $150,000 of the $400,000 payment is attributed to services performed by O in L's 2017 taxable year. L's next earliest taxable year to which any portion of the payment could be attributed is L's 2018 taxable year. Accordingly, the remaining $150,000 of the $400,000 payment is attributed to services performed by O in L's 2018 taxable year. Because the portion of the $400,000 payment attributed to L's

2018 taxable year is less than the total deferred deduction remuneration attributed to L's 2018 taxable year, the excess deferred deduction remuneration ($50,000) is treated as paid in a subsequent taxable year.

(iv) The portion of the deferred deduction remuneration attributed to services performed in a disqualified taxable year under paragraph (d) of this section that exceeds the deduction limitation for that disqualified taxable year, as reduced, is not deductible for any taxable year. For L's 2016 taxable year, the deduction limitation is reduced to zero by the $500,000 of applicable individual remuneration for that year. Because $100,000 exceeds the reduced deduction limitation of zero, the $100,000 of the deferred deduction remuneration is not deductible for L's 2019 taxable year, the year of payment, or any other taxable year. For L's 2017 taxable year, the deduction limitation is reduced to $200,000 by the $300,000 of applicable individual remuneration for that year. Because $150,000 does not exceed that reduced deduction limitation, the $150,000 of the deferred deduction remuneration is deductible for 2019, the year of payment. The deduction limitation for remuneration attributable to services performed by O in 2017 is then reduced to $50,000, and this reduced limitation is applied to any future payment of deferred deduction remuneration attributable to services performed by O in 2017. For L's 2018 taxable year, the deduction limitation is reduced to $50,000 by the $450,000 of applicable individual remuneration for that year. Because the $150,000 of deferred deduction remuneration exceeds the reduced deduction limitation of $50,000, $100,000 of the $150,000 attributable to services performed by O in L's 2018 taxable year is not deductible for L's 2019 taxable year, the year of payment, or any other taxable year. As a result, $200,000 of the $400,000 payment ($0 + $150,000 + $50,000) is deductible by L for L's 2019 taxable year, and the remaining $200,000 is not deductible by L for any taxable year.

(v) Applying the rules in paragraphs (d)(1)(ii) and (e)(2)(ii)(B) of this section to the January 1, 2020 payment of $200,000, the payment is deemed a payment of deferred deduction remuneration attributed to services performed by O in the earliest taxable year that the amount could be attributed under paragraph (d)(3)(i) of this section. L's first taxable year to which any portion of the payment could be attributed is L's 2018 taxable year because all of the deferred deduction remuneration attributed to earlier taxable years was deemed paid as part of the January 1, 2019 payment. Accordingly, $50,000 of the $200,000 payment is attributed to services performed by O in L's 2018 taxable year (because the remaining portion of the deferred deduction remuneration under the plan originally attributed to services performed by O in L's 2018 taxable year was deemed paid as part of the January 1, 2019 payment). L's next earliest taxable year to which any portion of the payment is attributed is L's 2019 taxable year. Accordingly, $150,000 of the $200,000 payment is attributed to services performed by O in L's 2019 taxable year.

(vi) The portion of the deferred deduction remuneration attributed to a disqualified taxable year under paragraph (d) of this section that exceeds the deduction limitation for that disqualified taxable year, as reduced, is not deductible for any taxable year. For L's 2018 taxable year, the deduction limitation is reduced to zero by the $450,000 of applicable individual remuneration for that year and the $50,000 of deferred deduction remuneration deducted in 2019. Because $50,000 exceeds the reduced deduction limitation of zero, $50,000 of the deferred deduction remuneration is not deductible for L's 2020 taxable year, the year of payment, or any other taxable year. For L's 2019 taxable year, the deduction limitation is not reduced because there is no applicable individual remuneration for that year. Because $150,000 does not exceed the unreduced $500,000 limitation, the $150,000 of the deferred deduction remuneration is deductible for L's 2020 taxable year, the year of payment. As a result, $150,000 of the $200,000 payment ($0 + $150,000) is deductible by L for L's 2020 taxable year, and the remaining $50,000 is not deductible by L for any taxable year.

Example 5 (Installment payments attributable to multiple taxable years from an account balance plan using the alternative attribution method for account balance plans). (i) The facts are the same as set forth in *Example 4,* paragraph (i), except as set forth in this paragraph (i). L uses the alternative method for attributing remuneration from an account balance plan. Principal additions under the plan are $50,000 in 2016 and 2017, $100,000 in 2018, and $125,000 in 2019. As of the January 1, 2019 initial payment date, earnings on the 2016, 2017, and 2018 are $125,000, $75,000, and $50,000 respectively.

(ii) To determine the extent to which L is entitled to a deduction for any portion of either payment under the plan, the payments to O under the plan must first be attributed to services performed by O in F's taxable years in accordance with the attribution rules set forth in paragraph (d) of this section. Under the alternative attribution method for account balance plans in paragraph (d)(3)(ii) of this section, the amount of remuneration under an account balance plan attributed to services performed in a taxable year is equal to the sum of the principal additions credited to the plan for that taxable year plus (or minus) the earnings (or losses) credited on those principal additions.

(iii) Under the rule in paragraphs (d)(1)(ii) and (e)(2)(ii)(B) of this section, the $400,000 payment on January 1, 2019, is deemed to constitute a payment of remuneration attributed to services performed by O in the earliest taxable year that the amount could be attributed under paragraph (d)(3)(ii) of this section. L's first taxable year to which any portion of the payment could be attributed is L's 2016 taxable year. Accordingly, $175,000 of the $400,000 payment is attributed to services performed by O in L's 2016 taxable year. The next earliest taxable year of L to which any portion of the payment could be attributed is L's 2017 taxable year. Accordingly, $125,000 of the $400,000 payment is attributed to services performed by O in L's 2017 taxable year. L's next earliest taxable year to which any portion of the payment could be attributed is L's 2018 taxable year. Accordingly, the remaining $100,000 of the $400,000 payment is attributed to services performed by O in L's 2018 taxable year. Because the portion of the $400,000 payment attributed to L's 2018 taxable year is less than the total deferred deduction remuneration attributable to services performed by O in L's 2018 taxable year, the excess deferred deduction remuneration ($50,000) is treated as paid in a subsequent taxable year.

(iv) The portion of the deferred deduction remuneration attributable to services performed in a disqualified taxable year under paragraph (d) of this section that exceeds the deduction limitation for that disqualified taxable year, as reduced, is not deductible for any taxable year. For L's 2016 taxable year, the deduction limitation is reduced to zero by the $500,000 of applicable individual remuneration for that year. Because $175,000 exceeds the reduced deduction limitation of zero, the $175,000 is not deductible for L's 2019 taxable year, the year of payment, or any other taxable year. For L's 2017 taxable year, the deduction limitation is reduced to $200,000 by the $300,000 of applicable individual remuneration for that year. Because $125,000 does not exceed the reduced deduction limitation, the $125,000 payment is deductible for 2019. For L's 2018 taxable year, the deduction limitation is reduced to $50,000 by the $450,000 of applicable individual remuneration for that year. Because $100,000 exceeds the reduced limitation of $50,000, $50,000 of the $100,000 attributable to L's 2018 taxable year is not deductible for 2019, the year of payment, or any other taxable year. As a result, $175,000 of the $400,000 payment ($0 + $125,000 + $50,000) is deductible by L for L's 2019 taxable year, and the remaining $225,000 is not deductible by L for any taxable year.

(v) Earnings through January 1, 2020 on the excess deferred deduction remuneration attributable to L's 2018 taxable year ($50,000) that was not paid as part of the January 1, 2019 payment are $10,000. Earnings through January 1, 2020 on the $100,000 in principal credited to O's account on January 1, 2019 are $15,000. Therefore, as of January 1, 2020, O's remaining deferred deduction remuneration under the plan is attributed to L's taxable years as follows: $60,000 ($50,000 + $10,000) to 2018 and $140,000 ($125,000 + $15,000) to 2019. Applying the rules in paragraphs (d)(1)(ii) and (e)(2)(ii)(B) to the January 1, 2020 payment of $200,000, the payment is deemed a payment of deferred deduction remuneration attributed to services performed by O in the earliest taxable year that the amount could be attributed under paragraph (d)(3)(ii) of this section. L's first taxable year to which any portion of the payment could be attributed is L's 2018 taxable year because all of the deferred deduction remuneration attributed to earlier taxable years was deemed paid as part of the January 1, 2019 payment. Accordingly, $60,000 of the $200,000 payment is attributed to services performed by O in L's 2018 taxable year. L's next taxable earliest taxable year to which any portion of the payment could be attributed is F's 2019 taxable year. Accordingly, $140,000 of the $200,000 payment is attributed to services performed by O in L's 2019 taxable year.

(vi) The portion of the deferred deduction remuneration attributed to a disqualified taxable year under paragraph (d) of this section that exceeds the deduction limitation for that disqualified taxable year, as reduced, is not deductible for any taxable year. For L's 2018 taxable year, the deductible limitation is reduced to zero by the $450,000 of applicable individual remuneration for that year and the payment of $50,000 of deferred deduction remuneration attributable to that year. Because $60,000 exceeds the reduced deduction limitation of zero, the $60,000 is not deductible for the year of payment (or any other taxable year). For L's 2019 taxable year, the deduction limitation is not reduced because there is no applicable individual remuneration for that year. Because $140,000 does not exceed the unreduced $500,000 limitation, the $140,000 is deductible for 2020, the year of payment. As a result, $140,000 of the $200,000 payment ($0 + $140,000) is deductible for L's 2020 taxable year, and the remaining $60,000 is not deductible by L for any taxable year.

(4) *Application of deduction limitation to aggregated groups of covered health insurance providers*—(i) *In general.* The total combined deduc-

tion for applicable individual remuneration and deferred deduction remuneration attributable to services performed by an applicable individual in a disqualified taxable year allowed for all members of an aggregated group that are treated as covered health insurance providers for any taxable year is limited to $500,000. Therefore, if two or more members of an aggregated group that are treated as covered health insurance providers may otherwise deduct applicable individual remuneration or deferred deduction remuneration attributable to services provided by an applicable individual in a disqualified taxable year, the applicable individual remuneration and deferred deduction remuneration otherwise deductible by all members of the aggregated group is combined, and the deduction limitation is applied to the total amount.

(ii) *Proration of deduction limitation.* If the total amount of applicable individual remuneration or deferred deduction remuneration attributable to services performed by an applicable individual in a disqualified taxable year that is otherwise deductible by two or more members of an aggregated group in any taxable year exceeds the $500,000 deduction limitation (as reduced by previous applications to applicable individual remuneration or deferred deduction remuneration, if applicable), the deduction limitation is prorated based on the applicable individual remuneration and deferred deduction remuneration otherwise deductible by the members of the aggregated group in the taxable year and allocated to each member of the aggregated group. The deduction limitation allocated to each member of the aggregated group is determined by multiplying the deduction limitation for the disqualified taxable year (as previously reduced, if applicable) by a ratio, the numerator of which is the applicable individual remuneration and deferred deduction remuneration otherwise deductible by that member in that taxable year that is attributable to services performed by the applicable individual in the disqualified taxable year, and the denominator of which is the total applicable individual remuneration and deferred deduction remuneration otherwise deductible by all members of the aggregated group in that taxable year that is attributable to services performed by the applicable individual in the disqualified taxable year. The amount of applicable individual remuneration or deferred deduction remuneration otherwise deductible by a member of the aggregated group in excess of the portion of the deduction limitation allocated to that member is not deductible in any taxable year.

(5) *Examples.* The following examples illustrate the rules of paragraph (e)(4) of this section. For purposes of these examples, each corporation has a taxable year that is the calendar year and is a covered health insurance provider for all relevant taxable years, and deferred deduction remuneration is otherwise deductible by the covered health insurance provider in the taxable year in which it is paid.

Example 1. (i) Corporations I, J, and K are members of the same aggregated group under paragraph (b)(3) of this section. In 2016, C is an employee of, and performs services for, I, J, and K. C's total applicable individual remuneration for 2016 is $1,500,000, which consists of $750,000 of applicable individual remuneration for services provided to K; $450,000 of applicable individual remuneration for services provided to J; and $300,000 of applicable individual remuneration for services to I.

(ii) Because I, J, and K are members of the same aggregated group, the applicable individual remuneration otherwise deductible by them is aggregated for purposes of applying the deduction limitation. Further, because the aggregate applicable individual remuneration otherwise deductible by I, J, and K for 2016 exceeds the deduction limitation for C for that taxable year, the deduction limitation is prorated and allocated to the members of the aggregated group in proportion to the applicable individual remuneration otherwise deductible by each member of the aggregated group for that taxable year. Therefore, the deduction limitation that applies to the applicable individual remuneration otherwise deductible by K is $250,000 ($500,000 × ($750,000/$1,500,000)); the deduction limitation that applies to the applicable individual remuneration otherwise deductible by J is $150,000 ($500,000 × ($450,000/$1,500,000)); and the deduction limitation that applies to applicable individual remuneration otherwise deductible by I is $100,000 ($500,000 × ($300,000/$1,500,000)). Therefore, for the 2016 taxable year, K may not deduct $500,000 of the $750,000 of applicable individual remuneration paid to C ($750,000 – $250,000); J may not deduct $300,000 of the $450,000 of applicable individual remuneration paid to C ($450,000 – $150,000); and I may not deduct $200,000 of the $300,000 of applicable individual remuneration paid to C ($300,000 – $100,000).

Example 2. (i) The facts are the same as *Example 1,* except that C's total applicable individual remuneration for 2016 is $400,000, which consists of $75,000 for services provided to K; $150,000 for services provided to J; and $175,000 for services provided to I. In addition, C becomes entitled to $60,000 of deferred deduction remuneration attributable to services provided to K in 2016, which is payable on April 1,

2018, and $75,000 of deferred deduction remuneration attributable to services provided to J in 2016, which is payable on April 1, 2019.

(ii) Because C's total applicable individual remuneration of $400,000 for 2016 for services provided to K, J, and I does not exceed the $500,000 limitation, K, J, and I may deduct $75,000, $150,000, and $175,000, respectively, for 2016. The deduction limitation is then reduced to $100,000 by the total applicable individual remuneration deductible by all members of the aggregated group ($500,000 – $400,000). The deduction limitation, as reduced, is then applied to any deferred deduction remuneration attributable to services provided by C in 2016 in the first subsequent taxable year that it becomes deductible, which is the $60,000 payment made on April 1, 2018. Because the $60,000 of deferred deduction remuneration otherwise deductible by K does not exceed the $100,000 deduction limitation, K may deduct the entire $60,000 for its 2018 taxable year. The $100,000 deduction limitation is then reduced by the $60,000 of deferred deduction remuneration deductible by K for 2018, and the reduced deduction limitation of $40,000 ($100,000 – $60,000) is applied to the $75,000 of deferred deduction remuneration that is otherwise deductible for 2019. Because the deferred deduction remuneration of $75,000 otherwise deductible by J exceeds the reduced deduction limitation of $40,000, J may deduct only $40,000, and the remaining $35,000 ($75,000 – $40,000) is not deductible by J for that taxable year or any other taxable year.

Example 3. (i) The facts are the same as *Example 2,* except that C's deferred deduction remuneration of $75,000 attributable to services performed by C in J's 2016 taxable year is payable on July 1, 2018.

(ii) The results are the same as *Example 2,* except that the reduced deduction limitation of $100,000 is prorated between K and J in proportion to the deferred deduction remuneration otherwise deductible by them for 2018. Accordingly, $44,444 of the remaining deduction limitation is allocated to K ($100,000 × ($60,000/$135,000)), and $55,556 of the remaining deduction limitation is allocated to J ($100,000 × ($75,000/$135,000)). Because the $60,000 of deferred deduction remuneration otherwise deductible by K exceeds the $44,444 deduction limitation applied to that remuneration, K may deduct only $44,444 of the $60,000 payment, and $15,556 may not be deducted by K for any taxable year. Similarly, because the $75,000 of deferred deduction remuneration otherwise deductible by J exceeds the $55,556 deduction limitation applied to that remuneration, J may deduct only $55,556 of the $75,000 payment, and $19,444 may not be deducted by J for that taxable year or any other taxable year.

(f) *Corporate transactions*—(1) *Treatment as a covered health insurance provider in connection with a corporate transaction*—(i) *In general.* Except as otherwise provided in this paragraph (f), a person that participates in a corporate transaction is a covered health insurance provider for the taxable year in which the corporate transaction occurs and any subsequent taxable year if it would otherwise be a covered health insurance provider under paragraph (b)(4) of this section for that taxable year. For example, if a member of an aggregated group purchases a health insurance issuer that is a covered health insurance provider (so that the health insurance issuer becomes a member of the aggregated group), each member of the acquiring aggregated group generally will be a covered health insurance provider for the taxable year in which the corporate transaction occurs and each subsequent taxable year in which the health insurance issuer continues to be a member of the group, unless the *de minimis* exception applies. For purposes of this paragraph (f), the term *corporate transaction* means a merger, acquisition of assets or stock, disposition, reorganization, consolidation, or separation, or any other transaction (including a purchase or sale of stock or other equity interest) resulting in a change in the composition of an aggregated group.

(ii) *Transition period relief for persons becoming covered health insurance providers solely as a result of a corporate transaction*—(A) *In general.* Except as provided in paragraph (f)(1)(ii)(B) of this section, a person that is not a covered health insurance provider before a corporate transaction, but would (except for application of this paragraph (f)(1)(ii)(A)) become a covered health insurance provider solely as a result of the corporate transaction, is not treated as a covered health insurance provider subject to the deduction limitation of section 162(m)(6) in the taxable year of that person in which the corporate transaction occurs (the transition period).

(B) *Certain applicable individuals.* The transition period relief described in paragraph (f)(1)(ii)(A) of this section does not apply with respect to the remuneration of any individual who is an applicable individual of a health insurance issuer that is a covered health insurance provider during its taxable year in which the corporate transaction occurs, even with respect to remuneration attributable to services performed by the applicable individual for a person that is eligible for the transition period relief described in paragraph (f)(1)(ii)(A) of this section. Therefore, each member of an acquiring aggregated group that would become a covered health insurance provider solely as a result of a corporate transaction, but is not treated as a covered health insurance provider under the transition period relief described in paragraph (f)(1)(ii)(A) of this section, is still subject to the deduction limitation of section 162(m)(6) for a taxable year during the transition period with respect to applicable individual remuneration and deferred deduction remuneration attributable to services performed by anyone who is an applicable individual of the acquired health insurance issuer that is a covered health insurance provider.

(iii) *Short taxable years*—(A) *Taxable year ending as a result of a corporate transaction.* As a result of a corporate transaction, a covered health insurance provider's taxable year may end, resulting in a short taxable year. For example, the taxable year of the covered health insurance provider ends if it becomes, or ceases to be, a member of a consolidated group by reason of § 1.1502-76(b)(1)(ii)(A)(1). A covered health insurance provider whose taxable year ends as a result of a corporate transaction is treated as a covered health insurance provider for that short taxable year if the covered health insurance provider is a covered health insurance provider within the meaning of paragraph (b)(4) of this section for the short taxable year that ends as a result of the corporate transaction, provided that, for purposes of this paragraph (f)(1)(iii)(A), the *de minimis* exception set forth in paragraph (b)(4)(iii)(A) of this section is available for that short taxable year only if it applied to the covered health insurance provider for the preceding taxable year.

(B) *Taxable year beginning as a result of a corporate transaction.* As a result of a corporate transaction, a covered health insurance provider may begin a new taxable year. For example, if as a result of a corporate transaction, a health insurance issuer that is a covered health insurance provider joins a consolidated group within the meaning of § 1.1502-1(h), or a covered health insurance provider ceases to be a member of an aggregated group as a result of a distribution to which section 355 applies, the covered health insurance provider begins a short taxable year. A health insurance issuer that is a covered health insurance provider whose taxable year begins as a result of a corporate transaction is treated as a covered health insurance provider for the taxable year that begins as a result of the corporate transaction if the covered health insurance provider is otherwise a covered health insurance provider within the meaning of paragraph (b)(4) of this section for the taxable year that begins as a result of a corporate transaction, even if it becomes a member of an acquiring aggregate group the other members of which are not treated as covered health insurance providers during that taxable year by reason of the transition period relief under paragraph (f)(1)(ii)(A) of this section, provided that, for purposes of this paragraph (f)(1)(iii)(B), the one-year grace period set forth in paragraph (b)(4)(ii)(B) of this section is available for that short taxable year.

(C) *Deduction limitation not prorated for short taxable years.* If a corporate transaction results in a short taxable year for a covered health insurance provider, the $500,000 deduction limitation for the short taxable year is neither prorated nor reduced. For example, if a corporate transaction results in a short taxable year of three months, the deduction limitation under section 162(m)(6) for that short taxable year is $500,000 (and is not reduced to $125,000).

(2) *Application to partnerships.* The rules in paragraph (f) of this section apply by analogy to transactions involving entities treated as partnerships for purposes of federal taxation.

(3) *Examples.* The following examples illustrate the principles of this paragraph (f). For purposes of these examples, each corporation has a taxable year that is the calendar year unless stated otherwise, and none of the corporations qualify for the *de minimis* exception under paragraph (b)(4)(iii) of this section.

Example 1. (i) Corporation J merges with and into corporation H on June 30, 2015, such that H is the surviving entity. As a result of the merger, J's taxable year ends on June 30, 2015. For its taxable year ending June 30, 2015, J is a covered health insurance provider. For all taxable years before the taxable year of the merger, H is not a covered health insurance provider. However, solely as a result of the merger, H becomes a covered health insurance provider for its 2015 taxable year.

(ii) Corporation J is a covered health insurance provider for its short taxable year ending June 30, 2015. Corporation H is not treated as a covered health insurance provider for its 2015 taxable year by reason of the transition period relief in paragraph (d)(1)(ii)(A) of this section. However, H will be a covered health insurance provider for its 2016 taxable year and all subsequent taxable years for which it is a covered health insurance provider under paragraph (b)(4) of this section.

Example 2. (i) On January 1, 2016, corporations D, E, and F are members of a controlled group within the meaning of section 414(b). F is a health insurance issuer that is a covered health insurance provider under paragraph (b)(4)(i)(B) of this section. D and E are not health insurance issuers (but are treated as covered health insurance providers pursuant to paragraph (b)(4)(i)(C) and (D) of this section). F's taxable year is a fiscal year ending on September 30. P is an applicable individual of F for all taxable years. On May 1, 2016, a controlled group within the meaning of section 414(b) consisting of corporations C and B purchases all of the stock of corporation F, resulting in a controlled group within the meaning of section 414(b) consisting of corporations C, B, and F. C and B are not health insurance issuers. The C, B, and F controlled group is a consolidated group within the meaning of § 1.1502-1(h). Thus, F's taxable year ends on May 1, 2016 by reason of § 1.1502-76(b)(1)(ii)(A)(*1*), and F becomes part of the C, B, and F consolidated group for the taxable year ending December 31, 2016.

(ii) D and E are covered health insurance providers for the taxable year ending December 31, 2016 because they were in an aggregated group with F for a portion of their taxable year. Accordingly, D and E are subject to the deduction limitation under section 162(m)(6) for their taxable years ending December 31, 2016. C and B are not treated as covered health insurance providers for their taxable year ending December 31, 2016, by reason of the transition period relief of paragraph (d)(1)(ii)(A) of this section. F, however, is a covered health insurance provider for its taxable year ending May 1, 2016, and for its taxable year ending December 31, 2016.

(iii) P is an applicable individual whose remuneration is subject to the deduction limitation under section 162(m)(6) for F's short taxable year ending May 1, 2016. In addition, remuneration for services by P for C, B or F after May 1, 2016, during the taxable year of the consolidated group ending December 31, 2016, is subject to the deduction limitation under section 162(m)(6), even though C and B are not treated as covered health insurance providers for their taxable year ending December 31, 2016 by reason of the transition period relief of paragraph (d)(1)(ii)(A) of this section.

Example 3. (i) The same facts as *Example 2,* except that E is a health insurance issuer that is a covered health insurance provider under paragraph (b)(4) of this section, and F is not a health insurance issuer.

(ii) F is a covered health insurance provider for its short taxable year ending May 1, 2016. However, because F is not a health insurance issuer that is a covered health insurance provider, F is not treated as a covered health insurance provider for its short, post-acquisition taxable year ending December 31, 2016, during which it is a member of the consolidated group comprised of C, B, and F.

(iii) P is an applicable individual whose remuneration is subject to the deduction limitation under section 162(m)(6) and paragraph (c) of this section for F's short taxable year ending May 1, 2016. However, because F is not a health insurance issuer, remuneration for P's services for C, B or F after May 1, 2016, during the taxable year of the consolidated group ending December 31, 2016, are not subject to the deduction limitation under section 162(m)(6).

(g) *Coordination*—(1) *Coordination with section 162(m)(1).* If section 162(m)(1) and section 162(m)(6) would both otherwise apply with respect to the remuneration of an applicable individual, the deduction limitation under section 162(m)(6) applies without regard to section 162(m)(1). For example, if an applicable individual is both a covered employee of a publicly held corporation (see sections 162(m)(2) and (3); § 1.162-27) and an applicable individual within the meaning of paragraph (b)(7) of this section, remuneration earned by the applicable individual that is attributable to a disqualified taxable year of a covered health insurance provider is subject to the $500,000 deduction limitation under section 162(m)(6) with respect to such disqualified taxable year, without regard to section 162(m)(1).

(2) *Coordination with disallowed excess parachute payments*—(i) *In general.* The $500,000 deduction limitation of section 162(m)(6) is reduced (but not below zero) by the amount (if any) that would have been included in the applicable individual remuneration or deferred deduction remuneration of the applicable individual for a taxable year but for being disallowed by reason of section 280G.

(ii) *Example.* The following example illustrates the rule of this paragraph (g)(2).

Example. Corporation A, a covered health insurance provider, pays $750,000 of applicable individual remuneration to P, an applicable individual, during A's disqualified taxable year ending December 31, 2016. Of the $750,000, $300,000 is an excess parachute payment as defined in section 280G(b)(1), the deduction for which is disallowed by reason of that section. The excess parachute payment reduces the $500,000 deduction limitation to $200,000 ($500,000—$300,000). There-

fore, A may deduct only $200,000 of the $750,000 in applicable individual remuneration, and $250,000 of the payment is not deductible by reason of section 162(m)(6).

(h) *Grandfathered amounts attributable to services performed in taxable years beginning before January 1, 2010*—(1) *In general.* The section 162(m)(6) deduction limitation does not apply to remuneration attributable to services performed in taxable years of a covered health insurance provider beginning before January 1, 2010. For purposes of this paragraph (h), whether remuneration is attributable to services performed in a taxable year beginning before January 1, 2010, is determined by applying an attribution method in paragraph (h)(2) of this section.

(2) *Identification of services performed in taxable years beginning before January 1, 2010*—(i) *Account balance plans.* Deferred deduction remuneration provided under an account balance plan (as defined in § 1.409A-1(c)(2)(i)(A) and (B)) is attributable to services performed in a taxable year beginning before January 1, 2010 if it is attributable to services performed before that date under paragraph (d)(3) of this section, without regard to whether that remuneration is subject to a substantial risk of forfeiture on or after that date.

(ii) *Nonaccount balance plans.* The amount of remuneration attributable to services performed in taxable years beginning before January 1, 2010 under a nonqualified deferred compensation plan that is a nonaccount balance plan (as defined in § 1.409A-1(c)(2)(i)(C)), equals the present value of the remuneration to which the applicable individual would have been entitled under the plan if the applicable individual voluntarily terminated services without cause on the last day of the first taxable year of the covered health insurance provider beginning before January 1, 2010 and received a payment of the benefit available from the plan on the earliest possible date allowed under the plan to receive a payment of benefits following the termination of service, and received the benefit in the form with the maximum value. Notwithstanding the foregoing, for any subsequent taxable year of the covered health insurance provider, this amount may increase to equal the present value of the benefit the applicable individual actually becomes entitled to receive, in the form and at the time actually paid, determined under the terms of the plan (including applicable limits under the Code) as in effect on the last day of the first taxable year beginning before January 1, 2010 without regard to any further services rendered by the individual after that date or any other events affecting the amount of, or the entitlement to, benefits (other than the applicable individual's election with respect to the time or form of an available benefit). For purposes of calculating the present value of remuneration under this paragraph (h)(2)(ii), reasonable actuarial assumptions and methods, determined as of the date the remuneration is valued, must be used. The present value as of the last day of the first taxable year beginning before January 1, 2010 is determined without regard to whether the remuneration under the nonaccount balance is subject to a substantial risk of forfeiture on or after that date.

(iii) *Equity-based remuneration.* For purposes of this section, all remuneration resulting from a stock option, stock appreciation right, restricted stock, or restricted stock unit and the right to any associated dividends or dividend equivalents (together, referred to as *equity-based remuneration*) granted before the first day of the taxable year of the covered health insurance provider beginning on or after January 1, 2010, is attributable to services performed in taxable years beginning before January 1, 2010, regardless of the date on which the equity-based remuneration is exercised (in the case of a stock option or SAR), the date on which the amounts due under the equity-based remuneration are paid or includible in income, or whether the equity-based remuneration is subject to a substantial risk of forfeiture on or after the first day of the taxable year of the covered health insurance provider beginning on or after January 1, 2010. For example, appreciation in the value of restricted shares granted before the first day of the taxable year beginning on or after January 1, 2010 is treated as remuneration that is attributable to services performed in taxable years beginning before January 1, 2010, regardless of whether the shares are vested at that time.

(i) *Transition rules for certain deferred deduction remuneration*—(1) *Transition rule for deferred deduction remuneration attributable to services performed in taxable years of the covered health insurance provider beginning after December 31, 2009 and before January 1, 2013.* The deduction limitation under section 162(m)(6) applies to deferred deduction remuneration attributable to services performed in a disqualified taxable year of a covered health insurance provider beginning after December 31, 2009 and before January 1, 2013, only if that remuneration is otherwise deductible in a disqualified taxable year of the covered health insurance provider beginning after December 31, 2012. However, if the deduction limitation applies to deferred deduction remuneration attributable to services performed by an applicable individual in a disqualified taxable year of a covered health insurance provider beginning after December 31, 2009 and before January 1, 2013, the deduction limitation is calculated as if it had been applied to the applicable individual's applicable individual remuneration and deferred deduction remuneration deductible in those taxable years.

(2) *Example.* The following examples illustrate the principles of this paragraph (i). For purposes of these examples, each corporation has a taxable year that is the calendar year, and deferred deduction remuneration is otherwise deductible by the covered health insurance provider in the taxable year in which it is paid.

Example 1. (i) Q is an applicable individual of corporation Z. Z's 2010, 2011, and 2012 taxable years are disqualified taxable years. Z's 2013, 2014, and 2015 taxable years are not disqualified taxable years. However, Z's 2016 taxable year and all subsequent taxable years are disqualified taxable years. Q receives $200,000 of applicable individual remuneration from Z for 2012, and becomes entitled to $800,000 of deferred deduction remuneration that is attributable to services performed by Q in 2012. Z pays Q $350,000 of the deferred deduction remuneration in 2015, and the remaining $450,000 of the deferred deduction remuneration in 2016. These payments are otherwise deductible by Z in 2015 and 2016, respectively.

(ii) Deferred deduction remuneration attributable to services performed by Q in Z's 2010, 2011, and 2012 taxable years that is otherwise deductible in Z's 2013, 2014, or 2015 taxable years is not subject to the deduction limitation under section 162(m)(6) by reason of the transition rule under paragraph (i)(1) of this section. However, deferred deduction remuneration attributable to services performed in Z's 2010, 2011, and 2012 taxable years that is otherwise deductible in a later taxable year that is a disqualified taxable year (in this case, Z's 2016 and subsequent taxable years) is subject to the deduction limitation under section 162(m)(6). Accordingly, the deduction limitation with respect to applicable individual remuneration and deferred deduction remuneration attributable to services performed by Q in 2012 is determined by reducing the $500,000 deduction limitation by the $200,000 of applicable individual remuneration paid to Q by Z for 2012 ($500,000-$200,000). Under the transition rule of paragraph (i)(1) of this section, no portion of the reduced deduction limitation of $300,000 for the 2012 taxable year is applied against the $350,000 payment made in 2015, and accordingly, the deduction limitation is not reduced by the amount of that payment. The reduced deduction limitation is then applied to Q's $450,000 of deferred deduction remuneration attributable to services performed by Q in 2012 that is paid to Q and becomes otherwise deductible in 2016. Because the reduced deduction limitation

of $300,000 is less than the $450,000 otherwise deductible by Z in 2016, Z may deduct only $300,000 of the deferred deduction remuneration, and $150,000 of the $450,000 payment is not deductible by Z in that taxable year or any taxable year.

Example 2. (i) R is an applicable individual of corporation Y, which is a covered health insurance provider for all relevant taxable years. During 2010, Y pays R $400,000 in salary and grants R a right to $200,000 in deferred deduction remuneration payable on a fixed schedule in 2011, 2012, and 2013. Pursuant to the fixed schedule, Y pays R $50,000 of deferred deduction remuneration in 2011, $50,000 of deferred deduction remuneration in 2012, and the remaining $100,000 of deferred deduction remuneration in 2013.

(ii) Because the deduction limitation for deferred deduction remuneration under section 162(m)(6)(A)(ii) is effective for deferred deduction remuneration that is attributable to services performed by an applicable individual during any disqualified taxable year beginning after December 31, 2009 that would otherwise be deductible in a taxable year beginning after December 31, 2012, only the deferred deduction remuneration paid by Y in 2013 is subject to the deduction limitation. However, the limitation is applied as if section 162(m)(6) and paragraph (c)(2) of this section were effective for taxable years beginning after December 31, 2009 and before January 1, 2013. Accordingly, the deduction limitation with respect to remuneration for services performed by R in 2010 is determined by reducing the $500,000 deduction limitation by the $400,000 of applicable individual remuneration paid to R for 2010 ($500,000-$400,000). The reduced deduction limitation of $100,000 is further reduced to zero by the $50,000 of deferred deduction remuneration attributable to services performed by R in Y's 2010 taxable year that is deductible in each of 2011 and 2012 (($100,000-$50,000-$50,000). Because the deduction limitation is reduced to zero, none of the $100,000 of deferred deduction remuneration attributable to services performed by R in Y's 2010 taxable year and paid to R in 2013 is deductible.

(j) *Effective/Applicability dates.* These regulations apply to taxable years that begin after December 31, 2012, and end on or after April 2, 2013. These regulations are effective on publication of final regulations in the **Federal Register**.

Steven T. Miller,

Deputy Commissioner for Services and Enforcement.

[FR Doc. 2013-07533 Filed 4-1-13; 8:45 am]

BILLING CODE 4830-01-P

¶ 20,263N

IRS: Affordable Insurance Exchanges: Health insurance coverage: Health insurance premium tax credit: Minimum value.—The IRS has issued proposed regulations on determining whether health coverage under an eligible employer-sponsored plan provides a minimum value, as required under the Patient Protection and Affordable Care Act (PPACA; P.L. 111-148). Under the PPACA, beginning in 2014, eligible individuals who purchase coverage through a health insurance exchange may receive a premium tax credit unless they are eligible for other minimum essential coverage, including coverage under an employer-sponsored plan that is affordable to the employee and provides at least minimum value. The proposed rules affect individuals who enroll in qualified health plans through Affordable Insurance Exchanges and claim the premium tax credit, exchanges that make qualified health plans available to individuals and employers, and employers that offer health coverage and their employees. The regulations are proposed to be effective for taxable years ending after December 31, 2013. However, taxpayers may apply the proposed regulations for taxable years ending before January 1, 2015.

The proposed regulation was published in the Federal Register on May 3, 2013 (78 FR 25909). The IRS has withdrawn portions of these proposed regulations—specifically, Reg. Sec. 1.36B-6(a) and (g)—and has replaced the withdrawn portions with new proposed regulations. See Pension Plan Guide ¶ 20,264E for the new proposed regulations. The regulations were finalized, in part, on December 18, 2015 (80 FR 78971). The preamble to the final regulations is at ¶ 23,321. The final regulations are at ¶ 11,112F-1, ¶ 11,112F-2, ¶ 11,112F-3, ¶ 11,112F-4, ¶ 11,112F-7, and ¶ 13,649E-15. The IRS states that some proposed regulations on the minimum value of eligible employer-sponsored plans have been reserved and will be finalized separately later.

DEPARTMENT OF THE TREASURY

Internal Revenue Service

26 CFR Part 1

[REG-125398-12]

RIN 1545-BL43

Minimum Value of Eligible Employer-Sponsored Plans and Other Rules Regarding the Health Insurance Premium Tax Credit

AGENCY: Internal Revenue Service (IRS), Treasury.

ACTION: Notice of proposed rulemaking.

SUMMARY: This document contains proposed regulations relating to the health insurance premium tax credit enacted by the Patient Protection and Affordable Care Act and the Health Care and Education Reconciliation Act of 2010, as amended by the Medicare and Medicaid Extenders Act of 2010, the Comprehensive 1099 Taxpayer Protection

and Repayment of Exchange Subsidy Overpayments Act of 2011, and the Department of Defense and Full-Year Continuing Appropriations Act, 2011. These proposed regulations affect individuals who enroll in qualified health plans through Affordable Insurance Exchanges (Exchanges) and claim the premium tax credit, and Exchanges that make qualified health plans available to individuals and employers. These proposed regulations also provide guidance on determining whether health coverage under an eligible employer-sponsored plan provides minimum value and affect employers that offer health coverage and their employees.

DATES: Written (including electronic) comments and requests for a public hearing must be received by July 2, 2013.

ADDRESSES: Send submissions to: CC:PA:LPD:PR (REG-125398-12), Room 5203, Internal Revenue Service, PO Box 7604, Ben Franklin Station, Washington, DC 20044. Submissions may be hand-delivered Monday through Friday between the hours of 8 a.m. and 4 p.m. to CC:PA:LPD:PR (REG-125398-12), Courier's Desk, Internal Revenue

Service, 1111 Constitution Avenue NW., Washington, DC, or sent electronically via the Federal eRulemaking Portal at *www.regulations.gov* (IRS REG-125398-12).

FOR FURTHER INFORMATION CONTACT: Concerning the proposed regulations, Andrew S. Braden, (202) 622-4960; concerning the submission of comments and/or requests for a public hearing, Oluwafunmilayo Taylor, (202) 622-7180 (not toll-free calls).

SUPPLEMENTARY INFORMATION:

Background

Beginning in 2014, under the Patient Protection and Affordable Care Act, Public Law 111-148 (124 Stat. 119 (2010)), and the Health Care and Education Reconciliation Act of 2010, Public Law 111-152 (124 Stat. 1029 (2010)) (collectively, the Affordable Care Act), eligible individuals who purchase coverage under a qualified health plan through an Affordable Insurance Exchange may receive a premium tax credit under section 36B of the Internal Revenue Code (Code). Section 36B was subsequently amended by the Medicare and Medicaid Extenders Act of 2010, Public Law 111-309 (124 Stat. 3285 (2010)); the Comprehensive 1099 Taxpayer Protection and Repayment of Exchange Subsidy Overpayments Act of 2011, Public Law 112-9 (125 Stat. 36 (2011)); and the Department of Defense and Full-Year Continuing Appropriations Act, 2011, Public Law 112-10 (125 Stat. 38 (2011)).

Notice 2012-31 (2012-20 IRB 910) requested comments on methods for determining whether health coverage under an eligible employer-sponsored plan provides minimum value (MV). Final regulations under section 36B (TD 9590) were published on May 23, 2012 (77 FR 30377). The final regulations requested comments on issues to be addressed in further guidance. The comments have been considered in developing these proposed regulations.

Minimum Value

Individuals generally may not receive a premium tax credit if they are eligible for affordable coverage under an eligible employer-sponsored plan that provides MV. An applicable large employer (as defined in section 4980H(c)(2)) may be liable for an assessable payment under section 4980H if a full-time employee receives a premium tax credit.

Under section 36B(c)(2)(C)(ii), a plan fails to provide MV if the plan's share of the total allowed costs of benefits provided under the plan is less than 60 percent of the costs. Section 1302(d)(2)(C) of the Affordable Care Act provides that, in determining the percentage of the total allowed costs of benefits provided under a group health plan, the regulations promulgated by the Secretary of Health and Human Services (HHS) under section 1302(d)(2) apply.

HHS published final regulations under section 1302(d)(2) on February 25, 2013 (78 FR 12834). The HHS regulations at 45 CFR 156.20 define the percentage of the total allowed costs of benefits provided under a group health plan as (1) The anticipated covered medical spending for essential health benefits (EHB) coverage (as defined in 45 CFR 156.110(a)) paid by a health plan for a standard population, (2) computed in accordance with the plan's cost-sharing, and (3) divided by the total anticipated allowed charges for EHB coverage provided to a standard population. In addition, 45 CFR 156.145(c) provides that the standard population used to compute this percentage for MV (as developed by HHS for this purpose) reflects the population covered by typical self-insured group health plans.

The HHS regulations describe several options for determining MV. Under 45 CFR 156.145(a)(1), plans may use the MV Calculator (available at *http://cciio.cms.gov/resources/regulations/index.html*). Alternatively, 45 CFR 156.145(a)(2) provides that a plan may determine MV through a safe harbor established by HHS and IRS. For plans with nonstandard features that are incompatible with the MV Calculator or a safe harbor, 45 CFR 156.145(a)(3) provides that the plan may determine MV through an actuarial certification from a member of the American Academy of Actuaries after performing an analysis in accordance with generally accepted actuarial principles and methodologies. Finally, 45 CFR 156.145(a)(4) provides that a plan in the small group market satisfies MV if it meets the requirements for any of the levels of metal coverage defined at 45 CFR 156.140(b) (bronze, silver, gold, or platinum).

Miscellaneous Provisions Under Section 36B

To be eligible for a premium tax credit, an individual must be an applicable taxpayer. Under section 36B(c)(1), an applicable taxpayer is a taxpayer whose household income for the taxable year is between 100 percent and 400 percent of the federal poverty line (FPL) for the taxpayer's family size.

¶20,263N

Section 36B(b)(1) provides that the premium assistance credit amount is the sum of the premium assistance amounts for all coverage months in the taxable year for individuals in the taxpayer's family. The premium assistance amount for a coverage month is the lesser of (1) the premiums for the month for one or more qualified health plans that cover a taxpayer or family member, or (2) the excess of the adjusted monthly premium for the second lowest cost silver plan (as described in section 1302(d)(1)(B) of the Affordable Care Act (42 U.S.C. 18022(d)(1)(B)) (the benchmark plan) that applies to the taxpayer over 1/12 of the product of the taxpayer's household income and the applicable percentage for the taxable year. The adjusted monthly premium, in general, is the premium an insurer would charge for the plan adjusted only for the ages of the covered individuals.

Under section 36B(c)(2)(A), a coverage month is any month for which the taxpayer or a family member is covered by a qualified health plan enrolled in through an Exchange and the premium is paid by the taxpayer or through an advance credit payment. Section 36B(c)(2) provides that a month is not a coverage month for an individual who is eligible for other minimum essential coverage. If the other coverage is eligible employer-sponsored coverage, however, it is treated as minimum essential coverage only if it is affordable and provides MV. Eligible employer-sponsored coverage is affordable for an employee and related individuals if the portion of the annual premium the employee must pay for self-only coverage does not exceed the required contribution percentage (9.5 percent for taxable years beginning before January 1, 2015) of the taxpayer's household income. The MV requirement is discussed in the Explanation of Provisions.

Any arrangement under which employees are required, as a condition of employment or otherwise, to be enrolled in an employer-sponsored plan that does not provide minimum value or is unaffordable, and that does not give the employees an effective opportunity to terminate or decline the coverage, raises a variety of issues. Proposed regulations under section 4980H indicate that if an employer maintains such an arrangement it would not be treated as having made an offer of coverage. As a result, an applicable large employer could be subject to an assessable payment under that section. See Proposed §54.4980H-4(b), 78 FR 250 (January 2, 2013). Such an arrangement would also raise additional concerns. For example, it is questionable whether the law permits interference with an individual's ability to apply for a section 36B premium tax credit by seeking to involuntarily impose coverage that does not provide minimum value. (See, for example, the Fair Labor Standards Act, as amended by section 1558 of the Affordable Care Act, 29 U.S.C. 218c(a).) If an employer sought to involuntarily impose on its employees coverage that did not provide minimum value or was unaffordable, the IRS and Treasury, as well as other relevant departments, may treat such arrangements as impermissible interference with an employee's ability to access premium tax credits, as contemplated by the Affordable Care Act.

Explanation of Provisions and Summary of Comments

1. Minimum Value

a. In General

The proposed regulations refer to the proportion of the total allowed costs of benefits provided to an employee that are paid by the plan as the plan's MV percentage. The MV percentage is determined by dividing the cost of certain benefits (described in paragraph b.) the plan would pay for a standard population by the total cost of certain benefits for the standard population, including amounts the plan pays and amounts the employee pays through cost-sharing, and then converting the result to a percentage.

b. Health Benefits Measured in Determining MV

Commentators sought clarification of the health benefits considered in determining the share of benefit costs paid by a plan. Some commentators maintained that MV should be based on the plan's share of the cost of coverage for all EHBs, including those a plan does not offer. Other commentators suggested that the MV percentage should be based on the plan's share of the costs of only those categories of EHBs the plan covers.

The proposed regulations do not require employer-sponsored self-insured and insured large group plans to cover every EHB category or conform their plans to an EHB benchmark that applies to qualified health plans. The preamble to the HHS regulations (see 78 FR 12833) notes that employer-sponsored group health plans are not required to offer EHBs unless they are health plans offered in the small group market subject to section 2707(a) of the Public Health Service Act. The preamble also states that, under section 1302(d)(2) of the Affordable Care Act, MV is measured based on the provision of EHBs to a standard population and plans may account for any benefits covered by the employer that also are covered in any one of the EHB-benchmark plans. See 45 CFR 156.145(b)(2).

Consistent with 45 CFR 156.145(a)–(c) and the assumptions described in Notice 2012-31, these proposed regulations provide that MV is based on the anticipated spending for a standard population. The plan's anticipated spending for benefits provided under any particular EHB-benchmark plan for any State counts towards MV.

c. Health reimbursement arrangements, health savings accounts, and wellness program incentives

i. Arrangements That Reduce Cost-Sharing

Some commentators suggested that current year health savings account (HSA) contributions and amounts newly made available under a health reimbursement arrangement (HRA) should be fully counted toward the plan's share of costs included in calculating MV. Some commentators suggested that only HRA contributions that may be used to pay for cost sharing and not HRAs restricted to other uses should be counted in the MV calculation.

Consistent with 45 CFR 156.135(c), the proposed regulations provide that all amounts contributed by an employer for the current plan year to an HSA are taken into account in determining the plan's share of costs for purposes of MV and are treated as amounts available for first dollar coverage. Amounts newly made available under an HRA that is integrated with an eligible employer-sponsored plan for the current plan year count for purposes of MV in the same manner if the amounts may be used only for cost-sharing and may not be used to pay insurance premiums. It is anticipated that regulations will provide that whether an HRA is integrated with an eligible employer-sponsored plan is determined under rules that apply for purposes of section 2711 of the Public Health Service Act (42 U.S.C. 300gg-11). Commentators offered differing opinions about how nondiscriminatory wellness program incentives that may affect an employee's cost sharing should be taken into account for purposes of the MV calculation. Some commentators noted that the rules governing wellness incentives require that they be available to all similarly situated individuals. These commentators suggested that because eligible individuals have the opportunity to reduce their cost-sharing if they choose, a plan's share of costs should be based on the costs paid by individuals who satisfy the terms of the wellness program. Other commentators expressed concern that, despite the safeguards of the regulations governing wellness incentives, certain individuals inevitably will face barriers to participation and fail to qualify for rewards. These commentators suggested that a plan's share of costs should be determined without assuming that individuals would qualify for the reduced cost-sharing available under a wellness program.

The proposed regulations provide that a plan's share of costs for MV purposes is determined without regard to reduced cost-sharing available under a nondiscriminatory wellness program. However, for nondiscriminatory wellness programs designed to prevent or reduce tobacco use, MV may be calculated assuming that every eligible individual satisfies the terms of the program relating to prevention or reduction of tobacco use. This exception is consistent with other Affordable Care Act provisions (such as the ability to charge higher premiums based on tobacco use) reflecting a policy about individual responsibility regarding tobacco use.

ii. Arrangements That Reduce Premiums

Section 36B(c)(2)(C)(i)(II) and the final regulations provide that eligible employer-sponsored coverage is affordable only if an employee's required contribution for self-only coverage does not exceed 9.5 percent of household income. The preamble to the final regulations indicated that rules for determining how HRAs and wellness program incentives are counted in determining the affordability of eligible employer-sponsored coverage would be provided in later guidance.

Some commentators asserted that an employer's entire annual contribution to an HRA plus prior year contributions should be taken into account in determining affordability. The proposed regulations provide that amounts newly made available under an HRA that is integrated with an eligible employer-sponsored plan for the current plan year are taken into account only in determining affordability if the employee may use the amounts only for premiums or may choose to use the amounts for either premiums or cost-sharing. Treating amounts that may be used either for premiums or cost-sharing only towards affordability prevents double counting the HRA amounts when assessing MV and affordability of eligible employer-sponsored coverage.

It is anticipated that regulations under section 5000A will provide that amounts newly made available under an HRA that is integrated

with an eligible employer-sponsored plan for the current plan year are also taken into account for purposes of the affordability exemption under section 5000A(e)(1) if the employee may use the amounts only for premiums or for either premiums or cost-sharing.

The final regulations requested specific comments on the nature of wellness incentives and how they should be treated for determining affordability. Commentators expressed similar views about the treatment of wellness incentives that affect the cost of premiums as about the treatment of wellness incentives that affect cost-sharing.

Like the rule for determining MV, the proposed regulations provide that the affordability of an employer-sponsored plan is determined by assuming that each employee fails to satisfy the requirements of a wellness program, except the requirements of a nondiscriminatory wellness program related to tobacco use. Thus, the affordability of a plan that charges a higher initial premium for tobacco users will be determined based on the premium that is charged to non-tobacco users, or tobacco users who complete the related wellness program, such as attending smoking cessation classes.

In many circumstances these rules relating to the effect of premium-related wellness program rewards on affordability will have no practical consequences. They matter only when the employer sets the level of the employee's required contribution to self-only premium, and establishes a wellness program that provides for a level of premium discount, in such a manner that the employee's required contribution to premium would exceed 9.5 percent of household income (or wages, under an affordability safe harbor under the section 4980H proposed regulations) but for the potential premium discount under the wellness program. If, for example, the employee's household income was at least $25,000, and the employee's required contribution for self-only coverage did not exceed $2,375 (9.5 percent of $25,000), the coverage would be affordable whether or not a wellness premium discount was taken into account to reduce the $2,375 required contribution.

It is anticipated that regulations under section 5000A will provide that nondiscriminatory wellness programs that affect premiums will be treated for purposes of the affordability exemption under section 5000A(e)(1) in the same manner as they are treated for purposes of determining affordability under section 36B.

Solely for purposes of applying section 4980H and solely for plan years of an employer's group health plan beginning before January 1, 2015, with respect to an employee described in the next sentence, an employer will not be subject to an assessable payment under section 4980H(b) with respect to an employee who received a premium tax credit because the offer of coverage was not affordable or did not satisfy MV, if the offer of coverage to the employee under the employer's group health plan would have been affordable or would have satisfied MV based on the total required employee premium and cost-sharing for that group health plan that would have applied to the employee if the employee satisfied the requirements of any wellness program described in the next sentence, including a wellness program with requirements unrelated to tobacco use. The rule in the preceding sentence applies only (1) To the extent of the reward as of May 3, 2013, expressed as either a dollar amount or a fraction of the total required employee contribution to the premium (or the employee cost-sharing, as applicable), (2) under the terms of a wellness program as in effect on May 3, 2013, and (3) with respect to an employee who is in a category of employees eligible under the terms of the wellness program as in effect on May 3, 2013 (regardless of whether the employee was hired before or after that date). Any required employee contribution to premium determined based upon assumed satisfaction of the requirements of a wellness program available under this transition relief may be applied to the use of an affordability safe harbor provided in the proposed regulations under section 4980H.

d. Standard Population and Utilization

Consistent with 45 CFR 156.145(c), the proposed regulations provide that the standard population used to determine MV reflects the population covered by self-insured group health plans. HHS has developed the MV standard population and described it through summary statistics (for example, continuance tables). MV continuance tables and an explanation of the MV Calculator methodology and the health claims data HHS has used to develop the continuance tables are available at *http://cciio.cms.gov/resources/regulations/index.html.*

e. Methods for Determining Minimum Value

Notice 2012-31 and 45 CFR 156.145(a) describe several methods for determining MV: the MV Calculator, a safe harbor, actuarial certification, and, for small group market plans, a metal level. Some commentators requested that plans be allowed to choose one of the four methods in determining MV. Other commentators favored requiring employers to use the most precise method for plans that may be close to the 60 percent threshold.

The proposed regulations provide that taxpayers may determine whether a plan provides MV by using the MV Calculator made available by HHS and the IRS. Taxpayers must use the MV Calculator to measure standard plan features (unless a safe harbor applies), but the percentage may be adjusted based on an actuarial analysis of plan features that are outside the parameters of the calculator.

Certain safe harbor plan designs that satisfy MV will be specified in additional guidance under section 36B or 4980H, see § 601.601(d). It is anticipated that the guidance will provide that the safe harbors are examples of plan designs that clearly would satisfy the 60 percent threshold if measured using the MV Calculator. The safe harbors are intended to provide an easy way for sponsors of typical employer-sponsored group health plans to determine whether a plan meets the MV threshold without having to use the MV Calculator.

Plan designs meeting the following specifications are proposed as safe harbors for determining MV if the plans cover all of the benefits included in the MV Calculator: (1) A plan with a $3,500 integrated medical and drug deductible, 80 percent plan cost-sharing, and a $6,000 maximum out-of-pocket limit for employee cost-sharing; (2) a plan with a $4,500 integrated medical and drug deductible, 70 percent plan cost-sharing, a $6,400 maximum out-of-pocket limit, and a $500 employer contribution to an HSA; and (3) a plan with a $3,500 medical deductible, $0 drug deductible, 60 percent plan medical expense cost-sharing, 75 percent plan drug cost-sharing, a $6,400 maximum out-of-pocket limit, and drug co-pays of $10/$20/$50 for the first, second and third prescription drug tiers, with 75 percent coinsurance for specialty drugs. Comments are requested on these and other common plan designs that would satisfy MV and should be designated as safe harbors.

Consistent with 45 CFR 156.145(a), the proposed regulations require plans with nonstandard features that cannot determine MV using the MV Calculator or a safe harbor to use the actuarial certification method. The actuary must be a member of the American Academy of Actuaries and must perform the analysis in accordance with generally accepted actuarial principles and methodologies and any additional standards that subsequent guidance requires.

f. Other Issues

Commentators suggested a de minimis exception to the MV 60 percent level of coverage, noting that similar de minimis variations are permitted in determining actuarial value for qualified health plans. However, as other commentators noted, permitting a de minimis exception would have the effect of lowering the minimum level of coverage to a percentage below 60 percent. Under section 36B(c)(2)(C)(ii), coverage below 60 percent does not provide MV. Accordingly, the proposed regulations do not provide for a de minimis exception.

2. Miscellaneous Issues Under Section 36B

a. Definition of Modified Adjusted Gross Income

Section 36B(d)(2) provides that the term *household income* means the modified adjusted gross income of the taxpayer plus the modified adjusted gross income of all members of the taxpayer's family required to file a tax return under section 1 for the taxable year. The final regulations provide that the determination of whether a family member is required to file a return is made without regard to section 1(g)(7). Under section 1(g)(7), a parent may, if certain requirements are met, elect to include in the parent's gross income, the gross income of his or her child. If the parent makes the election, the child is treated as having no gross income for the taxable year.

The proposed regulations remove "without regard to section 1(g)(7)" from the final regulations because that language implies that the child's gross income is included in both the parent's adjusted gross income and the child's adjusted gross income in determining household income. Thus, the proposed regulations clarify that if a parent makes an election under section 1(g)(7), household income includes the child's gross income included on the parent's return and the child is treated as having no gross income.

b. Rating Area

Section 36B(b)(3)(B) determines the applicable benchmark plan by reference to the rating area where a taxpayer resides. The final regulations reserved the definition of *rating area*. The proposed regulations provide that the term *rating area* has the same meaning as used in section 2701(a)(2) of the Public Health Service Act (42 U.S.C. 300gg) and 45 CFR 156.255.

c. Retiree Coverage

The section 36B final regulations provide that an individual who may enroll in continuation coverage required under Federal law or a State law that provides comparable continuation coverage is eligible for minimum essential coverage only for months that the individual is enrolled in the coverage. These proposed regulations apply this rule to former employees only. Active employees eligible for continuation coverage as a result of reduced hours should be subject to the same rules for eligibility of affordable employer-sponsored coverage offering MV as other active employees. The proposed regulations add a comparable rule for health coverage offered to retired employees (retiree coverage). Accordingly, an individual who may enroll in retiree coverage is eligible for minimum essential coverage under the coverage only for the months the individual is enrolled in the coverage.

d Coverage Month for Newborns and New Adoptees

Under section 36B(c)(2)(A)(i) and the final regulations, a month is a coverage month for an individual only if, as of the first day of the month, the individual is enrolled in a qualified health plan through an Exchange. A child born or adopted during the month is not enrolled in coverage on the first day and therefore would not be eligible for the premium tax credit or cost-sharing reductions for that month. Accordingly, the proposed regulations provide that a child enrolled in a qualified health plan in the month of the child's birth, adoption, or placement with the taxpayer for adoption or in foster care, is treated as enrolled as of the first day of the month.

e. Adjusted Monthly Premium for Family Members Enrolled for Less Than a Full Month

Under section 36B(c), the premium assistance amount for a coverage month is computed by reference to the adjusted monthly premium for an applicable benchmark plan. The final regulations provide that the applicable benchmark plan is the plan that applies to a taxpayer's coverage family. The final regulations do not address whether changes to a coverage family, for example as the result of the birth and enrollment of a child or the disenrollment of another family member, that occur during the month affect the premium assistance amount. The proposed regulations provide that the adjusted monthly premium is determined as if all members of the coverage family for that month were enrolled in a qualified health plan for the entire month.

f. Premium Assistance Amount for Partial Months of Coverage

The final regulations do not address the computation of the premium assistance amount if coverage under a qualified health plan is terminated during the month. The proposed regulations provide that when coverage under a qualified health plan is terminated before the last day of a month and, as a result, the issuer reduces or refunds a portion of the monthly premium the premium assistance amount for the month is prorated based on the number of days of coverage in the month.

g. Family Members Residing at Different Locations

The final regulations reserved rules on determining the premium for the applicable benchmark plan if family members are geographically separated and enroll in separate qualified health plans. The proposed regulations provide that the premium for the applicable benchmark plan in this situation is the sum of the premiums for the applicable benchmark plans for each group of family members residing in a different State.

h. Correction to Applicable Percentage Table

The applicable percentage table in the final regulations erroneously states that the 9.5 percentage applies only to taxpayers whose household income is less than 400 percent of the FPL. The proposed regulations clarify that the 9.5 percentage applies to taxpayers whose household income is not more than 400 percent of the FPL.

i. Additional Benefits and Applicable Benchmark Plan

Under section 36B(b)(3)(D) and the final regulations, only the portion of the premium for a qualified health plan properly allocable to EHBs determines a taxpayer's premium assistance amount. Premiums allocable to benefits other than EHBs (additional benefits) are disregarded. The final regulations do not address, however, whether a taxpayer's benchmark plan is determined before or after premiums have been allocated to additional benefits. The proposed regulations provide that premiums are allocated to additional benefits before determining the applicable benchmark plan. Thus, only essential health benefits are considered in determining the applicable benchmark plan, consistent with the requirement in section 36B(b)(3)(D) that only essential health benefits are considered in determining the premium assistance amount. In addition, allocating premium to benefits that exceed EHBs before determining the applicable benchmark plan results in a more accurate determination of the premium assistance amount.

j. Requirement To File a Return To Reconcile Advance Credit Payments

The final regulations provided that a taxpayer who receives advance credit payments must file an income tax return for that taxable year on or before the fifteenth day of the fourth month following the close of the taxable year. Under the proposed regulations, a taxpayer who receives advance credit payments must file an income tax return on or before the due date for the return (including extensions).

Effective/Applicability Date

These regulations are proposed to apply for taxable years ending after December 31, 2013. Taxpayers may apply the proposed regulations for taxable years ending before January 1, 2015.

Special Analyses

It has been determined that this notice of proposed rulemaking is not a significant regulatory action as defined in Executive Order 12866, as supplemented by Executive Order 13563. Therefore, a regulatory assessment is not required. It has also been determined that section 553(b) of the Administrative Procedure Act (5 U.S.C. chapter 5) does not apply to these regulations and, because the regulations do not impose a collection of information on small entities, the Regulatory Flexibility Act (5 U.S.C. chapter 6) does not apply. Pursuant to section 7805(f) of the Code, this notice of proposed rulemaking has been submitted to the Chief Counsel for Advocacy of the Small Business Administration for comment on its impact on small business.

Comments and Requests for Public Hearing

Before these proposed regulations are adopted as final regulations, consideration will be given to any comments that are submitted timely to the IRS as prescribed in this preamble under the "Addresses" heading. Treasury and the IRS request comments on all aspects of the proposed rules. All comments will be available at *www.regulations.gov* or upon request. A public hearing will be scheduled if requested in writing by any person who timely submits written comments. If a public hearing is scheduled, notice of the date, time and place for the hearing will be published in the **Federal Register**.

Drafting Information

The principal authors of these proposed regulations are Andrew S. Braden, Frank W. Dunham III, and Stephen J. Toomey of the Office of Associate Chief Counsel (Income Tax and Accounting). However, other personnel from the IRS and the Treasury Department participated in the development of the regulations.

Proposed Amendments to the Regulations

Accordingly, 26 CFR part 1 is proposed to be amended as follows:

PART 1—INCOME TAXES

■ **Paragraph 1.** The authority citation for part 1 continues to read in part as follows:

Authority: 26 U.S.C. 7805 * * *

■ **Par. 2.** Section 1.36B-0 is amended by:

■ 1. Revising the introductory text.

■ 2. Adding new entries for §§ 1.36B-2(c)(3)(iv) and (c)(3)(v)(A)(*5*) and 1.36B-3(c)(2) and (3), and (d)(1), (2), and (3).

■ 3. Revising the entries for §§ 1.36B-2(c)(3)(v)(A)(*4*) and 1.36B-3(c)(4).

■ 4. Adding new entries for § 1.36B-6.

The revisions and additions read as follows:

§ 1.36B-0 Table of contents.

This section lists the captions contained in §§ 1.36B-1 through 1.36B-6.

*****

§ 1.36B-2 Eligibility for premium tax credit.

*****

(c) * * *

(3) * * *

(iv) Post-employment coverage.

(v) * * *

(A) * * *

(*4*) Wellness incentives.

(*5*) Employer contributions to health reimbursement arrangements.

*****

§ 1.36B-3 Computing the premium assistance credit amount.

*****

(c) * * *

(2) Child born or adopted during a month.

(3) Premiums paid for a taxpayer.

(4) Examples.

(d) * * *

(1) In general.

(2) Mid-month termination of coverage.

(3) Example.

*****

§ 1.36B-6 Minimum value.

(a) In general.

(b) MV standard population.

(c) MV percentage.

(1) In general.

(2) Wellness incentives.

(i) In general.

(ii) Example.

(3) Health savings accounts.

(4) Health reimbursement arrangements.

(5) Expected spending adjustments for health savings accounts and health reimbursement arrangements.

(d) Methods for determining MV.

(e) Scope of essential health benefits and adjustment for benefits not included in MV Calculator.

(f) Actuarial certification.

(1) In general.

(2) Membership in American Academy of Actuaries.

(3) Actuarial analysis.

(4) Use of MV Calculator.

(g) Effective/applicability date.

■ **Par. 3.** Section 1.36B-1 is amended by revising paragraph (e)(1)(ii)(B) and adding paragraph (n) to read as follows:

§ 1.36B-1 Premium tax credit definitions.

*****

(e) * * *

(1) * * *

(ii) * * *

(B) Are required to file a return of tax imposed by section 1 for the taxable year.

*****

(n) *Rating area.* The term *rating area* has the same meaning as used in section 2701(a)(2) of the Public Health Service Act (42 U.S.C. 300gg(a)(2)) and 45 CFR 156.255.

*****

■ **Par. 4.** Section 1.36B-2 is amended by:

■ 1. Revising paragraphs (c)(3)(iv), (c)(3)(v)(A)(*4*), and (c)(3)(vi).

■ 2. Adding paragraphs (c)(3)(v)(A)(*5*) and (c)(3)(v)(D), Example 9.

The revisions and additions read as follows:

§ 1.36B-2 Eligibility for premium tax credit.

*****

(c) * * *

(3) * * *

(iv) *Post-employment coverage.* A former employee who may enroll in continuation coverage required under Federal law or a State law that provides comparable continuation coverage, and an individual who may enroll in retiree coverage under an eligible employer-sponsored plan, are eligible for minimum essential coverage under this coverage only for months that the individual is enrolled in the coverage.

*****

(v) * * *

(A) * * *

(*4*) *Wellness incentives.* Nondiscriminatory wellness program incentives offered by an eligible employer-sponsored plan that affect premiums are treated as earned in determining an employee's required contribution for purposes of affordability of an eligible employer-sponsored plan to the extent the incentives relate to tobacco use. Wellness program incentives that do not relate to tobacco use are treated as not earned for this purpose.

(*5*) *Employer contributions to health reimbursement arrangements.* Amounts newly made available for the current plan year under a health reimbursement arrangement that is integrated with an eligible employer-sponsored plan and that an employee may use to pay premiums are counted toward the employee's required contribution.

*****

(D) * * *

Example 9. Wellness incentives. (i) Employer X offers an eligible employer-sponsored plan with a nondiscriminatory wellness program that reduces premiums by $300 for employees who do not use tobacco products or who complete a smoking cessation course. Premiums are reduced by $200 if an employee completes cholesterol screening within the first six months of the plan year. Employee B does not use tobacco and the cost of his premiums is $3,700. Employee C uses tobacco and the cost of her premiums is $4,000.

(ii) Under paragraph (c)(3)(v)(A)(*4*) of this section, only the incentives related to tobacco use are counted toward the premium amount used to determine the affordability of X's plan. C is treated as having earned the $300 incentive for attending a smoking cessation course. Thus, the employee's required contribution to premium for determining affordability for both Employees B and C is $3,700. The $200 incentive for completing cholesterol screening is disregarded.

(vi) *Minimum value.* See § 1.36B-6 for rules for determining whether an eligible employer-sponsored plan provides minimum value.

*****

■ **Par. 5.** Section 1.36B-3 is amended by:

■ 1. Redesignating paragraphs (c)(2) and (c)(3) as paragraphs (c)(3) and (c)(4) and adding a new paragraph (c)(2).

■ 2. Revising paragraphs (d), (g)(2), (j)(1), and (j)(3).

■ 3. Adding a sentence to the end of paragraph (e).

■ 4. Adding paragraph (f)(4).

The revisions and additions read as follows:

§ 1.36B-3 Computing the premium assistance credit amount.

*****

(c) * * *

(2) *Child born or adopted during a month.* A child enrolled in a qualified health plan in the month of the child's birth, adoption, or placement with the taxpayer for adoption or in foster care, is treated as enrolled as of the first day of the month for purposes of this paragraph (c).

*****

(d) *Premium assistance amount*—(1) *In general.* Except as provided in paragraph (d)(2) of this section, the premium assistance amount for a coverage month is the lesser of—

(i) The premiums for the month for one or more qualified health plans in which a taxpayer or a member of the taxpayer's family enrolls; or

(ii) The excess of the adjusted monthly premium for the applicable benchmark plan over 1/12 of the product of a taxpayer's household income and the applicable percentage for the taxable year.

(2) *Mid-month termination of coverage.* If a qualified health plan is terminated before the last day of a month and, as a result, the issuer reduces or refunds a portion of the monthly premium, the premium assistance amount for the coverage month is the amount that would apply under paragraph (d)(1) of this section for the entire month multiplied by a fraction, the numerator of which is the number of days of enrollment in the month and the denominator of which is the number of days in the month.

(3) *Example.* The following example illustrates the provisions of this paragraph (d):

Example. (i) Taxpayer R is single and has no dependents. R enrolls in a qualified health plan for 2014 with a monthly premium of $450. The adjusted monthly premium for R's applicable benchmark plan is $490 and 1/12 of the product of R's household income and applicable percentage for 2014 (R's contribution amount) is $190. R takes a new job in September of 2014, enrolls in the employer-sponsored plan, and terminates his enrollment in the qualified health plan, effective on September 10, 2014. The issuer of R's qualified health plan refunds 2.3 of the September premium for R's coverage. (ii) Under paragraph (d)(1) of this section, R's premium assistance amount for the months January-August of 2014 is $300, the lesser of $450 (the monthly premium for the plan in which R enrolls) and $300 (the excess of the adjusted monthly premium for R's applicable benchmark plan ($490) over R's contribution amount ($190)). Under paragraph (d)(2) of this section, R's premium assistance amount for September is $100, the premium assistance amount for September had R been enrolled for the full month ($300), times 10/30 (the number of days R is enrolled in September, over the number of days in September).

(e) * * * The adjusted monthly premium is determined as if all members of the coverage family for that month were enrolled in the qualified health plan for the entire month.

(f) * * *

(4) *Family members residing at different locations.* The premium for the applicable benchmark plan determined under paragraphs (f)(1) and (f)(2) of this section for family members who live in different States and enroll in separate qualified health plans is the sum of the premiums for the applicable benchmark plans for each group of family members living in the same State.

*****

(g) * * *

(2) *Applicable percentage table.*

Household income percentage of Federal poverty line	Initial percentage	Final percentage
Less than 133%	2.0	2.0
At least 133% but less than 150%	3.0	4.0
At least 150% but less than 200%	4.0	6.3
At least 200% but less than 250%	6.3	8.05
At least 250% but less than 300%	8.05	9.5
At least 300% but not more than 400%	9.5	9.5

*****

(j) *Additional benefits*—(1) *In general.* If a qualified health plan offers benefits in addition to the essential health benefits a qualified health plan must provide under section 1302 of the Affordable Care Act (42 U.S.C. 18022), or a State requires a qualified health plan to cover benefits in addition to these essential health benefits, the portion of the premium for the plan properly allocable to the additional benefits is excluded from the monthly premiums under paragraph (d)(1) or (d)(2) of this section. Premiums are allocated to additional benefits before determining the applicable benchmark plan under paragraph (f) of this section.

*****

(3) *Examples.* The following examples illustrate the rules of this paragraph (j):

Example 1. (i) Taxpayer B enrolls in a qualified health plan that provides benefits in addition to essential health benefits (additional benefits). The monthly premium for the plan in which B enrolls is $370, of which $35 is allocable to additional benefits. The premium for B's applicable benchmark plan (determined after allocating premiums to additional benefits for all silver level plans) is $440, of which $40 is allocable to additional benefits. B's contribution amount, which is the product of B's household income and the applicable percentage, is $60.

(ii) Under this paragraph (j), the premium for the qualified health plan in which B enrolls and the applicable benchmark premium are reduced by the portion of the premium that is allocable to the additional benefits provided under that plan. Therefore, the premium for the qualified health plan in which B enrolls is reduced to $335 ($370–$35) and the premium for B's applicable benchmark plan is reduced to $400 ($440–$40). B's premium assistance amount for a coverage month is $335, the lesser of $335 (the premium for the qualified health plan in which B enrolls, reduced by the portion of the premium allocable to additional benefits) and $340 (the premium for B's applicable benchmark plan, reduced by the portion of the premium allocable to additional benefits ($400), minus B's $60 contribution amount).

Example 2. The facts are the same as in *Example 1,* except that the plan in which B enrolls provides no benefits in addition to the essential health benefits required to be provided by the plan. Thus, under paragraph (j) of this section, the premium for B's applicable benchmark plan ($440) is reduced by the portion of the premium allocable to additional benefits provided under that plan ($40). The premium for the plan in which B's enrolls ($370) is not reduced under this paragraph (j). B's premium assistance amount for a coverage month is $340, the lesser of $370 (the premium for the qualified health plan in which B enrolls) and $340 (the premium for B's applicable benchmark plan, reduced by the portion of the premium allocable to additional benefits ($400), minus B's $60 contribution amount).

*****

■ **Par. 6.** Section 1.36B-6 is added to read as follows:

§ 1.36B-6 Minimum value.

(a) *In general.* An eligible employer-sponsored plan provides minimum value (MV) only if the plan's share of the total allowed costs of benefits provided to an employee (the MV percentage) is at least 60 percent.

(b) *MV standard population.* The MV standard population is a standard population developed and described through summary statistics by the Department of Health and Human Services (HHS). The MV standard population is based on the population covered by typical self-insured group health plans.

(c) *MV percentage*—(1) *In general.* An eligible employer-sponsored plan's MV percentage is—

(i) The plan's anticipated covered medical spending for benefits provided under a particular essential health benefits (EHB) benchmark plan described in 45 CFR 156.110 (EHB coverage) for the MV standard population based on the plan's cost-sharing provisions;

(ii) Divided by the total anticipated allowed charges for EHB coverage provided to the MV standard population; and

(iii) Expressed as a percentage.

(2) *Wellness incentives*—(i) *In general.* Nondiscriminatory wellness program incentives offered by an eligible employer-sponsored plan that affect deductibles, copayments, or other cost-sharing are treated as earned in determining the plan's MV percentage to the extent the incentives relate to tobacco use. These wellness program incentives that do not relate to tobacco use are treated as not earned.

(ii) *Example.* The following example illustrates the rules of this paragraph (c)(2):

Example. (i) Employer X offers an eligible employer-sponsored plan that reduces the deductible by $300 for employees who do not use tobacco products or who complete a smoking cessation course. The deductible is reduced by $200 if an employee completes cholesterol screening within the first six months of the plan year. Employee B does not use tobacco and his deductible is $3,700. Employee C uses tobacco and her deductible is $4,000.

(ii) Under paragraph (c)(2)(i) of this section, only the incentives related to tobacco use are considered in determining the plan's MV percentage. C is treated as having earned the $300 incentive for

attending a smoking cessation course. Thus, the deductible for determining for the MV percentage for both Employees B and C is $3,700. The $200 incentive for completing cholesterol screening is disregarded.

(3) *Health savings accounts.* Employer contributions for the current plan year to health savings accounts that are offered with an eligible employer-sponsored plan are taken into account for that plan year towards the plan's MV percentage.

(4) *Health reimbursement arrangements.* Amounts newly made available for the current plan year under a health reimbursement arrangement that is integrated with an eligible employer-sponsored plan are taken into account for that plan year towards the plan's MV percentage if the amounts may be used only to reduce cost-sharing for covered medical expenses.

(5) *Expected spending adjustments for health savings accounts and health reimbursement arrangements.* The amount taken into account under paragraph (c)(3) or (c)(4) of this section is the amount of expected spending for health care costs in a benefit year.

(d) *Methods for determining MV.* An eligible employer-sponsored plan may use one of the following methods to determine whether the plan provides MV—

(1) The MV Calculator made available by HHS and IRS, with adjustments permitted by paragraph (e) of this section;

(2) One of the safe harbors established by HHS and IRS and described in published guidance, see § 601.601(d) of this chapter;

(3) Actuarial certification, as described in paragraph (f) of this section, if an eligible employer-sponsored plan has nonstandard features that are not compatible with the MV Calculator and may materially affect the MV percentage; or

(4) For plans in the small group market, conformance with the requirements for a level of metal coverage defined at 45 CFR 156.140(b) (bronze, silver, gold, or platinum).

(e) *Scope of essential health benefits and adjustment for benefits not included in MV Calculator.* An eligible employer-sponsored plan may include in calculating its MV percentage all benefits included in any EHB benchmark (as defined in 45 CFR part 156). An MV percentage that is calculated using the MV Calculator may be adjusted based on an actuarial analysis that complies with the requirements of paragraph (f) of this section to the extent of the value of these benefits that are outside the parameters of the MV Calculator.

(f) *Actuarial certification*—(1) *In general.* An actuarial certification under paragraph (d)(3) of this section must satisfy the requirements of this paragraph (f).

(2) *Membership in American Academy of Actuaries.* The actuary must be a member of the American Academy of Actuaries.

(3) *Actuarial analysis.* The actuary's analysis must be performed in accordance with generally accepted actuarial principles and methodologies and specific standards that may be provided in published guidance, see § 601.601(d) of this chapter.

(4) *Use of MV Calculator.* The actuary must use the MV Calculator to determine the plan's MV percentage for coverage the plan provides that is measurable by the MV Calculator. The actuary may perform an actuarial analysis of the plan's EHB coverage for the MV standard population for benefits not measured by the MV Calculator to determine the effect of nonstandard features that are not compatible with the MV Calculator. The actuary may certify the plan's MV percentage based on the MV percentage that results from use of the MV Calculator and the actuarial analysis of the plan's coverage that is not measured by the MV calculator.

(g) *Effective/applicability date.* This section applies for taxable years ending after December 31, 2013.

■ **Par. 7.** Section 1.6011-8 is amended by revising paragraph (a) to read as follows:

§ 1.6011-8 Requirement of income tax return for taxpayers who claim the premium tax credit under section 36B.

(a) *Requirement of return.* A taxpayer who receives advance payments of the premium tax credit under section 36B must file an income tax return for that taxable year on or before the due date for the return (including extensions of time for filing).

*****

Steven T. Miller,

Deputy Commissioner for Services and Enforcement.

[FR Doc. 2013-10463 Filed 4-30-13; 4:15 pm]   BILLING CODE 4830-01-P

¶ 20,263O

IRS: Affordable insurance exchanges: Health insurance coverage: Health insurance premium tax credit: Reporting and disclosure: Patient Protection and Affordable Care Act.—The IRS has issued proposed regulations on requirements for affordable insurance exchanges to report information relating to the health insurance premium tax credit enacted by the Patient Protection and Affordable Care Act (PPACA; P.L. 111-148). Specifically, the regulations propose detailed rules for information reporting by the exchanges, including information identified by the IRS that is necessary for efficient tax administration. Exchanges must report to the IRS and to taxpayers certain information required to reconcile the premium tax credit with advance credit payments and to administer the premium tax credit generally. The regulations are proposed to apply for taxable years ending after December 31, 2013. Exchanges and taxpayers may apply these proposed regulations until final regulations or other guidance is published.

The proposed regulation was published in the Federal Register on July 2, 2013 (78 FR 39644). The regulations were finalized on May 7, 2014 (79 FR 26113). The preamble to the final regulations is at ¶ 23,299. The final regulations are at ¶ 11,112F-1 and ¶ 11,112F-6.

¶ 20,263P

IRS: Tax credit: Small employers: Health insurance coverage: Patient Protection and Affordable Care Act.—The IRS has issued proposed regulations that provide guidance on the Code Sec. 45R tax credit added by the Patient Protection and Affordable Care Act (P.L. 111-148), which is available to certain small employers offering health insurance coverage to their employees. The proposed regulations are applicable to tax years beginning after December 31, 2013. To assist in transitioning to requirements applicable to tax years beginning after December 31, 2014, employers may also rely on the proposed regulations for tax years beginning after December 31, 2013 and before December 31, 2014.

The proposed regulations were published in the Federal Register on August 26, 2013 (78 FR 52719). The regulations were finalized on June 30, 2014 (79 FR 36640). The preamble to the final regulations is at ¶ 23,303. The final regulations are at ¶ 11,119A, ¶ 11,119B, ¶ 11,119C, ¶ 11,119D, ¶ 11,119E, and ¶ 11,119F.

DEPARTMENT OF THE TREASURY

Internal Revenue Service

26 CFR Part 1

[REG-113792-13]

RIN 1545-BL55

Tax Credit for Employee Health Insurance Expenses of Small Employers

AGENCY: Internal Revenue Service (IRS), Treasury.

ACTION: Notice of proposed rulemaking.

SUMMARY: This document contains proposed regulations provide guidance on the tax credit available to certain small employers that offer health insurance coverage to their employees under section 45R of the Internal Revenue Code (Code), enacted by the Patient Protection and Affordable Care Act. These proposed regulations affect certain taxable employers and certain tax-exempt employers.

DATES: Comments and request for a public hearing must be received by November 25, 2013.

ADDRESSES: Send submissions to: CC:PA:LPD:PR (REG-113792-13), Internal Revenue Service, room 5205, PO Box 7604, Ben Franklin Station, Washington, DC 20044. Submissions may be hand delivered Monday through Friday between the hours of 8:00 a.m. and 4:00 p.m. to CC:PA:LPD:PR (REG-113792-13), Courier's Desk, Internal Revenue Service, 1111 Constitution Avenue NW., Washington, DC, or sent electronically via the Federal eRulemaking Portal at *http:www.regulations.gov* (IRS113792-13).

FOR FURTHER INFORMATION CONTACT: Concerning these proposed regulations, call Stephanie Caden at (202) 927-9639; concerning submission of comments, and/or to request a hearing, Oluwafunmilayo Taylor at (202) 622-7180 (not toll-free numbers).

SUPPLEMENTARY INFORMATION:

Background

Section 45R of the Internal Revenue Code (Code) offers a tax credit to certain small employers that provide insured health coverage to their employees. Section 45R was added to the Code by section 1421 of the Patient Protection and Affordable Care Act, enacted March 23, 2010, Public Law No. 111-148 (as amended by section 10105(e) of the Patient Protection and Affordable Care Act, which was amended by the Health Care and Education Reconciliation Act of 2010, Public Law 111-152 (124 Stat. 1029)) (collectively, the "Affordable Care Act").

I. Section 45R

Section 45R(a) provides for a health insurance tax credit in the case of an eligible small employer for any taxable year in the credit period. Section 45R(d) provides that in order to be an eligible small employer with respect to any taxable year, an employer must have in effect a contribution arrangement that qualifies under section 45R(d)(4) and must have no more than 25 full-time equivalent employees (FTEs), and the average annual wages of its FTEs must not exceed an amount equal to twice the dollar amount determined under section 45R(d)(3)(B). The amount determined under section 45R(d)(3)(B) is $25,000 (as adjusted for inflation for taxable years beginning after December 31, 2013).

Section 45R(d)(4) states that a contribution arrangement qualifies if it requires an eligible small employer to make a nonelective contribution on behalf of each employee who enrolls in a qualified health plan (QHP) offered to employees by the employer through an Exchange in an amount equal to a uniform percentage (not less than 50 percent) of the premium cost of the QHP (referred to in this preamble as the uniform percentage requirement). For purposes of section 45R, an Exchange refers to a Small Business Health Options Program (SHOP) Exchange, established pursuant to section 1311 of the Affordable Care Act and defined in 45 CFR 155.20. For purposes of this preamble and the proposed regulations, a contribution arrangement that meets these requirements is referred to as a "qualifying arrangement." See also the section of this preamble entitled "Explanation of Provisions."

Section 45R(b) provides that, subject to the reductions described in section 45R(c), the amount of the credit is equal to 50 percent (35 percent in the case of a tax-exempt eligible small employer) of the lesser of: (1) The aggregate amount of nonelective contributions the employer made on behalf of its employees during the taxable year under the qualifying arrangement for premiums for QHPs offered by the employer to its employees through a SHOP Exchange, or (2) the aggregate amount of nonelective contributions the employer would have made during the taxable year under the arrangement if each employee taken into account under: (1) Of this sentence had enrolled in a QHP which had a premium equal to the average premium (as determined by the Secretary of Health and Human Services) for the small group market in the rating area in which the employee enrolls for coverage. Section 45R(c) phases out the credit based upon the number of the employer's FTEs in excess of 10 and the amount by which the average annual wages exceeds $25,000 (as adjusted for inflation for taxable years beginning after December 31, 2013 pursuant to section 45R(d)(3)(B)). Specifically, section 45R(c) provides that the credit amount determined under section 45R(b) is reduced (but not below zero) by the sum of: (1) The credit amount determined under section 45R(b) multiplied by a fraction, the numerator of which is the total number of FTEs of the employer in excess of 10 and the denominator of which is 15, and (2) the credit amount determined under section 45R(b) multiplied by a fraction, the numerator of which is the average annual wages of the employer in excess of the dollar amount in effect under section 45R(d)(3)(B) and the denominator of which is such dollar amount. Section 45R(d)(3) provides that the average annual wages of an eligible small employer for any taxable year is the amount determined by dividing the aggregate amount of wages that were paid by the employer to employees during the taxable year by the number of FTEs of the employer and rounding such amount to the next lowest multiple of $1,000.

Section 45R(e)(2) provides that for taxable years beginning in or after 2014, the credit period means the two-consecutive-taxable year period beginning with the first taxable year in which the employer (or any predecessor) offers one or more QHPs to its employees through a SHOP Exchange.

For taxable years beginning in 2010, 2011, 2012, and 2013, section 45R(g) provides that the credit is determined without regard to whether the taxable year is in a credit period, and no credit period is treated as beginning with a taxable year beginning before 2014. The amount of the credit is 35 percent (25 percent in the case of a tax-exempt eligible small employer) of an eligible small employer's nonelective contributions for premiums paid for health insurance coverage (within the meaning of section 9832(b)(1)) of an employee. Section 45R(g)(3) provides that an employer does not become ineligible for the tax credit solely because it arranges for the offering of insurance outside of a SHOP Exchange.

The Treasury Department and the IRS have published two notices addressing the application of section 45R. Each notice provides guidance that taxpayers may rely upon for taxable years beginning before January 1, 2014. See Notice 2010-44 (2010-22 IRB 717 (June 10, 2010)) and Notice 2010-82 (2010-51 IRB 857 (December 20, 2010)). Notice 2010-44 also provided transition relief for taxable years beginning in 2010 with respect to the requirements for a qualifying arrangement under section 45R.

II. Notice 2010-44

Notice 2010-44 addresses the eligibility requirements for employers to claim the credit, provides guidance on how to calculate and claim the credit, and explains the effect on estimated tax, alternative minimum tax, and deductions. The notice specifically describes the rules for how employees are taken into account in determining an employer's FTEs, average wages, and premiums paid, with certain individuals excluded and with employees of certain related employers included.

III. Notice 2010-82

Notice 2010-82 expands on the guidance provided in Notice 2010-44 and provides additional guidance on determining whether to take into account spouses and leased employees (as defined in section 414(n)) in computing an employer's FTEs, average annual wages, and premiums paid. The notice provides that employer contributions to health reimbursement arrangements (HRAs), health flexible spending arrangements (FSAs), and health savings accounts (HSAs) are not taken into account for purposes of the section 45R credit. The notice further explains the requirement that an eligible small employer must pay a uniform percentage (not less than 50 percent) of the premium for each employee enrolled in health insurance coverage offered by the employer. The notice provides rules for applying the uniform percentage requirement in taxable years beginning after December 31, 2009 and prior to 2014, and further provides that for taxable years beginning in 2010, an employer may satisfy the uniform percentage requirement either by meeting the requirements provided in Notice 2010-82 or by meeting the transition relief rules provided in Notice 2010-44. With respect to calculating the credit, the notice provides guidance on small group markets, taxpayers with employees in multiple States, the application of the average premium cap, and taxpayers with fiscal taxable years.

Explanation of Provisions

These proposed regulations generally incorporate the provisions of Notice 2010-44 and Notice 2010-82 as modified to reflect the differences between the statutory provisions applicable to years before 2014 and those applicable to years after 2013. As in Notices 2010-44 and 2010-82, these proposed regulations use the term "qualifying arrangement" to describe an arrangement under which an eligible small employer pays premiums for each employee enrolled in health insurance coverage offered by the employer in an amount equal to a uniform percentage (not less than 50 percent) of the premium cost of the coverage. Section 45R(d)(4) and these proposed regulations require that, for tax years beginning during or after 2014, the health insurance coverage described in a qualifying arrangement be a QHP offered by an employer to its employees through a SHOP Exchange (but see section II.I of this preamble for a description of certain transition guidance for 2014).

I. Eligibility for the Credit

A. Eligible Small Employer Defined

Section 45R and these proposed regulations provide that an eligible small employer is defined as an employer that has no more than 25 FTEs for the taxable year, whose employees have average annual wages of less than $50,000 per FTE (as adjusted for inflation for years

after December 31, 2013), and that has a qualifying arrangement in effect that requires the employer to pay a uniform percentage (not less than 50 percent) of the premium cost of a QHP offered by the employer to its employees through a SHOP Exchange. A tax-exempt eligible small employer is an eligible small employer that is described in section 501(c) and that is exempt from tax under section 501(a). An employer that is an agency or instrumentality of the Federal government, or of a State, local or Indian tribal government, is not an eligible small employer for purposes of section 45R unless it is an organization described in section 501(a) (and otherwise meets the requirements for an eligible small employer). However, a farmers' cooperative described in section 521 that is subject to tax pursuant to section 1381 and otherwise meets the requirements of this section is an eligible small employer.

Section 45R does not require that, in order for an employer to be an eligible small employer, the employees perform services in a trade or business. Thus, an employer that otherwise meets the requirements for the section 45R credit does not fail to be an eligible small employer merely because the employees of the employer are not performing services in a trade or business. For example, a household employer that otherwise satisfies the requirements of section 45R is an eligible small employer for purposes of the credit.

An employer located outside the United States (including a U.S. Territory) may be an eligible small employer if the employer has income effectively connected with the conduct of a trade or business in the United States, otherwise meets the requirements of this section and is able to offer a QHP to its employees through a SHOP Exchange.

B. Application of Section 414 Aggregation Rules

In accordance with section 45R(e)(5), these proposed regulations provide that all employers treated as a single employer under section 414(b), (c), (m), or (o) are treated as a single employer for purposes of section 45R. Thus, for example, all employees of the employers treated as a single employer are counted in computing the single employer's FTEs and average annual wages. This applies to employers that are corporations in a controlled group of corporations, employers that are members of an affiliated service group, and employers that are partnerships, sole proprietorships, etc. under common control under section 414(c). Section 414 also applies to tax-exempt eligible small employers under common control. See § 1.414(c)-5.

C. Determining Employees Taken Into Account

The proposed rules for determining employees taken into account are the same as those in the previous notices. In general, all employees (determined under the common law standard) who perform services for the employer during the taxable year are taken into account in determining FTEs and average annual wages, including those who are not performing services in the employer's trade or business. (But see special rules for seasonal employees described in this section of the preamble.) However, section 45R and these proposed regulations provide that certain individuals are not considered employees when calculating the credit, and hours and wages of these individuals are not counted when determining an employer's eligibility for the credit. The following individuals are not employees or are otherwise excluded for this purpose: independent contractors (including sole proprietors); partners in a partnership; shareholders owning more than two percent of an S corporation; owners of more than five percent of other businesses; family members of these owners and partners, including a child (or descendant of a child), a sibling or step sibling, a parent (or ancestor of a parent), a step-parent, a niece or nephew, an aunt or uncle, or a son-in-law, daughter-in-law, father-in-law, mother-in-law, brother-in-law, or a sister-in-law. A spouse is also considered a family member for this purpose, as is a member of the household who is not a family member but qualifies as a dependent on the individual income tax return of an excluded individual.

Section 45R(d)(5) and these proposed regulations provide that seasonal employees who work for 120 or fewer days during the taxable year are not considered employees when determining FTEs and average annual wages, but premiums paid on behalf of seasonal workers may be counted in determining the amount of the credit. Seasonal workers include retail workers employed exclusively during holiday seasons and workers employed exclusively during the summer.

Compensation paid to a minister performing services in the exercise of his or her ministry generally is subject to tax under the Self-Employment Contributions Act (SECA) and not under the Federal Insurance Contributions Act (FICA), whether the minister is an employee or self-employed under the common law. See sections 1402(c)(2)(d), 1402(c)(4), and 3121(b)(8)(A). For purposes of income taxes generally, including the credit under section 45R, whether a minister is an employee is determined under the common law standard for determining worker status. If under the common law a minister is not an employee, the minister is not taken into account in determining an employer's FTEs. If under the common law a minister is an employee, the minister is taken into account in determining an employer's FTEs. However, because a minister performing services in the exercise of his or her ministry is treated as not engaged in employment for purposes of FICA, compensation paid to a minister is not wages as defined under section 3121(a), and so is not included for purposes of computing an employer's average annual wages.

D. Determining Hours of Service

These proposed regulations provide that an employee's hours of service for a year include hours for which the employee is paid, or entitled to payment, for the performance of duties for the employer during the employer's taxable year. Hours of service also include hours for which the employee is paid for vacation, holiday, illness, incapacity (including disability), layoff, jury duty, military duty, or leave of absence. Hours of service do not include the hours of seasonal employees who work for 120 or fewer days during the taxable year, nor do they include hours worked for a year in excess of 2,080 for a single employee.

These proposed regulations describe three methods for calculating the total number of hours of service for a single employee for the taxable year: actual hours worked; days-worked equivalency; and weeks-worked equivalency. Employers need not use the same method for all employees and may apply different methods for different classifications of employees if the classifications are reasonable and consistently applied. For example, an employer may use the actual hours worked method for all hourly employees and the weeks-worked equivalency method for all salaried employees. These proposed rules are the same as those in the previous notices.

E. Determining FTEs

In accordance with section 45R(d)(2), these proposed regulations provide that FTEs are calculated by computing the total hours of service for the taxable year using a method described in section 1.D of this preamble, and dividing the total hours of service by 2,080. If the result is not a whole number (0, 1, 2, etc.), the result is rounded down to the next lowest whole number. The only exception to this rule is when the result is less than one; in this case, the employer rounds up to one FTE. In some circumstances, an employer with 25 or more employees may qualify for the credit if some of its employees work less than full-time. For example, an employer with 46 employees that each are paid wages for 1,040 hours per year has 23 FTEs and, therefore, may qualify for the credit. These proposed rules are the same as those in the previous notices.

F. Determining Average Annual FTE Wages

In accordance with section 45R(e)(4), these proposed regulations define wages, for purposes of the credit, as wages defined under section 3121(a) for purposes of FICA, determined without considering the social security wage base limitation. To calculate average annual FTE wages, an employer must figure the total wages paid during the taxable year to all employees, divide the total wages paid by the number of FTEs, and if the result is not a multiple of $1,000, round the result to the next lowest multiple of $1,000. For example, $30,699 is rounded down to $30,000. But see special rules for seasonal employees described in section I.C of this preamble. These proposed rules are the same as those in the previous notices.

II. Calculating the Credit

A. Maximum Credit

Under section 45R and these proposed regulations, for taxable years beginning during or after 2014, the maximum credit for an eligible small employer other than a tax-exempt eligible small employer is 50 percent of the eligible small employer's premium payments made on behalf of its employees under a qualifying arrangement for QHPs offered through a SHOP Exchange. For a tax-exempt eligible small employer for those years, the maximum credit is 35 percent. The employer's tax credit is subject to several adjustments and limitations as set forth in this preamble.

B. Average Premium Limitation

Under section 45R and these proposed regulations, for purposes of calculating the credit for taxable years beginning after 2013, the em-

ployer's premium payments are limited by the average premium in the small group market in the rating area in which the employee enrolls for coverage through a SHOP Exchange. The credit will be reduced by the excess of the credit calculated using the employer's premium payments over the credit calculated using the average premium. For example, if an employer pays 50 percent of the $7,000 premium for family coverage for its employees ($3,500), but the average premium for family coverage in the small group market in the rating area in which the employees enroll is $6,000, for purposes of calculating the credit the employer's premium payments are limited to 50 percent of $6,000 ($3,000).

C. Credit Phaseout

Under section 45R and these proposed regulations, the credit phases out for eligible small employers if the number of FTEs exceeds 10, or if the average annual wages for FTEs exceed $25,000 (as adjusted for inflation for taxable years beginning after December 31, 2013). For an employer with both more than 10 FTEs and average annual FTE wages exceeding $25,000, the credit will be reduced based on the sum of the two reductions. This may reduce the credit to zero for some employers with fewer than 25 FTEs and average annual FTE wages of less than double the $25,000 dollar amount (as adjusted for inflation).

D. State Subsidy and Tax Credit Limitation

Some States offer tax credits to a small employer that provides health insurance to its employees. Some of these credits are refundable credits and others are nonrefundable credits. In addition, some States offer premium subsidy programs for certain small employers under which the State makes a payment equal to a portion of the employees' health insurance premiums. Generally, the State pays this premium subsidy either directly to the employer or to the employer's insurance company (or another entity licensed under State law to engage in the business of insurance).

Under these proposed regulations, and consistent with previous notices, if the employer is entitled to a State tax credit or premium subsidy that is paid directly to the employer, the amount of employer premiums paid is not reduced for purposes of calculating the section 45R credit, but the amount of the credit cannot exceed the net premiums paid, which are the employer premiums paid minus the amount of any State tax credits or premium subsidies received. If a State makes premium payments directly to the insurance company, the State is treated as making these payments on behalf of the employer for purposes of determining whether the employer has satisfied the "qualifying arrangement" requirement to pay an amount equal to a uniform percentage (not less than 50 percent) of the premium cost of coverage. Also, these premium payments by the State are treated as an employer contribution under section 45R for purposes of calculating the credit, but the amount of the credit cannot exceed the premiums actually paid by the employer. Finally, if a State-administered program, such as Medicaid, makes payments on behalf of individuals and their families who meet certain eligibility requirements, these payments do not reduce the amount of employer premiums paid for purposes of calculating the credit.

E. Payroll Tax Limitation for Tax-Exempt Employers

Section 45R and these proposed regulations define the term "payroll taxes" as (1) amounts required to be withheld under section 3402[1] and (2) the employee's and employer's shares of Medicare tax required to be withheld and paid under sections 3101(b) and 3111(b) on employees' wages for the year. For a tax-exempt eligible small employer, the amount of the credit cannot exceed the amount of the payroll taxes of the employer during the calendar year in which the taxable year begins.

F. Two-Consecutive-Taxable Year Credit Period Limitation

These proposed regulations provide that the first year for which an eligible small employer files Form 8941, "Credit for Small Employer Health Insurance Premiums," claiming the credit, or files Form 990-T, "Exempt Organization Business Income Tax Return," with an attached Form 8941, is the first year of the two-consecutive-taxable year credit period. Even if the employer is only eligible to claim the credit for part of the first year, the filing of Form 8941 begins the first year of the two-consecutive-taxable year credit period. For application of the two-consecutive-taxable year credit period under the transition relief related to taxable years beginning in 2014, see § 1.45R-3(i) of these proposed regulations and section II.I of the Explanation of Provisions section of this preamble.

---

[1] Although section 45R(f)(3)(A)(i) cites to section 3401(a)(1) as imposing the obligation on employers to withhold income tax from employees, it is actually section 3402 that imposes the withholding obligation. We have cited to section 3402 throughout this preamble and in the proposed regulation.

Section 45R(i) provides that regulations shall be prescribed as necessary to prevent the avoidance of the two-year limit on the credit period through the use of successor entities and the avoidance of the credit phaseout limitations through the use of multiple entities. For purposes of identifying successor entities, these proposed regulations generally apply the rules for identifying successor employers applicable under the employment tax provisions for determining when wages paid by a predecessor may be attributed to a successor employer (see § 31.3121(a)(1)-1(b)). Accordingly, under the proposed regulations, an entity that would be treated as a successor employer for employment tax purposes will also be treated as a successor employer for purposes of the two-consecutive-taxable year credit period under section 45R. Therefore, if the predecessor employer had previously claimed the credit under section 45R for a period, that period will count towards the successor employer's two-consecutive-taxable year credit period.

G. Premium Payments by the Employer

In general, only premiums paid by the employer for employees enrolled in a QHP offered through a SHOP Exchange are counted when calculating the credit.[2] If the employer pays a portion of the premiums and the employees pay the rest, only the portion paid by the employer is taken into account. For this purpose, any premium paid through a salary reduction arrangement under a section 125 cafeteria plan is not treated as an employer-paid premium. Premiums paid with employer-provided flex credits that employees may elect to receive as cash or as a taxable benefit are treated as paid pursuant to a salary reduction arrangement under a section 125 cafeteria plan. See Notice 2012-40 (2012-26 IRB 1046 (June 25, 2012)). The proposed regulations further provide that amounts made available by an employer under or contributed by an employer to HRAs, FSAs and HSAs are not taken into account for purposes of determining premium payments by the employer.

The proposed regulations provide that if a minister is a common law employee and is taken into account in an employer's FTEs, the premiums paid by the employer for health insurance may be counted in calculating the credit.

A leased employee is defined in section 414(n)(2) as a person who is not an employee of the service recipient and who provides services to the service recipient pursuant to an agreement with the leasing organization. The person must have performed services for the service recipient on a substantially full-time basis for a period of at least one year under the primary direction and control of the service recipient. Leased employees are counted in computing a service recipient's FTEs and average annual wages. See section 45R(e)(1)(B).

See section II.I of this preamble for special rules related to taxable years beginning in 2014.

H. Trusts, Estates, Regulated Investment Companies, Real Estate Investment Trusts and Cooperative Organizations

Section 45R(e)(5)(B) provides that rules similar to the rules of section 52(c), (d) and (e) will apply. Because section 45R(f) explicitly provides that a tax-exempt eligible small employer may be eligible for the credit, these proposed regulations do not adopt a rule similar to section 52(c). However, these proposed regulations provide that rules similar to the rules of section 52(d) and (e) and the regulations thereunder apply in calculating and apportioning the credit with respect to trusts, estates, regulated investment companies, real estate investment trusts, and cooperative organizations.

I. Transition Rules

If an eligible small employer's plan year begins on a date other than the first day of its taxable year, it may not be practical or possible for the employer to offer insurance to its employees through a SHOP Exchange at the beginning of its first taxable year beginning in 2014. These proposed regulations provide that if: (1) As of August 26, 2013, a small employer offers coverage in a plan year that begins on a date other than the first day of its taxable year, (2) the employer offers coverage during the period before the first day of the plan year beginning in 2014 that would have qualified the employer for the credit under the rules otherwise applicable to the period before January 1, 2014, and (3) the employer begins offering coverage through a SHOP Exchange as of the first day of its plan year that begins in 2014, then it will be treated as offering coverage through a SHOP Exchange for its entire 2014 taxable year for purposes of eligibility for, and calculation of, a credit under section 45R. Thus, for an employer that meets these requirements, the credit will be calculated at the 50 percent rate (35

percent rate for tax-exempt eligible small employers) for the entire 2014 taxable year and the 2014 taxable year will be the start of the two-consecutive-taxable year credit period.

III. Application of Uniform Percentage Requirement

A. Uniform Premium

Section 45R and these proposed regulations require that to be eligible for the credit, an eligible small employer must generally pay a uniform percentage (not less than 50 percent) of the premium for each employee enrolled in a QHP offered to its employees through a SHOP Exchange. These proposed regulations set forth rules for applying this requirement in separate situations depending upon (1) whether the premium established for the QHP is based upon list billing or is based upon composite billing, (2) whether the QHP offers only self-only coverage, or other coverage (such as family coverage) for which a higher premium is charged, and (3) whether the employer offers one QHP or more than one QHP. The uniform percentage rule applies only to the employees offered coverage and does not impose a coverage requirement.

B. Composite Billing and List Billing

These proposed regulations define the term "composite billing" to mean a system of billing under which a health insurer charges a uniform premium for each of the employer's employees or charges a single aggregate premium for the group of covered employees that the employer may then divide by the number of covered employees to determine the uniform premium. In contrast, the term "list billing" is defined as a billing system under which a health insurer lists a separate premium for each employee based on the age of the employee or other factors.

C. Employers Offering One QHP

For an employer offering one QHP under a composite billing system with one level of self-only coverage, these proposed regulations provide that the uniform percentage requirement is met if an eligible small employer pays the same amount for each employee enrolled in coverage and that amount is equal to at least 50 percent of the premium for self-only coverage. For employers offering one QHP under a composite billing system with different tiers of coverage (for example, self-only, self plus one, and family coverage) for which different premiums are charged, the uniform percentage requirement is satisfied if the eligible small employer either: (1) Pays the same amount for each employee enrolled in that tier of coverage and that amount is equal to at least 50 percent of the premium for that tier of coverage, or (2) pays an amount for each employee enrolled in the more expensive tiers of coverage that is the same for all employees and is no less than the amount that the employer would have contributed toward self-only coverage for that employee (and is equal to at least 50 percent of the premium for self-only coverage).

For an employer offering one QHP under a list billing system that offers only self-only coverage, the uniform percentage requirement is satisfied if the eligible small employer either: (1) Pays an amount equal to a uniform percentage (not less than 50 percent) of the premium charged for each employee, or (2) determines an "employer-computed composite rate" and, if any employee contribution is required, each enrolled employee pays a uniform amount toward the self-only premium that is no more than 50 percent of the employer-computed composite rate for self-only coverage. The proposed regulations define "employer-computed composite rate" as the average rate determined by adding the premiums for that tier of coverage for all employees eligible to participate in the employer's health insurance plan (whether or not the eligible employee enrolls in coverage under the plan or in that tier of coverage under the plan) and dividing by the total number of such eligible employees.

For eligible small employers offering one QHP under list billing with different tiers of coverage for which different premiums are charged, the uniform percentage requirement is satisfied if the eligible small employer pays toward the premium for each employee covered under each tier of coverage an amount equal to or exceeding the amount the employer would have contributed with respect to that employee for self-only coverage, calculated either based on the actual premium that would have been charged by the insurer for that employee for self-only coverage, or based on the employer-computed composite rate for self-only coverage, and the employer premium payments within the same tier are uniform in percentage or amount. Alternatively, the eligible small employer may satisfy the uniform percentage requirement by

---

[2] In general a stand-alone dental health plan will be considered a qualifed health plan. Patient Protection and Affordable Care Act; Establishment of Exchanges and Qualified Health Plans; Exchange Standards for Employers, 77 Fed. Reg. 18310, 18315 (March 27, 2012).

meeting the uniform percentage requirement separately for each tier of coverage and substituting the employer-computed composite rate for that tier of coverage for the employer-computed composite rate for self-only coverage.

The proposed regulations provide examples of how the uniform percentage requirement is applied in all of these situations.

D. Employers Offering More Than One Plan

As set forth in these proposed regulations, if an employer offers more than one QHP through a SHOP Exchange, the uniform percentage requirement may be satisfied in one of two ways. The first is on a plan-by-plan basis, meaning that the employer's premium payments for each plan must individually satisfy the uniform percentage requirement stated above. The amounts or percentages of premiums paid toward each QHP do not have to be the same, but they must each satisfy the uniform percentage requirement if each QHP is tested separately. The other permissible method to satisfy the uniform percentage requirement is through the reference plan method. Under the reference plan method, the employer designates one of its QHPs as a reference plan. Then the employer either determines a level of employer contributions for each employee such that, if all eligible employees enrolled in the reference plan, the contributions would satisfy the uniform percentage requirement as applied to that reference plan, or the employer allows each employee to apply the minimum amount of employer contribution determined necessary to meet the uniform percentage requirement toward the reference plan or toward coverage under any other available QHP.

E. Employers Complying With State Law

The Treasury Department and the IRS understand that at least one State requires employers to contribute a certain percentage (50%) to an employee's premium cost, but also requires that the employee's contribution not exceed a certain percentage of monthly gross earnings so that, in some instances, the employer's required contribution for a particular employee may exceed 50 percent of the premium.[3] To satisfy the uniform percentage requirement under section 45R, that employer generally would be required to increase the employer contribution to all its employees' premiums to match the increase for that one employee, which may be difficult especially if the percentage increase is substantial. Accordingly, for taxable years beginning in 2014, an employer will be treated as meeting the uniform percentage requirement if the failure to satisfy the uniform percentage requirement is attributable to additional employer contributions made to certain employees solely to comply with an applicable State or local law.

IV. Claiming the Credit

A. Form 8941, Credit for Small Employer Health Insurance Premiums

For an eligible small employer that is not a tax-exempt eligible small employer, the credit is calculated on Form 8941, "Credit for Small Employer Health Insurance Premiums," and can be applied against both regular and alternative minimum tax. For tax-exempt eligible small employers, the credit is also calculated on Form 8941 and attached to Form 990-T, "Exempt Organization Business Income Tax Return." Filing Form 990-T with an attached Form 8941 is required for a tax-exempt eligible small employer to claim the credit, even if it is not otherwise required to file Form 990-T.

B. Estimated Tax Payments and Alternative Minimum Tax (AMT) Liability

These proposed regulations provide that the section 45R credit may be reflected in an eligible small employer's estimated tax payments in accordance with the estimated tax rules. The credit can also be used to offset an eligible small employer's AMT liability for the year, subject to certain limitations based on the amount of an employer's regular tax liability, AMT liability and other allowable credits. See section 38(c)(1), as modified by section 38(c)(4)(B)(vi), for these limitations.

C. Reduced Section 162 Deduction

No deduction is allowed under section 162 for that portion of the premiums paid equal to the amount of the credit claimed under section 45R. See section 280C(h).

Proposed Effective/Applicability Dates

These regulations are proposed to be effective the date the final regulations are published in the **Federal Register**, and apply to taxable years beginning after December 31, 2013. To assist with any prepara-

tion needed for transition to the requirements applicable to taxable years beginning after December 31, 2014, employers may also rely on these proposed regulations for guidance for taxable years beginning after December 31, 2013, and before December 31, 2014. If and to the extent future guidance is more restrictive than the guidance in these proposed regulations, the future guidance will be applied without retroactive effect and employers will be provided with time to come into compliance with the final regulations (and will in any case not be required to comply for taxable years beginning prior to January 1, 2015).

Availability of IRS Documents

IRS notices cited in this preamble are made available by the Superintendent of Documents, U.S. Government Printing Office, Washington, DC 20402.

Special Analyses

It has been determined that this notice of proposed rulemaking is not a significant regulatory action as defined in Executive Order 12866, as supplemented by Executive Order 13563. Therefore, a regulatory assessment is not required. It has also been determined that section 553(b) of the Administrative Procedure Act (5 U.S.C. chapter 5) does not apply to these regulations.

It is hereby certified that this regulation will not have a significant economic impact on a substantial number of small entities. Accordingly, a regulatory flexibility analysis is not required. While the number of small entities affected is substantial, the economic impact on the affected small entities is not significant. The information required to determine a small employer's eligibility for, and amount of, an applicable credit, generally consisting of the annual hours worked by its employees, the annual wages paid to its employees, the cost of the employees' premiums for qualified health plans and the employer's contribution towards those premiums, is information that the small employer generally will retain for business purposes and be readily available to accumulate for purposes of completing the necessary form for claiming the credit. In addition, this credit is available to any eligible small employer only twice (because the credit can be claimed by a small employer only for two consecutive taxable years beginning after December 31, 2013, beginning with the taxable year for which the small employer first claims the credit). Accordingly, no small employer will calculate the credit amount or complete the process for claiming the credit under this regulation more than two times.

Based on these facts, a Regulatory Flexibility Analysis under the Regulatory Flexibility Act (5 U.S.C. chapter 6) is not required.

Pursuant to section 7805(f) of the Code, this notice of proposed rulemaking has been submitted to the Chief Counsel for Advocacy of the Small Business Administration for comment on its impact on small business.

Comments and Requests for Public Hearing

Before these proposed regulations are adopted as final regulations, consideration will be given to any comments that are timely submitted to the IRS as prescribed in this preamble under the "Addresses" heading. The IRS and the Treasury Department request comments on all aspects of the proposed rules. All comments will be available at *www.regulations.gov* or upon request. A public hearing will be scheduled if requested in writing by any person that timely submits written or electronic comments. If a public hearing is scheduled, notice of the date, time, and place for the hearing will be published in the **Federal Register**.

Drafting Information

The principal author of these proposed regulations is Stephanie Caden, Office of the Division Counsel/Associate Chief Counsel (Tax Exempt and Government Entities). However, other personnel from the IRS and the Treasury Department participated in their development.

List of Subjects in 26 CFR Part 1

Income taxes, Reporting and recordkeeping requirements.

Proposed Amendments to the Regulations

Accordingly, 26 CFR part 1 is proposed to be amended as follows:

PART I—INCOME TAXES

■ **Paragraph 1.** The authority citation for part 1 continues to read as follows:

---

[3] See Hawaii Prepaid Health Care Act, Hawaii Revised Statutes Chapter 393 (1974).

Authority: 26 U.S.C. 7805 * * *

■ **Par. 2.** Section 1.45R-0 is added to read as follows:

§ 1.45R-0 Table of Contents

This section lists the table of contents for §§ 1.45R-1 through 1.45R-5.

■ **Par. 3.** Sections 1.45R-1, 1.45R-2, 1.45R-3, 1.45R-4 and 1.45R-5 are added to read as follows:

§ 1.45R-1 Definitions.

(a) *Definitions.* The definitions in this section apply to this section and §§ 1.45R-2, 1.45R-3, 1.45R-4, and 1.45R-5.

(1) *Average premium.* The term *average premium* means an average premium for the small group market in the rating area in which the employee enrolls for coverage. The average premium for the small group market in a rating area is determined by the Secretary of Health and Human Services.

(2) *Composite billing.* The term *composite billing* means a system of billing under which a health insurer charges a uniform premium for each of the employer's employees or charges a single aggregate premium for the group of covered employees that the employer then divides by the number of covered employees to determine the uniform premium.

(3) *Credit period*—(i) *In general.* The term *credit period* means, with respect to any eligible small employer (or any predecessor employer), the two-consecutive-taxable year period beginning with the first taxable year beginning after December 31, 2013, for which the eligible small employer files an income tax return with an attached Form 8941, "Credit for Small Employer Health Insurance Premiums" (or files a Form 990-T, "Exempt Organization Business Income Tax Return," with an attached Form 8941 in the case of a tax-exempt eligible employer). For a transition rule for 2014, see § 1.45R-3(i).

(ii) *Examples.* The following examples illustrate the provisions of paragraph (a)(3)(i) of this section:

Example 1. (i) *Facts.* In 2014, an eligible small employer (Employer) that uses a calendar year as its taxable year begins to offer insurance through a SHOP Exchange. Employer has 4 employees and otherwise qualifies for the credit, but none of the employees enroll in the coverage offered by Employer through the SHOP Exchange. In mid-2015, the 4 employees enroll for coverage through the SHOP Exchange but Employer does not file Form 8941 or claim the credit. In 2016, Employer has 20 employees and all are enrolled in coverage offered through the SHOP Exchange. Employer files Form 8941 with Employer's 2016 tax return to claim the credit.

(ii) *Conclusion.* Employer's taxable year 2016 is the first year of the credit period. Accordingly, Employer's two-year credit period is 2016 and 2017.

Example 2. (i) *Facts.* Same facts as *Example 1,* but Employer files Form 8941 with Employer's 2015 tax return.

(ii) *Conclusion.* Employer's taxable year 2015 is the first year of the credit period. Accordingly, Employer's two-year credit period is 2015 and 2016 (and does not include 2017). Employer is entitled to a credit based on a partial year of SHOP Exchange coverage for Employer's taxable year 2015.

(4) *Eligible small employer.* (i) The term *eligible small employer* means an employer that meets the requirements set forth in § 1.45R-2.

(ii) For the definition of tax-exempt eligible small employer, see paragraph (a)(19) of this section.

(iii) A farmers' cooperative described under section 521 that is subject to tax pursuant to section 1381, and otherwise meets the requirements of this paragraph (a)(4) and § 1.45R-2, is an eligible small employer.

(5) *Employee*—(i) *In general.* Except as otherwise specifically provided in this paragraph (a)(5), the term *employee* means an individual who is an employee of the eligible small employer under the common law standard. See § 31.3121(d)-1(c).

(ii) *Leased employees.* For purposes of this paragraph (a)(5), the term *employee* also includes a leased employee (as defined in section 414(n)).

(iii) *Certain individuals excluded.* The term *employee* does not include independent contractors (including sole proprietors), partners in a partnership, shareholders owning more than two percent of an S corporation, and any owners of more than five percent of other businesses. The term *employee* also does not include family members of these owners and partners including the employee-spouse of a shareholder owning more than two percent of the stock of an S corporation, the employee-spouse of an owner of more than five percent of a business, the employee-spouse of a partner owning more than a five percent interest in a partnership, and the employee-spouse of a sole proprietor.

(iv) *Seasonal employees.* The term *employee* does not include seasonal workers unless the seasonal worker provides services to the employer on more than 120 days during the taxable year.

(v) *Dependents.* The term *employee* does not include any other member of the household of owners and partners who qualifies as a dependent under section 152(d)(2)(H).

(vi) *Ministers.* Whether a minister is an employee is determined under the common law standard for determining worker status. If, under the common law standard, a minister is not an employee, the minister is not an employee for purposes of this paragraph (a)(5) and is not taken into account in determining an employer's FTEs, and premiums paid for the minister's health insurance coverage are not taken into account in computing the credit. If, under the common law standard, a minister is an employee, the minister is an employee for purposes of this paragraph (a)(5), and is taken into account in determining an employer's FTEs, and premiums paid by the employer for the minister's health insurance coverage can be taken into account in computing the credit. Because the performance of services by a minister in the exercise of his or her ministry is not treated as employment for purposes of the Federal Insurance Contributions Act (FICA), compensation paid to the minister is not wages as defined under section 3121(a), and is not counted as wages for purposes of computing an employer's average annual wages.

(6) *Employer-computed composite rate.* The term *employer-computed composite rate* refers to a rate for a tier of coverage (such as self-only or family) of a QHP that is the average rate determined by adding the premiums for that tier of coverage for all employees eligible to participate in the QHP (whether or not they actually receive coverage under the plan or under that tier of coverage) and dividing by the total number of such eligible employees. The employer-computed composite rate is used in list billing to convert individual premiums for a tier of coverage into an employer-computed composite rate for that tier of coverage.

(7) *Exchange.* The term *Exchange* means an exchange as defined in 45 CFR 155.20.

(8) *Family member.* The term *family member* is defined with respect to a taxpayer as a child (or descendant of a child); a sibling or step-sibling; a parent (or ancestor of a parent); a step-parent; a niece or nephew; an aunt or uncle; or a son-in-law, daughter-in-law, father-in-law, mother-in-law, brother-in-law or sister-in-law. A spouse of any of these family members is also considered a family member.

(9) *Full-time equivalent employee (FTE).* The number of *full-time equivalent employees (FTEs)* is determined by dividing the total number of hours of service for which wages were paid by the employer to employees during the taxable year by 2,080. See § 1.45-2(d) and (e) for permissible methods of calculating hours of service and the method for calculating the number of an employer's FTEs.

(10) *List billing.* The term *list billing* refers to a system of billing under which a health insurer lists a separate premium for each employee based on the age of the employee or other factors.

(11) *Net premium payments.* The term *net premium payments* means, in the case of an employer receiving a State tax credit or State subsidy for providing health insurance to its employees, the excess of the employer's actual premium payments over the State tax credit or State subsidy received by the employer. In the case of a State payment directly to an insurance company (or another entity licensed under State law to engage in the business of insurance), the employer's net premium payments are the employer's actual premium payments. If a State-administered program (such as Medicaid or another program that makes payments directly to a health care provider or insurance company on behalf of individuals and their families who meet certain eligibility guidelines) makes payments that are not contingent on the maintenance of an employer-provided group health plan, those payments are not taken into account in determining the employer's net premium payments.

(12) *Nonelective contribution.* The term *nonelective contribution* means an employer contribution other than a contribution pursuant to a salary reduction arrangement under section 125.

(13) *Payroll taxes.* For purposes of section 45R, the term *payroll taxes* means amounts required to be withheld as tax from the employees of a tax-exempt eligible small employer under section 3402, amounts required to be withheld from such employees under section 3101(b), and amounts of tax imposed on the tax-exempt eligible small employer under section 3111(b).

(14) *Qualified health plan (QHP).* The term *qualified health plan (QHP)* means a qualified health plan as defined in Affordable Care Act section 1301(a) (*see* 42 U.S.C. 18021(a)), but does not include a catastrophic plan described in Affordable Care Act section 1302(e) (*See* 42 U.S.C. 18022(e)).

(15) *Qualifying arrangement.* The term *qualifying arrangement* means an arrangement that requires an eligible small employer to make a nonelective contribution on behalf of each employee who enrolls in a QHP offered to employees by the employer through a SHOP Exchange in an amount equal to a uniform percentage (not less than 50 percent) of the premium cost of the QHP.

(16) *Seasonal worker.* The term *seasonal worker* means a worker who performs labor or services on a seasonal basis as defined by the Secretary of Labor, including (but not limited to) workers covered by 29 CFR 500.20(s)(1), and retail workers employed exclusively during holiday seasons.

(17) *Small Business Health Options Program (SHOP).* The term *Small Business Health Options Program (SHOP)* means an Exchange established pursuant to section 1311 of the Affordable Care Act and defined in 45 CFR 155.20.

(18) *State.* The term *State* means a State as defined in section 7701(a)(10), including the District of Columbia.

(19) *Tax-exempt eligible small employer.* The term *tax-exempt eligible small employer* means an eligible small employer that is exempt from federal income tax under section 501(a) as an organization described in section 501(c).

(20) *Tier.* The term *tier* refers to a category of coverage under a benefits package that varies only by the number of individuals covered. For example, self-only coverage, self plus one coverage, and family coverage would constitute three separate tiers of coverage.

(21) *United States.* The term *United States* means United States as defined in section 7701(a)(9).

(22) *Wages.* The term *wages* for purposes of section 45R means wages as defined under section 3121(a) for purposes of the Federal Insurance Contributions Act (FICA), determined without regard to the social security wage base limitation under section 3121(a)(1).

(b) *Effective/applicability date.* This section is applicable for periods after December 31, 2013.

§ 1.45R-2 Eligibility for the credit.

(a) *Eligible small employer.* To be eligible for the credit, an employer must be an eligible small employer. In order to be an eligible small employer, with respect to any taxable year, an employer must have no more than 25 full-time equivalent employees (FTEs), must have in effect a qualifying arrangement, and the average annual wages of its FTEs must not exceed an amount equal to twice the dollar amount in effect under § 1.45R-3(c)(2). To claim the credit for taxable years beginning in or after 2014, the qualifying arrangement is an arrangement that requires an employer to make a nonelective contribution on behalf of each employee who enrolls in a qualified health plan (QHP) offered to employees through a small business health options program (SHOP) Exchange in an amount equal to a uniform percentage (not less than 50 percent) of the premium cost of the QHP. Notwithstanding the foregoing, an employer that is an agency or instrumentality of the federal government, or of a State, local or Indian tribal government, is not an eligible small employer unless it is an organization described in section 501(c) that is exempt from tax under section 501(a). An employer does not fail to be an eligible small employer merely because its employees are not performing services in a trade or business of the employer. An employer located outside the United States (including a U.S. Territory) must have income effectively connected with the conduct of a trade or business in the United States, and otherwise meet the requirements of this section, to be an eligible small employer. For eligibility standards for SHOP related to foreign employers, see 45 CFR 155.710. Paragraphs (b) through (f) of this section provide the rules for determining whether the requirements to be an eligible small employer are met, including rules related to identifying and counting the employer's number of the employer's FTEs, counting the employees' hours of service, and determining the employer's average annual FTE wages for the taxable year. For rules on determining whether the uniform percentage requirement is met, see § 1.45R-4.

(b) *Application of section 414 employer aggregation rules.* All employers treated as a single employer under section 414(b), (c), (m) or (o) are treated as a single employer for purposes of this section. Thus, all employees of a controlled group under section 414(b), (c) or (o), or an affiliated service group under section 414(m), are taken into account in determining whether any member of the controlled group or affiliated service group is an eligible small employer. Similarly, all wages paid to, and premiums paid for, employees by the members of the controlled group or affiliated service group are taken into account when determining the amount of the credit for a group treated as a single employer under these rules.

(c) *Employees taken into account.* To be eligible for the credit, an employer must have employees as defined in § 1.45R-1(a)(5) during the taxable year. All employees of the eligible small employer are taken into account for purposes of determining the employer's FTEs and average annual FTE wages. Employees include former employees who terminated employment during the year for which the credit is being claimed, employees covered under a collective bargaining agreement, and employees who do not enroll in a QHP offered by the employer through a SHOP Exchange.

(d) *Determining the hours of service performed by employees*—(1) *In general.* An employee's hours of service for a year include each hour for which an employee is paid, or entitled to payment, for the performance of duties for the employer during the employer's taxable year. It also includes each hour for which an employee is paid, or entitled to payment, by the employer on account of a period of time during which no duties are performed due to vacation, holiday, illness, incapacity (including disability), layoff, jury duty, military duty or leave of absence (except that no more than 160 hours of service are required to be counted for an employee on account of any single continuous period during which the employee performs no duties).

(2) *Permissible methods.* In calculating the total number of hours of service that must be taken into account for an employee during the taxable year, eligible small employers need not use the same method for all employees, and may apply different methods for different classifications of employees if the classifications are reasonable and consistently applied. Eligible small employers may change the method for

calculating employees' hours of service for each taxable year. An eligible small employer may use any of the following three methods.

(i) *Actual hours worked.* An employer may use the actual hours of service provided by employees including hours worked and any other hours for which payment is made or due (as described in paragraph (d)(1) of this section).

(ii) *Days-worked equivalency.* An employer may use a days-worked equivalency whereby the employee is credited with 8 hours of service for each day for which the employee would be required to be credited with at least one hour of service under paragraph (d)(1) of this section.

(iii) *Weeks-worked equivalency.* An employer may use a weeks-worked equivalency whereby the employee is credited with 40 hours of service for each week for which the employee would be required to be credited with at least one hour of service under paragraph (d)(1) of this section.

(3) *Examples.* The following examples illustrate the rules of paragraph (d) of this section:

Example 1. Counting hours of service by hours actually worked or for which payment is made or due. (i) *Facts.* An eligible small employer (Employer) has payroll records that indicate that Employee A worked 2,000 hours and that Employer paid Employee A for an additional 80 hours on account of vacation, holiday and illness. Employer uses the actual hours worked method described in paragraph (d)(2)(i) of this section.

(ii) *Conclusion.* Under this method of counting hours, Employee A must be credited with 2,080 hours of service (2,000 hours worked and 80 hours for which payment was made or due).

Example 2. Counting hours of service under days-worked equivalency. (i) *Facts.* Employee B worked from 8:00 a.m. to 12:00 p.m. every day for 200 days. Employer uses the days-worked equivalency method described in paragraph (d)(2)(ii) of this section.

(ii) *Conclusion.* Under this method of counting hours, Employee B must be credited with 1,600 hours of service (8 hours for each day Employee B would otherwise be credited with at least 1 hour of service × 200 days).

Example 3. Counting hours of service under weeks-worked equivalency. (i) *Facts.* Employee C worked 49 weeks, took 2 weeks of vacation with pay, and took 1 week of leave without pay. Employer uses the weeks-worked equivalency method described in paragraph (d)(2)(iii) of this section.

(ii) *Conclusion.* Under this method of counting hours, Employee C must be credited with 2,040 hours of service (40 hours for each week during which Employee C would otherwise be credited with at least 1 hour of service × 51 weeks).

Example 4. Excluded employees. (i) *Facts.* Employee D worked 3 consecutive weeks at 32 hours per week during the holiday season. Employee D did not work during the remainder of the year. Employee E worked limited hours after school from time to time through the year for a total of 350 hours. Employee E does not work through the summer. Employer uses the actual hours worked method described in paragraph (d)(2)(i) of this section.

(ii) *Conclusion.* Employee D is a seasonal employee who worked for 120 days or less for Employer during the year. Employee D's hours are not counted when determining the hours of service of Employer's employees. Employee E works throughout most of the year and is not a seasonal employee. Employer counts Employee E's 350 hours of service during the year.

(e) *FTE Calculation*—(1) *In general.* The number of an employer's FTEs is determined by dividing the total hours of service, determined in accordance with paragraph (d) of this section, credited during the year to employees taken into account under paragraph (c) of this section (but not more than 2,080 hours for any employee) by 2,080. The result, if not a whole number, is then rounded to the next lowest whole number. If, however, after dividing the total hours of service by 2,080, the resulting number is less than one, the employer rounds up to one FTE.

(2) *Example.* The following example illustrates the provisions of paragraph (e) of this section:

Example. Determining the number of FTEs. (i) *Facts.* A sole proprietor pays 5 employees wages for 2,080 hours each, pays 3 employees wages for 1,040 hours each, and pays 1 employee wages for 2,300 hours. One of the employees working 2,080 hours is the sole proprietor's nephew. The sole proprietor's FTEs would be calculated as follows: 8,320 hours of service for the 4 employees paid for 2,080 hours each (4 × 2,080); the sole proprietor's nephew is excluded from the FTE calculation; 3,120 hours of service for the 3 employees paid for 1,040 hours each (3 ×

1,040); and 2,080 hours of service for the 1 employee paid for 2,300 hours (lesser of 2,300 and 2,080). The sum of the included hours of service equals 13,520 hours of service.

(ii) *Conclusion.* The sole proprietor's FTEs equal 6 (13,520 divided by 2,080 = 6.5, rounded to the next lowest whole number).

(f) *Determining the employer's average annual FTE wages*—(1) *In general.* All wages paid to employees (including overtime pay) are taken into account in computing an eligible small employer's average annual FTE wages. The average annual wages paid by an employer for a taxable year is determined by dividing the total wages paid by the eligible small employer during the employer's taxable year to employees taken into account under paragraph (c) of this section by the number of the employer's FTEs for the year. The result is then rounded down to the nearest $1,000 (if not otherwise a multiple of $1,000). For purposes of determining the employer's average annual wages for the taxable year, only wages that are paid for hours of service determined under paragraph (d) of this section are taken into account.

(2) *Example.* The following example illustrates the provision of paragraphs (e) and (f) of this section:

Example. (i) *Facts.* An employer has 26 FTEs with average annual wages of $23,000. Only 22 of the employer's employees enroll for coverage offered by the employer through a SHOP Exchange.

(ii) *Conclusion.* The hours of service and wages of all employees are taken into consideration in determining whether the employer is an eligible small employer for purposes of the credit. Because the employer does not have fewer than 25 FTEs for the taxable year, the employer is not an eligible small employer for purposes of this section, even if less than 25 employees (or FTEs) enroll for coverage through the SHOP Exchange.

(g) *Effective/applicability date.* This section is applicable for periods after December 31, 2013.

§ 1.45R-3 Calculating the credit.

(a) *In general.* The tax credit available to an eligible small employer equals 50 percent of the eligible small employer's premium payments made on behalf of its employees under a qualifying arrangement, or in the case of a tax-exempt eligible small employer, equals 35 percent of the employer's premium payments made on behalf of its employees under a qualifying arrangement. The employer's tax credit is subject to the following adjustments and limitations:

(1) The average premium limitation for the small group market in the rating area in which the employee enrolls for coverage, described in paragraph (b) of this section;

(2) The credit phaseout described in paragraph (c) of this section;

(3) The net premium payment limitation in the case of State credits or subsidies described in paragraph (d) of this section;

(4) The payroll tax limitation for a tax-exempt eligible small employer described in paragraph (e) of this section;

(5) The two-consecutive-taxable year credit period limitation, described in paragraph (f) of this section;

(6) The rules with respect to the premium payments taken into account, described in paragraph (g) of this section;

(7) The rules with respect to credits applicable to trusts, estates, regulated investment companies, real estate investment trusts and cooperatives described in paragraph (h) of this section; and

(8) The transition relief for 2014 described in paragraph (i) of this section.

(b) *Average premium limitation*—(1) *In general.* The amount of an eligible small employer's premium payments that are taken into account in calculating the credit is limited to the premium payments the employer would have made under the same arrangement if the average premium for the small group market in the rating area in which the employee enrolls for coverage were substituted for the actual premium.

(2) *Examples.* The following examples illustrate the provisions of paragraph (b)(1) of this section:

Example 1. Comparing premium payments to average premium for small group market. (i) *Facts.* An eligible small employer (Employer) offers a health insurance plan with self-only and family coverage through a small business options program (SHOP) Exchange. Employer has 9 full-time equivalent employees (FTEs) with average annual wages of $23,000 per FTE. All 9 employees are employees as defined under § 1.45R-1(a)(5). Four employees are enrolled in self-only coverage and 5 are enrolled in family coverage. Employer pays 50% of the premiums for all employees enrolled in self-only coverage and 50%

of the premiums for all employees enrolled in family coverage (and the employee is responsible for the remainder in each case). The premiums are $4,000 a year for self-only coverage and $10,000 a year for family coverage. The average premium for the small group market in Employer's rating area is $5,000 for self-only coverage and $12,000 for family coverage. Employer's premium payments for each FTE ($2,000 for self-only coverage and $5,000 for family coverage) do not exceed 50 percent of the average premium for the small group market in Employer's rating area ($2,500 for self-only coverage and $6,000 for family coverage).

(ii) *Conclusion.* The amount of premiums paid by Employer for purposes of computing the credit equals $33,000 ((4 × $2,000) plus (5 × $5,000)).

Example 2. Premium payments exceeding average premium for small group market. (i) *Facts.* Same facts as *Example* 1, except that the premiums are $6,000 for self-only coverage and $14,000 for family coverage. Employer's premium payments for each employee ($3,000 for self-only coverage and $7,000 for family coverage) exceed 50% of the average premium for the small group market in Employer's rating area ($2,500 for self-only coverage and $6,000 for family coverage).

(ii) *Conclusion.* The amount of premiums paid by Employer for purposes of computing the credit equals $40,000 ((4 × $2,500) plus (5 × $6,000)).

(c) *Credit phaseout*—(1) *In general.* The tax credit is subject to a reduction (but not reduced below zero) if the employer's FTEs exceed 10 or average annual FTE wages exceed $25,000. If the number of FTEs exceeds 10, the reduction is determined by multiplying the otherwise applicable credit amount by a fraction, the numerator of which is the number of FTEs in excess of 10 and the denominator of which is 15. If average annual FTE wages exceed $25,000, the reduction is determined by multiplying the otherwise applicable credit amount by a fraction, the numerator of which is the amount by which average annual FTE wages exceed $25,000 and the denominator of which is $25,000. In both cases, the result of the calculation is subtracted from the otherwise applicable credit to determine the credit to which the employer is entitled. For an employer with both more than 10 FTEs and average annual FTE wages exceeding $25,000, the total reduction is the sum of the two reductions.

(2) *$25,000 dollar amount adjusted for inflation.* For taxable years beginning in a calendar year after 2013, each reference to "$25,000" in paragraph (c)(1) of this section is replaced with a dollar amount equal to $25,000 multiplied by the cost-of-living adjustment under section 1(f)(3) for the calendar year, determined by substituting "calendar year 2012" for "calendar year 1992" in section 1(f)(3)(B).

(3) *Examples.* The following examples illustrate the provisions of paragraph (c) this section. For purposes of these examples, no employer is a tax-exempt organization and no other adjustments or limitations on the credit apply other than those adjustments and limitations explicitly set forth in the example.

Example 1. Calculating the maximum credit for an eligible small employer without an applicable credit phaseout. (i) *Facts.* An eligible small employer (Employer) has 9 FTEs with average annual wages of $23,000. Employer pays $72,000 in health insurance premiums for those employees (which does not exceed the total average premium for the small group market in the rating area), and otherwise meets the requirements for the credit.

(ii) *Conclusion.* Employer's credit equals $36,000 (50% × $72,000)

Example 2. Calculating the credit phaseout if the number of FTEs exceeds 10 or average annual wages exceed $25,000, as adjusted for inflation. (i) *Facts.* An eligible small employer (Employer) has 12 FTEs and average annual FTE wages of $30,000 in a year when the amount in paragraph (c)(1) of this section, as adjusted for inflation, is $25,000. Employer pays $96,000 in health insurance premiums for its employees (which does not exceed the average premium for the small group market in the rating area) and otherwise meets the requirements for the credit.

(ii) *Conclusion.* The initial amount of the credit is determined before any reduction (50% × $96,000) = $48,000. The credit reduction for FTEs in excess of 10 is $6,400 ($48,000 × 2/15). The credit reduction for average annual FTE wages in excess of $25,000 is $9,600 ($48,000 × $5,000/$25,000), resulting in a total credit reduction of $16,000 ($6,400 + $9,600). Employer's total tax credit equals $32,000 ($48,000-$16,000).

(d) *State credits and subsidies for health insurance*—(1) *Payments to employer.* If the employer is entitled to a State tax credit or a premium subsidy that is paid directly to the employer, the premium payment made by the employer is not reduced by the credit or subsidy for purposes of determining whether the employer has satisfied the requirement to pay an amount equal to a uniform percentage (not less than 50 percent) of the premium cost. Also, except as described in paragraph (d)(3) of this section, the maximum amount of the credit is not reduced by reason of a State tax credit or subsidy or by reason of payments by a State directly to an employer.

(2) *Payments to issuer.* If a State makes payments directly to an insurance company (or another entity licensed under State law to engage in the business of insurance) to pay a portion of the premium for coverage of an employee enrolled for coverage through a SHOP Exchange, the State is treated as making these payments on behalf of the employer for purposes of determining whether the employer has satisfied the requirement to pay an amount equal to a uniform percentage (not less than 50 percent) of the premium cost of coverage. Also, except as described below in paragraph (d)(3) of this section, these premium payments by the State are treated as an employer contribution under this section for purposes of calculating the credit.

(3) *Credits may not exceed net premium payment.* Regardless of the application of paragraphs (d)(1) and (d)(2) of this section, in no event may the amount of the credit exceed the amount of the employer's net premium payments as defined in § 1.45R-1(a)(11).

(4) *Examples.* The following examples illustrate the provisions of paragraphs (d)(1) through (d)(3) of this section. For purposes of these examples, the eligible small employer's taxable year and plan year begin during or after 2014. No other adjustments or limitations on the credit apply other than those adjustments and limitations explicitly set forth in the example.

Example 1. State premium subsidy paid directly to employer. (i) *Facts.* The State in which an eligible small employer (Employer) operates provides a health insurance premium subsidy of up to 40% of the health insurance premiums for each eligible employee. The State pays the subsidy directly to Employer. Employer has one employee, Employee D. Employee D's health insurance premiums are $100 per month and are paid as follows: $80 by Employer and $20 by Employee D through salary reductions to a cafeteria plan. The State pays Employer $40 per month as a subsidy for Employer's payment of insurance premiums on behalf of Employee D. Employer is otherwise an eligible small employer that meets the requirements for the credit.

(ii) *Conclusion.* For purposes of calculating the credit, the amount of premiums paid by the employer is $80 per month (the premium payment by the Employer without regard to the subsidy from the State). The maximum credit is $40 ($80 × 50%).

Example 2. State premium subsidy paid directly to insurance company. (i) *Facts.* The State in which Employer operates provides a health insurance premium subsidy of up to 30% for each eligible employee. Employer has one employee, Employee E. Employee E is enrolled in self-only coverage through a qualified health plan (QHP) offered by Employer through a SHOP Exchange. Employee E's health insurance premiums are $100 per month and are paid as follows: $50 by Employer; $30 by the State and $20 by the employee. The State pays the $30 per month directly to the insurance company and the insurance company bills Employer for the employer and employee's share, which equal $70 per month. Employer is otherwise an eligible small employer that meets the requirements for the credit.

(ii) *Conclusion.* For purposes of calculating the amount of the credit, the amount of premiums paid by Employer is $80 per month (the sum of Employer's payment and the State's payment). The maximum credit is $40 ($80 × 50%).

Example 3. Credit limited by employer's net premium payment. (i) *Facts.* Employer is an eligible small employer that is not a tax-exempt organization. The State in which Employer operates provides a health insurance premium subsidy of up to 50% for each eligible employee. Employer has one employee, Employee F. Employee F is enrolled in self-only coverage under the QHP offered to Employee F by Employer through a SHOP Exchange. Employee F's health insurance premiums are $100 per month and are paid as follows: $20 by Employer; $50 by the State and $30 by Employee F. The State pays the $50 per month directly to the insurance company and the insurance company bills Employer for the employer's and employee's shares, which total $50 per month. Employer is otherwise an eligible small employer that meets the requirements for the credit. The amount of premiums paid by Employer (the sum of Employer's payment and the State's payment) is $70 per month, which is more than 50% of the $100 monthly premium payment. The amount of the premium for calculating the credit is also $70 per month.

(ii) *Conclusion.* The maximum credit without adjustments or limitations is $35 ($70 × 50%). Employer's net premium payment is $20 (the amount actually paid by Employer excluding the State subsidy). Be-

cause the credit may not exceed Employer's net premium payment, the credit is $20 (the lesser of $35 or $20).

(e) *Payroll tax limitation for tax-exempt eligible small employers*—(1) *In general.* For a tax-exempt eligible employer, the amount of the credit claimed cannot exceed the total amount of payroll taxes (as defined in § 1.45R-1(a)(13)) of the employer during the calendar year in which the taxable year begins.

(2) *Example.* The following example illustrates the provisions of paragraph (e)(1) of this section. For purposes of this example, the eligible small employer's taxable year and plan year begin during or after 2014. No other adjustments or limitations on the credit apply other than those adjustments and limitations explicitly set forth in the example.

Example. Calculating the maximum credit for a tax-exempt eligible small employer. (i) *Facts.* Employer is a tax-exempt eligible small employer that has 10 FTEs with average annual wages of $21,000. Employer pays $80,000 in health insurance premiums for its employees (which does not exceed the average premium for the small group market in the rating area) and otherwise meets the requirements for the credit. The total amount of Employer's payroll taxes equals $30,000.

(ii) *Conclusion.* The initial amount of the credit is determined before any reduction: (35% × $80,000) = $28,000, and Employer's payroll taxes are $30,000. The total tax credit equals $28,000 (the lesser of $28,000 and $30,000).

(f) *Two-consecutive-taxable year credit period limitation.* The credit is only available to an eligible small employer, including a tax-exempt eligible small employer, during that employer's credit period. For a transition rule for 2014, see paragraph (i) of this section. To prevent the avoidance of the two-year limit on the credit period through the use of successor entities, a successor entity and a predecessor entity are treated as the same employer. For this purpose, the rules for identifying successor entities under § 31.3121(a)(1)-1(b) apply. Accordingly, for example, if an eligible small employer claims the credit for the 2014 and 2015 taxable years, that eligible small employer's credit period will have expired so that any successor employer to that eligible small employer will not be able to claim the credit for any subsequent taxable years.

(g) *Premium payments by the employer for a taxable year*—(1) *In general.* Only premiums paid by an eligible small employer or tax-exempt eligible small employer on behalf of each employee enrolled in a QHP or payments paid to the issuer in accordance with paragraph (d)(2) of this section are counted in calculating the credit. If an eligible small employer pays only a portion of the premiums for the coverage provided to employees (with employees paying the rest), only the portion paid by the employer is taken into account. Premiums paid on behalf of seasonal workers may be counted in determining the amount of the credit (even though seasonal worker wages and hours of service are not included in the FTE and average annual FTE wage calculation unless the seasonal worker works for the employer on more than 120 days during the taxable year).

(2) *Excluded amounts*—(i) *Salary reduction amounts.* Any premium paid pursuant to a salary reduction arrangement under a section 125 cafeteria plan is not treated as paid by the employer for purposes of section 45R and these regulations. For this purpose, premiums paid with employer-provided flex credits that employees may elect to receive as cash or other taxable benefit are treated as paid pursuant to a salary reduction arrangement under a section 125 cafeteria plan.

(ii) *HSAs, HRAs, and FSAs.* Employer contributions to, or amounts made available under, health savings accounts, reimbursement arrangements, and health flexible spending arrangements are not taken into account in determining the premium payments by the employer for a taxable year.

(h) *Rules applicable to trusts, estates, regulated investment companies, real estate investment trusts and cooperative organizations.* Rules similar to the rules of section 52(d) and (e) and the regulations thereunder apply in calculating and apportioning the credit with respect to a trust, estate, a regulated investment company or real estate investment trusts or cooperative organization.

(i) *Transition rule for 2014*—(1) *In general.* This paragraph (i) applies if as of August 26, 2013 an eligible small employer offers coverage on a plan year that begins on a date other than the first day of its taxable year. In such a case, if an eligible small employer has a health plan year beginning after January 1, 2014 but before January 1, 2015 (2014 health plan year) that begins after the start of its first taxable year beginning after January 1, 2014 (2014 taxable year), and the employer offers one or more QHPs to its employees through a SHOP Exchange as of the first day of its 2014 health plan year, then the eligible small employer is treated as offering coverage through a SHOP Exchange for its entire 2014 taxable year for purposes of section 45R if the health care coverage provided from the first day of the 2014 taxable year through the day immediately preceding the first day of the 2014 health plan year would have qualified for a credit under section 45R using the rules applicable to taxable years beginning before January 1, 2014. If the eligible small employer claims the section 45R credit in the 2014 taxable year, the 2014 taxable year begins the first year of the credit period.

(2) *Example.* The following example illustrates the rule of paragraph (i) of this section. For purposes of this example, the eligible small employer is not a tax-exempt organization. No other adjustments or limitations on the credit apply other than those adjustments and limitations explicitly set forth in the example.

Example. (i) *Facts.* An eligible small employer (Employer) has a 2014 taxable year that begins January 1, 2014 and ends on December 31, 2014, and a 2014 health plan year that begins July 1, 2014 and ends June 30, 2015. Employer offers a QHP through a SHOP Exchange the coverage under which begins July 1, 2014. Employer provides coverage from January 1, 2014 through June 30, 2014 that would have qualified for a credit under section 45R using the rules applicable to taxable years beginning before January 1, 2014.

(ii) *Conclusion.* Employer may claim the credit at the 50% rate under section 45R for the entire 2014 taxable year using the rules under paragraph (i) of this section. Accordingly, in calculating the credit, Employer may count premiums paid for coverage from January 1, 2014 through June 30, 2014, as well as premiums paid from July 1, 2014 through December 31, 2014. If Employer claims the credit for the 2014 taxable year, that taxable year is the first year of the credit period.

(j) *Effective/applicability date.* This section is applicable for periods after December 31, 2013.

§ 1.45R-4 Uniform percentage of premium paid.

(a) *In general.* An eligible small employer must pay a uniform percentage (not less than 50 percent) of the premium for each employee enrolled in a qualified health plan (QHP) offered to employees by the employer through a small business health options program (SHOP) Exchange.

(b) *Employers offering one QHP.* An employer that offers a single QHP through a SHOP Exchange must satisfy the requirements of this paragraph (b).

(1) *Employers offering one QHP, self-only coverage, composite billing.* For an eligible small employer offering self-only coverage and using composite billing, the employer satisfies the requirements of this paragraph if it pays the same amount toward the premium for each employee receiving self-only coverage under the QHP, and that amount is equal to at least 50 percent of the premium for self-only coverage.

(2) *Employers offering one QHP, other tiers of coverage, composite billing.* For an eligible small employer offering one QHP providing at least one tier of coverage with a higher premium than self-only coverage and using composite billing, the employer satisfies the requirements of this paragraph (b)(2) if it either—

(i) Pays an amount for each employee enrolled in that more expensive tier of coverage that is the same for all employees and that is no less than the amount that the employer would have contributed toward self-only coverage for that employee, or

(ii) Meets the requirements of paragraph (b)(1) of this section for each tier of coverage that if offers.

(3) *Employers offering one QHP, self-only coverage, list billing.* For an eligible small employer offering one QHP providing only self-only coverage and using list billing, the employer satisfies the requirements of this paragraph (b)(3) if either—

(i) The employer pays toward the premium an amount equal to a uniform percentage (not less than 50 percent) of the premium charged for each employee, or

(ii) The employer converts the individual premiums for self-only coverage into an employer-computed composite rate for self-only coverage, and, if an employee contribution is required, each employee who receives coverage under the QHP pays a uniform amount toward the self-only premium that is no more than 50 percent of the employer-computed composite rate for self-only coverage.

(4) *Employers offering one QHP, other tiers of coverage, list billing.* For an eligible small employer offering one QHP providing at least one tier of coverage with a higher premium than self-only coverage and using list billing, the employer satisfies the requirements of this paragraph (b)(4) if it either—

(i) Pays toward the premium for each employee covered under each tier of coverage an amount equal to or exceeding the amount that the employer would have contributed with respect to that employee for self-only coverage, calculated either based upon the actual premium that would have been charged by the insurer for that employee for self-only coverage or based upon the employer-computed composite rate for self-only coverage, or

(ii) Meets the requirements of paragraph (b)(3) of this section for each tier of coverage that it offers substituting the employer-computed composite rate for each tier of coverage for the employer-computed composite rate for self-only coverage.

(c) *Employers offering more than one QHP.* If an eligible small employer offers more than one QHP, the employer must satisfy the requirements of this paragraph (c). The employer may satisfy the requirements of this paragraph (c) in either of the following two ways:

(1) *QHP-by-QHP method.* The employer makes payments toward the premium with respect to each QHP for which the employer is claiming the credit that satisfy the uniform percentage requirement under paragraph (b) of this section on a QHP-by-QHP basis (so that the amounts or percentages of premium paid by the employer for each QHP need not be identical, but the payments with respect to each QHP must satisfy paragraph (b) of this section); or

(2) *Reference QHP method.* The employer designates a reference QHP and makes employer contributions in accordance with the following requirements—

(i) The employer determines a level of employer contributions for each employee such that, if all eligible employees enrolled in the reference QHP, the contributions would satisfy the uniform percentage requirement under paragraph (b) of this section, or

(ii) The employer allows each employee to apply the minimum amount of employer contribution determined necessary to meet the uniform percentage requirement under paragraph (b) of this section either toward the reference QHP or toward the cost of coverage under any of the other available QHPs.

(d) *Special rules regarding employer compliance with applicable State or local law.* An employer will be treated as satisfying the uniform percentage requirement if the failure to otherwise satisfy the uniform percentage requirement is attributable solely to additional employer contributions made to certain employees to comply with an applicable State or local law.

(e) *Examples.* The following examples illustrate the provisions of paragraphs (a) through (d) of this section:

Example 1. (i) *Facts.* An eligible small employer (Employer) offers a QHP on a SHOP Exchange, Plan A, which uses composite billing. The premiums for Plan A are $5,000 per year for self-only coverage, and $10,000 for family coverage. Employees can elect self-only or family coverage under Plan A. Employer pays $3,000 (60% of the premium) toward self-only coverage under Plan A and $6,000 (60% of the premium) toward family coverage under Plan A.

(ii) *Conclusion.* Employer's contributions of 60% of the premium for each tier of coverage satisfy the uniform percentage requirement.

Example 2. (i) *Facts.* Same facts as *Example 1*, except that Employer pays $3,000 (60% of the premium) for each employee electing self-only coverage under Plan A and pays $3,000 (30% of the premium) for each employee electing family coverage under Plan A.

(ii) *Conclusion.* Employer's contributions of 60% of the premium toward self-only coverage and the same dollar amount toward the premium for family coverage satisfy the uniform percentage requirement, even though the percentage is not the same.

Example 3. (i) *Facts.* Employer offers two QHPs, Plan A and Plan B, both of which use composite billing. The premiums for Plan A are $5,000 per year for self-only coverage and $10,000 for family coverage. The premiums for Plan B are $7,000 per year for self-only coverage and $13,000 for family coverage. Employees can elect self-only or family coverage under either Plan A or Plan B. Employer pays $3,000 (60% of the premium) for each employee electing self-only coverage under Plan A, $3,000 (30% of the premium) for each employee electing family coverage under Plan A, $3,500 (50% of the premium) for each employee electing self-only coverage under Plan B, and $3,500 (27% of the premium) for each employee electing family coverage under Plan B.

(ii) *Conclusion.* Employer's contributions of 60% (or $3,000) of the premiums for self-only coverage and the same dollar amounts toward the premium for family coverage under Plan A, and of 50% (or $3,500) of the premium for self-only of coverage and the same dollar amount toward the premium for family coverage under Plan B, satisfy the uniform percentage requirement on a QHP-by-QHP basis; therefore the employer's contributions to both plans satisfy the uniform percentage requirement.

Example 4. (i) *Facts.* Same facts as *Example 3,* except that Employer designates Plan A as the reference QHP. Employer pays $2,500 (50% of the premium) for each employee electing self-only coverage under Plan A and pays $2,500 of the premium for each employee electing family coverage under Plan A or either self-only or family coverage under Plan B.

(ii) *Conclusion.* Employer's contribution of 50% (or $2,500) toward the premium of each employee enrolled under Plan A or Plan B satisfies the uniform percentage requirement.

Example 5. (i) *Facts.* Employer receives a list billing premium quote with respect to Plan X, a QHP offered by Employer on a SHOP Exchange for health insurance coverage for each of Employer's four employees. For Employee L, age 20, the self-only premium is $3,000 per year, and the family premium is $8,000. For Employees M, N and O, each age 40, the self-only premium is $5,000 per year and the family premium is $10,000. The total self-only premium for the four employees is $18,000 ($3,000 + (3 × 5,000)). Employer calculates an employer-computed composite self-only rate of $4,500 ($18,000/4). Employer offers to make contributions such that each employee would need to pay $2,000 of the premium for self-only coverage. Under this arrangement, Employer would contribute $1,000 toward self-only coverage for L and $3,000 toward self-only coverage for M, N, and O. In the event an employee elects family coverage, Employer would make the same contribution ($1,000 for L or $3,000 for M, N, or O) toward the family premium.

(ii) *Conclusion.* Employer satisfies the uniform percentage requirement because it offers and makes contributions based on an employer-calculated composite self-only rate such that, to receive self-only coverage, each employee must pay a uniform amount which is not more than 50% of the composite rate, and it allows employees to use the same employer contributions toward family coverage.

Example 6. (i) *Facts.* Same facts as *Example 5,* except that Employer calculates an employer-computed composite family rate of $9,500 (($8,000 + 3 × 10,000)/4) and requires each employee to pay $4,000 of the premium for family coverage.

(ii) *Conclusion.* Employer satisfies the uniform percentage requirement because it offers and makes contributions based on a calculated self-only and family rate such that, to receive either self-only or family coverage, each employee must pay a uniform amount which is not more than 50% of the composite rate for coverage of that tier.

Example 7. (i) *Facts.* Same facts as *Example 5,* except that Employer also receives a list billing premium quote from Plan Y with respect to a second QHP offered by Employer on a SHOP Exchange for each of Employer's 4 employees. Plan Y's quote for Employee L, age 20, is $4,000 per year for self-only coverage or $12,000 per year for family coverage. For Employees M, N and O, each age 40, the premium is $7,000 per year for self-only coverage or $15,000 per year for family coverage. The total self-only premium under Plan Y is $25,000 ($4,000 + (3 × 7,000)). The employer-computed composite self-only rate is $6,250 ($25,000/4). Employer designates Plan X as the reference plan. Employer offers to make contributions based on the employer-calculated composite premium for the reference QHP (Plan X) such that each employee has to contribute $2,000 to receive self-only coverage through Plan X. Under this arrangement, Employer would contribute $1,000 toward self-only coverage for L and $3,000 toward self-only coverage for M, N, and O. In the event an employee elects family coverage through Plan X or either self-only or family coverage through Plan Y, Employer would make the same contributions ($1,000 for L or $3,000 for M, N, or O) toward that coverage.

(ii) *Conclusion.* Employer satisfies the uniform percentage requirement because it offers and makes contributions based on the employer-calculated composite self-only premium for the Plan X reference QHP such that, in order to receive self-only coverage, each employee must pay a uniform amount which is not more than 50% of the self-only composite premium of the reference QHP; it allows employees to use the same employer contributions toward family coverage in the reference QHP or coverage through another QHPs.

Example 8. (i) *Facts.* Employer has five employees. Employer is located in a State that requires employers to pay 50% of employees' premium costs, but also requires that an employee's contribution not exceed a certain percentage of the employee's monthly gross earnings from that employer. Employer offers to pay 50% of the premium costs for all its employees, and to comply with the State law, Employer contributes more than 50% of the premium costs for two of its employees.

(ii) *Conclusion.* Employer satisfies the uniform percentage requirement because its failure to otherwise satisfy the uniform percentage requirement is attributable solely to compliance with the applicable State or local law.

(f) *Effective/applicability date.* This section is applicable for periods after December 31, 2013.

§ 1.45R-5 Claiming the credit.

(a) *Claiming the credit.* The credit is a general business credit and is claimed on an eligible small employer's annual income tax return and offsets an employer's actual tax liability for the year. The credit is claimed by attaching Form 8941, "Credit for Small Employer Health Insurance Premiums," to the eligible small employer's income tax return or, in the case of a tax-exempt eligible small employer, by attaching Form 8941 to the employer's Form 990-T, "Exempt Organization Business Income Tax Return." To claim the credit, a tax-exempt eligible small employer must file a form 990-T with an attached Form 8941, even if a Form 990-T would not otherwise be required to be filed.

(b) *Estimated tax payments and alternative minimum tax (AMT) liability.* An eligible small employer may reflect the credit in determining estimated tax payments for the year in which the credit applies in accordance with the estimated tax rules as set forth in section 6654 and 6655 and the applicable regulations. An eligible small employer may also use the credit to offset the employer's alternative minimum tax (AMT) liability for the year, if any, subject to certain limitations based on the amount of an eligible small employer's regular tax liability, AMT liability and other allowable credits. See section 38(c)(1), as modified by section 38(c)(4)(B)(vi). However, an eligible small employer, including a tax-exempt eligible small employer, may not reduce its deposits and payments of employment tax (that is, income tax required to be withheld under section 3402, social security and Medicare tax under sections 3101 and 3111, and federal unemployment tax under section 3301) during the year in anticipation of the credit.

(c) *Reduction of section 162 deduction.* No deduction under section 162 is allowed for the eligible small employer for that portion of the health insurance premiums that is equal to the amount of the credit under § 1.45R-2.

(d) *Effective/applicability date.* This section is applicable for periods after December 31, 2013.

Heather C. Maloy,

Acting Deputy Commissioner for Services and Enforcement.

[FR Doc. 2013-20769 Filed 8-23-13; 8:45 am]

BILLING CODE 4830-01-P

¶ 20,263Q

IRS: Filing requirements: Retirement plans: Magnetic media: Electronic filing: Form 8955-SSA: Form 5500 series: Schedule SB: Schedule MB.—The IRS has issued proposed regulations that require the filing of certain retirement plan statements, returns, and reports under Code Sec. 6057, Code Sec. 6058, and Code Sec. 6059 (i.e., Form 8955-SSA, Form 5500 series, and Schedule SB and Schedule MB) on magnetic media. The term "magnetic media" includes electronic filing, as well as other magnetic media specifically permitted by the IRS. The proposed regulations provide that a plan administrator (or, in certain situations, an employer maintaining a plan) required to file at least 250 returns during the calendar year that includes the first day of the plan year must use magnetic media to file statements, returns, and reports under Code Sec. 6057, Code Sec. 6058, and Code Sec. 6059. The determination of whether a filer is required to file at least 250 returns is made by aggregating all returns, regardless of type, that the filer is required to file. These regulations are proposed to apply for retirement plan statements, notifications, returns, and reports required to be filed under Code Sec. 6057, Code Sec. 6058, and Code Sec. 6059 for plan years that begin on or after January 1, 2014, but only for filings with a filing deadline (not taking into account extensions) after December 31, 2014.

The proposed regulations were published in the Federal Register on August 30, 2013 (78 FR 53704). The regulations were finalized on September 29, 2014 (79 FR 58256). The preamble to the final regulations is at ¶ 23,308. The final regulations are at ¶ 13,735, ¶ 13,746, and ¶ 13,750G.

DEPARTMENT OF THE TREASURY

Internal Revenue Service

26 CFR Part 301

[REG-111837-13]

RIN 1545-BL54

Employee Retirement Benefit Plan Returns Required on Magnetic Media

AGENCY: Internal Revenue Service (IRS), Treasury.

ACTION: Notice of proposed rulemaking.

SUMMARY: This document contains proposed regulations relating to the requirements for filing certain employee retirement benefit plan statements, returns, and reports on magnetic media. The term magnetic media includes electronic filing, as well as other magnetic media specifically permitted under applicable regulations, revenue procedures, publications, forms, instructions, or other guidance on the IRS.gov Internet Web site. These regulations would affect plan administrators and employers maintaining retirement plans that are subject to various employee benefit reporting requirements under the Internal Revenue Code (Code).

DATES: Comments and requests for a public hearing must be received by October 29, 2013.

ADDRESSES: Send submissions relating to the proposed regulations to: CC:PA:LPD:PR (REG-111837-13), room 5205, Internal Revenue Service, PO Box 7604, Ben Franklin Station, Washington DC, 20044. Submissions may be hand delivered Monday through Friday, between the hours of 8 a.m. and 4 p.m. to CC:PA:LPD:PR (REG-111837-13), Courier's Desk, Internal Revenue Service, 1111 Constitution Avenue NW., Washington, DC.

Alternately, taxpayers may submit comments relating to the proposed regulations electronically via the Federal eRulemaking Portal at *www.regulations.gov* (IRS REG-111837-13).

FOR FURTHER INFORMATION CONTACT: Concerning the proposed regulations, William Gibbs or Pamela Kinard at (202) 622-6060; concerning the submission of comments or to request a public hearing, Oluwafunmilayo Taylor at (202) 622-7180 (not toll-free numbers).

SUPPLEMENTARY INFORMATION:

Background

Electronic filing of tax returns benefits taxpayers and the IRS by reducing errors that are more likely to occur during the manual preparation and processing of paper returns. Electronic filing results in faster settling of accounts and better customer service. Requiring that employee retirement benefit plan statements, returns, and reports be filed electronically improves the timeliness and accuracy of the information for both the public and the employee retirement benefit plan community.

Section 6011(e)(1) authorizes the Secretary to prescribe regulations providing the standards for determining which returns must be filed on magnetic media or in other machine-readable form. Section 6011(e)(2)(A) provides that the Secretary may not require any person to file returns on magnetic media unless the person is required to file at least 250 returns during the calendar year. Section 6011(e)(2)(B) requires that the Secretary, prior to issuing regulations requiring these entities to file returns on magnetic media, take into account (among other relevant factors) the ability of the taxpayer to comply at reasonable cost with the requirements of such regulations.

A statement, return, or report filed electronically with an electronic return transmitter in the manner and time prescribed by the Commissioner is deemed to be filed on the date of the electronic postmark given by the return transmitter (that is, a record of the date and time that an authorized electronic return transmitter receives the transmission of a taxpayer's electronically filed document on its host system). Accordingly, if the electronic postmark is timely, the document is considered filed timely although it is received by the IRS after the last date prescribed for filing. See § 301.7502-1(d). Section 414(g) defines a plan administrator as a person specifically so designated by the terms of the plan or, in the event no one is designated: (a) An employer for a single employer plan; (b) an association, committee, joint board of trustees, or other similar group of representatives for a plan maintained by two or more employers or jointly by one or more employers and one or more employee organizations; or (c) such other person as the Secretary of Treasury may prescribe in regulations.

Section 6057(a) requires the plan administrator (within the meaning of section 414(g)) of each plan to which the vesting standards of section 203 of the Employee Retirement Income Security Act of 1974 (ERISA) applies for a plan year to file, within the time prescribed by regulations, a registration statement with the Secretary of the Treasury. The registration statement must set forth the following information relating to the plan: (1) The name of the plan; (2) the name and address of the plan administrator; (3) the name and identifying information of plan participants who separated from service covered by the plan and are entitled to deferred vested retirement benefits; and (4) the nature, amount, and form of deferred vested retirement benefits to which the plan participants are entitled. The form used to file this registration statement is Form 8955-SSA, "Annual Registration Statement Identifying Separated Participants with Deferred Vested Benefits." Section 6057(b) requires that the plan administrator notify the Secretary of certain changes in the plan, including the name of the plan, the name and address of the plan administrator, the termination of the plan, or any merger or consolidation of the plan with another plan (or the plan's division into two or more plans).

Section 6058(a) generally requires that every employer maintaining a pension, annuity, stock bonus, profit-sharing, or other funded plan of deferred compensation, or the plan administrator within the meaning of section 414(g) of the plan, file an annual return stating such information as the Secretary may by regulations prescribe with respect to the qualification, financial condition, and operations of the plan. The reporting requirement under section 6058(a) is satisfied by filing a return on the Form 5500 series. The Form 5500, "Annual Return/Report of Employee Benefit Plan," the Form 5500-SF, "Short Form Annual Return/Report of Small Employee Benefit Plan," and Form 5500-EZ, "Annual Return of One-Participant (Owners and Their Spouses) Retirement Plan," make up the Form 5500 series.

Section 6059(a) generally requires that a plan administrator of each defined benefit plan to which section 412 applies file the actuarial report described in section 6059(b) for the first plan year for which section 412 applies to the plan and for each third plan year thereafter (or more frequently if the Secretary determines that more frequent reports are necessary). The schedules used to file these actuarial reports are the Schedule SB, "Single-Employer Defined Benefit Plan Actuarial Information," and the Schedule MB, "Multiemployer Defined Benefit Plan and Certain Money Purchase Plan Actuarial Information," which are required to be filed as part of the Form 5500 or Form 5500-SF.

On July 21, 2006, the Department of Labor (DOL) published a final rule in the **Federal Register** (71 FR 41359) requiring electronic filing of the Form 5500 and Form 5500-SF for plans covered by Title I of ERISA for plan years beginning on or after January 1, 2008. On November 16, 2007, the DOL published a final rule in the **Federal Register** (72 FR 64710) postponing the effective date of the electronic filing mandate so that the mandate applies to plan years beginning on or after January 1, 2009. See 29 CFR § 2520.104a-2. The electronic filing system mandated by DOL is the computerized ERISA Filing Acceptance System (EFAST2).

Filers of the Form 5500 and Form 5500-SF are required to file electronically through EFAST2. Currently, electronic filing is not available for the Form 5500-EZ. However, certain filers that would otherwise file the Form 5500-EZ on paper may instead file the Form 5500-SF electronically through EFAST2. Under the current requirements, plans that are eligible to use the Form 5500-SF to file electronically include plans that cover fewer than 100 participants at the beginning of the plan year and satisfy certain other requirements. See the Instructions to the Form 5500-EZ for information about filing the Form 5500-EZ.

In order to implement DOL's mandate for electronic filing of the Form 5500 and Form 5500-SF, certain items on these forms that relate solely to Code requirements were eliminated. Information on the forms, schedules, and attachments that were eliminated was used by the IRS for compliance purposes. By mandating electronic filing of information, the IRS can obtain valuable plan information that is not currently required to be filed through EFAST2.[1] In coordination with DOL, the IRS anticipates adding items on the Form 5500 and Form 5500-SF relating solely to Code requirements. For those filers that are not subject to IRS electronic filing requirements, the IRS plans to

---

[1] In its published report on September 20, 2011, the Treasury Inspector General for Tax Administration (TIGTA) recommended that the IRS explore regulatory options for mandating electronic filings of annual employee benefit returns for employee benefit retirement plans. TIGTA believed that this would assist the IRS in satisfying its tax administration responsibilities. See "The Employee Plans Function Should Continue Its Efforts to Obtain Needed Retirement Plan Information," Reference Number 3011-10-108 (September 20, 2011).

provide a paper-only form containing those Code-related items and an alternative method of filing with the IRS.

Explanation of Provisions

I. In General

These regulations provide that a plan administrator (or, in certain situations, an employer maintaining a plan) required by the Code or regulations to file at least 250 returns during the calendar year that includes the first day of the plan year must use magnetic media to file certain statements, returns, and reports under sections 6057, 6058, and 6059. Magnetic media is defined as electronic filing or other media specifically permitted under applicable regulations, revenue procedures, publications, forms, instructions, or other guidance on the IRS.gov Internet Web site. (See § 601.601(d)(2)(ii)(b) of this chapter.)

Filers of the Form 5500 and Form 5500-SF are already required to file the returns electronically through EFAST2. In addition, many filers of the Form 8955-SSA already voluntarily file electronically with the IRS and also are required to file the Form 5500 and Form 5500-SF electronically through EFAST2. The IRS and the Treasury Department have determined that taxpayers should be able to comply at a reasonable cost with the requirement to file statements, returns, and reports on magnetic media.

The determination of whether a filer is required to file at least 250 returns is made by aggregating all returns, regardless of type, that the filer is required to file, including for example, income tax returns, returns required under section 6033, information returns, excise tax returns, and employment tax returns.

II. Registration Statements and Notifications Required Under Section 6057(a) and (b)

The proposed regulations under section 6057 provide that a registration statement under section 6057(a) or notification required under section 6057(b) must be filed on magnetic media if the filer is required by the Code or regulations to file at least 250 returns during the calendar year that includes the first day of the plan year. For purposes of the regulations under section 6057, the term filer means the plan administrator within the meaning of section 414(g).

The proposed regulations under section 6057 provide that if a filer that is required to file electronically fails to do so, the filer is deemed to have failed to file the registration statement or other notification required under section 6057. Section 6652(d)(1) imposes a penalty on the plan administrator for the failure to file a registration statement required under section 6057(a). Section 6652(d)(2) imposes a penalty on the plan administrator for the failure to file a notification required under section 6057(b). The proposed regulations under section 6057 provide that rules under § 301.6652-3(b) apply for purposes of determining whether there is reasonable cause for failure to file a registration statement required under section 6057(a) or notification required under section 6057(b). In addition, rules similar to the rules in § 301.6724-1(c)(3)(ii), regarding undue economic hardship relating to filing on magnetic media, will apply.

III. Form 5500 Series

The proposed regulations under section 6058 provide that a return required under section 6058 must be filed on magnetic media if the filer is required by the Code or regulations to file at least 250 returns during the calendar year that includes the first day of the plan year. The term filer means the employer or employers maintaining the plan and the plan administrator within the meaning of section 414(g). Thus, in applying the 250-return requirement, the returns of the employer or employers maintaining the plan and of the plan administrator are aggregated.

The proposed regulations under section 6058 also provide that, in determining the 250-return requirement, the aggregation rules of section 414(b), (c), (m), and (o) apply to a filer that is, or includes, an employer. Thus, for example, a filer that is a member of a controlled group of corporations within the meaning of section 414(b) must file the Form 5500 series on magnetic media if the aggregate number of returns required to be filed by the controlled group of corporations is at least 250. These aggregation rules also apply to the regulations under sections 6057 and 6059 if the plan administrator is the employer.

The proposed regulations under section 6058 provide that if the filer is required to file electronically but fails to do so, the filer is deemed to have failed to file the Form 5500 series. For a failure to file the Form 5500 series, a penalty under section 6652(e) applies. The proposed regulations under section 6058 provide that rules under § 301.6652-3(b) apply for purposes of determining whether there is reasonable cause for failure to file a return. In addition, rules similar to the rules in § 301.6724-1(c)(3)(ii), regarding undue economic hardship relating to filing on magnetic media, will apply.

IV. Actuarial Reports

The proposed regulations under section 6059 provide that an actuarial report required under section 6059 must be filed on magnetic media if the filer is required by the Code or regulations to file at least 250 returns during the calendar year that includes the first day of the plan year. For purposes of the regulations under section 6059, the term filer means the plan administrator within the meaning of section 414(g).

The proposed regulations under section 6059 provide that if a filer that is required to file electronically fails to do so, the filer is deemed to have failed to file the actuarial report required under section 6059. Section 6692 provides that a plan administrator that fails to file the report required under section 6059 shall pay a penalty for each such failure, unless it is shown that there is reasonable cause for the failure. The proposed regulations under section 6059 provide that rules under § 301.6692-1(c) apply for purposes of determining whether there is reasonable cause for failure to file an actuarial report. In addition, rules similar to the rules in § 301.6724-1(c)(3)(ii), regarding undue economic hardship relating to filing on magnetic media, will apply.

V. Economic Hardship Waiver

These proposed regulations also provide that the Commissioner may waive the requirement to file electronically in cases of undue economic hardship. Because the Treasury Department and the IRS believe that electronic filing will not impose significant burdens on the taxpayers covered by these regulations, the Commissioner anticipates granting waivers of the electronic filing requirement in only exceptional cases. Waivers are anticipated to be particularly rare for the filers of Form 5500 and Form 5500-SF (as well as the schedules attached to those forms), because these filers are already required to file electronically under EFAST2.

Proposed Effective Date

These regulations are proposed to apply for employee retirement benefit plan statements, notifications, returns, and reports required to be filed under sections 6057, 6058, and 6059 for plan years that begin on or after January 1, 2014, but only for filings with a filing deadline (not taking into account extensions) after December 31, 2014.

Special Analyses

It has been determined that this notice of proposed rulemaking is not a significant regulatory action as defined in Executive Order 12866. Therefore, a regulatory assessment is not required. It has also been determined that 5 U.S.C. 533(b) of the Administrative Procedure Act (5 U.S.C. chapter 5) does not apply to these regulations. In addition, it is hereby certified that any collection of information contained in this regulation will not have a significant economic impact on a substantial number of small entities, and therefore no flexibility analysis under the Regulatory Flexibility Act (5 U.S.C. chapter 6) is required. Pursuant to section 7805(f) of the Internal Revenue Code, these regulations have been submitted to the Office of Chief Counsel for Advocacy of the Small Business Administration for comments on its impact on small businesses.

The certification is based on the fact that §§ 301.6057-1, 301.6058-1, and 301.6059-1 currently require filing with the IRS of information under sections 6057, 6058, and 6059 in accordance with applicable forms, schedules, and accompanying instructions. These proposed regulations merely require that this information be filed electronically by persons required to file at least 250 returns for the calendar year, consistent with section 6011(e)(2)(A), which provides that, in prescribing regulations providing standards for determining which returns must be filed on magnetic media or in other machine-readable form, the Secretary shall not require any person to file returns on magnetic media unless the person is required to file at least 250 returns during the calendar year. Many small entities are unlikely to file 250 returns or more during the calendar year. Filers of the Form 5500 and Form 5500-SF are already required to file the returns electronically through EFAST2 pursuant to DOL regulations. In addition, many filers of the Form 8955-SSA already voluntarily file electronically with the IRS.

Further, if a taxpayer's operations are computerized, reporting in accordance with the regulations should be less costly than filing on paper. The IRS and the Treasury Department have determined that taxpayers should be able to comply at a reasonable cost with the requirement in these regulations to file employee retirement statements, returns, and reports on magnetic media. In addition, the proposed regulations provide that the IRS may waive the electronic filing requirements upon a showing of hardship.

Comments and Requests for Public Hearing

Before these proposed regulations are adopted as final regulations, consideration will be given to any comments that are submitted timely to the IRS as prescribed in this preamble under the " **ADDRESSES**" heading. The IRS and the Treasury Department request comments on all aspects of the rules. All comments are available at *www.regulations.gov* or upon request. A public hearing will be scheduled if requested in writing by any person who timely submits written comments. If a public hearing is scheduled, notice of the date, time, and place of the public hearing will be published in the **Federal Register**.

Drafting Information

The principal authors of these regulations are William Gibbs and Pamela R. Kinard, Office of Division Counsel/Associate Chief Counsel (Tax Exempt and Government Entities). However, other personnel from the IRS and the Treasury Department participated in the development of these regulations.

List of Subjects in 26 CFR Part 301

Administrative practice and procedure, Alimony, Bankruptcy, Child support, Continental shelf, Courts, Crime, Employment taxes, Estate taxes, Excise taxes, Gift taxes, Income taxes, Investigations, Law enforcement, Oil pollution, Penalties, Pensions, Reporting and recordkeeping requirements, Seals and insignia, Statistics and taxes.

Proposed Amendments to the Regulations

Accordingly, 26 CFR part 301 is proposed to be amended as follows:

PART 301—PROCEDURE AND ADMINISTRATION

■ **Paragraph 1.** The authority for part 301 continues to read in part as follows:

Authority: 26 U.S.C. 7508 * * *

■ **Par. 2.** Section 301.6057-3 is added to read as follows:

§ 301.6057-3 Required use of magnetic media for filing requirements relating to deferred vested retirement benefit.

(a) *Magnetic media filing requirements under section 6057.* A registration statement required under section 6057(a) or a notification required under section 6057(b) with respect to an employee benefit plan must be filed on magnetic media if the filer is required by the Internal Revenue Code or regulations to file at least 250 returns during the calendar year ending with or within the plan year. Returns filed on magnetic media must be made in accordance with applicable revenue procedures, publications, forms, instructions, or other guidance on the IRS.gov Internet Web site. In prescribing revenue procedures, publications, forms, instructions, or other guidance on the IRS.gov Internet Web site, the Commissioner may direct the type of magnetic media filing. (See § 601.601(d)(2)(ii)(*b*) of this chapter.)

(b) *Economic hardship waiver.* The Commissioner may waive the requirements of this section in cases of undue economic hardship. The principal factor in determining hardship will be the amount, if any, by which the cost of filing the registration statements or notifications on magnetic media in accordance with this section exceeds the cost of filing the registration statements or notifications on paper or other media. A request for a waiver must be made in accordance with applicable published guidance, publications, forms, instructions, or other guidance on the IRS.gov Internet Web site. (See § 601.601(d)(2)(ii)(*b*) of this chapter.) The waiver will specify the type of filing (that is, a registration statement or notification under section 6057), and the period to which it applies, and will be subject to such terms and conditions regarding the method of filing as may be prescribed by the Commissioner.

(c) *Failure to file.* If a filer required to file a registration statement or other notification under section 6057 fails to file the statement or other notification on magnetic media when required to do so by this section, the filer is deemed to have failed to file the statement or other notification. See section 6652(d) for the amount imposed for the failure to file a registration statement or other notification under section 6057. In determining whether there is reasonable cause for the failure to file the registration statement or notification under section 6057, § 301.6652-3(b) and rules similar to the rules in § 301.6724-1(c)(3)(ii) (regarding undue economic hardship related to filing information returns on magnetic media) will apply.

(d) *Meaning of terms.* The following definitions apply for purposes of this section.

(1) *Magnetic media.* The term *magnetic media* means electronic filing, as well as other media specifically permitted under applicable regulations, revenue procedures, or publications, forms, instructions, or other guidance on the IRS.gov Internet Web site. (See § 601.601(d)(2)(ii)(*b*) of this chapter.)

(2) *Registration statement required under section 6057(a).* The term *registration statement required under section 6057(a)* means a Form 8955-SSA (or its successor).

(3) *Notification required under section 6057(b).* The term *notification required under section 6057(b)* means either a Form 8955-SSA (or its successor) or a Form 5500 series (or its successor).

(4) *Determination of 250 returns*—(i) *In general.* For purposes of this section, a filer is required to file at least 250 returns if, during the calendar year that includes the first day of the plan year, the filer is required to file at least 250 returns of any type, including information returns (for example, Forms W-2 and Forms 1099), income tax returns, employment tax returns, and excise tax returns.

(ii) *Definition of filer.* For purposes of this section, the term *filer* means the plan administrator within the meaning of section 414(g). If the plan administrator within the meaning of section 414(g) is the employer, the special rules in § 1.6058-2(d)(3)(iii) will apply.

(e) *Example.* The following example illustrates the provisions of paragraph (d)(4) of this section:

Example. In 2014, P, the plan administrator of Plan B, is required to file 252 returns (including Forms 1099-R, "Distributions From Pensions, Annuities, Retirement or Profit-Sharing Plans, IRAs, Insurance Contracts, etc.," Form 8955-SSA, "Annual Registration Statement Identifying Separated Participants with Deferred Vested Benefits," Form 5500, "Annual Return/Report of Employee Benefit Plan," and Form 945, "Annual Return of Withheld Federal Income Tax"). Plan B's plan year is the calendar year. Because P is required to file at least 250 returns during the 2014 calendar year, P must file the 2014 Form 8955-SSA for Plan B electronically.

(f) *Effective/applicability date.* This section is applicable for registration statements and other notifications required to be filed under section 6057 for plan years that begin on or after January 1, 2014, but only for filings with a filing deadline (not taking into account extensions) after December 31, 2014.

■ **Par. 3.** Section 301.6058-2 is added to read as follows:

§ 301.6058-2 Required use of magnetic media for filing requirements relating to information required in connection with certain plans of deferred compensation.

(a) *Magnetic media filing requirements under section 6058.* A return required under section 6058 with respect to an employee benefit plan must be filed on magnetic media if the filer is required by the Internal Revenue Code or regulations to file at least 250 returns during the calendar year ending with or within the plan year. Returns filed on magnetic media must be made in accordance with applicable revenue procedures, publications, forms, instructions, or other guidance on the IRS.gov Internet Web site. In prescribing revenue procedures, publications, forms, and instructions, or other guidance on the IRS.gov Internet site, the Commissioner may direct the type of magnetic media filing. (See § 601.601(d)(2)(ii)(*b*) of this chapter.)

(b) *Economic hardship waiver.* The Commissioner may waive the requirements of this section in cases of undue economic hardship. The principal factor in determining hardship will be the amount, if any, by which the cost of filing the return on magnetic media in accordance with this section exceeds the cost of filing the returns on paper or other media. A request for a waiver must be made in accordance with applicable published guidance, publications, forms, instructions, or other guidance on the IRS.gov Internet Web site. (See § 601.601(d)(2)(ii)(*b*) of this chapter.) The waiver will specify the type of filing (that is, a return required under section 6058) and the period to which it applies, and will be subject to such terms and conditions regarding the method of filing as may be prescribed by the Commissioner.

(c) *Failure to file.* If a filer required to file a return under section 6058 fails to file the return on magnetic media when required to do so by this section, the filer is deemed to have failed to file the return. See section 6652(e) for the addition to tax for failure to file a return. In determining whether there is reasonable cause for failure to file the return, § 301.6652-3(b) and rules similar to the rules in § 301.6724-1(c)(3)(ii) (regarding undue economic hardship related to filing information returns on magnetic media) will apply.

(d) *Meaning of terms.* The following definitions apply for purposes of this section.

(1) *Magnetic media.* The term *magnetic media* means electronic filing, as well as other media specifically permitted under applicable regulations, revenue procedures, or publications, forms, instructions, or other guidance on the IRS.gov Internet Web site. (See § 601.601(d)(2)(ii)(b) of this chapter.)

(2) *Return required under section 6058.* The term *return required under section 6058* means the Form 5500 series (or its successor).

(3) *Determination of 250 returns*—(i) *In general.* For purposes of this section, a filer is required to file at least 250 returns if, during the calendar year that includes the first day of the plan year, the filer is required to file at least 250 returns of any type, including information returns (for example, Forms W-2 and Forms 1099), income tax returns, employment tax returns, and excise tax returns.

(ii) *Definition of filer.* For purposes of this section, the term *filer* means the employer or employers maintaining the plan and the plan administrator within the meaning of section 414(g).

(iii) *Special rules relating to determining 250 returns.* For purposes of applying paragraph (d)(3)(ii) of this section, the aggregation rules of section 414(b), (c), (m), and (o) will apply to a filer that is or includes an employer. Thus, for example, a filer that is a member of a controlled group of corporations within the meaning of section 414(b) must file the Form 5500 series on magnetic media if the aggregate number of returns required to be filed by all members of the controlled group of corporations is at least 250.

(e) *Example.* The following example illustrates the provisions of paragraph (d)(3) of this section:

Example. In 2014, Employer X (the plan sponsor of Plan A) and P (the plan administrator of Plan A) are required to file 267 returns. Employer X is required to file the following: one Form 1120, "U.S. Corporation Income Tax Return," 195 Forms W-2, "Wage and Tax Statement," 25 Forms 1099-DIV, "Dividends and Distributions," one Form 940, "Employer's Annual Federal Unemployment (FUTA) Tax Return," and four Forms 941, "Employer's Quarterly Federal Tax Return." P is required to file 40 Forms 1099-R, "Distributions From Pensions, Annuities, Retirement, Profit-Sharing Plans, IRAs, Insurance Contracts, etc." P and Employer X are jointly required to file one Form 5500 series. Plan A's plan year is the calendar year. Because P and Employer X, in the aggregate, are required to file at least 250 returns during the calendar year, the 2014 Form 5500 for Plan A must be filed electronically.

(f) *Effective/applicability date.* This section is applicable for returns required to be filed under section 6058 for plan years that begin on or after January 1, 2014, but only for filings with a filing deadline (not taking into account extensions) after December 31, 2014.

■ **Par. 4.** Section 301.6059-2 is added to read as follows:

§ 301.6059-2 Required use of magnetic media for filing requirements relating to periodic report of actuary

(a) *Magnetic media filing requirements under section 6059.* An actuarial report required under section 6059 with respect to an employee benefit plan must be filed on magnetic media if the filer is required by the Internal Revenue Code or regulations to file at least 250 returns during the calendar year ending with or within the plan year. Actuarial reports filed on magnetic media must be made in accordance with applicable revenue procedures, publications, forms, instructions, or other guidance on the IRS.gov Internet Web site. In prescribing revenue procedures, publications, forms, instructions, or other guidance on the IRS.gov Internet Web site, the Commissioner may direct the type of magnetic media filing. (See § 601.601(d)(2)(ii)(b) of this chapter.)

(b) *Economic hardship waiver.* The Commissioner may waive the requirements of this section in cases of undue economic hardship. The principal factor in determining hardship will be the amount, if any, by which the cost of filing the reports on magnetic media in accordance

with this section exceeds the cost of filing the reports on paper or other media. A request for a waiver must be made in accordance with applicable published guidance, publications, forms, instructions, or other guidance on the IRS.gov Internet Web site. (See § 601.601(d)(2)(ii)(b) of this chapter.) The waiver will specify the type of filing (that is, an actuarial report required under section 6059) and the period to which it applies, and will be subject to such terms and conditions regarding the method of filing as may be prescribed by the Commissioner.

(c) *Failure to File.* If a filer required to file an actuarial report under section 6059 fails to file the report on magnetic media when required to do so by this section, the filer is deemed to have failed to file the report. See section 6692 for the penalty for the failure to file an actuarial report. In determining whether there is reasonable cause for failure to file the report, § 301.6692-1(c) and rules similar to the rules in § 301.6724-1(c)(3)(ii) (regarding undue economic hardship related to filing information returns on magnetic media) will apply.

(d) *Meaning of terms.* The following definitions apply for purposes of this section.

(1) *Magnetic media.* The term *magnetic media* means electronic filing, as well as other media specifically permitted under applicable regulations, revenue procedures, or publications, forms, instructions, or other guidance on the IRS.gov Internet Web site. (See § 601.601(d)(2)(ii)(b) of this chapter.)

(2) *Actuarial report required under section 6059*—(i) *Single employer plans.* For a single employer plan, the term *actuarial report required under section 6059* means the Schedule SB, "Single-Employer Defined Benefit Plan Actuarial Information," of the Form 5500 series (or its successor).

(ii) *Multiemployer and certain money purchase plans.* For multiemployer and certain money purchase plans, the term *actuarial report required under section 6059* means the Schedule MB, "Multiemployer Defined Benefit Plan and Certain Money Purchase Plan Actuarial Information," of the Form 5500 series (or its successor).

(3) *Determination of 250 returns*—(i) *In general.* For purposes of this section, a filer is required to file at least 250 returns if, during the calendar year that includes the first day of the plan year, the filer is required to file at least 250 returns of any type, including information returns (for example, Forms W-2 and Forms 1099), income tax returns, employment tax returns, and excise tax returns.

(ii) *Definition of filer.* For purposes of this section, the term *filer* means the plan administrator within the meaning of section 414(g). If the plan administrator within the meaning of section 414(g) is the employer, the special rules in § 1.6058-2(d)(3)(iii) will apply.

(e) *Example.* The following example illustrates the provisions of paragraph (d)(3) of this section:

Example. In 2014, P, the plan administrator of Plan B (a single employer defined benefit plan), is required to file 266 returns (including Forms 1099-R "Distributions From Pensions, Annuities, Retirement, Profit-Sharing Plans, IRAs, Insurance Contracts, etc." and one Form 5500 series). Plan B's plan year is the calendar year. Because P is required to file at least 250 returns during the calendar year, P must file the 2014 Schedule SB of the Form 5500 series for Plan B electronically.

(f) *Effective/applicability date.* This section is applicable for actuarial reports required to be filed under section 6059 for plan years that begin on or after January 1, 2014, but only for filings with a filing deadline (not taking into account extensions) after December 31, 2014.

Beth Tucker,

Deputy Commissioner for Operations Support.

[FR Doc. 2013-21159 Filed 8-29-13; 8:45 am]

BILLING CODE 4830-01-P

¶ 20,263R

IRS: Employee health insurance providers: Minimum essential coverage: Information reporting.—The IRS has issued proposed regulations that supply guidance to providers of minimum essential health coverage that are subject to the information reporting requirements of Code Sec. 6055. Health insurance issuers, certain employers, and others that provide minimum essential coverage to individuals must report to the IRS information about the type and period of coverage and furnish related statements to covered individuals. The regulations are proposed to apply for calendar years beginning after December 31, 2014. However, a reporting entity will not be subject to penalties if it first reports beginning in 2016 for 2015, including the furnishing of statements to covered individuals in 2016 with respect to 2015. Taxpayers are encouraged, however, to voluntarily comply with section 6055 information reporting for minimum essential coverage provided in 2014 by applying these regulations once finalized.

The proposed regulations were published in the Federal Register on September 9, 2013 (78 FR 54986). The regulations were finalized on March 10, 2014 (79 FR 13220). The preamble to the final regulations is at ¶ 23,297. The final regulations are at ¶ 13,724A, ¶ 13,724B, and ¶ 13,649D.

DEPARTMENT OF THE TREASURY

Internal Revenue Service

26 CFR Parts 1 and 301

[REG-132455-11]

RIN 1545-BL31

Information Reporting of Minimum Essential Coverage

AGENCY: Internal Revenue Service (IRS), Treasury.

ACTION: Notice of proposed rulemaking and notice of public hearing.

SUMMARY: This document contains proposed regulations providing guidance to providers of minimum essential health coverage that are subject to the information reporting requirements of section 6055 of the Internal Revenue Code (Code), enacted by the Affordable Care Act. Health insurance issuers, certain employers, and others that provide minimum essential coverage to individuals must report to the IRS information about the type and period of coverage and furnish related statements to covered individuals. These proposed regulations affect health insurance issuers, employers, governments, and other persons that provide minimum essential coverage to individuals.

DATES: Written or electronic comments must be received by November 8, 2013. Requests to speak and outlines of topics to be discussed at the public hearing scheduled for November 19, 2013, at 10 a.m., must be received by November 8, 2013.

ADDRESSES: Send submissions to: CC:PA:LPD:PR (REG-132455-11), Room 5203, Internal Revenue Service, P.O. Box 7604, Ben Franklin Station, Washington, DC 20044. Submissions may be hand-delivered Monday through Friday between the hours of 8 a.m. and 4 p.m. to CC:PA:LPD:PR (REG-132455-11), Courier's Desk, Internal Revenue Service, 1111 Constitution Avenue NW., Washington, DC, or sent electronically via the Federal eRulemaking Portal at *http://www.regulations.gov* (IRS REG-132455-11).

FOR FURTHER INFORMATION CONTACT: Concerning the proposed regulations, Andrew Braden, (202) 622-4960; concerning the submission of comments and/or to be placed on the building access list to attend the public hearing, Oluwafunmilayo (Funmi) Taylor, (202) 622-7180 (not toll-free calls).

SUPPLEMENTARY INFORMATION:

Paperwork Reduction Act

The collection of information contained in this notice of proposed rulemaking has been submitted to the Office of Management and Budget in accordance with the Paperwork Reduction Act of 1995 (44 U.S.C. 3507(d)). Comments on the collection of information should be sent to the Office of Management and Budget, Attn: Desk Officer for the Department of the Treasury, Office of Information and Regulatory Affairs, Washington, DC 20503, with copies to the Internal Revenue Service, Attn: IRS Reports Clearance Officer, SE:W:CAR:MP:T:T:SP, Washington, DC 20224. Comments on the collection of information should be received by November 8, 2013. Comments are specifically requested concerning:

Whether the proposed collection of information is necessary for the proper performance of the functions of the IRS, including whether the information will have practical utility;

How the quality, utility, and clarity of the information to be collected may be enhanced;

How the burden of complying with the proposed collection of information may be minimized, including through the application of automated collection techniques or other forms of information technology; and

Estimates of capital or start-up costs and costs of operation, maintenance, and purchase of services to provide information.

The collection of information in these proposed regulations is in §§ 1.6055-1 and 1.6055-2. The collection of information will be used to determine whether an individual has minimum essential coverage under section 1501(b) of the Patient Protection and Affordable Care Act (26 U.S.C. 5000A(f)). The collection of information is required to comply with the provisions of section 6055 of the Code. The likely respondents are health insurers, self-insured employers or other sponsors of self-insured health plans, and governments that provide minimum essential coverage.

The burden for the collection of information contained in these proposed regulations will be reflected in the burden on Form 1095-B or another form that the IRS designates, which will request the information in the proposed regulation.

An agency may not conduct or sponsor, and a person is not required to respond to, a collection of information unless it displays a valid control number assigned by the Office of Management and Budget.

Background

Beginning in 2014, under the Patient Protection and Affordable Care Act, Public Law 111-148 (124 Stat. 119 (2010)), and the Health Care and Education Reconciliation Act of 2010, Public Law 111-152 (124 Stat. 1029 (2010)) (collectively, the Affordable Care Act), nonexempt individuals have the choice of maintaining minimum essential coverage (as defined in section 5000A(f)) or paying an individual shared responsibility payment with their income tax returns. Minimum essential coverage may be health insurance coverage offered in the individual market (such as a qualified health plan offered through an Affordable Insurance Exchange (Exchange, also known as a Marketplace)), an employer-sponsored plan, or a government-sponsored program. Section 5000A(f)(1)(A) specifies that Medicare Part A, Medicaid, the Children's Health Insurance Program established under title XXI of the Social Security Act (42 U.S.C. 1397aa et seq.) (CHIP), TRICARE, certain health care programs for veterans and other individuals under chapter 17 or 18 of Title 38 U.S.C., coverage for Peace Corps volunteers under 22 USC 2504(e), and coverage under the Nonappropriated Fund Health Benefits Program under section 349 of Public Law 103-337, are government-sponsored programs that qualify as minimum essential coverage.

Section 1401 of the Affordable Care Act enacted section 36B, allowing certain taxpayers a refundable premium tax credit that will make minimum essential coverage in qualified health plans offered in the individual market through an Exchange more affordable.

Section 1502 of the Affordable Care Act enacted section 6055 regarding information reporting by any person that provides minimum essential coverage to an individual. Section 6055(b)(1)(B) requires providers of minimum essential coverage to report (1) the name, address, and taxpayer identification number (TIN) of the primary insured, (2) the name, dates of coverage, and TIN of each individual covered under a policy, (3) whether health insurance coverage is a qualified health plan offered through an Exchange, (4) for a qualified health plan, the amount of any advance payments of the premium tax credit under section 1412 of the Affordable Care Act and cost-sharing reductions under section 1402 of the Affordable Care Act, and (5) other information the Secretary requires.

Section 6055(b)(2) requires, for coverage through an employer's group health plan, reporting (1) the name, address, and employer identification number (EIN) of the employer maintaining the plan, (2) the portion of the premium (if any) paid by the employer, and (3) any other information that the Secretary requires for administering the credit under section 45R (the tax credit for employee health insurance expenses of small employers).

Section 6055(c) directs a person filing an information return under section 6055 to provide a written statement to each individual listed on the return that shows the name, address, and contact phone number of the reporting entity and information reported to the IRS for that individual. The statement must be furnished to the individual by January 31 of the year following the coverage year.

The information reported under section 6055 will allow taxpayers to establish and the IRS to verify that the taxpayers were covered by minimum essential coverage and their months of enrollment during a calendar year.

Under section 6724(d), as amended by the Affordable Care Act, a reporting entity that fails to comply with the filing and statement furnishing requirements of section 6055 may be subject to penalties for failure to file a correct information return (section 6721) and failure to furnish correct payee statements (section 6722). However, these penalties may be waived if the failure was due to reasonable cause and not to willful neglect (section 6724(a)).

Section 1514 of the Affordable Care Act enacted section 6056, which requires applicable large employers (generally employers with 50 or more full-time employees) to report to the IRS information about the coverage that they offer to their full-time employees and requires them to furnish related statements to employees.

Notice 2012-32 (2012-20 IRB 910) requested public comments on issues to be addressed in regulations under section 6055. In addition, Notice 2012-33 (2012-20 IRB 912) requested public comments on issues to be addressed in regulations under section 6056. As described later in this preamble, the written comments in response to Notice 2012-32 and other written comments have been considered in connection with the development of these proposed regulations.

As discussed in Notice 2013-45 (2013-31 IRB 116), Treasury and the IRS have engaged in dialogue with stakeholders in an effort to simplify section 6055 (and section 6056) reporting consistent with effective implementation of the law. This process has included discussions with stakeholders representing a wide range of interests to assist in the consideration of effective information reporting rules that will be as streamlined, simple, and workable as possible. The effort to develop these proposed information reporting rules has reflected a considered balancing of the importance of (1) providing individuals the information to complete their tax returns accurately, including with respect to the individual responsibility provisions and eligibility for the premium tax credit, (2) minimizing cost and administrative tasks for the reporting entities and individuals, and (3) providing the IRS with information needed for effective and efficient tax administration. As noted elsewhere in this preamble, the proposed regulations will be the subject of public comments, including comments that are specifically invited regarding particular issues identified in the preamble.

Notice 2013-45 provides as transition relief that section 6055 information reporting will be optional for 2014. The IRS will not impose penalties for failure to timely and accurately report under section 6055 for coverage in 2014. As stated in Notice 2013-45, the IRS encourages voluntary section 6055 reporting for coverage in 2014.

Explanation of Provisions and Summary of Comments

1. Persons Subject to Information Reporting Requirement

a. Plans in the individual market

Under section 36B(f)(3) and §1.36B-5, an Exchange must report information relating to enrollment in qualified health plans in the individual market to the IRS and taxpayers. This information includes the period coverage was in effect, the names and TINs of each individual covered, the amount of advance credit payments relating to the coverage, and the amount of premiums for the coverage. This reporting facilitates compliance with and administration of the premium tax credit under section 36B. A commenter suggested that issuers of qualified health plans should not be required to report under section 6055 regarding minimum essential coverage that they provide in the individual market through the Exchange because the Exchange reporting provides the IRS and taxpayers with the necessary information about this coverage.

In response to this comment and to reduce the burden associated with reporting under section 6055, the proposed regulations provide that issuers are not required to submit section 6055 information returns for coverage under a qualified health plan in the individual market enrolled in through an Exchange. For individuals enrolled in this coverage, the IRS and individuals will receive information necessary to administer or comply with the individual shared responsibility provision through information reporting by Exchanges under section 36B(f)(3). Issuers must report, however, on qualified health plans in the small group market enrolled in through the Small Business Health Options Program (SHOP), because annual information reporting by Exchanges under section 36B(f)(3) does not include these plans.

b. Employer-sponsored Insured Group Health Plans

Commenters recommended that the proposed regulations require employers rather than health insurance issuers to report under section 6055 for insured coverage under an employer-sponsored group health plan. The commenters suggested that employers have more direct access to information required to be reported for an employee enrolled in a group health plan.

Because section 6055(a) requires reporting by the entities providing the coverage, which for insured coverage is the issuer, the proposed regulations provide that health insurance issuers are responsible for reporting under section 6055 for all insured coverage, except coverage under certain government-sponsored programs (such as Medicaid and Medicare) that provide coverage through a health insurance issuer and coverage under qualified health plans in the individual market enrolled in through an Exchange.

Reporting entities are permitted to use third parties to facilitate filing returns and furnishing statements to comply with reporting requirements, including those under section 6055. These arrangements do not, however, transfer the potential liability for failure of the reporting entity to report and furnish under the regulations.

A party preparing returns or statements required under section 6055 that is a tax return preparer will be subject to the requirements that generally apply to return preparers.

c. Self-insured Group Health Plans

The proposed regulations provide that sponsors of self-insured health coverage are responsible for reporting under section 6055. The proposed regulations identify the employer as the plan sponsor and reporting entity for a self-insured group health plan established or maintained by a single employer. This rule is consistent with section 3(16)(B)(i) of the Employee Retirement Income Security Act of 1974 (ERISA), which states that the term "plan sponsor" means the employer in the case of an employee benefit plan established or maintained by a single employer.

Commenters noted that individuals may be covered under a self-insured arrangement that is a multiemployer plan and offered suggestions for identifying the entity responsible for reporting. Some commenters stated that employers that participate in a multiemployer plan do not have access to the information required to be reported under section 6055 and that the multiemployer plan or its administrator, for example, the joint board of trustees, should report for the participating employers. Another commenter suggested that labor unions report for multiemployer plans. Other commenters asserted that a plan's administrator or trustees generally are in the best position to report minimum essential coverage funded under a collective bargaining agreement unless the plan is funded by a single employer. A commenter asserted that each participating employer should be responsible for reporting under section 6055 for a multiple employer welfare arrangement (MEWA) under section 3(40) of ERISA (29 U.S.C. 1002(40)).

In response to these comments, the proposed regulations identify the sponsor and reporting entity for various types of self-insured arrangements (for example, the joint board of trustees for a multiemployer plan). For these purposes, the section 414 employer aggregation rules do not apply. Accordingly, a self-insured group health plan or arrangement covering employees of related corporations is treated as sponsored by more than one employer and each employer must report for its employees. However, one member of the group may assist the other members by filing returns and furnishing statements on behalf of all members.

Section 6055(d) provides that an appropriately designated person may report under section 6055 on behalf of a government employer. Accordingly, the proposed regulations allow a government employer providing self-insured coverage for its employees to report under section 6055 on its own behalf or to designate as the reporting entity another governmental unit or agency or instrumentality of a governmental unit that is part of or related to the same governmental unit as the government employer. If the designation is made before the filing deadline and the designee accepts it, the designated governmental unit, agency, or instrumentality is the sponsor responsible for section 6055 reporting. Comments are requested on issues specific to government employer plans and arrangements.

As noted, section 6056 requires applicable large employers to report information about the coverage that they offer to their full-time employees and to furnish related statements to employees. Commenters suggested that applicable large employers with self-insured health plans that must report under both sections 6055 and 6056 should be allowed to combine that reporting.

The general rules described in the proposed regulations assume separate reporting, but include other rules that reduce duplicative reporting and otherwise simplify reporting. For example, the proposed regulations allow the use of substitute forms and statements to individuals, which may permit self-insured health plans to furnish a single substitute statement to covered individuals for both sections 6055 and 6056.

In addition, the preamble to proposed regulations under section 6056 advises that the IRS and the Treasury Department are considering permitting applicable large employers with self-insured plans that provide mandatory, minimum value coverage to employees, and offer that coverage to spouses and dependents, all with no employee contribution, to forgo providing section 6056 statements to those covered employees. Because the section 6055 return would provide the individual taxpayers information to accurately file the taxpayers' income tax returns, and would provide the IRS the information concerning those employees to administer the premium tax credit and employer shared responsibility provisions, Treasury and the IRS are considering whether for those employees the employer could file and furnish only the return required under section 6055 and include a code on the employees' Forms W-2.

Comments are requested on other ways to simplify and combine reporting.

d. Foreign Employers That Provide Minimum Essential Coverage

Section 6055(b)(2)(A) requires that reporting for coverage under a group health plan include the employer's EIN. A commenter noted that a foreign employer may provide minimum essential coverage but may not have an EIN. Comments are requested on rules for reporting by foreign employers without EINs that sponsor self-insured plans and on any other issues specific to reporting coverage provided by foreign employers.

e. Government-Sponsored Programs

The proposed regulations provide that the executive department or agency of a governmental unit that provides coverage under a government-sponsored program (within the meaning of section 5000A(f)(1)(A)) is responsible for reporting under section 6055. For example, the Department of Defense is responsible for reporting coverage under the TRICARE program. The proposed regulations identify the State agency that administers the Medicaid or CHIP program, rather than the Department of Health and Human Services, as the reporting entity for these programs. Additionally, under the proposed regulations, the responsible government department or agency, and not the issuer, is the reporting entity for coverage under a government-sponsored program provided through a health insurance issuer (such as some Medicaid, CHIP, and Medicare programs). Comments are requested on issues specific to reporting coverage under government-sponsored programs.

f. Other Arrangements Designated as Minimum Essential Coverage

Section 5000A(f)(1)(E) provides that the Secretary of Health and Human Services (HHS), in coordination with the Secretary of the Treasury, may recognize other health benefits coverage as minimum essential coverage. On July 1, 2013, HHS published final regulations designating certain coverage as minimum essential coverage and outlining substantive and procedural requirements that other types of coverage must fulfill to be recognized as minimum essential coverage. Patient Protection and Affordable Care Act: Exchange Functions: Eligibility for Exemptions; Miscellaneous Minimum Essential Coverage Provisions, 78 FR 39494 (HHS MEC regulations). These regulations designate as minimum essential coverage (1) self-funded student health coverage for plan or policy years beginning on or before December 31, 2014, (2) Refugee Medical Assistance supported by the Administration for Children and Families, (3) Medicare Advantage plans, and (4) State high risk pools for plan or policy years beginning on or before December 31, 2014.

The proposed rule that designates the government department or agency as the reporting entity for coverage under a government-sponsored program provided through a health insurance issuer applies to Medicare Advantage plans. Comments are requested on appropriate rules for identifying the reporting entity for other arrangements recognized as minimum essential coverage under section 5000A(f)(1)(E).

2. Information Required To Be Reported

a. In General

The proposed regulations provide that the section 6055 information return must include the name of each individual enrolled in minimum essential coverage and the name and address of the primary insured or other related person (for example, a parent or spouse) who submits the application for coverage (the responsible individual). The proposed regulations use the term *responsible individual* rather than the term *primary insured* because minimum essential coverage may not be insured coverage (for example, health coverage provided by the Department of Veterans Affairs). The return also must report the TIN and months of coverage for each individual who is covered under the policy or program and other information specified in forms, instructions, or published guidance, see §§ 601.601(d) and 601.602. For employer-provided coverage, the proposed regulations require reporting the name, address, and EIN of the employer maintaining the plan and whether coverage was enrolled in through the SHOP.

As part of the effort to minimize the cost and administrative steps associated with the reporting requirements, the proposed regulations do not require reporting information that would not be needed by individual taxpayers or the IRS for purposes of administering the individual shared responsibility provisions or the credit for small employers. Accordingly, the proposed regulations do not require reporting the portion of the premium paid by an employer, which the IRS does not need to determine if an individual is covered by minimum essential coverage. The proposed regulations require reporting the months of coverage rather than the specific dates of coverage, because minimum essential coverage applies month by month. The proposed regulations do not require reporting the amount of any cost-sharing

reductions, which are not administered by the IRS. Finally, the proposed regulations do not require reporting the amount of advance payments or on coverage in a qualified health plan in the individual market enrolled in through an Exchange, since in both cases this information is reported to the IRS and provided to individuals by the Exchanges under section 36B(f)(3).

b. Identifying Information

Health insurance issuers and employers with self-funded plans expressed concern that they do not typically collect TINs from dependents covered under their policies and that they may have difficulty obtaining TINs for some covered individuals. Other commenters suggested allowing alternative means of identifying individuals, such as unique enrollee identification numbers similar to the method used by the Massachusetts Health Connector (the State-based exchange), or allowing reporting without TINs for individuals who enroll in coverage but decline to provide a TIN. Some commenters suggested simplifying reporting requirements for dependents or providing alternatives in reporting TINs for new beneficiaries and others who may not provide TINs at the time of enrollment.

The proposed regulations adopt TIN reporting, consistent with the statute. Section 6055 reporting allows individuals to confirm their coverage and the IRS to verify that coverage without the need to contact the individuals. The use of TINs to cross-check individuals against coverage months is the most efficient way for individuals and the IRS to avoid the need for follow-up. Accordingly, covered individuals have an interest in providing TINs to reporting entities.

Federal tax records for individuals for all purposes are maintained by TIN and individual taxpayers identify themselves on their returns by TIN. Establishing another method of identifying individuals for sections 5000A and 6055 purposes would require the IRS to create, and taxpayers to adapt to, an entire parallel identification system solely for this purpose.

While section 6055 and the proposed regulations require TINs for administering section 5000A, reporting entities that make reasonable efforts to collect TINs but do not receive them will not be subject to penalties under sections 6721 and 6722 for failure to timely and accurately report. In particular, section 6055 reporting is governed by the same procedures, limitations, and protections as other information reporting that requires obtaining and reporting TINs. Section 6724 and the regulations under that section waive penalties on reporting entities for a reasonable failure to include correct TIN information on a return or statement, including those required under section 6055. Penalties are waived if the reporting entity demonstrates that it acted in a responsible manner both before and after the failure occurred, and that the failure was due to significant mitigating factors or events beyond the reporting entity's control. In general, a reporting entity acts responsibly in attempting to solicit a TIN if after an initial, unsuccessful request for a TIN (for example, at the time of enrollment), the reporting entity makes two consecutive annual TIN solicitations. No section 6724 penalty is imposed unless the reporting entity fails to make the two additional solicitations. Accordingly, section 6055 reporting entities will not be unduly penalized for failing to report a TIN.

As a backstop to reporting a TIN, the proposed regulations allow reporting entities to report date of birth if a TIN is not available. This alternative should not be used, however, unless the reporting entity has made reasonable efforts to obtain the information by requesting that a covered individual provide the TIN.

A commenter requested that the proposed regulations provide rules authorizing reporting entities to request TINs. This authority exists under section 6109(a)(2) and § 301.6109-1(b)(1) of the Procedure and Administration Regulations, which require individuals to furnish TINs to persons that must file information returns.

A commenter noted that issuers and employers may have difficulty obtaining overseas addresses for individuals living abroad. The proposed regulations provide that only the last known address for the responsible individual must be reported.

c. Coverage Dates

For purposes of section 5000A, an individual who has coverage on any day in a month is treated as having minimum essential coverage for the entire month. See proposed § 1.5000A-1(b) (78 FR 7314). As a result, the specific coverage dates are not necessary for administering and complying with rules relating to minimum essential coverage. Accordingly, the proposed regulations do not require reporting of the specific dates of coverage. Instead, the proposed regulations generally require reporting of the months during which an individual is treated as having minimum essential coverage.

A commenter noted that coverage dates may be inaccurate because coverage may be terminated or reinstated after the reporting date for periods occurring before the reporting date. Under section 6724 and the regulations under that section, the IRS may waive penalties if there is reasonable cause for the failure to correct an information return for retroactive terminations or reinstatements that are determined after the calendar year in which coverage was terminated or reinstated.

A commenter recommended permitting separate returns or creating special forms to report coverage for individuals who change their coverage during the year to a different health plan with the same issuer. Although the proposed regulations do not adopt a rule addressing this situation, additional procedures that are responsive to this comment may be provided in IRS forms and instructions, see § 601.602.

A commenter noted that employers face challenges in determining coverage dates for employees and dependents, including seasonal and temporary workers whose term of employment changes during the year. The commenter recommended that the rules allow reporting an individual's enrollment in minimum essential coverage as of a fixed date each year to accommodate an employer's administrative, payroll, and recordkeeping procedures. The individual responsibility payment under section 5000A applies to individuals on a monthly basis, so reporting based on one day during the year would not be sufficient. Additionally, varying reporting dates would be difficult to administer and would produce information less useful to taxpayers, who generally file their tax returns and must determine their coverage based on a calendar year. Accordingly, the proposed regulations do not adopt this suggestion. Comments are welcome on potential alternative ways to address the challenges associated with determining coverage dates when employment changes.

d. Supplemental Coverage Arrangements

A commenter asked whether an employer and an issuer must coordinate section 6055 reporting for an employer-sponsored group health plan that consists of an insured high-deductible health plan (HDHP) and additional health benefits provided through a contribution to a health savings account. Health savings accounts are not minimum essential coverage, and therefore section 6055 reporting is not required for them. Additionally, the proposed regulations provide that reporting is not required for arrangements such as health reimbursement arrangements that supplement minimum essential coverage.

3. Time and Manner of Filing

a. Form of Return

The proposed regulations provide that the return under section 6055 may be made on Form 1095-B or another form the IRS designates, or on a substitute form. A substitute form must comply with revenue procedures or other published guidance, see § 601.601(d)(2), that apply to substitute forms. The proposed regulations require that information returns be submitted to the IRS with a transmittal form, Form 1094-B. In accordance with usual procedure, these forms will be made available in draft form at a later date.

b. Time for Filing Returns

The proposed regulations provide for reporting entities to file the return and transmittal form on or before February 28 (or March 31 if filed electronically) of the year following the calendar year in which they provided minimum essential coverage. Commenters suggested that the proposed regulations provide different reporting deadlines for fiscal year health plans to avoid calendar year reporting of data from multiple plan years. Since most individuals file calendar year returns, permitting fiscal year reporting would interfere with return preparation and processing for individuals potentially subject to the section 5000A individual shared responsibility payment. Therefore, the proposed regulations do not adopt this comment.

c. Electronic Reporting

Commenters recommended permitting electronic reporting under section 6055. Section 6011(e) and § 301.6011-2 require high-volume filers (those who file 250 or more returns during the calendar year) to file electronically. The proposed regulations provide that these electronic filing requirements apply to information returns under section 6055, but do not limit electronic filing to high-volume filers. Accordingly, any reporting entity may file electronically under section 6055.

4. Combined Reporting

As discussed earlier in this preamble, applicable large employers that provide minimum essential coverage on a self-insured basis are subject to the reporting requirements of sections 6055 and 6056, as well as the requirement under section 6051 to file Form W-2, Wage and Tax Statement, showing wages paid to employees and taxes withheld. Notices 2012-32 and 2012-33 requested comments on how to minimize duplication in reporting under these provisions.

Several commenters recommended that the regulations allow combined information reporting under sections 6055 and 6056 for applicable large employers that sponsor self-insured group health plans and must report under both sections. Other commenters recommended that employers be permitted to use a single information return to report under sections 6051 and 6055, for example by adding the information required under section 6055 to Form W-2.

As discussed elsewhere in this preamble, these proposed regulations seek to simplify reporting and reduce duplication through a number of approaches. In particular, the proposed regulations provide that issuers need not report under section 6055 for individual market qualified health plans enrolled in through an Exchange. The proposed regulations also provide relief from the requirement to report several items of information that are unnecessary for tax administration or are available from other reporting, and they allow the use of substitute forms and statements to individuals, which, under future guidance, may include furnishing a single substitute statement to covered individuals for both sections 6055 and 6056.

Accordingly, while the rules for section 6055 reporting in the proposed regulations do not assume full combined reporting under sections 6055, 6056 and 6051, they reflect other means of avoiding duplication and simplifying reporting. We continue to seek comments on other ways to streamline the reporting methods that would be permissible under the statute.

5. Statements Furnished to Individuals

The proposed regulations provide that a reporting entity must furnish a statement to the covered individual providing the policy number and the name, address, and a contact number for the reporting entity, and the information required to be reported to the IRS. The proposed regulations permit substitute statements that include the information required to be shown on the return filed with the IRS and comply with applicable requirements in published guidance relating to substitute statements. See § 601.601(d)(2) of this chapter. A substitute statement that includes the information required by both sections 6055 and 6056 in a single statement may be permitted by future guidance.

Commenters recommended permitting electronic delivery of statements to individuals. A commenter suggested that the regulations provide rules for electronic delivery of statements to individuals that are similar to the rules under section 2715 of the Public Health Service Act for providing a summary of benefits and coverage. The commenter suggested that these reporting regulations permit the furnishing of one electronic statement per home address rather than multiple statements per household. Another commenter requested guidance on procedures when an email notice is returned due to an incorrect address.

The proposed regulations permit electronic delivery of statements to individuals if the recipient consents. In response to concerns about the need to furnish a statement to each individual, the proposed regulations also permit furnishing only one statement per address. Comments are requested on whether and under what circumstances the regulations should direct reporting entities to provide a statement to another individual (who may, for example, need the statement to determine his or her tax liability).

Commenters expressed concern about protecting the privacy of individuals who provide TINs and about disclosure of the TINs to other parties. The regulations provide that section 6055 information reporting will be included in the IRS truncated TIN program. Accordingly, to protect the privacy of covered individuals, statements furnished to individuals under section 6055 are not required to disclose their complete TINs.

A commenter recommended that the statement to individuals should explain minimum essential coverage and advise taxpayers that they may be subject to a penalty for months in which they do not have minimum essential coverage. The proposed regulations do not include rules addressing educational content in the statement. However, information on the section 5000A individual shared responsibility payment may be included in IRS forms, instructions, and publications.

6. Penalties

Commenters recommended providing procedures for correcting errors in reporting and a safe harbor from penalties for an issuer that fails to report information that another entity fails to provide to the issuer. The proposed regulations provide that the provisions of section 6724(a) providing relief for a failure due to reasonable cause apply to reporting under section 6055. Because the procedures described in

§ 301.6721-1(b), which provide for reduced penalties for reporting errors that are timely corrected, will apply to corrections of errors in reporting under section 6055 that are not due to reasonable cause, the proposed regulations do not prescribe separate rules for correcting errors.

Proposed Effective/Applicability Date

These regulations are proposed to apply for calendar years beginning after December 31, 2014. Consistent with Notice 2013-45, reporting entities will not be subject to penalties for failure to comply with the section 6055 reporting requirements for coverage in 2014, which would have resulted in reporting in 2015 and furnishing statements to covered individuals in 2015.

Accordingly, a reporting entity will not be subject to penalties if it first reports beginning in 2016 for 2015, including the furnishing of statements to covered individuals in 2016 with respect to 2015. Taxpayers are encouraged, however, to voluntarily comply with section 6055 information reporting for minimum essential coverage provided in 2014 by applying these regulations once finalized.

Special Analyses

It has been determined that this notice of proposed rulemaking is not a significant regulatory action as defined in Executive Order 12866, as supplemented by Executive Order 13563. Therefore, a regulatory assessment is not required. It has also been determined that section 553(b) of the Administrative Procedure Act (5 U.S.C. chapter 5) does not apply to these regulations.

It is hereby certified that these regulations will not have a significant economic impact on a substantial number of small entities. This certification is based on the fact that the information collection required under these regulations is imposed under section 6055. Consistent with the statute, the proposed regulations require a person that provides minimum essential coverage to an individual to file a return with the IRS reporting certain information and to furnish a statement to the responsible individual who enrolled an individual or family in the coverage. These regulations primarily provide the method of filing and furnishing returns and statements under section 6055. Moreover, the proposed regulations attempt to minimize the burden associated with this collection of information by limiting reporting to the information that the IRS will use to verify minimum essential coverage and administer tax credits.

Based on these facts, a Regulatory Flexibility Analysis under the Regulatory Flexibility Act (5 U.S.C. chapter 6) is not required.

Pursuant to section 7805(f) of the Code, this notice of proposed rulemaking has been submitted to the Chief Counsel for Advocacy of the Small Business Administration for comment on its impact on small business.

Comments and Public Hearing

Before these proposed regulations are adopted as final regulations, consideration will be given to any comments that are submitted timely to the IRS as prescribed in this preamble under the **ADDRESSES** heading. The IRS and Treasury Department request comments on all aspects of the proposed rules. All comments will be available at *www.regulations.gov* or upon request.

A public hearing has been scheduled for November 19, 2013, at 10 a.m., in the auditorium, Internal Revenue Building, 1111 Constitution Avenue NW., Washington, DC. Due to building security procedures, visitors must enter at the Constitution Avenue entrance. All visitors must present photo identification to enter the building. Because of access restrictions, visitors will not be admitted beyond the immediate entrance more than 30 minutes before the hearing starts. For information about having your name placed on the building access list to attend the hearing, see the **FOR FURTHER INFORMATION CONTACT** section of this preamble.

The rules of 26 CFR 601.601(a)(3) apply to the hearing. Persons who wish to present oral comments at the hearing must submit written or electronic comments by November 8, 2013, an outline of topics to be discussed and the time to be devoted to each topic by (signed original and eight (8) copies by November 8, 2013. A period of 10 minutes will be allotted to each person for making comments.

An agenda showing the scheduling of the speakers will be prepared after the deadline for receiving outlines has passed. Copies of the agenda will be available free of charge at the hearing.

Drafting Information

The principal authors of these proposed regulations are Andrew Braden and Frank W. Dunham III of the Office of Associate Chief

Counsel (Income Tax and Accounting). However, other personnel from the IRS and the Treasury Department participated in the development of the regulations.

List of Subjects

26 CFR Part 1

Income taxes, Reporting and recordkeeping requirements.

26 CFR Part 301

Employment taxes, Estate taxes, Excise taxes, Gift taxes, Income taxes, Penalties, Reporting and recordkeeping requirements.

Proposed Amendments to the Regulations

Accordingly, 26 CFR parts 1 and 301 are proposed to be amended as follows:

PART 1—INCOME TAXES

■ **Paragraph 1.** The authority citation for part 1 is amended by adding entries in numerical order to read in part as follows:

Authority: 26 U.S.C. 7805 * * *

Sections 1.6055-1 and 1.6055-2 also issued under 26 U.S.C. 6055.

■ **Par. 2.** Sections 1.6055-1 and 1.6055-2 are added to read as follows:

§ 1.6055-1 Information reporting for minimum essential coverage.

(a) *Information reporting requirement.* Every person that provides minimum essential coverage to an individual during a calendar year must file an information return and a transmittal on forms prescribed by the Internal Revenue Service.

(b) *Definitions*—(1) *In general.* The definitions in this paragraph (b) apply for purposes of this section.

(2) *Affordable Care Act.* The term *Affordable Care Act* refers to the Patient Protection and Affordable Care Act, Public Law 111-148 (124 Stat. 119 (2010)), and the Health Care and Education Reconciliation Act of 2010, Public Law 111-152 (124 Stat. 1029 (2010)), and amendments to those acts.

(3) *ERISA.* The term *ERISA* means the Employee Retirement Income Security Act of 1974, as amended (29 U.S.C. 1001 et seq.).

(4) *Exchange.* Exchange has the same meaning as in 45 CFR 155.20.

(5) *Government employer.* The term *government employer* means an employer that is a governmental unit or an agency or instrumentality of a governmental unit.

(6) *Governmental unit.* The term *governmental unit* refers to the government of the United States, any State or political subdivision of a State, or any Indian tribal government (as defined in section 7701(a)(40)) or subdivision of an Indian tribal government (as defined in section 7871(d)).

(7) *Agency or instrumentality of a governmental unit.* [Reserved]

(8) *Minimum essential coverage.* Minimum essential coverage is defined in section 5000A(f) and regulations issued under that section.

(9) *Qualified health plan.* The term *qualified health plan* has the same meaning as in section 1301(a) of the Affordable Care Act (42 U.S.C. 18021(a)).

(10) *Reporting entity.* A reporting entity is any person that must report, under section 6055 and this section, minimum essential coverage provided to an individual.

(11) *Responsible individual.* A responsible individual is a primary insured, employee, former employee, uniformed services sponsor, parent, or other related person named on an application who enrolls one or more individuals in minimum essential coverage.

(12) *Taxpayer identifying number.* The term *taxpayer identifying number* (TIN) has the same meaning as in section 7701(a)(41).

(c) *Persons required to report*—(1) *In general.* The following persons must file the information return and transmittal form required under paragraph (a) of this section to report minimum essential coverage—

(i) Health insurance issuers, or carriers (as used in 5 U.S.C. 8901), for all insured coverage, except as provided in paragraph (c)(3)(ii) of this section;

(ii) Plan sponsors of self-insured group health plan coverage;

(iii) The executive department or agency of a governmental unit that provides coverage under a government-sponsored program (within the meaning of section 5000A(f)(1)(A)); and

(iv) Any other person that provides minimum essential coverage to an individual.

(2) *Plan sponsors of self-insured group health plan coverage*—(i) *In general.* For purposes of this section, a plan sponsor of self-insured group health plan coverage is—

(A) The employer for a self-insured group health plan or arrangement established or maintained by a single employer (determined without application of section 414(b), (c), (m) or (o)), including each participating employer with respect to a self-insured group health plan or arrangement established or maintained by more than one employer (other than a Multiple Employer Welfare Arrangement as defined in section 3(40) of ERISA);

(B) The association, committee, joint board of trustees, or other similar group of representatives of the parties who establish or maintain the plan for a self-insured group health plan or arrangement that is a multiemployer plan (as defined in section 3(37) of ERISA).

(C) The employee organization for a self-insured group health plan or arrangement maintained solely by an employee organization;

(D) Each participating employer for a self-insured group health plan or arrangement maintained by a Multiple Employer Welfare Arrangement (as defined in section 3(40) of ERISA) with respect to the participating employer's own employees; and

(E) For a self-insured group health plan or arrangement for which a plan sponsor is not otherwise identified in paragraphs (c)(2)(1)(A) through (c)(2)(1)(D) of this section, the person designated by plan terms as the plan sponsor or plan administrator or, if no person is designated as the administrator and a plan sponsor cannot be identified, each entity that maintains the plan or arrangement.

(ii) *Government employers.* Unless otherwise provided by statute or regulation, a government employer that maintains a self-insured group health plan or arrangement may enter into a written agreement with another governmental unit, or an agency or instrumentality of a governmental unit, that designates the other governmental unit, agency, or instrumentality as the person required to file the returns and to furnish the statements required by this section for some or all of the individuals receiving minimum essential coverage under that plan or arrangement. The designated governmental unit, agency, or instrumentality must be part of or related to the same governmental unit as the government employer (for example, a political subdivision of a state may designate the state or another political subdivision of the state) and agree to the designation. The government employer must make or revoke the designation before the earlier of the deadline for filing the returns or furnishing the statements required by this section. If the requirements of this paragraph (c)(2)(ii) are met, the designated governmental unit, agency, or instrumentality is the sponsor under paragraph (c)(2)(i) of this section. If no entity is designated, the government employer that maintains the self-insured group health plan or arrangement is the sponsor under paragraph (c)(2)(i) of this section.

(3) *Special rules for government-sponsored programs*—(i) *Medicaid and Children's Health Insurance Program (CHIP) coverage.* The State agency that administers the Medicaid program under title XIX of the Social Security Act (42 U.S.C. 1396 and following sections) or the CHIP program under title XXI of the Social Security Act (42 U.S.C. 1396 and following sections) must file the returns and furnish the statements required by this section for those programs.

(ii) *Government-sponsored coverage provided through health insurance issuers.* An executive department or agency of a governmental unit that provides coverage under a government-sponsored program through a health insurance issuer (such as Medicaid, CHIP, or Medicare) must file the returns and furnish the statements required by this section.

(iii) *Nonappropriated Fund Health Benefits Program.* The Secretary of Defense may designate the Department of Defense components (as used in DoD 7000.14-R, Department of Defense Financial Management Regulations) that must file the returns and furnish the statements required by this section for the Nonappropriated Fund Health Benefits Program.

(4) *Other arrangements recognized as minimum essential coverage.* The Commissioner may designate in published guidance, see § 601.601(d) of this chapter, the reporting entity for arrangements the Secretary of Health and Human Services, in coordination with the Secretary of the Treasury, recognizes under section 5000A(f)(1)(E) as minimum essential coverage.

(d) *Information required to be reported to the Internal Revenue Service*—(1) *In general.* All information returns required by this section must report the following information for the calendar year of coverage—

(i) Name, address, and employer identification number (EIN) for the person required to file the return;

(ii) Name, address, and TIN, or date of birth if a TIN is not available, of the responsible individual;

(iii) Name and TIN, or date of birth if a TIN is not available, of each individual covered under the policy or program;

(iv) For each covered individual, the months for which, for at least one day, the individual was enrolled in coverage and entitled to receive benefits; and

(v) Any other information specified in forms, instructions, or published guidance, see § § 601.601(d) and 601.602 of this chapter.

(2) *Information relating to employer-provided coverage.* In addition to the information described in paragraph (d)(1) of this section, information returns reporting minimum essential coverage provided to an individual that is coverage provided by a health insurance issuer through a group health plan must report—

(i) Name, address, and EIN of the employer sponsoring the plan;

(ii) Whether the coverage is a qualified health plan enrolled in through the Small Business Health Options Program (SHOP) and the SHOP's unique identifier; and

(iii) Other information specified in forms, instructions, or published guidance, see § § 601.601(d) and 601.602 of this chapter.

(e) *Reporting not required*—(1) *Qualified health plans.* A health insurance issuer is not required to file a return or furnish a report under this section for coverage in a qualified health plan in the individual market enrolled in through an Exchange.

(2) *Additional health benefits.* No information return is required to report arrangements that provide benefits in addition or as a supplement to a health plan or arrangement that constitutes minimum essential coverage.

(3) *Individuals not enrolled in coverage.* No reporting is required under this section for coverage offered to individuals who do not enroll.

(f) *Time and place for filing return*— (1) *In general.* A reporting entity must file the return and transmittal form required under paragraph (a) of this section on or before February 28 (March 31 if filed electronically) of the year following the calendar year in which it provided minimum essential coverage to an individual. A reporting entity must file the return and transmittal form at the address specified on the return form or in its instructions.

(2) *Extensions of time.* See § 1.6081-8 for rules relating to extensions of time to file.

(3) *Electronic filing.* See § 301.6011-8 of this chapter for rules relating to electronic filing.

(4) *Form of return.* A return required under this paragraph (f) may be made on Form 1095-B or other form designated by the Internal Revenue Service or on a substitute form. A substitute form must comply with revenue procedures or other published guidance (see § 601.601(d)(2) of this chapter) that apply to substitute forms.

(g) *Statements to be furnished to individuals*—(1) *In general.* Every person required to file a return under this section must furnish to the responsible individual identified on the return a written statement showing—

(i) Contact phone number for the person required to file the return and policy number, if applicable; and

(ii) Information described in paragraph (d) of this section for the reporting entity and each individual listed on the return.

(2) *Statements for individuals other than the responsible individual.* A reporting entity is not required to provide a statement described in paragraph (g)(1) of this section to an individual who is not the responsible individual.

(3) *Form of the statement.* A statement required under this paragraph (g) may be made either by furnishing to the responsible individual identified in the return a copy of the return filed with the IRS or on a substitute statement. A substitute statement must include the information required to be shown on the return filed with the IRS, and must comply with requirements in published guidance (see § 601.601(d)(2) of this chapter) relating to substitute statements. An IRS truncated taxpayer identifying number may be used as the identifying number for

an individual in lieu of the identifying number appearing on the corresponding information return filed with the IRS.

(4) *Time and manner for furnishing statements.* A reporting entity must furnish the statements required under this paragraph (g) on or before January 31 of the year following the calendar year in which minimum essential coverage is provided. If mailed, the statement must be sent to the individual's last known permanent address or, if no permanent address is known, to the individual's temporary address. A reporting entity may furnish the statement electronically in accordance with § 1.6055-2.

(h) *Penalties*—(1) *Failure to file correct returns.* The section 6721 penalty may apply to a person that fails to file information returns required by this section on or before the required filing date, fails to include all of the required information on the return, or includes incorrect information on the return. See section 6724 and the regulations under that section for rules relating to waivers of penalties for certain failures due to reasonable cause.

(2) *Failure to furnish correct information statements.* The section 6722 penalty may apply to a reporting entity that fails to furnish statements required by this section on or before the prescribed date, fails to include all the required information on the statement, or includes incorrect information on the statement. See section 6724 and the regulations under that section for rules relating to waivers of penalties for certain failures due to reasonable cause.

(i) *Effective/applicability date.* This section applies for calendar years beginning after December 31, 2014. Reporting entities will not be subject to penalties under section 6721 or 6722 with respect to the reporting requirements for 2014 (for information returns that would have been required to be filed and statements that would have been required to be furnished to covered individuals in 2015 with respect to 2014).

§ 1.6055-2 Electronic furnishing of statements reporting minimum essential coverage.

(a) *Electronic furnishing of statements*—(1) *In general.* A person required by section 6055 to furnish a statement (furnisher) to a responsible individual (a recipient) may furnish the statement in an electronic format in lieu of a paper format. A furnisher who meets the requirements of paragraphs (a)(2) through (a)(6) of this section is treated as furnishing the statement in a timely manner.

(2) *Consent*—(i) *In general.* The recipient must have affirmatively consented to receive the statement in an electronic format. The consent may be made electronically in any manner that reasonably demonstrates that the recipient can access the statement in the electronic format in which it will be furnished. Alternatively, the consent may be made in a paper document that is confirmed electronically.

(ii) *Withdrawal of consent.* The furnisher may provide in the disclosure furnished pursuant to paragraph (a)(3)(v) of this section that a withdrawal of consent takes effect either on the date the furnisher receives it or on another date no more than 60 days later. A furnisher may treat a request for a paper statement as a withdrawal of consent. If the furnisher provides a statement after the withdrawal of consent takes effect, the recipient has not consented to receive the statement in electronic format.

(iii) *Change in hardware or software requirements.* If a change in the hardware or software required to access the statement creates a material risk that the recipient will not be able to access a statement, a furnisher must, prior to changing the hardware or software, notify the recipient. The notice must describe the revised hardware and software required to access the statement and inform the recipient that a new consent to receive the statement in the revised electronic format must be provided to the furnisher. After implementing the revised hardware or software, the furnisher must obtain a new consent or confirmation of consent to receive the statement electronically from the recipient.

(iv) *Examples.* The following examples illustrate the rules of this paragraph (a)(2):

Example 1. Furnisher F sends Recipient R a letter stating that R may consent to receive the statement required under section 6055 electronically on a Web site instead of in a paper format. The letter contains instructions explaining how to consent to receive the statement electronically by accessing the Web site, downloading and completing the consent document, and emailing the completed consent back to F. The consent document posted on the Web site uses the same electronic format that F will use for the electronically furnished statement. R reads the instructions and submits the consent in the manner provided in the instructions. R has consented to receive the statement required under section 6055 electronically in the manner described in paragraph (a)(2)(i) of this section.

Example 2. Furnisher F sends Recipient R an email stating that R may consent to receive the statement required under section 6055 electronically instead of in a paper format. The email contains an attachment instructing R how to consent to receive the statement required under section 6055 electronically. The email attachment uses the same electronic format that F will use for the electronically furnished statement. R opens the attachment, reads the instructions, and submits the consent in the manner provided in the instructions. R has consented to receive the statement required under section 6055 electronically in the manner described in paragraph (a)(2)(i) of this section.

Example 3. Furnisher F posts a notice on its Web site stating that Recipient R may receive the statement required under section 6055 electronically instead of in a paper format. The Web site contains instructions on how R may access a secure Web page and consent to receive the statements electronically. R accesses the secure Web page and follows the instructions for giving consent. R has consented to receive the statement required under section 6055 electronically in the manner described in paragraph (a)(2)(i) of this section.

(3) *Required disclosures*—(i) *In general.* Prior to, or at the time of, a recipient's consent, a furnisher must provide to the recipient a clear and conspicuous disclosure statement containing each of the disclosures described in this paragraph (a)(3).

(ii) *Paper statement.* The furnisher must inform the recipient that the statement will be furnished on paper if the recipient does not consent to receive it electronically.

(iii) *Scope and duration of consent.* The furnisher must inform the recipient of the scope and duration of the consent. For example, the recipient must be informed whether the consent applies to each statement required to be furnished after the consent is given until it is withdrawn or only to the first statement required to be furnished following the consent.

(iv) *Post-consent request for a paper statement.* The furnisher must inform the recipient of any procedure for obtaining a paper copy of the recipient's statement after giving the consent described in paragraph (a)(2)(i) of this section and whether a request for a paper statement will be treated as a withdrawal of consent.

(v) *Withdrawal of consent.* The furnisher must inform the recipient that—

(A) The recipient may withdraw a consent by writing (electronically or on paper) to the person or department whose name, mailing address, telephone number, and email address is provided in the disclosure statement;

(B) The furnisher will confirm the withdrawal and the date on which it takes effect in writing (either electronically or on paper); and

(C) A withdrawal of consent does not apply to a statement that was furnished electronically in the manner described in this paragraph (a) before the date on which the withdrawal of consent takes effect.

(vi) *Notice of termination.* The furnisher must inform the recipient of the conditions under which the furnisher will cease furnishing statements electronically to the recipient (for example, termination of the recipient's employment with a furnisher who is the recipient's employer).

(vii) *Updating information.* The furnisher must inform the recipient of the procedures for updating the information needed to contact the recipient. The furnisher must inform the recipient of any change in the furnisher's contact information.

(viii) *Hardware and software requirements.* The furnisher must provide the recipient with a description of the hardware and software required to access, print, and retain the statement, and the date when the statement will no longer be available on the Web site. The furnisher must advise the recipient that the statement may be required to be printed and attached to a Federal, State, or local income tax return.

(4) *Format.* The electronic version of the statement must contain all required information and comply with applicable published guidance (see § 601.601(d) of this chapter) relating to substitute statements to recipients.

(5) *Notice*—(i) *In general.* If a statement is furnished on a Web site, the furnisher must notify the recipient. The notice may be delivered by mail, electronic mail, or in person. The notice must provide instructions on how to access and print the statement and include the following statement in capital letters, "IMPORTANT TAX RETURN DOCUMENT AVAILABLE." If the notice is provided by electronic mail, this statement must be on the subject line of the electronic mail.

(ii) *Undeliverable electronic address.* If an electronic notice described in paragraph (a)(5)(i) of this section is returned as undeliverable, and the furnisher cannot obtain the correct electronic address from the furnisher's records or from the recipient, the furnisher must furnish the notice by mail or in person within 30 days after the electronic notice is returned.

(iii) *Corrected statement.* The furnisher must furnish a corrected statement to the recipient electronically if the original statement was furnished electronically. If the original statement was furnished through a Web site posting, the furnisher must notify the recipient that it has posted the corrected statement on the Web site in the manner described in paragraph (a)(5)(i) of this section within 30 days of the posting. The corrected statement or the notice must be furnished by mail or in person if—

(A) An electronic notice of the Web site posting of an original statement or the corrected statement was returned as undeliverable; and

(B) The recipient has not provided a new email address.

(6) *Access period.* Statements furnished on a Web site must be retained on the Web site through October 15 of the year following the calendar year to which the statements relate (or the first business day after October 15, if October 15 falls on a Saturday, Sunday, or legal holiday). The furnisher must maintain access to corrected statements that are posted on the Web site through October 15 of the year following the calendar year to which the statements relate (or the first business day after such October 15, if October 15 falls on a Saturday, Sunday, or legal holiday) or the date 90 days after the corrected forms are posted, whichever is later.

(7) *Paper statements after withdrawal of consent.* A furnisher must furnish a paper statement if a recipient withdraws consent to receive a statement electronically and the withdrawal takes effect before the statement is furnished. A paper statement furnished after the statement due date under this paragraph (a)(7) is timely if furnished within 30 days after the date the furnisher receives the withdrawal of consent.

(b) *Effective/applicability date.* This section applies for calendar years beginning after December 31, 2014. Reporting entities will not be subject to penalties under section 6722 with respect to the reporting requirements for 2014 (for statements that would have been required to be furnished to covered individuals in 2015 with respect to 2014).

■ **Par. 3.** Section 1.6081-8 is amended by adding the language "1095 series" between the words "1042-S," and "1098" in paragraph (a).

PART 301—PROCEDURE AND ADMINISTRATION

■ **Par. 4.** The authority citation for part 301 continues to read in part as follows:

Authority: 26 U.S.C. 7805 * * *

■ **Par. 5.** Section 301.6011-8 is added to read as follows:

§ 301.6011-8 Required use of magnetic media to report minimum essential coverage.

(a) *Returns reporting minimum essential coverage must be filed on magnetic media.* A person required to file an information return reporting minimum essential coverage under § 1.6055-1 of this chapter must file the return on magnetic media if the person is required to file to least 250 returns during the calendar year. Returns filed on magnetic media must be made in accordance with applicable publications, forms, instructions, or published guidance, see §§ 601.601(d) and 601.602 of this chapter.

(b) *Magnetic media.* For purposes of this section, the term *magnetic media* has the same meaning as in § 301.6011-2(a)(1).

(c) *Determination of 250 returns.* For purposes of this section, a person is required to file at least 250 returns if, during the calendar year, the person is required to file at least 250 returns of any type, including information returns (for example, Forms W-2, Forms 1099), income tax returns, employment tax returns, and excise tax returns.

(d) *Waiver.* The Commissioner may waive the requirements of this section in cases of hardship in accordance with § 301.6011-2(c)(2)(i).

(e) *Failure to file.* If a person fails to file an information return on magnetic media when required by this section, the person is deemed to have failed to file the return. See section 6721 for penalties for failure to file returns and see section 6724 and the regulations under section 6721 for failure to file on magnetic media.

(f) *Effective/applicability date.* This section applies to returns on Form 1095-B or another form the IRS designates required to be filed after December 31, 2015. Reporting entities will not be subject to penalties under section 6721 with respect to the reporting requirements for 2014 (for information returns that would have been required to be filed in 2015 with respect to 2014).

■ **Par 6.** Section 301.6721-1 is amended by removing the word "or" after paragraph (g)(3)(xxii), removing the period and adding a semicolon in its place after paragraph (g)(3)(xxiii), and adding paragraphs (g)(3)(xxiv) and (g)(3)(xxv) to read as follows:

§ 301.6721-1 Failure to file correct information returns.

* * * * *

(g) * * *

(3) * * *

(xxiv) Section 6055 (relating to information returns reporting minimum essential coverage); or

(xxv) Section 6056 (relating to information returns reporting on offers of health insurance coverage by applicable large employer members).

* * * * *

■ **Par 7.** Section 301.6722-1 is amended by removing the word "or" after paragraph (d)(2)(xxxi), removing the period and adding a semicolon in its place after paragraph (d)(2)(xxxii), and adding paragraphs (d)(2)(xxxiii) and (d)(2)(xxxiv) to read as follows:

§ 301.6722-1 Failure to furnish correct payee statements.

* * * * *

(d) * * *

(2) * * *

(xxxiii) Section 6055 (relating to information returns reporting minimum essential coverage); or

(xxxiv) Section 6056 (relating to information returns reporting on offers of health insurance coverage by applicable large employer members).

* * * * *

Heather C. Maloy,

Acting Deputy Commissioner for Services and Enforcement.

[FR Doc. 2013-21783 Filed 9-5-13; 4:15 pm]

BILLING CODE 4830-01-P

¶ 20,263S

IRS: Employee health insurance coverage: Applicable large employers: Information reporting: Shared responsibility.—The IRS has issued proposed regulations that provide guidance to applicable large employers that are subject to the information reporting requirements under Code Sec. 6056. Code Sec. 6056 requires those employers to report to the IRS information about their compliance with the employer shared responsibility provisions of Code Sec. 4980H and about the health care coverage they have offered employees. The regulations are proposed to apply for calendar years beginning after December 31, 2014. However, a reporting entity will not be subject to penalties if it first reports beginning in 2016 for 2015, including the furnishing of statements to covered individuals in 2016 with respect to 2015. Taxpayers are encouraged, however, to voluntarily comply with section 6055 information reporting for minimum essential coverage provided in 2014 by applying these regulations once finalized.

The proposed regulations were published in the Federal Register on September 9, 2013 (78 FR 54996). The regulations were finalized on March 10, 2014 (79 FR 13231). The preamble to the final regulations is at ¶ 23,298. The final regulations are at ¶ 13,729A and ¶ 13,729B.

DEPARTMENT OF THE TREASURY

Internal Revenue Service

26 CFR Part 301

[REG-136630-12]

RIN 1545-BL26

Information Reporting by Applicable Large Employers on Health Insurance Coverage Offered Under Employer-Sponsored Plans

AGENCY: Internal Revenue Service (IRS), Treasury.

ACTION: Notice of proposed rulemaking and notice of public hearing.

SUMMARY: This document contains proposed regulations providing guidance to employers that are subject to the information reporting requirements under section 6056 of the Internal Revenue Code (Code), enacted by the Affordable Care Act. Section 6056 requires those employers to report to the IRS information about their compliance with the employer shared responsibility provisions of section 4980H of the Code and about the health care coverage they have offered employees. Section 6056 also requires those employers to furnish related statements to employees so that employees may use the statements to help determine whether, for each month of the calendar year, they can claim on their tax returns a premium tax credit under section 36B of the Code (premium tax credit). In addition, that information will be used to administer and ensure compliance with the eligibility requirements for the employer shared responsibility provisions and the premium tax credit. The proposed regulations affect applicable large employers (generally meaning employers with 50 or more full-time employees, including full-time equivalent employees, in the prior year), employees and other individuals.

This document also provides notice of a public hearing on these proposed rules.

DATES: Written or electronic comments must be received by November 8, 2013. Requests to speak and outlines of topics to be discussed at the public hearing scheduled for November 18, 2013, at 10 a.m., must be received by November 8, 2013.

ADDRESSES: Send submissions to: CC:PA:LPD:PR (REG-136630-12), Room 5205, Internal Revenue Service, PO Box 7604, Ben Franklin Station, Washington, DC 20044. Submissions may be hand-delivered Monday through Friday between the hours of 8 a.m. and 4 p.m. to CC:PA:LPD:PR (REG-136630-12), Courier's Desk, Internal Revenue Service, 1111 Constitution Avenue NW., Washington, DC, or sent electronically, via the Federal eRulemaking Portal at *www.regulations.gov* (IRS REG-136630-12). The public hearing will be held in the Auditorium, Internal Revenue Building, 1111 Constitution Avenue NW., Washington, DC.

FOR FURTHER INFORMATION CONTACT: Concerning the proposed regulations, Ligeia Donis (202) 927-9639; concerning submission of comments, the hearing, and/or to be placed on the building access list to attend the hearing, please contact Oluwafunmilayo (Funmi) Taylor at (202) 622-7180 (not toll-free numbers).

SUPPLEMENTARY INFORMATION:

Paperwork Reduction Act

The collection of information contained in this notice of proposed rulemaking has been submitted to the Office of Management and Budget for review in accordance with the Paperwork Reduction Act of 1995 (44 U.S.C. 3507(d)). Comments on the collection of information should be sent to the Office of Management and Budget, Attn: Desk Officer for the Department of the Treasury, Office of Information and Regulatory Affairs, Washington, DC 20503, with copies to the Internal Revenue Service, Attn: IRS Reports Clearance Officer, SE:W:CAR:MP:T:T:SP, Washington, DC 20224. Comments on the collection of information should be received by November 8, 2013. Comments are specifically requested concerning:

Whether the proposed collection of information is necessary for the proper performance of the functions of the IRS, including whether the information will have practical utility;

How the quality, utility, and clarity of the information to be collected may be enhanced;

How the burden of complying with the proposed collection of information may be minimized, including through the application of auto-

mated collection techniques or other forms of information technology; and

Estimates of capital or start-up costs and costs of operation, maintenance, and purchase of services to provide information.

The collection of information in these proposed regulations is in proposed regulation §§ 301.6011-9, 301.6056-1, and 301.6056-2. This information will be used by the IRS to verify compliance with the return and employee statement requirements under section 6056 for purposes of section 4980H, and with the eligibility requirements for the premium tax credit. This information will be used to determine whether the information has been reported and calculated correctly for purposes of section 4980H and section 6056, and whether claims for the premium tax credit are correct. The likely respondents are employers that are applicable large employers, as defined under section 4980H(c)(2).

An agency may not conduct or sponsor, and a person is not required to respond to, a collection of information unless it displays a valid control number assigned by the Office of Management and Budget.

Books or records relating to a collection of information must be retained as long as their contents may become material in the administration of any internal revenue law. Generally, tax returns and tax return information are confidential, as required by 26 U.S.C. 6103.

Background

Sections I through V of the preamble ("Background") describe the statutory provisions governing the information reporting requirements, as well as related statutory provisions. Sections VI through XIII of the preamble ("Explanation of Provisions and Summary of Comments") describe and explain how these regulations propose to implement the statutory provisions of section 6056 and include a discussion of a variety of potential simplified reporting methods that are under consideration. As is typical with regulations on information reporting, these proposed regulations refer generally to additional information that may be required under the applicable forms and instructions. Sections IX.B and C of this preamble set forth the specific data elements that Treasury and the IRS anticipate will be included with the reporting, including the data elements that Treasury and the IRS anticipate will be provided through the use of an indicator code.

Section 6056[1] requires applicable large employers, as defined in section 4980H(c)(2), to file returns at the time prescribed by the Secretary with respect to each full-time employee and furnish a statement to each full-time employee by January 31 of the calendar year following the calendar year for which the return must be filed. Section 6056 specifies certain information that must be reported on the section 6056 return and related statement, and authorizes the Secretary to require additional information and determine the form of the return. Section 6056 is effective for periods beginning after December 31, 2013; however, Notice 2013-45 (2013-31 IRB 116) provides transition relief for 2014 from the section 6056 information reporting requirements (as well as the section 6055 information reporting requirements relating to the section 5000A individual shared responsibility provisions and the section 4980H employer shared responsibility provisions).

I. Shared Responsibility for Employers (Section 4980H)

One of the purposes of section 6056 reporting is to assist with the administration of the employer shared responsibility provisions added by the Affordable Care Act as section 4980H of the Code. Section 4980H imposes an assessable payment on applicable large employers if certain requirements relating to the provision of health care coverage to full-time employees are not met and one or more full-time employees claim a premium tax credit. On December 28, 2012, Treasury and the IRS released proposed regulations under section 4980H. The proposed regulations under section 4980H were published in the **Federal Register** on January 2, 2013 (REG-138006-12 [78 FR 218]). Section 4980H is effective for months after December 31, 2013; however, Notice 2013-45, issued on July 9, 2013, provides transition relief for 2014 from the section 4980H employer shared responsibility provisions.

The reporting requirements under section 6056 apply only to employers that are subject to section 4980H (which the statute refers to as "applicable large employers"). Section 4980H(c)(2) defines the term "applicable large employer" as, with respect to a calendar year, an employer that employed an average of at least 50 full-time employees on business days during the preceding calendar year. Generally, for purposes of determining applicable large employer status, a full-time employee includes any employee who was employed on average at

---

[1] Section 6056 was enacted by section 1514(a) of the Patient Protection and Affordable Care Act, Public Law 111-148 (124 Stat. 119 (2010)), amended by the Health Care and Education Reconciliation Act of 2010, Public Law 111-152 (124 Stat. 1029 (2010)), and further amended by the Department of Defense and Full-Year Continuing Appropriations Act of 2011, Public Law 112-10 (125 Stat. 38 (2011)) (collectively, the Affordable Care Act).

least 30 hours of service per week and any full-time equivalents determined pursuant to section 4980H(c)(2)(E). All employers treated as a single employer under section 414(b), (c), (m), or (o) are treated as one employer for purposes of determining applicable large employer status. Section 4980H contains rules for determining whether an employer qualifies as an applicable large employer, including special rules addressing an employer's first year of existence and predecessor and successor employers. See section 4980H(c)(2)(C) and proposed §54.4980H-2. Proposed regulations under section 4980H provide guidance on determining applicable large employer status and determining full-time employee status, including defining and providing rules for calculating hours of service. See proposed §§54.4980H-1(a)(21) (definition of hours of service), 54.4980H-2 (determination of applicable large employer status), and 54.4980H-3 (determination of full-time employee status).

II. Premium Tax Credit (Section 36B)

Section 6056 reporting will also be used for the administration of the premium tax credit, which was added by the Affordable Care Act as section 36B of the Code. Section 36B allows an advanceable and refundable premium tax credit to help individuals and families afford health insurance coverage purchased through an Affordable Insurance Exchange (Exchange). An employee is not eligible for a premium tax credit to subsidize the cost of Exchange coverage if the employee is offered affordable coverage under an employer-sponsored plan that provides minimum value, or if the employee enrolls in an employer-sponsored plan. For this purpose, an employer-sponsored plan is affordable if the employee's required contribution for the lowest-cost self-only minimum value coverage offered does not exceed 9.5% of the employee's household income. Thus, an employee (and in the case of an employer-sponsored plan that offers coverage to an employee's spouse or dependents, the employee's spouse and dependents) who does not accept an offer of affordable minimum value coverage under an employer-sponsored plan and who purchase coverage on an Exchange may not be eligible for a premium tax credit. Individuals and the IRS will use the information on the cost of the lowest-cost employer-sponsored self-only coverage that provides minimum value to verify the individual's eligibility for the premium tax credit.[2]

III. Individual Shared Responsibility (Section 5000A)

In addition, the Affordable Care Act added section 5000A to the Code. Section 5000A provides nonexempt individuals with a choice: maintain minimum essential coverage for themselves and any nonexempt family members, or include an additional payment with their Federal income tax return. Section 5000A(f)(1)(B) provides that minimum essential coverage includes coverage under an eligible employer-sponsored plan. Under section 5000A(f)(2), an eligible employer-sponsored plan is, with respect to an employee, a group health plan or group health insurance coverage offered by an employer to the employee that is (1) a governmental plan, within the meaning of section 2791(d)(8) of the Public Health Service Act (42 U.S.C. 300gg-91(d)(8)), or (2) any other plan or coverage offered in the small or large group market within a State. An eligible employer-sponsored plan also includes a grandfathered health plan, as defined in section 5000A(f)(1)(D), offered in a group market. Group health plans within the meaning of section 1301(b)(3) of the Affordable Care Act (42 U.S.C. 18021(b)(3)) include both insured health plans and self-insured health plans. Accordingly, a self-insured group health plan is an eligible employer-sponsored plan. See the Questions and Answers on the Individual Shared Responsibility Provision available on the IRS Web site at *www.irs.gov.*

IV. Information Reporting by Providers of Coverage (Issuers, Self-Insuring Employers, and Sponsors of Certain Government-Sponsored Programs) (Section 6055)

The Affordable Care Act also added section 6055 to the Code, providing for information reporting for the administration of section 5000A. The section 6055 reporting requirements are effective for years beginning after December 31, 2013; however, Notice 2013-45 provides transition relief for 2014 from the section 6055 reporting requirements. Section 6055 requires information reporting by any person that pro-

vides minimum essential coverage to an individual during a calendar year, including coverage provided under an eligible employer-sponsored plan, and the furnishing to taxpayers of a related statement covering each individual listed on the section 6055 return. The information reported under section 6055 can be used by individuals and the IRS to verify the months (if any) in which they were covered by minimum essential coverage. Treasury and the IRS are issuing proposed regulations under section 6055 (REG-132455-11) concurrently with these proposed regulations.

V. Reporting Requirements for Applicable Large Employers (Section 6056)

Section 6056 directs an applicable large employer (within the meaning of section 4980H(c)(2)) to file a return with the IRS that reports for each employee who was a full-time employee for one or more months during the calendar year certain information described in section 6056(b) about the health care coverage the employer offered to that employee (or, if applicable, that the employer did not offer health care coverage to that employee). Section 6056 also requires such employers to furnish by January 31 of the calendar year following the calendar year for which the return must be filed a related statement described in section 6056(c) to each full-time employee for whom information is required to be included on the return.

Section 6056(b) describes the return required to be filed with the IRS under section 6056. It states that a return meets the requirements of section 6056 if the return is in such form as the Secretary may prescribe and contains (1) the name, date, and employer's employer identification number (EIN), (2) a certification as to whether the employer offers to its full-time employees (and their dependents) the opportunity to enroll in minimum essential coverage under an eligible employer-sponsored plan (as defined in section 5000A(f)(2)), (3) the number of full-time employees for each month during the calendar year, and (4) the name, address, and taxpayer identification number of each full-time employee during the calendar year and the months, if any, during which that employee (and any dependents) were covered under any such health benefits plans.

If the applicable large employer certifies that it offered to its full-time employees (and their dependents) the opportunity to enroll in minimum essential coverage under an eligible employer-sponsored plan (as defined in section 5000A(f)(2)), section 6056 specifies that the return must also include (1) the length of any waiting period (as defined in section 2701(b)(4) of the Public Health Service Act (42 U.S.C. 300gg(b)(4)) with respect to that coverage,[3] (2) the months during the calendar year for which coverage under the plan was available, (3) the monthly premium for the lowest cost option in each of the enrollment categories under the plan, and (4) the employer's share of the total allowed costs of benefits provided under the plan. Section 6056(b)(2)(F) provides that the return must include such other information as the Secretary may require. See section IX of this preamble for a discussion of the information proposed to be included in these proposed regulations as part of the reporting requirements, as well as additional information that may be required under the applicable forms and instructions, as is typical with regulations on information reporting.

Section 6056(c) requires that every person required to make a return under section 6056(a) furnish to each full-time employee whose name is required to be set forth in the return a written statement showing (1) the name and address of the person required to make that return and the phone number of the information contact for that person, and (2) the information required to be shown on the return with respect to that individual. The written statement must be furnished on or before January 31 of the year following the calendar year for which the return under section 6056(a) was required to be made.

As discussed in section IX.B of this preamble, the approach contemplated by these proposed regulations would give effect to these statutory provisions by limiting the information elements listed and other information that would be provided annually to those that are needed by individual taxpayers to accurately complete their tax returns or by the IRS to effectively administer other provisions of the Affordable Care Act. Treasury and the IRS seek comments on ways to achieve these goals efficiently and effectively.

---

[2] In connection with providing advance payment of the premium tax credit, the Exchanges will employ a verification process. Because the information concerning household income and other relevant factors that are known to the individual and the Exchanges at that time may differ from the information used to file the tax return after the close of the coverage year, an individual who receives an advance payment of the premium tax credit will also need to calculate the appropriate amount of the credit when filing his or her tax return, and the credit may be more or less than the advance payment.

[3] While section 6056(b)(2)(C)(i) refers to the term "waiting period" as defined in section 2701(b)(4) of the PHS Act, amendments made by section 1201 of the Affordable Care Act

moved this definition from section 2701(b)(4) of the PHS Act to section 2704(b)(4). Separately, section 2708 of the PHS Act prohibits a group health plan and a health insurance issuer offering group health insurance coverage from applying any waiting period that exceeds 90 days. The Affordable Care Act adds section 715(a)(1) to the Employee Retirement Income Security Act (ERISA) and section 9815(a)(1) to the Code to incorporate the provisions of part A of title XXVII of the PHS Act (specifically, PHS Act sections 2701 through 2728) into ERISA and the Code, and to make them applicable to group health plans and health insurance issuers providing health insurance coverage in connection with group health plans.

Section 6056(d) provides that to the maximum extent feasible, the Secretary may permit combined reporting under section 6056, section 6051 (employers filing and furnishing Forms W-2, Wage and Tax Statement, with respect to employees) or section 6055, and in the case of an applicable large employer offering health insurance coverage of a health insurance issuer, the employer may enter into an agreement with the issuer to include information required under section 6056 with the return and statement required to be provided by the issuer under section 6055.

Section 6056(e) generally permits governmental units, or any agency or instrumentality thereof, to designate a person to comply with the section 6056 requirements on behalf of the governmental unit, agency or instrumentality.

Under section 6724(d), as amended by the Affordable Care Act, an applicable large employer that fails to comply with the filing and statement furnishing requirements of section 6056 may be subject to penalties for failure to file a correct information return (section 6721) and failure to furnish correct payee statements (section 6722). However, these penalties may be waived if the failure is due to reasonable cause and not to willful neglect (section 6724).

Notice 2012-32 (2012-20 IRB 910) requested public comments on issues to be addressed in regulations under section 6055. Notice 2012-33 (2012-20 IRB 912) requested public comments on issues to be addressed in regulations under section 6056. In developing these proposed regulations and the proposed regulations under section 6055, including the potential further simplified reporting methods described in section XI of this preamble, Treasury and the IRS have considered the written comments submitted in response to these notices and other written comments received.

In addition, consistent with Notice 2013-45, Treasury and the IRS have engaged in further dialogue with stakeholders in an effort to simplify section 6056 and section 6055 reporting consistent with effective implementation of the law. This process has included discussions with stakeholders representing a wide range of interests to assist in the consideration of effective information reporting rules that will be as streamlined, simple, and workable as possible. The effort to develop these proposed information reporting rules has reflected a considered balancing of the importance of (1) providing individuals the information to complete their tax returns accurately, including with respect to the individual responsibility provisions and eligibility for the premium tax credit, (2) minimizing cost and administrative tasks for the reporting entities and individuals, and (3) providing the IRS with information to use for effective and efficient tax administration. As noted elsewhere in this preamble, the proposed regulations will be the subject of public comments, including comments that are specifically invited regarding particular issues identified in the preamble.

Explanation of Provisions and Summary of Comments

VI. Introduction

The Explanation of Provisions that follows (Sections VII through XIII of the preamble) describes the regulatory provisions proposed to implement the statutory reporting provisions described in the Background portion of the preamble. Specifically, this section includes the following:

VII. Key Terms

These proposed regulations under section 6056 use a number of terms that are defined in other Code provisions or regulations. For example, section 6056(f) provides that any term used in section 6056 that is also used in section 4980H shall have the same meaning given to the term by section 4980H. Relevant terms include the following:

A. Applicable Large Employer

The proposed regulations provide that the term *applicable large employer* has the same meaning as in section 4980H(c)(2) and any applicable guidance. See proposed § 54.4980H-1(a)(4).

B. ALE Member

All persons treated as a single employer under section 414(b), (c), (m), or (o) are treated as one employer for purposes of determining applicable large employer status.[4] Under the proposed regulations, the section 6056 filing and furnishing requirements are applied separately to each person comprising the applicable large employer consistent with the approach taken in the section 4980H proposed regulations (REG-138006-12 [78 FR 218]) with respect to the determination of any assessable payment under section 4980H. The person or persons that comprise the applicable large employer are referred to as ALE members. The proposed regulations define the term *ALE member* as a person that, together with one or more other persons, is treated as a single employer that is an applicable large employer. For this purpose, if a person, together with one or more other persons, is treated as a single employer that is an applicable large employer on any day of a calendar month, that person is an ALE member for that calendar month. This definition is the same as the definition provided in the proposed regulations under section 4980H. See § 54.4980H-1(a)(5).

C. Dependent

The proposed regulations provide that the term *dependent* has the same meaning as in section 4980H(a) and (b) and any applicable guidance. See proposed § 54.4980H-1(a)(11).

D. Eligible Employer-Sponsored Plan

The proposed regulations provide that the term *eligible employer-sponsored plan* has the same meaning as in section 5000A(f)(2) and any applicable guidance.

E. Full-time Employee

The proposed regulations provide that the term full-time employee has the same meaning as in section 4980H(c)(4) and any applicable guidance as applied to the determination and calculation of liability under section 4980H(a) and (b) with respect to any individual employee. See proposed § 54.4980H-1(a)(18).

F. Governmental Unit and Agency or Instrumentality of a Governmental Unit

The proposed regulations define the term *governmental unit* as the government of the United States, any State or political subdivision thereof, or any Indian tribal government (as defined in section 7701(a)(40)) or subdivision of an Indian tribal government (as defined in section 7871(d)). The proposed regulations do not define the term *agency or instrumentality of a governmental unit,* but rather reserve on the issue.

G. Minimum Essential Coverage

The proposed regulations provide that the term *minimum essential coverage* has the same meaning as in section 5000A(f)(1) and any applicable guidance.

H. Minimum Value

The proposed regulations provide that the term *minimum value* has the same meaning as in section 36B and any applicable guidance. See proposed § 1.36B-6.

I. Person

The proposed regulations provide that the term *person* has the same meaning as provided in section 7701(a)(1) and the regulations thereunder.

---

[4] As explained in section 1.A.2 of the preamble to the proposed regulations under section 4980H (REG-138006-12 [78 FR 218]), until further guidance is issued, government entities, churches, and a convention or association of churches may apply a reasonable, good faith interpretation of section 414(b), (c), (m), and (o) in determining whether a person or group of persons is an applicable large employer and whether a particular entity is an applicable large employer member. See proposed § 54.4980H-1(a)(5).

VIII. ALE Member Subject to Section 6056 Requirements With Respect to Full-Time Employees

As discussed earlier in section VII.B of this preamble, an ALE member is any person that is an applicable large employer or a member of an aggregated group (determined under section 414(b), 414(c), 414(m) or 414(o)) that is determined to be an applicable large employer. Under the proposed regulations, the section 6056 filing and statement furnishing requirements apply on a member-by-member basis to each ALE member, even though the determination of whether an entity is an applicable large employer is made at the aggregated group level. For example, if an applicable large employer is comprised of a parent corporation and 10 wholly-owned subsidiary corporations, there are 11 ALE members (the parent corporation and each of the 10 subsidiary corporations). Under the proposed regulations, each ALE member with full-time employees, rather than the group of entities that comprise the applicable large employer, is the entity responsible for filing and furnishing statements with respect to its full-time employees under section 6056. This is consistent with the manner in which any potential assessable payments under section 4980H will be calculated and administered.

Treasury and the IRS understand that ALE members may benefit from the assistance of a third party in preparing these returns, for example a third-party plan administrator or a related ALE member tasked with preparing the returns for all the members of that applicable large employer. For a discussion of how these third parties may help an ALE member fulfill its reporting obligations, see section XII.C of this preamble.

Whether an employee is a full-time employee is determined under section 4980H(c)(4) and any applicable guidance. See proposed §§ 54.4980H-1(a)(18) and 54.4980H-3. This includes any full-time employees who may perform services for multiple ALE members within the applicable large employer.[5] Under the proposed regulations, only ALE members with full-time employees are subject to the filing and statement furnishing requirements of section 6056 (and only with respect to their full-time employees).

Generally, the ALE member providing the section 6056 reporting is the common law employer. Disregarded entities are treated for section 4980H purposes, and therefore for section 6056 purposes, similarly to the way they are treated for employment tax purposes, so that the reporting requirements under section 6056 are imposed on a disregarded entity that is an applicable large employer, and not on its owner.[6]

IX. General Method—Content, Manner, and Timing of Information Required to be Reported to the IRS and Furnished to Full-Time Employees

This section describes the general method for reporting to the IRS and furnishing statements to employees pursuant to section 6056 that is set forth in the proposed regulations. This general method would be available for all employers and with respect to reporting for all employees. Treasury and the IRS are also considering certain simplified reporting methods, such as using codes on Form W-2 to report whether full-time employees, spouses, and their dependents have been offered coverage, which in some cases may be available only with respect to certain groups of employees. In those cases, with respect to those employees for whom the simplified reporting method was not available, the employer would use the general method. In any case, however, the simplified reporting methods under consideration would be optional so that an employer could choose to report for all of its full-time employees using the general method described in these proposed regulations even if a simplified reporting method is available. For a further description of the simplified reporting methods under consideration, see section XI of this preamble.

A. Information Reporting to the IRS

In accordance with section 6056, the proposed regulations provide for every ALE member to file a section 6056 return with respect to its full-time employees. Similar to the separate Form W-2, Wage and Tax Statement, filed by an employer for each employee and the Form W-3, Transmittal of Wage and Tax Statements, filed as a transmittal form for the Forms W-2, the proposed regulations provide that a separate return is required for each full-time employee, accompanied by a single transmittal form for all of the returns filed for a given calendar year.

As a general method, the proposed regulations further provide that the section 6056 return may be made by filing Form 1094-C (a transmittal) and Form 1095-C (an employee statement), or other forms the IRS designates. Alternatively, the section 6056 return may be made by filing other form(s) designated by the IRS or a substitute form. Under the proposed regulations, a substitute form must include all of the information required to be reported on Forms 1094-C and 1095-C or other forms the IRS designates and comply with applicable revenue procedures or other published guidance relating to substitute returns. See § 601.601(d)(2). In accordance with usual procedures, these forms will be made available in draft form at a later date.

B. Information Required To Be Reported and Furnished

The proposed regulations provide that every ALE member will report on the section 6056 information return the following information: (1) The name, address, and employer identification number of the ALE member, the name and telephone number of the applicable large employer's contact person, and the calendar year for which the information is reported; (2) a certification as to whether the ALE member offered to its full-time employees (and their dependents) the opportunity to enroll in minimum essential coverage under an eligible employer-sponsored plan (as defined in section 5000A(f)(2)), by calendar month; (3) the number of full-time employees for each month during the calendar year; (4) for each full-time employee, the months during the calendar year for which coverage under the plan was available; (5) for each full-time employee, the employee's share of the lowest cost monthly premium (self-only) for coverage providing minimum value offered to that full-time employee under an eligible employer-sponsored plan, by calendar month; and (6) the name, address, and taxpayer identification number of each full-time employee during the calendar year and the months, if any, during which the employee was covered under an eligible employer-sponsored plan. In addition, the proposed regulations provide, as with other information reporting, that the section 6056 information return may request such other information as the Secretary may prescribe or as may be required by the form or instructions.

As part of the effort to minimize the cost and administrative steps associated with the reporting requirements, Treasury and the IRS have sought to identify any information that would not be relevant to individual taxpayers or the IRS for purposes of administering the premium tax credit and employer shared responsibility provisions or that is already provided at the same time through other means. Specifically, the proposed regulations do not require the reporting of the following four data elements (a more detailed description of the data elements that Treasury and the IRS anticipate will be included is provided later in this section of the preamble).

First, the proposed regulations do not require the reporting of the length of any waiting period, because the length of the waiting period is not relevant for administration of the premium tax credit or employer shared responsibility provisions or for an individual in preparing his or her tax return. However, Treasury and the IRS anticipate that information will be requested, using an indicator code, regarding whether an employee's coverage was not effective during certain months because of a waiting period since this information is relevant to the administration of the employer shared responsibility provisions.

Second, the proposed regulations do not require reporting of the employer's share of the total allowed costs of benefits provided under the plan because this information also is not relevant to the administration of the premium tax credit and the employer shared responsibility provisions. In contrast, whether the employer-sponsored plan provides minimum value coverage is relevant information; accordingly, Treasury and the IRS anticipate that information will be requested, also using an indicator code.

Third, the proposed regulations do not require the reporting of the monthly premium for the lowest-cost option in each of the enrollment categories (such as self-only coverage or family coverage) under the plan. Rather, because only the lowest-cost option of self-only coverage offered under any of the enrollment categories for which the employee is eligible is relevant to the determination of whether coverage is affordable (and thus to the administration of the premium tax credit and employer shared responsibility provisions), that is the only cost information proposed to be requested.

---

[5] For example, if an employee performs services for two applicable large employer members within an applicable large employer and the combined hours of service for the two applicable large employer members are sufficient to trigger a reporting obligation under section 6056, each applicable large employer member is required to file and furnish a section 6056 return with respect to services performed by the employee for that applicable large employer member. See proposed § 54.4980H-5(d).

[6] Specifically, the proposed regulations under section 7701 (REG-138006-12 [78 FR 218]) treat the disregarded entity (as defined in § 301.7701-2) as a corporation with respect to the reporting requirements under section 6056. See proposed § 301.7701-2(c)(2)(v)(A)(5). These rules would also apply to a qualified subchapter S subsidiary. See proposed § 1.1361-4(a)(8)(i)(E).

Fourth, the proposed regulations do not require the reporting of the months, if any, during which any of the employee's dependents were covered under the plan. Instead, the proposed regulations require reporting only regarding whether the employee was covered under a plan. This is because information relating to the months during which any of the employee's dependents were covered under the plan will be reported on the section 6055 information return associated with that employee's coverage.

Under the proposed regulations, each ALE member must file and furnish the section 6056 return and employee statement using its EIN. Any ALE member that does not have an EIN may easily apply for one online, by telephone, fax, or mail. See Publication 1635, Employer Identification Number, for further information at *www.irs.gov*.

Having considered the information required by section 6056 and the information needed to verify employer-sponsored coverage and to administer the employer shared responsibility provisions under section 4980H and the premium tax credit, Treasury and the IRS anticipate that as part of the general method for section 6056 reporting, the IRS will need certain information not specifically set forth under section 6056 but authorized under section 6056(b)(2)(F). Accordingly, the proposed regulations provide, in a manner similar to other information reporting guidance, that additional information may be prescribed by guidance, forms, or instructions. Treasury and the IRS are also considering potential simplified reporting methods that in certain situations may permit an employer to provide less information than all data elements required under the general method for reporting. See section XI of this preamble.

Under the general method of section 6056 reporting, the following information is expected to be requested, through the use of indicator codes for some information, as part of the section 6056 return (as well as an indication of how many individual employee statements are being submitted):

(1) Information as to whether the coverage offered to employees and their dependents under an employer-sponsored plan meets minimum value and whether the employee had the opportunity to enroll his or her spouse in the coverage;

(2) the total number of employees, by calendar month;

(3) whether an employee's effective date of coverage was affected by a waiting period;

(4) if the ALE member was not conducting business during any particular month, by month;

(5) if the ALE member expects that it will not be an ALE member the following year;

(6) information regarding whether the ALE member is a person that is a member of an aggregated group, determined under section 414(b), 414(c), 414(m), or 414(o), and, if applicable, the name and EIN of each employer member of the aggregated group constituting the applicable large employer on any day of the calendar year for which the information is reported;

(7) if an appropriately designated entity is reporting on behalf of an ALE member that is a governmental unit or any agency or instrumentality thereof for purposes of section 6056, the name, address, and identification number of the appropriately designated person;

(8) if an ALE member is a contributing employer to a multiemployer plan, whether a full-time employee is treated as eligible to participate in a multiemployer plan due to the employer's contributions to the multiemployer plan; and

(9) if the administrator of a multiemployer plan is reporting on behalf of the ALE member with respect to the ALE member's full-time employees who are eligible for coverage under the multiemployer plan, the name, address, and identification number of the administrator of the multiemployer plan (in addition to the name, address, and EIN of the ALE member already required under the proposed regulations).

C. Use of Indicator Codes To Provide Information With Respect to a Particular Full-Time Employee

In an effort to simplify and streamline the section 6056 reporting process even under the general section 6056 reporting rules, Treasury and the IRS anticipate that certain of the information described above as applied to a particular full-time employee will be reported to the IRS, and furnished to the full-time employee, through the use of a code

rather than by providing specific or detailed information. Specifically, it is contemplated that the following information will be reported with respect to each full-time employee for each calendar month using a code:[7]

(1) minimum essential coverage meeting minimum value was offered to:

a. the employee only;

b. the employee and the employee's dependents only;

c. the employee and the employee's spouse only; or

d. the employee, the employee's spouse and dependents;

(2) coverage was not offered to the employee and:

a. the employee was in a waiting period that complies with the requirements of PHS Act section 2708 and its implementing regulations;

b. the employee was not a full-time employee;

c. the employee was not employed by the ALE member during that month; or

d. no other code or exception applies;

(3) coverage was offered to the employee for the month although the employee was not a full-time employee during that month; and

(4) the ALE member met one of the affordability safe harbors under proposed § 54.4980H-5(e)(2) with respect to the employee.

It is anticipated that if multiple codes apply with respect to a full-time employee for a particular calendar month, the reporting format will accommodate the necessary codes.

D. Section 6056 Statements to Full-Time Employees

Under the general section 6056 reporting rules set forth in the proposed regulations, every ALE member required to file a section 6056 return must furnish a section 6056 employee statement to each of its full-time employees that includes the name, address and EIN of the ALE member and the information required to be shown on the section 6056 return with respect to the full-time employee. The section 6056 employee statement is not required to include a copy of the transmittal form that accompanies the returns. As part of the potential simplified reporting methods Treasury and the IRS are also considering whether, in certain circumstances, other methods of furnishing information to an employee may be sufficient (for example, through the use of a code on the Form W-2). For a detailed description of these potential simplified reporting methods, see section XI of this preamble.

Some employers may wish to have the flexibility to use a substitute type of statement to provide the necessary information to full-time employees. The proposed regulations provide that the section 6056 employee statement may be made by furnishing a copy of the section 6056 return on Form 1095-C (or another form the IRS designates) or a substitute employee statement for that full-time employee. Under the proposed regulations, a substitute statement must include the information required to be shown on the section 6056 return filed with the IRS with respect to that employee and must comply with applicable revenue procedures or other published guidance relating to substitute statements. See § 601.601(d)(2). These proposed regulations provide that section 6056 employee statements filed using Form 1095-C or another form the IRS designates will be included in the proposed IRS truncated TIN program. Under this proposed program, an IRS truncated taxpayer identifying number may be used as the identifying number for an individual in lieu of the identifying number appearing on the corresponding information return filed with the IRS. See the proposed regulations on IRS Truncated Taxpayer Identification Numbers (REG-148873-09 [78 FR 913]).

E. Time for Filing Section 6056 Returns and Furnishing Employee Statements

The proposed regulations provide that section 6056 returns must be filed with the IRS annually, no later than February 28 (March 31 if filed electronically) of the year immediately following the calendar year to which the return relates. This is the same filing schedule applicable to other information returns with which employers are familiar such as Forms W-2 and 1099. Because Notice 2013-45 provided transition relief for section 6056 reporting for 2014, the first section 6056 returns required to be filed are for the 2015 calendar year and must be filed no

---

[7] Treasury and the IRS have received comments regarding whether transition relief previously provided in the section 4980H proposed regulations (REG-138006-12 [78 FR 218]) with respect to the transition from 2013 to 2014 will be extended to the transition from 2014 to 2015. The issue is currently under consideration and will be addressed in future guidance under section 4980H. If further transition relief is provided under section 4980H, it is expected that additional indicator codes will be available on the section 6056 return to indicate that an employer is using the transition relief.

later than March 1, 2016 (February 28, 2016, being a Sunday), or March 31, 2016, if filed electronically. In addition, the regulations propose that the section 6056 employee statements be furnished annually to full-time employees on or before January 31 of the year immediately following the calendar year to which the employee statements relate. This means that the first section 6056 employee statements (meaning the statements for 2015) must be furnished no later than February 1, 2016 (January 31, 2016, being a Sunday).

In preparation for the application of the section 4980H provisions beginning in 2015, employers are encouraged to voluntarily comply for 2014 (that is, for section 6056 returns and statements filed and furnished in 2015) with the information reporting provisions (once the information reporting rules have been issued) and to maintain or expand health coverage in 2014. Real-world testing of reporting systems and plan designs through voluntary compliance for 2014 will contribute to a smoother transition to full implementation for 2015.

Some commenters asked for use of an alternate filing date for employers whose health plan is not a calendar year plan. While Treasury and the IRS understand that employers may collect information on a plan year basis, employees generally will need to receive their section 6056 employee statements early in the calendar year in order to have the requisite information to correctly and completely file their income tax returns reflecting any available premium tax credit. For this reason, the proposed regulations do not adopt this suggestion. However, Treasury and the IRS are considering a simplified reporting method, described in section XI of this preamble, that in certain circumstances could permit the employer to report the required information on the Form W-2 which is already being furnished to an employee on the same schedule.

These proposed regulations do not include rules regarding extensions of the time to file section 6056 returns but this topic is addressed elsewhere. Specifically, the notice of proposed rulemaking under section 6055 (REG-132455-11) includes proposed amendments to the regulations under section 6081 relating to general rules on extensions of time to file to include returns under both sections 6055 and 6056. The final section 6056 regulations are expected to cross-reference the amendments to the regulations under section 6081. These proposed regulations reserve a paragraph for this cross-reference.

F. Manner of Filing of Section 6056 Information Returns and Furnishing of Section 6056 Employee Statements

Treasury and the IRS understand that electronic filing is often easier and more efficient for taxpayers, and several commenters requested that employers be permitted to file section 6056 returns electronically. The proposed regulations require electronic filing of section 6056 information returns except for an ALE member filing fewer than 250 returns during the calendar year. Each section 6056 return for a full-time employee is a separate return. Although an ALE member filing fewer than 250 returns during the calendar year may always choose to make the section 6056 returns on the prescribed paper form, that member is permitted (and encouraged) to file section 6056 returns electronically. This proposed requirement for electronic filing is the same as the current requirements for other information returns.

The proposed regulations provide that all returns are aggregated for the purpose of applying the 250-return threshold so that, for example, an ALE member required to file 150 section 6056 returns and 200 Forms W-2 will be required to electronically file section 6056 returns. A reporting entity must submit the prescribed form(s) to request authorization and obtain a Transmitter Control Code from the IRS to be able to file an information return electronically.

In addition to electronic filing, Treasury and the IRS understand that electronic methods are often a simpler and more efficient method to supply employees with the required information, and several commenters requested that employers be permitted to electronically furnish section 6056 employee statements to full-time employees. In response, the proposed regulations permit electronic furnishing of section 6056 employee statements if certain notice, consent, and hardware or software requirements are met. To provide rules for electronic furnishing with which employers are already familiar, the proposed regulations adopt by analogy the process currently in place for the electronic furnishing of employee statements (that is, Forms W-2) pursuant to section 6051 and applicable regulations.

X. Combined Reporting Under Section 6056 and Section 6051 or 6055

In addition to the reporting under section 6056, two other reporting provisions provide for annual reporting with respect to certain individuals and the furnishing of statements to those individuals. Specifically, section 6051 requires employers to provide Forms W-2 reporting wages paid and taxes withheld. Section 6055 requires information reporting by any person that provides minimum essential coverage to an individual. ALE members that provide minimum essential coverage on a self-insured basis are subject to the reporting requirements of all three sections (6051, 6055 and 6056). Notices 2012-32 and 2012-33 requested comments on how to minimize duplication in reporting under these provisions.

Several commenters recommended that the regulations allow combined information reporting under sections 6055 and 6056 for applicable large employers that sponsor self-insured plans and must report under both sections. Other commenters recommended that employers be permitted to use a single information return to report under sections 6051 (Form W-2) and 6055. Some commenters suggested adding section 6055 or section 6056 reporting to Form W-2.

Because not all employers are subject to each of these three reporting requirements, independent reporting methods under each section need to be available; otherwise, employers subject to only one reporting requirement may have to expend additional effort to use a combined reporting method. Optional combined reporting therefore would require development of multiple forms for each reporting requirement (some forms for combined reporting, other forms for separate reporting), which could create administrative complexity and create confusion for employees.

In addition, any consideration of combined reporting must take into account that sections 6051, 6055 and 6056 apply to different types of entities (subject to the various reporting requirements, which differ among the Code provisions), and require reporting of different types of information. Section 6051 requires reporting of certain wage and wage-related information on an annual basis by all employers for all employees (and only employees). Section 6055 requires reporting of certain health coverage information by various entities (issuers, employers sponsoring self-insured group health plans, and governmental units) only for individuals who are actually covered (and not for individuals who are offered coverage but do not enroll), and multiple covered individuals may be included on one return. Section 6056 requires reporting of information by applicable large employers on offers of coverage that have or have not been made only to full-time employees (whether or not the offer has been accepted). Further, unlike Form W-2 reporting under section 6051, which provides annual information, both sections 6055 and 6056 require reporting some information on a monthly basis. Accordingly, the general section 6056 reporting method under the proposed regulations does not assume overall combined reporting under sections 6051, 6055, and 6056.

However, as described more fully below in section XI of this preamble, Treasury and the IRS are considering whether it may be possible to permit a type of combined reporting under sections 6051 and 6056 by providing an option to use a code on the Form W-2 in certain circumstances to provide information needed by both the employee and the IRS rather than through the use of the section 6056 employee statement (with employer-level information being provided separately). In addition, in other limited circumstances involving no-cost or very low-cost coverage provided under a self-insured group health plan, Treasury and the IRS are considering whether the employee and the IRS could rely solely on the information provided by the employer on a section 6055 return and the Form W-2 without any further information reporting under section 6056. For further discussion of these potential approaches, see section XI of this preamble.

In response to comments, Treasury and the IRS also have considered suggestions to use, for section 6055 and 6056 reporting purposes, information that employers communicate to employees about employer-sponsored coverage prior to employees' potential enrollment in Exchange coverage. These comments have observed that, under the Affordable Care Act, employers are required to provide pre-enrollment information to employees by various means, including information in the Notice of Coverage Options provided to employees pursuant to the requirements under section 18B of the Fair Labor Standards Act[8] in the Exchanges and potentially via the Employer Coverage Tool developed by the Department of Health and Human Services (HHS) that supports

---

[8] On May 8, 2013, the Department of Labor issued Technical Release 2013-02 providing temporary guidance under Fair Labor Standards Act section 18B, as well as model notices. See Technical Release 2013-02, model notice for employers who offer a health plan to some or all employees, and model notice for employers who do not offer a health plan, available at *http://www.dol.gov/ebsa/healthreform/*. Guidance on the Notice to Employees of Coverage.

the application for enrollment in a qualified health plan and insurance affordability programs.[9]

Treasury and the IRS have considered and coordinated with the Departments of HHS and Labor regarding the various reporting provisions with a view to identifying ways to make the entire process as effective and efficient as possible for all parties. That said, the various reports are designed for different purposes, and pre-enrollment reporting regarding anticipated employer coverage in an upcoming coverage year is unlikely to be helpful to individual taxpayers in accurately completing their tax returns more than a year later, after the coverage year. Among other issues, the pre-enrollment information may not be readily available to individuals at the time they are filing their tax returns, could be confused with the more recently received pre-enrollment information that applies to the subsequent year (not the year for which the tax return is being filed), and is in a format that does not facilitate easy transfer to the appropriate location on the Federal income tax return. Notwithstanding these challenges, Treasury and the IRS continue to work with the other Departments and stakeholders to consider approaches that might help minimize cost and administrative complexity and realize efficiencies in the reporting process.

Both sections 6055 and 6056 require employers to furnish to employees information about health care coverage. Solely for the purpose of furnishing information to employees (as opposed to filing with the IRS), Treasury and the IRS are considering whether employers sponsoring self-insured group health plans could fulfill their obligation to furnish an employee statement under both sections 6055 and 6056 through the use of a single substitute statement, within the parameters of the rules provided in revenue procedures or other published guidance relating to substitute returns. See § 601.601(d)(2) of this chapter.

XI. Potential Simplified Methods for Section 6056 Information Reporting

In developing these regulations, Treasury and the IRS have sought to develop simplified reporting methods that will minimize the cost and administrative tasks for employers, consistent with the statutory requirements to file an information return and furnish an employee statement to each full-time employee. Comments have suggested that, at least for some employers, the collection, assembling and processing of the necessary data into an appropriate format for filing may not be necessary if the employer offers sufficient coverage to make it unlikely that the employer will be subject to an assessable payment under section 4980H because the employee will be ineligible for a premium tax credit. Treasury and the IRS have considered these comments in formulating the potential simplified reporting methods described in this section. If Treasury and the IRS adopt one or more of these simplified reporting methods, they would be optional alternatives to the general reporting method set forth in the proposed regulations, which could substantially reduce the data elements reported using the general method. It is anticipated that, if an employer uses one or more of the simplified reporting methods, the employer would indicate on its section 6056 transmittal which simplified reporting method(s) was used and the number of employees for which the particular method was used. Comments are invited on these potential simplified reporting methods and on other possible simplified approaches that would benefit employers while providing sufficient and timely information to individual taxpayers and the IRS.

The information provided to the IRS and the employee pursuant to section 6056 is important for administering the section 4980H shared employer responsibility provisions and the premium tax credit. However, in looking at the potential flow of information, Treasury and the IRS have determined that in some circumstances only some of the information required under the general method is necessary. Treasury and the IRS have attempted to identify the specific groups of employees for whom simplified reporting would provide sufficient information, and simplified reporting approaches for these groups are outlined below. In many situations, not every full-time employee of an employer would fit into the groups of employees for which simplified reporting would be available. In that case, the employer would continue to use the general reporting method in the proposed regulations for those full-time employees for whom the employers could not use a simplified method. However, it is anticipated that a significant number of employers will have a sufficient number of employees that fit into one or more of the categories described below to make use of the simplified reporting method preferable to the general reporting method.

Subsections A through F of this section XI of the preamble describe, and comments are invited on, possible simplified methods of reporting under section 6056. Each of these possible methods would be optional for the reporting employer, and, except where specifically noted, would not affect any reporting obligations under section 6055.

A. Eliminating Section 6056 Employee Statements in Favor of Form W-2 Reporting for Certain Groups of Employees Offered Coverage

In response to stakeholder comments, Treasury and the IRS are considering allowing employers in certain circumstances to report offers of minimum value coverage on an employee's Form W-2, instead of reporting the offers to the IRS on a section 6056 employee statement or furnishing a section 6056 employee statement to the employee. The reporting is envisioned as using an existing box on the Form W-2 to provide the monthly dollar amount of the required employee contribution for the lowest cost minimum value self-only coverage offered to the employee and using a letter code to describe the offer of coverage. Specifically, Treasury and the IRS anticipate that this approach could be used for any employee employed by the employer for the entire calendar year when the offer, the individuals to whom the offer is made, and the employee contribution for the lowest-cost option for self-only coverage all remained the same for all twelve months of the calendar year. The letter code could be used to indicate that minimum value coverage was offered to: (1) The employee, the employee's spouse and the employee's dependents, (2) the employee and the employee's dependents but not the employee's spouse; (3) the employee and the employee's spouse but not the employee's dependents; (4) the employee, but not the employee's spouse or the employee's dependents; or that the employee was (5) only offered coverage that was not minimum value coverage; or (6) not offered coverage. For this purpose, an employer is treated as offering coverage to the employee's spouse or dependents even if the employee does not have a spouse or dependent, if the employee could elect such coverage if the employee did have a spouse or dependent. If an employee was not offered coverage, it is anticipated that the dollar amount of the employee share of the lowest-cost employee-only coverage option would be shown as zero.

Example: Employer has 100 full-time employees, all of whom are employed for the entire year. Employer offers all of its full-time employees, spouses and dependents the opportunity to enroll in health care coverage that provides minimum value. Under the potential simplified reporting method, it is contemplated that, for all employees, Employer would be permitted to avoid filing or furnishing section 6056 employee statements if it used a letter code on the Form W-2 to report that an offer of coverage had been made to the employee, the employee's spouse (if any), and the employee's dependents (if any), and a dollar amount indicating the required monthly employee contribution to purchase the lowest cost option offered to the employee for self-only coverage.

Treasury and the IRS are also considering whether this or a similar simplified reporting method could be extended to cases in which the required monthly employee contribution is below a specified threshold. For example, if the annual employee cost of self-only coverage is $800 or less, the employer would be permitted to report zero as the employee cost. The $800 amount is less than 9.5 percent of the federal poverty line for a single individual. Thus, regardless of the size of the employee's household or the level of other income or loss of any member of the employee's household, either the employer's coverage will be affordable for purposes of section 36B(c)(2)(C)(i) or the employee's household income will be less than 100 percent of the federal poverty line and the employee will not be an applicable taxpayer under section 36B(c)(2) who is eligible for the credit. In addition, even if other income increases the employee's household income, the employee would not be entitled to the affordability exemption to the shared responsibility payment under section 5000A(e)(1) because the $800 amount would not exceed 8 percent of the employee's household income. Alternatively, if other losses reduce the employee's household income below the income tax filing threshold, the employee will qualify

---

[9] Available at *https://www.healthcare.gov/downloads/ECT_Application_508_130615.pdf*

for the exemption under section 5000A(e)(2), and the information otherwise reported under section 6056 would not be required to determine whether the employee satisfied section 5000A. Comments are also requested on the extent to which this approach could reasonably be combined with the other simplified reporting methods described in this section XI of the preamble.

An employer that decides to use this simplified reporting method would not be required to file or furnish a section 6056 employee statement with respect to the employees for whom this method was used. Instead, the employer would simply indicate on a section 6056 transmittal that it had chosen to use this method. If the Form W-2 for an employee used an EIN other than the employer's EIN (for example, a third-party payor treated as an employer under section 3401(d)(1) of the Code filed the Form W-2), the employer (that is, the ALE member) may be required as part of the 6056 transmittal to identify those employees for whom a third party reported on Form W-2 without the employer's EIN and to list the employees' social security numbers.

Stakeholders have inquired whether a similar optional Form W-2 reporting method could be used for employees offered coverage under their employer's plan for less than a full calendar year (for example for a new employee hired during the year), but offered no coverage for the remainder of the year. Treasury and the IRS note that this type of reporting would leave gaps in information that would otherwise be used for tax administration purposes. For example, the reporting would not provide any information regarding the particular calendar months during which coverage was offered (or not offered). Even if the employer represented that the coverage was offered during all periods of employment, the reporting would not be able to be reconciled, for example, with another Form W-2 received by the employee from another employer using the same reporting method. That is because while both employers would report the number of months coverage was offered, that information would not be sufficient to determine whether offers of coverage were overlapping (because the employee was employed simultaneously at both employers).

Additionally, for months for which coverage was not offered, information as to whether the employee was employed and also the reason coverage was not offered during certain months of the calendar year would not be captured (for example, the employee was in a waiting period or employed but not as a full-time employee). The specific reason coverage was not offered is relevant to the administration of the employer shared responsibility provisions since the failure to offer coverage for certain reasons does not result in an assessable payment under the employer shared responsibility provisions for a calendar month, even if the full-time employee receives a premium tax credit for that month. Comments are requested on whether this approach to reporting would be useful for employers and, if so, on possible ways to address issues concerning the information gaps that would exist in reporting on employees offered coverage for less than a full calendar year.

B. No Need To Determine Full-Time Employees If Minimum Value Coverage Is Offered to All Potentially Full-Time Employees

Treasury and the IRS understand that some employers offer coverage to all or nearly all of their employees, and are able to accurately represent that the only employees not offered coverage are not full-time employees. In that case, the employer will have determined that it would not owe an assessable payment under section 4980H(a) because it would have made an offer of coverage to all of its full-time employees. However, the employer might not have determined whether every employee to whom coverage is offered is or is not a full-time employee. Treasury and the IRS are considering whether these employers may provide section 6056 reporting that does not identify the number of full-time employees and that does not specify whether a particular employee offered coverage is a full-time employee, provided that the employer certifies that all of its employees to whom it did not offer coverage during the calendar year were not full-time employees (or were otherwise ineligible for coverage, for example because they were in the initial permitted waiting period following the date of hire). This method would permit the employer to forgo identifying the full-time status of its employees prior to filing a section 6056 return. However, if an employee who was offered coverage claimed a premium tax credit, the employer could be asked to confirm at a later date (after the filing of the section 6056 return and the relevant Form 1040 return) whether that employee was a full-time employee during that calendar year (in the same manner that an employer reporting only on behalf of full-time employees might later be asked about the status of an employee claiming the premium tax credit if the employee was not listed on that employer's section 6056 return). Treasury and the IRS recognize that this method often would result in over-reporting of certain elements in the sense that reporting would occur with respect to one or more employees who may not be full-time employees during the calendar year. But some employers have indicated that they anticipate relatively few of their employees will claim the premium tax credit, and that determining those few employees' status as full-time employees later would be administratively easier than determining the full-time employee status of all employees at the time of the initial filing.

Example: Employer has 100 employees. Employer makes an offer of minimum value coverage to 90 of the employees. Employer has determined that the ten employees to whom coverage is not offered are not full-time employees for any calendar month during the year. Employer has not determined which of the remaining 90 employees were full-time employees for one or more calendar months during the year. Employer certifies as part of its section 6056 transmittal return that the only employees to whom it did not offer coverage were not full-time employees or were otherwise not required to be offered coverage for all months of employment (for example, a full-time employee was hired in November and, under the terms of the plan, which comply with the Affordable Care Act, would not be initially offered coverage until the following calendar year). Employer would file a section 6056 return and furnish an employee statement for each of the 90 employees, but would not be required to report either the total number of full-time employees for the year or whether any particular employee was a full-time employee for any calendar month during the year. If one of the employees included as part of the return declined the offer of coverage and properly claimed a premium tax credit with respect to coverage provided through an Exchange, and the employer were contacted by the IRS to determine whether the employer did or did not owe an assessable payment under section 4980H(b), the employer could determine at that point whether the employee was a full-time employee for one or more months during that calendar year and supply that information to the IRS.

C. Self-Insured Employers Offering Employees, Their Spouses, and Dependents Mandatory No-Cost Minimum Value Coverage

Some employers may provide mandatory minimum value coverage under a self-insured group health plan to an employee, an employee's spouse, and an employee's dependents, with no employee contribution. In that case, none of those individuals would be eligible for a premium tax credit for any month during which the coverage was provided, and the employer would indicate on the return required under section 6055 for the employee all months for which that coverage was provided with respect to each individual in the employee's family. Because the section 6055 return would provide the individual taxpayers the necessary information to accurately file the taxpayers' income tax returns, and would provide the IRS the information concerning those employees to administer the premium tax credit and employer shared responsibility provisions, Treasury and the IRS are considering whether for those employees the employer could file and furnish only the return required under section 6055, a code on the Form W-2, the summary information provided in the section 6056 transmittal form, and no further information reporting under section 6056.

D. Voluntarily Reporting Section 6056 Elements During or Prior to the Year of Coverage

Some employers have expressed an interest in voluntarily reporting information about the coverage they offer their employees prior to the end of a coverage year, for example at their open enrollment or before the open enrollment at the Exchanges, on the theory that earlier section 6056 reporting to the IRS could lead to greater efficiency in the employer verification system employed by Exchanges to determine eligibility for premium tax credits. Under such an arrangement, they believe that if some employers chose to provide part of their section 6056 reporting to the IRS earlier in the process, the IRS, in turn, would be able to transmit any pertinent data to the Exchanges.

A proposal of this kind would need to address a number of issues. First, the regulations under section 6103 do not authorize the IRS to share taxpayer information in this manner. Even if this information sharing were permitted, information reporting plays a role in enabling individuals to file complete and accurate tax returns. Under the proposal, individuals would not receive the information for their tax return preparation proximate to when they are completing their tax returns. Employees may bear less burden and prepare more accurate tax returns when their employer furnishes a statement at the start of the relevant tax season reflecting all the information the employee needs to file a correct tax return for the prior year. Gaps in complete and timely information increase the need for additional follow-up communication among employers, employees, and the IRS.

Also, offering two sets of reporting alternatives with filing occurring at different time periods would present challenges. Because the reporting options would be voluntary, different reporting protocols and regimes would need to be established and would need to accommodate employer choices to change the method of reporting from year to year. The multiple forms, procedures, and protocols could create complexity and be difficult to administer.

In addition, the information about the offer of coverage made before the year starts may change during the calendar year. For example, during the year, an employee may be hired or may terminate employment, a part-time employee may become full-time and be eligible for different coverage options, or an employee may change positions during the year and no longer be offered coverage. Accordingly, disclosure before the coverage year does not adequately substitute for disclosure to employees and reporting to the IRS after the coverage year.

Employers, employees, and the IRS share the goal of aligning eligibility for advance payments of premium tax credits as closely as possible with eligibility for the premium tax credit on the employee's annual tax return filed after the coverage year. This would reduce confusion and minimize the risk of employees owing advance payments back as liabilities on their tax returns. Regardless of the final rules on section 6056 information reporting, employers are encouraged to make their pre-enrollment disclosures to employees and Exchanges as effective and helpful to individuals as possible.

Comments are invited on whether there could be a way to design such a voluntary partial early reporting arrangement that would reduce complexity and avoid confusion for employers and employees, be administrable for the IRS, and provide timely information to individuals so that they can meet their income tax filing obligation without undue burden or undue risk of inaccuracy.

E. Reporting for Employees Potentially Ineligible for the Premium Tax Credit

Some employers have indicated that, because many of their employees are relatively highly paid, they are unlikely to be eligible for a premium tax credit. The assumption is that the employee's household income is likely to exceed 400 percent of the Federal poverty line, and therefore the employee would not benefit from receiving the information otherwise included with a section 6056 employee statement. Further, because the employee is unlikely to qualify for a premium tax credit, employers have stated that the information will not be useful to the IRS in administering the employer shared responsibility provisions because the precondition of a section 4980H(b) assessable payment—that the employee receive a premium tax credit—is unlikely to be satisfied.

Treasury and the IRS have considered this request and welcome comments both on its potential usefulness to employers and its administrability. Employers would still need to report to the IRS the months during which the employee was a full-time employee, at least to the extent the employee being was included in a full-time employee count. Additionally, employers will not be in a position to know the correlation between an employee's Form W-2 wages and household income with sufficient accuracy to determine whether an employee may be eligible for the premium tax credit. The only pertinent information the employer retains is the employee's annual wages, yet the poverty level from which the premium tax credit income threshold is determined varies considerably based on family size (which employers will not necessarily know). In addition, employees for whom an employer may use an affordability safe harbor based on wages for purposes of compliance with the employer shared responsibility provisions under section 4980H might still be eligible for a premium tax credit based on their household income. Employers generally do not know employees' household income, and will not have information as to whether the employee (or another member of the employee's household) has incurred losses or expenses (such as alimony, casualty losses, Schedule C business deductions, and the like) that reduce the employee's household modified adjusted gross income below 400 percent of the Federal poverty line. Accordingly, it is unclear whether Form W-2 wages alone would provide sufficient information to determine eligibility for the premium tax credit because the employee's household income may be well below the employee's Form W-2 wages. Comments are requested as to whether there is a level of Form W-2 wages at which such a determination might be made with sufficient confidence, and whether that level of wages is so high as not to be of practical use to employers.

F. Combinations of Simplified Reporting Methods

The potential simplified reporting methods described above would apply to particular groups of employees that in many cases would not overlap. In such cases, two different potential simplified reporting methods could not be applied to the same employee. Treasury and the IRS anticipate that, to the extent any of these potential reporting methods are adopted in final regulations or other administrative guidance, including forms and instructions, an employer would be permitted to use different simplified methods for different employees at the employer's election.

XII. Person Responsible for Section 6056 Reporting

Under the proposed regulations, in general, each ALE member must file a section 6056 return with respect to its full-time employees for a calendar year.

A. Special Rules for Governmental Units: Designation

In accordance with section 6056(e), the proposed regulations provide that in the case of any ALE member that is a governmental unit or any agency or instrumentality thereof (together referred to in this preamble as a governmental unit), that governmental unit may report under section 6056 on its own behalf or may appropriately designate another person or persons to report on its behalf.[10] For purposes of designation, another person is appropriately designated for purposes of the filing and furnishing requirements of section 6056 if that other person is part of or related to the same governmental unit as the ALE member. For example, a political subdivision of a state may designate the state, another political subdivision of the state, or an agency or instrumentality of the foregoing as the designated person for purposes of section 6056 reporting. The person designated might be the governmental unit that operates the relevant health plan or the governmental unit that does other information reporting on behalf of the designating governmental unit. Further, the governmental unit may designate more than one governmental unit to file and furnish under section 6056 on its behalf, such as, for example, if different categories of employees are offered coverage under different health plans operated by different governmental units. In addition, a governmental unit may designate another person to file and furnish with respect to all or some of its full-time employees. If the designation is accepted by the designee and is made before the filing deadline, the designated governmental unit is the designated entity responsible for section 6056 reporting.

The person (or persons) appropriately designated for this purpose would report under section 6056 on behalf of the ALE member. Accordingly, the person (or persons) appropriately designated is (are) the person(s) responsible for section 6056 reporting on behalf of the ALE member and subject to the penalties for failure to comply with information return requirements under sections 6721 and 6722. However, the ALE member remains subject to the requirements of section 4980H.

Under the proposed regulations, a separate section 6056 return and transmittal must be filed for each ALE member for which the appropriately designated person is reporting. The designated entity must report its name, address, and EIN on the section 6056 return to indicate it is the appropriately designated person.

The proposed regulations further provide that the designation under section 6056(e) must be in writing and must contain certain language. Specifically, under the proposed regulations, the designation must be signed by both the ALE member and the designated person, and must be effective under all applicable laws. The proposed regulations also require that the designation set forth the name and EIN of the designated person, and appoint that person as the person responsible for reporting under section 6056 on behalf of the ALE member. The designation must contain information identifying the category of full-time employees (which may be full-time employees eligible for a specified health plan, or in a particular job category, provided that the specific employees covered by the designation can be identified) for which the designated person is responsible for reporting under section 6056 on behalf of the ALE member. If the designated person is responsible for reporting under section 6056 for all full-time employees of an ALE member, the designation should so indicate.

The designation must also contain language that the designated person agrees that it is the appropriately designated person under section 6056(e), and an acknowledgement that the designated person is responsible for reporting under section 6056 on behalf of the ALE member and subject to the requirements of section 6056, and the information reporting penalty provisions of sections 6721 and 6722. The designation must also set forth the name and EIN of the ALE member, identifying the ALE member as the person subject to the requirements of section 4980H. The proposed regulations provide that an equivalent applicable statutory or regulatory designation containing similar lan-

---

[10] Until further guidance is issued, government entities, churches, and a convention or association of churches may apply a reasonable, good faith interpretation of section 414(b), (c), (m), and (o) in determining whether a person or group of persons is an applicable large employer.

guage will be treated as a written designation for purposes of section 6056(e).

B. ALE Members Participating in Multiemployer Plans

Several commenters suggested that administrators of multiemployer plans may be willing to file section 6056 returns reporting information for coverage offered to full-time employees under the multiemployer plan and recommended in such cases that an ALE member not be required to report coverage information for those employees.

Treasury and the IRS understand that the plan administrator of a multiemployer plan may have better access than a participating employer to certain information on participating employees required to be included as part of section 6056 reporting. For this reason, Treasury and the IRS anticipate that the section 6056 reporting with respect to full-time employees eligible to participate in a multiemployer plan will be permitted to be provided in a bifurcated manner. Under the bifurcated approach, one return would pertain to the full-time employees eligible to participate in the multiemployer plan (or, if the employer participates in more than one multiemployer plan, one return for each relevant multiemployer plan in which full-time employees are eligible to participate), and another return would pertain to the remaining full-time employees (those who are not eligible to participate in a multiemployer plan). As in the case of other third parties, as discussed in section XII.C of this preamble, the administrator (or administrators, in the case of an employer contributing to two or more multiemployer plans) of a multiemployer plan is permitted to report on behalf of an ALE member that is a contributing employer, and is permitted to report with respect to the ALE member's full-time employees who are eligible for coverage under the multiemployer plan (but not with respect to any other full-time employees of the ALE member). The administrator of the multiemployer plan would file a separate section 6056 return for any ALE member that is a contributing employer on behalf of whom it files using the ALE member's EIN. The administrator of the multiemployer plan would also provide its own name, address, and identification number (in addition to the name, address, and EIN of the ALE member already required). The ALE member would remain the responsible person under section 6056 with respect to all of its full-time employees and accordingly would be required to sign the section 6056 return filed on its behalf and be subject to any potential liability for failure to properly file returns or furnish statements. To the extent the plan administrator that prepares returns or statements required under section 6056 is a tax return preparer, it will be subject to the requirements generally applicable to return preparers.

C. Section 6056 Reporting Facilitated by Third Parties

Treasury and the IRS understand that third party administrators or other third party service providers are integral to the operation of many employers' health plans, including with respect to compliance with any reporting requirements. As requested by several commenters, ALE members are permitted to contract with and use third parties to facilitate filing returns and furnishing employee statements to comply with section 6056. The proposed regulations make clear, however, that ALE members are responsible for reporting under section 6056, with the exception of certain governmental unit applicable large employers that properly designate under section 6056(e). While the proposed regulations do not provide guidance on contractual or other reporting arrangements between private ALE members and other parties, they do not prohibit these arrangements. Such contractual arrangements would not transfer the potential liability of the ALE member for failure to report and furnish under section 6056 and the regulations, or the ALE member's potential liability under section 4980H.

As one example, an applicable large employer that is a member of an aggregated group of related entities (determined under section 414(b), 414(c), 414(m) or 414(o)), may file returns and furnish employee statements on behalf of one or more of the other ALE members of the aggregated group. Each other ALE member of the group, for example, could have the ALE member that operates the employer-sponsored plan file section 6056 returns and furnish section 6056 employee statements on its behalf. However, a separate section 6056 return must be filed for each ALE member, providing that ALE member's EIN. Each ALE member in the aggregated group would continue to be the responsible person under section 6056, would be required to sign the return filed on its behalf, and would be subject to any potential liability for failure to properly file returns or furnish statements. To the extent the other party that prepares returns or statements required under section 6056 is a tax return preparer, it will be subject to the requirements generally applicable to return preparers.

XIII. Applicability of Information Return Requirements

The proposed regulations provide that an ALE member that fails to comply with the section 6056 information return and employee statement requirements may be subject to the general reporting penalty provisions under sections 6721 (failure to file correct information returns), and 6722 (failure to furnish correct payee statement). The proposed regulations also provide, however, that the waiver of penalty and special rules under section 6724 and the applicable regulations, including abatement of information return penalties for reasonable cause, apply. The proposed regulations under section 6055 (REG-132455-11) include proposed amendments to the regulations under sections 6721 and 6722 to include returns under both sections 6055 and 6056 in the definitions of information return and payee statement. Treasury and the IRS anticipate that the final regulations under section 6056 will cross-reference those amendments to the regulations under sections 6721 and 6722.

Proposed Effective/Applicability Dates

These regulations are proposed to be effective the date the final regulations are published in the **Federal Register**. These regulations are proposed to apply for calendar years beginning after December 31, 2014. Consistent with Notice 2013-45, reporting entities will not be subject to penalties for failure to comply with the section 6506 information reporting provisions for 2014 (including the furnishing of employee statements in 2015). Accordingly, a reporting entity will not be subject to penalties if it first reports beginning in 2016 for 2015 (including the furnishing of employee statements). Taxpayers are encouraged, however, to voluntarily comply with section 6056 information reporting for 2014 by using the general reporting method set forth in these regulations once finalized.

Special Analyses

It has been determined that this notice of proposed rulemaking is not a significant regulatory action as defined in Executive Order 12866, as supplemented by Executive Order 13563. Therefore, a regulatory assessment is not required. It has also been determined that section 553(b) of the Administrative Procedure Act (5 U.S.C. chapter 5) does not apply to these regulations.

It is hereby certified that these regulations will not have a significant economic impact on a substantial number of small entities. This certification is based on the fact that the regulations are consistent with the requirements imposed by section 6056. Consistent with the statute, the regulations require applicable large employers, as defined in section 4980H(c)(2), to file a return with the IRS, using either the prescribed form or a substitute form, for each full-time employee reporting certain information regarding the health care coverage offered and provided to the employee for the year. Consistent with the statute, the proposed regulations further require applicable large employers to furnish to each full-time employee a copy of the return, or a substitute statement, required to be filed by the applicable large employer with respect to the employee. Accordingly, these regulations merely prescribe the method of filing and furnishing returns and employee statements as required under section 6056. Moreover, the proposed regulations attempt to minimize the burden associated with this collection of information by requiring that applicable large employers file and furnish only information that the IRS will utilize to administer the shared employer responsibility provisions under section 4980H and administer the premium tax credit under section 36B, and information employees will need in order to complete their tax returns.

Based on these facts, a Regulatory Flexibility Analysis under the Regulatory Flexibility Act (5 U.S.C. chapter 6) is not required.

Pursuant to section 7805(f) of the Code, this notice of proposed rulemaking has been submitted to the Chief Counsel for Advocacy of the Small Business Administration for comment on its impact on small business.

Comments and a Public Hearing

Before these proposed regulations are adopted as final regulations, consideration will be given to any written comments (a signed original and eight (8) copies) or electronic comments that are submitted timely to the IRS as prescribed in this preamble under the **ADDRESSES** heading. Treasury and the IRS specifically request comments on the clarity of the proposed rules and how they can be made easier to understand. All comments will be available for public inspection at *www.regulations.gov* or upon request. A public hearing has been scheduled for November 18, 2013, in the Auditorium, Internal Revenue Building, 1111 Constitution Avenue NW., Washington, DC. Due to building security procedures, visitors must enter at the Constitution Avenue entrance. In addition, all visitors must present photo identification to enter the building. Because of access restrictions, visitors will not be admitted beyond the immediate entrance area more than 30 minutes before the hearing starts. For information about having your name placed on the building access list to attend the hearing, see the **FOR FURTHER INFORMATION CONTACT** section of this preamble.

The rules of 26 CFR 601.601(a)(3) apply to the hearing. Persons who wish to present oral comments at the hearing must submit written or electronic comments by November 8, 2013 and an outline of the topics to be discussed and the time to be devoted to each topic (signed original and eight (8) copies) by November 8, 2013.

A period of 10 minutes will be allotted to each person for making comments. An agenda showing the scheduling of the speakers will be prepared after the deadline for receiving outlines has passed. Copies of the agenda will be available free of charge at the hearing.

Drafting Information

The principal author of these proposed regulations is Ligeia M. Donis of the Office of the Division Counsel/Associate Chief Counsel (Tax Exempt and Government Entities). However, other personnel from the IRS and Treasury participated in their development.

List of Subjects in 26 CFR Part 301

Employment taxes, Estate taxes, Excise taxes, Gift taxes, Income taxes, Penalties, Reporting and recordkeeping requirements.

Proposed Amendments to the Regulations

Accordingly, 26 CFR part 301 is proposed to be amended as follows:

PART 301—PROCEDURE AND ADMINISTRATION

■**Paragraph 1.** The authority citation for part 301 continues to read in part as follows:

Authority: 26 U.S.C. 7805 * * *

■**Par. 2.** Section 301.6011-9 is added to read as follows:

§ 301.6011-9 Electronic filing of section 6056 returns.

(a) *Returns required under section 6056.* An applicable large employer member, as defined in § 301.6056-1(b)(2), is required to file electronically an information return under section 6056 and § 301.6056-1, except as otherwise provided in paragraph (b) of this section.

(b) *Exceptions*—(1) *Low-volume filers/250-return threshold*—(i) *In general.* An applicable large employer member will not be required to file electronically the section 6056 information return described in paragraph (a) of this section unless it is required to file 250 or more returns during the calendar year. Each section 6056 information return for a full-time employee is a separate return. For purposes of this section, an applicable large employer member is required to file at least 250 returns if, during the calendar year, the applicable large employer member is required to file at least 250 returns of any type, including information returns (for example, Forms W-2, Forms 1099), income tax returns, employment tax returns, and excise tax returns. An applicable large employer member filing fewer than 250 returns during the calendar year may make the returns on the prescribed paper form.

(ii) *Examples.* The following examples illustrate the provisions of paragraph (b)(1) of this section:

Example 1. Company X is an applicable large employer member. For the calendar year ending December 31, 2015, Company X is required to file 275 section 6056 returns. Company X is required to file section 6056 returns electronically for that calendar year because 275 section 6056 information returns exceed the 250-return threshold.

Example 2. Company Y is an applicable large employer member. For the calendar year ending December 31, 2015, Company Y is required to file 200 returns on Form W-2 and 150 section 6056 returns. Company Y is required to file the section 6056 returns electronically for that calendar year because it is required to file more than 250 returns (that is, the 200 Forms W-2 plus the 150 section 6056 returns).

(2) *Waiver*—(i) *In general.* The Commissioner may waive the requirements of this section if hardship is shown in a request for waiver filed in accordance with this paragraph (b)(2)(i). The principal factor in determining hardship will be the amount, if any, by which the cost of filing the section 6056 returns in accordance with this section exceeds the costs of filing the returns on other media. A request for waiver must be made in accordance with applicable revenue procedures or publications (see § 601.601(d)(2)(ii)(*b*) of this chapter). Pursuant to these procedures, a request for waiver should be filed at least 45 days before the due date of the section 6056 return in order for the IRS to

have adequate time to respond to the request for waiver. The waiver will specify the type of information return (that is, section 6056 information return) and the period to which it applies and will be subject to such terms and conditions regarding the method of reporting as may be prescribed by the Commissioner.

(ii) *Supplemental rules.* The Commissioner may prescribe rules that supplement the provisions of paragraph (b)(2)(i) of this section.

(c) *Effective/applicability date.* The rules of this section are effective as of the date of publication of the Treasury decision adopting these rules as final regulations in the **Federal Register**. This section applies to returns on "Form 1095-C" or another form the IRS designates required to be filed after December 31, 2014. However, reporting entities will not be subject to penalties under sections 6721 or 6722 with respect to the reporting requirements for 2014 (for information returns filed and for statements furnished to employees in 2015).

■**Par. 3.** Section 301.6056-1 is added to read as follows:

§ 301.6056-1 Rules relating to reporting by applicable large employers on health insurance coverage offered under employer-sponsored plans.

(a) *In general.* Section 6056 requires an applicable large employer subject to the requirements of section 4980H to report certain health insurance coverage information to the Internal Revenue Service, and to furnish certain related employee statements to its full-time employees. Paragraph (b) of this section contains definitions for purposes of this section. Paragraph (c) of this section prescribes general rules for filing the required information with the IRS and furnishing the required employee statements to employees. Paragraphs (d) and (e) of this section describe the information required to be reported on a section 6056 information return and the time and place for filing. Paragraph (f) of this section sets forth the mandatory electronic filing requirements for applicable large employer members. Paragraph (g) of this section provides information about the statement required to be furnished to a full-time employee. Paragraph (h) of this section prescribes the time and manner of furnishing the statement, including extensions of time to furnish. Paragraph (i) of this section prescribes the method for correcting information included in a statement required by section 6056(d) that has been furnished to an employee. Paragraph (j) of this section describes the information return requirements applicable to section 6056 returns. Paragraph (k) of this section describes special rules for certain applicable large employers.

(b) *Definitions*—(1) *Applicable large employer.* The term *applicable large employer* has the same meaning as in section 4980H(c)(2) and any applicable regulations.

(2) *Applicable large employer member.* The term *applicable large employer member* means a person that, together with one or more other persons, is treated as a single employer that is an applicable large employer. For this purpose, if a person, together with one or more other persons, is treated as a single employer that is an applicable large employer on any day of a calendar month, that person is an applicable large employer member for that calendar month. If the applicable large employer comprises one person, that one person is the applicable large employer member. An applicable large employer member does not include a person that is not an employer or only an employer of employees with no hours of service for the calendar year.

(3) *Dependent.* The term *dependent* has the same meaning as in section 4980H(a) and (b) and any applicable regulations.

(4) *Eligible employer-sponsored plan.* The term *eligible employer-sponsored plan* has the same meaning as in section 5000A(f)(2) and any applicable regulations.

(5) *Full-time employee.* The term *full-time employee* has the same meaning as in section 4980H and any applicable regulations, as applied to the determination and calculation of liability under section 4980H(a) and (b) with respect to any individual employee, and not as applied to the determination of status as an applicable large employer, if different.

(6) *Governmental unit.* The term *governmental unit* refers to the government of the United States, any State or political subdivision thereof, or any Indian tribal government (as defined in section 7701(a)(40)) or subdivision of an Indian tribal government (as defined in section 7871(d)).

(7) *Agency or instrumentality of a governmental unit.* [Reserved]

(8) *Minimum essential coverage.* The term *minimum essential coverage* has the same meaning as in section 5000A(f)(1) and any applicable regulations.

(9) *Minimum value.* The term *minimum value* has the same meaning as in section 36B and any applicable regulations.

(10) *Person.* The term *person* has the same meaning as in section 7701(a)(1) and applicable regulations.

(c) *Content and timing of reporting by applicable large employers.* Each applicable large employer member required to make a return and furnish a related statement to its full-time employees under section 6056 for a calendar year must make a return and furnish the related statement using such form(s) as may be prescribed by the Internal Revenue Service. An applicable large employer member will satisfy its reporting requirements under section 6056 if it files with the Internal Revenue Service a return for each full-time employee using Form 1095-C or another form the IRS designates, and a transmittal form using Form 1094-C or another form the IRS designates, as prescribed in this section and in the instructions to the forms.

(d) *Information required to be reported to the Internal Revenue Service*—(1) *In general.* Every applicable large employer member must make a section 6056 information return with respect to each full-time employee. Each section 6056 information return must show—

(i) The name, address, and employer identification number of the applicable large employer member,

(ii) The name and telephone number of the applicable large employer's contact person,

(iii) The calendar year for which the information is reported,

(iv) A certification as to whether the applicable large employer member offered to its full-time employees (and their dependents) the opportunity to enroll in minimum essential coverage under an eligible employer-sponsored plan (as defined in section 5000A(f)(2)), by calendar month,

(v) The months during the calendar year for which coverage under the plan was available,

(vi) Each full-time employee's share of the lowest cost monthly premium (self-only) for coverage providing minimum value offered to that full-time employee under an eligible employer-sponsored plan, by calendar month;

(vii) The number of full-time employees for each month during the calendar year,

(viii) The name, address, and taxpayer identification number of each full-time employee during the calendar year and the months, if any, during which the employee was covered under the plan, and

(ix) Such other information as the Secretary may prescribe or as may be required by the form or instructions.

(2) *Form of the return.* A return required under this paragraph (d) may be made on Forms 1094-C and 1095-C or other form(s) designated by the Internal Revenue Service, or a substitute form. A substitute form must include the information required to be reported on Forms 1094-C and 1095-C and must comply with applicable revenue procedures or other published guidance relating to substitute statements. See §601.601(d)(2) of this chapter.

(e) *Time and place for filing return*— (1) *In general.* An applicable large employer member must file each return and transmittal form required under paragraph (d)(2) of this section on or before February 28 (March 31 if filed electronically) of the year succeeding the calendar year to which it relates in accordance with any applicable guidance and the instructions to the form. An applicable large employer member must file the return and transmittal form at the address specified on the return form or its instructions.

(2) *Extensions of time for filing.* [Reserved]

(f) *Electronic filing of returns.* The section 6056 return is required to be filed electronically, except as otherwise provided in §301.6011-9.

(g) *Statements required to be furnished to full-time employees*—(1) *In general.* Every applicable large employer member required to file a return under section 6056 must furnish to each of its full-time employees identified on the return a written statement showing—

(i) The name, address and employer identification number of the applicable large employer member, and

(ii) The information required to be shown on the section 6056 return with respect to the full-time employee.

(2) *Form of the statement.* A statement required under this paragraph (g) may be made either by furnishing to the full-time employee a copy of Form 1095-C or another form the IRS designates as prescribed in this section and in the instructions to such forms, or a substitute statement. A substitute statement must include the information required to be shown on Form 1095-C or another form the IRS designates and must comply with applicable revenue procedures or other pub-

lished guidance relating to substitute statements. See §601.601(d)(2). An Internal Revenue Service truncated taxpayer identification number may be used as the identifying number for an individual in lieu of the identifying number appearing on the corresponding information return filed with the Internal Revenue Service.

(h) *Time and manner for furnishing statements*—(1) Each statement required by this section for a calendar year must be furnished to a full-time employee on or before January 31 of the year succeeding that calendar year in accordance with applicable Internal Revenue Service procedures and instructions or as provided in §301.6056-2.

(2) *Extensions of time*—(i) *In general.* For good cause upon written application of the person required to furnish statements under this section, the Internal Revenue Service may grant an extension of time not exceeding 30 days in which to furnish such statements. The application must be addressed to the Internal Revenue Service, and must contain a full recital of the reasons for requesting the extension to aid the Internal Revenue Service in determining the period of the extension, if any, that will be granted. Such a request in the form of a letter to the Internal Revenue Service, signed by the applicant, will suffice as an application. The application must be filed on or before the date prescribed in paragraph (h)(1) of this section.

(ii) *Automatic extension of time.* The Commissioner may, in appropriate cases, prescribe additional guidance or procedures, published in the Internal Revenue Bulletin (see §601.601(d)(2)(ii)(*b*)), for automatic extensions of time to furnish to one or more full-time employees the statement required under section 6056.

(i) *Correction of information return.* If the information reported on a return required pursuant to section 6056 for a full-time employee for a prior year was incomplete or incorrect, a corrected return accompanied by a transmittal form must be filed with the Internal Revenue Service as soon as possible after the correction is made. The return must be identified as corrected. A copy of the corrected return for the prior year reflecting the correct data must be furnished to the employee as soon as possible after the correction is made.

(j) *Information reporting penalties.* Section 6724(d)(1)(B)(xxv) and (d)(2)(HH) provides that for purposes of Subtitle F, Chapter 68, Subchapter B, Part II (sections 6721 et seq.), the terms *information return* and *payee statement* include the return required under section 6056 and the statement required to be furnished under section 6056(c). An applicable large employer member who fails to comply with the filing and statement requirements under section 6056 is subject to the penalties under sections 6721 (failure to file correct information returns) and 6722 (failure to furnish correct payee statement), and the waiver and special rules provisions under section 6724, and the applicable regulations.

(k) *Special rules for governmental units*—(1) *Person appropriately designated.* In the case of any applicable large employer member that is a governmental unit or any agency or instrumentality thereof, the person or persons appropriately designated under section 6056(e) for purposes of the filing and furnishing requirements of section 6056 must be part of or related to the same governmental unit as the applicable large employer member. The applicable large employer member must make (or revoke) the designation before the earlier of the deadline for filing the returns or furnishing the statements required by this section. A person that has been appropriately designated under section 6056(e) must file a separate section 6056 return and transmittal for each applicable large employer member for which the person is reporting. The person appropriately designated under section 6056(e) assumes responsibility for the section 6056 requirements on behalf of the applicable large employer member for which the person is designated.

(2) *Written designation.* The designation under section 6056(e) must be made in writing, must be signed by both the applicable large employer member and the designated person, and must be effective under all applicable laws. The designation must set forth the name and employer identification number of the designated person, and appoint such person as the person responsible for reporting under section 6056 on behalf of the applicable large employer member. The designation must contain information identifying the category of full-time employees (which may be full-time employees eligible for a specified health plan, or in a particular job category, as long as the specific employees covered by the designation can be identified) for which the designated person is responsible for reporting under section 6056 on behalf of the applicable large employer member. If the designated person is responsible for reporting under section 6056 for all full-time employees of an applicable large employer member, the designation must so indicate. The designation must contain language that the designated person agrees and certifies that it is the appropriately designated person under section 6056(e), and an acknowledgement that the designated person is responsible for reporting under section 6056 on behalf of the applica-

ble large employer member and subject to the requirements of section 6056, including for purposes of information reporting requirements under sections 6721, 6722, and 6724. The designation must also set forth the name and employer identification number of the applicable large employer member, identifying the applicable large employer member as the person subject to the requirements of section 4980H. An equivalent applicable statutory or regulatory designation containing the language described in this paragraph (k)(2) will be treated as a written designation for purposes of section 6056(e) and this section.

(l) *Additional guidance.* The Commissioner may prescribe additional guidance of general applicability, published in the Internal Revenue Bulletin (see § 601.601(d)(2)(ii)(*b*)) to provide additional rules under section 6056, including rules permitting use of alternate optional methods to meet reporting requirements.

(m) *Effective/applicability date.* The rules of this section are effective as of the date of publication of the Treasury decision adopting these rules as final regulations in the **Federal Register**. This section applies for calendar years beginning after December 31, 2014. Reporting entities will not be subject to penalties under sections 6721 or 6722 with respect to the reporting requirements for 2014 (for information returns filed and for statements furnished to employees in 2015).

■ **Par 4.** Section 301.6056-2 is added to read as follows:

§ 301.6056-2 Electronic furnishing of statements.

(a) *Electronic furnishing of statements*—(1) *In general.* An applicable large employer member required by § 301.6056-1 to furnish a statement (furnisher) to a full-time employee (a recipient) may furnish the statement in an electronic format in lieu of a paper format, provided that the employer meets the requirements of paragraphs (a)(2) through (a)(6) of this section. An applicable large employer member who meets the requirements of paragraphs (a)(2) through (6) of this section is treated as furnishing the statement in a timely manner.

(2) *Consent*—(i) *In general.* The recipient must have affirmatively consented to receive the statement in an electronic format. The consent may be made electronically in any manner that reasonably demonstrates that the recipient can access the statement in the electronic format in which it will be furnished to the recipient. Alternatively, the consent may be made in a paper document if it is confirmed electronically.

(ii) *Withdrawal of consent.* The consent requirement of this paragraph (a)(2) is not satisfied if the recipient withdraws the consent and the withdrawal takes effect before the statement is furnished. The furnisher may provide that a withdrawal of consent takes effect either on the date it is received by the furnisher or on a subsequent date. The furnisher may also provide that a request for a paper statement will be treated as a withdrawal of consent.

(iii) *Change in hardware or software requirements.* If a change in the hardware or software required to access the statement creates a material risk that the recipient will not be able to access the statement, the furnisher must, prior to changing the hardware or software, provide the recipient with a notice. The notice must describe the revised hardware and software required to access the statement and inform the recipient that a new consent to receive the statement in the revised electronic format must be provided to the furnisher. After implementing the revised hardware and software, the furnisher must obtain from the recipient, in the manner described in paragraph (a)(2)(i) of this section, a new consent or confirmation of consent to receive the statement electronically.

(iv) Examples. The following examples illustrate the rules of this paragraph (a)(2):

Example 1. Furnisher F sends Recipient R a letter stating that R may consent to receive section 6056 statements electronically on a Web site instead of in a paper format. The letter contains instructions explaining how to consent to receive section 6056 statements electronically by accessing the Web site, downloading the consent document, completing the consent document and emailing the completed consent back to F. The consent document posted on the Web site uses the same electronic format that F will use for the electronically furnished section 6056 statements. R reads the instructions and submits the consent to receive the statements electronically in the manner described in paragraph (a)(2)(i) of this section. R has consented to receive the statements electronically in the manner described in paragraph (a)(2)(i) of this section.

Example 2. Furnisher F sends Recipient R an email stating that R may consent to receive section 6056 statements electronically instead of in a paper format. The email contains an attachment instructing R how to consent to receive section 6056 statements electronically. The email attachment uses the same electronic format that F will use for the

electronically furnished section 6056 statements. R opens the attachment, reads the instructions, and submits the consent in the manner provided in the instructions. R has consented to receive section 6056 statements electronically in the manner described in paragraph (a)(2)(i) of this section.

Example 3. Furnisher F posts a notice on its Web site stating that Recipient R may receive section 6056 statements electronically instead of in a paper format. The Web site contains instructions on how R may access a secure Web page and consent to receive the statements electronically. By accessing the secure Web page and giving consent, R has consented to receive section 6056 statements electronically in the manner described in paragraph (a)(2)(i).

(3) *Required disclosures*—(i) *In general.* Prior to, or at the time of, a recipient's consent, the furnisher must provide to the recipient a clear and conspicuous disclosure statement containing each of the disclosures described in paragraphs (a)(3)(ii) through (viii) of this section.

(ii) *Paper statement.* The recipient must be informed that the statement will be furnished on paper if the recipient does not consent to receive it electronically.

(iii) *Scope and duration of consent.* The recipient must be informed of the scope and duration of the consent. For example, the recipient must be informed whether the consent applies to each statement required to be furnished after the consent is given until it is withdrawn in the manner described in paragraph (a)(3)(v)(A) of this section or only to the first statement required to be furnished following the date on which the consent is given.

(iv) *Post-consent request for a paper statement.* The recipient must be informed of any procedure for obtaining a paper copy of the recipient's statement after giving the consent described in paragraph (a)(2)(i) of this section and whether a request for a paper statement will be treated as a withdrawal of consent.

(v) *Withdrawal of consent.* The recipient must be informed that—

(A) The recipient may withdraw a consent by writing (electronically or on paper) to the person or department whose name, mailing address, telephone number, and email address is provided in the disclosure statement,

(B) The furnisher will confirm the withdrawal and the date on which it takes effect in writing (either electronically or on paper), and

(C) A withdrawal of consent does not apply to a statement that was furnished electronically in the manner described in this paragraph (a) before the date on which the withdrawal of consent takes effect.

(vi) *Notice of termination.* The recipient must be informed of the conditions under which a furnisher will cease furnishing statements electronically to the recipient (for example, termination of the recipient's employment with furnisher-employer).

(vii) *Updating information.* The recipient must be informed of the procedures for updating the information needed by the furnisher to contact the recipient. The furnisher must inform the recipient of any change in the furnisher's contact information.

(viii) *Hardware and software requirements.* The recipient must be provided with a description of the hardware and software required to access, print, and retain the statement, and the date when the statement will no longer be available on the Web site. The recipient must be informed that the statement may be required to be printed and attached to a Federal, State, or local income tax return.

(4) *Format.* The electronic version of the statement must contain all required information and comply with applicable revenue procedures relating to substitute statements to recipients.

(5) *Notice*—(i) *In general.* If the statement is furnished on a Web site, the furnisher must notify the recipient that the statement is posted on a Web site. The notice may be delivered by mail, electronic mail, or in person. The notice must provide instructions on how to access and print the statement. The notice must include the following statement in capital letters, "IMPORTANT TAX RETURN DOCUMENT AVAILABLE." If the notice is provided by electronic mail, the foregoing statement must be on the subject line of the electronic mail.

(ii) *Undeliverable electronic address.* If an electronic notice described in paragraph (a)(5)(i) of this section is returned as undeliverable, and the correct electronic address cannot be obtained from the furnisher's records or from the recipient, then the furnisher must furnish the notice by mail or in person within 30 days after the electronic notice is returned.

(iii) *Corrected statement.* If the furnisher has corrected a recipient's statement as directed in § 301.6056-1(k) and the statement was furnished electronically, the furnisher must furnish the corrected statement to the recipient electronically. If the recipient's statement was furnished through a Web site posting and the furnisher has corrected the statement, the furnisher must notify the recipient that it has posted the corrected statement on the Web site within 30 days of such posting in the manner described in paragraph (a)(5)(i) of this section. The corrected statement or the notice must be furnished by mail or in person if—

(A) An electronic notice of the Web site posting of an original statement or the corrected statement was returned as undeliverable, and

(B) The recipient has not provided a new email address.

(6) *Access period.* Statements furnished on a Web site must be retained on the Web site through October 15 of the year following the calendar year to which the statements relate (or the first business day after October 15, if October 15 falls on a Saturday, Sunday, or legal holiday). The furnisher must maintain access to corrected statements that are posted on the Web site through October 15 of the year following the calendar year to which the statements relate (or the first business day after such October 15, if October 15 falls on a Saturday, Sunday, or legal holiday) or the date 90 days after the corrected forms are posted, whichever is later.

(7) *Paper statements after withdrawal of consent.* If a recipient withdraws consent to receive a statement electronically and the withdrawal takes effect before the statement is furnished electronically, a paper statement must be furnished. A paper statement furnished after the statement due date under this paragraph (a)(7) will be considered timely if furnished within 30 days after the date the withdrawal of consent is received by the furnisher.

(b) *Effective/applicability date.* The rules of this section are effective as of the date of publication of the Treasury decision adopting these rules as final regulations in the **Federal Register**. This section applies for calendar years beginning after December 31, 2014. Reporting entities will not be subject to penalties under sections 6721 or 6722 with respect to the reporting requirements for 2014 (for information returns filed and for statements furnished to employees in 2015).

Heather C. Maloy,

Acting Deputy Commissioner for Services and Enforcement.

[FR Doc. 2013-21791 Filed 9-5-13; 4:15 pm]

BILLING CODE 4830-01-P

¶ 20,263T

IRS: Indian tribes: Compensation.—The IRS has issued proposed regulations clarifying that amounts paid to an Indian tribe member as remuneration for services performed in a fishing rights-related activity may be treated as compensation for purposes of applying the limits on qualified plan benefits and contributions under Code Sec. 415(c). Comments and hearing requests must be received by February 13, 2014.

The proposed regulation was published in the Federal Register on November 15, 2013 (78 FR 68780).

DEPARTMENT OF THE TREASURY

Internal Revenue Service

26 CFR Part 1

[REG-120927-13]

RIN-1545-BL61

Treatment of Income from Indian Fishing Rights-Related Activity as Compensation

AGENCY: Internal Revenue Service (IRS), Treasury

ACTION: Notice of proposed rulemaking.

SUMMARY: This document contains proposed regulations that would clarify that amounts paid to an Indian tribe member as remuneration for services performed in a fishing rights-related activity may be treated as compensation for purposes of applying the limits on qualified plan benefits and contributions. These regulations would affect sponsors of, and participants in, employee benefit plans of Indian tribal governments. DATES: Comments and requests for a public hearing must be received by February 13, 2014.

ADDRESSES: Send submissions to CC:PA:LPD:PR (REG-120927-13), room 5205, Internal Revenue Service, PO Box 7604, Ben Franklin Station, Washington D.C. 20044. Submissions may be hand-delivered Monday through Friday between the hours of 8 a.m. and 4 p.m. to CC:PA:LPD:PR (REG-120927-13), Courier's Desk, Internal Revenue Service, 1111 Constitution Avenue, N.W., Washington, DC, 20224, or sent electronically via the Federal eRulemaking Portal at *www.regulations.gov* (IRS REG-120927-13).

FOR FURTHER INFORMATION CONTACT: Concerning the proposed regulations, Sarah Bolen or Pamela Kinard at (202) 622-6060 or (202) 317-6700; concerning the submission of comments or to request a public hearing, Oluwafunmilayo Taylor, (202) 622-7180 or (202) 317-6901 (not toll-free numbers).

SUPPLEMENTARY INFORMATION:

Background

Indian tribal governments (ITGs) and individual tribe members conduct fishing activities to generate revenue, protect critical habitats, and preserve tribal customs and traditions. Various treaties, federal statutes, and Presidential executive orders reserve to Indian tribe members the right to fish for subsistence and commercial purposes both on and off reservations. Because many of the treaties, statutes, and executive orders were adopted before passage of the Federal income tax, they often do not expressly address the question of whether income derived by Indians and ITGs from protected fishing activities is exempt from taxation. *See* H.R. Rep. 100-1104, at p. 77 (1988).

Congress added section 7873 to the Internal Revenue Code as part of the Technical and Miscellaneous Revenue Act of 1988 (Public Law 100-647). Section 7873(a)(1) provides that no income tax shall be imposed on income derived from a fishing rights-related activity of an Indian tribe by (A) a member of the tribe directly or through a qualified Indian entity, or (B) a qualified Indian entity. Section 7873(a)(2) provides that no employment tax shall be imposed on remuneration paid for services performed in a fishing rights-related activity of an Indian tribe by a member of such tribe for another member of such tribe or for a qualified Indian entity. Thus, section 7873(a) exempts income derived from a fishing rights-related activity ("fishing rights-related income") from both income and employment taxes.

Section 7873(b)(1) defines fishing rights-related activity with respect to an Indian tribe as any activity directly related to harvesting, processing, or transporting fish harvested in the exercise of a recognized fishing right of the tribe or to selling such fish but only if substantially all of such harvesting was performed by members of such tribe.

Section 415(a)(1) provides that a trust that is part of a pension, profitsharing, or stock bonus plan shall not constitute a qualified trust under section 401(a) if (A) in the case of a defined benefit plan, the plan provides for the payment of benefits with respect to a participant which exceed the limitation of section 415(b), or (B) in the case of a defined contribution plan, contributions and other additions under the plan with respect to any participant for any taxable year exceed the limitation of section 415(c).

Section 415(b)(1) provides that benefits with respect to a participant exceed the annual limitation for defined benefit plans if, when expressed as an annual benefit (within the meaning of section 415(b)(2)), the participant's annual benefit is greater than the lesser of $160,000 (as adjusted in accordance with section 415(d)(1)) or 100 percent of the participant's average compensation for the participant's high 3 years.

Section 415(b)(3) provides that, for purposes of section 415(b)(1), a participant's high 3 years will be the period of consecutive calendar years (not more than 3) during which the participant had the greatest aggregate compensation from the employer. In the case of an employee within the meaning of section 401(c)(1) (that is, a self-employed individual treated as an employee), the preceding sentence is applied by substituting for "compensation from the employer" the following: "the participant's earned income (within the meaning of section 401(c)(2) but determined without regard to any exclusion under section 911)."

Section 415(c)(1) provides that contributions and other additions with respect to a participant exceed the annual limitation for defined contribution plans if, when expressed as an annual addition (within the meaning of section 415(c)(2)) to the participant's account, the participant's annual addition is greater than the lesser of $40,000 (as adjusted in accordance with section 415(d)(1)) or 100 percent of the participant's compensation. Section 415(c)(3) provides that the term "participant's compensation" means the compensation of the participant from the employer for the year. Section 1.415(c)-2(a) of the Income Tax Regulations generally provides that compensation from the employer within the meaning of section 415(c)(3) includes all items of remuneration described in § 1.415(c)-2(b), but excludes the items of remuneration described in § 1.415(c)-2(c).

Section 1.415(c)-2(b) generally provides that, for purposes of applying the limitations of section 415, the term compensation means remuneration for services. Specifically, under § 1.415(c)-2(b)(1), compensation includes employee wages, salaries, fees for professional services, and other amounts received (without regard to whether or not an amount is paid in cash) for personal services actually rendered in the course of employment with the employer maintaining the plan, to the extent that the amounts are includible in gross income. In addition, § 1.415(c)-2(b)(2) provides that in the case of an employee within the meaning of section 401(c)(1) (a self-employed employee), compensation includes the employee's earned income (as described in section 401(c)(2)) plus amounts deferred at the election of the employee that would be includible in gross income but for the rules of section 402(e)(3), 402(h)(1)(B), 402(k), or 457(b).

Section 1.415(c)-2(c) excludes certain items from the definition of compensation under section 415(c)(3). Specifically, § 1.415(c)-2(c)(1) excludes contributions (other than certain elective contributions) made by the employer to a plan of deferred compensation to the extent that the contributions are not includible in the gross income of the employee for the taxable year in which contributed. Likewise, distributions from plans (whether qualified or not) are generally not considered to be compensation for section 415 purposes. Section 1.415(c)-2(c)(2) excludes from compensation amounts realized from the exercise of nonstatutory options and amounts realized when restricted stock or other property held by an employee becomes freely transferable or is no longer subject to a substantial risk of forfeiture. Section 1.415(c)-2(c)(3) excludes from compensation amounts realized from the sale, exchange, or other disposition of stock acquired under a statutory stock option (as defined in § 1.421-1(b)). Finally, § 1.415(c)-2(c)(4) excludes from compensation other amounts that receive special tax benefits, such as certain premiums for group-term life insurance.

Section 1.415(c)-2(d) provides safe harbor definitions that a plan is permitted to use to define compensation in a manner that satisfies section 415(c)(3). Section 1.415(c)-2(d)(2) provides a safe harbor definition of compensation that includes only those items listed in § 1.415(c)-2(b)(1) or (b)(2) and excludes all the items listed in § 1.415(c)-2(c). Section 415(c)-2(d)(3) provides a separate safe harbor definition of compensation that includes wages within the meaning of section 3401(a), plus amounts that would be included in wages but for an election under section 125(a), 132(f)(4), 402(e)(3), 402(h)(1)(b), 402(k), or 457(b).

Explanation of Provisions

Because fishing rights-related income is not subject to income tax, an issue has been raised as to whether such income is included as compensation for purposes of section 415(c)(3) and § 1.415(c)-2(b). The proposed regulations would clarify that certain fishing rights-related income is included in the definition of compensation. Specifically, these regulations would provide that amounts paid to a member of an Indian tribe as remuneration for services performed in a fishing rights-related activity (as defined in section 7873(b)(1)) do not fail to be treated as compensation under § 1.415(c)-2(b)(1) and (b)(2) (and are not excluded from the definition of compensation pursuant to § 1.415(c)-2(c)(4)) merely because those amounts are not subject to income tax as a result of section 7873(a)(1). Thus, the determination of whether an amount constitutes wages, salaries, or earned income for purposes of § 1.415(c)-2(b)(1) or (b)(2) is made without regard to the exemption from taxation under section 7873(b)(1) and (b)(2). In addition, by permitting fishing rights-related income to be treated as wages, salaries, or earned income under § 1.415(c)-2(b)(1) and (b)(2), plans that accept contributions of fishing rights-related income would not be precluded from utilizing the safe harbor definitions of compensation under § 1.415(c)-2(d)(2) and (d)(3) of the regulations.

Proposed Applicability Date

These regulations are proposed to apply for taxable years ending on or after the date of publication of the Treasury decision adopting these rules as final regulations in the **Federal Register**. Taxpayers, however, may rely on these proposed regulations for periods preceding the effective date, pending the issuance of final regulations. If, and to the extent, the final regulations are more restrictive than the rules in these

proposed regulations, those provisions of the final regulations will be applied without retroactive effect.

Special Analyses

It has been determined that this notice of proposed rulemaking is not a significant regulatory action as defined in Executive Order 12866, as supplemented by Executive Order 13563. Therefore, a regulatory assessment is not required. It has also been determined that 5 U.S.C. 533(b) of the Administrative Procedure Act (5 U.S.C. chapter 5) does not apply to these regulations. Because these regulations do not impose a collection of information on small entities, the provisions of the Regulatory Flexibility Act (5 U.S.C. chapter 6) do not apply and a Regulatory Flexibility Analysis is not required. Pursuant to section 7805(f) of the Internal Revenue Code, these regulations have been submitted to the Office of Chief Counsel for Advocacy of the Small Business Administration for comments on its impact on small business.

Comments and Requests for Public Hearing

Before these proposed regulations are adopted as final regulations, consideration will be given to any comments that are submitted timely to the IRS as prescribed in this preamble under the "Addresses" heading. In addition to general comments on the proposed regulations, the IRS and the Treasury Department request comments on the taxation of qualified plan distributions that are attributable to fishing rights-related income, and the application of section 72(f)(2) (which treats certain amounts as basis for purposes of computing employee contributions if those amounts would have not been includible in income had they been paid directly to the employee). All comments are available at *www.regulations.gov* or upon request. A public hearing will be scheduled if requested in writing by any person who timely submits written comments. If a public hearing is scheduled, notice of the date, time, and place of the public hearing will be published in the **Federal Register**.

Consultation and Coordination with Indian Tribal Governments

These proposed regulations take into account comments provided through a number of general consultation sessions held with the Indian tribal community in recent years. Consistent with Executive Order 13175, the Treasury Department and the IRS expect to hold a telephone consultation on a date between *[INSERT DATE OF PUBLICATION OF THIS DOCUMENT IN THE FEDERAL REGISTER]* and *[INSERT DATE 90 DAYS AFTER PUBLICATION OF THIS DOCUMENT IN THE FEDERAL REGISTER]*. This telephone consultation session will focus principally on the contribution of section 7873 income to qualified retirement plans and the taxation of qualified plan distributions that are attributable to this income. Information relating to the consultation, including the date, time, registration requirements, and procedures for submitting written and oral comments, will be available on the IRS website relating to Indian tribal governments at: http://www.irs.gov/Government-Entities/Indian-Tribal-Governments.

Drafting Information

The principal author of these regulations is Sarah R. Bolen, Office of Division Counsel/Associate Chief Counsel (Tax Exempt and Government Entities). However, other personnel from the IRS and the Treasury Department participated in the development of these regulations.

List of subjects in 26 CFR Part 1

Income taxes, Reporting and recordkeeping requirements.

Proposed Amendments to the Regulations

Accordingly, 26 CFR part 1 is proposed to be amended as follows:

PART 1—INCOME TAXES

Paragraph 1. The authority citation for part 1 continues to read in part as follows:

Authority: 26 U.S.C. 7805 * * *

Par. 2. Section 1.415(c)-2 is amended by adding paragraphs (g)(9) and (h) to read as follows:

§ 1.415(c)-2 Compensation.

* * * * *

(g) * * *

(9) *Income derived by Indians from exercise of fishing rights.* Amounts paid to a member of an Indian tribe directly or through a qualified Indian entity (within the meaning of section 7873(b)(3)) as compensation for services performed in a fishing rights-related activity (as defined in section 7873(b)(1)) of the tribe do not fail to constitute

compensation under paragraphs (b)(1) and (b)(2) of this section and are not excluded from the definition of compensation pursuant to paragraph (c)(4) of this section merely because those amounts are not subject to income or employment taxes as a result of section 7873(a)(1) and (2). Thus, the determination of whether an amount constitutes wages, salaries, or earned income for purposes of paragraph (b)(1) or (a)(2) of this section is made without regard to the exemption from taxation under section 7873(a)(1) and (2).

(h) *Effective/applicability date.* Section 1.415(c)-2(g)(9) shall apply for plan years ending on or after the date of publication of the Treasury decision adopting these rules as final regulations in the **Federal Register**.

Heather C. Maloy

Acting Deputy Commissioner for Services and Enforcement.

¶ 20,263U

IRS: Proposed regulations: Employee Benefits Security Administration (EBSA): Group health plans: Excepted benefits.—The IRS, EBSA, and Department of Health and Human Services have issued proposed regulations that would amend Code and ERISA regulations regarding excepted benefits, which are generally exempt from the health reform requirements that were added by the Health Insurance Portability and Accountability Act of 1996 (HIPAA, P.L. 104-191) and the Patient Protection and Affordable Care Act (PPACA, P.L. 111-148). The proposed regulations would make amendments concerning dental and vision benefits, limited wraparound coverage, and employee assistance programs. The Departments seek comments on the proposed regulations. Until the regulations are finalized, through at least 2014, for purposes of enforcing the provisions of title XXVII of the Public Health Service Act, part 7 of ERISA, and chapter 100 of the Code, the Departments will consider dental and vision benefits and employee assistance program benefits as meeting the conditions of the proposed regulations to qualify as excepted benefits. To the extent that the final regulations or other guidance concerning vision or dental benefits or employee assistance programs is more restrictive that the proposed regulations, the final regulations or other guidance will not be effective before January 1, 2015.

The proposed regulations were published in the Federal Register on December 24, 2013 (78 FR 77632). All of the regulations, except the portion pertaining to limited wraparound coverage, were finalized on October 1, 2014 (79 FR 59130). The preamble to the final regulations is at ¶ 23,309. The final regulations are at ¶ 13,968W-10. New proposed regulations on limited wraparound coverage were published in the Federal Register on December 23, 2014. See ¶ 20,264.

¶ 20,263V

IRS: Employee health coverage: Minimum essential coverage: Shared responsibility.—The IRS has issued proposed regulations relating to the requirement for nonexempt individuals to maintain minimum essential coverage or make a shared responsibility payment under Code Sec. 5000A, as enacted by the Patient Protection and Affordable Care Act (P.L. 111-148) and amended by the TRICARE Affirmation Act of 2010 (P.L. 111-159) and P.L. 111-173. The proposed regulations provide that coverage under certain government-sponsored programs is not government-sponsored minimum essential coverage. The proposed regulations also address the determination, for purposes of the lack of an affordable coverage exemption, of the required contribution for individuals eligible to enroll in an eligible employer-sponsored plan that provides employer contributions to health reimbursement arrangements (HRAs) or wellness program incentives. In addition, the proposed regulations provide or clarify rules under Code Sec. 5000A addressing the definition of excepted benefits, hardship exemptions that may be claimed on a Federal income tax return, and the computation of the monthly penalty amount. The regulations are proposed to apply for months beginning after December 31, 2013.

The proposed regulations were published in the Federal Register on January 27, 2014 (79 FR 4302). The IRS corrected the proposed regulations on June 3, 2014 (79 FR 31893). The regulations were finalized on November 26, 2014 (79 FR 70464). The preamble to the final regulations is at ¶ 23,310. The final regulations are at ¶ 13,648Z-55, ¶ 13,648Z-57, ¶ 13,648Z-58, and ¶ 13,648Z-59.

¶ 20,263W

IRS: Proposed regulations: Employee Benefits Security Administration (EBSA): Patient Protection and Affordable Care Act (P.L. 111-148, PPACA): Group health plans: Waiting periods: Employment-based orientation periods.—The IRS, EBSA, and the Department of Health and Human Services have issued proposed regulations that would clarify the maximum allowed length of any reasonable and bona fide employment-based orientation period, consistent with the 90-day waiting period limitation for health insurance coverage as set forth in Sec. 2708 of the Public Health Service (PHS) Act, which was added by the PPACA and incorporated into the Code and ERISA. The proposed regulations would provide that one month is the maximum allowed length of any reasonable and bona fide employment-based orientation period. The Departments will consider compliance with these proposed regulations to constitute compliance with PHS Act Sec. 2708 at least through the end of 2014. To the extent final regulations or other guidance with respect to the application of the 90-day waiting period limitation to orientation periods is more restrictive on plans and issuers, the final regulations or other guidance will not be effective prior to January 1, 2015, and will provide plans and issuers a reasonable time period to comply.

The proposed regulations were published in the Federal Register on February 24, 2014 (79 FR 10319). The regulations were finalized on June 25, 2014 (79 FR 35942). The preamble to the final regulations is at ¶ 23,301. The final regulations are at ¶ 13,968V-20K.

FEDERAL REGISTER

DEPARTMENT OF THE TREASURY

Internal Revenue Service

26 CFR Part 54

[REG-122706-12]

RIN 1545-BL97

DEPARTMENT OF LABOR

Employee Benefits Security Administration

29 CFR Part 2590

RIN 1210-AB61

DEPARTMENT OF HEALTH AND HUMAN SERVICES

45 CFR Part 147

[CMS-9952-P2]

RIN 0938-AR77

Ninety-Day Waiting Period Limitation

AGENCY: Internal Revenue Service, Department of the Treasury; Employee Benefits Security Administration, Department of Labor; Centers for Medicare & Medicaid Services, Department of Health and Human Services.

ACTION: Proposed rules.

SUMMARY: These proposed regulations would clarify the maximum allowed length of any reasonable and bona fide employment-based orientation period, consistent with the 90-day waiting period limitation set forth in section 2708 of the Public Health Service Act, as added by the Patient Protection and Affordable Care Act (Affordable Care Act), as amended, and incorporated into the Employee Retirement Income Security Act of 1974 and the Internal Revenue Code.

DATES: Written comments on this notice of proposed rulemaking are invited and must be received by April 25, 2014.

ADDRESSES: Written comments may be submitted to the Department of Labor as specified below. Any comment that is submitted will be shared with the other Departments and will also be made available to the public. Warning: Do not include any personally identifiable information (such as name, address, or other contact information) or confidential business information that you do not want publicly disclosed. All comments may be posted on the Internet and can be retrieved by most Internet search engines. No deletions, modifications, or redactions will be made to the comments received, as they are public records. Comments may be submitted anonymously.

Comments, identified by "Ninety-day waiting period limitation," may be submitted by one of the following methods:

Federal eRulemaking Portal: http://www.regulations.gov. Follow the instructions for submitting comments.

Mail or Hand Delivery: Office of Health Plan Standards and Compliance Assistance, Employee Benefits Security Administration, Room N-5653, U.S. Department of Labor, 200 Constitution Avenue NW., Washington, DC 20210, Attention: Ninety-day waiting period limitation.

Comments received will be posted without change to *www.regulations.gov* and available for public inspection at the Public Disclosure Room, N-1513, Employee Benefits Security Administration, 200 Constitution Avenue NW., Washington, DC 20210, including any personal information provided.

FOR FURTHER INFORMATION CONTACT: Amy Turner or Elizabeth Schumacher, Employee Benefits Security Administration, Department of Labor, at (202) 693-8335; Karen Levin, Internal Revenue Service, Department of the Treasury, at (202) 317-6846; or Cam Moultrie Clemmons, Centers for Medicare & Medicaid Services, Department of Health and Human Services, at (410) 786-1565.

Customer service information: Individuals interested in obtaining information from the Department of Labor concerning employment-based health coverage laws may call the EBSA Toll-Free Hotline at 1-866-444-EBSA (3272) or visit the Department of Labor's Web site (*www.dol.gov/ebsa*). In addition, information from HHS on private health insurance for consumers can be found on the Centers for Medicare & Medicaid Services (CMS) Web site (*www.cciio.cms.gov/*) and information on health reform can be found at *www.HealthCare.gov.*

SUPPLEMENTARY INFORMATION:

I. Background

The Patient Protection and Affordable Care Act, Public Law 111-148, was enacted on March 23, 2010, and the Health Care and Education Reconciliation Act, Public Law 111- 152, was enacted on March 30, 2010. (They are collectively known as the "Affordable Care Act".) The Affordable Care Act reorganizes, amends, and adds to the provisions of part A of title XXVII of the Public Health Service Act (PHS Act) relating to group health plans and health insurance issuers in the group and individual markets. The term "group health plan" includes both insured and self-insured group health plans.[1] The Affordable Care Act adds section 715(a)(1) to the Employee Retirement Income Security Act (ERISA) and section 9815(a)(1) to the Internal Revenue Code (the Code) to incorporate the provisions of part A of title XXVII of the PHS Act into ERISA and the Code, and to make them applicable to group health plans and health insurance issuers providing health insurance coverage in connection with group health plans. The PHS Act sections incorporated by these references are sections 2701 through 2728.

PHS Act section 2708, as added by the Affordable Care Act and incorporated into ERISA and the Code, provides that a group health plan or health insurance issuer offering group health insurance coverage shall not apply any waiting period (as defined in PHS Act section 2704(b)(4)) that exceeds 90 days. PHS Act section 2704(b)(4), ERISA section 701(b)(4), and Code section 9801(b)(4) define a waiting period to be the period that must pass with respect to an individual before the individual is eligible to be covered for benefits under the terms of the plan. In 2004 regulations implementing the Health Insurance Portability and Accountability Act of 1996 (HIPAA) portability provisions (2004 HIPAA regulations), the Departments of Labor, Health and Human Services (HHS), and the Treasury (the Departments[2]) defined a waiting period to mean the period that must pass before coverage for an

employee or dependent who is otherwise eligible to enroll under the terms of a group health plan can become effective.[3] PHS Act section 2708 does not require an employer to offer coverage to any particular individual or class of individuals, including part-time employees. PHS Act section 2708 merely prevents an otherwise eligible individual from being required to wait more than 90 days before coverage becomes effective. PHS Act section 2708 applies to both grandfathered and non-grandfathered group health plans and group health insurance coverage for plan years beginning on or after January 1, 2014.

On February 9, 2012, the Departments issued guidance[4] outlining various approaches under consideration with respect to both the 90-day waiting period limitation and the employer shared responsibility provisions under Code section 4980H (February 2012 guidance) and requested public comment. On August 31, 2012, following their review of the comments on the February 2012 guidance, the Departments provided temporary guidance,[5] to remain in effect at least through the end of 2014, regarding the 90-day waiting period limitation, and described the approach they intended to propose in future rulemaking (August 2012 guidance). After consideration of all of the comments received in response to the February 2012 guidance and August 2012 guidance, the Departments issued proposed regulations on March 21, 2013 (78 FR 17313).

Under the proposed regulations, a group health plan, and a health insurance issuer offering group health insurance coverage may not apply any waiting period that exceeds 90 days. The regulations proposed to define "waiting period" as the period that must pass before coverage for an employee or dependent who is otherwise eligible to enroll under the terms of a group health plan can become effective. Being otherwise eligible to enroll in a plan means having met the plan's substantive eligibility conditions (such as being in an eligible job classification or achieving job-related licensure requirements specified in the plan's terms). After consideration of comments on the proposed regulations, the Departments are publishing final regulations elsewhere in this issue of the **Federal Register**. These proposed regulations address orientation periods under the 90-day waiting period limitation of PHS Act section 2708 and solicit comment before promulgation of final regulations on this discrete issue.

II. Overview of the Proposed Regulations

A. Orientation Periods

Final regulations published elsewhere in this edition of the **Federal Register** set forth rules governing the relationship between a plan's eligibility criteria and the 90-day waiting period limitation. Specifically, the final regulations provide that being otherwise eligible to enroll in a plan means having met the plan's substantive eligibility conditions (such as, for example, being in an eligible job classification, achieving job-related licensure requirements specified in the plan's terms, or satisfying a reasonable and bona fide employment-based orientation period). Under the final regulations, after an individual is determined to be otherwise eligible for coverage under the terms of the plan, any waiting period may not extend beyond 90 days, and all calendar days are counted beginning on the enrollment date, including weekends and holidays.[6]

The final regulations do not specify the facts and circumstances under which an employment-based orientation period would not be considered "reasonable and bona fide." These proposed regulations would provide that one month is the maximum allowed length of any reasonable and bona fide employment-based orientation period. During an orientation period, the Departments envision that an employer and employee could evaluate whether the employment situation was satisfactory for each party, and standard orientation and training processes would begin. Under these proposed regulations, one month would be determined by adding one calendar month and subtracting one calendar day, measured from an employee's start date in a position that is otherwise eligible for coverage. For example, if an employee's start date in an otherwise eligible position is May 3, the last permitted day of the orientation period is June 2. Similarly, if an employee's start date in an otherwise eligible position is October 1, the last permitted day of the orientation period is October 31. If there is not a corresponding date in the next calendar month upon adding a calendar month, the last

---

[1] The term "group health plan" is used in title XXVII of the PHS Act, part 7 of ERISA, and chapter 100 of the Code, and is distinct from the term "health plan," as used in other provisions of title I of the Affordable Care Act. The term "health plan" does not include self-insured group health plans.

[2] Note, however, that in the Economic Analysis and Paperwork Burden section of this preamble, in sections under headings listing only two of the three Departments, the term "Departments" generally refers only to the two Departments listed in the heading.

[3] 26 CFR 54.9801-3(a)(3)(iii), 29 CFR 2590.701-3(a)(3)(iii), and 45 CFR 146.111(a)(3)(iii).

[4] Department of Labor Technical Release 2012- 01, IRS Notice 2012-17, and HHS FAQs issued February 9, 2012.

[5] Department of Labor Technical Release 2012- 02, IRS Notice 2012-59, and HHS FAQs issued August 31, 2012.

[6] The final regulations also note that a plan or issuer that imposes a 90-day waiting period may, for administrative convenience, choose to permit coverage to become effective earlier than the 91st day if the 91st day is a weekend of holiday.

permitted day of the orientation period is the last day of the next calendar month. For example, if the employee's start date is January 30, the last permitted day of the orientation period is February 28 (or February 29 in a leap year). Similarly, if the employee's start date is August 31, the last permitted day of the orientation period is September 30. If a group health plan conditions eligibility on an employee's having completed a reasonable and bona fide employment-based orientation period, the eligibility condition would not be considered to be designed to avoid compliance with the 90-day waiting period limitation if the orientation period did not exceed one month and the maximum 90-day waiting period would begin on the first day after the orientation period.

B. Comment Invitation and Reliance

The Departments invite comments on these proposed regulations. The Departments will consider compliance with these proposed regulations to constitute compliance with PHS Act section 2708 at least through the end of 2014. To the extent final regulations or other guidance with respect to the application of the 90-day waiting period limitation to orientation periods is more restrictive on plans and issuers, the final regulations or other guidance will not be effective prior to January 1, 2015, and will provide plans and issuers a reasonable time period to comply.

III. Economic Impact and Paperwork Burden

A. Executive Order 12866 and 13563—Department of Labor and Department of Health and Human Services

Executive Order 13563 emphasizes the importance of quantifying both costs and benefits, of reducing costs, of harmonizing and streamlining rules, and of promoting flexibility. It also requires federal agencies to develop a plan under which the agencies will periodically review their existing significant regulations to make the agencies' regulatory programs more effective or less burdensome in achieving their regulatory objectives.

Under Executive Order 12866, a regulatory action deemed "significant" is subject to the requirements of the Executive Order and review by the Office of Management and Budget (OMB). Section 3(f) of the Executive Order defines a "significant regulatory action" as an action that is likely to result in a rule (1) having an annual effect on the economy of $100 million or more, or adversely and materially affecting a sector of the economy, productivity, competition, jobs, the environment, public health or safety, or State, local or tribal governments or communities (also referred to as "economically significant"); (2) creating serious inconsistency or otherwise interfering with an action taken or planned by another agency; (3) materially altering the budgetary impacts of entitlement grants, user fees, or loan programs or the rights and obligations of recipients thereof; or (4) raising novel legal or policy issues arising out of legal mandates, the President's priorities, or the principles set forth in the Executive Order.

These proposed regulations are not economically significant within the meaning of section 3(f)(1) of the Executive Order. However, OMB has determined that the actions are significant within the meaning of section 3(f)(4) of the Executive Order. Therefore, OMB has reviewed these proposed regulations, and the Departments[7] have provided the following assessment of their impact.

1. Summary

As stated earlier in this preamble, these proposed regulations address reasonable and bona fide employment-based orientation periods under the 90-day waiting period limitation of PHS Act section 2708. The Departments have crafted these proposed regulations to secure the protections intended by Congress in an economically efficient manner. The Departments lack sufficient data to quantify the regulations' economic cost or benefits. The proposed regulations implementing PHS Act section 2708[8] provided a qualitative discussion of economic impacts of proposed limits on waiting periods and requested detailed comments and data that would allow for quantification of the costs, benefits, and transfers. Comments were received expressing concern about the cost to employers that currently have waiting periods longer than 90 days, and explaining that they would have to change their practices and often have to provide coverage sooner than the 90-day waiting period limitation. No comments provided additional data that would help in estimating the economic impacts of the proposed regulations. The

Departments request comments that would allow them to quantify the impacts of these proposed regulations on the discrete issue of orientation periods.

2. Estimated Number of Affected Entities

The Departments estimate that 4.1 million new employees receive group health insurance coverage through private sector employers and 1.0 million new employees receive group health insurance coverage through public sector employers annually.[9] The 2013 Kaiser Family Foundation and Health Research and Education Trust Employer Health Benefits Annual Survey (the "2013 Kaiser Survey") finds that 30 percent of covered workers were subject to waiting periods of three months or more.[10] The Departments do not have any data, and therefore invite public comment, on the number of employees subject to orientation periods, as described earlier in this preamble.

2. Benefits

The final regulations provide that being otherwise eligible to enroll in a plan means having met the plan's substantive eligibility conditions (such as, for example, being in an eligible job classification, achieving job-related licensure requirements specified in the plan's terms, or satisfying a reasonable and bona fide employment-based orientation period). These proposed regulations would provide that one month is the maximum allowed length of any reasonable and bona fide employment-based orientation period. During an orientation period, the Departments envision that an employer and employee could evaluate whether the employment situation was satisfactory for each party, and standard orientation and training processes would begin. If a group health plan conditions eligibility on an employee's having completed a reasonable and bona fide employment-based orientation period, the eligibility condition would not be considered to be designed to avoid compliance with the 90-day waiting period limitation if the orientation period did not exceed one month and the maximum 90-day waiting period would begin on the first day after the orientation period.

3. Costs

These proposed regulations could extend the time between an employee beginning work and obtaining health care coverage relative to the time before the issuance of the final regulations and these proposed regulations. If employees delay health care treatment until the expiration of the orientation period and waiting period, detrimental health effects can result, especially for employees and their dependents requiring higher levels of health care, such as older Americans, pregnant women, young children, and those with chronic conditions. This could lead to lower work productivity and missed school days. Low-wage workers also are vulnerable, because they have less income to spend out-of-pocket to cover medical expenses. The Departments anticipate that these proposed regulations could lead to these effects, although the overall cost may be limited because few employees are likely to be affected and it is anticipated that conditioning eligibility on an employee's having completed an orientation period will not result in most employees facing a full additional month between being hired and obtaining coverage.

4. Transfers

The possible transfers associated with these proposed regulations would arise from employers beginning to pay their portion of premiums or contributions later than they did before the issuance of the final regulations and these proposed regulations. Recipients of the transfer would be employers who implement an orientation period in addition to the 90-day waiting period, thus delaying having to pay premiums. The source of the transfers would be covered employees who, after these proposed regulations become applicable, will have to wait longer between being employed and obtaining health coverage, during which they must forgo health coverage, purchase COBRA continuation coverage, or obtain an individual health insurance policy—all of which are options that could lead to higher out-of-pocket costs for employees to cover their healthcare expenditures.

The Departments believe that under these proposed regulations only a small number of employers would further delay offering coverage to their employees because a relatively small fraction of workers have an orientation period in addition to a waiting periods that runs for 90 days.

---

[7] In section III of this preamble, some subsections have a heading listing one or two of the three Departments. In those subsections, the term "Departments" generally refers only to the Departments listed in the heading.

[8] 78 FR 17313 (March 21, 2013).

[9] This estimate is based upon internal Department of Labor calculations derived from the 2009 Medical Expenditure Panel Survey.

[10] See e.g., Kaiser Family Foundation and Health Research and Education Trust, *Employer Health Benefits 2013 Annual Survey* (2013) available at *http://ehbs.kff.org/pdf/2013/8345.pdf.*

B. Regulatory Flexibility Act—Department of Labor and Department of Health and Human Services

The Regulatory Flexibility Act (5 U.S.C. 601 et seq.) (RFA) applies to most Federal rules that are subject to the notice and comment requirements of section 553(b) of the Administrative Procedure Act (5 U.S.C. 551 et seq.). Unless an agency certifies that such a rule will not have a significant economic impact on a substantial number of small entities, section 603 of the RFA requires the agency to present an initial regulatory flexibility analysis at the time of the publication of the notice of proposed rulemaking describing the impact of the rule on small entities. Small entities include small businesses, organizations and governmental jurisdictions.

For purposes of analysis under the RFA, the Departments propose to continue to consider a small entity to be an employee benefit plan with fewer than 100 participants. The basis of this definition is found in section 104(a)(3) of ERISA, which permits the Secretary of Labor to prescribe simplified annual reports for welfare benefit plans that cover fewer than 100 participants.[11]

Further, while some large employers may have small plans, in general, small employers maintain most small plans. Thus, the Departments believe that assessing the impact of these proposed regulations on small plans is an appropriate substitute for evaluating the effect on small entities.

The definition of small entity considered appropriate for this purpose differs, however, from a definition of small business that is based on size standards promulgated by the Small Business Administration (SBA) (13 CFR 121.201) pursuant to the Small Business Act (15 U.S.C. 631 et seq.). The Departments therefore request comments on the appropriateness of the size standard used in evaluating the impact of these proposed regulations on small entities.

The Departments carefully considered the likely impact of the rule on small entities in connection with their assessment under Executive Order 12866. The Departments lack data to focus only on the impacts on small business. However, the Departments believe that the proposed regulations include flexibility that would minimize the transfers in health insurance premiums that would occur due to the orientation period.

The Departments hereby certify that these proposed regulations will not have a significant economic impact on a substantial number of small entities. Consistent with the policy of the RFA, the Departments encourage the public to submit comments that would allow the Departments to assess the impacts specifically on small plans or suggest alternative rules that accomplish the stated purpose of PHS Act section 2708 and minimize the impact on small entities.

C. Special Analyses—Department of the Treasury

For purposes of the Department of the Treasury, it has been determined that this proposed rule is not a significant regulatory action as defined in Executive Order 12866, as supplemented by Executive Order 13563. Therefore, a regulatory assessment is not required. It has also been determined that section 553(b) of the Administrative Procedure Act (5 U.S.C. chapter 5) does not apply to these proposed regulations, and, because these proposed regulations do not impose a collection of information requirement on small entities, a regulatory flexibility analysis under the Regulatory Flexibility Act (5 U.S.C. chapter 6) is not required. Pursuant to Code section 7805(f), this proposed rule has been submitted to the Small Business Administration for comment on its impact on small business.

D. Congressional Review Act

These proposed regulations are subject to the Congressional Review Act provisions of the Small Business Regulatory Enforcement Fairness Act of 1996 (5 U.S.C. 801 et seq.) and, if finalized, will be transmitted to the Congress and the Comptroller General for review.

E. Unfunded Mandates Reform Act

For purposes of the Unfunded Mandates Reform Act of 1995 (Pub. L. 104-4), as well as Executive Order 12875, these proposed regulations do not include any Federal mandate that may result in expenditures by State, local, or tribal governments, or by the private sector, of $100 million or more adjusted for inflation.

F. Federalism Statement—Department of Labor and Department of Health and Human Services

Executive Order 13132 outlines fundamental principles of federalism, and requires the adherence to specific criteria by Federal agencies in the process of their formulation and implementation of policies that have "substantial direct effects" on the States, the relationship between the national government and States, or on the distribution of power and responsibilities among the various levels of government. Federal agencies promulgating regulations that have these federalism implications must consult with State and local officials, and describe the extent of their consultation and the nature of the concerns of State and local officials in the preamble to the regulation.

In the Departments' view, these proposed regulations have federalism implications, because they have direct effects on the States, the relationship between the national government and States, or on the distribution of power and responsibilities among various levels of government. In general, through section 514, ERISA supersedes State laws to the extent that they relate to any covered employee benefit plan, and preserves State laws that regulate insurance, banking, or securities. While ERISA prohibits States from regulating a plan as an insurance or investment company or bank, the preemption provisions of ERISA section 731 and PHS Act section 2724 (implemented in 29 CFR 2590.731(a) and 45 CFR 146.143(a)) apply so that the HIPAA requirements (including those of the Affordable Care Act) are not to be "construed to supersede any provision of State law which establishes, implements, or continues in effect any standard or requirement solely relating to health insurance issuers in connection with group health insurance coverage except to the extent that such standard or requirement prevents the application of a requirement" of a federal standard. The conference report accompanying HIPAA indicates that this is intended to be the "narrowest" preemption of State laws. (See House Conf. Rep. No. 104-736, at 205, reprinted in 1996 U.S. Code Cong. & Admin. News 2018.)

States may continue to apply State law requirements except to the extent that such requirements prevent the application of the Affordable Care Act requirements that are the subject of this rulemaking. State insurance laws that are more consumer protective than the Federal requirements are unlikely to "prevent the application of" the Affordable Care Act, and therefore are unlikely to be preempted. Accordingly, States have significant latitude to impose requirements on health insurance issuers that are more restrictive than the Federal law.

Guidance conveying this interpretation was published in the **Federal Register** on April 8, 1997 (62 FR 16904), and December 30, 2004 (69 FR 78720), and these proposed regulations would clarify and implement the statute's minimum standards and would not significantly reduce the discretion given the States by the statute.

In compliance with the requirement of Executive Order 13132 that agencies examine closely any policies that may have federalism implications or limit the policy making discretion of the States, the Departments have engaged in efforts to consult with and work cooperatively with affected State and local officials, including attending conferences of the National Association of Insurance Commissioners and consulting with State insurance officials on an individual basis.

Throughout the process of developing these proposed regulations, to the extent feasible within the specific preemption provisions of HIPAA as it applies to the Affordable Care Act, the Departments have attempted to balance the States' interests in regulating health insurance issuers, and Congress' intent to provide uniform minimum protections to consumers in every State. By doing so, it is the Departments' view that they have complied with the requirements of Executive Order 13132.

IV. Statutory Authority

The Department of the Treasury regulations are proposed to be adopted pursuant to the authority contained in sections 7805 and 9833 of the Code.

The Department of Labor regulations are proposed to be adopted pursuant to the authority contained in 29 U.S.C. 1027, 1059, 1135, 1161-1168, 1169, 1181-1183, 1181 note, 1185, 1185a, 1185b, 1185d, 1191, 1191a, 1191b, and 1191c; sec. 101(g), Public Law 104-191, 110 Stat. 1936; sec. 401(b), Public Law 105-200, 112 Stat. 645 (42 U.S.C. 651 note); sec. 512(d), Public Law 110-343, 122 Stat. 3881; sec. 1001, 1201, and 1562(e), Public Law 111-148, 124 Stat. 119, as amended by Public

---

[11] Under ERISA section 104(a)(2), the Secretary may also provide exemptions or simplified reporting and disclosure requirements for pension plans. Pursuant to the authority of ERISA section 104(a)(3), the Department of Labor has previously issued at 29 CFR 2520.104-20, 2520.104-21, 2520.104-41, 2520.104-46, and 2520.104b-10 certain simplified reporting provisions and limited exemptions from reporting and disclosure requirements for small plans, including unfunded or insured welfare plans, that cover fewer than 100 participants and satisfy certain other requirements.

Law 111- 152, 124 Stat. 1029; Secretary of Labor's Order 3-2010, 75 FR 55354 (September 10, 2010).

The Department of Health and Human Services regulations are proposed to be adopted pursuant to the authority contained in sections 2701 through 2763, 2791, and 2792 of the PHS Act (42 U.S.C. 300gg through 300gg-63, 300gg-91, and 300gg-92), as amended.

List of Subjects

26 CFR Part 54

Excise taxes, Health care, Health insurance, Pensions, Reporting and recordkeeping requirements.

29 CFR Part 2590

Continuation coverage, Disclosure, Employee benefit plans, Group health plans, Health care, Health insurance, Medical child support, Reporting and recordkeeping requirements.

45 CFR Part 147

Health care, Health insurance, Reporting and recordkeeping requirements, and State regulation of health insurance.

John Dalrymple,

Deputy Commissioner for Services and Enforcement, Internal Revenue Service.

Signed this 12th day of February, 2014.

Phyllis C. Borzi,

Assistant Secretary, Employee Benefits Security Administration, Department of Labor.

Dated: February 11, 2014.

Marilyn Tavenner,

Administrator, Centers for Medicare & Medicaid Services.

Dated: February 14, 2014.

Kathleen Sebelius,

Secretary, Department of Health and Human Services.

Department of the Treasury

Internal Revenue Service

Accordingly, 26 CFR Part 54, as amended by the final rule titled, Ninety-Day Waiting Period Limitation and Technical Amendments to Certain Health Coverage Requirements Under the Affordable Care Act, published elsewhere in this issue of the **Federal Register**, is proposed to be further amended as follows:

PART 54—PENSION EXCISE TAXES

■ **Paragraph 1.** The authority citation for Part 54 continues to read in part as follows:

Authority: 26 U.S.C. 7805. * * *

Section 54.9815-2708 is also issued under 26 U.S.C. 9833.

* * * * *

■ **Par. 2.** Section 54.9815-2708 is amended by adding paragraph (c)(3)(iii) and a new Example 11 in paragraph (f) to read as follows:

§54.9815-2708 Prohibition on waiting periods that exceed 90 days.

* * * * *

(c) * * *

(3) * * *

(iii) *Limitation on orientation periods.* To ensure that an orientation period is not used as a subterfuge for the passage of time, or designed to avoid compliance with the 90-day waiting period limitation, an orientation period is permitted only if it does not exceed one month. For this purpose, one month is determined by adding one calendar month and subtracting one calendar day, measured from an employee's start date in a position that is otherwise eligible for coverage. For example, if an employee's start date in an otherwise eligible position is May 3, the last permitted day of the orientation period is June 2. Similarly, if an employee's start date in an otherwise eligible position is October 1, the last permitted day of the orientation period is October 31. If there is not a corresponding date in the next calendar month upon adding a calendar month, the last permitted day of the orientation period is the last day of the next calendar month. For example, if the employee's start date is January 30, the last permitted day of the orientation period is February 28 (or February 29 in a leap year). Similarly, if the employee's start date is August 31, the last permitted day of the orientation period is September 30.

* * * * *

(f) * * *

Example 11. (i) *Facts.* Employee *H* begins working full time for Employer *Z* on October 16. *Z* sponsors a group health plan, under which full time employees are eligible for coverage after they have successfully completed a one-month orientation period. *H* completes the orientation period on November 15.

(ii) *Conclusion.* In this *Example 11,* the orientation period is not considered a subterfuge for the passage of time and is not considered to be designed to avoid compliance with the 90-day waiting period limitation. Accordingly, plan coverage for *H* must begin no later than February 14, which is the 91st day after *H* completes the orientation period. (If the orientation period was more than one month, it would be considered to be considered a subterfuge for the passage of time and designed to avoid compliance with the 90-day waiting period limitation. Accordingly it would violate the rules of this section.)

* * * * *

Department of Labor

Employee Benefits Security Administration

29 CFR Chapter XXV

For the reasons stated in the preamble, the Department of Labor proposes to further amend 29 CFR part 2590, as amended by the final rule titled, Ninety-Day Waiting Period Limitation and Technical Amendments to Certain Health Coverage Requirements Under the Affordable Care Act, published elsewhere in this issue of the **Federal Register**, as follows:

PART 2590—RULES AND REGULATIONS FOR GROUP HEALTH PLANS

■ 3. The authority citation for Part 2590 continues to read as follows:

Authority: 29 U.S.C. 1027, 1059, 1135, 1161-1168, 1169, 1181-1183, 1181 note, 1185, 1185a, 1185b, 1185c, 1185d, 1191, 1191a, 1191b, and 1191c; sec. 101(g), Pub. L.104-191, 110 Stat. 1936; sec. 401(b), Pub. L. 105-200, 112 Stat. 645 (42 U.S.C. 651 note); sec. 512(d), Pub. L. 110-343, 122 Stat. 3881; sec. 1001, 1201, and 1562(e), Pub. L. 111-148, 124 Stat. 119, as amended by Pub. L. 111-152, 124 Stat. 1029; Secretary of Labor's Order 3-2010, 75 FR 55354 (September 10, 2010).

■ 4. Section 2590.715-2708 is amended by adding paragraph (c)(3)(iii) and a new Example 11 in paragraph (f) to read as follows:

§2590.715-2708 Prohibition on waiting periods that exceed 90 days.

* * * * *

(c) * * *

(3) * * *

(iii) *Limitation on orientation periods.* To ensure that an orientation period is not used as a subterfuge for the passage of time, or designed to avoid compliance with the 90-day waiting period limitation, an orientation period is permitted only if it does not exceed one month. For this purpose, one month is determined by adding one calendar month and subtracting one calendar day, measured from an employee's start date in a position that is otherwise eligible for coverage. For example, if an employee's start date in an otherwise eligible position is May 3, the last permitted day of the orientation period is June 2. Similarly, if an employee's start date in an otherwise eligible position is October 1, the last permitted day of the orientation period is October 31. If there is not a corresponding date in the next calendar month upon adding a calendar month, the last permitted day of the orientation period is the last day of the next calendar month. For example, if the employee's start date is January 30, the last permitted day of the orientation period is February 28 (or February 29 in a leap year). Similarly, if the employee's start date is August 31, the last permitted day of the orientation period is September 30.

* * * * *

(f) * * *

Example 11. (i) *Facts.* Employee *H* begins working full time for Employer *Z* on October 16. *Z* sponsors a group health plan, under which full time employees are eligible for coverage after they have successfully completed a one-month orientation period. *H* completes the orientation period on November 15.

(ii) *Conclusion.* In this *Example 11,* the orientation period is not considered a subterfuge for the passage of time and is not considered to be designed to avoid compliance with the 90-day waiting period limitation. Accordingly, plan coverage for *H* must begin no later than February 14, which is the 91st day after *H* completes the orientation

period. (If the orientation period was more than one month, it would be considered to be considered a subterfuge for the passage of time and designed to avoid compliance with the 90-day waiting period limitation. Accordingly it would violate the rules of this section.)

* * * * *

[FR Doc. 2014-03811 Filed 2-20-14; 11:15 am]

BILLING CODE 4830-01-P; 4510-29-P; 4120-01-P; 6325-64-P

¶ 20,263X

IRS: Proposed rules: Employee Benefits Security Administration (EBSA): Group health plans: Preventive health services: Religious employers: Contraceptive services.—The IRS, EBSA, and the Department of Health and Human Services have issued proposed regulations that would extend the current religious employer accommodation for nonprofit entities that do not want to provide contraceptive services to certain closely held for-profit entities by changing the definition of an eligible organization that may use the accommodation.

The proposed regulations, which were published in the Federal Register on August 27, 2014 (79 FR 51118), are reproduced below. The proposed regulations were finalized on July 14, 2015 (80 FR 41317). The preamble to the final regulations is at ¶ 23,315. The IRS final regulations are at ¶ 13,968V-20PB. The EBSA final regulations are at ¶ 15,050R-50PB.

DEPARTMENT OF THE TREASURY

Internal Revenue Service

26 CFR Part 54

[REG 129786-14]

RIN 1545-BM39

DEPARTMENT OF LABOR

Employee Benefits Security Administration

29 CFR Part 2590

RIN 1210-AB67

DEPARTMENT OF HEALTH AND HUMAN SERVICES

45 CFR Part 147

[CMS-9940-P]

RIN 0938-AS50

Coverage of Certain Preventive Services Under the Affordable Care Act

AGENCIES: Internal Revenue Service, Department of the Treasury; Employee Benefits Security Administration, Department of Labor; Centers for Medicare & Medicaid Services, Department of Health and Human Services.

ACTION: Proposed rules.

SUMMARY: This document proposes a change to the definition of an eligible organization that can avail itself of an accommodation with respect to coverage of certain preventive services under section 2713 of the Public Health Service Act (PHS Act), added by the Patient Protection and Affordable Care Act, as amended, and incorporated into the Employee Retirement Income Security Act of 1974 and the Internal Revenue Code.

Section 2713 of the PHS Act requires coverage without cost sharing of certain preventive health services by non-grandfathered group health plans and health insurance coverage. Among these services are women's preventive health services, as specified in guidelines supported by the Health Resources and Services Administration (HRSA). As authorized by the current regulations, and consistent with the HRSA Guidelines, group health plans established or maintained by certain religious employers (and group health insurance coverage provided in connection with such plans) are exempt from the otherwise applicable requirement to cover certain contraceptive services. Additionally, under current regulations, accommodations are available with respect to the contraceptive coverage requirement for group health plans established or maintained by eligible organizations (and group health insurance coverage provided in connection with such plans), and student health insurance coverage arranged by eligible organizations that are institutions of higher education, that effectively exempt them from this requirement. The regulations establish a mechanism for separately furnishing payments for contraceptive services on behalf of participants and beneficiaries of the group health plans of eligible organizations that avail themselves of an accommodation, and enrollees and dependents of student health insurance coverage arranged by eligible organizations that are institutions of higher education that avail themselves of an accommodation.

These rules propose and seek comments on potential changes to the definition of "eligible organization" in the Departments' regulations in light of the Supreme Court's decision in *Burwell v. Hobby Lobby Stores, Inc.,* 134 S. Ct. 2751 (2014), to ensure that participants and beneficiaries in group health plans (and enrollees and dependents in student health insurance coverage arranged by institutions of higher education) obtain, without additional cost, coverage of the full range of Food and Drug Administration (FDA) approved contraceptive services, as prescribed by a health care provider, while respecting certain closely held for profit entities' religion based objections to contraceptive coverage. These proposed rules also seek comments on any additional steps the government should take to help ensure coverage of the full range of FDA approved contraceptives, as prescribed by a health care provider, without cost sharing, for participants and beneficiaries in group health plans of such entities (and enrollees and dependents in student health insurance coverage arranged by such entities that are institutions of higher education).

DATES: To be assured consideration, comments must be received at one of the addresses provided below, no later than 5 p.m. on October 21, 2014.

ADDRESSES: In commenting, please refer to file code CMS-9940-P. Because of staff and resource limitations, we cannot accept comments by facsimile (FAX) transmission.

You may submit comments in one of four ways (please choose only one of the ways listed):

1. *Electronically.* You may submit electronic comments on these regulations to *http://www.regulations.gov.* Follow the "Submit a comment" instructions.

2. *By regular mail.* You may mail written comments to the following address ONLY: Centers for Medicare & Medicaid Services, Department of Health and Human Services, Attention: CMS-9940-P, P.O. Box 8010, Baltimore, MD 21244-1850.

Please allow sufficient time for mailed comments to be received before the close of the comment period.

3. *By express or overnight mail.* You may send written comments to the following address ONLY: Centers for Medicare & Medicaid Services, Department of Health and Human Services, Attention: CMS-9940-P, Mail Stop C4-26-05, 7500 Security Boulevard, Baltimore, MD 21244-1850.

4. *By hand or courier.* Alternatively, you may deliver (by hand or courier) your written comments ONLY to any of the following addresses prior to the close of the comment period:

a. For delivery in Washington, DC—

Centers for Medicare & Medicaid Services, Department of Health and Human Services, Room 445-G, Hubert H. Humphrey Building, 200 Independence Avenue SW., Washington, DC 20201.

(Because access to the interior of the Hubert H. Humphrey Building is not readily available to persons without Federal government identification, commenters are encouraged to leave their comments in the CMS drop slots located in the main lobby of the building. A stamp-in clock is available for persons wishing to retain a proof of filing by stamping in and retaining an extra copy of the comments being filed.)

b. For delivery in Baltimore, MD—

Centers for Medicare & Medicaid Services, Department of Health and Human Services, 7500 Security Boulevard, Baltimore, MD 21244-1850.

If you intend to deliver your comments to the Baltimore address, call telephone number (410) 786-9994 in advance to schedule your arrival with one of our staff members.

Comments erroneously mailed to an address indicated as appropriate for hand or courier delivery may be delayed and received after the close of the comment period.

For information on viewing public comments, see the beginning of the **SUPPLEMENTARY INFORMATION** section.

FOR FURTHER INFORMATION CONTACT: David Mlawsky, Centers for Medicare & Medicaid Services (CMS), Department of Health and Human Services (HHS), at (410) 786-1565; Amy Turner or Beth Baum, Employee Benefits Security Administration (EBSA), Department of Labor, at (202) 693-8335; Karen Levin, Internal Revenue Service (IRS), Department of the Treasury, at (202) 927-9639.

Customer Service Information: Individuals interested in obtaining information from the Department of Labor concerning employment-based health coverage laws may call the EBSA Toll-Free Hotline at 1-866-444-EBSA (3272) or visit the Department of Labor's Web site (*www.dol.gov/ebsa*). Information from HHS on private health insurance coverage can be found on CMS's Web site (*www.cms.gov/cciio*), and information on health care reform can be found at *www.HealthCare.gov.*

SUPPLEMENTARY INFORMATION:

Inspection of Public Comments: All comments received before the close of the comment period will be available for viewing by the public, including any personally identifiable or confidential business information that is included in a comment. We post all comments received before the close of the comment period on the following Web site as soon as possible after they have been received: *http://www.regulations.gov.* Follow the search instructions on that Web site to view public comments.

Comments received timely will also be available for public inspection as they are received, generally beginning approximately 3 weeks after publication of a document, at the headquarters of the Centers for Medicare & Medicaid Services, 7500 Security Boulevard, Baltimore, Maryland 21244, Monday through Friday of each week from 8:30 a.m. to 4 p.m. To schedule an appointment to view public comments, phone 1-800-743-3951.

I. Background

The Patient Protection and Affordable Care Act (Pub. L. 111-148) was enacted on March 23, 2010. The Health Care and Education Reconciliation Act of 2010 (Pub. L. 111-152) was enacted on March 30, 2010. These statutes are collectively known as the Affordable Care Act. The Affordable Care Act reorganizes, amends, and adds to the provisions of part A of title XXVII of the Public Health Service Act (PHS Act) relating to group health plans and health insurance issuers in the group and individual markets. The Affordable Care Act adds section 715(a)(1) to the Employee Retirement Income Security Act of 1974 (ERISA) and section 9815(a)(1) to the Internal Revenue Code (Code) to incorporate the provisions of part A of title XXVII of the PHS Act into ERISA and the Code, and to make them applicable to group health plans and health insurance issuers providing health insurance coverage in connection with group health plans. The sections of the PHS Act incorporated into ERISA and the Code are sections 2701 through 2728.

Section 2713 of the PHS Act, as added by the Affordable Care Act and incorporated into ERISA and the Code, requires that non-grandfathered group health plans and health insurance issuers offering non-grandfathered group or individual health insurance coverage provide coverage of certain specified preventive services without cost sharing, including under paragraph (a)(4), benefits for certain women's preventive health services as provided for in comprehensive guidelines supported by the Health Resources and Services Administration (HRSA).

On August 1, 2011, HRSA adopted and released guidelines for women's preventive health services (HRSA Guidelines) based on recommendations of the independent Institute of Medicine. As relevant here, the HRSA Guidelines include all Food and Drug Administration (FDA)-approved contraceptives, sterilization procedures, and patient education and counseling for women with reproductive capacity, as prescribed by a health care provider (collectively, contraceptive services).[1] Except as discussed later in this section, non-grandfathered group health plans and health insurance coverage are required to provide coverage consistent with the HRSA Guidelines, without cost sharing, for plan years (or, in the individual market, policy years) beginning on or after August 1, 2012.[2]

Interim final regulations implementing section 2713 of the PHS Act were published on July 19, 2010 (75 FR 41726) (2010 interim final regulations). On August 1, 2011, the Departments of Health and Human Services (HHS), Labor, and the Treasury (collectively, the Departments) amended the 2010 interim final regulations to provide HRSA with authority to exempt group health plans established or maintained by certain religious employers (and group health insurance coverage provided in connection with such plans) from the requirement to cover contraceptive services consistent with the HRSA Guidelines (76 FR 46621) (2011 amended interim final regulations).[3] On the same date, HRSA exercised this authority in the HRSA Guidelines to exempt group health plans established or maintained by these religious employers (and group health insurance coverage provided in connection with such plans) from the HRSA Guidelines with respect to contraceptive services.[4] The 2011 amended interim final regulations specified that, for purposes of this exemption, a religious employer was one that: (1) Has the inculcation of religious values as its purpose; (2) primarily employs persons who share its religious tenets; (3) primarily serves persons who share its religious tenets; and (4) is a nonprofit organization described in section 6033(a)(1) and (a)(3)(A)(i) or (iii) of the Code. Section 6033(a)(3)(A)(i) and (iii) of the Code refers to churches, their integrated auxiliaries, and conventions or associations of churches, as well as to the exclusively religious activities of any religious order. Final regulations issued on February 10, 2012, adopted the definition of religious employer in the 2011 amended interim final regulations without modification (2012 final regulations).[5]

Contemporaneous with the issuance of the 2012 final regulations, HHS, with the agreement of the Departments of Labor and the Treasury, issued guidance establishing a temporary safe harbor from enforcement of the contraceptive coverage requirement by the Departments for group health plans established or maintained by certain nonprofit organizations with religious objections to contraceptive coverage (and group health insurance coverage provided in connection with such plans).[6] The guidance provided that the temporary enforcement safe harbor would remain in effect until the first plan year beginning on or after August 1, 2013. At the same time, the Departments committed to rulemaking to achieve the goals of providing coverage of recommended preventive services, including contraceptive services, without cost sharing, while simultaneously ensuring that certain additional nonprofit organizations with religious objections to contraceptive coverage would not have to contract, arrange, pay, or refer for such coverage.

On March 21, 2012, the Departments published an advance notice of proposed rulemaking (ANPRM) that described and solicited comments on possible approaches to achieve these goals (77 FR 16501).

On February 6, 2013, following review of the comments on the ANPRM, the Departments published proposed regulations at 78 FR 8456 (proposed regulations). The regulations proposed to simplify and clarify the definition of "religious employer" for purposes of the religious employer exemption. The regulations also proposed accommodations for group health plans established or maintained or arranged by certain nonprofit religious organizations with religious objections to contraceptive coverage (and group health insurance coverage provided

---

[1] The HRSA Guidelines for Women's Preventive Services do not include services relating to a man's reproductive capacity, such as vasectomies and condoms.

[2] Interim final regulations published by the Departments on July 19, 2010, generally provide that plans and issuers must cover a newly recommended preventive service starting with the first plan year (or, in the individual market, policy year) that begins on or after the date that is one year after the date on which the new recommendation is issued. 26 CFR 54.9815-2713T(b)(1); 29 CFR 2590.715-2713(b)(1); 45 CFR 147.130(b)(1).

[3] The 2011 amended interim final regulations were issued and effective on August 1, 2011, and published in the **Federal Register** on August 3, 2011 (76 FR 46621).

[4] HRSA subsequently amended the HRSA Guidelines to reflect the simplified definition of "religious employer" contained in the July 2013 final regulations. 78 FR 39870 (July 2, 2013) (discussed below), effective August 1, 2013.

[5] The 2012 final regulations were published in the **Federal Register** on February 15, 2012 (77 FR 8725).

[6] Guidance on the Temporary Enforcement Safe Harbor for Certain Employers, Group Health Plans, and Group Health Insurance Issuers with Respect to the Requirement to Cover Contraceptive Services Without Cost Sharing Under Section 2713 of the Public Health Service Act, Section 715(a)(1) of the Employee Retirement Income Security Act, and Section 9815(a)(1) of the Internal Revenue Code (originally issued on February 10, 2012, and reissued on August 15, 2012 and June 28, 2013), *available at: http://www.cms.gov/CCIIO/Resources/Regulations-and-Guidance/Downloads/preventive-services-guidance-6-28-2013.pdf.* The guidance clarified, among other things, that plans that took some action before February 10, 2012, to try, without success, to exclude or limit contraceptive coverage were not precluded from eligibility for the safe harbor. The temporary enforcement safe harbor was also available to student health insurance coverage arranged by nonprofit institutions of higher education with religious objections to contraceptive coverage that met the conditions set forth in the guidance. *See* "Student Health Insurance Coverage," 77 FR16457 (Mar. 21, 2012).

in connection with such plans). These organizations were referred to as "eligible organizations."

The regulations proposed that, in the case of an insured group health plan established or maintained by an eligible organization, the health insurance issuer providing group health insurance coverage in connection with the plan would be required to assume sole responsibility for providing contraceptive coverage to plan participants and beneficiaries without cost sharing, premium, fee, or other charge to plan participants or beneficiaries or to the eligible organization or its plan. The Departments proposed a comparable accommodation with respect to student health insurance coverage arranged by eligible organizations that are institutions of higher education.

In the case of a self-insured group health plan established or maintained by an eligible organization, the proposed regulations presented potential approaches under which the third party administrator of the plan would provide or arrange for a third party to provide contraceptive coverage to plan participants and beneficiaries without cost sharing, premium, fee, or other charge to plan participants or beneficiaries or to the eligible organization or its plan. An issuer (or its affiliate) would be able to offset the costs incurred by the third party administrator and the issuer in the course of arranging and providing such coverage by claiming an adjustment in the Federally-facilitated Exchange (FFE) user fee.

The Departments received over 400,000 comments (many of them standardized form letters) in response to the proposed regulations. After consideration of the comments, the Departments published final regulations on July 2, 2013 at 78 FR 39870 (July 2013 final regulations). The July 2013 final regulations simplified and clarified the definition of religious employer for purposes of the religious employer exemption and established accommodations for health coverage established or maintained or arranged by eligible organizations. A contemporaneously re-issued HHS guidance document extended the temporary safe harbor from enforcement of the contraceptive coverage requirement by the Departments to encompass plan years beginning on or after August 1, 2013, and before January 1, 2014. This guidance included a form to be used by an organization during this temporary period to self-certify that its plan qualified for the temporary enforcement safe harbor. In addition, HHS and the Department of Labor (DOL) issued a self-certification form, EBSA Form 700, to be executed by an organization seeking to be treated as an eligible organization for purposes of an accommodation under the July 2013 final regulations. This self-certification form was provided for use with the accommodation under the July 2013 final regulations, after the expiration of the temporary enforcement safe harbor (that is, for plan years beginning on or after January 1, 2014).

On June 30, 2014, the Supreme Court ruled in the case of *Burwell v. Hobby Lobby Stores, Inc.* that, under the Religious Freedom Restoration Act of 1993 (RFRA), the requirement to provide contraceptive coverage could not be applied to the closely held for-profit corporations before the Court because their owners had religious objections to providing such coverage, and because the Government's goal of guaranteeing coverage for contraceptive methods without cost sharing could be achieved in a less restrictive manner by offering such closely held for-profit entities the accommodation the Government already provided to religious nonprofit organizations with religious objections to contraceptive coverage. After describing this accommodation, the Court concluded that the accommodation "does not impinge on the plaintiffs' religious belief that providing insurance coverage for the contraceptives at issue here violates their religion, and it serves HHS' stated interests equally well."

On July 3, 2014, the Supreme Court issued an interim order in connection with an application for an injunction pending appeal in *Wheaton College v. Burwell,* 134 S. Ct. 2806 (2014) (the *Wheaton* order), in which Wheaton College challenged under RFRA the requirement in the July 2013 final regulations that an eligible organization invoking the accommodation send EBSA Form 700 to the insurance issuer or third party administrator. The Court's order stated that, "[i]f [Wheaton College] informs the Secretary of Health and Human Services in writing that it is a nonprofit organization that holds itself out as religious and has religious objections to providing coverage for contraceptive services, the [Departments of Labor, Health and Human Services, and the Treasury] are enjoined from enforcing against [Wheaton College]" certain provisions of the Affordable Care Act and related regulations requiring coverage without cost sharing of certain contraceptive services "pending final disposition of appellate review." 134 S. Ct. at 2807. The order stated that Wheaton College need not use EBSA Form 700 or send a copy of the executed form to its health insurance issuers or third party administrators to meet the condition for this injunctive relief. Id. The Court also stated that its interim order neither affected "the ability of [Wheaton College's] employees and students to obtain, without cost, the full range of FDA approved contraceptives,"

nor precluded the Government from relying on the notice by Wheaton College "to facilitate the provision of full contraceptive coverage under the Act." Id. The Court's order further stated that it "should not be construed as an expression of the Court's views on the merits" of Wheaton College's challenge to the accommodations. Id.

This notice of proposed rulemaking proposes and invites comments on changes to the definition of an eligible organization in the Departments' regulations in light of the Supreme Court's decision in *Hobby Lobby.* It also solicits comments on any other steps the Government should take to help ensure that participants and beneficiaries in group health plans or enrollees and dependents in student health insurance coverage arranged by institutions of higher education are able to obtain, without cost, the full range of FDA-approved contraceptives, as prescribed by a health care provider, without cost sharing, if enrolled in a group health plan or insurance coverage sponsored or arranged by a closely held for-profit entity that objects on religious grounds to covering contraceptive services. Given the importance of this coverage, initiating this proposed rulemaking now allows for public input and a pathway toward helping to ensure access to contraceptive coverage.

The Departments are publishing contemporaneously with this notice of proposed rulemaking interim final regulations in light of the Supreme Court's interim order in connection with the application for an injunction in the pending case of *Wheaton College v. Burwell.* The interim final regulations are published elsewhere in this edition of the **Federal Register**.

II. Provisions of the Proposed Regulations

As stated above, on June 30, 2014, the Supreme Court ruled in *Burwell v. Hobby Lobby Stores, Inc.* that, under RFRA, the requirement to provide contraceptive coverage could not be applied to certain closely held for-profit organizations. The individual plaintiffs in *Hobby Lobby* and the associated case *Conestoga Wood Specialties Corp. v. Burwell* run closely held businesses that are family-owned and operated and that have adopted statements of mission or purpose to conduct the companies' affairs in accordance with the owners' shared religious beliefs and values. See 134 S. Ct. at 2764-2766.

In light of the Court's decision in *Hobby Lobby,* the Departments propose to amend the definition of an eligible organization under the July 2013 final regulations to include a closely held for-profit entity that has a religious objection to providing coverage for some or all of the contraceptive services otherwise required to be covered. Under these proposed rules, a qualifying closely held for-profit entity that has a religious objection to providing coverage for some or all of the contraceptive services otherwise required to be covered would not be required to contract, arrange, pay or refer for contraceptive coverage; instead, payments for contraceptive services provided to participants and beneficiaries in the eligible organization's plan would be provided separately by an issuer (if the qualifying entity sponsors an insured group health plan, or if the qualifying entity is an institution of higher education that arranges student health insurance coverage) or arranged separately by a third party administrator (if the qualifying entity is self-insured), consistent with the July 2013 final regulations as amended by interim final regulations published in this same edition of the **Federal Register**. This proposed change would extend to participants and beneficiaries in group health plans established or maintained by certain closely held for-profit entities with religious objections to contraceptive coverage, and to enrollees and dependents enrolled in student health insurance coverage arranged by certain closely held for-profit entities that are institutions of higher education with religious objections to contraceptive coverage, the same, separate payments for contraceptive services provided to participants and beneficiaries of group health plans (and enrollees and dependents in student health insurance) established or maintained by certain nonprofit religious entities with such objections, while similarly respecting the religious objections of the closely held for-profit entities.

Defining a Closely Held For-Profit Entity

In considering inclusion of certain closely held for-profit entities among the eligible organizations that may avail themselves of the accommodations, the Departments are considering and seek comment on how to define a qualifying closely held for-profit entity. In *Hobby Lobby,* the Supreme Court noted that the companies at issue in the cases were not publicly traded and were owned and controlled by members of a single family and that the companies were operated in accordance with the owners' shared religious beliefs and values. 134 S. Ct. at 2764-2766.

In light of the Supreme Court's decision, the Departments are proposing for comment two possible approaches to defining a qualifying closely held for-profit entity, although the Departments invite comments on other approaches as well. In common understanding, a closely held corporation—a term often used interchangeably with a "close" or "closed" corporation—is a corporation the stock of which is owned by a small number of persons and for which no active trading market exists. See, for example, American Law Institute, Principles of Corporate Governances section 1.06; Black's Law Dictionary (9th ed. 2009) ("close corporation"); Del. Code Tit. 8, Ch.1, Sub. Ch. 14 ("close corporation"). The examples below are by way of illustration, and the maximum number of shareholders specified in particular examples would not necessarily be borrowed as the standard in this context.

Under the first proposed approach, a qualifying closely held for-profit entity would be an entity where none of the ownership interests in the entity is publicly traded and where the entity has fewer than a specified number of shareholders or owners.

There is precedent in other areas of federal law for limiting the definition of closely held entities in this context to those with a relatively small number of owners. For example, subchapter S treatment under section 1361 of the Code is currently limited to corporations with 100 or fewer shareholders who are generally individuals and has in the past been limited to corporations with 10 or fewer shareholders. Similarly, certain favorable estate tax treatment is limited to businesses with 45 or fewer partners or shareholders under section 6166 of the Code.

Under a second, alternative approach, a qualifying closely held entity would be a for-profit entity in which the ownership interests are not publicly traded, and in which a specified fraction of the ownership interest is concentrated in a limited and specified number of owners. This approach also has precedent in federal law. For example, certain rules governing the taxation of real estate investment trusts, passive activity losses, and certain income from foreign entities are limited to organizations that are more than 50 percent owned by or for not more than five individuals. See, for example, sections 856(h), 542(a)(2), and 469(j)(1) of the Code and regulations under these sections.

These approaches might serve to identify for-profit entities controlled and operated by individual owners who likely have associational ties, are personally identified with the entity, and can be regarded as conducting personal business affairs through the entity. These appear to be the types of entities the Court sought to accommodate in *Hobby Lobby*. There may also be useful definitions or principles in state laws governing close corporations, or other areas of law.

The Departments invite comments on the appropriate scope of the definition of a qualifying closely held for-profit entity, including but not limited to whether a closely held for-profit entity should be defined with reference to a maximum number of owners (and, if so, what that maximum number should be) or a minimum concentration of ownership (and if so, what that concentration should be) or with reference to additional or other criteria.

It would be helpful for comments to address how the selection of a particular approach can be informed by the purposes of the Affordable Care Act and the contraceptive coverage requirement; the range of business structures in the Nation's economy; background principles of federal and state law applicable to business entities and the relationship of the entities' owners to the entities; other related or analogous areas of the law; experience regarding accommodations of religion and religious beliefs in various contexts and the rationales for the scope and operation of such accommodations; *Hobby Lobby* and other court decisions that shed light on these issues; and any other relevant matters.

Religious Objection To Providing Coverage for Some or All of the Contraceptive Services Required To Be Covered.

In *Hobby Lobby,* the Supreme Court held that the closely held for-profit corporations at issue in that case could opt not to provide otherwise required contraceptive coverage if doing so runs counter to their owners' sincerely held religious beliefs. These proposed regulations would require that the qualifying closely held for-profit entity's objection, based on its owners' sincerely held religious beliefs, to covering some or all of the contraceptive services otherwise required to be covered, be made in accordance with the entity's applicable rules of governance. As discussed by the Court in *Hobby Lobby,* state corporate law dictates how a corporation may establish its governing structure.[7]

Under the Departments' proposal, valid corporate action (or similar action by a business that is not organized as a corporation) taken in accordance with the entity's governing structure in accordance with state law, stating its owners' religious objection to providing some or all contraceptive coverage otherwise required to be provided, can serve to establish that a closely held for-profit entity has religious objections to providing such coverage. In determining whether a closely held for-

profit entity's decision-making process followed the necessary rules and procedures, the laws of the state in which the entity is incorporated, or, for non-corporate entities, organized, would govern. The Departments invite comments on whether to require documentation of the decision-making process and disclosure of the decision.

The Departments seek comment on this approach to determining that a closely held for-profit entity opposes providing coverage for some or all of the contraceptive services otherwise required to be covered on account of the owners' religious objections.

Other Potential Changes

The Departments seek comment on other potential changes to the July 2013 final regulations in light of the proposed change to the definition of eligible organization. In particular, the Departments seek comment on applying the approach set forth in the July 2013 final regulations in the context of the expanded definition of eligible organization. The July 2013 final regulations provide for separate payments for contraceptive services for participants and beneficiaries in self-insured group health plans of eligible organizations in a manner that enables these organizations to completely separate themselves from administration and payment for contraceptive coverage. Specifically, the third party administrator must provide or arrange such payments, and can seek reimbursement for such costs (including an allowance for administrative costs and margin) by making an arrangement with a participating issuer—that is, an issuer offering coverage through a Federally-facilitated Exchange (FFE). The participating issuer can receive an adjustment to its FFE user fees to finance such costs.

The Departments seek comment on the likely number of closely held for-profit entities that would seek an accommodation, the number of participants and beneficiaries (or in the case of student health insurance coverage, enrollees and dependents) in the plans of such entities, and the number of issuers and third-party administrators affected by the proposed rules. Finally, the Departments seek comment on whether any other aspects of the accommodations in the July 2013 final regulations, including relevant definitions, should be modified in light of the proposed addition of closely held for-profit entities with religious objections to contraceptive coverage to the definition of eligible organization.

These proposed regulations, if finalized as proposed, would require a small number of conforming changes to cross-references in the regulations. Any such necessary conforming changes would be incorporated into final regulations.

III. Response to Comments

Because of the large number of public comments we normally receive on **Federal Register** documents, we are not able to acknowledge or respond to them individually. The Departments will consider all comments we receive by the date and time specified in the "DATES" section of this preamble, and, when we proceed with a subsequent document, we will respond to the comments in the preamble to that document.

IV. Economic Impact and Paperwork Burden

A. Executive Orders 12866 and 13563—Department of Health and Human Services and Department of Labor

Executive Orders 12866 and 13563 direct agencies to assess all costs and benefits of available regulatory alternatives and, if regulation is necessary, to select regulatory approaches that maximize net benefits (including potential economic, environmental, and public health and safety effects; distributive impacts; and equity). Executive Order 13563 emphasizes the importance of quantifying both costs and benefits, reducing costs, harmonizing rules, and promoting flexibility.

Section 3(f) of Executive Order 12866 defines a "significant regulatory action" as an action that is likely to result in a regulation: (1) Having an annual effect on the economy of $100 million or more in any 1 year, or adversely and materially affecting a sector of the economy, productivity, competition, jobs, the environment, public health or safety, or state, local, or tribal governments or communities (also referred to as "economically significant"); (2) creating a serious inconsistency or otherwise interfering with an action taken or planned by another agency; (3) materially altering the budgetary impacts of entitlement grants, user fees, or loan programs or the rights and obligations of recipients thereof; or (4) raising novel legal or policy issues arising out of legal mandates, the President's priorities, or the principles set forth in the Executive Order.

---

[7] 134 S. Ct. at 2774-2775.

A regulatory impact analysis must be prepared for major rules with economically significant effects ($100 million or more in any 1 year), and an "economically significant" regulatory action is subject to review by the Office of Management and Budget (OMB). The Departments anticipate that these proposed regulations are not likely to have economic impacts of $100 million or more in any 1 year, and therefore, do not meet the definition of "economically significant" under Executive Order 12866.

1. Need for Regulatory Action

The proposed rules would modify the July 2013 final regulations in light of the Supreme Court's decision in *Hobby Lobby*. That decision held that a closely held for-profit corporation is exempt from the requirement to provide contraceptive coverage if its owners have religious objections to such coverage, because there is a less restrictive means of furthering the law's interests, namely the accommodation the Government already provided to nonprofit religious organizations with such objections. Contraceptive coverage is crucial to women's health and equality for a number of reasons, including but not limited to the psychological toll and compromised financial position, and adverse health consequences, that can result from unplanned or unwanted pregnancies. As documented in a report of the Institute of Medicine, women experiencing an unintended pregnancy may not immediately be aware that they are pregnant, and thus delay prenatal care. They also may not be as motivated to discontinue behaviors that pose pregnancy-related risks (for example, smoking, consumption of alcohol).[8] Studies show a greater risk of preterm birth and low birth weight among unintended pregnancies compared with pregnancies that were planned.[9] Contraceptives also have medical benefits for women who are contraindicated for pregnancy, and there are demonstrated preventive health benefits from contraceptives relating to conditions other than pregnancy.[10] In addition, there are significant cost savings to employers from the coverage of contraceptives.[11] Providing this coverage to participants and beneficiaries affected by the Supreme Court decision is a priority.

2. Anticipated Effects

The Departments expect that these proposed regulations would not result in any additional significant burden on or costs to the affected entities.

B. Special Analyses—Department of the Treasury

For purposes of the Department of the Treasury, it has been determined that this proposed rule is not a significant regulatory action as defined in Executive Order 12866, as supplemented by Executive Order 13563. Therefore, a regulatory assessment is not required. It also has been determined that section 553(b) of the Administrative Procedure Act (5 U.S.C. chapter 5) does not apply to this proposed rule. Pursuant to the Regulatory Flexibility Act (5 U.S.C. chapter 6), it is hereby certified that this proposed rule will not have a significant economic impact on a substantial number of small entities. This certification is based on the fact that the regulations merely propose to modify the definition of eligible organization to include certain closely held for-profit entities. This modification, if adopted, would not increase costs to or burdens on the affected organizations. Pursuant to section 7805(f) of the Code, these regulations have been submitted to the Chief Counsel for Advocacy of the Small Business Administration for comment on their impact on small business.

C. Paperwork Reduction Act—Department of Health and Human Services

Under the Paperwork Reduction Act of 1995, we are required to provide 60-day notice in the **Federal Register** and solicit public comment before a collection of information requirement is submitted to the Office of Management and Budget (OMB) for review and approval. In order to fairly evaluate whether an information collection should be approved by OMB, section 3506(c)(2)(A) of the Paperwork Reduction Act of 1995 requires that we solicit comment on the following issues:

• The need for the information collection and its usefulness in carrying out the proper functions of our agency.

• The accuracy of our estimate of the information collection burden.

• The quality, utility, and clarity of the information to be collected.

• Recommendations to minimize the information collection burden on the affected public, including automated collection techniques.

We are soliciting public comment on each of these issues for the following sections of this document that contain information collection requirements (ICRs):

The 2013 final regulations require an eligible organization that seeks an accommodation to self-certify that it meets the definition of an eligible organization using the EBSA Form 700 and providing it directly to each third party administrator or issuer under the plan that would otherwise arrange for or provide the covered contraceptive services. The interim final regulations being published contemporaneously with these proposed regulations continue to allow such eligible organizations to use EBSA Form 700, as set forth in the 2013 final regulations and guidance. In addition, the interim final regulations permit an alternative process, consistent with the Supreme Court's interim order in *Wheaton College,* under which an eligible organization may notify HHS in writing of its religious objection to coverage of all or a subset of contraceptive services.

These proposed regulations do not change the requirement that an eligible organization that seeks accommodation self-certifies that it meets the definition of an eligible organization, either using the EBSA Form 700 method of self-certification or the alternative notice to HHS process.

HHS is anticipating that 71 for-profit organizations will seek an accommodation. This is based on the number of plaintiffs that are for-profit employers in recent litigation objecting on religious grounds to the provision of contraceptive services. We seek comments on this estimate and welcome any data that may assist us in estimating the number of entities affected by this provision. For each eligible organization it is assumed that, clerical staff will gather and enter the necessary information, send the self-certification or the notice to its issuer(s) or third party administrator(s) or to HHS electronically and retain a copy for recordkeeping, a manager and legal counsel will review it, and a senior executive will execute it. It is estimated that an organization will need approximately 50 minutes (30 minutes of clerical labor at a cost of $30.00 per hour, 10 minutes for a manager at a cost of $102 per hour, 5 minutes for legal counsel at a cost of $127 per hour, and 5 minutes for a senior executive at a cost of $121 per hour) to execute the self-certification. The certification may be electronically transmitted to the issuer or to HHS at minimal cost, but a cost burden of $38.34 is estimated for a paper filing calculated with 5 cents per page printing and material costs and 49 cents postage costs. Therefore, the total one-time burden for preparing and providing the information in the self-certification is estimated to be approximately $53 for each eligible organization.

Based on this estimate of 71 affected entities and the individual burden estimate of $53, we estimate the hour burden to be 59.2 hours with an equivalent cost of $3736 and a paper filing cost burden of $38.34. As the Department of Labor and the Department of Health and Human Services share jurisdiction they are splitting the hour burden so each will account for 29.6 burden hours and a cost burden of $19.17. We welcome comments on any aspect of this burden estimate.

If you comment on these information collection and recordkeeping requirements, please submit your comments electronically as specified in the **ADDRESSES** section of this proposed rule.

Comments must be received on/by October 27, 2014.

D. Paperwork Reduction Act—Department of Labor

As discussed above, the proposed regulations would revise the definition of eligible organization to include qualifying closely held for-profit entities. This action would amend the EBSA Form 700 information collection request (ICR), which is approved under OMB Control number 1210-NEW to allow qualified closely held for-profit entities to avail themselves of the accommodation by self-certifying that they meet the definition of an eligible organization, either using the EBSA Form 700 method of self-certification or the alternative notice to HHS process under the contemporaneous interim final regulations.

• Consistent with the HHS analysis presented above, DOL estimates that there will be 71 additional entities that would utilize the accommodation. The Departments are soliciting comments for 60 days regarding the likely number of additional entities seeking an accommodation, the number of participants and beneficiaries in the plans of such organizations, and the number of issuers and third party administrators impacted by the proposed regulations. The Departments will submit a copy of these proposed rules to OMB in accordance with 44 U.S.C.

---

[8] Inst. Of Med., *Clinical Preventive Services for Women: Closing the Gaps,* Wash., DC: Nat'l Acad. Press, 2011, at p. 16.

[9] Gipson, J.D. et al., The Effects of Unintended Pregnancy on Infant, Child and Parental Health: A Review of the Literature, *Studies on Family Planning,* 2008, 39(1):18-38.

[10] Inst. Of Med., *Clinical Preventive Services for Women: Closing the Gaps,* Wash., DC: Nat'l Acad. Press, 2011, at p. 107.

[11] See discussion at 77 FR 8727.

3507(d) for review of the proposed ICRs. The Departments and OMB are particularly interested in comments that:

• Evaluate whether the collection of information is necessary for the proper performance of the functions of the agency, including whether the information will have practical utility;

• Evaluate the accuracy of the agency's estimate of the burden of the collection of information, including the validity of the methodology and assumptions used;

• Enhance the quality, utility, and clarity of the information to be collected; and

• Minimize the burden of the collection of information on those who are to respond, including through the use of appropriate automated, electronic, mechanical, or other technological collection techniques or other forms of information technology, for example, by permitting electronic submission of responses.

Comments should be sent to the Office of Information and Regulatory Affairs, Attention: Desk Officer for the Employee Benefits Security Administration either by Fax to (202) 395-5806 or by email to *oira_submission@omb.eop.gov*. A copy of the proposed ICRs may be obtained by contacting the PRA addressee: G. Christopher Cosby, Office of Policy and Research, Department of Labor, Employee Benefits Security Administration, 200 Constitution Avenue NW., Room N-5718, Washington, DC 20210; telephone: (202) 693-8410; Fax: (202) 219-4745 (please note that these numbers are not toll-free numbers); email: *ebsa.opr@dol.gov*. Proposed ICRs submitted to OMB also are available at *www.reginfo.gov (http://www.reginfo.gov/public/do/PRAMain)*.

The Departments expect that qualified closely held for-profit entities will spend the same time (and incur the same cost) to prepare and send the EBSA Form 700 or the notification to the Secretary of HHS as other eligible organizations under the existing ICR (approximately 50 minutes in preparation time and $0.54 mailing costs). The Departments note that persons are not required to respond to, and generally are not subject to any penalty for failing to comply with, an ICR unless the ICR has a valid OMB control number. The paperwork burden estimates are summarized as follows:

Type of Review: Revised Collection.

Agencies: Employee Benefits Security Administration, Department of Labor.

Title: EBSA Form 700.

OMB Number: 1210-NEW.

Affected Public: Business or other for profit entity.

Total Respondents: 71.

Total Responses: 71.

Frequency of Response: Once, Variable.

Estimated Total Annual Burden Hours: 59 hours (DOL 29.5 hours, HHS 29.5 hours).

Estimated Total Annual Burden Cost: $38 (DOL $19, HHS $19).

V. Unfunded Mandates Reform Act

For purposes of the Unfunded Mandates Reform Act of 1995 (Pub. L. 104-4), as well as Executive Order 12875, these proposed regulations do not include any federal mandate that may result in expenditures by state, local, or tribal governments, nor do they include any federal mandates that may impose an annual burden of $100 million, adjusted for inflation, or more on the private sector.[12]

VI. Federalism—Department of Health and Human Services and Department of Labor

Executive Order 13132 outlines fundamental principles of federalism, and requires the adherence to specific criteria by federal agencies in the process of their formulation and implementation of policies that have "substantial direct effects" on states, the relationship between the federal government and states, or the distribution of power and responsibilities among the various levels of government. Federal agencies promulgating regulations that have these federalism implications must consult with state and local officials, and describe the extent of their consultation and the nature of the concerns of state and local officials in the preamble to the regulation.

In the Departments' view, these proposed regulations have federalism implications, but the federalism implications are substantially mitigated because, with respect to health insurance issuers, 45 states are either enforcing the requirements related to coverage of specified preventive services (including contraception) without cost sharing pursuant to state law or otherwise are working collaboratively with HHS to ensure that issuers meet these standards. In five states, HHS ensures that issuers comply with these requirements. Therefore, the proposed regulations are not likely to require substantial additional oversight of states by HHS.

In general, section 514 of ERISA provides that state laws are superseded to the extent that they relate to any covered employee benefit plan, and preserves state laws that regulate insurance, banking, or securities. ERISA also prohibits states from regulating a covered plan as an insurance or investment company or bank. The Health Insurance Portability and Accountability Act of 1996 (HIPAA) added a new preemption provision to ERISA (as well as to the PHS Act) narrowly preempting state requirements on group health insurance coverage. States may continue to apply state law requirements but not to the extent that such requirements prevent the application of the federal requirement that group health insurance coverage provided in connection with certain group health plans provide coverage for specified preventive services without cost sharing. HIPAA's Conference Report states that the conferees intended the narrowest preemption of state laws with regard to health insurance issuers (H.R. Conf. Rep. No. 104-736, 104th Cong. 2d Session 205, 1996). State insurance laws that are more stringent than the federal requirement are unlikely to "prevent the application of" the preventive services coverage provision, and therefore are unlikely to be preempted. Accordingly, states have significant latitude to impose requirements on health insurance issuers that are more restrictive than those in federal law.

Guidance conveying this interpretation was published in the **Federal Register** on April 8, 1997 (62 FR 16904) and December 30, 2004 (69 FR 78720), and these proposed regulations implement the preventive services coverage provision's minimum standards and do not significantly reduce the discretion given to states under the statutory scheme.

The PHS Act provides that states may enforce the provisions of title XXVII of the PHS Act as they pertain to issuers, but that the Secretary of HHS will enforce any provisions that a state does not have authority to enforce or that a state has failed to substantially enforce. When exercising its responsibility to enforce provisions of the PHS Act, HHS works cooperatively with the state to address the state's concerns and avoid conflicts with the state's exercise of its authority. HHS has developed procedures to implement its enforcement responsibilities, and to afford states the maximum opportunity to enforce the PHS Act's requirements in the first instance. In compliance with Executive Order 13132's requirement that agencies examine closely any policies that may have federalism implications or limit the policymaking discretion of states, the Departments have engaged in numerous efforts to consult and work cooperatively with affected state and local officials.

In conclusion, throughout the process of developing these proposed regulations, to the extent feasible within the specific preemption provisions of ERISA and the PHS Act, the Departments have attempted to balance states' interests in regulating health coverage and health insurance issuers, and the rights of those individuals intended to be protected in the PHS Act, ERISA, and the Code.

VII. Statutory Authority

The Department of the Treasury regulations are adopted pursuant to the authority contained in sections 7805 and 9833 of the Code.

The Department of Labor regulations are adopted pursuant to the authority contained in 29 U.S.C. 1002(16), 1027, 1059, 1135, 1161-1168, 1169, 1181- 1183, 1181 note, 1185, 1185a, 1185b, 1185d, 1191, 1191a, 1191b, and 1191c; sec. 101(g), Public Law 104-191, 110 Stat. 1936; sec. 401(b), Public Law 105- 200, 112 Stat. 645 (42 U.S.C. 651 note); sec. 512(d), Public Law 110-343, 122 Stat. 3881; sec. 1001, 1201, and 1562(e), Public Law 111-148, 124 Stat. 119, as amended by Public Law 111-152, 124 Stat. 1029; Secretary of Labor's Order 3- 2010, 75 FR 55354 (September 10, 2010).

The Department of Health and Human Services regulations are adopted pursuant to the authority contained in sections 2701 through 2763, 2791, and 2792 of the PHS Act (42 U.S.C. 300gg through 300gg-63, 300gg-91, and 300gg-92), as amended; and Title I of the Affordable Care Act, sections 1301- 1304, 1311-1312, 1321-1322, 1324, 1334, 1342-1343, 1401-1402, and 1412, Pub. L. 111-148, 124 Stat. 119 (42 U.S.C. 18021-18024, 18031-18032, 18041-18042, 18044, 18054, 18061, 18063, 18071, 18082, 26 U.S.C. 36B, and 31 U.S.C. 9701).

Signed this 20th day of August 2014.

---

[12] In 2014, that threshold level is approximately $141 million.

John Dalrymple,

Deputy Commissioner for Services and Enforcement, Internal Revenue Service.

Signed this 20th day of August 2014.

Phyllis C. Borzi,

Assistant Secretary, Employee Benefits Security Administration. Department of Labor.

Dated: August 19, 2014.

Marilyn Tavenner,

Administrator, Centers for Medicare & Medicaid Services.

Approved: August 20, 2014.

Sylvia M. Burwell,

Secretary, Department of Health and Human Services.

List of Subjects

26 CFR Part 54

Excise taxes, Health care, Health insurance, Pensions, Reporting and recordkeeping requirements.

29 CFR Part 2590

Continuation coverage, Disclosure, Employee benefit plans, Group health plans, Health care, Health insurance, Medical child support, Reporting and recordkeeping requirements.

45 CFR Part 147

Health care, Health insurance, Reporting and recordkeeping requirements, State regulation of health insurance.

DEPARTMENT OF THE TREASURY

Internal Revenue Service

Accordingly, 26 CFR part 54 is proposed to be amended as follows:

PART 54—PENSION EXCISE TAXES

■ **Paragraph 1.** The authority citation for part 54 continues to read, in part, as follows:

Authority: 26 U.S.C. 7805 * * *

■ **Par. 2.** Section 54.9815-2713A is amended by revising paragraph (a) to read as follows:

§ 54.9815-2713A Accommodations in connection with coverage of preventive health services.

(a) *Eligible organizations.* An eligible organization is an organization that meets the criteria of paragraph (a)(1) through (3) of this section.

(1) The organization opposes providing coverage for some or all of any contraceptive items or services required to be covered under § 54.9815-2713(a)(1)(iv) on account of religious objections.

(2)(i) The organization is organized and operates as a nonprofit entity and holds itself out as a religious organization; or

(ii) The organization is organized and operates as a closely held for-profit entity, as defined in paragraph (a)(4) of this section, and the entity's objection to covering some or all of the contraceptive services on account of its owners' sincerely held religious beliefs is made in accordance with the organization's applicable rules of governance, consistent with state law.

(3) The organization must self-certify in the form and manner specified by the Secretary or provide notice to the Secretary of Health and Human Services as described in paragraph (b) or (c) of this section. The organization must make such self-certification or notice available for examination upon request by the first day of the first plan year to which the accommodation in paragraph (b) or (c) of this section applies. The self-certification or notice must be executed by a person authorized to make the certification on behalf of the organization, and must be maintained in a manner consistent with the record retention requirements under section 107 of ERISA.

(4) [Reserved]

* * * * *

DEPARTMENT OF LABOR

Employee Benefits Security Administration

For the reasons stated in the preamble, the Department of Labor proposes to amend 29 CFR part 2590 as follows:

PART 2590—RULES AND REGULATIONS FOR GROUP HEALTH PLANS

■ 1. The authority citation for part 2590 is revised to read as follows:

Authority: 29 U.S.C. 1027, 1059, 1135, 1161-1168, 1169, 1181-1183, 1181 note, 1185, 1185a, 1185b, 1185d, 1191, 1191a, 1191b, and 1191c; sec. 101(g), Pub. L. 104- 191, 110 Stat. 1936; sec. 401(b), Pub. L. 105-200, 112 Stat. 645 (42 U.S.C. 651 note); sec. 512(d), Pub. L. 110-343, 122 Stat. 3881; sec. 1001, 1201, and 1562(e), Pub. L. 111-148, 124 Stat. 119, as amended by Pub. L. 11-152, 124 Stat. 1029; Secretary of Labor's Order 1- 2011, 77 FR 1088 (January 9, 2012).

■ 2. Section 2590.715-2713A is amended by revising paragraph (a) to read as follows:

§ 2590.715-2713A Accommodations in connection with coverage of preventive health services.

(a) *Eligible organizations.* An eligible organization is an organization that meets the criteria of paragraph (a)(1) through (3) of this section.

(1) The organization opposes providing coverage for some or all of any contraceptive items or services required to be covered under § 2590.715-2713(a)(1)(iv) on account of religious objections.

(2)(i) The organization is organized and operates as a nonprofit entity and holds itself out as a religious organization; or

(ii) The organization is organized and operates as a closely held for-profit entity, as defined in paragraph (a)(4) of this section, and the entity's objection to covering some or all of the contraceptive services on account of its owners' sincerely held religious beliefs is made in accordance with the organization's applicable rules of governance, consistent with state law.

(3) The organization must self-certify in the form and manner specified by the Secretary or provide notice to the Secretary of Health and Human Services as described in paragraph (b) or (c) of this section. The organization must make such self-certification or notice available for examination upon request by the first day of the first plan year to which the accommodation in paragraph (b) or (c) of this section applies. The self-certification or notice must be executed by a person authorized to make the certification on behalf of the organization, and must be maintained in a manner consistent with the record retention requirements under section 107 of ERISA.

(4) [Reserved]

* * * * *

¶ 20,263Y

IRS: Hybrid plans: Market rate of return: Transitional plan amendments.—The IRS has issued proposed regulations providing transition rules for satisfying the market rate of return requirement for hybrid plans included in the 2014 final hybrid plan regulations (see ¶ 23,306).

The proposed regulations, which were published in the Federal Register on September 19, 2014 (79 FR 56305), are reproduced below. The regulations were finalized on November 16, 2015 (80 FR 70680). The preamble to the final regulations is at ¶ 23,319. The final regulations are at ¶ 12,220 and ¶ 12,224.

DEPARTMENT OF THE TREASURY

Internal Revenue Service

26 CFR Part 1

REG-111839-13

RIN 1545-BL62

Transitional Amendments to Satisfy the Market Rate of Return Rules for Hybrid Retirement Plans

AGENCY: Internal Revenue Service (IRS), Treasury.

ACTION: Notice of proposed rulemaking and notice of public hearing.

SUMMARY: This document contains proposed regulations that would provide guidance regarding certain amendments to applicable defined benefit plans. Applicable defined benefit plans are defined benefit plans that use a lump sum-based benefit formula, including cash balance plans and pension equity plans, as well as other hybrid retirement plans that have a similar effect. These proposed regulations would permit an applicable defined benefit plan that does not comply with the requirement that the plan not provide for interest credits (or equivalent amounts) at an effective rate that is greater than a market rate of return to comply with that requirement by changing to an interest crediting rate that is permitted under the final hybrid plan regulations, without violating the anti-cutback rules of section 411(d)(6). These regulations would affect sponsors, administrators, participants, and beneficiaries of these plans. This document also provides a notice of a public hearing on these proposed regulations.

DATES: Written or electronic comments must be received by [*INSERT DATE 90 DAYS AFTER PUBLICATION IN THE FEDERAL REGISTER*]. Outlines of topics to be discussed at the public hearing scheduled for January 9, 2015, at 10 a.m. must be received by [*INSERT DATE 90 DAYS AFTER PUBLICATION IN THE FEDERAL REGISTER*].

ADDRESSES: Send submissions to: CC:PA:LPD:PR (REG-111839-13), Room 5203, Internal Revenue Service, PO Box 7604, Ben Franklin Station, Washington, DC 20044. Submissions may be hand-delivered Monday through Friday between the hours of 8 a.m. and 4 p.m. to: CC:PA:LPD:PR (REG-111839-13), Courier's Desk, Internal Revenue Service, 1111 Constitution Avenue, NW., Washington, DC, or sent electronically, via the Federal eRulemaking Portal at *http://www.regulations.gov* (IRS REG-111839-13). The public hearing will be held in the IRS Auditorium, Internal Revenue Building, 1111 Constitution Avenue, NW., Washington, DC.

FOR FURTHER INFORMATION CONTACT: Concerning the regulations, Neil S. Sandhu or Linda S. F. Marshall at (202) 317-6700; concerning submissions of comments, the hearing, and/or being placed on the building access list to attend the hearing, Oluwafunmilayo (Funmi) Taylor at (202) 317-6901 (not toll-free numbers).

SUPPLEMENTARY INFORMATION:

Background

I. *In general*

This document contains proposed amendments to the Income Tax Regulations (26 CFR part 1) under section 411(b)(5) of the Internal Revenue Code (Code).

Generally, a defined benefit pension plan must satisfy the requirements of section 411 in order to be qualified under section 401(a) of the Code. Section 411(b)(5), which modifies the accrual requirements of section 411(b), was added to the Code by section 701(b) of the Pension Protection Act of 2006, Public Law 109-280 (120 Stat. 780 (2006)) (PPA '06). Section 411(b)(5) and certain related effective date provisions were subsequently amended by the Worker, Retiree, and Employer Recovery Act of 2008, Public Law 110-458 (122 Stat. 5092 (2008)) (WRERA '08).

Under section 411(b)(5)(I3)(i), a statutory hybrid plan is treated as failing to satisfy the requirements of section 411(b)(1)(H) (which provides that the rate of an employee's benefit accrual must not be reduced because of the attainment of any age) if the terms of the plan provide any interest credit (or an equivalent amount) for any plan year at a rate that is in excess of a market rate of return. Section 411(b)(5)(I3)(i) is generally effective for plan years beginning after December 31, 2007.

Section 411(d)(6) provides generally that a plan does not satisfy section 411 if an amendment to the plan decreases a participant's accrued benefit. For this purpose, a plan amendment that has the effect of eliminating or reducing an early retirement benefit or a retirement-type subsidy or eliminating an optional form of benefit with respect to benefits attributable to service before the amendment is treated as reducing accrued benefits.

Sections 204(b)(5)(I3)'(i) and 204(g) of the Employee Retirement Income Security Act of 1974, Public Law 93-406 (88 Stat. 829 (1974)), as amended (ERISA), contain rules that are parallel to sections 411(b)(5)(I3)(i) and 411(d)(6), respectively. Under section 101 of Reorganization Plan No. 4 of 1978 (43 FR 47713), the Secretary of the Treasury has interpretive jurisdiction over the subject matter addressed in these proposed regulations for purposes of ERISA, as well as the Code. Thus, these proposed regulations would apply for purposes of sections 411(b)(5)(B)(i) and 411(d)(6) of the Code, as well as for purposes of sections 204(b)(5)(B)(i) and 204(g) of ERISA.

Section 1.411(d)-4, A-2(b)(1), of the Income Tax Regulations provides, in part, that the Commissioner may, consistent with the provisions of § 1.411(d)-4, provide for the elimination or reduction of section 411(d)(6) protected benefits that have already accrued to the extent that such elimination or reduction is necessary to permit compliance with other requirements of section 401(a). The Commissioner may exercise this authority only through the publication of revenue rulings, notices, and other documents of general applicability.

Section 1.411(d)-4, A-2(b)(2)(i), provides that a plan may be amended to eliminate or reduce a section 411(d)(6) protected benefit, within the meaning of § 1.411(d)-4, A-1, if the following three requirements are met: the amendment constitutes timely compliance with a change in law affecting plan qualification; there is an exercise of section 7805(b) relief by the Commissioner; and the elimination or reduction of the section 411(d)(6) protected benefit is made only to the extent necessary to enable the plan to continue to satisfy the requirements for qualified plans.

Final regulations (TD 9505) (2010 final hybrid plan regulations) were published by the Treasury Department and the IRS in the Federal Register on October 19, 2010 (75 FR 64123). The 2010 final hybrid plan regulations provide for certain interest crediting rates that satisfy the requirements of section 411(b)(5)(B)(i). The 2010 final hybrid plan regulations provide, effective for plan years that begin on or after January 1, 2012, a list of interest crediting rates and combinations of rates that satisfy the requirement of section 411(b)(5)(B)(i) that the plan not provide an effective rate of return in excess of a market rate of return, while not permitting other rates. The provisions that provide for a list of rates are set forth at § 1.411(b)(5)-1(d)(1)(iii), (d)(1)(vi), and (d)(6)(i).

Proposed regulations (REG-132554-08) (2010 proposed hybrid plan regulations) were also published by the Treasury Department and the IRS in the Federal Register on October 19, 2010 (75 FR 64197). The 2010 proposed hybrid plan regulations provide for additional interest crediting rates that satisfy the requirements of section 411(b)(5)(B)(i). The preamble to the 2010 proposed hybrid plan regulations solicited comments with respect to guidance needed to permit a plan to change its interest crediting rate to comply with the final hybrid plan regulations.

II. *Effective dates*

Notice 2011-85 (2011-44 IRB 605 (October 31, 2011)), (see § 601.601(d)(2)(ii)(b) of this chapter), announced delayed effective/applicability dates with respect to certain provisions in the hybrid plan regulations. Notice 2011-85 provided that the Treasury Department and the IRS intended to amend the hybrid plan regulations to postpone the effective/applicability date of § 1.411(b)(5)-1(d)(1)(iii), (d)(1)(vi), and (d)(6)(i), so that these provisions would be effective at a future date, not earlier than January 1, 2013.

Notice 2011-85 also provided that, when the 2010 proposed regulations were finalized, it was expected that relief from the requirements of section 411(d)(6) would be granted for certain plan amendments that eliminate or reduce a section 411(d)(6) protected benefit. A plan amendment would be eligible for this relief only if the plan amendment were adopted by the last day of the first plan year preceding the plan year for which the 2010 proposed regulations, once finalized, apply to the plan, and the elimination or reduction was made only to the extent necessary to enable the plan to meet the requirements of section 411(b)(5). In addition, Notice 2011-85 extended the deadline for amending cash balance and other applicable defined benefit plans, within the meaning of section 411(a)(13)(C), to meet the requirements of section 411(a)(13) (other than section 411(a)(13)(A)) and section 411(b)(5), relating to vesting and other special rules applicable to these plans. Under Notice 2011-85, the deadline for these amendments is the same as the deadline for an amendment that is eligible for the relief under section 411(d)(6) that is also announced in the notice.

Notice 2012-61 (2012-42 IRB 479 (October 15, 2012)), (see § 601.601(d)(2)(ii)(b) of this chapter), announced that the regulations described in Notice 2011-85 would not be effective for plan years beginning before January 1, 2014.

Final regulations (TD **9693**) (2014 final hybrid plan regulations) that finalize the 2010 proposed hybrid plan regulations are being issued at the same time as these proposed regulations. The 2014 final hybrid plan regulations amend the effective/applicability date of § 1.411(b)(5)-1(d)(1)(iii), (d)(1)(vi), and (d)(6)(i), so that these provisions apply to plan years that begin on or after January 1, 2016.

III. *Permissible interest crediting rates*

Interest crediting rates can be broadly characterized as either investment-based rates or rates that are not investment-based rates. An investment-based rate is a rate of return provided by actual investments, taking into account the return attributable to any change in the value of the underlying investments. A rate of return that is based on the rate of return for an index that measures the change in the value of investments can also be considered to be an investment-based rate. Rates that are not investment-based rates include fixed rates of interest and yields to maturity of bonds.

Sections 1.411(b)(5)-1(d)(3) and (d)(4) set forth permitted rates that are not investment-based rates, such as the third segment rate described in section 417(e)(3)(D) or 430(h)(2)(C)(iii), the yield on 30-year Treasury Constant Maturities, and a fixed 6 percent rate of interest. Section 1.411(b)(5)-1(d)(5) sets forth permitted investment-based rates, such as the rate of return on certain regulated investment companies (RICs), as defined in section 851, and the rate of return on plan assets. As provided in §1.411(b)(5)-1(d)(6), certain annual (or more frequent) floors are permitted in combination with the bond-based rates and cumulative floors (in excess of the cumulative zero floor required under section 411(b)(5)(i)(II)) are permitted in combination with either the bond-based rates or the investment-based rates.

Explanation of Provisions

Prior to the first day of the first plan year that begins on or after January 1, 2016, a plan that uses an interest crediting rate that is not permitted under the final hybrid plan regulations must be amended to change to an interest crediting rate that is permitted under those regulations. Although a plan is permitted to be amended to change the interest crediting rate with respect to benefits that have not yet accrued, an amendment that reduces the interest crediting rate with respect to benefits that have already accrued would ordinarily be impermissible under section 411(d)(6).

In order to resolve this conflict between the market rate of return rules of section 411(b)(5)(B)(i) and the anti-cutback rules of section 411(d)(6), these proposed regulations would permit a plan with a noncompliant interest crediting rate to be amended with respect to benefits that have already accrued so that its interest crediting rate complies with the market rate of return rules. If the applicable requirements of these regulations are satisfied, such an amendment is permitted with respect to benefits that have already accrued, but only with respect to interest credits that are credited for interest crediting periods that begin on or after the later of the effective date of the amendment or the date the amendment is adopted (the applicable amendment date within the meaning of §1.411(d)-3(g)(4)). To qualify for this treatment, the amendment would have to be adopted prior to and effective no later than the first day of the first plan year that begins on or after January 1, 2016.

These proposed regulations set forth amendments that would be eligible for this treatment by providing a specific correction for each noncompliant feature of a noncompliant interest crediting rate.[1] If the noncompliant interest crediting rate has more than one noncompliant feature, then each noncompliant feature must be addressed separately in the prescribed manner. Examples are included to illustrate the application of these rules.

The general approach in the regulations is to permit amendments that bring the plan into compliance by changing the specific feature that causes the plan's interest crediting rate to be noncompliant, while not changing other features of the existing rate. For example, if a plan uses what would otherwise be a permissible bond-based rate but provides for an impermissible lookback month to determine interest credits, then the plan must be amended to correct the lookback month to a permitted lookback month while retaining the underlying bond-based rate. The Treasury Department and the IRS believe this general approach is the most appropriate manner to resolve the conflict between the market rate of return rules of section 411(b)(5)(B)(i) and the anti-cutback rules of section 411(d)(6).[2]

The proposed regulations take a special approach with respect to a noncompliant composite interest crediting rate that is determined as the greatest of two or more component rates, because it is not always readily apparent which specific feature or component rate causes the composite rate to be noncompliant. Two types of composite rates are specifically addressed in the proposed regulations, and a comment request is included to solicit suggestions for appropriate corrective amendments with respect to a third type of composite rate.

A composite rate that is the greater of an otherwise permissible variable bond-based rate and a fixed minimum rate in excess of an annual interest crediting rate of 6 percent (the maximum permitted fixed rate) could be viewed either as: (1) a noncompliant fixed rate that must be brought into compliance by reducing the fixed rate and eliminating the variable bond-based rate component, or (2) a noncompliant bond-based rate that must be brought into compliance by reducing the fixed minimum rate to the highest permitted fixed minimum interest crediting rate that is permitted with the particular variable bond-based rate (4 or 5 percent, as applicable). As a result, in that particular case, the proposed regulations would give the plan sponsor the choice of either: (1) eliminating the variable rate while changing to an annual interest crediting rate of 6 percent or (2) retaining the variable rate while reducing the fixed minimum component to the extent necessary to bring the plan into compliance. These same options would apply if the fixed minimum interest crediting rate is greater than the highest permitted fixed minimum interest crediting rate that is permitted with the particular variable bond-based rate but is not greater than the highest permitted fixed rate (6 percent).

In the case of a composite rate that is the greatest of two or more otherwise permissible variable bond-based rates, it is also difficult to determine the most appropriate method to bring the plan into compliance. One reason for this difficulty is because, in most of these cases, the composite rate will not exceed the rate of interest on long-term investment grade corporate bonds. As a result, in such a case, the proposed regulations do not provide for the elimination of any of the variable bond-based components. Instead, the proposed regulations would provide that the noncompliant composite rate must be capped at a third segment rate.[3]

The proposed regulations also take a special approach with respect to a noncompliant interest crediting rate that is an impermissible investment-based rate. One example of an impermissible investment-based rate is an investment-based rate that is not equal to the rate of return on a RIC or the actual rate of return on the aggregate assets of a plan or a specified subset of plan assets (even if the rate of return is reasonably expected to be not significantly more volatile than the broad United States equities market or a similarly broad international equities market). Another example of an impermissible investment-based rate is the rate of return on a RIC that has most of its assets invested in securities of issuers (including other RICs) concentrated in an industry sector.

If an investment-based rate is noncompliant, the proposed regulations would require the plan sponsor to amend the plan to credit interest using a permitted investment-based rate with similar risk and return characteristics as the noncompliant rate, if possible. If it is not possible to select a permitted investment-based rate with similar risk and return characteristics as the noncompliant rate, then the proposed regulations would require the plan sponsor to amend the plan to credit interest using a permitted investment-based rate that is otherwise similar to the noncompliant rate (which would generally require the use of a rate that is less volatile than the noncompliant rate but is otherwise similar to the noncompliant rate).

Several commenters suggested that the IRS and the Treasury Department should permit a change from a noncompliant interest crediting rate to any of the maximum compliant interest crediting rates. However, this suggested approach was not taken in these proposed regulations because this approach would not require a sufficient connection between the correction and the specific feature that caused an interest crediting rate to be noncompliant, and would permit a plan sponsor to reduce the interest crediting rate more than is appropriate.

Proposed Effective/Applicability Dates

These regulations are proposed to apply to amendments adopted on or after the date regulations that finalize these proposed regulations are published in the **Federal Register**. In addition, it is proposed that taxpayers be permitted, pursuant to section 7805(b)(7), to elect to apply these regulations, as finalized, to plan amendments that are adopted during earlier periods.

---

[1] A plan may have been amended to change its interest crediting rate under the rules of section 1107 of PPA '06. Section 1107 of PPA '06 provided relief from the requirements of section 411(d)(6) for amendments made pursuant to a change in law under PPA '06, if the amendment was adopted by the last day of the first plan year that began on or after January 1, 2009 (or 2011, in the case of a governmental plan as defined in section 414(d)). If an interest crediting rate adopted under the rules of section 1107 of PPA '06 is not permitted under the final hybrid plan regulations, then these proposed regulations would permit a subsequent amendment to change the rate to a rate permitted under the final hybrid plan regulations.

[2] The standard in these proposed regulations for resolving this conflict between section 411(d)(6) and section 411(b)(5)(13)(i) is generally comparable to the standard under the rules of §1.411(d)-4, A-2(b)(1) and (b)(2)(i) with respect to the Commissioner's exercise of authority to resolve a conflict between section 411(d)(6) and another qualification requirement under section 401(a).

[3] Any of the rates that are denominated a third segment rate pursuant to §1.411(d)(5)-1(d)(3) can be specified by a plan for this purpose, as well as for other purposes under these proposed regulations for which a third segment rate is used.

Special Analyses

It has been determined that these proposed regulations are not a significant regulatory action as defined in Executive Order 12866. Therefore, a regulatory assessment is not required. It also has been determined that section 553(b) of the Administrative Procedure Act (5 U.S.C. chapter 5) does not apply to these regulations, and because the regulation does not impose a collection of information on small entities, the Regulatory Flexibility Act (5 U.S.C. chapter 6) does not apply. Pursuant to section 7805(f) of the Code, these regulations have been submitted to the Chief Counsel for Advocacy of the Small Business Administration for comment on its impact on small business.

Comments and Public Hearing

Before these proposed regulations are adopted as final regulations, consideration will be given to any written (a signed original and eight (8) copies) or electronic comments that are submitted timely to the IRS. The Treasury Department and the IRS request comments on all aspects of the proposed rules.

In addition, comments are specifically requested as to the amendment required to bring a plan into compliance if the plan credits interest using a composite rate that is an investment-based rate of return with an impermissible annual (or more frequent) fixed or variable minimum rate. Some of these plans might currently be applying a reduction to the investment-based rate of return, in order to take into account the value provided by the minimum rate. For a plan that credits interest using an investment-based rate of return with an impermissible minimum rate:

- Should the required amendment eliminate the minimum rate (and eliminate any reduction to the investment-based rate of return), so that the required rate after amendment is the unreduced investment-based rate of return?

- Should the required amendment change the interest crediting rate to another permitted rate that is less volatile than the unreduced investment-based rate (such as a rate described in § 1.411(b)(5)-1(d)(3) with a fixed minimum rate of 4 percent per year)?

- Should the required amendment depend on the level of the minimum rate and the extent of any reduction to the investment-based rate of return?

- Should the plan sponsor have a choice among alternative required amendments to bring the plan into compliance?

Comments are also requested as to whether there are statutory hybrid plans other than those described in the specific request for comments that use a noncompliant interest crediting rate that is not addressed in the regulations and for which an amendment is necessary to bring the plan into compliance with the market rate of return rules. If so, comments are requested as to the appropriate amendment to bring the plan into compliance in such a case.

All comments will be available for public inspection and copying at *www.regulations.gov* or upon request. A public hearing has been scheduled for January 9, 2015, beginning at 10 a.m. in the Auditorium, Internal Revenue Service, 1111 Constitution Avenue, NW., Washington, DC. Due to building security procedures, visitors must enter at the Constitution Avenue entrance. In addition, all visitors must present photo identification to enter the building. Because of access restrictions, visitors will not be admitted beyond the immediate entrance area more than 30 minutes before the hearing starts. For information about having your name placed on the building access list to attend the hearing, see the " **FOR FURTHER INFORMATION CONTACT**" section of this preamble.

The rules of 26 CFR 601.601(a)(3) apply to the hearing. Persons who wish to present oral comments at the hearing must submit written or electronic comments by **[*INSERT DATE 90 DAYS AFTER PUBLICATION IN THE FEDERAL REGISTER]* and submit an outline of topics to be discussed and the amount of time to be devoted to each topic (a signed original and eight (8) copies) by **[*INSERT DATE 90 DAYS AFTER PUBLICATION IN THE FEDERAL REGISTER]*.

A period of 10 minutes will be allotted to each person for making comments. An agenda showing the scheduling of the speakers will be prepared after the deadline for receiving outlines has passed. Copies of the agenda will be available free of charge at the hearing.

Drafting Information

The principal authors of these regulations are Neil S. Sandhu and Linda S. F. Marshall, Office of Division Counsel/Associate Chief Counsel (Tax Exempt and Government Entities). However, other personnel from the IRS and the Treasury Department participated in the development of these regulations.

List of Subjects in 26 CFR Part 1

Income taxes, Reporting and recordkeeping requirements.

Proposed Amendments to the Regulations

Accordingly, 26 CFR part 1 is proposed to be amended as follows:

PART 1–INCOME TAXES

Paragraph 1. The authority citation for part 1 continues to read in part as follows:

Authority: 26 U.S.C. 7805 * * *

Par. 2. Section 1.411(b)(5)-1 is amended by adding paragraph (e)(3)(vi) to read as follows:

§ 1.411(b)(5)-1 Reduction in rate of benefit accrual under a defined benefit plan.

* * * * *

(e) * * *

(3) * * *

(vi) *Transitional amendments needed to satisfy the market rate of return rules*–(A) *In general.* Notwithstanding the requirements of section 411(d)(6), if the requirements set forth in this paragraph (e)(3)(vi) are satisfied, a plan may be amended to change its interest crediting rate with respect to benefits that have already accrued in order to comply with the requirements of section 411(b)(5)(B)(i) and paragraph (d) of this section. A plan amendment is eligible for the treatment provided under this paragraph (e)(3)(vi)(A) to the extent that the amendment modifies an interest crediting rate that does not satisfy the requirements of section 411(b)(5)(B)(i) and paragraph (d) of this section in the manner specified in paragraph (e)(3)(vi)(C) of this section.

(B) *Rules of application*–(1) *Multiple noncompliant features.* If a plan's interest crediting rate has more than one noncompliant feature as described in paragraph (e)(3)(vi)(C) of this section, then each noncompliant feature must be addressed separately in the manner specified in paragraph (e)(3)(vi)(C) of this section.

(2) *Definition of investment-based rate.* The application of the rules of paragraph (e)(3)(vi)(C) of this section to an interest crediting rate depends on whether the interest crediting rate is an investment-based rate. For purposes of this paragraph (e)(3)(vi), an investment-based rate is either a rate of return provided by actual investments (taking into account the return attributable to any change in the value of the underlying investments) or a rate that is based on the rate of return for an index that measures the change in the value of investments.

(3) *Timing rules for permitted amendments.* The rules under this paragraph (e)(3)(vi) apply only to a plan amendment that is adopted prior to and effective no later than the first day of the first plan year described in paragraph (f)(2)(i)(B) of this section. In addition, the rules under this paragraph (e)(3)(vi) apply to a plan amendment only with respect to interest credits that are credited for interest crediting periods that begin after the applicable amendment date (within the meaning of § 1.411(d)-3(g)(4)).

(C) *Noncompliant feature and amendment to bring plan into compliance*–(1) *Timing rules not satisfied.* If a plan does not satisfy the timing rules relating to how interest credits are determined and credited (as set forth in paragraph (d)(1)(iv) of this section), then the plan must be amended to correct the aspect of the plan's interest crediting rate that fails to comply with those rules with respect to its underlying interest crediting rate.

(2) *Fixed rate in excess of 6 percent.* If a plan credits interest using a fixed rate in excess of the rate described in paragraph (d)(4)(v) of this section, then the plan must be amended to reduce the interest crediting rate to an annual interest crediting rate of 6 percent.

(3) *Bond-based rate with margin exceeding maximum permitted margin.* If a plan credits interest using a rate that would be described in paragraph (d)(3) or (d)(4) of this section except that the plan applies a margin that exceeds the maximum permitted margin under paragraph (d)(3) or (d)(4) of this section, then the plan must be amended to reduce the margin to the maximum permitted margin for the underlying rate used by the plan.

(4) *Bond-based rate with fixed minimum rate exceeding maximum permitted fixed minimum rate.* If a plan credits interest using a variable rate described in paragraph (d)(3) or (d)(4) of this section in combina-

tion with a fixed minimum rate in excess of the highest permitted fixed minimum rate under paragraph (d)(6)(ii)(A)(2) or (B)(2) of this section (as applicable), then the plan must be amended either–

(*i*) To reduce the fixed minimum rate to the highest permitted fixed minimum rate that can be used in combination with the plan's variable rate; or

(*ii*) To credit interest using an annual interest crediting rate of 6 percent.

(*5*) *Greatest of two or more variable bond-based rates.* If a plan credits interest using a composite rate that is the greatest of two or more variable rates described in paragraph (d)(3) or (d)(4) of this section, then the plan must be amended to credit interest using the lesser of the composite rate and a rate described in paragraph (d)(3) of this section.

(*6*) *Impermissible bond-based rate.* If a plan credits interest using a variable rate that is not an investment-based rate of return and is not described in paragraph (d)(3) or (d)(4) of this section (after application of the rule of paragraph (e)(3)(vi)(C)(3) of this section, if applicable), then–

(*i*) If a variable rate described in paragraph (d)(3) or (d)(4) of this section that has similar duration and quality characteristics as the plan's variable rate can be selected, then the plan must be amended to credit interest based on such a rate; or

(*ii*) If a variable rate described in paragraph (d)(3) or (d)(4) of this section that has similar duration and quality characteristics as the plan's variable rate cannot be selected, then the plan must be amended to provide that the plan credits interest using the lesser of the plan's variable rate and a rate described in paragraph (d)(3) of this section.

(*7*) *Impermissible investment-based rate.* If a plan credits interest using an investment-based rate of return that is not described in paragraph (d)(5) of this section, then–

(*i*) If a permitted investment-based rate described in paragraph (d)(5)(ii)(A), (d)(5)(ii)(B), or (d)(5)(iv) of this section that has similar risk and return characteristics as the plan's impermissible investment-based rate can be selected, then the plan must be amended to credit interest based on such a permitted investment-based rate; or

(*ii*) If a permitted investment-based rate described in paragraph (d)(5)(ii)(A) (d)(5)(ii)(B), or (d)(5)(iv) of this section that has similar risk and return characteristics as the plan's impermissible investment-based rate cannot be selected, then the plan must be amended to credit interest based on a rate of return described in paragraph (d)(5)(ii)(A), (d)(5)(ii)(B), or (d)(5)(iv) of this section that is otherwise similar to the plan's impermissible investment-based rate (generally requiring the use of a rate that is less volatile than the plan's impermissible investment-based rate but is otherwise similar to that rate).

(D) *Examples.* The following examples illustrate the application of the rules of this paragraph (e)(3)(vi). Each plan has a plan year that is the calendar year, and all amendments are adopted on October 1, 2015 and become effective for interest crediting periods beginning on or after January 1, 2016.

Example 1. (i) *Facts.* A plan determines interest credits for a plan year using the average yield on 30-year Treasury Constant Maturities for the last week of the preceding plan year (which is an impermissible period for this purpose pursuant to paragraph (d)(1)(iv)(B) of this section because it is not a month).

(ii) *Conclusion.* Pursuant to paragraph (e)(3)(vi)(C)(1) of this section, the plan must be amended to determine interest credits for a plan year using the average yield on 30-year Treasury Constant Maturities for a period that complies with the requirements of paragraph (d)(1)(iv)(B) of this section.

Example 2. (i) *Facts.* The facts are the same as in *Example 1,* except that the plan's interest crediting rate is determined as the average yield on 30-year Treasury Constant Maturities for the period, plus 50 basis points.

(ii) *Conclusion.* Pursuant to paragraph (e)(3)(vi)(B)(1) of this section, the plan must be amended to correct both the impermissible lookback period and the excess margin. Accordingly, pursuant to

paragraph (e)(3)(vi)(C)(1) and (3) of this section, the plan must be amended to determine interest credits for a plan year using the average yield on 30-year Treasury Constant Maturities (with no margin) for a period that complies with the requirements of paragraph (d)(1)(iv)(B) of this section.

Example 3. (i) *Facts.* A plan credits interest for a plan year using the rate of return on plan assets for the preceding plan year.

(ii) *Conclusion.* Pursuant to paragraph (e)(3)(vi)(C)(1) of this section, the plan must be amended to determine interest credits for each plan year using the rate of return on plan assets for that plan year.

Example 4. (i) *Facts.* A plan credits interest using the average yield on 30-year Treasury Constant Maturities for December of the preceding plan year with a minimum rate of 5.5 percent per year.

(ii) *Conclusion.* Pursuant to paragraph (e)(3)(vi)(C)(4) of this section, the plan must be amended to change the plan's interest crediting rate. The new interest crediting rate under the plan must be either the average yield on 30-year Treasury Constant Maturities for December of the preceding plan year with a minimum rate of 5 percent per year or an annual interest crediting rate of 6 percent.

Example 5. (i) *Facts.* A plan credits interest using the greater of the unadjusted yield on 30-year Treasury Constant Maturities and the yield on 1-year Treasury Constant Maturities plus 100 basis points.

(ii) *Conclusion.* Pursuant to paragraph (e)(3)(vi)(C)(5) of this section, the plan must be amended to credit interest using the lesser of a third segment rate described in paragraph (d)(3) of this section and the composite rate used under the plan before the amendment (the greater of the unadjusted yield on 30-year Treasury Constant Maturities and the yield on 1-year Treasury Constant Maturities plus 100 basis points).

Example 6. (i) *Facts.* A plan credits interest using a broad-based index that measures the yield to maturity on a group of long-term investment grade corporate bonds.

(ii) *Conclusion.* Pursuant to paragraph (e)(3)(vi)(C)(6)(i) of this section, the plan must be amended to credit interest using a third segment rate described in paragraph (d)(3) of this section.

Example 7. (i) *Facts.* A plan credits interest using the rate of return for a broad-based index that measures the yield to maturity on a group of short-term non-investment grade corporate bonds.

(ii) *Conclusion.* Pursuant to paragraph (e)(3)(vi)(C)(6)(ii) of this section, the plan must be amended to credit interest at the lesser of the rate of return for the index used under the plan before the amendment date and a third segment rate described in paragraph (d)(3) of this section.

Example 8. (i) *Facts.* A plan credits interest using the rate of return for the S&P 500 index. To bring the plan into compliance with the market rate of return rules, the plan sponsor amends the plan to credit interest based on the rate of return on a RIC that is designed to track the rate of return on the S&P 500 index.

(ii) *Conclusion.* The amendment satisfies the rule of paragraph (e)(3)(vi)(C)(7)(i) of this section.

Example 9. (i) *Facts.* A plan credits interest based on the rate of return on a collective trust that holds a balanced portfolio of equity and fixed income investments, which provides a rate of return that is reasonably expected to be not significantly more volatile than the broad U.S. equities market or a similarly broad international equities market. To bring the plan into compliance with the market rate of return rules, the plan sponsor amends the plan to credit interest based on the actual rate of return on the assets within a specified subset of the plan's assets that is invested in the collective trust.

(ii) *Conclusion.* The amendment satisfies the rule of paragraph (e)(3)(vi)(C)(7)(i) of this section.

* * * * *

John Dalrymple

Deputy Commissioner for Services and Enforcement.

¶ 20,263Z

IRS: Rollovers: After-tax funds: Allocation rule.—The IRS has proposed amending the requirement under IRS Reg. §1.402A-1, Q-5, that amounts from a designated Roth account that are paid in a direct rollover be treated as a separate distribution from any amount paid directly to the taxpayer. Under the proposed rules, applicable to distributions as early as September 18, 2014, the separate distribution requirement would no longer apply. The modified rule would effectively allow taxpayers to directly roll over after-tax funds held in a qualified plan, 403(b) plan, or 457 plan to a Roth IRA, while rolling over the pre-tax amounts to a traditional IRA.

The proposed regulations were published in the Federal Register on September 19, 2014 (79 FR 56310). The regulations were finalized on May 18, 2016 (81 FR 31165). The preamble to the final regulations is at ¶ 23,324. The final regulations are reproduced at ¶ 11,799A-1.

¶ 20,264

IRS: Proposed regulations: Employee Benefits Security Administration (EBSA): Group health plans: Excepted benefits: Limited wraparound coverage.—The IRS, EBSA, and Department of Health and Human Services have issued proposed regulations that would amend Code and ERISA regulations regarding "excepted benefits," which are generally exempt from the health reform requirements that were added by the Health Insurance Portability and Accountability Act of 1996 (HIPAA, P.L. 104-191) and the Patient Protection and Affordable Care Act (PPACA, P.L. 111-148). The Agencies are seeking public comment on the proposed rules that would amend the definition of excepted benefits to include certain limited wraparound coverage in response to suggestions made on a December 2013 proposed rule (PENSION PLAN GUIDE ¶ 20,263U) from a wide range of stakeholders. The proposed rule proposes a pilot program for wraparound coverage that will sunset.

The proposed regulations were published in the Federal Register on December 23, 2014 (79 FR 76931). The regulations were finalized on March 18, 2015 (80 FR 13995). The preamble to the final regulations is at ¶ 23,311. The final regulation is at ¶ 13,968W-10.

¶ 20,264A

IRS: Employee Benefits Security Administration (EBSA): Group health plans: Health insurance coverage: Summary of benefits and coverage: Uniform glossary: Disclosure requirements.—The IRS, EBSA, and Department of Health and Human Services have proposed changes to the regulations that implement the Patient Protection and Affordable Care Act (PPACA, P.L. 111-148) disclosure requirements under section 2715 of the Public Health Service Act to help plans and individuals better understand their health coverage, as well as to gain a better understanding of other coverage options for comparison. It proposes changes to the documents required for compliance with section 2715 of the Public Health Service Act, including a template for the summary of benefits and coverage (SBC), instructions, sample language, a guide for coverage example calculations and the uniform glossary. The proposed regulations, as well as a new set of proposed SBC templates, instructions, an updated uniform glossary, and other materials are being issued to incorporate some of the feedback received and to make some improvements to the template. These modifications clarify when and how a plan or issuer must provide an SBC, and streamline and shorten the SBC template while also adding certain additional elements that will be useful to consumers.

The proposed regulations were published in the Federal Register on December 30, 2014 (79 FR 78577). The regulations were finalized on June 16, 2015 (80 FR 34292). The preamble to the final regulations is at ¶ 23,313. The final regulations are at ¶ 13,968V-20R.

¶ 20,264B

IRS: Proposed regulations: Multiemployer Pension Reform Act of 2014 (MPRA): Multiemployer defined benefit (DB) plans: Critical and declining status: Suspension of benefits.—The IRS has issued proposed regulations governing the suspension of benefits by multiemployer DB plans under Code Sec. 432(e)(9), which was added by the Multiemployer Pension Reform Act of 2014 (MPRA), Division O of the Consolidated and Further Continuing Appropriations Act (P.L. 113-235). The proposed regulations provide guidance relating to the standards that will be applied in reviewing an application for suspension of benefits and the statutory limitations on a suspension of benefits. The proposed regulations would permit a phase-in of the reduction that is scheduled in a definite, pre-determined manner as of a specified future date(s). The proposed regulations are proposed to be effective on and after the date of publication in the Federal Register of the final regulations. Until the final regulations are issued, the proposed regulations may not be relied on.

The guidance provided in the proposed regulations is in addition to temporary regulations that were issued contemporaneously (see PENSION PLAN GUIDE ¶ 23,314). The proposed regulations together with the temporary regulations provide guidance in implementing the statutory provisions of MPRA, according to the IRS. After consideration of public comments on the temporary and proposed regulations, the IRS intends to integrate the two sets of regulations and issue a single set of final regulations. In addition, the IRS has released Rev. Proc. 2015-34 (see PENSION PLAN GUIDE ¶ 17,299U-85), which outlines the application process for a plan seeking approval of a reduction of benefits.

The proposed regulations were published in the Federal Register on June 19, 2015 (80 FR 35262). The proposed regulations were corrected by the IRS on August 6, 2015 (80 FR 46882). The temporary and proposed regulations were finalized on April 28, 2016 (81 FR 25539). The preamble to the final regulations is at ¶ 23,322. The IRS final regulations is reproduced at ¶ 13,151N-1 (Reg. Sec. 1.432(e)(9)-1). Temporary Reg. §1.432(e)(9)-1T at ¶ 13,151N-2 is removed. The IRS has also issued Rev. Proc. 2016-27 (¶ 17,299V-13), which modifies and supersedes Rev. Proc. 2015-34 and contains revised procedures for applying for a suspension of benefits in a multiemployer defined benefit plan that is in critical and declining status.

¶ 20,264C

IRS: Proposed regulations: Performance of services: Property as compensation transferred: Code Sec. 83(b) election: Reporting and disclosure.—The IRS has issued proposed regulations that would eliminate the requirement that a copy of a Code Sec. 83(b) election to include the fair market value of property transferred in connection with the performance of services at the time of transfer be submitted with an individual's tax return. These regulations are proposed to apply January 1, 2016, and would apply to property transferred on or after that date. However, taxpayers may rely on the proposed regulations for property transferred on or after January 1, 2015.

The proposed regulation was published in the Federal Register on July 17, 2015 (80 FR 42439). The proposed regulations were finalized without modification on July 26, 2016 (81 FR 48707). The preamble to the final regulations is at ¶ 23,325. The IRS final regulations are reproduced at ¶ 11,242 (Reg. Sec. 1.83-2).

¶ 20,264D

IRS: Proposed regulations: Reporting and disclosure: Information returns: Extension of time to file.—The IRS has issued proposed regulations in which the substance of accompanying temporary regulations (see ¶ 23,316) is included. The proposed regulation would also remove the automatic 30-day extension of time to file other information returns, including the Form 1099 series, Form 3921, Form 3922, and the Form 5498 series, and replace the automatic 30-day extension with a single non-automatic 30-day extension of time to file. The proposed regulations would affect information returns due January 1 of the calendar year beginning after the date of publication of final regulations in the Federal Register, but not any earlier than the 2018 filing season.

The proposed regulation was published in the Federal Register on August 13, 2015 (80 FR 48472).

DEPARTMENT OF THE TREASURY

Internal Revenue Service

26 CFR Part 1

[REG-132075-14]

RIN 1545-BM49

Extension of Time to File Certain Information Returns

AGENCY: Internal Revenue Service (IRS), Treasury.

ACTION: Notice of proposed rulemaking.

SUMMARY: In the Rules and Regulations section of this issue of the **Federal Register**, the IRS is issuing temporary regulations that will remove the automatic extension of time to file information returns on forms in the W-2 series (except Form W-2G). The temporary regulations will allow only a single 30-day non-automatic extension of time to file these information returns. In addition, the temporary regulations will update the list of information returns subject to the rules regarding extensions of time to file. These proposed regulations incorporate the temporary regulations with respect to extensions of time to file information returns on forms in the W-2 series (except Form W-2G). In addition, these proposed regulations would remove the automatic 30-day extension of time to file all information returns listed in the temporary regulation.

DATES: Written or electronic comments and requests for a public hearing must be received by November 12, 2015.

ADDRESSES: Send submissions to: CC:PA:LPD:PR (REG-132075-14), Room 5203, Internal Revenue Service, P.O. Box 7604, Ben Franklin Station, Washington, DC 20044. Submissions may be hand-delivered between the hours of 8 a.m. and 4 p.m. to CC:PA:LPD:PR (REG-132075-14), Courier's Desk, Internal Revenue Service, 1111 Constitution Avenue NW., Washington, DC, or sent via the Federal eRulemaking Portal at www.regulations.gov (IRS REG-132075-14).

FOR FURTHER INFORMATION CONTACT:

Concerning these proposed regulations, Jonathan R. Black, (202) 317-6845; concerning submissions of comments and/or requests for a hearing, Regina Johnson (202) 317-6901 (not toll-free numbers).

SUPPLEMENTARY INFORMATION:

Background and Explanation of Provisions

Temporary regulations § 1.6081-8T in the Rules and Regulations section of this issue of the **Federal Register** will amend 26 CFR part 1 by removing the automatic extension of time to file information returns on forms in the W-2 series (except Form W-2G), effective for filing season 2017. The temporary regulations will allow only a single 30-day non-automatic extension of time to file these information returns that the IRS may, in its discretion, grant if the IRS determines that an extension of time to file is warranted based on the filer's or transmitter's explanation attached to a Form 8809, "Application for Extension of Time to File Information Returns," signed under penalties of perjury. The temporary regulations will also add Forms 3921, 3922, 1094-C, and forms in the 1097 series to the list of information returns covered by § 1.6081-8T(a) and clarify that Forms 1095-B and 1095-C, but not Form 1095-A, are covered by the rules in § 1.6081-8T(a).

These proposed regulations would remove the automatic 30-day extension of time to file the information returns listed in § 1.6081-8T(a) and allow only a single non-automatic extension of time to file all information returns listed in § 1.6081-8T.

The IRS anticipates that, as described in the temporary regulations with respect to forms in the W-2 series (other than Forms W-2G), under the proposed regulations, the IRS will grant the nonautomatic 30-day extension of time to file information returns listed in § 1.6081-8(a) only in limited cases where the filer's or transmitter's explanation demonstrates that an extension of time to file is needed as a result of extraordinary circumstances or catastrophe, such as a natural disaster or fire destroying the books and records a filer needs for filing the information returns.

Treasury and the IRS request comments on the appropriate timing of the removal of the automatic 30-day extension of time to file information returns covered by these proposed regulations, such as Form 1042-S, including whether special transitional considerations should be given for any category or categories of forms or filers relative to other forms or filers. Although these regulations are proposed to be effective for requests for extensions of time to file information returns due on or after January 1 of the calendar year immediately following the date of publication of a Treasury decision adopting these rules as final regulations in the **Federal Register**, removal of the automatic 30-day extension of time to file will not apply to information returns (other than forms in the W-2 series except Forms W-2G) due any earlier than January 1, 2018. Please follow the instructions in the "Comments and Requests for Public Hearing" portion of this preamble.

The temporary regulations affect taxpayers who are required to file information returns on forms in the W-2 series (except Forms W-2G) and need an extension of time to file. These proposed regulations also affect taxpayers who need an extension of time to file any of the information returns listed in § 1.6081-8T(a).

The substance of the temporary regulations is incorporated in these proposed regulations. The preamble to the temporary regulations explains these amendments. These proposed regulations would also expand the rules in § 1.6081-8T(b) to the other information returns, which are listed in § 1.6081-8T(a).

Proposed Effective/Applicability Date

The regulations, as proposed, would apply to requests for extensions of time to file information returns due on or after January 1 of the calendar year immediately following the date of publication of a Treasury decision adopting these rules as final regulations in the **Federal Register**.

Special Analyses

Certain IRS regulations, including this one, are exempt from the requirements of Executive Order 12866, as supplemented and reaffirmed by Executive Order 13563. Therefore, a regulatory assessment is not required. It also has been determined that section 553(b) of the Administrative Procedure Act (5 U.S.C. chapter 5) does not apply to these proposed regulations.

Pursuant to the Regulatory Flexibility Act (5 U.S.C. chapter 6), it is hereby certified that this proposed rule, if adopted, would not have a significant economic impact on a substantial number of small entities. As stated in this preamble, the proposed regulations would remove the automatic 30-day extension of time to file certain information returns (Form W-2G, 1042-S, 1094-C, 1095-B, 1095-C, 1097 series, 1098 series, 1099 series, 3921, 3922, 5498 series, and 8027). Under the proposed regulations, filers and transmitters would be permitted to request only one 30-day extension of time to file these information returns by timely submitting a Form 8809, including an explanation of the reasons for requesting the extension and signed under penalty of perjury. Although the proposed regulation may potentially affect a substantial number of small entities, the economic impact on these entities is not expected to be significant because filers who are unable to timely file as a result of extraordinary circumstances or catastrophe may continue to obtain a 30-day extension through the Form 8809 process, which takes approximately 20 minutes to prepare and submit to the IRS. Pursuant to section 7805(f) of the Internal Revenue Code, this notice of proposed rulemaking has been submitted to the Chief Counsel for Advocacy of the Small Business Administration for comment on its impact on small business.

Comments and Requests for Public Hearing

Before these proposed regulations are adopted as final regulations, consideration will be given to any comments that are submitted timely to the IRS as prescribed in the preamble under the **ADDRESSES** heading. Treasury and the IRS request comments on all aspects of the proposed regulations. All comments submitted will be made available at www.regulations.gov or upon request. A public hearing will be scheduled if requested in writing by any person that timely submits written comments. If a public hearing is scheduled, notice of the date, time, and place for the public hearing will be published in the **Federal Register**.

Drafting Information

The principal author of these regulations is Jonathan R. Black of the Office of the Associate Chief Counsel (Procedure and Administration).

List of Subjects in 26 CFR Part 1

Income taxes, Reporting and recordkeeping requirements.

Proposed Amendments to the Regulations

Accordingly, 26 CFR part 1 is proposed to be amended as follows:

PART 1—INCOME TAXES

Paragraph 1. The authority citation for part 1 continues to read as follows:

Authority: 26 U.S.C. 7805 * * *

Par. 2. Section 1.6081-8 is revised to read as follows:

§ 1.6081-8 Extension of time to file certain information returns.

(a) *In general.* Except as provided in paragraph (e) of this section, a person required to file an information return (the filer) on forms in the W-2 series (including Forms W-2, W-2AS, W-2G, W-2GU, and W-2VI), 1097 series, 1098 series, 1099 series, or 5498 series, or on Forms 1042-S, 1094-C, 1095-B, 1095-C, 3921, 3922, or 8027, or the person transmitting the information return for the filer (the transmitter), may only request one non-automatic 30-day extension of time to file the information return beyond the due date for filing it. To make such a request, the filer or transmitter must submit an application for an extension of time to file in accordance with paragraph (b) of this section. No additional extension of time to file will be allowed pursuant to § 1.6081-1 beyond the 30-day extension of time to file provided by this paragraph.

(b) *Requirements.* To satisfy this paragraph (b), a filer or transmitter must—

(1) Submit a complete application on Form 8809, "Application for Extension of Time to File Information Returns," or in any other manner prescribed by the Commissioner, including a detailed explanation of why additional time is needed;

(2) File the application with the Internal Revenue Service in accordance with forms, instructions, or other appropriate guidance on or before the due date for filing the information return; and

(3) Sign the application under penalties of perjury.

(c) *Penalties.* See sections 6652, 6693, and 6721 through 6724 for failure to comply with information reporting requirements on information returns described in paragraph (a) of this section.

(d) *No effect on time to furnish statements.* An extension of time to file an information return under this section does not extend the time for furnishing a statement to the person with respect to whom the information is required to be reported.

(e) *Form W-2 filed on expedited basis.* This section does not apply to an information return on a form in the W-2 series if the procedures authorized in Rev. Proc. 96-57 (1996-2 CB 389) (or a successor revenue procedure) allow an automatic extension of time to file the information return. See § 601.601(d)(2)(ii)(b) of this chapter.

(f) *Effective/applicability date.* This section applies to requests for extensions of time to file information returns due on or after January 1 of the calendar year immediately following the date of publication of a Treasury decision adopting these rules as final regulations in the **Federal Register**.

§ 1.6081-8T [Removed]

Par. 3. Section 1.6081-8T is removed.

John Dalrymple,

Deputy Commissioner for Services and Enforcement.

[FR Doc. 2015-19933 Filed 8-12-15; 8:45 am]

BILLING CODE **4830-01-P**

¶ 20,264E

IRS: Health insurance coverage: Employer-sponsored group health plans: Minimum value.—The IRS has issued proposed regulations providing that an eligible employer-sponsored group health plan does not provide minimum value, as defined under Code Sec. 36B(c)(2)(C)(ii), if it excludes substantial coverage to employees for in-patient hospitalization services or physician services (or both). Specifically, the proposed regulations state that an eligible employer-sponsored plan provides minimum value only if the plan's share of the total allowed costs of benefits provided to an employee is at least 60 percent and the plan provides substantial coverage of inpatient hospital and physician services. Thus, these proposed regulations withdraw part of proposed regulations issued on May 3, 2013 (see Pension Plan Guide ¶ 20,263N)—proposed Reg. Sec. 1.36B-6(a) and (g)—and replaces the withdrawn portions with new versions. These regulations are proposed to apply for plan years beginning after November 3, 2014. However, for purposes of Code Sec. 4980H, the changes to the minimum value regulations may not apply before the end of the plan year beginning no later than March 1, 2015 under certain conditions.

The proposed regulation was published in the Federal Register on September 1, 2015 (80 FR 52678). The regulations were finalized, in part, on December 18, 2015 (80 FR 78971). The preamble to the final regulations is at ¶ 24,511J. The final regulations are at ¶ 11,112F-7. The IRS states that the portions of the proposed regulations that are not currently finalized will be finalized later.

DEPARTMENT OF THE TREASURY

Internal Revenue Service

26 CFR Part 1

[REG-143800-14]

RIN 1545-BM85

Minimum Value of Eligible Employer-Sponsored Health Plans

AGENCY: Internal Revenue Service (IRS), Treasury.

ACTION: Supplemental notice of proposed rulemaking.

SUMMARY: This document withdraws, in part, a notice of proposed rulemaking published on May 3, 2013, relating to the health insurance premium tax credit enacted by the Affordable Care Act (including guidance on determining whether health coverage under an eligible employer-sponsored plan provides minimum value) and replaces the withdrawn portion with new proposed regulations providing guidance on determining whether health coverage under an eligible employer-sponsored plan provides minimum value. The proposed regulations affect participants in eligible employer-sponsored health plans and employers that sponsor these plans.

DATES: Written (including electronic) comments and requests for a public hearing must be received by November 2, 2015.

ADDRESSES: Send submissions to: CC:PA:LPD:PR (REG-143800-14), Room 5203, Internal Revenue Service, P.O. Box 7604, Ben Franklin Station, Washington, DC 20044. Submissions may be hand-delivered Monday through Friday between the hours of 8 a.m. and 4 p.m. to CC:PA:LPD:PR (REG-143800-14), Courier's Desk, Internal Revenue Service, 1111 Constitution Avenue NW., Washington, DC, or sent electronically via the Federal eRulemaking Portal at *www.regulations.gov* (IRS REG-143800-14).

FOR FURTHER INFORMATION CONTACT: Concerning the proposed regulations, Andrew S. Braden, (202) 317-4725; concerning the submission of comments and/or requests for a public hearing, Oluwafunmilayo Taylor, (202) 317-5179 (not toll-free calls).

SUPPLEMENTARY INFORMATION:

Background

This document withdraws, in part, a notice of proposed rulemaking (REG-125398-12), which was published in the **Federal Register** on May 3, 2013 (78 FR 25909) and replaces the portion withdrawn with new proposed regulations. The 2013 proposed regulations added § 1.36B-6 of the Income Tax Regulations, providing rules for determining the minimum value of eligible employer-sponsored plans for purposes of the premium tax credit under section 36B of the Internal Revenue Code (Code). Notice 2014-69 (2014-48 IRB 903) advised taxpayers that the Department of Health and Human Service (HHS) and the Treasury Department and the IRS intended to propose regulations providing that plans that fail to provide substantial coverage for inpatient hospitalization or physician services do not provide minimum value. Accordingly, the proposed regulations under § 1.36B-6(a) and (g) are withdrawn.

Beginning in 2014, under the Patient Protection and Affordable Care Act, Public Law 111-148 (124 Stat. 119 (2010)), and the Health Care and Education Reconciliation Act of 2010, Public Law 111-152 (124 Stat. 1029 (2010)) (collectively, the Affordable Care Act), eligible individuals who enroll in, or whose family member enrolls in, coverage under a qualified health plan through an Affordable Insurance Exchange (Exchange), also known as a Health Insurance Marketplace, may receive a premium tax credit under section 36B of the Code.

Premium Tax Credit

Section 36B allows a refundable premium tax credit, which subsidizes the cost of health insurance coverage enrolled in through an Exchange. A taxpayer may claim the premium tax credit on the taxpayer's tax return only if the taxpayer or a member of the taxpayer's tax family (the persons for whom the taxpayer claims a personal exemption deduction on the taxpayer's tax return, generally the taxpayer, spouse, and dependents) has a coverage month. An individual has a coverage month only if the individual enrolls in a qualified health plan through an Exchange, is not eligible for minimum essential coverage other than coverage in the individual market, and premiums for the qualified health plan are paid. Section 36B(b) and (c)(2)(B). Minimum essential coverage includes coverage under an eligible employer-sponsored plan. See section 5000A(f)(1)(B). However, for purposes of the premium tax credit, an individual is not eligible for coverage under an eligible employer-sponsored plan unless the coverage is affordable and provides minimum value or unless the individual enrolls in the plan. Section 36B(c)(2)(C). Final regulations under section 36B (TD 9590) were published on May 23, 2012 (77 FR 30377).

Employer Shared Responsibility Provision

Section 4980H(b) imposes an assessable payment on applicable large employers (as defined in section 4980H(c)(2)) that offer minimum essential coverage under an eligible employer-sponsored plan that is not affordable or does not provide minimum value for one or more full-time employees who receive a premium tax credit subsidy. Final regulations under section 4980H (TD 9655) were published on February 12, 2014 (79 FR 8544).

Minimum Value

Under section 36B(c)(2)(C)(ii), an eligible employer-sponsored plan provides minimum value only if the plan's share of the total allowed costs of benefits provided under the plan is at least 60 percent. Section 1302(d)(2)(C) of the Affordable Care Act provides that, in determining the percentage of the total allowed costs of benefits provided under a group health plan, the regulations promulgated by HHS under section 1302(d)(2), dealing with actuarial value, apply.

HHS published final regulations under section 1302(d)(2) on February 25, 2013 (78 FR 12834). HHS regulations at 45 CFR 156.20, which apply to the actuarial value of plans required to provide coverage of all essential health benefits, define the percentage of the total allowed costs of benefits provided under a group health plan as (1) the anticipated covered medical spending for essential health benefits coverage (as defined in 45 CFR 156.110(a)) paid by a health plan for a standard population, computed in accordance with the plan's cost-sharing, divided by (2) the total anticipated allowed charges for essential health benefit coverage provided to a standard population.

Under section 1302(b) of the Affordable Care Act, only individual market and insured small group market health plans are required to cover the essential health benefits. Minimum value, however, applies to all eligible employer-sponsored plans, including self-insured plans and insured plans in the large group market. Accordingly, HHS regulations at 45 CFR 156.145(b)(2) and (c) apply the actuarial value definition in the context of minimum value by (1) defining the standard population as the population covered by typical self-insured group health plans, and (2) taking into account the benefits a plan provides that are included in any one benchmark plan a state uses to specify the benefits included in essential health benefits.

Notice 2014-69, advising taxpayers of the intent to propose regulations providing that plans that fail to provide substantial coverage for inpatient hospitalization or physician services do not provide minimum value, was released on November 4, 2014. Notice 2014-69 also advised that it was anticipated that, for purposes of section 4980H liability, the final regulations would not apply to certain plans (as described later in this preamble) before the end of a plan year beginning no later than March 1, 2015. However, an offer of coverage under these plans to an employee does not preclude the employee from obtaining a premium tax credit, if otherwise eligible.

As announced by Notice 2014-69, HHS published proposed regulations on November 26, 2014 (79 FR 70674, 70757), and final regulations on February 27, 2015 (80 FR 10872), amending 45 CFR 156.145(a). The HHS regulations provide that an eligible employer-sponsored plan provides minimum value only if, in addition to covering at least 60 percent of the total allowed costs of benefits provided under the plan, the plan benefits include substantial coverage of inpatient hospitalization and physician services. Consistent with Notice 2014-69, the HHS

regulations indicate that the changes to the minimum value regulations do not apply before the end of the plan year beginning no later than March 1, 2015 to a plan that fails to provide substantial coverage for inpatient hospitalization services or for physician services (or both), provided that the employer had entered into a binding written commitment to adopt, or had begun enrolling employees in, the plan before November 4, 2014. For this purpose, the plan year is the plan year in effect under the terms of the plan on November 3, 2014. Also for this purpose, a binding written commitment exists when an employer is contractually required to pay for an arrangement, and a plan begins enrolling employees when it begins accepting employee elections to participate in the plan. See 80 FR 10828.

Explanation of Provisions

The preamble to the HHS regulations acknowledges that self-insured and large group market group health plans are not required to cover the essential health benefits, but notes that a health plan that does not provide substantial coverage for inpatient hospitalization and physician services does not meet a universally accepted minimum standard of value expected from and inherent in any arrangement that can reasonably be called a health plan and that is intended to provide the primary health coverage for employees. The preamble concludes that it is evident in the structure of and policy underlying the Affordable Care Act that the minimum value standard may be interpreted to require that employer-sponsored plans cover critical benefits. See 80 FR 10827-10828.

As the preamble notes, allowing plans that fail to provide substantial coverage of inpatient hospital or physician services to be treated as providing minimum value would adversely affect employees (particularly those with significant health risks) who may find this coverage insufficient, by denying them access to a premium tax credit for individual coverage purchased through an Exchange, while at the same time avoiding the employer shared responsibility payment under section 4980H. Plans that omit critical benefits used disproportionately by individuals in poor health would likely enroll far fewer of these individuals, effectively driving down employer costs at the expense of those who, because of their individual health status, are discouraged from enrolling. See 80 FR 10827-10829.

Accordingly, these proposed regulations incorporate the substance of the rule in the HHS regulations. They provide that an eligible employer-sponsored plan provides minimum value only if the plan's share of the total allowed costs of benefits provided to an employee is at least 60 percent and the plan provides substantial coverage of inpatient hospital and physician services. Comments are requested on rules for determining whether a plan provides "substantial coverage" of inpatient hospital and physician services.

Effective/Applicability Date and Transition Relief

These regulations are proposed to apply for plan years beginning after November 3, 2014. However, for purposes of section 4980H(b), the changes to the minimum value regulations (in § 1.36B-6(a)(2) of these proposed regulations) do not apply before the end of the plan year beginning no later than March 1, 2015 to a plan that fails to provide substantial coverage for in-patient hospitalization services or for physician services (or both), provided that the employer had entered into a binding written commitment to adopt the noncompliant plan terms, or had begun enrolling employees in the plan with noncompliant plan terms, before November 4, 2014. For this purpose, the plan year is the plan year in effect under the terms of the plan on November 3, 2014. Also for this purpose, a binding written commitment exists when an employer is contractually required to pay for an arrangement, and a plan begins enrolling employees when it begins accepting employee elections to participate in the plan. The relief provided in this section does not apply to an applicable large employer that would have been liable for a payment under section 4980H without regard to § 1.36B-6(a)(2) of these proposed regulations.

An offer of coverage under an eligible employer-sponsored plan that does not comply with § 1.36B-6(a)(2) of these proposed regulations does not preclude an employee from obtaining a premium tax credit under section 36B, if otherwise eligible.

Special Analyses

Certain IRS regulations, including this one, are exempt from the requirements of Executive Order 12866, as supplemented and reaffirmed by Executive Order 13563. Therefore, a regulatory impact assessment is not required. It has been determined that section 553(b) of the Administrative Procedure Act (5 U.S.C. chapter 5) does not apply to these regulations and, because the regulations do not impose a collection of information on small entities, the Regulatory Flexibility Act (5 U.S.C. chapter 6) does not apply. Pursuant to section 7805(f) of the

Code, this notice of proposed rulemaking has been submitted to the Chief Counsel for Advocacy of the Small Business Administration for comment on its impact on small business.

Comments and Requests for Public Hearing

Before these proposed regulations are adopted as final regulations, consideration will be given to any comments that are submitted timely to the IRS as prescribed in this preamble under the **ADDRESSES** heading. The Treasury Department and the IRS request comments on all aspects of the proposed rules. All comments will be available at *www.regulations.gov* or upon request. A public hearing will be scheduled if requested in writing by any person who timely submits written comments. If a public hearing is scheduled, notice of the date, time, and place for the hearing will be published in the **Federal Register**.

Drafting Information

The principal author of these regulations is Andrew Braden of the Office of the Associate Chief Counsel (Income Tax and Accounting). However, other personnel from the Treasury Department and the IRS participated in their development.

List of Subjects in 26 CFR Part 1

Income taxes, Reporting and recordkeeping requirements.

Proposed Amendments

Accordingly, 26 CFR part 1 as proposed to be amended on May 3, 2013 (78 FR 25909), is proposed to be further amended as follows:

PART 1—INCOME TAXES

■ **Paragraph 1.** The authority citation for part 1 continues to read as follows:

Authority: 26 U.S.C. 7805 * * *

■ **Par. 2.** Section 1.36B-6, as proposed to be added May 3, 2013 (78 FR 25909), is amended by revising paragraphs (a) and (g) to read as follows:

§ 1.36B-6 Minimum value.

(a) *In general.* An eligible employer-sponsored plan provides minimum value (MV) only if—

(1) The plan's share of the total allowed costs of benefits provided to an employee (the MV percentage) is at least 60 percent; and

(2) The plan provides substantial coverage of inpatient hospital services and physician services.

* * * * *

(g) *Effective/applicability date*—(1) *In general.* Except as provided in paragraph (g)(2) of this section, this section applies for taxable years ending after December 31, 2013.

(2) *Exception.* Paragraph (a)(2) of this section applies for plan years beginning after November 3, 2014.

John Dalrymple,

Deputy Commissioner for Services and Enforcement.

[FR Doc. 2015-21427 Filed 8-31-15; 8:45 am]

BILLING CODE 4830-01-P

¶ 20,264F

IRS: Employee benefits: Qualified retirement plans: Same-sex marriages.—The IRS has issued proposed regulations that take into account recent changes in the law with respect to same-sex marriages affecting, among others, sponsors and administrators of employee benefit plans. The IRS has determined that marriages of couples of the same sex should be treated the same as marriages of couples of the opposite sex. Therefore, terms indicating sex, such as "husband," "wife," and "husband and wife" should be interpreted in a neutral way to include same-sex spouses as well as opposite-sex spouses.

The IRS states that taxpayers may continue to rely on guidance related to the application of Rev. Rul. 2013-17 (¶ 19,948Z-344) to employee benefit plans and the benefits provided under such plans, including Notices 2014-19 and 2014-37 (¶ 17,153O and ¶ 17,154B, respectively), until the issuance of the final regulations in the Federal Register. At that time, Rev. Rul. 2013-17 will be obsoleted.

The proposed regulations were published in the Federal Register on October 23, 2015 (80 FR 64378). The regulations were finalized on September 2, 2016 (81 FR 60609). The preamble to the final regulations is at ¶ 23,326. The final regulations are reproduced at ¶ 13,935.

¶ 20,264G

IRS: Governmental pension plans: Normal retirement age: Pre-ERISA vesting rules: Safe harbors.—The IRS has issued proposed regulations on which governmental plan sponsors may rely prior to the effective date, providing guidance and safe harbors with respect to the normal retirement age used by governmental plans. A governmental plan's normal retirement age must satisfy the pre-ERISA vesting rules. The proposed regulations would provide guidance relating to the determination of whether the normal retirement age under a governmental plan satisfies the requirements of Code Sec. 401(a) by amending the 2007 normal retirement age final regulations (see ¶ 24,508Q) to provide a number of additional safe harbors concerning normal retirement age designed solely for governmental plans that would be deemed to satisfy the reasonably representative requirement. The regulations are proposed to be effective for employees hired during plan years beginning on or after the later of (1) January 1, 2017, or (2) the close of the first regular legislative session of the legislative body with the authority to amend the plan that begins on or after the date that is three months after the final regulations are published in the Federal Register.

The proposed regulation was published in the Federal Register on January 27, 2016 (81 FR 4599).

DEPARTMENT OF THE TREASURY

Internal Revenue Service

26 CFR Part 1

[REG-147310-12]

RIN-1545-BM22

Applicability of Normal Retirement Age Regulations to Governmental Pension Plans

AGENCY: Internal Revenue Service (IRS), Treasury.

ACTION: Notice of proposed rulemaking.

SUMMARY: This document contains proposed regulations under section 401(a) of the Internal Revenue Code (Code). These regulations would provide rules relating to the determination of whether the normal retirement age under a governmental plan (within the meaning of section 414(d) of the Code) that is a pension plan satisfies the requirements of section 401(a) and whether the payment of definitely determinable benefits that commence at the plan's normal retirement age satisfies these requirements. These regulations would affect sponsors and administrators of governmental pension plans, as well as participants in such plans.

DATES: Comments and requests for a public hearing must be received by April 26, 2016.

ADDRESSES: Send submissions to CC:PA:LPD:PR (REG-147310-12), Room 5205, Internal Revenue Service, P.O. Box 7604, Ben Franklin Station, Washington, DC 20044. Submissions may be hand-delivered Monday through Friday between the hours of 8 a.m. and 4 p.m. to CC:PA:LPD:PR (REG-147310-12), Courier's Desk, Internal Revenue Service, 1111 Constitution Avenue NW., Washington, DC 20224, or sent electronically via the Federal eRulemaking Portal at *www.regulations.gov* (IRS REG-147310-12).

FOR FURTHER INFORMATION CONTACT: Concerning the proposed regulations, Pamela Kinard at (202) 317-4148 or Robert Walsh at

(202) 317-4102; concerning the submission of comments or to request a public hearing, Oluwafunmilayo (Funmi) Taylor, (202) 317-7180 or (202) 317-6901 (not toll-free numbers).

SUPPLEMENTARY INFORMATION:

Background

I. Normal Retirement Age Generally

This document contains proposed regulations under section 401(a) of the Internal Revenue Code (Code). Section 401(a) sets forth the qualification requirements for a trust forming part of a stock bonus, pension, or profit-sharing plan of an employer. Several of these qualification requirements are based on a plan's normal retirement age, including the regulatory interpretation of the requirement that the plan provide for definitely determinable benefits (generally after retirement). Final regulations defining normal retirement age for the definitely determinable requirement were published in the **Federal Register** as TD 9325 on May 22, 2007 (72 FR 28604) (2007 NRA regulations).

Section 1.401(a)-1(b)(1) of the 2007 NRA regulations generally requires that a pension plan be established and maintained primarily to provide systematically for the payment of definitely determinable benefits over a period of years, usually for life, after retirement. The 2007 NRA regulations include two exceptions to the general rule that payments commence after retirement: (1) Payments can commence after attainment of normal retirement age; and (2) in accordance with section 401(a)(36), payments can commence after an employee reaches age 62.

Section 1.401(a)-1(b)(2)(i) of the 2007 NRA regulations provides that, as a general rule, a normal retirement age under a pension plan must be an age that is not earlier than the earliest age that is reasonably representative of the typical retirement age for the industry in which the covered workforce is employed (reasonably representative requirement). Section 1.401(a)-1(b)(2)(ii) of the 2007 NRA regulations provides that a normal retirement age of age 62 or later is deemed to satisfy the reasonably representative requirement. Under section 1.401(a)-1(b)(2)(iii) of the 2007 NRA regulations, whether a normal retirement age that is not earlier than age 55 but is below age 62 satisfies the reasonably representative requirement is based on a facts and circumstances analysis. Section 1.401(a)-1(b)(2)(iv) of the 2007 NRA regulations provides that a normal retirement age that is lower than age 55 is presumed not to satisfy the reasonably representative requirement unless the Commissioner determines otherwise on the basis of facts and circumstances. Under §1.401(a)-1(b)(2)(v) of the 2007 NRA regulations, in the case of a pension plan in which substantially all of the participants are qualified public safety employees (within the meaning of section 72(t)(10)(B)), a normal retirement age of age 50 or later is deemed to satisfy the reasonably representative requirement.

As previously explained, normal retirement age is used by a pension plan in a variety of circumstances relating to plan qualification. Generally, in the case of a pension plan that is not a governmental plan under section 414(d) and is subject to the rules of section 411(a) through (d), normal retirement age is used in applying the rules under section 411(b) that are designed to preclude avoidance of the minimum vesting standards through the backloading of benefits (such as a benefit formula under which the rate of benefit accrual is increased disproportionately for employees with longer service). Normal retirement age is also relevant for such a plan for other purposes, including the application of the rules relating to suspension of benefits under section 411(a)(3)(B), plan offset rules under section 411(b)(1)(H)(iii), and the minimum benefit rules applicable to non-key employee participants in the case of a top-heavy defined benefit plan under section 416. In addition, for such a plan, section 411(a)(8) defines the term *normal retirement age* as the earlier of (a) the time a participant attains normal retirement age under the plan or (b) the later of the time a plan

participant attains age 65 or the 5th anniversary of the time a plan participant commenced participation in the plan.[1]

II. Normal Retirement Age Under a Governmental Plan

A. Application of Section 411 to Governmental Plans

Section 414(d) of the Code provides that the term *governmental plan* generally means a plan established and maintained for its employees by the Government of the United States, by the government of any State or political subdivision thereof, or by any agency or instrumentality of any of the foregoing.[2] See sections 3(32) and 4021(b)(2) of ERISA for definitions of the term *governmental plan* for purposes of title I and title IV of ERISA, respectively.

Section 411(e)(1) of the Code provides that the provisions of section 411, other than section 411(e)(2), do not apply to a governmental plan. Under section 411(e)(2), a governmental plan is treated as meeting the requirements of section 411, for purposes of section 401(a), if the plan meets the vesting requirements resulting from the application of sections 401(a)(4) and 401(a)(7) as in effect on September 1, 1974 (pre-ERISA vesting rules). The only requirements under section 411 that apply to a governmental plan are the pre-ERISA vesting rules under section 411(e)(2). Thus, the definition of normal retirement age under section 411(a)(8) does not apply to a governmental plan. In addition, other rules of section 411, including section 411(a)(3)(B) (related to suspension of benefits), section 411(b)(1) (related to backloading of benefits in a defined benefit plan), and section 411(b)(1)(H)(iii) (related to offsets after normal retirement age) do not apply to a governmental plan. Therefore, except for specific circumstances in which in-service benefit payments are permitted under §1.401(a)-1(b)(1), the definition of normal retirement age need not be used by a governmental plan for the same purposes that apply to a plan subject to section 411(a) through (d).[3]

B. Pre-ERISA Vesting Requirements for Governmental Plans

Under section 411(e)(2), a normal retirement age under a governmental plan must satisfy the pre-ERISA vesting rules. The pre-ERISA vesting rules applicable to governmental plans contain two basic components: (a) Rules relating to vesting and (b) rules relating to the right to commence benefits without reduction for early commencement. Rev. Rul. 66-11, 1966-1 C.B. 71, and Rev. Rul. 68-302, 1968-1 C.B. 163, illustrate the interplay between normal retirement age under the pre-ERISA vesting rules and section 401(a). As described in these rulings, to satisfy the requirements of section 401(a), a plan that is subject to the pre-ERISA vesting rules must provide for full vesting of the contributions made to or benefits payable under the plan for any employee who has attained normal retirement age under the plan and satisfied any reasonable and uniformly applicable requirements as to length of service or participation described in the plan. For more information about these rules, see Part 5(c) of Publication 778, *Guides for Qualification of Pension, Profit-Sharing, and Stock Bonus Plans (Pub. 778)*.

Rev. Rul. 71-24, 1971-1 C.B. 114, illustrates the application of the pre-ERISA vesting rules to benefits provided under a pension plan for employees who continue employment after normal retirement age. Rev. Rul. 71-24 includes an example under which benefits are permitted to commence during employment after normal retirement age.

As described in Rev. Rul. 71-147,[4] 1971-1 C.B. 116, the normal retirement age in a pension or annuity plan under the pre-ERISA vesting rules is generally the lowest age specified in the plan at which the employee has the right to retire without the consent of the employer and receive retirement benefits based on the amount of the employee's service to the date of retirement at the full rate set forth in the plan (that is, without actuarial or similar reduction because of retirement before some later specified age). Rev. Rul. 71-147 does not explicitly require a plan to include a provision defining normal retirement age. Instead, a plan's normal retirement age may be deduced

---

[1] Section 411(f) provides a special normal retirement age rule that applies only to certain defined benefit plans that are subject to section 411(a) through (d). Section 411(f) was added to the Code on December 16, 2014 by Section 2 of Division P of the Consolidated and Further Continuing Appropriations Act, 2015, Public Law 113-235 (128 Stat. 2130 (2014)), which also made a corresponding change to section 204 of the Employee Retirement Income Security Act of 1974, Public Law 93-406 (88 Stat. 829 (1974)), as amended (ERISA). Under section 101 of Reorganization Plan No. 4 of 1978 (92 Stat. 3790), the Secretary of the Treasury has interpretive jurisdiction over the subject matter addressed in section 411(f) for purposes of ERISA, as well as the Code.

[2] The term *governmental plan* also includes a plan that is established and maintained by an Indian tribal government (as defined in section 7701(a)(40)), a subdivision of an Indian tribal government (determined in accordance with section 7871(d)), or an agency or instrumentality of either, and all the participants of which are employees of such entity substantially all of whose services as such an employee are in the performance of essential governmental functions but not in the performance of commercial activities (whether or

not an essential government function). In addition, the term *governmental plan* includes any plan to which the Railroad Retirement Act of 1935 or 1937 (49 Stat. 967, as amended by 50 Stat. 307) applies and which is financed by contributions required under that Act and any plan of an international organization that is exempt from taxation by reason of the International Organizations Immunities Act, Public Law 79-291 (59 Stat. 669).

[3] Normal retirement age may also be relevant to participant eligibility for certain favorable tax treatment, including section 402(l) (providing an income exclusion of up to $3,000 annually for certain distributions for health insurance and longterm care insurance premiums to eligible retired public safety officers who separate from service by reason of disability or attainment of normal retirement age) and the special catch-up provisions under §1.457-4(c)(3)(v)(A).

[4] Even though Rev. Rul. 71-147 was superseded by Rev. Rul. 80-276, 1980-1 C.B. 131, for plans subject to section 411(a)(8), Rev. Rul. 71-147 remains valid guidance for purposes of the pre-ERISA vesting rules.

from other plan provisions. As described in Rev. Rul. 71-147, although normal retirement age under a pension or annuity plan is ordinarily age 65, a plan may specify a lower age at which the employee has the right to retire without the consent of the employer and to receive retirement benefits based on the amount of the employee's service at the full rate set forth in the plan if this lower age would be an age at which employees customarily retire in the particular company or industry, and if the provision permitting receipt of unreduced benefits at this age is not a device to accelerate funding. For more information about these rules, see also Part 5(e) of Pub. 778.

III. Application of the 2007 NRA Regulations to Governmental Plans

Notice 2007-69, 2007-2 C.B. 468, asked for comments "on whether and how a pension plan with a normal retirement age conditioned on the completion of a stated number of years of service satisfies the requirement in § 1.401(a)-1(b)(1)(i) that a pension plan be maintained primarily to provide for the payment of definitely determinable benefits after retirement or attainment of normal retirement age and how such a plan satisfies the pre-ERISA vesting rules." Comments were received on a variety of issues, including comments that guidance should be issued to (1) clarify that governmental plans are not required to define normal retirement age, (2) provide safe harbor rules that would permit a governmental plan to define normal retirement age that includes a service component, and (3) provide that the age-50 safe harbor rule in § 1.401(a)-1(b)(2)(v) for qualified public safety employees can apply to these employees even if less than substantially all of a plan's participants are qualified public safety employees.

The 2007 NRA regulations provided that, in the case of governmental plans, the regulations would be effective for plan years beginning on or after January 1, 2009. Notices 2008-98, 2008-44 I.R.B. 1080, and 2009-86, 2009-6 I.R.B. 629, provided that the Department of the Treasury and the IRS intended to amend the 2007 NRA regulations to change the effective date of the 2007 NRA regulations for governmental plans to January 1, 2013.

Notice 2012-29, 2012-18 I.R.B. 872, announced that the Department of the Treasury and the IRS intend to modify provisions of the 2007 NRA regulations as applied to governmental plans in two ways. First, Notice 2012-29 announced the intent to modify the regulations to clarify that a governmental plan that is not subject to section 411(a) through (d) and does not provide for the payment of in-service distributions before age 62 will not fail to satisfy the requirement that the plan provide definitely determinable benefits to employees after retirement or attainment of normal retirement age merely because the pension plan does not have a definition of normal retirement age or does not have a definition of normal retirement age that satisfies the requirements of the 2007 NRA regulations.

Second, Notice 2012-29 announced the intent to modify the 2007 NRA regulations to provide that the rule deeming age 50 or later to be a normal retirement age that satisfies the 2007 NRA regulations will apply to a group of employees substantially all of whom are qualified public safety employees, whether or not the group of qualified public safety employees are covered by a separate plan. Thus, under the intended modification, a governmental plan would be permitted to satisfy the reasonably representative requirement using a normal retirement age as low as 50 for a group substantially all of whom are qualified public safety employees and a later normal retirement age that otherwise satisfies the 2007 NRA requirements for all other participants.

Notice 2012-29 requested comments from governmental stakeholders on the guidance under consideration. Specific comments were requested on whether a new rule should be provided under which retirement after 20 to 30 years of service may be a normal retirement age that is reasonably representative of the typical retirement age for the industry in which qualified public safety employees are employed because these employees tend to have career spans that commence at a young age and continue over a limited number of years. Many commenters wrote that such a rule would be helpful and appropriate. Several commenters requested a rule that would permit a governmental plan to use the completion of 20 or more years of service as a normal retirement age for public safety employees.

Comments were also requested on whether there are other categories of governmental employees who have career spans similar to qualified public safety employees for whom a rule should be provided that is similar to the safe harbor for qualified public safety employees. Many commenters recommended a rule that would permit governmental plans to use the completion of a number of years of service as a normal retirement age for all employees, not just qualified public safety employees.

Notice 2012-29 also requested information on the overall retirement patterns of employees in government service to assist the Department of the Treasury and the IRS in determining the earliest age that is reasonably representative of the typical retirement ages for the industry in which these employees are employed. One commenter provided data on the retirement patterns and median normal retirement ages for participants in a state retirement system.

Notice 2012-29 also provided that the Department of the Treasury and the IRS intend to amend the 2007 NRA regulations to modify the effective date of the 2007 NRA regulations for governmental plans to annuity starting dates that occur in plan years beginning on or after the later of (1) January 1, 2015 or (2) the close of the first regular legislative session of the legislative body with the authority to amend the plan that begins on or after the date that is 3 months after the final regulations are published in the **Federal Register**.

Explanation of Provisions

I. Overview

These proposed regulations would provide guidance with respect to the applicability of the 2007 NRA regulations to governmental plans. These proposed regulations, when finalized, would provide guidance relating to the determination of whether the normal retirement age under a governmental plan satisfies the requirements of section 401(a) by amending the 2007 NRA regulations to provide additional rules for governmental plans. In addition, these proposed regulations would also include a minor change to the 2007 NRA regulations to reflect the addition of section 411(f), which provides a special rule for determining a permissible normal retirement age that applies only to certain defined benefit plans that are not governmental plans.

II. Use of Years of Service as a Component of the Pre-ERISA Vesting Rules

In response to Notice 2012-29, the Department of the Treasury and the IRS received a range of comments regarding the pre-ERISA vesting rules that apply to a governmental plan's normal retirement age. In particular, the Department of the Treasury and the IRS received many comments requesting rules that would permit governmental plans to define normal retirement age by reference to a period of service. Comments also focused on whether a governmental plan is required to include an explicit definition of normal retirement age.

As previously stated, a normal retirement age under a governmental plan must satisfy the pre-ERISA vesting rules. The Department of the Treasury and the IRS generally agree with those commenters who indicated that the pre-ERISA vesting rules applicable to normal retirement age may be read to permit a governmental plan to use a normal retirement age that reflects a period of service. Under pre-ERISA vesting rules, use of a period of service to determine normal retirement age under a governmental plan would be permissible if the period of service used is reasonable and uniformly applicable and the other pre-ERISA rules related to normal retirement age are satisfied. One of the pre-ERISA rules permits a governmental plan to specify a normal retirement age that is lower than age 65 if that age represents the age at which employees customarily retire in the industry.

Under the pre-ERISA rules related to normal retirement age, the terms of a governmental plan are not required to include an explicit definition of the term normal retirement age in order to satisfy section 401(a). However, in the absence of an explicit definition of normal retirement age, the terms of the plan must specify the earliest age at which a participant has the right to retire without the consent of the employer and to receive retirement benefits based upon the amount of the participant's service on the date of retirement at the full rate set forth in the plan (that is, without actuarial or similar reduction because of retirement before some later specified age). That age (the earliest age described in the preceding sentence) will be considered the plan's normal retirement age for purposes of any statutory or regulatory requirements based on a normal retirement age.

Consistent with Notice 2012-29, the proposed regulations would provide that a governmental plan that does not provide for the payment of in-service distributions before age 62 would not fail to satisfy § 1.401(a)-1(b)(1) under these proposed regulations merely because the pension plan has a normal retirement age that is earlier than otherwise permitted under the requirements of § 1.401(a)-1(b)(2) of the 2007 NRA regulations (as proposed to be amended by these proposed regulations). Instead, because section 411(a) through (d) does not apply, the earlier normal retirement age under such a plan is treated as the age as of which an unreduced early retirement benefit is payable for purposes of these regulations.

III. Normal Retirement Age Must Satisfy the Reasonably Representative Requirement

A. In General

These proposed regulations would apply the reasonably representative requirement in the 2007 NRA regulations to governmental plans. Thus, the normal retirement age under a governmental plan must be an age that is not earlier than the earliest age that is reasonably representative of the typical retirement age for the industry in which the covered workforce is employed.

B. General Safe Harbor

These proposed regulations would apply to governmental plans the safe harbor in the 2007 NRA regulations that a normal retirement age of at least age 62 is deemed to satisfy the reasonably representative requirement. Thus, a governmental plan satisfies this safe harbor if the normal retirement age under the plan is age 62 or if the normal retirement age is the later of age 62 or another specified date, such as the fifth anniversary of plan participation.

C. Safe Harbors for Governmental Plans

To address comments regarding the need for additional safe harbors for governmental plans, including safe harbors that reflect permissible periods of service, these proposed regulations would provide several additional alternative safe harbors that a governmental plan could satisfy. The safe harbors included in these proposed regulations were developed based upon feedback provided in comments received in response to Notices 2007-69 and 2012-29.

1. Age 60 and 5 Years of Service

Under these proposed regulations, a normal retirement age under a governmental plan that is the later of age 60 or the age at which the participant has been credited with at least 5 years of service would be deemed to satisfy the reasonably representative requirement.

2. Age 55 and 10 Years of Service

Similarly, a normal retirement age under a governmental plan that is the later of 55 or the age at which the participant has been credited with at least 10 years of service would be deemed to satisfy the reasonably representative requirement. Thus, for example, a normal retirement age under a governmental plan that is the later of age 55 or the age at which the participant has been credited with 12 years of service would satisfy this safe harbor.

3. Combined Age and Years of Service of 80 or More

A normal retirement age under a governmental plan that is the participant's age if the sum of the participant's age plus the number of years of service that have been credited to the participant under the plan equals 80 or more would also be deemed to satisfy the reasonably representative requirement. For example, a participant in a governmental plan who is age 55 and who has been credited with 25 years of service under the plan would satisfy this safe harbor.

4. Any Age With 25 years of Service (in Combination With a Safe Harbor That Includes an Age)

A governmental plan would also be permitted to combine any of the other safe harbors (except for the qualified public safety employee safe harbors) provided under the proposed regulations with 25 years of service, so that a participant's normal retirement age would be the participant's age when the number of years of service that have been credited to the participant under the plan equals 25 if that age is earlier than what the participant's normal retirement age would be under the other safe harbor(s). For example, a normal retirement age under a governmental plan would satisfy the reasonably representative requirement if the normal retirement age is the earlier of (1) the participant's age when the participant has been credited with 25 years of service under the plan and (2) the later of age 60 or the age when the participant has been credited with 5 years of service under the plan. Use of 25 years of service by a governmental plan for normal retirement age generally would not satisfy the pre-ERISA vesting require-

ment relating to normal retirement age, unless it is used in conjunction with an alternative normal retirement age that includes an age component and that otherwise satisfies the pre-ERISA rules. This is because the pre-ERISA vesting requirements allow for a service component only if that component does not unreasonably delay full vesting. For example, applying a 25 years of service requirement (without an alternative normal retirement age) to a newly-hired 63-year-old employee would not be reasonable because it would result in a normal retirement age of 88. See generally, Rev. Rul. 66-11.

D. Qualified Public Safety Employees

The proposed regulations include three safe harbors specifically for qualified public safety employees. The safe harbors were developed based upon feedback provided in comments received in response to Notices 2007-69 and 2012-29. Consistent with Notice 2012-29 and in response to comments, the proposed regulations would make clear that a governmental plan is permitted to use one or more of the safe harbors for qualified public safety employees to satisfy the reasonably representative requirement for those employees even if a different normal retirement age or ages is used under the plan for one or more other categories of participants who are not qualified public safety employees. The safe harbors for qualified public safety employees are not permitted to be used for these other categories of participants; a different normal retirement age (or ages) must be used for participants in a plan who are not qualified public safety employees.

As under the 2007 NRA regulations, the term *qualified public safety employee* would be defined by reference to section 72(t)(10)(B), under which a qualified public safety employee means any employee of a State or political subdivision of a State who provides police protection, firefighting services, or emergency medical services for any area within the jurisdiction of such State or political subdivision.[5] Defining qualified public safety employee by reference to section 72(t)(10)(B) has been retained because it is closely aligned with the categories of employees described in the Age Discrimination in Employment Act that an employer may refrain from hiring after a certain age.[6] Because qualified public safety employees typically commence plan participation at younger ages, the period of service required for full vesting at normal retirement age under each of the safe harbors for qualified public safety employees should be reasonable.

1. Age 50

The proposed regulations would modify the safe harbor for qualified public safety employees that was provided in the 2007 NRA regulations under which a normal retirement age of age 50 or later is deemed to satisfy the reasonably representative requirement and would expand on the guidance under consideration described in Notice 2012-29. The proposed regulations would make clear that a governmental plan is permitted to use the safe harbor (alone or together with one or both of the other safe harbors for qualified public safety employees described in this preamble) for one or more qualified public safety employees in a governmental plan without regard to any "substantially all" requirement (that is, without regard to whether substantially all of the participants in the plan or substantially all of the participants within a group of participants are qualified public safety employees).

2. Combined Age and Years of Service of 70 or More

The proposed regulations would add a safe harbor under which a normal retirement age for qualified public safety employees under a governmental plan that is the participant's age when the sum of the participant's age plus the number of years of service that have been credited to the participant under the plan equals 70 or more would be deemed to satisfy the reasonably representative requirement.

3. Any Age With 20 Years of Service

The proposed regulations would also add a safe harbor under which a normal retirement age for qualified public safety employees under a governmental plan that is the participant's age when the number of years of service that have been credited to the participant under the plan equals 20 or more would be deemed to satisfy the reasonably representative requirement. For example, a normal retirement age for qualified public safety employees under a plan that is 25 years of

---

[5] Section 72(t)(10)(B) was amended by section 2(a) of Defending Public Safety Employees' Retirement Act, Public Law 114-26 (129 Stat. 319) (2015)) and section 308 of Protecting Americans From Tax Hikes Act of 2015 (PATH Act), enacted as part of the Consolidated Appropriations Act, 2016, Public Law 114-113 (129 Stat. 2422), to include federal public safety employees as qualified public safety employees for purposes of the rules under section 72(t)(10). Thus, for distributions made after December 31, 2015, the term *qualified public safety employee* means any employee of a State or political subdivision of a State who provides police protection, firefighting services, or emergency medical services for any area within the jurisdiction of such State or political subdivision, or any Federal law

enforcement officer described in section 8331(20) or 8401(17) of title 5, United States Code, any Federal customs and border protection officer described in section 8331(31) or 8401(36) of such title, any Federal firefighter described in section 8331(21) or 8401(14) of such title, or any air traffic controller described in 8331(30) or 8401(35) of such title, any nuclear materials courier described in section 8331(27) or 8401(33) of such title, any member of the United States Capitol Police, any member of the Supreme Court Police, and any diplomatic security special agent of the Department of State.

[6] See section 4(j) of the Age Discrimination in Employment Act, 29 U.S.C. 623(j).

service would satisfy this safe harbor. The Department of the Treasury and the IRS agree with the comments received in response to Notice 2012-29 that indicated that a safe harbor based solely on a period of service would be appropriate for qualified public safety employees because these employees typically have career spans that commence at a young age and continue over a limited period of years.

E. Multiple Normal Retirement Ages in a Governmental Plan

Commenters on Notice 2012-29 stated that it is a common practice for governmental plans to have a normal retirement age that is a combination of age and years of service. In light of these comments, some of the safe harbors proposed in these regulations contemplate a combination of age and years of service, such as, for example, the use of a normal retirement age that is the earlier of (1) the participant's age when the participant has been credited with 30 years of service under the plan or (2) the later of age 60 or the age when the participant has been credited with 5 years of service under the plan. A normal retirement age under a governmental plan that is consistent with the safe harbors in these proposed regulations would not fail to satisfy the pre-ERISA requirements, including the requirement that any period of service required for vesting at normal retirement age be uniformly applicable to all employees in a plan, merely because the plan uses such a normal retirement age.

Commenters to Notice 2012-29 also stated that governmental plans typically provide multiple normal retirement ages, often based on different benefit structures or classifications of employees in a single plan. These comments expressed concern that certain language in Notice 2012-29[7] could be read to indicate that a governmental plan could only have two normal retirement ages if one of the normal retirement ages covered qualified public safety employees and the other normal retirement age covered all of the other participants in the plan.

Use of one normal retirement age for one classification of employees (such as qualified public safety employees) and one or more other normal retirement ages for one or more different classifications of employees would not be inconsistent with these proposed regulations and generally would not be inconsistent with the applicable pre-ERISA requirements, including the requirement that any period of service required for full vesting at normal retirement age be uniformly applicable. Similarly, the use of one normal retirement age under a governmental plan for employees hired before a certain date and another normal retirement age under the plan for employees hired on or after that date generally would not fail to satisfy the applicable pre-ERISA requirements.

F. Other Normal Retirement Ages

The proposed regulations would provide that in the case of a normal retirement age under a governmental plan that fails to satisfy any of the governmental plan safe harbors, whether the normal retirement age satisfies the reasonably representative requirement would be based on all of the relevant facts and circumstances. Similar to the treatment of normal retirement ages between ages 55 and 62 under the 2007 NRA regulations, it is generally expected that a good faith determination of the typical retirement age for the industry in which the covered workforce is employed that is made by the employer will be given deference, assuming that the determination is reasonable under the facts and circumstances and that the normal retirement age is otherwise consistent with the pre-ERISA vesting requirements.

Proposed Effective Date

These regulations are proposed to be effective for employees hired during plan years beginning on or after the later of (1) January 1, 2017 or (2) the close of the first regular legislative session of the legislative body with the authority to amend the plan that begins on or after the date that is 3 months after the final regulations are published in the **Federal Register**. Governmental plan sponsors may rely on these proposed regulations for periods preceding the effective date, pending the issuance of final regulations. If and to the extent the final regulations are more restrictive than the rules in these proposed regulations, those provisions of the final regulations will be applied without retroactive effect.

Statement of Availability for IRS Documents

For copies of recently issued Revenue Procedures, Revenue Rulings, Notices, and other guidance published in the Internal Revenue Bulletin or Cumulative Bulletin, please visit the IRS Web site at *http://*
www.irs.gov or the Superintendent of Documents, U.S. Government Publishing Office, Washington, DC 20402.

Special Analyses

Certain IRS regulations, including this one, are exempt from the requirements of Executive Order 12866, as supplemented and reaffirmed by Executive Order 13563. Therefore, a regulatory assessment is not required. It has also been determined that 5 U.S.C. 533(b) of the Administrative Procedure Act (5 U.S.C. chapter 5) does not apply to these regulations. In addition, because no collection of information is imposed on small entities, the provisions of the Regulatory Flexibility Act (5 U.S.C. chapter 6) do not apply and a Regulatory Flexibility Analysis is not required. Pursuant to section 7805(f) of the Internal Revenue Code, these regulations have been submitted to the Office of Chief Counsel for Advocacy of the Small Business Administration for comments on its impact on small business.

Comments and Requests for Public Hearing

Before these proposed regulations are adopted as final regulations, consideration will be given to any comments that are submitted timely to the IRS as prescribed in this preamble under the **ADDRESSES** heading. All comments are available at *www.regulations.gov* or upon request. A public hearing will be scheduled if requested in writing by any person who timely submits written comments. If a public hearing is scheduled, notice of the date, time, and place of the public hearing will be published in the **Federal Register**.

Drafting Information

The principal authors of these regulations are Sarah R. Bolen and Pamela R. Kinard, Office of Associate Chief Counsel (Tax Exempt and Government Entities). However, other personnel from the Department of the Treasury and the IRS participated in the development of these regulations.

List of Subjects in 26 CFR Part 1

Income taxes, Reporting and recordkeeping requirements.

Proposed Amendments to the Regulations

Accordingly, 26 CFR part 1 is proposed to be amended as follows:

PART 1—INCOME TAXES

■ **Paragraph 1.** The authority citation for part 1 continues to read in part as follows:

Authority: 26 U.S.C. 7805 * * *

■ **Par. 2.** Section 1.401(a)-1 is amended by:

■ 1. Revising paragraph (b)(2)(v).

■ 2. Adding paragraph (b)(2)(vi).

■ 3. Revising the heading and the second sentence of paragraph (b)(4).

The revisions read as follows:

§ 1.401(a)-1 Post-ERISA qualified plans and qualified trusts; in general.

* * * * *

(b) * * *

(2) * * *

(v) *Rules of application for governmental plans*—(A) *In general.* In the case of a governmental plan (within the meaning of section 414(d)) that provides for distributions before retirement, the general rule described in paragraph (b)(2)(i) of this section may be satisfied in accordance with paragraph (b)(2)(ii) of this section or this paragraph (b)(2)(v). In the case of a governmental plan that does not provide for distributions before retirement, the plan's normal retirement age is not required to comply with the general rule described in paragraph (b)(2)(i) of this section or this paragraph (b)(2)(v).

(B) *Age 60 and 5 years of service safe harbor.* A normal retirement age under a governmental plan that is the later of age 60 or the age at which the participant has been credited with at least 5 years of service under the plan is deemed to be not earlier than the earliest age that is reasonably representative of the typical retirement age for the industry in which the covered workforce is employed.

---

[7] Notice 2012-29 provided that, under an anticipated amendment to the 2007 NRA regulations, a governmental plan would be permitted to satisfy the reasonably representative requirement using a normal retirement age as low as 50 for a group substantially all of whom are qualified public safety employees and a later normal retirement age that otherwise satisfies the 2007 NRA requirements for all other participants.

(C) *Age 55 and 10 years of service safe harbor.* A normal retirement age under a governmental plan that is the later of age 55 or the age at which the participant has been credited with at least 10 years of service under the plan is deemed to be not earlier than the earliest age that is reasonably representative of the typical retirement age for the industry in which the covered workforce is employed.

(D) *Sum of 80 safe harbor.* A normal retirement age under a governmental plan that is the participant's age at which the sum of the participant's age plus the number of years of service that have been credited to the participant under the plan equals 80 or more is deemed to be not earlier than the earliest age that is reasonably representative of the typical retirement age for the industry in which the covered workforce is employed. For example, a normal retirement age under a governmental plan that is age 55 for a participant who has been credited with 25 years of service would satisfy the rule described in this paragraph.

(E) *Service-based combination safe harbor.* A normal retirement age under a governmental plan that is the earlier of the participant's age at which the participant has been credited with at least 25 years of service under the plan and an age that satisfies any other safe harbor provided under paragraphs (b)(2)(v)(B) through (D) of this section is deemed to be not earlier than the earliest age that is reasonably representative of the typical retirement age for the industry in which the covered workforce is employed. For example, a normal retirement age under a governmental plan that is the earlier of the participant's age at which the participant has been credited with 25 years of service under the plan and the later of age 60 or the age at which the participant has been credited with 5 years of service under the plan would satisfy this safe harbor.

(F) *Age 50 safe harbor for qualified public safety employees.* A normal retirement age under a governmental plan that is age 50 or later is deemed to be not earlier than the earliest age that is reasonably representative of the typical retirement age for the industry in which the covered workforce is employed if the participants to which this normal retirement age applies are qualified public safety employees (within the meaning of section 72(t)(10)(B)).

(G) *Sum of 70 safe harbor for qualified public safety employees.* A normal retirement age under a governmental plan that is the participant's age at which the sum of the participant's age plus the number of years of service that have been credited to the participant under the plan equals 70 or more, is deemed to be not earlier than the earliest age that is reasonably representative of the typical retirement age for the industry in which the covered workforce is employed if the participants to which this normal retirement age applies are qualified public safety employees (within the meaning of section 72(t)(10)(B)).

(H) *Service-based safe harbor for qualified public safety employees.* A normal retirement age under a governmental plan that is the age at which the participant has been credited with at least 20 years of service under the plan is deemed to be not earlier than the earliest age that is reasonably representative of the typical retirement age for the industry in which the covered workforce is employed if the participants to which this normal retirement age applies are qualified public safety employees (within the meaning of section 72(t)(10)(B)). For example, a normal retirement age that covers only qualified public safety employees and that is an employee's age when the employee has been credited with 25 years of service under a governmental plan would satisfy this safe harbor.

(I) *Reserved.*

(J) *Other normal retirement ages.* In the case of a normal retirement age under a governmental plan that fails to satisfy any safe harbor described in paragraph (b)(2)(ii) of this section or this paragraph (b)(2)(v), whether the age is not earlier than the earliest age that is reasonably representative of the typical retirement age for the industry in which the covered workforce is employed is based on all of the relevant facts and circumstances.

(vi) *Special normal retirement age rule for certain plans.* See section 411(f), which provides a special rule for determining a permissible normal retirement age under certain defined benefit plans.

* * * * *

(4) *Effective/applicability date.* * * * In the case of a governmental plan (as defined in section 414(d)), the rules in paragraph (b)(2)(v) of this section are effective for employees hired during plan years beginning on or after the later of: January 1, 2017; or the close of the first regular legislative session of the legislative body with the authority to amend the plan that begins on or after the date that is 3 months after the final regulations are published in the **Federal Register**. However, a governmental plan sponsor may elect to apply the rules of paragraph (b)(2)(v) of this section to earlier periods. * * *

John M. Dalrymple,

Deputy Commissioner for Services and Enforcement.

[FR Doc. 2016-01639 Filed 1-26-16; 8:45 am]

BILLING CODE 4830-01-P

¶ 20,264H

IRS: Nondiscrimination rules: Defined benefit plans: Defined benefit replacement allocations.—The IRS has issued proposed regulations that would add special rules that allow closed defined benefit plans to satisfy the nondiscrimination rules in additional situations. These special rules are based on the existing rules for defined benefit replacement allocations (DBRAs), as modified, which may be disregarded when determining whether a DC plan has broadly available allocation rates. Under the proposed regulations, the eligibility conditions set forth in the modified DBRA rules provide a framework for the eligibility conditions for the snapshot rule related to closed plans in a defined benefit/defined contribution (DB/DC) plan. The DBRA rules are also used as a basis for the special testing rule for benefits, rights, and features provided to a grandfathered group of employees. The above rules are proposed to apply to plan years beginning after the final rules are published, but may be relied upon to satisfy the nondiscrimination requirements of Code Sec. 401(a)(4) for plan years beginning on or after January 1, 2014, and until the corresponding final regulations become applicable.

The proposed regulations also provide a special rule for closed plans and similar arrangements that would ease the rules under which any DB/DC plan can satisfy the nondiscrimination in amount requirement on the basis of benefits. These changes are intended to ease the ongoing maintenance of a defined benefit plan that provides coverage to a group of employees that is determined using a reasonable business classification. These rules apply only after the proposed regulations are finalized, and cannot be relied upon before then.

The proposed regulation was published in the Federal Register on January 29, 2016 (81 FR 4976). The IRS has announced its intention to withdraw Proposed Reg. §1.401(a)(4)-2(c) and Proposed Reg. §1.401(a)(4)-3(c), which concern benefit formulas for individual employees or groups without a reasonable business purpose, in Announcement 2016-16, I.R.B. 2016-18, May 2, 2016.

[4830-01-p]

DEPARTMENT OF THE TREASURY

Internal Revenue Service

26 CFR Part 1

[REG-125761-14]

RIN 1545-BM58

Nondiscrimination Relief for Closed Defined Benefit Pension Plans and Additional Changes to the Retirement Plan Nondiscrimination Requirements

AGENCY: Internal Revenue Service (IRS), Treasury.

ACTION: Notice of proposed rulemaking and notice of public hearing.

SUMMARY: This document contains proposed regulations that modify the nondiscrimination requirements applicable to certain retirement plans that provide additional benefits to a grandfathered group of employees following certain changes in the coverage of a defined benefit plan or a defined benefit plan formula. The proposed regulations also make certain other changes to the nondiscrimination rules that are not limited to these plans. These regulations would affect participants in, beneficiaries of, employers maintaining, and administrators of tax-qualified retirement plans.

DATES: Written or electronic comments and must be received by April 28, 2016. Outlines of topics to be discussed at the public hearing scheduled for May 19, 2016 at 10 a.m., must be received by April 28, 2016.

ADDRESSES: Send submissions to: CC:PA:LPD:PR (REG-125761-14), room 5203, Internal Revenue Service, PO Box 7604, Ben Franklin Station, Washington D.C. 20044. Submissions may be hand-delivered Monday through Friday between the hours of 8 a.m. and 4 p.m. to: CC:PA:LPD:PR (REG-125761-14), Courier's Desk, Internal Revenue Service, 1111 Constitution Avenue, N.W., Washington, D.C., or sent electronically via the Federal eRulemaking Portal at *http:// www.regulations.gov* (IRS REG-125761-14).

FOR FURTHER INFORMATION CONTACT: Concerning the regulations, Kelly C. Scanlon and Linda S. F. Marshall at (202) 317-6700; concerning submissions of comments, the hearing, and/or being placed on the building access list to attend the hearing, Oluwafunmilayo (Funmi) Taylor at (202) 317-6901 (not toll-free numbers).

SUPPLEMENTARY INFORMATION:

Background

Section 401(a)(4) provides generally that a plan is a qualified plan only if the contributions or benefits provided under the plan do not discriminate in favor of highly compensated employees. In 1991, the Treasury Department and the IRS issued comprehensive regulations under section 401(a)(4) (TD 8360, 56 FR 47524) setting forth several alternative methods for testing compliance with this statutory requirement. In 1993, the Treasury Department and the IRS made significant amendments to those regulations (TD 8485, 58 FR 46773).

Under the section 401(a)(4) regulations, a plan is permitted to demonstrate that either the contributions or the benefits provided under the plan are nondiscriminatory in amount, regardless of whether the plan is a defined benefit or defined contribution plan. See § 1.401(a)(4)-1(b)(2). In order to test a defined contribution plan on the basis of benefits, the amounts allocated to employees under the plan must be converted to equivalent benefits. This conversion is done using an interest rate between 7.5% and 8.5%.[1] In addition, for purposes of section 401(a)(4), a defined benefit plan and a defined contribution plan are permitted to be aggregated and treated as a single plan pursuant to § 1.401(a)(4)-9, which refers to such an aggregated plan as a DB/DC plan.

After issuance of the final regulations, a new type of plan design developed. This type of plan is often referred to as a "new comparability" plan and is typically a defined contribution plan that provides higher allocation rates to an older and more highly compensated group of employees. This type of plan nonetheless satisfies the nondiscrimination requirements by testing the contributions on the basis of equivalent benefits because the conversion to equivalent benefits reflects assumed growth to normal retirement age and therefore results in relatively lower equivalent benefits for the highly compensated employees who are closer to normal retirement age. The Treasury Department and the IRS concluded that this type of plan was inconsistent with the intent behind the nondiscrimination regulations. Consequently, the Treasury Department and the IRS amended the section 401(a)(4) regulations in 2001 to require that a new comparability plan provide a higher minimum contribution to nonhighly compensated employees[2] in order for the plan to be eligible to demonstrate compliance with the nondiscrimination requirements of section 401(a)(4) on the basis of equivalent benefits (TD 8954, 66 FR 34535) (the "2001 amendments").

This higher minimum contribution requirement was directed at the new comparability plans. Other defined contribution plans that provide "broadly available allocation rates" or allocation rates that are "based on a gradual age or service schedule" are not subject to the higher minimum contribution requirement even if they demonstrate compliance with the nondiscrimination requirements of section 401(a)(4) on the basis of equivalent benefits.[3] In addition, under the 2001 amendments, defined benefit replacement allocations ("DBRAs") may be disregarded when determining whether a defined contribution plan has broadly available allocation rates. The 2001 amendments also prescribe rules regarding DB/DC plans that provide for benefits in a manner similar to new comparability plans. Under these rules (contained in § 1.401(a)(4)-9(b)(2)(v)), in order for a DB/DC plan to be eligible to demonstrate compliance with the section 401(a)(4) nondiscrimination requirements on the basis of equivalent benefits, it must satisfy a minimum aggregate allocation gateway unless the DB/DC plan either fits within the definition of "primarily defined benefit in character" or consists of "broadly available separate plans." This minimum aggregate allocation gateway requires a minimum allocation rate (or equivalent allocation rate) for each nonhighly compensated employee.

Since 2001, a number of employers have moved away from providing retirement benefits through traditional defined benefit plans. In many of these cases, employers have either significantly changed the type of benefit formula provided under the plan (such as in the case of a conversion to a cash balance plan), or have prohibited new employees from entering the plan entirely. The employers may then have allowed employees who had already begun participation in the defined benefit plan (or who are older or have been credited with longer service under the plan) to continue to earn pension benefits under the defined benefit plan while closing the plan or formula to all other employees. These defined benefit plans are sometimes referred to as "closed plans," and the employees who continue to earn pension benefits under the closed plan are often known as a "grandfathered group of employees." In situations in which new employees continue to earn benefits under the defined benefit plan, but are under a new formula, any formula that continues to apply to a grandfathered group of employees is sometimes referred to as a "closed formula."

Closed plans are required to meet the coverage rules under section 410(b) and the nondiscrimination rules under section 401(a)(4) (including a nondiscrimination requirement regarding the availability of benefits, rights, and features). Many closed plans, however, may eventually find it difficult to meet these requirements because the proportion of the grandfathered group of employees who are highly compensated employees compared to the employer's total workforce increases over time. This occurs because members of the grandfathered group of employees usually continue to receive pay raises (and so may become highly compensated employees), and new employees (who are generally nonhighly compensated employees) are not covered by the closed plan.

When a closed defined benefit plan can no longer meet the nondiscrimination requirements on a stand-alone basis because of the demographic changes previously described, it can demonstrate compliance with section 401(a)(4) by aggregating with the employer's defined contribution plan. In general, it is easier to meet the nondiscrimination requirements if the resulting DB/DC plan demonstrates compliance with section 401(a)(4) based on the benefits or equivalent benefits provided to the employees (rather than based on contributions).

On January 6, 2014, the Treasury Department and the IRS published Notice 2014-5, 2014-2 I.R.B. 276. Notice 2014-5 provided temporary nondiscrimination relief for certain closed plans. Specifically, under Notice 2014-5, if certain criteria are satisfied,[4] a plan sponsor is permitted to test a DB/DC plan that includes a closed plan that was closed before December 13, 2013, on a benefits basis for plan years beginning before January 1, 2016, without complying with the minimum aggregate allocation gateway, even if that would otherwise be required under the current regulations. Notice 2015-28, 2015-14 I.R.B. 848, extended that relief for an additional year by applying it to plan years beginning before 2017 provided that the conditions of Notice 2014-5 are satisfied.

Notice 2014-5 also requested comments on whether the section 401(a)(4) regulations should be amended to provide additional alternatives that would allow a DB/DC plan to satisfy the nondiscrimination in amount requirements on the basis of equivalent benefits, and whether certain other permanent changes should be made to the nondiscrimination regulations, such as modifications to the rules regarding nondiscriminatory benefits, rights, and features.[5] The comments received in response to Notice 2014-5 generally supported these types of changes. In addition, all of the commenters requested permanent changes to the nondiscrimination requirements in order to make it easier for closed plans to continue to satisfy the nondiscrimination requirements.

The Treasury Department and the IRS agree that permanent changes to the nondiscrimination rules should be made in order to

---

[1] See § 1.401(a)(4)-8(c)(2)(ii) and § 1.401(a)(4)-12 (definition of standard interest rate). This standard interest rate is used to determine assumed growth of a defined contribution plan account and to convert the projected account balance to an annuity at normal retirement age.

[2] This higher minimum contribution rate is required under § 1.401(a)(4)-8(b)(1)(i)(B)(3) and (b)(1)(vi)..

[3] See § 1.401(a)(4)-8(b)(1)(i)(B)(1) and (2), (b)(1)(iii), and (b)(1)(iv).

[4] Generally, in order to be eligible for the relief provided by Notice 2014-5, each defined benefit plan that is part of an aggregated DB/DC plan must have satisfied the requirements of section 401(a)(4) without using the minimum aggregate allocation gateway under

§ 1.401(a)(4)-9(b)(2)(v)(D). Thus, the defined benefit plan must have either been primarily defined benefit in character (within the meaning of § 1.401(a)(4)-9(b)(2)(v)(B)), consisted of broadly available separate plans (within the meaning of § 1.401(a)(4)-9(b)(2)(v)(C)), or satisfied the applicable nondiscrimination rules without being aggregated with a DC plan.

[5] Section 1.401(a)(4)-4 provides rules for determining whether the benefits, right, and features provided under a plan are made available in a nondiscriminatory manner. Under these rules, each benefit, right, or feature must satisfy the current availability requirement of § 1.401(a)(4)-4(b) (which requires testing of the group to which the benefit, right, or feature is currently available) and the effective availability requirement of § 1.401(a)(4)-4(c) (which requires that the group of employees to whom the benefit, right, or feature is effectively available must not substantially favor highly compensated employees).

help employers and plan sponsors preserve the retirement expectations of certain grandfathered groups of employees. These changes are meant to apply to situations in which the proportion of the grandfathered group of employees who are highly compensated employees compared to the employer's total workforce has increased due to ordinary demographic changes, as previously described in this preamble.

Explanation of Provisions

I. Overview

The proposed regulations modify a number of provisions in the existing regulations under section 401(a)(4) to address situations and plan designs, including closed plans and formulas, that were not contemplated in the development of the regulations and the 2001 amendments. While many of the changes in the proposed regulations provide nondiscrimination relief for certain closed plans and formulas, the proposed regulations also include other changes that are not limited to closed plans and formulas.

II. Rules related to closed plans and similar arrangements

The proposed regulations set forth special rules that allow closed plans and similar arrangements to satisfy the nondiscrimination rules in additional situations. These special rules are based on the existing rules for DBRAs, as modified to respond to concerns raised by stakeholders with respect to those existing rules.

Under the proposed regulations, the eligibility conditions set forth in the modified DBRA rules (described in section II.A of this portion of the preamble) provide a framework for the eligibility conditions for the snapshot rule related to closed plans in a DB/DC plan (described in section II.B of this portion of the preamble). The modified DBRA rules are also used as a basis for the special testing rule for benefits, rights, and features provided to a grandfathered group of employees (described in section II.C of this portion of the preamble). For example, the special testing rule for a benefit, right, or feature provided to a grandfathered group of employees under a defined contribution plan establishes nondiscrimination relief for matching contributions provided to a grandfathered group of employees who formerly participated in a defined benefit plan that is intended to be consistent with the nondiscrimination relief provided by the modified DBRA rules for nonelective contributions provided to such a grandfathered group of employees.

A. Modifications to the DBRA rules under § 1.401(a)(4)-8

The proposed regulations modify the rules applicable to DBRAs under § 1.401(a)(4)-8, which allow certain defined contribution plan allocations to be disregarded when determining whether a defined contribution plan has broadly available allocation rates. The rules applicable to DBRAs allow employers to provide, in a nondiscriminatory manner, certain allocations to replace defined benefit plan retirement benefits without having to satisfy the minimum aggregate allocation gateway. The modifications in the proposed regulations are intended to allow more allocations to fit within the DBRA rules. For example, under the existing regulations a DBRA must be reasonably designed to replace the benefits that would have been provided under the closed defined benefit plan. The proposed regulations provide greater flexibility in this respect and allow the allocations to be reasonably designed to replace some or all of the benefits that would have been provided under the closed plan, subject to a requirement that the allocations be provided in a consistent manner to all similarly situated employees.

The proposed regulations incorporate a modified version of the conditions for an allocation to be a DBRA that were reflected in Rev. Rul. 2001-30, 2001-2 C.B. 46. For example, under one of the conditions set forth in Rev. Rul. 2001-30, in order for an allocation to be a DBRA, the defined benefit plan's benefit formula for the group of employees who formerly benefitted under that plan must have generated equivalent normal allocation rates that increased from year to year as employees attained higher ages. The proposed regulations ease this restriction on the types of defined benefit plans with respect to which a DBRA can be provided by allowing a DBRA also to replace the benefit provided under a defined benefit plan with a benefit formula that generated equivalent normal allocation rates that increased from year to year as employees were credited with additional years of service (rather than only as the employees attained higher ages).

The existing regulation also requires that the group of employees who receive a DBRA must be a nondiscriminatory group of employees, and Rev. Rul. 2001-30 interprets this rule as requiring that the group of employees satisfy the minimum coverage requirements of section 410(b) (determined without regard to the average benefit percentage

test). The proposed regulations incorporate this interpretation, but limit its application so that the rule only applies for the first 5 years after the closure date. In addition, the proposed regulations incorporate the interpretation in Rev. Rul. 2001-30 regarding whether the defined benefit plan was an established nondiscriminatory defined benefit plan by requiring that the closed plan be in effect for 5 years before the closure date (with one year substituted for 5 years, as provided by Rev. Rul. 2001-30, in the case of a defined benefit plan maintained by a former employer) with no substantial change to the closed plan during that time (except for certain permitted amendments allowed by the proposed regulations).

In addition, the proposed regulations expand the list of permitted amendments to a closed plan that do not prevent allocations under a plan from being DBRAs. For example, the proposed regulations permit an amendment to a closed plan during the 5-year period before it was closed, provided that the amendment does not increase the accrued benefit or future accruals for any employee, does not expand coverage, and does not reduce the ratio-percentage under any applicable nondiscrimination test. In addition, under the proposed regulations, an amendment during this period could extend coverage to an acquired group of employees provided that all similarly situated employees within that group are treated in a consistent manner.

As under the existing regulations, the proposed regulations contain a general restriction on plan amendments relating to a DBRA; however, the proposed regulations expand the list of plan amendments that are excepted from this rule. The proposed regulations retain the exception from this restriction on plan amendments for an amendment that makes *de minimis* changes in the calculation of a DBRA and for an amendment that adds or removes a "greater-of" plan provision (under which a participant receives the greater of the otherwise applicable allocation and the DBRA). In addition, the proposed regulations provide an exception from this restriction for any plan amendment modifying a DBRA that does not reduce the ratio percentage under any applicable nondiscrimination test.

B. Closed plan rule added to the plan aggregation and restructuring rules under § 1.401(a)(4)-9

The proposed regulations add a new exception to the requirement that a DB/DC plan must satisfy the minimum aggregate allocation gateway once the other conditions under § 1.401(a)(4)-9 are not met (the "closed plan rule"). This closed plan rule, which applies to a DB/DC plan that includes a closed plan, provides an exception to the minimum aggregate allocation gateway that would otherwise apply, but only if the closed plan was in effect for 5 years before the closure date and no significant change was made to the closed plan during or since that time (except for certain permitted amendments).

The DB/DC plan may use this closed plan rule for a plan year that begins on or after the fifth anniversary of the closure date. To be eligible for the closed plan rule, during the 5-year period following the closure date, either the DB/DC plan must satisfy the nondiscrimination in amount requirement of section 401(a)(4) without using the minimum aggregate allocation gateway, or the closed plan must satisfy that requirement without aggregation with any defined contribution plan. This requirement is comparable to the requirement that the group of employees who receive DBRAs must be a group of employees who satisfy the minimum coverage requirements of section 410(b).

Under the proposed regulations, certain amendments to a closed defined benefit plan do not prevent the plan from using the closed plan rule. These plan amendments are intended to allow a plan sponsor of a closed plan to address changed circumstances. For example, under the proposed regulations, a plan amendment during the 5-year period ending on the closure date does not prevent the plan from later using the closed plan rule, provided that the plan amendment does not increase the accrued benefit or future accruals for any employee, does not expand coverage, and does not reduce the ratio percentage under any applicable nondiscrimination test. Similarly, an amendment to the closed plan is permitted after the closure date, provided that the amendment does not reduce the ratio percentage under any applicable nondiscrimination test. Thus, for example, under the proposed regulations, a plan sponsor may add nonhighly compensated employees to a coverage group after it is closed in order to satisfy the nondiscrimination rules. *De minimis* changes to the closed plan's benefit formula are also permitted under the proposed regulations.

C. Special testing rule for the nondiscriminatory availability of a benefit, right, or feature provided to a grandfathered group of employees under § 1.401(a)(4)-4

The proposed regulations establish a special nondiscrimination testing rule under § 1.401(a)(4)-4 that applies if a benefit, right, or feature is made available only to a grandfathered group of employees with respect to a closed plan. This special rule provides relief in certain circumstances from certain nondiscrimination testing for a benefit, right, or feature provided under the closed plan, or for a rate of matching contributions provided to a grandfathered group under a defined contribution plan.

If the eligibility conditions are satisfied, the special testing rule treats a benefit, right, or feature that is provided only to a grandfathered group of employees as satisfying the current and effective availability tests of § 1.401(a)(4)-4(b) and (c). The special testing rule applies to plan years beginning on or after the fifth anniversary of the closure date and applies on a plan-year by plan-year basis. To be eligible for the special testing rule, the benefit, right or feature must be currently available to a group of employees that satisfies the minimum coverage requirements of section 410(b) for the plan years that begin within 5 years after the closure date. Once the special testing rule applies to a benefit, right, or feature, the special testing rule continues to apply for purposes of that benefit, right, or feature indefinitely (unless a later amendment changes the eligibility for the benefit, right, or feature). If a plan amendment changes the eligibility for the benefit, right, or feature after the closure date, then the special testing rule will cease to apply (subject to certain specified exceptions).

If the benefit, right, or feature that is available solely to a grandfathered group of employees is provided under a defined benefit plan, then it must be provided under the closed plan (rather than a different defined benefit plan). This is because the purpose of the special rule is to accommodate a plan amendment under which the benefit formula has been changed, but the prior benefit formula has been preserved for a grandfathered group of employees and the benefit, right, or feature is made available only to the grandfathered group of employees who continue to accrue benefits under the prior benefit formula.[6] Accordingly, the special testing rule is available only if the amendment restricting the availability of the benefit, right, or feature also resulted in a significant change in the type of the defined benefit plan's formula. For example, a conversion to a cash balance plan would be a significant change in the type of benefit formula, so that the special testing rule would apply to facilitate preservation of any subsidized early retirement factors for the employees who continue to benefit under the prior benefit formula. By contrast, in the case of a benefit formula that determines benefits as a percentage of compensation, a change in that formula to reduce that percentage would not be considered a significant change in the type of benefit formula, even if the reduction is large.

The special testing rule for a benefit, right, or feature provided under the closed plan also requires that the benefit, right, or feature has been in effect without being amended for a 5-year period before the closure date (subject to a limited exception for acquired employees). This rule is designed to ensure that the special treatment is available only for a long-standing provision and cannot be used for a benefit, right, or feature that has not been provided long enough for participants to have established a reasonable expectation that it will continue. In addition, this rule prevents a plan sponsor from obtaining special treatment for a benefit, right, or feature added shortly before and in anticipation of the closure of the plan. The proposed regulations set forth a list of permitted plan amendments that do not result in the loss of this special testing rule that are generally comparable to the list of permitted amendments for other closed plan arrangements.

The special testing rule also applies to a rate of matching contributions under a defined contribution plan that meets certain requirements. In order to be eligible for this testing rule, the rate of matching contributions must be reasonably designed so that the matching contributions will replace some or all of the value of the benefit accruals that each employee in the grandfathered group of employees would have been provided under the closed plan in the absence of a closure amendment. In addition, the rate of matching contributions for the grandfathered group of employees must be provided in a consistent manner to all similarly situated employees.

III. Modification of testing options under § 1.401(a)(4)-9 for DB/DC plans, including DB/DC plans that do not include a closed plan

In addition to providing a special rule for closed plans and similar arrangements, the proposed regulations generally ease the rules under which any DB/DC plan can satisfy the nondiscrimination in amount requirement on the basis of benefits. These changes are intended to facilitate the ongoing maintenance of a defined benefit plan that provides coverage to a group of employees that is determined using a reasonable business classification.

The proposed regulations expand the ability to use the average of the equivalent allocation rates under the defined benefit plan for purposes of satisfying the minimum aggregate allocation gateway by permitting the averaging of allocation rates for nonhighly compensated employees under the defined contribution plan for this purpose. This modification is intended to better accommodate plan sponsors that have a defined contribution plan with service-or age-based allocation formulas. The Treasury Department and the IRS have determined that it is appropriate, in this context, to allow shorter-service nonhighly compensated employees to be provided less than the minimum aggregate allocation gateway rate, as long as longer-service nonhighly compensated employees are provided allocation rates that are sufficiently higher than the minimum aggregate allocation gateway rate. The Treasury Department and the IRS are considering whether any restrictions on this rule are appropriate so that the rule serves its intended purpose of facilitating formulas that provide higher allocation rates to longer-service nonhighly compensated employees, and invite comments on ways to permit appropriate flexibility while ensuring the provision is not used to circumvent the purpose of the nondiscrimination rules.

The proposed regulations also include a limitation on the averaging of rates that applies to both defined contribution and defined benefit plans in order to minimize the impact of outliers. In general, this special rule applies a cap under which any equivalent normal allocation rate or allocation rate in excess of 15% is treated as equal to 15%. However, this cap is raised to 25% for any allocation rate or equivalent normal allocation rate that results solely from a plan design providing allocation rates or generating equivalent normal allocation rates that are a function of age or service under which higher rates are provided to older or longer-service employees.

In addition, under the proposed regulations, the average of the matching contributions actually made for nonhighly compensated employees may be used to a limited extent (up to 3 percent of compensation) for purposes of determining whether each nonhighly compensated employee satisfies the minimum aggregate allocation gateway test. Thus, for example, if the minimum aggregate allocation gateway is 7% and the average of the matching contributions actually made for nonhighly compensated employees is 3%, then a non-elective contribution of 4% for each individual would be needed in order to satisfy the minimum aggregate allocation gateway under the proposed regulations. The regulations use the average matching contributions, rather than matching contributions allocated for each employee, in order to avoid diluting the incentive effect of an employer match.

The proposed regulations also provide a new alternative to the minimum aggregate allocation gateway. Under this alternative, a DB/DC plan is not required to satisfy the minimum aggregate allocation gateway if it can satisfy the nondiscrimination in amount requirement on the basis of equivalent benefits using an interest rate of 6%, rather than the current standard interest rate of between 7.5% and 8.5%.

IV. Benefit formulas for individual employees or groups without a reasonable business purpose; modifications to the amounts testing rules under § 1.401(a)(4)-2 and § 1.401(a)(4)-3

The proposed regulations also include changes to address certain arrangements that take advantage of the flexibility in the existing nondiscrimination rules[7] to provide a special benefit formula for selected employees without extending that formula to a classification of employees that is reasonable and is established under objective business criteria. A plan satisfies the minimum coverage requirements of section 410(b) if the plan's ratio percentage is 70% or higher or the plan satisfies the average benefit test. To satisfy the average benefit test, pursuant to § 1.410(b)-4, the group of employees must be determined using a classification that is reasonable and that is established under objective business criteria pursuant to § 1.410(b)-4(b) and must have a ratio percentage that is described in § 1.410(b)-4(c) (which includes safe harbor and unsafe harbor percentages). A classification of employees that is reasonable and is established under objective business criteria is referred to in this preamble as a "reasonable business classification." To the extent that a plan provides a special benefit formula and can still pass the nondiscrimination requirements, the plan sponsor can use a qualified retirement plan to provide benefits that would otherwise be provided under a nonqualified plan. These arrange-

---

[6] The existing regulations provide a special rule for current availability testing for a benefit, right, or feature that applies solely to benefits accrued before the amendment date. *See* § 1.401(a)(4)-4(d)(2).

[7] Under the existing regulations, the nondiscrimination requirements of section 401(a)(4) and the coverage rules of section 410(b) are coordinated. The general test under

the section 401(a)(4) regulations is applied by determining whether each rate group under the plan (that is, for each highly compensated employee, the group of employees with a benefit or contribution rate that is greater than or equal to the benefit or contribution rate for the highly compensated employee) satisfies section 410(b) as if it were a plan.

ments are sometimes referred to as qualified supplemental executive retirement plans (or QSERPs).

Under the general test in the existing regulations, if a plan satisfies the minimum coverage requirements of section 410(b) using the average benefit percentage test, then the rate group for each highly compensated employee is treated as satisfying the minimum coverage requirements if the ratio percentage for the rate group is equal to the midpoint between the safe harbor and the unsafe harbor percentages (or the ratio percentage for the plan as a whole, if less). This rule recognizes that the composition of a rate group may be unpredictable and so the rate group should not be subject to a reasonable business classification standard. However, that same consideration is not relevant if the group of employees to whom the allocation formula under a defined contribution plan (or benefit formula under a defined benefit plan) applies is not a reasonable business classification.

Accordingly, the proposed regulations limit the existing rule under which a rate group with respect to a highly compensated employee is treated as satisfying the average benefit percentage test to those situations in which the allocation formula (or benefit formula) that applies to the highly compensated employee also applies to a reasonable business classification. For example, if a benefit formula applies solely to a highly compensated employee who is identified by name, it does not apply to a reasonable business classification. See § 1.410(b)-4(b). In such a case, the proposed regulations would require that the rate group with respect to that individual satisfy the ratio percentage test.

Proposed Applicability Date

Except as described below, these regulations are proposed to be applicable to plan years beginning on or after the date of publication of the Treasury decision adopting these rules as final regulations in the **Federal Register**. Taxpayers are permitted to apply the provisions of these proposed regulations except for those described in section III of the Explanation of Provisions portion of the preamble for plan years beginning before this proposed applicability date, but not for plan years earlier than those beginning on or after January 1, 2014. Accordingly, the ability to rely on a provision of these proposed regulations for periods prior to the proposed applicability date for these regulations applies to the disregard of certain defined benefit replacement allocations in cross-testing; the exception from the minimum aggregate allocation gateway with respect to certain closed plans; the special testing rule for benefits, rights, and features with respect to certain closed plans; and the rule applying the ratio percentage test to a rate group in the case of a benefit formula that does not apply to a reasonable business classification. Taxpayers may rely on these provisions (that is, the provisions that the proposed regulations would permit a taxpayer to apply before the proposed applicability date for these regulations) in order to satisfy the nondiscrimination requirements of section 401(a)(4) for plan years beginning on or after January 1, 2014, and until the corresponding final regulations become applicable.

Special Analyses

Certain IRS regulations, including this one, are exempt from the requirements of Executive Order 12866, as supplemented and reaffirmed by Executive Order 13563. Therefore, a regulatory impact assessment is not required. It also has been determined that section 553(b) of the Administrative Procedure Act (5 U.S.C. chapter 5) does not apply to these regulations, and because the regulation does not impose a collection of information on small entities, the Regulatory Flexibility Act (5 U.S.C. chapter 6) does not apply. Pursuant to section 7805(f) of the Internal Revenue Code, these regulations have been submitted to the Chief Counsel for Advocacy of the Small Business Administration for comment on their impact on small business.

Comments and Public Hearing

Before these proposed regulations are adopted as final regulations, consideration will be given to any comments that are submitted timely to the IRS as prescribed in this preamble under the "ADDRESSES" heading. Treasury and the IRS request comments on all aspects of the proposed rules, including the proposed applicability date. Treasury and the IRS also request comments on the following issues:

- Whether guidance needs to be developed for a plan that has more than one closure or closure amendment?

- Whether the rules regarding transition allocations and successor employers are still needed in light of the modifications to the DBRA rules? All comments will be available for public inspection and copying at www.regulations.gov or upon request.

A public hearing has been scheduled for May 19, 2016, beginning at 10 a.m. in the Auditorium, Internal Revenue Service, 1111 Constitution

Avenue, N.W., Washington D.C. Because of building security procedures, visitors must enter at the Constitution Avenue entrance. In addition, all visitors must present photo identification to enter the building. Due to access restrictions, visitors will not be admitted beyond the immediate entrance area more than 30 minutes before the hearing starts. For information about having your name placed on the building access list to attend the hearing, see the "FOR FURTHER INFORMATION CONTACT" section of this preamble.

The rules of 26 CFR 601.601(a)(3) apply to the hearing. Persons who wish to present oral comments at the hearing must submit written or electronic comments by April 28, 2016 and an outline of the topics to be discussed and the time to be devoted to each topic by April 28, 2016. A signed paper or electronic copy of the outline should be submitted as prescribed in this preamble under the "ADDRESSES" heading. A period of 10 minutes will be allotted to each person for making comments. An agenda showing the scheduling of the speakers will be prepared after the deadline for receiving outlines has passed. Copies of the agenda will be available free of charge at the hearing.

Statement of Availability for IRS Documents

For copies of recently issued Revenue Procedures, Revenue Rulings, notices, and other guidance published in the Internal Revenue Bulletin, please visit the IRS website at http://irs.gov.

Drafting Information

The principal authors of these proposed regulations are Kelly C. Scanlon and Linda S. F. Marshall, IRS Office of Associate Chief Counsel (Tax Exempt and Government Entities). However, other personnel from the IRS and the Department of Treasury participated in the development of the proposed regulations.

List of Subjects in 26 CFR Part 1

Income taxes, reporting and recordkeeping requirements.

Proposed Amendments to the Regulations

Accordingly, 26 CFR part 1 is proposed to be amended as follows:

PART 1—INCOME TAXES

Paragraph 1. The authority citation for part 1 continues to read in part as follows:

Authority: 26 U.S.C. 7805 * * *

Par. 2. Section 1.401(a)(4)-0 is amended by:

1. Adding paragraph (c)(5) to the entry for § 1.401(a)(4)-2.

2. Adding paragraph (d)(8) to the entry for § 1.401(a)(4)-4.

3. Adding paragraph (a)(4) to the entry for § 1.401(a)(4)-13.

The additions read as follows:

§ 1.401(a)(4)-0 Table of contents.

* * * * *

§ 1.401(a)(4)-2 Nondiscrimination in amount of employer contributions under a defined contribution plan.

* * * * *

(c) * * *

(5) Effective/applicability date.

* * * * *

§ 1.401(a)(4)-4 Nondiscriminatory availability of benefits, rights, and features

* * * * *

(d) * * *

(8) Special testing rule for grandfathered group of employees.

* * * * *

§ 1.401(a)(4)-13 Effective dates and fresh-start rules.

(a) * * *

(4) Effective/applicability date.

* * * * *

Par. 3. Section 1.401(a)(4)-2 is amended by:

1. Revising paragraph (c)(3)(ii).

2. Revising *Examples 4* and *5* in paragraph (c)(4).

3. Adding *Examples 6* and *7* to paragraph (c)(4).

4. Adding paragraph (c)(5).

The revisions and additions read as follows:

§ 1.401(a)(4)-2 Nondiscrimination in amount of employer contributions under a defined contribution plan.

* * * * *

(c) * * *

(3) * * *

(ii) *Application of nondiscriminatory classification test.* A rate group satisfies the nondiscriminatory classification test of § 1.410(b)-4 if and only if—

(A) The formula that is used to determine the allocation for the HCE with respect to whom the rate group is established applies to a group of employees that satisfies the reasonable classification requirement of § 1.410(b)-4(b); and

(B) The ratio percentage of the rate group is greater than or equal to the midpoint between the safe and unsafe harbor percentages applicable to the plan (or the ratio percentage of the plan, if that percentage is less).

* * * * *

(4) * * *

Example 4. (a) The facts are the same as in *Example 3*, except that N4 has an allocation rate of 8.0 percent. In addition, the formula that is used to determine the allocation for H2 is the same formula that is used to determine the allocation for all other employees in Plan D.

(b) There are two rate groups in Plan D. Rate group 1 consists of H1 and all those employees who have an allocation rate greater than or equal to H1's allocation rate (5.0 percent). Thus, rate group 1 consists of H1, H2 and N1 through N4. Rate group 2 consists of H2, and all those employees who have an allocation rate greater than or equal to H2's allocation rate (7.5 percent). Thus, rate group 2 consists of H2 and N4.

(c) Rate group 1 satisfies the ratio percentage test under § 1.410(b)-2(b)(2) because the ratio percentage of the rate group is 100 percent—that is, 100 percent (the percentage of all nonhighly compensated nonexcludable employees who are in the rate group) divided by 100 percent (the percentage of all highly compensated nonexcludable employees who are in the rate group).

(d) Rate group 2 does not satisfy the ratio percentage test of § 1.410(b)-2(b)(2) because the ratio percentage of the rate group is 50 percent—that is, 25 percent (the percentage of all nonhighly compensated nonexcludable employees who are in the rate group) divided by 50 percent (the percentage of all highly compensated nonexcludable employees who are in the rate group).

(e) However, under paragraph (c)(3)(ii) of this section rate group 2 satisfies the nondiscriminatory classification test of § 1.410(b)-4 because (i) the formula that is used to determine the allocation for H2 applies to a group of employees that satisfies the reasonable classification requirement of § 1.410(b)-4(b) (in this case, because it applies to all the employees) and (ii) the ratio percentage of the rate group (50 percent) is greater than the midpoint between the safe harbor and unsafe harbor percentages applicable to the plan under § 1.410(b)-4(c)(4) (40.5 percent).

(f) Under paragraph (c)(3)(iii) of this section, rate group 2 satisfies the average benefit percentage test if Plan D satisfies the average benefit percentage test. (The requirement that Plan D satisfy the average benefit percentage test applies even though Plan D satisfies the ratio percentage test and would ordinarily not need to run the average benefit percentage test.) If Plan D satisfies the average benefit percentage test, then rate group 2 satisfies section 410(b); thus, Plan D satisfies the general test in paragraph (c)(1) of this section because each rate group under the plan satisfies section 410(b).

Example 5. (a) Plan E satisfies section 410(b) by satisfying the nondiscriminatory classification test of § 1.410(b)-4 and the average benefit percentage test of § 1.410(b)-5 (without regard to § 1.410(b)-5(f). See § 1.410(b)-2(b)(3). Plan E uses the facts-and-circumstances requirements of § 1.410(b)-4(c)(3) to satisfy the nondiscriminatory classification test of § 1.410(b)-4. The safe and unsafe harbor percentages applicable to the plan under § 1.410(b)-4(c)(4) are 29 and 20 percent, respectively. Plan E has a ratio percentage of 22 percent. Rate group 1 under Plan E has a ratio percentage of 23 percent. The formula that is used to determine the allocation for the HCE with respect to whom rate group 1 was formed applies to all other employees

(b) Under paragraph (c)(3)(ii) of this section, rate group 1 satisfies the nondiscriminatory classification requirement of § 1.410(b)-4, because (i) the formula that is used to determine the allocation for the HCE with respect to whom the rate group was formed applies to a group of employees that satisfies the reasonable classification requirement of § 1.410(b)-4(b) (in this case, because it applies to all the employees) and (ii) the ratio percentage of the rate group (23 percent) is greater than the lesser of—

(1) The ratio percentage for the plan as a whole (22 percent); and

(2) The midpoint between the safe and unsafe harbor percentages (24.5 percent).

(c) Under paragraph (c)(3)(iii) of this section, the rate group satisfies section 410(b) because the plan satisfies the average benefit percentage test of § 1.410(b)-5.

Example 6. (a) Employer Z maintains a defined contribution plan, Plan F. Employer Z has six nonexcludable employees, all of whom benefit under Plan F. There is one HCE (H1) and five NHCEs (N1 through N5). There is one rate group under Plan F. The formula that is used to determine the allocation for H1 is the greater of $20,000 or 10% of compensation for the year. The formula that applies to determine the allocation for N1 through N5 is 10% of compensation.

(b) Under paragraph (c)(3)(ii) of this section, the rate group with respect to H1 does not satisfy the nondiscriminatory classification test under § 1.410(b)-4 because the formula that is used to determine the allocation for H1 (with respect to whom the rate group is established) only applies to H1. Therefore, the rate group will satisfy paragraph (c)(3) of this section only if the ratio percentage of the rate group is greater than or equal to 70 percent. This ratio percentage test applies even if H1's compensation is greater than $200,000. In such a case, the rate group will pass the ratio percentage test (and accordingly the plan will satisfy the general test of this paragraph (c)) because each employee receives an allocation of 10% of compensation and therefore the ratio percentage for the rate group is equal to 100%.

Example 7. The facts are the same as in *Example 6*, except that the classification of employees who are entitled to benefit under the formula that applies to H1 includes N1 and N2, who are identified by name. Under paragraph (c)(3)(ii) of this section, the rate group with respect to H1 does not satisfy the nondiscriminatory classification test under § 1.410(b)-4 because the classification of H1, N1 and N2 by name does not satisfy the reasonable classification requirement of § 1.410(b)-4(b). Therefore, the rate group with respect to H1 will satisfy paragraph (c)(3) of this section only if the ratio percentage of the rate group is greater than or equal to 70 percent.

(5) *Effective/applicability date.* See § 1.401(a)(4)-13(a)(4) for rules on the effective/applicability date of this paragraph (c).

Par. 4. In § 1.401(a)(4)-3, paragraph (c)(2) is revised to read as follows:

§ 1.401(a)(4)-3 Nondiscrimination in amount of employer-provided benefits under a defined benefit plan.

* * * * *

(c) * * *

(2) *Satisfaction of section 410(b) by a rate group.* For purposes of determining whether a rate group satisfies section 410(b), the rules of § 1.401(a)(4)-2(c)(3) apply except that § 1.401(a)(4)-2(c)(3)(ii)(A) is applied by substituting "benefit formula" for "formula that is used to determine the allocation." See paragraph (c)(4) of this section and § 1.401(a)(4)-2(c)(4), *Example 3* through *Example 6*, for examples of this rule. See § 1.401(a)(4)-13(a)(4) for rules on the effective/applicability date of this paragraph (c)(2).

* * * * *

Par. 5. In § 1.401(a)(4)-4, paragraph (d)(8) is added to read as follows:

§ 1.401(a)(4)-4 Nondiscriminatory availability of benefits, rights, and features.

* * * * *

(d) * * *

(8) *Special testing rule for grandfathered group of employees*—(i) *General rule.* For a plan year that begins on or after the fifth anniversary of the closure date with respect to a closed defined benefit plan, a benefit, right, or feature under a defined benefit or defined contribution plan that is available only to a grandfathered group of employees with respect to the closed defined benefit plan is treated as satisfying paragraphs (b) and (c) of this section for the plan year, provided that—

(A) No plan amendment that affects the availability of the benefit, right, or feature (other than the closure amendment) has an applicable amendment date (within the meaning of §1.411(d)-3(g)(4)) that is within the period that begins on the closure date and ends on the last day of the plan year; and

(B) The additional requirements of paragraph (d)(8)(ii) or (iii) of this section, whichever is applicable, are satisfied.

(ii) *Additional requirements in the case of a benefit, right, or feature provided under a defined benefit plan.* If the benefit, right, or feature is provided under a defined benefit plan, then the following additional requirements apply—

(A) The defined benefit plan under which the benefit, right, or feature is provided is the closed defined benefit plan;

(B) No plan amendment that affects the availability of the benefit, right, or feature (other than the closure amendment) has an applicable amendment date that is within the 5-year period ending on the closure date; and

(C) The closure amendment that restricted the availability of the benefit, right, or feature, making it available only to the grandfathered group of employees, must also have provided for a significant change in the type of benefit formula under the plan (such as a change from a benefit formula that is not a statutory hybrid benefit formula to a lump sum-based benefit formula).

(iii) *Additional requirements in the case of a benefit, right, or feature provided under a defined contribution plan.* If the benefit, right, or feature is provided under a defined contribution plan, then the following additional requirements apply—

(A) The benefit, right, or feature must be a right to a rate of matching contributions provided under the defined contribution plan;

(B) The rate of matching contributions must be reasonably designed so that the matching contributions will replace some or all of the value of the benefit accruals that each employee in the grandfathered group of employees would have been provided under the closed defined benefit plan in the absence of a closure amendment (based on the terms of that plan and the section 415(b)(1)(A) dollar limit in effect immediately prior to the closure date);

(C) The closed defined benefit plan must satisfy the conditions set forth in §1.401(a)(4)-8(b)(1)(iii)(D)(*3*); and

(D) The rate of matching contributions must be provided in a consistent manner to all similarly situated employees.

(iv) *Certain amendments not taken into account.* For purposes of applying the rules under this paragraph (d)(8), the following plan amendments are not taken into account (and, in the case of an amendment described in paragraph (d)(8)(iv)(C) or (D) of this section, the rules of this paragraph (d)(8) are applied as if the benefit, right, or feature provided after the amendment were the benefit, right, or feature provided before the amendment):

(A) An amendment adopted during the 5-year period ending on the closure date that extends eligibility for the benefit, right, or feature to an acquired group of employees provided that all similarly situated employees within that group are treated in a consistent manner.

(B) An amendment adopted after the closure date that expands or restricts the eligibility for the benefit, right, or feature, provided that, as of the applicable amendment date, the ratio percentage of the group of employees eligible for the benefit, right, or feature (taking into account the plan amendment) is not less than the ratio percentage of the group of employees eligible for the benefit, right, or feature provided before the amendment.

(C) An amendment adopted after the closure date that results in a replacement of the benefit, right, or feature with another benefit, right, or feature that is available to the same group of employees as the original benefit, right, or feature, provided that the original benefit, right, or feature is of inherently equal or greater value (within the meaning of paragraph (d)(4)(i)(A) of this section) than the benefit, right, or feature that replaces it.

(D) An amendment adopted after the closure date that results in a replacement of the benefit, right, or feature with another benefit, right, or feature that is available to the same group of employees as the original benefit, right, or feature, provided that there is only a *de minimis* difference between the amount payable under the original benefit, right, or feature and the amount payable under the benefit, right, or feature that replaces it.

(E) An amendment that is permitted by guidance published by the Commissioner in the Internal Revenue Bulletin.

(v) *Examples.* The following examples illustrate the rules in this paragraph (d)(8):

Example 1—(i) *Pre-amendment defined benefit plan.* Employer A maintains Plan P, a defined benefit plan that provides for an annual benefit equal to 2% of an employee's average annual compensation multiplied by the employee's years of service. Plan P also provides for a subsidized early retirement benefit available to employees who retire between the ages of 55 and 65 with 20 years of service. Plan P was established in 2003. The plan year is a calendar year. For the 2015 plan year, Plan P satisfied the nondiscrimination requirements under sections 410(b) and 401(a)(4) without regard to the special rules under section 410(b)(6)(C) and without aggregation with any other plan.

(ii) *Plan conversion amendment.* On November 1, 2015, Employer A amends Plan P to cease future accruals under its benefit formula effective as of the close of the plan year ending December 31, 2015 and to provide future benefit accruals under a cash balance formula. The cash balance formula provides for pay credits equal to 5% of compensation and annual interest credits at an interest crediting rate of 6%. Early retirement benefits payable with respect to benefits accrued under the cash balance formula are determined as the actuarial equivalent of the hypothetical account balance, determined using reasonable actuarial assumptions that are specified in Plan P. Under the terms of the conversion amendment, an employee's benefit is equal to the employee's benefit under the prior benefit formula as of the close of the plan year ending December 31, 2015, plus the amount determined under the cash balance formula. However, any employee who had attained the age of 50 and had completed 15 years of service on or before December 31, 2015 is entitled to a plan benefit that is the greater of the benefit determined under the pre-amendment formula, or the benefit described in the prior sentence. Except for the closure amendment, there is no other plan amendment that affects the availability of Plan P's early retirement subsidy. No other significant change to Plan P's coverage or benefit formula is made with an applicable amendment date that is during the period beginning on January 1, 2011 and ending on December 31, 2015 (the 5-year period ending on the closure date).

(iii) *Applicability of special testing rule.* The plan conversion amendment is a closure amendment with a closure date of December 31, 2015. Plan P's subsidized early retirement benefit available solely to the grandfathered group of employees is a separate benefit, right, or feature that must be tested for current and effective availability under paragraphs (b) and (c) of this section. For a plan year that begins on or after January 1, 2021, Plan P's subsidized early retirement benefit is eligible for the relief provided by the special testing rule of this paragraph (d)(8) because all of the applicable requirements are satisfied. The requirement under paragraph (d)(8)(i)(A) of this section is satisfied because no other plan amendment that affects the availability of the subsidized early retirement benefit has an applicable amendment date that is on or after December 31, 2015. The additional requirements pertaining to a benefit, right, or feature provided under a defined benefit plan are also satisfied: the subsidized early retirement benefit is provided under a closed defined benefit plan as required by paragraph (d)(8)(ii)(A) of this section; no amendment that affected the availability of the subsidized early retirement benefit was made with an applicable amendment date during the 5-year period ending on the closure date as required by paragraph (d)(8)(ii)(B) of this section; and Plan P has undergone a significant change in benefit formula in connection with the closure amendment that resulted in a restriction on the availability of the subsidized early retirement benefit as required by paragraph (d)(8)(ii)(C) of this section.

Example 2—(i) *Closure of defined benefit plan.* The facts are the same as in *Example 1* of this paragraph (d)(8)(v), except that, instead of adopting a plan conversion amendment, Employer A amends Plan P to cease future accruals under the original benefit formula for all employees.

(ii) *Plan amendment to profit-sharing plan that provides enhanced rate of matching contributions.* Employer A has a profit-sharing plan that includes a qualified cash or deferred arrangement and matching contributions with respect to elective deferrals of up to 3% of compensation. On November 1, 2015, Employer A amends the plan to provide, effective January 1, 2016, for additional matching contributions of up to an additional 4% of compensation solely for employees who (1) were previously covered under the defined benefit plan, and (2) had attained the age of 50 and had 15 years of service on or before December 31, 2015. This enhanced rate of matching contributions is reasonably designed so that the matching contributions will replace some or all of the value of the benefit accruals that would have otherwise been provided to this grandfathered group of employees under Plan P. Employer A makes no other change to this enhanced rate of matching contribution after the enhanced rate is established.

(iii) *Applicability of special testing rule.* The plan amendment is a closure amendment with a closure date of December 31, 2015. The enhanced rate of matching contribution that is available solely to the grandfathered group of employees is a separate benefit, right, or feature that must be tested for current and effective availability under paragraphs (b) and (c) of this section. For a plan year that begins on or after January 1, 2021, Plan P's enhanced rate of matching contribution is eligible for the relief provided by the special testing rule of this paragraph (d)(8) because all applicable requirements are satisfied. The requirement under paragraph (d)(8)(i)(A) of this section is satisfied because no change was made to the enhanced rate of match with an applicable amendment date that is on or after December 31, 2015. The following applicable additional requirements are also satisfied: the benefit, right, or feature provided under the defined contribution plan is a rate of matching contribution as required by paragraph (d)(8)(iii)(A) of this section; the enhanced rate of matching contribution is reasonably designed so that the matching contributions will replace some of the value of the benefit accruals that each employee in the grandfathered group of employees would have otherwise been provided under Plan P immediately prior to the closure date as required by paragraph (d)(8)(iii)(B) of this section; and the rate of matching contributions is provided in a consistent manner to all similarly situated employees as required by paragraph (d)(8)(iii)(D) of this section.

(iv) *Applicability of § 1.401(a)(4)-8(b)(1)(iii)(D)(3).* In addition to the requirements described in paragraph (iii) of this *Example 2,* Plan P meets the conditions for a closed defined benefit plan specified in § 1.401(a)(4)-8(b)(1)(iii)(D)(3) as required by paragraph (d)(8)(iii)(C) of this section because Plan P's prior benefit formula generated equivalent normal allocation rates that increased as employees attained higher ages; Plan P satisfied the minimum coverage and nondiscrimination requirements under sections 410(b) and 401(a)(4) without regard to the special rules under section 410(b)(6)(C) and without aggregating with any other plan for the plan year preceding the closure date; and Plan P was in effect for the five-year period ending on the closure date and neither the benefit formula nor the coverage of the plan was significantly changed during this period.

(vi) *Effective/applicability dates.* The rules of this paragraph (d)(8) apply to plan years beginning on or after the date of publication of the Treasury decision adopting these rules as final in the **Federal Register.** Taxpayers may apply the rules of this paragraph (d)(8) for plan years beginning on or after January 1, 2014.

* * * * *

Par. 6. Section 1.401(a)(4)-8 is amended by:

1. Revising paragraphs (b)(1)(iii)(B) through (E).

2. Removing paragraph (b)(1)(iii)(F).

3. Adding paragraph (b)(1)(iv)(E).

The revisions and additions read as follows:

§ 1.401(a)(4)-8 Cross-testing.

* * * * *

(b) * * *

(1) * * *

(iii) * * *

(B) *Defined benefit replacement allocations disregarded.* In determining whether a plan has broadly available allocation rates for the plan year within the meaning of paragraph (b)(1)(iii)(A) of this section, the following rules in paragraphs (b)(1)(iii)(B)(1) and (2) of this section apply:

(1) If an employee receives a defined benefit replacement allocation (within the meaning of paragraph (b)(1)(iii)(D) of this section) for the plan year in addition to the employee's otherwise applicable allocation under the plan for the plan year, then the employee's allocation rate is determined without regard to the defined benefit replacement allocation.

(2) If an employee receives an allocation for the plan year that is the greater of the allocation for which the employee would otherwise be eligible and the defined benefit replacement allocation (within the meaning of paragraph (b)(1)(iii)(D) of this section), then the allocation for which the employee would otherwise be eligible is considered currently available to the employee, even if the employee's defined benefit replacement allocation is greater. See paragraph (b)(1)(iii)(C)(2) of this section for additional rules relating to "greater-of" plan provisions.

(C) *Plan provisions*—(1) *In general.* Plan provisions providing for defined benefit replacement allocations (within the meaning of paragraph (b)(1)(iii)(D) of this section) for the plan year must specify both the group of employees who are eligible for the defined benefit replacement allocations and the amount of the defined benefit replacement allocations.

(2) *"Greater-of" plan provisions.* An allocation does not fail to be a defined benefit replacement allocation within the meaning of paragraph (b)(1)(iii)(D) of this section merely because the plan provides that each employee who is eligible for a defined benefit replacement allocation receives the greater of that allocation and the allocation for which the employee would otherwise be eligible under the plan.

(3) *Limited plan amendments.* Except as provided in paragraph (b)(1)(iii)(D)(5) of this section, an allocation is not a defined benefit replacement allocation within the meaning of paragraph (b)(1)(iii)(D) of this section for the plan year if the plan provisions relating to the allocation are amended after the date those plan provisions are both adopted and effective.

(D) *Defined benefit replacement allocation*—(1) *In general.* A defined benefit replacement allocation is an allocation under a defined contribution plan provided only to a grandfathered group of employees with respect to a closed defined benefit plan. An allocation is treated as a defined benefit replacement allocation if—

(i) The allocation satisfies the conditions to be a replacement allocation with respect to a closed defined benefit plan in paragraph (b)(1)(iii)(D)(2) of this section;

(ii) The closed defined benefit plan satisfies the conditions in paragraph (b)(1)(iii)(D)(3) of this section; and

(iii) For each plan year that begins before the fifth anniversary of the closure date of the closed defined benefit plan, the grandfathered group of employees is a nondiscriminatory group of employees within the meaning of paragraph (b)(1)(iii)(D)(4) of this section.

(2) *Replacement allocation.* An allocation is a replacement allocation with respect to a closed defined benefit plan under this paragraph (b)(1)(iii)(D)(2) if—

(i) The allocation is designed so that it is reasonably expected to replace some or all of the value of the benefit accruals that each employee in the grandfathered group of employees would have been provided under the closed defined benefit plan in the absence of a closure amendment (based on the terms of that plan and the section 415(b)(1)(A) dollar limit in effect immediately prior to the closure date); and

(ii) The allocation is provided in a consistent manner to all similarly situated employees.

(3) *Closed defined benefit plan.* A closed defined benefit plan satisfies the conditions in this paragraph (b)(1)(iii)(D)(3) if—

(i) The closed defined benefit plan's benefit formula applicable to the grandfathered group of employees generated equivalent normal allocation rates that increased from year to year as employees attained higher ages or were credited with additional years of service;

(ii) The closed defined benefit plan satisfied the minimum coverage and nondiscrimination requirements under sections 410(b) and 401(a)(4) without regard to the special rules under section 410(b)(6)(C) and without aggregating with any other plan, for the plan year preceding the closure date; and

(iii) The closed defined benefit plan was in effect for the 5-year period ending on the closure date and neither the benefit formula nor the coverage of the plan was significantly changed by plan amendment with an effective date during this period.

(4) *Nondiscriminatory group of employees.* A group of employees is a nondiscriminatory group of employees for purposes of this paragraph (b)(1)(iii)(D)(4) if the group of employees satisfies section 410(b) for the plan year (without regard to § 1.410(b)-5).

(5) *Certain amendments not taken into account.* For purposes of determining whether the requirements of paragraphs (b)(1)(iii)(C)(3) and (b)(1)(iii)(D)(3) of this section are satisfied, the following plan amendments are not taken into account:

(i) An amendment to the closed defined benefit plan adopted during the 5-year period ending on the closure date, provided that the accrued benefit or future accruals for any employee are not increased, coverage is not expanded, and the amendment is not discriminatory within the meaning of paragraph (b)(1)(iii)(D)(6) of this section.

(ii) An amendment to the defined contribution plan under which the defined benefit replacement allocation is provided that makes *de* minimis changes in the calculation of that allocation (such as a change in the definition of compensation to include section 132(f) elective reductions).

(*iii*) An amendment to the defined contribution plan under which the defined benefit replacement allocation is provided that adds or removes a "greater-of" provision described under paragraph (b)(1)(iii)(C)(*2*) of this section.

(*iv*) An amendment to the defined contribution plan under which the defined benefit replacement allocation is provided that makes changes in the calculation of that allocation in a manner that is not discriminatory within the meaning of paragraph (b)(1)(iii)(D)(*6*) of this section.

(*v*) An amendment that guidance published by the Commissioner in the Internal Revenue Bulletin provides will not be taken into account.

(*6*) *Nondiscriminatory amendment—(i) General rule.* An amendment to a plan is not discriminatory if the ratio percentage of the plan is not decreased as a result of the amendment and, in the case of a plan that demonstrates compliance with the nondiscrimination in amount requirement of § 1.401(a)(4)-1(b)(2) using a method other than a safe harbor test under § 1.401(a)(4)-2(b), § 1.401(a)(4)-3(b), or paragraph (b)(3) or (c)(3) of this section, the ratio percentage for the rate group with respect to any HCE is not decreased as a result of the amendment.

(*ii*) *Timing of nondiscrimination testing.* In determining whether the ratio percentage of the plan or the rate group is decreased as a result of an amendment, an amendment that is not in effect for an entire plan year is treated as if it were in effect for the entire plan year. In the case of an amendment that has separate portions with separate effective dates, each portion of the amendment is treated as a separate amendment that must satisfy the requirements of paragraph (b)(1)(iii)(D)(*6*)(*i*) of this section for the plan year in which it takes effect.

(*7*) *Special rules for former employers and acquired employees.* The following special rules apply in the case of former employers and acquired employees:

(*i*) If the closed defined benefit plan was sponsored by a former employer and not by the employer, then the rules in paragraph (b)(1)(iii)(D)(*3*)(*ii*) of this section do not apply and one year is substituted for 5 years with respect to paragraph (b)(1)(iii)(D)(*3*)(*iii*) of this section;

(*ii*) An amendment adopted during the 5-year period ending on the closure date that extends the coverage or benefit formula of the closed defined benefit plan to an acquired group of employees may be applied (in addition to the amendments described in paragraph (b)(1)(iii)(D)(*5*) of this section) provided that all similarly situated employees within that group are treated in a consistent manner; and

(*iii*) If the employees of a former employer become the employees of the new employer as a result of a transaction that is a merger, acquisition, or similar event, then the transaction is treated as a closure amendment with respect to the former employer's plan as of the effective date of the acquisition.

(E) *Effective/applicability date.* See § 1.401(a)(4)-13(a)(4) for rules on the effective/applicability date of this section.

(iv) * * *

(E) *Defined benefit replacement allocation may be disregarded.* In determining whether a plan has a gradual age or service schedule for the plan year within the meaning of paragraph (b)(1)(iv)(A) of this section, if an employee receives a defined benefit replacement allocation (within the meaning of paragraph (b)(1)(iii)(D) of this section) for the plan year, then the plan's schedule is determined without regard to the defined benefit replacement allocation. For this purpose, the rules under paragraph (b)(1)(iii)(B) of this section apply. See § 1.401(a)(4)-13(a)(4) for rules on the effective/applicability date of this paragraph (b)(1)(iv)(E).

* * * * *

Par. 7. Section 1.401(a)(4)-9 is amended by:

1. Revising paragraphs (b)(2)(v)(A) and (b)(2)(v)(D)(*3*).

2. Adding paragraphs (b)(2)(v)(D)(*4*) and (*5*).

3. Redesignating paragraph (b)(2)(v)(F) as paragraph (b)(2)(v)(H).

4. Adding paragraphs (b)(2)(v)(F) and (b)(2)(v)(G). The revisions and additions read as follows:

§ 1.401(a)(4)-9 Plan aggregation and restructuring.

* * * * *

(b) * * *

(2) * * *

(*v*) *Eligibility for testing on a benefits basis—(A) General rule—(1) In general.* Unless, for the plan year, a DB/DC plan is primarily defined benefit in character (within the meaning of paragraph (b)(2)(v)(B) of this section) or consists of broadly available separate plans (within the meaning of paragraph (b)(2)(v)(C) of this section), in order to be permitted to demonstrate satisfaction of the nondiscrimination in amount requirement of § 1.401(a)(4)-1(b)(2) on the basis of benefits, the DB/DC plan must satisfy the minimum aggregate allocation gateway (as described in paragraph (b)(2)(v)(D) of this section) except as provided in paragraph (b)(2)(v)(A)(*2*) of this section.

(*2*) *Additional testing options.* A DB/DC plan that is not eligible to demonstrate satisfaction of the nondiscrimination in amount requirement of § 1.401(a)(4)-1(b)(2) on the basis of benefits under paragraph (b)(2)(v)(A)(*1*) of this section is permitted to demonstrate satisfaction of that requirement on the basis of benefits if the DB/DC plan satisfies either the closed plan rule of paragraph (b)(2)(v)(F) of this section or the lower interest rate rule of paragraph (b)(2)(v)(G) of this section.

(*3*) *Effective/applicability date.* See § 1.401(a)(4)-13(a)(4) for rules on the effective/applicability date of this paragraph (b)(2)(v)(A).

* * * * *

(D) * * *

(*3*) *Averaging of rates for NHCEs—(i) Defined benefit plan.* For purposes of this paragraph (b)(2)(v)(D), a plan is permitted to treat each NHCE who benefits under a defined benefit plan that is part of the DB/DC plan as having an equivalent normal allocation rate equal to the average of the equivalent normal allocation rates under the defined benefit plan for all NHCEs benefitting under that plan.

(*ii*) *Defined contribution plan.* For purposes of this paragraph (b)(2)(v)(D), a plan is permitted to treat each NHCE who benefits under a defined contribution plan that is part of the DB/DC plan as having an allocation rate equal to the average of the allocation rates under the defined contribution plan for all NHCEs benefitting under that plan.

(*iii*) *Limitations on the averaging of rates.* For purposes of applying paragraphs (b)(2)(v)(D)(3)(i) and (ii) of this section, any equivalent normal allocation rate or allocation rate in excess of 15% of plan year compensation is treated as being 15%. The preceding sentence is applied by substituting 25% for 15% each time it appears, but only if any allocation rate or equivalent normal allocation rate higher than 15% results solely from a plan design providing allocation rates or generating equivalent normal allocation rates that are a function of age or service under which higher rates are provided to older or longer-service employees.

(*4*) *Use of matching contributions.* For purposes of this paragraph (b)(2)(v)(D), if an NHCE is eligible for a matching contribution under a defined contribution plan that is part of the DB/DC plan, then the lesser of 3% and the average matching contribution percentage for the group of eligible NHCEs in that plan is permitted to be added to the allocation rate for that NHCE. For this purpose, the average matching contribution percentage for the group of eligible NHCEs in a plan is the actual contribution percentage (within the meaning of § 1.401(m)-5) for that group, determined without taking into account any employee contributions.

(*5*) *Effective/applicability date.* See § 1.401(a)(4)-13(a)(4) for rules on the effective/applicability date of this paragraph (b)(2)(v)(D).

* * * * *

(F) *Closed plan rule—(1) In general.* For a plan year that begins on or after the fifth anniversary of the closure date with respect to a closed defined benefit plan, a DB/DC plan that includes a closed defined benefit plan satisfies the closed plan rule of this paragraph (b)(2)(v)(F) for the plan year if—

(*i*) The closed defined benefit plan was in effect for the 5-year period ending on the closure date and neither the benefit formula nor the coverage of the plan was significantly changed by plan amendment (other than the closure amendment) with an effective date during the period that begins five years before the closure date and ends on the last day of the plan year; and

(*ii*) For each plan year that begins on or after the closure date and before the fifth anniversary of the closure date, one of the requirements in paragraph (b)(2)(v)(F)(*2*) of this section is satisfied.

(*2*) *Testing for 5 years post-closure.* A DB/DC plan meets the requirements of this paragraph (b)(2)(v)(F)(*2*) if—

(*i*) Each defined benefit plan that is part of the DB/DC plan satisfies the nondiscrimination in amount requirement of § 1.401(a)(4)-1(b)(2)

on the basis of benefits without aggregation with any defined contribution plan;

(*ii*) The DB/DC plan satisfies the nondiscrimination in amount requirement of § 1.401(a)(4)-1(b)(2) on the basis of contributions; or

(*iii*) The DB/DC plan satisfies the primarily defined benefit in character requirement of paragraph (b)(2)(v)(B) of this section, or the broadly available separate plans requirement of paragraph (b)(2)(v)(C) of this section.

(*3*) *Certain amendments not taken into account.* For purposes of this paragraph (b)(2)(v)(F), the following plan amendments are not taken into account:

(*i*) An amendment to the closed defined benefit plan adopted during the 5-year period ending on the closure date, provided that the accrued benefit or future accruals for any employee are not increased, coverage is not expanded, and the amendment is not discriminatory within the meaning of § 1.401(a)(4)-8(b)(1)(iii)(D)(*6*).

(*ii*) An amendment adopted during the 5-year period ending on the closure date that extends the benefit formula with respect to the closed defined benefit plan to an acquired group of employees provided that all similarly situated employees within that group are treated in a consistent manner.

(*iii*) An amendment to the closed defined benefit plan that is adopted after the closure date that is not discriminatory within the meaning of § 1.401(a)(4)-8(b)(1)(iii)(D)(*6*).

(*iv*) An amendment to the closed defined benefit plan that makes *de minimis* changes in the benefit formula

(*v*) An amendment that guidance published by the Commissioner in the Internal Revenue Bulletin provides will not be taken into account.

(G) *Lower interest rate rule.* A DB/DC plan satisfies the lower interest rate rule of this paragraph (b)(2)(v)(G) if the plan can demonstrate satisfaction of the nondiscrimination in amount requirement of § 1.401(a)(4)-1(b)(2) on the basis of benefits, provided that benefits are normalized using an interest rate of 6% rather than a standard interest rate.

* * * * *

Par. 8. In § 1.401(a)(4)-12, add definitions for *Closed defined benefit plan, Closure amendment, Closure date*, and *Grandfathered group of employees* in alphabetical order to read as follows:

§ 1.401(a)(4)-12 Definitions.

* * * * *

Closed defined benefit plan. Closed defined benefit plan means a defined benefit plan that has been amended to—

(1) Cease accruals under a benefit formula provided by the defined benefit plan for some or all employees whose benefits were previously determined under that benefit formula; or

(2) Limit participation in the defined benefit plan to a group of employees that consists of some or all of the plan participants who participated in the plan as of the closure date.

Closure amendment. A closure amendment is a plan amendment that results in a closed defined benefit plan.

Closure date. A closure date is the last day before accruals cease or participation is limited pursuant to the closure amendment.

* * * * *

Grandfathered group of employees. A grandfathered group of employees with respect to a closure amendment means the group of employees who, after the closure date, either continue accruals under the closed defined benefit plan's benefit formula or are entitled to an allocation formula under a defined contribution plan because those employees previously participated in the closed defined benefit plan.

* * * * *

Par. 9. In § 1.401(a)(4)-13, paragraph (a)(4) is added to read as follows:

§ 1.401(a)(4)-13 Effective dates and fresh-start rules.

(a) * * *

(4) *Effective/applicability date*—(i) *In general.* Except as otherwise provided in this paragraph (a)(4), the rules of § 1.401(a)(4)-2(c), § 1.401(a)(4)-3(c)(2), § 1.401(a)(4)-8(b), and § 1.401(a)(4)-9(b)(2)(v)(A) and (D) apply to plan years beginning on or after the date of publication of the Treasury decision adopting these rules as final in the **Federal Register**.

(ii) *Application for earlier plan years.* Except as provided in paragraph (a)(4)(iii) of this section, taxpayers may apply § 1.401(a)(4)-2(c), § 1.401(a)(4)-3(c)(2), § 1.401(a)(4)-8(b), or § 1.401(a)(4)-9(b)(2)(v)(A) and (D) for plan years beginning on or after January 1, 2014 and before the effective/applicability date specified under paragraph (a)(4)(i) of this section. Alternatively, for these plan years, taxpayers may apply § 1.401(a)(4)-2(c), § 1.401(a)(4)-3(c)(2), § 1.401(a)(4)-8(b), or § 1.401(a)(4)-9(b)(2)(v)(A) and (D) as contained in 26 CFR part 1 revised April 1, 2015.

(iii) *Certain rules not applicable until finalized.* The rules of § 1.401(a)(4)-9(b)(2)(v)(D)(3)(ii), (b)(2)(v)(D)(4), and (b)(2)(v)(G) are not permitted to be applied for plan years before the effective/applicability date specified in paragraph (a)(4)(i) of this section.

* * * * *

John Dalrymple,

Deputy Commissioner for Services and Enforcement.

¶ 20,264I

IRS: Multiemployer Pension Reform Act of 2014 (MPRA): Multiemployer defined benefit plans: Critical and declining status: Suspension of benefits: Employer withdrawal.—The IRS has issued proposed regulations under Code Sec. 432(e)(9), as added by the Multiemployer Pension Reform Act of 2014 (MPRA), Division O of the Consolidated and Further Continuing Appropriations Act (P.L. 113-235), relating to the ordering requirements for the suspension of benefits in certain multiemployer defined benefit plans in critical and declining status. The proposed regulations cover the order of the suspension of benefits under a plan that includes benefits that are directly attributable to a participant's service with any employer that has withdrawn, paid the full amount of its withdrawal liability and, pursuant to a collective bargaining agreement, assumed liability for providing benefits to participants and beneficiaries of the plan under a separate, single-employer plan sponsored by the employer, in an amount equal to any amount of benefits for such participants and beneficiaries reduced as a result of the financial status of the multiemployer plan. The regulations are proposed to be effective and apply with respect to suspensions for which an approval or denial is issued on or after final regulations are published in the Federal Register.

The proposed regulation was published in the Federal Register on February 11, 2016 (81 FR 7253). The regulation was finalized on May 5, 2016 (81 FR 27011). The preamble to the final regulations is at ¶ 23,323. The final regulation is at ¶ 13,151N-1.

¶ 20,264J

IRS: Employee Benefits Security Administration (EBSA): Group health plans: Expatriate health plans: Excepted benefits: Reporting and disclosure.—The IRS, EBSA, and Department of Health and Human Services have issued proposed regulations on the rules for expatriate health plans, expatriate health plan issuers, and qualified expatriates under the Expatriate Health Coverage Clarification Act of 2014 (EHCCA), which was enacted as Division M of the Consolidated and Further Continuing Appropriations Act, 2015 (P.L. 113-235). The proposed regulations also provide standards for travel insurance and supplemental health insurance coverage to be considered excepted benefits and require a notice to be furnished in connection with hospital indemnity and other fixed indemnity insurance in the group health insurance market for it to be considered excepted benefits. The regulations are proposed to be applicable for plan years (or, in the individual market, policy years) beginning on or after January 1, 2017. Issuers, employers, administrators, and individuals are permitted to rely on these proposed regulations pending the applicability date of final regulations.

The proposed regulations were published in the Federal Register on June 10, 2016 (81 FR 38019). The regulations concerning short-term, limited duration insurance, standards for travel insurance and supplemental health insurance coverage, and lifetime and annual limits were finalized on October 31, 2016 (81 FR 75316). The Departments intend to address hospital imdemnity or other fixed indemnity insurance, and expatriate health plans in future rulemaking. The preamble to the final regulations is at ¶ 23,328. The IRS final regulations are at ¶ 13,968Q-12, ¶ 13,968V-20NA, ¶ 13,968W-10, and ¶ 13,968Y-10. The EBSA final regulations are at ¶ 15,049J, ¶ 15,050R-50NA, ¶ 15,051B-1, and ¶ 15,051E-1.

FEDERAL REGISTER

Vol. 81 No. 112

Friday, June 10, 2016

Part VI Department of the Treasury

Internal Revenue Service

26 CFR Parts 1, 46, et al.

Department of Labor

Employee Benefits Security Administration

29 CFR Part 2590

Department of Health and Human Services

45 CFR Parts 144, 146, et al.

Expatriate Health Plans, Expatriate Health Plan Issuers, and Qualified Expatriates; Excepted Benefits; Lifetime and Annual Limits; and Short-Term, Limited-Duration Insurance; Proposed Rule

DEPARTMENT OF THE TREASURY

Internal Revenue Service

26 CFR Parts 1, 46, 54, 57, and 301

[REG-135702-15]

RIN 1545-BN44

DEPARTMENT OF LABOR

Employee Benefits Security Administration

29 CFR Part 2590

RIN 1210-AB75

DEPARTMENT OF HEALTH AND HUMAN SERVICES

45 CFR Parts 144, 146, 147, 148, and 158

[CMS-9932-P]

RIN 0938-AS93

Expatriate Health Plans, Expatriate Health Plan Issuers, and Qualified Expatriates; Excepted Benefits; Lifetime and Annual Limits; and Short-Term, Limited-Duration Insurance

AGENCY: Internal Revenue Service, Department of the Treasury; Employee Benefits Security Administration, Department of Labor; Centers for Medicare & Medicaid Services, Department of Health and Human Services.

ACTION: Proposed rule.

SUMMARY: This document contains proposed regulations on the rules for expatriate health plans, expatriate health plan issuers, and qualified expatriates under the Expatriate Health Coverage Clarification Act of 2014 (EHCCA). This document also includes proposed conforming amendments to certain regulations to implement the provisions of the EHCCA. Further, this document proposes standards for travel insurance and supplemental health insurance coverage to be considered excepted benefits and revisions to the definition of short-term, limited-duration insurance for purposes of the exclusion from the definition of individual health insurance coverage. These proposed regulations affect expatriates with health coverage under expatriate health plans and sponsors, issuers and administrators of expatriate health plans, individuals with and plan sponsors of travel insurance and supplemental health insurance coverage, and individuals with short-term, limited-duration insurance. In addition, this document proposes to amend a reference in the final regulations relating to prohibitions on lifetime and annual dollar limits and proposes to require that a notice be provided in connection with hospital indemnity and other fixed indemnity insurance in the group health insurance market for it to be considered excepted benefits.

DATES: Comments are due on or before August 9, 2016.

ADDRESSES: Comments, identified by "Expatriate Health Plans and other issues," may be submitted by one of the following methods:

Hand delivery or mail: Written comment submissions may be submitted to CC:PA:LPD:PR (REG-135702-15), Internal Revenue Service, P.O. Box 7604, Ben Franklin Station, Washington, DC 20044. Comment submissions may be hand-delivered Monday through Friday between the hours of 8 a.m. and 4 p.m. to CC:PA:LPD:PR (REG-135702-15).

Federal eRulemaking Portal: http://www.regulations.gov. Follow the instructions for submitting comments.

Comments received will be posted without change to *www.regulations.gov* and available for public inspection. Any comment that is submitted will be shared with the Department of Labor (DOL) and Department of Health and Human Services (HHS). Warning: Do not include any personally identifiable information (such as name, address, or other contact information) or confidential business information that you do not want publicly disclosed. All comments may be posted on the Internet and can be retrieved by most Internet search engines. No deletions, modifications, or redactions will be made to the comments received, as they are public records.

FOR FURTHER INFORMATION CONTACT: Concerning the proposed regulations, with respect to the treatment of expatriate health plan coverage as minimum essential coverage under section 5000A of the Internal Revenue Code, John Lovelace, at 202-317-7006; with respect to the provisions relating to the health insurance providers fee imposed by section 9010 of the Affordable Care Act, Rachel Smith, at 202-317-6855; with respect to the definition of expatriate health plans, expatriate health insurance issuers, and qualified expatriates, and the provisions relating to the market reforms (such as excepted benefits, and short-term, limited-duration coverage), R. Lisa Mojiri-Azad of the IRS Office of Chief Counsel, at 202-317-5500, Elizabeth Schumacher or Matthew Litton of the Department of Labor, at 202-693-8335, Jacob Ackerman of the Centers for Medicare & Medicaid Services, Department of Health and Human Services, at 301-492-4179. Concerning the submission of comments or to request a public hearing, Regina Johnson. (202) 317-6901 (not toll-free numbers).

Customer Service Information: Individuals interested in obtaining information from the Department of Labor concerning employment-based health coverage laws may call the EBSA Toll-Free Hotline, at 1-866-444-EBSA (3272) or visit the Department of Labor's Web site (*http://www.dol.gov/ebsa*). In addition, information from HHS on private health insurance for consumers can be found on the Centers for Medicare & Medicaid Services (CMS) Web site (*www.cms.gov/cciio*) and information on health reform can be found at *www.HealthCare.gov.*

SUPPLEMENTARY INFORMATION:

I. Background

This document contains proposed amendments to Department of the Treasury (Treasury Department) regulations at 26 CFR part 1 (Income taxes), 26 CFR part 46 (Excise taxes, Health care, Health insurance, Pensions, Reporting and recordkeeping requirements), 26 CFR part 54 (Pension and excise taxes), 26 CFR part 57 (Health insurance providers fee), and 26 CFR part 301 (relating to procedure and administration) to implement the rules for expatriate health plans, expatriate health plan issuers, and qualified expatriates under the Expatriate Health Coverage Clarification Act of 2014 (EHCCA), which was enacted as Division M of the Consolidated and Further Continuing Appropriations Act, 2015, Public Law 113-235 (128 Stat. 2130). This document also contains proposed amendments to DOL regulations at 29 CFR part 2590 and HHS regulations at 45 CFR part 147, which are substantively identical to the amendments to 26 CFR part 54.

The EHCCA generally provides that the requirements of the Affordable Care Act[1] (ACA) do not apply with respect to expatriate health plans, expatriate health insurance issuers for coverage under expatriate health plans, and employers in their capacity as plan sponsors of expatriate health plans, except that: (1) An expatriate health plan shall be treated as minimum essential coverage under section 5000A(f) of the Internal Revenue Code of 1986, as amended (the Code) and any other section of the Code that incorporates the definition of minimum

---

[1] The Patient Protection and Affordable Care Act, Public Law 111-148, was enacted on March 23, 2010, and the Health Care and Education Reconciliation Act, Public Law 111-152, was enacted on March 30, 2010. They are collectively known as the "Affordable Care Act."

essential coverage; (2) the employer shared responsibility provisions of section 4980H of the Code continue to apply; (3) the health care reporting provisions of sections 6055 and 6056 of the Code continue to apply but with certain modifications relating to the use of electronic media for required statements to enrollees; (4) the excise tax provisions of section 4980I of the Code continue to apply with respect to coverage of certain qualified expatriates who are assigned (rather than transferred) to work in the United States; and (5) the annual health insurance providers fee imposed by section 9010 of the ACA takes into account expatriate health insurance issuers for certain purposes for calendar years 2014 and 2015 only.

This document also contains proposed amendments to 26 CFR part 54, 29 CFR part 2590, and 45 CFR parts 146 and 148, which would specify conditions for travel insurance, supplemental health insurance coverage, and hospital indemnity and other fixed indemnity insurance to be considered excepted benefits. Excepted benefits are exempt from the requirements that generally apply under title XXVII of the Public Health Service Act (PHS Act), part 7 of the Employee Retirement Income Security Act of 1974, as amended (ERISA), and Chapter 100 of the Code. In addition, this document contains proposed amendments to (1) the definition of "short-term, limited-duration insurance," for purposes of the exclusion from the definition of "individual health insurance coverage" and (2) the definition of "essential health benefits," for purposes of the prohibition on annual and lifetime dollar limits in 26 CFR part 54, 29 CFR part 2590, and 45 CFR parts 144 and 147.

This document clarifies an exemption set forth in 45 CFR 153.400(a)(1)(iii) related to the transitional reinsurance program. Section 1341 of the Affordable Care Act provides for the establishment of a transitional reinsurance program in each State to help pay the cost of treating high-cost enrollees in the individual market in the 2014 through 2016 benefit years. Section 1341(b)(3)(B) of the ACA and 45 CFR 153.400(a)(1) require contributing entities to make reinsurance contributions for major medical coverage that is considered to be part of a commercial book of business.

This document also contains proposed conforming amendments to 45 CFR part 158 that address the separate medical loss ratio (MLR) reporting requirements for expatriate policies that are not expatriate health plans under the EHCCA.

General Statutory Background and Enactment of ACA

The Health Insurance Portability and Accountability Act of 1996 (HIPAA), Public Law 104-191 (110 Stat. 1936), added title XXVII of the PHS Act, part 7 of ERISA, and Chapter 100 of the Code, which impose portability and nondiscrimination rules with respect to health coverage. These provisions of the PHS Act, ERISA, and the Code were later augmented by other consumer protection laws, including the Mental Health Parity Act of 1996, the Paul Wellstone and Pete Domenici Mental Health Parity and Addiction Equity Act of 2008, the Newborns' and Mothers' Health Protection Act, the Women's Health and Cancer Rights Act, the Genetic Information Nondiscrimination Act of 2008, the Children's Health Insurance Program Reauthorization Act of 2009, Michelle's Law, and the ACA.

The ACA reorganizes, amends, and adds to the provisions of part A of title XXVII of the PHS Act relating to group health plans and health insurance issuers in the group and individual markets. For this purpose, the term "group health plan" includes both insured and self-insured group health plans.[2] The ACA added section 715(a)(1) of ERISA and section 9815(a)(1) of the Code to incorporate the provisions of part A of title XXVII of the PHS Act (generally, sections 2701 through 2728 of the PHS Act) into ERISA and the Code to make them applicable to group health plans and health insurance issuers providing health insurance coverage in connection with group health plans.

Expatriate Health Plans, Expatriate Health Plan Issuers and Qualified Expatriates

Prior to the enactment of the EHCCA, employers, issuers and covered individuals had expressed concerns about the application of the ACA market reform rules to expatriate health plans and whether coverage under expatriate health plans was minimum essential coverage for purposes of section 5000A of the Code. To address these concerns on an interim basis, on March 8, 2013, the Departments of Labor, HHS, and the Treasury (collectively, the Departments[3]) issued Affordable Care Act Implementation Frequently Asked Questions (FAQs) Part XIII, Q&A-1, providing relief from the ACA market reform requirements for certain expatriate group health insurance coverage.[4] For plan years ending on or before December 31, 2015, the FAQ provides that, with respect to expatriate health plans, the Departments will consider the requirements of subtitles A and C of title I of the ACA to be satisfied if the plan and issuer comply with the pre-ACA version of title XXVII of the PHS Act. For purposes of the relief, an expatriate health plan is an insured group health plan with respect to which enrollment is limited to primary insureds who reside outside of their home country for at least six months of the plan year and any covered dependents, and its associated group health insurance coverage. The FAQ also states that coverage provided under an expatriate group health plan is a form of minimum essential coverage under section 5000A of the Code. On January 9, 2014, the Departments issued Affordable Care Act Implementation FAQs Part XVIII, Q&A-6 and Q&A-7, which extended the relief of Affordable Care Act Implementation FAQs Part XIII, Q&A-1 for insured expatriate health plans to subtitle D of title I of the ACA and also provided that the relief from the requirements of subtitles A, C, and D of title I of the ACA would apply for plan years ending on or before December 31, 2016.[5]

Subsequently, the EHCCA was enacted on December 16, 2014. Section 3(a) of the EHCCA provides that the ACA generally does not apply to expatriate health plans, employers with respect to expatriate health plans but solely in their capacity as plan sponsors of these plans, and expatriate health insurance issuers with respect to coverage offered by such issuers under expatriate health plans. Under section 3(b) of the EHCCA, however, the ACA continues to apply to expatriate health plans with respect to the employer shared responsibility provisions of section 4980H of the Code, the reporting requirements of sections 6055 and 6056 of the Code, and the excise tax provisions of section 4980I of the Code. Section 3(b) of the EHCCA further provides that an expatriate health plan offered to primary enrollees described in sections 3(d)(3)(A) and (B) of the EHCCA shall be treated as an eligible employer sponsored plan under section 5000A(f)(2) of the Code, and that an expatriate health plan offered to primary enrollees described in section 3(d)(3)(C) of the EHCCA shall be treated as a plan in the individual market under section 5000A(f)(1)(C) of the Code. Section 3(c) of the EHCCA sets forth rules for expatriate health plans with respect to the annual health insurance providers fee imposed by section 9010 of the ACA.

Sections 4375 and 4376 of the Code impose the Patient-Centered Outcomes Research Trust Fund (PCORTF) fee only with respect to individuals residing in the United States. Final regulations regarding the PCORTF fee exempt any specified health insurance policy or applicable self-insured group health plan designed and issued specifically to cover employees who are working and residing outside the United States from the fee. The exclusion from the ACA for expatriate health plans, employers with respect to expatriate health plans but solely in their capacity as plan sponsors of these plans, and expatriate health insurance issuers with respect to coverage offered by such issuers under expatriate health plans would apply to the PCORTF fee to the extent an expatriate health plan was not already excluded from the fee.

Section 1341 of the ACA establishes a transitional reinsurance program to help stabilize premiums for non-grandfathered health insurance coverage in the individual health insurance market from 2014 through 2016. Section 1341(b)(3)(B) of the ACA and the implementing regulations at 45 CFR 153.400(a)(1) require health insurance issuers and certain self-insured group health plans ("contributing entities") to make reinsurance contributions for major medical coverage that is considered to be part of a commercial book of business. This language has been interpreted to exclude "expatriate health coverage."[6] As such, HHS regulation at 45 CFR 153.400(a)(1)(iii) provides that a contributing entity must make reinsurance contributions for lives covered by its self-insured group health plans and health insurance coverage, except to the extent that such plan or coverage is expatriate health coverage, as defined by the Secretary of HHS, or for the 2015 and 2016 benefit

---

[2] The term "group health plan" is used in title XXVII of the PHS Act, part 7 of ERISA, and Chapter 100 of the Code, and is distinct from the term "health plan," as used in other provisions of title I of the ACA. The term "health plan" does not include self-insured group health plans.

[3] Note, however, that in sections under headings listing only two of the three Departments, the term "Departments" generally refers only to the two Departments listed in the heading.

[4] Frequently Asked Questions about Affordable Care Act Implementation (Part XIII), available at *http://www.dol.gov/ebsa/pdf/faq-aca13.pdf* and *http://www.cms.gov/CCIIO/Resources/Fact-Sheets-andFAQs/ACA_implementation_faq13.html*.

[5] Frequently Asked Questions about Affordable Care Act Implementation (Part XVIII), available at *https://www.dol.gov/ebsa/faqs/faq-aca18.html* and *https://www.cms.gov/CCIIO/Resources/Fact-Sheets-and-FAQs/aca_implementation_faqs18.html*.

[6] See HHS Notice of Benefit and Payment Parameters for 2014 (78 FR 15410) (March 11, 2013) and HHS Notice of Benefit and Payment Parameters for 2016 (80 FR 10750) (February 27, 2015).

years only, is a self-insured group health plan with respect to which enrollment is limited to participants who reside outside of their home country for at least six months of the plan year and any covered dependents of such participants. As noted in the March 8, 2013 Affordable Care Act Implementation FAQs Part XIII, Q&A-1, the FAQ definition of "expatriate health plan" was extended to the definition of "expatriate health coverage" under 45 CFR 153.400(a)(1)(iii).

Section 3(a) of the EHCCA provides that the ACA generally does not apply to expatriate health plans, employers with respect to expatriate health plans but solely in their capacity as plan sponsors of expatriate health plans, and expatriate health insurance issuers with respect to coverage offered by such issuers under expatriate health plans. Accordingly, under the EHCCA, the transitional reinsurance program contribution obligation under section 1341 of the ACA does not apply to expatriate health plans.

Section 5000A of the Code, as added by section 1501 of the ACA, provides that, for each month, taxpayers must have minimum essential coverage, qualify for a health coverage exemption, or make an individual shared responsibility payment when filing a federal income tax return. Section 5000A(f)(1)(B) of the Code provides that minimum essential coverage includes coverage under an eligible employer-sponsored plan. Section 5000A(f)(2) of the Code and 26 CFR 1.5000A-2(c) provide that an eligible employer-sponsored plan means, with respect to an employee, group health insurance coverage that is a governmental plan or any other plan or coverage offered in the small or large group market within a State, or a self-insured group health plan. Under section 5000A(f)(1)(C) of the Code, minimum essential coverage includes coverage under a health plan offered in the individual market within a State.

Section 3(b)(1)(A) of the EHCCA provides that an expatriate health plan that is offered to primary enrollees who are qualified expatriates described in sections 3(d)(3)(A) and 3(d)(3)(B) of the EHCCA is treated as an eligible employer-sponsored plan within the meaning of section 5000A(f)(2) of the Code. Section 3(b)(1)(B) of the EHCCA provides that, in the case of an expatriate health plan that is offered to primary enrollees who are qualified expatriates described in section 3(d)(3)(C) of the EHCCA, the coverage is treated as a plan in the individual market within the meaning of section 5000A(f)(1)(C) of the Code, for purposes of sections 36B, 5000A and 6055 of the Code.

Under section 6055 of the Code, as added by section 1502 of the ACA, providers of minimum essential coverage must file an information return with the Internal Revenue Service (IRS) and furnish a written statement to covered individuals reporting the months that an individual had minimum essential coverage. Under section 6056 of the Code, as added by section 1514 of the ACA, an applicable large employer (as defined in section 4980H(c)(2) of the Code and 26 CFR 54.4980H-1(a)(4) and 54.4980H-2) must file an information return with the IRS and furnish a written statement to its full-time employees reporting details regarding the minimum essential coverage, if any, offered by the employer. Under both sections 6055 and 6056 of the Code, reporting entities may satisfy the requirement to furnish statements to covered individuals and employees, respectively, by electronic means only if the individual or employee affirmatively consents to receiving the statements electronically.[7]

Under section 4980H of the Code, as added by section 1513 of the ACA, an applicable large employer that does not offer minimum essential coverage to its full-time employees (and their dependents) or offers minimum essential coverage that does not meet the standards for affordability and minimum value will owe an assessable payment if a full-time employee is certified as having enrolled in a qualified health plan on an Exchange with respect to which a premium tax credit is allowed with respect to the employee.

Section 3(b)(2) of the EHCCA provides that the reporting requirements of sections 6055 and 6056 of the Code and the provisions of section 4980H of the Code relating to the employer shared responsibility provisions for applicable large employers continue to apply with respect to expatriate health plans and qualified expatriates. Section 3(b)(2) of the EHCCA provides a special rule for the use of electronic media for statements required under sections 6055 and 6056 of the Code. Specifically, the required statements may be provided to a primary insured for coverage under an expatriate health plan using electronic media unless the primary insured has explicitly refused to consent to receive the statement electronically.

Section 4980I of the Code, as added by section 9001 of the ACA, imposes an excise tax if the aggregate cost of applicable employer-sponsored coverage provided to an employee exceeds a statutory dollar limit. Section 3(b)(2) of the EHCCA provides that section 4980I of the Code continues to apply to applicable employer-sponsored coverage (as defined in section 4980I(d)(1) of the Code) of a qualified expatriate (as described in section 3(d)(3)(A)(i) of the EHCCA) who is assigned (rather than transferred) to work in the United States.

Section 9010 of the ACA imposes a fee on covered entities engaged in the business of providing health insurance for United States health risks. Section 3(c)(1) of the EHCCA excludes expatriate health plans from the health insurance providers fee imposed by section 9010 of the ACA by providing that, for calendar years after 2015, a qualified expatriate (and any spouse, dependent, or any other individual enrolled in the plan) enrolled in an expatriate health plan is not considered a United States health risk. Section 3(c)(2) of the EHCCA provides a special rule solely for purposes of determining the health insurance providers fee imposed by section 9010 of the ACA for the 2014 and 2015 fee years.

Section 162(m)(6) of the Code, as added by section 9014 of the ACA, in general, limits to $500,000 the allowable deduction for remuneration attributable to services performed by certain individuals for a covered health insurance provider. For taxable years beginning after December 31, 2012, section 162(m)(6)(C)(i) of the Code and 26 CFR 1.162-31(b)(4)(A) provide that a health insurance issuer is a covered health insurance provider if not less than 25 percent of the gross premiums that it receives from providing health insurance coverage during the taxable year are from minimum essential coverage. Section 3(a)(3) of the EHCCA provides that the provisions of the ACA (including section 162(m)(6) of the Code) do not apply to expatriate health insurance issuers with respect to coverage offered by such issuers under expatriate health plans.

Section 3(d)(2) of the EHCCA provides that an expatriate health plan means a group health plan, health insurance coverage offered in connection with a group health plan, or health insurance coverage offered to certain groups of similarly situated individuals, provided that the plan or coverage meets a number of specific requirements. Section 3(d)(2)(A) of the EHCCA provides that substantially all of the primary enrollees of an expatriate health plan must be qualified expatriates. For this purpose, primary enrollees do not include individuals who are not nationals of the United States and reside in the country of their citizenship. Section 3(d)(2)(B) of the EHCCA provides that substantially all of the benefits provided under a plan or coverage must be benefits that are not excepted benefits. Section 3(d)(2)(C) of the EHCCA provides that the plan or coverage must provide coverage for inpatient hospital services, outpatient facility services, physician services, and emergency services that are comparable to the emergency services coverage that was described in or offered under 5 U.S.C. 8903(1) for the 2009 plan year.[8] Also, coverage for these services must be provided in certain countries. For qualified expatriates described in section 3(d)(3)(A) of the EHCCA (category A) and qualified expatriates described in section 3(d)(3)(B) of the EHCCA (category B), coverage for these services must be provided in the country or countries where the individual is working, and such other country or countries as the Secretary of HHS, in consultation with the Secretary of the Treasury and the Secretary of Labor, may designate. For qualified expatriates who are members of a group of similarly situated individuals described in section 3(d)(3)(C) of the EHCCA (category C), the coverage must be provided in the country or countries that the Secretary of HHS, in consultation with the Secretary of the Treasury and the Secretary of Labor, may designate.

Section 3(d)(2)(D) of the EHCCA provides that a plan qualifies as an expatriate health plan under the EHCCA only if the plan sponsor reasonably believes that benefits under the plan satisfy a standard at least actuarially equivalent to the level provided for in section 36B(c)(2)(C)(ii) of the Code (that is, "minimum value"). Section 3(d)(2)(E) of the EHCCA provides that dependent coverage of children, if offered under the expatriate health plan, must continue to be available until the individual attains age 26 (unless the individual is the child of a child receiving dependent coverage). Section 3(d)(2)(G) of the EHCCA provides that an expatriate health plan must satisfy the provisions of title XXVII of the PHS Act, Chapter 100 of the Code, and part 7 of subtitle B of title I of ERISA, that would otherwise apply if the ACA had not been enacted. These provisions are sometimes referred to as the HIPAA portability and nondiscrimination requirements.

---

[7] See 26 CFR 1.6055-2(a)(2)(i) and 301.6056-2(a)(2)(i).

[8] These are emergency services comparable to emergency services offered under a government-wide comprehensive health plan under the Federal Employees Health Benefits (FEHB) program prior to the enactment of the ACA.

Section 3(d)(1) of the EHCCA provides that an expatriate health insurance issuer means a health insurance issuer that issues expatriate health plans. Section 3(d)(2)(F)(i) of the EHCCA provides that an expatriate health plan or coverage must be issued by an expatriate health plan issuer, or administered by an administrator, that together with any person in the issuer's or administrator's controlled group: (1) Maintains network provider agreements that provide for direct claims payments (directly or through third-party contracts), with health care providers in eight or more countries; (2) maintains call centers (directly or through third-party contracts) in three or more countries and accepts calls in eight or more languages; (3) processes at least $1 million in claims in foreign currency equivalents each year; (4) makes global evacuation/repatriation coverage available; (5) maintains legal and compliance resources in three or more countries; and (6) has licenses to sell insurance in more than two countries. In addition, section 3(d)(2)(F)(ii) of the EHCCA provides that the plan or coverage must offer reimbursement for items or services under such plan or coverage in the local currency in eight or more countries.

Section 3(d)(3) of the EHCCA describes three categories of qualified expatriates. A category A qualified expatriate, under section 3(d)(3)(A) of the EHCCA, is an individual whose skills, qualifications, job duties, or expertise has caused the individual's employer to transfer or assign the individual to the United States for a specific and temporary purpose or assignment tied to the individual's employment and who the plan sponsor has reasonably determined requires access to health insurance and other related services and support in multiple countries, and is offered other multinational benefits on a periodic basis (such as tax equalization, compensation for cross-border moving expenses, or compensation to enable the expatriate to return to the expatriate's home country). A category B qualified expatriate, under section 3(d)(3)(B) of the EHCCA, is a primary insured who is working outside the United States for at least 180 days during a consecutive 12-month period that overlaps with the plan year. A category C qualified expatriate, under section 3(d)(3)(C) of the EHCCA, is an individual who is a member of a group of similarly situated individuals that is formed for the purpose of traveling or relocating internationally in service of one or more of the purposes listed in section 501(c)(3) or (4) of the Code, or similarly situated organizations or groups, provided the group is not formed primarily for the sale of health insurance coverage and the Secretary of HHS, in consultation with the Secretary of the Treasury and the Secretary of Labor, determines the group requires access to health insurance and other related services and support in multiple countries.

Section 3(d)(4) of the EHCCA defines the United States as the 50 States, the District of Columbia, and Puerto Rico.

Section 3(f) of the EHCCA provides that, unless otherwise specified, the requirements of the EHCCA apply to expatriate health plans issued or renewed on or after July 1, 2015.

IRS Notice 2015-43

On July 20, 2015, the Treasury Department and the IRS issued Notice 2015-43 (2015-29 IRB 73) to provide interim guidance on the implementation of the EHCCA and the application of certain provisions of the ACA to expatriate health insurance issuers, expatriate health plans, and employers in their capacity as plan sponsors of expatriate health plans. The Departments of Labor and HHS reviewed and concurred with the interim guidance of Notice 2015-43. Comments were received in response to Notice 2015-43, and these comments have been considered in drafting these proposed regulations. The relevant portions of Notice 2015-43 and the related comments are discussed in the Overview of Proposed Regulations section of this preamble.[9]

IRS Notices 2015-29 and 2016-14

On March 30, 2015, the Treasury Department and the IRS issued Notice 2015-29 (2015-15 IRB 873) to provide guidance implementing the special rule of section 3(c)(2) of the EHCCA for fee years 2014 and 2015 with respect to the health insurance providers fee imposed by section 9010 of the ACA. Notice 2015-29 defines expatriate health plan by reference to the definition of expatriate policies in the MLR final rule issued by HHS[10] (MLR final rule definition) solely for the purpose of applying the special rule for fee years 2014 and 2015. The Treasury Department and the IRS determined that the MLR final rule definition of expatriate policies was sufficiently broad to cover potential expatriate health plans described in section 3(d)(2) of the EHCCA. The MLR final rule defines expatriate policies as predominantly group health insurance policies that provide coverage to employees, substantially all of whom are: (1) Working outside their country of citizenship; (2) working outside their country of citizenship and outside the employer's country of domicile; or (3) non-U.S. citizens working in their home country.

On January 29, 2016, the Treasury Department and the IRS issued Notice 2016-14 (2016-7 IRB 315) to provide guidance implementing the definition of expatriate health plan for fee year 2016 with respect to the health insurance providers fee imposed by section 9010 of the ACA. Like Notice 2015-29, Notice 2016-14 provides that the definition of expatriate health plan will be the same as provided in the MLR final rule definition, solely for the purpose of the health insurance providers fee imposed by section 9010 of the ACA for fee year 2016.[11]

The Consolidated Appropriations Act, 2016, Public Law 114-113, Division P, Title II, § 201, Moratorium on Annual Fee on Health Insurance Providers (the Consolidated Appropriations Act), suspends collection of the health insurance providers fee for the 2017 calendar year. Thus, health insurance issuers are not required to pay the fee for 2017.

Excepted Benefits

Sections 2722 and 2763 of the PHS Act, section 732 of ERISA, and section 9831 of the Code provide that the respective requirements of title XXVII of the PHS Act, part 7 of ERISA, and Chapter 100 of the Code generally do not apply to the provision of certain types of benefits, known as "excepted benefits." These excepted benefits are described in section 2791(c) of the PHS Act, section 733(c) of ERISA, and section 9832(c) of the Code.

There are four statutorily enumerated categories of excepted benefits. One category, under section 2791(c)(1) of the PHS Act, section 733(c)(1) of ERISA, and section 9832(c)(1) of the Code, identifies benefits that are excepted in all circumstances, including automobile insurance, liability insurance, workers compensation, and accidental death and dismemberment coverage. Under section 2791(c)(1)(H) of the PHS Act (and the parallel provisions of ERISA and the Code), this category of excepted benefits also includes "[o]ther similar insurance coverage, specified in regulations, under which benefits for medical care are secondary or incidental to other insurance benefits."

The second category of excepted benefits is limited excepted benefits, which may include limited scope vision or dental benefits, and benefits for long-term care, nursing home care, home health care, or community-based care. Section 2791(c)(2)(C) of the PHS Act, section 733(c)(2)(C) of ERISA, and section 9832(c)(2)(C) of the Code authorize the Secretaries of HHS, Labor, and the Treasury (collectively, the Secretaries) to issue regulations establishing other, similar limited benefits as excepted benefits. The Secretaries exercised this authority previously with respect to certain health flexible spending arrangements.[12] To be an excepted benefit under this second category, the statute provides that these limited benefits must either: (1) Be provided under a separate policy, certificate, or contract of insurance; or (2) otherwise not be an integral part of a group health plan, whether insured or self-insured.[13]

The third category of excepted benefits, referred to as "noncoordinated excepted benefits," includes both coverage for only a specified disease or illness (such as cancer-only policies), and hospital indemnity or other fixed indemnity insurance. These benefits are excepted under section 2722(c)(2) of the PHS Act, section 732(c)(2) of ERISA, and section 9831(c)(2) of the Code only if all of the following conditions are met: (1) The benefits are provided under a separate policy, certificate, or contract of insurance; (2) there is no coordination between the provision of such benefits and any exclusion of benefits under any group health plan maintained by the same plan sponsor; and (3) the benefits are paid with respect to any event without regard to whether benefits are provided under any group health plan maintained by the same plan sponsor. In the group market, the regulations further provide that to be hospital indemnity or other fixed indemnity insurance, the insurance must pay a fixed dollar amount per day (or per other time period) of hospitalization or illness (for example, $100/day) regardless of the amount of expenses incurred.[14]

Since the issuance of these regulations, the Departments have released FAQs to address various requests for clarification as to what types of coverage meet the conditions necessary to be hospital indemnity or other fixed indemnity insurance that are excepted benefits. Affordable Care Act Implementation FAQs Part XI, Q&A-7 clarified that group health insurance coverage in which benefits are provided in varying amounts based on the type of procedure or item, such as the

---

[9] See 26 CFR 601.601(d)(2)(ii)(B).

[10] 45 CFR 158.120(d)(4).

[11] See 26 CFR 601.601(d)(2)(ii)(B).

[12] 26 CFR 54.9831-1(c)(3)(v), 29 CFR 2590.732(c)(3)(v), 45 CFR 146.145(b)(3)(v).

[13] PHS Act section 2722(c)(1), ERISA section 732(c)(1), Code section 9831(c)(1).

[14] 26 CFR 54.9831-1(c)(4)(i), 29 CFR 2590.732(c)(4)(i), 45 CFR 146.145(b)(4)(i).

type of surgery actually performed or prescription drug provided is not a hospital indemnity or other fixed indemnity insurance excepted benefit because it does not meet the condition that benefits be provided on a per day (or per other time period, such as per week) basis, regardless of the amount of expenses incurred.[15]

The fourth category, under section 2791(c)(4) of the PHS Act, section 733(c)(4) of ERISA, and section 9832(c)(4) of the Code, is supplemental excepted benefits. Benefits are supplemental excepted benefits only if they are provided under a separate policy, certificate, or contract of insurance and are Medicare supplemental health insurance (also known as Medigap), TRICARE supplemental programs, or "similar supplemental coverage provided to coverage under a group health plan." The phrase "similar supplemental coverage provided to coverage under a group health plan" is not defined in the statute or regulations. However, the Departments' regulations clarify that one requirement to be similar supplemental coverage is that the coverage "must be specifically designed to fill gaps in primary coverage, such as coinsurance or deductibles."[16]

In 2007 and 2008, the Departments issued guidance on the circumstances under which supplemental health insurance would be considered excepted benefits under section 2791(c)(4) of the PHS Act (and the parallel provisions of ERISA, and the Code).[17] The guidance identifies several factors the Departments will apply when evaluating whether supplemental health insurance will be considered to be "similar supplemental coverage provided to coverage under a group health plan." Specifically the Departments' guidance provides that supplemental health insurance will be considered an excepted benefit if it is provided through a policy, certificate, or contract of insurance separate from the primary coverage under the plan and meets all of the following requirements: (1) The supplemental policy, certificate, or contract of insurance is issued by an entity that does not provide the primary coverage under the plan; (2) the supplemental policy, certificate, or contract of insurance is specifically designed to fill gaps in primary coverage, such as coinsurance or deductibles, but does not include a policy, certificate, or contract of insurance that becomes secondary or supplemental only under a coordination of benefits provision; (3) the cost of the supplemental coverage is 15 percent or less of the cost of primary coverage (determined in the same manner as the applicable premium is calculated under a COBRA continuation provision); and (4) the supplemental coverage sold in the group health insurance market does not differentiate among individuals in eligibility, benefits, or premiums based upon any health factor of the individual (or any dependents of the individual).

On February 13, 2015, the Departments issued Affordable Care Act Implementation FAQs Part XXIII, providing additional guidance on the circumstances under which health insurance coverage that supplements group health plan coverage may be considered supplemental excepted benefits.[18] The FAQ states that the Departments intend to propose regulations clarifying the circumstances under which supplemental insurance products that do not fill in cost-sharing under the primary plan are considered to be specifically designed to fill gaps in primary coverage. Specifically, the FAQ provides that health insurance coverage that supplements group health coverage by providing coverage of additional categories of benefits (as opposed to filling in cost-sharing gaps under the primary plan) would be considered to be designed to "fill in the gaps" of the primary coverage only if the benefits covered by the supplemental insurance product are not essential health benefits (EHB) in the State in which the product is being marketed. The FAQ further states that, until regulations are issued and effective, the Departments will not take enforcement action under certain conditions for failure to comply with the applicable insurance market reforms with respect to group or individual health insurance coverage that provides coverage of additional categories of benefits that are not EHBs in the applicable State. States were encouraged to exercise similar enforcement discretion.

Short-Term, Limited-Duration Insurance Coverage

Short-term limited duration insurance is a type of health insurance coverage that is designed to fill in temporary gaps in coverage when an individual is transitioning from one plan or coverage to another plan or coverage. Although short-term, limited-duration insurance is not an excepted benefit, it is similarly exempt from PHS Act requirements because it is not individual health insurance coverage. Section 2791(b)(5) of the PHS Act provides that the term "individual health insurance coverage" means health insurance coverage offered to individuals in the individual market, but does not include short-term, limited-duration insurance. The PHS Act does not define short-term, limited-duration insurance. Under existing regulations, short-term, limited-duration insurance means "health insurance coverage provided pursuant to a contract with an issuer that has an expiration date specified in the contract (taking into account any extensions that may be elected by the policyholder without the issuer's consent) that is less than 12 months after the original effective date of the contract."[19]

Prohibition on Lifetime and Annual Limits

Section 2711 of the PHS Act, as added by the ACA, generally prohibits group health plans and health insurance issuers offering group or individual health insurance coverage from imposing lifetime and annual dollar limits on EHB, as defined in section 1302(b) of the ACA. These prohibitions apply to both grandfathered and non-grandfathered health plans, except the annual limits prohibition does not apply to grandfathered individual health insurance coverage.

Under the ACA, self-insured group health plans, large group market health plans, and grandfathered health plans are not required to offer EHB, but they generally cannot place lifetime or annual dollar limits on covered services that are considered EHB. The Departments' regulations provide that, for plan years (in the individual market, policy years) beginning on or after January 1, 2017, a plan or issuer that is not required to provide EHB may select from among any of the 51 base-benchmark plans selected by a State or applied by default pursuant to 45 CFR 156.100, or one of the three FEHBP options specified at 45 CFR 156.100(a)(3), for purposes of complying with the lifetime and annual limits prohibition in section 2711 of the PHS Act.[20]

II. Overview of the Proposed Regulations

A. Expatriate Health Plans

In General

Section 3(a) of the EHCCA provides that the ACA generally does not apply to expatriate health plans, employers with respect to expatriate health plans but solely in their capacity as plan sponsors of expatriate health plans, and expatriate health insurance issuers with respect to coverage offered by such issuers under expatriate health plans. Consistent with this provision, the proposed regulations provide that the market reform provisions enacted or amended as part of the ACA, included in sections 2701 through 2728 of the PHS Act and incorporated into section 9815 of the Code and section 715 of ERISA, do not apply to an expatriate health plan, an employer, solely in its capacity as plan sponsor of an expatriate health plan, and an expatriate health insurance issuer with respect to coverage under an expatriate health plan. Similarly, section 162(m)(6) of the Code does not apply to an expatriate health insurance issuer with respect to premiums received for coverage under an expatriate health plan. In addition, under the EHCCA, the PCORTF fee under sections 4375 and 4376 of the Code and the transitional reinsurance program fee under section 1341 of the ACA do not apply to expatriate health plans. The EHCCA excludes expatriate health plans from the health insurance providers fee imposed by section 9010 except that the EHCCA provides a special rule solely for purposes of determining the fee for the 2014 and 2015 fee years. The EHCCA also designates certain coverage by an expatriate health plan as minimum essential coverage under section 5000A(f) of the Code, and provides special rules for the application of the reporting rules under sections 6055 and 6056 of the Code to expatriate health plans.

Definition of Expatriate Health Insurance Issuer

Consistent with sections 3(d)(1) and (d)(2)(F) of the EHCCA, the proposed regulations define "expatriate health insurance issuer" as a health insurance issuer (as defined under 26 CFR 54.9801-2, 29 CFR 2590.701-2 and 45 CFR 144.103) that issues expatriate health plans and

---

[15] Frequently Asked Questions about Affordable Care Act Implementation (Part XI), available at *http://www.dol.gov/ebsa/faqs/faq-aca11.html* and *http://www.cms.gov/CCIIO/Resources/Fact-Sheets-and-FAQs/aca_implementation_faqs11.html.*

[16] 26 CFR 54.9831-1(c)(5)(i)(C), 29 CFR 2590.732(c)(5)(i)(C), and 45 CFR 146.145(b)(5)(i)(C).

[17] See EBSA Field Assistance Bulletin No. 2007-04 (available at *http://www.dol.gov/ebsa/regs/fab2007-4.html*); CMS Insurance Standards Bulletin 08-01 (available at *http://*

www.cms.gov/CCIIO/Resources/Files/Downloads/hipaa_08_01_508.pdf); and IRS Notice 2008-23 (available at *http://www.irs.gov/irb/2008-07_IRB/ar09.html*).

[18] Frequently Asked Questions about Affordable Care Act Implementation (Part XXIII), available at *http://www.dol.gov/ebsa/pdf/faq-aca23.pdf* and *https://www.cms.gov/CCIIO/Resources/Fact-Sheets-and-FAQs/Downloads/Supplmental-FAQ_2-13-15-final.pdf.*

[19] 26 CFR 54.9801-2, 29 CFR 2590.701-2, 45 CFR 144.103.

[20] 26 CFR 54.9815-2711(c), 29 CFR 2590.715-2711(c), 45 CFR 147.126(c).

satisfies certain requirements.[21] The requirements for the issuer to be an expatriate health insurance issuer include that, in the course of its normal business operations, the issuer: (1) Maintains network provider agreements that provide for direct claims payments with health care providers in eight or more countries; (2) maintains call centers in three or more countries, and accepts calls from customers in eight or more languages; (3) processed at least $1 million in claims in foreign currency equivalents during the preceding calendar year; (4) makes global evacuation/repatriation coverage available; (5) maintains legal and compliance resources in three or more countries; and (6) has licenses or other authority to sell insurance in more than two countries, including the United States. For purposes of meeting the $1 million threshold for claims processed in foreign currency equivalents, the proposed regulations provide that the dollar value of claims processed is determined using the Treasury Department's currency exchange rate in effect on the last day of the preceding calendar year.[22] Comments are requested regarding whether use of the calendar year as the basis for measuring the dollar amount of claims processed presents administrative challenges, and how the resulting challenges, if any, may be addressed. The proposed regulations provide that each of the applicable requirements may be satisfied by two or more entities (including one entity that is the health insurance issuer) that are members of the health insurance issuer's controlled group or through contracts between the expatriate health insurance issuer and third parties.

Definition of Expatriate Health Plan

Consistent with section 3(d)(2) of the EHCCA, the proposed regulations define "expatriate health plan" as a plan offered to qualified expatriates and that satisfies certain requirements. With respect to qualified expatriates in categories A or B, the plan must be a group health plan (whether or not insured). In contrast, with respect to qualified expatriates in category C, the plan must be health insurance coverage that is not a group health plan. In addition, consistent with section 3(d)(2)(A) of the EHCCA, the proposed regulations require that substantially all primary enrollees in the expatriate health plan must be qualified expatriates. The proposed regulations define a primary enrollee as the individual covered by the plan or policy whose eligibility for coverage is not due to that individual's status as the spouse, dependent, or other beneficiary of another covered individual. However, notwithstanding this definition, an individual is not a primary enrollee if the individual is not a national of the United States and the individual resides in his or her country of citizenship. Further, the proposed regulations provide that, for this purpose, a "national of the United States" has the meaning used in the Immigration and Nationality Act (8 U.S.C. 1101 et. seq.) and 8 CFR parts 301 to 392, including U.S. citizens. Thus, for example, an individual born in American Samoa is a national of the United States at birth for purposes of the EHCCA and the proposed regulations.

Comments in response to Notice 2015-43 requested clarification of the "substantially all" enrollment requirement, with one comment suggesting that 93 percent of the enrollees would be an appropriate threshold. In response to the request for clarification, the proposed regulations provide that a plan satisfies the "substantially all" enrollment requirement if, on the first day of the plan year, less than 5 percent of the primary enrollees (or less than 5 primary enrollees if greater) are not qualified expatriates (effectively a 95 percent threshold). Consistent with section 3(d)(2)(B) of the EHCCA, the proposed regulations further provide that substantially all of the benefits provided under an expatriate health plan must be benefits that are not excepted benefits as described in 26 CFR 54.9831-1(c), 29 CFR 2590.732(c), 45 CFR 146.145(b) and 148.220, as applicable. The Departments intend that the first day of the plan year approach, which has been used in other contexts, will be simple to administer.[23] Moreover, the 95% threshold has been used in certain other circumstances in applying a "substantially all" standard.[24] The Departments solicit comment on this regulatory approach and whether the current regulatory language is sufficient to protect against potential abuses, or whether any further anti-abuse provision is necessary.

Consistent with section 3(d)(2)(C) of the EHCCA, the proposed regulations also require that an expatriate health plan cover certain types of services. Specifically, an expatriate health plan must provide coverage for inpatient hospital services, outpatient facility services, physician services, and emergency services (comparable to emergency services coverage that was described in and offered under section 8903(1) of title 5, United States Code for plan year 2009). Coverage for such services must be available in certain countries depending on the type of qualified expatriates covered by the plan. The statute authorizes the Secretary of HHS, in consultation with the Secretary of the Treasury and Secretary of Labor, to designate other countries where coverage for such services must be made available to the qualified expatriate.

Consistent with section 3(d)(2)(D) of the EHCCA, the proposed regulations provide that in the case of an expatriate health plan, the plan sponsor must reasonably believe that benefits provided by the plan satisfy the minimum value requirements of section 36B(c)(2)(C)(ii) of the Code.[25] For this purpose, the proposed regulations provide that the plan sponsor is permitted to rely on the reasonable representations of the issuer or administrator regarding whether benefits offered by the group health plan or issuer satisfy the minimum value requirements unless the plan sponsor knows or has reason to know that the benefits fail to satisfy the minimum value requirements. Consistent with section 3(d)(2)(D) of the EHCCA, in the case of an expatriate health plan that provides dependent coverage of children, the proposed regulations provide that such coverage must be available until the individual attains age 26, unless the individual is the child of a child receiving dependent coverage. Additionally, consistent with section 3(d)(2)(F)(ii) of the EHCCA, the plan or coverage must offer reimbursements for items or services in the local currency in eight or more countries.

Consistent with section 3(d)(2)(F) of the EHCCA, the proposed regulations also provide that the policy or coverage under an expatriate health plan must be issued by an expatriate health insurance issuer or administered by an expatriate health plan administrator. With respect to qualified expatriates in categories A or B (generally, individuals whose travel or relocation is related to their employment with an employer), the coverage must be under a group health plan (whether insured or self-insured). With respect to qualified expatriates in category C (generally, groups of similarly situated individuals travelling for certain tax-exempt purposes), the coverage must be under a policy issued by an expatriate health insurance issuer.

Finally, consistent with section 3(d)(2)(G) of the EHCCA, the proposed regulations provide that an expatriate health plan must satisfy the provisions of Chapter 100 of the Code, part 7 of subtitle B of title I of ERISA and title XXVII of the PHS Act that would otherwise apply if the ACA had not been enacted. Among other requirements, those provisions limited the ability of a group health plan or group health insurance issuer to impose preexisting condition exclusions (which are now prohibited for grandfathered and non-grandfathered group health plans and health insurance coverage offered in connection with such plans, and non-grandfathered individual health insurance coverage under the ACA), including a requirement that the period of any preexisting condition exclusion be reduced by the length of any period of creditable coverage the individual had without a 63-day break in coverage.

Prior to the enactment of the ACA, HIPAA and underlying regulations also generally required that plans and issuers provide certificates of creditable coverage when an individual ceased to be covered by a plan or policy and upon request. Following the enactment of the ACA, the regulations under these provisions have eliminated the requirement for providing certificates of creditable coverage beginning December 31, 2014, because the requirement is generally no longer relevant to plans and participants as a result of the prohibition on preexisting condition exclusions. The Departments recognize that reimposing the requirement to provide certificates of creditable coverage on expatriate health plans would only be useful in situations in which an individual transferred from one expatriate health plan to another and that reimposing the requirement on all health plans would require certificates that would be unnecessary except in limited cases, such as for an individual who ceased coverage with a health plan or policy and began coverage under an expatriate health plan that imposed a preexisting condition exclusion. Because reimposing the re-

---

[21] Section 3(d)(1) of the EHCCA provides that the term "expatriate health insurance issuer" means a health insurance issuer that issues expatriate health plans; section 3(d)(5)(A) of the EHCCA provides that the term "health insurance issuer" has the meaning given in section 2791 of the PHS Act. The definition of health insurance issuer in section 9832(b)(2) of the Code and section 733(b)(2) of ERISA and underlying regulations are substantively identical to the definition under section 2791 of the PHS Act and its underlying regulations.

As discussed in the section of this preamble entitled "Definition of Expatriate Health Plan" a health insurance issuer as defined in section 2791 of the PHS Act is limited to an entity licensed to engage in the business of insurance in a State and subject to State law that regulates insurance.

[22] The most recent Treasury Department currency exchange rate can be found at *https://www.fiscal.treasury.gov/fsreports/rpt/treasRptRateExch/currentRates.htm.*

[23] 26 CFR 54.9831-1(b), 29 CFR 2590.732(b), 45 CFR 146.145(b).

[24] See *e.g.*, 26 CFR 1.460-6(d)(4)(i)(D)(*1*).

[25] For this purpose, generally "minimum value" takes into account the provision of "essential health benefits" as defined in section 1302(b)(1) of the Affordable Care Act.

quirement to provide certificates of creditable coverage would be inefficient and overly broad, and relevant in only limited circumstances, the proposed regulations do not require expatriate health plans to provide certificates of creditable coverage. However, expatriate health plans imposing a preexisting condition exclusion must still comply with certain limitations on preexisting condition exclusions that would otherwise apply if the ACA had not been enacted. Therefore, the proposed regulations require expatriate health plans to ensure that individuals who enroll in the expatriate health plan are provided an opportunity to demonstrate creditable coverage to offset any preexisting condition exclusion. For example, an email from the prior issuer (or former plan administrator or plan sponsor) providing information about past coverage could be sufficient confirmation of prior creditable coverage.

Comments in response to Notice 2015-43 requested clarification of the treatment of health coverage provided by a foreign government. Specifically, comments requested that health coverage provided by a foreign government be treated as minimum essential coverage under section 5000A of the Code, and that, for purposes of the employer shared responsibility provision of section 4980H of the Code, an offer of such coverage be treated as an offer of minimum essential coverage for certain foreign employees working in the United States. These issues are generally beyond the scope of these proposed regulations. Under the existing regulations under section 5000A(f)(1)(E) of the Code, there are procedures for health benefits coverage not otherwise designated under section 5000A(f)(1) of the Code as minimum essential coverage to be recognized by the Secretary of HHS, in coordination with the Secretary of the Treasury, as minimum essential coverage. The Secretary of HHS has provided that coverage under a group health plan provided through insurance regulated by a foreign government is minimum essential coverage for expatriates who meet specified conditions.[26] Furthermore, plan sponsors of health coverage that is not recognized as minimum essential coverage through statute, regulation, or guidance may submit an application to CMS for minimum essential coverage recognition pursuant to 45 CFR 156.604.[27] For a complete list of coverage recognized by CMS as minimum essential coverage under section 5000A(f)(1)(E) of the Code, see *https://www.cms.gov/CCIIO/ Programs-and-Initiatives/Health-Insurance-Market-Reforms/minimum- essential-coverage.html*.

Comments also requested that policies sold by non-United States health insurance issuers be treated as minimum essential coverage under section 5000A of the Code, or as expatriate health plans. Section 3(d)(5)(A) of the EHCCA specifies that the terms "health insurance issuer" and "health insurance coverage" have the meanings given those terms by section 2791 of the PHS Act. Section 2791 of the PHS Act (and parallel provisions in section 9832(b) of the Code and section 733(b) of ERISA) define those terms by reference to an entity licensed to engage in the business of insurance in a State and subject to State law that regulates insurance. Under section 2791 of the PHS Act, the term "State" means each of the several States, the District of Columbia, Puerto Rico, the Virgin Islands, Guam, American Samoa, and the Northern Mariana Islands. Consistent with those provisions, these proposed regulations limit an expatriate health insurance issuer to a health insurance issuer within the meaning of those sections (and that meets the other requirements set forth in the proposed regulations). As such, a non-United States health insurance issuer does not qualify as an expatriate health insurance issuer within the meaning of the EHCCA, and coverage issued by a non-United States issuer that is not otherwise minimum essential coverage is not minimum essential coverage pursuant to the EHCCA.

Definition of Expatriate Health Plan Administrator

The proposed regulations define "expatriate health plan administrator," with respect to self-insured coverage, as an administrator of self-insured coverage that generally satisfies the same requirements as an "expatriate health insurance issuer."

Definition of Qualified Expatriate

Consistent with section 3(d)(3) of the EHCCA, the proposed regulations define "qualified expatriate" as one of three types of individuals. The first type of qualified expatriate, a category A expatriate, is an individual who has the skills, qualifications, job duties, or expertise that has caused the individual's employer to transfer or assign the individual to the United States for a specific and temporary purpose or assignment that is tied to the individual's employment with the employer. A category A expatriate may only be an individual who: (1) The plan sponsor has reasonably determined requires access to health coverage and other related services and support in multiple countries, (2) is offered other multinational benefits on a periodic basis (such as tax equalization, compensation for cross-border moving expenses, or compensation to enable the individual to return to the individual's home country), and (3) is not a national of the United States. The proposed regulations provide that an individual who is not expected to travel outside the United States at least one time per year during the coverage period would not reasonably "require access" to health coverage and other related services and support in multiple countries. Furthermore, under the proposed regulations, the offer of a one-time *de minimis* benefit would not meet the standard for the "periodic" offer of "other multinational benefits."

Section 3(d)(3)(B) of the EHCCA provides that a second type of qualified expatriate, a category B expatriate, is an individual who works outside the United States for a period of at least 180 days in a consecutive 12-month period that overlaps with the plan year. A comment requested that the regulations clarify that the 12-month period could either be within a single plan year, or across two consecutive plan years. Consistent with the statutory language, the proposed regulations provide that a category B expatriate is an individual who is a national of the United States and who works outside the United States for at least 180 days in a consecutive 12-month period that is within a single plan year, or across two consecutive plan years. Section 3(d)(2)(C)(ii) of the EHCCA requires an expatriate health plan provided to category B expatriates to cover certain specified services, such as inpatient and outpatient services, in the country in which the individual is "present in connection" with his employment. The Departments request comments on whether it would be helpful to provide further administrative clarification of this statutory language regarding the country or countries in which the services must be provided, and, if so, whether there are facts or circumstances that will present particular challenges in applying this rule.

Finally, consistent with section 3(d)(3)(C) of the EHCCA, the proposed regulations provide that a third type of qualified expatriate, a category C expatriate, is an individual who is a member of a group of similarly situated individuals that is formed for the purpose of traveling or relocating internationally in service of one or more of the purposes listed in section 501(c)(3) or (4) of the Code, or similarly situated organizations or groups, and meets certain other conditions.[28] A category C expatriate does not include an individual in a group that is formed primarily for the sale or purchase of health insurance coverage. To qualify as this type of qualified expatriate, the Secretary of HHS, in consultation with the Secretary of the Treasury and the Secretary of Labor, must determine that the group requires access to health coverage and other related services and support in multiple countries. The proposed regulations clarify that a category C expatriate does not include an individual whose international travel or relocation is related to employment. Thus, an individual whose travel is employment-related may be a qualified expatriate only in category A or B. The proposed regulations also provide that, in the case of a group organized to travel or relocate outside the United States, the individual must be expected to travel or reside outside the United States for at least 180 days in a consecutive 12-month period that overlaps with the policy year (or in the case of a policy year that is less than 12 months, at least half of the policy year), and in the case of a group organized to travel or relocate within the United States, the individual must be expected to travel or reside in the United States for not more than 12 months. The proposed regulations provide that a group of category C expatriates must also meet the test for having associational ties under section 2791(d)(3)(B) through (F) of the PHS Act (42 U.S.C. 300gg-91(d)(3)(B) through (F)).

For purposes of section 3(d)(3)(C)(iii) of the EHCCA, the proposed regulations provide that the Secretary of HHS, in consultation with the Secretary of the Treasury and the Secretary of Labor, has determined that, in the case of a group of similarly situated individuals that meets all of the criteria in the proposed regulations, the group requires access to health coverage and other related services and support in multiple countries.

---

[26] See CMS Insurance Standards Bulletin Series. CCIIO Sub-Regulatory Guidance: Process for Obtaining Recognition as Minimum Essential Coverage (Oct. 31, 2013), available at *https://www.cms.gov/CCIIO/Resources/Regulations-and-Guidance/Downloads/ mec-guidance-10-31-2013.pdf*.

[27] See CMS Insurance Standards Bulletin Series. CCIIO Sub-Regulatory Guidance: Process for Obtaining Recognition as Minimum Essential Coverage (Oct. 31, 2013), available at *https://www.cms.gov/CCIIO/Resources/Regulations-and-Guidance/Downloads/*

mec-guidance-10-31-2013.pdf. See also CMS Insurance Standards Bulletin Series. CCIIIO Sub-Regulatory Guidance: Minimum Essential Coverage.

[28] Code section 501(c)(3) describes an organization formed for religious, charitable, scientific, public safety, literary, or educational purposes, or to foster national or international amateur sports competition, or for the prevention of cruelty to children or animals, and not for political candidate campaign or legislative purposes or propaganda. Code section 501(c)(4) describes an organization operated exclusively for the promotion of social welfare.

Comments in response to Notice 2015-43 requested that category C expatriates not be limited to individuals expected to travel or reside in the United States for 12 or fewer months. While the EHCCA does not include a time limit for category C expatriates, section 3(e) of the EHCCA provides that the Departments "may promulgate regulations necessary to carry out this Act, including such rules as may be necessary to prevent inappropriate expansion of the exclusions under the Act from applicable laws and regulations." In the group market, the EHCCA and the proposed regulations define a category A expatriate with respect to a "specific and temporary purpose or assignment" tied to the individual's employment in the United States. It is the view of HHS, in consultation with the Departments of Labor and the Treasury, that similar safeguards are necessary in the individual market to prevent inappropriate expansion of the exception for category C expatriates.

Comments are requested on all aspects of the proposed definition of a category C expatriate. Comments are also requested on the time limit for category C expatriates being expected to travel or reside in the United States, and what standards, if any, may be adopted in lieu of the 12-month maximum that would ensure that the definition does not permit inappropriate expansion of the exception. For example, comments are requested on whether a "specific and temporary purpose" standard should be adopted for category C expatriates, consistent with the standard for category A expatriates, or whether category C expatriates should be expected to seek medical care outside the United States at least one time per year in order to be considered to reasonably require access to health coverage and other related services and support in multiple countries. Comments are also requested on the proposed standard with respect to category C expatriates being expected to travel or reside outside the United States for at least 180 days in a consecutive 12-month period that overlaps with the policy year, and whether there are fact patterns in which the 12-month period could either be within a single policy year, or across two consecutive policy years.

Definitions of Group Health Plan and United States

Consistent with section 3(d)(5)(A) of the EHCCA, for purposes of applying the definition of expatriate health plan, "group health plan" means a group health plan as defined under 26 CFR 54.9831-1(a)(1), 29 CFR 2590.732(a)(1) or 45 CFR 146.145(a)(1), as applicable. Consistent with section 3(d)(4) of the EHCCA, the proposed regulations define "United States" to mean the 50 States, the District of Columbia and Puerto Rico.

Section 9010 of the ACA

Section 3(c)(1) of the EHCCA provides that, for purposes of the health insurance providers fee imposed by section 9010 of the ACA, a qualified expatriate enrolled in an expatriate health plan is not a United States health risk for calendar years after 2015. Section 3(c)(2) of the EHCCA provides a special rule applicable to calendar years 2014 and 2015. The Treasury Department and the IRS issued Notices 2015-29 and 2016-14 to address the definition of expatriate health plan for purposes of the health insurance providers fee imposed by section 9010 for the 2014, 2015, and 2016 fee years. No fee is due in the 2017 fee year because the Consolidated Appropriations Act suspends collection of the health insurance providers fee imposed by section 9010 of ACA for 2017.

These proposed regulations provide that, for any fee that is due on or after the date final regulations are published in the **Federal Register**, a qualified expatriate enrolled in an expatriate health plan as defined in these proposed regulations is not a United States health risk. These proposed regulations also authorize the IRS to specify in guidance in the Internal Revenue Bulletin the manner of determining excluded premiums for qualified expatriates in expatriate health plans. Until the date the final regulations are published in the **Federal Register**, taxpayers may rely on these proposed regulations with respect to any fee that is due beginning with the 2018 fee year.

Federal Tax Provision: Section 162(m)(6) of the Code

Section 162(m)(6) of the Code, as added by section 9014 of the ACA, in general, limits to $500,000 the allowable deduction for remuneration attributable to services performed by certain individuals for a covered health insurance provider. For taxable years beginning after December 31, 2012, section 162(m)(6)(C)(i) of the Code and 26 CFR 1.162-31(b)(4)(A) provide that a health insurance issuer is a covered health insurance provider if not less than 25 percent of the gross premiums that it receives from providing health insurance coverage during the taxable year are from minimum essential coverage. Section 3(a)(3) of the EHCCA provides that the provisions of the ACA (which include section 162(m)(6) of the Code) do not apply to expatriate

health insurance issuers with respect to coverage offered by such issuers under expatriate health plans. Consistent with this rule, the proposed regulations exclude from the definition of the term "premium" for purposes of section 162(m)(6) of the Code amounts received in payment for coverage under an expatriate health plan. As a result, those amounts received are included in neither the numerator nor the denominator for purposes of determining whether the 25 percent standard under section 162(m)(6)(C)(i) of the Code and 26 CFR 1.162-31(b)(4)(A) is met, and they have no impact on whether a particular issuer is a covered health insurance provider.

Federal Tax Provision: Section 4980I of the Code

Section 3(b)(2) of the EHCCA provides that section 4980I of the Code applies to employer-sponsored coverage of a qualified expatriate who is assigned, rather than transferred, to work in the United States. As amended by section 101 of Division P of the Consolidated Appropriations Act, section 4980I of the Code first applies to coverage provided in taxable years beginning after December 31, 2019. Comments in response to Notice 2015-43 requested additional guidance on what it means for an employer to assign rather than transfer an employee. These proposed regulations do not address the interaction of the EHCCA and section 4980I of the Code because the Treasury Department and the IRS anticipate that this issue will be addressed in future guidance promulgated under section 4980I of the Code.

Federal Tax Provision: Section 5000A of the Code and Minimum Essential Coverage

The proposed regulations provide that, beginning January 1, 2017, coverage under an expatriate health plan that provides coverage for a qualified expatriate qualifies as minimum essential coverage for all participants in the plan. If the expatriate health plan provides coverage to category A or category B expatriates, the coverage of any participant in the plan is treated as an eligible employer-sponsored plan under section 5000A(f)(2) of the Code. If the expatriate health plan provides coverage to category C expatriates, the coverage of any enrollee in the plan is treated as a plan in the individual market under section 5000A(f)(1)(C) of the Code.

Federal Tax Provision: Sections 6055 and 6056 of the Code

Section 3(b)(2) of the EHCCA permits the use of electronic media to provide the statements required under sections 6055 and 6056 of the Code to individuals for coverage under an expatriate health plan unless the primary insured has explicitly refused to receive the statement electronically. The proposed regulations provide that, for an expatriate health plan, the recipient is treated as having consented to receive the required statement electronically unless the recipient has explicitly refused to receive the statement in an electronic format. In addition, the proposed regulations provide that the recipient may explicitly refuse either electronically or in a paper document. For a recipient to be treated as having consented under this special rule, the furnisher must provide a notice in compliance with the general disclosure requirements under sections 6055 and 6056 that informs the recipient that the statement will be furnished electronically unless the recipient explicitly refuses to consent to receive the statement in electronic form. The notice must be provided to the recipient at least 30 days prior to the due date for furnishing of the first statement the furnisher intends to furnish electronically to the recipient. Absent receipt of this notice, a recipient will not be treated as having consented to electronic furnishing of statements. Treasury and IRS request comments on further guidance that will assist issuers and plan sponsors in providing this notice in the least burdensome manner while still ensuring that the recipient has sufficient information and opportunity to opt out of the electronic reporting if the recipient desires. For example, Treasury and the IRS specifically request comments on whether the ability to provide this notice as part of the enrollment materials for the coverage would meet these goals.

Federal Tax Provision: PCORTF Fee

The proposed regulations provide that the excise tax under sections 4375 and 4376 of the Code (the PCORTF fee) does not apply to an expatriate health plan as defined at 26 CFR 54.9831-1(f)(3). Section 4375 of the Code limits the application of the fee to policies issued to individuals residing in the United States. Existing regulations under sections 4375, 4376, and 4377 of the Code exclude coverage under a plan from the fee if the plan is designed specifically to cover primarily employees who are working and residing outside the United States. A comment requested clarification about the existing PCORTF fee exemption for plans that primarily cover employees working and residing outside the United States. Consistent with the provisions of the EHCCA, the proposed regulations expand the exclusion from the PCORTF fee to also exclude an expatriate health plan regardless of whether the plan provides coverage for qualified expatriates residing or working in or outside the United States if the plan is an expatriate health plan.

Section 1341 of the ACA: Transitional Reinsurance Program

A comment also requested that the current exclusion under the PCORTF fee regulations for individuals working and residing outside the United States be applied to the transitional reinsurance fee under section 1341 of the ACA. Existing regulations relating to section 1341 of the ACA include an exception for certain expatriate health plans,[29] including expatriate group health coverage as defined by the Secretary of HHS and, for the 2015 and 2016 benefit years, self-insured group health plans with respect to which enrollment is limited to participants who reside outside their home country for at least six months of the plan year, and any covered dependents. HHS solicits comment on whether amendments are needed to 45 CFR 153.400(a)(1)(iii) to clarify the alignment with the EHCCA and exempt all expatriate plans from the requirement to make reinsurance contributions.

Section 2718 of the PHS Act: MLR Program

Section 2718 of the PHS Act, as added by sections 1001 and 10101 of the ACA, generally requires health insurance issuers to provide rebates to consumers if issuers do not achieve specified MLRs, as well as to submit an annual MLR report to HHS. The proposed regulations provide that expatriate policies described in 45 CFR 158.120(d)(4) continue to be subject to the reporting and rebate requirements of 45 CFR part 158, but update the description of expatriate policies in 45 CFR 158.120(d)(4) to exclude policies that are expatriate health plans under the EHCCA. Given this modification, issuers may find that the number of expatriate policies that remain subject to MLR requirements is low, and that it is administratively burdensome and there is no longer a qualitative justification for continuing separate reporting of such policies. Therefore, comments are requested on whether the treatment of expatriate policies for purposes of the MLR regulations should be amended so that expatriate policies that do not meet the definition of expatriate health plan under the EHCCA would not be required to be reported separately from other health insurance policies.

Section 833(c)(5) of the Code, as added by section 9016 of the ACA, and amended by section 102 of Division N of the Consolidated and Further Continuing Appropriations Act, 2015 (Pub. L. 113-235, 128 Stat. 2130), provides that section 833(a)(2) and (3) do not apply to any organization unless the organization's MLR for the taxable year was at least 85 percent. In describing the MLR computation under section 833(c)(5), the statute and implementing regulations provide that the elements in the MLR computation are to be "as reported under section 2718 of the Public Service Health Act." Accordingly, the proposed regulations under section 2718 of the PHS Act would effectively apply the EHCCA exemption to section 833(c)(5) of the Code by carving out expatriate health plans under the EHCCA from the section 833(c)(5) requirements as well.

Excepted Benefits

Supplemental Health Insurance Coverage

The proposed regulations incorporate the guidance from the Affordable Care Act Implementation FAQs Part XXIII addressing supplemental health insurance products that provide categories of benefits in addition to those in the primary coverage. Under the proposed regulations, if group or individual supplemental health insurance coverage provides benefits for items and services not covered by the primary coverage (referred to as providing "additional categories of benefits"), the coverage would be considered to be designed "to fill gaps in primary coverage," for purposes of being supplemental excepted benefits if none of the benefits provided by the supplemental policy are an EHB, as defined for purposes of section 1302(b) of the ACA, in the State in which the coverage is issued. Conversely, if any benefit provided by the supplemental policy is an EHB in the State where the coverage is issued, the insurance coverage would not be supplemental excepted benefits under the proposed regulations. This standard is proposed to apply only to the extent that the supplemental health insurance provides coverage of additional categories of benefits. Supplemental health insurance products that both fill in cost sharing in the primary coverage, such as coinsurance or deductibles, and cover additional categories of benefits that are not EHB, also would be considered supplemental excepted benefits under these proposed regulations provided all other criteria are met.

Travel Insurance

The Departments are aware that certain travel insurance products may include limited health benefits. However, these products typically are not designed as major medical coverage. Instead, the risks being insured relate primarily to: (1) The interruption or cancellation of a trip (2) the loss of baggage or personal effects; (3) damages to accommodations or rental vehicles; or (4) sickness, accident, disability, or death occurring during travel, with any health benefits usually incidental to other coverage.

Section 2791(c)(1)(H) of the PHS Act, section 733(c)(1)(H) of ERISA, and section 9832(c)(1)(H) of the Code provide that the Departments may, in regulations, designate as excepted benefits "benefits for medical care that are secondary or incidental to other insurance benefits." Pursuant to this authority, and to clarify which types of travel-related insurance products are excepted benefits under the PHS Act, ERISA, and the Code, the proposed regulations provide that certain travel-related products that provide only incidental health benefits are excepted benefits. The proposed regulations define the term "travel insurance" as insurance coverage for personal risks incident to planned travel, which may include, but is not limited to, interruption or cancellation of a trip or event, loss of baggage or personal effects, damages to accommodations or rental vehicles, and sickness, accident, disability, or death occurring during travel, provided that the health benefits are not offered on a stand-alone basis and are incidental to other coverage. For this purpose, travel insurance does not include major medical plans that provide comprehensive medical protection for travelers with trips lasting 6 months or longer, including, for example, those working overseas as an expatriate or military personnel being deployed. This definition is consistent with the definition of travel insurance under final regulations for the health insurance providers fee imposed by section 9010 of the ACA issued by the Treasury Department and the IRS,[30] which uses a modified version of the National Association of Insurance Commissioners (NAIC) definition of travel insurance.

Hospital Indemnity and Other Fixed Indemnity Insurance

These proposed regulations also include an amendment to the "noncoordinated excepted benefits" category as it relates to hospital indemnity and other fixed indemnity insurance in the group market. Since the issuance of final regulations defining excepted benefits, the Departments have become aware of some hospital indemnity and other fixed indemnity insurance policies that provide comprehensive benefits related to health care costs. In addition, although hospital indemnity and other fixed indemnity insurance under section 2791 of the PHS Act, section 733 of ERISA, and section 9832 of the Code is not intended to be major medical coverage, the Departments are aware that some group health plans that provide coverage through hospital indemnity or other fixed indemnity insurance policies that meet the conditions necessary to be an excepted benefit have made representations to participants that the coverage is minimum essential coverage under section 5000A of the Code. The Departments are concerned that some individuals may incorrectly understand these policies to be comprehensive major medical coverage that would be considered minimum essential coverage.

To avoid confusion among group health plan enrollees and potential enrollees, the proposed regulations revise the conditions necessary for hospital indemnity and other fixed indemnity insurance in the group market to be excepted benefits so that any application or enrollment materials provided to enrollees and potential enrollees at or before the time enrollees and potential enrollees are given the opportunity to enroll in the coverage must include a statement that the coverage is a supplement to, rather than a substitute for, major medical coverage and that a lack of minimum essential coverage may result in an additional tax payment. The proposed regulations include specific language that must be used by group health plans and issuers of group health insurance coverage to satisfy this notice requirement, which is consistent with the notice requirement for individual market fixed indemnity coverage under regulations issued by HHS.[31] The Departments request comments on this proposed notice requirement as well as whether any additional requirements should be added to prevent confusion among enrollees and potential enrollees regarding the limited coverage provided by hospital indemnity and other fixed indemnity insurance. The Departments anticipate that conforming changes will be made in the final regulations to ensure the notice language in the individual market is consistent with the notice language in the group market, and solicit comments on this approach.

---

[29] 45 CFR 153.400(a)(1)(iii).

[30] 26 CFR 57.2(h)(4).

[31] 45 CFR 148.220(b)(4)(iv).

Additionally, the Departments have become aware of hospital indemnity or other fixed indemnity insurance policies that provide benefits for doctors' visits at a fixed amount per visit, for prescription drugs at a fixed amount per drug, or for certain services at a fixed amount per day but in amounts that vary by the type of service. These types of policies do not meet the condition that benefits be provided on a per day (or per other time period, such as per week) basis. Accordingly, the proposed regulations clarify this standard by stating that the amount of benefits provided must be determined without regard to the type of items or services received. The proposed regulations add two examples demonstrating that group health plans and issuers of group health insurance coverage that provide coverage through hospital indemnity or fixed indemnity insurance policies that provide benefits based on the type of item or services received do not meet the conditions necessary to be an excepted benefit. The first example would incorporate into regulations guidance previously provided by the Departments in Affordable Care Act Implementation FAQs Part XI, which clarified that if a policy provides benefits in varying amounts based on the type of procedure or item received, the policy does not satisfy the condition that benefits be provided on a per day (or per other time period, such as per week) basis. The second example demonstrates that a hospital indemnity or other fixed indemnity insurance policy that provides benefits for certain services at a fixed amount per day, but in varying amounts depending on the type of service, does not meet the condition that benefits be provided on a per day (or per other time period, such as per week) basis. The Departments request comments on these examples specifically, as well as on the requirement that hospital indemnity and other fixed indemnity insurance in the group market that are excepted benefits must provide benefits on a per day (or per other time period, such as per week) basis in an amount that does not vary based on the type of items or services received. The Departments also request comments on whether the conditions for hospital indemnity or other fixed indemnity insurance to be considered excepted benefits should be more substantively aligned between the group and individual markets. For example, the requirements for hospital indemnity or other fixed indemnity insurance in the individual market could be modified to be consistent with the group market provisions of these proposed regulations by limiting payment strictly on a per-period basis and not on a per-service basis.

Specified Disease Coverage

The Departments have been asked whether a policy covering multiple specified diseases or illnesses may be considered to be excepted benefits. The statute provides that the noncoordinated excepted benefits category includes "coverage of a specified disease or illness" if the coverage meets the conditions for being offered as independent, noncoordinated benefits, and the Departments' implementing regulations identify cancer-only policies as one example of specified disease coverage.[32] The Departments are concerned that individuals who purchase a specified disease policy covering multiple diseases or illnesses (including policies that cover one overarching medical condition such as "mental illness" as opposed to a specific condition such as depression) may incorrectly believe they are purchasing comprehensive medical coverage when, in fact, these polices may not include many of the important consumer protections under the PHS Act, ERISA, and the Code. The Departments solicit comments on this issue and on whether, if such policies are permitted to be considered excepted benefits, protections are needed to ensure such policies are not mistaken for comprehensive medical coverage. For example, the Departments solicit comments on whether to limit the number of diseases or illnesses that may be covered in a specified disease policy that is considered to be excepted benefits or whether issuers should be required to disclose that such policies are not minimum essential coverage under section 5000A(f) of the Code.

Short-Term, Limited-Duration Insurance

Under existing regulations, short-term, limited-duration insurance means "health insurance coverage provided pursuant to a contract with an issuer that has an expiration date specified in the contract (taking into account any extensions that may be elected by the policyholder without the issuer's consent) that is less than 12 months after the original effective date of the contract."[33] Before enactment of the ACA, short-term, limited-duration insurance was an important means for individuals to obtain health coverage when transitioning from one job to another (and from one group health plan to another) or in a similar situation. But with the guaranteed availability of coverage and special enrollment period requirements in the individual health insurance market under the ACA, short-term, limited-duration insurance is no longer the only means to obtain transitional coverage.

The Departments recently have become aware that short-term, limited-duration insurance is being sold to address situations other than the situations that the exception was initially intended to address.[34] In some instances individuals are purchasing this coverage as their primary form of health coverage and, contrary to the intent of the 12-month coverage limitation in the current definition of short-term, limited-duration insurance, some issuers are providing renewals of the coverage that extend the duration beyond 12 months. The Departments are concerned that these policies, because they are exempt from market reforms, may have significant limitations, such as lifetime and annual dollar limits on EHBs and pre-existing condition exclusions, and therefore may not provide meaningful health coverage. Further, because these policies can be medically underwritten based on health status, healthier individuals may be targeted for this type of coverage, thus adversely impacting the risk pool for ACA-compliant coverage.

To address the issue of short-term, limited-duration insurance being sold as a type of primary coverage, the proposed regulations revise the definition of short-term, limited-duration insurance so that the coverage must be less than three months in duration, including any period for which the policyholder renews or has an option to renew with or without the issuer's consent. The proposed regulations also provide that a notice must be prominently displayed in the contract and in any application materials provided in connection with enrollment in such coverage with the following language: THIS IS NOT QUALIFYING HEALTH COVERAGE ("MINIMUM ESSENTIAL COVERAGE") THAT SATISFIES THE HEALTH COVERAGE REQUIREMENT OF THE AFFORDABLE CARE ACT. IF YOU DON'T HAVE MINIMUM ESSENTIAL COVERAGE, YOU MAY OWE AN ADDITIONAL PAYMENT WITH YOUR TAXES.

This change would align the definition more closely with the initial intent of the regulation: To refer to coverage intended to fill temporary coverage gaps when an individual transitions between primary coverage. Further, limiting the coverage to less than three months improves coordination with the exemption from the individual shared responsibility provision of section 5000A of the Code for gaps in coverage of less than three months (the short coverage gap exemption), 26 CFR 1.5000A-3. Under current law, individuals who are enrolled in short-term, limited-duration coverage instead of minimum essential coverage for three months or more are generally not eligible for the short coverage gap exemption. The proposed regulations help ensure that individuals who purchase short-term, limited-duration coverage will still be eligible for the short coverage gap exemption (assuming other requirements are met) during the temporary coverage period.

In addition to proposing to reduce the length of short-term, limited-duration insurance to less than three months, the proposed regulations add the words "with or" in front of "without the issuer's consent" to address the Departments' concern that some issuers are taking liberty with the current definition of short-term, limited-duration insurance either by automatically renewing such policies or having a simplified reapplication process with the result being that such coverage lasts much longer than 12 months and serves as an individual's primary coverage but does not contain the important protections of the ACA. As indicated above, this type of coverage should only be sold for the purpose of providing coverage on a short-term basis such as filling in coverage gaps as a result of transitioning from one group health plan to another. The addition of the words "with or" clarifies that short-term, limited-duration insurance must be less than 3 months in total taking into account any option to renew or to reapply for the same or similar coverage.

The Departments seek comment on this proposal, including information and data on the number of short-term, limited-duration insurance policies offered for sale in the market, the types of individuals who typically purchase this coverage, and the reasons for which they purchase it.

Definition of EHB for Purposes of the Prohibition on Lifetime and Annual Limits

On November 18, 2015, the Departments issued final regulations implementing section 2711 of the PHS Act.[35] The final regulations provide that, for plan years beginning on or after January 1, 2017, a plan or issuer that is not required to provide EHBs must define EHB, for

---

[32] 26 CFR 54.9831-1(c)(4), 29 CFR 2590.732(c)(4), 45 CFR 146.145(b)(4) and 148.220(b)(3).

[33] 26 CFR 54.9801-2, 29 CFR 2590.702-2, 45 CFR 144.103.

[34] See e.g., Mathews, Anna W. "Sales of Short-Term Health Policies Surge," The Wall Street Journal April 10, 2016, available at http://www.wsj.com/articles/sales-of-short-term-health-policies-surge-1460328539.

[35] 80 FR 72192.

purposes of the prohibition on lifetime and annual dollar limits, in a manner consistent with any of the 51 EHB base-benchmark plans applicable in a State or the District of Columbia, or one of the three FEHBP base-benchmarks, as specified under 45 CFR 156.100.

The final regulations under section 2711 of the PHS Act include a reference to selecting a "base-benchmark" plan, as specified under 45 CFR 156.100, for purposes of determining which benefits cannot be subject to lifetime or annual dollar limits. The base-benchmark plan selected by a State or applied by default under 45 CFR 156.100, however, may not reflect the complete definition of EHB in the applicable State. For that reason, the Departments propose to amend the regulations at 26 CFR 54.9815-2711(c), 29 CFR 2590.715-2711(c), and 45 CFR 147.126(c) to refer to the provisions that capture the complete definition of EHB in a State. Specifically, the Departments propose to replace the phrase "in a manner consistent with one of the three Federal Employees Health Benefit Program (FEHBP) options as defined by 45 CFR 156.100(a)(3) or one of the base-benchmark plans selected by a State or applied by default pursuant to 45 CFR 156.100" in each of the regulations with the following: "In a manner that is consistent with (1) one of the EHB-benchmark plans applicable in a State under 45 CFR 156.110, and includes coverage of any additional required benefits that are considered essential health benefits consistent with 45 CFR 155.170(a)(2); or (2) one of the three Federal Employees Health Benefit Program (FEHBP) options as defined by 45 CFR 156.100(a)(3), supplemented, as necessary, to meet the standards in 45 CFR 156.110." This change reflects the possibility that base-benchmark plans, including the FEHBP plan options, could require supplementation under 45 CFR 156.110, and ensures the inclusion of State-required benefit mandates enacted on or before December 31, 2011 in accordance with 45 CFR 155.170, which when coupled with a State's EHB-benchmark plan, establish the definition of EHB in that State under regulations implementing section 1302(b) of the ACA.[36] The Departments seek comment on the requirement that, when one of the FEHBP plan options is selected as the benchmark, it would be supplemented, as needed, to ensure coverage in all ten statutory EHB categories, and the benchmark plan options that should be available for this purpose.

Proposed Applicability Date and Reliance

Except as otherwise provided herein, these proposed regulations are proposed to be applicable for plan years (or, in the individual market, policy years) beginning on or after January 1, 2017. Issuers, employers, administrators, and individuals are permitted to rely on these proposed regulations pending the applicability date of final regulations in the **Federal Register**. To the extent final regulations or other guidance is more restrictive on issuers, employers, administrators, and individuals than these proposed regulations, the final regulations or other guidance will be applied without retroactive effect and issuers, employers, administrators, and individuals will be provided sufficient time to come into compliance with the final regulations.

III. Economic Impact and Paperwork Burden

A. Summary—Department of Labor and Department of Health and Human Services

As stated above, the proposed regulations would provide guidance on the rules for expatriate health plans, expatriate health plan issuers, and qualified expatriates under the EHCCA. The EHCCA generally provides that the requirements of the ACA do not apply with respect to expatriate health plans, expatriate health insurance issuers for coverage under expatriate health plans, and employers in their capacity as plan sponsors of expatriate health plans.

The proposed regulations address how certain requirements relating to minimum essential coverage under section 5000A of the Code, the health care reporting provisions of sections 6055 and 6056 of the Code, and the health insurance providers fee imposed by section 9010 of the ACA continue to apply subject to certain provisions while providing that the excise tax under sections 4375 and 4376 of the Code do not apply to expatriate health plans.

The proposed regulations also propose amendments to the Departments' regulations concerning excepted benefits, which would specify the conditions for supplemental health insurance products that are designed "to fill gaps in primary coverage" by providing additional

categories of benefits (as opposed to filling in gaps in cost sharing) to constitute supplemental excepted benefits, and clarify that certain travel-related insurance products that provide only incidental health benefits constitute excepted benefits. The proposed regulations also require that, to be considered hospital indemnity or other fixed indemnity insurance in the group market, any application or enrollment materials provided to participants at or before the time participants are given the opportunity to enroll in the coverage must include a statement that the coverage is a supplement to, rather than a substitute for, major medical coverage and that a lack of minimum essential coverage may result in an additional tax payment. Further, the regulations clarify that hospital indemnity and other fixed indemnity insurance must pay a fixed dollar amount per day (or per other time period, such as per week) regardless of the type of items or services received.

The regulations also propose revisions to the definition of short-term, limited-duration insurance so that the coverage has to be less than 3 months in duration (as opposed to the current definition of less than 12 months in duration), and that a notice must be prominently displayed in the contract and in any application materials provided in connection with the coverage that provides that such coverage is not minimum essential coverage.

The proposed regulations also include amendments to 45 CFR part 158 to clarify that the MLR reporting requirements do not apply to expatriate health plans under the EHCCA.

Finally, the proposed regulations propose to amend the definition of "essential health benefits" for purposes of the prohibition of annual and lifetime dollar limits for group health plans and health insurance issuers that are not required to provide essential health benefits.

The Departments are publishing these proposed regulations to implement the protections intended by the Congress in the most economically efficient manner possible. The Departments have examined the effects of this rule as required by Executive Order 13563 (76 FR 3821, January 21, 2011), Executive Order 12866 (58 FR 51735, September 1993, Regulatory Planning and Review), the Regulatory Flexibility Act (RFA) (September 19, 1980, Pub. L. 96-354), the Unfunded Mandates Reform Act of 1995 (Pub. L. 104-4), Executive Order 13132 on Federalism, and the Congressional Review Act (5 U.S.C. 804(2)).

B. Executive Orders 12866 and 13563—Department of Labor and Department of Health and Human Services

Executive Order 12866 (58 FR 51735) directs agencies to assess all costs and benefits of available regulatory alternatives and, if regulation is necessary, to select regulatory approaches that maximize net benefits (including potential economic, environmental, public health and safety effects; distributive impacts; and equity). Executive Order 13563 (76 FR 3821, January 21, 2011) is supplemental to and reaffirms the principles, structures, and definitions governing regulatory review as established in Executive Order 12866.

Section 3(f) of Executive Order 12866 defines a "significant regulatory action" as an action that is likely to result in a final rule—(1) having an annual effect on the economy of $100 million or more in any one year, or adversely and materially affecting a sector of the economy, productivity, competition, jobs, the environment, public health or safety, or state, local or tribal governments or communities (also referred to as "economically significant"); (2) creating a serious inconsistency or otherwise interfering with an action taken or planned by another agency; (3) materially altering the budgetary impacts of entitlement grants, user fees, or loan programs or the rights and obligations of recipients thereof; or (4) raising novel legal or policy issues arising out of legal mandates, the President's priorities, or the principles set forth in the Executive Order.

A regulatory impact analysis (RIA) must be prepared for rules with economically significant effects (for example, $100 million or more in any 1 year), and a "significant" regulatory action is subject to review by the OMB. The Departments have determined that this regulatory action is not likely to have economic impacts of $100 million or more in any one year, and therefore is not significant within the meaning of Executive Order 12866. The Departments expect the impact of these proposed regulations to be limited because they do not require any additional action or impose any requirements on issuers, employers and plan sponsors.

---

[36] In the HHS Notice of Benefit and Payment Parameters for 2016 published February 27, 2015 (80 FR 10750), HHS instructed States to select a new base-benchmark plan to take effect beginning with plan or policy years beginning in 2017. The new final EHB base-benchmark plans selected as a result of this process are publicly available at *downloads.cms.gov/cciio/Final%20List%20of%20BMPs_15_10_21.pdf*. Additional information about the new base-benchmark plans, including plan documents and summaries of

benefits, is available at *www.cms.gov/CCIIO/Resources/Data-Resources/ehb.html*. The definition of EHB in each of the 50 states and the District of Columbia is based on the base-benchmark plan, and takes into account any additions to the base-benchmark plan, such as supplementation under 45 CFR 156.110, and State-required benefit mandates in accordance with 45 CFR 155.170.

1. Need for Regulatory Action

Consistent with the EHCCA, enacted as Division M of the Consolidated Clarification Continuing Appropriations Act, 2015 Public Law 113-235 (128 Stat. 2130), these proposed regulations provide that the market reform provisions enacted as part of the ACA generally do not apply to expatriate health plans, any employer solely in its capacity as a plan sponsor of an expatriate health plan, and any expatriate health insurance issuer with respect to coverage under an expatriate health plan. Further, the proposed regulations define the benefit and administrative requirements for expatriate health issuers, expatriate health plans, and qualified expatriates and provide clarification regarding the applicability of certain fee and reporting requirements under the Code.

Consistent with section 2 of the EHCCA, these proposed regulations are necessary to carry out the intent of Congress that (1) American expatriate health insurance issuers should be permitted to compete on a level playing field in the global marketplace; (2) the global competitiveness of American companies should be encouraged; and (3) in implementing the health insurance providers fee imposed by section 9010 of the ACA and other provisions of the ACA, the unique and multinational features of expatriate health plans and the United States companies that operate such plans and the competitive pressures of such plans and companies should continue to be recognized.

In response to feedback the Departments have received from stakeholders, the proposed regulations would also clarify the conditions for supplemental health insurance and travel insurance to be considered excepted benefits. These clarifications will provide health insurance issuers offering supplemental insurance coverage and travel insurance products with a clearer understanding of whether these types of coverage are subject to the market reforms under title XXVII of the PHS Act, part 7 of ERISA, and Chapter 100 of the Code. The proposed regulations also would amend the definition of short-term, limited-duration insurance and impose a new notice requirement in response to recent reports that this type of coverage is being sold for purposes other than for which the exclusion for short-term, limited-duration insurance was initially intended to cover.

2. Summary of Impacts

These proposed regulations would implement the rules for expatriate health plans, expatriate health insurance issuers, and qualified expatriates under the EHCCA. The proposed regulations also outline the conditions for travel insurance and supplemental insurance coverage to be considered excepted benefits, and revise the definition of short-term, limited-duration insurance.

Based on the NAIC 2014 Supplemental Health Care Exhibit Report,[37] which generally uses the definition of expatriate coverage in the MLR final rule at 45 CFR 158.120(d)(4),[38] there are an estimated eight issuers (one issuer in the small group market and seven issuers in the large group market) domiciled in the United States that provide expatriate health plans for approximately 270,349 enrollees. While the Departments acknowledge that some expatriate health insurance issuers and employers in their capacity as plan sponsor of an expatriate health plan may incur costs in order to comply with certain provisions of the EHCCA and these proposed regulations, as discussed below, the Departments believe that these costs will be relatively insignificant and limited.

The vast majority of expatriate health plans described in the EHCCA would qualify as expatriate health plans under the transitional relief provided in the Departments' Affordable Care Act Implementation FAQs Part XVIII, Q&A-6 and Q&A-7. The FAQs provide that expatriate health plans with plan years ending on or before December 31, 2016 are exempt from the ACA market reforms and provide that coverage provided under an expatriate group health plan is a form of minimum essential coverage under section 5000A of the Code. The EHCCA permanently exempts expatriate health plans with plan or policy years beginning on or after July 1, 2015 from the ACA market reform requirements and provides that coverage provided under an expatriate health plan is a form of minimum essential coverage under section 5000A of the Code.

Because the Departments believe that most, if not all, expatriate health plans described in the EHCCA would qualify as expatriate health plans under the Departments' previous guidance, and the proposed regulations codify the provisions of the EHCCA by making the temporary relief in the Departments' Affordable Care Act Implementa-

tion FAQs Part XVIII, Q&A-6 and Q&A-7 permanent for specified expatriate health plans, the Departments believe that the proposed regulations will result in only marginal, if any, impact on these plans. Furthermore, the Departments believe the proposed regulations outlining the conditions for travel insurance and supplemental insurance coverage to be considered excepted benefits are consistent with prevailing industry practice and will not result in significant cost to health insurance issuers of these products.

The Departments believe that any costs incurred by issuers of short-term, limited-duration insurance and hospital indemnity and other fixed indemnity insurance to include the required notice in application or enrollment materials will be negligible since the Departments have provided the exact text for the notice. Further, the Departments note that issuers of hospital indemnity and other fixed indemnity insurance in the individual market already provide a similar notice.

As a result, the Departments have concluded that the impacts of these proposed regulations are not economically significant. The Departments request comments on the assumptions used to evaluate the economic impact of these proposed regulations, including specific data and information on the number of expatriate health plans.

C. Paperwork Reduction Act

1. Department of the Treasury

The collection of information in these proposed regulations are in 26 CFR 1.6055-2(a)(8) and 301.6056-2(a)(8). The collection of information in these proposed regulations relates to statements required to be furnished to a responsible individual under section 6055 of the Code and statements required to be furnished to an employee under section 6056 of the Code. The collection of information in these proposed regulations would, in accordance with the EHCCA, permit a furnisher to furnish the required statements electronically unless the recipient has explicitly refused to consent to receive the statement in an electronic format. The collection of information contained in this notice of proposed rulemaking will be taken into account and submitted to the Office of Management and Budget in accordance with the Paperwork Reduction Act of 1995 (44 U.S.C. 3507(d)) in connection with the next review of the collection of information for IRS Form 1095-B (OMB # 1545-2252) and IRS Form 1095-C (OMB # 1545-2251).

Comments on the collection of information should be sent to the Office of Management and Budget, Attn: Desk Officer for the Department of the Treasury, Office of Information and Regulatory Affairs, Washington, DC 20503, with copies to the Internal Revenue Service, Attn: IRS Reports Clearance Officer, SE:CAR:MP:T:T:SP, Washington, DC 20224. Comments on the collection of information should be received by August 9, 2016. Comments are sought on whether the proposed collection of information is necessary for the proper performance of the IRS, including whether the information will have practical utility; the accuracy of the estimated burden associated with the proposed collection of information; how the quality, utility, and clarity of the information to be collected may be enhanced; how the burden of complying with the proposed collection of information may be minimized, including through the application of automated collection techniques and other forms of information technology; and estimates of capital or start-up costs and costs of operation, maintenance, and purchase of service to provide information. Comments on the collection of information should be received by August 9, 2016.

An agency may not conduct or sponsor, and a person is not required to respond to, a collection of information unless it displays a valid control number assigned by the Office of Management and Budget.

Books or records relating to a collection of information must be retained as long as their contents may become material in the administration of any internal revenue law. Generally, tax returns and tax return information are confidential, as required by 26 U.S.C. 6103.

2. Department of the Treasury, Department of Labor, and Department of Health and Human Services

The proposed regulations provide that to be considered hospital or other fixed indemnity excepted benefits in the group market for plan years beginning on or after January 1, 2017, a notice must be included in any application or enrollment materials provided to participants at or before the time participants are given the opportunity to enroll in the coverage, indicating that the coverage is a supplement to, rather than a substitute for major medical coverage and that a lack of minimum

---

[37] NAIC, 2014 Supplemental Health Care Exhibit Report, Volume 1 (2015), available at *http://www.naic.org/documents/prod_serv_statistical_hcs_zb.pdf.*

[38] Section 45 CFR 158.120(d)(4) defines expatriate policies as predominantly group health insurance policies that provide coverage to employees, substantially all of whom are:

(1) Working outside their country of citizenship; (2) working outside their country of citizenship and outside the employer's country of domicile; or (3) non-U.S. citizens working in their home country.

essential coverage may result in an additional tax payment. The proposed regulations also provide that to be considered short-term, limited-duration insurance for policy years beginning on or after January 1, 2017, a notice must be prominently displayed in the contract and in any application materials, stating that the coverage is not minimum essential coverage and that failure to have minimum essential coverage may result in an additional tax payment. The Departments have provided the exact text for these notice requirements and the language will not need to be customized. The burden associated with these notices is not subject to the Paperwork Reduction Act of 1995 in accordance with 5 CFR 1320.3(c)(2) because they do not contain a "collection of information" as defined in 44 U.S.C. 3502(11).

D. Regulatory Flexibility Act

The Regulatory Flexibility Act (5 U.S.C. 601 *et seq.*) (RFA) imposes certain requirements with respect to Federal rules that are subject to the notice and comment requirements of section 553(b) of the Administrative Procedure Act (5 U.S.C. 551 *et seq.*) and that are likely to have a significant economic impact on a substantial number of small entities. Unless an agency certifies that a proposed rule is not likely to have a significant economic impact on a substantial number of small entities, section 603 of RFA requires that the agency present an initial regulatory flexibility analysis at the time of the publication of the notice of proposed rulemaking describing the impact of the rule on small entities and seeking public comment on such impact. Small entities include small businesses, organizations and governmental jurisdictions.

The RFA generally defines a "small entity" as (1) a proprietary firm meeting the size standards of the Small Business Administration (SBA) (13 CFR 121.201); (2) a nonprofit organization that is not dominant in its field; or (3) a small government jurisdiction with a population of less than 50,000. (States and individuals are not included in the definition of "small entity.") The Departments use as their measure of significant economic impact on a substantial number of small entities a change in revenues of more than 3 to 5 percent.

These proposed regulations are not likely to impose additional costs on small entities. According to SBA size standards, entities with average annual receipts of $38.5 million or less would be considered small entities for these North American Industry Classification System codes. The Departments believe that, since the majority of small issuers belong to larger holding groups, many if not all are likely to have non-health lines of business that would result in their revenues exceeding $38.5 million. Therefore, the Departments certify that the proposed regulations will not have a significant impact on a substantial number of small entities. In addition, section 1102(b) of the Social Security Act requires agencies to prepare a regulatory impact analysis if a rule may have a significant economic impact on the operations of a substantial number of small rural hospitals. This analysis must conform to the provisions of section 604 of the RFA. These proposed regulations would not affect small rural hospitals. Therefore, the Departments have determined that these proposed regulations would not have a significant impact on the operations of a substantial number of small rural hospitals.

E. Special Analysis—Department of the Treasury

Certain IRS regulations, including this one, are exempt from the requirements of Executive Order 12866, as supplemented and reaffirmed by Executive Order 13563. Therefore, a regulatory impact assessment is not required. It also has been determined that section 553(b) of the Administrative Procedure Act (5 U.S.C. Chapter 5) does not apply to these regulations. For applicability of RFA, see paragraph D of this section III.

Pursuant to section 7805(f) of the Code, these regulations have been submitted to the Chief Counsel for Advocacy of the Small Business Administration for comment on their impact on small business.

F. Unfunded Mandates Reform Act

For purposes of the Unfunded Mandates Reform Act of 1995 (2 U.S.C. 1501 *et seq.*), as well as Executive Order 12875, these proposed rules do not include any Federal mandate that may result in expenditures by State, local, or tribal governments, or the private sector, which may impose an annual burden of $146 million adjusted for inflation since 1995.

G. Federalism—Department of Labor and Department of Health and Human Services

Executive Order 13132 outlines fundamental principles of federalism. It requires adherence to specific criteria by Federal agencies in formulating and implementing policies that have "substantial direct effects" on the States, the relationship between the national government and States, or on the distribution of power and responsibilities among the various levels of government. Federal agencies promulgating regulations that have these federalism implications must consult with State and local officials, and describe the extent of their consultation and the nature of the concerns of State and local officials in the preamble to the final regulation.

In the Departments' view, these proposed regulations do not have federalism implications, because they do not have direct effects on the States, the relationship between the national government and States, or on the distribution of power and responsibilities among various levels of government.

H. Congressional Review Act

These proposed regulations are subject to the Congressional Review Act provisions of the Small Business Regulatory Enforcement Fairness Act of 1996 (5 U.S.C. 801 *et seq.*), and, if finalized, will be transmitted to the Congress and to the Comptroller General for review in accordance with such provisions.

I. Statement of Availability of IRS Documents

IRS Revenue Procedures, Revenue Rulings notices, and other guidance cited in this document are published in the Internal Revenue Bulletin (or Cumulative Bulletin) and are available from the Superintendent of Documents, U.S. Government Printing Office, Washington, DC 20402, or by visiting the IRS Web site at *http://www.irs.gov*.

IV. Statutory Authority

The Department of the Treasury regulations are proposed to be adopted pursuant to the authority contained in sections 7805 and 9833 of the Code.

The Department of Labor regulations are proposed pursuant to the authority contained in 29 U.S.C. 1135,and 1191c; Secretary of Labor's Order 1-2011, 77 FR 1088 (Jan. 9, 2012).

The Department of Health and Human Services regulations are proposed to be adopted pursuant to the authority contained in sections 2701 through 2763, 2791, and 2792 of the PHS Act (42 U.S.C. 300gg through 300gg-63, 300gg-91, and 300gg-92), as amended.

List of Subjects

26 CFR Part 1

Income taxes.

26 CFR Part 46

Excise taxes, Health care, Health insurance, Pensions, Reporting and recordkeeping requirements.

26 CFR Part 54

Pension and excise taxes.

26 CFR Part 57

Health insurance providers fee.

26 CFR Part 301

Procedure and administration.

29 CFR Part 2590

Continuation coverage, Disclosure, Employee benefit plans, Group health plans, Health care, Health insurance, Medical child support, Reporting and recordkeeping requirements.

45 CFR Parts 144, 146 and 147

Health care, Health insurance, Reporting and recordkeeping requirements.

45 CFR Part 148

Administrative practice and procedure, Health care, Health insurance, Penalties, Reporting and recordkeeping requirements.

45 CFR Part 158

Health insurance, Medical loss ratio, Reporting and rebate requirements.

John Dalrymple,

Deputy Commissioner for Services and Enforcement, Internal Revenue Service.

Signed this 1st day of June 2016.

Phyllis C. Borzi,

Assistant Secretary, Employee Benefits Security Administration, Department of Labor.

Dated: June 2, 2016.

Andrew M. Slavitt,

Acting Administrator, Centers for Medicare & Medicaid Services.

Dated: June 3, 2016.

Sylvia M. Burwell,

Secretary, Department of Health and Human Services.

DEPARTMENT OF THE TREASURY

Internal Revenue Service

Proposed Amendments to the Regulations

Accordingly, 26 CFR parts 1, 46, 54, 57, and 301 are proposed to be amended as follows:

PART 1—INCOME TAXES

■ 1. The authority citation for part 1 continues to read in part as follows:

Authority: 26 U.S.C. 7805.* * *

■ 2. Section 1.162-31 is amended by adding paragraph (b)(5)(v) to read as follows:

§1.162-31 The $500,000 deduction limitation for remuneration provided by certain health insurance providers.

*****

(b) * * *

(5) * * *

(v) *Expatriate health plan coverage.* For purposes of this section, amounts received in payment for expatriate health plan coverage, as defined in §54.9831-1(f)(3), are not premiums.

*****

■ 3. Section 1.5000A-2 is amended by adding paragraphs (c)(1)(i)(D) and (d)(3) to read as follows:

§1.5000A-2 Minimum essential coverage.

*****

(c) * * *

(1) * * *

(i) * * *

(D) A group health plan that is an expatriate health plan within the meaning of §54.9831-1(f)(3) of this chapter if the requirements of §54.9831-1(f)(3)(i) of this chapter are met by providing coverage for qualified expatriates described in §54.9831-1(f)(6)(i) or (ii) of this chapter.

*****

(d) * * *

(3) *Certain expatriate health plans.* An expatriate health plan within the meaning of §54.9831-1(f)(3) of this chapter that is not an eligible employer-sponsored plan under paragraph (c)(1)(i)(D) of this section is a plan in the individual market.

*****

■ 4. Section 1.6055-2 is amended by adding paragraph (a)(8) to read as follows:

§1.6055-2 Electronic furnishing of statements.

(a) * * *

(8) *Special rule for expatriate health plan coverage* —(i) *In general.* In the case of an individual covered under an expatriate health plan (within the meaning of §54.9831-1(f)(3) of this chapter), the recipient is treated as having consented under paragraph (a)(2) of this section unless the recipient has explicitly refused to consent to receive the statement in an electronic format. The refusal to consent may be made electronically or in a paper document. A recipient's request for a paper statement is treated as an explicit refusal to receive the statement in electronic format. A furnisher relying on this paragraph (a)(8) must satisfy the requirements of paragraphs (a)(3) through (7) of this section, except that the statement required under paragraph (a)(3) must

be provided at least 30 days prior to the time for furnishing under §1.6055-1(g)(4)(i)(A) of this chapter of the first statement that the furnisher intends to furnish electronically to the recipient, and the other requirements of paragraph (a)(3) are modified to reflect that the statement will be furnished electronically unless the recipient explicitly refuses to consent to receive the statement in an electronic format.

(ii) *Manner and time of notifying recipient.* The IRS may specify in other guidance published in the Internal Revenue Bulletin the manner and timing for the initial notification of recipients that the statement required under paragraph (a)(3) of this section will be furnished electronically unless the recipient explicitly refuses to consent to receive the statement in an electronic format. See §601.601(d)(2)(ii)(B) of this chapter.

(iii) *Effective/applicability date.* The provisions of this paragraph (a)(8) apply as of January 1, 2017.

*****

PART 46—EXCISE TAXES, HEALTH CARE, HEALTH INSURANCE, PENSIONS, REPORTING AND RECORDKEEPING

■ 5. The authority citation for part 46 continues to read as follows:

Authority: 26 U.S.C. 7805.

■ 6. Section 46.4377-1 is amended by redesignating paragraph (c) as paragraph (d) and adding new paragraph (c) to read as follows:

§46.4377-1. Definitions and special rules.

*****

(c) *Treatment of expatriate health plans.* For policy years and plan years that end after January 1, 2017, the fees imposed by sections 4375 and 4376 do not apply to an expatriate health plan within the meaning of §54.9831-1(f)(3).

*****

PART 54—PENSION AND EXCISE TAXES

■ 7. The authority citation for part 54 continues to read in part as follows:

Authority: 26 U.S.C. 7805* * *

■ 8. Section 54.9801-2 is amended by:

■ a. Adding in alphabetical order definitions for "expatriate health insurance issuer", "expatriate health plan", and "qualified expatriate;"

■ b. Revising the definition of "short-term, limited-duration insurance"; and

■ c. Adding in alphabetical order a definition for "travel insurance".

The additions and revisions read as follows:

§54.9801-2 Definitions.

*****

Expatriate health insurance issuer means an expatriate health insurance issuer within the meaning of §54.9831-1(f)(2).

Expatriate health plan means an expatriate health plan within the meaning of §54.9831-1(f)(3).

*****

Qualified expatriate means a qualified expatriate within the meaning of §54.9831-1(f)(6).

Short-term, limited-duration insurance means health insurance coverage provided pursuant to a contract with an issuer that:

(1) Has an expiration date specified in the contract (taking into account any extensions that may be elected by the policyholder with or without the issuer's consent) that is less than 3 months after the original effective date of the contract; and

(2) Displays prominently in the contract and in any application materials provided in connection with enrollment in such coverage in at least 14 point type the following: "THIS IS NOT QUALIFYING HEALTH COVERAGE ("MINIMUM ESSENTIAL COVERAGE") THAT SATISFIES THE HEALTH COVERAGE REQUIREMENT OF THE AFFORDABLE CARE ACT. IF YOU DON'T HAVE MINIMUM ESSENTIAL COVERAGE, YOU MAY OWE AN ADDITIONAL PAYMENT WITH YOUR TAXES."

*****

Travel insurance means insurance coverage for personal risks incident to planned travel, which may include, but is not limited to, interruption or cancellation of trip or event, loss of baggage or personal effects, damages to accommodations or rental vehicles, and sickness, accident, disability, or death occurring during travel, provided that the health benefits are not offered on a stand-alone basis and are incidental to other coverage. For this purpose, the term travel insurance does not include major medical plans that provide comprehensive medical protection for travelers with trips lasting 6 months or longer, including, for example, those working overseas as an expatriate or military personnel being deployed.

*****

■ 9. Section 54.9815-2711 is amended by revising paragraph (c) to read as follows:

§54.9815-2711 No lifetime or annual limits.

*****

(c) *Definition of essential health benefits.* The term "essential health benefits" means essential health benefits under section 1302(b) of the Patient Protection and Affordable Care Act and applicable regulations. For this purpose, a group health plan or a health insurance issuer that is not required to provide essential health benefits under section 1302(b) must define "essential health benefits" in a manner that is consistent with—

(1) One of the EHB-benchmark plans applicable in a State under 45 CFR 156.110, and includes coverage of any additional required benefits that are considered essential health benefits consistent with 45 CFR 155.170(a)(2); or

(2) One of the three Federal Employees Health Benefit Program (FEHBP) options as defined by 45 CFR 156.100(a)(3), supplemented, as necessary, to meet the standards in 45 CFR 156.110.

*****

§54.9831-1 [Amended]

■ 10. Section 54.9831-1 is amended in paragraph (b)(1) by removing the reference "54.9812-1T" and adding in its place the reference "54.9812-1, 54.9815-1251 through 54.9815-2719A," and in paragraph (c)(1) by removing the reference "54.9811-1T, 54.9812-1T" with the phrase "54.9811-1, 54.9812-1, 54.9815-1251 through 54.9815-2719A".

■ 11. Section 54.9831-1 is amended:

■ a. In paragraph (c)(2)(vii) by removing "and" at the end;

■ b. In paragraph (c)(2)(viii) by adding "and" at the end;

■ c. Adding paragraph (c)(2)(ix);

■ d. Revising paragraph (c)(4)(i);

■ e. Adding paragraph (c)(4)(ii)(D);

■ f. Revising paragraphs (c)(4)(iii) and (c)(5)(i)(C); and

■ g. Adding paragraph (f).

The revisions and additions read as follows:

§54.9831-1 Special rules relating to group health plans.

*****

(c) * * *

(2) * * *

(ix) Travel insurance within the meaning of §54.9801-2 of this section.

*****

(4) *Noncoordinated benefits* —(i) *Excepted benefits that are not coordinated.* Coverage for only a specified disease or illness (for example, cancer-only policies) or hospital indemnity or other fixed indemnity insurance is excepted only if the coverage meets each of the conditions specified in paragraph (c)(4)(ii) of this section.

(ii) * * *

(D) To be hospital indemnity or other fixed indemnity insurance, the insurance must pay a fixed dollar amount per day (or per other time period, such as per week) of hospitalization or illness (for example, $100/day) without regard to the amount of expenses incurred or the type of items or services received and—

(*1*) The plan or issuer must provide, in any application or enrollment materials provided to participants at or before the time participants are given the opportunity to enroll in the coverage, a notice that prominently displays in at least 14 point type the following language: "THIS IS A SUPPLEMENT TO HEALTH INSURANCE AND IS NOT A SUBSTITUTE FOR MAJOR MEDICAL COVERAGE. THIS IS NOT QUALIFYING HEALTH COVERAGE ("MINIMUM ESSENTIAL COVERAGE") THAT SATISFIES THE HEALTH COVERAGE REQUIREMENT OF THE AFFORDABLE CARE ACT. IF YOU DON'T HAVE MINIMUM ESSENTIAL COVERAGE, YOU MAY OWE AN ADDITIONAL PAYMENT WITH YOUR TAXES."

(*2*) If participants are required to reenroll (in either paper or electronic form) for renewal or reissuance, the notice described in paragraph (c)(4)(ii)(D)(*1*) of this section must be displayed in the reenrollment materials that are provided to the participants at or before the time participants are given the opportunity to reenroll in the coverage.

(*3*) If a notice satisfying the requirements of this paragraph (c)(4)(ii)(D) is timely provided to a participant, the obligation to provide the notice is satisfied for both the plan and the issuer.

(iii) *Examples.* The rules of this paragraph (c)(4) are illustrated by the following examples:

Example 1. (i) *Facts.* An employer sponsors a group health plan that provides coverage through an insurance policy. The policy provides benefits only for hospital stays at a fixed percentage of hospital expenses up to a maximum of $100 a day.

(ii) *Conclusion.* In this *Example 1*, because the policy pays a percentage of expenses incurred rather than a fixed dollar amount per day (or per other time period, such as per week), the policy is not hospital indemnity or other fixed indemnity insurance that is an excepted benefit under this paragraph (c)(4). This is the result even if, in practice, the policy pays the maximum of $100 for every day of hospitalization.

Example 2. (i) *Facts.* An employer sponsors a group health plan that provides coverage through an insurance policy. The policy provides benefits for doctors' visits at $50 per visit, hospitalization at $100 per day, various surgical procedures at different dollar rates per procedure, and prescription drugs at $15 per prescription.

(ii) *Conclusion.* In this *Example 2*, for doctors' visits, surgery, and prescription drugs, payment is not made on a per-period basis, but instead is based on whether a procedure or item is provided, such as whether an individual has surgery or a doctor visit or is prescribed a drug, and the amount of payment varies based on the type of procedure or item. Because benefits related to office visits, surgery, and prescription drugs are not paid based on a fixed dollar amount per day (or per other time period, such as per week), as required under paragraph (c)(4) of this section, the policy is not hospital indemnity or other fixed indemnity insurance that is an excepted benefit under this paragraph (c)(4).

Example 3. (i) *Facts.* An employer sponsors a group health plan that provides coverage through an insurance policy. The policy provides benefits for certain services at a fixed dollar amount per day, but the dollar amount varies by the type of service.

(ii) *Conclusion.* In this *Example 3*, because the policy provides benefits in a different amount per day depending on the type of service, rather than one specific dollar amount per day regardless of the type of service, the policy is not hospital indemnity or other fixed indemnity insurance that is an excepted benefit under this paragraph (c)(4).

(5) * * *

(i) * * *

(C) *Similar supplemental coverage provided to coverage under a group health plan.* To be similar supplemental coverage, the coverage must be specifically designed to fill gaps in the primary coverage. The preceding sentence is satisfied if the coverage is designed to fill gaps in cost sharing in the primary coverage, such as coinsurance or deductibles, or the coverage is designed to provide benefits for items and services not covered by the primary coverage and that are not essential health benefits in the State where the coverage is issued, or the coverage is designed to both fill such gaps in cost sharing under, and cover such benefits not covered by, the primary coverage. Similar supplemental coverage does not include coverage that becomes secondary or supplemental only under a coordination-of-benefits provision.

*****

(f) *Expatriate health plans and expatriate health insurance issuers* — (1) *In general.* With respect to coverage under an expatriate health plan, the requirements of section 9815 of the Code and implementing rules and regulations (incorporating sections 2701 through 2728 of the Public Health Service Act) do not apply to—

(i) An expatriate health plan (as defined in paragraph (f)(3) of this section),

(ii) An employer, solely in its capacity as plan sponsor of an expatriate health plan, and

(iii) An expatriate health insurance issuer (as defined in paragraph (f)(2) of this section) with respect to coverage under an expatriate health plan.

(2) *Definition of expatriate health insurance issuer* —(i) *In general.* Expatriate health insurance issuer means a health insurance issuer, within the meaning of §54.9801-2, that issues expatriate health plans and that in the course of its normal business operations—

(A) Maintains network provider agreements that provide for direct claims payments, with health care providers in eight or more countries;

(B) Maintains call centers in three or more countries, and accepts calls from customers in eight or more languages;

(C) Processed at least $1 million in claims in foreign currency equivalents during the preceding calendar year, determined using the Treasury Department's currency exchange rate in effect on the last day of the preceding calendar year;

(D) Makes global evacuation/repatriation coverage available;

(E) Maintains legal and compliance resources in three or more countries; and

(F) Has licenses or other authority to sell insurance in more than two countries, including in the United States.

(ii) *Additional rules.* For purposes of meeting the requirements of this paragraph (f)(2), two or more entities, including one entity that is the expatriate health insurance issuer, that are members of the expatriate health insurance issuer's controlled group (as determined under §57.2(c) of this chapter) are treated as one expatriate health insurance issuer. Alternatively, the requirements of this paragraph (f)(2) may be satisfied through contracts between an expatriate health insurance issuer and third parties.

(3) *Definition of expatriate health plan.* Expatriate health plan means a plan that satisfies the requirements of paragraphs (f)(3)(i) through (iii) of this section.

(i) *Substantially all qualified expatriates requirement.* Substantially all primary enrollees in the expatriate health plan must be qualified expatriates. For purposes of this paragraph (f)(3)(i), the primary enrollee is the individual covered by the plan or policy whose eligibility for coverage is not due to that individual's status as the spouse, dependent, or other beneficiary of another covered individual. Notwithstanding the foregoing, an individual is not a primary enrollee if the individual is not a national of the United States and the individual resides in his or her country of citizenship. A plan satisfies the requirement of this paragraph (f)(3)(i) for a plan or policy year only if, on the first day of the plan or policy year, less than 5 percent of the primary enrollees (or less than 5 primary enrollees if greater) are not qualified expatriates.

(ii) *Substantially all benefits not excepted benefits requirement.* Substantially all of the benefits provided under the plan or coverage must be benefits that are not excepted benefits described in §54.9831-1(c).

(iii) *Additional requirements.* To qualify as an expatriate health plan, the plan or coverage must also meet the following requirements:

(A) The plan or coverage provides coverage for inpatient hospital services, outpatient facility services, physician services, and emergency services (comparable to emergency services coverage that was described in and offered under section 8903(1) of title 5, United States Code for plan year 2009) in the following locations—

(*1*) In the case of individuals described in paragraph (f)(6)(i) of this section, in the United States and in the country or countries from which the individual was transferred or assigned, and such other country or countries the Secretary of Health and Human Services, in consultation with the Secretary of the Treasury and Secretary of Labor, may designate;

(*2*) In the case of individuals described in paragraph (f)(6)(ii) of this section, in the country or countries in which the individual is present in connection with his employment, and such other country or countries the Secretary of Health and Human Services, in consultation with the Secretary of the Treasury and Secretary of Labor, may designate; or

(*3*) In the case of individuals described in paragraph (f)(6)(iii) of this section, in the country or countries the Secretary of Health and Human Services, in consultation with the Secretary of the Treasury and Secretary of Labor, may designate.

(B) The plan sponsor reasonably believes that benefits provided by the plan or coverage satisfy the minimum value requirements of section 36B(c)(2)(C)(ii). For this purpose, a plan sponsor is permitted to rely on the reasonable representations of the issuer or administrator regarding whether benefits offered by the issuer or group health plan satisfy the minimum value requirements unless the plan sponsor knows or has reason to know that the benefits fail to satisfy the minimum value requirements.

(C) In the case of a plan or coverage that provides dependent coverage of children, such coverage must be available until an individual attains age 26, unless an individual is the child of a child receiving dependent coverage.

(D) The plan or coverage is:

(*1*) In the case of individuals described in paragraph (f)(6)(i) or (ii) of this section, a group health plan (including health insurance coverage offered in connection with a group health plan), issued by an expatriate health insurance issuer or administered by an expatriate health plan administrator. A group health plan will not fail to be an expatriate health plan merely because any portion of the coverage is provided through a self-insured arrangement.

(*2*) In the case of individuals described in paragraph (f)(6)(iii) of this section, health insurance coverage issued by an expatriate health insurance issuer.

(E) The plan or coverage offers reimbursements for items or services in local currency in eight or more countries.

(F) The plan or coverage satisfies the provisions of Chapter 100 and regulations thereunder as in effect on March 22, 2010. For this purpose, the plan or coverage is not required to comply with section 9801(e) (relating to certification of creditable coverage) and underlying regulations. However, to the extent the plan or coverage imposes a preexisting condition exclusion, the plan or coverage must ensure that individuals with prior creditable coverage who enroll in the plan or coverage have an opportunity to demonstrate that they have creditable coverage offsetting the preexisting condition exclusion.

(iv) *Example.* The rule of paragraph (f)(3)(i) of this section is illustrated by the following example:

Example.

(i) *Facts.* Business has health plan X for 250 U.S. citizens working outside of the United States in Country Y. All of the U.S. citizens working in Country Y satisfy the requirements to be qualified expatriates under §54.9831-1(f)(6)(ii). In addition to the 250 U.S. citizens, Business employs 100 citizens of Country Y who reside in Country Y and do not satisfy the requirements to be qualified expatriates under §54.9831-1(f)(6)(ii). Health plan X covers both the U.S. citizens and citizens of Country Y.

(ii) *Conclusion.* Health plan X satisfies the requirement of §54.9831-1(f)(3)(i) that substantially all primary enrollees of an expatriate health plan be qualified expatriates because 100 percent of the primary enrollees are qualified expatriates. The 100 citizens of Country Y who reside in Country Y are not treated as primary enrollees for purposes of the substantially all requirement of §54.9831-1(f)(3)(i) because they are not nationals of the United States and they reside in the country of their citizenship.

(4) *Definition of expatriate health plan administrator* —(i) *In general.* Expatriate health plan administrator means an administrator that in the course of its regular business operations—

(A) Maintains network provider agreements that provide for direct claims payments, with health care providers in eight or more countries,

(B) Maintains call centers, in three or more countries, and accepts calls from customers in eight or more languages,

(C) Processed at least $1 million in claims in foreign currency equivalents during the preceding calendar year, determined using the Treasury Department's currency exchange rate in effect on the last day of the preceding calendar year,

(D) Makes global evacuation/repatriation coverage available,

(E) Maintains legal and compliance resources in three or more countries, and

(F) Has licenses or other authority to sell insurance in more than two countries, including in the United States.

(ii) *Additional rules.* For purposes of meeting the requirements of this paragraph (f)(4), two or more entities, including one entity that is the expatriate health plan administrator, that are members of the expatriate health plan administrator's controlled group (as determined under §57.2(c) of this chapter) are treated as one expatriate health plan administrator. Alternatively, the requirements of this paragraph (f)(4) may be satisfied through contracts between an expatriate health plan administrator and third parties.

(5) *Definition of group health plan.* Group health plan, for purposes of this section, means a group health plan as defined in § 54.9831-1(a).

(6) *Definition of qualified expatriate.* Qualified expatriate, for purposes of this section, means an individual who is described in paragraph (f)(6)(i), (ii), or (iii) of this section.

(i) *Individuals transferred or assigned by their employer to work in the United States.* An individual is described in this paragraph (f)(6)(i) only if such individual has the skills, qualifications, job duties, or expertise that has caused the individual's employer to transfer or assign the individual to the United States for a specific and temporary purpose or assignment that is tied to the individual's employment with such employer. This paragraph (f)(6)(i) applies only to an individual who the plan sponsor has reasonably determined requires access to health coverage and other related services and support in multiple countries, and is offered other multinational benefits on a periodic basis (such as tax equalization, compensation for cross-border moving expenses, or compensation to enable the individual to return to the individual's home country), and does not apply to any individual who is a national of the United States. For purposes of this paragraph (f)(6)(i), an individual who is not expected to travel outside the United States at least one time per year during the coverage period would not reasonably require access to health coverage and other related services and support in multiple countries. Furthermore, the offer of a one-time *de minimis* benefit would not meet the standard for the offer of other multinational benefits on a periodic basis.

(ii) *Individuals working outside the United States.* An individual is described in this paragraph (f)(6)(ii) only if the individual is a national of the United States who is working outside the United States for at least 180 days in a consecutive 12-month period that overlaps with a single plan year, or across two consecutive plan years.

(iii) *Individuals within a group of similarly situated individuals.* (A) An individual is described in this paragraph (f)(6)(iii) only if:

(*1*) The individual is a member of a group of similarly situated individuals that is formed for the purpose of traveling or relocating internationally in service of one or more of the purposes listed in section 501(c)(3) or (4), or similarly situated organizations or groups. For example, a group of students that is formed for purposes of traveling and studying abroad for a 6-month period is described in this paragraph (f)(6)(iii);

(*2*) In the case of a group organized to travel or relocate outside the United States, the individual is expected to travel or reside outside the United States for at least 180 days in a consecutive 12-month period that overlaps with the policy year (or in the case of a policy year that is less than 12 months, at least half the policy year);

(*3*) In the case of a group organized to travel or relocate within the United States, the individual is expected to travel or reside in the United States for not more than 12 months;

(*4*) The individual is not traveling or relocating internationally in connection with an employment-related purpose; and

(*5*) The group meets the test for having associational ties under section 2791(d)(3)(B) through (F) of the PHS Act (42 U.S.C. 300gg-91(d)(3)(B) through (F)).

(B) This paragraph (f)(6)(iii) does not apply to a group that is formed primarily for the sale or purchase of health insurance coverage.

(C) If a group of similarly situated individuals satisfies the requirements of this paragraph (f)(6)(iii), the Secretary of Health and Human Services, in consultation with the Secretary and the Secretary of Labor, has determined that the group requires access to health coverage and other related services and support in multiple countries.

(7) *Definition of United States.* Solely for purposes of this paragraph (f), United States means the 50 States, the District of Columbia, and Puerto Rico.

(8) *National of the United States.* For purposes of this paragraph (f), national of the United States, when referring to an individual, has the meaning used in the Immigration and Nationality Act (8 U.S.C. 1101 *et seq.*) and includes U.S. citizens and non-citizen nationals. Thus, for example, an individual born in American Samoa is a national of the United States at birth.

■ 12. Section 54.9833-1 is amended by adding a sentence at the end to read as follows:

§ 54.9833-1 Effective dates.

* * * Notwithstanding the previous sentence, the definition of "short-term limited duration insurance" in §§ 54.9801-2 and

5.9831-1(c)(5)(i)(C) and (f) apply for policy years and plan years beginning on or after January 1, 2017.

*****

PART 301—PROCEDURE AND ADMINSTRATION

■ 17. The authority citation for part 301 continues to read in part as follows:

Authority: 26 U.S.C. 7805 * * *

■ 18. Section 301.6056-2 is amended by adding paragraph (a)(8) to read as follows:

§ 301.6056-2. Electronic furnishing of statements.

(a) * * *

(8) *Special rule for expatriate health plan coverage* —(i) *In general.* In the case of an individual covered under an expatriate health plan (within the meaning of § 54.9831-1(f)(3) of this chapter), the recipient is treated as having consented under paragraph (a)(2) of this section unless the recipient has explicitly refused to consent to receive the statement in an electronic format. The refusal to consent may be made electronically or in a paper document. A recipient's request for a paper statement is treated as an explicit refusal to receive the statement in electronic format. A furnisher relying on this paragraph (a)(8) must satisfy the requirements of paragraphs (a)(3) through (7) of this section, except that the statement required under paragraph (a)(3) must be provided at least 30 days prior to the time for furnishing under § 301.6056-1(g)(4)(i)(A) of this chapter of the first statement that the furnisher intends to furnish electronically to the recipient, and the other requirements of paragraph (a)(3) are modified to reflect that the statement will be furnished electronically unless the recipient explicitly refuses consent to receive the statement in an electronic format.

(ii) *Manner and time of notifying recipient.* The IRS may specify in other guidance published in the Internal Revenue Bulletin the manner and timing for the initial notification of recipients that the statement required under paragraph (a)(3) of this section will be furnished electronically unless the recipient explicitly refuses to consent to receive the statement in an electronic format. See § 601.601(d)(2)(ii)(B) of this chapter.

(iii) *Effective/applicability date.* The provisions of this paragraph (a)(8) apply as of January 1, 2017.

*****

DEPARTMENT OF LABOR

Employee Benefits Security Administration

29 CFR Chapter XXV

For the reasons stated in the preamble, the Department of Labor proposes to amend 29 CFR part 2590 as set forth below:

PART 2590—RULES AND REGULATIONS FOR GROUP HEALTH PLANS

■ 19. The authority citation for part 2590 is revised to read as follows:

Authority: 29 U.S.C. 1027, 1059, 1135, 1161-1168, 1169, 1181-1183, 1181 note, 1185, 1185a, 1185b, 1191, 1191a, 1191b, and 1191c; sec. 101(g), Pub. L. 104-191, 110 Stat. 1936; sec. 401(b), Pub. L. 105-200, 112 Stat. 645 (42 U.S.C. 651 note); sec. 512(d), Pub. L. 110-343, 122 Stat. 3881; sec. 1001, 1201, and 1562(e), Pub. L. 111-148, 124 Stat. 119, as amended by Pub. L. 111-152, 124 Stat. 1029; Division M, Pub. L. 113-235, 128 Stat. 2130; Secretary of Labor's Order 1-2011, 77 FR 1088 (Jan. 9, 2012).

■ 20. Section 2590.701-2 is amended by:

■ a. Adding in alphabetical order definitions for "expatriate health insurance issuer", "expatriate health plan", and "qualified expatriate";

■ b. Revising the definition of "short-term, limited-duration insurance"; and

■ c. Adding in alphabetical order a definition for "travel insurance".

The additions and revisions read as follows:

§ 2590.701-2 Definitions.

*****

Expatriate health insurance issuer means an expatriate health insurance issuer within the meaning of § 2590.732(f)(2).

Expatriate health plan means an expatriate health plan within the meaning of § 2590.732(f)(3).

*****

Qualified expatriate means a qualified expatriate within the meaning of § 2590.732(f)(6).

Short-term, limited-duration insurance means health insurance coverage provided pursuant to a contract with an issuer that:

(1) Has an expiration date specified in the contract (taking into account any extensions that may be elected by the policyholder with or without the issuer's consent) that is less than 3 months after the original effective date of the contract; and

(2) Displays prominently in the contract and in any application materials provided in connection with enrollment in such coverage in at least 14 point type the following: "THIS IS NOT QUALIFYING HEALTH COVERAGE ("MINIMUM ESSENTIAL COVERAGE") THAT SATISFIES THE HEALTH COVERAGE REQUIREMENT OF THE AFFORDABLE CARE ACT. IF YOU DON'T HAVE MINIMUM ESSENTIAL COVERAGE, YOU MAY OWE AN ADDITIONAL PAYMENT WITH YOUR TAXES."

*****

Travel insurance means insurance coverage for personal risks incident to planned travel, which may include, but is not limited to, interruption or cancellation of trip or event, loss of baggage or personal effects, damages to accommodations or rental vehicles, and sickness, accident, disability, or death occurring during travel, provided that the health benefits are not offered on a stand-alone basis and are incidental to other coverage. For this purpose, the term travel insurance does not include major medical plans that provide comprehensive medical protection for travelers with trips lasting 6 months or longer, including, for example, those working overseas as an expatriate or military personnel being deployed.

*****

■ 21. Section 2590.715-2711 is amended by revising paragraph (c) to read as follows:

§ 2590.715-2711 No lifetime or annual limits.

*****

(c) *Definition of essential health benefits.* The term "essential health benefits" means essential health benefits under section 1302(b) of the Patient Protection and Affordable Care Act and applicable regulations. For this purpose, a group health plan or a health insurance issuer that is not required to provide essential health benefits under section 1302(b) must define "essential health benefits" in a manner that is consistent with—

(1) One of the EHB-benchmark plans applicable in a State under 45 CFR 156.110, and includes coverage of any additional required benefits that are considered essential health benefits consistent with 45 CFR 155.170(a)(2); or

(2) One of the three Federal Employees Health Benefit Program (FEHBP) options as defined by 45 CFR 156.100(a)(3), supplemented, as necessary, to meet the standards in 45 CFR 156.110.

*****

■ 22. Section 2590.732 is amended:

■ a. In paragraph (c)(2)(vii) by removing "and" at the end;

■ b. In paragraph (c)(2)(viii) by adding "and" at the end;

■ c. Adding paragraph (c)(2)(ix);

■ d. Revising paragraph (c)(4)(i);

■ e. Adding paragraph (c)(4)(ii)(D);

■ f. Revising paragraphs (c)(4)(iii) and (c)(5)(i)(C); and

■ g. Adding paragraph (f).

The revisions and additions read as follows:

§ 2590.732 Special rules relating to group health plans.

*****

(c) * * *

(2) * * *

(ix) Travel insurance, within the meaning of § 2590.701-2 of this part.

*****

(4) *Noncoordinated benefits* —(i) *Excepted benefits that are not coordinated.* Coverage for only a specified disease or illness (for example, cancer-only policies) or hospital indemnity or other fixed indemnity

insurance is excepted only if the coverage meets each of the conditions specified in paragraph (c)(4)(ii) of this section.

(ii) * * *

(D) To be hospital indemnity or other fixed indemnity insurance, the insurance must pay a fixed dollar amount per day (or per other time period, such as per week) of hospitalization or illness (for example, $100/day) without regard to the amount of expenses incurred or the type of items or services received and—

(*1*) The plan or issuer must provide, in any application or enrollment materials provided to participants at or before the time participants are given the opportunity to enroll in the coverage, a notice that prominently displays in at least 14 point type the following language: "THIS IS A SUPPLEMENT TO HEALTH INSURANCE AND IS NOT A SUBSTITUTE FOR MAJOR MEDICAL COVERAGE. THIS IS NOT QUALIFYING HEALTH COVERAGE ("MINIMUM ESSENTIAL COVERAGE") THAT SATISFIES THE HEALTH COVERAGE REQUIREMENT OF THE AFFORDABLE CARE ACT. IF YOU DON'T HAVE MINIMUM ESSENTIAL COVERAGE, YOU MAY OWE AN ADDITIONAL PAYMENT WITH YOUR TAXES."

(*2*) If participants are required to reenroll (in either paper or electronic form) for renewal or reissuance, the notice described in paragraph (c)(4)(ii)(D)(*1*) of this section must be displayed in the reenrollment materials that are provided to the participants at or before the time participants are given the opportunity to reenroll in the coverage.

(*3*) If a notice satisfying the requirements of this paragraph (c)(4)(ii)(D) is timely provided to a participant, the obligation to provide the notice is satisfied for both the plan and the issuer.

(iii) *Examples.* The rules of this paragraph (c)(4) are illustrated by the following examples:

Example 1. (i) *Facts.* An employer sponsors a group health plan that provides coverage through an insurance policy. The policy provides benefits only for hospital stays at a fixed percentage of hospital expenses up to a maximum of $100 a day.

(ii) *Conclusion.* In this *Example 1*, because the policy pays a percentage of expenses incurred rather than a fixed dollar amount per day (or per other time period, such as per week), the policy is not hospital indemnity or other fixed indemnity insurance that is an excepted benefit under this paragraph (c)(4). This is the result even if, in practice, the policy pays the maximum of $100 for every day of hospitalization.

Example 2. (i) *Facts.* An employer sponsors a group health plan that provides coverage through an insurance policy. The policy provides benefits for doctors' visits at $50 per visit, hospitalization at $100 per day, various surgical procedures at different dollar rates per procedure, and prescription drugs at $15 per prescription.

(ii) *Conclusion.* In this *Example 2*, for doctors' visits, surgery, and prescription drugs, payment is not made on a per-period basis, but instead is based on whether a procedure or item is provided, such as whether an individual has surgery or a doctor visit or is prescribed a drug, and the amount of payment varies based on the type of procedure or item. Because benefits related to office visits, surgery, and prescription drugs are not paid based on a fixed dollar amount per day (or per other time period, such as per week), as required under paragraph (c)(4) of this section, the policy is not hospital indemnity or other fixed indemnity insurance that is an excepted benefit under this paragraph (c)(4).

Example 3. (i) *Facts.* An employer sponsors a group health plan that provides coverage through an insurance policy. The policy provides benefits for certain services at a fixed dollar amount per day, but the dollar amount varies by the type of service.

(ii) *Conclusion.* In this *Example 3*, because the policy provides benefits in a different amount per day depending on the type of service, rather than one specific dollar amount per day regardless of the type of service, the policy is not hospital indemnity or other fixed indemnity insurance that is an excepted benefit under this paragraph (c)(4).

(5) * * *

(i) * * *

(C) *Similar supplemental coverage provided to coverage under a group health plan.* To be similar supplemental coverage, the coverage must be specifically designed to fill gaps in the primary coverage. The preceding sentence is satisfied if the coverage is designed to fill gaps in cost sharing in the primary coverage, such as coinsurance or deductibles, or the coverage is designed to provide benefits for items and services not covered by the primary coverage and that are not essential health benefits in the State where the coverage is issued, or the coverage is designed to both fill such gaps in cost sharing under, and cover such benefits not covered by, the primary coverage. Similar supplemental coverage does not include coverage that becomes secondary or supplemental only under a coordination-of-benefits provision.

*****

(f) *Expatriate health plans and expatriate health insurance issuers* — (1) *In general.* With respect to coverage under an expatriate health plan, the requirements of section 715 of ERISA and implementing rules and regulations (incorporating sections 2701 through 2728 of the Public Health Service Act) do not apply to—

(i) An expatriate health plan (as defined in paragraph (f)(3) of this section),

(ii) An employer, solely in its capacity as plan sponsor of an expatriate health plan, and

(iii) An expatriate health insurance issuer (as defined in paragraph (f)(2) of this section) with respect to coverage under an expatriate health plan.

(2) *Definition of expatriate health insurance issuer* —(i) *In general.* Expatriate health insurance issuer means a health insurance issuer, within the meaning of § 2590.701-2, that issues expatriate health plans and that in the course of its normal business operations—

(A) Maintains network provider agreements that provide for direct claims payments, with health care providers in eight or more countries;

(B) Maintains call centers in three or more countries, and accepts calls from customers in eight or more languages;

(C) Processed at least $1 million in claims in foreign currency equivalents during the preceding calendar year, determined using the Treasury Department's currency exchange rate in effect on the last day of the preceding calendar year;

(D) Makes global evacuation/repatriation coverage available;

(E) Maintains legal and compliance resources in three or more countries; and

(F) Has licenses or other authority to sell insurance in more than two countries, including in the United States.

(ii) *Additional rules.* For purposes of meeting the requirements of this paragraph (f)(2), two or more entities, including one entity that is the expatriate health insurance issuer, that are members of the expatriate health insurance issuer's controlled group (as determined under 26 CFR 57.2(c)) are treated as one expatriate health insurance issuer. Alternatively, the requirements of this paragraph (f)(2) may be satisfied through contracts between an expatriate health insurance issuer and third parties.

(3) *Definition of expatriate health plan.* Expatriate health plan means a plan that satisfies the requirements of paragraphs (f)(3)(i) through (iii) of this section.

(i) *Substantially all qualified expatriates requirement.* Substantially all primary enrollees in the expatriate health plan must be qualified expatriates. For purposes of this paragraph (f)(3)(i), the primary enrollee is the individual covered by the plan or policy whose eligibility for coverage is not due to that individual's status as the spouse, dependent, or other beneficiary of another covered individual. Notwithstanding the foregoing, an individual is not a primary enrollee if the individual is not a national of the United States and the individual resides in his or her country of citizenship. A plan satisfies the requirement of this paragraph (f)(3)(i) for a plan or policy year only if, on the first day of the plan or policy year, less than 5 percent of the primary enrollees (or less than 5 primary enrollees if greater) are not qualified expatriates.

(ii) *Substantially all benefits not excepted benefits requirement.* Substantially all of the benefits provided under the plan or coverage must be benefits that are not excepted benefits described in § 2590.732(c).

(iii) *Additional requirements.* To qualify as an expatriate health plan, the plan or coverage must also meet the following requirements:

(A) The plan or coverage provides coverage for inpatient hospital services, outpatient facility services, physician services, and emergency services (comparable to emergency services coverage that was described in and offered under section 8903(1) of title 5, United States Code for plan year 2009) in the following locations—

(*1*) In the case of individuals described in paragraph (f)(6)(i) of this section, in the United States and in the country or countries from which the individual was transferred or assigned, and such other country or countries the Secretary of Health and Human Services, in consultation

with the Secretary of the Treasury and Secretary of Labor, may designate;

(*2*) In the case of individuals described in paragraph (f)(6)(ii) of this section, in the country or countries in which the individual is present in connection with his employment, and such other country or countries the Secretary of Health and Human Services, in consultation with the Secretary of the Treasury and Secretary of Labor, may designate; or

(*3*) In the case of individuals described in paragraph (f)(6)(iii) of this section, in the country or countries the Secretary of Health and Human Services, in consultation with the Secretary of the Treasury and Secretary of Labor, may designate.

(B) The plan sponsor reasonably believes that benefits provided by the plan or coverage satisfy the minimum value requirements of Internal Revenue Code section 36B(c)(2)(C)(ii). For this purpose, a plan sponsor is permitted to rely on the reasonable representations of the issuer or administrator regarding whether benefits offered by the issuer or group health plan satisfy the minimum value requirements unless the plan sponsor knows or has reason to know that the benefits fail to satisfy the minimum value requirements.

(C) In the case of a plan or coverage that provides dependent coverage of children, such coverage must be available until an individual attains age 26, unless an individual is the child of a child receiving dependent coverage.

(D) The plan or coverage is:

(*1*) In the case of individuals described in paragraph (f)(6)(i) or (ii) of this section, a group health plan (including health insurance coverage offered in connection with a group health plan), issued by an expatriate health insurance issuer or administered by an expatriate health plan administrator. A group health plan will not fail to be an expatriate health plan merely because any portion of the coverage is provided through a self-insured arrangement.

(*2*) In the case of individuals described in paragraph (f)(6)(iii) of this section, health insurance coverage issued by an expatriate health insurance issuer.

(E) The plan or coverage offers reimbursements for items or services in local currency in eight or more countries.

(F) The plan or coverage satisfies the provisions of this part as in effect on March 22, 2010. For this purpose, the plan or coverage is not required to comply with section 701(e) (relating to certification of creditable coverage) and underlying regulations. However, to the extent the plan or coverage imposes a preexisting condition exclusion, the plan or coverage must ensure that individuals with prior creditable coverage who enroll in the plan or coverage have an opportunity to demonstrate that they have creditable coverage offsetting the preexisting condition exclusion.

(iv) *Example.* The rule of paragraph (f)(3)(i) of this section is illustrated by the following example:

Example. (i) *Facts.* Business has health plan X for 250 U.S. citizens working outside of the United States in Country Y. All of the U.S. citizens working in Country Y satisfy the requirements to be qualified expatriates under § 2590.732(f)(6)(ii). In addition to the 250 U.S. citizens, Business employs 100 citizens of Country Y who reside in Country Y and do not satisfy the requirements to be qualified expatriates under § 2590.732(f)(6)(ii). Health plan X covers both the U.S. citizens and citizens of Country Y.

(ii) *Conclusion.* Health plan X satisfies the requirement of § 2590.732(f)(3)(i) that substantially all primary enrollees of an expatriate health plan be qualified expatriates because 100 percent of the primary enrollees are qualified expatriates. The 100 citizens of Country Y who reside in Country Y are not treated as primary enrollees for purposes of the substantially all requirement of § 2590.732(f)(3)(i) because they are not nationals of the United States and they reside in the country of their citizenship.

(4) *Definition of expatriate health plan administrator* —(i) *In general.* Expatriate health plan administrator means an administrator that in the course of its regular business operations—

(A) Maintains network provider agreements that provide for direct claims payments, with health care providers in eight or more countries,

(B) Maintains call centers, in three or more countries, and accepts calls from customers in eight or more languages,

(C) Processed at least $1 million in claims in foreign currency equivalents during the preceding calendar year, determined using the Treasury Department's currency exchange rate in effect on the last day of the preceding calendar year,

(D) Makes global evacuation/repatriation coverage available,

(E) Maintains legal and compliance resources in three or more countries, and

(F) Has licenses or other authority to sell insurance in more than two countries, including in the United States.

(ii) *Additional rules.* For purposes of meeting the requirements of this paragraph (f)(4), two or more entities, including one entity that is the expatriate health plan administrator, that are members of the expatriate health plan administrator's controlled group (as determined under 26 CFR 57.2(c)) are treated as one expatriate health plan administrator. Alternatively, the requirements of this paragraph (f)(4) may be satisfied through contracts between an expatriate health plan administrator and third parties.

(5) *Definition of group health plan.* Group health plan, for purposes of this section, means a group health plan as defined in §2590.732(a).

(6) *Definition of qualified expatriate.* Qualified expatriate, for purposes of this section, means an individual who is described in paragraph (f)(6)(i), (ii) or (iii) of this section.

(i) *Individuals transferred or assigned by their employer to work in the United States.* An individual is described in this paragraph (f)(6)(i) only if such individual has the skills, qualifications, job duties, or expertise that has caused the individual's employer to transfer or assign the individual to the United States for a specific and temporary purpose or assignment that is tied to the individual's employment with such employer. This paragraph (f)(6)(i) applies only to an individual who the plan sponsor has reasonably determined requires access to health coverage and other related services and support in multiple countries, and is offered other multinational benefits on a periodic basis (such as tax equalization, compensation for cross-border moving expenses, or compensation to enable the individual to return to the individual's home country), and does not apply to any individual who is a national of the United States. For purposes of this paragraph (f)(6)(i), an individual who is not expected to travel outside the United States at least one time per year during the coverage period would not reasonably require access to health coverage and other related services and support in multiple countries. Furthermore, the offer of a one-time *de minimis* benefit would not meet the standard for the offer of other multinational benefits on a periodic basis.

(ii) *Individuals working outside the United States.* An individual is described in this paragraph (f)(6)(ii) only if the individual is a national of the United States who is working outside the United States for at least 180 days in a consecutive 12-month period that overlaps with a single plan year, or across two consecutive plan years.

(iii) *Individuals within a group of similarly situated individuals.* (A) An individual is described in this paragraph (f)(6)(iii) only if:

(*1*) The individual is a member of a group of similarly situated individuals that is formed for the purpose of traveling or relocating internationally in service of one or more of the purposes listed in Internal Revenue Code section 501(c)(3) or (4), or similarly situated organizations or groups. For example, a group of students that is formed for purposes of traveling and studying abroad for a 6-month period is described in this paragraph (f)(6)(iii);

(*2*) In the case of a group organized to travel or relocate outside the United States, the individual is expected to travel or reside outside the United States for at least 180 days in a consecutive 12-month period that overlaps with the policy year (or in the case of a policy year that is less than 12 months, at least half the policy year);

(*3*) In the case of a group organized to travel or relocate within the United States, the individual is expected to travel or reside in the United States for not more than 12 months;

(*4*) The individual is not traveling or relocating internationally in connection with an employment-related purpose; and

(*5*) The group meets the test for having associational ties under section 2791(d)(3)(B) through (F) of the PHS Act (42 U.S.C. 300gg-91(d)(3)(B) through (F)).

(B) This paragraph (f)(6)(iii) does not apply to a group that is formed primarily for the sale or purchase of health insurance coverage.

(C) If a group of similarly situated individuals satisfies the requirements of this paragraph (f)(6)(iii), the Secretary of Health and Human Services, in consultation with the Secretary and the Secretary of the Treasury, has determined that the group requires access to health coverage and other related services and support in multiple countries.

(7) *Definition of United States.* Solely for purposes of this paragraph (f), United States means the 50 States, the District of Columbia, and Puerto Rico.

(8) *National of the United States.* For purposes of this paragraph (f), national of the United States, when referring to an individual, has the meaning used in the Immigration and Nationality Act (8 U.S.C. 1101 *et seq.*) and includes U.S. citizens and non-citizen nationals. Thus, for example, an individual born in American Samoa is a national of the United States at birth.

■ 23. Section 2590.736 is amended by adding a sentence at the end to read as follows:

§2590.736 Applicability dates.

* * * Notwithstanding the previous sentences, the definition of "short-term, limited-duration insurance" in §§2590.701-2 and 2590.732(c)(5)(i)(C) and (f) apply for plan years beginning on or after January 1, 2017.

*****

[FR Doc. 2016-13583 Filed 6-8-16; 11:15 am]

BILLING CODE **4830-01-P; 4510-29-P; 4120-01-P**

¶ 20,264K

IRS: 457 plans: State and local governmental deferred compensation plans: Taxable income.—The IRS has issued proposed regulations pursuant to Code Sec. 457 that provide rules for the taxation of compensation deferred under plans established and maintained by state and local governments, and tax-exempt entities. The proposed regulations include rules for determining when amounts deferred under these plans are includible in income, the amounts that are includible in income, and the types of plans that are not subject to these rules. The proposed regulations would amend final regulations issued in 2003 (see ¶ 24,507F) to reflect subsequent statutory changes, as well as new rules governing "ineligible" Code Sec. 457(f) plans. Generally, the proposed regulations may be relied upon until the application date of the finalized regulations.

The proposed regulation was published in the Federal Register on June 22, 2016 (81 FR 40548).

Proposed Rules

Federal Register

Vol. 81, No. 120

Wednesday, June 22, 2016

This section of the FEDERAL REGISTER contains notices to the public of the proposed issuance of rules and regulations. The purpose of these notices is to give interested persons an opportunity to participate in the rule making prior to the adoption of the final rules.

DEPARTMENT OF THE TREASURY

Internal Revenue Service

26 CFR Part 1

[REG-147196-07]

RIN 1545-BH72

Deferred Compensation Plans of State and Local Governments and Tax-Exempt Entities

AGENCY: Internal Revenue Service (IRS), Treasury.

ACTION: Notice of proposed rulemaking and notice of public hearing.

SUMMARY: This document contains proposed regulations prescribing rules under section 457 of the Internal Revenue Code for the taxation of compensation deferred under plans established and maintained by State or local governments or other tax exempt organizations. These proposed regulations include rules for determining when amounts deferred under these plans are includible in income, the amounts that are includible in income, and the types of plans that are not subject to these rules. The proposed regulations would affect participants, beneficiaries, sponsors, and administrators of certain plans sponsored by State or local governments or tax-exempt organizations that provide for a deferral of compensation. This document also provides a notice of a public hearing on the proposed regulations.

DATES: Written or electronic comments on these proposed regulations must be received by September 20, 2016. Outline of topics to be discussed at the public hearing scheduled for October 18, 2016 at 10 a.m. must be received by September 20, 2016.

ADDRESSES: Send submissions to: CC:PA:LPD:PR (REG-147196-07), Room 5203, Internal Revenue Service, P.O. Box 7604, Ben Franklin Station, Washington, DC 20044. Submissions may be hand delivered Monday through Friday, between the hours of 8 a.m. and 4 p.m. to CC:PA:LPD:PR (REG-147196-07), Courier's Desk, Internal Revenue Service, 1111 Constitution Avenue NW., Washington, DC 20224 or sent electronically, via the Federal eRulemaking Portal at *www.regulations.gov* (IRS REG-147196-07). The public hearing will be held in the IRS Auditorium, Internal Revenue Building, 1111 Constitution Avenue NW., Washington, DC 20224.

FOR FURTHER INFORMATION CONTACT: Concerning the proposed regulations under section 457, Keith Kost at (202) 317-6799 or Cheryl Press at (202) 317-4148, concerning submission of comments, the hearing, and/or to be placed on the building access list to attend the hearing, Regina Johnson at (202) 317-6901 (not toll-free numbers).

SUPPLEMENTARY INFORMATION:

Background

This document contains proposed amendments to the Income Tax Regulations (26 CFR part 1) under section 457(a), (b), and (f) of the Internal Revenue Code (Code), as well as proposed regulations under section 457(e)(11), (e)(12), and (g)(4). Generally, if a deferred compensation plan of a State or local government or tax-exempt entity does not satisfy the requirements of section 457(b), (c), (d), and, in the case of a plan that is maintained by a State or local government, (g), compensation deferred under the plan will be included in income in accordance with section 457(f) unless the plan is not subject to section 457 or is treated as not providing for a deferral of compensation for purposes of section 457. Section 457(e) includes certain definitions and special rules for purposes of section 457 and describes certain plans that either are not subject to section 457 or are treated as not providing for a deferral of compensation under section 457.[1]

Section 457(a)(1) provides that any amount of compensation deferred under an eligible deferred compensation plan as defined in section 457(b) (an eligible plan), and any income attributable to the amounts so deferred, is includible in gross income only for the taxable year in which the compensation or other income is paid to the participant or beneficiary in the case of an eligible employer described in section 457(e)(1)(A) or is paid or otherwise made available to the participant or beneficiary in the case of an eligible employer described in section 457(e)(1)(B). An eligible employer described in section 457(e)(1)(A) means a State, a political subdivision of a State, or any agency or instrumentality of a State or political subdivision of a State (a governmental entity). An eligible employer described in section 457(e)(1)(B) means any organization other than a governmental entity that is exempt from tax under subtitle A (a tax-exempt entity).

Section 457(f)(1)(A) provides that, in the case of a plan of an eligible employer providing for a deferral of compensation, if the plan is not an eligible plan, the compensation is included in gross income when the rights to payment of the compensation are not subject to a substantial risk of forfeiture, as defined in section 457(f)(3)(B).[2] Section 457(f)(1)(B) provides that the tax treatment of any amount made available under the plan will be determined under section 72. Section 457(f)(2) provides that section 457(f)(1) does not apply to a plan that is described in section 401(a) or an annuity plan or contract described in section 403, the portion of any plan that consists of a transfer of property described in section 83, the portion of a plan that consists of a trust described in section 402(b), a qualified governmental excess benefit arrangement described in section 415(m), or the portion of any applicable employment retention plan described in section 457(f)(4).

Section 457(e)(11) provides that certain plans are treated as not providing for a deferral of compensation. These plans include any bona fide vacation leave, sick leave, compensatory time, severance pay,

disability pay, or death benefit plan, as well as any plan paying solely length of service awards to certain bona fide volunteers (or their beneficiaries) and certain voluntary early retirement incentive plans.[3] Section 457(e)(12) provides that section 457 does not apply to certain nonelective deferred compensation of nonemployees.

On July 11, 2003, the Treasury Department and the IRS issued final regulations under section 457 (TD 9075) (68 FR 41230) (2003 final regulations). The 2003 final regulations provide guidance on deferred compensation plans of eligible employers, including eligible plans under section 457(b). The 2003 final regulations also reflect the changes made to section 457 by the Tax Reform Act of 1986, Public Law 99-514 (100 Stat. 2494), the Small Business Job Protection Act of 1996, Public Law 104-188 (110 Stat. 1755), the Taxpayer Relief Act of 1997, Public Law 105-34 (111 Stat. 788), the Economic Growth and Tax Relief Reconciliation Act of 2001, Public Law 107-16 (115 Stat. 38), and the Job Creation and Worker Assistance Act of 2002, Public Law 107-147 (116 Stat. 21). The proposed amendments to the 2003 final regulations under section 457(a), (b), and (g) contained in this document include amendments to reflect subsequent statutory changes made to section 457. The following sections of this preamble provide a chronological description of the relevant changes made after the 2003 final regulations were issued. (For a summary of the proposed changes to the 2003 final regulations, see the Explanation of Provisions section of this preamble.)

I. American Jobs Creation Act of 2004

Section 885 of the American Jobs Creation Act of 2004, Public Law 108-357 (118 Stat. 1418), added section 409A to the Code. Section 409A generally provides that, if at any time during a taxable year a nonqualified deferred compensation plan fails to meet the requirements of section 409A or is not operated in accordance with those requirements, all amounts deferred under the plan for the taxable year and all preceding taxable years are includible in gross income to the extent the amounts are not subject to a substantial risk of forfeiture and were not previously included in gross income.

On April 17, 2007, the Treasury Department and the IRS issued final regulations under section 409A (TD 9312) at 72 FR 19234 (final section 409A regulations). The final section 409A regulations provide guidance on the definition of certain terms and the types of plans covered under section 409A, permissible deferral elections under section 409A, and permissible payments under section 409A. The final section 409A regulations provide that a deferred compensation plan of a governmental entity or a tax-exempt entity that is subject to section 457(f) may constitute a nonqualified deferred compensation plan for purposes of section 409A and that the rules of section 409A apply separately and in addition to any requirements applicable to these plans under section 457(f).

On December 8, 2008, proposed regulations under section 409A were published in the **Federal Register** (73 FR 74380) (proposed section 409A regulations) that provide guidance on the calculation of amounts includible in income under section 409A(a) and the additional taxes imposed by that section with respect to arrangements that do not comply with the requirements of section 409A(a).

In Notice 2008-62 (2008-29 IRB 130 (July 21, 2008)), the Treasury Department and the IRS provided guidance under sections 409A and 457(f) regarding recurring part-year compensation. For this purpose, recurring part-year compensation is compensation paid for services rendered in a position that the employer and employee reasonably anticipate will continue under similar terms and conditions in subsequent years, and under which the employee will be required to provide services during successive service periods each of which comprises less than 12 months (for example, a teacher providing services during a school year comprised of 10 consecutive months) and each of which begins in one taxable year of the employee and ends in the next taxable year. Notice 2008-62 provides that an arrangement under which an employee or independent contractor receives recurring part-year compensation does not provide for the deferral of compensation for purposes of section 409A or for purposes of section 457(f) if (A) the

---

[1] Plans described in certain statutes that are not incorporated into the Code are not subject to section 457. See sections 1107(c)(3)(B), 1107(c)(4), and 1107(c)(5) of the Tax Reform Act of 1986, Public Law 99-514 (100 Stat. 2494 (1986)), as amended, and sections 1101(e)(6), 6064(d)(2), and 6064(d)(3) of the Technical and Miscellaneous Revenue Act of 1988, Public Law 100-647 (102 Stat. 3342 (1988)).

[2] In Notice 2007-62 (2007-2 CB 331 (August 6, 2007)), the Treasury Department and the IRS announced the intent to issue guidance under section 457, including providing definitions of a bona fide severance pay plan under section 457(e)(11) and substantial risk of forfeiture under section 457(f)(3)(B). In response to comments received in response to a request in Notice 2007-62 (on subjects including but not limited to severance pay, cove-

nants not to compete, and the definition of substantial risk of forfeiture), the rules in these proposed regulations have been modified from the proposals announced in that notice.

[3] Announcement 2000-1 (2000-1 CB 294 (January 1, 2000)), provides transitional guidance on the reporting requirements for certain broad-based, nonelective deferred compensation plans maintained by State or local governments. The announcement states that, pending the issuance of further guidance, a State or local government should not report amounts for any year before the year in which a participant or beneficiary is in actual or constructive receipt of those amounts if the amounts are provided under a plan that the State or local government has been treating as a bona fide severance pay plan under section 457(e)(11) for years before calendar year 1999. To be eligible for this transitional relief, the plan must satisfy certain requirements described in the announcement.

arrangement does not defer payment of any of the recurring part-year compensation beyond the last day of the 13th month following the beginning of the service period, and (B) the arrangement does not defer from one taxable year to the next taxable year the payment of more than the applicable dollar amount under section 402(g)(1)(B) ($18,000 for 2016). The notice provides that taxpayers may rely on this rule beginning in the first taxable year that includes July 1, 2008.

II. Pension Protection Act of 2006

The Pension Protection Act of 2006, Public Law 109-280 (120 Stat. 780) (PPA '06), permits a participant's designated beneficiary who is not a surviving spouse to roll over, in a direct trustee-to-trustee transfer, distributions from an eligible plan maintained by a governmental entity (an eligible governmental plan) to an individual retirement account or annuity (IRA). Section 829 of PPA '06 added section 402(c)(11) to the Code, which provides that this type of transfer is treated as an eligible rollover distribution for purposes of section 402(c).

Section 845(b)(3) of PPA '06 added section 457(a)(3) to the Code, which provides an exclusion from gross income for amounts that are distributed from an eligible governmental plan to the extent provided in section 402(l). Section 402(l) provides that distributions from certain governmental retirement plans are excluded from the gross income of an eligible retired public safety officer to the extent the distributions do not exceed the amount paid by the retired officer for qualified health insurance premiums for the year, up to a maximum of $3,000. See Notice 2007-7, part IV (2007-1 CB 395 (January 29, 2007)), as well as Notice 2007-99 (2007-2 CB 1243 (December 26, 2007)), for guidance on the application of section 402(l).

Section 1104(a)(1) of PPA '06 added section 457(e)(11)(D) to the Code, which treats applicable voluntary early retirement incentive plans as bona fide severance pay plans that do not provide for a deferral of compensation under section 457 with respect to payments or supplements that are an early retirement benefit, a retirement-type subsidy, or a social security supplement in coordination with a defined benefit pension plan. This treatment applies only to the extent the payments otherwise could have been provided under the defined benefit plan (determined as if section 411 applied to the defined benefit plan). Under section 457(e)(11)(D)(ii), an applicable voluntary early retirement incentive plan may be maintained only by a local educational agency or a tax-exempt education association.[4]

Section 1104(b)(1) of PPA '06 added section 457(f)(2)(F) to the Code, which provides that section 457(f)(1) does not apply to an applicable employment retention plan. Under section 457(f)(4), an applicable employment retention plan is a plan maintained by a local educational agency or a tax-exempt education association to pay additional compensation upon severance from employment for purposes of employee retention or rewarding employees to the extent that the benefits payable under the plan do not exceed twice the applicable annual dollar limit on deferrals in section 457(e)(15).[5]

III. Heroes Earnings Assistance and Relief Tax Act of 2008

Section 104(c) of the Heroes Earnings Assistance and Relief Tax Act of 2008, Public Law 110-245 (122 Stat. 1624) (HEART Act), amended section 457 to add section 457(g)(4) regarding benefits payable upon death during qualified active military service under the Uniformed Services Employment and Reemployment Rights Act of 1994, Public Law 103-353 (108 Stat. 3149). Section 457(g)(4) provides that an eligible governmental plan must meet the requirements of section 401(a)(37). Under section 401(a)(37), a plan is not treated as a qualified retirement plan unless the plan provides that, in the case of a participant who dies while performing qualified military service, the survivors of the participant are generally entitled to any additional benefits that would have been provided under the plan if the participant had resumed and then terminated employment on account of death. Section 105(b) of the HEART Act added section 414(u)(12) to the Code, which provides rules regarding (A) the treatment of differential wage payments as compensation and (B) the treatment of service in the uniformed services (as described in section 3401(h)(2)(A)) as a severance

from employment for purposes of plan distribution requirements, including the distribution requirements of section 457(d)(1)(A)(ii).

IV. Small Business Jobs Act of 2010 and American Taxpayer Relief Act of 2012

Section 2111 of the Small Business Jobs Act of 2010, Public Law 111-240 (124 Stat. 2504) (SBJA), amended section 402A of the Code to allow an eligible governmental plan to include a qualified Roth contribution program, effective for taxable years beginning after December 31, 2010. SBJA also amended section 402A to permit taxable in-plan rollovers to qualified Roth accounts under eligible governmental plans. Section 902 of the American Taxpayer Relief Act of 2012, Public Law 112-240 (126 Stat. 2313), expanded the types of amounts eligible for an in-plan Roth rollover. For guidance relating to in-plan rollovers to qualified Roth accounts, see Notice 2013-74 (2013-52 IRB 819 (December 23, 2013)) and Notice 2010-84 (2010-51 IRB 872 (July 19, 2010)).

Explanation of Provisions

I. Overview

These proposed regulations make certain changes to the 2003 final regulations under sections 457(a), 457(b), and 457(g) to reflect statutory changes to section 457 since the publication of those regulations. In addition, these proposed regulations provide guidance on certain issues under sections 457(e)(11) and 457(e)(12) that are not addressed in the 2003 final regulations and provide additional guidance under section 457(f). Consistent with the 2003 final regulations, although the rules under section 457 apply to plan participants and beneficiaries without regard to whether the related services are provided by an employee or independent contractor, these proposed regulations often use the terms employee and employer to describe a service provider and a service recipient, respectively, without regard to whether the service provider is an independent contractor.[6]

II. Regulatory Amendments To Reflect Statutory Changes to Section 457

A. Qualified Roth Contribution Program

Section 1.457-4 of the 2003 final regulations provides that annual deferrals to an eligible plan that satisfy certain requirements are excluded from the gross income of the participant in the year deferred or contributed and are not includable in gross income until paid to the participant, in the case of an eligible governmental plan, or until paid or otherwise made available to the participant, in the case of an eligible plan of a tax-exempt entity. These proposed regulations amend § 1.457-4(a) and (b) to reflect the change made by SBJA to allow an eligible governmental plan to include a qualified Roth contribution program, as defined in section 402A(c)(1), under which designated Roth contributions are included in income in the year of deferral. Consistent with section 402A(b)(2), these proposed regulations provide that contributions and withdrawals of a participant's designated Roth contributions must be credited and debited to a designated Roth account maintained for the participant, and that the plan must maintain a record of each participant's investment in the contract with respect to the account. In addition, the proposed regulations provide that no forfeitures may be allocated to a designated Roth account and that no contributions other than designated Roth contributions and rollover contributions described in section 402A(c)(3)(A) may be made to the account.

These proposed regulations also amend § 1.457-7(b)(1), which provides guidance regarding the circumstances under which amounts are included in income under an eligible governmental plan, to specify that qualified distributions from a designated Roth account are excluded from gross income.

B. Certain Distributions for Qualified Accident and Health Insurance Premiums

The proposed regulations amend the rules for the taxation of eligible governmental plan distributions under § 1.457-7(b) to reflect the change made by PPA '06 with respect to certain amounts distributed to an eligible public safety officer. The proposed regulations provide that

---

[4] A local education agency is defined in section 9101 of the Elementary and Secondary Education Act of 1965, Public Law 89-10 (79 Stat. 27), as a public board of education or other public authority legally constituted within a State for either administrative control or direction of, or to perform a service function for, public elementary schools or secondary schools in a city, county, township, school district, or other political subdivision of a State, or of or for a combination of school districts or counties that is recognized in a State as an administrative agency for its public elementary schools or secondary schools. A tax-exempt education association is an association that principally represents employees of one or more local education agencies and is an entity described in section 501(c)(5) or (6) that is exempt from tax under section 501(a).

[5] See also section 1104(c) of PPA '06, which amended section 3(2) of the Employee Retirement Income Security Act of 1974, Public Law 93-406 (88 Stat. 829) (ERISA), to provide that applicable voluntary early retirement incentive plans and applicable employment retention plans are treated as welfare plans (and not pension plans) for purposes of ERISA.

[6] Section 457(e)(2) provides that the performance of services for purposes of section 457 includes the performance of services as an independent contractor and that the person (or governmental entity) for whom these services are performed is treated as an employer.

distributions from an eligible governmental plan meeting the requirements of section 402(l) are excluded from gross income and are not subject to the general rule providing that amounts deferred under an eligible governmental plan are includable in the gross income of a participant or beneficiary for the taxable year in which they are paid. For this purpose, see section 402(l) for rules regarding the extent to which this income exclusion applies to a distribution (including the dollar limitation on the exclusion) and section 402(l)(4)(C) for the meaning of the term public safety officer.

C. Rules Related to Qualified Military Service

The proposed regulations amend §1.457-2(f) to implement the requirements of section 457(g)(4), which was added by the HEART Act and which provides that an eligible governmental plan must meet the requirements of section 401(a)(37) (providing that, in the case of a participant who dies while performing qualified military service, the survivors of the participant generally are entitled to any additional benefits that would have been provided under the plan if the participant had resumed and then terminated employment on account of death). In addition the proposed regulations amend §1.457-6(b)(1) to provide a cross reference to the rules under section 414(u)(12)(B) (providing that leave for certain military service is treated as a severance from employment for purposes of the plan distribution restrictions that apply to eligible plans).

III. Certain Plans That Are Not Subject to Section 457 or Are Not Treated as Providing for a Deferral of Compensation Under Section 457

A. In General

Section 1.457-2(k) of the 2003 final regulations defines the term plan for purposes of section 457 to include any plan, agreement, method, program, or other arrangement, including an individual employment agreement, of an eligible employer under which the payment of compensation is deferred. Section 1.457-2(k) of the 2003 regulations also identifies certain plans that are not subject to section 457 (pursuant to section 457(e)(12) and (f)(2) and statutes not incorporated into the Code) and certain plans that are treated as not providing for a deferral of compensation for purposes of section 457 (pursuant to section 457(e)(11)). These proposed regulations amend the definition of plan for purposes of section 457 to remove from §1.457-2(k) the provisions identifying plans that are not subject to section 457 and plans that are treated as not providing for a deferral of compensation for purposes of section 457, and move the provisions regarding most of these plans to §1.457-11 of the proposed regulations. In addition, §1.457-11 provides additional guidance on:

• Bona fide vacation leave, sick leave, compensatory time, severance pay, disability pay, and death benefit plans, as described in section 457(e)(11)(A)(i), which are treated as not providing for a deferral of compensation for purposes of section 457; and

• plans paying solely length of service awards to bona fide volunteers (or their beneficiaries), as described in section 457(e)(11)(A)(ii), that also are treated as not providing for a deferral of compensation for purposes of section 457.[7]

The proposed regulations also provide guidance in a new §1.457-12 on plans described in section 457(f)(2), to which section 457(f)(1) does not apply.

B. Bona Fide Severance Pay Plans

1. General Requirements

The proposed regulations provide that a plan must meet certain requirements to be a bona fide severance pay plan that is treated under section 457(e)(11)(A)(i) as not providing for the deferral of compensation (and therefore not subject to section 457). First, the benefits provided under the plan must be payable only upon a participant's involuntary severance from employment or pursuant to a window program or voluntary early retirement incentive plan. Second, the amount payable under the plan with respect to a participant must not exceed two times the participant's annualized compensation based upon the annual rate of pay for services provided to the eligible employer for the calendar year preceding the calendar year in which the participant has a severance from employment (or the current calendar year if the participant had no compensation from the eligible employer in the preceding calendar year), adjusted for any increase in compensation during the year used to measure the rate of pay that was expected to continue indefinitely if the participant had not had a severance from employment. Third, pursuant to the written terms of the plan, the severance benefits must be paid no later than the last day

of the second calendar year following the calendar year in which the severance from employment occurs. The rules in these proposed regulations for severance pay plans are similar to the rules for separation pay plans in §1.409A-1(b)(9) of the final section 409A regulations.

2. Involuntary Severance From Employment

a. In General

The proposed regulations require that benefits under a bona fide severance pay plan be payable only upon an involuntary severance from employment or pursuant to a window or voluntary early retirement incentive program. For this purpose, an involuntary severance from employment is a severance from employment due to the eligible employer's independent exercise of its authority to terminate the participant's services, other than due to the participant's implicit or explicit request, if the participant is willing and able to continue to perform services. The determination of whether a severance from employment is involuntary is based on the relevant facts and circumstances. If a severance from employment is designated as an involuntary severance from employment, but the facts and circumstances indicate otherwise, the severance from employment will not be treated as involuntary for purposes of section 457.

b. Severance From Employment for Good Reason

The proposed regulations provide that an employee's voluntary severance from employment may be treated as an involuntary severance from employment for purposes of section 457 if the severance from employment is for good reason. A severance from employment is for good reason if it occurs under certain bona fide conditions that are pre-specified in writing under circumstances in which the avoidance of section 457 is not the primary purpose of the inclusion of these conditions in the plan or of the actions by the employer in connection with the satisfaction of those conditions. Notwithstanding the previous sentence, once the bona fide conditions have been established, the elimination of one or more of the conditions may result in the extension of a substantial risk of forfeiture, the recognition of which would be subject to the rules discussed in section III.E of this preamble.

To be treated as an involuntary severance from employment, a severance from employment for good reason must result from unilateral action taken by the eligible employer resulting in a material adverse change to the working relationship (such as a material reduction in the employee's duties, working conditions, or pay). Other factors that may be taken into account in determining whether a termination for good reason effectively constitutes an involuntary severance from employment include the following:

• Whether the payments upon severance from employment for good reason are in the same amount and paid at the same time as payments conditioned upon an employer-initiated severance from employment without cause; and

• whether the employee is required to give notice to the employer of the material adverse change in conditions and provide the employer with an opportunity to remedy the adverse change.

The proposed regulations also provide a safe harbor under which a plan providing for the payment of amounts upon a voluntary severance from employment under certain conditions, that are specified in writing by the time the legally binding right to the payment arises, will be treated as providing for a payment upon a severance from employment for good reason.

c. Window Programs

The proposed regulations provide that the involuntary severance from employment requirement does not apply to window programs. The proposed regulations define the term window program to mean a program established by an employer to provide separation pay in connection with an impending severance from employment. To be a window program, the program must be offered for a limited period of time (typically no longer than 12 months), and the eligible employer must make the program available to employees who have a severance from employment during that period or who have a severance from employment during that period under specified circumstances. A program is not offered for a limited period of time (and, therefore, is not a window program) if there is a pattern of repeatedly providing similar programs. Whether the recurrence of programs constitutes a pattern of repeatedly providing similar programs is based on all of the relevant facts and circumstances, including whether the benefits are on account of a specific reduction in workforce (or other operational conditions), whether there is a relationship between the separation pay and an

---

[7] See section 457(e)(11)(B) for special rules relating to length of service award plans.

event or condition, and whether the event or condition is temporary and discrete or is a permanent aspect of the employer's operations.

d. Voluntary Early Retirement Incentive Plans

The proposed regulations also provide that the involuntary severance from employment requirement does not apply to an applicable voluntary early retirement incentive plan described in section 457(e)(11)(D)(ii). That section describes an applicable voluntary early retirement incentive plan as a bona fide severance pay plan for purposes of section 457 with respect to payments or supplements that are made as an early retirement benefit, a retirement-type subsidy, or an early retirement benefit that is greater than a normal retirement benefit, as described in section 411(a)(9), and that are paid in coordination with a defined benefit pension plan that is qualified under section 401(a) and maintained by an eligible employer that is a governmental entity or a tax-exempt education association as described in section 457(e)(11)(D)(ii)(II). Section 457(e)(11)(D) provides that these payments or supplements are treated as provided under a bona fide severance pay plan only to the extent that they otherwise could have been provided under the defined benefit plan with which the applicable voluntary early retirement incentive plan is coordinated (determined as if the rules in section 411 applied to the defined benefit plan).

e. Transitional Relief in Announcement 2000-1

Announcement 2000-1 provides transitional guidance on certain broad-based nonelective plans of State or local governments that were in existence before December 22, 1999, and were treated as bona fide severance pay plans for years before 1999. Under the announcement, an eligible employer that is a governmental entity is not required to report, including on Form W-2, "Wage and Tax Statement," or Form 1099-R "Distributions From Pensions, Annuities, Retirement or Profit-Sharing Plans, IRAs, Insurance Contracts, etc.," amounts payable under plans that meet certain requirements until the amounts are actually or constructively received. The rules described in these proposed regulations regarding bona fide severance pay plans, as modified when these proposed regulations are finalized and become applicable, will supersede the transitional guidance in Announcement 2000-1. See section V.B of this preamble for special applicability dates for governmental plans.

C. Bona Fide Death Benefit Plan

The proposed regulations provide that a bona fide death benefit plan, which is treated as not providing for the deferral of compensation pursuant to section 457(e)(11)(A)(i), is a plan providing for death benefits as defined in §31.3121(v)(2)-1(b)(4)(iv)(C) (relating to the application of the Federal Insurance Contributions Act to nonqualified deferred compensation). The proposed regulations further provide that benefits under a bona fide death benefit plan may be provided through insurance and that any lifetime benefits payable under the plan that may be includible in gross income will not be treated as including the value of any term life insurance coverage provided under the plan.

D. Bona Fide Disability Pay Plan

The proposed regulations provide that a bona fide disability pay plan, which is treated as not providing for the deferral of compensation pursuant to section 457(e)(11)(A)(i), is a plan that pays benefits only in the event of a participant's disability. For this purpose, the value of any taxable disability insurance coverage under the plan that is included in gross income is disregarded. These proposed regulations provide that a participant is disabled for this purpose if the participant meets any of the following three conditions:

• The participant is unable to engage in substantial gainful activity by reason of a medically determinable physical or mental impairment that can be expected to result in death or last for a continuous period of not less than 12 months;

• the participant is, by reason of any medically determinable physical or mental impairment that can be expected to result in death or last for a continuous period of not less than 12 months, receiving income replacement benefits for a continuous period of not less than three months under an accident or health plan covering employees of the eligible employer; or

• the participant is determined to be totally disabled by the Social Security Administration or the Railroad Retirement Board.

E. Bona Fide Sick Leave and Vacation Leave Plans

1. General Requirements

Under the proposed regulations, whether a sick or vacation leave plan is a bona fide sick or vacation leave plan, and therefore treated as

not providing for the deferral of compensation under section 457(e)(11)(A)(i), is determined based on the facts and circumstances. A sick or vacation leave plan is generally treated as bona fide, and not as a plan providing for the deferral of compensation, if the facts and circumstances demonstrate that the primary purpose of the plan is to provide employees with paid time off from work because of sickness, vacation, or other personal reasons. Factors used in determining whether a plan is a bona fide sick or vacation leave plan include the following:

• Whether the amount of leave provided could reasonably be expected to be used by the employee in the normal course (and before the cessation of services);

• limits, if any, on the ability to exchange unused accumulated leave for cash or other benefits and any applicable accrual restrictions (for example, where permissible under applicable law, the use of forfeiture provisions often referred to as use-or-lose rules);

• the amount and frequency of any in-service distributions of cash or other benefits offered in exchange for accumulated and unused leave;

• whether the payment of unused sick or vacation leave is made promptly upon severance from employment (or, instead, is paid over a period of time after severance from employment); and

• whether the sick leave, vacation leave, or combined sick and vacation leave offered under the plan is broadly applicable or is available only to certain employees.

2. Delegation of Authority to Commissioner

The Treasury Department and the IRS recognize that eligible employers sponsor a wide variety of sick and vacation leave plans and that additional rules on more specific arrangements or features of these plans may be beneficial. Accordingly, the proposed regulations provide that the Commissioner may issue additional rules regarding bona fide sick or vacation leave plans in revenue rulings, notices, or other guidance published in the Internal Revenue Bulletin, as the Commissioner determines to be necessary or appropriate.

F. Constructive Receipt

Bona fide sick or vacation leave plans (and certain other plans) are treated as not providing for the deferral of compensation for purposes of section 457, and the general federal tax principles for determining the timing and amount of income inclusion, including the constructive receipt rules of section 451, apply to these plans. See §§1.451-1 and 1.451-2 for rules regarding constructive receipt of income.

IV. Ineligible Plans Under Section 457(f)

A. Tax Treatment of Amounts Deferred Under Section 457(f)

Consistent with section 457(f)(1)(A), the proposed regulations provide that if a plan of an eligible employer provides for a deferral of compensation for the benefit of a participant or beneficiary and the plan is not an eligible plan (an ineligible plan), the compensation deferred under the plan is includible in the gross income of the participant or beneficiary under section 457(f)(1)(A) on the date (referred to in this preamble and the proposed regulations as the applicable date) that is the later of the date the participant or beneficiary obtains a legally binding right to the compensation or, if the compensation is subject to a substantial risk of forfeiture at that time, the date the substantial risk of forfeiture lapses. Generally, the amount of the compensation deferred under the plan that is includible in gross income on the applicable date is the present value, as of that date, of the amount of compensation deferred. For this purpose, the amount of compensation deferred under a plan as of an applicable date includes any earnings as of that date on amounts deferred under the plan.

Consistent with section 457(f)(1)(B), the proposed regulations provide that any earnings credited thereafter on compensation that was included in gross income under section 457(f)(1)(A) are includible in the gross income of a participant or beneficiary when paid or made available to the participant or beneficiary and are taxable under section 72. For purposes of section 72, the participant (or beneficiary) is treated as having an investment in the contract equal to the amount actually included in gross income on the applicable date.

Consistent with section 457(f)(2), the proposed regulations provide that section 457(f)(1) does not apply to a qualified plan described in section 401(a), an annuity plan or contract described in section 403, the portion of a plan that consists of a trust to which section 402(b) applies, a qualified governmental excess benefit arrangement described in section 415(m), the portion of a plan that consists of a transfer of property to which section 83 applies, or the portion of an applicable employment retention plan described in section 457(f)(4) with respect to any participant.

B. Calculation of the Present Value of Compensation Deferred Under an Ineligible Plan

1. Overview

The proposed regulations provide general rules for determining the present value of compensation deferred under an ineligible plan. The proposed regulations also include specific rules for determining the present value of compensation deferred under ineligible plans that are account balance plans. The rules for determining present value in the proposed regulations are similar to the rules for determining present value in the proposed section 409A regulations.[8]

The Treasury Department and the IRS expect that these regulations will be finalized after the proposed section 409A regulations are finalized and that these proposed regulations, when finalized, will adopt many provisions of § 1.409A-4 for ease of administration. Accordingly, these proposed regulations include cross references to certain provisions of § 1.409A-4 as currently proposed, including rules for determining present value under certain specific types of plans, such as reimbursement and in-kind benefit arrangements[9] and split-dollar life insurance arrangements,[10] and rules regarding the treatment of payment restrictions and alternative times and forms of a future payment. The Treasury Department and the IRS request comments on whether it is appropriate to provide any additional exceptions from the application of the rules currently described in the proposed section 409A regulations to amounts includible in income under section 457(f), to account for the different manners in which the two provisions apply to an amount deferred.

2. Present Value of Compensation Deferred Under an Account Balance Plan

The proposed regulations provide specific rules for calculating the present value of compensation deferred under an ineligible plan that is an account balance plan (as defined in § 31.3121(v)(2)-1(c)(1)(ii) and (iii)).[11] Provided that the account balance is determined using a predetermined actual investment or a reasonable rate of interest, the present value of an amount payable under an account balance plan as of an applicable date is generally the amount credited to the account, which includes both the principal and any earnings or losses through the applicable date. If the account balance is not determined using a predetermined actual investment or a reasonable rate of interest, the present value of compensation deferred under the plan as of an applicable date is equal to the amount credited to the participant's account as of that date, plus the present value of the excess (if any) of the earnings to be credited under the plan after the applicable date and through the projected payment date over the earnings that would be credited during that period using a reasonable rate of interest. If the present value of compensation deferred under the plan is not determined and is not taken into account by the taxpayer in this manner, the present value of the compensation deferred under the plan as of the applicable date will be treated as equal to the amount credited to the participant's account as of that date, plus the present value of the excess (if any) of the earnings to be credited under the plan through the projected payment date over the earnings that would be credited using the applicable Federal rate. The proposed regulations also provide that if the amount of earnings or losses credited under an account balance plan is based on the greater of the earnings on two or more investments or interest rates, then the amount included in income on the applicable date is the sum of the amount credited to the participant's account as of the applicable date and the present value (determined as described in section IV.B.3 of this preamble) of the right to future earnings.

3. Present Value of Compensation Deferred Under a Plan That Is Not an Account Balance Plan

a. Reasonable Actuarial Assumptions

The proposed regulations also set forth rules for calculating the present value of compensation deferred under an ineligible plan that is not an account balance plan. Under the proposed regulations, the present value of an amount deferred under such a plan as of an applicable date is the value, as of that date, of the right to receive payment of the compensation in the future, taking into account the time value of money and the probability that the payment will be made. Any actuarial assumptions used to calculate the present value of the compensation deferred must be reasonable as of the applicable date, determined based on all of the relevant facts and circumstances. For this purpose, taking into account the probability that a participant might die before receiving certain benefits is a reasonable actuarial assumption only if the plan provides that the benefits will be forfeited upon death. Discounts based on the probability that payments will not be made due to the unfunded status of the plan, the risk that the eligible employer or another party may be unwilling or unable to pay, the possibility of future plan amendments or changes in law, and other similar contingencies are not permitted for purposes of determining present value under the proposed regulations.

b. Treatment of Severance From Employment

If the present value of an amount depends on the time when a severance from employment occurs and the severance from employment has not occurred by the applicable date, then, for purposes of determining the present value of the amount, the severance from employment generally may be treated as occurring on any date on or before the fifth anniversary of the applicable date, unless, as of the applicable date, it would be unreasonable to use such an assumption. For example, if the applicable date occurs in 2017 and the employer knows on the applicable date that the severance from employment will occur in 2018, it would be unreasonable to use a date after the expected severance from employment date to determine the present value of the compensation.

c. Treatment of Payments Based on Formula Amounts

Some ineligible plans may provide that all or part of the amount payable under the plan is determined by reference to one or more factors that are indeterminable on the applicable date. For example, an amount payable may be dependent on a participant's final average compensation and total years of service. These proposed regulations refer to such an amount as a formula amount. The proposed regulations provide that the determination of the present value of a formula amount under an ineligible plan must be based on reasonable, good faith assumptions with respect to any contingencies as to the amount of the payment, with the assumptions based on all the facts and circumstances existing on the applicable date. The proposed regulations also provide that, if only a portion of the compensation deferred under the plan consists of a formula amount, the amount payable with respect to that portion is determined under the rules applicable to formula amounts, and the remaining balance is determined under the rules applicable to amounts that are not formula amounts.

d. Unreasonable Actuarial Assumptions

If the Commissioner determines that the actuarial assumptions used by an employer in determining present value are not reasonable, the proposed regulations provide that the Commissioner will determine the present value of the compensation deferred using actuarial assumptions and methods that the Commissioner determines to be reasonable based on all of the facts and circumstances.

4. Loss Deduction Rules

The proposed regulations contain rules similar to the loss deduction rules in the proposed section 409A regulations. Under the rules in these proposed regulations, if a participant includes an amount of deferred compensation in income under section 457(f)(1)(A), but the compensation that is subsequently paid or made available is less than the amount included in income because the participant has forfeited or lost some or all of the compensation due to death or some other reason (for example, due to investment performance), the participant is entitled to a deduction for the taxable year in which any remaining right to the amount is permanently forfeited under the plan's terms or otherwise permanently lost. The deduction allowed for the taxable year in which the permanent forfeiture or loss occurs is equal to the amount

---

[8] One difference between these proposed regulations and the proposed section 409A regulations is that income inclusion under section 457(f) and § 1.457-12(a)(2), and the present value calculation under these proposed regulations, is determined as of the applicable date, whereas income inclusion under section 409A, and the present value calculation under the proposed § 1.409A-4, is determined as of the end of the service provider's taxable year.

[9] A reimbursement or in-kind benefit arrangement is an arrangement in which benefits for a participant are provided under a nonqualified deferred compensation arrangement described in § 1.409A-1(c)(2)(i)(E).

[10] A split-dollar insurance arrangement is an arrangement in which benefits for a participant are provided under a nonqualified deferred compensation plan described in § 1.409A-1(c)(2)(i)(F).

[11] The rules in these regulations, however, do not apply with respect to Federal Insurance Contributions Act and Federal Unemployment Tax Act taxation liability under sections 3121(v)(2) and 3306(r)(2), respectively, and the regulations thereunder.

previously included in income under section 457(f)(1)(A), less the total amount of compensation that is actually paid or made available under the plan that constitutes a return of investment in the contract. In the case of an employee, the available deduction generally would be treated as a miscellaneous itemized deduction, subject to the deduction limitations applicable to such expenses under sections 67 and 68.[12]

5. Examples Illustrating the Present Value Rules

The proposed regulations include several examples illustrating the application of the present value rules to the more common types of plans providing for the deferral of compensation under section 457(f). The regulations do not illustrate the application of these valuation rules to plans that are more unusual for employees of governmental and tax-exempt entities, such as compensatory options to acquire stock or other property. The amount includible in income on the applicable date under these less common types of plans would be determined under the general rules for plans that are not account balance plans.

C. Definition of Deferral of Compensation

1. In General

The proposed regulations define the term deferral of compensation for purposes of determining whether section 457(f) applies to an arrangement because it provides for a deferral of compensation. In general, a plan provides for a deferral of compensation if a participant has a legally binding right during a taxable year to compensation that, pursuant to the terms of the plan, is or may be payable in a later taxable year. However, the proposed regulations generally provide that a participant does not have a legally binding right to compensation to the extent that it may be unilaterally reduced or eliminated by the employer after the services creating the right have been performed.

Whether a plan provides for a deferral of compensation is generally based on the terms of the plan and the relevant facts and circumstances at the time that the participant obtains a legally binding right to the compensation, or, if later, when a plan is amended to convert a right that does not provide for a deferral of compensation into a right that does provide for a deferral of compensation. For example, if a plan providing retiree health care does not initially provide for a deferral of compensation but is later amended to provide the ability to receive future cash payments instead of health benefits, it may become a plan that provides for the deferral of compensation at the time of the amendment.

Under the proposed regulations, an amount of compensation deferred under a plan that provides for the deferral of compensation does not cease to be an amount subject to section 457(f) by reason of any change to the plan that would recharacterize the right to the amount as a right that does not provide for the deferral of compensation. In addition, any change under the plan that results in an exchange of an amount deferred under the plan for some other right or benefit that would otherwise be excluded from the participants' gross income does not affect the characterization of the plan as one that provides for a deferral of compensation. Thus, for example, if a plan that provides for a deferral of compensation is amended to provide health benefits instead of cash, it will retain its character as a plan that provides for a deferral of compensation.

2. Short-Term Deferrals

The proposed regulations provide that a deferral of compensation does not occur with respect to any amount that would be a short-term deferral under § 1.409A-1(b)(4), substituting the definition of a substantial risk of forfeiture provided under these proposed regulations for the definition under § 1.409A-1(d). Accordingly, a deferral of compensation does not occur with respect to any payment that is not a deferred payment, provided that the participant actually or constructively receives the payment on or before the last day of the applicable 2 ½ month period. For this purpose, the applicable 2 ½ month period is the period ending on the later of the 15th day of the third month following the end of the first calendar year in which the right to the payment is no longer subject to a substantial risk of forfeiture or the 15th day of the third month following the end of the eligible employer's first taxable year in which the right to the payment is no longer subject to a substantial risk of forfeiture.

Because there is considerable overlap between the definition of substantial risk of forfeiture for purposes of section 457(f) and the definition of substantial risk of forfeiture for purposes of section 409A, in many cases amounts that, under this rule, are not deferred compen-

sation subject to section 457(f) are also not deferred compensation subject to section 409A. For example, if an arrangement provides for the payment of a bonus on or before March 15 of the year following the calendar year in which the right to the bonus is no longer subject to a substantial risk of forfeiture (within the meaning of both these proposed regulations and § 1.409A-1(d)) and the bonus is paid on or before that March 15, the arrangement would not be a plan providing for a deferral of compensation to which section 457(f) (or section 409A) applies. For circumstances in which a payment made under a plan after that March 15 may still qualify as a short-term deferral for purposes of sections 409A and 457(f) (due to incorporation of the section 409A regulatory provisions into these proposed regulations under section 457(f)), see § 1.409A-1(b)(4)(ii).

3. Recurring Part-Year Compensation

After issuance of the final section 409A regulations, commenters expressed concerns about the application of section 409A to situations involving certain recurring part-year compensation. For this purpose, recurring part-year compensation is compensation paid for services rendered in a position that the employer and employee reasonably anticipate will continue under similar terms and conditions in subsequent years, and under which the employee will be required to provide services during successive service periods each of which comprises less than 12 months (for example, a teacher providing services during a school year comprised of 10 consecutive months) and each of which begins in one taxable year of the employee and ends in the next taxable year. In general, commenters asserted that section 409A should not apply to situations involving recurring part-year compensation because the amount being deferred from one taxable year to the next taxable year is typically small and because most taxpayers view that type of arrangement as a method of managing cash flow, rather than a tax-deferral opportunity.

In response to these comments, Notice 2008-62 provided that an arrangement under which an employee or independent contractor receives recurring part-year compensation does not provide for the deferral of compensation for purposes of section 409A or for purposes of section 457(f) if (i) the arrangement does not defer payment of any of the recurring part-year compensation beyond the last day of the 13th month following the beginning of the service period, and (ii) the arrangement does not defer from one taxable year to the next taxable year the payment of more than the applicable dollar amount under section 402(g)(1)(B) ($18,000 for 2016).

Some commenters, however, subsequently expressed concerns that Notice 2008-62 does not adequately address some teaching positions, such as those of college and university faculty members. They asserted that, depending on several variables (such as the month in which the service period begins), the dollar limitation in the notice could result in adverse tax consequences to teachers with academic year compensation as low as $80,000. Commenters further observed that some of these arrangements are nonelective and, therefore, some employees cannot opt out of a recurring part-year compensation arrangement. Some commenters also contended that the rules set forth in the notice were difficult to apply.

To simplify the rule set forth in Notice 2008-62, and recognizing that educational employers frequently structure their pay plans to include recurring part-year compensation and that the main purpose of this design is to achieve an even cash flow for employees who do not work for a portion of the year, these proposed regulations modify the recurring part-year compensation rule for purposes of section 457(f). The proposed regulations provide that a plan or arrangement under which an employee receives recurring part-year compensation that is earned over a period of service does not provide for the deferral of compensation if the plan or arrangement does not defer payment of any of the recurring part-year compensation to a date beyond the last day of the 13th month following the first day of the service period for which the recurring part-year compensation is paid, and the amount of the recurring part-year compensation (not merely the amount deferred) does not exceed the annual compensation limit under section 401(a)(17) ($265,000 for 2016) for the calendar year in which the service period commences. A conforming change is included in proposed regulations under section 409A that are also published in the Proposed Rules section of this issue of the **Federal Register**.

D. Interaction of Section 457 With Section 409A

The proposed regulations also address the interaction of the rules under section 457(f) and section 409A. Section 409A(c) provides that nothing in section 409A is to be construed to prevent the inclusion of

---

[12] Section 1341 would not be applicable to this type of loss because inclusion of an amount in income as a result of section 457(f) would not constitute receipt of an amount to which it appeared that the taxpayer had an unrestricted right in the taxable year of inclusion.

amounts in gross income under any other provision of chapter 1 of subtitle A of the Code (Normal taxes and surtaxes) or any other rule of law earlier than the time provided in section 409A. In addition, it provides that any amount included in gross income under section 409A is not required to be included in gross income under any other provision of chapter 1 of subtitle A or any other rule of law later than the time provided in section 409A. The proposed regulations provide that the rules under section 457(f) apply to plans separately and in addition to the requirements under section 409A.[13] Thus, a deferred compensation plan of an eligible employer that is subject to section 457(f) may also be a nonqualified deferred compensation plan that is subject to section 409A. Section 1.457-12(d)(5)(iii) of the proposed regulations provides an example of the interaction of sections 409A and 457(f), and it is intended that this example will also be included in § 1.409A-4 when those currently proposed regulations are finalized.

E. Rules Relating to Substantial Risk of Forfeiture

The proposed regulations provide rules regarding the conditions that constitute a substantial risk of forfeiture for purposes of section 457(f). As discussed in section IV.A of this preamble, an amount to which an employee has a legally binding right under an ineligible plan is generally includible in gross income on the later of the date the employee obtains the legally binding right to the compensation or, if the compensation is subject to a substantial risk of forfeiture, the date the substantial risk of forfeiture lapses. The proposed regulations provide that an amount is generally subject to a substantial risk of forfeiture for this purpose only if entitlement to that amount is conditioned on the future performance of substantial services, or upon the occurrence of a condition that is related to a purpose of the compensation if the possibility of forfeiture is substantial. A special rule applies to determine whether initial deferrals of current compensation may be treated as subject to a substantial risk of forfeiture and whether a substantial risk of forfeiture can be extended. For this purpose, current compensation refers to compensation that is payable on a current basis such as salary, commissions, and certain bonuses, and does not include compensation that is deferred compensation.

Whether an amount is conditioned on the future performance of substantial services is based on all of the relevant facts and circumstances, such as whether the hours required to be performed during the relevant period are substantial in relation to the amount of compensation. A condition is related to a purpose of the compensation only if the condition relates to the employee's performance of services for the employer or to the employer's tax exempt or governmental activities, as applicable, or organizational goals. A substantial risk of forfeiture exists based on a condition related to the purpose of the compensation only if the likelihood that the forfeiture event will occur is substantial. Also, an amount is not subject to a substantial risk of forfeiture if the facts and circumstances indicate that the forfeiture condition is unlikely to be enforced. Factors considered for purposes of determining the likelihood that the forfeiture will be enforced include, but are not limited to, the past practices of the employer, the level of control or influence of the employee with respect to the organization and the individual(s) who would be responsible for enforcing the forfeiture, and the enforceability of the provisions under applicable law.

Under these proposed regulations, if a plan provides that entitlement to an amount is conditioned on an involuntary severance from employment without cause, the right is subject to a substantial risk of forfeiture if the possibility of forfeiture is substantial. For this purpose, a voluntary severance from employment that would be treated as an involuntary severance from employment under a bona fide severance pay plan for purposes of section 457(e)(11)(A)(i) (that is, a severance from employment for good reason) is also treated as an involuntary severance from employment without cause. See section III.B.2 of this preamble for a discussion of circumstances under which a severance from employment for good reason may be treated as an involuntary severance from employment for purposes of section 457(e)(11)(A)(i).

The proposed regulations provide that compensation is not considered to be subject to a substantial risk of forfeiture merely because it would be forfeited if the employee accepts a position with a competing employer unless certain conditions are satisfied. First, the right to the compensation must be expressly conditioned on the employee refraining from the performance of future services pursuant to a written agreement that is enforceable under applicable law. Second, the employer must consistently make reasonable efforts to verify compliance with all of the noncompetition agreements to which it is a party (including the noncompetition agreement at issue). Third, at the time the noncompetition agreement becomes binding, the facts and circumstances must show that the employer has a substantial and bona fide

interest in preventing the employee from performing the prohibited services and that the employee has a bona fide interest in engaging, and an ability to engage, in the prohibited services. The proposed regulations identify several factors that are relevant for this purpose.

Additional conditions apply with respect to the ability to treat initial deferrals of current compensation as being subject to a substantial risk of forfeiture. Similarly, an attempt to extend the period covered by a risk of forfeiture, often referred to as a rolling risk of forfeiture, is generally disregarded under the proposed regulations unless certain conditions are met.

Specifically, the proposed regulations permit initial deferrals of current compensation to be subject to a substantial risk of forfeiture and also allow an existing risk of forfeiture to be extended only if all of the following requirements are met. First, the present value of the amount to be paid upon the lapse of the substantial risk of forfeiture (as extended, if applicable) must be materially greater than the amount the employee otherwise would be paid in the absence of the substantial risk of forfeiture (or absence of the extension). The proposed regulations provide that an amount is materially greater for this purpose only if the present value of the amount to be paid upon the lapse of the substantial risk of forfeiture, measured as of the date the amount would have otherwise been paid (or in the case of an extension of the risk of forfeiture, the date that the substantial risk of forfeiture would have lapsed without regard to the extension), is more than 125 percent of the amount the participant otherwise would have received on that date in the absence of the new or extended substantial risk of forfeiture. (No implication is intended that this standard would also apply for purposes of § 1.409A-1(d)(1).)

Second, the initial or extended substantial risk of forfeiture must be based upon the future performance of substantial services or adherence to an agreement not to compete. It may not be based solely on the occurrence of a condition related to the purpose of the transfer (for example, a performance goal for the organization), though that type of condition may be combined with a sufficient service condition.

Third, the period for which substantial future services must be performed may not be less than two years (absent an intervening event such as death, disability, or involuntary severance from employment).

Fourth, the agreement subjecting the amount to a substantial risk of forfeiture must be made in writing before the beginning of the calendar year in which any services giving rise to the compensation are performed in the case of initial deferrals of current compensation or at least 90 days before the date on which an existing substantial risk of forfeiture would have lapsed in the absence of an extension. Special rules apply to new employees. The proposed regulations do not extend these special rules for new employees to employees who are newly eligible to participate in a plan. The Treasury Department and the IRS request comments on whether special provisions for newly eligible employees are needed in the context of arrangements subject to section 457(f), and if so whether the rules under §§ 1.409A-1(c)(2) and 1.409A-2(a)(7) would be a useful basis for similar rules under section 457(f) and how an aggregated single plan (versus multiple plans) should be defined for this purpose to ensure that the rules are not subject to manipulation.

V. Proposed Applicability Dates

A. General Applicability Date

Generally, these regulations are proposed to apply to compensation deferred under a plan for calendar years beginning after the date of publication of the Treasury decision adopting these rules as final regulations in the **Federal Register**, including deferred amounts to which the legally binding right arose during prior calendar years that were not previously included in income during one or more prior calendar years. No implication is intended regarding application of the law before these proposed regulations become applicable. Taxpayers may rely on these proposed regulations until the applicability date.

B. Special Applicability Dates

These regulations are proposed to include three special applicability dates for specific provisions. First, in the case of a plan that is maintained pursuant to one or more collective bargaining agreements that have been ratified and are in effect on the date of publication of the Treasury decision adopting these rules as final regulations in the **Federal Register**, these regulations would not apply to compensation deferred under the plan before the earlier of (1) the date on which the last of the collective bargaining agreements terminates (determined without regard to any extension thereof after the date of publication of

---

[13] See also § 1.409A-1(a)(4).

the Treasury decision adopting these rules as final regulations in the **Federal Register,** or (2) the date that is three years after the date of publication of the Treasury decision adopting these rules as final regulations in the **Federal Register.**

Second, for all plans, with respect to the rules regarding recurring part-year compensation for periods before the applicability date of these regulations, taxpayers may rely on either the rules set forth in these proposed regulations or the rules set forth in Notice 2008-62.

Third, to the extent that legislation is required to amend a governmental plan, the proposed regulations would apply only to compensation deferred under the plan in calendar years beginning on or after the close of the second regular legislative session of the legislative body with the authority to amend the plan that begins after the date of publication of the Treasury decision adopting these rules as final regulations in the **Federal Register.**

Special Analyses

Certain IRS regulations, including this one, are exempt from the requirements of Executive Order 12866, as supplemented and reaffirmed by Executive Order 13563. Therefore, a regulatory impact assessment is not required. It also has been determined that section 553(b) of the Administrative Procedure Act (5 U.S.C. chapter 5) does not apply to these regulations, and because the regulations do not impose a collection of information on small entities, the Regulatory Flexibility Act (5 U.S.C. chapter 6) does not apply. Pursuant to section 7805(f) of the Code, this notice of proposed rulemaking has been submitted to the Chief Counsel for Advocacy of the Small Business Administration for comment on its impact on small business.

Comments and Public Hearing

Before the proposed regulations are adopted as final regulations, consideration will be given to any written (a signed original and eight (8) copies) or electronic comments that are submitted timely to the IRS as prescribed in this preamble under the **ADDRESSES** heading. The Treasury Department and the IRS request comments on all aspects of the proposed rules, including whether special transition rules are needed for plans established before the proposed applicability dates of these regulations (including sick and vacation leave or severance pay plans that may be treated as providing deferred compensation subject to section 457, but that, under the proposed regulations, may be treated as providing deferred compensation subject to section 457(f), whether additional exceptions are appropriate to the general application of the rules currently described in the proposed section 409A regulations to determine the amounts includible in income under section 457(f), and whether special provisions for newly eligible employees are needed in the context of arrangements subject to section 457(f) (and if so whether the rules under §§ 1.409A-1(c)(2) and 1.409A-2(a)(7) would be a useful basis for similar rules under section 457(f)). All comments submitted by the public will be available at *www.regulations.gov* or upon request.

A public hearing has been scheduled for October 18, 2016, beginning at 10 a.m. in the Auditorium, Internal Revenue Service, 1111 Constitution Avenue NW., Washington, DC. Due to building security procedures, visitors must enter at the Constitution Avenue entrance. In addition, all visitors must present photo identification to enter the building. Because of access restrictions, visitors will not be admitted beyond the immediate entrance area more than 30 minutes before the hearing starts. For information about having your name placed on the building access list to attend the hearing, see the **FOR FURTHER INFORMATION CONTACT** section of this preamble.

The rules of 26 CFR 601.601(a)(3) apply to the hearing. Persons who wish to present oral comments at the hearing must submit written or electronic comments by September 20, 2016 and an outline of the topics to be discussed and the amount of time to be devoted to each topic (a signed original and eight (8) copies) by September 20, 2016. A period of 10 minutes will be allotted to each person for making comments. An agenda showing the scheduling of the speakers will be prepared after the deadline for receiving outlines has passed. Copies of the agenda will be available free of charge at the hearing.

Statement of Availability of IRS Documents

For copies of recently issued revenue procedures, revenue rulings, notices, and other guidance published in the Internal Revenue Bulletin, please visit the IRS Web site at *http://www.irs.gov* or contact the Superintendent of Documents, U.S. Government Printing Office, Washington, DC 20402.

Drafting Information

The principal author of the proposed regulations is Keith R. Kost, Office of Associate Chief Counsel (Tax Exempt and Government Entities). However, other personnel from the Treasury Department and the IRS participated in their development.

List of Subjects in 26 CFR Part 1

Income taxes, Reporting and recordkeeping requirements.

Proposed Amendments to the Regulations

Accordingly, 26 CFR part 1 is proposed to be amended as follows:

PART 1—INCOME TAXES

■ **Paragraph 1.** The authority citation for part 1 continues to read in part as follows:

Authority: 26 U.S.C. 7805 *   *   *

■ **Par. 2.** Section 1.457-1 is revised to read as follows:

§ 1.457-1 General overview of section 457.

Section 457 provides rules for nonqualified deferred compensation plans established by eligible employers as defined under § 1.457-2(d). Eligible employers may establish either deferred compensation plans that are eligible plans that meet the requirements of section 457(b) and §§ 1.457-3 through 1.457-10, or deferred compensation plans that do not meet the requirements of section 457(b) and §§ 1.457-3 through 1.457-10 (and therefore are ineligible plans which are generally subject to federal income tax treatment under section 457(f) and § 1.457-12(a)). Plans described in § 1.457-11 are not subject to section 457 or are treated as not providing for a deferral of compensation for purposes of section 457 (and, accordingly, the rules under §§ 1.457-3 through 1.457-10 and § 1.457-12(a) do not apply to these plans).

■ **Par. 3.** Section 1.457-2 is amended by:

■ 1. Revising the introductory text.

■ 2. Revising the second sentence of paragraph (f).

■ 3. Revising the last sentence of paragraph (i).

■ 4. Revising paragraph (k).

The revisions read as follows:

§ 1.457-2 Definitions.

This section sets forth the definitions that are used under §§ 1.457-1 through 1.457-12.

*   *   *   *   *

(f) *   *   * An eligible governmental plan is an eligible plan that is established and maintained by a State as defined in paragraph (l) of this section and that meets the requirements of section 401(a)(37). *   *   *

*   *   *   *   *

(i) *   *   * Solely for purposes of section 457 and §§ 1.457-2 through 1.457-12, the term *nonelective employer contribution* includes employer contributions that would be described in section 401(m) if they were contributions to a qualified plan.

*   *   *   *   *

(k) *Plan. Plan* includes any agreement, method, program, or other arrangement (including an individual employment agreement) under which the payment of compensation for services rendered to an eligible employer is deferred (whether by salary reduction, nonelective employer contribution, or otherwise). However, the plans described in § 1.457-11 are either not subject to section 457 or are treated as not providing for a deferral of compensation for purposes of section 457, even if the payment of compensation is deferred under the plan.

*   *   *   *   *

■ **Par. 4.** Section 1.457-4 is amended by:

■ 1. Revising paragraphs (a), (b), and the last sentence of (e)(1).

■ 2. Removing the language "§ 1.457-11" wherever it appears in paragraphs (e)(1), (e)(2), (e)(3), and (e)(5) *Example 1* and adding the language "§ 1.457-12" in its place.

The revisions read as follows:

§ 1.457-4 Annual deferrals, deferral limitations, and deferral agreements under eligible plans.

(a) *Taxation of annual deferrals.* With the exception of designated Roth contributions (which are not excludable from gross income), annual deferrals that satisfy the requirements of paragraphs (b) and (c) of this section are excluded from the gross income of a participant in the year deferred or contributed and are not includible in gross income until paid to the participant in the case of an eligible governmental plan, or until paid or otherwise made available to the participant in the case of an eligible plan of a tax-exempt entity. See § 1.457-7.

(b) *Agreement for deferral* —(1) *In general.* To be an eligible plan, the plan must provide that compensation for any calendar month may be deferred by salary reduction only if an agreement providing for the deferral has been entered into before the first day of the month in which the compensation to be deferred under the agreement would otherwise be paid or made available, and any modification or revocation of such an agreement may not become effective before the first day of the month following the month in which the modification or revocation occurs. However, a new employee may defer compensation in the first calendar month of employment if an agreement providing for the deferral is entered into on or before the first day the participant performs services for the eligible employer. An eligible plan may provide that if a participant enters into an agreement providing for deferral by salary reduction under the plan, the agreement will remain in effect until the participant revokes or alters the terms of the agreement. Nonelective employer contributions to an eligible plan are not subject to the timing rules for salary reduction agreements described in this paragraph (b)(1).

(2) *Designated Roth contributions in plans maintained by eligible governmental employers* —(i) *Elections.* An election by a participant to make a designated Roth contribution (as defined in section 402A(c)(1)) to an eligible governmental plan in lieu of all or a portion of the amount that the participant could elect to contribute to the plan on a pre-tax basis must be irrevocably designated as an elective deferral that is not excludable from gross income in accordance with the timing rules under paragraph (b)(1) of this section. Designated Roth contributions are treated the same as pre-tax contributions for purposes of §§ 1.457-1 through 1.457-10, except as otherwise specifically provided in those sections.

(ii) *Separate accounting.* Contributions and withdrawals of a participant's designated Roth contributions must be credited and debited to a designated Roth account maintained for the participant, and the plan must maintain a record of the participant's investment in the contract (that is, designated Roth contributions that have not been distributed) with respect to the participant's designated Roth account. In addition, gains, losses, and other credits or charges must be separately allocated on a reasonable and consistent basis to the designated Roth account and other accounts under the plan. However, forfeitures may not be allocated to the designated Roth account, and no contributions other than designated Roth contributions and rollover contributions described in section 402A(c)(3)(B) may be allocated to such account. The separate accounting requirement described in this paragraph applies to a plan at the time a designated Roth contribution is contributed to the plan and continues to apply until all designated Roth contributions (and the earnings attributable thereto) are distributed from the plan. See A-13 of § 1.402A-1 for additional requirements for separate accounting.

*   *   *   *   *

(e) *   *   *

(1) *   *   * Thus, an excess deferral is includible in gross income when deferred or, if later, when the excess deferral first ceases to be subject to a substantial risk of forfeiture, under the rules described in § 1.457-12(e).

*   *   *   *   *

■ **Par. 5.** Section 1.457-6 is amended by revising the first sentence of paragraph (b)(1) to read as follows:

§ 1.457-6 Timing of distributions under eligible plans.

*   *   *   *   *

(b) *   *   *

(1) *   *   * An employee has a severance from employment with the eligible employer if the employee dies, retires, or otherwise has a severance from employment (including as described in section 414(u)(12)(B)) with the eligible employer.*   *   *

*   *   *   *   *

■ **Par. 6.** Section 1.457-7 is amended by revising the section heading and paragraph (b)(1), redesignating paragraph (b)(4) as (b)(5), and adding a new paragraph (b)(4) to read as follows:

§ 1.457-7 Taxation of distributions under eligible plans.

*   *   *   *   *

(b) *   *   *

(1) *Amounts included in gross income in year paid under an eligible governmental plan.* Except as provided in paragraphs (b)(2), (3), and (4) of this section (or in § 1.457-10(c) relating to payments to a spouse or former spouse pursuant to a qualified domestic relations order), amounts deferred under an eligible governmental plan are includible in the gross income of a participant or beneficiary for the taxable year in which paid to the participant or beneficiary under the plan. Distributions from designated Roth accounts are excludable from gross income to the extent provided in section 402A and §§ 1.402A-1 and 1.402A-2.

*   *   *   *   *

(4) *Certain amounts from an eligible governmental plan not in excess of the amount paid for qualified health insurance premiums.* Amounts paid to a participant who is an eligible retired public safety officer from an eligible governmental plan are excludible from gross income to the extent provided in section 402(l).

*   *   *   *   *

■ **Par. 7.** Section 1.457-9 is amended by revising the third sentence of paragraph (a) and the last sentence of paragraph (b) to read as follows:

§ 1.457-9 Effect on eligible plans when not administered in accordance with eligibility requirements.

(a) *   *   * If a plan ceases to be an eligible governmental plan, amounts subsequently deferred by participants are includible in gross income when deferred, or, if later, when the amounts deferred first cease to be subject to a substantial risk of forfeiture, under the rules described in § 1.457-12(e). *   *   *

(b) *   *   * See § 1.457-12 for rules regarding the treatment of an ineligible plan.

§ 1.457-10 [Amended]

■ **Par. 8.** Section 1.457-10 is amended by removing the language "§ 1.457-11" wherever it appears in paragraphs (a)(2)(i), (a)(3) *Example 2* (ii), (c)(2) *Example 1* (ii) and *Example 2* (ii) and adding the language "§ 1.457-12" in its place.

§§ 1.457-11 and 1.457-12 [Redesignated as §§ 1.457-12 and 1.457-13]

■ **Par. 9.** Redesignate §§ 1.457-11 and 1.457-12 as §§ 1.457-12 and 1.457-13, respectively.

■ **Par. 10.** Add a new § 1.457-11 to read as follows:

§ 1.457-11 Exclusions and exceptions for certain plans.

(a) *In general.* The plans described in paragraphs (b) and (c) of this section either are not subject to section 457 or are treated as not providing for a deferral of compensation for purposes of section 457, and, accordingly, the provisions of §§ 1.457-3 through 1.457-10 and 1.457-12(a) do not apply to these plans.

(b) *Plans not subject to section 457.* The following plans are not subject to section 457:

(1) Any plan satisfying the conditions in section 1107(c)(4) of the Tax Reform Act of 1986, Public Law 99-514 (100 Stat. 2494) (TRA '86) (relating to certain plans for State judges);

(2) Any of the following plans (to which specific transitional statutory exclusions apply):

(i) A plan of a tax-exempt entity in existence prior to January 1, 1987, if the conditions of section 1107(c)(3)(B) of the TRA '86, as amended by section 1011(e)(6) of the Technical and Miscellaneous Revenue Act of 1988, Public Law 100-647 (102 Stat. 3342) (TAMRA), are satisfied (see § 1.457-2(b)(4) for a different rule that may apply to the annual deferrals permitted under this type of plan);

(ii) A collectively bargained nonelective deferred compensation plan in effect on December 31, 1987, if the conditions of section 6064(d)(2) of TAMRA are satisfied;

(iii) Amounts deferred under plans described in section 6064(d)(3) of TAMRA (relating to amounts deferred under certain nonelective deferred compensation plans in effect before 1989); and

(iv) Any plan satisfying the conditions in section 1107(c)(4) and (5) of TRA '86 (relating to certain plans for certain individuals with respect to which the IRS issued guidance before 1977); and

(3) Any plan described in section 457(e)(12) that provides only nonelective deferred compensation attributable to services not performed as an employee (for example, a plan providing nonelective deferred compensation attributable to services performed by indepen-

dent contractors). For this purpose, deferred compensation is nonelective only if all individuals, other than those who have not satisfied any applicable initial service requirement, with the same relationship to the payor are covered under the same plan with no individual variations or options under the plan.

(c) *Plans treated as not providing for a deferral of compensation.* The following plans are treated as not providing for a deferral of compensation for purposes of section 457, §§ 1.457-1 through 1.457-10, and § 1.457-12:

(1) A bona fide vacation leave, sick leave, compensatory time, severance pay, disability pay, or death benefit plan, as described in section 457(e)(11)(A)(i) (see paragraph (d) of this section for the definition of a bona fide severance pay plan, paragraph (e) of this section for the definitions of a bona fide death benefit plan and a bona fide disability pay plan, and paragraph (f) of this section for the requirements for a bona fide sick or vacation leave plan); and

(2) A plan described in section 457(e)(11)(A)(ii) paying solely length of service awards that are based on service accrued after December 31,1996, to bona fide volunteers (and their beneficiaries) on account of qualified services performed by those volunteers.

(d) *Definition of bona fide severance pay plan* —(1) *In general.* A bona fide severance pay plan is an arrangement that meets the following requirements:

(i) Except as provided in paragraph (d)(3) of this section, benefits are payable only upon involuntary severance from employment, as defined in paragraph (d)(2) of this section (see § 1.457-6(b) for the meaning of severance from employment);

(ii) The amount payable does not exceed two times the participant's annualized compensation based upon the annual rate of pay for services provided to the eligible employer for the calendar year preceding the calendar year in which the participant has a severance from employment with the eligible employer (or the current calendar year if the participant had no compensation for services provided to the eligible employer in the preceding calendar year), adjusted for any increase during the year used to measure the rate of pay that was expected to continue indefinitely if the participant had not had a severance from employment; and

(iii) The entire severance benefit must be paid to the participant no later than the last day of the second calendar year following the calendar year in which the severance from employment occurs, pursuant to a requirement contained in a written plan document.

(2) *Involuntary severance from employment* —(i) *In general.* For purposes of paragraph (d)(1) of this section, an *involuntary severance from employment* means a severance from employment due to the independent exercise of the eligible employer's unilateral authority to terminate the participant's services, other than due to the participant's implicit or explicit request, if the participant was willing and able to continue performing services. An involuntary severance from employment may include an eligible employer's failure to renew a contract at the time the contract expires, provided that the employee was willing and able to execute a new contract providing terms and conditions substantially similar to those in the expiring contract and to continue providing such services. The determination of whether a severance from employment is involuntary is based on all the facts and circumstances without regard to any characterization of the reason for the payment by the employer or participant.

(ii) *Severance from employment for good reason* —(A) *In general.* Notwithstanding paragraph (d)(2)(i) of this section, a participant's voluntary severance from employment will be treated as an involuntary severance from employment, for purposes of paragraph (d)(1)(i) of this section, if the severance occurs under certain bona fide conditions that are pre-specified in writing (referred to herein as a severance from employment for good reason), provided that the avoidance of the requirements of section 457 is not the primary purpose of the inclusion of the conditions or of the actions by the employer in connection with the satisfaction of the conditions, and a voluntary severance from employment under such conditions effectively constitutes an involuntary severance from employment. Notwithstanding the previous sentence, once the bona fide conditions have been established, the elimination of one or more of the conditions may result in the extension of a substantial risk of forfeiture, the recognition of which would be subject to the rules discussed in § 1.457-12(e)(2).

(B) *Material negative change required.* A severance from employment for good reason will be treated as an involuntary severance from employment only if the relevant facts and circumstances demonstrate that it was the result of unilateral employer action that caused a material negative change to the participant's relationship with the eligible employer. Some factors that may provide evidence of such a material negative change include a material reduction in the duties to be performed, a material negative change in the conditions under which the duties are to be performed, or a material reduction in the compensation to be received for performing such services. Other factors to be considered in determining whether a severance from employment due to good reason will be treated as an involuntary severance from employment include the extent to which the payments upon a severance from employment for good reason are in the same amount and made at the same time and in the same form as payments that would be made upon an actual involuntary severance from employment, and whether the employee is required to give the employer notice of the existence of the condition that would result in the treatment of a severance from employment as being for good reason and a reasonable opportunity to remedy the condition.

(C) *Safe harbor.* The requirements of paragraph (d)(2)(ii)(B) of this section are deemed to be satisfied if a severance from employment occurs under the conditions described in paragraph (d)(2)(ii)(C)(*1*) of this section, those conditions are specified in writing by the time the legally binding right to the payment arises, and the plan also satisfies the requirements in paragraphs (d)(2)(ii)(C)(*2*) and (*3*) of this section.

(*1*) The severance from employment occurs during a limited period of time not to exceed two years following the initial existence of one or more of the following conditions arising without the consent of the participant:

(*i*) A material diminution in the participant's base compensation;

(*ii*) A material diminution in the participant's authority, duties, or responsibilities;

(*iii*) A material diminution in the authority, duties, or responsibilities of the supervisor to whom the participant is required to report, including a requirement that a participant report to a corporate officer or employee instead of reporting directly to the board of directors (or similar governing body) of an organization;

(*iv*) A material diminution in the budget over which the participant retains authority;

(*v*) A material change in the geographic location at which the participant must perform services; or

(*vi*) Any other action or inaction that constitutes a material breach by the eligible employer of the agreement under which the participant provides services.

(*2*) The amount, time, and form of payment upon the severance from employment is substantially the same as the amount, time, and form of payment that would have been made upon an actual involuntary severance from employment, to the extent such right to payment exists.

(*3*) The participant is required to provide notice to the eligible employer of the existence of the applicable condition(s) described in paragraph (d)(2)(ii)(C)(*1*) of this section within a period not to exceed 90 days after the initial existence of the condition(s), upon the notice of which, the employer must be provided a period of at least 30 days during which it may remedy the condition(s) and not be required to pay the amount.

(3) *Window programs.* The requirement in paragraph (d)(1)(i) of this section that benefits be payable only upon involuntary severance from employment does not apply to a bona fide severance pay plan that provides benefits upon a severance from employment pursuant to a window program. For this purpose, a *window program* means a program established by an employer to provide separation pay in connection with an impending severance from employment, if the program is made available by the employer for a limited period of time (typically no longer than 12 months) to participants who have a severance from employment during that period or to participants who have a severance from employment during that period under specified circumstances. A program is not considered a window program for purposes of this paragraph if it is part of a pattern of multiple similar programs that, if offered as a single program, would not be a window program under this paragraph. Whether multiple programs constitute a pattern of similar programs is determined based on the relevant facts and circumstances. Although no one factor is determinative, relevant factors include whether the benefits are on account of a specific reduction in workforce (or some other entity-related operational condition), the degree to which the separation pay relates to an event or condition, and whether the event or condition is temporary or discrete or is a permanent aspect of the employer's practices.

(4) *Voluntary early retirement incentive plans* —(i) *In general.* Notwithstanding paragraph (d)(1) of this section, an applicable voluntary early retirement incentive plan (as defined in section 457(e)(11)(D)(ii)) is treated as a bona fide severance pay plan for purposes of this section with respect to payments or supplements made as an early retirement benefit, a retirement-type subsidy, or an early retirement benefit described in the last sentence of section 411(a)(9), if the payments or supplements are made in coordination with a defined benefit pension plan that is qualified under section 401(a) maintained by an eligible employer described in section 457(e)(1)(A) or by an education association described in section 457(e)(11)(D)(ii)(II). See section 1104(d)(4) of the Pension Protection Act of 2006, Public Law 109-280 (120 Stat. 780), regarding the application of the Internal Revenue Code and certain other laws to any plan, arrangement, or conduct to which section 457(e)(11)(D) does not apply.

(ii) *Definitions.* The definitions in § 1.411(d)-3(g)(6)(i) and (iv) apply for purposes of determining whether payments or supplements are an early retirement benefit or a retirement-type subsidy, and the definition in § 1.411(a)-7(c)(4) applies for purposes of determining whether payments or supplements are an early retirement benefit described in the last sentence of section 411(a)(9).

(e) *Bona fide death benefit or disability pay plans* —(1) *Bona fide death benefit plan.* For purposes of section 457(e)(11)(A)(i) and this section, a *bona fide death benefit plan* is a plan providing death benefits as defined in § 31.3121(v)(2)-1(b)(4)(iv)(C) of this chapter, provided that, for purposes of this paragraph (e)(1), the death benefits may be provided through insurance and the lifetime benefits payable under the plan are not treated as including the value of any term life insurance coverage provided under the plan that is includible in gross income.

(2) *Bona fide disability pay plan.* For purposes of section 457(e)(11)(A)(i) and this section, a *bona fide disability pay plan* is a plan that pays benefits (whether or not insured) only in the event that a participant is disabled, provided that, for purposes of this paragraph (e)(2), the value of any disability insurance coverage provided under the plan that is included in gross income is disregarded. For this purpose, a participant is considered disabled only if the participant meets one of the following conditions:

(i) The participant is unable to engage in any substantial gainful activity by reason of any medically determinable physical or mental impairment that can be expected to result in death or last for a continuous period of not less than 12 months;

(ii) The participant is, by reason of any medically determinable physical or mental impairment that can be expected to result in death or last for a continuous period of not less than 12 months, receiving income replacement benefits for a period of not less than three months under an accident and health plan covering employees of the eligible employer; or

(iii) The participant is determined to be totally disabled by the Social Security Administration or Railroad Retirement Board.

(f) *Bona fide sick and vacation leave plans* —(1) *In general.* For purposes of section 457(e)(11)(A)(i) and this section, the determination of whether a sick or vacation leave plan is a bona fide sick or vacation leave plan is made based on the relevant facts and circumstances. In general, a plan is treated as a bona fide sick or vacation leave plan, and not an arrangement to defer compensation, if the facts and circumstances demonstrate that the primary purpose of the plan is to provide participants with paid time off from work because of sickness, vacation, or other personal reasons. Factors used in determining whether a plan is a bona fide sick or vacation leave plan include whether the amount of leave provided could reasonably be expected to be used in the normal course by an employee (before the employee ceases to provide services to the eligible employer) absent unusual circumstances, the ability to exchange unused accumulated leave for cash or other benefits (including nontaxable benefits and the use of leave to postpone the date of termination of employment), the applicable restraints (if any) on the ability to accumulate unused leave and carry it forward to subsequent years in circumstances in which the accumulated leave may be exchanged for cash or other benefits, the amount and frequency of any in-service distributions of cash or other benefits offered in exchange for accumulated and unused leave, whether any payment of unused leave is made promptly upon severance from employment (or instead is paid over a period after severance from employment), and whether the program (or a particular feature of the program) is available only to a limited number of employees.

(2) *Delegation of authority to Commissioner.* The Commissioner may provide additional rules regarding the requirements of a bona fide sick or vacation leave plan under section 457, in revenue rulings, notices, or other guidance published in the Internal Revenue Bulletin (see

§ 601.601(d)(2)(ii)(*b*) of this chapter), as the Commissioner determines to be necessary or appropriate.

■ **Par. 11.** Newly-designated § 1.457-12 is revised to read as follows:

§ 1.457-12 Tax treatment of participants if plan is not an eligible plan.

(a) *Tax treatment of an ineligible plan under section 457(f)* —(1) *In general.* Pursuant to section 457(f)(1), if an eligible employer provides for a deferral of compensation under an ineligible plan, amounts will be included in income in accordance with paragraphs (a)(2) through (4) of this section, except as otherwise provided in this paragraph (a) or paragraph (b) of this section. See § 1.457-11 for plans that are not subject to section 457 or are not treated as providing for a deferral of compensation for purposes of section 457.

(2) *Income inclusion.* The present value of compensation deferred under an ineligible plan is includible in the gross income of a participant or beneficiary under section 457(f) on the applicable date. For this purpose, the applicable date is the later of the first date on which there is a legally binding right to the compensation or, if the compensation is subject to a substantial risk of forfeiture, the first date on which the substantial risk of forfeiture (within the meaning of section 457(f)(3)(B) and paragraph (e) of this section) lapses. Paragraph (c) of this section provides rules for determining the present value of the compensation deferred under the plan, including a requirement that the amount of compensation deferred under an ineligible plan as of an applicable date includes any earnings on the compensation as of that date.

(3) *Treatment of earnings after income inclusion.* Earnings credited on compensation deferred under an ineligible plan after the date on which the compensation is includible in gross income under section 457(f)(1) pursuant to paragraph (a)(2) of this section are includible in the gross income of a participant or beneficiary when paid or made available to the participant or beneficiary.

(4) *Income inclusion when compensation is paid or made available.* Amounts paid or made available to a participant or beneficiary under an ineligible plan are includible in the gross income of the participant or beneficiary under section 72, relating to annuities. For this purpose, an amount is paid or made available if there is actual or constructive receipt (within the meaning of § 1.451-2) of any taxable or nontaxable benefit, including a transfer of cash, a transfer of property includible in income under section 83, any other event that results in the inclusion in income under the economic benefit doctrine, a contribution to (or transfer or creation of a beneficial interest in) a trust described in section 402(b) at a time when contributions to the trust are includible in income under section 402(b), or inclusion of an amount in income under section 457A. An amount is also paid or made available for this purpose if there is a transfer, cancellation, or reduction of an amount of deferred compensation in exchange for benefits under a welfare benefit plan, a fringe benefit excludible under section 119 or section 132, or any other benefit that is excludible from gross income.

(5) *Investment in the contract.* For purposes of applying section 72 to amounts that are paid or made available as described in paragraph (a)(4) of this section, a participant is treated as having an investment in the contract to the extent that compensation has been included in gross income by the participant in accordance with paragraph (a)(2) of this section. An amount is treated as included in income for a taxable year only to the extent that the amount was properly includible in income and the participant actually included the amount in income (including on an original or amended federal income tax return or as a result of an IRS examination or a final decision of a court of competent jurisdiction).

(b) *Exceptions* —(1) *In general.* Section 457(f)(1) and paragraph (a) of this section do not apply to a plan or a portion of a plan described in this paragraph (b). The determination of whether a plan or a portion of a plan is described in this paragraph (b) is made as of the date on which the legally binding right to an amount arises. However, a plan or portion of a plan will cease to be a plan that is described in this paragraph (b) on the first date that it no longer meets the requirements described in this paragraph (b).

(2) *Certain retirement plans.* Annuity plans and contracts described in section 403 and plans described in section 401(a) are not subject to the provisions of section 457(f)(1) and paragraph (a) of this section.

(3) *Section 402(b) trusts* —(i) *Section 402(b).* The portion of a plan that consists of a trust to which section 402(b) applies is not subject to the provisions of section 457(f)(1) and paragraph (a) of this section.

(ii) *Example.* The provisions of this paragraph (b)(3) are illustrated in the following example:

Example. (i) *Facts.* On October 1, 2017, an eligible employer establishes an ineligible plan covering only one participant (a highly compensated employee under section 414(q)) under which the participant obtains an unconditional right to be paid $150,000 (plus interest at a specified reasonable rate) on October 1, 2021. As part of the plan, the employer simultaneously establishes a trust described in section 402(b) in the United States for the sole benefit of the participant. Under the terms of the plan and trust, the assets of the trust are also payable to the participant on October 1, 2021, and the amount that the employer is otherwise obligated to pay under the plan will be reduced (offset) by the amount paid to the participant from the trust. Section 402(b)(4) applies to the trust, and the trust has assets of $98,000 on October 1, 2017 and $100,000 on December 31, 2017.

(ii) *Conclusion.* Section 457(f) and this section apply only to the portion of the plan that is not funded through the section 402(b) trust. Thus, the participant has income under section 457(f) equal to the present value of the portion of the compensation deferred under the plan that is not funded through the section 402(b) trust on the date on which there is a legally binding right to the compensation (October 1, 2017). This present value is equal to $52,000 ($150,000—$98,000), which is included in the participant's gross income on October 1, 2017. The participant must also include $100,000 in gross income on December 31, 2017 pursuant to section 402(b)(4)(A).

(4) *Qualified governmental excess benefit arrangements under section 415(m).* A qualified governmental excess benefit arrangement described in section 415(m) is not subject to the provisions of section 457(f)(1) and paragraph (a) of this section.

(5) *Nonqualified annuities under section 403(c)* —(i) *Section 403(c) annuities.* The portion of a plan in which premiums are paid by an employer for an annuity contract to which section 403(c) applies is not subject to the provisions of section 457(f)(1) and paragraph (a) of this section.

(ii) *Examples.* The provisions of this paragraph (b)(5) are illustrated by the following examples:

Example 1. (i) *Facts.* A tax-exempt entity pays a premium for an annuity contract (described in section 403(c)) for the benefit of a participant. The annuity contract has a value of $135,000, and the participant is substantially vested (as defined in § 1.83-3(b)) at the time the premium is paid. The participant includes the full value ($135,000) in income under section 403(c) in the year the employer pays the premium.

(ii) *Conclusion.* Although the participant has a legally binding right to payments under the annuity contract that will be made in a subsequent taxable year, the participant's interest in the annuity contract is not subject to section 457(f)(1) and paragraph (a) of this section.

Example 2. (i) *Facts.* The facts are the same as in *Example 1 of this paragraph (b)(5),* except the participant's rights in the annuity contract are not substantially vested (as defined in § 1.83-3(b)) at the time the premium is paid and do not become substantially vested until a future taxable year. The participant does not include the full value of the contract in income under section 403(c) in the year the employer pays the premium.

(ii) *Conclusion.* Neither the payment of the premium nor the participant's interest in the annuity contract is subject to section 457(f)(1) or paragraph (a) of this section.

(6) *Transfer of property under section 83* —(i) *Section 83.* The portion of a plan that consists of a transfer of property to which section 83 applies is not subject to the provisions of section 457(f)(1) and paragraph (a) of this section. Specifically, section 457(f)(1) and paragraph (a) of this section do not apply if, on or before the first date on which compensation deferred under a plan is not subject to a substantial risk of forfeiture (within the meaning of section 457(f)(3)(B) and paragraph (e) of this section), the amount is paid through a transfer of property described in section 83. However, section 457(f)(1) and paragraph (a) of this section do apply if the first date on which compensation deferred under a plan is not subject to a substantial risk of forfeiture (as defined in section 457(f)(3)(B) and paragraph (e) of this section) precedes the date on which the amount is paid through a transfer of property described in section 83. If deferred compensation payable in property is includible in gross income under section 457(f)(1)(A), then, as provided in section 72, the amount includible in gross income when that property is later transferred or made available to the participant or beneficiary is the excess of the value of the property at that time over the amount previously included in gross income under section 457(f)(1)(A).

(ii) *Examples.* The provisions of this paragraph (b)(6) are illustrated by the following examples:

Example 1. (i) *Facts.* On December 1, 2017, an eligible employer agrees to transfer property that is substantially vested (within the meaning of § 1.83-3(b)) and has a fair market value equal to a specified dollar amount, to a participant on January 15, 2020. The participant's rights under the agreement are not subject to a substantial risk of forfeiture (within the meaning of section 457(f)(3)(B) and paragraph (e) of this section).

(ii) *Conclusion.* Because there is no substantial risk of forfeiture (within the meaning of section 457(f)(3)(B) and paragraph (e) of this section) with respect to the agreement to transfer property in 2020, the present value of the amount on the applicable date (December 1, 2017) is includible in the participant's gross income under section 457(f)(1)(A). Under paragraph (a)(4) of this section, when the substantially vested property is transferred to the participant on January 15, 2020, the amount includible in the participant's gross income is equal to the excess of the fair market value of the property on that date over the amount that was included in gross income for 2017.

Example 2. (i) *Facts.* Under a bonus plan, an eligible employer agrees in 2021 to transfer property that is substantially nonvested (within the meaning of § 1.83-3(b)) to Participants A and B in 2023 if they are continuously employed by the eligible employer through the date of the transfer (which condition constitutes a substantial risk of forfeiture within the meaning of section 457(f)(3)(B) and paragraph (e) of this section). In 2023, the eligible employer transfers the property to Participants A and B, subject to a substantial risk of forfeiture (within the meaning of § 1.83-3(c)), that lapses in 2025. Participant A makes a timely election to include the fair market value of the property in gross income under section 83(b). Participant B does not make this election.

(ii) *Conclusion.* The compensation deferred for both Participants A and B is not subject to section 457(f)(1) or paragraph (a) of this section because section 83 applies to the transfer of property on or before the date on which the property is not subject to a substantial risk of forfeiture (within the meaning of section 457(f)(3)(B) and paragraph (e) of this section). Because of the section 83(b) election, Participant A includes the fair market value of the property (disregarding lapse restrictions) in gross income for 2023 under section 83(b)(1). Participant B includes the value of the property in gross income when the substantial risk of forfeiture lapses in 2025 under section 83(a).

(7) *Applicable employment retention plan.* The portion of a plan that is an applicable employment retention plan as described in section 457(f)(4) with respect to any participant is not subject to the provisions of section 457(f)(1) and paragraph (a) of this section. See also section 1104(d)(4) of the Pension Protection Act of 2006, Public Law 109-280 (120 Stat. 780), regarding the application of the Internal Revenue Code and certain other laws to any plan, arrangement, or conduct to which section 457(f)(2)(F) does not apply.

(c) *Amount included in income* —(1) *Calculation of present value* —(i) *In general.* Except as otherwise provided in this paragraph (c), the present value of compensation deferred under an ineligible plan as of an applicable date equals the present value of the future payments to which the participant has a legally binding right (as described in paragraph (d) of this section). For this purpose, present value is determined in accordance with the provisions of this paragraph (c)(1)(i) by multiplying the amount of a payment (or the amount of each payment in a series of payments) by the probability that any condition or conditions on which the payment is contingent will be satisfied and discounting the amount using an assumed rate of interest to reflect the time value of money.

(ii) *Actuarial assumptions* —(A) *In general* —(*1*) *Reasonable actuarial assumptions.* For purposes of paragraph (c)(1)(i) of this section, present value is determined using actuarial assumptions and methods that, based on all of the facts and circumstances, are reasonable as of the applicable date, including an interest rate that is reasonable as of that date and other assumptions necessary to determine the present value (without regard to whether the present value of the compensation deferred under the plan is reasonably ascertainable as described in § 31.3121(v)(2)-1(e)(4)(i)(B) of this chapter).

(*2*) *Probability of death before the payment of benefits.* For purposes of paragraph (c)(1)(i) of this section, the probability that a participant will die before a payment is made is permitted to be taken into account only to the extent that the payment is forfeitable upon death.

(*3*) *Probability that the payment will not be made.* For purposes of paragraph (c)(1)(i) of this section, the probability that payments will not be made (or will be reduced) because of the unfunded status of a plan, the risk associated with any deemed or actual investment of compensation deferred under the plan, the risk that the eligible employer or another party will be unwilling or unable to pay, the possibility of future plan amendments, the possibility of a future change in the law, or similar risks or contingencies are not taken into account.

(B) *Payments made in foreign currency.* The rules in § 1.409A-4(b)(2)(i) apply for purposes of determining the treatment of payments in foreign currency.

(C) *Treatment of payment triggers based upon events* —(*1*) *In general.* Except as provided in paragraph (c)(1)(ii)(C)(*2*) of this section, the rules in § 1.409A-4(b)(2)(vii) apply for purposes of determining the treatment of payment triggers based upon events.

(*2*) *Treatment of severance from employment.* If the date on which a payment will be made depends on the date the participant has a severance from employment (as described in § 1.457-6(b)) and the participant has not had a severance from employment by the applicable date, then for purposes of paragraph (c)(1)(ii)(A)(*1*) of this section, the severance from employment may be treated as occurring on any date that is not later than the fifth anniversary of the applicable date, unless this assumption would be unreasonable under the facts and circumstances.

(iii) *Unreasonable assumptions.* If any actuarial assumption or method used to determine the present value of compensation deferred under the plan is not reasonable, as determined by the Commissioner, then the Commissioner will determine the present value using actuarial assumptions and methods that the Commissioner determines to be reasonable, including the AFR and the applicable mortality table under section 417(e)(3)(B) as of the applicable date. For purposes of this section, *AFR* means the mid-term applicable federal rate (as defined pursuant to section 1274(d)) for January 1 of the relevant calendar year, compounded annually.

(iv) *Account balance plans* —(A) *In general.* To the extent benefits are provided under an account balance plan, as defined in § 31.3121(v)(2)-1(c)(1)(ii) and (iii) of this chapter, to which earnings (or losses, if applicable) are credited at least annually, the present value of compensation deferred under the plan as of an applicable date is the amount credited to the participant's account, including both the principal amount credited to the account and any earnings or losses attributable to the principal amount that have been credited to the account, as of that date.

(B) *Unreasonable rates of return.* This paragraph (c)(1)(iv)(B) applies to an account balance plan under which the income credited is based on neither a predetermined actual investment, within the meaning of § 31.3121(v)(2)-1(d)(2)(i)(B) of this chapter, nor a rate of interest that is reasonable, within the meaning of § 31.3121(v)(2)-1(d)(2)(i)(C) of this chapter, as determined by the Commissioner. The present value of compensation deferred under that type of plan as of an applicable date is equal to the amount credited to the participant's account as of that date, plus the present value of the excess (if any) of the earnings to be credited under the plan over the earnings that would be credited through the projected payment date using a reasonable rate of interest. If the present value of compensation deferred under the plan is not determined and is not taken into account by the taxpayer in this manner, the present value of the compensation deferred under the plan will be treated as equal to the amount credited to the participant's account as of the applicable date, plus the present value of the excess (if any) of the earnings to be credited under the plan through the projected payment date over the earnings that would be credited using the AFR.

(C) *Combinations of predetermined actual investments or interest rates.* If the amount of earnings or losses credited under an account balance plan is based on the greater of two or more rates of return (each of which would be a predetermined actual investment or a reasonable interest rate if the earnings or losses credited were based on only one of those rates of return), then the amount included in income on the applicable date is the sum of the amount credited to the participant's account as of the applicable date and the present value (determined under paragraph (c)(1)(i) of this section) of the right to future earnings.

(D) *Examples.* The following examples illustrate the provisions of paragraphs (c)(1)(i) through (iv) of this section. For purposes of these examples, assume that the arrangements are either not subject to section 409A or 457A or otherwise comply with the requirements of those provisions, and that the parties are not under examination for any of the tax years in question.

Example 1. (i) *Facts.* On October 1, 2017, an eligible employer agrees to pay $100,000 to a participant on January 1, 2024, if the participant is alive on that date. The employer determines that the October 1, 2017 present value of that payment is $75,000 based on the second segment rate used for purposes of section 417(e)(3)(C) on October 1, 2017, and

using the mortality table applicable under section 417(e)(3)(B) on October 1, 2017.

(ii) *Conclusion.* The present value has been determined in accordance with paragraph (c)(1)(i) of this section.

Example 2. (i) *Facts.* On October 1, 2018, an eligible employer agrees to pay $100,000 to a participant at severance from employment. The assumptions that the employer uses to determine the present value are that the participant will have a severance from employment on October 1, 2023 (the fifth anniversary of the date the participant obtains the right to the payment in accordance with paragraph (c)(1)(ii)(C)(*2*) of this section) and that the present value will be determined using a rate of 4.5% compounded monthly.

(ii) *Conclusion.* Assuming, solely for purposes of this example, that the employer's severance from employment date and interest rate assumptions are reasonable, the value included in income on the applicable date (October 1, 2018) is $79,885.

Example 3. (i) *Facts.* On October 1, 2017, an eligible employer agrees to pay $100,000 to a participant at severance from employment, but no payment will be made if the severance from employment occurs on or after October 1, 2021.

(ii) *Conclusion.* Although paragraph (c)(1)(ii)(C)(*2*) of this section provides that for purposes of determining when a payment will be made, severance may be treated as if it occurred on the fifth anniversary of the applicable date, that assumption would be unreasonable under these facts and circumstances and would not be permitted under paragraph (c)(1)(ii)(C)(*2*) of this section. Accordingly, for purposes of determining the present value, an assumption that severance from employment would occur after September 30, 2021 would be unreasonable.

Example 4. (i) *Facts.* An eligible employer maintains a supplemental executive retirement plan that provides a subsidized early retirement benefit payable to participants between age 60 and 65. A 60 year old participant becomes vested in the right to the subsidized early retirement benefit on December 31, 2017.

(ii) *Conclusion.* The assumption under paragraph (c)(1)(ii)(C)(*2*) of this section would not be permitted for purposes of determining the amount to be included in income because the nature of the subsidized early retirement benefit causes it to decline in value until it becomes worthless upon attainment of age 65. In other words, the value of the subsidized early retirement benefit using the assumption permitted in paragraph (c)(1)(ii)(C)(*2*) of this section would result in a value of $0 and would be unreasonable under the facts and circumstances.

Example 5. (i) *Facts.* On October 1, 2017, an eligible employer agrees to provide compensation to an employee for prior services in an amount equal to $100,000, plus interest at a reasonable rate, with payment to be made at the time of the employee's severance from employment. The participant's right to the compensation is not subject to a substantial risk of forfeiture at any time.

(ii) *Conclusion.* Because the agreement provides for a reasonable rate of interest, the amount included in income on the applicable date (October 1, 2017) is $100,000.

Example 6. (i) *Facts.* The facts are the same as in *Example 5* of this paragraph (c)(1)(iv)(D), except that the right is subject to a requirement that the participant continue to provide substantial services for three additional years (which constitutes a substantial risk of forfeiture as described in paragraph (e) of this section). On October 1, 2020, when the substantial risk of forfeiture lapses, the account balance is $116,147.

(ii) *Conclusion.* The amount included in income on the applicable date (October 1, 2020) is $116,147.

Example 7. (i) *Facts.* The facts are the same as in *Example 5* of this paragraph (c)(1)(iv)(D), except that the rate of interest credited on the account is 5% above a reasonable rate of interest. On October 1, 2017, the sum of the $100,000 account balance, plus the present value of the right to receive the difference between a reasonable rate of return and the rate of return being credited on the account (from October 1, 2017 until October 1, 2022) is $128,336. The participant has a severance from employment on October 16, 2020, and is paid $135,379 on that date.

(ii) *Conclusion.* The amount included in income on the applicable date (October 1, 2017) is $128,336. Pursuant to paragraph (a)(5) of this section, the $128,336 is treated as investment in the contract for purposes of section 72 and, pursuant to paragraph (a)(4) of this section, the participant recognizes an additional $7,043 ($135,379, minus the $128,336 that was previously included in gross income for 2017) in income attributable to the payment on October 16, 2020.

Example 8. (i) *Facts.* The facts are the same as in *Example 5* of this paragraph (c)(1)(iv)(D), except that the employer also agrees to pay the participant an amount that is estimated to be equal to the federal, state, and local income taxes due (based on a fixed percentage that is pre-specified in the agreement) attributable to the amount included in income on the applicable date (October 1, 2017). In exchange for that tax payment, the amount payable upon severance from employment is to be reduced by an amount equal to the federal, state, and local income taxes for the taxable year of payment that the employer estimates would otherwise have been due but for the income inclusion in 2017. In satisfaction of this obligation to make the tax payment, the employer pays the participant $66,667 on April 15, 2018.

(ii) *Conclusion.* The present value on the applicable date (October 1, 2017) is $100,000, plus the present value of the $66,667 payment to be made on April 15, 2018, minus the present value of the reduction that will be applied at the time of payment (which, if reasonable, may be assumed to be October 1, 2022 in accordance with paragraph (c)(1)(ii)(C)(*2*) of this section).

Example 9. (i) *Facts.* An eligible employer credits $100,000 on December 31, 2017, to the account of a participant under an ineligible plan, subject to the condition that the amount will be forfeited if the participant voluntarily terminates employment before December 31, 2019. The account balance will be credited with notional annual earnings based on the greater of the return of a designated S&P 500 index fund or a specified rate of interest and will be paid on December 31, 2025.

(ii) *Conclusion.* Under paragraph (c)(1)(iv)(C) of this section, the sum of the amount credited to the participant's account as of the applicable date (December 31, 2019) and the present value (determined under paragraph (c)(1)(i) of this section) of the right to future earnings based on the greater of the return of the designated S&P 500 index fund or the specified rate of interest must be included in the participant's gross income on the applicable date.

(v) *Application of the general calculation rules to formula amounts.* With respect to a right to receive a formula amount, the amount or amounts of future payments under the plan, for purposes of determining the present value as of an applicable date, is determined based on all of the facts and circumstances existing as of that date. This determination must reflect reasonable, good faith assumptions with respect to any contingencies as to the amount of the payment, both with respect to each contingency and with respect to all contingencies in the aggregate. An assumption based on the facts and circumstances as of the applicable date may be reasonable even if the facts and circumstances change in the future so that when the amount payable is determined in a subsequent year, the amount payable is a greater (or lesser) amount. In such a case, the increase (or decrease) due to the change in the facts and circumstances is treated as earnings (or losses). For purposes of this paragraph (c)(1)(v), an amount payable is a formula amount to the extent that the amount payable in a future taxable year is dependent upon factors that, after applying the assumptions and other rules set forth in this section, are not determinable as of the applicable date, such that the amount payable may not be readily determined as of that date under the other provisions of this section. If some portion of an amount payable is not a formula amount, the amount payable with respect to such portion is determined under the rules applicable to amounts that are not formula amounts, and only the balance of the amount payable is determined under the rules applicable to formula amounts.

(vi) *Treatment of payment restrictions.* The rules in § 1.409A-4(b)(2)(v) apply for purposes of determining the treatment of payment restrictions.

(vii) *Treatment of alternative times and forms of a future payment.* The rules in § 1.409A-4(b)(2)(vi) apply for purposes of determining the treatment of alternative times and forms of a future payment.

(viii) *Reimbursement and in-kind benefit arrangements.* The rules in § 1.409A-4(b)(4) apply for purposes of determining the present value of reimbursement and in-kind benefit arrangements.

(ix) *Split-dollar life insurance arrangements.* The rules in § 1.409A-4(b)(5) apply for purposes of determining the present value of benefits provided under a split-dollar life insurance arrangement.

(2) *Forfeiture or other permanent loss of right to compensation previously included in income* —(i) *In general.* If a participant has included compensation under a plan in income pursuant to paragraph (a)(2) or (4) of this section, but all or a portion of that compensation is never paid under the plan, the participant is entitled to a deduction for the taxable year in which the entire remaining right to the payment of the compensation is permanently forfeited under the plan's terms or otherwise permanently lost. The deduction to which the participant is enti-

tled equals the excess of the amounts included in income under paragraphs (a)(2) and (4) of this section with respect to the compensation over the total amount of the compensation actually received that constitutes investment in the contract under paragraph (a)(5) of this section.

(ii) *Forfeiture or permanent loss of right.* For purposes of this paragraph (c)(2), a mere diminution in the amount payable under the plan due to a deemed investment loss, an actuarial reduction, or any other decrease in the amount deferred under the plan is not treated as a forfeiture or permanent loss of the right if the participant retains the right to any payment under the plan (whether or not such right is subject to a substantial risk of forfeiture as described in paragraph (e) of this section). In addition, an amount payable under a plan is not treated as forfeited or otherwise permanently lost if another amount or an obligation to make a payment in a future year is substituted for the original amount. However, an amount payable under a plan is treated as permanently lost if the participant's right to receive payment of the amount becomes wholly worthless during the taxable year. Whether the right to receive payment has become wholly worthless is determined based on the relevant facts and circumstances existing as of the last day of the relevant taxable year.

(iii) *Examples.* The provisions of this paragraph (c)(2) are illustrated in the following examples:

Example 1. (i) *Facts.* On October 1, 2017, an eligible employer establishes an ineligible plan for a participant under which the employer agrees to pay the amount credited to the participant's account when the participant has a severance from employment. The obligation to make the payment is not subject to a substantial risk of forfeiture. The account balance on October 1, 2017 is $125,000, and the participant includes $125,000 in income in 2017. The plan subsequently experiences notional investment losses, and the participant receives $75,000 from the plan in a lump-sum distribution in 2024, when the participant has a severance from employment. The $75,000 lump-sum distribution represents all amounts due to the participant under the plan.

(ii) *Conclusion.* For 2024, the participant is entitled to deduct $50,000 (the excess of the amount included in income under paragraph (a)(2) of this section ($125,000) over the amount actually received that constitutes investment in the contract under paragraph (a)(5) of this section ($75,000)).

Example 2. (i) *Facts.* The facts are the same facts as in *Example 1* of this paragraph (c)(2)(iii), except that the plan provides that the participant will receive the deferred compensation in three installments (1/3 of the account balance in 2024, 1/2 of the then remaining account balance in 2025, and the remaining balance in 2026), and that the sum of all three installments is $75,000.

(ii) *Conclusion.* The participant is entitled to deduct $50,000 in the taxable year of the last installment payment (2026) ($125,000, reduced by the sum of the amounts received in 2024, 2025, and 2026 ($75,000)).

(d) *Definition of deferral of compensation* —(1) *In general* —(i) *Legally binding right.* A plan provides for the deferral of compensation with respect to a participant for purposes of section 457(f) and this section if, under the terms of the plan and the relevant facts and circumstances, the participant has a legally binding right during a calendar year to compensation that, pursuant to the terms of the plan, is or may be payable to (or on behalf of) the participant in a later calendar year. Whether a plan provides for the deferral of compensation for purposes of section 457(f) and this section is determined based on the relevant facts and circumstances at the time that the participant obtains a legally binding right to the compensation, or, if later, when a plan is amended to convert a right that does not provide for a deferral of compensation into a right that does provide for a deferral of compensation. For example, if a plan providing for retiree health care does not initially provide for a deferral of compensation but is later amended to provide the ability to receive future cash payments instead of health benefits, it may become a plan that provides for the deferral of compensation at the time of the amendment. An amount of compensation deferred under a plan that provides for the deferral of compensation within the meaning of section 457(f) and this section does not cease to be an amount subject to section 457(f) and this section by reason of any change to the plan that would otherwise recharacterize the right to the amount as a right that does not provide for the deferral of compensation with respect to such amount. In addition, any change under the plan that results in an exchange of an amount deferred under the plan for some other right or benefit that would otherwise be excluded from the participant's gross income does not affect the characterization of the plan as one that provides for a deferral of compensation.

(ii) *Discretion to reduce or eliminate compensation.* A participant does not have a legally binding right to compensation to the extent that the compensation may be reduced or eliminated unilaterally by the employer or another person after the services creating the right to the compensation have been performed. However, if the facts and circumstances indicate that the discretion to reduce or eliminate the compensation is available or exercisable only upon a condition, or the discretion to reduce or eliminate the compensation lacks substantive significance, a participant is considered to have a legally binding right to the compensation. Whether the discretion to reduce or eliminate compensation lacks substantive significance depends on all the relevant facts and circumstances. However, if the participant to whom the compensation may be paid has effective control of the person retaining the discretion to reduce or eliminate the compensation, or has effective control over any portion of the compensation of the person retaining the discretion to reduce or eliminate the compensation, or is a member of the family (as defined in section 267(c)(4) but also including the spouse of any member of the family) of the person retaining the discretion to reduce or eliminate the compensation, the discretion to reduce or eliminate the compensation is not treated as having substantive significance. Compensation is not considered subject to unilateral reduction or elimination merely because it may be reduced or eliminated by operation of the objective terms of the plan, such as the application of a nondiscretionary, objective provision creating a substantial risk of forfeiture or the application of a formula that provides for benefits to be offset by benefits provided under another plan (such as a plan that is qualified under section 401(a)).

(2) *Short-term deferrals.* For purposes of section 457(f) and this section, a deferral of compensation does not occur under a plan with respect to any payment for which a deferral of compensation does not occur under section 409A pursuant to §1.409A-1(b)(4) (short-term deferrals), except that, for purposes of this paragraph, in applying the rules provided in §1.409A-1(b)(4) the meaning of *substantial risk of forfeiture* under §1.457-12(e) applies in each place that term is used (and not the meaning of *substantial risk of forfeiture* provided under §1.409A-1(d)).

(3) *Recurring part-year compensation.* For purposes of section 457(f) and this section and notwithstanding paragraph (d)(2) of this section, a deferral of compensation does not occur under a plan with respect to an amount that is recurring part-year compensation (as defined in §1.409A-2(a)(14)), if the plan does not defer payment of any of the recurring part-year compensation to a date beyond the last day of the 13th month following the first day of the service period for which the recurring part-year compensation is paid, and the amount of the recurring part-year compensation does not exceed the annual compensation limit under section 401(a)(17) for the calendar year in which the service period commences.

(4) *Certain other exceptions.* For purposes of section 457(f) and this section, a deferral of compensation does not occur to the extent that a plan provides for:

(i) The payment of expense reimbursements, medical benefits, or in-kind benefits, as described in §1.409A-1(b)(9)(v)(A), (B), or (C);

(ii) Certain indemnification rights, liability insurance, or legal settlements, as described in §1.409A-1(b)(10), or (11); or

(iii) Taxable educational benefits for an employee (which, for this purpose, means solely benefits consisting of educational assistance, as defined in section 127(c)(1) and the regulations thereunder, attributable to the education of an employee, and does not include any benefits provided for the education of any other person, including any spouse, child, or other family member of the employee).

(5) *Interaction with section 409A* —(i) *In general.* The rules of section 457(f) apply to an ineligible plan separately and in addition to any requirements applicable to the plan under section 409A.

(ii) *Acceleration of the time or schedule of a payment.* Although section 457(f) and this section do not preclude the acceleration of payments, see §1.409A-3(a) for the general rules and exceptions relating to the acceleration of payments that are subject to section 409A.

(iii) *Example.* The provisions of this paragraph (d)(5) are illustrated in the following example:

Example. (i) *Facts.* On December 1, 2017, an eligible employer establishes an account balance plan for an employee that is subject to section 457(f), under which an initial amount is credited to the account and is increased periodically by earnings based on a reasonable specified rate of interest. The entire account balance is subject to a substantial risk of forfeiture until December 1, 2021. Under the terms of the plan, the account balance will be paid in three annual installments on each January 15, beginning in 2024 (one third of the balance for the first installment, one half of the then remaining balance for the second installment, and the remaining balance for the third installment). How-

ever, in 2022, the plan is amended to provide for payments to begin in 2023, such that the plan fails to comply with the requirements of section 409A during 2022. The account balance is: $100,000 on December 1, 2021; $118,000 on December 31, 2022; $120,000 on January 15, 2023 (so that the payment made that day is $40,000 ($120,000/3)); $88,000 on January 15, 2024 (so that the payment made that day is $44,000 ($88,000/2)); and $50,000 on January 15, 2025 (so that the payment made that day is $50,000).

(ii) *Conclusion: Federal income tax treatment in 2021.* The plan provides for a deferral of compensation to which section 457(f) applies. Under section 457(f) and paragraph (a)(2) of this section, the $100,000 amount of the account balance on December 1, 2021, when the benefits cease to be subject to a substantial risk of forfeiture, is included in the employee's gross income on that date.

(iii) *Conclusion: Federal income tax treatment after 2021* —(*1*) *Treatment in 2022 under section 409A.* Because the arrangement fails to meet the requirements of section 409A in 2022, the employee has gross income under section 409A equal to the account balance on December 31, 2022, reduced by the amount previously included in income. Accordingly, the amount included in gross income under section 409A is equal to $18,000 (the $118,000 account balance on December 31, 2022, reduced by the $100,000 previously included in income under section 457(f) for 2021). The amount included in gross income under section 409A is subject to an additional 20 percent tax under section 409A(a)(1)(B)(i)(II) and a premium interest tax under section 409A(a)(1)(B)(i)(I).

(*2*) *Federal income tax treatment of first installment payment in 2023* —(*i*) *Earnings previously included under section 409A.* The first $18,000 of the $40,000 payment in 2023 is excluded from gross income under section 409A as a result of the earlier inclusion of that amount in income in 2022 due to the section 409A violation. See §1.409A-4(f).

(*ii*) *Deferral of compensation under section 457(f).* The amount of the investment in the contract (described in paragraph (a)(5) of this section) allocated to the remaining $22,000 of the installment paid in 2023 is $33,333 ($100,000/3), so no amount is included in gross income for 2023.

(*3*) *Federal income tax treatment of second installment payment in 2024.* The employee has unused investment in the contract from 2023 in the amount of $11,333 ($33,333-$22,000). Assuming that the employee elects to redetermine the amount recognized for the current and subsequent years in 2024 pursuant to §1.72-4(d)(3)(ii), the amount included in gross income for 2024 is $5,000 (the payment of $44,000, reduced by the portion of the remaining investment in the contract that is allocable to the installment, which is $39,000 (($100,000-$22,000)/2)).

(*4*) *Federal income tax treatment of third installment payment in 2025.* The amount included in gross income for 2025 is $11,000 (the payment of $50,000, reduced by the remaining investment in the contract of $39,000).

(e) *Rules relating to substantial risk of forfeiture* —(1) *Substantial risk of forfeiture* —(i) *In general.* An amount of compensation is subject to a substantial risk of forfeiture only if entitlement to the amount is conditioned on the future performance of substantial services, or upon the occurrence of a condition that is related to a purpose of the compensation if the possibility of forfeiture is substantial. An amount is not subject to a substantial risk of forfeiture if the facts and circumstances demonstrate that the forfeiture condition is unlikely to be enforced (see paragraph (e)(1)(v) of this section). If a plan provides that entitlement to an amount is conditioned on involuntary severance from employment without cause (which includes, for this purpose, a voluntary severance from employment that is treated as involuntary under §1.457-11(d)(2)(ii)), the right is subject to a substantial risk of forfeiture if the possibility of forfeiture is substantial.

(ii) *Substantial future services.* For purposes of paragraph (e)(1)(i) of this section, the determination of whether an amount of compensation is conditioned on the future performance of substantial services is based on the relevant facts and circumstances, such as whether the hours required to be performed during the relevant period are substantial in relation to the amount of compensation.

(iii) *Condition related to a purpose of the compensation.* For purposes of paragraph (e)(1)(i) of this section, a condition related to a purpose of the compensation must relate to the participant's performance of services for the employer or to the employer's governmental or tax-exempt activities (as applicable) or organizational goals.

(iv) *Noncompetition conditions.* For purposes of paragraph (e)(1)(i) of this section, an amount of compensation will not be treated as subject to a substantial risk of forfeiture merely because the right to payment of the amount is conditioned, directly or indirectly, upon the employee refraining from the future performance of certain services, unless each of the of the following conditions is satisfied:

(A) The right to payment of the amount is expressly conditioned upon the employee refraining from the future performance of services pursuant to an enforceable written agreement.

(B) The employer makes reasonable ongoing efforts to verify compliance with noncompetition agreements (including the noncompetition agreement applicable to the employee).

(C) At the time that the enforceable written agreement becomes binding, the facts and circumstances demonstrate that the employer has a substantial and bona fide interest in preventing the employee from performing the prohibited services and that the employee has bona fide interest in, and ability to, engage in the prohibited competition. Factors taken into account for this purpose include the employer's ability to show significant adverse economic consequences that would likely result from the prohibited services; the marketability of the employee based on specialized skills, reputation, or other factors; and the employee's interest, financial need, and ability to engage in the prohibited services.

(v) *Enforcement of forfeiture condition.* To constitute a substantial risk of forfeiture, the possibility of actual forfeiture in the event that the forfeiture condition occurs must be substantial based on the relevant facts and circumstances. Factors to be considered for this purpose include, but are not limited to, the extent to which the employer has enforced forfeiture conditions in the past, the level of control or influence of the employee with respect to the organization and the individual(s) who would be responsible for enforcing the forfeiture condition, and the likelihood that such provisions would be enforceable under applicable law.

(2) *Addition or extension of risk of forfeiture* —(i) *General rule.* The initial addition or extension of any risk of forfeiture after a legally binding right to compensation arises, including the application of a risk of forfeiture to a plan providing for deferrals of current compensation (an additional or extended risk of forfeiture), will be disregarded unless the plan meets the requirements of paragraphs (e)(2)(ii) through (v) of this section.

(ii) *Benefit must be materially greater.* A deferred amount will not be subject to a substantial risk of forfeiture for purposes of section 457 and this section after the date on which an employee could have received the amount, unless the present value of the amount made subject to the additional or extended substantial risk of forfeiture (disregarding the risk of forfeiture in determining the present value of the amount) is materially greater than the present value of the amount the employee otherwise would have received absent the initial or extended risk of forfeiture. For purposes of this paragraph (e)(2)(ii), present value is determined in accordance with the rules described in paragraph (c) of this section as of the applicable date for the amount the employee otherwise would have received absent the initial or extended risk of forfeiture. In addition, an amount is materially greater for purposes of this paragraph (e)(2)(ii) only if the present value of the amount subject to the additional or extended substantial risk of forfeiture is more than 125 percent of the present value of the amount that the employee would have received absent the additional or extended risk of forfeiture. For this purpose, compensation that the participant would receive for continuing to perform services, regardless of whether the deferred amount is subjected to an additional or extended substantial risk of forfeiture, is not taken into account.

(iii) *Minimum two years of substantial future services.* The employee must be required to perform substantial services in the future, or refrain from competing pursuant to an agreement that meets the requirements of paragraph (e)(1)(iv) of this section, for a minimum of two years after the date that the employee could have received the compensation in the absence of the additional or extended substantial risk of forfeiture. For example, if an employee elects to defer a fixed percentage from each semi-monthly payroll, the two year minimum applies to each semi-monthly payroll amount that would otherwise have been paid. Notwithstanding the two year minimum, a plan may provide that that the substantial future service condition will lapse upon death, disability, or involuntary severance from employment without cause.

(iv) *Timing.* The parties must agree in writing to any addition or extension of a substantial risk of forfeiture under this paragraph (e)(2). In the case of an initial addition of a substantial risk of forfeiture if none previously existed (for example, in the case of a deferral of current compensation), this written agreement must be entered into before the beginning of the calendar year in which any services that give rise to the compensation are performed, and, in the case of an extension of a substantial risk of forfeiture, the written agreement must be entered

into at least 90 days before an existing substantial risk of forfeiture would have lapsed. If an employee with respect to whom compensation is made subject to an initial or extended substantial risk of forfeiture was not providing services to the employer at least 90 days before the addition or extension, the addition or extension may be agreed to in writing within 30 days after commencement of employment but only with respect to amounts attributable to services rendered after the addition or extension is agreed to in writing.

(v) *Substitutions.* For purposes of paragraph (e)(2) of this section, if an amount is forfeited or relinquished and replaced, in whole or part, with a right to another amount (or benefit) that is a substitute for the amount that was forfeited or relinquished and that is subject to a risk of forfeiture, the risk of forfeiture will be disregarded unless the requirements of paragraphs (e)(2)(ii) through (iv) of this section are satisfied.

(3) *Examples.* The provisions of this paragraph (e) are illustrated in the following examples:

Example 1. (i) *Facts.* On January 15, 2017, an employee has a severance from employment with an eligible employer and enters into an agreement with the eligible employer under which the eligible employer agrees to pay the employee $250,000 on January 15, 2018, if the employee provides consulting services to the employer until that date. The consulting services required are insubstantial in relation to the payment. The employee provides the required consulting services for the employer through January 15, 2018.

(ii) *Conclusion.* The consulting services provided by the former employee do not constitute substantial services because they are insubstantial in relation to the payment. Accordingly, the present value of $250,000 payable on January 15, 2018 is includible in the employee's gross income on January 15, 2017.

Example 2. (i) *Facts.* On January 27, 2020, an eligible employer agrees to pay an employee an amount equal to $120,000 on January 1, 2023, provided that the employee continues to provide substantial services to the employer through that date. In 2021, the parties enter into a written agreement to extend the date through which substantial services must be performed to January 1, 2025, in which event, the employer will pay an amount that has a present value of $145,000 on January 1, 2023.

(ii) *Conclusion.* As of the date the initial risk of forfeiture would have lapsed, the present value of the compensation subject to the extended substantial risk of forfeiture is not materially greater than the present value of the amount previously deferred under the plan ($145,000 is not more than 125% of $120,000) and, therefore, the intended extension of the substantial risk of forfeiture is disregarded under the provisions of paragraph (e)(2) of this section. Accordingly, the employee will recognize income, on the applicable date (January 1, 2023) in an amount equal to $120,000 (the amount that is not subject to a substantial risk of forfeiture on that date, disregarding the intended extension). With respect to the amount that is ultimately paid under the plan on January 1, 2025, the employee is treated as having investment in the contract of $120,000 (pursuant to paragraph (a)(5) of this section).

Example 3. (i) *Facts.* On December 31, 2017, a participant enters into an agreement to defer $15,000 of the participant's current compensation that would otherwise be paid during 2018, with payment of the deferred amounts to be made on December 31, 2024, but only if the participant continues to provide substantial services until December 31, 2024. Under the terms of the agreement, the participant's periodic payments of current compensation are reduced, and a corresponding amount is credited (with a 30% employer match) to an account earning a reasonable rate of interest. The present value of the amount payable on December 31, 2024 is 130% of the present value of the amount deferred.

(ii) *Conclusion.* The amounts deferred are subject to a substantial risk of forfeiture because the plan satisfies the requirements of paragraphs (e)(2)(ii) through (v) of this section.

Example 4. (i) *Facts.* Employee A is a well-known college sports coach with a long history of success in a sports program at University X. University X reasonably expects that the loss of Employee A would be substantially detrimental to its sports program and would result in significant financial losses. Employee A has bona fide interest in continuing to work as a college sports coach and is highly marketable. On June 1, 2020, Employee A and University X enter into a written agreement under which Employee A agrees to provide substantial services to University X until June 1, 2023. The parties further agree that University X will pay $500,000 to Employee A on June 1, 2025 if Employee A has not performed services as a sports coach before that date for any other college or university with a sports program similar to that of University X. The agreement is enforceable under applicable law and University X would be reasonably expected to enforce it.

(ii) *Conclusion.* The $500,000 payable under the agreement is subject to a substantial risk of forfeiture until June 1, 2025, and includible in Employee A's gross income on that date.

■ **Par. 12**. Newly-designated § 1.457-13 is revised to read as follows:

§ 1.457-13 Applicability dates.

(a) *General applicability date.* Except as otherwise provided in paragraph (b) of this section, §§ 1.457-1 through 1.457-12 apply to compensation deferred under a plan for calendar years beginning after the date of publication of the Treasury decision adopting these rules as final regulations in the **Federal Register**, including deferred amounts to which the legally binding right arose during prior calendar years that were not previously included in income during one or more prior calendar years.

(b) *Special applicability dates* —(1) *Plans maintained pursuant to collective bargaining agreements.* In the case of a plan maintained pursuant to one or more collective bargaining agreements that have been ratified and are in effect on the date of publication of the Treasury decision adopting these rules as final regulations in the **Federal Register**, these regulations will not apply with respect to compensation deferred under the plan before the earlier of:

(i) The date on which the last of the collective bargaining agreements terminates (determined without regard to any extension thereof after the date of publication of the Treasury decision adopting these rules as final regulations in the **Federal Register**); or

(ii) The first day of the third calendar year beginning after the date of publication of the Treasury decision adopting these rules as final regulations in the **Federal Register**.

(2) *Governmental plans.* If legislation is required to amend a governmental plan, these regulations will not apply to compensation deferred under that plan in taxable years ending before the day following the end of the second legislative session of the legislative body with the authority to amend the plan that begins after the date of publication of the Treasury decision adopting these rules as final regulations in the **Federal Register**.

John Dalrymple,

Deputy Commissioner for Services and Enforcement.

[FR Doc. 2016-14329 Filed 6-21-16; 8:45 am]

BILLING CODE 4830-01-P

¶ 20,264L

IRS: Nonqualified deferred compensation plans: 409A compliance: Income inclusion.—The IRS has issued proposed regulations under Code Sec. 409A that modify and clarify certain features of the final regulations issued in 2007 (¶ 24,508O) and withdraw and replace Proposed Reg. § 1.409A-4(a)(1)(ii)(B) that was issued in 2008 (¶ 20,262S). The specific issues covered by the proposed regulations include the interaction between the rules under Code Sec. 409A and Code Sec. 457A, the short-term deferral rule, what is and is not a deferral of compensation, recurring part-time compensation, when a "payment" has been made, the conflict of interest exception to the prohibition on the acceleration of payments, and payments in connection with the termination and liquidation of a plan. The proposed regulations are proposed to be applicable on or after the date on which they are published as final regulations in the Federal Register. However, taxpayers may generally rely on the proposed regulations until finalized. Specifically, in the case of recurring part-year compensation, taxpayers may rely on either these proposed regulations or on IRS Notice 2008-62 (¶ 17,139X) for the taxable year in which these proposed regulations are published as final regulations and all prior taxable years.

The proposed regulation was published in the Federal Register on June 22, 2016 (81 FR 40569). The IRS issued corrections to Proposed Reg. § 1.409A-3 and Proposed Reg. § 1.409A-4 on August 4, 2016 (81 FR 51413).

DEPARTMENT OF THE TREASURY

Internal Revenue Service

26 CFR Part 1

[REG-123854-12]

RIN 1545-BL25

Application of Section 409A to Nonqualified Deferred Compensation Plans

AGENCY: Internal Revenue Service (IRS), Treasury.

ACTION: Partial withdrawal of notice of proposed rulemaking; notice of proposed rulemaking.

SUMMARY: This document contains proposed regulations that would clarify or modify certain specific provisions of the final regulations under section 409A (TD 9321, 72 FR 19234). This document also withdraws a specific provision of the notice of proposed rulemaking (REG-148326-05) published in the **Federal Register** on December 8, 2008 (73 FR 74380) regarding the calculation of amounts includible in income under section 409A(a)(1) and replaces that provision with revised proposed regulations. These proposed regulations would affect participants, beneficiaries, sponsors, and administrators of nonqualified deferred compensation plans.

DATES: Comments and requests for a public hearing must be received by September 20, 2016.

ADDRESSES: Send submissions to: CC:PA:LPD:PR (REG-123854-12), Room 5203, Internal Revenue Service, P.O. Box 7604, Ben Franklin Station, Washington, DC 20044. Submissions may be hand delivered Monday through Friday, between the hours of 8 a.m. and 4 p.m. to CC:PA:LPD:PR (REG-123854-12), Courier's Desk, Internal Revenue Service, 1111 Constitution Avenue NW., Washington, DC 20224 or sent electronically, via the Federal Rulemaking Portal at *www.regulations.gov* (IRS REG-123854-12).

FOR FURTHER INFORMATION CONTACT: Concerning these proposed regulations under section 409A, Gregory Burns at (202) 927-9639, concerning submission of comments and/or requests for a hearing, Regina Johnson at (202) 317-6901 (not toll-free numbers).

SUPPLEMENTARY INFORMATION:

Background

Section 885 of the American Jobs Creation Act of 2004, Public Law 108-357 (118 Stat. 1418) (AJCA'04) added section 409A to the Internal Revenue Code (Code). Section 409A(a)(1)(A) generally provides that, if certain requirements are not met at any time during a taxable year, amounts deferred under a nonqualified deferred compensation plan for that year and all previous taxable years are currently includible in gross income to the extent not subject to a substantial risk of forfeiture and not previously included in gross income.

On April 17, 2007 (72 FR 19234), the Treasury Department and the IRS issued final regulations under section 409A (TD 9321), which include §§ 1.409A-1, 1.409A-2, 1.409A-3, and 1.409A-6 (the final regulations). The final regulations define certain terms used in section 409A and in the final regulations, set forth the requirements for deferral elections and for the time and form of payments under nonqualified deferred compensation plans, and address certain other issues under section 409A.

On December 8, 2008 (73 FR 74380), the Treasury Department and the IRS issued additional proposed regulations under section 409A (REG-148326-05), which include proposed § 1.409A-4 (the proposed income inclusion regulations). The proposed income inclusion regulations provide guidance regarding the calculation of amounts includible in income under section 409A(a)(1) and the additional taxes imposed by section 409A with respect to service providers participating in certain nonqualified deferred compensation plans and other arrangements that do not comply with the requirements of section 409A(a).

Explanation of Provisions

I. Overview

The Treasury Department and the IRS have concluded that certain clarifications and modifications to the final regulations and the proposed income inclusion regulations will help taxpayers comply with the requirements of section 409A. These proposed regulations address certain specific provisions of the final regulations and the proposed income inclusion regulations and are not intended to propose a general revision of, or broad changes to, the final regulations or the proposed income inclusion regulations. The narrow and specific purpose of these proposed regulations should be taken into account when submitting comments on these proposed regulations. As provided in the section of this preamble titled "Proposed Effective Dates," taxpayers may rely upon these proposed regulations immediately.

These proposed regulations:

(1) Clarify that the rules under section 409A apply to nonqualified deferred compensation plans separately and in addition to the rules under section 457A.

(2) Modify the short-term deferral rule to permit a delay in payments to avoid violating Federal securities laws or other applicable law.

(3) Clarify that a stock right that does not otherwise provide for a deferral of compensation will not be treated as providing for a deferral of compensation solely because the amount payable under the stock right upon an involuntary separation from service for cause, or the occurrence of a condition within the service provider's control, is based on a measure that is less than fair market value.

(4) Modify the definition of the term "eligible issuer of service recipient stock" to provide that it includes a corporation (or other entity) for which a person is reasonably expected to begin, and actually begins, providing services within 12 months after the grant date of a stock right.

(5) Clarify that certain separation pay plans that do not provide for a deferral of compensation may apply to a service provider who had no compensation from the service recipient during the year preceding the year in which a separation from service occurs.

(6) Provide that a plan under which a service provider has a right to payment or reimbursement of reasonable attorneys' fees and other expenses incurred to pursue a bona fide legal claim against the service recipient with respect to the service relationship does not provide for a deferral of compensation.

(7) Modify the rules regarding recurring part-year compensation.

(8) Clarify that a stock purchase treated as a deemed asset sale under section 338 is not a sale or other disposition of assets for purposes of determining whether a service provider has a separation from service.

(9) Clarify that a service provider who ceases providing services as an employee and begins providing services as an independent contractor is treated as having a separation from service if, at the time of the change in employment status, the level of services reasonably anticipated to be provided after the change would result in a separation from service under the rules applicable to employees.

(10) Provide a rule that is generally applicable to determine when a "payment" has been made for purposes of section 409A.

(11) Modify the rules applicable to amounts payable following death.

(12) Clarify that the rules for transaction-based compensation apply to stock rights that do not provide for a deferral of compensation and statutory stock options.

(13) Provide that the addition of the death, disability, or unforeseeable emergency of a beneficiary who has become entitled to a payment due to a service provider's death as a potentially earlier or intervening payment event will not violate the prohibition on the acceleration of payments.

(14) Modify the conflict of interest exception to the prohibition on the acceleration of payments to permit the payment of all types of deferred compensation (and not only certain types of foreign earned income) to comply with bona fide foreign ethics or conflicts of interest laws.

(15) Clarify the provision permitting payments upon the termination and liquidation of a plan in connection with bankruptcy.

(16) Clarify other rules permitting payments in connection with the termination and liquidation of a plan.

(17) Provide that a plan may accelerate the time of payment to comply with Federal debt collection laws.

(18) Clarify and modify § 1.409A-4(a)(1)(ii)(B) of the proposed income inclusion regulations regarding the treatment of deferred amounts subject to a substantial risk of forfeiture for purposes of calculating the amount includible in income under section 409A(a)(1).

(19) Clarify various provisions of the final regulations to recognize that a service provider can be an entity as well as an individual.

II. Deferral of Compensation

A. Section 457(f) and Section 457A Plans

Section 457(f) generally provides that compensation deferred under a plan of an eligible employer (as that term is defined under section 457) is included in gross income in the first taxable year in which there is no substantial risk of forfeiture of the rights to the compensation. The final regulations provide that a deferred compensation plan subject to section 457(f) may be a nonqualified deferred compensation plan for purposes of section 409A and that the rules of section 409A apply to deferred compensation plans separately and in addition to any requirements applicable to such plans under section 457(f).

Similarly, section 457A, which was enacted more than a year after publication of the final regulations, generally provides that any compensation deferred under a nonqualified deferred compensation plan of a nonqualified entity (as these terms are defined under section 457A) is includible in gross income when there is no substantial risk of forfeiture of the rights to the compensation. These proposed regulations clarify that a nonqualified deferred compensation plan under section 457A, like a deferred compensation plan under section 457(f), may be a nonqualified deferred compensation plan for purposes of section 409A and that the rules of section 409A apply to such a plan separately and in addition to any requirements applicable to the plan under section 457A.

B. Short-Term Deferral Rule

The final regulations provide that a deferral of compensation does not occur for purposes of section 409A under a plan with respect to any payment that is not a deferred payment[1] provided that the service provider actually or constructively receives the payment on or before the later of: (1) The 15th day of the third month following the end of the service provider's first taxable year in which the right to the payment is no longer subject to a substantial risk of forfeiture, or (2) the 15th day of the third month following the end of the service recipient's first taxable year in which the right to the payment is no longer subject to a substantial risk of forfeiture (the applicable 2 ½ month period). A payment that meets these requirements of the short-term deferral rule (described more fully in § 1.409A-1(b)(4)) is referred to as a short-term deferral and is generally exempt from the requirements applicable to plans that provide for a deferral of compensation.

The final regulations provide that a payment that otherwise qualifies as a short-term deferral, but is made after the applicable 2 ½ month period, may continue to qualify as a short-term deferral if the payment is delayed for one of three reasons: (1) The taxpayer establishes that it was administratively impracticable for the service recipient to make the payment by the end of the applicable 2 ½ month period; (2) making the payment by the end of the applicable 2 ½ month period would have jeopardized the service recipient's ability to continue as a going concern; or (3) the service recipient reasonably anticipates that a deduction for the payment would not be permitted under section 162(m).

Similar exceptions apply under the general time and form of payment rules of section 409A. Under § 1.409A-3(d), a payment is treated as made on the date specified under the plan if the payment is delayed due to administrative impracticability or because making the payment would jeopardize the ability of the service recipient to continue as a going concern. Under § 1.409A-2(b)(7), a payment may be delayed to a date after the payment date designated in a plan without failing to meet the requirements of section 409A(a) if the service recipient reasonably anticipates that a deduction for the payment would not be permitted under section 162(m) or if making the payment would violate Federal securities laws or other applicable law. Together, these rules generally permit payments under section 409A to be delayed due to administrative impracticability or because making the payment would jeopardize the ability of the service recipient to continue as a going concern, the payment would not be deductible under section 162(m), or making the payment would violate Federal securities laws or other applicable law.

Some commenters have suggested that the exception for payments that would violate Federal securities laws or other applicable law should also apply to payments that are intended to be short-term deferrals. These commenters have noted that the policy reasons for excusing a timely payment when the payment would violate Federal securities laws or other applicable law apply equally to the general time and form of payment rules under section 409A and the short-term deferral rule. In response to these comments, the Treasury Department and the IRS have determined that it is appropriate to extend this exception to the short-term deferral rule. Accordingly, these proposed regulations provide that a payment that otherwise qualifies as a short-

---

[1] Under § 1.409A-1(b)(4)(i)(D), a payment is a deferred payment if it is made pursuant to a provision of a plan that provides for the payment to be made or completed on or after any date, or upon the occurrence of any event, that will or may occur later than the end of the applicable 2 ½ month period.

term deferral, but is made after the end of the applicable 2 ½ month period, may still qualify as a short-term deferral if the service recipient reasonably anticipates that making the payment during the applicable 2 ½ month period will violate Federal securities laws or other applicable law and the payment is made as soon as reasonably practicable following the first date on which the service recipient anticipates or reasonably should anticipate that making the payment would not cause a violation. For this purpose, making a payment that would cause inclusion in gross income or the application of any penalty provision or other provision of the Code is not treated as a violation of applicable law.

C. Stock Rights

1. Service Recipient Stock

The final regulations provide that certain stock options and stock appreciation rights (collectively, stock rights) granted with respect to service recipient stock do not provide for the deferral of compensation. The term "service recipient stock" means a class of stock that, as of the date of grant, is common stock for purposes of section 305 and the regulations thereunder of a corporation that is an eligible issuer of service recipient stock. For this purpose, service recipient stock does not include any stock that is subject to a mandatory repurchase obligation (other than a right of first refusal), or a permanent put or call right, if the stock price under such right or obligation is based on a measure other than the fair market value (disregarding lapse restrictions) of the equity interest in the corporation represented by the stock.

Commenters have noted that employers often want to deter employees from engaging in behavior that could be detrimental to the employer and have customarily reduced the amount that an employee receives under a stock rights arrangement if the employee is dismissed for cause or violates a noncompetition or nondisclosure agreement. These commenters have observed that this type of reduction is generally prohibited under the definition of service recipient stock in the final regulations but have argued that neither the statutory language nor the underlying policies of section 409A should prohibit a reduction under these circumstances. The Treasury Department and the IRS agree with these conclusions. Accordingly, these proposed regulations provide that a stock price will not be treated as based on a measure other than fair market value if the amount payable upon a service provider's involuntary separation from service for cause, or the occurrence of a condition that is within the control of the service provider, such as the violation of a covenant not to compete or a covenant not to disclose certain information, is based on a measure that is less than fair market value.

2. Eligible Issuer of Service Recipient Stock

Under the final regulations, the term "eligible issuer of service recipient stock" means the corporation or other entity for which the service provider provides direct services on the date of grant of the stock right and certain affiliated corporations or entities. Some commenters have asserted that this definition of "eligible issuer of service recipient stock" hinders employment negotiations because it prevents service recipients from granting stock rights to service providers before they are employed by the service recipient. In response to these comments, these proposed regulations provide that, if it is reasonably anticipated that a person will begin providing services to a corporation or other entity within 12 months after the date of grant of a stock right, and the person actually begins providing services to the corporation or other entity within 12 months after the date of grant (or, if services do not begin within that period, the stock right is forfeited), the corporation or other entity will be an eligible issuer of service recipient stock.

D. Separation Pay Plans

Under the final regulations, separation pay plans that provide for payment only upon an involuntary separation from service or pursuant to a window program do not provide for a deferral of compensation to the extent that they meet certain requirements. One of these requirements is that the separation pay generally not exceed two times the lesser of (1) the service provider's annualized compensation based upon the annual rate of pay for the service provider's taxable year preceding the service provider's taxable year in which the separation from service occurs, or (2) the limit under section 401(a)(17) for the year in which the service provider separates from service.

Some commenters have questioned whether this exception for separation pay plans is available for a service provider whose employment begins and ends during the same taxable year because the service provider was not employed by, and did not receive any compensation from, the service recipient for the taxable year preceding the taxable year in which the separation from service occurs. These proposed regulations clarify that the separation pay plan exception is available for service providers whose employment begins and ends in the same taxable year. In that circumstance, these proposed regulations provide that the service provider's annualized compensation for the taxable year in which the service provider separates from service may be used for purposes of this separation pay plan exception if the service provider had no compensation from the service recipient in the taxable year preceding the year in which the service provider separates from service.

E. Employment-Related Legal Fees and Expenses

Under the final regulations, an arrangement does not provide for a deferral of compensation to the extent that it provides for amounts to be paid as settlements or awards resolving bona fide legal claims based on wrongful termination, employment discrimination, the Fair Labor Standards Act, or workers' compensation statutes, including claims under applicable Federal, state, local, or foreign laws, or for reimbursements or payments of reasonable attorneys' fees or other reasonable expenses incurred by the service provider related to such bona fide legal claims.

Commenters have requested guidance on the application of section 409A(a) to provisions commonly included in employment agreements that provide for the reimbursement of attorneys' fees in connection with employment-related disputes and have asserted that there is no reason to distinguish between arrangements that provide for payment of reasonable attorneys' fees and expenses for the types of legal claims currently specified in the final regulations and any other bona fide legal claim with respect to the service relationship between a service provider and a service recipient. In response to these comments, these proposed regulations provide that an arrangement does not provide for a deferral of compensation to the extent that it provides for the payment or reimbursement of a service provider's reasonable attorneys' fees and other expenses incurred to enforce a claim by the service provider against the service recipient with respect to the service relationship.

F. Recurring Part-Year Compensation

After publication of the final regulations, commenters have expressed concerns about the application of section 409A to recurring part-year compensation. The final regulations define recurring part-year compensation as compensation paid for services rendered in a position that the service recipient and service provider reasonably anticipate will continue on similar terms and conditions in subsequent years, and will require services to be provided during successive service periods each of which comprises less than 12 months and each of which begins in one taxable year of the service provider and ends in the next taxable year. For example, a teacher providing services during school years comprised of 10 consecutive months would have recurring part-year compensation. See § 1.409A-2(a)(14). In general, commenters have asserted that section 409A should not apply to this situation because the amount being deferred from one taxable year to a subsequent taxable year is typically only a small amount and because most service providers who receive recurring part-year compensation (typically teachers and other educational workers) view an election to annualize this compensation as a cash flow decision, rather than a tax-deferral opportunity.

In response, the Treasury Department and the IRS issued Notice 2008-62 (2008-29 IRB 130), which provides that arrangements involving recurring part-year compensation do not provide for a deferral of compensation for purposes of section 409A or section 457(f) if: (1) The arrangement does not defer payment of any of the recurring part-year compensation beyond the last day of the 13th month following the beginning of the service period, and (2) the arrangement does not defer from one taxable year to the next taxable year the payment of more than the applicable dollar amount under section 402(g)(1)(B) in effect for the calendar year in which the service period begins ($18,000 for 2016). Notice 2008-62 also states that a conforming change is intended be made to the final regulations to reflect these rules.

Commenters have expressed concerns that Notice 2008-62 would not adequately address some teaching positions, such as college and university faculty members. They have noted that, depending on several variables (such as the calendar month in which a service provider commences service or the length of the service period), the dollar limitation in the notice may result in adverse tax consequences to service providers with annual compensation as low as $80,000. Commenters have further observed that some of these arrangements are nonelective, and therefore some service providers cannot opt out of a recurring part-year compensation arrangement. In recognition that service recipients in the field of education frequently structure their pay plans to include recurring part-year compensation and that the main purpose of this design is to provide uninterrupted cash flow for service providers who do not work for a portion of the year, these proposed regulations modify the recurring part-year compensation rule. These proposed regulations provide that a plan or arrangement under which a service provider receives recurring part-year compensation that is earned over a period of service does not provide for the deferral of compensation if the plan does not defer payment of any of the recurring part-year compensation to a date beyond the last day of the 13th month following the first day of the service period for which the recurring part-year compensation is paid, and the amount of the service provider's recurring part-year compensation (not merely the amount deferred) does not exceed the annual compensation limit under section 401(a)(17) ($265,000 for 2016) for the calendar year in which the service period commences. A conforming change is being made for purposes of section 457(f) under proposed section 457(f) regulations (REG-147196-07) that are also published in the Proposed Rules section of this issue of the **Federal Register**.

III. Separation From Service Definition

A. Asset Purchase Transactions

The final regulations permit the seller and an unrelated buyer in an asset purchase transaction to specify whether a person who is a service provider of the seller immediately before the transaction is treated as separating from service if the service provider provides services to the buyer after and as a result of the transaction. Commenters have asked whether this rule may be used with respect to a transaction that is treated as a deemed asset sale under section 338.

The provision of the final regulations giving buyers and sellers in asset transactions the discretion to treat employees as separating from service is based on the recognition that, while employees formally terminate employment with the seller and immediately recommence employment with the buyer in a typical asset transaction, the employees often experience no change in the type or level of services they provide. In a deemed asset sale under section 338, however, employees do not experience a termination of employment, formal or otherwise. Accordingly, the Treasury Department and the IRS have determined that it would be inconsistent with section 409A to permit the parties to a deemed asset sale to treat service providers as having separated from service upon the occurrence of the transaction. These proposed regulations affirm and make explicit that a stock purchase transaction that is treated as a deemed asset sale under section 338 is not a sale or other disposition of assets for purposes of this rule under section 409A.

B. Dual Status as Employee and Independent Contractor and Changes in Status From Employee to Independent Contractor (or Vice Versa)

The final regulations provide that an employee separates from service with an employer if the employee dies, retires, or otherwise has a termination of employment with the employer. Under the final regulations, a termination of employment generally occurs if the facts and circumstances indicate that the employer and employee reasonably anticipate that no further services would be performed after a certain date or that the level of *bona fide* services the employee would perform after that date (whether as an employee or as an independent contractor) would permanently decrease to no more than 20 percent of the average level of *bona fide* services performed (whether as an employee or an independent contractor) over the immediately preceding 36-month period (or if the employee has been providing services to the employer for less than 36 months, the full period of services). The final regulations provide that an independent contractor separates from service with a service recipient upon the expiration of the contract (or, if applicable, all contracts) under which services are performed for the service recipient if the expiration is a good-faith and complete termination of the contractual relationship.

The final regulations also provide that if a service provider provides services both as an employee and an independent contractor of a service recipient, the service provider must separate from service both as an employee and as an independent contractor to be treated as having separated from service. The final regulations further provide that "[i]f a service provider ceases providing services as an independent contractor and begins providing services as an employee, or ceases providing services as an employee and begins providing services as an independent contractor, the service provider will not be considered to have a separation from service until the service provider has ceased providing services in both capacities."

Some commenters have observed that the quoted sentence could be read to provide that a service provider who performs services for a service recipient as an employee, but who becomes an independent contractor for the same service recipient and whose anticipated level of services upon becoming an independent contractor are 20 percent or less than the average level of services performed during the immediately preceding 36-month period, would not have a separation from service because a complete termination of the contractual relationship with the service recipient has not occurred and, therefore, there is no separation from service as an independent contractor. Such a reading, however, would be inconsistent with the more specific rule that a service provider who is an employee separates from service if the employer and employee reasonably anticipate that the level of services to be performed after a certain date (whether as an employee or as an independent contractor) would permanently decrease to no more than 20 percent of the average level of services performed (whether as an employee or an independent contractor) over the immediately preceding 36-month period. To avoid potential confusion, these proposed regulations delete the quoted sentence from the regulations.

However, if a service provider, who performs services for a service recipient as an employee, becomes an independent contractor for the same service recipient but does not have a separation from service when he or she becomes an independent contractor (because at that time it is not reasonably anticipated that the level of services that would be provided by the service provider in the future would decrease to no more than 20 percent of the average level of services performed over the immediately preceding 36-month period), the service provider will have a separation from service in the future when the service provider has a separation from service based on the rules that apply to independent contractors.

IV. References to a Payment Being Made

As discussed in section II.B of this preamble entitled "Short-term Deferral Rule," the final regulations provide that a deferral of compensation does not occur under a plan if the service provider actually or constructively receives a payment that is not a deferred payment on or before the last day of the applicable 2 ½ month period. The final regulations further provide that, for this purpose, a payment is treated as actually or constructively received if the payment is includible in income, including if the payment is includible under the economic benefit doctrine, section 83, section 402(b), or section 457(f). Further, § 1.409A-2(b)(2) of the final regulations provides that, for purposes of subsequent changes in the time or form of payment, the term "payment" generally refers to each separately identified amount to which a service provider is entitled to payment under a plan on a determinable date. This section of the final regulations provides that a payment includes the provision of any taxable benefit, including cash or property. It also provides that a payment includes, but is not limited to, the transfer, cancellation, or reduction of an amount of deferred compensation in exchange for benefits under a welfare plan, a fringe benefit excludible from income, or any other benefit excludible from income. The final regulations, however, do not include a rule that is generally applicable for all purposes under section 409A to determine when a payment is made.

These proposed regulations add a generally applicable rule to determine when a payment has been made for all provisions of the regulations under section 409A. Under these proposed regulations, a payment is made, or the payment of an amount occurs, when any taxable benefit is actually or constructively received. Consistent with the final regulations, these proposed regulations provide that a payment includes a transfer of cash, any event that results in the inclusion of an amount in income under the economic benefit doctrine, a transfer of property includible in income under section 83, a contribution to a trust described in section 402(b) at the time includible in income under section 402(b), and the transfer or creation of a beneficial interest in a section 402(b) trust at the time includible in income under section 402(b). In addition, a payment is made upon the transfer, cancellation, or reduction of an amount of deferred compensation in exchange for benefits under a welfare plan, a non-taxable fringe benefit, or any other nontaxable benefit.

The final regulations generally provide that the inclusion of an amount in income under section 457(f)(1)(A) is treated as a payment under section 409A for purposes of the short-term deferral rule under § 1.409A-1(b)(4), but is generally not treated as a payment for other purposes under section 409A. Commenters, however, have observed that this treatment of income inclusion under section 457(f)(1)(A) is inconsistent with the rules under section 409A that generally treat the inclusion of any amount in income as a payment for all purposes under section 409A. These commenters have also noted that a primary purpose of section 409A is to limit the ability of a service provider or service recipient to change the time at which deferred compensation is included in income after the time of payment is established and that the failure to treat income inclusion under section 457(f)(1)(A) as a payment would be inconsistent with this purpose. In response to these observations, these proposed regulations provide that the inclusion of an amount in income under section 457(f)(1)(A) is treated a payment for all purposes under section 409A.

Under this rule, if the plan provides for a deferral of compensation under section 409A: (1) Plan terms that specify the conditions to which the payment is subject and thus when a substantial risk of forfeiture lapses for purposes of section 457(f)(1)(A) (and, consequently, determine when an amount is includible in income) would be treated as plan terms providing for the payment of the amount includible in income, and (2) all rules under section 409A applicable to the payment of an amount would apply to the inclusion of an amount under section 457(f)(1)(A). A plan would not be a deferred compensation plan within the meaning of section 409A to the extent that the amounts payable under the plan are short-term deferrals under § 1.409A-1(b)(4). However, in certain limited circumstances, amounts includible in income under section 457(f)(1)(A) may not be short-term deferrals under § 1.409A-1(b)(4). For example, under the proposed section 457(f) regulations (REG-147196-07), which are also published in the Proposed Rules section of this issue of the **Federal Register**, in certain circumstances conditioning a payment upon compliance with a noncompetition agreement will result in the payment being subject to a substantial risk of forfeiture for purposes of section 457(f)(1)(A), but that payment would not be treated as subject to a substantial risk of forfeiture for purposes of section 409A. In such cases, the amount payable at the end of the term of the noncompetition agreement upon compliance with the noncompete will be includible in income under section 457(f)(1)(A) only at the end of the term of the agreement under the section 457(f) regulations as proposed, but for purposes of section 409A will be deferred compensation (and not a short-term deferral), the payment of which is subject to the rules of section 409A.[2] See proposed § 1.457-12(e) (REG-147196-07); see also proposed § 1.457-12(a)(4) (REG-147196-07).

The Treasury Department and the IRS request comments on whether rules similar to those applicable to amounts included in income under section 457(f) should be adopted for amounts included in income under section 457A.

These proposed regulations also clarify that a transfer of property that is substantially nonvested (as defined under § 1.83-3(b)) to satisfy an obligation under a nonqualified deferred compensation plan is not a payment for purposes of section 409A unless the recipient makes an election under section 83(b) to include in income the fair market value of the property (disregarding lapse restrictions), less any amount paid for the property. These proposed regulations also make conforming clarifications to rules under § 1.409A-1(a)(4) regarding nonqualified deferred compensation plans subject to sections 457(f) and 457A, § 1.409A-1(b)(4) regarding the short-term deferral rule, and § 1.409A-2(b)(2) regarding the separate payment rule.

V. Permissible Payments

A. Death

The final regulations provide that an amount deferred under a nonqualified deferred compensation plan may be paid only at a specified time or upon an event set forth under the regulations. One of the permissible events upon which an amount may be paid is the service provider's death. The final regulations also provide that a payment is treated as made upon a date specified under the plan (including at the time a specified event occurs) if the payment is made on that date or on a later date within the same taxable year of the service provider or, if later, by the 15th day of the third calendar month following the date specified under the plan, provided that the service provider is not permitted, directly or indirectly, to designate the taxable year of the payment.

Some commenters have questioned whether these and other rules in the final regulations applicable to amounts payable upon the death of a service provider also apply in the case of the death of a beneficiary who has become entitled to the payment of an amount due to a service provider's death. These proposed regulations clarify that the rules applicable to amounts payable upon the death of a service provider also apply to amounts payable upon the death of a beneficiary.

Also, some commenters have indicated that the time periods for the payment of amounts following death often are not long enough to resolve certain issues related to the death (for example, confirming the death and completing probate). In view of the practical issues that often

arise following a death, these proposed regulations provide that an amount payable following the death of a service provider, or following the death of a beneficiary who has become entitled to payment due to the service provider's death, that is to be paid at any time during the period beginning on the date of death and ending on December 31 of the first calendar year following the calendar year during which the death occurs is treated as timely paid if it is paid at any time during this period. A plan is not required to specify any particular date within this period as the payment date and may rely on this rule if the plan provides that an amount will be paid at some time during this period, including if the plan provides that payment will be made upon death without defining the period for payment following death in any other manner, and including if the plan provides that payment will be made on a date within this period determined in the discretion of the beneficiary. These proposed regulations further provide that a plan providing for the payment of an amount at any time during this specified period may be amended to provide for the payment of that amount (or the payment of that amount may be made without amending the plan) at any other time during this period (including a time determined in the discretion of a beneficiary) without failing to meet the requirements of the deferral election provisions of § 1.409A-2 or the permissible payment provisions of § 1.409A-3, including the prohibition on the acceleration of payments under § 1.409A-3(j). For example, a plan that provides for a payment to be made during the first calendar year beginning after the death of a service provider may be amended to provide for the payment of the amount (or the payment may be made under the plan without such amendment) at any time during the period beginning on the date of death and ending on December 31 of the first calendar year following the calendar year during which the death occurs. For additional rules concerning payments due upon a beneficiary's death, see section VI.A of this preamble.

B. Certain Transaction-Based Compensation

The final regulations provide special rules for payments of transaction-based compensation. Transaction-based compensation payments are payments related to certain types of changes in control that (1) occur because a service recipient purchases its stock held by a service provider or because the service recipient or a third party purchases a stock right held by a service provider, or (2) are calculated by reference to the value of service recipient stock. Under the final regulations, transaction-based compensation may be treated as paid at a designated date or pursuant to a payment schedule that complies with the requirements of section 409A(a) if it is paid on the same schedule and under the same terms and conditions as apply to payments to shareholders generally with respect to stock of the service recipient pursuant to the change in control. Likewise, transaction-based compensation meeting these requirements will not fail to meet the requirements of the initial or subsequent deferral election rules under section 409A if it is paid not later than five years after the change in control event. These proposed regulations clarify that the special payment rules for transaction-based compensation apply to a statutory stock option or a stock right that did not otherwise provide for deferred compensation before the purchase or agreement to purchase the stock right. Accordingly, the purchase (or agreement to purchase) such a statutory stock option or stock right in a manner consistent with these rules does not result in the statutory stock option or stock right being treated as having provided for the deferral of compensation from the original grant date.

VI. Prohibition on Acceleration of Payments

A. Payments to Beneficiaries Upon Death, Disability, or Unforeseeable Emergency

Under the final regulations, a prohibited acceleration of a payment does not result from the addition of death, disability, or unforeseeable emergency as a potentially earlier alternative payment event for an amount previously deferred. However, under the final regulations, this exception applies only with respect to a service provider's death, disability, or unforeseeable emergency and does not apply with respect to the death, disability, or unforeseeable emergency of a beneficiary who has become entitled to a payment due to the service provider's death. These proposed regulations provide that this exception also applies to the payment of deferred amounts upon the death, disability, or unforeseeable emergency of a beneficiary who has become entitled to payment due to a service provider's death. These proposed regulations also clarify that a schedule of payments (including payments

---

[2] There may also be instances in which a portion of an amount payable under an arrangement that is subject to section 457(f) is a short-term deferral for purposes of both section 409A and section 457(f)(1)(A), while another portion of the amount is a deferral of compensation for purposes of section 409A. For example, assume an arrangement subject to section 457(f) provides for payment of a specified dollar amount plus earnings upon separation from service, with vesting to occur when the service provider has completed three years of service. The specified dollar amount plus earnings to date is includible in income under section 457(f)(1)(A) when the service provider completes three years of service, and that amount will be a short-term deferral under section 409A if the service provider includes it in income at that time. The service provider's right to receive a payment of additional earnings accruing after the vesting date is a deferred compensation plan under section 409A.

treated as a single payment) that has already commenced prior to a service provider's or a beneficiary's death, disability, or unforeseeable emergency may be accelerated upon the death, disability, or unforeseeable emergency.

B. Compliance With Bona Fide Foreign Ethics Laws or Conflicts of Interest Laws

Under the final regulations, a plan may provide for acceleration of the time or schedule of a payment, or a payment may be made under a plan, to the extent reasonably necessary to avoid the violation of a Federal, state, local, or foreign ethics or conflicts of interest law. However, with respect to a foreign ethics or conflicts of interest law, this exception applies only to foreign earned income from sources within the foreign country that promulgated the law. Commenters have suggested that this provision should not be limited to foreign earned income because the requirements of foreign ethics or conflicts of interest laws may affect both the payment of foreign and United States earned income. These proposed regulations expand the scope of this provision to permit the acceleration of any nonqualified deferred compensation if the acceleration is reasonably necessary to comply with a *bona fide* foreign ethics or conflicts of interest law.

C. Plan Terminations and Liquidations

Under the final regulations, a plan may provide for the acceleration of a payment made pursuant to the termination and liquidation of a plan under certain circumstances. Specifically, a plan may provide for the acceleration of a payment if the plan is terminated and liquidated within 12 months of a corporate dissolution taxed under section 331, or with the approval of a bankruptcy court pursuant to 11 U.S.C. 503(b)(1)(A) if certain other conditions are satisfied. The citation to 11 U.S.C. 503(b)(1)(A) is erroneous. These proposed regulations correct this provision by retaining the operative rule but deleting the section reference.

The final regulations also provide that a payment may be accelerated pursuant to a change in control event as described under § 1.409A-3(j)(4)(ix)(B) or in other circumstances provided certain requirements are satisfied, as described under § 1.409A-3(j)(4)(ix)(C). To terminate a plan pursuant to § 1.409A-3(j)(4)(ix)(C), the final regulations provide that the service recipient must terminate and liquidate all plans sponsored by the service recipient that would be aggregated with the terminated plan under the plan aggregation rules under § 1.409A-1(c) of the final regulations if the same service provider had deferrals of compensation under all such plans. The final regulations also provide that for three years following the date on which the service recipient took all necessary action to irrevocably terminate and liquidate the plan the service recipient cannot adopt a new plan that would be aggregated with the terminated and liquidated plan if the same service provider participated in both plans. Some commenters have asked whether these rules mean that only the plans of a particular category in which a particular service provider actually participates must be terminated if a plan in which that service provider participates is terminated.

The plan aggregation rules under § 1.409A-1(c)(2) of the final regulations identify nine different types of nonqualified deferred compensation plans—account balance plans providing for elective deferrals, account balance plans that do not provide for elective deferrals, nonaccount balance plans, separation pay plans, plans providing for in-kind benefits or reimbursements, split-dollar plans, foreign earned income plans, stock right plans, and plans that are not any of the foregoing. All plans of the same type in which the same service provider participates are treated as a single plan. The rule set forth under § 1.409A-3(j)(4)(ix)(C) that requires the termination and liquidation of all plans sponsored by the service recipient that would be aggregated with the terminated plan "if the same service provider had deferrals of compensation" under all of those plans is intended to require the termination of all plans in the same plan category sponsored by the service recipient. The reference to the "same service provider" having deferrals of compensation under all of those plans refers to participation of a hypothetical service provider in all such plans, which would be required to aggregate all of the plans under the section 409A plan aggregation rules.

The Treasury Department and the IRS have concluded that the meaning of the plan termination rule under § 1.409A-3(j)(4)(ix)(C) is not ambiguous. However, to address the questions raised by commenters, these proposed regulations further clarify that the acceleration of a payment pursuant to this rule is permitted only if the service recipient terminates and liquidates all plans of the same category that the service recipient sponsors, and not merely all plans of the same category in which a particular service provider actually participates. These proposed regulations also clarify that under this rule, for a

period of three years following the termination and liquidation of a plan, the service recipient cannot adopt a new plan of the same category as the terminated and liquidated plan, regardless of which service providers participate in the plan.

D. Offset Provisions

The final regulations provide that the payment of an amount as a substitute for a payment of deferred compensation is generally treated as a payment of the deferred compensation. They also provide that when the payment of an amount results in an actual or potential reduction of, or current or future offset to, an amount of deferred compensation, the payment is a substitute for the deferred compensation. Further, the final regulations provide that if a service provider's right to deferred compensation is made subject to anticipation, alienation, sale, transfer, assignment, pledge, encumbrance, attachment, or garnishment by the service provider's creditors, the deferred compensation is treated as having been paid. Under certain circumstances, these provisions may result in an amount being paid (or treated as paid) before the payment date or event specified in the plan in violation of the prohibition on the acceleration of payments under section 409A. The final regulations, however, include a de minimis exception to these rules pursuant to which a plan may provide for the acceleration of the time or schedule of a payment, or a payment may be made under a plan, in satisfaction of a debt of the service provider if the debt is incurred in the ordinary course of the service relationship, the entire offset in any taxable year does not exceed $5,000, and the offset is taken at the same time and in the same amount as the debt otherwise would have been due from the service provider.

Stakeholders have observed that the prohibition on offsets may conflict with certain laws regarding debt collection by the Federal government (for example, 31 U.S.C. 3711, *et. seq.*), and that the exception for small debts is insufficient to permit the enforcement of these laws. Because these laws would effectively prevent certain government entities from providing nonqualified deferred compensation in a manner that complies with the requirements of section 409A(a) and because of the limited applicability of Federal debt collection laws, the Treasury Department and the IRS have determined that it is appropriate to expand the current exception to the prohibition on accelerated payments for certain offsets to permit a plan to provide for the acceleration of the time or schedule of a payment, or to make a payment, to the extent reasonably necessary to comply with Federal laws regarding debt collection.

VII. Amount Includible in Income Under Section 409A

The proposed income inclusion regulations provide that the amount includible in income for a taxable year if a nonqualified deferred compensation plan fails to meet the requirements of section 409A(a) at any time during that taxable year equals the excess of (1) the total amount deferred under the plan for that taxable year, including any payments under the plan during that taxable year, over (2) the portion of that amount, if any, that is either subject to a substantial risk of forfeiture or has been previously included in income. The proposed income inclusion regulations, however, include an anti-abuse provision under § 1.409A-4(a)(1)(ii)(B), which provides that an amount otherwise subject to a substantial risk of forfeiture for purposes of determining the amount includible in income under a plan will be treated as not subject to a substantial risk of forfeiture for these purposes if the facts and circumstances indicate that a service recipient has a pattern or practice of permitting impermissible changes in the time or form of payment with respect to nonvested deferred amounts under one or more nonqualified deferred compensation plans and either (i) an impermissible change in the time or form of payment applies to the amount or (ii) the facts and circumstances indicate that the amount would be affected by the pattern or practice.

Although these rules permit the correction of certain plan provisions that fail to comply with the requirements of section 409A(a) while amounts are nonvested without including the amounts in income or incurring an additional tax, they were not intended to allow service recipients to change time or form of payment provisions that otherwise meet the requirements of section 409A(a) in a manner that fails to comply with section 409A(a), and they were not intended to permit service recipients to create errors in nonqualified deferred compensation plans with respect to nonvested amounts with the intention of using those errors as a pretext for establishing or changing a time or form of payment in a manner that fails to comply with section 409A(a). Accordingly, these proposed regulations clarify and modify the anti-abuse rule under § 1.409A-4(a)(1)(ii)(B) of the proposed income inclusion regulations to preclude changes of this nature.

First, these proposed regulations clarify that a deferred amount that is otherwise subject to a substantial risk of forfeiture is treated as not subject to a substantial risk of forfeiture for a service provider's taxable year during which there is a change in a plan provision (including an initial deferral election provision) that is not otherwise permitted under section 409A and the final regulations and that affects the time or form of payment of the amount if there is no reasonable, good faith basis for concluding that the original provision failed to meet the requirements of section 409A(a) and that the change is necessary to bring the plan into compliance with the requirements of section 409A(a).

Second, these proposed regulations provide examples of the types of facts and circumstances that indicate whether a service recipient has a pattern or practice of permitting impermissible changes in the time or form of payment with respect to nonvested deferred amounts under one or more plans. If the service recipient has such a pattern or practice that would affect a nonvested deferred amount, that amount is treated as not subject to a substantial risk of forfeiture. The facts and circumstances include: Whether a service recipient has taken commercially reasonable measures to identify and correct substantially similar failures promptly upon discovery; whether substantially similar failures have occurred with respect to nonvested deferred amounts to a greater extent than with respect to vested deferred amounts; whether substantially similar failures occur more frequently with respect to newly adopted plans; and whether substantially similar failures appear intentional, are numerous, or repeat common past failures that have since been corrected.

Third, these proposed regulations provide that, to the extent generally applicable guidance regarding the correction of section 409A failures prescribes a particular correction method (or methods) for a type of plan failure, that correction method (or one of the permissible correction methods) must be used if a service recipient chooses to correct that type of a failure with respect to a nonvested deferred amount. In addition, these proposed regulations provide that substantially similar failures affecting nonvested deferred amounts must be corrected in substantially the same manner.

A service recipient correcting a plan failure affecting a nonvested deferred amount is not required, solely with respect to the nonvested deferred amount, to comply with any requirement under generally applicable guidance regarding the correction of section 409A failures that is unrelated to the method for correcting the failure, such as general eligibility requirements, income inclusion, additional taxes, premium interest, or information reporting by the service recipient or service provider. Accordingly, a service recipient may amend a noncompliant plan term in a manner permitted under applicable correction guidance even though the failure may not have been eligible for correction under that guidance (for example, due to applicable timing requirements). In addition, the portion of the nonvested deferred amount that is affected by the correction is not subject to income inclusion, additional taxes, or applicable premium interest under section 409A(a)(1), and neither the service recipient nor the service provider is required to notify the IRS of the correction. For a description of the currently available corrections methods, see Notice 2008-113 (2008-51 IRB 1305), Notice 2010-6 (2010-3 IRB 275), and Notice 2010-80 (2010-51 IRB 853).

VIII. Individual and Entity Service Providers

Under the final regulations, the term service provider includes an individual, corporation, subchapter S corporation, partnership, personal service corporation, noncorporate entity that would be a personal service corporation if it were a corporation, qualified personal service corporation, and noncorporate entity that would be a qualified personal service corporation if it were a corporation. These proposed regulations clarify §§ 1.409A-1(b)(5)(vi)(A), 1.409A-1(b)(5)(vi)(E), 1.409A-1(b)(5)(vi)(F), and 1.409A-3(i)(5)(iii) of the final regulations to reflect that a service provider can be an entity as well as an individual. These proposed regulations also clarify § 1.409A-1(b)(3) of the final regulations to correct an erroneous reference to "service provider" that should be "service recipient."

Proposed Effective Dates

General Applicability Date for Amendments to Final Regulations

The provisions of these proposed regulations amending the final regulations are proposed to be applicable on or after the date on which they are published as final regulations in the **Federal Register**. For periods before this date, the existing final regulations and other applicable guidance apply (without regard to these proposed regulations). The applicability date for the existing final regulations in § 1.409A-6(b) is accordingly amended to reflect extension of certain transition relief through 2008 under Notice 2007-86, 2007-46 IRB 990. Taxpayers may, however, rely on these proposed regulations before they are published as final regulations, and until final regulations are published the IRS

will not assert positions that are contrary to the positions set forth in these proposed regulations.

Certain provisions of these proposed amendments to the final regulations are not intended as substantive changes to the current requirements under section 409A. Accordingly, the Treasury Department and the IRS have concluded that the following positions may not properly be taken under the existing final regulations: (1) That the transfer of restricted stock for which no section 83(b) election is made or the transfer of a stock option that does not have a readily ascertainable fair market value would result in a payment under a plan; (2) that a contribution to a section 402(b) trust includible in income under section 402(b) to fund an obligation under a plan would not result in a payment under a plan; (3) that a stock purchase treated as a deemed asset sale under section 338 is a sale or other disposition of assets for purposes of determining when a service provider separates from service as a result of an asset purchase transaction; or (4) that the exception to the prohibition on acceleration of a payment upon a termination and liquidation of a plan pursuant to § 1.409A-3(j)(4)(ix)(C) applies if the service recipient terminates and liquidates only the plans of the same category in which a particular service provider participates, rather than all plans of the same category that the service recipient sponsors.

General Applicability Date for Amendments to Proposed Income Inclusion Regulations

The proposed income inclusion regulations are proposed to be applicable on or after the date on which they are published as final regulations in the **Federal Register**. Notice 2008-115 provides that, until the Treasury Department and the IRS issue further guidance, compliance with the provisions of the proposed income inclusion regulations with respect to the calculation of the amount includible in income under section 409A(a)(1) and the calculation of the additional taxes under section 409A(a)(1) will be treated as compliance with the requirements of section 409A(a), provided that the taxpayer complies with all of the provisions of the proposed regulations. Until the Treasury Department and the IRS issue further guidance, taxpayers may rely on the proposed income inclusion regulations, as modified by the amendment of § 1.409A-4(a)(1)(ii)(B) in these proposed regulations, for purposes of calculating the amount includible in income under section 409A(a)(1) (including the identification and treatment of deferred amounts subject to a substantial risk of forfeiture) and the calculation of the additional taxes under section 409A(a)(1), and the IRS will not assert positions with respect to periods before the date final regulations are published in the **Federal Register** that are contrary to the positions set forth in the proposed income inclusion regulations as amended by these proposed regulations.

Special Applicability Dates for Amendments to Recurring Part-Year Compensation Rules

The rules set forth in these proposed regulations regarding recurring part-year compensation are proposed to be applicable on and after the date on which these proposed regulations are published as final regulations in the **Federal Register**. However, taxpayers may rely on either the rules in these proposed regulations or the rules in Notice 2008-62 relating to recurring part-year compensation for the taxable year in which these proposed regulations are published as final regulations and all prior taxable years.

Effect on Other Documents

These proposed regulations do not affect the applicability of other guidance issued with respect to section 409A, including Notice 2008-115, except that, for the permitted reliance on the proposed income inclusion regulations, these proposed regulations withdraw § 1.409A-4(a)(1)(ii)(B) of the proposed income inclusion regulations and replace it with a new § 1.409A-4(a)(1)(ii)(B).

Statement of Availability of IRS Documents

IRS Revenue Procedures, Revenue Rulings notices, and other guidance cited in this document are published in the Internal Revenue Bulletin (or Cumulative Bulletin) and are available from the Superintendent of Documents, U.S. Government Printing Office, Washington, DC 20402, or by visiting the IRS Web site at *http://www.irs.gov*. (See § 601.601(d)(2)(ii)(*b*) of this chapter.)

Special Analyses

Certain IRS regulations, including this one, are exempt from the requirements of Executive Order 12866, as supplemented and reaffirmed by Executive Order 13563. Therefore, a regulatory impact assessment is not required. It also has been determined that section 553(b) of the Administrative Procedure Act (5 U.S.C. chapter 5) does not apply to these proposed regulations. It is hereby certified that the collection of information in these proposed regulations would not have a significant impact on a substantial number of small entities. This certification is based on the fact that these proposed regulations only provide guidance on how to satisfy existing collection of information requirements. Accordingly, a Regulatory Flexibility Analysis is not required. Pursuant to section 7805(f) of the Code, these proposed regulations have been submitted to the Chief Counsel for Advocacy of the Small Business Administration for comment on its impact on small business.

Comments and Requests for Public Hearing

Before these proposed regulations are adopted as final regulations, consideration will be given to any comments that are submitted timely to the IRS as prescribed in this preamble under the *ADDRESSES* heading. The Treasury Department and the IRS request comments on all aspects of the rules proposed by these proposed regulations. All comments will be available at *www.regulations.gov* or upon request. A public hearing may be scheduled if requested by any person who timely submits comments. If a public hearing is scheduled, notice of the date, time and place for the hearing will be published in the **Federal Register**.

Drafting Information

The principal author of these proposed regulations is Gregory Burns, Office of Division Counsel/Associate Chief Counsel (Tax Exempt and Government Entities). However, other personnel from the Treasury Department and the IRS participated in their development.

List of Subjects in 26 CFR Part 1

Income taxes, Reporting and recordkeeping requirements.

Partial Withdrawal of Notice of Proposed Rulemaking

Accordingly, under the authority of 26 U.S.C. 7805, §1.409A-4(a)(1)(ii)(B) of the notice of proposed rulemaking (REG-148326-05) that was published in the **Federal Register** on December 8, 2008 (73 FR 74380) is withdrawn.

Proposed Amendments to the Regulations

Accordingly, 26 CFR parts 1 is proposed to be amended as follows:

PART 1—INCOME TAXES

■ **Paragraph 1**. The authority citation for part 1 continues to read in part as follows:

Authority: 26 U.S.C. 7805 * * *

■ **Par. 2**. Section 1.409A-0 is amended by:

■ 1. Revising the entry for §1.409A-1 by adding paragraph (b)(13).

■ 2. Redesignating paragraph (q) as paragraph (r), and revising paragraph (q) in §1.409A-1.

■ 3. Revising the entry to paragraph (d) in §1.409A-3.

■ 4. Revising the entry to (j)(4)(xiii) in §1.409A-3.

The revisions and addition read as follows:

§1.409A-0 Table of contents.

* * * * *

§1.409A-1 Definitions and covered plans.

* * * * *

(b) * * *

(13) Recurring part-year compensation.

* * * * *

(q) References to a payment being made.

(r) Application of definitions and rules.

* * * * *

§ 1.409A-3 Permissible Payments.

* * * * *

(d) * * *

(1) In general.

(2) Payments due following death.

* * * * *

(j) * * *

(4) * * *

(xiii) Certain offsets.

(A) De minimis offset.

(B) Compliance with Federal debt collection laws.

* * * * *

■ **Par. 3**. Section 1.409A-1 is amended by:

■ 1. Revising paragraph (a)(4).

■ 2. Revising the first sentence of paragraph (b)(1).

■ 3. Revising paragraphs (b)(3) and (b)(4)(i)(B).

■ 4. Revising paragraph (b)(4)(ii).

■ 5. Adding a last sentence to paragraph (b)(5)(iii)(A).

■ 6. Revising paragraph (b)(5)(iii)(E)(*1*).

■ 7. Revising the first sentence of paragraph (b)(5)(vi)(A).

■ 8. Revising paragraphs (b)(5)(vi)(E) and (b)(5)(vi)(F).

■ 9. Revising paragraph (b)(9)(iii)(A).

■ 10. Adding a last sentence to paragraph (b)(11).

■ 11. Adding paragraph (b)(13).

■ 12. Revising paragraphs (h)(4) and (h)(5).

■ 13. Redesignating paragraph (q) as paragraph (r) and revising paragraphs (q) and (r).

The revisions and additions read as follows:

§1.409A-1 Definitions and covered plans.

* * * * *

(a) * * *

(4) *Section 457(f) and section 457A plans.* A deferred compensation plan under section 457(f) or a nonqualified deferred compensation plan under section 457A may be a nonqualified deferred compensation plan for purposes of this paragraph (a). The rules of section 409A apply to nonqualified deferred compensation plans separately and in addition to any requirements applicable to such plans under section 457(f) or section 457A. In addition, nonelective deferred compensation of non-employees described in section 457(e)(12) and a grandfathered plan or arrangement described in §1.457-2(k)(4) may be a nonqualified deferred compensation plan for purposes of this paragraph (a). The term *nonqualified deferred compensation plan* does not include a length of service award to a *bona fide* volunteer under section 457(e)(11)(A)(ii).

* * * * *

(b) * * *

(1) * * Except as otherwise provided in paragraphs (b)(3) through (b)(13) of this section, a plan provides for the deferral of compensation if, under the terms of the plan and the relevant facts and circumstances, the service provider has a legally binding right during a taxable year to compensation that, pursuant to the terms of the plan, is or may be payable to (or on behalf of) the service provider in a later taxable year. * * *

* * * * *

(3) *Compensation payable pursuant to the service recipient's customary payment timing arrangement.* A deferral of compensation does not occur solely because compensation is paid after the last day of the service provider's taxable year pursuant to the timing arrangement under which the service recipient normally compensates service providers for services performed during a payroll period described in section 3401(b), or with respect to a non-employee service provider, a period not longer than the payroll period described in section 3401(b) or if no such payroll period exists, a period not longer than the earlier of the normal timing arrangement under which the service recipient normally compensates non-employee service providers or 30 days after the end of the service provider's taxable year.

(4) * * *

(i) * * *

(B) A payment is treated as actually or constructively received for purposes of this paragraph (b)(4) if it is made in accordance with the rules in §1.409A-1(q).

* * * * *

(ii) *Certain delayed payments.* A payment that otherwise qualifies as a short-term deferral under paragraph (b)(4)(i) of this section but is made after the applicable 2 ½ month period may continue to qualify as a short-term deferral if the taxpayer establishes that it was administratively impracticable for the service recipient to make the payment by the end of the applicable 2 ½ month period and, as of the date upon which the legally binding right to the compensation arose, such impracticability was unforeseeable, or the taxpayer establishes that making the payment by the end of the applicable 2 ½ month period would have jeopardized the ability of the service recipient to continue as a going concern, and provided further that the payment is made as soon as administratively practicable or as soon as the payment would no longer have such effect. For purposes of this paragraph (b)(4)(ii), an action or failure to act of the service provider or a person under the service provider's control, such as a failure to provide necessary information or documentation, is not an unforeseeable event. In addition, a payment that otherwise qualifies as a short-term deferral under paragraph (b)(4)(i) of this section but is made after the applicable 2 ½ month period may continue to qualify as a short-term deferral if the taxpayer establishes that the service recipient reasonably anticipated that the service recipient's deduction with respect to such payment otherwise would not be permitted by application of section 162(m), and, as of the date the legally binding right to the payment arose, a reasonable person would not have anticipated the application of section 162(m) at the time of the payment, and provided further that the payment is made as soon as reasonably practicable following the first date on which the service recipient anticipates or reasonably should anticipate that, if the payment were made on such date, the service recipient's deduction with respect to such payment would no longer be restricted due to the application of section 162(m). Further, a payment that otherwise qualifies as a short-term deferral under paragraph (b)(4)(i) of this section but is made after the applicable 2 ½ month period may continue to qualify as a short-term deferral if the taxpayer establishes that the service recipient reasonably anticipated that making the payment by the end of the applicable 2 ½ month period would have violated Federal securities laws or other applicable law, provided that the payment is made as soon as reasonably practicable following the first date on which the service recipient anticipates or reasonably should anticipate that making the payment would not cause such violation. The making of a payment that would cause inclusion in gross income or the application of any penalty provision or other provision of the Internal Revenue Code is not treated as a violation of applicable law. For additional rules applicable to certain transaction-based compensation, see § 1.409A-3(i)(5)(iv)(A).

*   *   *   *   *

(5) *   *   *

(iii) *   *   *

(A) *   *   * The stock price will not be treated as based on a measure other than the fair market value to the extent that the amount payable upon the service provider's involuntary separation from service for cause, or the occurrence of a condition within the service provider's control such as noncompliance with a noncompetition or nondisclosure agreement (whether or not the condition is specified at the time the stock right is granted), is based on a measure that results in a payment of less than fair market value.

*   *   *   *   *

(E) *Eligible issuer of service recipient stock* —(*1*) *In general.* The term *eligible issuer of service recipient stock* means the corporation or other entity for which the service provider provides direct services on the date of grant of the stock right or a corporation or other entity for which it is reasonably anticipated that the service provider will begin providing direct services within 12 months after the date of grant, and any corporation or other entity (a related corporation or other entity) in a chain of corporations or other entities in which each corporation or other entity has a controlling interest in another corporation or other entity in the chain, ending with the corporation or other entity that has a controlling interest in the corporation or other entity for which the service provider provides direct services on the date of grant of the stock right or the corporation or other entity for which it is reasonably anticipated that the service provider will begin providing direct services within 12 months after the date of grant. If it is reasonably anticipated that a service provider will begin providing services for a corporation or other entity within 12 months after the date of grant, that corporation or other entity (or a related corporation or other entity) will be an eligible issuer of service recipient stock only if the services in fact commence within 12 months after the date of grant and the stock otherwise is service recipient stock at the time the services begin or, if services do not commence within that 12 month period, the right is forfeited. For this purpose, the term *controlling interest* has the same

meaning as provided in § 1.414(c)-2(b)(2)(i), substituting the language "at least 50 percent" for "at least 80 percent" each place it appears in § 1.414(c)-2(b)(2)(i). In addition, if the use of such stock with respect to the grant of a stock right to a service provider is based upon legitimate business criteria, the term *controlling interest* has the same meaning as provided in § 1.414(c)-2(b)(2)(i), substituting the language "at least 20 percent" for "at least 80 percent" each place it appears in § 1.414(c)-2(b)(2)(i). For purposes of determining ownership of an interest in an organization, the rules of §§ 1.414(c)-3 and 1.414(c)-4 apply. The determination of whether a grant is based on legitimate business criteria is based on the facts and circumstances, focusing primarily on whether there is a sufficient nexus between the service provider and the issuer of the stock right so that the grant serves a legitimate non-tax business purpose other than simply providing compensation to the service provider that is excluded from the requirements of section 409A. For example, when stock of a corporation that owns an interest in a joint venture involving an operating business is granted to service providers of the joint venture who are former service providers of such corporation, that use is generally based upon legitimate business criteria, and therefore could be service recipient stock with respect to such service providers if the corporation owns at least 20 percent of the joint venture and the other requirements of this paragraph (b)(5)(iii) are met. Similarly, the legitimate business criteria requirement generally would be met if the corporate venturer issued such a right to a service provider of the joint venture who it reasonably expected would become a service provider of the corporate venturer. However, if a service provider has no real nexus with a corporate venturer, such as generally happens when the corporate venturer is a passive investor in the service recipient joint venture, a stock right issued to the service provider on the investor corporation's stock generally would not be based upon legitimate business criteria. Similarly, if a corporation holds only a minority interest in an entity that in turn holds a minority interest in the entity for which the service provider performs services, such that the corporation holds only an insubstantial indirect interest in the entity receiving the services, legitimate business criteria generally would not exist for issuing a stock right on the corporation's stock to the service provider.

*   *   *   *   *

(vi) *   *   *

(A) *   *   * The term *option* means the right or privilege of a person to purchase stock from a corporation by virtue of an offer of the corporation continuing for a stated period of time, whether or not irrevocable, to sell such stock at a price determined under paragraph (b)(5)(vi)(D) of this section, such person being under no obligation to purchase.

*   *   *   *   *

(E) *Exercise.* The term *exercise*, when used in reference to an option, means the act of acceptance by the holder of the option of the offer to sell contained in the option. In general, the time of exercise is the time when there is a sale or a contract to sell between the corporation and the holder. A promise to pay the exercise price is not an exercise of the option unless the holder of the option is subject to personal liability on such promise. An agreement or undertaking by the service provider to make payments under a stock purchase plan is not the exercise of an option to the extent the payments made remain subject to the withdrawal by or refund to the service provider.

(F) *Transfer.* The term *transfer*, when used in reference to the transfer to a person of a share of stock pursuant to the exercise of an option, means the transfer of ownership of such share, or the transfer of substantially all the rights of ownership. Such transfer must, within a reasonable time, be evidenced on the books of the corporation. A transfer may occur even if a share of stock is subject to a substantial risk of forfeiture or is not otherwise transferable immediately after the date of exercise. A transfer does not fail to occur merely because, under the terms of the arrangement, the person may not dispose of the share for a specified period of time, or the share is subject to a right of first refusal or a right to acquire the share at the share's fair market value at the time of the sale.

*   *   *   *   *

(9) *   *   *

(iii) *   *   *

(A) The separation pay (other than amounts described in paragraphs (b)(9)(iv) and (v) of this section) does not exceed two times the lesser of—

(*1*) The service provider's annualized compensation based upon the annual rate of pay for services provided to the service recipient for the service provider's taxable year preceding the taxable year in which the service provider has a separation from service with such service recipient (or for the taxable year in which the service provider has a separation from service if the service provider had no compensation from the service recipient in the preceding taxable year), adjusted for any increase during that year that was expected to continue indefinitely if the service provider had not separated from service; or

(*2*) The maximum amount that may be taken into account under a qualified retirement plan pursuant to section 401(a)(17) for the calendar year in which the service provider has a separation from service.

* * * * *

(11) * * * In addition, a plan does not provide for a deferral of compensation for purposes of this paragraph (b) to the extent it provides for a payment of reasonable attorneys' fees or other reasonable expenses incurred by the service provider to enforce any *bona fide* legal claim against the service recipient with respect to the service relationship between the service provider and the service recipient.

* * * * *

(13) *Recurring part-year compensation.* A plan in which a service provider participates that provides for the payment of recurring part-year compensation (as defined in §1.409A-2(a)(14)), whether or not at the service provider's election, does not provide for a deferral of compensation for purposes of this paragraph (b) if the plan does not defer payment of any of the recurring part-year compensation to a date beyond the last day of the 13th month following the first day of the service period for which the recurring part-year compensation is paid, and the amount of the service provider's recurring part-year compensation does not exceed the annual compensation limit under section 401(a)(17) for the calendar year in which the service period commences.

* * * * *

(h) * * *

(4) *Asset purchase transactions.* If as part of a sale or other disposition of assets by one service recipient (seller) to an unrelated service recipient (buyer), a service provider of the seller would otherwise experience a separation from service with the seller, the seller and the buyer may retain the discretion to specify, and may specify, whether a service provider providing services to the seller immediately before the asset purchase transaction and providing services to the buyer after and as a result of the asset purchase transaction has experienced a separation from service for purposes of this paragraph (h), provided that the asset purchase transaction results from *bona fide*, arm's length negotiations, all service providers providing services to the seller immediately before the asset purchase transaction and providing services to the buyer after and as a result of the asset purchase transaction are treated consistently (regardless of position at the seller) for purposes of applying the provisions of any nonqualified deferred compensation plan, and such treatment is specified in writing no later than the closing date of the asset purchase transaction. For purposes of this paragraph (h)(4), references to a sale or other disposition of assets, or an asset purchase transaction, refer only to a transfer of substantial assets, such as a plant or division or substantially all of the assets of a trade or business, and do not refer to a stock purchase treated as a deemed asset sale under section 338. For purposes of this paragraph (h)(4), whether a service recipient is related to another service recipient is determined under the rules provided in paragraph (f)(2)(ii) of this section.

(5) *Dual status.* If a service provider provides services both as an employee of a service recipient and as an independent contractor of the service recipient, the service provider must separate from service both as an employee and as an independent contractor to be treated as having separated from service. Notwithstanding the foregoing, if a service provider provides services both as an employee of a service recipient and as a member of the board of directors of a corporate service recipient (or an analogous position with respect to a non-corporate service recipient), the services provided as a director are not taken into account in determining whether the service provider has a separation from service as an employee for purposes of a nonqualified deferred compensation plan in which the service provider participates as an employee that is not aggregated with any plan in which the service provider participates as a director under paragraph (c)(2)(ii) of this section. In addition, if a service provider provides services both as an employee of a service recipient and as a member of the board of directors of a corporate service recipient (or an analogous position with respect to a non-corporate service recipient), the services provided as an employee are not taken into account in determining whether the service provider has a separation from service as a director for purposes of a nonqualified deferred compensation plan in which the service provider participates as a director that is not aggregated with

any plan in which the service provider participates as an employee under paragraph (c)(2)(ii) of this section.

* * * * *

(q) *References to a payment being made.* A payment is made or an amount is paid or received when any taxable benefit is actually or constructively received, which includes a transfer of cash, a transfer of property includible in income under section 83, any other event that results in the inclusion in income under the economic benefit doctrine, a contribution to a trust described in section 402(b) at the time includible in income under section 402(b), a transfer or creation of a beneficial interest in a section 402(b) trust at the time includible in income under section 402(b), and the inclusion of an amount in income under 457(f)(1)(A). In addition, a payment is made or an amount is paid or received upon the transfer, cancellation, or reduction of an amount of deferred compensation in exchange for benefits under a welfare benefit plan, a fringe benefit excludible under section 119 or section 132, or any other benefit that is excludible from gross income. Notwithstanding the foregoing, the occurrence of any of the following events is not a payment:

(1) a grant of an option that does not have a readily ascertainable fair market value (as defined under §1.83-7(b));

(2) a transfer of property (including an option that has a readily ascertainable fair market value) that is substantially nonvested (as defined under §1.83-3(b)) with respect to which the service provider does not make a valid election under section 83(b); or

(3) a contribution to a trust described in section 402(b) or a transfer or creation of a beneficial interest in a section 402(b) trust unless and until the amount is includible in income under section 402(b).

(r) *Application of definitions and rules.* The definitions and rules set forth in paragraphs (a) through (q) of this section apply for purposes of section 409A, this section, and §§1.409A-2 through 1.409A-6.

■ **Par. 4.** Section 1.409A-2 is amended by revising paragraph (b)(2)(i) to read as follows:

§1.409A-2 Deferral elections.

* * * * *

(b) * * *

(2) *Definitions of payments for purposes of subsequent changes in the time or form of payment* —(i) *In general.* Except as provided in paragraphs (b)(2)(ii) and (iii) of this section, the term *payment* refers to each separately identified amount to which a service provider is entitled to payment under a plan on a determinable date, and includes amounts applied for the benefit of the service provider. An amount is separately identified only if the amount may be objectively determined under a nondiscretionary formula. For example, an amount identified as 10 percent of the account balance as of a specified payment date would be a separately identified amount. The determination of whether a payment is or has been made for purposes of this paragraph (b) is made in accordance with the rules in §1.409A-1(q). For additional rules relating to the application of this paragraph (b) to amounts payable at a fixed time or pursuant to a fixed schedule, see §1.409A-3(i)(1).

* * * * *

■ **Par. 5.** Section 1.409A-3 is amended by:

■ 1. Revising paragraph (b).

■ 2. Redesignating paragraph (d) as paragraph (d)(1) and revising the heading of paragraph (d)(1).

■ 3. Adding paragraph (d)(2).

■ 4. Revising paragraphs (i)(5)(iii) and (i)(5)(iv)(A).

■ 5. Revising paragraphs (j)(1) and (j)(2).

■ 6. Revising paragraph (j)(4)(iii)(B).

■ 7. Revising paragraphs (j)(4)(ix)(A) and (j)(4)(ix)(C).

■ 8. Revising paragraph (j)(4)(xiii).

The revisions and additions read as follows:

§1.409A-3 Permissible payments.

* * * * *

(b) *Designation of payment upon a permissible payment event.* Except as otherwise specified in this section, a plan provides for the payment upon an event described in paragraph (a)(1), (2), (3), (5), or (6) of this section if the plan provides the date of the event is the payment date, or specifies another payment date that is objectively determinable and nondiscretionary at the time the event occurs. A plan may also provide that a payment upon an event described in paragraph (a)(1), (2), (3), (5), or (6) of this section is to be made in accordance with a schedule that is objectively determinable and nondiscretionary based on the date the event occurs and that would qualify as a fixed schedule under paragraph (i)(1) of this section if the payment event were instead a fixed date, provided that the schedule must be fixed at the time the permissible payment event is designated. In addition, a plan may provide that a payment, including a payment that is part of a schedule, is to be made during a designated taxable year of the service provider that is objectively determinable and nondiscretionary at the time the payment event occurs such as, for example, a schedule of three substantially equal payments payable during the first three taxable years following the taxable year in which a separation from service occurs. A plan may also provide that a payment, including a payment that is part of a schedule, is to be made during a designated period objectively determinable and nondiscretionary at the time the payment event occurs, but only if the designated period both begins and ends within one taxable year of the service provider or the designated period is not more than 90 days and the service provider does not have a right to designate the taxable year of the payment (other than an election that complies with the subsequent deferral election rules of §1.409A-2(b)). However, in the case of a payment to be made following the death of the service provider or a beneficiary who has become entitled to payment due to the service provider's death, in addition to the permitted designated periods described in the previous sentence, the designated period may begin on the date of death and end on December 31 of the first calendar year following the calendar year during which the death occurs, and the payment recipient may have the right to designate the taxable year of payment. If a plan provides for a period of more than one day following a payment event during which a payment may be made, such as permitting payment within 90 days following the date of the event, the payment date for purposes of the subsequent deferral rules under §1.409A-2(b) is treated as the first possible date upon which a payment could be made under the terms of the plan. A plan may provide for payment upon the earliest or latest of more than one event or time, provided that each event or time is described in paragraphs (a)(1) through (6) of this section. For examples illustrating the provisions of this paragraph, see paragraph (i)(1)(vi) of this section.

* * * * *

(d) *When a payment is treated as made upon the designated payment date*—(1) *In general.* * * *

(2) *Payments due following death.* A payment specified to be made under the plan on any date within the period beginning on the date of the death of the service provider, or of a beneficiary who has become entitled to payment due to the service provider's death, and ending on December 31 of the first calendar year following the calendar year during which the death occurs (including a payment specified to be made upon death) is treated as made on the date specified under the plan if the payment is made on any date during this period, regardless of whether the payment recipient designates the taxable year of payment. Further, any change to the time or form of a payment that is specified to be made under the plan during this period to provide that the payment will be made on any other date during this period will not be treated as a subsequent deferral election for purposes of §1.409A-2(b)(1) or an impermissible acceleration for purposes of §1.409A-3(j)(1):

* * * * *

(i) * * *

(5) * * *

(iii) *Attribution of stock ownership.* For purposes of paragraph (i)(5) of this section, section 318(a) applies to determine stock ownership. Stock underlying a vested option is considered owned by the person who holds the vested option (and the stock underlying a nonvested option is not considered owned by the person who holds the nonvested option). For purposes of the preceding sentence, however, if a vested option is exercisable for stock that is not substantially vested (as defined by §1.83-3(b) and (j)), the stock underlying the option is not treated as owned by the person who holds the option.

* * * * *

(iv) *Special rules for certain delayed payments pursuant to a change in control event*—(A) *Certain transaction-based compensation.* Payments of compensation related to a change in control event described in paragraph (i)(5)(v) of this section (change in the ownership of a corporation) or paragraph (i)(5)(vii) of this section (change in the ownership of a substantial portion of a corporation's assets) that occur because a service recipient purchases its stock held by the service provider or because the service recipient or a third party purchases a stock right or

a statutory stock option described in §1.409A-1(b)(5)(ii) held by a service provider, or that are calculated by reference to the value of stock of the service recipient (collectively, transaction-based compensation), may be treated as paid on a designated date or pursuant to a payment schedule that complies with the requirements of section 409A if the transaction-based compensation is paid on the same schedule and under the same terms and conditions as apply to payments to shareholders generally with respect to stock of the service recipient pursuant to a change in control event described in paragraph (i)(5)(v) of this section (change in the ownership of a corporation) or as apply to payments to the service recipient pursuant to a change in control event described in paragraph (i)(5)(vii) of this section (change in the ownership of a substantial portion of a corporation's assets). In addition, to the extent that the transaction-based compensation is paid not later than five years after the change in control event, the payment of such compensation will not violate the initial or subsequent deferral election rules set out in §1.409A-2(a) and (b) solely as a result of such transaction-based compensation being paid pursuant to such schedule and terms and conditions. The payment or agreement to pay transaction-based compensation payable with respect to a stock right described in §1.409A-1(b)(5)(i)(A) or (B) or a statutory stock option described in §1.409A-1(b)(5)(ii) also will not cause the stock right or statutory stock option to be treated as having provided for the deferral of compensation from the original grant date solely as a result of the transaction-based compensation being paid on the same schedule and under the same terms and conditions as apply to payments to shareholders generally with respect to stock of the service recipient pursuant to the change in control event described in paragraph (i)(5)(v) of this section (change in the ownership of a corporation) or as apply to payments to the service recipient pursuant to the change in control event described in paragraph (i)(5)(vii) of this section (change in the ownership of a substantial portion of a corporation's assets) and the transaction-based compensation is paid not later than five years after the change in control event. If before and in connection with a change in control event described in paragraph (i)(5)(v) or (i)(5)(vii) of this section, transaction-based compensation that would otherwise be payable as a result of such event is made subject to a condition on payment that is a substantial risk of forfeiture (as defined in §1.409A-1(d), without regard to the provisions of that section under which additions or extensions of forfeiture conditions are disregarded) and the transaction-based compensation is payable under the same terms and conditions as apply to payments made to shareholders generally with respect to stock of the service recipient pursuant to a change in control event described in paragraph (i)(5)(v) of this section or to payments to the service recipient pursuant to a change in control event described in paragraph (i)(5)(vii) of this section, for purposes of determining whether such transaction-based compensation is a short-term deferral the requirements of §1.409A-1(b)(4) are applied as if the legally binding right to such transaction-based compensation arose on the date that it became subject to such substantial risk of forfeiture. [Officially corrected 8/4/16 (81 FR 51413).]

* * * * *

(j) *Prohibition on acceleration of payments*—(1) *In general*—Except as provided in paragraph (j)(4) of this section, a nonqualified deferred compensation plan may not permit the acceleration of the time or schedule of any payment or amount scheduled to be paid pursuant to the terms of the plan, and no such accelerated payment may be made whether or not provided for under the terms of such plan. For purposes of determining whether a payment of deferred compensation has been made, the rules of paragraph (f) of this section (on substituted payments) apply. For purposes of this paragraph (j), an impermissible acceleration does not occur if payment is made in accordance with plan provisions or an election as to the time and form of payment in effect at the time of initial deferral (or added in accordance with the rules applicable to subsequent deferral elections under §1.409A-2(b)) pursuant to which payment is required to be made on an accelerated schedule as a result of an intervening payment event that is an event described in paragraph (a)(1), (2), (3), (5) or (6) of this section. For such purpose, the intervening payment event may apply with respect to either the service provider or, following the service provider's death, a beneficiary who becomes entitled to payment due to the service provider's death (substituting such beneficiary for the service provider in the definitions of *disability* in paragraph (i)(4) of this section and *unforeseeable emergency* in paragraph (i)(3) of this section, as applicable). For example, a plan may provide that a participant will receive six installment payments commencing at separation from service, and also provide that if the participant dies after such payments commence but before all payments have been made, all remaining amounts will be paid in a lump sum payment. Additionally, it is not an acceleration of the time or schedule of payment of a deferral of compensation if a service recipient waives or accelerates the satisfaction of a condition constituting a substantial risk of forfeiture applicable to such deferral of compensation, provided that the requirements of section 409A (including the requirement that the payment be made upon a permissible payment event) are otherwise satisfied with respect to such deferral of compensation. For example, if a nonqualified deferred compensation plan provides for a lump sum payment of the vested benefit upon separation from service, and the benefit vests under the plan only after 10 years of service, it is not a violation of the requirements of section 409A if the service recipient reduces the vesting requirement to five years of service, even if a service provider becomes vested as a result and receives a payment in connection with a separation from service before the service provider would have completed 10 years of service. However, if the plan in this example had provided for a payment on a fixed date, rather than at separation from service, the date of payment could not be accelerated due to the accelerated vesting. For the definition of a payment for purposes of this paragraph (j), see § 1.409A-2(b)(5) (coordination of the subsequent deferral election rules with the prohibition on acceleration of payments). For other permissible payments, see § 1.409A-2(b)(2)(iii) (certain immediate payments of remaining installments) and paragraph (d) of this section (certain payments made no more than 30 days before the designated payment date).

(2) *Application to multiple payment events.* The addition of a permissible payment event, the deletion of a permissible payment event, or the substitution of one permissible payment event for another permissible payment event, results in an acceleration of a payment if the addition, deletion, or substitution could result in the payment being made on an earlier date than such payment would have been made absent such addition, deletion, or substitution. Notwithstanding the previous sentence, the addition of death, disability (as defined in paragraph (i)(4) of this section), or an unforeseeable emergency (as defined in paragraph (i)(3) of this section), as a potentially earlier alternative or intervening payment event to an amount previously deferred will not be treated as resulting in an acceleration of a payment, even if such addition results in the payment being paid at an earlier time than such payment would have been made absent the addition of the payment event. For such purpose, the earlier alternative or intervening payment event may apply with respect to either the service provider or, following the service provider's death, a beneficiary who becomes entitled to payment due to the service provider's death (substituting such beneficiary for the service provider in the definitions of *disability* in paragraph (i)(4) of this section and *unforeseeable emergency* in paragraph (i)(3) of this section, as applicable). However, the addition of such a payment event as a potentially later alternative payment event generally is subject to the rules governing changes in the time and form of payment (see § 1.409A-2(b)).

* * * * *

(4) * * *

(iii) * * *

(B) *Compliance with ethics laws or conflicts of interest laws.* A plan may provide for acceleration of the time or schedule of a payment under the plan, or a payment may be made under a plan, to the extent reasonably necessary to avoid the violation of an applicable Federal, state, local, or *bona fide* foreign ethics law or conflicts of interest law (including under circumstances in which such payment is reasonably necessary to permit the service provider to participate in activities in the normal course of his or her position in which the service provider would otherwise not be able to participate under an applicable rule). A payment is reasonably necessary to avoid the violation of a Federal, state, local, or *bona fide* foreign ethics law or conflicts of interest law if the payment is a necessary part of a course of action that results in compliance with a Federal, state, local, or *bona fide* foreign ethics law or conflicts of interest law that would be violated absent such course of action, regardless of whether other actions would also result in compliance with the Federal, state, local, or *bona fide* foreign ethics law or conflicts of interest law.

* * * * *

(ix) * * *

(A) The service recipient's termination and liquidation of the plan within 12 months of a corporate dissolution taxed under section 331, or with the approval of a U.S. bankruptcy court, provided that the amounts deferred under the plan are included in the participants' gross incomes in the latest of the following years (or, if earlier, the taxable year in which the amount is actually or constructively received).

(1) The calendar year in which the plan termination and liquidation occurs;

(2) The first calendar year in which the amount is no longer subject to a substantial risk of forfeiture; or

(3) The first calendar year in which the payment is administratively practicable.

* * * * *

(C) The service recipient's termination and liquidation of the plan, provided that—

(1) The termination and liquidation does not occur proximate to a downturn in the financial health of the service recipient;

(2) The service recipient terminates and liquidates all agreements, methods, programs, and other arrangements sponsored by the service recipient that would be aggregated with any terminated and liquidated agreements, methods, programs, and other arrangements under § 1.409A-1(c) as if there were one service provider that had deferrals of compensation under every such agreement, method, program, and other arrangement sponsored by the service recipient (for example, all elective account balance plans that the service recipient sponsors);

(3) No payments in liquidation of the plan are made within 12 months of the date the service recipient takes all necessary action to irrevocably terminate and liquidate the plan other than payments that would be payable under the terms of the plan if the action to terminate and liquidate the plan had not occurred;

(4) All payments are made within 24 months of the date the service recipient takes all necessary action to irrevocably terminate and liquidate the plan; and

(5) The service recipient does not adopt any new agreement, method, program, or other arrangement described in paragraph (C)(2) of this subsection, at any time within three years following the date the service recipient takes all necessary action to irrevocably terminate and liquidate the plan.

* * * * *

(xiii) *Certain offsets* —(A) *De minimis offset.* A plan may provide for the acceleration of the time or schedule of a payment, or a payment may be made under such plan, as satisfaction of a debt of the service provider to the service recipient, if such debt is incurred in the ordinary course of the service relationship between the service recipient and the service provider, the entire amount of reduction in any of the service recipient's taxable years does not exceed $5,000, and the reduction is made at the same time and in the same amount as the debt otherwise would have been due and collected from the service provider.

(B) *Compliance with Federal debt collection laws.* A plan may provide for the acceleration of the time or schedule of a payment, or a payment may be made under such plan, as satisfaction of a debt of the service provider to the service recipient, to the extent reasonably necessary to comply with 31 U.S.C. 3711 et. seq. or similar Federal nontax law regarding debt collection relating to claims of the Federal government. A payment is reasonably necessary to comply with such a Federal debt collection law if the payment is a necessary part of a course of action that results in compliance with the Federal debt collection law that would be violated absent such course of action, regardless of whether other actions would also result in compliance with the Federal debt collection law.

* * * * *

■ **Par. 6**. Section 1.409A-4 (REG-148326-05), as proposed at 73 FR 74380 (December 8, 2008), is proposed to be amended by revising paragraph (a)(1)(ii)(B) to read as follows:

§ 1.409A-4 Calculation of amount includible in income and additional income taxes.

* * * * *

(B) *Treatment of certain deferred amounts otherwise subject to a substantial risk of forfeiture.* For purposes of determining the amount includible in income under section 409A(a)(1) and paragraph (a)(1)(i) of this section, an amount deferred under a plan that is otherwise subject to a substantial risk of forfeiture for a taxable year is treated as not subject to a substantial risk of forfeiture for the taxable year, if during the taxable year any of the following occur: [Officially corrected 8/4/16 (81 FR 51413).]

(1) A change (including an initial deferral election) that is not authorized under § 1.409A-1, § 1.409A-2, or § 1.409A-3 is made to a provision of the plan providing for the time or form of payment of the deferred amount, if the service recipient has not made a reasonable, good faith determination that, absent the change, the provision fails to comply with the requirements of section 409A(a). [Officially corrected 8/4/16 (81 FR 51413).]

(*2*) The service recipient has engaged in a pattern or practice of permitting substantially similar failures to comply with section 409A(a) under one or more nonqualified deferred compensation plans while amounts deferred under the plans are nonvested, and the facts and circumstances indicate that the deferred amount would be affected by the pattern or practice. Whether such a pattern or practice exists will depend on the facts and circumstances, including, but not limited to, whether the service recipient has taken commercially reasonable measures to identify and correct the substantially similar failures promptly upon discovery, whether the failures have affected nonvested deferred amounts with greater frequency than vested deferred amounts, whether the failures have occurred more frequently under newly adopted plans, and whether the failures appear intentional, are numerous, or repeat one or more similar past failures that were previously identified and corrected. [Officially corrected 8/4/16 (81 FR 51413).]

(*3*) The correction of a failure to comply with section 409A(a) affecting the deferred amount is not consistent with an applicable correction method (if one exists) set forth in applicable guidance issued by the Treasury Department and the IRS for correcting failures under section 409A(a), or the failure is not corrected in substantially the same manner as a substantially similar failure affecting a nonvested deferred amount under another plan sponsored by the service recipient. Solely with respect to the deferred amount, the requirements under applicable correction guidance with respect to eligibility, income inclusion, additional taxes, premium interest, and information reporting by the service recipient or service provider do not apply. [Officially corrected 8/4/16 (81 FR 51413).]

■ **Par. 7**. Section 1.409A-6 is amended by revising paragraph (b) to read as follows:

§ 1.409A-6 Application of section 409A and effective dates.

* * * * *

(b) *Regulatory applicability date.* Section 1.409A-0, § 1.409A-1, § 1.409A-2, § 1.409A-3 and this section, as amended, apply for taxable years beginning on or after publication of the Treasury decision adopting these rules as final regulations in the **Federal Register**. Section 1.409A-0, § 1.409A-1, § 1.409A-2, § 1.409A-3 and this section as they appeared in the April 2009 edition of 26 CFR part 1 apply for taxable years beginning on or after January 1, 2009 and before publication of the Treasury decision adopting these rules as final regulations in the **Federal Register**.

John M. Dalrymple,

Deputy Commissioner for Services and Enforcement.

[FR Doc. 2016-14331 Filed 6-21-16; 8:45 am]

BILLING CODE 4830-01-P

¶ 20,264M

IRS: Health insurance exchanges: Health insurance coverage: Health insurance premium tax credit: Opt-out arrangements: Benchmark plan premium: Reporting and disclosure.—The IRS has released proposed regulations relating to the health insurance premium tax credit (premium tax credit) and the individual shared responsibility provision of the Patient Protection and Affordable Care Act (PPACA, P.L. 111-148). The proposed regulations provide guidance and clarification on eligibility for the premium tax credit (including guidance on opt-out arrangements), the amount of the tax credit, determining the benchmark plan premium, and information reporting. The proposed regulations are generally proposed to apply for tax years beginning after December 31, 2016, though taxpayers may rely on certain provisions of the proposed regulations for tax years ending after December 31, 2013. In addition, several rules are proposed to apply for tax years beginning after December 31, 2018.

The proposed regulation was published in the Federal Register on July 8, 2016 (81 FR 44557). The IRS issued corrections on September 14, 2016 (81 FR 63154). All of the regulations, except for the regulations pertaining to opt-out arrangements, were finalized on December 19, 2016 (81 FR 91755). The preamble to the final regulations is at ¶ 23,329. The final regulations are reproduced at ¶ 11,112F-1, ¶ 11,112F-2, ¶ 11,112F-3, ¶ 11,112F-4, ¶ 11,112F-6, ¶ 13,648Z-58, ¶ 13,649E-15, and ¶ 13,649D.

DEPARTMENT OF THE TREASURY

Internal Revenue Service

26 CFR Parts 1 and 301

[REG-109086-15]

RIN 1545-BN50

Premium Tax Credit NPRM VI

AGENCY: Internal Revenue Service (IRS), Treasury.

ACTION: Notice of proposed rulemaking.

SUMMARY: This document contains proposed regulations relating to the health insurance premium tax credit (premium tax credit) and the individual shared responsibility provision. These proposed regulations affect individuals who enroll in qualified health plans through Health Insurance Exchanges (Exchanges, also called Marketplaces) and claim the premium tax credit, and Exchanges that make qualified health plans available to individuals and employers. These proposed regulations also affect individuals who are eligible for employer-sponsored health coverage and individuals who seek to claim an exemption from the individual shared responsibility provision because of unaffordable coverage. Although employers are not directly affected by rules governing the premium tax credit, these proposed regulations may indirectly affect employers through the employer shared responsibility provisions and the related information reporting provisions.

DATES: Written (including electronic) comments and requests for a public hearing must be received by September 6, 2016.

ADDRESSES: Send submissions to: CC:PA:LPD:PR (REG-109086-15), Room 5203, Internal Revenue Service, P.O. Box 7604, Ben Franklin Station, Washington, DC 20044. Submissions may be hand-delivered Monday through Friday between the hours of 8 a.m. and 4 p.m. to CC:PA:LPD:PR (REG-109086-15), Courier's Desk, Internal Revenue Service, 1111 Constitution Avenue NW., Washington, DC, or sent electronically via the Federal eRulemaking Portal at *http:// www.regulations.gov* (REG-109086-15).

FOR FURTHER INFORMATION CONTACT: Concerning the proposed regulations, Shareen Pflanz, (202) 317-4727; concerning the submission of comments and/or requests for a public hearing, Oluwafunmilayo Taylor, (202) 317-6901 (not toll-free calls).

SUPPLEMENTARY INFORMATION:

Paperwork Reduction Act

The collection of information contained in this notice of proposed rulemaking has been submitted to the Office of Management and Budget in accordance with the Paperwork Reduction Act of 1995 (44 U.S.C. 3507(d)). Comments on the collection of information should be sent to the Office of Management and Budget, Attn: Desk Officer for the Department of the Treasury, Office of Information and Regulatory Affairs, Washington, DC 20503, with copies to the Internal Revenue Service, Attn: IRS Reports Clearance Officer, SE:W:CAR:MP:T:T:SP, Washington, DC 20224. Comments on the collection of information should be received by September 6, 2016. Comments are specifically requested concerning:

Whether the proposed collection of information is necessary for the proper performance of the functions of the IRS, including whether the information will have practical utility;

How the quality, utility, and clarity of the information to be collected may be enhanced;

How the burden of complying with the proposed collection of information may be minimized, including through the application of automated collection techniques or other forms of information technology; and

Estimates of capital or start-up costs and costs of operation, maintenance, and purchase of services to provide information.

The collection of information in these proposed regulations is in § 1.36B-5. The collection of information is necessary to reconcile advance payments of the premium tax credit and determine the allowable premium tax credit. The collection of information is required to comply with the provisions of section 36B of the Internal Revenue Code (Code). The likely respondents are Marketplaces that enroll individuals in qualified health plans.

The burden for the collection of information contained in these proposed regulations will be reflected in the burden on Form 1095-A, *Health Insurance Marketplace Statement*, which is the form that will request the information from the Marketplaces in the proposed regulations.

An agency may not conduct or sponsor, and a person is not required to respond to, a collection of information unless it displays a valid control number assigned by the Office of Management and Budget.

Background

Beginning in 2014, under the Patient Protection and Affordable Care Act, Public Law 111-148 (124 Stat. 119 (2010)), and the Health Care and Education Reconciliation Act of 2010, Public Law 111-152 (124 Stat. 1029 (2010)) (collectively, the Affordable Care Act), eligible individuals who purchase coverage under a qualified health plan through an Exchange may claim a premium tax credit under section 36B of the Code. Section 36B was subsequently amended by the Medicare and Medicaid Extenders Act of 2010, Public Law 111-309 (124 Stat. 3285 (2010)); the Comprehensive 1099 Taxpayer Protection and Repayment of Exchange Subsidy Overpayments Act of 2011, Public Law 112-9 (125 Stat. 36 (2011)); and the Department of Defense and Full-Year Continuing Appropriations Act, 2011, Public Law 112-10 (125 Stat. 38 (2011)).

The Affordable Care Act also added section 5000A to the Code. Section 5000A was subsequently amended by the TRICARE Affirmation Act of 2010, Public Law 111-159 (124 Stat. 1123 (2010)) and Public Law 111-173 (124 Stat. 1215 (2010)). Section 5000A provides that, for months beginning after December 31, 2013, a nonexempt individual must have qualifying healthcare coverage (called minimum essential coverage) or make an individual shared responsibility payment.

Applicable Taxpayers

To be eligible for a premium tax credit, an individual must be an applicable taxpayer. Among other requirements, under section 36B(c)(1) an applicable taxpayer is a taxpayer whose household income for the taxable year is between 100 percent and 400 percent of the Federal poverty line (FPL) for the taxpayer's family size (or is a lawfully present non-citizen who has income below 100 percent of the FPL and is ineligible for Medicaid). A taxpayer's family size is equal to the number of individuals in the taxpayer's family. Under section 36B(d)(1), a taxpayer's family consists of the individuals for whom the taxpayer claims a personal exemption deduction under section 151 for the taxable year. Taxpayers may claim a personal exemption deduction for themselves, a spouse, and each of their dependents.

Under section 1412 of the Affordable Care Act, advance payments of the premium tax credit (advance credit payments) may be made directly to insurers on behalf of eligible individuals. The amount of advance credit payments made on behalf of a taxpayer in a taxable year is determined by a number of factors including projections of the taxpayer's household income and family size for the taxable year. Taxpayers who receive the benefit of advance credit payments are required to file an income tax return to reconcile the amount of advance credit payments made during the year with the amount of the credit allowable for the taxable year.

Under § 1.36B-2(b)(6), in general, a taxpayer whose household income for a taxable year is less than 100 percent of the applicable FPL is nonetheless treated as an applicable taxpayer if (1) the taxpayer or a family member enrolls in a qualified health plan, (2) an Exchange estimates at the time of enrollment that the taxpayer's household income for the taxable year will be between 100 and 400 percent of the applicable FPL, (3) advance credit payments are authorized and paid for one or more months during the taxable year, and (4) the taxpayer would be an applicable taxpayer but for the fact that the taxpayer's household income for the taxable year is below 100 percent of the applicable FPL.

Premium Assistance Credit Amount

Under section 36B(a), a taxpayer's premium tax credit is equal to the premium assistance credit amount for the taxable year. Section 36B(b)(1) and § 1.36B-3(d) generally provide that the premium assistance credit amount is the sum of the premium assistance amounts for all coverage months in the taxable year for individuals in the taxpayer's family. The premium assistance amount for a coverage month is the lesser of (1) the premiums for the month for one or more qualified health plans that cover a taxpayer or family member (enrollment premium), or (2) the excess of the adjusted monthly premium for the second lowest cost silver plan (as described in section 1302(d)(1)(B) of the Affordable Care Act (42 U.S.C. 18022(d)(1)(B))) offered through the Exchange for the rating area where the taxpayer resides that would provide coverage to the taxpayer's coverage family (the benchmark plan), over 1/12 of the product of the taxpayer's household income and the applicable percentage for the taxable year (the contribution amount). In general, the benchmark plan's adjusted monthly premium is the premium an insurer would charge for the plan adjusted only for the ages of the covered individuals. The applicable percentage is provided in a table that is updated annually and represents the portion of a taxpayer's household income that the taxpayer is expected to pay if the taxpayer's coverage family enrolls in the benchmark plan. See, for example, Rev. Proc. 2014-62, 2014-2 C.B. 948 (providing the applicable percentage table for taxable years beginning in 2016) and Rev. Proc. 2014-37, 2014-2 C.B. 363 (providing the applicable percentage table for taxable years beginning in 2015). A taxpayer's coverage family refers to all members of the taxpayer's family who enroll in a qualified health plan in a month and are not eligible for minimum essential coverage as defined in section 5000A(f) (other than coverage in the individual market) for that month.

Under section 1301(a)(1)(B) of the Affordable Care Act, a qualified health plan must offer the essential health benefits package described in section 1302(a). Under section 1302(b)(1)(J) of the Affordable Care Act, the essential health benefits package includes pediatric services, including oral and vision care. Section 1302(b)(4)(F) of the Affordable Care Act provides that, if an Exchange offers a plan described in section 1311(d)(2)(B)(ii)(I) of the Affordable Care Act (42 U.S.C. 13031(d)(2)(B)(ii)(I)) (a stand-alone dental plan), other health plans offered through the Exchange will not fail to be qualified health plans solely because the plans do not offer pediatric dental benefits.

For purposes of calculating the premium assistance amount for a taxpayer who enrolls in both a qualified health plan and a stand-alone dental plan, section 36B(b)(3)(E) provides that the enrollment premium includes the portion of the premium for the stand-alone dental plan properly allocable to pediatric dental benefits that are included in the essential health benefits required to be provided by a qualified health plan.

Section 36B(b)(3)(B) provides that the benchmark plan with respect to an applicable taxpayer is the second lowest cost silver plan offered by the Marketplace through which the applicable taxpayer (or a family member) enrolled and which provides (1) self-only coverage, in the case of unmarried individuals (other than a surviving spouse or head of household) who do not claim any dependents, or any other individual who enrolls in self-only coverage, and (2) family coverage, in the case of any other applicable taxpayer. Section 1.36B-1(l) provides that self-only coverage means health insurance that covers one individual. Section 1.36B-1(m) provides that family coverage means health insurance that covers more than one individual.

Under § 1.36B-3(f)(3), if there are one or more silver-level plans offered through the Exchange for the rating area where the taxpayer resides that do not cover all members of a taxpayer's coverage family under one policy (for example, because of the relationships within the family), the benchmark plan premium is the second lowest-cost option for covering all members of the taxpayer's family, which may be either a single silver-level policy or more than one silver-level policy.

Section 1.36B-3(d)(2) provides that, if a qualified health plan is terminated before the last day of a month or an individual is enrolled in coverage effective on the date of the individual's birth, adoption, or placement for adoption or in foster care, or on the effective date of a court order, the premium assistance amount for the month is the lesser of the enrollment premiums for the month (reduced by any amounts that were refunded) or the excess of the benchmark plan premium for a full month of coverage over the full contribution amount for the month.

Coverage Month

Under section 36B(c)(2)(A) and § 1.36B-3(c)(1), a coverage month is generally any month for which the taxpayer or a family member is covered by a qualified health plan enrolled in through an Exchange on the first day of the month and the premium is paid by the taxpayer or through an advance credit payment. However, section 36B(c)(2) provides that a month is not a coverage month for an individual who is eligible for minimum essential coverage other than coverage in the individual market. Under section 36B(c)(2)(B)(ii), minimum essential coverage is defined by reference to section 5000A(f). Minimum essential coverage includes government-sponsored programs such as most Medicaid coverage, Medicare part A, the Children's Health Insurance Program (CHIP), most TRICARE programs, most coverage provided to veterans under title 38 of the United States Code, and the Nonappropriated Fund Health Benefits Program of the Department of Defense. See section 5000A(f)(1) and § 1.5000A-2(b). Section 1.36B-2(c)(3)(i) provides that, for purposes of section 36B, the government-sponsored programs described in section 5000A(f)(1)(A) are not considered eligible employer-sponsored plans.

Under § 1.36B-2(c)(2)(i), an individual generally is treated as eligible for government-sponsored minimum essential coverage as of the first day of the first full month that the individual meets the criteria for coverage and is eligible to receive benefits under the government program. However, under § 1.36B-2(c)(2)(v) an individual is treated as not eligible for Medicaid, CHIP, or a similar program for a period of coverage under a qualified health plan if, when the individual enrolls in the qualified health plan, an Exchange determines or considers (within the meaning of 45 CFR 155.302(b)) the individual to be ineligible for such program. In addition, § 1.36B-2(c)(2)(iv) provides that if an individual receiving the benefit of advance credit payments is determined to be eligible for a government-sponsored program, and that eligibility is effective retroactively, then, for purposes of the premium tax credit, the individual is treated as eligible for the program no earlier than the first day of the first calendar month beginning after the approval.

Coverage under an eligible employer-sponsored plan is minimum essential coverage. In general, an eligible employer-sponsored plan is coverage provided by an employer to its employees (and their dependents) under a group health plan maintained by the employer. *See* section 5000A(f)(2) and § 1.5000A-2(c). Under section 5000A(f)(3) and § 1.5000A-2(g), minimum essential coverage does not include any coverage that consists solely of excepted benefits described in section 2791(c)(1), (c)(2), (c)(3), or (c)(4) of the Public Health Service Act (PHS Act) (42 U.S.C. 300gg-91(c)), or regulations issued under those provisions (45 CFR 148.220). In general, excepted benefits are benefits that are limited in scope or are conditional.

Under section 36B(c)(2)(C) and § 1.36B-2(c)(3)(i), except as provided in the next paragraph of this preamble, an individual is treated as eligible for coverage under an eligible employer-sponsored plan only if the employee's share of the premium is affordable and the coverage provides minimum value. Under section 36B(c)(2)(C), an eligible employer-sponsored plan is treated as affordable for an employee if the amount of the employee's required contribution (within the meaning of section 5000A(e)(1)(B)) for self-only coverage does not exceed a specified percentage of the employee's household income. The affordability of coverage for individuals related to an employee is determined in the same manner. Thus, under section 36B(c)(2)(C)(i) and § 1.36B-2(c)(3)(v)(A)(2), an eligible employer-sponsored plan is treated as affordable for an individual eligible for the plan because of a relationship to an employee if the amount of the employee's required contribution for self-only coverage does not exceed a specified percentage of the employee's household income.

Under § 1.36B-2(c)(3)(v)(A)(3), an eligible employer-sponsored plan is not considered affordable if, when an individual enrolls in a qualified health plan, the Marketplace determines that the eligible employer-sponsored plan is not affordable. However, that rule does not apply for an individual who, with reckless disregard for the facts, provides incorrect information to a Marketplace concerning the employee's portion of the annual premium for coverage under the eligible employer-sponsored plan. In addition, under section 36B(c)(2)(C)(iii) and § 1.36B-2(c)(3)(vii)(A), an individual is treated as eligible for employer-sponsored coverage if the individual actually enrolls in an eligible employer-sponsored plan, even if the coverage is not affordable or does not provide minimum value.

Section 1.36B-2(c)(3)(iii)(A) provides that, subject to the rules described above, an employee or related individual may be considered eligible for coverage under an eligible employer-sponsored plan for a month during a plan year if the employee or related individual could have enrolled in the plan for that month during an open or special enrollment period. Under § 1.36B-2(c)(3)(ii), plan year means an eligible employer-sponsored plan's regular 12-month coverage period (or the remainder of a 12-month coverage period for a new employee or an individual who enrolls during a special enrollment period).

Although coverage in the individual market is minimum essential coverage under section 5000A(f)(1)(C), under section 36B(c)(2)(B)(i), an individual who is eligible for or enrolled in coverage in the individual market (whether or not obtained through the Marketplace) nevertheless may have a coverage month for purposes of the premium tax credit.

Required Contribution for Employer-Sponsored Coverage

Under section 36B(c)(2)(C) and § 1.36B-2(c)(3)(v)(A)(1) and (2), an eligible employer-sponsored plan is treated as affordable for an employee or a related individual if the amount the employee must pay for self-only coverage whether by salary reduction or otherwise (the employee's required contribution) does not exceed a specified percentage of the employee's household income. Under section 36B(c)(2)(C)(i)(II), an employee's required contribution has the same meaning for purposes of the premium tax credit as in section 5000A(e)(1)(B).

Section 5000A provides that, for each month, taxpayers must have minimum essential coverage, qualify for a health coverage exemption, or make an individual shared responsibility payment when they file a Federal income tax return. Section 5000A(e)(1) and § 1.5000A-3(e)(1) provide that an individual is exempt for a month when the individual cannot afford minimum essential coverage. For this purpose, an individual cannot afford coverage if the individual's required contribution (determined on an annual basis) for minimum essential coverage exceeds a specified percentage of the individual's household income. Under section 5000A(e)(1)(B)(i) and § 1.5000A-3(e)(3)(ii)(A), for employees eligible for coverage under an eligible employer-sponsored plan, the employee's required contribution is the amount an employee would have to pay for self-only coverage (whether paid through salary reduction or otherwise) under the plan. For individuals eligible to enroll in employer-sponsored coverage because of a relationship to an employee (related individual), under section 5000A(e)(1)(C) and § 1.5000A-3(e)(3)(ii)(B), the required contribution is the portion of the annual premium that the employee would pay (whether through salary reduction or otherwise) for the lowest cost family coverage that would cover the employee and all related individuals who are included in the employee's family and are not otherwise exempt under § 1.5000A-3.

Notice 2015-87, 2015-52 I.R.B. 889, provides guidance on determining the affordability of an employer's offer of eligible employer-sponsored coverage for purposes of sections 36B, 5000A, and 4980H (and the related information reporting under section 6056).[1] In relevant part, Notice 2015-87 addresses how to determine the affordability of an employer's offer of eligible employer-sponsored coverage if an employer also makes available an opt-out payment, which is a payment that (1) is available only if the employee declines coverage (which includes waiving coverage in which the employee would otherwise be enrolled) under the employer-sponsored plan, and (2) cannot be used to pay for coverage under the employer-sponsored plan. The arrangement under which the opt-out payment is made available is an opt-out arrangement.

As Notice 2015-87 explains, the Treasury Department and the IRS have determined that it is generally appropriate to treat an opt-out payment that is made available under an unconditional opt-out arrangement in the same manner as a salary reduction contribution for purposes of determining an employee's required contribution under sections 36B and 5000A and any related consequences under sections 4980H(b) and 6056. Accordingly, Notice 2015-87 provides that the Treasury Department and the IRS intend to propose regulations reflecting this rule and to request comments on those regulations. For this purpose, an unconditional opt-out arrangement refers to an arrangement providing payments conditioned solely on an employee declining coverage under employer-sponsored coverage and not on an employee satisfying any other meaningful requirement related to the provision of health care to employees, such as a requirement to provide proof of coverage through a plan of a spouse's employer.

Notice 2015-87 also provides that the Treasury Department and the IRS anticipate requesting comments on the treatment of conditional opt-out arrangements, meaning opt-out arrangements under which payments are conditioned not only on the employee declining employer-sponsored coverage but also on satisfaction of one or more additional meaningful conditions (such as the employee providing proof of enrollment in coverage provided by a spouse's employer or other coverage).

Notice 2015-87 provides that, until the applicability date of any final regulations (and in any event for plan years beginning before 2017), individuals may treat opt-out payments made available under unconditional opt-out arrangements as increasing the employee's required

---

[1] An assessable payment under section 4980H(b) may arise if at least one full-time employee (as defined in § 54.4980H-1(a)(21)) of the applicable large employer (as defined in § 54.4980H-1(a)(4)) receives the premium tax credit. A full-time employee generally is ineligible for the premium tax credit if the employee is offered minimum essential coverage under an eligible employer-sponsored plan that is affordable and provides minimum value. The determination of whether an applicable large employer has made an offer of affordable coverage under an eligible employer-sponsored plan for purposes of section 4980H(b) generally is based on the standard set forth in section 36B, which provides that an offer is affordable if the employee's required contribution is at or below 9.5 percent (as indexed) of the employee's household income. However, because an employer generally will not know the taxpayer employee's household income, § 54.4980H-5(e)(2) sets forth three safe harbors under which an employer may determine affordability (solely for purposes of section 4980H) based on information that is readily available to the employer (that is, Form W-2 wages, the rate of pay, or the Federal poverty line).

contribution for purposes of sections 36B and 5000A.[2] In addition, for the same period, an individual who can demonstrate that he or she meets the condition(s) (in addition to declining the employer's health coverage) that must be satisfied to receive an opt-out payment (such as demonstrating that the employee has coverage under a spouse's group health plan) may treat the amount of the conditional opt-out payment as increasing the employee's required contribution for purposes of sections 36B and 5000A. See the section of this preamble entitled "*Effective/Applicability Date*" for additional related discussion.

Notice 2015-87 included a request for comments on opt-out arrangements. The Treasury Department and the IRS received a number of comments, and the comments are discussed in section 2.f. of this preamble entitled "*Opt-out arrangements and an employee's required contribution*."

Information Reporting

Section 36B(f)(3) provides that Exchanges must report to the IRS and to taxpayers certain information required to administer the premium tax credit. Section 1.36B-5(c)(1) provides that the information required to be reported annually includes (1) identifying information for each enrollee, (2) identifying information for the coverage, (3) the amount of enrollment premiums and advance credit payments for the coverage, (4) the premium for the benchmark plan used to calculate the amount of the advance credit payments made on behalf of the taxpayer or other enrollee, if advance credit payments were made, and the benchmark plan premium that would apply to all individuals enrolled in the coverage if advance credit payments were not made, and (5) the dates the coverage started and ended. Section 1.36B-5(c)(3)(i) provides that an Exchange must report this information for each family enrolled in the coverage.

Explanation of Provisions

1. Effective/Applicability Date

Except as otherwise provided in this section, these regulations are proposed to apply for taxable years beginning after December 31, 2016. As indicated in this section, taxpayers may rely on certain provisions of the proposed regulations for taxable years ending after December 31, 2013. In addition, several rules are proposed to apply for taxable years beginning after December 31, 2018. See the later section of this preamble entitled "*Effective/Applicability Date*" for information on the applicability date for the regulations on opt-out arrangements.

2. Eligibility

a. Applicable Taxpayers

To avoid repayments of advance credit payments for taxpayers who experience an unforeseen decline in income, the existing regulations provide that if an Exchange determines at enrollment that the taxpayer's household income will be at least 100 percent but will not exceed 400 percent of the applicable FPL, the taxpayer will not lose his or her status as an applicable taxpayer solely because household income for the year turns out to be below 100 percent of the applicable FPL. To reduce the likelihood that individuals who recklessly or intentionally provide inaccurate information to an Exchange will benefit from an Exchange determination, the proposed regulations provide that a taxpayer whose household income is below 100 percent of the FPL for the taxpayer's family size is not treated as an applicable taxpayer if, with intentional or reckless disregard for the facts, the taxpayer provided incorrect information to an Exchange for the year of coverage.

b. Exchange Determination of Ineligibility for Medicaid or CHIP

Similar to the rule for taxpayers who received the benefit of advance credit payments but ended the taxable year with household income below 100 percent of the applicable FPL, the existing regulations do not require a repayment of advance credit payments for taxpayers with household income within the range for eligibility for certain government-sponsored programs if an Exchange determined or considered

(within the meaning of 45 CFR 155.302(b)) the taxpayer or a member of the taxpayer's family to be ineligible for the program. To reduce the likelihood that individuals who recklessly or intentionally provide inaccurate information to an Exchange will benefit from an Exchange determination, the proposed regulations provide that an individual who was determined or considered by an Exchange to be ineligible for Medicaid, CHIP, or a similar program (such as a Basic Health Program) may be treated as eligible for coverage under the program if, with intentional or reckless disregard for the facts, the individual (or a person claiming a personal exemption for the individual) provided incorrect information to the Exchange.

c. Nonappropriated Fund Health Benefits Program

The existing regulations under section 36B provide that government-sponsored programs described in section 5000A(f)(1)(A), which include the Nonappropriated Fund Health Benefits Program of the Department of Defense, established under section 349 of the National Defense Authorization Act for Fiscal Year 1995 (Public Law 103-337; 10 U.S.C. 1587 note), are not eligible employer-sponsored plans. However, §1.5000A-2(c)(2) provides that, because the Nonappropriated Fund Health Benefits Program (Program) is offered by an instrumentality of the Department of Defense to its employees, the Program is an eligible employer-sponsored plan. The proposed regulations conform the section 36B regulations to the section 5000A regulations and provide that the Program is treated as an eligible employer-sponsored plan for purposes of determining if an individual is eligible for minimum essential coverage under section 36B. Thus, if coverage under the Program does not provide minimum value (under §1.36B-2(c)(3)(vi)) or is not affordable (under §36B-2(c)(3)(v)) for an individual who does not enroll in the coverage, he or she is not treated as eligible for minimum essential coverage under the Program for purposes of premium tax credit eligibility.

d. Eligibility for Employer-Sponsored Coverage for Months During a Plan Year

The existing regulations under section 36B provide that an individual is eligible for minimum essential coverage through an eligible employer-sponsored plan if the individual had the opportunity to enroll in the plan and the plan is affordable and provides minimum value. The Treasury Department and the IRS are aware that in some instances individuals may not be allowed an annual opportunity to decide whether to enroll in eligible employer-sponsored coverage. This lack of an annual opportunity to enroll in employer-sponsored coverage should not limit an individual's annual choice from available coverage options through the Marketplace with the possibility of benefitting from the premium tax credit. Thus, the proposed regulations clarify that if an individual declines to enroll in employer-sponsored coverage for a plan year and does not have the opportunity to enroll in that coverage for one or more succeeding plan years, for purposes of section 36B, the individual is treated as ineligible for that coverage for the succeeding plan year or years for which there is no enrollment opportunity.[3]

e. Excepted Benefits

Under section 36B and §1.36B-2(c)(3)(vii)(A), an individual is treated as eligible for minimum essential coverage through an eligible employer-sponsored plan if the individual actually enrolls in the coverage, even if the coverage is not affordable or does not provide minimum value. Although health coverage that consists solely of excepted benefits may be a group health plan and, therefore, is an eligible employer-sponsored plan under section 5000A(f)(2) and §1.5000A-2(c)(1), section 5000A(f)(3) provides that health coverage that consists solely of excepted benefits is not minimum essential coverage. Therefore, individuals enrolled in a plan consisting solely of excepted benefits still must obtain minimum essential coverage to satisfy the individual shared responsibility provision. The proposed regulations clarify that for purposes of section 36B an individual is considered eligible for coverage under an eligible employer-sponsored plan only if that plan is minimum essential coverage. Accordingly, an individual enrolled in or offered a plan consisting solely of excepted benefits is not denied the premium tax credit by virtue of that excepted

---

[2] Notice 2015-87 also provides that the Treasury Department and the IRS anticipate that the regulations generally will apply only for periods after the issuance of final regulations and that for the period prior to the applicability date of the final regulations, employers are not required to increase the amount of an employee's required contribution by the amount of an opt-out payment made available under an opt-out arrangement (other than a payment made available under a non-relief-eligible opt-out arrangement) for purposes of section 6056 (Form 1095-C), and an opt-out payment made available under an opt-out arrangement (other than a payment made available under a non-relief-eligible opt-out arrangement) will not be treated as increasing an employee's required contribution for purposes of any

potential consequences under section 4980H(b). For a discussion of non-relief-eligible opt-out arrangements see Notice 2015-87, Q&A-9.

[3] Note that for purposes of section 4980H, in general, an applicable large employer will not be treated as having made an offer of coverage to a full-time employee for a plan year if the employee does not have an effective opportunity to elect to enroll in the coverage at least once with respect to the plan year. For this purpose, a plan year must be twelve consecutive months, unless a short plan year of less than twelve consecutive months is permitted for a valid business purpose. For additional rules on the definition of "offer" and "plan year" under section 4980H, see §§54.4980H-1(a)(35), 54.4980H-4(b), and 54.4980H-5(b).

benefits offer or coverage. Taxpayers may rely on this rule for all taxable years beginning after December 31, 2013.

f. Opt-Out Arrangements and an Employee's Required Contribution

Sections 1.36B-2(c)(3)(v) and 1.5000A-3(e)(3)(ii)(A) provide that, in determining whether employer-sponsored coverage is affordable to an employee, an employee's required contribution for the coverage includes the amount by which the employee's salary would be reduced to enroll in the coverage.[4] If an employer makes an opt-out payment available to an employee, the choice between cash and health coverage presented by the opt-out arrangement is analogous to the cash-or-coverage choice presented by the option to pay for coverage by salary reduction. In both cases, the employee may purchase the employer-sponsored coverage only at the price of forgoing a specified amount of cash compensation that the employee would otherwise receive—salary, in the case of a salary reduction, or an equal amount of other compensation, in the case of an opt-out payment. Therefore, the economic cost to the employee of the employer-sponsored coverage is the same under both arrangements. Accordingly, the employee's required contribution generally should be determined similarly regardless of the type of payment that an employee must forgo.

Notice 2015-87 requested comments on the proposed treatment of opt-out arrangements outlined in Q&A-9 of that notice. Several commenters objected to the proposal that the amount of an available unconditional opt-out payment increases the employee's required contribution on the basis that forgoing opt-out payments as part of enrolling in coverage has not traditionally been viewed by employers or employees as economically equivalent to making a salary reduction election and that such a rule would discourage employers from making opt-out payments available. None of the commenters, however, offered a persuasive economic basis for distinguishing unconditional opt-out payments from other compensation that an employee must forgo to enroll in employer-sponsored coverage, such as a salary reduction. Because forgoing an unconditional opt-out payment is economically equivalent to forgoing salary pursuant to a salary reduction election, and because §§ 1.36B-2(c)(3)(v) and 1.5000A-3(e)(3)(ii)(A) provide that the employee's required contribution includes the amount of any salary reduction, the proposed regulations adopt the approach described in Notice 2015-87 for opt-out payments made available under unconditional opt-out arrangements and provide that the amount of an opt-out payment made available to the employee under an unconditional opt-out arrangement increases the employee's required contribution.[5]

Notice 2015-87 provides that, for periods prior to the applicability date of any final regulations, employers are not required to increase the amount of an employee's required contribution by amounts made available under an opt-out arrangement for purposes of section 4980H(b) or section 6056 (in particular Form 1095-C, *Employer-Provided Health Insurance Offer and Coverage*), except that, for periods after December 16, 2015, the employee's required contribution must include amounts made available under an unconditional opt-out arrangement that is adopted after December 16, 2015. However, Notice 2015-87 provided that, for this purpose, an opt-out arrangement will not be treated as adopted after December 16, 2015, under limited circumstances, including in cases in which a board, committee, or similar body or an authorized officer of the employer specifically adopted the opt-out arrangement before December 16, 2015.

Some commenters requested clarification that an unconditional opt-out arrangement that is required under the terms of a collective bargaining agreement in effect before December 16, 2015, should be treated as having been adopted prior to December 16, 2015, and that amounts made available under such an opt-out arrangement should not be included in an employee's required contribution for purposes of sections 4980H(b) or 6056 through the expiration of the collective bargaining agreement that provides for the opt-out arrangement. The Treasury Department and the IRS now clarify that, under Notice 2015-87, for purposes of sections 4980H(b) and 6056, an unconditional opt-out arrangement that is required under the terms of a collective bargaining agreement in effect before December 16, 2015, will be treated as having been adopted prior to December 16, 2015. In addi-

tion, until the later of (1) the beginning of the first plan year that begins following the expiration of the collective bargaining agreement in effect before December 16, 2015 (disregarding any extensions on or after December 16, 2015), or (2) the applicability date of these regulations with respect to sections 4980H and 6056, employers participating in the collective bargaining agreement are not required to increase the amount of an employee's required contribution by amounts made available under such an opt-out arrangement for purposes of sections 4980H(b) or 6056 (Form 1095-C). The Treasury Department and the IRS further adopt these commenters' request that this treatment apply to any successor employer adopting the opt-out arrangement before the expiration of the collective bargaining agreement in effect before December 16, 2015 (disregarding any extensions on or after December 16, 2015). Commenters raised the issue of whether other types of agreements covering employees may need a similar extension of the relief through the end of the agreement's term. The Treasury Department and the IRS request comments identifying the types of agreements raising this issue due to their similarity to collective bargaining agreements because, for example, the agreement is similar in scope to a collective bargaining agreement, binding on the parties involved for a multi-year period, and subject to a statutory or regulatory regime.

Several commenters suggested that, notwithstanding the proposal on unconditional opt-out arrangements, the amount of an opt-out payment made available should not increase an employee's required contribution if the opt-out payment is conditioned on the employee having minimum essential coverage through another source, such as a spouse's employer-sponsored plan. These commenters argued that the amount of such a conditional opt-out payment should not affect the affordability of an employer's offer of employer-sponsored coverage for an employee who does not satisfy the applicable condition because that employee is ineligible to receive the opt-out payment. Moreover, commenters argued that an employee who satisfies the condition (that is, who has alternative minimum essential coverage) is ineligible for the premium tax credit and does not need to determine the affordability of the employer's coverage offer. Thus, the commenters asserted, an amount made available under such an arrangement should be excluded from the required contribution.

While it is clear that the availability of an unconditional opt-out payment increases an individual's required contribution, the effect of the availability of a conditional opt-out payment is less obvious. In particular, under an unconditional opt-out arrangement, an individual who enrolls in the employer coverage loses the opt-out payment as a direct result of enrolling in the employer coverage. By contrast, in the case of a conditional opt-out arrangement, the availability of the opt-out payment may depend on information that is not generally available to the employer (who, if it is an applicable large employer, must report the required contribution under section 6056 and whose potential liability under section 4980H may be affected). Because of this difficulty of ascertaining which individuals could have met the condition and, therefore, would actually forgo the opt-out payment when enrolling in employer-sponsored coverage, it generally is not feasible to have a rule under which the required contribution perfectly captures the cost of coverage for each specific individual offered a conditional opt-out payment.

Similarly, another way to view opt-out payments that are conditioned on alternative coverage is that, rather than raising the cost to the employee of the employer's coverage, they reduce the cost to the employee of the alternative coverage. However, because employers generally do not have information about the existence and cost of other options available to the individual, it is not practical to take into account any offer of coverage other than the offer made by the employer in determining the required contribution with respect to the employer coverage (that is, the coverage that the employee must decline to receive the opt-out payment).

While commenters indicated that the required contribution with respect to the employer coverage does not matter for an individual enrolled in any other minimum essential coverage because the individual would be ineligible for the premium tax credit, this statement is not true if the other coverage is individual market coverage. In particular, while enrollment in most types of minimum essential coverage results in an individual being ineligible for a premium tax credit, that is not the

---

[4] Section 5000A(e)(1)(C) and § 1.5000A-3(e)(3)(ii)(B) provide that, for purposes of the individual shared responsibility provision, the required contribution for individuals eligible to enroll in employer coverage because of a relationship to an employee (related individual) is the portion of the annual premium that the employee would pay (whether through salary reduction or otherwise) for the lowest cost family coverage that would cover the employee and all related individuals who are included in the employee's family and are not otherwise exempt under § 1.5000A-3.

[5] To distinguish between opt-out payments and employer contributions to a section 125 cafeteria plan (which in some cases could be paid in cash to an employee who declines coverage in the health plan or other available benefits), the proposed regulations further clarify that an amount provided as an employer contribution to a cafeteria plan and that may be used by the employee to purchase minimum essential coverage is not an opt-out payment, whether or not the employee may receive the amount as a taxable benefit. This provision clarifies that the effect on an employee's required contribution of employer contributions to a cafeteria plan is determined under § 1.36B-2(c)(3)(v)(A)(6) rather than § 1.36B-2(c)(3)(v)(A)(7).

case for coverage in the individual market. Moreover, for individual market coverage offered through a Marketplace, the required contribution with respect to the employer coverage frequently will be relevant in determining whether the individual is eligible for a premium tax credit. In such cases, as in the case of an unconditional opt-out payment, the availability of a conditional opt-out payment effectively increases the cost to the individual of enrolling in the employer coverage (at least relative to Marketplace coverage).

Further, an opt-out arrangement that is conditioned on an employee's ability to obtain other coverage (if that coverage can be coverage in the individual market, whether inside or outside the Marketplace) does not generally raise the issues described earlier in this section of the preamble regarding the difficulty of ascertaining which individuals could meet the condition under a conditional opt-out arrangement. This is because generally all individuals are able to obtain coverage in the individual market, pursuant to the guaranteed issue requirements in section 2702 of the PHS Act. Thus, in the sense that all individuals can satisfy the applicable condition, such an opt-out arrangement is similar to an unconditional opt-out arrangement.

In an effort to provide a workable rule that balances these competing concerns, the proposed regulations provide that amounts made available under conditional opt-out arrangements are disregarded in determining the required contribution if the arrangement satisfies certain conditions (an "eligible opt-out arrangement"), but otherwise the amounts are taken into account. The proposed regulations define an "eligible opt-out arrangement" as an arrangement under which the employee's right to receive the opt-out payment is conditioned on (1) the employee declining to enroll in the employer-sponsored coverage and (2) the employee providing reasonable evidence that the employee and all other individuals for whom the employee reasonably expects to claim a personal exemption deduction for the taxable year or years that begin or end in or with the employer's plan year to which the opt-out arrangement applies (employee's expected tax family) have or will have minimum essential coverage (other than coverage in the individual market, whether or not obtained through the Marketplace) during the period of coverage to which the opt-out arrangement applies. For example, if an employee's expected tax family consists of the employee, the employee's spouse, and two children, the employee would meet this requirement by providing reasonable evidence that the employee, the employee's spouse, and the two children, will have coverage under the group health plan of the spouse's employer for the period to which the opt-out arrangement applies.[6]

The Treasury Department and the IRS invite comments on this proposed rule, including suggestions for other workable rules that result in the required contribution more accurately reflecting the individual's cost of coverage while minimizing undesirable consequences and incentives.

For purposes of the proposed eligible opt-out arrangement rule, reasonable evidence of alternative coverage includes the employee's attestation that the employee and all other members of the employee's expected tax family, if any, have or will have minimum essential coverage (other than coverage in the individual market, whether or not obtained through the Marketplace) or other reasonable evidence. Notwithstanding the evidence of alternative coverage required under the arrangement, to qualify as an eligible opt-out arrangement, the arrangement must also provide that any opt-out payment will not be made (and the payment must not in fact be made) if the employer knows or has reason to know that the employee or any other member of the employee's expected tax family does not have (or will not have) the required alternative coverage. An eligible opt-out arrangement must also require that the evidence of coverage be provided no less frequently than every plan year to which the eligible opt-out arrangement applies, and that the evidence be provided no earlier than a reasonable period before the commencement of the period of coverage to which the eligible opt-out arrangement applies. Obtaining the reasonable evidence (such as an attestation) as part of the regular annual open enrollment period that occurs within a few months before the commencement of the next plan year of employer-sponsored coverage meets this reasonable period requirement. Alternatively, the eligible opt-out arrangement would be permitted to require evidence of alternative coverage to be provided later, such as after the plan year starts, which would enable the employer to require evidence that the em-

ployee and other members of the employee's expected tax family have already obtained the alternative coverage.

Commenters on Notice 2015-87 generally stated that typical conditions under an opt-out arrangement include a requirement that the employee have alternative coverage through employer-sponsored coverage of a spouse or another relative, such as a parent. Provided that, as required under the opt-out arrangement, the employee provided reasonable evidence of this alternative coverage for the employee and the other members of the employee's expected tax family, and met the related conditions described in this preamble, these types of opt-out arrangements would be eligible opt-out arrangements, and opt-out payments made available under such arrangements would not increase the employee's required contribution.

The Treasury Department and the IRS did not receive comments on opt-out arrangements indicating that the meaningful conditions imposed include any requirement other than one relating to alternative coverage. Therefore, the proposed rules do not address other opt-out conditions and would not treat an opt-out arrangement based on other conditions as an eligible opt-out arrangement. However, the Treasury Department and the IRS invite comments on whether opt-out payments are made subject to additional types of conditions in some cases, whether those types of conditions should be addressed in further guidance, and, if so, how.

One commenter suggested that, if opt-out payments conditioned on alternative coverage are not included in an employee's required contribution, rules will be needed for cases in which an employee receives an opt-out payment and that employee's alternative coverage subsequently terminates. The commenter suggested that, in that case, the termination of the alternative coverage should have no impact on the determination of the employee's required contribution for the employer-sponsored coverage from which the employee opted out. In response, under the proposed regulations, provided that the reasonable evidence requirement is met, the amount of an opt-out payment made available under an eligible opt-out arrangement may continue to be excluded from the employee's required contribution for the remainder of the period of coverage to which the opt-out payment originally applied. The opt-out payment may be excluded for this period even if the alternative coverage subsequently terminates for the employee or any other member of the employee's expected tax family, regardless of whether the opt-out payment is required to be adjusted or terminated due to the loss of alternative coverage, and regardless of whether the employee is required to provide notice of the loss of alternative coverage to the employer.

The Treasury Department and the IRS are aware that the way in which opt-out arrangements affect the calculation of affordability is important not only to an employee and the other members of the employee's expected tax family in determining whether they may be eligible for a premium tax credit or whether an individual may be exempt under the individual shared responsibility provisions, but also to an employer subject to the employer shared responsibility provisions under section 4980H in determining whether the employer may be subject to an assessable payment under section 4980H(b). An employer subject to the employer shared responsibility provisions will be subject to a payment under section 4980H(b) only with respect to a full-time employee who receives a premium tax credit, and an employee will not be eligible for the premium tax credit if the employer's offer of coverage was affordable and provided minimum value.[7] Commenters expressed concern that if the rule adopted for conditional opt-outs required an employee to provide reasonable evidence that the employee has or will have minimum essential coverage, the employer may not know whether the employee is being truthful and has obtained (or will obtain) such coverage, or how long such coverage will continue. Under these proposed regulations, however, the employee's required contribution will not be increased by an opt-out payment made available under an eligible opt-out arrangement, provided that the arrangement provides that the employer makes the payment only if the employee provides reasonable evidence of alternative coverage and the employer does not know or have reason to know that the employee or any other member of the employee's expected tax family fails or will fail to meet the requirement to have alternative coverage (other than individual market coverage, whether or not obtained through the Marketplace).

---

[6] The Treasury Department and the IRS note that if an opt-out payment is conditioned on an employee obtaining individual market coverage, that opt-out arrangement could act as a reimbursement arrangement for some or all of the employee's premium for that individual market coverage; therefore, the opt-out arrangement could operate as an employer payment plan as discussed in Notice 2015-87, Notice 2015-17, 2015-14 I.R.B. 845, and Notice

2013-54, 2013-40 I.R.B. 287. Nothing in these proposed regulations is intended to affect the prior guidance on employer payment plans.

[7] The affordability rules under section 36B, including rules regarding opt-out payments, may also affect the application of section 4980H(a) because one element that is required for an applicable large employer to be subject to an assessable payment under section 4980H(a) is that at least one full-time employee must receive the premium tax credit.

Some commenters requested exceptions for special circumstances from the general rule that the employee's required contribution is increased by the amount of an opt-out payment made available. These circumstances include (1) conditional opt-out payments that are required under the terms of a collective bargaining agreement and (2) opt-out payments that are below a de minimis amount. Regarding opt-out arrangements contained in collective bargaining agreements, the Treasury Department and the IRS anticipate that the proposed treatment of eligible opt-out arrangements, generally, will address the concerns raised in the comments. Accordingly, the Treasury Department and the IRS do not propose to provide a permanent exception for opt-out arrangements provided under collective bargaining agreements. Earlier in this section of the preamble, however, the Treasury Department and the IRS clarify and expand the transition relief provided under Notice 2015-87 for opt-out arrangements provided under collective bargaining agreements in effect before December 16, 2015, As for an exception for de minimis amounts, the Treasury Department and the IRS decline to adopt such an exception because there is neither a statutory nor an economic basis for establishing a de minimis threshold under which an unconditional opt-out payment would be excluded from the employee's required contribution.

g. Effective Date of Eligibility for Minimum Essential Coverage When Advance Credit Payments Discontinuance Is Delayed

Section 36B and the regulations under section 36B provide that an individual who may enroll in minimum essential coverage outside the Marketplace (other than individual market coverage) for a month is generally not allowed a premium tax credit for that month. Consequently, individuals enrolled in a qualified health plan with advance credit payments must return to the Exchange to report eligibility for other minimum essential coverage so the Exchange can discontinue the advance credit payments for Marketplace coverage. Similarly, individuals enrolled in a qualified health plan with advance credit payments may be determined eligible for coverage under a government-sponsored program, such as Medicaid. In some cases, individuals may inform the Exchange of their opportunity to enroll in other minimum essential coverage or receive approval for coverage under a government-sponsored program after the time for which the Exchange can discontinue advance credit payments for the next month. Because taxpayers should generally not have to repay the advance credit payments for that next month in these circumstances, the proposed regulations provide a rule for situations in which an Exchange's discontinuance of advance credit payments is delayed. Under the proposed regulations, if an individual who is enrolled in a qualified health plan for which advance credit payments are made informs the Exchange that the individual is or will soon be eligible for other minimum essential coverage and that advance credit payments should be discontinued, but the Exchange does not discontinue advance credit payments for the first calendar month beginning after the month the individual notifies the Exchange, the individual is treated as eligible for the other minimum essential coverage no earlier than the first day of the second calendar month beginning after the first month the individual may enroll in the other minimum essential coverage. Similarly, if a determination is made that an individual is eligible for Medicaid or CHIP but advance credit payments are not discontinued for the first calendar month beginning after the eligibility determination, the individual is treated as eligible for Medicaid or CHIP no earlier than the first day of the second calendar month beginning after the determination. Taxpayers may rely on this rule for all taxable years beginning after December 31, 2013.

3. Premium Assistance Amount

a. Payment of Taxpayer's Share of Premiums for Advance Credit Payments Following Appeal Determinations

Under § 1.36B-3(c)(1)(ii), a month in which an individual who is enrolled in a qualified health plan is a coverage month for the individual only if the taxpayer's share of the premium for the individual's coverage for the month is paid by the unextended due date of the taxpayer's income tax return for the year of coverage, or the premium is fully paid by advance credit payments.

One of the functions of an Exchange is to make determinations as to whether an individual who enrolls in a qualified health plan is eligible for advance credit payments for the coverage. If an Exchange determines that the individual is not eligible for advance credit payments, the individual may appeal that decision. An individual who is initially determined ineligible for advance credit payments, does not enroll in a qualified health plan under the contested determination, and is later determined to be eligible for advance credit payments through the appeals process, may elect to be retroactively enrolled in a health plan through the Exchange. In that case, the individual is treated as having

been enrolled in the qualified health plan from the date on which the individual would have enrolled had he or she initially been determined eligible for advance credit payments. If retroactively enrolled, the deadline for paying premiums for the retroactive coverage may be after the unextended due date for filing an income tax return for the year of coverage. Consequently, the proposed regulations provide that a taxpayer who is eligible for advance credit payments pursuant to an eligibility appeal for a member of the taxpayer's coverage family who, based on the appeals decision, retroactively enrolls in a qualified health plan, is considered to have met the requirement in § 1.36B-3(c)(1)(ii) for a month if the taxpayer pays the taxpayer's share of the premium for coverage under the plan for the month on or before the 120th day following the date of the appeals decision. Taxpayers may rely on this rule for all taxable years beginning after December 31, 2013.

b. Month That Coverage Is Terminated

Section 1.36B-3(d)(2) provides that if a qualified health plan is terminated before the last day of a month, the premium assistance amount for the month is the lesser of the enrollment premiums for the month (reduced by any amounts that were refunded), or the excess of the benchmark plan premium for a full month of coverage over the full contribution amount for the month. Section 1.36B-3(c)(2) provides that an individual whose enrollment in a qualified health plan is effective on the date of the individual's birth or adoption, or placement for foster care, or upon the effective date of a court order, is treated as enrolled as of the first day of the month and, therefore, the month of enrollment may be a coverage month. The regulations, however, do not expressly address how the premium assistance amount is computed when a covered individual disenrolls before the last day of a month but the plan is not terminated because other individuals remain enrolled. For purposes of the premium tax credit, the premium assistance amount for an individual who is not enrolled for an entire month should be the same regardless of the circumstances causing the partial-month coverage, provided that the individual was enrolled, or is treated as enrolled, as of the first day of the month (that is, so long as the month is a coverage month). Accordingly, to provide consistency for all individuals who have a coverage month that is less than a full calendar month, the proposed regulations provide that the premium assistance amount for a month is the lesser of the enrollment premiums for the month (reduced by any amounts that were refunded), or the excess of the benchmark plan premium over the contribution amount for the month. Taxpayers may rely on this rule for all taxable years beginning after December 31, 2013.

4. Benchmark Plan Premium

a. Effective/Applicability Date of Benchmark Plan Rules

The rules relating to the benchmark plan in this section are proposed to apply for taxable years beginning after December 31, 2018.

b. Pediatric Dental Benefits

Under section 1311(d)(2)(B) of the Affordable Care Act, only qualified health plans, including stand-alone dental plans offering pediatric dental benefits, may be offered through a Marketplace. In general, a qualified health plan is required to provide coverage for all ten essential health benefits described in section 1302(b) of the Affordable Care Act, including pediatric dental coverage. However, under section 1302(b)(4)(F), a plan that does not provide pediatric dental benefits may nonetheless be a qualified health plan if it covers each essential health benefit described in section 1302(b) other than pediatric dental benefits and if it is offered through a Marketplace in which a stand-alone dental plan offering pediatric dental benefits is offered as well.

Section 36B(b)(3)(E) and § 1.36B-3(k) provide that if an individual enrolls in both a qualified health plan and a stand-alone dental plan, the portion of the premium for the stand-alone dental plan properly allocable to pediatric dental benefits is treated as a premium payable for the individual's qualified health plan. Thus, in determining a taxpayer's premium assistance amount for a month in which a member of the taxpayer's coverage family is enrolled in a stand-alone dental plan, the taxpayer's enrollment premium includes the portion of the premium for the stand-alone dental plan allocable to pediatric dental benefits. The existing regulations do not provide a similar adjustment for the taxpayer's applicable benchmark plan premium to reflect the cost of pediatric dental benefits in cases where the second-lowest cost silver plan does not provide pediatric dental benefits.

Section 36B(b)(3)(B) provides that the applicable benchmark plan with respect to a taxpayer is the second lowest cost silver plan available through the applicable Marketplace that provides "self-only coverage" or "family coverage," depending generally on whether the coverage family includes one or more individuals. Neither the Code nor the

Affordable Care Act defines the terms "self-only coverage" or "family coverage" for this purpose.

Under the existing regulations, the references in section 36B(b)(3)(B) to plans that provide self-only coverage and family coverage are interpreted to refer to all qualified health plans offered through the applicable Marketplace, regardless of whether the coverage offered by those plans includes all ten essential health benefits. Because qualified health plans that do not offer pediatric dental benefits tend to be cheaper than qualified health plans that cover all ten essential health benefits, the second lowest-cost silver plan (and therefore the premium tax credit) for taxpayers purchasing coverage through a Marketplace in which stand-alone dental plans are offered is likely to not account for the cost of obtaining pediatric dental coverage.

The Treasury Department and the IRS believe that the current rule frustrates the statute's goal of making coverage that provides the essential health benefits affordable to individuals eligible for the premium tax credit. Accordingly, the proposed regulations reflect a modification in the interpretation of the terms "self-only coverage" and "family coverage" in section 36B(b)(3)(B) to refer to coverage that provides each of the essential health benefits described in section 1302(b) of the Affordable Care Act. This coverage may be obtained from either a qualified health plan alone or from a qualified health plan in combination with a stand-alone dental plan. In particular, self-only coverage refers to coverage obtained from such plans where the coverage family is a single individual. Similarly, family coverage refers to coverage obtained from such plans where the coverage family includes more than one individual.

Consistent with this interpretation, the proposed regulations provide that for taxable years beginning after December 31, 2018, if an Exchange offers one or more silver-level qualified health plans that do not cover pediatric dental benefits, the applicable benchmark plan is determined by ranking (1) the premiums for the silver-level qualified health plans that include pediatric dental benefits offered by the Exchange and (2) the aggregate of the premiums for the silver-level qualified health plans offered by the Exchange that do not include pediatric dental benefits plus the portion of the premium allocable to pediatric dental benefits for stand-alone dental plans offered by the Exchange. In constructing this ranking, the premium for the lowest-cost silver plan that does not include pediatric dental benefits is added to the lowest-cost portion of the premium for a stand-alone dental plan that is allocable to pediatric dental benefits, and similarly, the premium for the second lowest-cost silver plan that does not include pediatric dental benefits is added to the second-lowest-cost portion of the premium for a stand-alone dental plan that is allocable to pediatric dental benefits. The second lowest-cost amount from this combined ranking is the taxpayer's applicable benchmark plan premium. [Officially corrected 9/14/16 (81 FR 63154).]

c. Coverage Family Members Residing in Different Locations

Under § 1.36B-3(f), a taxpayer's applicable benchmark plan is the second lowest cost silver plan offered at the time a taxpayer or family member enrolls in a qualified health plan through the Exchange for the rating area where the taxpayer resides. Under § 1.36B-3(f)(4), if members of a taxpayer's family reside in different states and enroll in separate qualified health plans, the premium for the taxpayer's applicable benchmark plan is the sum of the premiums for the applicable benchmark plans for each group of family members living in the same state.

Referring to the residence of the taxpayer to establish the cost for a benchmark health plan is appropriate when the taxpayer and all members of the taxpayer's coverage family live in the same location because it reflects the cost of available coverage for the taxpayer's coverage family. However, because premiums and plan availability may vary based on location, the existing rule for a taxpayer whose family members reside in different locations in the same state may not accurately reflect the cost of available coverage. In addition, the rules for calculating the premium tax credit should operate the same for families residing in multiple locations within a state and families residing in multiple states. Accordingly, § 1.36B-3(f)(4) of the proposed regulations provides that if a taxpayer's coverage family members reside in multiple locations, whether within the same state or in different states, the taxpayer's benchmark plan is determined based on the cost of available coverage in the locations where members of the taxpayer's coverage family reside. In particular, if members of a taxpayer's coverage family reside in different locations, the taxpayer's benchmark plan premium is the sum of the premiums for the applicable benchmark plans for each group of coverage family members residing in different locations, based on the plans offered to the group through the Exchange for the rating area where the group resides. If all members of a taxpayer's coverage family reside in a single location that is different from where

the taxpayer resides, the taxpayer's benchmark plan premium is the premium for the applicable benchmark plan for the coverage family, based on the plans offered to the taxpayer's coverage family through the Exchange for the rating area where the coverage family resides.

d. Aggregation of Silver-Level Policies

Section 1.36B-3(f)(3) provides that if one or more silver-level plans offered through an Exchange do not cover all members of a taxpayer's coverage family under one policy (for example, because an issuer will not cover a taxpayer's dependent parent on the same policy the taxpayer enrolls in), the premium for the applicable benchmark plan may be the premium for a single policy or for more than one policy, whichever is the second lowest-cost silver option. This rule does not specify which combinations of policies must be taken into account for this purpose, suggesting that all such combinations must be considered, which is unduly complex for taxpayers, difficult for Exchanges to implement, and difficult for the IRS to administer. Accordingly, to clarify and simplify the benchmark premium determination for situations in which a silver-level plan does not cover all the members of a taxpayer's coverage family under one policy, the proposed regulations delete the existing rule and provide a new rule in its place.

Under the proposed regulations, if a silver-level plan offers coverage to all members of a taxpayer's coverage family who reside in the same location under a single policy, the plan premium taken into account for purposes of determining the applicable benchmark plan is the premium for that policy. In contrast, if a silver-level plan would require multiple policies to cover all members of a taxpayer's coverage family who reside in the same location, the plan premium taken into account for purposes of determining the applicable benchmark plan is the sum of the premiums for self-only policies under the plan for each member of the coverage family who resides in the same location. Under the proposed regulations, similar rules would apply to the portion of premiums for stand-alone dental plans allocable to pediatric dental coverage taken into account for purposes of determining the premium for a taxpayer's applicable benchmark plan.

Comments are requested on the rule contained in the proposed regulations, as well as on an alternative rule under which the plan premium taken into account for purposes of determining a taxpayer's applicable benchmark plan would be equal to the sum of the self-only policies under a plan for each member of the taxpayer's coverage family, regardless of whether all members of the taxpayer's coverage family could be covered under a single policy under the plan.

e. Silver-Level Plan Not Available for Enrollment

Section 1.36B-3(f)(5) provides that if a qualified health plan is closed to enrollment for a taxpayer or a member of the taxpayer's coverage family, that plan is disregarded in determining the taxpayer's applicable benchmark plan. Similarly, § 1.36B-3(f)(6) provides that a plan that is the applicable benchmark plan for a taxpayer does not cease to be the applicable benchmark plan solely because the plan or a lower cost plan terminates or closes to enrollment during the taxable year. Because stand-alone dental plans are considered in determining a taxpayer's applicable benchmark plan under the proposed regulations, the proposed regulations provide consistency in the treatment of qualified health plans and stand-alone dental plans that are closed to enrollment or that terminate during the taxable year.

f. Only One Silver-Level Plan Offered to the Coverage Family

In general, § 1.36B-3(f)(1) provides that a taxpayer's applicable benchmark plan is the second lowest-cost silver-level plan available to the taxpayer for self-only or family coverage. However, for taxpayers who reside in certain locations, only one silver-level plan providing such coverage may be available. Section 1.36B-3(f)(8) of the proposed regulations clarifies that if there is only one silver-level qualified health plan offered through the Exchange that would cover all members of the taxpayer's coverage family (whether under one policy or multiple policies), that silver-level plan is used for purposes of the taxpayer's applicable benchmark plan. Similarly, if there is only one stand-alone dental plan offered through the Exchange that would cover all members of the taxpayer's coverage family (whether under one policy or multiple policies), the portion of the premium of that plan that is allocable to pediatric dental benefits is used for purposes of determining the taxpayer's applicable benchmark plan.

5. Reconciliation of Advance Credit Payments

Section 301.6011-8 provides that a taxpayer who receives the benefit of advance credit payments must file an income tax return for that taxable year on or before the due date for the return (including extensions of time for filing) and reconcile the advance credit payments. In addition, the regulations under section 36B provide that if advance credit payments are made for coverage of an individual for whom no taxpayer claims a personal exemption deduction, the taxpayer who attests to the Exchange to the intention to claim a personal exemption deduction for the individual as part of the determination that the taxpayer is eligible for advance credit payments for coverage of the individual must reconcile the advance credit payments.

Questions have been raised concerning how these two rules apply, and consequently which individual must reconcile advance credit payments, when a taxpayer (a parent, for example) attests that he or she will claim a personal exemption deduction for an individual, the advance payments are made with respect to coverage for the individual, the taxpayer does not claim a personal exemption deduction for the individual, and the individual does not file a tax return for the year. The intent of the existing regulation is that the taxpayer, not the individual for whose coverage advance credit payments were made, must reconcile the advance credit payments in situations in which a taxpayer attests to the intention to claim a personal exemption for the individual and no one claims a personal exemption deduction for the individual. Consequently, the proposed regulations clarify that if advance credit payments are made for coverage of an individual for whom no taxpayer claims a personal exemption deduction, the taxpayer who attests to the Exchange to the intention to claim a personal exemption deduction for the individual, not the individual for whose coverage the advance credit payments were made, must file a tax return and reconcile the advance credit payments.

6. Information Reporting

a. Two or More Families Enrolled in Single Qualified Health Plan

Section 1.36B-3(h) provides that if a qualified health plan covers more than one family under a single policy (for example, a plan covers a taxpayer and the taxpayer's child who is 25 and not a dependent of the taxpayer), the premium tax credit is computed for each applicable taxpayer covered by the plan. In addition, in computing the tax credit for each taxpayer, premiums for the qualified health plan the taxpayers purchase (the enrollment premiums) are allocated to each taxpayer in proportion to the premiums for each taxpayer's applicable benchmark plan.

The existing regulations provide that the Exchange must report the enrollment premiums for each family, but do not specify the manner in which the Exchange must divide the enrollment premiums among the families enrolled in the policy. Consequently, the proposed regulations clarify that when multiple families enroll in a single qualified health plan and advance credit payments are made for the coverage, the enrollment premiums reported by the Exchange for each family is the family's allocable share of the enrollment premiums, which is based on the proportion of each family's applicable benchmark plan premium.

b. Partial Months of Enrollment

The existing regulations do not specify how the enrollment premiums and benchmark plan premiums are reported in cases in which one or more individuals is enrolled or disenrolled in coverage mid-month. To ensure that this reporting is consistent with the rules for calculating the premium assistance amounts for partial months of coverage, the proposed regulations provide that, if an individual is enrolled in a qualified health plan after the first day of a month, generally no value should be reported for the individual's enrollment premium or benchmark plan premium for that month. However, if an individual's coverage in a qualified health plan is terminated before the last day of a month, or an individual is enrolled in coverage after the first day of a month and the coverage is effective on the date of the individual's birth, adoption, or placement for adoption or in foster care, or on the effective date of a court order, an Exchange must report the premium for the applicable benchmark plan for a full month of coverage (excluding the premium allocated to benefits in excess of essential health benefits). In addition, the proposed regulations provide that the Exchange must report the enrollment premiums for the month (excluding the premium allocated to benefits in excess of essential health benefits), reduced by any amount that was refunded due to the plan's termination.

c. Use of Electronic Media

Section 301.6011-2(b) provides that if the use of certain forms, including the Form 1095 series, is required by the applicable regulations or

revenue procedures for the purpose of making an information return, the information required by the form must be submitted on magnetic media. Form 1095-A should not have been included in §301.6011-2 because Form 1095-A is not an information return. Consequently, the proposed regulations replace the general reference in §301.6011-2(b) to the forms in the 1095 series with specific references to Forms 1095-B and 1095-C, but not Form 1095-A.

Effective/Applicability Date

Except as otherwise provided, these regulations are proposed to apply for taxable years beginning after December 31, 2016. In addition, taxpayers may rely on certain provisions of the proposed regulations for taxable years ending after December 31, 2013, as indicated earlier in this preamble. In addition, rules relating to the benchmark plan described in section 4 of this preamble are proposed to apply for taxable years beginning after December 31, 2018.

Notwithstanding the proposed applicability date, nothing in the proposed regulations is intended to limit any relief for opt-out arrangements provided in Notice 2015-87, Q&A 9, or in section 2.f of the preamble to these proposed regulations (regarding opt-out arrangements provided for in collective bargaining agreements). For purposes of sections 36B and 5000A, although under the proposed regulations amounts made available under an eligible opt-out arrangement are not added to an employee's required contribution, for periods before the final regulations are applicable and, if later, through the end of the most recent plan year beginning before January 1, 2017, an individual who can demonstrate that he or she meets the condition for an opt-out payment under an eligible opt-out arrangement is permitted to treat the opt-out payment as increasing the employee's required contribution.[8]

For purposes of the consequences of these regulations under sections 4980H and 6056 (and in particular Form 1095-C), the regulations regarding opt-out arrangements are proposed to be first applicable for plan years beginning on or after January 1, 2017,[9] and for the period prior to this applicability date employers are not required to increase the amount of an employee's required contribution by the amount of an opt-out payment made available under an opt-out arrangement (other than a payment made available under a non-relief-eligible opt-out arrangement[10]). See also section 2.f of this preamble for transition relief provided under Notice 2015-87 as clarified and expanded for opt-out arrangements contained in collective bargaining agreements in effect before December 16, 2015. See §601.601(d)(2)(ii)(b).

Special Analyses

Certain IRS regulations, including this one, are exempt from the requirements of Executive Order 12866, as supplemented and reaffirmed by Executive Order 13563. Therefore, a regulatory assessment is not required. It has also been determined that section 553(b) of the Administrative Procedure Act (5 U.S.C. chapter 5) does not apply to these regulations.

It is hereby certified that these regulations will not have a significant economic impact on a substantial number of small entities. This certification is based on the fact that the information collection required under these regulations is imposed under section 36B. Consistent with the statute, the proposed regulations require a person that provides minimum essential coverage to an individual to file a return with the IRS reporting certain information and to furnish a statement to the responsible individual who enrolled an individual or family in the coverage. These regulations merely provide the method of filing and furnishing returns and statements under section 36B. Moreover, the proposed regulations attempt to minimize the burden associated with this collection of information by limiting reporting to the information that the IRS requires to verify minimum essential coverage and administer tax credits.

Based on these facts, a Regulatory Flexibility Analysis under the Regulatory Flexibility Act (5 U.S.C. chapter 6) is not required.

Pursuant to section 7805(f) of the Code, this notice of proposed rulemaking has been submitted to the Chief Counsel for Advocacy of the Small Business Administration for comment on its impact on small business.

---

[8] For periods prior to the applicability date, an individual who cannot demonstrate that he or she meets the condition for an opt-out payment under an eligible opt-out arrangement is not permitted to treat the opt-out payment as increasing the employee's required contribution.

[9] Notice 2015-87, Q&A 9 provides that the Treasury Department and the IRS anticipate that the regulations on opt-out arrangements generally will apply only for periods after the

issuance of final regulations. The Treasury Department and the IRS anticipate finalizing these regulations prior to the end of 2016.

[10] For a discussion of non-relief-eligible opt-out arrangements see Notice 2015-87, Q&A-9.

Comments and Requests for Public Hearing

Before these proposed regulations are adopted as final regulations, consideration will be given to any comments that are submitted timely to the IRS as prescribed in this preamble under the *ADDRESSES* heading. Treasury and the IRS request comments on all aspects of the proposed rules. All comments will be available at *www.regulations.gov* or upon request. A public hearing will be scheduled if requested in writing by any person who timely submits written comments. If a public hearing is scheduled, notice of the date, time, and place for the hearing will be published in the **Federal Register**.

Drafting Information

The principal authors of these proposed regulations are Shareen S. Pflanz and Stephen J. Toomey of the Office of Associate Chief Counsel (Income Tax and Accounting). However, other personnel from the IRS and the Treasury Department participated in the development of the regulations.

List of Subjects

26 CFR Part 1

Income taxes, Reporting and recordkeeping requirements.

26 CFR Part 301

Employment taxes, Estate taxes, Excise taxes, Gift taxes, Income taxes, Penalties, Reporting and recordkeeping requirements.

Proposed Amendments to the Regulations

Accordingly, 26 CFR parts 1 and 301 are proposed to be amended as follows:

PART 1—INCOME TAXES

■ *Paragraph 1.* The authority citation for part 1 is amended by adding entries in numerical order to read in part as follows:

Authority: 26 U.S.C. 7805 * * *

■ *Par. 2.* Section 1.36B-0 is amended by:

■ 1. Adding the entries for § § 1.36B-2(b)(6)(i) and (ii).

■ 2. Adding entries for § § 1.36B-2(c)(3)(v)(A)(*7*), (v)(A)(*7*)(*i*), (*ii*), (*iii*), (*iii*)(*A*), (*iii*)(*B*), (*iii*)(*C*), and (*iv*).

■ 3. Redesignating entry for § 1.36B-2(c)(4) as (c)(5) and adding new entries for § 1.36B-2(c)(4), (c)(4)(i), (ii), (ii)(A), and (ii)(B).

■ 4. Redesignating entry for § 1.36B-3(c)(4) as (c)(5) and adding a new entry for § 1.36B-3(c)(4).

■ 5. Revising entries for § § 1.36B-3(d)(1) and (d)(2).

■ 6. Revising entries for § § 1.36B-3(f)(3), (4), (5), (6), and (7).

■ 7. Adding entries for § § 1.36B-3(f)(8), (9), and (10).

■ 8. Adding entries for § § 1.36B-5(c)(3)(iii).

The revisions and additions read as follows:

§ 1.36B-0 Table of contents.

* * * * *

§ 1.36B-2 Eligibility for premium tax credit.

* * * * *

(b) * * *

(6) * * *

(i) In general.

(ii) Exceptions.

* * * * *

(c) * * *

(3) * * *

(v) * * *

(A) * * *

(*7*) Opt-out arrangements.

(*i*) In general.

(*ii*) Eligible opt-out arrangements.

(*iii*) Definitions.

(*A*) Opt-out payment.

(*B*) Opt-out arrangement.

(*C*) Eligible opt-out arrangement.

(*iv*) Examples.

* * * * *

(4) Special eligibility rules.

(i) Related individuals not claimed as a personal exemption deduction.

(ii) Exchange unable to discontinue advance credit payments.

(A) In general.

(B) Medicaid or CHIP.

* * * * *

§ 1.36B-3 Computing the premium assistance credit amount.

* * * * *

(c) * * *

(4) Appeals of coverage eligibility.

(d) * * *

(1) Premium assistance amount.

(2) Examples.

* * * * *

(f) * * *

(3) Silver-level plan not covering pediatric dental benefits.

(4) Family members residing in different locations.

(5) Single or multiple policies needed to cover the family.

(i) Policy covering a taxpayer's family.

(ii) Policy not covering a taxpayer's family.

(6) Plan not available for enrollment.

(7) Benchmark plan terminates or closes to enrollment during the year.

(8) Only one silver-level plan offered to the coverage family.

(9) Examples. [Officially corrected 9/14/16 (81 FR 63154).]

* * * * *

(m) [Reserved]. [Added by official corrections 9/14/16 (81 FR 63154).]

(n) Effective/applicability date. [Added by official corrections 9/14/16 (81 FR 63154).]

* * * * *

§ 1.36B-5 Information reporting by Exchanges.

* * * * *

(c) * * *

(3) * * *

(iii) Partial month of coverage.

(A) In general.

(B) Certain mid-month enrollments.

* * * * *

■ *Par. 3.* Section 1.36B-1 is amended by revising paragraphs (l), (m), and (o) to read as follows:

§ 1.36B-1 Premium tax credit definitions.

* * * * *

(l) *Self-only coverage.* Self-only coverage means health insurance that covers one individual and provides coverage for the essential health benefits as defined in section 1302(b)(1) of the Affordable Care Act (42 U.S.C. 18022).

(m) *Family coverage.* Family coverage means health insurance that covers more than one individual and provides coverage for the essential health benefits as defined in section 1302(b)(1) of the Affordable Care Act (42 U.S.C. 18022).

* * * * *

(o) *Effective/applicability date.* Except for paragraphs (l) and (m), this section applies to taxable years ending after December 31, 2013. Paragraphs (l) and (m) of this section apply to taxable years beginning after December 31, 2018. Paragraphs (l) and (m) of § 1.36B-1 as contained in 26 CFR part I edition revised as of April 1, 2016, apply to taxable years ending after December 31, 2013, and beginning before January 1, 2019.

■ *Par. 4.* Section 1.36B-2 is amended by:

■ 1. Revise paragraph (b)(6) introductory text, (b)(6)(i) and (ii).

■ 2. Adding three new sentences to the end of paragraph (c)(2)(v).

■ 3. Revising paragraph (c)(3)(i).

■ 4. Revising paragraph (c)(3)(iii)(A).

■ 5. Adding three new sentences to the end of paragraph (c)(3)(v)(A)(*3*).

■ 6. Adding new paragraphs (c)(3)(v)(A)(*7*).

■ 7. Revising paragraph (c)(4).

■ 8. Adding a new paragraph (e).

§ 1.36B-2 Eligibility for premium tax credit.

* * * * *

(b) * * *

(6) *Special rule for taxpayers with household income below 100 percent of the Federal poverty line for the taxable year* —(i) *In general.* A taxpayer (other than a taxpayer described in paragraph (b)(5) of this section) whose household income for a taxable year is less than 100 percent of the Federal poverty line for the taxpayer's family size is treated as an applicable taxpayer for the taxable year if—

(A) The taxpayer or a family member enrolls in a qualified health plan through an Exchange for one or more months during the taxable year;

(B) An Exchange estimates at the time of enrollment that the taxpayer's household income will be at least 100 percent but not more than 400 percent of the Federal poverty line for the taxable year;

(C) Advance credit payments are authorized and paid for one or more months during the taxable year; and

(D) The taxpayer would be an applicable taxpayer if the taxpayer's household income for the taxable year was at least 100 but not more than 400 percent of the Federal poverty line for the taxpayer's family size.

(ii) *Exceptions.* This paragraph (b)(6) does not apply for an individual who, with intentional or reckless disregard for the facts, provides incorrect information to an Exchange for the year of coverage. A reckless disregard of the facts occurs if the taxpayer makes little or no effort to determine whether the information provided to the Exchange is accurate under circumstances that demonstrate a substantial deviation from the standard of conduct a reasonable person would observe. A disregard of the facts is intentional if the taxpayer knows the information provided to the Exchange is inaccurate.

* * * * *

(c) * * *

(2) * * *

(v) * * * This paragraph (c)(2)(v) does not apply for an individual who, with intentional or reckless disregard for the facts, provides incorrect information to an Exchange for the year of coverage. A reckless disregard of the facts occurs if the taxpayer makes little or no effort to determine whether the information provided to the Exchange is accurate under circumstances that demonstrate a substantial deviation from the standard of conduct a reasonable person would observe. A disregard of the facts is intentional if the taxpayer knows that information provided to the Exchange is inaccurate.

* * * * *

(3) * * *

(i) *In general.* For purposes of section 36B, an employee who may enroll in an eligible employer-sponsored plan (as defined in section 5000A(f)(2) and the regulations under that section) that is minimum essential coverage, and an individual who may enroll in the plan because of a relationship to the employee (a related individual), are eligible for minimum essential coverage under the plan for any month only if the plan is affordable and provides minimum value. Except for the Nonappropriated Fund Health Benefits Program of the Department of Defense, established under section 349 of the National Defense Authorization Act for Fiscal Year 1995 (Pub. L. 103-337; 10 U.S.C. 1587 note), government-sponsored minimum essential coverage is not an eligible employer-sponsored plan. The Nonappropriated Fund Health Benefits Program of the Department of Defense is considered eligible employer-sponsored coverage, but not government-sponsored cover-

age, for purposes of determining if an individual is eligible for minimum essential coverage under this section.

* * * * *

(iii) * * *

(A) *Failure to enroll in plan.* An employee or related individual may be eligible for minimum essential coverage under an eligible employer-sponsored plan for a month during a plan year if the employee or related individual could have enrolled in the plan for that month during an open or special enrollment period for the plan year. If an enrollment period relates to coverage for not only the upcoming plan year (or the current plan year in the case of an enrollment period other than an open enrollment period), but also coverage in one or more succeeding plan years, this paragraph (c)(3)(iii)(A) applies only to eligibility for the coverage in the upcoming plan year (or the current plan year in the case of an enrollment period other than an open enrollment period).

* * * * *

(v) * * *

(A) * * *

(*3*) * * * This paragraph (c)(3)(v)(A)(*3*) does not apply for an individual who, with intentional or reckless disregard for the facts, provides incorrect information to an Exchange concerning the portion of the annual premium for coverage for the employee or related individual under the plan. A reckless disregard of the facts occurs if the taxpayer makes little or no effort to determine whether the information provided to the Exchange is accurate under circumstances that demonstrate a substantial deviation from the standard of conduct a reasonable person would observe. A disregard of the facts is intentional if the taxpayer knows that the information provided to the Exchange is inaccurate.

* * * * *

(*7*) *Opt-out arrangements* —(*i*) *In general.* Except as otherwise provided in this paragraph (c)(3)(v)(A)(*7*), the amount of an opt-out payment made available to an employee under an opt-out arrangement increases the employee's required contribution for purposes of determining the affordability of the eligible employer-sponsored plan to which the opt-out arrangement relates, regardless of whether the employee enrolls in the eligible employer-sponsored plan or declines to enroll in that coverage and is paid the opt-out payment.

(*ii*) *Eligible opt-out arrangements.* The amount of an opt-out payment made available to an employee under an eligible opt-out arrangement does not increase the employee's required contribution for purposes of determining the affordability of the eligible employer-sponsored plan to which the eligible opt-out arrangement relates, regardless of whether the employee enrolls in the eligible employer-sponsored plan or is paid the opt-out payment.

(*iii*) *Definitions.* The following definitions apply for purposes of this paragraph (c)(3)(v)(A)(*7*):

(*A*) *Opt-out payment.* The term *opt-out payment* means a payment that is available only if an employee declines coverage, including waiving coverage in which the employee would otherwise be enrolled, under an eligible employer-sponsored plan and that is not permitted to be used to pay for coverage under the eligible employer-sponsored plan. An amount provided as an employer contribution to a cafeteria plan that is permitted to be used by the employee to purchase minimum essential coverage is not an opt-out payment, whether or not the employee may receive the amount as a taxable benefit. See paragraph (c)(3)(v)(A)(*6*) of this section for the treatment of employer contributions to a cafeteria plan.

(*B*) *Opt-out arrangement.* The term *opt-out arrangement* means the arrangement under which an opt-out payment is made available.

(*C*) *Eligible opt-out arrangement.* The term *eligible opt-out arrangement* means an arrangement under which an employee's right to receive an opt-out payment is conditioned on the employee providing reasonable evidence that the employee and all other individuals for whom the employee reasonably expects to claim a personal exemption deduction for the taxable year or years that begin or end in or with the employer's plan year to which the opt-out arrangement applies (employee's expected tax family) have or will have minimum essential coverage (other than coverage in the individual market, whether or not obtained through the Marketplace) during the period of coverage to which the opt-out arrangement applies. For this purpose, reasonable evidence of alternative coverage may include the employee's attestation that the employee and all other members of the employee's expected tax family have or will have minimum essential coverage (other than coverage in the individual market, whether or not obtained through the Marketplace) for the relevant period. Regardless of the evidence of alternative coverage required under the arrangement, to be an eligible opt-out arrangement, the arrangement must provide that the opt-out payment will not be made, and the employer in fact must not make the payment, if the employer knows or has reason to know that the employee or any other member of the employee's expected tax family does not have or will not have the alternative coverage. The arrangement must also require that the evidence of the alternative coverage be provided no less frequently than every plan year to which the eligible opt-out arrangement applies, and that it must be provided no earlier than a reasonable period of time before the commencement of the period of coverage to which the eligible opt-out arrangement applies. If the reasonable evidence (such as an attestation) is obtained as part of the regular annual open enrollment period that occurs within a few months before the commencement of the next plan year of employer-sponsored coverage, it will qualify as being provided no earlier than a reasonable period of time before commencement of the applicable period of coverage. An eligible opt-out arrangement is also permitted to require evidence of alternative coverage to be provided at a later date, such as after the plan year starts, which would enable the employer to require evidence that the employee and all other members of the employee's expected tax family have already obtained the alternative coverage. Nothing in this rule prohibits an employer from requiring reasonable evidence of alternative coverage other than an attestation in order for an employee to qualify for an opt-out payment under an eligible opt-out arrangement. Further, provided that the reasonable evidence requirement is met, the amount of an opt-out payment made available under an eligible opt-out arrangement continues to be excluded from the employee's required contribution for the remainder of the period of coverage to which the opt-out payment originally applied even if the alternative coverage subsequently terminates for the employee or for any other member of the employee's expected tax family, regardless of whether the opt-out payment is required to be adjusted or terminated due to the loss of alternative coverage, and regardless of whether the employee is required to provide notice of the loss of alternative coverage to the employer.

(*iv*) *Examples.* The following examples illustrate the provisions of this paragraph (c)(3)(v)(A)(*7*). In each example, the eligible employer-sponsored plan's plan year is the calendar year.

Example 1.

Taxpayer B is an employee of Employer X, which offers its employees coverage under an eligible employer-sponsored plan that requires B to contribute $3,000 for self-only coverage. X also makes available to B a payment of $500 if B declines to enroll in the eligible employer-sponsored plan. Therefore, the $500 opt-out payment made available to B under the opt-out arrangement increases B's required contribution under X's eligible employer-sponsored plan from $3,000 to $3,500, regardless of whether B enrolls in the eligible employer-sponsored plan or declines to enroll and is paid the opt-out payment.

Example 2

The facts are the same as in *Example 1*, except that availability of the $500 opt-out payment is conditioned not only on B declining to enroll in X's eligible employer-sponsored plan but also on B providing reasonable evidence no earlier than the regular annual open enrollment period for the next plan year that B and all other members of B's expected tax family are or will be enrolled in minimum essential coverage through another source (other than coverage in the individual market, whether or not obtained through the Marketplace). B's expected tax family consists of B and B's spouse, C, who is an employee of Employer Y. During the regular annual open enrollment period for the upcoming plan year, B declines coverage under X's eligible employer-sponsored plan and provides X with reasonable evidence that B and C will be enrolled in Y's employer-sponsored plan, which is minimum essential coverage. The opt-out arrangement provided by X is an eligible opt-out arrangement, and, therefore, the $500 opt-out payment made available to B does not increase B's required contribution under X's eligible employer-sponsored plan. B's required contribution for self-only coverage under X's eligible employer-sponsored plan is $3,000.

Example 3.

The facts are the same as in *Example 2*, except that B and C have two children that B expects to claim as dependents for the taxable year that coincides with the upcoming plan year. During the regular annual open enrollment period for the upcoming plan year, B declines coverage under X's eligible employer-sponsored plan and provides X with reasonable evidence that B and C will be enrolled in Y's employer-sponsored plan, which is minimum essential coverage. However, B does not provide reasonable evidence that B's children will be enrolled in minimum essential coverage (other than coverage in the individual market,

whether or not obtained through the Marketplace); therefore, X determines B is not eligible for the opt-out payment, and B does not receive it. The $500 opt-out payment made available under the opt-out arrangement does not increase B's required contribution under X's eligible employer-sponsored plan because the opt-out arrangement provided by X is an eligible opt-out arrangement. B's required contribution for self-only coverage under X's eligible employer-sponsored plan is $3,000.

Example 4.

Taxpayer D is married and is employed by Employer Z, which offers its employees coverage under an eligible employer-sponsored plan that requires D to contribute $2,000 for self-only coverage. Z also makes available to D a payment of $300 if D declines to enroll in the eligible employer-sponsored plan and provides reasonable evidence no earlier than the regular annual open enrollment period for the next plan year that D is or will be enrolled in minimum essential coverage through another source (other than coverage in the individual market, whether or not obtained through the Marketplace); the opt-out arrangement is not conditioned on whether the other members of D's expected tax family have other coverage. This opt-out arrangement is not an eligible opt-out arrangement because it does not condition the right to receive the opt-out payment on D providing reasonable evidence that D and the other members of D's expected tax family have (or will have) minimum essential coverage (other than coverage in the individual market, whether or not obtained through the Marketplace). Therefore, the $300 opt-out payment made available to D under the opt-out arrangement increases D's required contribution under Z's eligible employer-sponsored plan. D's required contribution for self-only coverage under Z's eligible employer-sponsored plan is $2,300.

* * * * *

(4) *Special eligibility rules* —(i) *Related individual not claimed as a personal exemption deduction.* An individual who may enroll in minimum essential coverage because of a relationship to another person eligible for the coverage, but for whom the other eligible person does not claim a personal exemption deduction under section 151, is treated as eligible for minimum essential coverage under the coverage only for months that the related individual is enrolled in the coverage.

(ii) *Exchange unable to discontinue advance credit payments* —(A) *In general.* If an individual who is enrolled in a qualified health plan for which advance credit payments are made informs the Exchange that the individual is or will soon be eligible for other minimum essential coverage and that advance credit payments should be discontinued, but the Exchange does not discontinue advance credit payments for the first calendar month beginning after the month the individual informs the Exchange, the individual is treated as eligible for the other minimum essential coverage no earlier than the first day of the second calendar month beginning after the first month the individual may enroll in the other minimum essential coverage.

(B) *Medicaid or CHIP.* If a determination is made that an individual who is enrolled in a qualified health plan for which advance credit payments are made is eligible for Medicaid or CHIP but the advance credit payments are not discontinued for the first calendar month beginning after the eligibility determination, the individual is treated as eligible for the Medicaid or CHIP no earlier than the first day of the second calendar month beginning after the eligibility determination.

* * * * *

(e) *Effective/applicability date.* (1) Except as provided in paragraph (e)(2) of this section, this section applies to taxable years ending after December 31, 2013. [Officially corrected 9/14/16 (81 FR 63154).]

(2) Paragraph (b)(6)(ii), the last three sentences of paragraph (c)(2)(v), paragraph (c)(3)(i), paragraph (c)(3)(iii)(A), the last three sentences of paragraph (c)(3)(v)(A)(*3*), paragraph (c)(3)(v)(A)(*7*), and paragraph (c)(4) of this section apply to taxable years beginning after December 31, 2016. Paragraphs (b)(6), (c)(3)(i), (c)(3)(iii)(A), and (c)(4) of §1.36B-2 as contained in 26 CFR part I edition revised as of April 1, 2016, apply to taxable years ending after December 31, 2013, and beginning before January 1, 2017.

■ *Par. 5.* Section 1.36B-3 is amended by:

■ 1. Redesignating paragraph (c)(4) as paragraph (c)(5) and adding a new paragraph (c)(4).

■ 2. Revising paragraph (d)(1).

■ 3. Revising paragraph (d)(2).

■ 4. Revising paragraph (f)

■ 5. Adding paragraph (n).

§1.36B-3 Computing the premium tax credit amount.

* * * * *

(c) * * *

(4) *Appeals of coverage eligibility.* A taxpayer who is eligible for advance credit payments pursuant to an eligibility appeal decision implemented under 45 CFR 155.545(c)(1)(ii) for coverage of a member of the taxpayer's coverage family who, based on the appeal decision, retroactively enrolls in a qualified health plan is considered to have met the requirement in paragraph (c)(1)(ii) of this section for a month if the taxpayer pays the taxpayer's share of the premiums for coverage under the plan for the month on or before the 120th day following the date of the appeals decision.

* * * * *

(d) * * *

(1) *Premium assistance amount.* The premium assistance amount for a coverage month is the lesser of—

(i) The premiums for the month, reduced by any amounts that were refunded, for one or more qualified health plans in which a taxpayer or a member of the taxpayer's family enrolls (enrollment premiums); or

(ii) The excess of the adjusted monthly premium for the applicable benchmark plan (benchmark plan premium) over 1/12 of the product of a taxpayer's household income and the applicable percentage for the taxable year (the taxpayer's contribution amount).

(2) *Examples.* The following examples illustrate the rules of paragraph (d)(1) of this section.

Example 1.

Taxpayer Q is single and has no dependents. Q enrolls in a qualified health plan with a monthly premium of $400. Q's monthly benchmark plan premium is $500, and his monthly contribution amount is $80. Q's premium assistance amount for a coverage month is $400 (the lesser of $400, Q's monthly enrollment premium, and $420, the difference between Q's monthly benchmark plan premium and Q's contribution amount).

Example 2.

(i) Taxpayer R is single and has no dependents. R enrolls in a qualified health plan with a monthly premium of $450. The difference between R's benchmark plan premium and contribution amount for the month is $420. R's premium assistance amount for a coverage month is $420 (the lesser of $450 and $420).

(ii) The issuer of R's qualified health plan is notified that R died on September 20. The issuer terminates coverage as of that date and refunds the remaining portion of the September enrollment premiums ($150) for R's coverage.

(iii) Under paragraph (d)(1) of this section, R's premium assistance amount for September is the lesser of the enrollment premiums for the month, reduced by any amounts that were refunded ($300 ($450 – $150)) or the difference between the benchmark plan premium and the contribution amount for the month ($420). R's premium assistance amount for September is $300, the lesser of $420 and $300.

Example 3.

The facts are the same as in Example 2 of this paragraph (d)(2), except that the qualified health plan issuer does not refund any enrollment premiums for September. Under paragraph (d)(1) of this section, R's premium assistance amount for September is $420, the lesser of $450 and $420.

* * * * *

(f) *Applicable benchmark plan* —(1) *In general.* Except as otherwise provided in this paragraph (f), the applicable benchmark plan for each coverage month is the second-lowest-cost silver plan (as described in section 1302(d)(1)(B) of the Affordable Care Act (42 U.S.C. 18022(d)(1)(B))) offered to the taxpayer's coverage family through the Exchange for the rating area where the taxpayer resides for—

(i) Self-only coverage for a taxpayer—

(A) Who computes tax under section 1(c) (unmarried individuals other than surviving spouses and heads of household) and is not allowed a deduction under section 151 for a dependent for the taxable year;

(B) Who purchases only self-only coverage for one individual; or

(C) Whose coverage family includes only one individual; and

(ii) Family coverage for all other taxpayers.

(2) *Family coverage.* The applicable benchmark plan for family coverage is the second lowest-cost silver plan that would cover the members of the taxpayer's coverage family (such as a plan covering two adults if the members of a taxpayer's coverage family are two adults).

(3) *Silver-level plan not covering pediatric dental benefits.* If one or more silver-level qualified health plans offered through an Exchange do not cover pediatric dental benefits, the premium for the applicable benchmark plan is determined based on the second lowest-cost option among—

(i) The silver-level qualified health plans that provide pediatric dental benefits offered by the Exchange to the members of the coverage family;

(ii) The lowest-cost silver-level qualified health plan that does not provide pediatric dental benefits offered by the Exchange to the members of the coverage family in conjunction with the lowest-cost portion of the premium for a stand-alone dental plan (within the meaning of section 1311(d)(2)(B)(ii) of the Affordable Care Act (42 U.S.C. 13031(d)(2)(B)(ii)) offered through the Exchange to the members of the coverage family that is properly allocable to pediatric dental benefits determined under guidance issued by the Secretary of Health and Human Services; and

(iii) The second-lowest-cost silver-level qualified health plan that does not provide pediatric dental benefits offered by the Exchange to the members of the coverage family in conjunction with the second-lowest-cost portion of the premium for a stand-alone dental plan (within the meaning of section 1311(d)(2)(B)(ii) of the Affordable Care Act (42 U.S.C. 13031(d)(2)(B)(ii)) offered through the Exchange to the members of the coverage family that is properly allocable to pediatric dental benefits determined under guidance issued by the Secretary of Health and Human Services.

(4) *Family members residing in different locations.* If members of a taxpayer's coverage family reside in different locations, the taxpayer's benchmark plan premium is the sum of the premiums for the applicable benchmark plans for each group of coverage family members residing in different locations, based on the plans offered to the group through the Exchange where the group resides. If all members of a taxpayer's coverage family reside in a single location that is different from where the taxpayer resides, the taxpayer's benchmark plan premium is the premium for the applicable benchmark plan for the coverage family, based on the plans offered through the Exchange to the taxpayer's coverage family for the rating area where the coverage family resides.

(5) *Single or multiple policies needed to cover the family* —(i) *Policy covering a taxpayer's family.* If a silver-level plan or a stand-alone dental plan offers coverage to all members of a taxpayer's coverage family who reside in the same location under a single policy, the premium (or allocable portion thereof, in the case of a stand-alone dental plan) taken into account for the plan for purposes of determining the applicable benchmark plan under paragraphs (f)(1), (f)(2), and (f)(3) of this section is the premium for this single policy.

(ii) *Policy not covering a taxpayer's family.* If a silver-level qualified health plan or a stand-alone dental plan would require multiple policies to cover all members of a taxpayer's coverage family who reside in the same location (for example, because of the relationships within the family), the premium (or allocable portion thereof, in the case of a standalone dental plan) taken into account for the plan for purposes of determining the applicable benchmark plan under paragraphs (f)(1), (f)(2), and (f)(3) of this section is the sum of the premiums (or allocable portion thereof, in the case of a stand-alone dental plan) for self-only policies under the plan for each member of the coverage family who resides in the same location.

(6) *Plan not available for enrollment.* A silver-level qualified health plan or a stand-alone dental plan that is not open to enrollment by a taxpayer or family member at the time the taxpayer or family member enrolls in a qualified health plan is disregarded in determining the applicable benchmark plan.

(7) *Benchmark plan terminates or closes to enrollment during the year.* A silver-level qualified health plan or a stand-alone dental plan that is used for purposes of determining the applicable benchmark plan under this paragraph (f) for a taxpayer does not cease to be the applicable benchmark plan for a taxable year solely because the plan or a lower cost plan terminates or closes to enrollment during the taxable year.

(8) *Only one silver-level plan offered to the coverage family.* If there is only one silver-level qualified health plan providing pediatric dental benefits, one silver-level qualified health plan not providing pediatric dental benefits, or one stand-alone dental plan offered through an Exchange that would cover all members of a taxpayer's coverage family

who reside in the same location (whether under one policy or multiple policies), that plan is used for purposes of determining the taxpayer's applicable benchmark plan.

(9) *Examples.* The following examples illustrate the rules of this paragraph (f). Unless otherwise stated, in each example the plans are open to enrollment to a taxpayer or family member at the time of enrollment and are offered through the Exchange for the rating area where the taxpayer resides:

Example 1. Single taxpayer enrolls in a qualified health plan. Taxpayer A is single, has no dependents, and enrolls in a qualified health plan. The Exchange in the rating area in which A resides offers only silver-level qualified health plans that provide pediatric dental benefits. Under paragraphs (f)(1) and (f)(2) of this section, A's applicable benchmark plan is the second lowest cost silver plan providing self-only coverage for A.

Example 2. Single taxpayer enrolls with dependent in a qualified health plan. Taxpayer B is single and claims her daughter, C, as a dependent. B purchases family coverage for herself and C. The Exchange in the rating area in which B and C reside offers qualified health plans that provide pediatric dental benefits but does not offer qualified health plans without pediatric dental benefits. Under paragraphs (f)(1) and (f)(2) of this section, B's applicable benchmark plan is the second lowest-cost silver plan providing family coverage to B and C.

Example 3. Benchmark plan for a coverage family with a family member eligible for pediatric dental benefits. (i) Taxpayer D's coverage family consists of D and D's 10-year old son, E, who is a dependent of D and eligible for pediatric dental benefits. The Exchange in the rating area in which D and E reside offers three silver-level qualified health plans, two of which provide pediatric dental benefits (S1 and S2) and one of which does not (S3), in which D and E may enroll. The Exchange also offers two stand-alone dental plans (DP1 and DP2) available to D and E. The monthly premiums allocable to essential health benefits for the silver-level plans are as follows:

S1—$1,250

S2—$1,200

S3—$1,180

(ii) The monthly premiums, and the portion of the premium allocable to pediatric dental benefits, for the two dental plans are as follows:

DP1—$100 ($25 allocable to pediatric dental benefits)

DP2—$80 ($40 allocable to pediatric dental benefits).

(iii) Under paragraph (f)(3) of this section, D's applicable benchmark plan is the second lowest cost option among the following offered by the rating area in which D resides: silver-level qualified health plans providing pediatric dental benefits ($1,250 for S1 and $1,200 for S2); the lowest-cost silver-level qualified health plan not providing pediatric dental benefits, in conjunction with the lowest-cost portion of the premium for a stand-alone dental plan properly allocable to pediatric dental benefits ($1,180 for S3 in conjunction with $25 for DP1 = $1,205); and the second lowest cost silver-level qualified health plan not providing pediatric health benefits, in conjunction with the second lowest-cost portion of the premium for a stand-alone dental plan allocable to pediatric dental benefits ($1,180 for S3 in conjunction with $40 for DP2 = $1,220). Under paragraph (f)(8) of this section, S3, as the lone silver-level qualified health plan not providing pediatric dental benefits offered by the Exchange, is treated as the second lowest-cost silver-level qualified health plan not providing pediatric dental benefits. Under paragraph (e) of this section, the adjusted monthly premium for D's applicable benchmark plan is $1,205.

Example 4. Benchmark plan for a coverage family with no family members eligible for pediatric dental coverage. (i) The facts are the same as in *Example 3*, except Taxpayer D's coverage family consists of D and D's 22-year old son, F, who is a dependent of D and not eligible for pediatric dental coverage and the monthly premiums allocable to essential health benefits for the silver-level plans are as follows:

S1—$1,210

S2—$1,190

S3—$1,180

(ii) Because no one in D's coverage family is eligible for pediatric dental benefits, $0 of the premium for a stand-alone dental plan is allocable to pediatric dental benefits in determining A's applicable benchmark plan. Consequently, under paragraphs (f)(1), (f)(2), and (f)(3) of this section, D's applicable benchmark plan is the second lowest-cost option among the following options offered by the rating area in which D resides: silver-level qualified health plans providing

pediatric dental benefits ($1,210 for S1 and $1,190 for S2), the lowest-cost silver-level qualified health plan not providing pediatric dental benefits, in conjunction with the lowest-cost portion of the premium for a stand-alone dental plan properly allocable to pediatric dental benefits ($1,180 for S3 in conjunction with $0 for DP1 = $1,180), and the second lowest cost silver-level qualified health plan not providing pediatric health benefits, in conjunction with the second lowest-cost portion of the premium for a stand-alone dental plan allocable to pediatric dental benefits ($1,180 for S3 in conjunction with $0 for DP2 = $1,180). Under paragraph (e) of this section, the adjusted monthly premium for D's applicable benchmark plan is $1,180.

Example 5. Single taxpayer enrolls with dependent and nondependent in a qualified health plan. Taxpayer G is single and resides with his daughter, H, and with his teenage son, I, but may only claim I as a dependent. G, H, and I enroll in coverage through the Exchange in the rating area in which they all reside. The Exchange offers only silver-level plans providing pediatric dental benefits. Under paragraphs (f)(1) and (f)(2) of this section, G's applicable benchmark plan is the second lowest-cost silver plan covering G and I. However, H may qualify for a premium tax credit if H is otherwise eligible. See paragraph (h) of this section.

Example 6. Change in coverage family. Taxpayer J is single and has no dependents when she enrolls in a qualified health plan. The Exchange in the rating area in which she resides offers only silver-level plans that provide pediatric dental benefits. On August 1, J has a child, K, whom she claims as a dependent. J enrolls in a qualified health plan covering J and K effective August 1. Under paragraphs (f)(1) and (f)(2) of this section, J's applicable benchmark plan for January through July is the second lowest-cost silver plan providing self-only coverage for J, and J's applicable benchmark plan for the months August through December is the second lowest-cost silver plan covering J and K.

Example 7. Minimum essential coverage for some coverage months. Taxpayer L claims his daughter, M, as a dependent. L and M enroll in a qualified health plan through an Exchange that offers only silver-level plans that provide pediatric dental benefits. L, but not M, is eligible for government-sponsored minimum essential coverage for September to December. Thus, under paragraph (c)(1)(iii) of this section, January through December are coverage months for M, and January through August are coverage months for L. Because, under paragraphs (d) and (f)(1) of this section, the premium assistance amount for a coverage month is computed based on the applicable benchmark plan for that coverage month, L's applicable benchmark plan for January through August is the second lowest-cost option covering L and M. Under paragraph (f)(1)(i)(C) of this section, L's applicable benchmark plan for September through December is the second lowest-cost silver plan providing self-only coverage for M.

Example 8. Family member eligible for minimum essential coverage for the taxable year. The facts are the same as in Example 7, except that L is not eligible for government-sponsored minimum essential coverage for any months and M is eligible for government sponsored minimum essential coverage for the entire year. Under paragraph (f)(1)(i)(C) of this section, L's applicable benchmark plan is the second lowest-cost silver plan providing self-only coverage for L.

Example 9. Benchmark plan premium for a coverage family with family members who reside in different locations. (i) Taxpayer N's coverage family consists of N and her three dependents O, P, and Q. N, O, and P reside together but Q resides in a different location. Under paragraphs (f)(1), (f)(2), and (f)(3) of this section, the monthly applicable benchmark plan premium for N, O, and P is $1,000 and the monthly applicable benchmark plan premium for Q is $220.

(ii) Under paragraph (f)(4) of this section, because the members of N's coverage family reside in different locations, the monthly premium for N's applicable benchmark plan is the sum of $1,000, the monthly premiums for the applicable benchmark plan for N, O, and P, who reside together, and $220, the monthly applicable benchmark plan premium for Q, who resides in a different location than N, O, and P. Consequently, the premium for N's applicable benchmark plan is $1,220.

Example 10. Aggregation of silver-level policies for plans not covering a family under a single policy. (i) Taxpayers R and S are married and live with S's mother, T, whom they claim as a dependent. The Exchange for their rating area offers self-only and family coverage at the silver level through Issuers A, B, and C, which each offer only one silver-level plan. The silver-level plans offered by Issuers A and B do not cover R, S, and T under a single policy. The silver-level plan offered by Issuer A costs the following monthly amounts for self-only coverage of R, S, and T, respectively: $400, $450, and $600. The silver-level plan offered by Issuer B costs the following monthly amounts for self-only coverage of R, S, and T, respectively: $250, $300, and $450. The silver-level plan offered by Issuer C provides coverage for R, S, and T under one policy for a $1,200 monthly premium.

(ii) Under paragraph (f)(5) of this section, Issuer C's silver-level plan that covers R, S, and T under one policy ($1,200 monthly premium) and Issuer A's and Issuer B's silver-level plans that do not cover R, S and T under one policy are considered in determining R's and S's applicable benchmark plan. In addition, under paragraph (f)(5)(ii) of this section, in determining R's and S's applicable benchmark plan, the premium taken into account for Issuer A's plan is $1,450 (the aggregate premiums for self-only policies covering R ($400), S ($450), and T ($600) and the premium taken into account for Issuer B's plan is $1,000 (the aggregate premiums for self-only policies covering R ($250), S ($300), and T ($450). Consequently, R's and S's applicable benchmark plan is the Issuer C silver-level plan covering R's and S's coverage family and the premium for their applicable benchmark plan is $1,200.

Example 11. Benchmark plan premium for a taxpayer with family members who cannot enroll in one policy and who reside in different locations. (i) Taxpayer U's coverage family consists of U, U's mother, V, and U's two daughters, W and X. U and V reside together in Location 1 and W and X reside together in Location 2. The Exchange in the rating area in which U and V reside does not offer a silver-level plan that covers U and V under a single policy, whereas all the silver-level plans offered through the Exchange in the rating area in which W and X reside cover W and X under a single policy. Both Exchanges offer only silver-level plans that provide pediatric dental benefits. The silver plan offered by the Exchange for the rating area in which U and V reside that would cover U and V under self-only policies with the second-lowest aggregate premium costs $400 a month for self-only coverage for U and $600 a month for self-only coverage for V. The monthly premium for the second-lowest cost silver plan covering W and X that is offered by the Exchange for the rating area in which W and X reside is $500.

(ii) Under paragraph (f)(5)(ii) of this section, because multiple policies are required to cover U and V, the members of U's coverage family who reside together in Location 1, the premium taken into account in determining U's benchmark plan is $1,000, the sum of the premiums for the second-lowest aggregate cost of self-only policies covering U ($400) and V ($600) offered by the Exchange to U and V for the rating area in which U and V reside. Under paragraph (f)(5)(i) of this section, because all silver-level plans offered by the Exchange in which W and X reside cover W and X under a single policy, the premium for W and X's coverage that is taken into account in determining U's benchmark plan is $500, the second-lowest cost silver policy covering W and X that is offered by the Exchange for the rating area in which W and X reside. Under paragraph (f)(4) of this section, because the members of U's coverage family reside in different locations, U's monthly benchmark plan premium is $1,500, the sum of the premiums for the applicable benchmark plans for each group of family members residing in different locations ($1,000 for U and V, who reside in Location 1, plus $500 for W and X, who reside in Location 2).

Example 12. Qualified health plan closed to enrollment. Taxpayer Y has two dependents, Z and AA. Y, Z, and AA enroll in a qualified health plan through the Exchange for the rating area where the family resides. The Exchange, which offers only qualified health plans that include pediatric dental benefits, offers silver-level plans J, K, L, and M, which are, respectively, the first, second, third, and fourth lowest cost silver plans covering Y's family. When Y's family enrolls, Plan J is closed to enrollment. Under paragraph (f)(6) of this section, Plan J is disregarded in determining Y's applicable benchmark plan, and Plan L is used in determining Y's applicable benchmark plan.

Example 13. Benchmark plan closes to new enrollees during the year. (i) Taxpayers BB, CC, and DD each have coverage families consisting of two adults. In that rating area, Plan 2 is the second lowest cost silver plan and Plan 3 is the third lowest cost silver plan covering the two adults in each coverage family offered through the Exchange. The BB and CC families each enroll in a qualified health plan that is not the applicable benchmark plan (Plan 4) in November during the annual open enrollment period. Plan 2 closes to new enrollees the following June. Thus, on July 1, Plan 3 is the second lowest cost silver plan available to new enrollees through the Exchange. The DD family enrolls in a qualified health plan in July.

(ii) Under paragraphs (f)(1), (f)(2), (f)(3), and (f)(7) of this section, the silver-level plan that BB and CC use to determine their applicable benchmark plan for all coverage months during the year is Plan 2. The applicable benchmark plan that DD uses to determine DD's applicable benchmark plan is Plan 3, because Plan 2 is not open to enrollment through the Exchange when the DD family enrolls.

Example 14. Benchmark plan terminates for all enrollees during the year. The facts are the same as in *Example 13*, except that Plan 2

terminates for all enrollees on June 30. Under paragraphs (f)(1), (f)(2), (f)(3), and (f)(7) of this section, Plan 2 is the silver-level plan that BB and CC use to determine their applicable benchmark plan for all coverage months during the year, and Plan 3 is the applicable benchmark plan that DD uses.

Example 15. Exchange offers only one silver-level plan. Taxpayer EE's coverage family consists of EE, his spouse FF, and their two dependent children GG and HH, who all reside together. The Exchange for the rating area in which they reside offers only one silver-level plan that EE's family may enroll in and the plan does not provide pediatric dental benefits. The Exchange also offers one stand-alone dental plan in which the family may enroll. Under paragraph (f)(8) of this section, the silver-level plan and the stand-alone dental plan offered by the Exchange are used for purposes of determining EE's applicable benchmark plan under paragraph (f)(3) of this section. Moreover, the lone silver-level plan and the lone stand-alone dental plan offered by the Exchange are used for purposes of determining EE's applicable benchmark plan regardless of whether these plans cover EE's family under a single policy or multiples policies.

* * * * *

(n) *Effective/applicability date.* (1) Except as provided in paragraph (n)(2) of this section, this section applies to taxable years ending after December 31, 2013. [Officially corrected 9/14/16 (81 FR 63154).]

(2) Paragraphs (c)(4), (d)(1) and (2) apply to taxable years beginning after December 31, 2016. Paragraph (f) of this section applies to taxable years beginning after December 31, 2018. Paragraphs (d)(1) and (2) of § 1.36B–3 as contained in 26 CFR part I edition revised as of April 1, 2016, apply to taxable years ending after December 31, 2013, and beginning before January 1, 2017. Paragraph (f) of § 1.36B–3 as contained in 26 CFR part I edition revised as of April 1, 2016, applies to taxable years ending after December 31, 2013, and beginning before January 1, 2019. [Officially corrected 9/14/16 (81 FR 63154).]

■ *Par. 6.* Section 1.36B-5 is amended by:

■ 1. Adding a new sentence to the end of paragraph (c)(3)(i).

■ 2. Adding paragraphs (c)(3)(iii) and (h).

§ 1.36B-5 Information reporting by Exchanges.

* * * * *

(c) * * *

(3) —* * *

(i) * * * If advance credit payments are made for coverage under the plan, the enrollment premiums reported to each family under paragraph (c)(1)(viii) of this section are the premiums allocated to the family under § 1.36B-3(h) (allocating enrollment premiums to each taxpayer in proportion to the premiums for each taxpayer's applicable benchmark plan).

* * * * *

(iii) *Partial month of coverage* —(A) *In general.* Except as provided in paragraph (c)(iii)(B) of this section, if an individual is enrolled in a qualified health plan after the first day of a month, the amount reported for that month under paragraphs (c)(1)(iv), (c)(1)(v), and (c)(1)(viii) of this section is $0.

(B) *Certain mid-month enrollments.* If an individual's qualified health plan is terminated before the last day of a month, or if an individual is enrolled in coverage after the first day of a month and the coverage is effective on the date of the individual's birth, adoption, or placement for adoption or in foster care, or on the effective date of a court order, the amount reported under paragraphs (c)(1)(iv) and (c)(1)(v) of this section is the premium for the applicable benchmark plan for a full month of coverage (excluding the premium allocated to benefits in excess of essential health benefits) and the amount reported under paragraph (c)(1)(viii) of this section is the enrollment premium for the month, reduced by any amounts that were refunded.

* * * * *

(h) *Effective/applicability date.* Except for the last sentence of paragraph (c)(3)(i) of this section and paragraph (c)(3)(iii) of this section, this section applies to taxable years ending after December 31, 2013. The last sentence of paragraph (c)(3)(i) of this section and paragraph (c)(3)(iii) of this section apply to taxable years beginning after December 31, 2016. Paragraph (c)(3)(iii) of § 1.36B-5 as contained in 26 CFR part I edition revised as of April 1, 2016, applies to taxable years ending after December 31, 2013, and beginning before January 1, 2017.

■ *Par. 7.* Section 1.5000A-3 is amended by adding a new paragraph (e)(3)(ii)(G) to read as follows:

§ 1.5000A-3 Exempt individuals.

* * * * *

(e) * * *

(3) * * *

(ii) * * *

(G) *Opt-out arrangements* —(*1*) *In general.* Except as otherwise provided in this paragraph (e)(3)(ii)(G), the amount of an opt-out payment made available to an employee under an opt-out arrangement increases the employee's (or related individual's) required contribution for purposes of determining the affordability of the eligible employer-sponsored plan to which the opt-out arrangement relates, regardless of whether the employee (or related individual) enrolls in the eligible employer-sponsored plan or declines to enroll in that coverage and is paid the opt-out payment.

(*2*) *Eligible opt-out arrangements.* The amount of an opt-out payment made available to an employee under an eligible opt-out arrangement does not increase the employee's (or related individual's) required contribution for purposes of determining the affordability of the eligible employer-sponsored plan to which the eligible opt-out arrangement relates, regardless of whether the employee (or related individual) enrolls in the eligible employer-sponsored plan or is paid the opt-out payment.

(*3*) *Definitions.* The following definitions apply for purposes of this paragraph (e)(3)(ii)(G):

(*A*) *Opt-out payment.* The term *opt-out payment* means a payment that is available only if an employee declines coverage, including waiving coverage in which the employee would otherwise be enrolled, under an eligible employer-sponsored plan and that is not permitted to be used to pay for coverage under the eligible employer-sponsored plan. An amount provided as an employer contribution to a cafeteria plan that is permitted to be used by the employee to purchase minimum essential coverage is not an opt-out payment, whether or not the employee may receive the amount as a taxable benefit. See paragraph (e)(3)(ii)(E) of this section for the treatment of employer contributions to a cafeteria plan.

(*B*) *Opt-out arrangement.* The term *opt-out arrangement* means the arrangement under which an opt-out payment is made available.

(*C*) *Eligible opt-out arrangement.* The term *eligible opt-out arrangement* means an arrangement under which an employee's right to receive an opt-out payment is conditioned on the employee providing reasonable evidence that the employee and all other individuals for whom the employee reasonably expects to claim a personal exemption deduction for the taxable year or years that begin or end in or with the employer's plan year to which the opt-out arrangement applies (employee's expected tax family) have, or will have, minimum essential coverage (other than coverage in the individual market, whether or not obtained through the Marketplace) during the period of coverage to which the opt-out arrangement applies. For this purpose, reasonable evidence of alternative coverage may include the employee's attestation that the employee and all other members of the employee's expected tax family have, or will have, minimum essential coverage (other than coverage in the individual market, whether or not obtained through the Marketplace) for the relevant period. Regardless of the evidence of alternative coverage required under the arrangement, to be an eligible opt-out arrangement, the arrangement must provide that the opt-out payment will not be made, and the employer in fact must not make the payment, if the employer knows or has reason to know that the employee or any other member of the employee's expected tax family does not have, or will not have, the alternative coverage. The arrangement must also require that the evidence of the alternative coverage be provided no less frequently than every plan year to which the eligible opt-out arrangement applies, and that it must be provided no earlier than a reasonable period of time before the commencement of the period of coverage to which the eligible opt-out arrangement applies. If the reasonable evidence (such as an attestation) is obtained as part of the regular annual open enrollment period that occurs within a few months before the commencement of the next plan year of employer-sponsored coverage, it will qualify as being provided no earlier than a reasonable period of time before commencement of the applicable period of coverage. An eligible opt-out arrangement is also permitted to require evidence of alternative coverage to be provided at a later date, such as after the plan year starts, which would enable the employer to require evidence that the employee and all other members of the employee's expected tax family have already obtained the alternative coverage. Nothing in this rule prohibits an employer from requiring reasonable evidence of alternative coverage other than an attestation in order for an employee to qualify for an opt-out payment under an eligible opt-out arrangement. Further, provided that the reasonable evidence requirement is met, the amount of an opt-out payment made available under an eligible opt-out arrangement continues to be excluded from the employee's required contribution for the remainder of the period of coverage to which the opt-out payment originally applied even if the alternative coverage subsequently terminates for the employee or for any other member of the employee's expected tax family, regardless of whether the opt-out payment is required to be adjusted or terminated due to the loss of alternative coverage, and regardless of whether the employee is required to provide notice of the loss of alternative coverage to the employer.

* * * * *

■ *Par. 8.* Section 1.5000A-5 is amended by revising paragraph (c).

§ 1.5000A-5 Administration and procedure.

* * * * *

(c) *Effective/applicability date.* (1) Except as provided in paragraph (c)(2), this section and §§ 1.5000A-1 through 1.5000A-4 apply for months beginning after December 31, 2013.

(2) Paragraph (e)(3)(ii)(G) of § 1.5000A-3 applies to months beginning after December 31, 2016.

■ *Par. 9.* Revise § 1.6011-8 to read as follows:

§ 1.6011-8 Requirement of income tax return for taxpayers who claim the premium tax credit under section 36B.

(a) *Requirement of return.* Except as otherwise provided in this paragraph (a), a taxpayer who receives the benefit of advance payments of the premium tax credit under section 36B must file an income tax return for that taxable year on or before the due date for the return (including extensions of time for filing) and reconcile the advance credit payments. However, if advance credit payments are made for coverage of an individual for whom no taxpayer claims a personal exemption deduction, the taxpayer who attests to the Exchange to the intention to claim a personal exemption deduction for the individual as part of the determination that the taxpayer is eligible for advance credit payments must file a tax return and reconcile the advance credit payments.

(b) *Effective/applicability date.* Except as otherwise provided, this section applies for taxable years beginning after December 31, 2016. Paragraph (a) of § 1.6011-8 as contained in 26 CFR part I edition revised as of April 1, 2016, applies to taxable years ending after December 31, 2013, and beginning before January 1, 2017.

§ 301.6011-2 [Amended]

■ *Par. 10.* Section 301.6011-2(b)(1) is amended by adding "1095-B, 1095-C" after "1094 series", and removing "1095 series".

John Dalrymple,

Deputy Commissioner for Services and Enforcement.

[FR Doc. 2016-15940 Filed 7-6-16; 11:15 am]

BILLING CODE 4830-01-P

¶ 20,264N

IRS: Group health plans: Minimum essential coverage: Reporting and disclosure: Information returns: Catastrophic health coverage.—The IRS has issued proposed regulations relating to information reporting of minimum essential coverage under Code Sec. 6055. Health insurance issuers, certain employers, and others that provide minimum essential coverage to individuals must report to the IRS information about the type and period of coverage and furnish related statements to covered individuals. The proposed regulations clarify issues relating to reporting of certain plans and taxpayer identification number (TIN) solicitation and truncation. The proposed regulations are generally proposed to apply for tax years ending after December 31, 2015 and may be relied on for calendar years ending after December 31, 2013, with the exception of rules on reporting of coverage under catastrophic plans.

The proposed regulation was published in the Federal Register on August 2, 2016 (81 FR 50671).

DEPARTMENT OF THE TREASURY

Internal Revenue Service

26 CFR Parts 1 and 301

[REG-103058-16]

RIN 1545-BN23

Information Reporting of Catastrophic Health Coverage and Other Issues Under Section 6055

AGENCY: Internal Revenue Service (IRS), Treasury.

ACTION: Notice of proposed rulemaking.

SUMMARY: This document contains proposed regulations relating to information reporting of minimum essential coverage under section 6055 of the Internal Revenue Code (Code). Health insurance issuers, certain employers, and others that provide minimum essential coverage to individuals must report to the IRS information about the type and period of coverage and furnish related statements to covered individuals. These proposed regulations affect health insurance issuers, employers, governments, and other persons that provide minimum essential coverage to individuals.

DATES: Written or electronic comments and requests for a public hearing must be received by October 3, 2016.

ADDRESSES: Send submissions to: CC:PA:LPD:PR (REG-103058-16), Room 5203, Internal Revenue Service, P.O. Box 7604, Ben Franklin Station, Washington, DC 20044. Submissions may be hand-delivered Monday through Friday between the hours of 8 a.m. and 4 p.m. to CC:PA:LPD:PR (REG-103058-16), Courier's Desk, Internal Revenue Service, 1111 Constitution Avenue NW., Washington, DC 20224, or sent electronically via the Federal eRulemaking Portal at *http://www.regulations.gov* (IRS REG-103058-16).

FOR FURTHER INFORMATION CONTACT: Concerning the proposed regulations under section 6055, John B. Lovelace, (202) 317-7006; concerning the proposed regulations under section 6724, Hollie Marx, (202) 317-6844; concerning the submission of comments, Regina Johnson, (202) 317-6901 (not toll-free calls).

SUPPLEMENTARY INFORMATION:

Paperwork Reduction Act

The collection of information contained in this notice of proposed rulemaking has been submitted to the Office of Management and Budget in accordance with the Paperwork Reduction Act of 1995 (44 U.S.C. 3507(d)). Comments on the collection of information should be sent to the Office of Management and Budget, Attn: Desk Officer for the Department of the Treasury, Office of Information and Regulatory Affairs, Washington, DC 20503, with copies to the Internal Revenue Service, Attn: IRS Reports Clearance Officer, SE:W:CAR:MP:T:T:SP, Washington, DC 20224. Comments on the collection of information should be received by October 3, 2016. Comments are specifically requested concerning:

Whether the proposed collection of information is necessary for the proper performance of the functions of the IRS, including whether the information will have practical utility;

How the quality, utility, and clarity of the information to be collected may be enhanced;

How the burden of complying with the proposed collection of information may be minimized, including through the application of automated collection techniques or other forms of information technology; and

Estimates of capital or start-up costs and costs of operation, maintenance, and purchase of services to provide information.

The collection of information in these proposed regulations is in § 1.6055-1. The collection of information will be used to determine whether an individual has minimum essential coverage under section 1501(b) of the Patient Protection and Affordable Care Act (26 U.S.C. 5000A(f)). The collection of information is required to comply with the provisions of section 6055. The likely respondents are health insurers, self-insured employers or other sponsors of self-insured health plans, and governments that provide minimum essential coverage.

The burden for the collection of information contained in these proposed regulations will be reflected in the burden on Form 1095-B, Health Coverage, or another form that the IRS designates, which will request the information in the proposed regulation.

An agency may not conduct or sponsor, and a person is not required to respond to, a collection of information unless it displays a valid control number assigned by the Office of Management and Budget.

Background

Under section 5000A, individuals must for each month have minimum essential coverage, qualify for a health coverage exemption, or make an individual shared responsibility payment with their income tax returns. Section 6055 provides that all persons who provide minimum essential coverage to an individual must report certain information to the IRS that identifies covered individuals and the period of coverage, and must furnish a statement to the covered individuals containing the same information. The information reported under section 6055 allows individuals to establish, and the IRS to verify, that the individuals were covered by minimum essential coverage for months during the year.

Information returns under section 6055 generally are filed using Form 1095-B. A separate and distinct health coverage-related reporting requirement under section 6056 requires that certain large employers report information on Form 1095-C, Employer-Provided Health Insurance Offer and Coverage. Self-insured employers required to file Form 1095-C use Part III of that form, rather than Form 1095-B, to report information required under section 6055 for individuals enrolled in the self-insured employer-sponsored coverage. These proposed regulations provide guidance under section 6055 only, which relates to Form 1095-B and Form 1095-C, Part III. These proposed regulations do not affect information reporting under section 6056 on Form 1095-C, Parts I and II.

Under section 5000A(f)(1), various types of health plans and programs are minimum essential coverage, including: (1) Specified government-sponsored programs such as Medicare Part A, the Medicaid program under Title XIX of the Social Security Act (42 U.S.C. 1936 and following sections), the Children's Health Insurance Program under Title XXI of the Social Security Act (42 U.S.C. 1397aa and following sections) (CHIP), the TRICARE program under chapter 55 of Title 10, U.S.C., health care programs for veterans and other individuals under chapter 17 or 18 of Title 38 U.S.C., coverage for Peace Corps volunteers under 22 U.S.C. 2504(e), and coverage under the Nonappropriated Fund Health Benefits Program under section 349 of Public Law 103-337, (2) coverage under an eligible employer-sponsored plan, (3) coverage under a plan in the individual market (such as a qualified health plan offered through an Affordable Insurance Exchange (Exchange, also known as a Marketplace)), (4) coverage under a grandfathered health plan, and (5) other coverage recognized as minimum essential coverage by the Secretary of Health and Human Services, in coordination with the Secretary of the Treasury.

Under section 5000A(f)(3) and § 1.5000A-2(g) of the Income Tax Regulations, coverage that consists solely of excepted benefits described in section 2791(c)(1), (c)(2), (c)(3), or (c)(4) of the Public Health Service Act (42 U.S.C. 300gg-91(c)), and the regulations under that section, is not minimum essential coverage. Section 1.5000A-2(b)(2) lists government-sponsored programs that provide limited benefits and which are not minimum essential coverage.

Under section 5000A(f)(4), an individual who is a bona fide resident of a United States possession for a month is treated as having minimum essential coverage for that month.

Notice 2015-68, 2015-41 I.R.B. 547, provides guidance on various issues under section 6055. In Notice 2015-68, the Treasury Department and the IRS stated that they intend to propose regulations under section 6055 addressing certain of these issues and requested comments. Comments were requested about the application of the reasonable cause rules under section 6724 to section 6055 reporting, in particular as applied to taxpayer identification number (TIN) solicitation and reporting.

Persons Required To Report

Under § 1.6055-1(c)(1)(iii), the executive department or agency of the governmental unit that provides coverage under a government-sponsored program is the reporting entity for government-sponsored minimum essential coverage. Section 1.6055-1(c)(3)(i) specifically provides that the State agency that administers the Medicaid or CHIP program, respectively, must report government-sponsored coverage under section 6055. Notice 2015-68 provides that Medicaid and CHIP agencies in U.S. possessions or territories are not required to report Medicaid and CHIP coverage because an individual eligible for that coverage is generally a bona fide resident of the possession or territory who is deemed to have minimum essential coverage under section 5000A(f)(4) and, therefore, does not require reporting under section 6055 to verify compliance with section 5000A.

In general, under § 1.6055-1(c)(1)(ii) the reporting entity for coverage under a self-insured group health plan is the plan sponsor. Section 1.6055-1(c)(2) provides rules for identifying which entity is the plan sponsor of a self-insured group health plan for purposes of section 6055. For this purpose, the employer is the plan sponsor of a self-insured group health plan established by a single employer (determined without aggregating related entities under section 414). If the plan or arrangement is established or maintained by more than one employer (including a Multiple Employer Welfare Arrangement (as defined in section 3(40) of the Employee Retirement Income Security Act of 1974 (ERISA)), and the plan is not a multiemployer plan (as defined in section 3(37) of ERISA), each participating employer is a plan sponsor with respect to that employer's employees. For a self-insured group health plan or arrangement that is a multiemployer plan, the plan sponsor is the association, committee, joint board of trustees, or other similar group of representatives of the parties who establish or maintain the plan. For a self-insured group health plan or arrangement maintained solely by an employee organization, the plan sponsor is the employee organization.

The existing regulations at § 1.6055-1(d)(2) provide that no reporting is required for minimum essential coverage that provides benefits in addition or as a supplement to other coverage that is minimum essential coverage if the primary and supplemental coverage have the same plan sponsor or the coverage supplements government-sponsored minimum essential coverage. Notice 2015-68 explained that this rule had proven to be confusing, and, accordingly, the Treasury Department and the IRS intended to propose regulations providing that (1) if an individual is covered by multiple minimum essential coverage plans or programs provided by the same provider, reporting is only required for one of the plans or programs; and (2) reporting generally is not required for an individual's minimum essential coverage to the extent that the individual is eligible for that coverage only if the individual is also covered by other minimum essential coverage for which section 6055 reporting is required.

Information Required To Be Reported

Under section 6055(b) and § 1.6055-1(e)(1), providers of minimum essential coverage must report to the IRS (1) the name, address, and employer identification number (EIN) of the reporting entity required to file the return; (2) the name, address, and TIN, or date of birth if a TIN is not available, of the responsible individual (except that a reporting entity may, but is not required to, report the TIN of a responsible individual not enrolled in the coverage); (3) the name and TIN, or date of birth if a TIN is not available, of each individual who is covered under the policy or program; and (4) the months of coverage for each covered individual.[1] Section 1.6055-1(b)(11) provides that the responsible individual includes a primary insured, employee, former employee, uniformed services sponsor, parent, or other related person named on an application who enrolls one or more individuals, including him or herself, in minimum essential coverage.

In addition, under § 1.6055-1(e)(2), for coverage provided by a health insurance issuer through a group health plan, information returns must report (1) the name, address, and EIN of the employer maintaining the plan, and (2) any other information that the Secretary requires for administering the credit under section 45R (relating to the tax credit for employee health insurance expenses of small employers).

A reporting entity that fails to comply with the filing and statement furnishing requirements of section 6055 may be subject to penalties for failure to file timely a correct information return (section 6721) or failure to furnish timely a correct statement (section 6722). See section 6724(d); see also § 1.6055-1(h)(1). These penalties may be waived if the failure is due to reasonable cause and is not due to willful neglect. See section 6724(a). In particular, under § 301.6724-1(a)(2) of the Procedure and Administration Regulations penalties are waived if a reporting entity demonstrates that it acted in a responsible manner and that the failure is due to significant mitigating factors or events beyond the reporting entity's control. For purposes of section 6055 reporting, if the information reported on a return is incomplete or incorrect as a result of a change in circumstances (such as a retroactive change in coverage), a failure to timely file or furnish a corrected document is a failure to file a correct return or furnish a correct statement under sections 6721 and 6722. See § 1.6055-1(h)(2).

In general, under § 301.6724-1(e) a person will be treated as acting in a responsible manner if the person properly solicits a TIN but does not receive it. For this purpose, proper solicitation of a TIN involves an initial solicitation and two subsequent annual solicitations. In general, an initial solicitation is made when the relationship between the reporting entity and the taxpayer is established. If the reporting entity does not receive the TIN, the first annual solicitation is generally required by December 31 of the year in which the relationship with the taxpayer begins (January 31 of the following year if the relationship begins in December). Generally, if the TIN is still not provided, a second annual solicitation is required by December 31 of the following year. Similar rules applying to filers who file or furnish information reports with incorrect TINs are in § 301.6724-1(f).

The preamble to the section 6055 regulations (T.D. 9660, 79 FR 13220) provides short-term relief from reporting penalties for 2015 coverage. Specifically, the IRS will not impose penalties under sections 6721 and 6722 on reporting entities that can show that they have made good faith efforts to comply with the information reporting requirements. This relief applies to incorrect or incomplete information, including TINs or dates of birth, reported on a return or statement.

Explanation of Provisions and Summary of Comments

1. Reporting of Catastrophic Plans

Under § 1.36B-5(a), Exchanges must report to the IRS information relating to qualified health plans in which individuals enroll through the Exchange. Under section 36B(c)(3)(A), the term qualified health plan has the same meaning as defined in section 1301 of the Affordable Care Act except that it does not include a catastrophic plan described in section 1302 of the Affordable Care Act. Thus, Exchanges are not required to report on catastrophic coverage. Section 1.6055-1(d) provides that health insurance issuers need not report on coverage in a qualified health plan in the individual market enrolled in through an Exchange, because that information is generally reported by Exchanges pursuant to § 1.36B-5. Thus, currently neither the Exchanges nor health insurance issuers are responsible for reporting coverage under a catastrophic plan.

Effective administration of section 5000A generally requires reporting of all minimum essential coverage, including catastrophic plans in which individuals enroll through an Exchange. Accordingly, Notice 2015-68 indicated that the Treasury Department and the IRS intended to propose regulations under section 6055 to narrow the relief provided to issuers in § 1.6055-1(d) by requiring issuers of catastrophic plans to report catastrophic plan coverage on Form 1095-B, effective for coverage in 2016 and returns and statements filed and furnished in 2017. Consistent with Notice 2015-68, the proposed regulations include this requirement but, to allow reporting entities sufficient time to implement these reporting requirements, are proposed to be effective for coverage in 2017 and returns and statements filed and furnished in 2018.

Notice 2015-68 indicated that health insurance issuers could voluntarily report on 2015 catastrophic coverage (on returns and statements filed and furnished in 2016) and were encouraged to do so. Notice 2015-68 further provided that an issuer that reports on 2015 catastrophic coverage will not be subject to penalties for these returns. Given the 2017 effective date for reporting of catastrophic coverage provided in these proposed regulations, health insurance issuers similarly may voluntarily report on 2016 catastrophic coverage (on returns and statements filed and furnished in 2017) and are encouraged to do so. An issuer that reports on 2016 catastrophic coverage will not be subject to penalties for these returns.

2. Reporting of Coverage Under Basic Health Programs

Section 1331 of the Affordable Care Act allows states to establish a Basic Health Program to provide an additional healthcare coverage option to certain individuals not eligible for Medicaid. See 42 CFR part 600. The Basic Health Program is designated as minimum essential coverage under 42 CFR 600.5.

Section 5000A(f) does not identify the Basic Health Program as a government-sponsored program, but it closely resembles government-sponsored coverage such as Medicaid and CHIP. Accordingly, Notice 2015-68 indicated that the state agency that administers the Basic Health Program is the entity that must report that coverage under section 6055. Consistent with Notice 2015-68, these proposed regulations provide that the State agency administering coverage under the

---

[1] The Affordable Care Act also added section 6056, which requires that applicable large employers file and furnish statements containing information related to offers of coverage, if any, made to each full-time employee. To complete these statements properly, employers must have each employee's TIN. In accordance with the requirements of a different Code section (section 3402(f)(2)(A)), employers should have already sought each employee's TIN in advance of the deadline for filing and furnishing statements required under section 6056. Therefore, the TIN solicitation rules in these proposed regulations *only apply* to information reporting under section 6055 (which in the case of an applicable large employer providing coverage under a self-insured plan, includes information reporting on Form 1095-C, Part III).

Basic Health Program is required to report that coverage under section 6055.

3. Truncated TINs

Section 6055(b) and §1.6055-1(e) require that health insurance issuers and carriers reporting coverage under insured group health plans report information about the employer sponsoring the plan, including the employer's EIN, to the IRS. Section 6055(c) and §1.6055-1(g) require that health insurance issuers and carriers reporting information to the IRS furnish a statement to a taxpayer providing information about the filer and the covered individuals. Section 301.6109-4(b)(1) provides that the TIN of a person other than the filer, including an EIN, may be truncated on statements furnished to recipients unless, among other reasons, such truncation is otherwise prohibited by statute or regulations. Thus, under §1.6055-1(g)(3) of the existing regulations, a recipient's TIN may appear in the form of an IRS truncated taxpayer identification number (TTIN) on a statement furnished to the recipient. These proposed regulations amend the existing regulations to clarify that a TTIN is not an alternative identifying number; rather, it is one of the ways that a TIN may appear, subject to the rules in §301.6109-4(b)(1).

Existing regulations do not address whether health insurance issuers and carriers are permitted to truncate a sponsoring employer's EIN on statements furnished to taxpayers. Notice 2015-68 advised that the Treasury Department and the IRS intended to propose regulations to clarify that the EIN of the employer sponsoring the plan may be truncated to appear as an IRS TTIN on statements health insurance issuers and carriers furnish to taxpayers. Consistent with Notice 2015-68, the proposed regulations clarify that the EIN of the employer sponsoring the plan may be truncated to appear as an IRS TTIN on statements health insurance issuers and carriers furnish to taxpayers. Section 301.6109-4(b)(2)(ii) prohibits using TTINs if, among other things, a statute specifically requires the use of an EIN. While section 6055(b)(2)(A) requires that the information return filed with the IRS includes the employer's EIN, and section 6055(c)(1)(B) requires that the statement furnished to a taxpayer includes the information required to be shown on the information return with respect to such individual, the statute does not require that the full EIN appear on the statement furnished to taxpayers and the employer's EIN may be truncated to appear in the form of an IRS TTIN.

4. Plans for Which Reporting Is Not Required

Information reporting under section 6055(a) is generally required of every person who provides minimum essential coverage to an individual during the year. In certain instances where the reporting would be duplicative, the existing regulations allow the person who provides supplemental coverage to forgo information reporting. This supplemental coverage rule in §1.6055-1(d)(2) was intended to eliminate duplicate reporting of an individual's minimum essential coverage under circumstances when there is reasonable certainty that the provider of the "primary" coverage will report. This rule has proven to be confusing.

The Treasury Department and the IRS indicated in Notice 2015-68 that regulations would be proposed to replace the existing rules. Accordingly, the proposed regulations provide that (1) if an individual is covered by more than one minimum essential coverage plan or program provided by the same reporting entity, reporting is required for only one of the plans or programs; and (2) reporting is not required for an individual's minimum essential coverage to the extent that the individual is eligible for that coverage only if the individual is also covered by other minimum essential coverage for which section 6055 reporting is required. As in Notice 2015-68, the proposed regulations provide that the second rule applies to eligible employer-sponsored coverage only if the supplemental coverage is offered by the same employer that offered the eligible employer-sponsored coverage for which section 6055 reporting is required. These rules apply month by month and individual by individual.

Thus, under the proposed regulations, applying the first rule, if for a month an individual is enrolled in a self-insured group health plan provided by an employer and also is enrolled in a self-insured health reimbursement arrangement (HRA) provided by the same employer, the reporting entity (the employer) is required to report only one type of coverage for that individual. If an employee is covered under both self-insured arrangements for some months of the year but retires or otherwise drops coverage under the non-HRA group health plan and is covered only under the HRA for other months, the employer must report coverage under the HRA for the months after the employee retires or drops the non-HRA coverage.

Applying the second rule, reporting is not required for minimum essential coverage for a month if that coverage is offered only to individuals who are also covered by other minimum essential coverage,

including Medicare, TRICARE, Medicaid, or certain employer-sponsored coverage, for which reporting is required. In these arrangements, the program for which reporting is required represents the primary coverage while the other minimum essential coverage is supplemental to the primary plan.

Under the application of the second rule to eligible employer-sponsored coverage, if an employer offers both an insured group health plan and an HRA for which an employee is eligible if enrolled in the insured group health plan, and an employee enrolls in both, the employer is not required to report the employee's coverage under the HRA. However, if an employee is enrolled in his or her employer's HRA and in a spouse's non-HRA group health plan, the employee's employer is required to report for the HRA, and the employee's spouse's employer (or the health insurance issuer or carrier, if the plan is insured) is required to report for the non-HRA group health plan coverage. The proposed regulations clarify that, for purposes of this rule, an employer is treated as offering minimum essential coverage that is offered by another employer with whom the employer is treated as a single employer under section 414(b), (c), (m), or (o).

Separately, Notice 2015-68 also stated that, because Medicaid and CHIP coverage provided by the governments of American Samoa, the Commonwealth of the Northern Mariana Islands, Guam, Puerto Rico, and the U.S. Virgin Islands is generally made available only to individuals who are treated as having minimum essential coverage under section 5000A(f)(4) (and, therefore, do not need section 6055 reporting to verify minimum essential coverage), the Medicaid and CHIP agencies in those U.S. possessions or territories are not required to report that coverage under section 6055. Consistent with that rule, the proposed regulations provide that reporting under section 6055 is not required with respect to Medicaid and CHIP agencies in U.S. possessions or territories.

5. TIN Solicitation

Information reporting under section 6055 is subject to the penalty provisions of sections 6721 and 6722 for failure to file timely a correct information return or failure to furnish timely a correct statement to the individual. See §1.6055-1(h). The penalties may be waived under section 6724(a) if the failure is due to reasonable cause and not due to willful neglect; that is, if a reporting entity demonstrates that it acted in a responsible manner and that the failure is due to significant mitigating factors or events beyond the reporting entity's control. See §301.6724-1(a)(2). Under §301.6724-1(e), in cases of a missing TIN, the reporting entity is treated as acting in a responsible manner in soliciting a TIN if the reporting entity makes (1) an initial solicitation when an account is opened or a relationship is established, (2) a first annual solicitation by December 31 of the year the account is opened (or January 31 of the following year if the account is opened in December), and (3) a second annual solicitation by December 31 of the year following the year in which the account is opened. Similar rules apply regarding incorrect TINs under §301.6724-1(f). The rules in §301.6724-1(e) and (f) were issued prior to the enactment of section 6055 and apply to most forms of information reporting.

Comments received in response to the first notice of proposed rulemaking (REG-132455-11) under section 6055, published in the **Federal Register** (78 FR 54986) on September 9, 2013, raised concerns about the application of the TIN solicitation rules to section 6055 reporting. Accordingly, Notice 2015-68 provided that, pending the issuance of additional guidance, reporting entities will not be subject to penalties for failure to report a TIN if they comply with the requirements of §301.6724-1(e) with the following modifications: (1) The initial solicitation is made at an individual's first enrollment or, if already enrolled on September 17, 2015, the next open season, (2) the second solicitation (the first annual solicitation) is made at a reasonable time thereafter, and (3) the third solicitation (the second annual solicitation) is made by December 31 of the year following the initial solicitation. Notice 2015-68 also requested comments on the application of the reasonable cause rules under section 6724 to section 6055 reporting.

In response to the request for comments in Notice 2015-68, one commenter requested that the proposed regulations include detailed rules tailored to TIN solicitation for information returns required by section 6055. This commenter expressed concern that, because the current rules were designed primarily to apply to financial relationships, they are difficult to apply to section 6055 reporting, particularly the rules for demonstrating that the filer acted in a responsible manner as described in §301.6724-1(e) and (f). The Treasury Department and the IRS agree with the commenter that some modification to the rules in §301.6724-1(e) is warranted to account for the differences between information reporting under section 6055 and information reporting under other provisions of the Code. Accordingly, the Treasury Department and the IRS propose regulations to provide specific TIN solicitation rules for section 6055 reporting. Until final regulations are released, reporting entities may rely on these proposed rules and Notice 2015-68. The preamble below also includes some additional transition rules that apply to reporting entities in certain situations.

Section 301.6724-1(e)(1)(i) provides that an initial TIN solicitation must occur when an account (which includes accounts, relationships, and other transactions) is opened. Section 301.6724-1(e) does not define the term "opened" for this purpose. Commenters requested clarification as to how the term "opened" should be interpreted for purposes of reporting under section 6055. In the context of financial accounts, an account is generally considered opened on the first day it is available for use by its owner. In most cases, this would be shortly after the application to open that account is received, and this day would be no earlier than the day the application was received. Health coverage does not work in the same way. In some cases, the first effective date of health coverage is before the day the application was received, making it impractical to solicit TINs before the coverage takes effect. In other cases, the effective date of coverage may be months after the day the application was received. To account for this different timing, the proposed regulations provide that, for purposes of section 6055 reporting, an account is considered "opened" on the date the filer receives a substantially complete application for new coverage or to add an individual to existing coverage. Accordingly, health coverage providers may generally satisfy the requirement for the initial solicitation by requesting enrollees' TINs as part of the application for coverage.

To address differences in the way financial accounts and health coverage are opened, the proposed regulations also change the timing of the first annual solicitation (the second solicitation overall) with respect to missing TINs. Under §301.6724-1(e)(1)(ii), a first annual solicitation must be made by December 31 of the year the account is opened (or by January 31 of the following calendar year if the account is opened in December). The timing of the first annual solicitation is dictated by the need to have accurate reporting of information to taxpayers and the IRS in preparation for the filing of an income tax return. Accounts, relationships, and other transactions may be opened or begun throughout the year, and may remain active indefinitely. It is beneficial to the IRS, filers, and taxpayers in the context of accounts, relationships, and other transactions to have a single deadline for the first annual solicitation at the end of the calendar year (or January if the account is opened in December).

By contrast, health coverage is generally offered on an annual basis. While individuals may, depending on their circumstances, enroll in coverage at any point during the year, many covered individuals enroll in coverage during the open enrollment period, which is in advance of the beginning of the coverage year. The most common coverage year is the calendar year and many individuals enroll late each year for coverage the following year. For such individuals, requiring the first annual solicitation (the second solicitation overall) by December 31 of the year in which the application is received is earlier than is necessary (because reporting is not due until more than a year later) and coincides with the end of a plan year, which is already the busiest time of year for coverage providers. To address these considerations, the proposed regulations require that the first annual solicitation be made no later than seventy-five days after the date on which the account was "opened" (*i.e.*, the day the filer received the substantially complete application for coverage), or, if the coverage is retroactive, no later than the seventy-fifth day after the determination of retroactive coverage is made. The deadline for the second annual solicitation (third solicitation overall) remains December 31 of the year following the year the account is opened as required by §301.6724-1(e)(1)(iii).

As noted above, taxpayers may rely on these proposed regulations and on Notice 2015-68 until final regulations are published. To provide additional relief and ensure that the requirements for the first annual and second annual solicitations may be satisfied with respect to individuals already enrolled in coverage, an additional rule is provided. Under this rule, if an individual was enrolled in coverage on any day before July 29, 2016, the account is considered opened on July 29, 2016. Accordingly, reporting entities have satisfied the requirement for the initial solicitation with respect to already enrolled individuals so long as they requested enrollee TINs either as part of the application for coverage or at any other point before July 29, 2016. The deadlines for the first and second annual solicitations are set by reference to the date the account is opened. Thus, the rule above that treats all accounts for individuals currently enrolled in coverage for which a TIN has not been provided as opened on July 29, 2016, provides additional time for the

annual solicitations as well. Specifically, consistent with Notice 2015-68, the first annual solicitation should be made at a reasonable time after July 29, 2016. For this purpose, a reporting entity that makes the first annual solicitation within 75 days of the initial solicitation will be treated as having made the second solicitation within a reasonable time. Reporting entities that have not made the initial solicitation before July 29, 2016 should comply with the first annual solicitation requirement by making a solicitation within a reasonable time of July 29, 2016. Notice 2015-68 also provided that a reporting entity is deemed to have satisfied the initial, first annual, and second annual solicitations for an individual whose coverage was terminated prior to September 17, 2015, and taxpayers may continue to rely on this rule as well.

Section 301.6724-1(e)(1)(v) provides that the initial and first annual solicitations relate to failures on returns filed for the year in which the account is opened (meaning that showing reasonable cause with respect to the year the account is opened generally requires making the initial and first annual solicitations in the year the account is opened). Because these proposed regulations provide that an account is considered opened for section 6055 purposes when a substantially complete application for that account is received, an account would, in some cases, be considered open in a year prior to the year for which coverage is actually effective and for which reporting is required. This would occur, for example, when a reporting entity receives an application during open enrollment for coverage effective as of the first day of the next coverage year. To ensure that reporting entities that make the initial solicitation and first annual solicitation are eligible for relief for the first year for which reporting is required, the proposed regulations provide that, for purposes of reporting under section 6055, the initial and first annual solicitations relate to failures on returns required to be filed for the year that includes the day that is the first effective date of coverage for a covered individual. Similarly, §301.6724-1(e)(1)(v) provides that the second annual solicitation relates to failures on returns filed for the year immediately following the year in which the account is opened and succeeding calendar years (meaning that showing reasonable cause with respect to years after the account is opened generally requires making the second annual solicitation during the year following the year the account is opened). As with the initial and first annual solicitations, the existing rule under §301.6724-1(e)(1)(v) could provide relief for the wrong year when combined with the proposed definition of account opening under section 6055. Accordingly, the proposed regulations provide that the second annual solicitation relates to failures on returns filed for the year immediately following the year to which the first annual solicitation relates, and succeeding calendar years.

In contrast to missing TINs, the Treasury Department and the IRS do not recognize a similar need to modify the existing first annual solicitation rules for incorrect TINs in §301.6724-1(f)(1)(ii). As with many other types of information reports, information reports of health coverage are generally filed after the end of the tax year, and thus, it is only after the tax year that a filer would generally receive notice of an incorrect TIN. Because the end of the tax year typically corresponds with the end of the coverage year, there is no reason to distinguish the timing of the correction of incorrect TINs for health coverage from all other types of accounts for which information reporting is required. Consequently, the proposed regulations do not alter the rules for incorrect TINs in §301.6724-1(f)(1)(ii) and (iii) as applied to information reporting under section 6055. However, as with the rules regarding missing TINs under §301.6724-1(e)(1)(ii), the rules regarding incorrect TINs in §301.6724-1(f)(1)(i) make reference to the time an account is "opened." Accordingly, the proposed regulations, which provides that for purposes of section 6055 reporting an account is considered "opened" at the time the filer receives an application for new coverage or to add an individual to existing coverage, also applies for purposes of the initial solicitation for incorrect TINs in §301.6724-1(f)(1)(i).[2]

a. Application of the TIN Solicitation Rules to "Responsible Individuals" and "Covered Individuals"

A commenter requested clarification that the initial and annual solicitations of §301.6724-1(e)(1)(i) and (ii) need be made only to the responsible individual for all individuals covered under a single policy. The commenter further suggested that TIN solicitations made to a responsible individual be treated as TIN solicitations made to all individuals named on the responsible individual's policy.

Under §1.6055-1(e)(1)(ii) and (iii), filers must report the TIN of each covered individual (who, under §301.6721-1(g)(5), are also "payees"), and §1.6055-1(g)(1) requires that the TIN of each covered individual

---

[2] A filer of the information return required under §1.6055-1 may receive an error message from the IRS indicating that a TIN and name provided on the return do not match IRS records. An error message is neither a Notice 972CG, Notice of Proposed Civil Penalty, nor a requirement that the filer must solicit a TIN in response to the error message.

be shown on statements furnished to the responsible individual. Current § 1.6055-1(g)(1) provides that, for purposes of the penalties under section 6722, the furnishing of a statement to the responsible individual is treated as the furnishing of a statement to a covered individual. This rule is intended to allow reporting entities to satisfy the section 6722 requirements for all covered individuals by furnishing the required statement only to the responsible individual. The Treasury Department and the IRS also intend for a similar rule to apply to the TIN solicitation rules under the section 6724 regulations. To clarify that this is how these rules apply, the proposed regulations expressly provide that TIN solicitations (both initial and annual) made to the responsible individual for a policy or plan are treated as TIN solicitations of every covered individual on the policy or plan for purposes of § 301.6724-1(e)(1) and (f)(1). The filer does not need to make separate solicitations from the responsible individual for each covered individual nor does it need to separately solicit the TINs of each covered individual by contacting each covered individual directly. However, we decline to adopt the commenter's suggestion that a TIN solicitation made to a responsible individual be treated as a TIN solicitation made to all individuals named on that responsible individual's policy at any time, including those individuals added to a policy after the TIN solicitations. When a new individual is added to a policy, the coverage provider establishes a relationship with that individual. The individual is new to the filer, and it is the filer's responsibility to solicit that individual's TIN. Accordingly, to qualify for the penalty waiver, filers must solicit TINs for each individual added to a policy under the procedures outlined in § 301.6724-1(e)(1)(i) and (f)(1)(i); however, any other individual for whom the filer already has a TIN or already has solicited a TIN the prescribed amount of times need not be solicited again regardless of what changes take place during the filer's coverage of that individual.

b. Different Forms of TIN Solicitations

A commenter to Notice 2015-68 requested that the provision of renewal applications to enrollees be permitted to satisfy the annual solicitation requirement for purposes of § 301.6724-1(e)(1)(ii) and (iii) and (f)(1)(ii) and (iii) if those renewal applications request TINs from covered individuals. Under current law, TIN requests may be made in a number of different formats. The provision of a renewal application that requests TINs for all covered individuals satisfies the annual solicitation provisions of § 301.6724-1(e)(1)(ii) and (iii) and (f)(1)(ii) and (iii) if it is sent by the deadline for those annual solicitations. Thus, no changes to the regulations are necessary for renewal applications to satisfy the annual solicitation requirement.

The same commenter requested that the requirement in § 301.6724-1(e)(2)(i)(B) to provide the responsible individual with a Form W-9 should be eliminated. The commenter was concerned that this requirement imposes burdens on responsible individuals that make it less likely that they will respond to a TIN solicitation. Section 301.6724-1(e)(2)(i)(B) requires that an annual solicitation include a "Form W-9 or an acceptable substitute . . . " Thus, the existing regulations do not require that Form W-9 be sent. Filers are allowed to request TINs on an acceptable substitute for Form W-9, which includes a renewal application or other request for a TIN. Thus, this comment is not adopted.

This commenter also requested that the requirement in § 301.6724-1(e)(2)(i)(C) that annual solicitations include a return envelope be eliminated, and, if not eliminated, that clarification be provided as to how this requirement applies to multiple TINs. Existing regulations include this requirement because individuals are more likely to comply with a TIN solicitation if that solicitation includes a return envelope. We see no reason that the requirement to include a return envelope, which exists for other information reporting provisions, should be removed for reporting under section 6055. Thus, the proposed regulations do not adopt this comment. However, filers may request more than one TIN at the same time and do not need to send separate envelopes with each request. For example, on a renewal application requesting the TINs for all covered individuals, filers need only provide one return envelope for that application or request.

c. Solicitations by Employers

A commenter requested that employers be permitted to make TIN solicitations on behalf of filers. The commenter offered that employers are frequently in a better position than coverage providers to request TINs from the employers' employees and the employees' dependents, and, for practical reasons, it would make sense to allow employers to step in the shoes of the coverage provider for purposes of making the solicitations under § 301.6724-1(e)(1) and (f)(1).

Under existing regulations, actions taken by employers may satisfy the requirement for making an initial or annual TIN solicitation. Employers may, for example, provide their employees with applications for health coverage. If these applications request that the applicants provide TINs for all individuals to be covered, the coverage provider has made an initial solicitation for these individuals' TINs.

The commenter further requested that a filer that arranges to have an employer take on responsibility for the TIN solicitations be treated as having met the penalty waiver requirements of § 301.6724-1(e)(1) and (f)(1). Under existing regulations, qualifying for a penalty waiver requires that the solicitations actually be made. To avoid creating a less stringent standard in cases where an employer is acting on the filer's behalf, the proposed regulations do not adopt the commenter's proposal.

d. Electronic TIN Solicitations

A commenter requested that filers be permitted to make annual TIN solicitations by electronic means if the responsible individual has consented to the receipt of information concerning his or her coverage in the same electronic format in which the annual solicitation is made. IRS Publication 1586, Reasonable Cause Regulations and Requirements for Missing and Incorrect Name/TINs (including instructions for reading CD/DVDs), provides that filers may establish an electronic system for payees (including covered individuals) to receive and respond to TIN solicitations, provided certain listed requirements are met. IRS Publication 1586 can be found at *www.irs.gov/forms-pubs*. Because filers are already able to solicit TINs electronically, it is unnecessary to address the commenter's recommendation for electronic TIN solicitations with these proposed regulations.

Proposed Effective/Applicability Date

These regulations are generally proposed to apply for taxable years ending after December 31, 2015, and may be relied on for calendar years ending after December 31, 2013.

The only exception is the rules in section 1 of this preamble relating to reporting of coverage under catastrophic plans. Those rules are proposed to apply for calendar years beginning after December 31, 2016. Health insurance issuers may voluntarily report on 2015 and 2016 catastrophic coverage (on returns and statements filed and furnished in 2016 and 2017 respectively). An issuer that reports on 2015 and/or 2016 catastrophic coverage will not be subject to penalties for these returns.

In addition, until these the proposed regulations are finalized, taxpayers may continue to rely on the rules provided in Notice 2015-68.

Special Analyses

Certain IRS regulations, including this one, are exempt from the requirements of Executive Order 12866, as supplemented and reaffirmed by Executive Order 13563. Therefore, a regulatory impact assessment is not required.

It has also been determined that section 553(b) of the Administrative Procedure Act (5 U.S.C. chapter 5) does not apply to these regulations.

It is hereby certified that these regulations will not have a significant economic impact on a substantial number of small entities. This certification is based on the fact that the information collection required under these regulations is imposed under section 6055. Consistent with the statute, the proposed regulations require a person that provides minimum essential coverage to an individual to file a return with the IRS reporting certain information and to furnish a statement to the responsible individual who enrolled an individual or family in the coverage. These regulations primarily provide the method of filing and furnishing returns and statements under section 6055. Moreover, the proposed regulations attempt to minimize the burden associated with this collection of information by limiting reporting to the information that the IRS will use to verify minimum essential coverage and administer tax credits.

Based on these facts, a Regulatory Flexibility Analysis under the Regulatory Flexibility Act (5 U.S.C. chapter 6) is not required.

Pursuant to section 7805(f), this notice of proposed rulemaking will be submitted to the Chief Counsel for Advocacy of the Small Business Administration for comment on its impact on small business.

Statement of Availability of IRS Documents

IRS Revenue Procedures, Revenue Rulings notices, notices and other guidance cited in this preamble are published in the Internal Revenue Bulletin (or Cumulative Bulletin) and are available from the Superintendent of Documents, U.S. Government Printing Office, Washington, DC 20402, or by visiting the IRS Web site at *http://www.irs.gov*.

Comments and Requests for Public Hearing

Before these proposed regulations are adopted as final regulations, consideration will be given to any comments that are submitted timely to the IRS as prescribed in this preamble under the " **ADDRESSES**" heading. The Treasury Department and the IRS request comments on all aspects of the proposed rules. All comments will be available for public inspection at *www.regulations.gov* or upon request. A public hearing will be scheduled if requested in writing by any person that timely submits written comments. If a public hearing is scheduled, notice of the date, time, and place for the public hearing will be published in the **Federal Register**.

Drafting Information

The principal author of these proposed regulations is John B. Lovelace of the Office of Associate Chief Counsel (Income Tax and Accounting). However, other personnel from the IRS and the Treasury Department participated in the development of the regulations.

List of Subjects

26 CFR Part 1

Income taxes, Reporting and recordkeeping requirements.

26 CFR Part 301

Employment taxes, Estate taxes, Excise taxes, Gift taxes, Income taxes, Penalties, Reporting and recordkeeping requirements.

Proposed Amendments to the Regulations

Accordingly, 26 CFR parts 1 and 301 are proposed to be amended as follows:

PART 1—INCOME TAXES

■ **Paragraph 1**. The authority citation for part 1 continues to read in part as follows:

Authority: 26 U.S.C. 7805 * * *

■ **Par. 2**. Section 1.6055-1 is amended by:

■ 1. Adding paragraphs (b)(13) and (14).

■ 2. Redesignating paragraph (c)(1)(iv) as (c)(1)(v) and adding a new paragraph (c)(1)(iv).

■ 3. Revising paragraphs (d)(1) and (2).

■ 4. Redesignating paragraph (d)(3) as (d)(5) and adding a new paragraph (d)(3).

■ 5. Adding paragraphs (d)(4) and (6).

■ 6. Revising paragraph (g)(3).

■ 7. Revising paragraph (h)(1).

■ 8. Adding paragraph (h)(3).

■ 9. Revising paragraph (j).

The revisions and additions read as follows:

§ 1.6055-1 Information reporting for minimum essential coverage.

* * * * *

(b) * * *

(13) *Catastrophic plan*. The term catastrophic plan has the same meaning as in section 1302(e) of the Affordable Care Act (42 U.S.C. 18022(e)).

(14) *Basic health program*. The term basic health program means a basic health program established under section 1331 of the Affordable Care Act (42 U.S.C. 18051).

(c) * * *

(1) * * *

(iv) The state agency that administers a Basic Health Program;

* * * * *

(d) *Reporting not required* —(1) *Qualified health plans*. Except for coverage under a catastrophic plan, a health insurance issuer is not required to file a return or furnish a report under this section for coverage in a qualified health plan in the individual market enrolled in through an Exchange.

(2) *Duplicative coverage*. If an individual is covered for a month by more than one minimum essential coverage plan or program provided by the same reporting entity, reporting is required for only one of the plans or programs for that month.

(3) *Supplemental coverage*. Reporting is not required for minimum essential coverage of an individual for a month if that individual is eligible for that coverage only if enrolled in other minimum essential coverage for which section 6055 reporting is required and is not waived under this paragraph (d)(3). This paragraph (d)(3) applies with respect to eligible employer-sponsored coverage only if the supplemental coverage is offered by the same employer that offered the eligible employer-sponsored coverage for which reporting is required. For this purpose, an employer is treated as offering minimum essential coverage offered by any other person that is a member of a controlled group of entities under section 414(b) or (c), an affiliated service group under section 414(m), or an entity in an arrangement described under section 414(o) of which the employer is also a member.

(4) *Certain coverage provided by Territories and Possessions*. The agencies that administer Medicaid and the Children's Health Insurance Program in American Samoa, the Commonwealth of the Northern Mariana Islands, Guam, Puerto Rico, and the United States Virgin Islands are not required to report that coverage under section 6055.

* * * * *

(6) *Examples*. The following examples illustrate the rules of this paragraph (d).

Example 1. Upon being hired, Taxpayer A enrolls in a self-insured major medical group health plan and a health reimbursement arrangement (HRA), both offered by A's employer, V. Both the group health plan and the HRA are minimum essential coverage, and V is the reporting entity for both. Because V is the reporting entity for both the self-insured major medical group health plan and the HRA, under paragraph (d)(2) of this section V must report under paragraph (a) of this section for either its self-insured major medical group health plan or its HRA for A for the months in which A is enrolled in both plans.

Example 2. Taxpayer B is enrolled in an insured employer-sponsored group health plan offered by B's employer, W. B is also covered by an HRA offered by W. Under the terms of the HRA, B is eligible for the HRA because B is enrolled in W's insured employer-sponsored group health plan. W's insured employer-sponsored group health plan is minimum essential coverage and, under paragraphs (a) and (c)(1)(i) of this section, the issuer of the insured employer-sponsored group health plan must report coverage under the plan. Therefore, for the months in which B is enrolled in both plans, under paragraph (d)(3) of this section, W does not need to report the HRA for B because the issuer is required to report on coverage for B in the insured employer-sponsored group health plan offered by W for those months.

Example 3. Taxpayer C enrolls in a Medicare Savings Program administered by X, a state Medicaid agency, which provides financial assistance with Medicare Part A premiums. Only individuals enrolled in Medicare Part A are offered coverage in this Medicare Savings Program. Medicare Part A is government-sponsored minimum essential coverage and, under paragraphs (a) and (c)(1)(iii) of this section, Medicare must report coverage under the program. Therefore, under paragraph (d)(3) of this section, X does not need to report under paragraph (a) of this section for C's coverage under the Medicare Savings Program.

Example 4. Taxpayer E obtains a Medicare supplemental insurance (Medigap) policy that provides financial assistance with costs not covered by Medicare Part A from Z, a health insurance issuer. Only individuals enrolled in Medicare Part A are offered coverage under this Medigap policy. Medicare Part A is minimum essential coverage and, under paragraphs (a) and (c)(1)(iii) of this section, Medicare is required to report E's coverage under Medicare Part A. Therefore, under paragraph (d)(3) of this section, Z does not need to report E's coverage under the Medigap policy.

Example 5. Taxpayer F is covered by an HRA offered by F's employer, P. F is also enrolled in a non-HRA group health plan that is self-insured and sponsored by F's spouse's employer, Q. P and Q are not treated as one employer under section 414(b), (c), (m), or (o). Under the terms of the HRA, F is eligible for the HRA only because F is enrolled in a non-HRA group health plan, which in this case is the group health plan offered by Q. However, because the HRA and the non-HRA group health plan are offered by different employers, paragraph (d)(3) of this section does not apply. Accordingly, under paragraphs (a) and (c)(2)(i)(A) of this section, P must report F's enrollment in the HRA, and Q must report F's (and F's spouse's) enrollment in the non-HRA group health plan.

* * * * *

(g) * * *

(3) *Form of the statement.* A statement required under this paragraph (g) may be made either by furnishing to the responsible individual a copy of the return filed with the Internal Revenue Service or on a substitute statement. A substitute statement must include the information required to be shown on the return filed with the Internal Revenue Service and must comply with requirements in published guidance (see § 601.601(d)(2) of this chapter) relating to substitute statements. An individual's identifying number may be truncated to appear in the form of an IRS truncated taxpayer identification number (TTIN) on the statement furnished to the responsible individual. The identifying number of the employer may also be truncated to appear in the form of a TTIN on the statement furnished to the responsible individual. For provisions relating to the use of TTINs, see § 301.6109-4 of this chapter (Procedure and Administration Regulations).

* * * * *

(h) * * * (1) *In general.* For provisions relating to the penalty for failure to file timely a correct information return required under section 6055, see section 6721 and the regulations under that section. For provisions relating to the penalty for failure to furnish timely a correct statement to responsible individuals required under section 6055, see section 6722 and the regulations under that section. See section 6724, and the regulations thereunder, and paragraph (h)(3) of this section for provisions relating to the waiver of penalties if a failure to file or furnish timely or accurately is due to reasonable cause and not due to willful neglect.

* * * * *

(3) *Application of section 6724 waiver of penalties to section 6055 reporting* —(i) *In general.* Paragraphs (e) and (f) of § 301.6724-1 of this chapter, as modified by this paragraph (h)(3), apply to reasonable cause waivers of penalties under sections 6721 and 6722 for failure to file timely or accurate information returns or to furnish individual statements required to be filed or furnished under section 6055.

(ii) *Account opened.* For purposes of section 6055 reporting and the solicitation rules contained in paragraphs (i), (ii), (iii), and (v) of § 301.6724-1(e) of this chapter and paragraph (i) of § 301.6724-1(f)(1) of this chapter, an account is considered opened at the time the reporting entity receives a substantially complete application for coverage (including an application to add an individual to existing coverage) from or on behalf of an individual for whom the reporting entity does not already provide coverage.

(iii) *First annual solicitation deadline for missing TINs.* In lieu of the deadline for the first annual solicitation contained in paragraph (ii) of § 301.6724-1(e)(1) of this chapter, the first annual solicitation must be made on or before the seventy-fifth day after the date on which an account is opened (or, in the case of retroactive coverage, the seventy-fifth day after the determination of retroactive coverage is made). The period from the date on which the reporting entity receives an application for coverage to the last day on which the first annual solicitation may be made is the first annual solicitation period.

(iv) *Failures to which a solicitation relates* —(A) *Missing TIN.* For purposes of reporting under section 6055 and the solicitation rules contained in paragraph (1) of § 301.6724-1(e) of this chapter, the initial and first annual solicitations relate to failures on returns required to be filed for the year which includes the first effective date of coverage for a covered individual. The second annual solicitation relates to failures on returns filed for the year immediately following the year to which the first annual solicitation relates and for succeeding calendar years.

(B) *Incorrect TIN.* For purposes of reporting under section 6055 and the solicitation rules contained in paragraph (i) of § 301.6724-1(f)(1) of this chapter, the initial solicitation relates to failures on returns required to be filed for the year which includes the first effective date of coverage for a covered individual.

(v) *Solicitations made to responsible individual.* For purposes of reporting under section 6055 and the solicitation rules contained in § 301.6724-1(e) and (f) of this chapter, an initial or annual solicitation made to the responsible individual is treated as a solicitation made to a covered individual.

* * * * *

(j) *Applicability date* —(1) Except as provided in paragraphs (j)(2) and (3) of this section, this section applies for calendar years ending after December 31, 2014.

(2) Paragraphs (b)(14), (c)(1)(v), (d)(2) through (6), and (g)(3) of this section apply to calendar years ending after December 31, 2015. Paragraphs (d)(2), (d)(3), and (g)(3) of § 1.6055-1 as contained in 26 CFR part 1 edition revision as of April 1, 2016, apply to calendar years ending after December 31, 2014 and beginning before January 1, 2016.

(3) Paragraphs (b)(13) and (d)(1) of this section apply to calendar years beginning after December 31, 2016. Paragraph (d)(1) of § 1.6055-1 as contained in 26 CFR part 1 edition revised as of April 1, 2016, applies to calendar years ending after December 31, 2015 and beginning before January 1, 2017.

* * * * *

John Dalrymple,

Deputy Commissioner for Services and Enforcement.

[FR Doc. 2016-18100 Filed 7-29-16; 11:15 am]

BILLING CODE **4830-01-P**

¶ 20,264O

IRS: Defined benefit plans: Distributions: Minimum present value requirements.—The IRS has issued proposed regulations that would update the current final regulations regarding the minimum present value requirements of Code Sec. 417(e)(3) that applicable to certain defined benefit (DB) plans for changes made by the Pension Protection Act of 2006 (PPA, P.L. 109-280) and to eliminate certain obsolete provisions. In addition, the proposed regulations would provide other clarifying changes. The changes are proposed to apply to distributions with annuity starting dates in plan years beginning on or after the date regulations that finalize the proposed regulations are published in the Federal Register.

The proposed regulation was published in the Federal Register on November 25, 2016 (81 FR 85190).

DEPARTMENT OF THE TREASURY

Internal Revenue Service

26 CFR Part 1

[REG-107424-12]

RIN 1545-BK95

Update to Minimum Present Value Requirements for Defined Benefit Plan Distributions

AGENCY: Internal Revenue Service (IRS), Treasury.

ACTION: Notice of proposed rulemaking and notice of public hearing.

SUMMARY: This document contains proposed regulations providing guidance relating to the minimum present value requirements applicable to certain defined benefit pension plans. These proposed regulations would provide guidance on changes made by the Pension Protection Act of 2006 and would provide other modifications to these rules as well. These regulations would affect participants, beneficiaries, sponsors, and administrators of defined benefit pension plans. This document also provides a notice of a public hearing on these proposed regulations.

DATES: Written or electronic comments must be received by February 23, 2017. Outlines of topics to be discussed at the public hearing scheduled for March 7, 2017, must be received by February 23, 2017.

ADDRESSES: Send submissions to: CC:PA:LPD:PR (REG-107424-12), Room 5203, Internal Revenue Service, P.O. Box 7604, Ben Franklin Station, Washington, DC 20044. Submissions may be hand-delivered Monday through Friday between the hours of 8 a.m. and 4 p.m. to: CC:PA:LPD:PR (REG-107424-12), Courier's Desk, Internal Revenue Service, 1111 Constitution Avenue NW., Washington, DC, or sent electronically, via the Federal eRulemaking Portal at *http://www.regulations.gov* (IRS REG-107424-12). The public hearing will be held in the IRS Auditorium, Internal Revenue Building, 1111 Constitution Avenue NW., Washington, DC.

FOR FURTHER INFORMATION CONTACT: Concerning the regulations, Neil S. Sandhu or Linda S.F. Marshall at (202) 317-6700; concerning submissions of comments, the hearing, and/or being placed on the building access list to attend the hearing, Oluwafunmilayo (Funmi) Taylor at (202) 317-6901 (not toll-free numbers).

SUPPLEMENTARY INFORMATION:

Background

Section 401(a)(11) of the Internal Revenue Code (Code) provides that, in order for a defined benefit plan to qualify under section 401(a), except as provided under section 417, in the case of a vested participant who does not die before the annuity starting date, the accrued benefit payable to such participant must be provided in the form of a qualified joint and survivor annuity. In the case of a vested participant who dies before the annuity starting date and who has a surviving spouse, a defined benefit plan must provide a qualified preretirement survivor annuity to the surviving spouse of such participant, except as provided under section 417.

Section 411(d)(6)(B) provides that a plan amendment that has the effect of eliminating or reducing an early retirement benefit or a retirement-type subsidy, or eliminating an optional form of benefit, with respect to benefits attributable to service before the amendment is treated as impermissibly reducing accrued benefits. However, the last sentence of section 411(d)(6)(B) provides that the Secretary may by regulations provide that section 411(d)(6)(B) does not apply to a plan amendment that eliminates an optional form of benefit (other than a plan amendment that has the effect of eliminating or reducing an early retirement benefit or a retirement-type subsidy).

Section 417(e)(1) provides that a plan may provide that the present value of a qualified joint and survivor annuity or a qualified preretirement survivor annuity will be immediately distributed if that present value does not exceed the amount that can be distributed without the participant's consent under section 411(a)(11). Section 417(e)(2) provides that, if the present value of the qualified joint and survivor annuity or the qualified preretirement survivor annuity exceeds the amount that can be distributed without the participant's consent under section 411(a)(11), then a plan may immediately distribute the present value of a qualified joint and survivor annuity or the qualified preretirement survivor annuity only if the participant and the spouse of the participant (or where the participant has died, the surviving spouse) consent in writing to the distribution.

Section 417(e)(3)(A) provides that the present value shall not be less than the present value calculated by using the applicable mortality table and the applicable interest rate.[1]

Section 417(e)(3)(B) of the Code, as amended by section 302 of the Pension Protection Act of 2006 (PPA '06), Public Law 109-280, 120 Stat. 780 (2006), provides that the term "applicable mortality table" means a mortality table, modified as appropriate by the Secretary, based on the mortality table specified for the plan year under section 430(h)(3)(A) (without regard to section 430(h)(3)(C) or (3)(D)).

Section 417(e)(3)(C) of the Code, as amended by section 302 of PPA '06, provides that the term "applicable interest rate" means the adjusted first, second, and third segment rates applied under rules similar to the rules of section 430(h)(2)(C) of the Code for the month before the date of the distribution or such other time as the Secretary may prescribe by regulations. However, for purposes of section 417(e)(3), these rates are to be determined without regard to the segment rate stabilization rules of section 430(h)(2)(C)(iv). In addition, under section 417(e)(3)(D), these rates are to be determined using the average yields for a month, rather than the 24-month average used under section 430(h)(2)(D).

Section 411(a)(13) of the Code, as added by section 701(b) of PPA '06, provides that an "applicable defined benefit plan," as defined by section 411(a)(13)(C), is not treated as failing to meet the requirements of section 417(e) with respect to accrued benefits derived from employer contributions solely because the present value of a participant's accrued benefit (or any portion thereof) may be, under the terms of the plan, equal to the amount expressed as the hypothetical account balance or as an accumulated percentage of such participant's final average compensation.

Section 1107(a)(2) of PPA '06 provides that a pension plan does not fail to meet the requirements of section 411(d)(6) by reason of a plan amendment to which section 1107 applies, except as provided by the Secretary of the Treasury. Section 1107 of PPA '06 applies to plan amendments made pursuant to the provisions of PPA '06 or regulations issued thereunder that are adopted no later than a specified date, generally the last day of the first plan year beginning on or after January 1, 2009.

Final regulations under section 417 relating to the qualified joint and survivor and qualified preretirement survivor annuity requirements have not been amended to reflect PPA '06. The regulations, which were issued on August 22, 1988, were amended on April 3, 1998, to reflect changes enacted by the Uruguay Round Agreements Act, Public Law 103-465 (GATT).

Section 1.417(e)-1(d)(1) provides that a defined benefit plan generally must provide that the present value of any accrued benefit and the amount of any distribution, including a single sum, must not be less than the amount calculated using the specified applicable interest rate and the specified applicable mortality table. The present value of any optional form of benefit cannot be less than the present value of the accrued benefit determined in accordance with the preceding sentence.

Section 1.417(e)-1(d)(6) provides an exception from the minimum present value requirements of section 417(e) and § 1.417(e)-1(d). This exception applies to the amount of a distribution paid in the form of an annual benefit that either does not decrease during the life of the participant (or, in the case of a qualified preretirement survivor annuity, the life of the participant's spouse), or that decreases during the life of the participant merely because of the death of the survivor annuitant (but only if the reduction is to a level not below 50 percent of the annual benefit payable before the death of such survivor annuitant) or the cessation or reduction of Social Security supplements or qualified disability benefits.

Notice 2007-81, 2007-2 CB 899 (see 26 CFR 601.601(d)(2)(ii)(b)), provides guidance on the applicable interest rate. Rev. Rul. 2007-67, 2007-2 CB 1047 (see 26 CFR 601.601(d)(2)(ii)(b)), provides guidance on the applicable mortality table[2] and the timing rules that apply to the determination of the applicable interest rate and the applicable mortality table.

The Worker, Retiree, and Employer Recovery Act of 2008, Public Law 109-280 (120 Stat. 780), amended section 415(b)(2)(E)(v) to provide that the applicable mortality table under section 417(e)(3)(B) applies for purposes of adjusting a benefit or limitation pursuant to section 415(b)(2)(B), (C), or (D).

Sections 205(g), 203(e), and 204(g) of the Employee Retirement Income Security Act of 1974 (ERISA) contain rules that are parallel to Code sections 417(e), 411(a)(11), and 411(d)(6), respectively. Under section 101 of Reorganization Plan No. 4 of 1978 (43 FR 47713), the Secretary of the Treasury has interpretive jurisdiction over the subject matter addressed in these regulations for purposes of ERISA, as well as the Code. Thus, these regulations apply for purposes of the Code and the corresponding provisions of ERISA.

In *West* v. *AK Steel Corporation Retirement Accumulation Pension Plan*, 484 F.3d 395 (6th Cir. 2007), the court held that a preretirement mortality discount could not be used in the computation of the present value of a participant's single-sum distribution under a cash balance plan if the death benefit under the plan was equal in value to the participant's accrued benefit under the plan. The court found that, if a participant's beneficiary is entitled to the participant's entire accrued benefit upon the participant's death before attainment of normal retirement age, the use of a mortality discount for the period before normal retirement age would result in a partial forfeiture of benefits in violation of the ERISA vesting rules that correspond to the rules of section 411(a). See also *Berger* v. *Xerox Corporation Retirement Income Guarantee Plan*, 338 F.3d 755 (7th Cir. 2003); *Crosby* v. *Bowater, Inc. Ret. Plan*, 212 FRD. 350 (W.D. Mich. 2002), rev'd on other grounds, 382 F.3d 587 (6th Cir. 2004) (accrued benefits include not only retirement benefits themselves, but also death benefits which are directly related to the value of the retirement benefits). In *Stewart* v. *AT&T Inc.*, 354 Fed. Appx. 111 (5th Cir. 2009), however, the court held that a preretirement mortality discount was appropriately applied to determine a single-sum distribution under a traditional defined benefit plan. The court distinguished *AK Steel* and *Berger* on the basis that the plans at issue in those cases did not provide for a forfeiture of the accrued benefit on the death of the participant before retirement, whereas the plan at issue in *Stewart* provided for such a forfeiture.

Final regulations (TD 9783) under section 417(e) that permit defined benefit plans to simplify the treatment of certain optional forms of benefit that are paid partly in the form of an annuity and partly in a more accelerated form were published by the Treasury Department and the IRS in the **Federal Register** on September 9, 2016 (81 FR 62359).

---

[1] Under section 411(a)(11)(B), the same applicable mortality table and applicable interest rate are used for purposes of determining whether the present value of a participant's nonforfeitable accrued benefit exceeds the maximum amount that can be immediately distributed without the participant's consent.

[2] Notice 2008-85, 2008-2 CB 905, Notice 2013-49, 2013-32 IRB 127, Notice 2015-53, 2015-33 IRB 190, and Notice 2016-50, 2016-38 IRB 371, set forth the section 417(e)(3) applicable mortality tables for 2009 through 2017.

Explanation of Provisions

Overview

These proposed regulations would amend the current final regulations under section 417(e) regarding the minimum present value requirements of section 417(e)(3) in several areas. Specifically, the proposed regulations would update the regulations for changes made by PPA '06 and to eliminate certain obsolete provisions. The proposed regulations also contain a few other clarifying changes.

Updates To Reflect Statutory and Regulatory Changes

The proposed regulations would update the existing regulatory provisions to reflect the statutory changes made by PPA '06, including the new interest rates and mortality tables set forth in section 417(e)(3) and the exception from the valuation rules for certain applicable defined benefit plans set forth in section 411(a)(13). The proposed regulations clarify that the interest rates that are published by the Commissioner pursuant to the provisions as modified by PPA '06 are to be used without further adjustment. In addition, the proposed regulations would eliminate obsolete provisions of the regulations relating to the transition from pre-1995 law to the interest rates and mortality assumptions provided by GATT. Furthermore, the proposed regulations make conforming changes to reflect the final regulations under section 417(e) that permit defined benefit plans to simplify the treatment of certain optional forms of benefit that are paid partly in the form of an annuity and partly in a more accelerated form.

Other Clarifying Changes

A. Treatment of Preretirement Mortality

The proposed regulations would include rules relating to the treatment of preretirement mortality discounts in determining the minimum present value of accrued benefits under the regulations to address the issue raised by *AK Steel* and *Berger* of whether a plan that provides a death benefit equal in value to the accrued benefit may apply a preretirement mortality discount for the probability of death when determining the amount of a single-sum distribution.

Section 411(a) generally prohibits forfeitures of accrued benefits. Under section 411(a)(1), an employee's rights in his accrued benefit derived from employee contributions must be nonforfeitable, and under section 411(a)(2), an employee's rights in his accrued benefit derived from employer contributions must become nonforfeitable in accordance with a vesting schedule that is specified in the statute. Section 411(a)(3)(A) provides that a right to an accrued benefit derived from employer contributions is not treated as forfeitable solely because the plan provides that it is not payable if the participant dies (except in the case of a survivor annuity which is payable as provided in section 401(a)(11)).

Section 411(a)(7)(A)(i) defines a participant's accrued benefit under a defined benefit plan as the employee's accrued benefit determined under the plan and, except as provided in section 411(c)(3), expressed in the form of an annual benefit commencing at normal retirement age. Section 1.411(a)-7(a)(1) defines a participant's accrued benefit under a defined benefit plan as the annual benefit commencing at normal retirement age if the plan provides an accrued benefit in that form. If a defined benefit plan does not provide an accrued benefit in the form of an annual benefit commencing at normal retirement age, § 1.411(a)-7(a)(1)(ii) defines the accrued benefit as an annual benefit commencing at normal retirement age which is the actuarial equivalent of the accrued benefit determined under the plan. The regulation further clarifies that the term "accrued benefits" refers only to pension or retirement benefits. Consequently, accrued benefits do not include ancillary benefits not directly related to retirement benefits, such as incidental death benefits.

Section 411(d)(6)(A) prohibits a plan amendment that decreases a participant's accrued benefit. Section 411(d)(6)(B) provides that a plan amendment that has the effect of eliminating or reducing an early retirement benefit or retirement-type subsidy or eliminating an optional form of benefit with respect to benefits attributable to service before the amendment is treated as reducing accrued benefits for this purpose. Section 1.411(d)-3(g)(2)(v) provides that a death benefit under a defined benefit plan other than a death benefit that is part of an optional form of benefit is an ancillary benefit. Section 1.411(d)-3(g)(6)(ii)(B) describes death benefits payable after the annuity starting date that are considered part of an optional form of benefit. Pursuant to § 1.411(d)-3(g)(14) and (15), section 411(d)(6) protected benefits do not include a death benefit under a defined benefit plan that is an ancillary benefit and not part of an optional form of benefit.

A death benefit under a defined benefit plan that is payable when the participant dies before attaining normal retirement age and before

benefits commence is not part of the participant's accrued benefit within the meaning of section 411(a)(7). Accordingly, the anti-forfeiture rules of section 411(a) do not apply to such a death benefit. This is the case even if the amount of the death benefit is the same as the amount the participant would have received had the participant separated from service and elected to receive a distribution immediately before death. Moreover, such a death benefit is an ancillary benefit within the meaning of § 1.411(d)-3(g)(2)(v)—rather than a section 411(d)(6) protected benefit—and therefore can be eliminated by plan amendment (provided that a qualified preretirement survivor annuity for a surviving spouse is preserved, pursuant to section 401(a)(11)).

The minimum present value requirements of section 417(e)(3) do not take into account the value of ancillary benefits that are not part of the participant's accrued benefit under the plan. Consistent with this, § 1.417(e)-1(d)(1)(i) does not require ancillary death benefits to be taken into account in the required minimum present value calculation. Because questions have arisen regarding this rule, the proposed regulations would clarify that the probability of death under the applicable mortality table is generally taken into account for purposes of determining the present value under section 417(e)(3), without regard to the death benefits provided under the plan other than a death benefit that is part of the normal form of benefit or part of another optional form of benefit (as described in § 1.411(d)-3(g)(6)(ii)(B)) for which present value is determined.

However, a different rule applies with respect to whether the probability of death under the applicable mortality table is taken into account for purposes of determining the present value with respect to the accrued benefit derived from contributions made by an employee. This is because an employee's rights in the accrued benefit derived from the employee's own contributions are nonforfeitable under section 411(a)(1), and the exception for death under section 411(a)(3)(A) to the nonforfeitability of accrued benefits does not apply to the accrued benefit derived from employee contributions. As a result, for purposes of determining the present value under section 417(e)(3) with respect to the accrued benefit derived from contributions made by an employee (that is computed in accordance with the requirements of section 411(c)(3)), the probability of death during the assumed deferral period, if any, is not taken into account. For purposes of the preceding sentence, the assumed deferral period is the period between the date of the present value determination and the assumed commencement date for the annuity attributable to contributions made by an employee.

The proposed regulations include an example to illustrate the application of the minimum present value requirements of section 417(e)(3) in the case of a single-sum distribution of a participant's entire accrued benefit that consists both of an accrued benefit derived from employee contributions and an employer-provided accrued benefit. Consistent with the rules in these proposed regulations, the example illustrates that a single-sum distribution of the participant's entire accrued benefit in such a case must equal the sum of the minimum present value of the accrued benefit derived from employee contributions, determined under section 417(e)(3) (applying the special rules set forth in the preceding paragraph), and the minimum present value of the employer-provided accrued benefit, determined under section 417(e)(3). Note that Rev. Rul. 89-60, 1989-1 CB 113 (1989) suggests that it is sufficient for a single-sum distribution in such a case to merely equal the greater of the minimum present value of the accrued benefit derived from employee contributions and the minimum present value of the participant's entire accrued benefit. To the extent the guidance under Rev. Rul. 89-60 is inconsistent with the final regulations that adopt these proposed regulations, the regulations would supersede the guidance in Rev. Rul. 89-60.

B. Social Security Level Income Options

Questions have arisen regarding whether the minimum present value requirements of section 417(e)(3) apply to a social security level income option. As noted above, § 1.417(e)-1(d)(6) provides that the minimum present value requirements of section 417(e)(3) do not apply to the amount of a distribution paid in the form of an annual benefit that does not decrease during the life of the participant, or that decreases during the life of the participant merely because of the death of the survivor annuitant or the cessation or reduction of social security supplements or qualified disability benefits.

A social security supplement is defined in § 1.411(a)-7(c)(4) as a benefit for plan participants that commences before and terminates before the age when participants are entitled to old-age insurance benefits, unreduced on account of age, under title II of the Social Security Act, and does not exceed such old-age insurance benefit. A social security supplement (other than a QSUPP as defined in § 1.401(a)(4)-12) is an ancillary benefit that is not a section 411(d)(6) protected benefit.

A social security level income option is an optional form of benefit (protected under section 411(d)(6)) under which a participant's accrued benefit is paid in the form of an annuity with larger payments in earlier years, before an assumed social security commencement age, to provide the participant with approximately level retirement income when the assumed social security payments are taken into account. It is appropriate to subject a social security level income option to the rules of section 417(e)(3) because, when a participant's accrued benefit is paid as a social security level income option, a portion of the participant's accrued benefit (which may be substantial) is accelerated and paid over a short period of time until social security retirement age. Because the periodic payments under a social security level income option decrease during the lifetime of the participant and the decrease is not the result of the cessation of an ancillary social security supplement, § 1.417(e)-1(d)(6) does not provide an exception from the minimum present value requirements of section 417(e)(3) for such a distribution. These proposed regulations contain an example that illustrates this point.

C. Application of Required Assumptions to the Accrued Benefit

The proposed regulations would clarify the scope of the rule of § 1.417(e)-1(d)(1) under which the present value of any optional form of benefit cannot be less than the present value of the normal retirement benefit (with both values determined using the applicable interest rate and the applicable mortality table). The proposed regulations would require that the present value of any optional form of benefit cannot be less than the present value of the accrued benefit payable at normal retirement age, and would provide an exception for an optional form of benefit payable after normal retirement age to the extent that a suspension of benefits applies pursuant to section 411(a)(3)(B).

Effective/Applicability Dates

The changes under the proposed regulations are proposed to apply to distributions with annuity starting dates in plan years beginning on or after the date regulations that finalize these proposed regulations are published in the **Federal Register**. Prior to this applicability date, taxpayers must continue to apply existing regulations relating to section 417(e), modified to reflect the relevant statutory provisions during the applicable period (and guidance of general applicability relating to those statutory provisions, such as Rev. Rul. 2007-67).

Special Analyses

Certain IRS regulations, including this one, are exempt from the requirements of Executive Order 12866, as supplemented and reaffirmed by Executive Order 13563. Therefore, a regulatory assessment is not required. It also has been determined that section 553(b) of the Administrative Procedure Act (5 U.S.C. chapter 5) does not apply to these regulations, and because the proposed regulation does not impose a collection of information on small entities, the Regulatory Flexibility Act (5 U.S.C. chapter 6) does not apply. Pursuant to section 7805(f) of the Code, this notice of proposed rulemaking has been submitted to the Chief Counsel for Advocacy of the Small Business Administration for comment on its impact on small business.

Comments and Public Hearing

Before these proposed regulations are adopted as final regulations, consideration will be given to any written (a signed original and eight (8) copies) or electronic comments that are submitted timely to the IRS. The Treasury Department and the IRS request comments on all aspects of these proposed regulations. In addition, the Treasury Department and the IRS specifically request comments on whether, in the case of a plan that provides a subsidized annuity payable upon early retirement and determines a single-sum distribution as the present value of the early retirement annuity, the present-value determination should be required to be calculated using the applicable interest rate and the applicable mortality table applied to the early retirement annuity (or whether the requirement to have a minimum present value that is equal to the present value of the annuity payable at normal retirement age determined in accordance with section 417(e)(3) provides the level of protection for the participant that is required by section 417(e)(3)). See *Rybarczyk* v. *TRW*, 235 F.3d 975 (6th Cir. 2000).

All comments will be available at *www.regulations.gov* or upon request. A public hearing has been scheduled for March 7, 2017, beginning at 10 a.m. in the Auditorium, Internal Revenue Service, 1111 Constitution Avenue NW., Washington, DC. Due to building security procedures, visitors must enter at the Constitution Avenue entrance. In addition, all visitors must present photo identification to enter the building. Because of access restrictions, visitors will not be admitted beyond the immediate entrance area more than 30 minutes before the hearing starts. For information about having your name placed on the building access list to attend the hearing, see the **FOR FURTHER INFORMATION CONTACT** section of this preamble.

The rules of 26 CFR 601.601(a)(3) apply to the hearing. Persons who wish to present oral comments at the hearing must submit written or electronic comments by February 23, 2017, and an outline of topics to be discussed and the amount of time to be devoted to each topic (a signed original and eight (8) copies) by February 23, 2017. A period of 10 minutes will be allotted to each person for making comments. An agenda showing the scheduling of the speakers will be prepared after the deadline for receiving outlines has passed. Copies of the agenda will be available free of charge at the hearing.

Drafting Information

The principal authors of these regulations are Neil S. Sandhu and Linda S.F. Marshall, Office of Division Counsel/Associate Chief Counsel (Tax Exempt and Government Entities). However, other personnel from the IRS and the Treasury Department participated in the development of these regulations.

List of Subjects in 26 CFR Part 1

Income taxes, Reporting and recordkeeping requirements.

Proposed Amendments to the Regulations

Accordingly, 26 CFR part 1 is proposed to be amended as follows:

PART 1—INCOME TAXES

■ **Par. 1**. The authority citation for part 1 continues to read in part as follows:

Authority: 26 U.S.C. 7805 * * *

■ **Par. 2**. Section 1.417(e)-1 is amended by:

■ 1. Revising paragraphs (d)(1)(i), (d)(2), (d)(3), (d)(4), and (d)(6).

■ 2. Adding paragraph (d)(8)(vi).

■ 3. Revising paragraph (d)(9).

■ 4. Removing paragraph (d)(10).

The addition and revisions read as follows:

§ 1.417(e)-1 Restrictions and valuations of distributions from plans subject to sections 401(a)(11) and 417.

* * * * *

(d) *Present value requirement*—(1) *General rule*—(i) *Defined benefit plans*—(A) *In general*. A defined benefit plan must provide that the present value of any accrued benefit and the amount (subject to sections 411(c)(3) and 415) of any distribution, including a single sum, must not be less than the amount calculated using the applicable mortality table described in paragraph (d)(2) of this section and the applicable interest rate described in paragraph (d)(3) of this section, as determined for the month described in paragraph (d)(4) of this section. The present value of any optional form of benefit, determined in accordance with the preceding sentence, cannot be less than the present value of the accrued benefit payable at normal retirement age, except to the extent that, for an optional form of benefit payable after normal retirement age, the requirements for suspension of benefits under section 411(a)(3)(B) are satisfied. The same rules used for the plan under this paragraph (d) must also be used to compute the present value of the benefit for purposes of determining whether consent for a distribution is required under paragraph (b) of this section.

(B) *Payment of a portion of a participant's benefit*. The rules of this paragraph (d)(1) apply with respect to a payment of only a portion of the accrued benefit in the same manner as these rules would apply to a distribution of the entire accrued benefit. See paragraph (d)(7) of this section.

(C) *Special rules for applicable defined benefit plans*. See section 411(a)(13) and the regulations thereunder for an exception from the rules of section 417(e)(3) and this paragraph (d) that applies to certain distributions from certain applicable defined benefit plans.

* * * * *

(2) *Applicable mortality table*—(i) *In general*. The applicable mortality table for a calendar year is the mortality table that is prescribed by the Commissioner in guidance published in the Internal Revenue Bulletin. See § 601.601(d)(2) of this chapter. This mortality table is to be based on the table specified under section 430(h)(3)(A), but without regard to section 430(h)(3)(C) or (D).

(ii) *Mortality discounts* —(A) *In general.* Except as provided under paragraph (d)(2)(ii)(B) of this section, the probability of death under the applicable mortality table is taken into account for purposes of determining the present value under this paragraph (d) without regard to the death benefits provided under the plan (other than a death benefit that is part of the normal form of benefit or part of another optional form of benefit, as described in § 1.411(d)-3(g)(6)(ii)(B), for which present value is determined).

(B) *Special rule for employee-provided benefit.* For purposes of determining the present value under this paragraph (d) with respect to the accrued benefit derived from employee contributions (that is determined in accordance with the requirements of section 411(c)(3)), the probability of death during the assumed deferral period, if any, is not taken into account. For purposes of the preceding sentence, the assumed deferral period is the period between the date of the present value determination and the assumed commencement date for the annuity attributable to contributions made by an employee.

(3) *Applicable interest rate* —(i) *In general.* The applicable interest rate for a month is determined using the first, second, and third segment rates for that month under section 430(h)(2)(C), as modified pursuant to section 417(e)(3)(D) (and without regard to the segment rate stabilization rules of section 430(h)(2)(C)(iv)). The applicable interest rate is specified by the Commissioner in revenue rulings, notices, or other guidance published in the Internal Revenue Bulletin, and is applied under rules similar to the rules under § 1.430(h)(2)-1(b). Thus, for example, in determining the present value of a straight life annuity, the first segment is applied with respect to payments expected to be made during the 5-year period beginning on the annuity starting date, the second segment rate is applied with respect to payments expected to be made during the 15-year period following the end of that 5-year period, and the third segment rate is applied with respect to payments expected to be made after the end of that 15-year period. The interest rates that are published by the Commissioner are to be used for this purpose without further adjustment.

(ii) *Examples.* The following examples illustrate the rules of paragraphs (d)(2) and (3) of this section.

Example 1. (i) Plan A is a non-contributory single-employer defined benefit plan with a calendar-year plan year, a one-year stability period coinciding with the calendar year, and a two-month lookback used for determining the applicable interest rate. The normal retirement age is 65, and all participant elections are made with proper spousal consent. Plan A provides for optional single sum payments equal to the present value of the participant's accrued benefit. Plan A provides that the applicable interest rates are the segment rates as specified by the Commissioner for the second full calendar month preceding the calendar year that contains the annuity starting date. The applicable mortality table is the table specified by the Commissioner for the calendar year that contains the annuity starting date.

(ii) Participant P retires in May 2017 at age 60 and elects (with spousal consent) to receive a single-sum payment. P has an accrued benefit of $2,000 per month payable as a life annuity beginning at the plan's normal retirement age of 65. The applicable mortality rates for 2017 apply. The applicable interest rates published by the Commissioner for November 2016 are 1.57%, 3.45%, and 4.39% for the first, second, and third segment rates, respectively. The deferred annuity factor calculated based on these interest rates and the applicable mortality table for 2017 is 10.931 for a participant age 60. To satisfy the requirements of section 417(e)(3) and this paragraph (d), the single-sum payment received by P cannot be less than $262,344 (that is, $2,000 × 12 × 10.931).

Example 2. (i) The facts are the same as for *Example 1* of this paragraph (d)(3)(ii), except that Plan A provides for mandatory employee contributions. Participant Q retires in May 2017 at age 60 and elects (with spousal consent) to receive a single-sum payment of Q's entire accrued benefit. Q has an accrued benefit of $2,000 per month payable as a life annuity beginning at Plan A's normal retirement age of 65, consisting of an accrued benefit derived from employee contributions determined in accordance with section 411(c)(2) (Q's employee-provided accrued benefit) of $500 per month and an accrued benefit derived from employer contributions (Q's employer-provided accrued benefit) of $1,500 per month.

(ii) Pursuant to paragraph (d)(2)(ii)(B) of this section, the single-sum payment used to settle Q's employee-provided accrued benefit cannot be less than the present value of that portion of Q's accrued benefit determined using the applicable interest and mortality rates described in paragraphs (d)(3)(i) and (d)(2)(ii) of this section, determined without taking the probability of death during the assumed deferral period into account. The deferred annuity factor calculated

based on the interest and mortality rates specified in *Example 1* of this paragraph (d)(3)(ii) (taking the probability of death only after age 65 into account) is 11.266 for a participant age 60. To satisfy the requirement of section 417(e)(3) and this paragraph (d), the single-sum payment received by Q with respect to the employee-provided portion of the accrued benefit cannot be less than the minimum present value of $67,596 (that is, $500 × 12 × 11.266).

(iii) The single-sum payment used to settle Q's employer-provided accrued benefit cannot be less than the present value of that portion of Q's accrued benefit determined using the applicable interest and mortality rates. However, for this purpose, Plan A is permitted to take the probability of death during the assumed deferral period into account. The single-sum payment received by Q with respect to the employer-provided portion of the accrued benefit cannot be less than $196,758 (that is, $1,500 × 12 × 10.931).

(iv) The total single-sum payment received by Q cannot be less than the sum of the minimum present value of Q's employee- and employer-provided accrued benefits, or $264,354 ($67,596 + $196,758).

(4) *Time for determining interest rate and mortality table* —(i) *Interest rate general rule.* Except as provided in paragraph (d)(4)(v) or (vi) of this section, the applicable interest rate to be used for a distribution is the applicable interest rate determined under paragraph (d)(3) of this section for the applicable lookback month. The applicable lookback month for a distribution is the lookback month (as described in paragraph (d)(4)(iv) of this section) for the stability period (as described in paragraph (d)(4)(iii) of this section) that contains the annuity starting date for the distribution. The time and method for determining the applicable interest rate for each participant's distribution must be determined in a consistent manner that is applied uniformly to all participants in the plan.

(ii) *Mortality table general rule.* The applicable mortality table to be used for a distribution is the mortality table that is published for the calendar year during which the stability period containing the annuity starting date begins.

(iii) *Stability period.* A plan must specify the period for which the applicable interest rate remains constant (the stability period). This stability period may be one calendar month, one plan quarter, one calendar quarter, one plan year, or one calendar year. This same stability period also applies to the applicable mortality table.

(iv) *Lookback month.* A plan must specify the lookback month that is used to determine the applicable interest rate with respect to a stability period. The lookback month may be the first, second, third, fourth, or fifth full calendar month preceding the first day of the stability period.

(v) *Permitted average interest rate.* A plan may apply the rules of paragraph (d)(4)(i) of this section by substituting a permitted average applicable interest rate with respect to the plan's stability period for the applicable interest rate determined under paragraph (d)(3) of this section for the applicable lookback month for the stability period. For this purpose, a permitted average applicable interest rate with respect to a stability period is the applicable interest rate that is computed by averaging the applicable interest rates determined under paragraph (d)(3) of this section for two or more consecutive months from among the first, second, third, fourth, and fifth calendar months preceding the first day of the stability period. For this paragraph (d)(4)(v) to apply, a plan must specify the manner in which the permitted average interest rate is computed.

(vi) *Additional determination dates.* The Commissioner may prescribe, in guidance published in the Internal Revenue Bulletin, other times that a plan may provide for determining the applicable interest rate.

(vii) *Example.* The following example illustrates the rules of this paragraph (d)(4):

Example. (i) The facts are the same as *Example 1* of paragraph (d)(3)(ii) of this section, except that Plan A provides that the applicable interest rates are the rates for the third full calendar month preceding the beginning of the plan quarter that contains the annuity starting date. Plan A also provides that the applicable mortality table is the table specified by the Commissioner for the calendar year that contains the beginning of the stability period.

(ii) The segment interest rates that apply for annuity starting dates during the period beginning April 1, 2017 and ending June 30, 2017 are the segment rates for January 2017. This plan design permits the applicable interest rate to be fixed for each plan quarter and for the applicable interest rate for all distributions made during each plan quarter to be determined before the beginning of the plan quarter.

* * * * *

(6) *Exceptions* —(i) *In general.* This paragraph (d) (other than the provisions relating to section 411(d)(6) requirements in paragraph (d)(9) of this section) does not apply to the amount of a distribution paid in the form of an annual benefit that—

(A) Does not decrease during the life of the participant, or, in the case of a QPSA, the life of the participant's spouse; or

(B) Decreases during the life of the participant merely because of—

(*1*) The death of the survivor annuitant (but only if the reduction is to a level not below 50 percent of the annual benefit payable before the death of the survivor annuitant): or

(*2*) The cessation or reduction of a social security supplement or qualified disability benefit (as defined in section 411(a)(9)).

(ii) *Example.* The following example illustrates the rules of this paragraph (d)(6).

Example. (i) The facts are the same as *Example 1* of paragraph (d)(3)(ii) of this section. Plan A also provides an optional distribution in the form of a Social Security level income option. Under this provision, the participant's benefit is adjusted so that a larger amount is payable until age 65, at which time it is reduced to provide a level social income in combination with the participant's estimated social security benefit beginning at age 65. Participant R's reduced early retirement benefit payable as a straight life annuity benefit commencing at age 60 is $1,300 per month (which is less than the actuarially equivalent benefit that would have been determined using the applicable interest and mortality rates under section 417(e)(3)) and R's estimated social security benefit is $1,000 per month beginning at age 65.

(ii) Because the benefit payable under the social security level income option decreases at age 65 and the decrease is not on account of the death of the participant or a beneficiary or the cessation or reduction of social security supplements or qualified disability benefits, the benefits payable under the social security level income option are subject to the minimum present value requirements of section 417(e)(3). As illustrated in *Example 1* of paragraph (d)(3)(ii) of this section, the minimum present value of Participant R's benefits under section 417(e)(3) is $262,344, which is based on the present value of R's accrued benefit, not R's benefit that would be payable as a straight life annuity at the annuity starting date.

(iii) The deferred annuity factor for a participant age 60 with lifetime benefits commencing at age 65, based on the November 2016 segment rates and the applicable mortality table for 2017, is 10.931. The corresponding temporary annuity factor to age 65 is 4.752. The minimum benefits payable to Participant R in the form of a social security level income option (with a decrease of $1,000—equal to the participant's estimated social security benefit—occurring at age 65) are $2,090.99 per month until age 65 and $1,090.99 per month thereafter. Any amounts less than this would have a present value smaller than the required amount of $262,344, and thus would fail to satisfy the minimum present value requirement of section 417(e)(3).

* * * * *

(8) * * *

(vi) *Applicability date for provisions reflecting PPA '06 updates and other rules.* Paragraphs (d)(1) through (4) of this section apply to distributions with annuity starting dates in plan years beginning on or after the date regulations that finalize these proposed regulations are published in the **Federal Register**. Prior to this applicability date, taxpayers must continue to apply the provisions of §1.417(e)-1(d) as contained in 26 CFR part 1 as in effect immediately before publication of those final regulations, except to the extent superseded by statutory changes and guidance of general applicability relating to those statutory changes.

(9) *Relationship with section 411(d)(6)* —(i) *In general.* A plan amendment that changes the interest rate or the mortality assumptions used for the purposes described in paragraph (d)(1) of this section (including a plan amendment that changes the time for determining those assumptions) is generally subject to section 411(d)(6). However, for certain exceptions to the rule in the preceding sentence, see paragraph (d)(7)(iv) of this section, §1.411(d)-4, Q&A-2(b)(2)(v) (with respect to plan amendments relating to involuntary distributions), and section 1107(a)(2) of the Pension Protection Act of 2006, Public Law 109-280, 120 Stat. 780 (2006) (PPA '06) (with respect to certain plan amendments that were made pursuant to a change to the Internal Revenue Code by PPA '06 or regulations issued thereunder).

(ii) *Section 411(d)(6) relief for change in time for determining interest rate and mortality table.* Notwithstanding the general rule of paragraph (d)(9)(i) of this section, if a plan amendment changes the time for determining the applicable interest rate (and, if the amendment changes the stability period described in paragraph (d)(4)(iii) of this section, the time for determining the applicable mortality table), including an indirect change as a result of a change in plan year, the amendment will not be treated as reducing accrued benefits in violation of section 411(d)(6) merely on account of this change if the conditions of this paragraph (d)(9)(ii) are satisfied. If the plan amendment is effective on or after the date the amendment is adopted, any distribution for which the annuity starting date occurs in the one-year period commencing at the time the amendment is effective must be determined using the interest rate and mortality table provided under the plan determined at either the date for determining the interest rate and mortality table before the amendment or the date for determining the interest rate and mortality table after the amendment, whichever results in the larger distribution. If the plan amendment is adopted retroactively (that is, the amendment is effective prior to the adoption date), the plan must use the interest rate and mortality table determination dates resulting in the larger distribution for distributions with annuity starting dates occurring during the period beginning with the effective date and ending one year after the adoption date.

* * * * *

John Dalrymple,

Deputy Commissioner for Services and Enforcement.

[FR Doc. 2016-27907 Filed 11-23-16; 8:45 am]

BILLING CODE 4830-01-P

¶ 20,264P

IRS: Defined benefit plans: Funding requirements: Mortality tables.—The IRS has issued proposed regulations that provide updated mortality tables to be used by most defined benefit plans to calculate the present value of a stream of expected future benefit payments for determining the plan's minimum funding requirements. The proposed regulations also update the requirements that a plan sponsor must meet to obtain IRS approval to use substitute mortality tables that are specific to the plan, rather than generally applicable mortality tables. The changes are proposed to apply to plan years beginning on or after January 1, 2018.

The proposed regulation was published in the Federal Register on December 29, 2016 (81 FR 95911). The regulations were finalized on October 5, 2017 (82 FR 46388). The preamble to the final regulations is at ¶ 23,331. The final regulations are reproduced at ¶ 13,151L-20A, ¶ 13,151L-22A, ¶ 13,151M-15A, and ¶ 13,151N-20.

¶ 20,264Q

IRS proposed regulations: Qualified matching contributions (QMACs): Qualified nonelective contributions (QNECs): 401(k) plans.—The IRS has issued proposed regulations amending the definitions of qualified matching contributions (QMACs) and qualified nonelective contributions (QNECs) to allow employers with 40(k) plans that permit the use of amounts in plan forfeiture accounts to offset future employer contributions under the plan to use the amounts to fund QMACs and QNECs. Under the proposed regulations, employer contributions would qualify as QMACs or QNECs if they satisfied applicable nonforfeitability and distribution requirements at the time they are allocated to participants' accounts, but need not meet these requirements when they are contributed to the plan. These regulations are proposed to apply to tax years beginning on or after the date final regulations are published in the Federal Register, but may be relied upon for periods preceding the proposed applicability date.

The proposed regulations were published in the Federal Register on January 18, 2017 (82 FR 5477).

DEPARTMENT OF THE TREASURY

Internal Revenue Service

26 CFR Part 1

[REG-131643-15]

RIN-1545-BN05

Definitions of Qualified Matching Contributions and Qualified Nonelective Contributions

AGENCY: Internal Revenue Service (IRS), Treasury.

ACTION: Notice of proposed rulemaking.

SUMMARY: This document contains proposed amendments to the definitions of qualified matching contributions (QMACs) and qualified nonelective contributions (QNECs) under regulations relating to certain qualified retirement plans that contain cash or deferred arrangements under section 401(k) or that provide for matching contributions or employee contributions under section 401(m). Under these regulations, employer contributions to a plan would be able to qualify as QMACs or QNECs if they satisfy applicable nonforfeitability and distribution requirements at the time they are allocated to participants' accounts, but need not meet these requirements when they are contributed to the plan. These regulations would affect participants in, beneficiaries of, employers maintaining, and administrators of tax-qualified plans that contain cash or deferred arrangements or provide for matching contributions or employee contributions.

DATES: Comments and requests for a public hearing must be received by April 18, 2017.

ADDRESSES: Send submissions to CC:PA:LPD:PR (REG-131643-15) Room 5203, Internal Revenue Service, P.O. Box 7604, Ben Franklin Station, Washington, DC 20044. Submissions may be hand-delivered Monday through Friday between the hours of 8 a.m. and 4 p.m. to CC:PA:LPD:PR (REG-131643-15), Courier's Desk, Internal Revenue Service, 1111 Constitution Avenue NW., Washington, DC 20224, or sent electronically via the Federal eRulemaking Portal at *www.regulations.gov* (IRS REG-131643-15).

FOR FURTHER INFORMATION CONTACT: Concerning the proposed regulations, Rosemary Y. Oluwo at (202) 317-6060; concerning submissions of comments or to request a hearing, Regina Johnson at (202) 317-6901 (not toll-free numbers).

SUPPLEMENTARY INFORMATION:

Background

Section 401(k)(1) provides that a profit-sharing or stock bonus plan, a pre-ERISA money purchase plan, or a rural cooperative plan shall not be considered as failing to satisfy the requirements of section 401(a) merely because the plan includes a qualified cash or deferred arrangement (CODA). To be considered a qualified CODA, a plan must satisfy several requirements, including: (i) Under section 401(k)(2)(B), amounts held by the plan's trust that are attributable to employer contributions made pursuant to an employee's election must satisfy certain distribution requirements; (ii) under section 401(k)(2)(C), an employees' right to such employer contributions must be nonforfeitable; and (iii) under section 401(k)(3), such employer contributions must satisfy certain nondiscrimination requirements.

Under section 401(k)(3)(D)(ii), the employer contributions taken into account for purposes of applying the nondiscrimination requirements may, under such rules as the Secretary may provide and at the election of the employer, include, in addition to contributions made pursuant to an employee's election, matching contributions that meet the distribution and nonforfeitability requirements of section 401(k)(2)(B) and (C) and qualified nonelective contributions within the meaning of section 401(m)(4)(C). Under section 401(m)(4)(C), a qualified nonelective contribution is an employer contribution, other than a matching contribution, with respect to which the distribution and nonforfeitability requirements of section 401(k)(2)(B) and (C) are met.

Under § 1.401(k)-1(b)(1)(ii), a CODA satisfies the applicable nondiscrimination requirements if it satisfies the actual deferral percentage (ADP) test of section 401(k)(3), described in § 1.401(k)-2. The ADP test limits the degree of disparity permitted between the percentage of compensation made as employer contributions to the plan for a plan year on behalf of eligible highly compensated employees and the percentage of compensation made as employer contributions on behalf of eligible nonhighly compensated employees. If the ADP test limits are exceeded, the employer must take corrective action to ensure that the limits are met. In determining the amount of employer contributions made on behalf of an eligible employee, employers are allowed to take into account certain qualified matching contributions (QMACs)

and qualified nonelective contributions (QNECs) made on behalf of the employee by the employer.

In lieu of applying the ADP test, an employer may choose to design its plan to satisfy an ADP safe harbor, including the ADP safe harbor provisions of section 401(k)(12), described in § 1.401(k)-3. Under § 1.401(k)-3, a plan satisfies the ADP safe harbor provisions of section 401(k)(12) if, among other things, it satisfies certain contribution requirements. With respect to the safe harbor under section 401(k)(12), an employer may choose to satisfy the contribution requirement by providing a certain level of QMACs or QNECs to eligible nonhighly compensated employees under the plan.

A defined contribution plan that provides for matching or employee after-tax contributions must satisfy the nondiscrimination requirements under section 401(m) with respect to those contributions for any plan year. Under § 1.401(m)-1(b)(1), the matching contributions and employee contributions under a plan satisfy the nondiscrimination requirements for a plan year if the plan satisfies the actual contribution percentage (ACP) test of section 401(m)(2) described in § 1.401(m)-2.

The ACP test limits the degree of disparity permitted between the percentage of compensation made as matching contributions and after-tax employee contributions for or by eligible highly compensated employees under the plan and the percentage of compensation made as matching contributions and after-tax employee contributions for or by eligible nonhighly compensated employees under the plan. If the ACP test limits are exceeded, the employer must take corrective action to ensure that the limits are met. In determining the amount of employer contributions made on behalf of an eligible employee, employers are allowed to take into account certain QNECs made on behalf of the employee by the employer. Employers must also take into account QMACs made on behalf of the employee by the employer unless an exclusion applies (including an exclusion for QMACs that are taken into account under the ADP test).

If an employer designs its plan to satisfy the ADP safe harbor of section 401(k)(12), it may avoid performing the ACP test with respect to matching contributions under the plan, as long as the additional requirements of the ACP safe harbor of section 401(m)(11) are met.

Under § 1.401(k)-6, QMACs and QNECs are matching contributions and employer contributions (other than elective or matching contributions) that satisfy the nonforfeitability requirements of § 1.401(k)-1(c) and the distribution requirements of § 1.401(k)-1(d) "when they are contributed to the plan." Similarly, § 1.401(m)-5 includes independent definitions of QMACs and QNECs, which are matching contributions and employer contributions (other than elective or matching contributions) that satisfy the nonforfeitability and distribution requirements of § 1.401(k)-1(c) and (d) "at the time the contribution is made."

The Treasury Department and the IRS have received comments with respect to the definitions of QMACs and QNECs in §§ 1.401(k)-6 and 1.401(m)-5. In particular, commenters assert that employer contributions should be able to qualify as QMACs and QNECs as long as they satisfy applicable nonforfeitability and distribution requirements at the time they are allocated to participants' accounts, rather than when they are first contributed to the plan. Commenters contend that interpreting sections 401(k)(3)(D)(ii) and 401(m)(4)(C) to require satisfaction of applicable nonforfeitability and distribution requirements at the time amounts are first contributed to the plan would preclude plan sponsors with plans that permit the use of amounts in plan forfeiture accounts to offset future employer contributions under the plan from applying such amounts to fund QMACs and QNECs. This is because the amounts would have been allocated to the forfeiture accounts only after a participant incurred a forfeiture of benefits and, thus, generally would have been subject to a vesting schedule when they were first contributed to the plan. Commenters have requested that QMAC and QNEC requirements not be interpreted to prevent the use of plan forfeitures to fund QMACs and QNECs. The commenters urge that the nonforfeitability and distribution requirements under § 1.401(k)-6 should apply when QMACs and QNECs are allocated to participants' accounts and not when the contributions are first made to the plan.

Explanation of Provisions

After consideration of the comments described in this preamble in the "Background" section, the Treasury Department and the IRS are proposing to amend § 1.401(k)-6 to provide that amounts used to fund QMACs and QNECs must be nonforfeitable and subject to distribution restrictions in accordance with § 1.401(k)-1(c) and (d) when allocated to participants' accounts, and to no longer require that amounts used to fund QMACs and QNECs satisfy the nonforfeitability and distribution requirements when they are first contributed to the plan. Treasury and IRS note that while the second sentence of each of the current definitions of QMACs and QNECs refers to the "vesting" requirements of

§ 1.401(k)-1(c), those requirements are more appropriately characterized as "nonforfeitability" requirements consistent with section 401(k)(2)(C) and the title of § 1.401(k)-1(c). Accordingly, these proposed regulations would amend these definitions to clarify those references by replacing the word "vesting" with "nonforfeitability" in each definition; these changes are not otherwise intended to have any substantive impact on this or any other section of the regulations. These proposed regulations would also amend the definitions of QMACs and QNECs in § 1.401(m)-5 to provide cross-references to the definitions of QMACs and QNECs under § 1.401(k)-6. These amendments to § 1.401(m)-5 are being made to ensure a consistent definition of QMACs and QNECs in § 1.401(k)-6 and § 1.401(m)-5 (including the requirement that amounts used to fund QMACs and QNECs be made subject to nonforfeitability and distribution requirements when they are allocated to participants' accounts as QMACs or QNECs) and are not otherwise intended to have any substantive impact on this or any other section of the regulations.

Proposed Effective/Applicability Date

These regulations are proposed to apply to taxable years beginning on or after the date of publication of the Treasury decision adopting these rules as final regulations in the **Federal Register**. Taxpayers, however, may rely on these proposed regulations for periods preceding the proposed applicability date. If, and to the extent, the final regulations are more restrictive than the rules in these proposed regulations, those provisions of the final regulations will be applied without retroactive effect.

Special Analyses

Certain IRS regulations, including this one, are exempt from the requirements of Executive Order 12866, as supplemented and reaffirmed by Executive Order 13563. Therefore, a regulatory impact assessment is not required. Because the regulation does not impose a collection of information on small entities, the Regulatory Flexibility Act (5 U.S.C. chapter 6) does not apply. Pursuant to section 7805(f) of the Internal Revenue Code, these regulations will be submitted to the Chief Counsel for Advocacy of the Small Business Administration for comment on their impact on small business.

Comments and Requests for Public Hearing

Before these proposed regulations are adopted as final regulations, consideration will be given to any comments that are submitted timely to the IRS as prescribed in this preamble under the **Addresses** heading. Treasury and the IRS request comments on all aspects of the proposed rules. All comments will be available at *www.regulations.gov* or upon request. A public hearing will be scheduled if requested in writing by any person who timely submits written comments. If a public hearing is scheduled, notice of the date, time, and place for the public hearing will be published in the **Federal Register**.

Drafting Information

The principal author of these regulations is Rosemary Y. Oluwo, Office of Associate Chief Counsel (Tax Exempt and Governmental Entities). However, other personnel from the IRS and Treasury Department participated in the development of these regulations.

List of Subjects in 26 CFR Part 1

Income taxes, Reporting and recordkeeping requirements.

Proposed Amendments to the Regulations

Accordingly, 26 CFR part 1 is proposed to be amended as follows:

PART 1—INCOME TAXES

■ **Paragraph 1**. The authority citation for part 1 continues to read in part as follows:

Authority: 26 U.S.C. 7805 * * *

■ **Par. 2**. Section 1.401(k)-1 is amended by adding paragraph (g)(5) to read as follows:

§ 1.401(k)-1 Certain cash or deferred arrangements.

* * * * *

(g) * * *

(5) *Effective date for definitions of qualified matching contributions (QMACs) and qualified nonelective contributions (QNECs)*. The revisions to the second sentence in the definitions of QMACs and QNECs in § 1.401(k)-6 apply to taxable years ending on or after the date of publication of the Treasury decision adopting these rules as final regulations in the **Federal Register**.

■ **Par. 3**. Section 1.401(k)-6 is amended by revising the second sentence in the definitions of *Qualified matching contributions (QMACs)* and *Qualified nonelective contributions (QNECs)* to read as follows:

§ 1.401(k)-6 Definitions.

* * * * *

Qualified matching contributions (QMACs). * * * Thus, the matching contributions must satisfy the nonforfeitability requirements of § 1.401(k)-1(c) and be subject to the distribution requirements of § 1.401(k)-1(d) when they are allocated to participants' accounts. * * *

Qualified nonelective contributions (QNECs). * * * Thus, the nonelective contributions must satisfy the nonforfeitability requirements of § 1.401(k)-1(c) and be subject to the distribution requirements of § 1.401(k)-1(d) when they are allocated to participants' accounts. * * *

* * * * *

■ **Par. 4**. Section 1.401(m)-1 is amended by adding paragraph (d)(4) to read as follows:

§ 1.401(m)-1 Employee contributions and matching contributions.

* * * * *

(d) * * *

(4) *Effective date for definitions of qualified matching contributions (QMACs) and qualified nonelective contributions (QNECs)*. The revisions to the definitions of QMACs and QNECs in § 1.401(m)-5 apply to taxable years ending on or after the date of publication of the Treasury decision adopting these rules as final regulations in the **Federal Register**.

■ **Par. 5**. Section 1.401(m)-5 is amended by revising the definitions of *Qualified matching contributions (QMACs)* and *Qualified nonelective contributions (QNECs)* to read as follows:

§ 1.401(m)-5 Definitions.

* * * * *

Qualified matching contributions (QMACs). Qualified matching contributions or QMACs means qualified matching contributions or QMACs as defined in § 1.401(k)-6.

Qualified nonelective contributions (QNECs). Qualified nonelective contributions or QNECs means qualified nonelective contributions or QNECs as defined in § 1.401(k)-6.

John Dalrymple,

Deputy Commissioner for Services and Enforcement.

[FR Doc. 2017-00876 Filed 1-17-17; 8:45 am]

BILLING CODE 4830-01-P

¶ 20,264R

IRS proposed regulations: Reporting and disclosure: Form W-2: Social security numbers: IRS taxpayer identification numbers: Truncated numbers.—The IRS has issued proposed regulations that permit employers to voluntarily truncate employees' social security numbers (SSNs) on copies of Forms W-2 (Wage and Tax Statement) that are furnished to employees so that they appear as IRS truncated taxpayer identification numbers (TTINs). The proposed regulations also clarify how the truncation rules apply to Forms W-2, add an illustrating example, and delete obsolete provisions and update cross references in related regulations under Code Secs. 6051 and 6052.

The proposed regulations will be effective on the date the final regulations are published in the Federal Register. However, due to the request of several state tax administrators for more time to develop systems to process Forms W-2 with truncated SSNs that are filed with state income tax returns, the proposed regulations will not apply to Forms W-2 required to be furnished before January 1, 2019, but will apply to statements required to be filed and furnished after December 31, 2018.

The proposed regulation was published in the Federal Register on September 20, 2017 (82 FR 43920).

DEPARTMENT OF THE TREASURY

Internal Revenue Service

26 CFR Parts 1, 31, and 301

[REG-105004-16]

RIN 1545-BK35

Use of Truncated Taxpayer Identification Numbers on Forms W-2, Wage and Tax Statement, Furnished to Employees

AGENCY: Internal Revenue Service (IRS), Treasury.

ACTION: Notice of proposed rulemaking.

SUMMARY: This document contains proposed amendments to the regulations under sections 6051 and 6052 of the Internal Revenue Code (Code). To aid employers' efforts to protect employees from identity theft, these proposed regulations would amend existing regulations to permit employers to voluntarily truncate employees' social security numbers (SSNs) on copies of Forms W-2, Wage and Tax Statement, that are furnished to employees so that the truncated SSNs appear in the form of IRS truncated taxpayer identification numbers (TTINs). These proposed regulations also would amend the regulations under section 6109 to clarify the application of the truncation rules to Forms W-2 and to add an example illustrating the application of these rules. Additionally, these proposed amendments would delete obsolete provisions and update cross references in the regulations under sections 6051 and 6052. These proposed regulations affect employers who are required to furnish Forms W-2 and employees who receive Forms W-2.

DATES: Written or electronic comments and requests for a public hearing must be received by December 18, 2017.

ADDRESSES: Send submissions to: CC:PA:LPD:PR (REG-105004-16), Room 5203, Internal Revenue Service, P.O. Box 7604, Ben Franklin Station, Washington, DC 20044. Submissions may be hand-delivered between the hours of 8 a.m. and 4 p.m. to CC:PA:LPD:PR (REG-105004-16), Courier's Desk, Internal Revenue Service, 1111 Constitution Avenue NW., Washington, DC, or sent via the Federal eRulemaking Portal at *www.regulations.gov* (REG-105004-16).

FOR FURTHER INFORMATION CONTACT: Concerning these proposed regulations, Eliezer Mishory, (202) 317-6844; concerning submissions of comments and/or requests for a hearing, Regina Johnson, (202) 317-6901 (not toll-free numbers).

SUPPLEMENTARY INFORMATION:

Background

This document contains proposed amendments to the Income Tax Regulations (26 CFR part 1), the Employment Taxes and Collection of Income Tax at Source Regulations (26 CFR part 31), and the Procedure and Administration Regulations (26 CFR part 301) regarding statements that are required to be furnished to employees by employers or other persons under sections 6051 and 6052 of the Code. Section 6051(a) generally requires that an employer provide to each employee on or before January 31st of the succeeding year a written statement that shows the employee's total amount of wages and the total amount deducted and withheld as tax from those wages, along with other information, for each calendar year. Employers must use Form W-2 (or a substitute statement that complies with applicable revenue procedures relating to such statements) to provide the information required by section 6051(a) to employees. See §31.6051-1(a)(1)(i); Rev. Proc. 2016-54, 2016-45 I.R.B. 685, also published as Publication 1141, "General Rules and Specifications for Substitute Forms W-2 and W-3," or any successor guidance. Section 6051(d) provides that, when required to do so by regulations, employers must file with the Secretary duplicates of the forms required to be furnished to employees under section 6051. Section 31.6051-2(a) generally requires employers to file Social Security Administration copies of Forms W-2 with the Social Security Administration. A person making a payment of third-party sick pay to an employee of another employer (payee) is required under section 6051(f)(1) to furnish a written statement to the employer for whom services are normally rendered containing certain information, including the payee's SSN. Under certain conditions, the employer for whom services are normally rendered is required under section 6051(f)(2) to furnish a Form W-2 to the payee. This situation may arise, for example, when an insurance company is making payments to an employee of another employer because the employee is temporarily absent from work due to injury, sickness or disability, and the insurance company has satisfied the necessary requirements under §32.1(e) of the Temporary Employment Tax Regulations under the Act of December 29, 1981

(Pub. L. 97-123) to transfer the obligation to do Form W-2 reporting to the employer. Employers also must use Form W-2 to file and furnish information regarding payment of wages in the form of group-term life insurance under section 6052.

Section 6109(a) authorizes the Secretary to prescribe regulations with respect to the inclusion in returns, statements, or other documents of an identifying number as may be prescribed for securing proper identification of a person. On July 15, 2014, the Treasury Department and the IRS published in the **Federal Register** (79 FR 41127-02) final regulations (TD 9675) authorizing the use of TTINs on certain payee statements and certain other documents. These final regulations were in response to concerns about the risks of identity theft, including its effect on tax administration.

Section 301.6109-4(b) generally provides that a TTIN may be used to identify any person on any statement or other document that the internal revenue laws require to be furnished to another person. Under §301.6109-4(a), a TTIN is an individual's SSN, IRS individual taxpayer identification number (ITIN), IRS adoption taxpayer identification number (ATIN), or IRS employer identification number (EIN) in which the first five digits of the nine-digit number are replaced with Xs or asterisks. For example, a TTIN replacing an SSN appears in the form XXX-XX-1234 or ***-**-1234. Section 301.6109-4(b)(2)(ii) prohibits using TTINs if, among other things, a statute, regulation, other guidance published in the Internal Revenue Bulletin, form, or instructions specifically requires the use of an SSN. Additionally, §301.6109-4(b)(2)(iii) prohibits the use of TTINs on any return, statement, or other document that is required to be filed with or furnished to the IRS.

Prior to being amended by the Protecting Americans from Tax Hikes (PATH) Act of 2015, Public Law 114-113, div. Q, title IV, 129 Stat. 2242, section 6051(a)(2) specifically required employers to include their employees' SSNs on copies of Forms W-2 that are furnished to employees. In addition, current regulations under §31.6051-1, as well as forms and instructions, require employers to include their employees' SSNs on copies of Forms W-2 that are furnished to employees. Section 409 of the PATH Act amended section 6051(a)(2) by striking "his social security account number" from the list of information required on Form W-2 and inserting "an identifying number for the employee" instead. This statutory amendment is effective for statements issued after December 18, 2015, the date that the PATH Act was signed into law. Because an SSN is no longer required by section 6051, the Treasury Department and the IRS propose amending the regulations to permit employers to truncate employees' SSNs to appear in the form of TTINs on copies of Forms W-2 that are furnished to employees. If the proposed regulations are finalized without change, the IRS intends to incorporate the revised regulations into forms and instructions, permitting employers to use a TTIN on the employee copy of the Form W-2. See §301.6109-4(b)(2)(i) and (ii).

Explanation of Provisions

Truncated SSN Permitted on Employee's Copies of Form W-2

These proposed regulations amend §31.6051-1 to permit employers to truncate employees' SSNs to appear in the form of a TTIN on copies of Forms W-2 that are furnished to employees under section 6051. Consistent with the rule in §301.6109-4(b)(2)(iii), prohibiting the use of TTINs on any return, statement, or other document that is required to be filed with or furnished to the IRS, these proposed regulations amend §31.6051-2 to clarify that employers may not truncate an employee's SSN to appear in the form of a TTIN on a copy of a Form W-2 that is filed with the Social Security Administration. This result is appropriate because both the IRS and the SSA need to utilize Forms W-2 to properly identify individuals to be able to carry out their respective duties.

Consistent with the rule in §301.6109-4(b)(2)(ii) that prohibits using TTINs if, among other things, a statute specifically requires the use of an SSN, the proposed regulations also amend §31.6051-3 to clarify that a payee's SSN may not be truncated to appear in the form of a TTIN on a statement furnished to the employer of the payee who received sick pay from a third party because section 6051(f)(1)(A)(i) specifically requires such a statement to contain the employee's SSN. Nonetheless, these proposed regulations permit employers to truncate payees' SSNs to appear in the form of TTINs on copies of Forms W-2 that are furnished under section 6051(f)(2) to payees that report such third-party sick pay, in accordance with the general rule governing the reporting of wages to employees on Forms W-2 under section 6051(a), because section 6051(f)(2) does not specifically require the use of an SSN.

Further, these proposed regulations amend § 1.6052-2 to permit employers to truncate employees' SSNs to appear in the form of TTINs on copies of Forms W-2 that are furnished to employees under section 6052(b) regarding payment of wages in the form of group-term life insurance.

These proposed regulations amend § 301.6109-4 to clarify that truncation is not allowed on any return, statement, or other document that is required to be filed with or furnished to the Social Security Administration under the internal revenue laws. These proposed regulations also clarify the rule prohibiting truncation if a statute, regulation, other guidance published in the Internal Revenue Bulletin, form, or instructions, specifically requires use of a SSN, ITIN, ATIN, or EIN. The proposed regulations provide that truncation is allowed if a statute or IRS guidance (*e.g.*, regulations, forms, instructions), that specifically requires use of a SSN, ITIN, ATIN, or EIN, also specifically states that the taxpayer identifying number may be truncated. These proposed regulations also add an example illustrating the application of these rules to Forms W-2. These proposed regulations also amend the existing example for clarity.

Miscellaneous Updates to Regulations Under Sections 6051 and 6052

In addition to the amendments relating to the truncation of employees' SSNs to appear in the form of TTINs in specific circumstances, these proposed regulations eliminate obsolete provisions and update cross references in the regulations under sections 6051 and 6052, as explained below.

First, these proposed regulations amend § 31.6051-1 to remove obsolete provisions regarding compensation, as defined in the Railroad Retirement Tax Act, paid during 1968, 1969, 1970, and 1971 and reported on the now obsolete Form W-2 (RR); the special rule for statements with respect to the refundable earned income credit for Form W-2 for 1987 and 1988; and references to the annual contribution base (repealed in 1993) for wages subject to the Hospital Insurance tax (commonly known as Medicare tax).

Second, these proposed regulations amend § 31.6051-1 to remove obsolete cross references, including a cross reference to former § 301.6676-1 relating to the penalty for failure to report an identification number or an account number, and a cross reference to section 6723 (prior to its amendment in 1989) that was relevant for Forms W-2 that were due from the beginning of 1987 through the end of 1989.

Third, these proposed regulations amend § 31.6051-2 to update now inaccurate cross references resulting from statutory and regulatory changes regarding penalties for failures to file, and to remove a cross reference to section 6723 (prior to its amendment in 1989) that was relevant for Forms W-2 that were due from the beginning of 1987 through the end of 1989. These proposed regulations also change the title of § 31.6051-2 from "Information returns on Form W-3 and Internal Revenue Service copies of Forms W-2" to "Information returns on Form W-3 and Social Security Administration copies of Forms W-2," to conform with the text of the regulation that refers to the Social Security Administration copies of Form W-2. In addition, these proposed regulations remove obsolete references in § 31.6051-2 to the requirements to submit information on magnetic tape and insert a reference to the requirements to submit information on magnetic media.

Fourth, these proposed regulations amend § 31.6051-3 to remove the obsolete transition rule for third-party sick pay that was paid to a payee after December 31, 1980, and before May 1, 1981.

Fifth, these proposed regulations amend § 1.6052-2 to remove an obsolete rule that allowed employers to use a statement other than a Form W-2 to satisfy the requirement to furnish a statement to an employee with respect to wages paid in the form of group-term life insurance. This rule was relevant for years prior to 1973, before § 1.6052-1 was amended to require employers to report wages in the form of group-term life insurance on Form W-2. At the same time, to conform to this new requirement, § 1.6052-2 was amended to provide that the requirement to furnish a statement to an employee with respect to wages paid in the form of group-term life insurance may be satisfied by furnishing to the employee the employee's copy of Form W-2 that was filed pursuant to § 1.6052-1. Because the transition period to require employers to file Form W-2 has long since passed and because the Treasury Department and the IRS understand that copies of Forms W-2 are used to satisfy the requirement to furnish statements to employees under § 1.6052-2, these proposed regulations require employers to furnish to employees the employees' copies of Forms W-2 that were filed pursuant to § 1.6052-1, and these proposed regulations make conforming changes throughout that section.

Finally, these proposed regulations update the now inaccurate cross reference resulting from statutory changes regarding penalties for failures to furnish statements under section 6052 and remove the deemed compliance rule, which applied only to years before 1972.

Proposed Effective/Applicability Date

These proposed regulations will be effective on the date of the publication of the Treasury Decision adopting these rules as final in the **Federal Register**. These proposed regulations amend the effective/applicability date provisions in § 31.6051-1, § 31.6051-3, and § 301.6109-4, and add applicability date provisions to § 1.6052-2 and § 31.6051-2. Several state tax administrators have requested additional time to develop systems to process the copies of Forms W-2 filed with state income tax returns that may contain truncated SSNs. In light of this request, these proposed regulations will not apply to Forms W-2 required to be furnished before January 1, 2019. Accordingly, these proposed regulations provide that these regulations, as amended, will be applicable for statements required to be filed and furnished under sections 6051 and 6052 after December 31, 2018.

Statement of Availability of IRS Documents

IRS Revenue Procedures, Revenue Rulings notices, and other guidance cited in this preamble are published in the Internal Revenue Bulletin (or Cumulative Bulletin) and are available from the Superintendent of Documents, U.S. Government Printing Office, Washington, DC 20402, or by visiting the IRS Web site at *www.irs.gov*.

Special Analyses

Certain IRS regulations, including this one, are exempt from the requirements of Executive Order 12866, as supplemented and reaffirmed by Executive Order 13563. Therefore, a regulatory assessment is not required. Because these proposed regulations do not impose a collection of information on small entities, the Regulatory Flexibility Act (5 U.S.C. chapter 6) does not apply. Pursuant to section 7805(f) of the Code, this notice of proposed rulemaking has been submitted to the Chief Counsel for Advocacy of the Small Business Administration for comment on its impact on small business.

Comments and Requests for Public Hearing

Before these proposed regulations are adopted as final regulations, consideration will be given to any comments that are submitted timely to the IRS as prescribed in the preamble under the **ADDRESSES** section. The Treasury Department and the IRS request comments on all aspects of these proposed regulations. All comments submitted will be made available at *www.regulations.gov* or upon request. A public hearing may be scheduled if requested in writing by any person that timely submits written comments. If a public hearing is scheduled, notice of the date, time, and place for the hearing will be published in the **Federal Register**.

Drafting Information

The principal author of these proposed regulations is Eliezer Mishory of the Office of the Associate Chief Counsel (Procedure and Administration).

List of Subjects

26 CFR Part 1

Income taxes, Reporting and recordkeeping requirements.

26 CFR Part 31

Employment taxes, Income taxes, Penalties, Pensions, Railroad Retirement, Reporting and recordkeeping requirements, Social Security, Unemployment compensation.

26 CFR Part 301

Employment taxes, Estate taxes, Excise taxes, Gift taxes, Income taxes, Penalties, Reporting and recordkeeping requirements.

Proposed Amendments to the Regulations

Accordingly, 26 CFR parts 1, 31 and 301 are proposed to be amended as follows:

PART 1—INCOME TAXES

■ *Paragraph 1.* The authority citation for part 1continues to read in part as follows:

Authority: 26 U.S.C. 7805, unless otherwise noted.

* * * * *

■ *Par. 2.* Section 1.6052-2 is amended by:

■ 1. Revising paragraph (a).

■ 2. Removing paragraph (b).

■ 3. Redesignating paragraph (e) as new paragraph (b).

■ 4. Revising paragraphs (c) and (d).

■ 5. Removing paragraphs (f) and (g).

The revisions read as follows:

§ 1.6052-2 Statements to be furnished employees with respect to wages paid in the form of group-term life insurance.

(a) *Requirement.* Every employer filing a return under section 6052(a) and § 1.6052-1, with respect to group-term life insurance on the life of an employee, shall furnish to the employee whose name is set forth in such return the tax return copy and the employee's copy of Form W-2. Each copy of Form W-2 must show the information required to be shown on the Form W-2 filed under § 1.6052-1. An employer may truncate an employee's social security number to appear in the form of an IRS truncated taxpayer identification number (TTIN) on copies of Form W-2 furnished to the employee. For provisions relating to the use of TTINs, see § 301.6109-4 of this chapter (Procedure and Administration Regulations). The rules in § 31.6051-1 of this chapter (Employment Taxes and Collection of Income Tax at Source Regulations) shall apply with respect to the means and time (including extensions thereof) for furnishing the employee's copy of Form W-2 required by this section to the employee and making corrections to such form.

* * * * *

(c) *Penalty.* For provisions relating to the penalty provided for failure to furnish a statement under this section, see section 6722 and the regulations thereunder.

(d) *Applicability date.* This section is applicable for statements required to be furnished under section 6052 after December 31, 2018.

PART 31—EMPLOYMENT TAXES AND COLLECTION OF INCOME TAX AT SOURCE

■ *Par. 3.* The authority citation for part 31 is amended by adding an entry in numerical order to read in part as follows:

Authority: 26 U.S.C. 7805 * * *

Section 31.6051-3 also issued under 26 U.S.C. 6051.

* * * * *

■ *Par. 4.* Section 31.6051-1 is amended by:

* * * * *

■ 4. Removing paragraph (j)(8).

* * * * *

■ *Par. 6.* Section 31.6051-3 is amended by revising paragraphs (a)(1)(i), (b)(1), (e)(3), and (f) and removing paragraph (g) to read as follows:

§ 31.6051-3 Statements required in case of sick pay paid by third parties.

(a) * * *

(1) * * *

(i) The name and, if there is withholding from sick pay under section 3402(o) and the regulations thereunder, the social security account number of the payee (the payee's social security number may not be truncated to appear in the form of an IRS truncated taxpayer identification number (TTIN)),

(b) * * *

(1) All of the information required to be furnished under paragraph (a) of this section, but the employer may truncate the payee's social security number to appear in the form of an IRS truncated taxpayer identification number (TTIN) on copies of Forms W-2 that are furnished to the payee (for provisions relating to the use of TTINs, see § 301.6109-4 of this chapter (Procedure and Administration Regulations)),

* * * * *

(e) * * *

(3) The provisions of section 6109 (relating to identifying numbers) and the regulations thereunder shall be applicable to Form W-2 and to any payee of sick pay to whom a statement on Form W-2 is required by this section to be furnished. The employer must include the social security number of the payee on all copies of Forms W-2. The employer may truncate the payee's social security number to appear in the form of an IRS truncated taxpayer identification number (TTIN) on copies of Forms W-2 that are furnished to the payee. For provisions relating to the use of truncated taxpayer identification numbers (TTINs), see § 301.6109-4 of this chapter (Procedure and Administration Regulations).

(f) *Applicability date.* This section is applicable for statements required to be furnished under section 6051 after December 31, 2018.

* * * * *

Kirsten Wielobob,

Deputy Commissioner for Services and Enforcement.

[FR Doc. 2017-19910 Filed 9-18-17; 11:15 am]

BILLING CODE 4830-01-P

¶ 20,519L

Proposed regulations on 29 CFR Parts 2520 and 2530.—Reproduced below is the text of proposed regulations on 29 CFR Parts 2520 and 2530 that deal with reports that must be furnished to participants, and their beneficiaries, of single pension plans only, regarding benefits to which they are entitled or will become entitled at retirement and with records that must be maintained to provide the information necessary for these reports. These proposed regs are in place of earlier proposals (dated February 9, 1979) which were withdrawn by the Department of Labor.

The regulations were filed with the *Federal Register* on July 29, 1980.

DEPARTMENT OF LABOR

Office of Pension and Welfare Benefit Programs

29 CFR Parts 2520 and 2530

Reporting and Disclosure and Minimum Standards for Employee Pension Benefit Plans; Individual Benefit Reporting and Record-keeping for Single Employer Plans.

AGENCY: Department of Labor.

ACTION: Proposed rulemaking and withdrawal of previously proposed regulations.

SUMMARY: This document (1) withdraws previously proposed regulations (44 FR 8294, February 9, 1979), which dealt with reports that must be furnished to participants in pension plans (and, in some cases, to their beneficiaries) regarding their benefit entitlements, and with records that must be maintained to provide the information necessary for these reports, and (2) contains new proposed regulations applicable only to single employer plans (defined herein to include plans maintained by groups of employers under common control). The Employee Retirement Income Security Act of 1974 (the Act) imposes on certain pension plans the duty to furnish reports and maintain records regarding participants' benefit entitlements and authorizes the Secretary of Labor to prescribe regulations under these provisions. The proposed regulations, if adopted, would provide necessary guidance to employers maintaining such single employer pension plans and to plan administrators of such plans for compliance with the statutory provisions, and would enable participants in single employer plans to receive accurate, timely, and useful information.

DATES: Written comments and requests for a public hearing must be received by the Department of Labor (the Department) on or before October 1, 1980. These regulations, if adopted, would become effective 120 days after adoption.

ADDRESSES: Written comments (preferably three copies) should be submitted to the Division of Reporting and Disclosure, Pension and Welfare Benefit Programs, Room N-4508, U.S. Department of Labor, Washington, D.C. 20216, Attention: Single Employer Individual Benefit Reporting and Recordkeeping Regulations. All comments should be clearly referenced to the section of the regulations to which they apply. All written comments will be available for public inspection at the Public Documents Room, Pension and Welfare Benefit Programs, Department of Labor, Room N-4677, 200 Constitution Avenue NW., Washington, D.C. 20216.

FOR FURTHER INFORMATION CONTACT: Mary O. Lin, Plan Benefits Security Division, Office of the Solicitor, U.S. Department of Labor, Washington, D.C. 20210, (202) 523-9595, or Ronald D. Allen, Pension and Welfare Benefit Programs, U.S. Department of Labor, Washington, D.C. 20216, (202) 523-8515. (These are not toll-free numbers.)

SUPPLEMENTARY INFORMATION: Notice is hereby given that the Department of Labor is withdrawing previously proposed regulations (44 FR 8294, February 9, 1979), and has under consideration new proposed regulations applicable to single-employer plans[1] dealing with reports that must be furnished to individual participants (and, in some cases, their beneficiaries) regarding their benefit entitlements under employee pension benefit plans, and with records that must be maintained to provide the information necessary for these reports. These regulations are proposed under the authority contained in sections 105, 209, and 505 of the Act (Pub. L. 93-406, 88 Stat. 849, 865, and 894, 29 U.S.C. 1025, 1059, and 1135).

The Department has determined that these proposed regulations are "significant" within the meaning of Department of Labor guidelines (44 FR 5570, January 26, 1979) issued to implement Executive Order 12044 (43 FR 12661, March 23, 1978).

Statutory Provisions

Sections 105(a) of the Act generally requires each administrator of an employee pension benefit plan to furnish to any plan participant or beneficiary who so requests in writing, a statement indicating, on the basis of the latest available information, the total benefits accrued and the nonforfeitable pension benefits, if any, which have accrued, or the earliest date on which such benefits will become nonforfeitable. Similarly, section 209(a)(1) of the Act generally requires the plan administrator of a pension plan subject to Part 2 of Title I of the Act to make a report, in accordance with regulations of the Secretary of Labor, to each employee who is a participant under the plan and who requests such report. The report required under section 209(a)(1) must be sufficient to inform the employee of his accrued benefits which are nonforfeitable. Under both sections 105(a) and 209(a)(1), no participant is entitled to more than one report on request during any single 12-month period. Section 209(a) also requires similar reports to be provided to a participant who terminates service with the employer or has a one-year break in service. Sections 105(d) and 209(a)(2) authorize the Secretary of Labor to prescribe regulations specifying the extent to which these reporting requirements apply to plans adopted by more than one employer. In addition, section 105(c) of the Act requires plan administrators to provide to participants with respect to whom registration statements are filed with the Internal Revenue Service under section 6057 of the Internal Revenue Code of 1954 (the Code) individual statements setting forth the information contained in the registration statements.

In order to enable employees' benefits to be determined, so that the reporting requirements of section 209 can be met, section 209(a)(1) generally requires records to be maintained by employers and authorizes the Secretary of Labor to prescribe regulations governing such records. The information necessary for individual benefit reporting is to be furnished by the employer to the plan administrator. In the case of a plan adopted by more than one employer, however, section 209(a)(2) requires records to be maintained by the plan administrator, based on information to be provided by each such employer.

Background

On February 9, 1979 (44 FR 8294), the Department published proposed regulations with respect to individual benefit statements and recordkeeping (referred to herein as "the 1979 proposal"). These regulations would have applied both to single employer plans and to multiple employer plans. A large number of public comments on the 1979 proposal were filed. Many of these comments suggested that substantial revisions should be made to the 1979 proposal. In particular, comments filed on behalf of single and multiple employer plans raised distinct issues.

Upon consideration of those comments, the Department has determined to withdraw the 1979 proposal and to propose the regulations set forth below which pertain only to single employer plans. Reporting and recordkeeping questions relating to multiple employer plans, including multiemployer plans, are still under consideration by the Department. The Department contemplates that proposed regulations dealing with reporting and recordkeeping requirements for multiple employer plans will be published in the *Federal Register* in the future.

Of the regulations now being proposed, 29 CFR 2520.105-1 through 2520.105-2 deal with individual benefit reporting to participants and beneficiaries, while 29 CFR 2530.209-1 through 2530.209-2 deal with the maintenance by plans of records to serve as a basis for individual benefit statements.

In addition to substantive changes from the 1979 proposal, this new proposal contains language changes designed to clarify provisions or to improve readability.

These regulations are proposed under the authority in section 105, 209, and 505 of the Act (Pub. L. 93-446, 88 Stat. 349, 865, and 894, 29 U.S.C. 1025, 1059, and 1135).

Discussion of Proposed Individual Benefit Reporting Regulations

[1] The term "single employer plan" is defined in the proposed regulations to include plans maintained by a group of employers under common control. In discussions of the proposal throughout this document, the term "single employer plan" generally should be read to be consistent with this definition.

1. *Benefit statement.* Under these proposed regulations, the benefit statement is the basic document to be used for providing individual benefit information to participants upon request, upon termination or upon a one-year break in service. The benefit statement must state the amount of a participant's accrued benefit regardless of the extent to which it is nonforfeitable (i.e., "vested"), the percentage of the accrued benefit which is vested, and the amount of such accrued vested benefit. The regulations specify the form in which accrued benefits and accrued vested benefits must be reported. The new proposal is designed to ensure that the information provided to an individual participant is presented in a meaningful fashion, without imposing excessive administrative costs on plans.

Some of the comments received by the Department on the 1979 proposal raised objections to the degree to which that proposal would have required benefit statements to provide individualized information geared to each participant's particular circumstances. These comments suggested that the degree of individualization that would have been required would entail significant additional costs for plans, and that ultimately these costs would be borne to some extent by participants. These commentators pointed out that, in some cases, the individualized information might be misleading or of little value to recipients of benefit statements as a result of changes in participants' circumstances. At the same time, it appears to the Department that some degree of individualization is necessary if individual benefit statements are to serve the purposes which underlie the statutory requirements. In the new proposal the Department has struck what it believes to be a better balance between the need for individualization of benefit statements and the costs that individualization imposes.

In the case of defined benefit plans, the accrued benefit and the amount of the participant's accrued vested benefit may be expressed either in terms of a straight life annuity payable at normal retirement age, or in terms of the normal form of benefits offered by the plan (e.g., annuity for a term of years, lump sum distribution, etc.). By contrast, the 1979 proposal would have required accrued benefits to be stated either in the form of a straight life annuity payable at normal retirement age or, if the plan did not offer such a benefit, in the form of the primary option offered by the plan. If a participant had made any elections affecting the manner of payment of benefits, the 1979 proposal generally would have required accrued benefits to be stated in the form elected by the participant. The elimination in the new proposal of the requirement to state accrued benefits in the form elected by the participant is in keeping with the goal of reducing costs resulting from excessive individualization. It also reflects comments to the effect that the requirement to state accrued benefits in the form of a straight life annuity payable at normal retirement age might prove misleading to participants when this is not the normal form of benefits payable under the plan. One of the comments on the 1979 proposal suggested that the Department should prohibit explicitly inclusion in the benefit statement of benefit projections predicated on the assumption that a participant will work until retirement. The comment suggested that such projections would not satisfy the requirement that a benefit statement must report accrued benefits, vested percentage and accrued vested benefits as of the date of the statement. The Department has decided not to prohibit the inclusion of such projections, but notes that the benefit statement must be written in a manner calculated to be understood by the average plan participant or beneficiary and its format must not have the effect of misleading or misinforming participants or beneficiaries.

The new proposal would require the benefit statement to indicate that election of options under the plan might affect the participant's accrued benefits, and to refer the participant to the Summary Plan Description for information on available options. In addition, if the accrued benefit and accrued vested benefit are not expressed as amounts payable in the form of a joint and survivor annuity, the benefit statement must explain that the periodic benefit the participant will receive at retirement may be reduced on account of survivor benefits.

Social security offset plans must furnish the net benefit. In the case of benefit statements furnished on request or under the annual benefit statement alternative, the net benefit may be determined on the basis of assumptions about participants' earnings in service not covered by the plan, provided that the benefit statement indicates that the reported amounts are approximate. Benefit statements furnished upon termination or after a break in service must report the actual amounts of benefits to which the participant is entitled.

In the case of an individual account plan, the regulations make it clear that the participant's account balance is considered to be the accrued benefit.

In accordance with the statutory requirements, the benefit statement would be required to indicate the nonforfeitable (vested) percentage of the participant's accrued benefit. If the participant has no vested ac-

crued benefits, the benefit statement must indicate the earliest date on which any benefits will become vested. Consistent with the goal of avoiding excessive administrative costs, the new proposal eliminates the requirement in the 1979 proposal that plans with "graded" vesting indicate the earliest dates on which a participant may attain each subsequent level of nonforfeitable accrued benefits derived from employer contributions. The new proposal also provides that class year plans would be required to indicate the nonforfeitable percentage of each portion of the participant's account balance, to which a separate nonforfeitable percentage applies.

The benefit statement would also be required to indicate the amount of the participant's nonforfeitable accrued benefit, in the same form as that in which the accrued benefit is reported.

The new proposal requires only a general reference to the Summary Plan Description. The 1979 proposal required more detailed information regarding circumstances that might result in the reduction or elimination of accrued or nonforfeitable benefits, including detailed references to the Summary Plan Description. The new proposal also eliminates the requirement in the 1979 proposal that the benefit statement include certain information concerning a participant's work history used as a basis for calculation of the participant's benefits. This change was made to reduce the degree to which benefit statements must be individualized. The eliminated information, however, must be available to a participant under the provisions of these regulations regarding inspection of records (§ 2530.209-2(f)), and, as under the 1979 proposal, the benefit statement must so indicate. As under the 1979 proposal, the benefit statement would be required to include a statement urging the participant to bring promptly to the attention of the plan administrator anything in the benefit statement that does not appear correct; information regarding the availability of plan records for inspection; the date as of which information is reported; and the participant's social security number (for the purpose of verification by the participant).

Like its predecessor, the new proposal would provide that the benefit statement must be written in a manner calculated to be understood by the average plan participant or beneficiary and that the format of the benefit statement must not have the effect of misleading or misinforming the participant or beneficiary. Under certain circumstances, plans must offer foreign language assistance to participants who are not literate in English to aid them in understanding their benefit statements, as is required under regulations relating to the Summary Plan Description (see 29 CFR 2520.102-2(c)).

The benefit statement must be based on the latest available information. As under the 1979 proposal, benefit statements based on records that meet the standards of sufficiency set forth in the proposed record-keeping regulations will be deemed to be based on the latest available information Although "sufficient", a plan's records may nevertheless be incomplete (i.e., if they do not include all items necessary to determine participants' benefit entitlements) if, for example, a plan did not maintain complete records prior to the adoption of these regulations. In these instances, the benefit statement must indicate that the records on which it is based are incomplete and the participant or beneficiary must be offered an opportunity to provide other information relating to his benefit entitlements. The plan administrator must prepare a benefit statement based on such information although, to the extent that a benefit statement is based on such information, it may indicate that it is conditioned upon the accuracy of that information.

In the 1979 proposal the Department solicited comments on whether and to what extent it should adopt regulations concerning circumstances under which liability should be imposed for payment of benefits in accordance with the information provided in the benefit statement. Some comments supported the adoption of regulations imposing liability, while others suggested that liability should be limited, or objected to the imposition of any liability. Upon consideration of the comments, the Department has concluded that a judgment concerning the consequences of an incorrect benefit statement can properly be made only after account has been taken of all the facts and circumstances. The Department believes, therefore, that it would be more appropriate to leave determinations of this sort to plan fiduciaries, whose actions are subject to review by means of the judicial process, than to attempt to deal with all conceivable factual situations in the context of regulations.

In the 1979 proposal, the Department also solicited comments on whether it should publish model benefit statements. In view of the multiplicity of plan provisions, it would be difficult for the Department to ensure that the format of a model statement would not be misleading under any circumstances. Accordingly, the Department has made a decision at this time not to publish model benefit statements.

2. *Furnishing benefit statements on request.* Both sections 105(a) and 209(a)(1)(A) of the Act require plan administrators of pension plans to furnish individual benefit information on request. The requirements of both statutory provisions are substantially similar in this regard; accordingly, these requirements are dealt with in a single section of the regulations (§ 2520.105-2(a)). The only significant difference between the two statutory provisions is that section 105(a) applies to requests by both participants and their designated beneficiaries, while section 209(a)(1)(A) applies only to requests by participants. The regulations, therefore, apply to requests by both participants and beneficiaries, so as to cover the broadest range of circumstances under which benefit statements must be furnished on request.

In response to suggestions made in comments on the 1979 proposal, the new proposal provides that a plan administrator subject to these regulations need not provide a benefit statement upon request to certain classes of participants and beneficiaries. These include participants and beneficiaries currently receiving benefits; participants and beneficiaries to whom paid up insurance policies representing their full benefit entitlements have been distributed; participants and beneficiaries who have received a full distribution of their benefits or who are receiving benefits under the plan; beneficiaries of participants who are entitled to benefit statements; and participants with deferred vested benefits who have received benefit statements on termination or after having incurred a one-year break in service without returning to service with any employer maintaining the plan, and their beneficiaries. The Department believes that it would be superfluous to require benefit statements to be furnished to these participants and beneficiaries.

The plan administrator may establish a simple and convenient procedure for the submission of requests for benefit statements. If such a procedure is established and communicated to participants and beneficiaries (for example, in the Summary Plan Description), the plan administrator, under certain conditions, need not comply with requests that do not conform to the procedure. If no such procedure is established, however, the plan administrator must comply with any request in writing by a participant or beneficiary. The plan administrator may not require information regarding a participant's employment record as a condition for furnishing the benefit statement (although such information may be requested). The new proposal would, however, allow plan administrators to require the furnishing of certain items of information identifying the participant about whom information is requested.

Many of the comments on the 1979 proposal urged that the Department permit benefit statements to report benefits as of the end of the plan year. The comments suggested that this approach would relieve individual account plans of the expense of conducting a valuation whenever a participant or beneficiary requests a benefit statement. Defined benefit plans might also face lower administrative costs if an end-of-plan-year approach were adopted because it might enable these plans to gear data processing systems to a single date. In light of these comments, the new proposal would require a benefit statement to report benefits as of a date not earlier than the end of the plan year preceding the plan year in which a participant or beneficiary requests the statement.

The end-of-plan-year approach, however, entails changes in the deadlines for furnishing benefit statements on request. The new proposal is designed to permit a reasonable period of time after the end of the plan year for the processing of information. Under the new proposal, a benefit statement must be furnished to a participant or beneficiary on request within the later of 60 days of the date of the request or 120 days after the end of the plan year which immediately precedes the year in which the request was made. The Department recognizes that this scheme would provide participants and beneficiaries who request benefit statements towards the end of the plan year with a statement that contains relatively old information based on the prior plan year (as much as 14 months old), while participants and beneficiaries who request statements during the earlier part of the plan year may be required to wait a substantial period (up to four months) to receive their statements.

Nevertheless, the Department believes that the proposed scheme strikes an appropriate balance between providing participants with timely information and reducing administrative costs.

As under the 1979 proposal the plan administrator would not be required to furnish more than one benefit statement to a participant or beneficiary on request during any 12-month period.

The original proposal appeared to require plans to furnish a complete benefit statement to a non-vested participant if the annual alternative was used. The new proposal would permit a plan to provide annually, as an alternative to furnishing benefit statements on request, a benefit statement to each vested participant and a statement of non-vested status to each non-vested participant. Permitting the furnishing of a statement of non-vested status under the annual alternative should reduce costs to plans electing the alternative, while providing sufficient disclosure to a non-vested participant The plan administrator must furnish a complete benefit statement, however, to any non-vested participant who requests one after receiving the statement of non-vested status.

The annual benefit statement must be furnished within 180 days after the end of the plan year.

Despite comments objecting to the requirement in the 1979 proposal that the plan administrator furnish at least one duplicate of the annual benefit statement to any participant or beneficiary who requests it during the year, the Department has not eliminated this requirement. In some cases a participant or beneficiary may not receive an annual benefit statement mailed to him. Since it would be impracticable and unfair to require a participant or beneficiary to prove that he did not receive an annual statement in order to obtain a duplicate, the regulations allow all participants or beneficiaries entitled to receive a benefit statement on request at least one duplicate if the annual alternative is used.

3. *Furnishing benefit statements upon termination and after one-year breaks in service.* The benefit statement must report benefits as of the end of the plan year in which the termination or the one-year break in service occurs. Consistent with end-of-the-year benefit reporting, the new proposal requires statements to be furnished within 180 days after the end of the plan year in which the termination or break in service occurs. The 180 day period would allow plans to satisfy the requirement to furnish benefit statements upon termination or break in service through the use of the annual benefit statement alternative, which is required to be furnished in the same time period.

A participant who receives a benefit statement in connection with termination of service, and thereafter incurs a one-year break in service, is not entitled to receive an additional benefit statement if the information in the second benefit statement would be the same as in the first. Similarly, a participant who receives a benefit statement upon incurring a one-year break in service and thereafter terminates service with the employer, or incurs a subsequent one-year break in service, is not entitled to receive an additional benefit statement if the information in the second benefit statement would be the same as that in the first.

In the case of participants who have no vested benefits, the new proposal, like the 1979 proposal, would permit plan administrators of single employer plans to satisfy the requirements to furnish individual benefit information upon termination by furnishing a statement of non-vested status. The statement of non-vested status informs the participant that he has no nonforfeitable benefits. It does not, however, provide information regarding accrued benefits. Thus, the statement of non-vested status does not require extensive calculations and may be presented to all participants entitled to it in a standardized form, with no need for preparation of an individual statement for each. However, the statement of non-vested status must inform the participant that he may request a benefit statement with more detailed information regarding his individual accrued (non-vested) benefits. Such a request must be treated as a request for a benefit statement.

4. *Corrections in the benefit statement.* As under the 1979 proposal, a participant who raises a question with regard to the accuracy of a benefit statement must be given an opportunity to furnish information regarding his benefit entitlements to the plan administrator. Within a reasonable time, the plan administrator must make a decision with regard to the question raised by the participant and notify the participant of the decision, the basis for the decision, and any change in benefit entitlements as a result of the decision. The plan administrator is not required to prepare a benefit statement based on the information furnished by the participant except, as noted above, in situations where the benefit statement is based on incomplete records.

5. *Statement of deferred vested benefits.* Under section 105(c) of the Act, each plan administrator required to register with the Internal Revenue Service under section 6057 of the Code shall furnish a statement of deferred vested benefits to each participant described in section 6057(a)(2)(C) (i.e., to each participant who, during the plan year for which registration is required, is separated from service covered under the plan, is entitled to a deferred vested benefit under the plan as of the end of the plan year, and with respect to whom retirement benefits were not paid under the plan). Section 6057(e) of the Code requires plan administrators to furnish similar individual statements to the same class of participants. The requirements of section 105(c) will be deemed to be satisfied if, in accordance with section 6057(e) of the Code and regulations thereunder, the plan administrator furnishes to the participant the individual statement required under the latter section.

6. *Manner of furnishing individual benefit reporting documents.* Like the 1979 proposal, the new proposal would require a plan to furnish individual benefit documents to a participant or beneficiary either by first class mail to his last known address, or by personal delivery. The new proposal makes it clear that personal delivery may be accomplished by another party under the plan administrator's supervision.

The new recordkeeping proposal would require a participant's individual benefit records to include current address information. Although some comments suggested that plans should not be required to maintain current address information on file, and should be permitted to use less reliable modes of delivery than first-class mail and personal delivery, the Department believes that these requirements represent the only means of assuring that individual benefit reporting documents will actually reach participants and beneficiaries in most cases.

Proposed Individual Benefit Recordkeeping Regulations

1. *Duty to maintain records.* In the case of a single employer plan, the duty to maintain individual benefits records would be imposed on the employer maintaining the plan. As under the 1979 proposal, the employer would be required to furnish to the plan administrator the information necessary to enable the latter to comply with the individual benefit reporting requirements.

2. *Sufficiency of records.* The individual benefit records maintained in connection with a single employer plan will be deemed to be sufficient if they contain all information relevant to the determination of each employee's benefit entitlements under the plan with respect to service with the employer who maintains the plan after the effective date of the regulations. In the case of a plan adopted after the effective date, records must contain all information relevant to a determination of each employee's benefit entitlements under the plan relating to such service after the date of adoption. Certain information with respect to service before the initial recordkeeping date specified in the regulations will be relevant in determining vested accrued benefits. The proposed regulations would not require records of this information to be compiled, but if such records were in existence as of February 9, 1979, the date on which the 1979 proposal was published in the Federal Register, they must be retained. In the Department's view, the 1979 proposal was sufficient to put plan administrators on notice that existing records would not be permitted to be destroyed.

3. *Retention, preservation and inspection of records.* As under the 1979 proposal, individual benefit records must be retained as long as a possibility exists that they might be relevant to a determination of the benefit entitlements of a participant or beneficiary. However, if they are lost or destroyed due to circumstances beyond the control of the person responsible for their maintenance, they will not be deemed insufficient solely for that reason. They must be maintained in a safe and accessible place at the offices of the employer, or at special recordkeeping offices.

The proposal makes clear that original records may be disposed of at any time if microfilm, microfiche or similarly reproduced records which are clear reproductions of the original documents are retained, and adequate viewing equipment is available for inspecting them. (The 1979 proposal appeared to allow microfilm reproduction only.)

Individual benefit records, including original documents must be available for inspection by participants, beneficiaries, and their representatives.

The period within which plan records must be made available for inspection after a request to do so has been extended from 72 hours, as under the 1979 proposal, to 10 working days. This change was made in response to comments noting the difficulties which would have been involved under the previous proposal.

In response to some public comments, provisions have been added to this proposal requiring the employer maintaining the records to bear the cost of converting records into a form accessible for inspection, although reasonable charges for copying may be imposed, not exceeding the actual cost. Inspection of records may be made only by those persons entitled to receive a benefit statement, and their representatives. Representatives of the Department have the authority to inspect plan records under the circumstances specified in section 504 of ERISA.

If an employer ceases to be responsible for the maintenance of individual benefit records, they must be transferred to the person who becomes responsible for their maintenance.

4. *Definition of "single employer plan".* The Department has tentatively decided to extend the term "single employer plan", for the purposes of these regulations, to a plan adopted by a group of employers under common control. In the case of these plans, the new proposal

would impose the recordkeeping requirements on the individual employers, rather than on a central recordkeeping agent such as the plan administrator, but would make it clear that the individual employers may enter into cooperative centralized recordkeeping arrangements. The Department believes that for these plans it is unnecessary to impose on the employers a legal obligation, such as might be appropriate in the case of a plan maintained by a group of unaffiliated employers, to participate in such arrangements because the central management of the control group is able to require employers maintaining the plan to adhere to efficient recordkeeping arrangements.

Effective Dates

The Department has received a number of comments in response to the 1979 proposal suggesting that some plans may need to effect changes to their existing reporting and recordkeeping systems to comply with the proposed regulations. In order to allow for orderly preparations for compliance with the regulations, the Department contemplates providing that these regulations would not become effective with respect to collectively bargained multiple employer plans until nine months after the expiration of the collective bargaining agreement or agreements in effect on the date of adoption of these regulations, but in no case more than 45 months after the date of adoption. For multiple employer plans which are not collectively bargained, the regulations, if adopted, would become effective 120 days after adoption.

Drafting Information

The principal author of these proposed regulations is Mary O. Lin of the Plan Benefits Security Division, Office of the Solicitor, Department of Labor. However, other persons in the Department of Labor participated in developing the proposed regulations, both on matters of substance and style.

Proposed Regulation

Accordingly, proposed regulations 29 CFR 2520.105-1 through 2520.105-2 and proposed regulations 29 CFR 2530.209-1 through 2530.209-2 (44 FR 8294, February 9, 1979) are hereby withdrawn, and it is proposed to amend Chapter XXV of Title 29 of the Code of Federal Regulations as follows:

1. By adding to Part 2520 new §§ 2520.105-1, 2520.105-2, and 2520.105-3 to read as follows:

Subpart G—Individual Benefit Reporting

Sec.

2520.105-1 General.

2520.105-2 Individual Benefit Reporting for Single-Employer Plans.

2520.105-3 [Reserved].

Authority: Secs. 105, 209 and 505 of the Act (Pub. L. 93-406; 88 Stat. 849, 865 and 894, 29 U.S.C. 1025, 1059 and 1135).

§ 2520.105-1 General.—(a) *Scope and purpose.* Sections 105 and 209 of the Employee Retirement Income Security Act of 1974 (the Act) impose on plan administrators of employee pension benefit plans certain requirements to report to plan participants and beneficiaries information regarding their individual benefit entitlements. Section 105 of the Act provides, among other things, that each plan administrator of an employee pension benefit plan shall furnish to any plan participant or beneficiary who so requests in writing, a statement of certain information relating to his individual benefit entitlements. Section 209(a) of the Act provides, among other things, that the plan administrator shall make a report regarding individual benefit entitlements, in accordance with regulations prescribed by the Secretary of Labor, to each employee who is a participant under the plan and who either requests such report in accordance with regulations issued by the Secretary of Labor, terminates service with the employer, or has a one-year break in service (as defined in section 203(b)(3)(A) of the Act). In addition, section 105(c) provides that a plan administrator who is required to register under section 6057 of the Internal Revenue Code of 1954 (the Code) shall furnish to certain plan participants individual statements relating to their deferred vested benefits. Section 2520.105-2 and 2520.105-3 contain provisions relating to the reporting of individual benefit entitlements under sections 105 and 209(a) of the Act. Section 2520.105-2 applies to "single employer plans", while section 2520.105-3 applies to "multiple employer plans". The paragraphs of §§ 2520.105-2 and 2520.105-3 are parallel. Recordkeeping requirements relating to information necessary for determining individual benefit entitlements are set forth in §§ 2530.209-1, 2530.209-2 and 2530.209-3.

(b) *Individual benefit reporting documents.* Sections 2520.105-2 and 2520.105-3 deal with three types of documents, collectively referred to as "individual benefit reporting documents":

(1) The benefit statement that must be furnished to plan participants or beneficiaries upon request, upon termination of employment or upon a one-year break in service;

(2) The statement of non-vested status that may be substituted for the benefit statement under certain circumstances; and

(3) The statement of referred vested retirement benefits that must be furnished to participants in connection with certain filing by the plan administrator under section 6057 of the Code.

§ 2520.105-2 Individual benefit reporting for single employer plans.

(a) *Finishing statements on request.*—(1) *General.* The administrator of a single employer employee pension benefit plan (as defined in § 2520.105-2(k)) subject to Part 1 or 2 of Title I of the Act shall furnish a benefit statement which satisfies the requirements of this paragraph and paragraphs (c) through (i) of § 2520.105-2 to all plan participants or beneficiaries who request in writing information regarding their individual benefit entitlements under the plan, except:

(i) Participants and beneficiaries who are currently receiving benefits under the plan;

(ii) Participants and beneficiaries whose entire benefit entitlements under the plan are fully guaranteed by an insurance company, insurance service or insurance organization qualified to do business in a State: *Provided,* That the benefits are paid under an insurance policy or contract on which no further premiums are payable and which has been distributed to the participant or beneficiary;

(iii) Participants and beneficiaries who have received all benefits to which they are entitled under the plan;

(iv) Beneficiaries of a participant who is entitled to a benefit statement on request; and

(v) Participants with deferred vested benefits who have received benefit statements on termination or after incurring a one year break in service and who have not returned to service with any employer maintaining the plan, and beneficiaries of such participants.

(2) *Procedure for submission of requests for benefit statements.* The plan administrator may establish a simple procedure, convenient to participants' and beneficiaries. for the submission of requests for benefits statements. The plan administrator will not be required to comply with a request made in a manner which does not conform to such a procedure which has been communicated in writing to participants and beneficiaries, provided that the plan administrator informs the requesting participant or beneficiary that he had failed to comply with the procedure and explains how to comply with the procedure. A procedure shall be deemed to be communicated to participants and beneficiaries if a description of the procedure is included in the Summary Plan Description of the plan or in any other document distributed to all plan participants. If no such procedure is established, any request in writing to the plan administrator or plan office by a participant or beneficiary for information regarding his benefit entitlements under the plan administrator for the purposes of this section.

(3) *Information obtained from participant or beneficiary.* A participant or beneficiary who requests a benefit statement may not be required to furnish information regarding the participant's employment record as a condition to receiving the benefit statement, but may be required to furnish the following information: Name, address, date of birth, Social Security account number and, if relevant to information provided in the benefit statement, marital status and date of birth of spouse.

(4) *Date of furnishing.* A benefit statement shall be furnished to a participant or beneficiary who requests such a statement, no later than (i) 60 days after receipt of the request or (ii) 120 days after the end of the plan year which immediately precedes the plan year in which the request is made, whichever is later.

(5) *Date as of which information is provided.* A benefit statement furnished at the request of a participant or beneficiary shall report benefits as of a date not earlier than the end of the plan year preceding the plan year in which the request is made.

(6) *Annual benefit statement alternative.* (i) The requirement of furnish a benefit statement on request to a participant or beneficiary as set forth in § 2520.105-2(a)(1), shall not apply if within one year before the request the plan administrator has furnished to such participant or beneficiary an annual benefit statement, or a "statement on non-vested status" described in § 2520.105-2(f), as appropriate, which is based on information as of the end of the plan year preceding the plan year in which it is furnished, and it is furnished within 180 days after the end of that plan year.

(ii) Notwithstanding the provisions of paragraph (a)(6)(i) of this section, the plan administrator shall furnish a complete benefit state-ment meeting the requirements of § 2520.105-2(d) and (e) to a participant who requests information on his accrued benefits after receiving a statement of non-vested status, and shall furnish upon request a duplicate of the most recent annual benefit statement, or statement of non-vested status, as appropriate, to any participant or beneficiary who was entitled to such a statement but claims not to have received one.

(b) *Furnishing statements upon termination and after one-year breaks in service.*—(1) *Furnishing statements upon termination*—(i) *General.* Except as provided in § 2520.105-2(c), the plan administrator of a single employer employee pension benefit plan that is subject to Part 2 of Title I of the Act shall furnish a benefit statement to a participant who terminates service with the employer, unless the participant is reemployed by the employer before the date on which the benefit statement must be furnished under paragraph (b)(1)(iii) of this section.

(ii) *Non-vested participants.* In the case of a terminated participant who has no nonforfeitable benefits under the plan, the plan administrator will comply with the requirements of section 209(a)(1)(B) of the Act and this section if the plan furnishes such participant a "statement of non-vested status" described in § 2520.105-2(f).

If a participant is furnished a statement of non-vested status under this paragraph, and request information concerning his accrued benefits under the plan, the plan administrator shall furnish a benefit statement meeting the requirements of § 2520.105-2(d) and (e) to the participant no later than the later of 60 days after such request or 180 days after the end of the plan year in which the participant's termination occurred.

(iii) *Date of furnishing.* A benefit statement or statement of non-vested status shall be furnished within 180 days after the end of the plan year in which the participant terminates service with the employer. This requirement may be satisfied by furnishing to the participant an annual benefit statement described in § 2520.105-2(a)(6), which reports the participants' benefits as of the end of the plan year in which termination occurred.

(iv) *Date as of which information is provided.* A benefit statement furnished upon termination of service shall report benefits as of a date no earlier than the date of termination.

(2) *Furnishing statements after one-year breaks in service*—(i) *General.* Except as provided in § 2520.105-2(c), a plan administrator of a single employer employee pension benefit plan, that is subject to Part 2 of Title I of the Act and provides that participants may suffer adverse consequences on incurring a one-year break in service, shall furnish a benefit statement to a participant who incurs a "one-year break in service", as defined in paragraph (b)(2)(v) of this section.

(ii) *Non-vested participants.* In the case of a participant who has no nonforfeitable benefits under the plan and who incurs a one-year break in service, the plan administrator will comply with the requirements of section 209(a)(1)(B) of the Act and this section if the plan furnishes such participant a "statement of non-vested status" as described in § 2520.105-2(f).

If a participant who incurs a one-year break in service is furnished a statement of non-vested status under this paragraph, and requests information concerning his accrued benefits under the plan, the plan administrator shall furnish a benefit statement meeting the requirements of § 2520.105-2(d) and (e) to the participant no later than the later of 60 days after such request or 180 days after the end of the plan in which he incurs a one-year break in service.

(iii) *Date of furnishing.* A benefit statement or statement of non-vested status shall be furnished within 18O days after the end of the plan year in which a participant incurs a one-year break in service. This requirement may be satisfied by furnishing to the participant an annual benefit statement described in § 2520.105-2(a)(6), which reports the participant's benefits as of the end of the plan year in which the one-year break in service occurred.

(iv) *Date as of which information is provided.* A benefit statement furnished after a one-year break in service shall report benefits as of the end of the plan year in which the one-year break in service occurs.

(v) *Definition of "one-year break in service".* For purposes of this section, the term "one-year break in service" shall mean a one-year break in service or vesting purposes as defined in the plan documents, or in the case of a plan under which service is credited for purposes of vesting according to the elapsed time method permitted under 26 CFR 1.410(a)-7, a one-year period of severance for vesting purposes, as defined in 26 CFR 1.410(a)-7(c)(4).

(c) *Frequency of benefit statements.*—(1) A plan administrator is not required to furnish a participant or beneficiary more than one benefit statement upon request under § 2520.105-2(a) in any 12-month period.

(2) Where a participant receives a benefit statement upon termination or upon incurring a one-year break in service, a plan administrator is not required to furnish a second benefit statement upon a subsequent one-year break in service or termination, respectively, or upon a request by the participant, if the information that would be contained in a second benefit statement would be the same as that contained in the earlier benefit statement.

(d) *Style and format of benefit statements.*—(1) *General.* Individual benefit reporting documents shall be written in a manner calculated to be understood by the average plan participant or beneficiary. The format of these documents must not have the effect of misleading or misinforming the participant or beneficiary.

(2) *Foreign language assistance*—(i) The plan administrator of a plan described in paragraph (d)(2)(ii) of this section shall communicate to plan participants, in the non-English language common to such participants, information relating to any procedure for requesting benefit statements that may have been established by the plan administrator in accordance with § 2520.105-2(a)(2). In addition, the plan administrator shall provide these participants with either a benefit statement in such non-English language, or an English language benefit statement or statement of non-vested status which prominently displays a notice, in the non-English language common to these participants, explaining how they may obtain assistance. The assistance provided need not involve written materials, but shall be given in the non-English language common to these participants.

(ii) The plan administrators of the following plans are subject to the foreign language requirement of paragraph (d)(2)(i) above:

(A) A plan that covers fewer than 100 participants at the beginning of the plan year, and in which 25 percent or more of plan participants are not literate in English and are all literate in the same non-English language, or

(B) A plan which covers 100 or more participants at the beginning of the plan year, and in which the lesser of 500 or more participants, or 10% or more of all plan participants, are not literate in English and are all literate in the same non-English language.

(e) *Contents of the benefit statement.*—(1) *General.* In accordance with paragraphs (e)(2), (e)(3), (e)(4) and (e)(5) of this section, each benefit statement shall contain the following information:

(i) The participant's total accrued benefits;

(ii) The nonforfeitable percentage of the participant's accrued benefits;

(iii) The amount of the participant's nonforfeitable accrued benefits; and

(iv) Additional information specified in § 2520.105-2(e)(5) below.

(2) *Total accrued benefits*—(i) *Defined benefit plans.*—(A) *General.* In the case of a defined benefit plan, the accrued benefit shall be stated in the form of a straight life annuity payable at normal retirement age or in the normal form of benefit provided by the plan.

(B) *Contributory plans.* If a defined benefit plan requires contributions to be made by employees, the benefit statement shall separately indicate, in addition to the participant's total accrued benefit, either the amount of the participant's accrued benefit derived from employee contributions and the amount of the accrued benefit derived from employer contributions, or the percentages of the participant's total accrued benefit derived from employee contributions and from employer contributions. The portion of the accrual benefit derived from employer contributions and the portion derived from employee contributions shall be determined in accordance with section 204(c) of the Act (section 411(c) of the Internal Revenue Code of 1954 and Treasury Regulations thereunder).

(C) *Social Security offset plans.* If a participant's benefits under the plan are offset by a percentage of the participant's benefits under the Social Security Act, the benefit statement shall state the participant's accrued benefit after reduction by the applicable amount. In the case of a benefit statement furnished upon request or under the annual benefit statement alternative permitted under paragraph (a)(6) of this section, the amount of the offset may be determined on the basis of assumptions about the participant's earnings from service not covered under the plan, provided that the statement indicates that the stated amounts of the accrued and nonforfeitable accrued benefit are approximate. A benefit statement furnished when an employee terminates employment or incurs a break in service must indicate the actual amounts of the accrued benefit and nonforfeitable accrued benefit to which the participant is entitled.

(ii) *Individual account plans.* In the case of an individual account plan, the participant's accrued benefit shall be the fair market value of

the participant's account balance on the date as of which benefits are reported.

(3) *Nonforfeitable percentage.*—(i) *General.* The benefit statement shall indicate the percentage of a participant's accrued benefit which is nonforfeitable within the meaning of section 203 of the Act (and section 411(a) of the Internal Revenue Code of 1954 and Treasury Regulations thereunder). Except in the case of a plan described in paragraph (e)(3)(ii) of this section, if a participant has no nonforfeitable benefits, the benefit statement shall indicate the earliest date on which any benefits may become nonforfeitable; and if less than 100 percent of the participant's benefits are nonforfeitable, the benefit statement shall indicate the earliest date on which 100 percent of the participant's benefits may be nonforfeitable.

(ii) *Class year plans.* In the case of an individual account plan which provides for the separate nonforfeitability of benefits derived from contributions for each plan year, the benefit statement shall state each nonforfeitable percentage applicable to a portion of the participant's account balance and the value of that portion of the account balance.

(iii) *Contributory plans.* In the case of a plan which provides for employee contributions, the benefit statement shall indicate that the portion of the accrued benefits derived from the participant's contribution to the plan is nonforfeitable.

(4) *Nonforfeitable benefits.*—(i) *Defined benefit plans.* The benefit statement shall indicate the amount of the participant's nonforfeitable benefit in the same form as the participant's total accrued benefit is reported under paragraph (b) of this section.

(ii) *Individual account plans.* In the case of an individual account plan, the benefit statement shall indicate the fair market value of the nonforfeitable portion of the participant's account balance on the date as of which benefits are reported.

(5) *Other information.* A benefit statement shall include the following information:

(i) In the case of a defined benefit plan, a statement to the effect that the amount of benefits which may be received under the plan may be affected as a result of electing any option under the plan, and that further information on such options is contained in the Summary Plan Description.

(ii) In the case of a defined benefit plan, if the accrued benefit and nonforfeitable benefit are not stated in the form of an annuity for the joint lives of the participant and his spouse, an explanation to the effect that unless a married participant elects not to receive benefits in that form, the participant's nonforfeitable benefit may be reduced;

(iii) A statement to the effect that further information on the circumstances, if any, which may result in a reduction or elimination of accrued benefits or of nonforfeitable benefits is contained in the Summary Plan Description;

(iv) A statement urging the participant or beneficiary to bring promptly to the attention of the plan administrator anything in the statement that does not appear correct;

(v) A statement informing the participant or beneficiary that plan records upon which information in the benefit statement is based are available for inspection upon request, and the name, address and telephone number of the person or office to whom requests should be directed;

(vi) The date as of which benefit entitlements are reported; and

(vii) The participant's Social Security Account Number.

(f) *Statement of non-vested status.*—A statement of non-vested status shall inform the participant that he does not have any nonforfeitable benefits under the plan, and that he may obtain upon request a benefit statement indicating his accrued benefits, if any, and the earliest date on which any benefits may become nonforfeitable.

(g) *Basis of benefit statement.*—(1) *General.* A benefit statement shall be based on the latest available information. A benefit statement will be deemed to be based on the latest available information if it reports benefit entitlements as of the date benefits must be reported under paragraphs (a) or (b) of § 2520.105-2, as appropriate, or any subsequent date, and if it is based on plan records which comply with the requirements of paragraphs (b) and (c) of § 2530.209-2.

(2) *Benefit statement based on incomplete plan records.* A benefit statement based on incomplete plan records (i.e. records that do not contain all information necessary to determine the participant's benefit entitlements) shall so indicate. To the extent that the records of a plan are incomplete, an opportunity to provide information relating to benefit entitlements shall be offered to a participant or beneficiary entitled to a benefit statement, and the benefit statement shall be based on such

¶ 20,519L

information. A benefit statement based in whole or in part on information supplied by a participating [sic] may state that it is conditioned upon the accuracy of such information.

(h) *Manner of furnishing individual benefit reporting documents.*— Individual benefit reporting documents shall be furnished either by first class mail to the participant or beneficiary at his last known address, or by personal delivery to the participant or beneficiary by the plan administrator or an individual under the plan administrator's supervision. In the event that the plan administrator learns that the participant or beneficiary has failed to receive a document by mail or personal delivery, the plan administrator shall employ any means of delivery reasonably likely to ensure the receipt by such participant or beneficiary of the document.

(i) *Corrections to the Benefit Statement.*—A participant or beneficiary who raises questions regarding the accuracy of the benefit statement shall be given a reasonable opportunity to point out information in the benefit statement that he believes inaccurate, and to furnish to the plan administrator information which such participant or beneficiary believes relevant in determining his benefit entitlements. The plan administrator shall make reasonable attempts to determine whether the plan's records or the benefit statement are inaccurate and to verify the information furnished by the participant or beneficiary. Within a reasonable time after the plan administrator receives such a communication from a participant or beneficiary, the plan administrator shall notify him in writing of the plan's decision with respect to such matter, the basis for such decision, and any change in benefit entitlements as a result of the decision.

(j) *Statement of Deferred Vested Benefits.*—Section 105(c) of the Act provides that each administrator required to file a registration statement under section 6057 of the Internal Revenue Code of 1954 (the Code) shall furnish to each participant described in section 6057(a)(2)(C) of the Code an individual statement setting forth the information with respect to such participant which is required to be contained in the registration statement. The requirements of section 105(c) of the Act will be satisfied if an individual statement is furnished to a participant in accordance with section 6057(e) of the Code and the regulations thereunder.

(k) *Definition of "single employer plan."*—For purposes of §§ 2520.105-1 and 2510.105-2, the term "single employer plan" shall mean a plan adopted by a single employer or by a group of employers which are under common control.

§ 2520.105-3 [Reserved]

2. By adding to part 2530 new §§ 2530.209-1, 2530.209-2, and 2530.209-3 to read as follows:

Subpart E—Individual Benefit Recordkeeping

Sec.

2530.209-1 General.

2530.200-2 Individual benefit recordkeeping for single employer plans.

2530.209-3 [Reserved].

Subpart E—Individual Benefit Recordkeeping

§ 2530.209-1 General.

Section 209 of the Employee Retirement Income Security Act of 1974 (the Act) contains certain requirements relating to the maintenance of records for determining the benefits to which individual participants in employee pension benefit plans subject to Part 2 of Title I of the Act are or may become entitled. Section 2530.209-2 contains regulations applicable to single employer plans with respect to the individual benefit recordkeeping requirements set forth in section 209 of the Act. Section 2530.209-3 contains individual benefit recordkeeping regulations under section 209 of the Act applicable to multiple employer plans. The paragraphs of §§ 2530.209-2 and 2530.209-3 are parallel. In addition to individual benefit recordkeeping requirements, section 209 also contains provisions dealing with individual benefit reporting. Regulations relating to the individual benefit reporting provisions of section 209 are set forth in §§ 2520.105-1, 2520.105-2 and 2520.105-3.

§ 2530.209-2 Individual benefit recordkeeping for single employer plans.

(a) *Recordkeeping requirement.* For every single employer/employee pension benefit plan (as defined in § 2530.209-2(h)) subject to Part 2 of Title I of the Act, records shall be maintained with respect to each employee covered under the plan. These records shall be sufficient to determine the benefits which are, or may become, due to such employee and shall include the name and address of each such employee.

(b) *Maintenance of records and furnishing of information.* The employer or employers maintaining the plan shall maintain the records

required to be maintained by a single employer plan under § 2530.209-2(a). The employer shall furnish to the plan administrator information necessary to enable the plan administrator to comply with the individual benefit reporting requirements set forth in § 2520.105-2. If the plan is maintained by more than one employer, the employers may enter into arrangements under which the necessary records are furnished by the employers to the plan administrator and maintained by the plan administrator. Each employer, however, shall remain responsible for ensuring that the records are properly maintained.

(c) *Sufficiency of records.* Records required to be maintained by a single employer plan under § 2530.209-2(a) will be deemed to be sufficient if:

(1) With respect to service from the later of the date the employer adopts the plan or [effective date of regulation], they contain all information with respect to service with that employer that is relevant to a determination of each employee's benefit entitlements under the plan, and

(2) With respect to service before [effective date of regulation], if any, they include all records maintained by the employer on and after February 9, 1979, for the purpose of determining employee's benefit entitlements under the provisions of the plan.

(3) *Loss or destruction of records.* Notwithstanding the preceding paragraphs, records shall not be deemed to be insufficient solely because they have been lost or destroyed due to circumstances beyond the control of the person responsible for their maintenance under § 2530.209-2(b).

(d) *Period for which records must be retained.* The records which are required to be maintained under § 2530.209-2(a) shall be retained in a manner described in § 2530.209-2(e) as long as any possibility exists that they might be relevant to a determination of benefit entitlements. When it is no longer possible that records might be relevant to a determination of benefit entitlements, the records may be disposed of, unless they are required to be maintained for a longer period under any other law.

(e) *Preservation of records by employer and plan administrator.*—(1) *General.* The records which are required to be maintained under § 2530.209-2(a) shall be maintained in reasonable order in a safe and accessible place at the main offices of the plan administrator or the employer, or at recordkeeping offices established by the employer or the plan and customarily used for the maintenance of records.

(2) *Reproduction of records; disposal of original documents.* Original documents may be disposed of at any time if microfilm, microfiche, or similarly reproduced records which are clear reproductions of the original documents are retained, and adequate projection or other viewing equipment is available for inspecting such reproductions.

(3) *Electronic data processing.* Nothing in this section precludes the use of punch cards, magnetic tape or other electronic information storage material for processing information.

(f) *Inspection and copying.* The records required to be maintained under § 2530.209-2(a) with respect to any participant or beneficiary, including any original documents or reproductions thereof maintained under § 2530.209-2(e), shall be made available free of charge to such participant or beneficiary, or his representative, in a reasonably accessible form for inspection and copying. The records shall be made available during normal business hours within 10 working days after receipt of a request. A reasonable charge may be imposed for copying records, not exceeding the actual cost of copying them.

(g) *Transfer of records.* In the event that an employer ceases to be responsible under § 2530.209-2(b) for maintaining records, such employer shall transfer any records which continue to be potentially relevant to the determination of benefit entitlements to the appropriate successor employer or plan administrator responsible for their maintenance. The employer transferring such records is not required to retain copies of the records transferred. Nothing in this section, however, shall relieve an employer from any responsibility or liability for violations of the requirements of § 2520.209-1 through § 2530.209-2 which occur during the time such employer has control of and is responsible for maintaining, retaining or transferring the records as required by those sections.

(h) *Definition of "Single Employer Plan".* For purposes of this section, the term "single employer plan" shall mean a plan adopted by a single employer or by a group of employers which are under common control.

§ 2530.209-3 [Reserved]

Signed at Washington, D. C., this 25th day of July, 1980.

Ian D. Lanoff,

Administrator, Pension and Welfare Benefit Programs, Labor-Management Services Administration, Department of Labor.

[FR Doc. 80-22911 Filed 7-29-80; 8:45 am]

¶ 20,519M Reserved.

[Proposed regulation under 29 CFR Part 2520 prescribing an alternative method of compliance with the reporting and disclosure requirements for simplified employee pension plans using the model IRS Form 5305-SEP was formerly reproduced at this point. The final regulation appears at ¶ 14,247ZB.]

¶ 20,519N Reserved.

Formerly reproduced at this point were proposed regulations issued by the Equal Employment Opportunity Commission under the Age Discrimination in Employment Act of 1967. The final regulations are at ¶ 15,750A—15,750F and 15,750I.]

¶ 20,519O Reserved.

Formerly produced at this point were proposed regulations issued by the Equal Employment Opportunity Commission relating to the interpretation of the Equal Pay Act of 1963. The final regulations appear at ¶ 15,767-15,769B.]

¶ 20,519P Reserved.

Proposed regulations relating to the reduction of benefit payments after plan termination and the recoupment of benefit overpayments were formerly reproduced at this point. The final regulations appear at ¶ 15,429G—15,429G-27.]

¶ 20,519Q Reserved.

Formerly reproduced at this paragraph were proposed DOL regulations relating to the definition of plan assets. The final regulations appear at ¶ 14,139M and 14,876.]

¶ 20,519R

Proposed regulations on 29 CFR Part 2620: Valuation of plan assets: Termination of non-multiemployer plans.—Following below are proposed regulations setting forth rules for valuing the assets of terminating non-multiemployer pension plans. The proposed regulations were published in the *Federal Register* on May 8, 1985 (50 FR 19386).

ERISA Sec. 4044.

PENSION BENEFIT GUARANTY CORPORATION

29 CFR Part 2620

Valuation of Plan Assets

AGENCY: Pension Benefit Guaranty Corporation.

ACTION: Proposed rule.

SUMMARY: This proposed regulation sets forth rules for valuing the assets of terminating non-multiemployer pension plans that are covered by Title IV of the Employee Retirement Income Security Act of 1974, *as amended,* (the "Act"). Under Title IV of the Act, the assets of a terminating plan must be valued and allocated to the plan's benefits. Because plan assets are often held in forms that are subject to different valuation methods, this regulation is necessary to provide uniform standards for plan administrators and employers to use in determining the value of plan assets. The effect of this regulation would be to ensure that the parties involved in plan terminations are provided with the guidance necessary to comply with the provisions of Title IV of the Act.

DATES: Comments must be received on or before July 8, 1985.

ADDRESSES: Comments should be addressed to the Director, Corporate Policy and Regulations Department, Code 611, Pension Benefit Guaranty Corporation, Suite 7300, 2020 K Street, NW., Washington, D.C. 20006. Written comments will be available for public inspection in Suite 7100, at the above address, between the hours of 9:00 a.m. and 4:00 p.m.

FOR FURTHER INFORMATION CONTACT: Renae R. Hubbard, Special Counsel, Corporate Policy and Regulations Department, Code 611, Pension Benefit Guaranty Corporation, 2020 K Street, NW., Washington, D.C. 20006, 202-254-6476 (202-254-8010 for TTY and TDD). These are not toll-free numbers.

SUPPLEMENTARY INFORMATION:

Background

On May 7, 1976, the Pension Benefit Guaranty Corporation (the "PBGC") published in the Federal Register a final regulation on Valuation of Plan Assets, 41 FR 18992 (codified at 29 CFR Part 2611, recodified as Part 2620). The regulation sets forth standards for valuing the assets of a terminating pension plan. In the preamble to the regulation, the PBGC noted that specific rules for the valuation of insurance contracts when they are held as plan assets were not included and that it would provide guidance on that issue in the future. Accordingly, on April 18, 1977, the PBGC published proposed amendments to the Valuation of Plan Assets regulation, setting forth rules for determining the value of insurance contracts and insurance contract rights that are held as plan assets (42 FR 20158).

Because of the passage of time, the PBGC is publishing new proposed rules for valuing insurance contracts and insurance contract rights, in order to receive current public comment on the issues presented. The rules proposed in this document differ substantively from the 1977 proposal in several respects. Additionally, non-substantive changes have been made to simplify the regulation.

In the discussion that follows, unless otherwise stated, references are to sections of the proposed regulation set forth in this document.

Overview of the Regulation

As in the 1977 proposal, this proposed rule would restructure the regulation. For the sake of clarity, the regulation has been divided into three subparts. Subpart A contains the general provisions of the regulation. Subpart B contains the rules for valuing plan assets other than insurance contracts and insurance contract rights. Subpart C sets forth

¶ 20,519M

rules for identifying insurance contracts and insurance contract rights that are plan assets and for determining their value.

It should be noted that the scope of this regulation also would be changed by this amendment. Unlike the original rules, this proposal does not apply to multiemployer pension plans (§ 2620.1(b)). The Multiemployer Pension Plan Amendments Act of 1980, Pub. L. 96-364 (Sept. 26, 1980), 94 Stat. 1208, established a new insurance program for multiemployer plans, and regulations dealing with valuation of assets by such plans will be issued in the future.

In addition, this regulation has been coordinated with the PBGC's regulation on Determination of Plan Sufficiency and Termination of Sufficient Plans, which was published on January 28, 1981, 46 FR 9532 (codified at 29 CFR Part 2615, recodified as Part 2617). The "Sufficiency" regulation sets forth a procedure for plan administrators to follow in order to demonstrate whether the value of the plan's assets will be sufficient to provide plan benefits on the date the plan's assets are distributed, rather than the date of plan termination which is the valuation date for insufficient plans. Proposed § 2620.3 recognizes that alternate valuation date for sufficient plans.

With those exceptions, the provisions of Subparts A and B of this proposal do not differ substantively from the provisions of the final regulation published on May 7, 1976. Accordingly, the remainder of this preamble addresses Subpart C exclusively.

Valuation and Plan Sufficiency

Because the Sufficiency regulation provides that a plan administrator who demonstrates sufficiency may distribute plan assets to participants in the form elected by the participants, certain of the valuation rules proposed in 1977 are inapposite to a plan that is closing out pursuant to the Sufficiency regulation. For example, in the 1977 proposal, § 2611.12(a) provided that, in order to determine the value of an insurance contract, the contract's greatest cash settlement value had to be determined. Under § 2611.12(c) of that proposal, the greatest cash settlement value was to be either (1) the amount of a lump sum payment or (2) the fair market value of a series of installment payments. It is not productive, however, to require a plan administrator to determine the fair market value of a series of installment payments if the participants have elected to receive immediate lump sum distributions.

Accordingly, this proposal includes a rule to ensure that plan administrators who are demonstrating sufficiency or closing out a plan under the Sufficiency regulation are not forced to follow unnecessary valuation procedures. Under § 2620.13 of this proposal, for purposes of demonstrating sufficiency under Subpart B of the Sufficiency regulation and closing out a plan under Subpart C of that regulation, the plan administrator shall value insurance contracts and participation rights in the manner that reflects the highest value that can be realized in a form that will enable the plan administrator to close out the plan as required by the Sufficiency regulation.

Contract Provisions

Under the 1977 proposed amendments, the value of an insurance contract would have depended upon the alternatives expressly available under the contract as of the valuation date (1977 proposal § 2611.10—definition of "settlement options"). The PBGC reviewed this rule and determined that it was unnecessarily restrictive because the contractholder may be able to negotiate with the insurer for a higher value than the contract provides. Accordingly, a new § 2620.14 provides that the valuation of plan assets shall be based upon the provisions of the insurance contract as of the valuation date or upon other options available from the insurer as of the valuation date.

The existence of options other than those expressly contained in the insurance contract must be demonstrated by means of a written statement by the insurer. That section also makes clear that the plan administrator has the responsibility for obtaining the factual basis for the insurer's computations underlying its determination of value. Where the factual basis used by the insurer would lead to an unreasonable determination of value, the plan administrator is responsible for taking whatever action is necessary to arrive at a fair and reasonable determination of value.

Cash Settlement Value

Under the 1977 proposal, as well as this proposed rule, the basic method for determining the value of an insurance contract is to compare the contract's greatest cash settlement value with the present value of the benefits that can be purchased with the contract funds (1977 proposal § 2611.12(a); this proposal § 2620.15(a)). In the preamble to the proposed 1977 amendments, the PBGC noted that many insurance contacts give the insurer some discretion in calculating the amount of a cash settlement. It was and is the PBGC's expectation that

insurers will be fair and reasonable in interpreting and implementing their contracts. This expectation does not in any way, however, affect the plan administrator's responsibility to scrutinize the basis upon which the insurer has made its determination and to negotiate a settlement that is both fair and reasonable in light of the factors relevant to a determination of value, *e.g.*, mortality rates, interest rates, the value of future dividend streams and comparable contract prices.

The PBGC did, however, invite suggestions from the public on the need for special safeguards and the type of safeguards that might be adopted. In response to this invitation, one comment stated that many insurance contracts provide that the cash amount available upon liquidation of the contract is determined by means of a formula that is subject to periodic modification called, in insurance parlance, a "secretary formula." The comment suggested that the regulation require the insurer to use the formula in effect during the five-year period preceding plan termination that would produce the highest cash settlement. The PBGC has considered this suggestion but has not adopted it in this new proposal because that formula may no longer be available and, thus, would be irrelevant to an accurate determination of the fair value of the asset.

In the 1977 proposal, § 2611.12(c)(2) provided that "[t]he value of a settlement option requiring cash payments by the insurer in installments is the fair market value, determined in accordance with Subpart B of this part, of the right to receive that stream of future payments." The PBGC has made three changes in this provision. First, one public comment on the 1977 proposal objected to the use of the term "settlement option" on the ground that its use might cause confusion since it is a term of art referring to the various ways in which the proceeds of life insurance policies can be paid other than in a lump sum. In light of the comment, the PBGC has eliminated from this proposed rule the term "settlement option" and, in its place, uses the term "cash settlement" (§ 2620.15(b)).

Second, in reviewing § 2611.12(c)(2) of the 1977 proposal, the PBGC decided that the fair market value concept set forth in Subpart B of the regulation might not be particularly helpful in valuing the right to receive the stream of future payments from the insurer. Subpart B's fair market value concept depends upon the existence of a market for the asset to be valued. The PBGC is not aware of a market for the right to receive the stream of future payments from the insurer. Accordingly, this proposal sets forth a new method for determining the value of a cash settlement that provides cash installment payments by the insurer. Proposed § 2620.15(b)(2) provides that the value of these installment payments is the present value of the payments calculated as of the valuation date, determined by applying an interest rate that is the sum of the PBGC's interest rate for valuing immediate annuities in effect on the valuation date plus one-half of one percent. The resulting interest rate is the rate the PBGC uses to value immediate annuities before adjusting for benefit administration costs.

Finally, the PBGC has clarified § 2620.15(b)(2) of the proposal to make explicit the fact that it applies to a deferred lump sum cash payment as well as to a series of installment payments.

Value of Participation Rights

The 1977 proposal provided in § 2611.14 that the value of participation rights was to be determined solely by reference to the cancellation of such rights. The PBGC received a number of public comments that were critical of this provision. As suggested by some of the comments, this proposal now provides a method for valuing participant rights that cannot be cancelled.

Section 2620.16(b) provides that if a participation right cannot be cancelled, the value of the right is the present value of the future stream of payments determined by reference to all relevant factors, such as interest rates, mortality rates, the past practice of the insurer regarding participation rights and comparable contract prices. The contractholder is responsible for negotiating with the insurer to make clear, in the contract, that the rights must either be cancellable or, if not, that the insurer must provide information with respect to the future stream of payments based on past dividend practice that is adequate for the plan administrator to determine the fair value of such rights.

Additionally, the rules dealing with the valuation of participation rights that can be cancelled has been slightly modified. Proposed § 2611.14 provided that the value of a participation right was the greater of the cash amount payable by the insurer upon cancellation of the right or the value of the benefits provided by the insurer upon cancellation of the right. Section 2620.16(a) of this proposed rule provides that the value of a participation right is the greater of the cash amount or the value of the additional benefits negotiated by the parties upon cancellation of the right.

In the preamble to the 1977 proposed amendments, the PBGC invited public suggestions on appropriate measures that the PBGC might take to assure that an insurer attributes a reasonable value to a plan's participation rights. In response, one comment suggested that "if abuse really occurs, PBGC might move to requiring prior disclosure of an insurer's practices upon contract termination in . . . greater detail that is now usually provided." The PBGC would be interested in public reaction to that suggestion.

Two comments suggested that, if a participation right cannot be cancelled, the PBGC should become the holder of the right, even in the sufficient plan context. While the PBGC might become the holder of participation rights when it becomes trustee of a plan, a possibility contemplated by this regulation, the situation is different in the case of plans that are not trusteed by the PBGC. Generally, it is the PBGC's view that its involvement with plans that can be closed out in the private sector should be kept to a minimum. It would be inconsistent with this view of the PBGC's responsibilities under Title IV of the Act for the PBGC to become the holder of a plan's participation rights when the plan is sufficient.

Comments Invited

Interested persons are invited to submit written comments on this proposed regulation. Comments should be addressed to: Director, Corporate Policy and Regulations Department, Code 611, Pension Benefit Guaranty Corporation, 2020 K Street, NW., Washington, D.C. 20006. Written comments will be available for public inspection at the above address, Suite 7100, between the hours of 9:00 a.m. and 4:00 p.m. Each comment should identify this regulation and should include the name and address of the person submitting it and the reasons for any recommendation. This proposal may be changed in light of the comments received.

Classification: E.O. 12291 and Regulatory Flexibility Act

The PBGC has determined that this rule is not a "major rule" within the meaning of Executive Order 12291 because it will not have an annual effect on the economy of $100 million or more; nor will it create a major increase in costs or prices for consumers, individual industries, or geographic regions; nor will it have significant adverse effects on competition, employment, investment, innovation or on the ability of United States-based enterprises to compete with foreign-based enterprises in domestic or export markets.

Under section 605(b) of the Regulatory Flexibility Act, the PBGC certifies that this regulation will not have a significant economic effect on a substantial number of small entities. All pension plans that terminate under Title IV of the Employee Retirement Income Security Act of 1974 must value their assets. By setting forth valuation methods, this regulation will make it easier for administrators of such plans to comply with the law. Compliance with sections 603 and 604 of the Regulatory Flexibility Act is accordingly waived.

List of Subjects in 29 CFR Part 2620

Employee benefit plans, Pension insurance, and Pensions.

In consideration of the foregoing, it is proposed to revise Part 2620 of Chapter XXVI of Title 29, Code of Federal Regulations, to read as follows:

PART 2620—VALUATION OF PLANS ASSETS IN NON-MULTIEMPLOYER PENSION PLANS

Subpart A—General

Sec.

2620.1 Purpose and scope.

2620.2 Definitions.

2620.3 Valuation date.

Subpart B—Assets Other Than Insurance Contracts

2620.5 Purpose and scope.

2620.6 Definitions.

2620.7 General rule.

2620.8 Fair market value presumptions.

Subpart C—Insurance Contracts

2620.10 Purpose and scope.

2620.11 Definitions.

2620.12 Plan assets.

2620.13 Special rule applicable to demonstrating sufficiency and closing out a plan under Subpart C of Part 2617.

2620.14 Contract provisions.

2620.15 Value of insurance contracts.

2620.16 Value of participation rights.

Authority: Secs. 4002(b)(3), 4141, 4044 and 4062, Pub. L. 93—406, 88 Stat. 1004, 1020, 1025 and 1029 (1974), as amended by secs. 403(1), 403(d), 402(a)(7) and 403(g), Pub. L. 96-364, 94 Stat. 1302, 1301, 1299 and 1301 (1980) (29 U.S.C. 1302(b)(3), 1341, 1344 and 1362).

Subpart A—General

§ 2620.1 Purpose and scope.

(a) *Purpose.* This part sets forth rules governing the valuation of the assets of a terminating pension plan for purposes of Title IV of the Act.

(b) *Scope.* This part applies to non-multiemployer pension plans for which a Notice of Intent to Terminate is filed on or after the effective date of this part, or for which the PBGC commences a termination action on or after the effective date of this part.

§ 2620.2 Definitions.

For purposes of this part:

"Act" means the Employee Retirement Income Security Act of 1974 (29 U.S.C. § 1001 *et seq.*), *as amended.*

"Date of plan termination" means the date of plan termination established under section 4048 of the Act.

"Notice of Intent to Terminate" means a notice filed with the PBGC pursuant to section 4041(a) of the Act and Part 2616 of this chapter.

"PBGC" means the Pension Benefit Guaranty Corporation.

"Non-multiemployer plan" means a pension plan described in section 4021(a) of the Act that is maintained by one trade or business (whether or not incorporated), or by more than one trade or business (whether or not incorporated) all of which are under control within the meaning of Part 2612 of this chapter, or a plan maintained by more than one trade or business not under common control that is not a multiemployer plan as defined in section 4001(a)(3) of the Act.

§ 2620.3 Valuation date.

Except as otherwise provided, the assets of a plan that has been placed into trusteeship by the PBGC shall be valued as of the date of plan termination and the assets of a plan that closes out in accordance with Part 2617 of this chapter shall be valued as of the date plan assets are to be distributed.

Subpart B—Assets Other Than Insurance Contracts

§ 2620.5 Purpose and Scope.

This subpart sets forth rules for valuing plan assets other than plan assets described in § 2620.12.

§ 2620.6 Definitions.

For purposes of this subpart:

"Exchange" means a national securities exchange registered with the Securities and Exchange Commission under section 6 of the Securities Exchange Act of 1934.

"Fair market value" means the price at which property would change hands between a willing buyer and a willing seller, neither being under any compulsion to buy or to sell and both having reasonable knowledge of relevant facts.

"National Association of Securities Dealers Automated Quotations Systems" means the automated quotations system sponsored by the National Association of Securities Dealers, Inc., a national securities association registered with the Securities and Exchange Commission under section 15A of the Securities Exchange Act of 1934.

"Principally traded" means the market place at which the greatest volume of trades normally occurs.

§ 2620.7 General rule.

Plan assets to which this subpart applies shall be valued at their fair market value on the plan's valuation date, using the method of valuation that most accurately reflects fair market value.

§ 2620.8 Fair market value presumptions.

(a) *Treasury bills.* The fair market value of Treasury bills is presumed to be the value computed from the average of the bid and asked discount for the bill on the valuation date, as nationally published in a general circulation daily newspaper.

(b) *Treasury notes, bonds and Federal agency securities.* The fair market value of Treasury notes, bonds and Federal agency securities is presumed to be the value computed from the average of bid and asked prices for the security on the valuation date, as nationally published in a general circulation daily newspaper.

(c) *Shares in open-end mutual funds.* The fair market value of shares in open-end mutual funds is presumed to be the net asset value (the redemption value) per share of the mutual fund on the valuation date, as nationally published in a general circulation daily newspaper.

(d) *Units of participation in a common trust fund or collective investment fund.* The fair market value of units of participation in a common trust fund or collective investment fund is presumed to be the value per unit of the fund as reflected on a statement of account prepared by the manager of the fund. The value per unit of the fund is to be determined in accordance with the procedures normally employed by the manager of the fund purusant to the terms of the fund, and federal and state law and regulations, as applicable, and as of the normal date on which the fund is valued if that date is on or within 31 days after the valuation date. This presumption will apply only if there were no distributions from the fund in relation to units of the fund in the interval between the plan's valuation date and the normal valuation date of the fund.

(e) *Common and preferred stocks, warrants and closed-end mutual funds.* The fair market value of common and preferred stocks, warrants, and closed-end mutual funds is presumed to be the value determined in accordance with the rules set forth in Paragraphs (e)(1) through (e)(4) of this section, as follows:

(1) If the security is traded on the New York Stock Exchange and the plan's valuation date is on or before January 26, 1976, or traded on the American Stock Exchange and the valuation date is on or after March 1, 1976, the fair market value is presumed to be the closing sale price on the valuation date as reported by the consolidated last sale reporting system established pursuant to Rule 11Aa3-1, promulgated by the Securities and Exchange Commission under the Securities Exchange Act of 1934, as nationally published in a general circulation daily newspaper.

(2) If the security is principally traded on an exchange, other than as set forth in Paragraph (e)(1), the fair market value is presumed to be the closing sale price on the valuation date on the exchange where the security is principally traded, as nationally published in a general circulation daily newspaper.

(3) If the security is principally traded otherwise than on an exchange, and is quoted on the National Association of Securities Dealers Automated Quotations System, the fair market value is presumed to be the average of the end-of-day bid and asked prices for the security on the valuation date, as made available for publication by such system and nationally published in a general circulation daily newspaper.

(4) If there is no nationally published closing sale price or end-of-day bid and asked prices on the valuation date, the fair market value of the security is presumed to be—

(i) For securities traded principally on an exchange, the average of the nationally published closing sale price on the date nearest the valuation date and within five trading days before the valuation date and the nationally published closing sale price on the date nearest the valuation date and within five trading days after the valuation date; and

(ii) For securities principally traded otherwise than on an exchange, the average of (1) the average of the nationally published end-of-day bid and asked prices on the date nearest the valuation date and within five trading days before the valuation date and (2) the average of the nationally published end-of-day bid and asked prices on the date nearest the valuation date and within five trading days after the valuation date.

(f) *State and municipal obligations.* The fair market value of state and municipal obligations is presumed to be the average of bid and asked prices for the security on the valuation date, as nationally published in a general circulation daily newspaper. If there are no such nationally published bid and asked prices on the valuation date, the fair market value of the security is presumed to be the average of (1) the average of the nationally published bid and asked prices on the date nearest the valuation date and within five trading days before the valuation date and (2) the average of the nationally published bid and asked prices on the date nearest the valuation date and within five trading days after the valuation date.

Subpart C—Insurance Contracts

§ 2620.10 Purpose and scope.

This subpart sets forth rules for identifying insurance contracts and insurance contract rights that are plan assets and for determining their value.

§ 2620.11 Definitions.

For purposes of this subpart:

"Contractholder" means the owner of an insurance contract purchased with funds contributed to or under a plan. A participant who has received an insurance contract from or under a plan is not a "contractholder" for purposes of this subpart.

"Insurance contract" or "contract" means a valid written agreement between an insurer and a contractholder pursuant to which the insurer agrees to perform services including the payment of specified benefits or their equivalent in return for the payment of premiums or similar consideration. References in this subpart to "an insurance contract" include more than one contract, unless the plural is clearly inappropriate.

"Insurer" means a company authorized to do business as an insurance carrier under the laws of a State or the District of Columbia.

"Participation right" means the right of a contractholder or plan, under an insurance contract, to receive future dividends, rate credits, interest, experience credits or other earnings or distributions from the insurer.

§ 2620.12 Plan assets.

(a) *Insurance contracts.* An insurance contract purchased with funds contributed to or under a plan is a plan asset for purposes of this part if, on the valuation date, the contract has not been distributed to a participant and the insurer's obligations under the contract have not been cancelled.

(b) *Participation rights.* A participation right under an insurance contract purchased with funds contributed to or under a plan is a plan asset for purposes of this part to the extent that the value of the participation right is not included in the value of an insurance contract that is a plan asset.

§ 2620.13 Special rule applicable to demonstrating sufficiency and closing out a plan under Subpart C of Part 2617.

Notwithstanding §§ 2620.14 through 2620.16, for purposes of demonstrating sufficiency under Subpart B of Part 2617 of this chapter and closing out a plan under Subpart C of Part 2617 of this chapter, the plan administrator shall value insurance contracts and participation rights in the manner that best reflects the highest value that can be realized in a form that will enable the plan administrator to close out the plan as required by § 2617.21 of this chapter.

§ 2620.14 Contract provisions.

(a) *General.* The valuation of plan assets under this subpart shall be based upon the provisions of the insurance contract as of the valuation date or upon other options available from the insurer as of the valuation date. The existence of such other options must be demonstrated by means of a written statement by the insurer.

(b) *Responsibilities of plan administrator.* In determining the value of an insurance contract as of the valuation date, the plan administrator is responsible for critically assessing the reasonableness of the factors underlying the insurer's determination of the contract's cash value or the value of other options provided in lieu thereof. Where the factors underlying the determination are unreasonable, the plan administrator is responsible for taking whatever action is necessary to reach a reasonable value for the asset.

§ 2620.15 Value of insurance contracts.

(a) *General.* The value of an insurance contract is the greater of—

(1) The contract's greatest cash settlement value, determined in accordance with paragraph (b) of this section, as of the valuation date; or

(2) The present value, determined in accordance with Part 2619 of this chapter, of the benefits that can be purchased under the contract as of the valuation date by application of the contract assets described in Paragraph (c) of this section to the purchase of benefits in accordance with the order of priorities prescribed by section 4044 of the Act.

(b) *Cash settlement value.* (1) The value of a cash settlement that provides and immediate lump sum cash payment by the insurer is the dollar amount of the cash payment (including the value of participation rights under § 2620.16).

(2) The value of a cash settlement that provides a deferred lump sum cash payment (including the value of participation rights, if there are any, under § 2620.16) by the insurer or cash payments by the insurer in installments is the present value of such payments calculated as of the valuation date, determined by applying an interest rate that is the sum of—

(i) The PBGC's interest rate for valuing immediate annuities in effect on the valuation date, set forth in Appendix B of Part 2619 of this chapter, and

(ii) .5 (one-half) percent.

(c) *Contract assets.* (1) Contract assets are the funds credited to an insurance contract as of the valuation date that are available to provide benefits, including funds becoming available to provide benefits upon the cancellation of any participation rights held under the insurance contract.

(2) Contract assets do not include—

(i) Funds that the insurer is entitled, under the insurance contract, to withdraw in payment for an irrevocable commitment made by the insurer prior to the date of plan termination;

(ii) Funds that the insurer is entitled, under the insurance contract, to withdraw to satisfy liabilities of the plan that became due and owing prior to the valuation date;

Funds that the insurer is entitled, under the insurance contract, to withdraw to pay for administrative or other services performed by the insurer; and

(iv) Funds that have been paid to the insurer prior to the valuation date in return for benefits or services, which are credited to an account under the contract solely for the purpose of computing amounts payable pursuant to the plan's participation rights.

(d) *Exclusive plan asset test.* Except as provided in Paragraph (e) of this section, the benefits that can be provided under the contract be determined as if each insurance contract that is a plan asset were the plan's only asset on the valuation date. If two or more insurance contracts owned by a plan expressly provide a basis for coordinated allocation of contract assets in conformance with section 4044 of the Act, the benefits that can be provided under the contracts shall be determined as prescribed by the contracts.

(e) *Optional valuation procedure.* (1) When an insurance contract is not a plan's only asset on the valuation date, the plan administrator may value the contract by applying the contract assets to purchase benefits under the insurance contract without regard to the order of priorities prescribed by section 4044 of the Act, if the plan administrator demonstrates to the PBGC that—

(i) All of the plan's assets on the valuation date, taken together, can be allocated in a manner that complies with section 4044 of the Act;

(ii) Under the combined allocation described in Paragraph (e)(1)(i) of this section, the plan's assets will provide benefits with a total

present value that equals or exceeds the total present value of the benefits that could otherwise be provided by the plan's assets; and

(iii) In the case of a plan that receives a Notice of Inability to Determine Sufficiency under Part 2617 of this chapter, arrangements for a specific combined allocation that satisfies section 4044 of the Act were made prior to the date of plan termination.

(2) A plan administrator who elects this optional valuation procedure must furnish the PBGC with evidence, including supporting computations, that the optional valuation meets all of the requirements of Paragraph (e)(1) of this section.

(3) When this optional valuation procedure is used, the total value of the plan's assets is the total present value of the benefits that can be provided through the combined allocation of the plan's assets described in Paragraph (e)(1)(i) of this section.

§ 2620.16 Value of participation rights.

(a) If a participation right can be cancelled, the value of the participation right is the greater of—

(1) The dollar amount negotiated by the parties in accordance with § 2620.14(b) of this part, as payable upon cancellation of the participation right as of the valuation date; or

(2) The present value, determined in accordance with Part 2619 of this chapter, of the additional benefits, negotiated by the parties in accordance with § 2620.14(b) of this part, to be provided upon cancellation of the participation right as of the valuation date.

(b) If a participation right cannot be cancelled, the value of the participation right is present value, determined by applying the interest rate described in § 2620.15(b)(2), of the future stream of payments, taking into account all relevant factors, including but not limited to the past practice of the insurer with respect to participation rights, mortality rates, interest rates and comparable contract prices.

Approved, pursuant to 29 U.S.C. 552, as an exercise of the duties of the Secretary of Labor and Chairman of the Board of Directors, Pension Benefit Guaranty Corporation.

Ford B. Ford,

Under Secretary of Labor.

Issued pursuant to a resolution of the Board of Directors approving this regulation and authorizing its chairman to issue same.

Edward R. Mackiewicz,

Secretary, Pension Benefit Guaranty Corporation.

[FR Doc. 85-11044 Filed 5-7-85; 8:45 am]

¶ 20,520   Reserved.

Proposed Reg. §§ 2608.1—2608.12, on the allocation of assets of terminating pension plans, were formerly reproduced at this point. The final regulations appear at ¶ 15,472—15,473F.]

¶ 20,520A   Reserved.

Proposed Reg. §§ 2520.103-1 and 2520.103-12 on an alternate method of annual reporting for plans investing in certain entities, were formerly reproduced at this point. The final regulations appear at ¶ 14,231A and 14,231L.]

¶ 20,520B   Reserved.

Proposed Reg. §§ 2676.1—2676.31, relating to valuation of plan benefits and plan assets following mass withdrawal, were formerly reproduced at this point. The final regulations appear at ¶ 15,687D—15,687V.]

¶ 20,520C   Reserved.

Proposed Regs. § 2640.8 and 2649.1—8, relating to adjusting liability for withdrawal subsequent to a partial withdrawal, were formerly reproduced at this point. The final regulations appear at ¶ 15,663H and 15,670A—I.]

¶20,520

¶ 20,521   Reserved.

Proposed Reg. §§ 2609.1—2609.8, Part 2609, on limitations on guaranteed benefits, were formerly reproduced at this point. The final regulations appear at ¶ 15,429—15,429G.]

¶ 20,521A   Reserved.

PBGC illustrative examples on the proposed regulations, relating to benefit payments under Pension Reform Act Sec. 4022(b), formerly reproduced at ¶ 20,521 were formerly reproduced at this point. The final regulations appear at ¶ 15,429—15,429G.]

¶ 20,521B   Reserved.

Proposed Reg. §§ 2550.414c-1—2550.414c-3, relating to certain loans, leases, and dispositions of property prior to June 30, 1984 where an employee benefit plan is involved in a transaction, were formerly reproduced at this point. The final regulations appear at ¶ 14,844A—14,844C.]

¶ 20,521C   Reserved.

Proposed regulations on 29 CFR 2520, which provide exemptions from the reporting and disclosure requirements of ERISA for apprenticeship and other training plans were formerly reproduced at this point. The final regulations appear at ¶ 14,221, 14,247B and 14,248A.]

¶ 20,521D   Reserved.

Proposed regulations relating to limited relief from reporting, disclosure and claims procedure requirements with respect to welfare plans offering membership in a qualified health maintenance organization were formerly reproduced at this point. The final regulations appear at ¶ 14,225, 14,247, 14,247X and 14,931.]

¶ 20,521E   Reserved.

Proposed regulations relating to certain acquisitions, sales, or leases of property by an employee benefit plan were formerly reproduced at this point. The final regulations are at ¶ 14,789.]

¶ 20,521F   Reserved.

Proposed regulations which prescribe rules for the determination and payment of employer liability under ERISA Sec. 4062 and 4067 were formerly reproduced at this point. The final regulations are at ¶ 15,623.]

¶ 20,522   Reserved.

Proposed regulations on 29 CFR Part 2520, relating to the preparation of annual return/report forms, were formerly reported at this point. Temporary and proposed regulations now appear at ¶ 14,231A.]

¶ 20,523   Reserved.

Proposed Reg. §§ 2611.1—2611.5, relating to valuation of plan assets were formerly reproduced at this point. The final regulations now appear at ¶ 15,621—15,621D.]

¶ 20,524   Reserved.

Proposed regulations on 29 CFR Part 2610 on the valuation of plan benefits for the purposes of the Pension Benefit Guaranty Corporation, were formerly reproduced at this point. The proposed regulations now appear at ¶ 15,620A—15,620L.]

¶ 20,525   Reserved.

The proposed regulations on 29 CFR Part 2602, relating to premium payment and declaration under the Pension Benefit Guaranty Corporation, were formerly reproduced at this point. The final regulations are at ¶ 15,371A, and the paragraphs following thereafter.]

¶ 20,525A   Reserved.

Proposed regulations relating to the definition of the term "pension plan" under ERISA were formerly reproduced at this paragraph. The final regulations are at ¶ 14,132.]

¶ 20,525B

Proposed regulations on 29 CFR Part 2530.—Reproduced below is the text of proposed regulations relating to certain circumstances in which it is permissible for a plan to suspend the payment of pension benefits to a retiree. The proposed regulations were published in the *Federal Register* on January 27, 1981 (46 FR 8906).

DEPARTMENT OF LABOR

Office of Pension and Welfare Benefit Programs

29 CFR Part 2530

Rules and Regulations for Minimum Standards for Employee Benefit Plans; Suspension of Benefit Rules

AGENCY: Department of Labor.

ACTION: Notice of proposed rulemaking.

SUMMARY: This document sets forth a proposed amendment to a rule relating to certain circumstances in which it is permissible for a plan to suspend the payment of pension benefits to a retiree. The Employee Retirement Income Security Act of 1974 (the Act) authorizes the Secretary of Labor to prescribe regulations setting forth the circumstances and conditions under which the right of a retiree to a benefit payment is not treated as forfeitable solely because the plan provides that benefit payments are suspended during certain periods of reemployment. The proposal would affect employees in maritime industries covered under employee pension benefit plans.

DATE: Written comments on proposed paragraph (c)(2)(iii)(B) must be received by the Department of Labor (the Department) on or before March 30, 1981.

ADDRESSES: Written comments (preferably at least three copies) should be submitted to the Office of Reporting and Plan Standards, Pension and Welfare Benefit Programs, Room N-4508, U.S. Department of Labor, Washington, D.C. 20216, Attention: § 2530.203-3(c)(2)(ii)(B). All written comments will be available for public inspection at the Public Documents Room, Pension and Welfare Benefit Programs, Department of Labor, Room N-4677, 200 Constitution Avenue NW., Washington, D.C.

FOR FURTHER INFORMATION CONTACT: Jay S. Neuman, Esq., Office of the Solicitor of Labor, (202) 523-8658; or Judith Bleich Kahn, Pension and Welfare Benefit Programs. (202-523-8430). These telephone numbers are not toll free.

SUPPLEMENTARY INFORMATION: On December 19, 1978, notice was published in the **Federal Register** (43 FR 59098) that the Department had under consideration a proposal to adopt a regulation. 29 CFR 2530.203-3, under section 203(a)(3)(B) of the Act, relating to suspension of pension benefit payments under certain circumstances. As part of the proposal, the Department requested specific comment regarding whether and to what extent the "geographic area covered by the plan" should be specially defined for purposes of plans covering employees in the maritime industries.[1] In response to comments which suggested the need for such a special definition, the Department is publishing for comment proposed paragraph (c)(2)(iii)(B). The proposal defines the geographic area covered by plans covering employees in the maritime industries in terms of ports of embarkation because it appears that these are the most appropriate territorial reference points for such plans. The proposal provides that the geographic area covered by a plan that covers employees in a maritime industry consists of any port of embarkation at which employers hired employees for whom contributions have been made or have been required to be made as of the time that the payment of benefits commenced or would have commenced if the employee had not returned to employment.

It should be noted that the Department has decided to adopt, with certain modifications, § 2530.203-3 as proposed. This final regulation appears elsewhere in this issue of the **Federal Register.** Persons who are interested in commenting on proposed § 2530.203-3(c)(2)(iii)(B) should refer to the adopted portions of § 2530.203-3 in order to appreciate how this proposed paragraph would operate in the context of the regulation as a whole.

Statutory Authority

Paragraph (c)(2)(iii)(B) is proposed under the authority contained in sections 203(a)(3)(B) and 505 of the Act (Pub. L. 93-406, 88 Stat. 854, 894, 29 U.S.C. 1053, 1135) and section 411(a)(3)(B) of the Internal Revenue Code of 1954.

§ 2520.203-3 Suspension of pension benefits upon reemployment of retirees.

* * * * *

(c) *Section 203(a)(3)(B) Service.* * * *

(2) *Multiemployer plans.* * * *

(iii) *Geographic area covered by the plan.* * * *

(B) The geographic area covered by a plan that covers employees in a maritime industry consists of any port of embarkation at which employers hired employees for whom contributions were made or were required to be made as of the time the payment of benefits commenced or would have commenced if the employee had not returned to employment.

* * * * *

Signed at Washington, D.C. this 19th day of January 1981.

Ian D. Lanoff,

Administrator, Pension and Welfare Benefit Programs, Labor-Management Services Administration.

[FR Doc. 81-2444. Filed 1-26-81; 8:45 am]

¶ 20,525C   Reserved.

Proposed amendments relating to the suspension of pension benefit payments to reemployed retirees were formerly reproduced at this point. The amendments, as adopted, are at ¶ 14,433.]

¶ 20,525D

Proposed regulations on 29 CFR Parts 2690 through 2695.—Reproduced below are proposed regulations on 29 CFR Parts 2690 through 2695, which would establish a supplemental program to guarantee benefits under multiemployer plans that would otherwise be guaranteed but for the dollar or percentage limitations on guaranteed benefits under ERISA. Under this voluntary program, benefits under multiemployer plans could be guaranteed at the level provided for single-employer plan.

The proposed regulations were published in the *Federal Register* on February 1, 1983 (48 FR 4632).

---

[1] In relevant part, section 203(a)(3)(B) provides that—
(B) A right to an accrued benefit from employer contributions shall not be treated as forfeitable solely because the plan provides that the payment of benefits is suspended for such period as the employee is employed, subsequent to the commencement of payment of such benefits—

(ii) In the case of a multiemployer plan, in the same industry, in the same trade or craft, and the same geographic area covered by the plan, as when such benefits commenced.

PENSION BENEFIT GUARANTY CORPORATION

29 CFR Parts 2690 through 2695

Supplemental Guarantee Program

AGENCY: Pension Benefit Guaranty Corporation.

ACTION: Proposed rule.

SUMMARY: This proposed regulation if adopted would establish a supplemental program to guarantee benefits under multiemployer plans that would otherwise be guaranteed but for the dollar or percentage limitations on guaranteed benefits in the Employee Retirement Income Security Act of 1974, as amended. That law requires the Pension Benefit Guaranty Corporation to establish a supplemental guarantee program, coverage under which must be available by January 1, 1983. Participation by plans in this supplemental program is optional. The regulation is needed to establish a supplemental guarantee program, as required by law, in order to afford participants in multiemployer plans and their beneficiaries the fullest feasible benefit guarantee. The effect of this regulation would be to provide multiemployer plans with the opportunity to obtain a greater benefit guarantee for participants.

DATE: Comments must be received on or before April 4, 1983.

ADDRESSES: Comments should be addressed to the Assistant Executive Director for Policy and Planning (140), Pension Benefit Guaranty Corporation, Suite 7300, 2020 K Street, NW., Washington, D.C. 20006. Written comments will be available for public inspection at the PBGC, Suite 7100, at the above address, between the hours of 9:00 a.m. and 4:00 p.m.

FOR FURTHER INFORMATION CONTACT: J. Ronald Goldstein, Office of the Executive Director, Policy and Planning (140), 2020 K Street, NW., Washington, D.C. 20006; 202-254-4862. [This is not a toll-free number].

SUPPLEMENTARY INFORMATION:

The Statute

The Multiemployer Pension Plan Amendments Act of 1980, Pub. L. 96-364, 94 Stat. 1208 ("Multiemployer Act"), became law on September 26, 1980 and amended the Employee Retirement Income Security Act of 1974 ("ERISA"). (As used herein, "ERISA" means the Act as amended, unless the context requires otherwise.) The Multiemployer Act revised the rules under which the Pension Benefit Guaranty Corporation (the "PBGC") guarantees benefits under a multiemployer plan.

Under section 4022A(a) of ERISA, the PBGC guarantees the payment of certain nonforfeitable benefits ("basic benefits" or "guaranteed benefits") under a multiemployer plan that is insolvent. A plan is insolvent if it is unable to pay benefits when due for the plan year. A plan terminated by a mass withdrawal is not insolvent until it has first been amended to eliminate all benefits that are not eligible for the PBGC's guarantee under section 4022A(b).

Under section 4022A(b), only nonforfeitable benefits or benefit increases that have been in effect for 60 months or more are eligible for PBGC's guarantee ("guaranteeable benefits"). Section 4022A(c) limits the maximum monthly guaranteed benefit to the product of (a) 100 percent of the first $5 of a participant's benefit accrual rate and 75 percent of the next $15 of a participant's benefit accrual rate, and (b) the participant's number of years of credited service. A participant's benefit accrual rate is computed by dividing a participant's monthly guaranteeable benefit by the participant's number of years of credited service under the plan for benefit accrual purposes. In this fraction, the guaranteeable benefit may not exceed the plan benefit payable at normal retirement age as a life annuity and is determined without regard to past service benefit reductions permitted to be made on account of the cessation of contributions by the participant's employer. The 75 percent guarantee is reduced to 65 percent under plans that did not satisfy pre-ERISA funding requirements.[1]

These rules for determining guaranteed benefits are applied without regard to past service benefit reductions permitted to be made on account of the cessation of contributions by an employer (section 4022A(c)(3)). Under section 4022A(d), if a past-service benefit is reduced because of the cessation of contributions by an employer, the guaranteed benefit is the lesser of the benefit determined under section 4022A(c) or the benefit determined under the plan's past service disregard rule. Section 4022A(h) contains a special rule for participants

or beneficiaries under a multiemployer plan who, on July 29, 1980, were in pay status or were within 36 months of the plan's normal retirement age and had a nonforfeitable right to a pension. The PBGC will guarantee those individuals' nonforfeitable accrued benefits as of that date under the single-employer rules in section 4022 of the Act, except for plan years following a plan year in which substantially all employers withdrew pursuant to an agreement to withdraw or the plan terminates by mass withdrawal under section 4041A(a)(2).

Section 4022A(g)(2) requires the PBGC to establish a supplemental program to guarantee benefits that would otherwise be guaranteed but for the limitations in section 4022A(c) ("supplemental benefits"). The supplemental benefits of a participant that are guaranteed by the PBGC under section 4022A(g)(2) are nonbasic benefits under Title IV.

The PBGC is required under section 4022A(g)(2) to establish a program to guarantee supplemental benefits, coverage under which must be available by January 1, 1983. Under the Act, participation by plans in this program is voluntary. Supplemental benefits under a plan are guaranteed only if and to the extent the plan elects coverage under the supplemental program. A plan's election to participate in the program can be made only within the time specified by PBGC regulations and cannot be made unless plan assets as of the end of the plan year preceding the election are at least 15 times benefit payments made for that year. Section 4022A(g)(2) also provides that the PBGC regulations, in addition to prescribing exceptions, if any, to the latter rule, shall provide "such other reasonable terms and conditions for supplemental coverage, including funding standards and any other reasonable limitations with respect to plans or benefits covered or to means of program financing, as the corporation determines are necessary and appropriate for a feasible supplemental program consistent with the purposes of [Title IV]."

The supplemental guarantee program is a self-financing program. To this end, a separate revolving fund on the books of the United States Treasury is established by section 4005(e). This fund is one of six revolving funds established on the books of the United States Treasury to be used by PBGC in carrying out its duties under Title IV.

Monies in this fund are to be used exclusively for the purpose of making payments under the supplemental guarantee program. These monies are not available to make loans to or on behalf of any other fund. Similarly, monies in other funds are not available for the supplemental guarantee program. In addition, no money borrowed by PBGC from the United States Treasury pursuant to section 4005(c) is available for the supplemental guarantee program (section 4005(f)(2)).

Under section 4006(a)(5)(B), the PBGC is authorized to prescribe premium rates for multiemployer plans for supplemental coverage that "reflect any reasonable considerations which the corporation determines to be appropriate." No revised schedule of premiums may go into effect without Congressional approval.

Finally, section 4022A(g)(5) authorizes the PBGC regulation to include rules that supersede the requirements of section 4245 (relating to insolvent plans), section 4261 (relating to financial assistance) and section 4281 (relating to multiemployer plans terminated by mass withdrawal), but only with respect to nonbasic benefits guaranteed under section 4022A(g).

The Regulation

Overview

In designing the supplemental guarantee program, the PBGC attempted to achieve the following goals:

(1) To minimize premiums and the PBGC's administrative expenses, especially in the early years of the program;

(2) To minimize the potential for antiselection by a plan;

(3) To structure a program that is simple to understand and administer; and

(4) To afford plans flexibility, *e.g.,* the ability to choose the desired amount of coverage.

The proposed regulation sets forth rules under six parts in Subchapter I—Supplemental Guarantee Program for Multiemployer Plans, of the PBGC's regulations. Part 2690 contains all the definitions for Subchapter I. Part 2691 establishes the requirements for PBGC's guarantee of supplemental benefits and for coverage of a multiemployer plan under the supplemental guarantee program. Part 2692 prescribes

---

[1] The insurance limits in section 4022(b) of the Act (other than the limits in section 4022(b)(6), relating to benefit accruals under a plan that ceases to meet the requirements of Internal Revenue Code section 401(a)) apply only to single-employer plans.

rules for determining the amount of coverage for a participant and for a multiemployer plan under the supplemental guarantee program. Part 2693 prescribes the premiums for coverage under the supplemental guarantee program. Part 2693 also establishes a late entry fee for a plan that applies for its initial coverage after the plan year in which it is first eligible for coverage under the supplemental program. Part 2694 prescribes the requirements of PBGC financial assistance under the supplemental guarantee program. Finally, Part 2695 prescribes special rules for multiemployer plans covered by the program that experience a mass withdrawal.

Part 2690—Definitions

Part 2690 contains all the definitions for Subchapter I. Section 2690.2 contains definitions of terms of general applicability. The subsequent sections contain definitions of terms specific to each part within the subchapter.

Two of the definitions in § 2690.2 are fundamental to an understanding of the supplemental guarantee program: "supplemental benefit" and "guaranteed supplemental benefit". These benefits may vary from one plan participant to another and may be different amounts for any individual participant.

"Supplemental benefit" is "the monthly benefit under the plan, except for the nonforfeitable benefit accrued prior to July 30, 1980 by participants and beneficiaries to whom section 4022A(h) of the Act applies, that would be guaranteed under section 4022A of the Act, determined without regard to section 4022A(c), reduced by the benefit guaranteed under section 4022A(c) of the Act." As discussed earlier, under section 4022A(c) of the Act, the maximum monthly guaranteed benefit is limited to the product of a) 100 percent of the first $5 of a participant's benefit accrual rate and, generally, 75 percent of the next $15 of a participant's benefit accrual rate, and b) a participant's number of years of credited service. Supplemental benefits are benefits in excess of the section 4022A(c) limits, *i.e.,* 25 percent of a participant's benefit accrual rate between $5.01 and $20, and 100 percent of a participant's benefit accrual rate above $20. The following examples illustrate how to determine a participant's supplemental benefit:

Participant A has 20 years of credited service under a multiemployer plan and a monthly benefit of $300 (based on the benefit in effect for at least five years). The benefit has not been reduced under section 411(a)(3)(E) of the Code. Participant A has a guaranteed monthly benefit of $250. This is based on an accrual rate for purposes of section 4022A, without regard to the section 4022A(c) limits, of $15; *i.e.,* $300, the benefit in effect for five years or more, divided by 20, the number of years of credited service. This $15 rate is reduced by the limits in section 4022A(c) to a guaranteed accrual rate of $12.50; *i.e.,* 100 percent of the first $5 = $5, plus 75 percent of the remaining $10 = $7.50. The $12.50 accrual rate is then multiplied by 20, the number of years of credited service, to determine Participant A's guaranteed benefit. Participant A's supplemental benefit is $50 per month; *i.e.,* $2.50, the excess of his or her accrual rate under section 4022A without regard to the section 4022A(c) limits ($15), over his or her accrual rate taking into account the section 4022A(c) limits ($12.50), multiplied by 20, the participant's years of credited service.

Participant B has 20 years of credited service under a multiemployer plan and a monthly benefit of $600 (based on the benefit in effect for at least five years). The benefit has not been reduced under section 411(a)(3)(E) of the Code. Participant B has a guaranteed monthly benefit of $325. This is based on an accrual rate for purposes of section 4022A, without regard to the section 4022A(c) limits, of $30; i.e., $600, the benefit in effect for five years or more, divided by 20, the number of years of credited service. This $30 accrual rate is reduced by the limits in section 4022A(c) to a guaranteed accrual rate of $16.25; *i.e.,* 100 percent of the first $5 = $5, plus 75 percent of the net $15 = $11.25. The $16.25 accrual rate is then multiplied by 20, the number of years of credited service, to determine participant B's guaranteed benefit.

Participant B's supplemental benefit is $275 per month; *i.e.,* $13.75, the excess of his or her accrual rate under section 4022A without regard to the section 4022A(c) limits ($30), over his or her accrual rate taking into account the section 4022A(c) limits ($16.25), multiplied by 20, the participant's years of credited service. Note in this example that while no portion of a participant's accrual rate in excess of $20 per month is subject to PBGC's basic benefit guarantee the entire amount is guaranteeable under this supplemental guarantee program.

"Guaranteed supplemental benefit" is "the supplemental benefit payable with respect to a participant that is guaranteed by the PBGC under the supplemental guarantee program, as determined under § 2692.3 of this subchapter." That section provides that a participant's guaranteed supplemental benefit is the lesser of his or her supplemental benefit or the number of units of supplemental coverage purchased by the plan

multiplied by the participant's service multiplier. Under § 2692.3(b), the service multiplier is normally the participant's total number of years of credited service, although there is a special rule for a participant whose benefit has been reduced under section 411(a)(3)(E) of the Code (relating to a past-service disregard provision in a plan). Thus, PBGC will guarantee a participant's supplemental benefit only to the extent of the number of units of supplemental coverage purchased by his or her plan. In the first example above, PBGC will guarantee the participant's entire supplemental benefit only if his or her plan has purchased at least 3 units of coverage (3 × (the number of years of credited service) = $60 of supplemental coverage).

Part 2691—Requirements for Coverage

Part 2691 establishes the requirements for PBGC's guarantee of supplemental benefits and for coverage of a multiemployer plan under the supplemental guarantee program.

Section 2691.2 Provides that PBGC will guarantee the payment of supplemental benefits under a multiemployer plan if the plan (1) is covered by Title IV of ERISA, (2) is eligible for coverage, (3) satisfies the requirements for initial coverage, (4) pays its premiums when due, and (5) is insolvent.

A plan is eligible for coverage under § 2691.3 if (1) the fair market value of the plan assets as of the end of the pre-eligibility year equals at least 15 times the total amount of the benefit payments and expenses under the plan for that year ("15-year asset test"); (2) the fair market value of the plan's assets as of the end of the pre-eligibility year, plus expected investment earnings on those assets for the next ten plan years equal or exceed the total amount of expected benefit payments and expected expenses under the plan for that ten-year period ("10-year benefit payment test"); (3) the plan has not experienced a mass withdrawal on or before the date the plan's application for coverage is filed ("mass withdrawal test"); and (4) the maximum supplemental benefit under the plan, as of the date the plan's application for coverage is filed, is greater than zero. "Pre-eligibility year" is defined in § 2690.3 as "the plan year preceding the plan year in which an application for coverage that conforms with the requirements of § 2691.5 is filed."

The 15-year asset test is derived from section 4022A(g)(2)(B)(i) of the Act. That section provides that "unless the corporation determines otherwise, a plan may not elect supplemental coverage unless the value of the assets of the plan as of the end of the plan year preceding the plan year in which the election must be made is an amount equal to 15 times the total amount of the benefit payments made under the plan for that year." In order to reduce plan costs, the regulation provides that the plan's Form 5500 or Form 5500-C filed for the pre-eligibility year is used to determine whether this test is met. For example, under the Form 5500 for plan years beginning in 1981, the value of plan assets as of the end of the 1981 plan year is stated on line 13(h) of the Form 5500 and the total of benefit payments and other expenses for the 1981 plan year is stated on line 14(l). A special rule is included for small plans that have filed or are going to file a Form 5500-R (which does not include this information) for the pre-eligibility plan year. For such plans, the plan sponsor must submit a certification that the plan satisfies the 15-year asset test.

The 15-year asset test is a conservative means for determining eligibility. In view of the fact that this program is voluntary and self-financing, it is necessary, at least at the outset, to adopt a conservative approach to coverage under the program in order to preserve its financial integrity. The 15-year asset test is also necessary to avoid adverse selection by plans that will require financial assistance from PBGC in the near future.

PBGC believes that the 15-year asset test and the fact that this program is voluntary are indicative of Congress' intent that coverage under this program be made aviable only to plans in good financial condition that are able to pay benefits when due in the near future.

However, satisfaction of the 15-year asset test does not necessarily indicate that a plan can pay future benefits when due. Accordingly PBGC is proposing two additional eligibility tests: the mass withdrawal test and the 10-year benefit payment test. The mass withdrawal test is necessary to protect the supplemental insurance program because a mass withdrawal is the result of a shrinkage in the plan's contribution base, and therefore will increase the likelihood that the plan will require financial assistance. The 10-year benefit payment test is intended for those rare situations where a plan that satisfies the 15-year asset test, nevertheless faces an imminent cash flow problem because of a significant increase in the benefits expected to be payable under the plan.

For example, assume that all the retirees in a multiemployer plan are "spunoff" to a new plan, with the multiemployer plan transferring the retirees' entire accrued benefit liabilities and substantially all of the plan's assets to the new plan. As a result of this transaction the multiemployer plan satisfies the 15-year asset test. However, the plan has a significant number of active participants who are expected to enter pay status within the next several years. Because of this, the plan may be unable to pay benefits in the near future. In this situation, PBGC believes that the plan should be ineligible for coverage under the supplemental guarantee program.

Finally, a plan is eligible for coverage under §2691.3 only if the maximum supplemental benefit under the plan, as of the date the plan's application for coverage is filed, is greater than zero. "Maximum supplemental benefit" is defined in §2690.2 as "the supplemental benefit to which an individual who is or could be a participant under the plan would be entitled at the earlier of age 65 or the plan's normal retirement age if he or she commenced participation at the earlier of the earliest possible entry age under the plan or age 22 and served continuously until the earlier of age 65 or the plan's normal retirement age, based on plan provisions currently in effect five years or more (under which such amount would be the highest)." Under this, a plan is eligible for coverage even if no actual plan participant has yet accrued a supplemental benefit. The purpose of this rule is to enable plans that are otherwise eligible and will have supplemental benefits based on the current plan provisions, to apply for coverage at the earliest possible date. (As will be explained more fully in the discussion of the late entry fee, a plan may defer applying for coverage without penalty until such time as it has participants in pay status who are entitled to supplemental benefits. It may nevertheless be to the plan's advantage to enroll sooner.)

Section 2691.4(a) of the regulation provides that a plan that is eligible for coverage shall become covered under the supplemental guarantee program upon filing with PBGC a written application for coverage, including the initial premium, and any late entry fee, due under Part 2693, and thereafter, approval by PBGC of the application. (See discussion of late entry fee under Part 2693 (relating to premiums)). Coverage is effective under the supplemental guarantee program as of the first day of the plan year during which a complete application is filed by the plan and the initial premium, and if applicable, late entry fee, is paid (§2691.4(c)).

Section 2691.4(d) of the regulation relates to changes in coverage. To preserve the fiscal integrity of the program, increases in units of supplemental coverage will be approved by PBGC only if the plan satisfies the requirements for initial coverage. A plan seeking an increase in coverage must satisfy anew the eligibility requirements in §2691.3(a)(1) and (a)(2) (*i.e.*, the 15-year asset test and the insolvency test; the plan by definition already satisfies the maximum supplemental benefit requirement in §2691.3(a)(3)) and comply with the requirements for coverage in §2691.4 (§2691.4(d)(1)). That is, the plan must file an application, pay the premium for the additional unit or units, and thereafter obtain PBGC approval.

Decreases in coverage, on the other hand, do not create a potential for abuse of the supplemental insurance program, because such decreases reduce the exposure of the program. Accordingly, a plan may decrease its coverage without PBGC approval (§2691.4(d)(2)). A plan may decrease its coverage no more than once a year, by so indicating on the PBGC-1 and paying the reduced premium. A plan that has already filed its PBGC-1 for a plan year must wait until the following plan year to decrease its coverage. A plan may not decrease coverage in any plan year during which it is receiving financial assistance from PBGC under Part 2694 of this subchapter.

Requirements concerning the application for coverage are set forth in §2691.5. In addition to paying the initial premium and any late entry fee, the application must include the information specified in §2691.5(d). Among the information required is information that will enable PBGC to determine whether the eligibility tests in §2691.3 are satisfied and to apply the maximum plan coverage limitation in §2692.4:

(1) A copy of the plan's Form 5500, 5500-C or 5500-R filed for the pre-eligibility plan year. In addition, for a plan that filed a Form 5500-R for the pre-eligibility plan year, the application shall include the plan's most recent Form 5500 or Form 5500-C. (PBGC notes that a plan will be unable to submit an application for coverage until it has submitted its annual report form for the pre-eligibility plan year.)

(2) A copy of the two most recent actuarial reports.

(3) A statement updating the most recent actuarial report to show any material changes.

(4) A statement of the number of units of supplemental coverage necessary to guarantee the maximum supplemental benefit under the plan, determined as of the date the plan's application for coverage is filed, including supporting documentation.

(5) A certification by the plan sponsor that the plan has not experienced a mass withdrawal on or before the date the plan's application for coverage is filed.

(6) A certification by an enrolled actuary that the plan satisfies the test described in §2691.3(a)(2), including supporting assumptions and method, and a statement that, in making the certification, due consideration was given to the distribution of benefit liabilities under the plan.

In addition, the plan sponsor must submit a certification indicating whether the plan is subject to a late entry fee, and, if so, the amount of the fee (including interest), with supporting calculations. This certification shall include a statement of the year in which the plan first satisfied the 15-year asset test, and for that year and each year thereafter, the amount of the missed premium or a statement that there is no missed premium due for that year, including, calculations or other evidence supporting the statement. (Calculation of the late entry fee is discussed in greater detail later in this preamble.) PBGC may request any additional information it needs, including information to verify the late entry fee (§2691.5(e)).

PBGC is required under §2691.6(a) to accept a plan for coverage if it determines that the plan is eligible for coverage and has submitted a complete application. PBGC may, however, approve lower coverage than the plan requested, if it determines that the plan requested coverage greater than that allowed under §2692.4 of this subchapter. PBGC's decision to approve or reject an application will be in writing (§2691.6(b)). If PBGC rejects the application, in whole or in part, PBGC's decision will state the reasons for the decision and advise the plan sponsor of its right to appeal the decision pursuant to Part 2606 of PBGC's regulations.

Section 2691.7 of the regulation contains rules relating to cancellation of coverage under the supplemental guarantee program. PBGC may cancel coverage if the plan fails to pay a premium when due (§2691.7(a)), or if PBGC determines that the plan's application contained a material misrepresentation (§2691.7(b)). A plan may cancel coverage upon notice to PBGC (§2691.7(c)).

If a plan fails to pay the full amount of any premium due by the last date prescribed for payment under Part 2693, PBGC shall issue the plan a notice of cancellation. A notice of cancellation is effective on the 31st day after it is issued, unless the plan pays its full premium before that date.

PBGC may cancel coverage if it determines that the application contained a material misrepresentation of fact, and that it would have rejected the application had not that fact been misrepresented (§2691.7(b)). PBGC will cancel a plan's coverage under this provision only after reviewing all the facts and circumstances, and coverage is cancelled as of the first day the plan was covered under the supplemental guarantee program. If coverage is cancelled, PBGC will refund premiums (and any late entry fee) paid by the plan (§2691.7(b)(1)). PBGC's decision to cancel coverage is subject to appeal pursuant to Part 2606 of PBGC's regulations (§2691.7(b)(2)). However, the filing of an appeal did not stay the cancellation decision. If the plan appeals the decision and PBGC's Appeals Board determines that the initial determination to cancel coverage was erroneous, the Appeals Board will order that coverage be reinstated upon the plan's repayment of any amounts refunded and payment of any premium subsequently due. These same rules on cancellation also apply to an application for an increase in coverage.

Coverage will become incontestable as to the statements in the application after coverage (or the increased coverage) has been in effect for 10 years (§2691.7(b)(3)). PBGC believes that it is reasonable for plans and participants to be able to rely on supplemental guarantee program coverage after coverage has been in effect for this length of time. However, any individual who knowingly and willfully falsifies a material fact in the application will be subject to applicable criminal penalties under 18 U.S.C. 1001, no matter when the false statement is discovered.

Section 4022A(g)(2) of the Act provides that coverage "shall be irrevocable, except to the extent otherwise provided by regulations prescribed by the corporation." This regulation provides that a plan may cancel coverage without PBGC approval in accordance with the rules in §2691.7(c). A plan may cancel its coverage by so indicating on the Form PBGC-1. A plan may not cancel coverage in any plan year in which it is receiving financial assistance from PBGC under Part 2694; nor may a plan cancel coverage in any plan year in which it has already filed its Form PBGC-1 and paid its premium pursuant to Part 2693. Finally, a plan that cancels its coverage shall not be eligible to re-enter the supplemental guarantee program.

PBGC believes that revocable coverage is consistent with traditional insurance principles and with the concept of a voluntary insurance program. In addition, PBGC is concerned that requiring an irrevocable election of coverage by a plan might deter participation by plans that are uncertain about their long-term interest in the program.

PBGC recognizes that making coverage revocable may increase its administrative burden by making it more difficult to anticipate future experience under the program. This will make it more difficult to prescribe a reasonable and adequate initial premium rate and to recommend appropriate adjustments to Congress. Moreover, PBGC understands that revocable coverage could be disruptive to plans and participants because the decision to participate could be subject to yearly reevaluation. Nevertheless, the PBGC believes, on balance, that revocable coverage is preferable. The bar on re-entering the program after voluntarily cancelling coverage is necessary, in PBGC's view, to prevent abuse of the supplemental program and to provide some greater measure of stability to the program.

PBGC specifically requests public comment on these issues.

Part 2692—Coverage Limitation for Participants and Multiemployer Plans

Part 2692 prescribes rules for determining the amount of coverage of a participant and a multiemployer plan under the supplemental guarantee program. Section 2692.2 provides that the guaranteed supplemental benefit of a participant is the lesser of the participant's supplemental benefit or the number of units of supplemental coverage of the plan, multiplied by the participant's service multiplier. Each unit of supplemental coverage is equal to a monthly benefit of $1.00 times a participant's "service multiplier" (§ 2692.3(a)). As discussed earlier in this preamble, a participant's "service multiplier" is normally a participant's total number of years of credited service under the plan (§ 2692.3(b)).

Units of supplemental coverage are available only in whole number increments (§ 2692.3(a)). Thus, to insure the entire supplemental benefit of a participant whose supplemental benefit is $75 per month and who has 30 years of credited service under the plan, a plan must purchase 3 units ($75÷30=$2.50 supplemental accrual rate).

A plan may apply for any number of units of supplemental coverage, up to the limit described in § 2692.4, for the plan as a whole (§ 2692.3(a)). That is, a plan must purchase the same number of units for all participants in the plan, even though the guaranteeable supplemental benefits of the participants will be different amounts. In deciding to propose this guarantee structure, PBGC first considered and rejected two other alternatives. First, PBGC considered a guarantee structure that would make coverage available for all supplemental benefits, regardless of amount, under the plan. Under this structure a plan would pay a single premium for coverage of all participants' full supplemental benefit. PBGC also considered a guarantee structure that would permit a plan to vary coverage for specific groups of participants, *e.g.*, by bargaining units or regions. This structure might be attractive to plans that vary benefit levels for such groups.

PBGC has decided to propose only one guarantee structure at this time in the interest of simplicity and administrative ease. PBGC chose the plan-wide unit benefit guarantee structure, rather than the other two structures, because this structure is comparatively easy to administer, while still providing a plan with the flexibility to select the coverage it wants and the ability to obtain full coverage. Moreover, this structure is attractive because coverage of the plan as a whole will work in the same manner as under the basic benefits program.

Section 2692.4 of the regulation contains a limitation on the number of units of supplemental coverage a plan may purchase. A multiemployer plan that is eligible for coverage under § 2691.3 may apply for any number of units of supplemental coverage, up to the number of units necessary to guarantee the maximum supplemental benefit under the plan, determined as of the date the plan's application for coverage is filed. This rule is designed to make it impossible for plans to circumvent the requirement in § 2691.4(d)(1) that a plan that wants to increase its coverage must satisfy anew the eligibility requirements in § 2691.3, by prohibiting a plan from purchasing more units of supplemental coverage than it currently needs in anticipation of future benefit increases.

Part 2693—Premiums

Part 2693 prescribes the premium for coverage under the supplemental guarantee program. It also requires a late entry fee in certain instances for a plan that applies for initial coverage after the first year it is eligible for coverage under the supplemental program.

To participate in the supplemental program, a multiemployer plan is required to pay an annual premium. (Payment of the premium will not, however, result in coverage under the supplemental guarantee program for plans that have not satisfied the requirements for coverage under the program.) The premium is based on the number of plan participants, the number of units of supplemental coverage elected by the plan, and the supplemental premium rate (§ 2693.4(a)). The definition of "participant" for this purpose is the same definition as that used for payment of premiums for basic benefits guaranteed by PBGC. The supplemental premium rate is $.30.

The premium rate for the supplemental program is based on the ultimate premium rate for multiemployer plans for basic benefits under section 4006(a)(3)(A)(iii)(IV) of the Act. To determine the supplemental premium rate, the premium rate for basic benefits was converted to a premium per $1.00 of basic benefits guaranteed, based on the highest average guaranteed benefit payable under a multiemployer plan covered by Title IV. The cost of one unit of supplemental coverage is a prorata portion of the premium for the underlying basic benefits.

The form prescribed in Part 2693 for payment of premiums is Form PBGC-1 (§ 2693.2). A plan must use the same Form PBGC-1 for its premium payment under the supplemental guarantee program and for its premium for basic benefits;

The plan sponsor must file the plan's initial premium payment as part of its application for coverage (§ 2693.3(a)). No Form PBGC-1 is necessary with this premium payment. The filing may be made at any time. The plan administrator must make subsequent premium payments concurrently with premium payments for basic benefits *i.e.*, no later than the last day of the seventh month following the close of the prior plan year (§ 2693.3(b)).

As noted above, under § 2691.7(a), if a plan fails to pay a premium when due, after the initial premium, PBGC shall issue a notice of cancellation. The notice is effective on the 31st day after it is issued, unless the plan pays the premium due on or before the 30th day. Under this proposed regulation, no interest or penalty charges are assessed for a premium payment made during the 30-day period, although a late payment charge will be imposed with respect to a premium for basic benefits paid during that time. (*See* Part 2610 of PBGC's regulations.) PBGC is considering assessing late payment interest and penalty charges for a premium payment under the supplemental program during the 30-day period in order to discourage routine late payments. PBGC specifically requests comments on this issue.

If PBGC determines that a plan has paid less than its full premium, it will issue a notice of cancellation, requiring that the amount due be paid within 30 days. The plan may appeal PBGC's determination. However, filing of an appeal will not stay PBGC's notice of cancellation; the plan must pay the amount determined due by PBGC within the 30-day period in order to avoid cancellation (§ 2693.3(f)). If the plan's appeal is successful, PBGC will refund the overpayment with interest (§ 2693.7(c)).

As discussed earlier, § 2693.5 generally requires a late entry fee, in addition to an initial premium, for a plan that fails to apply for coverage during the first year in which it is eligible for coverage. The late entry fee equals the plan's missed premiums plus interest (§ 2692.5(a)).

The late entry fee is intended to encourage early entry into the supplemental guarantee program. It is consistent with and authorized by section 4022A(g)(2)(B)(i) and (iii) of the Act, which provide "that a plan must elect coverage under the supplemental program within the time permitted by the [PBGC] regulations" and that the PBGC regulations shall include "such other reasonable terms and conditions for supplemental coverage, including funding standards and any other reasonable limitations with respect to plans or benefits covered or to means of program financing, as the corporation determines are necessary and appropriate for a feasible supplemental program consistent with the purposes of this title." Section 4022A(g)(4)(B)(i) contemplates time limits within which a plan may enter the program. Accordingly, with the exceptions noted below, a plan that enters after the plan year in which it is first eligible is assessed a charge for late entry based on the premiums it would have paid had it applied when first eligible.

Moreover, PBGC believes it is necessary and appropriate for a viable program to charge a late entry fee. First, a late entry fee will encourage early entry. By doing so, it should enable PBGC to identify, at an early date, the majority of the plans interested in the program. This will assist PBGC in determining the viability of the program. Second, the fees will help finance the cost of the program. (Had the plan joined the program and paid premiums from when it was first eligible, those monies would have been available for the program.)

The late entry fee rules assume that a plan that satisfies the 15-year asset test is eligible for coverage under § 2691.3(a), unless the plan can demonstrate to the contrary. Accordingly, a plan that fails to file an application for coverage on or before the last day of the first plan year in which it satisfies the 15-year asset test described in § 2691.3(a)(1) is presumptively liable for a late entry fee based on the plan's missed premiums for each "missed premium year" (§ 2693.5(a)). A "missed premium year" is defined in §2690.4 as "any plan year in which the plan satisfies the 15-year asset test described in §2691.3(a)(1) of this subchapter but does not apply for coverage in accordance with §2691.5 of this subchapter." (As discussed hereafter, however, there is no missed premium due for any year for which the plan can demonstrate it was not, in fact, eligible for coverage under §2691.3(a).) Because the effective date of the supplemental guarantee program is January 1, 1983, a plan's first missed premium year cannot be earlier than its plan year beginning in 1983.

Section 2693.5(b) provides that the amount of the missed premium for each missed premium year is the premium determined under §2693.4 that would have been due had coverage been in effect for that year. For this purpose, the number of participants is the number reported on the plan's Form PBGC-1 filed for that year. The number of units of supplemental coverage used in this calculation is the lesser of (a) one-half the number of units necessary to guarantee the maximum supplemental benefit under the plan as of the date the plan's application for coverage is filed, or (b) the number of units of supplemental coverage actually necessary in each year to guarantee the highest supplemental benefit for a participant in pay status as of the last day of that year, as demonstrated by the plan sponsor to the satisfaction of PBGC.

PBGC considered several other rules for determining missed premium amounts. For example, PBGC considered basing the computation on the number of units of supplemental coverage for which the plan applies in its initial application. This rule was rejected because it is easily subject to abuse: a plan could apply for 1 unit of coverage in its initial application and apply for additional units the following year. PBGC also considered basing the missed premium amounts on one unit of supplemental coverage for each missed premium year. This rule was rejected because it would not adequately encourage early entry into the supplemental guarantee program. Finally, PBGC considered using the maximum supplemental benefit under the plan in each missed premium year. This rule was rejected as too harsh.

Consequently, PBGC has decided to propose a rule that normally assumes that the number of units in effect for each missed premium year is one-half the maximum number of units the plan could purchase, *i.e.*, one-half the units necessary to guarantee the maximum supplemental benefit under the plan as of the date the plan's application for coverage is filed. However, if for any given year, the plan sponsor can demonstrate that the number of units of supplemental coverage necessary to guarantee the highest supplemental benefit for a participant in pay status on the last day of that year is lower than one-half the maximum, then this lower number of units shall be used to compute the missed premiums. If the plan sponsor demonstrates that no participant in pay status as of the last day of a plan year had a supplemental benefit, then the missed premium for that year is zero (see discussion below).

Section 2693.5(b) contains special rules which provide, among other things, that a plan that satisfies the 15-year asset test described in §2691.3(a)(1) will not have a missed premium due for any year for which it can show that it did not satisfy either of the other two eligibility requirements, and therefore, was not actually eligible for coverage in that year. Section 2693.5(b)(1) provides that there is no missed premium due for a missed premium year if the plan sponsor demonstrates to the satisfaction of PBGC that, as of the last day of that plan year, the plan could not satisfy the insolvency test described in §2691.3(a)(2).

Section 2693.5(b)(2) gives somewhat broader relief and provides that there is no missed premium due for a missed premium year if the plan sponsor demonstrates to the satisfaction of PBGC that, as of the last day of that year, there was no participant in pay status entitled to a supplemental benefit. Thus, under this rule, even though a plan was eligible for coverage in a particular year, because the maximum supplemental benefit was greater than zero, it will not be charged a late entry fee with respect to that year if no pay status participant was receiving a supplemental benefit. PBGC believes that this rule achieves a fair result.

As discussed earlier, the maximum supplemental benefit test is used as an eligibility requirement in order to make the supplemental program available to more plans sooner. However, PBGC does not believe it is fair to assess a late entry fee with respect to a year in which a plan did not actually have benefits that would be insured under the program. Thus, PBGC concluded that a missed premium should accrue only for a plan year in which an eligible plan had either participants in pay status with supplemental benefits or participants whose accrued benefits included supplemental benefits. The latter alternative was rejected because of the administrative burden it would have placed on a

plan to demonstrate that no participant had accrued a supplemental benefit, in order to avoid a missed premium charge for a given year.

PBGC expects that in many cases a plan sponsor will be able to demonstrate that there is no missed premium due for a year based on the maximum supplemental benefit under the plan for that year. That is, in any year when the maximum supplemental benefit is zero, it automatically follows that no actual plan participant could have a supplemental benefit. In those cases where the maximum supplemental benefit for a missed premium year is greater than zero, the plan would have to review the benefits of only those participants in pay status to determine whether it can satisfy this exception.

Finally, it should be noted that if a plan can demonstrate that the maximum supplemental benefit in a given year was zero, that demonstration will cover all prior missed premium years as well. This is because it is extremely unlikely that a plan with a maximum supplemental benefit of zero in one year, had a maximum supplemental benefit greater than zero in an earlier year.

Similarly, if a plan can demonstrate for a given year that it had no pay status participants with supplemental benefits, that demonstration will also cover prior years. PBGC believes that the possibility that there was a participant in pay status with a supplemental benefit in an earlier year is too remote to warrant the administrative expense of making a plan prove that fact for each prior year.

Section 2693.5(b)(3) contains a special rule for multiemployer plans classified as "small" in any missed premium year. A plan is a small plan for a missed premium year is the plan filed a Form 5500-R or Form 5500-C for the preceding plan year. For all such years, there is no missed premium due.

PBGC believes this rule is appropriate because it would be relatively costly for these plans to attempt to determine and demonstrate that no participant in pay status had a supplemental benefit for a prior year. In addition, PBGC is concerned that the late entry fee would operate as a powerful disincentive for a small plan to apply for coverage under the supplemental guarantee program. Finally, PBGC believes that the amount of money involved (potentially waived) under this rule is relatively small.

Under §2693.5(c), interest accrues on the amount of the missed premium for each missed premium year until the late entry fee is paid, at the rate prescribed in section 6621(b) of the Internal Revenue Code. Interest is compounded annually. This interest rate is the same rate applicable to late payments of basic benefits premiums. The rate is currently 20 percent per year, but it is variable and will change whenever the rate under section 6621(b) of the Code changes. The date from which interest accrues for each missed premium year is the last day of that year.

Section 2693.6 of the regulation provides that premiums due from a multiemployer plan for coverage under the supplemental guarantee program for any plan year during which the plan receives financial assistance from the PBGC, either for guarantee supplemental benefits or for basic benefits, are not required to be paid, but instead shall be treated as financial assistance. This is consistent with the rule on payment of the basic benefits premium by multiemployer plans receiving financial assistance for basic benefits.

Section 2693.7 of the regulation sets forth rules for PBGC refunds of overpayments. Under §2693.7(a), if PBGC rejects an application for coverage, PBGC shall refund to the plan the initial premium and late entry fee, if any. Section 2693.7(b) provides that if the PBGC cancels a plan's coverage for a material misrepresentation or a mass withdrawal, PBGC shall likewise refund to the plan any amounts paid for plan years beginning on or after the effective date of cancellation. If the plan miscalculates the premium or late entry fee and overpays, PBGC shall refund to the plan the excess payment (§2693.7(c)). Finally, under §2693.7(d), if in response to a notice of cancellation a plan pays the premium demanded by PBGC but appeals that determination, and PBGC's Appeals Board finds that the plan did overpay, PBGC shall refund the overpayment amount with interest. Interest will be paid at the rate prescribed in section 6621(b) of the Code.

Part 2694—Financial Assistance

Part 2694 prescribes the rules for PBGC financial assistance to multiemployer plans covered by the supplemental guarantee program that are or will be insolvent and unable to pay when due supplemental benefits (§2694.1(a)). Part 2694 also establishes the procedure under which plan sponsors shall file an application for financial assistance with PBGC and the terms and conditions under which PBGC shall provide financial assistance (§2694.1(a)).

Section 2694.2 provides that the plan sponsor of a multiemployer plan covered by the supplemental guarantee program who determines that the plan is or will be insolvent and unable to pay supplemental benefits when due may apply to PBGC for financial assistance. Section 2694.2 also provides that the plan sponsor shall submit any information the PBGC determines it needs to review the application.

PBGC expects to promulgate, at a later date, specific information required to be included in an application. PBGC notes that there is little need to prescribe this information requirement at this time because of the remote possibility that a plan that is covered by the supplemental guarantee program and which thus satisfies the 15-year asset test, will require financial assistance within at least 10 years after coverage under the program is effective. PBGC believes it important in developing these information requirements to minimize reporting requirements and to avoid requiring the submission of duplicative information. Accordingly, PBGC will coordinate the information required to be submitted in an application for financial assistance under the supplemental guarantee program with the information required to be submitted in an application for financial assistance for basic benefits.

If, upon receipt of an application for financial assistance, PBGC verifies that the plan is or will be insolvent and unable to pay supplemental benefits when due, PBGC shall provide the plan financial assistance in an amount sufficient to enable the plan to pay guaranteed supplemental benefits under the plan (§ 2694.3(a)). PBGC decisions on applications for financial assistance shall be in writing. A PBGC decision to disapprove an application shall state the reasons for the determination and state that the plan may file an administrative appeal in accordance with Part 2606 (§ 2694.3(b)).

The rules in §§ 2669.4 and 2694.5 of the regulation for financial assistance for guaranteed supplemental benefits are virtually identical to the rules in section 4261(b) of the Act for financial assistance for basic benefits. Under § 2694.4(a), financial assistance shall be provided under such conditions as PBGC determines are equitable and are appropriate to prevent unreasonable loss to PBGC with respect to the plan. Financial assistance is a loan by PBGC to the plan. A plan which has received financial assistance shall repay the amount of such assistance to PBGC on such reasonable terms and for such periods as PBGC deems equitable and appropriate in the particular case. (*See* section 4067 of the Act; cf. section 4261(b)(2) of the Act, which requires financial assistance to be repaid to PBGC on reasonable terms consistent with regulations prescribed by PBGC.) PBGC may provide interim financial assistance under § 2694.5, pending determination of the proper amount of financial assistance, in such amounts as it considers appropriate in order to avoid undue hardship to plan participants and beneficiaries.

Sections 4005(e) and 4005(f) of the Act establish a supplemental guarantee program fund on the books of the U.S. Treasury and require the fund to be self-supporting. In addition, no amounts borrowed from the U.S. Treasury pursuant to PBGC's borrowing authority may be used for the supplemental guarantee fund. Accordingly, § 2694.6 of the regulation provides that PBGC shall pay guaranteed supplemental benefits only to the extent there is money available in the supplemental benefit program fund to pay those benefits. PBGC specifically requests public comment on what rules should be adopted to deal with the situation where the program is expected not to have sufficient funds to pay all benefits when due. For example, should a reduction in financial assistance apply to all plans receiving assistance, or only to those that apply after the guarantee fund is exhausted?

One alternative for dealing with the potential insolvency problem would be to establish a much higher premium rate, in order to minimize the likelihood of benefit cutback. PBGC is disinclined to adopt this approach because of the difficulty in determining what that premium rate should be and because a much higher premium might deter many plans from entering the program. But PBGC requests comments on this alternative.

Part 2695—Mass Withdrawals

Part 2695 prescribes special rules for multiemployer plans covered by the supplemental guarantee program that experience a mass withdrawal. Section 2695.2(a) of the regulation provides that PBGC shall cancel the coverage of a multiemployer plan with respect to which there is a mass withdrawal if the mass withdrawal date occurs on or before the earlier of (1) the date on which the last collective bargaining agreement providing for employer contributions under the plan, which has an effective date on or after the plan's initial coverage date, expires, or (2) six years after the plan's initial coverage date.

A "mass withdrawal" is defined in § 2690.5 as "a withdrawal or withdrawals from a multiemployer plan as a result of which the plan is subject to section 4219(c)(1)(D) of the Act, and includes a termination by mass withdrawal under section 4041A(a)(2) of the Act and the withdrawal of substantially all the employers pursuant to an agreement

or agreements to withdraw". Section 4219(c)(1)(D) of the Act requires that when a multiemployer plan terminates by the withdrawal of every employer from a plan or where substantially all the employers withdraw from a plan pursuant to an agreement or agreements to withdraw from the plan, the plan's total unfunded vested benefits must be allocated among all such employers. "Initial coverage date" is defined in § 2690.5 as "the date as of which coverage under the supplemental guarantee program is first effective for a plan pursuant to § 2691.4(c)". "Mass withdrawal date" means—"(a) in the case of a termination by mass withdrawal, the date determined under section 4041A(b)(2) of the Act; or (b) in any other case, the earliest employer withdrawal date for an employer subject to section 4219(c)(1)(D) of the Act, as determined under section 4203(e) of the Act" (§ 2690.5).

PBGC believes it necessary to establish a minimum period of participation during which a plan is covered by the supplemental guarantee program before which a plan may experience a mass withdrawal and continue to be covered. PBGC notes that a mass withdrawal will generally increase the likelihood that a plan will require financial assistance under the supplemental guarantee program. The existence of coverage under the supplemental guarantee program may encourage a mass withdrawal. Therefore, a minimum period of program participation is necessary to deter a plan from electing coverage under the supplemental guarantee program in anticipation of the withdrawal of all or substantially all of the employers in the plan.

Because a mass withdrawal is most likley to occur on the date on which one or more collective bargaining agreements expire, the minimum participation period is tied to the bargaining cycle. The minimum participation period runs from the plan's initial coverage date and in the usual case, will not expire until each collective bargaining agreement under which the plan is maintained has been re-negotiated and thereafter expires. Thus, if the mass withdrawal date is before the date on which the last collective bargaining agreement providing for employer contributions under the plan, which has an effective date on or after the plan's initial coverage date, expires, the plan's coverage will be cancelled. However, in no event will PBGC cancel a plan's coverage because of a mass withdrawal, if the mass withdrawal date is more than six years after the plan's initial coverage date. PBGC believes that six years is a sufficiently long period to deter possible abuse of the insurance system.

PBGC's decision to cancel a plan's coverage as the result of a mass withdrawal shall be in writing. The decision shall state the reasons for the determination, include a statement of the plan's right to appeal the decision pursuant to Part 2606 of PBGC's regulations, and state that the decision is effective on the date of issuance. The decision shall also state the date as of which the plan's coverage is cancelled. The cancellation date shall be the last day of the plan year preceding the plan year in which PBGC notifies the plan that its coverage is cancelled. PBGC shall refund to the plan any amount paid for plan years beginning after the date as of which the plan's coverage is cancelled. If the plan appeals PBGC's decision and PBGC's Appeals Board finds that the initial determination is erroneous the Appeals Board will order the plan reinstated subject to payment of any amounts refunded and any premium due.

PBGC believes it will be necessary for the supplemental guarantee program to contain certain special rules relating to mergers, spinoffs or transfers of assets or liabilities. These rules would address plan coverage in the event a covered plan engaged in one of these transactions. Special rules are necessary because a merger, spinoff or transfer may create a significant risk to the supplemental guarantee program, as for example, in the case of the merger of a financially weak, non-covered plan into a covered plan, as well as create substantial administrative problems.

Special rules would need to address the following issues: Under what circumstances, if any, should a plan covered by the program continue to be covered when it is involved in a merger, spinoff or transfer? Should the result be different if the other plan involved in the transaction is a non-covered plan? In this latter situation, should coverage be continued only for those participants who were previously covered by the program? If so, what administrative problems would this create, and how might they be handled?

PBGC currently believes that, except for a *de minimis* transaction, the resulting plans or plan should be treated as new plans that must satisfy the eligibility requirements of § 2691.3(a) and the coverage requirements of § 2691.4 anew in order to participate in the program. Consistent with this rule, participants who, because of a merger, spinoff or transfer, are no longer in a plan covered by the program would not continue to be covered by the program.

This would avoid a tremendous administrative burden on both the non-covered plan and the guarantee program.

A tentative cut-off for whether a transaction is *de minimis* would be if the transaction affects less than 3% of the total assets or liabilities. For example, in the case of a merger, a transaction would be *de minimis* if the present value of the accrued benefits of the merging plan not covered by the program is less than three percent of the fair market value of the assets of the covered plan.

Finally, under these rules, the merger of two covered plans would not result in cancellation of coverage. However, this raises the issue of the level of coverage, if the two plans had different levels. The approach which would seem to provide the greatest protection to the supplemental guarantee program would be to cover the merged plan at whatever was the lowest level of coverage of the merging plans.

PBGC specifically invites comments on these issues.

The Pension Benefit Guaranty Corporation has determined that this regulation is not a "major rule" for the purposes of Executive Order 12291, because it will not have an annual effect on the economy of $100 million or more; or create a major increase in costs or prices for consumers, individual industries, or geographic regions; or have significant adverse effects on competition, employment, investment, innovation, or on the ability of United States-based enterprises to compete with foreign-based enterprises in domestic or export markets. The PBGC expects that the total annual premiums collected in the first few years of the program will be less than $10 million. Moreover, this regulation is required by statute.

Under section 605(b) of the Regulatory Flexibility Act the Pension Benefit Guaranty Corporation certifies that this rule will not have a significant economic impact on a substantial number of small entities. Pension plans with fewer than 100 participants have traditionally been treated as small plans. The proposed regulation affects only multiemployer plans covered by PBGC. Defining "small plans" as those with under 100 participants, such plans represent only 10% of all multiemployer plans covered by PBGC (200 out of 2,000). Further, small multiemployer plans represent only .3% of all small plans covered by the PBGC (200 out of 61,200) and less than .05% of all small plans (200 out of 427,900). Moreover, the PBGC expects that a significant number of multiemployer plans are currently ineligible for coverage under this program because of the 15-year asset test. In addition, the program is voluntary. Therefore, compliance with sections 603 and 604 of the Regulatory Flexibility Act is waived.

Interested parties are invited to submit comments on this proposed regulation. Comments should be addressed to: Assistant Executive Director for Policy and Planning, Pension Benefit Guaranty Corporation (140), 2020 K Street, NW., Washington, D.C. 20006. Written comments will be available for public inspection at the above address, Suite 7100, between the hours of 9:00 a.m. and 4:00 p.m. Each person submitting comments should include his or her name and address, identify this proposed regulation, and give reasons for any recommendation. This proposal may be changed in light of the comments received.

In developing this proposed regulation, PBGC solicited comments from knowledgeable individuals outside the corporation. Copies of these comments are available for public inspection at the above address.

List of Subjects in 29 CFR Parts §§ 2690—2695

Employee benefit plans, Pensions, Pension insurance.

In consideration of the foregoing, it is proposed to amend Chapter XXVI of Title 29, Code of Federal Regulations by adding a new Subchapter I consisting of Parts 2690 through 2695 to read as follows:

Subchapter I—Supplemental Guarantee Program For Multiemployer Plans

PART 2690—DEFINITIONS

2691—Requirements for Coverage

2692—Coverage Limitations for Participants and Multiemployer Plans

2693—Premiums

2694—Financial Assistance

2695—Mass Withdrawals

Subchapter I—Supplemental Guarantee Program For Multiemployer Plans

PART 2690—DEFINITIONS

Sec. 2690.1—Purpose and scope.

2690.2—General definitions.

2690.3—Requirements for coverage.

2690.4—Premiums.

2690.5—Mass withdrawals.

Authority: Secs. 4002(b)(3), 4002A(g)(2), Pub. L. 93-406, as amended by secs. 403(1) and 102 (respectively), Pub. L. 96-364, 94 Stat. 1302, 1214-15 (1980) [29 U.S.C. 1302, 1322a].

§ 2690.1 Purpose and scope.

This part sets forth the definitions used in Subchapter I. Section 2690.2 contains definitions of terms of general applicability. The subsequent sections contain definitions of terms specific to each part within the subchapter.

§ 2690.2 General definitions.

For purposes of Subchapter I—

"Act" means the Employee Retirement Income Security Act of 1974, as amended.

"Actuarial report" means a report submitted to the plan in connection with a valuation of plan assets and liabilities, for purposes of section 412 of the Code.

"Code" means the Internal Revenue Code of 1954, as amended.

"Guaranteed supplemental benefit" means the supplemental benefit payable with respect to a participant that is guaranteed by the PBGC under the supplemental guarantee program set forth in this subchapter, as determined under § 2692.2 of this subchapter.

"Insolvent" means that a plan is unable to pay benefits when due for the plan year. A plan terminated by mass withdrawal is not insolvent until it has first been amended to eliminate all benefits that are not eligible for the PBGC's guarantee under section 4022A(b) of the Act.

"Maximum supplemental benefit" means the supplemental benefit to which an individual who is or could be a participant under the plan would be entitled at the earlier of age 65 or the plan's normal retirement age if he or she commenced participation at the earlier of the earliest possible entry age under the plan or age 22 and served continuously until the earlier of age 65 or the plan's normal retirement age, based on plan provisions in effect five years or more (under which such amount would be the highest.)

"Multiemployer plan" means a pension plan described in section 4001(a)(3) of the Act.

"Participant" means any individual who is included in one of the categories below:

(a) *Active.*—(1) Any individual who is currently in employment covered by the plan and who is earning or retaining credited service under the plan. This category includes any individual who is currently below the integration level in a plan that is integrated with Social Security.

(2) Any non-vested individual who is not currently in employment covered by the plan but who is earning or retaining credited service under the plan. This category does not include a non-vested former employee who has incurred a break in service of the greater of one year or the break in service period specified in the plan.

(b) *Inactive.*—(1) *Inactive receiving benefits.* Any individual who is retired or separated from employment covered by the plan and who is receiving benefits under the plan. This category does not include an individual to whom an insurance company has made an irrevocable commitment to pay all the benefits to which the individual is entitled under the plan.

(2) *Inactive entitled to future benefits.* Any individual who is retired or separated from employment covered by the plan and who is entitled to begin receiving benefits under the plan in the future. This category does not include an individual to whom an insurance company has made an irrevocable commitment to pay all the benefits to which the individual is entitled under the plan.

(c) *Deceased.* Any deceased individual who has one or more beneficiaries who are receiving or entitled to receive benefits under the plan. This category does not include an individual if an insurance company has made an irrevocable commitment to pay all the benefits to which the beneficiaries of that individual are entitled under the plan.

"PBGC" means the Pension Benefit Guaranty Corporation.

"Plan administrator" means the plan administrator, as defined in sections 4001(a)(1) and 3(16) of the Act.

"Plan sponsor" means the plan sponsor, as defined in section 4001(a)(10) of the Act.

"Plan year" means the calendar, policy or fiscal year on which the records of the plan are kept.

"Supplemental benefit" means the monthly benefit under the plan, except for the nonforfeitable benefit accrued prior to July 30, 1980 by a participant to whom section 4022A(h) of the Act applies, that would be guaranteed under section 4022A of the Act without regard to the limitations in section 4022A(c), reduced by the benefit guaranteed under section 4022A(c) of the Act.

"Supplemental guarantee program" means the program described in section 4022A(g)(2) of the Act and established in this subchapter, under which the PBGC guarantees the payment of supplemental benefits.

"Terminate by mass withdrawal" means to terminate under section 4041A(a)(2) of the Act.

§ 2690.3 Requirements for coverage.

For purposes of Part 2691—

"Last entry date" means the last day of the first plan year beginning on or after January 1, 1983, in which a plan satisfies the 15-year asset test described in § 2691.3(a)(1) of this subchapter.

"Pre-eligibility year" means the plan year preceding the plan year in which an application for coverage that conforms with the requirements of § 2691.5 is filed.

§ 2690.4 Premiums.

For purposes of Part 2693—

"Missed premium year" means any plan year in which the plan satisfies the 15-year asset test described in § 2691.3(a)(1) of this subchapter but does not apply for coverage in accordance with § 2691.5.

§ 2690.5 Mass withdrawals.

For purposes of Part 2695—

"Initial coverage date" means the date as of which coverage under the supplemental guarantee program is first effective for a plan pursuant to § 2691.4(c).

"Mass withdrawal" means a withdrawal or withdrawals from a multiemployer plan as a result of which the plan is subject to section 4219(c)(1)(D) of the Act, and includes a termination by mass withdrawal under section 4041A(a)(2) of the Act and the withdrawal of substantially all the employers pursuant to an agreement or agreements to withdraw.

"Mass withdrawal date" means (a) in the case of a termination by mass withdrawal, the date determined under section 4041A(b)(2) of the Act; or (b) in any other case, the earliest employer withdrawal date for an employer subject to section 4219(c)(1)(D) of the Act, as determined under section 4203(e) of the Act.

PART 2691—REQUIREMENTS FOR COVERAGE

Sec. 2691.1—Purpose and scope.

2691.2—Benefits guaranteed under supplemental guarantee program.

2691.3—Eligibility for coverage.

2691.4—Requirements for coverage.

2691.5—Application.

2691.6—PBGC action on application.

2691.7—Cancellation of coverage.

Authority: Secs. 4002(b)(3), 4022A(g)(2), Pub. L. 93-406, as amended by secs. 403(1) and 102 (respectively), Pub. L. 96-364, 94 Stat. 1302, 1214-15 (1980) [29 U.S.C. 1302, 1322a].

§ 2691.1 Purpose and scope.

(a) *Purpose.* The purpose of this part is to set forth the requirements for PBGC's guarantee of supplemental benefits and for coverage of a multiemployer plan under the supplemental guarantee program established in this subchapter.

(b) *Scope.* This part applies to each multiemployer plan covered under section 4021(a) of the Act and not excluded by section 4021(b), that applies for coverage or is covered under the supplemental guarantee program.

§ 2691.2 Benefits guaranteed under supplemental guarantee program.

(a) *General requirements.* PBGC shall guarantee, in accordance with this subchapter, the payment of supplemental benefits under a multiemployer plan—

(1) To which section 4021 of the Act applies;

(2) Which is eligible for coverage in accordance with § 2691.3;

(3) Which satisfies the requirements for coverage in accordance with § 2691.4;

(4) Which pays all premiums when due in accordance with Part 2693 of this subchapter; and

(5) Which is insolvent.

(b) *Benefits guaranteed for a participant.* The supplemental benefits of a participant in a plan described in paragraph (a) of this section that are guaranteed by PBGC under the supplemental guarantee program shall be determined in accordance with § 2692.2 of this subchapter.

§ 2691.3 Eligibility for coverage.

(a) *General requirement.* Except as provided in paragraph (b) of this section, a multiemployer plan is eligible for coverage under the supplemental guarantee program if it satisfies the following requirements:

(1) The fair market value of the plan's assets as of the end of the pre-eligibility plan year equals or exceeds 15 times the total amount of the benefit payments and expenses under the plan for that year.

(i) For a plan that has filed or is going to file a Form 5500 or Form 5500-C for the pre-eligibility plan year, that form shall be used to demonstrate satisfaction of the test described in paragraph (a)(1).

(ii) For a plan that has filed or is going to file a Form 5500-R for the pre-eligibility plan year, the plan sponsor's certification in accordance with § 2691.5(d)(12) shall be used to demonstrate satisfaction of the test described in paragraph (a)(1).

(2) The fair market value of the plan's assets as of the end of the pre-eligibility plan year, plus expected investment earnings on those assets for the next ten plan years, equal or exceed the total amount of expected benefit payments and expected expenses under the plan for that ten-year period.

(i) For a plan that has filed or is going to file a Form 5500 or Form 5500-C for the pre-eligibility plan year, that form shall be used to determine the fair market value of plan assets.

(ii) For a plan that has filed or is going to file a Form 5500-R for the pre-eligibility plan year, the fair market value of plan assets shall be the fair market value reported by the plan sponsor in accordance with § 2691.5(d)(12).

(iii) Expected investment earnings shall be determined using the same interest assumption used for determining the minimum funding requirement under section 412 of the Code.

(iv) Expected benefit payments shall be determined by assuming that current benefits remain in effect and that all scheduled increases in benefits occur.

(v) Expected expenses shall be determined using expenses in the pre-eligibility plan year, adjusted to reflect any anticipated changes.

(3) The plan has not experienced a mass withdrawal on or before the date the plan's application for coverage is filed.

(4) The maximum supplemental benefit under the plan, as defined in § 2690.2, is greater than zero, as of the date the plan's application for coverage is filed.

(b) *Re-entry.* A multiemployer plan is not eligible for coverage under the supplemental guarantee program if it was previously covered by the program and its coverage was cancelled in accordance with § 2691.7(a) or (c) of this part, or § 2695.2 of this subchapter. If coverage was cancelled pursuant to § 2691.7(b), the plan shall be eligible for re-entry if it meets the requirements in paragraph (a) of this section.

§ 2691.4 Requirements for coverage.

(a) *General rule.* Except as provided in paragraph (b) of this section, a plan that is eligible for coverage under § 2691.3 shall become covered under the supplemental guarantee program upon—

(1) Filing with PBGC a written application that comforms with the requirements of § 2691.5, including payment of the initial premium and any late entry fee due under Part 2693 of this subchapter; and

(2) Approval by PBGC of the application.

(b) *Late entry fee.* If a plan fails to apply for coverage before its last entry date, as defined in § 2690.3, its application for coverage under the supplemental guarantee program shall include a late entry fee determined in accordance with § 2693.5 of this subchapter.

(c) *Effective date of coverage.* A plan whose application is approved by PBGC is covered under the supplemental guarantee program as of the first day of the plan year during which it files a complete application with PBGC.

(d) *Changes in coverage.*—(1) *Increase coverage.* A plan that is covered under the supplemental guarantee program may increase its coverage at any time upon satisfaction of the requirements of paragraph (a) of this section. When a plan applies for increased coverage, the premium described in paragraph (a)(1) is the premium owed for the plan's existing coverage plus the increased coverage requested. The effective date of increased coverage, if approved by PBGC, shall be the first day of the plan year in which the complete application is filed.

(2) *Decreased coverage.* A plan that is covered under the supplemental guarantee program may decrease its coverage without PBGC's approval by following the procedures, including time limits, for cancellation of coverage set forth in § 2691.7(c) of this part. A plan may not decrease coverage in any plan year during which it is receiving financial assistance from PBGC under Part 2694 of this subchapter.

§ 2691.5 Application.

(a) *General.* Subject to the rule in § 2691.4(b) on late entry, an application for initial or increased coverage may be filed with PBGC at any time. In addition to the initial premium, and any late entry fee, due under Part 2693, the application shall include the information specified in paragraph (d) of this section.

(b) *Who shall file.* The plan sponsor, or a duly authorized representative acting on behalf of the plan sponsor, shall sign the application.

(c) *Where to file.* The application shall be delivered by mail or submitted by hand to the Division of Case Classification and Control (540), Office of Program Operations, Pension Benefit Guaranty Corporation, 2020 K Street, N.W., Washington, D.C. 20006.

(d) *Information.* Each application shall contain the following information:

(1) The name of the plan.

(2) The name, address and telephone number of the plan sponsor, and of the duly authorized representative, if any, of the plan sponsor.

(3) The nine-digit Employer Identification Number (EIN) assigned by the Internal Revenue Service to the plan sponsor and the three-digit Plan Identification Number (PIN) assigned by the plan sponsor to the plan, and, if different, the EIN or PIN last filed with the PBGC. The notice should indicate of no EIN or PIN has been assigned.

(4) A copy of the most recent IRS determination letter, if any, relating to the plan.

(5) A statement that the plan is applying for coverage (or increased coverage) under the supplemental guarantee program, indicating the number of units of supplemental coverage for which the plan is applying, *i.e.,* the number of $1.00 units requested.

(6) A statement of the number of units of supplemental coverage necessary to guarantee the maximum supplemental benefit under the plan, determined as of the date the plan's application for coverage is filed, including supporting documentation.

(7) A copy of the plan document currently in effect, *i.e.,* a copy of the last restatement of the plan and all subsequent amendments.

(8) If not included in item 7, a copy of any amendment to the plan adopted or effective within the 5-year period preceding the beginning of the plan year during which the application is filed.

(9) A copy of the two most recent actuarial reports relating to the plan. The reports shall include a complete description of the actuarial assumptions and methods used; an age and service distribution of active and retired lives, and the associated liability distributions for retired lives; the number of contribution base units for the five most recent plan years; all asset and liability figures used to complete Schedule B of the Annual Report Form (Form 5500 series), including the value of vested benefits; and the contribution rates in effect.

(10) A statement updating the most recent actuarial report described in item 9 to show any material changes.

(11) A copy of the plan's Annual Report Form (Form 5500 series) for the pre-eligibility plan year, including schedules. In addition, for a plan that has filed a Form 5500-R for the pre-eligibility plan year, the application shall contain the plan's most recent Form 5500 or Form 5500-C, including schedules.

(12) For a plan that has filed a Form 5500-R for the pre-eligibility plan year, a certification by the plan sponsor that the plan satisfies the 15-year asset test described in § 2691.3(a)(1). The certification shall include a statement as to the fair market value of the plan's assets as of

the end of the pre-eligibility year and the total amount of the benefit payments and expenses under the plan for that year.

(13) A certification by the plan sponsor that the plan has not experienced a mass withdrawal on or before the date the plan's application for coverage is filed.

(14) A certification by an enrolled actuary that the plan satisfies the test described in § 2691.3(a)(3), including supporting assumptions and methods, and a statement that in making the certification due consideration was given to the distribution of benefit liabilities under the plan.

(15) The amount of the initial premium, paid to PBGC in the application, including supporting calculations.

(16) A certification by the plan, sponsor indicating whether the plan is subject to a late entry fee, and, if so, the amount of the fee (including interest). The certification shall include a statement as to the year in which the plan first satisfied the 15-year asset test described in § 2691.3(a)(1), and for that year and each year thereafter, a statement with calculations as to the amount of missed premium or a statement that there is no missed premium due for that year, including evidence supporting the statement.

(e) *Additional information.* In addition to the information described in paragraph (d) of this section, PBGC may require the plan sponsor to submit any other information PBGC determines it needs to review an application.

(f) *Duplicate information.* In the case of plan applying for additional units of supplemental coverage, any of the information required by paragraph (d) of this section may be omitted if the identical information was previously filed with PBGC. When information is omitted pursuant to this paragraph, the application shall so indicate and shall state the date on which the information was submitted and that the information is still accurate and complete.

(g) *Date of filing.* An application is not considered filed until all the information required by paragraph (d) of this section and the initial premium, and, if applicable, late entry fee due have been submitted. The date of filing is the date on which all the information (or the final portion of the required information), the premium and late entry fee, if any, are hand-delivered or mailed, or the last such date if these items are submitted separately. An application shall be presumed to have been mailed on the date on which it is postmarked by the United States Postal Service, or three days prior to the date on which it is received by the PBGC if it does not contain a legible United States Postal Service postmark.

§ 2691.6 PBGC action on application.

(a) *General.* PBGC shall accept a plan for coverage if it determines that the plan is eligible for coverage under § 2691.3 and has submitted an application that complies with § 2691.5. PBGC may, however, approve lower coverage than the plan requested, if it determines that the plan requested coverage greater than that allowed under § 2692.4 of this subchapter.

(b) *PBGC decision.* PBGC shall notify the plan sponsor in writing of its decision on the application. If PBGC approves the application, the decision shall state that the plan is covered under the supplemental guarantee program and specify the amount of coverage the plan will receive. If PBGC rejects the application, in whole or in part, the decision shall state the reasons for the rejection and include a statement of the plan sponsor's right to appeal the decision pursuant to Part 2606 of this chapter. Filing of an appeal shall not stay the effectiveness of a decision granting coverage for less than the amount applied for.

§ 2691.7 Cancellation of coverage.

(a) *Missed premiums.* Unless the premium due is not payable under § 2693.6 of this subchapter because the plan is receiving financial assistance from PBGC, if the plan fails to pay any premium due under Part 2693 by the last date prescribed for payment in § 2693.3(b) or (c), PBGC shall issue the plan a notice of cancellation. The notice shall advise the plan that unless the full amount due is paid within 30 days after the date of the notice, the plan's coverage under the supplemental guarantee program shall be cancelled. Cancellation shall be effective on the 31st day after the date of the notice. If a plan's coverage is cancelled pursuant to this paragraph, it shall not be entitled to a refund of premiums paid, nor shall it be eligible to re-apply for coverage.

(b) *Material misrepresentation.* Except as provided in paragraph (b)(3) of this section, if PBGC determines that a plan's application for initial coverage or an increase in coverage contained a misrepresentation as to a material fact that would have caused PBGC to reject the application had not that fact been misrepresented, the plan's coverage shall be cancelled by PBGC. Cancellation shall be effective as of the

¶ 20,525D

plan's effective date under § 2691.4(c) of initial coverage or increased coverage, as applicable.

(1) *Effect of cancellation.* A plan whose coverage is cancelled pursuant to paragraph (b) of this section shall be entitled to a refund of amounts paid under the supplemental guarantee program, in accordance with § 2693.7(b) of this subchapter. The plan shall be eligible to re-apply for coverage if it meets the tests in § 2691.3(a).

(2) *PBGC decision.* PBGC shall notify the plan in writing of its decision to cancel the plan's coverage. The decision shall state the reasons for the determination, the date as of which a plan's coverage is cancelled, include a statement of the plan's right to appeal the decision pursuant to Part 2606 of this chapter, and state that the decision is effective on the date of issuance.

(3) *Restriction on right to cancel.* After initial coverage or an increase in coverage has been in effect for 10 years, it shall be incontestable as to the statements contained in the application.

(c) *Cancellation by plan.* Except as provided in paragraph (c)(2) of this section, a plan may cancel coverage, without PBGC approval, by so indicating on its Form PBGC-1 filed in accordance with Part 2693 of this subchapter. To be effective, the form must be filed within the time limits for filing set forth in Part 2693. Cancellation of coverage shall be effective as of the last day of the plan year preceding the plan year for which the Form PBGC-1 is filed.

(1) *Effect of cancellation.* A plan that cancels its coverage pursuant to paragraph (c) of this section shall not be entitled to a refund of premiums (or any late entry fee) paid for plan years when coverage was in effect, nor shall it be eligible to re-apply for coverage.

(2) *Restrictions on right to cancel.* A plan may not cancel coverage in any plan year in which it is receiving financial assistance from PBGC under Part 2694 of this subchapter, nor in any plan year in which it has already filed its Form PBGC-1 and paid its premium pursuant to Part 2693.

PART 2692—COVERAGE LIMITATIONS FOR PARTICIPANTS AND MULTIEMPLOYER PLANS

Sec. 2692.1—Purpose and scope.

2692.2—Guaranteed supplemental benfits.

2692.3—Plan coverage.

2692.4—Maximum plan coverage.

Authority: Secs. 4002(b)(3), 4022A(g)(2), Pub. L. 93-406, as amended by secs. 403(1) and 102 (respectively), Pub. L. 96-364, 94 Stat. 1302, 1214-15 (1980) (29 U.S.C. 1302, 1322).

§ 2692.1 Purpose and scope.

(a) *Purpose.* The purpose of this part is to prescribe rules for determining the amount of coverage for a participant and a multiemployer plan under the supplemental guarantee program.

(b) *Scope.* This part applies to each multiemployer plan covered under section 4021(a) of the Act and not excluded by section 4021(b), that applies for coverage or is covered under the supplemental guarantee program and to participants and beneficiaries in those plans.

§ 2692.2 Guarantees supplemental benefits.

The PBGC shall guarantee the payment with respect to a participant of a supplemental benefit provided under a multiemployer plan covered by the supplemental guarantee program equal to the lesser of the participant's supplemental benefit, or the number of units of supplemental coverage purchased by the plan multiplied by the participant's service multiplier (as defined in § 2692.3(b)).

§ 2692.3 Plan coverage.

(a) *General.* Subject to the limitation in § 2962.4, a multiemployer plan that is eligible for coverage under § 2691.3 may apply for any number of units of supplemental coverage. The same number of units shall be purchased for all participants in the plan. Units may only be purchased in whole number increments. Each unit is equal to a monthly benefit with respect to a participant in the amount of $1.00 times the participant's service multiplier.

(b) *Service multiplier.* Except as provided in the next sentence, a participant's service multiplier is the participant's total number of years of credited service, determined in accordance with section 4022A(c)(4) of the Act. In the case of a participant whose benefit under the plan has been reduced under section 411(a)(3)(E) of the Code and whose benefit guaranteed under section 4022A is determined under section 4022A(d)(1), the participant's service multiplier is the amount determined under section 4022A(d)(1) of the Act, divided by the amount determined under section 4022A(c)(1)(A) of the Act.

§ 2692.4 Maximum plan coverage.

A multiemployer plan may not purchase more than the number of units of coverage necessary to guarantee the maximum supplemental benefit under the plan, determined as of the date the plan's application for coverage (or increased coverage) is filed.

PART 2693—PREMIUMS

Sec. 2693.1—Purpose and scope.

2693.2—Form.

2693.3—Requirement to pay premiums.

2693.4—Premium rate.

2693.5—Late entry fee.

2693.6—Premium for plan year during which plan receives financial assistance.

2693.7—Overpayments.

2693.8—Date of filing or payment.

2693.9—Computation of time.

Authority: Secs. 4002(b)(3), 4006(a), 4022A(g)(2), Pub. L. 93-406, as amended by secs. 403(1), 105(a) and 102 (respectively), Pub. L. 96-364, 94 Stat. 1302, 1264-66, 1214-15 (1980) (29 U.S.C. 1302, 1306, 1322a).

§ 2693.1 Purpose and scope.

(a) *Purpose.* The purpose of this part is to prescribe the premiums for coverage of multiemployer plans under the supplemental guarantee program established in this subchapter. This part also prescribes the late entry fee for a plan that applies for coverage after its last entry date.

(b) *Scope.* This part applies to each multiemployer plan that applies for coverage or is covered under the supplemental guarantee program.

§ 2693.2 Form.

The form prescribed by this part for the payment of premiums in Form PBGC-1. A completed Form PBGC-1 shall accompany all payments of premiums under this part (other than the initial premium payment). A plan shall use a single Form PBGC-1 for both is premium payment under this part and under Part 2610 (premium for basic benefit coverage) of this chapter.

§ 2693.3 Requirement to pay premiums.

(a) *Initial premium.* The plan sponsor of a plan that is applying under § 2691.4 of this subchapter for coverage under the supplemental guarantee program shall pay the initial premium due as part of its application for coverage. The payment check shall be made payable to PBGC and shall show the name of the plan and the EIN-PIN with respect to the plan on its face.

(b) *Premium for covered plan.* The plan administrator of each plan covered under the supplemental guarantee program shall file Form PBGC-1 and pay the premium due, in accordance with the instructions accompanying the form, no later than the last day of the seventh month following the close of the prior plan year.

(c) *Change of plan year.* Notwithstanding paragraph (b) of this section, the plan administrator of a plan that is covered under the supplemental guarantee program and that changes its plan year, shall file Form PBGC-1 and pay the premium due for the short plan year, in accordance with the instructions accompanying the form, no later than the later of—

(1) The last day of the seventh month following the close of the short plan year; or

(2) 30 days after the date on which the amendment changing the plan year was adopted.

(d) *Non-payment of premium.* Except as provided in paragraphs (d)(1) and (d)(2), the failure of the plan administrator of a plan covered by the supplemental guarantee program to pay the full premium due under this part within the time limits prescribed in this section shall result in the cancellation of that plan's coverage under the program, in accordance with § 2691.7.

(1) *Non-payment of initial premium.* A plan has not satisfied the requirement for coverage under § 2691.4(a)(1) (filing a complete application), until it has paid the full initial premium due pursuant to this part.

(2) *Financial assistance.* Paragraph (d) of this section shall not apply to a premium that need not be paid pursuant to § 2693.6 of this part for a year in which the plan is receiving financial assistance under Part 2694 of this subchapter or financial assistance under section 4261 of the Act.

¶ 20,525D

(e) *Duration of obligation to pay premiums.* Premiums shall continue to accrue under this part for each plan year until the end of the plan year in which a multiemployer plan's coverage is cancelled in accordance with §2691.7 or §2695.2 of this subchapter or until the plan's assets are distributed in connection with the termination of the plan.

(f) *Contested premium amounts.* If PBGC determines that a plan has paid less than the full premium due under this part, it shall so notify the plan, as described in §2691.7(a) of this subchapter. The plan may appeal PBGC's determination pursuant to Part 2606 of this chapter. However, filing of an appeal shall not stay the effect of a notice of cancellation issued under §2691.7(a) of this subchapter.

§2693.4 Premium rate.

(a) *General.* A multiemployer plan shall pay for each plan year a premium to PBGC for coverage under the supplemental guarantee program in an amount equal to the product of—

(1) The number of individuals who were participants in the plan on the last day of the preceding plan year;

(2) The number of units of supplemental coverage in effect for the year, or for which the plan is applying; and

(3) The supplemental premium rate of $.30.

(b) *Short plan year.* For any plan that changes its plan year, the plan shall pay the applicable premium under paragraph (a) for each individual who is a participant in the plan on the last day of the short plan year.

§2693.5 Late entry fee.

(a) *General.* A multiemployer plan that fails to apply for initial coverage on or before the last day of the first plan year in which the plan satisfies the 15-year asset test set forth in §2691.3(a)(1) shall be presumptively liable for a late entry fee determined under this section. The late entry fee shall equal the total amount of the plan's missed premiums, determined under paragraph (b) of this section, plus interest, determined under paragraph (c) of this section, for each missed premium year. However, there is no missed premium due for any year in which the plan did not, in fact, satisfy all of the eligibility requirements in §2691.3(a), as demonstrated in accordance with paragraphs (b)(1) and (b)(2) of this section.

(b) *Computation of missed premiums.* Except as provided in paragraphs (b)(1), (b)(2) and (b)(3) of this section, the amount of the missed premium for each missed premium year is equal to the premium determined under §2693.4 of this part that would have been due had coverage been in effect for each missed premium year, based on the plan's Form PBGC-1 filed for that year and assuming coverage in each year of the lesser of one-half the number of units of supplemental coverage necessary to guarantee the maximum supplemental benefit under the plan as of the date the plan's application for coverage is filed, or the number of units of supplemental coverage actually necessary to guarantee the highest supplemental benefit for any participant in pay status under the plan as of the last day of that year, as demonstrated by the plan sponsor to the satisfaction of PBGC.

(1) There is no missed premium for any missed premium year if the plan sponsor demonstrates to the satisfaction of PBGC that, as of the last day of that plan year, the plan could not satisfy the plan solvency requirement described in §2691.3(a)(2).

(2) There is no missed premium for any missed premium year (and all prior missed premium years) if the plan sponsor demonstrates to the satisfaction of PBGC that there is no supplemental benefit payable with respect to any participant in pay status as of the last day of that year.

(3) There is no missed premium for any missed premium year if the plan filed a Form 5500-R or Form 5500-C for the preceding plan year.

(c) *Interest.* Interest shall accrue on the amount of the missed premium for each missed premium year from the last day of the year until the late entry fee is paid. Interest shall be at the rate prescribed in section 6621(b) of the Code and shall be compounded annually.

(d) *Contested amount.* In any case where the plan disputes PBGC's determination of the amount due under this section, the plan may appeal PBGC's determination pursuant to Part 2606 of this chapter. However, notwithstanding the filing of an appeal, a plan shall not be covered under the supplemental guarantee program until it has paid the late entry determined due by PBGC.

§2693.6 Premium for plan year during which plan receives financial assistance.

The premium due under this part need not be paid for any plan year during which a plan receives financial assistance from PBGC pursuant

to Part 2694 of this subchapter or section 4261 of the Act. Any premium not paid pursuant to this section shall be treated as financial assistance under Part 2694.

§2693.7 Overpayments.

(a) *Rejected applications.* If a plan files an application for coverage and pays its initial premium and late entry fee, if any, and thereafter PBGC rejects the application, PBGC shall refund to the plan the total amount paid.

(b) *Cancellation for material misrepresentation or mass withdrawal.* If PBGC cancels a plan's coverage under the supplemental guarantee program under §2691.7(b) (for a material misrepresentation) or under §2695.2(a) (for a mass withdrawal), the PBGC shall refund to the plan any amounts paid by the plan under the supplemental guarantee program for plan years beginning on or after the effective date of cancellation.

(c) *Erroneous computation by plan.* If a plan computes and pays an amount that exceeds the premium payment or late entry fee due under this part, PBGC shall refund to the plan the excess amount.

(d) *Contested amounts.* If a plan pays a premium or late entry fee and then appeals the amount of the premium or late entry fee pursuant to §2693.3(f) or §2693.5(d), respectively, and the decision on the appeal finds that there has been an overpayment, PBGC shall refund to the plan the excess amount, with interest at the rate specified in section 6621(b) of the Code from the date of the overpayment to the date of the refund.

§2693.8 Date of filling or payment.

Any form required to be filed and any payment required to be made under the provisions of this part shall be considered to have been filed or made on the date on which it is hand-delivered or mailed. A form or payment shall be presumed to have been mailed on the date on which it is postmarked by the United States Postal Service, or three days prior to the date on which it is received by the PBGC if it does not contain a legible United States Postal Service postmark.

§2693.9 Computations of time.

In computing any period of time under this part, the day of the act, event or default from which the designated period of time begins to run is not counted. The last day of the period so computed shall be included, unless it is a Saturday, Sunday or federal holiday, in which event the period runs until the end of the next day which is not a Saturday, Sunday or a federal holiday. For the purpose of computing interest under §2693.5, a Saturday, Sunday or federal holiday referred to in the previous sentence shall be included.

PART 2694—FINANCIAL ASSISTANCE

Authority: Secs. 4002(b)(3), 4022A(g)(2), Pub. L. 93-406, as amended by secs. 403(1) and 102 (respectively), Pub. L. 96-364, 94 Stat. 1302, 1214-15 (1980) (29 U.S.C. 1302, 1322a).

§2694.1 Purpose and scope.

(a) *Purpose.* The purpose of this part is to prescribe the rules for PBGC financial assistance to multiemployer plans covered by the supplemental guarantee program that are or will be insolvent and unable to pay when due supplemental benefits. This part establishes the procedure under which plan sponsors shall file an application for financial assistance with PBGC and the terms and conditions under which PBGC shall provide financial assistance.

(b) *Scope.* This part applies to multiemployer plans that are covered by the supplemental guarantee program and are or will be insolvent and unable to pay when due supplemental benefits.

§2694.2 Application for financial assistance.

A plan sponsor of a multiemployer plan covered by the supplemental guarantee program who determines that the plan is or will be insolvent and unable to pay supplemental benefits when due may apply to PBGC for financial assistance. Thereafter, the plan sponsor shall submit any information PBGC determines it needs to review the application.

§2694.3 PBGC action on application.

(a) *General.* If, upon receipt of an application for financial assistance under § 2694.2, PBGC verifies that the plan is insolvent and unable to pay supplemental benefits when due, PBGC shall provide the plan financial assistance in an amount sufficient to enable the plan to pay guaranteed supplemental benefits due under the plan.

(b) *PBGC decision.* PBGC's decision under this section approving or disapproving an application, in whole or in part, shall be in writing. If PBGC disapproves an application, in whole or in part, the decision shall state the reasons for the determination, include a statement of the plan's right to appeal the decision pursuant to Part 2606 of this chapter and state that the decision is effective on the date of issuance.

§ 2694.4 Financial assistance.

(a) *Terms and conditions.* Financial assistance shall be provided under such conditions as PBGC determines are equitable and are appropriate to prevent unreasonable loss to PBGC with respect to the plan.

(b) *Repayment.* A plan which has received financial assistance shall repay the amount of such assistance to PBGC on such reasonable terms and for such periods as PBGC deems equitable and appropriate in the particular case.

§ 2694.5 Interim financial assistance.

Pending determination of the proper amount of financial assistance under § 2694.3(a), PBGC may provide interim financial assistance in such amounts as it considers appropriate in order to avoid undue hardship to plan participants and beneficiaries.

§ 2694.6 Limitation on payment of supplemental benefits.

Notwithstanding §§ 2694.3(a) and 2694.5 of this part, PBGC shall provide financial assistance to pay supplemental benefits guaranteed under the supplemental guarantee program only to the extent that there is money available to do so in the supplemental guarantee program fund established under section 4005(e) of the Act.

§ 2694.7 Prohibition on changes in coverage.

A plan may not cancel or decrease its coverage under the supplemental guarantee program in a year during which the plan receives financial assistance under this part.

PART 2695—MASS WITHDRAWALS

Sec. 2695.1—Purpose and scope.

2695.2—Mass withdrawals.

Authority: Secs. 4002(b)(3), 4022A(g)(2), Pub. L. 93-406, as amended by secs. 403(1) and 102 (respectively), Pub. L. 96-364, 94 Stat. 1302, 1214-15 (1980) [29 U.S.C. 1302, 1322a].

§ 2695.1 Purpose and scope.

(a) *Purpose.* The purpose of this part is to prescribe special rules for multiemployer plans that are covered by the supplemental guarantee program that experience a mass withdrawal.

(b) *Scope.* This part applies to mass withdrawals, including a termination by mass withdrawal under section 4041A(a)(2) of the Act and the withdrawal of substantially all employers in a plan pursuant to an agreement or agreements to withdraw.

§ 2695.2 Mass withdrawals.

(a) *General rule.* PBGC shall cancel the coverage under the supplemental guarantee program of a multiemployer plan with respect to which there is a mass withdrawal if the mass withdrawal date occurs on or before the earlier of—

(1) The date on which the last collective bargaining agreement providing for employer contributions under the plan, which has an effective date on or after the plan's initial coverage date, expires; or

(2) Six years after the plan's initial coverage data.

(b) *Cancellation of coverage.* Cancellation shall be effective as of the last day of the plan year preceding the plan year in which PBGC notifies the plan that its coverage is cancelled. PBGC shall make a refund to the plan for any overpayment in accordance with § 2693.7(b) of this subchapter. If a plan's coverage is cancelled pursuant to this paragraph, it shall not be eligible to reapply for coverage.

(c) *PBGC decision.* PBGC's decision to cancel a plan's coverage under this section shall be in writing. PBGC's decision shall state the reasons for the determination, the date as of which the plan's coverage is cancelled, include a statement of the plan's right to appeal the decision pursuant to Part 2606 of this chapter and state that the decision is effective on the date of issuance.

Issued at Washington, D.C., this 26th day of January 1983.

Raymond Donovan,

Chairman, Board of Directors, Pension Benefit Guaranty Corporation.

Issued on the date set forth above, pursuant to a resolution of the Board of Directors authorizing its Chairman to issue this Notice of Proposed Rulemaking.

Henry Rose,

Secretary, Pension Benefit Guaranty Corporation.

[FR Doc. 83-2752 Filed 1-31-83; 8:45 am]

¶ 20,525E   Reserved.

Formerly reproduced at this paragraph were proposed regulations prescribing variances from the bond/escrow and sale of assets requirements that pertain to an employer who contributes to a multiemployer plan. The regulations were finalized and appear at ¶ 15,668A, 15,668B and 15,668J—15,668O.]

¶ 20,525F   Reserved.

Proposed regulations establishing the interest rate to be charged by multiemployer plans on overdue and defaulted withdrawal liability were formerly reproduced at this paragraph. The final regulations are at ¶ 15,687—15,687C.]

¶ 20,525G   Reserved.

Proposed regulations providing an alternative means to comply with the requirements of furnishing updated summary plan descriptions were formerly reproduced here. The proposed rules have been withdrawn. For the notice of withdrawal, see 49 FR 27954 (7/9/1984).]

¶ 20,525H

Proposed regulations on 29 CFR Part 2606.—Following is the text of proposed Pension Benefit Guaranty Corporation regulations relating to Administrative Review of Agency Decisions.

The proposed regulations were published in the *Federal Register* of May 18, 1983 (48 FR 22330).

PENSION BENEFIT GUARANTY CORPORATION

29 CFR Part 2606

¶ 20,525E

Rules for Administrative Review of Agency Decisions

AGENCY: Pension Benefit Guaranty Corporation.

ACTION: Proposed Rule

SUMMARY: The Pension Benefit Guaranty Corporation's regulation on Administrative Review of Agency Decisions sets forth the rules governing the issuance of certain initial determinations made by the Pension Benefit Guaranty Corporation (the "PBGC") and the procedures for requesting and obtaining administrative reviews by the PBGC of those determinations. This proposed amendment makes a number of modifications to the final regulation. The regulations, as the agency proposes to amend it, is reprinted in full for the convenience of the public. The modifications are being proposed to take into account agency experience during the three years this rule has been in effect. The amendments are intended to streamline the review process, clarify issues that have created confusion in the past, and modify the Appeals Board procedures to more effectively utilize the agency's resources. The amendments would also conform the regulation with the multiemployer Pension Plan Amendments Act of 1980.

DATE: Comments must be received on or before July 18, 1983.

ADDRESSES: Comments should be addressed to the Office of the General Counsel, Pension Benefit Guaranty Corporation, Suite 7200, 2020 K Street, N.W., Washington, D.C. 20006. Written comments will be available for public inspection at the PBGC, Suite 7100, at the above address, between the hours of 9:00 A.M. and 4:00 P.M. on regular business days.

FOR FURTHER INFORMATION CONTACT: Deborah West, Attorney, Office of the General Counsel, Pension Benefit Guaranty Corporation, 2020 K Street, N.W., Washington, D.C. 20006; (202) 254-3010. (This is not a toll-free number.)

SUPPLEMENTARY INFORMATION: On July 19, 1979, the PBGC published a final rule regarding administrative review of agency decisions (44 FR 42181). The purpose of the regulation was to ensure that persons who are adversely affected by certain determinations of the PBGC are provided with an opportunity to contest and to obtain review of those determinations. The current regulation applies to eleven types of determinations and provides for two types of agency review. Seven types of determinations are subject to appeal; four are subject to reconsideration. An Appeals Board was established to consider appeals. On April 25, 1983, the PBGC amended the regulation to change the composition of the Appeals Board, 48 FR 17070.

This proposal, if adopted would regulation in several ways. First, the formal reconsideration process under the regulation would be eliminated. This action is being proposed because the PBGC now believes a formal reconsideration procedure is unnecessary. The PBGC may informally reconsider determinations not subject to the regulation and will, of course, correct erroneous determinations, however discovered, without reference to the formal administrative review process. The amendment adds additional PBGC determinations to the list of determinations subject to administrative appeal. The regulation's provision concerning requests for assistance in obtaining information is modified in the proposed rule to make it clear that this provision applies to information in the possession of parties other than the PBGC and not to information available from the PBGC. The regulation is clarified to indicate that there is no appeal of determinations made final upon issuance.

The proposed rule provides that determinations regarding benefit entitlement of participants and beneficiaries under single employer plans (sections 4022(a) and (b), and 4022B of the Act) shall be effective upon issuance. The regulation's provision on late-filed appeals is changed to provide that such appeals shall be reviewed by the Appeals Board if the Board determines that good cause is shown for the late filing.

The amendment makes technical changes that are necessary to clarify the regulation by conforming the regulation to the Multiemployer Act. Finally, minor clarifying

Elimination of Reconsideration Process; Additional Determinations Subject to Administrative Appeal

The formal reconsideration process under the regulation is eliminated in this proposal. PBGC now believes a formal reconsideration procedure is unnecessary. The current dichotomy between appeals and reconsideration has proven cumbersome and confusing. Determinations not subject to appeal may be informally reconsidered on request, and, of course, the PBGC will correct erroneous determinations, however discovered, whether or not subject to appeal.

The proposed amendment adds a new item to the list of PBGC determinations subject to appeal: determinations under section 4022B of the Act regarding limitations on guaranteed benefit entitlement under single employer plans.

If the amendment is adopted, cases in which a determination was made prior to the regulation's effective date will be processed pursuant to the current administrative review procedure.

Appeals Board Jurisdiction

The proposed regulation provides, at §2606.3, that there shall be within the PBGC an Appeals Board to consider determinations listed as appealable at §2606.1(b) of the regulation, other than those determinations made final upon issuance under §2606.23(b). The Appeals Board shall consider, in reaching its decision, applicable law and policy, relevant facts, and equity.

PBGC Assistance in Obtaining Information

Section 2603.3 of the current regulation provides for PBGC assistance in obtaining information necessary to file an appeal (or necessary to a decision whether to file an appeal). This provision is intended to apply only to situations where the needed information is in the possession of a party other than the PBGC (for example, a bank or insurance company). Where the PBGC is in possession of relevant records, an appellant may make a request under the Freedom of Information Act or the Privacy Act. Thus, the provision, at §2606.4 of the proposed rule, is being modified so that it is clear that this provision applies only to information in the possession of parties other than the PBGC.

Effective Date of Determinations Under Sections 4022(a) and (b), and 4022B of the Act

Under the current regulation, the effective date of a determination that is subject to appeal and that is not made "immediately effective" under current §2606.23(b) is stayed until the Appeals Board disposition of the appeal. Thus, when a participant who is receiving a benefit in excess of the amount guaranteed by Title IV of the Act files an appeal, the current regulation obligates the PBGC to continue paying the higher benefits until the Appeals Board rules on the appeal. Often these excess amounts paid are not recovered by PBGC. The result is that plan assets are depleted, and a greater expenditure of PBGC's insurance funds is required. To alleviate this problem, the proposed regulation provides, at §2606.23, initial determinations of benefit amounts under sections 4022(a) and (b) and 4022B of the Act shall be effective upon issuance. Should the Appeals Board determine that an appellant is entitled to a greater amount than the PBGC initially determined, appellant will be reimbursed for underpayments made during the period after the plan terminated.

The PBGC believes that the likelihood of an erroneous determination is small. Moreover, the proposed regulation provides that the effective date of the determination regarding benefit entitlement under sections 4022(a) and (b) and 4022B of the Act may be stayed by the Appeals Board until the Board's disposition of the appeal. A temporary stay may be granted by the Appeals Board. Stays will be granted only where there exist extraordinary circumstances.

Review of Determinations Made Final on the Date of Issuance

Section 2606.23(b) of the current regulation provides that the PBGC may, in its discretion, make an initial determination "effective" on the date it is issued, and that, in such cases, there is no obligation to exhaust administrative remedies with respect to that determination by filing an appeal. As discussed above, the proposed regulation provides that PBGC benefit determinations are generally "effective" upon issuance. However, such determinations are still subject to Appeals Board review and thus even though effective immediately do not constitute the final agency action on the matter. To avoid confusion regarding terminology, the provision, renumbered §2606.24(b), is changed to provide that when the PBGC intends a decision to be final agency action, that determination is "final" on the date of issuance.

As the preamble to the current regulation noted, there may be cases where it is warranted to make a determination final immediately. However, the preamble to the final regulation stated that "administrative review of the determination would still be available to the person if he or she requests it." The PBGC believes it necessary to clarify this statement. This statement does not mean that an administrative appeal is available. The words "administrative review" nean that the PBGC may informally review a determination under current §2606.23(b), but would not stay the decision pending review. The same factors that lead the PBGC to make a determination final upon issuance will normally require that the delay resulting from the appeals process be avoided. Accordingly, in appropriate cases, PBGC will make a determination final upon issuance, eliminating Appeals Board review. To make this clear, the proposed amendment stated that there is no PBGC Appeals Board review of determinations that are made final on the date of issuance.

Nothing in the proposed regulation is intended to limit settlement discussions between the PBGC and the aggrieved party even while an appeal is pending. PBGC proposes to amend the regulation to state (1), at §2606.23(b), that determinations under that subsection are final upon issuance, and (2) at §2606.3, that the Appeals Board has no jurisdiction over such determinations. This is consistent with PBGC's regulation on employer liability for single employer plan terminations, which provides, at 29 CFR 2622.9(c), that there is no right to appeal the assessment of liability when a determination is made "immediately effective."

Finally, no determination issued by the Executive Director is subject to appeal under this part.

Non-timely Requests for Review

The current regulation provides that the PBGC will process a late-filed appeal if (1) the person requesting review demonstrates in his or her request that he or she did not file a timely appeal because he or she neither knew nor could have known of the initial determination, and (2) the appeal was filed within 45 days of the date the person first learned of the initial determination. The proposed regulation provides, at §2606.36, that late-filed appeals, i.e., appeals filed after the 45-day appeals period plus any additional time granted by the Appeals Board pursuant to §2606.35, may be processed if the Appeals Board determines that good cause is shown for the late filing.

Record Before the Appeals Board

The present regulation does not provide for a uniform method by which appellants may fully understand the basis for a disputed initial determination. The proposed regulation would add such a procedure. It provides that the Appeals Board shall serve the appeal upon the office within the PBGC that issued the disputed initial determination. The office shall, within 30 days, compile and submit to the Board a copy of the initial determination and any other documents which the office believes are necessary to support the initial determination. The office may also submit supporting statements within this 30 day period.

The Appeals Board shall then send all material submitted by the office to the appellant except such material as the appellant has already been provided. The appellant must file any response to the material within 15 days of the date of the Appeals Board letter transmitting the material. This change, then, is to ensure that all appellants have an opportunity to review and comment upon the records relied upon by the PBGC in making its initial determination.

Changes Due to the Enactment of the Multiempioyer Pension Plan Amendments Act of 1980

Certain technical changes in the regulation are being made to conform the citations in the regulation to the proper section numbers of the Employee Retirement Income Security Act of 1974, as amended by the Multiemployer Act.

The regulation currently provides that determinations with respect to benefit entitlement under a plan under section 4022(a) and determinations of the amount of guaranteed benefits under section 4022(b) are subject to appeal. The Multiemployer Act added a new section on rules for aggregate limits on guaranteed benefits (section 4022B), which rules are essentially those previously contained in section 4022(b)(5). Accordingly, the proposed regulation authorizes appeal of determinations under section 4022B by the PBGC regarding limitations on guaranteed benefit entitlement under a covered single employer plan.

The regulation currently provides that coverage determinations under section 4082(b) of ERISA are subject to administrative review. Under the Multiemployer Act, section 4082(b) is redesignated as section 4402(b). The proposed rcgulation makes the necessary conforming changes.

Other Changes

Nonsubstantive clarifying changes were made in the language of several sections. To accommodate the changes discussed above and to make the regulation clearer and more useful to the public, the regulation has been reorganized. The subpart on reconsiderations has been deleted, along with all other references to reconsideration.

The Pension Benefit Guaranty Corporation has determined that this regulation is not a "major rule" for the purposes of Executive Order 12291, because it will not have an annual effect on the economy of $100 million or more; or create a major increase in costs or prices for consumers, individual industries, or geographic regions; or have significant adverse effects on competition, employment, investment, innovation, or on the ability of United States-based enterprises to compete with foreign-based enterprises in domestic or export markets. This conclusion is based on the fact that this regulation is merely a procedural regulation which provides an administrative appeal route for aggrieved persons so that they may avoid, in certain instances, expensive federal court litigation.

Under section 605(b) of the Regulatory Flexibility Act, the Pension Benefit Guaranty Corporation certifies that this rule will not have a significant economic impact on a substantial number of small entities. The reason for this certification is that the rule is essentially procedural in nature. In addition, this regulation will have little or no adverse economic impact on small entities and will, in many cases, substantially lessen the financial burden of contesting agency action in expensive court proceedings by providing an avenue for expediting inexpensive administrative review. Therefore compliance with sections 603 and 604 of the Regulatory Flexibility Act is waived.

Interested parties are invited to submit comments on this proposed regulation. Comments should be addressed to: Deborah West, Office of the General Counsel, Pension Benefit Guaranty Corporation (240), Suite 7200, 2020 K Street, NW., Washington, D.C. 20006. Written comments will be available for public inspection at the above address, Suite 7100, between the hours of 9:00 a.m. and 4:00 p.m. Each person submitting comments should include his or her name and address, identify this proposed regulation, and give reasons for any recommendation. This proposal may be changed in light of the comments received.

For the convenience of the public and to have the entire proposed amended rule in one place, the regulation is being reprinted below in its entirety.

List of Subjects in 29 CFR Part 2606

Administrative practice and procedure, Conflict of interests, Penalties.

In consideration of the foregoing, the PBGC proposes to amend Chapter XXVI of Title 29, Code of Federal Regulations, by revising Part 2606 as follows:

PART 2606—RULES FOR ADMINISTRATIVE REVIEW OF AGENCY DECISIONS

Subpart A—General Provisions

Sec.

2606.1	Purpose and scope.
2606.2	Definitions.
2606.3	Appeals Board jurisdiction.
2606.4	PBGC assistance in obtaining information.
2606.5	Representation.
2606.6	Request for confidential treatment.
2606.7	Exhaustion of administrative remedies.

Subpart B—Determinations

2606.21	Purpose and scope.
2606.22	Form and contents of determinations.
2606.23	Effective date of determinations; final agency action.

Subpart C—Administrative Appeals

2606.31	Purpose and scope.
2606.32	Who may appeal or participate in appeals.
2606.33	When to file.
2606.34	Filing of documents.
2606.35	Extension of time.
2606.36	Non-timely request for review.
2606.37	Computation of time.
2606.38	Contents of appeal.
2606.39	Record before the Appeals Board.
2606.40	Opportunity to appear and to present witnesses.
2606.41	Consolidation of appeals.
2606.42	Appeals affecting third parties.
2606.43	Powers of the Appeals Board.
2606.44	Decision by the Appeals Board.
2606.45	Referral of appeal to the Executive Director.

Authority: Sec. 4002(b)(3), Pub. L. 93-406, as amended by Sec. 403(1), Pub. L. 96-364, 94 Stat. 1208, 1302 (1980) (29 U.S.C. 1302(b)(3)).

Subpart A—General Provisions

§ 2606.1 Purpose and scope.

(a) *Purpose.* This part sets forth the rules governing the issuance of all determinations issued on or after the effective date of this part by the PBGC involving the matters set forth in paragraph (b) of this section and the procedures for requesting and obtaining administrative review by the PBGC of those determinations.

(b) *Scope.* This part applies to the following determinations made by the PBGC on or after the effective date of this part and to the review of those determinations:

(1) Determinations that a plan is not covered under section 4021 or section 4402(b) of the Act;

(2) Determinations under section 4022(a) of the Act with respect to benefit entitlement of participants and beneficiaries under covered single employer plans;

(3) Determinations regarding the amount of guaranteed benefits of participants and beneficiaries under covered single employer plans under sections 4022(b) or 4022B of the Act;

(4) Determinations of the amount of money subject to recapture pursuant to section 4045 of the Act;

(5) Determinations of the amount of employer liability under section 4062 of the Act;

(6) Determinations of the amount of contingent liability under section 4063 of the Act;

(7) Determinations of the amount of employer liability under section 4064 of the Act;

(c) *Determinations not covered by this part.* Nothing contained in this part shall limit the authority of the PBGC to review informally, either upon request or on its own motion, determinations that are not subject to this part when the PBGC determines, in its discretion, that it is appropriate to do so.

§ 2606.2 Definitions.

As used in this part:

"Act" means the Employee Retirement Income Security Act of 1974, as amended.

"Aggrieved person" means any participant, beneficiary, plan administrator, plan sponsor, or employer, adversely affected by a determination of the PBGC covered by this part with respect to a pension plan in which such participant, beneficiary, plan administrator, plan sponsor, or employer has an interest. The term "employer" includes all trades and businesses under common control within the meaning of Part 2612 of this chapter, and all employers who contribute to or have contributed to a pension plan to which more than one employer contributes.

"Appeals Board" means a board consisting of a Chairperson appointed by the Executive Director of the PBGC and two senior agency officials appointed by the Executive Director to serve as regular members. Other senior agency officials may serve as alternate members in the event that a regular member is not available to serve or is unable to serve. Such alternates may be appointed pursuant to a list designated by the Executive Director and shall serve in the order designated in that list. The General Counsel, and the Executive Director or the Deputy Executive Director, in the absence of the Executive Director, shall be ex officio members of the Appeals Board. The General Counsel may, as an ex officio member of the Appeals Board, if he or she chooses, vote on any matter before the Board. Appeals shall be decided by a majority vote of the Board members, but if the General Counsel's vote on an appeal results in a tie vote, the appeal shall be referred to the Executive Director as specified in § 2606.45. The Executive Director may designate the Deputy Executive Director to decide any appeal referred to the Executive Director from the Appeals Board under this section in accordance with § 2606.45. A person may not serve on the Appeals Board with respect to any case in which he or she made a determination with respect to the merits of the determination subject to appeal.

"Appellant" means any person filing an appeal under Subpart C of this part.

"PBGC" means the Pension Benefit Guaranty Corporation.

§ 2606.3 Appeals Board jurisdiction.

There shall be within the Pension Benefit Guaranty Corporation an Appeals Board to consider administrative appeals from determinations listed at § 2606.1(b), other than those determinations made final upon issuance under § 2606.23(b) of this part.

§ 2606.4 PBGC assistance in obtaining information.

A person who lacks information or documents necessary to file an appeal pursuant to Subpart C of this part, or necessary to a decision whether to seek review, or necessary to participate in an appeal pursuant to § 2606.42 of this part, or necessary to a decision whether to participate, may request the Appeals Board's assistance in obtaining the information or documents when the information or documents are in the possession of a party other than the PBGC. The request shall state or describe the missing information or data, the reason why the person needs the information or documents, and the reason why the person needs the assistance of the Appeals Board in obtaining the

information or documents. The request may also include a request for an extension of time to file an appeal pursuant to § 2606.35 of this part.

§ 2606.5 Representation.

A person may file any document or make any appearance that is required or permitted by this part on his or her own behalf or he or she may designate a representative. When the representative is not an attorney-at-law, a notarized power of attorney signed by the person making the designation authorizing the representation shall be filed with the Appeals Board in accordance with § 2606.34(b) of this part.

§ 2606.6 Request for confidential treatment.

If any person filing a document with the Appeals Board believes that some or all of the information contained in the document is exempt from the mandatory public disclosure requirements of the Freedom of Information Act, 5 U.S.C. § 552, and wishes such material to be withheld by the PBGC, he or she shall specify the information with respect to which he or she requests confidentiality and the grounds therefore.

§ 2606.7 Exhaustion of administrative remedies.

Except as provided in § 2606.23(b), a person aggrieved by a determination of the PBGC covered by this part has not exhausted his or her administrative remedies until he or she has filed an appeal under Subpart C of this part, and a decision granting or denying the relief requested has been issued.

Subpart B—Determinations

§ 2606.21 Purpose and scope.

This subpart sets forth rules governing the issuance of determinations of the PBGC on matters covered by this part.

§ 2606.22 Form and contents of determinations.

All determinations to which this part applies shall be in writing and shall state the reason for the determination. All determinations to which this part applies, other than determinations made final upon issuance under § 2606.23(b) of this part, shall include notice of the right to request review of the determination pursuant to Subpart C of this part and a brief description of the procedures review.

§ 2606.23 Effective date of determinations; final action.

(a) *General rule.* Except as provided in Paragraph (c) of this section, determinations regarding benefit entitlement under sections 4022(a) and (b), and 4022B of the Act shall be effective upon issuance. Except as provided in Paragraph (b) of this section, all determinations covered by this part will not become final until the prescribed period of time for filing an appeal under Subpart C of this part has elapsed, or if an appeal is filed, until the date of the Appeals Board decision regarding the appeal.

(b) *Exception.* The PBGC may, in its discretion, order that a determination is final on the date it is issued. When the PBGC makes such an order, the determination shall state that it is the final agency action with respect to the matter.

(c) *Stay.* The Appeals Board may order that the effective date of a determination regarding benefit entitlement or amount under sections 4022(a) and (b), and 4022B of the Act be stayed until the Appeals Board disposition of the appeal. Such an order may provide for complete or partial relief from the immediate implementation of the determination. A temporary stay may be granted by the Appeals Board.

Subpart C—Administrative Appeals

§ 2606.31 Purpose and Scope.

This subpart establishes procedures governing administrative appeals to the Appeals Board from determinations relating to the matters set forth in § 2606.1(b) of this part, other than those determinations made final upon issuance under § 2606.23(b) of this part.

§ 2606.32 Who may appeal or participate in appeals.

Any person aggrieved by a determination of the PBGC to which this subpart applies may file an appeal. Any person who will be aggrieved by a decision of the Appeals Board under this part granting the relief requested in whole or in part may participate in the appeal as provided in § 2606.42.

§ 2606.33 When to file.

Except as provided in § § 2606.35 and 2606.36, an appeal under this subpart must be filed within 45 days after the date of the determination being appealed.

§ 2606.34 Filing of documents.

(a) *Date of filing.* Any document required or permitted to be filed under this part is considered filed on the date of the United States postmark stamped on the cover in which the document is mailed, provided that the document was mailed postage prepaid properly packaged and addressed to the Appeals Board. If these conditions are not met, the document is considered filed on the date it is received by the PBGC. Documents received after regular business hours are considered filed on the next regular business day.

(b) *Where to file.* Any document required or permitted to be filed under this part in connection with an appeal shall be submitted to the Appeals Board, Pension Benefit Guaranty Corporation, 2020 K Street, N.W., Washington, D.C. 20006.

§ *2606.35 Extension of time.*

When a document is required under this part to be filed within a prescribed period of time, an extension of time to file will be granted only upon good cause shown. The request for an extension of time shall be filed before the expiration of the time prescribed. The request for an extension shall be in writing and shall state why additional time is needed and the amount of additional time requested. The filing of a request for an extension shall stop the running of the prescribed period of time. When a request for an extension is granted, the Appeals Board shall notify the person requesting the extension, in writing, of the amount of additional time granted. When a request for an extension is denied, the Appeals Board shall so notify the requestor in writing, and the prescribed period of time shall resume running from the date of the letter denying the request. A request for an extension of time that is filed after the expiration of the time prescribed shall be considered only if good cause is shown for the late filing.

§ *2606.36 Non-timely request for review.*

The Appeals Board shall process a request for review of a determination that was not filed within the prescribed period of time for requesting review in § 2606.33 if the Board, in its discretion, determines that good cause is shown for the late filing.

§ *2606.37 Computation of time.*

In computing any period of time prescribed or allowed by this part, the day of the act, event, or default from which the designated period of time begins to run is not counted. The last day of the period so computed shall be included, unless it is a Saturday, Sunday, or Federal holiday, in which event the period runs until the end of the next day which is not a Saturday, Sunday, or a Federal holiday.

§ *2606.38 Contents of appeal.*

(a) An appeal shall—

(1) Be in writing;

(2) Be designated as an appeal;

(3) Contain a statement of the grounds upon which it is brought and the relief sought;

(4) Reference all pertinent information known to be in the possession of the PBGC; and

(5) Include any additional information believed to be relevant.

(b) In any case where the appellant believes that another person may be aggrieved if the PBGC grants the relief sought, the appeal shall also include the name(s) and address(es), if known, of such other person(s).

§ *2606.39 Record before the Appeals Board.*

(a) Upon receipt of an appeal, the Appeals Board shall furnish a copy of the appeal to the office of the PBGC that issued the initial determination. The office shall compile and submit to the Board within 30 days a copy of the initial determination being appealed and a copy of any other documents which the office believes are necessary to support the initial determination. Supporting statements may accompany such material.

(b) All material submitted by the office pursuant to subsection (a) except that already provided to appellant shall be sent to appellant and to any person identified under § 2606.42 for response. Appellant and any third party under § 2606.42 shall file any response to the material submitted by the office with the Appeals Board within 30 days of the date of the letter transmitting the material.

(c) The Chairperson may, upon good cause shown, extend the time limits in paragraphs (a) and (b) of this section.

§ *2606.40 Opportunity to appear and to present witnesses.*

(a) An opportunity to appear before the Appeals Board and an opportunity to present witnesses may be permitted at the discretion of the Appeals Board.

(b) Appearances permitted under this section will take place at the main offices of the PBGC, 2020 K Street, N.W., Washington, D.C., unless the Appeals Board, in its discretion, designates a different location.

(c) An appearance permitted under this subpart may be before a hearing officer designated by the Appeals Board.

§ *2606.41 Consolidation of appeals.*

(a) *When consolidation may be required.* Whenever multiple appeals are filed that arise out of the same or similar facts and seek the same or similar relief, the Appeals Board may, in its discretion, order the consolidation of all or some of the appeals.

(b) *Decision by Appeals Board.* The decision of the Appeals Board in a consolidated appeal shall be binding on all appellants whose appeals were consolidated.

§ *2606.42 Appeals affecting third parties.*

(a) When the Appeals Board makes a preliminary finding that the relief requested in an appeal should be granted in whole or in part, before issuing a decision the Board shall make a reasonable effort to notify third persons who will be aggrieved by the decision of the pendency of the appeal, of the grounds upon which the Appeals Board is considering reversing the initial determination, of the right to submit written comments on the appeal, and that no further opportunity to present information to the PBGC with respect to the determination under appeal will be provided.

(b) Written comments and a request to appear before the Appeals Board must be filed within 45 days after the date of the notice from the Appeals Board.

(c) Appellant shall be notified of material submitted by any third party under this section. Such material, to the extent permitted by law, will be made available to appellant upon request.

(d) If more than one third party is involved, their participation in the appeal may be consolidated pursuant to § 2606.41.

§ *2606.43 Powers of the Appeals Board.*

In addition to the powers specifically described in this part, the Appeals Board, in its discretion, may cause additional information to be obtained, may request the submission of any information or the appearance of any person it considers necessary to resolve a matter before it and may enter any order it considers necessary for or appropriate to the disposition of any matter before it.

§ *2606.44 Decision by the Appeals Board.*

(a) In reaching its decision, the Appeals Board shall consider those portions of the PBGC file relating to the issues raised by the appeal, material submitted by the appellant and third parties in connection with the appeal, and written statements or documents, if any, filed with the Appeal Board that are made available to the appellant.

(b) The decision of the Appeals Board constitutes the final agency action with respect to the determination which was the subject of the appeal and is binding on all parties who participated in the appeal and on all parties who were notified pursuant to § 2606.42 of their right to participate in the appeal.

(c) The decision of the Appeals Board shall be in writing, specify the relief granted, if any, state the reasons for the decision, and state that the appellant has exhausted his or her administrative remedies.

§ *2606.45 Referral of appeal to the Executive Director.*

If the Appeals Board finds that an appeal presents a major unresolved policy issue for the PBGC, the Appeals Board shall refer such appeal to the Executive Director of the PBGC for appropriate action. The Executive Director may designate the Deputy Executive Director to decide any appeal referred to the Executive Director from the Appeals Board under this section. When acting on appeals which are referred by the Appeals Board under this section or § 2606.02, the Executive Director and the Deputy Executive Director shall have, in addition to all the powers vested in their offices, all the powers vested in the Appeals Board by this part. The decision of the Executive Director or the Deputy Executive Director shall meet the requirements of and have the effect of a decision issued under § 2606.44 of this part.

Issued this 13th day of May, 1983.

Charles C. Tharp,

Acting Executive Director, Pension Benefit Guaranty Corporation

[FR Doc. 83-13284 Filed 5-17-83 8:45 am]

¶ 20,525I   Reserved.

Formerly reproduced at this paragraph were proposed regulations prescribing rules and procedures for the arbitration of disputes between employers and multiemployer plan sponsors concerning employer withdrawal liability under ERISA. The regulations were finalized and appear at ¶ 15,663C and ¶ 15,689A—15,689M.]

¶ 20,525J   Reserved.

Formerly reproduced at this paragraph were proposed amendments to PBGC regulations governing the events that require notice to the PBGC. The regulations were finalized and appear at ¶ 15,461, 15,461C, 15,463B, 15,463C and 15,464.]

¶ 20,525K   Reserved.

Formerly reproduced at this paragraph were proposed regulations relating to the reduction or waiver of the liability of an employer that has withdrawn completely from a multiemployer plan. The final PBGC regulations are at ¶ 15,663F and 15,671A—15,671H.]

¶ 20,525L   Reserved.

Formerly reproduced at this paragraph were proposed DOL regulations relating to the definition of plan assets. The final regulations appear at ¶ 14,139M and 14,876.]

¶ 20,525M   Reserved.

Formerly reproduced at this paragraph were proposed PBGC regulations relating to the powers and duties of a sponsor of a plan that has terminated by mass withdrawal. The regulations were finalized and appear at ¶ 15,715A—15,715Z and 15,718D-2.]

¶ 20,525N   Reserved.

Proposed regulations relating to an increase in the Pension Benefit Guaranty Corporation's fees for document search and duplication under the Freedom of Information Act were formerly reproduced at this paragraph. The final regulation is at ¶ 15,322.]

¶ 20,525O   Reserved.

A proposed regulation defining the terms "amount involved" and "correction" as used in the assessment of civil penalties under ERISA against parties in interest who engage in a prohibited transaction with certain employee benefit plans was formerly reproduced at this paragraph. The final regulation is at ¶ 14,926.]

¶ 20,525P   Reserved.

Proposed regulations that set forth procedures for the imposition of civil sanctions under ERISA against parties in interest who engaged in prohibited transactions involving welfare plans and unqualified pension plans were formerly reproduced here. The final regulations are reproduced at ¶ 14,928.]

¶ 20,525Q   Reserved.

Proposed Reg. §§ 2613.2, 2613.8, 2617.4, and 2619.26, relating to the limit on benefit amounts that may be paid in a form other than an annuity, were formerly reproduced at this point. The final regulations appear at ¶ 15,422, 15,428, 15,447C, and 15,620I.]

¶ 20,525R   Reserved.

Proposed regulations necessary to conform existing regulations to proposed revisions to the annual return/report forms (Form 5500 series) filed by administrators of employee pension and welfare benefit plans were formerly reproduced here.

The final regulations are at ¶ 14,231A, ¶ 14,231B, ¶ 14,231F, ¶ 14,231J, ¶ 14,247B, ¶ 14,247C, ¶ 14,247U, ¶ 14,247Z, ¶ 14,248B, ¶ 14,248C and ¶ 14,249H.]

¶ 20,525S   Reserved.

EEOC proposed Reg. § 1625.21, relating to the cessation of contributions and accruals to pension plans for employees who continue to work beyond normal retirement age, was formerly reproduced here. The EEOC had been ordered to issue the proposed rule by the U.S. District Court. However, the U.S. Court of Appeals reversed that decision. Because the EEOC felt that the proposal should become effective for plan years beginning after January 1, 1988, and rules under the Omnibus Budget Reconciliation Act of 1986 (P.L. 99-509) superseded the provisions of ADEA Sec. 4(f)(2) under which Reg. § 1625.21 was promulgated, the EEOC terminated and withdrew the notice of proposed rulemaking.]

¶ 20,526 Reserved.

Reg. §§ 2550.407d-5, 2550.407d-6, and 2550.408d-3, relating to employee stock ownership plans, were formerly reproduced at this point.

The final regulations are at ¶ 14,776E, ¶ 14,776F, and ¶ 14,783.]

¶ 20,526A Reserved.

Proposed amendment to 29 CFR Part 2610 on rates and factors used for valuing plan benefits for plans that terminated on or after June 1, 1977, but before December 1, 1977, was formerly reproduced at this point. The final regulation was at ¶ 15,620L. 29 CFR Part 2610 was later completely revised effective April 1, 1981. Under the revised regulations, the rates and factors used for valuation are at ¶ 15,620Z.]

¶ 20,526B Reserved.

Proposed amendment to 29 CFR Part 2610 on rates and factors used for valuing plan benefits for plans that terminated on or after December 1, 1977, but before March 1, 1978, was formerly reproduced at this point.

The final regulation was at ¶ 15,620L. 29 CFR Part 2610 was later completely revised effective April 1, 1981. Under the revised regulations, the rates and factors used for valuation are at ¶ 15,620Z.]

¶ 20,526C Reserved.

Proposed amendment to 29 CFR Part 2610 on rates and factors used for valuing plan benefits for plans that terminated on or after March 1, 1978, but before June 1, 1978, was formerly reproduced at this point.

The final regulation was at ¶ 15,620L. 29 CFR Part 2610 was later completely revised effective April 1, 1981. Under the revised regulations, the rates and factors used for valuation are at ¶ 15,620Z.]

¶ 20,526D Reserved.

Proposed amendments to 29 CFR Part 2618 on rules for administrative review of agency decisions were formerly reproduced at this point.

The final regulations appear at ¶ 15,325.]

¶ 20,526E Reserved.

Proposed amendments to 29 CFR Part 2618 on rules for administrative review of agency decisions were formerly reproduced at this point.

The final regulations appear at ¶ 15,325.]

¶ 20,526F Reserved.

Proposed amendment to 29 CFR Part 2610 on rates and factors used for valuing plan benefits for plans that terminated on or after September 1, 1978, but before March 1, 1979, was formerly reproduced at this point.

The final regulation was at ¶ 15,620L. 29 CFR Part 2610 was later completely revised effective April 1, 1981. Under the revised regulations, the rates and factors used for valuation are at ¶ 15,620Z.

¶ 20,526G Reserved.

Proposed amendments to interim regulations that establish new mortality rates for disabled plan participants under 29 CFR Part 2610 were formerly reproduced at this point.

The amended interim regulations were at ¶ 15,620L. However, 29 CFR Part 2610 was later completely revised effective April 1, 1981. Under the revised regulations, the mortality tables for disabled plan participants are at ¶ 15,620Z.]

¶ 20,526H Reserved.

¶20,526

Proposed regulations relating to a revised method of filing a Notice of Intent to Terminate a pension plan were formerly reproduced at this paragraph.

The regulations, which were originally proposed as Reg. §§ 2604.1—2604.6, have been finalized and redesignated as Reg. §§ 2616.1—2616.7. The final regulations are reproduced at ¶ 15,441—15,446A.]

¶ 20,526I   Reserved.

Proposed regulations to 29 CFR 2520, relating to reporting and disclosure requirements for certain simplified employee pension plans other than those created by use of Internal Revenue Service Form 5305-SEP, were formerly reproduced here. The final regulations appear at ¶ 14,247ZC.]

¶ 20,526J   Reserved.

Proposed regulations relating to the definition of "assets" of an employee benefit plan under ERISA were formerly reproduced here. The proposed rules were withdrawn.

¶ 20,526K   Reserved.

Proposed regulations relating to the maintenance of indicia of ownership of plan assets outside the jurisdiction of the district courts of the United States were formerly reproduced at this point.

The final regulations are at ¶ 14,743.]

¶ 20,526L

Proposed regulations on 29 CFR Parts 2520 and 2530.—Reproduced below is the text of proposed regulations, applicable to certain multiple employer pension plans, which deal with reports that must be furnished to participants regarding their benefit entitlements and records that must be maintained to provide the information necessary for these reports.

The proposed regulations were published in the *Federal Register* on August 8, 1980 (45 FR 52824).

DEPARTMENT OF LABOR

Office of Pension and Welfare Benefit Programs

29 CFR Parts 2520 and 2530

Rules and Regulations for Reporting and Disclosure and Minimum Standards for Employee Pension Benefit Plans; Individual Benefit Reporting and Recordkeeping for Multiple Employer Plans

AGENCY: Department of Labor.

ACTION: Proposed rulemaking.

SUMMARY: This document contains proposed regulations, applicable to certain multiple employer pension plans, which deal with reports that must be furnished to participants in such plans (and, in some cases, to their beneficiaries) regarding their benefit entitlements, and with records that must be maintained to provide the information necessary for these reports. The Employee Retirement Income Security Act of 1974 (the Act) authorizes the Secretary of Labor to prescribe regulations regarding individual benefit reporting to participants and beneficiaries and individual benefit recordkeeping. The proposed regulations, if adopted, would provide necessary guidance to employers maintaining certain multiple employer pension plans and to plan administrators of such plans, and would enable participants in such plans to receive accurate, timely and useful information.

DATES: Written comments and requests for a public hearing must be received by the Department of Labor (the Department) on or before October 7, 1980. These regulations, if adopted, would generally become effective 120 days after adoption. However, with respect to collectively bargained multiple employer plans, the regulations would not become effective until nine months after the expiration of current collective bargaining agreements (but in no case more than 45 months after adoption).

ADDRESSES: Written comments (preferably three copies) should be submitted to the Division of Reporting and Disclosure, Pension and Welfare Benefit Programs, Room N-4508, U.S. Department of Labor, Washington, D.C. 20216. Attention: Multiple Employer Individual Benefit Reporting and Recordkeeping Regulations. All comments should be clearly referenced to the section of the regulations to which they apply. All written comments will be available for public inspection at the Public Documents Room, Pension and Welfare Benefit Programs, Department of Labor, Room N-4677, 200 Constitution Avenue, NW., Washington, D.C. 20216.

FOR FURTHER INFORMATION CONTACT: Mary O. Lin, Plan Benefits Security Division, Office of the Solicitor, U.S. Department of Labor, Washington, D.C. 20210, (202) 523-9595, or Joseph L. Roberts III, Pension and Welfare Benefit Programs, U.S. Department of Labor, Washington, D.C. 20216, (202) 523-8685. (These are not toll-free numbers.)

SUPPLEMENTARY INFORMATION: Notice is hereby given that the Department of Labor has under consideration proposed regulations applicable to multiple employer pension plans[1] dealing with reports that must be furnished to individual participants (and, in some cases, to their beneficiaries) regarding their benefit entitlements under employee pension benefit plans, and with records that must be maintained to provide the information necessary for these reports. These regulations are proposed under the authority contained in sections 105, 209 and 505 of the Act (Pub. L. 93-406, 88 Stat. 849, 865 and 894, 29 U.S.C. 1025, 1059 and 1135). Parallel regulations relative to single employer plans[2] have already been proposed (45 FR 51231, August 1, 1980).

The Department has determined that these proposed regulations are "significant" within the meaning of Department of Labor guidelines (44 FR 5570, January 26, 1979) issued to implement Executive Order (44 FR 12661, March 24, 1978).

Statutory Provisions

Section 105(a) of the Act generally requires each administrator of an employee pension benefit plan to furnish to any plan participant or beneficiary who so requests in writing, a statement indicating, on the basis of the latest available information, the total benefits accrued and the nonforfeitable pension benefits which have accrued, if any, or the earliest date on which such benefits will become nonforfeitable. Similarly, section 209(a)(1) of the Act generally requires the plan administrator of a plan subject to Part 2 of Title I of the Act to make a report, in accordance with regulations of the Secretary of Labor, to each employee who is a participant under the plan and who requests such report. The report required under section 209(a)(1) must be sufficient to inform the employee of his accrued benefits which are nonforfeitable. Under both sections 105(a) and 209(a)(1), no participant is enti-

---

[1] The term "multiple employer plan" is defined in the proposed regulation to mean a plan adopted by more than one employer other than a plan maintained by employers under common control. In discussions of the proposal throughout this document, the term "multiple employer plan" generally should be read to be consistent with this definition.

[2] The term "single employer plan" has been defined in such proposal to include plans maintained by a group of employers under common control. Throughout this document the term "single employer plan" generally should be read to be consistent with his definition.

tled to more than one report on request during any single 12-month period. Section 209(a) also requires similar reports to be provided to a participant who terminates service with the employer or has a one-year break in service. Sections 105(d) and 209(a)(2) authorize the Secretary of Labor to prescribe regulations specifying the extent to which these reporting requirements apply to plans adopted by more than one employer. In addition, section 105(c) of the Act requires plan administrators to provide to participants with respect to whom registration statements are filed with the Internal Revenue Service under section 6057 of the Internal Revenue Code of 1954 (the Code) individual statements setting forth the information contained in the registration statements.

In order to enable employees' benefits to be determined, so that the reporting requirements of section 209 can be met, section 209(a)(1) generally requires records to be maintained by employers and authorizes the Secretary of Labor to prescribe regulations governing such recordkeeping. The information necessary for individual benefit reporting is to be furnished by the employer to the plan administrator. In the case of a plan adopted by more than one employer, however, section 209(a)(2) requires records to be maintained by the plan administrator, based on information to be provided by each such employer.

Background

On February 9, 1979 (44 FR 8294), the Department published proposed regulations with respect to individual benefit statements and recordkeeping (referred to herein as "the 1979 proposal"). These regulations would have applied both to single and multiple employer plans. A large number of public comments on the 1979 proposal were filed. Many of these comments suggested that substantial revisions should be made in the 1979 proposal. Comments filed on behalf of single and multiple employer plans raised distinct issues.

Upon consideration of those comments, the Department decided to withdraw the 1979 proposal and to propose separately regulations pertaining to single employer plans and to multiple employer plans. On August 1, 1980, (45 FR 51231), the Department published a document which withdrew the 1979 proposal and which contained new proposed regulations applicable only to single employer plans. That document also contained general provisions with respect to recordkeeping and individual benefit statement requirements. In addition, the Department announced in that document that proposed regulations dealing with multiple employer plans would be published in the **Federal Register** in the future. Accordingly, the regulations now being proposed contain provisions which pertain only to multiple employer plans. Many of these provisions are similar to the proposed regulations pertaining to single employer plans. As a result, many of the same considerations are applicable to these proposed regulations as were applicable to the single employer plan regulations. Although the discussion of the multiple employer plan regulations in this preamble is to a certain extent duplicative of the discussion in the preamble of the single employer proposal, the multiple employer plan regulations are discussed here in full in order to avoid making it necessary to refer to the single employer document for a discussion of the regulations proposed in this document.

Of the regulations now being proposed, 29 CFR § 2520.105-3 deals with individual benefit reporting to participants and beneficiaries, while 29 CFR § 2530.209-3 deals with the maintenance by plans of records to serve as a basis for individual benefit statements.

In addition to substantive changes from the 1979 proposal, this new proposal contains language changes designed to clarify provisions or to improve readability.

These regulations are proposed under the authority in sections 105, 209, and 505 of the Act (Pub. L. 93-466, 88 Stat. 849, 865, and 894, 29 U.S.C. 1025, 1059, and 1135).

Discussion of Proposed Individual Benefit Reporting Regulations

1. *Benefit statement.* Under these proposed regulations, the benefit statement is the basic document to be used for providing individual benefit information to participants upon request, upon termination or upon a one-year break in service. The benefit statement must state the amount of a participant's accrued benefit regardless of the extent to which it is nonforfeitable (i.e., "vested"), the percentage of the accrued benefit which is vested, and the amount of such accrued vested benefit. The regulations specify the form in which accrued benefits and accrued vested benefits must be reported. The new proposal is designed to ensure that the information provided to an individual participant is presented in a meaningful fashion, without imposing excessive administrative costs on plans.

Some of the comments received by the Department on the 1979 proposal raised objections to the degree to which that proposal would

have required benefit statements to provide individualized information geared to each participant's particular circumstances. These comments suggested that the degree of individualization that would have been required would entail significant additional costs for plans, and that ultimately these costs would be borne to some extent by participants. These commentators pointed out that, in some cases, the individualized information might be misleading or of little value to recipients of benefit statements as a result of changes in participants' circumstances. At the same time, it appears to the Department that some degree of individualization is necessary if individual benefit statements are to serve the purposes which underlie the statutory requirements. In the new proposal the Department has struck what it believes to be a better balance between the need for individualization of benefit statements and the costs that individualization imposes.

In the case of defined benefit plans, the accrued benefit and the amount of the participant's accrued vested benefit may be expressed either in terms of a straight life annuity payable at normal retirement age, or in terms of the normal form of benefits offered by the plan (e.g., annuity for a term of years, lump-sum distribution, etc.). By contrast, the 1979 proposal would have required accrued benefits to be stated either in the form of a straight life annuity payable at normal retirement age or, if the plan did not offer such a benefit, in the form of the primary option offered by the plan. If a participant had made any elections affecting the manner of payment of benefits, the 1979 proposal generally would have required accrued benefits to be stated in the form elected by the participant. The elimination in the new proposal of the requirement to state accrued benefits in the form elected by the participant is in keeping with the goal of reducing costs resulting from excessive individualization. It also reflects comments to the effect that the requirement to state accrued benefits in the form of a straight life annuity payable at normal retirement age might prove misleading to participants when this is not the normal form of benefits payable under the plan. One of the comments on the 1979 proposal suggested that the Department should explicitly prohibit inclusion in the benefit statement of benefit projections predicated on the assumption that a participant will work until retirement. The comment suggested that such projections would not satisfy the requirement that a benefit statement must report accrued benefits, vested percentage and accrued vested benefits as of the date of the statement. The Department has decided not to prohibit the inclusion of such projections, but notes that the benefit statement must be written in a manner calculated to be understood by the average plan participant or beneficiary and its format must not have the effect of misleading or misinforming participants or beneficiaries.

The new proposal would require the benefit statement to indicate that election of options under the plan might affect the participant's accrued benefits, and to refer the participant to the Summary Plan Description for information on available options. In addition, if the accrued benefit and accrued vested benefit are not expressed as amounts payable in the form of a joint and survivor annuity, the benefit statement must explain that the periodic benefit the participant will receive at retirement may be reduced on account of survivor benefits.

"Social Security offset plans" must furnish the net benefit. In the case of benefit statements furnished on request or under the annual benefit statement alternative, the net benefit may be determined on the basis of assumptions about participants' earnings in service not covered by the plan, provided that the benefit statement indicates that the reported amounts are approximate. Benefit statements furnished after a break in service (or after a "severance," as described below) must report the actual amounts of benefits to which the participant is entitled.

In the case of an individual account plan, the regulations make it clear that the participant's account balance is considered to be accrued benefit.

In accordance with the statutory requirements, the benefit statement would be required to indicate the nonforfeitable (vested) percentage of the participant's accrued benefit. If the participant has no vested accrued benefits, the benefit statement must indicate the earliest date on which any benefits will become vested. Consistent with the goal of avoiding excessive administrative costs, the new proposal eliminates the requirement in the 1979 proposal that plans with "graded" vesting indicate the earliest dates on which a participant may attain each subsequent level of nonforfeitable accrued benefits derived from employer contributions. The new proposal also provides that class year plans would be required to indicate the nonforfeitable percentage of each portion of the participant's account balance to which a separate nonforfeitable percentage applies.

The benefit statement would also be required to indicate the amount of the participant's nonforfeitable accrued benefit, in the same form as that in which the accrued benefit is reported.

The new proposal requires only a general reference to the Summary Plan Description. The 1979 proposal required more detailed information regarding circumstances that might result in the reduction or elimination of accrued or nonforfeitable benefits, including detailed references to the Summary Plan Description. The new proposal also eliminates the requirement contained in the 1979 proposal that the benefit statement include certain information concerning a participant's work history used as a basis for calculation of the participant's benefits. This change was made to reduce the degree to which benefit statements must be individualized. The eliminated information, however, must be available to a participant under the provisions of these regulations regarding inspection of records (§ 2530.209-3(f)), and, as under the 1979 proposal, the benefit statement must so indicate. As under the 1979 proposal, the benefit statement would be required to include a statement urging the participant to bring promptly to the attention of the plan administrator anything in the benefit statement that does not appear correct, information regarding the availability of plan records for inspection, the date as of which information is reported, and the participant's social security number (for the purpose of verification by the participant).

Like its predecessor, the new proposal would provide that the benefit statement must be written in a manner calculated to be understood by the average plan participant or beneficiary and that the format of the benefit statement must not have the effect of misleading or misinforming the participant or beneficiary. Under certain circumstances, plans must offer foreign language assistance to participants who are not literate in English to aid them in understanding their benefit statements, as is required under regulations relating to the Summary Plan Description (see 29 CFR § 2520-102.2(c)).

The benefit statement must be based on the latest available information. As under the 1979 proposal, benefit statements based on records that meet the standards of sufficiency set forth in the proposed recordkeeping regulations will be deemed to be based on the latest available information. Although "sufficient", a plan's records may nevertheless be incomplete (i.e., if they do not include all items necessary to determine participants' benefit entitlements) if, for example, a plan did not maintain complete records prior to the adoption of these regulations. In these instances, the benefit statement must indicate that the records on which it is based are incomplete, and the participant or beneficiary must be offered an opportunity to provide other information relating to his benefit entitlements. The plan administrator must prepare a benefit statement based on such information although, to the extent that a benefit statement is based on such information, it may indicate that it is conditioned upon the accuracy of that information.

In the 1979 proposal the Department solicited comments on whether and to what extent it should adopt regulations concerning circumstances under which liability should be imposed for the payment of benefits in accordance with the information provided in the benefit statement. Some comments supported the adoption of regulations imposing liability, while others suggested that liability should be limited, or objected to the imposition of any liability. Upon consideration of the comments, the Department has concluded that a judgment concerning the consequences of an incorrect benefit statement can properly be made only after account has been taken of all of the facts and circumstances. The Department believes, therefore, that it would be more appropriate to leave determinations of this sort to plan fiduciaries, whose actions are subject to review by the judicial process, rather than to attempt to deal with all conceivable factual situations in the context of regulations.

In the 1979 proposal, the Department also solicited comments on whether it should publish model benefit statements. In view of the multiplicity of plan provisions, it would be difficult for the Department to ensure that the format of a model statement would not be misleading under any circumstances. Accordingly, the Department has made a decision at this time not to publish model benefit statements.

2. *Furnishing benefit statements on request.* Both sections 105(a) and 209(a)(1)(A) of the Act require plan administrators of pension plans to furnish individual benefit information on request. The requirements of both statutory provisions are substantially similar in this regard; accordingly, these requirements are dealt with in a single section of the regulations (§ 2520.105-3(a)). The only significant difference between the two statutory provisions is that section 105(a) applies to requests by both participants and their designated beneficiaries, while section 209(a)(1)(A) applies only to requests by participants.

The regulations, therefore, apply to requests by both participants and beneficiaries, so as to cover the broadest range of circumstances under which benefit statements must be furnished on request.

In response to suggestions made in comments on the 1979 proposal, the new proposal provides that a plan administrator subject to these regulations need not provide a benefit statement upon request to certain classes of participants and beneficiaries. These include participants and beneficiaries currently receiving benefits; participants and beneficiaries to whom paid up insurance policies representing their full benefit entitlements have been distributed; participants and beneficiaries who have received a full distribution of their benefits; beneficiaries of participants who are entitled to benefit statements; and participants with deferred vested benefits who have received benefit statements upon termination or after having incurred a one-year break in service without returning to service with any employer maintaining the plan, and their beneficiaries. The Department believes that it would be superfluous to require benefit statements to be furnished to these participants and beneficiaries.

The plan administrator may establish a simple and convenient procedure for the submission of requests for benefit statements. If such a procedure is established and communicated to participants and beneficiaries (for example, in the Summary Plan Description), the plan administrator, under certain conditions, need not comply with requests that do not conform to the procedure. If no such procedure is established, however, the plan administrator must comply with any request in writing by a participant or beneficiary. The plan administrator may not require information regarding a participant's employment record as a condition for furnishing the benefit statement (although such information may be requested). The new proposal would, however, allow plan administrators to require the furnishing of certain items of information identifying the participant about whom information is requested.

Many of the comments on the 1979 proposal urged that the Department permit benefit statements to report benefits as of the end of the plan year. The comments suggested that this approach would relieve individual account plans of the expense of conducting a valuation whenever a participant or beneficiary requests a benefit statement. Defined benefit plans might also face lower administrative costs if an end-of-plan-year approach were adopted because it might enable these plans to gear data processing systems to a single date. In light of these comments, the new proposal would require a benefit statement to report benefits as of a date not earlier than the end of the plan year preceding the plan year in which a participant or beneficiary requests the statement.

The end-of-year approach, however, entails changes in the deadlines for furnishing benefit statements on request. The new proposal is designed to permit a reasonable period of time after the end of the plan year for the processing of information. Under the new proposal, a benefit statement must be furnished to a participant or beneficiary on request within the later of 60 days of the date of the request or 120 days after the end of the plan year which immediately precedes the year in which the request was made. The Department recognizes that this scheme would provide participants and beneficiaries who request benefit statements towards the end of the plan year with a statement that contains relatively old information (as much as 14 months old), while participants and beneficiaries who request statements during the earlier part of the plan year may be required to wait a substantial period (up to four months) to receive their statements. Nevertheless, the Department believes that the proposed scheme strikes an appropriate balance between providing participants with timely information and reducing administrative costs.

As under the 1979 proposal, the plan administrator would not be required to furnish more than one benefit statement to a participant or beneficiary on request during any 12-month period.

The original proposal appeared to require plans to furnish a complete benefit statement to a non-vested participant if the annual alternative was used. The new proposal would permit a plan to provide annually, as an alternative to furnishing benefit statements on request, a benefit statement to each vested participant and a statement of non-vested status to each non-vested participant. Permitting the furnishing of a statement of non-vested status under the annual alternative should reduce costs to plans electing the alternative, while providing sufficient disclosure to a non-vested participant. The plan administrator must furnish a complete benefit statement, however, to any non-vested participant who requests one after receiving the statement of non-vested status.

The annual benefit statement must be furnished within 180 days after the end of the plan year.

Despite comments objecting to the requirement in the 1979 proposal that the plan administrator furnish at least one duplicate of the annual benefit statement to any participant or beneficiary who requests it during the year, the Department has not eliminated this requirement. In some cases a participant or beneficiary may not receive an annual benefit statement mailed to him. Since it would be impracticable and unfair to require a participant or beneficiary to prove that he did not receive an annual statement in order to obtain a duplicate, the regulations allow all participants or beneficiaries entitled to receive a benefit statement on request at least one duplicate if the annual alternative is used.

3. *Furnishing benefit statements after one-year breaks in service.* The benefit statement must report benefits as of the end of the plan year in which a one-year break in service occurs. Consistent with end-of-the-year benefit reporting, the new proposal requires statements to be furnished within 180 days after the end of the plan year in which the break in service occurs. The 180 day period also would allow plans to satisfy the requirement to furnish benefit statements after a one-year break in service through the use of the annual benefit statement alternative, which is required to be furnished in the same time period.

A participant who receives a benefit statement upon incurring a one-year break in service, and thereafter incurs a subsequent one-year break in service, is not entitled to receive an additional benefit statement if the information in the second benefit statement would be the same as that in the first.

As under the 1979 proposal, plan administrators of multiple employer plans are not required to furnish benefit statements upon termination. However, if a multiple employer plan does not provide that a participant may suffer adverse consequences upon incurring a one-year break in service, the plan administrator is required to furnish a benefit statement to a participant if the participant is not listed on any Service Report furnished to the plan administrator by an employer for two consecutive plan years. The fact that the participant has not appeared on a Service Report for an extended period of time suggests that such participant has ceased to participate actively in the plan. In the Department's view, such a participant should be furnished a benefit statement for the same reasons as a participant who incurs a one-year break in service (or a participant in a single employer plan who terminates service with the employer).

In the case of participants who have no vested benefits, the new proposal, like the 1979 proposal, would permit plan administrators of multiple employer plans to satisfy the requirements to furnish individual benefit information after a one-year break in service by furnishing a statement of non-vested status. The statement of non-vested status informs the participant that he has no nonforfeitable benefits. It does not, however, provide information regarding accrued benefits. Thus, the statement of non-vested status does not require extensive calculations and may be presented to all participants entitled to it in a standardized form, with no need for preparation of an individual statement for each. However, the statement of non-vested status must inform the participant that he may request a benefit statement with more detailed information regarding his individual accrued (non-vested) benefits. Such a request must be treated as a request for a benefit statement.

4. *Corrections to the benefit statement.* As under the 1979 proposal, a participant who raises a question with regard to the accuracy of a benefit statement must be given an opportunity to furnish information regarding his benefit entitlements to the plan administrator. Within a reasonable time, the plan administrator must make a decision with regard to the question raised by the participant and notify the participant of the decision, the basis for the decision, and any change in benefit entitlements as a result of the decision. The plan administrator is not required to prepare a benefit statement based on the information furnished by the participant except, as noted above, in situations where the benefit statement is based on incomplete records.

5. *Statement of deferred vested benefits.* Under section 105(c) of the Act, each plan administrator required to register with the Internal Revenue Service under section 6057 of the Code shall furnish a statement of deferred vested benefits to each participant described in section 6057(a)(C) (i.e., to each participant who, during the plan year for which registration is required, is separated from service covered under the plan, is entitled to a deferred vested benefit under the plan as of the end of the plan year, and with respect to whom retirement benefits were not paid under the plan). Section 6057(e) of the Code requires plan administrators to furnish similar individual statements to the same class of participants. The requirements of section 105(c) will be deemed to be satisfied if, in accordance with section 6057(e) of the Code and regulations thereunder, the plan administrator furnishes to the participant the individual statement required under the latter section.

6. *Manner of furnishing individual benefit reporting documents.* Like the 1979 proposal, the new proposal would require a plan to furnish individual benefit documents to a participant or beneficiary either by first class mail to his last known address, or by personal delivery. The

new proposal makes it clear that personal delivery may be accomplished by another party under the plan administrator's supervision.

The new recordkeeping proposal would require participants' individual benefit records to include current address information. Although some comments suggested that plans should not be required to maintain current address information on file, and should be permitted to use less reliable modes of delivery than first-class mail and personal delivery, the Department believes that these requirements represent the only means of assuring that individual benefit reporting documents will actually reach participants and beneficiaries in most cases.

Proposed Individual Benefit Recordkeeping Regulations

1. *Duty to maintain records.* In the case of a multiple employer plan, the duty to maintain individual benefit records would be imposed on the plan administrator. As under the 1979 proposal, the records are to be based on information in Service Reports furnished to the plan administrator by employers within 45 days (rather than 30, as under the 1979 proposal) after the end of a reporting period. The reporting period may be up to three months in duration. The new proposal makes it clear that a shorter reporting period may be established by agreement. The new proposal, like the 1979 proposal, requires Service Reports to contain information on all employees in service covered under the plan and all employees who have moved from covered to noncovered service after having met the plan's eligibility requirements for participation.

The new proposal imposes the duty to provide Service Reports upon every employer required to make contributions to the plan in respect of work performed by the employer's employees during the reporting period. (As in the 1979 proposal, however, employers are not required to provide Service Reports on employees in non-covered job classifications who have never performed service covered under the plan.) In addition, an employer is generally required to file Service Reports if another party is required to make contributions in respect of work performed by the employer's employees. This requirement is designed to cover a situation brought to the Department's attention in comments on the 1979 proposal in which contributions are made to the plan not by the employers of covered employees, but by firms that contract with these employers for their output, and similar situations if they exist. Further, the language of the new proposal should make it clear that employers will not be required to furnish Service Reports to a plan if their employees accumulate service credits under the plan solely by virtue of a reciprocity agreement with another plan.

If the plan administrator fails to receive an employer's Service Report, or an employer's Service Report does not contain all the necessary information, or the plan administrator has reason to believe that the information in the Service Report is inaccurate, the plan administrator must make reasonable efforts to obtain accurate and complete information. The plan administrator may prescribe reasonable rules and regulations regarding the format, manner of reporting and reportable information, and may prescribe forms and worksheets for reporting.

2. *Sufficiency of records.* Records maintained by the plan administrator of a multiple employer plan will be deemed to be sufficient under the proposed regulations if such records accurately reflect the Service Reports furnished by employers to the plan administrator. In general, Service Reports must contain the same information as the records maintained by an employer in connection with a single employer plan (i.e., they must include all information relating to service with such employer during the reporting period which would be relevant to a determination of the benefit entitlements of each employee covered under the plan). This may include information regarding service in a job classification not covered by the plan during the quarter. Under certain circcumstances, section 210 of the Act requires service not performed in job classifications covered by a multiple employer plan to be credited to a participant, particularly for purposes of vesting. These circumstances generally occur when an employee moves between a covered and a non-covered job classification. When an employee moves from a covered to a non-covered job classification, the employee must continue to report information regarding the employee to the plan administrator although the employee no longer performs service in a covered job classification, if this information is relevant to a determination of the employee's individual benefit entitlements. Under the proposal, an employer would not be required to furnish Service Reports on an employee who has not met the Plan's requirements for eligibility for participation in the plan. Since service in a covered job classification is always a requirement for eligibility to participate in a plan, the regulation would not require Service Reports to be furnished with respect to employees in non-covered job classifications merely because they might later move to covered job classifications and thereby become eligible to participate (with the result that their non-covered service would then be required to be credited for vesting or other purposes).

As in the case of single employer plans, there is no requirement to develop records relating to service before the effective date of the regulations, but records in existence on February 9, 1979 must be retained. In the Department's view, the 1979 proposal was sufficient to put plan administrators on notice that existing records would not be permitted to be destroyed.

3. *Retention, preservation and inspection of records.* As under the 1979 proposal, individual benefit records must be retained as long as a possibility exists that they might be relevant to a determination of the benefit entitlements of a participant or beneficiary. However, if they are lost or destroyed due to circumstances beyond the control of the person responsible for their maintenance, they will not be deemed insufficient solely for that reason. They must be maintained in a safe and accessible place at the offices of the plan administrator, or at special recordkeeping offices.

The proposal makes clear that original records may be disposed of at any time if microfilm, microfiche or similarly reproduced records which are clear reproductions of the original documents are retained, and adequate viewing equipment is available for inspecting them. (The 1979 proposal appeared to allow microfilm reproduction only.) The regulations do not preclude electronic data processing of records.

Individual benefit records, including original documents, must be available for inspection by participants, beneficiaries, and their representatives.

The period within which plan records must be made available for inspection after a request to do so has been extended from 72 hours, as under the 1979 proposal, to 10 working days. This change was made in response to comments noting the difficulties which would have been involved under the previous proposal.

In response to some public comments, provisions have been added to this proposal requiring the plan to bear the cost of converting records into a form accessible for inspection, although reasonable charges for copying may be imposed, not exceeding the actual cost. Inspection of records may be made only by those persons entitled to receive a benefit statement, and by their representatives. Representatives of the Department have the authority to inspect plan records under the circumstances specified in section 504(a)(2) of ERISA.

If a plan administrator ceases to be responsible for the maintenance of individual benefit records, they must be transferred to the person who becomes responsible for their maintenance.

4. *Definition of "multiple employer plans".* The Department has decided to limit the term "multiple employer plan", for the purposes of these regulations, to a plan adopted by more than one employer, other than a plan adopted by employers under common control.

5. *Reliance on Social Security records; variances for multiple employer plans.* Comments on the 1979 proposal indicate that a number of multiple employer plans have hitherto relied on records maintained by the Social Security Administration, among other sources of information, as a basis for making benefit determinations. The commentators suggest that these plans should be permitted to continue to rely on Social Security Administration records. The Department believes that adequate pre-retirement individual benefit reporting cannot be provided to participants and beneficiaries unless plans develop and maintain recordkeeping systems of their own. Consequently, the new proposal does not permit reliance on Social Security records as a substitute for recordkeeping by employers or plan administrators.

The comments indicate, however, that there may be a few multiple employer plans that operate under extraordinary circumstances that would make compliance with the multiple employer reporting and recordkeeping requirements in this proposal virtually impossible. The Department solicits detailed comments from these multiple employer plans with respect to any such special circumstances. If warranted by the comments, the Department might consider a procedure under which such plans would be granted variances which would permit them to use alternative methods of complying with the individual benefit reporting and recordkeeping requirements of the Act and these regulations.

Effective Dates

A number of comments on the 1979 proposal suggested that some multiple employer plans may need additional time to make preparations for compliance. In order to allow for orderly preparations for compliance with the regulations would not become effective with respect to collectively bargained multiple employer plans until nine months after the expiration of the collective bargaining agreement or agreements in effect on the date of adoption of these regulations, but in no case more than 45 months after the date of adoption. For multiple

employer plans which are not collectively bargained, the regulations, if adopted, would become effective 120 days after adoption.

Drafting Information

The principal author of these proposed regulations is Mary O. Lin of the Plan Benefits Security Division, Office of the Solicitor, Department of Labor. However, other persons in the Department of Labor participated in developing the proposed regulations, both on matters of substance and style.

Proposed Regulation

Accordingly, it is proposed to amend Chapter XXV of Title 29 of the Code of Federal Regulations as follows:

1. By adding to Part 2520 new § 2520.105-3 to read as follows:

PART 2520—RULES AND REGULATIONS FOR REPORTING AND DISCLOSURE

Subpart G—Individual Benefit Reporting

Sec. 2520.105-3—Individual Benefit Reporting for Multiple Employer Plans.

Authority: Secs. 105, 209 and 505 of the Act, (Pub. L. 93-406; 88 Stat. 849, 865 and 894, 29 U.S.C. 1025, 1059 and 1135).

Subpart G—Individual Benefit Reporting

§ 2520.105-3 Individual benefit reporting for multiple employer plans.

(a) *Furnishing benefit statements on request.*—(1) *General.* The administrator of a multiple employer employee pension benefit plan (as defined in paragraph (k) of this section) subject to Parts 1 or 2 of Title I of the Act shall furnish a benefit statement which satisfies the requirements of this paragraph and paragraphs (c) through (i) of this section to all plan participants or beneficiaries who request in writing information regarding their individual benefit entitlements under the plan, except:

(i) Participants and beneficiaries who are currently receiving benefits under the plan;

(ii) Participants and beneficiaries whose entire benefit entitlements under the plan are fully guaranteed by an insurance company, insurance service or insurance organization qualified to do business in a State, provided that the benefits are paid under an insurance policy or contract on which no further premiums are payable and which has been distributed to the participant or beneficiary;

(iii) Participants and beneficiaries who have received all benefits to which they are entitled under the plan;

(iv) Beneficiaries of a participant who is entitled to a benefit statement on request; and

(v) Participants with deferred vested benefits who have received benefit statements on termination or after incurring a one year break in service and who have not returned to service with any employer maintaining the plan, and beneficiaries of such participants.

(2) *Procedure for submission of requests for benefit statements.* The plan administrator may establish a simple procedure, convenient to participants and beneficiaries, for the submission of requests for benefit statements. The plan administrator will not be required to comply with a request made in a manner which does not conform to such a procedure which has been communicated in writing to participants and beneficiaries, provided that the plan administrator informs the requesting participant or beneficiary that he has failed to comply with the procedure and explains how to comply with the procedure. A procedure shall be deemed to be communicated to participants and beneficiaries if a description of the procedure is included in the Summary Plan Description of the plan or in any other document distributed to all plan participants. If no such procedure is established, any request in writing to the plan administrator or plan office by a participant or beneficiary for information regarding his benefit entitlements under the plan shall be deemed a request to the plan administrator for the purposes of this section.

(3) *Information obtained from participant or beneficiary.* A participant or beneficiary who requests a benefit statement may not be required to furnish information regarding the participant's employment record as a condition to receiving the benefit statement, but may be required to furnish the following information: name, address, date of birth, Social Security account number, and, if relevant to information provided in the benefit statement, marital status and date of birth of spouse.

(4) *Date of furnishing.* A benefit statement shall be furnished to a participant or beneficiary who requests such a statement, no later than (i) 60 days after receipt of the request or (ii) 120 days after the end of

the plan year which immediately precedes the plan year in which the request is made, whichever is later.

(5) *Date as of which information is provided.* A benefit statement furnished at the request of a participant or beneficiary shall report benefits as of a date not earlier than the end of the plan year preceding the plan year in which the request is made.

(6) *Annual benefit statement alternative.* (i) the requirement to furnish a benefit statement on request to a participant or beneficiary, as set forth in paragraph (a)(1) of this section, shall not apply if within one year before the request the plan administrator has furnished to such participant or beneficiary an annual benefit statement, or a "statement of non-vested status" described in paragraph (f) of this section, as appropriate, which is based on information as of the end of the plan year preceding the plan year in which it is furnished, and it is furnished within 180 days after the end of that plan year.

(ii) Notwithstanding the provisions of paragraph (a)(6)(i) of this section, the plan administrator shall furnish a complete benefit statement meeting the requirements of paragraph (d) and (e) of this section to a participant who requests information on his accrued benefits after receiving a statement of non-vested status, and shall furnish upon request a duplicate of the most recent annual benefit statement, or statement of non-vested status, as appropriate, to any participant or beneficiary who was entitled to such a statement but claims not to have received one.

(b) *Furnishing statements after one-year breaks in service or severance*—(1) *General.* Except as provided in paragraph (c) of this section, the plan administrator of a multiple employer pension plan that is subject to Part 2 of Title I of the act shall furnish a benefit statement to a participant who incurs a one-year break in service as defined in paragraph (b)(5) of this section. If, however, the plan does not provide that participants may suffer adverse consequences on incurring a one-year break in service, such plan administrator shall furnish a benefit statement to a participant who incurs a severance as defined in paragraph (b)(6) of this section.

(2) *Date of furnishing.* A benefit statement or statement of non-vested status shall be furnished within 180 days after the end of the plan year in which a participant incurs a one-year break in service or a severance. This requirement may be satisfied by furnishing to the participant an annual benefit statement described in paragraph (a)(6) of this section, which reports the participant's benefits as of the end of the plan year in which the one-year break in service or the severance occurred.

(3) *Non-vested participants.* In the case of a participant who has no nonforfeitable benefits under the plan and who incurs a one-year break in service or a severance, the plan administrator will comply with the requirements of section 209(a)(1)(B) of the Act and this section if the plan furnishes such participant a "statement of non-vested status" as described in paragraph (f) of this section.

If a participant who incurs a one-year break in service is furnished a statement of non-vested status under this paragraph, and requests information concerning his accrued benefits under the plan, the plan administrator shall furnish a benefit statement meeting the requirements of paragraph (d) and (e) of this section to the participant no later than the later of 60 days after such request or 180 days after the end of the plan year in which he incurs a one-year break in service.

(4) *Date as of which information is provided.* A benefit statement furnished after a one-year break in service or a severance shall report benefits as of the end of the plan year in which the one-year break in service or the severance occurs.

(5) *Definition of "one-year break in service".* For purposes of this section, the term "one-year break in service" shall mean a one-year break in service for vesting purposes as defined in the plan documents, or in the case of a plan under which service is credited for purposes of vesting according to the elapsed time method permitted under 26 CFR 1.410(a)-7, a one-year period of severance for vesting purposes, as defined in 26 CFR 1.410(a)-7(c)(4).

(6) *Definition of "severance".* For purposes of this section, a participant shall be deemed to incur a "severance" in the second of two consecutive plan years in which the participant is not listed on any Service Report furnished by an employer to the plan administrator in accordance with paragraph (b) of this section.

(c) *Frequency of benefit statements.* (1) A plan administrator is not required to furnish to a participant or beneficiary more than one benefit statement upon request under paragraph (a) of this section in any 12-month period.

(2) Where a participant receives a benefit statement upon incurring a one-year break in service or a severance, the plan administrator is not

required to furnish a second benefit statement upon a subsequent one-year break in service or severance, or upon a request by the participant, if the information that would be contained in a second benefit statement would be the same as that contained in the earlier benefit statement.

(d) *Style and format of benefit statements.*—(1) *General.* Individual benefit reporting documents shall be written in a manner calculated to be understood by the average plan participant or beneficiary. The format of these documents must not have the effect of misleading or misinforming the participant or beneficiary.

(2) *Foreign language assistance.* (i) The plan administrator of a plan described in paragraph (d)(2)(ii) of this section shall communicate to plan participants, in the non-English language common to such participants, information relating to any procedure for requesting benefit statements that may have been established by the plan administrator in accordance with paragraph (a)(2) of this section. In addition, the plan administrator shall provide these participants with either a benefit statement in such non-English language, or an English language benefit statement or statement of non-vested status which prominently displays a notice, in the non-English language common to these participants, explaining how they may obtain assistance. The assistance provided need not involve written materials, but shall be given in the non-English language common to these participants.

(ii) The plan administrators of the following plans are subject to the foreign language requirements of paragraph (d)(2)(i) of this section:

(A) A plan that covers fewer than 100 participants at the beginning of the plan year, and in which 25 percent or more of plan participants are not literate in English and are all literate in the same non-English language, or

(B) A plan which covers 100 or more participants at the beginning of the plan year, and in which the lesser of 500 or more participants, or 10% or more of all plan participants, are not literate in English and are all literate in the same non-English language.

(e) *Contents of the benefit statement.*—(1) *General.* In accordance with paragraphs (e)(2), (e)(3), (e)(4) and (e)(5) of this section, each benefit statement shall contain the following information:

(i) The participant's total accrued benefits;

(ii) The nonforfeitable percentage of the participant's accrued benefits;

(iii) The amount of the participant's nonforfeitable accrued benefits; and

(iv) Additional information specified in paragraph (e)(5) of this section.

(2) *Total accrued benefits.*—(i) *Defined benefit plans.*—(a) *General.* In the case of a defined benefit plan, the accrued benefit shall be stated in the form of a straight life annuity payable at normal retirement age or in the normal form of benefit provided by the plan.

(B) *Contributory plans.* If a defined benefit plan requires contributions to be made by employees, the benefit statement shall separately indicate, in addition to the participant's total accrued benefit, either the amount of the participant's accrued benefit derived from employee contributions and the amount of the accrued benefit derived from employer contributions, or the percentages of the participant's total accrued benefit derived from employee contributions and from employer contributions. The portion of the accrued benefit derived from employer contributions and the portion derived from employee contributions shall be determined in accordance with section 204(c) of the Act (section 411(c) of the Internal Revenue Code of 1954 and Treasury Regulations thereunder).

(C) *Social Security offset plans.* If a participant's benefits under the plan are offset by a percentage of the participant's old-age insurance benefit under the Social Security Act, the benefit statement shall state the participant's accrued benefit after reduction by the applicable amount. In the case of a benefit statement furnished upon request or under the annual benefit statement alternative permitted under paragraph (a)(6) of this section, the amount of the offset may be determined on the basis of assumptions about the participant's earnings from service not covered under the plan, provided that the statement indicates that the stated amounts of the accrued and nonforfeitable accrued benefit are approximate. A benefit statement furnished when an employee terminates employment or incurs a break in service must indicate the actual amounts of the accrued benefit and nonforfeitable accrued benefit to which the participant is entitled.

(ii) *Individual account plans.* In the case of an individual account plan, the participant's accrued benefit shall be the fair market value of the participant's account balance on the date as of which benefits are reported.

(3) *Nonforfeitable percentage.*—(i) *General.* The benefit statement shall indicate the percentage of a participant's accrued benefit which is nonforfeitable within the meaning of section 203 of the Act (and sections 411(a) of the Internal Revenue Code of 1954 and Treasury Regulations thereunder). Except in the case of a plan described in paragraph (e)(3)(ii) of this section, if a participant has no nonforfeitable benefits the benefit statement shall indicate the earliest date on which any benefits may become nonforfeitable; and if less than 100 percent of the participant's benefits are nonforfeitable, the benefit statement shall indicate the earliest date on which 100 percent of the participant's benefits may be nonforfeitable.

(ii) *Class year plans.* In the case of an individual account plan which provides for the separate nonforfeitability of benefits derived from contributions for each plan year, the benefit statement shall state each nonforfeitable percentage applicable to a portion of the participant's account balance and the value of that portion of the account balance.

(iii) *Contributory plans.* In the case of a plan which provides for employee contributions, the benefit statement shall indicate that the portion of the accrued benefits derived from the participant's contribution to the plan is nonforfeitable.

(4) *Nonforfeitable benefits.*—(i) *Defined benefit plans.* The benefit statement shall indicate the amount of the participant's nonforfeitable benefit in the same form as the participant's total accrued benefit is reported under paragraph (e)(2) of this section.

(ii) *Individual account plans.* In the case of an individual account plan, the benefit statement shall indicate the fair market value of the nonforfeitable portion of the participant's account balance on the date as of which benefits are reported.

(5) *Other information.* A benefit statement shall include the following information.

(i) In the case of a defined benefit plan, a statement to the effect that the amount of benefits which may be received under the plan may be affected as a result of electing any option under the plan, and that further information on such options is contained in the Summary Plan Description;

(ii) In the case of a defined benefit plan, if the accrued benefit and nonforfeitable benefit are not stated in the form of an annuity for the joint lives of the participant and his spouse, an explanation to the effect that unless a married participant elects not to receive benefits in that form, the participant's nonforfeitable benefit may be reduced;

(iii) A statement to the effect that further information on the circumstances, if any, which may result in a reduction or elimination of accrued benefits or of nonforfeitable benefits is contained in the Summary Plan Description;

(iv) A statement urging the participant or beneficiary to bring promptly to the attention of the plan administrator anything in the statement that does not appear correct;

(v) A statement informing the participant or beneficiary that plan records upon which information in the benefit statement is based are available for inspection upon request, and the name, address and telephone number of the person or office to whom requests should be directed;

(vi) The date as of which benefit entitlements are reported; and

(vii) The participant's Social Security account number.

(f) *Statement of non-vested status.* A statement of non-vested status shall inform the participant that he does not have any nonforfeitable benefits under the plan and that he may obtain upon request a benefit statement indicating his accrued benefits, if any, and the earliest date on which any benefits may become nonforfeitable.

(g) *Basis of benefit statement.* (1) *General.* A benefit statement shall be based on the latest available information. A benefit statement will be deemed to be based on the latest available information if it reports benefit entitlements as of the date benefits must be reported under paragraphs (a) or (b) of this section, as appropriate, or any subsequent date, and if it is based on plan records which comply with the requirements of paragraphs (b) and (c) of this section.

(2) *Benefit statement based on incomplete plan records.* A benefit statement based on incomplete plan records (i.e., records that do not contain all items of information necessary to determine the participant's benefit entitlements) shall so indicate. To the extent that the records of a plan are incomplete, an opportunity to provide information relating to benefit entitlements shall be offered to a participant or beneficiary

entitled to a benefit statement, and the benefit statement shall be based on such information. A benefit statement based in whole or in part on information supplied by a participant may state that it is conditioned upon the accuracy of such information.

(h) *Manner of furnishing individual benefit reporting documents.* Individual benefit reporting documents shall be furnished either by first class mail to the participant or beneficiary at his last known address, or by personal delivery to the participant or beneficiary by the plan administrator or an individual under the plan administrator's supervision. In the event that the plan administrator learns that the participant or beneficiary has failed to receive a document by mail or personal delivery, the plan administrator shall employ any means of delivery reasonably likely to ensure the receipt by such participant or beneficiary of the document.

(i) *Corrections to the benefit statement.* A participant or beneficiary who raises questions regarding the accuracy of the benefit statement shall be given a reasonable opportunity to point out information in the benefit statement that he believes inaccurate, and to furnish to the plan administrator information which such participant or beneficiary believes relevant in determining his benefit entitlements. The plan administrator shall make reasonable attempts to determine whether the plan's records or the benefit statement are inaccurate and to verify the information furnished by the participant or beneficiary. Within a reasonable time after the plan administrator receives such a communication from a participant or beneficiary, the plan administrator shall notify him in writing of the plan's decision with respect to such matter, the basis for such decision, and any change in benefit entitlements as a result of the decision.

(j) *Statement of deferred vested benefits.* Section 105(c) of the Act provides that each plan administrator required to file a registration statement under section 6057 of the Internal Revenue Code of 1954 (the Code) shall furnish to each participant described in section 6057(a)(2)(C) of the Code an individual statement setting forth the information with respect to such participant which is contained in the registration statement. The requirements of section 105(c) of the Act will be satisfied if an individual statement is furnished to a participant in accordance with section 6057(e) of the Code and the regulations thereunder.

(k) *Definition of "Multiple Employer Plan".* For purposes of paragraphs (a) through (j) of this section, the term "multiple employer plan" shall mean a plan adopted by more than one employer, other than a plan adopted by employers which are under common control.

PART 2530—RULES AND REGULATIONS FOR MINIMUM STANDARDS FOR EMPLOYEE PENSION BENEFITS PLANS

2. By adding to Part 2530 new § 2530.209-3 to read as follows:

Subpart E—Individual Benefit and Recordkeeping

Sec. 2530.209-3—Individual Benefit Recordkeeping.

Authority: Secs. 105, 209 and 505 of the Act (Pub. L. 93-406; 88 Stat. 849, 865 and 894 (29 U.S.C. 1025, 1059 and 1135)).

Subpart E—Individual Benefit and Recordkeeping

§ 2530.209-3 *Individual benefit recordkeeping for multiple employer plans.*

(a) *Recordkeeping requirement.* For every multiple employer pension plan (as defined in paragraph (h) of this section) subject to Part 2 of Title I of the Act, records shall be maintained with respect to each employee covered under the plan. These records shall be sufficient to determine the benefits which are, or may become, due to such employee and shall include the name and address of each such employee.

(b) *Maintenance of records and furnishing of information.*—(1) *Maintenance of records.* The plan administrator shall maintain the records required to be maintained by a multiple employer plan under paragraph (a) of this section.

(2) *Reporting by Sponsoring Employer.* Each employer who is a sponsoring employer of a multiple employer plan shall furnish written Service Reports to the plan administrator on a regular basis. The Service Reports shall cover a reporting period of no longer than one quarter of a year. A reporting period of less than one quarter of a year may be established by agreement, and different reporting periods may be established for different employers or different classes of employers sponsoring the same plan. A Service Report shall be furnished to the plan administrator no later than 45 days after the end of the reporting period to which it relates. The Service Reports shall be furnished in accordance with any rules prescribed under paragraph (b)(6) of this section and shall be prepared on any forms and worksheets prescribed thereunder.

(3) *Contents of Service Reports.* A Service Report shall contain all information that relates to service for, or other employment relationship with, the employer during the reporting period which it covers and that is relevant to a determination of the benefit entitlements of—

(i) Any of the employer's employees who has met the plan's requirements for eligibility to participate in the plan (including any requirement regarding service in a job classification covered by the plan), whether or not such employee performs service in a job classification covered under the plan during the reporting period; and

(ii) Any of the employer's employees who performs service in a job classification covered under the plan during the reporting period, whether or not such employee has met the plan's requirements for eligibility to participate during such reporting period.

(4) *Definition of "sponsoring employer".* For purposes of this paragraph, an employer shall be deemed to be a "sponsoring employer" of a plan for any reporting period where during such reporting period the employer or another party (other than another plan pursuant to a reciprocity arrangement) is required to make contributions to the plan in respect of work performed by such employer's employees (whether measured in service time or in output).

(5) *Duty of plan administrator to seek information.* The plan administrator shall make reasonable efforts to obtain complete and accurate information where a sponsoring employer of a multiple employer plan fails to furnish a Service Report to the plan administrator; or such an employer fails to include in a Service Report information required under paragraph (b)(3) of this section; or the plan administrator has reason to believe that the information furnished by such an employer is inaccurate.

(6) *Reasonable rules prescribed by plan administrator.* The plan administrator of a multiple employer plan may prescribe in writing reasonable rules concerning the format of reports, the manner of reporting, and reportable information. The plan administrator also may prescribe forms or worksheets to be used by employers for purposes of reporting under paragraph (b) of this section.

(c) *Sufficiency of records.* Records required to be maintained by a multiple employer plan under paragraph (a) of this section will be deemed to be sufficient if:

(1) They accurately reflect all the information contained in the Service Reports furnished to the plan administrator by participating employers under paragraph (b)(2) of this section, and the plan administrator has made reasonable attempts to obtain accurate and complete information under the circumstances described in paragraph (b)(5) of this section, and

(2) With respect to service before [effective date of regulation], if any, they include all records maintained by the administrator on and after February 9, 1979, for the purpose of determining employees' benefit entitlements under the provisions of the plan.

(3) *Loss or destruction of records.* Notwithstanding the preceding paragraphs, records shall not be deemed to be insufficient solely because they have been lost or destroyed due to circumstances beyond the control of the person responsible for their maintenance under paragraph (b)(1) of this section.

(d) *Period for which records must be retained.* The records which are required to be maintained under paragraph (a) of this section shall be retained in a manner described in paragraph (e) of this section as long as any possibility exists that they might be relevant to a determination of benefit entitlements. When it is no longer possible that records might be relevant to a determination of benefit entitlements, the records may be disposed of, unless they are required to be maintained for a longer period under any other law.

(e) *Preservation of records by plan administrator.*—(1) *General.* The records which are required to be maintained under paragraph (a) of this section shall be maintained in reasonable order in a safe and accessible place at the main offices of the plan administrator, or at recordkeeping offices established by the plan administrator and customarily used for the maintenance of records.

(2) *Reproduction of records; disposal of original documents.* Original documents may be disposed of at any time if microfilm, microfiche, or similarly reproduced records which are clear reproductions of the original documents are retained, and adequate projection or other viewing equipment is available for inspecting such reproductions.

(3) *Electronic data processing.* Nothing in this section precludes the use of punch cards, magnetic tape or other electronic information storage material for processing information.

(f) *Inspection and copying.* The records required to be maintained under paragraph (a) of this section with respect to any participant or beneficiary (including any original documents or reproductions thereof maintained under paragraph (e) of this section) shall be made available free of charge to such participant or beneficiary, or his representative, in a reasonably accessible form for inspection and copying. The records shall be made available during normal business hours within 10 working days after receipt of a request. A reasonable charge may be imposed for copying records, not exceeding the actual cost of copying them.

(g) *Transfer of records.* In the event that a plan administrator ceases to be responsible under paragraph (b) of this section for maintaining records, such plan administrator shall transfer any records which continue to be potentially relevant to the determination of benefit entitlements to the appropriate successor plan administrator responsible for their maintenance. The plan administrator transferring such records is not required to retain copies of the records transferred. Nothing in this section, however, shall relieve a plan administrator from any responsibility or liability for violations of the requirements of paragraphs (a) through (h) of this section which occur during the time such plan administrator has control of and is responsible for maintaining, retaining or transferring the records as required by those sections.

(h) *Definition of "Multiple Employer Plan."* For purposes of this section, the term "multiple employer plan" shall mean a plan adopted by more than one employer, other than a plan adopted by employers which are under common control.

Signed at Washington, D.C. this 4th day of August, 1980.

Ian D. Lanoff,

Administrator, Pension and Welfare Benefit Programs, Labor-Management Services Administration, U.S. Department of Labor.

¶ 20,526N   Reserved.

Proposed revisions of annual return/reports and regulations regarding plans which participate in a master trust were formerly reproduced at this point. The regulations, as revised are at ¶ 14,231A.

¶ 20,526O   Reserved.

Proposed amendments to the regulation governing the summary annual report (SAR) in order to accommodate the SAR requirements to the triennial filing system recently implemented for certain small employee benefit plans filing the annual report were formerly reproduced at this point. The regulations, as revised, are at ¶ 14,249H.

¶ 20,526P   Reserved.

Formerly reproduced at this paragraph were proposed regulations that provided guidance for determining whether a merger or transfer of assets of liabilities between multiemployer plans complied with ERISA. The regulations were finalized and appear at ¶ 15,700A—15,700I and 15,718D-1.]

¶20,526N

¶ 20,526Q   Reserved.

Proposed regulations to the deferral of distribution of updated summary plan descriptions were formerly reproduced at this point. The final regulations are at ¶ 14,249A.]

¶ 20,526R   Reserved.

Proposed regulations relating to the powers and duties of a plan sponsor of a plan terminated by a mass withdrawal and benefit reductions and suspensions were formerly reproduced at this paragraph. The final regulations are at ¶ 15,715A—15,715I and 15,718D-2.]

¶ 20,527   Reserved.

Proposed Reg. §§ 2550.408b-2, 2550.408b-4, 2550.408b-6, 2550.408c-2, and 2550.408c-4, on exemptions from prohibited transactions for the provision of services and office space to employee benefit plans, were formerly reproduced at this point. The final regulations appear at ¶ 14,782, 14,784, 14,786, 14,788, and 14,845.]

¶ 20,528   Reserved.

Proposed Reg. §§ 2615.1—2615.7, on the manner for determining whether a terminating plan is sufficient and the procedure for winding up the affairs of such plans, were formerly reproduced at this point. The regulations now appear at ¶ 15,447—15,448D.]

¶ 20,529   Reserved.

Proposed Reg. § 2550.404b-1, relating to the maintenance of the indicia of ownership of plan assets outside the jurisdiction of the district courts of the United States, was formerly reproduced at this point. The final regulation is at ¶ 14,745.]

¶ 20,530   Reserved.

Proposed Reg. §§ 2550.407a-1—2550.407a-4, relating to the acquisition and holding of employer securities and employer real property, were formerly reproduced at this point. The final regulations now appear at ¶ 14,771—14,771C.]

¶ 20,530A   Reserved.

Proposed Reg. § 2520.104-47, relating to the requirement of filing insurance company financial reports with the Department of Labor only upon request, was formerly reproduced at this point. The final regulation is at ¶ 14,247ZA.]

¶ 20,530B   Reserved.

Proposed Reg. §§ 2642.1, 2642.2, 2642.5—2642.8, and 2642.11—2642.14, relating to the change in the method of allocating unfunded vested benefits to employers withdrawing from a multiemployer plan, were formerly reproduced at this paragraph. The final regulations appear at ¶ 15,678—15,678H.]

¶ 20,530C   Reserved.

Proposed Reg. §§ 2646.1-8, relating to the waiver or reduction of partial withdrawal liability, were formerly reproduced at this paragraph. The final regulations appear at ¶ 15,663F and 15,673A-15,673H.]

¶ 20,530D

Proposed regulations on 29 CFR Part 2580: ERISA bonding requirement: Exemption for certain broker-dealers and investment advisers.—Reproduced below is the text of proposed regulations designed to provide certain broker dealers and investment advisers with an exemption from the bonding requirements imposed by ERISA Sec. 412.

The proposed regulations were published in the *Federal Register* on August 19, 1987 (52 FR 31039).

DEPARTMENT OF LABOR

Pension and Welfare Benefits Administration

29 CFR Part 2580

Proposed Regulation Exempting Certain Broker-Dealers and Investment Advisers From Bonding Requirements

AGENCY: Department of Labor.

ACTION: Notice of proposed rulemaking.

SUMMARY: This document contains a proposed regulation under the Employee Retirement Income Security Act of 1974 (ERISA, or the Act) which would provide certain broker-dealers and investment advisers with an exemption from the bond otherwise required under section 412 of ERISA. The proposed regulation, if adopted, would affect participants and beneficiaries of employee benefit plans, officials of employee benefit plans and employees of broker-dealers and investment advisers.

DATE: Written comments concerning the proposed regulation must be received by October 19, 1987.

ADDRESS: All written comments (at least three copies) should be sent to the Office of Regulations and Interpretations, Pension and Welfare Benefits Administration, Room N-5669, U.S. Department of Labor, 200 Constitution Avenue N.W., Washington, D.C. 20210, Attention: Proposed Bonding Regulation. The application relating to the proposed regulation herein and any comments received will be available for public inspection in the Public Documents Room of the Pension and Welfare Benefits Administration, U.S. Department of Labor, Room N-4677, 200 Constitution Avenue N.W., Washington, D.C. 20210.

FOR FURTHER INFORMATION CONTACT: Linda Shore, Office of Regulations and Interpretations, Pension and Welfare Benefits Administration, U.S. Department of Labor, (202) 523-8671. This is not a toll-free number.

SUPPLEMENTARY INFORMATION: This document contains a proposed regulation which would provide an alternative to the bonding requirements of section 412 of ERISA for certain broker-dealers and investment advisers. The proposed exemption was requested in an application filed on November 30, 1982 by the Securities Industry Association (SIA), which was later clarified by letters dated September 11, 1983, June 5, 1986, and September 24, 1986. The Department is proposing the regulation pursuant to the authority contained in section 412(e) of ERISA.

Background

Section 412(a) of ERISA generally requires that every fiduciary of an employee benefit plan and every person who "handles" funds or other property of any plan (plan official) be bonded in an amount equal to not less than 10 percent of the amount of each plan's funds and other property "handled" by such person. In no case shall the bond with respect to each plan be less than $1,000 nor more than $500,000 (see 29 CFR 2580.412.16).

Temporary bonding regulation section 29 CFR 2580.412-6 defines the term "handling" to encompass more than actual physical contact with plan funds. "Handling" occurs whenever the duties or activities of the plan official with respect to given funds or other property are such that there is a risk that such funds or other property could be lost in the event of fraud or dishonesty on the part of the plan official, acting either alone or in collusion with others. This section further provides that a person would be considered to be "handling" where, as a result of such person's decisionmaking responsibility with respect to given funds or other property, the person exercises such close control over the plan's investment policy that the person, in effect, determines all specific investments.

In this regard, the Department has stated (question FR-8, 29 CFR 2509.75-5) that a person who, under ERISA section 3(21)(A) renders investment advice to a plan for a fee or other compensation, direct or indirect, but who does not exercise or have the right to exercise discretionary authority with respect to plan assets, is not considered to be "handling" funds or other property of such plan and, accordingly, is not required to be bonded solely by reason of the provision of such investment advice. However, if the person, in addition to rendering investment advice, exercises or has the right to exercise discretionary authority or control and thereby makes specific investment decisions, such person is considered to be "handling" funds or other property, and accordingly, must be bonded.

Section 412(e) of ERISA provides that when, in the opinion of the Secretary of Labor, the administrator of a plan offers adequate evidence of the financial responsibility of the plan, or that other bonding arrangements would provide adequate protection of the beneficiaries and participants, the Secretary may provide an exemption from the requirements of section 412 of ERISA. The Conference Report, H.R. Report No. 93-1280, 93rd Cong. 2nd Sess. 324 (1974), in explaining this provision, indicates that Congress contemplated that the Department would provide an exemption for plans where other bonding arrangements of the employer, employee organization, investment manager or other fiduciaries or the overall financial condition of the plan or the fiduciaries meet standards deemed adequate to protect the interests of the beneficiaries and participants, including bonds subject to a reasona-

ble maximum for professional investment managers supervising large aggregation of clients' funds.

Proposed regulation 29 CFR 2580.412-33, discussed in detail below, would provide an exemption for certain broker-dealers and investment advisers which meet standards that the Department believes are adequate to protect the interests of the beneficiaries and participants. This proposed regulation would permit an alternative to the bond required by section 412(a) of the Act if the alternative bonding arrangement comes within the terms of the proposed regulation.

Discussion of Application

The representations of the applicant are summarized below. Interested persons are referred to the application on file with the Department for the complete representations of the applicant.

1. The SIA represents that its members engage in diverse facets of the securities business within the United States and Canada, including the provision of brokerage and investment advisory services. All SIA members doing business in the United States are broker-dealers registered with the Securities and Exchange Commission (SEC) under the Securities Exchange Act of 1934 (Exchange Act). Some SIA members perform investment advisory functions within the same entity as their broker-dealer operations while others perform these functions through an entity affiliated with the broker-dealer. SIA members that provide investment advice for separate nontransactional compensation must be registered with the SEC as investment advisers under the Investment Advisers Act of 1940 (Advisers Act).[2]

2. The applicant requests an exemption from the bonding requirements contained in section 412 of ERISA for two classes of entities: Registered broker-dealers; and those registered investment advisers which are: (1) Affiliates of registered broker-dealers and (2) do not maintain actual custody or possession of plan assets.[3]

The applicant states that to comply with the bonding requirements of section 412 of ERISA, broker-dealers and investment advisers often obtain bonding coverage through the use of an "agent's rider" attached to the bond otherwise secured by a plan. Broker-dealers and investment advisers which desire to secure their own fidelity bonding coverage find thta such coverage is generally available only through the use of an individual or schedule bond, at greatly increased cost. The applicant represents that such bonds are typically two party bonds naming the broker-dealer as insured, rather than the client plan as required by section 412 of ERISA.[4] The applicant further represents that third party fidelity bonds naming client plans as insureds are not presently offered by fidelity insurance companies and have not been offered in the past. To the extent that bonding coverage complying with section 412 could be procured, that section would require a progressively larger bond as the number of client plans to which the broker-dealer provides services increases. As a consequence, the SIA requests exemptive relief for broker-dealers and their investment adviser affiliates that are covered by the two party blanket bonds required by the self-regulatory organization (SRO) of which the broker-dealer is a member.[5] The SIA asserts that the requested exemption will adequately protect the interests of plan participants and beneficiaries.

3. The applicant represents that, in addition to the bonding arrangement (described below) required for broker-dealers by each of the SROs, plans are also protected by the extensive regulation of broker-dealers by the SEC. Such regulation includes requirements for registration, recordkeeping, net capital, customer protection and insurance. The SIA states that these substantive requirements provide customers of broker-dealers with protections similar to those afforded to customers of banks and insurance companies which are exempt from the bonding requirements of section 412 of ERISA.

4. Since December 6, 1983, all registered broker-dealers have been subject to a two-tiered system of regulation and inspection under the general supervision of the SEC. A broker-dealer, in addition to being registered with the SEC, must be a member of one or more SROs.[6] Under this regulatory system, broker-dealers are regulated primarily by one or more SROs which, in turn, are subject to intensive oversight by the SEC. Periodic examinations of broker-dealers are conducted by the SEC and the SROs under this system without prior notification. It is not unusual for a broker-dealer to be examined several times a year by the various examining authorities.

---

[2] We note that the definition of investment adviser contained in section 202(a)(11) of the Advisers Act may encompass persons who exercise the type of discretion described in section 3(21)(A)(i) of ERISA rather than merely providing advice about investment decisions. Such persons would be considered to be "handling" funds or other property of a plan so as to require bonding under section 412 of ERISA.

[3] We note that the applicant's request for relief is specifically limited to those broker-dealers and investment advisers described above.

[4] See 29 CFR 2580.412-18.

[5] American Stock Exchange, Boston Stock Exchange, Midwest Stock Exchange, New York Stock Exchange, Pacific Stock Exchange, Philadelphia Stock Exchange, Chicago Board of Options Exchange and National Association of Securities Dealers.

[6] 15 U.S.C. 78(o)(b)(8).

5. Registration subjects broker-dealers to the recordkeeping rules adopted by the SEC pursuant to the Exchange Act. These rules require broker-dealers to make and preserve accurate books and records to provide a basis upon which the SEC or SRO may monitor compliance with the applicable regulatory requirements. In accordance with these rules, broker-dealers are required to file with the SRO and/or the SEC a standard form of report, partially completed on a monthly basis and fully completed quarterly. In addition, all broker-dealers must file audited financial statements on an annual basis.

6. The net capital rule [Securities Exchange Act of 1934, Rule 15c3-1, 17 CFR 240.15c3-1 (1974)] imposes minimum financial requirements on broker-dealers. The customer protection rule [Securities Exchange Act of 1934, Rule 15c3-3, 17 CFR 240.15c3-3 (1974)] establishes reserve and segregation requirements for broker-dealers which limit the use of customers' funds by broker-dealers in their business and requires broker-dealers to obtain and maintain physical possession or control of all fully paid and excess margin securities carried in accounts of customers. The purpose of the customer protection rule is to safeguard customers' funds and prevent unsound use of customers' assets by ensuring that such funds are deployed in limited areas of a broker-dealer's business. The Securities Investor Protection Act of 1970 established a fund, administered by the Securities Investor Protection Corporation (SIPC), to ensure the reimbursement of customers of insolvent broker-dealers for up to $500,000 in losses arising out of the insolvency. In this regard, the SIA represents that SIPC would have no defenses against the reimbursement of a pension plan for up to the maximum insured amount where a broker-dealer holding securities as customer property for such plan became insolvent and was put into a SIPC receivership. With certain limited exceptions, all registered brokers-dealers are required to contribute to the fund and to be members of SIPC.

7. Broker-dealers are required under the Exchange Act to maintain a blanket fidelity bond covering all of their officers and employees. Each of the SROs has adopted it own bonding requirements. Currently, the amount of the bond is based on a percentage of the net capital of the broker-dealer. At the present time, the various SRO bonding rules are substantially similar. However, the New York Stock Exchange (NYSE) has proposed to increase its minimum bonding requirements for its members and to base such requirements on total securities and money values in the possession and control of a member.[7] The minimum coverage for member firms that carry customer accounts or clear transactions would range from $1 million for firms with under $50 million of securities and money values in possession and control, to $50 million for firms with over $2 billion of securities and money values in possession and control. The SIA represents that a solvent broker-dealer would be strictly liable to a plan if the broker-dealer issued a receipt evidencing that it was holding securities for the account of the plan and subsequently could not deliver such securities.

8. If the investment adviser and broker-dealer functions of the SIA member are performed within the same entity, the investment adviser is subject to the regulation and examination requirements, including the bonding requirements, of the broker-dealer. Registered investment advisers that do business through entities affiliated with a broker-dealer are subject to the regulation and examination requirements of the Advisers Act. Pursuant to the registration requirements of the Advisers Act, investment advisers must file Form ADV. Form ADV provides information concerning the ownership and business of the investment adviser, the nature and scope of its authority with respect to client funds and accounts, its methods of analysis, sources of information and investment strategies; and the background, including prior securities violations, of its officers and directors and any person who controls the investment adviser. Information on Form ADV must be kept up to date. The Advisers Act requires that investment advisers keep accurate and current books and records which are subject to examination by the SEC, without prior notice at irregular intervals every several years. Although the Advisers Act does not have a bonding requirement, the applicant represents that most sureties are willing to extend the broker-dealer's blanket bond to cover all of the investment advisory activities of an affiliated investment adviser, thereby extending fidelity bond protection to the clients of the affiliated investment adviser.

Discussion of Proposed Regulation

The Department has in the past exercised its statutory authority under section 13(e) of the Welfare and Pension Plans Disclosure Act (WPPDA) to grant exemptions from the bonding requirements of that statute where the parties seeking exemptive relief were subject to other bonding requirements that included minimum bonding amounts and periodic examination and review by supervisory authorities.[8] Section 412(e) of ERISA contains provisions substantially similar to those contained in section 13(e) of the WPPDA.

After consideration of the representations of the applicant, the Department has tentatively determined that, as modified below, the bonding arrangements imposed by the various SROs on their member firms constitute other bonding arrangements that would adequately protect the beneficiaries and participants of employee benefit plans under section 412(e) of ERISA.

However, the Department recognizes that the present bonding requirements of the various SROs set the amount of the bond based on the net capital of the broker-dealer. In the Department's view, a bonding requirement based on the total securities and money in the possession and control of the broker-dealer is a more appropriate basis on which to propose exemptive relief since it would more closely parallel the requirement of section 412(a) of ERISA. For this reason, the Department has included a condition in the proposed exemption which requires minimum bonding coverage similar to that proposed under the NYSE rule. In all other respects, the proposed exemption provides flexibility by permitting broker-dealers and investment adviser affiliates to satisfy the bond required under section 412 of ERISA by maintaining a fidelity bond that complies with the rules of the broker-dealer's SRO.

Finally, the Department has determined to provide only limited relief from sections 412(a) and 412(b) of ERISA. The exemption retains the requirement contained in section 412(a) that the surety on a fidelity bond must be a corporate surety company which is an acceptable surety on Federal bonds under authority granted by the Secretary of the Treasury pursuant to sections 9304 through 9308 of title 31, United States Code.

In addition, the exemption retains the prohibitions of section 412(b) which make it unlawful for a plan official to "handle" funds or other property without being bonded as required by section 412(a) or to permit the "handling" of funds or other property by another plan official who is not similarly bonded. However, broker-dealers and investment adviser affiliates which comply with the requirements of this exemption shall be deemed to be bonded as required by section 412(a) of ERISA. The exemption provides no relief from section 412(c) which makes it unlawful for anyone to procure a bond required by ERISA from any surety or through an agent or broker in whose business operations the plan or any party in interest with respect to the plan has any control or significant financial interest, direct or indirect. In the Department's view, the exemption as proposed will adequately address the concerns of the SIA.

Regulatory Flexibility Act

The Department has determined that this regulation would not have a significant economic effect on small plans or other small entities. The proposed regulation would exempt certain broker-dealers and investment advisers from bonding requirements that, in the absence of this exemption, would be imposed by section 412(a) of ERISA. The regulation does not impose paperwork or other types of costs and burdens on those broker-dealers and investment advisers who meet the criteria for exemptive relief.

Executive Order 12291 Statement

The Department has determined that the proposed regulatory action would not constitute a "major rule" as that term is used in Executive Order 12291 because the action would not result in: an annual effect on the economy of $100 million; a major increase in costs or prices for consumers, individual industries, government agencies, or geographical regions; or significant adverse effects on competition, employment, investment, productivity, innovation, or on the ability of United States based enterprises to compete with foreign based enterprises in domestic or export markets.

Paperwork Reduction Act Statement

This proposed regulation does not contain any new information collection requirements and does not modify any existing requirements.

Statutory Authority

The proposed regulation set forth herein is issued pursuant to sections 412(e) (Pub. L. 93-406, 88 Stat. 889, 29 U.S.C. 1112(3)) and 505 of ERISA (Pub. L. 93-406, 88 Stat. 894, 29 U.S.C. 1135); and under Secretary of Labor's Order No. 1-86.

List of Subjects in 29 CFR Part 2580

---

[7] SEC File No. SR-NYSE-83-13, 48 FR 20837, May 9, 1983.

[8] See EXR-179, St. Louis Union Trust Company, March 9, 1972.

Employee benefit plans, Employee Retirement Income Security Act, Pension plans, Welfare plans, Bonding, Exemptions.

In view of the foregoing, the Department proposes to amend Part 2580 of Chapter XXV of Title 29 of the Code of Federal Regulations as follows:

PART 2580—TEMPORARY BONDING RULES

1. By revising the authority citation for Part 2580 to read as set forth below:

Authority: Sec. 505, Pub. L. 93-406, 88 Stat. 894 (29 U.S.C. 1135); Sec. 412(e), Pub. L. 93-406, 88 Stat. 889 (29 U.S.C. 1112), Secretary of Labor's Order No. 1-86.

§§ 2580.412-33 through 2580.412-36 [Redesignated as §§ 2580.412-45 through 2580.412-48]

2. By redesignating §§ 2580.412-33 through 2580.412-36, which constitute subpart G, as §§ 2580.412-45 through 2580.412-48 respectively.

3. By adding to subpart F of Part 2580 a new centered heading and a new § 2580.412-33 to read as follows:

Broker-Dealers and Investment Advisers Subject to Federal Regulation

§ 2580.412-33 Exemption.

(a) *Persons covered.* If the alternative bonding arrangement set forth in paragraph (b) of this section is satisfied, the bond required by section 412(a) of ERISA shall not apply to the following persons:

(a) Any broker-dealer registered under the Securities Exchange Act of 1934 (Exchange Act),

(2) Any investment adviser registered under the Investment Advisers Act of 1940 which—

(A) Controls, is controlled by, or is under common control with a broker-dealer registered under the Exchange Act (investment adviser affiliate),

(B) Does not maintain actual custody or possession of assets of employee benefit plans, and

(C) Is named as an additional insured on the registered broker-dealer's bond described in paragraph (b) of this section. Persons complying with the alternative bonding arrangement set forth in paragraph (b) of this section shall be deemed to be bonded as required by section 412(a) of ERISA.

(b) *Alternative bonding arrangement.* (1) Each broker-dealer relying on the exemption in paragraph (a) of this section shall maintain a fidelity bond covering the broker-dealer and/or its investment adviser affiliate in the form required by each self-regulatory organization (SRO) of which the broker-dealer is a member, except that the following minimum limits of coverage are substituted for any other limits otherwise prescribed by the SRO.

Securities and money values in possession and control	Basic minimum coverage
$0-50 million	$ 1 million
50-100 million	3 million
100-500 million	5 million
500 million-1 billion	10 million
1-2 billion	25 million
Above $2 billion	50 million

(2) The surety on any bond procured in accordance with this exemption must be a corporate surety company which is an acceptable surety on Federal bonds under authority granted by the Secretary of the Treasury pursuant to sections 9304 through 9308 of title 31, United States Code.

(c) *Definitions.* For the purposes of this exemption:

(1) The terms "broker-dealer" and "investment adviser" include any partner, director, officer or employee of such broker-dealer or investment adviser.

(2) The term "control" means the power to exercise a controlling influence over the management or policies of a person other than an individual.

Signed at Washington, D.C., this 13th day of August 1987.

David M. Walker,

Deputy Assistant Secretary, Pension and Welfare Benefits Administration, United States Department of Labor.

[FR Doc. 87-18922; Filed 8-18-87; 8:45 am]

¶ 20,530E   Reserved.

Proposed regulations relating to the statutory exemption to ERISA's prohibition of loans by plans to participants and beneficiaries who are parties in interest with respect to the plan were formerly reproduced at this paragraph. The final regulations appear at ¶ 14,781.]

¶ 20,531   Reserved.

Proposed regulations on 29 CFR Part 2610, providing valuation factors for plans that terminate on or after September 1, 1976, but before December 1, 1976, were formerly reproduced at this point.

The final regulations are at ¶ 15,620L.]

¶ 20,531A   Reserved.

Proposed regulations relating to the enforcement of the prohibition of discrimination on the basis of a handicap as it applies to the programs and activities of the PBGC were formerly reproduced at this paragraph.

The final regulations appear at ¶ 15,326.]

¶ 20,531B   Reserved.

Proposed regulations relating to an alternative method for demonstrating plan sufficiency under the PBGC's regulation on Determination of Plan Sufficiency and Termination of Sufficient Plans were formerly reproduced at this paragraph.

The final regulations appear at ¶ 15,447A, ¶ 15,447B, ¶ 15,447K, ¶ 15,447L, ¶ 15,447M, and ¶ 15,447V.]

¶ 20,531C   Reserved.

Proposed regulations on redetermining withdrawal liability upon mass withdrawal. were formerly reproduced at this paragraph.

¶20,530E

The final regulations appear at ¶ 15,669A—15,669J.]

¶ 20,531D   Reserved.

Proposed Reg. §§ 2610.2, 2610.3, 2610.5, 2610.6, and 2610.9, relating to a change in the filing and premium payment due date from the last day of the seventh month following the close of the prior plan year to the last day of the second month following the close of the prior plan year, were formerly reproduced at this point.

The final regulations are at ¶ 15,371A, ¶ 15,371B, ¶ 15,371D, ¶ 15,371E, and ¶ 15,371H.]

¶ 20,531E

Proposed regulations: Definition of "adequate consideration": Assets other than securities: Fair market valuation: Fiduciaries and plan trustees.—Reproduced below is the text of a proposed regulation which clarifies the definition of "adequate consideration" for assets other than securities for which there is a generally recognized market and provides the certainty necessary for a plan fiduciary or trustee to determine in good faith the fair market value of assets other than securities. The proposed regulations were published in the *Federal Register* on May 17, 1988.

DEPARTMENT OF LABOR

Pension and Welfare Benefits Administration

29 CFR Part 2510

Proposed Regulation Relating to the Definition of Adequate Consideration

AGENCY: Pension and Welfare Benefits Administration, Department of Labor.

ACTION: Notice of proposed rulemaking.

SUMMARY: This document contains a notice of a proposed regulation under the Employee Retirement Income Security Act of 1974 (the Act or ERISA) and the Federal Employees' Retirement System Act of 1986 (FERSA). The proposal clarifies the definition of the term "adequate consideration" provided in section 3(18)(B) of the Act and section 8477(a)(2)(B) of FERSA for assets other than securities for which there is a generally recognized market. Section 3(18)(B) and section 8477(a)(2)(B) provided that the term "adequate consideration" for such assets means the fair market value of the asset as determined in good faith by the trustee or named fiduciary (or, in the case of FERSA, a fiduciary) pursuant to the terms of the plan and in accordance with regulations promulgated by the Secretary of Labor. Because valuation questions of this nature arise in a variety of contexts, the Department is proposing this regulation in order to provide the certainty necessary for plan fiduciaries to fulfill their statutory duties. If adopted, the regulation would affect plans investing in assets other than securities for which there is a generally recognized market.

DATES: Written comments on the proposed regulation must be received by July 18, 1988. If adopted, the regulation will be effective for transactions taking place after the date 30 days following publication of the regulation in final form.

ADDRESS: Written comments on the proposed regulation (preferably three copies) should be submitted to: Office of Regulations and Interpretations, Pension and Welfare Benefits Administration, Room N-5671, U. S. Department of Labor, 200 Constitution Avenue NW., Washington, DC 20216, Attention: Adequate Consideration Proposal. All written comments will be available for public inspection at the Public Disclosure Room, Pension and Welfare Benefits Administration, U. S. Department of Labor, Room N-5507, 200 Constitution Avenue NW., Washington, DC.

FOR FURTHER INFORMATION CONTACT: Daniel J. Maguire, Esq., Plan Benefits Security Division, Office of the Solicitor, U. S. Department of Labor, Washington, DC 20210, (202) 523-9596 (not a toll-free number) or Mark A. Greenstein, Office of Regulations and Interpretations, Pension and Welfare Benefits Administration, (202) 523-7901 (not a toll-free number).

SUPPLEMENTARY INFORMATION:

Background

Notice is hereby given of a proposed regulation under section 3(18)(B) of the Act and section 8477(a)(2)(B) of FERSA. Section 3(18) of the Act provides the definition for the term "adequate consideration," and states:

"The term 'adequate consideration' when used in part 4 of subtitle B means (A) in the case of a security for which there is a generally recognized market, either (i) the price of the security prevailing on a national securities exchange which is registered under section 6 of the Securities Exchange Act of 1934, or (ii) if the security is not traded on such a national securities exchange, a price not less favorable to the plan than the offering price for the security as established by the current bid and asked prices quoted by persons independent of the issuer and of any party in interest; and (B) in the case of an asset other than a security for which there is a generally recognized market, the fair market value of the asset as determined in good faith by the trustee or named fiduciary pursuant to the terms of the plan and in accordance with regulations promulgated by the Secretary."

The term "adequate consideration" appears four times in part 4 of subtitle B of Title I of the Act, and each time represents a central requirement for a statutory exemption from the prohibited transaction restrictions of the Act. Under section 408(b)(5), a plan may purchase insurance contracts from certain parties in interest if, among other conditions, the plan pays no more than adequate consideration. Section 408(b)(7) provides that the prohibited transaction provisions of section 406 shall not apply to the exercise of a privilege to convert securities, to the extent provided in regulations of the Secretary of Labor, only if the plan receives no less than adequate consideration pursuant to such conversion. Section 406(e) of the Act provides that the prohibitions in sections 406 and 407(a) of the Act shall not apply to the acquisition or sale by a plan of qualifying employer securities, or the acquisition, sale or lease by a plan of qualifying employer real property if, among other conditions, the acquisition, sale or lease is for adequate consideration. Section 414(c)(5) of the Act states that sections 406 and 407(a) of the Act shall not apply to the sale, exchange, or other disposition of property which is owned by a plan on June 30, 1974, and all times thereafter, to a party in interest, if such plan is required to dispose of the property in order to comply with the provisions of section 407(a) (relating to the prohibition against holding excess employer securities and employer real property), and if the plan receives not less than adequate consideration.

Public utilization of these statutory exemptions requires a determination of "adequate consideration" in accordance with the definition contained in section 3(18) of the Act. Guidance is especially important in this area because many of the transactions covered by these statutory exemptions involve plan dealings with the plan sponsor. A fiduciary's determination of the adequacy of consideration paid under such circumstances represents a major safeguard for plans against the potential for abuse inherent in such transactions.

The Federal Employees' Retirement System Act of 1986 (FERSA) established the Federal Retirement Thrift Investment Board whose members act as fiduciaries with regard to the assets of the Thrift Savings Fund. In general. FERSA contains fiduciary obligation and prohibited transaction provisions similar to ERISA. However, unlike ERISA, FERSA prohibits party in interest transactions similar to those described in section 406(a) of ERISA only in those circumstances where adequate consideration is not exchanged between the Fund and the party in interest. Specifically, section 8477(c)(1) of FERSA provides that, except in exchange for adequate consideration, a fiduciary shall not permit the Thrift Savings Fund to engage in: transfers of its assets to, acquisition of property from or sales of property to, or transfers or exchanges of services with any person the fiduciary knows or should know to be a party in interest. Section 8477(a)(2) provides the FERSA definition for the term "adequate consideration" which is virtually identical to that contained in section 3(18) of ERISA. Thus, the proposal would apply to both section 3(18) of ERISA and section 8477(a)(2) of FERSA.

When the asset being valued is a security for which there is a generally recognized market, the plan fiduciary must determine "adequate consideration" by reference to the provisions of section 3(18)(A) of the Act (or with regard to FERSA, section 8477(a)(2)(A)). Section 3(18)(A) and section 8477(a)(2)(A) provide detailed reference points for the valuation of securities within its coverage, and in effect provides that adequate consideration for such securities is the prevailing market price. It is not the Department's intention to analyze the requirements of section 3(18)(A) or 8477(a)(2)(A) in this proposal. Fiduciaries must, however, determine whether a security is subject to the specific provisions of section 3(18)(A) (or section 8477(a)(2)(A) of FERSA) or the more general requirements of section 3(18)(B) (or section 8477(a)(2)(B)) as interpreted in this proposal. The question of whether a security is one for which there is a generally recognized market requires a factual determination in light of the character of the security and the nature and extent of market activity with regard to the security. Generally, the Department will examine whether a security is being actively traded so as to provide the benchmarks Congress intended. Isolated trading activity, or trades between related parties, generally will not be sufficient to show the existence of a generally recognized market for the purposes of section 3(18)(A) or section 8477(a)(2)(A).

In the case of all assets other than securities for which there is a generally recognized market, fiduciaries must determine adequate consideration pursuant to section 3(18)(B) of the Act (or, in the case of FERSA, section 8477(a)(2)(B)). Because it is designed to deal with all but a narrow class of assets, section 3(18)(B) and section 8477(a)(2)(B) are by their nature more general than section 3(18)(A) or section 8477(a)(2)(A). Although the Department has indicated that it will not issue advisory opinions stating whether certain stated consideration is "adequate consideration" for the purposes of section 3(18), ERISA Procedure 76-1, § 5.02(a) (41 FR 36281, 36282, August 27, 1976), the Department recognizes that plan fiduciaries have a need for guidance in valuing assets, and that standards to guide fiduciaries in this area may be particularly elusive with respect to assets other than securities for which there is a generally recognized market. *See,* for example, *Donovan v. Cunningham,* 716 F. 2d 1455 (5th Cir. 1983) (court encourages the Department to adopt regulations under section 3(18)(B)). The Department has therefore determined to propose a regulation only under section 3(18)(B) and section 8477(a)(2)(B). This proposal is described more fully below.

It should be noted that it is not the Department's intention by this proposed regulation to relieve fiduciaries of the responsibility for making the required determinations of "adequate consideration" where applicable under the Act or FERSA Nothing in the proposal should be construed as justifying a fiduciary's failure to take into account all relevant facts and circumstances in determining adequate consideration. Rather, the proposal is designed to provide a framework within which fiduciaries can fulfill their statutory duties. Further, fiduciaries should be aware that, even where a determination of adequate consideration comports with the requirements of section 3(18)(B) (or section 8477(a)(2)(B) of FERSA) and any regulation adopted thereunder, the investment of plan assets made pursuant to such determination will still be subject to the fiduciary requirements of Part 4 of Subtitle B of Title I of the Act, including the provisions of sections 403 and 404 of the Act, or the fiduciary responsibility provisions of FERSA.

Description of the Proposal

Proposed regulation 29 CFR 2510.3-18(b) is divided into four major parts. Proposed § 2510.3-18(b)(1) states the general rule and delineates the scope of the regulation. Proposed § 2510.3-18(b)(2) addresses the concept of fair market value as it relates to a determination of "adequate consideration" under section 3(18)(B) of the Act. Proposed § 2510.3-18(b)(3) deals with the requirement in section 3(18)(B) that valuing fiduciary act in good faith, and specifically discusses the use of an independent appraisal in connection with the determination of good faith. Proposed § 2510.3-18(b)(4) sets forth the content requirements for written valuations used as the basis for a determination of fair market value, with a special rule for the valuation of securities other than securities for which there is a generally recognized market. Each subsection is discussed in detail below.

1. General Rule and Scope.

Proposed § 2510.3-18(b)(1)(i) essentially follows the language of section 3(18)(B) of the Act and section 8477(a)(2)(B) of FERSA and states that, in the case of a plan asset other than a security for which there is a generally recognized market, the term "adequate consideration" means the fair market value of the asset as determined in good faith by the trustee or named fiduciary (or, in the case of FERSA, a fiduciary) pursuant to the terms of the plan and in accordance with regulations promulgated by the Secretary of Labor. Proposed § 2510.3-18(b)(1)(ii) delineates the scope of this regulation by establishing two criteria, both of which must be met for a valid determination of adequate consideration. First, the value assigned to an asset must reflect its fair market value as determined pursuant to proposed § 2510.3-18(b)(2). Second, the value assigned to an asset must be the product of a determination made by the fiduciary in good faith as defined in proposed § 2510.3-18(b)(3). The Department will consider that a fiduciary has determined adequate consideration in accordance with section 3(18)(B) of the Act or section 8477(a)(2)(B) of FERSA only if both of these requirements are satisfied.

The Department has proposed this two part test for several reasons. First, Congress incorporated the concept of fair market value into the definition of adequate consideration. As explained more fully below, fair market value is an often used concept having an established meaning in the field of asset valuation. By reference to this term, it would appear that Congress did not intend to allow parties to a transaction to set an arbitrary value for the assets involved. Therefore, a valuation determination which fails to reflect the market forces embodied in the concept of fair market value would also fail to meet the requirements of section 3(18)(B) of the Act or section 8477(a)(2)(B) of FERSA.

Second, it would appear that Congress intended to allow a fiduciary a limited degree of latitude so long as that fiduciary acted in good faith. However, a fiduciary would clearly fail to fulfill the fiduciary duties delineated in Part 4 of Subtitle B of Title I of the Act if that fiduciary acted solely on the basis of native or uninformed good intentions. See *Donovan v. Cunningham, supra,* 716 F. 2d at 1467 ("[A] pure heart and an empty head are not enough.") The Department has therefore proposed standards for a determination of a fiduciary's good faith which must be satisfied in order to meet the requirements of section 3(18)(B) or section 8477(a)(2)(B) of FERSA.

Third, even if a fiduciary were to meet the good faith standards contained in this proposed regulation, there may be circumstances in which good faith alone fails to insure an equitable result. For example, errors in calculation or honest failure to consider certain information could produce valuation figures outside of the range of acceptable valuations of a given asset. Because the determination of adequate consideration is a central requirement of the statutory exemptions discussed above, the Department believes it must assure that such exemptions are made available only for those transactions possessing all the external safeguards envisioned by Congress. To achieve this end, the Department's proposed regulation links the fair market value and good faith requirements to assure that the resulting valuation reflects market considerations and is the product of a valuation process conducted in good faith.

2. Fair Market Value

The first part of the Department's proposed two part test under section 3(18)(B) and section 8477(a)(2)(B) requires that a determination of adequate consideration reflect the asset's fair market value. The term "fair market value" is defined in proposed § 2510.3-18(b)(2)(i) as the price at which an asset would change hands between a willing buyer and a willing seller when the former is not under any compulsion to buy and the latter is not under any compulsion to sell, and both parties are able, as well as willing, to trade and are well-informed about the asset and the market for that asset. This proposed definition essentially reflects the well-established meaning of this term in the area of asset valuation. *See,* for example, 26 CFR 20.2031-1 (estate tax regulations); Rev. Rul. 59-60, 1959-1 Cum. Bull. 237; *United States v. Cartwright,* 411 U. S. 546, 551 (1973): *Estate of Bright v. United States,* 658 F. 2d 999, 1005 (5th Cir. 1981). It should specifically be noted that comparable valuations reflecting transactions resulting from other than free and equal negotiations (*e.g.,* a distress sale) will fail to establish fair market value. *See Hooker Industries, Inc. v. Commissioner,* 3 EBC 1849, 1854-55 (T. C. June 24, 1982). Similarly, the extent to which the Department will view a valuation as reflecting fair market value will be affected by an assessment of the level of expertise demonstrated by the parties making the valuation. *See Donovan v. Cunningham, supra,* 716 F. 2d at 1468 (failure to apply sound business principles of evaluation, for whatever reason, may result in a valuation that does not reflect fair market value).[1]

---

[1] Whether in any particular transaction a plan fiduciary is in fact well-informed about the asset in question and the market for that asset, including any specific circumstances which may affect the value of the asset, will be determined on a facts and circumstances basis. If, however, the fiduciary negotiating on behalf of the plan has or should have specific knowledge concerning either the particular asset or the market for that asset. It is the view of the Department that the fiduciary must take into account that specific knowledge in negotiating the price of the asset in order to meet the fair market value standard of this regulation. For example, a sale of plan-owned real estate at a negotiated price consistent with valuations of comparable property will not be a sale for adequate consideration if the negotiating fiduciary does not take into account any special knowledge which he has or

The Department is aware that the fair market value of an asset will ordinarily be identified by a range of valuations rather than a specific, set figure. It is not the Department's intention that only one valuation figure will be acceptable as the fair market value of a specified asset. Rather, this proposal would require that the valuation assigned to an asset must reflect a figure within an acceptable range of valuations for that asset.

In addition to this general formulation of the definition of fair market value, the Department is proposing two specific requirements for the determination of fair market value for the purposes of section 3(18)(B) and section 8477(a)(2)(B). First, proposed § 2510.3-18(b)(2)(ii) requires that fair market value must be determined as of the date of the transaction involving that asset. This requirement is designed to prevent situations such as arose in *Donovan v. Cunningham, supra.* In that case, the plan fiduciaries relied on a 1975 appraisal to set the value of employer securities purchased by an ESOP during 1976 and thereafter, and failed to take into account significant changes in the company's business condition in the interim. The court found that this reliance was unwarranted, and therefore the fiduciaries' valuation failed to reflect adequate consideration under section 3(18)(B). *Id.* at 1468-69.

Second, proposed § 2510.3-18(b)(2)(iii) states that the determination of fair market value must be reflected in written documentation of valuation[2] meeting the content requirements set forth in § 2510.3-18(b)(4). (The valuation content requirements are discussed below.) The Department has proposed this requirement in light of the role the adequate consideration requirement plays in a number of statutory exemptions from the prohibited transaction provisions of the Act. In determining whether a statutory exemption applies to a particular transaction, the burden of proof is upon the party seeking to make use of the statutory exemption to show that all the requirements of the provision are met. *Donovan v. Cunningham, supra,* 716 F. 2d at 1467 n. 27. In the Department's view, written documentation relating to the valuation is necessary for a determination of how, and on what basis, an asset was valued, and therefore whether that valuation reflected an asset's fair market value. In addition, the Department believes that it would be contrary to prudent business practices for a fiduciary to act in the absence of such written documentation of fair market value.

3. Good Faith

The second part of the Department's proposed two-part test under section 3(18)(B) and section 8477(a)(2)(B) requires that an assessment of adequate consideration be the product of a determination made in good faith by the plan trustee or named fiduciary (or under FERSA, a fiduciary). Proposed § 2510.3-18(b)(3)(i) states that as a general matter this good faith requirement establishes an objective standard of conduct, rather than mandating an inquiry into the intent or state of mind of the plan trustee or named fiduciary. In this regard, the proposal is consistent with the opinion in *Donovan v. Cunningham, supra,* where the court stated that the good faith requirement in section 3(18)(B):

is not a search for subjective good faith * * * The statutory reference to good faith in Section 3(18) must be read in light of the overriding duties of Section 404.

716 F. 2d at 1467. The inquiry into good faith under the proposal therefore focuses on the fiduciary's conduct in determining fair market value. An examination of all relevant facts and circumstances is necessary for a determination of whether a fiduciary has met this objective good faith standard.

Proposed § 2510.3-18(b)(3)(ii) focuses on two factors which must be present in order for the Department to be satisfied, that the fiduciary has acted in good faith. First, this section would require a fiduciary to apply sound business principles of evaluation and to conduct a prudent investigation of the circumstances prevailing at the time of the valuation. This requirement reflects the *Cunningham* court's emphasis on the use of prudent business practices in valuing plan assets.

Second, this section states that either the fiduciary making the valuation must itself be independent of all the parties to the transaction

(other than the plan), or the fiduciary must rely on the report of an appraiser who is independent of all the parties to the transaction (other than the plan). (The criteria for determining independence are discussed below.) As noted above, under ERISA, the determination of adequate consideration is a central safeguard in many statutory exemptions applicable to plan transactions with the plan sponsor. The close relationship between the plan and the plan sponsor in such situations raises a significant potential for conflicts of interest as the fiduciary values assets which are the subject of transactions between the plan and the plan sponsor. In light of this possibility, the Department believes that good faith may only be demonstrated when the valuation is made by persons independent of the parties to the transaction (other than the plan), *i.e.,* a valuation made by an independent fiduciary or by a fiduciary acting pursuant to the report of an independent appraiser.

The Department emphasizes that the two requirements of proposed § 2510.3-18(b)(3)(ii) are designed to work in concert. For example, a plan fiduciary charged with valuation may be independent of all the parties to a transaction and may, in light of the requirement of proposed § 2510.3-18(b)(3)(ii)(B), decide to undertake the valuation process itself. However, if the independent fiduciary has neither the experience, facilities nor expertise to make the type of valuation under consideration, the decision by that fiduciary to make the valuation would fail to meet the prudent investigation and sound business principles of proposed § 2510.3-18(b)(3)(ii)(A).

Proposed § 2510.3-18(b)(3)(iii) defines the circumstances under which a fiduciary or an appraiser will be deemed to be independent for the purposes of subparagraph (3)(ii)(B), above. The proposal notes that the fiduciary or the appraiser must in fact be independent of all parties participating in the transaction other than the plan. The proposal also notes that a determination of independence must be made in light of all relevant facts and circumstances, and then delineates certain circumstances under which this independence will be lacking. These circumstances reflect the definitions of the terms "affiliate" and "control" in Departmental regulation 29 CFR 2510.3-21(c) (defining the circumstances under which an investment adviser is a fiduciary). It should be noted that, under these proposed provisions, an appraiser will be considered independent of all parties to a transaction (other than the plan) only if a plan fiduciary has chosen the appraiser and has the right to terminate that appointment, and the plan is thereby established as the appraiser's client.[3] Absent such circumstances, the appraiser may be unable to be completely neutral in the exercise of his function.[4]

4. Valuation Content—General

Proposed § 2510.3-18(b)(4)(i) sets the content requirements for the written documentation of valuation required for a determination of fair market value under proposed § 2510.3-18(b)(2)(iii). The proposal follows to a large extent the requirements of Rev. Proc. 66-49, 1966-2 C. B. 1257, which sets forth the format required by the IRS for the valuation of donated property. The Department believes that this format is a familiar one, and will therefore facilitate compliance. Several additions to the IRS requirement merit brief explanation.

First, proposed paragraph (b)(4)(i)(E) requires a statement of the purpose for which the valuation was made. A valuation undertaken, for example, for a yearly financial report may prove an inadequate basis for any sale of the asset in question. This requirement is intended to facilitate review of the valuation in the correct context.

Second, proposed paragraph (b)(4)(i)(F) requires a statement as to the relative weight accorded to relevant valuation methodologies. The Department's experience in this area indicates that there are a number of different methodologies used within the appraisal industry. By varying the treatment given and emphasis accorded relevant information, these methodologies directly affect the result of the appraiser's analysis. It is the Department's understanding that appraisers will often use different methodologies to cross-check their results. A statement of the method or methods used would allow for a more accurate assessment of the validity of the valuation.

(Footnote Continued)

should have about the asset or its market, e. g., that the property's value should reflect a premium due to a certain developer's specific land development plans.

[2] It should be noted that the written valuation required by this section of the proposal need not be a written report of an independent appraiser. Rather, it should be documentation sufficient to allow the Department to determine whether the content requirements of § 2510.3-18(b)(4) have been satisfied. The use of an independent appraiser may be relevant to a determination of good faith, as discussed with regard to proposed § 2510.3-18(b)(3), *infra,* but it is not required to satisfy the fair market value criterion in § 2510.3-18(b)(2)(i).

[3] The independence of an appraiser will not be affected solely because the plan sponsor pays the appraiser's fee.

[4] With regard to this independence requirement the Department notes that new section 401(a)(28) of the Code (added by section 1175(a) of the Tax Reform Act of 1986) requires that, in the case of an employee stock ownership plan, employer securities which are not readily tradable on established securities markets must be valued by an independent appraiser. New section 401(a)(28)(C) states that the term "independent appraiser" means an appraiser meeting requirements similar to the requirements of regulations under section 170(a)(1) of the Code (relating to IRS verification of the value assigned for deduction purposes to assets donated to charitable organizations). The Department notes that the requirements of proposed regulation § 2510.3-18(b)(3)(iii) are not the same as the requirements of the regulations issued by the IRS under section 170(a)(1) of the Code. The IRS has not yet promulgated rules under Code section 401(a)(28).

Finally, proposed subparagraph (b)(4)(i)(G) requires a statement of the valuation's effective date. This reflects the requirement in proposed § 2510.3-18(b)(ii) that fair market value must be determined as of the date of the transaction in question.

5. Valuation Content—Special Rule

Proposed § 2510.3-18(b)(4)(ii) establishes additional content requirements for written documentation of valuation when the asset being appraised is a security other than a security for which there is a generally recognized market. In other words, the requirements of the proposed special rule supplement, rather than supplant, the requirements of paragraph (b)(4)(i). The proposed special rule establishes a nonexclusive list of factors to be considered when the asset being valued is a security not covered by section 3(18)(A) of the Act or section 8477(a)(2)(A) of FERSA. Such securities pose special valuation problems because they are not traded or are so thinly traded that it is difficult to assess the effect on such securities of the market forces usually considered in determining fair market value. The Internal Revenue Service has had occasion to address the valuation problems posed by one type of such securities—securities issued by closely held corporations. Rev. Rul. 59-60. 1959-1 Cum. Bull. 237, lists a variety of factors to be considered when valuing securities of closely held corporation for tax purposes.[5] The Department's experience indicates that Rev. Rul. 59-60 is familiar to plan fiduciaries, plan sponsors and the corporate community in general. The Department has, therefore, modeled this proposed special rule after Rev. Rul. 59-60 with certain additions and changes discussed below. It should be emphasized, however, that this is a non-exclusive list of factors to be considered. Certain of the factors listed may not be relevant to every valuation inquiry, although the fiduciary will bear the burden of demonstrating such irrelevance. Similarly, reliance on this list will not relieve fiduciaries from the duty to consider all relevant facts and circumstances when valuing such securities. The purpose of the proposed list is to guide fiduciaries in the course of their inquiry.

Several of the factors listed in proposed § 2510.3-18(b)(4)(ii) merit special comment and explanation. Proposed subparagraph (G) states that the fair market value of securities other than those for which there is a generally recognized market may be established by reference to the market price of similar securities of corporations engaged in the same or a similar line of business whose securities are actively traded in a free and open market, either on an exchange or over the counter. The Department intends that the degree of comparability must be assessed in order to approximate as closely as possible the market forces at work with regard to the corporation issuing the securities in question.

Proposed subparagraph (H) requires an assessment of the effect of the securities' marketability or lack thereof. Rev. Rul. 59-60 does not explicitly require such an assessment, but the Department believes that the marketability of these types of securities will directly affect their price. In this regard, the Department is aware that, especially in situations involving employee stock ownership plans (ESOPs),[6] the employer securities held by the ESOP will provide a "put" option whereby individual participants may upon retirement sell their shares back to the employer.[7] It has been argued that some kinds of "put" options may diminish the need to discount the value of the securities due to lack of marketability. The Department believes that the existence of the "put" option should be considered for valuation purposes only to the extent it is enforceable and the employer has and may reasonably be expected to continue to have, adequate resources to meet its obligations. Thus, the Department proposes to require that the plan fiduciary assess whether these "put" rights are actually enforceable, and whether the employer will be able to pay for the securities when and if the "put" is exercised.

Finally, proposed subparagraph (I) deals with the role of control premiums in valuing securities other than those for which there is a generally recognized market. The Department proposes that a plan purchasing control may pay a control premium, and a plan selling control should receive a control premium. Specifically, the Department proposes that a plan may pay such a premium only to the extent a third party would pay a control premium. In this regard, the Department's

position is that the payment of a control premium is unwarranted unless the plan obtains both voting control and control in fact. The Department will therefore carefully scrutinize situations to ascertain whether the transtion involving payment of such a premium actually results in the passing of control to the plan. For example, it may be difficult to determine that a plan paying a control premium has received control in fact where it is reasonable to assume at the time of acquisition that distribution of shares to plan participants will cause the plan's control of the company to be dissipated within a short period of time subsequent to acquisition.[8] In the Department's view, however, a plan would not fail to receive control merely because individuals who were previously officers, directors or shareholders of the corporation continue as plan fiduciaries or corporate officials after the plan has acquired the securities. Nonetheless, the retention of management and the utilization of corporate officials as plan fiduciaries, when viewed in conjunction with other facts, may indicate that actual control has not passed to the plan within the meaning of paragraph (b)(4)(ii)(I) of the proposed regulation. Similarly, if the plan purchases employer securities in small increments pursuant to an understanding with the employer that the employer will eventually sell a controlling portion of shares to the plan, a control premium would be warranted only to the extent that the understanding with the employer was actually a binding agreement obligating the employer to pass control within a reasonable time. See *Donovan v. Cunningham, supra,* 716 F. 2d at 1472-74 (mere intention to transfer control not sufficient).

6. Service Arrangements Subject to FERSA

Section 8477(c)(1)(C) of FERSA permits the exchange of services between the Thrift Savings Fund and a party in interest only in exchange for adequate consideration. In this context, the proposal defines the term "adequate consideration" as "reasonable compensation" , as that term is described in sections 408(b)(2) and 408(c)(2) of ERISA and the regulations promulgated thereunder. By so doing, the proposal would establish a consistent standard of exemptive relief for both ERISA and FERSA with regard to what otherwise would be prohibited service arrangements.

Regulatory Flexibility Act

The Department has determined that this regulation would not have a significant economic effect on small plans. In conducting the analysis required under the Regulatory Flexibility Act, it was estimated that approximately 6,250 small plans may be affected by the regulation. The total additional cost to these plans, over and above the costs already being incurred under established valuation practices, are estimated not to exceed $875,000 per year, or $140 per plan for small plans choosing to engage in otherwise prohibited transactions that are exempted under the statute conditioned on a finding of adequate consideration.

Executive Order 12291

The Department has determined that the proposed regulatory action would not constitute a "major role" as that term is used in Executive Order 12291 because the action would not result in an annual effect on the economy of $100 million; a major increase in costs of prices for consumers, individual industries, government agencies, or geographical regions; or significant adverse effects on competition, employment, investment, productivity, innovation, or on the ability of United States based enterprises to compete with foreign based enterprises in domestic or export markets.

Paperwork Reduction Act

This proposed regulation contains several paperwork requirements. The regulation has been forwarded for approval to the Office of Management and Budget under the provisions of the Paperwork Reduction Act of 1980 (Pub. L. 96-511). A control number has not yet been assigned.

Statutory Authority

This regulation is proposed under section 3(18) and 505 of the Act (29 U. S. C. 1003(18) and 1135); Secretary of Labor's Order No. 1-87; and sections 8477(a)(2)(B) and 8477(f) of FERSA.

List of Subjects in 29 CFR Part 2510

---

[5] Rev. Rul. 89-60 was modified by Rev. Rul. 65-193 (1965-2 C. B. 370) regarding the valuation of tangible and intangible corporate assets. The provisions of Rev. Rul. 59-60, as modified, were extended to the valuation of corporate securities for income and other tax purposes by Rev. Rul. 68-809 (1968-3 C. B. 327). In addition, Rev. Rul. 77-287 (1977-2 C. B. 319), amplified. Rev. Rul. 59-60 by indicating the ways in which the factors listed in Rev. Rul. 59-60 should be applied when valuing restricted securities.

[6] The definition of the term "adequate consideration" under ERISA is of particular Importance to the establishment and maintenance of ESOPs because, pursuant to section 408(e) of the Act, an ESOP may acquire employer securities from a party in interest only

under certain conditions, including that the plan pay no more than adequate consideration for the securities.

[7] Regulation 29 CFR 2550.406b-(j) requires such a put option in order for a loan from a party in Interest to the ESOP to qualify for the statutory exemption in section 406(b)(3) of ERISA from the prohibited transactions provisions of ERISA.

[8] However, the Department notes that the mere pass-through of voting rights to participants would not in itself effect a determination that a plan has received control in fact, notwithstanding the existence of participant voting rights, if the plan fiduciaries having control over plan assets ordinarily may resell the shares to a third party and command a control premium, without the need to secure the approval of the plan participants.

Employee benefit plans, Employee Retirement Income Security Act, Pensions, Pension and Welfare Benefit Administration.

Proposed Regulation

For the reasons set out in the preamble, the Department proposes to amend Part 2510 of Chapter XXV of Title 29 of the Code of Federal Regulations as follows:

PART 2510—[AMENDED]

1. The authority for Part 2510 is revised to read as follows:

Authority: Sec. 3(2), 111(c), 505, Pub. L. 93-406, 88 Stat. 852, 894, (29 U. S. C. 1002(2), 1031, 1135); Secretary of Labor's Order No. 27-74, 1-86, 1-87, and Labor Management Services Administration Order No. 2-6.

Section 2510.3-18 is also issued under sec. 3(18) of the Act (29 U. S. C. 1003(18)) and secs. 8477(a)(2)(B) and (f) of FERSA (5 U. S. C. 8477).

Section 2510.3-101 is also issued under sec. 102 of Reorganization Plan No. 4 of 1978 (43 FR 47713, October 17, 1978), effective December 31, 1978 (44 FR 1065, January 3, 1978); 3 CFR 1978 Comp. 332, and sec. 11018(d) of Pub. L. 99-272, 100 Stat. 82.

Section 2510.3-102 is also issued under sec. 102 of Reorganization Plan No. 4 of 1978 (43 FR 47713, October 17, 1978), effective December 31, 1978 (44 FR 1065, January 3, 1978), and 3 CFR 1978 Comp. 332.

2. Section 2510.3-18 is added to read as follows:

§ 2510.3-18 Adequate Consideration.

(a) [Reserved]

(b)(1)(i) *General.* (A) Section 3(18)(B) of the Employee Retirement Income Security Act of 1974 (the Act) provides that, in the case of a plan asset other than a security for which there is a generally recognized market, the term "adequate consideration" when used in Part 4 of Subtitle B of Title I of the Act means the fair market value of the asset as determined in good faith by the trustee or named fiduciary pursuant to the terms of the plan and in accordance with regulations promulgated by the Secretary of Labor.

(B) Section 8477(a)(2)(B) of the Federal Employees' Retirement System Act of 1986 (FERSA) provides that, in the case of an asset other than a security for which there is a generally recognized market, the term "adequate consideration" means the fair market value of the asset as determined in good faith by a fiduciary or fiduciaries in accordance with regulations prescribed by the Secretary of Labor.

(ii) *Scope.* The requirements of section 3(18)(B) of the Act and section 8477(a)(2)(B) of FERSA will not be met unless the value assigned to a plan asset both reflects the asset's fair market value as defined in paragraph (b)(2) of this section and results from a determination made by the plan trustee or named fiduciary (or, in the case of FERSA, a fiduciary) in good faith as described in paragraph (b)(3) of this section. Paragraph (b)(5) of this section contains a special rule for service contracts subject to FERSA.

(2) *Fair Market Value.* (i) Except as otherwise specified in this section, the term "fair market value" as used in section 3(18)(B) of the Act and section 8477(a)(2)(B) of FERSA means the price at which an asset would change hands between a willing buyer and a willing seller when the former is not under any compulsion to buy and the latter is not under any compulsion to sell, and both parties are able, as well as willing, to trade and are well informed about the asset and the market for such asset.

(ii) The fair market value of an asset for the purposes of section 3(18)(B) of the Act and section 8477(a)(2)(B) of FERSA must be determined as of the date of the transaction involving that asset.

(iii) The fair market value of an asset for the purposes of section 3(18)(B) of the Act and section 8477(a)(2)(B) of FERSA must be reflected in written documentation of valuation meeting the requirements set forth in paragraph (b)(4), of this section.

(3) *Good Faith*—(i) *General Rule.* The requirement in section 3(18)(B) of the Act and section 8477(a)(2)(B) of FERSA that the fiduciary must determine fair market value in good faith establishes an objective, rather than a subjective, standard of conduct. Subject to the conditions in paragraphs (b)(3)(ii) and (iii) of this section, an assessment of whether the fiduciary has acted in good faith will be made in light of all relevant facts and circumstances.

(ii) In considering all relevant facts and circumstances, the Department will not view a fiduciary as having acted in good faith unless

(A) The fiduciary has arrived at a determination of fair market value by way of a prudent investigation of circumstances prevailing at the

time of the valuation, and the application of sound business principles of evaluation; and

(B) The fiduciary making the valuation either,

(1) Is independent of all parties to the transaction (other than the plan), or

(2) Relies on the report of an appraiser who is independent of all parties to the transaction (other than the plan).

(iii) In order to satisfy the independence requirement of paragraph (b)(3)(ii)(B), of this section, a person must in fact be independent of all parties (other than the plan) participating in the transaction. For the purposes of this section, an assessment of independence will be made in light of all relevant facts and circumstances. However, a person will not be considered to be independent of all parties to the transaction if that person—

(1) Is directly or indirectly, through one or more intermediaries, controlling, controlled by, or under common control with any of the parties to the transaction (other than the plan);

(2) Is an officer, director, partner, employee, employer or relative (as defined in section 3(15) of the Act, and including siblings) of any such parties (other than the plan);

(3) Is a corporation or partnership of which any such party (other than the plan) is an officer, director or partner.

For the purposes of this subparagraph, the term "control," in connection with a person other than an individual, means the power to exercise a controlling influence over the management or policies of that person.

(4) *Valuation Content.* (i) In order to comply with the requirement in paragraph (b)(2)(iii), of this section, that the determination of fair market value be reflected in written documentation of valuation, such written documentation must contain, at a minimum, the following information:

(A) A summary of the qualifications to evaluate assets of the type being valued of the person or persons making the valuation;

(B) A statement of the asset's value, a statement of the methods used in determining that value, and the reasons for the valuation in light of those methods;

(C) A full description of the asset being valued;

(D) The factors taken into account in making the valuation, including any restrictions, understandings, agreements or obligations limiting the use or disposition of the property;

(E) The purpose for which the valuation was made;

(F) The relevance or significance accorded to the valuation methodologies taken into account;

(G) The effective date of the valuation; and

(H) In cases where a valuation report has been prepared, the signature of the person making the valuation and the date the report was signed.

(ii) *Special Rule.* When the asset being valued is a security other than a security covered by section 3(18)(A) of the Act or section 8477(a)(2)(A) of FERSA, the written valuation required by paragraph (b)(2)(iii) of this section, must contain the information required in paragraph (b)(4)(i) of this section, and must include, in addition to an assessment of all other relevant factors, an assessment of the factors listed below:

(A) The nature of the business and the history of the enterprise from its inception;

(B) The economic outlook in general, and the condition and outlook of the specific industry in particular;

(C) The book value of the securities and the financial condition of the business;

(D) The earning capacity of the company;

(E) The dividend-paying capacity of the company;

(F) Whether or not the enterprise has goodwill or other intangible value;

(G) The market price of securities of corporations engaged in the same or a similar line of business, which are actively traded in a free and open market, either on an exchange or over-the-counter;

(H) The marketability, or lack thereof, of the securities. Where the plan is the purchaser of securities that are subject to "put" rights and such rights are taken into account in reducing the discount for lack of marketability, such assessment shall include consideration of the extent to which such rights are enforceable, as well as the company's ability to meet its obligations with respect to the "put" rights (taking into account the company's financial strength and liquidity);

(I) Whether or not the seller would be able to obtain a control premium from an unrelated third party with regard to the block of securities being valued, provided that in cases where a control premium is taken into account:

(*1*) Actual control (both in form and in substance) is passed to the purchaser with the sale, or will be passed to the purchaser within a reasonable time pursuant to a binding agreement in effect at the time of the sale, and

(*2*) It is reasonable to assume that the purchaser's control will not be dissipated within a short period of time subsequent to acquisition.

¶ 20,531F   Reserved.

Proposed Department of Labor regulations on procedures for filing and processing applications for exemptions from the prohibited transaction provisions of ERISA, the Internal Revenue Code, and the Federal Employees' Retirement System Act of 1986 formerly appeared here.

The final regulations are at ¶ 14,789C to ¶ 14,789Y.]

¶ 20,531G   Reserved.

Formerly reproduced at this paragraph were proposed PBGC regulations relating to insurance premiums for single-employer plans.

The final regulations appear at ¶ 15,371—15,371V.]

¶ 20,532   Reserved.

Proposed Reg. § § 2608.2—2608.7 were formerly reproduced at this point.

The final regulations appear at ¶ 15,472—15,473V.]

¶ 20,532A

Proposed regulation on 29 CFR Part 2619—Valuation— Single-employer plans.—Reproduced below is the text of a proposed rule which would amend the PBGC final regulations on Valuation of Plan Benefits in Non-Multiemployer Plans to change the interest assumption for the immediate and deferred annuity rates, so as to make it the same as that under the multiemployer regulation.

The proposed regulation was published in the *Federal Register* on March 25, 1986 (51 FR 10334).

PENSION BENEFIT GUARANTY CORPORATION

29 CFR Part 2619

Valuation of Plan Benefit In Non-Multiemployer Plan

AGENCY: Pension Benefit Guaranty Corporation.

ACTION: Proposed rule.

SUMMARY: This is a proposed amendment to the Pension Benefit Guaranty Corporation's regulation on Valuation of Plan Benefits in Non-Multiemployer Plans. If adopted, this amendment would change the interests assumption prescribed by the regulation, and make corresponding changes in the actuarial formulas used under the regulation, to eliminate inaccuracies inherent in the existing assumption and to achieve uniformity with the interest assumption and formulas proposed for multiemployer plans.

DATES: Comments must be received on or before May 27, 1986.

ADDRESSES: Comments should be addressed to Director, Corporate Policy and Regulations Department (611), Pension Benefit Guaranty Corporation, 2020 K Street, NW., Washington, DC 20006. Written comments will be available for public inspection at the PBGC, Suite 7100, at the above address, between 9:00 a.m. and 4:00 p.m.

FOR FURTHER INFORMATION CONTACT: Deborah Murphy, Attorney, Corporate Policy and Regulations Department (611), 2020 K Street, NW., Washington, DC 20006, 202-254-4860 (202-254-8010 for TTY and TDD). These are not toll free numbers.

SUPPLEMENTARY INFORMATION:

Background

The Pension Benefit Guaranty Corporation ("PBGC") published a final regulation on Valuation of Plan Benefits in Non-Multiemployer

(5) *Service Arrangements Subject to FERSA.* For purposes of determinations pursuant to section 8477(c)(1)(C) of FERSA (relating to the provision of services) the term "adequate consideration" under section 8477(a)(2)(B) of FERSA means "reasonable compensation" as defined in sections 408(b)(2) and 408(c)(2) of the Act and § § 2550.408b-2(d) and 2550.408e-2 of this chapter.

(6) *Effective Date.* This section will be effective for transactions taking place after the date 30 days following publication of the final regulation in the *Federal Register*.

Signed in Washington, DC, this 11th day of May 1988.

David M. Walker,

Assistant Secretary, Pension and Welfare Benefits Administration, U. S. Department of Labor.

[FR Doc. 88-10934 Filed 5-16-88; 8:45 am]

Plans (the "Single-employer regulation") on January 28, 1981 (40 FR 9497). The regulation was subsequently amended and is now codified as 29 CFR Part 2619. On February 19, 1985 (50 FR 6956), the PBGC published a proposed regulation on Valuation of Plan Assets and Plan Benefits Following Mass Withdrawal (The "multiemployer regulation"). As proposed, the multiemployer regulation would be codified as 29 CFR Part 2676. For reasons discussed below, this proposed amendment would change the interest assumption under the existing single-employer regulation to make it the same as that under the multi employer regulation.

Under the single-employer regulation, benefits in pay status on the valuation date are valued using a flat rate of interest (the immediate annuity rate). Benefits that are to start after the valuation date are valued in two steps. First, the benefit is valued as of its deferred starting date using the immediate annuity rate. Second, an adjustment is made for the period of deferral. The adjustment is represented by a factor that has the effect of reducing the assumed interest rate. The amount of reduction is greater for longer periods of deferral. The particular interest rates that are applicable from time to time, together with the manner of applying them to the valuation of benefits as summarized above. constitute the single.employer regulation's interest assumption.

The preamble to the original proposal version of the single-employer regulation (40 FR 57960. December 12, 1975), in discussing the adjustment factor for deferred benefits, noted that "[i]t is common financial practice to assume that the rate of return on investments made in the future will be lower than that for investments made in the present or near future." (40 FR at 57983.)

When the regulation was published as an interim rule. however (41 FR 46460, November 3, 1976). the preamble warned, in response to comments on the proposed rule, that the deferred benefit adjustment factor should not be "misconstrued as an investment model which actually reflects the investment yields which the PBGC expects to realize during a particular year of deferment. Rather, the current value of annuities obtained by applying the [factor] is in line with price data for such annuities received from the industry." (41 FR at 46485.)

Clearly, an interest assumption that applies the same rate (the immediate annuity rate) to every payment under a pay status annuity. as the single-employer regulation does, is not to be regarded as "an investment model." The design of the deferred benefit adjustment factor used in the regulation merely highlights that fact. As noted in the preamble to the proposed multiemployer regulation. the single-employer interest assumption "represents an appropriate compromise between actuarial theory . . . and administrative convenience." (50 FR at 6957.)

In this context, "administrative convenience" means primarily ease of computation. Although many single-employer plans have been valued by computer for years. some (mostly small) plan valuations have not been computerized. The present single-employer interest assumption "facilitates the valuation of benefits 'by hand' (*i.e.,* using nothing more sophisticated than a desk calculator) from tables of relatively small bulk." (50 FR at 6957.)

In introducing the proposed multiemployer regulation, on the other hand, the PBGC indicated that, "[b]ecause of economies of scale, valuations by computer are not merely cost-justified but, in general, a financial, as well as logistical, necessity" for multiemployer plans. (50 FR at 6957.) This was one reason why the PBGC considered it appropriate to propose a select and ultimate interest assumption for multiemployer valuations. The primary motivation for proposing such an assumption, of course, was that the use of select and ultimate interest yields results that exhibit better internal consistency and closer agreement with marketplace values, both in the aggregate and for individual streams of payments. A select and ultimate interest assumption applies to each payment under a benefit an individually determined interest rate that depends on the amount of time between the valuation date and the date of payment. As a practical matter, therefore, the select and ultimate interest assumption makes valuations without the use of a computer impossible. On the other hand, it comes much closer to being an "investment model." Thus, in the PBGC's view, the multiemployer assumption leads to more realistic valuations than the single-employer assumption does.

A further problem with valuations under the existing single-employer regulation is that, as pointed out in the preamble to that regulation (46 FR at 9495), the adjustment factor for deferred benefits ignores the mortality of the beneficiary where joint and survivor benefits are being valued. Leaving the beneficiary's mortality out of the factor simplifies calculations that use the factor, but reduces the accuracy of values generated with the factor. The need for this distorting simplification would disappear if a computerized valuation method were adopted.

Until 1964, the provisions of the single-employer regulation that would be affected by this amendment applied almost exclusively to the PBGC itself, rather than to plan administrators. Thus, any administrative inconvenience arising from the adoption of this amendment would have been confined to a very few plans, primarily those for which the PBGC assumed the burden of paying certain deferred benefits.

Under sections 103 and 203 of the Retirement Equity Act of 1984, the interest rate assumption that the PBGC would use to value benefits on plan termination became the standard for determining the value of a participant's benefit in situations where the benefit is or may be cashed out. The PBGC specifically invites public comment on the administrative difficulty of processing cashouts using the proposed select and ultimate interest assumption as opposed to the existing single-employer interest assumption and on the number of cashouts that are processed by plans each year and that would be affected by the proposed assumption.

It appears that the valuation standards that would be changed by this amendment have been voluntarily adopted in some cases where their use is not legally mandated. The PBGC does not know what effect the proposed amendment might have on such situations, nor how many such situations there are. Comments are invited on the impact of the amendment on such cases and the extent to which any such impact should be considered by the PBGC.

Even for plans affected by this amendment, administrative inconvenience should be minimal. The single-employer regulation has been in effect, in interim and final form, since 1976, before the microcomputer had become the ubiquitous business tool that it is today. Microcomputers capable of handling actuarial computations with select and ultimate interest are as common now as electronic calculators were when the single-employer regulation was first drafted. The PBGC has

thus concluded that accuracy need no longer make the concessions to administrative convenience that the existing single-employer interest assumption reflects.

Accordingly, the PBGC proposes to amend the single-employer regulation to substitute for the existing interest assumption the select and ultimate interest assumption used in the recently proposed multiemployer regulation. To reflect this change, the actuarial formulas in the single-employer regulation would be replaced by the corresponding formulas from the proposed multiemployer regulation.

The PBGC recognizes that microcomputer programs to evaluate actuarial formulas with select and ultimate interest may not be widely available, and that some people, including perhaps even some actuaries, may not feel confident about writing such programs for themselves. The PBGC is therefore considering the possibility of developing such programs and making them available to the public at cost. Public comment on this possibility is invited.

The Amendment

The major changes made by the amendment would be in Subpart C of the single-employer regulation (existing § § 2619.41 through 2619.48). However, § § 2619.3(a) and 2619.25(b)(2), which refer to certain Subpart C provisions, would be revised, and a new § 2619.25(c) would be added, simply to reflect changes that the amendment would make in Subpart C. Appendices A, B, and C, which contain mortality and interest tables, would be deleted, because mortality and interest tables in the amended regulation would be included in Subpart C.

The amendment would have no effect on the first section (§ 2619.41, *Purpose and scope*) or the last section (existing § 2619.48, *Withdrawal of employee contributions*) of Subpart C, except to renumber the latter as § 2619.46. All of the other sections of Subpart C would be deleted and replaced by slightly reworded versions of § § 2676.12 through 2676.15 from the multiemployer regulation.

New § 2619.42(a) restates the rule from existing § 2619.43(b) regarding the form of benefit to be valued. New § 2619.42(b) restates the rule regarding the timing of benefits from existing § 2619.46(b). (Note that the latter rule is not the same as the corresponding provision of the proposed multiemployer regulation (§ 2676.12(b)).)

New § 2619.43(a) carries over the substance of existing § § 2619.43(a) and (c) and 2619.44(a). Like existing § 2619.43(a) (and unlike § 2676.13(a) in the multiemployer regulation), the new section makes clear that the actuarial formulas set forth in the regulation are to be regarded as standards of accuracy, not as absolute requirements.

Paragraphs (b) through (i) of new § 2619.43 contain actuarial formulas that would replace the formulas now set forth in existing § § 2619.44, 2619.45, and 2619.47. The new formulas in paragraphs (b) through (h) are identical with those in multiemployer § 2676.13(b) through (h). Paragraph (i) supplies new formulas for the death benefits described in existing § 2619.47(d) through (f), which were not included in the proposed multiemployer regulation.

The following table shows the location of the proposed new formula corresponding to each valuation provision in the existing regulation.

Existing provision	Proposed provision
§ 2619.44(c)	§ 2619.43(c)(2)
§ 2619.44(d)	§ 2619.43(c)(1)
§ 2619.44(e)	§ 2619.43(g)(2)
§ 2619.44(f)	§ 2619.43(g)(1)
§ 2619.44(g)	§ 2619.43(c)(3)
§ 2619.44(h)	§ 2619.43(e)(2)
§ 2619.44(i)	§ 2619.43(e)(1)
§ 2619.44(j)	§ 2619.43(e)(4)
§ 2619.44(k)	§ 2619.43(e)(4)
§ 2619.44(l)	§ 2619.43(e)(3)
§ 2619.45	§ 2619.43(b), (d), (f), (g)(3), (g)(4)
§ 2619.47(b)	§ 2619.43(h)(1)
§ 2619.47(c)	§ 2619.43(h)(2)
§ 2619.47(d)	§ 2619.43(i)(1)
§ 2619.47(e)	§ 2619.43(i)(1)
§ 2619.47(f)	§ 2619.43(i)(2)

Paragraphs (m) and (n) of existing § 2619.44 are no longer considered necessary and accordingly have no counterparts in the amended regulation. (Those provisions merely explained that two common forms of benefit—cash refund and installment refund annuities—could be analyzed in terms of other benefits listed elsewhere in the regulations.) The benefits described in existing § § 2619.44(j) and 2619.47(d) are simply special cases of the benefits described in amended § 2619.43(e)(4) and (i)(1) respectively.

New § 2619.44 contains the prescribed mortality tables currently found in appendix C. (Appendix A, containing data from which the mortality tables in Appendix C can be derived, is no longer considered necessary. Thus both Appendices A and C are replaced by new § 2619.44.) New § 2619.44 also contains provisions derived from existing § 2619.44(b) concerning the circumstances under which each table is to be used.

The select and ultimate rate series that is at the heart of the amendment would be set forth in new § 2619.45. The series used in this regulation would be identical with the series used in the multiemployer regulation. A new series would be promulgated each month as necessary to respond to changes in current rates of investment return and expectations regarding future rates. The rates series would be constructed so as to produce values, for a typical plan, within a few percent of the cost of commercial annuities covering the plan's benefits—the same criterion used in setting rates under the existing single-employer regulation. Existing Appendix B, which contains interest rates applicable under the current regulation, would be superseded by new § 2619.45.

E.O. 12291 and the Regulatory Flexibility Act

The PBGC has determined that this proposed regulation is not a "major rule" for the purposes of Executive Order 12291, because it will not have an annual effect on the economy of $100 million or more; or create a major increase in costs or prices for consumers, individual industries, or geographic regions; or have significant adverse effects on competition, employment, investment, innovation, or the ability of United States-based enterprises to compete with foreign-based enterprises in domestic or export markets.

Under section 605(b) of the Regulatory Flexibility Act, the PBGC certifies that this rule will not have a significant economic impact on a substantial number of small entities. Pension plans with fewer than 100 participants have traditionally been treated as small plans. Such plans typically contract with actuarial firms, insurance companies, and other service providers for actuarial services. The larger providers of actuarial services perform valuations by computer, and such providers serve the great majority of small plans. For such service providers, the proposed amendment would necessitate a one-time programming expense that would be amortized over a period of time and spread among not only small plan clients but larger plan clients as well. The economic impact of the amendment on each such small plan would thus be insignificant. While the amendment might have a significant economic impact on small plans that are not currently valued by computer, the number of such plans is considered to be insignificant. Therefore, compliance with sections 603 and 604 of the Regulatory Flexibility Act is waived.

Public Comments

Interested parties are invited to submit comments on this proposed regulation. Comments should be addressed to: Director, Corporate Policy and Regulations Department (611), Pension Benefit Guaranty Corporation, 2020 K Street, NW., Washington, DC 20006. Written comments will be available for public inspection at the above address, Suite 7100, between the hours of 9:00 a.m. and 4:00 p.m. Comments should include the commenter's name and address, identify this proposed regulation, and give reasons for any recommendation. This proposal may be changed in light of the comments received.

List of Subjects in 29 CFR Part 2619

Employee benefits plans, Pension insurance, Pensions.

PART 2619—[AMENDED]

In consideration of the foregoing, it is proposed that 29 CFR Part 2619 be amended as follows:

1. The authority citation for Part 2619 continues to read as follows:

Authority: Secs. 4002(b)(3), 4041(b), 4044, 4062(b)(1)(A), Pub. L. 93-406, 88 Stat. 1004, 1020, 1025, 1029, as amended by secs. 403(1), 403(d), 402(a)(7), Pub. L. 96-364, 94 Stat. 1302, 1301, 1299 (29 U.S.C. 1302, 1341, 1344, 1362).

2. In § 2619.3, paragraph (a) is revised to read as follows:

§ 2619.3 General valuation rules.

(a) *Non-trusteed plans.* Plan administrators of non-trusteed plans shall value plan benefits in accordance with Subpart B of this part, except for any early retirement benefits to be provided by PBGC, which shall be valued in accordance with Subpart C. If a plan with respect to which PBGC has issued a Notice of Sufficiency is unable to satisfy all benefits assigned to priority categories 1 through 4 on the date of distribution,

the PBGC will place it into trusteeship and the plan administrator shall re-value the benefits in accordance with Subpart C of this part.

* * *

3. In § 2619.25, paragraph (b)(2) is revised, and a new paragraph (c) is added, to read as follows:

§ 2619.25 Early retirement benefits.

* * *

(b) * * *

(2) If the plan administrator is unable to obtain a qualifying bid described in paragraph (b)(1), then the plan administrator may arrange for the PBGC to become responsible for the payment of such benefits in accordance with Subpart D of Part 2617 of this chapter. If such an arrangement is made, the plan administrator shall calculate the value of all such early retirement benefits in accordance with paragraph (c) of this section, and the PBGC will provide these benefits as set forth in Part 2617 of this chapter. If the PBGC does not provide these benefits, the value of each early retirement benefit is its cost under the qualifying bid.

(c) *Valuation of early retirement benefits.* An early retirement benefit that is to be provided by an insurer pursuant to a qualifying bid is valued in accordance with paragraph (a) of this section. An early retirement benefit that is to be provided by PBGC in accordance with Part 2617 is valued as an annuity in accordance with Subpart C of this part.

4. Sections 2619.42 through 2619.45 are revised to read as follows:

§ 2619.42 Benefits to be valued.

(a) *Form of benefit.* The plan administrator shall determine the form of each benefit to be valued, without regard to the form of benefit valued in any prior year, in accordance with the following rules:

(1) If a benefit is in pay status as of the valuation date, the plan administrator shall value the form of benefit being paid.

(2) If a benefit is not in pay status as of the valuation date but a valid election with respect to the form of benefit has been made on or before the valuation date, the plan administrator shall value the form of benefit so elected.

(3) If a benefit is not in pay status as of the valuation date and no valid election with respect to the form of benefit has been made on or before the valuation date, the plan administrator shall value the form of benefit that is payable under the terms of the plan in the absence of a valid election.

(b) *Timing of benefit.* The plan administrator shall value benefits whose starting date is subject to election using the assumption specified in paragraph (b)(1) or (b)(2) of this section.

(1) *Where election made.* If a valid election of the starting date of a benefit has been made on or before the valuation date, the plan administrator shall assume that the starting date of the benefit is the starting date so elected.

(2) *Where no election made.* If no valid election of the starting date of a benefit has been made on or before the valuation date, the plan administrator shall assume that the starting date of the benefit is the later of—

(i) The expected retirement age, as determined under Subpart D of this part, of the participant with respect to whom the benefit is payable, or

(ii) The valuation date.

§ 2619.43 Valuation methods.

(a) *General rule.* The plan administrator shall value benefits as of the valuation date using—

(1) The mortality and interest assumptions prescribed by § § 2619.44 and 2619.45,

(2) Interpolation methods, where necessary, at least as accurate as linear interpolation, and

(3) Formulas that are at least as accurate as the formulas set forth in paragraphs (b)-(i) of this section.

(b) *Single-sum payments (other than death benefits).* The present value of a single-sum payment of 1 to be made 11 years after the valuation date may be found as follows:

(1) If the payment is not contingent on the survival of any person:

$$1 \quad \frac{k}{\underline{\hspace{2cm}}} \quad 1$$

$$V^{0:n} = \left(\frac{}{1+i_{k+1}} \right) j. \quad \sigma \quad \left(\frac{}{1+i_t} \right)_{t=1}$$

where $n = k + j$, k is an integer, $0 \le j < 1$, $v^{0:0} = 1$, and i_k is the interest rate determined under §2619.45 applicable to the year ending on the kth anniversary of the valuation date.

(2) If the payment is contingent on the survival of a person aged x on the valuation date:

$$_np_x \cdot v^{0:n} = \frac{l_{x+n}}{l_x} \cdot v^{0:n},$$

where l_x and l_{x+n} are the numbers of persons living at ages x and $x + n$ respectively, as determined under §2619.44.

(3) If the payment is contingent on the survival of two persons aged x and v respectively on the valuation date:

$$_np_x \cdot {}_np_v \cdot v^{0:n}.$$

(c) *Basic annuities in pay status.* The present value of an annuity due providing payments of $1/m$, m times per year, starting on the valuation date, may be found as follows:

(1) If the annuity is for a term certain of r years after the valuation date and is not contingent on the survival of any person:

$$\overset{(m)}{\ddot{a}}_r = \frac{1}{m} \sum_{t=0}^{r-1} \frac{v^{0:t} (v^{0:t} - v^{0:t+1})}{v^{0:t} - v^{0:t + (1/m)}}.$$

(2) If the annuity is for the life of a person aged x on the valuation date:

$$\overset{(m)}{a}_x = \sum_{t=0}^{\infty} v^{0:t} \cdot {}_tp_x - \frac{m-1}{2m}.$$

$$\overset{(m)}{_nI\ddot{a}}_{xy} = \sum_{t=n}^{\infty} v^{0:t} \cdot {}_tp_x \cdot {}_tp_y - v^{0:n} \cdot {}_np_x \cdot {}_np_y$$

(e) *Joint and survivor annuities in pay status.* The present value of an annuity due providing payments m times per year, starting on the valuation date, in an initial amount of $1/m$ per payment, and in an ultimate amount of s/m per payment, may be found as follows:

(1) If the annuity is payable in the initial amount for the life of a person aged x on the valuation date and, after the death of that person, in the ultimate amount for the life of a person aged y on the valuation date:

$$\overset{(m)}{\ddot{a}}_x + s(\overset{(m)}{\ddot{a}}_y - \overset{(m)}{\ddot{a}}_{xy}).$$

(2) If the annuity is payable in the initial amount for the joint lives of two persons aged x and y on the valuation date and, after the death of either of those persons, in the ultimate amount for the life of the survivor:

$$\overset{(m)}{\ddot{a}}_{r1} + {}_{r|}\overset{(m)}{\ddot{a}}_{xy} + s\,({}_{r|}\overset{(m)}{\ddot{a}}_x$$

(f) *Deferred joint and survivor annuities.* The present value of an annuity due providing payments m times per year, starting n years after the valuation date, in an initial amount of $1/m$ per payment, and in an ultimate amount of s/m per payment, contingent on the survival for n years of a person aged x on the valuation date, may be found as follows:

(1) If the annuity is payable in the initial amount for the life of the person and, after the death of that person, in the ultimate amount for the life of a person aged y on the valuation date:

$$_n|\overset{(m)}{\ddot{a}}_{xy} + s\,({}_n|\overset{(m)}{\ddot{a}}_x$$

(3) If the annuity is payable in the initial amount for a term certain of r years or for the life of the person (whichever of those two periods is longer) and, after the expiration of the term certain and the death of that person, in the ultimate amount for the life of a person aged y on the valuation date:

$$_np_{x \cdot n}|\overset{(m)}{\ddot{a}}_{r1} + {}_{n+r|}\overset{(m)}{\ddot{a}}_x$$

(4) If the annuity is payable in the initial amount for a term certain of r years or for the joint lives of the person and a person aged y on the valuation date (whichever of those two periods is longer) and, after the

$$_np_{x \cdot n}|\overset{(m)}{\ddot{a}}_r + {}_{n+r|}\overset{(m)}{\ddot{a}}_{xy} + s\,({}_{n+r|}\overset{(m)}{\ddot{a}}_x$$

(3) If the annuity is for the joint lives of two persons aged x and y on the valuation date:

$$\overset{(m)}{a}_{xy} = \sum_{t=0}^{\infty} v^{0:t} \cdot {}_tp_x \cdot {}_tp_y - \frac{m-1}{2m}.$$

(d) *Basic deferred annuities.* The present value of an annuity due providing payments of $1/m$, m times per year, starting n years after the valuation date, may be found as follows:

(1) If the annuity is for a term certain of r years and is not contingent on the survival of any person:

$$_n\overset{(m)}{\ddot{a}}_r = \overset{(m)}{\ddot{a}}_{n+r} - \overset{(m)}{\ddot{a}}_n.$$

(2) If the annuity is for a term certain of r years and is contingent on the survival for n years of a person aged x on the valuation date:

$$_np_x \cdot {}_n\overset{(m)}{I\ddot{a}}_r$$

(3) If the annuity is for the life of a person aged x on the valuation date:

$$_n\overset{(m)}{I\ddot{a}}_x = \sum_{t=n}^{\infty} \frac{v^{0:t} \cdot {}_tp_x - v^{0:n} \cdot {}_np_x}{} \cdot \frac{m-1}{2m}.$$

(4) If the annuity is for the life of a person aged y on the valuation date and is contingent on the survival for n years of a person aged x on the valuation date:

$$_np_x \cdot {}_n\overset{(m)}{\ddot{a}}_y.$$

(5) If the annuity is for the joint lives of two persons aged x and y on the valuation date:

$$\frac{m-1}{2m}.$$

$$\overset{(m)}{\ddot{a}}_{xy} + s\,(\overset{(m)}{\ddot{a}}_x + \overset{(m)}{\ddot{a}}_y - 2.\overset{(m)}{\ddot{a}}_{xy}).$$

(3) If the annuity is payable in the initial amount for a term certain of r years after the valuation date or for the life of a person aged x on the valuation date (whichever of those two periods is longer) and, after the expiration of the term certain and the death of that person, in the ultimate amount for the life of a person aged y on the valuation date:

$$\overset{(m)}{\ddot{a}}_{r1} + {}_{r|}\overset{(m)}{\ddot{a}}_x + s\,({}_{r|}\overset{(m)}{\ddot{a}}_y - {}_{r|}\overset{(m)}{\ddot{a}}_{xy}).$$

(4) If the annuity is payable in the initial amount for a term certain of r years after the valuation date or for the joint lives of two persons aged x and y on the valuation date (whichever of those two periods is longer) and, after the expiration of the term certain and the death of either of the persons, in the ultimate amount for the life of the survivor:

$$_{r|}\overset{(m)}{\ddot{a}}_y - 2.\,{}_{r|}\overset{(m)}{\ddot{a}}_{xy}).$$

$$_n|\overset{(m)}{\ddot{a}}_x + s\,({}_n|\overset{(m)}{\frac{p_x}{a_y}} - {}_n|\overset{(m)}{\ddot{a}}_{xy}).$$

(2) If the annuity is payable in the initial amount for the joint lives of the person and a person aged y on the valuation date and, after the death of either of those persons, in the ultimate amount for the life of the survivor:

$$+ {}_np_x \cdot {}_n|\overset{(m)}{\ddot{a}}_y - 2.\,{}_n|\overset{(m)}{\ddot{a}}_{xy}).$$

that person, in the ultimate amount for the life of a person aged y on the valuation date:

$$+ s\,({}_np_{x \cdot n+r|}\overset{(m)}{\ddot{a}}_y - {}_{n+r|}\overset{(m)}{\ddot{a}}_{xy}).$$

expiration of the term certain and the death of either of those persons, in the ultimate amount for the life of the survivor:

$$+ {}_np_{x \cdot n+r|}\overset{(m)}{\ddot{a}}_y - 2.\,{}_{n+r|}\overset{(m)}{\ddot{a}}_{xy}).$$

(g) *Single life or certain annuities.* The present value of an annuity due providing payment of $1/m$, m times per year, for the life of a person aged x on the valuation date or a term certain of r years, may be found as follows:

(1) If the annuity starts on the valuation date and is for the shorter of those two periods:

$$\ddot{a}^{(m)}_x - {}_r\ddot{a}^{(m)}_x .$$

(2) If the annuity starts on the valuation date and is for the longer of those two periods:

$$\ddot{a}^{(m)}_r + {}_{r|}\ddot{a}^{(m)}_x .$$

(3) If, contingent on the survival of the person for n years, the annuity starts n years after the valuation date and is for the shorter of those two periods:

$$_n|\ddot{a}^{(m)}_x - {}_{n+r|}\ddot{a}^{(m)}_x .$$

(4) If, contingent on the survival of the person for n years, the annuity starts n years after the valuation date and is for the longer of those two periods:

$$_n p_x \cdot {}_{n|}\ddot{a}^{(m)}_{r|} + {}_{n+r|}\ddot{a}^{(m)}_x .$$

(h) *Fixed single-sum death benefits.* The present value of a fixed single-sum payment of 1 to be made upon the death of a person aged x on the valuation date may be found as follows:

(1) If the payment is to be made whenever death occurs:

$$\bar{A}_x = \sum_{t=0}^{\infty} v^{0:t+\frac{1}{2}} ({}_t p_x - {}_{t+1} p_x).$$

(2) If the payment is to be made only if the person dies within r years after the valuation date:

$$A^1_{x:r|} = \sum_{t=0}^{r-1} v^{0:t+\frac{1}{2}} ({}_t p_x - {}_{t+1} p_x).$$

(3) If the payment is to be made only if the person dies at least n years after the valuation date:

$$\bar{A}^{1}_{x:n+r} - \bar{A}^{1}_{x:n} .$$

(4) If the payment is to be made only if the person dies at least n years, but within $n + r$ years, after the valuation date:

$$\bar{A}^{1}_{x:n+r} - \bar{A}^{1}_{x:n} .$$

(i) *Variable single-sum death benefits.* The present value of a single-sum payment to be made upon the death of a payment to be made upon the death of a person aged x on the valuation date, if the person dies within r years after the valuation date, may be found as follows:

(1) If the amount payable is initially $r - 1/m$ and decreases by $1/m$, m times per year:

$$\sum_{t=0}^{r-1} \left(r - t - \frac{m+1}{2m} \right) \cdot v^{0:t+\frac{1}{2}} \cdot ({}_t p_x - {}_{t+1} p_x).$$

(2) If the amount payable is initially and increases at an effective interest rate of j, compounded annually:

$$\sum_{t=0}^{r-1} (1+j)^{t+\frac{1}{2}} \cdot v^{0:t+\frac{1}{2}} \cdot ({}_t p_x - {}_{t+1} p_x).$$

§ 2619.44 Mortality.

(a) *General rule.* In determining the value of mortality factors of the form ${}_n\rho_x$ (as defined in §2619.43(b)(2)) for purposes of applying the formulas set forth in §2619.43(b)-(i), and in determining the value of any mortality factor used in valuing benefits under this subpart, the plan administrator shall use the values of lx prescribed in paragraphs (d), (e) and (f) of this section.

(b) *Certain death benefits.* If an annuity for one person is in pay status on the valuation date, and if the payment of a death benefit after the valuation date to another person, who need not be identifiable on the valuation date, depends in whole or in part on the death of the pay status annuitant, then to determine the mortality factors involved in the valuation of the death benefit—

(1) In the case of factors that represent the mortality of the pay status annuitant, the plan administrator shall apply the mortality rates that are applicable to the annuity in pay status under paragraph (d), (e) or (f) of this section; and

(2) In the case of factors that represent the mortality of the death beneficiary, the plan administrator shall apply the mortality rates applicable to annuities not in pay status and to deferred benefits other than annuities, under paragraph (d) of this section.

(c) *Description of mortality tables.* The tables in paragraphs (d), (e) and (f) of this section tabulate, for each age (denoted by x, $x \geq 15$], the number of persons assumed to be living at that age (denoted by l_x) out of a closed group consisting originally of 10,000 persons aged 15 years.

(d) *Health lives.* The values of l_x applicable to annuities in pay status on the valuation date that are not being received as disability benefits, to annuities not in pay status on the valuation date, and to deferred benefits other than annuities, are as follows:

MORTALITY TABLE FOR HEALTHY MALE PARTICIPANTS

Age x	l_x
15	10,000,000.
16	9,985.6300
17	9,971.5103
18	9,957.6998
19	9,944.2469
20	9,931.2100
21	9,918.6272
22	9,906.5364
23	9,894.9755
24	9,883.6062
25	9,872.4476
26	9,861.5188
27	9,850.8388
28	9,840.4166
29	9,829.7594
30	9,818.8385
31	9,807.6352
32	9,796.1308
33	9,784.2971
34	9,771.6069
35	9,757.9462
36	9,743.1824
37	9,727.1744
38	9,709.7433
39	9,690.8287
40	9,670.2357
41	9,674.7331
42	9,623.0735
43	9,595.9557
44	9,566.2562
45	9,533.6353
46	9,497.7030
47	9,458.0026
48	9,414.1648
49	9,366.1243
50	9,313.5241
51	9,255.8175
52	9,192.3874
53	9,123.0492
54	9,047.5286
55	8,965.8023
56	8,877.2650
57	8,781.2663
58	8,677.0941
59	8,564.7084
60	8,443.4150
61	8,312.4661
62	8,171.0711
63	8,018.3946
64	7,853.8812
65	7,676.6819
66	7,485.9394
67	7,282.0823
68	7,066.2851
69	6,839.6481
70	6,602.0182
71	6,353.3400
72	6,093.6726
73	5,822.4798
74	5,540.0662
75	5,246.9247
76	4,943.7836
77	4,631.6232
78	4,313.7642
79	3,991.7503
80	3,667.3966
81	3,342.7660
82	3,021.1317
83	2,705.9975
84	2,400.7177
85	2,107.6405
86	1,829.0352
87	1,567.1815
88	1,324.0380

Age x	l_x
89	1,101.3242
90	900.3755
91	722.0741
92	566.8029
93	434.7475
94	324.9542
95	235.9564
96	165.8415
97	112.3488
98	73.0823
99	45.3940
100	26.7427
101	14.8217
102	7.6505
103	3.6393
104	1.5708
105	0.6026
106	0.1996
107	0.0547
108	0.0117
109	0.0017
110	0.0001

MORTALITY TABLE FOR HEALTHY FEMALE PARTICIPANTS

Age x	l_x
15	10,000.0000
16	10,000.0000
17	10,000.0000
18	10,000.0000
19	10,000.0000
20	10,000.0000
21	9,985.6300
22	9,971.5103
23	9,957.6998
24	9,944.2469
25	9,931.2100
26	9,918.6272
27	9,906.5364
28	9,894.9755
29	9,883.6062
30	9,872.4476
31	9,861.5188
32	9,850.8388
33	9,840.4166
34	9,829.7594
35	9,818.8385
36	9,807.6352
37	9,796.1308
38	9,784.2971
39	9,771.6069
40	9,757.9462
41	9,743.1824
42	9,727.1744
43	9,709.7433
44	9,690.8287
45	9,670.2357
46	9,647.7331
47	9,623.0735
48	9,595.9557
49	9,566.2562
50	9,533.6353
51	9,497.7030
52	9,458.0026
53	9,414.1648
54	9,366.1243
55	9,313.5241
56	9,255.8175
57	9,192.3874
58	9,123.0492
59	9,047.5286
60	8,965.8023
61	8,877.2650
62	8,781.2663
63	8,677.0941
64	8,564.7084
65	8,443.4150
66	8,312.4661
67	8,171.0711
68	8,018.3946
69	7,853.8812
70	7,676.6819
71	7,485.9394
72	7,282.0823
73	7,066.2851
74	6,839.6481
75	6,602.0182
76	6,353.3400
77	6,093.6726
78	5,822.4798
79	5,540.0662
80	5,246.9247
81	4,943.7836
82	4,631.6232
83	4,313.7642
84	3,991.7503
85	3,667.3966
86	3,342.7660
87	3,021.1317
88	2,705.9975

Age x	l_x
89	2,400.7177
90	2,107.6405
91	1,829.0652
92	1,567.1815
93	1,324.0380
94	1,101.3242
95	900.3755
96	722.0741
97	566.8029
98	434.7475
99	324.9542
100	235.9564
101	165.8415
102	112.3488
103	73.0823
104	45.3940
105	26.7427
106	14.8217
107	7.6505
108	3.6393
109	1.5708
110	0.6026

(e) *Disabled lives (other than Social Security disability).* The values of l_x applicable to annuities in pay status on the valuation date that are being received as disability benefits and for which neither eligibility for, nor receipt of, Social Security disability benefits is a prerequisite, are as follows:

MORTALITY TABLE FOR DISABLED MALE PARTICIPANTS NOT RECEIVING SOCIAL SECURITY DISABILITY BENEFIT PAYMENTS

Age x	l_x
15	10,000.0000
16	9,986.4900
17	9,973.3977
18	9,960.7614
19	9,948.6192
20	9,937.0092
21	9,925.5916
22	9,914.3856
23	9,903.4104
24	9,892.6850
25	9,882.2165
26	9,871.5161
27	9,860.5488
28	9,849.2979
29	9,837.7447
30	9,825.8607
31	9,813.1166
32	9,799.3979
33	9,784.5714
34	9,768.4953
35	9,750.9902
36	9,731.9953
37	9,711.3148
38	9,688.7166
39	9,663.9522
40	9,636.7192
41	9,606.8936
42	9,574.1341
43	9,538.0492
44	9,498.1802
45	9,454.1561
46	9,405.9115
47	9,353.0879
48	9,295.1362
49	9,231.4366
50	9,161.8039
51	9,085.9625
52	9,003.8890
53	8,914.9756
54	8,818.5691
55	8,713.9544
56	8,601.0913
57	8,479.2826
58	8,347.7774
59	8,205.7817
60	8,052.4567
61	7,887.2444
62	7,709.2924
63	7,517.7396
64	7,313.0165
65	7,096.3026
66	6,868.7029
67	6,630.0636
68	6,380.3290
69	6,119.5586
70	5,847.2138
71	5,563.6005
72	5,269.2137
73	4,964.7849
74	4,651.2985
75	4,332.0892
76	4,008.7074
77	3,682.9759
78	3,356.9662
79	3,033.9656
80	2,717.4926
81	2,410.9160
82	2,116.5938
83	1,836.8351
84	1,573.8389
85	1,329.6625

Age x	l_x
86	1,106.0026
87	904.2003
88	725.1415
89	569.2107
90	436.5943
91	326.3346
92	236.9587
93	166.5459
94	112.8260
95	73.3927
96	45.5868
97	26.8563
98	14.8846
99	7.6830
100	3.6548
101	1.5775
102	0.6052
103	0.2005
104	0.0550
105	0.0117
106	0.0017
107	0.0001

MORTALITY TABLE FOR DISABLED FEMALE PARTICIPANTS NOT RECEIVING SOCIAL SECURITY DISABILITY BENEFIT PAYMENTS

Age x	l_x
15	10,000.0000
16	10,000.0000
17	10,000.0000
18	10,000.0000
19	10,000.0000
20	10,000.0000
21	9,986.4900
22	9,973.3977
23	9,960.7614
24	9,948.6192
25	9,937.0092
26	9,925.5916
27	9,914.3856
28	9,903.4104
29	9,692.6850
30	9,882.2185
31	9,871.5161
32	9,860.5488
33	9,849.2979
34	9,837.7447
35	9,825.8607
36	9,813.1166
37	9,799.3979
38	9,784.5714
39	9,768.4953
40	9,750.9902
41	9,731.9953
42	9,711.3148
43	9,688.7166
44	9,663.9522
45	9,636.7192
46	9,606.8936
47	9,574.1341
48	9,538.0492
49	9,498.1802
50	9,454.1561
51	9,405.9115
52	9,353.0879
53	9,295.1362
54	9,231.4366
55	9,161.8039
56	9,085.9625
57	9,003.8890
58	8,914.9756
59	8,818.5691
60	8,713.9544
61	8,601.0913
62	8,479.2826
63	8,347.7774
64	8,205.7817
65	8,052.4567
66	7,887.2444
67	7,709.2924
68	7,517.7396
69	7,313.0165
70	7,096.3026
71	6,868.7029
72	6,630.0636
73	6,380.3290
74	6,119.5586
75	5,847.2138
76	5,563.6005
77	5,269.2137
78	4,964.7849
79	4,651.2985
80	4,332.0892
81	4,008.7074
82	3,682.9759
83	3,356.9662
84	3,033.9656
85	2,717.4926
86	2,410.9160
87	2,116.5938
88	1,836.8351

Age x	l_x
89	1,573.8389
90	1,329.6625
91	1,106.0026
92	904.2003
93	725.1415
94	569.2107
95	436.5943
96	326.3346
97	236.9587
98	166.5459
99	112.8260
100	73.3927
101	45.5868
102	26.8563
103	14.8846
104	7.6830
105	3.6548
106	1.5775
107	0.6052
108	0.2005
109	0.0550
110	0.0117

(f) *Disabled lives (Social Security disability).* The values of l_x applicable to annuities in pay status on the valuation date that are being received as disability benefits and for which either eligibility for, or receipt of, Social Security disability benefits is a prerequisite, are as follows:

MORTALITY TABLE FOR DISABLED MALE PARTICIPANTS RECEIVING SOCIAL SECURITY DISABILITY BENEFIT PAYMENTS

Age x	l_x
15	10,000.0000
16	10,000.0000
17	10,000.0000
18	10,000.0000
19	10,000.0000
20	10,000.0000
21	9,517.0000
22	9,057.3289
23	8,619.8599
24	8,203.5207
25	7,807.2906
26	7,430.1985
27	7,087.6663
28	6,778.6441
29	6,500.0418
30	6,249.1402
31	6,022.9213
32	5,818.7443
33	5,632.5445
34	5,462.4416
35	5,305.1233
36	5,157.6409
37	5,017.3531
38	4,881.3228
39	4,748.1210
40	4,617.0729
41	4,486.8714
42	4,357.6495
43	4,228.2274
44	4,099.2664
45	3,970.5495
46	3,842.6978
47	3,715.8887
48	3,589.5485
49	3,462.8375
50	3,335.7513
51	3,207.9920
52	3,079.3516
53	2,950.0188
54	2,820.5130
55	2,690.7694
56	2,561.0743
57	2,431.4839
58	2,302.3721
59	2,174.5905
60	2,048.2468
61	1,924.7375
62	1,804.6339
63	1,688.5959
64	1,577.6552
65	1,472.2678
66	1,372.4480
67	1,278.1609
68	1,189.0731
69	1,104.7678
70	1,024.8931
71	949.1535
72	877.3025
73	809.2239
74	744.8096
75	683.8842
76	626.3012
77	571.8756
78	519.9493
79	469.9302
80	420.9165
81	373.4371
82	327.8404
83	284.4999
84	243.7595
85	205.9524

Age x		l_x
86		171.3112
87		140.0469
88		112.3176
89		88.1693
90		67.6259
91		50.5503
92		36.7046
93		25.7960
94		17.4742
95		11.3670
96		7.0600
97		4.1591
98		2.3050
99		1.1898
100		.5660
101		.2443
102		.0937
103		.0310
104		.0085
105		.0018
106		.0003

MORTALITY TABLE FOR DISABLED FEMALE PARTICIPANTS RECEIVING SOCIAL SECURITY DISABILITY BENEFIT PAYMENTS

Age x	l_x
15	10,000.0000
16	10,000.0000
17	10,000.0000
18	10,000.0000
19	10,000.0000
20	10,000.0000
21	9,737.0000
22	9,480.9169
23	9,231.5688
24	8,988.7785
25	8,752.3737
26	8,522.1862
27	8,303.1660
28	8,098.0959
29	7,893.1965
30	7,702.1811
31	7,519.6394
32	7,345.1838
33	7,178.4481
34	7,019.0866
35	6,866.0705
36	6,719.1366
37	6,576.6909
38	6,438.5804
39	6,304.6579
40	6,173.5210
41	6,044.4944
42	5,917.5600
43	5,791.5160
44	5,666.4193
45	5,542.3247
46	5,418.1766
47	5,294.1004
48	5,169.6890
49	5,044.5825
50	4,918.9724
51	4,792.5548
52	4,666.0314
53	4,539.1153
54	4,411.5662
55	4,284.5131
56	4,158.1200
57	4,032.9605
58	3,909.1487
59	3,786.0105
60	3,663.7223
61	3,542.4531
62	3,422.3640
63	3,303.6079
64	3,186.3299
65	3,070.9847
66	2,957.3583
67	2,845.5701
68	2,735.7311
69	2,627.9433
70	2,522.3000
71	2,418.6335
72	2,316.8090
73	2,216.4912
74	2,117.4140
75	2,018.9543
76	1,919.6217
77	1,818.0737
78	1,712.9891
79	1,604.8995
80	1,494.8034
81	1,383.2910
82	1,270.8295
83	1,158.3611
84	1,046.9267
85	937.7323
86	831.9561
87	730.3742
88	633.8188

Age x	l_x
89	543.0559
90	458.8279
91	381.6531
92	312.0014
93	250.2251
94	196.4267
95	150.6593
96	112.6178
97	81.7718
98	57.4692
99	38.9297
100	25.3237
101	15.7266
102	9.2657
103	5.1351
104	2.6507
105	1.2609
106	.5542
107	.2088
108	.0692
109	.0190
110	.0041

MORTALITY TABLE FOR DISABLED FEMALE
PARTICIPANTS NOT RECEIVING SOCIAL SECURITY

Age x	l_x
51	9,405.9115
52	9,353.0879
53	9,295.1362
54	9,231.4366
55	9,161.8039
56	9,085.9625
57	9,003.8890
58	8,914.9756
59	8,818.5691
60	8,713.9544
61	8,601.0913
62	8,479.2826
99	112.8260
100	73.3927
101	45.5868
102	26.8563
103	14.8846
104	7.6830
105	3.6548
106	1.5775
107	0.6052
108	0.2005
109	0.0550
110	0.0117

§ 2619.45 Interest.

(a) *General rule.* In determining the value of interest factors of the form $v^{o:n}$ (as defined in § 2619.43(b)(1)) for purposes of applying the formulas set forth in § 2619.43(b)-(i) and in determining the value of any interest factor used in valuing benefits under this subpart, the plan administrator shall use the values of i_k prescribed in paragraph (c) of this section.

(b) *Description of interest table.* The table in paragraph (c) of this section tabulates, for each calendar month ending after the effective date of this part, the interest rates (denoted by i_1, i_2, ..., i_{15}, i_u, and referred to generally as i_k assumed to be in effect during each one-year period ending on an anniversary (the first, second, ..., fifteenth, and subsequent anniversaries, respectively, and referred to generally as the k_{th} of a valuation date that occurs within that calendar month; the rate i_u is assumed to be in effect during the sixteenth and all subsequent years. For example, the interest rate assumed to be in effect during the one-year ending on the seventh anniversary of the valuation date is tabulated as i_7, and the rate assumed to be in effect during the one-year period ending on the seventeenth anniversary of the valuation date is tabulated as i_u.

(c) *Interest rates.*

For valuation dates occurring in the month:	The values of i_k are:															
	i_1	i_2	i_3	i_4	i_5	i_6	i_7	i_8	i_9	i_{10}	i_{11}	i_{12}	i_{13}	i_{14}	i_{15}	i_u
X/85	.IIII	.IIII	.IIII	.IIII	.IIII	.IIII	.IIII	.IIII	.IIII	.IIII	.IIII	.IIII	.IIII	.IIII	.IIII	.IIII

§ § 2619.46 and 2619.47 [Removed]

§ 2619.48 [Redesignated as § 2619.46]

5. Sections 2619.46 and 2619.47 are removed, and § 2619.48 is redesignated as § 2619.46.

Appendices A, B, and C [Removed]

6. Apppendices A, B and C are removed.

Issued in Washington, DC, on February 27, 1986.

William E. Brock,

Chairman of the Board of Directors, Pension Benefit Guaranty Corporation.

Issued pursuant to a resolution of the Board of Directors approving, and authorizing its chairman to issue, this notice of proposed rulemaking.

Edward R. Mackiewicz,

Secretary to the Board of Directors, Pension Benefit Guaranty Corporation.

¶ 20,532B   Reserved.

Proposed regulations that would have established rules and procedures for terminating a single-employer pension plan in standard and distress terminations were formerly reproduced here. The final regulations are at ¶ 15,441-15,446C, 15,446O-15,446W, 15,447-15,447I, and 15,447T-15,448.]

¶ 20,532C   Reserved.

Proposed regulations that would have established criteria for determining whether a plan is an individual account plan which permits participants to exercise independent control over assets in their account was withdrawn and replaced by revised regulations. The revised regulations, including the notice of withdrawal, are at ¶ 20,532G.]

¶ 20,532D   Reserved.

Proposed regulations that would have established rules to govern the allocation of unfunded vested benefits to an employer that had withdrawn from a multiemployer pension plan following the merger of the plan with another multiemployer plan were formerly reproduced here. The final regulations are at ¶ 15,663D, 15,678, and 15,678O-15,678U.]

¶ 20,532E

Proposed regulations on 29 CFR Part 1625: Equal Employment Opportunity Commission: Age Discrimination in Employment Act of 1967: Benefits under employee pension benefit plans.—Reproduced below is the text of proposed regulations that would implement amendments made to the Age Discrimination in Employment Act by the Omnibus Budget Reconciliation Act of 1986 (OBRA) (P.L. 99-509). This Act requires continuing contributions, allocations, and accruals in pension plans regardless of an employee's age.

The proposed regulations were published in the *Federal Register* on November 27, 1987 (52 FR 45360).

EQUAL EMPLOYMENT OPPORTUNITY COMMISSION

29 CFR Part 1625

Employee Pension Benefit Plans

AGENCY: Equal Employment Opportunity Commission (EEOC)

ACTION: Notice of Proposed Rulemaking

SUMMARY: The Commission hereby provides notice of its proposed legislative regulation under section 9 of the Age Discrimination in Employment Act of 1967 (ADEA), 29 U.S.C. § 621 *et seq.*, relating to the prohibition against discrimination on the basis of age in employee pension benefit plans (hereafter, "pension plans") in section 4(i) of the ADEA, 29 U.S.C. § 623(i).

DATES: Written comments must be received by December 28, 1987 and must be submitted in quadruplicate. It is anticipated that final rules will be effective thirty days after publication.

ADDRESS: Comments may be mailed to: Executive Secretariat, Equal Employment Opportunity Commission, Room 507, 2401 E Street, N.W., Washington, D.C. 20507.

FOR FURTHER INFORMATION CONTACT: Paul E. Boymel, Office of Legal Counsel, Room 214, EEOC, 2401 E Street, N.W., Washington, D.C. 20507, (202) 634-6423.

SUPPLEMENTARY INFORMATION: The Commission has determined that this proposed rule is not a major rule as defined in Executive Order 12291 and that a regulatory impact analysis is not required. The rule has been coordinated with the Office of Management and Budget pursuant to Executive Order 12291.

Pursuant to 5 U.S.C. § 605(b), the Chairman, EEOC, certifies that the rule will not have a significant economic impact on a substantial number of small entities. Accordingly, the Commission is not required to prepare an initial or a final regulatory flexibility analysis of the proposed rule.

Background

Congress, in section 4(a)(1) of the ADEA, described the employer conduct that is prohibited (unlawful discrimination by employment agencies and labor organizations is described in sections 4(b) and 4(c) of the ADEA, respectively):

(a) It shall be unlawful for an employer—

(1) to fail or refuse to hire or to discharge any individual or otherwise discriminate against any individual with respect to his compensation, terms, conditions, or privileges of employment, because of such individual's age;

However, Congress fashioned an exception to the general prohibitions in section 4(a) of the ADEA. That exception in section 4(f)(2) of the ADEA provides:

It shall not be unlawful for an employer, employment agency, or labor organization—

(2) to observe the terms of a bona fide seniority system or any bona fide employee benefit plan such as a retirement, pension, or insurance plan, which is not a subterfuge to evade the purposes of this Act, except that no such employee benefit plan shall excuse the failure to hire any individual, and no such seniority system or employee benefit plan shall require or permit the involuntary retirement of any individual specified by section 12(a) of this Act because of the age of such individual.

The ADEA was amended in 1978 to preclude mandatory retirement of covered employees and to raise the upper age limit for coverage under the ADEA from 65 to 70. Because these amendments potentially affected pension plans, in 1979 the Department of Labor (DOL), at the urging of Congress, published the "Employee Benefit Plans: Amend-

ment to Interpretive Bulletin," 29 C.F.R. § 860.120, 44 FR 30648 (May 25, 1979), which provided guidance on employee benefit plans covered under the ADEA. The Interpretive Bulletin contained special rules that allowed employers to cease contributions and accruals to pension plans for employees who continued to work beyond normal retirement age, whether or not the employers could make a cost justification for such cessation.

On October 17, 1986, Congress passed the Omnibus Budget Reconciliation Act of 1986 (OBRA), Pub. L. 99-509. In sections 9201-9204 of OBRA, Congress added section 4(i) to the ADEA and added essentially identical provisions to ERISA and the Internal Revenue Code (IRC) to require continuing contributions, allocations, and accruals in a pension plan regardless of an employee's age. The amendments require such contributions, allocations, and accruals without regard to the cost of such benefits. These proposed regulations are promulgated as the result of the passage of sections 9201-9204 of OBRA.

Interagency Coordination Process

Since sections 9201-9202 of OBRA amended the ADEA, ERISA, and the IRC almost identically, section 9204(d) of OBRA provides that the regulations and rulings of the Commission, the Internal Revenue Service (IRS) and DOL, the three agencies with jurisdiction over the three statutes, "shall each be consistent with the others." Since IRS was given lead regulatory authority on a major portion of the OBRA regulations, the three agencies decided initially that IRS would prepare the regulations and that EEOC and DOL would, to the extent necessary, adapt and incorporate such regulations. Accordingly, the proposed regulations published herein by the Commission have been coordinated with IRS and DOL extensively. However, since IRS is not yet ready to publish proposed or final rules, EEOC's rules do not address in detail such issues as actuarial equivalency (ADEA section 4(i)(3)), highly compensated employees (ADEA section 4(i)(5)), and IRC limits on contributions, benefits, or deductions (ADEA section 4(i)(7)). Under OBRA, IRS was given the exclusive regulatory authority for such issues. As soon as final IRS regulations are promulgated, the regulations herein can be amended appropriately. While IRS regulations will relate to the IRC and ERISA provisions of OBRA and the Commission's proposed regulations relate to the ADEA, it is the clear intent of Congress, and therefore of the Commission, that the regulatory provisions be construed as identical wherever possible.

Discussion And Comparison Of EEOC And IRS Rules

(a) *Remedies*—IRS rules will relate to the determination of whether a pension plan qualifies for favorable tax treatment under the IRC. The Commission rules relate to the determination of whether a pension plan's sponsor (whether an employer, an employment agency, a labor organization, or any combination thereof) is in violation of the ADEA and subject to the sanctions set forth therein. (See section 7 of the ADEA).

(b) *Statutory Scope*—The OBRA provisions apply to "employee pension benefit plans," as defined by section 3(2) of ERISA:

. . . the terms "employee pension benefit plan" and "pension plan" mean any plan, fund, or program which was heretofore or is hereafter established or maintained by an employer or by an employee organization, or by both, to the extent that by its express terms or as a result of surrounding circumstances such plan, fund, or program—

(i) provides retirement income to employees, or

(ii) results in a deferral of income by employees for periods extending to the termination of covered employment or beyond, regardless of the method of calculating the contributions made to the plan, the method of calculating the benefits under the plan or the method of distributing benefits from the plan . . .

The ADEA, ERISA, and the IRC contain provisions limiting the jurisdiction of each statute. Pursuant to section 4(b) of ERISA and IRC section 411(e), any IRS regulations would not apply to most state and local governmental plans, church plans, or excess benefit plans, as defined in sections 3(32), 3(33) and 3(36) of ERISA, respectively. However, to the extent that such plans' sponsors are not exempt from coverage under the ADEA, the same rules applicable under the ADEA to plans other than such plans are also applicable to governmental plans, church plans and excess benefits plans. (Participation rules for such plans are discussed in section (c), below).

Secondly, sections 11 and 12 of the ADEA set forth the jurisdictional limits on ADEA coverage. Section 11(b), for example, provides in effect that employers with fewer than twenty employees would not be covered by the ADEA. ERISA and the IRC have no such jurisdictional limits.

(c) *Participation Rules*—Section 9203 of OBRA sets forth rules relating to maximum age conditions for participation in pension plans (age-related exclusion from participation is no longer permitted). Although that section amended ERISA and the IRC, but not the ADEA, the Commission believes such participation rules have equal validity with regard to the ADEA. See the 1979 Interpretative Bulletin, 29 C.F.R. § 860.120(f)(1)(iv)(A), implementing a consistent approach regarding ERISA participation rules and ADEA enforcement. Accordingly, a violation of the section 9203 participation rules would be considered a violation of section 4(a)(1) of the ADEA, whether or not the pension plan is excluded from IRC coverage by IRC section 411(e). These rules do not address the validity of vesting requirements in ERISA section 4(b) plans which do not comply with the standards set in IRC section 411(a).

(d) *Scope of Section 4(i)*—Section 4(i)(4) of the ADEA provides that compliance with the requirements of section 4(i) with regard to benefit accruals under a pension plan satisfies all pension benefits accrual requirements in section 4 of the ADEA. Accordingly, after the effective date of section 4(i), sections 4(a)(1) and 4(f)(2) will no longer apply to such benefit accrual issues.

Explanation Of Provisions

Section 9201 of OBRA added section 4(i)(1)(A) to the ADEA to provide rules for continued accruals under defined benefit plans beyond normal retirement age and added section 4(i)(1)(B) to provide rules for allocations to the accounts of participants in defined contribution plans without regard to age.

Effective for plan years beginning after December 31, 1987, section 4(i)(1)(A) provides the general rule that it shall be unlawful for an employer, an employment agency, or a labor organization, or any combination thereof, to establish or maintain a defined benefit plan under which an employee's benefit accrual is ceased, or the rate of an employee's benefit accrual is reduced, because of the employee's age. Similarly, effective for plan years beginning after December 31, 1987, section 4(i)(1)(B) provides that a defined contribution plan will not be in compliance with the ADEA if allocations to an employee's account are ceased, or the rate at which allocations to an employee's account is reduced, because of the attainment of any age.

Section 4(i)(2) provides that a pension plan will not be treated as failing to satisfy the general rule in section 4(i)(1) merely because the plan contains a limitation on the maximum number of years of service or participation that are taken into account in determining benefits under the plan or merely because the plan contains a limitation on the amount of benefits a participant will receive under the plan, as long as such a limitation is not on account of age. The proposed regulations provide that these limitations apply to both defined benefit plans and defined contribution plans (including target benefit plans).

Section 4(i)(3) provides that, with respect to an employee who, as of the end of a plan year, has attained normal retirement age under a defined benefit plan, certain adjustments may be made to the benefit accrual for the plan year if the plan distributes benefits to the employee during the plan year or if the plan adjusts the amount of the benefits payable to take into account delayed payment.

Section 4(i)(4) provides that compliance with the requirements of section 4(i) with regard to a pension plan shall constitute compliance with the requirements of section 4 relating to pension benefit accruals under such plan. The provisions of sections 4(a)(1) and 4(f)(2) will no longer apply to such accruals.

Section 4(i)(5) provides that the Secretary of the Treasury shall prescribe regulations relating to the treatment of highly compensated employees.

Section 4(i)(6) provides that a pension plan will not be treated as failing to satisfy the general rule of section 4(i)(1) merely because the

subsidized portion of an early retirement benefit is disregarded in determining benefit accruals under the plan.

Section 4(i)(7) provides that the Secretary of the Treasury shall prescribe regulations coordinating the requirements of section 4(i)(1) with the requirements of IRC sections 411(a), 404, 410, 415, and the anti-discrimination provisions of IRC subchapter D of Chapter 1 (IRC sections 401 through 425).

Section 4(i)(8) permits a pension plan to provide a "normal retirement age."

Section 4(i)(9) adopts the ERISA definitions of such terms as "employee pension benefit plan", "defined benefit plan," and "defined contribution plan." In addition, the term "target benefit plan" shall have the same meaning as provided in IRS regulations under IRC section 410. List of Subjects in 29 C.F.R. Part 1625:

Advertising, Aged, Employee benefit plans, Equal employment opportunity, Retirement.

Substantive Rules

Therefore, it is proposed that 29 C.F.R. Part 1625 is amended as follows:

PART 1625—[AMENDED]

1. The authority citation for Part 1625 continues to read as follows:

Authority: 81 Stat. 602; 29 U.S.C. § 621; 5 U.S.C. § 301; Secretary's Order No. 10-68; Secretary's Order No. 11-68; and Sec. 2, Reorg. Plan No. 1 of 1978, 43 FR 19807.

2. Section 1625.21 is added to Subpart B to read as follows:

§ 1625.21 Benefits under employee pension benefit plans—Application of section 4(i) of the ADEA.—(a) *In general.* Section 4(i)(1)(A) of the ADEA provides that a defined benefit plan does not satisfy the requirements of section 4(i), if, under the plan, benefit accruals on behalf of a participant are reduced or discontinued because of the participant's age. Section 4(i)(1)(B) provides that a defined contribution plan does not satisfy the requirements of section 4(i) if, under the plan, allocations to a participant's account are reduced or discontinued because of the participant's age.

(b) *Defined benefit plans*—(1) *In general.* Under section 4(i), except as provided in paragraph (b)(2) of this section, a defined benefit plan does not satisfy the requirements of section 4(i) if, because of a participant's age, a participant's accrual of benefits is discontinued, the rate of a participant's accrual of benefits is decreased, or a participant's compensation is not taken into account in determining the participant's accrual of benefits.

(2) *Certain limitations permitted.* A defined benefit plan does not fail to satisfy section 4(i) solely because under the plan a limitation is placed on the amount of benefits a participant may accrue or a limitation is placed on the number of years of service or participation taken into account for purposes of determining the accrual of benefits under the plan. For this purpose, a limitation expressed as a percentage of compensation (whether averaged over a participant's total years of credited service or over a shorter period) is treated as a permissible limitation on the amount of benefits a participant may accrue under the plan. However, any limitation on the amount of benefits a participant may accrue under the plan and any limitation on the number of years of credited service taken into account under the plan may not be based on the attainment of any age. A limitation that is determined by reference to age or that is not determinable except by reference to age is considered a limitation based on age. For example, a plan provision that, for purposes of benefit accrual, disregards years of credited service completed after a participant becomes eligible to receive Social Security benefits is considered a limitation based on age. Whether a limitation is based on age is determined with reference to all the facts and circumstances.

(c) *Rate of benefit accruals before normal retirement age.* [RESERVED]

(d) *Certain adjustments for delayed retirement.* [RESERVED]

(e) *Benefit subsidies disregarded.* A pension plan does not fail to satisfy section 4(i)(1) and paragraphs (b) and (f) of this section solely because the subsidized portion of any early retirement benefit provided under the plan is disregarded in determining the accrual of benefits or account allocations under the plan.

(f) *Defined contribution Plans*—(1) *In general.* Under section 4(i)(1)(B), except as provided in paragraph (f)(2) of this section, a defined contribution plan will not satisfy the requirements of section 4(i), if, because of the participant's age—

(i) The allocation of employer contributions or forfeitures to the accounts of participants is discontinued,

(ii) The rate at which the allocation of employer contributions or forfeitures is made to the accounts of participants is decreased, or

(iii) The basis upon which gains, losses, or income of the trust is allocated to the accounts of participants is modified.

(2) *Certain limitations permitted.* (i) Notwithstanding paragraph (f)(1) of this section, a defined contribution plan (including a target benefit plan) does not fail to satisfy the requirements of section 4(i) solely because, for purposes of determining benefits under the plan, a limitation is placed on the total amount of employer contributions and forfeitures that may be allocated to a participant's account (for a particular plan year or for the participant's total years of credited service under the plan) or solely because a limitation is placed on the total number of years of credited service or participation for which a participant may receive allocations of employer contributions and forfeitures. However, the limitation described in the preceding sentence may not be applied with respect to the allocation of gains, losses, or income of the trust to the account of a participant.

(ii) A defined contribution plan (including a target benefit plan) does not fail to satisfy section 4(i)(1)(B) solely because the plan limits the number of years of credited service which may be taken into account for purposes of determining the amount of, or the rate at which, employer contributions and forfeitures are allocated to a participant's account for a particular plan year.

(iii) Any limitation described in paragraph (f)(2)(i) and (ii) of this section must not be based on the attainment of any age. The provisions of paragraph (b)(2) of this section shall also apply for purposes of this paragraph (f).

(g) *Amendment reducing accruals.* Any amendment to a defined benefit plan or a defined contribution plan that reduces the rate of benefit accruals for a plan year may not vary the rate of such reduction based on the age of a participant.

(h) *Coordination with certain IRC provisions.*

[RESERVED]

(i) *Effective dates*—(1) *In general.* Except as otherwise provided in paragraph (i)(2) of this section, section 4(i) is effective for plan years beginning on or after January 1, 1988, and is applicable to an employee who is credited with at least one hour of service in a plan year to which

section 4(i) applies. Accordingly, section 4(i) is not applicable to an employee who is not credited with at least one hour of service in a plan year beginning on or after January 1, 1988. Also, section 4(i) is not applicable to an employee for any plan year beginning before January 1, 1988, even if the employee is credited with at least one hour of service in a plan year beginning on or after January 1, 1988.

(2) *Collectively bargained plans.* (i) In the case of a plan maintained pursuant to one or more collective bargaining agreements, between employee representatives and one or more employers, ratified before March 1, 1986, section 4(i) is applicable for plan years beginning on or after the later of—

(A) January 1, 1988, or

(B) the date on which the last of such collective bargaining agreements terminate (determined without regard to any extension of any such agreement occurring on or after March 1, 1986). However, notwithstanding the previous sentence, section 4(i) shall be applicable to plans described in this paragraph (i)(2)(i) no later than the first plan year beginning on or after January 1, 1990.

(ii) For purposes of paragraph (i)(2)(i) of this section, the service crediting rules of paragraph (i)(1) of this section shall apply to a plan described in paragraph (i)(2)(i) of this section, except that in applying such rules the effective date determined under paragraph (i)(2)(i) of this section shall be substituted for the effective date determined under paragraph (i)(1) of this section.

(3) *Amendments to plans.* Plan amendments required by section 4(i) shall not be required to be made before the first plan year beginning on or after January 1, 1989, if the following requirements are met—

(i) the plan is operated in accordance with the requirements of section 4(i) for all periods before the first plan year beginning on or after January 1, 1989, for which such section is effective with respect to the plan; and

(ii) such plan amendments are adopted no later than the last day of the first plan year beginning on or after January 1, 1989, and are made effective retroactively for all periods for which section 4(i) is effective with respect to the plan.

Dated: November 20, 1987.

Clarence Thomas, Chairman

Equal Employment Opportunity Commission

[FR Doc. 87-27243 Filed 11-25-87; 8:45 am]

¶ 20,532F   Reserved.

Proposed regulations related to available civil penalties under ERISA Sec. 502(l) were formerly reproduced at this paragrph. The regulations were withdrawn by the PWBA, effective February 1, 1995 (May 8, 1995 60 FR 23546)].

¶ 20,532G   Reserved.

Proposed regulations on participant-directed accounts were formerly reproduced here.

The PWBA has issued final regulations which are located at ¶ 14,744.]

¶ 20,532H

Proposed regulations on 29 CFR Part 2628: Annual Financial and Actuarial Information Reporting.—Reproduced below is the text of proposed regulations on 29 CFR Part 2628 concerning annual reporting and actuarial reporting by contributing plan sponsors to the Pension Benefit Guaranty Corporation. The information must be filed if the total pension underfunding in the corporate group exceeds $50 million, if a pension contribution exceeding $1 million has been missed in any of the corporate group's pension plans, or if a minimum funding waiver in excess of $1 million has been granted to any of the corporate group's pension plans.

The proposed regulations were filed with the *Federal Register* on July 5, 1995, and published in the *Federal Register* on July 6, 1995 (60 FR 35308).

PENSION BENEFIT GUARANTY CORPORATION

29 CFR Part 2628

RIN 1212-AA78

Annual Financial and Actuarial Information Reporting

AGENCY: Pension Benefit Guaranty Corporation.

ACTION: Proposed rule.

SUMMARY: The Pension Benefit Guaranty Corporation is proposing regulations to implement a new requirement under section 4010 of the Employee Retirement Income Security Act of 1974. Section 4010 requires controlled groups maintaining plans with large amounts of underfunding to submit annually to the PBGC financial and actuarial information as prescribed by the PBGC.

DATE: Comments must be received on or before September 5, 1995.

¶20,532F

ADDRESSES: Comments may be mailed to the Office of the General Counsel, Pension Benefit Guaranty Corporation, 1200 K Street, NW., Washington, DC 20005-4026, or hand-delivered to Suite 340 at the above address. Comments will be available for inspection at the PBGC's Communications and Public Affairs Department, Suite 240, 1200 K Street, NW., Washington, DC 20005-4026.

FOR FURTHER INFORMATION CONTACT: Frank H. McCulloch, Senior Counsel, Office of the General Counsel, Pension Benefit Guaranty Corporation, 1200 K Street, NW., Washington, DC 20005-4026; 202326-4116 (202-326-4179 for TTY and TDD).

SUPPLEMENTARY INFORMATION:

Background

Section 772(a) of the Retirement Protection Act of 1994 (subtitle F of title VII of the Uruguay Round Agreements Act, Pub. L. No. 103-465, 108 Stat. 4809 (1994)) added section 4010 to ERISA. Under section 4010, certain contributing sponsors and all members of their controlled groups must submit annually to the PBGC financial and actuarial information as prescribed by the PBGC in regulations.

Who Must File

Under section 4010 of ERISA, each contributing sponsor of a pension plan and each member of its controlled group is obligated to submit information to the PBGC if (1) the aggregate unfunded vested benefits of all plans maintained by the members of the controlled group exceed $50 million; (2) the conditions specified in section 302(f) of ERISA and section 412(n) of the Internal Revenue Code for imposing a lien for missed contributions exceeding $1 million have been met with respect to any plan maintained by any member of the controlled group; or (3) the Internal Revenue Service has granted minimum funding waivers in excess of $1 million to any plan maintained by any member of the controlled group, and any portion of the waivers is still outstanding. The regulation defines each entity obligated to submit information to the PBGC as a "Filer" (§ 2628.4).

"Unfunded vested benefits" for the $50 million test are determined in the same manner used to determine unfunded vested benefits for purposes of calculating the PBGC's variable rate premium (but without reference to the exemptions or special rules provided in the PBGC's premium regulation (29 CFR 2610.24)).

Information Years

The regulation introduces the concept of an Information Year for a person (§ 2628.6). The Information Year serves four purposes. First, it will help persons determine which plan years and fiscal years to use to identify Filers. Second, it will help Filers determine whether a pension plan qualifies for a filing exemption. Third, it is used to identify the information to be submitted by a Filer. Fourth, it establishes the due date for submission of required information by a Filer.

The regulation does not require a Filer to change its fiscal year or the plan year of any pension plan. Further, the regulation does not require a Filer to report financial information on any accounting period other than an existing fiscal year or to report actuarial information for any period other than the existing plan year of a pension plan.

Generally, the Information Year is the fiscal year of the Filer. If all members of a controlled group do not report financial information on the same fiscal year, the Information Year is the calendar year.

Required Submissions

Section 4010(a) of ERISA requires each Filer annually to provide to the PBGC audited financial statements and other financial and actuarial information required by regulation. Section 2628.3(b) of the regulation allows information to be submitted by a representative of a Filer so that, for example, a Filer can submit required information to the PBGC on behalf of itself and all other members of its controlled group and satisfy their obligations under the regulation.

Exemptions

A Filer is not required to submit actuarial information for a pension plan ("Exempt Plan") if, at the end of the plan year ending within the Filer's Information Year, the plan has no unfunded benefit liabilities or has fewer than 500 participants. The amount of "unfunded benefit liabilities" is determined as of the end of that plan year by subtracting the market value of plan assets, without regard to any contributions receivable, from the value of the plan's benefit liabilities. The regulation requires that the "value of benefit liabilities" be calculated as of the end of that plan year using (1) the PBGC's termination assumptions in effect at the end of that plan year and (2) plan census data as of the end of that plan year or the beginning of the next plan year. If that census data is not available, the value of benefit liabilities may be based on a projection of census data from a date within the plan year. This

projection must be consistent with projections used to measure pension obligations for financial statement purposes and produce a result appropriate to the measurement date for these obligations. Adjustments to this projection process may be required where there have been significant events (such as plan amendments or curtailments) which were not reflected in the projection assumptions. Plans that have minimum funding waivers outstanding at the end of the plan year ending within the Filer's Information Year or that have any missed minimum funding payments in any amount that were required to be made during the Information Year are not Exempt Plans.

Section 2628.4(b) requires that all single-employer plans covered by Title IV of ERISA in a controlled group, including Exempt Plans, be taken into account in determining whether a person is a Filer. For example, a contributing sponsor has two plans—Plan A with unfunded vested benefits of $45 million and more than 500 participants, and Plan B with unfunded vested benefits of $6 million and fewer than 500 participants. Because the aggregate unfunded vested benefits of the two plans will exceed $50 million, the contributing sponsor and each of its controlled group members are Filers. (Because Plan B has fewer than 500 participants, no actuarial information for the plan need be submitted.)

The PBGC also may waive some or all of the filing requirements for Filers in appropriate cases where the PBGC finds convincing evidence for such a waiver (§ 2628.5(b)). Waivers may be conditioned on the submission of substitute information or the execution of an agreement protective of plan participants and the PBGC. A Filer that seeks a waiver must file its request in writing no less than fifteen days before the applicable due date for required information.

The PBGC invites members of the public to express their views concerning other factors or criteria that could warrant additional exemptions for individual Filers, for classes of Filers, or for plans.

Information to be Submitted

Section 2628.7 describes the information that Filers must submit to the PBGC. Although each Filer is subject to the obligation to submit information on each controlled group member and plan (to the extent no exemptions apply), the regulation allows for a single consolidated filing for the controlled group.

Identifying Information

Section 2628.7(b) specifies identifying information for each Filer (the Filer's name, address, telephone number, and the Employer Identification Number (EIN), if any, assigned by the IRS) and for each pension plan (the name of the plan, EIN, and the Plan Number assigned by the plan's contributing sponsor). Also, each Filer (or one Filer for the entire controlled group) must identify all members of the controlled group and the legal relationship of each entity to the others (parent, wholly-owned subsidiary, etc.).

Actuarial Information

Section 2628.7(c) specifies the actuarial information that a Filer must provide as follows: (1) the market value of plan assets (without regard to any contributions receivable) at the end of the plan year ending within the Filer's Information Year, (2) the value of benefit liabilities as of the same date, (3) certain participant data, and (4) the actuarial valuation report ("AVR") for that plan year, which must contain or be supplemented by certain required actuarial information. Generally, this actuarial information is developed and maintained by the plan's enrolled actuary for purposes of, among other things, completing Schedule B of the plan's Form 5500. A plan's enrolled actuary must certify that all actuarial information submitted is accurate and complete

If the AVR or any of the supplementary actuarial information is not available by the due date, § 2628.7(d) allows a Filer to submit the unavailable information by an alternative date—15 days after the deadline for filing the plan's Form 5500 for the plan year ending within the Filer's Information Year (see 29 CFR 2520.104a-5(a)(2)).

Financial Information

Section 4010(a)(2) of ERISA requires each Filer to provide to the PBGC copies of audited financial statements (or, if not available, unaudited statements). Financial statements include balance sheets, income statements and cash flow statements. Under § 2628.7(e)(1)(iii), if audited or unaudited financial statements are not prepared, the Filer may satisfy the financial information requirement by submitting copies of federal tax returns for the tax year ending within its Information Year.

For most controlled group members whose financial information is combined with that of other group members, the submission of the consolidated financial statement for the group will satisfy the obligation to submit individual financial statements (§ 2628.7(e)(2)(i)). Limited

¶20,532H

financial information a group member's revenues and operating income for the Information Year, and its assets as of the end of the Information Year—is required for each contributing sponsor of a non-Exempt Plan included in such a consolidated financial statement (§ 2628.(e)(2)(ii)).

If the required financial information of a controlled group member has been filed with the Securities and Exchange Commission, or has otherwise been made publicly available, the Filer need not submit it to PBGC. Section 2628.7(e)(3) requires only that the Filer include a statement in its submission to the PBGC indicating when the information was made available to the public and where the PBGC may obtain it.

The PBGC may request additional information from any Filer to determine plan assets and liabilities and a Filer's financial status (§ 2628.7(f)). For example, after a controlled group's parent submits consolidated financial statements in accordance with § 2628.7(e)(2)(i), it proposes to sell one of its subsidiaries. In that instance, the PBGC would normally request financial information relating to the subsidiary that was to be sold. Nothing in this proposed regulation limits the PBGC's authority under section 4003 of ERISA to seek any information from a Filer by any means provided thereunder.

Previously provided information

Any information previously submitted to the PBGC need not be resubmitted. Section 2628.7(g) allows the Filer to incorporate the previous submission by reference. For example, some of the required actuarial information with respect to a Filer's plans may have already been submitted to the PBGC in a reportable event filing; the Filer can make a reference to the reportable event filing in its submission.

When To File

Under § 2628.8(a), a Filer must submit the required information to the PBGC on or before the one hundred and fifth day after the end of the Filer's Information Year. (This due date is designed to be fifteen days after the Securities and Exchange Commission's annual reporting date for public companies.) If a plan's AVR or any of the related supplementary actuarial information is not available by this due date, the Filer may submit the unavailable information by the alternative due date—15 days after the deadline for filing the plan's Form 5500 for the plan year ending within the Filer's Information Year (§ 2628.8(b)).

Filers may submit required information by mail, by overnight and express delivery services, by hand, or by other means that are acceptable to the PBGC. The PBGC invites Filers to offer suggestions regarding procedures to electronically transmit some or all of the required information.

Confidentiality

Generally, required information submitted to the PBGC by a Filer in accordance with this regulation will not be made available or disclosed to the public. This restriction on disclosure shall not apply to publicly available information. For example, if a Filer submits required information to the PBGC, part of which is also publicly available, only that information that is not publicly available will be subject to confidentiality. Further, as provided in section 4010(c) of ERISA, these confidentiality strictures shall not apply to information disclosed by the PBGC in administrative or judicial proceedings or to Congress.

Penalties for Non-Compliance

Failure to provide information to the PBGC in accordance with the requirements of this part would constitute a violation of Title IV of ERISA. Section 4071 authorizes the PEGC to assess a penalty against any person who fails, within the specified time limits, to provide material information to the PBGC. All required information under this regulation is deemed material by the PBGC. The PBGC may assess a penalty on a pension plan's contributing sponsor and on each member of its controlled group of up to $1,000 for each day for which a failure to submit required information continues. The PBGC has the right to pursue other equitable or legal remedies available to it under the law.

Effective Date

The regulation applies for Information Years ending on or after December 31, 1995.

Paperwork Reduction Act

The PBGC has submitted the collection of information requirements in this proposed regulation to the Office of Management and Budget for review under section 3504(h) of the Paperwork Reduction Act (44 U.S.C. chapter 35). The PBGC needs this information, and will use it, to identify controlled groups with severely underfunded plans, to determine the financial status of controlled group members and evaluate the potential risk of future losses resulting from corporate transactions and the need to take legal action, and to negotiate agreements under which

controlled groups would provide additional plan funding. The PBGC estimates the public reporting burden for this collection of information to average 215.3 hours for each of approximately 100 controlled groups.

Comments concerning this collection of information should be submitted to the Office of Management and Budget, Office of Information and Regulatory Affairs, Room 10235, New Executive Office Building, Washington, DC 20503; Attention: PBGC Desk Officer.

E.O. 12866 and Regulatory Flexibility Act

The PBGC has determined that this action is not a "significant regulatory action" under the criteria set forth in Executive Order 12866. The provisions of this proposed regulation would implement policy decisions made by Congress in requiring Filers to provide audited financial statements and other required information annually to the PBGC. Those provisions reflect the PBGC's interpretation of the statutory standards and prescribe the form, time, and manner in which the required information should be submitted.

Under section 605(b) of the Regulatory Flexibility Act, the PBGC certifies that, if adopted, this proposed regulation would not have a significant economic impact on a substantial number of small entities. The tests for identifying Filers under section 4010(b) of ERISA limit the filing requirements to large companies and their controlled groups. With respect to many of those groups, the PBGC will obtain audited financial statements from public sources (such as the Securities and Exchange Commission), rather than require each of the companies to file the information with the PBGC. Further, the proposed regulation will exempt plans with fewer than 500 participants from the actuarial information requirements. The regulation would not require individual financial information with respect to many of the companies within controlled groups. In addition, the PEGC intends to develop the means to allow Filers to submit required information electronically. Accordingly, as provided in section 605 of the Regulatory Flexibility Act (5 U.S.C. 601, *et seq.*), sections 603 and 604 do not apply.

List of Subjects in 29 CFR Part 2628

Employee benefit plans, Pension Insurance, Pensions, Reporting and record keeping requirements.

For the reasons set forth above, the PBGC proposes to amend subchapter C, chapter XXVI of 29 CFR by adding a new part 2628 to read as follows:

PART 2628—ANNUAL FINANCIAL AND ACTUARIAL INFORMATION REPORTING

2628.1 Purpose and scope.

2628.2 Definitions.

2628.3 Required submission of information.

2628.4 Filers.

2628.5 Exemptions.

2628.6 Information Year.

2628.7 Required information.

2628.8 Due date and filing with the PBGC.

2628.9 Date of filing.

2628.10 Confidentiality of information submitted.

Authority: 29 U.S.C. 1302(b)(3); 29 U.S.C. 1310

§ 2628.1 Purpose and scope.

(a) *Purpose.* This part prescribes the procedures and the information that Filers (as described in § 2628.4(a) of this part) must submit annually to the PBGC under section 4010 of the Act.

(b) *Scope.* This part applies to Filers for any Information Year ending on or after December 31, 1995.

§ 2628.2 Definitions.

For purposes of this part—

Act means the Employee Retirement Income Security Act of 1974, as amended.

Code means the Internal Revenue Code of 1986, as amended.

Contributing sponsor means a person who is a contributing sponsor as defined in section 4001(a)(13) of the Act.

Controlled group means, in connection with any person, a group consisting of that person and all other persons under common control with such person, determined under part 2612 of this chapter.

Information Year means the year determined under § 2628.6 of this part.

Exempt Plan means a plan as described in § 2628.5(a) of this part.

Filer means a person who is a Filer as described in § 2628.4 of this part.

Fiscal year means, with respect to a person, the annual accounting period or, if the person has not adopted a closing date, a calendar year (*i.e.*, the year ending on December 31).

Person means an individual, partnership, joint venture, corporation, mutual company, joint-stock company, trust, estate, unincorporated organization, association, or employee organization representing any group of participants for purposes of collective bargaining.

Plan means a single-employer plan (as defined in section 4001(a)(15) of the Act) that is covered by section 4021(a) and not excluded under section 4021(b) of the Act.

Plan year means the calendar, policy, or fiscal year on which the records of a Plan are kept.

Unfunded vested benefits means the amount determined under section 4006(a)(3)(E)(iii) of the Act and § 2610.23 of this chapter (without reference to § 2610.24 of this chapter)

Value of benefit liabilities means the value of a Plan's benefit liabilities (as defined in section 4001(a)(16) of the Act), as of the end of the plan year ending within the Filer's Information Year, using:

(1) The PBGC's valuation assumptions for trusteed plans terminating as of the end of that plan year, as prescribed in 29 CFR part 2619, subpart C, and

(2) Plan census data as of the end of that plan year or the beginning of the next plan year.

If such census data are not available, a projection of plan census data from a date within the plan year must be used. The projection must be consistent with projections used to measure pension obligations of the Plan for financial statement purposes and must give a result appropriate to the measurement date for these obligations. Thus, for example, adjustments to the projection process may be required where there has been a significant event (e.g., a plan amendment or a curtailment) which has not been reflected in the projection assumptions.

§ 2628.3 Required submission of information.

(a) *General requirement.* Except as provided in § 2628.5, each person who is a Filer as described in § 2628.4(a) shall submit to the PBGC annually on or before the date specified in § 2628.8(a) all information specified in § 2628.7 of this part.

(b) *Submission by representative.* One or more Filers or other persons may act as a representative and submit the information specified in § 2628.7 on behalf of some or all Filers within a controlled group. Representatives, other than Filers, must also submit a written power of attorney signed by the Filer authorizing the representative to act on the Filer's behalf in connection with the required information.

§ 2628.4 Filers.

(a) *General.* A Filer is a contributing sponsor of a Plan and each member of the contributing sponsor's controlled group if, for an Information Year,

(1) The aggregate unfunded vested benefits of all Plans maintained by the contributing sponsor and other members of the contributing sponsor's controlled group exceed $50 million (disregarding those Plans with no unfunded vested benefits) at the end of the plan year or years ending within the Filer's Information Year;

(2) The conditions for imposition of a lien described in section 302(f)(1)(A) and (B) of the Act or section 412(n)(1)(A) and (B) of the Code have been met during the plan year ending within the Filer's Information Year with respect to any Plan maintained by the contributing sponsor or any member of its controlled group; or

(3) The Internal Revenue Service has granted a waiver or waivers of the minimum funding standards, as defined in section 303 of the Act and section 412(d) of the Code, in excess of $1 million with respect to any Plan maintained by the contributing sponsor or any member of its controlled group, and any portion thereof is still outstanding at the end of the plan year ending within the Filer's Information Year.

(b) All Plans, including any Exempt Plan as described in § 2628.5(a), maintained by members of a controlled group must be taken into account in determining the persons who are Filers under this section.

§ 2628.5 Exemptions.

(a) *Exempt Plan.* The actuarial information specified in § 2628.7(c) of this part is not required for a Plan (an "Exempt Plan") that—

(1) Has no minimum funding waivers outstanding at the end of the plan year ending within the Filer's Information Year,

(2) Has received all payments required to be made during the Information Year under section 302 of the Act and Section 412 of the Code, and

(3) Satisfies at least one of the following conditions—

(i) The Plan has no unfunded benefit liabilities, determined using the market value of assets in the Plan (without regard to any contributions receivable) at the end of the plan year ending within the Filer's Information Year and the value of benefit liabilities; or

(ii) The Plan has fewer than 500 participants as of the end of the plan year ending within the Filer's Information Year.

(b) *Waiver of information requirements.* The PBGC may waive the requirement to submit required information with respect to a Filer, a Plan, or groups thereof. The PBGC will exercise this discretion in appropriate cases where it finds convincing evidence for such a waiver, and any such waiver may be subject to conditions. A request for a waiver must be filed in writing with the PBGC at the address provided in § 2628.8(d) no later than fifteen days prior to the applicable date specified in § 2628.8 of this part, and must state the facts and circumstances on which the request is based.

§ 2628.6 Information Year.

(a) *Determinations based on Information Year.* An Information Year is used under this part to determine which fiscal year and plan year should be used to determine whether members of a controlled group are Filers (§ 2628.4) and whether a Plan is an Exempt Plan (§ 2628.5(a)), and to identify the information that a Filer must submit (§ 2628.7) and the due date for submitting that information (§ 2628.8(a)). A Filer is not required to change its fiscal year or the plan year of a Plan, to report financial information on any accounting period other than an existing fiscal year, or to report actuarial information for any plan year other than the existing plan year of a Plan.

(b) *General.* Except as provided in paragraph (c) of this section, the Information Year shall be the fiscal year of the Filer or the consolidated fiscal year of the Filer's controlled group.

(c) *Controlled groups with different fiscal years.* If members of a controlled group report financial information for different fiscal years, the Information Year shall be the calendar year. Example: Filers A and B are members of the same controlled group. Filer A has a July 1 fiscal year, and Filer B has an October 1 fiscal year. The Information Year is the calendar year. Filer A's financial information with respect to its fiscal year beginning July 1, 1995, and Filer B's financial information with respect to its fiscal year beginning October 1, 1995, must be submitted to the PBGC following the end of the 1996 calendar year (the calendar year in which those fiscal years end).

§ 2628.7 Required information.

(a) *General.* Except as otherwise provided in section 2628.5 of this part, the information to be submitted by a Filer is that specified in paragraphs (b), (c), and (e) of this section with respect to each member of the Filer's controlled group and each Plan maintained by any member of the controlled group.

(b) *Identifying information.*

(1) The name, address, and telephone number of the Filer.

(2) The nine-digit Employer Identification Number (EIN) assigned by the Internal Revenue Service to the Filer (if there is no EIN, explain).

(3) If the Filer is a contributing sponsor of a Plan or Plans—

(i) The name of each Plan.

(ii) The EIN and the three-digit Plan Number (PN) assigned by the contributing sponsor to each Plan, but—

(A) If the EIN-PN has changed since the beginning of the Information Year, the previous EIN-PN and an explanation; or

(B) If there is no EIN-PN for the Plan, an explanation.

(4) The name and address of each other member of the Filer's controlled group and the legal relationships of each (for example, parent, subsidiary).

(c) *Plan actuarial information.*

(1) The market value of Plan assets (determined without regard to any contributions receivable) at the end of the plan year ending within the Filer's Information Year.

(2) The value of benefit liabilities.

(3) Schedules or listings with the following information as of the first day of the plan year ending within the Filer's Information Year:

(i) The distribution of active participants by 5-year age and service groupings and, if benefits are based (in whole or in part) on compensation, each grouping's average compensation;

(ii) The distribution of retirees by 5-year age groupings with each grouping's average benefit amounts; and

(iii) The distribution of deferred vested participants by 5-year age groupings with each grouping's average benefit amount to be paid at normal retirement age.

(4) A copy of the actuarial valuation report for the plan year ending within the Filer's Information Year that contains or is supplemented by the following information:

(i) Each amortization base and related amortization charge or credit to the funding standard account (as defined in section 302(b) of the Act and section 412(b) of the Code) for that plan year (excluding the amount considered contributed to the Plan as described in section 302(b)(3)(A) of the Act and section 412(b)(3)(A) of the Code);

(ii) The itemized development of the additional funding charge payable for that plan year pursuant to section 412(l) of the Code;

(iii) The minimum funding contribution and the maximum deductible contribution for that plan year;

(iv) The actuarial assumptions and actuarial methods used for that plan year for purposes of section 302(b) and (d) of the Act and section 412(b) and (l) of the Code (and any change in those assumptions and methods since the previous valuation and justifications for any change); and

(v) A summary of the principal eligibility and benefit provisions on which the valuation of the Plan was based (and any change(s) to those provisions since the previous valuation), along with descriptions of any benefits not included in the valuation, any significant events that occurred during that plan year, and the Plan's early retirement factors.

(5) A written certification by the Plan's enrolled actuary that, to the best of his or her knowledge and belief, the actuarial information submitted is true, correct, and complete and conforms to all applicable laws and regulations.

(d) *Alternative compliance for plan actuarial information.* If any of the information specified in paragraph (c)(4) of this section is not available by the date specified in § 2628.8(a) of this part, a Filer may satisfy the requirement to provide such information by—

(1) Including a statement, with the material that is submitted to the PEGC, that the Filer will file the unavailable information by the alternative due date specified in § 2628.8(b), and

(2) Filing such information and a certification by the Plan's enrolled actuary as described in paragraph (c)(5) of this section with the PBGC by that alternative due date.

(e) *Financial information.*

(1) Except as provided in paragraph (e)(2) of this section, required financial information for each controlled group member consists of—

(i) Audited financial statements for the fiscal year ending within the Information Year (including balance sheets, income statements, cash flow statements, and notes to the financial statements); or

(ii) If no audited financial statements are prepared, unaudited financial statements for the fiscal year ending within the Information Year; or

(iii) If neither audited nor unaudited financial statements are prepared, copies of federal tax returns for the tax year ending within the Information Year.

(2) If the financial information of a controlled group member is combined with the information of other group members in a consolidated financial statement, required financial information consists of—

(i) The consolidated, audited (or, if unavailable, unaudited) financial statement for the Information Year; and

(ii) For each controlled group member included in such consolidated financial statement that is a contributing sponsor of a Plan that is not an Exempt Plan, the contributing sponsor's revenues and operating in-

come for the Information Year, and assets as of the end of the Information Year.

(3) If any of the financial information required by paragraphs (e)(1) or (e)(2) of this section is publicly available (for example, the controlled group member has filed audited financial statements with the Securities and Exchange Commission), the Filer, in lieu of submitting such information to the PBGC, may include a statement with the other information that is submitted to the PBGC indicating when such financial information was made available to the public and where the PBGC may obtain it.

(f) *Additional information.* The PBGC may, by written notification, require any Filer to submit additional actuarial or financial information that is necessary to determine Plan assets and liabilities or the financial status of a Filer. Such information must be submitted within 10 days after the date of the written notification or by a different time specified therein.

(g) *Previous submissions.* If any required information has been previously submitted to the PBGC, a Filer may incorporate such information into the required submission by referring to the previous submission.

(h) *Penalties for non-compliance.* If all of the information required under this section is not provided within the specified time limit, the PBGC may assess a separate penalty under section 4071 of the Act against the Filer and each member of the Filer's controlled group of up to $1,000 a day for each day that the failure continues. The PBGC may also pursue other equitable or legal remedies available to it under the law.

§ 2628.8 Due date and filing with the PBGC.

(a) *Due date.* Except as permitted under paragraph (b) of this section, a Filer shall file the information required under this part with the PBGC on or before the 105th day after the close of the Filer's Information Year.

(b) *Alternative due date.* A Filer that includes the statement specified in § 2628.7(d)(1) with its submission to the PBGC by the date specified in paragraph (a) of this section must submit the actuarial information specified in § 2628.7(d)(2) within 15 days after the deadline for filing the Plan's annual report for the plan year ending within the Filer's Information Year (see § 2520.104a-5(a)(2) of this title).

(c) *Extensions.* When the President of the United States declares that, under the Disaster Relief Act of 1974, as amended (42 U.S.C. 5121, 5122(2), 5141(b)), a major disaster exists, the PBGC may extend the due dates provided under paragraphs (a) and (b) of this section by up to 180 days.

(d) *How to file.* Requests and information may be delivered by mail, by overnight and express delivery services, by hand, or by any other method acceptable to the PBGC, to: Corporate Finance and Negotiations Department, Pension Benefit Guaranty Corporation, 1200 K Street, N.W., Washington, DC 20005-4026.

§ 2628.9 Date of filing.

(a) Information filed under this part is considered filed on the date of the United States postmark stamped on the cover in which the information is mailed, if—

(1) The postmark was made by the United States Postal Service; and

(2) The document was mailed postage prepaid, properly addressed to the PBGC.

(b) If the Filer sends or transmits the information to the PBGC by means other than the United States Postal Service, the information is considered filed on the date it is received by the PBGC. Information received on a weekend or Federal holiday or after 5:00 p.m. on a weekday is considered filed on the next regular business day.

(c) In computing any period of time under this part, the day of the act or event from which the designated period of time begins to run shall not be included. The last day of the period so computed shall be included, unless it is a weekend or Federal holiday, in which event the period runs until the end of the next day that is not a weekend or Federal holiday.

§ 2628.10 Confidentiality of information submitted.

In accordance with § 2603.15(b) of this chapter and section 4010(c) of the Act, any information or documentary material that is not publicly available and is submitted to the PBGC pursuant to this part shall not be made public, except as may be relevant to any administrative or judicial action or proceeding or for disclosures to either body of Congress or to any duly authorized committee or subcommittee of the Congress.

Issued in Washington, DC this 30th day of June, 1995.

Martin Slate,   Pension Benefit Guaranty Corporation
Executive Director,

¶ 20,533

Proposed regulations on 29 CFR Part 2611: Valuation of insurance contracts.—Reproduced below is the text of proposed regulations on 29 CFR Part 2611 to provide rules for identifying insurance contracts or contract rights that are assets of terminating pension plans and for determining their asset value.

The regulations were filed with the *Federal Register* on April 15, 1977.

VALUATION OF PLAN ASSETS

[29 CFR Part 2611]

Proposed Amendments—Insurance Contracts

AGENCY: Pension Benefit Guaranty Corporation.

ACTION: Proposed rule.

SUMMARY: The proposed amendments create special rules for identifying insurance contracts or contract rights that are assets of terminating pension plans and for determining their asset value. These special rules are needed because the pension plan termination insurance provisions of the Employee Retirement Income Security Act of 1974 require that the assets of a covered pension plan be valued at plan termination, and the value of insurance contracts is not readily established. The basic effect of the proposed amendment is first, to provide that the value of an irrevocable promise made by an insurance company directly to a pension plan participant is not counted in the value of the pension plan's assets, and second, to provide that an insurance contract is worth the benefits it can be used to provide.

DATE: Comments due by June 2, 1977.

ADDRESS: Comments should be sent to the Office of the General Counsel, Pension Benefit Guaranty Corporation, 2020 K Street, N.W., Washington, D.C. 20006. Copies of written comments will be available for public inspection in the PBGC's Office of Communications, at the same address, between 9 a.m. and 4 p.m. Each person submitting comments should include his or her name and address, identify this notice and give reasons for any recommendations.

FOR FURTHER INFORMATION CONTACT: Judith F. Mazo, Special Counsel, Office of the General Counsel, Pension Benefit Guaranty Corporation, 2020 K. Street, N.W., Washington, D.C. 20006, 202-354-4868.

SUPPLEMENTARY INFORMATION: On May 7, 1976, the Pension Benefit Guaranty Corporation (the "PBGC") published a regulation (41 FR 18992, codified at 29 CFR Part 2611) that prescribes standards for valuing the assets of a pension plan covered under Title IV of the Employee Retirement Income Security Act of 1974 (the "Act") when the plan terminates. Under the regulation plan assets are valued at their fair market value. The preamble to the regulation noted that special valuation considerations apply to insurance contracts held as plan assets, and that PBGC would provide guidance on that issue in the future. Because an insurance contract has a unique value to a plan that is not freely transferable, traditional fair market value concepts cannot measure such a contract's value appropriately. Therefore the PBGC proposes to amend its asset-valuation regulation to provide special rules for computing the value of insurance contracts for Title IV purposes.

Several essentially technical amendments that do not affect existing substantive rules are proposed. They would restructure the present regulation and revise the language of two of its sections. Those amendments are necessary to accommodate the new rules, contained in proposed Subpart C of this part, for valuing insurance contracts. Because proposed Subpart C represents the only substantively significant aspect of the proposed amendments, the remainder of this preamble discusses that proposed Subpart exclusively.

General Approach

1. *Introduction.* A pension plan that owns an insurance contract owns the right to enforce the promises that the insurer has made in the contract. The plan's asset is the insurance contract, rather than the premiums paid to purchase the insurer's contractual obligations. Proposed Subpart C of this part ("Subpart C") measures an insurance contract's value by the value of the benefits that the contract can be used to provide, either directly or after liquidation of the contract for cash.

Subpart C covers individual and group insurance contracts issued by any company authorized to do business as an insurance carrier under State (or District of Columbia) law. Within this broad spectrum, con-

tracts use widely varying language to define similar legal relationships. In addition, Title IV of the Act sometimes expresses uniquely statutory ideas in words that have a different connotation when used in private insurance contracts. To avoid misleading the public and the insurance industry, Subpart C uses its own uniform terms to describe certain fundamental concepts. Those terms and the related concepts are discussed in greater detail below.

2. *What Must Be Valued.* A terminating plan's assets are primarily relevant under Title IV of the Act to the extent they can be used to meet outstanding plan liabilities. Thus § 4044(a) of the Act requires allocation of those assets that are "available to provide benefits," and employer liability under § 4062(b) of the Act is based, in part, on the "current value of the plan's assets allocable to [guaranteed] benefits * * *" For this reason, only those contractual promises that offer a means of satisfying the plan's future benefit payment obligations are included among the plan assets to be valued under Subpart C.

A plan that has distributed an insurance contract to a participant before plan termination does not own that contract on the termination date. A plan that has arranged, under group insurance contract, for an insurer to make an irrevocable commitment to pay benefits to a specific participant has in effect distributed that commitment to the participant. In either case, the plan cannot alter the insurer's direct commitment to the participant, or use the value of the commitment to provide benefits for other participants. Therefore, the value of a distributed contract or of an insurer's irrevocable commitment to a participant is not part of the value of a plan's assets under Subpart C. (If, under § 4045 of the Act, a trustee recaptures part of a distribution that was made to a participant in the form of an insurance contract or commitment, the net amount recaptured would be a plan asset. It would not, however, be part of the asset value of the plan's insurance contracts.)

The PBGC is publishing in the FEDERAL REGISTER today (42 FR 20156) proposed amendments to Part 2608 of this chapter, "Allocation of Plan Assets," to make sure that a terminating plan does not allocate its assets to benefits that are or will be paid under an insurer's irrevocable commitment.

One type of promise made to a plan by an insurer has value as a plan asset, even if its value is not part of the asset value of an insurance contract owned by the plan. In connection with the purchase of benefits or services a plan might purchase the right to receive future interest, dividends or similar payments from the insurer. Those payments can be used to provide benefits, and the right to receive that future income (called a "participation right") is a plan asset to be valued under Subpart C.

3. *Valuation Rules.* In many cases an insurance contract owned by a terminating pension plan can be used to provide benefits in two ways: the plan can either direct that the funds credited to the contract be used to buy the insurer's irrevocable commitment to pay participants' benefits, or it can cash the contract in and provide benefits with the proceeds. Under Subpart C, the value of an insurance contract is the greater of the present value of the irrevocable benefit commitments that can be purchased under the contract or the contract's liquidation value. Because insurance contracts do not invariably offer a choice between the purchase of benefit commitments or cancellation for cash, an insurance contract's asset value depends on the alternatives expressly available under the contract as of the valuation date.

Upon termination, a plan covered under Title IV of the Act must allocate its assets to provide benefits in the order prescribed by § 4044 of the Act. Therefore, for valuation purposes, the purchase of irrevocable commitments under a contract must follow the statutory order of priorities, whether or not the particular contract so provides. The cost of those irrevocable commitments is set by the contract. Under Subpart C, the present value of the benefits that can be provided through those irrevocable commitments is determined according to PBGC's rules for valuing plan benefits, which are contained in Part 2610 of this chapter.

In most cases the value of a plan's participation rights will be reflected in the asset value of an insurance contract owned by the plan. Under Subpart C, participation rights that must be valued separately are worth the value of the amount realizable by the plan, in cash or in the form of additional irrevocable benefit commitments, upon cancellation of the participation rights.

As a general rule, under Subpart C each insurance contract is valued separately, and the benefits that it can provide are determined by applying § 4044 of the Act as if the contract were the plan's only asset. If the plan owns two or more contracts that provide for the coordinated purchase of irrevocable commitments in accordance with the statutory allocation requirements, the benefits that the contracts can provide will be determined under that contractual formula. In addition, the plan administrator may elect an optional procedure by which benefits could be provided under separate contracts in any order, as long as a combined allocation of all of the plan's assets complies with the statutory priority scheme. This option is not available unless it would yield benefits worth at least as much as the plan's assets could otherwise provide and, for insufficient plans, unless it had been arranged with the insurer before the plan termination date. To take advantage of the optional valuation procedure the plan administrator must demonstrate exactly how the combined allocation will meet Subpart C's requirements.

Basic Concepts

1. *Irrevocable Commitment.* Whether a particular commitment made by an insurer is irrevocable depends on the specific contract language. For example, a retired participant may be "eligible" to receive benefits from an insurer but not contractually "entitled" to continue receiving them, because the contract requires an additional premium payment before the entitlement arises. A contract provision limiting the insurer's liability to those benefits for which the insurer actually receives payment could create a similar problem, if by the plan termination date the funds held under the contract had dropped below the level necessary to cover the cost of annuities for participants who had begun receiving benefits from the insurer. If an insurer claims the right to cut back benefits to any participant in that situation, that would indicate that all similar benefit payment obligations of the insurer under that contract are fully revocable.

An insurance contract might specifically identify a portion of the insurer's commitment as irrevocable. For example, some deposit administration group annuity contracts contain "post-funding riders," which authorize the insurer to pay full benefits to a retired participant while the participant's irrevocable annuity from the insurer is being purchased in installments after the participant's retirement. Under Subpart C, only that portion of the retiree's annuity that had been purchased from the insurer before the plan terminated would be treated as covered by an irrevocable commitment. Similarly, the insurance contract might state that annuity commitments made to certain plan participants are subject to reduction if required by the Internal Revenue Service to prevent prohibited discrimination on plan termination. Unless the benefit cut-back is in fact required, the full annuity commitment would be irrevocable.

An insurer's commitment is considered irrevocable under Subpart C even though it can be cancelled with the participant's consent, as in the case of a commitment that offers the participant an option to receive a lump sum in lieu of future benefit payments. Similarly, an insurer's commitment is not considered revocable solely because it provides for assignment of future benefit payments as authorized or required by law.

2. *Contractholder.* The contractholder is the identifiable owner of an insurance contract purchased with funds contributed to or under a plan. Although plan participants may be third-party beneficiaries of such a contract, the contractholder is the party to whom all of the insurer's promises are made directly, regardless of how that party is designated in the contract. For example, an insurance contract might identify a named corporation as "the Employer," and then define the insurer's obligations in terms of duties owed to, or rights exercisable by, the Employer. The Employer is the owner of the contract, and thus the contractholder within the meaning of Subpart C.

As all insurance contracts that are plan assets need not be held in a trust fund (see, 403(b) of the Act), the holder of a plan's insurance contract is often not a plan trustee. Nevertheless, the contractholder represents the plan's interests with regard to the insurance contract, so Subpart C treats the rights of the plan and the rights of the contractholder interchangeably.

Because a contract that has been distributed to a participant is not considered a plan asset, a plan participant who has become the owner of a contract bought by the plan is not "the contractholder" for purposes of Subpart C.

3. *Contract Assets.* Under many of the insurance contracts in which pension plans invest, the insurer agrees to make a specified amount of money available in the future to support benefit payments. Ordinarily those amounts are based to some extent on the premiums paid by the plan, and are credited to the contract in some defined form, such as the cash surrender value of an individual contract. Group contracts often contain one or more accounts to which funds that will be used to cover future plan liabilities are credited. Subpart C uses the term "contract assets" to describe the funds credited to the plan's account that are available to meet outstanding plan benefit obligations.

Under Subpart C, funds are not treated as contract assets if they have been used to purchase an irrevocable commitment from the insurer prior to the date of plan termination, or if the insurer has a contractual right to use those funds to pay for previously-issued irrevocable commitments. Money credited to the plan that must be used to pay pretermination plan debts (such as accrued but unpaid benefits to retirees who do not have an irrevocable commitment from the insurer) is also excluded from the contract assets, as are funds to which the insurer is contractually entitled in payment for administrative or other services performed on behalf of the plan. Subpart C makes clear that funds credited to the special accounts kept under some types of group contracts solely for determining the credits due under a plan's participation rights are not contract assets.

The proposed amendment includes as contract assets the additional funds that will be credited to the plan upon cancellation, as provided in the contract, of any outstanding participation rights owned by the plan under the contract. Subpart C values a plan's participation rights, to the extent they are not included in an insurance contract's asset value, at the amount realizable by the plan upon cancellation of those participation rights. An insurance contract might indicate the cancellation value of participation rights, or an insurer might be able to determine their value by comparing the cost of similar contracts issued on a non-participating basis. Nevertheless, the PBGC recognizes that in many cases it might be difficult for the contractholder to assess the reasonableness of the insurer's determination of the cancellation value of participation rights. The PBGC therefore invites public suggestions on appropriate measures that the PBGC might take to assure that a reasonable value is attributed to a plan's participation rights when those rights must be cancelled at plan termination.

4. *Present Value of Benefits.* Under Subpart C, the value of the irrevocable benefit commitments that can be bought under a contract is to be determined in accordance with Part 2610 of this chapter "Valuation of Plan Benefits" (at present, proposed Part 2610, 41 FR 48499, November 3, 1976). That part sets forth actuarial factors and assumptions, which are periodically revised, to be used to determine the present value of plan benefits. Proposed § 2610.3(c) contains a special valuation rule for determining plan sufficiency and allocating plan assets under proposed Part 2615 of this chapter, "Determination of Sufficiency" (41 FR 48504, November 3, 1976). Under proposed § 2611.8, proposed § 2610.3(c) would apply to determine the asset value of an insurance contract for purposes of proposed Part 2615 as well.

This means that, for a plan that does not receive a Notice of Inability to Determine Sufficiency under proposed Part 2615, an insurance contract's value will be measured in part by the actual cost to the plan of purchasing in the private sector the benefits that the contract could provide. As that cost may have changed by the date that assets must be distributed under proposed § 2615.6(d), a revaluation for allocation purposes may be necessary. For all other plans, the value of the benefits that can be provided by an insurance contract will be determined at PBGC rates applicable for the valuation date, and the contract's value as of the plan termination date will be used for all purposes under Title IV of the Act.

Under customary contract terms, an individual insurance contract cannot be converted into an irrevocable commitment for the benefit of anyone other than the participant covered under the contract. Since each contract held by a plan is valued as if it were the plan's only asset, benefits under most individual contracts cannot be allocated in accordance with § 4044 of the Act. Contract liquidation would therefore be the only acceptable valuation alternative available, unless the plan administrator elects the optional valuation procedure.

5. *Cash Settlement Value.* The contractholder's choices with respect to disposition of contract assets upon discontinuance of an insurance contract are labelled "settlement options" in Subpart C. The value of an option that requires a cash payment by the insurer is its "cash settlement value." Under Subpart C, the greatest cash settlement value (expressly available under the contract as of the valuation date) is compared to the present value of benefits that can be provided under a contract to determine the contract's value as a plan asset.

Individual insurance contracts usually offer one option that entails a cash payment: the cancellation of the contract in return for its cash surrender value, less any outstanding policy loans. A group contract might include several options, depending on whether the cash is withdrawn immediately or in installments. Under the Subpart C, the value of a cash installment option is its fair market value, that is, the amount a willing buyer would pay a willing seller for the right to receive those future payments from the insurance company.

Insurance contracts frequently authorize the transfer of funds to an alternative funding agent, usually upon certification that the transfer will not impair the plan's tax qualification. A terminating plan might wish to exercise that right in order to purchase annuities from another insurer. If the PBGC has become trustee of a terminating plan, it might choose to have the funds transferred to a custodian bank. The cash settlement options to be considered in determining a contract's asset value under Subpart C include the option to have funds transferred to such alternative funding agents, as well as provisions for other types of cash payments.

Many insurance contracts give the insurer some discretion in calculating the cash amount available under settlement options. The PBGC anticipates that most insurers will be fair and reasonable in interpreting and implementing their contracts, and will not discriminate against small employers in discharging their contractual obligations. The PBGC invites suggestions from the public on the need for special safeguards, and the type of safeguards that PBGC might adopt, in this context.

In consideration of the foregoing, it is proposed to amend Part 2611 of Chapter XXVI of Title 29, Code of Federal Regulations by:

§ 2611.2-2611.5 [Redesignated]

1. Redesignating §§ 2611.2-2611.5 as follows:

Old § 2611.2—§ 2611.5.

Old § 2611.3—§ 2611.6.

Old § 2611.4—§ 2611.2.

Old § 2611.5—§ 2611.7.

2. Revising paragraph (a) of § 2611.1 as follows:

§ 2611.1 Purpose and scope.

(a) This part sets forth standards for valuing plan assets in connection with the determination of plan asset sufficiency under section 4041(b) of the Act, the allocation of plan assets under section 4044 of the Act and the determination of employer liability under § 4062 of the Act.

* * *

3. Revising § 2611.6 as follows:

§ 2611.6 Valuation of plan assets.

Except as provided in Subpart C of this part, plan assets shall be valued at their fair market value on the valuation date, based on the method of valuation that most accurately reflects such fair market value.

4. Designating §§ 2611.1 and 2611.2 as "Subpart A General;" designating §§ 2611.5-2611.7 as "Subpart B—Assets Other Than Insurance Contracts;" and adding a new Subpart C as follows:

Subpart C—Insurance Contracts

Sec.

Appendix A—Examples: Valuation of insurance contracts.

Authority: Secs. 4002(b)(3), 4041, 4044, 4062(b)(1)(B), Pub. L. 93-406; 88 Stat. 1004, 1020-21, 1025-27, 1029 (29 U.S.C. 1302(b)(3), 1341(b), 1344, 1362(b)(1)(B)).

§ 2611.10 Definitions.

For purposes of this subpart, "Act" means the Employee Retirement Income Security Act of 1974, 29 U.S.C. 1001 et seq.

"Cash settlement value" means the value of any settlement option that requires a cash payment by the insurer.

"Contractholder" means the owner of an insurance contract purchased with funds contributed to or under a plan. References in this subpart to a plan's interests, obligations or rights under an insurance contract include the interests, obligations or rights of the contractholder. A participant who has received an insurance contract from or under a plan is not a "contractholder" for purposes of this subpart.

"Insurance contract" or "contract" means a valid written agreement between an insurer and a contractholder pursuant to which the insurer agrees to perform services including the payment of specified benefits or their equivalent in return for the payment of premiums or similar consideration. References in this subpart to "an insurance contract" include more than one contract, unless the plural is clearly inappropriate in this context.

"Insurer" means a company authorized to do business as an insurance carrier under the laws of a State or the District of Columbia.

"Irrevocable commitment" means an insurer's obligation to pay benefits or their equivalent to a named plan participant, which cannot be cancelled under the terms of the insurance contract without the consent of the participant (except for fraud or mistake) and which is legally enforceable by the participant. An otherwise irrevocable commitment that authorizes the assignment of benefit payments as permitted or required by law is an irrevocable commitment.

"Participation right" means a plan's right under an insurance contract to receive future dividends, rate credits, interest, experience credits or other earnings from the insurer.

"Participant" means a person who is or has been a participant as defined under the terms of a plan, and includes the beneficiary of a plan participant.

"PBGC" means Pension Benefit Guaranty Corporation.

"Plan" means a pension plan to which section 4021 of the Act applies.

"Plan termination date" means the termination date established under section 4048 of the Act.

"Present value of benefits" means the present value determined in accordance with Part 2610 of this chapter, as applicable for the valuation date.

"Settlement options" means the alternatives available to the contractholder under the express terms of an insurance contract, as of the valuation date, with respect to disposition of contract assets upon discontinuance of the insurance contract.

§ 2611.11 Plan assets.

For purposes of this subpart, the following are plan assets on the date of plan termination:

(a) An insurance contract purchased with funds contributed to or under the plan, if on the date of plan termination the contract has not been distributed to a participant and the insurer's obligations under the contract have not been cancelled.

(b) Participation rights under any insurance contract purchased with funds contributed to or under the plan, to the extent the value of those participation rights is not included in the value of an insurance contract that is a plan asset.

§ 2611.12 Value of insurance contracts.

(a) *General.* The value of an insurance contract is the greater of:

(1) The contract's greatest cash settlement value, or

(2) The present value of the benefits that can be provided under the contract by application of the contract assets to the purchase of benefits in accordance with the order of priorities prescribed by section 4044 of the Act.

(b) *Exclusive plan asset test.* Except as provided in paragraph (d) of this section, the benefits that can be provided under the contract shall be determined as if each insurance contract that is a plan asset were the plan's only asset on the date of plan termination. If two or more insurance contracts owned by a plan expressly provide a basis for coordinated allocation of contract assets in conformance with § 4044 of the Act, the benefits that can be provided under the contracts shall be determined as prescribed by the contracts.

(c) *Cash settlement value.* (1) The value of a settlement option requiring an immediate, lump sum cash payment by the insurer is the dollar amount of the cash payment.

(2) The value of a settlement option requiring cash payments by the insurer in installments is the fair market value, determined in accordance with Subpart B of this part, of the right to receive that stream of future payments.

(d) *Optional valuation procedure.* (1) When an insurance contract is not a plan's only asset on the plan termination date, the plan administrator may value the contract by applying the contract assets to purchase benefits under the insurance contract without regard to the order of priorities prescribed by section 4044 of the Act, if the plan administrator demonstrates to the PBGC that:

(i) All of the plan's assets on the date of plan termination, taken together, can be allocated in a manner that complies with section 4044 of the Act;

(ii) Under the combined allocation, the plan's assets will provide benefits with a total present value that equals or exceeds the total present value of the benefits that could otherwise be provided by the plan's assets, and

(iii) In the case of a plan that receives a Notice of Inability to Determine Sufficiency under Part 2615 of this chapter, arrangements for a specific combined allocation that satisfies section 4044 of the Act were made prior to the plan termination date.

(2) A plan administrator who elects the valuation procedure described in paragraph (c)(1) of this section must furnish the PBGC with evidence, including supporting computations, that the optional valuation meets all of the requirements of that paragraph.

(3) When a plan administrator elects the valuation procedure described in paragraph (c)(1) of this section, the total value of the plan's assets is the total present value of the benefits that can be provided through the combined allocation of the plan's assets pursuant to that paragraph.

§ 2611.13 Contract assets.

(a) Contract assets are the funds credited to an insurance contract as of the plan termination date that are available to provide benefits, including funds that will become available to provide benefits upon the exercise of the contractholder's rights under the insurance contract to cancel any participation rights held by the plan under the insurance contract.

(b) Contract assets do not include:

(1) Funds that the insurer is entitled, under the insurance contract, to withdraw in payment for an irrevocable commitment made by the insurer prior to the date of plan termination;

(2) Funds that the insurer is entitled, under the insurance contract, to withdraw to satisfy liabilities of the plan that became due and owing prior to the date of plan termination;

(3) Funds that the insurer is entitled, under the insurance contract, to withdraw to pay for administrative or other services performed by the insurer; and

(4) Funds that have been paid to the insurer prior to the date of plan termination in return for benefits or services, which are credited to an account under the contract solely for the purpose of computing amounts payable pursuant to the plan's participation rights.

§ 2611.14 Value of participation rights.

The value of a participation right is the greater of:

(a) The dollar amount payable by the insurer upon cancellation of the participation right as of the plan termination date, or

(b) The present value of the additional benefits that the insurer offers to provide, pursuant to irrevocable commitments, upon cancellation of the participation right as of the plan termination date.

Appendix A—Examples: Valuation of Insurance Contracts

The following examples assume that no amounts are recapturable on behalf of the plan under 4045 of the Act.

(a) *Trusteed plan.* Contributions to the ABC plan are deposited in a trust fund, through which the plan's assets are invested in bonds and common stocks. From time to time the trustee uses plan funds to purchase an irrevocable commitment from an insurer for a participant who retires or leaves employment with vested rights under the plan. For purposes of this part, that irrevocable commitment is the property of the participant and is not a plan asset. If the plan has participation rights based on the purchase of that irrevocable commitment, they are plan assets to be valued under § 2611.14 of this part. The plan's other assets will be valued in accordance with Subpart B of this part.

(b) *Fully insured plan.* The trustees of the DEF Plan invest the plan's assets exclusively in individual insurance contracts, each covering a named participant. A portion of the annual premium paid to the insurer is credited to the cash surrender value of the contract, which accumulates cash value at a rate designed to amortize the cost of an annuity for the covered participant at retirement. The insurer makes no irrevocable commitment until an insurance contract is distributed to a participant, either directly or after conversion to an annuity. For purposes of this part, once an insurance contract is distributed to a participant it is no longer a plan asset, although any participation rights the plan may have in distributed contracts are plan assets.

The cash surrender values of the individual contracts held by the plan on its termination date are the contract assets. Although an individual contract may provide for conversion to an annuity at contractually-specified rates, each contract may only be used to purchase benefits for the participant named in the contract. As the application of the contract assets to purchase benefits through this contractual mechanism would not comply with § 4044 of the Act, under § 2611.12(a) the value of the contracts as plan assets is the sum of their individual cash surrender values on the date of plan termination. The plan administrator could elect the optional valuation procedure described in § 2611.12(d) if that would yield an equal or higher total value for the plan assets.

(c) *Split-funded plan.* (1) The trustee of the GHI Plan uses part of the plan's assets to purchase individual life insurance contracts covering each participant, and holds the remaining plan assets in a "side fund," which it invests in equity and fixed-income securities. When a participant with vested rights leaves employment before retirement age, the trustee gives the participant the insurance contract on his or her life plus a share of the side fund. For participants who retire, the trustee purchases irrevocable commitments from the insurer, using the cash value of the insurance contracts on their lives supplemented as needed by withdrawals from the side fund. The trustee is the contractholder, who owns the individual contracts of insurance on active participants. Those contracts may be cancelled at the contractholder's option even though a covered participant has vested rights under the plan.

For purposes of this part, the assets of the GHI Plan consist of the side fund, the individual insurance contracts held by the trustee, and any participation rights held by the plan. As in paragraph (b) of this Appendix, the value of the individual life insurance contracts is the sum of their cash surrender values on the plan termination date. The assets in the side fund are valued in accordance with Subpart B of this part.

(2) The trustees of the JKL Plan pay all contributions received under the plan to an insurer, which issues individual life insurance contracts to the trustees and credits the remainder of the money received from the plan to a side fund managed by the insurer. As liquidation of the side fund is subject to contractual restraints, the side fund must be valued in accordance with § 2611.8 (a) and (c), rather than Subpart B of this part.

(d) *Deposit administration contract.* The sole asset of the MNO Plan is a group insurance contract of the deposit administration ("DA") type, which the employer purchases directly from the insurer with funds contributed under the plan. The insurer credits premiums (contributions) to an account maintained under the contract (the "active life fund") in which funds for the benefits of active participants accumulate. The insurer makes an irrevocable commitment when a participant retires, withdrawing the amount needed to purchase the promised benefits from the active life fund, pursuant to the contract, at that time.

The active life fund contains the bulk of the contract assets. Because the plan has participation rights based on previously purchased benefits, the insurer maintains an experience account under the contract to compute the earnings due the plan. Under paragraph (b)(4) of § 2611.13, the experience account would not contain contract assets, except for amounts owed to the plan that had not yet been credited to the active life fund.

Under § 2611.13(b)(2), the balance in the active life fund must be reduced to reflect outstanding claims against the fund (e.g., accrued benefits payable to retirees that are chargeable to the fund under the contract). The fund balance may also be increased, pursuant to § 2611.13(a), as the result of liquidation of any separate investment accounts maintained for the plan under the contract or cancellation of the plan's participation rights. The value of the participation rights is included in the contract assets even though the contract states that the earnings may be paid to the employer, because the employer is the contractholder.

Under § 2611.12, the contract is valued by:

(1) Determining the benefits that can be provided by applying the assets in the active life fund (adjusted as described above) to the purchase of irrevocable commitments from the insurer at rates specified in the contract, in accordance with the benefit priority categories established by § 4044 of the Act, and

(2) Comparing the present value of the benefits so purchased with the most valuable cash settlement option available on the date of plan termination.

(e) *Immediate participation guarantee ("IPG") contract.* The Board of Trustees of the PQR Plan has invested all contributions made to the plan in an IPG contract, which is a specialized form of DA contract that enables the contractholder (the Board of Trustees) to share directly in the insurer's experience gains and losses on the plan's retired and terminated-vested participants. Under the plan's IPG contract the insurer issues irrevocable commitments to participants as they retire or leave employment with vested rights under the plan. However, the insurer does not withdraw the cost of the benefits covered by the irrevocable commitments until the contract is discontinued. The insurer maintains an IPG account under the contract, which contains funds to support benefits currently payable to retired participants as well as active participants' future benefits.

Because the PQR Plan's insurance contract entitles the insurer to withdraw from the IPG account the amount necessary to pay for previously issued irrevocable commitments at the date of contract discontinuance, under paragraph (b)(2) of § 2611.13 those amounts are not included in the contract assets. Once the withdrawals are made the discontinued IPG contract operates like a conventional DA contract, and would be valued in the manner described in paragraph (d) of this Appendix.

(f) *Group deferred annuity contract.* The trustees of the RST Plan own a group deferred annuity contract, under which the premiums paid by the plan are used to purchase deferred annuities for active participants in increments as benefits accrue. Before the participants' rights to benefits become vested under the plan, the insurer's commitment to pay the annuities can be revoked. For purposes of this part, the contract assets under the RST Plan's group deferred annuity contract consist of: (1) the cash surrender values of the deferred annuity units purchased to cover benefits that are not vested on the earlier of the date of discontinuance of the contract or the plan termination date, and (2) any participation rights held by the plan.

(g) *Optional valuation procedure.* The XYZ Plan owns two DA contracts, No. 111 and No. 222, each issued by the same insurer and held by the employer as contractholder. In addition, a corporate trustee holds $100,000 worth of plan assets, invested in corporate bonds. Under § 2611.12 (a), (b) and (c), the value of Contract No. 111 is determined by computing the present value of the benefits that could be provided by applying the contract assets to the purchase of benefits in the priority sequence prescribed by § 4044 of the Act, beginning with the first priority category, and comparing that figure with the greatest amount realizable under a settlement option. The value of Contract No. 222 is determined in the same manner. So valued, each contract is worth $100,000.

However, because the rates for deferred annuities are different under the two contracts, benefits in the statutory fourth priority category may be purchased more cheaply from the insurer under Contract No. 222 than under Contract No. 111. If the plan administrator agrees to purchase additional benefits from the insurer with the funds held by the corporate trustee, the insurer is willing to allow the plan to use all of the contract assets under Contract No. 222 to purchase category four benefits, applying the Contract No. 111 contract assets plus the trust fund money to higher priority benefits. This arrangement will enable the plan assets to provide $400,000 worth of benefits.

The plan administrator may elect the optional valuation procedure described in § 2611.12(d), by demonstrating to the PBGC that the result would comply with § 4044 of the Act and would equal or increase the total amount of benefits that the plan's assets can provide. If the plan's assets would still not be sufficient to satisfy all guaranteed benefits, in order to qualify for the optional valuation procedure, the plan administrator must demonstrate to the PBGC that the arrangement with the insurer had been worked out prior to the date of plan termination.

Issued in Washington, D.C. this 8th day of April 1977.

Ray Marshall,

Chairman, Board of Director, Pension Benefit Guaranty Corporation.

Issued on the date set forth above, pursuant to a resolution of the Board of Directors authorizing its Chairman to issue this Notice of Proposed Rulemaking.

Henry Rose,

Secretary, Pension Benefit Guaranty Corporation.

[FR Doc. 77-11226 Filed 4-15-77; 8:45 am]

¶ 20,533A   Reserved.

Proposed rules that would have imposed certain notice requirements on plan administrators of plans undergoing standard terminations were formerly reproduced here.

The final regulations are at ¶ 15,448P—¶ 15,448S.]

¶ 20,533B

Proposed regulations on 29 CFR Part 2610: Premium payment requirements: Simplification.—The PBGC has issued newly proposed rules that are designed to reduce the burden and administrative costs of complying with the PBGC premium payment requirements for most of the defined benefit pension plans that it insures.

The proposals were filed with the *Federal Register* on April 9, 1992, and published in the *Federal Register* (57 FR 12666) on April 10, 1992.

[Caution: The PBGC has extended the effective date of the proposed amendment to the premium payment regulations by one year to plan years beginning after 1993. The deferred effective date extends the comment period until November 16, 1992. The announcement of the extended effective date was published in the *Federal Register* (57 FR 42910) on September 17, 1992.]

[NOTE: The PBGC has adopted final regulations relating to Prop. Regs. § 2610.25(b)(1), § 2610.25(b)(2)(ii), and § 2610.25(b)(3)(i). *The change in the premium filing due date was originally proposed for the 1993 plan year. However, the finalized change is effective beginning with the 1999 plan year. PBGC Final Reg. § 4007.11 was published in the Federal Register on December 14, 1998 (63 FR 68684) and is at ¶ 15,371J.]*

PENSION BENEFIT GUARANTY CORPORATION

29 CFR Part 2610

RIN 1212-AA58

Payment of Premiums

AGENCY: Pension Benefit Guaranty Corporation.

ACTION: Proposed rule.

SUMMARY: This is a proposed amendment to the Pension Benefit Guaranty Corporation's regulation on Payment of Premiums (29 CFR part 2610). Comments on the existing regulation by premium payers in recent years and studies by PBGC staff have persuaded the PBGC that the regulation can be simplified to reduce the public burden of compliance and the PBGC's burden of administration. The proposed amendment would make a number of simplifying changes suggested by those comments and studies.

For example, the proposed amendment would replace the existing alternative calculation method with a new simplified filing method using tables of adjustment factors instead of formulas (and would place restrictions on the new method's use by large plans). The definition of the term "participant" in the regulation would be changed to agree with that used for the Form 5500 series annual report. The proposed amendment would also defer the final filing due date (so that it would be closer to the extended Form 5500 due date), raise the number of participants a plan must have in order to be required to make the early premium payment (so that fewer plans would have to file twice a year), and eliminate both penalties and interest on early payments that equal at least a definitely determinable amount (so that both estimates and special safe harbor rules would be unnecessary). It would also accelerate the early filing due date to an earlier date in the premium payment year and widen the scope of the early payment to cover the variable rate, as well as the flat rate, portion of the premium.

DATES: Comments on the proposed amendment must be received on or before May 26, 1992.

ADDRESSES: Comments may be mailed to the Office of the General Counsel (22500), Pension Benefit Guaranty Corporation, 2020 K Street, NW., Washington DC, 20006-1860, or delivered to suite 7200 at that address between 9 a.m. and 5 p.m. on business days. Written comments will be available for public inspection at the PBGC's Communications and Public Affairs Department, suite 7100 at the same address, between 9 a.m. and 4 p.m. on business days.

FOR FURTHER INFORMATION CONTACT: Harold J. Ashner, Assistant General Counsel, or Deborah C. Murphy, Attorney, Office of the General Counsel (22500), Pension Benefit Guaranty Corporation, 2020 K Street, NW., Washington DC 20006-1860; 202-778-8850 (202-778-1958 for TTY and TDD). (These are not toll-free numbers.)

SUPPLEMENTARY INFORMATION:

Background

Section 4006 of the Employee Retirement Income Security Act of 1974 ("ERISA") sets forth the premium rates to be charged by the Pension Benefit Guaranty Corporation ("PBGC"). Section 4007 of ERISA makes the premiums payable "at the time, and on an estimated, advance, or other basis, as determined by the [PBGC]," and provides for the imposition of interest and penalties on premiums not timely paid. Pursuant to these provisions and to section 4002(b)(3) of ERISA, the PBGC has issued its regulation on Payment of Premiums (29 CFR part 2610). The regulation and related forms and instructions describe in detail how to compute and pay premiums, interest, and penalties.

Under section 4006, the multiemployer plan premium for a premium payment year beginning after September 26, 1988, is $2.60 per participant. The single-employer plan premium for a premium payment year beginning after 1987 is composed of a flat rate per capita assessment and a variable rate assessment that is based on the value of a plan's unfunded vested benefits and is also determined on a per-participant basis. The flat rate assessment (for post-1990 years) is $19 per participant.

The basic formula for the variable rate assessment for each participant (for post-1990 years) is $9 for each $1,000 (or fraction thereof) of a plan's unfunded vested benefits (determined as of the last day of the year before the premium payment year) with that product divided by the number of participants in the plan as of that same date. This variable rate assessment is subject to a statutory ceiling of $53 per participant, resulting in a maximum per participant premium of $72.

The formula for computing the variable rate assessment is based, in large part, on the determination of the plan's unfunded vested benefits, defined by statute as the amount that would be the plan's "unfunded current liability" (within the meaning of ERISA section 302(d)(8)(A)) as of the close of the preceding plan year, subject to two qualifications, viz., that only vested benefits are taken into account in the calculation, and that the interest rate used in valuing vested benefits must equal 80% of the annual yield on 30-year Treasury securities for the month preceding the month in which the plan year begins.

The premium regulation provides two methods for determining the amount of a plan's unfunded vested benefits. Under the "general rule" (§ 2610.23(a)), an enrolled actuary must determine the amount of the plan's unfunded vested benefits as of the last day of the plan year preceding the premium payment year based on the plan's provisions and population as of that date, and must certify that the determination was made in a manner consistent with generally accepted actuarial principles and practices. Under the "alternative calculation method" (§ 2610.23(c)), the plan administrator must calculate the amount of the plan's unfunded vested benefits based on certain data from the plan's Form 5500 Schedule B for the plan year preceding the premium payment year, using formulas specified in the regulation. The regulation also provides a number of exemptions and special rules regarding the variable rate portion of the premium.

While the current premium regulation exhibits a degree of complexity, much of this is simply a reflection of the complexity inherent in the statute's variable rate premium provisions, as well as the PBGC's desire to reduce compliance burdens and costs as much as possible by providing options, exemptions, and special rules to simplify or, in some cases, eliminate calculation requirements. Nevertheless, PBGC staff studies have identified a number of possible simplifying changes that would be implemented by this proposed amendment. The PBGC envisions making these proposed changes effective generally for premium payment years beginning after 1992, contingent on implementation of a new computerized premium accounting system by the end of 1992. The proposed changes are discussed below.

General Provisions

The premium regulation is divided into three subparts. Subpart A (General Provisions) contains rules that apply generally to both single-employer and multiemployer plans for all plan years (although some of these rules are more limited in scope or take different forms depending on the plan year involved). Subpart B currently contains rules governing only single-employer plans for plan years beginning after 1987; the rules in Subpart C currently cover single-employer plans for plan years beginning before 1988 and multiemployer plans for all plan years.

The proposed amendments would make a minor change to the general organization of the premium regulation by transferring the rules governing multiemployer plan premiums for premium payment years beginning after 1987 from subpart C to subpart B. This would avoid duplication (in subparts B and C) of several provisions that apply to both single-employer and multiemployer plans for post-1987 years only, consolidate current (that is, post-1987) rules in subpart B, and permit most filers to ignore subpart C completely. A minor rewording of § 2610.1(a) would reflect this organizational change; §§ 2610.21 and 2610.31 would be correspondingly reworded.

Similarly, § 2610.22 (Premium rates) would be revised to include multiemployer as well as single-employer premium rate rules for the post-1987 period. Existing § 2610.22(b) (dealing with new and newly covered plans) would be redesignated as § 2610.22(c); a new § 2610.22(b) would be added to set forth the multiemployer premium rates (now found in § 2610.33(a)(1)); and § 2610.22(d) would be modified to reflect the difference between the refund rules for multiemployer plans (currently set forth in § 2610.33(d)) and those for single-employer plans, which form the subject of existing § 2610.22(d). (The provision in existing § 2610.22(c), that the prescribed premiums are payable for short as well as normal plan years, is considered obvious and would simply be removed.)

In addition, the variable rate premium cap reduction rules that make up most of existing § 2610.22(a)(3)—and that apply only to premium payment years beginning before 1993—would be moved to a new paragraph (§ 2610.22(f)) at the end of the section because they would no longer be of current interest to most premium payers. The special rule for new and newly covered plans (moved to § 2610.22(c)) would be modified to refer to both the single-employer and multiemployer premium rate provisions (in § 2610.22(a) and new § 2610.22(b) respectively), and the parallel rule in § 2610.33(b)(2) covering multiemployer plans only would be deleted.

The penalty waiver rule now in § 2610.8(b)(5) would be moved to § 2610.8(b)(4). This rule, which waives penalties accruing within 30 days after the date of a PBGC bill that is paid within the 30-day period, would be reworded to make its effect clearer.

(Other organizational changes, relating to substantive rule revisions, are discussed below in the context of those revisions.)

Definition of "Participant"

The wording of the PBGC's definition of "participant" in § 2610.2 (Definitions) for the purpose of filing and paying PBGC premiums has differed for several years from the wording of the definition prescribed in the instructions for Form 5500. (For example, the definition in the 1990 instructions for Form 5500 excludes "nonvested former employees who have incurred the break in service period specified in the plan," while the corresponding exclusion in existing § 2610.2 applies to "a non-vested former employee who has incurred a break in service the greater of one year or the break in service period specified in the plan." (Emphasis added.)) The difference in wording, coupled with uncertainty about how the two definitions might be interpreted for purposes of the two different filings, has caused concern for many plan administrators that the participant count for PBGC premiums may differ from the Form 5500 participant count in certain cases.

The amendment would redefine the term "participant" for premium payment years beginning after 1992 while retaining the existing definition for premium payment years beginning before 1993 (including those with premium filing dates in 1993). To accommodate the change, § 2610.2 would be reorganized to place most of the defined terms in a new paragraph (a) and the new and old definitions of "participant" in new paragraphs (b) and (c) (respectively). In paragraph (a), definitions would be added for the terms "Form 5500" and "single-employer plan."

The new definition of "participant" in § 2610.2(b) would simply adopt the definition prescribed for purposes of the Form 5500. This change would allow most premium payers to use the same participant count determined for the Form 5500 without having to worry that the difference in definitions might make the count wrong for premium purposes. Since the Form 5500 definition may change (as it has in the past), § 2610.2(b) would refer specifically to the Form 5500 applicable to the plan year preceding the premium payment year. In general, premiums are based on the participant count for the last day of the plan year preceding the premium payment year. New and newly covered plans, and certain plans involved in mergers and spinoffs, base their premiums on the participant count as of the first day of the premium payment year, but it would be impossible to wait for the issuance of the Form 5500 for the premium payment year and still pay premiums on time. (For new plans, and newly covered plans that were not required to file Form 5500 for the plan year preceding the premium payment year, the definition the plan would use would be the one for the Form 5500 that would have been used for a plan year beginning one year before the first day of the premium payment year.)

For purposes of determining whether a plan is a "large plan" required to make an early premium payment, the participant count comes from the prior year's premium filing. For premium payment years beginning after 1993, this would generally be the same as the participant count on the Form 5500 for the year before the prior year. For example, to determine whether a plan is a "large plan" for the 1994 premium payment year, the plan administrator would note the number of participants for whom premiums had to be paid for the 1993 plan year; since that plan year would have been covered by the new definition of "participant," the participant count for premium purposes would probably have been the same as that on the 1992 Form 5500. (Exceptions would occur where, for example, a plan used the special rule for mergers and spinoffs in § 2610.10 and counted participants as of a date other than the Form 5500's participant count date.)

However, the 1993 premium payment year would be a special case, because the number of participants for whom premiums were payable for 1992 (the prior plan year) might be different than the 1991 Form 5500 participant count (even if the dates were the same). This is because the 1992 plan year would not have been covered by the new "participant" definition—so the 1992 participant count for premium purposes would not necessarily have agreed with the participant count on the 1991 Form sponsors, were formerly reproduced at this paragraph. The final regulations appear at ¶ 15,328A—15,328G.]

Miscellaneous Filing Rules

The amendment would revise § 2610.4 to provide expressly for modification of the premium filing address in the PBGC's Annual Premium Payment Package. This would allow the PBGC to change the address quickly if necessary before completion of the formal procedure of amending the regulation.

Section 2610.5 would be revised to liberalize slightly the rule about when a premium filing or payment is considered to have been made. This rule is used to determine whether a premium filing is timely, when interest on a late payment stops accruing, etc. The current rule, which would be retained in § 2610.5(b) for premium payment years beginning before 1993, is that filings are deemed made when mailed, as evidenced by a legible U.S. Postal Service postmark, or three days before receipt by the PBGC if they do not contain a legible U.S. Postal Service postmark.

In new § 2610.5(a)(1), the proposed rule would increase the assumed transit time (between when a filing is received and when it is deemed to have been sent) from three days to five and make it applicable to all filings, including those with legible U.S. Postal Service postmarks. It would also make clear that the PBGC would accept other evidence of the date of mailing besides legible postmarks.

In addition, new § 2610.5(a)(2) would clarify that where a filing is received on the first business day following a period of one or more non-business days (Saturday, Sundays, or holidays), it would be deemed received on the first day of the non-business period—i.e., the earliest day when it might have been received but for the non-business period.

Application of the transit time assumption to filings with legible U.S.P.S. postmarks would eliminate an anomaly under the existing rule. Currently, a filing mailed one day late with a legible U.S.P.S postmark would be considered late even if it were received the next day, whereas a filing mailed a day late bearing a legible postage meter postmark (but no U.S.P.S. postmark) would be considered timely if it arrived the following day.

The new rule would be effective only for filings and payments for premium payment years beginning after 1992; thus the current rule would continue to apply (for example) to filings due in 1993 for the 1992 premium payment year.

In subpart B of the regulation, the amendment would simplify the certification that is required of fully insured plans taking advantage of the exemption from the variable rate premium under § 2610.24(a)(3). Currently, the plan administrator must certify to the plan's satisfaction of the requirements of section 412(i) of the Internal Revenue Code and regulations thereunder throughout the plan year preceding the premium payment year or (for new or newly covered plans) throughout the premium payment year up to the premium due date.

The PBGC has reconsidered these provisions in light of the general principle that liability for the variable rate premium is determined as of a single "snapshot date," rather than on the basis of a plan's status over on extended period of time. Consistent with that general principle, the PBGC has decided that the certification required of a section 412(i) plan administrator under § 2610.24(a)(3) should be limited to the "snapshot date." (This certification as of the premium "snapshot date" would be relevant only for premium purposes, and would not govern the plan's status under section 412(i) and the regulations thereunder.) Such a change would also avoid the current rule's implication that the plan administrator of a new or newly covered plan must either wait until the premium due date to file, or certify to the status of the plan for a period of time that is still in the future when the certification is made.

Since § 2610.24(e) automatically corrects § 2610.24(e) "snapshot dates" for new or newly covered plans, amended § 2610.24(a)(3) would no longer have to include an explicit special provision for such plans.

Short Plan Year Credits

The amendment would supplement the special refund rule in § 2610.22(d) with a new special credit rule for short plan years of new and newly covered plans and plans that change their plan years. Under the existing premium regulation, the refund rule in §§ 2610.22(d) and 2610.33(d) is the only mechanism available to such a plan for recovering a prorated portion of the premium for the short year. The plan must prepare and submit a refund request, and the PBGC must process the request and issue the refund. Under proposed new § 2610.22(e), these two burdens would be eliminated. The plan would simply compute the credit, in the same manner as a refund under § 2610.22(d), and claim it on its premium payment form. (The refund rule under § 2610.22(d)—with some rewording to make it applicable to multiemployer as well as single-employer plans and to clarify its operation—would remain as an option.)

A new or newly covered plan would be allowed to take the credit against the short first year's premium; a plan that changed its plan year could take the credit against the premium for the following full-length year. The difference in treatment reflects differences between the two classes of plans. For a new or newly covered plan, it is the beginning of the plan year—the portion before the plan becomes effective for premium purposes—that generates the credit, and the plan knows from the start how long its first plan year will be. In contrast, changes in plan year are typically made after the beginning of what will turn out to be the short year (and often after the short year is over), and it is the end of the plan year—the portion overlapped by the following full year— that generates the credit. (By the same token, the credit rule would not apply to final short years (of terminating plans described in § 2610.22(d)(3) and (4)) because the date of the short year's end would not generally be known until it arrived and because there would be no following year's premium to apply the credit to.)

Under the proposed new credit rule, the credit could be taken against the premium for a premium payment year beginning after 1992. Accordingly, it would apply to a new or newly covered plan's short first year beginning after 1992 (since the credit would be taken against that same year's premium). For a plan changing plan years, the new rule would permit a credit to be taken against the premium for a full plan year beginning after 1992 with respect to an immediately preceding short year.

Simplified Filing Method

The alternative calculation method ("ACM") for unfunded vested benefits, provided for in current § 2610.23(c), is an easier, though less accurate, method of calculating the amount of unfunded vested benefits ("UVBs")—on which the variable rate premium is based—than the general rule described in § 2610.23(a) and (b). Whereas the general rule prescribes standards for the actuarial determination of UVBs from basic data, the ACM provides formulas (and optional tables of substitution factors that may be used in place of one expression in one of the formulas) for calculating UVBs from data reported on Form 5500 Schedule B for the prior year.

Both the general rule and the ACM yield values for UVBs as of the last day of the plan year preceding the premium payment year, the "snapshot date" for computing the variable rate premium. The Schedule B data on which the ACM is based, however, are as of the first, not the last, day of that prior year. In addition to other adjustments that may be necessary, therefore, the ACM must "bring forward" the data to the end of the prior year. Rather than bring each figure forward separately, the ACM uses the data to calculate UVBs as of the first day of the prior year, then brings just the UVB figure forward by adding interest.

The ACM begins with the values of the current liability for vested benefits reported on Schedule B as of the beginning of the plan year preceding the premium payment year. In § 2610.23(c)(1), it increases those benefit values to reflect accruals for active participants during that plan year. Then, in § 2610.23(c)(2), it adjusts the benefit values to account for any difference between the current liability interest rate (or rates) actually used to determine them (the "Funding Interest Rate(s)") and the interest rate prescribed by the statute and § 2610.23(b)(1) for premium purposes (the "Premium Interest Rate"). The adjusted vested benefit values are added together to give a single figure reflecting all adjusted vested benefits as of the first day of the plan year preceding the premium payment year.

In § 2610.23(c)(4), the ACM begins with the asset value reported on Schedule B as of the beginning of the plan year preceding the premium payment year and increases that value to reflect contributions made since the beginning of the preceding plan year. The result is an adjusted value of assets as of the beginning of that year. The difference between adjusted vested benefits as of the beginning of the year before the premium payment year and the adjusted asset value as of the same date is the UVBs as of that date. Finally, in § 2610.23(c)(5), the ACM adjusts that UVB figure by adding interest (at the Premium Interest Rate) from the first day of the year before the premium payment year (i.e., the day as of which the UVBs were calculated) to the end of that year (i.e., the day before the beginning of the premium payment year). This in effect produces a value of UVBs as of the last day of the plan year preceding the premium payment year.

Small plans (which, for this purpose, means those paying premiums for fewer than 500 participants) use this UVB value directly as the basis for determining the amount of the variable rate premium. Under § 2610.23(d), however, large plans (those paying premiums for 500 or more participants) must correct this UVB value for any significant events, as defined in § 2610.23(d), that may have occurred during the prior year (i.e., between the date of the Schedule B data and the premium "snapshot date"). (The same significant events must be taken into account under the general rule.)

The PBGC introduced the ACM, when the variable rate premium was first added to ERISA, in response to its concern that the method described in the statute for determining UVBs (which is tracked by the general rule in the regulation) would be quite expensive and time-consuming to apply, especially for smaller plans. The ACM was designed for ease of use, with the thought that it would give small plan administrators a way to calculate variable rate premiums from Form 5500 Schedule B data without the services of an actuary. Indeed, the PBGC expected most plans, including large plans, to use the ACM routinely and to resort to the more difficult general rule only when unusual circumstances made it apparent that the general rule results would be much more favorable than the ACM results.

Of course, achieving simplicity meant sacrificing accuracy. The ACM was devised on the basis of the soundest actuarial principles and most effective actuarial techniques available to be an unbiased surrogate for the general rule both in the aggregate and for most plans individually. However, the PBGC recognized that UVBs (and thus premiums) calculated with the ACM would vary from what they would be under the general rule, and would in some cases be substantially different. Weighing the expected magnitude of premium variations under the ACM against the perceived need for relief from the burdens of the general rule, the PBGC concluded that the risks arising from the ACM's inaccuracy were acceptable. Having reassessed these considerations in connection with its premium simplification efforts, the PBGC now believes that the balance has shifted. On the one hand, the major premium increase in 1991 means that the effect on premiums of any given variation in UVBs is half again as great as it was in 1988. On the other hand, a number of actuarial consulting firms report that many large plans that expect to pay variable rate premiums routinely calculate them under both the ACM and the general rule and pay the smaller amount, thus suggesting that general rule determinations are considerably less burdensome than the PBGC initially feared, at least for larger plans. Accordingly, there now appears to be cause for concern that the PBGC may be exposed to possibly significant revenue loss in individual cases where the ACM is selected over the general rule specifically because the former yields a lower premium than the latter.

In addition, it appears that the ACM is not as easy to use as the PBGC initially thought. Adjustment of the Schedule B data under the ACM requires the use of formulas with several terms and factors, including expressions with negative and/or fractional exponents, that some small plan administrators evidently find daunting. Despite the ACM's ease of use in comparison to the general rule, the PBGC has received complaints about its complexity.

The PBGC proposes to address these problems by replacing the ACM with a simpler procedure and restricting the new procedure's use by large plans. The PBGC has devised a simplified filing method ("SFM") that is even easier to use than the ACM, with the hope that more small plan administrators will be able to use the SFM to compute premiums without the assistance of an actuary than appears to be the case with the ACM. The new SFM eliminates all of the existing ACM formulas and replaces them with tables of adjustment factors and simple arithmetical rules. Under the proposed amendment, the SFM would replace the ACM for all plan years beginning after 1992. However, as discussed in detail below, plans paying premiums for 500 or more participants would not be allowed to use the SFM if their UVBs as determined under the SFM were less than if they had used the general rule.

(The PBGC invites public comment regarding what proportion of plans of various sizes routinely determine UVBs under both the ACM and the general rule before they decide which method to use for paying premiums, whether they do it in all cases or only, for example, when an ACM calculation shows some amount of UVBs, and whether the general rule determinations made for this purpose are full final determinations on which a premium filing could be based or merely trial determinations that cost substantially less than full determinations and that are intended only as a basis for deciding whether full determinations should be made. Similarly, the PBGC invites comment regarding whether a significant number of plans that currently calculate UVBs under the ACM without making a general rule determination would encounter obstacles to timely filing (involving, e.g., general rule data collection) under the PBGC's proposed restriction on the use of the SFM by larger plans and what (if anything) might be done in the context of this proposed amendment to alleviate any such problems.)

Overview of the SFM

Like the ACM, the SFM would start from figures reported on Form 5500 Schedule B as of the beginning of the plan year preceding the premium payment year; add accruals and contributions for that year; correct for any difference between the current liability interest rate(s) (the "Funding Interest Rate(s)") actually used and the required interest rate under § 2610.23(b)(1) (the "Premium Interest Rate"); and bring the resulting UVB figure forward to the end of the plan year preceding the premium payment year by adding interest at the Premium Interest Rate. Unlike the ACM, however, the SFM would use no formulas. Instead, it would provide two tables of factors for adjusting the Form 5500 vested benefit figures to reflect the difference between the Premium Interest Rate and the Funding Interest Rate and give additional simple arithmetic rules (involving only addition, subtraction, and multiplication) for making other adjustments to the Form 5500 figures and the resulting UVB figure. The factors in the tables would replace the ACM interest adjustment formula and related tables in current § 2610.23(c)(2) and (3). The additional simple arithmetical rules would replace the provision that adjusts assets for contributions under current § 2610.23(c)(4) and the formula in current § 2610.23(c)(5) that adjusts UVBs for the passage of time. The ACM adjustment for accruals in current § 2610.23(c)(1), which is now based on a percentage of vested benefits, would be replaced by an adjustment based on the amount of accruals reported on the Schedule B.

Perhaps the best way to introduce the proposed SFM is to work through an example showing how it would be used to compute UVBs in a simulated premium filing. Accordingly, assume that a small calendar year plan, for which the plan administrator is computing the 1993 variable rate premium using the SFM, has the following data on its Schedule B for 1992:

Item 6d (current liability for vested benefits as of 1/1/92)—

(i) (retirees and beneficiaries): $40,000;

(ii) (terminated vested participants): $10,000;

(iii) (active participants): $110,000;

Item 6e (increase in current liabilities for accruals in 1992): $8,000;

Item 7 (total employer and employee contributions for 1992): $10,000;

Item 8b (actuarial value of assets—assume as of 1/1/92): $100,000;

Item 12c(i) (current liability interest rates (Funding Interest Rates))—

Pre-retirement: 8.0 percent; Post-retirement: 7.625 percent;

Item 12d (assumed retirement age): 62.

The interest rate required under § 2610.23(b)(1) (the Premium Interest Rate) that the plan administrator would use would be that for January 1993; assume that it is 7.91 percent. Finally, the plan administrator would have to refer to the tables of adjustment factors in proposed §2610.23(c)(3). For convenience, a portion of each table is reproduced here; their use is explained as the example proceeds.

TABLE 1

Column A		Column B	Column C			
If the Funding Interest Rate minus the Premium Interest Rate (to the nearest hundreth of a percent) is—		The factor for pay-status benefits is—	The factor for pre-pay-status benefits (based on the plan's assumed retirement age) is—			
at least	but not over	for ages under 60	for ages 60-61	for ages 62-63	for ages over 63
0.01	0.25	1.02	1.04	1.04	1.05	1.05
.26	.50	1.03	1.08	1.09	1.10	1.11
.51	.75	1.05	1.12	1.13	1.15	1.16

TABLE 2

Column A		Column B	Column C			
If the Premium Interest Rate minus the Funding Interest Rate (to the nearest hundreth of a percent) is—		The factor for pay-status benefits is—	The factor for pre-pay-status benefits (based on the plan's assumed retirement age) is—			
at least	but not over	for ages under 60	for ages 60-61	for ages 62-63	for ages over 63
0.00	0.25	1.00	1.00	1.00	1.00	1.00
.26	.50	.98	.97	.96	.96	.95
.51	.75	.97	.95	.92	.91	.91

To find the plan's 12/31/92 UVBs in order to compute the 1993 variable rate premium, the plan administrator would take the following steps:

Step 1: Adjust the 1/1/92 Benefit Value for Retirees and Beneficiaries

The plan administrator's first step is to adjust the 1/1/92 value of vested benefits for retirees and beneficiaries to reflect the difference between the Funding Interest Rate used to value those benefits and the Premium Interest Rate mandated by the statute. The unadjusted benefits value is on line 6d(i) of the Schedule B: $40,000. The adjustment factor depends on the difference between the Funding Interest Rate and the Premium Interest Rate; for retiree benefits, the Premium Interest Rate is compared with the post-retirement Funding Interest Rate. The SFM table headings tell which table the adjustment factor should come from. In this case, the factor comes from Table 2, because the Premium Interest Rate (7.91 percent) is greater than the applicable Funding Interest Rate (7.625 percent). The adjustment factor comes from the second row of Table 2, because the difference between the Premium Interest Rate and the Funding Interest Rate is in the 0.26-0.50 range on the second row of column A of Table 2 (7.91 minus 7.625 is 0.285, which rounds up to 0.29 percentage points). Following this row over to column B leads to the adjustment factor for the line 6d(i) amount. The factor is 0.98. Multiplying $40,000 by 0.98 gives $39,200. This is the adjusted 1/1/92 value of vested benefits for retirees and beneficiaries.

Step 2: Adjust the 1/1/92 Benefit Value for Terminated Vested Participants

The second step is very much like the first. Here, the plan administrator adjusts the 1/1/92 value of vested benefits for terminated vested participants to reflect the difference between the Funding Interest Rate and the Premium Interest Rate. This unadjusted benefits value is on line 6d(ii) of the Schedule B: $10,000. Once again, the adjustment factor depends on the difference between the Funding Interest Rate and the Premium Interest Rate, but where (as here) the pre- and post-retirement Funding Interest Rates are different, the plan administrator must compare the greater of the two Funding Interest Rates with the Premium Interest Rate to get the adjustment factor for terminated vested participants' benefits. In this case, the pre-retirement Funding Interest Rate (8.0 percent) is greater than the post-retirement Funding Interest Rate (7.625 percent). For this step, therefore, the adjustment factor comes from Table 1, because the Premium Interest Rate (7.91 percent) is less than the applicable Funding Interest Rate (8.0 percent). The adjustment factor comes from the first row of Table 1, because the difference between the Premium Interest Rate and the Funding Interest Rate is in the 0.01-0.25 range on the first row of column A of Table 1 (8.0 minus 7.91 is 0.09 percentage points).

Since terminated vested participants have not yet retired, the adjustment factor for the value of their benefits also depends on the plan's assumed retirement age. The assumed retirement age for this plan is 62. So the plan administrator follows the first row of Table 1 over to

column C and then looks in the subcolumn headed "for ages 62-63" for the adjustment factor for the line 6d(ii) amount. The factor is 1.05. Multiplying $10,000 by 1.05 gives $10,500. This is the adjusted 1/1/92 value of vested benefits for terminated vested participants.

Step 3: Adjust the 1/1/92 Benefit Value for Active Participants

The third step is almost the same as the second. Here, the plan administrator adds accruals for 1992 to the 1/1/92 value of vested benefits for active participants and adjusts the sum to reflect the difference between the Funding Interest Rate and the Premium Interest Rate. The unadjusted benefits value for active participants is on line 6d(iii) of the Schedule B: $110,000. The current liability increase for 1992 accruals is on line 6e of the Schedule B: $8,000. The sum of these two figures is $118,000. The plan administrator uses the same Funding Interest Rate, and thus the same table (Table 1) and row (the first row), to find the adjustment factor for active participants' benefits as was used for terminated vested participants' benefits in step 2. The plan administrator also uses the same column (C) and subcolumn (for ages 62-63) as in step 2. So the adjustment factor for the line 6d(iii) amount is the same as that for the line 6d(ii) amount: 1.05. Multiplying $118,000 by 1.05 gives $123,900. This is the adjusted 1/1/92 value of vested benefits for active participants.

The sum of the three adjusted 1/1/92 vested benefits values is therefore $173,600 ($39,200 + $10,500 + $123,900), and this is the total value of vested benefits as of 1/1/92 that will be used in computing 1/1/92 UVBs in step 5 below.

Step 4: Adjust the 1/1/92 Value of Plan Assets

In this step, the plan administrator adjusts the 1/1/92 value of plan assets to reflect contributions for 1992. The unadjusted plan asset value comes from line 8b of the Schedule B: $100,000. The total 1992 contributions come from item 7 of the Schedule B: $10,000. The contributions (which may have been made on various dates in 1992 and 1993) are discounted back to 1/1/92 by multiplying them by 0.95. (The SFM uses this same discount factor no matter what the Premium Interest Rate is and no matter when the contributions were actually made.) Multiplying $10,000 by 0.95 gives $9,500 as the discounted value of the contributions. Then adding the discounted contributions to the unadjusted assets value gives $109,500 ($100,000 plus $9,500). This is the adjusted value of plan assets as of 1/1/92.

Step 5: Compute the UVBs

In this step, the plan administrator computes the 1/1/92 UVBs and then adjusts them so that the adjusted figure can be used as 12/31/92 UVBs. The 1/1/92 UVBs are equal to the total adjusted 1/1/92 vested benefits (from steps 1, 2, and 3) minus the total adjusted 1/1/92 assets (from step 4). At the end of step 3, the total adjusted 1/1/92 benefits were found to be $173,600; in step 4, the total adjusted 1/1/92 assets were found to be $109,500. So the 1/1/92 UVBs are $64,100 ($173,600 minus $109,500). To adjust this 1/1/92 figure for use as a 12/31/92 figure, the plan administrator adds interest using the Premium Interest Rate as the interest rate. Since the Premium Interest Rate is 7.91

percent, the 1/1/92 UVBs are multiplied by 1.0791 (1 plus the Premium Interest Rate) to yield $69,170.31. This is the UVBs as of 12/31/92. The plan administrator then uses this UVB figure to determine the plan's variable rate premium.

Details of the SFM

The SFM, applicable to premium payment years beginning after 1992, would be set forth in §2610.23(c), and the ACM, limited to premium payment years beginning before 1993, would be transferred to a new §2610.23(f). New §2610.23(c)(1), like the introductory text of existing §2610.23(c), would be a summary or general statement of how the method would work, and §2610.23(c)(2)-(7) would provide the detailed rules. The tables of factors to be applied to the vested benefit values, and general rules for their use, would be in §2610.23(c)(2). (To avoid possible confusion, the SFM tables would be called Tables 1 and 2 to distinguish them from ACM Tables A and B.) Section 2610.23(c)(3)-(5) would contain specific adjustment rules for the vested benefits of retirees and beneficiaries, terminated vested participants, and active participants respectively. Section 2610.23(c)(6) would provide for adjusting plan assets, and §2610.23(c)(7) for determining and adjusting UVBs.

Use of the SFM, as of the ACM, would be restricted for plans paying premiums for 500 or more participants, but the restrictions would now be more stringent. The ACM requires such plans to make adjustments for any significant events described in §2610.23(d), and the SFM would continue this requirement, which would be stated explicitly in new §2610.23(c)(1) instead of just in §2610.23(d) as at present. In addition, §2610.23(c)(1) would allow such plans to use the SFM only if the amount of their UVBs determined under the general rule were not greater than that calculated with the SFM. An enrolled actuary would be required to certify to that fact if the SFM were used, and if an audit found that the general rule UVBs were greater, the amount of any premium deficiency (and related interest and penalties) would be based on the (higher) general rule figure.

As discussed above, this new restriction is proposed as a response to concerns that the PBGC may be exposed to significant revenue losses in individual cases where large plans select the ACM over the general rule because calculations with both methods show that use of the ACM minimizes UVBs. The PBGC believes that the new rule will solve this problem without imposing substantial additional administrative costs on plans. A study of premium filings suggests that more than four-fifths of single-employer plans pay no variable rate premiums; for most of those plans, the absence of UBVs is likely to be obvious even before any calculations are done. As for large plans whose funding status is not so clear, the PBGC has reason to believe, as noted above, that calculations under both the general rule and the ACM are already routinely done as part of the premium payment process.

The SFM would also include another new limitation (applicable to all plans). Section 2610.23(c)(1) would provide that the SFM could be used only if the Premium Interest Rate prescribed under §2610.23(b)(1) were not more than six percentage points less than the plan's Funding Interest Rates from its Schedule B. This limitation would be needed because use of the tables in new §2610.23(c)(3) would be mandatory under the SFM (unlike the ACM, in which use of the tables is optional), and Table 1 would only cover Funding Interest Rates up to six percentage points higher than the Premium Interest Rate. The restriction of Table 1 to a six-point rate spread reflects two considerations. One is that the SFM makes simplifying assumptions about interest rates, and these assumptions introduce inaccuracies that, though relatively small when the Funding Interest Rate is close to the Premium Interest Rate, become more significant when the rates diverge further. The other is that, because of the way the Premium Interest Rate and the permissible range of the Funding Interest Rate are set by statute, a six-point spread between them is extremely unlikely. (Although no limitation would be placed on use of the SFM by a plan whose Funding Interest Rate (or Funding Interest Rates) was (or were) lower than the Premium Interest Rate, no matter how great the spread, the adjustment factors provided for spreads greater than six points would be the same as for a six-point spread. A six-point spread when the Funding Interest Rate is lower than the Premium Interest Rate is considered even less likely than when the Funding Interest Rate is higher.)

In addition to setting forth the two tables of vested benefit adjustment factors, proposed §2610.23(c)(2) would describe how to select a table and a row within a table in finding each adjustment factor. The benefit adjustment factors would adjust the vested benefit values for the difference between the Premium Interest Rate and the Funding Interest Rate, and this difference would accordingly determine the table and row from which each adjustment factor would be taken. The Premium Interest Rate in the SFM is the same as the quantity called

"RIR" in the ACM, viz., the rate prescribed in §2610.23(b)(1) for the month in which the premium payment year began. The Funding Interest Rate would be one of the rates entered in the pre- or post-retirement column of line 12c(i) on the Schedule B. The pre- and post-retirement Funding Interest Rates are the same as the ACM's BIA and BIR respectively.

Since choosing a table and row would depend on the Funding Interest Rate applicable to each vested benefit amount, §2610.23(c)(2) would refer to the specific adjustment rules for the three vested benefits amounts (in §2610.23(c)(3)-(5)) for the Funding Interest Rate to be used for each adjustment. If the Premium Interest Rate were less than the applicable Funding Interest Rate, Table 1 would be used; if the Premium Interest Rate were equal to or greater than the Funding Interest Rate, Table 2 would be used. To find the proper row in the table, the difference between the Funding Interest Rate and the Premium Interest Rate (determined by subtracting the smaller of the two from the larger) would be rounded to the nearest hundredth of a percent. (For example, 1.035 percentage points would round to 1.04 points, and 0.374 percentage points would round to 0.37 points.) One would then locate the rate range in column A of the table that included the difference between the Premium Interest Rate and the applicable Funding Interest Rate. Each row would cover a difference range of one-quarter of one percent. The appropriate factor for the particular combination of Premium Interest Rate and Funding Interest Rate would be found on that row in the appropriate column of the table. The specific adjustment rules for the three vested benefits amounts in §2610.23(c)(3)-(5) would also tell which column (and, for line 6d(ii) and 6d(iii) adjustments, which subcolumn) of the appropriate table to use for each adjustment.

Under §2610.23(c)(3), the post-retirement Funding Interest Rate would be used to find the factor for adjusting the value from line 6d(i) of the Schedule B, since that is the rate used to value retiree benefits for the Schedule B. The appropriate column for the line 6d(i) adjustment factor would be column B. The adjusted line 6d(i) amount under §2610.23(c)(3) would simply be the unadjusted amount from that line multiplied by the factor found in the appropriate table following the rules in §2610.23(c)(2) and (3).

The benefits of active and terminated vested participants may be valued using two rates, one for the pre-retirement period and another for the post-retirement period. To simplify the SFM, only one rate would be used to find the adjustment factors for these values. In order to avoid premium losses to the PBGC, §2610.23(c)(4) and (5) would require that the greater of the pre- and post-retirement Funding Interest Rates be used to find the adjustment factors for the values from lines 6d(ii) and 6d(iii) of the Schedule B.

The appropriate column for the line 6d(ii) and 6d(iii) adjustment factors would be column C. To find the factors, the assumed retirement age reported on line 12d of the Schedule B would be used to select the proper subcolumn of column C. (The assumed retirement age in the SFM is the same as the assumed retirement age used in the ACM.) Each subcolumn is headed by a range of ages: under 60, 60-61, 62-63, and over 63. The subcolumn used would be the one whose heading included the assumed retirement age.

In addition to specifying the Funding Interest Rate, column, and subcolumn to be used in adjusting the line 6d(ii) amount, §2610.23(c)(4) would provide simply that the adjusted line 6d(ii) amount would be the unadjusted amount from that line multiplied by the factor found in the appropriate table following the rules in §2610.23(c)(2) and (4). Section 2610.23(c)(5), on the other hand, would require that the unadjusted line 6d(iii) amount be increased by the amount of the expected current liability increase for benefits accruing during the plan year preceding the premium payment year—from line 6e of the Schedule B—before being multiplied by the adjustment factor. The line 6d(iii) factor would be the same as the line 6d(ii) factor because it would be based on the same Funding Interest Rate and assumed retirement age.

The use of the expected current liability increase figure from line 6e of the Schedule B represents a change from the ACM, which approximated accruals as an amount equal to seven percent of the combined vested benefits of active and terminated vested participants—no accrual figure having been available on the Schedule B when the ACM was devised. While the line 6e figure is typically determined as of the first day of the plan year, it need not be; the use of a later date would make benefit liabilities under the SFM higher than if the determination were made as of the beginning of the plan year, because the SFM would add the line 6e figure, without discount, to the value of active participants' vested benefits as of the first day of the plan year from the line 6d(iii) of the Schedule B. The line 6e figure may also include nonvested as well as vested accruals, and this also would tend to inflate benefit liabilities. However, the PBGC believes that the amount of any such inflation would typically be minimal. In any event, a plan would be free to use the general rule to avoid any disadvantage that the SFM might cause either by not providing a discount or by including nonvested accruals.

The three adjusted vested benefits values determined under § 2610.23(c)(2)-(5) would be added together to give a total adjusted value of vested benefits for computing UVBs under proposed § 2610.23(c)(7).

The factors in Tables 1 and 2 in § 2610.23(c)(2) have been derived from formulas similar to the formulas prescribed under the ACM. Each column B factor is equal to 0.94^D, where D is equal to the Premium Interest Rate minus the Funding Interest Rate. However, the factor in each row is used for a range of D's—the ranges shown in column A of each table. To avoid premium losses to the PBGC, the Table 1 factors are derived using the highest percentage point difference in each range, while the Table 2 factors are derived using the lowest difference in each range. For example, in the third row of Table 1, D would be -0.75, but in the third row of Table 2, D would be 0.51.

Similarly, each column C factor is equal to the column B factor from the same row multiplied by $((107-D)/107)^{(ARA-50)}$ (with "ARA" standing for the plan's assumed retirement age). However, the factor in each subcolumn of column C is used for a range of assumed retirement ages—the ranges shown in the subcolumn headings. To avoid premium losses to the PBGC, the Table 1 factors are derived using assumed retirement ages from the high end of each range, while Table 2 factors are derived using assumed retirement ages from the low end of each range. (The low end of the under-60 range is assumed to be 55, and the high end of the over-63 range is assumed to be 65.) Thus, for example, in the 60-61 subcolumn of Table 1, an assumed retirement age of 61 is used, but in the same subcolumn of Table 2, the assumed retirement age used is 60.

While the ACM uses both pre- and post-retirement interest corrections in its formula for adjusting the benefit values for active and terminated vested participants, the formulas used to generate the SFM tables refer to only one interest figure for these participants—either the pre- or post-retirement Funding Interest Rate, whichever is greater. To avoid having different tables for different values of Premium Interest Rate, the SFM formulas also use a simplified version of the fraction expressing the ratio of the Funding Interest Rate to the Premium Interest Rate. Since the value of this fraction depends mostly on the spread between the Funding Interest Rate and the Premium Interest Rate, rather than on their actual values, the SFM formulas use a fraction based on the actual spread and an assumed Premium Interest Rate of 7.00 percent. This assumed value of Premium Interest Rate represents a rough historical average of actual Premium Interest Rates; if Premium Interest Rates begin to deviate significantly from the assumed value, the PBGC may find it appropriate to issue new tables based on a different assumed value.

Proposed § 2610.23(c)(6) would provide rules for adjusting the value of plan assets taken from Schedule B. As under the ACM (§ 2610.23(c)(4) of the existing regulation), the basic figure would come from line 8b, unless that figure were determined as of a date other than the first day of the prior plan year, in which case the figure would come from line 6c. However, the SFM would provide a simplied procedure for adjusting that basic figure.

Like the existing adjustment procedure, the new procedure in proposed § 2610.23(c)(6) would correct for any contributions made for the plan year preceding the premium payment year. The value of assets as of the first day of that prior year, whether from line 8b or line 6c of the Schedule B, must exclude any contributions made for that year. (Of course, contributions for the year before the prior year are includible in the value of assets as of the beginning of the prior year only if actually made before the Schedule B for the prior year is filed.) The assets figure must therefore be increased to reflect contributions for the prior year.

The amount of contributions made for the prior year would be taken from columns (b) and (c) of item 7 of the Schedule B. The contributions would then have to be discounted to reflect the fact that they were paid after the date as of which the plan assets figure was determined (the beginning of the prior year). In order to simplify this step, § 2610.23(c)(6)(i) would use a flat discount factor of 0.95, so that the discounted contributions amount would be the total contributions amount times 0.95. This flat discount factor reflects an assumption that all of the contributions being discounted would have been made about three-quarters of the way through the prior year and that the discount rate would be about 7.00 percent (the same value assumed for the Premium Interest Rate in the simplified ratio between the Funding Interest Rate and the Premium Interest Rate that is used in the

formulas for generating the benefit adjustment tables in § 2610.23(c)(2)). To the extent that the weighted average contribution date were earlier or the Premium Interest Rate were lower, these assumptions would result in a higher variable rate premium. However, the PBGC believes that relatively few plans receive contributions so early as to be seriously disadvantaged by the SFM's assumed weighted average contribution date. In any event, the SFM is an optional procedure that plans need not use. (The flat discount factor, like the tables of benefit adjustment factors in § 2610.23(c)(2), might be changed if Premium Interest Rates were to deviate significantly from historical values.)

Under proposed § 2610.23(c)(7), the adjusted assets value (computed under proposed § 2610.23(c)(6)) would be subtracted from the adjusted benefits value (computed under proposed § 2610.23(c)(2)-(5)) to yield the value of UVBs at the beginning of the plan year preceding the premium payment year, and this figure would be brought forward to the end of the prior year by multiplying it by the sum of one plus the Premium Interest Rate (expressing the Premium Interest Rate as a decimal fraction of 1, not as a percentage).

The ACM uses a somewhat more complicated method for adjusting the UVBs figure, expressed in a formula that compensates for the possibility that the plan year preceding the premium payment year may be a short year. By ignoring that possibility, the SFM would be simpler, but would produce a higher UVB amount, and therefore a higher variable rate premium, for a premium payment year that followed a short plan year. The PBGC believes that the increased simplicity of the SMF in this regard outweighs the detriment to plans in the relatively infrequent situations where there is a short plan year, especially in view of the fact that the SFM (like the ACM) would be an optional computation method.

Taking into account the aggregate effect of all of the differences between the ACM and the SFM, the PBGC believes that its aggregate premium receipts from plans using the SFM would be neither less than nor significantly greater than if the ACM were used instead. For most plans, the results produced by the SFM would differ from those produced by the ACM primarily because of the shift from the ACM's assumed value of benefit accruals (in current § 2610.23(c)(1)) to the SFM's actual value (in proposed § 2610.23(c)(5)). Any such difference for an individual plan would be in the direction of improved accuracy and should thus be unobjectionable.

Aside from the change in accounting for accruals, the PBGC believes that for the vast majority of plans, the results produced by the SFM would not differ significantly from those that would be produced by the ACM. While there would be a relatively small number of plans for which the SFM would produce a significantly higher premium than the ACM, such a plan could avoid paying an unnecessarily high premium by using the general rule.

The other proposed amendments to § 2610.23 reflect technical, clarifying, and conforming changes that are not intended to have any substantive effect.

SFM for Distress or Involuntary Terminations

Section 2610.24(c) currently contains a special version of the ACM for plans undergoing distress or involuntary termination. Following the same pattern as in § 2610.23, the amendment would move this special ACM rule to the end of § 2610.24 and preserve it (as § 2610.24(h)) for premium payment years beginning after 1988 and before 1993. In its place, a new § 2610.24(c) would provide a special version of the SFM for plans in involuntary or distress terminations. (As in § 2610.23, there would also be a number of technical and conforming changes.)

New § 2610.24(c) would be much like the existing provision, except that it would tie into the SFM rather than the ACM. Aside from the new restriction (discussed above) on use of the SFM by large plans, the plans permitted to use the new special rule would be the same as under the existing rule, and the Schedule B they could use would be determined in the same way as it is now. However, because the SFM would adjust benefits for additional accruals, and UVBs for the passage of time, differently than the ACM does, new § 2610.24(c)(3), (4), and (6), which deal with these adjustments, would be restructured to conform to the new SFM rules. In particular, § 2610.24(c)(3) and (4) would provide different modifications of the SFM rules, depending on whether or not the Schedule B being used included separate entries for active and terminated vested participants' vested benefits and an entry for accruals (features that were added in 1989).

Also, § 2610.24(c)(5) would provide that the new simpler method for adjusting plan assets in proposed § 2610.23(c)(6) could not be used; instead, a method that tracks the current ACM asset adjustment method in existing § 2610.23(c)(4) would be required. This provision is prompted by the difficulty of devising an adaptation of the simple new

§ 2610.23(c)(6) rule that would appropriately discount contributions that might cover multiple years and that might have been made before the full phase-in of the quarterly contribution requirement in section 302(e) of ERISA and section 412(m) of the Internal Revenue Code of 1986.

Due Dates

ERISA section 4007 specified a due date of 30 days after the beginning of the premium payment year for premiums for the first premium payment year beginning after ERISA's effective date. The premium regulation retained this due date rule until 1978, when the due date was changed to seven months after the end of the preceding plan year; for 1981 through 1984, the due date was the end of the seventh month of the premium payment year. In 1985, it was changed to the end of the second month of the premium payment year for large plans only, in response to recommendations of the Grace Commission (the President's Private Sector Survey on Cost Control) (see the preambles to the proposed and final 1985 amemdment to the premium regulation, 50 FR 1065 at 1066 (January 9, 1985) and 50 FR 12533 at 12534-5 (March 29, 1985)). (For the first year of the new rule, large plans were defined as those with at least 10,000 participants; beginning in 1986, the threshold was dropped to 500 participants.) However, the end of the seventh month was retained in 1985 as the small plan due date.

The PBGC recognized that some large plans might have problems computing their premiums by the new, earlier due date because of difficulty in determining participant counts as of the required determination date (the last day of the prior year). The PBGC therefore made provision for the estimation of early payments, established safe harbor rules to give large plans a means of avoiding penalties on underpayments resulting from low estimates, and established explicit rules in the premium regulation for the reconciliation of estimated early premium payments with the final participant count. The reconciliation date was made the same as the later due date that remained applicable to small plans.

In 1988, the variable rate premium for single-employer plans was introduced. The flat rate premium due date for large plans remained the end of the second month of the premium payment year (e.g., February 28th for calendar year plans); however, the due date for the new variable rate premium was made the same for large plans as for small plans (and the same as the reconciliation date for large plans), and was deferred to the fifteenth day of the eighth month after the beginning of the premium payment year (e.g., September 15th for calendar year plans). (The use of the later due date for large plans' variable rate premiums—an anomaly in the context of the Grace Commission recommendations—reflected concern for plans' ability to make realistic variable rate premium estimates by the early due date, in view particularly of the variable rate premium computation rules prescribed in the regulation, which relied heavily on data developed for the Form 5500 and Schedule B thereto.)

Thus, although the premium regulation does not actually require two annual premium filings by large plans, the due date structure makes filing twice a year a practical necessity for most large plans. This is true for those plans that find it necessary (or administratively convenient) to pay an estimate at the early filing date, which they must later reconcile; and also for those single-employer plans that find it impossible (or administratively inconvenient) to compute the variable rate premium in time to pay it at the same time the flat rate premium is due. The need for two filings each year by most large plans is a burden for them and for the PBGC.

Moreover, a large plan that underestimates its flat rate premium on the early due date must pay interest to the PBGC on the amount of the underpayment, even if it satisfies the safe harbor rules. The safe harbor rules provide protection only from penalties, not from interest charges; the PBGC does not have the authority to waive interest charges. If an estimated payment turns out to be higher than the flat rate amount finally determined to be due, the plan may receive a credit or refund, but the PBGC lacks the authority to pay interest on overpayments.

Furthermore, although the safe harbor rules give large plans an opportunity to avoid penalties on underpayment of the flat rate premium by paying a definitely determinable amount (last year's participant count times the current year's flat rate) and making up any shortfall by the reconciliation due date, the safe harbor rules make the premium regulation more complex by providing a different rule for penalties than is provided for interest. The safe harbor rules are also an administrative burden for the PBGC, which must treat plans that fail the safe harbor tests differently than those that pass the tests but nonetheless underpay the flat rate premium at the early due date, assessing both interest and penalties against the former but charging the latter for interest only. Where a penalty is assessed, it is based on the full difference between the early payment actually made and the

final flat-rate amount due (rather than just the difference between the actual early payment and the safe harbor amount).

Finally, while variable rate premiums are due after the nominal due date for the Form 5500 (and Schedule B), the Form 5500 due date is often extended by two-and-a-half months, making it later than the premium due date. Thus, single-employer plans must often pay variable rate premiums a whole month before they are required to report on Form 5500 the data on which those premiums are based (although of course the data ultimately reported on Form 5500 may be used to determine premiums before the Form 5500 is in fact filed). This discrepancy has been of particular concern for plans using the alternative calculation method, which refers explicitly to Schedule B line items. (The same comment would apply to the simplified filing method that the PBGC proposes to substitute for the existing alternative calculation method.)

The PBGC proposes to address these problems by deferring the final filing due date (to just 15 days before the extended Form 5500 due date), raising the number of participants a plan must have in order to be required to make the early premium payment (so that fewer plans must file twice a year), and charging neither penalties nor interest on early payments that equal at least a definitely determinable amount (so that both estimates and special safe harbor rules are unnecessary). Providing a definite amount for the early payment would also obviate the need for even estimated data determinations before the early payment was made. This would make it possible to accelerate the early filing due date to nearer the beginning of the premium payment year and to widen the scope of the early payment to cover the variable rate, as well as the flat rate, portion of the premium—changes that would balance those described above in order to achieve approximate revenue neutrality for the PBGC.

Structurally, the existing due date rules in § 2610.25(b), (c), and (d) (and those in § 2610.34(a) and (b) for premium payment years of multiemployer plans beginning after 1987) would be consolidated, moved to the end of § 2610.25 (as § 2610.25(e)), and preserved for premium payment years beginning after 1987 and before 1993. (These rules would be significantly reworded to make them consistent in format with the new rules being proposed for premium payment years beginning after 1992, but without the intent to make any substantive changes in the old rules.) Current § 2610.25(e) and (f) would be redesignated as § 2610.25(c) and (d). The new due date rules, for premium payment years beginning after 1992, would be set forth in a new § 2610.25(b).

Although the proposed amendment would eliminate prospectively the need for the safe harbor rules (currently in § 2610.8(b)(4)), these rules would need to be preserved for premium payment years beginning before 1993. Accordingly, the safe harbor rules would be moved to the end of § 2610.8(b) (that is, redesignated as § 2610.8(b)(5)) and reworded slightly to make them applicable only to premium payment years beginning before 1993 and to conform references to other provisions of the amended premium regulation.

Under the current due date rules, the plans that must pay the flat rate premium by the early due date are those that were required to pay premiums for at least 500 participants for the plan year preceding the premium payment year (the current "large plan threshold," which would be preserved in § 2610.25(e)(5)). Under the new rules, the number of plans required to file by the early due date would be reduced by increasing the large plan threshold to 5,000 participants. This would be reflected in the definitions (for purposes of the new due date rules) of the terms "large plan" and "small plan" in proposed § 2610.25(b)(5). For the 1989 premium payment year, there were about 8,000 plans at or above the 500-participant threshold, but only about 1,000 plans that had at least 5,000 participants; thus, the PBGC estimates that the proposed increase in the large plan threshold would reduce by about 7,000 (or 87 percent) the number of plans that would potentially need to make two filings per year.

The amendment would also change both annual due dates (that is, the early date applicable only to the new, smaller group of "large plans" and the later date applicable to the new, larger group of "small plans" and to reconciliation filings by the large plans). Under proposed new § 2610.25(b)(1), the small plan due date would be the last day of the ninth full calendar month following the end of the plan year preceding the premium payment year (i.e., September 30th for calendar year plans, October 31st for plans with plan years beginning January 2d-February 1st, etc.). Under proposed § 2610.25(b)(2)(ii), this would also be the reconciliation due date for large plans. This is only 15 days before the due date for the Form 5500 with the typical two-and-a-half-month extension. This change would relieve plans of the need to compute premiums a full month before the underlying data have to be reported on Form 5500 and Schedule B thereto.

Under new § 2610.25(b)(2)(i), the early due date for large plans would be advanced to the fifteenth day of the first full calendar month following the end of the plan year preceding the premium payment year (i.e., January 15th for calendar year plans, February 15th for plans with plan years beginning January 2d-February 1st, etc.). If large plans were still to be required to pay their (actual or estimated) flat rate premiums for the premium payment year by the early filing date, advancing the date would worsen the existing problems with early filing. However, as mentioned briefly above and discussed in detail below, the amendment would also provide large plans with a definitely determinable amount to pay at the early filing date, thus making estimation unnecessary. In view of this latter change, there would no longer be any reason not to collect the preliminary payment close to the beginning of the premium payment year. This practice would be more in line with the practices of commercial insurance companies.

New § 2610.25(b)(2)(i) would also prescribe the amount due from large plans on the early filing date. This would be either the dollar amount of the total (flat and variable rate) premium payable for the plan year preceding the premium payment year—a definitely determinable amount that would be known well in advance of the early due date—or, at the plan's option, the total (flat and variable rate) premium due for the premium payment year (which the plan could estimate if it chose). If the early payment fell short of the total premium finally determined to be payable for the premium payment year, the amount of the shortfall would be due by the reconciliation due date under new § 2610.25(b)(2)(ii).

It should be noted that under this proposal, the scope of the early payment for large plans would not be limited to the flat rate portion of the premium, as it has been up to now. As mentioned above, problems with estimating the variable rate premium militated against including it in the initial payment when it was introduced in 1988. Since estimating would no longer be required under this proposal, however, the PBGC sees no reason to continue deferring large plans' variable rate payments to a date close to the end of the premium payment year.

It should also be noted that the proposed early payment would be based on the dollar amount of the previous year's premium, rather than on the previous year's plan data and the current year's premium rates, as under the existing regulation's safe harbor rules. The proposed approach has been taken in the interest of simplicity, even though it would mean that the PBGC would lose the benefit of any future premium rate increases in the initial premium filing.

A third point to note is that in determining the amount of the previous year's premium, refunds and credits under existing § 2610.22(d) and proposed new § 2610.22(e) would be disregarded. Thus, the early payment obligation would not be artificially reduced by the circumstance that the preceding plan year was a short year.

The key feature of the proposed new early payment requirement, however, would be the elimination of the need to estimate, and with it the need for special safe harbor rules and the risk of interest charges. Currently, safe harbor rules are needed to relieve plans from penalties that would otherwise accrue for even small good faith underestimates of their flat rate premiums at the early filing date. But even the safe harbor rules provide no relief from interest charges on underestimates. Under the proposal, a plan that paid the same amount as the previous year's final total premium by the early filing date would be assured of avoiding not only penalties (as under the existing safe harbor rules) but also interest on any amount by which the early payment fell short of the final total premium.

However, the proposal would still allow a plan to pay an estimate of the current year's premium at the early filing date if it so chose. Choosing to pay an estimate would open the plan to the risk of interest and penalty charges if the estimate proved to be too low, but a plan would presumably accept this risk if it believed that its current year's premium would end up being substantially less than its previous year's premium (as, for example, if it had lost many of its participants or had substantially improved its funding during the preceding year).

Upon reconciliation, a plan would owe the amount (if any) by which its early payment was less than the premium finally determined to be due. However, no penalty or interest on the amount of the shortfall would be owed as long as the early payment were at least equal to the previous year's premium. If the early payment were less than both the previous year's final amount and the current year's final amount, interest and penalty would be imposed only on the amount by which the early payment fell short of the lesser of the previous year's final premium or the current year's final premium. (If the early payment were more than the current year's final amount, a refund or credit would be available under the same rules applicable to overpayments generally.)

For example, suppose that a plan's final total premium obligation for 1995 were $1,000 and that the plan made an early premium payment (using an estimate) of $700 for 1996. If its final 1996 premium were $1,200, it would owe penalty and interest only on $300, the amount by which its early payment fell short of $1,000 (the lesser of 1995's or 1996's final premium obligation). But if its final 1996 premium were $900, it would owe interest and payment only on $200, the shortfall for $900 (again, the lesser of the 1995 or the 1996 final premium). Of course, if the plan made an early payment of $1,000, it would owe no penalty or interest no matter how large its final 1996 obligation turned out to be.

The PBGC now permits large plans to file a Form 1 instead of a Form 1-ES at the early filing date; single-employer plans are allowed to file this early Form 1 without a Schedule A. This practice is consistent with the fact that the early payment under the current rules is an estimate of only the flat rate portion of the final premium. By filing Form 1 early without Schedule A, therefore, a plan is simply substituting a final flat rate figure for an estimate of the same figure. Under the proposed system, however, the early payment would be keyed to the total premium liability (either the previous year's figure or an estimate of the current year's). Thus, the PBGC would continue to accept advance filing of a final premium payment (either instead of the early payment or after the early payment was made) only if the advance filing were a complete final filing including (in the case of a single-employer plan) Schedule A and payment of both the flat and variable rate premiums.

The proposed due date rules for new and newly covered plans (in new § 2610.25(b)(3)) would be the same as the existing rules for such plans (which would be preserved in § 2610.25(e)(3)). The proposed due date rules for plans changing plan years (in new § 2610.25(b)(4)) would be almost the same as the corresponding rules in the existing regulation (which would be preserved in § 2610.25(e)(4)), except that a plan would have at least 90 days, instead of the 30 days now allowed, to pay its premium after adopting the amendment changing the plan year. The purpose of this change would be simply to make the filing rule for plans that change plan years more consistent with the rule for new and newly covered plans (which permits filing 90 days after plan adoption or the beginning of title IV coverage), and thus remove a potential source of confusion.

As alluded to briefly above, the new due date provisions would embody a combination of changes (some representing financial losses for the PBGC and others representing financial gains) that the PBGC has designed to have no substantial net revenue effect for the PBGC. Obviously, however, the new rules would shift financial burdens among premium payers to some degree, primarily away from smaller "large plans" that would no longer be required to pay premiums by the early due date and toward larger "large plans" that would be required to pay more of their premiums by an earlier due date. (The policy of requiring earlier payment from larger plans than from smaller plans was discussed in the preamble to the final 1985 amendment to the premium regulation, 50 FR 12533 at 12535 (March 29, 1985).)

In the process of devising the new premium payment system embodied in the proposed changes to the due date rules in § 2610.25, the PBGC considered and rejected several alternative approaches to the premium payment problems discussed above. For example, the early payment required of large plans might have remained limited to the flat rate portion of the premium only. However, the proposal's substantial reduction in the number of plans required to make the early filing would not then have been possible without significant revenue loss to the PBGC. Another possibility would have been to base the early payment required of large plans on the amount of the previous year's premium only, without the option of paying an estimate. However, the lack of an estimation option might have created problems for plans that underwent very substantial contraction (as through spinoff of most of their participants) or substantially improved their funding during the year preceding the premium payment year.

Another approach (the "maximum simplicity" approach) would have returned to the pre-Grace Commission practice of having all plans pay their premiums on the same schedule, with the due date for all plans deferred to the Form 5500 due date. This approach would have solved all the due date problems discussed above. However, it would have entailed an unacceptable loss of revenue to the PBGC, due to the deferral of premium receipts from large plans.

A third approach (the "legislative change" approach) would have sought a statutory amendment moving the premium determination date back one year, from the last day of the plan year preceding the premium payment year to the last day of the plan year *before* the plan year preceding the premium payment year. The premium due date would then have been accelerated to the beginning of the premium payment year for all plans.

Since the extended due date of the applicable Form 5500 would have fallen in the tenth month of the preceding plan year, this approach would have avoided the need to pay premiums before the relevant data had to be filed on Form 5500. It would also have eliminated estimated premium payments and reconciliation by making the early payment the only payment. However, it would have involved a substantial additional cost for small plans, which currently pay relatively late in the premium payment year.

Also, the use of older determination data would have made premiums lag behind changes in participant counts and funding levels. This would have tended to favor plans with increasing participant counts and single-employer plans with deteriorating funding levels by making their premiums lower than under the current system. But plans with declining participant counts and single-employer plans with improving funding levels would have been disadvantaged because their premiums would have been higher than under the current system.

In addition, creating a one-year gap between the premium determination date and the beginning of the premium payment year would have created significant complexities regarding the premium obligations of plans involved in mergers, consolidations and spinoffs during the period between the earlier determination date and the beginning of the premium payment year.

A fourth approach (the "combined filing" approach) would also have called for all plans to pay premiums just once a year, at the beginning of each premium payment year. The payment would have been a combination of two components. One component would have been a reconciliation for the prior year, based on the Form 5500 data filed during the prior year for the year preceding the prior year. The second component would have been a preliminary payment for the current year equal to the prior year's total premium. If the reconciliation involved an additional payment, it would have been added to the preliminary premium for the current year, without any penalties or interest. If the reconciliation generated a credit, it would have been subtracted from the preliminary payment for the current year.

As with the legislative change approach, the applicable Form 5500 due date under the combined filing approach would have been well before the premium due date when the Form 5500 data would be needed. Estimates would also have been avoided, and although there would have been reconciliation filings, they would have been combined with the preliminary premium filings so that plans would not have had to file twice a year. But accelerating most of the premium to the beginning of the year would have meant increased costs for plans, particularly for small plans.

Furthermore, plans with declining participant counts and single-employer plans with improving funding would have been disadvantaged under the combined filing approach in much the same way as under the legislative change approach because, although the preliminary payment would eventually have been reconciled, the reconciliation date would have been a whole year after the preliminary payment. (A plan would have been allowed to reconcile earlier only if it also paid the preliminary premium for the following year at the same time.)

A fifth approach (the "two-system" approach) would have combined the maximum simplicity approach for small plans with the combined filing approach for large plans, giving the advantages of both approaches. However, large plans with declining participant counts and large single-employer plans with improving funding would have had the same kinds of problems as under the combined filing approach. In addition, the difference in payment rules for large and small plans would have been great enough so that different forms and instructions for large and small plans might have been needed.

Compliance with Rulemaking Guidelines

The PBGC has determined that this amendment is not a "major rule" for purposes of Executive Order 12291 (46 FR 13193 (February 17, 1981)) because it will not have an annual effect on the economy of $100 million or more; or create a major increase in costs or prices for consumers, individual industries, or geographic regions; or have significant adverse effects on competition, employment, investment, or innovation, or on the ability of United States-based enterprises to compete with foreign-based enterprises in domestic or export markets. This determination is based on the fact that this amendment would have no significant effect on the overall financial burden of PBGC premiums on plans in general, but rather would only shift those burdens to a limited extent among classes of plans, primarily away from smaller plans and toward larger plans (especially larger underfunded plans); and on the fact that this amendment would tend to decrease the nonfinancial burden of paying PBGC premiums by making the premium payment process simpler.

Under section 605(b) of the Regulatory Flexibility Act, the PBGC certifies that this amendment will not have a significant economic impact on a substantial number of small entities. The amendment will tend to shift the financial burden of PBGC premiums away from smaller plans and toward larger plans (especially larger underfunded plans), and will tend to decrease the non-financial burden of paying PBGC premiums by making the premium payment process simpler. For these reasons, compliance with sections 603 and 604 of the Regulatory Flexibility Act is waived.

List of Subjects in 29 CFR Part 2610

Employee benefit plans, Penalties, Pension insurance, Pensions, and Reporting and recordkeeping requirements.

In consideration of the foregoing, the PBGC proposes to amend part 2610 of subchapter H of chapter XXVI of title 29, Code of Federal Regulations, as follows:

PART 2610—PAYMENT OF PREMIUMS

1. The authority citation for part 2610 continues to read as follows:

Authority: 29 U.S.C. 1302(b)(3), 1306, 1307 (1988 & Supp. I 1989), as amended by sec. 12021, Public Law 101-508, 104 Stat. 1388, 1388-573.

2. In § 2610.1, the second sentence and the last three sentences of paragraph (a) are revised to read as follows:

§ 2610.1 Purpose and scope.

(a) *Purpose.* * * * Subpart A contains rules that apply to both single-employer and multiemployer plans with respect to all premium payment years. * * *

Subpart B contains the premium rates, due dates and computational rules for premium payment years beginning after 1987. Subpart C contains the premium rates and due dates for premium payment years beginning before 1988.

* * *

3. Section 2610.2 is revised to read as follows:

§ 2610.2 Definitions.

(a) *In general.* For purposes of this part:

Act means the Employee Retirement Income Security Act of 1974, as amended.

Code means the Internal Revenue Code of 1986, as amended.

Form 5500 means the Form 5500 series annual report prescribed by the Internal Revenue Service, the Department of Labor and the PBGC.

Multiemployer plan means a plan described in section 4001(a)(3) of the Act.

New plan means a plan that became effective within the premium payment year and includes a plan resulting from a consolidation or spinoff. A plan that meets this definition is considered to be a new plan for purposes of this part even if the plan constitutes a successor plan within the meaning of section 4021(a) of the Act.

Newly covered plan means a plan that is not a new plan and that was not covered by title IV of the Act pursuant to section 4021 of the Act immediately before the premium payment year.

PBGC means the Pension Benefit Guaranty Corporation.

Plan year means the calendar, policy or fiscal year on which the records of the plan are kept.

Premium payment year means the plan year for which the premium is being paid.

Short plan year means a plan year that is less than twelve full months.

Single-employer plan means a plan described in section 4001(a)(15) of the Act.

(b) *"Participant" for premium payment years beginning after 1992.* For purposes of this part, for a premium payment year beginning after 1992, "participant" means the same as it does for purposes of the Form 5500 for the plan year preceding the premium payment year (or, in the case of a new plan, or a newly covered plan that was not required to file Form 5500 for the plan year preceding the premium payment year, the Form 5500 prescribed for plan years beginning one year before the first day of the plan's first premium payment year).

(c) *"Participant" for premium payment years beginning before 1993.* For purposes of this part, for a premium payment year beginning before 1993, "participant" means any individual who is included in one of the categories described in paragraphs (c)(1)-(c)(3) of this section, subject to the provisions of paragraph (c)(4) of this section.

(1) *Active.* (i) Any individual who is currently in employment covered by the plan and who is earning or retaining credited service under the plan. This category includes any individual who is considered covered under the plan for purposes of meeting the minimum coverage requirements, but who, because of offset or other provisions (including integration with Social Security benefits), does not have any accrued benefits.

(ii) Any non-vested individual who is not currently in employment covered by the plan but who is earning or retaining credited service under the plan. This category does not include a non-vested former employee who has incurred a break in service the greater of one year or the break in service period specified in the plan.

(2) *Inactive*—(i) *Inactive receiving benefits.* Any individual who is retired or separated from employment covered by the plan and who is receiving benefits under the plan. This category does not include an individual to whom an insurer has made an irrevocable commitment to pay all the benefits to which the individual is entitled under the plan.

(ii) *Inactive entitled to future benefits.* Any individual who is retired or separated from employment covered by the plan and who is entitled to begin receiving benefits under the plan in the future. This category does not include an individual to whom an insurer has made an irrevocable commitment to pay all the benefits to which the individual is entitled under the plan.

(3) *Deceased.* Any deceased individual who has one or more beneficiaries who are receiving or entitled to receive benefits under the plan. This category does not include an individual if an insurer has made an irrevocable commitment to pay all the benefits to which the beneficiaries of that individual are entitled under the plan.

(4) For plan years beginning before September 2, 1975, a retiree or former employee for whom a fully paid-up immediate or deferred annuity has been purchased shall be treated as a "participant" for purposes of this part if such individual retains a legal claim against the plan for benefits or if the plan retains a participating interest in the annuity policy.

4. Section 2610.4 is revised to read as follows:

§ *2610.4 Filing address.*

Except as may otherwise be provided by instructions in the PBGC Annual Premium Payment Package, any form or payment required to be filed or paid under the provisions of this part shall be mailed to Pension Benefit Guaranty Corporation, P.O. Box 105655, Atlanta, GA 30348-5655, or delivered to Nations Bank Retail Lockbox Processing Center, PBGC Lockbox 105655, 6000 Feldwood Road, 5 Southside East, College Park, GA 30349.

5. Section 2610.5 is revised to read as follows:

§ *2610.5 Date of filing.*

(a) *Premium payment years beginning after 1992.* (1) Any form or payment required to be filed or paid under the provisions of this part with respect to a premium payment year beginning after 1992 shall be deemed filed or paid on the earlier of—

(i) The date on which it is mailed, as evidenced by a legible United States Postal Service postmark, registered mail receipt, or other proof of the date of mailing with the United States Postal Service, or

(ii) Five days before the date on which it is received by the PBGC.

(2) For purposes of this section, if the PBGC receives a form or payment on the first business day following a weekend or a federal holiday, then the PBGC shall be deemed to have received the form or payment on the day after the last business day preceding the weekend or holiday. The term *business day* as used in this section means any day that is not a Saturday, a Sunday, or a federal holiday.

(b) *Premium payment years beginning before 1993.* (1) Any form or payment required to be filed or paid under the provisions of this part with respect to a premium payment year beginning before 1993 shall be deemed filed or paid on the date on which it is mailed.

(2) For purposes of this paragraph (b), a form or payment shall be presumed to have been mailed on the date on which it is postmarked by the United States Postal Service, or three days prior to the date on which it is received by the PBGC if it does not contain a legible United States Postal Service postmark.

6. In § 2610.8, paragraphs (b)(4) and (b)(5) are revised to read as follows:

§ *2610.8 Late payment penalty charges.*

* * *

(b) *Waiver of penalty charge.* * * *

(4) With respect to the period of 30 days after the date of any PBGC bill for the premium payment necessary to reconcile the premium paid with the actual premium due, if the bill is paid within that 30-day period; or

(5) With respect to any premium payment (excluding any variable rate portion of the premium under § 2610.22(a)(2)) for a premium payment year beginning before 1993, if a plan that is required to make a reconciliation filing described in § 2610.25(e)(2)(iii) or § 2610.34(b)—

(i) paid at least 90 percent of the flat rate portion of the premium due for the premium payment year by the due date specified in § 2610.25(e)(2)(i) or § 2610.34(a); or

(ii) paid by the due date specified in § 2610.25(e)(2)(i) or § 2610.34(a) an amount equal to the premium that would be due for the premium payment year, computed using the flat per capita premium rate for the premium payment year and the participant count upon which the prior year's premium was based; and

(iii) pays 100 percent of the premium due for the premium payment year under § 2610.22 (excluding any variable rate portion of the premium under § 2610.22(a)(2)), § 2610.32, or § 2610.33, as applicable, on or before the due date for the reconciliation filing under § 2610.25(e)(2)(iii) or § 2610.34(b), as applicable.

7. Section 2610.21 is revised to read as follows:

§ *2610.21 Purpose and scope.*

This subpart provides rules for computing and procedures for paying premiums for plan years beginning after 1987.

8. In § 2610.22, paragraph (a) is amended by revising its heading; paragraphs (a)(3) introductory text and (a)(3)(i)-(a)(3)(v) are redesignated as paragraphs (f) introductory text and (f)(1)-(f)(5) respectively; redesignated paragraphs (f) introductory text and (f)(5) are amended by revising the references "(a)(3)", "(a)(3)(i)", "(a)(3)(ii)", "(a)(3)(iii)", "(a)(3)(iv)", and "(a)(3)(v)" (wherever they appear) to read "(f)", "(f)(1)", "(f)(2)", "(f)(3)", "(f)(4)", and "(f)(5)" respectively; paragraph (c) is removed; paragraph (b) is redesignated as paragraph (c); redesignated paragraph (c) is amended by revising the reference "paragraph (a)" to read "paragraphs (a) and (b)"; redesignated paragraph (f) is amended by revising its heading and by removing the first sentence of its introductory text; paragraph (d) is revised; and new paragraphs (a)(3), (b), and (e) are added, to read as follows:

§ *2610.22 Premium rates.*

(a) *Single-employer plans.* * * *

(3) *Cap on variable rate amount.* In no event shall the variable rate amount determined under paragraph (a)(2) of this section exceed $34 per participant (for premium payment years beginning in 1988, 1989, or 1990) or $53 per participant (for premium payment years beginning after 1990), or (for premium payment years beginning before 1993) such lesser amount as may be determined under paragraph (f) of this section.

(b) *Multiemployer plans.* For a premium payment year beginning on or after January 1, 1988, the premium paid by a multiemployer plan for basic benefits guaranteed under section 4022A(a) of the Act is equal to the number of participants in the plan on the last day of the plan year preceding the premium payment year multiplied by:

(1) For premium payment years beginning before September 27, 1988, $2.20; and

(2) For premium payment years beginning after September 26, 1988, $2.60.

* * *

(d) *Special refund rule for certain short plan years.* A plan described in this paragraph that pays the full premium due for a short plan year that begins after 1988 is entitled, upon request, to a refund of a portion of the premium. The amount of the refund will be determined by prorating the premium for the short plan year by the number of months (treating a part of a month as a month) in the short plan year. A plan is described in this paragraph if—

(1) the plan is a new or newly covered plan that becomes effective for premium purposes on a date other than the first day of its first plan year;

(2) the plan adopts an amendment changing its plan year, resulting in a short plan year;

(3) the plan's assets are distributed pursuant to the plan's termination, in which case the short plan year for purposes of computing the amount of the refund under this paragraph shall be deemed to end on the asset distribution date or, if later (in the case of a single-employer

plan), the date 30 days before the PBGC receives the plan's post-distribution certification; or

(4) the plan is a single-employer plan, and a trustee of the plan is appointed pursuant to section 4042 of the Act, in which case the short plan year for purposes of computing the amount of the refund under this paragraph shall be deemed to end on the date of appointment.

(e) *Special credit rule for certain short plan years.* A plan described in paragraph (d)(1) or (d)(2) of this section is entitled at its option to a credit for a portion of the premium for a short plan year, in lieu of a refund under paragraph (d) of this section, under the circumstances described in this paragraph (e). A plan described in paragraph (d)(1) of this section may claim the credit against the premium due for an initial short plan year that begins after 1992. A plan described in paragraph (d)(2) of this section that pays the full premium due for a short plan year may claim the credit for the short plan year against the premium due for the following full plan year if the full plan year begins after 1992. In either case, the amount of the credit shall be determined in the same manner as the amount of a refund under paragraph (d) of this section, and the credit shall be claimed in accordance with instructions in the PBGC Annual Premium Payment Package.

(f) *Variable rate cap reduction for premium payment years beginning before 1993.*

* * *

9. In §2610.23, paragraph (a) is amended by adding, after the reference "paragraph (c)" in the first sentence of the introductory text, the reference "or (f)"; paragraph (c) is redesignated as paragraph (f); paragraph (e) is amended by adding, after the reference "paragraphs (a) through (d)", the reference "and (f)"; redesignated paragraph (f) is amended by revising the references "(c)(1)", "(c)(2)", "(c)(3)", "(c)(4)", and "(c)(5)" (wherever they appear) to read "(f)(1)", "(f)(2)", "(f)(3)", "(f)(4)", and "(f)(5)" respectively; paragraph (b)(2) is amended by revising the second, third and fourth sentences; paragraph (d) is amended by revising the heading and introductory text; redesignated paragraph (f) is amended by revising the heading and the first sentence of the introductory text; and paragraph (c) is added, to read as follows:

§ *2610.23 Determination of unfunded vested benefits.*

* * *

(b) *Unfunded vested benefits.* * * *

(2) *Actuarial value of assets.* * * *

Contributions owed for any plan year preceding the premium payment year shall be included for premium payment years beginning during 1988 and, for premium payment years beginning after 1988, shall be included for plans with 500 or more participants as of the last day of the plan year preceding the premium payment year and may be included for any other plan. However, contributions may be included only to the extent such contributions have been paid into the plan on or before the earlier of the due date specified in § 2610.25(b)(1), (b)(2)(ii), (e)(1), or (e)(2)(ii) (as applicable) or the date that the full amount of the premium (including any variable rate portion) is paid. Contributions included that are paid after the last day of the plan year preceding the premium payment year shall be discounted at the plan asset valuation rate (on a simple or compound basis in accordance with the plan's discounting rules) to the last day of the plan year preced ing the premium payment year to reflect the date(s) of payment. * * *

(c) *Simplified filing method for premium payment years after 1992—* (1) *In general.* In lieu of determining the amount of a plan's unfunded

vested benefits pursuant to paragraph (a) of this section for a premium payment year beginning after 1992, the plan administrator may, subject to the restrictions in paragraphs (c)(1)(i) and (c)(1)(ii) of this section, calculate the amount of the plan's unfunded vested benefits under this paragraph (c). The computation shall be done, using the plan's Form 5500 Schedule B for the plan year preceding the premium payment year, as follows. The value of the plan's vested benefits shall be adjusted in accordance with paragraphs (c)(2) through (c)(5) of this section to reflect accruals for the plan year preceding the premium payment year and the difference between the interest rate prescribed in paragarph (b)(1) of this section and the plan's current liability interest rate or rates. The value of plan assets shall be adjusted in accordance with paragraph (c)(6) of this section to reflect contributions for the plan year preceding the premium payment year. The resulting unfunded vested benefits amount (the adjusted value of vested benefits minus the adjusted value of assets) shall be further adjusted in accordance with paragraph (c)(7) of this section to reflect the passage of time from the date of the adjusted Schedule B data (the first day of the plan year preceding the premium payment year) to the last day of the plan year preceding the premium payment year. (An alternative calculation method for premium payment years beginning before 1993 is described in paragraph (f) of this section.)

(i) A plan's unfunded vested benefits may be calculated under this paragraph (c) only if neither of the plan's current liability interest rates required to be entered in line 12c(i) of the plan's Form 5500 Schedule B for the plan year preceding the premium payment year exceeds the interest rate prescribed in paragraph (b)(1) of this section by more than six percentage points.

(ii) The unfunded vested benefits of a plan with 500 or more participants as of the last day of the plan year preceding the premium payment year may be calculated under this paragraph (c) only in accordance with the provisions of paragraph (d) of this section, and only if the amount of the plan's unfunded vested benefits determined pursuant to paragraph (a) of this section does not exceed the amount of such unfunded vested benefits calculated under this paragraph (c) and an enrolled actuary so certifies in accordance with the Premium Payment Package.

(2) *Vested benefits adjustment factors.* In the simplified filing method described in this paragraph (c), the vested benefits values required to be entered in item 6d of Schedule B shall be adjusted in accordance with paragraphs (c)(3), (c)(4), and (c)(5) of this section using factors from the tables set forth in this paragraph (c)(2), and the sum of the three vested benefits values as so adjusted shall be used in determining unfunded vested benefits under paragraph (c)(7) of this section. For each adjustment, a Table 1 factor shall be used if the required interest rate prescribed in paragraph (b)(1) of this section (the "Premium Interest Rate") is less than the applicable current liability interest rate specified in paragraph (c)(3), (c)(4), or (c)(5) of this section (the "Funding Interest Rate"), and a Table 2 factor shall be used if the Premium Interest Rate equals or exceeds the applicable Funding Interest Rate. The factor for each adjustment shall be taken from the line in the appropriate table on which appears, in column A, the range of values that includes the amount (expressed as a percentage, rounded to the nearest hundredth of one percent) by which the Premium Interest Rate differs from the applicable Funding Interest Rate, and from the column specified in paragraph (c)(3), (c)(4), or (c)(5) of this section (based, in the case of paragraphs (c)(4) and (c)(5) of this section, on the assumed retirement age required to be entered in line 12d of Schedule B).

TABLE 1

If the Funding Interest Rate minus the Premium Interest Rate (to the nearest hundredth of a percent) is—		The factor for pay-status benefits is—	The factor for pre-pay-status benefits (based on the plan's assumed retirement age) is—			
Column A		**Column B**	**Column C**			
at least	but not over		for ages under 60	for ages 60-61	for ages 62-63	for ages over 63
0.01	0.25	1.02	1.04	1.04	1.05	1.05
.26	.50	1.03	1.08	1.09	1.10	1.11
.51	.75	1.05	1.12	1.13	1.15	1.16
.76	1.00	1.06	1.16	1.18	1.20	1.22
1.01	1.25	1.08	1.20	1.23	1.26	1.29
1.26	1.50	1.10	1.24	1.28	1.31	1.35
1.51	1.75	1.11	1.29	1.33	1.38	1.42
1.76	2.00	1.13	1.34	1.39	1.44	1.49
2.01	2.25	1.15	1.39	1.45	1.51	1.57
2.26	2.50	1.17	1.44	1.50	1.58	1.65

Column A		Column B	Column C			
If the Funding Interest Rate minus the Premium Interest Rate (to the nearest hundredth of a percent) is—		The factor for pay-status benefits is—	The factor for pre-pay-status benefits (based on the plan's assumed retirement age) is—			
at least	but not over		for ages under 60	for ages 60-61	for ages 62-63	for ages over 63
2.51	2.75	1.19	1.49	1.57	1.65	1.73
2.76	3.00	1.20	1.54	1.63	1.72	1.82
3.01	3.25	1.22	1.60	1.70	1.80	1.92
3.26	3.50	1.24	1.66	1.77	1.89	2.01
3.51	3.75	1.26	1.72	1.84	1.97	2.11
3.76	4.00	1.28	1.78	1.92	2.06	2.22
4.01	4.25	1.30	1.85	2.00	2.16	2.33
4.20	4.50	1.32	1.91	2.08	2.26	2.45
4.51	4.75	1.34	1.98	2.16	2.36	2.57
4.76	5.00	1.36	2.06	2.25	2.47	2.70
5.01	5.25	1.38	2.13	2.34	2.58	2.84
5.26	5.50	1.41	2.21	2.44	2.70	2.98
5.51	5.75	1.43	2.29	2.54	2.82	3.13
5.76	6.00	1.45	2.37	2.64	2.95	3.29

TABLE 2

Column A		Column B	Column C			
If the Premium Interest Rate minus the Funding Interest Rate (to the nearest hundredth of a percent) is—		The factor for pay-status benefits is—	The factor for pre-pay-status benefits (based on the plan's assumed retirement age) is—			
at least	but not over		for ages under 60	for ages 60-61	for ages 62-63	for ages over 63
0.00	0.25	1.00	1.00	1.00	1.00	1.00
.26	.50	.98	.97	.96	.96	.95
.51	.75	.97	.95	.92	.91	.91
.76	1.00	.95	.92	.89	.88	.86
1.01	1.25	.94	.90	.85	.84	.82
1.26	1.50	.92	.87	.82	.80	.78
1.51	1.75	.91	.85	.79	.77	.75
1.76	2.00	.90	.83	.76	.73	.71
2.01	2.25	.88	.80	.73	.70	.68
2.26	2.50	.87	.78	.70	.67	.64
2.51	2.75	.86	.76	.68	.64	.61
2.76	3.00	.84	.74	.65	.62	.58
3.01	3.25	.83	.72	.62	.59	.56
3.26	3.50	.83	.70	.60	.56	.53
3.51	3.75	.80	.68	.58	.54	.50
3.76	4.00	.79	.66	.55	.52	.48??
4.01	4.25	.78	.64	.53	.49	.46
4.26	4.50	.77	.63	.51	.47	.44
4.51	4.75	.76	.61	.49	.45	.41
4.76	5.00	.74	.59	.47	.43	.39
5.01	5.25	.73	.58	.45	.41	.37
5.26	5.50	.72	.56	.44	.39	.36
5.51	5.75	.71	.55	.42	.38	.34
>5.75	>5.75	.70	.53	.40	.36	.32

(3) *Adjusted value of vested benefits—retirees and beneficiaries.* In the simplified filing method described in this paragraph (c), the adjusted value of vested benefits for retirees and beneficiaries shall be the value of such benefits required to be entered in column (2) on line 6d(i) of Schedule B, multiplied by the appropriate factor determined under paragraph (c)(2) of this section. The factor shall be determined using the Funding Interest Rate required to be entered in the post-retirement column on line 12c(i) of Schedule B and shall be taken from column B of the appropriate table in paragraph (c)(2) of this section.

(4) *Adjusted value of vested benefits—terminated vested participants.* In the simplified filing method described in this paragraph (c), the adjusted value of vested benefits for terminated vested participants shall be the value of such benefits required to be entered in column (2) on line 6d(ii) of Schedule B, multiplied by the appropriate factor determined under paragraph (c)(2) of this section. The factor shall be determined using the greater of the Funding Interest Rates required to be entered in the pre-retirement and post-retirement columns on line 12c(i) of Schedule B and shall be taken from column C of the appropriate table in paragraph (c)(2) of this section and from the subcolumn of column C that is headed by the age range that includes the plan's assumed retirement age.

(5) *Adjusted value of vested benefits—active participants.* In the simplified filing method described in this paragraph (c), the adjusted value of vested benefits for active participants shall be the sum of the value of such benefits required to be entered in column (2) on line 6d(iii) of Schedule B and the expected accruals for the plan year preceding the premium payment year required to be entered on line 6e of Schedule B, multiplied by the appropriate factor determined under paragraph (c)(2) of this section. The factor shall be determined using the same Funding Interest Rate, and shall be taken from the same column and subcolumn, as specified for terminated vested participants' benefits under paragraph (c)(4) of this section.

(6) *Adjusted value of plan assets.* In the simplified filing method described in this paragraph (c), the adjusted value of plan assets that shall be used in determining unfunded vested benefits under paragraph (c)(7) of this section shall be the sum of—

(i) the value of such assets required to be entered on line 8b of Schedule B (if the amount on line 8b was determined as of the first day of the plan year preceding the premium payment year) or on line 6c of Schedule B (if the amount on line 8b was determined as of a date other than the first day of the plan year preceding the premium payment year), plus

¶20,533B

(ii) an amount equal to 0.95 times the total amount of contributions required to be entered in columns (b) and (c) of item 7 of Schedule B.

(7) *Adjusted value of unfunded vested benefits.* In the simplified filing method described in this paragraph (c), the amount of the plan's unfunded vested benefits shall be the product of—

(i) the sum of the adjusted values of vested benefits determined under paragraphs (c)(3), (c)(4), and (c)(5) of this section minus the adjusted value of plan assets determined under paragraph (c)(6) of this section, multiplied by

(ii) the sum of 1 plus the required interest rate prescribed in paragraph (b)(1) of this section (expressed as a decimal fraction of 1, not as a percentage).

(d) *Significant events.* The significant events described in this paragraph shall be reflected in the assumptions used in determining a plan's unfunded vested benefits under paragraph (a) of this section to the extent required by paragraph (a) of this section. A plan with 500 or more participants as of the last day of the plan year preceding the premium payment year may use the simplified filing method described in paragraph (c) of this section or the alternative calculation method described in paragraph (f) of this section if no significant event, as described in this paragraph, has occurred between the first day and the last day of the plan year preceding the premium payment year and an enrolled actuary so certifies in accordance with the Premium Payment Package. If a significant event has occurred between those dates, such a plan may use the simplified filing method or alternative calculation method only if an enrolled actuary makes an appropriate adjustment to the value of unfunded vested benefits to reflect the occurrence of the signficant event and certifies to that fact in accordance with the Premium Payment Package. The significant events described in this paragraph are—

* * *

(f) *Alternative calculation method for premium payment years before 1993.* In lieu of determining the amount of a plan's unfunded vested benefits pursuant to paragraph (a) of this section for a premium payment year beginning before 1993, the plan administrator may calculate the amount of the plan's unfunded vested benefits under this paragraph (f) using the plan's Form 5500, Schedule B, for the plan year preceding the premium payment year. * * *

* * *

10. In § 2610.24, paragraph (c) is redesignated as paragraph (h); paragraph (d) is amended by revising the reference "§ 2610.22(a)(3)" to read "§ 2610.22(f)"; paragraph (g) is amended by revising the reference "(e)(1) and (e)(2)" to read "(f)(1) and (f)(2)"; redesignated paragraph (h) is amended by adding, after the words *"unfunded vested benefits"* in the heading, the words *"for premium payment years beginning before 1993"* and by revising the words "on or after January 1, 1989" in the first sentence of the introductory text to read "after 1988 and before 1993"; redesignated paragraphs (h) introductory text, (h)(2), (h)(3), and (h)(4) are amended by revising the references "§ 2610.23(c)", "§ 2610.23(c)(1)", and "§ 2610.23(c)(5)" (wherever they appear) to read "§ 2610.23(f)", "§ 2610.23(f)(1)", and "§ 2610.23(f)(5)", respectively; paragraph (a)(3) is revised; and new paragraph (c) is added, to read as follows:

§ 2610.24 Variable rate exemptions and special rules.

(a) *Exemptions.* * * *

(3) *Section 412(i) plans.* A plan is described in this paragraph if the plan satisfied all criteria listed in section 412(i) of the Code and the regulations thereunder on the last day of the plan year preceding the premium payment year and the plan administrator so certifies, in accordance with the Premium Payment Package.

* * *

(c) *Special rule for determining unfunded vested benefits for premium payment years beginning after 1992 for plans terminating in distress or involuntary terminations.* With respect to premium payment years beginning after 1992, a plan described in this paragraph (c) may determine its unfunded vested benefits by using the special simplified filing method set forth in this paragraph, but only if neither of the plan's current liability interest rates required to be entered in line 12c(i) of the Schedule B described in paragraph (c)(1) of this section exceeds the interest rate prescribed in § 2610.23(b)(1) by more than six percentage points; and, in the case of a plan with 500 or more participants as of the last day of the plan year preceding the premium payment year, only in accordance with the provisions of § 2610.23(d), and only if the amount of the plan's unfunded vested benefits determined pursuant to § 2610.23(a) does not exceed the amount of such unfunded vested

benefits determined under this paragraph (c) and an enrolled actuary so certifies in accordance with the Premium Payment Package. (A similar special rule for premium payment years beginning before 1993 is described in paragraph (h) of this section.) A plan is described in this paragraph if it has issued notices of intent to terminate in a distress termination in accordance with section 4041(a)(2) of the Act with a proposed termination date on or before the last day of the plan year preceding the premium payment year, or if the PBGC has instituted proceedings to terminate the plan in accordance with section 4042 of the Act and has sought a termination date on or before the last day of the plan year preceding the premium payment year. Pursuant to this paragraph, a plan shall determine its unfunded vested benefits in accordance with the simplified filing method in § 2610.23(c), except that—

(1) The calculation shall be based on the plan's Form 5500 Schedule B for the plan year that includes (in the case of a distress termination) the proposed termination date or (in the case of an involuntary termination) the termination date sought by the PBGC, or, if no Schedule B is filed for that plan year, on the Schedule B for the immediately preceding plan year;

(2) All references in § 2610.23(c) and § 2610.23(d) to the first day of the plan year preceding the premium payment year shall be deemed to refer to the first day of the plan year for which the Schedule B was filed;

(3) If the Schedule B described in paragraph (c)(1) of this section is for a plan year beginning after 1988, then § 2610.23(c)(5) shall be applied by using, instead of the amount required to be entered on line 6e of Schedule B, an amount equal to the product of—

(i) The amount required to be entered on line 6e of Schedule B, multiplied by

(ii) the number of years (rounded to the nearest hundredth of a year) between the date of the Schedule B data and (in the case of a distress termination) the proposed termination date or (in the case of an involuntary termination) the termination date sought by the PBGC;

(4) If the Schedule B described in paragraph (c)(1) of this section is for a plan year beginning before 1989, then—

(i) the reference to "column (2)" in § 2610.23(c)(3) shall be ignored;

(ii) Section 2610.23(c)(4) shall not be applied; and

(iii) Section 2610.23(c)(5) shall be applied by using, instead of the amount required to be entered in column (2) on line 6d(iii) of Schedule B, the amount required to be entered on line 6d(ii) of Schedule B, and instead of the amount required to be entered on line 6e of Schedule B, an amount equal to the product of—

(A) Seven percent of the amount required to be entered on line 6d(ii) of Schedule B, multiplied by

(B) The number of years (rounded to the nearest hundredth of a year) between the date of the Schedule B data and (in the case of a distress termination) the proposed termination date or (in the case of an involuntary termination) the termination date sought by the PBGC;

(5) Section 2610.23(c)(6) shall not be applied, and the adjusted value of plan assets shall be the value of such assets required to be entered on line 8b of Schedule B (if the amount on line 8b was determined as of the first day of the plan year preceding the premium payment year) or on line 6c of Schedule B (if the amount on line 8b was determined as of a date other than the first day of the plan year preceding the premium payment year), adjusted in accordance with § 2610.23(b)(2); except that the amount of all contributions that are included in the value of assets and that were made after the first day of the plan year preceding the premium payment year shall be discounted to such first day at the interest rate prescribed in § 2610.23(b)(1) for the premium payment year, compounded annually except that simple interest may be used for any partial years; and

(6) For purposes of applying § 2610.23(c)(7), the quantity described in § 2610.23(c)(7)(ii) shall be modified by raising it to a power, the exponent being the number of years (rounded to the nearest hundredth of a year) between the date of the Schedule B data and the last day of the plan year preceding the premium payment year.

* * *

11. In § 2610.25, paragraphs (b), (c), and (d) are removed; paragraphs (e) and (f) are redesignated as paragraphs (c) and (d); paragraph (a) is amended by revising the last sentence; redesignated paragraph (c) is amended by revising the last sentence; and new paragraphs (b) and (e) are added, to read as follows:

§ 2610.25 Filing requirement.

[NOTE: The PBGC has adopted final regulations relating to Prop. Regs. §2610.25(b)(1), §2610.25(b)(2)(ii), and §2610.25(b)(3)(i). The change in the premium filing due date was originally proposed for the 1993 plan year. However, the finalized change is effective beginning with the 1999 plan year. PBGC Final Reg. §4007.11 was published in the Federal Register on December 14, 1998 (63 FR 68684) and is at ¶ 15,371J.]

(a) *General rule.* * * * The premium forms and payments shall be filed no later than the applicable due dates specified in paragraph (b) of this section (for premium payment years beginning after 1992) or paragraph (e) of this section (for premium payment years beginning after 1987 and before 1993).

(b) *Due dates for premium payment years beginning after 1992.* For premium payment years beginning after 1992, the due date generally applicable to small plans is prescribed in paragraph (b)(1) of this section and the due dates generally applicable to large plans are prescribed in paragraph (b)(2) of this section; paragraphs (b)(3) and (b)(4) of this section prescribe special rules for new and newly covered plans and for plans that change plan years; and paragraph (b)(5) of this section defines the terms "large plan" and "small plan" for purposes of this paragraph (b).

(1) *Small plans; in general.* The due date for a small plan (except as provided in paragraphs (b)(3) and (b)(4) of this section) is the last day of the ninth full calendar month following the end of the plan year preceding the premium payment year.

(2) *Large plans; in general.* For a large plan (except as provided in paragraphs (b)(3) and (b)(4) of this section)—

(i) The fifteenth day of the first full calendar month following the end of the plan year preceding the premium payment year is the due date for so much of the premium as does not exceed the amount of the premium required to be paid for the plan year preceding the premium payment year (determined without regard to any refund or credit for a short premium payment year under §2610.22(d) or (e)); and

(ii) the due date for any portion of the premium that exceeds the amount described in paragraph (b)(2)(i) of this section is the last day of the ninth full calendar month following the end of the plan year preceding the premium payment year.

(3) *New and newly covered plans.* The due date for the first premium payment year of coverage of any new plan or newly covered plan (as defined in §2610.2) is the latest of—

(i) The last day of the ninth full calendar month that begins on or after the later of—

(A) The first day of the premium payment year, or

(B) The day on which the plan becomes effective for benefit accruals for future service;

(ii) 90 days after the date of the plan's adoption; or

(iii) 90 days after the date on which the plan becomes covered by title IV of the Act pursuant to section 4021 of the Act.

(4) *Plans that change plan years.* For a plan that changes its plan year, each due date for the short plan year shall be the applicable due date specified in paragraph (b)(1), (b)(2), or (b)(3) of this section, and each due date for the plan year that follows the short plan year shall be the later of—

(i) The applicable due date specified in paragraph (b)(1) or (b)(2) of this section; or

(ii) 90 days after the date on which the amendment changing the plan year was adopted.

(5) *Definition of "large plan" and "small plan."* For purposes of this paragraph (b), a "large plan" is a plan that was required to pay premiums for 5,000 or more participants for the plan year preceding the premium payment year, and a "small plan" is a plan that was required to pay premiums for fewer than 5,000 participants for the plan year preceding the premium payment year.

(c) *Continuing obligation to file.* * * * The entire premium computed under this subpart must be paid for that plan year, whether or not the plan is entitled to a refund for a short plan year pursuant to §2610.22(d)(3) or (4).

* * *

(e) *Due dates for premium payment years beginning after 1987 and before 1993.* For premium payment years beginning after 1987 and before 1993, the due date generally applicable to small plans is prescribed in paragraph (e)(1) of this section and the due dates generally applicable to large plans are prescribed in paragraph (e)(2) of this section; paragraphs (e)(3) and (e)(4) of this section prescribe special rules for new and newly covered plans and for plans that change plan years; and paragraph (e)(5) of this section defines the terms "large plan" and "small plan" for purposes of this paragraph (e).

(1) *Small plans; in general.* The due date for a small plan (except as provided in paragraphs (e)(3) and (e)(4) of this section) is the fifteenth day of the eighth full calendar month following the month in which the premium payment year begins.

(2) *Large plans; in general.* For a large plan (except as provided in paragraphs (e)(3) and (e)(4) of this section)—

(i) The due date for the multiemployer premium required by §2610.22(b) and for the flat rate portion of the single-employer premium required by §2610.22(a)(1) is the last day of the second full calendar month following the close of the plan year preceding the premium payment year; and

(ii) The due date for the variable rate portion of the single-employer premium required by §2610.22(a)(2) is the fifteenth day of the eighth full calendar month following the month in which the premium payment year begins.

(iii) If the number of plan participants on the last day of the plan year preceding the premium payment year is not known by the date specified in paragraph (e)(2)(i) of this section, a reconciliation filing (on the form prescribed by this part) and any required premium payment or request for refund shall be made by the date specified in paragraph (e)(2)(ii) of this section.

(3) *New and newly covered plans.* The due date for the first premium payment year of coverage of any new plan or newly covered plan (as defined in §2610.2) is the latest of—

(i) The fifteenth day of the eighth full calendar month following the month in which the plan year begins or, if later, in which the plan becomes effective for benefit accruals for future service;

(ii) 90 days after the date of the plan's adoption; or

(iii) 90 days after the date on which the plan becomes covered by Title IV of the Act pursuant to section 4021 of the Act.

(4) *Plans that change plan years.* For a plan that changes its plan year, each due date for the short plan year shall be the applicable due date specified in paragraph (e)(1), (e)(2), or (e)(3) of this section, and each due date for the plan year that follows the short plan year shall be the later of—

(i) The applicable due date specified in paragraph (e)(1) or (e)(2) of this section; or

(ii) 30 days after the date on which the amendment changing the plan year was adopted.

(5) *Definition of "large plan" and "small plan."* For purposes of this paragraph (e), a "large plan" is a plan that was required to pay premiums for 500 or more participants for the plan year preceding the premium payment year, and a "small plan" is a plan that was required to pay premiums for fewer than 500 participants for the plan year preceding the premium payment year.

* * *

12. Section 2610.31 is revised to read as follows:

§2610.31 Purpose and scope.

This subpart provides rules for calculating and procedures for paying premiums for plan years beginning before 1988.

13. In §2610.33, paragraph (d) is removed; paragraph (a)(1) is amended by revising the table; and paragraph (b) is revised, to read as follows:

§2610.33 Multiemployer premium rates.

(a) * * *

(1) * * *

For premium payment years	Rate
After Sept. 26, 1980, and before Sept. 27, 1984	$1.40
After Sept. 26, 1984, and before Sept. 27, 1986	1.80
After Sept. 26, 1986, and before 1988	2.20

* * *

(b) *New and newly covered plans.* For any new plan or newly covered plan (as defined in § 2610.2), the plan administrator shall pay the applicable premium under paragraph (a) of this section for each individual who is a participant in the plan on the date the plan becomes covered by section 4021(a) of the Act.

* * *

14. In § 2610.34, paragraphs (a)(7), (a)(8)(ii), (a)(9)(iv), and (b)(6) are removed; paragraph (a)(8)(i) is amended by removing the introductory text and by redesignating paragraphs (a)(8)(i)(A)-(D) as paragraphs (a)(8)(i)-(iv) respectively; paragraphs (a)(8), (a)(9), and (a)(10) are redesignated respectively as paragraphs (a)(7), (a)(8), and (a)(9); paragraphs (a) introductory text, (a)(5)(i), (a)(5)(ii), (a)(6)(i), and (a)(6)(ii), and redesignated paragraphs (a)(7), (a)(8) introductory text, (a)(8)(ii)(A), (a)(8)(ii)(B), (a)(8)(iii)(A), and (a)(8)(iii)(B) are amended by revising the references "(a)(7)", "(a)(7)(ii)", "(a)(8)", "(a)(9)", and "(a)(10)" (wherever they appear) to read "(a)(6)", "(a)(6)", "(a)(7)", "(a)(8)", and "(a)(9)" respectively; redesignated paragraph (a)(9) is amended by revising the introductory text; and paragraph (c) is amended by revising the last sentence, to read as follows:

§ 2610.34 Filing requirement.

(a) * * *

¶ 20,533C   Reserved.

Proposed Reg. § § 2647.1, 2647.2, and 2647.9, relating to the reduction or waiver of complete withdrawal liability, were formerly reproduced at this paragraph.

The final regulations appear at ¶ 15,671A, ¶ 15,671B, and ¶ 15,671I.]

¶ 20,533D   Reserved.

Proposed regulations designed to conform 29 CFR Parts 2606, 2612, 2615, 2622, and 2623 to current law, including the Single Employer Pension Plan Amendments Act of 1986 and the Pension Protection Act, were formerly reproduced at this paragraph.

The final regulations are at ¶ 15,315, ¶ 15,325, ¶ 15,429G-21— ¶ 15,429G-26, ¶ 15,461— ¶ 15,465B, and ¶ 15,623— ¶ 15,623I.]

¶ 20,533E   Reserved.

Proposed regulations that would update the mortality assumptions used in valuing plan benefits in terminated single-employer pension plans trusteed by the PBGC were formerly reproduced at this paragraph.

The final regulations are at ¶ 15,620C, ¶ 15,620H, ¶ 15,620M— ¶ 15,620O, ¶ 15,620Z, ¶ 15,687H and ¶ 15,687W.]

¶ 20,533F   Reserved.

Proposed Reg. § § 2609.1—2609.6, governing the PBGC's use of administrative offset in collecting late premiums, late payment penalties, and other debts owed to it by plan sponsors, were formerly reproduced at this paragraph.

The final regulations appear at ¶ 15,328A—¶ 15,328G.]

¶ 20,533G   Reserved.

Proposed Regs. § § 2671.1—2671.9 regarding the PBGC's notice requirements for underfunded plans were formally reproduced at this paragraph.

The final regulations appear at ¶ 15,403A—¶ 15,403L]

(9) For purposes of paragraphs (a)(5), (a)(6), (a)(8), (b)(4), and (b)(5) of this section, the number of participants in a plan year is determined as of the following dates:

* * *

(c) *Continuing obligation to file.* * * * The entire premium computed under this subpart must be paid for that plan year.

* * *

15. Appendix B to part 2610 is amended by revising the introductory text preceding the table to read as follows:

Appendix B—Interest Rates for Valuing Vested Benefits

The following table lists the required interest rates to be used in valuing a plan's vested benefits under § 2610.23(b) and in calculating a plan's adjusted vested benefits under § 2610.23(c)(2) and (e)(1):

* * *

Issued in Washington, DC, this 6th day of April, 1992.

James B. Lockhart III,

Executive Director, Pension Benefit Guaranty Corporation.

[FR Doc. 92-8242 Filed 4-9-92; 8:45 am]

¶ 20,533H

Proposed regulation on 29 CFR Part 2510: Multiple Employer Welfare Arrangements: Collective Bargaining Agreements.—Reproduced below is the text of proposed regulations concerning when an employee benefit plan is established or maintained pursuant to a collective bargaining agreement and, therefore, is excluded from the definition of a multiple employer welfare arrangement (MEWA). Such plans are not subject to state insurance law regulation under ERISA Sec. 514(b)(6). The proposed regulations establish specific criteria for determining that an agreement is a collective bargaining agreement and criteria for determining when an employee benefit plan or other arrangement is established or maintained pursuant to such an agreement.

The proposed regulations were published in the *Federal Register* on August 1, 1995 (60 FR 39208). The comment period was extended to November 16, 1995 on September 29, 1995 by 60 FR 50508. The proposed regulations are reproduced with the preamble below.

DEPARTMENT OF LABOR

Pension and Welfare Benefits Administration

29 CFR Part 2510

RIN 1210-AA48

Proposed Regulation for Plans Established or Maintained Pursuant to Collective Bargaining Agreements Under Section 3(40)(A)

AGENCY: Pension and Welfare Benefits Administration, Department of Labor.

ACTION: Notice of Proposed Rulemaking.

SUMMARY: This document contains a proposed regulation under the Employee Retirement Income Security Act of 1974, as amended, 29 U.S.C. 1001-1461 (ERISA or the Act), setting forth specific criteria that must be met in order for the Secretary of Labor (the Secretary) to find that an agreement is a collective bargaining agreement for purposes of this section. The proposed regulation also sets forth criteria for determining when an employee benefit plan is established or maintained under or pursuant to such an agreement. Employee benefit plans that meet the requirements of the proposed regulation are excluded from the definition of "multiple employer welfare arrangements" under section 3(40) of ERISA and consequently are not subject to state regulation of multiple employer welfare arrangements as provided for by the Act. If adopted, the proposed regulation would affect employee welfare benefit plans, their sponsors, participants, and beneficiaries as well as service providers to plans.

DATES: Written comments concerning this proposed rule must be received by November 16, 1995. [Extended 9/29/95 by 60 FR 50508].

ADDRESSES: Interested persons are invited to submit written comments (preferably three copies) concerning the proposals herein to: Pension and Welfare Benefits Administration, Room N-5669, U.S. Department of Labor, 200 Constitution Ave., N.W., Washington, DC 20210. Attention: Proposed Regulation Under Section 3(40). All submissions will be open to public inspection at the Public Documents Room, Pension and Welfare Benefits Administration, U.S. Department of Labor, Room N-5638, 200 Constitution Ave., N.W., Washington, DC 20210.

FOR FURTHER INFORMATION CONTACT: Mark Connor, Office of Regulations and Interpretations, Pension and Welfare Benefits Administration, U.S. Department of Labor, Rm N-5669, 200 Constitution Ave., N.W., Washington, D.C. 20210 (telephone (202) 219-8671) or Cynthia Caldwell Weglicki, Office of the Solicitor, Plan Benefits Security Division, U.S. Department of Labor, Rm N-4611, 200 Constitution Ave., N.W., Washington, D.C. 20210 (telephone (202) 219-4592). These are not toll-free numbers.

SUPPLEMENTARY INFORMATION:

Background

Notice is hereby given of a proposed regulation under section 3(40) of ERISA, 29 U.S.C. 1002(40). Section 3(40)(A) defines the term multiple employer welfare arrangement (MEWA) in pertinent part as follows:

The term "multiple employer welfare arrangement" means an employee welfare benefit plan, or any other arrangement (other than an employee welfare benefit plan), which is established or maintained for the purpose of offering or providing any benefit described in paragraph (1) [of section 3 of the Act] to the employees of two or more employers (including one or more self-employed individuals), or to their benefi-

ciaries, except that such term does not include any such plan or other arrangement which is established or maintained—

(i) under or pursuant to one or more agreements which the Secretary finds to be collective bargaining agreements . . . .

This provision was added to ERISA by the Multiple Employer Welfare Arrangement Act of 1983, Sec. 302(b), Pub. L. 97-473, 96 Stat. 2611, 2612 (29 U.S.C. 1002(40)), which also amended section 514(b) of ERISA. Section 514(a) of the Act provides that state laws which relate to employee benefit plans are generally preempted by ERISA. Section 514(b) sets forth exceptions to the general rule of section 514(a) and subjects employee benefit plans that are MEWAs to various levels of state regulation depending on whether or not the MEWA is fully insured. Sec. 302(b), Pub. L. 97-473, 96 Stat. 2611, 2613 (29 U.S.C. 1144(b)(6)).[1]

The Multiple Employer Welfare Arrangement Act legislation was introduced to counter what the Congressional drafters termed abuse by the "operators of bogus 'insurance' trusts." 128 Cong. Rec. E2407 (1982) (Statement of Congressman Erlenborn). In his comments, Congressman Erlenborn noted that certain MEWA operators had been successful in thwarting timely investigations and enforcement activities of state agencies by asserting that such entities were ERISA plans exempt from state regulation by the terms of section 514 of ERISA. The goal of the bill, according to Congressman Erlenborn, was to remove "any potential obstacle that might exist under current law which could hinder the ability of the States to regulate multiple employer welfare arrangements to assure the financial soundness and timely payment of benefits under such arrangements." *Id*. This concern was also expressed by the Committee on Education and Labor in the Activity Report of the Pension Task Force (94th Congress, 2d Session, 1977) cited by Congressman Erlenborn:

It has come to our attention, through the good offices of the National Association of State Insurance Commissioners, that certain entrepreneurs have undertaken to market insurance products to employers and employees at large, claiming these products to be ERISA covered plans. For instance, persons whose primary interest is in the profiting from the provision of administrative services are establishing insurance companies and related enterprises. The entrepreneur will then argue that his enterprise is an ERISA benefit plan which is protected under ERISA's preemption provision from state regulation.

Id. As a result of the addition of section 514(b)(6), certain state laws regulating insurance apply to employee benefit plans that are MEWAs. However, the definition of a MEWA in section 3(40) provides that an employee benefit plan is not a MEWA if it is established or maintained pursuant to an agreement which the Secretary finds to be a collective bargaining agreement. Such a plan is therefore not subject to state insurance law regulation under section 514(b)(6). This exclusion is necessary to avoid disrupting the activities of legitimate Taft-Hartley plans.

While the Multiple Employer Welfare Arrangement Act of 1983 significantly enhanced the states' ability to regulate MEWAs, problems in this area continue to exist as the result of the exception for collectively bargained plans contained in the 1983 amendments. This exception is now being exploited by some MEWA operators who, through the use of sham unions and collective bargaining agreements, market fraudulent insurance schemes under the guise of collectively bargained welfare plans exempt from state insurance regulation.[2] Another problem in this area involves the use of collectively bargained arrangements as vehicles for marketing health care coverage nationwide to employ-

---

[1] The Multiple Employer Welfare Arrangement Act of 1983 added section 514(b)(6) which provides a limited exception to ERISA's preemption of state insurance laws that allows states to exercise regulatory authority over employee welfare benefit plans that are MEWAs. Section 514(b) provides, in relevant part, that:

(6)(A) Notwithstanding any other provision of this section—(i) in the case of an employee welfare benefit plan which is a multiple employer welfare arrangement and is fully insured (or which is a multiple employer welfare arrangement subject to an exemption under subparagraph (B)), any law of any State which regulates insurance may apply to such arrangement to the extent that such law provides—

(I) standards, requiring the maintenance of specified levels of reserves and specified levels of contributions, which any such plan, or any trust established under such a plan, must meet in order to be considered under such law able to pay benefits in full when due, and

(II) provisions to enforce such standards, and

(ii) in the case of any other employee welfare benefit plan which is a multiple employer welfare arrangement, in addition to this title, any law of any State which regulates insurance may apply to the extent not inconsistent with the preceding sections of this title.

Thus an employee welfare benefit plan that is a MEWA remains subject to state regulation to the extent provided in section 514(b)(6)(A). MEWAs which are not employee benefit plans are unconditionally subject to state law.

[2] In addition, the Department has received requests to make individual determinations concerning the status of particular plans under section 3(40). *See, e.g., Ocean Breeze Festival Park v. Reich*, 853 F. Supp. 906, 910 (1994) (denying motion for mandamus and granting leave to amend complaint), *summary judgement granted sub nom. Virginia Beach Policemen's Benevolent Association, et al. v. Reich* 881 F. Supp. 1059 (E.D.Va. 1995); *Amalgamated Local Union No. 355 v. Gallagher*, No. 91 CIV 0193(RR) (E.D.N.Y. April 15, 1991).

ees and employers with no relationship to the bargaining process or the underlying agreement.

The Department believes that regulatory guidance in this area is necessary to ensure that (1) state insurance regulators have ascertainable guidelines to help identify and regulate MEWAs operating in their jurisdiction and (2) sponsors of employee health benefit programs will be able to determine independently whether their plans are established or maintained pursuant to collective bargaining agreements for purposes of section 3(40)(A) without imposing the additional burden of having to apply to the Secretary for an individual finding.[3]

The proposed regulation first establishes specific criteria that the Secretary finds must be present in order for an agreement to be a collective bargaining agreement for purposes of section 3(40) and, second, establishes certain criteria applicable to determining when an employee benefit plan or other arrangement is established or maintained under or pursuant to such an agreement for purposes of section 3(40). In this regard, the Department notes that section 3(40) not only requires the existence of a *bona fide* collective bargaining agreement, but also requires that the plan be "established or maintained" pursuant to such an agreement. The Department believes that, in establishing the exception under section 3(40)(A)(i) of the Act, Congress intended to accommodate only those plans established or maintained to provide benefits to bargaining unit employees on whose behalf the plans where collectively bargained. For this reason, the Department believes that the exception under section 3(40)(A)(i) should be limited to plans providing coverage primarily to those individuals covered under collective bargaining agreements. Accordingly, the criteria in the proposed regulation relating to whether a plan or other arrangement qualifies as "established or maintained" is intended to ensure that the statutory exception is only available to plans whose participant base is predominately comprised of the bargaining unit employees on whose behalf such benefits were negotiated.

The proposed regulation would, upon adoption, constitute the Secretary's finding for purposes of determining whether an agreement is a collective bargaining agreement pursuant to section 3(40) of the Act. The Department does not intend to make individual findings or determinations concerning an entity's compliance with the proposed regulation. The criteria contained in the proposed regulation are designed to enable entities and state insurance regulatory agencies to determine whether the requirements of the statute are met. Under the proposed regulation, entities seeking to comply with these criteria must, upon request, provide documentation of their compliance with the criteria to the state or state agency charged with investigating and enforcing state insurance laws.

Description of the Proposal

Proposed § 2510.3-40(a) follows the language of section 3(40)(A) of the Act and states that the term multiple employer welfare arrangement does not include an employee welfare benefit plan which is established or maintained under or pursuant to one or more agreements which the Secretary finds to be collective bargaining agreements. Proposed § 2510.3-40(b) provides criteria which the Secretary finds to be essential for an agreement to be collectively bargained for purposes of section 3(40)(A) of the Act. Proposed § 2510.3-40(c) sets forth requirements concerning individuals covered by the employee welfare benefit plan that must be satisfied in order for an employee welfare benefit plan to be considered established or maintained under or pursuant to a collective bargaining agreement as defined in § 2510.3-40(b). Proposed § 2510.3-40(d) provides definitions of the terms "employee labor organization" and "supervisors and managers" for purposes of this section. Proposed § 2510.3-40(e) explains that a plan does not satisfy the requirements of this section if the plan or any entity associated with the plan (such as the employee labor organization or the employer) fails or refuses to comply with the requests of a state or state agency with respect to any documents or other evidence in its possession or control that are necessary to make a determination concerning the extent to which the plan is subject to state insurance

law. Proposed § 2510.3-40(f) provides that, in a proceeding brought by a state or state agency to enforce the insurance laws of the state, nothing in the proposed regulation shall be construed to prohibit allocation of the burden of proving the existence of all the criteria required by this section to the entity seeking to be treated as other than a MEWA.

Under the proposed regulation, a plan that fails to meet the applicable criteria would be a MEWA and thus subject to state insurance laws as provided in section 514(b)(6) of ERISA.

Each subsection of the proposed regulation is described in detail below.

1. General Rule and Scope

Proposed regulation 29 CFR 2510.3-40 establishes criteria which must be met for a plan to be established or maintained under or pursuant to one or more agreements which the Secretary finds to be collective bargaining agreements for purposes of section 3(40) of the Act. The proposed regulation is not intended to apply to or affect any other provision of federal law.[4]

In the Department's view, the exclusion of collectively bargained plans or other arrangements from the definition of a MEWA in section 3(40)(A) is an exception to the general statutory rule. Thus the entity asserting the applicability of the provisions concerning collectively bargained plans in section 3(40) has the burden of providing evidence of compliance with the conditions of the statutory exception and the criteria set forth in the proposed regulation.[5] Accordingly, if an entity's status as established or maintained pursuant to one or more agreements which satisfy the criteria of the proposed regulation is challenged by a state or state agency, the entity seeking to be treated as other than a MEWA must produce sufficient evidence to establish that all of the requirements of the proposed regulation have been met.[6]

2. Definition of a Collective Bargaining Agreement

Proposed § 2510.3-40(b) establishes criteria that an agreement must meet in order to be a collective bargaining agreement for purposes of this section. An agreement constitutes a collective bargaining agreement only if the agreement is in writing and is executed by or on behalf of an employer of employees described in § 2510.3-40(c)(1) and by representatives of an employee labor organization meeting the requirements of § 2510.3-40(d)(1). In addition, the agreement must also be the result of good faith, arms-length bargaining binding signatory employers and the employee labor organization to the terms of the agreement for a specified project or period of time, and the agreement must be one which cannot be unilaterally amended or terminated. The Department notes that agreements in which an employer adopts all provisions of an existing agreement binding an employer and an employee labor organization to the terms and conditions of a collective bargaining agreement, such as a pattern agreement, will not fail to satisfy the requirements of proposed § 2510.3-40(b) if the original agreement as initially adopted satisfied the requirements of this section. The Department has also determined that collective bargaining agreements containing an agreement not to strike and providing that the collective bargaining agreement will terminate upon the initiation of a strike, often called "no strike" provisions, will not fail to satisfy the proposed regulation solely by reason of such provisions.

Proposed § 2510.3-40(b)(6) requires that a collective bargaining agreement may not provide for termination of the agreement solely as a result of the failure to make contributions to the plan. Proposed § 2510.3-40(b)(7) provides that an agreement will not constitute a collective bargaining agreement under this section if, in addition to the provision of health coverage, the agreement encompasses only the minimum requirements mandated by law with respect to the terms and conditions of employment (*e.g.*, minimum wage and workers' compensation). The phrase "terms and conditions of employment" as used in the proposed regulation is intended to have the same meaning and application as in case law decided under the National Labor Relations Act, 29 U.S.C. § 151 *et seq.* (NLRA), and would include wages, hours of

---

[3] It is the Department's position that the language of section 3(40) of ERISA does not require the Secretary to make individual findings that specific agreements are collective bargaining agreements. Moreover, a district court recently found that the Secretary has no "statutory responsibility" to make individualized findings. *Virginia Beach Policeman's Benevolent Association v. Reich*, 881 F. Supp. 1059, 1069-70 (E.D.Va. 1995).

[4] The Department notes that section 3(40) of ERISA is not the only provision that provides special rules to be applied to agreements that the Secretary finds to be collectively bargained. For example, sections 404(a)(1)(B) and (C) of the Internal Revenue Code (Code) provide special rules to determine the maximum amount of deductible contributions in the case of amendments to plans that the Secretary of Labor finds to be collectively bargained. In addition, Code sections 410(b)(3) and 413(a) exclude from minimum coverage requirements certain employees covered by an agreement that the Secretary finds to be a collective bargaining agreement.

[5] 2A Sutherland Statutory Construction § 47.11 (Norman J. Singer ed. 5th ed. 1992); *United States v. First City National Bank of Houston*, 386 U.S. 361, 366 (1967) (burden of establishing applicability of statutory exception is on entity that asserts it); *Federal Trade Commission v. Morton Salt Co.*, 334 U.S. 37, 44-45 (1948) ("First, the general rule of statutory construction [is] that the burden of proving justification or exemption under a special exception to the prohibitions of a statute generally rests on one who claims its benefits . . . .").

[6] *See Donovan v. Cunningham*, 716 F. 2d 1455, 1467-68 n.27 (5th Cir. 1983) (citing *Securities and Exchange Commission v. Ralston Purina Co.*, 346 U.S. 119, 126 (1953), "As the Supreme Court has observed in a different context, it seems 'fair and reasonable' to place the burden of proof upon a party who seeks to bring his conduct within a statutory exception to a broad remedial scheme.")

work and other matters of employment such as grievance procedures and seniority rights. For purposes of this section, the expiration of a collective bargaining agreement will not in and of itself prevent the agreement from satisfying the requirements under the proposed regulation if the agreement, although expired, continues in force.

3. Plans Established or Maintained

The proposed regulation also establishes certain criteria to determine when a plan is established or maintained under or pursuant to one or more collective bargaining agreements for purposes of section 3(40). Proposed § 2510.3-40(c) provides that in situations where a plan covers both individuals who are members of a group or bargaining unit represented by an employee labor organization as defined in proposed § 2510.3-40(d)(1) as well as other individuals, the plan will not be considered to be established or maintained pursuant to one or more collective bargaining agreements unless no less than 85% of the individuals covered by the plan are present or certain former employees and their beneficiaries, excluding supervisors and managers as defined in paragraph (d)(2), who are currently or who were previously covered by a collective bargaining agreement.[7] In addition, three groups of individuals may participate in the plan but are not counted in determining the total number of individuals covered by the plan for purposes of calculating the 85% limitation: (1) present or former employees of the plan or of a related plan established or maintained pursuant to the same collective bargaining agreement; (2) present or former employees of the employee labor organization as defined in paragraph (d)(1) that is a signatory to the collective bargaining agreement pursuant to which the plan is maintained, and (3) beneficiaries of individuals in groups (1) and (2).

For purposes of the proposed regulation, the term "former employee" is limited to individuals who are receiving workers' compensation or disability benefits, continuation coverage pursuant to the Consolidated Omnibus Budget Reconciliation Act (COBRA) (Part 6 of title I of ERISA, 29 U.S.C. §§ 1161-1168), or who have retired or separated from employment after working for more than 1000 hours a year for at least three years for a signatory employer or employee organization, or the plan or related plan. For purposes of paragraph (c)(4), to be considered an employee of the plan, a related plan, or the signatory employee labor organization, an individual must work at least (A) 15 hours a week or 60 hours a month during the period of coverage under the plan, or (B) have worked at least 1000 hours in the last year and currently be on *bona fide* leave based on sickness or disability of the individual or the individual's family or on earned vacation time.

The proposed regulation requires that the plan satisfy the 85% limitation on the last day of each of the previous five calendar quarters unless the plan has not been in existence for five calendar quarters. If the plan or other arrangement has been in existence for a shorter period of time, it must satisfy the 85% limitation on the last day of each calendar quarter during which it has been in existence.

Through the requirement that no less than 85% of individuals covered by the plan be present or former bargaining unit members, the proposed regulation intends to treat as MEWAs arrangements that permit individuals to participate in an employee welfare benefit plan solely as a result of membership or affiliation with an entity and not as a result of the individuals being legitimately represented in collective bargaining by a *bona fide* employee labor organization.[8] The Department believes that the 85% limitation in the proposed regulation is consistent with the purpose of the statutory exception in section 3(40)(A)(i) of ERISA for employee welfare benefit plans which are established or maintained as the result of collective bargaining on behalf of employees concerning the terms and conditions of their employment. To the extent that the Department's position as indicated in Advisory Opinion 91-06A (January 15, 1991) to Gerald Grimes, Oklahoma Insurance Commissioner (concerning a trust that provided health care and other benefits to "associate members" of a labor organization who were not represented by the organization in collective bargaining), appears to express a different position, it would be superseded by the adoption of a final regulation that incorporates this requirement.

4. Definition of Employee Labor Organization

Proposed § 2510.3-40(d)(1) defines the term "employee labor organization" for purposes of this section. Proposed § 2510.3-40(d)(1)(i) pro-

vides that, with respect to a particular collective bargaining agreement, an employee labor organization must represent the employees of each signatory employer in one of two ways. All of a signatory employer's bargaining units covered by the collective bargaining agreement must either be certified by the National Labor Relations Board, or the employee labor organization must be lawfully recognized by the signatory employer as the exclusive representative for the employer's bargaining unit employees covered by the collective bargaining agreement. Such representation must take place without employer interference or domination. For purposes of the proposed regulation, employer interference or domination in the formation, administration, or operation of the employee labor organization includes taking an active part in organizing an employee organization or committee to represent employees; bringing pressure upon employees to join an employee organization; improperly favoring one of two or more employee organizations that are competing to represent employees; or otherwise unlawfully promoting or assisting in the formation or operation of the employee organization.

Under proposed § 2510.3-40(d)(1)(ii), an employee labor organization must operate for a substantial purpose other than that of offering or providing health coverage. Proposed § 2510.3-40(d)(1)(iii) states that an employee labor organization may not pay commissions, fees, or bonuses to individuals other than full-time employees of the employee labor organization in connection with the solicitation of employers or participants with regard to a collectively bargained plan. In addition, under subsection (d)(1)(iv), the term "employee labor organization" does not include an organization that utilizes the services of licensed insurance agents or brokers for soliciting employers or participants in connection with a collectively bargained plan. Proposed § 2510.3-40(d)(1)(v) requires an employee labor organization to be a "labor organization" as defined in section 3(i) of the Labor-Management Reporting and Disclosure Act, 29 U.S.C. § 402(i). Proposed § 2510.3-40(d)(1)(vi) also requires an employee labor organization to qualify as a tax-exempt labor organization under section 501(c)(5) of the Internal Revenue Code of 1986. It is the view of the Department that these criteria are necessary to distinguish organizations that provide benefits through legitimate employee representation from organizations that are primarily in the business of marketing commercial insurance products.

5. Supervisors and Managers

Proposed § 2510.3-40(d)(2) defines the terms "supervisors and managers" for purposes of this section. Proposed § 2510.3-40(d)(2) defines as "supervisors and managers" those employees of a signatory employer to a collective bargaining agreement who, acting on behalf of the employer, have the authority to hire, transfer, suspend, layoff, recall, promote, discharge, assign, reward, or discipline other employees, or who have responsibility to direct other employees or to adjust their grievances, or who have power to make effective recommendations concerning any of the actions described above. In order to be considered a supervisor or manager, an individual must be able to use independent judgement in the exercise of authority, responsibility, and power, and that exercise must be more than a routine or clerical function.

6. Failure to Provide Documents

The proposed regulation provides that even if a plan meets the requirements of subsections 2510.3-40(b) and (c) of this section, it will not be considered to be established or maintained pursuant to an agreement that the Secretary finds to be a collective bargaining agreement if an entity, plan, employee labor organization or employer which is a party to the agreement fails or refuses to provide documents or evidence in its possession or control to a state or state agency which reasonably requests documents or evidence in order to determine the status of any entity either under the proposed regulation or under state insurance laws. While the proposed regulation enumerates criteria designed to enable entities to determine whether the requirements of the statute are met, the Department intends that, when requested to do so, entities will provide documentation of their compliance with the criteria to the state or state agency charged with investigating and enforcing state insurance laws. An entity seeking to be treated as other than a MEWA under the provisions of the proposed regulation has the burden of producing sufficient documents and other evidence to prove that it meets the criteria of the proposed regulation and is therefore

---

[7] Although the proposed regulation itself does not impose any specific restrictions concerning individuals who may be included in the 15%, the entity as a whole must comply with the requirements of section 3(1) of ERISA in order to be an employee welfare benefit plan covered by the Act. Section 3(1) provides that status as an ERISA covered plan is dependent on the composition and attributes of the participant base as well as the characteristics of the employer and employee organization. *See, e.g., Bell v. Employee Security Benefits Association*, 437 F. Supp. 382 (1977); Advisory Opinion 93-32 (letter to Mr.

Kevin Long, December 16, 1993); Advisory Opinion 85-03A (letter to Mr. James Ray, January 15, 1985); Advisory Opinion 77-59 (letter to Mr. William Hager, August 26, 1977).

[8] A number of instances have been brought to the Department's attention where entities have attempted to utilize purported collective bargaining agreements as a basis for marketing insurance coverage, generally under the guise of "associate membership," to non-bargaining unit individuals and unrelated employers. *See, e.g., Empire Blue Cross and Blue Shield v. Consolidated Welfare*, 830 F. Supp. 170 (E.D.N.Y. 1993).

entitled to application of the statutory exemption from the definition of a MEWA.

The Department anticipates that states or state agencies, including any commission, board or committee charged with investigating and enforcing state insurance laws, will utilize existing jurisdiction under state laws to require the production of documents and other evidence. Where the entity's compliance with the criteria of the proposed regulation is disputed by a state or state agency, the Department expects that the state or state agency will use its existing authority under state law to bring the matter before the appropriate state adjudicatory body to determine the facts. The proposed regulation does not restrict the authority of the state or state agency to reinvestigate the entity at any time if it believes the entity is not in compliance with the proposed regulation or with state laws.

7. Allocation of Burden of Proof

The proposed regulation provides that, in a proceeding brought by a state or a state agency to enforce the insurance laws of the state, nothing in the proposed regulation shall be read or construed to prohibit the allocation of the burden of proving the existence of all criteria required by this section to the entity seeking to be treated as other than a MEWA. The proposed regulation enumerates criteria designed to enable entities to determine whether the requirements of the statute are met. However, as discussed in paragraph 1. General Rule and Scope, supra, the Department believes that when challenged, the entity asserting the applicability of an exception has the burden of providing evidence of compliance with each of the terms of the proposed regulation.

Regulatory Flexibility Act

The Regulatory Flexibility Act of 1980 requires each Federal agency to perform a Regulatory Flexibility Analysis for all rules that are likely to have a significant economic impact on a substantial number of small entities. Small entities include small businesses, organizations, and governmental jurisdictions. The Pension and Welfare Benefits Administration has determined that, if adopted, this proposed rule may have a significant economic impact on a substantial number of small entities. Accordingly, as provided in section 603 of the Regulatory Flexibility Act (5 U.S.C. § 601, et seq.), the following initial regulatory flexibility analysis is provided:

(1) PWBA is considering the proposed regulation because it believes that regulatory guidance in this area is necessary to ensure (a) that state insurance regulators have ascertainable guidelines to help identify and regulate MEWAs operating in their jurisdictions, and (b) that sponsors of employee welfare benefit plans will be able to determine independently whether their plans are excepted plans under section 3(40)(A) of ERISA. A more detailed discussion of the agency's reasoning for issuing the proposed regulation is found in the Background section, above.

(2) The objective of the proposed regulation is to provide guidance on the application of an exception to the definition of the term "multiple employer welfare arrangement" (MEWA) which is found in section 3(40) of ERISA and applies to certain employee welfare benefit plans. The legal basis for the proposed regulation is found at ERISA section 3(40) (29 U.S.C. 1002(40)); an extensive list of authority may be found in the Statutory Authority section, below.

(3) No accurate estimate of the number of small entities affected by the proposed regulation is available. No small governmental jurisdictions will be affected. It is estimated that a substantial number of small businesses and organizations will be affected, due to the fact that it is precisely those entities, seeking group health care coverage, that are most harmed by unscrupulous entrepreneurs who purport to provide employee health benefits. In a report entitled "Employee Benefits: States Need Labor's Help Regulating Multiple Employer Welfare Arrangements," the United States General Accounting Office (GAO) calculated that between January 1988 and June 1991, fraudulent MEWAs left at least 398,000 participants and their beneficiaries with $123 million in unpaid medical claims and left many other participants without the health insurance they had paid for.[9] By restricting fraudulent and financially unsound MEWAs, the proposed regulation may limit the sources of health care coverage offered to small businesses. On the other hand, MEWAs that either meet the section 3(40) criteria or meet state regulatory standards are less likely to demonstrate the type of fraudulent or imprudent activity that prompted Congressional action. The GAO Report indicated that, during the January 1988 and June 1991 period, more than 600 MEWAs failed to comply with state insurance laws and some violated criminal statutes.[10] Consequently, small entities will receive a benefit from the reduced incidence of fraud

and insolvency among the pool of MEWAs in the marketplace. To the extent that MEWAs themselves are small entities, they too will be affected by the proposed regulation.

(4) No identical reporting or recordkeeping is required under the proposed rule. However, this regulation clarifies the information that must be provided upon request to state authorities by those MEWAs wishing to take advantage of the exception under section 3(40)(A) of ERISA. The information to be provided will vary depending upon the entity involved but will include a written collective bargaining agreement and records on the individuals covered by the plan for at least the last five calendar quarters. Such information is routinely prepared and held in the ordinary course of business under current law by most small entities. It is anticipated that the preparation of some of these documents would require the professional skills of an attorney, accountant, or other health benefit plan professional; however, the majority of the recordkeeping may be handled by clerical staff.

(5) No federal rules have been identified that duplicate, overlap or conflict with the proposed rule.

(6) No significant alternatives which would minimize the impact on small entities have been identified. The proposed regulation is less costly in comparison with the alternative methods of determining compliance with section 3(40), such as case-by-case analysis by PWBA of each employee welfare benefit plan, or litigation. The costs of such alternatives would be unduly burdensome on small entities. No federal reporting is required. Instead, the proposed regulation would create standards by which the MEWAs may be reviewed by the states. It would be inappropriate to create an alternative with lower compliance criteria, or an exemption under the proposed regulation, for small MEWAs because those are the entities which pose a higher degree of risk of non-performance due to their increased likelihood of being under-funded or otherwise having inadequate reserves to meet the benefits claims submitted for payment.

Executive Order 12866 Statement

Under Executive Order 12866 (58 FR 51735, Oct. 4, 1993), the Department must determine whether the regulatory action is "significant" and therefore subject to review by the Office of Management and Budget (OMB) and the requirements of the Executive Order. Under section 3(f), the order defines a "significant regulatory action" as an action that is likely to result in a rule (1) having an annual effect on the economy of $100 million or more, or adversely and materially affecting a sector of the economy, productivity, competition, jobs, the environment, public health or safety, or State, local or tribal governments or communities (also referred to as "economically significant"); (2) creating a serious inconsistency or otherwise interfering with an action taken or planned by another agency; (3) materially altering the budgetary impacts of entitlement, grants, user fees, or loan programs or the rights and obligations of recipients thereof; or (4) raising novel legal or policy issues arising out of legal mandates, the President's priorities, or the principles set forth in the Executive Order.

Pursuant to the terms of the Executive Order, the Department has determined that this program creates a improved method for statutory compliance that will reduce paperwork and regulatory compliance burdens on state governments, businesses, including small businesses and organizations, and make better use of scarce federal resources, in accord with the mandates of the Paperwork Reduction Act, the Regulatory Flexibility Act, and the President's priorities. The Department believes this notice is "significant" under category (4), supra, and subject to OMB review on that basis.

Paperwork Reduction Act

The proposed regulation does not contain any information collection or recordkeeping requirements as those terms are defined under the Paperwork Reduction Act because the information to be provided on request to state authorities will vary in each instance depending on the entity involved. Consequently, there is no requirement that the entities comply with identical reporting or recordkeeping requirements. 5 CFR § 1320.7(c). Thus, the proposed regulation imposes no additional federal paperwork burden and the Paperwork Reduction Act does not apply.

Statutory Authority

This regulation is proposed pursuant to section 3(40) of ERISA (Pub. L. 97-473, 96 Stat. 2611, 2612, 29 U.S.C. 1002(40)) and section 505 (Pub. L. 93-406, 88 Stat. 892, 894, 29 U.S.C. 1135) of ERISA and under Secretary of Labor's Order No. 1-87, 52 FR 13139, April 21, 1987.

List of Subjects in 29 CFR Part 2510

---

[9] GAO/HRD-92-40 (March 1992) at 2.

[10] Id.

Employee benefit plans, Employee Retirement Income Security Act, Pension and Welfare Benefit Administration.

Proposed Regulation

For the reasons set out in the preamble, the Department proposes to amend Part 2510 of Chapter XXV of Title 29 of the Code of Federal Regulations as follows:

PART 2510—[AMENDED]

1. The authority for Part 2510 is revised to read:

Authority: Secs. 3(2), 111(c), 505, Pub. L. 93-406, 88 Stat. 852, 894 (29 U.S.C. 1002(2), 1031, 1135); Secretary of Labor's Order No. 27-74, 1-86 (51 FR 3521, January 28, 1986), 1-87 (52 FR 13139, April 21, 1987), and Labor Management Services Administration Order No. 2-6.

Section 2510.3-40 is also issued under sec. 3(40), Pub. L. 97-473, 96 Stat. 2611, 2612, (29 U.S.C. 1002(40)).

Section 2510.3-101 is also issued under sec. 102 of Reorganization Plan No. 4 of 1978, 43 FR 47713, 3 CFR 1978 Comp., p. 332, effective under E.O. 12108, 44 FR 1065, 3 CFR 1978 Comp. p. 275 and sec. 11018(d) of Pub. L. 99-272, 100 Stat. 82.

Section 2510.3-102 is also issued under sec. 102 of Reorganization Plan No. 4 of 1978, 43 FR 47713, 3 CFR 1978 Comp., p. 332, effective under E.O. 12108, 44 FR 1065, 3 CFR Comp., p. 275.

2. Part 2510 is amended by adding new Section 2510.3-40 to read:

§ 2510.3-40 Plans Established or Maintained Pursuant to One or More Collective Bargaining Agreements.

(a) *General.* Section 3(40)(A) of the Employee Retirement Income Security Act of 1974 (the Act) provides that the term "multiple employer welfare arrangement" (MEWA) does not include an employee welfare benefit plan or other arrangement which is established or maintained under or pursuant to one or more agreements which the Secretary of Labor (the Secretary) finds to be a collective bargaining agreement(s). The purposes of the proposed regulation are to establish specific criteria that the Secretary finds must be met for an agreement to be a collective bargaining agreement and to establish criteria for determining when an employee benefit plan is established or maintained pursuant to such an agreement.

(b) *Collective Bargaining Agreement.* The Secretary finds, for purposes of section 3(40)(A) of the Act, that an agreement constitutes a collective bargaining agreement only if the agreement—

(1) is in writing;

(2) is executed by, or on behalf of, an employer of employees represented by an employee labor organization;

(3) is executed by an employee labor organization;

(4) is the product of good faith, arms-length bargaining between one or more employers and an employee labor organization or uniformly incorporates and binds one or more employers and an employee labor organization to the terms and conditions of another agreement which as originally negotiated and adopted satisfies the requirements of this section;

(5) binds signatory employers and the employee labor organization to the terms of the agreement for a specified project or period of time, cannot be unilaterally amended or terminated and contains procedures for amending the terms and conditions of the agreement;

(6) does not terminate solely as a result of failure to make contributions to the plan; and

(7) in addition to the provision of health coverage, provides more than the minimum requirements mandated by law with respect to the terms and conditions of employment (*e.g.,* provides for more than minimum wage and workers' compensation).

(c) *Established or Maintained.* An employee benefit plan is not established or maintained under or pursuant to one or more collective bargaining agreements for purposes of section 3(40)(A) of the Act unless not less than 85 percent of the individuals covered by the plan are—

(1) employees, excluding supervisors and managers, currently included in one or more groups or bargaining units of employees covered by one or more collective bargaining agreements as defined in paragraph (b) of this section which expressly refer to the plan and provide for contributions thereto; or

(2) persons who were formerly employees described in paragraph (c)(1) of this section who are receiving workers' compensation or disability benefits, COBRA continuation coverage pursuant to Part 6 of title I of ERISA, 29 U.S.C. 1161-1168, or who have retired or separated

from employment after working more than 1,000 hours a year for at least three years; or

(3) beneficiaries of individuals included in paragraphs (c)(1) and (2) of this section.

(4) For purposes of this subsection, the following individuals covered by the plan or other arrangement shall not be counted in determining the total number of individuals covered by the plan—

(i) employees of the plan or another plan established or maintained pursuant to the same collective bargaining agreement(s);

(ii) employees of an employee labor organization that meets the requirements of paragraph (d)(1) of this section and that is a signatory to the collective bargaining agreement(s) pursuant to which the plan is maintained;

(iii) persons who were formerly employees described in paragraphs (c)(4)(i) and (ii) of this section who are receiving workers' compensation or disability benefits, COBRA continuation coverage pursuant to Part 6 of title I of ERISA, 29 U.S.C. §§ 1161-1168, or who have retired or separated from employment after working more than 1,000 hours a year for at least three years; or

(iv) beneficiaries of individuals included in paragraphs (c)(4)(i), (ii) and (iii);

(v) provided that, for purposes of paragraphs (c)(4)(i) and (ii) of this section, in order to be an employee, an individual must work at least:

(A) 15 hours a week or 60 hours a month during the period of coverage under the plan, or

(B) have worked more than 1,000 hours in the last year and currently be on *bona fide* leave based on sickness or disability of the individual or the individual's family or on earned vacation time.

(5) For purposes of calculating whether the 85% limitation has been met, a plan or other arrangement must satisfy the requirements of paragraphs (c)(1) through (4) of this section on the last day of—

(i) each of the previous five calendar quarters; or

(ii) if the plan has been in existence for fewer than five calendar quarters, every calendar quarter during which the plan has been in existence.

(d) *Definitions.*

(1) *Employee Labor Organization.* For purposes of this section, an "employee labor organization" shall mean an organization that—

(i) represents, with respect to a particular collective bargaining agreement, the employees of each signatory employer to the agreement where:

(A) all of the employer's bargaining units covered by the agreement are certified by the National Labor Relations Board, or

(B) the employee labor organization is lawfully recognized by the signatory employer (*e.g.,* without employer interference or domination) as the exclusive bargaining representative for the employer's bargaining unit employees covered by the agreement;

(ii) provides substantial representational services to employees regarding the terms and conditions of their employment in addition to health coverage;

(iii) does not pay commissions, fees, or bonuses to individuals, other than full-time employees of the employee labor organization, in connection with the solicitation of employers or participants;

(iv) does not utilize the services of licensed insurance agents or brokers for soliciting employers or participants;

(v) is a "labor organization" as defined in section 3(i) of the Labor-Management Reporting and Disclosure Act, 29 U.S.C. section 402(i); and

(vi) qualifies as a tax-exempt labor organization under section 501(c)(5) of the Internal Revenue Code of 1986.

(2) *Supervisors and Managers.* For purposes of this section, "supervisors and managers" shall mean any employees of a signatory employer to an agreement described in paragraph (b) of this section who, acting in the interest of the employer, have—

(i) authority to hire, transfer, suspend, layoff, recall, promote, discharge, assign, reward or discipline other employees; or

(ii) responsibility to direct other employees or to adjust their grievances; or

(iii) power to make effective recommendations concerning the actions described in paragraphs (d)(2)(i) and (ii) of this section; as long as the exercise of the authority, responsibility and power in paragraphs (d)(2)(i), (ii) or (iii) of this section is not of a merely routine or clerical nature, but requires the use of independent judgment.

(e) *Failure to Provide Documents or Other Necessary Evidence.* This section shall not apply to any plan or other arrangement if, in conjunction with an investigation or proceeding by a state or state agency, the plan, arrangement, any employee labor organization or employer which is a party to the agreement(s) at issue fails or refuses to provide the state or state agency with any document or other evidence in its possession or control that is reasonably requested by the state or state agency for the purpose of determining the status of the plan or other arrangement under state insurance laws or under this section.

(f) *Allocation of Burden of Proof*

In a proceeding brought to enforce state insurance laws, nothing in the proposed regulation shall be construed to prohibit a state or state agency from allocating the burden of proving the existence of all the criteria required by this section to the entity seeking to be treated as other than a MEWA.

Signed at Washington, DC, this 26th day of July 1995.

Olena Berg

Assistant Secretary,

Pension and Welfare Benefits Administration

¶ 20,533I   Reserved.

Proposed Reg. §§ 2629.1-2629.12 relating to the PBGC Missing Participant Program were formerly reproduced at this paragraph. The final regulations begin at ¶ 15,530A. Schedule MP and its instructions appear at ¶ 10,818.]

¶ 20,533J

Proposed rule on 29 CFR Parts 2509, 2520 and 2550: Obsolete rulings.—Reproduced below is a proposed rule issued by the Pension and Welfare Benefits Administration to remove certain interpretive bulletins and regulations under ERISA that the DOL believes are obsolete. These generally provided transitional relief for plan sponsors, plan administrators and others subject to Title 1 of ERISA during the first several years after ERISA was enacted. They are considered obsolete because the periods or dates of applicability have expired, they merely provide notice of a rescission or withdrawal of prior guidance or regulations, or were rendered ineffective by a subsequent Supreme Court decision.

The proposed rule was filed with the *Federal Register* on April 2, 1996 and published in the *Federal Register* on April 3, 1996. (61 FR 14690).

The regulations were finalized effective July 1, 1996 (61 FR 33847). The changes implemented by the final regulations are reflected at ¶ 14,231F, ¶ 14,231G, ¶ 14,244, ¶ 14,245, ¶ 14,246, ¶ 14,246A, ¶ 14,247H, ¶ 14,247Y, ¶ 14,249A, ¶ 14,249C, ¶ 14,249D, ¶ 14,249K, ¶ 14,521, ¶ 14,522, ¶ 14,771B, ¶ 14,771C, ¶ 14,775, ¶ 14,841, ¶ 14,844A, ¶ 14,844B, and ¶ 14,845, ¶ 14,875, ¶ 14,876, ¶ 14,881.

¶ 20,533K

Pension Benefit Guaranty Corporation: Proposed rule: Reportable events: Retirement Protection Act of 1994.—Reproduced below is the preamble and text of a proposed rule issued by the Pension Benefit Guaranty Corporation that revises reportable event regulations to conform to changes made by the Retirement Protection Act of 1994. The proposed rule also add three new reportable events and discusses waivers and timing of filing requirements.

The proposed regulations were filed with the *Federal Register* on July 23, 1996 and published in the *Federal Register* on July 24, 1996 (61 FR 38409).

The regulations were finalized December 2, 1996 (61 FR 63988). The regulations are reproduced at ¶ 15,315A, ¶ 15,461, ¶ 15,461A, ¶ 15,461B, ¶ 15,461C, ¶ 15,461D, ¶ 15,461E, ¶ 15,461F, ¶ 15,461G, ¶ 15,462, ¶ 15,462A, ¶ 15,462B, ¶ 15,462C, ¶ 15,462D, ¶ 15,462E, ¶ 15,462F, ¶ 15,462G, ¶ 15,462H, ¶ 15,462I, ¶ 15,462J, ¶ 15,462K, ¶ 15,462L, ¶ 15,462M, ¶ 15,462N, ¶ 15,462O, ¶ 15,463, ¶ 15,463A, ¶ 15,463B, ¶ 15,463C, ¶ 15,463D, ¶ 15,463E, ¶ 15,463F, ¶ 15,463G, ¶ 15,464 and ¶ 15,651B. The preamble is reproduced at ¶ 24,177.

¶ 20,533L

Proposed Regulation: Premium audit program: Penalty assessment policy.—Reproduced below is the preamble and text of a proposed rule issued by the Pension Benefit Guaranty Corporation (PBGC) that will require plan administrators to make available to the agency certain plan records supporting premium filings, such as records relating to the number of plan participants as well as records reflecting any plan underfunding. The PBGC proposes to amend the existing regulation to provide for such submission within 30 days of receipt of the PBGC's request.

The proposed regulation was published in the *Federal Register* on December 17, 1996 (61 FR 66247).

The regulation was finalized August 8, 1997 (62 FR 36663). The regulation is reproduced at ¶ 15,371I. The preamble is reproduced at ¶ 24,179.

¶ 20,533M

Proposed regulations: Equal Employment Opportunity Commission: Age Discrimination in Employment Act of 1967: Benefits waivers.—The Equal Employment Opportunity Commission has issued a proposed regulation to provide guidance on waivers of rights and claims under the Age Discrimination in Employment Act (ADEA) as amended by the Older Workers Benefit Protection Act of 1990 (OWBPA) (P.L. 101-433). The OWBPA requires that all waivers to ADEA rights and claims be knowing and voluntary.

Under the proposed regulation, exit incentive programs and other employment termination programs need not constitute an employee benefit plan for purposes of ERISA. An employer may or may not have an ERISA severance plan in connection with its OWBPA program.

The proposed regulations were published in the *Federal Register* on March 10, 1997 (62 FR 10787).

The final regulations were finalized June 6, 1998 (63 FR 30624). The regulations are reproduced at ¶ 15,750J.

¶ 20,533N

Pension Benefit Guarantee Corporation: Proposed rule: Standard termination process: Single-employer plans.—Reproduced below is a proposed rule issued by the PBGC to extend deadlines and simplify the standard termination process for single-employer plans. Specifically, the filing deadline for a standard termination notice would be extended from 120 days to 180 days after the proposed termination date. Plan administrators would have 120 days, instead of 60 days, to distribute plan assets after receipt of an IRS clearance letter. There would be a new requirement that administrators must inform participants of state guarantees applicable to their benefits. Also, standard termination packages would include a model notice of intent to terminate. Effective March 14, 1997, penalties are waived for late filing of post-distribution certification if it is filed within 90 days after the distribution deadline.

The proposed regulation was filed with the *Federal Register* on March 11, 1997 and published in the *Federal Register* on March 14, 1997 (62 FR 12508).

The regulations were finalized November 7, 1997 (62 FR 60424). The regulations are reproduced at ¶ 15,315A, ¶ 15,361D, ¶ 15,423, ¶ 15,440A, ¶ 15,440A-1, ¶ 15,440A-2, ¶ 15,440A-3, ¶ 15,440A-4, ¶ 15,440A-5, ¶ 15,440A-6, ¶ 15,440A-7, ¶ 15,440F, ¶ 15,440F-1, ¶ 15,440F-2, ¶ 15,440F-3, ¶ 15,440F-4, ¶ 15,440F-5, ¶ 15,440F-6, ¶ 15,440F-7, ¶ 15,440F-8, ¶ 15,440F-9, ¶ 15,440F-10, ¶ 15,440J, ¶ 15,440J-1, ¶ 15,440J-2, ¶ 15,440J-3, ¶ 15,440J-4, ¶ 15,440J-5, ¶ 15,440J-6, ¶ 15,440J-7, ¶ 15,440J-8, ¶ 15,440J-9, ¶ 15,530A, ¶ 15,530B, ¶ 15,530C, ¶ 15,530D, ¶ 15,530E, ¶ 15,530F, ¶ 15,530G, ¶ 15,530H, ¶ 15,530I, ¶ 15,530J, ¶ 15,530K, ¶ 15,530L, ¶ 15,530M, and ¶ 15,530N. The preamble is reproduced at ¶ 24,182.

¶ 20,533O

Proposed rules: Pension and Welfare Benefits Administration: Definition of ERISA plan assets: SIMPLE IRAs: Salary reduction elective contributions.—The Pension and Welfare Benefits Administration has issued a proposed amendment to a final regulation which would clarify when salary reduction elective contributions to SIMPLE IRAs must become plan assets. The amendment would harmonize the ERISA Title I definition of plan assets (with respect to participant contributions) with Code rules that govern the timing of deposits for SIMPLE IRAs. The proposed amendment aims to simplify plan establishment and administration for small businesses.

The proposed regulation was published in the *Federal Register* on March 27, 1997 (62 FR 14760).

The regulation was finalized effective November 25, 1997 (62 FR 62934). The regulation is reproduced at ¶ 14,139N.

¶ 20,533P

Proposed rules: Pension and Welfare Benefits Administration: Civil monetary penalties.—The Pension and Welfare Benefits Administration has issued proposed regulations to adjust civil monetary penalties under ERISA pursuant to the requirements of the Federal Civil Penalties Inflation Adjustment Act of 1990, as amended by the Debt Collection Improvement Act of 1996 (the Act). The Act requires that certain penalties, which are listed as dollar amounts under ERISA, be adjusted for inflation. Penalties listed as percentages are not required to be adjusted. The adjusted penalties will apply only to violations taking place after the new penalty is effective.

The proposed regulation was published in the *Federal Register* on April 18, 1997 (62 FR 19078).

The regulations were finalized effective July 29, 1997 (62 FR 40696). The regulation is reproduced at ¶ 14,929A, ¶ 14,929B, ¶ 14,929C, ¶ 14,929D, and ¶ 14,929E. The preamble is reproduced at ¶ 24,181.

¶ 20,533Q

Proposed rules: Pension Benefit Guaranty Corporation: Mergers and transfers: Multiemployer plans.—The PBGC has issued proposed regulations to clarify the application of current PBGC regulations on mergers and transfers between multiemployer plans to plans terminated by mass withdrawal. Under the proposed regs, transactions involving plans that have been terminated by mass withdrawal under ERISA are subject to the merger and transfer rules, and, unless they are *de minimis* transactions, the transactions are governed by the higher-level valuation standard and "safe harbor" solvency test.

The proposed regulations were published in the *Federal Register* on May 1, 1997 (62 FR 23700).

The regulations were finalized May 4, 1998 (63 FR 24421). The regulations are reproduced at ¶ 15,700A, ¶ 15,700B, ¶ 15,700C, ¶ 15,700D, ¶ 15,700E, ¶ 15,700F, ¶ 15,700G, ¶ 15,700H, ¶ 15,700I and ¶ 15,700J. The preamble is reproduced at ¶ 24,184.

¶ 20,533R

Pension Benefit Guaranty Corporation: Proposed rule: Recoupment: Overpayment.—The PBGC has proposed amendments to its existing regulation governing recoupment of benefit overpayments that would stop the reduction of monthly benefits once the overpayment has been repaid.

The proposed regulations, were published in the *Federal Register* on December 18, 1997 (62 FR 66319).

The regulations were finalized May 28, 1998 (63 FR 29353). The regulations are reproduced at ¶ 15,424, ¶ 15,424A, ¶ 15,424B, ¶ 15,440J-1 and ¶ 15,530B. The preamble is reproduced at ¶ 24,185.

¶ 20,533S

Proposed rules: Pension and Welfare Benefits Administration: Insurance company general accounts.—The PWBA has issued proposed regulations to clarify which assets held by an insurer are plan assets for purposes of Title I of ERISA in instances where an insurer issues policies to or for the benefit of an employee benefit plan, and such policies are supported by assets of the insurer's general account. The proposed regulations also provide guidance with respect to the application of Title I to the general account assets of insurers. The proposed regulations were introduced as a result of amendments to ERISA Sec. 401 made by the Small Business Job Protection Act of 1996, which mandated the guidance.

The proposed regulations, which were published in the *Federal Register* on December 22, 1997 (62 FR 66908), are reproduced below.

The regulations were finalized January 5, 2000 (65 FR 613). The regulations are reproduced at ¶ 14,714. The preamble is reproduced at ¶ 24,192.

¶ 20,533T

Pension Benefit Guaranty Corporation: Proposed rule: Terminations: Single-employer plan: Guaranteed benefits: Lump sum payments.—The PBGC has issued proposed regulations to increase the maximum value of benefits payable by the PBGC as a lump sum from $3,500 to $5,000. ERISA Sec. 203(e), which specifies the maximum amount that a plan may pay in a single installment to a participant or a surviving spouse without their consent, was amended to increase the maximum value from $3,500 to $5,000. Accordingly, the PBGC has proposed to amend its regulations to increase various thresholds from $3,500 to $5,000.

The proposed regulations were published in the *Federal Register* on April 30, 1998 (63 FR 23693)

The regulations were finalized July 15, 1998 (63 FR 38305). The regulations are reproduced at ¶ 15,421F, ¶ 15,449U, ¶ 15,475A, ¶ 15,475C, ¶ 15,531A, ¶ 15,531D ¶ 15,715G, ¶ 15,715H, ¶ 15,715I. The preamble is reproduced at ¶ 24,186.

¶ 20,533U

PWBA proposed regulations: Pension and welfare benefit plans: Summary plan descriptions (SPDs).—The Pension and Welfare Benefits Administration (PWBA) has proposed regulations that would change ERISA's summary plan description (SPD) requirements for pension and welfare benefit plans. These changes would clarify the information that must be included in a group health plan SPD and would require the SPD to identify whether the plan is intended to comply with ERISA Sec. 404(c), if it is a pension plan, or ERISA Sec. 733(a), if it is a welfare plan. These changes would also require that SPDs include a description of QDRO and QMCSO procedures, respectively; the authority of all ERISA plan sponsors to terminate, amend or eliminate benefits under the plan; and a description of the rights and obligations of participants and beneficiaries on termination, amendment or elimination of benefits.

The proposed regulations and preamble, were published in the *Federal Register* on September 9, 1998 (63 FR 48376), are reproduced below.

The PWBA has extended the deadline for comments to December 9, 1998 (63 FR 58335, October 30, 1998).

The regulations were finalized November 21, 2000 (65 FR 70225). The regulations are reproduced at ¶ 14,223, ¶ 14,225 and ¶ 14,429B. The preamble is reproduced at ¶ 24,208.

¶ 20,533V

Proposed rules: Pension and Welfare Benefits Administration: Employee Retirement Income Security Act of 1974; Rules and Regulations for Administration and Enforcement; Claims Procedure.—The Pension and Welfare Benefits Administration has issued proposed regulations revising the minimum requirements for benefit claims procedures of employee benefit plans covered by Title I of the Employee Retirement Income Security Act of 1974. The proposed regulations establish new standards for the processing of group health disability, pension, and other employee benefit plan claims filed by participants and beneficiaries.

For group health plans and certain plans providing disability benefits, the new standards are intended to ensure more timely benefit determinations, improved access to information on which a benefit determination is made, and greater assurance that participants and beneficiaries will be afforded a full and fair review of denied claims.

The proposed regulations were published in the *Federal Register* on September 9, 1998 (63 FR 48390).

The regulations were finalized November 21, 2000 (65FR 70246). The regulations are reproduced at ¶ 14,931. The preamble is reproduced at ¶ 24,209.

¶ 20,533W

PBGC: Proposed Rule: Valuation of Benefits: Use of Single Set of Assumptions for All Benefits.—The PBGC is proposing an amendment to its regulations to provide for the use of a single, modified version of its annuity assumptions for allocating assets to lump-sum and annuity benefits. Use of the modified version will be implemented some time after the year 2000. Existing lump-sum assumptions will be used at least through the year 2000.

The proposed rule was published in the *Federal Register* on October 26, 1998 (63 FR 57229) and is reproduced below.

The regulations were finalized on March 17, 2000 (65 FR 14751, 14753). The regulations are reproduced at ¶ 15,421F, ¶ 15,424C, ¶ 15,475A—15,475C, ¶ 15,475E—15,475G and ¶ 15,530B. The preamble is reproduced at ¶ 24,202.

¶ 20,533X

PWBA: Annual reporting regulations: Form 5500 series: Proposed revisions.—The PWBA has issued proposed amendments to ERISA's annual reporting and disclosure requirements. The amendments are necessary to ensure that the regulations conform to the revisions to the annual return/report forms in the Form 5500 series that employee pension and welfare benefit plan administrators are required to file.

The proposed amendments were published in the *Federal Register* on December 10, 1998 (63 FR 68370).

The regulations were finalized on April 19, 2000 (65 FR 21067). The regulations are reproduced at ¶ 14,231A, ¶ 14,231B, ¶ 14,231C, ¶ 14,231D, ¶ 14,231E, ¶ 14,231F, ¶ 14,231I, ¶ 14,231J, ¶ 14,231K, ¶ 14,231L, ¶ 14,247A, ¶ 14,247U, ¶ 14,247W, ¶ 14,247X, ¶ 14,247Z and ¶ 14,249H. The preamble is reproduced at ¶ 24,206.

¶ 20,533Y

PWBA: Proposed rules: Electronic technology: Communication and recordkeeping.—The PWBA has issued proposed rules addressing electronic communications of certain information by employee benefit plans and minimum standards for maintenance and retention of employee benefit records in electronic form.

The proposed rules were published in the *Federal Register* on January 28, 1999 (64 FR 4505). The regulations were finalized on April 9, 2002 (67 FR 17264) and are reproduced at ¶ 14,249 and ¶ 14,270B.

¶ 20,533T

¶ 20,533Z

PBGC: Proposed rules: Premium payments: Late payment penalty: Safe harbors.—The PBGC has issued proposed regulations which would expand current safe-harbor rules regarding the payment of premiums. The goal of the proposed rules is to expand the existing safe harbors (CCH PENSION PLAN GUIDE ¶ 15,371G) and encourage self-correction of incorrect premium payments in three situations, which are outlined in detail in the full text below.

The proposed rules were published in the *Federal Register* on April 27, 1999 (64 FR 22589).

The regulations were finalized on November 26, 1999 (64 FR 66383). The regulations are reproduced at ¶ 15,371G. The preamble is reproduced at ¶ 24,190.

¶ 20,534

Proposed regulations: Equal Employment Opportunity Commission (EEOC): Age Discrimination in Employment Act (ADEA): Older Workers Benefit Protection Act (OWBPA): Severance pay: Waivers.—The EEOC has issued proposed regulations to address issues related to the United States Supreme Court's decision in *Oubre v. Entergy Operations, Inc.* (CCH ¶ 23,939T). Under the regulations, an individual alleging that a waiver agreement was not knowing and voluntary under the ADEA is not required to tender back any consideration received as a precondition for challenging that waiver agreement. As was the case in *Oubre v. Entergy Operations, Inc.*, consideration for such a waiver may include severance benefits or other employee benefits.

The proposed regulations were published in the *Federal Register* on April 23, 1999 (64 FR 19952).

The regulations were finalized on December 11, 2000 (65 FR 77438). The regulations are reproduced at ¶ 15,750K. The preamble is reproduced at ¶ 24,211.

¶ 20,534A

Proposed regulations: Summary plan descriptions (SPDs): Summaries of material modifications (SMMs): Plan descriptions.—The PWBA has issued proposed regulations to remove certain superseded regulations from the Code of Federal Regulations. The superseded regulations pertain to filing SPDs, SMMs and plan descriptions with the DOL. The Taxpayer Relief Act of 1997 created amendments to ERISA and these documents are no longer required to be filed with the DOL, but are to be made available to the DOL upon request.

The preamble and text of the proposed regulations reproduced below were published in the *Federal Register* on August 5, 1999 (64 FR 42792).

DEPARTMENT OF LABOR

Pension and Welfare Benefits Administration

29 CFR Parts 2520 and 2560

RIN 1210-AA66

Removal of Superseded Regulations Relating to Plan Descriptions and Summary Plan Descriptions, and Other Technical Conforming Amendments

AGENCY: Pension and Welfare Benefits Administration, Department of Labor.

ACTION: Notice of Proposed Rulemaking.

SUMMARY: This document sets forth a proposed rule that would remove certain provisions from the Code of Federal Regulations (CFR) that were superseded, in whole or in part, by amendments of the Employee Retirement Income Security Act of 1974 (ERISA) enacted as part of the Taxpayer Relief Act of 1997 (TRA '97). These TRA '97 amendments eliminated the requirements that plan administrators file summary plan descriptions (SPDs) and summaries of material modifications (SMMs) with the Department of Labor (Department). The amendments also eliminated all requirements pertaining to plan descriptions. In addition to removing superseded regulations from the CFR, this proposed rule would make miscellaneous technical amendments to the CFR designed to correct affected cross-references.

DATES: Written comments concerning the proposed regulation must be received by October 4, 1999.

ADDRESSES: Written comments (preferably three copies) should be sent to: Office of Regulations and Interpretations, Room N-5669, Pension and Welfare Benefits Administration, U.S. Department of Labor, 200 Constitution Avenue, NW, Washington, DC 20210; Attention: Proposed SPD/Plan Description Regulations. All submissions will be open to public inspection at the Public Documents Room, Pension and Welfare Benefits Administration, Room N-5638, 200 Constitution Avenue, NW, Washington, DC.

FOR FURTHER INFORMATION CONTACT: Jeffrey J. Turner, Office of Regulations and Interpretations, Pension and Welfare Benefits Administration, U.S. Department of Labor, (202) 219-8671 (not a toll-free number).

SUPPLEMENTARY INFORMATION:

Overview

TRA '97 amended sections 101(b), 102, and 104(a)(1) of ERISA to eliminate the requirements that plan administrators file SPDs, SMMs, and plan descriptions with the Department.[1] TRA '97 also amended section 104(b) of ERISA to eliminate the requirement that plan administrators furnish plan descriptions to participants and beneficiaries. These statutory amendments superseded, in whole or in part, the Department's regulations that implemented the SPD, SMM, and plan description filing requirements. This proposed rule would remove those superseded regulations from the CFR.[2] This proposed rule also would make several technical conforming amendments to reflect the fact that regulatory relief from certain plan description, SPD, and SMM requirements is no longer needed in light of TRA '97 and to correct affected regulatory and statutory cross-references in parts 2520 and 2560 of Chapter XXV of Title 29 of the CFR. A chart identifying each regulation that would be changed by this proposed rule is printed below.

Removal of Superseded Regulations

This proposed rule would remove, in whole or in part, the following superseded regulations from 29 CFR part 2520, which pertain to reporting and disclosure under ERISA. This proposed rule also would reserve certain removed sections of the CFR to preserve the continuity of codification in the CFR.

Regulations Superseded in Whole

This proposed rule would remove and reserve §§ 2520.102-1 and 2520.104a-2. These sections require plan administrators to file a plan description with the Department in accordance with §§ 101(b)(2) and 104(a)(1)(B) of ERISA.[3] They were superseded by paragraphs (a) and

---

[1] Prior to 1979, the administrator of an employee benefit plan subject to the provisions of Part 1 of Title I of ERISA was required to file with the Department a plan description (Form EBS-1) to satisfy the statutory filing requirements of section 104(a) and 29 CFR 2520.104a-2. *See* 41 FR 16957 (April 23, 1976). In 1979, the Department amended 29 CFR 2520.104a-2 (44 FR 31639 (June 1, 1979)), to provide that the administrator of an employee benefit plan would satisfy the plan description filing requirements of section 104(a)(1)(B) by filing with the Department a SPD and an updated SPD in accordance with section 104(a)(1)(C) and the regulations thereunder.

[2] Under a separate notice, the Department will promulgate proposed regulations to implement new sections 502(c)(6) and 104(a)(6) of ERISA. Section 502(c)(6) provides that

if, within 30 days of a request by the Department to a plan administrator for documents under section 104(a)(6), the plan administrator fails to furnish the material requested to the Department, the Department may assess a civil penalty against the plan administrator of up to $100 a day from the date of such failure, but in no event in excess of $1,000 per request. Section 104(a)(6) provides that the administrator of any employee benefit plan must furnish to the Department, upon request, any documents relating to the employee benefit plan, including but not limited to, the latest SPD, and the bargaining agreement, trust agreement, contract, or other instrument under which the plan is established or operated.

[3] *See supra* note 1.

(c) of § 1503 of TRA '97, which eliminated § § 101 (b) (2) and 104 (a) (1) (B) of ERISA.

This proposed rule would remove and reserve § 2520.104a-3. This section implements sections 101 (b) (1) and 104 (a) (1) (C) of ERISA, which require plan administrators to file with the Department a copy of any SPD that is required to be furnished to participants covered under the plan and beneficiaries receiving benefits under the plan. Section 2520.104a-3 was superseded by paragraphs (a) and (c) of section 1503 of TRA '97, which eliminated sections 101 (b) (1) and 104 (a) (1) (C) of ERISA.

This proposed rule would remove and reserve § § 2520.104a-4 and 2520.104a-7. These sections implement § § 101 (b) (3), 102 (a) (2), and 104 (a) (1) (D) of ERISA, which require plan administrators to file with the Department a copy of summaries of material modifications in the terms of the plan and summaries of any changes in the information required to be in the SPD. Sections 2520.104a-4 and 2520.104a-7 were superseded by paragraphs (a) and (c) of § 1503 of TRA '97, which eliminated § § 101 (b) (3), 102 (a) (2), and 104 (a) (1) (D) of ERISA.

Regulations Superseded in Part

This proposed rule would amend § 2520.104-20 to reflect the fact that certain of the reporting relief granted by that regulation is no longer needed in light of TRA '97. Specifically, § 2520.104-20 exempts certain unfunded or insured welfare plans with fewer than 100 participants from, among others, the requirements to file plan descriptions, SPDs, and SMMs with the Department. Inasmuch as plan descriptions, SPDs, and SMMs are no longer required to be filed under ERISA as amended by TRA '97, this proposed rule would amend § 2520.104-20(a) to remove the provisions that grant relief from such filing requirements. The amendments made by this proposed rule would not otherwise change the relief available in § 2520.104-20.

This proposed rule would similarly amend § 2520.104-21 to reflect the fact that the SPD, SMM, and plan description filing relief granted by that regulation is no longer needed in light of the TRA '97 elimination of those filing requirements. Specifically, § 2520.104-21 provides a limited exemption from, among others, the requirements to file SPDs, SMMs, and plan descriptions with the Department for welfare benefit plans that cover fewer than 100 participants at the beginning of the plan year, are part of a group insurance arrangement, and that otherwise satisfy the conditions of § 2520.104-21(b). This proposed rule would amend § 2520.104-21(a) by removing the provisions on SPDs, SMMs, and plan descriptions because these documents are no longer required to be filed under ERISA as amended by TRA '97. The amendments made by this proposed rule would not otherwise change the relief available in § 2520.104-21.[4]

This proposed rule would further amend § § 2520.104-20 and 2520.104-21 to reflect the fact that the need for relief under ERISA from the requirement to disclose plan descriptions was eliminated by TRA '97. These section exempt eligible welfare plans from the requirement to: (1) Furnish upon written request of any participant or beneficiary a copy of the plan description, and (2) make copies of the plan description available in the principle office of the administrator and such other places as may be necessary for examination by any participant or beneficiary. This proposed rule would amend § § 2520.104-20(a) (2) and (3) and 2520.104-21(a) (1) and (2) by removing the provisions on disclosing plan descriptions because plan descriptions are nolonger required to be furnished or made available under ERISA as amended by TRA '97.

This proposed rule would amend § § 2520.104-26 and 2520.104-27 to reflect the fact that the need for relief under ERISA from the requirement to file plan descriptions, SPDs, and SMMs was eliminated by TRA '97. These regulations provide certain unfunded dues financed welfare and pension plans maintained by employee organizations with a limited exemption from, among others, the requirement to file plan descriptions and a simplified option for complying with the filing and disclosure requirements applicable to SPDs. This proposed rule would amend § § 2520.104-26 and 2520.104-27 by removing the provisions on plan descriptions and would further amend § § 2520.104-26 and 2520.104-27 to remove the simplified option provisions for filing SPDs because plan descriptions and SPDs are no longer required to be filed with the Department under ERISA as amended by TRA '97. The proposal is not otherwise intended to change the relief available under these sections.

Technical Conforming Amendments

This proposal also would make technical changes that are needed to conform certain cross references in the CFR to sections of ERISA as amended by TRA '97. For example, § 2520.104a-5 refers to section 104 (a) (1) (A) of ERISA as the authority for the requirement to file annual reports with the Department. After TRA '97, the correct citation is to § 104 (a) (1) of ERISA. Similar technical changes are also being made to conform internal CFR cross references.

Effective Date

This regulation is proposed to be effective 60 days after publication of a final rule in the **Federal Register.** If adopted, the proposed amendments implementing TRA '97 would be applicable as of the August 5, 1997, effective date of section 1503 of TRA '97.

Quick Reference Chart

The chart below lists each section of 29 CFR parts 2520 and 2560 that would be affected by this proposed rule and includes a brief description of the proposed change.

QUICK REFERENCE CHART

CFR section(s)	Remove	Add	Reason(s)
2520.102-1	The whole section	"Reserved"	All "plan description" requirements eliminated from ERISA.
2520.102-4	The last sentence	Nothing	SPD filing requirement eliminated.
2520.103-1(a)	"section 104(a)(1)(A)"	"section 104(a)(1)"	Cross reference correction.
2520.103-5(a), (c)(1)(i), (c)(1)(iii), (c)(2)(ii), (c)(2)(iii), and (c)(3).	"section 104(a)(1)(A)"	"section 104(a)(1)"	Cross reference correction.
2520.103-12(a)	"section 104(a)(1)(A)"	"section 104(a)(1)"	Cross reference correction.
2520.104-4(a)	Last sentence	Nothing	SPD filing requirement eliminated.
2520.104-20(a) (introductory text)	"any of the following documents: Plan description, copy of summary plan description, description of material modification in the terms of a plan or change in the information required to be included in the plan description,".	Nothing	All "plan description" requirements eliminated from ERISA, SPD filing requirement eliminated, and SMM filing requirement eliminated.
2520.104-20(a)(2)	"plan description,"	Nothing	All "plan description" requirements eliminated from ERISA.
2520.104-20(a)(3)	"plan description and"	Nothing	All "plan description" requirements eliminated from ERISA.
2520.104-20(c)	"(section 104(a)(1))"	"(section 104(a)(6))"	Requirement to furnish documents to the Department upon request—moved to different paragraph of ERISA section 104.
2520.104-21(a) (introductory text)	"with the Secretary any of the following documents: Plan description, copy of summary plan description, description of material modification in the terms of a plan or change in the information required to be included in the plan description, and terminal report. In addition, the administrator of a plan exempted under this section:".	After the word file, add: "with the Secretary a terminal report or furnish upon written request of any participant or beneficiary a copy of any terminal report as required by section 104(b)(4) of the Act.".	All "plan description" requirements eliminated from ERISA, SPD filing requirement eliminated, and SMM filing requirement eliminated.

---

[4] *See* 63 FR 68370, 68388 (Dec. 10, 1998) (eliminating references to requirements to file plan descriptions, SPDs, and SMMs in § 2520.104-21-(d)(3) as part of proposed amendments to annual reporting regulations).

CFR section(s)	Remove	Add	Reason(s)
2520.104-21(a)(1)	All of (a)(1)	Nothing	All "plan description" requirements eliminated from ERISA.
2520.104-21(a)(2)	All of (a)(2)	Nothing	All "plan description" requirements eliminated from ERISA.
2520.104-21(c) (second parenthetical).	"section 104(a)(1)(A)"	"section 104(a)(1)"	Cross reference correction.
2520.104-21(c) (third parenthetical).	"section 104(a)(1)"	"section 104(a)(6)"	Requirement to furnish documents to the Department upon request—moved to different paragraph of ERISA section 104.
2520.104-23(b)(2)	"104(a)(1)"	"104(a)(6)"	Requirement to furnish documents to the Department upon request—moved to different paragraph of ERISA section 104.
2520.104-24(b)	"104(a)(1)"	104(a)(6)"	Requirement to furnish documents to the Department upon request—moved to different paragraph of ERISA section 104.
2520.104-25	"104(a)(1)"	"104(a)(6)"	Requirement to furnish documents to the Department upon request—moved to different paragraph of ERISA section 104.
2520.104-26(a)	All of paragraph (a), (a)(1), (a)(2), and (a)(3).	New paragraph (a), (a)(1), and (a)(2).	Paragraph (a) needed to be restructured to reflect the fact that all "plan description" requirements and the SPD filing requirement were eliminated from ERISA.
2520.104-27(a)	All of paragraph (a), (a)(1), (a)(2), and (a)(3).	New paragraph (a), (a)(1), and (a)(2).	Paragraph (a) needed to be restructured to reflect the fact that all "plan description" requirements and the SPD filing requirement were eliminated from ERISA.
2520.104-41(b)	"section 104(a)(1)(A)"	"section 104(a)(1)"	Cross reference correction.
2520.104-43(a)	"section 104(a)(1)(A)"	"section 104(a)(1)"	Cross reference correction.
2520.104-44(d)	"section 104(a)(1)(A)"	"section 104(a)(1)"	Cross reference correction.
2520.104a-2	Whole section	"Reserved"	All "plan description" requirements eliminated from ERISA.
2520.104a-3	Whole section	"Reserved"	SPD filing requirement eliminated.
2520.104a-4	Whole section	"Reserved"	SMM filing requirement eliminated.
2520.104a-5(a)	"section 104(a)(1)(A)"	"section 104(a)(1)"	Cross reference correction.
2520.104a-5(a)(1)	All text in paragraph (a)(1)	"Reserved"	Provision obsolete.
2520.104a-7	Whole section	"Reserved"	SMM filing requirement eliminated.
2520.104b-1(b)(3)	"plan description"	Nothing	All "plan description" requirements eliminated from ERISA.
2520.104b-3(f)	All of para. (f)	Nothing	Part of paragraph (f) was superseded by TRA '97 and the rest of the paragraph has become obsolete as a result of the removal of § 2520.104a-3 by this rule.
2520.104b-3(g)	All of para. (g)	Nothing	Paragraph (g) was superseded by TRA '97 and as a result of the removal of § 2520.104a-3 by this rule.
2560.502c-2(a)	"section 101(b)(4)"	"section 101(b)(1)"	Cross reference correction.

Executive Order 12866 Statement

Under Executive Order 12866, the Department must determine whether the regulatory action is "significant" and therefore subject to the requirements of the Executive Order and subject to review by the Office of Management and Budget (OMB). Under section 3(f), the order defines a "significant regulatory action" as an action that is likely to result in a rule: (1) Having an annual effect on the economy of $100 million or more, or adversely and materially affecting a sector of the economy, productivity, competition, jobs, the environment, public health or safety, or State, local or tribal governments or communities (also referred to as "economically significant"); (2) creating serious inconsistency or otherwise interfering with an action taken or planned by another agency; (3) materially altering the budgetary impacts of entitlement grants, user fees, or loan programs or the rights and obligations of recipients thereof; or (4) raising novel legal or policy issues arising out of legal mandates, the President's priorities, or the principles set forth in the Executive Order. Pursuant to the terms of the Executive Order, it has been determined that this action is not significant within the meaning of the Executive Order.

Paperwork Reduction Act

The rule being issued here is not subject to the requirements of the Paperwork Reduction Act of 1995 (44 U.S.C. 3501 *et seq.*) because it does not contain an "information collection request" as defined in 44 U.S.C. 3502(3).

Regulatory Flexibility Act

The Regulatory Flexibility Act, 5 U.S.C. 601 *et seq.*, requires each Federal agency to perform an initial regulatory flexibility analysis for all proposed rules unless the head of the agency certifies that the rule will not, if promulgated, have a significant economic impact on a substantial number of small entities. Small entities include small businesses, organizations, and governmental jurisdictions. Because this proposed rule would remove certain provisions of the CFR and make a number of technical amendments to the CFR designed to correct cross-references affected by amendments to ERISA enacted as part of TRA '97, the proposed rule would have no impact, independent of the statutory change eliminating the SPD and SMM filing requirements, on small plans. As a result, the undersigned certifies that this proposed rule, if promulgated, would not have a significant impact on a substantial number of small entities. The factual basis for this certification is the same regardless of whether one uses the definition of small entity found in regulations issued by the Small Business Administration (13 CFR 121.201) or one defines small entity, on the basis of section 104(a)(2) of ERISA, as an employee benefit plan with fewer than 100 participants.

Small Business Regulatory Enforcement Fairness Act

The proposed rule being issued here is subject to the provisions of the Small Business Regulatory Enforcement Fairness Act of 1996 (5 U.S.C. 801 *et seq.*) and, if finalized, will be transmitted to Congress and the Comptroller General for review. The rule is not a "major rule" as that term is defined in 5 U.S.C. 804, because it is not likely to result in: (1) An annual effect on the economy of $100 million or more; (2) a major increase in costs or prices for consumers, individual industries, or federal, State, or local government agencies, or geographic regions; or (3) significant adverse effects on competition, employment, investment, productivity, innovation, or on the ability of United States-based enterprises to compete with foreign-based enterprises in domestic or export markets.

Unfunded Mandates Reform Act

For purposes of the Unfunded Mandates Reform Act of 1995 (Pub. L. 104-4), as well as Executive Order 12875, this proposed rule does not include any Federal mandate that may result in expenditures by State, local, or tribal governments, and will not impose an annual burden of $100 million or more on the private sector.

Statutory Authority

This proposed rule is promulgated pursuant to the authority contained in section 505 of ERISA (Pub. L. 93-406, 88 Stat. 894, 29 U.S.C. 1135) and sections 101(b) and 104(a)(1) of ERISA, as amended, and under the Secretary of Labor's Order No. 1-87, 52 FR 13139, April 21, 1987.

List of Subjects

29 CFR Part 2520

Employee benefit plans, Employee Retirement Income Security Act, Group health plans, Pension plans, Welfare benefit plans.

29 CFR Part 2560

Claims, Employee benefit plans, Employee Retirement Income Security Act, Law enforcement, Pensions.

For the reasons set forth above, parts 2520 and 2560 of Chapter XXV of Title 29 of the Code of Federal Regulations are amended as follows:

PART 2520—RULES AND REGULATIONS FOR REPORTING AND DISCLOSURE

1. The authority citation for Part 2520 continues to read as follows:

Authority: Secs. 101, 102, 103, 104, 105, 109, 110, 111 (b) (2), 111(c), and 505, Pub. L. 93-406, 88 Stat. 840-52 and 894 (29 U.S.C. 1021-1025, 1029-31, and 1135); Secretary of Labor's Order No. 27-74, 13-76, 1-87, and Labor Management Services Administration Order 2-6.

Sections 2520.102-3, 2520.104b-1 and 2520.104b-3 also are issued under sec. 101(a), (c) and (g)(4) of Pub. L. 104-191, 110 Stat. 1936, 1939, 1951 and 1955 and, sec. 603 of Pub. L. 104-204, 110 Stat. 2935 (29 U.S.C. 1185 and 1191(c)).

2. Section 2520.102-1 is removed and reserved.

3. Revise section 2520.102-4 to read as follows:

§ 2520.102-4 Option for different summary plan descriptions.

In some cases an employee benefit plan may provide different benefits for various classes of participants and beneficiaries. For example, a plan amendment altering benefits may apply to only those participants who are employees of an employer when the amendment is adopted and to employees who later become participants, but not to participants who no longer are employees when the amendment is adopted. (See § 2520.104b-4). Similarly, a plan may provide for different benefits for participants employed at different plants of the employer, or for different classes of participants in the same plant. In such cases the plan administrator may fulfill the requirement to furnish a summary plan description to participants covered under the plan and beneficiaries receiving benefits under the plan by furnishing to each member of each class of participants and beneficiaries a copy of a summary plan description appropriate to that class. Each summary plan description so prepared shall follow the style and format prescribed in § 2520.102-2, and shall contain all information which is required to be contained in the summary plan description under § 2520.102-3. It may omit information which is not applicable to the class of participants or beneficiaries to which it is furnished. It should also clearly identify on the first page of the text the class of participants and beneficiaries for which it has been prepared and the plan's coverage of other classes. If the classes which the employee benefit plan covers are too numerous to be listed adequately on the first page of the text of the summary plan description, they may be listed elsewhere in the text so long as the first page of the text contains a reference to the page or pages in the text which contain this information.

4. Section 2520.103-1(a), introductory text, is amended by removing the term "section 104(a)(1)(A)" and adding, in its place, the term "section 104(a)(1)".

5. Section 2520.103-5 is amended by removing the term "section 104(a)(1)(A)" from paragraphs (a), introductory text, (c)(1)(i), (c)(1)(iii), (c)(2)(ii), (c)(2)(iii) and (c)(3) and adding, in their place, the term "section 104(a)(1)".

6. Section 2520.103-12 is amended by removing from paragraph (a) the term "section 104(a)(1)(A)" and adding, in its place, the term "section 104(a)(1)".

7. Revise paragraph (a) of § 2520.104-4 to read as follows:

§ 2520.104-4 Alternative method of compliance for certain successor pension plans.

(a) *General.* Under the authority of section 110 of the Act, this section sets forth an alternative method of compliance for certain successor pension plans in which some participants and beneficiaries not only have their rights set out in the plan, but also retain eligibility for certain benefits under the terms of a former plan which has been merged into the successor. This section is applicable only to plan mergers which occur after the issuance by the successor plan of the initial summary plan description under the Act. Under the alternative method, the plan administrator of the successor plan is not required to describe relevant provisions of merged plans in summary plan descriptions of the successor plan furnished after the merger to that class of participants and beneficiaries still affected by the terms of the merged plans.

* * * * *

8. Revise the introductory text in paragraph (a) and paragraphs (a)(2), (a)(3), and (c) of § 2520.104-20 to read as follows:

§ 2520.104-20 Limited exemption for certain small welfare plans.

(a) *Scope.* Under the authority of section 104(a)(3) of the Act, the administrator of any employee welfare benefit plan which covers fewer than 100 participants at the beginning of the plan year and which meets the requirements of paragraph (b) of this section is exempted from certain reporting and disclosure provisions of the Act. Specifically, the administrator of such plan is not required to file with the Secretary an annual or terminal report. In addition, the administrator of a plan exempted under this section—

* * * * *

(2) Is not required to furnish upon written request of any participant or beneficiary a copy of the annual report and any terminal report, as required by section 104(b)(4) of the Act;

(3) Is not required to make copies of the annual report available for examination by any participant or beneficiary in the principal office of the administrator and such other places as may be necessary, as required by section 104(b)(2) of the Act.

(b) * * *

(c) *Limitations.* This exemption does not exempt the administrator of an employee benefit plan from any other requirement of Title I of the Act, including the provisions which require that plan administrators furnish copies of the summary plan description to participants and beneficiaries (section 104(b)(1)) and furnish certain documents to the Secretary of Labor upon request (section 104(a)(6)), and which authorize the Secretary of Labor to collect information and data from employee benefit plans for research and analysis (section 513).

* * * * *

9. Amend § 2520.104-21 by revising paragraphs (a) and (c) to read as follows:

§ 2520.104-21 Limited exemption for certain group insurance arrangements.

(a) *Scope.* Under the authority of section 104(a)(3) of the Act, the administrator of any employee welfare benefit plan which covers fewer than 100 participants at the beginning of the plan year and which meets the requirements of paragraph (b) of this section is exempted from certain reporting and disclosure provisions of the Act. Specifically, the administrator of such plan is not required to file with the Secretary a terminal report or furnish upon written request of any participant or beneficiary a copy of any terminal report as required by section 104(b)(4) of the Act.

* * * * *

(c) *Limitations.* This exemption does not exempt the administrator of an employee benefit plan from any other requirement of title I of the Act, including the provisions which require that plan administrators furnish copies of the summary plan description to participants and beneficiaries (section 104(b)(1)), file an annual report with the Secretary of Labor (section 104(a)(1)) and furnish certain documents to the Secretary of Labor upon request (section 104(a)(6)), and authorize the Secretary of Labor to collect information and data from employee benefit plans for research and analysis (section 513).

* * * * *

10. Section 2520.104-23 is amended by removing from paragraph (b)(2) the term "104(a)(1)" and adding, in its place, the term "104(a)(6)".

11. Section 2520.104-24 is amended by removing from paragraph (b) the term "104(a)(1)" and adding, in its place, the term "104(a)(6)".

12. Section 2520.104-25 is amended by removing the term "104(a)(1)" and adding, in its place, the term "104(a)(6)".

13. In § 2520.104-26, revise paragraph (a) to read as follows:

§ 2520.104-26 Limited exemption for certain unfunded dues financed welfare plans maintained by employee organizations.

(a) *Scope.* Under the authority of section 104(a)(3) of the Act, a welfare benefit plan that meets the requirements of paragraph (b) of this section is exempted from the provisions of the Act that require filing with the Secretary an annual report and furnishing a summary annual report to participants and beneficiaries. Such plans may use a simplified method of reporting and disclosure to comply with the requirement to furnish a summary plan description to participants and beneficiaries, as follows:

(1) In lieu of filing an annual report with the Secretary or distributing a summary annual report, a filing is made of Report Form LM-2 or LM-3, pursuant to the LMRDA and regulations thereunder, and

(2) In lieu of a summary plan description, the employee organization constitution or by-laws may be furnished in accordance with § 2520.104b-2 to participants and beneficiaries together with any supplement to such document necessary to meet the requirements of §§ 2520.102-2 and 2520.102-3.

* * * * *

14. In § 2520.104-27, revise paragraph (a) to read as follows:

§ 2520.104-27 Alternative method of compliance for certain unfunded dues financed pension plans maintained by employee organizations.

(a) *Scope.* Under the authority of section 110 of the Act, a pension benefit plan that meets the requirements of paragraph (b) of this section is exempted from the provisions of the Act that require filing with the Secretary an annual report and furnishing a summary annual report to participants and beneficiaries. Such plans may use a simplified method of reporting and disclosure to comply with the requirement to furnish a summary plan description to participants and beneficiaries, as follows:

(1) In lieu of filing an annual report with the Secretary or distributing a summary annual report, a filing is made of Report Form LM-2 or LM-3, pursuant to the LMRDA and regulations thereunder, and

(2) In lieu of a summary plan description, the employee organization constitution or by-laws may be furnished in accordance with § 2520.104b-2 to participants and beneficiaries together with any supplement to such document necessary to meet the requirements of §§ 2520.102-2 and 2520.102-3.

* * * * *

15. Section 2520.104-41 is amended by removing from paragraph (b) the term "section 104(a)(1)(A)" and adding, in its place, the term "section 104(a)(1)".

16. Section 2520.104-43 is amended by removing from paragraph (a) the term "section 104(a)(1)(A)" and adding, in its place, "section 104(a)(1)".

17. Section 2520.104-44 is amended by removing from paragraph (d) the term "section 104(a)(1)(A)" and adding, in its place, "section 104(a)(1)".

18. Section 2520.104a-2 is removed and reserved.

19. Section 2520.104a-3 is removed and reserved.

20. Section 2520.104a-4 is removed and reserved.

21. Section 2520.104a-5 is amended by removing the term "section 104(a)(1)(A)" and adding, in its place, the term "section 104(a)(1)".

22. Section 2520.104a-5 is amended by removing and reserving paragraph (a)(1).

23. Section 2520.104a-7 is removed and reserved.

24. Section 2520.104b-1 is amended by removing from the second sentence of paragraph (b)(3) the term "plan description,".

25. In § 2520.104b-3 paragraphs (f) and (g) are removed and reserved.

PART 2560—RULES AND REGULATIONS FOR ADMINISTRATION AND ENFORCEMENT

26. The authority citation for part 2560 continues to read as follows:

Authority: Secs. 502, 505 of ERISA, 29 U.S.C. 1132, 1135, and Secretary's Order 1-87, 52 FR 13139 (April 21, 1987).

Section 2560.502-1 also issued under sec. 502(b)(2), 29 U.S.C. 1132(b)(2).

Section 2560.502i-1 also issued under sec. 502(i), 29 U.S.C. 1132(i).

Section 2560.503-1 also issued under sec. 503, 29 U.S.C. 1133.

§ 2560.502c-21 [Amended]

27. Section 2560.502c-2 is amended by removing from paragraph (a)(1) and (a)(2) the term "section 101(b)(4)" each time it appears and adding, in its place, the term "section 101(b)(1)".

Signed at Washington, D.C., this 28th day of July 1999.

Richard M. McGahey,

Assistant Secretary,

Pension and Welfare Benefits Administration,

Department of Labor.

[FR Doc. 99-19860 Filed 8-4-99; 8:45 am]

¶ 20,534B

Proposed regulations: Summary plan descriptions (SPDs): Summaries of material modifications (SMMs): Plan descriptions: Civil penalties: Liability.—The Taxpayer Relief Act of 1997 (TRA '97) created amendments to ERISA relating to filing of SPDs, SMMs and plan descriptions. Under TRA '97, these documents are no longer required to be filed with the DOL, but are to be made available to the DOL upon request. The PWBA has proposed civil penalties against administrators for a failure or refusal to provide plan documents to the DOL upon request. Administrators will be jointly and severally liable for all assessed penalties. The liability will be a personal liability of the administrator, not a liability of the plan.

The proposed regulations were published in the *Federal Register* on August 5, 1999 (64 FR 42797). The final regulations were published in the *Federal Register* on January 7, 2002 (67 FR 777) and are reproduced at ¶ 14,248G, ¶ 14,925E, and ¶ 14,928Q. The preamble to the final regulations is reproduced at ¶ 24,217.

ERISA Sec. 104 and ERISA Sec. 502.

¶ 20,534C

PWBA: Department of Health and Human Services (HHS): Proposed regulations: National Medical Support Notice: Qualified medical child support order (QMCSO): Group health plans.—The PWBA and HHS have jointly issued a proposed regulation that introduces a National Medical Support Notice (Notice) to be used by state agencies in enforcing health care coverage provisions of child support orders. The DOL and HHS developed this Notice pursuant to the Child Support Performance and Incentive Act of 1998 (CSPIA). This regulation would amend ERISA Sec. 609(a) and require administrators of group health plans to treat the Notice as a qualified medical child support order.

The preamble and text of the proposed regulations were published in the *Federal Register* on November 15, 1999 (64 FR 62054). The regulations were finalized December 27, 2000 (65 FR 82127), effective January 26, 2001. The regulations are reproduced at ¶ 15,047H and ¶ 15,047I. The preamble is reproduced at ¶ 24,212.

¶ 20,534D

PWBA: Proposed regulations: Small pension plans: Annual report: Form 5500: Independent qualified public accountant (IQPA): Audit: Waiver.—The PWBA has issued proposed regulations increasing the eligibility requirements for plans with 100 or fewer participants to qualify for a waiver of the annual examination and report of IQPA's. Under the proposed regulations, the PWBA is also requiring enhanced disclosure to participants and beneficiaries and increased bonding, under certain circumstances, as further conditions of eligibility for a waiver.

The preamble and text of the proposed regulations were published in the *Federal Register* on December 1, 1999 (64 FR 67436). The regulations were finalized October 19, 2000 (65 FR 62957), effective December 18, 2000. The regulations are reproduced at ¶ 14,247U and ¶ 14,247Z. The preamble is reproduced at ¶ 24,207.

¶ 20,534E

PWBA/DOL: Proposed regulations: Multiple employer welfare arrangements (MEWAs): Collective bargaining agreements.—The Department of Labor has issued proposed regulations setting forth criteria for the exclusion of certain welfare benefit plans from the definition of MEWAs. The criteria would be used to determine if an employee welfare benefit plan was established or maintained under one or more collective bargaining agreements, thereby triggering ERISA preemption.

The proposed regulations were published in the *Federal Register* on October 27, 2000 (65 FR 64481). The regulations were finalized April 9, 2003 (68 FR 17471). The regulations are reproduced at ¶ 14,139C. The preamble is reproduced at ¶ 24,231.

¶ 20,534F

PWBA/DOL: Proposed regulations: Administrative hearings: Multiple employer welfare arrangements (MEWAs): Collective bargaining agreements.—The Department of Labor has issued proposed regulations regarding administrative hearings, to accompany proposed regulations setting forth criteria for the exclusion of certain welfare benefit plans from state regulation. The hearings would only be available to plans against whom a state's jurisdiction or law has been asserted, and that are claiming ERISA preemption as collectively bargained plans, as opposed to being MEWAs.

The proposed regulations were published in the *Federal Register* on October 27, 2000 (65 FR 64498). The final regulations were published in the *Federal Register* on April 9, 2003 (68 FR 17484) and are effective June 9, 2003. The preamble to the final regulations is reproduced at ¶ 24,229; the final regulations are reproduced at ¶ 14,789Z-1 through ¶ 14,789Z-10.

¶ 20,534G

PBGC: Proposed regulations: Benefit payments: Amendment of current payments method.—The PBGC has issued proposed regulations to amend its current benefit method payment. The proposed amendments give participants more choices of annuity benefit forms, add rules regarding distribution of payments the PBGC owes to a participant at the time of death, and clarify what it means to be able to retire under plan provisions within Title IV of ERISA. The proposed regulations amend the PBGC's current regulations on Benefits Payable in Terminated Single-Employer Plans, Aggregate Limits on Guaranteed Benefits, and Allocation of Assets in Single-Employer Plans.

The proposed regulation was published in the *Federal Register* on December 26, 2000 (65 FR 81456).

The preamble to the final regulations, which was published in the *Federal Register* on April 8, 2002 (67 FR 16949), can be found at ¶ 24,219. The regulations are reproduced at ¶ 15,421C , ¶ 15,421E , ¶ 15,421F , ¶ 15,421G , ¶ 15,421H , ¶ 15,421I , ¶ 15,422 , ¶ 15,422D , ¶ 15,424 , ¶ 15,425 , ¶ 15,425A , ¶ 15,425B , ¶ 15,425C , ¶ 15,425D , ¶ 15,426 , ¶ 15,426A , ¶ 15,426B , ¶ 15,426C , ¶ 15,429M , ¶ 15,471A , and ¶ 15,472C .

ERISA Sec. 4022, ERISA Sec. 4022B, ERISA Sec. 4044.

¶ 20,534H

Pension and Welfare Benefits Administration (PWBA) proposed regulations: IRS: Bona fide wellness programs: Health Insurance Portability and Accountability Act of 1996 (HIPAA): Nondiscrimination requirements.—The PWBA, in conjunction with the IRS and the Department of Health and Human Services, has issued proposed regulations to establish and elucidate the meaning of "bona fide wellness program" with regard to nondiscrimination provisions of the Code and ERISA, as added by HIPAA.

The proposed regulations were published in the *Federal Register* on January 8, 2001 (66 FR 1421). The IRS's proposed regulations were at ¶ 20,255. The regulations were finalized December 13, 2006 (71 FR 75014). The final regulations are reproduced at ¶ 15,050A-1 (ERISA Reg. Sec. 2590.702). The preamble to the final regulations is at ¶ 23,240.

¶ 20,534I

PBGC: Proposed regulations: Penalties: Late payments: Information penalty: Reasonable cause: Aggravating and mitigating factors.—The PBGC has issued proposed regulations concerning the assessment of penalties against a plan for late payments or failing to provide certain notices or other material information that is required under ERISA Sec. 4071. The proposed regulations state that penalties for late payments may be waived "for reasonable cause" and that the PBGC may take "aggravating and mitigating factors" into account when assessing an information penalty.

The proposed regulations reproduced below were published in the *Federal Register* on January 12, 2001 (66 FR 2856). The portion of the proposed regulations concerning premium payment penalty waivers was finalized on November 17, 2006 (71 FR 66867). The preamble to the final regulations is reproduced at ¶ 24,252. The final regulations are at ¶ 15,371G (Reg. §4007.8) and ¶ 15,373 (Appendix to Part 4007). The portion of the proposed regulations that amends the PBGC's administrative review rules to make them applicable to assessments for failure to timely provide certain notices was finalized on April 16, 2012 (77 FR 22488). The preamble to the final regulations is reproduced at ¶ 24,311. The final regulations are at ¶ 15,331 (Reg. §4003.1).

Federal Register Volume 66, Number 9 (Friday, January 12, 2001)]

[Proposed Rules]

[Pages 2856-2866]

From the Federal Register Online via the Government Printing Office [*www.gpo.gov*]

[FR Doc No: 01-686]

PENSION BENEFIT GUARANTY CORPORATION

29 CFR Parts 4003, 4007, and 4071

RIN 1212-AA95

Assessment of and Relief From Penalties

AGENCY: Pension Benefit Guaranty Corporation.

ACTION: Proposed rule.

SUMMARY: The PBGC has issued a number of policy statements about penalties over the last few years. Some of these policy statements have been incorporated into the PBGC's regulations. For the convenience of the public, the PBGC is now proposing to codify in its regulations an expanded version of the remaining penalty policy statements. Among other things, this expanded version of the PBGC's penalty policies would explain in general terms the meaning of "reasonable cause" for penalty waivers and the guidelines for assessing penalties under ERISA section 4071.

DATES: Comments must be received on or before March 13, 2001.

ADDRESSES: Comments may be mailed to the Office of the General Counsel, Pension Benefit Guaranty Corporation, 1200 K Street, NW., Washington, DC 20005-4026, or delivered to Suite 340 at the above address. Comments also may be sent by Internet e-mail to *reg.comments@pbgc.gov*. Comments will be available for inspection at the PBGC's Communications and Public Affairs Department in Suite 240 at the above address during normal business hours.

FOR FURTHER INFORMATION CONTACT: Harold J. Ashner, Assistant General Counsel, or Deborah C. Murphy, Attorney, Pension Benefit Guaranty Corporation, Office of the General Counsel, Suite 340, 1200 K Street, NW., Washington, DC 20005-4026, 202-326-4024. (For TTY/TTD users, call the Federal relay service toll-free at 1-800-877-8339 and ask to be connected to 202-326-4024.)

SUPPLEMENTARY INFORMATION: The PBGC administers the pension plan termination insurance program under Title IV of the Employee Retirement Income Security Act of 1974 (ERISA). When a single-employer plan terminates without sufficient assets to provide all benefits, the PBGC steps in to ensure that participants and beneficiaries receive their plan benefits, subject to certain legal limits. The PBGC also provides financial assistance to multiemployer plans that become unable to pay benefits.

ERISA and the PBGC's regulations require the payment of premiums to the PBGC and the providing of certain information to the PBGC and to other persons. To promote the effective operation of the insurance program under Title IV, ERISA authorizes the PBGC to assess penalties if premiums are paid late and if certain notices and other material information are not timely provided. (See ERISA sections 4007 and 4071 and the PBGC's regulations on Payment of Premiums (29 CFR Part 4007) and Penalties for Failure to Provide Certain Notices or Other Material Information (29 CFR Part 4071).) The PBGC has published four notices in the Federal Register since mid-1995 describing its penalty policies under sections 4007 and 4071.

This proposed rule would expand and codify the policies described in two of those notices: those published July 18, 1995 (60 FR 36837), and December 17, 1996 (61 FR 66338). (The 1995 notice in turn replaced an earlier penalty policy notice published March 3, 1992 (at 57 FR 7605).) The policy guidance would be placed in appendices to the premium payment regulation and the regulation on Penalties for Failure to Provide Certain Notices or Other Material Information. In addition, the PBGC's regulation on Rules for Administrative Review of Agency Decisions (29 CFR Part 4003) would be amended to cover penalties assessed under section 4071.

The policies described in the other two notices have already been codified in PBGC regulations.

The PBGC's regulations on Termination of Single-Employer Plans (29 CFR Part 4041) and Missing Participants (29 CFR Part 4050) reflect the PBGC's Statement of Policy published March 14, 1997 (at 62 FR 12521), announcing penalty relief for late filing of post-distribution certifications in connection with a plan termination.

Section 4007.8 of the PBGC's premium payment regulation reflects the PBGC's Statement of Policy published December 2, 1996 (at 61 FR 63874), announcing a new policy regarding the rate at which premium penalties accrue (1 percent or 5 percent per month depending on whether the premium underpayment is self-corrected).

Thus, once the amendments in this rule became effective, all of the PBGC's penalty policies under sections 4007 and 4071 would be in the Code of Federal Regulations. (This rule does not deal with penalties under ERISA section 4302, which applies only to multiemployer plans.)

This rule would not affect the use of any other remedies available to the PBGC and would not address the settlement of legal disputes involving penalties, either alone or in the context of other legal issues.

Compliance With Rulemaking Guidelines

The PBGC has determined that this action is not a "significant regulatory action" under the criteria set forth in Executive Order 12866.

Although the PBGC is publishing this rule as a proposed rule, the rule is not subject to notice and comment rulemaking requirements under section 553 of the Administrative Procedure Act because it deals only with general statements of PBGC policy and with PBGC procedural rules. Because no general notice of proposed rulemaking is required, the Regulatory Flexibility Act does not apply. See 5 U.S.C. 601(2), 603, 604.

List of Subjects

29 CFR Part 4003

Administrative practice and procedure, Organization and functions (Government agencies), Pension insurance, Pensions.

29 CFR Part 4007

Penalties, Pension insurance, Pensions, Reporting and recordkeeping requirements.

29 CFR Part 4071

Penalties.

For the reasons given above, the PBGC proposes to amend 29 CFR parts 4003, 4007, and 4071 as follows.

PART 4003—RULES FOR ADMINISTRATIVE REVIEW OF AGENCY DECISIONS

1. The authority citation for part 4003 continues to read as follows:

Authority: 29 U.S.C. 1302(b)(3).

2. In Sec. 4003.1, paragraph (a) is amended by removing the words "(b)(1) through (b)(4)" and adding in their place the words "(b)(1) through (b)(5)" and by removing the words "(b)(5) through (b)(10)" and adding in their place the words "(b)(6) through (b)(11)"; paragraphs (b)(5) through (b)(10) are redesignated as paragraphs (b)(6) through (b)(11); and a new paragraph (b)(5) is added to read as follows:

Sec. 4003.1 Purpose and scope.

* * * * *

(b) Scope. * * *

* * * * *

(5) Determinations with respect to penalties under section 4071 of ERISA.

* * * * *

PART 4007—PAYMENT OF PREMIUMS

3. The authority citation for part 4007 continues to read as follows:

Authority: 29 U.S.C. 1302(b)(3), 1303(a), 1306, 1307.

4. In Sec. 4007.8, the introductory text of paragraph (a) is amended by removing the words "The charge will be based on" and adding in their place the words "The amount determined under this paragraph (a) will be based on"; and paragraphs (c) and (d) are revised to read as follows:

Sec. 4007.8 Late payment penalty charges.

* * * * *

(c) Reasonable cause waivers. The PBGC will waive all or part of a late payment penalty charge if the PBGC determines that there is reasonable cause for the late payment. Policy guidelines for applying the "reasonable cause" standard are in Secs. 32 through 35 of the Appendix to this part.

(d) Other waivers. The PBGC may waive all or part of a late payment penalty charge in other circumstances without regard to whether there is reasonable cause. Policy guidelines for waivers without reasonable cause are in Sec. 31(b)(1), (b)(3), and (b)(4) of the Appendix to this part.

* * * * *

5. An appendix is added to part 4007 to read as follows:

Appendix to Part 4007—Policy Guidelines on Penalties

Sec.

General Provisions

1 What is the purpose of this Appendix?

2 What defined terms are used in this Appendix?

3 What is the purpose of a premium penalty?

Procedures

11 What are the basic rules for assessing and reviewing premium penalties?

12 What should I know about preliminary notices of premium penalties?

13 What should I know about premium penalty determinations?

14 What should I know about review of premium penalty determinations?

Premium Penalty Assessment

21 What are the rules for assessing a premium penalty?

22 How do premium penalties apply to small plans?

Waiver Standards

31 What are the standards for waiving a premium penalty?

32 What is "reasonable cause"?

33 What kinds of facts does the PBGC consider in determining whether there is reasonable cause for a failure to pay a premium?

34 What are some situations that might justify a "reasonable cause" waiver?

35 What are some situations that might justify a partial "reasonable cause" waiver?

General Provisions

Section 1 What Is the Purpose of this Appendix?

This appendix sets forth principles and guidelines that we intend to follow in assessing, reviewing, and waiving premium penalties. However, this is only general policy guidance. Our action in each case is guided by the facts and circumstances of the case.

Section 2 What Defined Terms Are Used in This Appendix?

The following terms are defined in part 4001 of this chapter: contributing sponsor, ERISA, PBGC, person, plan, and plan administrator. In addition, in this appendix:

(a) Premium penalty means a penalty under ERISA section 4007 and Sec. 4007.8 of this part for failing to pay all or part of a premium on time.

(b) Waiver means reduction or elimination of a premium penalty that is being or has been assessed.

(c) We means the PBGC.

(d) You means (according to the context) —

(1) A plan administrator, contributing sponsor, or other person, if —

(i) The person's action or inaction may be the basis for a premium penalty assessment,

(ii) The person may be required to pay the premium penalty, or

(iii) The person is requesting review of the premium penalty; or

(2) An employee or agent of, or advisor to, any of these persons.

Section 3 What Is the Purpose of a Premium Penalty?

The basic purpose of a premium penalty is to encourage you to pay premiums on time. Premium penalties should be fair, simple, effective, and easy to administer. Therefore,—

(a) We assess a lower (one percent) premium penalty if you correct a premium underpayment yourself before we issue a written notice that there is or may be a premium delinquency;

(b) We assess a higher (five percent) premium penalty if you do not self-correct before we issue a notice; and

(c) We waive premium penalties, in whole or in part, if there is reasonable cause or in other appropriate circumstances.

Procedures

Section 11 What Are the Basic Steps for Assessing and Reviewing Premium Penalties?

(a) Overview. There are typically three steps in the premium penalty assessment and review process:

(1) A preliminary notice (discussed in Sec. 12), which gives you an opportunity to submit information relating to the premium penalty assessment, or to simply pay the amount owed;

(2) A premium penalty determination (discussed in Sec. 13) that assesses the premium penalty; and

(3) A review of the premium penalty determination (discussed in Sec. 14).

(b) Relationship to premium procedures. (1) When we assess a premium penalty for a late premium payment, the late payment often has already been made. However, if the premium has not been paid when we assess a premium penalty, we will generally assess and review the premium (and any related interest) at the same time as we assess and review the penalty. Differences in premium penalty procedures depending on whether the premium has or has not been paid are noted in Secs. 12 and 13.

(2) A premium penalty stops accruing when the premium is paid.

(c) Debt collection. Our regulation on Debt Collection (29 CFR Part 4903) provides that we may collect amounts that you owe to us (such as premium penalties) by reducing other amounts that the government owes to you (such as tax refunds). Procedures under our debt collection regulation may run separately or together with the premium penalty assessment and review procedures.

(d) Decision-making standards and guidelines. At each stage of the premium penalty assessment and review process, we evaluate the circumstances by the same standards and apply the same guidelines in deciding whether to assess or waive a premium penalty and how much the premium penalty should be. However, we may have more information when we review a premium penalty than we had when we originally assessed it, and that may make our decision on review different from our original premium penalty determination.

(e) Providing information to the PBGC. (1) It is your responsibility to raise any facts and issues that you want us to consider in making premium penalty assessment or waiver decisions and to support your contentions with documentation such as correspondence and police, fire, or insurance reports. If you want us to consider information that you believe we already have in connection with another case, you should identify the information specifically enough so that we can determine whether we have the information, locate it in our files, and review it.

(2) Since premium penalties are assessed for paying a premium late, it is important that you bring to our attention any information or arguments that tend to show that you were not required to pay a premium or that you paid the premium on time.

(f) Terminology. There is a slight difference between the terminology we use in this appendix and the terminology we use in our regulation on Rules for Administrative Review of Agency Decisions (29 CFR Part 4003), which governs our issuance and review of premium penalty determinations:

(1) "Initial determination" in the administrative review regulation means the same as "premium penalty determination" in this appendix, and

(2) "Reconsideration of an initial determination" in the administrative review regulation means the same as "review of a premium penalty determination" in this appendix.

Section 12 What Should I Know About Preliminary Notices of Premium Penalties?

Before we make a premium penalty determination, we want you to have an opportunity to give us any information you think we should consider. In most cases, therefore, we send a preliminary notice to tell you that we intend to assess a premium penalty and the reason for the premium penalty. (In some cases, we may skip this preliminary step— for example, if we contact you by telephone to discuss the matter or if we need to make the assessment quickly in order to preserve our right to collect the premium penalty in court.) You may respond to a preliminary notice by submitting any information you want us to consider before we make a premium penalty determination. The preliminary notice will state the time within which you should respond (typically 30 days).

(a) If premium already paid. If, by the time we issue a preliminary notice stating that we intend to assess a premium penalty, you have already paid the late premium, the notice ordinarily tells you the amount of the premium penalty that we intend to assess. (The notice also ordinarily tells you the amount of any interest due on the late premium.) If you pay the amount stated in the preliminary notice without requesting relief, that is the end of the matter.

(b) If premium not already paid. If, by the time we issue a preliminary notice stating that we intend to assess a premium penalty, you have not already paid the late premium, the notice ordinarily tells you the amount of premium due and the amount of the premium penalty that has accrued up through the date of the preliminary notice. (The preliminary notice also ordinarily tells you the amount of interest that has accrued on the late premium up through the date of the preliminary notice.) If you pay the amount stated in the preliminary notice within 30 days after the date of the preliminary notice without requesting relief, that is the end of the matter. If you do not pay the amount of unpaid premium within 30 days after the date of the preliminary notice, the premium penalty will continue to accrue (subject to the premium penalty cap).

Section 13 What Should I Know About Premium Penalty Determinations?

As the second step in the premium penalty assessment and review process—after a preliminary notice—we make a premium penalty determination (unless, in response to the preliminary notice, you pay the full premium penalty without requesting relief). (If we skip the preliminary notice step, the premium penalty assessment is the first step in the process.) The premium penalty determination notifies you of the reason for the premium penalty (even if we have already issued a preliminary notice stating the reason) and takes into account any information you may have submitted to us in response to a preliminary notice. We also tell you when and where to send your payment, and we tell you about requesting review of the premium penalty determination. (Complete rules for premium penalty determinations and for requesting review are in part 4003 of this chapter.)

(a) If premium already paid. If, by the time we issue a premium penalty determination, you have already paid the late premium, the determination tells you the amount of the premium penalty that we are assessing (taking into account any waiver of all or part of the premium penalty) and how we determined the amount of the premium penalty. (The premium penalty determination also ordinarily tells you the amount of any interest due on the late premium.) If you pay the amount stated in the premium penalty determination without requesting review, that is the end of the matter.

(b) If premium not already paid. If, by the time we issue a premium penalty determination, you have not already paid the late premium, the premium penalty determination tells you the amount of premium due and the amount of the premium penalty that has accrued up through the date of the premium penalty determination. (The premium penalty determination also ordinarily tells you the amount of interest that has accrued on the late premium up through the date of the premium penalty determination.) If you pay the amount stated in the premium penalty determination within 30 days after the date of the premium penalty determination without requesting review, that is the end of the matter. If you do not pay the amount of unpaid premium within 30 days after the date of the premium penalty determination, the premium penalty will continue to accrue (subject to the premium penalty cap).

Section 14 What Should I Know About Review of Premium Penalty Determinations?

(a) Timing. (1) General rule. In general, you must request review of a premium penalty determination within 30 days after the date of the determination; if you do not do so, the determination becomes effective, and we may take steps to collect the premium penalty. In addition, you may not be able to raise in court some legal defenses that you might have against collection of the premium penalty, because you have failed to exhaust administrative remedies. (In some cases, the 30-day limitation for requesting review may be extended or waived. See Secs. 4003.4 and 4003.5 of the administrative review regulation. If we notify you that we may attempt to collect a debt resulting from a premium penalty determination by referring it for offset against federal payments that may be due you, you will have at least 60 days to request review. See Sec. 4003.32 of the administrative review regulation.)

(2) Determinations effective immediately. We may, in our discretion, make a premium penalty determination effective on the date we issue it—for example, if our ability to bring a collection action in court is about to be cut off by the statute of limitations. If we make a premium penalty determination effective immediately, you are not required to request review by us in order to exhaust your administrative remedies. This means that you have the right to raise legal defenses against collection of the premium penalty in court even if you do not request that we review the determination. (See Sec. 4003.22(b) of the administrative review regulation.) If you do request review by the PBGC, we may review the determination.

(b) Review of determination. If you request review of a premium penalty determination within the required time, we review the determi-

nation and notify you of the results of the review. This review takes into account any information you may have submitted to us in response to a preliminary notice or a premium penalty determination notice or with your request for review.

(c) Premium penalty accrual during review. Requesting review of a premium penalty does not make the premium penalty stop accruing. A premium penalty stops accruing on the date when you pay the premium or, if you pay the premium within 30 days after the date of a PBGC bill for the premium, on the date of the bill. In addition, if you request review of a premium penalty, we may waive the portion of the premium penalty that accrues during review if you make a non-frivolous argument that you were not required to pay the premium, as described in Sec. 31(b)(4) of this Appendix.

Premium Penalty Assessment

Section 21 What Are the Rules for Assessing a Premium Penalty?

The rules for assessing a premium penalty are in Sec. 4007.8 of this part. A premium penalty is assessed for failure to pay a premium on time. In general, the amount of a premium penalty is based on the number of months from the due date to the date of payment, subject to a floor of $25 and a ceiling of 100 percent of the unpaid premium. The premium penalty rate is generally—

(a) 1 percent per month (for all months) on any amount of unpaid premium that you pay on or before the date we issue a written notice that there is or may be a premium delinquency (e.g., a premium bill, a letter initiating a premium compliance review, or a letter questioning a failure to make a premium filing), or

(b) 5 percent per month (for all months) on any amount of unpaid premium that you pay after that date.

Section 22 How Do Premium Penalties Apply to Small Plans?

Since small plan premiums are generally lower than large plan premiums, premium penalties are also generally lower for small plans than for large plans. This is because premium penalties accrue (each month) as a percentage of your premium underpayment.

Waiver Standards

Section 31 What Are the Standards for Waiving a Premium Penalty?

(a) Facts and circumstances. In deciding whether to waive a premium penalty in whole or in part, we consider the facts and circumstances of each case.

(b) Waivers. (1) Provisions of law. We waive all or part of a premium penalty if a statute or regulation requires that we do so. For example, ERISA section 4007(b) and Sec. 4007.8(b) of this part provide for a waiver in certain circumstances involving business hardship; Sec. 4007.8(f) and (g) of this part provides for waivers if certain "safe harbor" tests are met; and Sec. 4007.8(e) of this part provides for a waiver of any premium penalty that accrues after the date of a premium bill if you pay the premium within 30 days after the date of the bill.

(2) Reasonable cause. We waive a premium penalty if you show reasonable cause for a failure to pay a premium on time. See Secs. 32 through 35 for guidelines on "reasonable cause" waivers. If there is reasonable cause for only part of a failure to pay a premium, we waive the premium penalty only for that part. In determining whether "reasonable cause" exists, we do not consider either—

(i) The likelihood or cost of collecting the premium penalty, or

(ii) The costs and risks of enforcing the premium penalty by litigation.

(3) Erroneous legal interpretations. We may waive all or part of a premium penalty if the failure to pay a premium on time that gives rise to the premium penalty is based on your reliance on an erroneous interpretation of the law.

(i) If you disclose the interpretation to us. If a failure to pay a premium on time results from your reliance on an erroneous interpretation of the law, we will waive a premium penalty that arises from the failure if you promptly and adequately call our attention to the interpretation and the relevant facts, and the erroneous interpretation is not frivolous. If the interpretation affects a filing that you make with us, you should call our attention to the interpretation with the filing. If you rely on the interpretation to justify not making a filing with us, you should call our attention to the interpretation in a notice submitted to us by the time and in the manner prescribed for the filing not made.

(ii) If you do not disclose the interpretation to us. If a failure to pay a premium on time results from your reliance on an erroneous interpretation of the law, and you do not promptly and adequately call our attention to the interpretation and the relevant facts, we may nevertheless waive a premium penalty if the weight of authority supporting the interpretation is substantial in relation to the weight of opposing authority and it is reasonable for you to rely on the interpretation.

(4) Pendency of review. If you request review of a premium penalty (as described in Sec. 14 of this Appendix), and you make a non-frivolous argument in your request for review that you were not required to pay the premium, we waive the portion of the premium penalty that accrues during the review process. (If you make a non-frivolous argument that you were not required to pay a portion of the premium, we apply this rule to that portion.)

(5) Other circumstances. We may waive all or part of a premium penalty in other circumstances if we determine that it is appropriate to do so. We intend to exercise this waiver authority only in narrow circumstances, primarily if we determine that assessing a premium penalty, or assessing the full amount of a premium penalty, would be inconsistent with the purposes of Title IV of ERISA. For example—

(i) We may waive all or part of a premium penalty if a premium underpayment reflected on a premium form is insignificant and is caused by an inadvertent mathematical error (such as a transposition of digits) on the form. In determining whether and to what extent to grant a waiver in a case of this kind, we consider such factors as how insignificant the underpayment is, whether you have a history of compliance, and whether the underpayment results from an isolated error rather than from a number of errors.

(ii) We may waive all or part of a premium penalty if the law changes shortly before the date a premium payment is due and the premium payment that you make by the due date would have been correct under the law as in effect before the change. In determining whether and to what extent to grant a waiver in a case of this kind, we consider such factors as the length of time between the change in the law and the premium due date, the nature and timing of any publicity given to the change in the law, the complexity of the legal issues, and your general familiarity with those issues.

(c) Action or inaction of outside parties. If an accountant, actuary, lawyer, pension consultant, or other individual or firm that is not part of your organization assists you in complying with PBGC requirements, we apply our waiver authority as if the outside individual or firm were part of your organization, as described in Sec. 32(c) of this Appendix.

Section 32 What Is "Reasonable Cause"?

(a) General rule. In general, there is "reasonable cause" for a failure to pay a premium on time to the extent that—

(1) The failure arises from circumstances beyond your control, and

(2) You could not avoid the failure by the exercise of ordinary business care and prudence.

(b) Overlooking legal requirements. Overlooking legal requirements does not constitute reasonable cause.

(c) Action or inaction of outside parties. In some cases an accountant, actuary, lawyer, pension consultant, or other individual or firm that is not part of your organization may assist you in complying with PBGC requirements. If the outside individual's or firm's action, inaction, or advice causes or contributes to a failure to pay a premium on time, our analysis is generally the same as if the outside individual or firm were part of your organization. (In the case of an outside individual who is part of a firm, we generally consider both the individual and the firm to be part of your organization.) Thus, if a failure to pay a premium on time arises from circumstances within the control of the outside individual or firm, or could be avoided by the exercise of ordinary business care and prudence by the outside individual or firm, there is generally no reasonable cause for the failure. The fact that you exercised care and prudence in selecting and monitoring the outside individual or firm is not a basis for a reasonable cause waiver. (However, you may have recourse against the outside individual or firm.)

(d) Size of organization. If an organization or one or more of its employees is responsible for taking action, the size of the organization may affect what ordinary business care and prudence would require. For example, ordinary business care and prudence would typically require a larger organization to establish more comprehensive backup procedures than a smaller organization for dealing with situations such as computer failure, the loss of important records, and the inability of an individual to carry out assigned responsibilities. Thus, there may be reasonable cause for a small organization's failure to pay a premium on time even though, if the organization were larger, the exercise of ordinary business care and prudence would have avoided the failure.

(e) Amount of premium underpayment. In general, the larger a premium, the more care and prudence you should use to make sure that you pay it on time. Thus, there may be reasonable cause for a small underpayment even though, under the same circumstances, we would conclude that a larger underpayment could have been avoided by the exercise of ordinary business care and prudence.

Section 33 What Kinds of Facts Does the PBGC Consider in Determining Whether There is Reasonable Cause for a Failure to Pay a Premium?

In determining whether a failure to pay a premium on time arose from circumstances beyond your control and whether you could have avoided the failure by the exercise of ordinary business care and prudence—and thus whether waiver of a premium penalty for reasonable cause is appropriate—we consider facts such as the following:

(a) What event or circumstance caused the underpayment and when the event happened or the circumstance arose. The dates you give should clearly correspond with the underpayment upon which the premium penalty is based.

(b) How that event or circumstance kept you from paying the premium on time. The explanation you give should relate directly to the failure to pay a premium that is the subject of the premium penalty.

(c) Whether the event or circumstance was beyond your control.

(d) Whether you could have anticipated the event or circumstance.

(e) How you responded to the event or circumstance, including what steps you took (and how quickly you took them) to pay the premium and how you conducted other business affairs. Knowing how you responded to the event or circumstance may help us determine what degree of business care and prudence you were capable of exercising during that period and thus whether the failure to pay the premium could or could not have been avoided by the exercise of ordinary business care and prudence.

Section 34 What Are Some Situations That Might Justify a "Reasonable Cause" Waiver?

The following examples illustrate some of the reasons often given for failures to pay premiums for which we may assess penalties. The situation described in each example may constitute reasonable cause, and each example lists factors we consider in determining whether to grant a premium penalty waiver for reasonable cause in a case of that kind.

(a) An individual with responsibility for taking action was suddenly and unexpectedly absent or unable to act. We consider such factors as the following: the nature of the event that caused the individual's absence or inability to act (for example, the resignation of the individual or the death or serious illness of the individual or a member of the individual's immediate family); the size of the organization and what kind of backup procedures it had to cope with such events; how close the event was to the deadline that was missed; how abrupt and unanticipated the event was; how the individual's absence or inability to act prevented compliance; how expensive it would have been to comply without the absent individual; whether and how other business operations and obligations were affected; how quickly and prudently a replacement for the absent individual was selected or other arrangements for compliance were made; and how quickly a replacement for the absent individual took appropriate action.

(b) A fire or other casualty or natural disaster destroyed relevant records or prevented compliance in some other way. We consider such factors as the following: the nature of the event; how close the event was to the deadline that was missed; how the event caused the failure to pay the premium; whether other efforts were made to get needed information; how expensive it would have been to comply; and how you responded to the event.

(c) You reasonably relied on erroneous oral or written advice given by a PBGC employee. We consider such factors as the following: whether there was a clear relationship between your situation and the advice sought; whether you provided the PBGC employee with adequate and accurate information; and whether the surrounding circumstances should have led you to question the correctness of the advice or information provided.

(d) You were unable to obtain information (including records and calculations) needed to comply. We consider such factors as the following: what information was needed; why the information was unavailable; when and how you discovered that the information was not available; what attempts you made to get the information or reconstruct it through other means; and how much it would have cost to comply.

Section 35 What Are Some Situations That Might Justify a Partial "Reasonable Cause" Waiver?

(a) Assume that a fire destroyed the records needed to compute a premium payment. If in the exercise of ordinary business care and prudence it should take you one month to reconstruct the records and pay the premium, but the payment was made two months late, it might be appropriate to waive that part of the premium penalty attributable to the first month the payment was late, but not the part attributable to the second month.

(b) Assume that a plan administrator underpaid the plan's flat-rate premium because of reasonable reliance on erroneous advice from a PBGC employee, and also underpaid the plan's variable-rate premium because the plan actuary used the wrong interest rate. A PBGC audit revealed both errors. The PBGC billed the plan for a premium penalty of $5,000—$1,000 for underpayment of the flat-rate premium and $4,000 for underpayment of the variable-rate premium. The plan administrator requested a waiver of the premium penalty. While the erroneous PBGC advice constituted reasonable cause for underpaying the flat-rate premium, there was no showing of reasonable cause for the error in the variable-rate premium. Therefore, we would waive only the part of the premium penalty based on underpayment of the flat-rate portion of the premium ($1,000).

PART 4071—PENALTIES FOR FAILURE TO PROVIDE CERTAIN NOTICES OR OTHER MATERIAL INFORMATION

6. The authority citation for part 4071 is revised to read as follows:

Authority: 28 U.S.C. 2461 note; 29 U.S.C. 1302(b)(3), 1371.

7. Section 4071.1 is amended by adding at the end of the section the following sentence:

Sec. 4071.1 Purpose and scope.

* * * This part also provides policy guidelines for assessing and reviewing penalties under ERISA section 4071.

8. A new Sec. 4071.4 and a new appendix are added to part 4071 to read as follows:

Sec. 4071.4 Assessment and review of penalties.

Policy guidelines for assessing, reviewing, and waiving penalties under ERISA section 4071 are in the Appendix to this part.

Appendix to Part 4071—Policy Guidelines on Penalties

Sec.

General Provisions

1 What is the purpose of this Appendix?

2 What defined terms are used in this Appendix?

3 What is the purpose of an information penalty?

Procedures

11 What are the basic rules for assessing and reviewing information penalties?

12 What should I know about preliminary notices of information penalties?

13 What should I know about information penalty determinations?

14 What should I know about review of information penalty determinations?

Information Penalty Assessment

21 Where can I find the general principles that the PBGC follows in assessing information penalties and how the PBGC applies those principles to specific cases?

22 What are the general principles that the PBGC follows in deciding whether to assess an information penalty and, if so, the amount or rate of information penalty to assess?

23 What aggravating factors does the PBGC consider?

24 What mitigating factors does the PBGC consider?

25 What if multiple persons must give a notice?

26 What if multiple persons must get a notice?

27 What if a single event or circumstance leads to multiple failures to provide section 4071 information?

28 What special guidance is there for specific types of cases?

Waiver Standards

31 What are the standards for waiving an information penalty?

32 What is "reasonable cause"?

33 What kinds of facts does the PBGC consider in determining whether there is reasonable cause for a failure to provide section 4071 information?

34 What are some situations that might justify a "reasonable cause" waiver?

35 What is a situation that might justify a partial "reasonable cause" waiver?

General Provisions

Section 1 What Is the Purpose of This Appendix?

Section 4071 of ERISA authorizes us to assess a penalty if you do not provide certain notices or other material information within the time limit specified in ERISA or in PBGC regulations. Some of the notices and other material information covered by section 4071 have to be provided to us, and some have to be provided to other parties, such as plan participants. This appendix sets forth principles and guidelines that we intend to follow in assessing, reviewing, and waiving information penalties. However, this is only general policy guidance. Our action in each case is guided by the facts and circumstances of the case.

Section 2 What Defined Terms are Used in This Appendix?

The following terms are defined in part 4001 of this chapter: contributing sponsor, controlled group, employer, ERISA, PBGC, person, plan, plan administrator, and standard termination. In addition, in this appendix:

(a) Information penalty means a penalty under ERISA section 4071 for failing to provide section 4071 information on time.

(b) Section 4071 information means any notice or other material information that you are required to provide to us or to another party under subtitles A-D of title IV of ERISA, or under section 302(f)(4) or 307(e) of Title I of ERISA, or under PBGC regulations implementing any of these provisions. Whether a particular item of information is "material" depends on the facts and circumstances.

(c) Waiver means reduction or elimination of an information penalty that is being or has been assessed.

(d) We means the PBGC.

(e) You means (according to the context)—

(1) A plan administrator, contributing sponsor, or other person, if—

(i) The person's action or inaction may be the basis for an information penalty assessment,

(ii) The person may be required to pay the information penalty, or

(iii) The person is requesting review of the information penalty; or

(2) An employee or agent of, or advisor to, any of these persons.

Section 3 What Is the Purpose of an Information Penalty?

The basic purpose of an information penalty is to encourage you to provide section 4071 information on time. Information penalties should be fair, simple, effective, and easy to administer. Therefore—

(a) We assess lower information penalties for plans of small businesses and for failures to provide section 4071 information that are speedily corrected;

(b) We assess higher information penalties if the facts and circumstances warrant it; and

(c) We waive information penalties, in whole or in part, if there is reasonable cause or in other appropriate circumstances.

Procedures

Section 11 What Are the Basic Steps for Assessing and Reviewing Information Penalties?

(a) Overview. There are typically three steps in the information penalty assessment and review process:

(1) A preliminary notice (discussed in Sec. 12), which gives you an opportunity to submit information bearing on the information penalty assessment;

(2) An information penalty determination (discussed in Sec. 13) that assesses the information penalty; and

(3) A review of the information penalty determination (discussed in Sec. 14).

(b) Debt collection. Our regulation on Debt Collection (29 CFR Part 4903) provides that we may collect amounts that you owe to us (such as information penalties) by reducing other amounts that the government owes to you (such as tax refunds). Procedures under our debt collection regulation may run separately or together with the information penalty assessment and review procedures.

(c) Decision-making standards and guidelines. At each stage of the information penalty assessment and review process, we evaluate the circumstances by the same standards and apply the same guidelines in deciding whether to assess or waive an information penalty and how much the information penalty should be. However, we may have more information when we review an information penalty than we had when we originally assessed it, and that may make our decision on review different from our original information penalty determination.

(d) Providing information to the PBGC. (1) It is your responsibility to raise any facts and issues that you want us to consider in making information penalty assessment or waiver decisions and to support your contentions with documentation such as correspondence and police, fire, or insurance reports. If you want us to consider information that you believe we already have in connection with another case, you should identify the information specifically enough so that we can determine whether we have the information, locate it in our files, and review it.

(2) Since information penalties are assessed for providing section 4071 information late, it is important that you bring to our attention any information or arguments that tend to show that you were not required to provide the section 4071 information or that you provided the section 4071 information on time.

(e) Terminology. There is a slight difference between the terminology we use in this appendix and the terminology we use in our regulation on Rules for Administrative Review of Agency Decisions (29 CFR Part 4003), which governs our issuance and review of information penalty determinations:

(1) "Initial determination" in the administrative review regulation means the same as "information penalty determination" in this appendix, and

(2) "Reconsideration of an initial determination" in the administrative review regulation means the same as "review of an information penalty determination" in this appendix.

Section 12 What Should I Know About Preliminary Notices of Information Penalties?

Before we make an information penalty determination, we want you to have an opportunity to give us any information you think we should consider. In most cases, therefore, we send a preliminary notice to tell you that we intend to assess an information penalty and the reason for the information penalty. (In some cases, we may skip this preliminary step—for example, if we contact you by telephone to discuss the matter or if we need to make the assessment quickly in order to preserve our right to collect the information penalty in court.) You may respond to a preliminary notice by submitting any information you want us to consider before we make an information penalty determination. The preliminary notice will state the time within which you should respond (typically 30 days).

(a) If section 4071 information already provided. If, by the time we issue a preliminary notice stating that we intend to assess an information penalty, you have already provided the late section 4071 information, the notice ordinarily tells you the amount of the information penalty that we intend to assess. If the preliminary notice states an amount of information penalty and you pay the amount stated in the preliminary notice without requesting relief, that is the end of the matter.

(b) If section 4071 information not already provided. If, by the time we issue a preliminary notice stating that we intend to assess an information penalty, you have not already provided the late section 4071 information, the notice ordinarily tells you the rate of penalty that we intend to assess. Providing the section 4071 information will cut off further accrual of the information penalty.

Section 13 What Should I Know About Information Penalty Determinations?

As the second step in the information penalty assessment and review process—after a preliminary notice—we make an information penalty determination (unless, in response to a preliminary notice that states an amount of information penalty, you pay the full information penalty

without requesting relief). (If we skip the preliminary notice step, the information penalty assessment is the first step in the process.) The information penalty determination notifies you of the reason for the information penalty (even if we have already issued a preliminary notice stating the reason) and takes into account any information you may have submitted to us in response to a preliminary notice. We also tell you when and where to send your payment, and we tell you about requesting review of the information penalty determination. (Complete rules for information penalty determinations and for requesting review are in part 4003 of this chapter.)

(a) If section 4071 information already provided. If, by the time we issue an information penalty determination, you have already provided the late section 4071 information, the determination tells you the amount of the information penalty that we are assessing (taking into account any waiver of all or part of the information penalty) and how we determined the amount of the information penalty. If the information penalty determination states an amount of information penalty and you pay the amount stated in the information penalty determination without requesting review, that is the end of the matter.

(b) If section 4071 information not already provided. If, by the time we issue an information penalty determination, you have not already provided the late section 4071 information, the determination ordinarily tells you the rate of penalty we intend to assess. Providing the section 4071 information will cut off further accrual of the information penalty.

Section 14 What Should I Know About Review of Information Penalty Determinations?

(a) Timing. (1) General rule. In general, you must request review of an information penalty determination within 30 days after the date of the determination; if you do not do so, the determination becomes effective, and we may take steps to collect the information penalty. In addition, you may not be able to raise in court some legal defenses that you might have against collection of the information penalty, because you have failed to exhaust administrative remedies. (In some cases, the 30-day limitation for requesting review may be extended or waived. See Secs. 4003.4 and 4003.5 of the administrative review regulation. If we notify you that we may attempt to collect a debt resulting from an information penalty determination by referring it for offset against federal payments that may be due you, you will have at least 60 days to request review. See Sec. 4003.32 of the administrative review regulation.)

(2) Determinations effective immediately. We may, in our discretion, make an information penalty determination effective on the date we issue it—for example, if our ability to bring a collection action in court is about to be cut off by the statute of limitations. If we make an information penalty determination effective immediately, you are not required to request review by us in order to exhaust your administrative remedies. This means that you have the right to raise legal defenses against collection of the information penalty in court even if you do not request that we review the determination. (See Sec. 4003.22(b) of the administrative review regulation.) If you do request review by the PBGC, we may review the determination.

(b) Review of determination. If you request review of an information penalty determination within the required time, we review the determination and notify you of the results of the review. This review takes into account any information you may have submitted to us in response to a preliminary notice or an information penalty determination notice or with your request for review.

(c) Information penalty accrual during review. Requesting review of an information penalty does not make the information penalty stop accruing. An information penalty stops accruing when you provide the section 4071 information. In addition, if you request review of an information penalty, we may waive the portion of the information penalty that accrues during review if you make a non-frivolous argument that you were not required to provide the section 4071 information or that you were (and still are) unable to provide it, as described in Sec. 31(b)(4) of this Appendix.

Information Penalty Assessment

Section 21 Where Can I Find the General Principles That the PBGC Follows in Assessing Information Penalties and how the PBGC Applies Those Principles to Specific Cases?

The general principles that we follow in deciding whether to assess an information penalty and, if so, the amount or rate of information penalty to assess are explained in the following sections of this Appendix:

(1) Section 22 contains basic guidance.

(2) Sections 23 and 24 describe some aggravating and mitigating factors.

(3) Sections 25 through 27 describe how we generally treat situations involving multiple persons and multiple failures to provide section 4071 information.

(4) Section 28 contains special guidance for specific types of cases.

Section 22 What Are the General Principles That the PBGC Follows in Deciding Whether To Assess an Information Penalty and, if so, the Amount or Rate of Information Penalty to Assess?

(a) Facts and circumstances. In deciding whether to assess an information penalty for a failure to provide section 4071 information on time and, if so, what rate or amount of information penalty to assess, we consider the facts and circumstances of the failure.

(b) Aggravating and mitigating factors. Among the facts and circumstances we consider are aggravating and mitigating factors such as those described in Secs. 23 and 24 of this Appendix. Aggravating factors tend to make it more likely that we will assess an information penalty, and mitigating factors tend to make it less likely. If we do assess an information penalty, aggravating factors tend to increase the rate or amount of the information penalty we assess, and mitigating factors tend to decrease the rate or amount. An aggravating or mitigating factor may apply to all or only some of the section 4071 information that is not provided and to all or only some days of a delinquency.

(c) Effect of plan size.

(1) Likelihood of assessment. In general, the likelihood that we will assess an information penalty is strongly influenced by the number of participants in your plan (as determined under paragraph (e)(2) of this section). Thus, for example, we are much less likely to assess an information penalty if your plan has fewer than 100 participants (especially for a first violation) than if your plan has more than 1,000 participants (whether or not it is a first violation). This reflects differences in the ordinary business care and prudence standard for large and small plans (see Sec. 32(c)) and in their access to professional help in monitoring their activities and meeting PBGC requirements.

(2) Amount or rate of information penalty. The effect of plan size on the amount or rate of an information penalty is explained in paragraphs (e)(1)(ii) and (e)(1)(iii) of this section.

(d) Waivers. We may also reduce or eliminate an information penalty if we have information showing that a partial or complete waiver of the information penalty is appropriate. Waivers are explained in Secs. 31 through 35 of this Appendix.

(e) Basic amount or rate of information penalty. If we assess an information penalty, the starting point for determining the rate or amount of the information penalty is the rate or amount determined under this section. The amount or rate may be higher or lower based on considerations such as those described in paragraphs (a) through (c) of this section and Secs. 23 through 28 of this Appendix.

(1) Basic guidelines. Although ERISA section 4071 allows us to assess an information penalty up to $1,100 per day for each failure to provide section 4071 information, the information penalties we assess are generally much lower under the following guidelines.

(i) Daily amount. The information penalty is generally $25 a day for the first 90 days that the section 4071 information is late, and $50 for each day thereafter.

(ii) Limit on total information penalty. The total information penalty generally does not exceed $100 times the number of participants.

(iii) Reduction for small plans. If there are fewer than 100 participants in your plan, we generally reduce the daily information penalty based on the ratio of the number of participants to 100, subject to a floor of $5 a day.

(2) How we count the number of participants. For purposes of the per-participant cap and the small plan reduction described in paragraphs (e)(1)(ii) and (e)(1)(iii) of this section, we generally count participants in the following ways:

(i) In plan terminations. For a failure to provide section 4071 information under part 4041 of this chapter (dealing with standard and distress plan terminations), we generally use the number of persons entitled to distributions of benefits in the plan termination. For example, if you are a plan administrator, and you are late in certifying to us that all benefits were properly distributed in a plan termination, the information penalty generally should not exceed $100 times the number of persons entitled to distributions of benefits in the plan termination.

(ii) In other cases. For any other failure to provide section 4071 information, we generally use the number of participants reported on the PBGC Form 1 premium declaration that you most recently filed before the date of the failure, unless the number of participants has changed significantly since the Form 1 was filed. However, if clearly appropriate in a particular case, we may use a different method of determining the number of participants (e.g., adding up the number of participants in two or more plans).

(3) Examples. The following examples illustrate the basic guidelines for assessing information penalties under this section. In these examples, assume that you are the plan administrator of a terminating plan and that you file your post-distribution certification late.

(i) General rule. If your plan has 112 participants, and you file 306 days after the last day on which you could have made an information-penalty-free filing, the total information penalty would ordinarily be $11,200, as shown in the following table. (Note that in this example, the cap of $100 times the number of participants applies.)

	Daily rate	Total information penalty
Days 1-90	$25	$2,250 ($25 × 90 days).
Days 91-306	$50	$10,800 ($50 × 216 days).
Total for all days (uncapped)		$13,050 ($2,250 + $10,800).
Total capped information penalty.		$11,200 ($100 × 112 participants).

(ii) Small plan rule. If your plan has 15 participants, and you file 100 days after the last day on which you could have made an information-penalty-free filing, the total information penalty should ordinarily be $525, as shown in the following table. (Note that in this example, the total information penalty is less than the cap of $100 times the number of participants, i.e., $1,500 ($100 x 15).)

	Daily rate	Total information penalty
Days 1-90	$5 (minimum daily information penalty, since 15/100 × $25 = $3.75).	$450 ($5 × 90 days).
Days 91-100	$7.50 (15/100 × $50)	$75 ($7.50 × 10 days).
Total for all days		$525 ($450 + $75).

Section 23 What Aggravating Factors Does the PBGC Consider?

The aggravating factors that we consider are the following. (We do not consider the absence of mitigating factors to be an aggravating factor.)

(a) Harmfulness. Failure to provide section 4071 information on time where the failure is—or has the potential of being—particularly harmful to participants or the PBGC is an aggravating factor. (This may be true even though, by the time we receive the information, any possible harm has been avoided.) Harmfulness may depend on the importance, time-sensitivity, and quantity of section 4071 information you fail to provide on time and on the size of your plan.

(b) Pattern or practice. A pattern or practice of failure to provide section 4071 information is an aggravating factor.

(c) Willfulness. Willful failure to comply is an aggravating factor.

Section 24 What Mitigating Factors Does the PBGC Consider?

(a) The mitigating factors that we consider are the following (We do not consider the absence of aggravating factors to be a mitigating factor.):

(1) First-time requirement. It is a mitigating factor if your failure to provide section 4071 information is a violation of a requirement that applies to you for the first time.

(2) Self-correction. It is a mitigating factor if you—

(i) Correct your failure to provide section 4071 information promptly after you discover the failure, and

(ii) Notify us on your own initiative of your failure to provide the section 4071 information before we notify you that you have or may have failed to provide the section 4071 information.

(3) Corrective action. It is a mitigating factor if you cooperate with us by taking appropriate corrective action and establishing procedures designed to ensure future compliance.

(b) Example. A mid-size company with a pension plan covering 750 participants mistakenly made a quarterly contribution that was too low. The company did not immediately realize that the contribution was too low and did not make a reportable events report to the PBGC. As soon as the company discovered its error, it made a corrective contribution, telephoned the PBGC to alert us to the problem, and promptly filed the required reportable event notice. The company had never before failed to make all required contributions, and both the plan and the company were financially healthy. At the PBGC's request, the plan administrator put in place new procedures to avoid future reporting failures. Under the circumstances, the PBGC might assess no information penalty or might assess an information penalty of less than the amount that would be called for under Sec. 22.

Section 25 What if Multiple Persons Must Give a Notice?

If each of two or more persons is responsible for providing substantially identical section 4071 information to us or to another person or persons, and the information is not provided as required, we may—

(a) Assess an information penalty against any one or more of the persons without regard to whether we assess an information penalty against any other of the persons; and

(b) Determine the amount of information penalty assessed against any person without regard to the amount assessed against any other person.

Section 26 What if Multiple Persons Must Get a Notice?

In general, if you have to give substantially identical notices to multiple persons, we generally assess only a single information penalty for failure to provide the notices as required, regardless of how many persons did not receive a notice as required. However:

(a) The number of persons you did not provide notice to as required may affect the amount of daily information penalty we assess. For example, if you are a plan administrator and you fail to give a Participant Notice under Part 4011 of this chapter as required, we generally assess only one information penalty. But if your plan is quite large, the information penalty we assess is likely to be greater than if the plan were small.

(b) If there are aggravating factors, we may, in addition to assessing a higher information penalty under Sec. 22(b), assess a separate information penalty for each person to whom you failed to give a notice.

Section 27 What if a Single Event or Circumstance Leads to Multiple Failures to Provide Section 4071 Information?

If there are multiple failures to provide section 4071 information relating to a single event or circumstance, we generally assess a separate information penalty for each failure. For example, suppose you are a contributing sponsor of a plan and you fail to make several required contributions to the plan because of a single failure to determine that contributions are necessary for the year. The failure to notify us of each missed contribution is a separate failure for which we generally assess a separate information penalty.

Section 28 What Special Guidance is There for Specific Types of Cases?

The following is special guidance for applying the general assessment principles in specific types of cases:

(a) Premium information requirements. If you file a complete, correct premium form (Form 1, Schedule A, Form 1-ES) late, with the full premium payment, we do not assess an information penalty except in unusual cases. The premium penalty for late payment is usually an adequate penalty.

(b) Plan termination information requirements. If you fail to file or issue a notice required for a plan termination under Part 4041 of this chapter on time, and we issue a notice of noncompliance nullifying the termination, we do not also assess an information penalty for your failure to file or issue the required notice on time.

(c) Reportable event post-event notice requirements. If we assess an information penalty for a failure by a large plan or employer to file a notice of a reportable event under ERISA section 4043, other than an advance notice under ERISA section 4043(b) (which is discussed in paragraph (d) of this section), the amount or rate may be much higher than the basic amount or rate that would be determined under Sec.

22(e) of this Appendix. Such failures usually are—or have the potential of being—particularly harmful to participants or the PBGC if they involve large plans or employers. For example, if you do not give us a required notice of a controlled group member's bankruptcy filing, the controlled group member's assets may be distributed to other creditors before we can file our claims for plan underfunding, and we may therefore be unable to recover on our claims or otherwise participate in the bankruptcy proceedings.

(d) Reportable event advance notice requirements. We virtually always assess an information penalty if you fail to file an advance notice of a reportable event under ERISA section 4043(b), and we generally assess the full $1,100-per-day information penalty. This information is generally so time-sensitive and significant that the maximum information penalty is warranted in virtually every case, without regard to whether there are aggravating circumstances in the particular case, because of the need for strong deterrence of violations of this kind.

(e) Missed contribution notice requirements. We virtually always assess an information penalty if you fail to file a missed contribution notice (Form 200) under ERISA section 302(f)(4), and we generally assess the full $1,100-per-day information penalty. This information is very time-sensitive because it is the basis for filing a lien under section 302(f) for the protection of the plan. Thus, the maximum information penalty is warranted in virtually every case, without regard to whether there are aggravating circumstances in the particular case, because of the need for strong deterrence of violations of this kind. The fact that the contribution is ultimately made does not undo the potential for harm that exists while the contribution is outstanding. However, we may reduce the information penalty rate for any period during which the notice remains unfiled after the missed contribution is made—for example, from $1,100 per day to $100 per day.

(f) Employer reporting requirements. We virtually always assess an information penalty if you fail to file a financial and actuarial information report under ERISA section 4010, covering plans with very high underfunding, and we generally assess the full $1,100-per-day information penalty. Failures to file financial and actuarial information reports generally are—or have the potential of being—so harmful to participants or the PBGC that the maximum information penalty is warranted in virtually every case, without regard to whether there are aggravating circumstances in the particular case, because of the need for strong deterrence of violations of this kind.

Waiver Standards

Section 31 What are the Standards for Waiving an Information Penalty?

(a) Facts and circumstances. In deciding whether to waive an information penalty in whole or in part, we consider the facts and circumstances of each case.

(b) Waivers. (1) Provisions of law. We waive all or part of an information penalty if a statute or regulation requires that we do so. For example, Sec. 4041.29(b) of this chapter provides that we do not assess an information penalty for a late post-distribution certification except to the extent that you file it more than 90 days after the distribution deadline under Sec. 4041.28(a) of this chapter; and 4050.6(b)(2) of this chapter contains a similar provision for the late filing of information and certifications regarding missing participants in a terminating plan.

(2) Reasonable cause. We waive an information penalty if you show reasonable cause for a failure to provide section 4071 information on time. See Secs. 32 through 35 for guidelines on "reasonable cause" waivers. If there is reasonable cause for only part of a failure to provide section 4071 information, we waive the information penalty only for that part. In determining whether "reasonable cause" exists, we do not consider either —

(i) The likelihood or cost of collecting the information penalty, or

(ii) The costs and risks of enforcing the information penalty by litigation.

(3) Erroneous legal interpretations. We may waive all or part of an information penalty if the failure to provide section 4071 information on time that gives rise to the information penalty is based on your reliance on an erroneous interpretation of the law.

(i) If you disclose the interpretation to us. If a failure to provide section 4071 information on time results from your reliance on an erroneous interpretation of the law, we will waive an information penalty that arises from the failure if you promptly and adequately call our attention to the interpretation and the relevant facts, and the erroneous interpretation is not frivolous. If the interpretation affects a filing that you make with us, you should call our attention to the interpretation with the filing. If you rely on the interpretation to justify not making a filing with us, you should call our attention to the interpretation in a notice submitted to us by the time and in the manner prescribed for the filing not made. If the interpretation affects information that you provide to persons other than us, you should call our attention to the interpretation when you provide the information by sending us a notice addressed to Technical Assistance Branch, Insurance Operations Department, PBGC, 1200 K Street, NW., Washington, DC 20005-4026. If you rely on the interpretation to justify not providing information to persons other than us, you should call our attention to the interpretation by sending a notice to the above address by the time prescribed for providing the information that is not provided.

(ii) If you do not disclose the interpretation to us. If a failure to provide section 4071 information on time results from your reliance on an erroneous interpretation of the law, and you do not promptly and adequately call our attention to the interpretation and the relevant facts, we may waive an information penalty that arises from the failure if the weight of authority supporting the interpretation is substantial in relation to the weight of opposing authority and it is reasonable for you to rely on the interpretation.

(4) Pendency of review. If you request review of an information penalty (as described in Sec. 14 of this Appendix), and you make a non-frivolous argument that you were not required to provide the section 4071 information or that you were (and still are) unable to provide it, we waive the portion of the information penalty that accrues during the review process. (If you make a non-frivolous argument that you were not required (or were unable) to provide a portion of the section 4071 information, we apply this rule to that portion.) The waiver also applies to the post-review period (the period after we complete our review) if you pay the information penalty within 30 days after the date of our decision and provide the section 4071 information by the time specified in the notice of our decision, which is normally also 30 days after the date of the decision, but may be less depending on the importance of the information. Otherwise, the waiver does not apply to the period from the date of our decision until you provide the section 4071 information.

(5) Other circumstances. We may waive all or part of an information penalty in other circumstances if we determine that it is appropriate to do so. We intend to exercise this waiver authority only in narrow circumstances, primarily if we determine that assessing an information penalty, or assessing the full amount of information penalty that might otherwise be appropriate under the guidelines in this appendix, would be inconsistent with the purposes of Title IV of ERISA. For example, we may waive all or part of an information penalty if the law changes shortly before the date when section 4071 information must be provided and the information you provide by that date would have been correct under the law as in effect before the change. In determining whether and to what extent to grant a waiver in a case of this kind, we consider such factors as the length of time between the change in the law and the date by which the section 4071 information must be provided, the nature and timing of any publicity given to the change in the law, the complexity of the legal issues, and your general familiarity with those issues.

(c) Action or inaction of outside parties. If an accountant, actuary, lawyer, pension consultant, or other individual or firm that is not part of your organization assists you in complying with PBGC requirements, we apply our waiver authority as if the outside individual or firm were part of your organization, as described in Sec. 32(c) of this Appendix.

Section 32 What Is "Reasonable Cause"?

(a) General rule. In general, there is "reasonable cause" for a failure to provide section 4071 information on time to the extent that—

(1) The failure arises from circumstances beyond your control, and

(2) You could not avoid the failure by the exercise of ordinary business care and prudence.

(b) Overlooking legal requirements. Overlooking legal requirements does not constitute reasonable cause.

(c) Action or inaction of outside parties. In some cases an accountant, actuary, lawyer, pension consultant, or other individual or firm that is not part of your organization may assist you in complying with PBGC requirements. If the outside individual's or firm's action, inaction, or advice causes or contributes to a failure to provide section 4071 information on time, our analysis is generally the same as if the outside individual or firm were part of your organization. (In the case of an outside individual who is part of a firm, we generally consider both the individual and the firm to be part of your organization.) Thus, if a failure to provide section 4071 information on time arises from circumstances within the control of the outside individual or firm, or could be avoided by the exercise of ordinary business care and prudence by the

outside individual or firm, there is generally no reasonable cause for the failure. The fact that you exercised care and prudence in selecting and monitoring the outside individual or firm is not a basis for a reasonable cause waiver. (However, you may have recourse against the outside individual or firm.)

(d) Size of organization. If an organization or one or more of its employees is responsible for taking action, the size of the organization may affect what ordinary business care and prudence would require. For example, ordinary business care and prudence would typically require a larger organization to establish more comprehensive backup procedures than a smaller organization for dealing with situations such as computer failure, the loss of important records, and the inability of an individual to carry out assigned responsibilities. Thus, there may be reasonable cause for a small organization's failure to provide section 4071 information on time even though, if the organization were larger, the exercise of ordinary business care and prudence would have avoided the failure.

(e) Potential seriousness of failure to provide section 4071 information on time. In general, the more potentially serious or harmful a failure to provide section 4071 information on time would be, the more care and prudence you should use to make sure that you provide it on time. Thus, there may be reasonable cause for a minor failure even though, under the same circumstances, we would conclude that a more serious failure could have been avoided by the exercise of ordinary business care and prudence.

Section 33 What Kinds of Facts Does the PBGC Consider in Determining Whether There is Reasonable Cause for a Failure to Provide Section 4071 Information?

In determining whether a failure to provide section 4071 information on time arose from circumstances beyond your control and whether you could have avoided the failure by the exercise of ordinary business care and prudence—and thus whether waiver of an information penalty for reasonable cause is appropriate—we consider facts such as the following:

(a) What event or circumstance caused the failure and when the event happened or the circumstance arose. The dates you give should clearly correspond with the failure upon which the information penalty is based.

(b) How that event or circumstance kept you from providing the section 4071 information on time. The explanation you give should relate directly to the failure to provide section 4071 information that is the subject of the information penalty.

(c) Whether the event or circumstance was beyond your control.

(d) Whether you could have anticipated the event or circumstance.

(e) How you responded to the event or circumstance, including what steps you took (and how quickly you took them) to provide the section 4071 information and how you conducted other business affairs. Knowing how you responded to the event or circumstance may help us determine what degree of business care and prudence you were capable of exercising during that period and thus whether the failure to provide section 4071 information could or could not have been avoided by the exercise of ordinary business care and prudence.

Section 34 What Are Some Situations That Might Justify a "Reasonable Cause" Waiver?

The following examples illustrate some of the reasons often given for failures to provide section 4071 information for which we may assess penalties. The situation described in each example may constitute reasonable cause, and each example lists factors we consider in determining whether we should grant an information penalty waiver for reasonable cause in a case of that kind.

(a) An individual with responsibility for taking action was suddenly and unexpectedly absent or unable to act. We consider such factors as the following: the nature of the event that caused the individual's absence or inability to act (for example, the resignation of the individual or the death or serious illness of the individual or a member of the individual's immediate family); the size of the organization and what kind of backup procedures it had to cope with such events; how close the event was to the deadline that was missed; how abrupt and unanticipated the event was; how the individual's absence or inability to act prevented compliance; how expensive it would have been to comply without the absent individual; whether and how other business operations and obligations were affected; how quickly and prudently a replacement for the absent individual was selected or other arrangements for compliance were made; and how quickly a replacement for the absent individual took appropriate action.

(b) A fire or other casualty or natural disaster destroyed relevant records or prevented compliance in some other way. We consider such factors as the following: the nature of the event; how close the event was to the deadline that was missed; how the event caused the failure to provide section 4071 information; whether other efforts were made to get needed information; how expensive it would have been to comply; and how you responded to the event.

(c) You reasonably relied on erroneous oral or written advice given by a PBGC employee. We consider such factors as the following: whether there was a clear relationship between your situation and the advice sought; whether you provided the PBGC employee with adequate and accurate information; and whether the surrounding circumstances should have led you to question the correctness of the advice or information provided.

(d) You were unable to obtain information (including records and calculations) needed to comply. We consider such factors as the following: what information was needed; why the information was unavailable; when and how you discovered that the information was not available; what attempts you made to get the information or reconstruct it through other means; and how much it would have cost to comply.

Section 35 What Is a Siuation That Might Justify a Partial "Reasonable Cause" Waiver?

Assume that a fire destroyed the records needed for a required filing of section 4071 information. If in the exercise of ordinary business care and prudence it should take you one month to reconstruct the records and prepare the filing, but the filing was made two months late, it might be appropriate to waive that part of the information penalty attributable to the first month the filing was late, but not the part attributable to the second month.

Issued in Washington, D.C., this 5th day of January, 2001.

David M. Strauss,

Executive Director, Pension Benefit Guaranty Corporation.

[FR Doc. 01-686 Filed 1-11-01; 8:45 am]

BILLING CODE 7708-01-P

¶ 20,534J

PBGC proposed regulations: System of Records: Personnel Security Investigation Records: Contract employees: Privacy Act of 1974.—The PBGC has issued a proposed regulation which would amend its current regulations to protect the identity of sources of confidential background information on individuals who work for, or who are being considered for work for the PBGC as contractors or as employees of contractors.

The proposed regulation was published in the *Federal Register* on April 2, 2001 (66 FR 17518).

The preamble to the final regulations, which was published in the *Federal Register* on June 14, 2001 (66 FR 32221), can be found at ¶ 24,215. The amended portion of the regulations appears at ¶ 15,721B.

¶ 20,534K

PBGC proposed regulations: Appeals board: Administrative review.—The PBGC has proposed to amend its regulation on Administrative Review of Agency Decisions to expedite the appeals process by authorizing a single member of the PBGC's Appeals Board to decide routine appeals. The PBGC would continue to use three-member panels for cases that involve a significant issue of law or a precedent-setting issue.

The proposed regulation was published in the *Federal Register* on March 27, 2002 (67 FR 14663).

The regulation was finalized on July 22, 2002 (67 FR 47694). The final regulation is at ¶ 15,334J. The preamble is at ¶ 24,221.

¶ 20,534L

PBGC proposed regulations: Electronic filing: Electronic filing: Computation-of-time rules: Electronic record retention rules.—The PBGC is attempting to provide filers with increased flexibility with regard to electronic filing as set forth in Title IV of ERISA by issuing proposed regulations designed to minimize existing electronic filing limitations. Filing addresses currently set forth in existing regulations would be put in PBGC form instructions and on the PBGC website at www.pbgc.gov. Additionally, the existing distribution and derivation tables in ERISA Part 4000 would also be moved to the PBGC website.

The proposed regulations, which were published in the *Federal Register* on February 14, 2003 (68 FR 7454), are reproduced below.

PENSION BENEFIT GUARANTY CORPORATION

29 CFR Parts 4000, 4003, 4007, 4010, 4011, 4022, 4041, 4041A, 4043, 4050, 4062, 4203, 4204, 4207, 4208, 4211, 4219, 4220, 4221, 4231, 4245, 4281, 4901, 4902, 4903 and 4907

RIN 1212-AA89

Rules on Filings, Issuances, Computation of Time, and Electronic Means of Record Retention

AGENCY: Pension Benefit Guaranty Corporation.

ACTION: Proposed rule.

SUMMARY: We propose, consistent with the Government Paperwork Elimination Act, to remove requirements from our regulations that might limit electronic filing with us or electronic issuances to others. The proposed rules will give us flexibility to keep pace with ever-changing technology. In addition, they simplify and consolidate our rules on what methods you may use to send us a filing or provide an issuance to someone other than us, on how to determine the date we treat you as having made your filing or provided your issuance, and on how to compute various periods of time (including those for filings with us and for issuances to third parties). Finally, they provide rules for maintaining records by electronic means.

DATES: Comments must be received by April 15, 2003.

ADDRESSES: Comments may be mailed to the Office of the General Counsel, Pension Benefit Guaranty Corporation, 1200 K Street, NW., Washington, DC 20005-4026, or delivered to Suite 340 at the above address. Comments also may be sent by Internet e-mail to reg.comments@pbgc.gov, or by fax to 202-326-4112. We will make all comments available on our Web site, http://www.pbgc.gov. Copies of comments also may be obtained by writing the PBGC's Communications and Public Affairs Department (CPAD) at Suite 240 at the above address or by visiting or calling CPAD during normal business hours (202-326-4040).

FOR FURTHER INFORMATION CONTACT: Harold J. Ashner, Assistant General Counsel, or Thomas H. Gabriel, Attorney, Office of the General Counsel, PBGC, 1200 K Street, NW., Washington, DC 20005-4026; 202-326-4024. (For TTY/TDD users, call the Federal relay service toll-free at 1-800-877-8339 and ask to be connected to 202-326-4024.)

SUPPLEMENTARY INFORMATION: These proposed rules are part of our ongoing implementation of the Government Paperwork Elimination Act (GPEA) and are consistent with the Office of Management and Budget directive to remove regulatory impediments to electronic transactions. They address electronic means for filings with us, issuances to third parties, and recordkeeping. They build in the flexibility needed to allow us to continue to expand the availability of electronic options as technology advances. Under the proposal, much of the detailed information on permitted electronic means will be on our Web site, http://www.pbgc.gov, which will be updated from time to time.

The proposed rules make it easier for you to make a filing or provide an issuance on time by treating most types of submissions as filed or issued on the date sent (provided you meet certain requirements) rather than on the date received. In addition, under the proposal, the rules are easier to use—they are simpler, more uniform, and appear together in a single part of the regulations. The proposal makes similar simplifying changes to the rules for computing periods of time.

Under this proposal, our filing, issuance, computation-of-time, and electronic record-retention rules are consolidated in new subparts A through E of part 4000.

• New subpart A tells you what methods you may use for sending a filing to us. These new rules will apply to any filing with us under our regulations where the particular regulation calls for their application. For these purposes, we treat any payment to us under our regulations as a filing.

• New subpart B tells you what methods you may use to issue a notice or otherwise provide information to any person other than us. These new rules will apply to any issuance (except a payment) under our regulations where the particular regulation calls for their application.

• New subpart C tells you how we will determine the date you send us a filing and the date you provide an issuance to someone other than us (such as a participant). These new rules will apply to any filing or issuance under our regulations where the particular regulation calls for their application.

• New subpart D tells you how to compute time periods. These new rules will apply to any time period under our regulations (e.g., for filings with us and issuances to third parties) where the particular regulation calls for their application.

• New subpart E tells you how to comply with any recordkeeping requirement under our regulations using electronic means.

Existing Part 4000's distribution and derivation tables, which show the changes that occurred as a result of the PBGC's July 1, 1996, reorganization and renumbering of its regulations (61 FR 32574), will be moved to the PBGC's Web site at http://www.pbgc.gov, and combined with similar tables showing the changes that occurred as a result of the PBGC's June 29, 1981, reorganization and renumbering of its regulations (46 FR 32574). A note at the beginning of the PBGC's regulations will refer users to the PBGC's Web site for the tables.

Method of Filing

We are trying to provide as much flexibility as possible in filing methods. The proposed rules allow you to file any submission with us by hand, mail, or commercial delivery service, and refer you to our Web site, http://www.pbgc.gov, for current information on electronic filing, including permitted methods, fax numbers, and e-mail addresses. The instruction booklets and forms used for certain filings with us also will describe electronic and other filing methods, as appropriate, and will be available on our Web site.

Where To File

Under the proposed rule, we are removing the filing addresses from our regulations and putting them on our Web site, http://www.pbgc.gov, and in the instructions to our forms; addresses will also be available through our Customer Service Center, 1-800-400-7242 (for participants), or 1-800-736-2444 (for practitioners). (TTY/TDD users may call the Federal relay service toll-free at 1-800-877-8339 and ask to be connected to the appropriate number.) Because we have different addresses for different types of filings, you should make sure to use the appropriate address for your type of filing. For example, some filings (such as premium payments) must be sent to a bank, while other filings (such as the Standard Termination Notice (Form 500)) must be sent to the appropriate department at our offices in Washington, DC.

Method of Issuance

The proposed rules on methods of issuance permit you to use any method of issuance, provided you use measures reasonably calculated to ensure actual receipt of the material by the intended recipient. Posting is not a permissible method of issuance under the rules of this part. (However, for certain issuances, posting is specifically permitted by the regulation governing the particular issuance.)

The proposed rules include a safe-harbor method for providing an issuance by electronic media. The proposed safe-harbor method generally tracks the Department of Labor's final rules (67 FR 17264 (April 9, 2002)) concerning disclosure of certain employee benefit plan information through electronic media, as set out at 29 CFR 2520.104b-1. Our safe-harbor method would be available to any person using electronic media to satisfy issuance obligations under our regulations.

These proposed rules on methods of issuance do not address compliance with the Electronic Signatures in Global and National Commerce

Act, Pub. L. 106-229, 114 Stat. 464 (2000) (codified at 15 U.S.C. 7001-7006) ("E-SIGN").

Date of Filing or Issuance

The proposed rules tell you how we will determine the date you filed your submission with us and the date you provided your issuance to someone other than us (such as a participant). In some cases, other PBGC rules relating to issuances to third parties refer to when an issuance is received. (For instance, when there is a request for abatement (regulation §4207.3), interest is credited to the employer if the plan sponsor does not issue a revised payment schedule reflecting the credit or make the required refund within 60 days after receipt by the plan sponsor of a complete abatement application action.) These proposed rules would not affect those other receipt rules for issuances to third parties. Similarly, these proposed rules would not affect any receipt rule for filings with the PBGC, except to the extent these rules describe how to determine when a document is received (for instance, filings received by the PBGC after 5 p.m. are treated as received on the next business day).

Date of Filing in General

Under the proposed rule, we will treat most types of submissions as filed on the date you send the submission to us if you comply with certain requirements. The requirements vary depending on the method of filing you use. We may ask you for evidence of when you sent a submission to us.

There are a few types of submissions to us that we always treat as filed when received (not when sent), no matter what method you use: (1) Applications for benefits and related submissions (unless the instructions for the applicable forms provide for an earlier date), (2) advance notices of reportable event (under subpart C of section 4043), (3) notices of missed contributions exceeding $1 million (under subpart D of section 4043), and (4) requests for approval of a multiemployer plan amendment. The "filed-when-received" rule is necessary for these submissions because we may need to act quickly to provide benefit payments, to protect participants or premium payers, or to act within a statutory time frame.

In these cases, as well as cases where you do not meet the requirements for your filing date to be the date you send your submission, your filing date is the date we receive your submission. However, if we receive your submission after 5 p.m. (our time) on a business day, or anytime on a weekend or Federal holiday, we will treat it as received on the next business day.

Date of Issuance in General

Under the proposed rule, we will treat most types of issuances to third parties as provided on the date you send the issuance if you comply with certain requirements. The requirements vary depending on the method of issuance you use. The proposed rules for determining the date of an issuance generally track the proposed rules for determining the date of a filing; however, there are some differences for issuances using electronic means. An electronic issuance meeting the proposed safe harbor will have the benefit of the "send-date" rule. An electronic issuance that meets the general standard for issuances (i.e., using measures reasonably calculated to ensure actual receipt), but not the safe harbor, will be deemed issued on the date received by the intended recipient.

Filing and Issuance by U.S. Postal Service

If you send your submission to us, or provide an issuance to someone else, by First-Class Mail (or another at least equivalent class), and you properly mail it by the last scheduled collection of the day, your filing or issuance date is the date you mail it. If you properly mail it later than the last scheduled collection or on a day when there is no scheduled collection, your filing or issuance date is the date of the next scheduled collection.

If your submission or issuance has a legible U.S. Postal Service postmark, we will presume your filing or issuance date is the date of the postmark. However, you may prove an earlier date. The same rules apply if your submission or issuance has a legible postmark made by a private postage meter (but no legible U.S. Postal Service postmark) and arrives at the proper address by the time reasonably expected.

Filing and Issuance Using the Postal Service of a Foreign Country

If you send your submission to us, or provide an issuance to someone else, using the postal service of a foreign country, your filing or issuance date is the date of receipt at the proper address.

Filing and Issuance by Commercial Delivery Service

If you send your submission to us, or provide an issuance to someone else, by a commercial delivery service that meets certain requirements (described below) and you properly deposit your submission or issuance by the last scheduled collection of the day, your filing or issuance date is the date you deposit your submission or issuance; if you properly deposit it later than the last scheduled collection or on a day when there is no scheduled collection, your filing or issuance date is the date of the next scheduled collection.

To benefit from this "send-date" rule, you must use: (1) A "designated delivery service" under Internal Revenue Code §7502(f) (our Web site, http://www.pbgc.gov, will list the designated delivery services), or (2) a service for which it is reasonable to expect that your submission or issuance will arrive at the proper address by 5 p.m. on the second business day after the date of collection.

Filing and Issuance by Hand Delivery

If you hand deliver your submission or issuance, your filing or issuance date is the date of receipt at the proper address. A hand-delivered issuance need not be delivered while the intended recipient is physically present. For example, unless you have reason to believe that the intended recipient will not receive the notice within a reasonable amount of time, a notice is deemed to be received when you place it in the intended recipient's office mailbox.

Filing and Issuance by Electronic Delivery

You may submit most types of filings to PBGC electronically. If you do, the filing date for your submission is the date you transmit it to us at the proper address, provided (1) you comply with the technical requirements for that type of submission (our Web site, http://www.pbgc.gov, tells you when electronic filing is permitted and, if so, identifies the technical requirements for each type of submission), and (2) when sending an e-mail with an attachment, you include, in the body of the e-mail, the name and telephone number of the person for us to contact if we are unable to read the attachment.

Under certain circumstances, you may provide issuances electronically. An electronic issuance meeting the proposed safe harbor will have the benefit of a "send-date" rule. An electronic issuance that meets the general standard for issuances (i.e., using measures reasonably calculated to ensure actual receipt), but not the safe harbor for electronic filings, will be deemed issued on the date received by the intended recipient. For any issuance in the form of an e-mail, you must include, in the body of the e-mail, the name and telephone number of the person to contact if the recipient is unable to read the attachment.

Filing and Issuance by Submission of Computer Disk

For most types of filings with PBGC, you may send us your submission on a computer disk (e.g., a CD-ROM or floppy diskette). Similarly, you may be able to provide certain issuances on computer disk. For filings, you must comply with the technical requirements for that type of submission. For issuances, you must meet certain safe-harbor requirements. For both filings and issuances, you must include, in a paper cover letter or on the disk's label, the name and telephone number of the person to contact if we or the intended recipient is unable to read the disk. The rules for determining the filing or issuance date of your submission of a computer disk will apply as if you sent us a paper version of your submission.

Requirement To Resend

If you have reason to believe that we or the intended recipient has not received your electronic or paper filing or issuance (or has received it in a form that is not useable), you must promptly resend it. If you do so, we will treat it as filed or issued on the original filing or issuance date. If you are not prompt, your filing or issuance date will be the filing or issuance date of the resubmission or reissuance.

De Minimis Issuance Errors

We will not treat your issuance as untimely based on your failure to provide it to a participant or beneficiary in a timely manner if the failure resulted from administrative error and involved only a de minimis percentage of intended recipients, provided that you resend the issuance to the intended recipient promptly after discovering the error. (Under our existing regulations, this rule applies only to standard and distress termination issuances; the proposed rule applies it to all our issuances under our regulations.)

Computation of Time

The proposed computation-of-time rules tell you how to compute time periods under our regulations (e.g., for filings with us and issuances to third parties) where the particular regulation calls for their application. (Some of our regulations will contain specific exceptions or modifications to these proposed rules.)

When computing a time period (whether counting forwards or backwards) under these rules, exclude the day of the act, event, or default that begins the period; include the last day of the period; and if the last day is a weekend or Federal holiday, extend or shorten the period (whichever benefits you in complying with the time requirement) to the next regular business day. The weekend and holiday rule also applies to deadlines for which counting is not required, such as "the last day" of a plan year.

For example, suppose that you miss a required minimum funding contribution of $2 million that has a November 13, 2003, due date. Under our regulations, you are required to file a notice of a missed contribution (Form 200) no later than 10 days after the due date for the missed contribution. To determine your deadline, count November 14 as day 1, November 15 as day 2, November 16 as day 3, and so on. Therefore, November 23 is day 10. Since November 23, 2003, is a Sunday, you will have until Monday, November 24, 2003, to file the notice.

As another example, suppose you are required to file an advance notice of reportable event for a transaction that is effective December 16, 2003. Under our regulations, the notice is due at least 30 days before the effective date of the event. To determine your deadline, count December 15 as day 1, December 14 as day 2, December 13 as day 3, and so on. Therefore, November 16 is day 30. Since November 16, 2003, is a Sunday, you will have until Monday, November 17, 2003, to file the notice.

If a time period is measured in months, you would first identify the day of the calendar month on which you start counting (i.e., the date of the act, event, or default that triggers the period). Then you would look to the corresponding day of the calendar month in which you stop counting. For example, a one-month period measured from January 15 ends (if counting forward) on February 15 or (if counting backward) on December 15. In this example, as in most cases where you are counting months, the day of the calendar month in which the period starts (the 15th) corresponds to the same numbered day of the calendar month in which the period ends. There are two special rules that apply where you start counting on a day that is at or near the end of a calendar month:

• If you start counting on the last day of a calendar month, the corresponding day of any later (or earlier) calendar month is the last day of that calendar month. For example, for a three-month period measured from November 30, the corresponding day (if counting forward) is the last day of February (the 28th or 29th) or (if counting backward) the last day of August (the 31st).

• If you start counting on the 29th or 30th of a calendar month, the corresponding day of February is the last day of February. For example, for a one-month period measured from January 29, the corresponding day is the last day of February (the 28th or 29th).

Electronic Means of Record Retention

The proposed rule provides guidance on record maintenance and retention using electronic means. The proposed rule generally tracks the Department of Labor's final rules (67 FR 17264 (April 9, 2002)) for retaining records by electronic means, set out at 29 CFR 2520.107-1.

You remain responsible for following our electronic recordkeeping rules, even if you rely on others for help. For example, if a service provider to a plan administrator creates, maintains, retains, prepares, or keeps physical custody of the plan's records, the plan administrator must ensure that the service provider complies with these rules.

The proposed recordkeeping requirements are consistent with the goals of E-SIGN and are designed to facilitate voluntary use of electronic records while ensuring continued accuracy, integrity and accessibility of records required to be kept under our regulations. The requirements are justified by the importance of the records involved, are substantially equivalent to the requirements imposed on records that are not electronic records, will not impose unreasonable costs on the acceptance and use of electronic records, and do not require, or accord greater legal status or effect to, the implementation or application of a specific technology or technical specification for performing the functions of creating, storing, generating, receiving, communicating, or authenticating electronic records.

Paperwork Reduction Act

Under the Paperwork Reduction Act (PRA), 44 U.S.C. 3501-3520, an agency may not conduct or sponsor, and a person is not required to respond to, a collection of information unless it displays a currently valid Office of Management and Budget (OMB) control number. The information collection requirements related to the regulations that would be affected by this proposed action were previously approved by

OMB. We are requesting OMB's approval of the proposed changes in our filing, issuance, computation-of-time, and recordkeeping rules.

The proposed rules will promote the use of appropriate automated, electronic, or other technological collection techniques or other forms of information technology in connection with the approved information collections. Although the proposed rules are expected to make the information collections more convenient to the public by allowing use of electronic means, expanding the choice of filing, issuance, and recordkeeping methods, and giving the benefit of a "when-sent" filing or issuance date for most types of submissions, we do not expect the changes to materially affect burden and are therefore not revising the annual burden estimates currently approved by OMB for each of our regulations.

We invite comment from the public on any issues arising under the Paperwork Reduction Act relating to this proposed rule. We specifically seek public comments to:

• Evaluate whether the proposed collection of information is necessary for the proper performance of the functions of the agency, including whether the information will have practical utility;

• Evaluate the accuracy of the estimate of the burden of the proposed collection of information, including the validity of the methodology and assumptions used;

• Enhance the quality, utility, and clarity of the information to be collected; and

• Minimize the burden of the collection of information on those who are to respond, including through the use of appropriate automated, electronic, mechanical, or other technological collection techniques or other forms of information technology, e.g., permitting electronic submission of responses.

Compliance With Rulemaking Guidelines

The PBGC has determined, in consultation with the Office of Management and Budget, that this proposed rule is not a "significant regulatory action" under Executive Order 12866.

We certify under section 605(b) of the Regulatory Flexibility Act that the proposed rule will not have a significant economic impact on a substantial number of small entities. The proposed rule does not affect the underlying requirements (e.g., to file a submission with us, provide an issuance to a third party, or retain records) to which the proposed rules would apply. Nor does the final rule require any plan or other entity to make use of electronic media for either disclosure or recordkeeping purposes or to change the method it currently uses. Entities may avoid both any marginal cost and any beneficial impacts by simply retaining their existing paper-based or electronic methods of compliance with disclosure requirements or existing paper-based methods of compliance with recordkeeping requirements. (For those entities that already use electronic media for recordkeeping purposes, any expense associated with conforming their procedures to the minimum standards in this proposal would be marginal.) We do not expect the economic impact (if any) associated with the proposed changes to be significant for entities of any size, and therefore certify that the proposed rule would not have a significant economic impact on a substantial number of small entities. Accordingly, sections 603 and 604 of the Regulatory Flexibility Act do not apply.

List of Subjects

29 CFR Part 4000

Pension insurance, Pensions, Reporting and recordkeeping requirements.

29 CFR Part 4003

Administrative practice and procedure, Pension insurance.

29 CFR Part 4007

Employee benefit plans, Penalties, Pension insurance, Reporting and recordkeeping requirements.

29 CFR Part 4010

Employee benefit plans; Penalties; Pension insurance; Reporting and recordkeeping requirements.

29 CFR Part 4011

Employee benefit plans, Pension insurance, Reporting and recordkeeping requirements.

29 CFR Part 4022

Employee benefit plans, Pension insurance, Reporting and recordkeeping requirements.

29 CFR Part 4041

Employee benefit plans, Pension insurance, Reporting and recordkeeping requirements.

29 CFR Part 4041A

Employee benefit plans, Pension insurance, Reporting and recordkeeping requirements.

29 CFR Part 4043

Employee benefit plans, Pension insurance, Reporting and recordkeeping requirements.

29 CFR Part 4050

Employee benefit plans, Pension insurance, Reporting and recordkeeping requirements.

29 CFR Part 4062

Employee benefit plans, Pension insurance, Reporting and recordkeeping requirements.

29 CFR Part 4203

Employee benefit plans, Pension insurance, Reporting and recordkeeping requirements.

29 CFR Part 4204

Employee benefit plans, Pension insurance, Reporting and recordkeeping requirements.

29 CFR Part 4207

Employee benefit plans, Pension insurance.

29 CFR Part 4208

Employee benefit plans, Pension insurance, Reporting and recordkeeping requirements.

29 CFR Part 4211

Employee benefit plans, Pension insurance, Reporting and recordkeeping requirements.

29 CFR Part 4219

Employee benefit plans, Pension insurance, Reporting and recordkeeping requirements.

29 CFR Part 4220

Employee benefit plans, Pension insurance, Reporting and recordkeeping requirements.

29 CFR Part 4221

Employee benefit plans, Pension insurance.

29 CFR Part 4231

Employee benefit plans, Pension insurance, Reporting and recordkeeping requirements.

29 CFR Part 4245

Employee benefit plans, Pension insurance, Reporting and recordkeeping requirements.

29 CFR Part 4281

Employee benefit plans, Pension insurance, Reporting and recordkeeping requirements.

29 CFR Part 4901

Freedom of information.

29 CFR Part 4902

Privacy.

29 CFR Part 4903

Claims, Government employees, Income taxes.

29 CFR Part 4907

Administrative practice and procedure, Civil rights, Equal employment opportunity, Federal buildings and facilities, Individuals with disabilities.

For the reasons set forth above, the PBGC proposes to amend 29 CFR parts 4000, 4003, 4007, 4010, 4011, 4022, 4041, 4041A, 4043, 4050, 4062, 4203, 4204, 4207, 4208, 4211, 4219, 4220, 4221, 4231, 4245, 4281, 4901, 4902, 4903 and 4907 of 29 CFR chapter XL as follows:

1. Add the following note above the heading for Subchapter A of Chapter XL:

Note: PBGC's regulations were substantially reorganized and renumbered effective June 29, 1981 (at 46 FR 32574) and July 1, 1996 (at 61 FR 34002). Distribution and derivation tables showing the changes that occurred as a result of these amendments are available on the PBGC's Web site at http://www.pbgc.gov.

2. Revise part 4000 to read as follows:

PART 4000—FILING, ISSUANCE, COMPUTATION OF TIME, AND RECORD RETENTION

Subpart A—Filing Rules §

4000.1 What are these filing rules about?

4000.2 What definitions do I need to know for these rules?

4000.3 What methods of filing may I use?

4000.4 Where do I file my submission?

4000.5 Does the PBGC have discretion to waive these filing requirements?

Subpart B—Issuance Rules

4000.11 What are these issuance rules about?

4000.12 What definitions do I need to know for these rules?

4000.13 What methods of issuance may I use?

4000.14 What is the safe-harbor method for providing an issuance by electronic media?

4000.15 Does the PBGC have discretion to waive these issuance requirements?

Subpart C—Determining Filing and Issuance Dates

4000.21 What are these rules for determining the date of a filing or issuance about?

4000.22 What definitions do I need to know for these rules?

4000.23 When is my submission or issuance treated as filed or issued?

4000.24 What if I mail my submission or issuance using the U.S. Postal Service?

4000.25 What if I use the postal service of a foreign country?

4000.26 What if I use a commercial delivery service?

4000.27 What if I hand deliver my submission or issuance?

4000.28 What if I send a computer disk?

4000.29 What if I use electronic delivery?

4000.30 What if I need to resend my filing or issuance for technical reasons?

4000.31 Is my issuance untimely if I miss a few participants or beneficiaries?

4000.32 Does the PBGC have discretion to waive any requirements under this part?

Subpart D—Computation of Time

4000.41 What are these computation-of-time rules about?

4000.42 What definitions do I need to know for these rules?

4000.43 How do I compute a time period?

Subpart E—Electronic Means of Record Retention

4000.51 What are these record retention rules about?

4000.52 What definitions do I need to know for these rules?

4000.53 May I use electronic media to satisfy PBGC's record retention requirements?

4000.54 May I dispose of original paper records if I keep electronic copies?

Authority: 29 U.S.C. 1082(f), 1302(b)(3).

Subpart A—Filing Rules

§ *4000.1 What are these filing rules about?*

Where a particular regulation calls for their application, the rules in this subpart A of part 4000 tell you what filing methods you may use for any submission (including a payment) to us. They do not cover an issuance from you to anyone other than the PBGC, such as a notice to participants. Also, they do not cover filings with us that are not made under our regulations, such as procurement filings, litigation filings, and applications for employment with us. (Subpart B tells you what

methods you may use to issue a notice or otherwise provide information to any person other than us. Subpart C tells you how we determine your filing or issuance date. Subpart D tells you how to compute various periods of time. Subpart E tells you how to maintain required records in electronic form.)

§ *4000.2 What definitions do I need to know for these rules?*

You need to know two definitions from § 4001.2 of this chapter: *PBGC* and *person*. You also need to know the following definitions:

Filing means any notice, information, or payment that you submit to us under our regulations.

Issuance means any notice or other information you provide to any person other than us under our regulations.

We means the PBGC.

You means the person filing with us.

§ *4000.3 What methods of filing may I use?*

(a) *Paper filings.* You may file any submission with us by hand, mail, or commercial delivery service.

(b) *Electronic filings.* Current information on electronic filings, including permitted methods, fax numbers, and e-mail addresses, is—

(1) On our Web site, http://www.pbgc.gov;

(2) In our various printed forms and instructions packages; and

(3) Available by contacting our Customer Service Center at 1200 K Street, NW, Washington, DC, 20005-4026; telephone 1-800-400-7242 (for participants), or 1-800-736-2444 (for practitioners). (TTY/TDD users may call the Federal relay service toll-free at 1-800-877-8339 and ask to be connected to the appropriate number.)

§ *4000.4 Where do I file my submission?*

To find out where to send your submission, visit our Web site at http://www.pbgc.gov, see the instructions to our forms, or call our Customer Service Center (1-800-400-7242 for participants, or 1-800-736-2444 for practitioners; TTY/TDD users may call the Federal relay service toll-free at 1-800-877-8339 and ask to be connected to the appropriate number.) Because we have different addresses for different types of filings, you should make sure to use the appropriate address for your type of filing. For example, some filings (such as premium payments) must be sent to a specified bank, while other filings (such as the Standard Termination Notice (Form 500)) must be sent to the appropriate department at our offices in Washington, DC.

§ *4000.5 Does the PBGC have discretion to waive these filing requirements?*

We retain the discretion to waive any requirement under this part, at any time, if warranted by the facts and circumstances.

Subpart B—Issuance Rules

§ *4000.11 What are these issuance rules about?*

Where a particular regulation calls for their application, the rules in this subpart B of part 4000 tell you what methods you may use to issue a notice or otherwise provide information to any person other than us (e.g., a participant or beneficiary). They do not cover payments to third parties. In some cases, the PBGC regulations tell you to comply with requirements that are found somewhere other than in the PBGC's own regulations (e.g., requirements under the Internal Revenue Code (Title 26 of the United States Code)). If so, you must comply with any applicable issuance rules under those other requirements. (Subpart A tells you what filing methods you may use for filings with us. Subpart C tells you how we determine your filing or issuance date. Subpart D tells you how to compute various periods of time. Subpart E tells you how to maintain required records in electronic form.)

§ *4000.12 What definitions do I need to know for these rules?*

You need to know two definitions from § 4001.2 of this chapter: *PBGC* and *person*. You also need to know the following definitions:

Filing means any notice, information, or payment that you submit to us under our regulations.

Issuance means any notice or other information you provide to any person other than us under our regulations.

We means the PBGC.

You means the person providing the issuance to a third party.

§ *4000.13 What methods of issuance may I use?*

(a) *In general.* You may use any method of issuance, provided you use measures reasonably calculated to ensure actual receipt of the material by the intended recipient. Posting is not a permissible method of issuance under the rules of this part.

(b) *Electronic safe-harbor method.* Section 4000.14 provides a safe-harbor method for meeting the requirements of paragraph (a) of this section when providing an issuance using electronic media.

§ 4000.14 What is the safe harbor method for providing an issuance by electronic media?

(a) *In general.* Except as otherwise provided by applicable law, rule or regulation, you satisfy the requirements of § 4000.13 if you follow the methods described at paragraph (b) of this section when providing an issuance by electronic media to any person described in paragraph (c) or (d) of this section.

(b) *Issuance requirements.* (1) You must take appropriate and necessary measures reasonably calculated to ensure that the system for furnishing documents—

(i) Results in actual receipt of transmitted information (e.g., using return-receipt or notice of undelivered electronic mail features, conducting periodic reviews or surveys to confirm receipt of the transmitted information); and

(ii) Protects confidential information relating to the intended recipient (e.g., incorporating into the system measures designed to preclude unauthorized receipt of or access to such information by anyone other than the intended recipient);

(2) You prepare and furnish electronically delivered documents in a manner that is consistent with the style, format and content requirements applicable to the particular document;

(3) You provide each intended recipient with a notice, in electronic or non-electronic form, at the time a document is furnished electronically, that apprises the intended recipient of—

(i) The significance of the document when it is not otherwise reasonably evident as transmitted (e.g., "The attached participant notice contains information on the funding level of your defined benefit pension plan and the benefits guaranteed by the Pension Benefit Guaranty Corporation."); and

(ii) The intended recipient's right to request and obtain a paper version of such document; and

(4) You give the intended recipient, upon request, a paper version of the electronically furnished documents.

(c) *Employees with electronic access.* This section applies to a participant who—

(1) Has the ability to effectively access the document furnished in electronic form at any location where the participant is reasonably expected to perform duties as an employee; and

(2) With respect to whom access to the employer's electronic information system is an integral part of those duties.

(d) *Any person.* This section applies to any person who—

(1) Except as provided in paragraph (d)(2) of this section, has affirmatively consented, in electronic or non-electronic form, to receiving documents through electronic media and has not withdrawn such consent;

(2) In the case of documents to be furnished through the Internet or other electronic communication network, has affirmatively consented or confirmed consent electronically, in a manner that reasonably demonstrates the person's ability to access information in the electronic form that will be used to provide the information that is the subject of the consent, and has provided an address for the receipt of electronically furnished documents;

(3) Prior to consenting, is provided, in electronic or non-electronic form, a clear and conspicuous statement indicating:

(i) The types of documents to which the consent would apply;

(ii) That consent can be withdrawn at any time without charge;

(iii) The procedures for withdrawing consent and for updating the participant's, beneficiary's or other person's address for receipt of electronically furnished documents or other information;

(iv) The right to request and obtain a paper version of an electronically furnished document, including whether the paper version will be provided free of charge;

(v) Any hardware and software requirements for accessing and retaining the documents; and

(4) Following consent, if a change in hardware or software requirements needed to access or retain electronic documents creates a material risk that the person will be unable to access or retain electronically furnished documents,

(i) Is provided with a statement of the revised hardware or software requirements for access to and retention of electronically furnished documents;

(ii) Is given the right to withdraw consent without charge and without the imposition of any condition or consequence that was not disclosed at the time of the initial consent; and

(iii) Again consents, in accordance with the requirements of paragraph (d)(1) or paragraph (d)(2) of this section, as applicable, to the receipt of documents through electronic media.

§ 4000.15 Does the PBGC have discretion to waive these issuance requirements?

We retain the discretion to waive any requirement under this part, at any time, if warranted by the facts and circumstances.

Subpart C—Determining Filing and Issuance Dates

§ 4000.21 What are these rules for determining the filing or issuance date about?

Where the particular regulation calls for their application, the rules in this subpart C of part 4000 tell you how we will determine the date you send us a filing and the date you provide an issuance to someone other than us (such as a participant). These rules do not cover payments to third parties. In addition, they do not cover filings with us that are not made under our regulations, such as procurement filings, litigation filings, and applications for employment with us. In some cases, the PBGC regulations tell you to comply with requirements that are found somewhere other than in the PBGC's own regulations (e.g., requirements under the Internal Revenue Code (Title 26 of the United States Code)). In meeting those requirements, you should follow any applicable rules under those requirements for determining the filing and issuance date. (Subpart A tells you what filing methods you may use for filings with us. Subpart B tells you what methods you may use to issue a notice or otherwise provide information to any person other than us. Subpart D tells you how to compute various periods of time. Subpart E tells you how to maintain required records in electronic form.)

§ 4000.22 What definitions do I need to know for these rules?

You need to know two definitions from § 4001.2 of this chapter: *PBGC* and *person.* You also need to know the following definitions:

Business day means a day other than a Saturday, Sunday, or Federal holiday.

We means the PBGC.

You means the person filing with us or the person providing the issuance to a third party.

§ 4000.23 When is my submission or issuance treated as filed or issued?

(a) *Filed or issued when sent.* Generally, we treat your submission as filed, or your issuance as provided, on the date you send it, if you meet certain requirements. The requirements depend upon the method you use to send your submission or issuance (see §§ 4000.24 through 4000.29). (Certain filings are always treated as filed when received, as explained in paragraph (b)(2) of this section.)

(b) *Filed or issued when received.* (1) *In general.* If you do not meet the requirements for your submission or issuance to be treated as filed or issued when sent (see §§ 4000.24 through 4000.32), we treat it as filed or issued on the date received in a permitted format at the proper address.

(2) *Certain filings always treated as filed when received.* We treat the following submissions as filed on the date we receive your submission, no matter what method you use:

(i) *Applications for benefits.* An application for benefits or related submission (unless the instructions for the applicable forms provide for an earlier date);

(ii) *Advance notices of reportable events.* Information required under subpart C of part 4043 of this chapter, dealing with advance notice of reportable events;

(iii) *Form 200 filings.* Information required under subpart D of part 4043 of this chapter, dealing with notice of certain missed minimum funding contributions; and

(iv) *Requests for approval of multiemployer plan amendments.* A request for approval of an amendment filed with the PBGC pursuant to part 4220 of this chapter.

(3) *Determining our receipt date for your filing.* If we receive your submission at the correct address by 5 p.m. (our time) on a business day, we treat it as received on that date. If we receive your submission at the correct address after 5 p.m. on a business day, or anytime on a weekend or Federal holiday, we treat it as received on the next business day. For example, if you send your fax or e-mail of a Form 200 filing to us in Washington, DC, on Friday, March 15, from California at 3 p.m. (Pacific standard time), and we receive it immediately at 6 p.m. (our time), we treat it as received on Monday, March 18.

§ 4000.24 What if I mail my submission or issuance using the U.S. Postal Service?

(a) *In general.* Your filing or issuance date is the date you mail your submission or issuance using the U.S. Postal Service if you meet the requirements of paragraph (b) of this section, and you mail it by the last scheduled collection of the day. If you mail it later than that, or if there is no scheduled collection that day, your filing or issuance date is the date of the next scheduled collection. If you do not meet the requirements of paragraph (b), your filing or issuance date is the date of receipt at the proper address.

(b) *Requirements for "send date."* Your submission or issuance must meet the applicable postal requirements, be properly addressed, and you must use First-Class Mail (or a U.S. Postal Service mail class that is at least the equivalent of First-Class Mail, such as Priority Mail or Express Mail). However, if you are filing an advance notice of reportable event or a Form 200 (notice of certain missed contributions), see § 4000.23(b); these filings are always treated as filed when received.

(c) *Presumptions.* We make the following presumptions—

(1) *U.S. Postal Service postmark.* If you meet the requirements of paragraph (b) of this section and your submission or issuance has a legible U.S. Postal Service postmark, we presume that the postmark date is the filing or issuance date. However, you may prove an earlier date under paragraph (a) of this section.

(2) *Private meter postmark.* If you meet the requirements of paragraph (b) of this section and your submission or issuance has a legible postmark made by a private postage meter (but no legible U.S. Postal Service postmark) and arrives at the proper address by the time reasonably expected, we presume that the metered postmark date is your filing or issuance date. However, you may prove an earlier date under paragraph (a) of this section.

(d) *Examples.* (1) You mail your issuance using the U.S. Postal Service and meet the requirements of paragraph (b) of this section. You deposit your issuance in a mailbox at 4 p.m. on Friday, March 15 and the next scheduled collection at that mailbox is 5 p.m. that day. Your issuance date is March 15. If on the other hand you deposit it at 6 p.m. and the next collection at that mailbox is not until Monday, March 18, your issuance date is March 18.

(2) You mail your submission using the U.S. Postal Service and meet the requirements of paragraph (b) of this section. You deposit your submission in the mailbox at 4 p.m. on Friday, March 15, and the next scheduled collection at that mailbox is 5 p.m. that day. If your submission does not show a March 15 postmark, then you may prove to us that you mailed your submission by the last scheduled collection on March 15.

§ 4000.25 What if I use the postal service of a foreign country?

If you send your submission or issuance using the postal service of a foreign country, your filing or issuance date is the date of receipt at the proper address.

§ 4000.26 What if I use a commercial delivery service?

(a) *In general.* Your filing or issuance date is the date you deposit your submission or issuance with the commercial delivery service if you meet the requirements of paragraph (b) of this section, and you deposit it by the last scheduled collection of the day for the type of delivery you use (such as two-day delivery or overnight delivery). If you deposit it later than that, or if there is no scheduled collection that day, your filing or issuance date is the date of the next scheduled collection. If you do not meet the requirements of paragraph (b), your filing or issuance date is the date of receipt at the proper address. However, if you are filing an advance notice of reportable event or a Form 200 (notice of certain missed contributions), see § 4000.23(b); these filings are always treated as filed when received.

(b) *Requirements for "send date."* Your submission or issuance must meet the applicable requirements of the commercial delivery service, be properly addressed, and—

(1) *Delivery within two days.* It must be reasonable to expect your submission or issuance will arrive at the proper address by 5 p.m. on the second business day after the next scheduled collection; or

(2) *Designated delivery service.* You must use a "designated delivery service" under section 7502(f) of the Internal Revenue Code (Title 26 of the United States Code). Our Web site, http://www.pbgc.gov, lists those designated delivery services. You should make sure that both the provider and the particular type of delivery (such as two-day delivery) are designated.

(c) *Example.* You send your submission by commercial delivery service using two-day delivery. In addition, you meet the requirements of paragraph (b). Suppose the deadline for two-day delivery at the place you make your deposit is 8 p.m. on Friday, March 15. If you deposit your submission by the deadline, your filing date is March 15. If, instead, you deposit it after the 8 p.m. deadline and the next collection at that site for two-day delivery is on Monday, March 18, your filing date is March 18.

§ 4000.27 What if I hand deliver my submission or issuance?

Your filing or issuance date is the date of receipt of your hand-delivered submission or issuance at the proper address. A hand-delivered issuance need not be delivered while the intended recipient is physically present. For example, unless you have reason to believe that the intended recipient will not receive the notice within a reasonable amount of time, a notice is deemed to be received when you place it in the intended recipient's office mailbox. Our Web site, http://www.pbgc.gov, and the instructions to our forms, identify the proper addresses for filings with us.

§ 4000.28 What if I send a computer disk?

(a) *In general.* We determine your filing or issuance date for a computer disk as if you had sent a paper version of your submission or issuances if you meet the requirements of paragraph (b) of this section.

(1) *Filings.* For computer-disk filings, we may treat your submission as invalid if you fail to meet the requirements of paragraph (b)(1) or (b)(3) of this section.

(2) *Issuances.* For computer-disk issuances, we may treat your issuance as invalid if—

(i) You fail to meet the requirements ("using measures reasonably calculated to ensure actual receipt") of § 4000.13(a), or

(ii) You fail to meet the contact information requirements of paragraph (b)(3) of this section.

(b) *Requirements.* To get the filing date under paragraph (a) of this section, you must meet the requirements of paragraphs (b)(1) and (b)(3) To get the issuance date under paragraph (a), you must meet the requirements of paragraphs (b)(2) and (b)(3).

(1) *Technical requirements for filings.* For filings, your electronic disk must comply with any technical requirements for that type of submission (our Web site, http://www.pbgc.gov, identifies the technical requirements for each type of filing).

(2) *Technical requirements for issuances.* For issuances, you must meet the safe-harbor requirements of § 4000.14.

(3) *Identify contact person.* For filings and issuances, you must include, in a paper cover letter or on the disk's label, the name and telephone number of the person to contact if we or the intended recipient is unable to read the disk.

§ 4000.29 What if I use electronic delivery?

(a) *In general.* Your filing or issuance date is the date you electronically transmit your submission or issuance to the proper address if you meet the requirements of paragraph (b) of this section. Note that we always treat an advance notice of reportable event and a Form 200 (notice of certain missed contributions) as filed when received.

(1) *Filings.* For electronic filings, if you fail to meet the requirements of paragraph (b)(1) or (b)(3) of this section, we may treat your submission as invalid.

(2) *Issuances.* For electronic issuances, we may treat your issuance as invalid if—

(i) You fail to meet the requirements ("using measures reasonably calculated to ensure actual receipt") of § 4000.13(a), or

(ii) You fail to meet the contact information requirements of paragraph (b)(3) of this section.

(b) *Requirements.* To get the filing date under paragraph (a), you must meet the requirements of paragraphs (b)(1) and (b)(3). To get the issuance date under paragraph (a), you must meet the requirement of paragraphs (b)(2) and (b)(3).

(1) *Technical requirements for filings.* For filings, your electronic submission must comply with any technical requirements for that type

of submission (our Web site, http://www.pbgc.gov, identifies the technical requirements for each type of filing).

(2) *Technical requirements for issuances.* For issuances, you must meet the safe-harbor requirements of § 4000.14.

(3) *Identify contact person.* For an e-mail submission or issuance with an attachment, you must include, in the body of your e-mail, the name and telephone number of the person to contact if we or the intended recipient needs you to resubmit your filing or issuance.

(c) *Failure to meet address requirement.* If you send your electronic submission or issuance to the wrong address (but you meet the requirements of paragraph (b) of this section), your filing or issuance date is the date of receipt at the proper address.

§ *4000.30 What if I need to resend my filing or issuance for technical reasons?*

(a) *Request to resubmit.* (1) *Filing.* We may ask you to resubmit all or a portion of your filing for technical reasons (for example, because we are unable to open an attachment to your e-mail). In that case, your submission (or portion) is invalid. However, if you comply with the request or otherwise resolve the problem (e.g., by providing advice that allows us to open the attachment to your e-mail) by the date we specify, your filing date for the submission (or portion) that we asked you to resubmit is the date you filed your original submission. If you comply with our request late, your submission (or portion) will be treated as filed on the date of your resubmission.

(2) *Issuance.* The intended recipient may, for good reason (of a technical nature), ask you to resend all or a portion of your issuance (for example, because of a technical problem in opening an attachment to your e-mail). In that case, your issuance (or portion) is invalid. However, if you comply with the request or otherwise resolve the problem (e.g., by providing advice that the recipient uses to open the attachment to your e-mail), within a reasonable time, your issuance date for the issuance (or portion) that the intended recipient asked you to resend is the date you provided your original issuance. If you comply with the request late, your issuance (or portion) will be treated as provided on the date of your reissuance.

(b) *Reason to believe submission or issuance not received or defective.* If you have reason to believe that we have not received your submission (or have received it in a form that is not useable), or that the intended recipient has not received your issuance (or has received it in a form that is not useable), you must promptly resend your submission or issuance to get your original filing or issuance date. However, we may require evidence to support your original filing or issuance date. If you are not prompt, or you do not provide us with any evidence we may require to support your original filing or issuance date, your filing or issuance date is the filing or issuance date of your resubmission or reissuance.

§ *4000.31 Is my issuance untimely if I miss a few participants or beneficiaries?*

The PBGC will not treat your issuance as untimely based on your failure to provide the issuance to a participant or beneficiary in a timely manner if—

(a) The failure resulted from administrative error;

(b) The failure involved only a de minimis percentage of intended recipients; and

(c) You resend the issuance to the intended recipient promptly after discovering the error.

§ *4000.32 Does the PBGC have discretion to waive any requirements under this part?*

We retain the discretion to waive any requirement under this part, at any time, if warranted by the facts and circumstances.

Subpart D—Computation of Time

§ *4000.41 What are these computation-of-time rules about?*

The rules in this subpart D of part 4000 tell you how to compute time periods under our regulations (e.g., for filings with us and issuances to third parties) where the particular regulation calls for their application. (There are specific exceptions or modifications to these rules in § 4007.6 of this chapter (premium payments), § 4050.6(d)(3) of this chapter (payment of designated benefits for missing participants), and § 4062.10 of this chapter (employer liability payments). In some cases, the PBGC regulations tell you to comply with requirements that are found somewhere other than in the PBGC's own regulations (e.g., requirements under the Internal Revenue Code (Title 26 of the United States Code)). In meeting those requirements, you should follow any applicable computation-of-time rules under those other requirements.

(Subpart A tells you what filing methods you may use for filings with us. Subpart B tells you what methods you may use to issue a notice or otherwise provide information to any person other than us. Subpart C tells you how we determine your filing or issuance date. Subpart E tells you how to maintain required records in electronic form.)

§ *4000.42 What definitions do I need to know for these rules?*

You need to know two definitions from § 4001.2 of this chapter: *PBGC* and *person.* You also need to know the following definitions:

Business da y means a day other than a Saturday, Sunday, or Federal holiday.

We means the PBGC.

You means the person responsible, under our regulations, for the filing or issuance to which these rules apply.

§ *4000.43 How do I compute a time period?*

(a) *In general.* If you are computing a time period to which this part applies, whether you are counting forwards or backwards, the day after (or before) the act, event, or default that begins the period is day one, the next day is day two, and so on. Count all days, including weekends and Federal holidays. However, if the last day you count is a weekend or Federal holiday, extend or shorten the period (whichever benefits you in complying with the time requirement) to the next regular business day. The examples in paragraph (d) of this section illustrate these rules.

(b) *When date is designated.* In some cases, our regulations designate a specific day as the end of a time period, such as "the last day" of a plan year or "the fifteenth day" of a calendar month. In these cases, you simply use the designated day, together with the weekend and holiday rule of paragraph (a) of this section.

(c) *When counting months.* If a time period is measured in months, first identify the date (day, month, and year) of the act, event, or default that begins the period. The corresponding day of the following (or preceding) month is one month later (or earlier), and so on. For example, two months after July 15 is September 15. If the period ends on a weekend or Federal holiday, follow the weekend and holiday rule of paragraph (a) of this section. There are two special rules for determining what the corresponding day is when you start counting on a day that is at or near the end of a calendar month:

(1) *Special "last-day" rule.* If you start counting on the last day of a calendar month, the corresponding day of any calendar month is the last day of that calendar month. For example, a three-month period measured from November 30 ends (if counting forward) on the last day of February (the 28th and 29th) or (if counting backward) on the last day of August (the 31st).

(2) *Special February rule.* If you start counting on the 29th or 30th of a calendar month, the corresponding day of February is the last day of February. For example, a one-month period measured from January 29 ends on the last day of February (the 28th or 29th).

(d) *Examples.* (1) *Counting backwards.* Suppose you are required to file an advance notice of reportable event for a transaction that is effective December 31. Under our regulations, the notice is due at least 30 days before the effective date of the event. To determine your deadline, count December 30 as day 1, December 29 as day 2, December 28 as day 3, and so on. Therefore, December 1 is day 30. Assuming that day is not a weekend or holiday, your notice is timely if you file it on or before December 1.

(2) *Weekend or holiday rule.* Suppose you are filing a notice of intent to terminate. The notice must be issued at least 60 days and no more than 90 days before the proposed termination date. Suppose the 60th day before the proposed termination date is a Saturday. Your notice is timely if you issue it on the following Monday even though that is only 58 days before the proposed termination date. Similarly, if the 90th day before the proposed termination date is Wednesday, July 4 (a Federal holiday), your notice is timely if you issue it on Tuesday, July 3, even though that is 91 days before the proposed termination date.

(3) *Counting months.* Suppose you are required to issue a Participant Notice two months after December 31. The deadline for the Participant Notice is the last day of February (the 28th or 29th). If the last day of February is a weekend or Federal holiday, your deadline is extended until the next day that is not a weekend or Federal holiday.

Subpart E—Electronic Means of Record Retention

§ *4000.51 What are these record retention rules about?*

The rules in this subpart E of part 4000 tell you what methods you may use to meet any record retention requirement under our regulations if you choose to use electronic means. The rules for who must retain the records, how long the records must be maintained, and how records must be made available to us are contained in the specific part where the record retention requirement is found. (Subpart A tells you what filing methods you may use for filings with us and how we determine your filing date. Subpart B tells you what methods you may use to issue a notice or otherwise provide information to any person other than us. Subpart C tells you how we determine your filing or issuance date. Subpart D tells you how to compute various periods of time.)

§ 4000.52 What definitions do I need to know for these rules?

You need to know two definitions from § 4001.2 of this chapter: *PBGC* and *person*. You also need to know the following definitions:

We means the PBGC.

You means the person subject to the record retention requirement.

§ 4000.53 May I use electronic media to satisfy PBGC's record retention requirements?

General requirements. You may use electronic media to satisfy the record maintenance and retention requirements of this chapter if:

(a) The electronic recordkeeping system has reasonable controls to ensure the integrity, accuracy, authenticity and reliability of the records kept in electronic form;

(b) The electronic records are maintained in reasonable order and in a safe and accessible place, and in such manner as they may be readily inspected or examined (for example, the recordkeeping system should be capable of indexing, retaining, preserving, retrieving and reproducing the electronic records);

(c) The electronic records are readily convertible into legible and readable paper copy as may be needed to satisfy reporting and disclosure requirements or any other obligation under section 302(f)(4), section 307(e), or Title IV of ERISA;

(d) The electronic recordkeeping system is not subject, in whole or in part, to any agreement or restriction that would, directly or indirectly, compromise or limit a person's ability to comply with any reporting and disclosure requirement or any other obligation under section 302(f)(4), section 307(e), or Title IV of ERISA;

(e) Adequate records management practices are established and implemented (for example, following procedures for labeling of electronically maintained or retained records, providing a secure storage environment, creating back-up electronic copies and selecting an off-site storage location, observing a quality assurance program evidenced by regular evaluations of the electronic recordkeeping system including periodic checks of electronically maintained or retained records; and retaining paper copies of records that cannot be clearly, accurately or completely transferred to an electronic recordkeeping system); and

(f) All electronic records exhibit a high degree of legibility and readability when displayed on a video display terminal or other method of electronic transmission and when reproduced in paper form. The term "legibility" means the observer must be able to identify all letters and numerals positively and quickly to the exclusion of all other letters or numerals. The term "readability" means that the observer must be able to recognize a group of letters or numerals as words or complete numbers.

§ 4000.54 May I dispose of original paper records if I keep electronic copies?

You may dispose of original paper records any time after they are transferred to an electronic recordkeeping system that complies with the requirements of this subpart, except such original records may not be discarded if the electronic record would not constitute a duplicate or substitute record under the terms of the plan and applicable federal or state law.

PART 4003—RULES FOR ADMINISTRATIVE REVIEW OF AGENCY DECISIONS

3. The authority citation for part 4003 continues to read as follows:

Authority: 29 U.S.C. 1302(b)(3).

4. Revise § 4003.9 to read as follows:

§ 4003.9 Method and date of filing.

(a) *Method of filing.* The PBGC applies the rules in subpart A of part 4000 of this chapter to determine permissible methods of filing with the PBGC under this part.

(b) *Date of filing.* The PBGC applies the rules in subpart C of part 4000 of this chapter to determine the date that a submission under this part was filed with the PBGC.

5. Revise § 4003.10 to read as follows:

§ 4003.10 Computation of time.

The PBGC applies the rules in subpart D of part 4000 of this chapter to compute any time period under this part.

§ 4003.33 [Amended]

6. Amend § 4003.33 to add the sentence "See § 4000.4 of this chapter for information on where to file." to the end of the paragraph.

§ 4003.53 [Amended]

7. Amend § 4003.53 to add the sentence "See § 4000.4 of this chapter for information on where to file." to the end of the paragraph.

PART 4007—PAYMENT OF PREMIUMS

8. The authority citation for part 4007 continues to read as follows:

Authority: 29 U.S.C. 1302(b)(3), 1303(a), 1306, 1307.

9. Revise § 4007.3 to read as follows:

§ 4007.3 Filing requirements; method of filing.

(a) *Filing requirements.* The estimation, declaration, reconciliation and payment of premiums shall be made using the forms prescribed by and in accordance with the instructions in the PBGC annual Premium Payment Package. The plan administrator of each covered plan must file the prescribed form or forms, and any premium payments due, no later than the applicable due date specified in § 4007.11.

(b) *Method of filing.* The PBGC applies the rules in subpart A of part 4000 of this chapter to determine permissible methods of filing with the PBGC under this part.

10. Revise § 4007.5 to read as follows:

§ 4007.5 Date of filing.

The PBGC applies the rules in subpart C of part 4000 of this chapter to determine the date that you filed your submission under this part with the PBGC.

11. Revise § 4007.6 to read as follows:

§ 4007.6 Computation of time.

The PBGC applies the rules in subpart D of part 4000 of this chapter to compute any time period under this part. However, for purposes of determining the amount of a late payment interest charge under § 4007.7 or of a late payment penalty charge under § 4007.8, the rules in part 4000.43 of this chapter governing weekends and Federal holidays do not apply.

12. Revise paragraphs (a) and (c)(1) of § 4007.10 to read as follows:

§ 4007.10 Recordkeeping; audits; disclosure of information.

(a) *Retention of records to support premium payments.* (1) *In general.* All plan records, including calculations and other data prepared by an enrolled actuary or, for a plan described in section 412(i) of the Internal Revenue Code (Title 26 of the United States Code), by the insurer from which the insurance contracts are purchased, that are necessary to support or to validate premium payments under this part shall be retained by the plan administrator for a period of six years after the premium due date. Records that must be retained pursuant to this paragraph include, but are not limited to, records that establish the number of plan participants and that reconcile the calculation of the plan's unfunded vested benefits with the actuarial valuation upon which the calculation was based.

(2) *Electronic recordkeeping.* The plan administrator may use electronic media for maintenance and retention of records required by this part in accordance with the requirements of subpart E of part 4000 of this chapter.

* * * * *

(c) *Providing record information.* (1) *In general.* The plan administrator shall make the records retained pursuant to paragraph (a) of this section available to the PBGC upon request for inspection and photocopying (or, for electronic records, inspection, electronic copying, and printout) at the location where they are kept (or another, mutually agreeable, location) and shall submit information in such records to the PBGC within 45 days of the date of the PBGC's written request therefor, or by a different time specified therein.

* * * * *

PART 4010—ANNUAL FINANCIAL AND ACTUARIAL INFORMATION REPORTING

13. Revise the authority citation for part 4010 to read as follows:

Authority: 29 U.S.C. 1302(b)(3), 1310.

14. Revise paragraphs (c), (d) and (e) of §4010.10 to read as follows:

§4010.10 Due date and filing with the PBGC.

* * * * *

(c) *How and where to file.* The PBGC applies the rules in subpart A of part 4000 of this chapter to determine permissible methods of filing with the PBGC under this part. See §4000.4 for information on where to file.

(d) *Date of filing.* The PBGC applies the rules in subpart C of part 4000 of this chapter to determine the date that a submission under this part was filed with the PBGC.

(e) *Computation of time.* The PBGC applies the rules in subpart D of part 4000 of this chapter to compute any time period under this part.

PART 4011—DISCLOSURE TO PARTICIPANTS

15. The authority citation for part 4011 continues to read as follows:

Authority: 29 U.S.C. 1302(b)(3), 1311.

16. Revise §4011.9 to read as follows:

§4011.9 Method and date of issuance of notice; computation of time.

(a) *Method of issuance.* The PBGC applies the rules in subpart B of part 4000 of this chapter to determine permissible methods of delivery of the Participant Notice. The Participant Notice may be issued together with another document, such as the summary annual report required under section 104(b)(3) of ERISA for the prior plan year, but must be in a separate document.

(b) *Issuance date.* The PBGC applies the rules in subpart C of part 4000 of this chapter to determine the date the Participant Notice was issued.

(c) *Computation of time.* The PBGC applies the rules in subpart D of part 4000 of this chapter to compute any time period for issuances under this part.

PART 4022—BENEFITS PAYABLE IN TERMINATED SINGLE-EMPLOYER PLANS

17. The authority citation for part 4022 continues to read as follows:

Authority: 29 U.S.C. 1302, 1322, 1322b, 1341(c)(3)(D), and 1344.

18. Amend §4022.9 by adding paragraph (d) to read as follows:

§4022.9 Time of payment; benefit applications.

* * * * *

(d) *Filing with the PBGC.* (1) *Method and date of filing.* The PBGC applies the rules in subpart A of part 4000 of this chapter to determine permissible methods of filing with the PBGC under this part. Benefit applications and related submissions are treated as filed on the date received by the PBGC unless the instructions for the applicable form provide for an earlier date. Subpart C of part 4000 of this chapter provides rules for determining when the PBGC receives a submission.

(2) *Where to file.* See §4000.4 of this chapter for information on where to file.

(3) *Computation of time.* The PBGC applies the rules in subpart D of part 4000 of this chapter to compute any time period for filing under this part.

PART 4041—TERMINATION OF SINGLE-EMPLOYER PLANS

19. The authority citation for part 4041 continues to read as follows:

Authority: 29 U.S.C. 1302(b)(3), 1341, 1344, 1350.

20. Amend §4041.3 as follows:

a. Revise paragraphs (a), (b), and (c)(1) to read as follows:

b. Remove paragraph (c)(2);

c. Add the word "or" to the end of paragraph (c)(3)(i);

d. Remove paragraph (c)(3)(ii) and redesignate paragraph (c)(3)(iii) as paragraph (c)(3)(ii);

e. Redesignate paragraphs (c)(3) through (c)(6) as paragraphs (c)(2) through (c)(5).

§4041.3 Computation of time; filing and issuance rules.

(a) *Computation of time.* The PBGC applies the rules in subpart D of part 4000 of this chapter to compute any time period under this part. A proposed termination date may be any day, including a weekend or Federal holiday.

(b) *Filing with the PBGC.* (1) *Method and date of filing.* The PBGC applies the rules in subpart A of part 4000 of this chapter to determine permissible methods of filing with the PBGC under this part. The PBGC applies the rules in subpart C of part 4000 of this chapter to determine the date that a submission under this part was filed with the PBGC.

(2) *Where to file.* See §4000.4 of this chapter for information on where to file.

(c) *Issuance to third parties.* The following rules apply to affected parties (other than the PBGC). For purposes of this paragraph (c), a person entitled to notice under the spin-off/termination transaction rules of §4041.23(c) or §4041.24(f) is treated as an affected party.

(1) *Method and date of issuance.* The PBGC applies the rules in subpart B of part 4000 of this chapter to determine permissible methods of issuance under this part. The PBGC applies the rules in subpart C of part 4000 of this chapter to determine the date that an issuance under this part was provided.

* * * * *

21. Revise §4041.5 to read as follows:

§4041.5 Record retention and availability.

(a) *Retention requirement.* (1) *Persons subject to requirement; records to be retained.* Each contributing sponsor and the plan administrator of a plan terminating in a standard termination, or in a distress termination that closes out in accordance with §4041.50, must maintain all records necessary to demonstrate compliance with section 4041 of ERISA and this part. If a contributing sponsor or the plan administrator maintains information in accordance with this section, the other(s) need not maintain that information.

(2) *Retention period.* The records described in paragraph (a)(1) of this section must be preserved for six years after the date when the post-distribution certification under this part is filed with the PBGC.

(3) *Electronic recordkeeping.* The contributing sponsor or plan administrator may use electronic media for maintenance and retention of records required by this part in accordance with the requirements of subpart E of part 4000 of this chapter.

(b) *Availability of records.* The contributing sponsor or plan administrator must make all records needed to determine compliance with section 4041 of ERISA and this part available to the PBGC upon request for inspection and photocopying (or, for electronic records, inspection, electronic copying, and printout) at the location where they are kept (or another, mutually agreeable, location) and must submit such records to the PBGC within 30 days after the date of a written request by the PBGC or by a later date specified therein.

PART 4041A—TERMINATION OF MULTIEMPLOYER PLANS

22. The authority citation for part 4041A continues to read as follows:

Authority: 29 U.S.C. 1302(b)(3), 1341a, 1441.

23. Revise §4041A.3 to read as follows:

§4041A.3 Method and date of filing; where to file; computation of time; issuances to third parties.

(a) *Method and date of filing.* The PBGC applies the rules in subpart A of part 4000 of this chapter to determine permissible methods of filing with the PBGC under this part. The PBGC applies the rules in subpart C of part 4000 of this chapter to determine the date that a submission under this part was filed with the PBGC.

(b) *Where to file.* See §4000.4 of this chapter for information on where to file.

(c) *Computation of time.* The PBGC applies the rules in subpart D of part 4000 of this chapter to compute any time period for filing or issuance under this part.

(d) *Method and date of issuance.* The PBGC applies the rules in subpart B of part 4000 of this chapter to determine permissible methods of issuance under this part. The PBGC applies the rules in subpart C of part 4000 of this chapter to determine the date that an issuance under this part was provided.

PART 4043—REPORTABLE EVENTS AND CERTAIN OTHER NOTIFICATION REQUIREMENTS

24. The authority citation for part 4043 continues to read as follows:

Authority: 29 U.S.C. 1082(f), 1302(b)(3), 1443.

25. Revise §4043.5 to read as follows:

§4043.5 How and where to file.

The PBGC applies the rules in the instructions to the applicable PBGC reporting form and subpart A of part 4000 of this chapter to determine permissible methods of filing with the PBGC under this part. See §4000.4 for information on where to file.

26. Amend §4043.6 by removing paragraph (d) and revising paragraphs (a) and (b) and the paragraph heading of paragraph (c) to read as follows:

§4043.6 Date of filing.

(a) *Post-event notice filings.* The PBGC applies the rules in subpart C of part 4000 of this chapter to determine the date that a submission under subpart B of this part was filed with the PBGC.

(b) *Advance notice and Form 200 filings.* Information filed under subpart C or D of this part is treated as filed on the date it is received by the PBGC. Subpart C of part 4000 of this chapter provides rules for determining when the PBGC receives a submission.

(c) *Partial electronic filing; deemed filing date.* * * *

* * * * *

27. Revise §4043.7 to read as follows:

§4043.7 Computation of time.

The PBGC applies the rules in subpart D of part 4000 of this chapter to compute any time period under this part.

PART 4050—MISSING PARTICIPANTS

28. The authority citation for part 4050 continues to read as follows:

Authority: 29 U.S.C. 1302(b)(3), 1350.

29. Amend §4050.6 by revising paragraph (d) to read as follows:

§4050.6 Payment and required documentation.

* * * * *

(d) *Filing with the PBGC.* (1) *Method and date of filing.* The PBGC applies the rules in subpart A of part 4000 of this chapter to determine permissible methods of filing with the PBGC under this part. The PBGC applies the rules in subpart C of part 4000 of this chapter to determine the date that a submission under this part was filed with the PBGC.

(2) *Where to file.* See §4000.4 of this chapter for information on where to file.

(3) *Computation of time.* The PBGC applies the rules in subpart D of part 4000 of this chapter to compute any time period for filing under this part. However, for purposes of determining the amount of an interest charge under §4050.6(b) or §4050.12(c)(2)(iii), the rules in §4000.43 of this chapter governing weekends and Federal holidays do not apply.

PART 4062—LIABILITY FOR TERMINATION OF SINGLE-EMPLOYER PLANS

30. The authority citation for part 4062 continues to read as follows:

Authority: 29 U.S.C. 1302(b)(3), 1362-1364, 1367, 1368.

31. Revise §4062.9 to read as follows:

§4062.9 Method and date of filing; where to file.

(a) *Method of filing.* The PBGC applies the rules in subpart A of part 4000 of this chapter to determine permissible methods of filing with the PBGC under this part. Payment of liability must be clearly designated as such and include the name of the plan.

(b) *Filing date.* The PBGC applies the rules in subpart C of part 4000 of this chapter to determine the date that a submission under this part was filed with the PBGC.

(c) *Where to file.* See §4000.4 of this chapter for information on where to file.

32. Revise §4062.10 to read as follows:

§4062.10 Computation of time.

The PBGC applies the rules in subpart D of part 4000 of this chapter to compute any time period under this part. However, for purposes of determining the amount of an interest charge under §4062.7, the rules in §4000.43 of this chapter governing weekends and Federal holidays do not apply.

PART 4203—EXTENSION OF SPECIAL WITHDRAWAL LIABILITY RULES

33. The authority citation for part 4203 continues to read as follows:

Authority: 29 U.S.C. 1302(b)(3).

34. Amend §4203.4 by revising paragraphs (a) and (c) to read as follows:

§4203.4 Requests for PBGC approval of plan amendments.

(a) *Filing of request.* (1) *In general.* A plan shall apply to the PBGC for approval of a plan amendment which establishes special complete or partial withdrawal liability rules. The request for approval shall be filed after the amendment is adopted. PBGC approval shall also be required for any subsequent modification of the plan amendment, other than a repeal of the amendment which results in employers being subject to the general statutory rules on withdrawal.

(2) *Method and date of filing.* The PBGC applies the rules in subpart A of part 4000 of this chapter to determine permissible methods of filing with the PBGC under this part. The PBGC applies the rules in subpart C of part 4000 of this chapter to determine the date that a submission under this part was filed with the PBGC.

* * * * *

(c) *Where to file.* See §4000.4 of this chapter for information on where to file.

* * * * *

PART 4204—VARIANCES FOR SALE OF ASSETS

35. The authority citation for part 4204 continues to read as follows:

Authority: 29 U.S.C. 1302(b)(3), 1384(c).

36. Amend §4204.11 as follows:

a. In the first sentence of paragraph (b), remove the word "filed" and add in its place the word "submitted".

b. Add new paragraph (e) to read as follows:

§4204.11 Variance of the bond/escrow and sale-contract requirements.

* * * * *

(e) *Method and date of issuance.* The PBGC applies the rules in subpart B of part 4000 of this chapter to determine permissible methods of issuance under this subpart. The PBGC applies the rules in subpart C of part 4000 of this chapter to determine the date that an issuance under this subpart was provided.

37. Amend §4204.21 by revising paragraphs (a) and (c) to read as follows:

§4204.21 Requests to PBGC for variances and exemptions.

(a) *Filing of request.* (1) *In general.* If a transaction covered by this part does not satisfy the conditions set forth in subpart B of this part, or if the parties decline to provide to the plan privileged or confidential financial information within the meaning of section 552(b)(4) of the Freedom of Information Act (5 U.S.C. 552), the purchaser or seller may request from the PBGC an exemption or variance from the requirements of section 4204(a)(1)(B) and (C) of ERISA.

(2) *Method of filing.* The PBGC applies the rules in subpart A of part 4000 of this chapter to determine permissible methods of filing with the PBGC under this subpart.

* * * * *

(c) *Where to file.* See §4000.4 of this chapter for information on where to file.

* * * * *

PART 4207—REDUCTION OR WAIVER OF COMPLETE WITHDRAWAL LIABILITY

38. The authority citation for part 4207 continues to read as follows:

Authority: 29 U.S.C. 1302(b)(3), 1387.

39. Amend §4207.10 by revising paragraph (c) to read as follows:

§4207.10 Plan rules for abatement.

* * * * *

(c) *Where to file.* See §4000.4 of this chapter for information on where to file.

* * * * *

40. Add §4207.11 to read as follows:

§4207.11 Method and date of filing and issuance; computation of time.

(a) *Method of filing.* The PBGC applies the rules in subpart A of part 4000 of this chapter to determine permissible methods of filing with the PBGC under this part.

(b) *Method of issuance.* The PBGC applies the rules in subpart B of part 4000 of this chapter to determine permissible methods of issuance under this part.

(c) *Date of issuance.* The PBGC applies the rules in subpart C of part 4000 of this chapter to determine the date that an issuance under this part was provided.

PART 4208—REDUCTION OR WAIVER OF PARTIAL WITHDRAWAL LIABILITY

41. Revise the authority citation for part 4208 to read as follows:

Authority: 29 U.S.C. 1302(b)(3), 1388(c) and (e).

42. Amend § 4208.9 by revising paragraph (c) to read as follows:

§ 4208.9 Plan adoption of additional abatement conditions.

* * * * *

(c) *Where to file.* See § 4000.4 of this chapter for information on where to file.

* * * * *

43. Add § 4208.10 to read as follows:

§ 4208.10 Method and date of filing and issuance; computation of time.

(a) *Method of filing.* The PBGC applies the rules in subpart A of part 4000 of this chapter to determine permissible methods of filing with the PBGC under this part.

(b) *Method of issuance.* The PBGC applies the rules in subpart B of part 4000 of this chapter to determine permissible methods of issuance under this part.

(c) *Date of issuance.* The PBGC applies the rules in subpart C of part 4000 of this chapter to determine the date that an issuance under this part was provided.

PART 4211—ALLOCATING UNFUNDED VESTED BENEFITS TO WITHDRAWING EMPLOYERS

44. Revise the authority citation for part 4211 to read as follows:

Authority: 29 U.S.C. 1302(b)(3), 1391(c)(1), (c)(2)(d), (c)(5)(B), (c)(5)(D), and (f).

45. Amend § 4211.22 by revising paragraphs (a) and (c) to read as follows:

§ 4211.22 Requests for PBGC approval.

(a) *Filing of request.* (1) *In general.* A plan shall submit a request for approval of an alternative allocation method or modification to an allocation method to the PBGC in accordance with the requirements of this section as soon as practicable after the adoption of the amendment.

(2) *Method of filing.* The PBGC applies the rules in subpart A of part 4000 of this chapter to determine permissible methods of filing with the PBGC under this subpart.

* * * * *

(c) *Where to submit.* See § 4000.4 of this chapter for information on where to file.

* * * * *

PART 4219—NOTICE, COLLECTION AND REDETERMINATION OF WITHDRAWAL LIABILITY

46. The authority citation for part 4219 continues to read as follows:

Authority: 29 U.S.C. 1302(b)(3), 1388(c) and (e).

47. Amend § 4219.17 by revising paragraphs (a), (d) and (e) to read as follows:

§ 4219.17 Filings with PBGC.

(a) *Filing requirements.* (1) *In general.* The plan sponsor shall file with PBGC a notice that a mass withdrawal has occurred and separate certifications that determinations of redetermination liability and reallocation liability have been made and notices provided to employers in accordance with this subpart.

(2) *Method of filing.* The PBGC applies the rules in subpart A of part 4000 of this chapter to determine permissible methods of filing with the PBGC under this subpart.

(3) *Computation of time.* The PBGC applies the rules in subpart D of part 4000 of this chapter to compute any time period under this subpart for filing with the PBGC.

* * * * *

(d) *Where to file.* See § 4000.4 for information on where to file.

(e) *Date of filing.* The PBGC applies the rules in subpart C of part 4000 of this chapter to determine the date that a submission under this part was filed with the PBGC.

* * * * *

§ 4219.19 [Redesignated as § 4219.20]

48. Redesignate § 4219.19 as § 4219.20.

49. Add a new § 4219.19 to read as follows:

§ 4219.19 Issuances to third parties; methods and dates.

The PBGC applies the rules in subpart B of part 4000 of this chapter to determine permissible methods of issuance under this subpart. The PBGC applies the rules in subpart C of part 4000 of this chapter to determine the date that an issuance under this subpart was provided. The PBGC applies the rules in subpart D of part 4000 of this chapter to compute any time period for issuances to third parties under this subpart.

PART 4220—PROCEDURES FOR PBGC APPROVAL OF PLAN AMENDMENTS

50. The authority citation for part 4220 continues to read as follows:

Authority: 29 U.S.C. 1302(b)(3), 1400.

51. Amend § 4220.3 by revising paragraphs (a) and (c) and adding paragraph (f) to read as follows:

§ 4220.3 Requests for PBGC approval.

(a) *Filing of request.* (1) *In general.* A request for approval of an amendment filed with the PBGC in accordance with this section shall constitute notice to the PBGC for purposes of the 90-day period specified in section 4220 of ERISA. A request is treated as filed on the date on which a request containing all information required by paragraph (d) of this section is received by the PBGC. Subpart C of part 4000 of this chapter provides rules for determining when the PBGC receives a submission.

(2) *Method and date of filing.* The PBGC applies the rules in subpart A of part 4000 of this chapter to determine permissible methods of filing with the PBGC under this part.

* * * * *

(c) *Where to file.* See § 4000.4 of this chapter for information on where to file.

* * * * *

(f) *Computation of time.* The PBGC applies the rules in subpart D of part 4000 of this chapter to compute any time period under this part.

PART 4221—ARBITRATION OF DISPUTES IN MULTIEMPLOYER PLANS

52. The authority citation for part 4221 continues to read as follows:

Authority: 29 U.S.C. 1302(b)(3), 1401.

§ 4221.4 Appointment of the arbitrator. [Amended]

53. Amend paragraph (c) of § 4221.4 by revising the second sentence to read as follows:

* * * * *

(c) *Challenge and withdrawal.* * * * The request for withdrawal shall be served on all other parties and the arbitrator by hand or by certified or registered mail (or by any other method that includes verification or acknowledgment of receipt and meets the requirements of § 4000.14 of this chapter) and shall include a statement of the circumstances that, in the requesting party's view, affect the arbitrator's impartiality and a statement that the requesting party has brought these circumstances to the attention of the arbitrator and the other parties at the earliest practicable point in the proceedings. * * *

* * * * *

54. Amend § 4221.6 by revising paragraph (b) to read as follows:

§ 4221.6 Hearing.

* * * * *

(b) After the time and place for the hearing have been established, the arbitrator shall serve a written notice of the hearing on the parties by hand, by certified or registered mail, or by any other method that includes verification or acknowledgment of receipt and meets the requirements of § 4000.14 of this chapter.

* * * * *

55. Revise § 4221.12 to read as follows:

§ 4221.12 Calculation of periods of time.

The PBGC applies the rules in subpart D of part 4000 of this chapter to compute any time period under this part.

56. Revise § 4221.13 to read as follows:

§ 4221.13 Filing and issuance rules.

(a) *Method and date of filing.* The PBGC applies the rules in subpart A of part 4000 of this chapter to determine permissible methods of filing with the PBGC under this part. The PBGC applies the rules in subpart C of part 4000 of this chapter to determine the date that a submission under this part was filed with the PBGC.

(b) *Where to file.* See § 4000.4 of this chapter for information on where to file.

(c) *Method and date of issuance.* The PBGC applies the rules in subpart B of part 4000 of this chapter to determine permissible methods of issuance under this part. The PBGC applies the rules in subpart C of part 4000 of this chapter to determine the date that an issuance under this part was provided.

§ 4221.14 PBGC-approved arbitration procedures. [Amended]

57. Revise the third sentence of paragraph (c) of § 4221.14 to read: "The application shall include:".

PART 4231—MERGERS AND TRANSFERS BETWEEN MULTIEMPLOYER PLANS

58. The authority citation for part 4231 continues to read as follows:

Authority: 29 U.S.C. 1302(b)(3), 1411.

59. Amend § 4231.8 by revising paragraphs (a), (c), and (d) to read as follows:

§ 4231.8 Notice of merger or transfer.

(a) *Filing of request.* (1) *When to file.* Except as provided in paragraph (f) of this section, a notice of a proposed merger or transfer must be filed not less than 120 days before the effective date of the transaction. For purposes of this part, the effective date of a merger or transfer is the earlier of—

(i) The date on which one plan assumes liability for benefits accrued under another plan involved in the transaction; or

(ii) The date on which one plan transfers assets to another plan involved in the transaction.

(2) *Method of filing.* The PBGC applies the rules in subpart A of part 4000 of this chapter to determine permissible methods of filing with the PBGC under this part.

(3) *Computation of time.* The PBGC applies the rules in subpart D of part 4000 of this chapter to compute any time period for filing under this part.

* * * * *

(c) *Where to file.* See § 4000.4 of this chapter for information on where to file.

(d) *Date of filing.* The PBGC applies the rules in subpart C of part 4000 of this chapter to determine the date that a submission under this part was filed with the PBGC. For purposes of paragraph (a) of this section, the notice is not considered filed until all of the information required by paragraph (e) of this section has been submitted.

* * * * *

PART 4245—NOTICE OF INSOLVENCY

60. The authority citation for part 4245 continues to read as follows:

Authority: 29 U.S.C. 1302(b)(3), 1426(e).

61. Amend § 4245.3 as follows:

a. In the first sentence of paragraph (a) remove the words "interested parties, as defined in paragraph (d) of this section" and add in their place the words "interested parties, as defined in paragraph (e) of this section".

b. Redesignate paragraph (d) as paragraph (e).

c. Revise paragraph (c) and add new paragraph (d) to read as follows:

§ 4245.3 Notice of insolvency.

* * * * *

(c) *Delivery to PBGC; filing date.* (1) *Method of delivery.* The PBGC applies the rules in subpart A of part 4000 of this chapter to determine permissible methods of filing with the PBGC under this part.

(2) *Filing date.* The PBGC applies the rules in subpart C of part 4000 of this chapter to determine the date that a submission under this part was filed with the PBGC.

(d) *Delivery to interested parties; issuance date.* (1) *Method of delivery.* The PBGC applies the rules in subpart B of part 4000 of this chapter to determine permissible methods of delivery for the notice of insolvency. In addition to the methods permitted under subpart B of part 4000, the plan sponsor may notify interested parties, other than participants and beneficiaries who are in pay status when the notice is required to be delivered, by posting the notice at participants' work sites or publishing the notice in a union newsletter or in a newspaper of general circulation in the area or areas where participants reside. Notice to a participant shall be deemed notice to that participant's beneficiary or beneficiaries.

(2) *Issuance date.* The PBGC applies the rules in subpart C of part 4000 of this chapter to determine the date that the notice of insolvency was issued.

* * * * *

§ 4245.4 [Amended]

62. Amend the introductory language of paragraph (b) by removing the words "an interested party, as defined in § 4245.3(d)" and adding in their place the words "interested parties, as defined in § 4245.3(e)".

§ 4245.5 [Amended]

63. Amend § 4245.5 as follows:

a. In the first sentence of paragraph (a) remove the words "interested parties, as defined in § 4245.3(d)" and add in their place the words "interested parties, as defined in § 4245.3(e)".

b. Revise paragraph (d) and add paragraph (e) to read as follows:

§ 4245.5 Notice of insolvency benefit level.

* * * * *

(d) *Method of delivery to PBGC; filing date.* (1) *Method of delivery.* The PBGC applies the rules in subpart A of part 4000 of this chapter to determine permissible methods of filing with the PBGC under this part.

(2) *Filing date.* The PBGC applies the rules in subpart C of part 4000 of this chapter to determine the date that a submission under this part was filed with the PBGC.

(e) *Method of delivery to interested parties; issuance date.* (1) *Method of delivery.* The PBGC applies the rules in subpart B of part 4000 of this chapter to determine permissible methods of delivery for the notice of insolvency benefit levels. In addition to the methods permitted under subpart B of part 4000, the plan sponsor may notify interested parties, other than participants and beneficiaries who are in pay status or reasonably expected to enter pay status during the insolvency year for which the notice is given, by posting the notice at participants' work sites or publishing the notice in a union newsletter or in a newspaper of general circulation in the 'area or areas where participants reside. Notice to a participant shall be deemed notice to that participant's beneficiary or beneficiaries.

(2) *Issuance date.* The PBGC applies the rules in subpart C of part 4000 of this chapter to determine the date that the notice of insolvency benefit levels was issued.

§ 4245.6 [Amended]

64. In § 4245.6, amend the introductory language of paragraph (b) by removing the words "interested parties, as defined in § 4245.3(d)" and adding in their place the words "interested parties, as defined in § 4245.3(e)".

65. Revise § 4245.7 to read as follows:

§ 4245.7 PBGC address.

See § 4000.4 of this chapter for information on where to file.

66. Add § 4245.8 to read as follows:

§ 4245.8 Computation of time.

The PBGC applies the rules in subpart D of part 4000 of this chapter to compute any time period for filing or issuance under this part.

PART 4281—DUTIES OF PLAN SPONSOR FOLLOWING MASS WITHDRAWAL

67. Revise the authority citation for part 4281 to read as follows:

Authority: 29 U.S.C. 1302(b)(3), 1341(a), 1399(c)(1)(D), and 1441.

68. Revise § 4281.3 to read as follows:

§ 4281.3 Filing and issuance rules.

(a) *Method of filing.* The PBGC applies the rules in subpart A of part 4000 of this chapter to determine permissible methods of delivery for filings with the PBGC under this part.

(b) *Method of issuance.* See § 4281.32(c) for notices of benefit reductions, § 4281.43(e) for notices of insolvency, and § 4281.45(c) for notices of insolvency benefit level.

(c) *Date of filing.* The PBGC applies the rules in subpart C of part 4000 of this chapter to determine the date that a submission under this part was filed with the PBGC.

(d) *Date of issuance.* The PBGC applies the rules in subpart C of part 4000 of this chapter to determine the date that an issuance under this part was provided.

(e) *Where to file.* See § 4000.4 of this chapter for information on where to file.

(f) *Computation of tim e.* The PBGC applies the rules in subpart D of part 4000 of this chapter to compute any time period for filing or issuance under this part.

69. Revise paragraph (c) of § 4281.32 to read as follows:

§ 4281.32 Notices of benefit reductions.

* * * * *

(c) *Method of issuance to interested parties.* The PBGC applies the rules in subpart B of part 4000 of this chapter to determine permissible methods of delivery for the notice of benefit reduction. In addition to the methods permitted under subpart B of part 4000, the plan sponsor may notify interested parties, other than participants and beneficiaries who are in pay status when the notice is required to be delivered or who are reasonably expected to enter pay status before the end of the plan year after the plan year in which the amendment is adopted, by posting the notice at participants' work sites or publishing the notice in a union newsletter or in a newspaper of general circulation in the area or areas where participants reside. Notice to a participant shall be deemed notice to that participant's beneficiary or beneficiaries.

* * * * *

70. Revise paragraphs (e) and (f) of § 4281.43 to read as follows:

§ 4281.43 Notices of insolvency and annual updates.

* * * * *

(e) *Notices of insolvency—method of issuance to interested parties.* The PBGC applies the rules in subpart B of part 4000 of this chapter to determine permissible methods of delivery for the notice of insolvency. In addition to the methods permitted under subpart B of part 4000, the plan sponsor may notify interested parties, other than participants and beneficiaries who are in pay status when the notice is required to be delivered, by posting the notice at participants' work sites or publishing the notice in a union newsletter or in a newspaper of general circulation in the area or areas where participants reside. Notice to a participant shall be deemed notice to that participant's beneficiary or beneficiaries.

(f) *Annual updates—method of issuance.* The PBGC applies the rules in subpart B of part 4000 of this chapter to determine permissible methods of delivery for the annual update to participants and beneficiaries. In addition to the methods permitted under subpart B of part 4000, the plan sponsor may notify interested parties by posting the notice at participants' work sites or publishing the notice in a union newsletter or in a newspaper of general circulation in the area or areas where participants reside. Notice to a participant shall be deemed notice to that participant's beneficiary or beneficiaries.

71. Revise paragraph (c) of § 4281.45 to read as follows:

§ 4281.45 Notices of insolvency benefit level.

* * * * *

(c) *Method of issuance.* The notices of insolvency benefit level shall be delivered to the PBGC and to plan participants and beneficiaries in pay status or reasonably expected to enter pay status during the insolvency year. The PBGC applies the rules in subpart B of part 4000 of this chapter to determine permissible methods of delivery for the notice of insolvency benefit levels.

PART 4901—EXAMINATION AND COPYING OF PENSION BENE-FIT GUARANTY CORPORATION RECORDS

72. Revise the authority citation for part 4901 to read as follows:

Authority: 5 U.S.C. 552, 29 U.S.C. 1302(b)(3), E.O. 12600, 52 FR 23781, 3 CFR, 1987 Comp., p.235.

73. Add § 4901.6 to read as follows:

§ 4901.6 Filing rules; computation of time.

* * * * *

(a) *Filing rules.* (1) *Where to file.* See § 4000.4 of this chapter for information on where to file a submission under this part with the PBGC.

(2) *Method of filing.* The PBGC applies the rules in subpart A of part 4000 of this chapter to determine permissible methods of filing with the PBGC under this part.

(3) *Date of filing.* The PBGC applies the rules in subpart C of part 4000 of this chapter to determine the date that a submission under this part was filed with the PBGC.

(b) *Computation of time.* The PBGC applies the rules in subpart D of part 4000 of this chapter to compute any time period under this part.

74. Revise § 4901.11 to read as follows:

§ 4901.11 Submittal of requests for access to records.

A request to inspect or copy any record subject to this subpart shall be submitted to the Disclosure Officer, Pension Benefit Guaranty Corporation. Such a request may be sent to the Disclosure Officer or made in person between the hours of 9 a.m. and 4 p.m. on any working day in the Communications and Public Affairs Department, PBGC, 1200 K Street, NW., Suite 240, Washington, DC 20005-4026. To expedite processing, the request should be prominently identified as a "FOIA request."

75. Revise paragraph (a) of § 4901.15 to read as follows:

§ 4901.15 Appeals from denial of requests.

(a) *Submittal of appeals.* If a disclosure request is denied in whole or in part by the disclosure officer, the requester may file a written appeal within 30 days from the date of the denial or, if later (in the case of a partial denial), 30 days from the date the requester receives the disclosed material. The appeal shall state the grounds for appeal and any supporting statements or arguments, and shall be addressed to the General Counsel, Pension Benefit Guaranty Corporation. See part 4000.4 of this chapter for information on where to file. To expedite processing, the words "FOIA appeal" should appear prominently on the request.

* * * * *

76. Revise paragraph (c) of § 4901.33 to read as follows:

§ 4901.33 Payment of fees.

* * * * *

(c) *Late payment interest charges.* The PBGC may assess late payment interest charges on any amounts unpaid by the 31st day after the date a bill is sent to a requester. Interest will be assessed at the rate prescribed in 31 U.S.C. 3717 and will accrue from the date the bill is sent.

PART 4902—DISCLOSURE AND AMENDMENT OF RECORDS PERTAINING TO INDIVIDUALS UNDER THE PRIVACY ACT

77. The authority citation for part 4902 continues to read as follows:

Authority: 5 U.S.C. 552a.

78. Revise paragraphs (a) and (b) of § 4902.3 to read as follows:

§ 4902.3 Procedures for determining existence of and requesting access to records.

(a) Any individual may submit a request to the Disclosure Officer, Pension Benefit Guaranty Corporation, for the purpose of learning whether a system of records maintained by the PBGC contains any record pertaining to the requestor or obtaining access to such a record. Such a request may be sent to the Disclosure Officer or made in person between the hours of 9 a.m. and 4 p.m. on any working day in the Communications and Public Affairs Department, PBGC, 1200 K Street, NW., Suite 240, Washington, DC 20005-4026.

(b) Each request submitted pursuant to paragraph (a) of this section shall include the name of the system of records to which the request pertains and the requester's full name, home address and date of birth, and shall prominently state the words, "Privacy Act Request." If this information is insufficient to enable the PBGC to identify the record in question, or to determine the identity of the requester (to ensure the privacy of the subject of the record), the disclosure officer shall request such further identifying data as the disclosure officer deems necessary to locate the record or to determine the identity of the requester.

* * * * *

79. Revise paragraph (c) of § 4902.5 to read as follows:

§ 4902.5 Procedures for requesting amendment of a record.

* * * * *

(c) An individual who desires assistance in the preparation of a request for amendment of a record shall submit such request for assistance in writing to the Deputy General Counsel, Pension Benefit Guaranty Corporation. The Deputy General Counsel shall respond to such request as promptly as possible.

80. Revise paragraph (c) of § 4902.6 to read as follows:

§ 4902.6 Action on request for amendment of a record.

* * * * *

(c) An individual who desires assistance in preparing an appeal of a denial under this section shall submit a request to the Deputy General Counsel, Pension Benefit Guaranty Corporation. The Deputy General Counsel shall respond to the request as promptly as possible, but in no event more than 30 days after receipt.

81. Revise paragraph (a) of § 4902.7 to read as follows:

§ 4902.7 Appeal of a denial of a request for amendment of a record.

(a) An appeal from a denial of a request for amendment of a record under § 4902.6 shall be submitted, within 45 days of receipt of the denial, to the General Counsel, Pension Benefit Guaranty Corporation, unless the record subject to such request is one maintained by the Office of the General Counsel, in which event the appeal shall be submitted to the Deputy Executive Director, Pension Benefit Guaranty Corporation. The appeal shall state in detail the basis on which it is made and shall clearly state "Privacy Act Request" on the first page. In addition, the submission shall clearly state "Privacy Act Request" on the envelope (for mail, hand delivery, or commercial delivery), in the subject line (for e-mail), or on the cover sheet (for fax).

* * * * *

82. Add § 4902.10 to read as follows:

§ 4902.10 Filing rules; computation of time.

(a) *Filing rules.* (1) *Where to file.* See § 4000.4 of this chapter for information on where to file a submission under this part with the PBGC.

(2) *Method of filing.* The PBGC applies the rules in subpart A of part 4000 of this chapter to determine permissible methods of filing with the PBGC under this part.

(3) *Date of filing.* The PBGC applies the rules in subpart C of part 4000 of this chapter to determine the date that a submission under this part was filed with the PBGC.

(b) *Computation of time.* The PBGC applies the rules in subpart D of part 4000 of this chapter to compute any time period for filing under this part.

PART 4903—DEBT COLLECTION

83. The authority citation for part 4903 continues to read as follows:

Authority: 29 U.S.C. 1302(b); 31 U.S.C. 3701, 3711(f), 3720A; 4 CFR part 102; 26 CFR 301.6402-6.

84. Amend § 4903.2 by adding paragraphs (c) and (d) to read as follows:

§ 4903.2 General.

* * * * *

(c) The PBGC applies the rules in subpart A of part 4000 of this chapter to determine permissible methods of filing with the PBGC under this part. The PBGC applies the rules in subpart C of part 4000 of this chapter to determine the date that a submission under this part was filed with the PBGC. See § 4000.4 for information on where to file.

(d) The PBGC applies the rules in subpart D of part 4000 of this chapter to compute any time period for filing under this part.

85. Revise paragraph (b)(2) of § 4903.24 to read as follows:

§ 4903.24 Request for offset from other agencies.

* * * * *

(b)(1) * * *

(2) All such requests should be directed to the Director, Financial Operations Department. See § 4000.4 of this chapter for information on where to file.

* * * * *

PART 4907—ENFORCEMENT OF NONDISCRIMINATION ON THE BASIS OF HANDICAP IN PROGRAMS OR ACTIVITIES CONDUCTED BY THE PENSION BENEFIT GUARANTY CORPORATION

86. The authority citation for part 4907 continues to read as follows:

Authority: 29 U.S.C. 794, 1302(b)(3).

87. Revise paragraph (c) of § 4907.170 to read as follows:

§ 4907.170 Compliance procedures.

* * * * *

(c) The Equal Opportunity Manager shall be responsible for coordinating implementation of this section.

(1) *Where to file.* See § 4000.4 of this chapter for information on where to file complaints under this part.

(2) *Method of filing.* The PBGC applies the rules in subpart A of part 4000 of this chapter to determine permissible methods of filing with the PBGC under this part.

(3) *Date of filing.* The PBGC applies the rules in subpart C of part 4000 of this chapter to determine the date that a submission under this part was filed with the PBGC.

(4) *Computation of time.* The PBGC applies the rules in subpart D of part 4000 of this chapter to compute any time period under this part.

* * * * *

Issued in Washington, DC, this 4th day of February, 2003.

Steven A. Kandarian,

Executive Director,

Pension Benefit Guaranty Corporation.

¶ 20,534M

EBSA proposed regulations: COBRA: Notice requirements: Health care continuation coverage: Model notices.—EBSA has issued proposed rules setting minimum standards for the notices required of group health plans to participants and beneficiaries who would lose coverage, regarding their opportunity to obtain continued coverage at group rates for a limited period of time. The proposed rules include model notices. Final regulations were issued, effective July 26, 2004 and applicable to notice obligations that arise on or after the first day of the first plan year beginning on or after November 26, 2004. See ¶ 15,046B-1, ¶ 15,046B-2, ¶ 15,046B-3, ¶ 15,046B-4, ¶ 15,046B-5, ¶ 15,046B-6, and ¶ 24,234. According to the final regulation preamble, pending the applicability of the final rules, EBSA will view compliance with either the proposed rules or the final rules to constitute good faith compliance with the COBRA statutory notice requirements.

The proposed regulations, which were published in the *Federal Register* on May 28, 2003 (68 FR 31832), were previously reproduced below.

¶ 20,534N

Equal Employment Opportunity Commission (EEOC): Proposed regulations: Age Discrimination in Employment Act: Retiree health benefits: Medicare: State-sponsored retiree health benefits program.—The EEOC has issued proposed regulations that exempt from the prohibitions of the Age Discrimination in Employment Act of 1967 the altering, reducing, or eliminating of employer-provided retiree health benefits when retirees become eligible for Medicare or a state-sponsored retiree health benefits program.

The proposed regulations, which were published in the *Federal Register* on July 14, 2003 (68 FR 41542), are reproduced below.

EQUAL EMPLOYMENT OPPORTUNITY COMMISSION

29. CFR Parts 1625 and 1627

RIN 3046-AA72

Age Discrimination in Employment Act; Retiree Health Benefits

AGENCY: U.S. Equal Employment Opportunity Commission.

ACTION: Notice of proposed rulemaking.

SUMMARY: The U.S. Equal Employment Opportunity Commission (Commission or EEOC) proposes to amend its regulations governing age discrimination in employment to exempt from the prohibitions of the Age Discrimination in Employment Act of 1967 the practice of altering, reducing or eliminating employer-sponsored retiree health benefits when retirees become eligible for Medicare or a State-sponsored retiree health benefits program. This exemption will ensure that the application of the ADEA does not discourage employers from providing health benefits to their retirees.

DATES: Comments must be received by September 12, 2003. The Commission will consider any comments received on or before the closing date and thereafter adopt final regulations. Comments received after the closing date will be considered to the extent practicable.

ADDRESSES: Written comments should be submitted to Frances M. Hart, Executive Officer, Office of the Executive Secretariat, U.S. Equal Employment Opportunity Commission, 1801 L Street, NW., Washington, DC 20507. As a convenience to commentators, the Executive Secretariat will accept comments transmitted by facsimile ("FAX") machine. The telephone number of the FAX receiver is (202) 663-4114 (This is not a toll free number). Only comments of six or fewer pages will be accepted via FAX transmittal. This limitation is necessary to assure access to the equipment. Receipt of fax transmittals will not be acknowledged, except that the sender may request confirmation of receipt by calling the Executive Secretariat staff at (202) 663-4078 (voice) or (202) 663-4077 (TTY). (These are not toll free numbers). Copies of comments submitted by the public will be available for review on weekdays, except federal holidays, at the Commission's library, Room 6502, 1801 L Street, NW., Washington, DC, between the hours of 9:30 a.m. and 5 p.m.

FOR FURTHER INFORMATION CONTACT: Lynn A. Clements, Special Assistant to the Legal Counsel, Office of Legal Counsel, at (202) 663-4624 (voice) or (202) 663-7026 (TTY) (These are not toll free numbers). This notice is also available in the following formats: large print, braille, audio tape, and electronic file on computer disk. Requests for this notice in an alternative format should be made to the Publications Information Center at 1-800-669-3362.

SUPPLEMENTARY INFORMATION: Section 9 of the Age Discrimination in Employment Act of 1967, 29 U.S.C. 621 et seq. (ADEA or Act), provides that EEOC "may establish such reasonable exemptions to and from any or all provisions of [the Act] as it may find necessary and proper in the public interest." Implicit in this authority is the recognition that the application of the ADEA could, in certain circumstances, foster unintended consequences that are not consistent with the purposes of the law and are not in the public interest. Such circumstances are rare. Accordingly, EEOC's exercise of this authority has been limited and tempered with great discretion.

After an in-depth study, the Commission believes that the practice of altering, reducing or eliminating employer-sponsored retiree health benefits when retirees become eligible for Medicare or a State-sponsored retiree health benefits program presents a circumstance that warrants Commission exercise of its ADEA exemption authority. For the reasons that follow, and pursuant to its authority under Section 9 of the Act, the EEOC proposes in this notice of proposed rulemaking (NPRM) to add a new section 32 to part 1625 of Title 29 of the Code of Federal Regulations exempting such coordination of employer-sponsored retiree health benefits with Medicare or a State-sponsored retiree health benefits program from all prohibitions of the ADEA.

Basis for Exemption

In August 2001, the Commission announced that it would study the relationship between the ADEA and employer-sponsored retiree health benefit plans that alter, reduce or eliminate benefits upon eligibility for Medicare or a comparable State-sponsored retiree health benefits program. To begin the process, EEOC developed an internal Retiree Health Benefits Task Force headed by its Legal Counsel. The Task Force met with a wide range of Commission stakeholders, including employers, employee groups, labor unions, human resource consultants, benefit consultants, actuaries and state and local government representatives. The Task Force also reviewed available survey data regarding employer-sponsored retiree health benefits; analyzed the May 2001 United States General Accounting Office's Report to the Chairman of the United States's Senate Committee on Health, Education, Labor and Pensions entitled "Retiree Health Benefits: Employer-Sponsored Benefits May Be Vulnerable to Further Erosion;" and reviewed numerous professional articles discussing the continued erosion of retiree health benefits.

As a result of its study, the Commission has concluded, as discussed in greater detail below, that the number of employers providing retiree health benefits has declined considerably over the last ten years, even though many retired individuals rely on such employer-sponsored plans for affordable health coverage. Various factors have contributed to this erosion, including the increased cost of health care coverage, an increased demand for such coverage as large numbers of workers near retirement age, and changes in the way accounting rules treat the long-term costs of providing retiree health benefits. The Commission believes that concern about the potential application of the ADEA to employer-sponsored retiree health benefits is adversely affecting the continued provision of this important retirement benefit.

Employers Are Not Obligated To Provide Retiree Health Care

Employers are not legally obligated to provide retiree health benefits and many do not. In fact, in 2001, only about "one-third of large employers and less than 10% of small employers offer[ed]retiree health benefits."[1] Employers who choose to provide retiree health benefits are not required to provide such benefits indefinitely, absent some contractual agreement to the contrary. Employers that do offer retiree health benefits, however, often do so to maintain a competitive advantage in the marketplace—using these and other benefits to attract and retain the best talent available to work for their organizations.

Likewise, employer-sponsored retiree health benefits clearly benefit employees. In many cases, employers offer retiree health benefits as a bridge to Medicare so that younger retirees have access to affordable health care benefits when they leave the workforce before reaching the age of Medicare eligibility. Often those benefits are more generous than Medicare benefits because, for example, the employer simply includes younger retirees in its group plan for existing employees. In other cases, employers wish to offer their retirees age 65 and older health benefit plans that supplement the coverage provided under Medicare so that these retirees have access to comprehensive health care benefits at a time when their health care needs may be greatest. The Commission believes that it is in the best interest of both employers and employees for the Commission to pursue a policy that permits employers to offer these benefits to the greatest extent possible.

The Rising Cost of Health Care

The cost of employee health care has increased consistently for several years, making it difficult for employers to continue to provide retiree health benefits. One report estimates that employers will experience a double-digit increase in their health care costs in 2003 for the third consecutive year.[2] Two widely-cited surveys of employer-sponsored health plans—(1) the Health Research and Educational Trust survey sponsored by The Henry J. Kaiser Family Foundation (Kaiser/HRET) and (2) the William M. Mercer, Incorporated survey (formerly produced by Foster Higgins) (Mercer/Foster Higgins)—estimate that premiums for employer-sponsored health insurance increased an average of about 11% in 2001.[3] The 2002 Kaiser/HRET study found monthly premium costs for employer-sponsored health insurance rose 12.7% between the Spring of 2001 and 2002, while early results from the 2002 Mercer/Foster Higgins study estimate that health care costs increased almost 15% in 2002.[4] The 2001 Kaiser/HRET survey found that these large changes in premiums would affect small employers, defined as those employing between 3-199 workers, at a greater rate than larger

[1] Hearing Before the House Comm. on Education and the Workforce, 107th Cong. (2001) (statement of William J. Scanlon, Director of Health Care Services, GAO).

[2] Hewitt Associates LLC, "Health Care Cost Increases Expected to Continue Double-Digit Pace in 2003," (Lincolnshire, IL: Hewitt Associates LLC Oct. 14, 2002).

[3] The Henry J. Kaiser Family Foundation & Health Research and Educational Trust, "Employer Health Benefits, 2001 Annual Survey" (Menlo Park, CA: The Henry J. Kaiser Family Foundation and Health Research and Educational Trust 2001); William M. Mercer, "Mercer/Foster Higgins National Survey of Employer-Sponsored Health Plans 2001" (New York, N.Y.: William M. Mercer Inc. 2002). The 2001 Kaiser/HRET study, conducted between January and May 2001, surveyed more than 2,500 randomly selected public and

private companies in the United States. The 2001 Mercer/Foster Higgins study used a national probability sampling of public and private employers and the results represent about 600,000 employers.

[4] The Henry J. Kaiser Family Foundation & Health Research and Educational Trust, "Employer Health Benefits, 2002 Annual Survey" (Menlo Park, CA: The Henry J. Kaiser Family Foundation and Health Research and Educational Trust 2002); Mercer Human Resource Consulting LLC, "Rate Hikes pushed employers to drop health plans, cut benefits in 2002—but average cost still rose," (New York, N.Y.: Mercer Human Resource Consulting LLC December 9, 2002). The 2002 Kaiser/HRET study surveyed 3,262 randomly selected public and private employers.

employers.[5] Indeed, the 2002 Kaiser/HRET survey suggests that there may be evidence of erosion in the number of small employers offering health benefits; the study reports that the number of small employers offering such benefits dropped 6% between 2000 and 2002.[6] Many employers and benefit experts believe that the rising cost of prescription drug coverage, in particular, has heavily contributed to the rising cost of health care, with 64% of employers responding to the 2001 Kaiser/HRET study citing "higher spending for drugs" as a significant factor in health insurance premium increases.[7]

In addition to the rising cost of health care generally, increased longevity and, thus, increased numbers of retirees, will continue to mean larger and more frequent payments for health care services on behalf of retired workers. The United States General Accounting Office (GAO) projects that, by 2030, the number of people age 65 or older will be double what it is today, while the number of individuals between the ages of 55 and 64 will increase 75 percent by 2020.[8] It is well-established that utilization of health care services generally rises with age.[9] Thus, the demand for and cost of retiree health coverage is likely to grow significantly in the next few years, while there will be comparatively fewer active workers to subsidize such benefits.[10] The 2000 Mercer/Foster Higgins National Survey of Employer-Sponsored Health Plans showed substantial cost increases for retiree health care coverage between 1999 and 2000, with a 10.6 percent increase for retirees under age 65 and a 17 percent increase for those over 65.[11] A 2002 study by The Henry J. Kaiser Family Foundation and Hewitt Associates (Kaiser/Hewitt) found that retiree health care costs increased an average of 16% between 2001 and 2002 for employers with at least 1000 employees.[12]

Changes in accounting rules also have dramatically impacted the way employers account for the long-term costs of providing retiree health benefits.[13] In 1990, the Financial Accounting Standards Board, which is charged with establishing U.S. standards of financial accounting and reporting, promulgated new rules for retiree health accounting, referred to as Financial Accounting Standards Number 106 or FAS 106. FAS 106 requires employers to apportion the costs of retiree health over the working lifetime of employees and to report unfunded retiree health benefit liabilities in accordance with generally accepted accounting principles beginning with fiscal years after December 15, 1992. Because "the recognition of these liabilities in financial statements dramatically impacts a company's calculation of its profits and losses,"[14] some companies have said that FAS 106 led to reductions in reported income, thus creating an incentive to reduce expenditures for employee benefits such as retiree health.

The Incentive for Employers To Reduce Health Care Costs

As a result of these increased costs and accounting changes, employers have actively examined ways to reduce health care costs, including by reducing, altering or eliminating retiree health coverage.[15] During hearings before the U.S. House of Representative's Committee on Education and the Workforce in November 2001, the GAO's Director of Health Care Services testified that only "one-third of large employers and less than 10% of small employers offer retiree health benefits."[16] The 2001 Mercer/Foster Higgins study shows that the number of employers with 500 or more workers who offer retiree health coverage decreased by 17 percent between 1993 and 2001 for both pre- and post-Medicare eligible retirees.[17] The 2002 Kaiser/HRET survey similarly found that a declining percentage of large companies (those with at least 200 employees) offer retiree health benefits; only 34 percent of such employers offered retiree health coverage in 2002, compared to 66 percent of similar companies in 1988.[18] Another survey completed by Hewitt Associates LLC estimates a 15 percent decline in the number of large employers providing pre-age 65 retiree health coverage between 1991 and 2000 and an 18 percent decrease in the number of large employers providing health benefits to retirees age 65 or older during the same period.[19] The 2002 Kaiser/Hewitt retiree health study concluded that this trend will continue, with one in five large employers likely to eliminate retiree health coverage for future retirees within the next three years.[20]

Of those employers offering retiree health benefits, most are more likely to offer such benefits to early retirees and not to Medicare-eligible retirees. A report issued by Kaiser, HRET and The Commonwealth Fund (Kaiser/HRET/Commonwealth) estimates that only 23% of employers with at least 200 workers offered retiree health benefits to Medicare-age retirees in 2001. This is a decline of more than 10 percentage points in a three-year period.[21]

As the number of employers offering retiree health coverage declines, so has the incentive to provide future retirees with such coverage. Unions report that meaningful negotiations about the future provision of employer-sponsored retiree health benefits are becoming increasingly futile. Union representatives have informed EEOC that increasing numbers of employers have refused to include retiree health among the benefits to be provided to employees. A significant number of employers have agreed to provide retiree health only if the benefit terminates when the retiree becomes eligible for Medicare.

Alternatives to employer-sponsored retiree health coverage are costly, offer fewer benefits, and may be limited in availability, particularly for retirees not yet eligible for Medicare.[22] Under provisions of the Consolidated Omnibus Budget Reconciliation Act of 1985, 29 U.S.C. 1161 et seq. (COBRA), retirees under the age of 65 may be eligible for temporary health coverage from either their spouse's employer or their former employer, although the retiree may be required to pay the entire premium. Other retirees under age 65 must obtain coverage in the private individual insurance market, which often is prohibitively

[5] The Henry J. Kaiser Family Foundation & Health Research and Educational Trust, "Employer Health Benefits, 2001 Annual Survey" (Menlo Park, CA: The Henry J. Kaiser Family Foundation and Health Research and Educational Trust 2001).

[6] The Henry J. Kaiser Family Foundation & Health Research and Educational Trust, "Employer Health Benefits, 2002 Annual Survey" (Menlo Park, CA: The Henry J. Kaiser Family Foundation and Health Research and Educational Trust 2002).

[7] The Henry J. Kaiser Family Foundation & Health Research and Educational Trust, "Employer Health Benefits, 2001 Annual Survey" (Menlo Park, CA: The Henry J. Kaiser Family Foundation and Health Research and Educational Trust 2001).

[8] U.S. General Accounting Office, "Retiree Health Benefits: Employer-Sponsored Benefits May Be Vulnerable to Further Erosion," GAO Doc. No. GAO-01-374, at 17 (May 2001).

[9] Anna M. Rappaport, "Planning for Health Care Needs in Retirement," in Forecasting Retirement Needs and Retirement Wealth, 288, 288-294 (Olivia S. Mitchell et al. eds., University of Pennsylvania Press 2000).

[10] U.S. General Accounting Office, "Retiree Health Benefits: Employer-Sponsored Benefits May Be Vulnerable to Further Erosion," GAO Doc. No. GAO-01-374, at 17-18 (May 2001).

[11] Anna M. Rappaport, "Postemployment Benefits: Retiree Health Challenges and Trends—2001 and Beyond," in Compensation and Benefits Management, 52, 56 (Autumn 2001) (citing William M. Mercer, "Mercer/Foster Higgins National Survey of Employer-Sponsored Health Plans 2000" (New York, N.Y.: William M. Mercer Inc. 2001).

[12] The Henry J. Kaiser Family Foundation & Hewitt Associates LLC, "Kaiser/Hewitt 2002 Retiree Health Survey" (Menlo Park, CA: The Henry J. Kaiser Family Foundation and Hewitt Associates LLC 2002). This online survey, conducted between July and September 2002, represents information from 435 private employers (with at least 1000 employees) that currently offer retiree health benefits.

[13] Anna M. Rappaport, "FAS 106 and Strategies for Managing Retiree Health Benefits," in Compensation and Benefits Management, 37 (Spring 2001); Paul Fronstin, "Retiree Health Benefits: Trends and Outlook," EBRI Issue Brief No. 236 (Employee Benefit Research Institute Aug. 2001).

[14] Paul Fronstin, "Retiree Health Benefits: Trends and Outlook," EBRI Issue Brief No. 236, at 3 (Employee Benefit Research Institute Aug. 2001).

[15] A survey by THAP!, Andersen and CalPERS found that both public and private employers considered controlling health care costs as a top business issue for the next two

to three years. THAP! et al., "Productive Workforce Survey: Report of Findings Private Employer/Public Agency" (THAP!, Andersen and CalPERS Aug. 2001); see also Anna M. Rappaport, "Postemployment Benefits: Retiree Health Challenges and Trends—2001 and Beyond," in Compensation and Benefits Management, 52, 56 (Autumn 2001) ("Companies seeking to reduce costs are closely examining retiree medical benefits.").

[16] Hearing Before the House Comm. on Education and the Workforce, 107th Cong. (2001) (statement of William J. Scanlon, Director of Health Care Services, GAO).

[17] William M. Mercer, "Mercer/Foster Higgins National Survey of Employer-Sponsored Health Plans 2001" (New York, NY: William M. Mercer, Inc. 2002).

[18] The Henry J. Kaiser Family Foundation & Health Research and Educational Trust, "Employer Health Benefits, 2002 Annual Survey" (Menlo Park, CA: The Henry J. Kaiser Family Foundation and Health Research and Educational Trust 2002).

[19] Hewitt Associates LLC, "Trends in Retiree Health Plans" (Lincolnshire, IL: Hewitt Associates LLC 2001). This conclusion is based on information from Hewitt Associates database of 1,020 large employers, including 85% of Fortune 100 companies and 57% of Fortune 500 companies.

[20] The Henry J. Kaiser Family Foundation & Hewitt Associates LLC, "Kaiser/Hewitt 2002 Retiree Health Survey" (Menlo Park, CA: The Henry J. Kaiser Family Foundation and Hewitt Associates LLC 2002); see also The Henry J. Kaiser Family Foundation & Health Research and Educational Trust, "Employer Health Benefits, 2002 Annual Survey" (Menlo Park, CA: The Henry J. Kaiser Family Foundation and Health Research and Educational Trust 2002) (11% of large employers predict they will eliminate retiree health benefits for future retirees).

[21] The Henry J. Kaiser Family Foundation et al., "Erosion of Private Health Insurance Coverage For Retirees: Findings from the 2000 and 2001 Retiree Health and Prescription Drug Coverage Survey" (Menlo Park, CA: The Henry J. Kaiser Family Foundation, Health Research and Educational Trust, and The Commonwealth Fund 2002); see also The Henry J. Kaiser Family Foundation & Health Research and Educational Trust, "Employer Health Benefits, 2002 Annual Survey" (Menlo Park, CA: The Henry J. Kaiser Family Foundation and Health Research and Educational Trust 2002) (96% of employers with at least 200 employees offer health benefits to pre-age 65 retirees, while only 72% of large employers offer health benefits to retirees age 65 and above).

[22] U.S. General Accounting Office, "Retiree Health Benefits: Employer-Sponsored Benefits May Be Vulnerable to Further Erosion," GAO Doc. No. GAO-01-374, at 20-24 (May 2001).

expensive or provides limited benefits.[23] Those unable to afford coverage in the private insurance market rely on public insurance, pay for health care out of pocket, or are uninsured. Retirees age 65 or older often rely on Medicare as their primary source of health coverage. Nonetheless, many retirees in this age group rely on employer-sponsored benefits to cover Medicare's cost-sharing requirements or gaps in Medicare coverage. Retirees who do not have access to employer-sponsored supplemental coverage must obtain private individual "Medicare supplement" insurance, which can be prohibitively expensive, particularly if prescription drug coverage is desired.[24] For these reasons, employer-sponsored retiree health coverage is a valuable benefit for older persons that should be protected and preserved to the greatest extent possible.

Interplay Between the ADEA and Employer-Sponsored Retiree Health Benefits

Section 4 of the ADEA makes it unlawful for an employer to discriminate against any individual with respect to "compensation, terms, conditions, or privileges or employment, because of such individual's age." 29 U.S.C. 623(a)(1). In 1989, the Supreme Court held in Public Employees Retirement Sys. of Ohio v. Betts, 492 U.S. 158, 109 S. Ct. 256 (1989), that the ADEA, nevertheless, did not prohibit discrimination in employee benefits, such as health insurance. In response to the Supreme Court's decision in Betts, Congress enacted the Older Workers Benefit Protection Act of 1990, Pub. L. No. 101-433, 104 Stat. 978 (1990) (OWBPA), which amended the ADEA and defined the term "compensation, terms, conditions or privileges of employment" in Section 4 of the Act as including employee benefits. 29 U.S.C. 630(l).

For many years after, however, there was little discussion about the interplay between the ADEA and the provision of retiree health benefits by employers. Many employers relied on legislative history to the OWBPA which states that the practice of eliminating, reducing, or altering employer-sponsored retiree health benefits with Medicare eligibility is lawful under the ADEA. Specifically, employers looked to a joint "Statement of Managers" clarifying several proposed amendments to the OWBPA, which was entered into the congressional records of both the House and Senate and accompanied the final compromise bill. On the subject of "retiree health," the Statement says:

Many employer-sponsored retiree medical plans provide medical coverage for retirees only until the retiree becomes eligible for Medicare. In many of these cases, where coverage is provided to retirees only until they attain Medicare eligibility, the value of the employer-provided retiree medical benefits exceeds the value of the retiree's Medicare benefits. Other employers provide medical coverage to retirees at a relatively high level until the retirees become eligible for Medicare and at a lower level thereafter. In many of these cases, the value of the medical benefits that the retiree receives before becoming eligible for Medicare exceeds the total value of the retiree's Medicare benefits and the medical benefits that the employer provides after the retirees attains Medicare eligibility. These practices are not prohibited by this substitute. Similarly, nothing in this substitute should be construed as authorizing a claim on behalf of a retiree on the basis that the actuarial value of employer-provided health benefits available to that retiree not yet eligible for Medicare is less than the actuarial value of the same benefits available to a younger retiree.

Final Substitute: Statement of Managers, 136 Cong. Rec. S25353 (Sept. 24, 1990); 136 Cong. Rec. H27062 (Oct. 2, 1990).

In August 2000, the United States Court of Appeals for the Third Circuit became the first federal court of appeals to examine whether an employer's coordination of its retiree health plans with Medicare eligibility violated the ADEA. Erie County Retirees Ass'n v. County of Erie, 220 F.3d 193 (3rd Cir. 2000). Prior to 1992, Erie County offered current employees and retirees separate but similar traditional indemnity health insurance coverage. Id. at 196. In February 1998, however, in an effort to control escalating health benefit costs, the county began to

require all eligible retirees over age 65 to accept a coordinated health care plan provided through a health maintenance organization (HMO) and Medicare. Eligible retirees had to have Medicare Part B Medical Insurance in order to participate in the plan. Id. at 197. Retirees not yet eligible for Medicare continued to be covered by a traditional indemnity plan until October 1998 when they were transferred to a hybrid point of service plan where each insured could select between an HMO and the traditional indemnity option on an as-needed basis. Id. In a class action lawsuit, the Medicare-eligible retirees alleged that the county violated the ADEA by offering them health insurance coverage that was inferior to that offered to the county's younger retirees. Id. at 193. In examining whether the county's practice violated the Act, the Third Circuit held that the Statement of Managers language was not controlling and that the ADEA prohibits an employer from treating "retirees differently with respect to health benefits based on Medicare eligibility," unless the employer can meet any of the affirmative defenses provided in section 4 of the ADEA. Id. at 213-14.[25] The one affirmative defense examined in detail by the Third Circuit was the equal benefit/equal cost defense set forth in 29 U.S.C. 623(f)(2)(B)(i). The equal benefit/equal cost defense has been part of the ADEA's regulatory framework since 1967.[26] Consistent with Congress' concern that employers might not hire older workers because many employee benefits become more costly with age, Department of Labor and EEOC regulations interpreted section 4(f)(2) of the ADEA as permitting employers to offer lower levels of certain employee benefits to older workers as long as the benefit cost incurred on behalf of older workers is no less than that incurred for younger workers. 29 CFR 1625.10. In the OWBPA, Congress adopted this test in section 4(f)(2)(B)(i) of the ADEA, thereby codifying the EEOC's equal benefit/equal cost rule.

In Erie County, the Third Circuit found that the costs Medicare incurs on behalf of retirees over age 65 cannot be considered when evaluating whether an employer has satisfied the equal cost prong and remanded the case so the district court could determine whether the county could nonetheless meet the equal benefit/equal cost test. Id. at 216. On remand, the county conceded that it could not meet the equal cost prong using the Third Circuit's formulation of the test. Erie County Retirees Ass'n v. County of Erie, 140 F. Supp.2d 466, 477 (W.D. Pa. 2001). The district court then found that the county did not provide equal benefits to its retirees because (1) age 65 retirees were required to pay a greater portion of the total cost of their health insurance premiums than younger retirees; (2) the health plan offered to older retirees did not allow participants to alternate between different forms of coverage, while the plan offered to younger retirees did; and (3) the health plan for younger retirees did not restrict participants to a prescription drug formulary, while the plan for older retirees did contain such a restriction. Id. at 475-77.

Many benefit experts cautioned that the Erie County decision would exacerbate the erosion of employer-sponsored retiree health benefits.[27] The Erie County decision means, among other things, that an employer who voluntarily provides its pre-age 65 retirees with a bridge to Medicare (with the intent to terminate all employer-sponsored retiree coverage at that time) can do so without ADEA implications only if the benefits provided by the bridge coverage are either the same as or less generous than those provided by Medicare. Stated otherwise, in every instance where employer-provided bridge coverage exceeds Medicare coverage, the employer would be prevented by the ADEA from ending its coverage when retirees become eligible for Medicare. The Commission is concerned that many employers will respond to this outcome, given the dramatic cost increases for retiree health benefits, not by incurring additional costs for retiree benefits that supplement Medicare, but rather by reducing or eliminating health coverage for retirees who are not yet eligible for Medicare.

In fact, this is ultimately what happened in Erie County. In an attempt to comply with the court's ruling, the county transferred younger retirees from the hybrid point of service plan—where each

---

[23] U.S. General Accounting Office, "Retiree Health Benefits: Employer-Sponsored Benefits May Be Vulnerable to Further Erosion," GAO Doc. No. GAO-01-374, at 20-22 (May 2001).

[24] U.S. General Accounting Office, "Retiree Health Benefits: Employer-Sponsored Benefits May Be Vulnerable to Further Erosion," GAO Doc. No. GAO-01-374, at 22-24 (May 2001). GAO estimates that Medigap coverage costs an average of $1,300 per year. Hearing Before the House Comm. on Education and the Workforce, 107th Cong. (2001) (statement of William J. Scanlon, Director of Health Care Services, GAO).

[25] The Commission submitted an amicus curiae brief in Erie County, asserting, based on the plain language of the ADEA, that (1) retirees are covered by the ADEA and (2) employer reliance on Medicare eligibility in making distinctions in employee benefits violated the ADEA, unless the employer satisfied one of the Act's specified defenses or exemptions. In its October 2000 Compliance Manual Chapter on "Employee Benefits," the Commission explicitly adopted the position taken by the Third Circuit in Erie County as its national enforcement policy. When the Commission announced in August 2001 that it

wished to further study the relationship between the ADEA and employer-sponsored retiree health plans, the Commission unanimously voted to rescind those portions of its Compliance Manual that discussed the Erie County decision.

[26] In Public Employees Retirement Sys. of Ohio v. Betts, 492 U.S. 158, 109 S. Ct. 256 (1989), the Supreme Court held that the equal benefit/equal cost test did not apply to the ADEA. Congress believed the test should apply, and the regulatory equal benefit/equal cost test was codified in the OWBPA.

[27] See Anna M. Rappaport, "Postemployment Benefits: Retiree Health Challenges and Trends—2001 and Beyond," in Compensation and Benefits Management, 52, 55 (Autumn 2001) (Erie County will force employers to examine the application of the ADEA to their retiree health plans with "little or no legal precedent"); Paul Fronstin, "Retiree Health Benefits: Trends and Outlook," EBRI Issue Brief No. 236, at 12-14 (Employee Benefit Research Institute Aug. 2001) ("because of the legal and cost concerns raised by the Erie County decision, [employers] are more likely to cut back on benefits for early retirees" or eliminate retiree health benefits).

retiree had the ability to select between HMO or traditional indemnity plan coverage on an as-needed basis—to an HMO plan similar to that available to retirees over age 65 that did not provide such an option. Erie County Retirees Ass'n v. County of Erie, 192 F. Supp.2d 369, 372 (W.D. Pa. 2002). The county also required employees not yet eligible for Medicare to pay a monthly amount for such coverage equal to the monthly amount of Medicare Part B premiums that retirees over age 65 paid. Id. The result, therefore, is a decrease in health benefits for retirees generally; older retirees receive no better health benefits, while younger retirees must pay more for health benefits that offer fewer choices.

Alternative Proposals

In considering the proper regulatory approach, EEOC closely examined whether it would be possible to apply the equal benefit/equal cost test in its regulations to the practice of coordinating employer-sponsored retiree health benefits with Medicare or a State-sponsored retiree health benefits program. The Commission evaluated various proposals that would have allowed employers to take the cost of Medicare into account when assessing whether they satisfied the equal cost test. The Commission also considered the feasibility of implementing regulations under the ADEA that would require employers to adopt or maintain benefits programs that supplement Medicare in order to satisfy the equal benefits test.

After extensive study, however, it does not appear that retiree health costs or benefits can be reasonably quantified in a regulation. Unlike valuation of costs associated with life insurance or long-term disability benefits, calculating retiree health costs is complex due to the multitude of variables, including types of plans, levels and types of coverage, deductibles, and geographical areas covered. In addition, the subjective nature of some health benefits, such as a greater choice in providers, makes any such valuation more complicated.

Even allowing an employer to take into account the "cost" of Medicare is problematic because the government's cost to provide Medicare services does not reflect what similar benefits would cost an employer in the marketplace. Nor can an employer's Medicare tax obligation, pursuant to the Federal Insurance Contributions Act, 26 U.S.C. 3101 et seq. (FICA), be considered the "cost" of any specific retiree's Medicare benefits inasmuch as most retirees have been employed by multiple employers over the course of their careers and employer FICA contributions are paid into a general Medicare fund that is not employee-specific. Additionally, the fact that employees themselves pay for a portion of the cost of Medicare further complicates cost valuation.

The Commission therefore believes that quantifying the cost to employers of post-Medicare retiree health benefits under any formulation of the equal cost test would not be practicable. This is particularly true for employers who maintain multiple plans for different categories of employees. Even for employers with only one plan, the variability in health claims data from year to year can be great. As a result, calculating retiree health benefit expenses would be cost prohibitive for many employers. Thus, even if it were possible to capture the myriad of complexities involved in a retiree health cost analysis in a regulation, the likelihood is that far too many employers might simply reduce or eliminate existing retiree health benefit plans instead of attempting to comply with such a regulation.

Further complicating compliance with many of the alternative proposals considered by the Commission is the fact that employers do not have the same flexibility in designing retiree health benefit programs as they do when designing other types of retirement benefit programs, such as cash-based retirement incentives. For example, providing supplemental health benefits to retirees who are eligible for Medicare may require that the employer obtain and administer a separate policy just for that coverage. Many employers are unable or unwilling to bear such a burden. Instead, if faced with such a choice, employers are more likely to simply eliminate retiree health coverage altogether—for retirees under and over age 65. Furthermore, future changes in the private health insurance market or in Medicare likely would necessitate further regulatory action were the Commission to adopt many of the alternative proposals considered. The Commission does not believe

that it is possible to apply the equal benefit/equal cost test, or a variant of that rule, to the rapidly changing landscape of retiree health care.

The Commission therefore believes that application of the equal cost/equal benefit rule, or a variant of that rule, to the practice of coordinating retiree health benefits with Medicare or a State-sponsored retiree health benefits program would not allow employers to readily and cost-efficiently determine which practices are, and are not, permissible and therefore would not fully alleviate employers' concerns about offering retiree health benefits. It is clear that small and medium-sized employers, and those unable to hire sophisticated employee benefit professionals, would be most affected by a complicated rule. In light of the other factors affecting an employer's decision to provide retiree health benefits, the Commission believes that the current regulatory framework of the ADEA does not provide a sufficient safe harbor to protect and preserve the important employer practice of providing health coverage for retirees.

This lack of regulatory protection may cause a class of people—retirees not yet 65—to be left without any health insurance. It also may contribute to the loss of valuable employer-sponsored coverage that supplements Medicare for retirees age 65 and over. Because almost 60% of retirees between the ages of 55 to 64 rely on employer-sponsored health coverage as their primary source of health coverage,[28] and about one-third of retirees over age 65 rely on employer-provided retiree health plans to supplement Medicare,[29] the Commission believes that such a result is contrary to the public interest and necessitates regulatory action.

The Commission's Proposed Exemption

When enacting the ADEA, Congress recognized that enforcement of the Act required a case-by-case examination of employment practices.[30] In light of this recognition, Congress authorized the Commission to "establish such reasonable exemptions to and from any or all provisions of [the Act] as it may find necessary and proper in the public interest." 29 U.S.C. 628. Pursuant to that authority, the Commission proposes a narrowly drawn exemption that permits the practice of coordinating employer-provided retiree health coverage with eligibility for Medicare or a State-sponsored retiree health benefits program and shows due regard for the remedial purposes of the ADEA. Section 2(b) of the Act firmly establishes the goal of "encouraging employers and workers [to] find ways of meeting problems arising from the impact of age on employment." 29 U.S.C. 621(b). Unrestricted coordination of employer-sponsored retiree health benefits with Medicare or a State-Sponsored health benefits program permits employers to provide a valuable benefit to early retirees who otherwise might not be able to afford health insurance coverage and allows employers to provide valuable supplemental health benefits to retirees who are eligible for Medicare.

The proposed exemption shows due regard for the Act's prohibition against arbitrary age discrimination in employment—a central concern of Congress when it enacted the ADEA. The exemption also is consistent with the Act's purpose of promoting the employment of older persons and is in accord with the Statement of Managers. See Final Substitute: Statement of Managers, 136 Cong. Rec. 25353 (Sept. 24, 1990); 126 Cong. Rec. H.27062 (Oct. 2, 1990).[31] Therefore, the Commission believes that the remedial purposes of the Act will be better served by allowing employers to coordinate retiree health benefits with Medicare or a State-sponsored retiree health benefits program.

Effect of Exemption

As with any exemption from remedial legislation, the proposal is a narrow exemption from the prohibitions of the ADEA. The exemption permits employee benefit plans to lawfully provide health benefits for retired participants that are altered, reduced or eliminated when the participant is eligible for Medicare health benefits or for health benefits under a State-sponsored retiree health benefits program. No other aspects of ADEA coverage or benefits other than retiree health benefits are affected by this exemption.

The proposed exemption would become effective on the date of publication of a final rule in the Federal Register. It is intended that the exemption shall apply to existing, as well as newly created, employer-

---

[28] Hearing Before the House Comm. on Education and the Workforce, 107th Cong. (2001) (statement of William J. Scanlon, Director of Health Care Services, GAO). Of the 56.8% of retirees covered by employer-sponsored health coverage in 1999, 36.3% were covered in their own name and 20.5% received health benefits through a spouse. Paul Fronstin, "Retiree Health Benefits: Trends and Outlook," EBRI Issue Brief No. 236, at 6-7 (Employee Benefit Research Institute Aug. 2001).

[29] The Henry J. Kaiser Family Foundation et al., "Erosion of Private Health Insurance Coverage For Retirees: Findings from the 2000 and 2001 Retiree Health and Prescription

Drug Coverage Survey," at iv (Menlo Park, CA: The Henry J. Kaiser Family Foundation, Health and Research Educational Trust and The Commonwealth Fund April 2002).

[30] H.R. Rep. No. 90-805 (1967), reprinted in 1967 U.S.C.C.A.N. 2213; S. Rep. 90-723 (1967).

[31] While the Third Circuit in Erie County did not find the Statement of Managers controlling, the Commission, in the exercise of its exemption authority, is free to take a broader look at the legislative record in determining whether the proposed exemption is consistent with the Act's purpose of promoting the employment of older persons. The Statement of Managers strongly suggests that it is.

provided retiree health benefit plans. As the Appendix to the proposed exemption indicates, it also is intended that the exemption shall apply to dependent and/or spousal health benefits that are included as part of the health benefits provided to retired participants. However, dependent and/or spousal benefits need not be identical to the health benefits provided for retired participants. Consequently, dependent and/or spousal benefits may be altered, reduced or eliminated pursuant to the exemption whether or not the health benefits provided for retired participants are similarly altered, reduced or eliminated.

Additional Amendments

In addition to the proposed exemption discussed above, the Commission proposes to redesignate subpart C of part 1627 as subpart C of part 1625 of Chapter XIV of Title 29 of the Code of Federal of Regulations. Subpart C of part 1627 currently includes two sections. The first, which will be redesignated as section 1625.30, outlines procedures by which the Commission may exercise its exemption authority under Section 9 of the ADEA. The second, redesignated as section 1625.31, explains the parameters of an already existing exemption for special employment programs. Redesignation does not alter either the procedures by which the Commission may exercise its exemption authority under Section 9 of the ADEA or the Special Employment Programs exemption.

Comments

The Commission invites comments on this proposed exemption from all interested parties, including employee rights organizations, labor unions, employers, benefits groups, actuaries, and state and local governments. In particular, the Commission would welcome comments on other types of government-sponsored retiree health benefit programs, including state and local government retiree health plans, that are comparable to Medicare.

In proposing this exemption, the Commission coordinated with other federal agencies in accord with Executive Order 12067, and incorporated, where appropriate, agency comments in the proposal.

Executive Order 12866 and Regulatory Flexibility Act

The proposed rule has been drafted and reviewed in accordance with Executive Order 12866, section 1(b), Principles of Regulation. This rule is considered a "significant regulatory action" under section 3(f)(4) of that Order and was reviewed by the Office of Management and Budget (OMB). The Commission does not believe that the proposed exemption will have a significant impact on small business entities under the Regulatory Flexibility Act because it imposes no economic or reporting burdens on such firms.

The ADEA applies to all employers with at least 20 employees. 29 U.S.C. 630(b). The Act prohibits covered employers from discriminating in employment against any individual who is at least 40 years of age. 29 U.S.C. 623, 631. The Bureau of Labor Statistics estimates that there are 74,347,000 individuals in the U.S. labor force that are age 40 or above.[32] According to Census Bureau information, approximately 1,976,216 establishments employed 20 or more employees in 2000.[33]

The proposed exemption would apply to all covered employers who provide health benefits to their retirees. In 2001, the GAO concluded that about one-third of large employers and less than 10% of small employers provided such benefits to current retirees.[34] According to the GAO, in 1999, such employer-sponsored health plans were relied on by 10 million retired individuals aged 55 and over as either their primary source of coverage or a supplement to Medicare coverage.[35]

The proposal—which exempts certain practices from regulation—will decrease, not increase, costs to covered employers by reducing the risks of liability for noncompliance with the statute. When the Third Circuit held that the practice of coordinating retiree health benefits with Medicare eligibility was unlawful unless an employer could meet the equal benefit/equal cost test, there was widespread concern that employers who currently provide such retiree health benefits would either have to provide greater benefits to older retirees or reduce benefits for younger retirees to comply. The Commission believes that, if required to make a choice between paying more or less to comply with the ADEA, many employers will choose to pay less by reducing or eliminating health coverage for retirees who are not yet eligible for Medicare. This result is particularly likely given the rising costs of health care in general. The proposed exemption seeks to eliminate this incentive by making clear that the ADEA permits employers to freely coordinate the provision of retiree health benefits with Medicare eligibility. This approach also benefits the significant number of employees

who rely on employer-sponsored retiree health coverage and otherwise would have to obtain retiree health coverage in the private individual marketplace at substantial personal expense.

The proposed exemption has no reporting requirements. A major concern regarding the inequitable impact of regulation on small firms is that reporting and accompanying record keeping requirements can be as costly to smaller firms as large ones. The absence of reporting requirements eliminates this concern.

It is not likely that the proposed regulation will disrupt the efficient functioning of the economy and private market forces. Until recently, when structuring retiree health benefits, many employers relied on legislative history to the OWBPA which states that the practice of eliminating, reducing, or altering employer-sponsored retiree health benefits with Medicare eligibility is lawful under the ADEA. The proposed regulation permits the practice of unrestricted coordination of retiree health benefits with Medicare eligibility to continue.

Under other proposals considered by the Commission, many employers would have been forced to discontinue retiree health coverage if they could not afford the required actuarial analysis. It is clear that small and medium-sized employers, and those unable to hire sophisticated employee benefit professionals, would be most affected by a complicated rule. Larger employers who maintain multiple plans for different categories of employees also would face significant expense complying with alternative proposals. Even for employers with only one plan, the variability in health claims data from year to year can be great. As a result, calculating retiree health benefit expenses under alternative proposals considered by the Commission would have been cost prohibitive for many employers.

List of Subjects

29. CFR Part 1625

Advertising, Aged, Employee benefit plans, Equal employment opportunity, Retirement.

29. CFR Part 1627

Aged, Equal employment opportunity, Reporting and recordkeeping requirements.

For the Commission.

Cari M. Dominguez, Chair.

For the reasons discussed in the preamble, the Equal Employment Opportunity Commission proposes to amend 29 CFR chapter XIV as follows:

PART 1627—RECORDS TO BE MADE OR KEPT RELATING TO AGE: NOTICES TO BE POSTED

1. Revise the heading of Part 1627 to read as set forth above.

2. The authority citation for 29 CFR Part 1627 shall continue to read as follows:

Authority: §7, 81 Stat. 604; 29 U.S.C. 626; sec. 11, 52 Stat. 1066, 29 U.S.C. 211; sec. 12, 29 U.S.C. 631, Pub L. 99-592, 100 Stat. 3342; sec. 2, Reorg. Plan No. 1 of 1978, 43 FR 19807.

3. In §1627.1, remove paragraph (b) and redesignate paragraph (c) as new paragraph (b).

4. In Part 1627, redesignate Subpart C and sections 1627.15 and 1627.16 as Subpart C of Part 1625 and sections 1625.30 and 1625.31, respectively.

PART 1625—AGE DISCRIMINATION IN EMPLOYMENT ACT

5. The authority citation for 29 CFR Part 1625 is revised to read as follows:

Authority: 81 Stat. 602; 29 U.S.C. 621; 5 U.S.C. 301; Secretary's Order No. 10-68; Secretary's Order No. 11-68; §9, 81 Stat. 605; 29 U.S.C. 628; sec. 12, 29 U.S.C. 631, Pub. L. 99-592, 100 Stat. 3342; sec. 2, Reorg. Plan No. 1 of 1978, 43 FR 19807.

6. In newly redesignated Subpart C of Part 1625, revise the heading of newly redesignated §1625.31 and the first sentence of paragraph (a) to read as follows:

§1625.31 Special employment programs.

(a) Pursuant to the authority contained in section 9 of the Act and in accordance with the procedure provided therein and in §1625.30(b) of

---

[32] Bureau of Labor Statistics, U.S. Department of Labor, Current Population Survey (April 2003).

[33] Census Bureau, U.S. Department of Commerce, Statistics of U.S. Businesses (2000).

[34] Hearing Before the House Comm. on Education and the Workforce, 107th Cong. (2001) (statement of William J. Scanlon, Director of Health Care Services, GAO).

[35] U.S. General Accounting Office, "Retiree Health Benefits: Employer-Sponsored Benefits May Be Vulnerable to Further Erosion," GAO Doc. No. GAO-01-374, at 1 (May 2001).

this part, it has been found necessary and proper in the public interest to exempt from all prohibitions of the Act all activities and programs under Federal contracts or grants, or carried out by the public employment services of the several States, designed exclusively to provide employment for, or to encourage the employment of, persons with special employment problems, including employment activities and programs under the Manpower Development and Training Act of 1962, Public Law No. 87-415, 76 Stat. 23 (1962), as amended, and the Economic Opportunity Act of 1964, Public Law No. 88-452, 78 Stat. 508 (1964), as amended, for persons among the long-term unemployed, handicapped, members of minority groups, older workers, or youth. * * *

* * * * *

7. Add section 1625.32 to Subpart C of Part 1625 to read as follows:

§ 1625.32 Coordination of retiree health benefits with Medicare and State health benefits.

(a) *Definitions.* (1) Employee benefit plan means an employee benefit plan as defined in 29 U.S.C. 1002(3).

(2) Medicare means the health insurance program available pursuant to Title XVIII of the Social Security Act, 42 U.S.C. 1395 et seq.

(3) Comparable State health benefit plan means a State-sponsored health benefit plan that, like Medicare, provides retired participants who have attained a minimum age with health benefits, whether or not the type, amount or value of those benefits are equivalent to the type, amount or value of the health benefits provided under Medicare.

(b) *Exemption.* Some employee benefit plans provide health benefits for retired participants that are altered, reduced or eliminated when the participant is eligible for Medicare health benefits or for health benefits under a comparable State health benefit plan. Pursuant to the authority contained in section 9 of the Act, and in accordance with the procedures provided therein and in § 1625.30(b) of this part, it is hereby found necessary and proper in the public interest to exempt from all prohibitions of the Act such coordination of retiree health benefits with Medicare or a comparable State health benefit plan.

(c) *Scope of exemption.* This exemption shall be narrowly construed. It does not apply to the use of eligibility for Medicare or a comparable State health benefit plan in connection with any act, practice or benefit of employment not specified in paragraph (b) of this section. Nor does it apply to the use of the age of eligibility for Medicare or a comparable State health benefit plan in connection with any act, practice or benefit of employment not specified in paragraph (b) of this section.

Appendix to § 1625.32—Questions and Answers Regarding Coordination of Retiree Health Benefits with Medicare and State Health Benefits

Q1. Why is the Commission issuing an exemption from the Act?

A1. The Commission recognizes that while employers are under no legal obligation to offer retiree health benefits, some employers choose to do so in order to maintain a competitive advantage in the marketplace—using these and other benefits to attract and retain the best talent available to work for their organizations. Further, retiree health benefits clearly benefit workers, allowing such individuals to acquire affordable health insurance coverage at a time when private health insurance coverage might otherwise be cost prohibitive. The Commission believes that it is in the best interest of both employers and employees for the Commission to pursue a policy that permits employers to offer these benefits to the greatest extent possible.

Q2. Does the exemption mean that the Act no longer applies to retirees?

A2. No. Only the practice of coordinating retiree health benefits with Medicare (or a comparable State health benefit plan) as specified in paragraph (b) of this section is exempt from the Act. In all other contexts, the Act continues to apply to retirees to the same extent that it did prior to the issuance of this section.

Q3. May employers continue to offer "Medicare carve-out plans" that deduct from the health benefits provided to Medicare-eligible retirees those health benefits that Medicare provides, while continuing to provide to Medicare-eligible retirees those health benefits that Medicare does not provide?

A3. Yes. Employers may continue to offer such "carve-out plans'and make Medicare the primary payer of health benefits for Medicare-eligible retirees. Employers may also continue to offer "carve-out plans" to those retirees eligible for health benefits pursuant to a comparable State health benefit plan and make the comparable State health plan the primary payer of health benefits for these State-eligible retirees.

Q4. Does the exemption also apply to dependent and/or spousal health benefits that are included as part of the health benefits provided for retired participants?

A4. Yes. Because dependent and/or spousal health benefits are benefits provided to the retired participant, the exemption applies to these benefits, just as it does to the health benefits for the retired participant. However, dependent and/or spousal benefits need not be identical to the health benefits provided for retired participants. Consequently, dependent and/or spousal benefits may be altered, reduced or eliminated pursuant to the exemption whether or not the health benefits provided for retired participants are similarly altered, reduced or eliminated.

Q5. Does the exemption permit employers to use Medicare (or comparable State health benefit plan) eligibility, or the age of Medicare eligibility (or the age of eligibility for a comparable State health benefit plan) as a basis for other acts, practices or decisions regarding retirees?

A5. No. Employer use of Medicare (or comparable State health benefit plan) eligibility or the age of Medicare eligibility (or the age of eligibility for a comparable State health benefit plan) in a manner other than as specified in paragraph (b) of this section likely would be considered reliance upon an age-defined factor. Reliance upon an age-defined factor in making distinctions in employee benefits violates the Act, unless the employer satisfies one of the Act's specified defenses or exemptions.

Q6. Does the exemption apply to existing, as well as to newly created, employee benefit plans?

A6. Yes. The exemption applies to all retiree health benefits that coordinate with Medicare (or a comparable State health benefit plan) as specified in paragraph (b) of this section, whether those benefits are provided for in an existing or newly created employee benefit plan.

Q7. Does the exemption apply to health benefits that are provided to current employees who are at or over the age of Medicare eligibility (or the age of eligibility for a comparable State health benefit plan)?

A7. No. The exemption applies only to retiree health benefits, not to health benefits that are provided to current employees. Thus, health benefits for current employees must be provided in a manner that comports with the requirements of the Act. Moreover, under the laws governing the Medicare program, an employer must offer to current employees who are at or over the age of Medicare eligibility the same health benefits, under the same conditions, that it offers to any current employee under the age of Medicare eligibility.

[FR Doc. 03-17738 Filed 7-11-03; 8:45 am]

¶ 20,5340

Employee Benefits Security Administration (EBSA): Investment advisers: State registration: Securities and Exchange Commission (SEC)..—Reproduced below is the text of a proposed rule which would require state-registered investment advisers that wish to obtain or maintain investment manager status under ERISA to electronically register through a centralized electronic filing system established by the SEC in conjunction with state securities authorities. The electronic system, known as the Investment Adviser Registration Depository (IARD), would become the only way which state-registered investment advisers could satisfy ERISA's filing requirements for investment adviser status.

The proposed regulation was published in the Federal Register on December 9, 2003 (68 FR 68709) and was finalized on August 24, 2004 (69 FR 52119). The final regulations appear at ¶ 14,139A and ¶ 14,879. The preamble is reproduced at ¶ 24,236.

ERISA § 3(38)(B)(ii).

Part III

Department of Labor

¶20,5340

Employee Benefits Security Administration

29 CFR Part 2510

Electronic Registration Requirements for Investment Advisers To Be Investment Managers Under Title I of ERISA; Proposed Rule

DEPARTMENT OF LABOR

Employee Benefits Security Administration

29 CFR Part 2510

RIN 1210-AA94

Electronic Registration Requirements for Investment Advisers To Be Investment Managers Under Title I of ERISA

AGENCY: Employee Benefits Security Administration, Department of Labor.

ACTION: Notice of proposed rulemaking.

SUMMARY: This document contains a proposed regulation relating to the definition of investment manager in section 3(38)(B) of Title I of the Employee Retirement Income Security Act of 1974 (ERISA). Under the proposed regulation, in lieu of filing a copy of their state registration forms with the Secretary of Labor, state-registered investment advisers seeking to obtain or maintain investment manager status under Title I of ERISA would have to electronically register through the Investment Adviser Registration Depository (IARD) as an investment adviser with the state in which they maintain their principal office and place of business. The IARD is a centralized electronic filing system, established by the Securities and Exchange Commission (SEC) in conjunction with state securities authorities. The IARD enables investment advisers to satisfy SEC and state registration obligations through the use of the Internet, and current filing information in the IARD database is readily available to the Department and the general public via the Internet. If adopted, the proposed regulation would make electronic registration through the IARD the exclusive method for state-registered investment advisers to satisfy filing requirements for investment manager status under section 3(38)(B)(ii) of Title I of ERISA. The proposed regulation would affect plan trustees, investment managers, other fiduciaries, and plan participants and beneficiaries.

DATES: Written comments (either in print or electronic format) are invited and must be submitted to the Department of Labor on or before February 9, 2004.

ADDRESSES: Interested persons are invited to submit written comments (preferably with three copies) to the Office of Regulations and Interpretations, Room N-5669, Employee Benefits Security Administration, U.S. Department of Labor, 200 Constitution Ave., NW., Washington, DC 20210, Attention: ERISA Investment Manager Electronic Registration NPRM. Written comments may also be sent by Internet to the following address: E-ORI.EBSA@dol.gov. All submissions received will be available for public inspection and copying from 8:30 a.m. to 4:30 p.m. at the Public Disclosure Room, Employee Benefits Security Administration, U.S. Department of Labor, Room N-1513, 200 Constitution Ave. NW., Washington, DC 20210.

FOR FURTHER INFORMATION CONTACT: Florence M. Novellino, Office of Regulations and Interpretations, Employee Benefits Security Administration, U.S. Department of Labor, Washington, DC 20210, telephone (202) 693-8518 (not a toll free number).

SUPPLEMENTARY INFORMATION:

Background

Under Title I of the Employee Retirement Income Security Act of 1974 (ERISA), named fiduciaries of plans may appoint investment managers to manage assets of the plan. If the investment manager is a registered investment adviser, bank or insurance company, and meets the other requirements for being an "investment manager" as defined in section 3(38) of ERISA, the plan trustees are relieved from certain liabilities relating to the investment manager's performance.[1]

In 1996, the National Securities Market Improvement Act (NSMIA) amended the Investment Advisers Act of 1940 (Advisers Act) to divide certain investment adviser regulatory responsibilities, including the registration requirements, between the Securities and Exchange Commission (SEC) and the states. Prior to 1996, most investment advisers were required to register with the SEC and in each state in which they were doing business. Pursuant to paragraph (1) of section 203A(a) of the Advisers Act, and SEC rule at 17 CFR 275.203A-1, certain investment advisers are prohibited from registering with the SEC but must register with the state in which the adviser maintains it principal office and place of business.[2] The legislative history of NSMIA indicates that this division of regulatory responsibilities was intended, among other things, to encourage the SEC and state regulators to create a uniform system for "one-stop" filing that would benefit investors, reduce regulatory and paperwork burdens for registered investment advisers, and facilitate supervision of investment advisers.[3]

The SEC implemented that legislative intent at the federal level by publishing a final rule in September of 2000 at 17 CFR 275.203-1 which made electronic filing with the Investment Adviser Registration Depository (IARD) mandatory for SEC-registered advisers. Additionally, all states accept forms filed via the IARD to satisfy state registration requirements, and many mandate state registration via the IARD.[4] Accordingly, the IARD has become a "one-stop" Internet-based centralized filing system that enables investment advisers to satisfy filing obligations with both federal and state securities regulators. Pertinent state registration information in the IARD database is available on the Internet to the general public through the Investment Adviser Public Disclosure (IAPD) Web site that may be directly accessed through the SEC's Web site or through links from various state and investor Web sites. The IAPD Web site contains investment adviser registration data, including information about current registration forms, registration status, services provided, fees charged, and disclosures about certain conflicts of interest and disciplinary events, if any. The IAPD Web site includes information on investment advisers that currently are registered with the SEC or a state, and also contains information on investment advisers that were registered in the previous two years but are no longer registered.

Section 3(38)(B) of Title I of ERISA was also amended to reflect the above-described changes to the investment adviser registration requirements under the Advisers Act.[5] Specifically, section 3(38)(B) of ERISA requires that, to be an investment manager under Title I, an investment adviser must: (i) be registered with the SEC under the Advisers Act of 1940, or (ii) if not registered under such Act by reason of paragraph (1) of section 203A(a) of such Act, be registered as an investment adviser under the laws of the state in which it maintains its principal office and place of business and, at the time the investment adviser last filed the registration form it most recently filed with such state in order to maintain its registration under the laws of such state, it also filed a copy of such form with the Secretary of Labor.

To implement the filing requirements in section 3(38)(B)(ii) of ERISA, the Department announced on January 14, 1998, that state-registered investment advisers seeking to qualify, or remain qualified, as investment managers must file a copy of their most recent state registration form for the state in which it maintains its principal office and place of business with the Department prior to November 10, 1998, and thereafter file with the Department copies of any subsequent filings with that state. The ongoing obligation to file copies with the Department was, however, to be temporary in nature and remain in effect until a centralized database containing the state registration forms, or substantially similar information, was available to the Department.[6]

The current requirement to file with the Department copies of state registration filings already accessible to the Department and the general public via the IAPD Web site places an unnecessary administrative burden on the regulated community. The requirement also results in the Department allocating resources to receive, sort, and store paper

---

[1] Section 402(c)(3) of ERISA states that a plan may provide that with respect to control or management of plan assets a named fiduciary may appoint an investment manager or managers to manage (including the power to acquire and dispose of) plan assets. Section 405(d) of ERISA provides in part that, if an investment manager or managers have been appointed under section 402(c)(3), then no trustee shall be liable for the acts or omissions of such investment manager or managers, or be under an obligation to invest or otherwise manage any asset of the plan which is subject to the management of such investment manager.

[2] Specifically, subject to certain exceptions, investment advisers fall into three categories under the NSMIA amendments. First, investment advisers having assets under management of less than $25 million generally are prohibited from registering with the SEC but must register with the state regulatory authority in the state where the investment adviser maintains its principal office and place of business. Those with at least $25 million but less than $30 million may register with the SEC in lieu of filing with state authorities. Those

with $30 million or more must register with the SEC. Section 203A(a) of the Advisers Act is codified at 15 U.S.C. 80b-3a(a). See also 17 CFR 275.203A-2 for exemptions from the prohibition for certain investment advisers registering with the SEC.

[3] S. Rep. No. 104-293, at 5 (1996).

[4] The State of Wyoming has not promulgated a state investment adviser regulation requirement; therefore all Wyoming-based investment advisers are required to register under the Advisers Act with the SEC via the IARD. See 65 FR 57438, 57445 (Sept. 22, 2000).

[5] See sec. 308(b)(1) of Title III of NSMIA and Act of November 10, 1997, § 1, Pub. L. 105-72, 111 Stat. 1457.

[6] Pub. L. 105-72 provided that a fiduciary shall be treated as meeting the requirement for filing a copy of the required state registration form with the Secretary if a copy of the form (or substantially similar information) is available to the Secretary from a centralized electronic or other record-keeping database. See Act of November 10, 1997, § 1(b), Pub. L. 105-72, 111 Stat. 1457.

copies of information readily available in electronic form. It is the Department's view that use of the IARD as a centralized electronic database would improve the ability of the Department, plan fiduciaries, and plan participants and beneficiaries to readily access registration information regarding investment advisers eligible to be investment managers of ERISA-covered plans. As noted above, not only does the SEC require electronic filing through the IARD for registration under the Advisers Act, but most states also require IARD filing for compliance with state investment adviser registration requirements. While a few states do not make electronic filing through the IARD mandatory, as noted above, all states permit investment advisers to use the IARD to satisfy registration requirements. As described more fully below, the Department believes the majority of investment managers of ERISA-covered plans already file registration forms electronically through the IARD under the Advisers Act or under applicable state securities laws. In the Department's view, the benefits to plan trustees, plan participants and beneficiaries, and the Department of this proposed regulation outweigh the relatively small incremental cost that some investment managers may incur to file state registration filings through the IARD.

Summary of the Proposed Regulation

The proposed regulation would add § 2510.3-38 to title 29 of the Code of Federal Regulations. Section 2510.3-38(a) would describe the general filing requirement with the Secretary set forth in section 3(38)(B)(ii) applicable to state-registered investment advisers seeking to become or remain investment managers under Title I of ERISA. The regulation would also make clear that its purpose is to establish the exclusive means to satisfy that filing obligation. Section 2510.3-38(b) would provide that, for a state-registered investment adviser to satisfy the filing requirement in section 3(38)(B)(ii) of ERISA, it must electronically file the required registration forms through the IARD. Section 2510.3-38(b) would also provide that submitting a copy of state registration forms to the Secretary does not constitute compliance with section 3(38)(B)(ii) of ERISA. Section 2510.3-38(c) would define the term "Investment Adviser Registration Depository" and "IARD" for purposes of the regulation as the centralized electronic depository described in 17 CFR 275.203-1. Finally, § 2510.3-38(d) would provide a cross-reference to the SEC Internet site at http://www.sec.gov/iard for information on filing investment advisor registration forms with the IARD.

Effective Date and Interim Reliance

This regulation is proposed to be effective 60 days after publication of a final rule in the Federal Register. If adopted, the proposed regulation would be applicable to investment adviser registration filings due after the effective date of the final regulation. Until the effective date of the final regulation, investment advisers seeking to obtain or maintain investment manager status under Title I of ERISA will be treated as having met the filing obligations with the Secretary of Labor described in section 3(38)(B)(ii) of ERISA for any registration filing due on or after the date the proposed regulation is published in the Federal Register if they satisfy the conditions of the proposed regulation.

Regulatory Impact Analysis

Summary

The Department has undertaken this proposed rulemaking for the purpose of establishing a single and readily accessible source of consistent information about the registration of investment advisers that are investment managers by virtue of meeting the requirements of section 3(38)(B)(ii) of ERISA. The Department believes the regulation, if implemented as proposed, would benefit plan fiduciaries, investment advisers, and ultimately the participants and beneficiaries of employee benefit plans. Although the anticipated benefits of the proposal are not quantified here, they are expected to more than justify its relatively modest estimated cost.

The estimated cost of the implementation of electronic registration through the IARD for approximately 500 advisers that submitted copies of their state registrations to the Secretary of Labor, and that currently register in only those states that do not mandate IARD filing, is just under $400,000. Ongoing annual costs are estimated at $50,000. These costs will be offset by efficiency gains for plan fiduciaries and for investment advisers that wish to be appointed by plan fiduciaries. As a result of the electronic registration requirement, plan fiduciaries will be able to access a single source of registration information regardless of

the size or location of the adviser, and advisers may more readily demonstrate their eligibility to be investment managers in order to gain appointments by plan fiduciaries. Over time, these investment managers may also reduce the handling of paper and the time required to complete the Form ADV, which is the joint SEC and state registration form that is also currently accepted by all the states for State registration purposes. Electronic availability of registration information will also support better and more transparent decision making with respect to the appointment of investment managers, which ultimately benefits the participants and beneficiaries of the plans involved.

Discussion

The proposal would benefit plan fiduciaries that wish to appoint an investment manager pursuant to section 402(c)(3) of ERISA. Under section 405(d)(1) of ERISA, plan fiduciaries are not liable for the acts or omissions of the investment manager, and have no obligation to invest assets subject to management by the investment manager. The centralized source of readily accessible registration information offered by the IARD will help plan fiduciaries more efficiently locate information needed to determine whether advisers they may consider appointing are eligible to be an investment manager under ERISA. The source and format of information will no longer differ based on the size or principal business location of the adviser.

Uniform use of the IARD for all advisers who wish to be or remain as investment managers under ERISA will benefit these advisers as well. The change to electronic filing will not change the incentives for investment advisers to become investment managers under ERISA, but should promote increased efficiency for doing so. Advisers are not required to be an investment manager to conduct advisory activities for any customer. The Department assumes that an adviser's decision whether to meet the definition of investment manager under ERISA is based on factors unrelated to the form or format of their registration. It is therefore expected that those state-registered advisers who filed paper copies of their state registration forms with the Secretary chose to do so to gain an advantage in securing appointments by plan fiduciaries.

In any case, this proposed regulation will not change the content of the filings for these advisers because all states accept the joint SEC and state filing form (Form ADV) for state registration, and with certain exceptions, all of the copies submitted to the Secretary were made on Form ADV.[7] Mandatory use of the IARD will, however, change the format and manner in which the information is transmitted. While the Department expects advisers to incur a cost to establish a procedure for electronic filing through the IARD plus an annual fee, the change to an electronic format and transmission method is expected to be more efficient and less costly over time. Use of the IARD will reduce the paper handling, filing, and mailing costs associated with providing copies to the State or States as well as to the Secretary, and reduce handling to obtain and reproduce signatures. The SEC cited similar efficiency gains in its regulatory impact analysis of the final rule implementing mandatory electronic filing for federally regulated advisers. Securities and Exchange Commission, Electronic Filing by Investment Advisers; Final Rule, 65 FR 57438, Sept. 22, 2000.

The proposed regulation will directly affect only those investment advisers who wish to become or remain as investment managers under section 3(38) of ERISA, who generally have $25 million or less under management and consequently do not register with the SEC, and who register only in states that do not mandate use of the IARD to satisfy state registration requirements. Copies of registration forms submitted to the Secretary by State-registered investment advisers indicate that about 500 State-registered advisers have registered in only a non-IARD state.[8] Prior to the implementation of the IARD and many States' decisions to mandate use of the IARD to meet state adviser registration requirements, about 1,500 advisers provided paper copies of their state registration forms to the Secretary. Based on the data contained in those filings, about 1,000 of these already have the capability to file electronically because they are required to register in states that mandate use of the IARD. The Department therefore assumes that this proposed regulation would affect only those advisers that register only in non-IARD states.

Under existing requirements, State-registered advisers incur a State registration filing fee with every State in which they are required to register, plus postage and handling fees for their submissions. Such fees vary by State. Most if not all of the 500 advisers potentially affected by this proposed regulation now register in only one state. When

---

[7] Several exceptions were observed; in those cases, the adviser submitted a copy of the State's action on their registration, such as a license or approval form, rather than the registration form itself. In each case, other advisers' filings for the same State were examined to confirm that the state did accept Form ADV filings.

[8] California, Florida, Kentucky, South Carolina, and West Virginia at the time of this writing.

advisers registered only in non-IARD States register through the IARD, the appropriate state registration fee will be forwarded to the state, such that there will be no net change in state filing fees.

The Advisers Act and Form ADV allow for the requirement that states be provided registration statements. To facilitate state registration, the registrant checks the appropriate boxes on the form for each applicable state, and the IARD then distributes the required information electronically to those states. States will be unaffected because they will continue to receive existing fees, although they will be transmitted in a different manner.

These advisers would, however, newly incur the IARD initial filing fee of $150 for advisers of the size under consideration here, and an annual filing fee of $100. It is also expected that the 500 state-registered advisers will incur a cost for the set-up of the electronic filing capability, and an expenditure of time to adjust internal procedures and put existing information into an electronic format. Filing fees for the first year are expected to total $75,000 in the first year and $50,000 in each subsequent year for these advisers.

The cost of the electronic filing set-up is not known. The SEC did not quantify the cost of set-up in the final rule cited above that pertained to mandatory use of the IARD for registration with the SEC. However, for the purpose of this discussion, the cost for establishment of electronic filing capability has been estimated to be $500, or $250,000 for the 500 advisers affected. This is a one-time cost based on available information on annual fees charged to SEC registrants by commercial providers of service in the industry.[9] An examination of a sample of the 500 individual filings showed that many of the advisers in question already use the software of a single provider for completing their Form ADV. Because this provider performs services to IARD filers who are currently SEC registrants as well, we have assumed that their range of services includes a method of facilitating electronic filing. It is also assumed that all advisers make use of electronic technology in the normal course of business and will not be required to make substantial technological changes as a result of this proposal.

A one-time cost is also estimated for the time required for the adviser to adjust its internal procedures to input data electronically, if necessary. A comparison of a sample of the paper filings received with IARD data indicated that these advisers had not also filed electronically with IARD. It seems likely that many advisers already prepare the forms electronically, regardless of whether they submit them electronically. To account for preparation for electronic transmission, it has been estimated that the advisers will incur the cost of two hours of a financial professional's time at $68 per hour, for a cost of $136 per adviser and a total of $68,000.

The estimated one-time cost of this proposal totals $393,000. The ongoing cost of maintaining registration information and completing and filing Form ADV is not accounted for here because the advisers prepare and file such forms to meet state registration requirements and would continue to do so without regard to this proposed regulation. The ongoing incremental cost of this proposal is therefore $100 per adviser per year, or $50,000.

The Department considered alternatives to this proposal, including issuing no guidance and implementing a standard that would provide the adviser an option to either file a print copy of its state registration or make use of the IARD. The value of greater efficiency through the elimination of dual sources of registration information and promotion of greater accessibility of consistent information through electronic methods was considered to outweigh the relatively modest estimated cost of about $800 per adviser in the first year, and $100 per adviser in each subsequent year. As a result, the Department elected to issue this proposal and seek public comment on its views.

Executive Order 12866

Under Executive Order 12866, the Department must determine whether the regulatory action is "significant" and therefore subject to the requirements of the Executive Order and subject to review by the Office of Management and Budget (OMB). Under section 3(f), the order defines a "significant regulatory action" as an action that is likely to result in a rule (1) having an annual effect on the economy of $100 million or more, or adversely and materially affecting a sector of the economy, productivity, competition, jobs, the environment, public health or safety, or State, local or tribal governments or communities (also referred to as "economically significant"); (2) creating serious inconsistency or otherwise interfering with an action taken or planned by another agency; (3) materially altering the budgetary impacts of entitlement grants, user fees, or loan programs or the rights and

obligations of recipients thereof; or (4) raising novel legal or policy issues arising out of legal mandates, the President's priorities, or the principles set forth in the Executive Order.

Pursuant to the terms of the Executive Order, it has been determined that this action is "significant" within the meaning of section 3(f)(4) of the Executive Order and has therefore been reviewed by OMB. The Department has also undertaken the assessment of the costs and benefits of this regulatory action presented above.

Paperwork Reduction Act

As part of its continuing effort to reduce paperwork and respondent burden, the Department of Labor conducts a preclearance consultation program to provide the general public and federal agencies with an opportunity to comment on proposed and continuing collections of information in accordance with the Paperwork Reduction Act of 1995 (PRA 95) (44 U.S.C. 3506(c)(2)(A)). This helps to ensure that requested data can be provided in the desired format, reporting burden (time and financial resources) is minimized, collection instruments are clearly understood, and the impact of collection requirements on respondents can be properly assessed.

Currently, EBSA is soliciting comments concerning the proposed information collection request (ICR) included in this Notice of Proposed Rulemaking concerning Electronic Registration Requirements for Investment Advisers to be Investment Managers Under Title I of ERISA (ERISA Investment Manager Electronic Registration). A copy of the ICR may be obtained by contacting the individual identified in the PRA Addresses section below.

The Department has submitted a copy of the proposed information collection to OMB in accordance with 44 U.S.C. 3507(d) for review of its information collections. The Department and OMB are particularly interested in comments that:

• Evaluate whether the proposed collection of information is necessary for the proper performance of the functions of the agency, including whether the information will have practical utility;

• Evaluate the accuracy of the agency's estimate of the burden of the collection of information, including the validity of the methodology and assumptions used;

• Enhance the quality, utility, and clarity of the information to be collected; and

• Minimize the burden of the collection of information on those who are to respond, including through the use of appropriate automated, electronic, mechanical, or other technological collection techniques or other forms of information technology, e.g., permitting electronic submission of responses.

Comments should be sent to the Office of Information and Regulatory Affairs, Office of Management and Budget, Room 10235, New Executive Office Building, Washington, DC 20503; Attention: Desk Officer for the Employee Benefits Security Administration. Although comments may be submitted through February 9, 2004, OMB requests that comments be received within 30 days of publication of the Notice of Proposed Rulemaking to ensure their consideration.

PRA Addresses: Address requests for copies of the ICR to Joseph S. Piacentini, Office of Policy and Research, U.S. Department of Labor, Employee Benefits Security Administration, 200 Constitution Avenue, NW., Room N-5718, Washington, DC 20210. Telephone (202) 693-8410; Fax: (202) 219-5333. These are not toll-free numbers.

The Department is issuing these proposed rules to establish the uniform availability of investment adviser registration information in a centralized electronic database. The proposed rule would affect investment advisers that register with the states rather than SEC by virtue of the requirements of NSMIA, who do not currently register electronically through the IARD, and who wish to fall within the definition of investment manager for purposes of ERISA section 3(38)(B). Such advisers currently file a paper copy of the applicable state registration form with the Secretary of Labor pursuant to section 3(38)(B)(ii) of the statute. The information collection is found in the proposed regulation at section 2520.3-38(b). The basis for the burden estimates is found in the discussion above.

Type of Review: New collection.

Agency: Employee Benefits Security Administration, Department of Labor.

Title: ERISA Investment Manager Electronic Registration.

---

[9] Such fees are used here as a proxy only; the fees do not pertain specifically to electronic set-up or transmission.

OMB Number: 1210-0NEW.

Affected Public: Individuals or households; Business or other for-profit.

Respondents: 500.

Frequency of Response: Annually.

Responses: 500.

Estimated Total Burden Hours: 1,000.

Total Annualized Capital/Startup Costs: $275,000.

Total Burden Cost (Operating and Maintenance): $50,000.

Total Annualized Cost: $325,000.

After the year of implementation, the startup cost will be fully defrayed.The ongoing annual operating and maintenance cost will be $50,000.

Unfunded Mandates Reform Act

For purposes of the Unfunded Mandates Reform Act of 1995 (Pub. L. 104-4), as well as Executive Order 12875, this proposed rule does not include any federal mandate that may result in expenditures by State, local, or tribal governments in the aggregate of more than $100 million, or increased expenditures by the private sector of more than $100 million.

Small Business Regulatory Enforcement Fairness Act

The rule being issued here is subject to the Congressional Review Act provisions of the Small Business Regulatory Enforcement Fairness Act of 1996 (5 U.S.C. 801 et seq.) and, if finalized, will be transmitted to Congress and the Comptroller General for review. The rule is not a "major rule" as that term is defined in 5 U.S.C. 804, because it is not likely to result in (1) an annual effect on the economy of $100 million or more; (2) a major increase in costs or prices for consumers, individual industries, or Federal, State, or local government agencies, or geographic regions; or (3) significant adverse effects on competition, employment, investment, productivity, innovation, or on the ability of United States-based enterprises to compete with foreign-based enterprises in domestic or export markets.

Regulatory Flexibility Act

The Regulatory Flexibility Act (5 U.S.C. 601 et seq.) (RFA) imposes certain requirements with respect to federal rules that are subject to the notice and comment requirements of section 553(b) of the Administrative Procedure Act (5 U.S.C. 551 et seq.) and that are likely to have a significant economic impact on a substantial number of small entities. Unless an agency certifies that a proposed rule will not have a significant economic impact on a substantial number of small entities, section 603 of the RFA requires that the agency present an initial regulatory flexibility analysis at the time of the publication of the notice of proposed rulemaking describing the impact of the rule on small entities and seeking public comment on such impact. Small entities include small businesses, organizations and governmental jurisdictions.

For purposes of analysis under the RFA, EBSA normally considers a small entity to be an employee benefit plan with fewer than 100 participants, on the basis of the definition found in section 104(a)(2) of ERISA. However, this proposed regulation pertains to investment advisers that are prohibited from registering with the SEC pursuant to section 203(A) of the Advisers Act and SEC rules. This generally includes those advisers that have assets of less than $25 million under management. In its final rule relating to Electronic Filing by Investment Advisers (65 FR 57445, note 86), the SEC states that for purposes of the Advisers Act and the RFA, an investment adviser generally is a small entity if (a) it manages assets of less than $25 million reported on its most recent Schedule I to Form ADV, (b) it does not have total assets of $5 million or more on the last day of the most recent fiscal year, and (c) it is not in a control relationship with another investment adviser that is not a small entity (Rule 0-7 under the Advisers Act).

Because the entities potentially affected by this rule are similar if not identical to those that fall within the SEC definition of small entity for RFA purposes, and because the regulation is expected to have a direct impact on an existing cost of doing business that investment advisers would assume without regard to this proposal, but no economic impact that would be passed on to employee benefit plans, the Department considers it appropriate in this limited circumstance to use the SEC definition for evaluating potential impacts on small entities. The Department invites comments on its election to use this definition. Using this definition, the Department certifies that this proposed regulation would not have a significant economic impact on a substantial number of small entities. The factual basis for this conclusion is described below.

The SEC States that of about 20,000 investment advisers in the United States, some 12,000 do not file with them. As discussed above, approximately 500 investment advisers are expected to incur costs under this regulation. This represents 2.5 percent of the approximately 20,000 advisers doing business in the U.S., or 4 percent of the 12,000 small advisers that do not currently file with the SEC. Thus the number of advisers that will incur costs under this regulation is substantial neither in absolute terms nor as a fraction of the universe of all or of small advisers.

In addition, the economic impact of the proposal is not expected to be significant for any small entity. Seeking investment manager status for purposes of ERISA is not mandatory; small advisers presumably make efforts to meet the terms of the ERISA investment manager definition only when they compute a net benefit for doing so. The proposed regulation will mandate electronic submission of small adviser's registration information, but will not change the content or other requirements for those registrations. The average cost for affected advisers is estimated to be small: about $800 in the initial year, and $100 in each following year. It is possible that some portion of this cost will be passed on to plans.

On this basis, the Department certifies that this proposed regulation would not have a significant economic impact on a substantial number of small entities. The Department invites comments on the potential impact of this proposed regulation on small entities, and on ways in which costs may be limited within the stated objectives of this proposal.

Federalism Statement

Executive Order 13132 (August 4, 1999) outlines fundamental principles of federalism and requires the adherence to specific criteria by federal agencies in the process of their formulation and implementation of policies that have substantial direct effects on the States, on the relationship between the national government and the States, or on the distribution of power and responsibilities among the various levels of government. This proposed rule does not have federalism implications because it has no substantial direct effect on the States, on the relationship between the national government and the States, or on the distribution of power and responsibilities among the various levels of government. Section 514 of ERISA provides, with certain exceptions specifically enumerated, that the provisions of Titles I and IV of ERISA supersede any and all laws of the States as they relate to any employee benefit plan covered under ERISA. Although the requirements in this proposed rule do alter the fundamental reporting and disclosure requirements of section 3(38)(B) of ERISA with respect to state-registered investment managers, because the duty of these state-registered advisers to report to the states exists independently of ERISA, and the proposed rule merely prescribes that investment advisers seeking ERISA investment manager status use a specific filing method that is accepted by all states and available as a choice in all states for registration purposes, there is neither a direct implication for the States, nor is there a direct effect on the relationship or distribution of power between the national government and the States. This proposal only affects those State-registered investment advisers who choose to seek investment manager status under section 3(38) of ERISA, advisers not seeking such status are unaffected by this proposed regulation.

Statutory Authority

The proposed regulation would be adopted pursuant to the authority contained in section 505 of ERISA (Pub. L. 93-406, 88 Stat. 894; 29 U.S.C. 1135), and the Act of November 10, 1997, § 1, Pub. L. 105-72, 111 Stat. 1457, and under Secretary of Labor's Order 1-2003, 68 FR 5374 (Feb. 3, 2003).

List of Subjects in 29 CFR Part 2510

Employee benefit plans, Employee Retirement Income Security Act, Pensions, Plan assets.

PART 2510—[AMENDED]

1. The authority citation for part 2510 is revised to read as follows:

Authority: 29 U.S.C. 1002(2), 1002(21), 1002(37), 1002(38), 1002(40), 1031, and 1135; Secretary of Labor's Order 1-2003, 68 FR 5374; § 2510.3-101 also issued under sec. 102 of Reorganization Plan No. 4 of 1978, 43 FR 47713, 3 CFR, 1978 Comp., p. 332 and E.O. 12108, 44 FR 1065, 3 CFR, 1978 Comp., p. 275, and 29 U.S.C. 1135 note. § 2510.3-102 also issued under sec. 102 of Reorganization Plan No. 4 of 1978, 43 FR 47713, 3 CFR, 1978 Comp., p. 332 and E.O. 12108, 44 FR 1065, 3 CFR, 1978 Comp., p. 275. Section 2510.3-38 is also issued under § 1, Pub. L. 105-72, 111 Stat. 1457.

2. Add § 2510.3-38 to read as follows:

§ 2510.3-38 *Filing requirements for State registered investment advisers to be investment managers.*

(a) *General.* Section 3(38) of the Act sets forth the criteria for a fiduciary to be an investment manager for purposes of section 405 of the Act. Subparagraph (B)(ii) of section 3(38) of the Act provides that, in the case of a fiduciary who is not registered under the Investment Advisers Act of 1940 by reason of paragraph (1) of section 203A(a) of such Act, the fiduciary must be registered as an investment adviser under the laws of the State in which it maintains its principal office and place of business, and, at the time the fiduciary files registration forms with such State to maintain the fiduciary's registration under the laws of such State, also files a copy of such forms with the Secretary of Labor. The purpose of this section is to set forth the exclusive means for investment advisers to satisfy the filing obligation with the Secretary described in subparagraph (B)(ii) of section 3(38) of the Act.

(b) *Filing requirement.* To satisfy the filing requirement with the Secretary in section 3(38)(B)(ii) of the Act, a fiduciary must be registered as an investment adviser with the State in which it maintains its principal office and place of business and file through the Investment Adviser Registration Depository (IARD), in accordance with applicable IARD requirements, the information required to be registered and maintain the fiduciary's registration as an investment adviser in such State. Submitting to the Secretary investment adviser registration forms filed with a State does not constitute compliance with the filing requirement in section 3(38)(B)(ii) of the Act.

(c) *Definitions.* For purposes of this section, the term "Investment Adviser Registration Depository" or "IARD" means the centralized electronic depository described in 17 CFR 275.203-1.

(d) *Cross reference.* Information for investment advisers on how to file through the IARD is available on the Securities and Exchange Commission Web site at http://www.sec.gov/iard.

Signed at Washington, DC this 3rd day of December, 2003.

Ann L. Combs,

Assistant Secretary, Employee Benefits Security Administration, U.S. Department of Labor.

[FR Doc. 03-30435 Filed 12-8-03; 8:45 am]

¶ 20,534P

Employee Benefits Security Administration (EBSA): Mandatory distributions: Automatic rollovers: Safe harbors: Individual retirement accounts (IRAs).—The proposed ruleprovides guidance from EBSA that facilitates the satisfaction of fiduciary responsibilities with regard to automatic rollovers of certain mandatory distributions to IRAs. The safe harbor set forth in the proposed rule requires the proper selection of an individual retirement plan provider and provides conditions for the proper investment of funds in connection with the automatic rollover.

The proposed regulation was published in the *Federal Register* on March 2, 2004 (69 FR 9899) and was previously reproduced below.

The regulations were finalized and published in the *Federal Register* on September 28, 2004 (69 FR 58017). The final rules are effective March 28, 2005. The regulations appear at ¶ 14,742A and the preamble is reproduced at ¶ 24,238.

¶ 20,534Q

Veterans' Employment and Training Service: Uniformed Services Employment and Reemployment Rights Act of 1994: Protected pension benefits: Protections against discrimination and retaliation: Employer statutory defenses.—The Department of Labor has issued proposed regulations that are designed to clarify the rights of employees and the attendant responsibilities of employers under the Uniformed Services Employment and Reemployment Rights Act of 1994 (USERRA). In addition to reemployment rights and protections from retaliation and discrimination, USERRA entitles veterans returning to employment from uniformed military service to the restoration of pension and profit-sharing benefits that would have accrued but for the employee's military service. Specifically, the reemployed veterans military service is considered served with the employer for purposes of benefit accrual. A reemployed veteran is also entitled to accrued benefits that are contingent on the making of, or derived from, employee contributions or elective deferrals, to the extent that the employee makes payments to the plan with respect to contributions or deferrals.

The proposed regulations were published in the *Federal Register* on September 20, 2004 (69 FR 56265). The final regulations were published in the *Federal Register* on December 19, 2005 (70 FR 75246). The preamble to the final regulations is reproduced at ¶ 24,243.

¶ 20,534R

Pension Benefit Guaranty Corporation (PBGC): Electronic filing requirements: Financial statements: Actuarial information.—The PBGC has issued a proposed rule which would: require that certain identifying, financial and actuarial information be filed electronically in a standardized format; require the filing of additional items of supporting information that are readily available to the filer; and require a filer for the previous year, who does not believe a filing is required for the current year, to demonstrate why there is no current filing requirement.

The proposed regulation, which was reproduced here, was published in the *Federal Register on* December 28, 2004 (69 FR 77679), and corrected on January 12, 2005 (70 FR 2080). The final regulations were published in the *Federal Register* on March 9, 2005 (70 FR 11540). The preamble to the final regulations is reproduced at ¶ 24,239.

¶ 20,534S

Employee Benefits Security Administration: Health plans: HIPAA: Family and Medical Leave Act: Tolling of time periods: Creditable coverage.—The Employee Benefits Security Administration has issued proposed regulations relating to the interaction between the Health Insurance Portability and Accountability Act (HIPAA) and the Family and Medical Leave Act (FMLA). Under the proposed regulations, the beginning of the period that is used for determining whether a significant break in coverage has occurred (generally 63 days) is tolled in cases in which a certificate of creditable coverage is not provided on or before the day coverage ceases. In those cases, the significant break-in-coverage period is tolled until a certificate is provided but not beyond 44 days after the coverage ceases. These rules are being jointly issued with the Internal Revenue Service. Comments must be received by March 30, 2005.

The proposed regulations, which were published in the *Federal Register* on December 30, 2004 (69 FR 78799), are reproduced below.

DEPARTMENT OF LABOR

Employee Benefits Security Administration

29 CFR Part 2590

RIN 1210-AA54

Notice of Proposed Rulemaking for Health Coverage Portability: Tolling Certain Time Periods and Interaction With the Family and Medical Leave Act Under HIPAA Titles I and IV

¶20,534S

AGENCIES: Internal Revenue Service, Department of the Treasury; Employee Benefits Security Administration, Department of Labor; Centers for Medicare & Medicaid Services, Department of Health and Human Services.

ACTION: Notice of proposed rulemaking and request for comments.

SUMMARY: These proposed rules would clarify certain portability requirements for group health plans and issuers of health insurance coverage offered in connection with a group health plan. These rules propose to implement changes made to the Internal Revenue Code, the Employee Retirement Income Security Act, and the Public Health Service Act enacted as part of the Health Insurance Portability and Accountability Act of 1996.

DATES: Written comments on this notice of proposed rulemaking are invited and must be received by the Departments on or before March 30, 2005.

ADDRESSES: Written comments should be submitted with a signed original and three copies (except for electronic submissions) to any of the addresses specified below. Any comment that is submitted to any Department will be shared with the other Departments.

Comments to the IRS can be addressed to: CC:PA:LPD:PR (REG-130370-04), Room 5203, Internal Revenue Service, POB 7604, Ben Franklin Station, Washington, DC 20044.

In the alternative, comments may be hand-delivered between the hours of 8 a.m. and 4 p.m. to: CC:PA:LPD:PR (REG-130370-04), Courier's Desk, Internal Revenue Service, 1111 Constitution Avenue, NW., Washington, DC 20224.

Alternatively, comments may be transmitted electronically via the IRS or via the Federal eRulemaking Portal at *www.regulations.gov* (IRS-REG-130370-04).

Comments to the Department of Labor can be addressed to: U.S. Department of Labor, Employee Benefits Security Administration, 200 Constitution Avenue NW., Room C-5331, Washington, DC 20210, *Attention:* Proposed Portability Requirements.

Alternatively, comments may be hand-delivered between the hours of 9 a.m. and 5 p.m. to the same address. Comments may also be transmitted by e-mail to: *e-ohpsca.ebsa@dol.gov.*

Comments to HHS can be submitted as described below: In commenting, please refer to file code CMS-2158-P. Because of staff and resource limitations, we cannot accept comments by facsimile (FAX) transmission.

You may submit comments in one of three ways (no duplicates, please):

1. *Electronically.* You may submit electronic comments on specific issues in this regulation to *http://www.cms.hhs.gov/regulations/ecomments.* (Attachments should be in Microsoft Word, WordPerfect, or Excel; however, we prefer Microsoft Word.)

2. *By mail.* You may mail written comments (one original and two copies) to the following address ONLY:

Centers for Medicare & Medicaid Services, Department of Health and Human Services, Attention: CMS-2158-P, P.O. Box 8017, Baltimore, MD 21244-8010.

Please allow sufficient time for mailed comments to be received before the close of the comment period.

3. *By hand or courier.* If you prefer, you may deliver (by hand or courier) your written comments (one original and two copies) before the close of the comment period to one of the following addresses. If you intend to deliver your comments to the Baltimore address, please call telephone number (410) 786-7195 in advance to schedule your arrival with one of our staff members. Room 445-G, Hubert H. Humphrey Building, 200 Independence Avenue, SW., Washington, DC 20201; or 7500 Security Boulevard, Baltimore, MD 21244-1850.

(Because access to the interior of the HHH Building is not readily available to persons without Federal Government identification, commenters are encouraged to leave their comments in the CMS drop slots located in the main lobby of the building. A stamp-in clock is available for persons wishing to retain a proof of filing by stamping in and retaining an extra copy of the comments being filed.)

Comments mailed to the addresses indicated as appropriate for hand or courier delivery may be delayed and received after the comment period.

Submission of comments on paperwork requirements. You may submit comments on this document's paperwork requirements by mailing

your comments to the addresses provided at the end of the "Collection of Information Requirements" section in this document.

All submissions to the IRS will be open to public inspection and copying in room 1621, 1111 Constitution Avenue, NW., Washington, DC from 9 a.m. to 4 p.m.

All submissions to the Department of Labor will be open to public inspection and copying in the Public Disclosure Room, Employee Benefits Security Administration, U.S. Department of Labor, Room N-1513, 200 Constitution Avenue, NW., Washington, DC from 8:30 a.m. to 4:30 p.m.

All submissions timely submitted to HHS will be available for public inspection as they are received, generally beginning approximately three weeks after publication of a document, at the headquarters for the Centers for Medicare & Medicaid Services, 7500 Security Boulevard, Baltimore, MD 21244, Monday through Friday of each week from 8:30 a.m. to 4:00 p.m. To schedule an appointment to view public comments, phone 410-786-7195.

FOR FURTHER INFORMATION CONTACT:

Dave Mlawsky, Centers for Medicare & Medicaid Services (CMS), Department of Health and Human Services, at 1-877-267-2323 ext. 61565; Amy Turner, Employee Benefits Security Administration, Department of Labor, at (202) 693-8335; or Russ Weinheimer, Internal Revenue Service, Department of the Treasury, at (202) 622-6080.

SUPPLEMENTARY INFORMATION:

Customer Service Information

To assist consumers and the regulated community, the Departments have issued questions and answers concerning HIPAA. Individuals interested in obtaining copies of Department of Labor publications concerning changes in health care law may call a toll free number, 1-866-444-EBSA (3272), or access the publications on-line at *www.dol.gov/ebsa,* the Department of Labor's Web site. These regulations as well as other information on the new health care laws are also available on the Department of Labor's interactive web pages, Health *E* laws. In addition, CMS's publication entitled "Protecting Your Health Insurance Coverage" is available by calling 1-800-633-4227 or on the Department of Health and Human Services' Web site (www.cms.hhs.gov/hipaa1), which includes the interactive webpages, HIPAA Online. Copies of the HIPAA regulations, as well as notices and press releases related to HIPAA and other health care laws, are also available at the above-referenced Web sites.

Background

The Health Insurance Portability and Accountability Act of 1996 (HIPAA), Public Law 104-191, was enacted on August 21, 1996. HIPAA amended the Internal Revenue Code of 1986 (Code), the Employee Retirement Income Security Act of 1974 (ERISA), and the Public Health Service Act (PHS Act) to provide for, among other things, improved portability and continuity of health coverage. Interim final regulations implementing the HIPAA provisions were first made available to the public on April 1, 1997 (published in the **Federal Register** on April 8, 1997, 62 FR 16894) (April 1997 interim rules). On December 29, 1997, the Departments published a clarification of the April 1997 interim rules as they relate to excepted benefits. On October 25, 1999, the Departments published a notice in the **Federal Register** (64 FR 57520) soliciting additional comments on the portability requirements based on the experience of plans and issuers operating under the April 1997 interim rules.

After consideration of all the comments received on the portability provisions, the Departments are publishing final regulations elsewhere in this issue of the **Federal Register**. These proposed rules address additional and discrete issues for which the Departments are soliciting further comment before promulgating final regulations.

Overview of the Proposed Regulations

1. Rules Relating to Creditable Coverage—26 CFR 54.9801-4, 29 CFR 2590.701-4, 45 CFR 146.113

Tolling of the 63-Day Break-in-Coverage Rule

These proposed rules would modify the 63-day break-in-coverage rules with one significant substantive change. Under the proposed rules, the beginning of the period that is used for determining whether a significant break in coverage has occurred (generally 63 days) is tolled in cases in which a certificate of creditable coverage is not provided on or before the day coverage ceases. In those cases, the significant-break-in-coverage period is tolled until a certificate is provided but not beyond 44 days after the coverage ceases.

The Departments have fashioned this tolling rule (and a similar tolling rule for the 30-day period for requesting special enrollment) in an effort to address the inequity of individuals' losing coverage without being aware that the coverage has ended while minimizing the burdens on subsequent plans and issuers that are not responsible for providing the missing or untimely certificates. Numerous situations have come to the attention of the Departments in which an individual's health coverage is terminated but in which the individual does not learn of the termination of coverage until well after it occurs. The statute generally requires that a certificate of creditable coverage be provided at the time an individual ceases to be covered under a plan. The statute, the April 1997 interim rules, and the final regulations (published elsewhere in this issue of the **Federal Register**) all permit a plan or issuer to provide the certificate at a later date if it is provided at a time consistent with notices required under a COBRA continuation provision. The statute also directs the Secretaries to establish rules to prevent a plan or issuer's failure to provide a certificate timely from adversely affecting the individual's subsequent coverage. If a plan or issuer chooses to provide a certificate later than the date an individual loses coverage, as the regulations permit in certain circumstances, these proposed rules provide that an individual should not suffer from this rule of convenience for the plan or issuer. However, to prevent the abuse that might result from an open-ended tolling rule, an outside limit of 44 days is placed on this relief. This reflects the fact that, in most cases, plans and issuers are required to provide certificates within 44 days (although some plans and issuers may be required to provide certificates sooner than 44 days after coverage ceases and some entities are not required to provide certificates at all). The Departments have adopted this uniform limit on the tolling rule for purposes of consistency. New examples have been added to illustrate the tolling rule.

2. Evidence of Creditable Coverage—26 CFR 54.9801-5, 29 CFR 2590.701-5, 45 CFR 146.115

Information in Certificate and Model Certificate

These proposed rules would modify the required elements for the educational statement in certificates of creditable coverage to require a disclosure about the Family and Medical Leave Act. Use of the first model certificate below by group health plans and group health insurance issuers, or use of the appropriate model certificate that appears in the preamble to the related final regulations published elsewhere in this issue of the **Federal Register**, will satisfy the requirements of paragraph (a)(3)(ii) in this section of the final regulations. Similarly, for purposes of complying with those final regulations, State Medicaid programs may use the second version below, or may use the appropriate model certificate that appears in the preamble to those final regulations. Thus, until this proposed regulation is published as a final regulation, entities may use either the model certificates published below, or those published elsewhere in this issue of the **Federal Register**. For entities that choose not to use the model certificates below until this proposed regulation is published as a final regulation, we welcome comments as to the applicability date for using them.

BILLING CODE 4830-01-P

CERTIFICATE OF GROUP HEALTH PLAN COVERAGE

1. Date of this certificate: _____

2. Name of group health plan: _____
_____

3. Name of participant: _____

4. Identification number of participant: _____

5 Name of individuals to whom this certificate
applies: _____
_____

6. Name, address, and telephone number of
plan administrator or issuer responsible
for providing this certificate:_____
_____
_____

7. For further information, call: _____

8. If the individual(s) identified in line 5 has (have)
at least 18 months of creditable coverage
(disregarding periods of coverage before
a 63-day break), check here and skip lines 9 and
10: ___

9. Date waiting period or affiliation period
(if any) began: _____

10. Date coverage began: _____

11. Date coverage ended (or if coverage has not
ended, enter "continuing"): _____

[Note: separate certificates will be furnished if information is not identical for the participant and each beneficiary.]

Statement of HIPAA Portability Rights

IMPORTANT — KEEP THIS CERTIFICATE. This certificate is evidence of your coverage under this plan. Under a federal law known as HIPAA, you may need evidence of your coverage to reduce a preexisting condition exclusion period under another plan, to help you get special enrollment in another plan, or to get certain types of individual health coverage even if you have health problems.

Preexisting condition exclusions. Some group health plans restrict coverage for medical conditions present before an individual's enrollment. These restrictions are known as "preexisting condition exclusions." A preexisting condition exclusion can apply only to conditions for which medical advice, diagnosis, care, or treatment was recommended or received within the 6 months before your "enrollment date." Your enrollment date is your first day of coverage under the plan, or, if there is a waiting period, the first day of your waiting period (typically, your first day of work). In addition, a preexisting condition exclusion cannot last for more than 12 months after your enrollment date (18 months if you are a late enrollee). Finally, a preexisting condition exclusion cannot apply to pregnancy and cannot apply to a child who is enrolled in health coverage within 30 days after birth, adoption, or placement for adoption.

If a plan imposes a preexisting condition exclusion, the length of the exclusion must be reduced by the amount of your prior creditable coverage. Most health coverage is creditable coverage, including group health plan coverage, COBRA continuation coverage, coverage under an individual health policy, Medicare, Medicaid, State Children's Health Insurance Program (SCHIP), and coverage through high-risk pools and the Peace Corps. Not all forms of creditable coverage are required to provide certificates like this one. If you do not receive a certificate for past coverage, talk to your new plan administrator.

You can add up any creditable coverage you have, including the coverage shown on this certificate. However, if at any time you went for 63 days or more without any coverage (called a break in coverage) a plan may not have to count the coverage you had before the break.

➔ Therefore, once your coverage ends, you should try to obtain alternative coverage as soon as possible to avoid a 63-day break. You may use this certificate as evidence of your creditable coverage to reduce the length of any preexisting condition exclusion if you enroll in another plan.

Right to get special enrollment in another plan. Under HIPAA, if you lose your group health plan coverage, you may be able to get into another group health plan for which you are eligible (such as a spouse's plan), even if the plan generally does not accept late enrollees, if you request enrollment within 30 days. (Additional special enrollment rights are triggered by marriage, birth, adoption, and placement for adoption.)

➔ Therefore, once your coverage ends, if you are eligible for coverage in another plan (such as a spouse's plan), you should request special enrollment as soon as possible.

Prohibition against discrimination based on a health factor. Under HIPAA, a group health plan may not keep you (or your dependents) out of the plan based on anything related to your health. Also, a group health plan may no charge you (or your dependents) more for coverage, based on health, than the amount charged a similarly situated individual.

Right to individual health coverage. Under HIPAA, if you are an "eligible individual," you have a right to buy certain individual health policies (or in some states, to buy coverage through a high-risk pool) without a preexisting condition exclusion. To be an eligible individual, you must meet the following requirements:

• You have had coverage for at least 18 months without a break in coverage of 63 days or more;
• Your most recent coverage was under a group health plan (which can be shown by this certificate);
• Your group coverage was not terminated because of fraud or nonpayment of premiums;
• You are not eligible for COBRA continuation coverage or you have exhausted your COBRA benefits (or continuation coverage under a similar state provision); and
• You are not eligible for another group health plan, Medicare, or Medicaid, and do not have any other health insurance coverage.

The right to buy individual coverage is the same whether you are laid off, fired, or quit your job.

➔ Therefore, if you are interested in obtaining individual coverage and you meet the other criteria to be an eligible individual, you should apply for this coverage as soon as possible to avoid losing your eligible individual status due to a 63-day break.

Special information for people on FMLA leave. If you are taking leave under the Family and Medical Leave Act (FMLA) and you drop health coverage during your leave, any days without health coverage while on FMLA leave will not count towards a 63-day break in coverage. In addition, if you do not return from leave, the 30-day period to request special enrollment in another plan will not start before your FMLA leave ends.

➔ Therefore, when you apply for other health coverage, you should tell your plan administrator or health insurer about any prior FMLA leave.

State flexibility. This certificate describes minimum HIPAA protections under federal law. States may require insurers and HMOs to provide additional protections to individuals in that state.

For more information. If you have questions about your HIPAA rights, you may contact your state insurance department or the U.S. Department of Labor, Employee Benefits Security Administration (EBSA) toll-free at 1-866-444-3272 (for free HIPAA publications ask for publications concerning changes in health care laws). You may also contact the CMS publication hotline at 1-800-633-4227 (ask for "Protecting Your Health Insurance Coverage"). These publications and other useful information are also available on the Internet at: http://www.dol.gov/ebsa, the DOL's interactive web pages - Health *E*laws, or http://www.cms.hhs.gov/hipaa1.

CERTIFICATE OF MEDICAID COVERAGE

1. Date of this certificate: _____

2. Name of state Medicaid program: _____

3. Name of recipient: _____

4. Identification number of recipient: _____

5. Name of individuals to whom this certificate applies: _____ _____

6. Name, address, and telephone number of state Medicaid agency responsible for providing this certificate: _____ _____ _____

7. For further information call: _____

8. If the individual(s) identified in line 5 has (have) at least 18 months of creditable coverage (disregarding periods of coverage before a 63-day break), check here and skip line 9. ____

9. Date coverage began: _____

10. Date coverage ended (or if coverage has not ended, enter "continuing"): _____

[Note: separate certificates will be furnished if information is not identical for the recipient and each dependent.]

Statement of HIPAA Portability Rights

IMPORTANT — KEEP THIS CERTIFICATE. This certificate is evidence of your coverage under this state Medicaid program. Under a federal law known as HIPAA, you may need evidence of your coverage to reduce a preexisting condition exclusion period under a group health plan, to help you get special enrollment in a group health plan, or to get certain types of individual health coverage even if you have health problems.

Preexisting condition exclusions. Some group health plans restrict coverage for medical conditions present before an individual's enrollment. These restrictions are known as "preexisting condition exclusions." A preexisting condition exclusion can apply only to conditions for which medical advice, diagnosis, care, or treatment was recommended or received within the 6 months before your "enrollment date." Your enrollment date is your first day of coverage under the plan, or, if there is a waiting period, the first day of your waiting period (typically, your first day of work). In addition, a preexisting condition exclusion cannot last for more than 12 months after your enrollment date (18 months if you are a late enrollee). Finally, a preexisting condition exclusion cannot apply to pregnancy and cannot apply to a child who is enrolled in health coverage within 30 days after birth, adoption, or placement for adoption.

If a plan imposes a preexisting condition exclusion, the length of the exclusion must be reduced by the amount of your prior creditable coverage. Most health coverage is creditable coverage, including group health plan coverage, COBRA continuation coverage, coverage under an individual health policy, Medicare, Medicaid, State Children's Health Insurance Program (SCHIP), and coverage through high-risk pools and the Peace Corps. Not all forms of creditable coverage are required to provide certificates like this one. If you do not receive a certificate for past coverage, talk to your new plan administrator.

You can add up any creditable coverage you have, including the coverage shown on this certificate. However, if at any time you went for 63 days or more without any coverage (called a break in coverage) a plan may not have to count the coverage you had before the break.

→ Therefore, once your coverage ends, you should try to obtain alternative coverage as soon as possible to avoid a 63-day break. You may use this certificate as evidence of your creditable coverage to reduce the length of any preexisting condition exclusion if you enroll in a group health plan.

Right to get special enrollment in another plan. Under HIPAA, if you lose your group health plan coverage, you may be able to get into another group health plan for which you are eligible (such as a spouse's plan), even if the plan generally does not accept late enrollees, if you request enrollment within 30 days. (Additional special enrollment rights are triggered by marriage, birth, adoption, and placement for adoption.)

→ Therefore, once your coverage in a group health plan ends, if you are eligible for coverage in another plan (such as a spouse's plan), you should request special enrollment as soon as possible.

Prohibition against discrimination based on a health factor. Under HIPAA, a group health plan may not keep you (or your dependents) out of the plan based on anything related to your health. Also, a group health plan may not charge you (or your dependents) more for coverage, based on health, than the amount charged a similarly situated individual.

Right to individual health coverage. Under HIPAA, if you are an "eligible individual," you have a right to buy certain individual health policies (or in some states, to buy coverage through a high-risk pool) without a preexisting condition exclusion. To be an eligible individual, you must meet the following requirements:

- You have had coverage for at least 18 months without a break in coverage of 63 days or more;
- Your most recent coverage was under a group health plan;
- Your group coverage was not terminated because of fraud or nonpayment of premiums;
- You are not eligible for COBRA continuation coverage or you have exhausted your COBRA benefits (or continuation coverage under a similar state provision); and
- You are not eligible for another group health plan, Medicare, or Medicaid, and do not have any other health insurance coverage.

The right to buy individual coverage is the same whether you are laid off, fired, or quit your job.

→ Therefore, if you are interested in obtaining individual coverage and you meet the other criteria to be an eligible individual, you should apply for this coverage as soon as possible to avoid losing your eligible individual status due to a 63-day break.

Special information for people on FMLA leave. If you are taking leave under the Family and Medical Leave Act (FMLA) and you drop health coverage during your leave, any days without health coverage while on FMLA leave will not count towards a 63-day break in coverage. In addition, if you do not return from leave, the 30-day period to request special enrollment in another plan will not start before your FMLA leave ends.

→ Therefore, when you apply for other health coverage, you should tell your plan administrator or health insurer about any prior FMLA leave.

State flexibility. This certificate describes minimum HIPAA protections under federal law. States may require insurers and HMOs to provide additional protections to individuals in that state.

For more information. If you have questions about your HIPAA rights, you may contact your state insurance department or the U.S. Department of Labor, Employee Benefits Security Administration (EBSA) toll-free at 1-866-444-3272 (for free HIPAA publications ask for publications concerning changes in health care laws). You may also contact the CMS publication hotline at 1-800-633-4227 (ask for "Protecting Your Health Insurance Coverage"). These publications and other useful information are also available on the Internet at: http://www.dol.gov/ebsa or http://www.cms.hhs.gov/hipaa1.

3. Special Enrollment Periods—26 CFR 54.9801-6, 29 CFR 2590.701-6, 45 CFR 146.117

Tolling of the Special Enrollment Period

Under HIPAA, the April 1997 interim rules, and the final regulations, an individual wishing to special enroll following a loss of coverage is generally required to request enrollment not later than 30 days after the loss of eligibility, termination of employer contributions, or exhaustion of COBRA continuation coverage. For individuals whose coverage ceases and a certificate of creditable coverage is not provided on or before the date coverage ceases, this regulation provides for proposed tolling rules similar to those described above for determining a significant break. That is, the special enrollment period terminates at the end of the 30-day period that begins on the first day after the earlier of the date that a certificate of creditable coverage is provided or the date 44 days after coverage ceases.

Modification of Special Enrollment Procedures and When Coverage Begins Under Special Enrollment

The April 1997 interim rules did not establish procedures for processing requests for special enrollment beyond affirming the statutory requirement that requests be made not later than 30 days after the event giving rise to the special enrollment right and providing that the same requirements could be imposed on special enrollees that were imposed on other enrollees (*e.g.,* that the request be made in writing). Some examples in the April 1997 interim rules could be read to suggest that plans and issuers could require individuals requesting special enrollment to file completed applications for health coverage by the end of the special enrollment period.

It has been brought to the Departments' attention that some plans and issuers were imposing application requirements that could not reasonably be completed within the special enrollment period (for example, requiring the social security number of a newborn within 30 days of the birth), effectively denying individuals their right to special enroll their dependents. In this regard, the statute merely requires an employee to request special enrollment, or an individual to seek to enroll, during the special enrollment period. These proposed regulations preserve individuals' access to special enrollment by clarifying that during the special enrollment period individuals are only required to make an oral or written request for special enrollment.

The proposed regulations provide further that after a timely request, the plan or issuer may require the individual to complete all enrollment materials within a reasonable time after the end of the special enrollment period. However, the enrollment procedure may only require information required from individuals who enroll when first eligible and information about the event giving rise to the special enrollment right. While a plan can impose a deadline for submitting the completed enrollment materials, the deadline must be extended for information that an individual making reasonable efforts cannot obtain within that deadline.

Thus, even where a plan requires social security numbers from individuals who enroll when first eligible, the plan must provide an extended deadline for receiving the social security number in the case of a newborn. In no event could a plan deny special enrollment for newborns because an employee could not provide a social security number for the newborn within the special enrollment period.

As regards the effective date of coverage for special enrollments, the proposed rules generally follow the statute, the April 1997 interim final rules, and the final regulations being published elsewhere in this issue of the **Federal Register.** However clarifications of the effective date of coverage are added to conform to the clarification of the special enrollment procedures. Where the special enrollment right results from a loss of eligibility for coverage or marriage, coverage generally must begin no later than the first day of the first calendar month after the date the plan or issuer receives the request for special enrollment. However, if the plan or issuer requires completion of additional enrollment materials, coverage must begin no later than the first day of the first calendar month after the plan or issuer receives enrollment materials that are substantially complete.

Where the special enrollment right results from a birth, coverage must begin on the date of birth. In the case of adoption or placement for adoption, coverage must begin no later than the date of such adoption or placement for adoption. If a plan or issuer requires completion of additional enrollment materials, the plan or issuer must provide benefits once the plan or issuer receives substantially complete enrollment materials. However, the benefits provided at that time must be retroactive to the date of birth, adoption, or placement for adoption.

The Departments welcome comments on these aspects of the proposed rule.

¶20,534S

4. Interaction With the Family and Medical Leave Act—26 CFR 54.9801-7, 29 CFR 701-8, 45 CFR 146.120

The proposed rules address how the HIPAA portability requirements apply in situations where a person is on leave under the Family and Medical Leave Act of 1993 (FMLA). A general principle of FMLA is that an employee returning from leave under FMLA should generally be in the same position the employee was in before taking leave. At issue is how to reconcile that principle of FMLA with the HIPAA rights and requirements that are triggered by an individual ending coverage under a group health plan. These proposed regulations provide specific rules that clarify how HIPAA and FMLA interact when the coverage of an employee or an employee's dependent ends in connection with an employee taking leave under FMLA.

With respect to the rules concerning a significant break in coverage, if an employee takes FMLA leave and does not continue group health coverage for any part of the leave, the period of FMLA leave without coverage is not taken into account in determining whether a significant break in coverage has occurred for the employee or any dependents. To the extent an individual needs to demonstrate that coverage ceased in connection with FMLA leave (which would toll any significant break with respect to another plan or issuer), these regulations provide that a plan or issuer must take into account all information that it obtains about an employee's FMLA leave. Further, if an individual attests to the period of FMLA leave and the individual cooperates with a plan's or issuer's efforts to verify the individual's FMLA leave, the plan or issuer must treat the individual as having been on FMLA leave for the period attested to for purposes of determining if the individual had a significant break in coverage. Nonetheless, a plan or issuer is not prevented from modifying its initial determination of FMLA leave if it determines that the individual did not have the claimed FMLA leave, provided that the plan or issuer follows procedures for reconsideration similar to those set forth in the final rules governing determinations of creditable coverage.

The question has arisen whether it would be appropriate to waive the general requirement to provide automatic certificates of creditable coverage in the case of an individual who declines coverage when electing FMLA leave if the individual will be reinstated at the end of FMLA leave. At the time an employee elects FMLA leave, the employer (as well as the employee) may not know if the employee will later return from FMLA leave and elect to be reinstated. Requiring plans and issuers to provide certificates when individuals cease health coverage in connection with FMLA leave may result in some certificates being issued when individuals ceasing coverage will not need the certificates as evidence of coverage (because of later reinstatement). However, automatic issuance likely imposes less burden because the plan or issuer does not need to determine whether a certificate is required. Moreover, automatic issuance eliminates the need for remedial measures if an individual expected to be reinstated in fact is not later reinstated. Thus, these proposed regulations clarify there is no exception to the general rule requiring automatic certificates when coverage ends and provide that if an individual covered under a group health plan takes FMLA leave and ceases coverage under the plan, an automatic certificate must be provided.

With respect to the special enrollment rules, an individual (or a dependent of the individual) who is covered under a group health plan and who takes FMLA leave has a loss of eligibility that results in a special enrollment period if the individual's group health coverage is terminated at any time during FMLA leave and the individual does not return to work for the employer at the end of FMLA leave. This special enrollment period begins when the period of FMLA leave ends. Moreover, the rules that delay the start of the special enrollment period until the receipt of a certificate of creditable coverage continue to operate.

5. Special Rules—Excepted Plans and Excepted Benefits—26 CFR 54.9831-1, 29 CFR 2590.732, 45 CFR 146.145

Determination of Number of Plans

Various provisions in Chapter 100 of the Code, Part 7 of Subtitle B of Title I of ERISA, and Title XXVII of the PHS Act apply when an individual commences coverage or terminates coverage under a group health plan. For example, a certificate of creditable coverage must be provided when an individual ceases to be covered under a group health plan. Under the April 1997 interim rules, it was not always clear whether an individual changing benefit elections among those offered by an employer or employee organization was merely switching between benefit packages under a single plan or was switching from one plan to another. These proposed regulations add rules to remove this uncertainty.

Under these proposed regulations, all medical care benefits made available by an employer or employee organization (including a board of trustees of a multiemployer trust) are generally considered to constitute one group health plan (the default rule). However, the employer or employee organization can establish more than one group health plan if it is clear from the instruments governing the arrangements to provide medical care benefits that the benefits are being provided under separate plans and if the arrangements are operated pursuant to the instruments as separate plans. A multiemployer plan and a nonmultiemployer plan are always separate plans. Under an anti-abuse rule, separate plans are aggregated to the extent necessary to prevent the evasion of any legal requirement.

These rules provide plan sponsors great flexibility while minimizing the burden of making decisions about how many plans to maintain. For example, many employers may wish to minimize the number of certificates of creditable coverage required to be furnished to continuing employees. Under the default rule, because all health benefits provided by an employer are considered a single group health plan, there is no need to furnish a certificate of creditable coverage when an employee merely switches coverage among the options made available by the employer. This need would arise only if the employer designated separate benefit packages as separate plans in the plan documents and only if the benefit packages were also operated pursuant to the plan documents as separate plans.

The anti-abuse rule limits the flexibility of these rules to prevent evasions. For example, a plan sponsor might design an arrangement under which the participation of each of many employees in the arrangement would be considered a separate plan. On the face of it, such an arrangement might appear to satisfy the requirement for a plan being exempt from the requirements of Chapter 100 of the Code, Part 7 of ERISA, and Title XXVII of the PHS Act because on the first day of the plan year each plan would have fewer than two participants who are current employees. This would give the impression that the plans would not have to comply with the prohibitions against discriminating based on one or more health factors, with the restrictions on preexisting condition exclusions, nor with any of the other requirements of Chapter 100 of the Code, Part 7 of ERISA, and Title XXVII of the PHS Act. The anti-abuse rule would require the aggregation of plans under such an arrangement to the extent necessary to make the plans subject to the requirements of Chapter 100 of the Code, Part 7 of ERISA, and Title XXVII of the PHS Act. The anti-abuse rule would apply in similar fashion to prevent the evasion of any other law that applies to group health plans or to the parties administering them or providing benefits under them.

Counting the Average Number of Employees

These proposed regulations add rules for counting the average number of employees employed by an employer during a year.[1] Various rules in Chapter 100 of the Code, Part 7 of ERISA, and Title XXVII of the PHS Act require the determination of such an average number, including the Mental Health Parity Act provisions, the guaranteed access provisions under the PHS Act for small employers, and the exemption from the excise tax under the Code for certain small employers.

Under these proposed regulations, the average number of employees employed by an employer is determined by using a full-time equivalents method. Each full-time employee employed for the entire previous calendar year counts as one employee. Full-time employees employed less than the entire previous calendar year and part-time employees are counted by totaling their employment hours in the previous calendar year (but not to exceed 40 hours for any week) and dividing that number by the annual full-time hours under the employer's general employment practices (but not exceeding 40 hours per week). Any resulting fraction is disregarded. For example, if these calculations produce a result of 50.9, the average number of employees is considered to be 50. If an employer existed for less than the entire previous calendar year (including not being in existence at all), then the determination of the average number of employees is made by estimating the average number of employees that it is reasonably expected that the employer will employ on business days in the current calendar year. For a multiemployer plan, the number of employees employed by the employer with the most employees is attributed to each employer with at least one employee participating in the plan.

Economic Impact and Paperwork Burden

Summary—Department of Labor and Department of Health and Human Services

HIPAA's group market portability provisions, which limit the scope and application of preexisting condition exclusions and establish special enrollment rights, provide a minimum standard of protection designed to increase access to health coverage. The Departments crafted these proposed regulations to secure these protections under certain special circumstances, consistent with the intent of Congress, and to do so in a manner that is economically efficient. The Departments are unable to quantify the regulations' economic benefits and costs, but believe that their benefits will justify their costs.

HIPAA's primary economic effects ensue directly from its statutory provisions. HIPAA's statutory group market portability provisions extend coverage to certain individuals and preexisting conditions not otherwise covered. This extension of coverage entails both benefits and costs. Individuals enjoying expanded coverage will realize benefits, sometimes including improvements in health and relief from so-called "job lock." The costs of HIPAA's portability provisions generally include the cost of extending coverage, as well as certain attendant administrative costs. The Departments believe that the benefits of HIPAA are concentrated in a relatively small population, while the costs are distributed broadly across group plan enrollees. The economic effects of HIPAA's statutory portability provisions are discussed in detail in the preamble to the final regulation under the "Effects of the Statute" of the "Basis for Assessment of Economic Impact" section, published elsewhere in this issue of the **Federal Register**.

By clarifying and securing HIPAA's statutory portability protections, these proposed regulations will help ensure that HIPAA rights are fully realized. The result is likely to be a small increase at the margin in the economic effects of HIPAA's statutory portability provisions.

These proposed regulations are intended to secure and implement HIPAA's group market portability and special enrollment provisions under certain special circumstances. The regulations will secure HIPAA's portability rights for individuals who are not timely notified that their coverage has ended and for individuals whose coverage ends in connection with the taking of leave that is guaranteed under FMLA. The regulations also will clarify and thereby secure individuals' special enrollment rights under HIPAA, and clarify the methodologies to be used by employers to determine the number of plans offered and the average number of individuals employed during a given year.

Additional economic benefits derive from the regulations' clarifications of HIPAA requirements. The regulations will reduce uncertainty and costly disputes between employees, employers and issuers, and promote confidence among employees in health benefits' value, thereby promoting labor market efficiency and fostering the establishment and continuation by employers of group health plans.

Benefits under these regulations will be concentrated among a small number of affected individuals while costs will be spread thinly across group plan enrollees.

Affected individuals will generally include those who would have lost access to coverage for needed medical care after being denied HIPAA portability and/or special enrollment rights due to time spent without coverage prior to receiving a certificate or while on FMLA-guaranteed leave. The benefits of these regulations for any particular affected individual may be significant. As noted above and under "Effects of the Statute" in the "Basis for Assessment of Economic Impact" section of the preamble to the final regulation, published elsewhere in this issue of the **Federal Register**, access to coverage for needed medical care is important to individuals' health and productivity. However, the number of affected individuals, and therefore the aggregate cost of extended access to coverage under these regulations, is expected to be small, for several reasons. First, these regulations extend HIPAA rights only in instances where individuals are not timely notified that their coverage has ended or their coverage ends in connection with the taking of FMLA-guaranteed leave. Second, the period over which this regulation extends rights will often be short, insofar as certificates are often provided promptly after coverage ends and many family leave periods are far shorter than the guaranteed 12 weeks. Third, it is generally in individuals' interest to minimize periods of uninsurance. Individuals are likely to exercise their portability and special enrollment rights as soon as possible after coverage ends, which will often be before any extension of such rights under these regulations becomes effective. Fourth, only a portion of individuals who enroll in health plans in circum-

---

[1] The rules for determining the average number of employees employed by an employer during a year are not used for counting the number employed by the employer on a given day, such as the first day of a plan year.

stances where these regulations alone guarantee their special enrollment or portability rights would otherwise have been denied such rights. Fifth, only a small minority of individuals who avoid a significant break in coverage as a direct result of these regulations would otherwise have lost coverage for needed medical care. (The affected minority would be those who suffer from preexisting conditions, join health plans that exclude coverage for such conditions, and require treatment of such conditions during the exclusion periods.)

Affected individuals may also include some who would have been denied special enrollment rights if plans or issuers failed to recognize their requests for special enrollment or imposed unreasonable deadlines or requirements for completion of enrollment materials.

As noted above, the Departments expect that these regulations will increase at the margin the economic effects of HIPAA's statutory portability provisions. For the reasons stated immediately above, the Departments believe that these increases will be small on aggregate, adding only a small increment to the costs attributable to HIPAA's statutory portability provisions, which themselves amount to a small fraction of one percent of health plan expenditures. Additionally, as with the cost of HIPAA's statutory portability provisions, the majority of these costs will be borne by group plan enrollees. The Departments expect these regulations to have little or no perceptible negative impact on employers' propensity to offer health benefit plans or on the generosity of those plans. In sum, the Departments expect that the benefits of these regulations, which can be very large for a particular affected individual, will justify their costs. The basis for the Departments' conclusions is detailed below.

The Departments solicit comments on their conclusions and their basis for them, and empirical data or other information that would support a fuller or more accurate analysis.

Executive Order 12866—Department of Labor and Department of Health and Human Services

Under Executive Order 12866 (58 FR 551735, Oct. 4, 1993), the Departments must determine whether a regulatory action is "significant" and therefore subject to the requirements of the Executive Order and subject to review by the Office of Management and Budget (OMB). Under section 3(f), the order defines a "significant regulatory action" as an action that is likely to result in a rule: (1) Having an annual effect on the economy of $100 million or more, or adversely and materially affecting a sector of the economy, productivity, competition, jobs, the environment, public health or safety, or state, local or tribal governments or communities (also referred to as "economically significant"); (2) creating serious inconsistency or otherwise interfering with an action taken or planned by another agency; (3) materially altering the budgetary impacts of entitlement grants, user fees, or loan programs or the rights and obligations of recipients thereof; or (4) raising novel legal or policy issues arising out of legal mandates, the President's priorities, or the principles set forth in the Executive Order.

Pursuant to the terms of the Executive Order, the Departments have determined that this action raises novel policy issues arising out of legal mandates. Therefore, this notice is "significant" and subject to OMB review under Section 3(f)(4) of the Executive Order. Consistent with the Executive Order, the Departments have assessed the costs and benefits of this regulatory action. The Departments' assessment, and the analysis underlying that assessment, is detailed below. The Departments performed a comprehensive, unified analysis to estimate the costs and benefits attributable to the regulations for purposes of compliance with Executive Order 12866, the Regulatory Flexibility Act, and the Paperwork Reduction Act.

Statement of Need for Proposed Action

These proposed regulations clarify and interpret the HIPAA portability provisions under Section 701 of the Employee Retirement Income Security Act of 1974 (ERISA), Section 2701 of the Public Health Service Act, and Section 9801 of the Internal Revenue Code of 1986. The regulations are needed to secure and implement HIPAA's portability rights for individuals who are not timely notified that their coverage has ended and for individuals whose coverage ends in connection with the taking of leave that is guaranteed under FMLA, and to clarify and secure individuals' special enrollment rights under HIPAA.

Economic Effects

As noted above, HIPAA's primary economic effects ensue directly from its statutory provisions. HIPAA's statutory group market portability provisions extend coverage to certain individuals and preexisting conditions not otherwise covered. This extension of coverage entails both benefits and costs. The economic effects of HIPAA's statutory portability provisions is summarized above and discussed in detail under the "Basis for Assessment of Economic Impact" section of the preamble to the final regulation, published elsewhere in this issue of the **Federal Register**.

Also as noted above, by clarifying and securing HIPAA's statutory portability protections, these regulations will help ensure that HIPAA rights are fully realized. The result is likely to be a small increase at the margin in the economic effects of HIPAA's statutory portability provisions. The benefits of these regulations will be concentrated among a small number of affected individuals, while their costs will be spread thinly across plans and issuers. The regulations also will reduce uncertainty about health benefits' scope and value, thereby promoting employee health benefit coverage and labor market efficiency. The Departments believe that the regulations' benefits will justify their cost. The Departments assessment of the expected economic effects of the regulation are summarized above and discussed in detail below.

Regulatory Flexibility Act—The Department of Labor and Department of Health and Human Services

The Regulatory Flexibility Act (5 U.S.C. 601 *et seq.*) (RFA), imposes certain requirements with respect to Federal rules that are subject to the notice and comment requirements of section 553(b) of the Administrative Procedure Act (5 U.S.C. 551 *et seq.*) and which are likely to have a significant economic impact on a substantial number of small entities. Section 603 of the RFA stipulates that an agency, unless it certifies that a proposed rule will not have a significant economic impact on a substantial number of small entities, must present an initial regulatory flexibility analysis at the time of publication of the notice of proposed rulemaking that describes the impact of the rule on small entities and seeks public comment on such impact. Small entities include small businesses, organizations, and governmental jurisdictions.

For purposes of analysis under the RFA, the Departments consider a small entity to be an employee benefit plan with fewer than 100 participants. The basis for this definition is found in section 104(a)(2) of ERISA, which permits the Secretary of Labor to prescribe simplified annual reports for pension plans which cover fewer than 100 participants. Under section 104(a)(3), the Secretary may also provide for simplified annual reporting and disclosure if the statutory requirements of part 1 of Title I of ERISA would otherwise be inappropriate for welfare benefit plans. Pursuant to the authority of section 104(a)(3), the Department of Labor has previously issued at 29 CFR 2520.104-20, 2520.104-21, 2520.104-41, 2520.104-46 and 2520.104b-10 certain simplified reporting provisions and limited exemptions from reporting and disclosure requirements for small plans, including unfunded or insured welfare plans covering fewer than 100 participants and which satisfy certain other requirements.

Further, while some small plans are maintained by large employers, most are maintained by small employers. Both small and large plans may enlist small third party service providers to perform administrative functions, but it is generally understood that third party service providers transfer their costs to their plan clients in the form of fees. Thus, the Departments believe that assessing the impact of this rule on small plans is an appropriate substitute for evaluating the effect on small entities. The definition of small entity considered appropriate for this purpose differs, however, from a definition of small business based on size standards promulgated by the Small Business Administration (SBA) (13 CFR 121.201) pursuant to the Small Business Act (5 U.S.C. 631 *et seq.*). The Department of Labor solicited comments on the use of this standard for evaluating the effects of the proposal on small entities. No comments were received with respect to the standard. Therefore, a summary of the initial regulatory flexibility analysis based on the 100 participant size standard is presented below.

The economic effects of HIPAA's statutory provisions on small plans are discussed extensively under the "Regulatory Flexibility Act—Department of Labor and Department of Health and Human Services" section of the preamble to the final regulation, published elsewhere in this issue of the **Federal Register**.

By clarifying and securing HIPAA's statutory portability protections, these regulations will help ensure that these benefits are fully realized. The result is likely to be a small increase in the economic effects of HIPAA's statutory provisions. The Departments were unable to estimate the amount of this increase. However, the direct financial value of coverage extensions pursuant to HIPAA's statutory portability provisions are estimated to be approximately $180 million for small plans, or a small fraction of one percent of total small plan expenditures.[2]

The regulations also will reduce uncertainty about health benefits' scope and value, thereby promoting employee health benefit coverage, including coverage under small plans, and labor market efficiency.

The benefits of these regulations will be concentrated among a small number of affected small group plan enrollees, while their costs will be spread thinly across small group plans enrollees. The benefits of these regulations for any particular affected individual, which may include improved health and productivity, may be significant. However, as previously noted, the number of affected individuals, and therefore the aggregate cost of these regulations, is expected to be small. The Departments believe that the benefits to affected individuals of the application of these regulations to small plans justify the cost to small plans of such application. The basis for the Departments' conclusions is detailed below.

The Departments generally expect the impact of the regulations on any particular small plan to be small. A very large majority of small plans are fully insured, so the cost will fall nominally on issuers rather than from plans. Issuers are expected to pass this cost back to plans and enrollees, but will spread much of it across a large number of plans, thereby minimizing the impact on any particular plan. However, it is possible that small plans that self-insure, or fully insured small plans whose premiums are tied closely to their particular claims experience, might bear all or most of the cost associated with extensions of coverage attributable directly to these regulations. The Departments have no way to quantify the incidence or magnitude of such costs, and solicit comments on such incidence and magnitude, and on whether these regulations would have a significant impact on a substantial number of small plans.

Special Analyses—Department of the Treasury

Notwithstanding the determinations of the Departments of Labor and of Health and Human Services, for purposes of the Department of the Treasury this notice of proposed rulemaking is not a significant regulatory action. Because this notice of proposed rulemaking does not impose a collection of information on small entities and is not subject to section 553(b) of the Administrative Procedure Act (5 U.S.C. chapter 5), the Regulatory Flexibility Act (5 U.S.C. chapter 6) does not apply pursuant to 5 U.S.C. 603(a), which exempts from the Regulatory Flexibility Act's requirements certain rules involving the internal revenue laws. Pursuant to section 7805(f) of the Internal Revenue Code, this notice of proposed rulemaking will be submitted to the Chief Counsel for Advocacy of the Small Business Administration for comment on its impact on small business.

Paperwork Reduction Act

Department of Labor

These proposed regulations include three separate collections of information as that term is defined in the Paperwork Reduction Act of 1995 (PRA 95), 44 U.S.C. 3502(3): the Notice of Enrollment Rights, Notice of Preexisting Condition Exclusion, and Certificate of Creditable Coverage. Each of these disclosures is currently approved by the Office of Management and Budget (OMB) through October 31, 2006 in accordance with PRA 95 under control numbers 1210-0101, 1210-0102, and 1210-0103.

Department of the Treasury

These proposed regulations include a collection of information as that term is defined in PRA 95: the Notice of Enrollment Rights, Notice of Preexisting Condition Exclusion, and Certificate of Creditable Coverage. Each of these disclosures is currently approved by OMB under control number 1545-1537.

Department of Health and Human Services

These proposed regulations include three separate collections of information as that term is defined in PRA 95: the Notice of Enrollment Rights, Notice of Preexisting Condition Exclusion, and Certificate of Creditable Coverage. Each of these disclosures is currently approved

by OMB through June 30, 2006 in accordance with PRA 95 under control number 0938-0702.

Small Business Regulatory Enforcement Fairness Act

The rule being issued here is subject to the provisions of the Small Business Regulatory Enforcement Fairness Act of 1996 (5 U.S.C. 801 et seq.) and, if finalized, will be transmitted to Congress and the Comptroller General for review. The rule is not a "major rule" as that term is defined in 5 U.S.C. 804, because it is not likely to result in (1) an annual effect on the economy of $100 million or more; (2) a major increase in costs or prices for consumers, individual industries, or federal, state, or local government agencies, or geographic regions; or (3) significant adverse effects on competition, employment, investment, productivity, innovation, or on the ability of United States-based enterprises to compete with foreign-based enterprises in domestic or export markets.

Unfunded Mandates Reform Act

Section 202 of the Unfunded Mandates Reform Act of 1995 requires that agencies assess anticipated costs and benefits before issuing any rule that may result in an expenditure in any 1 year by state, local, or tribal governments, in the aggregate, or by the private sector, of $100 million. These proposed regulations have no such mandated consequential effect on state, local, or tribal governments, or on the private sector.

Federalism Statement Under Executive Order 13132— Department of Labor and Department of Health and Human Services

Executive Order 13132 outlines fundamental principles of federalism. It requires adherence to specific criteria by federal agencies in formulating and implementing policies that have "substantial direct effects" on the States, the relationship between the national government and States, or on the distribution of power and responsibilities among the various levels of government. Federal agencies promulgating regulations that have these federalism implications must consult with State and local officials, and describe the extent of their consultation and the nature of the concerns of State and local officials in the preamble to the regulation.

In the Departments' view, these proposed regulations have federalism implications because they may have substantial direct effects on the States, the relationship between the national government and States, or on the distribution of power and responsibilities among the various levels of government. However, in the Departments' view, the federalism implications of these proposed regulations are substantially mitigated because, with respect to health insurance issuers, the vast majority of States have enacted laws which meet or exceed the federal HIPAA portability standards.

In general, through section 514, ERISA supersedes State laws to the extent that they relate to any covered employee benefit plan, and preserves State laws that regulate insurance, banking or securities. While ERISA prohibits States from regulating a plan as an insurance or investment company or bank, HIPAA added a new section to ERISA (as well as to the PHS Act) narrowly preempting State requirements for issuers of group health insurance coverage. Specifically, with respect to seven provisions of the HIPAA portability rules, states may impose stricter obligations on health insurance issuers.[3] Moreover, with respect to other requirements for health insurance issuers, states may continue to apply state law requirements except to the extent that such requirements prevent the application of HIPAA's portability, access, and renewability provisions.

In enacting these new preemption provisions, Congress intended to preempt State insurance requirements only to the extent that they prevent the application of the basic protections set forth in HIPAA. HIPAA's conference report states that the conferees intended the narrowest preemption of State laws with regard to health insurance issuers. H.R. Conf. Rep. No. 736, 104th Cong. 2d Session 205 (1996). State insurance laws that are more stringent than the federal requirements are unlikely to "prevent the application of" the HIPAA portability provisions, and be preempted. Accordingly, States have significant latitude to impose requirements on health insurance insurers that are more restrictive than the federal law.

---

[2] Computer runs using Medical Expenditure Survey Household Component (MEPS-HC) and the Robert Wood Johnson Employer Health Benefits Survey determined that the share of covered private-sector job leavers at small firms average 35 percent of all covered private sector job leavers. From this, we inferred that the financial burden borne by small plans is approximately 35 percent of the total expenditures by private-sector group health plans which was estimated to be $515 million.

[3] States may shorten the six-month look-back period prior to the enrollment date; shorten the 12-month and 18-month maximum preexisting condition exclusion periods;

increase the 63-day significant break in coverage period; increase the 30-day period for newborns, adopted children, and children placed for adoption to enroll in the plan with no preexisting condition exclusion; further limit the circumstances in which a preexisting condition exclusion may be applied (beyond the federal exceptions for certain newborns, adopted children, children placed for adoption, pregnancy, and genetic information in the absence of a diagnosis; require additional special enrollment periods; and reduce the HMO affiliation period to less than 2 months (3 months for late enrollees).

Guidance conveying this interpretation of HIPAA's preemption provisions was published in the **Federal Register** on April 8, 1997, 62 FR 16904. These proposed regulations clarify and implement the statute's minimum standards and do not significantly reduce the discretion given the States by the statute. Moreover, the Departments understand that the vast majority of States have requirements that meet or exceed the minimum requirements of the HIPAA portability provisions.

HIPAA provides that the States may enforce the provisions of HIPAA as they pertain to issuers, but that the Secretary of Health and Human Services must enforce any provisions that a State fails to substantially enforce. To date, CMS enforces the HIPAA portability provisions in only one State in accordance with that State's specific request to do so. When exercising its responsibility to enforce the provisions of HIPAA, CMS works cooperatively with the State for the purpose of addressing the State's concerns and avoiding conflicts with the exercise of State authority. CMS has developed procedures to implement its enforcement responsibilities, and to afford the States the maximum opportunity to enforce HIPAA's requirements in the first instance. CMS's procedures address the handling of reports that States may not be enforcing HIPAA's requirements, and the mechanism for allocating responsibility between the States and CMS. In compliance with Executive Order 13132's requirement that agencies examine closely any policies that may have federalism implications or limit the policymaking discretion of the States, the Department of Labor and CMS have engaged in numerous efforts to consult and work cooperatively with affected State and local officials.

For example, the Departments sought and received input from State insurance regulators and the National Association of Insurance Commissioners (NAIC). The NAIC is a non-profit corporation established by the insurance commissioners of the 50 States, the District of Columbia, and the four U.S. territories. In most States the Insurance Commissioner is appointed by the Governor, in approximately 14 States, the insurance commissioner is an elected official. Among other activities, it provides a forum for the development of uniform policy when uniformity is appropriate. Its members meet, discuss and offer solutions to mutual problems. The NAIC sponsors quarterly meetings to provide a forum for the exchange of ideas and in-depth consideration of insurance issues by regulators, industry representatives and consumers. CMS and the Department of Labor staff have consistently attended these quarterly meetings to listen to the concerns of the State Insurance Departments regarding HIPAA portability issues. In addition to the general discussions, committee meetings, and task groups, the NAIC sponsors the standing CMS/DOL meeting on HIPAA issues for members during the quarterly conferences. This meeting provides CMS and the Department of Labor with the opportunity to provide updates on regulations, bulletins, enforcement actions, and outreach efforts regarding HIPAA.

The Departments received written comments on the interim regulation from the NAIC and from ten States. In general, these comments raised technical issues that the Departments considered in conjunction with similar issues raised by other commenters. In a letter sent before issuance of the interim regulation, the NAIC expressed concerns that the Departments interpret the new preemption provisions of HIPAA narrowly so as to give the States flexibility to impose more stringent requirements. As discussed above, the Departments address this concern in the preamble to the interim regulation.

In addition, the Departments specifically consulted with the NAIC in developing these proposed regulations. Through the NAIC, the Departments sought and received the input of State insurance departments regarding certain insurance industry definitions, enrollment procedures and standard coverage terms. This input is generally reflected in the discussion of comments received and changes made in Section B—Overview of the Regulations of the preamble to the final regulations published elsewhere in this issue of the **Federal Register**.

The Departments have also cooperated with the States in several ongoing outreach initiatives, through which information on HIPAA is shared among federal regulators, State regulators and the regulated community. In particular, the Department of Labor has established a Health Benefits Education Campaign with more than 70 partners, including CMS, NAIC and many business and consumer groups. CMS has sponsored conferences with the States—the Consumer Outreach and Advocacy conferences in March 1999 and June 2000, and the Implementation and Enforcement of HIPAA National State-Federal Conferences in August 1999, 2000, 2001, 2002, and 2003. Furthermore, both the Department of Labor and CMS Web sites offer links to important State web sites and other resources, facilitating coordination between the State and federal regulators and the regulated community.

Throughout the process of developing these regulations, to the extent feasible within the specific preemption provisions of HIPAA, the Departments have attempted to balance the States' interests in regulating health insurance issuers, and the Congress' intent to provide uniform minimum protections to consumers in every State. By doing so, it is the Departments' view that they have complied with the requirements of Executive Order 13132.

Pursuant to the requirements set forth in Section 8(a) of Executive Order 13132, and by the signatures affixed to proposed final regulations, the Departments certify that the Employee Benefits Security Administration and the Centers for Medicare & Medicaid Services have complied with the requirements of Executive Order 13132 for the attached proposed regulation, Notice of Proposed Rulemaking for Health Coverage Portability: Tolling and Certain Time Periods and Interaction with the Family and Medical Leave Act under HIPAA Titles I & IV (RIN 1210-AA54 and RIN 0938-AL88), in a meaningful and timely manner.

Basis for Assessment of Economic Impact—Department of Labor and Department of Health and Human Services

As noted above, the primary economic effects of HIPAA's portability provisions ensue directly from the statute. The Department's assessment of the economic effects of HIPAA's statutory portability provisions and the basis for the assessment is presented in detail under the "Basis for Assessment of Economic Impact" section of the preamble to the final regulation, published elsewhere in this issue of the **Federal Register**. By clarifying and securing HIPAA's statutory portability protections, these regulations will help ensure that HIPAA rights are fully realized. The result is likely to be a small increase in the economic effects of HIPAA's statutory portability provisions.

Additional economic benefits derive from the regulations' clarifications of HIPAA's portability requirements. The regulations provide clarity through both their provisions and their examples of how those provisions apply in various circumstances. By clarifying employees' rights and plan sponsors' obligations under HIPAA's portability provisions, the regulations will reduce uncertainty and costly disputes over these rights and obligations. They will promote employers' and employees' common understanding of the value of group health plan benefits and confidence in the security and predictability of those benefits, thereby improving labor market efficiency and fostering the establishment and continuation of group health plans by employers.[4]

These proposed regulations are intended to secure and implement HIPAA's group market portability provisions under certain special circumstances. The regulations will secure HIPAA's portability rights for individuals who are not timely notified that their coverage has ended and for individuals whose coverage ends in connection with the taking of leave that is guaranteed under FMLA. The regulations also will clarify and thereby secure individuals' special enrollment rights under HIPAA, and clarify the methodologies to be used by employers to determine the number of plans offered and the average number of individuals employed during a given year.

The benefits of these regulations will be concentrated among a small number of affected individuals.

Affected individuals will generally include those who would have lost access to coverage for needed medical care after forfeiting HIPAA portability and/or special enrollment rights due to time spent without

---

[4] The voluntary nature of the employment-based health benefit system in conjunction with the open and dynamic character of labor markets make explicit as well as implicit negotiations on compensation a key determinant of the prevalence of employee benefits coverage. It is likely that 80% to 100% of the cost of employee benefits is borne by workers through reduced wages (see for example Jonathan Gruber and Alan B. Krueger, "The Incidence of Mandated Employer-Provided Insurance: Lessons from Workers Compensation Insurance," in, David Bradford, ed., *Tax Policy and Economy*, pp:111-143 (Cambridge, MA: MIT Press, 1991); Jonathan Gruber, "The Incidence of Mandated Maternity Benefits," *American Economic Review*, Vol. 84 no. 3 (June 1994), pp. 622-641; Lawrence H. Summers, "Some Simple Economics of Mandated Benefits," *American Economic Review*, Vol. 79, No. 2 (May 1989), pp:177-183; Louise Sheiner, "Health Care Costs, Wages, and Aging," Federal Reserve Board of Governors working paper, April 1999; Mark Pauly and Brad Herring, *Pooling Health Insurance Risks* (Washington, DC: AEI Press, 1999), Gail A. Jensen and Michael A. Morrisey, "Endogenous Fringe Benefits, Compensating Wage Differentials and Older Workers," *International Journal of Health Care Finance and Economics* Vol 1, No. 3-4 (forthcoming), and Edward Montgomery, Kathryn Shaw, and Mary Ellen Benedict, "Pensions and Wages: An Hedonic Price Theory Approach," *International Economic Review*, Vol. 33 No. 1 (Feb. 1992.), pp:111-128.) The prevalence of benefits is therefore largely dependent on the efficacy of this exchange. If workers perceive that there is the potential for inappropriate denial of benefits they will discount their value to adjust for this risk. This discount drives a wedge in the compensation negotiation, limiting its efficiency. With workers unwilling to bear the full cost of the benefit, fewer benefits will be provided. The extent to which workers perceive a federal regulation supported by enforcement authority to improve the security and quality of benefits, the differential between the employers costs and workers willingness to accept wage offsets is minimized.

coverage prior to receiving a certificate or while on FMLA-guaranteed leave. Affected individuals may also include some who would have been denied special enrollment rights if plans or issuers failed to recognize their requests for special enrollment or imposed unreasonable deadlines or requirements for completion of enrollment materials. The benefits of these regulations for any particular affected individual may be large. As noted above, access to coverage for needed medical care is important to individuals' health and productivity. However, the number of affected individuals, and therefore the aggregate cost of extended access to coverage under these regulations, is expected to be small, for several reasons.

First, these regulations extend HIPAA rights only in instances where individuals do not receive certificates immediately when coverage ends or their coverage ends in connection with the taking of FMLA-guaranteed leave. The Departments know of no source of data on the timeliness with which certificates are typically provided. The final regulations that accompany these proposed regulations permit plans to provide certificates with COBRA notices, up to 44 days after coverage ends. Plans, however, often do have the option of providing certificates immediately when coverage ends or even in advance, for example as part of exit packages given to terminating employees or in mailings to covered dependents in advance of birthdays that will end their eligibility for coverage. With respect to FMLA-protected leave, data provided in a 1996 report to Congress suggests that the number of employees who lose coverage in connection with FMLA-protected leave is likely to be small. The report notes that over an 18-month period just 1.2 percent of surveyed employees took what they reported to be FMLA leave. A similar survey of employers found that 3.6 percent of employees took such leave. Nearly all of those taking leave continued their health coverage. (This is not surprising, given that FMLA requires covered employers to extend eligibility for health insurance to employees on FMLA-protected leave on the same terms that applied when the employees were not on leave.) Just 9 percent of leave-takers reported that they lost some kind of employee benefit, with one-third of these reporting that they lost health insurance.[5] Putting these numbers together and converting to an annual basis, in a given year between 0.02 percent and 0.07 percent of employees, or well under one in one thousand, might lose health coverage in connection with FMLA-protected leave. Many of these will ultimately exercise their right to be reinstated in the job from which they took leave and to exercise their FMLA-guaranteed right to resume their previous health coverage. Therefore, the number of employees who will lose coverage and then, later and at the conclusion of FMLA-protected leave, enjoy extended portability rights under HIPAA as a result of these regulations, is likely to be very small.

Second, the period over which this regulation extends rights will often be short, insofar as certificates are often provided promptly after coverage ends and many family leave periods are far shorter than the guaranteed 12 weeks. As noted above, plans generally are required to provide certificates no later than 44 days after coverage ends and may provide them sooner. According to the aforementioned report to Congress on FMLA-protected leave, 41 percent of employees taking FMLA-protected leave did so for less than 8 days. Fifty-eight percent were on leave for less than 15 days, and two-thirds were on leave for less than 29 days. (FMLA protects leaves of up to 12 weeks, or 84 days.)

Third, it is generally in individuals' interest to minimize periods of uninsurance. Individuals are likely to exercise their portability and special enrollment rights as soon as possible after coverage ends, which will often be before any extension of such rights under these regulations becomes effective. Over one 36-month period prior to HIPAA, 71 percent of Americans had continuous coverage—that is, incurred not even a single, one-month break in coverage. Just 4 percent were uninsured for the entire period. About one-half of observed spells without insurance lasted less than 5 months. As noted above, few employees taking FMLA-protected leave had a lapse in health coverage.

Fourth, only a portion of individuals who enroll in health plans in circumstances where these regulations alone guarantee their special enrollment or portability rights would otherwise have been denied such rights. HIPAA special enrollment and portability requirements, both as specified under the final regulations and as modified under these proposed regulations, are minimum standards. Plans are free to provide additional enrollment opportunities.

Fifth, only a small minority of individuals who avoid a significant break in coverage solely as a direct result of these regulations would otherwise have lost coverage for needed medical care. The affected minority would be those who suffer from preexisting conditions, join health plans that exclude coverage for such conditions, and require treatment of such conditions during the exclusion periods. GAO estimated that HIPAA could ensure continued coverage for up to 25 million Americans.[6] More recent estimates suggest that the number of individual policy holders and their dependents which could be helped by HIPAA's portability provisions are more in the 14 million range.[7] As noted above, however, the number of workers and dependents actually gaining coverage for a preexisting condition due to credit for prior coverage following a job change under HIPAA will be smaller than this. Both GAO's and our estimates of people who could benefit include all job changers with prior coverage and their dependents, irrespective of whether their new employer offers a plan, whether their new plan imposed a preexisting condition exclusion period, and whether they actually suffer from a preexisting condition. Accounting for these narrower criteria, CBO estimated that, at any point in time, about 100,000 individuals would have a preexisting condition exclusion reduced for prior creditable coverage. An additional 45,000 would gain added coverage in the individual market. The CBO estimate demonstrates that the number of individuals actually gaining coverage for needed medical services will be a small fraction of all those whose right to such coverage HIPAA's portability provisions guarantee. Accordingly, the Departments expect that the number gaining coverage for needed services as a direct result of these regulations will be a small fraction of the already small number whose right to such coverage these regulations would establish.

The Departments attempted to estimate the number of individuals who might avoid a break in coverage because of the provision of these proposed regulations that tolls the break until the individual receives a certification but not more than 44 days. The Departments examined coverage patterns evident in the Survey of Income and Program Participation (SIPP), a longitudinal household survey that tracks transitions in coverage. SIPP interviews households once every four months. The Departments estimate that, in a given year, about 7 million individuals have breaks in coverage lasting 4 months or less. The survey data suffer from so-called "seam bias"—respondents tend to report that status as unchanged over 4-month increments. Of the 7 million reporting breaks of 4 months or less, 6.5 million report breaks of exactly 4 months. This finding is consistent with the more general finding that breaks of 4 months or less are far more common than longer breaks. It seems likely that the 7 million breaks of 4 months or less actually included proportionate or disproportionately large shares of breaks of 1 or 2 months. Assuming the breaks are actually distributed evenly by length between 1 day and 4 months, then about one-half of the breaks, or 3.5 million breaks, would have lasted less than 63 days and therefore would not have constituted breaks for purposes of HIPAA's portability protections even without reference to the provision of this proposed regulation that tolls the break until the individual receives a certification but not more than 44 days. Approximately three-fourths of the remaining breaks or about 2.6 million breaks, would have lasted between 1 and 44 additional days and thereby potentially have been tolled until the individuals received their certifications but not more than 44 days. Thus 2.6 million provides a reasonable upper bound on the number of individuals who might avoid a break in coverage in a given year because of this tolling provision. It is not known what fraction of these would subsequently join group health plans that include preexisting condition exclusions while suffering from and requiring additional care for preexisting conditions. Comparing GAO's (20 million or more) and our (14 million) estimates of the number of individuals who could potentially benefit from HIPAA's portability protections (individuals with prior creditable coverage who join new health plans in a given year) with the CBO estimate of the number who might actually have added group coverage for needed care (100,000) produces a ratio of about 1 percent. If this proportion holds for group health plan enrollees who avoid breaks because of this tolling provision, then an upper bound of about 26,000 individuals annually might gain coverage for needed care under the proposed regulation's provision treating coverage under such programs as creditable coverage.

---

[5] Commission on Family and Medical Leave and U.S. Department of Labor, *A Workable Balance: Report to Congress on Family and Medical Leave Policies,* transmitted April 30, 1996.

[6] U.S. General Accounting Office, Report HEHS-95-257, "Health Insurance Portability: Reform Could Ensure Continued Coverage for up to 25 Million Americans," September 1995.

[7] We calculated these estimates using internal runs off the MEPS-HC. These runs gave the number of total job changers, total job changers that had employer-sponsored insurance (ESI), and whether this coverage had been for less than 12 months or not. Estimates for dependents were based off the ratio of policy-holders to total dependents from the March 2003 Current Population Survey (March CPS). It should be noted, however, that the EBSA estimate of 14 million does not include estimate of individuals no longer eligible for COBRA continuation coverage or individuals facing job lock, while the GAO numbers do.

The Departments considered whether certain individuals whose HIPAA portability rights these proposed regulations would extend may be disproportionately likely to be in (or have dependents who are in) poor health. Specifically, individuals taking FMLA-protected leave, especially those who elect not to be reinstated in their prior jobs following FMLA-protected leave, may be so likely. On the other hand, individuals in such circumstances are also particularly unlikely to allow their health insurance from their prior job to lapse while they are on leave. Accordingly, most such individuals' special enrollment periods and countable breaks in coverage (if any) would probably have begun at the conclusion of the FMLA-protected leave even in absence of these proposed regulations. The Departments are therefore uncertain whether individuals who would exercise HIPAA portability rights extended solely by these regulations would be more costly to insure than others exercising HIPAA portability rights, and solicit comments on this question.

Affected individuals may also include some who would have been denied special enrollment rights if plans or issuers failed to recognize their requests for special enrollment or imposed unreasonable deadlines or requirements for completion of enrollment materials.

As noted above, the Departments expect that these regulations will result in a small increase in the economic effects of HIPAA's statutory provisions. For the reasons stated immediately above, the Departments believe that this increase will be small on aggregate, adding only a small increment to the cost attributable to HIPAA's statutory portability provisions, which themselves amount to a small fraction of one percent of health plan expenditures. Thus the increase will be negligible relative to typical year-to-year increases in premiums charged by issuers, which can amount to several percentage points or more. Therefore, the Departments expect these regulations to have little or no perceptible negative impact on employers' propensity to offer health benefit plans or on the generosity of those plans. In sum, the Departments expect that the benefits of these regulations, which can be very large for a particular affected individual, will justify their costs.

List of Subjects

26 CFR Part 54

Excise taxes, Health care, Health insurance, Pensions, Reporting and recordkeeping requirements.

29 CFR Part 2590

Continuation coverage, Disclosure, Employee benefit plans, Group health plans, Health care, Health insurance, Medical child support, Reporting and recordkeeping requirements.

45 CFR Part 146

Health care, Health insurance, Reporting and recordkeeping requirements, and State regulation of health insurance.

Proposed Amendments to the Regulations

Employee Benefits Security Administration

29 CFR Chapter XXV

For the reasons set forth above, 29 CFR Part 2590 is proposed to be amended as follows:

PART 2590—RULES AND REGULATIONS FOR GROUP HEALTH PLANS

1. The authority citation for Part 2590 continues to read as follows:

Authority: 29 U.S.C. 1027, 1059, 1135, 1161-1168, 1169, 1181-1183, 1181 note, 1185, 1185a, 1185b, 1191, 1191a, 1191b, and 1191c, sec. 101(g), Pub. L. 104-191, 101 Stat. 1936; sec. 401(b), Pub. L. 105-200, 112 Stat. 645 (42 U.S.C. 651 note); Secretary of Labor's Order 1-2003, 68 FR 5374 (Feb. 3, 2003).

2. Section 2590.701-4 is amended by revising paragraphs (b)(2)(iii) and (b)(2)(iv) and adding *Examples 4* and *6* in paragraph (b)(2)(v) as follows:

§ *2590.701-4 Rules relating to creditable coverage.*

* * * * *

(b) *Standard method.* * * *

(2) *Counting creditable coverage.* * * *

(iii) *Significant break in coverage defined.* A *significant break in coverage* means a period of 63 consecutive days during each of which an individual does not have any creditable coverage, except that periods described in paragraph (b)(2)(iv) of this section are not taken into account in determining a significant break in coverage. (See also § 2590.731(c)(2)(iii) regarding the applicability to issuers of state insur-

ance laws that require a break of more than 63 days before an individual has a significant break in coverage for purposes of state insurance law.)

(iv) *Periods that toll a significant break.* Days in a waiting period and days in an affiliation period are not taken into account in determining whether a significant break in coverage has occurred. In addition, for an individual who elects COBRA continuation coverage during the second election period provided under the Trade Act of 2002, the days between the date the individual lost group health plan coverage and the first day of the second COBRA election period are not taken into account in determining whether a significant break in coverage has occurred. Moreover, in the case of an individual whose coverage ceases, if a certificate of creditable coverage with respect to that cessation is not provided on or before the date coverage ceases, then the period that begins on the first date that an individual has no creditable coverage and that continues through the earlier of the following two dates is not taken into account in determining whether a significant break in coverage has occurred:

(A) The date that a certificate of creditable coverage with respect to that cessation is provided; or

(B) The date 44 days after coverage ceases.

(v) *Examples.* The rules of this paragraph (b)(2) are illustrated by the following examples:

* * * * *

Example 4. (i) *Facts.* Individual *B* terminates coverage under a group health plan, and a certificate of creditable coverage is provided 10 days later. *B* begins employment with Employer *R* and begins enrollment in *R*'s plan 60 days after the certificate is provided.

(ii) *Conclusion.* In this *Example 4*, even though *B* had no coverage for 69 days, the 10 days before the certificate of creditable coverage is provided are not taken into account in determining a significant break in coverage. Therefore, *B*'s break in coverage is only 59 days and is not a significant break in coverage. Accordingly, B's prior coverage must be counted by *R*'s plan.

* * * * *

Example 6. (i) *Facts.* Employer *V* sponsors a group health plan. Under the terms of the plan, the only benefits provided are those provided under an insurance policy. Individual *D* works for *V* and has creditable coverage under *V*'s plan. *V* fails to pay the issuer the premiums for the coverage period beginning March 1. Consistent with applicable state law, the issuer terminates the policy so that the last day of coverage is April 30. *V* goes out of business on July 31. On August 15 *D* begins employment with Employer *W* and enrolls in *W*'s group health plan. *W*'s plan imposes a 12-month preexisting condition exclusion on all enrollees. *D* never receives a certificate of creditable coverage for coverage under *V*'s plan.

(ii) *Conclusion.* In this *Example 6*, the period from May 1 (the first day without coverage) through June 13 (the date 44 days after coverage under *V*'s plan ceases) is not taken into account in determining a 63-day break in coverage. This is because, in cases in which a certificate of creditable coverage is not provided by the date coverage is lost, the break begins on the date the certificate is provided, or the date 44 days after coverage ceases, if earlier. Therefore, even though *D*'s actual period without coverage was 106 days (May 1 through August 14), because the period from May 1 through June 13 is not taken into account, *D*'s break in coverage is only 62 days (June 14 through August 14). Thus, *D* has not experienced a significant break in coverage, and *D*'s prior coverage must be counted by *W*'s plan.

* * * * *

3. Section 2590.701-5 is amended by redesignating paragraphs (a)(3)(ii)(H)(*5*) and (*6*) as paragraphs (a)(3)(ii)(H)(*6*) and (*7*), respectively, and by adding a new paragraph (a)(3)(ii)(H)(*5*) as follows:

§ *2590.701-5 Evidence of creditable coverage.*

(a) *Certificate of creditable coverage.* * * *

(3) *Form and content of certificate.* * * *

(ii) *Required information.* * * *

(H) * * *

(*5*) The interaction with the Family and Medical Leave Act;

* * * * *

4. Section 2590.701-6 is amended by revising paragraphs (a)(1), (a)(4), (b)(1), (b)(3), and *Example 2* in paragraph (b)(4), and adding *Examples 3*, *4*, and *5* in paragraph (b)(4) as follows:

§ 2590.701-6 Special enrollment periods.

(a) *Special enrollment for certain individuals who lose coverage*—(1) *In general.* A group health plan, and a health insurance issuer offering health insurance coverage in connection with a group health plan, is required to permit current employees and dependents (as defined in § 2590.701-2) who are described in paragraph (a)(2) of this section to enroll for coverage under the terms of the plan if the conditions in paragraph (a)(3) of this section are satisfied. Paragraph (a)(4) of this section describes procedures that a plan or issuer may require an employee to follow and describes the date by which coverage must begin. The special enrollment rights under this paragraph (a) apply without regard to the dates on which an individual would otherwise be able to enroll under the plan.

* * * * *

(4) *Applying for special enrollment and effective date of coverage*—(i) *Request.* A plan or issuer must allow an employee a period of at least 30 days after an event described in paragraph (a)(3) of this section (loss of eligibility for coverage, termination of employer contributions, or exhaustion of COBRA continuation coverage) to request enrollment (for the employee or the employee's dependent). For this purpose, any written or oral request made to any of the following constitutes a request for enrollment—

(A) The plan administrator;

(B) The issuer;

(C) A person who customarily handles claims for the plan (such as a third party administrator); or

(D) Any other designated representative.

(ii) *Tolling of period for requesting special enrollment.* (A) In the case of an individual whose coverage ceases, if a certificate of creditable coverage with respect to that cessation is not provided on or before the date coverage ceases, then the period for requesting special enrollment described in paragraph (a)(4)(i) of this section does not end until 30 days after the earlier of —

(*1*) The date that a certificate of creditable coverage with respect to that cessation is provided; or

(*2*) The date 44 days after coverage ceases.

(B) For purposes of this paragraph (a)(4), if an individual's coverage ceases due to the operation of a lifetime limit on all benefits, coverage is considered to cease on the earliest date that a claim is denied due to the operation of the lifetime limit. (Nonetheless, the date of a loss of eligibility for coverage is determined under the rules of paragraph (a)(3) of this section, which provides that a loss of eligibility occurs when a claim that would meet or exceed a lifetime limit on all benefits is incurred, not when it is denied.)

(C) The rules of this paragraph (a)(4)(ii) are illustrated by the following examples:

Example 1. (i) *Facts.* Employer *V* provides group health coverage through a policy provided by Issuer *M*. Individual *D* works for *V* and is covered under *V*'s plan. *V* fails to pay *M* the premiums for the coverage period beginning March 1. Consistent with applicable state law, *M* terminates the policy so that the last day of coverage is April 30. On May 15, *M* provides *D* with a certificate of creditable coverage with respect to *D*'s cessation of coverage under *V*'s plan.

(ii) *Conclusion.* In this *Example 1,* the period to request special enrollment ends no earlier than June 14 (which is 30 days after May 15, the day a certificate of creditable coverage is provided with respect to *D*).

Example 2. (i) *Facts.* Same facts as *Example 1,* except *D* is never provided with a certificate of creditable coverage.

(ii) *Conclusion.* In this *Example 2,* the period to request special enrollment ends no earlier than July 13. (July 13 is 74 days after April 30, the date coverage ceases. That is, July 13 is 30 days after the end of the 44-day maximum tolling period.)

Example 3. (i) *Facts.* Individual *E* works for Employer *W* and has coverage under *W*'s plan. *W*'s plan has a lifetime limit of $1 million on all benefits under the plan. On September 13, *E* incurs a claim that would exceed the plan's lifetime limit. On September 28, *W* denies the claim due to the operation of the lifetime limit and a certificate of creditable coverage is provided on October 3. *E* is otherwise eligible to enroll in the group health plan of the employer of *E*'s spouse.

(ii) *Conclusion.* In this *Example 3,* the period to request special enrollment in the plan of the employer of *E*'s spouse ends no earlier than November 2 (30 days after the date the certificate is provided) and

begins not later than September 13, the date *E* lost eligibility for coverage.

(iii) *Reasonable procedures for special enrollment.* After an individual has requested enrollment under paragraph (a)(4)(i) of this section, a plan or issuer may require the individual to complete enrollment materials within a reasonable time after the end of the 30-day period described in paragraph (a)(4)(i) of this section. In these enrollment materials, the plan or issuer may require the individual only to provide information required of individuals who enroll when first eligible and information about the event giving rise to the special enrollment right. A plan or issuer may establish a deadline for receiving completed enrollment materials, but such a deadline must be extended for information that an individual making reasonable efforts does not obtain by that deadline.

(iv) *Date coverage must begin.* If the plan or issuer requires completion of additional enrollment materials in accordance with paragraph (a)(4)(iii) of this section, coverage must begin no later than the first day of the first calendar month beginning after the date the plan or issuer receives enrollment materials that are substantially complete. If the plan or issuer does not require completion of additional enrollment materials, coverage must begin no later than the first day of the first calendar month beginning after the date the plan or issuer receives the request for special enrollment under paragraph (a)(4)(i) of this section.

(b) *Special enrollment with respect to certain dependent beneficiaries*—(1) *In general.* A group health plan, and a health insurance issuer offering health insurance coverage in connection with a group health plan, that makes coverage available with respect to dependents is required to permit individuals described in paragraph (b)(2) of this section to be enrolled for coverage in a benefit package under the terms of the plan. Paragraph (b)(3) of this section describes procedures that a plan or issuer may require an individual to follow and describes the date by which coverage must begin. The special enrollment rights under this paragraph (b) apply without regard to the dates on which an individual would otherwise be able to enroll under the plan.

* * * * *

(3) *Applying for special enrollment and effective date of coverage*—(i) *Request.* A plan or issuer must allow an individual a period of at least 30 days after the date of the marriage, birth, adoption, or placement for adoption (or, if dependent coverage is not generally made available at the time of the marriage, birth, adoption, or placement for adoption, a period of at least 30 days after the date the plan makes dependent coverage generally available) to request enrollment (for the individual or the individual's dependent). For this purpose, any written or oral request made to any of the following constitutes a request for enrollment—

(A) The plan administrator;

(B) The issuer;

(C) A person who customarily handles claims for the plan (such as a third party administrator); or

(D) Any other designated representative.

(ii) *Reasonable procedures for special enrollment.* After an individual has requested enrollment under paragraph (b)(3)(i) of this section, a plan or issuer may require the individual to complete enrollment materials within a reasonable time after the end of the 30-day period described in paragraph (b)(3)(i) of this section. In these enrollment materials, the plan or issuer may require the individual only to provide information required of individuals who enroll when first eligible and information about the event giving rise to the special enrollment right. A plan or issuer may establish a deadline for receiving completed enrollment materials, but such a deadline must be extended for information that an individual making reasonable efforts does not obtain by that deadline.

(iii) *Date coverage must begin*—(A) *Marriage.* In the case of marriage, if the plan or issuer requires completion of additional enrollment materials in accordance with paragraph (b)(3)(ii) of this section, coverage must begin no later than the first day of the first calendar month beginning after the date the plan or issuer receives enrollment materials that are substantially complete. If the plan or issuer does not require such additional enrollment materials, coverage must begin no later than the first day of the first calendar month beginning after the date the plan or issuer receives the request for special enrollment under paragraph (b)(3)(i) of this section.

(B) *Birth, adoption, or placement for adoption.* Coverage must begin in the case of a dependent's birth on the date of birth and in the case of a dependent's adoption or placement for adoption no later than the date of such adoption or placement for adoption (or, if dependent coverage is not made generally available at the time of the birth, adoption, or placement for adoption, the date the plan makes dependent coverage available). If the plan or issuer requires completion of additional enrollment materials in accordance with paragraph (b)(3)(ii) of this section, the plan or issuer must provide benefits (including benefits retroactively to the date of birth, adoption, or placement for adoption) once the plan or issuer receives enrollment materials that are substantially complete.

(4) *Examples.* * * *

Example 2. (i) *Facts.* Individual *D* works for Employer *X*. *X* maintains a group health plan with two benefit packages—an HMO option and an indemnity option. Self-only and family coverage are available under both options. *D* enrolls for self-only coverage in the HMO option. Then, a child, *E*, is placed for adoption with *D*. Within 30 days of the placement of *E* for adoption, *D* requests enrollment for *D* and *E* under the plan's indemnity option and submits completed enrollment materials timely.

(ii) *Conclusion.* In this *Example 2*, *D* and *E* satisfy the conditions for special enrollment under paragraphs (b)(2)(v) and (b)(3) of this section. Therefore, the plan must allow *D* and *E* to enroll in the indemnity coverage, effective as of the date of the placement for adoption.

Example 3. (i) *Facts.* Same facts as *Example 1*. On March 17 (two days after the birth of *C*), *A* telephones the plan administrator and requests special enrollment of *A*, *B*, and *C*. The plan administrator sends *A* an enrollment form. Under the terms of the plan, enrollment is denied unless a completed form is submitted within 30 days of the event giving rise to the special enrollment right (in this case, *C*'s birth).

(ii) *Conclusion.* In this *Example 3*, the plan does not satisfy paragraph (b)(3) of this section. The plan may require only that *A* request enrollment during the 30-day period after *C*'s birth. *A* did so by telephoning the plan administrator. The plan may not condition special enrollment on filing additional enrollment materials during the 30-day period. To comply with paragraph (b)(3) of this section, the plan must allow *A* a reasonable time after the end of the 30-day period to submit any additional enrollment materials. Once these enrollment materials are received, the plan must allow whatever coverage is chosen to begin on March 15, the date of *C*'s birth.

Example 4. (i) *Facts.* Same facts as *Example 3*, except that *A* telephones the plan administrator to request enrollment on April 13 (29 days after *C*'s birth). Also, under the terms of the plan, the deadline for submitting the enrollment form is 14 days after the end of the 30-day period for requesting special enrollment (thus, in this case, April 28, which is 44 days after *C*'s birth). The form requests the same information for *A*, *B*, and *C* (name, date of birth, and place of birth) as well as a copy of *C*'s birth certificate. *A* fills out the enrollment form and delivers it to the plan administrator on April 28. At that time *A* does not have a birth certificate for *C* but applies on that day for one from the appropriate government office. *A* receives the birth certificate on June 1 and furnishes a copy of the birth certificate to the plan administrator shortly thereafter.

(ii) *Conclusion.* In this *Example 4*, *A*, *B*, and *C* are entitled to special enrollment under the plan even though *A* did not satisfy the plan's requirement of providing a copy of *C*'s birth certificate by the plan's 14-day deadline. While a plan may establish such a deadline, the plan must extend the deadline for information that an individual making reasonable efforts does not obtain by that deadline. *A* delivered the enrollment form to the plan administrator by the deadline and made reasonable efforts to furnish the birth certificate that the plan requires.

Example 5. (i) *Facts.* Same facts as *Example 4*. On May 3 (after *A* has delivered the enrollment form to the plan administrator but before *A* provides the birth certificate), *A* submits claims for all medical expenses incurred for *B* and *C* from the date of *C*'s birth.

(ii) *Conclusion.* In this *Example 5*, the plan must pay all of the claims submitted by *A*. Because the plan requires that individuals seeking special enrollment complete additional enrollment materials, it is required to provide benefits once it receives enrollment materials that are substantially complete. The form that *A* submitted on April 28 was substantially complete. Because *C*'s birth is the event giving rise to the special enrollment right, on April 28 *A*, *B*, and *C* become entitled to benefits under the plan retroactive to the date of *C*'s birth.

* * * * *

5. Section 2590.701-8 is added to read as follows:

§ *2590.701-8 Interaction with the Family and Medical Leave Act.*

(a) *In general.* The rules of §§ 2590.701-1 through 2590.701-7 apply with respect to an individual on leave under the Family and Medical Leave Act of 1993 (29 U.S.C. 2601) (FMLA), and apply with respect to a dependent of such an individual, except to the extent otherwise provided in this section.

(b) *Tolling of significant break in coverage during FMLA leave.* In the case of an individual (or a dependent of the individual) who is covered under a group health plan, if the individual takes FMLA leave and does not continue group health coverage for any period of FMLA leave, that period is not taken into account in determining whether a significant break in coverage has occurred under § 2590.701-4(b)(2)(iii).

(c) *Application of certification provisions*—(1) *Timing of issuance of certificate*—(i) In the case of an individual (or a dependent of the individual) who is covered under a group health plan, if the individual takes FMLA leave and the individual's group health coverage is terminated during FMLA leave, an automatic certificate must be provided in accordance with the timing rules set forth in § 2590.701-5(a)(2)(ii)(B) (which generally require plans and issuers to provide certificates within a reasonable time after coverage ceases).

(ii) In the case of an individual (or a dependent of the individual) who is covered under a group health plan, if the individual takes FMLA leave and continues group health coverage for the period of FMLA leave, but then ceases coverage under the plan at the end of FMLA leave, an automatic certificate must be provided in accordance with the timing rules set forth in § 2590.701-5(a)(2)(ii)(A) (which generally require plans and issuers to provide a certificate no later than the time a notice is required to be furnished for a qualifying event under a COBRA continuation provision).

(2) *Demonstrating FMLA leave.* (i) A plan or issuer is required to take into account all information about FMLA leave that it obtains or that is presented on behalf of an individual. A plan or issuer must treat the individual as having been on FMLA leave for a period if—

(A) The individual attests to the period of FMLA leave; and

(B) The individual cooperates with the plan's or issuer's efforts to verify the individual's FMLA leave.

(ii) Nothing in this section prevents a plan or issuer from modifying its initial determination of FMLA leave if it determines that the individual did not have the claimed FMLA leave, provided that the plan or issuer follows procedures for reconsideration similar to those set forth in § 2590.701-3(f).

(d) *Relationship to loss of eligibility special enrollment rules.* In the case of an individual (or a dependent of the individual) who is covered under a group health plan and who takes FMLA leave, a loss of eligibility for coverage under § 2590.701-6(a) occurs when the period of FMLA leave ends if —

(1) The individual's group health coverage is terminated at any time during FMLA leave; and

(2) The individual does not return to work for the employer at the end of FMLA leave.

6. Section 2590.732 is amended by adding paragraphs (a)(2) and (e) to read as follows:

§ *2590.732 Special rules relating to group health plans.*

(a) *Group health plan.* * * *

(2) *Determination of number of plans.* The number of group health plans that an employer or employee organization (including for this purpose a joint board of trustees of a multiemployer trust affiliated with one or more multiemployer plans) maintains is determined under the rules of this paragraph (a)(2).

(i) Except as provided in paragraph (a)(2)(ii) or (iii) of this section, medical care benefits provided by a corporation, partnership, or other entity or trade or business, or by an employee organization, constitute one group health plan, unless—

(A) It is clear from the instruments governing the arrangement or arrangements to provide medical care benefits that the benefits are being provided under separate plans; and

(B) The arrangement or arrangements are operated pursuant to such instruments as separate plans.

(ii) A multiemployer plan and a nonmultiemployer plan are always separate plans.

(iii) If a principal purpose of establishing separate plans is to evade any requirement of law, then the separate plans will be considered a single plan to the extent necessary to prevent the evasion.

* * * * *

(e) *Determining the average number of employees*—(1) *Scope.* Whenever the application of a rule in this part depends upon the average number of employees employed by an employer, the determination of that number is made in accordance with the rules of this paragraph (e).

(2) *Full-time equivalents.* The average number of employees is determined by calculating the average number of full-time equivalents on business days during the preceding calendar year.

(3) *Methodology.* For the preceding calendar year, the average number of full-time equivalents is determined by—

(i) Determining the number of employees who were employed full-time by the employer throughout the entire calendar year;

(ii) Totaling all employment hours (not to exceed 40 hours per week) for each part-time employee, and for each full-time employee who was not employed full-time with the employer throughout the entire calendar year;

(iii) Dividing the total determined under paragraph (e)(3)(ii) of this section by a figure that represents the annual full-time hours under the employer's general employment practices, such as 2,080 hours (although for this purpose not more than 40 hours per week may be used); and

(iv) Adding the quotient determined under paragraph (e)(3)(iii) of this section to the number determined under paragraph (e)(3)(i).

(4) *Rounding.* For purposes of paragraph (e)(3)(iv) of this section, all fractions are disregarded. For instance, a figure of 50.9 is deemed to be 50.

(5) *Employers not in existence in the preceding year.* In the case of an employer that was in existence for less than the entire preceding calendar year (including an employer that was not in existence at all), a determination of the average number of employees that the employer employs is based on the average number of employees that it is reasonably expected the employer will employ on business days in the current calendar year.

(6) *Scope of the term "employer".* For purposes of this paragraph (e), employer includes any predecessor of the employer. In addition, all persons treated as a single employer under section 414(b), (c), (m), or (o) of the Internal Revenue Code are treated as one employer.

(7) *Special rule for multiemployer plans.* (i) With respect to the application of a rule in this part to a multiemployer plan (as defined in section 3(37) of the Act), each employer with at least one employee participating in the plan is considered to employ the same average number of employees. That number is the highest number that results by applying the rules of paragraphs (e)(1) through (6) of this section separately to each of the employers.

(ii) The rules of this paragraph (e)(7) are illustrated by the following example:

Example. (i) *Facts.* Twenty five employers have at least one employee who participates in Multiemployer Plan *M.* Among these 25 employers, Employer *K* has 51 employees, determined under the rules of paragraphs (e)(1) through (6) of this section. Each of the other 24 employers has fewer than 50 employees.

(ii) *Conclusion.* With respect to the application of a rule in this part to *M,* each of the 25 employers is considered to employ 51 employees.

Signed at Washington, DC, this 1st day of December, 2004.

Ann L. Combs,

Assistant Secretary, Employee Benefits Security Administration, U.S. Department of Labor.

¶ 20,534T

Employee Benefits Security Administration (EBSA): Defined benefit plans: Multiemployer plans: Annual Funding Notice.— The Employee Benefits Security Administration (EBSA) has released a proposed regulation that would provide increased financial disclosure to participants and beneficiaries of multiemployer defined benefit plans. The annual funding notice, which would also be sent to relevant labor organizations, employers, and the PBGC, would include a statement noting whether the plan's funded current liability percentage was at least 100 percent.

The proposed regulations, which were published in the *Federal Register* on February 4, 2005 (70 FR 6305), were finalized on January 11, 2006 (71 FR 1904). See preamble to the final regulation at ¶ 24,244. The regulation is reproduced at ¶ 14,214.

¶ 20,534U

Pension Benefit Guaranty Corporation (PBGC): Cessation of operations: Single employer: Withdrawal liability.—The PBGC has proposed regulations for computing liability under ERISA § 4063(b) when there is a plant shutdown or substantial cessation of operations by an employer in an " ERISA § 4062(e) event." Such an event occurs when more than 20% of employee-participants in an employer-sponsored plan are separated from employment when the employer ceases operations at a facility in any of its locations without terminating the plan for remaining employees. When such an event occurs, the employer is treated as if it were a substantial employer withdrawing from a multiemployer plan.

The proposed regulations, published in the *Federal Register* on February 25, 2005 (70 FR 9258), were finalized on June 16, 2006 (71 FR 34819). The preamble to the final regulations appears at ¶ 24,248, and the final regulation appear at ¶ 15,621, ¶ 15,621B, ¶ 15,621F, ¶ 15,621G, ¶ 15,621H, ¶ 15,621I, ¶ 15,621J, and ¶ 15,631.

¶ 20,534V

Pension Benefit Guaranty Corporation (PBGC): Electronic filing requirements: Financial statements: Actuarial information.—The PBGC has issued a proposed rule which would require that certain identifying, financial and actuarial information be filed electronically in a standardized format and would also require the filing of additional items of supporting information that are readily available to the filer.

The proposed regulation, which was reproduced here, was published in the Federal Register on March 9, 2005 (70 FR 11592). The final regulation was published in the Federal Register on June 1, 2006 (71 FR 31077). The preamble to the final regulation is reproduced at ¶ 24,247.

¶ 20,534W

Employee Benefits Security Administration (EBSA): Prohibited transactions: Qualified termination administrators (QTAs): Plan termination: Individual retirement plans.—The full text of an EBSA proposed rule that establishes standards for determining when an individual account plan has been abandoned, guidelines for winding up the plan's affairs and distributing benefits, and guidance with regard to who may initiate and carry out the termination process was previously reproduced below. The proposed rule was issued in conjunction with a proposed prohibited transaction class exemption (see ¶ 16,707). The proposed regulation was published in the *Federal Register* on March 10, 2005 (70 FR 12045).

The final version of the regulations were issued on April 21, 2006 (71 FR 20820). The preamble to the final regulations appears at ¶ 24,246; the final regulations appear at ¶ 14,231M, ¶ 14,742B and ¶ 14,929S.

¶ 20,534X

Pension Benefit Guaranty Corporation: Benefit valuation: Terminating plans: Mortality assumptions.—The Pension Benefit Guaranty Corporation has issued proposed regulations relating to the mortality assumptions used in its benefit valuation regulations, which provide rules for valuing benefits in a single-employer plan that terminates in a distress or voluntary termination. According to the PBGC, the updated mortality assumptions would better conform to those used by private-sector insurers in pricing group annuities. Under the proposed regulations, the PBGC's mortality tables contained in Appendix A to Part 4044 would be updated from a version of the 1983 Group Annuity Mortality (GAM-83) Tables to a version of 1994 Group Annuity Mortality Basic (GAM-94 Basic) Tables, in order to reflect longer life expectancies and to conform to updated tables used by insurance companies. Comments must be received on or before May 13, 2005.

The proposed regulations, published in the *Federal Register* on March 14, 2005 (70 FR 12429), were previously reproduced below. The final regulations were published in the *Federal Register* on December 2, 2005 (70 FR 72205); the preamble to the final regulations is reproduced at ¶ 24,241.

¶ 20,534Y

Employee Benefits Security Administration (EBSA): Form 5500: Defined benefit plans: Welfare plans: Multiemployer plans: Electronic filing.— The DOL and the Employee Benefits Security Administration (EBSA) have released proposed regulations which would require Form 5500 filers to transmit 100% of annual returns/reports electronically, for plan years beginning on or after January 1, 2007. Therefore, the 100% electronic filing requirement would affect Form 5500 filings due in 2008. Upon adoption, the regulations would impact employee pension and welfare benefit plans, plan sponsors, administrators, and service providers to plans subject to Title I of ERISA.

The proposed regulations, which were published in the *Federal Register* on August 30, 2005 (70 FR 51542), are reproduced below.

DEPARTMENT OF LABOR

Employee Benefits Security Administration

29 CFR Part 2520

RIN 1210-AB04

Electronic Filing of Annual Reports

AGENCY: Employee Benefits Security Administration, Department of Labor.

ACTION: Proposed regulation.

SUMMARY: This document contains a proposed regulation that, upon adoption, would establish an electronic filing requirement for certain annual reports required to be filed with the Department of Labor by plan administrators and other entities. The Employee Retirement Income Security Act of 1974 (ERISA) and the Internal Revenue Code (the Code), and the regulations issued thereunder, impose certain annual reporting obligations on pension and welfare benefit plans, as well as on certain other entities. These annual reporting obligations generally are satisfied by filing the Form 5500 Series. Currently, the Department of Labor, the Pension Benefit Guaranty Corporation, and the Internal Revenue Service (the Agencies) use an automated document processing system — the ERISA Filing Acceptance System — to process the Form 5500 Series filings. As part of the Department's efforts to update and streamline the current processing system, the Department has determined that improvements and cost savings in the filing processes can best be achieved by adopting a wholly electronic filing processing system and eliminating the currently accepted paper filings. The Department believes that a wholly electronic system will result in, among other things, reduced filer errors and, therefore, reduced correspondence and potential for filer penalties; more timely data for public disclosure and enforcement, thereby enhancing the protections for participants and beneficiaries; and lower annual report processing costs, benefiting taxpayers generally. As part of the move to a wholly electronic filing system, the regulation contained in this document would, upon adoption, require Form 5500 filings made to satisfy the annual reporting obligations under Title I of ERISA to be made electronically. In order to ensure an orderly and cost-effective migration to an electronic filing system by both the Department and Form 5500 filers, under the proposal the requirement to file electronically would not apply until plan years beginning on or after January 1, 2007, with the first electronically filed forms due in 2008. Upon adoption, this regulation would affect employee pension and welfare benefit plans, plan sponsors, administrators, and service providers to plans subject to Title I of ERISA.

DATES: Written comments must be received by the Department of Labor on or before October 31, 2005.

ADDRESSES: Comments should be addressed to the Office of Regulations and Interpretations, Employee Benefits Security Administration (EBSA), Room N-5669, U.S. Department of Labor, 200 Constitution Avenue, NW, Washington, D.C. 20210. Attn: Form 5500 E-filing regulation (RIN 1210-AB04). Comments also may be submitted electronically to *e-ori@dol.gov* or by using the Federal eRulemaking Portal: *www.regulations.gov* (follow instructions provided for submission of comments). EBSA will make all comments available to the public on its website at *www.dol.gov/ebsa*. The comments also will be available for public inspection at the Public Disclosure Room, N-1513, EBSA, U.S. Department of Labor, 200 Constitution Avenue, NW, Washington, D.C. 20210.

FOR FURTHER INFORMATION CONTACT: Yolanda R. Wartenberg, Office of Regulations and Interpretations, Employee Benefits Security Administration, (202) 693-8510. This is not a toll-free number.

SUPPLEMENTARY INFORMATION:

Background

Sections 104(a) and 4065 of the Employee Retirement Income Security Act of 1974, as amended (ERISA), and sections 6057(b) and 6058(a) of the Internal Revenue Code of 1986, as amended (the Code), and the regulations issued under those sections, impose certain annual reporting and filing obligations on pension and welfare benefit plans, as well as on certain other entities.[1] Plan administrators, employers, and others generally satisfy these annual reporting obligations by filing the Form 5500 Annual Return/Report of Employee Benefit Plan, together with any required attachments and schedules for the particular plan (Form 5500).[2]

Currently, the Department of Labor, the Pension Benefit Guaranty Corporation, and the Internal Revenue Service (the Agencies) use an automated document processing system — the ERISA Filing Acceptance System (EFAST) - maintained by the Department of Labor (the Department) to process annual reports. Using the EFAST system, the Department annually receives and processes approximately 1.4 million filings. For the 2002 plan year, these filings translated into approximately 25 million paper pages.

Developed in 1998 and 1999, the EFAST system relies on a mixture of filing and processing methods to accept, compile, and monitor the Form 5500 filings. The EFAST system currently accepts filings generated using any of three different formats: (1) government printed "hand-print" forms, which must be filed on paper; (2) computer-generated paper forms identical in format to government-printed hand-print forms, which also must be filed on paper and are treated in processing the same as hand-print forms; and (3) computer-generated forms in which 2D bar code technology is used to encode filer data (known as the "machine-print" version of the forms), which may be filed either on

---

[1] Other filing requirements may apply to employee benefit plans under ERISA or to other benefit arrangements under the Code, and such other filing requirements are not within the scope of this proposal. For example, Code sec. 6033(a) imposes an additional reporting and filing obligation on organizations exempt from tax under Code sec. 501(a), which may be related to retirement trusts that are qualified under sec. 401(a) of the Code. Code sec. 6047(e) also imposes an additional reporting and filing obligation on pension benefit plans that are employee stock ownership plans (ESOPs).

[2] For purposes of the annual reporting requirements under the Code, certain pension benefit arrangements that cover only business owners or partners (and their spouses), which are not employee benefit plans under Title I of ERISA, are permitted to file the Form 5500-EZ to satisfy filing requirements under the Code. *See* instructions to the Form 5500-EZ to determine who may currently file the Form 5500-EZ.

paper or electronically. As indicated, only the computer-generated machine-print forms may be filed electronically, and the Agencies currently accept machine-print filings through any of the following electronic methods of transmission: (1) via modem using file transfer protocol (FTP), or (2) on magnetic or optical media, such as CD-ROM, computer diskette, or magnetic tape. To process the different filing formats, the system uses a variety of computer technologies, such as optical character recognition technology to read data from the hand-print forms; 2D bar-coding technology to read coded filer information printed on the "machine-print" forms submitted on paper; scanning technology to retain images of paper filings; etc.

A private contractor performs the EFAST processing under a time-limited contract with EBSA. The end of the time-limited contracting cycle and the beginning of another contracting cycle present a significant opportunity for EBSA to evaluate the system and to make changes to take advantage of technological advances. In connection with that process, in March, 2004, the Department posted a request for public comments (Request for Comment) on its website relating to updating the current EFAST processing system.[3]

The Request for Comment set out the Department's preference for enhanced electronic filing and described in detail its understanding of the deficiencies in the EFAST design that impede use of the current electronic filing option. The Request for Comment stated that the Department's goal in developing a new processing system is to make it "more accessible to its user base through Internet and Web-based technology, devoid of paper to the greatest extent possible, faster, less expensive, and more accurate" and to ensure that "electronic filing becomes more convenient and beneficial for all users and stakeholders." The Department noted that "[t]he full benefits of electronic processing have not . . . been realized . . . because [EFAST's]electronic filing option has been underutilized."[4] The Request for Comment noted the benefits to be gained from electronic filing, explaining that, compared with electronic filings, using paper-based forms is less accurate in terms of data capture and less efficient in terms of processing — paper filings take three times as long as electronic filings to process and have nearly twice as many errors, which often trigger follow-up letters from the Agencies seeking corrections or clarifications concerning the filed information. Such filings may also result in the imposition of penalties under ERISA and the Code.

Signaling the Department's interest in moving to an electronic filing system for the Form 5500 Series, the Request for Comment specifically requested comment on whether a reduction in the available filing methods, up to and including adoption of an electronic filing mandate, would be an appropriate solution to the problems caused by underutilization of electronic filing.

In response to the Request for Comment, the Department received many constructive and useful comments from a diverse group of interested parties, including small business owners, sponsors and administrators of small and large plans, actuaries, accountants, entrepreneurs involved in the development and sale of EFAST-approved software, and firms that prepare Form 5500 filings for a wide variety of employee benefit plans.[5] Public comment was largely in accord with the Department's analysis of EFAST's technical deficiencies as laid out in the Request for Comment.

Based on what appears to be a consensus as to the current technical deficiencies of EFAST, the Department has begun the technical process necessary for the development of a new processing system. At the same time, the Agencies separately are undertaking a comprehensive review of the Form 5500 Series in an effort to determine what, if any, design or data changes should be made, in anticipation of the new processing system. Neither the technical project for development of a new processing system, nor the Form 5500 Series project, however, is the subject of this proposal.[6] Any Form or related regulation changes will be proposed for public comment as part of a separate rulemaking.

The subject of this proposal is the Department's determination that any new processing system designed to replace EFAST must have as its core component a requirement that all Form 5500s be submitted through electronic means. The Department's determination that electronic filing must be the sole method available under the new processing system is not dependent on the extent or type of data that will be required of filers or the form or forms in which it must be provided; nor is it dependent on the exact software or hardware that will ultimately be devised to accommodate electronic filing, either by the Federal government or by the private sector. Rather, this determination arises from the Department's conclusion that electronic filing will benefit plan sponsors, participants and beneficiaries, and the taxpayer, based on the Department's investigation and analysis, described more fully below, of the practical alternatives. The proposal for an electronic filing requirement contained in this notice is therefore being published in advance of the other projects related to the Form 5500 Series and processing because the Department has concluded, based on considerations explained more fully below, that it is essential to the success of any redesign of EFAST that it provide filers and other affected parties adequate time to make the transition to a fully electronic method of filing the Form 5500 Series. Given the importance of the contemplated transition, the Department is publishing this proposal separately to describe the reasoning behind its conclusion and to solicit public comment on how best to proceed with the transition to electronic filing.

Public Comment and Alternatives

Virtually all of the public comments submitted in response to the Request for Comment recognized the value of electronic filing over paper filing and expressed support for increasing the use of electronic filing. The majority of comments also endorsed the concept of a gradual transition to 100 percent electronic filing. A clear consensus among commenters further favored the development of a secure Internet website on which a filer could file the Form 5500 through direct input of data, provided it was cost-free to the filer. Nonetheless, the commenters opposed an immediate mandate of electronic filing as the next step in EFAST development. The commenters argued that an immediate mandate would impose economic burdens on small businesses and small plans, which may not have easy access to the Internet. The commenters urged the Department to make only incremental changes, building on the current system and taking into account the substantial investments that the filing public has already made to accommodate EFAST. One representative commenter, speaking on behalf of a large number of large employers and service providers to employers of all sizes, suggested that, although electronic filing provides many advantages to both the public and the government, the Department should phase in any mandate over time by market segment, starting first with the largest employers who are already familiar with electronic filing, such as is required by the Securities and Exchange Commission. Other commenters asked the Department to allow sufficient time for experimentation and testing before inaugurating a mandate.

In developing this proposed regulation, the Department sought to advance two main goals. One was to maximize the speed, efficiency, and accuracy with which annual reports are transmitted, accepted, and processed, thereby enhancing the protection of participants' rights. The other was to minimize the burden placed on filers. In pursuit of these goals, the Department considered and analyzed several alternatives, taking into account the costs and benefits attendant to each. These included the following: (1) creating a new processing system that could continue to process both electronic and paper submissions without limitation; (2) continuing the present, primarily paperbased processing system on an interim basis alongside a new, solely electronic processing system; (3) developing a new, primarily electronic processing system with a temporary capacity to process a limited number of paper filings, which would be made available under criteria targeting those filers most likely to desire a longer transition period; and (4) transitioning to a new, solely electronic processing system under a uniformly applicable requirement to file electronically.

The Department considered the costs and benefits of each of these alternatives, and its economic analysis is described below under the heading "Regulatory Impact Analysis." Based on its analysis of the alternatives, the Department has concluded that the maintenance of any paper filing system, even on a reduced scale and/or for limited

---

[3] The Request for Comment may be reviewed at: http://www.efast.dol.gov/efastrfc.html.

[4] The Department specifically identified technical deficiencies involving the process for obtaining and using electronic signatures, the use of outdated transmission methods, and the continued use of paper for post-filing communications. The Request for Comment suggested various technical design changes to address these and other deficiencies, including creating an Internet-based method of filing; requiring that approved software be designed only for Internet transmission of computer-generated filings; adopting improved data exchange technology based on widely-accepted standards, such as XML; improving the technical handling of third-party attachments and attestations; and eliminating differences in treatment between paper and electronic filings with respect to acceptance and rejection.

[5] Comments received in response to the Request for Comment may be reviewed at: http://www.dol.gov/ebsa/regs/cmt_efastrfc.html.

[6] In connection with this proposal, the Department is providing in this document further information respecting the technical design and Form 5500 content projects underway within the Department concerning the Form 5500 Series. The Department believes the information about those two other projects will assist the public in evaluating this proposal; however, the Department notes that it is not asking for public comment at this time on those two separate projects. The proposal contained in this notice concerns only the mandate of electronic filing. The public will have adequate separate opportunity for public comment on the Form 5500 regulatory initiative prior to its finalization and ample time to make necessary practical changes prior to implementation of the new processing system.

periods of time, which would be required under any of the first three alternatives, would be inherently inefficient and unnecessarily costly. It is also the Department's view that any economic benefit that might accrue to some class of filers under those alternatives would be outweighed by the benefits to participants and beneficiaries at large, and to the Department and taxpayers generally, of implementing a single, wholly electronic system. Accordingly, the Department has decided to propose adoption of a uniform requirement to file electronically, as detailed further below.[7]

In so doing, the Department believes that transitioning to a new wholly electronic processing system will not present the problems suggested by the public responses to the Request for Comment. First, as explained more fully below, the Department intends to ensure that the new processing system will remedy the existing technical difficulties that underlie the perceived limitations of EFAST's current electronic filing design and will provide an electronic filing process that will be simpler, easier, and more attractive to filers.

Second, the Department does not believe that transitioning to the new processing system will impose undue burdens on small plans or small employers. Rather, the Department's analysis indicates that filers' costs of transitioning from paper filing to electronic transmission will be relatively modest and surpassed by benefits that will accrue in subsequent years.

Finally, the Department intends to delay implementation of any electronic mandate until the due date for the filing of Form 5500 Series for the plan year beginning in 2007, generally July 2008 or later. The Department believes that this substantial time delay of the proposed full electronic mandate will provide the public with adequate time to make adjustments in advance of the implementation of the new filing system.

The Department's conclusions concerning the public comments and alternatives are grounded in the Regulatory Impact Analysis presented below.

The Department invites comment on the need for an exception to accommodate any potentially significant impediments to some filers' transition to electronic filing. Commenters are encouraged to provide specific examples of such impediments, as well as to address the specific conditions for, and necessary scope of, relief under a hardship exception.

Electronic Filing

After careful consideration of the comments on the Request for Comment, as well as the need to develop a more efficient, cost-effective processing system for annual return/reports, the Department has determined, consistent with the goals of E-government, as recognized by the Government Paperwork Elimination Act[8] and the E-Government Act of 2002,[9] to require electronic filing of the Form 5500 to satisfy the reporting requirements of section 104(a) of Title I of ERISA. A mandate of electronic filing of benefit plan information, among other program strategies, will facilitate EBSA's achievement of its Strategic Goal of "enhancing pension and health benefits of American workers." EBSA's strategic goal directly supports the Secretary of Labor's Strategic Goals of "protecting workers benefits" and of "a competitive workforce," as well as promoting job flexibility and minimizing regulatory burden.[10] A cornerstone of our enforcement program is the collection, analysis, and disclosure of benefit plan information. Requiring electronic filing of benefit plan information, with the resulting improvement in the timeliness and accuracy of the information, would, in part, assist EBSA in its enforcement, oversight, and disclosure roles, which ultimately enhance the security of plan benefits. As the Government Accountability Office noted in its June, 2005, report on the Form 5500 Series,[11] the current necessity for handling paper filings under EFAST creates a substantial delay between receipt of a filing and the availability of its information for any enforcement and oversight purposes. Stating that "the abundance of paper filings results in long processing times," the GAO estimated, for purposes of illustration, that the processing time for a

paper filing under EFAST averages 90 days from date of receipt where no filing errors are detected.[12] Electronic filing would eliminate virtually all of this processing time, improving outcomes for all of the users of the Form 5500 information. In this regard, the PBGC has advised the Department that electronic filing will enable PBGC to receive important information about defined benefit plans more quickly and efficiently, improving the PBGC's ability to monitor plan funding; calculate bankruptcy claims; estimate the impact of non-bankruptcy reportable events; evaluate exposure and expected claims; study plan formation and termination trends; and assess compliance with PBGC premium requirements.

In order to ensure an orderly and cost-effective migration to an electronic filing requirement and a new processing system, the requirement to file the Form 5500 electronically would apply only to annual return/reports required to be filed under ERISA section 104(a) for plan years beginning on or after January 1, 2007.

For purposes of the annual reporting requirements under section 4065 of Title IV of ERISA, the Pension Benefit Guaranty Corporation (PBGC) has advised the Department that a plan administrator's electronic filing of a Form 5500 for purposes of ERISA section 104(a), together with the required attachments and schedules and otherwise in accordance with the instructions to the Form, will be treated as satisfying the administrator's annual reporting obligation under section 4065 of Title IV of ERISA.[13] Similarly, for purposes of the annual filing and reporting requirements of the Code, the Internal Revenue Service (IRS) has advised the Department that, although there are no mandatory electronic filing requirements for a Form 5500 under the Code or the regulations issued thereunder, the electronic filing of a Form 5500 by plan administrators, employers, and certain other entities for purposes of ERISA section 104(a), together with the required attachments and schedules and otherwise in accordance with the instructions to the Form, will be treated as satisfying the annual filing and reporting requirements under Code sections 6058(a) and 6059(a). The IRS intends that plan administrators, employers, and certain other entities that are subject to various other filing and reporting requirements under Code sections 6033(a), 6047(e), and 6057(b) must continue to satisfy these requirements in accordance with IRS revenue procedures, publications, forms, and instructions.

With respect to annual reporting and filing obligations imposed by the Code but not required under section 104(a) of ERISA, such as are currently satisfied by the filing of the Form 5500-EZ, the IRS has advised the Department that it is currently working with taxpayers to explore how best to make a transition from paper filing to electronic filing in a manner that minimizes the burdens on taxpayers and practitioners. In this regard, the IRS has promulgated regulations mandating or permitting electronic filing of certain returns filed by pension and welfare benefit plans.[14]

With regard to the development of a new annual return/report electronic processing system, the Department is committed to resolving the electronic filing impediments identified by commenters on the Request for Comment, in particular those impediments relating to electronic signatures, attachments, and attestations furnished by third parties (e.g., accountants, actuaries, etc.).

It is anticipated that the new electronic filing system will incorporate the Internet as the sole medium for transmission of all filings and that the system will incorporate immediate validity and accuracy checks that will reduce both the error and rejection rate of filings and eliminate much of the costly post-filing paper correspondence and related potential penalties. The Department does not anticipate charging any filing fees in connection with the new system.

It is intended that the new electronic filing system will provide more than one vehicle for the electronic submission of annual return/reports. First, it is intended that the new filing system will offer users of approved, privately developed Form 5500 computer software (service providers to plans as well as plan administrators) a secure Internet-based method for transmission of Form 5500s created through the use

---

[7] This approach is congruent with recommendations of the Government Accountability Office, which, in a June, 2005, Report to Congressional Committees, stated that "[g]iven the improved timeliness and reduced errors associated with electronic filing, Labor, IRS and PBGC should require the electronic filing of the Form 5500." See *Private Pension - Government Actions Could Improve the Timeliness and Content of Form 5500 Pension Information* (GAO-05-491) at 44. The Report went on to state "[i]n doing so, Labor should also make improvements to the current electronic filing process to make it less burdensome, such as revising the procedure for signing and authenticating an electronic filing."

[8] Title XVII, Pub. L. 105-277, 112 Stat. 2681 (Oct. 21, 1998).

[9] Pub. L. 107-347, 116 Stat. 2899 (Dec. 17, 2002).

[10] For further information on the Department of Labor's Strategic Plan and EBSA's relationship to it, *see* http://www.dol.gov/_sec/stratplan/main.htm.

[11] *See* fn. 7, above.

[12] *See Private Pensions - Government Actions Could Improve the Timeliness and Content of Form 5500 Pension Information* (GAO-05-491) at 28, fig. 9 at 32. GAO also noted that, where errors in a filing are detected, additional processing delays of up to 120 more days occur.

[13] It should be noted that all administrators of plans required to file reports under ERISA sec. 4065 also are required to file reports for purposes of sec. 104(a) of ERISA.

[14] *See,* e.g., 26 CFR 301.6033-4T (mandating electronic filing of certain corporate income tax returns and returns of organizations required to be filed under Code sec. 6033); 26 CFR 1.6033-4T (returns required to be filed on magnetic media under 26 CFR 301.6033-4T must be filed in accordance with IRS revenue procedures, publications, forms, or instructions).

of the software. This Internet-based transmission process will supercede all of the other currently available methods of transmitting machine-print versions of the Form 5500, including use of computer diskette, CD-ROM, magnetic tape, and modem. As the Department made clear in the Request for Comment, in making a transition to 100 percent electronic filing, the Department does not intend to supplant private software developers, vendors, or service providers to plans. Rather, it is contemplated that the new system will continue to provide support to these private industries, and the Department believes that filers will continue to rely on a variety of privately developed software products and services to facilitate plan administration, including the preparation and filing of the annual return/report. Indeed, it is expected that third-party software will remain the primary means of producing Form 5500s, with the simple difference that the reports will be filed electronically rather than through the use of paper. It is intended that service providers and software developers that provide value-added services for plan sponsors will be able to incorporate the new system's method of transmission into their services effectively and efficiently. Software file specifications will be non-proprietary so that users of different software may freely share information across different platforms. In this regard, the Department specifically invites public comment on how best to configure the new electronic filing architecture to provide the necessary flexibility to accommodate the needs of the diverse community of employee benefit plans.

Second, the Department also intends to include in the new system, as a separate filing method, a dedicated, secure Internet website through which plan administrators (or other return/report preparers) will be able to input data and to complete and submit Form 5500 filings on an individual plan-by-plan basis. It is anticipated that the Internet website will provide the filer with the capability of entering and saving data for an individual filing through multiple sessions, authorizing input for that filing from multiple parties (service providers, accountants, actuaries, etc.), uploading attachments, saving return/reports to a repository, and retrieving, updating, and editing stored filings, as well as creating and submitting amended filing data to EBSA.

As mentioned above, in connection with implementation of the redesign of EFAST, the Department, in coordination with the IRS and the PBGC, is conducting a thorough content review of the Form 5500. This review will be conducted as a three-agency regulatory initiative and will provide notice and comment opportunities for the public. The Department intends to consider, in conducting the content review of the Form 5500, changes that would facilitate electronic filing, as well as recommendations made by the ERISA Advisory Council on electronic reporting and on reporting by health and welfare plans.[15] That regulatory project would undertake to produce revised forms to be used for annual return/reports for the 2007 plan year, which will be due to be filed in 2008, when the new processing system will be implemented and the electronic filing requirement will begin to apply. Within the next few months, the Department intends to publish a separate notice inviting public comment on proposed changes to the Form 5500 and related rules.

Proposed Rule

The proposed rule contained in this notice is necessary to establish a requirement for the electronic filing of the Form 5500 for purposes of the annual reporting provisions of Title I of ERISA. Although at this time it is not possible to provide full technical details regarding the new electronic filing system, as many of the technological aspects of the redesign are still in development, filing requirements and compliance instructions will be provided to filers in advance of any due date for filing the Form 5500 under a final regulation requiring electronic submissions.

The proposal, upon adoption, would add a new section 2520.104a-2, Electronic Filing of Annual Reports, to Subpart E of Part 2520 of Title 29 of the Code of Federal Regulations. The proposal provides that any Form 5500 Annual Return/Report to be filed with the Secretary of Labor (Secretary) for any plan year beginning on or after January 1, 2007, shall be filed electronically in accordance with instructions and such other guidance as the Secretary may provide, applicable to such annual report. Because the Form 5500 is also filed by certain non-plan entities, such as common or collective trusts, pooled separate accounts, and entities described in 29 CFR 2520.103-12, which file for the fiscal year ending with or within the plan year for which a plan's annual report is filed, the proposal makes further reference to the first "reporting year" beginning on or after January 1, 2007, for such entities.

The proposal is intended to ensure that all Form 5500s filed with the Department, as well as any statements or schedules required to be attached to the report, including those filed by administrators (29 CFR 2520.103-1(a)(2) and (e)), group insurance arrangements (29 CFR 2520.103-2), common or collective trusts and pooled separate accounts (29 CFR 2520.103-3, 2520.103-4, and 2520.103-9), and entities described in 29 CFR 2520.103-12, are required (to the extent of the Department's authority) to be filed electronically. Following the development of a new electronic filing system, the Department intends to provide specific instructions and guidance concerning methods of filing in the instructions for the annual report form(s) and via its website.

As indicated above in the discussion under "Electronic Filing," the proposal would not apply to any reporting requirements imposed solely under the Code (i.e., not required under section 104(a) of ERISA). As discussed above, issues relating to transition from paper filing to electronic filing for such reporting requirements are under consideration at the IRS. Accordingly, the regulation would not apply to any attachment, schedule, or report required to be completed by a tax-qualified pension benefit plan solely in order to provide the IRS with information concerning compliance with Code section 410(b) for a plan year, even if such attachment, schedule, or report is required to accompany the Form 5500 Annual Report/Return for that year. The proposal also would not apply to attachments, schedules, or reports that the IRS requires (1) under Code section 6033(a) to be filed by a trustee of a trust created as part of an employee benefit plan described in Code section 401(a) or by a custodian of a custodial account described in Code section 401(f), or (2) under Code section 6047(e) to be filed with respect to an employee stock ownership plan (ESOP).

The proposal, at 29 CFR 2520.104a-2(b), makes clear that the requirement to file annual reports electronically does not affect a person's record retention or disclosure obligations. In other words, the obligations of persons to retain records for purposes of sections 107 and 209 of ERISA would not be altered by the fact that the annual report would be required to be filed in electronic form. Similarly, a plan administrator's obligation to make the latest annual report available for examination and to furnish copies upon request, in accordance with sections 104(b)(2) and 104(b)(4) of ERISA, will not be affected by an electronic filing requirement.

Conforming changes are being proposed to 29 CFR 2520.103-1(f) [contents of the annual report], 2520.103-2(c) [contents of the annual report for a group insurance arrangement], 2520.103-9(d) [direct filing for bank or insurance carrier trusts and accounts], and 2520.103-12(f) [limited exception and alternative method of compliance for annual reporting of investments in certain entities].

Regulatory Impact Analysis

Summary

The Department has considered the potential costs and benefits of this proposed regulation. Costs to plans would consist mainly of a one-time, transition or start-up cost to make the change to electronic filing, generally to be incurred in 2008, which is estimated to be $23 million. Benefits to plans would include ongoing savings on material and postage and efficiency gains from the early detection and correction of more potential filing errors in the course of electronic filing, estimated to total $10 million annually, and realized each succeeding year beginning in 2008. Over time the ongoing savings attributable to this proposed regulation are expected to outweigh its one-time transition costs. Aggregate savings are estimated to exceed aggregate costs by $23 million over the first five years (discounting future savings at a rate of 7 percent).

Additional benefits are expected to accrue to the government and the public in the forms of substantially reduced processing costs and more timely availability of accurate filing data for use in enforcement and for other purposes of benefit to plans and participants.

Executive Order 12866 Statement

Under Executive Order 12866, the Department must determine whether a regulatory action is "significant" and therefore subject to the requirements of the Executive Order and subject to review by the Office of Management and Budget (OMB). Under section 3(f) of the Executive Order, a "significant regulatory action" is an action that is likely to result in a rule (1) having an annual effect on the economy of $100 million or more, or adversely and materially affecting a sector of the economy, productivity, competition, jobs, the environment, public health or safety, or State, local or tribal governments or communities

---

[15] *See, e.g., Report of the ERISA Advisory Council Working Group on Electronic Reporting* (Nov. 8, 2002), at http://www.dol.gov/ebsa/publications/AC_1108a02_report.html.

(also referred to as "economically significant"); (2) creating serious inconsistency or otherwise interfering with an action taken or planned by another agency; (3) materially altering the budgetary impacts of entitlement grants, user fees, or loan programs or the rights and obligations of recipients thereof; or (4) raising novel legal or policy issues arising out of legal mandates, the President's priorities, or the principles set forth in the Executive Order. OMB has determined that this action is significant under section 3(f)(4) because it raises novel legal or policy issues arising from the President's priorities. Accordingly, the Department has undertaken below an analysis of the costs and benefits of the proposed regulation.

Regulatory Flexibility Act

The Regulatory Flexibility Act (5 U.S.C. 601 et seq.) (RFA) imposes certain requirements with respect to Federal rules that are subject to the notice and comment requirements of section 553(b) of the Administrative Procedure Act (5 U.S.C. 551 et seq.) and which are likely to have a significant economic impact on a substantial number of small entities. Unless an agency determines that a proposed rule is not likely to have a significant economic impact on a substantial number of small entities, section 603 of the RFA requires that the agency present an initial regulatory flexibility analysis at the time of the publication of the notice of proposed rulemaking describing the impact of the rule on small entities and seeking public comment on such impact. Small entities include small businesses, organizations, and governmental jurisdictions.

For purposes of analysis under the RFA, EBSA proposes to continue to consider a small entity to be an employee benefit plan with fewer than 100 participants. The basis of this definition is found in section 104(a)(2) of ERISA, which permits the Secretary to prescribe simplified annual reports for pension plans that cover fewer than 100 participants. Under section 104(a)(3) of ERISA, the Secretary may also provide for exemptions or simplified annual reporting and disclosure for welfare benefit plans. Pursuant to the authority of section 104(a)(3), the Department has previously issued at 29 CFR 2520.104-20, 2520.104-21, 2520.104-41, 2520.104-46, and 2520.104b-10 certain simplified reporting provisions and limited exemptions from reporting and disclosure requirements for small plans, including unfunded or insured welfare plans that cover fewer than 100 participants and satisfy certain other requirements.

Further, while some large employers may have small plans, in general small employers maintain most small plans. Thus, EBSA believes that assessing the impact of these proposed rules on small plans is an appropriate substitute for evaluating the effect on small entities. The definition of small entity considered appropriate for this purpose differs, however, from a definition of small business that is based on size standards promulgated by the Small Business Administration (SBA) (13 CFR 121.201) pursuant to the Small Business Act (15 U.S.C. 631 et seq.). EBSA therefore requests comments on the appropriateness of the size standard used in evaluating the impact of these proposed rules on small entities.

These proposed rules may have a significant impact on a substantial number of small entities. The Department has therefore prepared an initial regulatory flexibility analysis, presented below under the heading "Small Plans." Additional relevant material also appears below under the heading "Alternatives Considered."

Costs and Benefits

The Department has considered the potential costs and benefits of this proposed regulation. Costs to plans would include a one-time transition or start-up cost to make the change to electronic filing, estimated to be $23 million. Benefits would include ongoing savings on material and postage and efficiency gains from the early detection and correction of more potential filing errors in the course of electronic filing, estimated to total $10 million annually. Over time the ongoing savings attributable to this proposed regulation are expected to outweigh its one-time transition costs. Aggregate savings are estimated to exceed aggregate costs by $23 million over the first five year (discount-

ing future savings at a rate of 7 percent). Additional benefits are expected to accrue to the government and the public in the forms of reduced processing costs and more timely availability of accurate filing data. Beyond that, it is not immediately clear how the costs and benefits of mandatory electronic filing will compare with that of current filing modes, and the Department invites comments on this point.

The costs and benefits of this proposed regulation would accrue primarily to 832,000 plans that file Form 5500.[16] Non-plan entities that file Form 5500 generally do so in their capacity as service providers to plans and therefore are expected to pass their own costs and benefits from the regulation on to the plans they serve.[17]

Transition Costs

The proposed regulation would entail some one-time transition costs, incurred in making the transition to electronic filing. The magnitude of the transition costs is likely to vary with filers' previous filing methods, reflecting the extent to which their existing filing infrastructure supports electronic filing. It is also expected that different filers will make the transition to electronic filing in different ways, depending on their circumstances and preferences. It is intended that all filers will have a number of methods of electronic filing from which to choose. For example, filers may enter information directly into a government-provided website (using their own Internet service or one available for a fee at a local business center or free of charge at a public library or other facility). They may use commercial software equipped for electronic filing. They may hire a service provider (or rely on an existing relationship with a service provider) to provide electronic filing services.

In 2002, the bulk of all filings, 87 percent, were submitted on machine-print forms; 12 percent were submitted on hand-print forms; and 1 percent were submitted electronically.

Hand-print Filers - Hand-print filers as a group are likely to face larger transition costs than others. These filers by and large currently file government printed forms, filled out by hand or by using a typewriter.[18] Like all other filers, they will have the option of preparing and submitting their filings via a government provided website. It is likely that many (but not all) already have the electronic infrastructure (mainly a personal computer and Internet service) to support electronic filing. It is also likely that others will have access to the Internet at no charge at a local library or other location.[19] Nonetheless, hand-print filers are likely to incur some expense to learn about the new requirement, and some will incur additional costs, such as in locating and becoming familiar with Internet access, as well as in establishing a secured filing account.

For the 104,000 current hand-print filers, the Department estimates a onetime, aggregate transition cost to electronic filing of $12 million. This assumes that a professional-level employee, who costs the plans on average $58.80 per hour in wages, benefits, and overhead,[20] would require on average two hours to make the transition to electronic filing. The cost might be devoted to one or more one-time, transition activities such as learning about the electronic filing system, registering for a secure filing account, selecting and acquiring software, selecting and hiring a service provider, or locating an Internet access site and becoming familiar with a web-based interface. Different types of transition activities will have different costs. Selecting and hiring a service provider might be an example of a potential activity that would cost more than average, while registering for a secure account might be an example of one that would cost less. The activities and the cost will vary from filer to filer. For example, transition activities might be limited and costs low for a filer that is a highly experienced Internet user already carrying out other aspects of business management (such as buying supplies and selling products, reporting wages to SSA, etc.) on line. Activities might be more extensive and costs higher for a filer lacking Internet and computing expertise who needs to acquire a computer and Internet connection or select and hire a service provider. The Department invites comments on transitional activities and costs.

Machine-print Filers - Machine-print filers as a group are likely to incur smaller transition costs than hand-print filers. It is likely that a

---

[16] The economic analysis of the proposed regulation pertains only to those plans that file a Form 5500 to satisfy filing requirements under Title I of ERISA. Because the Form 5500-EZ is filed to satisfy filing requirements under the Code, data related to Form 5500-EZ filers is not included in this analysis.

[17] Economic theory predicts that producers in competitive markets pass costs and savings on to buyers.

[18] A very small fraction of all hand-print filers, typically a few percent, files computer-generated forms that are similar to and processed in the same way as government printed forms. These filers might tend to incur smaller transition costs than other hand-print filers. Because of their small numbers and the difficulties in separately identifying them in the data used for this analysis, the Department did not attempt to adjust its estimates to reflect

this possible difference. This omission may slightly bias upwards the estimated aggregate transition cost for hand-print filers.

[19] This assumption is consistent with observations made by the ERISA Advisory Council Working Group on Electronic Reporting in its Nov. 8 Report. *See* fn. 15, above.

[20] The total labor cost is derived from wage and compensation data from the Bureau of Labor Statistics' (BLS) 2004 National Occupational Employment and Wage Estimates from the Occupational Employment Survey and BLS 2004 Employment Cost for Compensation. This data can be found at: http://www.bls.gov/news.release/ocwage.t01.htm and http://www.bls.gov/news.release/archives/ecec_09152004.pdf. The estimate assumes a 3 percent annual rate of compensation growth and includes an overhead component, which is a multiple of compensation based on the Government Cost Estimate.

large proportion of machine-print filings are prepared by service providers, while the remainder are prepared by filers using commercial software. Filers that currently rely on service providers to prepare and submit their filings may opt to continue in this manner, relying on the service provider to file electronically. Service providers' transition costs will be passed back to and spread across the filers they serve. Other machine-print filers may rely on the vendors of their software to incorporate electronic filing features into the 2007 plan-year software (probably as part of an otherwise normal annual software update typically carried out to incorporate any form and instruction changes). It is likely that a majority already have the Internet service required for such software features to function, and some that currently do not have such service would have acquired it by the time the plan-year 2007 filings are due (for reasons unrelated to this regulation). For many machine-print filers the transition to electronic filing will be largely transparent, but will nonetheless entail at least some activities, such as registration for a secure filing account.

For the 726,000 current machine-print filers, the Department estimates a one-time, aggregate transition cost to electronic filing of $11 million. This assumes that one-half of machine-print filers will rely entirely on their existing service providers to make the transition and that the service providers will spread their own transition costs across the filers they serve. The Department, lacking data on the number of affected service providers, did not attempt to estimate their transition cost, and such costs are not included here. Because these costs would be spread across filers, the amount passed on to any single filer is expected to be minimal. The remaining one-half of machine-print filers are assumed to shoulder the transition costs themselves. The Department's estimate assumes that these filers will require on average thirty minutes of a professionallevel employee's time to make the transition to electronic filing. The Department invites comments on these transition costs.

Ongoing Costs and Benefits

Preparation Costs - This proposed regulation pertains to the filing, and not to the preparation, of the Form 5500. However, it is possible that, for some filers, mandatory electronic filing would prompt changes in preparation methods. For example, hand-print filers may currently prepare their filings using a government printed form and a typewriter. Such filers might prepare future filings by entering information into a government website. The Department considered the cost of making such transitions in preparation methods to be part of the overall transition cost of the proposed regulation, included in the estimates presented above.

With respect to ongoing preparation costs, it is likely that some filers will incur higher costs in connection with new preparation methods prompted by this regulation and enabled by the new electronic filing system than with their current methods, but that others will incur lower costs. For example, it is not immediately determinable whether entering information into a website will take more or less time than typing it onto a paper form. The Department expects that commercial preparation software will incorporate features that ease preparation, such as integrated access to form instructions and automatic filling of data fields based on entries in other fields or in prior filings. The Department also intends that the new government filing website interface will be designed with attention to ease of preparation. Lacking an immediate basis to quantify the magnitude or costs and savings from possible changes in preparation methods, the Department did not attribute any such costs or savings to this proposed regulation, but invites comments on the potential magnitude of any such costs and benefits.

Filing Cost Savings - Filing costs generally are expected to be reduced by the implementation of this proposed regulation. Savings are foreseen from the elimination of materials and mailing costs and from a reduction in filing errors and subsequent corrections.

Electronic transmission will eliminate certain costs otherwise attendant to paper filing, including materials and postage. The Department estimates that, by changing to electronic filing, 829,000 plans will benefit from approximately $900,000 in cost-savings annually, assuming savings of $0.0167 per sheet of paper and $0.57 for postage per filing.

In addition, automated checks for errors and omissions upon electronic transmission, together with automated error checks and integrated instructions common to filing preparation software, will ease compliance with reporting requirements. Importantly, these features will reduce the need for subsequent amendments to submitted filings, as well as helping to avoid reporting penalties that might otherwise be assessed for deficient filings.

Historically, filers that use a software-based system generally have fewer filing errors. In 2002, 7 percent and 16 percent of electronic and machine-print filings, respectively, had filing errors compared to 40 percent of hand-print filings. The filing errors include items such as missing signatures, attestations, schedules, or back-up documents that resulted in an incomplete filing. As a result of filer errors and the need for additional information or clarifications about Form 5500 filings for the 2002 plan year, the Department mailed 160,000 letters to filers requesting corrections or additions. This process ultimately delays the final submission and requires plans to incur additional costs to address deficiencies. The electronic filing system's intended error detection capability may largely eliminate the Department's need to forward correspondence to plans with deficient filings. This enhancement is likely to save time for filers. If the need for correspondence can be eliminated, the aggregate annual cost savings to affected filers could be as high as $10 million, assuming elimination of correspondence with the Department saves an average of one hour of a professional's time, at an average of $58.80 per hour, plus the value of associated postage and materials. A disproportionate share of this savings, estimated at $2.4 million, would accrue to current hand-print filers (reflecting their historically higher filing error rates), while $7.1 million would accrue to machine-print filers. The Department (and by extension taxpayers) would realize additional savings from this reduced need to correct filing errors.

Societal Benefits

Additional benefits are expected to accrue to the government and the public in the forms of reduced processing costs and more timely availability of accurate filing data.

Participants will benefit from the transition to a fully electronic method of filing. The new filing procedures will provide participants and beneficiaries with access to more accurate plan information since software-based forms are generally less prone to error, the new system will process filings more quickly, and reports disclosing information about plans' administrative and financial status will be available to the public sooner than would otherwise be possible. This improved access can enhance the quality of interaction between plans, participants, and beneficiaries.

The Federal government and the public at large will also benefit from the change to electronic filing. The decrease in correspondence will constitute immediate savings to the Federal government that will, in turn, yield savings to the taxpayers. Finally, improvements in the accuracy of the data contained in submitted filings and the expected acceleration in processing may make possible more timely production of reliable national statistics on private employee benefit plans. Such statistics historically have been produced at a substantial lag of up to four years after the end of the filing year.

Additional Considerations

Proliferation of Technology - In proposing this regulation, and in assessing its economic impacts, the Department took into consideration the high and increasing rates of use of electronic information technologies by businesses, including by small businesses in particular. Such technologies include office computing hardware and software that process, organize, store, and transmit information electronically. The proliferation of such technologies, and of expertise and familiarity with using them, is expected to moderate the cost of compliance with this proposed regulation.

The Department believes that most filers already have access to a computer and the Internet. The use of computers and the Internet has become the norm among U.S. businesses. Most or all industries in the economy are beginning to use the Internet as a means of conducting at least some of their daily operations and to remain competitive. Moreover, it is possible that plan sponsors as a group are more likely than other companies to be using information technologies. The Department believes that few, if any, plan sponsors will purchase a computer or subscribe to Internet service for the sole purpose of electronically filing their Form 5500. (If some do, they may realize collateral benefits as they put their newly acquired technologies to additional uses.) Furthermore, the Department believes that the number of firms offering pension and welfare plans that do not have a computer and/or Internet access is a relatively small number, especially given the substantial growth of computer and Internet usage over the past decade. The Department also believes that the number of plans that will not have a computer or Internet access by the year 2008 will be small.

The Department's views on the proliferation of technologies are grounded in its review of various studies of the topic.

According to a 2002 study for the SBA,[21] the Internet offers unparalleled new opportunities for small businesses. Fifty-seven percent of small businesses already used the Internet; of those most had their own websites; and more than one-third were selling their products on line.[22] Of those not using the Internet, two-thirds did use computers.[23]

The most popular uses of the Internet among small firm users were communicating with customers and suppliers (83 percent), gathering business information (80 percent), and purchasing goods and services (61 percent).[24] Some also used the Internet to conduct banking or other financial transactions (27 percent) or bid on contracts (21 percent). Most firms with websites either broke even financially or made money through use of the sites.

Also according to this study, use of Internet technology is growing. Among small firms with websites, two-thirds had been operating the site for less than one year.[25] Business use of on-line technologies is being driven up by increasing use of such technologies by consumers. Increasing availability and use of affordable, fast broad-band Internet services is helping to drive both trends. Market forecasters predicted rapid growth in world e-commerce, reaching as much as several trillion dollars by 2004.[26]

A 2003 report by SBA[27] found that self-employed computer users numbered 10.5 million in 2000, up from 9.2 million two years earlier. Over the same two years, self-employed individuals' access to the Internet increased by 50 percent, reaching 83 percent of all such individuals.

A 2004 study for SBA[28] of small firms with fewer than 500 employees found that only 27 percent did not currently subscribe to Internet service.

Benefits of E-government - The proposed regulation will advance the goals of administration articulated in the Government Paperwork Elimination Act and the E-Government Act of 2002.

The Department expects this proposed regulation to advance the general trend toward the efficiencies of E-government. Federal, State, and local government agencies have already implemented numerous E-government initiatives.[29] These initiatives reduce the government's burden on businesses by eliminating redundant collection of data. Citizens receive faster, more convenient services from a more responsive and informed government.[30] According to one study, citizens see the most important benefits of E-government as increased government accountability to citizens (36 percent), greater public access to information (23 percent), and more efficient/cost-effective government (21 percent).[31] The GAO has indicated that government agencies that reported using the Internet as a medium for core business operations delivered information and services more quickly, less expensively, and to wider groups of users.[32]

Another study suggests that one of the most powerful ways to reduce compliance costs is through E-government. Web-enabling can save businesses and citizens a considerable amount of time and money, as the following examples demonstrate: (1) The State of Oregon's on-line permitting and reporting process for building construction approvals saved Oregon's construction industry $100 million annually. Deloitte's estimate suggests that if governments at all levels were to follow Oregon's lead, the United States' construction industry, as a whole, could save in the range of $15 billion to $20 billion annually. (2) The SBA's Business Compliance One Stop website saves businesses about $526 million a year, by helping them find, understand, and comply with regulations. (3) In Canada, the province of British Columbia's OneStopBC website cuts down on government paperwork costs for businesses by allowing on-line business license registrations. The cost savings to businesses are estimated to be in the range of $14 million to $27 million annually.[33]

Time Rebates - Time considerations affect all interactions and activities in business. When citizens and businesses can go on line, instead of waiting in line, they can obtain faster, more convenient access to government services.[34] E-government can provide what has come to be described as a "time rebate" — cutting down on the time it takes to comply with government regulations and to complete transactions.

For example, the Commonwealth of Pennsylvania's "PA Open for Business" website allows a business to enter all the information needed to register with the State in one place, instead of having to go to five different agencies. A process that once took days or weeks has been reduced to one hour.[35]

The Department intends that the new electronic filing system will be equipped to streamline submissions and reduce time and burden on filers. The proposed regulation should benefit all parties because the information contained in the Form 5500 would be directly entered into the Department's records. This would improve transaction accuracy, reduce cycle times, improve cost efficiencies, enhance information accessibility, and provide more timely availability of the information contained in the Form 5500 return/reports.

Alternatives Considered

As noted earlier in this preamble, before electing to pursue the approach taken in this proposed regulation, the Department considered alternative options for reconfiguring the filing methods for the Form 5500 Series, focusing in particular on the gradual approach advocated generally in the public comments. The following discusses three such alternatives that the Department considered but rejected, along with the reasons why each was rejected in favor of a uniform requirement to file electronically beginning with filings for the 2007 plan year. Fuller discussion of the third alternative, which would provide a time-limited exception from mandatory electronic filing for certain small plans, follows under the heading "Small Plans."

First, the Department considered developing a new processing system that could continue to process both electronic and paper submissions without limitation. Such a system might be popular with the filing public and might result over time in virtually complete conversion to electronic filing, provided that the new system successfully incorporated the contemplated technological advances. Such a "dual method" processing system would permit filers to choose between electronic and paper filing. It therefore would likely appear to some filers to be more cost-efficient than the uniform requirement to file electronically that the Department is proposing. However, while a "dual method" processing system might be popular with some filers, such a system would perpetuate the inefficiencies inherent in paper filings - larger number of filing errors, required correspondence with filers, increased likelihood of civil penalties, delays in reviews of filings, and increased risks to participants and beneficiaries resulting from erroneous data or delayed enforcement. It therefore does not appear to be in the interest of plans or participants to maintain such a system. In addition, the maintenance of such a system would entail additional costs for the Federal government (and by extension taxpayers) because it would be necessary to incorporate into the system the ability to receive and process a potentially large number of paper filings. In the Department's view, the additional costs for such a complex processing system would be virtually prohibitive for the Federal government in light of current budgetary constraints on the Federal government generally and on the Department in particular. Under such constraints, maintaining a paper filing system would consume resources that would be better devoted to enhancing the system's electronic filing capabilities or carrying out other Department functions.

Second, the Department considered the alternative of continuing the present paper processing system on a short-term interim basis during

[21] Joanne H. Pratt, "E-Biz: Strategies for Small Business Success" 32 (2002) (prepared for the SBA Office of Advocacy), available at http://www.sba.gov/advo/research/rs220tot.pdf.

[22] Id. at 6.

[23] Id.

[24] Id. at 6-8.

[25] Id. at 11.

[26] Id. at 23-24.

[27] SBA Office of Advocacy, "Self Employment and Computer Usage," 3 (2003), available at http://www.sba.gov/ADVO/stats/sepc.pdf.

[28] Stephen B. Pociask, TeleNomic Research, LLC, "A Survey of Small Businesses' Telecommunications Use and Spending" 71 (2004) (prepared for SBA Office of Advocacy), available at http://www.sba.gov/advo/research/rs236tot.pdf.

[29] *See*, e.g., "Electronic Government: Challenges Must Be Addressed with Effective Leadership and Management," Hearing on S.803 Before the Senate Comm. in Governmental Affairs, 106th Cong. 1 (July 11, 2001) (statement of David McClure, Director, Informa-

tion Technology Management Issues, GAO), available at http://www.gao.gov/new.items/d01959t.pdf.

[30] Susie Trinkle, Capella Univ., "Moving Citizens from in line to Online: How the Internet is Changing How Government Serves its Citizens" (Sept. 10, 2001, available at http://oma.od.nih.gov/ma/bps/bpkm/Resource/Y_MovingCitizensFromLineOn.doc.

[31] Hart-Teeter, "E-Government: the Next American Revolution" (Sept. 28, 2000) available at http://www.excelgov.org/displaycontent.asp?keyword=mReleases&NewsItemID=2559.

[32] Testimony of David A. McClure, GAO, before the Subcommittee on Government Management, Information and Technology, Committee on Government Reform, House of Representatives (2000), as reported in Karen Laynea and Jungwoo Leeb, *Government Information Quarterly* 18 (2001), 122-136.

[33] William D. Eggers, Global Director, Deloitte Research-Public Sector, "Citizen Advantage: Enhancing Economic Competitiveness Through e-Government" 1 (2004).

[34] Gassan Al-Kibsi; Kito de Boer; Mona Mourshed; Nigel P. Rea; "Putting citizens on-line, not in line," McKinsey Quarterly 2001 no. 2.

[35] *See* Eggers, supra note 25 at 7, 14.

the initial years of operating a new, solely electronic processing system. This alternative would enable filers to gain familiarity with the new paperless system as part of the transition process. As with the prior approach, this approach would continue, albeit for a limited period, the current inefficiencies of a paper system and the substantial costs of maintaining tandem operations, particularly since continuing the old processing system would require "sole source" non-competitive yearly contractual negotiations with the current contractor, with ever increasing additional costs. For example, in fiscal year 2006 the Department requested an additional $2.1 million to maintain current operations in the first year of a sole source contract.

Third, the Department considered developing a new processing system that would have the temporary capacity to process paper filings from a targeted group of filers under an exception from the electronic filing requirement. For reasons described below under "Small Plans," the Department considered it appropriate to limit the exception to small plans that had previously filed government printed "hand-print" forms and that are not subject to the audit requirement. The Department believes that making such an exception available, at least for the first few years of operating the new processing system, might provide a small net benefit to at least some proportion of this class of filers. However, the Department believes this potential benefit, which could amount (as explained further below) to as little as $14 per plan on average for 74,000 plans or as much as $249 per plan on average for 7,400 plans, is outweighed by the benefits to participants and beneficiaries at large, and to the Department and taxpayers generally, of implementing a single, wholly electronic filing system beginning with reports for the 2007 plan year. The maintenance of any paper system, even on a reduced scale, is inherently inefficient and unnecessarily costly and could undermine full realization of the potential benefits of electronic filing for ERISA compliance and enforcement, thereby exposing some plans and participants to unnecessary risk. Accordingly, the Department rejected this alternative, along with the other two considered alternatives, in favor of a uniform requirement to file electronically.

The Department's consideration of this third alternative, and its basis for rejecting it in favor of a uniform requirement to file electronically, is detailed below under the heading "Small Plans."

Small Plans

The Department believes this regulation may have a significant impact on a substantial number of small plans. As for all other plans, costs and benefits for small plans are expected to vary with the plans' circumstances. Most will likely incur moderate transition costs and subsequently realize moderate ongoing savings. Some, however, may experience larger impacts, including both larger transition costs and/or ongoing net cost increases rather than ongoing net savings. For example, some small plans may lack experience with or easy access to the Internet. Such plans may incur larger than typical transition costs to gain access to the Internet (or to enlist a service provider with access) and may find it more time consuming, and therefore more costly, to prepare their filing on a government website (or to interact with a service provider) than to prepare their filing using a government printed form that is completed "by hand" and filed on paper through the mails. The Department expects that only a minority of plans might be so affected, but that minority might nonetheless represent a substantial number.

The Department therefore conducted an initial regulatory flexibility analysis, repeating the above analysis while limiting the scope to include only small plans - that is, those with fewer than 100 participants. On that basis, it is estimated that 667,000 small plans will incur one-time transition costs of $18 million, including $9 million for 78,000 current hand-print filers and $9 million for 589,000 current machine-print filers. It is further estimated that small plans would realize ongoing materials and postage savings of approximately $700,000 annually and could realize up to $7 million in savings annually from the elimination of the need to correct deficient filings (including $2 million accruing to hand-print filers and $5 million to machine-print), for a total of approximately $8 million in annual savings. As with all other plans, over time the aggregate ongoing savings realized by small plans are expected to outweigh their aggregate one-time transition costs. Over five years, savings are estimated to exceed costs by $17 million (discounting future savings at a rate of 7 percent). The Department believes that impacts may vary among small plans, depending for example on their (or their service providers') access to and familiarity with associated technologies, and possibly on their size. The Department, however, lacks a basis on which to estimate such variations. The Department

invites comments on this assessment of the impact of the proposed regulation on small plans.

The Department also assessed the costs and benefits of alternative approaches. As noted above, the Department considered proposing a temporary exception from the requirement to file electronically for certain small plans. The Department undertook to develop as an alternative to a uniform electronic filing requirement an exception provision that would maximize benefits and minimize costs to affected parties including plans, participants, and taxpayers.

The Department first considered the criteria that should be adopted to designate filers eligible to continue to file on paper under the exception. The Department selected as the first criterion plan size. Small plans (and the small businesses that sponsor them) may be less likely than large ones to use computers and the Internet or to have current expertise in such usage. They may be harder pressed to devote resources to making a transition to electronic filing. Moreover, transition costs may be largely fixed costs (invariant to plan size) and therefore more burdensome to small than to large plans. The Department considered alternative plan size thresholds, including plans with fewer than 100, fewer than 25, or fewer than 10 participants. The threshold of fewer than 100 participants seemed most desirable. It is consistent with the threshold used for other distinctions in annual reporting requirements and therefore would not add additional complexity to reporting requirements. In addition, the overall systems requirements associated with an exception for plans with fewer than 100 participants would be expected to differ little from those associated with an exception limited to smaller plans. The cost of building, maintaining and periodically updating a system capable of accepting and processing paper filings is largely invariant to the number of paper filings to be accepted. Moreover, the number of plans eligible for the exception would not vary much across the thresholds considered. Among plans not subject to the audit requirement and filing by the hand-print method, the Department estimates that 74,000 have fewer than 100 participants, 59,000 fewer than 25, and 46,000 fewer than 10.

The second criterion identified by the Department was past filing method. As noted above, it is likely that hand-print filers will confront higher average transition costs than machine-print filers. Machine-print filers currently prepare their filings electronically, even if they do not file them electronically. In contrast, some fraction of hand-print filers may be entirely without computing infrastructure.

A third criterion identified by the Department was potential risk to participants. As noted above, hand-print filings are more prone to error than machine-print or electronic filings. In addition, processing of paper filings is inherently slower than processing of electronic filings. Therefore, continued acceptance of paper filings has the potential to slow both detection of ERISA violations and enforcement actions to address such violations.[36] The Department therefore considered approaches that would limit the exception to situations where risks of violations (and associated threats to participants) were less, such as in connection with plans that, because of the presence of other safeguards and/or absence of certain risks, were not required to provide financial audits with their annual reports.

Finally, the Department considered the appropriate duration of such an exception. To accommodate such an exception, the Department's new processing system would need to incorporate an ability to receive and process some number of paper filings. The incorporation of this ability into the system would entail a relatively large, up-front development cost, followed by smaller but substantial ongoing costs to process paper filings. It therefore seemed reasonable to consider as the duration of such an exception the expected minimum "lifetime" of the new system (which corresponds to the expected duration of the contract that will develop and maintain it), which is five years. The Department next considered whether a five-year exception would be sufficient to accomplish the exception's goal of easing small plans' transition to electronic filing. Assuming continued rapid proliferation of computer and Internet usage, it seems likely that five years would be sufficient to accomplish this goal.

Based on this reasoning, the Department considered, as an alternative to a uniform 100 percent electronic filing requirement, a five-year exception for plans that: (1) have fewer than 100 participants, (2) previously filed their annual reports using government printed "hand-print" forms, and (3) are not subject to the audit requirement for annual reporting under Title I of ERISA. The Department estimates that use of these criteria would create a class of 74,000 filers eligible for the temporary exception from electronic filing.

---

[36] This concerns not merely reporting violations, but all potential ERISA violations, including those which might directly jeopardize plan assets or participants' benefits.

As noted above, small plans are estimated to face an aggregate transition cost of $18 million, followed by ongoing annual savings of $8 million. Over time the aggregate savings will outweigh the cost. But, also as noted above, a disproportionate share of the transition cost, $9 million, is estimated to accrue to the small minority of small plans that file via the hand-print method. The savings accruing to these filers, being attributable to reduced materials and postage and, more important, reduced filing errors, if proportionate to their numbers, will amount to $2 million.

The Department undertook to carefully consider the potential costs and benefits to small plans of the exception defined above. Approximately 74,000 plans could be eligible for the exception. The Department considered two potential scenarios.

In the first scenario, the Department assumed that all eligible plans would file on paper, for an average of three of the five years for which paper filings would be permitted. The Department assumed further that these plans' average transition costs and ongoing savings would be the same as the average assumed earlier for all small plan hand-print filers.[37] The Department also assumed that, by taking advantage of the exception, these filers would reduce their transition cost to the level assumed earlier to be incurred by machine-print filers, but would delay commencement of the ongoing savings available through electronic filing until they began filing electronically (on average after three years). In this scenario, the 74,000 filers taking advantage of the exception would reduce their transition costs by $6.5 million on aggregate, while sacrificing $5.5 million in potential ongoing savings, thereby realizing a net benefit of approximately $1 million, or $14 per filer.

In the second scenario, the Department considered the possibility that the transition cost might vary widely across filers. The Department assumed that just 10 percent of eligible filers would take advantage of the exception (again for an average of three years), but that these filers would face a transition cost (absent the exception) of three times the average assumed for all hand-print filers. Other assumptions were the same as in the first scenario. In this scenario, 7,400 filers taking advantage of the exception would reduce their transition costs by $2.4 million on aggregate, while sacrificing $550,000 in potential ongoing savings, thereby realizing a net benefit of approximately $1.8 million, or $249 per filer.

On the basis of these scenarios, the Department believes that some filers would likely benefit from the exception. However, as noted above, the potential net benefit to a given filer from the exception would be modest. In the first scenario, the average net benefit would amount to just $12 per plan using the exception; in the second, $249 per plan. Further, the availability of the exception would create significant risks to participants and costs to the government (and taxpayers). As discussed above, the maintenance of any paper system, even on a relatively small scale, is inherently inefficient and costly. Also, as discussed above, paper filings take longer to process and therefore pose unnecessary compliance risks. Therefore, the Department concluded that the potential benefit of a limited exception would be outweighed by the associated cost to the government (and to taxpayers) and the potential risks to participants and that adoption of a limited exception could not be justified. For these reasons, the Department rejected the alternative of providing an exception in favor of a uniform requirement to file electronically.

Paperwork Reduction Act

This proposed regulation does not introduce, or materially modify, any information collection requirement, but furthers the Department's goal of automating the submission of the Form 5500 return/report. As such, this notice of proposed rulemaking is not subject to the requirements of the Paperwork Reduction Act of 1995 (44 U.S.C. 3501 et seq.) because it does not contain a "collection of information" as defined in 44 U.S.C. 3502(3).

Congressional Review Act

The notice of proposed rulemaking being issued here is subject to the provisions of the Congressional Review Act provisions of the Small Business Regulatory Enforcement Fairness Act of 1996 (5 U.S.C. 801 et seq.) and, if finalized, will be transmitted to the Congress and the Comptroller General for review.

Unfunded Mandates Reform Act

Pursuant to provisions of the Unfunded Mandates Reform Act of 1995 (Pub. L. 104-4), this rule does not include any Federal mandate that may result in expenditures by State, local, or tribal governments, or the private sector, which may impose an annual burden of $100 million or more.

List of Subjects in 29 CFR Part 2520

Employee benefit plans, pensions, reporting and recordkeeping requirements

For the reasons set forth in the preamble, the Department proposes to amend 29 CFR part 2520 as follows:

1. The authority section of Part 2520 continues to read as follows:

Authority: 29 U.S.C. 1021-1025, 1027, 1029-31, 1059, 1134, and 1135; Secretary of Labor's Order 1-2003, 68 FR 5374 (Feb. 3, 2003). Sec. 2520.101-2 also issued under 29 U.S.C. 1132, 1181-1183, 1181 note, 1185, 1185a-b, 1191, and 1191a-c. Secs. 2520.102-3, 2520.104b-1, and 2520.104b-3 also issued under 29 U.S.C. 1003, 1181-1183, 1181 note, 1185, 1185a-b, 1191, and 1191a-c. Secs. 2520.104b-1 and 2520.107 also issued under 26 U.S.C. 401 note, 111 Stat. 788.

2. Add § 2520.104a-2 after § 2520.104a-1 to read as follows:

§ 2520.104a-2 Electronic Filing of Annual Reports.

(a) Any Form 5500 Annual Return/Report (including accompanying statements or schedules) to be filed with the Secretary for any plan year (or reporting year, in the case of common or collective trusts, pooled separate accounts, and similar non-plan entities) beginning on or after January 1, 2007, shall be filed electronically in accordance with the instructions, and such other guidance as the Secretary may provide, applicable to such report.

(b) Nothing in paragraph (a) of this section is intended to alter or affect the duties of any person to retain records or to disclose information to participants, beneficiaries, or the Secretary.

3. Amend § 2520.103-1 by revising paragraph (f) as follows:

§ 2520.103-1 Contents of the annual report.

* * * * *

(f) *Electronic filing.* Except as provided in § 2520.104a-2 of this chapter, the Form 5500 "Annual Return/Report of Employee Benefit Plan" may be filed electronically or through other media in accordance with the instructions accompanying the form, provided the plan administrator maintains an original copy, with all required signatures, as part of the plan's records.

4. Amend § 2520.103-2 by revising paragraph (c) as follows:

§ 2520.103-2 Contents of the annual report for a group insurance arrangement.

* * * * *

(c) *Electronic filing.* Except as provided in § 2520.104a-2 of this chapter, the Form 5500 "Annual Return/Report of Employee Benefit Plan" may be filed electronically or through other media in accordance with the instructions accompanying the form, provided the trust or other entity described in § 2520.104-43(b) maintains an original copy, with all required signatures, as part of the trust's or entity's records.

5. Amend § 2520.103-9 by revising paragraph (d) as follows:

§ 2520.103-9 Direct filing for bank or insurance carrier trusts and accounts.

* * * * *

(d) *Method of filing.* Except as provided in § 2520.104a-2 of this chapter, the Form 5500 "Annual Return/Report of Employee Benefit Plan" may be filed electronically or through other media in accordance with the instructions accompanying the form, provided the bank or insurance company which maintains the common or collective trust or pooled separate account maintains an original copy, with all required signatures, as part of its records.

6. Amend § 2520.103-12 by revising paragraph (f) as follows:

§ 2520.103-12 Limited exemption and alternative method of compliance for annual reporting of investments in certain entities.

* * * * *

(f) *Method of filing.* Except as provided in § 2520.104a-2 of this chapter, the Form 5500 "Annual Return/Report of Employee Benefit Plan" may

---

[37] This assumption seems reasonable insofar as an estimated 94 percent of all small hand-print filers were not subject to the audit requirement and therefore would be eligible for the exception.

be filed electronically or through other media in accordance with the instructions accompanying the form provided the entity described in paragraph (c) of this section maintains an original copy, with all required signatures, as part of its records.

Signed at Washington, D.C., this *23d* day of *August*, 2005.

Ann L. Combs

Assistant Secretary

Employee Benefits Security Administration

¶ 20,534Z

EBSA proposed regulations: Form 5500: Annual reporting: Electronic filing .—EBSA has proposed amendments to annual reporting regulations to conform them to Form 5500 electronic filing requirements.

The proposed regulations, which were published in the *Federal Register* on July 21, 2006 (71 FR 41392), are reproduced below.

DEPARTMENT OF LABOR

Employee Benefits Security Administration

29 CFR Part 2520

RIN 1210-AB06

Annual Reporting and Disclosure

AGENCY: Employee Benefits Security Administration, Labor.

ACTION: Proposed rule.

SUMMARY: This document contains proposed amendments to Department of Labor (Department) regulations relating to annual reporting and disclosure requirements under Part 1 of Subtitle B of Title I of the Employee Retirement Income Security Act of 1974, as amended (ERISA or Act). The proposed amendments contained in this document are necessary to conform the annual reporting and disclosure regulations to proposed revisions to the Form 5500 Annual Return/Report of Employee Benefit Plan forms and instructions. The proposed changes to the Form 5500 and implementing regulatory amendments are intended to facilitate the transition to an electronic filing system, separately proposed at 70 FR 51542 (August 30, 2005), reduce and streamline annual reporting burdens, especially for small businesses, and update the annual reporting forms to reflect current issues and agency priorities. The regulatory amendments thus would, upon adoption, apply for the reporting year for which the electronic filing requirement is implemented. The proposed regulatory amendments will affect the financial and other information required to be reported and disclosed by employee benefit plans filing the Form 5500 Annual Return/Report of Employee Benefit Plan under Part 1 of Subtitle B of Title I of ERISA.

DATES: Written comments must be received by the Department of Labor on or before September 19, 2006.

ADDRESSES: Comments should be addressed to the Office of Regulations and Interpretations, Employee Benefits Security Administration (EBSA), Room N-5669, U.S. Department of Labor, 200 Constitution Avenue, NW., Washington, DC 20210. Attn: Form 5500 Regulation Revisions (RIN 1210-AB06). Comments also may be submitted electronically to *e-ori@dol.gov* or by using the Federal eRulemaking Portal *http://www.regulations.gov* (follow instructions for submission of comments). EBSA will make all comments available to the public on its Web site at *http://www.dol.gov/ebsa*. The comments also will be available for public inspection at the Public Disclosure Room, N-1513, EBSA, U.S. Department of Labor, 200 Constitution Avenue, NW., Washington, DC 20210.

FOR FURTHER INFORMATION CONTACT: Elizabeth A. Goodman or Michael Baird, Office of Regulations and Interpretations, Employee Benefits Security Administration, U.S. Department of Labor, (202) 693-8523 (not a toll-free number).

SUPPLEMENTARY INFORMATION:

A. Background

Under Titles I and IV of ERISA, and the Internal Revenue Code (Code), as amended, pension and other employee benefit plans are generally required to file annual returns/reports concerning, among other things, the financial condition and operations of the plan. Filing the Form 5500 "Annual Return/Report of Employee Benefit Plan," together with any required attachments and schedules (Form 5500 Annual Return/Report) generally satisfies these annual reporting requirements. The Form 5500 Annual Return/Report is the primary source of information concerning the operation, funding, assets, and investments of pension and other employee benefit plans. In addition to

being an important disclosure document for plan participants and beneficiaries, the Form 5500 Annual Return/Report is a compliance and research tool for the Department and a source of information and data for use by other federal agencies, Congress, and the private sector in assessing employee benefit, tax, and economic trends and policies.

B. Discussion of the Proposed Revisions to Part 2520

1. Section 2520.103-1

The Department of Labor (Department) annual reporting regulations, including § 2520.103-1, are promulgated under the provisions of ERISA that authorize the creation of limited exemptions and simplified reporting and disclosure for welfare plans under ERISA section 104(a)(3), simplified annual reports under ERISA section 104(a)(2)(A) for pension plans that cover fewer than 100 participants, and alternative methods of compliance for all pension plans under ERISA section 110(a). Various changes are being proposed to the Form 5500 Annual Return/Report and its instructions in a Notice of Proposed Form Revisions published today in the **Federal Register**. To accommodate those form and instruction changes, the regulatory amendments to 29 CFR 2520.103-1 are being proposed to update the references to the annual report to reflect the new structure and components of the Form 5500 Annual Return/Report.

The following subsections outline major changes to the Form 5500. A more comprehensive discussion of the form and instructions changes is in the above-referenced Notice of Proposed Forms Revisions. Facsimiles of the proposed form revisions and proposed form instructions can be viewed on the EBSA's Web site at *http://www.dol.gov/ebsa*.[1] To avoid unnecessary duplication, only a general summary of the form and instruction changes is included in this notice as background for the required cost/benefit and regulatory analysis discussions. For a comprehensive discussion of form and instruction changes, see the Notice of Proposed Forms Revisions published concurrently in today's **Federal Register**.

(a) Short Form 5500 (Eligible Small Plan Filers)

A new two-page Form 5500 Annual Return/Report of Employee Benefit Plan—the Form 5500-SF (Short Form 5500)—is being proposed in an effort to streamline the reporting requirements for certain small pension and welfare plans (generally, plans with fewer than 100 participants) that have investment portfolios in which their assets are held by regulated financial institutions and the investments have a readily determinable fair market value as described in the proposed regulation at § 2520.103-1(c)(2)(iii). A detailed description of the proposed Form 5500-SF and a facsimile of the form is in the Notice of Proposed Forms Revisions being published concurrently in today's **Federal Register**. Substantially all of the information required to be reported by employee benefit plans on the proposed Short Form 5500 currently is included in that information required to be reported as part of the Form 5500 Annual Return/Report under the simplified reporting options presently available to small plans. The proposal would not eliminate the existing simplified reporting options for small plans but, rather, would add the Short Form 5500 as another simplified reporting option for eligible small plans.

The Internal Revenue Service (IRS) has advised the Department that, although there are no mandatory electronic filing requirements for the Form 5500 under the Code or the regulations issued thereunder, to ease the burdens on plans that are not subject to Title I of ERISA but that file the Form 5500-EZ to satisfy the annual reporting and filing obligations imposed by the Code, the IRS is proposing to permit certain Form 5500-EZ filers to satisfy the requirement to file the Form 5500-EZ with the IRS by filing the proposed Short Form 5500 electronically through the EFAST processing system. Therefore, under

---

[1] Paper copies of the proposed form revisions and proposed instructions may be obtained by telephoning 1-866-444-EBSA (3272) (this is a toll-free number).

the IRS' proposal, certain Form 5500-EZ filers will be provided both electronic and paper filing options. The electronic option will allow 5500-EZ filers to complete and electronically file with EFAST selected information on the Short Form 5500. 5500-EZ filers will also be able to choose instead to file a Form 5500-EZ on paper with the IRS.[2]

(b) Removal of Internal Revenue Service-Only Schedules From the Form 5500 Annual Return/Report

Under the proposal the Form 5500 Annual Return/Report will no longer include any of the schedules from the current Form 5500 Annual Return/Report that are required only for the IRS. This will effectuate the adoption of a wholly electronic filing requirement for the Form 5500 Annual Return/Report given the current limitations on the IRS's authority to mandate electronic filing of certain tax returns. Accordingly, under the proposal, the following schedules will no longer be required to be filed as part of the Form 5500 Annual Return/Report: Schedule E (ESOP Annual Information), Schedule P (Annual Return of Fiduciary of Employee Benefit Trust), and Schedule SSA (Annual Registration Statement Identifying Separated Participants With Deferred Vested Benefits). The IRS, however, has advised the Department that it intends that plan administrators, employers, and certain other entities that are subject to filing and reporting requirements under the Code will have to continue to satisfy any applicable requirements in accordance with IRS revenue procedures, regulations, publications, forms, and instructions. In that regard, the IRS has independently eliminated the Schedule P from the 2006 Form 5500 in anticipation of the transition to a wholly electronic filing environment. Further, as described elsewhere in this document, the Department is proposing to move to the Schedule R three questions on ESOP information formerly reported on the Schedule E, and the IRS has advised the Department that it does not anticipate requiring separate filings by ESOPs on the remaining questions from the Schedule E. The IRS is evaluating the information collected on Schedule SSA, and considering whether other existing information collections could be used in place of the Form 5500 Annual Return/Report.

(c) Schedule A (Insurance Information)

Schedule A must be attached to the Form 5500 Annual Return/ Report for an ERISA-covered plan if any pension or welfare benefits under the plan are provided by, or if the plan holds any investment contracts with, an insurance company or other similar organization. Although the proposal would retain most of the Schedule A data substantially unchanged, the Department is proposing to add a line item to give administrators a specific space on the Schedule A to report the failure by an insurance carrier to provide necessary information. Certain other technical changes are being proposed to the Schedule A form and instructions to improve Schedule A as a tool for disclosure of insurance fees and commissions.

(d) Schedule B (Actuarial Information)

Schedule B is required for defined benefit pension plans subject to the minimum funding standards (see Code section 412 and Part 3 of Title I of ERISA). The Pension Benefit Guaranty Corporation (PBGC) proposes adding questions to the Schedule B designed to obtain a "look-through" allocation of plan investments in certain pooled investment funds for certain very large defined benefit plans. Under the proposal, defined benefits plans with more than 1,000 participants would be required to breakout the percentage of total plan assets held as "stock," "debt," "real estate," and "other." The underlying investments in master trusts, common or collective trusts, pooled separate accounts, and other pooled investment vehicles, would be required to be broken out and could not be treated merely as "other," regardless of how they are listed on Schedule H. For investments in "debt," plans would be required to provide the "Macaulay duration" and break out the percentages held as government debt, investment-grade corporate debt, and high-yield corporate debt.

(e) Schedule C (Service Provider Information)

Schedule C must be attached to the Form 5500 Annual Return/ Report filed by large plan filers to report any person who rendered services to the plan that received directly or indirectly $5,000 or more in compensation from the plan during the plan year, and to report terminated accountants or actuaries. Consistent with recommendations of the ERISA Advisory Council Working Groups and the Government Accountability Office (GAO), EBSA has concluded that more information should be disclosed on the Form 5500 Annual Return/Report regarding plan fees and expenses. *See ERISA Advisory Council Report of*

the Working Group on Plan Fees and Reporting on Form 5500 (November 10, 2004) (available on the Internet at: *http://www.dol.gov/ebsa/ publications*) and the Government Accountability Office (*See Private Pensions: Government Actions Could Improve the Timeliness and Content of Form 5500 Pension Information,* GAO-05-491) (available on the Internet at: *http://www.gao.gov*). EBSA's proposal would continue to limit Schedule C reporting to large plan filers and would retain the $5,000 reporting threshold, but would revise the Schedule C and accompanying instructions to clarify the requirements regarding reporting of direct and indirect compensation (*i.e.,* money or anything else of value) received during the plan year in connection with services rendered to the plan or the person's position with the plan. Also, a new section would be added requiring that the source and nature of compensation in excess of $1,000 received from parties other than the plan or the plan sponsor be disclosed for certain key service providers, including, among others, investment managers, consultants, brokers, and trustees, as well as all other fiduciaries.

(f) Schedule R (Retirement Plan Information)

In light of the proposed removal of the Schedule E (ESOP Annual Information), certain questions from the Schedule E are being incorporated into the Schedule R in order to continue to collect certain information regarding ESOPs as part of the Form 5500 Annual Return/ Report. In addition, multiemployer defined benefit pension plans would have to provide a list identifying each employer contributing an annual amount equal to or greater than five percent of all annual contributions to the plan (measured in dollars) and setting forth (1) the name of the contributing employer; (2) employer's employer identification number (EIN); (3) dollar amount contributed; (4) contribution rate; (5) whether the contribution base unit measure was hourly, weekly, unit of product, or other; and (6) expiration date for the collective bargaining agreement pursuant to which contributions are required to be made to the plan.

(g) Technical and Conforming Changes for Forms and Instructions

Various other technical and conforming changes are being proposed as part of the restructuring of the Form 5500 Annual Return/Report. Several of the more significant changes include: (1) Revision of the instructions for the Form 5500 Annual Return/Report and development of instructions for the Short Form 5500 to reflect the new structure of the reports and electronic filing requirements; (2) addition of questions regarding compliance with the Department's blackout notice regulation in 29 CFR 2510.101-3; (3) addition of a compliance question on whether the plan failed to pay benefits when due under the plan; (4) expansion of the use of codes to report plan feature information on pension and welfare benefit plans; (5) elimination of the optional entry of the name and the EIN of the preparer; (6) requiring administrative expenses to be reported separately from other expenses on the Schedule I; (7) addition of a question on whether any minimum funding amount reported for a pension plan will be met by the funding deadline; and (8) adoption of a standard format for use in connection with an independent qualified public accountant (IQPA) rendering an opinion on the supplemental schedule information on Line 4a of Schedule H and I relating to delinquent participant contributions.

2. Section 2520.104-44

Section 2520.104-44 and the current Form 5500 Annual Return/ Report instructions provide for limited reporting for pension plans exclusively using a tax deferred annuity arrangement under Code section 403(b)(1), custodial accounts for regulated investment company stock under Code section 403(b)(7), or a combination of both. Under the proposal, the exemption in § 2520.104-44(b)(3) would be eliminated, with the result that Code section 403(b) pension plans subject to Title I would be treated the same as any other Title I pension plan for purposes of the annual reporting requirements under Title I of ERISA. With the growth in the size and number of Code section 403(b) arrangements, and the advent of Code section 401(k) plans, the Code 403(b) arrangements have become more like Code section 401(k) plans. In this regard, the IRS has undertaken to update certain of its regulations. *See* 69 FR 67075, 67076 (November 16, 2004). For those section 403(b) plans that are subject to Title I of ERISA, the Department has detected violations in a high percentage of its investigations of Code section 403(b) plans. The predominant issue has been improper handling of employee contributions. The Department believes that these developments warrant amending the annual reporting requirements to put Code section 403(b) plans on par with other ERISA-covered pension plans. Small Code section 403(b) plans generally

---

[2] Under the voluntary electronic filing option, 5500-EZ filers filing an amended return for a plan year must file the amended return electronically using the Form 5500-SF if they initially filed electronically for the plan year and must file with the IRS using the paper Form 5500-EZ if they filed for plan year with the IRS on a paper Form 5500-EZ.

would be 100 percent invested in eligible assets for purposes of filing the proposed Short Form 5500.

3. Section 2520.104-46

In accordance with the Department's authority under section 104(a)(2)(A) and 104(a)(3) of ERISA, the Department has adopted, at 29 CFR 2520.104-41, simplified annual reporting requirements for pension and welfare benefit plans with fewer than 100 participants. In addition, the Department, at 29 CFR 2520.104-46, has prescribed for such small plans a waiver from the requirements of section 103(a)(3)(A) to engage an IQPA and to include the opinion of the accountant as part of the plan's annual report. The waiver of the IQPA requirements for pension plans was conditioned, among other requirements, on enhanced disclosure in the Summary Annual Report (SAR) provided to participants and beneficiaries. In that regard, the Department prepared a model notice that plans could use to satisfy the enhanced SAR disclosure conditions. That model notice has been available at the EBSA's Web site at *http://www.dol.gov/ebsa*. In order to provide plan administrators with additional access to the model notice and facilitate compliance with the audit waiver and Short Form 5500 eligibility conditions, the Department is proposing to add the model notice as an appendix to § 2520.104-46.

4. Section 2520.104b-10

Section 104(b)(3) of ERISA provides in part that, each year, administrators must furnish to participants and beneficiaries receiving benefits under a plan materials that fairly summarize the plan's annual report. Section 2520.104b-10 sets forth the requirements for the SAR and prescribes formats for such reports. The amendments being proposed do not include any change to the SAR requirements. However, in order to facilitate compliance with the SAR requirement for Short Form 5500 filers, the Department is updating its cross-reference guide to correspond to the line items of the SAR to the relevant line items on the Short Form 5500. The cross-reference guide, as before, would continue to be an appendix to § 2520.104b-10.

C. Findings on the Revised Form 5500 Annual Return/Report (including Short Form 5500) as a Limited Exemption and Alternative Method of Compliance

Section 104(a)(2)(A) of the Act authorizes the Secretary of Labor (Secretary) to prescribe by regulation simplified reporting for pension plans that cover fewer than 100 participants. Section 104(a)(3) authorizes the Secretary to exempt any welfare plan from all or part of the reporting and disclosure requirements of Title I of ERISA or to provide simplified reporting and disclosure if the Secretary finds that such requirements are inappropriate as applied to such plans. Section 110 permits the Secretary to prescribe for pension plans alternative methods of complying with any of the reporting and disclosure requirements if the Secretary finds that: (1) The use of the alternative method is consistent with the purposes of Title I of ERISA, provides adequate disclosure to plan participants and beneficiaries, and provides adequate reporting to the Secretary; (2) application of the statutory reporting and disclosure requirements would increase costs to the plan or impose unreasonable administrative burdens with respect to the operation of the plan; and (3) the application of the statutory reporting and disclosure requirements would be adverse to the interests of plan participants in the aggregate.

For purposes of Title I of ERISA, the filing of a completed Form 5500 Return/Report, including the filing of the proposed Short Form 5500, in accordance with the instructions and related regulations, generally would constitute compliance with the limited exemption and alternative method of compliance in 29 CFR 2520.103-1(b). The findings required under ERISA sections 104(a)(3) and 110 relating to the use of the proposed revised Form 5500 Annual Return/Report, including the proposed Short Form 5500, as alternative methods of compliance, simplified report, and limited exemption from the reporting and disclosure requirements of part 1 of Title I of ERISA are set forth below.

In proposing revisions to the Form 5500 Annual Return/Report and the amendments in this proposed rulemaking, the Department has attempted to balance the needs of participants, beneficiaries, and of the Department to obtain information necessary to protect ERISA rights and interests with the needs of administrators to minimize costs attendant with the reporting of information to the federal government. The Department makes the following findings under sections 104(a)(3) and 110 of the Act with regard to the use of the revised Form 5500 Annual Return/Report as a simplified report, alternative method of compliance, and limited exemption pursuant to 29 CFR 2520.103-1(b).

The use of the proposed revised Form 5500 Annual Return/Report, including the proposed Short Form 5500, is consistent with the purposes of Title I of ERISA and provides adequate disclosure to participants and beneficiaries and adequate reporting to the Secretary. While the information that would be required to be reported on or in connection with the revised Form 5500 Annual Return/Report and the proposed Short Form 5500 deviates, as before, in some respects, from that delineated in section 103 of the Act, the information essential to ensuring adequate disclosure and reporting under Title I is required to be included on or as part of the Form 5500 Annual Return/Report, as proposed to be revised, and the proposed Short Form 5500.

The use of Form 5500 Annual Return/Report, as revised, or the proposed Short Form 5500 will relieve plans subject to the annual reporting requirements from increased costs and unreasonable administrative burdens by providing a standardized format that facilitates reporting, eliminates duplicative reporting requirements, and simplifies the content of the annual report in general. The Form 5500 Annual Return/Report, under the proposed revision, including the proposed Short Form, is intended to further reduce the administrative burdens and costs attributable to compliance with the annual reporting requirements.

Taking into account the above, the Department has determined that application of the statutory annual reporting and disclosure requirements without the availability of the Form 5500 Annual Return/Report, including the proposed Short Form 5500, would be adverse to the interests of participants in the aggregate. The proposed revised Form 5500 Annual Return/Report provides for the reporting and disclosure of basic financial and other plan information described in section 103 of ERISA in a uniform, efficient, and understandable manner, thereby facilitating the disclosure of such information to plan participants and beneficiaries.

Finally, the Department has determined under section 104(a)(3) of ERISA that a strict application of the statutory reporting requirements, without taking into account the proposed revisions to the Form 5500 Annual Return/Report and the proposed Short Form 5500, would be inappropriate in the context of welfare plans for the same reasons discussed above (i.e., the streamlined form reduces filing burdens without impairing enforcement, research, and policy needs, while at the same time providing adequate disclosure to participants and beneficiaries).

D. Regulatory Impact Analysis

Executive Order 12866 Statement

Under Executive Order 12866, the Department must determine whether the regulatory action is "significant" and therefore subject to the requirements of the Executive Order and subject to review by the Office of Management and Budget (OMB). Under section 3(f) of Executive Order 12866, the order defines a "significant regulatory action" as an action that is likely to result in a rule (1) having an annual effect on the economy of $100 million or more, or adversely and materially affecting a sector of the economy, productivity, competition, jobs, the environment, public health or safety, or State, local or tribal governments or communities (also referred to as "economically significant"); (2) creating serious inconsistency or otherwise interfering with an action taken or planned by another agency; (3) materially altering the budgetary impacts of entitlement grants, user fees, or loan programs or the rights and obligations of recipients thereof; or (4) raising novel legal or policy issues arising out of legal mandates, the President's priorities, or the principles set forth in the Executive Order.

Pursuant to the terms of the Executive Order, it has been determined that this regulatory action will have an annual effect on the economy of more than $100 million. Therefore, this action is "economically significant" and subject to OMB review under section 3(f)(4) of Executive Order 12866. The Department accordingly has undertaken to assess the costs and benefits of this regulatory action in satisfaction of the applicable requirements of the Executive Order.

In accordance with OMB Circular A-4 (available at *http://www.whitehouse.gov/omb/circulars/a004/a-4.pdf*), Table 1 below depicts an accounting statement showing the net annual cost reduction associated with the provisions of this proposed rule. The Department believes that some employee benefit plans will see a decrease in costs and others might see an increase in costs due to this proposed rule. Further information about the amount of increase and decrease in costs for particular plan types is displayed in the cost section later on in this document. On aggregate, the Department estimates a cost reduction of up to $174 million in the first year.

TABLE 1.—ACCOUNTING STATEMENT: ESTIMATED COST REDUCTION FROM THE CURRENT REPORTING REQUIREMENTS TO THE PROPOSED 2008 REPORTING REQUIREMENTS

Category	Net cost reduction
Annualized Monetized Benefit	$174

Need for Regulatory Action

The annual reporting regulations for which amendments are being proposed provide specific limited exceptions, for certain types of welfare benefit plans, from the statutory reporting requirements; simplified reporting and disclosure requirements for other types of small plans; and an alternative method of compliance in general for all pension plans. In providing these special rules, the Department and the other Agencies intend to reduce the overall burden of the statutory reporting requirements without sacrificing the quality of the information collected.

As described in the preamble to the Department's proposal to require electronic filing of the Form 5500 (70 FR 51542) (E-Filing Proposal), the Department is in the process of creating a fully electronic filing system to receive the annual reports filed by employee benefit plans. In addition, as noted above, the Department has received reports from the GAO and the ERISA Advisory Council that suggest the need for some substantive changes to the annual reporting forms and the reporting regulations. The Department, in coordination with the IRS, and the PBGC (Agencies), also conducted a thorough review of the content requirements for the Form 5500. The Agencies believe the proposed regulatory and form changes, in conjunction with adoption of the electronic filing system, will substantially reduce plan administrators' reporting compliance burdens and also enhance the utility and accessibility of reported information to the government, participants and beneficiaries, and others.

The Form 5500 Annual Return/Report serves as the primary source of information concerning the operation, funding, assets, and investments of pension and other employee benefit plans. The Form 5500 Annual Return/Report is an important disclosure document for participants and beneficiaries, an enforcement and research tool for the Department, and a source of information and data for use by other federal agencies, Congress, and the private sector in assessing employee benefit, tax, and economic trends and policies. The Department in this proposal has attempted to balance the interests of participants, beneficiaries, and the Department in the protection of ERISA rights, as well as the public's interest in the availability of information on benefit plans, with plan administrators' and sponsors' interest in minimizing costs attendant with the reporting of information to the federal government. The Department believes that the proposed regulations' benefits justify the costs. The basis for this conclusion is explained below.

As stated in this preamble, the Department has determined that the use of the revised Form 5500 Annual Return/Report, including the proposed new Short Form 5500, would relieve plans subject to the annual reporting requirements from increased costs and administrative burdens by providing a standardized format that facilitates reporting, eliminates duplicative reporting requirements, and simplifies the content of the annual report in general.

Moreover, the Department believes that the revisions to the Form 5500 Annual Return/Report implemented by these proposed regulations, as compared to the existing form and schedules, will both reduce the cost of reporting, on aggregate and for a large majority of affected plans, and enhance the protection of ERISA rights.

Regulatory Alternatives

Executive Order 12866 directs Federal Agencies promulgating regulations to evaluate regulatory alternatives. The Department has concluded that, in connection with its proposal to move to a wholly electronic filing environment for employee benefit plan annual reports, form revisions and implementing regulatory changes should be made to facilitate the transition to an electronic filing system, reduce and streamline annual reporting burdens, especially for small businesses, and update the annual reporting forms to reflect current issues and agency priorities.

In developing the forms revisions and implementing regulatory changes, the Department was informed by recommendations made by GAO and the ERISA Advisory Council and conducted a thorough-going review of the current regulations and the scope of information collected, which included consideration of alternative methods of reaching its goals. The Department's consideration included, for example, different approaches to eligibility for the Short Form 5500, (see discussion in preamble to the Notice of Proposed Forms Revisions under the heading "Short Form 5500 as New Simplified Report for Certain Small Plans"), different approaches to reporting for welfare plans (see id. under the heading "F. Other Welfare Plan Issues"), and different approaches to improving the reporting of direct and indirect compensation paid to service providers (see id. under the heading "Schedule C: Compensation received by plan service providers"). Similarly, the Notice of Proposed Forms Revision discusses the assessments on how to balance the need for information to help the PBGC evaluate the financial solvency of multiemployer plans and the potential burden on administrators of multiemployer plans (see id. under the heading "Schedule R: Contributors to Multiemployer Pension Plans"). Inasmuch as the regulatory amendments contained in this Notice are intended to implement the forms revisions contained in the Notice of Proposed Forms Revisions, the discussions in the Notice of Proposed Forms Revisions are directly relevant to the Department's analysis under Executive Order 12866 and should be read as part of the Department's compliance with the requirements of the Executive Order. The Department therefore incorporates those discussions by this reference.

The public is invited to comment specifically on the decision points for the several categories of proposed revisions, and on the adequacy of the models, assumptions, and data developed in order to evaluate regulatory burden. In considering these alternatives, the Department weighted the objective of reduced regulatory burden against the need for adequate reporting and disclosure to insure the protection of plan participants, quantifying impacts where possible. For example:

• *Establishment of a Short Form 5500 for certain small plans:* In considering criteria of eligibility for filing the Short Form 5500 the Department evaluated both less stringent and more stringent criteria. If, for example, the Department had relied solely on the conditions for a waiver of the audit requirements for small plans, the Department believes that as many as 95 percent of small plans (612,000 plans) would meet the Short Form 5500 requirements. Because of concern about the need to limit eligibility to small plans with easy to value investment portfolios, however, the Department added the requirements of small plans that invest in secure assets that are held or issued by regulated financial institutions and that have a fair market value that is easily determined. In so doing, the Department estimates that approximately 90 percent of small plans (571,000 plans) that formerly were able to file under the simplified requirements would qualify as eligible to file the Short Form 5500. An additional 9,000 small Code section 403(b) plans would also qualify.

• *Addition of certain asset allocation and duration information to Schedule B:* Schedule B is filed by defined benefit pension plans subject to the minimum funding standards. As noted below, this revision will increase reporting costs for affected plans. The Agencies, however, believe that these costs are justified by the need to better monitor plan funding. In developing this proposed revision, the PBGC considered the approach that could balance the need for better monitoring of plan funding and the increased burden that would be incurred to provide additional information on the breakdown of assets and duration of debt instruments held by defined benefit plans. While the PBGC initially considered the application of the additional requirements to all large defined benefit plans (15,000 plans), it subsequently determined that additional information for the largest plans, i.e., those with more than 1,000 participants (5,000 plans), on the level and types of assets in the plan and the sensitivity of these assets to changes in market conditions would suffice for the desired improvement in the monitoring of plan funding.

Benefits and Costs

Benefits —These regulations and the Form 5500 Annual Return/Report and Short Form 5500 that the regulations implement will provide a standardized, streamlined alternative means of compliance with applicable statutory reporting requirements. In so doing, they will both ease plan administrators' compliance with reporting requirements and greatly enhance the utility and accessibility of information reported to the government, participants and beneficiaries, and others. In particular, the regulations and forms, together with the Department's planned program for assisting filers in the preparation and electronic submission of filings, will give plan administrators clear guidance and a supportive, routine mechanism for satisfying their reporting obligations. They also will make it possible to efficiently capture and assemble the information into an electronic data system. The data can then be processed and analyzed in the service of many beneficial activities. These include monitoring compliance with ERISA's reporting and other requirements, targeting, and carrying out prompt and effective enforcement actions; informing participants and beneficiaries of the characteristics, operations, and financial status of their benefit plans; producing statistics on the employee benefit system and monitoring trends therein and informing the public; and assembling information and conducting research that advances knowledge and fosters the formulation of sound public policies toward employee benefits. The Department believes that the benefits of the proposed regulations justify the costs.

The Department further believes that the revisions to the existing reporting requirements contained in the proposed regulations will both reduce aggregate reporting costs and enhance protection of ERISA rights. The former anticipated effect is quantified in the discussion of costs below. With respect to the latter, the Department developed each of the revisions contained in the proposed regulations either to enhance protections, or to reduce costs in ways that do not compromise protections. The revisions are considered separately below.

Removal of the IRS-only schedules: As explained in the Notice of Proposed Forms Revisions published simultaneously with these proposed regulations, this change is intended partly to facilitate a change to mandatory electronic filing—a change which is expected to yield substantial benefits. As also explained therein, to the extent that some Title I information may have been collected in these schedules, these proposed regulations provide for the ongoing collection of that information in other parts of the Annual Return/Report. In addition, it is the Department's understanding that some of the IRS-only information that will no longer be collected as part of the annual return/report may be collected in the future via other Treasury or IRS vehicles. The Department expects this revision to preserve protections of ERISA rights, while reducing Form 5500 Return/Report filing reporting costs as estimated below. From a broader societal perspective, the reduction in reporting costs may be less than what has been assumed here if IRS elects to collect some of this information through other channels.

Establishment of a Short Form 5500 for certain small plans: The Short Form 5500 is being developed with the specific intent of reducing reporting costs (as estimated below) while continuing to collect sufficient information to preserve ERISA protections, satisfying the enforcement, research, and regulatory needs of the Department and the other Agencies, and the disclosure needs of participants and beneficiaries. The Agencies determined that less information is needed in the case of small plans that invest in secure assets that are held or issued by regulated financial institutions and that have a fair market value that is easily determined. The Agencies believe that the eligibility conditions for Short Form 5500 filers, including the requirements relating to security and valuation of the plan's investments, ensure that the Short Form 5500 will provide adequate disclosure to the participants and beneficiaries in the plan and adequate annual reporting to the Agencies. The Notice of Proposed Forms Revisions published simultaneously with these proposed regulations details the content of the Short Form 5500 and elaborates on its adequacy for its intended purpose. Small plans that are not eligible to file the Short Form 5500 would continue to be able to file simplified reports as under the current system.

Elimination of the special reporting rules for Code section 403(b) plans: As noted below, this revision is expected to increase reporting costs for affected plans. However, the Department believes these added costs are justified by the need to enhance ERISA protections in connection with these plans the Department believes that developments with respect to Code section 403(b) plans, described above in connection with the proposed amendment to 2520.104-44, warrant amending the annual reporting requirements to put Code section 403(b) plans on par with other ERISA-covered pension plans. Small Code section 403(b) plans generally would be 100 percent invested in eligible assets for purposes of filing the proposed Short Form 5500. This would result in only a modest increase in the annual reporting burden on small Code section 403(b) plan filers.

Addition of certain asset allocation and duration information to Schedule B: As noted below, this revision will increase reporting costs for affected plans. The Agencies, however, believe that these costs are justified by the need to better monitor plan funding. The PBGC has found that it needs more information on the breakdown of assets and duration of debt instruments held by defined benefit plans. A plan's funded status is highly dependent on the level and types of assets in the plan and the sensitivity of these assets to changes in market conditions. Thus, the additional information required by this revision will improve the PBGC's ability to estimate the impact of economic changes on the financial status of the plans it insures, and by extension, on the future financial status of the PBGC. Much of the information newly required by this revision is typically in the immediate possession of the committee or authority that oversees the investments of plans sponsored by privately held companies, and generally is already required to be provided to the United States Securities and Exchange Commission by public company sponsors of defined benefit plans.

Adding Multiemployer Plan Contributing Employer Information: The Form 5500 Annual Return/Report currently does not require plans to state the number or identities of employers participating in a multiemployer plan. Multiemployer plans are, however, currently required to keep a list of participating employers on file and to make such information available to participants on request. Accordingly, requiring multiemployer plans to provide the number of participating employers will not create any new recordkeeping requirements. This information will be useful to various governmental and private firms that use the Form 5500 Annual Return/Report data for policy and research purposes. The Form 5500 Annual Return/Report also currently lacks information that shows a multiemployer plan's basis for employer contributions. This information is particularly important with respect to multiemployer defined benefit pension plans, as this information is needed by the PBGC in order for it to assess the financial risk posed to the plan by the financial collapse or withdrawal of one or more contributing employers. Over the past several years, the financial condition of many multiemployer plans has been deteriorating. The PBGC believes it is prudent to begin monitoring those companies that are major contributors to the multiemployer plans. To do so, the PBGC must be able to identify these companies. Because multiemployer plans are most at risk when a major contributing sponsor encounters financial difficulties, this proposed revision would require identification only of major contributors.

Other Improvements and Clarifications of Existing Form 5500 Reporting Requirements: Some of the revisions that come under this heading are technical clarifications or conforming changes to more substantive proposed revisions. These entail no material benefits or costs. Other revisions make small adjustments to the instructions or reporting requirements to reflect changing market or compliance trends. Some of these entail small increases in reporting costs that are justified by the need to stay current. These include, for example, the addition of feature codes to identify plans with certain default features, compliance questions directed at the provision of blackout notices, and fuller instruction on the reporting of certain indirect plan expenses. Others, such as the elimination of the requirement for self-insured health benefit plans to separately report certain payments to individual health care providers, may reduce reporting costs without compromising protections. These revisions and their respective intents are detailed in the Notice of Proposed Forms Revisions published simultaneously with these proposed regulations.

Costs

Although the costs to plans of satisfying their annual reporting obligations will be lower under these proposed regulations than they would be under existing regulations, they will still be substantial.[3] As shown in Table 2 below, the aggregate cost of such reporting under the existing regulations is estimated to be $1,062 million annually, shared across the 833,000 filers subject to the filing requirement. The Department estimates that the proposed regulations, however, impose an annual cost burden on the 833,000 filers of only $888 million.[4]

---

[3] The Department believes, however, that the annual cost burden on filers would be higher still in the absence of the existing regulations, because the filers would then be required to comply with the statutory filing requirements without the benefit of any regulatory exceptions, simplified reporting, or alternative methods of compliance.

[4] More detail about the cost estimates can be found in the section "Assumptions, Methodology, and Uncertainty".

TABLE 2.—SUMMARY OF COSTS: CURRENT REQUIREMENTS VS. PROPOSED REQUIREMENTS

	Total costs (in millions)	Total burden hours (in millions)
Current Reporting Requirements	$1,062	13.51
Change due to Revisions for 2008	174	2.26
Proposed Reporting Requirement, 2008	888	11.25

Note: Number of affected plans: 833,000.

Because these proposed regulations make substantial revisions to the existing reporting requirements, they will entail some one-time transition costs. The Department examined such transition costs in connection with the last major revision to the Form 5500 Annual Return/Report, which revised the Annual Return/Report for plan years beginning in 1999. *See* 65 FR 5026 (Feb. 2, 2000). Based on information provided by plan service providers and Form 5500 Annual Return/Report software developers at that time, the Department concluded that such costs are generally loaded into the prices paid by plans for affected services and products, spread both across plans and across the expected life of the service and product changes. The Department's estimates provided here are therefore intended to reflect such spreading and loading of these transition costs. That is, the gradual defrayal of the transition costs is included in the annual cost estimates here.

In addition to estimating the total impact of the proposed revisions on aggregate costs, the Department has broken down the change in cost by individual revisions. This apportioning of costs to individual revisions could be potentially done in several ways, as some types of plans are affected by more than one revision and therefore sequencing of the changes becomes important for the calculations. For example, large and small Code section 403(b) plans are affected by the elimination of the special reporting rules, but small Code section 403(b) plans are affected also by the introduction of the Short Form 5500. For the purpose of quantifying the impact of the individual law changes, the Department carried out the calculations in the following way:

1. Removal of the IRS-only schedules: Under the proposed regulations some of the information formerly collected in these schedules will be collected by the Department elsewhere in the Form 5500 Annual Return/Report filing. On net, however, this revision will substantially reduce the amount of information collected. Relative to the current filing requirement, this revision will reduce the total annual burden hours for 740,000 affected filers by 1.2 million hours. Applying an hourly labor rate of $84 for service providers and $59 for plan sponsors, the Department estimates that this will lower the aggregate annual reporting cost by an estimated $90 million.[5]

2. Establishment of a Short Form 5500 for certain small plans: A large majority of small plans, or 580,000 of the 640,000 total small plan filers, are estimated to be eligible to use the Short Form 5500, thereby saving an estimated $154 million (1.9 million hours) annually. This estimate includes about 9,000 small Code section 403(b) plans that

under the proposed rule would be subjected to increased filing requirements.

3. Addition of certain asset allocation and duration information to Schedule B: The provision of this information, and its certification by an actuary, will entail estimated additional annual costs of $1.5 million (19,000 hours) for 5,000 affected defined benefit pension plans with more than 1,000 participants.

4. Revision of Schedule C (Service Provider Information): This revision intends to clarify the reporting requirements and improve the information plan officials receive regarding amounts being received by plan service providers. This is anticipated to add an estimated $3 million (41,000 hours) for 79,000 affected plans to annual reporting costs.

5. Addition of requirements for certain multi-employer plans to report certain information about contributing employers: This is anticipated to add an estimated $300,000 (3,500 hours) to annual reporting costs for 10,000 multiemployer plans.

6. Adoption of various technical revisions and other miscellaneous revisions to the Form 5500 Annual Return/Report to improve and clarify existing reporting requirements: Together these are estimated to add an estimated $12 million (154,000 hours) to annual reporting costs and affect approximately 250,000 plans.

7. Elimination of the special reporting rules for Code section 403(b) plans: Approximately eighteen thousand Code section 403(b) plans are subject to the annual reporting requirements. It is anticipated that all 9,000 small Code section 403(b) plans will be eligible to use the new Short Form and will be eligible for waiver of the audit requirement. The impact of the proposed changes on the small Code section 403(b) plans is quantified above. Nine thousand large Code section 403(b) plans will be newly subject to the audit requirement and required to file a Form 5500 Annual Return/Report similar to those filed by similar Code section 401(k) plans. This revision will increase annual reporting costs for large Code section 403(b) plans by an estimated $54 million (or 690,000 hours).

A summary of the changes in costs and burden hours that were allocated to the groups of proposed changes as outlined above, as well as the number of affected employee benefit plans, can be found in Table 3 below.

TABLE 3.—SUMMARY OF PROPOSED CHANGES TO THE REPORTING REQUIREMENTS: COST, BURDEN, AND AFFECTED PLANS

Revisions for 2008	Change in costs (in millions)	Change in burden hours	Number of affected plans
IRS-only Schedules, Short Form and small	−$90.1	−1,226,000	739,000
Code Section 403(b) plans	−154.3	−1,938,000	580,000
Schedule B	1.5	19,000	5,000
Schedule C	3.2	41,000	79,000
Multi-employer plans	0.3	3,500	10,000
Technical and Miscellaneous Revisions	11.9	154,000	253,000
Large Code Section 403(b) plans	53.9	689,000	9,000
Total	−173.6	(2,258.30)	833,000

Note: The displayed numbers might not sum up to the totals due to rounding.

The proposed regulation otherwise generally does not alter reporting costs. Plans currently exempt from annual reporting requirements (such as certain small unfunded or fully insured welfare plans and certain Simplified Employer Pensions) will remain exempt. Also, except for Code section 403(b) plans, plans eligible for limited reporting options (such as certain IRA-based pension plans) will continue to be eligible for that annual reporting relief. The revisions continue the Form 5500 Annual Return/Report structure that is familiar to individual and corporate taxpayers—a simple two-page main form with basic information necessary to identify the plan for which the report is filed,

along with a checklist of the schedules being filed that are applicable to the filer's plan type. The structure is designed to aid filers by allowing them to assemble and file a return customized to their plan.

Assumptions, Methodology, and Uncertainty

The cost and burden associated with the annual reporting requirement for any given plan will vary according to a variety of factors, including the plan's characteristics, practices, and operations, which in turn determine what information must be provided. A small, single-employer defined contribution pension plan filing a new Short Form

---

[5] A discussion on the appropriateness of the labor rates used in the calculations as well as on other assumptions can be found in the Technical Appendix.

5500 generally will incur far lower costs than a large, multiemployer defined benefit pension plan that holds multiple insurance contracts, engages in numerous reportable transactions, and pays large fees to a number of service providers. Therefore, in arriving at its aggregate cost estimates, the Department separately considered the cost to different types of plans of providing different types of information. The basis for the Department's estimates is elaborated below.

Assumptions Underlying this Analysis —The Department's analysis of the costs and benefits of these proposed amendments assumes that all benefits and costs will be realized in the first year of the reporting cycle to which the amendments apply and within each year thereafter. This assumption is based on the nature of the statutory reporting provisions, which require that each plan complete a filing within a yearly period. The Department has used a "status quo" baseline for this analysis, assuming that the world absent the regulations will resemble the present.[6]

Methodology —The underlying cost data was developed by Mathematica Policy Research, Inc. (MPR), and has been used by the Agencies in various burden estimates related to the Form 5500 Annual Return/Report during recent years. *See,* 65 FR 21068, 21077-78 (April 19, 2000); Borden, William S., "Estimates of the Burden for Filing Form 5500: The Change in Burden from the 1997 to the 1999 Forms," Mathematica Policy Research, submitted to U.S. Dept. of Labor May 25, 1999.[7] It is grounded in surveys of filers and their service providers, which measured the unit cost burden of providing various types of information. Aggregate estimates were produced by interacting these unit cost measures with historical counts of Form 5500 Annual Return/Report filers.

A new burden estimating model, based on the Form 5500 Burden Model that MPR most recently used for estimating burdens in October

2004, was assembled by Actuarial Research Corporation (ARC). ARC assembled a simplified model, drawing on implied burdens associated with subsets of filer groups represented in the MPR model. The model used the level of detail consistent with reflecting burden differences associated with the various proposed forms revisions. In the following, the ARC model is described in broad terms. Further details about the model are explained in the Technical Appendix that can be accessed at the Department's Web site at *http://www.dol.gov/ebsa.*

To estimate aggregate burdens, the types of plans that have similar reporting requirements were grouped together. Thus, calculations were prepared for different subsets of types of plans as appropriate based on the specifics of the revisions to the reporting requirements. Table 4 below shows the particular types of plans considered, the number of plans affected by the proposed revisions, as well as the aggregate costs under current and proposed requirements. As can be seen from the Total line in Table 4, aggregate cost under current and proposed regulations add up to $1,062 million and $888 million, respectively. The universe of filers was divided into three basic plan types: Defined benefit pension plans, defined contribution pension plans, and welfare plans, and each of these major plan types was further subdivided into multiemployer and single-employer plans. Defined contribution Code section 403(b) plans were treated separately from other defined contribution plans. Since the filing requirements differ substantially for small and large plans, the plan types were also divided by plan size. For large plans (100 or more participants), the defined benefit plans were further divided between very large (1000 or more participants) and other large plans (at least 100 participants, but less than 1000 participants). For each of these sets of respondents, burden hours per respondent were estimated for the Form 5500 Annual Return/Report itself and for up to eight schedules.

TABLE 4.—NUMBER OF AFFECTED FILERS AND COST UNDER CURRENT VS. PROPOSED REQUIREMENTS

Type of plan	Number affected	Aggregate cost under current requirements (in millions)	Aggregate cost under proposed requirements (in millions)
5500 Large Plans (> = 100 participants)—189,000:			
DB, ME, 100-1,000 participants	800	7.600	7.200
DB, ME, > 1,000 participants	1,100	13.300	13.200
DB, SE, 100-1,000 participants	8,900	80.200	74.200
DB, SE, > 1,000 participants	4,200	38.800	39.200
DC, ME, non-403(b)	2,300	14.400	13.700
DC, ME, 403(b)	400	0.016	2.400
DC, SE, non-403(b)	70,000	437.100	401.300
DC, SE, 403(b)	8,600	0.350	51.900
Welfare, ME	5,700	14.300	14.800
Welfare, SE	86,600	124.300	127.900
5500 Small Short Form Eligible—580,000:			
DB	30,800	30.300	21.200
DC, non-403(b)	533,000	263.900	87.800
DC, 403(b)	8,800	0.360	1.400
Welfare	7,000	3.400	1.200
5500 Small Short Form Ineligible—64,000:			
DB	4,000	3.800	3.700
DC, non-403(b)	60,200	29.300	26.900
DC, 403(b)			
Welfare	100	0.079	0.080
Total	832,500	1,061.500	888.080

Note: The displayed numbers might not sum up to the totals due to rounding.

DB—defined benefit plans.

SE—single-employer plans.

Large plans—100 participants or more.

DC—defined contribution plans

ME—multi employer plans.

Small plans—less than 100 participants.

In addition to separating plans by type and size, costs were estimated separately for the form and for each schedule. When items on a Form 5500 Annual Return/Report schedule are required by more than one Agency, the estimated burden associated with that schedule is allocated among the Agencies. This allocation is based on whether only a single item on a schedule is required by more than one agency or whether several or all of the items are required by more than one agency. Filers must read not only the instructions for particular items

but also instructions pertaining to the general filing requirements, and the burden associated with reading the instructions is tallied and allocated accordingly.

A plan's reporting burden is estimated in light of the specific items and schedules it must complete as well as its size, funding method, and investment structures. For example, the annual report for a large fully insured welfare plan generally would consist of only a few questions on

---

[6] Further detail can be found in the Technical Appendix.

[7] The Mathematica report can be accessed at the Department's Web site at *http://www.dol.gov/ebsa.*

the Form 5500 and the Schedule A (Insurance Information). The requirement that this plan provide very limited information on the Form 5500 Annual Return/Report is reflected in the estimates of reporting burden time. By contrast, a large defined benefit pension plan that is intended to be tax-qualified and that uses a trust fund and invests in insurance contracts would be required to submit an annual report completing almost all the line items of the Form 5500, plus Schedule A (Insurance Information), Schedule B (Actuarial Information), Schedule C (Service Provider Information), Schedule D (DFE/ Participating Plan Information), Schedule H (Financial Information), and Schedule R (Retirement Plan Information), and would be required to submit an IQPA's report and opinion. The Agencies' methodology attempts to capture, through its categorization, these different reporting burdens, thereby providing meaningful estimates of significant differences in the burdens placed on different categories of filers.

Burden estimates for each schedule were adjusted for the proposed revisions, reflecting the numbers of items added or deleted in each schedule or moved from one schedule to another, and the average burden currently attributable to items on each of the corresponding current schedules. The burden for the proposed Short Form 5500 was built from the estimated current burden associated with the various line items included in it.

The Department has not attributed a recordkeeping burden to the Form 5500 Annual Return/Report either here or in its Paperwork Reduction Act analysis because it believes that plan administrators' practice of keeping financial records necessary to complete the Form 5500 Annual Return/Report arises from usual and customary management practices that would be used by any financial entity, and does not result from ERISA or Code annual reporting and filing requirements.

The aggregate baseline burden is the sum of the burden per form and schedule filed multiplied by the estimated aggregate number of forms and schedules. The simplified model draws on Form 5500 Annual Return/Report data representing each plan's filing for plan year 2002 (the most recent year for which complete data is available), both for estimating the impact of changes in the numbers of filings associated with the introduction of the Short Form 5500 for most small filers as well as for estimating the impact of changes in filing obligations associated with other schedules. In summary, the model estimates that due to $174 million in cost reductions the proposed revisions would lead to aggregate costs of $888 million. While there is a net reduction in costs, the Department estimates that some large plans might experience cost increases, while small plans will experience cost reductions. The total burden estimates, as well as the burden broken out by type of plan can be found in Table 4 above.

Uncertainty within Estimates —The Department acknowledges that there are several areas of uncertainty that might affect the estimates, in particular the unit cost estimates. While the Department has a good sense for the filing universe and for the number of filers that file the different schedules of the Form 5500, the unit costs under the current requirements as well as the way they would change due to the proposed revisions are more uncertain. The Department has no direct measure for the unit costs, but rather uses a proxy adapted from the existing MPR model, which was developed in the late 1990s. Additional uncertainty is added due to the proposed revisions. Some of the revisions delete items or move them from certain schedules to others. The impact of these changes can be estimated more accurately than the impact of the revisions that require the reporting of new items like fees. Consequently, the unit cost estimates would benefit from updated information and the Department welcomes comments that would provide information on this matter.

Peer Review

In December 2004, the Office of Management and Budget (OMB) issued a Final Information Quality Bulletin for Peer Review, 70 FR 2664 (January 14, 2005) (Peer Review Bulletin), establishing that important scientific information shall be peer reviewed before it is disseminated by the Federal government. The Peer Review Bulletin applies to original data and formal analytic models used by agencies in Regulatory Impact Analyses. The Department determined that the data and methods employed in its regulatory analysis of this proposal constitutes "influential scientific information" as defined in the Peer Review Bulletin. Accordingly, a peer review was conducted under Section II of the Bulletin. The peer review report concluded that the methodology and data generally were sound and produced plausible estimates, which supports the Department's conclusion that the proposed form changes should reduce the aggregate burden relative to the previous forms. The Peer Review Report can be accessed at the Department's Web site at *http://www.dol.gov/ebsa*.

Regulatory Flexibility Act

The Regulatory Flexibility Act (5 U.S.C. 601 *et seq.*) (RFA) imposes certain requirements with respect to Federal rules that are subject to the notice and comment requirements of section 553(b) of the Administrative Procedure Act (5 U.S.C. 551 *et seq.*) and that are likely to have a significant economic impact on a substantial number of small entities. Unless an agency certifies that a proposed rule will not, if promulgated, have a significant economic impact on a substantial number of small entities, section 603 of the RFA requires that the agency present an initial regulatory flexibility analysis at the time of the publication of the notice of proposed rulemaking describing the impact of the rule on small entities and seeking public comment on such impact. Small entities include small businesses, organizations, and governmental jurisdictions.

For purposes of analysis under the RFA, EBSA proposes to continue to consider a small entity to be an employee benefit plan with fewer than 100 participants. The basis of this definition is found in section 104(a)(2) of ERISA, which permits the Secretary to prescribe simplified annual reports for pension plans that cover fewer than 100 participants. Under ERISA section 104(a)(3), the Secretary may also provide for exemptions or for simplified reporting and disclosure for welfare benefit plans. Pursuant to the authority of ERISA section 104(a)(3), the Department has previously issued at 29 CFR 2520.104-20, 2520.104-21, 2520.104-41, 2520.104-46, and 2520.104b-10 certain simplified reporting provisions and limited exemptions from reporting and disclosure requirements for small plans, including unfunded or insured welfare plans, that cover fewer than 100 participants and satisfy certain other requirements.

Further, while some large employers may have small plans, in general small employers maintain most small plans. Thus, EBSA believes that assessing the impact of these proposed rules on small plans is an appropriate substitute for evaluating the effect on small entities. The definition of small entity considered appropriate for this purpose differs, however, from a definition of small business that is based on size standards promulgated by the Small Business Administration (SBA) (13 CFR 121.201) pursuant to the Small Business Act (15 U.S.C. 631 et seq.). EBSA therefore requests comments on the appropriateness of the size standard used in evaluating the impact of these proposed rules on small entities. EBSA has consulted with the SBA Office of Advocacy concerning use of this participant count standard for RFA purposes. *See* 13 CFR 121.902(b)(4). The following seven subsections address specific requirements of the RFA.

(1) The Department is proposing to amend the regulations relating to the annual reporting and disclosure requirements of section 103 of ERISA to conform existing regulations to proposed revisions to the Form 5500 Annual Return/Report forms that are included in the Notice of Proposed Forms Revisions published simultaneously with these regulations.

The Department continually strives to tailor reporting requirements to minimize reporting costs while ensuring that the information necessary to secure ERISA rights is adequately available. The optimal design for reporting requirements to satisfy these objectives changes over time. Benefit plan designs and practices evolve over time in response to market trends, including trends in labor markets, financial markets, health care and insurance markets, and markets for various services used by plans. Partly as a result, the nature and mix of compliance issues and risks to ERISA rights change over time. Frequent amendments to ERISA, the Code, and to associated regulations also change the parameters of ERISA rights and the methods needed to protect those rights. In addition, the technologies available to manage and transmit information continually advance. It is incumbent on the Department to revise its reporting requirements from time to time to keep pace with such changes. The Department is proposing these regulations and associated forms revisions to readjust its reporting requirements to take into account certain recent changes in markets, the law, and technology, many of which are referenced above in this preamble and/or in the Notice of Proposed Forms Revision published simultaneously with these regulations.

(2) Section 103 of ERISA requires every employee benefit plan covered under part 1 of Subtitle B of Title I of ERISA to publish and file an annual report concerning, among other things, the financial conditions and operations of the plan. Section 109 of ERISA authorizes the Secretary to prescribe forms for the reporting of information that is required to be included in the annual report. Section 104(a)(2)(A) of ERISA authorizes the Secretary to prescribe by regulation simplified annual reporting for pension plans that cover fewer than 100 participants. Section 104(a)(3) of ERISA authorizes the Secretary to exempt any welfare plan from all or part of the reporting and disclosure requirements of Title I of ERISA or to provide simplified reporting and

disclosure if the Secretary finds that such requirements are inappropriate as applied to such plans. Section 110 of ERISA permits the Secretary to prescribe for pension plans alternative methods of complying with any of the reporting and disclosure requirements if the Secretary finds that: (1) The use of the alternative method is consistent with the purposes of Title I of ERISA, and it provides adequate disclosure to plan participants and beneficiaries and adequate reporting to the Secretary; (2) application of the statutory reporting and disclosure requirements would increase costs to the plan or impose unreasonable administrative burdens with respect to the operation of the plan; and (3) the application of the statutory reporting and disclosure requirements would be adverse to the interests of plan participants in the aggregate.

The Department proposes to find that use of the Form 5500 Annual Return/Report, as revised, along with the proposed Short Form 5500, constitutes an alternative method of compliance, an exemption, and/or a simplified report, as applicable, consistent with these conditions. Generally, the Department believes that use of the revised Form 5500 Annual Return/Report and the proposed Short Form 5500 would relieve plans of all sizes of increased costs and burdens by providing a standard format that facilitates reporting required by the statute, eliminating duplicative reporting requirements, and streamlining the content of the annual return/report.

The objectives of these proposed, amended regulations and the associated proposed forms revisions are to streamline reporting and reduce aggregate reporting costs, particularly for small plans, while preserving and enhancing protection of ERISA rights. These purposes are detailed above in this preamble and in the Notice of Proposed Forms Revisions published simultaneously with these regulations.

(3) These proposed regulatory amendments do not alter the number of small plans required to comply with the annual reporting requirements, but do implement a new Short Form 5500, which is designed specifically to further streamline the limited reporting requirements presently applicable to small plans. The Department estimates that more than six million small, private-sector employee pension and welfare benefit plans are covered under Title I of ERISA. However, a large majority of these are fully insured or unfunded welfare benefit plans, which currently are exempt from annual reporting requirements and will continue to be exempt under these proposed regulations and the associated forms revisions. Approximately 644,000 small plans, including small pension plans and small funded welfare plans, currently are required to file annual reports and will continue to be so required under these proposed regulations and the associated forms revisions. Of these, an estimated 580,000 will be eligible to use the proposed new Short Form 5500. Use of the Short Form 5500 is expected to reduce

these plans' reporting costs while preserving or enhancing the protection of their participants' ERISA rights.

Among small plans, perhaps the most acutely affected will be the approximately 9,000 small Code section 403(b) plans. As explained above, such plans are currently subject only to limited annual reporting requirements. These proposed regulations and associated forms revisions, which will subject these plans to the same requirements as other covered small plans, will increase these plans' reporting costs. As discussed above, the Department believes these added costs are justified by the need to strengthen protections for affected participants' ERISA rights. The numbers and types of small plans affected by these proposed regulations and the magnitude and nature of the proposed regulations' effects are further elaborated below.

(4) The proposed regulations' reporting requirements applicable to small plans are detailed above and in the associated Notice of Proposed Forms Revisions. For a large majority of the 644,000 small plans subject to annual reporting requirements, or an estimated 549,000 plans, submission of the Short Form 5500 alone will fully satisfy their annual reporting requirements. All of these plans are eligible for the waiver of audit requirements, and none are defined benefit pension plans. Therefore, for such plans satisfaction of their applicable annual reporting requirements is not expected to require the services of an IQPA or auditor, but will require the use of a mix of clerical and professional administrative skills. For an additional 31,000 small defined benefit pension plans that would be eligible to use the streamlined Short Form 5500, satisfaction of the reporting requirements also will require services of an actuary and submission of Schedule B. The remaining 64,000 small plans will not be eligible to use the Short Form 5500 and will continue to be required to file the Form 5500 Annual Return/Report. Of these, 4,000 are defined benefit plans that must use an actuary and file Schedule B, and 32,000 are ineligible for waiver of the audit requirement and are required to employ an IQPA and submit an IQPA's report. All will require a mix of clerical and professional administrative skills to satisfy their reporting requirements.

Satisfaction of annual reporting requirements under these proposed regulations is not expected to require any additional recordkeeping that would not otherwise be part of normal business practices.

Table 5 below compares the Department's estimates of small plans' reporting costs under the current requirements with those under the proposed requirements for various classes of affected plans. As shown, costs under the proposed requirements will be lower on aggregate and for most classes of plans. These estimates take account of the quantity and mix of clerical and professional skills required to satisfy the reporting requirements for various classes of plans.

TABLE 5.—SMALL PLAN REPORTING COSTS UNDER CURRENT VS. PROPOSED REQUIREMENTS

Class of plan	Number affected	Aggregate cost under current requirements (In millions)	Aggregate cost under proposed requirements (In millions)
Defined Benefit Pension, Short Form eligible	31,000	$30.34	$21.24
Defined Benefit Pension, Short Form ineligible	4,000	3.77	3.67
Code Section 403(b)	All of 9,000	0.36	1.45
Other Defined Contribution, Short Form eligible	533,000	263.94	87.84
Other Defined Contribution Pension, Short Form ineligible.	60,000	29.32	26.92
Funded Welfare	All of 7,000	3.52	1.24
Other Welfare	None of approximately 6 million		
Total for All Affected Small Plans	644,000	331.26	142.35

The Department notes that the estimated reporting costs amount to $221 on average for each of the 644,000 small plans subject to annual reporting requirements, or just $22 if averaged across all of the approximately 6.6 million small plans covered by Title I of ERISA. This compares with roughly $4,000 on average for each of the 189,000 affected large filers.

(5) The Department is unaware of any relevant federal rules for small plans that duplicate, overlap, or conflict with these proposed regulations.

(6) In developing these proposed regulations and the associated forms revisions, the Department considered a number of alternative provisions directed at small plans. For example, as discussed in the Notice of Proposed Forms Revisions published simultaneously with these regulations, the ERISA Advisory Council suggested that the Department consider exempting welfare plans from reporting requirements, or, alternatively, subjecting all welfare plans to new, separately designed reporting requirements. The Department opted instead to

retain both the requirement that small funded welfare plans submit annual reports and the exception from annual reporting requirements for other small welfare plans. Annual reporting by the relatively small number of small funded welfare plans is necessary, in the Department's view, to protect ERISA rights in connection with the assets that they hold. A requirement that the remaining approximately six million small welfare plans report annually is not justified insofar as these plans have no assets to protect and insofar as the vast majority of these plans are fully insured and therefore separately protected by State oversight of the insurance contracts they hold and the insurers that issue them. The Department also considered both narrower and broader eligibility criteria for use of the Short Form 5500, settling on criteria that limit eligibility to plans holding relatively safe and protected assets, which nonetheless includes a large majority of small plans. The Department also considered the inclusion of more or fewer of the items of information formerly collected from small plans in the Form 5500 Annual Return/Report, retaining only those items it believes to be necessary and adequate to the protection of small plan participants' ERISA rights.

¶ 20,534Z

(7) The Department invites interested persons to submit comments regarding the impact on small plans of these proposed regulations and the associated forms revisions, and on the Department's assessment thereof. The Department also requests comments on the alternatives it considered and its conclusions regarding those alternatives; on any additional alternatives it should have considered; on what, if any, special problems small plans might encounter if the proposal were to be adopted; and what changes, if any, could be made to minimize those problems. To avoid duplication of comments, comments submitted in response to the Notice of Proposed Form Revisions published simultaneously with these proposed regulations will be treated as comments on this proposed rulemaking.

Paperwork Reduction Act Statement

The Department, as part of its continuing efforts to reduce paperwork and respondent burden, invites the general public and Federal agencies to comment on proposed and/or continuing collections of information in accordance with the Paperwork Reduction Act of 1995 (PRA) (44 U.S.C. 3506(c)(2)(A)). This helps to ensure that requested data are provided in the desired format, reporting burden (time and financial resources) is minimized, collection instruments are clearly understood, and the impact of collection requirements on respondents is properly assessed. The Department solicits comments on the information collection request (ICR) included in this proposed regulatory action, as well as the Notice of Proposed Forms Revisions published simultaneously with this Notice. In order to avoid unnecessary duplication of public comments, the PRA information published in the associated Notice of Proposed Forms Revisions is incorporated herein by this reference in its entirety, and comments submitted in response to the **Federal Register** publications will be treated as comments on these proposed rules. A copy of the ICR may be obtained by contacting the office listed under the heading "PRA Addressee."

The Department has submitted a copy of the proposed information collection to OMB, in accordance with 44 U.S.C. 3507(d), for its review of the information collection. The Department is particularly interested in comments that:

• Evaluate whether the proposed collection of information is necessary for the proper performance of the functions of the Agencies, including whether the information will have practical utility;

• Evaluate the accuracy of the Agencies' estimate of the burden of the proposed collection of information, including the validity of the methodology and assumptions used;

• Enhance the quality, utility, and clarity of the information to be collected; and

• Minimize the burden of the collection of information on those who are to respond, including through the use of appropriate automated, electronic, mechanical, or other technological collection techniques or other forms of information technology, *e.g.*, permitting electronic submission of responses.

Comments should be sent to the Office of Information and Regulatory Affairs, OMB, Room 10235, New Executive Office Building, Washington, DC 20503; Attention: Desk Officer for the Employee Benefits Security Administration, Department of Labor. Although comments may be submitted through September 19, 2006, OMB requests that comments be received within 30 days of publication of these proposed regulations to ensure their consideration.

PRA Addressee: Written comments regarding only PRA and the ICR should be sent to Gerald B. Lindrew, U.S. Department of Labor, EBSA/OPR, Room N-5718, 200 Constitution Avenue, NW., Washington, DC 20210, Telephone: (202) 693-8410; Fax: (202) 219-4745. These are not toll-free numbers. Written comments must be submitted on or before September 19, 2006 to be assured of consideration.

Congressional Review Act

The notice of proposed rulemaking being issued here is subject to the Congressional Review Act provisions of the Small Business Regulatory Enforcement Fairness Act of 1996 (5 U.S.C. 801 *et seq.*) and, if finalized, will be transmitted to the Congress and the Comptroller General for review.

Unfunded Mandates Reform Act

For purposes of the Unfunded Mandates Reform Act of 1995 (Pub. L. 104-4), as well as Executive Order 12875, the proposed rules do not include any Federal mandate that may result in expenditures by state, local, or tribal governments in the aggregate of more than $100 million, or increased expenditures by the private sector of more than $100 million.

Federalism Statement

Executive Order 13132 (August 4, 1999) outlines fundamental principles of federalism and requires adherence to specific criteria by federal agencies in the process of their formulation and implementation of policies that have substantial direct effects on the States, the relationship between the national government and the States, or on the distribution of power and responsibilities among the various levels of government. These proposed rules do not have federalism implications because they would have no substantial direct effect on the States, on the relationship between the national government and the States, or on the distribution of power and responsibilities among the various levels of government. Section 514 of ERISA provides, with certain exceptions specifically enumerated, that the provisions of Titles I and IV of ERISA supersede any and all laws of the States as they relate to any employee benefit plan covered under ERISA. The requirements implemented in these proposed rules do not alter the fundamental provisions of the statute with respect to employee benefit plans, and as such would have no implications for the States or the relationship or distribution of power between the national government and the States.

List of Subjects in 29 CFR Part 2520

Accountants, Disclosure requirements, Employee benefit plans, Employee Retirement Income Security Act, Pension plans, Pension and welfare plans, Reporting and recordkeeping requirements, and Welfare benefit plans.

In view of the foregoing, the Department of Labor proposes to amend 29 CFR part 2520 as set forth below:

PART 2520—RULES AND REGULATIONS FOR REPORTING AND DISCLOSURE

1. The authority citation for part 2520 continues to read as follows:

Authority: 29 U.S.C. 1021-1025, 1027, 1029-31, 1059, 1134, and 1135; Secretary of Labor's Order 1-2003, 68 FR 5374 (February 3, 2003). Sec. 2520.101-2 also issued under 29 U.S.C. 1132, 1181-1183, 1181 note, 1185, 1185a-b, 1191, and 1191a-c.

Secs. 2520.102-3, 2520.104b-1, and 2520.104b-3 also issued under 29 U.S.C. 1003, 1181-1183, 1181 note, 1185, 1185a-b, 1191, and 1191a-c. Secs. 2520.104b-1 and 2520.107 also issued under 26 U.S.C. 401 note, 111 Stat. 788.

2. In § 2520.103-1, revise paragraphs (a)(2) and (c) to read as follows:

§ 2520.103-1 Contents of the annual report.

(a) * * *

(2) Under the authority of subsections 104(a)(2), 104(a)(3) and 110 of the Act, a simplified report, limited exemption or alternative method of compliance is prescribed for employee welfare and pension benefit plans, as applicable. A plan filing a simplified report or electing the limited exemption or alternative method of compliance shall file an annual report containing the information prescribed in paragraph (b) or paragraph (c) of this section, as applicable, and shall furnish a summary annual report as prescribed in § 2520.104b-10.

* * * * *

(c) *Contents of the annual report for plans with fewer than 100 participants.* (1) Except as provided in paragraph (c)(2) of this section and in paragraph (d) of this section, and in §§ 2520.104-43 and 2520.104a-6, the annual report of an employee benefit plan that covers fewer than 100 participants at the beginning of the plan year shall include a Form 5500 "Annual Return/Report of Employee Benefit Plan" and any statements or schedules required to be attached to the form, completed in accordance with the instructions for the form, including Schedule A (Insurance Information), Schedule B (Actuarial Information), Schedule D (DFE/Participating Plan Information), Schedule I (Financial Information—Small Plan), and Schedule R (Retirement Plan Information). See the instructions for this form.

(2)(i) The annual report of an employee benefit plan that covers fewer than 100 participants at the beginning of the plan year and that meets the conditions in paragraph (c)(2)(ii) of this section with respect to a plan year may, as an alternative to the requirements of paragraph (c)(1) of this section, meet its annual reporting requirements by filing the Form 5500-SF "Short Form 5500 Annual Return/Report of Employee Benefit Plan" and any statements or schedules required to be attached to the form, including Schedule B (Actuarial Information), completed in accordance with the instructions for the form. See the instructions for this form.

(ii) A plan meets the conditions in this paragraph (c)(2)(ii) with respect to the year if the plan:

(A) Does not hold any employer securities at any time during the year;

(B) Satisfies the audit waiver conditions in §§ 2520.104-46(b)(1)(i)(A)(*1*) and 2520.104-46(b)(1)(i)(B) and (b)(1)(i)(C); and

(iii) Had at all times during the plan year 100 percent of the plan's assets held for investment purposes invested in assets that have a readily ascertainable fair market value. For purposes of this section, the following shall be treated as assets that have a readily ascertainable fair market value: Shares issued by an investment company registered under the Investment Company Act of 1940; investment and annuity contracts issued by any insurance company, qualified to do business under the laws of a State, that provides valuation information at least annually to the plan administrator; bank investment contracts issued by a bank or similar financial institution, as defined in § 2550.408b-4(c) of this chapter, that provides valuation information at least annually to the plan administrator; securities (except employer securities) traded on a public exchange; government securities issued by the United States or by a State; cash or cash equivalents held by a bank or similar financial institution, as defined in § 2550.408b-4(c) of this chapter; by an insurance company, qualified to do business under the law of a State; by an organization registered as a broker-dealer under the Securities Exchange Act of 1934; or by any other organization authorized to act as a trustee for individual retirement accounts under section 408 of the Internal Revenue Code; and any loan meeting the requirements of section 408(b)(1) of the Act and the regulations issued thereunder.

* * * * *

3. In § 2520.104-44, remove paragraph (b)(3).

4. In § 2520.104-46, add a new paragraph (e) and a new appendix to the section to read as follows:

§ 2520.104-46 Waiver of examination and report of an independent qualified public accountant for employee benefits plans with fewer than 100 participants.

* * * * *

(e) *Model notice.* The appendix to this section contains model language for inclusion in the summary annual report to assist plan administrators in complying with the requirements of paragraph (b)(1)(i)(B) of this section to avail themselves of the waiver of examination and report of the independent qualified public accountant for employee benefit plans with fewer than 100 participants. Use of the model language is not mandatory. In order to use the model language in the plan's summary annual report, administrators must, in addition to any other information required to be in the summary annual report, select among alternative language and add relevant information where appropriate in the model language. Items of information that are not applicable to a particular plan may be deleted. Use of the model language, appropriately modified and supplemented, will be deemed to satisfy the notice content requirements of paragraph (b)(1)(i)(B) of this section.

Appendix to § 2520.104-46—Model Summary Annual Report Notice (Plan Administrators Will Need To Modify the Model To Omit Information That Is Not Applicable to the Plan)

The U.S. Department of Labor's regulations require that an independent qualified public accountant audit the plan's financial statements unless certain conditions are met for the audit requirement to be waived. This plan met the audit waiver conditions for the plan year beginning (insert year) and therefore has not had an audit performed. Instead, the following information is provided to assist you in verifying that the assets reported on the (Form 5500 or Form 5500-SF-select as applicable) were actually held by the plan.

At the end of the (insert year) plan year, the plan had (include separate entries for each regulated financial institution holding or issuing qualifying plan assets):

[Set forth amounts and names of institutions as applicable where indicated]

[(insert $ amount) in assets held by (insert name of bank)],

[(insert $ amount) in securities held by (insert name of registered broker-dealer)],

[(insert $ amount) in shares issued by (insert name of registered investment company)],

[(insert $ amount) in investment or annuity contract issued by (insert name of insurance company)].

The plan receives year-end statements from these regulated financial institutions that confirm the above information. [Insert as applicable— The remainder of the plan's assets were (1) qualifying employer securities, (2) loans to participants, (3) held in individual participant accounts with investments directed by participants and beneficiaries and with account statements from regulated financial institutions furnished to the participant or beneficiary at least annually, or (4) other assets covered by a fidelity bond at least equal to the value of the assets and issued by an approved surety company.]

Plan participants and beneficiaries have a right, on request and free of charge, to get copies of the financial institution year-end statements and evidence of the fidelity bond. If you want to examine or get copies of the financial institution year-end statements or evidence of the fidelity bond, please contact [insert mailing address and any other available way to request copies such as e-mail and phone number].

If you are unable to obtain or examine copies of the regulated financial institution statements or evidence of the fidelity bond, you may contact the regional office of the U.S. Department of Labor's Employee Benefits Security Administration (EBSA) for assistance by calling toll-free 1.866.444.EBSA (3272). A listing of EBSA regional offices can be found at *http://www.dol.gov/ebsa.* General information regarding the audit waiver conditions applicable to the plan can be found on the U.S. Department of Labor Web site at *http://www.dol.gov/ebsa* under the heading "Frequently Asked Questions."

5. Revise the Appendix to § 2520.104b-10 to read as follows:

§ 2520.104b-10 Summary Annual Report.

* * * * *

APPENDIX TO § 2520.104b-10.-THE SUMMARY ANNUAL REPORT (SAR) UNDER ERISA: A CROSS-REFERENCE TO THE ANNUAL REPORT

APPENDIX TO § 2520.104B-10.—THE SUMMARY ANNUAL REPORT (SAR) UNDER ERISA: A CROSS-REFERENCE TO THE ANNUAL REPORT

SAR item	Form 5500—large plan filer line items	Form 5500—small plan filer line items	Form 5500-SF—filer line items
A. Pension Plan:			
1. Funding arrangement	Form 5500-9a	Same	Not applicable.
2. Total plan expenses	Sch. H—2j	Sch. I—2j	Line 8h.
3. Administrative expenses	Sch. H—2i(5)	Sch. I—2h	Line 8f.
4. Benefits paid	Sch. H—2e(4)	Sch. I—2e	Line 8d.
5. Other expenses	Sch. H—Subtract the sum of 2e(4) & 2i(5) from 2j.	Sch. I—2i	Line 8g.
6. Total participants	Form 5500—6f	Same	Line 5b.
7. Value of plan assets (net):			
a. End of plan year	Sch. H—1l [Col. (b)]	Sch. I—1c [Col. (b)]	Line 7a [Col. (b)].
b. Beginning of plan year	Sch. H—1l [Col. (a)]	Sch. I—1c [Col. (a)]	Line 7a [Col. (a)].
8. Change in net assets	Sch. H—Subtract 1l [Col. (a)] from 1l [Col. (b)].	Sch. I—Subtract 1c [Col. (a)] from 1c [Col. (b)].	Line 7c—Subtract Col. (a) from Col. (b).
9. Total income	Sch. H—2d	Sch. I—2d	Line 8c.
a. Employer contributions	Sch. H—2a(1)(A) & 2a(2)—if applicable	Sch. I—2a(1) & 2b if applicable	Line 8a(1) if applicable.
b. Employee contributions	Sch. H—2a(1)(B) & 2a(2) if applicable.	Sch. I—2a(2) & 2b if applicable	Line 8a(2) if applicable.
c. Gains (losses) from sale of assets.	Sch. H—2b(4)(C)	Not applicable	Not applicable.

SAR item	Form 5500—large plan filer line items	Form 5500—small plan filer line items	Form 5500-SF—filer line items
d. Earnings from investments.	Sch. H—Subtract the sum of 2a(3), 2b(4)(C) and 2c from 2d.	Sch. I—2c	Line 8b.
10. Total insurance premiums	Total of all Schs.A—5b	Total of all Schs.A—5b	Not applicable.
11. Funding deficiency:			
a. Defined benefit plans	Sch. B—10	Same	Same.
b. Defined contribution plans.	Sch. R—6c, if more than zero	Same	Line 12c.
B. Welfare Plan:			
1. Name of insurance carrier	All Schs. A—1(a)	Same	Not applicable.
2. Total (experience rated and non-experienced rated) insurance premiums.	All Schs. A—Sum of 8a(4) and 9(a).	Same	Not applicable.
3. Experience rated premiums	All Schs. A—8a(4)	Same	Not applicable.
4. Experience rated claims	All Schs. A—8b(4)	Same	Not applicable.
5. Value of plan assets (net):			
a. End of plan year	Sch. H—1l [Col. (b)]	Sch. I—1c [Col. (b)]	Line 7c—[Col. (b)].
b. Beginning of plan year	Sch. H—1l [Col. (a)]	Sch. I—1c [Col. (a)]	Line 7c—[Col. (a)].
6. Change in net assets	Sch. H—Subtract 1l [Col. (a)] from 1l [Col. (b)].	Sch. I—Subtract 1c [Col. (a)] from 1c [Col. (b)].	Line 7c—Subtract [Col. (a)] from [Col. (b)].
7. Total income	Sch. H—2d	Sch. I—2d	Line 8c.
a. Employer contributions	Sch. H—2a(1)(A) & 2a(2) if applicable.	Sch. I—2a(1) & 2b if applicable	Line 8a(1) if applicable.
b. Employee contributions	Sch. H—2a(1)(B) & 2a(2) if applicable.	Sch. I—2a(2) & 2b if applicable	Line 8a(2) if applicable.
c. Gains (losses) from sale of assets.	Sch. H—2b(4)(C)	Not applicable	Not applicable.
d. Earnings from investments.	Sch. H—Subtract the sum of 2a(3), 2b(4)(C) and 2c from 2d.	Sch. I—2c	Line 8b.
8. Total plan expenses	Sch. H—2j	Sch. I—2j	Line 8h.
9. Administrative expenses	Sch. H—2i(5)	Sch. I, line 2h	Line 8f.
10. Benefits paid	Sch. H—2e(4)	Sch. I—2e	Line 8d.
11. Other expenses	Sch. H—Subtract the sum of 2e(4) & 2i(5) from 2j.	Sch. I—2i	Line 8g.

Signed at Washington, DC, this 13th day of July 2006.

Ann C. Combs,

Assistant Secretary, Employee Benefits Security Administration, U.S. Department of Labor.

[FR Doc. 06-6330 Filed 7-20-06; 8:45 am]

BILLING CODE 4510-29-P

¶ 20,535

Employee Benefits Security Administration (EBSA): Defined contribution plans: Participant-directed accounts: Qualified default investment alternative.— The Employee Benefits Security Administration (EBSA) issued proposed regulations implementing amendments to ERISA enacted by the Pension Protection Act of 2006 (PPA, P.L. 109-280) pursuant to which a participant in a participant-directed individual account plan (*e.g.*, a 401(k) plan) will be deemed to have exercised control over the assets in his or her account if, in the absence of investment directions from the participant, the plan invests in a qualified default investment alternative.

The proposed regulations, published in the Federal Register on September 27, 2006 (71 FR 56806), were previously reproduced below. The preamble to the final regulations, published in the Federal Register on October 24, 2007 (72 FR 60452) appears at ¶ 24,262.

¶ 20,536

Pension Benefit Guaranty Corporation (PBGC): Proposed rule: Mortality assumptions: Missing participants: Mass withdrawals.— The Pension Benefit Guaranty Corporation (PBGC) has issued a proposed rule, as a companion to a direct final rule, to change the mortality assumptions in its regulations under parts 4050 (Missing Participants) and 4281 (Duties of Plan Sponsor Following Mass Withdrawal).

The related direct final rule was published in the Federal Register on December 14, 2006 at 71 FR 75115 (see ¶ 24,253). The proposed regulations, which were published in the Federal Register on December 14, 2006 at 71 FR 75181, are reproduced below.

PENSION BENEFIT GUARANTY CORPORATION

29 CFR Parts 4050 and 4281

RIN 1212-AB08

Mortality Assumptions

AGENCY: Pension Benefit Guaranty Corporation.

ACTION: Proposed rule.

SUMMARY: This proposed rule is a companion to PBGC's direct final rule (published today in the "Rules and Regulations" section of the Federal Register) making changes to the mortality assumptions under parts 4050 (Missing Participants) and 4281 (Duties of Plan Sponsor Following Mass Withdrawal) of its regulations. PBGC is making these changes as a direct final rule without prior proposal because we view them as non-controversial revisions and anticipate no significant adverse comment. We have explained our reasons in the preamble to the direct final rule. If we receive no significant adverse comment, no further action on this proposed rule will be taken. However, if we receive significant adverse comment, we will withdraw the direct final rule and it will not take effect. In that case, we will address all public comments in a subsequent final rule based on this proposed rule. We

will not institute a second comment period on this rule. Any parties interested in commenting must do so at this time.

DATES: Comments must be received on or before January 16, 2007.

ADDRESSES: Comments, identified by RIN number 1212-AB08, may be submitted by any of the following methods:

• Federal eRulemaking Portal: http://www.regulations.gov.

Follow the Web site instructions for submitting comments.

• E-mail: reg.comments@pbgc.gov.

• Fax: 202-326-4224.

• Mail or Hand Delivery: Legislative and Regulatory Department, Pension Benefit Guaranty Corporation, 1200 K Street, NW., Washington, DC 20005-4026. All submissions must include the Regulatory Information Number for this rulemaking (RIN number 1212-AB08). Comments received, including personal information provided, will be posted to http://www.pbgc.gov.

Copies of comments may also be obtained by writing to Disclosure Division, Office of the General Counsel, Pension Benefit Guaranty Corp., 1200 K Street, NW, Washington, DC 20005-4026 or calling 202-326-4040 during normal business hours. (TTY and TDD users may call the Federal relay service toll-free at 1-800-877-8339 and ask to be connected to 202-326-4040.)

FOR FURTHER INFORMATION CONTACT: Catherine B. Klion, Manager, or James L. Beller, Jr., Attorney, Regulatory and Policy Division, Legislative and Regulatory Department, Pension Benefit Guaranty Corp., 1200 K Street, NW., Suite 1200, Washington, DC 20005-4026; 202-326-4024. (TTY/ TDD users may call the Federal relay service toll-free at 1-800-877-8339 and ask to be connected to 202-326-4024.)

SUPPLEMENTARY INFORMATION: In the "Rules and Regulations" section of today's Federal Register, PBGC is publishing a direct final rule making changes to the mortality assumptions under parts

4050 (Missing Participants) and 4281 (Duties of Plan Sponsor Following Mass Withdrawal) of its regulations. The provisions proposed here are those contained in the direct final rule. Please refer to the preamble and regulatory text of the direct final rule for further information and the actual text of the revisions. Additionally, all information regarding Statutory and Executive Orders for this proposed rule can be found in the Supplementary Information section of the direct final rule.

Issued in Washington, DC, this 8th day of December, 2006.

Vincent K. Snowbarger, Interim Director, Pension Benefit Guaranty Corporation.

[FR Doc. E6-21279 Filed 12-13-06; 8:45 am]

¶ 20,537

Pension Benefit Guaranty Corporation (PBGC): Proposed rule: Flat premium rates: Variable rate premium cap: Termination premium.— the Pension Benefit Guaranty Corporation (PBGC) has issued proposed amendments to its regulations on premium rates and the payment of premiums to implement certain provisions of the Deficit Reduction Act of 2005 (DRA; P.L. 109-171) and the Pension Protection Act of 2006 (PPA; P.L. 109-280) that are effective beginning in 2006 or 2007. The provisions that would be implemented by the proposed regulations change the PBGC's flat-rate premium rate, cap the variable-rate premium in some cases, and create a new "termination premium" that is payable in connection with certain distress and involuntary plan terminations.

The proposed regulations, which were published in the Federal Register on February 20, 2007 (72 FR 7755), are reproduced below.

PENSION BENEFIT GUARANTY CORPORATION

29 CFR Parts 4006 and 4007

RIN 1212-AB10

Premium Rates; Payment of Premiums; Flat Premium Rates, Variable-Rate Premium Cap, and Termination Premium; Deficit Reduction Act of 2005; Pension Protection Act of 2006

AGENCY: Pension Benefit Guaranty Corporation.

ACTION: Proposed rule.

SUMMARY: This is a proposed rule to amend PBGC's regulations on Premium Rates and Payment of Premiums to implement certain provisions of the Deficit Reduction Act of 2005 (Pub. L. 109-171) and the Pension Protection Act of 2006 (Pub. L. 109-280) that are effective beginning in 2006 or 2007. The provisions that would be implemented by this rule change the flat premium rate, cap the variable-rate premium in some cases, and create a new "termination premium" that is payable in connection with certain distress and involuntary plan terminations. This rule does not address other provisions of the Pension Protection Act of 2006 that deal with PBGC premiums.

DATES: Comments must be submitted on or before April 23, 2007.

ADDRESSES: Comments, identified by RIN number 1212-AB10, may be submitted by any of the following methods:

Federal eRulemaking Portal: *http://www.regulations.gov.*

Follow the Web site instructions for submitting comments.

E-mail: *reg.comments@pbgc.gov.*

Fax: 202-326-4224.

Mail or Hand Delivery: Legislative and Regulatory Department, Pension Benefit Guaranty Corporation, 1200 K Street, NW., Washington, DC 20005-4026.

All submissions must include the Regulatory Information Number for this rulemaking (RIN 1212-AB10). Comments received, including personal information provided, will be posted to *http://www.pbgc.gov.* Copies of comments may also be obtained by writing to Disclosure Division, Office of the General Counsel, Pension Benefit Guaranty Corporation, 1200 K Street, NW., Washington DC 20005-4026, or calling 202-326-4040 during normal business hours. (TTY and TDD users may call the Federal relay service toll-free at 1-800-877-8339 and ask to be connected to 202-326-4040.)

FOR FURTHER INFORMATION CONTACT: John H. Hanley, Director, Legislative and Regulatory Department; or Catherine B. Klion, Manager, or Deborah C. Murphy, Attorney, Regulatory and Policy Division, Legislative and Regulatory Department, Pension Benefit Guaranty Corporation, 1200 K Street, NW., Washington DC 20005-4026; 202-326-4024. (TTY/TDD users may call the Federal relay service toll-free at 1-800-877-8339 and ask to be connected to 202-326-4024.)

SUPPLEMENTARY INFORMATION:

Background

Pension Benefit Guaranty Corporation (PBGC) administers the pension plan termination insurance program under Title IV of the Employee Retirement Income Security Act of 1974 (ERISA). Pension plans covered by Title IV must pay premiums to PBGC. Section 4006 of ERISA deals with premium rates, and section 4007 of ERISA deals with the payment of premiums, including premium due dates, interest and penalties on premiums not timely paid, and persons liable for premiums.

On February 8, 2006, the President signed into law the Deficit Reduction Act of 2005, Pub. L. 109-171 (DRA 2005). Section 8101 of DRA 2005 amends section 4006 of ERISA. Section 8101(a) changes the per-participant flat premium rate for plan years beginning in 2006 from $19 to $30 for single-employer plans and from $2.60 to $8 for multiemployer plans and provides for inflation adjustments to the flat rates for future years. Section 8101(b) creates a new "termination premium" (in addition to the flat-rate and variable-rate premiums under section 4006(a)(3)(A) and (E) of ERISA) that is payable for three years following certain distress and involuntary plan terminations that occur after 2005.

On August 17, 2006, the President signed into law the Pension Protection Act of 2006, Pub. L. 109-280 (PPA 2006). Sections 401(b) and 402(g)(2)(B) of PPA 2006 make changes to the termination premium rules of DRA 2005. Section 405 of PPA 2006 amends section 4006 of ERISA to cap the variable-rate premium for plans of certain small employers beginning in 2007. (PPA 2006 also makes other changes affecting PBGC premiums that are not addressed in this rule.)

This rule would amend PBGC's regulations on Premium Rates (29 CFR Part 4006) and Payment of Premiums (29 CFR Part 4007) to conform to these requirements of DRA 2005 and PPA 2006 and to clarify how the requirements apply.

Flat-Rate Premium

Until the enactment of DRA 2005, the flat-rate premium had remained unchanged for single-employer plans since 1991 and for multiemployer plans since 1989. Section 8101(a) of DRA 2005 amends section 4006(a)(3)(A) of ERISA and adds new subparagraphs (F) and (G) to the end of section 4006(a)(3) of ERISA to raise the flat premium rates for 2006 for both single- and multiemployer plans and to provide for inflation indexing for future years.

Applicability

Before amendment by DRA 2005, section 4006(a)(3)(A) of ERISA provided (in part) that "*** the annual premium rate *** is *** in the case of a single-employer plan, for plan years beginning after December 31, 1990, an amount equal to the sum of $19 plus the [per-participant variable-rate premium] under subparagraph (E) for each *** participant ***" Section 8101(a)(1)(A) of DRA 2005 changes "$19" to read "$30." Thus, the amended text of ERISA, read literally, makes it appear that the $30 single-employer flat-rate premium applies to plan years beginning after 1990. However, section 8101(d)(1) of DRA 2005 (which does not amend ERISA) says that this change applies to plan years beginning after December 31, 2005. Accordingly, PBGC considers single-employer flat premium rates for plan years beginning before 2006 to be unaffected by DRA 2005.

Participant Count

Section 8101(a)(2)(A)(ii) of DRA 2005 adds a new clause (iv) to section 4006(a)(3)(A) of ERISA providing that the flat premium rate for a multiemployer plan for a post-2005 plan year is "$8.00 for each individual who is a participant in such plan during the applicable plan year." PBGC interprets this to mean that the participant count is to be taken as of the premium snapshot date described in the premium rates regulation and PBGC's premium instructions (generally the last day of the plan year preceding the premium payment year). This is consistent with PBGC's interpretation of the nearly identical language in existing section 4006(a)(3)(A)(i) of ERISA.

Inflation Adjustments

Section 8101(a)(1)(B) and (2)(B) of DRA 2005 add to section 4006(a)(3) of ERISA substantially identical new subparagraphs (F) and (G) providing for inflation adjustments to the $30 and $8 flat rates for plan years beginning after 2006. The adjustments are based on changes in the national average wage index as defined in section 209(k)(1) of the Social Security Act, with a two-year lag—for example, for 2007, it will be the 2005 index that will be compared to the baseline (the 2004 index). However, new subparagraphs (F) and (G) are written in such a way that the premium rate can never go down; if the change in the national average wage index is negative, the premium rate remains the same as in the preceding year. Also, under new subparagraphs (F) and (G), premium rates are rounded to the nearest whole dollar. PBGC interprets this to mean that if the adjustment formula would produce an unrounded premium rate of some number of dollars plus 50 cents, the premium rate will be rounded up.

Regulatory Provisions

This rule would amend § 4006.3 of the premium rates regulation to reflect the changes to the flat-rate premium made by section 8101(a) of DRA 2005. Existing paragraphs (a)(1) and (a)(2) of § 4006.3 (setting forth the $19 and $2.60 flat rates) would be removed, and a cross-reference to new § 4006.3(c) would be provided instead. Paragraph (1) of new § 4006.3(c) provides pre-2006 rates ($19 and $2.60); paragraph (2) provides 2006 rates ($30 and $8); and paragraph (3) provides post-2006 rates (the greater of the preceding year's rate or the inflation-adjusted rate). The inflation adjustment is described in new § 4006.3(d).

Variable-Rate Premium

Section 405 of PPA 2006 amends section 4006(a)(3)(E)(i) of ERISA and adds new subparagraph (H) to the end of section 4006(a)(3) to cap the variable-rate premium for certain plans, effective for plan years beginning after 2006.

Plans Covered

Clause (i) of new section 4006(a)(3)(H) of ERISA says that the new variable-rate premium cap applies "[i]n the case of an employer who has 25 or fewer employees on the first day of the plan year." But clause (ii) of new section 4006(a)(3)(H) of ERISA makes clear that the applicability of the new cap does not necessarily depend on the size of a single employer, but rather depends on the size of a plan's controlled group, that is, the aggregate size of "all contributing sponsors and their controlled groups." (See the definition of "controlled group" in § 4001.2 of PBGC's regulation on Terminology (29 CFR Part 4001), which provides that "[a]ny reference to a plan's controlled group means all contributing sponsors of the plan and all members of each contributing sponsor's controlled group"). Since a plan maintained by one contributing sponsor may or may not also be maintained by one or more other contributing sponsors that are not in the first sponsor's controlled group, the applicability of the cap must be determined plan by plan, not employer by employer.

Meaning of "employee"

New section 4006(a)(3)(H) of ERISA does not give guidance as to the meaning of the term "employee." PBGC proposes to define "employee" for this purpose by reference to section 410(b)(1) of the Internal Revenue Code, which deals with minimum coverage requirements for qualified plans and requires that employees be counted to evaluate the breadth of coverage of a plan. For this purpose, certain individuals may be counted as "employees" although they might not be considered common law employees of the employer—for example, affiliated service group employees (under Code section 414(m)) and leased employees (under Code section 414(n)). PBGC considers this approach appropriate to prevent an employer from qualifying for the

cap by artificially lowering its employee count through the use of sophisticated business structuring devices. In addition, in order to ensure that all employees are counted, PBGC proposes that the employee count be determined without regard to Code section 410(b)(3), (4), and (5), which might be considered to exclude from the count collective bargaining employees, employees not meeting a plan's age and service requirements, and employees in separate lines of business.

Cap Amount

Under new section 4006(a)(3)(H)(i) of ERISA, the per-participant variable-rate premium is capped at "$5 multiplied by the number of participants in the plan as of the close of the preceding plan year." PBGC interprets this to mean that the participant count is to be taken as of the premium snapshot date described in the premium rates regulation and PBGC's premium instructions (generally the last day of the plan year preceding the premium payment year). This is consistent with PBGC's interpretation of the nearly identical language in existing section 4006(a)(3)(E)(i) of ERISA. This participant count is the same as the count used as a multiplier under section 4006(a)(3)(A)(i) of ERISA for purposes of both the flat- and variable-rate premiums. Thus, an eligible plan's total variable-rate premium is capped at an amount equal to $5 multiplied by the square of the participant count.

Regulatory Provisions

This rule would revise § 4006.3(b) of the premium rates regulation to reflect the new cap on the variable-rate premium added by section 405 of PPA 2006. The existing variable-rate premium is described in new paragraph (b)(1) of § 4006.3. The cap is described in new paragraph (b)(2); plans eligible for the cap in new paragraph (b)(3); and the meaning of the term "employee" in new paragraph (b)(4). Paragraph (b)(2) includes an example of the computation of the cap taken from page 95 of the Technical Explanation of H.R. 4, the "Pension Protection Act of 2006," as Passed by the House on July 28, 2006, and as Considered by the Senate on August 3, 2006, Prepared by the Staff of the Joint Committee on Taxation (August 3, 2006) (*http://www.house.gov/jct/x-38-06.pdf*).

Termination Premium

Section 8101(b) of DRA 2005 adds a new paragraph (7) to the end of section 4006(a) of ERISA, creating a new "termination premium" that applies only where certain distress and involuntary terminations occur and then only for three years. However, although only section 4006 of ERISA is amended, subparagraph (D) of new paragraph (7) in effect modifies section 4007 of ERISA as well. Sections 401(b) and 402(g)(2)(B) of PPA 2006 make changes to the termination premium rules of DRA 2005.

Termination Dates Covered

Section 8101(d)(2)(A) of DRA 2005 (which does not amend ERISA) restricts the new termination premium to "plans terminated after December 31, 2005." (Section 401(b)(1) of PPA 2006 repeals new section 4006(a)(7)(E) of ERISA, added by DRA 2005, which provided that the termination premium would not apply "with respect to any plan terminated after December 31, 2010.")

Section 8101(d)(2)(B) of DRA 2005 further restricts the application of the new termination premium in certain bankruptcy situations. If a plan "is terminated during the pendency of any bankruptcy reorganization proceeding under chapter 11 of title 11, United States Code (or under any similar law of a State or political subdivision of a State)," the new premium does not apply "if the proceeding is pursuant to a bankruptcy filing occurring before October 18, 2005." Under section 402(g)(2)(B)(ii) of PPA 2006, this limitation does not apply to an "eligible plan" under section 402(c)(1) of PPA 2006 (generally a plan of a commercial passenger airline or airline catering service) while a funding election under section 402(a)(1) of PPA 2006 is in effect for the plan.

These time restrictions on the applicability of the new premium turn on when a plan is "terminated." PBGC believes that the most natural reading of these provisions is that the date to look to is the termination date under section 4048 of ERISA. Focusing on the section 4048 termination date is also consistent with other provisions of DRA 2005 and implementing regulations discussed below.

Types of Terminations Covered

Under new section 4006(a)(7)(A) of ERISA, the termination premium applies where "there is a termination of a single-employer plan under clause (ii) or (iii) of section 4041(c)(2)(B) [of ERISA] or section 4042 [of ERISA]." Section 4041(c) of ERISA provides for distress terminations; ERISA section 4042 provides for involuntary terminations.

Under ERISA section 4041(c)(1), a distress termination of a plan may occur only if each contributing sponsor and each member of any contributing sponsor's controlled group meets one of the "distress tests" in clauses (i), (ii), and (iii) of section 4041(c)(2)(B). The tests are that the person is the subject of a bankruptcy liquidation proceeding (clause (i)), that the person is the subject of a bankruptcy reorganization proceeding (clause (ii)), or that the person is suffering business hardship (clause (iii)).

Although typically all contributing sponsors and controlled group members meet the same distress test, that is not required for a distress termination under section 4041(c). Thus, while terminations where all contributing sponsors and controlled group members meet the test in clause (i) seem to be excluded from applicability of the termination premium, it is not clear from the statutory language whether the termination premium is to apply to terminations where one or more contributing sponsors and/or controlled group members meet the clause (i) test but others meet the tests in clauses (ii) and/or (iii). Examples of such situations would be where there are two contributing sponsors, one liquidating and one reorganizing; where the sole contributing sponsor is liquidating but there are controlled group members that are reorganizing; and where the sole contributing sponsor is reorganizing but the controlled group members are liquidating.

The statutory language provides no basis for distinguishing among these examples or others that might be cited. All contributing sponsors and controlled group members are liable for plan underfunding under ERISA section 4062 and (as discussed below) for the termination premium (if it applies), and they must all satisfy one or another distress test under ERISA section 4041(c)(2)(B) for a distress termination to take place. This suggests that all these entities should be considered responsible as a group for the consequences of plan termination and that the fact that one entity among several is liquidating should not shield the others from liability. PBGC thus interprets new section 4006(a)(7)(A) of ERISA as applying the termination premium in any distress termination case where at least one contributing sponsor or controlled group member meets the distress test in either clause (ii) or (iii) of section 4041(c)(2)(B) (i.e., is not liquidating).

Payers

Section 4007(a) of ERISA places responsibility for paying PBGC premiums on the "designated payor" of a plan, and section 4007(e)(1)(A) of ERISA identifies the designated payor of a single-employer plan as the contributing sponsor or plan administrator. However, new section 4006(a)(7)(D)(i)(II) of ERISA, as added by section 8101(b) of DRA 2005, provides that notwithstanding section 4007, the designated payor of the new termination premium is "the person who is the contributing sponsor as of immediately before the termination date." It thus appears that the designated payor is to be identified as of the day before the termination date under section 4048 of ERISA. Similarly, this rule provides for identification of members of the contributing sponsor's controlled group (which are jointly and severally liable for premiums under section 4007(e)(2) of ERISA) as of the same day.

Participants

Under new section 4006(a)(7)(A) of ERISA, the termination premium is based on the number of "participants in the plan immediately before the termination date." It thus appears that participants are to be counted—for purposes of computing the termination premium—as of the day before the termination date under section 4048 of ERISA (the same day on which the contributing sponsor and controlled group members are determined). Section 4006.6 of the premium rates regulation already includes a definition of "participant" (which is used in computing the flat-rate premium), and DRA 2005 suggests no reason to depart from that definition for purposes of the termination premium.

Due Dates

The termination premium is payable each year for three years. Under new section 4006(a)(7)(D)(i)(I) of ERISA, as added by section 8101(b) of DRA 2005, the new premium is due within 30 days after the beginning of each of three "applicable 12-month periods," which are in turn described in new section 4006(a)(7)(C). New section 4006(a)(7)(C)(i)(I) provides that in general, the first applicable 12-month period starts with "the first month following the month in which the termination date occurs." (From this it is evident that calendar months are meant.) Under new section 4006(a)(7)(C)(i)(II), the second and third applicable 12-month periods are simply the two 12-month periods that follow the first applicable 12-month period.

But new section 4006(a)(7)(C)(ii) of ERISA defers the beginning of the first applicable 12-month period (and thus the due dates) in certain bankruptcy reorganization cases. This deferral rule comes into play where "the requirements of subparagraph (B) [of new section 4006(a)(7) of ERISA] are met in connection with the termination of the plan ***." (Section 401(b)(2) of PPA 2006 corrected an erroneous reference to "subparagraph (B)(i)(I)" in new section 4006(a)(7)(C)(ii) of ERISA.) Subparagraph (B) of new section 4006(a)(7)(B) of ERISA defers the applicability of the termination premium for distress or involuntary plan terminations that occur when bankruptcy reorganization proceedings are pending for terminations "under section 4041(c)(2)(B)(ii) [of ERISA] or under section 4042 [of ERISA]." Following the same reasoning discussed above regarding new section 4006(a)(7)(A) of ERISA (the general termination premium applicability provision), PBGC concludes that the bankruptcy reorganization deferral provision in new section 4006(a)(7)(B) of ERISA is meant to apply to a distress termination only when at least one contributing sponsor or controlled group member satisfies the bankruptcy reorganization test in section 4041(c)(2)(B)(ii).

In order for the due date deferral rule in new section 4006(a)(7)(C)(ii) of ERISA to apply, the requirements of subparagraph (B) of section 4006(a)(7) of ERISA must be met "with respect to 1 or more persons described in such subparagraph" (that is, one or more persons must be reorganizing in bankruptcy as described in subparagraph (B)). If so, then the first applicable 12-month period begins with "the first month following the month which includes the earliest date as of which each such person is discharged or dismissed in the case described in such clause [sic] in connection with such person." (The only clause mentioned in section 4006(a)(7)(C)(ii) of ERISA is clause (i)(I) of section 4006(a)(7)(C), which describes the first applicable 12-month period that applies if special bankruptcy rule does not. Thus the reference to "such clause" appears to be intended to refer to "such subparagraph"—that is, subparagraph (B)—and PBGC so interprets the reference.)

However, although subparagraph (B) of new section 4006(a)(7) of ERISA describes a case—a bankruptcy case—it does not describe a person. The only person mentioned in subparagraph (B) is "such person," with no cross-reference to another place where the person is described. Nonetheless, it seems clear that the person referred to must be a person that has a relationship to both the plan and the bankruptcy proceeding mentioned in subparagraph (B). Subparagraph (B) contains parenthetical language that is essentially identical to parenthetical language that appears in section 4041(c)(2)(B)(ii) of ERISA (which describes the bankruptcy reorganization test for distress terminations). In section 4041(c)(2)(B)(ii), the words "such person" in the parenthetical language refer to a contributing sponsor or member of a contributing sponsor's controlled group. PBGC infers that "such person" in new section 4006(a)(7)(B) of ERISA is meant to refer likewise to a contributing sponsor of the terminated plan or member of a contributing sponsor's controlled group—determined (consistent with the designated payor provision in new section 4007(a)(7)(D)(i)(II)) as of the day before the termination date under section 4048 of ERISA.

This inference is supported by the observation that these same persons—contributing sponsors and controlled group members—are the persons liable for the termination premium. It appears that Congress' intent was to defer the due date for the termination premium until the persons liable to pay it were not in bankruptcy proceedings. Accordingly, where the special bankruptcy rule for due dates applies, it is necessary to identify every contributing sponsor and controlled group member that was involved in bankruptcy reorganization proceedings on the termination date and determine the date when each one left bankruptcy—through dismissal of or discharge from the proceeding—or ceased to exist. (If an entity ceases to exist, its failure to emerge from bankruptcy should not postpone the termination premium due date.) Under new section 4006(a)(7)(C)(ii), the first applicable 12-month period for the termination will then begin with the calendar month that next begins following the last such date.

One due date issue not addressed by the statute is that the agreement or court action establishing a plan's termination date under ERISA section 4048 may occur well after the termination date so established. Where a termination date is thus "retroactively" set, one or more statutory due dates for the termination premium may already have passed when the termination date becomes known. Thus, termination premium payments could be overdue before it was determined that they were owed.

In cases of that kind, PBGC considers it appropriate to provide that where the termination date is set retroactively, the first applicable 12-month period does not begin immediately after the month in which the termination date falls, but rather begins immediately after the month in which the termination date is established. Where the special bankruptcy rule for due dates applies, this rule would come into play if the termination date was established after all contributing sponsors and controlled group members were out of bankruptcy reorganization proceedings, and would defer the beginning of the first applicable 12-month period until immediately after the month in which the termination date was established.

Other Bankruptcy Issues

The parenthetical language in new section 4006(a)(7)(B) of ERISA—"(or a case described in section 4041(c)(2)(B)(i) filed by or against such person has been converted, as of such date, to such a case in which reorganization is sought)"—shows that Congress focused on the fact that bankruptcy proceedings can be converted back and forth between liquidation and reorganization proceedings. But neither section 4006(a)(7)(B) nor section 4006(a)(7)(C)(ii) (which describes the special first applicable 12-month period) mentions conversion of a reorganization case to a liquidation case as being sufficient to trigger the beginning of the first applicable 12-month period. It thus appears that even after such a conversion, the first applicable 12-month period would be postponed until the (liquidation) bankruptcy proceeding were dismissed or the contributing sponsor or controlled group member discharged. This could be of significance where there were other persons liable for the termination premium that were not (or were no longer) in bankruptcy.

Section 8101(d)(2)(B) of DRA 2005 (which, as discussed above, excludes from the termination premium terminations that occur during the pendency of bankruptcy reorganization proceedings pursuant to a filing before October 18, 2005) says nothing about the persons involved in such proceedings. Following the reasoning above, PBGC concludes that section 8101(d)(2)(B) is intended to apply only where the subject of a pending bankruptcy proceeding is a contributing sponsor of the terminated plan or a member of a contributing sponsor's controlled group (and that these persons are to be identified as of the day before the termination date under section 4048 of ERISA). Section 8101(d)(2)(B) also does not mention conversion of a bankruptcy case from a liquidation proceeding to a reorganization, as new section 4006(a)(7)(B) of ERISA does. But the language of section 8101(d)(2)(B) is consistent with the interpretation that—like section 4006(a)(7)(B)—it covers bankruptcy proceedings begun as liquidation proceedings and converted to reorganization proceedings before the termination date under section 4048 of ERISA.

Termination Premium Rate

Under new section 4006(a)(7) of ERISA as added by section 8101(b) of DRA 2005, the termination premium is $1,250 per participant per year for three years. But under section 402(g)(2)(B) of PPA 2006 (which does not amend ERISA), the rate is increased from $1,250 to $2,500 where a commercial passenger airline or airline catering service elects funding relief (an extended underfunding amortization period and lenient assumptions for valuing liabilities) for a frozen plan under section 402(a)(1) of PPA 2006, if the plan terminates during the first five years of the funding relief period, unless the Secretary of Labor determines that the termination resulted from extraordinary circumstances such as a terrorist attack or other similar event.

Regulatory Provisions

This rule would add a new § 4006.7 to the premium rates regulation providing that the amount of the termination premium with respect to each applicable 12-month period is the premium rate (generally $1,250) times the number of participants, determined as of the day before the termination date, with a cross-reference from § 4006.3 (where the flat and variable premium rates are set forth). New § 4006.7(b) also explains the circumstances in which the termination premium rate is $2,500 rather than $1,250. In addition, the rule would add a new § 4007.13 to the premium payment regulation (with a cross-reference from § 4006.7), where the rest of the provisions about the termination premium are found.

New § 4007.13 contains provisions specific to the termination premium, and it supplements provisions in existing sections of Part 4007 that also apply to the termination premium. Section 4007.13(a) describes when the termination premium applies; § 4007.13 (d), (e), and (f) deal with due dates; § 4007.13(g) deals with what persons are liable for the termination premium. The provisions on these three topics reflect the discussions above.

Section 4007.13(b) makes each contributing sponsor and controlled group member (determined as of the day before the termination date under section 4048 of ERISA) responsible for filing required termination premium information and payments, and (where there is more than one such person) provides that any one can file on behalf of all of them. This provision ensures that, so long as there is at least one person still in existence that is liable for the termination premium, there will be at least one identifiable entity with responsibility to file.

This provision is similar to § 4010.3 of PBGC's regulation on Annual Financial and Actuarial Information Reporting (Part 4010 of PBGC's regulations) and § 4043.3(a) of PBGC's regulation on Reportable Events and Certain Other Notification Requirements (Part 4043 of PBGC's regulations). Thus, only a single filing of the premium and required premium information is required, but if it is not timely made, PBGC could seek enforcement against any or all contributing sponsors and controlled group members.

Section 4007.13(c) provides for a discretionary "facts-and-circumstances" penalty for failure to pay the termination premium timely, instead of the automatic 1 percent or 5 percent penalty that applies to late payment of flat- and variable-rate premiums under § 4007.8(a). PBGC wants to preserve flexibility in penalizing failures to pay the new premium in full and on time while it gains experience with the new premium. The penalty is limited to 100 percent of the amount of termination premium not timely filed.

In addition, this rule would amend several sections in the existing premium payment regulation to eliminate inconsistencies or potential inconsistencies between existing language in those sections and the termination premium provisions.

Technical Changes

PBGC is taking this opportunity to make some technical changes (unrelated to DRA 2005 or PPA 2006) to its regulations on Premium Rates and Payment of Premiums.

Section 4006.3 of the premium rates regulation refers to basic benefits guaranteed under section 4022(a) of ERISA (which relates only to single-employer plans) and omits mention of section 4022A(a) of ERISA (which relates to multi-employer plans). This rule would add a reference to section 4022A(a).

Section 4007.11(d) of the premium payment regulation states that where proration of the flat- and variable-rate premiums is available under § 4006.5(f) of the premium rates regulation, the un-prorated premium must be paid in full (even if the plan would be entitled to a refund). This provision is anachronistic: PBGC now permits payment of the prorated amount under § 4006.5(f), rather than requiring that a filer pay the un-prorated amount and request a refund. This rule would remove the outdated provision.

Section 4007.11(e) of the premium payment regulation permits PBGC to return improper filings and consider them not made. PBGC is not exercising this authority, and the provision is unnecessary; PBGC has authority to assess penalties under ERISA section 4071 for failure to submit material information under the premium payment regulation. This rule would remove § 4007.11(e).

Applicability

The regulatory changes made by this rule to implement the provisions of section 8101 of DRA 2005 would apply (as section 8101 of DRA 2005 does) to plan years beginning after 2005 and to terminations with termination dates after 2005 (subject to the special rule for bankruptcies filed before October 18, 2005). The regulatory changes made by this rule to implement the provisions of section 405 of PPA 2006 would apply (as section 405 of PPA 2006 does) to plan years beginning after 2006.

Compliance With Rulemaking Guidelines

The PBGC has determined, in consultation with the Office of Management and Budget, that this proposed rule is a "significant regulatory action" under Executive Order 12866. The Office of Management and Budget, therefore, has reviewed the rule under Executive Order 12866.

PBGC certifies under section 605(b) of the Regulatory Flexibility Act that the amendments in this rule will not have a significant economic impact on a substantial number of small entities. This rule implements statutory changes made by Congress. It provides guidance on how to calculate, pay, and substantiate the premiums prescribed by statute and imposes no significant burden beyond the burden imposed by statute. Furthermore:

The statutorily imposed increase in the flat-rate premium is at most $11 per participant per year, which does not constitute a significant economic impact where a plan has a small number of participants. Although the flat-rate premium will increase as the number of participants increases, the economic impact of the flat-rate premium relative to the size of the entity will remain fairly constant and will not be significant for a substantial number of entities of any size.

The statutorily imposed cap on the variable-rate premium will save qualifying plans money. The rule simply interprets the statutory provisions.

The statutorily imposed termination premium will not affect a substantial number of entities of any size.

Accordingly, as provided in section 605 of the Regulatory Flexibility Act (5 U.S.C. 601 et seq.), sections 603 and 604 do not apply.

The information requirements relating to the flat-rate and variable-rate premiums have been approved by the Office of Management and Budget under the Paperwork Reduction Act (OMB control number 1212-0009, expires April 30, 2008).

PBGC is submitting the information requirements relating to the termination premium to the Office of Management and Budget for review and approval under the Paperwork Reduction Act. Copies of PBGC's request may be obtained free of charge by contacting the Disclosure Division of the Office of the General Counsel of PBGC, 1200 K Street, NW., Washington, DC 20005, 202-326-4040.

PBGC needs this information to identify the plan for which a termination premium is paid to PBGC, to verify the determination of the premium, and to identify the persons liable for the premium.

PBGC expects that it will receive termination premium filings from about 30 contributing sponsors or controlled group members annually and that the total annual burden of the collection of information will be about 40 hours and $264,000.

Comments on the paperwork provisions under this proposed rule should be mailed to the Office of Information and Regulatory Affairs, Office of Management and Budget, Attention: Desk Officer for Pension Benefit Guaranty Corporation, Washington, DC 20503. Although comments may be submitted through April 23, 2007, the Office of Management and Budget requests that comments be received on or before March 22, 2007 to ensure their consideration. Comments may address (among other things)—

Whether the proposed collection of information is needed for the proper performance of PBGC's functions and will have practical utility;

The accuracy of PBGC's estimate of the burden of the proposed collection of information, including the validity of the methodology and assumptions used;

Enhancement of the quality, utility, and clarity of the information to be collected; and

Minimizing the burden of the collection of information on those who are to respond, including through the use of appropriate automated, electronic, mechanical, or other technological collection techniques or other forms of information technology, e.g., permitting electronic submission of responses.

List of Subjects

29 CFR Part 4006

Pension insurance, Pensions.

29 CFR Part 4007

Penalties, Pension insurance, Pensions, Reporting and recordkeeping requirements.

For the reasons given above, PBGC is amending 29 CFR parts 4006 and 4007 as follows.

PART 4006—PREMIUM RATES

1. The authority citation for part 4006 continues to read as follows:

Authority: 29 U.S.C. 1302(b)(3), 1306, 1307.

2. In § 4006.3:

a. The introductory text is amended by removing the words "§ 4006.5 (dealing with exemptions and special rules)" and adding in their place the words "§ 4006.5 (dealing with exemptions and special rules) and § 4006.7 (dealing with premiums for certain terminated single-employer plans)"; and by removing the words "section 4022(a)" and adding in their place the words "section 4022(a) or section 4022A(a)".

b. Paragraph (a) introductory text is amended by removing the words "multiplied by—" and adding in their place the words "multiplied by the applicable flat premium rate determined under paragraph (c) of this section.".

c. Paragraphs (a)(1) and (a)(2) are removed.

d. Paragraph (b) is revised, and new paragraphs (c) and (d) are added, to read as follows:

§ 4006.3 Premium rate.

*****

(b) Variable-rate premium.

(1) In general. Subject to the limitation in paragraph (b)(2) of this section, the variable-rate premium is $9 for each $1,000 of a single-employer plan's unfunded vested benefits, as determined under § 4006.4.

(2) Cap on variable-rate premium. If a plan is described in paragraph (b)(3) of this section for the premium payment year, the variable-rate premium does not exceed $5 multiplied by the square of the number of participants in the plan on the last day of the plan year preceding the premium payment year. For example, if the number of participants in the plan on the last day of the plan year preceding the premium payment year is 20, the variable-rate premium does not exceed $2,000 ($5 x 20\2\ = $5 x 400 = $2,000).

(3) Plans eligible for cap. A plan is described in this paragraph (b)(3) for the premium payment year if the aggregate number of employees of all employers in the plan's controlled group on the first day of the premium payment year is 25 or fewer.

(4) Meaning of "employee." For purposes of paragraph (b)(3) of this section, the aggregate number of employees is determined in the same manner as under section 410(b)(1) of the Code, taking into account the provisions of section 414(m) and (n) of the Code, but without regard to section 410(b)(3), (4), and (5) of the Code.

(c) Applicable flat premium rate. The applicable flat premium rate is:

(1) For a premium payment year beginning before 2006—

(i) For a single-employer plan, $19, and

(ii) For a multiemployer plan, $2.60.

(2) For a premium payment year beginning in 2006—

(i) For a single-employer plan, $30, and

(ii) For a multiemployer plan, $8.

(3) For a premium payment year beginning after 2006, the greater of—

(i) The applicable flat premium rate for plan years beginning in the calendar year preceding the calendar year in which the premium payment year begins, or

(ii) The adjusted flat rate determined under paragraph (d) of this section for the premium payment year.

(d) Adjusted flat rate. The adjusted flat rate for a premium payment year beginning after 2006 is determined by—

(1) Multiplying the applicable flat premium rate for 2006 by the ratio of—

(i) The national average wage index (as defined in section 209(k)(1) of the Social Security Act) for the first of the two calendar years preceding the calendar year in which the premium payment year begins, to

(ii) The national average wage index (as so defined) for 2004; and

(2) Rounding the result to the nearest multiple of $1 (rounding up any unrounded result that equals some whole number of dollars plus 50 cents).

3. New § 4006.7 is added to read as follows:

§ 4006.7 Premium rate for certain terminated single-employer plans.

(a) The premium under this section ("termination premium") applies to a DRA 2005 termination described in § 4007.13 of this chapter.

(b) The amount of the premium under this section that is payable with respect to each applicable 12-month period (as described in § 4007.13 of this chapter) is the number of participants in the plan, determined as of the day before the termination date under section 4048 of ERISA, multiplied by the termination premium rate. In general, the termination premium rate is $1,250. However, the termination premium rate is $2,500 for an "eligible plan" under section 402(c)(1) of the Pension Protection Act of 2006 (dealing with certain plans of commercial passenger airlines and airline catering services) while an election under section 402(a)(1) of the Pension Protection Act of 2006 (dealing with alternative funding schedules) is in effect for the plan if the plan terminates during the five-year period beginning on the first day of the first applicable plan year (as defined in section 402(c)(2) of that Act) with respect to the plan, unless the Secretary of Labor determines that the plan terminated as a result of extraordinary circumstances such as a terrorist attack or other similar event.

(c) The premium under this section is in addition to any other premium under this part.

(d) See § 4007.13 of this chapter for further rules about termination premiums.

PART 4007—PAYMENT OF PREMIUMS

4. The authority citation for part 4007 continues to read as follows:

Authority: 29 U.S.C. 1302(b)(3), 1303(a), 1306, 1307.

5. Section 4007.3 is amended by removing the words "The plan administrator" and adding in their place the words "Subject to the provisions of § 4007.13, the plan administrator"; and by removing "§ 4007.11" and adding in its place the words "this part".

6. In § 4007.7, paragraph (a) is amended by removing "§ 4007.11" and adding in its place the words "this part".

7. In § 4007.8:

a. Paragraph (a) introductory text is amended by removing the words "If any premium payment due" and adding in their place the words "Subject to the provisions of § 4007.13, if any premium payment due"; and by removing "§ 4007.11" and adding in its place the words "this part".

b. Paragraph (a)(1)(i) is amended by removing the word "plan's".

c. Paragraph (a)(1) introductory text is revised to read as follows:

§ 4007.8 Late payment penalty charges.

(a) Penalty charge. ***

(1) Penalty rate; in general. Except as provided in paragraph (a)(2) of this section, the penalty rate is—

*****

8. In § 4007.9, paragraph (a) is amended by removing the words "by a plan administrator"; and by removing the words "that plan's" and adding in their place the words "a plan's".

9. In § 4007.10:

a. Paragraph (a)(1) is amended by removing the words "plan administrator" and adding in their place the words "designated recordkeeper under paragraph (a)(3) of this section".

b. Paragraph (a)(2) is amended by removing the words "The plan administrator" and adding in their place the words "A designated recordkeeper".

c. Paragraph (b) is amended by removing the words "for any premium payment year".

d. Paragraph (c)(1) is amended by removing the words "The plan administrator" and adding in their place the words "A designated recordkeeper".

e. Paragraph (c)(2) is amended by removing the words "the plan administrator" and adding in their place the words "a designated recordkeeper".

f. Paragraph (c)(2)(ii) is amended by removing the words "plan administrator" and adding in their place the words "designated recordkeeper".

g. New paragraph (a)(3) is added to read as follows:

§ 4007.10 Recordkeeping; audits; disclosure of information.

(a) Retention of records to support premium payments.

*****

(3) Designated recordkeepers.

(i) With respect to the flat-rate and variable-rate premiums described in § 4006.3 of this chapter, the plan administrator is the designated recordkeeper.

(ii) With respect to the premium for certain terminated single-employer plans described in § 4006.7 of this chapter, each person who was a contributing sponsor of such a plan, or was a member of a contributing sponsor's controlled group, as of the day before the plan's termination date is a designated recordkeeper.

*****

10. In § 4007.11:

a. Paragraph (a) introductory text is amended by removing the words "The premium filing due date for small plans" and adding in their place the words "For flat-rate and variable-rate premiums, the premium filing due date for small plans".

b. Paragraph (a)(3) introductory text is amended by removing the words "the premium form or forms and payment or payments for the short plan year shall be filed by" and adding in their place the words "the due date or dates for the flat-rate premium and any variable-rate premium for the short plan year are"; and by removing the words "for the premium forms and payments".

c. Paragraph (c) introductory text is amended by removing the words "the premium form and all premium payments due for the first plan year of coverage of any new plan or newly covered plan shall be filed on or before" and adding in their place the words "the due date for the flat-rate premium and any variable-rate premium for the first plan year of coverage of any new plan or newly covered plan shall be".

d. Paragraph (d) is amended by removing the words "to file the forms or forms prescribed by this part and to pay any premiums due" and adding in their place the words "to make flat-rate and (as applicable) variable-rate premium filings and payments under this part"; and by removing the last sentence of the paragraph (beginning "The entire ***" and ending "*** § 4006.5(f).").

e. Paragraph (e) is removed.

11. In § 4007.12, paragraph (a) is amended by removing the words "to file the applicable forms and to submit the premium payment" and adding in their place the words "to make flat-rate and variable-rate premium filings and payments under this part"; and by removing the words "liable for premium payments" and adding in their place "liable for flat-rate and variable-rate premium payments".

12. New § 4007.13 is added to read as follows:

§ 4007.13 Premiums for certain terminated single-employer plans.

(a) Applicability.

(1) In general. This section applies where there is a "DRA 2005 termination" of a plan. Subject to paragraph (a)(2) of this section, there is a DRA 2005 termination where a single-employer plan's termination date under section 4048 of ERISA is after 2005 and either—

(i) The plan terminates under section 4042 of ERISA, or

(ii) The plan terminates under section 4041(c) of ERISA and at least one contributing sponsor or member of a contributing sponsor's controlled group meets the requirements of section 4041(c)(2)(B)(ii) or (iii) of ERISA.

(2) Plans terminated during reorganization proceedings. Except as provided in paragraph (a)(3) of this section, a DRA 2005 termination of a plan does not occur where as of the plan's termination date under section 4048 of ERISA—

(i) A bankruptcy proceeding has been filed by or against any person that was a contributing sponsor of the plan on the day before the plan's termination date or that was on that day a member of any controlled group of which any such contributing sponsor was a member,

(ii) The proceeding is pending as a reorganization proceeding under chapter 11 of title 11, United States Code (or under any similar law of a State or political subdivision of a State),

(iii) The person has not been discharged from the proceeding, and

(iv) The proceeding was filed before October 18, 2005.

(3) Special rule for certain airline-related plans. Paragraph (a)(2) of this section does not apply to an "eligible plan" under section 402(c)(1) of the Pension Protection Act of 2006 (dealing with certain plans of commercial passenger airlines and airline catering services) while an election under section 402(a)(1) of the Pension Protection Act of 2006 (dealing with alternative funding schedules) is in effect for the plan.

(4) Termination premium. A premium as described in § 4006.7 of this chapter is payable to PBGC with respect to a DRA 2005 termination each year for three years after the termination (the "termination premium").

(b) Filing requirements; method of filing. Notwithstanding § 4007.3, in the case of a DRA 2005 termination of a plan, each person that was a contributing sponsor of the plan on the day before the plan's termination date or that was on that day a member of any controlled group of which any such contributing sponsor was a member is responsible for filing prescribed termination premium information and payments. Any such person may file on behalf of all such persons.

(c) Late payment penalty charges. Notwithstanding § 4007.8(a), if any required termination premium payment is not filed by the due date under paragraph (d) of this section, PBGC may assess a late payment penalty charge based on the facts and circumstances, subject to waiver under § 4007.8(b), (c), (d), or (e). The charge will not exceed the amount of termination premium not timely filed.

(d) Due dates. Notwithstanding § 4007.11, the due date for the termination premium is the 30th day of each of three applicable 12-month periods. The three applicable 12-month periods with respect to a DRA 2005 termination of a plan are—

(1) First applicable 12-month period. Except as provided in paragraph (e) or (f) of this section, the period of 12 calendar months beginning with the first calendar month following the calendar month in which occurs the plan's termination date under section 4048 of ERISA, and

(2) Subsequent applicable 12-month periods. Each of the first two periods of 12 calendar months that immediately follow the first applicable 12-month period.

(e) Certain reorganization cases.

(1) This paragraph (e) applies with respect to a DRA 2005 termination of a plan if the conditions in both paragraph (e)(2) and paragraph (e)(3) of this section are satisfied.

(2) The condition of this paragraph (e)(2) is that either—

(i) The plan terminates under section 4042 of ERISA, or

(ii) The plan terminates under section 4041(c) of ERISA and at least one contributing sponsor or member of a contributing sponsor's controlled group meets the requirements of section 4041(c)(2)(B)(ii) of ERISA.

(3) The condition of this paragraph (e)(3) is that as of the plan's termination date under section 4048 of ERISA—

(i) A bankruptcy proceeding has been filed by or against any person that was a contributing sponsor of the plan on the day before the plan's termination date or that was on that day a member of any controlled group of which any such contributing sponsor was a member,

(ii) The proceeding is pending as a reorganization proceeding under chapter 11 of title 11, United States Code (or under any similar law of a State or political subdivision of a State), and

(iii) The person has not been discharged from the proceeding.

(4) If this paragraph (e) applies with respect to a DRA 2005 termination of a plan, then except as provided in paragraph (f) of this section, the first applicable 12-month period with respect to the plan is the period of 12 calendar months beginning with the first calendar month following the calendar month in which occurs the earliest date when, for every person that was a contributing sponsor of the plan on the day before the plan's termination date under section 4048 of ERISA, or that was on that day a member of any controlled group of which any such contributing sponsor was a member, either—

(i) There is not pending any bankruptcy proceeding that was filed by or against such person and that was, as of the plan's termination date under section 4048 of ERISA, a reorganization proceeding under chapter 11 of title 11, United States Code (or under any similar law of a State or political subdivision of a State), or

(ii) The person has been discharged from any such proceeding, or

(iii) The person no longer exists.

(f) Retroactive plan termination date. If a plan's termination date under section 4048 of ERISA is in the past when it is established by agreement or court action as described in section 4048 of ERISA, then the first applicable 12-month period for determining the due dates of the termination premium begins with the later of—

(1) The first calendar month following the calendar month in which the termination date is established by agreement or court action as described in section 4048 of ERISA, or

(2) The first calendar month specified in paragraph (d)(1) of this section or (if paragraph (e) of this section applies) paragraph (e)(4) of this section.

(g) Liability for termination premiums. In the case of a DRA 2005 termination of a plan, each person that was a contributing sponsor of the plan on the day before the plan's termination date, or that was on that day a member of any controlled group of which any such contributing sponsor was a member, is jointly and severally liable for termination premiums with respect to the plan.

Issued in Washington, DC, this 13th day of February, 2007.

Vincent K. Snowbarger, Interim Director, Pension Benefit Guaranty Corporation.

[FR Doc. E7-2812 Filed 2-16-07; 8:45 am]

¶ 20,537A

Pension Benefit Guaranty Corporation (PBGC): Proposed rule: Variable rate premium: Pension Protection Act of 2006 (PPA).—The Pension Benefit Guaranty Corporation (PBGC) has issued proposed amendments to its regulations on variable premium rates to implement provisions of the Pension Protection Act of 2006 (PPA; P.L. 109-280) under ERISA §4006 (Premium Rates) and ERISA §4007 (Payment of Premiums) that are effective beginning in 2008. The proposed regulations streamline and make consistent measurement dates and definitions for calculating variable rate premiums (VRPs) to comply with the PPA. The proposed rules would also alter due dates of variable rate premiums (in some cases) to better coincide with the new definitions of "unfunded vested benefits" (UVB) and "premium funding target."

The proposed regulations, which were published in the Federal Register on May 31, 2007 (72 FR 30308), are reproduced below.

The preamble to the final regulations, which was published in the Federal Register on March 21, 2008 (73 FR 15065), is reproduced at ¶ 24,266. The changes made by the final regulations are reflected at ¶ 15,361A, ¶ 15,361B, ¶ 15,361C, ¶ 15,361D, ¶ 15,361E, ¶ 15,371A, ¶ 15,371B, ¶ 15,371F, ¶ 15,371G, ¶ 15,371I, and ¶ 15,371J.

¶ 20,537B

Employee Benefit Security Administration (EBSA): Proposed rule: Individual account plans: Annuities: Selection of provider: Pension Protection Act of 2006 (PPA).—The Employee Benefit Security Administration (EBSA) has released interim final and proposed regulations to comply with provisions of the Pension Protection Act of 2006 (PPA; P.L. 109-280) concerning annuity provider selection. The proposed regulation provides a new safe harbor applicable to annuity provider selection by fiduciaries of defined contribution individual plan accounts, such as 401(k) plan accounts.

The proposed regulations, which were published in the Federal Register on September 12, 2007 (72 FR 52021), are reproduced below. The preamble to the final interim regulation, which limits prior annuity provider selection standards to defined benefit plans, is reproduced at ¶ 24,261.

DEPARTMENT OF LABOR

Employee Benefits Security Administration

29 CFR Part 2550

RIN 1210-AB19

Selection of Annuity Providers for Individual Account Plans

AGENCY: Employee Benefits Security Administration, Department of Labor.

ACTION: Proposed regulation.

SUMMARY: This document contains a proposed regulation that, upon adoption, would establish a safe harbor for the selection of annuity providers for the purpose of benefit distributions from individual account plans covered by title I of the Employee Retirement Income Security Act (ERISA). Also appearing in today's Federal Register is an interim final rule amending Interpretive Bulletin 95-1 to limit the application of the Bulletin to the selection of annuity providers for defined benefit plans. The proposed regulation, upon adoption, will affect plan sponsors and fiduciaries of individual account plans, and the participants and beneficiaries covered by such plans.

DATES: Written comments on the proposed regulation should be received by the Department of Labor on or before November 13, 2007.

ADDRESSES: To facilitate the receipt and processing of comments, the Department encourages interested persons to submit their comments electronically to http://www.regulations.gov. (follow instructions for submission of comments) or e-ORI@dol.gov. Persons submitting comments electronically are encouraged not to submit paper copies. Persons interested in submitting comments on paper should send or deliver their comments to: Office of Regulations and Interpretations, Employee Benefits Security Administration, Room N-5669, U.S. Department of Labor, 200 Constitution Avenue, NW., Washington, DC 20210. Attention: Annuity Regulation. Comments received will be posted without change, including any personal information provided, to http://www.regulations.gov and http://www.dol.gov/ebsa, and also available for public inspection at the Public Disclosure Room, Employee Benefits Security Administration, U.S. Department of Labor, Room N-1513, 200 Constitution Avenue, NW., Washington, DC 20210.

FOR FURTHER INFORMATION CONTACT: Janet A. Walters or Allison E. Wielobob, Office of Regulations and Interpretations, Employee Benefits Security Administration, U.S. Department of Labor, Washington, DC 20210, (202) 693-8510. This is not a toll-free number.

SUPPLEMENTARY INFORMATION:

A. Background

In 1995, the Department issued Interpretive Bulletin 95-1 (29 CFR 2509.95-1) (the IB), providing guidance concerning the fiduciary standards under Part 4 of Title I of ERISA applicable to the selection of annuity providers for purposes of pension plan benefit distributions. In general, the IB makes clear that the selection of an annuity provider in connection with benefit distributions is a fiduciary act governed by the fiduciary standards of section 404(a)(1), including the duty to act prudently and solely in the interest of the plan's participants and beneficiaries. In this regard, the IB provides that plan fiduciaries must take steps calculated to obtain the safest annuity available, unless under the circumstances it would be in the interest of the participants and beneficiaries to do otherwise. The IB also provides that fiduciaries must conduct an objective, thorough and analytical search for purposes of identifying providers from which to purchase annuities and sets forth six factors that should be considered by fiduciaries in evaluating a provider's claims paying ability and creditworthiness.

In Advisory Opinion 2002-14A (Dec. 18, 2002) the Department expressed the view that the general fiduciary principles set forth in the IB with regard to the selection of annuity providers apply equally to defined benefit and defined contribution plans. The opinion recognized that, the selection of annuity providers by the fiduciary of a defined contribution plan would be governed by section 404(a)(1) and, therefore, such fiduciary, in evaluating claims paying ability and creditworthiness of an annuity provider, should take into account the six factors set forth in 29 CFR 2509.95-1(c).

The Pension Protection Act of 2006 (the PPA) (Pub. L. 109-280, 120 Stat. 780) was enacted on August 17, 2006. Section 625 of the PPA directs the Secretary to issue final regulations within one year of the date of enactment, clarifying that the selection of an annuity contract as an optional form of distribution from an individual account plan is not subject to the safest available annuity standard under Interpretive Bulletin 95-1 and is subject to all otherwise applicable fiduciary standards. Consistent with section 625 of the PPA, the Department is amending Interpretive Bulletin 95-1, also published in today's Federal Register, to limit its application to defined benefit plans.

Given that the fiduciary standards in Interpretive Bulletin 95-1 would not apply to the selection of an annuity contract as an optional form of distribution from an individual account plan, the Department is proposing the adoption of this regulation that, in the form of a safe harbor, provides guidance concerning the fiduciary considerations attendant to the selection of annuity providers and contracts for purposes of benefit distributions from individual account plans. An overview of the proposed regulation follows.

B. Overview of Proposal

Scope of the Proposal

Paragraph (a) of § 2550.404a-4 provides that the scope of the proposed regulation is to provide guidance concerning ERISA's fiduciary standards applicable to the selection of annuity providers for the purpose of benefit distributions from an individual account plan and benefit distribution options made available to participants and beneficiaries under such plans. Paragraph (a) also includes a reference to § 2509.95-1 for guidance concerning the selection of annuity providers for defined benefit plans.

Application of General Fiduciary Standards

Paragraph (b) of § 2550.404a-4 provides that selecting an annuity provider in connection with a benefit distribution, or a benefit distribution option made available to plan participants and beneficiaries, is a fiduciary act governed by the fiduciary standards of section 404(a)(1) of ERISA, pursuant to which fiduciaries must discharge their duties with respect to the plan solely in the interest of the participants and beneficiaries. Section 404(a)(1)(A) provides that the fiduciary must act for the exclusive purpose of providing benefits to the participants and beneficiaries and defraying reasonable plan administration expenses. Section 404(a)(1)(B) requires a fiduciary to act with the care, skill, prudence and diligence under the prevailing circumstances that a prudent person acting in a like capacity and familiar with such matters would use.

Selection of Annuity Providers and Contracts

Pursuant to paragraph (c) of § 2550.404a-4, a fiduciary will have acted prudently in selecting an annuity provider and contract for purposes of benefit distributions, or benefit distribution options made available to participants and beneficiaries under the plan, if the conditions of that paragraph are satisfied. The specific conditions of this safe harbor are set forth in paragraph (c)(1)(A)-(F) of the proposal.

Consistent with the requirements applicable to the selection of service providers generally, paragraph (c)(1)(A) requires the fiduciary to engage in an objective, thorough and analytical search for the purpose of identifying and selecting providers from which to purchase annuities. Any such process must avoid self dealing, conflicts of interest or other improper influence, and should, to the extent feasible, involve consideration of competing annuity providers.

Paragraph (c)(1)(B) requires that the fiduciary responsible for the selection of the annuity provider appropriately determine whether he or she has the expertise or knowledge to meaningfully evaluate the annuity provider consistent with the requirements of the regulation. In those instances where the fiduciary appropriately determines that he or she has such expertise or knowledge, the fiduciary is not required to engage an independent expert (i.e., an expert independent of the annuity provider) to evaluate the annuity provider.

Paragraph (c)(1)(C) requires that the fiduciary appropriately consider information sufficient to assess the ability of the annuity provider to make all future payments under the annuity contract. Paragraph (c)(1)(D) requires that the fiduciary appropriately consider the cost of the annuity contract in relation to the benefits and administrative services to be provided under the contract. Paragraph (c)(1)(E) requires that the fiduciary appropriately conclude that, at the time of the selection, the annuity provider is financially able to make all future payments under the annuity contract and the cost of the annuity contract is reasonable in relation to the benefits and services to be provided under the contract.

Paragraph (c)(1)(F) requires that, for annuity providers selected to provide multiple annuities over time, the fiduciary periodically review the appropriateness of the conclusion described in paragraph (c)(1)(E), taking into account the factors described in paragraph (c)(1)(C) and (D). However, paragraph (c)(1)(F) does not require the fiduciary to review the appropriateness of an annuity provider with respect to an annuity contract after it is purchased for an individual participant or beneficiary.

Paragraph (c)(2) provides additional guidance regarding how the fiduciary can meet the requirements of paragraphs (c)(1)(C) and (D). For example, paragraph (c)(2)(C) requires consideration of the annuity provider's experience and financial expertise. Paragraph (c)(2)(D) requires consideration of the annuity provider's level of capital, surplus, and reserves available to make payments under the annuity contract. Paragraph (c)(2)(E) requires that the fiduciary consider whether an annuity provider's rating (as determined by an appropriate rating service(s)) demonstrate or raise questions regarding the provider's ability to make future payments under the annuity contract. And, paragraph (c)(2)(G) requires that the fiduciary consider the availability of additional protections through state guaranty associations and the extent of their guarantees. In this regard, the type of information that the fiduciary should consider is information that is available to the public and easily accessible through such associations as well as state insurance departments. If known facts call into question the ability of a state association offering guarantees to meet its obligations under the guarantee, it would be incumbent on the fiduciary to weigh that information when selecting an annuity provider.

Lastly, paragraph (c)(2)(H) requires consideration of any other information that the fiduciary knows or should know would be relevant to an evaluation of paragraphs (c)(1)(C) and (D). Such information would include that information which may not otherwise be described in paragraph (c)(2) or information surrounding events which, because of timing, may not yet have been reflected in those factors. For example, if a fiduciary learned through public indicators, such as the news media, that a corporate event affecting an annuity provider could call into serious question the provider's ability to make future payments under its contracts, or if the provider publicly stated that it was unlikely to survive the event in a manner that would ensure its ability to meet its financial commitments, the fiduciary would have an obligation to consider that information in evaluating paragraphs (c)(1)(C) and (D).

C. Request for Comments

The Department invites comments from interested persons on all aspects of the proposed regulation. To facilitate the receipt and processing of comments, EBSA encourages interested persons to submit their comments electronically to http://www.regulations.gov. (follow instructions for the submission of comments) or e-ORI@dol.gov. Persons submitting comments electronically are encouraged not to submit paper copies. Persons interested in submitting comments on paper should send or deliver their comments to: Office of Regulations and Interpretations, Employee Benefits Security Administration, Room N-5669, U.S. Department of Labor, 200 Constitution Avenue, NW., Washington, DC 20210. Attention: Annuity Regulation. All comments will be available to the public, without charge, online at www.regulations.gov and http://www.dol.gov/ebsa, and at the Public Disclosure Room, Employee Benefits Security Administration, U.S. Department of Labor, Room N-1513, 200 Constitution Avenue, NW., Washington, DC, 20210 from 8 a.m. to 4:30 p.m. (Monday-Friday).

D. Effective Date

The Department proposes to make the regulation effective 60 days after the date of publication of the final rule in the Federal Register.

E. Regulatory Impact Analysis

Executive Order 12866 Statement

Under Executive Order 12866 (58 FR 51735), the Department must determine whether a regulatory action is "significant" and therefore subject to review by the Office of Management and Budget (OMB). Section 3(f) of the Executive Order defines a "significant regulatory action" as an action that is likely to result in a rule (1) having an annual effect on the economy of $100 million or more, or adversely and materially affecting a sector of the economy, productivity, competition, jobs, the environment, public health or safety, or State, local or tribal governments or communities (also referred to as "economically significant"); (2) creating serious inconsistency or otherwise interfering with an action taken or planned by another agency; (3) materially altering the budgetary impacts of entitlement grants, user fees, or loan programs or the rights and obligations of recipients thereof; or (4) raising novel legal or policy issues arising out of legal mandates, the President's priorities, or the principles set forth in the Executive Order. For purposes of Executive Order 12866, the Department has determined that it is appropriate to review the proposed regulation contained in this document, which, upon adoption, will provide, in the form of a safe harbor, standards for the selection of annuity providers by fiduciaries of individual account plans, in conjunction with the amendment to Interpretive Bulletin 95-1, also appearing in today's Federal Register, that, consistent with Congressional intent, establishes that the standards of the Bulletin no longer apply to individual account plans. These regulatory actions together implement section 625 of the Pension Protection Act of 2006. Having considered these regulatory actions in

the aggregate, the Department believes that these actions are not economically significant within the meaning of section 3(f)(1) the Executive Order. The actions, however, have been determined to be significant within the meaning of section 3(f)(4) of the Executive Order, and the Department accordingly provides the following assessment of the potential benefits and costs. As elaborated below, the Department believes that the benefits of the regulation will justify its costs.

There is growing concern that, with increases in life expectancy, many retirees may outlive their retirement savings. In this environment, annuities offer one means by which retirees may ensure a lifetime income.[1] While a number of possible factors may influence a plan sponsor's decision not to offer an annuity distribution option as part of its plan, an often cited factor is concern about the fiduciary liability attendant to selecting the "safest available" annuity, as required by Interpretive Bulletin 95-1.[2] The Department believes that many of those plan sponsors that viewed fiduciary liability attendant to compliance with the "safest available" annuity standard as the primary impediment to including an annuity option in their plan will be more willing to consider the addition of such an option with the amendment of Interpretive Bulletin 95-1 and the establishment of fiduciary standards, in the form of a safe harbor, for the prudent selection of annuity providers for individual account plans. Providing such a safe harbor to plan sponsors is unlikely to discourage plans that currently offer an annuity option from continuing to do so, and it may encourage more plans to offer an annuity alternative. This will give more participants the opportunity to annuitize their retirement savings, while not impeding them from choosing other distribution options.

The proposed regulation could affect demand for annuities in two ways: by lowering the price of annuities, and by encouraging more plans to offer annuities by providing a safe harbor. Current research on annuities suggests that individual demand is largely price inelastic, which implies that a lower price would not result in a significant increase in individuals choosing an annuity. Holding the propensity of eligible individuals electing annuities constant but increasing the number of plans offering annuities, however, would result in an increase in the total number of individuals electing annuities.

The Department estimates that in response to the safe harbor, the share of participants offered an annuity option for their withdrawal would increase by 1 percentage point, from 25 to 26 percent,[3] while the share of eligible participants electing an annuity would remain at 6 percent.[4] The resulting total amount transferred into annuities by DC participants annually would be $2.41 billion, $93 million of which would be attributable to the regulation.[5] While the estimated annual effect of this regulatory action is not considered "economically significant," it is sensitive to assumptions regarding average separation rates, election rates and account balances.[6] The Department invites comments from interested persons on the appropriateness of these assumptions.

Regulatory Flexibility Act

The Regulatory Flexibility Act (5 U.S.C. 601 et seq.) (RFA) imposes certain requirements with respect to Federal rules that are subject to the notice and comment requirements of section 553(b) of the Administrative Procedure Act (5 U.S.C. 551 et seq.) and that are likely to have a significant economic impact on a substantial number of small entities. Unless an agency certifies that a proposed rule will not have a significant economic impact on a substantial number of small entities, section 603 of the RFA requires that the agency present an initial regulatory flexibility analysis at the time of the publication of the notice of proposed rulemaking describing the impact of the rule on small entities and seeking public comment on such impact. The Department has considered the likely impact of the proposed regulation on small entities in connection with its assessment under Executive Order 12866, described above, and believes this rule will not have a significant impact on a substantial number of small entities. See foregoing analysis.

---

[1] See GAO-03-810 Private Pensions: Participants Need Information on Risks They Face in Managing Pension Assets at and during Retirement (July 2003) at http://www.gao.gov/htext/d03810.html. Also see Report of Working Group on Retirement Distributions & Options (November 2005), Advisory Council on Employee Welfare and Pension Benefit Plans, at http://www.dol.gov/ebsa/publications/AC_1105A_report.html.

[2] Such factors may include burdens attendant to administering qualified joint and survivor annuity options and spousal consent requirements, complexity of communications, need for participant education, lack of participant interest. See GAO-03-810 Private Pensions: Participants Need Information on Risks They Face in Managing Pension Assets at and during Retirement (July 2003) at http://www.gao.gov/htext/d03810.html. Also see Report of Working Group on Retirement Distributions & Options (November 2005), Advisory Council on Employee Welfare and Pension Benefit Plans, at http://www.dol.gov/ebsa/publications/AC_1105A_report.html.

[3] Form 5500 data reports the number of participants in a DC plan that use insurance for at least one method of benefit payouts. This information was used to estimate the share of participants currently offered an annuity option for withdrawal, 25 percent in 2003.

[4] Hewitt Associates. "Survey Findings: Trends and Experiences in 401(k) Plans, 2005";.

[5] Estimate based on the average total balance of DC withdrawals as reported in Fidelity Investments', "Building Futures: How Workplace Savings are Shaping the Future of Retirement," A Report on Corporate Defined Contribution Plans: 2006.

[6] The reported analysis used separation rates reported in, Poterba, James, Steven Venti and David A. Wise. "Demographic Change, Retirement Saving and Financial Market Returns: Part I," December 19, 2005. An alternative analysis, using withdrawal rates reported in Fidelity Investments', "Building Futures: How Workplace Savings are Shaping the Future of Retirement," A Report on Corporate Defined Contribution Plans: 2006 generated an increase of $158 million.

Paperwork Reduction Act

This rulemaking is not subject to the requirements of the Paperwork Reduction Act of 1995 (44 U.S.C. § 301 et seq.) because it does not contain "collection of information" requirements as defined in 44 U.S.C. § 3502(3). Accordingly, this proposed regulation is not being submitted to the OMB for review under the Paperwork Reduction Act.

Unfunded Mandates Reform Act

For purposes of the Unfunded Mandates Reform Act of 1995 (Pub. L. 104-4), the proposed regulation does not include any Federal mandate that may result in expenditures by State, local, or tribal governments, or impose an annual burden exceeding $100 million on the private sector.

Federalism Statement

Executive Order 13132 (August 4, 1999) outlines fundamental principles of federalism and requires Federal agencies to adhere to specific criteria in the process of their formulation and implementation of policies that have substantial direct effects on the States, the relationship between the national government and the States, or on the distribution of power and responsibilities among the various levels of government. This proposed regulation does not have federalism implications because it has no substantial direct effect on the States, on the relationship between the national government and the States, or on the distribution of power and responsibilities among the various levels of government. Section 514 of ERISA provides, with certain exceptions specifically enumerated, that the provisions of Titles I and IV of ERISA supersede any and all laws of the States as they relate to any employee benefit plan covered under ERISA. The requirements implemented in the proposed regulation do not alter the fundamental provisions of the statute with respect to employee benefit plans, and as such would have no implications for the States or the relationship or distribution of power between the national government and the States.

List of Subjects in 29 CFR Part 2550

Annuities, Employee benefit plans, Fiduciaries, Pensions.

For the reasons set forth in the preamble, the Department proposes to amend Chapter XXV of Title 29 of the Code of Federal Regulations as follows:

PART 2550—RULES AND REGULATIONS FOR FIDUCIARY RESPONSIBILITY

1. The authority citation for part 2550 is revised to read as follows:

Authority: 29 U.S.C. 1135; sec. 657, Pub. L. 107-16, 115 Stat. 38; and Secretary of Labor's Order No. 1-2003, 68 FR 5374 (Feb. 3, 2003). § 2550.401b-1 also issued under sec. 102, Reorganization Plan No. 4 of 1978, 43 FR 47713 (Oct. 17, 1978), 3 CFR, 1978 Comp. 332, effective Dec. 31, 1978, 44 FR 1065 (Jan. 3, 1978), 3 CFR, 1978 Comp. 332. § 2550.401c-1 also issued under 29 U.S.C. 1101. Sections 2550.404c-1 and 2550.404c-5 also issued under 29 U.S.C. 1104. § 2550.407c-3 also issued under 29 U.S.C. 1107. § 2550.408b-1 also issued under 29 U.S.C. 1108(b)(1) and sec. 102, Reorganization Plan No. 4 of 1978, 3 CFR, 1978 Comp. p. 332, effective Dec. 31, 1978, 44 FR 1065 (Jan. 3, 1978), and 3 CFR, 1978 Comp. 332. § 2550.412-1 also issued under 29 U.S.C. 1112. § 2550.404a-4 also issued under sec. 625, Pub. L. 109-280, 120 Stat. 780.

2. Add § 2550.404a-4 to read as follows:

§ 2550.404a-4 Selection of annuity providers for individual account plans.

(a) Scope. This section provides guidance concerning the fiduciary standards under part 4 of title I of the Employee Retirement Income Security Act of 1974 (ERISA), 29 U.S.C. 1104-1114, applicable to the selection of an annuity provider for the purpose of benefit distributions from an individual account plan or benefit distribution options made available to participants and beneficiaries under such a plan. For guidance concerning the selection of an annuity provider for defined benefit plans see 29 CFR 2509.95-1.

(b) In general. When an individual account plan purchases an annuity from an insurer as a distribution of benefits to a participant or beneficiary, the plan's liability for the payment of those benefits is transferred to the annuity provider. The selection of an annuity provider in connection with a benefit distribution, or a benefit distribution option made available to participants and beneficiaries under the plan, is governed by the fiduciary standards of section 404(a)(1) of ERISA.

Pursuant to ERISA section 404(a)(1), fiduciaries must discharge their duties with respect to the plan solely in the interest of the participants and beneficiaries. Section 404(a)(1)(A) provides that the fiduciary must act for the exclusive purpose of providing benefits to the participants and beneficiaries and defraying reasonable plan administration expenses. In addition, section 404(a)(1)(B) requires a fiduciary to act with the care, skill, prudence and diligence under the prevailing circumstances that a prudent person acting in a like capacity and familiar with such matters would use.

(c) Selection of annuity providers and contracts. (1) With regard to a fiduciary's selection of an annuity provider for purposes of benefit distributions from an individual account plan or benefit distribution options made available to participants and beneficiaries under such a plan, the requirements of section 404(a)(1)(B) of ERISA are satisfied if the fiduciary:

(i) Engages in an objective, thorough and analytical search for the purpose of identifying and selecting providers from which to purchase annuities;

(ii) Appropriately determines either that the fiduciary had, at the time of the selection, the appropriate expertise to evaluate the selection or that the advice of a qualified, independent expert was necessary;

(iii) Gives appropriate consideration to information sufficient to assess the ability of the annuity provider to make all future payments under the annuity contract;

(iv) Appropriately considers the cost of the annuity contract in relation to the benefits and administrative services to be provided under such contract;

(v) Appropriately concludes that, at the time of the selection, the annuity provider is financially able to make all future payments under the annuity contract and the cost of the annuity contract is reasonable in relation to the benefits and services to be provided under the contract; and

(vi) In the case of an annuity provider selected to provide multiple contracts over time, periodically reviews the appropriateness of the conclusion described in paragraph (c)(1)(v) of this section, taking into account the factors described in paragraph (c)(1)(iii) and (iv) of this section. For purposes of this paragraph, a fiduciary is not required to review the appropriateness of an annuity provider with respect to an annuity contract purchased for an individual participant or beneficiary.

(2) For purposes of paragraphs (c)(1)(iii) and (iv) of this section, a fiduciary shall consider information pertaining to the following:

(i) The ability of the annuity provider to administer the payments of benefits under the annuity to the participants and beneficiaries and to perform any other services in connection with the annuity, if applicable;

(ii) The cost of the annuity contract in relation to the benefits and administrative services to be provided under such contract, taking into account the amount and nature of any fees and commissions;

(iii) The annuity provider's experience and financial expertise in providing annuities of the type being selected or offered;

(iv) The annuity provider's level of capital, surplus and reserves available to make payments under the annuity contract;

(v) The annuity provider's ratings by insurance ratings services. Consideration should be given to whether an annuity provider's ratings demonstrate or raise questions regarding the provider's ability to make future payments under the annuity contract;

(vi) The structure of the annuity contract and benefit guarantees provided, and the use of separate accounts to underwrite the provider's benefit obligations;

(vii) The availability and extent of additional protection through state guaranty associations; and

(viii) Any other information that the fiduciary knows or should know would be relevant to an evaluation of paragraphs (c)(1)(iii) and (iv) of this section.

Signed at Washington, DC, this 31st day of August, 2007.

Bradford P. Campbell, Assistant Secretary, Employee Benefits Security Administration, Department of Labor.

[FR Doc. E7-17743 Filed 9-11-07; 8:45 am]

¶ 20,537C

EBSA proposed regulations: Disclosures: Multiemployer plans .—The Employee Benefits Security Administration (EBSA) has released proposed regulations on the obligation of multiemployer plan administrators to disclose certain actuarial and financial information to plan participants, beneficiaries, employee representatives, and employers with an obligation to contribute to the plan.

The proposed regulations were published in the *Federal Register* on September 14, 2007 (72 FR 52527).

The regulations were finalized and published in the *Federal Register* on March 2, 2010 (75 FR 9334). The regulations are effective April 1, 2010. The regulations appear at ¶ 14,215, ¶ 14,216, and ¶ 14,249Z. The preamble is at ¶ 24,290.

¶ 20,537D

Pension Benefit Guaranty Corporation (PBGC): Proposed rule: PBGC Appeals Board: Administrative Review of Agency Decisions.— The Pension Benefit Guaranty Corporation (PBGC) has issued proposed regulations which would amend its regulations on Administrative Review of Agency Decisions (29 CFR Part 4003) to clarify that the PBGC's Appeals Board may refer certain categories of appeals to other PBGC departments for a written response and to remove determinations under ERISA § 4022A from the scope of part 4003.

The proposed regulations, which were published in the Federal Register on October 18, 2007 (72 FR 59050), were previously reproduced below.

The preamble to the final regulations, which was published in the Federal Register on July 3, 2008 (73 FR 38117), is reproduced at ¶ 24,268. The changes to the final regulations are reflected at ¶ 15,331, ¶ 15,331A, ¶ 15,331C, ¶ 15,333B, ¶ 15,333D, ¶ 15,334B, ¶ 15,334C, ¶ 15,334G, and ¶ 15,334I.

¶ 20,537E

Pension Benefit Guaranty Corporation (PBGC): Proposed rule: Plan terminations: Disclosures.— The Pension Benefit Guaranty Corporation (PBGC) has issued proposed regulations which would amend its regulations on required disclosures in plan terminations. The proposed regulations define and clarify the disclosure requirements which were added to ERISA § 4041 and ERISA § 4042 by the Pension Protection Act of 2006 (P.L. 109-280).

The proposed regulations, which were published in the Federal Register on December 5, 2007 (72 FR 68542), were previously reproduced below. The final regulations, published in the Federal Register on November 18, 2008 (73 FR 68333), appear at ¶ 15,440J-10, ¶ 15,451, ¶ 15,451A, ¶ 15,451B, ¶ 15,451C and ¶ 15,451D. The preamble to the final regulations appears at ¶ 24,274.

¶ 20,537F

EBSA proposed regulations: Fee disclosures: Plan fiduciaries: Service providers.— The Employee Benefits Security Administration (EBSA) has released proposed regulations designed to provide plan fiduciaries with sufficient information to evaluate the reasonableness of compensation and fees directly and indirectly paid to certain service providers, and assess the potential for conflicts of interest that may affect the performance of a service provider. Absent compliance by the service provider with the disclosure requirements, the plan fiduciary would be subject to liability for engaging in a prohibited transaction. However, concurrent with the proposed regulations, EBSA has issued a proposed class prohibited transaction exemption (see ¶ 16,712) that would relieve a fiduciary of liability for a prohibited transaction resulting from a service provider's failure to comply with the notice requirements.

The proposed regulations, which were published in the *Federal Register* on December 13, 2007 (72 FR 70988), are reproduced below.

Interim final regulations were issued on July 16, 2010 (75 FR 41600), effective on July 16, 2011. The preamble to the interim final regulations is at ¶ 24,295. The regulations (ERISA Reg. § 2550.408b-2(c)) are at ¶ 14,782.

Federal Register

Thursday, December 13, 2007

Part III Department of Labor

Employee Benefits Security Administration

29 CFR Part 2550

Reasonable Contract or Arrangement Under Section 408(b)(2)—Fee Disclosure; Proposed Rule

DEPARTMENT OF LABOR

Employee Benefits Security Administration

29 CFR Part 2550

RIN 1210-AB08

Reasonable Contract or Arrangement Under Section 408(b)(2)— Fee Disclosure

AGENCY: Employee Benefits Security Administration, DOL.

ACTION: Proposed regulation.

SUMMARY: This document contains a proposed regulation under the Employee Retirement Income Security Act of 1974 (ERISA) that, upon adoption, would require that contracts and arrangements between employee benefit plans and certain providers of services to such plans include provisions that will ensure the disclosure of information to assist plan fiduciaries in assessing the reasonableness of the compensation or fees paid for services that are rendered to the plan and the potential for conflicts of interest that may affect a service provider's

performance of services. The proposed regulation will redefine what constitutes a "reasonable contract or arrangement" for purposes of the statutory exemption from certain prohibited transaction provisions of ERISA. The regulation, upon adoption, will affect employee benefit plan sponsors and fiduciaries and the service providers to such plans.

DATES: Written comments on the proposed regulation should be received by the Department of Labor on or before February 11, 2008.

ADDRESSES: To facilitate the receipt and processing of comment letters, the Employee Benefits Security Administration (EBSA) encourages interested persons to submit their comments electronically by e-mail to *e-ORI@dol.gov*, or by using the Federal eRulemaking portal at *http://www.regulations.gov*. Persons submitting comments electronically are encouraged not to submit paper copies. Persons interested in submitting paper copies should send or deliver their comments (preferably at least three copies) to the Office of Regulations and Interpretations, Employee Benefits Security Administration, Attn: 408(b)(2) Amendment, Room N-5655, U.S. Department of Labor, 200 Constitution Avenue, NW., Washington, DC 20210. All comments will be available to the public, without charge, online at *http://www.regulations.gov* and *http://www.dol.gov/ebsa* and at the Public Disclosure Room, N-1513, Employee Benefits Security Administration, U.S. Department of Labor, 200 Constitution Avenue, NW., Washington, DC 20210.

FOR FURTHER INFORMATION CONTACT:

Kristen L. Zarenko, Office of Regulations and Interpretations, Employee Benefits Security Administration, (202) 693-8510. This is not a toll-free number.

SUPPLEMENTARY INFORMATION:

A. Background

(1) General

In recent years, there have been a number of changes in the way services are provided to employee benefit plans and in the way service providers are compensated. Many of these changes may have improved efficiency and reduced the costs of administrative services and benefits for plans and their participants. However, the complexity of these changes also has made it more difficult for plan sponsors and fiduciaries to understand what the plan actually pays for the specific services rendered and the extent to which compensation arrangements among service providers present potential conflicts of interest that may affect not only administrative costs, but the quality of services provided.

Despite these complexities, section 404(a)(1) of ERISA requires plan fiduciaries, when selecting or monitoring service providers, to act prudently and solely in the interest of the plan's participants and beneficiaries and for the exclusive purposes of providing benefits and defraying reasonable expenses of administering the plan. Fundamental to a fiduciary's ability to discharge these obligations is the availability of information sufficient to enable the fiduciary to make informed decisions about the services, the costs, and the service provider. In this regard, the Department of Labor (Department) has published interpretive guidance concerning the disclosure and other obligations of plan fiduciaries and service providers under ERISA.[1]

In addition to technical guidance, the Department makes available on its Web site various materials intended to assist plan fiduciaries and others in understanding their obligations, the importance of fees, and the assessment of service provider relationships.[2] The Department's Web site also provides a Model Plan Fee Disclosure Form to assist fiduciaries of individual account pension plans when analyzing and comparing the costs associated with selecting service providers and investment products.[3]

Although the Department has issued technical guidance and compliance assistance materials relating to the selection and monitoring of service providers, the Department nevertheless believes that, given plan fiduciaries' need for complete and accurate information about compensation and revenue sharing, both plan fiduciaries and service providers would benefit from regulatory guidance in this area. For this reason, the Department proposes the amendment described below relating to the conditions for a "reasonable contract or arrangement" under section 408(b)(2) of ERISA, as set forth in 29 CFR § 2550.408b-2.[4]

(2) The Statutory Exemption for Services

Section 406(a)(1)(C) of ERISA generally prohibits the furnishing of goods, services, or facilities between a plan and a party in interest to the plan. As a result, absent relief, a service relationship between a plan and a service provider would constitute a prohibited transaction, because any person providing services to the plan is defined by ERISA to be a "party in interest" to the plan.[5] However, section 408(b)(2) of ERISA exempts certain arrangements between plans and service providers that otherwise would be prohibited transactions under section 406 of ERISA. Specifically, section 408(b)(2) provides relief from ERISA's prohibited transaction rules for service contracts or arrangements between a plan and a party in interest if the contract or arrangement is reasonable, the services are necessary for the establishment or operation of the plan, and no more than reasonable compensation is paid for the services.[6] Regulations issued by the Department clarify each of these conditions to the exemption.[7]

In this Notice, the Department proposes to amend the regulations under ERISA section 408(b)(2) to clarify the meaning of a "reasonable" contract or arrangement. Currently, the regulation at 29 CFR § 2550.408b-2(c) states only that a contract or arrangement is not reasonable unless it permits the plan to terminate without penalty on reasonably short notice.[8] In the amendment described below, the Department proposes to add that, in order for a contract or arrangement for services to be reasonable, it must require that certain information be disclosed by the service provider to the responsible plan fiduciary. The Department believes that in order to satisfy their ERISA

obligations, plan fiduciaries need information concerning all compensation to be received by the service provider and any conflicts of interest that may adversely affect the service provider's performance under the contract or arrangement. Accordingly, under the proposal, an arrangement would not be reasonable unless the service provider agrees to furnish, and in fact does furnish, the required information to the responsible plan fiduciary. The "responsible plan fiduciary" is the fiduciary with authority to cause the plan to enter into, or extend or renew, a contract or arrangement for the provision of services to the plan.

B. Proposed Amendment to Regulations Under ERISA Section 408(b)(2)

(1) Overview of Proposed Regulation

In general, the proposal amends paragraph (c) of § 2550.408b-2 by moving, without change, the current provisions of paragraph (c) to a newly designated paragraph (c)(2) and adding a new paragraph (c)(1) to address the disclosure requirements applicable to a "reasonable contract or arrangement." The new paragraph (c)(1) of § 2550.408b-2 generally requires that, in order to be reasonable, any contract or arrangement between an employee benefit plan and certain service providers must require the service provider to disclose the compensation it will receive, directly or indirectly, and any conflicts of interest that may arise in connection with its services to the plan.

(a) Scope of the Proposal

Paragraph (c)(1)(i) of the proposal describes the scope of the regulation's disclosure requirements. The Department recognizes that responsible plan fiduciaries may not always need all of the required disclosures from every type of service provider in order to evaluate the reasonableness of the service provider's compensation. Thus, this paragraph limits the proposal's application to contracts or arrangements to provide services by service providers that fall within one or more of three categories. The first category, described in paragraph (c)(1)(i)(A), includes within the scope of the regulation service providers who provide services as a fiduciary under ERISA or under the Investment Advisers Act of 1940. Paragraph (c)(1)(i)(B) includes service providers who provide banking, consulting, custodial, insurance, investment advisory (plan or participants), investment management, recordkeeping, securities or other investment brokerage, or third party administration services, regardless of the type of compensation or fees that they receive. Finally, paragraph (c)(1)(i)(C) includes service providers who receive any indirect compensation in connection with accounting, actuarial, appraisal, auditing, legal, or valuation services.

The Department believes that the compensation arrangements for services provided by the service providers enumerated in paragraphs (c)(1)(i)(A) and (B) are most likely to give rise to conflicts of interest. As to the service providers enumerated in paragraph (c)(1)(i)(C), the Department believes that requiring every service contract or arrangement with these providers to satisfy the requirements of the proposed regulation may not be appropriate or yield helpful information to plan fiduciaries. However, the Department believes that these providers perform some of the most important and potentially influential services to plans and, to the extent these service providers receive indirect compensation in connection with their services, similar conflict of interest concerns would be raised, as with other enumerated service providers.

If a contract or arrangement meets the threshold scope requirement in paragraph (c)(1)(i), then the terms of such contract or arrangement must satisfy the proposal's disclosure requirements in order to be reasonable for purposes of paragraph (c)(1), regardless of the nature of any other services provided or whether the plan is a pension plan, group health plan, or other type of welfare benefit plan. Nevertheless, the proposal's application to contracts or arrangements between plans and the listed categories of service providers should not be construed to imply that responsible plan fiduciaries do not need to obtain and consider appropriate disclosures before contracting with service providers who *do not* fall within these categories. Responsible plan fiduciaries must continue to satisfy their general fiduciary obligations under

---

[1] *See, e.g.*, Field Assistance Bulletin 2002-3 (November 5, 2002) and Advisory Opinions 97-16A (May 22, 1997) and 97-15A (May 22, 1997).

[2] *See http://www.dol.gov/ebsa/publications/undrstndgrtrmnt.html* and *http://www.dol.gov/ebsa/newsroom/fs053105.html.*

[3] *http://www.dol.gov/ebsa/pdf/401kfefm.pdf.* This model form was developed jointly by the American Bankers Association, the Investment Company Institute, and the American Council of Life Insurers.

[4] The Department also implemented changes to the information required to be reported concerning service provider compensation and compensation arrangements as part of the

Form 5500 Annual Report. These changes to Schedule C of the Form 5500 complement the amendment proposed in this Notice in assuring that plan fiduciaries have the information they need to monitor their service providers consistent with their duties under section 404(a)(1) of ERISA. *See* 72 FR 64731.

[5] *See* ERISA § 3(14)(B).

[6] *See* ERISA § 408(b)(2).

[7] *See* 29 CFR § 2550.408b-2.

[8] *See* 29 CFR § 2550.408b-2(c).

ERISA with respect to the selection and monitoring of all service providers. Further, contracts or arrangements with these service providers must be "reasonable" and otherwise satisfy the requirements of section 408(b)(2) of ERISA.

The proposal also applies only to contracts or arrangements for services to employee benefit plans. The proposed regulation, if adopted, would not apply to contracts or arrangements with entities that are merely providing plan benefits to participants and beneficiaries, rather than providing services to the plan itself. For example, a pharmacy benefit manager that contracts with an employee benefit plan to manage the plan's prescription drug program would be covered as a service provider to the plan providing third party administration or recordkeeping, and possibly consulting, services. However, if a fiduciary contracts on behalf of a welfare plan with a medical provider network, for example an HMO, a doctor that is part of the network and that has no separate agreement or arrangement with the plan would not be a service provider to the plan; the doctor merely provides medical benefits to the plan's participants and beneficiaries.

(b) Disclosure Concerning Compensation and Services

If a contract or arrangement for services falls within the scope of the proposed regulation, the contract or arrangement must comply with paragraphs (c)(1)(ii) through (vi) of the proposal. Paragraph (c)(1)(ii) requires that the contract or arrangement be in writing. The proposal requires specific disclosures and representations from the service provider, and the Department believes they must be made in writing to ensure a meeting of the minds between the service provider and the responsible plan fiduciary.

The proposed regulation next provides in paragraph (c)(1)(iii) that the terms of the contract or arrangement must specifically require the service provider to disclose in writing, to the best of its knowledge, the information set forth in the proposal. The Department believes it is important for the responsible plan fiduciary to obtain assurance from the service provider that it has disclosed complete and accurate information. To ensure that the responsible plan fiduciary has the opportunity to consider all required disclosures before entering into a contract or arrangement with a service provider to the plan, the proposal requires that the contract or arrangement include a representation by the service provider that, before the contract or arrangement was entered into, all required information was provided to the responsible plan fiduciary.

The proposal does not prescribe the manner in which such disclosures should be presented to the plan fiduciary, other than requiring a statement by the service provider that the disclosures have been made. All of the required disclosures need not be contained in the same document, as long as all of the required information is presented to the responsible plan fiduciary in writing before such fiduciary enters into the contract or arrangement. Written disclosures may be provided in separate documents from separate sources and may be provided in electronic format, as long as these documents, collectively, contain all of the elements of disclosure required by the regulation. For example, a prospectus required by Federal securities laws, or a Form ADV required to be filed by a registered investment adviser, may include some of the indirect fee or conflict of interest information that a service provider would be required to disclose under this proposal. In these circumstances, the contracting parties are free to incorporate such materials by reference. The Department expects that the service provider will clearly describe these additional materials and explain to the responsible plan fiduciary the information they contain. The Department invites comments on whether, and the extent to which, duplicate disclosures can be avoided, while at the same time ensuring that responsible plan fiduciaries receive comprehensive, straightforward, and helpful information concerning the service provider's compensation and possible conflicts of interest.

The proposal also does not designate any specific time period prior to entering into the contract or arrangement for receipt of the required disclosures, other than requiring a representation by the service provider that all information was provided in writing before the parties entered into the contract. The Department believes it would be incumbent on the service provider to furnish current and accurate information to the plan fiduciary. Further, the responsible plan fiduciary, consistent with its general fiduciary obligations under ERISA, must ensure in its negotiations with a service provider that he or she obtains current and accurate information from the service provider sufficiently in advance of entering into the contract or arrangement to allow the fiduciary to prudently consider the information.

To facilitate the responsible plan fiduciary's determination that the service provider will receive no more than reasonable compensation, paragraph (c)(1)(iii)(A) of the proposal provides that the contract or arrangement must require the service provider to disclose the services to be provided to the plan and all compensation it will receive in connection with the services. A service provider must describe all services that it will provide, regardless of whether such services are described in the proposal's applicable scope provision. For example, if a plan consultant will provide appraisal, legal, and administrative services to the employee benefit plan in addition to its consulting services, then all of these services must be described. The subsections that follow in paragraph (c)(1)(iii)(A)(*1*) through (*4*) of the proposal clarify the requirement that the service provider disclose all compensation or fees that it will receive for its services.

Paragraph (c)(1)(iii)(A)(*1*) broadly defines compensation or fees to include money and any other thing of monetary value received by the service provider or its affiliate in connection with the services provided to the plan or the financial products in which plan assets are invested. Examples of compensation or fees that are covered by this definition include, but are not limited to: gifts, awards, and trips for employees, research, finder's fees, placement fees, commissions or other fees related to investment products, sub-transfer agency fees, shareholder servicing fees, Rule 12b-1 fees, soft dollar payments, float income, fees deducted from investment returns, fees based on a share of gains or appreciation of plan assets, and fees based upon a percentage of the plan's assets. The Department believes that an investment of plan assets or the purchase of insurance is not, in and of itself, compensation to a service provider for purposes of this regulation. However, persons or entities that provide investment management, recordkeeping, participant communication and other services to the plan as a result of an investment of plan assets will be treated as providing services to the plan.

Consistent with recommendations of the ERISA Advisory Council Working Group, the Department concludes that plan fiduciaries must receive more comprehensive information about the compensation or fees involved in plan administration and investments, including indirect compensation.[9] Indirect compensation includes fees that service providers receive from parties other than the plan, the plan sponsor, or the service provider.

Service providers also must disclose compensation or fees received by their affiliates from third parties. For purposes of the proposal, an "affiliate" of a service provider is defined in paragraph (c)(1)(iii)(A)(*1*) to be any person directly or indirectly (through one or more intermediaries), controlling, controlled by, or under common control with the service provider, or any officer, director, agent, or employee of, or partner in, the service provider. The Department does not intend this requirement to result in any "double counting" of compensation. For instance, an employee's salary or a bonus that is paid to an employee from the general assets of his or her employer (i.e., the service provider) would not need to be separately disclosed, even if the employee is paid in connection with services to an employee benefit plan. The proposal merely clarifies that disclosure of any direct or indirect compensation that otherwise is required under the proposal cannot be avoided merely because such compensation is paid to an employee or agent of the service provider or an affiliate, rather than directly to such service provider or affiliate.

The proposal next provides in paragraph (c)(1)(iii)(A)(*2*) that if a service provider cannot disclose compensation or fees in terms of a specific monetary amount, then the service provider may disclose compensation or fees by using a formula, a percentage of the plan's assets, or a per capita charge for each participant or beneficiary. The Department understands that it is not always possible at the time the parties enter into a service contract or arrangement to know the exact amount of compensation, whether direct or indirect, that the service provider will receive for its services. However, the service provider must describe its compensation or fees in such a way that the responsible plan fiduciary can evaluate its reasonableness. For instance, the service provider must clearly explain any assumptions that would be used in determining the compensation or fees according to any such formula or other charge.

Paragraph (c)(1)(iii)(A)(*3*) of the proposed regulation clarifies the nature of disclosures that must be provided concerning bundled arrangements. In many cases, administrative and investment services are provided to employee benefit plans in "bundled" arrangements, whereby a package or "bundle" of services is provided, either directly or through affiliates or subcontractors of a service provider. These

---

[9] *See* ERISA Advisory Council Working Group report at *http://www.dol.gov/ebsa/ publications.*

bundles are priced to the plan by a single service provider as a package, rather than on a service-by-service basis. For example, rather than hiring separate service providers for investment management, recordkeeping, Form 5500 annual report preparation, participant communications and statement preparation, payroll processing, and other functions, a plan fiduciary may arrange for one service provider to have all of these services performed as a bundle. The provider of the bundle may in turn use other affiliated service providers, or unaffiliated subcontractors, to provide some of the services in the bundle. However, the responsible plan fiduciary obtains a "package deal" and will negotiate only with the provider of the bundle.

Under paragraph (c)(1)(iii)(A)(3) of the proposed regulation, if a service provider offers a bundle of services, then a contract or arrangement must require only that the provider of the bundle make the prescribed disclosures. This bundled service provider must disclose information concerning all services to be provided in the bundle, regardless of who provides them. Further, the bundled service provider must disclose the aggregate direct compensation or fees that will be paid for the bundle, as well as all indirect compensation that will be received by the service provider, or its affiliates or subcontractors within the bundle, from third parties. Generally, the bundled provider is not required to break down this aggregate compensation or fees among the individual services comprising the bundle. For instance, the service provider would not have to break down the aggregate fee into the amount that will be charged for preparing the Form 5500 annual report and the amount that will be charged for preparing participant statements. Also, the bundled provider generally is not required to disclose the allocation of revenue sharing or other payments among affiliates or subcontractors within the bundle.

There are, however, exceptions to these rules. Specifically, paragraph (c)(1)(iii)(A)(3) requires the bundled provider to disclose separately the compensation or fees of any party providing services under the bundle that receives a separate fee charged directly against the plan's investment reflected in the net value of the investment, such as management fees paid by mutual funds to their investment advisers, float revenue, and other asset-based fees such as 12b-1 distribution fees, wrap fees, and shareholder servicing fees if charged in addition to the investment management fee. Also, paragraph (c)(1)(iii)(A)(3) requires the separate disclosure of compensation or fees of any service provider under the bundle that are set on a transaction basis, such as finder's fees, brokerage commissions, or soft dollars. Soft dollars include research or other products or services, other than execution, received from a broker-dealer or other third party in connection with securities transactions. Compensation or fees that are charged on a transaction basis must be separately disclosed even if paid from mutual fund management fees or other similar fees. The Department does not believe that disclosure of these fees would require bundled providers to disclose any revenue sharing arrangements or bookkeeping practices among affiliates that could legitimately be classified as proprietary or confidential. Further, the Department believes that investment-based charges, commissions, and other transaction-based fees paid to affiliates are just as likely to be relevant to the responsible plan fiduciary's evaluation of potential conflicts of interest, whether or not they are part of a bundled service arrangement.

Paragraph (c)(1)(iii)(A)(4) requires that the service provider also explain the manner of receipt of compensation, for example whether the service provider will bill the plan, deduct fees directly from plan accounts, or reflect a charge against the plan investment. The description also must explain how any pre-paid fees will be calculated and refunded when the contract or arrangement terminates.

(c) Disclosure Concerning Conflicts of Interest

The subsections that follow in (B) through (F) of paragraph (c)(1)(iii) are intended to inform the responsible plan fiduciary of the service provider's relationships or interests that may raise conflicts of interest for the service provider in its performance of services for the plan. As service arrangements have become more complex, so have the ways that service providers are compensated, as well as the relationships among different players in the plan service provider industry.

Plan fiduciaries must know of these relationships and indirect sources of compensation because they may impact the manner in which the provider performs services for the plan. There may be other, oftentimes subtle, influences on the service provider or its affiliates that may be relevant to a plan fiduciary's assessment of the objectivity of a service provider's decisions or recommendations.

The Department's attention to service providers' potential conflicts of interest is not new. For example, in 2005 the Department issued guidance with the Securities and Exchange Commission concerning potential conflicts of interest involved in pension consultant relationships.[10] This guidance provides a list of tips and related explanations to help plan fiduciaries obtain the information necessary to ensure that engagement of the pension consultant serves the best interest of the plan's participants and beneficiaries. The Department believes that the engagement of many plan service providers presents similar issues for the plan fiduciary. Accordingly, under the proposal, a contract or arrangement must require that the service provider disclose specific information that will help the responsible plan fiduciary assess any real or potential conflicts of interest.

Subsection (B) of paragraph (c)(1)(iii) requires that the service provider identify whether it will provide services to the plan as a fiduciary, either as an ERISA fiduciary under section 3(21) of ERISA or as a fiduciary under the Investment Advisers Act of 1940. The Department believes it is important for the responsible plan fiduciary and the service provider to understand at the outset of their relationship whether or not the service provider considers itself a fiduciary and how this status affects the nature of the services to be provided.[11]

Subsection (C) requires that the service provider disclose any financial or other interest in transactions in which the plan will partake in connection with the contract or arrangement. For example, if a service provider will be buying (or advising on the purchase of) a parcel of real estate for the plan, and an affiliate of the service provider owns an interest in the real estate, the service provider will have to state that it has an interest in the transaction and describe its affiliate's ownership of the real estate. The responsible plan fiduciary can then weigh the nature and extent of the conflict in analyzing the objectivity of the service provider when making the recommendations.

The proposal also provides that a reasonable contract or arrangement must require the service provider to disclose its relationships with other parties that may give rise to conflicts of interest. Specifically, subsection (D) obligates the service provider to describe any material financial, referral, or other relationship it has with various parties (such as investment professionals, other service providers, or clients) that creates or may create a conflict of interest for the service provider in performing services pursuant to the contract or arrangement. If the relationship between the service provider and this third party is one that a reasonable plan fiduciary would consider to be significant in its evaluation of whether an actual or potential conflict of interest exists, then the service provider must disclose the relationship.

Conflicts also may arise when a service provider can affect its own compensation in connection with its services. Under subsection (E) of the proposal, a contract or arrangement must require the service provider to identify whether it can affect its own compensation without the prior approval of an independent plan fiduciary and to describe the nature of this compensation. A common example of this potential conflict of interest is the receipt of "float" compensation.[12] If the amount a service provider receives in float compensation will not be approved by an independent plan fiduciary, then the service provider must state that it will receive float compensation and explain the nature of this compensation.[13]

Finally, the Department recognizes that service providers may have policies or procedures to manage these real or potential conflicts of interest. For example, a fiduciary service provider may have procedures for offsetting fees received from third parties (through revenue sharing or other indirect payment arrangements) against the amount that it otherwise would charge a plan client. Accordingly, subsection (F) of paragraph (c)(1)(iii) of the proposal provides that a reasonable contract or arrangement must require service providers to state

---

[10] *See* "Selecting and Monitoring Pension Consultants—Tips for Plan Fiduciaries" at *http://www.dol.gov/ebsa/newsroom/fs053105.html.*

[11] The Department notes that persons who perform one or more of the functions described in section 3(21)(A) of ERISA with respect to a plan are fiduciaries. *See* 29 CFR § 2509.75-8. Thus, fiduciary status depends on a factual analysis of a person's activities with respect to a plan. Formal agreements stating whether a person is a fiduciary are not dispositive of whether the person actually is a fiduciary under ERISA by virtue of the functions performed.

[12] Many financial service providers, such as banks and trust companies, maintain omnibus accounts to facilitate the transactions of employee benefit plan clients. The service

provider may retain earnings ("float") that result from the anticipated short-term investment of funds held in these accounts. These accounts generally hold contributions and other assets pending investment. Plan fiduciaries also may transfer funds to an omnibus account in connection with issuance of a check to make a plan distribution or other disbursement.

[13] For more information concerning "float" compensation and the information concerning such compensation that plan fiduciaries should obtain from service providers, see the Department's Field Assistance Bulletin 2002-3 (Nov. 5, 2002) at *http://www.dol.gov/ebsa/regs/fab_2002-3.html.*

whether or not any such policies or procedures exist and, if so, to provide an explanation of these policies or procedures and how they address conflicts of interest. The Department views this requirement as an opportunity for service providers to educate plan fiduciaries about how they address potential conflicts of interest.

(d) Material Changes to Disclosed Information

Paragraph (c)(1)(iv) of the proposal provides that a reasonable contract or arrangement must require that, during the term of the contract or arrangement, service providers must disclose to responsible plan fiduciaries any material changes to the information that is required by paragraph (c)(1)(iii), subsections (A) through (F). Changes on the part of a service provider or its employee benefit plan business may occasionally occur and may alter the information previously disclosed by the service provider. If any resulting change to the information previously disclosed to a plan fiduciary would be viewed by a reasonable plan fiduciary as significantly altering the "total mix" of information made available to the fiduciary, or as significantly affecting a reasonable plan fiduciary's decision to hire or retain the service provider, then the change is material. To ensure that plan fiduciaries continue to be well-informed concerning the compensation and conflict of interest issues affecting their service provider relationships, a contract or arrangement must require service providers to notify fiduciaries of material changes within 30 days of the service provider's knowledge of the change.

(e) Reporting and Disclosure Requirements

The proposed regulation under paragraph (c)(1)(v) requires that a reasonable contract or arrangement obligate the service provider to furnish all information related to the contract or arrangement and the service provider's receipt of compensation or fees thereunder that is requested by the responsible plan fiduciary or plan administrator in order to comply with the reporting and disclosure requirements of Title I of ERISA and the regulations, forms, and schedules issued thereunder. For example, this provision would obligate the service provider to furnish information that is necessary for the plan administrator to complete the annual report on Form 5500, and information that is necessary for the responsible plan fiduciary to comply with disclosure obligations to plan participants and beneficiaries.

Of course, detailed reporting concerning some service providers may not be required for annual reporting purposes, for example because the amount or nature of the compensation paid to the service provider does not fall within the threshold or other requirements of the annual report on Form 5500. Further, not all employee benefit plans are subject to the same annual reporting requirements, for example small plans and certain self-funded welfare plans. This does not mean that service providers to these plans would not be required to fully satisfy the disclosure requirements of this proposed regulation, assuming they otherwise fall within the scope of the proposal. The Department anticipates that this proposal would apply more broadly to relationships between service providers and employee benefit plans that are not necessarily covered by ERISA's reporting requirements. The primary goal of this proposal—to provide comprehensive and useful information to responsible plan fiduciaries when entering service contracts or arrangements—is different than that of ERISA's annual reporting and disclosure requirements, which provide more limited retrospective financial information on direct and indirect service provider compensation to facilitate and reinforce the broader fiduciary obligations imposed by this proposal.

(f) Compliance by Service Providers

The proposal's final requirement is contained in paragraph (c)(1)(vi). This condition provides explicitly that a service provider must comply with its obligations under the contract or arrangement as described in the proposed regulation. Not only must a contract or arrangement require disclosure from the service provider, but the service provider must actually provide all of the required disclosures in order for the contract or arrangement to be reasonable. Similarly, it is not enough for a service provider to commit in the written contract to later notify the responsible plan fiduciary of material changes to the disclosures contained in the contract; subsection (vi) requires that the service provider in fact provide such notification.

Subsection (vi) also refers to relief that may be available to a responsible plan fiduciary when a service provider fails to comply with this requirement. In addition to this proposed regulation, the Department is publishing a proposed Class Exemption in today's **Federal Register**. Subject to certain conditions, this Class Exemption will provide relief

from ERISA's prohibited transaction rules for a responsible plan fiduciary when a contract or arrangement fails to be "reasonable," through no fault of the responsible plan fiduciary, but due to a service provider's failure to satisfy its disclosure obligations under this regulation. The proposed Class Exemption is discussed below in paragraph (2), "Consequences of Failure to Satisfy the Proposed Regulation."

(g) Relationship Between Disclosures and the Plan Fiduciary's ERISA Section 404(a) Duties

The parties to a service contract or arrangement that falls within the scope of paragraph (c)(1)(i) of the proposal must, at a minimum, satisfy the requirements contained in this proposal and the other conditions to ERISA section 408(b)(2) in order for the provision of services under the contract or arrangement to be exempt from ERISA's prohibited transaction rules. However, the engagement of any particular service provider will not necessarily satisfy the fiduciary's obligations under section 404(a) of ERISA to act prudently and solely in the best interest of the plan's participants and beneficiaries merely because the service provider furnishes the information described in the proposed regulation.

Section 404(a) of ERISA requires that the responsible plan fiduciary engage in an objective process designed to elicit information necessary to assess not only the reasonableness of the compensation or fees to be paid for services, but also the qualifications of the service provider and the quality of the services that will be provided.[14] Although the steps taken by a responsible plan fiduciary may vary depending on the facts and circumstances, solicitation of bids among service providers is a means by which the responsible plan fiduciary can obtain information relevant to the decision-making process. A responsible plan fiduciary should not consider any one factor, including the fees or compensation to be paid to the service provider, to the exclusion of other factors. Further, a fiduciary need not necessarily select the lowest-cost service provider, so long as the compensation or fees paid to the service provider are determined to be reasonable in light of the particular facts and circumstances.

Further, plan fiduciaries are not limited by the disclosures required in this proposal. Plan fiduciaries may ask service providers for any additional information that they feel is necessary to their decision. For example, a responsible plan fiduciary may have questions for a service provider concerning the specific personnel that will be assigned to manage or perform services under the contract or arrangement.

Finally, although this proposal looks to disclosures made at the time a service contract or arrangement is entered into or renewed, responsible plan fiduciaries must continue to monitor service arrangements and the performance of service providers. Receipt of the disclosures described in this proposed regulation at the onset of a service relationship will not relieve plan fiduciaries of this ongoing obligation.

(h) Existing Requirement Concerning Termination of Contract or Arrangement

Paragraph (c)(2) of the regulation continues to require that service contracts or arrangements permit termination by the plan without penalty and on reasonably short notice. This requirement has not been changed, though the Department invites comments from the public as to any practical issues relating to the current regulation's requirements concerning contract termination. Specifically, the Department would like to know whether the current regulatory framework presents practical problems and whether further regulatory or interpretive guidance could address these problems.

(i) Other Statutory Exemptions Concerning Service Providers

The Department understands that, in certain circumstances, plans and service providers to such plans must rely on statutory exemptions other than section 408(b)(2) of ERISA in order to conduct business without violating ERISA's prohibited transaction provisions. Therefore, the Department invites comment on the extent to which the application of the disclosure requirements contained in this proposed regulation will affect, or may be affected by, other ERISA statutory exemptions that may relate to plan service arrangements.

(2) Consequences of Failure To Satisfy the Proposed Regulation

If the contract or arrangement fails to require disclosure of the information described in the proposed regulation, or if the service provider fails to disclose such information, then the contract or arrangement will not be "reasonable." Therefore, the service arrangement will not qualify for the relief from ERISA's prohibited transaction

---

[14] *See, e.g.,* Information Letters to D. Ceresi (Feb. 19, 1998) and to T. Konshak (Dec. 1, 1997).

rules provided by section 408(b)(2). The resulting prohibited transaction would have consequences for both the responsible plan fiduciary and the service provider. The responsible plan fiduciary, by participating in the prohibited transaction, will have violated section 406(a)(1)(C) of ERISA's prohibited transaction rules.[15] The service provider, as a "disqualified person" under the Internal Revenue Code's (Code) prohibited transaction rules, will be subject to the excise taxes that result from the service provider's participation in a prohibited transaction under Code section 4975.[16]

The Department believes that this significant result will provide incentives for all parties to service contracts or arrangements to cooperate in exchanging the disclosures required by the proposed regulation. However, the Department also believes that, in certain circumstances, a responsible plan fiduciary should not be held liable for a prohibited transaction that results when a service provider, unbeknownst to the plan fiduciary, fails to satisfy its disclosure obligations as required by the proposed regulation. Accordingly, the Department also published a proposed Class Exemption in today's **Federal Register**. The scope of the relief provided by the Class Exemption and the conditions that must be satisfied by a responsible plan fiduciary in order to obtain such relief are discussed in the preamble to the proposed Class Exemption. The Department notes that, in general, the parties seeking to avail themselves of either the statutory exemption provided by ERISA section 408(b)(2), or the administrative exemption provided in the Department's proposed Class Exemption, will bear the burden of establishing compliance with the conditions of these exemptions.

C. Effective Date

The Department proposes that its amendments to regulation section 2550.408b-2 be effective 90 days after publication of the final regulation in the **Federal Register**. The Department invites comments on whether the final regulation should be made effective on a different date.

D. Request for Comments

The Department invites comments from interested persons on the proposed regulation and other issues discussed in this Notice. Comments should be submitted electronically by e-mail to *e-ORI@dol.gov*, or by using the Federal eRulemaking portal at *http://www.regulations.gov*. Persons wishing to submit paper copies should address them to the Office of Regulations and Interpretations, Employee Benefits Security Administration, Room N-5655, U.S. Department of Labor, 200 Constitution Avenue, NW., Washington, DC 20210, Attn: 408(b)(2) Amendment. All comments received will be available for public inspection, without charge, at *http://www.regulations.gov* or at *http://www.dol.gov/ ebsa* and in the Public Disclosure Room, N-1513, Employee Benefits Security Administration, 200 Constitution Avenue, NW., Washington, DC 20210.

The comment period for this proposed regulation will end 60 days after publication of the proposed rule in the **Federal Register**. The Department believes that this period of time will afford interested persons an adequate amount of time to analyze the proposal and submit comments.

E. Regulatory Impact Analysis

(1) Overview of the Proposal

Under section 406(a)(1)(C) of ERISA's prohibited transaction rules, the furnishing of goods, services, or facilities between a plan and a party in interest to the plan is generally prohibited.[17] A service relationship between a plan and a service provider would thus constitute a prohibited transaction in the absence of regulatory relief, because ERISA defines any person providing services to the plan as a "party in interest" to the plan.[18] Section 408(b)(2) of ERISA, however, exempts certain arrangements between plans and service providers that otherwise would be prohibited transactions. To obtain relief under that section, the arrangement must be reasonable, the services must be necessary for the establishment or operation of the plan, and no more than reasonable compensation must be paid for the services.[19] Regulations issued by the Department clarify each of these conditions to the exemption.[20]

To further clarify the meaning of a "reasonable" contract or arrangement under section 408(b)(2), the Department proposes to amend the regulation at 29 CFR § 2550.408b-2(c). Under the proposal, a contract or arrangement to provide covered services to a plan would not be reasonable unless it requires the service provider to disclose, in writing, certain information before the contract or arrangement is entered into, extended, or renewed. The Department believes that, in order to satisfy their ERISA obligations, plan fiduciaries need information concerning all compensation to be received by the service provider and any conflicts of interest that may adversely affect the service provider's performance of the contract or arrangement.

The proposal requires that, in order to be considered a reasonable contract or arrangement, the contract must require the service provider to furnish the specified information to the responsible plan fiduciary. The rule also would require that the service provider comply with its contractual obligation and actually furnish the specified information. These disclosures are intended to enable the responsible plan fiduciary to ensure that no more than reasonable compensation is paid to the service provider for the services and to illustrate any actual or potential conflicts of interest that may affect the service provider's judgment.

Once adopted, these requirements will apply to all contracts or arrangements between plans (including pension plans, group health plans, and other types of welfare benefit plans) and service providers who are fiduciaries; who provide banking, consulting, custodial, insurance, investment advisory, investment management, recordkeeping, securities or other investment brokerage, or third party administration services; or who receive indirect compensation for accounting, actuarial, appraisal, auditing, legal, or valuation services to the plan (collectively "covered services" or "covered providers").

The Department's interest in this proposal stems from concerns about the fees paid for by employee benefit plans, and the ability of plan sponsors and fiduciaries to understand these fees which may be paid directly or indirectly by plans. The Department believes that greater understanding of these fees by the affected parties will increase efficiency and competition in the service provider market and generate benefits to plans and thus to plan participants. Although the Department believes this rule will have the greatest effect on service providers to pension plans, the Department identified other employee benefit plans, such as health and welfare plans, that would be affected by this regulation and could realize benefits from the proposal similar to the benefits realized by pension plans.

In a separate regulatory effort, the Department has revised Schedule C of the annual Form 5500, which is filed by most large plans. Schedule C collects information about plan service providers that were compensated in excess of $5,000. These revisions are intended to improve the reported information on compensation and revenue sharing arrangements of service providers to employee benefit plans. Similar to the proposed revisions under section 408(b)(2) of ERISA, the revisions to Schedule C are intended to help plan sponsors and fiduciaries in determining the reasonableness of the fees they pay to service providers and to help assess any potential conflicts of interest. While the proposed regulation under section 408(b)(2) of ERISA concerns the disclosure of information during the decision-making process, the changes to Schedule C concern the provision of retrospective information as part of a plan's annual reporting obligations.

The Department is also publishing, simultaneously with this regulatory initiative, a proposed class exemption for plan fiduciaries in certain circumstances when plan service arrangements fail to comply with ERISA section 408(b)(2). The exemption is published elsewhere in this issue of the **Federal Register**. In the preamble to the exemption, the Department describes how it has taken into account the availability of conditional relief under the exemption in assessing the economic costs and benefits of the regulation. The Department believes that the exemption is essential to achieve the purposes underlying the regulation.

(2) Executive Order 12866 Statement

Under Executive Order 12866, the Department must determine whether a regulatory action is "significant" and therefore subject to the requirements of the Executive Order and subject to review by the Office of Management and Budget (OMB). Under section 3(f) of the Executive Order, a "significant regulatory action" is an action that is

---

[15] *See* ERISA § 406(a)(1)(C).

[16] The Internal Revenue Code (Code) also provides statutory relief for transactions between a plan and a service provider that otherwise would be prohibited. Any excise taxes imposed by Code section 4975(a) and (b) for failure to satisfy the statutory exemption are paid by the disqualified person who participates in the prohibited transaction, in this case

the service provider, not the plan fiduciary. *See* Code § 4975(a), (b), (c)(1)(C), (d)(2), and (e)(2)(B).

[17] *See* ERISA § 406(a)(1)(C).

[18] *See* ERISA § 3(14)(B).

[19] *See* ERISA § 408(b)(2).

[20] *See* 29 CFR 2550.408b-2.

likely to result in a rule (1) having an annual effect on the economy of $100 million or more, or adversely and materially affecting a sector of the economy, productivity, competition, jobs, the environment, public health or safety, or State, local or tribal governments or communities (also referred to as "economically significant"); (2) creating serious inconsistency or otherwise interfering with an action taken or planned by another agency; (3) materially altering the budgetary impacts of entitlement grants, user fees, or loan programs or the rights and obligations of recipients thereof; or (4) raising novel legal or policy issues arising out of legal mandates, the President's priorities, or the principles set forth in the Executive Order. OMB has determined that this action is significant under section 3(f)(1) because it is likely to materially affect a sector of the economy. Accordingly, the Department has undertaken, as described below, an analysis of the costs and benefits of the proposed regulation in satisfaction of the requirements of the Executive Order. The Department believes that the proposed regulation's benefits justify its costs.

(3) Need for Regulatory Action

Employee benefit plans have evolved over the past several years, resulting in changes to both the services provided to the plans and the compensation received by service providers. Fee structures for service providers have, in some cases, become more complex and less transparent for plan sponsors or fiduciaries determining what is actually paid for services. This increased complexity also makes it more difficult to discern the service provider's potential conflicts of interest. It has also become more difficult to determine the impacts of these potential conflicts of interest on the fees paid by, or the quality of the services provided to, the plan.

Despite these complexities, when selecting or monitoring service providers, plan fiduciaries must act prudently and solely in the interest of the plan's participants and beneficiaries and for the exclusive purpose of providing benefits and defraying reasonable expenses of administering the plan. To meet these obligations, it is vital that fiduciaries have enough information to make informed assessments and decisions about the services, the costs and the providers. In this regard, the Department has published interpretive guidance concerning the disclosure and other obligations of plan fiduciaries and service providers under sections 404, 406(b) and 408(b) of ERISA.[21]

To the extent that plan fiduciaries are unable to obtain this information, or unable to use it to choose among service providers in a manner that upholds their fiduciary duty, a failure exists in the market for services for employee benefit plans. This market failure results from information asymmetry between the providers of plan services who possess information about their fee structures and potential conflicts of interest and plan fiduciaries that lack this information but need it to act in the best interest of their plans. The Department believes that both responsible plan fiduciaries and service providers will benefit from this proposed regulation, which will promote the efficiency of plan fiduciaries finding and using the information they need to search for service providers. This action furthers important public policy goals of increased transparency and increased competition in the service provider market.

(4) Regulatory Alternatives

Executive Order 12866 directs Federal Agencies promulgating regulations to evaluate regulatory alternatives. The Department considered the following alternatives: Remaining with the status quo, a general regulatory framework, broad applicability, and a specific framework with limited application. These alternatives are described further below:

• Remain with status quo

The Department weighed the option of remaining with the status quo and relying on the current regulatory framework. ERISA's existing fiduciary duties imposed by sections 404 and 408(b)(2) already require plan fiduciaries to ensure that fees paid to service providers are reasonable. As part of this duty, fiduciaries must obtain information about fees and conflicts of interest. Absent a regulation, the status quo framework relies upon these more general fiduciary requirements to ensure that plans pay reasonable service fees.

The status quo alternative was rejected. Although the Department has issued technical guidance concerning plan fiduciaries' obligations to assess all compensation received by service providers, issues remain concerning the adequacy of current disclosures made to plans. The Department believes that plan fiduciaries would benefit from a clear and uniform regulatory standard for disclosure. Additionally, under the "status quo" alternative, it is unclear whether non-fiduciary service providers are obligated by law to provide the information the Department believes fiduciaries need in order to evaluate whether a provider's fees are reasonable.

• General regulatory framework

Second, the Department considered establishing a general regulatory framework requiring service providers to furnish, and plan fiduciaries to obtain, information on fee structures and conflicts of interest. This alternative would not have specified in detail the exact information that must be exchanged, but would have left this up to the parties to the contract or arrangement. The Department rejected this alternative because it believes both responsible plan fiduciaries and service providers would benefit from additional guidance concerning the information that must be exchanged. The Department felt that, although this alternative would create an obligation on the part of the parties to exchange information that relates to the reasonableness of fees, parties may be left with ongoing ambiguity about exactly what information is necessary to fully evaluate a service provider contract or arrangement. The Department therefore believes that this alternative would fail to generate significant benefits in the form of greater efficiency with higher costs than the status quo.

• Broad applicability

Third, the Department considered applying the proposed regulation broadly to all service arrangements that rely on the section 408(b)(2) service provider exemption for relief from ERISA's prohibited transaction rules. Upon further consideration, this alternative was rejected because the Department believed that the proposal's written disclosure requirements should be targeted to a more specifically defined group of service providers. The Department believes that certain service arrangements generally do not involve complex compensation arrangements or conflicts of interest, and therefore need not be separately regulated in order to ensure that compensation information is disclosed. Benefits from this alternative and the proposed rule would be similar and benefits would be accruing primarily to those plans with complex service provider arrangements. This alternative would be more costly than the proposed framework as more service providers would be affected.

• Specific framework with limited application

Lastly, the Department considered, and ultimately has adopted as its proposal, a rule requiring that, in order to be reasonable, a contract or arrangement for services must mandate that certain sets of service providers disclose specified information about their compensation and conflicts of interest. The proposal covers typical plan service providers that are most likely to have complex compensation arrangements or conflicts of interest. They include: fiduciary service providers; providers furnishing banking, consulting, custodial, insurance, investment advisory or management, recordkeeping, securities or other investment brokerage, or third party administration services; or providers who receive indirect compensation for accounting, actuarial, appraisal, auditing, legal or valuation services. The Department believes this framework will yield the information that plan fiduciaries need in order to assess the reasonableness of compensation paid for services from these service providers. Absent the regulation, such information may be difficult to obtain. The Department believes that the proposed rule provides the largest benefit among the four alternatives, while also limiting the costs.

(5) Characterization of Affected Entities

(a) Interaction of Affected Entities

The Department considered the costs and benefits of the proposed regulation over a 10-year time frame beginning in 2008. The proposed regulation will apply to all contracts or arrangements between plan fiduciaries and service providers that fall within its scope. The Department believes that other entities also may be affected either directly or indirectly by the proposal, including plan participants and plan sponsors. Using data from plan year 2003 submissions of Form 5500 and Schedule C, the Department developed a detailed industry profile to obtain information on these entities and their growth over the analysis period. The industry profile also describes the interactions among these entities and the influence of the proposed regulation on these interactions.[22]

[21] *See, e.g.* Field Assistance Bulletin 2002-3 (Nov. 5, 2002) and Advisory Opinions 97-16A (May 22, 1997) and 97-15A (May 22, 1997).

[22] See Technical Appendix A to the 408(b)(2) Regulatory Impact Analysis, which is available as part of the public docket associated with this regulation, for details.

(b) Growth of Affected Entities Over Time

To estimate the costs of the rule in future years, it is necessary to project the growth of the affected entities. To estimate this growth, the Department calculated a growth rate from past data on pension plans and participants. This growth rate was used to project the numbers of potentially affected entities in future years out to 2020. In the absence of more specific information, the Department assumed a growth in pension plans and participants equal to that of the labor force and the economy. The estimated growth rate was thus based on industry-wide trends in pension plans and participants.

The Department used data from 1985 to 2005 on numbers of defined benefit (DB) and defined contribution (DC) plans.[23] Since 1985, there has been a dramatic increase in the number of 401(k) plans, while other DC and DB plans show a marked decrease. Overall, there are slight increases in the total number of plans and participants. These increases are driven by the growth of 401(k) plans.

The Department estimated a growth rate model based on fitting an exponential curve function through the data points. This growth rate model was then used to predict future numbers of plans and participants. The results showed steady increases in the total number of plans (from about 800,000 in 2010 to 850,000 in 2020) and participants (from around 81,800,000 in 2010 to 90,800,000 in 2020) for the years 2010 through 2020.

(c) Quantitative Characterization of Affected Entities

The Department undertook a quantitative characterization of the benefit plan industry to gain additional information on the entities the Department believes would be affected by the rule. This subset of employer-sponsored plans was used for this characterization due to the availability of data on these types of plans. Data from plan year 2003 submissions of Form 5500, a yearly filing required for many benefit plans, were used for this analysis. The general approach of this characterization was to look at the two major plan types, pension (defined benefit and defined contribution) and welfare, and, where appropriate, subcategories within each plan type.

For plan year 2003, there were around 762,000 benefit plans for which a Form 5500 was filed, 676,000 of which were pension plans and roughly 86,000 of which were welfare plans. This population of benefit plans can be divided into large plans (≥100 participants) and small plans (< 100 participants), according to the filing instructions for Form 5500. For plan year 2003, there were nearly 153,000 large plans and nearly 610,000 small plans. Thus, most employee benefit plans have fewer than 100 participants.

The Department made a rough characterization of the plan sponsor population using data collected via Form 5500. For all plans filed that year, there were over 622,000 plan sponsors, with about 86 percent of sponsors having only one benefit plan. Among plans filed for 2003, there were nearly 79,000 sponsors of large plans and over 555,000 sponsors of small plans. The Department believes, however, that these numbers might be slightly overestimated due to some plan sponsors filing under more than one employer identification number.

The Department characterized data for service providers to benefit plans from Schedule C submissions for plan year 2003. Compared to plan sponsor data, the data on service providers was very limited, as only a subset of plans must file Schedule C. For example, data for services and service providers to small plans, which account for over 80 percent of all plans, are not represented in the Schedule C filings. In terms of the number of service providers per plan, almost three quarters (72 percent) of the plans listed using one or two service providers, and 95 percent of the plans used 10 or less service providers. Only 14 plans used 40 or more unique service providers.

The Department also characterized the number of affected services provided by plan type and size (based on the number of participants) for all plans that filed Schedule C for plan year 2003, or the number of plan-provider arrangements. There were nearly 55,000 affected plan-provider arrangements for pension plans, and nearly 31,000 affected plan-provider arrangements for welfare plans. This analysis resulted in an estimate of the number of affected service providers to pension plans as nearly 9,878, and to welfare plans as 7,519, for a total number of about 15,600 affected service providers (providers that service both markets are counted only once). Although this analysis only covered a subset of the service provider market, the Department believes that this analysis included most of the affected service providers. Additional characterizations of service providers in terms of the services provided

and compensation received are presented in Technical Appendix A to the 408(b)(2) Regulatory Impact Analysis.

The Department characterized benefit plan participants from Form 5500 submissions for plan year 2003. This analysis showed roughly 151.8 million pension plan participants and 162.7 million welfare plan participants. The totals for pension plans and welfare plans may overlap, as individuals may participate in more than one type of plan.

(6) Benefits

As an example of the kind of benefits that could arise from this rule, the Department considered the possible benefits to defined contribution pension plans. The Department considered these benefits of the proposal from a qualitative perspective due to the ambiguous nature of the benefits arising from the proposal and the difficulty of quantifying them. Primary benefits of the proposal were thought to result from the potential for reduced unit costs incurred by plans for fiduciaries to search for service providers. This potential reduced unit cost of searching would encourage plan fiduciaries to obtain information from a larger set of service providers when they were making decisions about which provider to engage. Additionally, fiduciaries would have fewer barriers to changing service providers if they were not happy with their current fees or the returns they were receiving.

The social benefits arising from the proposal would be the sum of three different possible categories of primary benefits: possible lower fees paid by plans, possible increased efficiency due to reduced conflicts of interest, and possible higher returns due to reduced unit search costs incurred by plans. The magnitude of these benefits would depend in part on the degree to which the proposal actually resulted in lower search costs, and the degree to which different kinds of inefficiency currently exist in the market for service providers. A graphical analysis of these primary benefits is provided in Technical Appendix A to the 408(b)(2) Regulatory Impact Analysis which shows how the proposal lowers the marginal search costs for plans and how this cost reduction results in a greater amount of searching effort performed at a lower cost. The graphical analysis also shows the total net benefits to plans from the increased search effort by fiduciaries and the total societal net benefits of the reduction in unit search costs for service providers.

In addition to the potential primary benefits of the proposal, the Department identified potential secondary benefits due to possible higher rates of investment by participants in defined contribution pension plans. These secondary benefits could potentially arise from increased plan efficiencies and better investment choices by plan fiduciaries, and possibly from increases in plan participants' confidence in their plans as well. With greater transparency of fee structures, plan participants may have increased levels of confidence in their plans and may feel that their investment opportunities are more attractive. This increased confidence and attractiveness of investments could in turn result in a higher rate of investment in plans by plan participants. The existence and magnitude of these secondary benefits would depend on the preferences of employees in trading current for future consumption. Possible increases in rates of investment would be a benefit to society if the rate of return on capital investment were greater than the social rate of time preference between current and future consumption. Both of these issues are covered in Technical Appendix B to the 408(b)(2) Regulatory Impact Analysis.

(7) Costs

The Department estimated costs for the proposal over the 10-year time frame for the analysis. The primary costs of the rule are seen to accrue to service providers.[24] The Department used information from the quantitative characterization of the service provider market presented above as a basis for these cost estimates. This characterization did not account for all service providers, but did provide information on the segments of the service provider industry that are likely to be most affected by the proposal (*i.e.*, those who service pension plans). In addition to the costs to service providers, the Department also considered other potential costs and savings from the proposal, including savings to plan participants and costs to the plan due to its fiduciaries' review of any additional material they receive as part of the required disclosures.

(a) Costs to Service Providers

(i) *Initial costs.* When the Department publishes the proposal, affected service providers will need to evaluate whether their current disclosure practices comply with the proposal and, if not, how their

---

[23] Investment Company Institute, *401(k) Plans: A 25-Year Retrospective (Dec. 2006)* at 3.

[24] Costs to service providers might be ultimately borne by plans and their participants.

practices must be changed to be compliant. The Department projected this as a cost incurred in the year in which the rule takes effect.

The Department assumed that all affected service providers will incur a cost for rule familiarization, and estimated this cost to be one hour per service provider. The Department assumed that the rule familiarization would be performed by an in-house professional-level employee at a cost of $56 per hour.[25] Using the number of unique service providers identified in the quantitative analysis presented earlier (15,600), this cost was estimated to be about $870,000 (15,600×1× $56).

Although all affected service providers are assumed to incur these initial costs, it is more likely that only service providers with complex fee arrangements and conflicts of interest would find a formal review process to be necessary. The Department assumed that the number of service providers undertaking this kind of formal review is similar to the number of unique service providers who are reported on the Schedule C as having received $1 million or more in compensation (2,100). Assuming that 24 working hours would be required to read the proposal, review a service provider's current disclosure practices, and describe needed changes, if any, the initial cost of legal review is around $5.4 million (2,100 service providers× 24 hours×$106 in-house lawyer rate).

Affected service providers must also develop or update their current disclosure statements. This activity includes developing formulae and algorithms to estimate direct and indirect compensation that will be applied in a pro forma projection for each plan with which the provider will contract. The Department again assumed that the majority of this cost would be incurred by service providers in the first year of the analysis period. The existing amount of disclosure supplied by many service providers is likely to be adequate for compliance with the new rule. For example, a service provider offering unbundled trustee services or unbundled participant communications services is likely to stipulate a single direct payment that is already being adequately disclosed in the absence of the new rule. For this calculation, the Department assumed that the number of unique service providers reported on the Schedule C as having received $1 million or more in compensation (2,100) is a reasonable proxy for the number of service providers that will need to update their current disclosure statements.

The Department assumed that 80 working hours would be required to implement changes to disclosure statements, producing a cost of about $9.4 million (2,100 service providers×80 hours×$56 in-house professional rate).

(ii) *Recurring costs.*

In addition to the initial costs identified above, the Department estimated the burden for two recurring costs that would accrue during each subsequent year of the analysis period. The first recurring cost was for service providers entering the market (either for the first time or by re-entry) to provide service to plans after the first year of applicability. These firms incur the initial cost of rule familiarization. The Department has assumed that one-twelfth (1,300=15,600×1/12) of all service providers are new in each year subsequent to the first.[26] Familiarization costs then equal around $73,000 (1,300 service providers×1 hour×$56 in-house professional rate).

The second recurring cost arises from affected service providers needing to develop the written disclosure statement each time the "contracts and arrangements entered into," are "extended, or renewed." Many contracts between plans and service providers have multi-year terms, automatic annual renewals, or no specific term (having instead a provision for either party to terminate at will).[27] Despite these longer contract terms, though, even these contract types are likely to include, at least annually, material changes to elements such as unit costs. The Department thus estimated one disclosure per year per contract between a plan and service provider.[28] Service providers may provide similar written disclosures as plan administrators ask for multiple bids for a single service or as plan administrators ask for costs for multiple investment or service options from a single provider. These additional written disclosures are not strictly subject to the proposal because they are not directly related to a transaction. For this reason, these additional disclosures were not included in the estimated costs of the rule.

Exhibit 7—1 presents an estimate of the number of contracts using Form 5500 data from plan year 2003. The projection assumes that those who are not Schedule C filers have as many providers on average as Schedule C filers. Firms such as insurance companies that may be service providers for purposes of the proposal may have been reported on Schedule A. These firms are not included in this estimate.

EXHIBIT 7-1.—NUMBER OF DISCLOSURES PER YEAR

Type and number of participants	Number of plans	Schedule C filers	Affected schedule C filers	Affected provider-plan arrangements	Affected providers per plan	Affected service provider arrangements (projected)
Pension (DB, DC) <100 participants	596,641	526	444	613	1.38	823,741
Pension (DB, DC) 100-499 participants	57,961	16,680	15,289	18,846	1.23	71,446
Pension (DB, DC) 500-1,000 participants	8,958	4,774	4,488	7,470	1.66	14,910
Pension (DB, DC) >1,000 participants	12,427	8,478	8,077	28,255	3.50	43,472
All Pension (DB, DC) . .	675,987	30,458	28,298	55,227	. . . .	953,569
Welfare <100 participants	13,095	801	738	913	1.24	16,200
Welfare 100-499 participants	46,224	7,366	6,736	8,811	1.31	60,463
Welfare 500-1,000 participants	10,475	2,558	2,377	4,286	1.80	18,888
Welfare >1,000 participants	16,670	5,075	4,780	16,946	3.55	59,098
All Welfare	86,464	15,800	14,631	31,025	. . . .	154,649
All Plans	762,451	46,258	42,929	86,692	. . . .	1,108,218

The Department assumed that many written disclosure statements under the proposal could be made routine and automatic. In the absence of good data on the number of easily automated versus not easily automated disclosure statements, the Department estimated that 70 percent are easy and would not require any significant time to produce, and 30 percent are complex, requiring 1 hour and 40 minutes to produce. The weighted average for the time needed is therefore 0.5

hours per written disclosure, yielding a recurring contracting disclosure cost of around $31 million (1,108,000 disclosures×0.5 hours×$56 in-house professional rate). The Department invites the public to comment on these assumptions.

A summary of the initial and recurring labor costs is shown below in Exhibit 7-2.

---

[25] The hourly wage estimates used in this analysis are estimates for 2007 and are based on data from the Bureau of Labor Statistics National Occupational Employment Survey (May 2005) and the Bureau of Labor Statistics Employment Cost Index (Sept. 2006).

[26] Industry growth, and therefore the growth in the number of service providers over time, has been addressed in Exhibit 7-4. For example, in 2009 the Department has assumed that there are 12% more service providers than in 2003.

[27] Please note that 29 CFR 2550.408b-2(c) provides, in part, that a contract or arrangement for services must be terminable, on reasonably short notice, by a plan.

[28] These recurring costs are assumed to accrue every year, starting with the first year.

EXHIBIT 7-2.—SUMMARY OF INITIAL AND RECURRING LABOR COSTS

	Affected quantity (2003 data)	Hours	Labor rate (2007$s)	Total (2007$s)
Initial Cost 1 (First Year)	15,609	1	$56	$874,104
Initial Cost 2 (First Year)	2,101	24	106	5,344,944
Initial Cost 3 (First Year)	2,101	80	56	9,412,480
Subtotal Initial Cost				15,631,528
Recurring Cost 1 (Subsequent Years)	1,300	1	56	72,800
Recurring Cost 2 (All Years)	1,108,218	0.5	56	31,030,104

Lastly, the Department estimated annual materials costs attributable to the disclosures required under the proposal. The Department's proposal does not provide detailed guidance on the format of the disclosure. However, the Department previously made available on its Web site (*http://www.dol.gov/ebsa*) a Model Fee Disclosure Form developed in cooperation with industry representatives that reflects similar types of information and runs to 11 pages. The disclosures are thus assumed to add 11 pages to existing written materials in each year. Paper and printing costs are estimated at $0.05 per page. The

Department assumed that there would be no significant additional postage costs because the disclosures, in most cases, could be included with other written materials given to the plan before the contract is entered into.

[Total material costs are therefore roughly $609,500 ($0.05 per page× 11 additional pages×1,108,000 disclosures).]

This materials cost was then added to the initial and recurring costs to estimate the total costs of the rule. These calculations are summarized below in Exhibit 7-3.

EXHIBIT 7-3.—SUMMARY OF TOTAL INITIAL AND RECURRING COSTS BY YEAR

	Labor costs	Materials costs	Total costs
First Year: Initial Costs	$15,631,528	....	....
First Year: Recurring Costs 2	31,030,104	$609,520	....
First Year: Cost Total	46,661,632	609,520	47,271,152
Subsequent Years: Recurring Costs 1	72,800	....	....
Subsequent Years: Recurring Costs 2	31,030,104	609,520	....
Subsequent Years: Cost Total	31,102,904	609,520	31,712,424

Exhibit 7-4 below shows the projection of costs over the 10-year time horizon for the proposal. The number of service providers is expected to grow above the number projected from plan year 2003 Form 5500 data. In order to quantify the increase in affected service providers over time, the Department has used 1997 and 2002 Economic Census data from the U.S. Census Bureau. The growth in "Portfolio Managers" (NAICS 523920) between the 1997 and 2002 Economic Census represents a compound annual growth rate of 3.8 percent and was utilized for this analysis as an approximation of the growth rate for all affected service providers. The Department applied a conservative growth rate

of half that historical value, 1.9 percent, to the plan year 2003 Form 5500 data. A real discount rate of 7 percent, as recommended in OMB Circulars A-94 and A-4, was applied to the ten-year stream of costs to obtain an estimate of the net present value of the costs. The 7 percent rate is an estimate of the average before-tax rate of return to private capital in the U.S. economy. The analysis is relatively insensitive to the value of the discount rate. Since the benefits of the proposal are not quantified, this net present value of the costs is also equal to the Department's estimate of the quantified net costs of the rule.

EXHIBIT 7-4.—CALCULATION OF NET PRESENT VALUE

Year	Real 2007 dollars	Growth in service providers from 2003	Real 2007 constant dollars with growth	Discount factor	Discounted 2007 dollars
2008	$47,271,152	1.099	$51,950,996	0.935	$48,574,181
2009	31,712,424	1.120	35,517,915	0.873	31,007,140
2010	31,712,424	1.141	36,183,876	0.816	29,526,043
2011	31,712,424	1.163	36,881,549	0.763	28,140,622
2012	31,712,424	1.185	37,579,222	0.713	26,793,986
2013	31,712,424	1.207	38,276,896	0.666	25,492,413
2014	31,712,424	1.230	39,006,282	0.623	24,300,913
2015	31,712,424	1.253	39,735,667	0.582	23,126,158
2016	31,712,424	1.277	40,496,765	0.544	22,030,240
2017	31,712,424	1.301	41,257,864	0.508	20,958,995
Total					279,950,691

(b) Cost Savings for Plan Participants

The proposal may allow fiduciaries to make even better choices among offers from competing service providers and among options offered by any service provider. Since the fiduciary makes these choices in the best interest of the participants and beneficiaries, cost savings generally accrue to the plan and thus plan participants. The Department cannot directly quantify the amount of savings. The Department can, however, calculate a threshold value for the point at which the cost savings equal the costs identified above.

Because the largest costs to plans generally are investment management costs, it is useful to express the threshold in terms of a percent against assets. Total assets held in private defined benefit and defined contribution plans in 2005 were $4.9 trillion.[29] If more than 8 percent of plans realize expense reductions of 1 basis point (one one-hundredth of a percent), then cost savings will exceed costs. The Department assumes that at least 8 percent of plans will experience a reduction of at least 1 basis point. Therefore, cost savings are expected to exceed costs. These results are summarized below in Exhibit 7-5. The Department invites the public to comment on these assumptions.

---

[29] Investment Company Institute, *401(k) Plans: A 25-Year Retrospective (Dec. 2006)* at 3.

EXHIBIT 7-5.—CALCULATION OF THRESHOLD VALUE AT WHICH COST SAVINGS EQUAL COSTS

A	Annuity Equivalent to $280.0 M	$39,858,680
B	Total Assets	$4,861,000,000,000
C	Assets × 1 basis point	$486,100,000
D = A/C	Threshold Percent of Firms	8%

(c) Costs to Plans

Plan fiduciaries already have a fiduciary duty to evaluate the reasonableness of offers from service providers, and they already have access to tools like the Model Plan Fee Disclosure Form to assist them in asking service providers questions in order to encourage disclosure. The proposed changes to the Department's regulation under section 408(b)(2) of the Act attempt to facilitate this duty by providing a framework as to what must be disclosed concerning service arrangements and by requiring service providers to provide such disclosures in order to benefit from the section 408(b)(2) statutory exemption.

On the other hand, some plans may incur costs under the proposal. First, the new written disclosures are likely to become longer and more detailed than what fiduciaries are currently receiving. The prudent fiduciary may spend additional hours reviewing the longer written disclosure document, resulting in costs to their plan. In addition, some fiduciaries may be concerned that the availability of the detailed written disclosures exposes them to potential fiduciary liability. Fiduciaries could go so far as to hire outside consultants to review and evaluate the new written disclosures, which would again result in costs to their plans.

On the whole, the Department projects that the amount of time saved by fiduciaries in gathering data is offset by the additional time spent by them in reviewing additional data. These potential costs to plans were thus not included in the estimates. The amount of time spent by fiduciaries is likely to be similar with or without the proposal, though: As was previously discussed in the benefits section, the time spent under the proposal evaluating and documenting fees as reasonable is likely to be more efficient than in the baseline.

(8) Initial Regulatory Flexibility Analysis

The Regulatory Flexibility Act (5 U.S.C. 601, *et seq.*) (RFA) imposes certain requirements with respect to Federal rules that are subject to the notice and comment requirements of section 553(b) of the Administrative Procedure Act (5 U.S.C. 551, *et seq.*) and which are likely to have a significant economic impact on a substantial number of small entities. Unless an agency determines that a proposal is not likely to have a significant economic impact on a substantial number of small entities, section 603 of the RFA requires that the agency present an initial regulatory flexibility analysis (IRFA) at the time of the publication of the notice of proposed rulemaking describing the impact of the rule on small entities and seeking public comment on such impact. Small entities include small businesses, organizations and governmental jurisdictions.

In response to this request, the Department prepared an IRFA of the proposal because, although the Department considers it unlikely that the rule will have a significant effect on a substantial number of small entities, the Department does not have enough information to certify to that effect.

(a) Reasons for and Objectives of the Proposal

Employee benefit plans have evolved over the past several years, resulting in service providers having more complex compensation arrangements and conflicts of interest. Thus, plan fiduciaries face greater difficulty in assessing whether the compensation paid to their service providers is reasonable. This proposal is intended to help plan fiduciaries get the information they need to negotiate with and select service providers who offer high quality services at reasonable rates.

The reasons for and objectives of this proposed regulation are discussed in detail in Section A of this preamble, "Background," and in section 3 of the Regulatory Impact Analysis (RIA), "Need for Regulatory Action." The legal basis for the proposal is set forth in the "Authority" section of this preamble, below.

(b) Estimating Compliance Requirements for Small Entities

The Department estimated the number of small entities that would be required to make disclosures under the proposal by examining 2002 Economic Census data for industries in North American Industry

Classification System (NAICS) codes for activities affected by the proposal. Next, the Department used information on firms in the affected NAICS codes to estimate the population of affected firms. From this analysis, the Department estimated that about 14,600 small firms would incur costs under the proposal. Further detail on this estimation procedure is provided in Technical Appendix C to the 408(b)(2) Regulatory Impact Analysis.

To determine the impact of the rule on small entities, the Department examined the initial and recurring costs that would be borne by small firms in further detail. As discussed in Section 7, the initial costs are estimated to amount to $56 for every small entity for rule familiarization, and roughly $7,000 for more in-depth review and changes to disclosure practices for small entities at the larger end of the range, or those with over $1,000,000 in annual revenues. These costs, which are at most less than one percent of a single year's revenues, should be easily affordable for all small entities.

The impact of recurring costs will depend on the number of plans served by each firm, and the fraction of plans requiring complex disclosures. In an attempt to determine the numbers of plans served by small service providers relative to large ones, the Department examined data from Form 5500 filings for plan year 2003. These data showed a strong tendency for smaller service providers (measured in terms of the total number of participants served) to serve plans of smaller average size. The Department found that, if all plans with 5 or fewer participants are served by the smallest of the service providers, it is possible that up around 5,150 small entities could face costs equal to one percent of revenues. Comparing this maximum to the total number of small entities bearing costs under this rule (about 14,600), or roughly one third of affected small entities could possibly bear ongoing costs equal to one percent of revenues as a result of the proposal. Because these magnitudes are above the thresholds commonly used to measure impacts on small entities, the Department considered it inappropriate to certify that the rule would not cause a "significant impact on a substantial number of small entities."

In conclusion, the Department believes that the rule is very likely to result in costs that are insignificant in comparison to revenues for all but the smallest affected entities. This conclusion, however, is subject to considerable uncertainty, due largely to a lack of data on both small plans and small service providers. The Department believes that it is at least possible for a substantial number of small entities to bear costs that could be considered significant, and therefore, the Department examined the issue in detail. Additional detail on the Department's analysis of this issue can be found in Technical Appendix C to the 408(b)(2) Regulatory Impact Analysis.

(c) Considered Alternatives

In accordance with the RFA, the Department considered whether several alternatives to the proposed regulation would minimize the economic impact on affected small entities. The Department also considered the anticipated benefits of the proposal for these entities. These alternatives are described further below, followed by a discussion of the Department's chosen alternative.

(i) *Exemption for Small Entities.*

The Department considered exempting from the requirements of the proposed regulation small service providers with a threshold of $6.5 million in annual revenue. The threshold of $6.5 million follows from the Small Business Administration's definition of small firms.[30] An exemption may lessen the burden on small service providers, to the extent such small service providers are not already providing written disclosures that would comply with the requirements of the proposed regulation. The Department believes, however, that such an exemption would not comport with the rule's objectives of providing plan fiduciaries with the information they need to assess the reasonableness of service fees. There is no indication that small service providers are any less likely to have complex fee arrangements or conflicts of interest. Instead, the Department has determined that the likely existence of complex fee structures and conflicts of interest depends more on the

---

[30] U.S. Small Business Administration, "Table of Small Business Size Standards Matched to North American Industry Classification System Codes." Available online at: *http://www.sba.gov/idc/groups/public/documents/sba _ homepage/serv _ sstd _ tablepdf.pdf.*

For further discussion please see the Technical Appendix Section C which can be accessed at the Department's Web site at *www.dol.gov/ebsa.*

nature of the service provided than upon the size of the service provider. Accordingly, the Department has narrowed the proposal's scope to providers of a limited set of services, such as investment advice and management.

The Department believes that small providers and the plans they serve will benefit from the proposal, because it will clarify the information that must be disclosed to responsible plan fiduciaries.

(ii) *Delaying Implementation for Small Service Providers.*

The Department also considered delaying implementation of the proposal for small service providers and small plans. This delay would provide these parties with more time to become familiar with the disclosure requirements, over a period of up to two years beyond the rule's generally applicable effective date. However, similar to the Department's rationale for deciding not to provide an exemption for small entities, the Department believes that plans, large and small, contracting with small service providers need the information required by the proposal in order to determine the reasonableness of service provider fees. Further, the Department does not believe there is any benefit to delaying application of this proposal, because doing so would delay the benefits to all plans of the proposal's required disclosures. Failure to obtain such information could cause plans to pay too much for services.

(iii) *Benefits of the Proposal to Small Plans.*

The Department believes that small plans will benefit significantly from the proposal. Fiduciaries to small plans may sometimes have trouble obtaining complete disclosures from potential service providers. Because the proposal is conditioned on compliance by both responsible plan fiduciaries and service providers, the Department believes that it will assist small plan fiduciaries in obtaining the information they need to make informed decisions when selecting service providers. Additionally, responsible plan fiduciaries for plans, both large and small, will benefit from the clarity that the proposal provides concerning the specific information that the Department believes is relevant to these decisions.

(d) The Selected Alternative

The Department considered and selected a disclosure framework that outlines what disclosures must be included in a "reasonable" contract or arrangement. As indicated above, small plans will benefit from this increased information at least as much as large plans will. Because there is no standard form for the disclosure, small service providers with relatively simple compensation arrangements and few, if any, conflicts of interest can provide a relatively simple, short written disclosure. The Department also limited the application of the rule to certain classes of services providers, as discussed above in the "Scope" section of the preamble. By limiting the scope of the regulation to contracts or arrangements with service providers that are more likely to have complicated fee structures and conflicts of interest, the Department believes that the proposal will avoid unnecessary burdens on small service providers that will not be subject to its written disclosure requirements.

(e) Duplicative, Overlapping, and Conflicting Rules

The Department identified two rules that potentially overlap or duplicate the proposal: Changes to the Form 5500, Schedule C, and The Investment Advisers Act of 1940.

(i) *Changes to the Form 5500, Schedule C.*

Recent changes to the Form 5500, Schedule C, clarify the requirements for the reporting of direct and indirect compensation received by service providers. Also, Schedule C requires that the source and nature of compensation in excess of $1,000 received from parties other than the plan or the plan sponsor be disclosed for certain key service providers.

Both the revised Schedule C requirements and the proposal aim to make indirect compensation received by service providers more transparent. The proposal, however, requires disclosure of compensation and fees in advance of contract performance so that the fiduciary can assess their reasonableness before they are paid. The Form 5500 revisions, on the other hand, require disclosure of actual compensation and fees after contract performance.

Small plans need not file the Schedule C, so the rule does not overlap for over 90 percent of plans. In addition, because small plans may tend to use small service providers, the existing relief for small plans from filing the Schedule C also minimizes the burden on small service providers.

(ii) *The Investment Advisers Act of 1940.*

The Investment Adviser's Act of 1940 authorizes the U.S. Securities Exchange Commission (SEC) to regulate investment advisors. The SEC requires SEC-registered investment advisers to disclose compensation and conflicts of interest to clients using the SEC Form ADV.

Some of the information disclosed on Form ADV may be similar to disclosures required by this proposal, which also will elicit information about indirect compensation and conflicts of interest. However, the Department clarifies above in the preamble that parties may satisfy the proposal's disclosure requirements by incorporating other written materials. This flexibility is afforded to parties in order to avoid unnecessary duplication. Thus, the Form ADV may serve as part of the disclosure made by service providers to comply with the proposal. Further, many of the service providers covered by the proposal are not subject to the Investment Advisers Act.

(f) Congressional Review Act Statement

This notice of proposed rulemaking is subject to the Congressional Review Act provisions of the Small Business Regulatory Enforcement Fairness Act of 1996 (5 U.S.C. 801 *et seq.*) and, if finalized, will be transmitted to the Congress and the Comptroller General for review.

(g) Unfunded Mandates Reform Act Statement

For purposes of the Unfunded Mandates Reform Act of 1995 (Pub. L. 104-4), as well as Executive Order 12875, the notice of proposed rulemaking does not include any federal mandate that will result in expenditures by state, local, or tribal governments in the aggregate of more than $100 million, adjusted for inflation, or increased expenditures by the private sector of more than $100 million, adjusted for inflation.

(9) *Paperwork Reduction Act*

As part of its continuing effort to reduce paperwork and respondent burden, the Department of Labor conducts a preclearance consultation program to provide the general public and Federal agencies with an opportunity to comment on proposed and continuing collections of information in accordance with the Paperwork Reduction Act of 1995 (PRA 95) (44 U.S.C. 3506(c)(2)(A)). This helps to ensure that the public understands the Department's collection instructions; respondents can provide the requested data in the desired format, the reporting burden (time and financial resources) is minimized, and the Department can properly assess the impact of collection requirements on respondents.

Currently, the Department is soliciting comments concerning the information collection request (ICR) included in the Proposed Rule on Reasonable Contract or Arrangement Under Section 408(b)(2). A copy of the ICR may be obtained by contacting the person listed in the PRA Addressee section below. The Department has submitted a copy of the proposal to OMB in accordance with 44 U.S.C. 3507(d) for review of its information collections. The Department and OMB are particularly interested in comments that:

- Evaluate whether the proposed collection of information is necessary for the proper performance of the functions of the agency, including whether the information will have practical utility;

- Evaluate the accuracy of the agency's estimate of the burden of the collection of information, including the validity of the methodology and assumptions used;

- Enhance the quality, utility, and clarity of the information to be collected; and

- Minimize the burden of the collection of information on those who are to respond, including through the use of automated, electronic, mechanical, or other technological collection techniques, e.g., by permitting electronic submission of responses.

Comments should be sent to the Office of Information and Regulatory Affairs, Office of Management and Budget, Room 10235, New Executive Office Building, Washington, DC 20503; Attention: Desk Officer for the Employee Benefits Security Administration. Although comments may be submitted through February 11, 2008, OMB requests that comments be received within 30 days of publication of the Notice of Proposed Rulemaking to ensure their consideration. Please note that comments submitted to OMB are a matter of the public record.

PRA Addressee: Address requests for copies of the ICR to Gerald B. Lindrew, Office of Policy and Research, U.S. Department of Labor, Employee Benefits Security Administration, 200 Constitution Avenue, NW., Room N-5718, Washington, DC 20210. Telephone: (202) 693-8410; Fax: (202) 219-4745. These are not toll-free numbers. ICRs submitted to OMB are also available at reginfo.gov (*http://www.reginfo.gov/public/do/PRAMain*).

(a) The Proposal

The ICRs are contained in paragraph (c)(1)(iii) of the proposal and pertain to the written disclosure requirements that the service provider must make whenever a contract or arrangement is entered into, extended, or renewed as a condition to the relief provided by the proposal. The written disclosure must include a description of the specific services to be provided, the direct and indirect compensation or fees to be received by the service provider, and the manner of receipt of such compensation or fees. It must also include a statement concerning whether the service provider will provide any services to the plan as a fiduciary and statements about the potential for conflicts of interest.

The Department estimates that about 15,600 affected service providers would need to review the rule and their current disclosure practices in the first year. The Department assumed that the rule familiarization would require one hour and be performed by an in-house professional-level employee at a cost of $56 per hour.

In years subsequent to the first year of applicability, the Department estimates that providers newly entering the market for plan services will need to become familiar with the rule. One-twelfth (around 1,300) of all service providers are assumed to be new to the market for plan services in each year subsequent to the first.[31] The Department again assumed that the rule familiarization would take one hour and would be performed by an in-house professional-level employee at a cost of $56 per hour.

The Department assumed that 2,100 affected service providers would have more complex fee arrangements and would therefore need to undertake a more formal review of their disclosure practices in the first year. The Department assumed that this formal review would require 24 working hours and be performed by an in-house lawyer at an estimated cost of $106 per hour.

The Department assumed that the same affected providers (2,100) would also need to update templates and processes for disclosure in the first year. This update is assumed to require 80 working hours and be performed by a in-house profession-level employee at a cost of $56 per hour, as described above.

The Department estimates that 1,108,000 contracts or arrangements exist between service providers and plans and that each contract or arrangement will require a written disclosure. It is assumed that contracts or arrangements are either entered into or renewed once in each of the first three years after the regulation would become effective. Preparation and delivery of the required disclosure is assumed to add, on average, one half hour to the process of entering into a contract or arrangement. Preparation and delivery are assumed to be performed by an in-house professional-level employee at a cost of $56 per hour. The average annual burden hours across the first three years is therefore estimated as 633,000 hours. The equivalent cost for this burden hour estimate is about $36,290,000 per year.

In addition to burden hours, the Department has estimated annual materials costs attributable to the disclosure. The Department's proposal does not provide detailed guidance on the content or format of the disclosure. However, the Department makes available a model 401(k) plan fee disclosure form that represents similar types of information and runs to 11 pages. The disclosures are assumed to add 11 pages to existing written contracts in each year. Paper and printing costs were estimated at $0.05 per page. It is assumed that there are no postage costs because, in most cases, the disclosures simply add content to what would generally be a written contract even absent the proposal. For each of the first three years, materials costs are therefore estimated to be roughly $609,500 (1,108,000 disclosures×11 pages×$0.05 per page cost).

(b) The Proposed Class Exemption

Not only does the proposal provide that the terms of the service contract must require the service provider to disclose its compensation and conflicts of interest, the service provider must also comply with the contract on an on-going basis and actually disclose this information in writing to the responsible plan fiduciary. If the service provider fails to disclose the data, then the provision of services will constitute a prohibited transaction under ERISA section 406(a)(1)(C) because it will not be considered a "reasonable contract or arrangement" exempted by ERISA section 408(b)(2). Therefore, in such instances, the responsible plan fiduciary will have violated section 406(a)(1)(C) even if it made every effort to comply with the proposed regulation by entering into, or extending or renewing, a written contract that required such disclosures. The failure to make the required disclosures also would result in a prohibited transaction by the service provider under section 4975(c)(1)(C) of the Internal Revenue Code.

Therefore, as an accompaniment to the proposed regulation, the Department also proposes a Class Exemption that will relieve such fiduciaries from liability for a prohibited transaction under ERISA section 406(a)(1)(C) in cases where the contract or arrangement requires the specified disclosures but the service provider fails to make them. This proposed Class Exemption is published in today's **Federal Register**.

The ICR contained in the proposed exemption requires that the responsible plan fiduciary, upon discovering a service provider's failure to make the required disclosures, must submit a written request to the provider for all information that the provider should have disclosed. It also requires the responsible plan fiduciary to report a service provider's refusal or failure to comply with the request in certain situations. As discussed below, the Department has determined that this ICR imposes a small paperwork burden on responsible plan fiduciaries in addition to the ICR imposed by the proposal.

To estimate this burden, the Department started with the number of disclosures made in the first year of the analysis (1,108,000) and assumed that 10 percent (111,000) of these disclosures would result in a concern by the responsible plan fiduciary after the contract or arrangement was solidified. According to the requirements of the exemption, the responsible plan fiduciary must, upon discovering a failure to disclose, submit a written request to the service provider for all information that it should have disclosed. The Department thus assumed that 111,000 written requests to service providers would be made for additional disclosure in the first year of the analysis. The Department assumed that the number of written requests would decrease in future years as service providers became more accustomed to the new disclosure requirements. Thus, in years two and three of the analysis, it was assumed that only five percent (about 55,500) of the total number of disclosures would be questioned. The Department averaged the number of exemption related requests over three years to obtain an average annual total of roughly 74,000 written disclosures.

Upon receipt of the written request by the responsible plan fiduciary, the service provider then has 90 days to comply with the request. If the service provider fails or refuses to comply with the responsible plan fiduciary's request in this timeframe, the exemption requires the responsible fiduciary to notify the Department of the service provider's failure or refusal. The Department estimates the number of notifications they would expect to receive as ten percent of the total number of written requests received by service providers, or nearly 11,000 the first year and 5,500 in the two succeeding years. Averaging this number of notifications over the three years resulted in an annual number of notifications of around 7,400.

The Department next estimated the total annual hour burden for the additional tasks required of plan fiduciaries under the exemption. The Department assumed that the written request to service providers would take a half hour of a fiduciary's time, resulting in a total annual hour burden of about 37,000 hours (74,000 requests ×0.5 hours). The Department next assumed that a notification to the Department of a service provider's failure or refusal to comply with a written request by the responsible fiduciary would take one hour of the responsible fiduciary's time, resulting in a total annual hour burden of 7,400 (7,400× 1 hour). Summing the burden of these two tasks resulted in a total annual hour burden estimate for plan fiduciaries of roughly 44,000 hours. The equivalent costs of these annual burden hours are about $2,070,000 ($56 in-house professional labor rate×37,000 hours) and $783,000 ($106 in-house lawyer rate×7,400 hours) for a total equivalent cost of around $2,850,000.

In addition to burden hours, the Department has estimated annual materials costs for plan fiduciaries to comply with the requirements of the exemption. Paper and printing costs are estimated at $0.05 per page. The Department assumed that both requests to service providers and notifications to the Department would be two pages. Since 81,300 of these requests and notifications are expected annually, the annual material cost is about $8,100 (81,300×$0.05×2), plus an annual postage cost of $33,300 (83,100×$0.41), totaling around $41,400.

These paperwork burden estimates are summarized as follows:

---

[31] Industry growth, and therefore the growth in the number of service providers over time, has been addressed in Exhibit 7-4. For example, in 2009 the Department has assumed that there are 12% more service providers than in 2003

Type of Review: New collection (Request for new OMB control number).

Agency: Employee Benefits Security Administration, Department of Labor.

Title: Reasonable Contract or Arrangement Under Section 408(b)(2)—Fee Disclosure.

OMB Control Number: 1210-New.

Affected Public: Business or other for-profit; not-for-profit institutions.

Estimated Number of Respondents: 79,500.

Estimated Number of Responses: 1,189,000.

Frequency of Response: Annually; occasionally.

Estimated Average Annual Burden Hours: 677,000.

Estimated Average Annual Burden Cost: $651,000.

F. Federalism Statement

Executive Order 13132 (August 4, 1999) outlines fundamental principles of federalism and requires the adherence to specific criteria by Federal agencies in the process of their formulation and implementation of policies that have substantial direct effects on the States, the relationship between the national government and the States, or on the distribution of power and responsibilities among the various levels of government. The proposed regulation would not have federalism implications because it has no substantial direct effect on the States, on the relationship between the national government and the States, or on the distribution of power and responsibilities among the various levels of government. Section 514 of ERISA provides, with certain exceptions specifically enumerated that are not pertinent here, that the provisions of Titles I and IV of ERISA supersede State laws that relate to any employee benefit plan covered by ERISA. The requirements implemented in the proposed regulation do not alter the fundamental provisions of the statute with respect to employee benefit plans, and as such would have no implications for the States or the relationship or distribution of power between the national government and the States.

List of Subjects in 29 CFR Part 2550

Employee benefit plans, Exemptions, Fiduciaries, Investments, Pensions, Prohibited transactions, Reporting and recordkeeping requirements, and Securities.

For the reasons set forth in the preamble, the Department proposes to amend Chapter XXV, subchapter F, part 2550 of Title 29 of the Code of Federal Regulations as follows:

SUBCHAPTER F—FIDUCIARY RESPONSIBILITY UNDER THE EMPLOYEE RETIREMENT INCOME SECURITY ACT OF 1974

PART 2550—RULES AND REGULATIONS FOR FIDUCIARY RESPONSIBILITY

1. The authority citation for part 2550 continues to read as follows:

Authority: 29 U.S.C. 1135; and Secretary of Labor's Order No. 1-2003, 68 FR 5374 (Feb. 3, 2003). Sec. 2550.401b-1 also issued under sec. 102, Reorganization Plan No. 4 of 1978, 43 FR 47713 (Oct. 17, 1978), 3 CFR, 1978 Comp. 332, effective Dec. 31, 1978, 44 FR 1065 (Jan. 3, 1978), 3 CFR, 1978 Comp. 332. Sec. 2550.401c-1 also issued under 29 U.S.C. 1101. Sec. 2550.404c-1 also issued under 29 U.S.C. 1104. Sec. 2550.407c-3 also issued under 29 U.S.C. 1107. Sec. 2550.404a-2 also issued under 26 U.S.C. 401 note (sec. 657, Pub. L. 107-16, 115 Stat. 38). Sec. 2550.408b-1 also issued under 29 U.S.C. 1108(b)(1) and sec. 102, Reorganization Plan No. 4 of 1978, 3 CFR, 1978 Comp. p. 332, effective Dec. 31, 1978, 44 FR 1065 (Jan. 3, 1978), and 3 CFR, 1978 Comp. 332. Sec. 2550.412-1 also issued under 29 U.S.C. 1112.

2. Section 2550.408b-2(c) is revised to read as follows:

§ 2550.408b-2 General statutory exemption for services or office space.

* * * * *

(c) *Reasonable contract or arrangement* —(1) *Disclosure concerning contract or arrangement.* (i) No contract or arrangement to provide services to an employee benefit plan, nor any extension or renewal of such contract or arrangement, by:

(A) A service provider who provides or may provide any services to the plan pursuant to the contract or arrangement as a fiduciary either within the meaning of section 3(21) of the Act or under the Investment Advisers Act of 1940;

(B) A service provider who provides or may provide any one or more of the following services to the plan pursuant to the contract or arrangement: banking, consulting, custodial, insurance, investment advisory (plan or participants), investment management, recordkeeping, securities or other investment brokerage, or third party administration; or

(C) A service provider who receives or may receive indirect compensation or fees, as described in paragraph (c)(1)(iii)(A)(*1*) of this section, in connection with providing any one or more of the following services to the plan pursuant to the contract or arrangement: accounting, actuarial, appraisal, auditing, legal, or valuation; is reasonable within the meaning of section 408(b)(2) of the Act and Sec. 2550.408b-2(a)(2) unless the requirements of paragraphs (c)(1)(ii) through (vi) of this section are satisfied.

(ii) The terms of the contract or arrangement shall be in writing.

(iii) The terms of the contract or arrangement (including any extension or renewal of such contract or arrangement) shall require the service provider to disclose in writing, to the best of the service provider's knowledge, the information set forth in this paragraph (c)(1)(iii) and shall include a representation by the service provider that, before the contract or arrangement was entered into (or extended or renewed), all such information was provided to the fiduciary with authority to cause the employee benefit plan to enter into (or extend or renew) the contract or arrangement (the "responsible plan fiduciary"):

(A) All services to be provided to the plan pursuant to the contract or arrangement and, with respect to each such service, the compensation or fees to be received by the service provider, and the manner of receipt of such compensation or fees. For purposes of this paragraph (c)(1)(iii):

(*1*) "Compensation or fees" include money or any other thing of monetary value (for example, gifts, awards, and trips) received, or to be received, directly from the plan or plan sponsor or indirectly (i.e., from any source other than the plan, the plan sponsor, or the service provider) by the service provider or its affiliate in connection with the services to be provided pursuant to the contract or arrangement or because of the service provider's or affiliate's position with the plan. An "affiliate" of a service provider is any person directly or indirectly (through one or more intermediaries) controlling, controlled by, or under common control with the service provider, or any officer, director, agent, or employee of, or partner with, the service provider.

(*2*) Compensation or fees may be expressed in terms of a monetary amount, formula, percentage of the plan's assets, or per capita charge for each participant or beneficiary of the plan. The manner in which compensation or fees are expressed shall contain sufficient information to enable the responsible plan fiduciary to evaluate the reasonableness of such compensation or fees.

(*3*) If a service provider offers a bundle of services to the plan that is priced as a package, rather than on a service-by-service basis, then only the service provider offering the bundle of services must provide the disclosures required by this paragraph (c)(1). The service provider must disclose all services and the aggregate compensation or fees to be received, directly or indirectly, by the service provider, any affiliate or subcontractor of such service provider, or any other party in connection with the bundle of services. The service provider shall not be required to disclose the allocation of such compensation or fees among its affiliates, subcontractors, or other parties, except to the extent such party receives or may receive compensation or fees that are a separate charge directly against the plan's investment reflected in the net value of the investment or that are set on a transaction basis, such as finder's fees, brokerage commissions, and soft dollars (research or other products or services other than execution in connection with securities transactions).

(*4*) A description of the manner of receipt of compensation or fees shall state whether the service provider will bill the plan, deduct fees directly from plan accounts, or reflect a charge against the plan investment and shall describe how any prepaid fees will be calculated and refunded when a contract or arrangement terminates.

(B) Whether the service provider (or an affiliate) will provide any services to the plan as a fiduciary either within the meaning of section 3(21) of the Act or under the Investment Advisers Act of 1940,

(C) Whether the service provider (or an affiliate) expects to participate in, or otherwise acquire a financial or other interest in, any transaction to be entered into by the plan in connection with the contract or arrangement and, if so, a description of the transaction and the service provider's participation or interest therein,

(D) Whether the service provider (or an affiliate) has any material financial, referral, or other relationship or arrangement with a money manager, broker, other client of the service provider, other service provider to the plan, or any other entity that creates or may create a conflict of interest for the service provider in performing services pursuant to the contract or arrangement and, if so, a description of such relationship or arrangement,

(E) Whether the service provider (or an affiliate) will be able to affect its own compensation or fees, from whatever source, without the prior approval of an independent plan fiduciary, in connection with the provision of services pursuant to the contract or arrangement (for example, as a result of incentive, performance-based, float, or other contingent compensation) and, if so, a description of the nature of such compensation, and

(F) Whether the service provider (or an affiliate) has any policies or procedures that address actual or potential conflicts of interest or that are designed to prevent either the compensation or fees described in paragraph (c)(1)(iii)(A) of this section or the relationships or arrangements described in paragraph (c)(1)(iii)(C), (D), and (E) of this section from adversely affecting the provision of services to the plan pursuant to the contract or arrangement, and, if so, an explanation of these policies or procedures and how they address such conflicts of interest or prevent an adverse effect on the provision of services.

(iv) The terms of the contract or arrangement shall require that the service provider must disclose to the responsible plan fiduciary any material change to the information required to be disclosed in paragraph (c)(1)(iii) of this section not later than 30 days from the date on which the service provider acquires knowledge of the material change.

(v) The terms of the contract or arrangement shall require that the service provider must disclose all information related to the contract or arrangement and any compensation or fees received thereunder that is requested by the responsible plan fiduciary or plan administrator in order to comply with the reporting and disclosure requirements of Title I of the Act and the regulations, forms, and schedules issued thereunder.

(vi) The service provider shall comply with its disclosure obligations under the contract or arrangement as described in this paragraph (c)(1). Prohibited Transaction Class Exemption 2008-XX will provide relief for a responsible plan fiduciary from the prohibitions of section 406(a)(1)(C) of the Act as a result of a service provider's failure to comply with this paragraph (c)(1)(vi).

(2) *Termination of contract or arrangement.* No contract or arrangement is reasonable within the meaning of section 408(b)(2) of the Act and Sec. 2550.408b-2(a)(2) if it does not permit termination by the plan without penalty to the plan on reasonably short notice under the circumstances to prevent the plan from becoming locked into an arrangement that has become disadvantageous. A long-term lease which may be terminated prior to its expiration (without penalty to the plan) on reasonably short notice under the circumstances is not generally an unreasonable arrangement merely because of its long term. A provision in a contract or other arrangement which reasonably compensates the service provider or lessor for loss upon early termination of the contract, arrangement, or lease is not a penalty. For example, a minimal fee in a service contract which is charged to allow recoupment of reasonable start-up costs is not a penalty. Similarly, a provision in a lease for a termination fee that covers reasonably foreseeable expenses related to the vacancy and reletting of the office space upon early termination of the lease is not a penalty. Such a provision does not reasonably compensate for loss if it provides for payment in excess of actual loss or if it fails to require mitigation of damages.

* * * * *

Signed at Washington, DC, this 7th day of December, 2007.

Bradford P. Campbell,

Assistant Secretary, Employee Benefits Security Administration, Department of Labor.

[FR Doc. E7-24064 Filed 12-12-07; 8:45 am]

BILLING CODE 4510-29-P

¶ 20,537G

EBSA proposed regulations: Disclosures: Civil penalties.—The Employee Benefits Security Administration (EBSA) has issued proposed regulations on the assessment of civil penalties by the Department of Labor under ERISA § 502(c)(4) for disclosure failures. The proposed regulations explain how the maximum penalty amounts are computed, identifies the circumstances under which penalties are assessed, sets forth certain procedural rules for service and filing, and provides a plan administrator a means to contest a penalty assessment by requesting an administrative hearing.

The proposed regulations were published in the *Federal Register* on December 19, 2007 (72 FR 71842). The final regulations were published in the Federal Register on January 2, 2009 (74 FR 17). The preamble to the final regulations is reproduced at ¶ 24,277. The regulation is at ¶ 14,925C.

¶ 20,537H

Pension Benefit Guaranty Corporation (PBGC): Proposed rule: Financial reporting: Actuarial reporting: Controlled groups: Underfunding: Pension Protection Act of 2006 (PPA).—The Pension Benefit Guaranty Corporation (PBGC) has proposed rules amending its regulation on annual financial and actuarial information reporting to implement provisions of the Pension Protection Act of 2006 (P.L. 109-280; PPA). The PPA changed the standards for reporting for underfunded controlled groups under ERISA § 4010 (Authority to Require Certain Information). In addition to providing proposed guidance on implementing PPA changes, PBGC proposes waiving reporting in certain cases for controlled groups with aggregate plan underfunding of $15 million or less, modifying the standards for determining which plans are exempted from the actuarial information requirements, and revising the actuarial information requirements to conform with other PPA changes. The proposed rules also clarify the use of the term "information year", as well as provide reporting relief for certain multiple employer plans.

The proposed regulations, which were published in the Federal Register on February 20, 2008 (73 FR 9243), are reproduced below. The final regulations were published in the *Federal Register* on March 16, 2009 (74 FR 11022). The preamble to the final regulations is reproduced at ¶ 24,279. See the preamble for the final regulations.

¶ 20,537I

EBSA proposed regulations: Safe harbor: Small plans: Employee contributions: Plan remittances.—The Employee Benefits Security Administration (EBSA) has issued proposed regulations, applicable primarily to defined-contribution plans with fewer than 100 participants, providing a seven business-day safe harbor period for employers to remit contributions from participants into retirement plans.

The proposed regulations, which were published in the *Federal Register* on February 29, 2008 (73 FR 11072), are reproduced below. The final regulations were published in the Federal Register on January 14, 2010 (75 FR 2068). The preamble to the final regulations is reproduced at ¶ 24,287. The regulation is at ¶ 14,139N.

¶ 20,537J

Department of Labor (DOL): Proposed rule: Family and Medical Leave Act of 1993 (FMLA).—The Department of Labor (DOL) has issued proposed amendments to its regulations on the Family and Medical Leave Act of 1993 (P.L. 103-3; FMLA).

The proposed regulations, which were published in the Federal Register on February 11, 2008 (73 FR 7876), were formerly reproduced below in relevant part. The final regulations were published in the Federal Register on November 17, 2008. The preamble to the final regulations is reproduced at ¶ 24,275.

¶ 20,537K

Pension Benefit Guaranty Corporation (PBGC): Proposed rule: Multiemployer plans: Withdrawal liability: Pension Protection Act of 2006 (PPA).—The Pension Benefit Guaranty Corporation (PBGC) has proposed a regulation implementing provisions of the Pension Protection Act of 2006 (P.L. 109-280; PPA) to change the allocation of unfunded vested benefits to withdrawing employers from a multiemployer pension plan and make adjustments in determining an employer's withdrawal liability when a multiemployer plan is in critical status.

The proposed regulations, which were published in the Federal Register on March 19, 2008 (73 FR 14735), are reproduced below. Final regulations, effective January 29, 2009, were published in the Federal Register on December 30, 2008 (73 FR 79628). The preamble to the final regulations is at ¶ 24,276.

PENSION BENEFIT GUARANTY CORPORATION

29 CFR Parts 4001, 4211, and 4219

RIN 1212-AB07

Methods for Computing Withdrawal Liability; Reallocation Liability Upon Mass Withdrawal; Pension Protection Act of 2006

AGENCY: Pension Benefit Guaranty Corporation.

ACTION: Proposed rule.

SUMMARY: This proposed rule amends PBGC's regulation on Allocating Unfunded Vested Benefits to Withdrawing Employers (29 CFR part 4211) to implement provisions of the Pension Protection Act of 2006 (Pub. L. c109-280) that provide for changes in the allocation of unfunded vested benefits to withdrawing employers from a multiemployer pension plan, and that require adjustments in determining an employer's withdrawal liability when a multiemployer plan is in critical status. Pursuant to PBGC's authority under section 4211(c)(5) of ERISA to prescribe standard approaches for alternative methods, the proposed rule would also amend this regulation to provide additional modifications to the statutory methods for determining an employer's allocable share of unfunded vested benefits. In addition, pursuant to PBGC's authority under section 4219(c)(1)(D) of ERISA, this proposed rule would amend PBGC's regulation on Notice, Collection, and Redetermination of Withdrawal Liability (29 CFR part 4219) to improve the process of fully allocating a plan's total unfunded vested benefits among all liable employers in a mass withdrawal. Finally, this proposed rule would amend PBGC's regulation on Terminology (29 CFR part 4001) to reflect a definition of a "multiemployer plan" added by the Pension Protection Act of 2006.

DATES: Comments must be submitted on or before May 19, 2008.

ADDRESSES: Comments, identified by Regulation Information Number (RIN 1212-AB07), may be submitted by any of the following methods:

- *Federal eRulemaking Portal: http://www.regulations.gov.* Follow the Web site instructions for submitting comments.

- *E-mail: reg.comments@pbgc.gov.*

- *Fax:* 202-326-4224.

- *Mail or Hand Delivery:* Legislative and Regulatory Department, Pension Benefit Guaranty Corporation, 1200 K Street, NW., Washington, DC 20005-4026.

Comments received, including personal information provided, will be posted to *http://www.pbgc.gov.* Copies of comments may also be obtained by writing to Disclosure Division, Office of the General Counsel, Pension Benefit Guaranty Corporation, 1200 K Street, NW., Washington, DC 20005-4026, or calling 202-326-4040 during normal business hours. (TTY and TDD users may call the Federal relay service toll-free at 1-800-877-8339 and ask to be connected to 202-326-4040.)

FOR FURTHER INFORMATION CONTACT: John H. Hanley, Director; Catherine B. Klion, Manager; or Constance Markakis, Attorney; Legislative and Regulatory Department, Pension Benefit Guaranty Corporation, 1200 K Street, NW., Washington, DC 20005-4026; 202-326-4024. (TTY and TDD users may call the Federal relay service toll-free at 1-800-877-8339 and ask to be connected to 202-326-4024.)

SUPPLEMENTARY INFORMATION:

Background

Under section 4201 of the Employee Retirement Income Security Act of 1974, as amended by the Multiemployer Pension Plan Amendments Act of 1980 ("ERISA"), an employer that withdraws from a multiemployer pension plan may incur withdrawal liability to the plan. Withdrawal liability represents the employer's allocable share of the plan's unfunded vested benefits determined under section 4211 of ERISA, and adjusted in accordance with other provisions in sections 4201 through 4225 of ERISA. Section 4211 prescribes four methods that a plan may use to allocate a share of unfunded vested benefits to a withdrawing employer, and also provides for possible modifications of those methods and for the use of allocation methods other than those prescribed. In general, changes to a plan's allocation methods are subject to the approval of the Pension Benefit Guaranty Corporation ("PBGC").

Under section 4211(b)(1) of ERISA (the "presumptive method"), the amount of unfunded vested benefits allocable to a withdrawing employer is the sum of the employer's proportional share of: (i) The unamortized amount of the change in the plan's unfunded vested benefits for each plan year for which the employer has an obligation to contribute under the plan (*i.e.,* multiple-year liability pools) ending with the plan year preceding the plan year of employer's withdrawal; (ii) the unamortized amount of the unfunded vested benefits at the end of the last plan year ending before September 26, 1980, with respect to employers who had an obligation to contribute under the plan for the first plan year ending after such date; and (iii) the unamortized amount of the reallocated unfunded vested benefits (amounts the plan sponsor determines to be uncollectible or unassessable) for each plan year ending before the employer's withdrawal. Each amount described in (i) through (iii) is reduced by 5 percent for each plan year after the plan year for which it arose. An employer's proportional share is based on a fraction equal to the sum of the contributions required to be made under the plan by the employer over total contributions made by all employers who had an obligation to contribute under the plan, for the five plan years ending with the plan year in which such change arose, the five plan years preceding September 26, 1980, and the five plan years ending with the plan year such reallocation liability arose, respectively (the "allocation fraction").

Section 4211(c)(1) of ERISA generally prohibits the adoption of any allocation method other than the presumptive method by a plan that primarily covers employees in the building and construction industry ("construction industry plan"), subject to regulations that allow certain adjustments in the denominator of an allocation fraction.

Under section 4211(c)(2) of ERISA (the "modified presumptive method"), a withdrawing employer is liable for a proportional share of: (i) The plan's unfunded vested benefits as of the end of the plan year preceding the withdrawal (less outstanding claims for withdrawal liability that can reasonably be expected to be collected and the amounts set forth in (ii) below allocable to employers obligated to contribute in the plan year preceding the employer's withdrawal and who had an obligation to contribute in the first plan year ending after September 26, 1980); and (ii) the plan's unfunded vested benefits as of the end of the last plan year ending before September 26, 1980 (amortized over 15 years), if the employer had an obligation to contribute under the plan for the first plan year ending on or after such date. An employer's proportional share is based on the employer's share of total plan contributions over the five plan years preceding the plan year of the employer's withdrawal and over the five plan years preceding September 26, 1980, respectively. Plans that use this method fully amortize their first pool as of 1995. Then, employers that withdraw after 1995 are subject to the allocation of unfunded vested benefits as if the plan used the "rolling-5 method" discussed below.

Under section 4211(c)(3) of ERISA (the "rolling-5 method"), a withdrawing employer is liable for a share of the plan's unfunded vested benefits as of the end of the plan year preceding the employer's withdrawal (less outstanding claims for withdrawal liability that can reasonably be expected to be collected), allocated in proportion to the employer's share of total plan contributions for the last five plan years ending before the withdrawal.

Under section 4211(c)(4) of ERISA (the "direct attribution method"), an employer's withdrawal liability is based generally on the benefits and assets attributable to participants' service with the employer, as of the end of the plan year preceding the employer's withdrawal; the employer is also liable for a proportional share of any unfunded vested benefits that are not attributable to service with employers who have an obligation to contribute under the plan in the plan year preceding the withdrawal.

Section 4211(c)(5)(B) of ERISA authorizes PBGC to prescribe by regulation standard approaches for alternative methods for determining an employer's allocable share of unfunded vested benefits, and adjustments in any denominator of an allocation fraction under the withdrawal liability methods. PBGC has prescribed, in §4211.12 of its regulation on Allocating Unfunded Vested Benefits to Withdrawing Employers, changes that a plan may adopt, without PBGC approval, in the denominator of the allocation fractions used to determine a withdrawing employer's share of unfunded vested benefits under the presumptive, modified presumptive and rolling-5 methods.

Pension Protection Act of 2006 Changes

The Pension Protection Act of 2006, Public Law 109-280 ("PPA 2006"), which became law on August 17, 2006, makes various changes to ERISA withdrawal liability provisions. Section 204(c)(2) of PPA 2006 added section 4211(c)(5)(E) of ERISA, which permits a plan, including a construction industry plan, to adopt an amendment that applies the presumptive method by substituting a different plan year (for which the plan has no unfunded vested benefits) for the plan year ending before September 26, 1980. Such an amendment would enable a plan to erase a large part of the plan's unfunded vested benefits attributable to plan years before the end of the designated plan year, and to start fresh with liabilities that arise in plan years after the designated plan year.

Additionally, sections 202(a) and 212(a) of PPA 2006 create new funding rules for multiemployer plans in "critical" status, allowing these plans to reduce benefits and making the plans' contributing employers subject to surcharges. New section 305(e)(9) of ERISA and section 432(e)(9) of the Internal Revenue Code ("Code") provide that such benefit adjustments and employer surcharges are disregarded in determining a plan's unfunded vested benefits and allocation fraction for purposes of determining an employer's withdrawal liability, and direct PBGC to prescribe simplified methods for the application of these provisions in determining withdrawal liability. (PPA 2006 also makes other changes affecting the withdrawal liability provisions under ERISA that are not addressed in this proposed rule.)

Overview of Proposed Rule

This proposed rule would amend PBGC's regulation on Allocating Unfunded Vested Benefits to Withdrawing Employers (29 CFR part 4211) to implement the above-described changes made by PPA 2006.

The proposed rule would also make changes unrelated to PPA 2006. Under its authority to prescribe alternatives to the statutory methods for determining an employer's allocable share of unfunded vested benefits, the proposed rule would also amend part 4211 to broaden the rules and provide more flexibility in applying the statutory methods. PBGC has identified certain modifications that may be advantageous to plans because they reduce administrative burdens for plans using the presumptive method and may assist plans in attracting new employers in the case of the modified presumptive method.

In addition, in the case of a plan termination by mass withdrawal, section 4219(c)(1)(D) of ERISA provides that the total unfunded vested benefits of the plan must be fully allocated among all liable employers in a manner not inconsistent with regulations prescribed by PBGC. PBGC has determined that the fraction for allocating this "reallocation liability" under PBGC's regulation on Notice, Collection, and Redetermination of Withdrawal Liability (20 CFR part 4219) does not adequately capture the liability of employers who had little or no initial withdrawal liability. Accordingly, this proposed rule would amend part 4219 to revise the allocation fraction for reallocation liability.

Proposed Regulatory Changes

Withdrawal Liability Methods

Under section 4211(c)(5)(E) of ERISA, added by PPA 2006, a plan using the presumptive withdrawal liability method in section 4211(b) of

ERISA, including a construction industry plan, may be amended to substitute a plan year that is designated in a plan amendment and for which the plan has no unfunded vested benefits, for the plan year ending before September 26, 1980. For plan years ending before the designated plan year and for the designated plan year, the plan will be relieved of the burden of calculating changes in unfunded vested benefits separately for each plan year and allocating those changes to the employers that contributed to the plan in the year of the change. As the plan must have no unfunded vested benefits for the designated plan year, employers withdrawing from the plan after the modification is effective will have no liability for unfunded vested benefits arising in plan years ending before the designated plan year. PBGC proposes to amend §4211.12 of its regulation on Allocating Unfunded Vested Benefits to Withdrawing Employers to reflect this new statutory modification to the presumptive method.

In addition, PBGC proposes to expand §4211.12 to permit plans to substitute a new plan year for the plan year ending before September 26, 1980, *without regard* to the amount of a plan's unfunded vested benefits at the end of the newly designated plan year. This change would allow plans using the presumptive method to aggregate the multiple liability pools attributable to prior plan years and the designated plan year. It would thus allow such plans to allocate the plan's unfunded vested benefits as of the end of the designated plan year among the employers who have an obligation to contribute under the plan for the first plan year ending on or after such date, based on the employer's share of the plan's contributions for the five-year period ending before the designated plan year. Thereafter, the plan would apply the regular rules under the presumptive method to segregate changes in the plan's unfunded vested benefits by plan year and to allocate individual plan year liabilities among the employers obligated to contribute under the plan in that plan year.

PBGC believes this modification to the presumptive method will ease the administrative burdens of plans that lack the actuarial and contributions data necessary to compute each employer's allocable share of annual changes in unfunded vested benefits occurring in plan years as far back as 1980. Note, however, that this modification does not apply to a construction industry plan, because PBGC may prescribe only adjustments in the denominators of the allocation fractions for such plans.[1]

PBGC also proposes to amend §4211.12 to permit plans using the modified presumptive method to designate a plan year that would substitute for the last plan year ending before September 26, 1980. This proposal provides for the allocation of substantially all of a plan's unfunded vested benefits among employers who have an obligation to contribute under the plan, while enabling plans to split a single liability pool for plan years ending after September 25, 1980, into two liability pools. The first pool based on the plan's unfunded vested benefits as of the end of the newly designated plan year, allocated among employers who have an obligation to contribute under the plan for the plan year immediately following the designated plan year, and a second pool based on the unfunded vested benefits as of the end of the plan year prior to the withdrawal (offset in the manner described above for the modified presumptive method). For a period of time, this modification would reduce new employers' liability for unfunded vested benefits of the plan before the employer's participation, which could assist plans in attracting new employers and preserving the plan's contribution base. The proposal would not require PBGC approval for adoption.

For each of these modifications, the proposed rule would clarify that a plan's unfunded vested benefits, determined with respect to plan years ending after the plan year designated in the plan amendment, are reduced by the value of the outstanding claims for withdrawal liability that can reasonably be expected to be collected for employers who withdrew from the plan in or before the designated plan year.

Withdrawal Liability Computations for Plans in Critical Status— Adjustable Benefits

PPA 2006 establishes additional funding rules for multiemployer plans in "endangered" or "critical" status under section 305 of ERISA and section 432 of the Code. The sponsor of a plan in critical status (less than 65 percent funded and/or meets any of the other defined tests) is required to adopt a rehabilitation plan that will enable the plan to cease to be in critical status within a specified period of time. Notwithstanding section 204(g) of ERISA or section 411(d)(6) of the Code, as deemed appropriate by the plan sponsor, based upon the outcome of collective bargaining over benefit and contribution schedules, the rehabilitation plan may include reductions to "adjustable

---

[1] Under ERISA section 4211(c)(1), construction industry plans are limited to the presumptive allocation method, except that PBGC may by regulation permit adjustments in any denominator under section 4211 (including the denominator of a fraction used in the presumptive method by construction industry plans) where such adjustment would be appropriate to ease the administrative burdens of plan sponsors. See ERISA section 4211(c)(5)(D), 29 CFR 4211.11(b) and 4211.12.

benefits," within the meaning of section 305(e)(8) of ERISA and section 432(e)(8) of the Code. New section 305(e)(9) of ERISA and section 432(e)(9) of the Code provide, however, that any benefit reductions under subsection (e) must be disregarded in determining a plan's unfunded vested benefits for purposes of an employer's withdrawal liability under section 4201 of ERISA. (Also, under ERISA sections 305(f)(2) and (f)(3), and Code sections 432(f)(2) and (f)(3), a plan is limited in its payment of lump sums and similar benefits after a notice of the plan's critical status is sent, but any such benefit limits must be disregarded in determining a plan's unfunded vested benefits for purposes of determining an employer's withdrawal liability.)

Adjustable benefits under section 305(e)(8) of ERISA and section 432(e)(8) of the Code include benefits, rights and features under the plan, such as post-retirement death benefits, 60-month guarantees, disability benefits not yet in pay status; certain early retirement benefits, retirement-type subsidies and benefit payment options; and benefit increases that would not be eligible for a guarantee under section 4022A of ERISA on the first day of the initial critical year because the increases were adopted (or, if later, took effect) less than 60 months before such date. An amendment reducing adjustable benefits may not affect the benefits of any participant or beneficiary whose benefit commencement date is before the date on which the plan provides notice that the plan is or will be in critical status for a plan year; the level of a participant's accrued benefit at normal retirement age also is protected.

Under section 4213 of ERISA, a plan actuary must use actuarial assumptions that, in the aggregate, are reasonable and, in combination, offer the actuary's best estimate of anticipated experience in determining the unfunded vested benefits of a plan for purposes of determining an employer's withdrawal liability (absent regulations setting forth such methods and assumptions). Section 4213(c) provides that, for purposes of determining withdrawal liability, the term "unfunded vested benefits" means the amount by which the value of nonforfeitable benefits under the plan exceeds the value of plan assets.

The proposed rule amends the definition of "nonforfeitable benefits" in § 4211.2 of PBGC's regulation on Allocating Unfunded Vested Benefits to Withdrawing Employers, and the definition of "unfunded vested benefits" in § 4219.2 of PBGC's regulation on Notice, Collection, and Redetermination of Withdrawal Liability, to include adjustable benefits that have been reduced by a plan sponsor pursuant to ERISA section 305(e)(8) or Code section 432(e)(8), to the extent such benefits would otherwise be nonforfeitable benefits.

Section 305(e)(9)(C) of ERISA and section 432(e)(9)(C) of the Code direct PBGC to prescribe simplified methods for the application of this provision in determining withdrawal liability. PBGC intends to issue guidance on simplified methods at a later date.

Withdrawal Liability Computations for Plans in Critical Status— Employer Surcharges

Under section 305(e)(7) of ERISA, added by section 202(a) of PPA 2006, and under section 432(e)(7) of the Code, added by section 212(a) of PPA 2006, each employer otherwise obligated to make contributions for the initial plan year and any subsequent plan year that a plan is in critical status must pay to the plan for such plan year a surcharge, until the effective date of a collective bargaining agreement that includes terms consistent with the rehabilitation plan adopted by the plan sponsor. Section 305(e)(9) of ERISA and section 432(e)(9) of the Code provide, however, that any employer surcharges under paragraph (7) must be disregarded in determining an employer's withdrawal liability under section 4211 of ERISA, except for purposes of determining the unfunded vested benefits attributable to an employer under section 4211(c)(4) (the direct attribution method) or a comparable method approved under section 4211(c)(5) of ERISA.

The presumptive, modified presumptive and rolling-5 methods of allocating unfunded vested benefits allocate the liability pools among participating employers based on the employers' contribution obligations for the five-year period preceding the date the liability pool was established or the year of the employer's withdrawal (depending on the method or liability pool). Under section 4211 of ERISA, the numerator of the allocation fraction is the total amount required to be contributed by the withdrawing employer for the five-year period, and the denominator of the allocation fraction is the total amount contributed by all employers under the plan for the five-year period.

The proposed rule amends PBGC's regulation on Allocating Unfunded Vested Benefits to Withdrawing Employers (part 4211) by adding a new § 4211.4 that excludes amounts attributable to the employer surcharge under section 305(e)(7) of ERISA and section 432(e)(7) of the Code from the contributions that are otherwise includable in the numerator and the denominator of the allocation fraction under the presumptive, modified presumptive and rolling-5 methods. Pursuant to section 305(e)(9) of ERISA and section 432(e)(9) of the Code, a simplified method for the application of this principle is provided below in the form of an illustration of the exclusion of employer surcharge amounts from the allocation fraction.

Example: Plan X is a multiemployer plan that has vested benefit liabilities of $200 million and assets of $130 million as of the end of its 2015 plan year. During the 2015 plan year, there were three contributing employers. Two of three employers were in the plan for the entire five-year period ending with the 2015 plan year. One employer was in the plan during the 2014 and 2015 plan years only. Each employer had a $4 million contribution obligation each year under a collective bargaining agreement. In addition, for the 2011, 2012, and 2013 plan years, employers were liable for the automatic employer surcharge under section 305(e)(7) of ERISA and section 432(e)(7) of the Code, at a rate of 5% of required contributions in 2011 and 10% of required contributions in 2012 and 2013. The following table shows the contributions and surcharges owed for the five-year period.

Year	Employer A ($ in millions)		Employer B ($ in millions)		Employer C ($ in millions)	
	Contribution	Surcharge	Contribution	Surcharge	Contribution	Surcharge
2011	$4	$0.2	$4	$0.2	. . . .	. . . .
2012	4	0.4	4	0.4	. . . .	. . . .
2013	4	0.4	4	0.4	. . . .	. . . .
2014	4	0	4	0	$4	$0
2015	4	0	4	0	4	0
5-year total	20	1.0	20	1.0	8	0

Employers A, B and C contributed $48 million during the five-year period, excluding surcharges, and $50 million including surcharges. Under the rolling-5 method, the unfunded vested benefits allocable to an employer are equal to the plan's unfunded vested benefits as of the end of the last plan year preceding the withdrawal, multiplied by a fraction equal to the amount the employer was required to contribute to the plan for the last five plan years preceding the withdrawal over the total amount contributed by all employers for those five plan years (other adjustments are also required).

Employer A's share of the plan's unfunded vested benefits in the event it withdraws in 2016 is $29.17 million, determined by multiplying $70 million (the plan's unfunded vested benefits at the end of 2015) by the ratio of $20 million to $48 million. Employer B's allocable unfunded vested benefits are identical to Employer A's, and the amount allocable to Employer C is $11.66 million ($70 million multiplied by the ratio of $8 million over $48 million). The $2.0 million attributable to the auto-

matic employer surcharge is excluded from contributions in the allocation fraction.

Reallocation Liability Upon Mass Withdrawal

Section 4219(c)(1)(D) of ERISA applies special withdrawal liability rules when a multiemployer plan terminates because of mass withdrawal (*i.e.,* the withdrawal of every employer under the plan) or when substantially all employers withdraw pursuant to an agreement or arrangement to withdraw, including a requirement that the total unfunded vested benefits of the plan be fully allocated among all employers in a manner not inconsistent with PBGC regulations. To ensure that all unfunded vested benefits are fully allocated among all liable employers, § 4219.15(b) of PBGC's regulation on Notice, Collection, and Redetermination of Withdrawal Liability requires a determination of the plan's unfunded vested benefits as of end of the plan year of the plan termination, based on the value of the plan's nonforfeitable benefits as of that date less the value of plan assets (benefits and assets valued in accordance with assumptions specified by PBGC), less the outstanding balance of any initial withdrawal liability (assessments without regard to the occurrence of a mass withdrawal) and any redetermination liability (assessments for de minimis and 20-year cap reduction amounts) that can reasonably be expected to be collected.

Pursuant to § 4219.15(c)(1), each liable employer's share of this "reallocation liability" is equal to the amount of the reallocation liability multiplied by a fraction—

(i) The numerator of which is the sum of the employer's initial withdrawal liability and any redetermination liability, and

(ii) The denominator of which is the sum of all initial withdrawal liabilities and all the redetermination liabilities of all liable employers.

PBGC believes the current allocation fraction for reallocation liability must be modified to address those situations in which employers—who would otherwise be liable for reallocation liability—have little or no initial withdrawal liability or redetermination liability and, therefore, have a zero (or understated) reallocation liability. Such situations may arise, for example, where an employer withdraws from the plan before the mass withdrawal valuation date, but has no withdrawal liability under the modified presumptive and rolling-5 methods because either (i) the plan has no unfunded vested benefits as of the end of the plan year preceding the plan year in which the employer withdrew, or (ii) the plan did not require the employer to make contributions for the five-year period preceding the plan year of withdrawal. In these cases, if the employer's withdrawal is later determined to be part of a mass withdrawal for which reallocation liability applies under section 4219 of ERISA, the employer would not be liable for any portion of the reallocation liability.

A plan's status may change from funded to underfunded between the end of the plan year before the employer withdraws and the mass withdrawal valuation date as a result of differences in the actuarial assumptions used by the plan's actuary in determining unfunded vested benefits under sections 4211 and 4219 of ERISA, or due to investment losses that reduce the value of the plan's assets, among other reasons. Likewise, an employer may not have paid contributions for purposes of the allocation fraction used to determine the employer's initial withdrawal liability if the plan provided for a "contribution holiday" under which employers were not required to make contributions.

PBGC believes the absence of initial withdrawal liability should not generally exempt an otherwise liable employer from reallocation liability. By shifting reallocation liability away from some employers, the allocable share of other employers in a mass withdrawal is increased, and the risk of a loss of benefits to participants and to PBGC is increased. To ensure that reallocation liability is allocated broadly among all liable employers, PBGC proposes to amend § 4219.15(c) of the Notice, Collection, and Redetermination of Withdrawal Liability regulation to replace the current allocation fraction based on initial withdrawal liability with a new allocation fraction for determining an employer's allocable share of reallocation liability.

The proposed formula would allocate the plan's unfunded vested benefits based on the employer's contribution base units relative to the plan's total contribution base units for the three plan years preceding the employer's withdrawal from the plan. The numerator would consist of the withdrawing employer's average contribution base units during the three plan years preceding the withdrawal, and the denominator would consist of the average of all the employers' contribution base units during the three plan years preceding the withdrawal. Section 4001(a)(11) of ERISA defines a "contribution base unit" as a unit with respect to which an employer has an obligation to contribute under a multiemployer plan, e.g., an hour worked. PBGC proposes a similar definition for purposes of § 4219.15 of the Notice, Collection, and Redetermination of Withdrawal Liability regulation.

PBGC also proposes to amend § 4219.1 of the regulation on Notice, Collection, and Redetermination of Withdrawal Liability to implement a provision under new section 4221(g) of ERISA, added by section 204(d)(1) of PPA 2006, which relieves an employer in certain narrowly defined circumstances of the obligation to make withdrawal liability payments until a final decision in the arbitration proceeding, or in court, upholds the plan sponsor's determination that the employer is liable for withdrawal liability based in part or in whole on section 4212(c) of ERISA. The regulation would state that an employer that complies with the specific procedures of section 4221(g) (or a similar provision in section 4221(f) of ERISA, added by Pub. L. 108-218) is not in default under section 4219(c)(5)(A).

Definition of Multiemployer Plan

Section 1106 of PPA 2006 amended the definition of a "multiemployer" plan in section 3(37)(G) of ERISA and section 414(f)(6) of the

Code to allow certain plans to elect to be multiemployer plans for all purposes under ERISA and the Code, pursuant to procedures prescribed by PBGC. PBGC proposes to amend the definition of a "multiemployer plan" under § 4001.2 of its regulation on Terminology (29 CFR part 4001) to add a definition that is parallel to the definition in section 3(37)(G) of ERISA and section 414(f)(6) of the Code.

Applicability

The changes relating to modifications to the statutory methods prescribed by PBGC for determining an employer's share of unfunded vested benefits would be applicable to employer withdrawals from a plan that occur on or after the effective date of the final rule, subject to section 4214 of ERISA (relating to plan amendments). Changes in the fraction for allocating reallocation liability would be applicable to plan terminations by mass withdrawals (or by withdrawals of substantially all employers pursuant to an agreement or arrangement to withdraw) that occur on or after the effective date of the final rule.

The change relating to the presumptive method made by PPA 2006 would be applicable to employer withdrawals occurring on or after January 1, 2007, subject to section 4214 of ERISA.

The changes relating to the effect of PPA 2006 benefit adjustments and employer surcharges for purposes of determining an employer's withdrawal liability would be applicable to employer withdrawals from a plan and plan terminations by mass withdrawals (or withdrawals of substantially all employers pursuant to an agreement or arrangement to withdraw) occurring for plan years beginning on or after January 1, 2008.

The change in the definition of a multiemployer plan is effective August 17, 2006. The change in section 4221(g) of ERISA made by PPA 2006 would be effective for any person that receives a notification under ERISA section 4219(b)(1) on or after August 17, 2006, with respect to a transaction that occurred after December 31, 1998.

Compliance With Rulemaking Requirements

E.O. 12866

The PBGC has determined, in consultation with the Office of Management and Budget, that this rule is a "significant regulatory action" under Executive Order 12866. The Office of Management and Budget has therefore reviewed this notice under E.O. 12866. Pursuant to section 1(b)(1) of E.O. 12866 (as amended by E.O. 13422), PBGC identifies the following specific problems that warrant this agency action:

• This regulatory action implements the PPA 2006 amendment to section 4211(c)(5) of ERISA that permits a plan using the presumptive method to substitute a specified plan year for which the plan has no unfunded vested benefits for the plan year ending before September 26, 1980. The proposed rule would provide necessary guidance on the application of this modification to the specific provisions of the presumptive method under section 4211(b) of ERISA. Also, because the statutory amendment lacks specificity in describing how to compute unfunded vested benefits, the rule clarifies the need to reduce the plan's unfunded vested benefits for plan years ending on or after the last day of the designated plan year by the value of all outstanding claims for withdrawal liability reasonably expected to be collected from withdrawn employers as of the end of the designated plan year.

• Existing modifications to the statutory withdrawal liability methods not subject to PBGC approval are outmoded and restrictive and an expansion of the modifications is consistent with statutory changes under PPA 2006. This problem is significant because the current rules impose significant administrative burdens on plans and impede flexibility needed by multiemployer plans to attract new employers.

• This regulatory action implements the PPA 2006 amendment to section 305(e)(9) of ERISA and section 432(e)(9) of the Code requiring plans in critical status to disregard reductions in adjustable benefits and employer surcharges in determining a plan's unfunded vested benefits for purposes of an employer's withdrawal liability. The rule is necessary to conform the definition of nonforfeitable benefits and the allocation fraction based on employer contributions under PBGC's regulations to the statutory changes.

• The rule would revise the allocation fraction for reallocation liability, which applies when a multiemployer plan terminates by mass withdrawal, to ensure that reallocation liability is allocated broadly among all liable employers.

Regulatory Flexibility Act

PBGC certifies under section 605(b) of the Regulatory Flexibility Act (5 U.S.C. 601 et seq.) that the amendments in this proposed rule would not have a significant economic impact on a substantial number of small entities. Specifically, the amendments would have the following effect:

• A statutory change under PPA 2006 provides plans with a "fresh start" option in determining withdrawal liability when an employer withdraws from a multiemployer plan. This rule clarifies the application of this fresh start option and extends the option to other withdrawal liability calculations. Under these amendments, plans may avoid costly and burdensome year-by-year calculations of unfunded vested benefits and employers' allocable shares of such benefits for years as far back as 1980; alternatively, these amendments may help plans attract new employers by shielding them from unfunded liabilities that arose in the past. Any changes to a plan's withdrawal liability method are adopted at the discretion of each plan's governing board of trustees. Accordingly, there is no cost to compliance.

• A statutory change under PPA requires plans in "critical" status to disregard reductions in adjustable benefits and employer surcharges in determining an employer's withdrawal liability. This rule would clarify the exclusion of any surcharges from the allocation fraction consisting of employer contributions, and the exclusion of the cost of any reduced benefits from the plan's unfunded vested benefits. The rule simply applies the statutory provisions and imposes no significant burden beyond the burden imposed by statute. Furthermore, more than 88 percent of all multiemployer pension plans have 250 or more participants.

• Another amendment in the rule would revise the fraction for allocating reallocation liability (unfunded vested benefits as of the end of the plan year of a plan's termination) among employers when a plan terminates in a mass withdrawal. Plans routinely maintain the contribution records necessary to apply the new fraction in place of the old fraction for this purpose. Moreover, a majority of all plans that terminate in a mass withdrawal have more than 250 participants at the time of termination. Accordingly, as provided in section 605 of the Regulatory Flexibility Act (5 U.S.C 601 *et seq.*), sections 603 and 604 do not apply.

List of Subjects

20 CFR Part 4001

Business and industry, Organization and functions (Government agencies), Pension insurance, Pensions, Small businesses.

29 CFR Part 4211

Pension insurance, Pensions, Reporting and recordkeeping. requirements.

29 CFR Part 4219

Pensions, Reporting and recordkeeping requirements.

For the reasons given above, PBGC proposes to amend 29 CFR parts 4001, 4211 and 4219 as follows:

PART 4001—TERMINOLOGY

1. The authority citation for part 4001 continues to read as follows:

Authority: 29 U.S.C. 1301, 1302(b)(3).

§4001.2 [Amended]

2. In §4001.2, the definition of *Multiemployer plan* is amended by adding at the end the sentence "Multiemployer plan also means a plan that elects to be a multiemployer plan under ERISA section 3(37)(G) and Code section 414(f)(6), pursuant to procedures prescribed by PBGC and the approval of an election by PBGC."

PART 4211—ALLOCATING UNFUNDED VESTED BENEFITS TO WITHDRAWING EMPLOYERS

3. The authority citation for part 4211 continues to read as follows:

Authority: 29 U.S.C. 1302(b)(3); 1391(c)(1), (c)(2)(D), (c)(5)(A), (c)(5)(B), (c)(5)(D), and (f).

4. In §4211.2—

a. The first sentence is amended by removing the words "nonforfeitable benefit,".

b. The definition of *Unfunded vested benefits* is amended to add the words ", as defined for purposes of this section," between the words "plan" and "exceeds".

c. A new definition is added in alphabetical order to read as follows:

§4211.2 Definitions.

*****

Nonforfeitable benefit means a benefit described in §4001.2 of this chapter plus, for purposes of this part, any adjustable benefit that has been reduced by the plan sponsor pursuant to section 305(e)(8) of ERISA or section 432(e)(8) of the Code that would otherwise have been includable as a nonforfeitable benefit for purposes of determining an employer's allocable share of unfunded vested benefits.

*****

5. A new §4211.4 is added to read as follows:

§4211.4 Contributions for purposes of the numerator and denominator of the allocation fractions.

Each of the allocation fractions used in the presumptive, modified presumptive and rolling-5 methods is based on contributions that certain employers have made to the plan for a five-year period.

(a) The numerator of the allocation fraction, with respect to a withdrawing employer, is based on the "sum of the contributions required to be made" or the "total amount required to be contributed" by the employer for the specified period. For purposes of these methods, this means the amount that is required to be contributed under one or more collective bargaining agreements or other agreements pursuant to which the employer contributes under the plan, other than withdrawal liability payments or amounts that an employer is obligated to pay to the plan pursuant to section 305(e)(7) of ERISA or section 432(e)(7) of the Code (automatic employer surcharge). Employee contributions, if any, shall be excluded from the totals.

(b) The denominator of the allocation fraction is based on contributions that certain employers have made to the plan for a specified period. For purposes of these methods, and except as provided in §4211.12, "the sum of all contributions made" or "total amount contributed" by employers for a plan year means the amounts considered contributed to the plan for purposes of section 412(b)(3)(A) of the Code, other than withdrawal liability payments or amounts that an employer is obligated to pay to the plan pursuant to section 305(e)(7) of ERISA or section 432(e)(7) of the Code (automatic employer surcharge). For plan years before section 412 applies to the plan, "the sum of all contributions made" or "total amount contributed" means the amount reported to the IRS or the Department of Labor as total contributions for the plan year; for example, the plan years in which the plan filed the Form 5500, the amount reported as total contributions on that form. Employee contributions, if any, shall be excluded from the totals.

6. In §4211.12—

a. Paragraph (a) is removed and paragraph (b) is redesignated as paragraph (a).

b. Paragraph (c) is redesignated as paragraph (b).

c. Add new paragraphs (c) and (d) to read as follows:

§4211.12 Modifications to the presumptive, modified presumptive and rolling-5 methods.

*****

(c) *"Fresh start" rules under presumptive method.*

(1) The plan sponsor of a plan using the presumptive method (including a plan that primarily covers employees in the building and construction industry) may amend the plan to provide—

(i) A designated plan year ending after September 26, 1980 will substitute for the plan year ending before September 26, 1980, in applying section 4211(b)(1)(B), section 4211(b)(2)(B)(ii)(I), section 4211(b)(2)(D), section 4211(b)(3), and section 4211(b)(3)(B) of ERISA, and

(ii) Plan years ending after the end of the designated plan year in paragraph (c)(1)(i) will substitute for plan years ending after September 25, 1980, in applying section 4211(b)(1)(A), section 4211(b)(2)(A), and section 4211(b)(2)(B)(ii)(II) of ERISA.

(2) A plan amendment made pursuant to paragraph (c)(1) of this section must provide that the plan's unfunded vested benefits for plan years ending after the designated plan year are reduced by the value of all outstanding claims for withdrawal liability that can reasonably be expected to be collected from employers that had withdrawn from the plan as of the end of the designated plan year.

(3) In the case of a plan that primarily covers employees in the building and construction industry, the plan year designated by a plan

amendment pursuant to paragraph (c)(1) of this section must be a plan year for which the plan has no unfunded vested benefits.

(d) *"Fresh start" rules under modified presumptive method.*

(1) The plan sponsor of a plan using the modified presumptive method may amend the plan to provide—

(i) A designated plan year ending after September 26, 1980 will substitute for the plan year ending before September 26, 1980, in applying section 4211(c)(2)(B)(i) and section 4211(c)(2)(B)(ii)(I) and (II) of ERISA, and

(ii) Plan years ending after the end of the designated plan year will substitute for plan years ending after September 25, 1980, in applying section 4211(c)(2)(B)(ii)(II) and section 4211(c)(2)(C)(i)(II) of ERISA.

(2) A plan amendment made pursuant to paragraph (d)(1) of this section must provide that the plan's unfunded vested benefits for plan years ending after the designated plan year are reduced by the value of all outstanding claims for withdrawal liability that can reasonably be expected to be collected from employers that had withdrawn from the plan as of the end of the designated plan year.

PART 4219—NOTICE, COLLECTION, AND REDETERMINATION OF WITHDRAWAL LIABILITY

7. The authority citation for part 4219 continues to read as follows:

Authority: 29 U.S.C. 1302(b)(3) and 1399(c)(6).

8. In § 4219.1, paragraph (c) is amended by removing the words "after April 28, 1980 (May 2, 1979, for certain employees in the seagoing industry)" and adding in their place the words "on or after September 26, 1980, except employers with respect to whom section 4221(f) or section 4221(g) of ERISA applies (provided that such employers are in compliance with the provisions of those sections, as applicable)."

9. In § 4219.2—

a. Paragraph (a) is amended by removing the words "nonforfeitable benefit,".

b. Paragraph (b) is amended by adding the word "nonforfeitable" between the words "vested" and "benefits" and the words "(as defined for purposes of this section)" between the words "benefits" and "exceeds" in the definition of *Unfunded vested benefits.*

c. Paragraph (b) is amended by adding a new definition in alphabetical order to read as follows:

§ 4219.2 Definitions.

*****

"Nonforfeitable benefit means a benefit described in § 4001.2 of this chapter plus, for purposes of this part, any adjustable benefit that has been reduced by the plan sponsor pursuant to section 305(e)(8) of ERISA and section 432(e)(8) of the Code that would otherwise have been includable as a nonforfeitable benefit."

*****

10. In § 4219.15, revise paragraph (c)(1) and add a new paragraph (c)(4) to read as follows:

§ 4219.15 Determination of reallocation liability.

*****

(c) ***

(1) *Initial allocable share.* Except as otherwise provided in rules adopted by the plan pursuant to paragraph (d) of this section, and in accordance with paragraph (c)(3) of this section, an employer's initial allocable share shall be equal to the product of the plan's unfunded vested benefits to be reallocated, multiplied by a fraction—

(i) The numerator of which is a yearly average of the employer's contribution base units during the three plan years preceding the employer's withdrawal; and

(ii) The denominator of which is a yearly average of the total contribution base units of all employers liable for reallocation liability during the three plan years preceding the employer's withdrawal.

*****

(4) *Contribution base unit.* For purposes of paragraph (c)(1) of this section, a contribution base unit means a unit with respect to which an employer has an obligation to contribute, such as an hour worked or shift worked or a unit of production, under the applicable collective bargaining agreement (or other agreement pursuant to which the employer contributes) or with respect to which the employer would have an obligation to contribute if the contribution requirement with respect to the plan were greater than zero.

*****

Issued in Washington, DC, this 11th day of March, 2008.

Charles E.F. Millard,

Director, Pension Benefit Guaranty Corporation.

[FR Doc. E8-5541 Filed 3-18-08; 8:45 am]

BILLING CODE 7709-01-P

¶ 20,537L

EBSA proposed regulations: Critical status: Multiemployer plans.—The Employee Benefits Security Administration (EBSA) has issued a proposed regulation containing a model notice, entitled "Notice of Critical Status", that a multiemployer plan may use to satisfy the content requirements of ERISA § 305(b)(3)(D)(iii).

The proposed regulations, which were published in the *Federal Register* on March 25, 2008 (73 FR 15688), are reproduced below.

Fr. Doc. E8-5855

DEPARTMENT OF LABOR

Employee Benefits Security Administration

29 CFR Part 2540

RIN 1210-AB26

Model Notice of Multiemployer Plan in Critical Status

AGENCY: Employee Benefits Security Administration, Labor.

ACTION: Proposed rule.

SUMMARY: The Pension Protection Act of 2006 amended the Employee Retirement Income Security Act (ERISA) and the Internal Revenue Code (Code) to require that sponsors of multiemployer defined benefit pension plans that are in, or will be in, endangered or critical status for a plan year provide notice of this status to participants, beneficiaries, the bargaining parties, the Pension Benefit Guaranty Corporation and the Department of Labor. This document contains a model notice that is intended to facilitate compliance with this notification requirement under ERISA and the Code.

DATES: Written comments should be received by the Department of Labor on or before April 24, 2008.

ADDRESSES: You may submit comments, identified by RIN 1210-AB26, by one of the following methods:

- Federal eRulemaking Portal: http://www.regulations.gov. Follow the instructions for submitting comments.

- E-mail: e-ORI@dol.gov. Include "Notice of Critical Status: RIN 1210-AB26" in the subject line of the message.

- Mail: Office of Regulations and Interpretations, Employee Benefits Security Administration, Room N-5655, U.S. Department of Labor, 200 Constitution Avenue NW., Washington, DC 20210, Attention: Model Notice of Critical Status.

Instructions: All submissions received must include the agency name and Regulatory Information Number (RIN) for this rulemaking. Comments received will be posted without change to http://www.regulations.gov and http://www.dol.gov/ebsa, and available for public inspection at the Public Disclosure Room, N-1513, Employee Benefits Security Administration, 200 Constitution Avenue, NW., Washington, DC 20210, including any personal information provided. Persons submitting comments electronically are encouraged not to submit paper copies.

FOR FURTHER INFORMATION CONTACT: Susan Elizabeth Rees, Office of Regulations and Interpretations, Employee Benefits Security Administration (EBSA), U.S. Department of Labor, (202) 693-8500. This is not a toll-free number.

SUPPLEMENTARY INFORMATION:

A. Background

Section 202 of the Pension Protection Act of 2006, Public Law 109-280 (PPA), amended the Employee Retirement Income Security Act of 1974 (ERISA or Act) by adding section 305, and section 212 of the PPA amended the Internal Revenue Code (Code) by adding section 432, to provide additional rules for multiemployer defined benefit pension plans in endangered status or critical status. All references to section 305 of ERISA should be read to include section 432 of the Code. Pursuant to Reorganization Plan No. 4, the Department of the Treasury has interpretive authority over the minimum funding rules of Title I of ERISA, including section 305 of ERISA.[1]

In general, section 305(b)(3)(A) of ERISA provides that not later than the 90th day of each plan year, the actuary of a multiemployer defined benefit pension plan shall certify to the Secretary of the Treasury and to the plan sponsor[2] -(i) whether or not the plan is in endangered status for such plan year and whether or not the plan is or will be in critical status for such plan year, and (ii) in the case of a plan which is in a funding improvement or rehabilitation period, whether or not the plan is making the scheduled progress in meeting the requirements of its funding improvement or rehabilitation plan.

Section 305(b)(3)(D)(i) of ERISA provides that, in any case in which it is certified under section 305(b)(3)(A) that a multiemployer plan is or will be in endangered or critical status for a plan year, the plan sponsor shall, not later than 30 days after the date of the certification, provide notification of the endangered or critical status to participants and beneficiaries, the bargaining parties, the Pension Benefit Guaranty Corporation, and the Secretary of Labor.

Section 305(b)(3)(D)(ii) of ERISA provides that if it is certified under section 305(b)(3)(A) that a multiemployer plan is or will be in critical status, the plan sponsor shall include in the notice an explanation of the possibility that - (i) adjustable benefits (as defined in section 305(e)(8) of ERISA) may be reduced, and (ii) such reductions may apply to participants and beneficiaries whose benefit commencement date is on or after the date such notice is provided for the first plan year in which the plan is in critical status.

Section 305(b)(3)(D)(iii) provides that the Secretary of Labor shall prescribe a model notice that a multiemployer plan may use to satisfy the requirements of section 305(b)(3)(D)(ii) of ERISA. The Department consulted with both the PBGC and the IRS in developing the model notice.

Other provisions in section 305 define when a plan is in endangered or critical status and what corrective steps must be taken, by when, and by whom. These other provisions are beyond the scope of this notice. The Department of the Treasury and IRS have advised that they are developing guidance on these other provisions.

Section 202(f)(1) of the PPA provides, generally, that the amendments made by this section shall apply with respect to plan years beginning after 2007, while section 202(f)(3) provides a special rule in the case of plans having certain restored benefits.

Section 202(f)(2) of the PPA provides that in any case in which a plan's actuary certifies that it is reasonably expected that a multiemployer plan will be in critical status under section 305(b)(3) of the ERISA, with respect to the first plan year beginning after 2007, the notice required under section 305(b)(3)(D) of ERISA may be provided at any time after the date of enactment, so long as it is provided on or before the last date for providing the notice under such subparagraph.

B. Model

Pursuant to section 305(b)(3)(D)(iii) of ERISA, the Department is publishing a model notice, entitled Notice of Critical Status, that a multiemployer plan may use to satisfy the content requirements of section 305(b)(3)(D) of ERISA.[3] The IRS advises that it will consider the sponsor of a plan in critical status who uses the model notice to notify participants and others of the status of the plan to have satisfied its content obligations under 432(b)(3)(D) of the Code. While the model notice contained in this document specifically relates to plans in critical status, the Department believes that the model may be useful in preparing notices required to be furnished by plans in endangered status.

To discharge the obligation to furnish a notice to the Department of Labor, plans may mail notices to U.S. Department of Labor, Employee Benefits Security Administration, Public Disclosure Room, N-1513, 200 Constitution Ave., NW., Washington, DC 20210. Alternatively, notices may be e-mailed to criticalstatusnotice@dol.gov. Critical Status notices received by the Department will be available for public inspection at the Public Disclosure Room, and accessible on EBSA's Web site at: http://www.dol.gov/ebsa.

To discharge the obligation to furnish a notice to the Pension Benefit Guaranty Corporation, plans may mail notices to Multiemployer Program Division, Pension Benefit Guaranty Corporation, 1200 K Street, NW., Suite 930, Washington, DC, 20005. Alternatively, notices may be e-mailed to multiemployerprogram@pbgc.gov.

C. Effective Date

This regulation will be effective 60 days after the date of publication of the final regulation in the Federal Register. However, because section 305(b)(3)(D) of ERISA and section 432(b)(3)(D) of the Code are effective with respect to plan years beginning after 2007, the Department, as well as Treasury and IRS, will, for purposes of notices required to be furnished prior the effective date of a final regulation, view utilization of the model notice contained in this document, if accurately completed and timely furnished, as satisfying the notice requirements of section 305(b)(3)(D) of ERISA and 432(b)(3)(D) of the Code.

D. Regulatory Impact Analysis

Summary

The Notice of Critical Status ("Model Notice") in paragraph (b) of the proposed regulation will help sponsors of plans in critical status who use the model notice to satisfy their obligations under section 305(b)(3)(D) of ERISA and section 432(b)(3)(D) of the Code. While the Model Notice is not mandatory, the sponsor of a plan in critical status who uses the model notice to notify participants and others of the status of the plan will be considered to have satisfied its obligations under ERISA and the Code. The anticipated benefit of the Model Notice, therefore, is to help plan sponsors fulfill their disclosure responsibilities with greater certainty and less cost.

Executive Order 12866

Under Executive Order 12866 (58 FR 51735), the Department must determine whether a regulatory action is "significant" and therefore subject to review by the Office of Management and Budget (OMB). Section 3(f) of the Executive Order defines a "significant regulatory action" as an action that is likely to result in a rule (1) having an annual effect on the economy of $100 million or more, or adversely and materially affecting a sector of the economy, productivity, competition, jobs, the environment, public health or safety, or State, local or tribal governments or communities (also referred to as "economically significant"); (2) creating serious inconsistency or otherwise interfering with an action taken or planned by another agency; (3) materially altering the budgetary impacts of entitlement grants, user fees, or loan programs or the rights and obligations of recipients thereof; or (4) raising novel legal or policy issues arising

out of legal mandates, the President's priorities, or the principles set forth in the Executive Order. It has been determined that this action is not significant under section 3(f) of the Executive Order.

Paperwork Reduction Act

As part of its continuing effort to reduce paperwork and respondent burden, the Department conducts a preclearance consultation program to provide the general public and federal agencies with an opportunity to comment on proposed and continuing collections of information in accordance with the Paperwork Reduction Act of 1995 (PRA) (44 U.S.C. 3506(c)(2)(A)). This helps to ensure that requested data can be provided in the desired format, reporting burden (time and financial resources) is minimized, collection instruments are clearly understood, and the impact of collection requirements on respondents can be properly assessed.

The Department is not soliciting comments concerning an information collection request (ICR) pertaining to the Model Notice. As noted above, pursuant to Reorganization Plan No. 4, the Department of the Treasury has interpretive authority over the minimum funding rules of Title I of ERISA, including section 305 of ERISA, and it has advised that

---

[1] Reorganization Plan No. 4 of 1978, 43 FR 47713 (Oct. 17, 1978).

[2] Section 3(16)(B)(ii) of ERISA defines the term "plan sponsor" to mean, in the case of a plan established or maintained by two or more employers or jointly by one or more employers and one or more employee organizations, the association, committee, joint board of trustees, or other similar group of representatives of the parties who establish or maintain the plan.

[3] Plans may not use the model notice published herein to satisfy the notice requirement under section 305(e)(8)(C) of ERISA.

it is developing guidance under this provision. Costs and burdens associated with complying with the notice requirement in section 305(b)(3)(D) of ERISA and section 432(b)(3)(D) of the Code, therefore, will be accounted for in an ICR associated with the Treasury guidance. To the extent the Model Notice includes an ICR, persons are not required to respond to, and generally are not subject to any penalty for failing to comply with, the ICR unless the ICR has a valid OMB control number.[4]

Regulatory Flexibility Act

The Regulatory Flexibility Act (5 U.S.C. 601 et. seq.) (RFA) imposes certain requirements with respect to Federal rules that are subject to the notice and comment requirements of section 553(b) of the Administrative Procedure Act (5 U.S.C. 551 et. seq.) and which are likely to have a significant economic impact on a substantial number of small entities. Unless an agency certifies that a proposed rule is not likely to have a significant econcmic impact on a substantial number of small entities, section 603 of RFA requires that the agency present an initial regulatory flexibility analysis at the time of the publication of the notice of proposed rulemaking describing the impact of the rule on small entities and seeking public comment on such impact. Small entities include small businesses, organizations and governmental jurisdictions.

The Department has deemed that an employee benefit plan shall be considered a small entity if it has fewer than 100 participants.[5] By this standard, data from the EBSA Private Pension Bulletin 2004 (the latest available information) show that only 67 multiemployer pension plans or 4% of all multiemployer pension plans are small entities. The Department does not consider this to be a substantial number of small entities. Therefore, pursuant to section 605(b) of RFA, the Department hereby certifies that the proposed rule is not likely to have a significant economic impact on a substantial number of small entities. Further, to the Department's knowledge, there are no federal regulations that might duplicate, overlap, or conflict with the proposed rule.

Congressional Review Act

The Model Notice being issued here is subject to the Congressional Review Act provisions of the Small Business Regulatory Enforcement Fairness Act of 1996 (5 U.S.C. 801 et seq.) and, if finalized, will be transmitted to Congress and the Comptroller General for review.

Unfunded Mandates Reform Act

For purposes of the Unfunded Mandates Reform Act of 1995 (Pub. L. 104-4), as well as Executive Order 12875, the proposal does not include any Federal mandate that may result in expenditures by State, local, or tribal governments, and does not impose an annual burden exceeding $100 million on the private sector, adjusted for inflation.

Federalism Statement

Executive Order 13132 (August 4, 1999) outlines fundamental principles of federalism, and requires the adherence to specific criteria by Federal agencies in the process of their formulation and implementation of policies that have substantial direct effects on the States, the relationship between the national government and States, or on the distribution of power and responsibilities among the various levels of government. This proposed rule does not have federalism implications because it has no substantial direct effect on the States, on the relationship between the national government and the States, or on the distribution of power and responsibilities among the various levels of government. Section 514 of ERISA provides, with certain exceptions specifically enumerated, that the provisions of Titles I and IV of ERISA supersede any and all laws of the States as they relate to any employee benefit plan covered under ERISA. The proposed rule does not alter the fundamental reporting and disclosure requirements of the statute with respect to employee benefit plans, and as such have no implications for the States or the relationship or distribution of power between the national government and the States.

List of Subjects in 29 CFR Part 2540

Employee benefit plans, Pension plans, Multiemployer plans.

For the reasons set forth above, the Department proposes to amend Chapter XXV of Title 29 of the Code of Federal Regulations by adding Subchapter E to read as follows:

Subchapter E - Funding

PART 2540—MINIMUM FUNDING STANDARDS

Authority: 29 U.S.C. 1135 and Secretary of Labor's Order No. 1- 2003, 68 FR 5374 (Feb. 3, 2003). Section 2540.305-1 is also issued under 29 U.S.C. 1085(b)(3)(D)(iii).

§ 2540.305-1 Model Notice of Critical Status for Multiemployer Plans.

(a) Pursuant to section 305(b)(3)(D)(iii) of the Employee Retirement Income Security Act of 1974 (ERISA or Act), paragraph (b) of this section provides a model notice that a multiemployer plan may use to satisfy the content requirements under section 305(b)(3)(D) of ERISA and section 432(b)(3)(D) of the Code. Use of the model notice is not mandatory. However, the plan sponsor of a plan in critical status who uses the model notice to notify participants and others of the status of the plan is considered to have satisfied its content obligations under section 305(b)(3)(D) of ERISA and section 432(b)(3)(D) of the Code.

(b) Model notice:

[GPO: PHOTOGRAPH PAGES 11-13]

Notice of Critical Status

For

[Insert name of pension plan]

This is to inform you that on [enter date]the plan actuary certified to the U.S. Department of the Treasury, and also to the plan sponsor, that the plan [enter "is" or "will be"] in critical status for the plan year beginning [enter beginning date of plan year]. Federal law requires that you receive this notice.

Critical Status

The plan is considered to be in critical status because it has funding or liquidity problems, or both. More specifically, the plan's actuary determined that [complete and insert appropriate explanation(s) from the options below].

[Option one: "the plan's funded percentage for [enter plan year] is less than 65 %, and the sum of the fair market value of its current assets plus the present value of expected employer contributions through [enter end of the 6th plan year following the current plan year] is less than the present value of all benefits projected to be payable (plus administrative expenses) through [enter end of the 6th plan year following the current plan year."]

[Option two: "the plan has an accumulated funding deficiency for the current plan year."]

[Option three: "over the next three plan years, the plan is projected to have an accumulated funding deficiency for the [enter appropriate plan year or years]."]

[Option four: "the funded percentage of the plan is 65% or less, and over the next four plan years, the plan is projected to have an accumulated funding deficiency for the [enter appropriate plan year or years]."]

[Option five: "the sum of the plan's normal cost and interest on the unfunded benefits for the current plan year exceeds the present value of all expected contributions for the year; the present value of vested benefits of inactive participants is greater than the present value of vested benefits of active participants; and the plan has an accumulated funding deficiency for the current plan year."]

[Option six: "the sum of the plan's normal cost and interest on the unfunded benefits for the current plan year exceeds the present value of all expected contributions for the year; the present value of vested benefits of inactive participants is greater than the present value of vested benefits of active participants; and over the next four plan years, the plan is projected to have an accumulated funding deficiency for the [enter appropriate plan year or years]."].

[Option seven: "the sum of the fair market value of the plan's current assets plus the present value of expected employer contributions through [enter date that is the end of the plan year that is the 4th plan year following the current plan year]is less than the present value of all benefits payable through [enter date that is the end of the plan year that is the 4th plan year following the current plan year]."]

---

[4] See 5 CFR 1320.1 through 1320.18.

[5] The basis for this definition is found in section 104(a)(2) of the Act, which permits the Secretary of Labor to prescribe simplified annual reports for pension plans that cover fewer than 100 participants

[Option eight: "the plan was in critical status last year and over the next 9 years, the plan is projected to have an accumulated funding deficiency for the [enter appropriate plan year or years]."]

[Instructions: Insert the following discussion entitled Rehabilitation Plan and Possibility of Reduction in Benefits only if the plan is in critical status and adjustable benefits have not yet been reduced (e.g., the initial critical status year). Where adjustable benefits have already been reduced, insert the discussion below entitled Rehabilitation Plan.]

Rehabilitation Plan and Possibility of Reduction in Benefits

Federal law requires pension plans in critical status to adopt a rehabilitation plan aimed at restoring the financial health of the plan. The law permits pension plans to reduce, or even eliminate, benefits called "adjustable benefits" as part of a rehabilitation plan. If the trustees of the plan determine that benefit reductions are necessary, you will receive a separate notice in the future identifying and explaining the effect of those reductions. Any reduction of adjustable benefits (other than a repeal of a recent benefit increase, as described below) will not reduce the level of a participant's basic benefit payable at normal retirement. In addition, the reductions may only apply to participants and beneficiaries whose benefit commencement date is on or after [enter the date notice is or was provided for the first plan year in which the plan is in critical status]. But you should know that whether or not the plan reduces adjustable benefits in the future, effective as of [enter date notice is or was provided for the first plan year in which the plan is in critical status or January 1, 2008, whichever is later], the plan is not permitted to pay lump sum benefits (or any other payment in excess of the monthly amount paid under a single life annuity) while it is in critical status.

Rehabilitation Plan

Federal law requires pension plans in critical status to adopt a rehabilitation plan aimed at restoring the financial health of the plan. This is the [enter number] year the plan has been in critical status. The law permits pension plans to reduce, or even eliminate, benefits called "adjustable benefits" as part of a rehabilitation plan. On [enter date], you were notified that the plan reduced or eliminated adjustable benefits. On [enter date of initial critical status notice], you were notified that as of [enter date] the plan is not permitted to pay lump sum benefits (or any other payment in excess of the monthly amount paid under a single life annuity) while it is in critical status. If the trustees of the plan determine that further benefit reductions are necessary, you will receive a separate notice in the future identifying and explaining the effect of those reductions. Any reduction of adjustable benefits (other than a repeal of a recent benefit increase, as described below) will not reduce the level of a participant's basic benefit payable at normal retirement. In addition, the reductions may only apply to partici-

pants and beneficiaries whose benefit commencement date is on or after [enter the date notice is or was provided for the first plan year in which the plan is in critical status].

Adjustable Benefits

The plan offers the following adjustable benefits which may be reduced or eliminated as part of any rehabilitation plan the pension plan may adopt [check appropriate box or boxes]:

Post-retirement death benefits;

Sixty-month payment guarantees;

Disability benefits (if not yet in pay status);

Early retirement benefit or retirement-type subsidy;

Benefit payment options other than a qualified joint-and survivor annuity (QJSA);

Recent benefit increases (i.e, occurring in past 5 years);

Other similar benefits, rights, or features under the plan [provide identification]

Employer Surcharge

The law requires that all contributing employers pay to the plan a surcharge to help correct the plan's financial situation. The amount of the surcharge is equal to a percentage of the amount an employer is otherwise required to contribute to the plan under the applicable collective bargaining agreement. With some exceptions, a 5% surcharge is applicable in the initial critical year and a 10% surcharge is applicable for each succeeding plan year thereafter in which the plan is in critical status.

Where to Get More Information

For more information about this Notice, you may contact [enter name of plan administrator] at [enter phone number and address (including e- mail address if appropriate)]. You have a right to receive a copy of the rehabilitation plan from the plan.

[GPO: END PHOTOGRAPH]

Signed at Washington, DC, this 18th day of March, 2008.

Bradford P. Campbell,

Assistant Secretary,

Employee Benefits Security Administration,

Department of Labor.

[FR Doc. E8-5855 Filed 3-24-08; 8:45 am]

BILLING CODE 4510-29-P

¶ 20,537M

Equal Employment Opportunity Commission (EEOC): Proposed rule: Age Discrimination in Employment Act (ADEA): Reasonable factor other than age (RFOA).—The Equal Employment Opportunity Commission (EEOC) has released proposed rules incorporating the holding from the U.S. Supreme Court's decision in the *Smith v. City of Jackson* age discrimination case. The EEOC now proposes to revise its regulations in accordance with the Court's "reasonable factor other than age" standard. The Court held that an employment practice that has an adverse impact on individuals within the protected age group on the basis of older age is discriminatory unless the practice is justified by a "reasonable factor other than age" (RFOA). The Court concluded that disparate impact claims are cognizable under the Age Discrimination in Employment Act (ADEA) and that the RFOA test, rather than the business-necessity test, is the appropriate standard for determining the lawfulness of a practice that disproportionately affects older workers.

The proposed regulations, which were published in the *Federal Register* on March 31, 2008 (73 FR 16807), were reproduced below. The final regulations were published in the Federal Register on March 30, 2012 (77 FR 19080). The final regulations are reproduced at ¶ 15,750C.

¶ 20,537N

PBGC proposed regulations: Plan terminations: Termination date: Bankruptcy filing date.—The Pension Benefit Guaranty Corporation (PBGC) has issued proposed regulations which treat the bankruptcy filing date as the termination date for many purposes, for terminations occurring during a bankruptcy proceeding of the plan sponsor that was initiated on or after September 16, 2006.

The proposed regulations, which were published in the *Federal Register* on July 1, 2008 (73 FR 37390), were reproduced below. The final regulations were published in the *Federal Register* on June 14, 2011 (76 FR 34590). The preamble to the final regulations is at ¶ 24,302. The final regulations are reproduced at ¶ 15,421A, ¶ 15,421B, ¶ 15,421C, ¶ 15,521E, ¶ 15,422, ¶ 15,422A, ¶ 15,422B, ¶ 15,422C, ¶ 15,422D, ¶ 15,422DD, ¶ 15,423, ¶ 15,423A, ¶ 15,423B, ¶ 15,424, ¶ 15,424A, ¶ 15,471, ¶ 15,471A, ¶ 15,471B, ¶ 15,472, ¶ 15,472C, ¶ 15,472D, ¶ 15,474, ¶ 15,476, ¶ 15,476A, ¶ 15,476B, and ¶ 15,476D.

¶ 20,537O

Employee Benefits Security Administration (EBSA): Proposed rule: Fiduciary requirements: Fee disclosure: Participant-directed accounts.—The Employee Benefits Security Administration (EBSA) has issued proposed regulations that would require employers and plan administrators, in satisfaction of their fiduciary duties under ERISA, to provide participants and beneficiaries in participant-directed plans with plan and investment-related information. The proposed rules, when finalized, would specifically require the disclosure of investment-related fee and expense information (e.g., sales loads, deferred sales charges, redemption fees, service charges, exchange fees, account fees, purchase fees, and the expense ratio for the total operating expenses of the investment) to be made in a chart or similar format that would allow for a comparison of the plan's investment options. The proposed regs provide a model chart for this purpose.

The proposed regulations, which were published in the Federal Register on July 23, 2008 (73 FR 43014), are reproduced below. These regulations were finalized October 20, 2010 (75 FR 64910). The preamble to the final regulations appears at ¶ 24,298. The final regulations are at ¶ 14,742D and ¶ 14,744.

PRORULE

PREAMB

AGENCY TYPE'S' DEPARTMENT OF LABOR

SUBAGY Employee Benefits Security Administration

CFR 29 CFR Part 2550

RIN RIN 1210-AB07

SUBJECT Fiduciary Requirements for Disclosure in Participant-Directed Individual Account Plans

AGENCY: Employee Benefits Security Administration.

ACTION: Proposed regulation.

SUMMARY: This document contains a proposed regulation under the Employee Retirement Income Security Act of 1974 (ERISA) that, upon adoption, would require the disclosure of certain plan and investment-related information, including fee and expense information, to participants and beneficiaries in participant-directed individual account plans (e.g., 401(k) plans). This proposal is intended to ensure that all participants and beneficiaries in participant-directed individual account plans have the information they need to make informed decisions about the management of their individual accounts and the investment of their retirement savings. This document also contains proposed conforming changes to the regulations applicable to ERISA section 404(c) plans (29 CFR 2550.404c-1). Upon adoption, these proposals will affect plan sponsors, fiduciaries, participants and beneficiaries of participant-directed individual account plans, as well as providers of services to such plans.

DATES: Written comments on the proposed regulation should be received by the Department of Labor on or before September 8, 2008.

ADDRESSES: To facilitate the receipt and processing of comment letters, the Employee Benefits Security Administration (EBSA) encourages interested persons to submit their comments electronically by e-mail to *e-ORI@dol.gov* (enter into subject line: Participant Fee Disclosure Project) or by using the Federal eRulemaking portal at *http://www.regulations.gov*. Persons submitting comments electronically are encouraged not to submit paper copies. Persons interested in submitting paper copies should send or deliver their comments to the Office of Regulations and Interpretations, Employee Benefits Security Administration, Attn: Participant Fee Disclosure Project, Room N-5655, U.S. Department of Labor, 200 Constitution Avenue, NW., Washington, DC 20210. All comments will be available to the public, without charge, online at *http://www.regulations.gov* and *http://www.dol.gov/ebsa* and at the Public Disclosure Room, N-1513, Employee Benefits Security Administration, U.S. Department of Labor, 200 Constitution Avenue, NW., Washington, DC 20210.

FOR FURTHER INFORMATION CONTACT: Susan M. Halliday or Kristen L. Zarenko, Office of Regulations and Interpretations, Employee Benefits Security Administration, (202) 693-8510. This is not a toll-free number.

SUPPLEMENTARY INFORMATION:

A. Background

According to the Department's most recent data, there are an estimated 437,000 participant-directed individual account plans, covering an estimated 65 million participants, and holding almost $2.3 trillion in assets.[1] With the proliferation of these plans, which afford participants and beneficiaries the opportunity to direct the investment of all or a portion of the assets held in their individual plan accounts, participants and beneficiaries are increasingly responsible for making their own retirement savings decisions. This increased responsibility has led to a growing concern that participants and beneficiaries may not have access to, or if accessible, may not be considering information critical to making informed decisions about the management of their accounts, particularly information on investment choices, including attendant fees and expenses.

Under ERISA, the investment of plan assets is a fiduciary act governed by the fiduciary standards in ERISA section 404(a)(1)(A) and (B), which require fiduciaries to act prudently and solely in the interest of the plan's participants and beneficiaries. Where a plan assigns investment responsibilities to the plan's participants and beneficiaries, it is the view of the Department that plan fiduciaries must take steps to ensure that participants and beneficiaries are made aware of their rights and responsibilities with respect to managing their individual plan accounts and are provided sufficient information regarding the plan, including its fees and expenses, and designated investment alternatives, including fees and expenses attendant thereto, to make informed decisions about the management of their individual accounts. To some extent, such disclosures are already required by plans that elect to comply with the requirements of section 404(c) (see § 2550.404c-1(b)(2)(i)(B)). However, compliance with section 404(c)'s disclosure requirements is voluntary and does not extend to participants and beneficiaries in all participant-directed individual account plans.

The Department believes that all participants and beneficiaries with the right to direct the investment of assets held in their individual plan accounts should have access to basic plan and investment information. For this reason, the Department is issuing this proposed regulation under section 404(a), with conforming amendments to the regulations under section 404(c). These proposals would establish uniform, basic disclosures for such participants and beneficiaries, without regard to whether the plan in which they participate is a section 404(c) plan. In addition, the proposal would require participants and beneficiaries to be provided investment-related information in a form that encourages and facilitates a comparative review among investment options.

To facilitate the development of a proposed regulation, the Department published, on April 25, 2007, a Request for Information (RFI) in the E T='04' Federal Register /E[2] requesting suggestions, comments and views from interested persons on a variety of issues relating to the disclosure of plan and investment-related fee and expense and other information to participants and beneficiaries in participant-directed individual account plans. The Department received and reviewed 106 comment letters on these important issues. Copies of these letters are posted on the Department's Web site at *http://www.dol.gov/ebsa/regs/cmt-feedisclosures.html*.

The RFI encouraged persons preparing comments to consider a 2004 report and recommendations of a working group of the ERISA Advisory Council. The Employee Welfare and Pension Benefit Plans' Working Group on Fee and Related Disclosures to Participants reviewed the disclosure requirements applicable to participant-directed individual account plans. The Working Group assessed the adequacy and usefulness of such requirements and recommended changes to the requirements to help participants more effectively manage their retirement savings.[3]

Additionally, the RFI encouraged commenters to consider the Government Accountability Office's (GAO) 2006 report and recommendations contained in "Private Pensions: Changes Needed to Provide 401(k) Plan Participants and the Department of Labor Better Information on Fees."[4] Also relevant to the Department's consideration was the work of the Securities and Exchange Commission (Commission). The Commission has proposed, among other matters, the use of a summary

---

[1] 2005 Form 5500 Data, U.S. Department of Labor. The estimated 437,000 plans include plans that permit participants to direct the investment of all or a portion of their individual accounts.

[2] 72 FR 20457 (April 25, 2007).

[3] This report may be accessed at *www.dol.gov/ebsa/publications/AC_111704_report.html*.

[4] The GAO report, GAO-07-21, referenced above may be accessed at *www.gao.gov/htext/d0721.html*.

prospectus with additional information provided on an Internet Web site. The proposal is intended to improve mutual fund disclosure by providing investors with key information in plain English in a clear and concise format, while enhancing the means of delivering more detailed information to investors.[5] Following consultation with the Commission, the Department's proposal is coordinated with the Commission's summary prospectus approach where feasible. As ERISA plan investment options include many products not subject to the Commission's disclosure requirements, the Department seeks comments addressing the application of this proposed regulation to funds and investment products not subject to the securities laws.

B. Overview of Proposal § 2550.404a-5

1. *General*

Paragraph (a) of proposed § 2550.404a-5 sets forth the general principle that, where documents and instruments governing an individual account plan provide for the allocation of investment responsibilities to participants and beneficiaries, plan fiduciaries, consistent with ERISA section 404(a)(1)(A) and (B), must take steps to ensure that such participants and beneficiaries, on a regular and periodic basis, are made aware of their rights and responsibilities with respect to the investment of assets held in, or contributed to, their accounts and are provided sufficient information regarding the plan, including plan fees and expenses, and regarding designated investment alternatives available under the plan, including fees and expenses attendant thereto, to make informed decisions with regard to the management of their individual accounts. As discussed below, the proposal addresses the information that must be provided participants and beneficiaries, as well as timeframes for providing that information.

Paragraph (b) of the proposal addresses the disclosure requirements that must be met by plan fiduciaries for plan years beginning on or after January 1, 2009. Under this paragraph, plan fiduciaries must comply with the requirements of paragraph (c), dealing with plan-related information, and paragraph (d), dealing with investment-related information. Paragraph (e) describes the form in which the required information may be disclosed, such as via the plan's summary plan description, a quarterly benefit statement, or the use of the provided model, depending on the specific information. Paragraph (e) merely recognizes various acceptable means of disclosure; it does not preclude other means for satisfying disclosure duties under the proposed regulation. Fiduciaries that meet the requirements of paragraphs (c) and (d) will have satisfied the duty to make the regular and periodic disclosures described in paragraph (a) of this section.

The Department believes, as an interpretive matter, that ERISA section 404(a)(1)(A) and (B) impose on fiduciaries of all participant-directed individual account plans a duty to furnish participants and beneficiaries information necessary to carry out their account management and investment responsibilities in an informed manner. In the case of plans that elected to comply with section 404(c) before finalization of this proposal, the requirements of section 404(a)(1)(A) and (B) typically would have been satisfied by compliance with the disclosure requirements set forth at 29 CFR § 2550.404c-1(b)(2)(i)(B). However, the Department expresses no view with respect to plans that did not comply with section 404(c) and the regulations thereunder as to the specific information that should have been furnished to participants and beneficiaries in any time period before this regulation is finalized.

2. *Plan-Related Information*

In general, paragraph (c) of the proposal sets forth what is characterized as "plan-related" information. This information falls into three categories - general plan information, administrative expense information and individual expense information. Paragraph (c) also describes when this information must be provided to participants and beneficiaries and requires that it be based on the latest information available to the plan.

First, paragraph (c)(1) of the proposal provides for the disclosure of general plan information regarding: how participants and beneficiaries may give investment instructions; any specified limitations on such instructions, including any restrictions on transfer to or from a designated investment alternative; the exercise of voting, tender and similar rights appurtenant to an investment in a designated investment alternative as well as any restrictions on such rights; the specific designated investment alternatives offered under the plan; and any designated investment managers to whom participants and beneficiaries may give investment directions. Under the proposal, this information is required to be furnished to an individual on or before the date he or she becomes eligible to be a participant or beneficiary under the plan and at

least annually thereafter. In addition, the proposal requires that participants and beneficiaries be furnished a description of any material changes to the required information not later than 30 days after the date of adoption of such changes. The Department believes that, by referencing the "date of adoption," the regulation will increase the likelihood that participants and beneficiaries will be provided notification of material changes in advance of the changes becoming effective, thereby putting them in a better position to consider such changes (e.g., changes in designated investment alternatives) in managing their accounts. Paragraph (e)(1) of the proposal provides that the disclosures required by this paragraph (c)(1) may be made as part of the plan's summary plan description, provided that the applicable timing requirements are satisfied.

Second, paragraph (c)(2)(i) sets out the required disclosures for administrative expenses. Specifically, it provides that, on or before the date of an individual's eligibility to become a participant or beneficiary under the plan, and at least annually thereafter, participants and beneficiaries must be furnished an explanation of any fees and expenses for plan administrative services (e.g., legal, accounting, recordkeeping) that, to the extent not included in investment-related fees and expenses, may be charged against the individual accounts of participants or beneficiaries and the basis on which such charges will be allocated to, or affect the balance of, each individual account (e.g., pro rata, per capita). This requirement is intended to ensure that the plan fiduciary informs all participants and beneficiaries about the plan's day-to-day operational expenses that will be charged against their accounts. Because of its general nature, the information described in paragraph (c)(2)(i) may, pursuant to paragraph (e)(1) of the proposal, be disclosed as part of the plan's summary plan description, provided that the applicable timing requirements are met.

In addition to the general disclosures concerning plan administrative expenses, paragraph (c)(2)(ii) of the proposal requires that, at least quarterly, participants and beneficiaries be furnished statements of the dollar amounts actually charged during the preceding quarter to the participants' or beneficiaries' accounts for administrative services, and general descriptions of the services to which the charges relate. The statements should be sufficiently specific to inform the participants or beneficiaries of the actual charge(s) to their accounts and enable them to distinguish the administrative services from other charges and services that may be assessed against their accounts. An identification of the total administrative fees and expenses assessed during the quarter, with, for example, an indication that the charges for plan administrative expenses include legal, accounting, and recordkeeping costs to the plan, would be sufficient. The Department does not believe that it is necessary, or particularly useful, for participants to have administrative charges broken out and listed on a service-by-service basis. Commenters on the Department's RFI argued that an overly detailed breakdown of administrative fees may overwhelm participants and that meaningful information would not be conveyed by such a breakdown. Many commenters explicitly supported the disclosure of "aggregate" or summary fees. The requirement to furnish the information described in paragraph (c)(2)(ii) of the proposal may be satisfied by including the information as part of a quarterly benefit statement furnished pursuant to ERISA section 105(a)(1)(A)(i). See paragraph (e)(2) of the proposal.

Third, paragraph (c)(3) describes the required disclosures for individual expenses. This is identical to paragraph (c)(2) except that it focuses on the disclosure of information relating to individual expenses, i.e., expenses that are assessed on an individual-by-individual, rather than plan-wide, basis. Such expenses might be attendant to a qualified domestic relations order, a participant loan, or investment advice services. Paragraph (c)(3)(i) requires the disclosure of information concerning what expenses might be assessed and paragraph (c)(3)(ii) requires the disclosure of amounts actually assessed and identification of the service to which an expense relates. Also, like paragraph (c)(2), information described in paragraph (c)(3)(i) may be disclosed in the plan's summary plan description and the information described in paragraph (c)(3)(ii) may be included in a quarterly benefit statement.

The Department invites comments on the type of information required to be disclosed, the timing of the information required to be disclosed and the form in which the information may be disclosed.

3. *Investment-Related Information*

Paragraph (d) of the proposal sets forth the investment-related information required to be furnished or made accessible to participants and beneficiaries in participant-directed individual account plans. Paragraph

---

[5] 72 FR 67790 (November 30, 2007).

(d)(1) sets forth the investment-related information required to be automatically furnished to each participant and beneficiary. Paragraph (d)(2) addresses the format of the required information. Paragraph (d)(3) addresses the furnishing of post-investment information. And paragraph (d)(4) sets forth information required to be furnished only upon the request of a participant or beneficiary.

Paragraph (d)(1) provides that, on or before the date of eligibility and at least annually thereafter, participants and beneficiaries must be furnished certain basic information with respect to each designated investment alternative offered under the plan. For purposes of the proposal, paragraph (h)(1) defines the term "designated investment alternative" to mean any investment alternative designated by the plan into which participants and beneficiaries may direct the investment of assets held in, or contributed to, their individual accounts. The term "designated investment alternative" does not include "brokerage windows," "self-directed brokerage accounts," or similar plan arrangements that enable participants and beneficiaries to select investments beyond those designated by the plan.

For purposes of identifying the information essential for participants and beneficiaries to consider in evaluating their investment choices under the plan, the Department carefully reviewed the many comments received in response to the RFI, as well as the Commission's proposal for a summary prospectus. The majority of RFI commenters believe that, in addition to basic fee and expense information, participants and beneficiaries need additional disclosure to put fee-related information into context and to educate them about a plan's investment alternatives. On the basis of its review, the Department concluded that fee and expense information, although important, is only one of the factors to be considered in making informed investment decisions along with investment performance and other information relating to a designated investment alternative. Also, the Department is persuaded by RFI commenters that most participants and beneficiaries will probably not review large amounts of detailed investment information. Information that is too detailed may overwhelm participants, and commenters are concerned that the costs associated with providing overly detailed information, which ultimately will be borne by participants, significantly outweigh any possible benefits. However, the Department also is persuaded that the form in which information is required to be presented should serve to encourage and facilitate its review by participants and beneficiaries. Many commenters on the RFI, for example, supported the disclosure of fee information in a format that would facilitate comparison across a plan's investment alternatives. For this reason, paragraph (d)(2) of the proposal, as discussed later, requires the investment-related information set forth in paragraph (d)(1) to be presented in a comparative format.

Specifically, paragraph (d)(1) requires the following disclosures with respect to each designated investment alternative under the plan:

Paragraph (d)(1)(i) requires, among other items, the name and category (e.g., money market mutual fund, balanced fund, index fund, and whether the investment alternative is actively or passively managed) of the designated investment alternative and an Internet Web site address that is sufficiently specific to lead participants and beneficiaries to supplemental information regarding the investment alternative, including its principal strategies, risks, performance and costs. For example, such information may be contained in a Commission-required prospectus (or other document) made available at a Web site address. The Department believes that ready access to such information via the Internet alleviates the need to automatically furnish otherwise important, detailed investment-related information directly to every participant and beneficiary. This accommodates different levels of participant interest in such information. The Department recognizes that, while many investment fund providers do maintain Web sites to inform interested investors concerning specific investment funds, other providers of investment funds and products may not. The Department specifically invites comments on what, if any, challenges this proposed requirement may present for service providers and employers, such as in the case of in-house managed funds that might be offered as a designated investment alternative under a plan. The Department also is interested in comments on whether this proposed requirement raises any issues under the Department's rules on the use of electronic media (29 CFR 2520.104b-1(c)), given that plan fiduciaries may, in some cases, have to provide paper copies of the supplemental information listed in this requirement (i.e., information that would otherwise be accessible through the Internet Web site address) to participants who fail to affirmatively consent to receiving such information electronically.

Paragraph (d)(1)(ii) of the proposal requires the disclosure of specified performance data for each of the plan's designated investment alternatives. For designated investment alternatives with respect to which the return is not fixed, e.g., an equity index fund, the fiduciary (or designee) must provide the average annual total return (expressed as a percentage) of the investment for the following periods, if available: 1-year, 5-year, and 10-year, measured as of the end of the applicable calendar year; as well as a statement indicating that an investment's past performance is not necessarily an indication of how the investment will perform in the future. For this purpose, the term "if available" is intended merely to reflect that some plan investments may not have been in existence for 1, 5, or 10 years. In such cases, plans are expected to explain that the data is not available for this reason (e.g., "not applicable" or "not available"). In the case of designated investment alternatives for which the return is fixed for the term of the investment, e.g., a guaranteed investment contract, the fiduciary (or designee) must provide both the fixed rate of return and the term of the investment. For purposes of paragraph (d)(1)(ii), the term "average annual total return" is defined in section (h)(2) of the proposal by reference to standards applicable to open-end management investment companies registered under the Investment Company Act of 1940 (the 1940 Act). The Department specifically invites comments on what, if any, problems the proposed definition presents for investment funds and products that are not subject to the 1940 Act and, if problematic, suggestions for alternative definitions or approaches.

As a corollary to the disclosure of performance data, paragraph (d)(1)(iii) requires disclosure of performance data for an appropriate broad-based benchmark over time periods that are comparable to the performance data periods required under paragraph (d)(1)(ii). As structured, the proposal provides flexibility in identifying an appropriate benchmark. In general, the Department expects that most plans will simply identify the performance benchmark already being used for the investment option pursuant to the Commission's prospectus requirements, if applicable. The Department seeks comments on whether and how the proposed requirement may need to be modified to include a more narrowly based index that reflects the financial market sector for ERISA plan investment options that are not subject to the securities laws.

Paragraph (d)(1)(iv) specifically addresses the disclosure of fees and expenses attendant to the purchase, holding and sale of each of the plan's designated investment alternatives. For designated investment alternatives with respect to which the return is not fixed, the fiduciary (or designee) must provide: (A) The amount and a description of each shareholder-type fee (i.e., fees charged directly against a participant's or beneficiary's investment), such as sales loads, sales charges, deferred sales charges, redemption fees, surrender charges, exchange fees, account fees, purchase fees, and mortality and expense fees; (B) the total annual operating expenses of the investment expressed as a percentage (e.g., expense ratio); and (C) a statement indicating that fees and expenses are only one of several factors that participants and beneficiaries should consider when making investment decisions. In the case of designated investment alternatives with respect to which the return is fixed for the term of the investment, the fiduciary (or designee) must provide the amount and a description of any shareholder-type fees that may be applicable to a purchase, transfer or withdrawal of the investment in whole or in part. The description of each shareholder-type fee must include the amount on which the charge is applied, e.g., 4% of amount invested. For purposes of paragraph (d)(1)(iv), the term "total annual operating expenses" is defined in paragraph (h)(3) of the proposal by reference to standards applicable to open-end management investment companies registered under the 1940 Act. The Department specifically invites comments on what, if any, problems the proposed definition presents for investment funds and products that are not subject to the 1940 Act and, any suggestions for alternative definitions or approaches.

The Department has differentiated the fee and expense disclosures required for designated investment alternatives with returns that vary over time from alternatives with fixed returns based on the financial nature of each of these investment types. While the disclosure requirements for investments with respect to which the return is not fixed are more comprehensive, the Department decided that the most essential information for participants who choose to invest in fixed investment alternatives is the contractual interest rate paid to their accounts and the term of the investment during which their monies are shielded from market price fluctuations and reinvestment risks. Any fees assessed, of course, are factored into determining the contractual interest rate and RFI commentary suggested that there would be little benefit to participants to disclosing such fees for investments with fixed returns.

Paragraph (d)(1)(v) provides that, for purposes of the requirement that participants be provided information on or before the date they are eligible to be covered under the plan, plan fiduciaries may provide such participants the most recent annual disclosure furnished to participants and beneficiaries pursuant to paragraph (d)(1), in addition to any material changes to the information described in paragraph (c)(1)(i). This provision ensures that new participants receive at least the same information that has been furnished to other plan participants and beneficiaries with respect to the designated investment alternatives under the plan. It also avoids the possible burdens and costs of a requirement that fiduciaries update the required disclosures for each new plan participant, which could result in a daily updating requirement for many plans.

Paragraph (d)(2) of the proposal requires the fiduciary to furnish the information required by paragraph (d)(1) in a chart or similar format that will permit straightforward comparison of the plan's designated investment alternatives by participants and beneficiaries. Many commenters on the RFI supported this requirement and agreed that any required disclosure should enable participants and beneficiaries to easily compare data across a plan's menu of designated investment alternatives. Further, GAO indicated in its 2006 report that plan sponsors should be required to disclose fee information on each 401(k) investment option in a way that facilitates comparison among the options.[6] The fiduciary's name and contact information must also be provided so that participants and beneficiaries may request the additional information listed in paragraph (d)(4). The chart or similar document also must include a statement informing participants and beneficiaries that more current information about a designated investment alternative, including performance and cost updates, may be available on the Web site for the investment alternative.

In response to commenters on the RFI, the Department has developed a model disclosure form that can be used for purposes of satisfying the disclosure requirements of paragraph (d)(2) of the proposal. The model appears in the Appendix to this regulation. Paragraph (e)(3) of the proposal specifically provides that a fiduciary that uses and accurately completes the model format set forth in the Appendix will be deemed to have satisfied the requirements of paragraph (d)(2) relating to the disclosure of the information in paragraph (d)(1) in a comparative form.[7] The Department notes that the proposal would not mandate use of the model as the exclusive means for satisfying the requirement to provide a chart or similar format that facilitates comparison. This proposal provides fiduciaries with the flexibility to create a chart or comparative format of their own design, provided the required information is displayed in a manner facilitating comparisons.

Paragraph (d)(3) of the proposal requires that when a plan provides for the pass-through of voting, tender and similar rights, the fiduciary must furnish participants and beneficiaries who have invested in a designated investment alternative with these features any materials about such rights that have been provided to the plan. This requirement is similar to the requirement currently applicable to section 404(c) plans. See § 2550.404c-1(b)(2)(i)(B)(1)(ix).

Paragraph (d)(4) of the proposal requires a fiduciary to furnish certain identified information either automatically or upon request by participants and beneficiaries, based on the latest information available to the plan. This provision is modeled on the requirements currently applicable to section 404(c) plans with respect to information to be furnished upon request of a participant or beneficiary. See § 2550.404c-1(b)(2)(i)(B)(2).

4. *Timing of Disclosures*

As discussed above, each of the various disclosures must be made within specific timeframes. The plan-related information concerning certain administrative procedures and expenses required by subparagraphs (c)(1)(i), (c)(2)(i), (c)(3)(i), and the investment-related information required by subparagraph (d)(1) must be provided to each participant or beneficiary "on or before the date of plan eligibility" and "at least annually thereafter." The proposal defines "at least annually thereafter" in paragraph (h)(4) to mean at least once in any 12-month period, without regard to whether the plan operates on a calendar or fiscal year basis.

The proposal also requires that certain information be provided to participants and beneficiaries on a more frequent basis. Specifically, the actual dollar amounts charged to an individual's account during the preceding quarter for administrative and individual services must be disclosed in a statement to participants and beneficiaries "at least quarterly" pursuant to subparagraphs (c)(2)(ii) and (c)(3)(ii) of the proposal. The proposal defines "at least quarterly" in paragraph (h)(5) to mean at least once in any 3-month period.

5. *Other Fiduciary Duties*

Paragraph (f) makes clear that nothing in the regulation would relieve a fiduciary of its responsibilities to prudently select and monitor service providers to the plan and the investments made available under the plan (i.e., designated investment alternatives).[8]

C. Proposed Amendments to § 2550.404c-1

Also included in this notice are proposed amendments to the regulation under section 404(c) of ERISA, 29 CFR § 2550.404c-1. The proposed amendments to section 2550.404c-1(b), (c) and (f) would integrate the disclosure requirements in the section 404(c) regulation with the new proposed section 2550.404a-5 disclosure requirements and thereby avoid having different disclosure rules for plans intending to comply with the section 404(c) requirements. In brief, the proposed amendments to the section 404(c) regulation eliminate references to disclosures encompassed in the new § 2550.404a-5 proposal and incorporate cross-references to the new proposal, thereby establishing a uniform disclosure framework for all participant-directed individual account plans. The Department also is taking this opportunity to reiterate its long held position that the relief afforded by section 404(c) and the regulation thereunder does not extend to a fiduciary's duty to prudently select and monitor designated investment managers and designated investment alternatives under the plan. Accordingly, it is the Department's view that a fiduciary breach or an investment loss in connection with the plan's selection of a designated investment alternative is not afforded relief under section 404(c) because it is not the result of a participant's or beneficiary's exercise of control.[9] The Department is proposing to amend paragraph (d)(2) (entitled "Limitation on liability of plan fiduciaries") of § 2550.404c-1 to add a new subparagraph (iv) providing that, "[P]aragraph (d)(2)(i) does not relieve a fiduciary from the duty to prudently select and monitor any "designated investment manager or designated investment alternative offered under the plan."

D. Effective Date

The Department proposes that the regulations and amendments contained in this notice be effective for plan years beginning on or after January 1, 2009. The Department specifically invites comments on the earliest date on which the proposed regulation and amendments can or should be effective, addressing any administrative or programming costs or other issues that should be considered in establishing an effective date.

E. Regulatory Impact Analysis

As discussed in the preceding sections, the proposed regulation would establish a uniform basic disclosure regime for participant-directed plans. Many of the disclosures contained in the proposed regulation are similar to those required for participant-directed individual account plans that currently comply with section 404(c) and the Department's regulations issued thereunder. For other participant-directed plans which choose not to be section 404(c) compliant there is some uncertainty as to what information is provided to participants; accordingly, the Department is assuming for purposes of this analysis that for some of the plans that choose not to be 404(c) compliant the proposal's disclosure requirements are new.

Given the foregoing assumptions, the average incremental costs and benefits for participants in plans that provide section 404(c) compliant or similar disclosures will be smaller than for those in plans that do not provide this information. Participants in section 404(c) compliant plans or in plans that provide similar information will not receive as large an added benefit from the proposal's new disclosure requirements because they are already receiving some of the information that would be required under the proposed regulation.

---

[6] *See supra* note 4.

[7] The Department notes that the model set forth in the Appendix includes information and statements that are merely illustrative of the type of information that might appear in the required disclosure. It is the responsibility of each plan fiduciary to assure itself that the information contained in its disclosure statement is complete and accurate. However, such fiduciaries shall not be liable for their reasonable and good faith reliance on information furnished by their service providers with respect to those disclosures required by paragraph (d)(1).

[8] Also, with regard to ERISA's general fiduciary standards, it should be noted that there may be extraordinary situations when fiduciaries will have a disclosure obligation beyond those addressed by this regulation. For example, if a plan fiduciary knew that, due to a fraud, information contained in a public financial report would mislead investors concerning the value of a designated investment alternative, the fiduciary would have an obligation to take appropriate steps to protect the plan's participants, such as disclosing the information or preventing additional investments in that alternative by plan participants until the relevant information is made public. *See also Varity Corp.* v. *Howe,* 516 U.S. 489 (1996) (plan fiduciary has a duty not to misrepresent to participants and beneficiaries material information relating to a plan).

[9] See 57 FR 46906, 46924, n.27 (preamble to § 2550.404c-1) (October 13, 1992).

Executive Order 12866 Statement

Under Executive Order 12866, the Department must determine whether a regulatory action is "significant" and therefore subject to the requirements of the Executive Order and subject to review by the Office of Management and Budget (OMB). Under section 3(f) of the Executive Order, a "significant regulatory action" is an action that is likely to result in a rule (1) having an effect on the economy of $100 million or more in any one year, or adversely and materially affecting a sector of the economy, productivity, competition, jobs, the environment, public health or safety, or State, local or tribal governments or communities (also referred to as "economically significant"); (2) creating serious inconsistency or otherwise interfering with an action taken or planned by another agency; (3) materially altering the budgetary impacts of entitlement grants, user fees, or loan programs or the rights and obligations of recipients thereof; or (4) raising novel legal or policy issues arising out of legal mandates, the President's priorities, or the principles set forth in the Executive Order. The Department has determined that this action is "significant" under section 3(f)(1) because it is likely to have an effect on the economy of more than $100 million in any one year.

Accordingly, the Department has undertaken, as described below, an analysis of the costs and benefits of the proposed regulation in satisfaction of the requirements of the Executive Order and OMB Circular A-4. The Department believes that the proposed regulation's benefits justify its costs. The present value of the benefits over the ten year period is expected to be about $6.9 billion. The present value of the costs over the same time period is expected to be $759 million. Overall, the Department estimates that the proposed regulation will generate a net present value (or net present benefit) of almost $6.1 billion over the time period 2009-2018, as is shown in Table 1.

TABLE 1.—*Summary of Discounted Benefits and Costs*

Year	Benefits ($Millions/Year)	Costs ($Millions/Year)
1 2009	914.9	127.3
2 2010	855.0	90.7
3 2011	799.1	84.7
4 2012	746.8	79.2
5 2013	698.0	74.0
6 2014	652.3	69.2
7 2015	609.6	64.7
8 2016	569.8	60.4
9 2017	532.5	56.5
10 2018	497.6	52.8
Total with 7% Discounting	6875.6	759.4
Net Present Value 7% Discounting		6,116
Net Present Value 3% Discounting		7,158

Need for Regulatory Action

A growing number of workers are preparing for retirement by participating in ERISA governed retirement plans that allow for participant direction of investments. How well plan participants are prepared for retirement is partly determined by how well they have invested their retirement savings. Among the key determinants of the return on an investment are fees and expenses. A one percentage point difference in fees can result in an 18 percent difference in savings.[10]

In developing this proposed regulation, the Department considered why the market alone does not provide transparent fee disclosure to participants comparable to that prescribed by this regulation. In general, the market delivers products that are deemed valuable by consumers. The lack of transparent fee disclosure in this market suggests to the Department that individuals may underestimate the impact that fees and expenses can have on their account balances, and thus undervalue transparent fee disclosure. The Department believes that this causes individuals to make uninformed investment decisions that result in inferior outcomes to those that would result from making investment decisions based on full information. Retirement plan characteristics, including disclosure practices, are shaped in significant measure by labor market forces. Employers want to attract and retain productive employees and minimize cost. If employees undervalue disclosure, plans sponsors might under-provide it. Sub-optimal levels of disclosure translate into inefficiencies in participant's choices of investment products and services. Evidence for this undervaluation includes a wide dispersion of fees paid in 401(k) plans. As supported by a report of the Investment Company Institute,[11] the fees that plans pay vary over a wide range. According to their study, 23% of 401(k) stock mutual fund assets are in funds with an expense ratio of less than 50 basis points, while an equal amount of assets are in funds with an expense ratio of over 100 basis points. Some of this variation could be explained by the varying amount of assets in plans and their accompanying economies of scale. In addition, some plans might offer more, or more expensive, plan features. The Department believes, however, that a significant portion of the variation in plan fees is due to market inefficiencies.

Understanding and comparing investment options available in a 401(k) plan can be complicated and confusing for many participants. The magnitude of complexity and confusion may be defined by reference to the number of available investment options and the materials utilized for communicating investment-related information. For example, in plans that offer a large number of investment options, for which the primary communication is a full prospectus-like disclosure, understanding and comparing investment options may be challenging for the less financially savvy or less interested plan participants.[12] Moreover, the process of gathering and comparing information may itself be time consuming.

The proposed regulation will help a large number of plan participants by placing investment-related information in a format that facilitates comparison of investment alternatives. This simplified format will make it easier and less time consuming for participants to find and compare the needed information. As a result, plan participants may make better investment decisions and may be better financially prepared for retirement.

---

[10] The Commission reported that a $10,000 investment with an expense ratio of 1.5% invested for 20 years and having an annual return of 10% before fees will return roughly $49,725, while a similar investment with lower fees of 0.5% will return $60,858—an 18% difference. Invest Wisely: An Introduction to Mutual Funds, *http://www.sec.gov/investor/pubs/inwsmf.htm.*

[11] Investment Company Institute, "The Economics of Providing 401(k) Plans: Services, Fees, and Expenses, 2006," *http://www.ici.org/pdf/fm-v16n4.pdf.*

[12] For example, the ERISA Advisory Council Working group reported that "The Working Group questions the utility of the prospectus as a source of investment information. While its delivery is required under SEC rules for investment, it lacks any marginal utility to a plan participant in terms of making an investment decision," Report of the Working Group on Prudent Investment Process, 2006, *http://www.dol.gov/ebsa/publications/AC_1106A_report.html.* The Department also received similar comments in response to its Request of Information regarding Fee Disclosures to 401(k) Plan Participants from service providers and trade organizations. These comments can be accessed at *http://www.dol.gov/ebsa/regs/cmt-feedisclosures.html.*

Benefits

The proposed regulation's disclosure requirements will provide important benefits to society. The provision of investment-related information in a comparative format is a new requirement for all participant directed individual account plans, including section 404(c) compliant plans, and is anticipated to be especially beneficial to plan participants. The Department believes that such information will enable participants to make better decisions on how to structure their investments on a prospective basis. These benefits with respect to the provision of investment-related information are quantified in more detail below.

(a) Reduction in Fees

A review of the relevant literature suggests that plan participants on average pay fees that are higher than necessary by 11.3 basis points per year.[13] The proposal's required disclosure of fees and expenses is expected to result in the payment of lower fees for many participants, assuming that participants will more consistently pick the lower cost comparable investment alternatives under their plans.[14] Selection of the lower cost comparable investment alternatives will, in turn, result in increased plan participant account investment returns. In addition, the required disclosure could lead to reduced fees[15] in the investment alternatives market as more fee transparency fosters more price competition in the market. Furthermore, the fee disclosure requirements may lead plan fiduciaries to give additional scrutiny to fees, and consequently to select less expensive comparable investment alternatives.

Although participants in section 404(c) compliant plans already receive much of the information that would be required under the proposed regulation, they are expected to receive a substantial incremental benefit. Participants in section 404(c) compliant plans, as well as many participants in plans that are not choosing to be section 404(c) compliant, who invest in mutual funds that are designated investment alternatives under the plan already receive the fee information in the related funds' prospectuses. The proposal's required disclosure of a summary of fee and performance information in a comparable format may nevertheless be beneficial in assisting plan participants to make better investment decisions. Thus, the Department assumes that participants in plans that are not providing disclosures similar to that required under section 404(c) receive a larger added benefit from the proposal's disclosures than plan participants that receive section 404(c) compliant or similar disclosures.[16]

The Department estimates that there will be assets of about $2.6 trillion in participant-directed individual account plans in 2009[17] and that about $3.0 billion in higher than necessary fees are being paid by plan participants. Assuming the proposal's fee disclosures will reduce the amount of higher than necessary fees paid on average (a) by 10% (11.3 basis points*10%=1.13 basis points)[18] for participants in section 404(c) compliant plans or plans that provide similar information, and (b) by 15% (11.3 basis points*15 %=1.70 basis points) for participants in plans that do not receive section 404(c) compliant or similar information, the Department believes that the proposal's fee disclosures will result in $307 million in fee savings for plan participants in 2009 as shown in Table 2.

TABLE 2.—*Benefits Due to Reduction in Fees (2009)*

Type of Plan	Total Amount of Assets in Plans (in Millions of 2009 Dollars) (A)	Basis Points of Higher Than Necessary Fees (B)	Percent Correction Due to Disclosure (C)	Benefits From Reduction in Fees (A * B * C)
404(c) Plans and Plans with Similar Information	2,500,000	0.11%	10%	$282,754,000
Non-404(c) Plans without Similar Information	144,000	0.11%	15%	24,487,000
Total Undiscounted Benefits				307,241,000

Note: The displayed numbers are rounded to the nearest thousand and therefore may not add up to the totals.

There is some question as to whether some reductions in fees might represent transfers (such as consumer surpluses being recaptured by participants from investment managers) rather than efficiency gains. The Department believes that fee reductions attributable to this proposed regulation will mostly reflect efficiency gains, especially in the longer run. Downward pressure on fees will favor more efficient means of producing investment and other plan services. It will also reflect a diminution of the market for services whose costs exceeds their benefits (such as movement from more active to more passive investment

management in cases where the latter is more efficient). However, it is possible that some fraction of reduced fees could reflect a transfer.[19] The Department invites comments on this possibility. Since a purpose of the proposed regulation is to help plan participants increase their retirement savings, and because the expected fee reduction furthers this goal, the Department's motivation is the same irrespective of whether fee savings reflect transfers or efficiency gains. In the absence of information of what portion of fee savings might reflect transfers, for purposes of this assessment all such savings is counted as benefits.

---

[13] "Higher than necessary" here means that the participant could have obtained equal value without incurring the expense. This calculation, based on fees paid in 401(k) plans, assumes that participants on average pay 11 or more basis points in unnecessary fees and expenses, in the form of expense ratios or loads. This assumption is conservative in light of evidence on the distribution of investor expense levels presented in: Brad M. Barber, Terrance Odean and Lu Zheng, "Out of Sight, Out of Mind, The Effects of Expenses on Mutual Fund Flows," Journal of Business Vol. 79, No. 6 p. 2095-2119 (2005); James J Choi, David I. Laibson, and Brigitte C. Madrian, "Why Does the Law of One Price Fail? An Experiment on Index Mutual Funds," NBER Working Paper No. W12261 (May 2006); Report, Deloitte Financial Advisory Services LLP. "Fees and Revenue Sharing in Defined Contribution Retirement Plans," (December 6, 2007) (on file with the Department); Edwin J Elton, Martin J. Gruber, and Jeffrey A. Busse, "Are Investors Rational? Choices Among Index Funds," NYU Working Paper, Social Science Research Network Abstract 340482 (June 2002); Sarah Holden and Michael Hadley, Investment Company Institute, "The Economics of Providing 401(k) Plans: Services, Fees and Expenses 2006," 16 Research Fundamentals, No. 4. (September 2007). This estimate of excess expense does not take into account less visible expenses such as mutual funds' internal transaction costs (including explicit brokerage commissions and implicit trading costs), which are sometimes larger than funds' expense ratios. Deloitte, supra; Jason Karceski, Miles Livingston, and Edward O'Neal, "Portfolio Transactions Costs at U.S. Equity Mutual Funds," University of Florida Working Paper (2004) at E T='03' http://thefloat.typepad.com/the_float/files/2004_zag_study_on_mutual_fund_trading_costs.pdf /E

[14] While increased disclosure to plan participants is expected to reduce fees, it is not clear by how much. Some participants may not make optimal use of the disclosed information to reduce fees when making investment decisions. Also, the proposal's disclosures are limited to plan's designated investment alternatives chosen by plan fiduciaries rather than by plan participants.

[15] In their mutual fund experiment, Choi et al. found that presenting the participants with a comparison fee chart, and not just a prospectus, reduced the fees paid by 12% to 49%

depending on the group studied. Choi, James J., David I. Laibson, and Brigitte C. Madrian. May 2006. "Why Does the Law of One Price Fail? An Experiment on Index Mutual Funds." NBER Working Paper No. W12261.

[16] The Department assumes that plan participants that already receive the section 404(c) required information will receive a benefit from the proposal that is two thirds of that received by participants that do not already receive this information. In addition, the Department assumes that at least 80% of participants in plans that choose not to be 404(c) compliant, nevertheless, receive similar disclosures to participants in section 404(c) compliant plans. The Department specifically requests comments on the percentage of participants that already receive this information and the additional benefits that plan participants will receive due to the proposed regulation.

[17] The Department estimates, using 2005 Form 5500 data, that in 2005 $2.3 trillion in assets were held in participant directed accounts. To arrive at a 2009 dollar estimate, this number is then adjusted for inflation. This estimate does not include growth due to new participants or contributions and it also ignores increases or decreases due to the returns on the assets. Overall, the Department believes it under estimates the total amount of assets in 2009.

[18] Choi et al. (2006) found that providing comparative fee information to the treatment groups reduced fees by 12% to 49%. While this estimate originated from an experiment using young educated subjects, the Department believes that the assumptions made here are reasonable as they were selected from the lower range of values.

[19] Fees vary due to the number and type of investment alternatives selected by the plan fiduciary. Nevertheless, plan participants can still influence the amount of fees they pay. Participants can choose among, on average almost 19 alternatives (Vanguard. "How America Saves 2006.") in the plan and select lower cost investment options or change their allocation percentages. Participants can also ask the plan fiduciaries to offer lower cost alternatives.

(b) Reduction in Participant Search Time

The proposed regulation will benefit plan participants by reducing the time they spend searching for and compiling fee and expense information. Although it is possible that all of these 65 million participants in participant directed individual account plans could benefit from increased disclosure, only a subset will choose to act on the disclosed information. The Department estimates that about at least 29 percent of plan participants will spend time researching their plans' designated investment alternatives fee and expense information and are, therefore, likely to benefit from reduced search time and corresponding reduced costs. This estimate is based on an EBRI survey[20] which found that 29 percent of the respondents that received educational materials from their plans read the materials and made a change in their retirement plan investments. This assumption results in nearly 19 million plan participants that could benefit from reduced search costs. The Department seeks comments on the extent to which this proposal may increase the percentage of plan participants who will spend time researching their plans.

The same EBRI study found that respondents spent 19 hours per year on average planning for retirement. Of these 19 hours, the Depart-ment assumes that one-and-a-half hours could be saved on average for participants that are not receiving information like that required in section 404(c) and one hour for participants that are receiving section 404(c) compliant or similar disclosures based on the proposal's increased fee disclosure information. This assumption results in approximately 19 million hours being saved by affected plan participants as a result of the proposed regulation. The Department seeks comments on this assumption.

In order to convert the time-savings into a dollar estimate, the Department estimated how much the average participants would value the time saved. Since the search time is assumed to be spent during leisure time and in order to adjust for the difference that plan participants attribute to leisure time versus work time, an average total wage rate for private sector workers participating in a pension plan with individual accounts was reduced by 10 percent to derive at an average value rate of leisure time.[21] Using a wage rate of a little less than $35[22] for private sector workers participating in a pension plan with individual accounts results in an average value of an hour of leisure time of $31 for 2009. Thus, the benefits from reduced search time for plan participants are estimated at $608 million for 2009 as shown in Table 3 below.

TABLE 3.—*Benefits from Reduced Participant Search Time (2009)*

Type of Plan	Number of (affected) Participants in Participant-directed Accounts (A)	Percentage of Participants Predicted to Make a Change in Allocation to Lower Fee Investments (B)	Number of Search Hours Saved by Participant (C)	Average Hourly Value of Participants' Leisure Time (in 2009 Dollars) (D)	Total Benefits From Reduced Participant Search Time (A * B * C * D)
404(c) Plans and Plans with Similar Information	62,058,000	29%	1.0	$31.33	$563,884,000
Non-404(c) Plans without Similar Information	3,211,000	29%	1.5	$31.33	43,770,000
Total Undiscounted Benefits					607,654,000

Note: The displayed numbers are rounded to the nearest thousand and therefore may not add up to the totals.

(c) Summary of Benefits

The quantified benefits of the proposed regulation consist of benefits from the reduction in fees and from the reductions in search time for participants seeking information on fees, which will occur primarily as a result of the comparative disclosure of investment-related information, and secondarily due to the disclosure of noninvestment-related fee and expense disclosures. Estimates of these total benefits due to prospective fee disclosure are presented in Table 4 and amount to a total net present value of $6.9 billion over the 10-year period.

TABLE 4.—*Total Discounted Benefits of the Proposal*

Year	Benefits from Reduction in Fees (A)	Benefits from Reduced Participant Search Time (B)	Total Benefits (A + B)
2009	$307,241,000	$607,654,000	$914,895,000
2010	287,141,000	567,901,000	855,042,000
2011	268,356,000	530,748,000	799,105,000
2012	250,800,000	496,027,000	746,827,000
2013	234,393,000	463,576,000	697,969,000
2014	219,059,000	433,249,000	652,308,000
2015	204,728,000	404,905,000	609,633,000
2016	191,334,000	378,416,000	569,751,000
2017	178,817,000	353,660,000	532,477,000
2018	167,119,000	330,523,000	497,642,000

[20] Employee Benefit Research Institute Issue Brief #292, April, 2006.

[21] Feather and Shaw (1999), using an econometric model, found that the opportunity cost of leisure time is 10 percent less than observed wages for employed workers. See Feather, P. and Shaw, W.D., "Estimating the Cost of Leisure Time for Recreation Demand Models," *Journal of Environmental Economics and Management*, Volume 38, Issue 1, July 1999, Pages 49-65.

[22] This wage rate estimate is based on hourly wages from Panel 7 of the 2001 wave from the Survey of Income Program Participation (SIPP) and on wage growth data for private-sector workers that participate in a pension plan with individual accounts from the Bureau of Labor Statistics (BLS).

Year	Benefits from Reduction in Fees (A)	Benefits from Reduced Participant Search Time (B)	Total Benefits (A + B)
Total with 7% Discounting			6,875,649,000
Total with 3% Discounting			8,038,368,000

Note: The displayed numbers are rounded to the nearest thousand and therefore may not add up to the totals.

In addition to the benefits that will derive from the disclosure of investment-related information in a comparative format, which are quantified above, participants also will benefit from a retrospective disclosure of plan administrative fees actually charged to their accounts in the prior quarter. The Department believes that participants who are trying to plan for retirement are entitled to a comprehensive disclosure that includes not only information about fee and expenses that may occur depending on investment options selected, but also information on other fees that were actually assessed against their accounts in the previous quarter. RFI commentary indicates that participant advocates, plan sponsors and service providers, support such a disclosure requirement.[23] Information about actual charges to participants' accounts may, among other things, help participants understand their current reported account balance, help detect errors in prior charges by the plan, help them in relation to their general household budgeting and retirement planning, and help insure the reasonableness of the charges. The Department seeks comments that would help quantify the benefits of the retrospective disclosure.

Costs

The regulation may result in increased administrative burdens and costs for plans (or plan sponsors).

(a) Increased Administrative Burden

Costs Due to Upfront Review and Updating of Plan Documents

Plans are likely to incur administrative burdens and costs in order to comply with the requirements of the regulation. The proposed regulation will require each plan to incur an upfront cost to have the regulation reviewed by professionals, such as lawyers. This cost will be incurred by all participant-directed individual account plans. The Department assumes it will require a professional to spend one half hour to perform the review.[24] Using in-house labor rates for a legal professional of nearly $113[25], the up-front legal review cost is estimated at $24.6 million. In addition, the Department estimates that each plan will spend one-half hour of clerical time at an (in-house) hourly rate of $26 preparing the disclosures. This would result in a cost of $5.7 million for 2009. The costs of reviewing and preparing plan related information are summarized in Table 5. The Department seeks comments on its assumptions regarding hourly rates and number of hours in the table below.

TABLE 5.—Review and Prepare Plan Related Information, (2009)

Year	Number of Participant-Directed Plans (A)	Legal Professional Hours Required to Review each Plan (B)	Hourly Labor Cost for Legal Professional (in 2009 dollars) (C)	Clerical Professional Hours Required to Prepare Plan Documents (D)	Hourly Labor Cost for Clerical Professional (in 2009 dollars) (E)	Review Cost (A*B*C) + (A*D*E)
2009	436,862	0.5	$113	0.5	$26	$30,322,591
Total Undiscounted Costs						30,322,591

Note: The displayed numbers are rounded to the nearest thousand and therefore may not add up to the totals.

Based on the 2005 Form 5500 data, the Department estimates that approximately 59,000 new participant-directed individual account plans would be required to disclose general plan information each year. The Department assumes that writing a new disclosure notice for these plans would require, on average, one-half hour of legal professional time and one-half hour of clerical time per plan leading to a cost estimate of $4 million annually. The Department estimates that about 378,000 existing plans will require one-quarter hour of legal professional time and one-quarter hour of clerical staff time to update plan documents to take into account plan changes, such as new investment alternatives, in subsequent years. This results in a cost of approximately $13 million as summarized in Table 6. The Department seeks comments on the assumptions used to develop this figure.

TABLE 6.—Review and Update Plan Related Information, (Subsequent Years)

Type of Plan	Number of Participant-Directed Plans (A)	Legal Professional Hours Required to Review each Plan (B)	Hourly Labor Cost for Legal Professional (in 2009 dollars) (C)	Clerical Professional Hours Required to Prepare Plan Documents (D)	Hourly Labor Cost for Clerical Professional (in 2009 dollars) (E)	Review Cost (A*B*C) + (A*D*E)
Existing Plans	378,000	0.25	$113	0.25	$26	$13,107,000
New Plans	59,000	0.50	113	0.50	26	4,109,000
Total Undiscounted Costs						17,216,000

[23] These comments can be found under *http://www.dol.gov/ebsa/regs/cmt-feedisclosures.html*.

[24] This estimate reflects that plans may employ service providers for making disclosures and that these service providers are likely to spread fixed and start-up costs across many plan clients.

[25] EBSA wage estimates are based on the National Occupational Employment Survey (May 2006, Bureau of Labor Statistics) and the Employment Cost Index (March, 2007, Bureau of Labor Statistics), unless otherwise noted.

Type of Plan	Number of Participant-Directed Plans	Legal Professional Hours Required to Review each Plan	Hourly Labor Cost for Legal Professional (in 2009 dollars)	Clerical Professional Hours Required to Prepare Plan Documents	Hourly Labor Cost for Clerical Professional (in 2009 dollars)	Review Cost
	(A)	(B)	(C)	(D)	(E)	(A*B*C) + (A*D*E)

Note: The displayed numbers are rounded to the nearest thousand and therefore may not add up to the totals.

Costs Due to Production of Quarterly Dollar Amount Disclosures

The proposed regulation will require plan administrators to send out disclosures about administrative charges - on a plan-wide as well as a participant-specific basis - to participants' accounts and engage in record keeping. The increase in administrative costs resulting from disclosing actual dollar fee and expense disclosure is derived from a GAO report that measures the cost of the disclosures of the actual dollar amount of mutual fund investment expenses on a participant level.[26] The GAO report estimates the initial cost to generate these disclosures in 2001 at $1 per account,[27] and the annual cost of continued compliance at $0.35 per account.[28] The cost to plans to calculate administrative fees for purposes of this proposed regulation is expected to be less, because most of the expense information to be disclosed under the regulation is already tracked. The Department assumes it will cost both section 404(c) compliant and non-section 404(c) compliant plans one-third of the costs of disclosure of investment costs by mutual funds to disclose actual dollars charged, leading to cost estimates of about $0.41 per plan participant in the first year and $0.14 thereafter.[29] Thus, the cost to produce the actual dollar disclosure is estimated at $26.5 million for 2009 as shown in Table 7.[30] The Department invites comments on the cost to plans to produce actual dollar disclosures of the required fees, including the extent to which the costs differ for plans that are already making actual dollar disclosures and plans that are not.

TABLE 7.—*Cost of Additional Record Keeping and of Producing Actual Dollar Disclosures*

Year	Number of (Affected) Participants in Participant-Directed Accounts	Per Participant Cost from GAO Report	Percent of Cost for Calculating Administrative Fees	Cost of Record Keeping and of Producing Actual Dollar Disclosures
	(A)	(B)	(C)	(A * B * C)
2009	65,269,000	$1.22	33%	$26,543,000
Subsequent Year	65,269,000	0.43	33%	9,355,000

Note: The displayed numbers are rounded to the nearest thousand and therefore may not add up to the totals.

Costs Due to Consolidation of Fee Information

Additional administrative burdens and costs are likely to arise because of the need for plans to consolidate information from more than one source to prepare the required comparative chart. The Department estimates that it takes a staff person with some financial background about one hour per plan to consolidate the information from multiple sources for the comparative chart. Using a wage rate of about $60 for such an employee, results in estimated costs for the consolidation of fee information from multiple sources of approximately $26 million for 2009 as shown in Table 8.

TABLE 8.—*Cost of Consolidation of Fee Information*

Year	Number of Participant-Directed Plans	Average Plan Staff Time (Hours) Required to Consolidate Fee Information From Multiple Sources for Comparative Format	Accountant Hourly Labor Cost (in 2009 Dollars)	Cost of Consolidation of Fee Information for Comparative Format
	(A)	(B)	(C)	(A * B * C)
2009	437,000	1	$60	$26,290,000
Total Undiscounted Costs				26,290,000

Note: The displayed numbers are rounded to the nearest thousand and therefore may not add up to the totals.

Costs of Distribution and Materials Due to the Disclosure of Plan and Fee Information

These disclosures must be sent to plan participants on an annual or quarterly basis.[31] The Department assumes that it takes clerical staff two additional minutes to assemble and send out disclosures. The Department also assumes that 38% of disclosures will be sent electronically and therefore require only a de minimis amount of time to prepare. With wage rates of about $26 for clerical personnel, these

---

[26] GAO-03-551T, "Mutual Funds: Information on Trends in Fees and Their Related Disclosure," March 12, 2003, p.14.

[27] As a reference, Investment Management Consultants (IMC) has indicated that the cost to plan sponsors of producing an Internet report to comply with PPA ranges from $0.50 per participant per year for the largest plans to $3.00 per participant per year for the smallest plans. This cost, representing what IMC charges plan sponsors for industry-wide information on fees, is based on their data set containing 15,000 plans through September 2007, but does not include costs associated with printing reports, such as postage, stationary, and envelopes.

[28] The GAO report estimates that implementing specific dollar disclosures of fees would cost $1.00 per participant in the initial year (in 2001 dollars). In subsequent years this would annually cost about $0.35 (in 2001 dollars). This cost estimate includes the cost to enhance the current data processing systems, modify investor communication systems and media, develop new policies and procedures and implement employee training and customer support programs. This estimate does not include the reportedly significant costs that would be borne by third party financial institutions that maintain accounts on behalf of individual mutual fund shareholders.

[29] The Department used a) historical CPI data to inflate the $1.00 estimate to $1.19 (in 2007 dollars) and the $0.35 estimate to $0.42 (in 2007 dollars) and b) the projected inflation rate from the November 2007 President's Economic Forecast for 2008 (2.1 percent) to inflate the $1.19 value to $1.22 and the $0.42 value to $0.43 (in 2009 dollars). The President's Economic Forecast can be found at: *http://www.whitehouse.gov/cea/econ-outlook20071129.html*.

[30] The Department did not account for additional paper costs, given that no additional pages need be added as long as this information is included as part of the quarterly benefit statement.

[31] This section does not include distribution or material costs for the disclosures of administrative fees charged to participants' accounts as the Department assumes that this information can be included as part of the quarterly benefit statement.

dissemination labor costs are estimated at $35.1 million in 2009, as shown in Table 9.

Following a participant's investment in an investment alternative, the plan must provide any materials it receives regarding voting, tender or similar rights in the alternative ("pass-through materials") (29 CFR 2550.404a-5(d)(3)). This information is already required for 404(c) compliant plans and by the Department's Qualified Default Investment Alternative regulation. In addition, a large majority of plans voluntarily provide this information to its participants. As a result only an esti-

mated number of 699,000 participants will be receiving this information for the first time because of the proposed regulation.

The Department assumes that clerical staff will prepare and send the required materials. It may take the clerical staff on average one and one-half minutes to prepare and mail the post-investment materials. The Department assumes that this information will be sent annually resulting in nearly 699,000 disclosures. The Department expects that 38 percent of the disclosures will be sent electronically. Table 9 reports the cost of $283,000 to prepare and send the required post-investment information.

TABLE 9.—*Cost of Distributing Disclosures*

Type of Disclosure	Number of Disclosures to be Sent (A)	Percentage of Disclosures not Transmitted Via E-mail (B)	Hourly Labor Cost (in 2009 dollars) (C)	Hours Per Disclosure (D)	Materials Costs for Distribution of Disclosures (A * B * C * D)
Annual Disclosures	65,269,000	62%	$26.07	0.033	$35,166,000
Pass-Though Materials	699,000	62%	26.07	0.025	283,000
Total Undiscounted Costs					35,448,000

Note: The displayed numbers are rounded to the nearest thousand and therefore may not add up to the totals.

In addition to labor costs associated with the disclosure, plans will also bear materials and postage costs. The annual disclosure is assumed to include 13 pages for plans that are not already providing disclosures similar to section 404(c) disclosures. Plans already providing section 404(c) compliant or similar disclosures are assumed to already be making annual disclosure of information and are therefore assumed to need to add only three pages of additional information to what they are already disclosing to participants.[32] The pass-through

information is assumed to be ten pages and sent on an annual basis to plan participants as described above. Paper and printing costs are assumed to be $0.05 a page and mailing costs to be $0.42.[33] It is further assumed that 38 percent of statements will be available electronically. In total, this leads to an estimate for materials and postage of $8.2 million in 2009 for the annual disclosures as shown in Table 10 and $473 thousand for the post-investment pass-through information as shown in Table 11.

TABLE 10.—*Annual Disclosures Materials and Postage Costs (2009)*

Type of Plan	Number of (Affected) Participants in Participant-Directed Accounts (A)	Percentage of Disclosures not Transmitted Via E-mail (B)	Number of Pages For Annual Disclosure (C)	Paper and Printing Cost per Page (D)	Mailing Costs (E)	Materials Costs for Distribution of Disclosures (A*B) * (C*D+E)
404(c) Plans and Plans with Similar Information	62,058,000	62%	3	$0.05	$0.00	$5,771,000
Non-404(c) Plans without Similar Information	3,211,000	62%	13	0.05	0.59	2,468,000
Total Undiscounted Costs						8,240,000

Note: The displayed numbers are rounded to the nearest thousand and therefore may not add up to the totals.

TABLE 11.—*Pass-Through Materials and Postage Costs (2009)*

Number of Disclosures to be Sent (A)	Percentage of Disclosures not Transmitted Via E-mail (B)	Number of Pages For Annual Disclosure (C)	Paper and Printing Cost per Page (D)	Mailing Costs (E)	Materials Costs for Distribution of Disclosures (A*B) * (C*D+E)
699,000	62%	10	$0.05	$0.59	$473,000
Total Undiscounted Costs					473,000

Note: The displayed numbers are rounded to the nearest thousand and therefore may not add up to the totals.

In total, the Department estimates that in 2009 participant-directed plans incur increased administrative costs of approximately $127 million.

(b) Discouragement of Some Employers from Sponsoring a Retirement Plan

Increased administrative burdens may discourage some employers, particularly small employers, from sponsoring a retirement plan. For

small plan sponsors, the administrative burden is felt disproportionately because of their limited resources. Small business owners who do not have the resources to analyze plan fees or to hire an analyst may be discouraged from offering a plan at all.

Regulatory burden is one among many reasons for small businesses not to sponsor a retirement plan. According to the 2000, 2001, and 2002 Employee Benefit Research Institute (EBRI)'s Small Employer Retirement Surveys, about 2.7 percent of small employers cited "too many

---

[32] The proposed regulation would amend the regulation under ERISA section 404(c), 29 CFR 2550.404c-1, to make the disclosure requirements for section 404(c) compliant plans consistent with those that would apply to participant directed individual account plans generally. The Department assumes for purposes of the economic and paperwork analysis

that the disclosure costs of 404(c) compliant plans under the amended regulation would be similar to those absent the proposed regulation.

[33] The postage rate for First-Class Mail is increasing to $0.42 as of May 12, 2008 (E T='03' http://pe.usps.com/2008_RateCase/RateCharts/R08_Rate_Charts.htm /E).

government regulations" as the most important reason for not offering a retirement plan.[34] Due to very limited data in this area, the Department is not able to quantitatively estimate this impact. The Department seeks comments on the extent to which this proposal discourages small employers from offering retirement plans.

(c) Summary of Costs

The quantified total costs of the proposed regulation include costs due to the increased administrative burden. Columns (A) and (B) of

Table 12 below show the estimated costs of up-front review of the regulation and updating of plan documents. Column (C) shows the costs of producing quarterly Dollar amounts for administrative fees charged to participant accounts. The largest cost of the regulation, though, results from the disclosure of the administrative expenses and investment-related fees that may be charged to participants' accounts-the consolidation of fee information costs, and the distribution and material costs as can be seen in columns (D), (E), and (F). Table 12 reports that the total present value of theses costs is estimated at $759 million over the ten year period.

TABLE 12.—*Total Discounted Costs of Proposal*

Year	Up-front Review Cost	Update Plan Documents	Consolidation of Fee Information	Production of Quarterly Dollar Amount Disclosures	Distribution Materials Costs	Staff Cost to Distribute Disclosures	Total Costs
	(A)	(B)	(C)	(D)	(E)	(F)	(A + B + C + D+ E + F)
2009	$30,323,000	0	$26,290,000	$26,543,000	$8,713,000	$35,448,000	$127,317,000
2010	3,840,000	$ 12,250,000	24,570,000	8,743,000	8,143,000	33,129,000	90,675,000
2011	3,589,000	11,448,000	22,963,000	8,171,000	7,610,000	30,962,000	84,743,000
2012	3,353,000	10,699,000	21,461,000	7,637,000	7,112,000	28,936,000	79,199,000
2013	3,134,000	9,999,000	20,057,000	7,137,000	6,647,000	27,043,000	74,018,000
2014	2,929,000	9,345,000	18,745,000	6,670,000	6,212,000	25,274,000	69,176,000
2015	2,738,000	8,734,000	17,518,000	6,234,000	5,806,000	23,621,000	64,650,000
2016	2,559,000	8,162,000	16,372,000	5,826,000	5,426,000	22,075,000	60,421,000
2017	2,391,000	7,628,000	15,301,000	5,445,000	5,071,000	20,631,000	56,468,000
2018	2,234,000	7,129,000	14,300,000	5,089,000	4,739,000	19,281,000	52,774,000
Total with 7% Discounting							759,440,000
Total with 3% Discounting							880,339,000

Note: The displayed numbers are rounded to the nearest thousand and therefore may not add up to the totals.

Summary

As shown in Table 1 above, the Department concludes that the estimated benefits ($6.9 billion) of the proposed regulation outweigh its estimated costs ($759 million) by almost $6.1 billion over the ten-year period.

Uncertainty

Although the Department sought to anchor its analysis on empirical evidence, there are a number of variables that are subject to uncertainty. While the Department is confident that increased fee disclosures can induce changes in participant behavior and reductions in plan fees, it is uncertain about the exact magnitude of these changes. The variables with the most uncertainty in the analysis are:

- The percentage of plan fees that could be saved,

- The percentage of participants that would save search time for fee information,

- The amount of search time saved per participant,

- The time required for legal professionals, clerical professionals[35] and accountants to perform their tasks,

- And the cost to obtain the actual dollar amounts of participant's plan and administrative expenses.

To estimate the influence of these variables on the analysis, the Department reestimated the costs and benefits of the proposed regulation under different assumptions for these uncertain variables.

Table 13 presents the effects of changing the variables of interest. The first two variables on the list were decreased, while the remaining variables were increased. Changing the variables of concern by 25 percent still resulted in a net present value of $5.1 billion. Changing the variables by 50 percent still resulted in a net present value of $3.6 billion. Even after changing the key variables by 75 percent the net present value of the proposed regulation was $1.5 billion. The Department, however, does not believe that a change of 75% in these variables is a very likely scenario.

TABLE 13.—*Sensitivity of Benefits and Costs to Key Variables*

Percent Change in Variables	Benefits ($Millions/Year)	Costs ($Millions/Year)	Net Present Value ($Millions/Year)
25	6,013	866	5,147
50	4,579	973	3,606
75	2,575	1,080	1,495

Note: The displayed numbers are rounded to the nearest million.

---

[34] The survey defines small employers as those having up to 100 full-time workers. Other reasons small employers do not offer a retirement plan are that workers prefer wages or other benefits, that a large portion of employees are seasonal, part-time, or high turnover, and that revenue is too low or uncertain. See *http://www.ebri.org/surveys/sers* for more detail.

[35] The clerical time to distribute disclosures remains unchanged in this sensitivity analysis.

Regulatory Alternatives

Executive Order 12866 directs Federal Agencies promulgating regulations to evaluate regulatory alternatives. The Department considered the following alternatives to the proposed regulation, and will also briefly discuss the status quo baseline:

- Extending the existing section 404(c) regulation disclosure requirements to all participant-directed individual account plans;

- Establishing a general, non specific disclosure requirement; or

- Requiring more extensive and detailed disclosures.

These alternatives, and the status quo baseline, are described further below:

• Keeping the status quo

OMB Circular A-4 recommends that "benefits and costs are defined in comparison with a clearly stated alternative. This normally will be a 'no action' baseline: what the world will be like if the proposed rule is not adopted." The Department followed this recommendation, and weighed the option of keeping the status quo and relying on the current regulatory framework. By definition, as the regulatory baseline, this "alternative" would have zero costs and benefits; however, the Department feels it is useful to briefly describe the status quo, and the reasons for rejecting it in favor of a regulation, before we discuss regulatory alternatives. As stated above, regulations already exist specifying the information that must be provided to participants of 404(c) compliant plans in order to relieve plan fiduciaries of responsibility for participant investment decisions (see § 2550.404c-1(b)(2)(i)(B)). Many of the proposal's disclosures are identical or similar to the required disclosures of section 404(c) and the regulations issued thereunder. However, compliance with section 404(c) is elective and according to 2005 Form 5500 data only about 275,000 plans covering 49 million participants and beneficiaries make this election. About 16 million participants and beneficiaries are participating in 49,000 participant-directed individual account plans that are choosing not to be section

404(c) compliant and a significant number of these individuals may not receive disclosures in compliance with section 404(c), and, therefore, may not receive the information the Department believes they need to make informed account management and investment decisions.[36] More importantly, the section 404(c) disclosure of investment-related information is not required to be in a comparative format that encourages and facilitates review by plan participants and beneficiaries. Neither does such a requirement exist for any other type of participant-directed individual account plan.

• Extending the existing 404(c) disclosure requirements to all participant-directed individual account plans

The Department considered requiring all participant-directed individual account plans to comply with section 404(c) and the regulations issued thereunder. This would not have required any additional disclosures to participants in existing section 404(c) compliant plans, and, therefore, may have required less extensive effort by such plans, such as review of the proposed regulation and development of materials in order to come into compliance. Participants and Beneficiaries, however, would also not have had the benefit of receiving critical information in a comparative chart.[37]

Compared to the status quo, only participants in participant-directed individual account plans that do not receive similar information to the required 404(c) disclosures would experience additional benefits by extending the existing 404(c) disclosures. As noted above, the Department assumes that only 20% of the participants of plans that are presently not choosing to be section 404(c) compliant are not receiving similar information. These participants would experience benefits from a reduction in fees (5% of 0.113% of their assets, as shown in Table 14 below) and from a reduction in their search time (0.5 hour for 29% of the affected participants, as shown in Table 15 below). This would lead to annual benefits of approximately $8.1 million due to the reduction in fees and of about $14.6 million for the reduction in participant search time. In total, benefits add up to about $22.8 million, a much smaller amount than the expected benefits of the proposal.

TABLE 14.—*Annual Benefits Due to Mandatory 404(c) Compliance, Reduction in Fees*

Type of Plan	Total Amount of Assets in Affected Plans (in Millions of 2009 Dollars) (A)	Basis Points of Higher Than Necessary Fees (B)	Percent Correction Due to 404(c) Disclosure (C)	Benefits From Reduction in Fees Due to 404(c) Disclosures (A * B * C)
Non-404(c) Plans without Similar Information	144,000	0.11%	5%	$8,162,000
Total Undiscounted Benefits				8,162,000

Note: The displayed numbers are rounded to the nearest thousand and therefore may not add up to the totals.

TABLE 15.—*Annual Benefits Due to Mandatory 404(c) Compliance, Reduced Participant Search Time*

Type of Plan	Number of (affected) Participants in Participantdirected Accounts (A)	Percentage of Participants Predicted to Make a Change in Allocation to Lower Fee Investments (B)	Number of Search Hours Saved by Participant (C)	Average Hourly Value of Participants' Leisure Time (in 2009 Dollars) (D)	Total Benefits From Reduced Participant Search Time Due to 404(c) Disclosures (A * B * C * D)
Non-404(c) Plans without Similar Information	3,211,000	29%	0.5	$31.33	$14,590,000
Total Undiscounted Benefits					14,590,000

Note: The displayed numbers are rounded to the nearest thousand and therefore may not add up to the totals.

Additional costs for review, update and preparation of related information, as compared to the status quo, would fall on all participant-directed individual account plans that are presently not choosing to

comply with section 404(c).[38] The Department estimates that these costs would amount to about $11.3 million in the first year and would fall to $9.0 million in subsequent years, as shown in Table 16 below.

---

[36] However, the Department recognizes that many plan participants in participant-directed individual account plans that choose not to comply with all of the section 404(c) requirements are receiving similar information to what they would receive if the plans had chosen to comply with all requirements of section 404(c).

[37] Under the proposal, plans would be required to disclose specified identifying information, past performance data, comparable benchmark returns, and fee and expense informa-

tion for each investment alternative. Under the existing 404(c) rule, plans only have to provide past performance data and operating expense information directly or upon request and benchmark returns do not have to be provided.

[38] In subsequent years, these costs fall on newly created 404(c) plans and reduced costs for updates are expected for existing 404(c) plans.

TABLE 16.—*Annual Costs Due to Additional Review, Update, and Preparation of Plan Related Information*

Type of Plan	Number of Affected Participant-Directed Plans	Legal Professional Hours Required to Review each Plan	Hourly Labor Cost for Legal Professional (in 2009 dollars)	Clerical Professional Hours Required to Prepare Plan Documents	Hourly Labor Cost for Clerical Professional (in 2009 dollars)	Review Cost
	(A)	(B)	(C)	(D)	(E)	(A*B*C) + (A*D*E)
First Year (2009)						
Existing and New Plans	162,000	0.5	$113	0.5	$26	$11,250,000
Total Undiscounted Costs First Year						11,250,000
Subsequent Years, Annually						
Existing Plans	140,000	0.25	$113	0.25	$26	$4,863,000
New Plans	59,000	0.5	113	0.5	26	4,109,000
Total Undiscounted Costs Subsequent Years						8,971,000

Note: The displayed numbers are rounded to the nearest thousand and therefore may not add up to the totals.

In addition to costs for review, updating, and preparation of information, plans would also incur material and postage costs and labor costs for sending out the required disclosures to participants that presently are not receiving similar information and would receive the disclosures by mail, rather than via electronic means. As shown in Table 17 and Table 18 below, the Department estimates postage and material costs of about $2.6 million and labor costs of about $2 million.

TABLE 17.—*Annual Costs for Annual Additional Disclosures Materials and Postage and Pass-Through Materials*

Type of Plan	Number of (Affected) Participants in Participant-Directed Accounts	Percentage of Disclosures not Transmitted Via E-mail	Number of Pages For Annual Disclosure	Paper and Printing Cost per Page	Mailing Costs	Materials Costs for Distribution of Disclosures
	(A)	(B)	(C)	(D)	(E)	(A*B) * (C*D+E)
Annual Disclosures	3,211,000	62%	10	$0.05	$0.59	$2,170,000
Pass Through Material	699,000	62%	10	0.05	0.59	473,000
Total Undiscounted Costs						2,643,000

Note: The displayed numbers are rounded to the nearest thousand and therefore may not add up to the totals.

TABLE 18.—*Annual Costs of Additional Distributing Disclosures*

Type of Disclosure	Number of Disclosures to be Sent	Percentage of Disclosures not Transmitted Via E-mail	Hourly Labor Cost (in 2009 dollars)	Hours Per Disclosure	Materials Costs for Distribution of Disclosures
	(A)	(B)	(C)	(D)	(A * B * C * D)
Annual Disclosures	3,211,000	62%	$26	0.033	$1,730,000
Pass-Though Materials	699,000	62%	26	0.025	283,000
Total Undiscounted Costs					2,013,000

Note: The displayed numbers are rounded to the nearest thousand and therefore may not add up to the totals.

Table 19 below shows the annual costs and benefits and Table 20 below presents the net present benefit. The Department estimates that extending the existing 404(c) requirements would have resulted in ten-year costs of about $105 million and benefits of approximately $171 million. The ten-year net present value would have been about $66 million (in 2009 dollars).

TABLE 19.—*Additional Benefits and Costs of Mandatory 404(c) Compliance for all Participant-Directed Individual Account Plans*

	2009 Annual	2010-2018 Annual
Benefits		
Fee Reduction	$8,162,000	$8,162,000
Reduction in Participant Search Time	14,590,000	14,590,000
Total Benefits	22,752,000	22,752,000
Costs		
Review, Update, and Preparation of Documents	11,250,000	8,971,000

	2009 Annual	2010-2018 Annual
Annual Disclosures and Pass-Through Information	2,643,000	2,643,000
Distribution	2,013,000	2,013,000
Total Costs	15,905,000	13,627,000
Net Benefits in 2009	6,847,000	

Note: The displayed numbers are rounded to the nearest thousand and therefore may not add up to the totals.

TABLE 20.—*Total (Additional) Discounted Benefits of the Alternative*

Year	Additional Benefits from Extending 404(c), 7% Discounting (A)	Additional Costs from Extending 404(c), 7% Discounting (B)	Additional Net Benefits, 7% Discounting (A - B)
2009	$22,752,000	$15,905,000	$6,847,000
2010	21,264,000	12,736,000	8,528,000
2011	19,873,000	11,902,000	7,970,000
2012	18,573,000	11,124,000	7,449,000
2013	17,358,000	10,396,000	6,962,000
2014	16,222,000	9,716,000	6,506,000
2015	15,161,000	9,080,000	6,081,000
2016	14,169,000	8,486,000	5,683,000
2017	13,242,000	7,931,000	5,311,000
2018	12,376,000	7,412,000	4,964,000
Total with 7% Discounting	170,989,000	104,689,000	66,301,000
Total with 3% Discounting	$199,905,000	$122,007,000	77,898,000

Note: The displayed numbers are rounded to the nearest thousand and therefore may not add up to the totals.

• Establishing a general non-specific disclosure requirement

The Department considered establishing a general, non-specific disclosure rule requiring that plan fiduciaries take steps to ensure that participants and beneficiaries of participant-directed individual account plans are provided sufficient information to make informed decisions about the management of their individual accounts without further specifying what information would have to be disclosed. This alternative would have provided fiduciaries with more flexibility in providing disclosures to participants and beneficiaries, but may have also created uncertainty as to the scope of the required disclosures. It is possible that the costs to fiduciaries, and consequently plans, would be lower than the costs under the proposed regulation, but not all participants and beneficiaries may have received the critical information required under the proposed regulation. This approach also may have had the negative effect of having fiduciaries err on the side of being conservative and providing more, but not necessarily useful or meaningful, information to plan participants, creating a disincentive for participants and beneficiaries to review the furnished material.

• Requiring more extensive and detailed disclosures

The Department considered requiring more extensive and detailed prospectus-like disclosure of investment-related information to participants and beneficiaries. However, based on a review of RFI comments and the Commission's summary prospectus initiative, the Department concluded that a user-friendly summary of key information would be more beneficial than more extensive and detailed disclosures. In this regard, the Department attempted to define the most essential information about available investment options that should be automatically furnished in a comparative format to participants and beneficiaries, and included that information in the proposal. That information includes historical and benchmark performance, and fees and expenses. In addition, the Department considered including information on risk, but

believes that risk information is not easily translated into a simple uniform comparative format that can be described in a regulatory standard. The Department notes that in most cases more detailed information, including information on risk is readily available to participants and beneficiaries through Internet Web sites, should they decide to review such information in assessing the various investment options available under their plan. Importantly, under the proposed regulation participants and beneficiaries will be advised that risks exist, and will be directed and encouraged to review more detailed information prior to making decisions concerning the investment options most appropriate for them. The Department invites comments on any additional information that should be required.

Regulatory Flexibility Act

The Regulatory Flexibility Act (5 U.S.C. 601 *et seq.*) (RFA) imposes certain requirements with respect to Federal rules that are subject to the notice and comment requirements of section 553(b) of the Administrative Procedure Act (5 U.S.C. 551 *et seq.*) and that are likely to have a significant economic impact on a substantial number of small entities. Unless an agency certifies that a proposed rule will not, if promulgated, have a significant economic impact on a substantial number of small entities, section 603 of the RFA requires that the agency present an initial regulatory flexibility analysis at the time of the publication of the notice of proposed rulemaking describing the impact of the rule on small entities and seeking public comment on such impact. Small entities include small businesses, organizations, and governmental jurisdictions. For purposes of analysis under the RFA, EBSA proposes to continue to consider a small entity to be an employee benefit plan with fewer than 100 participants. The basis of this definition is found in section 104(a)(2) of ERISA, which permits the Secretary to prescribe simplified annual reports for pension plans that cover fewer than 100 participants.[39]

[39] Under ERISA section 104(a)(3), the Secretary may also provide exemptions or simplified reporting and disclosure requirements for welfare benefit plans. Pursuant to the authority of ERISA section 104(a)(3), the Department has previously issued at 29 CFR 2520.104-20, 2520.104-21, 2520.104-41, 2520.104-46, and 2520.104b-10 certain simplified

Further, while some large employers may have small plans, in general small employers maintain most small plans. Thus, EBSA believes that assessing the impact of these proposed rules on small plans is an appropriate substitute for evaluating the effect on small entities. The definition of small entity considered appropriate for this purpose differs, however, from a definition of small business that is based on size standards promulgated by the Small Business Administration (SBA) (13 CFR 121.201) pursuant to the Small Business Act (15 U.S.C. 631 *et seq.*). EBSA therefore requests comments on the appropriateness of the size standard used in evaluating the impact of these proposed rules on small entities. EBSA has consulted with the SBA Office of Advocacy concerning use of this participant count standard for RFA purposes. See 13 CFR 121.902(b)(4).

The Department prepared an initial RFA of the proposal because, although the Department considers it unlikely that the rule will have a significant effect on a substantial number of small plans, the Department does not have enough information to certify to that effect. The following subsections address specific requirements of the RFA.

(a) Reasons for and Objectives of the Proposal

A growing number of workers are preparing for retirement by participating in participant-directed plans that are governed by ERISA. Key determinants of the return on an investment include the fees and expenses paid. This proposal is intended to improve the information that is available to participants in participant-directed individual account plans and thereby enable participants to make good investment decisions.

The reasons for and objectives of this proposed regulation are discussed in detail in Section A of this preamble, "Background," and in section "Need for Regulatory Action" of the Regulatory Impact analysis (RIA) above. The legal basis for the proposal is set forth in the "Authority" section of this preamble, below.

(b) Estimating Compliance Requirements for Small Entities/Plans

The Department believes that the effects of this proposed regulation will be to increase retirement savings by reducing investment fees paid by participants. The Department also believes that small plans will

benefit from the proposal, because it will clarify what information must be disclosed to plan participants.

While small and large plans will incur administrative costs due to the proposed regulation, these costs are reasonable compared to the benefits and will probably be borne by the participants who will also receive the benefits of the proposed regulation. From industry comments, the Department inferred that participants in larger plans more often than participants in smaller plans have access to needed investment information. The Department believes that participants in small plans need as much information about their plan investments as participants in larger plans.

Some expenses, like the legal review of the proposal that plans may incur due to the disclosure requirements of the regulation do not increase proportionally with plan size. Nonetheless, it is possible that small plans incur smaller costs per participant than larger plans. In general, small plans offer fewer and less complex plan investment options than large plans. Less complex plan investments require less extensive disclosures and make disclosures less expensive. Thus, it is possible that smaller plans will experience lower per-participant disclosure costs than larger plans. The Department invites comments on the validity of this hypothesis.

Assuming that the plan incurs the average costs for all disclosure activities that are considered in the RIA section above, the following calculation illustrates how large the costs of the disclosures would be for a very small plan (one-participant plan). As can be seen in Table 21, the total cost of compliance for a one-participant plan amounts to less than $134 in the first year and less than that amount in the subsequent years. The costs in 2009 include a review cost of about $69 per plan (one-half hour of a legal professional's time plus one-half hour of a clerical professional's time), labor costs of $60 for consolidating the information for the comparative chart (one hour), costs of on average $0.40 per participant for record keeping and disclosure of information, additional annual labor cost for distribution of $0.90 in section 404(c) compliant plans or plans that already provide similar information ($1.50 in plans that do not already provide section 404(c) compliant or similar information), and material and postage costs of $0.15 in 404(c) compliant plans or plans that already provide similar information ($2.30 in plans that do not already provide section 404(c) compliant or similar information).

TABLE 21.—*Costs For One-Participant Plan (Undiscounted)*

Type of Cost	404(c) Plans and Plans with Similar Information		Non-404(c) Plans without Similar Information	
	Initial Year	Subsequent Year	Initial Year	Subsequent Year
Plan Review	69.00	35.00	69.00	35.00
Consolidation of Information	60.00	60.00	60.00	60.00
Actual Dollar Disclosure	0.40	0.15	0.40	0.15
Labor Cost for Distribution	0.90	0.90	1.50	1.50
Material Cost	0.15	0.15	2.30	2.30
Total	$131.00	$96.00	$134.00	$99.00

Note: The displayed numbers are rounded to the nearest thousand and therefore may not add up to the totals.

(c) Considered Alternatives

The Department considered several alternatives that would have required broader or narrower disclosures and which in turn would have increased or decreased the burden on plans. Exempting small plans from the disclosure requirements or limiting the disclosures from small plans would have reduced the costs small plans may incur, but would have also failed to ensure that participants in small plans receive the information that they need to make good investment decisions.

(d) Duplicative, Overlapping, and Conflicting Rules

ERISA section 404(c) and the regulations thereunder contain disclosure requirements for plan fiduciaries of certain participant-directed account plans that are to some extent similar to the ones that are contained in the proposed regulation. As explained in more detail in section "A. Background" of this preamble the Department amended the

regulations under section 404(c) in order to establish a uniform set of basic disclosure requirements and to ensure that all participants and beneficiaries in participant-directed individual account plans have access to the same investment-related information.

In addition, the Department has consulted the Securities and Exchange Commission to avoid duplicative, overlapping, or conflicting requirements.

The Department is unaware of any additional relevant federal rules for small plans that duplicate, overlap, or conflict with these proposed regulations.

(e) Comments

The Department invites interested persons to submit comments regarding the impact on small plans of the proposed regulation and on the Department's assessment thereof. The Department also requests

(Footnote Continued)

---

reporting provisions and limited exemptions from reporting and disclosure requirements for small plans, including unfunded or insured welfare plans, that cover fewer than 100 participants and satisfy certain other requirements.

comments on the alternatives considered and its conclusions regarding those alternatives; on any additional alternatives it should have considered; on what, if any, special problems small plans might encounter if the proposal were to be adopted; and what changes, if any, could be made to minimize those problems.

Paperwork Reduction Act

As part of its continuing effort to reduce paperwork and respondent burden, the Department of Labor conducts a pre-clearance consultation program to provide the general public and Federal agencies with an opportunity to comment on proposed and continuing collections of information in accordance with the Paperwork Reduction Act of 1995 (PRA 95) (44 U.S.C. 3506(c)(2)(A)). This helps to ensure that the public understands the Department's collection instructions; respondents can provide the requested data in the desired format, reporting burden (time and financial resources) is minimized, collection instruments are clearly understood, and the Department can properly assess the impact of collection requirements on respondents.

Currently, the Department is soliciting comments concerning the proposed information collection request (ICR) included in the proposed regulation. A copy of the ICR may be obtained by contacting the PRA addressee shown below or at *http://www.RegInfo.gov*.

The Department has submitted a copy of the proposed regulation to OMB in accordance with 44 U.S.C. 3507(d) for review of its information collections. The Department and OMB are particularly interested in comments that:

- Evaluate whether the collection of information is necessary for the proper performance of the functions of the agency, including whether the information will have practical utility;

- Evaluate the accuracy of the agency's estimate of the burden of the collection of information, including the validity of the methodology and assumptions used;

- Enhance the quality, utility, and clarity of the information to be collected; and

- Minimize the burden of the collection of information on those who are to respond, including through the use of appropriate automated, electronic, mechanical, or other technological collection techniques or other forms of information technology, *e.g.,* permitting electronic submission of responses.

Comments should be sent to the Office of Information and Regulatory Affairs, Office of Management and Budget, Room 10235, New Executive Office Building, Washington, DC 20503; Attention: Desk Officer for the Employee Benefits Security Administration. OMB requests that comments be received within 30 days of publication of the Notice of Proposed Rulemaking to ensure their consideration. Please note that comments submitted to OMB are a matter of public record.

PRA Addressee: Gerald B. Lindrew, Office of Policy and Research, U.S. Department of Labor, Employee Benefits Security Administration, 200 Constitution Avenue, NW., Room N-5718, Washington, DC 20210. Telephone (202) 693-8410; Fax: (202) 219-4745. These are not toll-free numbers.

In connection with publication of this proposed rule, the Department has submitted an ICR to OMB for its request of a revised information collection under OMB Control number 1210-0090. This is the control number for the Department's existing regulation under ERISA section 404(c), which would be amended by the proposal.[40] The public is advised that an agency may not conduct or sponsor, and a person is not required to respond to, a collection of information unless it displays a currently valid OMB control number. The Department will include a notice announcing OMB's action at the final rule stage.

The proposed regulation on Fiduciary Requirements for Disclosure in Participant-Directed Individual Account Plans would require the disclosure of plan and investmentrelated fee and expense information to participants and beneficiaries in participant-directed individual account plans. This ICR pertains to two categories of information that is required to be disclosed: "plan-related" and "investment-related" information. The information collection provisions of the proposal are intended to ensure that fiduciaries provide participants and beneficiaries with sufficient information regarding plan fees and expenses and designated investment alternatives to make informed decisions regarding the management of their individual accounts.

The estimates of respondents and responses are derived primarily from the Form 5500 Series filings for the 2005 plan year, which is the most recent reliable data available to the Department. The burden for the preparation and distribution of the disclosures is treated as an hour burden. Additional cost burden derives from materials and postage and costs to track and report required information. It is assumed that electronic means of communication will be used in 38 percent of the responses pertaining to annual notices and that such communications will make use of existing systems that comply with the Department's electronic media disclosure guidance (29 CFR 2520.104b-1(c)). Accordingly, no cost has been attributed to the electronic distribution of the information.

The Department estimates that approximately 437,000 participant directed individual account plans[41] covering 65,269,000 participants would be affected by the proposed regulation. Of these plans, 275,000 plans, covering 49,212,000 participants and beneficiaries are reported to comply with ERISA section 404(c), and the remaining 162,000 plans covering 16,057,000 participants and beneficiaries are not. The Department's estimates of the number of plans and participants are summarized in Table 22 below.

TABLE 22.—*Number of Plans and Participants*

Type of Plan	Plans	Participants
404(c)	275,000	49,212,000
Non-404(c)	162,000	16,057,000
Total	437,000	65,269,000

Note: The displayed numbers are rounded to the nearest thousand and therefore may not add up to the totals.

Plan-related Information-29 CFR 2550.404a-5(c). The proposal requires three subcategories of Plan-related information to be provided to participants and beneficiaries. The first sub-category is General Plan Information, which provides: how participants and beneficiaries may give investment instructions; any specified limitations on such instructions, including any restrictions on transfer to or from a designated investment alternative; the exercise of voting, tender and similar rights appurtenant to an investment in a designated investment alternative as well as any restrictions on such rights; the specific designated investment alternatives offered under the plan; and any designated investment managers to whom participants and beneficiaries may give investment directions. (§2550.404a-5(c)(1)(i)). This information must be provided on or before the date a participant becomes eligible to participate in the plan, and afterwards at least annually. Material changes to this information must be disclosed not more than 30 days after adoption. Plans may make these disclosures in the summary plan description.

The second subcategory of Plan-related Information is Administrative Expense Information, which refers to an explanation of any fees and expenses for plan administrative services (e.g., legal, accounting, recordkeeping) that, to the extent not included in investment-related fees and expenses, may be charged against the individual accounts of participants or beneficiaries and the basis on which such charges will be allocated to, or affect the balance of, each individual account (e.g., pro rata, per capita). (§2550.404a-5(c)(2)). This information must be provided on or before the date a participant becomes eligible to participate in the plan, and afterwards at least annually. At least quarterly, plans must furnish statements of the aggregate dollar amount charged to each participant's account for these services. Plans may make the initial and annual disclosures in the summary plan description or the

---

[40] See 29 CFR 2550.404c-1. The information collection provisions of the NPRM impose new hour and cost burdens on all participant directed individual account plans, and the Department intends to include the burden imposed by the proposal on 404(c) and not-404(c) compliant participant directed individual account plans under one control number.

[41] All numbers stated in this document have been rounded to the nearest 1,000. Any apparent discrepancy in the calculations described here is due to this rounding.

quarterly benefit statement, and the quarterly information may be included in the plan's quarterly benefit statements.

The third subcategory of Plan-related Information is Individual Expense Information, which describes expenses charged to individual accounts based on the actions taken by individual participants or beneficiaries. This would include charges for processing participant loans and qualified domestic relations orders. (§ 2550.404a-5(c)(3)). Information describing these charges must be furnished on or before the date a participant's eligibility and annually thereafter. Plans must provide quarterly statements identifying and showing the dollar amounts of each expense actually charged to an account. Plans may make the initial and annual disclosures in the summary plan description or the quarterly benefit statement, and the quarterly information may be included in the plan's quarterly benefit statements.

First Year

Annual Disclosure: The Department assumes that in the year of implementation, all 437,000 affected plans will conduct a legal review to verify their compliance with the proposed regulation and prepare the required disclosures. The Department estimates that the review would, on average, take one-half hour of a legal professional's time at an (inhouse) hourly rate[42] of $113 resulting in a total aggregate estimate of approximately 218,000 legal hours at an equivalent cost of approximately $24,628,000. In addition, the Department estimates that each plan will spend one-half hour of clerical time at an (inhouse) hourly rate of $26 preparing the disclosures. This would result in an hour burden of about 218,000 clerical burden hours with an equivalent cost of approximately $5,694,000. These estimates are summarized in Table 23 below.

TABLE 23.—*Plan-Related Information, General Information, First Year*

Type of Plan	Number of Affected Plans	Professional Hours	Clerical Hours	Total Professional Hours	Total Clerical Hours	Equivalent Cost-Professional	Equivalent Cost-Clerical
404(c)	275,000	0.5	0.5	137,000	137,000	$15,491,000	$3,582,000
Non-404(c)	162,000	0.5	0.5	81,000	81,000	91,370,200	2,112,000
Total	437,000			218,000	218,000	24,628,000	5,694,000

Note: The displayed numbers are rounded to the nearest thousand and therefore may not add up to the totals.

The Department assumes that plans will send 65,269,000 copies of the required plan information[43] to plan participants and beneficiaries, which will contain an average of 10 pages. Paper and printing costs are expected to be 5 cents per page and mailing costs are expected to be 76 cents per mailed disclosure. It is assumed that 38 percent of the disclosures will be delivered electronically. This results in a cost burden of $50,988,000, as shown in Table 24.

TABLE 24.—*Plan Related Information, Annual, Cost Burden*

Type of Plan	Number of Disclosures	Percent Sent by Mail	Number of Pages	Paper and Printing Cost per Page	Mailing Cost	Cost Burden
404(c)	49,212,000	62%	10	$0.05	$0.76	$38,444,000
Non-404(c)	16,057,000	62%	10	0.05	0.76	12,544,000
Total	65,269,000					50,988,000

Note: The displayed numbers are rounded to the nearest thousand and therefore may not add up to the totals.

Quarterly Disclosure: Plans will also have to determine the administrative and individual fees that will be charged directly against participants' accounts on a quarterly basis.[44] The Department estimates a cost burden of approximately $26,543,000 in the first year to establish new information systems or accounting practices that will collect, track and report the actual dollar amounts charged to the individual accounts. This cost is shown in Table 25.[45]

TABLE 25.—*Plan-Related Information, Cost Burden, First Year*

Type of Plan	Number of Disclosures	Per Participant Cost From GAO Report	Percent of Cost for Calculating Administrative Fees	Cost Burden
404(c)	49,212,000	$1.22	1/3	$20,013,000
Non-404(c)	16,057,000	1.22	1/3	6,530,000
Total	65,269,000			26,543,000

Note: The displayed numbers are rounded to the nearest thousand and therefore may not add up to the totals.

Subsequent Years

Annual Disclosure: Based on the 2005 Form 5500 data the Department estimates that approximately 74,000 new participant-directed individual account plans would be required to disclose general plan information each year.[46] The Department assumes that on average writing a new disclosure notice for these plans would require one-half

---

[42] The hourly wage estimates used in this analysis are estimates for 2009 and are based on data from the Bureau of Labor Statistics National Occupational Employment Survey (May 2005) and the Bureau of Labor Statistics Employment Cost Index (Sept. 2006).

[43] While plans are allowed to provide the disclosure in the SPD or quarterly benefit statement, the paperwork analysis assumes that plans would provide the required disclosures in a separate mailing to reduce costs as they otherwise are not required to send the SPD every year.

[44] It is assumed that the inclusion of the actual dollar disclosure will add a minimal burden that has not been quantified.

[45] The increase in administrative costs resulting from disclosing actual dollar fee and expense disclosure is derived from a GAO report (GAO-03-551T, "Mutual Funds: Informa-

tion on Trends in Fees and Their Related Disclosure," March 12, 2003, p.14), which measures the cost of the disclosures of the actual dollar amount of mutual fund investment expenses on a participant level. The GAO report estimates the initial cost to generate these disclosures in 2001 at $1 per account, and the annual cost of continued compliance at $0.35 per account. The cost to plans to calculate administrative fees for purposes of the NPRM is expected to be less, because most of the expense information to be disclosed under the regulation is already tracked. The Department assumes it may cost plans one-third less to provide these administrative disclosures than it does for mutual funds to disclose investment costs, leading to cost estimates in 2009 dollars of about 41 cents per plan participant in the first year and 14 cents thereafter.

[46] The 74,000 new plans include newly created participant directed account plans as well as some existing participant directed account plans that newly elect to be 404(c) compliant

hour of legal professional time and one-half hour of clerical time per plan.

This results in an hour burden of nearly 37,000 hours for legal professional work and 37,000 hours of clerical work. The hour burden

has an equivalent cost of approximately $4,168,000 for legal professional time at $113 per hour and $964,000 for clerical time at $26 per hour. These estimates are summarized in Table 26 below.

TABLE 26.—*Plan-Related Information, General Information, New Plans, Annual, Subsequent Years*

Type of New Plans	Number of New Plans	Professional Hours	Clerical Hours	Total Professional Hours	Total Clerical Hours	Equivalent Cost - Professional	Equivalent Cost- Clerical
404(c)	46,000	0.5	0.5	23,000	23,000	$2,621,000	$606,000
Non-404(c)	27,000	0.5	0.5	14,000	14,000	1,546,000	3,578,000
Total	74,000			37,000	37,000	4,168,000	964,000

Note: The displayed numbers are rounded to the nearest thousand and therefore may not add up to the totals.

The Department also estimates that 363,000 existing plans will require one-quarter hour of legal professional time and one-quarter hour of clerical staff time to update plan documents to take into account plan changes, such as new investment alternatives, in subsequent years.

This results in an hour burden of approximately 91,000 hours for professional time and 91,000 hours for clerical time with an equivalent cost of approximately $10,230,000 for professional time and $2,365,000 for clerical time as summarized in Table 27 below.

TABLE 27.—*Plan-Related Information, General Information, Existing Plans, Annual, Subsequent Years*

Existing Plans	Number of Revised Disclosures	Professional Hours	Clerical Hours	Total Professional Hours	Total Clerical Hours	Equivalent Cost- Professional	Equivalent Cost- Clerical
404(c)	228,000	0.25	0.25	57,000	57,000	$6,435,000	$1,488,000
Non-404(c)	135,000	0.25	0.25	34,000	34,000	3,795,000	878,000
Total	363,000			91,000	91,000	10,230,000	2,365,000

Note: The displayed numbers are rounded to the nearest thousand and therefore may not add up to the totals.

As with the first year, the Department assumes that plans will send 65,269,000 copies of the required plan information to plan participants and beneficiaries in all subsequent years, resulting in a cost burden of $50,988,000.

Quarterly Disclosures: In subsequent years plans will also have to determine the administrative and individual fees that will be charged

directly against participants' accounts on a quarterly basis. The Department estimates a cost burden of approximately $9,355,000 in the subsequent years to maintain the information systems or accounting practices that will collect, track and report the actual dollar amounts charged to the individual accounts. This cost is shown in Table 28.

TABLE 28.—*Plan-Related Information, Cost Burden, Annual, Subsequent Years*

Type of Plan	Number of Disclosures	Per Participant Cost From GAO Report	Percent of Cost for Calculating Administrative Fees	Cost Burden
404(c)	49,212,000	$0.43	1/3	$7,054,000
Non-404(c)	16,057,000	0.43	1/3	2,302,000
Total	65,269,000			9,355,000

Note: The displayed numbers are rounded to the nearest thousand and therefore may not add up to the totals.

Investment-related Information— 29 CFR 2550.404a-5(d). The proposal requires three sub-categories of Investment-related Information to be disclosed, which relates to the plans designated investment alternatives.

Sub-Category 1: Information to be Provided Automatically

The first subcategory is information to be provided automatically. (§ 2550.404a-5(d)(1)). For each designated investment alternative, the plan, based on the latest information available, must disclose specified identifying information, past performance data, comparable benchmark returns, and fee and expense information. This information must be furnished on or before the date of a participant's eligibility and annually

thereafter. This information must be furnished in a chart or similar format designed to help participants compare the plan's investment alternatives. (§ 2550.404a-5(d)(2)). To facilitate compliance, the proposal includes a model disclosure form that may be used by plan fiduciaries.

Preparation : The Department assumes that the preparation of a comparative chart containing specified identifying information, past performance data, comparable benchmark returns, and fee and expense information will require one hour of accountant or financial professional time at an hourly rate of $60, which would result in an hour burden of approximately 437,000 hours at an equivalent cost of about $26,290,000. These estimates are summarized in Table 29 below.

TABLE 29.—*Investment-Related Information, Information Provided Automatically, Preparation*

Type of Plan	Number of Plans	Professional Hours	Total Professional Hours	Equivalent Cost- Professional
404(c)	275,000	1	275,000	$16,537,000

(Footnote Continued)

in subsequent years. Plans that newly elect to be 404(c) compliant in subsequent years had to previously comply with the new requirements and therefore might need to spend

slightly less time on the review of the 404(c) requirements than the time indicated in Table 19.

Type of Plan	Number of Plans	Professional Hours	Total Professional Hours	Equivalent Cost- Professional
Non-404(c)	162,000	1	162,000	9,754,000
Total	437,000		437,000	26,290,000

Note: The displayed numbers are rounded to the nearest thousand and therefore may not add up to the totals.

Distribution: The comparative chart needs to be sent to all participants (65.3 million). Given that 38 percent (24.8 million) of all disclosures are made electronically, only 62 percent will be sent by mail (40.5 million). The Department assumes that clerical staff could spend, on average, two minutes per disclosure to copy and mail this information. This burden is shown in Table 30.

TABLE 30.—I *nvestment-Related Information, Information Provided Automatically, Annual, Distribution*

Type of Plan	Total Number of Participants	Disclosures by Mail	Number of Disclosures	Clerical Hours Per Disclosure	Total Clerical Hours	Equivalent Cost - Clerical
404(c)	49,212,000	62%	30,511,000	0.033	1,017,000	$26,514,000
Non-404(c)	16,057,000	62%	9,955,000	0.033	332,000	8,651,000
Total	65,269,000		40,467,000		1,349,000	35,166,000

Note: The displayed numbers are rounded to the nearest thousand and therefore may not add up to the totals.

It is assumed this disclosure will be three pages. As this information is required to be sent on an annual basis, the Department assumes it will be sent with the plan-related information required pursuant to § 2550.404a-5(c). Mailing costs are already accounted for in the calculation of the cost burden for delivery of the plan-related information. Table 31 shows the resulting annual cost burden of $6,070,000.

TABLE 31.—*Investment-Related Information, Information Provided Automatically, Cost Burden*

Type of Plan	Number of Disclosures	Percent Sent by Mail	Number of Pages	Paper and Printing Cost per Page	Cost Burden
404(c)	49,212,000	62%	3	$0.05	$4,577,000
Non-404(c)	16,057,000	62%	3	0.05	1,493,000
Total	65,269,000				6,070,000

Note: The displayed numbers are rounded to the nearest thousand and therefore may not add up to the totals.

Sub-Category 2: Post-Investment Information

The second sub-category is post-investment information. The proposal requires that when a plan provides for the pass-through of voting, tender and similar rights, the fiduciary must furnish participants and beneficiaries who have invested in a designated investment alternative with these features any materials about such rights that have been provided to the plan. See § 2550.404a-5(d)(3). This requirement is similar to the requirement currently applicable to section 404(c) plans ("pass-through materials").

Distribution: The Department assumes that clerical staff will prepare and send the required materials. It may take the clerical staff on average one and one-half minutes to prepare and mail the post-investment materials. It is further assumed that this disclosure will be sent to about 15,153,000 plan participants in plans that have assets invested in employer securities. This number was reduced to reflect that some participants already receive this information pursuant to the Department's Qualified Default Investment Alternative regulation (QDIA)[47] and the burden is counted under OMB Control Number 1210-0132. The Department expects 38 percent of the disclosures will be sent electronically resulting in no burden. This results in an hour burden of approximately 235,000 hours of clerical staff time, with an equivalent cost of $6,123,000. Table 32 reports the estimates of the burden.

TABLE 32.—*Investment-Related Information, Post Investment Information, Distribution*

Type of Plan	Number of Disclosures	Clerical Hours	Total Clerical Hours	Equivalent Cost - Clerical
404(c)	11,656,000	0.025	181,000	$4,710,000
Non-404(c)	3,497,000	0.025	54,000	1,413,000
Total	15,153,000		235,000	6,123,000

Note: The displayed numbers are rounded to the nearest thousand and therefore may not add up to the totals.

The required post-investment information is assumed to be, on average, ten pages long, with mailing costs of $0.59 per disclosure. As Table 33 shows, this results in an annual cost burden of $10,240,000.

[47] 29 CFR 2550.404c-5 (Oct. 24, 2007).

TABLE 33.—*Investment-Related Information, Post-Investment Information, Cost Burden*

Type of Plan	Number of Disclosures	Percent Sent by Mail	Number of Pages	Paper and Printing Cost per Page	Mailing Cost	Cost Burden
404(c)	11,656,000	62%	10	$0.05	$0.59	$7,877,000
Non-404(c)	3,497,000	62%	10	0.05	0.59	2,363,000
Total	15,153,000					10,240,000

Note: The displayed numbers are rounded to the nearest thousand and therefore may not add up to the totals.

Sub-Category 3: Information to be Provided Upon Request

The third subcategory is information to be provided upon request. (§ 2550.404a-5(d)(4)). Participants may request the plan to provide prospectuses, financial reports, as well as statements of valuation and of assets held by an investment alternative.

Preparation: Plans must be prepared to provide the required information on request. The Department expects all plans to receive, on average, one request per year for the information. The Department estimates that plans will need to devote, on average, one clerical staff hour to comply with this requirement. Paperwork burden for this requirement is divided between § 2550.404c-5 (Fiduciary relief for investments in qualified default investment alternatives), which was accounted for previously under OMB Control Number 1210-0132 (QDIA regulation), and § 2550.404c-1 (ERISA section 404(c) plans), which is reflected in Table 34 below.

TABLE 34.—*Investment-Related Information, Information on Request, Annual, Preparation*

Type of Plan	Number of Disclosures	Clerical Hours	Total Clerical Hours	Equivalent Cost - Clerical
404(c)	275,000	1	275,000	$7,164,000
Non-404(c)	0	1	0	0
Total	275,000		275,000	7,164,000

Note: The displayed numbers are rounded to the nearest thousand and therefore may not add up to the totals.

Distribution: The Department estimates that in total, plans will respond to approximately 275,000 requests for information annually. It is assumed that 38 percent of the disclosures will be delivered electronically. For the remaining 62 percent of disclosures (170,000 requests annually), the Department has assumed that these disclosures will be sent by mail and estimates that reproduction and distribution of these disclosures will take 2 minutes of clerical time per request. Plans will therefore have an additional annual hour burden of 5,700 hours (170,000 requests notices x 0.033 hours). The equivalent cost of these hours is $148,000. Table 35 contains the estimates of the burden.

TABLE 35.—*Investment-Related Information, Information on Request, Annual, Distribution*

Type of Plan	Number of Disclosures by Mail	Clerical Hours	Total Clerical Hours	Equivalent Cost - Clerical
404(c)	170,000	0.033	6,000	$148,000
Non-404(c)	. . . .	. . . .	. . . .	. . . .
Total	170,000		6,000	148,000

Note: The displayed numbers are rounded to the nearest thousand and therefore may not add up to the totals.

As some of these disclosures are accounted for under the QDIA regulation, the cost burden for the remainder is estimated at approximately $271,000 based on an average page length of 20 pages and mailing costs of $0.59 as shown in Table 36, below.

TABLE 36.—*Investment Related Information, Information on Request, Annual, Cost Burden*

Type of Plan	Number of Disclosures	Percent Sent by Mail	Number of Pages	Paper and Printing Cost per Page	Mailing Cost	Cost Burden
404(c)	275,000	62%	20	$0.05	$0.59	$271,000
Non-404(c)	0	62%	20	0.05	0.59	0
Total	275,000					271,000

Note: The displayed numbers are rounded to the nearest thousand and therefore may not add up to the totals.

Summary

The Department has estimated the hour burden in the first year to be 2,732,000 hours with an equivalent cost of $105,065,000, as shown in Table 37. The hour burden in the subsequent years is estimated to be 2,551,000 hours with an equivalent cost of $92,470,000, as shown Table 38.

TABLE 37.—*Hour Burden for First Year*

Type of Plan	Professional Hour Burden	Clerical Hour Burden	Total Hours	Equivalent Cost- Professional	Equivalent Cost - Clerical	Total Equivalent Cost
404(c)	412,000	1,610,000	2,022,000	32,028,000	$41,970,000	$73,998,000
Non-404(c)	243,000	467,000	710,000	18,891,000	12,177,000	31,068,000
Total	655,000	2,077,000	2,732,000	50,918,000	54,147,000	105,065,000

Note: The displayed numbers are rounded to the nearest thousand and therefore may not add up to the totals.

TABLE 38.—*Hour Burden for Years Two and Three*

Type of Plan	Professional Hour Burden	Clerical Hour Burden	Total Hours	Equivalent Cost- Professional	Equivalent Cost - Clerical	Total Equivalent Cost
404(c)	355,000	1,553,000	1,908,000	25,593,000	$40,482,000	$66,075,000
Non-404(c)	209,000	433,000	643,000	15,095,000	11,299,000	26,395,000
Total	565,000	1,986,000	2,551,000	40,688,000	51,781,000	92,470,000

Note: The displayed numbers are rounded to the nearest thousand and therefore may not add up to the totals.

The Department has estimated the cost burden in the first year to be $94,112,000; and $76,925,000 in the subsequent years. These estimates are shown in Table39.

TABLE 39.—*Total Cost Burden*

Type of Plan	First Year - Total Cost Burden	Subsequent Years - Total Cost Burden
404(c)	$71,182,000	$58,223,000
Non-404(c)	22,930,000	18,702,000
Total	94,112,000	76,925,000

Note: The displayed numbers are rounded to the nearest thousand and therefore may not add up to the totals.

Type of Review : Revised collection.

Agency : Employee Benefits Security Administration, Department of Labor.

Title : Fiduciary Requirements for Disclosure in Participant-Directed Individual Account Plans

OMB Number : 1210-0090.

Affected Public : Business or other for-profit; not-for-profit institutions.

Respondents : 437,000

Responses : 407,042,000

Frequency of Response : Annually; quarterly.

Estimated Annual Burden Hours : 2,732,000 hours in the first year; 2,551,000 hours in each subsequent year.

Estimated Annual Burden Cost : $94,112,000 in the first year; $76,925,000 in each subsequent year.

Congressional Review Act Statement

This notice of proposed rulemaking is subject to the Congressional Review Act provisions of the Small Business Regulatory Enforcement Fairness Act of 1996 (5 U.S.C. 801 *et seq.*) and, if finalized, will be transmitted to the Congress and the Comptroller General for review.

Unfunded Mandates Reform Act Statement

For purposes of the Unfunded Mandates Reform Act of 1995 (Pub. L. 104-4), as well as Executive Order 12875, the notice of proposed rulemaking does not include any federal mandate that will result in expenditures by state, local, or tribal governments in the aggregate of more than $100 million, adjusted for inflation, or increase expenditures by the private sector of more than $100 million, adjusted for inflation.

Federalism Statement

Executive Order 13132 (August 4, 1999) outlines fundamental principles of federalism and requires the adherence to specific criteria by Federal agencies in the process of their formulation and implementation of policies that have substantial direct effects on the States, the relationship between the national government and the States, or on the distribution of power and responsibilities among the various levels of government. The proposed regulations would not have federalism implications because they have no substantial direct effect on the States, on the relationship between the national government and the States, or on the distribution of power and responsibilities among the various levels of government. Section 514 of ERISA provides, with certain exceptions specifically enumerated that are not pertinent here, that the provisions of Titles I and IV of ERISA supersede State laws that relate to any employee benefit plan covered by ERISA. The requirements implemented in the proposed regulations do not alter the fundamental provisions of the statute with respect to employee benefit plans, and as such would have no implications for the States or the relationship or distribution of power between the national government and the States.

List of Subjects in 29 CFR Part 2550

Employee benefit plans, Fiduciaries, Investments, Pensions, Disclosure, Reporting and recordkeeping requirements, and Securities.

For the reasons set forth in the preamble, the Department proposes to amend Subchapter F, Part 2550 of Title 29 of the Code of Federal Regulations as follows:

SUBCHAPTER F—FIDUCIARY RESPONSIBILITY UNDER THE EMPLOYEE RETIREMENT INCOME SECURITY ACT OF 1974

PART 2550—RULES AND REGULATIONS FOR FIDUCIARY RESPONSIBILITY

1. The authority citation for part 2550 continues to read as follows:

Authority: 29 U.S.C. 1135; sec. 657, Pub. L. 107-16, 115 Stat.38; and Secretary of Labor's Order No. 1-2003, 68 FR 5374 (Feb. 3, 2003). Sec. 2550.401b-1 also issued under sec. 102, Reorganization Plan No. 4 of 1978, 43 FR 47713 (Oct. 17, 1978), 3 CFR, 1978 Comp. 332, effective Dec. 31, 1978, 44 FR 1065 (Jan. 3, 1978), 3 CFR, 1978 Comp. 332. Sec. 2550.401c-1 also issued under 29 U.S.C. 1101. Sections 2550.404c-1 and 2550.404c-5 also issued under 29 U.S.C. 1104. Sec. 2550.407c-3 also issued under 29 U.S.C. 1107. Sec. 2550.408b-1 also issued under 29 U.S.C. 1108(b)(1) and sec. 102, Reorganization Plan No. 4 of 1978, 3

CFR, 1978 Comp. p. 332, effective Dec. 31, 1978, 44 FR 1065 (Jan. 3, 1978), and 3 CFR, 1978 Comp. 332. Sec. 2550.412-1 also issued under 29 U.S.C. 1112.

2. Add § 2550.404a-5 to read as follows:

§ 2550.404a-5—Fiduciary requirements for disclosure in participant-directed individual account plans.

(a) *General.* The investment of plan assets is a fiduciary act governed by the fiduciary standards of section 404(a)(1)(A) and (B) of the Employee Retirement Income Security Act of 1974, as amended (ERISA), 29 U.S.C. 1001 *et seq.* (all section references herein are references to ERISA unless otherwise indicated). Pursuant to section 404(a)(1)(A) and (B), fiduciaries must discharge their duties with respect to the plan prudently and solely in the interest of participants and beneficiaries. Where the documents and instruments governing an individual account plan, as defined in section (3)(34), provide for the allocation of investment responsibilities to participants or beneficiaries, fiduciaries, consistent with section 404(a)(1)(A) and (B), must take steps to ensure that such participants and beneficiaries, on a regular and periodic basis, are made aware of their rights and responsibilities with respect to the investment of assets held in, or contributed to, their accounts and are provided sufficient information regarding the plan, including fees and expenses, and regarding designated investment alternatives, including fees and expenses attendant thereto, to make informed decisions with regard to the management of their individual accounts.

(b) *Satisfaction of duty to disclose.* For plan years beginning on or after January 1, 2009, the fiduciary (or fiduciaries) of an individual account plan must comply with the disclosure requirements set forth in paragraphs (c) and (d) of this section with respect to each participant or beneficiary that, pursuant to the terms of the plan, has the right to direct the investment of assets held in, or contributed to, his or her individual account. Compliance with paragraphs (c) and (d) of this section will satisfy the duty to make the regular and periodic disclosures described in paragraph (a) of this section.

(c) *Disclosure of plan-related information.* A fiduciary (or a person or persons designated by the fiduciary to act on its behalf) shall provide to each participant or beneficiary the plan-related information described in paragraphs (c)(1) through (3) of this section, based on the latest information available to the plan.

(1) *General.*

(i) On or before the date of plan eligibility and at least annually thereafter:

(A) An explanation of the circumstances under which participants and beneficiaries may give investment instructions;

(B) An explanation of any specified limitations on such instructions under the terms of the plan, including any restrictions on transfer to or from a designated investment alternative;

(C) A description of or reference to plan provisions relating to the exercise of voting, tender and similar rights appurtenant to an investment in a designated investment alternative as well as any restrictions on such rights;

(D) An identification of any designated investment alternatives offered under the plan; and

(E) An identification of any designated investment managers; and

(ii) Not later than 30 days after the date of adoption of any material change to the information described in paragraph (c)(1)(i) of this section, each participant and beneficiary shall be furnished a description of such change.

(2) *Administrative expenses.*

(i) On or before the date of plan eligibility and at least annually thereafter, an explanation of any fees and expenses for plan administrative services (e.g., legal, accounting, recordkeeping) that, to the extent not otherwise included in investment-related fees and expenses, may be charged to the plan and the basis on which such charges will be allocated (e.g., pro rata, per capita) to, or affect the balance of, each individual account, and

(ii) At least quarterly, a statement that includes:

(A) The dollar amount actually charged during the preceding quarter to the participant's or beneficiary's account for administrative services, and

(B) A description of the services provided to the participant or beneficiary for such amount (e.g., recordkeeping).

(3) *Individual expenses.*

(i) On or before the date of plan eligibility and at least annually thereafter, an explanation of any fees and expenses that may be charged against the individual account of a participant or beneficiary for services provided on an individual, rather than plan, basis (e.g., fees attendant to processing plan loans or qualified domestic relations orders, fees for investment advice or similar services charged on an individual basis), and

(ii) At least quarterly, a statement that includes:

(A) The dollar amount actually charged during the preceding quarter to the participant's or beneficiary's account for individual services, and

(B) A description of the services provided to the participant or beneficiary for such amount (e.g., fees attendant to processing plan loans).

(d) *Disclosure of investment-related information.* A fiduciary (or a person or persons designated by the fiduciary to act on its behalf), based on the latest information available to the plan, shall:

(1) *Information to be provided automatically.* Provide to each participant or beneficiary, on or before the date of plan eligibility and at least annually thereafter, the following information with respect to each designated investment alternative offered under the plan—

(i) *Identifying information.* Such information shall include:

(A) The name of the designated investment alternative;

(B) An Internet Web site address that is sufficiently specific to lead participants and beneficiaries to supplemental information regarding the designated investment alternative, including the name of the investment's issuer or provider, the investment's principal strategies and attendant risks, the assets comprising the investment's portfolio, the investment's portfolio turnover, the investment's performance and related fees and expenses;

(C) The type or category of the investment (e.g., money market fund, balanced (stocks and bonds) fund, large-cap fund); and,

(D) The type of management utilized by the investment (e.g., actively managed, passively managed);

(ii) *Performance data.* For designated investment alternatives with respect to which the return is not fixed, the average annual total return (percentage) of the investment for the following periods, if available: 1-year, 5-year, and 10-year, measured as of the end of the applicable calendar year; as well as a statement indicating that an investment's past performance is not necessarily an indication of how the investment will perform in the future. In the case of designated investment alternatives with respect to which the return is fixed for the term of the investment, both the fixed rate of return and the term of the investment;

(iii) *Benchmarks.* For designated investment alternatives with respect to which the return is not fixed, the name and returns of an appropriate broad-based securities market index over the 1-year, 5-year, and 10-year periods comparable to the performance data periods provided under paragraph (d)(1)(ii) of this section, and which is not administered by an affiliate of the investment provider, its investment adviser, or a principal underwriter, unless the index is widely recognized and used;

(iv) *Fee and expense information.* For designated investment alternatives with respect to which the return is not fixed:

(A) The amount and a description of each shareholder-type fee (i.e., fees charged directly against a participant's or beneficiary's investment), such as sales loads, sales charges, deferred sales charges, redemption fees, surrender charges, exchange fees, account fees, purchase fees, and mortality and expense fees;

(B) The total annual operating expenses of the investment expressed as a percentage (e.g., expense ratio); and

(C) A statement indicating that fees and expenses are only one of several factors that participants and beneficiaries should consider when making investment decisions. In the case of designated investment alternatives with respect to which the return is fixed for the term of the investment, the amount and a description of any shareholder-type fees that may be applicable to a purchase, transfer or withdrawal of the investment in whole or in part;

(v) *Disclosure on or before date of plan eligibility.* The requirement in paragraph (d)(1) of this section to provide information to a participant on or before the date of plan eligibility may be satisfied by furnishing to the participant the most recent annual disclosure furnished to participants and beneficiaries pursuant to paragraph (d)(1) of this section and any material changes to the information furnished to participants and beneficiaries pursuant to paragraph (c)(1)(ii) of this section.

(2) *Comparative format.* Furnish the information described in paragraph (d)(1) of this section in a chart or similar format that is designed to facilitate a comparison of such information for each designated investment alternative available under the plan; as well as:

(i) a statement indicating the name, address, and telephone number of the fiduciary (or a person or persons designated by the fiduciary to act on its behalf) to contact for the provision of the information required by paragraph (d)(4) of this section, and

(ii) A statement that more current investment-related information (e.g., fee and expense and performance information) may be available at the listed Internet Web site addresses (see paragraph (d)(1)(i)(B) of this section). Nothing herein, however, shall preclude a fiduciary from including additional information that the fiduciary determines appropriate for such comparisons, provided such information is not inaccurate or misleading;

(3) *Information to be provided subsequent to investment.* Provide to each investing participant or beneficiary, subsequent to an investment in a designated investment alternative, any materials provided to the plan relating to the exercise of voting, tender and similar rights appurtenant to the investment, to the extent that such rights are passed through to such participant or beneficiary under the terms of the plan;

(4) *Information to be provided upon request.* Provide to each participant or beneficiary, either at the times specified in paragraph (d)(1), or upon request, the following information relating to designated investment alternatives—

(i) Copies of prospectuses (or any short-form or summary prospectus, the form of which has been approved by the Securities and Exchange Commission) for the disclosure of information to investors by entities registered under either the Securities Act of 1933 or the Investment Company Act of 1940, or similar documents relating to designated investment alternatives that are provided by entities that are not registered under either of these Acts.

(ii) Copies of any financial statements or reports, such as statements of additional information and shareholder reports, and of any other similar materials relating to the plan's designated investment alternatives, to the extent such materials are provided to the plan;

(iii) A statement of the value of a share or unit of each designated investment alternative as well as the date of the valuation; and

(iv) A list of the assets comprising the portfolio of each designated investment alternative which constitute plan assets within the meaning of 29 CFR 2510.3-101 and the value of each such asset (or the proportion of the investment which it comprises);

(e) *Form of disclosure.* (1) The information required to be disclosed pursuant to paragraphs (c)(1), (c)(2)(i), and (c)(3)(i) of this section may be provided as part of the plan's summary plan description furnished pursuant to ERISA section 102 or as part of a pension benefit statement furnished pursuant to ERISA section 105(a)(1)(A)(i), if such summary plan description or pension benefit statement is furnished at a frequency that comports with paragraph (c)(1) of this section.

(2) The information required to be disclosed pursuant to paragraphs (c)(2)(ii) and (c)(3)(ii) of this section may be included as part of a pension benefit statement furnished pursuant to ERISA section 105(a)(1)(A)(i).

(3) A fiduciary that uses and accurately completes the model format set forth in the Appendix will be deemed to have satisfied the requirements of paragraph (d)(2) of this section.

(4) Except with respect to the dollar amounts required to be included under paragraphs (c)(2)(ii)(A) and (c)(3)(ii)(A) of this section, fees and expenses may be expressed in terms of a monetary amount, formula, percentage of assets, or per capita charge.

(5) The information required to be prepared by the fiduciary for disclosure under this section shall be written in a manner calculated to be understood by the average plan participant.

(f) *Selection and monitoring.* Nothing herein is intended to relieve a fiduciary from its duty to prudently select and monitor providers of services to the plan or designated investment alternatives offered under the plan.

(g) *Manner of furnishing.* Disclosures under this section shall be furnished in any manner consistent with the requirements of 29 CFR 2520.104b-1 of this chapter, including paragraph (c) of that section relating to the use of electronic media.

(h) *Definitions.* For purposes of this section, the term—

(1) *Designated investment alternative* means any investment alternative designated by the plan into which participants and beneficiaries may direct the investment of assets held in, or contributed to, their individual accounts. The term "designated investment alternative" shall not include "brokerage windows," "self-directed brokerage accounts," or similar plan arrangements that enable participants and beneficiaries to select investments beyond those designated by the plan.

(2) *Average annual total return* means the average annual profit or loss realized by a designated investment alternative at the end of a specified period, calculated in the same manner as average annual total return is calculated under Item 21 of Securities and Exchange Commission Form N-1A with respect to an open-end management investment company registered under the Investment Company Act of 1940.

(3) *Total annual operating expenses* means annual operating expenses of the designated investment alternative (e.g., investment management fees, distribution, service, and administrative expenses) that reduce the rate of return to participants and beneficiaries, expressed as a percentage, calculated in the same manner as total annual operating expenses is calculated under Instruction 3 to Item 3 of Securities and Exchange Commission Form N-1A with respect to an open-end management investment company registered under the Investment Company Act of 1940.

(4) *At least annually thereafter* means at least once in any 12-month period, without regard to whether the plan operates on a calendar or fiscal year basis.

(5) *At least quarterly* means at least once in any 3-month period, without regard to whether the plan operates on a calendar or fiscal year basis.

APPENDIX to § 2550.404a-5—Model Comparative Chart

ABC Corporation 401k Savings Plan

Investment Options—January 1, 200X

Whether you will have adequate savings at retirement will depend in large part on how much you choose to save and how you invest your savings. The following information will assist you in comparing the designated investment options available to you under the **ABC Corporation 401k Savings Plan**.

While the information furnished below is important to making informed investment decisions, you should carefully review all available information about an investment option prior to directing your retirement savings into an investment option. Internet Web site addresses are provided to help you access additional information (such as investment strategies and risks, portfolio holdings and turnover) about each of the plan's investment options. You may also contact your plan representative, [insert name of fiduciary or designee] at [insert telephone number and address] for additional information or visit the Department of Labor's Web site for general information on investing for retirement. See www.dol.gov/ebsa/investing.html

Part I. Performance Information

This chart shows each option's performance over several time periods and compares the performance with a recognized benchmark. For options with returns that vary over time, past performance does not guarantee how your investment in the option will perform in the future; your investment in these options could lose money.

Name/ Type of Option	Mgmt.	Fixed Return/ Term	Average Annual Total Return as of 12/31/0X 1yr. 5yr. 10yr.	Benchmark/Index as of 12/31/0X 1yr. 5yr. 10yr.
Stock Funds				
A Fund/S&P 500 Index www.Web site.com	Passive	NA	15.6% 6.1% 8.3%	15.8% 6.2% 8.4% S&P 500
B Fund/Large Cap www.Web site.com	Active	NA	8.9% .22% NA	-8.9% 5.9% 12.2% Russell 1000
C Fund/Int'l Stock www.Web site.com	Active	NA	4.3% 5.2% 11.2%	26.9% 15.4% 8.1% MSCI EAFE

Name/ Type of Option	Mgmt.	Fixed Return/ Term	Average Annual Total Return as of 12/31/0X 1yr. 5yr. 10yr.	Benchmark/Index as of 12/31/0X 1yr. 5yr. 10yr.
D Fund/Mid Cap ETF www.Web site.com	Passive	NA	15% 12.7% 11.4%	15% 13% 12% Russell Midcap
Bond Funds				
E Fund/Bond Index www.Web site.com	Passive	NA	4.3% 5.2% 6.2%	4.3% 5.1% 6.2% LBA U.S. Aggr. Bd.
Other				
F Fund/ GICs www.Web site.com	Active	NA	4.7% 4.4% 5%	5% 3% 3.8% US 91 Day T Bill
G Fund/Stable Value www.Web site.com	Active	NA	4.3% 4.0% 4.9%	4.7% 3.4% 4.3% Treasury CM
H 200X GIC www.Web site.com	NA	4% 2 yr.	NA NA NA	NA

Part II. Fees and Expense Information

This chart shows only investment-related fees and expenses for investment options offered in your plan. Fees and expenses are only one of many factors to consider when you decide to invest in an option. You may also want to think about whether an investment in a particular option, along with your other investments, will help you achieve your financial goals.

Name/ Type of Option	Total Annual Operating Expenses*	Shareholder/Shareholder-type Fees**
Stock Funds		
A Fund / S&P 500 Index	0.18%	$20 annual service fee assessed for accounts holding less than $10,000. May be waived in certain circumstances.
B Fund / Large Cap	2.45%	4.25% deferred sales charge against amounts redeemed within 12 months of purchase.
C Fund/International Stock	0.79%	5.75% sales charge against amounts invested.
D Fund/ Mid Cap ETF	0.20%	4.25% sales charge against amounts invested or redeemed.
Bond Funds		
E Fund/ Bond Index	0.50%	N/A
Other		
F Fund/ GICs	0.46%	10% charge against amounts withdrawn within 18 mos. of initial investment.
G Fund/ Stable Value	0.65%	Dollars withdrawn may not be transferred to a competing fund for 90 days after withdrawal.
H 200X GIC	NA	12% charge against amounts withdrawn before maturity.

* Total Annual Operating Expenses are ongoing expenses paid indirectly from your investment in this option each year, expressed as a percentage of the value of your investment in the option (*e.g.*, expense ratio).

** Shareholder/Shareholder-type Fees are fees paid directly from your investment in this option (*e.g.*, sales loads, sales charges, deferred sales charges, redemption fees, exchange fees, account fees, purchase fees, transfer or withdrawal fees, surrender charges, contract maintenance fees, and mortality and expense charges).

For an explanation of non investment-related fees and expenses, such as recordkeeping or loan processing fees that may be charged against your account, you may consult your [SPD], [insert name of annual disclosure used to satisfy §2550.404a-5(c)], [and][quarterly benefit statement]. The dollar amount actually charged to your account during the preceding quarter for such administrative or individual expenses will be reported to you on a quarterly basis.

NOTE: More current information about your plan's investment options, including fees and expenses and performance updates, may be available at the listed Internet Web site addresses.

3. In §2550.404c-1 revise (b)(2)(i)(B), (c)(1)(ii), and (f)(1), and add (d)(2)(iv) to read as follows:

§2550.404c-1—ERISA section 404(c) plans.

* * * * *

(b) * * *

(2) * * *

(i) * * *

(B) The participant or beneficiary is provided or has the opportunity to obtain sufficient information to make informed investment decisions with regard to investment alternatives available under the plan, and incidents of ownership appurtenant to such investments. For purposes of this subparagraph, a participant or beneficiary will be considered to have sufficient information if the participant or beneficiary is provided by an identified plan fiduciary (or a person or persons designated by the plan fiduciary to act on his behalf):

(*1*) An explanation that the plan is intended to constitute a plan described in section 404(c) of the Employee Retirement Income Security Act, and 29 CFR 2550.404c-1, and that the fiduciaries of the plan may be relieved of liability for any losses which are the direct and necessary result of investment instructions given by such participant or beneficiary;

(*2*) Identification of any designated investment managers;

(*3*) The information required pursuant to 29 CFR 2550.404a-5; and

(*4*) In the case of plans which offer an investment alternative which is designed to permit a participant or beneficiary to directly or indirectly acquire or sell any employer security (employer security alternative), a description of the procedures established to provide for the confidentiality of information relating to the purchase, holding and sale of employer securities, and the exercise of voting, tender and similar rights, by participants and beneficiaries, and the name, address and phone number of the plan fiduciary responsible for monitoring compliance with the procedures (see paragraphs (d)(2)(ii)(E)(4)(vii), (viii) and (ix) of this section).

* * * * *

(c) * * *

(1) * * *

(ii) For purposes of sections 404(c)(1) and 404(c)(2) of the Act and paragraphs (a) and (d) of this section, a participant or beneficiary will be deemed to have exercised control with respect to voting, tender or similar rights appurtenant to the participant's or beneficiary's ownership interest in an investment alternative, provided that the participant's or beneficiary's investment in the investment alternative was itself the result of an exercise of control; the participant or beneficiary was provided a reasonable opportunity to give instruction with respect to such incidents of ownership, including the provision of the information described in 29 CFR 2550.404a-5(d)(3); and the participant or beneficiary has not failed to exercise control by reason of the circumstances described in paragraph (c)(2) of this section with respect to such incidents of ownership.

* * * * *

(d) * * *

(2) * * *

(iv) Paragraph (d)(2)(i) of this section does not serve to relieve a fiduciary from its duty to prudently select and monitor any designated investment manager or designated investment alternative offered under the plan.

* * * * *

(f) * * *

(1) A plan is an individual account plan described in section 3(34) of the Act. The plan states that a plan participant or beneficiary may direct the plan administrator to invest any portion of his individual account in a particular diversified equity fund managed by an entity which is not affiliated with the plan sponsor, or any other asset administratively feasible for the plan to hold. However, the plan provides that the plan administrator will not implement certain listed instructions for which plan fiduciaries would not be relieved of liability under section 404(c) (see paragraph (d)(2)(ii) of this section). Plan participants and beneficiaries are permitted to give investment instructions during the first week of each month with respect to the equity fund and at any time with respect to other investments. The plan provides for the pass-through of voting, tender and similar rights incidental to the holding in the account of a participant or beneficiary of an ownership interest in the equity fund or any other investment alternative available under the plan. The plan administrator of Plan A provides each participant and beneficiary with the information described in paragraph (b)(2)(i)(B) of this section upon their entry into the plan (including the information that must be provided on or before plan eligibility pursuant to 29 CFR

2550.404a-5), and provides updated information in the event of any material change in the information provided. Subsequent to any investment by a participant or beneficiary, the plan administrator forwards to the investing participant or beneficiary any materials provided to the plan relating to the exercise of voting, tender or similar rights attendant to ownership of an interest in such investment (see paragraph (b)(2)(i)(B)(3) of this section and 29 CFR 2550.404a-5(d)(3)). Upon request, the plan administrator provides each participant or beneficiary with copies of any prospectuses (or similar documents relating to designated investment alternatives that are provided by entities that are not registered under the Securities Act of 1933 or the Investment Company Act of 1940), financial statements and reports, and any other materials relating to the designated investment alternatives available under the plan in accordance with 29 CFR 2550.404a-5(d)(4)(i) and (ii). Also upon request, the plan administrator provides each participant and beneficiary with other information required by 29 CFR 2550.404a-5(d)(4) with respect to the equity fund, which is a designated investment alternative, including information concerning the latest available value of the participant's or beneficiary's interest in the equity fund. Plan A meets the requirements of paragraph (b)(2)(i)(B) of this section regarding the provision of investment information. Note: The regulation imposes no additional obligation on the administrator to furnish or make available materials relating to the companies in which the equity fund invests (e.g., prospectuses, proxies, etc.).

* * * * *

Signed at Washington, DC, this 15t day of July, 2008.

Bradford P. Campbell ,

Assistant Secretary, Employee Benefits Security Administration, Department of Labor.

BILLING CODE 4510-29-P

[FR Doc. E8–16541 Filed 7–22–08; 8:45 am]

BILLING CODE 4510–29–P

[FR Doc. 2008-16541 Filed 07/22/2008 at 8:45 am; Publication Date: 07/23/2008]

¶ 20,537P

EBSA proposed regulations: Investment advice: Self-directed plans: IRAs: Fee leveling: Computer-modeling.—The Employee Benefits Security Administration (EBSA) has issued proposed regulations and a proposed class prohibited transaction exemption (Class PTE) (see CCH ¶ 16,713) on the provision of investment advice for self-directed individual account plans and individual retirement accounts (IRAs). They are intended to expand opportunities for plan fiduciaries to provide investment advice to such plan participants and beneficiaries without running afoul of prohibited transactions rules.

The proposed regulations, which were published in the *Federal Register* on August 22, 2008 (73 FR 49896), were reproduced below. The regulations were finalized January 21, 2009 (74 FR 3822). The preamble to the final regulations is at ¶ 24,278. The final regulations were withdrawn on November 20, 2009 (see ¶ 24,286).

¶ 20,537Q

Employee Benefits Security Administration (EBSA): Proposed rule: Self-directed plans: IRAs: Investment advice: Fiduciary adviser.—EBSA has issued a proposed extension of the effective date and applicability date of final regulations on investment advice provided to participants and beneficiaries of 401(k) plans and IRAs. The final regulations (CCH PENSION PLAN GUIDE ¶ 24,808C) are effective and apply to transactions occurring on or after March 23, 2009. EBSA proposes to extend for 60 days the effective and applicability date consistent with the January 20, 2009 memorandum from Rahm Emanuel, Chief of Staff for President Obama, directing all government agencies to consider extending the effective date of regulations already published in the Federal Register, which have not yet taken effect. Thus, the new effective and applicability date would be May 22, 2009.

The proposed regulation, which was published in the *Federal Register* on February 4, 2009 (74 FR 6007), was reproduced below. The final regulation was published in the Federal Register on March 20, 2009 (74 FR 11847). The preamble to the final regulation is reproduced at ¶ 24,280. The regulation is at ¶ 14,789B-1.

¶ 20,537R

Pension Benefit Guaranty Corporation (PBGC): Proposed rule: Privacy Act of 1974.—The Pension Benefit Guaranty Corporation (PBGC) has proposed amending its regulations implementing the Privacy Act of 1974, as amended, to exempt certain records that will be maintained in a system of records entitled "PBGC-17, Office of Inspector General Investigative File System)--PBGC" from the access, contest, and certain other provisions of the Privacy Act. The amendment would protect the information gathered to carry out the Office of Inspector General's law enforcement mission to investigate criminal, civil, and administrative matters.

The proposed regulations, which were published in the *Federal Register* on March 30, 2009 (74 FR 14100), were reproduced below. The final regulations were published in the *Federal Register* on June 8, 2009 (74 FR 27080). The preamble to the final regulations is reproduced at ¶ 24,282. The regulations are at ¶ 15,315A, ¶ 15,720B, ¶ 15,720F, ¶ 15,720U, ¶ 15,720V, ¶ 15,720W, ¶ 15,720X, ¶ 15,720Z, ¶ 15,721, ¶ 15,721B, ¶ 15,721B-1, ¶ 15,721B-2, and ¶ 15,721B-3.

¶ 20,537S

Pension Benefit Guaranty Corporation (PBGC): Proposed regulations: Uniformed Services Employment and Reemployment Rights Act of 1994 (USERRA): Guaranteed benefits.—The Pension Benefit Guaranty Corporation (PBGC) has issued proposed regulations that would harmonize the requirements of ERISA Title IV that guaranteed benefits be nonforfeitable on the plan termination date with the reemployment rights of service members under USERRA. The proposed rules would apply to reemployments under USERRA initiated on or after December 12, 1994.

The proposed regulations, which were published in the Federal Register on July 29, 2009 (74 FR 37666), were reproduced below. The final regulations were published in the Federal Register on November 17, 2009 (74 FR 59093). The preamble to the final regulations is at ¶ 24,284. The final regulations are reproduced at ¶ 15,315A and ¶ 15,421J.

¶ 20,537T

Employee Benefits Security Administration (EBSA): Proposed rule: Multiemployer plans: Endangered or critical status: Civil penalties under Pension Protection Act of 2006 (PPA).—The Employee Benefits Security Administration (EBSA) has issued proposed regulations that would establish procedures relating to the assessment of civil penalties under ERISA §502(c)(8). Under ERISA §502(c)(8), which was added by the Pension Protection Act of 2006 (PPA; P.L. 109-280), the Secretary of Labor is authorized to assess civil penalties against sponsors of multiemployer defined benefit plans that fail to adopt a funding improvement or rehabilitation plan in accordance with ERISA §305.

The proposed regulations, which were published in the Federal Register on September 4, 2009 (74 FR 45791), were reproduced below. The final regulations were published in the Federal Register on February 26, 2010 (75 FR 8796). The preamble to the final regulations is at ¶ 24,289. The final regulations are reproduced at ¶ 14,925G, ¶ 14,928YY-1, ¶ 14,928YY-2, ¶ 14,928YY-3, ¶ 14,928YY-4, ¶ 14,928YY-5, ¶ 14,928YY-6, ¶ 14,928YY-7, ¶ 14,928YY-8, ¶ 14,928YY-9, ¶ 14,928YY-10, ¶ 14,928YY-11, and ¶ 14,928YY-12.

¶ 20,537U

Pension Benefit Guaranty Corporation (PBGC): Proposed regulations: Reportable events: Pension Protection Act of 2006 (PPA).— The Pension Benefit Guaranty Corporation (PBGC) has issued proposed regulations that would amend the reportable events rules under ERISA §4043 to accommodate the changes to the funding and premium rules made by the Pension Protection Act of 2006 (P.L. 109-280). The proposed rules would eliminate most automatic waivers and filing extensions, add two new reportable events, and make other modifications to PBGC regulations.

The proposed regulations, which were published in the Federal Register on November 23, 2009 (74 FR 61248), are reproduced below.

Federal Register

Monday,

November 23, 2009

Part IV

Pension Benefit Guaranty Corporation

29 CFR Parts 4000, 4001, 4043, et al. Pension Protection Act of 2006; Conforming Amendments; Reportable Events and Certain Other Notification Requirements; Proposed Rule

PENSION BENEFIT GUARANTY CORPORATION

29 CFR Parts 4000, 4001, 4043, 4204, 4206, 4211, and 4231

RIN 1212-AB06

Pension Protection Act of 2006; Conforming Amendments; Reportable Events and Certain Other Notification Requirements

AGENCY: Pension Benefit Guaranty Corporation.

ACTION: Proposed rule.

SUMMARY: This is a proposed rule to conform PBGC's reportable events regulation under section 4043 of ERISA and a number of other PBGC regulations to statutory changes made by the Pension Protection Act of 2006 (PPA 2006) and to revisions of other PBGC regulations that implement the statutory changes. The rule would also eliminate most of the automatic waivers and filing extensions currently provided under the reportable events regulation and make other amendments to the regulation. For example, the rule would create two new reportable events based on provisions in PPA 2006 dealing with funding-based benefit limits and with asset transfers to retiree health benefits accounts.

DATES: Comments must be submitted on or before January 22, 2010.

ADDRESSES: Comments, identified by Regulation Identifier Number (RIN) 1212-AB06, may be submitted by any of the following methods:

• *Federal eRulemaking Portal: http://www.regulations.gov.* Follow the web site instructions for submitting comments.

• *E-mail: reg.comments@pbgc.gov.*

• *Fax:* 202-326-4224.

• *Mail or Hand Delivery:* Legislative and Regulatory Department, Pension Benefit Guaranty Corporation, 1200 K Street, NW., Washington, DC 20005-4026.

All submissions must include the Regulation Identifier Number for this rulemaking (RIN 1212-AB06). Comments received, including personal information provided, will be posted to *http://www.pbgc.gov.* Copies of comments may also be obtained by writing to Disclosure Division, Office of the General Counsel, Pension Benefit Guaranty Corporation, 1200 K Street, NW., Washington, DC 20005-4026, or calling 202-326-4040 during normal business hours. (TTY and TDD users may call the Federal relay service toll-free at 1-800-877-8339 and ask to be connected to 202-326-4040.)

FOR FURTHER INFORMATION CONTACT: John H. Hanley, Director, Legislative and Regulatory Department; or Catherine B. Klion, Manager, or Deborah C. Murphy, Attorney, Regulatory and Policy Division, Legislative and Regulatory Department, Pension Benefit Guaranty Corporation, 1200 K Street, NW., Washington, DC 20005-4026; 202-326-4024. (TTY/TDD users may call the Federal relay service toll-free at 1-800-877-8339 and ask to be connected to 202-326-4024.)

SUPPLEMENTARY INFORMATION:

Background

Pension Benefit Guaranty Corporation (PBGC) administers the pension plan termination insurance program under Title IV of the Employee Retirement Income Security Act of 1974 (ERISA). Under section 4007 of ERISA, pension plans covered by Title IV must pay premiums to PBGC. Section 4006 of ERISA establishes the premium rates and includes provisions for determining the variable-rate premium (VRP), which is based on plan funding rules. PBGC has regulations on Premium Rates (29 CFR part 4006) and Payment of Premiums (29 CFR part 4007) that implement the premium rules. A number of other provisions of ERISA, and of PBGC's other regulations, refer to funding and premium rules. Thus, changes in the funding and premium rules may require changes in some other PBGC regulations, such as PBGC's regulation on Reportable Events and Certain Other Notification Requirements (29 CFR part 4043), which implements section 4043 of ERISA (requiring that PBGC be notified of the occurrence of certain "reportable events").

On August 17, 2006, the Pension Protection Act of 2006 (PPA 2006), Public Law 109-280, was signed into law. PPA 2006 makes changes to the plan funding rules in Title I of ERISA and in the Internal Revenue Code of 1986 (Code) and amends the VRP provisions of section 4006 of ERISA to conform to the changes in the funding rules. On March 21, 2008, PBGC published in the **Federal Register** (at 73 FR 15065) a final rule amending its premium rates regulation and its premium payment regulation to implement the changes to ERISA and the Code made by PPA 2006. The changes to the funding and premium rules are effective for plan years beginning after 2007.

On November 28, 2007, PBGC issued Technical Update 07-2 (revised December 7, 2007 (corrected December 15, 2007)) (*http://www.pbgc.gov/practitioners/law-regulations-informal-guidance/content/tu16267.html*), providing transitional guidance on the applicability of the changes made by PPA 2006, and the corresponding changes proposed for PBGC premium regulations, to the determination of funding-related amounts for purposes of the reportable events regulation. On March 24, 2008, PBGC issued Technical Update 08-2 (*http://www.pbgc.gov/practitioners/law-regulations-informal-guidance/content/tu16372.html*), providing a waiver for reporting of missed quarterly contributions by certain small employers in 2008. On January 9, 2009, PBGC issued Technical Update 09-1 (*http://www.pbgc.gov/practitioners/law-regulations-informal-guidance/content/tu16637.html*), providing interim guidance on compliance with reportable events requirements for plan years beginning in 2009. On April 30, 2009, PBGC issued Technical Update 09-3 (*http://www.pbgc.gov/practitioners/law-regulations-informal-guidance/content/tu16725.html*), providing a waiver or alternative compliance method (depending on plan size) for reporting of missed quarterly contributions by certain small employers in 2009.

Overview of Proposed Regulatory Changes

This proposed rule would amend PBGC's reportable events regulation to make the advance reporting threshold test consistent with the PPA 2006 funding rules and PBGC's new variable-rate premium rules; eliminate most automatic waivers and filing extensions; create two new reportable events based on provisions in PPA 2006 dealing with funding-based benefit limits and with asset transfers to retiree health benefits accounts; reduce reporting of active participant reductions; clarify the provisions dealing with missed contributions and inability to pay benefits when due; clarify the benefit liability transfer event; remove from the regulation the lists of information items to be submitted (which are listed in the filing instructions); require filers to use PBGC forms to file reportable events notices; and eliminate the special "partial electronic filing" provision.

The rule would also amend six other PBGC regulations to revise statutory cross-references and otherwise accommodate the statutory and regulatory changes in the premium rules: the regulations on Filing, Issuance, Computation of Time, and Record Retention (29 CFR part 4000); Terminology (29 CFR part 4001); Variances for Sale of Assets (29 CFR part 4204); Adjustment of Liability for a Withdrawal Subsequent to a Partial Withdrawal (29 CFR part 4206); Allocating Unfunded Vested Benefits to Withdrawing Employers (29 CFR part 4211); and Mergers and Transfers Between Multiemployer Plans (29 CFR part 4231).

Reportable Events

PBGC proposes to amend the reportable events regulation to accommodate the changes to the funding and premium rules, to eliminate most automatic waivers and filing extensions, to add two new reportable events, and to make other modifications.

Advance Reporting Test

Under section 4043(a) of ERISA, plan administrators and contributing sponsors must notify PBGC of certain "reportable events" within 30 days after they occur. Section 4043(b) of ERISA requires advance reporting by a contributing sponsor for certain reportable events if a "threshold test" is met, unless the contributing sponsor or controlled group member to which an event relates is a public company. The advance reporting threshold test is based on the aggregate funding level of plans maintained by the contributing sponsor and members of the contributing sponsor's controlled group. The funding level criteria are expressed by reference to calculated values that are used to determine VRPs under section 4006 of ERISA. The reportable events regulation ties the statutory threshold test to the related provisions of the premium rates regulation.

The advance reporting threshold test in ERISA section 4043(b)(1) says: "The [advance reporting] requirements of this subsection shall be

applicable to a contributing sponsor if, as of the close of the preceding plan year—

• The aggregate unfunded vested benefits [(UVBs)] (as determined under [ERISA] section 4006(a)(3)(E)(iii)) of plans subject to this title which are maintained by such sponsor and members of such sponsor's controlled groups (disregarding plans with no unfunded vested benefits) exceed $50,000,000, and

• The funded vested benefit percentage for such plans is less than 90 percent.

—For purposes of the second bullet above, the funded vested benefit percentage means the percentage which the aggregate value of the assets of such plans bears to the aggregate vested benefits of such plans (determined in accordance with [ERISA]section 4006(a)(3)(E)(iii))."

PPA 2006 revised ERISA section 4006(a)(3)(E)(iii) to say that UVBs—"means, for a plan year, the excess (if any) of * * * the funding target of the plan as determined under [ERISA] section 303(d) for the plan year by only taking into account vested benefits and by using the interest rate described in [ERISA section 4006(a)(3)(E)(iv)], over * * * the fair market value of plan assets for the plan year which are held by the plan on the valuation date."

The section 303 of ERISA referred to here is a completely new section added by PPA 2006. Under new ERISA section 303(g)(1), the value of plan assets and the funding target of a plan for a plan year are determined as of the valuation date of the plan for the plan year. Under new ERISA section 303(g)(2), the valuation date for virtually all plans subject to advance reporting under ERISA section 4043 will be the first day of the plan year. Thus, while ERISA section 4043(b)(1) refers to UVBs, assets, and vested benefits "as of the close of the preceding plan year," in nearly all cases these quantities must, with respect to plan years beginning after 2007, be calculated as of the beginning of a plan year. This creates an ambiguity with regard to the date as of which the advance reporting threshold test is to be applied.

The proposed rule would resolve this ambiguity by requiring that the advance reporting threshold test be applied as of the valuation date for "the preceding plan year." That is the same date as of which UVBs, assets, and vested benefits must be determined for premium purposes for the preceding plan year under the premium rates regulation as amended by PBGC's final rule on VRPs under PPA 2006. Measuring these quantities as of that date for purposes of the advanced reporting threshold test will thus be less burdensome than requiring that separate computations be made as of the close of that year. It will also enable a plan to determine before a reportable event occurs (and before an advance report is due) whether it is subject to the advance reporting requirement.

The proposed rule would make a number of editorial changes to the advance reporting threshold provisions with a view to improving clarity and simplicity as well as accommodating the changes discussed above. It would also provide that the plans whose funding status is taken into account in applying the threshold test are determined as of the due date for the report, and that the "public company" status of a contributing sponsor or controlled group member to which the event relates is also determined as of that date. Although the existing regulation does not explicitly address this issue, PBGC believes it is implicit that these determinations be current. Requiring that they be made as of the due date for the report ensures currency.

Automatic Waivers and Extensions

Section 4043.4 of the reportable events regulation provides that PBGC may grant waivers and extensions case by case. In addition, the existing regulation provides automatic waivers and extensions for most of the reportable events. For example, waivers are provided for small plans, for well-funded plans, and for events affecting *de minimis* segments of controlled groups or foreign entities. In many cases, where it may be impossible to know by the filing due date whether criteria for a particular waiver are met, an extension gives a potential filer an opportunity to determine whether the waiver applies.

PBGC proposes to eliminate most of these automatic waivers and extensions, as indicated in the following tables. The complete waivers provided for certain statutory events in §§ 4043.21 (disqualification or noncompliance), 4043.22 (amendment decreasing benefits), 4043.24 (termination), and 4043.28 (merger, consolidation, or transfer) would be retained.

POST-EVENT NOTICES

Event	Current waivers	Proposed waivers	Current extensions	Proposed extensions
Active participant reduction (§ 4043.23).	• Small plan • Well-funded plan.	• Prior event reported within 1 year.	• 30 days after current VRP due date. • 30 days after next 5500 due date. • Following year flat-rate premium due date.	None.
Missed contribution (§ 4043.25).	• Payment within 30 days of due date.	None	None	None.
Inability to pay benefits when due (§ 4043.26).	• Large plan	• Large plan	None	None.
Distribution to substantial owner (§ 4043.27).	• Distribution up to § 415 limit. • Distribution up to 1% of assets. • Well-funded plan.	None	• 30 days after current VRP due date.	None.
Change in contributing sponsor or controlled group (§ 4043.29).	• *De minimis* transaction • Foreign entity • Well-funded plan	• *De minimis* transaction	• 30 days after current VRP due date. • 30 days after next 5500 due date. • 30 days after Form 10Q or press release.	None.
Liquidation (§ 4043.30)	• De minimis transaction • Foreign entity • Well-funded plan	None	• 30 days after current VRP due date. • 30 days after next 5500 due date. • 30 days after Form 10Q or press release.	None.
Extraordinary distribution or stock redemption (§ 4043.31).	• Statutory event • *De minimis* transaction • Foreign entity • Well-funded plan	• Statutory event • *De minimis* transaction	• 30 days after current VRP due date. • 30 days after next 5500 due date. • 30 days after Form 10Q or press release.	None.
Transfer of benefit liabilities (§ 4043.32).	• Transfer of all assets and liabilities. • *De minimis* transfer. • § 414(*l*) safe harbor. • Plans fully funded.	None	None	None.
Funding waiver application (§ 4043.33).	None	None	None	None.
Loan default (§ 4043.34)	• Cure or waiver • Foreign entity • Well-funded plan	• Cure or waiver	• 30 days after current VRP due date. • 30 days after next 5500 due date. • 1 day after cure period, acceleration, or default notice.	• 1 day after cure period, acceleration, or default notice.
Bankruptcy (§ 4043.35)	• Foreign entity	None	• 30 days after filer has actual knowledge.	None.

ADVANCE NOTICES

Event	Current waivers	Proposed waivers	Current extensions	Proposed extensions
Change in contributing sponsor or controlled group (§ 4043.62).	• Change in sponsor of small plan. • *De minimis* transaction.	• *De minimis* transaction	None	None.
Liquidation (§ 4043.63)	• *De minimis* transaction	None	None	None.
Extraordinary distributions or stock redemption (§ 4043.64).	• *De minimis* transaction	• *De minimis* transaction	None	None.
Transfer of benefit liabilities (§ 4043.65).	• Transfer of all assets and liabilities. • *De minimis* transfer. • § 414(*l*) safe harbor. • Plans fully funded.	None	None	None.
Funding waiver application (§ 4043.66).	None	None	10 days after event	Same day as event.
Loan default (§ 4043.67)	• Cure or waiver	• Cure or waiver	• 10 days after default • 1 day after cure period, acceleration, or default notice.	• 10 days after default. • 1 day after cure period, acceleration, or default notice.
Bankruptcy (§ 4043.68)			• 10 days after event	• 10 days after event.

Reportable events often signal financial distress and possible plan termination. When PBGC has timely information about a reportable event, it can take steps to encourage plan continuation—for example, by exploring alternative funding options with the plan sponsor—or, if plan termination is called for, to minimize the plan's potential funding shortfall through involuntary termination and maximize recovery of the shortfall from all possible sources. Without such timely information, PBGC typically learns that a plan is in danger only when most opportunities for protecting participants and the pension insurance system may have been lost.

PBGC believes that many of the automatic waivers and extensions in the existing reportable events regulation are depriving it of early warnings that would enable it to mitigate distress situations. For example, of the 88 small plans terminated in 2007, 21 involved situations where, but for an automatic waiver, an active participant reduction reportable event notice would have been required an average of three years before termination. Had those notices been filed, the need for some of those terminations might have been avoided, and PBGC might have been able to reduce the impact of other terminations on the pension insurance system.

PBGC believes that the increased reporting burden stemming from the elimination of most of the automatic waivers and extensions is justified by PBGC's need for timely information that may contribute to plan continuation or the minimizing of funding shortfalls. However, PBGC plans to monitor reportable events filings to determine whether some automatic waivers and extensions can be restored (or newly crafted waivers or extensions provided) without jeopardizing efforts to protect the benefits of participants in troubled plans and the pension insurance program. For each waiver and extension eliminated, PBGC solicits public comment on whether it has struck the correct balance between ensuring relevant information is received timely and increased reporting burden on the regulated community.

Active Participant Reduction—Facility Closings

An active participant reduction may occur as the result of a substantial cessation of operations under ERISA section 4062(e) or a substantial employer withdrawal under ERISA section 4063(a). Events covered by section 4062(e) or 4063(a) must be reported to PBGC under section 4063(a). With a view to avoiding duplicative reporting, PBGC proposes to limit the active participant reduction event by excluding from consideration—in determining whether a reportable active-participant-reduction event has occurred—active participant reductions to the extent that they (1) fall within the provisions of section 4062(e) or 4063(a) and (2) are timely reported to PBGC as required under ERISA section 4063(a).

Active Participant Reduction—Frequency of Reporting

The description of the active participant reduction event in the statute and the existing regulation suggests that reporting could be required multiple times in the course of a year if multiple reductions occurred. In fact, any such report leads PBGC to monitor the situation for an extended period of time; while that monitoring continues, additional formal reports of active participant reductions are unnecessary. Accordingly, the proposed rule would waive reporting for this event if another active participant reduction was reported within the past year.

Failure To Contribute—Clarification

PBGC proposes to clarify the language in § 4043.25, dealing with the reportable event of failure to make required contributions. This reportable event does not apply only to contributions required by statute (including quarterly contributions under ERISA section 303(j)(3) and Code section 430(j)(3), liquidity shortfall contributions under ERISA section 303(j)(4) and Code section 430(j)(4), and contributions to amortize funding waivers under ERISA section 303(e) and Code section 430(e)). It also applies to contributions required as a condition of a funding waiver that do not fall within the statutory provisions on waiver amortization charges. The proposed revision would make this point clearer. (Note that such "non-statutory" contributions are not considered under § 4043.81, dealing with missed contributions that give rise to liens under ERISA section 303(k) and Code section 430(k).)

Inability To Pay Benefits When Due—Clarification

PBGC proposes to clarify the language in the provision dealing with automatic waiver of the reporting requirement for inability to pay benefits when due. This provision reflects PBGC's judgment that it need not require reporting of this event by larger plans that are subject to the "liquidity shortfall" rules imposing more stringent contribution requirements where liquid assets are insufficient to cover anticipated disbursement requirements. For these larger plans, (1) if the contributions required by the liquidity shortfall rules are made, the inability to pay benefits when due is resolved, and (2) if the required contributions are not made, that fact is reportable to PBGC as a failure to make required contributions. Accordingly, this provision waives reporting unless the plan is a small plan that is exempt from the liquidity shortfall provisions.

Transfer of Benefit Liabilities—Cashouts and Annuitizations

Section 4043(c)(12) of ERISA requires reporting to PBGC when, in any 12-month period, three percent or more of a plan's benefit liabilities are transferred to a person outside the transferor plan's controlled group or to a plan or plans maintained by a person or persons outside the transferor plan's controlled group. Transfers of benefit liabilities are of concern to PBGC because they may reduce the transferor plan's funded percentage and because the transferee may not be as financially healthy as the transferor.

The existing text of the reportable events regulation does not make clear whether the satisfaction of benefit liabilities through the payment of a lump sum or the purchase of an irrevocable commitment to provide an annuity constitutes a transfer of benefit liabilities for purposes of this reporting requirement. PBGC has received inquiries seeking clarification of this point. PBGC proposes to provide that such cashouts and annuitizations do not constitute transfers of benefit liabilities that must be reported under the regulation.

Section 436 of the Code and section 206(g) of ERISA (as added by PPA 2006) prohibit or limit cashouts and annuitizations by significantly underfunded plans. These provisions thus tend to prevent cashouts and annuitizations that would most seriously reduce a transferor plan's funded percentage. And since cashouts and annuitizations satisfy benefit liabilities (rather than transferring them to another plan), there is no concern about a transferee plan's financial health.

Transfer of Benefit Liabilities—Plans of Other Controlled Group Members

Section 4043.32(a) of the existing reportable events regulation requires post-event reporting not only for the plan that transfers benefit liabilities, but also for every other plan maintained by a member of the transferor plan's controlled group. However, existing § 4043.32(d) provides a waiver that in effect limits the post-event reporting obligation to the transferor plan. Existing § 4043.65 (dealing with advance reporting of benefit liability transfers) does not provide a similar waiver.

PBGC has concluded that it is unnecessary to extend the advance reporting requirement for benefit liability transfers beyond the transferor plan. Accordingly, PBGC proposes to revise § 4043.32(a) to narrow the reporting requirement to the transferor plan; to remove § 4043.32(d) (which would be redundant); and to revise § 4043.65(a) to remove the provision requiring that § 4043.32(d) be disregarded. The effect of these changes would be to leave the post-event notice requirement unchanged and to limit the advance notice requirement to the transferor plan.

New Reportable Event—Low Adjusted Funding Target Attainment Percentage

Section 436 of the Code and section 206(g) of ERISA (as added by PPA 2006) provide that if a plan's "adjusted funding target attainment percentage" is less than 60 percent, the plan in general must cease benefit accruals; may not be amended to increase benefits, establish new benefits, or increase accrual or vesting rates; and may not pay unpredictable contingent event benefits (such as shut-down benefits) or lump sums, or annuitize benefits. "Adjusted funding target attainment percentage" (a variant of the funding target attainment percentage) is defined in Code section 436(j)(2) and ERISA section 206(g)(9)(B). Code section 436(h) and ERISA section 206(g)(7) provide a number of rules under which the adjusted funding target attainment percentage (AFTAP) is presumed in specified circumstances to have specified values.

PBGC shares Congress's concern about the financial health of plans with AFTAPs below 60 percent and believes that a funding percentage that low may (depending on the financial condition of the contributing sponsor and controlled group members) be indicative of a need to terminate the plan. Accordingly, PBGC proposes to create a new reportable event under ERISA section 4043(c)(13) that would occur when an enrolled actuary certifies that a plan's AFTAP is less than 60 percent or when the AFTAP is presumed to be less than 60 percent under one of the rules in Code section 436(h) and ERISA section 206(g)(7). This would be both a post-event notice event and an advance notice event (although the due date for the advance notice would be extended until ten days after the event occurs).

New Reportable Event—Transfer to Retiree Health Account

Section 420(f) of the Internal Revenue Code (as added by PPA 2006) permits a pension plan to transfer "excess pension assets" to a health benefits account under the plan to fund health benefits for a "transfer period" of up to 10 years. The term "excess pension assets" is defined for this purpose as the amount by which plan assets exceed 120 percent of plan liabilities for benefits (including benefits accruing during the year). If the ratio of assets to liabilities falls below 120 percent at any valuation date during the transfer period, additional contributions must be made to the pension plan, or assets must be transferred back from the health benefits account to the pension plan, to restore the funding ratio to 120 percent.

The 120-percent required funding ratio in this new provision is less than the 125-percent ratio previously required under Code section 420, and the transfer period can be much longer, entailing potentially the transfer of significantly greater amounts of plan assets. Furthermore, because the actuarial assumptions used to apply the 120-percent test under Code section 420 may differ significantly from the assumptions that would be used to value plan liabilities if a plan termination were to occur during the transfer period, a plan could be underfunded for termination purposes even if it could pass the 120-percent funding test in Code section 420. PBGC is accordingly concerned that large transfers under Code section 420(f), especially if the funded ratio falls below 120 percent during the transfer period, may indicate a need to terminate the plan.

PBGC therefore proposes to create a new reportable event that would occur if a section 420(f) transfer of $10 million or more is made or if, following such a transfer, the funded ratio falls below 120 percent during the transfer period. This would be a post-event notice event only. (Even with advance notice, PBGC could not prevent such a transfer if it complied with the law; post-event reporting would give PBGC an opportunity to monitor the plan going forward.)

Requiring Use of Forms; Putting Data Submission Requirements in Instructions

PBGC issues three reporting forms for use under the reportable events regulation. Form 10 is for post-event reporting under subpart B of the regulation; Form 10-Advance is for advance reporting under subpart C of the regulation; and Form 200 is for reporting under subpart D of the regulation.

Under the existing regulation, use of PBGC forms for reporting events under subparts B and C of the regulation is optional. The data items in the forms do not correspond exactly with those in the regulation, and the regulation recognizes that filers that use the forms may report different information from those that do not use the forms. With a view to greater uniformity in the reporting process and attendant administrative simplicity for PBGC, PBGC proposes to make use of prescribed reportable events forms mandatory. PBGC also proposes to revise the forms and instructions (see the discussion of Paperwork Reduction Act requirements infra).

Consistent with this change, PBGC proposes to eliminate from the regulation the lists of information items that must be reported, so that the information to be reported would be described in the filing instructions only (rather than in both the filing instructions and the regulation). PBGC anticipates that as uncertainties about the operation of new PPA 2006 provisions are resolved, it may be appropriate to make changes in the information required to be submitted with reportable events notices, particularly those for failures to make required contributions timely.

"Partial Electronic Filing" Rule

The existing regulation contains a "partial electronic filing" provision under which a filing is considered timely made if certain basic information (specified in PBGC's reporting instructions) is submitted on time electronically and followed up within one or two business days (depending on the type of report) with the remaining required information. This provision has facilitated last-minute filing where some required information consisted of documents that could not conveniently be sent electronically. But in the years since the regulation was issued, it has become common for documents to be created electronically and easy to create electronic images of documents that do not exist in electronic form. Thus PBGC believes that the "partial electronic filing" provision is no longer needed and that it is reasonable to require that all the information required for a filing be submitted on time, either electronically or on paper. Accordingly, PBGC proposes to eliminate the "partial electronic filing" provision. In the case of Form 200 filings, PBGC will accept an imaged signature, so that Form 200 filers need not submit a paper filing with ink signatures. (Forms 10 and 10-Advance do not require signatures.)

Other Changes

The proposed rule would make a number of editorial and clarifying changes to part 4043 and would add definitional cross-references, change statutory cross-references to track changes made by PPA 2006, and update language to conform to usage in PPA 2006 and regulations and reporting requirements thereunder. Some definitions of terms used in only one section of the regulation would be moved to the sections where they are used.

The proposed changes to the reportable events regulation make it unnecessary to define a number of terms at the beginning of the regulation. Accordingly, the definitions of "de minimis 10-percent segment," "fair market value of the plan's assets," "foreign entity," "foreign-linked entity," "foreign parent," "Form 5500 due date," "public company," "testing date," "ultimate parent," "unfunded vested benefits," "variable-rate premium," and "vested benefits amount" would be removed from § 4043.2. The definition of " *de minimis* 5-percent segment" (a term that in the existing regulation is defined by reference to the definition of " *de minimis* 10-percent segment") would be made self-contained.

PBGC recognizes that the changes made by PPA 2006 in the statutory provisions dealing with missed contributions—which are reportable under §§ 4043.25 and 4043.81—affect the computation of interest on missed contributions, which in turn affects the reporting requirements. This proposed rule includes no amendment to the reportable events regulation dealing with such issues, but PBGC may provide further guidance on this subject, taking into account as appropriate any relevant guidance from the Internal Revenue Service.

Other Regulations

Several other PBGC regulations also refer to plan funding concepts: The regulations on Filing, Issuance, Computation of Time, and Record Retention (29 CFR part 4000); Terminology (29 CFR part 4001); Vari-

ances for Sale of Assets (29 CFR part 4204); Adjustment of Liability for a Withdrawal Subsequent to a Partial Withdrawal (29 CFR part 4206); Allocating Unfunded Vested Benefits to Withdrawing Employers (29 CFR part 4211); and Mergers and Transfers Between Multiemployer Plans (29 CFR part 4231). Thus, these regulations must also be revised to be consistent with ERISA and the Code as amended by PPA 2006 and with the revised premium regulations. This proposed rule would make the necessary conforming revisions.

Applicability

In general, the changes to the reportable events regulation made by this rule would apply to post-event reports for reportable events occurring on or after the effective date of this rule and to advance reports due on or after the effective date of this rule. Technical Updates 07-2, 08-2, 09-1, and 09-3 would be superseded by this rule with respect to any circumstances to which this rule would apply.

Compliance With Rulemaking Guidelines

E.O. 12866

The PBGC has determined, in consultation with the Office of Management and Budget, that this rule is a "significant regulatory action" under Executive Order 12866. The Office of Management and Budget has therefore reviewed this notice under E.O. 12866.

Regulatory Flexibility Act

PBGC certifies under section 605(b) of the Regulatory Flexibility Act (5 U.S.C. 601 *et seq.*) that the amendments in this rule will not have a significant economic impact on a substantial number of small entities. Accordingly, as provided in section 605 of the Regulatory Flexibility Act (5 U.S.C. 601 *et seq.*), sections 603 and 604 do not apply. This certification is based on the fact that the reportable events regulation requires only the filing of notices and that the economic impact of filing is not significant.

Paperwork Reduction Act

PBGC is submitting the information requirements under this proposed rule to the Office of Management and Budget for review and approval under the Paperwork Reduction Act. There are two information collections under the reportable events regulation, approved under OMB control number 1212-0013 (covering subparts B and C) and OMB control number 1212-0041 (covering subpart D), both of which expire March 31, 2012. Copies of PBGC's requests may be obtained free of charge by contacting the Disclosure Division of the Office of the General Counsel of PBGC, 1200 K Street, NW., Washington, DC 20005, 202-326-4040.

PBGC is proposing the following changes to these information requirements:

• PBGC's experience is that in order to assess the significance of virtually every reportable events filing, it must obtain from the filer the most recent month-end statement of the market value of plan assets, the most recent adjusted funding target attainment percentage (AFTAP) certification, and the most recent actuarial valuation report that contains or is supplemented with all the items of information described in § 4010.8(a)(11) of PBGC's regulation on Annual Financial and Actuarial Information Reporting (29 CFR part 4010). Accordingly, PBGC proposes to require that every reportable events filing include these items.

• To provide better identification of controlled group members, PBGC proposes to require that lists of controlled group members include addresses as well as names.

• PBGC has found that some filers that should file Form 200 under § 4043.81 of the reportable events regulation (missed contributions totaling over $1 million) file only Form 10 under § 4043.25 (missed contributions of any amount). This has led to delays in enforcing liens under ERISA section 302(f) and Code section 412(n) (corresponding to ERISA section 303(k) and Code section 430(k) as amended by PPA 2006). To address this issue, PBGC proposes that the information collections under the reportable events regulation include a requirement to report the aggregate outstanding balance (with interest) of all prior contributions not timely made.

• In missed contribution cases, there is sometimes a credit balance that is available for application to a contribution that is due. PBGC needs to be able to determine whether all or a portion of the credit balance has been properly applied toward payment of the contribution. Accordingly, PBGC proposes to require filers of both Form 10 and Form 200 to indicate how much (if any) of the carryover balance or prefunding balance was used for partial payment of the missed contribution and submit copies of election letters relating to application of the carryover balance and prefunding balance to the contribution.

• To assist PBGC in assessing the impact of a change in contributing sponsor or controlled group, PBGC proposes to require submission of "before-and-after" financial statements for post-event as well as advance reporting. Where the event is the loss of one or more controlled group members, financial statements would be required for the controlled group before and after the loss of the departing member(s). Where the event is a transfer of a plan to another controlled group, financial statements would be required for the old and new controlled groups. (Filers would not be penalized if they were unable to obtain financial statements from controlled groups other than their own.)

• To help PBGC assess the significance of a loan default or an extraordinary distribution or stock redemption, PBGC proposes to require filings for these events to include financial statements for all controlled group members to the extent not publicly available.

• PBGC Form 10-Advance (used for advance reporting under subpart C of the reportable events regulation) currently includes a requirement for the benefit liability transfer event that both the transferor and the transferee (and contributing sponsors) be identified. Form 10 (used for post-event reporting under subpart B) calls only for the identity of the transferee. PBGC proposes to change the Form 10 requirement to correspond to the requirement of Form 10-Advance.

• To assist PBGC in assessing the impact of a transfer of benefit liabilities, PBGC proposes to require submission of financial statements for both the transferor controlled group and the transferee controlled group. (Filers would not be penalized if they were unable to obtain financial statements from controlled groups other than their own.)

• PBGC Form 10 currently requires for the bankruptcy event that the bankruptcy petition and docket (or similar documents) be submitted. Form 10-Advance requires that all documents filed in the relevant proceeding be submitted. Both forms require that the last date for filing claims be reported if known. PBGC proposes to replace these requirements with a requirement that filers simply identify the judicial district where the bankruptcy petition was filed and the docket number of the filing.

• When an advance report of an extraordinary dividend or stock redemption is made, PBGC has a 30-day window in which to determine whether there is a basis for taking action before the dividend is paid and, if so, to act. In order to do so, PBGC needs information about contributing sponsors' financial health. Accordingly, PBGC proposes to add a requirement for contributing sponsor financial statements to the information submission requirements for advance reporting of extraordinary dividends and stock redemptions.

• PBGC proposes to require that the notice of a low adjusted funding target attainment percentage certified by an enrolled actuary include a copy of the enrolled actuary's certification.

• If a section 420(f) transfer of $10 million or more is made, PBGC proposes to require that the notice to PBGC include a calculation demonstrating that the transfer does not reduce pension assets below 120 percent of liabilities for pension benefits.

• If, following a section 420(f) transfer of $10 million or more, the funded ratio falls below 120 percent during the transfer period, PBGC proposes to require that the notice to PBGC include a calculation demonstrating how (by making additional pension plan contributions or by transferring assets back from the health benefits account to the pension plan) pension assets were restored to an amount not less than 120 percent of liabilities for pension benefits.

PBGC needs the information in reportable events filings under subparts B and C of part 4043 (Forms 10 and 10-Advance) to determine whether it should terminate plans that experience events that indicate plan or contributing sponsor financial problems. PBGC estimates that it will receive such filings from about 1,615 respondents each year and that the total annual burden of the collection of information will be about 6,890 hours and $2,411,500.

PBGC needs the information in missed contribution filings under subpart D of part 4043 (Form 200) to determine the amounts of statutory liens arising under ERISA section 303(k) and Code section 430(k) and to evaluate the funding status of plans with respect to which such liens arise and the financial condition of the persons responsible for their funding. PBGC estimates that it will receive such filings from about 797 respondents each year and that the total annual burden of the collection of information will be about 1,636 hours and $572,600.

Comments on the paperwork provisions under this proposed rule should be sent to the Office of Information and Regulatory Affairs, Office of Management and Budget, Attention: Desk Officer for Pension Benefit Guaranty Corporation, via electronic mail at *OIRA_DOCKET@omb.eop.gov* or by fax to (202) 395-6974. Although comments may be submitted through January 22, 2010, the Office of Management and Budget requests that comments be received on or before December 23, 2009 to ensure their consideration. Comments may address (among other things)—

• Whether each proposed collection of information is needed for the proper performance of PBGC's functions and will have practical utility;

• The accuracy of PBGC's estimate of the burden of each proposed collection of information, including the validity of the methodology and assumptions used;

• Enhancement of the quality, utility, and clarity of the information to be collected; and

• Minimizing the burden of each collection of information on those who are to respond, including through the use of appropriate automated, electronic, mechanical, or other technological collection techniques or other forms of information technology, *e.g.,* permitting electronic submission of responses.

List of Subjects

29 CFR Part 4000

Employee benefit plans, Pension insurance, Reporting and recordkeeping requirements.

29 CFR Part 4001

Employee benefit plans, Pension insurance.

29 CFR Part 4043

Employee benefit plans, Pension insurance, Reporting and recordkeeping requirements.

29 CFR Part 4204

Employee benefit plans, Pension insurance, Reporting and recordkeeping requirements.

29 CFR Part 4206

Employee benefit plans, Pension insurance.

29 CFR Part 4211

Employee benefit plans, Pension insurance, Reporting and recordkeeping requirements.

29 CFR Part 4231

Employee benefit plans, Pension insurance, Reporting and recordkeeping requirements.

For the reasons given above, PBGC proposes to amend 29 CFR parts 4000, 4001, 4043, 4204, 4206, 4211, and 4231 as follows.

PART 4000—FILING, ISSUANCE, COMPUTATION OF TIME, AND RECORD RETENTION

1. The authority citation for part 4000 is revised to read as follows:

Authority: 29 U.S.C. 1083(k), 1302(b)(3).

§ 4000.53 [Amended]

2. In § 4000.53, paragraphs (c) and (d) are amended by removing the words "section 302(f)(4), section 307(e), and" where they occur in each paragraph and adding in their place the words "section 101(f), section 303(k)(4), and".

PART 4001—TERMINOLOGY

3. The authority citation for part 4001 continues to read as follows:

Authority: 29 U.S.C. 1301, 1302(b)(3).

§ 4001.2 [Amended]

4. In § 4001.2:

a. The definition of "controlled group" is amended by removing the words "section 412(c)(11)(B) of the Code or section 302(c)(11)(B) of ERISA" and adding in their place the words "section 412(b)(2) of the Code or section 302(b)(2) of ERISA".

b. The definition of "funding standard account" is amended by removing the words "section 302(b) of ERISA or section 412(b) of the Code" and adding in their place the words "section 304(b) of ERISA or section 431(b) of the Code".

c. The definition of "substantial owner" is amended by removing the words "section 4022(b)(5)(A)" and adding in their place the words "section 4021(d)".

PART 4043—REPORTABLE EVENTS AND CERTAIN OTHER NOTIFICATION REQUIREMENTS

5. The authority citation for part 4043 is revised to read as follows:

Authority: 29 U.S.C. 1083(k), 1302(b)(3), 1343.

§ 4043.1 [Amended]

6. Section 4043.1 is amended by removing the reference "302(f)(4)" and adding in its place the reference "303(k)(4)"; and by removing the reference "412(n)(4)" and adding in its place the reference "430(k)(4)".

7. In § 4043.2:

a. The introductory text is amended by removing the word "Code" and adding in its place the words "benefit liabilities, Code"; and by removing the words "plan administrator, proposed termination date" and adding in their place the words "plan administrator, plan year, proposed termination date".

b. The definitions of *de minimis 10-percent segment, fair market value of the plan's assets, foreign entity, foreign-linked entity, foreign parent, Form 5500 due date, public company, testing date, ultimate parent, unfunded vested benefits, variable-rate premium,* and *vested benefits* are removed.

c. The definitions of *event year* and *notice date* are amended by removing the words "the reportable event" and adding in their place the words "a reportable event" in each of the two definitions.

d. The definition of *de minimis 5-percent segment* is revised to read as follows:

§ 4043.2 Definitions.

* * * * *

De minimis 5-percent segment means, in connection with a plan's controlled group, one or more entities that in the aggregate have for a fiscal year—

(1) Revenue not exceeding 5 percent of the controlled group's revenue;

(2) Annual operating income not exceeding the greatest of—

(i) 5 percent of the controlled group's annual operating income;

(ii) 5 percent of the controlled group's first $200 million in net tangible assets at the end of the fiscal year(s); or

(iii) $5 million; and

(3) Net tangible assets at the end of the fiscal year(s) not exceeding the greater of—

(i) 5 percent of the controlled group's net tangible assets at the end of the fiscal year(s); or

(ii) $5 million.

* * * * *

8. In § 4043.3:

a. Paragraph (a)(1) is amended by removing the words "by this part" and adding in their place the words "under this part".

b. Paragraph (d) is amended by removing the words "submission of additional information" and adding in their place the words "submission of additional information not specified in its forms and instructions".

c. Paragraphs (b) and (c) are revised to read as follows:

§ 4043.3 Requirement of notice.

* * * * *

(b) *Contents of reportable event notice.* A person required to file a reportable event notice under subpart B or C of this part shall file, by the notice date, the form specified by PBGC for that purpose, with the information specified in PBGC's reportable events instructions.

(c) *Reportable event forms and instructions.* The PBGC shall issue reportable events forms and instructions and make them available on its Web site.

* * * * *

9. In § 4043.4:

a. Paragraphs (a), (b), (c), and (d) are redesignated as paragraphs (b), (c), (d), and (a) respectively.

b. Newly redesignated paragraph (a) is amended by removing the heading " *Other waivers and extensions."* and adding in its place the heading " *Waivers and extensions—in general.".*

c. Newly redesignated paragraph (b) is revised to read as follows:

§ 4043.4 Waivers and extensions.

* * * * *

(b) *Waivers and extensions—specific events.* For some reportable events, automatic waivers from reporting and information requirements and extensions of time are provided in subparts B and C of this part. If an occurrence constitutes two or more reportable events, reporting requirements for each event are determined independently. For example, reporting is automatically waived for an occurrence that constitutes a reportable event under more than one section only if the requirements for an automatic waiver under each section are satisfied.

* * * * *

10. Section 4043.5 is amended by adding the following sentence at the beginning of the text of the section:

§ 4043.5 How and where to file.

Reportable event notices required under this part must be filed using the forms and in accordance with the instructions promulgated by PBGC, which are posted on PBGC's Web site.

* * *

§ 4043.6 [Amended]

11. In § 4043.6:

a. Paragraph (a) is amended by removing the heading " *Post-Event notice filings."* and adding in its place the heading " *Post-event notice filings.".*

b. Paragraph (b) is amended by removing the heading " *Advance notice and Form 200 Filings."* and adding in its place the heading " *Advance notice and Form 200 filings.".*

c. Paragraph (c) is removed.

12. In § 4043.23:

a. The text of paragraph (a) is designated as paragraph (a)(1) and a paragraph heading is added.

b. New paragraph (a)(2) is added.

c. Paragraphs (b) and (d) are removed.

d. Paragraph (e) is redesignated as paragraph (b).

e. And paragraph (c) is revised.

The addition and revision read as follows:

§ 4043.23 Active participant reduction.

(a *) Reportable event—*(1) *In general.* * * *.

(2) *Certain participant reductions disregarded.* For purposes of paragraph (a)(1) of this section, a reduction in the number of active participants is to be disregarded to the extent that the reduction—

(i) Is attributable to a substantial cessation of operations under ERISA section 4062(e) or to the withdrawal of a substantial employer under ERISA section 4063(a), and

(ii) Is timely reported to PBGC under ERISA section 4063(a).

* * * * *

(c) *Waiver.* Notice is waived for an event (the "current event") if the notice date for another event (the "prior event") under paragraph (a) of this section was not more than 12 months before the notice date for the current event and the prior event was reported to PBGC in accordance with the requirements of this part.

13. Section 4043.25 is revised to read as follows:

§ 4043.25 Failure to make required funding payment.

(a) *Reportable event.* A reportable event occurs when—

(1) A contribution required under sections 302 and 303 of ERISA or sections 412 and 430 of the Code is not made by the due date for the payment under ERISA section 303(j) or Code section 430(j), or

(2) Any other contribution required as a condition of a funding waiver is not made when due.

(b) *Alternative method of compliance—Form 200 filed.* If, with respect to the same failure, a filing is made in accordance with § 4043.81, that filing satisfies the requirements of this section.

14. In § 4043.26:

a. Paragraph (a)(2) is amended in the second sentence by removing the words "Liquid assets and disbursements from the plan" and adding in their place the words " 'Liquid assets' and 'disbursements from the plan' "; by removing the reference "302(e)(5)(E)" and adding in its place the reference "303(j)(4)(E)"; and by removing the reference "412(m)(5)(E)" and adding in its place the reference "430(j)(4)(E)".

b. Paragraph (c) is removed.

c. Paragraph (b) is revised to read as follows:

§ 4043.26 Inability to pay benefits when due.

* * * * *

(b) *Waiver.* Notice is waived unless the reportable event occurs during a plan year for which the plan is exempt from the liquidity shortfall rules in section 303(j)(4) of ERISA and section 430(j)(4) of the Code because it is described in section 303(g)(2)(B) of ERISA and section 430(g)(2)(B) of the Code.

§ 4043.27 [Amended]

15. In § 4043.27:

a. Paragraph (a)(4) is amended by removing the words "as provided in § 4022.5" and adding in their place the words "as provided in § 4022.5 of this chapter".

b. Paragraphs (b), (c), and (d) are removed, and paragraph (e) is redesignated as paragraph (b).

16. In § 4043.29:

a. Paragraphs (c) and (d) are removed, and paragraph (e) is redesignated as paragraph (c).

b. The introductory text of newly redesignated paragraph (c) is amended by removing the words "waivers apply" and adding in their place the words "waiver applies".

c. Paragraph (b) is revised to read as follows:

§ 4043.29 Change in contributing sponsor or controlled group.

* * * * *

(b) *Waiver; de minimis 10-percent segment.* Notice is waived if the person or persons that will cease to be members of the plan's controlled group represent a *de minimis* 10-percent segment of the plan's old controlled group for the most recent fiscal year(s) ending on or before the date the reportable event occurs. For this purpose, " *de minimis* 10-percent segment" means, in connection with a plan's controlled group, one or more entities that in the aggregate have for a fiscal year—

(1) Revenue not exceeding 10 percent of the controlled group's revenue;

(2) Annual operating income not exceeding the greatest of—

(i) 10 percent of the controlled group's annual operating income;

(ii) 5 percent of the controlled group's first $200 million in net tangible assets at the end of the fiscal year(s); or

(iii) $5 million; and

(3) Net tangible assets at the end of the fiscal year(s) not exceeding the greater of—

(i) 10 percent of the controlled group's net tangible assets at the end of the fiscal year(s); or

(ii) $5 million.

* * * * *

§ 4043.30 [Amended]

17. In § 4043.30:

a. The heading of paragraph (a) is removed, and the introductory text of paragraph (a) is redesignated as the introductory text of § 4043.30.

b. Paragraphs (b), (c), and (d) are removed.

c. Paragraphs (a)(1), (a)(2), and (a)(3) are redesignated as paragraphs (a), (b), and (c).

§ 4043.31 [Amended]

18. In § 4043.31:

a. Paragraphs (b), (c)(3), (c)(4), (c)(5), and (d) are removed.

b. Paragraph (c) is redesignated as paragraph (b).

c. Paragraph (e) is redesignated as paragraph (c).

d. The reference "(e)" is removed and the reference "(c)" is added in its place once in paragraph (a) introductory text, once in paragraph (a)(1)(i), once in paragraph (a)(1)(ii), twice in paragraph (a)(2), twice in paragraph (a)(3), once in newly redesignated paragraph (c)(2)(i), once in newly redesignated paragraph (c)(2)(ii), once in newly redesignated paragraph (c)(5), and once in newly redesignated paragraph (c)(6)(iii).

19. In § 4043.32:

a. Paragraphs (b) and (d) are removed.

b. Paragraph (a)(2) is redesignated as paragraph (b).

c. The heading of paragraph (a)(1) is removed, and the introductory text of paragraph (a)(1) is redesignated as the introductory text of paragraph (a).

d. Paragraphs (a)(1)(i) and (a)(1)(ii) are redesignated as paragraphs (a)(1) and (a)(2).

e. Redesignated paragraph (a)(1) is amended by removing the words "or any other plan maintained by a person in the plan's controlled group".

f. Paragraph (c) is revised to read as follows:

§ 4043.32 Transfer of benefit liabilities.

* * * * *

(c) *Distributions of lump sums and annuities.* For purposes of paragraph (a) of this section, the payment of a lump sum, or purchase of an irrevocable commitment to provide an annuity, in satisfaction of benefit liabilities is not a transfer of benefit liabilities.

§ 4043.33 [Amended]

20. In § 4043.33:

a. Paragraph (b) is removed.

b. The heading of paragraph (a) is removed, and the text of paragraph (a) is redesignated as the text of § 4043.33.

c. The figures "303" are removed and the figures "302(c)" are added in their place; and the figures "412(d)" are removed and the figures "412(c)" are added in their place.

§ 4043.34 [Amended]

21. In § 4043.34:

a. Paragraph (a) introductory text is amended by removing the words "default by" and adding in their place the words "default under a loan agreement by".

b. Paragraph (a)(3) introductory text is amended by removing the colon and adding in its place a dash.

c. Paragraphs (b), (c)(2), (c)(3), (d)(3), and (d)(4) are removed.

d. The heading of paragraph (c) introductory text is removed.

e. Paragraph (c)(1) is redesignated as paragraph (b).

f. Newly redesignated paragraph (b) is amended by removing the heading " *Default cured.*" and adding in its place the heading " *Waiver for cure of default.*".

g. Paragraph (d)(5) is redesignated as paragraph (d)(3), and paragraph (d) is redesignated as paragraph (c).

h. Redesignated paragraph (c)(1) is amended by removing the words "(d)(2) or (d)(3)" and adding in their place the figures "(c)(2)".

i. Redesignated paragraph (c)(2) is amended by removing the heading " *Cure period extensions.*" and adding in its place the heading " *Extensions.*".

§ 4043.35 [Amended]

22. In § 4043.35:

a. Paragraphs (b), (c), and (d) are removed.

b. The heading of paragraph (a) introductory text is removed, and the introductory text of paragraph (a) is redesignated as the introductory text of § 4043.35.

c. Paragraphs (a)(1), (a)(2), (a)(3), (a)(4), and (a)(5) are redesignated as paragraphs (a), (b), (c), (d), and (e).

23. New §§ 4043.36 and 4043.37 are added to subpart B to read as follows:

§ 4043.36 Adjusted funding target attainment percentage under 60 percent.

A reportable event occurs for a plan when the plan's adjusted funding target attainment percentage under Code section 436(j)(2) and ERISA section 206(g)(9)(B) either—

(a) Is certified by an enrolled actuary to be less than 60 percent, or

(b) Is presumed under Code section 436(h) and ERISA section 206(g)(7) to be less than 60 percent.

§ 4043.37 Transfer of assets to retiree health account or subsequent reduction in funding ratio.

A reportable event occurs for a plan when either—

(a) The plan makes a qualified future transfer or a collectively bargained transfer under Code section 420(f) of $10 million dollars or more, or

(b) On any valuation date of the plan during the transfer period described in Code section 420(f)(5) following any transfer described in paragraph (a) of this section, 120 percent of the sum of the funding target and the target normal cost determined under Code section 430 for the plan year exceeds the lesser of—

(1) The fair market value of the plan's assets (reduced by the prefunding balance and funding standard account carryover balance determined under Code section 430(f)), or

(2) The value of plan assets as determined under Code section 430(g)(3) after reduction under Code section 430(f).

24. In § 4043.61, paragraphs (a), (b), and (c) are revised to read as follows:

§ 4043.61 Advance reporting filing obligation.

(a) *In general.* Unless a waiver or extension applies with respect to the plan, each contributing sponsor of a plan is required to notify the PBGC no later than 30 days before the effective date of a reportable event described in this subpart C if the contributing sponsor is subject to advance reporting for the reportable event. If there is a change in contributing sponsor, the reporting obligation applies to the person who is the contributing sponsor of the plan on the notice date.

(b) *Persons subject to advance reporting.* A contributing sponsor of a plan is subject to the advance reporting requirement under paragraph (a) of this section for a reportable event if—

(1) On the notice date, neither the contributing sponsor nor any member of the plan's controlled group to which the event relates is a person subject to the reporting requirements of section 13 or 15(d) of the Securities Exchange Act of 1934 or a subsidiary (as defined for purposes of the Securities Exchange Act of 1934) of a person subject to such reporting requirements; and

(2) The aggregate unfunded vested benefits, determined in accordance with paragraph (c) of this section, are more than $50 million; and

(3) The aggregate value of plan assets, determined in accordance with paragraph (c) of this section, is less than 90 percent of the aggregate premium funding target, determined in accordance with paragraph (c) of this section.

(c) *Funding determinations.* For purposes of paragraph (b) of this section, the aggregate unfunded vested benefits, aggregate value of plan assets, and aggregate premium funding target are determined by aggregating the unfunded vested benefits, values of plan assets, and premium funding targets (respectively), as determined for premium purposes in accordance with part 4006 of this chapter for the plan year preceding the effective date of the event, of plans maintained (on the notice date) by the contributing sponsor and any members of the contributing sponsor's controlled group, disregarding plans with no unfunded vested benefits (as so determined).

* * * * *

§ 4043.62 [Amended]

25. In § 4043.62:

a. Paragraph (a) is amended by removing the words " *and information required*" from the paragraph heading; and by removing the words

"§ 4043.29(a), and the notice shall include the information described in § 4043.29(b) and, if known, the expected effective date of the reportable event" and adding in their place the figures "§ 4043.29(a)".

b. Paragraph (b) is amended by removing the heading.

c. Paragraph (b)(1) is removed.

d. Paragraph (b)(2) is amended by removing the heading " *De minimis 5-percent segment.*" and adding in its place the heading " *Waiver; de minimis 5-percent segment.*".

e. Paragraph (b)(2) is redesignated as paragraph (b).

§ 4043.63 [Amended]

26. In § 4043.63:

a. Paragraph (a) is amended by removing the paragraph heading; and by removing the words "§ 4043.30(a), and the notice shall include the information described in § 4043.30(b) and, if known, the expected effective date of the reportable event" and adding in their place the reference "§ 4043.30".

b. Paragraph (b) is removed.

c. The text of paragraph (a) is redesignated as the text of § 4043.63.

§ 4043.64 [Amended]

27. In § 4043.64:

a. Paragraph (a) is amended by removing the words " *and information required*" from the paragraph heading; and by removing the last sentence of the paragraph.

b. Paragraph (b) is amended by removing the word " *Waiver*" from the paragraph heading and adding in its place the words " *Waiver; de minimis 5-percent segment*".

§ 4043.65 [Amended]

28. In § 4043.65:

a. Paragraph (a) is amended by removing the paragraph heading; and by removing the words "§ 4043.32(a) (determined without regard to § 4043.32(d)), and the notice shall include the information described in § 4043.32(b)" and adding in their place the reference "4043.32(a)".

b. Paragraph (b) is removed.

c. The text of paragraph (a) is redesignated as the text of § 4043.65.

§ 4043.66 [Amended]

29. In 4043.66:

a. Paragraph (a) is amended by removing the words " *and information required*" from the heading; and by removing the words "§ 4043.33(a), and the notice shall include the information described in § 4043.33(b)" and adding in their place the reference "§ 4043.33".

b. Paragraph (b) is amended by removing the words "10 days after" and adding in their place the words "the day"; and by removing the words "has occurred" and adding in their place the word "occurs".

§ 4043.67 [Amended]

30. In § 4043.67, paragraph (a) is amended by removing the words " *and information required*" from the heading; and by removing the last sentence of the paragraph.

§ 4043.68 [Amended]

31. In § 4043.68, paragraph (a) is amended by removing the words " *and information required*" from the heading; and by removing the words "§ 4043.35(a), and the notice shall include the information described in § 4043.35(b)" and adding in their place the reference "§ 4043.35".

32. New §§ 4043.69 and 4043.70 are added to subpart C to read as follows:

§ 4043.69 Adjusted funding target attainment percentage under 60 percent.

(a) *Reportable event.* Advance notice is required when a plan's adjusted funding target attainment percentage is certified or presumed to be less than 60 percent, as described in § 4043.36.

(b) *Extension.* The notice date is extended until 10 days after the reportable event has occurred.

§ 4043.70 Transfer of assets to retiree health account or subsequent reduction in funding ratio.

Advance notice is waived for a reportable event described in § 4043.37.

33. In § 4043.81:

a. Paragraph (a) introductory text is amended by removing the reference "302(f)(4)" and adding in its place the reference "303(k)(4)"; by removing the reference "412(n)(4)" and adding in its place the reference "430(k)(4)"; by removing the words "required installment or any other" and adding in their place the word "contribution"; by removing the words "section 302 of ERISA and section 412 of the Code" and adding in their place the words "sections 302 and 303 of ERISA and sections 412 and 430 of the Code"; and by removing the words "installments or other".

b. Paragraph (a)(2) is amended by removing the reference "302(f)(4)" and adding in its place the reference "303(k)(4)"; and by removing the reference "412(n)(4)" and adding in its place the reference "430(k)(4)".

c. Paragraph (b) is amended by removing the reference "302(f)" and adding in its place the reference "303(k)"; and by removing the reference "412(n)" and adding in its place the reference "430(k)".

d. Paragraph (c) is added to read as follows:

§ 4043.81 PBGC Form 200, notice of failure to make required contributions; supplementary information.

* * * * *

(c) *Ultimate parent.* For purposes of this section, the term "ultimate parent" means the parent at the highest level in the chain of corporations and/or other organizations constituting a parent-subsidiary controlled group.

PART 4204—VARIANCES FOR SALE OF ASSETS

34. The authority citation for part 4204 continues to read as follows:

Authority: 29 U.S.C. 1302(b)(3), 1384(c).

§ 4204.12 [Amended]

35. Section 4204.12 is amended by removing the reference "412(b)(3)(A)" and adding in its place the reference "431(b)(3)(A)".

PART 4206—ADJUSTMENT OF LIABILITY FOR A WITHDRAWAL SUBSEQUENT TO A PARTIAL WITHDRAWAL

36. The authority citation for part 4206 continues to read as follows:

Authority: 29 U.S.C. 1302(b)(3) and 1386(b).

§ 4206.7 [Amended]

37. Section 4206.7 is amended by removing the reference "412(b)(4)" and adding in its place the reference "431(b)(5)".

PART 4211—ALLOCATING UNFUNDED VESTED BENEFITS TO WITHDRAWING EMPLOYERS

38. The authority citation for part 4211 continues to read as follows:

Authority: 29 U.S.C. 1302(b)(3); 1391(c)(1), (c)(2)(D), (c)(5)(A), (c)(5)(B), (c)(5)(D), and (f).

PART 4231—MERGERS AND TRANSFERS BETWEEN MULTIEMPLOYER PLANS

39. The authority citation for part 4231 continues to read as follows:

Authority: 29 U.S.C. 1302(b)(3), 1411.

§ 4231.2 [Amended]

40. In § 4231.2, the definitions of "actuarial valuation" and "fair market value of assets" are amended by removing the words "section 302 of ERISA and section 412 of the Code" wherever they appear in each definition and adding in their place the words "section 304 of ERISA and section 431 of the Code".

§ 4231.6 [Amended]

41. In § 4231.6:

a. Paragraph (b)(4)(ii) is amended by removing the reference "412(b)(4)" and adding in its place the reference "431(b)(5)".

b. Paragraph (c)(2) is amended by removing the words "section 412 of the Code (which requires that such assumptions be reasonable in the aggregate)" and adding in their place the words "section 431 of the Code (which requires that each such assumption be reasonable)".

c. Paragraph (c)(5) is amended by removing the figure "412" and adding in their place the figure "431".

Issued in Washington, DC, this 18th day of November, 2009.

Vincent K. Snowbarger,

Acting Director, Pension Benefit Guaranty Corporation.

[FR Doc. E9-28056 Filed 11-20-09; 8:45 am]

BILLING CODE 7709-01-P

¶ 20,537V

Employee Benefits Security Administration (EBSA): Proposed regulations: Investment advice: Individual account plans IRAs.—The Employee Benefits Security Administration (EBSA) has issued proposed regulations on the provision of investment advice to participants and beneficiaries of individual account plans, such as 401(k) plans, and individual retirement accounts (IRAs).

The proposed regulations, which were published in the Federal Register on March 2, 2010 (75 FR 9360) are reproduced below. The final regulations were published in the Federal Register on October 25, 2011 (76 FR 66136). The preamble to the final regulations is at ¶ 24,306. The final regulations are reproduced at ¶ 14,789B, ¶ 14,789B-1, and ¶ 14,789B-2.

DEPARTMENT OF LABOR

Employee Benefits Security Administration

29 CFR 2550

RIN 1210-AB35

Investment Advice - Participants and Beneficiaries

AGENCY: Employee Benefits Security Administration, Labor.

ACTION: Proposed rule.

SUMMARY: This document contains a proposed rule under the Employee Retirement Income Security Act, and parallel provisions of the Internal Revenue Code of 1986, relating to the provision of investment advice to participants and beneficiaries in individual account plans, such as 401(k) plans, and beneficiaries of individual retirement accounts (and certain similar plans). Upon adoption, the proposed rule would implement provisions of a statutory prohibited transaction exemption, and would replace guidance contained in a final rule, published in the **Federal Register** on January 21, 2009, that was withdrawn by the Department pursuant to a Notice published in the **Federal Register** on November 20, 2009. Upon adoption, the proposed rule affects sponsors, fiduciaries, participants and beneficiaries of par-

ticipant-directed individual account plans, as well as providers of investment and investment advice related services to such plans.

DATES: Written comments on the proposed regulations should be submitted to the Department of Labor on or before May 5, 2010.

FOR FURTHER INFORMATION CONTACT: Fred Wong, Office of Regulations and Interpretations, Employee Benefits Security Administration (EBSA), (202) 693-8500. This is not a toll-free number.

ADDRESSES: To facilitate the receipt and processing of comment letters, the EBSA encourages interested persons to submit their comments electronically by e-mail to *e-ORI@dol.gov* (enter into subject line: 2010 Investment Advice Proposed Rule) or by using the Federal eRulemaking portal at *http://www.regulations.gov*. Persons submitting comments electronically are encouraged not to submit paper copies. Persons interested in submitting paper copies should send or deliver their comments to the Office of Regulations and Interpretations, Employee Benefits Security Administration, *Attn*: 2010 Investment Advice Proposed Rule, Room N-5655, U.S. Department of Labor, 200 Constitution Avenue, NW., Washington, DC 20210. All comments will be available to the public, without charge, online at *http://www.regulations.gov* and *http://www.dol.gov/ebsa* and at the Public Disclosure Room, N-1513, Employee Benefits Security Administration, U.S. Department of Labor, 200 Constitution Avenue, NW., Washington, DC 20210.

SUPPLEMENTARY INFORMATION:

A. Background

On January 21, 2009, the Department of Labor published final rules on the provision of investment advice to participants and beneficiaries of participant-directed individual account plans and to beneficiaries of individual retirement accounts and certain similar plans (IRAs) (74 FR 3822). The rules implement a statutory prohibited transaction exemption under ERISA Sec. 408(b)(14) and Sec. 408(g), and under section 4975 of the Internal Revenue Code of 1986 (Code),[1] and also contain an administrative class exemption granting additional relief. As published, these rules were to be effective on March 23, 2009. On February 4, 2009, the Department published in the **Federal Register (**74 FR 6007) an invitation for public comment on a proposed 60 day extension of the effective dates of the final rules in order to afford the Agency the opportunity to review legal and policy issues relating to the final rules. The Department also invited public comments on the provisions of those rules and on the merits of rescinding, modifying or retaining the rules. In response to this invitation, the Department received 28 comment letters.[2] On March 20, 2009, the Department adopted a 60 day extension of the final rule. (*See* 74 FR 11847). In order to afford the Department additional time to consider the issues raised by commenters, the effective and applicability dates were further delayed until November 18, 2009 (74 FR 23951), and then until May 17, 2010 (74 FR 59092).

B. Comments Received

A number of the commenters expressed the view that the final rule raises significant issues of law and policy, and should be withdrawn. Several of these commenters argued that the class exemption contained in the final rule permits financial interests that would cause a fiduciary adviser, and individuals providing investment advice on behalf of a fiduciary adviser, to have conflicts of interest, but does not contain conditions that would adequately mitigate such conflicts. They asserted that investment advice provided under the class exemption therefore might be tainted by the fiduciary adviser's conflicts. Other commenters expressed concerns about those provisions of the rule relating to the "fee-leveling" requirement under the statutory exemption. In particular, some opined that the Department's interpretation of the statutory exemption's fee-leveling requirement is incorrect for permitting the receipt of varying fees by an affiliate of a fiduciary adviser. As a result, they argued, a fiduciary adviser under such a feeleveling arrangement has a conflict of interest, and the final rule does not adequately protect against investment advice that is influenced by the financial interests of the fiduciary adviser's affiliates. Commenters who advocated retention of the final rule argued that it contains strong safeguards that would protect the interests of plan participants and beneficiaries.

C. Analysis and determination

As documented in the Department's regulatory impact analysis (RIA) of the January 2009 final regulation and class exemption, defined contribution (DC) plan participants and IRA beneficiaries often make costly investment errors. Those who receive and follow quality investment advice can reduce such errors and thereby reap substantial financial benefit. The Department estimated that the PPA statutory exemption as implemented by the final regulation, together with the final class exemption, would extend investment advice to 21 million previously unadvised participants and beneficiaries, generating $13 billion in annual financial benefits at a cost of $5 billion, for a net annual financial benefit of $8 billion.

In arriving at its estimates, the Department assumed that on average participants and beneficiaries who are advised make investment errors at one-half the rate of those who are not. The Department further assumed that different types of investment advice arrangements on average would be equally effective: arrangements operating without need for exemptive relief, those operating pursuant to the PPA, and those operating pursuant to the class exemption all would reduce investment errors by one-half on average.

The Department's assumptions regarding the effectiveness of different advice arrangements were subject to uncertainty, particularly as applied to its assessment of the final class exemption's effects. The Department has determined that the issues raised by commenters are sufficient to cast doubt as to whether the class exemption's conditions are adequate to mitigate advisers' conflicts. Based on this determination regarding the class exemption, the Department has decided to withdraw the final rule. Notice of the withdrawal of the final rule was published in the **Federal Register** on November 20, 2009 (74 FR 60156).

In order to address the absence of regulatory guidance on the statutory exemption that results from withdrawal of the January 2009 final rule, the Department is publishing in this notice proposed regulations that, upon adoption, implement the statutory prohibited transaction exemption under ERISA Sec. 408(b)(14) and Sec. 408(g), and parallel provisions in the Code. The proposed regulations do not include a class exemption. The Department notes that, while relief would have been available under the withdrawn class exemption, the statutory exemption does not provide prohibited transaction relief for any individualized advice rendered to individuals following the furnishing of investment recommendations generated by a computer model described in the statute unless such advice on its own meets the requirements of the statute (i.e., is generated by a computer model under a computer-model arrangement or is rendered under a fee-leveling arrangement).

D. Overview of Proposed Regulations

Proposed Sec. 2550.408g-1 tracks the requirements under section 408(g) of ERISA that must be satisfied in order for the investment advice-related transactions described in section 408(b)(14) to be exempt from the prohibitions of section 406. Paragraph (a) of the proposal describes the general scope of the statutory exemption and regulation. Paragraph (b) of the proposal sets forth the requirements that must be satisfied for an arrangement to qualify as an "eligible investment advice arrangement" and for the exemption to apply. Paragraph (c) of the proposal defines certain terms used in the regulation. The Appendix to the proposal contains a non-mandatory model disclosure form that may be used to satisfy certain of the requirements contained in paragraph (b). Proposed Sec. 2550.408g-2 addresses the requirements for electing to be treated as the only fiduciary and fiduciary adviser by reason of developing or marketing a computer model or an investment advice program used in an "eligible investment advice arrangement." *See* ERISA section 408(g)(11)(A).

The proposed regulations are nearly identical to the provisions of the January 2009 final rule that implement the statutory exemption. The Department's explanations of such provisions provided in the publication of the January 2009 final rule and in the publication of the related August 2008 proposed rule (73 FR 49896 (Aug. 22, 2008)), to the extent not modified or superseded in the January 2009 publication, should be read as applicable to the regulations being proposed in this notice. The Department is not providing a new description of the provisions.

The Department notes, however, that the proposed regulations contain clarifying language intended to address comment letters, mentioned above, that expressed concerns with the provisions of the final rule that interpret the statutory exemption's fee-leveling requirement. In particular, some commenters observed that the final rule would permit the receipt of varying fees by an affiliate of a fiduciary adviser, and further opined that this would permit an affiliate of a fiduciary adviser to establish economic incentives for either the fiduciary adviser, or individuals providing investment advice on its behalf, to recommend investments that pay varying fees to the affiliate. Therefore, commenters argued, the final rule would not adequately protect participants and beneficiaries from advice influenced by the affiliates' interests. In response, the Department is emphasizing in the proposal that, as stated in Field Assistance Bulletin 2007-1 (February 2, 2007) (FAB 2007-1), the receipt by a fiduciary adviser of any payment from any party (including an affiliate of the fiduciary adviser), or used for the benefit of such fiduciary adviser, that is based, in whole or part, on investments selected by participants or beneficiaries would be inconsistent with the fee-leveling requirement of the statutory exemption.[3] The Department also is further clarifying that this limitation applies both to an entity that is retained to render advice, and to any employee, agent, or registered representative of such an entity. Thus, even though an affiliate of a fiduciary adviser may receive fees that vary depending on investment options selected, any provision of financial or economic

---

[1] Section 601 of the Pension Protection Act of 2006 (PPA) added sections 408(b)(14) and 408(g) of ERISA. The PPA also added parallel provisions to the Code at sections 4975(d)(17) and 4975(f)(8). Under Reorganization Plan No. 4 of 1978 (43 FR 47713, Oct. 17, 1978), 5 U.S.C. App. 1, 92 Stat. 3790, the authority of the Secretary of the Treasury to issue rulings under section 4975 of the Code has been transferred, with certain exceptions not here relevant, to the Secretary of Labor. Therefore, the references in this notice to specific sections of ERISA should be taken as referring also to the corresponding sections of the Code.

[2] These comments are available on the Department's website at: *http://www.dol.gov/ ebsa/regs/cmtinvestmentadvicefinalrule.html.*

[3] FAB 2007-1 provides that "the fees or other compensation (including salary, bonuses, awards, promotions or any other thing of value) received, directly or indirectly *from an employer, affiliate or other party,* by a fiduciary adviser (or used for the adviser's benefit) may not be based, in whole or part, on the investment options selected by participants or beneficiaries." *See* FAB 2007-1, footnote 11 (emphasis added).

incentives by an affiliate (or any other party) to a fiduciary adviser or any individual employed by such fiduciary adviser (e.g., an employee providing advice on its behalf or an individual responsible for supervising such an employee) to favor certain investments would be impermissible. These are reflected in the proposal at paragraph (b)(3)(i)(D) of Sec. 2550.408g-1.

The proposed regulation also provides, in connection with investment advice arrangements that use computer models, that a computer model shall be designed and operated to avoid investment recommendations that inappropriately distinguish among investment options within a single asset class on the basis of a factor that cannot confidently be expected to persist in the future (paragraph (b)(4)(i)(E)(3)). While some differences between investment options within a single asset class, such as differences in fees and expenses or management style, are likely to persist in the future and therefore to constitute appropriate criteria for asset allocation, other differences, such as differences in historical performance, are less likely to persist and therefore less likely to constitute appropriate criteria for asset allocation. Asset classes, in contrast, can more often be distinguished from one another on the basis of differences in their historical risk and return characteristics.

E. Effective Date

The Department proposes that the regulations contained in this notice will be effective 60 days after publication of the final regulations in the **Federal Register**. The Department invites comments on whether the final regulations should be made effective on a different date.

F. Request for Comment

The Department invites comments from interested persons on the proposed regulations. In particular, the Department solicits comments on the conditions applicable to investment advice arrangements that use computer models under proposed § 2550.408g-1(b)(4)(i), including responses to the following questions.

What investment theories are generally accepted for purposes of § 2550.408g-1(b)(4)(i)(A), and what investment practices are consistent or inconsistent with such theories? Should this regulation specify such theories and require their application? Should the regulation dictate the bases for model parameters such as the probability distribution of future returns to assets classes or particular investments? Should the regulation specify certain practices as required by generally accepted investment theories, or certain other practices as proscribed by such theories? What are examples of investment theories that are not generally accepted? Should this regulation expressly proscribe the application of certain such theories?

What historical data should be taken into account in determining a model's expectation for future performance of asset classes and specific investment alternatives? Should the regulation specify minimum standards for the data, such as a minimum number of years of experience to be included in the data?

What types of criteria are appropriate and objective bases for asset allocation pursuant to proposed § 2550.408g-1(b)(4)(i)(D)? Should this regulation expressly designate some criteria as appropriate and objective and/or other criteria as not appropriate or not objective? Should it do both, thereby establishing a list of criteria that models must consider to the exclusion of all others? For example, the regulation could provide that computer models must consider only the historical risks and returns of different asset classes as a whole, information about the participants, and the expenses and asset allocation of each investment option under the plan. Is a fund's past performance relative to the average for its asset class an appropriate criterion for allocating assets to the fund? Under what if any conditions would it be consistent with generally accepted investment theories and with consideration of fees pursuant to § 2550.408g-1(b)(4)(i)(B) to recommend a fund with superior past performance over an alternative fund in the same asset class with average performance but lower fees? Should the regulation specify such conditions? On what if any bases can a fund's superior past performance be demonstrated to derive not from chance but from factors that are likely to persist and continue to affect performance in the future? Should the use of a fund's superior past performance as a criterion for allocating assets to the fund be conditioned on such demonstration? How, if at all, should a model take into account investment management style? For example, all else equal, should a model ascribe different levels of risk to passively and actively managed investment options?

To facilitate the receipt and processing of comment letters, the EBSA encourages interested persons to submit their comments electronically by e-mail to *e-ORI@dol.gov* (enter into subject line: 2010 Investment Advice Proposed Rule) or by using the Federal eRulemaking portal at *http://www.regulations.gov*. Persons submitting comments electronically are encouraged not to submit paper copies. Persons interested in submitting paper copies should send or deliver their comments to the Office of Regulations and Interpretations, Employee Benefits Security Administration, *Attn*: 2010 Investment Advice Proposed Rule, Room N-5655, U.S. Department of Labor, 200 Constitution Avenue, NW., Washington, DC 20210. All comments will be available to the public, without charge, online at *http://www.regulations.gov* and *http://www.dol.gov/ebsa* and at the Public Disclosure Room, N-1513, Employee Benefits Security Administration, U.S. Department of Labor, 200 Constitution Avenue, NW., Washington, DC 20210.

The comment period for the proposed regulations will end May 5, 2010. The Department believes that this period of time will afford interested persons an adequate amount of time to analyze the proposal and submit comments. Written comments on the proposed regulations should be submitted to the Department on or before May 5, 2010.

G. Regulatory Impact Analysis

Need for Regulatory Action

As documented in the Department's regulatory impact analysis of the August 2008 proposed regulation, there is evidence that many participants in participant-directed defined contribution (DC) plans and beneficiaries of individual retirement accounts (IRAs) (collectively hereafter, "participants") make poor investment decisions due to flawed information or reasoning. These participants may pay higher fees and expenses than necessary for investment products and services, engage in excessive or poorly timed trading or fail to adequately diversify their portfolios and thereby assume uncompensated risk, take more or less than optimal levels of compensated risk, and/or pay unnecessarily high taxes. Financial losses (including foregone earnings) from such mistakes likely amounted to more than $85 billion in 2009. These losses compound and grow larger as workers progress toward and into retirement.

The Department anticipates that full implementation of the PPA under this proposed regulation will ensure that quality, expert investment advice is provided to the greatest number of participants. The Department further anticipates that the increased investment advice resulting from the rule will improve participants investment decisions and results and reduce investment related errors and expenses.

In the statutory exemption, Congress called on the Department to provide regulatory guidance addressing the certification of computer model investment advice programs, a model form for disclosure of fees and other compensation received by the fiduciary adviser or an affiliate, and rules under which only one fiduciary adviser may elect to be treated as a fiduciary.[4] This proposed regulation addressed these issues, as well as additional questions raised by employers and other fiduciaries regarding their responsibilities in connection with other provisions of the statutory exemption.

Alternatives

Executive Order 12866 requires an economically significant regulation to include an assessment of the costs and benefits of potentially effective and reasonably feasible alternatives to a planned regulation, and an explanation of why the planned regulatory action is preferable to the identified potential alternatives. In formulating this proposed regulation, the Department considered two alternative approaches that are discussed below.

Detailed, Prescriptive Substantive Standards for Computer Model Design

To assure the quality of investment advice provided pursuant to the statutory exemption, this proposed regulation relies primarily on safeguards against bias that might otherwise arise from advisers' conflicts of interest. These safeguards include, for example, strong procedural standards for certification of computer models and audits of investment advice programs, and strict, carefully drawn standards for level-fee arrangements that broadly proscribe all manner of variable payments to advisers.

As an additional approach to ensuring that investment advice is not tainted by conflicts of interest, the Department considered requiring that a computer model consider only the historical risks and returns of different asset classes as a whole, information about the participants,

---

[4] *See* sections 408(g)(3)(C), 408(g)(8)(B), and 408(g)(11)(A) (flush language) of ERISA.

and the expenses and asset allocation of each investment option under the plan. However, the Department believes that the approach it has taken will effectively ensure that advice is not tainted by conflicts of interest, so the addition of such a restriction would be unnecessary. The Department also believes that such a restriction may inhibit innovations in investment advice that utilizes additional information, which could reduce the economic benefits of the statutory exemption. Nonetheless, the Department, as reflected in questions appearing earlier in this preamble, is interested in further exploring the merits of adopting such an alternative approach.

Additional Exemptive Relief

The Department's January 2009 final rule included a class exemption that would establish alternative conditions for granting prohibited transaction relief in connection with the provision of investment advice. The Department considered retaining such a class exemption in this new proposed rule. However, after considering issues raised by public comments received in response to the Department's February 4, 2009, notice, the Department decided to withdraw the class exemption. As discussed earlier, a number of commenters questioned the adequacy of the final class exemption's conditions to mitigate the potential for investment adviser selfdealing. The Department decided not to retain the class exemption in this proposal, because it found that the questions raised in these comments cast sufficient doubt on the conditions' adequacy to mitigate advisers' conflicts. The regulatory impact of the decision to withdraw the class exemption is discussed below.

Withdrawal of the Class Exemption

As documented in the Department's regulatory impact analysis (RIA) of the January 2009 final regulation and class exemption, defined contribution (DC) plan participants and IRA beneficiaries often make costly investment errors. Those who receive and follow quality investment advice can reduce such errors and thereby reap substantial financial benefit. Although the Department anticipated that the final rule would increase the availability of investment advice to DC plan participants and the use of advice by IRA beneficiaries, the Department stated that it was uncertain how changing market conditions might affect the incidence and magnitude of investment errors, as well as the availability, use, and effect of investment advice. The Department estimated that the PPA statutory exemption as implemented by the final regulation, together with the final class exemption, would extend investment advice to 21 million previously unadvised participants and beneficiaries, potentially generating as much as $13 billion in annual financial benefits at a cost of $5 billion, for a net annual financial benefit of $8 billion. In the 2009 final rule's RIA, Department stated its belief that the approach used in the analysis could reflect the long-term effects of these actions.

In arriving at its estimates, the Department assumed that on average participants and beneficiaries who are advised make investment errors at one-half the rate of those who are not. The Department further assumed that different types of investment advice arrangements on average would be equally effective: arrangements operating without need for exemptive relief, those operating pursuant to the PPA, and those operating pursuant to the class exemption all would reduce investment errors by one-half on average.

The Department's assumptions regarding the effectiveness of different advice arrangements were subject to uncertainty, particularly as applied to its assessment of the final class exemption's effects. In the preamble to the January 2009 final regulation and class exemption, the Department noted evidence that conflicts of interest, such as those that might be attendant to advice arrangements operating pursuant to the class exemption, can sometimes taint advice. Conflicted advisers pursu-

ing their own interests, and the investment managers who compensate them, may profit at the expense of participants and beneficiaries. The conditions attached to the class exemption were intended to ensure that advisers operating pursuant to the class exemption would honor the interests of participants and beneficiaries.

In its February 4, 2009, notice proposing to extend the effective dates of the final regulation and class exemption, the Department solicited public comments on the provisions of those rules and on the merits of rescinding, modifying or retaining the rules. As discussed earlier, a number of commenters raised legal and policy issues concerning the exemption and, in particular, questioned the adequacy of the final class exemption's conditions to mitigate the potential for investment adviser self-dealing.

The Department believes that the questions raised in these comments are sufficient to cast doubt on the conditions' adequacy to mitigate advisers' conflicts. If conflicts are not mitigated, advice might be tainted. Therefore, the Department has set aside its previous assumption that participants and beneficiaries who follow advice delivered pursuant to the final class exemption will commit investment errors at one-half the rate of those who are unadvised, together with its previous conclusion that the final class exemption's benefits justify its cost. Instead, the Department believes that doubts as to whether the final class exemption's conditions are adequate to mitigate conflicts justify withdrawal of the final class exemption.

Impact Assessment

In arriving at its January 2009 estimates of the combined effects of the final regulation and class exemption, the Department assumed that the incidence of investment advice arrangements permissible prior to the PPA would remain unchanged, while investment advice arrangements operating pursuant to the PPA statutory exemption and those operating pursuant to the class exemption would claim equal shares of the estimated growth of advice arrangements.

The Department has now updated its estimates of the costs and benefits of the proposed regulation to reflect the withdrawal of the class exemption. It is likely that some previously unadvised participants and beneficiaries who would have received advice pursuant to the class exemption will instead receive advice pursuant to the PPA statutory exemption, while others will remain unadvised.

Recently the Administration has taken major steps toward broad financial regulatory reform. On June 17, 2009, the President announced the Administration's proposal for "21 st Century Financial Regulatory Reform." The proposal includes provisions designed to strengthen investor protections in ways that the Department believes may beneficially influence the market for investment advice. Comprehensive reforms to the market for financial products and services, together with the PPA's exemptive relief as implemented by the Department's final regulation, may promote the availability of quality, affordable investment advice more than the latter would alone.

The estimates provided in the table below show three possible impacts for the proposed regulation: "low" estimates assume that all of those who would have received advice pursuant to the class exemption instead remain unadvised, "mid" estimates assume that one-half receive advice pursuant to the PPA statutory exemption, and "high" estimates assume that all receive such advice. The Department has updated its estimates to reflect year-end 2008 DC plan and IRA assets. Otherwise, the assumptions and calculations remain the same as presented in the preamble to the January 2009 final regulation and class exemption. The Department's low middle, and high estimates are presented in Table 1, below.

Table 1. Effect of PPA statutory exemption as implemented by proposed regulation $Billions, annual, in 2008 dollars and at 2008 asset levels

	Investment errors eliminated	Cost of advice	Net effect
Low	$5.5	$1.5	$3.9
Mid	8.2	2.3	5.9
High	10.9	3.1	7.8

On the basis of these estimates the Department believes that this proposed regulation, in isolation from the withdrawn class exemption, will yield benefits sufficient to justify its costs. The Department continues to believe that DC plan participants and IRA beneficiaries often make costly investment errors, and that those who receive and follow quality investment advice can reduce such errors and thereby reap substantial financial benefit.

H. Executive Order 12866 Statement

Under Executive Order 12866, the Department must designate a regulatory action it believes is "significant'" and therefore subject to the requirements of the Executive Order and OMB review. Under section 3(f), the order defines a "significant regulatory action" as an action that is likely to result in a rule (1) having an annual effect on the economy of $100 million or more, or adversely and materially affecting a sector of the economy, productivity, competition, jobs, the environment, public health or safety, or State, local or tribal governments or communities (also referred to as "economically significant"); (2) creating serious inconsistency or otherwise interfering with an action taken or planned by another agency; (3) materially altering the budgetary impacts of entitlement grants, user fees, or loan programs or the rights and obligations of recipients thereof; or (4) raising novel legal or policy issues arising out of legal mandates, the President's priorities, or the principles set forth in the Executive Order.

Pursuant to the terms of the Executive Order, this action, comprising this proposed rule, is economically significant under section 3(f)(1) of the Executive Order because it is likely to have an effect on the economy of $100 million or more in any one year. Accordingly, the Department undertook the foregoing analysis of the action's impact. On the basis of that analysis, the Department believes that the action's benefits justify its costs.

I. Regulatory Flexibility Act

As it did in the January 2009 final rule, the Department hereby certifies that this proposed rule will not have a significant economic impact on a substantial number of small entities. For purposes of the analysis, the Department proposed to continue its usual practice of considering a small entity to be an employee benefit plan with fewer than 100 participants. The Department consulted with the Small Business Administration Office of Advocacy concerning use of this participant count standard for Regulatory Flexibility Act purposes and requested public comment on this issue in the January 2009 final rule. The Department did not receive any comments that address its use of the participant count standard and continues to consider a small entity to be an employee benefit plan with fewer than 100 participants.

J. Congressional Review Act

This proposed regulation is a major rule is subject to the Congressional Review Act provisions of the Small Business Regulatory Enforcement Fairness Act of 1996 (5 U.S.C. 801 *et seq.*) and, if finalized, will be transmitted to the Congress and the Comptroller General for review.

K. Unfunded Mandates Reform Act

For purposes of the Unfunded Mandates Reform Act of 1995 (Pub. L. 104-4), as well as Executive Order 12875, the proposed rule does not include any federal mandate that will result in expenditures by state, local, or tribal governments in the aggregate of more than $100 million, adjusted for inflation, or increase expenditures by the private sector of more than $100 million, adjusted for inflation.

L. Federalism Statement

Executive Order 13132 (August 4, 1999) outlines fundamental principles of federalism and requires the adherence to specific criteria by federal agencies in the process of their formulation and implementation of policies that have substantial direct effects on the States, the relationship between the national government and the States, or on the distribution of power and responsibilities among the various levels of government. This proposed rule does not have federalism implications because it has no substantial direct effect on the States, on the relationship between the national government and the States, or on the distribution of power and responsibilities among the various levels of government. Section 514 of ERISA provides, with certain exceptions specifically enumerated, that the provisions of Titles I and IV of ERISA supersede any and all laws of the States as they relate to any employee benefit plan covered under ERISA. The requirements implemented in the rule do not alter the fundamental provisions of the statute with respect to employee benefit plans, and as such would have no implications for the States or the relationship or distribution of power between the national government and the States.

M. Paperwork Reduction Act

In accordance with the requirements of the Paperwork Reduction Act of 1995 (PRA) (44 U.S.C. 3506(c)(2)), the Department submitted an ICR to OMB for its request of a new information collection for the previous final rule. OMB approved the ICR on January 9, 2009, under

OMB Control Number 1210-0134, which will expire on January 31, 2012.

In connection with the issuance of this proposed rule, the Department submitted a revised ICR to OMB on October 23, 2009, reflecting information collection requirements associated with the PPA statutory exemption. In order to use the statutory exemption to provide investment advice to participants and beneficiaries in participant-directed DC plans and beneficiaries of IRAs (collectively hereafter, "participants"), investment advisory firms are required to make disclosures to participants, hire an independent auditor to conduct a compliance audit, and issue an audit report every year. Investment advice firms following the conditions of the exemption based on computer model-generated investment advice are required to obtain certification of the model from an eligible investment expert. These information collection requirements are designed to safeguard the interests of participants in connection with investment advice covered by the exemption.

This paperwork burden analysis reflects a very minor increase to the estimated number of DC plan sponsors offering advice, the number of DC plan participants utilizing advice, the labor hour rates used to estimate the hour burden, and the postage rate used to estimate the cost burden.[5] All other calculations remain the same as in the January 2009 final rule.

Statutory exemption hour and cost burden

For purposes of determining the hour and cost burden associated with the statutory exemption, the Department's analysis uses the "mid" estimate discussed under the section above, which assumes that one-half of participants who would have received advice pursuant to the class exemption now will receive advice pursuant to the PPA statutory exemption. The Department estimates that the third-party disclosures, computer model certification, and audit requirements for the statutory exemption will require approximately 4.5 million burden hours with an equivalent cost of approximately $486.7 million and a cost burden of approximately $579.8 million in the first year. In each subsequent year, the total labor burden hours are estimated to be approximately 2.4 million hours with an equivalent cost of approximately $252.6 million and the cost burden is estimated at approximately $430.5 million per year.[6]

These paperwork burden estimates are summarized as follows:

Type of Review: Revised Collection.

Agency: Employee Benefits Security Administration, Department of Labor.

Titles: Statutory Exemption for the Provision of Investment Advice to Participants and Beneficiaries of Participant-Directed Individual Account Plans and IRAs.

OMB Control Number: 1210-0134.

Affected Public: Business or other for-profit.

Estimated Number of Respondents: 16,000.

Estimated Number of Annual Responses: 15,156,000.

Frequency of Response: Initially, Annually, Upon Request, when a material change.

Estimated Total Annual Burden Hours: 4,453,000 hours in the first year; 2,428,000 hours in each subsequent year.

Estimated Total Annual Burden Cost: $579,808,000 in the first year; $430,508,000 for each subsequent year.

List of Subjects in 29 CFR Part 2550

Employee benefit plans, Exemptions, Fiduciaries, Investments, Pensions, Prohibited transactions, Reporting and recordkeeping requirements, and Securities.

For the reasons set forth in the preamble, Chapter XXV, subchapter F, part 2550 of Title 29 of the Code of Federal Regulations is proposed to be amended as follows:

---

[5] The increase in the estimated number of DC plans offering advice and DC plan participants utilizing advice is due to updating the count to reflect 2006 Form 5500 data, the latest year for which Form 5500 data is available. The counts in the 2009 Final Rule were based on 2005 Form 5500 data. The postage rate was increased to $0.44 from $0.42 due to the January 2009 increase. The labor hour rates were updated to reflect 2009 rates instead of 2008 rates, which were used in the 2009 Final Rule.

[6] If the 'low' estimate were used, which assumes that all of the participants who would have received advice pursuant to the class exemption instead remain unadvised, the statutory exemption will require approximately 4 million burden hours with an equivalent cost of approximately $444.7 million and a cost burden of approximately $579.4 million in

the first year. In each subsequent year, the total labor burden hours are estimated to be approximately 2.2 million hours with an equivalent cost of approximately $229.9 million and the cost burden is estimated at approximately $430.1 million per year. If the 'high' estimate were used, which assumes that all of the participants who would have received advice pursuant to the class exemption will receive advice under the statutory exemption, the statutory exemption will require approximately 4.9 million burden hours with an equivalent cost of approximately $528.7 million and a cost burden of approximately $580.2 million in the first year. In each subsequent year, the total labor burden hours are estimated to be approximately 2.7 million hours with an equivalent cost of approximately $275.3 million and the cost burden is estimated at approximately $430.9 million per year.

PART 2550—RULES AND REGULATIONS FOR FIDUCIARY RESPONSIBILITY

1. The authority citation for part 2550 is revised to read as follows:

Authority: 29 U.S.C. 1135; and Secretary of Labor's Order No. 6-2009, 74 FR 21524 (May 7, 2009). Secs. 2550.401b-1, 2550.408b-1, 2550.408b-19, 2550.408g-1, and 2550.408g-2 also issued under sec. 102, Reorganization Plan No. 4 of 1978, 5 U.S.C. App. Sec. 2550.401c-1 also issued under 29 U.S.C. 1101. Sections 2550.404c-1 and 2550.404c-5 also issued under 29 U.S.C. 1104. Sec. 2550.407c-3 also issued under 29 U.S.C. 1107. Sec. 2550.404a-2 also issued under 26 U.S.C. 401 note (sec. 657(c)(2), Pub. L. 107-16, 115 Stat. 38, 136 (2001)). Sec. 2550.408b-1 also issued under 29 U.S.C. 1108(b)(1). Sec. 2550.408b-19 also issued under sec. 611(g)(3), Public Law 109-280, 120 Stat. 780, 975 (2006).

2. Add § 2550.408g-1 to read as follows:

§ 2550.408g-1 Investment advice - participants and beneficiaries.

(a) In general. (1) This section provides relief from the prohibitions of section 406 of the Employee Retirement Income Security Act of 1974, as amended (ERISA or the Act), and section 4975 of the Internal Revenue Code of 1986, as amended (the Code), for certain transactions in connection with the provision of investment advice to participants and beneficiaries. This section, at paragraph (b), implements the statutory exemption set forth at sections 408(b)(14) and 408(g)(1) of ERISA and sections 4975(d)(17) and 4975(f)(8) of the Code. The requirements and conditions set forth in this section apply solely for the relief described in paragraph (b) of this section and, accordingly, no inferences should be drawn with respect to requirements applicable to the provision of investment advice not addressed by this section.

(2) Nothing contained in ERISA section 408(g)(1), Code section 4975(f)(8), or this regulation imposes an obligation on a plan fiduciary or any other party to offer, provide or otherwise make available any investment advice to a participant or beneficiary.

(3) Nothing contained in ERISA section 408(g)(1), Code section 4975(f)(8), or this regulation invalidates or otherwise affects prior regulations, exemptions, interpretive or other guidance issued by the Department of Labor pertaining to the provision of investment advice and the circumstances under which such advice may or may not constitute a prohibited transaction under section 406 of ERISA or section 4975 of the Code.

(b) Statutory exemption. (1) *General.* Sections 408(b)(14) and 408(g)(1) of ERISA provide an exemption from the prohibitions of section 406 of ERISA for transactions described in section 408(b)(14) of ERISA in connection with the provision of investment advice to a participant or a beneficiary if the investment advice is provided by a fiduciary adviser under an "eligible investment advice arrangement." Sections 4975(d)(17) and (f)(8) of the Code contain parallel provisions to ERISA sections 408(b)(14) and (g)(1).

(2) *Eligible investment advice.* For purposes of section 408(g)(1) of ERISA and section 4975(f)(8) of the Code, an "eligible investment advice arrangement" means an arrangement that meets either the requirements of paragraph (b)(3) of this section or paragraph (b)(4) of this section, or both.

(3) *Arrangements that use fee-leveling.* For purposes of this section, an arrangement is an eligible investment advice arrangement if —

(i)(A) Any investment advice is based on generally accepted investment theories that take into account the historic risks and returns of different asset classes over defined periods of time, although nothing herein shall preclude any investment advice from being based on generally accepted investment theories that take into account additional considerations;

(B) Any investment advice takes into account investment management and other fees and expenses attendant to the recommended investments;

(C) Any investment advice takes into account, to the extent furnished by a plan, participant or beneficiary, information relating to age, time horizons (e.g., life expectancy, retirement age), risk tolerance, current investments in designated investment options, other assets or sources of income, and investment preferences of the participant or beneficiary. A fiduciary adviser shall request such information, but nothing in this paragraph (b)(3)(i)(C) shall require that any investment advice take into account information requested, but not furnished by a participant or beneficiary, nor preclude requesting and taking into account additional information that a plan or participant or beneficiary may provide;

(D) No fiduciary adviser (including any employee, agent, or registered representative) that provides investment advice receives from any party (including an affiliate of the fiduciary adviser), directly or indirectly, any fee or other compensation (including commissions, salary, bonuses, awards, promotions, or other things of value) that is based in whole or in part on a participant's or beneficiary's selection of an investment option; and

(ii) The requirements of paragraphs (b)(5), (6), (7), and (8) and paragraph (d) of this section are met.

(4) *Arrangements that use computer models.* For purposes of this section, an arrangement is an eligible investment advice arrangement if the only investment advice provided under the arrangement is advice that is generated by a computer model described in paragraphs (b)(4)(i) and (ii) of this section under an investment advice program and with respect to which the requirements of paragraphs (b)(5), (6), (7), and (8) and paragraph (d) are met.

(i) A computer model shall be designed and operated to —

(A) Apply generally accepted investment theories that take into account the historic risks and returns of different asset classes over defined periods of time, although nothing herein shall preclude a computer model from applying generally accepted investment theories that take into account additional considerations;

(B) Take into account investment management and other fees and expenses attendant to the recommended investments;

(C) Request from a participant or beneficiary and, to the extent furnished, utilize information relating to age, time horizons (e.g., life expectancy, retirement age), risk tolerance, current investments in designated investment options, other assets or sources of income, and investment preferences; provided, however, that nothing herein shall preclude a computer model from requesting and taking into account additional information that a plan or a participant or beneficiary may provide;

(D) Utilize appropriate objective criteria to provide asset allocation portfolios comprised of investment options available under the plan;

(E) Avoid investment recommendations that:

(1) Inappropriately favor investment options offered by the fiduciary adviser or a person with a material affiliation or material contractual relationship with the fiduciary adviser over other investment options, if any, available under the plan;

(2) Inappropriately favor investment options that may generate greater income for the fiduciary adviser or a person with a material affiliation or material contractual relationship with the fiduciary adviser; or

(3) Inappropriately distinguish among investment options within a single asset class on the basis of a factor that cannot confidently be expected to persist in the future; and

(F)(1) Except as provided in paragraph (b)(4)(i)(F) *(2)* of this section, take into account all designated investment options, within the meaning of paragraph (c)(1) of this section, available under the plan without giving inappropriate weight to any investment option.

(2) A computer model shall not be treated as failing to meet the requirements of this paragraph merely because it does not make recommendations relating to the acquisition, holding or sale of an investment option that:

(i) Constitutes an investment primarily in qualifying employer securities;

(ii) Constitutes an investment fund, product or service that allocates the invested assets of a participant or beneficiary to achieve varying degrees of long-term appreciation and capital preservation through equity and fixed income exposures, based on a defined time horizon (such as retirement age or life expectancy) or level of risk of the participant or beneficiary, provided that, contemporaneous with the provision of investment advice generated by the computer model, the participant or beneficiary is also furnished a general description of such funds, products or services and how they operate; or

(iii) Constitutes an annuity option with respect to which a participant or beneficiary may allocate assets toward the purchase of a stream of retirement income payments guaranteed by an insurance company, provided that, contemporaneous with the provision of investment advice generated by the computer model, the participant or beneficiary is also furnished a general description of such options and how they operate.

(ii) Prior to utilization of the computer model, the fiduciary adviser shall obtain a written certification, meeting the requirements of paragraph (b)(4)(iv) of this section, from an eligible investment expert, within the meaning of paragraph (b)(4)(iii) of this section, that the computer model meets the requirements of paragraph (b)(4)(i) of this section. If, following certification, a computer model is modified in a manner that may affect its ability to meet the requirements of paragraph (b)(4)(i), the fiduciary adviser shall, prior to utilization of the modified model, obtain a new certification from an eligible investment expert that the computer model, as modified, meets the requirements of paragraph (b)(4)(i).

(iii) The term "eligible investment expert" means a person that, through employees or otherwise, has the appropriate technical training or experience and proficiency to analyze, determine and certify, in a manner consistent with paragraph (b)(4)(iv) of this section, whether a computer model meets the requirements of paragraph (b)(4)(i) of this section; except that the term "eligible investment expert" does not include any person that has any material affiliation or material contractual relationship with the fiduciary adviser, with a person with a material affiliation or material contractual relationship with the fiduciary adviser, or with any employee, agent, or registered representative of the foregoing.

(iv) A certification by an eligible investment expert shall -

(A) Be in writing;

(B) Contain —

(1) An identification of the methodology or methodologies applied in determining whether the computer model meets the requirements of paragraph (b)(4)(i) of this section;

(2) An explanation of how the applied methodology or methodologies demonstrated that the computer model met the requirements of paragraph (b)(4)(i) of this section;

(3) A description of any limitations that were imposed by any person on the eligible investment expert's selection or application of methodologies for determining whether the computer model meets the requirements of paragraph (b)(4)(i) of this section;

(4) A representation that the methodology or methodologies were applied by a person or persons with the educational background, technical training or experience necessary to analyze and determine whether the computer model meets the requirements of paragraph (b)(4)(i); and

(5) A statement certifying that the eligible investment expert has determined that the computer model meets the requirements of paragraph (b)(4)(i) of this section; and

(C) Be signed by the eligible investment expert.

(v) The selection of an eligible investment expert as required by this section is a fiduciary act governed by section 404(a)(1) of ERISA.

(5) Arrangement must be authorized by a plan fiduciary. (i) Except as provided in paragraph (b)(5)(ii), the arrangement pursuant to which investment advice is provided to participants and beneficiaries pursuant to this section must be expressly authorized by a plan fiduciary (or, in the case of an Individual Retirement Account (IRA), the IRA beneficiary) other than: the person offering the arrangement; any person providing designated investment options under the plan; or any affiliate of either. Provided, however, that for purposes of the preceding, in the case of an IRA, an IRA beneficiary will not be treated as an affiliate of a person solely by reason of being an employee of such person.

(ii) In the case of an arrangement pursuant to which investment advice is provided to participants and beneficiaries of a plan sponsored by the person offering the arrangement or a plan sponsored by an affiliate of such person, the authorization described in paragraph (b)(5)(i) may be provided by the plan sponsor of such plan, provided that the person or affiliate offers the same arrangement to participants and beneficiaries of unaffiliated plans in the ordinary course of its business.

(iii) For purposes of the authorization described in paragraph (b)(5)(i), a plan sponsor shall not be treated as a person providing a designated investment option under the plan merely because one of the designated investment options of the plan is an option that permits investment in securities of the plan sponsor or an affiliate.

(6) **Annual audit.** (i) The fiduciary adviser shall, at least annually, engage an independent auditor, who has appropriate technical training or experience and proficiency, and so represents in writing to the fiduciary adviser, to:

(A) Conduct an audit of the investment advice arrangements for compliance with the requirements of this section; and

(B) Within 60 days following completion of the audit, issue a written report to the fiduciary adviser and, except with respect to an arrangement with an IRA, to each fiduciary who authorized the use of the investment advice arrangement, in accordance with paragraph (b)(5) of this section, setting forth the specific findings of the auditor regarding compliance of the arrangement with the requirements of this section.

(ii) With respect to an arrangement with an IRA, the fiduciary adviser:

(A) Within 30 days following receipt of the report from the auditor, as described in paragraph (b)(6)(i)(B) of this section, shall furnish a copy of the report to the IRA beneficiary or make such report available on its website, provided that such beneficiaries are provided information, with the information required to be disclosed pursuant to paragraph (b)(7) of this section, concerning the purpose of the report, and how and where to locate the report applicable to their account; and

(B) In the event that the report of the auditor identifies noncompliance with the requirements of this section, within 30 days following receipt of the report from the auditor, shall send a copy of the report to the Department of Labor at the following address: Investment Advice Exemption Notification, U.S. Department of Labor, Employee Benefits Security Administration, Room N-1513, 200 Constitution Ave., NW., Washington, DC, 20210.

(iii) For purposes of this paragraph (b)(6), an auditor is considered independent if it does not have a material affiliation or material contractual relationship with the person offering the investment advice arrangement to the plan or with any designated investment options under the plan.

(iv) For purposes of this paragraph (b)(6), the auditor shall review sufficient relevant information to formulate an opinion as to whether the investment advice arrangements, and the advice provided pursuant thereto, offered by the fiduciary adviser during the audit period were in compliance with this section. Nothing in this paragraph shall preclude an auditor from using information obtained by sampling, as reasonably determined appropriate by the auditor, investment advice arrangements, and the advice pursuant thereto, during the audit period.

(v) The selection of an auditor for purposes of this paragraph (b)(6) is a fiduciary act governed by section 404(a)(1) of ERISA.

(7) Disclosure. (i) The fiduciary adviser must provide, without charge, to a participant or a beneficiary before the initial provision of investment advice with regard to any security or other property offered as an investment option, a written notification of:

(A) The role of any party that has a material affiliation or material contractual relationship with the fiduciary adviser in the development of the investment advice program, and in the selection of investment options available under the plan;

(B) The past performance and historical rates of return of the designated investment options available under the plan, to the extent that such information is not otherwise provided;

(C) All fees or other compensation that the fiduciary adviser or any affiliate thereof is to receive (including compensation provided by any third party) in connection with -

(1) The provision of the advice;

(2) The sale, acquisition, or holding of any security or other property pursuant to such advice; or

(3) Any rollover or other distribution of plan assets or the investment of distributed assets in any security or other property pursuant to such advice;

(D) Any material affiliation or material contractual relationship of the fiduciary adviser or affiliates thereof in the security or other property;

(E) The manner, and under what circumstances, any participant or beneficiary information provided under the arrangement will be used or disclosed;

(F) The types of services provided by the fiduciary adviser in connection with the provision of investment advice by the fiduciary adviser, including, with respect to a computer model arrangement referred to in paragraph (b)(4) of this section, any limitations on the ability of a computer model to take into account an investment primarily in qualifying employer securities;

(G) The adviser is acting as a fiduciary of the plan in connection with the provision of the advice; and

(H) That a recipient of the advice may separately arrange for the provision of advice by another adviser that could have no material affiliation with and receive no fees or other compensation in connection with the security or other property.

(ii)(A) The notification required under paragraph (b)(7)(i) of this section must be written in a clear and conspicuous manner and in a manner calculated to be understood by the average plan participant and must be sufficiently accurate and comprehensive to reasonably apprise such participants and beneficiaries of the information required to be provided in the notification.

(B) The appendix to this section contains a model disclosure form that may be used to provide notification of the information described in paragraph (b)(7)(i)(C) of this section. Use of the model form is not mandatory. However, use of an appropriately completed model disclosure form will be deemed to satisfy the requirements of paragraphs (b)(7)(i) and (ii) of this section with respect to such information.

(iii) The notification required under paragraph (b)(7)(i) of this section may, in accordance with 29 CFR 2520.104b-1, be provided in written or electronic form.

(iv) With respect to the information required to be disclosed pursuant to paragraph (b)(7)(i) of this section, the fiduciary adviser shall, at all times during the provision of advisory services to the participant or beneficiary pursuant to the arrangement, —

(A) Maintain accurate, up-to-date information in a form that is consistent with paragraph (b)(7)(ii) of this section,

(B) Provide, without charge, accurate, up-to-date information to the recipient of the advice no less frequently than annually,

(C) Provide, without charge, accurate information to the recipient of the advice upon request of the recipient, and

(D) Provide, without charge, to the recipient of the advice any material change to the information described in paragraph (b)(7)(i) at a time reasonably contemporaneous to the change in information.

(8) *Other Conditions.* The requirements of this paragraph are met if—

(i) The fiduciary adviser provides appropriate disclosure, in connection with the sale, acquisition, or holding of the security or other property, in accordance with all applicable securities laws,

(ii) Any sale, acquisition, or holding of a security or other property occurs solely at the direction of the recipient of the advice,

(iii) The compensation received by the fiduciary adviser and affiliates thereof in connection with the sale, acquisition, or holding of the security or other property is reasonable, and

(iv) The terms of the sale, acquisition, or holding of the security or other property are at least as favorable to the plan as an arm's length transaction would be.

(c) Definitions. For purposes of this section:

(1) The term "*designated investment option*" means any investment option designated by the plan into which participants and beneficiaries may direct the investment of assets held in, or contributed to, their individual accounts. The term "designated investment option" shall not include "brokerage windows," "self-directed brokerage accounts," or similar plan arrangements that enable participants and beneficiaries to select investments beyond those designated by the plan.

(2)(i) The term "*fiduciary adviser*" means, with respect to a plan, a person who is a fiduciary of the plan by reason of the provision of investment advice referred to in section 3(21)(A)(ii) of ERISA by the person to the participant or beneficiary of the plan and who is -

(A) Registered as an investment adviser under the Investment Advisers Act of 1940 (15 U.S.C. 80b-1 et seq.) or under the laws of the State in which the fiduciary maintains its principal office and place of business,

(B) A bank or similar financial institution referred to in section 408(b)(4) of ERISA or a savings association (as defined in section 3(b)(1) of the Federal Deposit Insurance Act (12 U.S.C. 1813(b)(1)), but only if the advice is provided through a trust department of the bank or similar financial institution or savings association which is subject to periodic examination and review by Federal or State banking authorities,

(C) An insurance company qualified to do business under the laws of a State,

(D) A person registered as a broker or dealer under the Securities Exchange Act of 1934 (15 U.S.C. 78a *et seq.*),

(E) An affiliate of a person described in paragraphs (c)(2)(i)(A) through (D), or

(F) An employee, agent, or registered representative of a person described in paragraphs (c)(2)(i)(A) through (E) of this section who

satisfies the requirements of applicable insurance, banking, and securities laws relating to the provision of advice.

(ii) Except as provided under 29 CFR 2550.408g-2, a fiduciary adviser includes any person who develops the computer model, or markets the computer model or investment advice program, utilized in satisfaction of paragraph (b)(4) of this section.

(3) A "registered representative" of another entity means a person described in section 3(a)(18) of the Securities Exchange Act of 1934 (15 U.S.C. 78c(a)(18)) (substituting the entity for the broker or dealer referred to in such section) or a person described in section 202(a)(17) of the Investment Advisers Act of 1940 (15 U.S.C. 80b-2(a)(17)) (substituting the entity for the investment adviser referred to in such section).

(4) "Individual Retirement Account" or "*IRA*" means-

(i) An individual retirement account described in section 408(a) of the Code;

(ii) An individual retirement annuity described in section 408(b) of the Code;

(iii) An Archer MSA described in section 220(d) of the Code;

(iv) A health savings account described in section 223(d) of the Code;

(v) A Coverdell education savings account described in section 530 of the Code; or

(vi) A trust, plan, account, or annuity which, at any time, has been determined by the Secretary of the Treasury to be described in any of paragraphs (c)(4)(i) through (v) of this section.

(5) An "*affiliate*" of another person means -

(i) Any person directly or indirectly owning, controlling, or holding with power to vote, 5 percent or more of the outstanding voting securities of such other person;

(ii) Any person 5 percent or more of whose outstanding voting securities are directly or indirectly owned, controlled, or held with power to vote, by such other person;

(iii) Any person directly or indirectly controlling, controlled by, or under common control with, such other person; and

(iv) Any officer, director, partner, copartner, or employee of such other person.

(6)(i) A person with a "*material affiliation*" with another person means -

(A) Any affiliate of the other person;

(B) Any person directly or indirectly owning, controlling, or holding, 5 percent or more of the interests of such other person; and

(C) Any person 5 percent or more of whose interests are directly or indirectly owned, controlled, or held, by such other person.

(ii) For purposes of paragraph (c)(6)(i) of this section, "interest" means with respect to an entity -

(A) The combined voting power of all classes of stock entitled to vote or the total value of the shares of all classes of stock of the entity if the entity is a corporation;

(B) The capital interest or the profits interest of the entity if the entity is a partnership; or

(C) The beneficial interest of the entity if the entity is a trust or unincorporated enterprise.

(7) Persons have a "material contractual relationship" if payments made by one person to the other person pursuant to contracts or agreements between the persons exceed 10 percent of the gross revenue, on an annual basis, of such other person.

(8) "Control" means the power to exercise a controlling influence over the management or policies of a person other than an individual.

(d) Retention of records. The fiduciary adviser must maintain, for a period of not less than 6 years after the provision of investment advice under this section any records necessary for determining whether the applicable requirements of this section have been met. A transaction prohibited under section 406 of ERISA shall not be considered to have occurred solely because the records are lost or destroyed prior to the end of the 6-year period due to circumstances beyond the control of the fiduciary adviser.

(e) Noncompliance. (1) The relief from the prohibited transaction provisions of section 406 of ERISA and the sanctions resulting from the application of section 4975 of the Code described in paragraph (b) of this section shall not apply to any transaction described in such paragraphs in connection with the provision of investment advice to an individual participant or beneficiary with respect to which the applicable conditions of this section have not been satisfied.

(2) In the case of a pattern or practice of noncompliance with any of the applicable conditions of this section, the relief described in paragraph (b) shall not apply to any transaction in connection with the provision of investment advice provided by the fiduciary adviser during the period over which the pattern or practice extended.

(f) Effective date and applicability date. This section shall be effective [ENTER DATE 60 DAYS AFTER THE DATE OF PUBICATION OF THE FINAL RULE]. This section shall apply to transactions described in paragraph (b) of this section occurring on or after [ENTER DATE 60 DAYS AFTER THE DATE OF PUBLICATION OF THE FINAL RULE].

APPENDIX to § 2550.408g-1

Fiduciary Adviser Disclosure

This document contains important information about [*enter name of* Fiduciary Adviser] and how it is compensated for the investment advice provided to you. You should carefully consider this information in your evaluation of that advice.

[*enter name of* Fiduciary Adviser] has been selected to provide investment advisory services for the [*enter name of* Plan]. [*enter name of* Fiduciary Adviser] will be providing these services as a fiduciary under the Employee Retirement Income Security Act (ERISA). [*enter name of* Fiduciary Adviser], therefore, must act prudently and with only your interest in mind when providing you recommendations on how to invest your retirement assets.

Compensation of the Fiduciary Adviser and Related Parties

[*enter name of* Fiduciary Adviser] (is/is not) compensated by the plan for the advice it provides. *(if compensated by the plan, explain what and how compensation is charged (e.g., asset-based fee, flat fee, per advice)). (If applicable,* [*enter name of* Fiduciary Adviser] is not compensated on the basis of the investment(s) selected by you.)

Affiliates of [*enter name of* Fiduciary Adviser] (*if applicable enter,* and other parties with whom [*enter name of* Fiduciary Adviser] is related or has a material financial relationship) also will be providing services for which they will be compensated. These services include: [*enter description of services, e.g., investment management, transfer agent, custodial, and shareholder services for some/all the investment funds available under the plan.*]

When [*enter name of* Fiduciary Adviser] recommends that you invest your assets in an investment fund of its own or one of its affiliates and you follow that advice, [*enter name of* Fiduciary Adviser] or that affiliate will receive compensation from the investment fund based on the amount you invest. The amounts that will be paid by you will vary depending on the particular fund in which you invest your assets and may range from ___% to ___%. Specific information concerning the fees and other charges of each investment fund is available from [*enter source, such as: your plan administrator, investment fund provider (possibly with Internet website address)*]. This information should be reviewed carefully before you make an investment decision.

(*if applicable enter,* [*enter name of* Fiduciary Adviser] or affiliates of [*enter name of* Fiduciary Adviser]also receive compensation from non-affiliated investment funds as a result of investments you make as a result of recommendations of [*enter name of* Fiduciary Adviser]. The amount of this compensation also may vary depending on the particular fund in which you invest. This compensation may range from ___% to ___%. Specific information concerning the fees and other charges of each investment fund is available from [*enter source, such as: your plan administrator, investment fund provider (possibly with Internet website address)*]. This information should be reviewed carefully before you make an investment decision.

(*if applicable enter,* In addition to the above, [*enter name of* Fiduciary Adviser] or affiliates of [*enter name of* Fiduciary Adviser] also receive other fees or compensation, such as commissions, in connection with the sale, acquisition or holding of investments selected by you as a result of recommendations of [*enter name of* Fiduciary Adviser]. These amounts are: [*enter description of all other fees or compensation to be received in connection with sale, acquisition or holding of investments*]. This information should be reviewed carefully before you make an investment decision.

(*if applicable enter,* When [*enter name of* Fiduciary Adviser] recommends that you take a rollover or other distribution of assets from the plan, or recommends how those assets should subsequently be invested, [*enter name of* Fiduciary Adviser] or affiliates of [*enter name of*

Fiduciary Adviser] will receive additional fees or compensation. These amounts are: [*enter description of all other fees or compensation to be received in connection with any rollover or other distribution of plan assets or the investment of distributed assets*]. This information should be reviewed carefully before you make a decision to take a distribution.

Consider Impact of Compensation on Advice

The fees and other compensation that [*enter name of* Fiduciary Adviser] and its affiliates receive on account of assets in [*enter name of* Fiduciary Adviser] (*enter if applicable,* and non-[*enter name of* Fiduciary Adviser]) investment funds are a significant source of revenue for the [*enter name of* Fiduciary Adviser] and its affiliates. You should carefully consider the impact of any such fees and compensation in your evaluation of the investment advice that [*enter name of* Fiduciary Adviser] provides to you. In this regard, you may arrange for the provision of advice by another adviser that may have no material affiliation with or receive no compensation in connection with the investment funds or products offered under the plan. This type of advice is/is not available through your plan.

Investment Returns

While understanding investment-related fees and expenses is important in making informed investment decisions, it is also important to consider additional information about your investment options, such as performance, investment strategies and risks. Specific information related to the past performance and historical rates of return of the investment options available under the plan (has/has not) been provided to you by [*enter source, such as: your plan administrator, investment fund provider*]. (*if applicable enter,* If not provided to you, the information is attached to this document.)

For options with returns that vary over time, past performance does not guarantee how your investment in the option will perform in the future; your investment in these options could lose money.

Parties Participating in Development of Advice Program or Selection of Investment Options

Name, and describe role of, affiliates or other parties with whom the fiduciary adviser has a material affiliation or contractual relationship that participated in the development of the investment advice program (if this is an arrangement that uses computer models) or the selection of investment options available under the plan.

Use of Personal Information

Include a brief explanation of the following -

What personal information will be collected;

How the information will be used;

Parties with whom information will be shared;

How the information will be protected; and

When and how notice of the Fiduciary Adviser's privacy statement will be available to participants and beneficiaries.

Should you have any questions about [*enter name of* Fiduciary Adviser] or the information contained in this document, you may contact [*enter name of contact person for fiduciary adviser, telephone number, address*].

3. Add § 2550.408g-2 to read as follows:

§ 2550.408g-2 Investment advice - fiduciary election.

(a) General. Section 408(g)(11)(A) of the Employee Retirement Income Security Act, as amended (ERISA), provides that a person who develops a computer model or who markets a computer model or investment advice program used in an "eligible investment advice arrangement" shall be treated as a fiduciary of a plan by reason of the provision of investment advice referred to in ERISA section 3(21)(A)(ii) to the plan participant or beneficiary, and shall be treated as a "fiduciary adviser" for purposes of ERISA sections 408(b)(14) and 408(g), except that the Secretary of Labor may prescribe rules under which only one fiduciary adviser may elect to be treated as a fiduciary with respect to the plan. Section 4975(f)(8)(J)(i) of the Internal Revenue Code, as amended (the Code), contains a parallel provision to ERISA section 408(g)(11)(A) that applies for purposes of Code sections 4975(d)(17) and 4975(f)(8). This section sets forth requirements that must be satisfied in order for one such fiduciary adviser to elect to be treated as a fiduciary with respect to a plan under an eligible investment advice arrangement.

(b)(1) If an election meets the requirements in paragraph (b)(2) of this section, then the person identified in the election shall be the sole fiduciary adviser treated as a fiduciary by reason of developing or marketing the computer model, or marketing the investment advice program, used in an eligible investment advice arrangement.

(2) An election satisfies the requirements of this subparagraph with respect to an eligible investment advice arrangement if the election is in writing and such writing —

(i) Identifies the investment advice arrangement, and the person offering the arrangement, with respect to which the election is to be effective;

(ii) Identifies a person who -

(A) Is described in any of 29 CFR 2550.408g-1(c)(2)(i)(A) through (E),

(B) Develops the computer model, or markets the computer model or investment advice program, utilized in satisfaction of 29 CFR 2550.408g-1(b)(4) with respect to the arrangement, and

(C) Acknowledges that it elects to be treated as the only fiduciary, and fiduciary adviser, by reason of developing such computer model, or marketing such computer model or investment advice program;

(iii) Is signed by the person identified in paragraph (b)(2)(ii) of this section;

(iv) Is furnished to the fiduciary who authorized the arrangement, in accordance with 29 CFR 2550.408g-1(b)(5); and

(v) Is maintained in accordance with 29 CFR 2550.408g-1(d).

Signed at Washington, DC, this 24th day of February, 2010.

Phyllis C. Borzi,

¶ 20,537W

Pension Benefit Guaranty Corporation (PBGC): Proposed regulations: Debt collection.—The Pension Benefit Guaranty Corporation (PBGC) has issued proposed rules that would revise the Agency's regulations on debt collection. The proposed rules would add salary offset and administrative wage garnishment to the collection methods allowed under the current regulations and make other changes designed to strengthen the PBGC's debt collection program.

The proposed regulations, which were published in the Federal Register on July 22, 2010 (75 FR 42662), were reproduced below. The final regulations were published in the Federal Register on November 5, 2010 (75 FR 68203). The preamble to the final regulations is at ¶ 24,299. The final regulations are reproduced at ¶ 15,333A, ¶ 15,334A, ¶ 15,721C, ¶ 15,721D, ¶ 15,721E, ¶ 15,721F, ¶ 15,721G, ¶ 15,721H, ¶ 15,721I, ¶ 15,731J, ¶ 15,721K, ¶ 15,721L, ¶ 15,721L-1, ¶ 15,721L-2, ¶ 15,721L-3, ¶ 15,721L-4, ¶ 15,721L-5, ¶ 15,721L-6, ¶ 15,721L-7, ¶ 15,721L-8, ¶ 15,721L-9, ¶ 15,721L-10, ¶ 15,721L-11, and ¶ 15,721L-12.

¶ 20,537X

Pension Benefit Guaranty Corporation (PBGC): Proposed regulations: Single-employer plans: Substantial cessations of operations by employers.—The Pension Benefit Guaranty Corporation (PBGC) has issued proposed regulations that would amend its current rules on the reporting of and liability for certain substantial cessations of operations by employers that maintain single-employer plans under ERISA § 4062(e). The proposed regulations address the applicability and enforcement of ERISA § 4062(e). The applicability provisions of the proposed regulations provide guidance on whether and when a "4062(e) event" occurs. The enforcement provisions describe the PBGC's 4062(e) investigatory program, provide rules for notifying the PBGC of 4062(e) events, explain how 4062(e) liability is calculated and how it is to be satisfied, and require the preservation of records about events that may be 4062(e) events. The proposed rules also provide for waivers in appropriate circumstances.

The proposed regulations, which were published in the Federal Register on August 10, 2010 (75 FR 48283), are reproduced below.

The comment period was extended to November 12, 2010 by 75 FR 64683.

FR Doc 2010-19627[Federal Register: August 10, 2010 (Volume 75, Number 153)]

[Proposed Rules]

[Page 48283-48294]

From the Federal Register Online via GPO Access [wais.access.gpo.gov]

[DOCID:fr10au10-11]

PENSION BENEFIT GUARANTY CORPORATION

29 CFR Parts 4062 and 4063

RIN 1212-AB20

Liability for Termination of Single-Employer Plans; Treatment of Substantial Cessation of Operations

AGENCY: Pension Benefit Guaranty Corporation.

ACTION: Proposed rule.

SUMMARY: ERISA section 4062(e) provides for reporting of and liability for certain substantial cessations of operations by employers that maintain single-employer plans. PBGC proposes to amend its current regulation on Liability for Termination of Single-Employer Plans to provide guidance on the applicability and enforcement of ERISA section 4062(e).

DATES: Comments must be submitted on or before October 12, 2010.

ADDRESSES: Comments, identified by Regulation Identifier Number (RIN) 1212-AB20, may be submitted by any of the following methods:

Federal eRulemaking Portal: http://www.regulations.gov. Follow the Web site instructions for submitting comments.

E-mail: reg.comments@pbgc.gov.

Fax: 202-326-4224.

Mail or Hand Delivery: Legislative and Regulatory Department, Pension Benefit Guaranty Corporation, 1200 K Street, NW., Washington, DC 20005-4026.

All submissions must include the Regulation Identifier Number for this rulemaking (RIN 1212-AB20). Comments received, including personal information provided, will be posted to http://www.pbgc.gov. Copies of comments may also be obtained by writing to Disclosure Division, Office of the General Counsel, Pension Benefit Guaranty Corporation, 1200 K Street, NW., Washington, DC 20005-4026, or calling 202-326-4040 during normal business hours. (TTY and TDD users may call the Federal relay service toll-free at 1-800-877-8339 and ask to be connected to 202-326-4040.)

FOR FURTHER INFORMATION CONTACT: Catherine B. Klion, Manager, or Deborah C. Murphy, Attorney, Regulatory and Policy Division, Legislative and Regulatory Department, Pension Benefit Guaranty Corporation, 1200 K Street, NW., Washington, DC 20005-4026; 202-326-4024. (TTY/TDD users may call the Federal relay service toll-free at 1-800-877-8339 and ask to be connected to 202-326-4024.)

SUPPLEMENTARY INFORMATION:

Introduction

Pension Benefit Guaranty Corporation (PBGC) administers the pension plan termination insurance program under title IV of the Employee Retirement Income Security Act of 1974 (ERISA). Under ERISA section 4002(b)(3), PBGC has authority to adopt, amend, and repeal regulations to carry out the purposes of title IV.

Background of Proposed Rule

ERISA section 4062(e) provides that "[i]f an employer ceases operations at a facility in any location and, as a result of such cessation of operations, more than 20 percent of the total number of his employees who are participants under a plan established and maintained by him are separated from employment, the employer shall be treated with respect to that plan as if he were a substantial employer under a plan under which more than one employer makes contributions and the provisions of [ERISA sections] 4063, 4064, and 4065 shall apply."

ERISA section 4063(a) requires the plan administrator of a multiple employer plan (that is, a single-employer plan with at least two contributing sponsors that are not under common control) to notify PBGC within 60 days after a substantial employer withdraws from the plan, and section 4063(b) and (c) makes the withdrawn employer liable to provide a bond or escrow in a specified amount for five years from the date of withdrawal, to be applied—if the plan terminates within that period—against the plan's underfunding. Section 4063(e) allows PBGC to waive this liability if there is an appropriate indemnity agreement among contributing sponsors of the plan, and ERISA section 4067 authorizes PBGC to make alternative arrangements for satisfaction of liability under sections 4062 and 4063. (ERISA sections 4064 and 4065 deal with plan termination liability and annual reports by plan administrators.)

The method described in section 4063(b) for computing the amount of liability focuses on relative amounts of contributions by more than one employer and is thus impracticable for calculating liability triggered by an event involving a plan of a single employer under section 4062(e). However, section 4063(b) provides that PBGC "may also determine the liability on any other equitable basis prescribed by [PBGC] in regulations." Pursuant to that authority, on June 16, 2006 (at 71 FR 34819), PBGC published a final rule providing a formula for computing liability under section 4063(b) when there is an event described in section 4062(e). The formula provided by the 2006 rule apportions to an employer affected by an event under section 4062(e) a fraction of plan termination liability based on the number of participants affected by the event. Over the next three-and-a-half years, PBGC resolved 37 cases under section 4062(e) through negotiated settlements valued at nearly $600 million, providing protection to over 65,000 participants.

Overview of Proposed Regulation

The proposed rule would create a new subpart B of PBGC's regulation on Liability for Termination of Single-Employer Plans (29 CFR part 4062) that would focus on section 4062(e). The liability computation rules that were added to part 4062 by PBGC's 2006 final rule (now in Sec. 4062.8) would be moved to this new subpart B. The purpose and scope section of part 4062 and the cross-references section of part 4063 (Withdrawal Liability; Plans Under Multiple Controlled Groups) would be revised to reflect the proposed regulation, and the references to the applicability date of part 4062 (now over 20 years in the past) would be removed.

Proposed subpart B addresses two general topics: The applicability and enforcement of section 4062(e). The provisions on applicability provide guidance on the kinds of events section 4062(e) applies to (i.e., on what a "section 4062(e) event" is). The enforcement provisions describe PBGC's section 4062(e) investigatory program, provide rules for notifying PBGC of section 4062(e) events, explain how section 4062(e) liability is calculated and how it is to be satisfied, and require the preservation of records about events that may be section 4062(e) events. Subpart B would also provide for waivers in appropriate circumstances.

Adoption of the regulatory provisions in this proposed rule will reduce uncertainty about PBGC's interpretation of the statute, thereby permitting more rapid resolution of cases. Clearer rules, together with specific, detailed reporting provisions, should encourage self-reporting of events that PBGC now learns of only through its own investigations and may enable PBGC to process section 4062(e) cases more quickly, thereby protecting more participants.

Further clarification of section 4062(e) is also warranted by requests from the public. Although PBGC's 2006 rule on section 4062(e) was limited to the issue of the liability formula, several commenters asked for additional guidance to clarify the meaning of statutory terms used to describe when an event covered by section 4062(e) occurs. PBGC also regularly receives requests from pension professionals for interpretive guidance on section 4062(e). This proposed rule provides such guidance.

Applicability of Section 4062(e)

PBGC proposes to provide guidance on whether and when a "section 4062(e) event" occurs by explaining each of the key terms that appear in the statute and in the proposed regulation: "operation," "facility," "cease," "separate," and "result." The term "active participant base" would be introduced to describe the baseline number of active participants against which the statutorily required decline in active participants would be measured and to serve as the denominator of the apportionment fraction used in calculating liability for a section 4062(e) event. Discussions of the subpart B explanations of these terms follow.

"Section 4062(e) Event"

New subpart B would use the term "section 4062(e) event" to refer to an event to which section 4062(e) applies.

The proposed regulation would apply only to events involving single-employer plans that are not multiple employer plans. ERISA section 4062(e) provides that if a section 4062(e) event occurs, the affected employer "shall be treated with respect to [the affected] plan as if he were a substantial employer under a plan under which more than one employer makes contributions." The phrase "as if" implies that section 4062(e) does not itself apply to events involving plans under which more than one employer makes contributions. From the context and language of section 4062(e), therefore, PBGC concludes that the term "plan" in section 4062(e) means a single-employer plan that is not a multiple employer plan. Furthermore, the liability formula adopted by PBGC in 2006 would produce anomalous results if applied to an event involving a multiple employer plan.

The proposed regulation would require only that a plan be maintained by an employer—not both established and maintained—to come within the provisions of section 4062(e). In Rose v. Long Island R.R. Pension Plan, 828 F.2d 910 (2nd Cir. 1987), the Second Circuit reasoned that a plan whose sponsorship has changed may be considered "established" (or "re-established") by the new sponsor, notwithstanding that it has not first been formally "terminated." In addition, in PBGC Opinion Letter 90-6, PBGC noted that it had "declined to interpret the conjunction of the terms 'established and maintained' strictly in the context of the exemption from Title IV coverage for governmental plans [under] ERISA section 4021(b)(2) * * * because doing so would frustrate the intent of Congress in providing the exemption." The opinion letter quoted from the Rose case, sanctioning that approach on the basis that "the status of the entity which currently maintains a particular pension plan bears more relation to Congress' goals in enacting ERISA and its various exemptions than does the status of the entity which established the plan."[1] The opinion letter applied the same principle to the exemption for substantial owner plans under ERISA section 4021(b)(9).

PBGC believes that similar reasoning applies to ERISA section 4062(e), which also uses the phrase "established and maintained." PBGC believes the textual analysis in the Rose case would be appropriate in interpreting this phrase in ERISA section 4062(e). In addition, Congress's goal in enacting section 4062(e) would appear to be frustrated, rather than promoted, by excluding from the ambit of that provision any case involving a plan established by a different employer from the employer maintaining the plan when the event occurred. Indeed, such an interpretation would seem to open a formalistic loophole that could be exploited where, by chance or foresight, a plan's sponsorship changed.

The proposed regulation would provide explicitly that evaluation of risk is not an element in deciding whether a section 4062(e) event has occurred. Sections 4062(e) and 4063 call for self-reporting by plan administrators. Each section describes a class of events that is to be reported. Neither section provides or even suggests that a plan administrator is to make a risk assessment and report an event to PBGC only if it creates risk for the plan or its participants or for PBGC. PBGC believes that section 4062(e) reflects a judgment that as a class, events described therein are indicative of increased risk of underfunded plan termination within five years—whether or not any particular risk factors appear to be present in particular cases. PBGC's experience bears out this view. For example, in a recent section 4062(e) case, an employer opposed the assessment of liability under section 4062(e) on the ground that its financial resources eliminated any risk to the termination insurance program. But shortly after reaching accord with PBGC, the employer entered bankruptcy with its plan underfunded because of an economic downturn in the industry.

Thus PBGC believes that risk is not relevant in deciding whether a section 4062(e) event has occurred, and the proposed regulation would provide that such decisions be made without regard to whether there might in a particular case be (or appear to be) no risk to the plan, participants, or PBGC. However, as discussed below under Liability for section 4062(e) events, in making arrangements for the satisfaction of liability arising from section 4062(e) events, PBGC may take account of such circumstances as employer financial strength.

---

[1] A contrary case is Hightower v. Texas Hospital Association, 65 F.3d 443 (5th Cir. 1995). The Hightower case does not discuss the actions an employer assuming sponsorship of an existing plan might take to be treated as having "established" (or "re-established") the plan.

The proposed regulation would also note that if an employer has two or more plans, section 4062(e) is applied separately to each plan, not on an aggregate basis. This principle is clear from section 4062(e)'s references to "a plan" and "that plan."

"Operation"

The proposed regulation uses the term "operation" (singular rather than plural) to refer to a set of activities that constitutes an organizationally, operationally, or functionally distinct unit of an employer. PBGC proposes that section 4062(e) apply to cessation of an operation in this sense. This approach is consistent with PBGC's practice and experience in its current enforcement activities under section 4062(e). The regulation would also suggest some criteria that might be considered in identifying a set of activities as an operation, such as whether it is so treated by the employer or its employees or customers, by the public, or within the relevant industry.

"Facility"

Section 4062(e) applies to cessation of an operation "at a facility in any location." PBGC thinks that section 4062(e) should be read as applying to an employer's cessation of an operation at a "facility in any location," even if the employer continues or resumes the operation at another "facility in any location." Accordingly, under the proposed rule, the facility (or facility in any location) associated with an operation would simply be the place or places where the operation is performed. This would typically be a building or buildings, but could be or include any one or more enclosed or open areas or structures where one or more employees were engaged in the performance of the operation.

PBGC's view of "operation" and "facility" means that a facility (a building, for example) may be the site of more than one operation. Under the proposed regulation, therefore, section 4062(e) might apply where some but not all activity at a facility ceased, if the activity that ceased constituted an operation distinct from other activities in the facility.[2]

"Cessation"

PBGC proposes that where an employer discontinues activity that constitutes an operation at a facility, deciding whether a cessation has occurred for purposes of section 4062(e) should involve assessment of whether the discontinuance represents a mere cutback or contraction, or is so thorough that the employer's conduct of the operation at the facility can no longer be considered on-going. The proposed regulation would address this issue for both voluntary and involuntary discontinuances.

PBGC believes that whether an employer's conduct of an operation at a facility ceases or remains on-going (though perhaps curtailed) depends on the degree to which the purpose of the operation continues to be fulfilled by the employer's activity at the facility. PBGC thus proposes that an employer's cessation of an operation at a facility be considered to occur only if the employer discontinues all significant activity at the facility in furtherance of the purpose of the operation.

Thus, an employer might cease an operation at a facility even though insignificant activity at the facility in furtherance of the purpose of the operation continued. For example, while continued processing of materials on hand would typically constitute significant activity in furtherance of the purpose of an operation, desultory sales of left-over inventory would typically not. Continuing activity that does not further an operation's purpose would be disregarded. For example, although maintenance and security activities may be important to a manufacturing operation, they do not further the purpose of the operation. Thus, a cessation of such an operation could occur even though there was a continuance of maintenance and guard services.

While this approach is apt for "voluntary" discontinuances pursuant to employer decision,[3] it is less suitable for "involuntary" discontinuances caused by events outside the employer's control. Where a discontinuance of activity is thrust upon an employer, rather than stemming from the employer's will, PBGC believes that the employer should have an opportunity to react—to resume or to decide not to resume the activity—before the discontinuance is characterized as a cessation under section 4062(e).

PBGC proposes to provide two rules for involuntary discontinuances. In each situation, cessation would occur not when all significant activity stopped, but at a later date—unless the employer in the meantime resumed the operation at the facility (in which case there would be no cessation) or decided not to resume it (in which case the cessation would occur when the decision was made). One situation would be where the discontinuance of activity was caused by employee action, such as a strike or sickout. In this case, the cessation date would be put off until the employee action ended (and the employer would have a week in which to resume activity). The other situation would be where the discontinuance was caused by a sudden and unanticipated event (other than an employee action) such as a natural disaster. In this case, the cessation date would be deferred for 30 days—time enough to resume work if the event causing the discontinuance left the operation viable.

As indicated in the discussion of "facility" above, PBGC believes that section 4062(e) may apply to an employer's cessation of an operation at one facility even if the employer continues or resumes the operation at another facility. For example, where an employer has been performing manufacturing, shipping, and administrative functions under a single roof, section 4062(e) could apply where the employer moves the manufacturing operation outside the United States and has manufactured goods shipped in bulk to the original U.S. facility for distribution using the employer's own existing shipping operation.

Similarly, PBGC believes that section 4062(e) applies to an employer's cessation of an operation at a facility even if the operation is continued or resumed by another employer at the same or another facility. One example of this would be the not uncommon situation where one employer sells the assets used in an operation to another employer that continues or resumes the operation.

The proposed regulation would thus provide that continuance or resumption of an operation at another facility or by another employer is to be disregarded in deciding whether a cessation has occurred.

The proposed regulation would also reflect PBGC's view that it is irrelevant whether an employer begins a new operation contemporaneously with its discontinuance of an existing operation, either at the same or another facility. A section 4062(e) event concerns itself with the cessation of one operation and the effect of that cessation on the employment of participants in the affected plan. Undertaking a second operation does not nullify the discontinuance of the first or the impact of that discontinuance on those participants. Of course, if enough of those participants were retained by the employer in connection with the new operation to avoid a drop of more than 20 percent in the active participant-count, there would be no section 4062(e) event.

Under the proposed regulation, any hope or expectation the employer may have that the discontinued work will be resumed would be irrelevant to whether the discontinuance is a cessation. A cessation does not ripen into a section 4062(e) event unless it results in a decline of more than 20 percent in the number of active participants in the affected plan. Where such a decline occurs because an employer discontinues activities constituting an operation at a facility, PBGC believes that the event should not fail to be covered by section 4062(e) because the activity may resume.

The proposed regulation would use the term "cessation date" for the date when a cessation occurs as discussed above. Since an employer's cessation of an operation at a facility is only part of what constitutes a section 4062(e) event (the other part being a resultant drop of more than 20 percent in the active participant-count), the date of a section 4062(e) event might be later than the associated cessation date.[4]

"Separation"

The fact that an employer ceases an operation at a facility does not in itself constitute a section 4062(e) event. Under section 4062(e), it must also be true that "as a result of such cessation of operations, more than 20 percent of the total number of [the employer's] employees who are participants under [the affected plan] are separated from employment." PBGC believes that "separation" as used here logically and naturally refers to separation from employment with the employer, rather than separation from employment in the operation.

---

[2] For example, an employer might conduct a manufacturing operation under the same roof with shipping and administrative functions—or with another, distinct manufacturing operation. If the employer ceased the manufacturing operation (or one of the two manufacturing operations) at the facility, the cessation might come within the scope of section 4062(e), even though the employer continued its other activity at the facility.

[3] "Voluntary" as used here does not connote something desirable or preferable, but merely refers to a discontinuance of activity that is not involuntary as described below. Thus, for example, a discontinuance of activity in response to an economic downturn is considered "voluntary" because it does not fall within the description of an involuntary discontinuance.

[4] For example, assume that the workers in an operation represent 21 percent of active participants in a plan and that when all activity in furtherance of the purpose of the operation stops, 19 percent (out of the 21 percent) lose their jobs but the remaining 2 percent keep working until the machinery used in the operation has been crated for disposal. A section 4062(e) event would not occur on the cessation date, but only when the over-20-percent active participant reduction requirement was satisfied.

Thus, PBGC believes that the requirement of separation is not satisfied if an employee is merely transferred within the employer's organization—for example, from work in the ceasing operation to work outside it—even if the transfer takes the employee out of the category of employees covered by the plan.[5] By the same token, PBGC believes that if an employer ceases an operation, but the operation is continued or resumed by a new employer, the fact that a person previously employed by the original employer continues to work in the operation as an employee of the new employer does not mean that the person has not separated from employment (with the original employer). Accordingly, the proposed regulation's discussion of separation would be couched in terms of the employment relationship between the employer and the employee.

The 60-day period within which notice of a section 4062(e) event must be given does not begin to run until a section 4062(e) event has occurred—that is, until there has been both a cessation by an employer of an operation at a facility and a separation from employment of more than 20 percent of the active participants in the affected plan. To know the reporting deadline, therefore, it is as important for the plan administrator to fix promptly the dates when participants separate from employment as it is to fix the cessation date promptly. In some cases (e.g., discharges and quits), fixing the separation date is relatively straightforward. Other cases (e.g., layoffs) may raise doubt about whether or when a separation has occurred. It is important to avoid having doubt of this kind delay decisions about whether the 20-percent threshold has been exceeded and a section 4062(e) event has thus occurred.

The proposed regulation would provide that an employee separates from employment when the employee discontinues the active performance, pursuant to the employee's employment relationship with the employer, of activities in furtherance of any of the employer's operations, unless, when the discontinuance occurs, it is reasonably certain that the employee will resume such active work within 30 days—for example, after a two-week holiday shutdown. This standard would allow a plan administrator to decide immediately whether a separation occurred when an employee discontinued active work. If, however, the 30 days pass without the employee's having returned, the employee would be considered to have separated from employment when active work stopped. The focus on active performance of activities pursuant to the employment relationship would mean that continued provision of benefits to an employee, such as the continued granting of credited service for pension purposes, would be disregarded in deciding whether a separation from employment occurred.

The proposed regulation would also include a special rule under which an employee's separation before a cessation was complete would be ignored if, by the cessation date, (1) the employee was rehired or a replacement was hired, and (2) the rehired or replacement employee was a participant in the plan.

"Result"

The proposed regulation would provide that a separation from employment results from the cessation of an operation if the separation would not have occurred when it did had the cessation not occurred. Thus, for example, if an employee had been planning to retire in a year or two but chose to retire sooner upon learning of a shutdown that would eliminate her job, the separation would be the result of the shutdown; whereas if (before learning of the shutdown) she had been planning to retire immediately and retired as planned after she learned of the shutdown, the separation would not be a result of the shutdown.

The proposed regulation would provide that whether a separation occurs before, on, or after the cessation date is not considered decisive of whether the separation is the result of the cessation. An operation may not cease instantaneously, and some employees may leave before the cessation date because the operation in which they are employed is in the process of shutting down, although significant activity in furtherance of the purpose of the operation is still ongoing. Yet other employees may continue to work after the cessation date—for example, disassembling machinery and guarding the premises until the plant and equipment can be sold—before they finally leave.

The proposed regulation would also provide that an employee's separation may result from the cessation of an operation at a facility even if the employee's employment has been in another operation or even at another facility. Ceasing one operation can have an impact on other operations, whether or not they also cease. For example, an employer might have one operation to assemble widgets from pre-

fabricated parts, and another operation to fabricate widget parts for use in the employer's own widget manufactory or for sale to other widget manufacturers. If the employer shut down the widget assembly operation, there would be reduced demand for widget parts, the fabrication operation would cut back, and some fabrication employees would lose their jobs—as a result of the shutdown of the widget assembly operation. And if there was reduced demand for widget parts in the industry generally, the shutdown of the employer's widget assembly operation might even cause the shutdown of its fabrication operation, and thus all of the fabrication employees might be separated as a result of the shutdown of the assembly operation.

To supplement the general rule on when separation from employment results from an employer's cessation of an operation at a facility, PBGC is proposing four presumptions based on the relationship between the timing of a separation and the timing of events involved in a cessation.

The first presumption (applicable to a voluntary cessation) would be that if an employee is employed in an operation at a facility and involuntarily separates from employment on or after the date when the employer decides to cease the operation at the facility, the employee has separated from employment as a result of the cessation.

The second presumption (also applicable to a voluntary cessation) would be that if an employee in an operation at a facility voluntarily separates from employment after the employer decision to cease the operation at the facility becomes known (to the employee, to employees generally, or to the public), the separation results from the cessation.

The third presumption would be that if a cessation is involuntary, and an employee in the operation voluntarily or involuntarily separates from employment on or after the date of the event that caused the cessation, the separation results from the cessation.

The fourth presumption would be that if an employee employed in an operation becomes employed by a new employer that continues or resumes the operation, the employee has separated from employment with the original employer as a result of the cessation.

PBGC believes that these four presumptions reflect reasonable inferences and will simplify application of the proposed regulation; nonetheless, any of the presumptions could be rebutted by appropriate evidence.

"Active Participant Base"

A section 4062(e) event occurs only if "as a result of [a]cessation of operations, more than 20 percent of the total number of [the employer's] employees who are participants under [the affected plan] are separated from employment." To apply the 20-percent test, one must know the base number against which the 20 percent is measured. The statute provides that this base number is "the total number of [the employer's] employees who are participants under [the affected plan]," but it does not say as of what point in time the number is to be fixed, although one may infer that it is to be a pre-cessation number.

The formula for calculating liability for a section 4062(e) event that PBGC added to the termination liability regulation in 2006 also refers to a base number—the denominator of a fraction that is applied to total termination liability to find the liability for a section 4062(e) event. Section 4062.8(a)(2) of the current regulation describes this base number as "the total number of the employer's current employees, as determined immediately before the cessation of operations, who are participants under the plan." This description is consistent with the description of a base number in section 4062(e), and administrative convenience is clearly served by using the same number for the statutory 20-percent threshold test and for the apportionment fraction in the regulatory formula for liability.

However, the existing regulatory language—"immediately before the cessation"—does not provide as much specificity about timing as PBGC thinks desirable. PBGC thus proposes to prescribe rules that are consistent with, but more specific than, the existing statutory and regulatory language, describing when to count active participants for purposes of fixing a single base number for both the 20-percent test and the liability formula. PBGC proposes to call this number the "active participant base."

The key to PBGC's proposal is to identify when a cessation begins, and employment starts to be affected by the cessation process, so that active participants can be counted just before then. For a voluntary

---

[5] In general, such a transfer would not terminate the transferred employee's participation in the plan, although it would typically mean that the employee would accrue no further benefits under the plan.

cessation, carried out pursuant to an employer decision, that decision marks the beginning of the cessation process, and the active participant base would be measured immediately before that decision. For an involuntary cessation, the active participant base would be measured immediately before the event that causes the cessation (strike, natural disaster, etc.).

In counting active participants, the proposed regulation would use the same formulation for describing active employment as in the provision on separation from employment: Active performance, pursuant to the employment relationship with the employer, of activities in furtherance of the employer's operations (or reasonable certainty of resuming such active work within 30 days, with a "reality check" if 30 days have passed). Thus, the active participant base would be measured on a basis consistent with the rules about measuring the number of participants who separate from employment.

In response to a public comment, PBGC's 2006 final rule prescribing the section 4062(e) liability computation formula clarified that, in calculating the denominator of the fraction in the formula (the number of employee participants immediately before the cessation), only current employees are included. The proposed formulation of the active participant base would make this point more clearly.

The proposal would also clarify that an employee need not be accruing benefits under a plan to be a participant in the plan.[6] Freezing a plan should not make the employer immune from section 4062(e).

Enforcement of Section 4062(e)

Proposed subpart B would describe two processes for PBGC to learn about section 4062(e) events: PBGC investigations and reports to PBGC by plan administrators. It would also describe the liability that arises when a section 4062(e) event occurs and how the liability is satisfied and would prescribe recordkeeping requirements. Provision would also be made for waivers in appropriate circumstances.

PBGC Investigations

Under ERISA section 4003(a), PBGC has authority to make such investigations as it deems necessary to enforce title IV and regulations thereunder (such as the regulation under section 4062(e) that PBGC is here proposing). PBGC's section 4062(e) enforcement has been strongly supported by investigations, and PBGC expects its section 4062(e) investigatory activity to continue, notwithstanding the inclusion in the proposed regulation of detailed reporting requirements.

The investigation provision in proposed subpart B would include a deadline for responding to PBGC information requests, and failure to respond by the deadline could result in the assessment of penalties under ERISA section 4071 (see Late filing penalties below). There would also be a requirement to correct or update information submitted to PBGC that was or became materially wrong or outdated.

Notice Requirement

Under ERISA section 4063(a), the plan administrator of a multiple employer plan must report the withdrawal of a substantial employer from the plan to PBGC within 60 days after the withdrawal. Since section 4062(e) refers to section 4063 for the procedures to be followed for section 4062(e) events, the proposed rule would provide, consistent with the statute, that notice of a section 4062(e) event must be filed with PBGC by the plan administrator of the affected plan within 60 days. The 60 days would run from the later of the cessation date or the date when the number of active participant separations resulting from the cessation exceeds 20 percent of the active participant base.

Filing forms and instructions, including filing methods, filing addresses, required data, etc., would be posted on PBGC's Web site.[7] The proposed regulation would also provide cross-references to filing rules in PBGC's regulation on Filing, Issuance, Computation of Time, and Record Retention (29 CFR part 4000). PBGC could require submission of supplementary information, ordinarily with a 45-day response period, which could be shortened if necessary to avoid prejudice to PBGC, the plan, or participants. The affected employer would be required to furnish necessary information to the plan administrator of the affected plan. Any filed information that a filer discovered to be materially wrong or outdated would have to be promptly corrected. Thus, for example, if more employees separated from employment as a result of

a cessation after the cessation had been reported to PBGC, and the number of additional separations would materially affect liability, the additional separations would have to be reported to PBGC.

To simplify section 4062(e) reporting, PBGC proposes to permit a plan administrator to disregard affected participants who were not employed at the facility where the affected operation was carried out. PBGC's experience suggests that effective and efficient enforcement of section 4062(e) is not usually best served by focusing the administrative resources of PBGC and plan administrators on tracing the effects of a cessation on employment at facilities beyond the one associated with the ceased operation. Accordingly, the proposed regulation would permit a plan administrator to ignore separations at other facilities in deciding whether a section 4062(e) event had occurred, when to file notice of an event, and how many affected participants to report in the notice. Only if PBGC specifically requested information about separations at other facilities would they need to be reported. In that case, however, or if identified in a PBGC investigation, separations at other facilities that were caused by a cessation would be counted in both the 20-percent threshold test and the liability calculation for the cessation.

Information submitted to PBGC under the proposed regulation would be protected from disclosure to the extent provided in the Freedom of Information Act and 18 U.S.C. 1905 (dealing with commercial and financial information).

Late Filing Penalties

ERISA section 4071 authorizes PBGC to assess a penalty against any person that fails to timely provide any notice or other material information required under section 4062(e) or 4063 or regulations thereunder (which would include the proposed regulation).[8] Under section 4071 and the Federal Civil Monetary Penalty Inflation Adjustment Act of 1990, as amended by the Debt Collection Improvement Act of 1996, the maximum penalty is currently $1,100 per day. See PBGC's regulation on Penalties for Failure To Provide Certain Notices or Other Material Information (29 CFR part 4071).

On July 18, 1995 (at 60 FR 36837), PBGC issued a statement of policy on penalties for failure to provide required information in a timely manner. The statement said that PBGC would—

consider the facts and circumstances of each case to assure that the penalty fits the violation. Among the factors the PBGC will consider are the importance and time-sensitivity of the required information, the extent of the omission of information, the willfulness of the failure to provide the required information, the length of delay in providing the information, and the size of the plan.

In general, the policy statement said that PBGC would assess penalties much lower than $1,100 per day—$25 per day for the first 90 days of delinquency and $50 per day thereafter, with limitations based on plan size. However, it also said that PBGC may assess larger penalties if circumstances warrant, such as "if the harm to participants or the PBGC resulting from a failure to timely provide material information is substantial." Such "larger penalties" would of course be subject to the $1,100-per-day limitation. (The policy statement noted in particular that penalties for violations under subparts C and D of PBGC's reportable events regulation would generally be at the $1,100-per-day level.) PBGC believes similarly that violations of the notice requirement under sections 4062(e) and 4063 may well result in substantial harm to participants and PBGC, especially because of the five-year limitation on maintaining a bond or escrow under ERISA section 4063(c)(2). Thus, such violations may well warrant section 4071 penalties larger than the "general" ($25/$50-per-day) penalty, subject to the $1,100-per-day limitation.

Liability for Section 4062(e) Events

The liability formula for section 4062(e) events that PBGC added to the termination liability regulation in 2006 would be preserved under this proposed rule,[9] with clarification about how the calculation is done and some editorial changes (including rewording for consistency with terminology used in the rest of subpart B).

The proposed clarification relates to the provision (in both the existing and proposed regulation) that liability for a section 4062(e) event is based on a computation of termination liability performed as if the plan had been terminated by PBGC immediately after the cessation

---

[6] See the definition of "active participant" in Sec. 4043.23 of PBGC's regulation on Reportable Events and Certain Other Notification Requirements (29 CFR part 4043).

[7] The absence heretofore of a section 4062(e) event reporting form made it possible to combine a section 4062(e) event notice with a reportable event notice under Sec. 4043.23 of PBGC's reportable events regulation. PBGC's proposal to require the use of prescribed forms to file notice of section 4062(e) events would make this unworkable. However,

information already submitted to PBGC in a reportable event notice would not need to be resubmitted in a section 4062(e) event notice.

[8] Section 4071 penalties are not the only applicable enforcement mechanism.

[9] In particular, no change would be made to the requirement to measure termination liability (on which section 4062(e) liability is based) as of the cessation date rather than as of the section 4062(e) event date.

date. PBGC believes that termination liability for this purpose should be fixed and determinable as of the cessation date and should not take account of changes in assets or liabilities after the cessation date, such as from the receipt of contributions or the accrual of additional benefits. Ignoring post-cessation-date changes will promote simplicity and avoid the possibility that the liability calculation might differ depending on how long after the cessation date it was actually performed. This provision reflects PBGC's current practice.

PBGC proposes to remove the example in the current regulation that illustrates the computation of the fraction that is applied to termination liability to arrive at the liability that arises from a section 4062(e) event. The example was intended to make clear that the number of pre-event active participants does not include participants who are not currently working for the employer when the pre-event participant-count is measured. PBGC believes that its proposed formulation of the active participant base makes this point clear without the need for an example.

In general, PBGC proposes that it would prescribe one of the statutory methods (described in ERISA section 4063(b) and (c)(1)) for satisfying liability arising from a section 4062(e) event. However, the proposed regulation would permit the continuation of PBGC's practice, as authorized by ERISA section 4067, of negotiating with affected employers in appropriate cases on the manner in which the liability is to be satisfied, with a view to accommodating employer interests to the extent consistent with protecting the plan, participants, and PBGC as contemplated by the statute. For example, in some cases section 4062(e) liability might be satisfied through additional plan funding contributions that would not be added to the plan's prefunding balance. Or, in appropriate cases, where a new, financially sound employer continues or resumes an operation, and the original employer's workers are employed by the new employer, the proposed regulation would enable PBGC to consider the original employer's liability satisfied through the new employer's adoption of the original employer's plan (or the portion of the plan covering the affected operation).

Recordkeeping and Waivers

PBGC proposes to require that employers and plan administrators preserve records about potential section 4062(e) events that tend to show whether a section 4062(e) event in fact occurred and if so how much the resultant liability is. The recordkeeping provision would also permit PBGC to proceed on the basis of reasonable assumptions if employer or plan records were insufficient. The proposed record retention period would be five years, which matches the period for which the security provided by an employer with respect to a section 4062(e) event can be held—and thus PBGC's window for enforcing section 4062(e).

New subpart B would also include a provision explicitly authorizing PBGC to grant waivers where warranted by the circumstances. PBGC's experience with section 4062(e) enforcement suggests that PBGC may encounter situations it does not now foresee, and this waiver provision is meant to provide a measure of flexibility in interpreting and applying the law.

Provisions Not in the Rule

The proposal does not include an exemption for small plans. Such an exemption was suggested by a commenter on PBGC's 2006 rulemaking that codified the section 4062(e) liability formula. PBGC believes that the protection afforded by section 4062(e) is appropriate for small plans (and their participants) as well as for large plans. Furthermore, to the extent that small plans present less underfunding potential than large plans (and thus less potential exposure for the pension insurance system), the liability under section 4062(e) will also be less, and thus the burden of satisfying it should not be disproportionate. Finally, PBGC believes that the guidance in this proposed rule should make compliance relatively easy for small and large plans alike. These considerations militate against an exemption for small plans.

The proposal also includes no exemption for well-funded plans. As noted above for small plans, the better a plan is funded, the lower (other things being equal) would be its liability for a section 4062(e) event under the formula provided in the regulation. If a plan were so well funded that it had no termination liability under ERISA section 4062, its liability for a section 4062(e) event would be zero. But termination liability computations are complex, and PBGC would not expect plans to make such computations simply to claim exemption from the section 4062(e) event reporting requirement.

The fact that a plan is undergoing a standard termination would likewise be ignored under the proposed rule. Until distributions pursu-

ant to a standard termination are complete, there is the possibility that plan assets will be found insufficient to complete the standard termination process and that the plan will remain ongoing. However, PBGC might forbear to pursue section 4062(e) liability where a standard termination was in process. And if distributions under a standard termination are complete by the deadline for giving notice of a section 4062(e) event, PBGC generally would not enforce the notice requirement.

Effect on Prior Opinions

PBGC has in the past issued a number of opinion letters dealing with ERISA section 4062(e).[10] While this proposed regulation does not explicitly address all details relating to section 4062(e), PBGC's intent in issuing the regulation is to set forth all of its current section 4062(e) guidance, supported by the discussion in this preamble. Accordingly, the regulation would displace and supersede all of PBGC's prior opinion letter pronouncements addressing section 4062(e).

Applicability

PBGC proposes that the amendments made by this rule apply to section 4062(e) events with cessation dates on or after the effective date of the amendments.

Compliance With Rulemaking Guidelines

E.O. 12866

The PBGC has determined, in consultation with the Office of Management and Budget, that this proposed rule is a "significant regulatory action" under Executive Order 12866. The Office of Management and Budget has therefore reviewed this proposed rule under E.O. 12866.

Regulatory Flexibility Act

PBGC certifies under section 605(b) of the Regulatory Flexibility Act (5 U.S.C. 601 et seq.) that the amendments in this rule will not have a significant economic impact on a substantial number of small entities. Accordingly, as provided in section 605 of the Regulatory Flexibility Act (5 U.S.C. 601 et seq.), sections 603 and 604 do not apply. This certification is based on the fact that the proposed regulatory amendments require only the filing of notices and that the economic impact of filing is not significant. Furthermore, section 4062(e) is generally not relevant for small employers. Small employers tend not to have multiple operations. For a small employer with a defined benefit pension plan, the cessation of an operation almost always would be accompanied by plan termination. Section 4062(e) protection is only relevant when the plan is ongoing after the cessation of operations. Since publication of PBGC's 2006 final rule on calculation of liability under section 4062(e), only a handful of the potential section 4062(e) cases reviewed by PBGC involved plans with 100 or fewer participants.

Paperwork Reduction Act

PBGC is submitting the information requirements under this proposed rule to the Office of Management and Budget for review and approval under the Paperwork Reduction Act. Copies of PBGC's request may be obtained free of charge by contacting the Disclosure Division of the Office of the General Counsel of PBGC, 1200 K Street, NW., Washington, DC 20005, 202-326-4040. The proposed information collection will also be available on PBGC's Web site.

PBGC is proposing to require that notices of section 4062(e) events be filed using a PBGC form and include the following information:

Identifying and contact information for the affected plan, the plan administrator, other plans covering affected participants, the contributing sponsor, and members of the contributing sponsor's controlled group.

A description of current and proposed plan provisions dealing with lump sum options, shutdowns, and early retirement benefits.

A description of any current or proposed plan termination proceedings, plan mergers, or changes in contributing sponsor or controlled group.

A description of the affected operation and associated facility.

A general description of the section 4062(e) event, including whether the affected operation is to be continued or resumed by the affected employer or a new employer at the same or another facility.

The date used to calculate the active participant base, the date of any employer decision to cease the affected operation, the date (and na-

---

[10] See for example PBGC Opinion Letters 76-8, 76-52, 77-123, 77-134, 77-147, 78-29, 82-29, 85-8, and 86-13.

ture) of any event that caused the cessation (other than an employer decision), the cessation date, and the date when the number of affected participants exceeded 20 percent of the active participant base.

A copy of any press release or other announcement of the employer's cessation decision (including any notice issued pursuant to the Worker Adjustment and Retraining Notification (WARN) Act) and the date when it was issued.

A description of any severance or retirement incentives offered since the date one year before the date of the employer decision to cease the operation.

The active participant base.

The number of affected participants as of the date when the filing was prepared.

The number of participants in the affected plan who have not separated from employment as of the date when the filing was prepared but who the employer believes will separate from employment as a result of the section 4062(e) event.

The number of active participants in the affected plan who had separated from employment as of the date when the filing was prepared but who were not counted as affected participants.

The name and address of each union representing affected participants.

A copy of each collective bargaining agreement covering affected participants.

The affected plan's most recent adjusted funding target attainment percentage (AFTAP) certification and most recent actuarial valuation report, including or supplemented by all of the information described in Sec. 4010.8(a)(11) of PBGC's regulation on Annual Financial and Actuarial Information Reporting (29 CFR part 4010).

A summary of plan amendments, significant changes in plan population, changes in plan assumptions, and amounts and dates of lump sums paid that are not reflected in the most recent actuarial valuation report.

The market value of plan assets as of, or as close as possible to, the cessation date.

PBGC needs this information to calculate the liability arising from a section 4062(e) event and decide how that liability should be satisfied. PBGC estimates that it will receive filings from about 200 respondents each year and that the total annual burden of the collection of information will be about 1,000 hours and $350,000.

Comments on the paperwork provisions under this proposed rule should be sent to the Office of Information and Regulatory Affairs, Office of Management and Budget, Attention: Desk Officer for Pension Benefit Guaranty Corporation, via electronic mail at OIRA_DOCKET@omb.eop.gov or by fax to (202) 395-6974. Although comments may be submitted through October 12, 2010, the Office of Management and Budget requests that comments be received on or before September 9, 2010 to ensure their consideration. Comments may address (among other things)—

Whether the proposed collection of information is needed for the proper performance of PBGC's functions and will have practical utility;

The accuracy of PBGC's estimate of the burden of the proposed collection of information, including the validity of the methodology and assumptions used;

Enhancement of the quality, utility, and clarity of the information to be collected; and

Minimizing the burden of the collection of information on those who are to respond, including through the use of appropriate automated, electronic, mechanical, or other technological collection techniques or other forms of information technology, e.g., permitting electronic submission of responses.

List of Subjects

29 CFR Part 4062

Employee benefit plans, Pension insurance, Reporting and recordkeeping requirements.

29 CFR Part 4063

Employee benefit plans, Pension insurance.

For the reasons given above, PBGC proposes to amend 29 CFR parts 4062 and 4063 as follows.

PART 4062—LIABILITY FOR TERMINATION OF SINGLE-EMPLOYER PLANS

1. The authority citation for part 4062 is revised to read as follows:

Authority: 29 U.S.C. 1302(b)(3), 1303(a), 1362-1364, 1367, 1368.

2. Section 4062.1 is revised to read as follows:

§ 4062.1 Purpose and scope.

Subpart A of this part sets forth rules for calculation and payment of the liability incurred, under section 4062(b) of ERISA, upon termination of any single-employer plan and, to the extent appropriate, calculation of the liability incurred with respect to multiple employer plans under sections 4063 and 4064 of ERISA. Subpart B of this part sets forth rules under section 4062(e) of ERISA, including rules for reporting section 4062(e) events and for calculating and satisfying liability arising from such events.

§ 4062.3 [Amended]

3. In § 4062.3, paragraph (b) is amended by removing the reference "§ 4062.9(c)" and adding in its place the reference "§ 4062.8(c)"; and by removing the reference "§ 4062.9(b)" and adding in its place the reference "§ 4062.8(b)".

§ 4062.7 [Amended]

4. In § 4062.7, paragraph (a) is amended by removing the reference "§ 4062.9" and adding in its place the reference "§ 4062.8".

§ 4062.8 [Removed]

5. Section 4062.8 is removed.

§§ 4062.9, 4062.10, and 4062.11 [Redesignated as §§ 4062.8, 4062.9, and 4062.10]

6. Sections 4062.9, 4062.10, and 4062.11 are redesignated as §§ 4062.8, 4062.9, and 4062.10 respectively.

§ 4062.1 through § 4062.10 [Designated]

7. Newly redesignated §§ 4062.1 through 4062.10 are designated as subpart A with the heading "Subpart A—General Termination Liability Rules".

8. A new subpart B is added to read as follows:

Subpart B—Treatment of Substantial Cessation of Operations

§

4062.21 Purpose and scope.

4062.22 Definitions.

4062.23 "Section 4062(e) event."

4062.24 "Operation."

4062.25 "Facility" or "facility in any location."

4062.26 "Cease" and "cessation."

4062.27 "Separate" and "separation."

4062.28 "Result."

4062.29 "Active participant base."

4062.30 PBGC investigations.

4062.31 Reporting requirement.

4062.32 Amount of liability.

4062.33 Manner of satisfying liability.

4062.34 Recordkeeping.

4062.35 Waivers.

Subpart B—Treatment of Substantial Cessation of Operations

§ 4062.21 Purpose and scope.

This subpart B provides guidance about the applicability and enforcement of ERISA section 4062(e).

§ 4062.22 Definitions.

For purposes of this subpart B:

Active participant base has the meaning described in § 4062.29.

Affected employer means an employer that ceases an operation at a facility.

Affected operation means the operation that an affected employer ceases.

Affected participant means an employee of an affected employer who is a participant in an affected plan and who separates from employment with the affected employer as a result of the affected employer's ceasing the affected operation.

Affected plan means a single-employer plan that is maintained by an affected employer, that is not a multiple employer plan, and that includes as participants employees of the affected employer who separate from employment as a result of the affected employer's ceasing the affected operation.

Cease and cessation have the meaning described in § 4062.26.

Cessation date means the date when an employer ceases an operation at a facility as described in § 4062.26.

Employer has the meaning described in § 4001.2 of this chapter.

Facility and facility in any location have the meaning described in § 4062.25.

Operation has the meaning described in § 4062.24.

Result has the meaning described in § 4062.28.

Section 4062(e) event has the meaning described in § 4062.23.

Separate and separation have the meaning described in § 4062.27.

§ 4062.23 "Section 4062(e) event."

(a) In general. A section 4062(e) event occurs if—

(1) An employer maintains a single-employer plan that is not a multiple employer plan;

(2) The employer ceases an operation at a facility in any location;

(3) As a result of the cessation, one or more persons who are employees of the employer and participants in the plan are separated from employment; and

(4) The number of such persons who are so separated is more than 20 percent of the active participant base associated with the cessation.

(b) Risk disregarded. Whether a section 4062(e) event has occurred is decided without regard to the existence or non-existence, when the event occurs or when the decision is made, of risk or apparent risk to a plan, its participants, or PBGC. However, PBGC may assess risk in making arrangements for satisfaction of liability for a section 4062(e) event.

(c) Plan-by-plan application. This subpart B applies separately to each plan of an affected employer.

§ 4062.24 "Operation."

An operation is a set of activities that constitutes an organizationally, operationally, or functionally distinct unit of an employer. Whether a set of activities is an operation may depend on whether it is (or similar sets of activities are) so considered or treated in the relevant industry, in the employer's organizational structure or accounts, in relevant collective bargaining agreements, by the employer's employees or customers, or by the public.

§ 4062.25 "Facility" or "facility in any location."

The facility (or facility in any location) associated with an operation is the place or places where the operation is performed. A facility is typically a building or buildings. However, a facility may be or include any one or more enclosed or open areas or structures. The same facility may be associated with more than one operation.

§ 4062.26 "Cease" and "cessation."

(a) Voluntary cessation. Unless paragraph (b) of this section applies, an employer is considered to cease an operation at a facility when the employer discontinues all significant activity at the facility in furtherance of the purpose of the operation.

(b) Involuntary cessation.

(1) Cessation caused by employee action. If a discontinuance of activity described in paragraph (a) of this section is caused by employee action such as a strike or sickout, then the employer is considered to cease the operation at the facility on the earlier of—

(i) The date when the employee action ends, unless within one week after that date the employer has resumed significant activity at the facility in furtherance of the purpose of the operation, or

(ii) The date when the employer decides not to resume significant activity at the facility in furtherance of the purpose of the operation.

(2) Other involuntary cessation. If a discontinuance of activity described in paragraph (a) of this section is caused by a sudden and unanticipated event (other than an employee action) such as a natural disaster, then the employer is considered to cease the operation at the facility on the earlier of—

(i) The date that is 30 days after the discontinuance, unless on that date the employer has resumed significant activity at the facility in furtherance of the purpose of the operation, or

(ii) The date when the employer decides not to resume significant activity at the facility in furtherance of the purpose of the operation.

(c) Follow-on operations disregarded. Whether an employer ceases an operation at a facility is decided without regard to whether—

(1) The operation is continued or resumed—

(i) At another facility, or

(ii) By another employer; or

(2) When the operation is discontinued, a different operation is undertaken.

§ 4062.27 "Separate" and "separation."

(a) In general. An employee of an employer separates from employment when the employee discontinues the active performance, pursuant to the employee's employment relationship with the employer, of activities in furtherance of any of the employer's operations, unless, when the discontinuance occurs, it is reasonably certain that the employee will resume such active work for the employer within 30 days. However, if the 30-day period passes and the employee has not resumed active work for the employer, the employee will be considered to have separated from employment when the discontinuance occurred.

(b) Employees rehired or replaced. If an employer ceases an operation at a facility, the separation from employment of an employee who is a participant in the affected plan is disregarded in computing the number of affected participants if the separation is before the cessation date and, as of the cessation date, either—

(1) The employee has been rehired and is an employee of the employer and a participant in the affected plan, or

(2) The employee has been replaced and the replacement is an employee of the employer and a participant in the affected plan.

§ 4062.28 "Result."

(a) In general. An employee separates from employment as a result of an employer's cessation of an operation at a facility if—

(1) The employee separates from employment with the employer, and

(2) The separation would not have occurred when it did if the employer's cessation of the operation at the facility had not occurred.

(b) Circumstances not decisive. An employee's separation from employment may result from an employer's cessation of an operation at a facility—

(1) Whether separation occurs before, on, or after the cessation date,

(2) Whether or not the employee is employed in the operation that ceases, and

(3) Whether or not the employee is employed at the facility associated with the operation that ceases.

(c) Presumption; voluntary cessation; involuntary separation. An employee's separation from employment with an employer is presumed to be a result of the employer's cessation of an operation at a facility if—

(1) The employee is employed by the employer in the operation,

(2) The cessation is described in § 4062.26(a) and not in § 4062.26(b), and

(3) The employee involuntarily separates from employment with the employer on or after the date of the employer decision pursuant to which the cessation occurred.

(d) Presumption; voluntary cessation; voluntary separation. An employee's separation from employment with an employer is presumed to be a result of the employer's cessation of an operation at a facility if—

(1) The employee is employed by the employer in the operation,

(2) The cessation is described in § 4062.26(a) and not in § 4062.26(b), and

(3) The employee voluntarily separates from employment with the employer on or after the earliest date when the employer decision pursuant to which the cessation occurred becomes known to the employee, to employees generally, or to the public.

(e) Presumption; involuntary cessation. An employee's separation from employment with an employer is presumed to be a result of the employer's cessation of an operation at a facility if—

(1) The employee is employed by the employer in the operation,

(2) The cessation is described in § 4062.26(b), and

(3) The employee voluntarily or involuntarily separates from employment with the employer on or after the date of the event that causes the cessation.

(f) Presumption; employment by new employer. An employee's separation from employment with an employer is presumed to be a result of the employer's cessation of an operation at a facility if—

(1) The employee is employed by the employer in the operation,

(2) Another employer (the "new employer") continues or resumes the operation at the same or another facility, and

(3) The employee becomes employed by the new employer.

§ 4062.29 "Active participant base."

(a) In general. The active participant base associated with a cessation is the total number of persons who, immediately before the applicable date in paragraph (b) of this section, were—

(1) Participants in the affected plan, and

(2) Employees of the affected employer either—

(i) Engaged in the active performance, pursuant to their employment relationship with the employer, of activities in furtherance of the employer's operations, or

(ii) Reasonably certain to resume such active work for the employer within 30 days, but a person is not counted in the active participant base under this paragraph (a)(2)(ii) if the 30-day period passes and the employee has not resumed active work for the employer.

(b) Applicable date. For purposes of paragraph (a) of this section, the applicable date is—

(1) For a cessation described in § 4062.26(a) and not in § 4062.26(b), the date of the employer decision pursuant to which the cessation occurred, and

(2) For a cessation described in § 4062.26(b), the date of the event that caused the cessation.

(c) "Participant." For purposes of this subpart B, whether an individual is a participant in a plan at a particular time is decided without regard to whether the individual is accruing benefits under the plan at that time.

§ 4062.30 PBGC investigations.

(a) In general. PBGC may make such investigations as it considers necessary to enforce section 4062(e) and this subpart B and in particular to discover whether section 4062(e) events have occurred and whether notices required under § 4062.31 have been timely filed.

(b) PBGC information requests. If PBGC requests from any person information about any event that may be a section 4062(e) event, the person must file the requested information within 45 days after PBGC's request or within a different time specified in the request. PBGC may specify a shorter time where it finds that the interests of PBGC, participants, or the pension insurance system may be prejudiced by a delay in the receipt of the information (for example, where timely enforcement of section 4062(e) of ERISA may be jeopardized).

(c) Duty to update or correct. If a person that has filed information with PBGC pursuant to a request under paragraph (b) of this section discovers that any information so filed (including the number of affected participants) is materially erroneous or has become materially outdated, the person must promptly file with PBGC the correct or updated information.

(d) PBGC determinations. On the basis of information gleaned from an investigation or otherwise obtained, PBGC may determine that a section 4062(e) event has occurred and determine the amount of liability arising from the event.

§ 4062.31 Reporting requirement.

(a) Notice required; who must file. If a section 4062(e) event occurs, the plan administrator of the affected plan must file a notice of the event with PBGC. The filing of the notice constitutes a request that PBGC determine the liability with respect to the event.

(b) When to file.

(1) In general. Notice of a section 4062(e) event must be filed with PBGC within 60 days after the later of—

(i) The cessation date, or

(ii) The date when the number of affected participants is more than 20 percent of the active participant base.

(2) Filing date; computation of time. See subparts C and D of part 4000 of this chapter for information on ascertaining filing dates and computing periods of time.

(c) How to file. See §§ 4000.3 and 4000.4 of this chapter for information on how and where to file. Notice of a section 4062(e) event must be filed in accordance with PBGC's instructions for filing section 4062(e) event notices, posted on PBGC's Web site (http://www.pbgc.gov).

(d) Additional information. If PBGC requests additional information from the plan administrator of an affected plan about a section 4062(e) event of which the plan administrator has given notice, the plan administrator must file the requested information within 45 days after PBGC's request or within a different time specified in the request. PBGC may specify a shorter time where it finds that the interests of PBGC, participants, or the pension insurance system may be prejudiced by a delay in the receipt of the information (for example, where timely enforcement of section 4062(e) of ERISA may be jeopardized).

(e) Requirement for employer to provide information. An employer that may be an affected employer must timely provide to the plan administrator of any plan that may be an affected plan any information that the plan administrator needs—

(1) To decide whether and when a section 4062(e) event has occurred, and

(2) To file under this section.

(f) Duty to update or correct. If the plan administrator of an affected plan discovers or is notified by the affected employer that any information filed with PBGC under this section (including the number of affected participants) is materially erroneous or has become materially outdated, the plan administrator must promptly file with PBGC the correct or updated information.

(g) Disregarding certain affected participants for notice purposes. In deciding whether notice of a section 4062(e) event is required, the due date of the notice, and the number of affected participants to be reported in the notice (and any update or correction of the notice under paragraph (f) of this section), a plan administrator may disregard affected participants who were not employed at the facility associated with the affected operation. This provision does not apply to—

(1) PBGC investigations under § 4062.30, or

(2) A request under paragraph (d) of this section for information about affected participants who were not employed at the facility associated with the affected operation (or any update or correction under paragraph (f) of this section of information provided in response to such a request).

§ 4062.32 Amount of liability.

(a) Determination of liability. PBGC will determine the amount of liability with respect to a section 4062(e) event in accordance with this section.

(b) Amount of liability. The amount of liability for a section 4062(e) event is the amount that PBGC determines to be the amount described in section 4062 of ERISA for the entire affected plan, computed as if the plan had been terminated by PBGC immediately after the cessation date, multiplied by a fraction—

(1) The numerator of which is the number of affected participants, and

(2) The denominator of which is the active participant base.

(c) Post-cessation changes disregarded. For purposes of paragraph (b) of this section, the amount described in section 4062 of ERISA for the entire affected plan is calculated without regard to any change in the affected plan's assets or benefit liabilities after the cessation date, such as an increase in assets due to receipt of contributions after the cessation date or an increase in liabilities due to accruals after that date.

§ 4062.33 Manner of satisfying liability.

(a) In general. PBGC will decide in accordance with ERISA how the liability for a section 4062(e) event is to be satisfied. In general, PBGC will require that liability for a section 4062(e) event be satisfied either—

(1) By paying the amount of the liability to PBGC to be held in escrow under section 4063(b) of ERISA, or

(2) By furnishing a bond in an amount not exceeding 150 percent of the amount of the liability under section 4063(c)(1) of ERISA.

(b) Other arrangements. PBGC may make arrangements for satisfaction of liability for a section 4062(e) event other than those in paragraph (a) of this section. For example, in appropriate cases:

(1) PBGC may permit liability for a section 4062(e) event to be satisfied through one or more additional plan funding contributions that would not be added to the plan's prefunding balance.

(2) If an affected operation is continued or resumed by another employer (the "new employer"), and the new employer employs in the operation persons who were employed by the affected employer in the operation, PBGC may permit the liability for the section 4062(e) event to be satisfied by the new employer's adoption or maintenance of the affected plan or of a plan that holds substantially all of the liabilities and assets of the affected plan attributable to employees employed in the affected operation.

§ 4062.34 Recordkeeping.

(a) Each employer that maintains a single-employer plan that is not a multiple employer plan, and the plan administrator of each such plan, must keep for five years, with respect to any discontinuance of all significant activity in furtherance of the purpose of an operation of the employer at a facility, all records that bear on whether there was a section 4062(e) event and on the calculation of liability with respect to the event.

(b) If PBGC finds that an employer or plan administrator referred to in paragraph (a) of this section has failed to keep records sufficient to determine whether a section 4062(e) event has occurred or the amount of liability arising from such an event, PBGC may make such determination on the basis of reasonable assumptions not inconsistent with information that PBGC knows of and considers reliable.

§ 4062.35 Waivers.

PBGC may waive any provision of this subpart B to accommodate the facts and circumstances of particular cases and promote the equitable and rational interpretation and application of title IV.

PART 4063—WITHDRAWAL LIABILITY; PLANS UNDER MULTIPLE CONTROLLED GROUPS

9. The authority citation for part 4063 continues to read as follows:

Authority: 29 U.S.C. 1302(b)(3).

10. In section 4063.1, paragraph (a) is amended by revising the second sentence to read as follows:

§ 4063.1 Cross references.

(a) *** Part 4062 also sets forth rules under section 4062(e) of ERISA, including rules for reporting section 4062(e) events and for calculating and satisfying liability arising from such events.

*****

Issued in Washington, DC, August 4, 2010.

Joshua Gotbaum, Director, Pension Benefit Guaranty Corporation.

[FR Doc. 2010-19627 Filed 8-9-10; 8:45 am]

¶ 20,537Y

Employee Benefits Security Administration (EBSA): Proposed regulations: Prohibited transactions: Exemption procedures.—The Employee Benefits Security Administration (EBSA) has issued proposed regulations that would update the procedures governing the filing and processing of applications for exemptions from the prohibited transaction provisions of ERISA. The amended procedures would consolidate existing policies, clarify the types of information and documentation required to submit a complete filing, expand the methods for transmitting filings to include electronic submissions, and make the exemptions more understandable to participants and other interested parties.

The proposed regulations, which were published in the Federal Register on August 30, 2010 (75 FR 53172), were previously reproduced below. An Official correction to the proposed regulations was issued on September 8, 2010 (75 FR 54542). The final regulations were published in the Federal Register on October 27, 2011 and appear beginning at ¶ 14,789B-5. The preamble to the final regulations appears at ¶ 24,307.

¶ 20,537Z

Employee Benefits Security Administration (EBSA): Proposed regulations: Fiduciary: Investment advice.—The Employee Benefits Security Administration (EBSA) has issued proposed regulations that would more broadly define the circumstances under which a person is considered a "fiduciary" under ERISA by reason of giving investment advice to an employee benefit plan. Written comments on the proposed regulations are due on or before January 20, 2011.

The proposed regulations were published in the Federal Register on October 22, 2010 (75 FR 65263). These proposed regulations were withdrawn and replaced with another set of proposed regulations on April 20, 2015 (80 FR 21927). See PENSION PLAN GUIDE ¶ 20,538Z for the new set of proposed regulations.

¶ 20,538

Employee Benefits Security Administration (EBSA): Proposed regulations: Defined benefit plans: Annual funding notice: Reporting and disclosure.—The Employee Benefits Security Administration (EBSA) has issued proposed regulations that would implement the annual funding notice requirements for defined benefit plans in ERISA § 101(f), as amended by the Pension Protection Act of 2006 (PPA) and the Worker, Retiree, and Employer Recovery Act of 2008 (WRERA). In February 2009, EBSA issued Field Assistance Bulletin 2009-01 (Pension Plan Guide ¶ 19,981Z-5) to provide interim guidance to plan administrators on the annual funding notice requirements under ERISA § 101(f). Much of this guidance has been incorporated into the proposed regulations. EBSA advises that the guidance will remain in effect until the rules or finalized (or if the Department adopts any additional guidance other than final regulations). Comments are sought by January 18, 2011.

The proposed regulations, which were published in the Federal Register on November 18, 2010 (75 FR 70625), are reproduced below. These regulations were finalized February 2, 2015 (80 FR 5625). The preamble to the final regulations appears at ¶ 24,326. The final regulations are at ¶ 14,214, ¶ 14,215, ¶ 14,215A, ¶ 14,215B, ¶ 14,247Z, and ¶ 14,249H.

DEPARTMENT OF LABOR

Employee Benefits Security Administration

29 CFR Part 2520

RIN 1210-AB18

Annual Funding Notice for Defined Benefit Plans

AGENCY: Employee Benefits Security Administration, Labor.

ACTION: Proposed rule.

SUMMARY: This document contains a proposed regulation that, on adoption, would implement the annual funding notice requirement in the Employee Retirement Income Security Act of 1974 (ERISA), as amended by the Pension Protection Act of 2006 (PPA) and the Worker, Retiree, and Employer Recovery Act of 2008 (WRERA). As amended, section 101(f) of ERISA generally requires the administrators of all defined benefit plans, not just multiemployer defined benefit plans, to furnish an annual funding notice to the Pension Benefit Guaranty Corporation (PBGC), participants, beneficiaries, and certain other persons. A funding notice must include, among other information, the plan's funding target attainment percentage or funded percentage, as applicable, over a period of time, as well as other information relevant to the plan's funded status. This document also contains proposed conforming amendments to other regulations under ERISA, such as the summary annual report regulation, which became necessary when the PPA amended section 101(f) of ERISA. The proposed regulation would affect plan administrators and participants and beneficiaries of defined benefit pension plans, as well as labor organizations representing participants and beneficiaries and contributing employers of multiemployer plans.

DATES: Written comments on the proposed regulation should be received by the Department of Labor on or before January 18, 2011.

ADDRESSES: You may submit comments, identified by RIN 1210-AB18, by one of the following methods:

• *Federal eRulemaking Portal: http://www.regulations.gov.* Follow the instructions for submitting comments.

• *E-mail: e-ORI@dol.gov.* Include RIN 1210-AB18 in the subject line of the message.

• *Mail:* Office of Regulations and Interpretations, Employee Benefits Security Administration, Room N-5655, U.S. Department of Labor, 200 Constitution Avenue, NW., Washington, DC 20210, Attention: Annual Funding Notice for Defined Benefit Plans.

Instructions: All submissions received must include the agency name and Regulation Identifier Number (RIN) for this rulemaking. Comments received will be posted without change to *http://www.regulations.gov* and *http://www.dol.gov/ebsa,* and made available for public inspection at the Public Disclosure Room, N-1513, Employee Benefits Security Administration, 200 Constitution Avenue, NW., Washington, DC 20210, including any personal information provided. Do not include any personally identifiable information (such as name, address, or other contact information) or confidential business information that you do not want publicly disclosed. Comments posted on the Internet can be retrieved by most Internet search engines. Comments may be submitted anonymously. Persons submitting comments electronically are encouraged not to submit paper copies.

FOR FURTHER INFORMATION CONTACT: Thomas M. Hindmarch or Stephanie L. Ward, Office of Regulations and Interpretations, Employee Benefits Security Administration, (202) 693-8500. This is not a toll-free number.

SUPPLEMENTARY INFORMATION:

A. Background

In 2004, the Pension Funding Equity Act (PFEA '04), Public Law 108-218, amended title I of the Employee Retirement Income Security Act of 1974 (ERISA) by adding section 101(f), which required multiemployer defined benefit plans to furnish a plan funding notice annually to each participant and beneficiary, to each labor organization representing such participants or beneficiaries, to each employer that has an obligation to contribute under the plan, and to the Pension Benefit Guaranty Corporation (PBGC).[1]

In 2006, section 501(a) of the Pension Protection Act of 2006, Public Law 109-280 (PPA), significantly amended section 101(f) of ERISA. For example, section 101(f) of ERISA now requires administrators of all defined benefit plans that are subject to title IV of ERISA, not only multiemployer plans, to furnish annual funding notices. In addition, the PPA shortened the time frame for providing funding notices and enhanced the notice content requirements. These changes are discussed

in detail below. Pursuant to section 501(d) of the PPA, the amendments to section 101(f) apply to plan years beginning after December 31, 2007.[2]

On February 10, 2009, the Department issued Field Assistance Bulletin 2009-01 (FAB 2009-01) as interim guidance under section 101(f) of ERISA in order to assist plan administrators in discharging their obligations under the new annual funding notice requirements. FAB 2009-01 provides question and answer guidance on a number of issues under section 101(f) of ERISA. It also includes model funding notices. Much of the guidance in FAB 2009-01 has been incorporated into the proposed regulation contained in this document. That guidance remains in effect until the Department adopts final regulations under section 101(f) of ERISA (or if the Department were to publish any other guidance under section 101(f) other than final regulations).[3]

B. Overview of Proposed 29 CFR 2520.101-5—Annual Funding Notice for Defined Benefit Pension Plans

1. Scope

Paragraph (a) of the proposed regulation implements the requirements set forth in section 101(f) of ERISA. This section in general requires the administrator of a defined benefit plan to which title IV of ERISA applies to furnish annually a funding notice to the PBGC, to each plan participant and beneficiary, to each labor organization representing such participants or beneficiaries, and, in the case of a multiemployer plan, to each employer that has an obligation to contribute to the plan. Those persons entitled to the funding notice are further clarified in paragraph (f) of the proposed regulation.

Paragraphs (a)(2) and (3) of the proposed regulation provide limited exceptions to the requirement to furnish a funding notice.

Under the exception in paragraph (a)(2)(i) of the proposal, the plan administrator of an insolvent multiemployer plan that is in compliance with the insolvency notice requirements of sections 4245(e) or 4281(d)(3) of ERISA before the due date of the funding notice for a plan year is not, for such year, required to furnish the funding notice to the parties otherwise entitled to such notice. This exception is effectively the same as the exception that currently exists in § 2520.101-4(a)(2) for multiemployer plans receiving financial assistance from the PBGC. The rationale for the exception was articulated in the final regulation under § 2520.101-4.[4] The exception in the proposal is phrased slightly differently than the exception in § 2520.101-4 at the request of the PBGC. Inasmuch as this exception is predicated on sufficient alternative notification under sections 4245(e) and 4281(d)(3), the exception would cease to be available with respect to a plan that emerges from insolvency or ceases to comply with the insolvency notice requirements under title IV of ERISA.

Under the exception in paragraph (a)(2)(ii) of the proposal, the plan administrator of a single-employer plan is not required to furnish a funding notice for a plan year if the due date for such notice is on or after the date the PBGC is appointed trustee of the plan pursuant to section 4042 of ERISA, or the plan has distributed assets in satisfaction of all benefit liabilities in a standard termination pursuant to section 4041(b) or in a distress termination pursuant to section 4041(c)(3)(B)(i), or of all guaranteed benefits in a distress termination pursuant to section 4041(c)(3)(B)(ii) of ERISA. The Department believes, because of the separate disclosure requirements applicable to such plans under title IV of ERISA, a funding notice may be unnecessary or confusing to participants where the PBGC is appointed trustee of a terminated single-employer plan or where a terminated single-employer plan has already satisfied all benefit liabilities or all guaranteed benefits.[5]

Under the exception in paragraph (a)(3) of the proposal, relief is provided in the case of a merger or consolidation of two or more plans. In such circumstances, the plan administrator of the plan that has legally transferred control of its assets to a successor plan (hereafter the "non-successor plan") shall not be required to furnish a funding notice for its final plan year that ends coincident with or immediately

---

[1] On January 11, 2006, the Department of Labor published a final regulation implementing the requirements of section 101(f) of ERISA as amended by PFEA '04. *See* 29 CFR 2520.101-4.

[2] Prior to the applicability date of the PPA amendments to section 101(f) of ERISA, a multiemployer plan was required to furnish a funding notice consistent with § 2520.101-4 (for plan years beginning prior to January 1, 2008). For plan years beginning after December 31, 2007, multiemployer plans must comply with section 101(f) as amended, and when final, the regulations under § 2520.101-5, rather than § 2520.101-4. The Department will remove § 2520.101-4 from the Code of Federal Regulations in conjunction with the promulgation of a final rule.

[3] FAB 2009-01 is available on the Department's Web site at *http://www.dol.gov/ebsa/regs/fab2009-1.html.*

[4] The annual funding notice would be of little, if any, value to recipients in light of the PBGC's authority and responsibility under title IV of ERISA with respect to insolvent multiemployer plans. *See* 71 FR 1904, n.1 (Jan. 11, 2006). *See also* 70 FR 6306, n.1 (Feb. 4, 2005).

[5] For example, under a standard termination, participants are provided a notice of intent to terminate 60 to 90 days prior to the proposed termination date (29 CFR 4041.23), a notice of plan benefits by the time PBGC Form 500 is filed with the PBGC (29 CFR 4041.24), and a notice of annuity information in the notice of intent to terminate or, in certain cases, 45 days prior to the distribution date (29 CFR 4041.23(b)(5) and 29 CFR 4041.27).

prior to the merger. Thus, for example, if plan A were to merge with plan B in 2010 and plan B is the successor plan (*i.e.,* the plan to which control of the assets of plan A was legally transferred), then the plan administrator of plan A is not required to furnish a funding notice for plan A for its final plan year that ends upon the occurrence of the merger in 2010. However, the funding notice of plan B (*i.e.,* the plan to which control of the assets of plan A was legally transferred) must satisfy the general content requirements in paragraph (b) of the proposed regulation and, in addition, contain a general explanation of the merger. The general explanation must include the effective date of, and identify each plan involved with, the merger or consolidation. Given that participants and beneficiaries will look to the successor plan for their pension benefits following the merger or consolidation, rather than the plan whose assets and liabilities were transferred to the successor plan, the Department believes that participants and beneficiaries would realize little, if any, benefit from receiving a funding notice from the non-successor plan. In addition, including an explanation of the merger in the funding notice of the successor plan should abate any participant confusion that might exist by virtue of not receiving a funding notice from the non-successor plan.

2. Content Requirements

a. Identifying Information (Proposed § 2520.105-1(b)(1))

Paragraph (b)(1) of the proposed regulation provides that a funding notice must include the name of the plan and the name, address and telephone number of the plan administrator (and the name, address and phone number of the plan's principal administrative officer if the principal administrative officer is different from the plan administrator). A funding notice also must include each plan sponsor's name and employer identification number and the plan number. For purposes of this requirement, employer identification numbers, name of plan sponsor, and plan numbers are the same as those used in the annual report filed in accordance with section 104(a) of ERISA.

b. Funding Percentage (Proposed § 2520.105-1(b)(2))

Paragraph (b)(2) of the proposed regulation requires disclosure of a plan's funding percentage. Specifically, in the case of a single-employer plan, paragraph (b)(2)(i) of the proposal provides that a notice must include a statement as to whether the plan's funding target attainment percentage for the plan year to which the notice relates (the "notice year"), and for each of the two preceding plan years, is at least 100 percent (and, if not, the actual percentages). The term "funding target attainment percentage" is defined in section 303(d)(2) of ERISA, which corresponds to Internal Revenue Code (Code) section 430(d)(2). Guidance issued by the Department of the Treasury under Code section 430 also applies for purposes of section 303 of ERISA. Treasury regulations under Code section 430 provide that the funding target attainment percentage of a plan for a plan year is a fraction (expressed as a percentage), the numerator of which is the value of plan assets for the plan year (determined under the rules of 26 CFR 1.430(g)-1) after subtraction of the prefunding balance and the funding standard carryover balance under section 430(f)(4)(B) of the Code and § 1.430(f)-1(c) and the denominator of which is the funding target of the plan for the plan year (determined without regard to the at-risk rules of section 430(i) of the Code and § 1.430(i)-1).[6] Thus, this percentage for a plan year is calculated by dividing the value of the plan's assets for that year (after subtracting the prefunding and funding standard carryover balances, if any) by the funding target of the plan for that year (disregarding the at-risk rules).

Similarly, in the case of a multiemployer plan, paragraph (b)(2)(ii) of the proposed regulation provides that a notice must include a statement as to whether the plan's funded percentage for the notice year, and for each of the two preceding plan years, is at least 100 percent (and, if not, the actual percentages). The term "funded percentage" is defined in section 305(i) of ERISA, which corresponds to section 432(i) of the Code. Guidance issued by the Department of the Treasury under section 432 of the Code also applies for purposes of section 305 of ERISA. Proposed Treasury regulations under Code section 432 provide that the funded percentage of a plan for a plan year is a fraction (expressed as a percentage), the numerator of which is the actuarial value of the plan's assets as determined under section 431(c)(2) of the Code and the denominator of which is the accrued liability of the plan, determined using the actuarial assumptions described in section 431(c)(3) of the Code and the unit credit funding method.[7] Thus, this percentage for a plan year is calculated by dividing the plan's assets for that year by the accrued liability of the plan for that year, determined using the unit credit funding method.

c. Assets and Liabilities (Proposed § 2520.101-5(b)(3))

(i) Single-Employer Plans—Assets and Liabilities as of the Valuation Date

In the case of a single-employer plan, paragraph (b)(3)(i)(A) of the proposed regulation requires that a funding notice include a statement of the total assets (separately stating the prefunding balance and the funding standard carryover balance) and liabilities of the plan for the notice year and each of the two preceding plan years. Like the statute, under section 101(f)(2)(B)(ii)(I)(aa), the proposed regulation provides that assets and liabilities are to be determined "in the same manner as under section 303" of ERISA. The Department interprets this reference to mean the assets and liabilities used to determine a plan's funding target attainment percentage (as well as the plan's "at-risk" liabilities pursuant to section 303(i) of ERISA, taking into account section 303(i)(5), if the plan is in "at-risk" status). This approach makes transparent the assets and liabilities used to determine the funding target attainment percentage of the plan, as well as the plan's liabilities (*i.e.,* funding target) actually used for funding purposes.

(ii) Single-Employer Plans—Assets and Liabilities as of the Last Day of the Plan Year

Section 101(f)(2)(B)(ii)(I)(bb) of ERISA states that a funding notice must include, in the case of a single-employer plan, "the value of the plan's assets and liabilities for the plan year to which the notice relates as of the last day of the plan year to which the notice relates determined using the asset valuation under subclause (II) of section 4006(a)(3)(E)(iii) and the interest rate under section 4006(a)(3)(E)(iv)[.]"

Based on the foregoing, paragraph (b)(3)(i)(B) of the proposed regulation provides that a single-employer plan must include a statement of the value of the plan's assets and liabilities determined as of the last day of the notice year. For purposes of this statement, plan administrators must report the fair market value of assets as of the last day of the plan year. In addition, a plan's liabilities as of the last day of the plan year are equal to the present value, as of the last day of the plan year, of benefits accrued as of that same date. With the exception of the interest rate assumption, the present value should be determined using the assumptions used to determine the funding target under section 303. The interest rate assumption is the segment interest rate provided under section 4006(a)(3)(E)(iv) of ERISA in effect for the last month of the notice year rather than the rate in effect for the month preceding the first month of the notice year.

The Department recognizes that in their funding notices some plans may need to estimate their year-end liability for the notice year. In this regard, the statute does not specifically set forth any standards to govern such estimations. Therefore, pending further guidance, plan administrators may, in a reasonable manner, project liabilities to year-end using standard actuarial techniques. The Department, however, specifically invites comment on this issue.

(iii) Multiemployer Plans—Assets and Liabilities as of the Valuation Date

In the case of a multiemployer plan, paragraph (b)(3)(ii)(A) of the proposed regulation requires a statement of the value of the plan's assets (determined in the same manner as under section 304(c)(2) of ERISA) and liabilities (determined in the same manner as under section 305(i)(8) of ERISA, using reasonable actuarial assumptions as required under section 304(c)(3) of ERISA) for the notice year and each of the two plan years preceding the notice year. The assets and liabilities are to be measured as of the valuation date in each of these three years. These are the same assets and liabilities used to determine the plan's funded percentage required to be disclosed under paragraph (b)(2)(ii) of the proposed regulation. Thus, the recipients of a funding notice will receive not only their plans' funded percentage, pursuant to paragraph (b)(2)(ii) of the proposal, but, pursuant to paragraph (b)(3)(ii)(A), they also will receive the numbers behind that percentage. Under section 305(i)(8) of ERISA, liabilities are determined using the unit credit funding method whether or not that actuarial method is used for the plan's actuarial valuation in general.

(iv) Multiemployer Plans—Assets as of the Last Day of the Plan Year

In the case of a multiemployer plan, paragraph (b)(3)(ii)(B) of the proposed regulation requires a statement of the fair market value of plan assets as of the last day of the notice year, and as of the last day of

---

[6] *See* 26 CFR 1.430(d)-1(b)(3)(i); 74 FR 53004, 53036 (Oct. 15, 2009).

[7] *See* proposed Treasury regulation 26 CFR 1.432(a)-1(b)(7); 73 FR 14417, 14423 (March 18, 2008).

each of the two preceding plan years as reported in the annual report filed under section 104(a) of ERISA for each such preceding plan year.[8]

(v) Year-End Statement of Plan Assets

As discussed above, all funding notices must contain a statement of the fair market value of plan assets as of the last day of the notice year. Plans may receive contributions for the notice year after the close of that year but before the funding notice is sent to recipients. In such circumstances, these contributions may be included in the fair market value of assets. Inclusion is permissive; the proposed regulation does not require these contributions to be included in the year-end asset statement. If they are included, however, they may be included only if they are attributable to the notice year for funding purposes.

In the case of a single-employer plan, such contributions must be discounted back to the last day of the notice year using the effective interest rate. The effective interest rate is defined under section 303(h)(2)(A) of ERISA (section 430(h)(2)(A) of the Code). This approach ensures consistency with section 303(g)(4) of ERISA (section 430(g)(4) of the Code) relating to prior year contributions.[9] For example: Plan X is a calendar year plan. The plan's funding notice for 2011 was timely furnished in 2012. The year-end statement of assets was based on December 31, 2011, fair market value. The plan administrator included the present value of contributions made to the plan on February 14, 2012, in the year-end statement of assets. The "effective interest rate" for the plan was five percent in 2011 and four percent in 2012. The contributions would be discounted from February 14, 2012, to December 31, 2011, using a discount rate of five percent per annum, which was the "effective interest rate" for 2011.

In the case of a multiemployer plan, section 304(c)(8) of ERISA provides that contributions made by an employer for the plan year after the last day of the plan year, but not later than two and one-half months after such day (which may be extended for not more than six months under regulations prescribed by the Secretary of the Treasury), shall be deemed made on the last day of the plan year. Section 304(c)(8) of ERISA corresponds to section 431(c)(8) of the Code. Section 431(c)(8) of the Code is the post-PPA counterpart to former section 412(c)(10)(B) of the Code. Pursuant to the Treasury regulations under former section 412(c)(10)(B) of the Code (26 CFR 11.412(c)-12), contributions for a plan year that are made within eight and one-half months after the end of a plan year are deemed to have been made on the last day of that plan year. Therefore, consistent with section 304(c)(8) of ERISA and the corresponding section 431(c)(8) of the Code, and Treasury regulations under the former section 412(c)(10)(B) of the Code, it is not necessary for a multiemployer plan to discount such contributions for interest when stating its year-end asset value in a funding notice.

d. Demographic Information (Proposed § 2520.101-5(b)(4))

Paragraph (b)(4) of the proposed regulation provides for disclosure of a plan's participant population based on the employment status of those participants. Specifically, it requires a statement of the number of participants who, as of the valuation date of the notice year, are: (i) Retired or separated from service and receiving benefits; (ii) retired or separated and entitled to future benefits (but currently not receiving benefits); or (iii) active participants under the plan. Plan administrators must state the number of participants in each of these categories and the sum of all such participants. For purposes of this statement, the terms "active" and "retired or separated" in relation to participants shall have the same meaning given to those terms in instructions to the latest annual report filed under section 104(a) of the Act (currently, instructions relating to lines 5 and 6 of the 2009 Form 5500 Annual Return/Report).

Neither section 101(f) of ERISA nor paragraph (b)(4) of the proposed regulation specifically address whether, or how, to account for deceased participants who have one or more beneficiaries who are receiving or are entitled to benefits under a plan. For purposes of the annual funding notice requirements, however, these participants

would appear to be similar to retired or separated participants who are themselves receiving, or are entitled to receive, benefits under the plan in that the plan retains liability for benefits accrued by such deceased participants. Accordingly, the Department solicits comments on whether such individuals should be reflected in the participant count required under paragraph (b)(4) of the proposal and, if so, how. For example, such individuals could be included in the respective "retired or separated" categories under paragraph (b)(4) of the proposal or in a stand-alone category.[10]

The statute does not specify the date for counting the participants required by paragraph (b)(4) of the proposed regulation. The Department has chosen the valuation date of the notice year to provide consistency with the measurement date of the plan's funding target attainment percentage or funded percentage, as applicable. The Department solicits comments on whether a different date would be more appropriate, such as the last day of the notice year. Comments should explain why a different date would be more appropriate.

As explained above, the demographic information required by paragraph (b)(4) of the proposal is limited to the notice year. The Department solicits comments on whether, and to what extent, notice recipients would benefit from demographic information covering a longer period of time, such as the notice year and two preceding plan years. Commentary is requested on whether such information, in conjunction with other information required by section 101(f) and the proposed regulation would assist notice recipients in fully understanding the financial health and condition of the plan.

e. Funding and Investment Policies; Asset Allocation (Proposed § 2520.101-5(b)(5))

Section 101(f)(2)(B)(iv) of ERISA provides that a funding notice must include "a statement setting forth the funding policy of the plan and the asset allocation of investments under the plan (expressed as percentages of total assets) as of the end of the plan year to which the notice relates[.]" Paragraph (b)(5) of the proposal directly incorporates these requirements. See paragraphs (b)(5)(i) and (ii) of the proposal. Paragraph (b)(5) of the proposal adds the requirement that a notice also must set forth a general description of any investment policy of the plan as it relates to the funding policy and the asset allocation. See paragraph (b)(5)(iii) of the proposal. The purpose of this addition is to provide participants and beneficiaries with contextual information not explicitly required by section 101(f) of ERISA so that they may better understand and appreciate the plan's approach to funding benefits.[11] Use of the word "any" in paragraph (b)(5)(ii) reflects that the maintenance of a written statement of investment policy is not specifically required under ERISA, although the Department expects that it would be rare for a plan subject to section 101(f) of ERISA not to have such a policy. The Department specifically requests comment on the costs and benefits associated with the disclosure of such additional information.

A plan administrator may satisfy the asset allocation requirement in paragraph (b)(5)(ii) of the proposal by using the table of asset classes set forth in the model notice published in the appendices to this proposal. The asset classes identified in the model are based on the asset classes listed in Part 1 of the Asset and Liability Statement of the latest Schedule H of the Form 5500 Annual Return/Report (see Lines 1a, 1c(1)-(15), 1d(1)-(2) and 1(e) of the 2009 Schedule H).[12] With respect to each asset class, plan administrators should insert an appropriate percentage. For this purpose, a plan administrator should use the same valuation and accounting methods as for Form 5500 Schedule H reporting purposes. The master trust investment account (MTIA), common/collective trust (CCT), pooled separate account (PSA), and 103-12 investment entity (103-12IE) investment categories have the same definitions as for the Form 5500 instructions. In addition, if a plan held at year-end an interest in one or more direct filing entities (DFEs), i.e., MTIAs, CCTs, PSAs, or 103-12IEs, the plan administrator should include in the model notice a statement apprising recipients how to obtain more information regarding the plan's DFE investments (e.g., a plan's Schedule D and R and/or the DFE's schedule H). For this purpose, the model notice provides a statement immediately following

---

[8] See Joint Committee on Taxation Technical Explanation (JCX 85-08, Dec. 11, 2008) of H.R. 7327, the "Worker, Retiree, and Employer Recovery Act of 2008" explaining that section 105 of this Act amended section 101(f)(2)(B)(ii)(II) of ERISA to conform the asset and liability information provided for a multiemployer plan to the information that must be provided for a single-employer plan.

[9] This approach is consistent with the position taken by the PBGC regarding the treatment of subsequent contributions in determining the fair market value of assets under section 4006(a)(3)(E)(iii). See page 18 of the PBGC's 2010 Comprehensive Premium Payment Instructions.

[10] See, e.g., line 6(e) of the 2009 Form 5500 Annual Return/Report (for listing the number of deceased participants whose beneficiaries are receiving or entitled to receive benefits).

[11] A requisite feature of every employee benefit plan is a procedure for establishing a funding policy to carry out plan objectives. See section 402(b)(1) of ERISA. The maintenance by an employee benefit plan of a statement of investment policy is consistent with the fiduciary obligations set forth in ERISA section 404(a)(1)(A) and (B). A statement of investment policy is a written statement that provides the fiduciaries who are responsible for plan investments with guidelines or general instructions concerning various types or categories of investment management decisions. A statement of investment policy is distinguished from directions as to the purchase or sale of a specific investment at a specific time. See 29 CFR 2509.08-2(2) (formerly 29 CFR 2509.94-2).

[12] The asset classes identified in the models do not include any receivables reportable on Schedule H of the Form 5500 (see lines 1b(1)-(3) of the 2009 Schedule H).

the asset allocation table for contact information, which a plan administrator should complete and include if the plan held an interest in one or more DFEs, in order to inform participants how to get additional investment information. The Department specifically requests comment on whether this approach (*i.e.,* based on the Schedule H) to stating the asset allocation of a plan's investments as of the last day of the notice year provides sufficient information to participants regarding the plan's investments, or whether there is a more effective way of communicating this required information in the funding notice, and if so, how.

f. Endangered or Critical Status (Proposed § 2520.101-5(b)(6))

Paragraph (b)(6) of the proposed regulation, which is limited to multiemployer plans, requires that the funding notice for such plans indicate whether the plan was in endangered or critical status for the notice year. For this purpose, "endangered or critical status" is determined in accordance with section 305 of ERISA, which corresponds to section 432 of the Code. Pursuant to paragraph (b)(6)(i) of the proposal, if the plan was in endangered or critical status for the notice year, the funding notice must describe how a person may obtain a copy of the plan's funding improvement or rehabilitation plan, as appropriate, and the actuarial and financial data that demonstrate any action taken by the plan toward fiscal improvement. Pursuant to paragraph (b)(6)(ii) of the proposal, if the plan was in endangered or critical status for the notice year, the notice must contain a summary of the plan's funding improvement or rehabilitation plan. This summary is required to include, when applicable, a description of any updates or modifications to such funding improvement or rehabilitation plan adopted during the notice year. Paragraph (b)(6)(ii) clarifies that a summary is required not only for the notice year in which the funding improvement or rehabilitation plan was adopted, but for every plan year thereafter until the funding improvement or rehabilitation plan ceases to be in effect. This proposed clarification resolves any ambiguity in section 101(f)(2)(B)(v)(II) regarding whether a summary is only required to be included for the notice year in which the funding improvement or rehabilitation plan is first adopted and then again if subsequently modified, as opposed to every plan year the funding improvement or rehabilitation plan is in effect.

g. Material Effect Events (Proposed § 2520.101-5(b)(7))

Paragraph (b)(7) of the proposed regulation directly incorporates the requirements of section 101(f)(2)(B)(vi) of ERISA. That section of ERISA requires an explanation of any plan amendment, scheduled benefit increase or reduction, or other known event taking effect in the current plan year and having a material effect on plan liabilities or assets for the year, as well as a projection to the end of such plan year of the effect of the amendment, scheduled increase or reduction, or event on plan liabilities. The Department believes there is ambiguity with respect to the term "current plan year" in section 101(f)(2)(B)(vi) of ERISA. The question is whether this term refers to the notice year or the plan year following the notice year. The proposed regulation adopts the view that such term means the plan year following the notice year (*i.e.,* the plan year in which the notice is due). Thus, for a calendar year plan that must furnish its 2010 annual funding notice no later than the 120th day of 2011, the "notice year" is the 2010 plan year and the "current plan year" for purposes of paragraph (b)(7) of the proposal is the 2011 plan year. It is difficult to find meaning in the phrase "a projection to the end of such year" if "current plan year" is interpreted to mean the notice year because the notice year has already ended. On the other hand, the Department is interested in ensuring that the proposal results in all material effect events being disclosed and, therefore, specifically requests comments on the approach taken in the proposal.

Section 101(f)(2)(B)(vi) of ERISA also provides that the Department will define by regulations when an event (*i.e.,* plan amendment, scheduled benefit increase or reduction, or other known event) has a material effect on plan liabilities or assets for the year. Pursuant to this provision, paragraph (g)(1) of the proposed regulation provides that a plan amendment, scheduled benefit increase (or reduction), or other known event has a material effect on plan liabilities or assets for the current plan year if it results, or is projected to result, in an increase or decrease of five percent or more in the value of assets or liabilities from the valuation date of the notice year. For example, if the liabilities of a calendar year plan were $100 million on January 1, 2010, (the valuation date for the 2010 notice year), a scheduled increase in benefits taking effect in 2011 will have a material effect if the present value of the increase, determined using the same actuarial assumptions used to determine the $100 million in liabilities, equals or exceeds $5 million.

Alternatively, an event has a material effect on plan liabilities or assets for the current plan year if, in the judgment of the plan's enrolled actuary, the event is material for purposes of the plan's funding status under section 430 or 431 of the Code, without regard to an increase or decrease of five percent or more in the value of assets or liabilities from the prior plan year. Paragraph (g)(3) of the proposal provides that, for purposes of paragraph (g)(1), assets and liabilities should be measured in the same manner that assets and liabilities are measured for purposes of establishing the plan's funding target attainment percentage or funded percentage under paragraph (b)(2) of the proposal.

Paragraph (g)(2) of the proposal provides guidance on the type of events that could constitute an "other known event" for purposes of paragraph (b)(7) of the regulation. Such events include, but are not limited to, an extension of coverage under the existing terms of the plan to a new group of employees; a plan merger, consolidation, or spinoff pursuant to regulations under section 414(l) of the Code; a shutdown of any facility, plant, store, or such other similar corporate event that creates immediate eligibility for benefits that would not otherwise be immediately payable for participants separating from service; an offer by the plan for a temporary period to permit participants to retire at benefit levels greater than that to which they would otherwise be entitled; or a cost-of-living adjustment for retirees.

In FAB 2009-01 (February 10, 2009), the Department provided interim guidance under section 101(f) of ERISA in the form of an enforcement policy. With respect to the material effect event provision in section 101(f)(2)(B)(vi) of ERISA, the Department, in addressing when an amendment, scheduled increase, or other known event would have a "material effect" on plan liabilities or assets, stated that "as part of this enforcement policy, if an otherwise disclosable event first becomes known to the plan administrator 120 days or less before the due date for furnishing the notice, such event is not required to be included in the notice." *See* Question 12 of FAB 2009-01. The rationale behind this policy is that at some close point in time before the due date for furnishing the notice, it becomes impracticable for, and unreasonable to expect, plan administrators to satisfy the detailed material effect provisions even though an otherwise disclosable event is known. In addition, the event's effect on the plan's assets and liabilities will in any event be reflected in the next annual funding notice. While the Department has not included this policy in the proposed regulation, the Department nonetheless requests comments on whether it or a similar approach should be included in the final regulation.

h. Rules on Termination, Reorganization or Insolvency (Proposed § 2520.101-5(b)(8))

Paragraph (b)(8) of the proposed regulation requires a summary of the rules under title IV of ERISA relating to plan termination, reorganization, or insolvency, as applicable. Specifically, in the case of single-employer plans, the proposal provides that a notice shall include a summary of the rules governing termination of single-employer plans under subtitle C of title IV of ERISA. *See* proposed § 2520.101-5(b)(8)(i). In the case of multiemployer plans, the proposed regulation provides that a notice shall include a summary of the rules governing reorganization or insolvency, including limitations on benefit payments. *See* proposed § 2520.101-5(b)(8)(ii).

i. PBGC Guarantees (Proposed § 2520.101-5(b)(9))

Paragraph (b)(9) of the proposed regulation requires a funding notice to include a general description of the benefits under the plan that are eligible to be guaranteed by the PBGC, and an explanation of the limitations on the guarantee and the circumstances under which such limitations apply.

j. Annual Report Information (Proposed § 2520.101-5(b)(10))

Paragraph (b)(10) of the proposed regulation provides that a funding notice shall include a statement that a person, including, in the case of a multiemployer plan, any labor organization representing plan participants and beneficiaries and any employer that has an obligation to contribute to the plan, may obtain a copy of the annual report of the plan filed under section 104(a) of ERISA upon request, through the Internet Web site of the Department of Labor (*http:// www.efast.dol.gov*), or through any Intranet Web site maintained by the applicable plan sponsor (or plan administrator on behalf of the plan sponsor). Under paragraph (b)(10), a plan administrator must furnish, on request, only copies of filed annual reports. Thus, for example, if, following the receipt of a funding notice in April 2011 for the 2010 plan year a plan participant requests a copy of the plan's 2010 annual report, which is completed, but not yet filed, the plan administrator is not required under section 101(f) of ERISA to furnish the 2010 report to the requesting participant. Consistent with paragraph (b)(12) of the proposed regulation, plans may include language in a funding notice explaining that the annual report for the plan for the notice year has not yet been filed and when such report is expected to be filed.

k. Information Disclosed to PBGC (Proposed § 2520.101-5(b)(11))

Paragraph (b)(11) of the proposed regulation, which applies only to single-employer plans, provides that, if applicable, a funding notice must include a statement that the contributing sponsor of the plan, and each member of the contributing sponsor's controlled group (other than an exempt entity within the meaning of 29 CFR 4010.4(c)), was required to provide to the PBGC the information under section 4010 of ERISA for the notice year. However, if the contributing sponsor of the plan is itself an exempt entity within the meaning of 29 CFR 4010.4(c), paragraph (b)(11) instead requires a statement that each member of the contributing sponsor's controlled group (other than an exempt entity) was required to provide the information under section 4010 of ERISA for the notice year. Section 4010 of ERISA generally requires sponsors (and each member of their controlled group) of certain underfunded plans (*e.g.,* a plan with a funding target attainment percentage of less than 80 percent, a plan with a minimum funding waiver in excess of $1 million any portion of which is still outstanding, or a plan that has met the conditions for imposition of a lien for failure to make required contributions (including interest) with an unpaid balance in excess of $1 million) to report identifying, financial, and actuarial information about themselves and their plans to the PBGC. The statement required by paragraph (b)(11) of the proposed regulation is required only if there was a reporting obligation under section 4010 of ERISA for the notice year. In this regard, the Department specifically requests comment on whether, and to what extent, the differences in the timing requirements under sections 4010 and 101(f) of ERISA present any compliance problems for plan administrators, *e.g.,* circumstances where, because of the potential differences between a plan year and an information year, as defined in 29 CFR 4010.5, a plan administrator will not know of the plan sponsor's 4010 reporting obligation for a particular information year by the deadline for furnishing the annual funding notice for a plan year that ends within such information year. Commenters are encouraged to provide specific examples of any compliance problems presented by paragraph (b)(11) of the proposal, as well as suggestions on how to address such problems.

l. Additional Information (Proposed § 2520.101-5(b)(12))

Paragraph (b)(12) of the proposed regulation permits the plan administrator to include in a funding notice any additional information that the administrator determines would be necessary or helpful to understanding the information required to be contained in the notice. Paragraph (b)(12) of the proposal does not include the rule in 29 CFR 2520.101-4(b)(9) (the Department's regulation implementing the pre-PPA annual funding notice requirements for multiemployer plans, which ceased being effective for plan years beginning after December 31, 2007) that required additional information, even if necessary or helpful, to be posted at the end of the funding notice under the heading "Additional Explanation." This rule is not being included in the proposed regulation because of negative feedback received by the Department on the former rule following its promulgation. Representatives of plans commented that placing additional or explanatory information at the end of a funding notice disconnects the information being explained from the explanation itself, often making it more difficult, instead of making it easier, for participants to understand the information being explained. These individuals also commented that the rule is being viewed by some as an obstruction to furnishing a funding notice along with, or as part of, other plan disclosures or communications, resulting in stand-alone disclosure of the annual funding notice and increased administrative expenses to the plan.

In addition to information that is "necessary or helpful," paragraph (b)(12) of the proposed regulation also provides for inclusion of information that is "otherwise permitted by law." This clause reflects the fact that some plan administrators may elect to satisfy the requirements of section 101(f) and other disclosure requirements through a combined notification. For example, where a plan elects the waiver described in 29 CFR 2520.104-46 (small pension plan audit waiver regulation), the plan administrator must include specified information about the waiver in the funding notice in order to satisfy the requirements of § 2520.104-46. *See* section C of this preamble discussing § 2520.104-46, as amended.

3. Form and Manner Requirements (Proposed § 2520.101-5(c) and (e))

Paragraphs (c) and (e) of the proposed regulation, respectively, set forth the style and format requirements and the manner of furnishing requirements relating to the funding notice. Paragraph (c) of the proposed regulation provides that funding notices shall be written in a manner that is consistent with the style and format requirements of 29 CFR 2520.102-2. Thus, notices shall be written in a manner calculated to be understood by the average plan participant and in a format that does not have the effect of misleading or misinforming recipients.

Paragraph (e) of the proposal relates to how annual funding notices must be furnished to recipients, with paragraph (e)(1) addressing how notices must be furnished to participants and beneficiaries and paragraph (e)(2) addressing how notices must be furnished to the PBGC. The Department, however, has decided to reserve paragraph (e)(1) of the proposal for the same reason the Department reserved the manner of furnishing requirements in the recently published final participant-level disclosure regulation, § 2550.404a-5 (75 FR 64910, October 20, 2010). In the preamble to the final participant-level disclosure regulation, the Department explained that, given the differing views on the use of and standards for electronic disclosure, it would be undertaking a review of the safe harbor applicable to the use of electronic media for furnishing information to plan participants and beneficiaries (29 CFR 2520.104b-1(c)). The Department further indicated that, in the very near future, it will be publishing a **Federal Register** notice requesting public comments, views, and data relating to the electronic distribution of plan information to plan participants and beneficiaries.

Accordingly, as with the final participant-level disclosure regulation, pending the completion of its review and the issuance of further guidance, the general disclosure regulation at 29 CFR 2520.104b-1 applies to annual funding notices required to be furnished to participants and beneficiaries, including the safe harbor for electronic disclosures at paragraph (c) of the general disclosure regulation. The Department anticipates that resolution of the issues involved with the electronic disclosure of plan information will directly affect the manner in which the annual funding notice may be furnished to participants and beneficiaries. Accordingly, interested persons are encouraged to participate in the Department's forthcoming solicitation of comments on the use of electronic media for furnishing plan information.

Paragraph (e)(2) of the proposal provides that funding notices shall be furnished to the PBGC consistent with the requirements of 29 CFR part 4000. The PBGC has advised the Department that it will accept electronic or hard copies of funding notices at the following postal and e-mail addresses: (1) For single-employer plans, hard copies of funding notices may be mailed to Pension Benefit Guaranty Corporation, ATTN: Single-Employer AFN Coordinator, 1200 K Street, NW., Suite 270, Washington, DC 20005-4026. Electronic copies of funding notices may be e-mailed to *Single-employerAFN@PBGC.gov.* (2) For multiemployer plans, hard copies of funding notices may be mailed to Pension Benefit Guaranty Corporation, ATTN: Multiemployer Data Coordinator, 1200 K Street, NW., Suite 930, Washington, DC 20005-4026. Electronic copies of funding notices may be e-mailed to *Multiemployerprogram@PBGC.gov.*

4. Timing Requirements (Proposed § 2520.101-5(d))

Paragraph (d) of the proposed regulation describes when a funding notice must be furnished to recipients. Paragraph (d)(1) of the proposal provides that notices generally must be furnished not later than 120 days after the end of the notice year. However, paragraph (d)(2) of the proposal provides that in the case of small plans, notices must be furnished no later than the earlier of the date on which the annual report is filed or the latest date the report could be filed (with granted filing extensions). For this purpose, a plan is a small plan if it had 100 or fewer participants on each day during the plan year preceding the notice year. *See* section 101(f)(3)(B) of ERISA (referencing section 303(g)(2)(B) of ERISA). Although section 303(g)(2)(B) of ERISA relates to single-employer plans only, the Department interprets section 101(f)(3)(B) of ERISA as applying the 100 or fewer participant standard in section 303(g)(2)(B) of ERISA to both single-employer and multiemployer plans.

5. Persons Entitled to Notice (Proposed § 2520.101(5)(f))

Paragraph (f) of the proposed regulation defines a person entitled to receive a funding notice as: Each participant covered under the plan on the last day of the notice year, each beneficiary receiving benefits under the plan on the last day of the notice year, each labor organization representing participants under the plan on the last day of the notice year, the PBGC, and, in the case of a multiemployer plan, each employer that, as of the last day of the notice year, is a party to the collective bargaining agreement(s) pursuant to which the plan is maintained or who otherwise may be subject to withdrawal liability pursuant to section 4203 of ERISA.

6. Model Notices (Proposed § 2520.101-5(h))

The appendices to § 2520.101-5 include two model notices (one for single-employer plans and one for multiemployer plans) that may be used by plan administrators for section 101(f) of ERISA purposes. The model in Appendix A is for single-employer plans (including multiple employer plans) and the model in Appendix B is for multiemployer plans. These models are intended to assist plan administrators in discharging their notice obligations under section 101(f) of ERISA and the regulation. Use of a model notice is not mandatory. However, the proposed regulation provides that use of a model notice will be deemed to satisfy the content requirements in paragraph (b) of the regulation, as well as the style and format requirements in paragraph (c) of the regulation. To the extent a plan administrator elects to include in a model notice additional information described in paragraph (b)(12) of the proposed regulation, such additional information must be consistent with the style and format requirements in paragraph (c) of the proposed regulation. Thus, such additional information should not have the effect of misleading or misinforming recipients.

In drafting the models, the Department attempted to develop and organize the models in a manner that will help the average plan participant understand and comprehend the information mandated by section 101(f) of ERISA, some of which is technical in nature. Nonetheless, the Department solicits comments on whether, and if so, how, the organization of the proposed models could be improved to enhance understandability and comprehensibility. For example, if a plan's funding percentage is the most important information for participants, does the chart format of the model adequately highlight this information or could other presentation techniques more effectively highlight this information?

7. Limited Alternative Method of Compliance for Furnishing Notice to PBGC (Proposed § 2520.101-5(i))

Section 101(f)(1) of ERISA provides that a plan administrator of a defined benefit plan to which title IV of ERISA applies shall, for each plan year, provide a funding notice to the PBGC, to each plan participant and beneficiary, to each labor organization representing such participants or beneficiaries, and, in the case of a multiemployer plan, to each employer with an obligation to contribute to the plan. Pursuant to section 110 of ERISA, paragraph (i) of the proposed regulation includes an alternative method of compliance pertaining to the requirement to furnish notice to the PBGC. Under this alternative, the plan administrator of a single-employer plan with liabilities that do not exceed plan assets by more than $50 million is not required to furnish a funding notice to the PBGC provided that the administrator furnishes the latest available funding notice to the PBGC within 30 days of receiving a written request from the PBGC. In determining whether a plan's liabilities exceed its assets by more than $50 million, the proposed regulation provides that plan administrators should subtract the plan's total assets from its liabilities, using the assets and liabilities disclosed in the funding notice in accordance with paragraph (b)(3)(i)(A) of this proposed regulation.

The Department has created this alternative method of compliance after consulting with the PBGC. The PBGC has determined that, in light of the extended funding notice due date for small plans, it will have electronic access to the information included on the funding notice for most single-employer plans as a result of ERISA's annual reporting requirement under section 104(a) on or around the time it would receive a copy of a funding notice under section 101(f) of ERISA and the proposed regulation. In addition, under the PBGC's Reportable Events regulation (29 CFR part 4043), the PBGC typically would receive information about certain events that might indicate increased exposure or risk before it would receive information under either ERISA section 101(f) or 104(a). Also, the Department believes the alternative method of compliance will reduce administrative burden for plans that meet the conditions of paragraph (i) of the proposed regulation.

At the request of the PBGC, the Department has limited the scope of the alternative method of compliance to single-employer plans. Because multiemployer plans are not subject to ERISA section 4043 and because very few multiemployer plans will qualify for the extended annual funding notice due date, the annual funding notice will provide a useful and non-duplicative source of information to the PBGC. The alternative method of compliance does not have any effect on the plan administrator's obligation to furnish notices to parties other than the PBGC.

Section 110 of ERISA permits the Department to prescribe alternative methods of complying with any of the reporting and disclosure requirements of ERISA if it finds: (1) That the use of the alternative is consistent with the purposes of ERISA and that it provides adequate disclosure to plan participants and beneficiaries and to the Department; (2) that application of the statutory reporting and disclosure requirements would increase the costs to the plan or impose unreasonable administrative burdens with respect to the operation of the plan; and

(3) that the application of the statutory reporting and disclosure requirements would be adverse to the interests of plan participants in the aggregate. Based on the discussion above, the Department finds these three conditions to be satisfied in this context.

8. Plans Not Immediately Subject to New Funding Rules or to Which Special Funding Rules Apply

Sections 104, 105, and 106 of the PPA defer the effective date of the amendments made by title I of the PPA for certain plans described in those sections, i.e. certain plans of cooperatives, plans affected by settlement agreements with the PBGC, and plans of government contractors.[13] Section 402 of the PPA applies special funding rules to certain plans of commercial passenger airlines and airline caterers. Section 402 of the PPA was amended by the U.S. Troop Readiness, Veterans' Care, Katrina Recovery, and Iraq Accountability Appropriations Act, 2007, Public Law 110-28. None of these provisions affects the applicability of the PPA amendments to section 101(f) of ERISA. Accordingly, the funding notice requirements of section 101(f) of ERISA apply to these plans for plan years beginning on or after January 1, 2008. These plans should disclose their funding target attainment percentage (and related asset and liability information) in accordance with guidance provided by the Secretary of the Treasury. For example, for a plan described in section 104, 105, or 106 of the PPA, the funding target attainment percentage of such plan is determined in accordance with paragraph (b)(2)(i) of the proposed regulation, except that the value of plan assets is determined without subtraction of the funding standard carryover balance or prefunding balance (credit balance under the funding standard account). See 26 CFR 1.430(d)-1(b)(3)(ii). The model in Appendix A is available to such plans, but the portions of the model entitled "Credit Balances" and "At-Risk Status" should be deleted from the model before use for notice years beginning prior to the delayed effective date.

The Department requests comment on whether, and to what extent, these plans would need special rules under section 101(f) of ERISA, if applicable, to reflect the delayed effective dates (in sections 104, 105, or 106 of the PPA) or special funding rules (in section 402 of the PPA). Comments on this issue should explain why the delayed effective dates or special funding rules under the PPA necessitate a special rule or rules under section 101(f) of ERISA and the regulation being adopted herein, and whether, and how, the model notices in the appendices to the regulation could be modified for use by these plans.

9. Multiemployer Plans Terminated by Mass Withdrawal

The proposed regulation does not provide an exemption or other relief for multiemployer plans that terminate by mass withdrawal pursuant to section 4041A(a)(2) of ERISA. Section 4041A(a)(2) provides that the termination of a multiemployer plan occurs as a result of the withdrawal of every employer from the plan or the cessation of the obligation of all employers to contribute under the plan.

Plans that terminate in this fashion typically continue to pay benefits from a declining trust as payments come due and have no new contributions other than withdrawal liability payments. Therefore, the Department recognizes that some information required by the regulation may not be relevant (e.g., the plan's funded percentages) for plans that have terminated by mass withdrawal. Other mandated information, such as PBGC benefit guarantee levels, assets and liabilities, numbers and status of participants, and insolvency information, however, may be very important to participants and beneficiaries receiving benefits from such plans. Accordingly, the Department solicits comment on whether the final regulation should provide special rules for such plans. Comments should be specific regarding what, if any, information otherwise required by the regulation should not be included in the funding notice, and why, and what, if any, alternative information might be disclosed in its place. Comments should provide any data that would demonstrate cost savings to such plans as a result of alternative reporting under special rules.

10. Code Section 412(e)(3) Insurance Contract Plans

The proposed regulation does not provide an exemption or any other relief for certain insurance contract plans to which section 412(e)(3) of the Code applies. "Code section 412(e)(3) insurance contracts" are contracts that provide retirement benefits under a plan that are guaranteed by an insurance carrier. In general, such contracts must provide for level premium payments over the individual's period of participation in the plan (to retirement age), premiums must be timely paid as currently required under the contract, no rights under the contract may be subject to a security interest, and no policy loans may be outstanding. If a plan is funded exclusively by the purchase of such contracts, the otherwise applicable minimum funding requirements of section 412 of the Code and section 302 of ERISA do not apply for the year and neither the Schedule MB nor the Schedule SB is required to be filed.[14]

Therefore, the Department recognizes that information regarding a plan's funded status required in the proposed regulation (*e.g.,* the plan's funding target attainment percentage or funded percentage) may not be applicable to certain of these plans. Other required information, such as PBGC benefit guarantee levels, termination rules, fair market value of assets, and numbers and status of participants, however, may be important to participants and beneficiaries receiving benefits from such plans. Other information not required by section 101(f) of ERISA and this proposed regulation could be important to persons receiving the funding notice of these plans. Accordingly, the Department solicits comment on whether the final regulation should provide special rules for such plans. Comments should be specific regarding what information otherwise required by the proposed regulation should not be included in the funding notice, and why, and what, if any, alternative information might be disclosed in its place. Comments should explain the benefit to plan participants and provide any data that would demonstrate cost savings to such plans as a result of alternative reporting under special rules.

11. Multiple Employer Pension Plans

After the Department issued FAB 2009-01, a number of plan administrators of multiple employer plans raised questions regarding whether, and how, the new annual funding notice requirements apply to such plans. The central question was whether all participants in such a plan must receive the same funding notice containing funding data at the plan level or whether each participant must receive a notice that reflects funding information relevant to his employer. It is the view of the Department that if all assets of the multiple employer pension plan are, on an ongoing basis, available to pay benefits to all plan participants and beneficiaries covered under the plan, then the information in the funding notice should be reflective of the plan as a whole. The plan administrator need not create a separate funding notice for the employees of each participating employer in the multiple employer plan containing the funding information (assets, liabilities, *etc.*) pertaining to that employer in the case of a multiple employer plan to which section 413(c)(4)(A) of the Code applies. Based on the foregoing, the proposal does not contain any special rules for multiple employer pension plans. Nonetheless, comments are requested on whether funding notices for such plans should alert participants to the fact that some funding rules under the Code, *e.g.,* benefit restrictions under Code section 436, may apply on an employer-by-employer basis. Thus, a participant in a multiple employer pension plan could have his benefits restricted even though the plan as a whole has a funding target attainment percentage well above what one would consider to be close to a percentage that would trigger a benefit restriction under Code section 436.

C. Overview of Amendments to 29 CFR 2520.104-46—Waiver of Examination and Report of an Independent Qualified Public Accountant for Employee Benefit Plans With Fewer Than 100 Participants

Department of Labor regulation 29 CFR 2520.104-46 governs the circumstances under which small pension plans (plans with fewer than 100 participants at the beginning of the plan year) are exempt from the requirements to engage an independent qualified public accountant (IQPA) and to include a report of the accountant as part of the plan's annual report under title I of ERISA. The waiver of the requirement to engage an accountant is conditioned on, among other things, the disclosure of certain information to participants and beneficiaries. A requirement of § 2520.104-46 is that such disclosure must be included in the summary annual report (SAR) of a plan electing the waiver. However, section 503(c) of the PPA amended section 104(b)(3) of ERISA by repealing the SAR requirement for defined benefit plans to which the annual funding notice requirements of section 101(f) of ERISA apply.[15] Therefore, in conjunction with the annual funding notice regulation (29 CFR 2520.101-5), discussed in section B of this preamble, above, the Department is adopting conforming amendments to § 2520.104-46 to enable plans subject to section 101(f) of ERISA to

elect to use the waiver provision in § 2520.104-46. Under § 2520.104-46, as amended, a plan subject to section 101(f) of ERISA must include the information in § 2520.104-46(b)(1)(i)(B)(1)-(4) in the plan's annual funding notice. Model language is included in the Appendix to § 2520.104-46 and provided on the Department's Web site at *http:// www.dol.gov/ebsa/faqs/faq_auditwaiver.html.*

D. Overview of Amendments to 29 CFR 2520.104b-10— Summary Annual Report

As discussed in section C of this preamble, the PPA repealed the summary annual report (SAR) requirement for plans subject to section 101(f) of ERISA, effective for plan years beginning after December 31, 2007. The Department, therefore, is making technical conforming amendments to the SAR regulation (§ 2520.104b-10) to give effect to the repeal. Specifically, a new paragraph (g)(9) is being added to provide that an SAR is not required to be furnished with respect to a plan to which title IV of ERISA applies. In this rulemaking, the Department is not making conforming changes to the form prescribed in paragraph (d)(3) of § 2520.104b-10, or to the appendix of the regulation, to reflect paragraph (g)(9), because such form and appendix continue to be applicable for plans not subject to title IV of ERISA. Nonetheless, the Department recognizes that some items and language in the form and appendix became irrelevant on and after the effective date of the repeal and, therefore, is requesting comments on how best to revise the form and appendix to eliminate unnecessary information.

E. Regulatory Impact Analysis

Summary

The proposed rule contains a model notice and other guidance necessary to implement section 101(f) of ERISA as amended by PPA and WRERA. Section 101(f) and the proposed rule increase the transparency of information about the funding status of plans, affording all parties interested in the financial viability of these plans with a greater opportunity to monitor their funding status and take action where necessary. In addition, the rule offers a model notice to administrators of single-employer and multiemployer defined benefit pension plans, which is expected to mitigate burden and contribute to the efficiency of compliance. Another benefit is that the rule would afford plan administrators greater certainty that they have discharged their notice obligation under section 101(f) by clarifying certain terms used in the statute. The Department has concluded that the benefits of the rule justify their costs. These benefits—increased transparency, greater efficiency, certainty, and clarity—are expected to be substantial, but cannot be specifically quantified.

The cost of the proposed rule is expected to amount to $57.2 million in the year of implementation, and $52.8 million in each subsequent year.[16] The total estimated cost includes the one-time development of a notice by each plan and the annual preparation and mailing of the notices to the required recipients.[17] The first year estimate is higher to account for the time required for plan administrators to adapt and review the model notice. The Department also makes the following additional estimates regarding the cost of the proposal:

—The total mailing costs are estimated to be about $20.0 million annually in the first three years;

—In addition to the mailing costs, the Department estimates that firms will spend about $37.2 million in the year of implementation and $32.9 million in subsequent years on labor costs.[18]

The Department has attempted to provide guidance in the proposed rule to assist administrators in meeting their responsibilities in the most economically efficient manner possible. Because the costs of the rule arise only from notice provisions in PPA, the data and methodology used in developing these estimates are more fully described in the Paperwork Reduction Act section of this analysis of regulatory impact.

The cost estimates of the proposal are based on the informational content requirements in paragraph (b) of the proposal. The Department is accepting comment on whether there is information or indicators, not already included in paragraph (b) of the proposal, that help explain a plan's financial condition and that may be helpful to notice recipients, *e.g.,* the ratio of plan assets to the present value of retired

---

[14] *See* the Instructions to the latest Form 5500 Annual Return/Report of Employee Benefit Plan.

[15] The repeal is effective for plan years beginning after December 31, 2007.

[16] All numbers used in this Regulatory Impact Analysis have been rounded to the nearest thousand.

[17] As discussed earlier in this preamble, this proposed regulation, when finalized, will implement the statutory requirement for defined benefit pension plan administrators to provide an annual funding notice that meets the requirements of ERISA section 101(f).

Because plans were required to comply with ERISA section 101(f) before the issuance of implementing regulations, and taking into account guidance previously issued by the Department in Field Assistance Bulletin 2009-01, this regulatory impact analysis includes a small initial cost for plans to make adjustments that would be necessary to ensure compliance with implementing regulations. These estimates then take into account the ongoing annual costs for plan administrators to create and send the annual funding notices.

[18] The total hour burden is estimated to be about 1,046,000 hours in the year of implementation and 1,003,000 hours in each subsequent year.

participants' benefits. Comments should be specific as to what other information or indicators could be included in the funding notice, the reasons why, and a cost/benefit analysis.

Executive Order 12866

Under Executive Order 12866 (58 FR 51735), the Department must determine whether a regulatory action is "significant" and therefore subject to review by the Office of Management and Budget (OMB). Section 3(f) of the Executive Order defines a "significant regulatory action" as an action that is likely to result in a rule (1) having an annual effect on the economy of $100 million or more, or adversely and materially affecting a sector of the economy, productivity, competition, jobs, the environment, public health or safety, or State, local or Tribal governments or communities (also referred to as "economically significant"); (2) creating serious inconsistency or otherwise interfering with an action taken or planned by another agency; (3) materially altering the budgetary impacts of entitlement grants, user fees, or loan programs or the rights and obligations of recipients thereof; or (4) raising novel legal or policy issues arising out of legal mandates, the President's priorities, or the principles set forth in the Executive Order. It has been determined that this action is significant under section 3(f)(4) of the Executive Order; therefore, OMB has reviewed this regulatory action pursuant to the Executive Order.

Paperwork Reduction Act

As part of its continuing effort to reduce paperwork and respondent burden, the Department of Labor conducts a preclearance consultation program to provide the general public and Federal agencies with an opportunity to comment on proposed and continuing collections of information in accordance with the Paperwork Reduction Act of 1995 (PRA 95) (44 U.S.C. 3506(c)(2)(A)). This helps to ensure that requested data can be provided in the desired format, reporting burden (time and financial resources) is minimized, collection instruments are clearly understood, and the impact of collection requirements on respondents can be properly assessed.

Currently, EBSA is soliciting comments concerning the information collection request (ICR) included in the Proposed Rule on the Annual Funding Notice for Defined Benefit Plans. A copy of the ICR may be obtained by contacting the PRA addressee shown below.

The Department has submitted a copy of the proposed rule to OMB in accordance with 44 U.S.C. 3507(d) for review of its information collections. The Department and OMB are particularly interested in comments that:

• Evaluate whether the collection of information is necessary for the proper performance of the functions of the agency, including whether the information will have practical utility;

• Evaluate the accuracy of the agency's estimate of the burden of the collection of information, including the validity of the methodology and assumptions used;

• Enhance the quality, utility, and clarity of the information to be collected; and

• Minimize the burden of the collection of information on those who are to respond, including through the use of appropriate automated, electronic, mechanical, or other technological collection techniques or other forms of information technology, *e.g.,* permitting electronic submission of responses.

Comments should be sent to the Office of Information and Regulatory Affairs, Office of Management and Budget, Room 10235, New Executive Office Building, Washington, DC 20503; Attention: Desk Officer for the Employee Benefits Security Administration. OMB requests that comments be received within 30 days of publication of the proposed rule to ensure their consideration.

PRA Addressee: Address requests for copies of the ICR to G. Christopher Cosby, Office of Policy and Research, U.S. Department of Labor, Employee Benefits Security Administration, 200 Constitution Avenue, NW., Room N-5718, Washington, DC 20210. Telephone (202) 693-8410; Fax: (202) 219-5333. These are not toll-free numbers. ICRs submitted to OMB also are available at *http://www.RegInfo.gov.*

The proposed rule implements the disclosure requirements of section 101(f) of ERISA, as amended by section 501 of the PPA. As described earlier in the preamble, section 101(f) of ERISA requires the administrator of a defined benefit plan to which title IV of ERISA applies to furnish an annual funding notice to the PBGC, each partici-

pant and beneficiary, each labor organization representing participants and beneficiaries, and for multiemployer plans only, each employer with an obligation to contribute to the plan.

The information collection provisions of the proposed rule are found in section 2520.101-5(b). Model notices are provided in the appendices to the rule to facilitate compliance and moderate the burden attendant to supplying notices to participants and beneficiaries, labor organizations, contributing employers, and PBGC. Use of the model notice is not mandatory; however, use of the model will be deemed to satisfy the requirements for content, style, and format of the notice, except with respect to any other information the plan administrator elects to include. The proposed rule also is intended to clarify several statutory requirements with respect to content, style and format, manner of furnishing, and persons entitled to receive the annual funding notice. Increasing the transparency of information about the funding status of defined benefit plans for participants and beneficiaries, labor organizations, contributing employers, and the PBGC will afford all parties interested in the financial viability of these plans greater opportunity to monitor their funding status.

In order to estimate the potential costs of the notice provisions of section 101(f) of ERISA and the proposed rule, the Department estimated the number of single-employer and multiemployer defined benefit plans, and the numbers of participants, beneficiaries receiving benefits, labor organizations representing participants, and employers with an obligation to contribute to these plans.

The PBGC Pension Insurance Data Book 2008 indicates that there are about 1,500 multiemployer defined benefit plans with approximately 10.1 million participants and beneficiaries receiving benefits. These estimates are based on premium filings with PBGC for 2007, projected by PBGC to 2008, generally the most recent information currently available. This total has been adjusted slightly to reflect the exception from the requirement to furnish annual funding notices to plans that are receiving financial assistance from PBGC.[19] The PBGC Pension Insurance Data Book 2008 also indicates that there are approximately 28,000 single-employer defined benefit plans with approximately 33.8 million participants.

The Department is not aware of a direct source of information as to the number of labor organizations that represent participants of multiemployer defined benefit plans and that would be entitled to receive notice under section 101(f). As a proxy for this number, the Department has relied on information supplied by the Department's Employment Standards Administration, Office of Labor Management Standards, as to the number of labor organizations that filed required annual reports for their most recent fiscal year, generally 2008, at this time. The Department adjusted the number provided by excluding labor organizations that appeared to represent only State, local, and Federal governmental employees to account for the fact that such employees are generally unlikely to be participants in plans covered under title I of ERISA. The resulting estimate of labor organizations that could be entitled to receive notice is almost 18,500.

The Department also is unaware of a source of information for the current number of employers obligated to contribute to multiemployer defined benefit plans. PBGC assisted with development of an estimate of this number by providing the Department with a tabulation on their 1987 premium filings of the number of employers contributing to multiemployer defined benefit plans at that time. This was the last year this data element was required to be reported on the Form 5500. The Department has attempted to validate that 1987 figure by dividing the number of participants in multiemployer defined benefit plans in the industries in which these plans are most concentrated, such as construction, trucking, and retail food sales,[20] by the average number of employees per firm in those industries based on data published by the Office of Advocacy, U.S. Small Business Administration for 2001. This computation resulted in a figure that was similar in magnitude, but somewhat higher than the 277,600 employers reported in the 1987 PBGC premium filing data. As a result, the Department has used 300,000 for its conservative estimate of the number of contributing employers to whom the required notice will be sent.

For purposes of its estimates of regulatory impact, the Department has assumed that each plan will develop a notice, and that each year approximately 44.3 million notices will be prepared and sent. The 44.3 million estimate breaks down as follows: 10.1 million notices to participants and beneficiaries of close to 1,500 multiemployer defined benefit plans; 33.8 million notices to participants and beneficiaries of close to 28,000 single employer plans; 39,000 notices to labor organizations;

---

[19] According to the PBGC Pension Insurance Data Book 2008, there were 1,513 multiemployer defined benefit plans in 2006. This number was reduced by 42 in order to account for the 42 plans that received financial assistance.

[20] *See* GAO-04-423 Private Pensions: Multiemployer Plans Face Short- and Long-Term Challenges. U.S. General Accounting Office, March 2004. The General Accounting Office's name changed to the Government Accountability Office effective July 7, 2004.

300,000 notices to contributing employers of multiemployer plans; and 30,000 notices to the PBGC.

Estimates of notice preparations are based on the assumption that plan service providers, actuaries, lawyers, and financial professionals will produce the notices. It is assumed that the availability of a model notice will lessen the time otherwise required by a plan administrator to draft a required notice. The Department has made the following estimate regarding preparation of the notice: Actuaries will spend three hours in the first year and two hours in each succeeding year for single-employer plans and two hours in the first year and one hour in each succeeding year for multiemployer plans making specific calculations for information that must be provided in the notice; legal professionals will spend one hour in the first year and 0.5 hours in each succeeding year reviewing the notice; and financial professionals will spend one hour in the first year and thereafter drafting the notice for single-employer plans and two hours per year for multiemployer plans. The final preparation and distribution of the notice will be done by a clerical professional using an estimated two minutes per notice mailed. The Department welcomes comments regarding these estimates.

Assuming 44.3 million notices are distributed,[21] the burden hours for that initial year of implementation are 87,000 actuarial hours, 31,000 financial professional hours, and 29,000 legal professional hours. Total clerical professional hours are calculated based on the total number of notices mailed and the preparation time of 2 minutes per notice resulting in 915,000 hours. The total hour burden for the year of implementation is 1,061,000 hours. Each subsequent year requires 57,000 actuarial hours, 915,000 clerical hours, 31,000 financial professional hours, and 15,000 legal professional hours for a total of 1,018,000 hours.[22]

Hourly labor rates were calculated using the rates based on the Bureau of Labor Statistics, National Occupational Employment Survey (May 2008) and the Bureau of Labor Statistics, Employment Cost Index (June 2009).[23] Calculations of the 2010 hourly labor costs were $26.14 for a clerical professional, $62.81 for a financial professional, $91.56 for an actuary, and $119.03 for plan legal counsel.

Based on the foregoing, the total equivalent cost for the initial year is estimated at approximately $7,937,000 for actuarial services, $23,915,000 for clerical services, $1,942,000 for financial professional services, and $3,409,000 for legal professional services. The total equivalent cost is approximately $37,203,000 in the initial year.

The total equivalent cost in each subsequent year is estimated at approximately $5,245,000 for actuarial services, $23,915,000 for clerical services, $1,942,000 for financial professional services, and $1,750,000 for legal professional services. The total equivalent cost is estimated at approximately $32,852,000 in each subsequent year.

The cost of mailing the notices was based on the assumption that each notice would be six pages for single-employer plans and five pages for multiemployer plans, with printing costs of 5 cents per page and postage of 44 cents resulting in an estimated 74 cent cost per paper notice for single-employer plans and a 69 cent cost per paper notice for multiemployer plans. It was further assumed that 38 percent of notices would be sent electronically. The Department has not estimated any additional burden for preparation or distribution of notices via electronic means because the Department assumes that plans will utilize pre-existing electronic communications systems and e-mail lists for these purposes and the process of preparation and distribution involves only a de minimis additional effort, *e.g.,* a few computer key strokes or the equivalent. This assumption will result in a total of approximately 16.8 million notices being sent electronically by multiemployer and single-employer plans. Single-employer plans will mail out approximately 21.0 million paper notices and multiemployer plans will mail out approximately 6.5 million paper notices. Total annual paper mailing costs are estimated to be approximately $20.0 million.

These paperwork burden estimates are summarized as follows:

Type of Review: Revised collection.

Agency: Employee Benefits Security Administration, Department of Labor.

Title: Annual Funding Notice for Defined Benefit Plans.

OMB Control Number: 1210-0126.

Affected Public: Business or other for-profit; not-for-profit institutions.

Respondents: 29,000.

Responses: 44,269,000.

Frequency of Response: Annually.

Estimated Total Annual Burden Hours: 1,032,000 (average over first three years); 1,061,000 (first year) (1,018,000 subsequent years).

Estimated Total Annual Burden Cost: $19,988,000 (first year and subsequent years).

Regulatory Flexibility Act

The Regulatory Flexibility Act (5 U.S.C. 601 *et seq.*) (RFA) imposes certain requirements with respect to Federal rules that are subject to the notice and comment requirements of section 553(b) of the Administrative Procedure Act (5 U.S.C. 551 *et seq.*) and which are likely to have a significant economic impact on a substantial number of small entities. Unless the head of an agency certifies that a proposed rule is not likely to have a significant economic impact on a substantial number of small entities, section 603 of the RFA requires that the agency present an initial regulatory flexibility analysis at the time of the publication of the notice of proposed rulemaking describing the impact of the rule on small entities and seeking public comment on such impact.

For purposes of the RFA, the Department continues to consider a small entity to be an employee benefit plan with fewer than 100 participants.[24] Further, while some large employers may have small plans, in general small employers maintain most small plans. Thus, the Department believes that assessing the impact of this proposed rule on small plans is an appropriate substitute for evaluating the effect on small entities. The definition of small entity considered appropriate for this purpose differs, however, from a definition of small business that is based on size standards promulgated by the Small Business Administration (SBA) (13 CFR 121.201) pursuant to the Small Business Act (15 U.S.C. 631 *et seq.*). The Department therefore requests comments on the appropriateness of the size standard used in evaluating the impact of this proposed rule on small entities.

By this standard, data from the 2007 Form 5500 (the latest available data) indicates that for over 88 percent of small affected plans, the average per plan compliance cost would be $1,265 ($37 million/29,400 plans) plus plan specific mailing cost (74 cents per participant, which cannot exceed $74 per plan because small plans have less than 100 participants). This amount is less than one percent of plan assets.

Based on the foregoing, the Department has preliminarily determined that while the rule is likely to impact a substantial number of small entities, the economic impact on such entities will not be significant. Therefore, pursuant to section 605(b) of RFA, the Assistant Secretary of the Employee Benefits Security Administration hereby certifies that the proposed rule, if promulgated, will not have a significant economic impact on a substantial number of small entities. The Department invites comments on this certification and the potential impact of the rule on small entities.

Congressional Review Act

The proposed rule is subject to the Congressional Review Act provisions of the Small Business Regulatory Enforcement Fairness Act of 1996 (5 U.S.C. 801 *et seq.*) and, if finalized, will be transmitted to Congress and the Comptroller General for review. The proposed rule is not a "major rule" as that term is defined in 5 U.S.C. 804, because it is not likely to result in (1) an annual effect on the economy of $100 million or more; (2) a major increase in costs or prices for consumers, individual industries, or Federal, State, or local government agencies, or geographic regions; or (3) significant adverse effects on competition, employment, investment, productivity, innovation, or on the ability of United States-based enterprises to compete with foreign-based enterprises in domestic and export markets.

Unfunded Mandates Reform Act

For purposes of the Unfunded Mandates Reform Act of 1995 (Pub. L. 104-4), as well as Executive Order 12875, the proposed rule does not include any Federal mandate that may result in expenditures by State, local, or Tribal governments in the aggregate of more than $100 million, adjusted for inflation, or increase expenditures by the private sector of more than $100 million, adjusted for inflation.

Federalism Statement

Executive Order 13132 (August 4, 1999) outlines fundamental principles of federalism, and requires the adherence to specific criteria by

---

[21] The Department assumes that 38 percent of notices are sent electronically and result in only a de minimis cost.

[22] The average Total Annual Burden Hours over the first three years is 1,032,000.

[23] EBSA estimates of labor rates include wages, other benefits, and overhead.

[24] The basis for this definition is found in section 104(a)(2) of the Act, which permits the Secretary of Labor to prescribe simplified annual reports for pension plans that cover fewer than 100 participants.

Federal agencies in the process of their formulation and implementation of policies that have substantial direct effects on the States, the relationship between the national government and States, or on the distribution of power and responsibilities among the various levels of government. The proposed rule does not have federalism implications because it has no substantial direct effect on the States, on the relationship between the national government and the States, or on the distribution of power and responsibilities among the various levels of government. Section 514 of ERISA provides, with certain exceptions specifically enumerated, that the provisions of titles I and IV of ERISA supersede any and all laws of the States as they relate to any employee benefit plan covered under ERISA. The requirements that would be implemented in the proposed rule do not alter the fundamental reporting and disclosure requirements of the statute with respect to employee benefit plans, and as such have no implications for the States or the relationship or distribution of power between the national government and the States.

List of Subjects in 29 CFR Part 2520

Accounting, Employee benefit plans, Employee Retirement Income Security Act, Pensions, Reporting and recordkeeping requirements.

For the reasons set forth in the preamble, the Department of Labor proposes to amend 29 CFR part 2520 as follows:

PART 2520—RULES AND REGULATIONS FOR REPORTING AND DISCLOSURE

1. The Authority citation for part 2520 is revised to read as follows:

Authority: 29 U.S.C. 1021-1025, 1027, 1029-31, 1059, 1134 and 1135; and Secretary of Labor's Order 1-2003, 68 FR 5374 (Feb. 3, 2003). Sec. 2520.101-2 also issued under 29 U.S.C. 1132, 1181-1183, 1181 note, 1185, 1185a-b, 1191, and 1191a-c. Secs. 2520.102-3, 2520.104b-1 and 2520.104b-3 also issued under 29 U.S.C. 1003, 1181-1183, 1181 note, 1185, 1185a-b, 1191, and 1191a-c. Secs. 2520.104b-1 and 2520.107 also issued under 26 U.S.C. 401 note, 111 Stat. 788. Sec. 2520.101-4 also issued under sec. 103 of Pub. L. 108-218, 118 Stat. 596. Sec. 2520.101-5 also issued under sec. 503 of Pub. L. 109-280, 120 Stat. 780 and sec. 105(a), Pub. L. 110-458, 122 Stat. 5104.

2. Add § 2520.101-5 to subpart A to read as follows:

§ 2520.101-5 Annual funding notice for defined benefit pension plans.

(a) *In general.* (1) Except as provided in paragraphs (a)(2) and (3) of this section, pursuant to section 101(f) of the Act, the administrator of a defined benefit plan to which title IV of the Act applies shall furnish annually to each person specified in paragraph (f) of this section a funding notice that conforms to the requirements of this section.

(2) A plan administrator shall not be required to furnish a funding notice—

(i) In the case of a multiemployer plan, for a plan year if the due date for such notice is on or after the date the plan complies with the insolvency notice requirements of section 4245(e) or 4281(d)(3) of the Act and regulations thereunder.

(ii) In the case of a single-employer plan, for a plan year if the due date for such notice is on or after the date:

(A) The Pension Benefit Guaranty Corporation is appointed as trustee of the plan pursuant to section 4042 of the Act; or

(B) The plan has distributed assets in satisfaction of all benefit liabilities in a standard termination pursuant to section 4041(b) or in a distress termination pursuant to section 4041(c)(3)(B)(i) or of all guaranteed benefits in a distress termination pursuant to section 4041(c)(3)(B)(ii) of the Act.

(3) In the case of a merger or consolidation of two or more plans—

(i) The plan administrator of a non-successor plan shall not be required to furnish a funding notice for the plan year in which the merger occurred, and

(ii) The funding notice of the successor plan, for the plan year in which the merger occurred, must, in addition to the requirements of paragraph (b) of this section, contain a general explanation, including the effective date, of the merger and an identification of each plan (*e.g.,* name and plan number) involved in the merger or consolidation.

(b) *Content of notice.* A funding notice shall include the following information:

(1) *Identifying information.* The name of the plan, the name, address, and phone number of the plan administrator and the plan's principal administrative officer (if different than the plan administrator), each plan sponsor's name and employer identification number, and the plan number.

(2) *Funding percentage.* (i) *Single-employer plans.* For single-employer plans, a statement as to whether the plan's funding target attainment percentage (as defined in section 303(d)(2) of the Act) for the notice year, and for each of the two preceding plan years, is at least 100 percent (and, if not, the actual percentages).

(ii) *Multiemployer plans.* For multiemployer plans, a statement as to whether the plan's funded percentage (as defined in section 305(i) of the Act) for the notice year, and for each of the two preceding plan years, is at least 100 percent (and, if not, the actual percentages).

(3) *Assets and liabilities.* (i) *Single-employer plans.* For single-employer plans—

(A) A statement of the total assets (separately stating the prefunding balance and the funding standard carryover balance) and liabilities of the plan, determined in the same manner as under section 303 of the Act as of the valuation date of the notice year and for each of the two preceding plan years, as reported in the annual report filed under section 104 of the Act for each such preceding plan year, and

(B) A statement of the value of the plan's assets and liabilities determined as of the last day of the notice year. For purposes of this statement, the value of the plan's assets is the fair market value of plan assets. Plan liabilities are equal to the present value of benefits accrued through the last day of the notice year determined in the same manner as liabilities are calculated under section 303 of the Act (including actuarial assumptions and methods), but using the interest rate under section 4006(a)(3)(E)(iv) of the Act in effect for the last month of the notice year.

(ii) *Multiemployer plans.* For multiemployer plans—

(A) A statement of the value of the plan's assets (determined in the same manner as under section 304(c)(2) of the Act) and liabilities (determined in the same manner as under section 305(i)(8) of the Act, using reasonable actuarial assumptions as required under section 304(c)(3) of the Act) as of the valuation date of the notice year and each of the two preceding plan years, and

(B) A statement of the fair market value of plan assets as of the last day of the notice year, and as of the last day of each of the two preceding plan years as reported in the annual report filed under section 104(a) of the Act for each such preceding plan year.

(4) *Demographic information.* A statement of the number of participants who, as of the valuation date of the notice year, are: retired or separated from service and receiving benefits; retired or separated from service and entitled to future benefits (but currently not receiving benefits); and active participants under the plan. The statement shall indicate the number of participants in each such category and the sum of all such participants. The terms "active" and "retired or separated" shall have the same meaning given to those terms in instructions to the annual report filed under section 104(a) of the Act.

(5) *Funding policy.* A statement setting forth—

(i) The funding policy of the plan;

(ii) The asset allocation of investments under the plan (expressed as percentages of total assets) as of the end of the notice year; and

(iii) A general description of any investment policy of the plan as it relates to the funding policy in paragraph (b)(5)(i) of this section and the asset allocation of investments under paragraph (b)(5)(ii) of this section.

(6) *Endangered or critical status.* In the case of a multiemployer plan, a statement whether the plan was in endangered or critical status under section 305 of the Act for the notice year and, if so—

(i) A statement describing how a person may obtain a copy of the plan's funding improvement plan or rehabilitation plan, as appropriate, adopted under section 305 of the Act and the actuarial and financial data that demonstrate any action taken by the plan toward fiscal improvement, and

(ii) A summary of the plan's funding improvement plan or rehabilitation plan, including any update or modification of such funding improvement or rehabilitation plan adopted under section 305 of the Act during the notice year.

(7) *Events having a material effects on liabilities or assets.* In the case of any plan amendment, scheduled benefit increase or reduction, or other known event taking effect in the current plan year and having a material effect on plan liabilities or assets for the year (as defined in paragraph (g) of this section), an explanation of the amendment, scheduled increase or reduction, or event, and a projection to the end

of such plan year of the effect of the amendment, scheduled increase or reduction, or event on plan liabilities.

(8) *Rules on termination, reorganization or insolvency.* (i) *Single-employer plans.* In the case of a single-employer plan, a summary of the rules governing termination of single-employer plans under subtitle C of title IV of the Act.

(ii) *Multiemployer plans.* In the case of a multiemployer plan, a summary of the rules governing reorganization or insolvency, including the limitations on benefit payments.

(9) *PBGC guarantees.* A general description of the benefits under the plan which are eligible to be guaranteed by the Pension Benefit Guaranty Corporation, along with an explanation of the limitations on the guarantee and the circumstances under which such limitations apply.

(10) *Annual report information.* A statement that a person entitled to notice under paragraph (f) of this section may obtain a copy of the annual report of the plan filed under section 104(a) of the Act upon request, through the Internet Web site of the Department of Labor, or through any Intranet Web site maintained by the applicable plan sponsor (or plan administrator on behalf of the plan sponsor).

(11) *Information disclosed to PBGC.* In the case of a single-employer plan, if applicable, a statement that the contributing sponsor of the plan, and each member of the contributing sponsor's controlled group (other than an exempt entity within the meaning of 29 CFR 4010.4(c)), was required to provide the information under section 4010 of the Act for the notice year. If the contributing sponsor of the plan is itself an exempt entity within the meaning of 29 CFR 4010.4(c), in lieu of the preceding sentence, a statement that each member of the contributing sponsor's controlled group (other than an exempt entity within the meaning of 29 CFR 4010.4(c)) was required to provide the information under section 4010 of the Act for the notice year.

(12) *Additional information.* Any additional information that the plan administrator elects to include, provided that such information is necessary or helpful to understanding the mandatory information in the notice, or is otherwise permitted by law.

(c) *Style and format of notice.* Funding notices shall be written in a manner that is consistent with the style and format requirements of § 2520.102-2 of this chapter.

(d) *When to furnish notice.* (1) Except as provided in paragraph (d)(2) of this section, a funding notice shall be provided not later than 120 days after the end of the notice year.

(2) In the case of a small plan, a funding notice shall be provided not later than the earlier of the date on which the annual report is filed under section 104(a) of the Act or the latest date the annual report must be filed under that section (including extensions). For this purpose, a single-employer plan is a small plan if it meets the exception in section 303(g)(2)(B) of the Act, and a multiemployer plan is a small plan if it had 100 or fewer participants on each day during the plan year preceding the notice year.

(e) *Manner of furnishing notice.* (1) [Reserved].

(2) A funding notice must be furnished to the Pension Benefit Guaranty Corporation in a manner consistent with the requirements of part 4000 of this title. The date that the notice is furnished to the Pension Benefit Guaranty Corporation is determined consistent with that part.

(f) *Persons entitled to notice.* Persons entitled to a funding notice under this section are:

(1) Each participant covered under the plan on the last day of the notice year;

(2) Each beneficiary receiving benefits under the plan on the last day of the notice year;

(3) Each labor organization representing participants under the plan on the last day of the notice year;

(4) In the case of a multiemployer plan, each employer that, as of the last day of the notice year, is a party to the collective bargaining agreement(s) pursuant to which the plan is maintained or who otherwise may be subject to withdrawal liability pursuant to section 4203 of the Act; and

(5) The Pension Benefit Guaranty Corporation.

(g) *Material effect definition.* (1) For purposes of paragraph (b)(7) of this section, a plan amendment, scheduled benefit increase (or reduction), or other known event has a material effect on plan liabilities or assets for the current plan year (*i.e.,* plan year following the notice year) if such amendment, benefit increase (or reduction), or event—

(i) Results, or is projected to result, in an increase or decrease of five percent or more in the value of assets or liabilities from the valuation date of the notice year; or

(ii) In the judgment of the plan's enrolled actuary, is material for purposes of the plan's funding status under section 430 or 431, as applicable, of the Internal Revenue Code, without regard to paragraph (g)(1)(i) of this section.

(2) For purposes of paragraph (b)(7) of this section, the term "other known event" includes, but is not limited to—

(i) An extension of coverage under the existing terms of the plan to a new group of employees;

(ii) A plan merger, consolidation, or spinoff pursuant to regulations under section 414(l) of the Internal Revenue Code;

(iii) A shutdown of any facility, plant, store, or such other similar corporate event that creates immediate eligibility for benefits that would not otherwise be immediately payable for participants separating from service;

(iv) An offer by the plan for a temporary period to permit participants to retire at benefit levels greater than that to which they would otherwise be entitled; or

(v) A cost-of-living adjustment for retirees.

(3) For purposes of paragraph (g)(1)(i) of this section, calculate assets and liabilities in the same manner as under paragraph (b)(2) of this section.

(h) *Model notices.* (1) The appendices to this section contain a model notice for single-employer plans and a model notice for multiemployer plans. These models are intended to assist plan administrators in discharging their notice obligations under this section. Use of a model notice is not mandatory. However, subject to paragraph (h)(2) of this section, use of a model notice will be deemed to satisfy the requirements of paragraphs (b)(1) through (11) and paragraph (c) of this section.

(2) To the extent a plan administrator elects to include in a model notice information described in paragraph (b)(12) of this section, such additional information must be consistent with the style and format requirements in paragraph (c) of this section.

(i) *Limited alternative method of compliance for furnishing notice to PBGC.* Notwithstanding any other provision of this section, the plan administrator of a single-employer plan is not required to furnish a notice to the Pension Benefit Guaranty Corporation annually if, based on the data described in paragraph (b)(3)(i)(A) of this section for the notice year, plan liabilities do not exceed total plan assets by more than $50 million, provided that the plan administrator furnishes the latest available funding notice to the Pension Benefit Guaranty Corporation within 30 days of a written request.

(j) *Notice year.* For purposes of this section, the term "notice year" means the plan year to which the notice relates. For example, for a calendar year plan that must furnish its 2010 funding notice no later than the 120th day of 2011, the "notice year" is the 2010 plan year.

BILLING CODE 4510-29-P

APPENDIX A TO § 2520.101-5—SINGLE-EMPLOYER PLANS
ANNUAL FUNDING NOTICE
For

[insert name of pension plan]

Introduction

This notice includes important information about the funding status of your pension plan ("the Plan") and general information about the benefit payments guaranteed by the Pension Benefit Guaranty Corporation ("PBGC"), a federal insurance agency. All traditional pension plans (called "defined benefit pension plans") must provide this notice every year regardless of their funding status. This notice does not mean that the Plan is terminating. It is provided for informational purposes and you are not required to respond in any way. This notice is for the plan year beginning [*insert beginning date*] and ending [*insert ending date*] ("Plan Year").

How Well Funded Is Your Plan

Under federal law, the plan must report how well it is funded by using a measure called the "funding target attainment percentage." This percentage is obtained by dividing the Plan's Net Plan Assets by Plan Liabilities on the Valuation Date for the plan year. In general, the higher the percentage, the better funded the plan. Your Plan's funding target attainment percentage for the Plan Year and each of the two preceding plan years is shown in the chart below, along with a statement of the value of the Plan's assets and liabilities for the same period.

	Funding Target Attainment Percentage		
	[insert Plan Year, e.g., 2011]	[insert plan year preceding Plan Year, e.g., 2010]	[insert plan year 2 years preceding Plan year, e.g., 2009]
1. Valuation Date	[insert date]	[insert date]	[insert date]
2. Plan Assets			
a. Total Plan Assets	[insert amount]	[insert amount]	[insert amount]
b. Funding Standard Carryover Balance	[insert amount]	[insert amount]	[insert amount]
c. Prefunding Balance	[insert amount]	[insert amount]	[insert amount]
d. Net Plan Assets (a) - (b) - (c) = (d)	[insert amount]	[insert amount]	[insert amount]
3. Plan Liabilities	[insert amount]	[insert amount]	[insert amount]
4. At-Risk Liabilities	[insert amount]	[insert amount]	[insert amount]
5. Funding Target Attainment Percentage (2d)/(3)	**[insert percentage]**	**[insert percentage]**	**[insert percentage]**

{Instructions: Report Valuation Date entries in accordance with section 303(g)(2) of ERISA. Report Total Plan Assets in accordance with section 303(g)(3) of ERISA. Report credit balances (i.e., funding standard carryover balance and prefunding balance) in accordance with section 303(f) of ERISA. Report Net Plan Assets, Plan Liabilities (i.e., funding target), and Funding Target Attainment Percentage in accordance with section 303(d)(2) of ERISA. The amount reported as "Plan Liabilities" should be the funding target determined without regard to at-risk assumptions, even if the plan is in at-risk status. At-Risk Liabilities are determined under section 303(i) of ERISA (taking into account section 303(i)(5) of ERISA). Report At-Risk Liabilities for any year covered by this chart in which the Plan was in "at-risk" status within the meaning of section 303(i) of ERISA, only if At-Risk Liabilities are greater than Plan Liabilities; otherwise delete the entire row designated as number 4. Round off all amounts in this notice to the nearest dollar.}

Plan Assets and Credit Balances

Total Plan Assets is the value of the Plan's assets on the Valuation Date (see line 2 in the chart above). Credit balances were subtracted from Total Plan Assets to determine Net Plan Assets (line 2 d) used in the calculation of the funding target attainment percentage shown in the chart above. While pension plans are permitted to maintain credit balances (also called "funding standard carryover balances" or "prefunding balances" see 2 b & c in the chart above) for funding purposes, they may not be taken into account when calculating a plan's funding target attainment percentage. A plan might have a credit balance, for example, if in a prior year an employer made contributions to the plan above the minimum level required by law. Generally, the excess contributions are counted as "credits" and may be applied in future years toward the minimum level of contributions a plan sponsor is required to make by law.

Plan Liabilities

Plan Liabilities shown in line 3 of the chart above are the liabilities used to determine the Plan's Funding Target Attainment Percentage. This figure is an estimate of the amount of assets the Plan needs on the Valuation Date to pay for promised benefits under the plan.

At-Risk Liabilities

If a plan's funding target attainment percentage for the prior plan year is below a specified legal threshold, the plan is considered under law to be in "at-risk" status. This means that the plan is required to use actuarial assumptions that result in a higher value of plan liabilities and, as a consequence, requires the employer to contribute more money to the plan. For example, plans in "at-risk" status are required to assume that all workers eligible to retire in the next 10 years will do so as soon as they can, and that they will take their distribution in whatever form would create the highest cost to the plan, without regard to whether those workers actually do so. The additional funding that results from "at-risk" status may then remove the plan from this status. The Plan has been determined to be in "at-risk" status in *[enter year or years covered by the chart above]*. The increased liabilities to the Plan as a result of being in "at-risk" status are reflected in the At-Risk Liabilities row in the chart above.

{Instructions: Include the preceding discussion, entitled At-Risk Liabilities, only in the case of a plan required to report At-Risk Liabilities. Delete the entire row designated as number 4 in the chart above if the At-Risk Liabilities discussion is not being included in the notice.}

Year-End Assets and Liabilities

The asset values in the chart above are measured as of the first day of the Plan Year and are actuarial values. Because market values can fluctuate daily based on factors in the marketplace, such as changes in the stock market, pension law allows plans to use actuarial values that are designed to smooth out those fluctuations for funding purposes. The asset values below are market values and are measured as of the last day of the plan year. Market values tend to show a clearer picture of a plan's funded status as of a given point in time. As of *[enter the last day of the Plan Year]*, the fair market value of the Plan's assets was *[enter amount]*. On this same date, the Plan's liabilities were *[enter amount]*.

{Instructions: Insert the fair market value of the plan's assets as of the last day of the plan year. You may include contributions made after the end of the plan year to which the notice relates and before the date the notice is timely furnished but only if such contributions are attributable to such plan year for funding purposes. A plan's liabilities as of the last day of the plan year are equal to the present value, as of the last day of the plan year, of benefits accrued as of that same date. With the exception of the interest rate assumption, the present value should be determined using assumptions used to determine the funding target under section 303. The interest rate assumption is the rate provided under section 4006(a)(3)(E)(iv), but using the last month of the year to which the notice relates rather than the month preceding the first month of the year to which the notice relates. If, consistent with section 303(g)(2) of ERISA, the plan's valuation date is not the first day of the plan year, make appropriate modifications to the preceding paragraph, e.g., replace "first day of" with "valuation date for."}

{Instructions: If, pursuant to section 303(g)(3) of ERISA, the value of the plan's assets in the chart above is fair market value, include the paragraph below rather than the paragraph above, but otherwise follow the instructions above.}

The asset values in the chart above are measured as of the first day of the Plan Year. As of *[enter the last day of the Plan Year]*, the fair market value of the Plan's assets was *[enter amount]*. On this same date, the Plan's liabilities were *[enter amount]*.

Participant Information

The total number of participants in the Plan as of the Plan's valuation date was *[insert number]*. Of this number, *[insert number]* were active participants, *[insert number]* were retired or separated from service and receiving benefits, and *[insert number]* were retired or separated from service and entitled to future benefits.

Funding & Investment Policies

Every pension plan must have a procedure for establishing a funding policy to carry out plan objectives. A funding policy relates to the level of assets needed to pay for promised benefits. The funding policy of the Plan is *[insert a summary statement of the Plan's funding policy]*.

Once money is contributed to the Plan, the money is invested by plan officials, called fiduciaries, who make specific investments in accordance with the Plan's investment policy. Generally speaking, an investment policy is a written statement that provides the fiduciaries who are responsible for plan investments with guidelines or general instructions concerning investment management decisions. The investment policy of the Plan is [*insert a summary statement of the Plan's investment policy*].

Under the Plan's investment policy, the Plan's assets were allocated among the following categories of investments, as of the end of the Plan Year. These allocations are percentages of total assets:

Asset Allocations		Percentage
1. Cash (interest bearing and non-interest bearing)		_____
2. U.S. Government securities		_____
3. Corporate debt instruments (other than employer securities):		
	Preferred	_____
	All other	_____
4. Corporate stocks (other than employer securities):		
	Preferred	_____
	Common	_____
5. Partnership/joint venture interests		_____
6. Real estate (other than employer real property)		_____
7. Loans (other than to participants)		_____
8. Participant loans		_____
9. Value of interest in common/collective trusts		_____
10. Value of interest in pooled separate accounts		_____
11. Value of interest in master trust investment accounts		_____
12. Value of interest in 103-12 investment entities		_____
13. Value of interest in registered investment companies (e.g., mutual funds)		_____
14. Value of funds held in insurance co. general account (unallocated contracts)		_____
15. Employer-related investments:		
	Employer Securities	_____
	Employer real property	_____
16. Buildings and other property used in plan operation		_____
17. Other		_____

For information about the plan's investment in any of the following types of investments as described in the chart above - common/collective trusts, pooled separate accounts, master trust investment accounts, or 103-12 investment entities - contact [*insert the name, telephone number, email address or mailing address of the plan administrator or designated representative*].

Instructions: If a plan holds an interest in one or more of the direct filing entities (DFEs) noted above, i.e., MTIAs, CCTs, PSAs, or 103-12IEs, immediately following the asset allocation chart include the paragraph above informing recipients how to obtain more information regarding the plan's DFE investments (e.g., the plan's Schedule D and/or the DFE's Schedule H). If a plan does not hold an interest in a DFE, do not include the above paragraph.

Events Having a Material Effect on Assets or Liabilities

Federal law requires the plan administrator to provide in this notice a written explanation of events, taking effect in the current plan year, which are expected to have a material effect on plan liabilities or assets. Material effect events are occurrences that tend to have a significant impact on a plan's funding condition. An event is material if it, for example, is expected to increase or decrease Total Plan Assets or Plan Liabilities by five percent or more. For the plan year beginning on [*insert the first day of the current plan year (i.e., the year after the notice year)*] and ending on [*insert the last day of the current plan year*], the following events are expected to have such an effect: [*insert explanation of any plan amendment, scheduled benefit increase or reduction, or other known event taking effect in the current plan year and having a material effect on plan liabilities or assets for the year, as well as a projection to the end of the current plan year of the effect of the amendment, scheduled increase or reduction, or event on plan liabilities*].

{Instructions: Include the preceding discussion, entitled Events having a Material Effect on Assets or Liabilities, only if applicable.}

Right to Request a Copy of the Annual Report

A pension plan is required to file with the US Department of Labor an annual report called the Form 5500 that contains financial and other information about the plan. Copies of the annual report are available from the US Department of Labor, Employee Benefits Security Administration's Public Disclosure Room at 200 Constitution Avenue, NW, Room N-1513, Washington, DC 20210, or by calling 202.693.8673. For 2009 and subsequent plan years, you may obtain an electronic copy of the plan's annual report by going to *www.efast.dol.gov* and using the Form 5500 search function. Or you may obtain a copy of the Plan's annual report by making a written request to the plan administrator. [*If*

the Plan's annual report is available on an Intranet website maintained by the plan sponsor (or plan administrator on behalf of the plan sponsor), modify the preceding sentence to include a statement that the annual report also may be obtained through that website and include the website address.] Individual information, such as the amount of your accrued benefit under the plan, is not contained in the annual report. If you are seeking information regarding your benefits under the plan, contact the plan administrator identified below under "Where To Get More Information."

Summary of Rules Governing Termination of Single-Employer Plans

If a plan is terminated, there are specific termination rules that must be followed under federal law. A summary of these rules follows.

There are two ways an employer can terminate its pension plan. First, the employer can end the plan in a "standard termination" but only after showing the PBGC that the plan has enough money to pay all benefits owed to participants. Under a standard termination, the plan must either purchase an annuity from an insurance company (which will provide you with periodic retirement benefits, such as monthly, for life or for a set period of time when you retire) or, if your plan allows, issue one lump-sum payment that covers your entire benefit. Your plan administrator must give you advance notice that identifies the insurance company (or companies) that your employer may select to provide the annuity. The PBGC's guarantee ends when your employer purchases your annuity or gives you the lump-sum payment.

Second, if the plan is not fully-funded, the employer may apply for a distress termination. To do so, however, the employer must be in financial distress and prove to a bankruptcy court or to the PBGC that the employer cannot remain in business unless the plan is terminated. If the application is granted, the PBGC will take over the plan as trustee and pay plan benefits, up to the legal limits, using plan assets and PBGC guarantee funds.

Under certain circumstances, the PBGC may take action on its own to end a pension plan. Most terminations initiated by the PBGC occur when the PBGC determines that plan termination is needed to protect the interests of plan participants or of the PBGC insurance program. The PBGC can do so if, for example, a plan does not have enough money to pay benefits currently due.

Benefit Payments Guaranteed by the PBGC

When the PBGC takes over a plan, it pays pension benefits through its insurance program. Only benefits that you have earned a right to receive and that cannot be forfeited (called vested benefits) are guaranteed. Most participants and beneficiaries receive all of the pension benefits they would have received under their plan, but some people may lose certain benefits that are not guaranteed.

The amount of benefits that PBGC guarantees is determined as of the plan termination date. However, if a plan terminates during a plan sponsor's bankruptcy and the bankruptcy proceeding began on or after September 16, 2006, then the amount guaranteed is determined as of the date the sponsor entered bankruptcy.

The PBGC maximum benefit guarantee is set by law and is updated each calendar year. For a plan with a termination date or sponsor bankruptcy date, as applicable in [*insert current calendar year*], the maximum guarantee is [*insert amount from PBGC web site, www.pbgc.gov, applicable for the current calendar year*]per month, or [*insert amount from PBGC web site, www.pbgc.gov, applicable for the current calendar year*] per year, for a benefit paid to a 65-year-old retiree with no survivor benefit. If a plan terminates during a plan sponsor's bankruptcy, and the bankruptcy proceeding began on or after September 16, 2006, the maximum guarantee is fixed as of the calendar year in which the sponsor entered bankruptcy. The maximum guarantee is lower for an individual who begins receiving benefits from PBGC before age 65; the maximum guarantee by age can be found on PBGC's website, *www.pbgc.gov*. [*If the Plan does not provide for commencement of benefits before age 65, you may omit this sentence.*] The guaranteed amount is also reduced if a benefit will be provided to a survivor of the plan participant.

The PBGC guarantees "basic benefits" earned before a plan is terminated, which includes [*Include the following guarantees that apply to benefits available under the Plan.*]:

- pension benefits at normal retirement age;

- most early retirement benefits;

- annuity benefits for survivors of plan participants; and

- disability benefits for a disability that occurred before the date the plan terminated or the date the sponsor entered bankruptcy, as applicable.

The PBGC does not guarantee certain types of benefits [*Include the following guarantee limits that apply to the benefits available under the Plan.*]:

- The PBGC does not guarantee benefits for which you do not have a vested right, usually because you have not worked enough years for the company.

- The PBGC does not guarantee benefits for which you have not met all age, service, or other requirements.

- Benefit increases and new benefits that have been in place for less than one year are not guaranteed. Those that have been in place for less than five years are only partly guaranteed.

- Early retirement payments that are greater than payments at normal retirement age may not be guaranteed. For example, a supplemental benefit that stops when you become eligible for Social Security may not be guaranteed.

- Benefits other than pension benefits, such as health insurance, life insurance, death benefits, vacation pay, or severance pay, are not guaranteed.

- The PBGC generally does not pay lump sums exceeding $5,000.

In some circumstances, participants and beneficiaries still may receive some benefits that are not guaranteed. This depends on how much money the terminated plan has and how much the PBGC recovers from employers for plan underfunding.

Corporate and Actuarial Information on File with PBGC

A plan sponsor must provide the PBGC with financial information about itself and actuarial information about the plan under certain circumstances, such as when the funding target attainment percentage of the plan (or any other pension plan sponsored by a member of the sponsor's controlled group) falls below 80 percent (other triggers may also apply). The sponsor of the Plan, [*enter name of plan sponsor*], and members of its controlled group, if any, were subject to this requirement to provide corporate financial information and plan actuarial information to the PBGC. The PBGC uses this information for oversight and monitoring purposes.

{Instructions: Insert the preceding paragraph entitled "Corporate and Actuarial Information on File with PBGC" only if a reporting under section 4010 of ERISA was required for the Plan Year. Modify the preceding paragraph, as appropriate, if the plan sponsor (as distinguished from the members of its controlled group) is exempt from the ERISA 4010 reporting requirement pursuant to 29 CFR 4010.4(c).}

Where to Get More Information

For more information about this notice, you may contact [*enter name of plan administrator and if applicable, principal administrative officer*], at [*enter phone number and address and insert email address if appropriate*]. For identification purposes, the official plan number is [*enter plan number*]and the plan sponsor's name and employer identification number or "EIN" is [*enter name and EIN of plan sponsor*]. For more information about the PBGC, go to PBGC's website, *www.pbgc.gov*.

APPENDIX B TO § 2520.101-5—MULTIEMPLOYER PLANS

ANNUAL FUNDING NOTICE

For

[*insert name of pension plan*]

Introduction

This notice includes important information about the funding status of your pension plan ("the Plan") and general information about the benefit payments guaranteed by the Pension Benefit Guaranty Corporation ("PBGC"), a federal insurance agency. All traditional pension plans (called "defined benefit pension plans") must provide this notice every year regardless of their funding status. This notice does not mean that the Plan is terminating. It is provided for informational purposes and you are not required to respond in any way. This notice is for the plan year beginning [*insert beginning date*] and ending [*insert ending date*] ("Plan Year").

How Well Funded Is Your Plan

Under federal law, the plan must report how well it is funded by using a measure called the "funded percentage." This percentage is obtained by dividing the Plan's assets by its liabilities on the Valuation Date for the plan year. In general, the higher the percentage, the better funded the plan. Your Plan's funded percentage for the Plan Year and each of the two preceding plan years is set forth in the chart below, along with a statement of the value of the Plan's assets and liabilities for the same period.

Funded Percentage			
	[insert Plan Year, e.g., 2011]	[insert plan year preceding Plan Year, e.g., 2010]	[insert plan year 2 years preceding Plan Year, e.g., 2009]
Valuation Date	[insert date]	[insert date]	[insert date]
Funded Percentage	[insert percentage]	[insert percentage]	[insert percentage]
Value of Assets	[insert amount]	[insert amount]	[insert amount]
Value of Liabilities	[insert amount]	[insert amount]	[insert amount]

{Instructions: The plan's "funded percentage" is equal to a fraction, the numerator of which is the actuarial value of the plan's assets {determined in the same manner as under section 304(c)(2) of ERISA} and the denominator of which is the accrued liability of the plan (under section 305(i)(8) of ERISA, using reasonable actuarial assumptions as required under section 304(c)(3) of ERISA. Report the value of the plan's assets and liabilities in the same manner as under section 304 of ERISA (but determining the plan's liabilities under section 305(i)(8) of ERISA, using

reasonable actuarial assumptions as required under section 304(c)(3) of ERISA) as of the plan's valuation date for the plan year.}

Year-End Fair Market Value of Assets

The asset values in the chart above are measured as of the Valuation Date for the plan year and are actuarial values. Because market values can fluctuate daily based on factors in the marketplace, such as changes in the stock market, pension law allows plans to use actuarial values that are designed to smooth out those fluctuations for funding purposes. The asset values below are market values and are measured as of the last day of the plan year, rather than as of the Valuation Date. Substituting the market value of assets for the actuarial value used in

	[insert last day of Plan Year, e.g., 2011]	[insert last day of plan year preceding Plan Year, e.g., 2010]	[insert last day of plan year 2 years preceding Plan Year, e.g., 2009]
Fair Market Value of Assets	[insert amount]	[insert amount]	[insert amount]

{Instructions: Insert the fair market value of the plan's assets as of the last day of the plan year. You may include contributions made after the end of the plan year to which the notice relates and before the date the notice is timely furnished but only if such contributions are attributable to such plan year for funding purposes. For each of the two preceding plan years, you may use the fair market value of assets on the last day of the plan year as reported in the annual report for such plan year.}

Critical or Endangered Status

Under federal pension law a plan generally will be considered to be in "endangered" status if, at the beginning of the plan year, the funded percentage of the plan is less than 80 percent or in "critical" status if the percentage is less than 65 percent (other factors may also apply). If a pension plan enters endangered status, the trustees of the plan are required to adopt a funding improvement plan. Similarly, if a pension plan enters critical status, the trustees of the plan are required to adopt a rehabilitation plan. Rehabilitation and funding improvement plans establish steps and benchmarks for pension plans to improve their funding status over a specified period of time.

{Instructions: Select and complete the appropriate option below.}

{Option one}

The Plan was not in endangered or critical status in the Plan Year.

{Option two}

The Plan was in *[insert* "endangered" *or* "critical" *]* status in the Plan Year ending [*insert last day of Plan Year*] because [*insert summary description of why plan was in this status based on statutory factors*]. In an effort to improve the Plan's funding situation, the trustees adopted [*insert summary of Plan's funding improvement or rehabilitation plan, including when adopted and expected duration, and a description of any modification or update to the plan adopted during the plan year to which the notice relates]*. You may obtain a copy of the Plan's funding improvement or rehabilitation plan and the actuarial and financial data that

demonstrate any action taken by the plan toward fiscal improvement by contacting the plan administrator. [*If applicable, insert:* "Or you may obtain this information at [*insert Intranet address of plan sponsor (or plan administrator on behalf of the plan sponsor)*].]

If the Plan is in endangered or critical status for the plan year ending [*insert the last day of the plan year following the Plan Year]*, separate notification of that status has or will be provided.

Participant Information

The total number of participants in the Plan as of the Plan's valuation date was [*insert number*]. Of this number, [*insert number*] were active participants, [*insert number*] were retired or separated from service and receiving benefits, and [*insert number*] were retired or separated from service and entitled to future benefits.

Funding & Investment Policies

Every pension plan must have a procedure for establishing a funding policy to carry out plan objectives. A funding policy relates to the level of assets needed to pay for benefits promised under the plan currently and over the years. The funding policy of the Plan is [*insert a summary statement of the Plan's funding policy*].

Once money is contributed to the Plan, the money is invested by plan officials called fiduciaries, who make specific investments in accordance with the Plan's investment policy. Generally speaking, an investment policy is a written statement that provides the fiduciaries who are responsible for plan investments with guidelines or general instructions concerning investment management decisions. The investment policy of the Plan is [*insert a summary statement of the Plan's investment policy*].

Under the Plan's investment policy, the Plan's assets were allocated among the following categories of investments, as of the end of the Plan Year. These allocations are percentages of total assets:

Asset Allocations		Percentage
1. Cash (Interest bearing and non-interest bearing)		_____
2. U.S. Government securities		_____
3. Corporate debt instruments (other than employer securities):		
	Preferred	_____
	All other	_____
4. Corporate stocks (other than employer securities):		
	Preferred	_____
	Common	_____
5. Partnership/joint venture interests		_____
6. Real estate (other than employer real property)		_____
7. Loans (other than to participants)		_____
8. Participant loans		_____
9. Value of interest in common/collective trusts		_____
10. Value of interest in pooled separate accounts		_____
11. Value of interest in master trust investment accounts		_____
12. Value of interest in 103-12 investment entities		_____
13. Value of interest in registered investment companies (e.g., mutual funds)		_____
14. Value of funds held in insurance co. general account (unallocated contracts)		_____
15. Employer-related investments:		
	Employer Securities	_____
	Employer real property	_____
16. Buildings and other property used in plan operation		_____
17. Other		_____

For information about the plan's investment in any of the following types of investments as described in the chart above - common/ collective trusts, pooled separate accounts, master trust investment accounts, or 103-12 investment entities - contact [*insert the name, telephone number, email address or mailing address of the plan administrator or designated representative*].

Instructions: If a plan holds an interest in one or more of the direct filing entities (DFEs) noted above, i.e., MTIAs, CCTs, PSAs, or 103-12IEs, immediately following the asset allocation chart include the paragraph above informing recipients how to obtain more information regarding the plan's DFE investments (e.g., the plan's Schedule D and/or the DFE's Schedule H). If a plan does not hold an interest in a DFE, do not include the above paragraph.

Events Having a Material Effect on Assets or Liabilities

Federal law requires the plan administrator to provide in this notice a written explanation of events, taking effect in the current plan year, which are expected to have a material effect on plan liabilities or assets. Material effect events are occurrences that tend to have a significant impact on a plan's funding condition. An event is material if it, for example, is expected to increase or decrease Total Plan Assets or Plan Liabilities by five percent or more. For the plan year beginning on [*insert the first day of the current plan year (i.e., the year after the notice year)*]and ending on [*insert the last day of the current plan year*], the following events are expected to have such an effect: [*insert explanation of any plan amendment, scheduled benefit increase or reduction, or other known event taking effect in the current plan year and having a material effect on plan liabilities and assets for the year, as well as a projection to the end of the current plan year of the effect of the amendment, scheduled increase or reduction, or event on plan liabilities*].

{Instructions: Include the preceding discussion, entitled Events having a Material Effect on Assets or Liabilities, only if applicable.}

Right to Request a Copy of the Annual Report

A pension plan is required to file with the US Department of Labor an annual report called the Form 5500 that contains financial and other information about the plan. Copies of the annual report are available from the US Department of Labor, Employee Benefits Security Administration's Public Disclosure Room at 200 Constitution Avenue, NW, Room N-1513, Washington, DC 20210, or by calling 202.693.8673. For 2009 and subsequent plan years, you may obtain an electronic copy of the plan's annual report by going to *www.efast.dol.gov* and using the Form 5500 search function. Or you may obtain a copy of the Plan's annual report by making a written request to the plan administrator. [*If the Plan's annual report is available on an Intranet website maintained by the plan sponsor (or plan administrator on behalf of the plan sponsor), modify the preceding sentence to include a statement that the annual report also may be obtained through that website and include the website address.*] Individual information, such as the amount of your accrued benefit under the plan, is not contained in the annual report. If you are seeking information regarding your benefits under the plan, contact the plan administrator identified below under "Where To Get More Information."

Summary of Rules Governing Plans in Reorganization and Insolvent Plans

Federal law has a number of special rules that apply to financially troubled multiemployer plans. The plan administrator is required by law to include a summary of these rules in the annual funding notice. Under so-called "plan reorganization rules," a plan with adverse financial experience may need to increase required contributions and may, under certain circumstances, reduce benefits that are not eligible for the PBGC's guarantee (generally, benefits that have been in effect for less than 60 months). If a plan is in reorganization status, it must provide notification that the plan is in reorganization status and that, if contributions are not increased, accrued benefits under the plan may be reduced or an excise tax may be imposed (or both). The plan is required to furnish this notification to each contributing employer and the labor organization.

Despite these special plan reorganization rules, a plan in reorganization could become insolvent. A plan is insolvent for a plan year if its available financial resources are not sufficient to pay benefits when due for that plan year. An insolvent plan must reduce benefit payments to the highest level that can be paid from the plan's available resources. If such resources are not enough to pay benefits at the level specified by law (see Benefit Payments Guaranteed by the PBGC, below), the plan must apply to the PBGC for financial assistance. The PBGC will loan the plan the amount necessary to pay benefits at the guaranteed level. Reduced benefits may be restored if the plan's financial condition improves.

A plan that becomes insolvent must provide prompt notice of its status to participants and beneficiaries, contributing employers, labor unions representing participants, and PBGC. In addition, participants and beneficiaries also must receive information regarding whether, and how, their benefits will be reduced or affected, including loss of a lump sum option. This information will be provided for each year the plan is insolvent.

Benefit Payments Guaranteed by the PBGC

The maximum benefit that the PBGC guarantees is set by law. Only benefits that you have earned a right to receive and that can not be forfeited (called vested benefits) are guaranteed. Specifically, the PBGC guarantees a monthly benefit payment equal to 100 percent of the first $11 of the Plan's monthly benefit accrual rate, plus 75 percent of the next $33 of the accrual rate, times each year of credited service. The PBGC's maximum guarantee, therefore, is $35.75 per month times a participant's years of credited service.

Example 1: If a participant with 10 years of credited service has an accrued monthly benefit of $500, the accrual rate for purposes of determining the PBGC guarantee would be determined by dividing the monthly benefit by the participant's years of service ($500/10), which equals $50. The guaranteed amount for a $50 monthly accrual rate is equal to the sum of $11 plus $24.75 (.75 × $33), or $35.75. Thus, the participant's guaranteed monthly benefit is $357.50 ($35.75 × 10).

Example 2: If the participant in Example 1 has an accrued monthly benefit of $200, the accrual rate for purposes of determining the guarantee would be $20 (or $200/10). The guaranteed amount for a $20 monthly accrual rate is equal to the sum of $11 plus $6.75 (.75 x $9), or $17.75. Thus, the participant's guaranteed monthly benefit would be $177.50 ($17.75 x 10).

The PBGC guarantees pension benefits payable at normal retirement age and some early retirement benefits. In calculating a person's monthly payment, the PBGC will disregard any benefit increases that were made under the plan within 60 months before the earlier of the plan's termination or insolvency (or benefits that were in effect for less than 60 months at the time of termination or insolvency). Similarly, the PBGC does not guarantee pre-retirement death benefits to a spouse or beneficiary (e.g., a qualified pre-retirement survivor annuity) if the participant dies after the plan terminates, benefits above the normal retirement benefit, disability benefits not in pay status, or non-pension benefits, such as health insurance, life insurance, death benefits, vacation pay, or severance pay.

Where to Get More Information

For more information about this notice, you may contact [*enter name of plan administrator and if applicable, principal administrative officer*], at [*enter phone number and address and insert email address if appropriate*]. For identification purposes, the official plan number is [*enter plan number*]and the plan sponsor's name and employer identification number or "EIN" is [*enter name and EIN of plan sponsor*]. For more information about the PBGC, go to PBGC's website, *www.pbgc.gov*.

BILLING CODE 4510-29-C

3. Amend § 2520.104-46 by revising paragraph (b)(1)(i)(B) introductory text to read as follows:

§ 2520.104-46 Waiver of examination and report of an independent qualified public accountant for employee benefit plans with fewer than 100 participants.

* * * * *

(b) * * *

(1) * * *

(i) * * *

(B) The summary annual report (described in § 2520.104b-10) or, in the case of plans subject to section 101(f) of the Act, the annual funding notice (described in § 2520.101-5), includes, in addition to any other required information:

* * * * *

4. Amend § 2520.104b-10, by revising paragraphs (g)(7) and (g)(8) and adding paragraph (g)(9) to read as follows:

§ 2520.104b-10 Summary Annual Report.

* * * * *

(g) * * *

(7) A dues financed welfare plan which meets the requirements of 29 CFR 2520.104-26;

(8) A dues financed pension plan which meets the requirements of 29 CFR 2520.104-27; and

(9) A plan to which title IV of the Act applies.

* * * * *

Signed at Washington, DC, on November 8, 2010.

Phyllis C. Borzi,

Assistant Secretary, Employee Benefits Security Administration, Department of Labor.

¶20,538

[FR Doc. 2010-28890 Filed 11-17-10; 8:45 am]   BILLING CODE 4510-29-P

¶ 20,538A

Employee Benefits Security Administration (EBSA): 401(k) plans: Disclosures: Target date funds.—The Employee Benefits Security Administration has issued proposed regulations that would amend the rules on qualified default investment alternatives and participant-level disclosures to enhance and provide more specificity regarding the information that must be disclosed to participants and beneficiaries concerning investments in target date funds. Comments on the proposed regulations are due by January 14, 2011.

NOTE: The comment period was reopened and extended to July 9, 2012 (77 FR 30928, May 24, 2012).

The proposed regulations, which were published in the Federal Register on November 30, 2010 (75 FR 73987), are reproduced below.

DEPARTMENT OF LABOR

Employee Benefits Security Administration

29 CFR Part 2550

RIN 1210-AB38

Target Date Disclosure

AGENCY: Employee Benefits Security Administration, Labor.

ACTION: Proposed regulation.

SUMMARY: The Department published in the **Federal Register** of October 24, 2007 a final regulation (the qualified default investment alternative regulation) providing relief from certain fiduciary responsibilities for fiduciaries of participant-directed individual account plans who, in the absence of directions from a participant, invest the participant's account in a qualified default investment alternative. On October 20, 2010, the Department published a final regulation that requires the disclosure of certain plan and investment-related information, including fee and expense information, to participants and beneficiaries in participant-directed individual account plans (the participant-level disclosure regulation). This document contains proposed amendments to the qualified default investment alternative regulation to provide more specificity as to the information that must be disclosed in the required notice to participants and beneficiaries concerning investments in qualified default investment alternatives, including target date or similar investments. This document also contains a proposed amendment to the participant-level disclosure regulation that would require the disclosure of the same information concerning target date or similar investments to all participants and beneficiaries in participant-directed individual account plans.

DATES: Written comments on the proposed regulation should be received by the Department of Labor no later than January 14, 2011.

ADDRESSES: To facilitate the receipt and processing of comments, EBSA encourages interested persons to submit their comments electronically to *e-ORI@dol.gov,* or by using the Federal eRulemaking portal *http://www.regulations.gov* (following instructions for submission of comments). Persons submitting comments electronically are encouraged not to submit paper copies. Persons interested in submitting comments on paper should send or deliver their comments (preferably three copies) to: Office of Regulations and Interpretations, Employee Benefits Security Administration, Room N-5655, U.S. Department of Labor, 200 Constitution Avenue, NW., Washington, DC 20210, Attention: Target Date Amendments. All comments will be available to the public, without charge, online at *http://www.regulations.gov* and *http://www.dol.gov/ebsa,* and at the Public Disclosure Room, Employee Benefits Security Administration, U.S. Department of Labor, Room N-1513, 200 Constitution Avenue, NW., Washington, DC 20210.

FOR FURTHER INFORMATION CONTACT: Kristen L. Zarenko, Office of Regulations and Interpretations, Employee Benefits Security Administration, (202) 693-8500. This is not a toll-free number.

SUPPLEMENTARY INFORMATION:

A. Background

Section 624(a) of the Pension Protection Act of 2006 (Pension Protection Act) added a new section 404(c)(5) to ERISA. Section 404(c)(5)(A) of ERISA provides that, for purposes of section 404(c)(1) of ERISA, a participant in an individual account plan shall be treated as exercising control over the assets in the account with respect to the amount of contributions and earnings which, in the absence of an investment election by the participant, are invested by the plan in accordance with

regulations prescribed by the Secretary of Labor. On October 24, 2007, the Department of Labor (Department) published a final regulation implementing the provisions of section 404(c)(5) of ERISA.[1] Correcting amendments to the final regulation were published on April 30, 2008.[2] A fiduciary of a plan that complies with the final regulation, as amended, will not be liable for any loss, or by reason of any breach, that occurs as a result of investment in a qualified default investment alternative. The regulation describes the types of investments that qualify as default investment alternatives under section 404(c)(5) of ERISA and the other requirements that must be satisfied in order for a fiduciary to obtain the relief from liability described above.

The final regulation provides that, in order for a fiduciary to obtain relief, participants and beneficiaries must receive information concerning the investments that may be made on their behalf. Specifically, paragraph (c)(3) of the final rule requires that participants and beneficiaries be furnished both an initial notice (generally thirty days in advance of a participant's eligibility to participate in the plan) and an annual notice for subsequent plan years. Paragraph (d) of the final rule sets forth the information that must be included in these notices. In addition to the notice requirement, paragraph (c)(4) of the final regulation required that fiduciaries provide certain investment-related information that must be disclosed under the Department's 404(c) regulation. Specifically, paragraph (c)(4) requires fiduciaries to provide to defaulted participants or beneficiaries the material described in sections 2550.404c-1(b)(2)(i)(B)(*1*)(*viii*) and (*ix*) and 2550.404c-1(b)(2)(i)(B)(*2*).

Since publication of the final rule, the Department has received many questions about the notice requirement, for example concerning the timing requirements for the notice and how much information must be disclosed concerning investment fees and expenses. The Department addressed these and other issues in a series of questions and answers concerning the final rule that was published in a Field Assistance Bulletin in April 2008.[3] With respect to the disclosure of investment fee and expense information, the Department indicated at that time that it was developing a regulation to establish disclosure requirements for all participant-directed individual account plans. The Department anticipated that furnishing the investment information required by such regulation, when finalized, would satisfy the investment-related fee and expense disclosures required by the qualified default investment alternative regulation. Nonetheless, the Department continues to receive requests for more formal guidance as to how the content requirements of the qualified default investment alternative notice may be satisfied. As discussed below, the Department proposes amending the qualified default investment alternative regulation to provide more specificity as to the information that must be disclosed.

In addition to questions about the notice requirement, recent attention has been paid to the increased use of "target date" or "lifecycle" funds and other similar investments (TDFs) as an investment alternative in participant-directed retirement plans, such as 401(k) plans.[4] The Department's final regulation included TDFs as one of the permissible categories of investment funds or products that may be used as a qualified default investment alternative, if all of the requirements of the final rule have been satisfied. The growing popularity of these products led to a focus in recent years on issues relating to the design, operation, and selection of TDFs for 401(k) plans, both as investment alternatives for plans generally and as qualified default investment alternatives for participants that do not provide investment direction. The designation of all investment alternatives, including TDFs, to be made available under a private sector retirement plan is governed by the fiduciary responsibility provisions of ERISA. Persons with this responsibility must prudently select and monitor investment alternatives, including alternatives intended to be qualified default investment alternatives.

---

[1] 72 FR 60452 (Oct. 24, 2007).

[2] 73 FR 23349 (Apr. 30, 2008).

[3] *See* Field Assistance Bulletin No. 2008-03 (April 29, 2008).

[4] Employee Benefits Research Institute Issue Brief #327, March 2009.

In 2008, the Department's ERISA Advisory Council studied several aspects of TDFs as 401(k) plan investment alternatives, including the challenges and risks they may pose to participants who invest in TDFs, the different types of TDFs, and appropriate criteria for selecting and monitoring TDFs. In its report to the Secretary of Labor, the Council recommended that the Department provide additional guidance to both plan fiduciaries and plan participants to enhance understanding of TDFs and the risks associated with TDF investing.[5] In addition, there has been Congressional interest in target date fund issues.[6] In June 2009, the Department and the Securities and Exchange Commission (Commission) held a joint public hearing to explore issues related to TDFs, including how they are managed at the investment level, how they are selected by plan fiduciaries and by investors, and how information about them is disclosed to plan participants and investors.

Following the public hearing and extensive review of the testimony presented and supplemental materials concerning TDFs, the Department was persuaded that both plan fiduciaries and plan participants would benefit from additional guidance concerning TDFs. Accordingly, the Department and the Commission recently published a joint Investor Bulletin to better educate investors and plan participants who are considering investing in TDFs.[7] The Commission also recently proposed rules to address concerns regarding the potential for investor misunderstandings about TDFs.[8] The Department further intends to publish a series of tips intended to assist plan fiduciaries in obtaining and evaluating relevant information when selecting and monitoring TDFs as investment options for participant-directed retirement plans.

The Department also determined that improvements can be made in the information that is disclosed to participants and beneficiaries concerning their plan investment in TDFs, whether by their own investment direction or pursuant to the qualified default investment alternative regulation. To ensure that consistent information concerning TDFs is furnished to defaulted participants and to participants who give investment directions, the Department is publishing in this Notice proposed amendments to both the qualified default investment alternative regulation and the participant-level disclosure regulation. The amendment to the participant-level disclosure regulation, at § 2550.404a-5 (75 FR 64910, October 20, 2010), will be included in paragraph (i)(4) of that regulation, which was reserved for this purpose. More detailed information about the participant-level disclosure regulation, including the general investment-related disclosure requirements, can be found in the Supplementary Information for that regulation.

B. Description of Amendments

This proposal amends paragraphs (c)(4) and (d)(3), (4), and (5) of the qualified default investment alternative regulation to more specifically describe certain investment-related information that must be included in the required notice to participants and beneficiaries. This information is intended to complement the new investment-related disclosure requirements contained in the participant-level disclosure regulation.

Paragraph (c)(4) of the rule is being revised to reflect amendments to the Department's 404(c) regulation that were made as part of the participant-level disclosure regulation. Rather than referring to requirements previously contained in the 404(c) regulation, this paragraph of the qualified default investment alternative regulation now requires fiduciaries to provide the comparable materials that are described in section 2550.404a-5(d)(3) and (4) of the participant-level disclosure regulation.[9]

Paragraph (d)(3) of the rule requires that the notice include: "[a]Description of the qualified default investment alternative, including a description of the investment objectives, risk and return characteristics (if applicable), and fees and expenses attendant to the investment alternative[.]"[10] To ensure that plan fiduciaries understand the specific investment information that must be disclosed to defaulted participants and beneficiaries about qualified default investment alternatives, and to better conform these requirements to those of all participant-directed individual account plans pursuant to the Department's participant-level disclosure regulation, proposed paragraph (d)(3) contains six separate elements. The description of the qualified default investment alternative must first include the name of the invest-

ment's issuer. Second, the description must include the investment's objectives or goals. Third, the description must include the investment's principal strategies (including a general description of the types of assets held by the investment), and principal risks (e.g., as required by Securities and Exchange Commission Form N-1A). Fourth, the description must include the investment's historical performance data (e.g., 1-, 5-, and 10-year returns) and, if applicable, any fixed return, annuity, guarantee, death benefit, or other ancillary features; as well as a statement indicating that an investment's past performance is not necessarily an indication of how the investment will perform in the future. Fifth, the description must include the investment's attendant fees and expenses, including: Any fees charged directly against the amount invested in connection with acquisition, sale, transfer of, or withdrawal (e.g., sales loads, sales charges, deferred sales charges, redemption fees, surrender charges, exchange fees, account fees, and purchase fees); any annual operating expenses (e.g., expense ratio); and any ongoing expenses in addition to annual operating expenses (e.g., mortality and expense fees). For purposes of these requirements to disclose an investment's objectives or goals, principal strategies and principal risks, historical performance, and fees and expenses, the Department requests comment on the extent to which these requirements should conform to the final participant-level disclosure regulation; for example, should the more specific standards for investment-related information contained in the participant-level disclosure regulation be incorporated by reference into the qualified default investment alternative regulation? The Department believes that conforming the requirements will make it easier for plan fiduciaries and administrators to comply and help to avoid confusion among participants and beneficiaries who will receive the required disclosures.

The sixth requirement will ensure that participants and beneficiaries obtain comprehensive information about TDFs that apply age or target retirement-based asset allocations, described in paragraph (e)(4)(i) of the qualified default investment alternative regulation. Specifically, to the extent the information is not already disclosed pursuant to the preceding requirements of paragraph (d)(3) of the rule, the description must satisfy three requirements. The first is an explanation of the asset allocation, how the asset allocation will change over time, and the point in time when the investment will reach its most conservative asset allocation, including a chart, table, or other graphical representation that illustrates such change in asset allocation over time and that does not obscure or impede a participant's or beneficiary's understanding of the information explained pursuant to this requirement. The Department understands that many investment issuers and service providers already include simple and straight-forward graphs, pie chart series, or other illustrations to assist investors by showing them how asset allocations in TDFs change over time. To the extent such illustrations are not already furnished to participants and beneficiaries, the Department is persuaded that any additional burden associated with preparation of a compliant illustration will prove highly beneficial to enhance participants' and beneficiaries' understanding of a TDF's asset allocation and how it will change over time.

The second requirement depends on whether the alternative is named, or otherwise described, with reference to a particular date (e.g., a target date). For example, many funds include a target retirement date in the name itself (e.g., a "2030 fund" or a "2040 fund"). In some cases the name of the alternative may not include a date, but a retirement or other target date may be referenced or implied in the description of the alternative's objectives or goals, or principal strategies or principal risks; this requirement applies to those alternatives as well. The notice must explain the age group for whom the investment is designed, the relevance of the date, and any assumptions about a participant's or beneficiary's contribution and withdrawal intentions on or after such date. The third requirement is a statement that the participant or beneficiary may lose money by investing in the qualified default investment alternative, including losses near and following retirement, and that there is no guarantee that investment in the qualified default investment alternative will provide adequate retirement income. All of the information required to be disclosed concerning TDFs and similar products is consistent with the analysis discussed in the Department's recent guidance to plan participants and expected guidance to plan fiduciaries concerning the factors that must be taken into account when selecting and monitoring, or investing in, these products. The Department is interested in comments as to whether,

---

[5] See 2008 ERISA Advisory Council Working Group Report on Hard to Value Assets and Target Date Funds, found at: http://www.dol.gov/ebsa/publications/2008ACreport1.html.

[6] See http://aging.senate.gov/record.cfm?id=308665&&; http://aging.senate.gov/hearing_detail.cfm?id=309027& and http://aging.senate.gov/hearing_detail.cfm?id=319426&.

[7] The Investor Bulletin, published May 6, 2010, is available at: http://www.dol.gov/ebsa/pdf/TDFInvestorBulletin.pdf.

[8] Commission Release Nos. 33-9126, 34-62300, IC-29301, at http://www.sec.gov/comments/s7-12-10/s71210.shtml.

[9] Consistent with the participant-level disclosure regulation, the material required by section 2550.404a-5(d)(4), which is referred to in paragraph (c)(4) of this amendment, must be furnished upon request.

[10] § 2550.404(c)-5(d)(3).

and to what extent, the final rule should include disclosure elements or concepts contained in the Commission's rulemaking.[11]

To ensure that all participants and beneficiaries in participant-directed individual account plans, not only participant and beneficiaries who are invested in a qualified default investment alternative, receive the same information about TDFs, the Department also is proposing in this Notice to include the same three disclosure requirements concerning TDFs in the participant-level disclosure regulation. Specifically, these new requirements, if adopted, will be added to paragraph § 2550.404a-5(i)(4) of the participant-level disclosure regulation, which was reserved for this purpose. To ensure consistency between these regulations, the Department expects that any changes made to the TDF disclosure requirements in response to comments on this Notice will be reflected in both the qualified default investment alternative regulation and the participant-level disclosure regulation.

Paragraph (d)(4) of the qualified default investment alternative regulation requires that the notice to participants contain a "description of the right of the participants and beneficiaries on whose behalf assets are invested in a qualified default investment alternative to direct the investment of those assets to any other investment alternative under the plan, including a description of any applicable restrictions, fees or expenses in connection with such transfer[.]"[12] In the proposal published today, this paragraph has been modified. If any such fees or restrictions are applicable, this paragraph would only require a statement that certain fees and limitations may apply in connection with such transfer. The requirement to disclose the fees and expenses themselves would be moved to paragraph (d)(3)(v), discussed above; if other limitations may apply, the notice must so state.

Finally, paragraph (d)(5) of the qualified default investment alternative regulation would be broadened to clarify that comprehensive information about the qualified default investment alternative, as well as the other investment alternatives available under the plan, is available to participants and beneficiaries. Currently, paragraph (d)(5) only requires "[a]n explanation of where the participants and beneficiaries can obtain investment information concerning the other investment alternatives available under the plan."[13] As amended by this proposal, this paragraph requires an explanation of where the participants and beneficiaries can obtain additional investment information concerning *the qualified default investment alternative and the other* investment alternatives available under the plan. The Department included this modification to conform to the participant-level disclosure regulation. Specifically, the Department expects that paragraph (d)(5), if adopted in final form, will ensure that defaulted participants and beneficiaries know where to obtain any additional investment information required to be disclosed pursuant to the final participant-level disclosure regulation concerning all of the plan's investment alternatives, including qualified default investment alternatives.

C. Furnishing Required Disclosures

In conjunction with the adoption of the final participant-level disclosure regulation, § 2550.404a-5 (75 FR 64910, October 20, 2010), the Department explained in the Supplementary Information that, given the differing views on the use of and standards for electronic disclosure, it would be undertaking a review of the safe harbor applicable to the use of electronic media for furnishing information to plan participants and beneficiaries (29 CFR 2520.104b-1(c)). The Department further indicated that, in the very near future, it will be publishing a **Federal Register** notice requesting public comments, views, and data relating to the electronic distribution of plan information to plan participants and beneficiaries. The Department also noted that, pending the completion of its review and the issuance of further guidance, the general disclosure regulation at 29 CFR 2520.104b-1 applies to material furnished under the participant-level disclosure regulation, including the safe harbor for electronic disclosures at paragraph (c) of the general disclosure regulation. The Department anticipates that resolution of the issues involved with the electronic disclosure of plan information will directly affect the manner in which materials required by the amendments contained in this notice may be furnished to participants and beneficiaries. Accordingly, interested persons are en-

couraged to participate in the Department's forthcoming solicitation of comments on the use of electronic media for furnishing plan information.

D. Effective Date

The Department proposes that the amendments to regulation sections 2550.404a-5 and 2550.404c-5 contained in this notice will be effective 90 days after publication of the final rule in the **Federal Register**. The Department invites comment on whether the final rule should be effective on a different date.

E. Regulatory Impact Analysis

Executive Order 12866 Statement

Under Executive Order 12866, the Department must determine whether a regulatory action is "significant" and therefore subject to the requirements of the Executive Order and subject to review by the Office of Management and Budget (OMB). Under section 3(f) of the Executive Order, a "significant regulatory action" is an action that is likely to result in a rule (1) Having an effect on the economy of $100 million or more in any one year, or adversely and materially affecting a sector of the economy, productivity, competition, jobs, the environment, public health or safety, or State, local or tribal governments or communities (also referred to as "economically significant"); (2) creating serious inconsistency or otherwise interfering with an action taken or planned by another agency; (3) materially altering the budgetary impacts of entitlement grants, user fees, or loan programs or the rights and obligations of recipients thereof; or (4) raising novel legal or policy issues arising out of legal mandates, the President's priorities, or the principles set forth in the Executive Order. Although the Department believes that this regulatory action is not economically significant within the meaning of section 3(f)(1) of the Executive Order, the action has been determined to be significant within the meaning of section 3(f)(4) of the Executive Order, and accordingly, OMB has reviewed this notice of proposed rulemaking pursuant to the Executive Order. The Department provides the following assessment of the potential costs and benefits associated with the proposed regulation below.

Need for Regulatory Action

As discussed earlier in this preamble, on October 24, 2007, the Department published a final regulation implementing the provisions of section 404(c)(5) of ERISA.[14] A fiduciary of a plan that complies with the final regulation, as amended, will not be liable for any loss, or by reason of any breach, that is the direct and necessary result of investing all or a part of a participant's or beneficiary's account in a qualified default investment alternative. As noted in the regulation, this relief does not apply to fiduciary duties or liability related to the selection or monitoring of particular qualified default investment alternatives. The regulation describes the types of investments that qualify as default investment alternatives under section 404(c)(5) of ERISA and the other requirements that must be satisfied in order for a fiduciary to obtain the relief from liability described above.

As discussed earlier, the Department's final qualified default investment alternative regulation includes TDFs as one of the permissible categories of investment funds or products that may be used as a qualified default investment alternative, if all of the requirements of the final rule have been satisfied. Since the issuance of the Department's final qualified default investment alternative regulation, plans have increased their use of TDFs as an investment alternative.[15] At the end of the first quarter of 2009, the amount of employer sponsored defined contribution plan assets invested in TDFs totaled $145 billion, compared to $37 billion in 2003.[16] A recent survey found that nearly 60 percent of plans have made TDFs the qualified default investment alternative for participants that do not provide investment direction and nearly 60 percent of participant-directed individual account plans, such as 401(k) plans, offer TDFs as an investment alternative.[17]

The financial market downturn that started in 2008 increased volatility and lowered returns of TDFs.[18] Many TDFs designed for people recently nearing or entering retirement suffered large losses. For

---

[11] See footnote 8, above.

[12] § 2550.404(c)-5(d)(4).

[13] § 2550.404(c)-5(d)(5).

[14] 72 FR 60452 (Oct. 24, 2007). Correcting amendments to the final regulation were published on April 30, 2008 (73 FR 23349).

[15] Donahue, Andrew. Testimony Concerning Target Date Funds. *Before the United States Senate Special Committee on Aging.* October 28, 2009.

[16] Borzi, Phyllis. Testimony of Phyllis C. Borzi. *Before the United States Senate Special Committee on Aging.* October 28, 2009.

[17] Profit Sharing/401k Council of America, 52nd Annual Survey of Profit Sharing and 401(k) plans, for plan year 2008.

[18] Deloitte Financial Advisory Services LLP, *Target Date Funds: Historical Volatility/Return Profiles,* unpublished presentation to the U.S. Department of Labor, Employee Benefits Security Administration (Sept. 30, 2009). In particular, the research found that the 1-year volatility was generally greater than the 3-year volatility and the 1-year returns were lower than the 3-year returns. Deloitte also found that funds with target date 2010 were more volatile in 2008 than they were in 2007. In addition, Deloitte reports that volatility among 2010 TDFs correlated with the fraction of the funds that are invested in stock and small 2010 funds are more heterogeneous in rates of return and in volatility than large funds.

example, on average, participants invested in TDFs dated 2010 and 2015 lost about a quarter of their value in 2008. Many of these funds typically held about half of the holdings in stocks, following glide paths that did not significantly reduce that percentage for 5 years or more after the average investor retired.[19] The Background discussion, above, summarizes responses to this development, for example from the U.S. Senate Special Committee on Aging, and activities undertaken by the Department and the Securities and Exchange Commission since then.

Experts within the investment community agree that TDF disclosures to participants and beneficiaries need to be improved. For example, the Investment Company Institute (ICI) Target Date Fund Disclosure Working Group reviewed existing TDF disclosures and in a June 2009 Report, recommended that TDFs display prominently five key pieces of information to help enhance investors' understanding such as the relevance of the target date used in a fund's name, the assumptions the fund makes regarding the investor's withdrawal intentions at and after the target date, the age group for whom the fund is designed, an illustration of the glide path that the TDF follows to reduce its equity exposure and become more conservative over time, and a statement that the risks associated with a TDF include the risk of loss near, at, or after the target date and that there is no guarantee that the fund will provide adequate income at and through the investor's retirement.[20]

Based on the foregoing, the Department is proposing to amend its final qualified default investment alternative and participant-level disclosure regulations to improve the information that is disclosed to participants and beneficiaries regarding TDFs.

Affected Entities

Based on the latest available information, the Department estimates that there are approximately 483,000 participant-directed individual account plans.[21] The Department's proposed amendment to its final qualified default investment alternative rule would affect the approximately 114,000 participant-directed individual account plans that use TDFs as their qualified default investment alternative and the proposed amendment to its participant-level disclosure final rule would affect 278,000 participant-directed individual account plans that offer TDFs as an investment alternative.[22] The Department also estimates that 43.6 million participants and beneficiaries are covered by plans using TDFs as an investment alternative.

Benefits

The Department expects that the enhanced disclosures required by the proposed regulation would benefit participants and beneficiaries by providing them with critical information they need to evaluate the quality of TDFs and how specific TDFs match their risk profile. This should lead to improved investment results and retirement planning decisions. The TDF disclosures would foster a better understanding of how TDFs operate and the glide path that is associated with each fund. The Department believes that the disclosures under this proposed regulation, combined with the greater transparency required by the Department's participant-level disclosure regulation, would allow participants and beneficiaries to determine whether the efficient way in which TDFs allow them to invest in a mix of asset classes and rebalance their asset allocation periodically is worth the price differential they generally pay for such funds.[23]

Although the Department is unable to quantify the benefits associated with the proposed regulation, it is confident that the benefits justify their costs.

Costs

The Department estimates that the proposed regulation would result in 66.2 million TDF disclosures being distributed. The associated total hour burden for affected plans is estimated to be 29,000 hours with an equivalent cost of $1.8 million annually. The estimated cost burden for plans to distribute the notices is $4.1 million annually. Because these costs are associated with information collection requests covered by

the Paperwork Reduction Act, the data and methodology used in developing the cost estimates are more fully discussed in the Paperwork Reduction Act section, below.

Paperwork Reduction Act

As part of its continuing effort to reduce paperwork and respondent burden, the Department of Labor conducts a preclearance consultation program to provide the general public and federal agencies with an opportunity to comment on proposed and continuing collections of information in accordance with the Paperwork Reduction Act of 1995 (PRA 95) (44 U.S.C. 3506(c)(2)(A)). This helps to ensure that requested data can be provided in the desired format, reporting burden (time and financial resources) is minimized, collection instruments are clearly understood, and the impact of collection requirements on respondents can be properly assessed.

Currently, EBSA is soliciting comments concerning the information collection request (ICR) included in the Proposed Rule on the Fiduciary Requirements for Disclosure and Default Investment Alternatives Under Participant Directed Individual Account Plans. A copy of the ICR may be obtained by contacting the PRA addressee shown below.

The Department has submitted a copy of the proposed rule to OMB in accordance with 44 U.S.C. 3507(d) for review of its information collections. The Department and OMB are particularly interested in comments that:

• Evaluate whether the collection of information is necessary for the proper performance of the functions of the agency, including whether the information will have practical utility;

• Evaluate the accuracy of the agency's estimate of the burden of the collection of information, including the validity of the methodology and assumptions used;

• Enhance the quality, utility, and clarity of the information to be collected; and

• Minimize the burden of the collection of information on those who are to respond, including through the use of appropriate automated, electronic, mechanical, or other technological collection techniques or other forms of information technology, *e.g.,* permitting electronic submission of responses.

Comments should be sent to the Office of Information and Regulatory Affairs, Office of Management and Budget, Room 10235, New Executive Office Building, Washington, DC 20503; Attention: Desk Officer for the Employee Benefits Security Administration. OMB requests that comments be received within 30 days of publication of the proposed rule to ensure their consideration.

PRA Addressee: Address requests for copies of the ICR to G. Christopher Cosby, Office of Policy and Research, U.S. Department of Labor, Employee Benefits Security Administration, 200 Constitution Avenue, NW., Room N-5718, Washington, DC 20210.

Telephone (202) 693-8410; Fax: (202) 219-5333. These are not toll-free numbers. ICRs submitted to OMB also are available at *http://www.RegInfo.gov.*

(a) Proposed Amendment to Qualified Default Investment Alternative Regulation

Under the proposed amendment to paragraph (d)(3) of the Department's qualified default investment alternative regulation, the notice provided to participants and beneficiaries that use TDFs as a qualified default investment alternative (the QDIA notice) would be required to contain comprehensive information about TDFs. This information is described in detail earlier in this preamble, along with other changes to the information required to be disclosed in the QDIA notice that do not relate specifically to TDFs.

The Department understands that many investment issuers and service providers currently furnish straight-forward graphs, pie chart series, and other illustrations to demonstrate to investors how asset

---

[19] Borzi, Phyllis. Testimony of Phyllis C. Borzi. Before the United States Senate Special Committee on Aging. October 28, 2009.

[20] See *e.g.* Principles to Enhance Understanding of Target Date Funds: Recommended by the ICI Target Date Fund Disclosure Working Group. June 18, 2009. *http://www.ici.org/pdf/ppr_09_principles.pdf.*

In order to address some of the deficiencies in communication relating to TDFs, the Investment Company Institute made a series of recommendations for disclosure, many of which overlap with the requirements contained in these proposed regulations. See *e.g.* Charlson, Josh et al. Target Date Series Research Paper: 2010 Industry Survey, *Morningstar,* 2010. *http://corporate.morningstar.com/US/documents/MethodologyDocuments/MethodologyPapers/TargetDateFundSurvey_2010.pdf.*

[21] Based on 2007 Form 5500 filings.

[22] The Department's estimate is based on the Profit Sharing/401k Council of America, 52nd Annual Survey of Profit Sharing and 401(k) plans, for plan year 2008. This survey finds that 57.7 percent of participant-directed individual account plans offer TDFs as an investment option (483,000 * .577 = 278,691). It also finds that 39.6 percent of participant-directed individual account plans have automatic enrollment and that 59.7 percent of those plans use TDFs as the QDIA (483,000 * .396 * .597 = 114,187).

[23] Collins, Margaret. Target-Date Funds May Miss Mark for Unsavvy Savers. Bloomberg *http://www.bloomberg.com/apps/news?pid=20603037&sid=aSGY6tmw7IXs.* The author finds that the median fee for TDFs is approximately .85 (depending on the age of the saver). However, some expense ratios are as low as .19 percent, while others are as high as 1.50 percent.

allocations in TDFs change over time and other information that would be required to be disclosed in the QDIA notice by the proposed regulation. Therefore, the burden that would be imposed by this proposed regulation stems primarily from incorporating the more comprehensive TDF disclosure into the QDIA notice. The Department invites comments regarding this assumption.

The Department believes that a financial professional should be able to incorporate the TDF disclosures into the QDIA notice, on average, in approximately 15 minutes at a labor rate of approximately $63 per hour.[24] The Department estimates that the hour burden imposed on the approximately 114,000 affected plans would be 28,520 hours (114,079 plans * 0.25 hours) with an equivalent cost of $1.79 million (114,079 plans * .25 hours per plan * $62.81/hour).

The Department estimates that the disclosure would add two pages to the QDIA notice, and that an estimated 18.4 million participants would be required to receive the disclosures.[25] The Department expects that 38 percent of participants would receive the disclosure by electronic means, leaving an estimated 11.4 million paper disclosures that would be sent via mail. The Department estimates that 6.8 percent of participants are new to a plan[26] in a given year; therefore, 780,000[27] participants generally would be required to receive the QDIA notice at least 30 days in advance of the date of plan eligibility. No mailing costs are included in the cost estimates, because the TDF disclosure would be incorporated into the QDIA notice. In total, 12.2 million paper disclosures would be required. Assuming paper costs of $.05 per page, the Department estimates that the cost burden associated with this proposed regulation's amendment to the QDIA notice would be $1.2 million.

(b) Proposed Amendment to Participant-Level Disclosure Regulation

The proposed amendment to the Department's participant-level disclosure regulation would require participant-directed individual account plans that offer TDFs as a designated investment alternative to include the TDF disclosures as an appendix to the participant-level disclosures required by 29 CFR 2550.404a-5(d)(1) and (d)(2).

The Department assumes that plans would incur a de minimis cost to prepare the appendix, because, as stated above, investment issuers and service providers already have the TDF information readily available to provide to plans. No additional mailing costs are expected, because the TDF disclosures would be attached as an appendix to, and distributed with, the participant-level disclosure. Thus, the only anticipated additional costs would pertain to the additional paper costs associated with including the additional TDF appendix with the participant-level disclosure.

The TDF appendix is expected, on average, to add two pages to the participant-level disclosure. As discussed above, the Department estimates that 43.6 million participants are covered by participant-directed individual account plans that offer TDFs as an investment alternative.[28] The Department estimates that 6.8 percent of participants are new to a plan in a given year; therefore, 2.96 million additional disclosures would be required[29] resulting in a total of 46.5 million TDF fund appendices being distributed annually. The Department estimates that 38 percent of the disclosures would be distributed electronically at a de minimis cost, leaving 28.8 million paper disclosures to be distributed via mail. Assuming paper costs of $0.10 per participant ($.05 per page), the proposed amendment to the participant-level disclosure regulation would impose an additional cost of approximately $2.9 million to the participant-level disclosure.

(c) Summary

Overall, the proposed amendments to the qualified default investment alternative and participant-level disclosure regulations would result in approximately 66.2 million TDF disclosures being distributed. The total hour burden associated with the additional disclosures would be an estimated 29,000 hours with an equivalent cost of $1.8 million (all allocated to the qualified default investment alternative regulation). The Department estimates that the total cost burden for the disclosures

would be $4.1 million ($1,217,000 (qualified default investment alternative); $2,884,000 (participant-level disclosure)).

These paperwork burden estimates are summarized as follows:

Type of Review: Revised collections.

Agency: Employee Benefits Security Administration, Department of Labor.

Title: Default Investment Alternatives Under Participant Directed Individual Account Plans (QDIA Regulation Amendment) and Fiduciary Requirements for Disclosure in Participant-Directed Individual Account Plans (Participant-Level Disclosure Regulation Amendment).

OMB Control Number: 1210-0132; 1210-0090.

Affected Public: Business or other for-profit; not-for-profit institutions.

Respondents: 114,000 (QDIA Regulation Amendment); 278,000 (Participant-Level Disclosure Amendment).

Responses: 66,157,539 (19,636,964 QDIA Regulation Amendment; 46,520,575 Participant-Level Disclosure Regulation Amendment).

Frequency of Response: Annually.

Estimated Total Annual Burden Hours: 29,000 hours (first year and subsequent years; all allocated to QDIA Regulation Amendment).

Estimated Total Annual Burden Cost: $4,102,000 (first year and subsequent years); $1,217,500 (QDIA Regulation Amendment); $2,884,500 (Participant-Level Disclosure Regulation Amendment).

Regulatory Flexibility Act

The Regulatory Flexibility Act (5 U.S.C. 601 *et seq.*) (RFA) imposes certain requirements with respect to Federal rules that are subject to the notice and comment requirements of section 553(b) of the Administrative Procedure Act (5 U.S.C. 551 *et seq.*) and which are likely to have a significant economic impact on a substantial number of small entities. Unless the head of an agency certifies that a proposed rule is not likely to have a significant economic impact on a substantial number of small entities, section 603 of the RFA requires that the agency present an initial regulatory flexibility analysis at the time of the publication of the notice of proposed rulemaking describing the impact of the rule on small entities and seeking public comment on such impact.

For purposes of the RFA, the Department continues to consider a small entity to be an employee benefit plan with fewer than 100 participants.[30] Further, while some large employers may have small plans, in general small employers maintain most small plans. Thus, the Department believes that assessing the impact of this proposed rule on small plans is an appropriate substitute for evaluating the effect on small entities. The definition of small entity considered appropriate for this purpose differs, however, from a definition of small business that is based on size standards promulgated by the Small Business Administration (SBA) (13 CFR 121.201) pursuant to the Small Business Act (15 U.S.C. 631 *et seq.*). The Department therefore requests comments on the appropriateness of the size standard used in evaluating the impact of this proposed rule on small entities.

The Department certifies, as required by the RFA, that while the proposed regulation would impact a substantial number of small entities, the economic impact of the proposed rule would not be significant. The Department estimates that the cost per plan to prepare the notice would be less than $20, because much of the required information is expected to be readily available from service providers. Moreover, the anticipated cost per participant for plans to send the qualified default investment alternative and participant-level fee TDF disclosures are estimated to be $0.20 annually.

Based on industry survey data, the Department believes that small plans would be less likely to be affected by this regulation, because while small plans are slightly more likely to be participant-directed, they are less likely to default participants into TDFs or provide access to such funds as an investment alternative. The survey showed that 56.3 percent of plans with 5,000 or more participants have automatic enrollment compared to just 15.8 percent of plans with 1-49 partici-

---

[24] EBSA estimates of labor rates include wages, other benefits, and overhead based on the National Occupational Employment Survey (May 2008, Bureau of Labor Statistics) and the Employment Cost Index (June 2009, Bureau of Labor Statistics).

[25] The Department estimate of 18.4 million participants is derived as follows: 76.6 percent of eligible workers participate in employer-sponsored pension plans. Based on 2007 Form 5500 data, the Department estimates that 59.6 million individuals are active participants in participant-directed individual account plans. Using those two numbers, the Department estimates that 77.8 million workers are eligible to participate in participant-directed individual account plans (77.8 million * .766 = 59.6 million). The Department estimates that 39.6 percent of plans have automatic enrollment, and 59.7 percent of these plans use TDFs as their QDIA (77.8 million*.396 * .597=18.4 million).

[26] These individuals receive the QDIA notice twice in their first year of participation: Once when they are eligible to participate in the plan and once when all participants receive the plan's annual QDIA notice.

[27] 18.4 million * .062 * .068=.78 million (rounded).

[28] The Department's estimate is based on the Profit Sharing/401k Council of America, 52nd Annual Survey of Profit Sharing and 401(k) plans, for plan year 2008.

[29] 43.6 million * .068 = 2.96 million.

[30] The basis for this definition is found in section 104(a)(2) of the Act, which permits the Secretary of Labor to prescribe simplified annual reports for pension plans that cover fewer than 100 participants..

pants, and that while 64 percent of participant-directed plans with more than 5,000 participants offer TDFs as an investment option, only 47.9 percent of such plans with 1-49 participants offer TDFs as an investment option.[31] The burden that would be imposed by the proposed regulation on small plans also would be mitigated by the fact that most of the information required for the TDF disclosures is expected to be readily available from service providers.

Congressional Review Act

The proposed rule is subject to the Congressional Review Act provisions of the Small Business Regulatory Enforcement Fairness Act of 1996 (5 U.S.C. 801 *et seq.*) and, if finalized, will be transmitted to Congress and the Comptroller General for review. The proposed rule is not a "major rule" as that term is defined in 5 U.S.C. 804, because it is not likely to result in (1) An annual effect on the economy of $100 million or more; (2) a major increase in costs or prices for consumers, individual industries, or Federal, State, or local government agencies, or geographic regions; or (3) significant adverse effects on competition, employment, investment, productivity, innovation, or on the ability of United States-based enterprises to compete with foreign-based enterprises in domestic and export markets.

Unfunded Mandates Reform Act

For purposes of the Unfunded Mandates Reform Act of 1995 (Pub. L. 104-4), as well as Executive Order 12875, the proposed rule does not include any Federal mandate that may result in expenditures by State, local, or tribal governments in the aggregate of more than $100 million, adjusted for inflation, or increase expenditures by the private sector of more than $100 million, adjusted for inflation.

Federalism Statement

Executive Order 13132 (August 4, 1999) outlines fundamental principles of federalism, and requires the adherence to specific criteria by Federal agencies in the process of their formulation and implementation of policies that have substantial direct effects on the States, the relationship between the national government and States, or on the distribution of power and responsibilities among the various levels of government. The proposed regulation does not have federalism implications because it has no substantial direct effect on the States, on the relationship between the national government and the States, or on the distribution of power and responsibilities among the various levels of government. Section 514 of ERISA provides, with certain exceptions specifically enumerated, that the provisions of Titles I and IV of ERISA supersede any and all laws of the States as they relate to any employee benefit plan covered under ERISA. The requirements that would be implemented in the proposed rule do not alter the fundamental reporting and disclosure requirements of the statute with respect to employee benefit plans, and as such have no implications for the States or the relationship or distribution of power between the national government and the States.

List of Subjects in 29 CFR Part 2550

Employee benefit plans, Exemptions, Fiduciaries, Investments, Pensions, Prohibited transactions, Real estate, Securities, Surety bonds, Trusts and Trustees.

For the reasons set forth in the preamble, the Department of Labor proposes to amend 29 CFR part 2550 as follows:

PART 2550—RULES AND REGULATIONS FOR FIDUCIARY RESPONSIBILITY

1. The authority citation for part 2550 is revised to read as follows:

Authority: 29 U.S.C. 1135 and Secretary of Labor's Order No. 6-2009, 74 FR 21524 (May 7, 2009). Sec. 2550.401c-1 also issued under 29 U.S.C. 1101. Sec. 2550.404a-1 also issued under sec. 657, Pub. L. 107-16, 115 Stat. 38. Sections 2550.404c-1 and 2550.404c-5 also issued under 29 U.S.C. 1104. Sec. 2550.408b-1 also issued under 29 U.S.C. 1108(b)(1) and sec. 102, Reorganization Plan No. 4 of 1978, 5 U.S.C. App. 1. Sec. 2550.408b-19 also issued under sec. 611, Pub. L. 109-280, 120 Stat. 780, 972, and sec. 102, Reorganization Plan No. 4 of 1978, 5 U.S.C. App. 1. Sec. 2550.412-1 also issued under 29 U.S.C. 1112.

2. Amend § 2550.404a-5 by revising paragraph (i)(4) to read as follows:

§ 2550.404a-5 Fiduciary requirements for disclosure in participant-directed individual account plans.

* * * * *

(i) * * *

(4) *Target date or similar funds.* In the case of a designated investment alternative that is described in 29 CFR 2550.404c-5(e)(4)(1) (*e.g.,* "life-cycle" or "target date" funds) the plan administrator shall, in addition to the information required by paragraph (d)(1) and, if applicable, paragraph (i) of this section, furnish to each participant or beneficiary the following information as an appendix or appendices to the chart or similar document intended to satisfy paragraph (d)(2) of this section—

(i) An explanation of the alternative's asset allocation, how the asset allocation will change over time, and the point in time when the alternative will reach its most conservative asset allocation; including a chart, table, or other graphical representation that illustrates such change in asset allocation over time and that does not obscure or impede a participant's or beneficiary's understanding of the information explained pursuant to this paragraph (i)(4)(i);

(ii) If the alternative is named, or otherwise described, with reference to a particular date (*e.g.,* a target date), an explanation of the age group for whom the alternative is designed, the relevance of the date, and any assumptions about a participant's or beneficiary's contribution and withdrawal intentions on or after such date; and

(iii) A statement that the participant or beneficiary may lose money by investing in the alternative, including losses near and following retirement, and that there is no guarantee that the alternative will provide adequate retirement income.

* * * * *

3. Amend § 2550.404c-5 by revising paragraphs (c)(4), (d)(3), (d)(4), and (d)(5) to read as follows:

§ 2550.404c-5 Fiduciary relief for investments in qualified default investment alternatives.

* * * * *

(c) * * *

(4) A fiduciary provides to a participant or beneficiary the material set forth in 29 CFR 2550.404a-5(d)(3) and (4) relating to a participant's or beneficiary's investment in a qualified default investment alternative;

* * * * *

(d) * * *

(3) A description of the qualified default investment alternative, including:

(i) The name of the investment's issuer;

(ii) The investment's objectives or goals;

(iii) The investment's principal strategies (including a general description of the types of assets held by the investment) and principal risks;

(iv) The investment's historical performance data and a statement indicating that an investment's past performance is not necessarily an indication of how the investment will perform in the future; and, if applicable, a description of any fixed return, annuity, guarantee, death benefit, or other ancillary features;

(v) The investment's attendant fees and expenses, including:

(A) Any fees charged directly against the amount invested in connection with acquisition, sale, transfer of, or withdrawal (*e.g.,* commissions, sales loads, sales charges, deferred sales charges, redemption fees, surrender charges, exchange fees, account fees, and purchase fees);

(B) Any annual operating expenses (*e.g.,* expense ratio); and

(C) Any ongoing expenses in addition to annual operating expenses (*e.g.,* mortality and expense fees); and

(vi) For an investment fund product or model portfolio intended to satisfy paragraph (e)(4)(i) of this section, and to the extent not already disclosed pursuant to this paragraph (d)(3):

(A) An explanation of the asset allocation, how the asset allocation will change over time, and the point in time when the qualified default

---

[31] Profit Sharing/401k Council of America, 52nd Annual Survey of Profit Sharing and 401(k) Plans, for plan year 2008.

investment alternative will reach its most conservative asset allocation; including a chart, table, or other graphical representation that illustrates such change in asset allocation over time and that does not obscure or impede a participant's or beneficiary's understanding of the information explained pursuant to this paragraph (d)(3)(vi)(A);

(B) If the qualified default investment alternative is named, or otherwise described, with reference to a particular date (*e.g.,* a target date), an explanation of the age group for whom the investment is designed, the relevance of the date, and any assumptions about a participant's or beneficiary's contribution and withdrawal intentions on or after such date; and

(C) If applicable, a statement that the participant or beneficiary may lose money by investing in the qualified default investment alternative, including losses near and following retirement, and that there is no guarantee that the investment will provide adequate retirement income.

(4) A description of the right of the participants and beneficiaries on whose behalf assets are invested in a qualified default investment alternative to direct the investment of those assets to any other investment alternative under the plan and, if applicable, a statement that certain fees and limitations may apply in connection with such transfer; and

(5) An explanation of where the participants and beneficiaries can obtain additional investment information concerning the qualified default investment alternative and the other investment alternatives available under the plan.

* * * * *

Signed at Washington, DC, this 16th day of November, 2010.

Phyllis C. Borzi

Assistant Secretary, Employee Benefits Security Administration, Department of Labor.

[FR Doc. 2010-29509 Filed 11-29-10; 8:45 am]

BILLING CODE 4510-29-P

¶ 20,538B

Pension Benefit Guaranty Corporation (PBGC): Proposed rule: Guaranteed benefits: Unpredictable contingent event benefits Pension Protection Act of 2006 (PPA).—The Pension Benefit Guaranty Corporation (PBGC) has issued proposed amendments to its regulations on Benefits Payable in Terminated Single-Employer Plans. The proposed regulations provide guidance on the phase-in period for the guarantee of benefits that are contingent upon the occurrence of an "unpredictable contingent event." The proposed rules would implement changes made by the Pension Protection Act of 2006 (PPA; P.L. 109-280). Comments are due by May 10, 2011.

The proposed regulations, which were published in the Federal Register on March 11, 2011 (76 FR 13304), were reproduced below. The final regulations were published in the Federal Register on May 6, 2014 (79 FR 25667). The preamble to the final regulations is at ¶ 24,320. The final regulations are reproduced at ¶ 15,421A, ¶ 15,422C, ¶ 15,422F, ¶ 15,422G, and ¶ 15,423A.

¶ 20,538C

Employee Benefits Security Administration (EBSA): Proposed regulations: Disclosure of plan fees: Applicability dates.—The Employee Benefits Security Administration (EBSA) has issued proposed regulations that would extend and align the applicability dates for its retirement plan fee disclosure rules.

Interim final regulations, issued on July 16, 2010, require plan service providers to disclose comprehensive information about their fees and potential conflicts of interest to plan fiduciaries (see ¶ 24,295). The requirements are scheduled to apply to plan contracts or arrangements for services in existence on or after July 16, 2011. The proposed regulations would extend deadline to January 1, 2012. Final regulations issued on October 20, 2010, require that employers disclose information about plan and investment costs to employees who direct their own investments (see ¶ 24,298). The regulations apply for plan years beginning on or after November 1, 2011, with a 60-day transition provision. The proposed rules would amend the regulations' transitional rule so that employers would have up to 120 days to furnish initial disclosures to workers.

The proposed regulations, which were published in the Federal Register on June 1, 2011 (76 FR 31544), were reproduced below. The final regulations were published in the Federal Register on July 19, 2011 (76 FR 42539). The preamble to the final regulations is at ¶ 24,304. The final regulations are reproduced at ¶ 14,742D and ¶ 14,782.

¶ 20,538C-5

Employee Benefits Security Administration (EBSA): Proposed rule: Group health plans: Health insurance coverage: Summary of benefits and coverage: Uniform glossary: Disclosure requirements.—The EBSA, IRS, and Department of Health and Human Services have issued proposed amendments that implement disclosure requirements under the Patient Protection and Affordable Care Act (PPACA) concerning the provision of a summary of benefits and coverage and a uniform glossary for group health plans and health insurance coverage in the group and individual markets. The disclosures are intended to help plans and individuals better understand their health coverage and other coverage options. The Agencies also have issued templates, instructions, and sample language for making the disclosures, and a uniform glossary.

The proposed regulations, which were published in the Federal Register on August 22, 2007 (76 FR 52442), and the templates, instructions, sample language, and glossary, which were published in the Federal Register August 22, 2011 (76 FR 52475), are reproduced at CCH Pension Plan Guide ¶ 20,262Y.

The regulations were finalized on February 14, 2012 (77 FR 8668). The preamble to the final regulations is at ¶ 23,282. The final regulations are at ¶ 15,050R-50RR. As to the templates, instructions, sample language, and glossary, the Agencies issued a separate document, Guidance for Compliance and Notice of Availability of Templates, Instructions, and Related Materials, explaining where to find the materials (77 FR 8706, February 14, 2012).

¶ 20,538D

Pension Benefit Guaranty Corporation (PBGC): Proposed rule: Hybrid plans: Benefit determinations: Plan valuations: Pension Protection Act of 2006 (PPA).—The Pension Benefit Guaranty Corporation (PBGC) has issued proposed regulations implementing provisions of the Pension Protection Act of 2006 (PPA; P.L. 109-280) that change the rules for determining benefits upon the termination of a hybrid plan, such as a cash balance plan. The proposed regulations would amend the PBGC's regulations to conform the rules for determining allocations of assets and the amount of benefits payable under ERISA Title IV to reflect the PPA changes in the benefit determination rules for hybrid plans. The proposed regulations would also implement a PPA change for determining the present value of an accrued benefit under a hybrid plan and would provide guidance on benefits payable under a hybrid plan that terminates in a standard termination.

The proposed regulations, which were published in the Federal Register on October 31, 2011 (76 FR 67105), are reproduced below.

[Billing Code 7709-01-P]

Pension Benefit Guaranty Corporation

29 CFR Parts 4001, 4022, 4041, and 4044

RIN 1212-AB17

Cash Balance Plans; Benefit Determinations and Plan Valuations for Statutory Hybrid Plans; Pension Protection Act of 2006

AGENCY: Pension Benefit Guaranty Corporation

Action: Proposed rule

SUMMARY: This proposed rule would implement provisions of the Pension Protection Act of 2006 (PPA 2006) that change the rules for determining benefits upon the termination of a statutory hybrid plan, such as a cash balance plan. PPA 2006 provides that, when such a plan terminates, a variable rate used under the plan to determine accrued benefits will be equal to the average of the rates of interest used under the plan during the five-year period ending on the termination date. Further, the amount of the benefit payable in the form of an annuity payable at normal retirement age will be determined using the interest rate and mortality table specified under the plan for that purpose as of the termination date (or an average interest rate if the plan rate is a variable rate). For a plan terminated and trusteed by PBGC, the proposed rule would amend PBGC's regulations to conform the rules for determining the allocation of assets and the amount of benefits payable under Title IV of ERISA to the PPA 2006 changes in the benefit determination rules for statutory hybrid plans. The proposed rule would also implement a PPA 2006 change for determining the present value of the accrued benefit under a statutory hybrid plan. Finally, the proposed rule would provide guidance on benefits payable under a statutory hybrid plan that terminates in a standard termination.

DATES: Comments must be submitted on or before [insert date 60 days after publication in the Federal Register].

ADDRESSES: Comments, identified by Regulatory Information Number (RIN 1212-AB17) may be submitted by any of the following methods

- Federal eRulemaking Portal: *http://www.regulations.gov*. Follow the web site instructions for submitting comments.

- E-mail: *reg.comments@pbgc.gov*.

- Fax: 202-326-4224.

- Mail or Hand Delivery: Legislative and Regulatory Department, Pension Benefit

Guaranty Corporation, 1200 K Street N.W., Washington, DC 20005-4026. Comments received, including personal information provided, will be posted to *www.pbgc.gov*. Copies of comments may also be obtained by writing to Disclosure Division, Office of the General Counsel, Pension Benefit Guaranty Corporation, 1200 K Street, N.W., Washington, DC 20005-4026, or calling 202-326-4040 during normal business hours. (TTY and TDD users may call the Federal relay service toll free at 1-800-877-8339 and ask to be connected to 202-326-4040.)

FOR FURTHER INFORMATION CONTACT: John H. Hanley, Director, or Constance Markakis, Attorney; Legislative and Regulatory Department, Pension Benefit Guaranty Corporation, 1200 K Street N.W., Washington, DC 20005-4026; 202-326-4024. (TTY and TDD users may call the Federal relay service toll free at 1-800-877-8339 and ask to be connected to 202-326-4024.)

SUPPLEMENTARY INFORMATION:

Background

When Pension Benefit Guaranty Corporation (PBGC) becomes trustee of a plan that terminates in a distress termination under section 4041 of the Employee Retirement Income Security Act of 1974, as amended (ERISA), or an involuntary termination (one initiated by PBGC) under section 4042 of ERISA, PBGC determines the amount of the annuity benefit that will be paid to a participant or beneficiary and whether the participant or beneficiary is eligible for a de minimis lump-sum payment. Guaranteed benefit determinations are made under section 4022 of ERISA. PBGC also values the benefits payable under the plan for purposes of allocating the plan's assets to priority categories in accordance with section 4044 of ERISA, determines employer liability under sections 4062 through 4064 of ERISA, and determines the amount of any unfunded nonguaranteed benefits payable under section 4022(c) of ERISA. These benefit determinations and plan valuations are generally made as of the plan's termination date.[1]

The termination of a cash balance plan presents unique issues for PBGC.[2] In contrast to a traditional defined benefit plan, which defines a participant's benefit under the plan as an annuity commencing at normal retirement age, a cash balance plan defines a participant's benefit as the balance of a hypothetical account maintained for the participant. The balance of a participant's hypothetical account consists generally of annual pay credits (*e.g.*, a percentage of the participant's pay for the year) and annual interest credits (*i.e.*, the hypothetical earnings on the account balance) at rates specified under the plan. The plan also provides an interest rate and mortality table (or factor) used for converting the participant's hypothetical account balance into a benefit payable as an annuity. Upon the termination of a cash balance plan (or an earlier freeze), the pay credits to a participant's hypothetical account cease, but interest credits generally continue to be added to the participant's hypothetical account until the participant begins to receive benefits.

If a cash balance plan uses a fixed interest rate as of the plan's termination date to determine accrued benefits or the amount of a benefit payable in the form of an annuity payable at normal retirement age, PBGC uses the plan's fixed rate when calculating benefits for valuation and payment purposes. PBGC has encountered difficult payment and valuation issues, however, when a cash balance plan uses a variable interest rate - *e.g.*, a rate that changes annually under the plan based on changes in an underlying index plus a margin. Many plans using variable rates adopted the standard indices and associated margins set forth in IRS Notice 96-8 (1996-1 C.B. 359) - which are based on the yields on Department of the Treasury (Treasury) constant maturities of various durations - to determine the plan's interest crediting rate or annuity conversion rate.

Under PBGC's operating policy on cash balance plans (established pre-PPA 2006), when PBGC performs its plan valuation under ERISA section 4044 of ERISA (for plans that terminated before the effective date of the relevant PPA 2006 changes), it fixes the plan's variable index at the plan's termination date. To calculate the value, as of the plan's termination date, of a participant's annuity commencing at the expected retirement age, PBGC derives a fixed rate equal to the average of the annual yields for 30-year Treasury constant maturities for the month specified in the plan, decreased by the associated margin in IRS Notice 96-8 for the variable index used by the plan, and adjusted by any plan margin.[3]

Under this operating policy, however, PBGC does not derive a fixed interest rate from a variable rate to determine benefits for payment purposes. Instead, PBGC pays a participant's pension benefit using the actual interest crediting rates in effect under the plan's variable index for periods after the plan's termination date. Until a participant commences benefits, PBGC estimates annuity payments using the most recent interest rate under the variable index used by the plan to determine the participant's projected benefit. The fact that a participant's exact benefit can be determined only when the participant begins receiving benefits has frequently resulted in benefit calculations for payment purposes that vary both from previously provided estimates and from benefit calculations for valuation purposes.

PBGC pays benefits in a single installment if the lump sum value of a benefit payable by PBGC is de minimis (currently $5,000 or less). See § 4022.7(b). In the case of cash balance plans, the payment of de minimis lump sums has posed difficult issues for PBGC due to PBGC's policy of determining lump sums using a present value calculation of the participant's benefit. Cash balance plans typically pay benefits in the form of a lump sum and often pay an amount equal to the hypotheti-

---

[1] As described below, section 404 of PPA 2006 added sections 4022(g) and 4044(a)(3) of ERISA, which treat the date the sponsor's bankruptcy petition was filed as the termination date of the plan for specified purposes. These changes apply for plan terminations that occur during the bankruptcy of the plan sponsor, if the bankruptcy filing date is on or after September 16, 2006. For convenience, this preamble generally refers to the plan's termination date, although in some cases this reference will instead apply to the bankruptcy filing date.

[2] Statutory hybrid plans other than cash balance plans, such as pension equity plans, also raise unique issues. For convenience, and because cash balance plans are the most common type of underfunded statutory hybrid plan trusteed by PBGC, this preamble generally refers to cash balance plans, although the regulatory changes would apply to all statutory hybrid plans.

[3] This policy applied only for plans that used a variable interest rate based on an index specified in IRS Notice 96-8, and that used either no plan margin or a plan margin that is constant.

cal account balance.[4] In contrast, in accordance with its operating policy on cash balance plans, PBGC uses the present value methodology in § 4022.7(d) to determine the lump sum value of a benefit, and, if either the present value or the participant's hypothetical account balance (or accumulated percentage of final average compensation) as of the termination date is de minimis, PBGC generally pays the greater of the two amounts.

Pension Protection Act of 2006

In the Pension Protection Act of 2006, Pub. L. 109-280 (PPA 2006), which became law on August 17, 2006, Congress sought to address, among other things, the problems encountered by terminating plans that use a variable interest rate. Under sections 701(a)(1) and 701(b)(1) of PPA 2006, which added section 411(b)(5)(B)(vi) of the Internal Revenue Code (Code) and section 204(b)(5)(B)(vi) of ERISA, an applicable defined benefit plan must include the following provisions that would apply upon termination of the plan:

- If the interest crediting rate (or equivalent amount) is a variable rate, the rate of interest used to determine accrued benefits under the plan will equal the average of the rates of interest used under the plan during the five-year period ending on the termination date.

- The interest rate and mortality table used to determine the amount of any benefit under the plan payable in the form of an annuity payable at normal retirement age is the rate and table specified under the plan for such purpose as of the termination date. If the interest rate is a variable rate, the rate used must be the average of the rates used under the plan during the five-year period ending on the termination date.

This change was intended to facilitate the calculation of benefits and provide participants with greater certainty about their benefit amounts when a plan terminates. This change is part of a more general interest rate requirement imposed by sections 701(a)(1) and 701(b)(1) of PPA 2006, which treats an applicable defined benefit plan as failing to meet accrual requirements related to age if the terms of the plan provide for an interest credit (or an equivalent amount) for any plan year that is greater than a market rate of return.

Sections 701(a)(2) and 701(b)(2) of PPA 2006 also create special rules for computing benefits under an applicable defined benefit plan by reference to the hypothetical account balance. Under new sections 411(a)(13)(A) of the Code and 203(f)(1) of ERISA, a plan is not treated as failing to meet the present value requirements of sections 417(e) of the Code or 205(g) of ERISA (and certain other vesting and accrued benefit rules) if the present value of the accrued benefit of any participant is equal to the amount expressed as the balance in the hypothetical account or as an accumulated percentage of the participant's final average compensation.

New sections 411(a)(13)(C) of the Code and 203(f)(3) of ERISA define an "applicable defined benefit plan" as a defined benefit plan under which the accrued benefit (or any portion thereof) for a participant is calculated as the balance of a hypothetical account maintained for the participant or as an accumulated percentage of the participant's final average compensation. The term also describes any plan that has an effect similar to an applicable defined benefit plan under regulations issued by Treasury.

The changes to the plan termination requirements made by sections 701(a)(1) and 701(b)(1) of PPA 2006 are effective for years beginning after December 31, 2007, unless the plan sponsor elects the earlier application of such requirements for any period after June 29, 2005.[5] A special rule for collectively bargained plans provides a delayed effective date.[6] The changes to the present value rules made by sections 701(a)(2) and 701(b)(2) of PPA 2006 are effective for distributions made after August 17, 2006.

Treasury issued final regulations on Hybrid Retirement Plans (2010 final Treasury regulations), 75 FR 64123 (Oct. 19, 2010), and simultaneously issued proposed Additional Rules Regarding Hybrid Retirement Plans (2010 proposed Treasury regulations), 75 FR 64197 (Oct. 19, 2010). These regulations provide guidance on changes made by PPA 2006 under sections 411(a)(13) and 411(b)(5) of the Code.

The other PPA 2006 provisions relevant to this proposed rule are in section 404, which added sections 4022(g) and 4044(e) of ERISA. These provisions provide that, when an underfunded pension plan terminates during the bankruptcy of the plan sponsor, the date that the sponsor's bankruptcy petition was filed is treated as the plan's termination date for purposes of determining (1) the amount of benefits PBGC guarantees, and (2) the amount of benefits in priority category 3 in the section 4044 asset allocation. These changes apply for plan terminations that occur during the bankruptcy of the plan sponsor, if the bankruptcy filing date was on or after September 16, 2006. On June 14, 2011 (at 76 FR 34590), PBGC published a final rule on Bankruptcy Filing Date Treated as Plan Termination Date for Certain Purposes that implements section 404 of PPA 2006.

Overview of Proposed Rule

This proposed rule would amend PBGC's regulation on Benefits Payable in Terminated Single-Employer Plans (29 CFR part 4022) to implement the above-described changes made by PPA 2006 upon the termination of a statutory hybrid plan. This proposed rule is intended to be consistent with the proposed Treasury rules under section 411(b)(5) of the Code that apply upon termination of a statutory hybrid plan (included in the 2010 proposed Treasury regulations at Treas. Reg. § 1.411(b)(5)-1(e)(2)). No inference should be drawn from the language in this proposed rule as to any changes that may be made to the Treasury rules when the 2010 proposed Treasury regulations are issued as final regulations. After the 2010 proposed Treasury regulations are finalized, PBGC intends to take those final Treasury regulations into account, so that the rules that finalize these proposed regulations are consistent with the final rules in the Treasury regulations.

Under the proposed rule, PBGC would generally determine plan benefits based on plan terms as of the plan's termination date; if, however, the plan used a variable rate during the five-year period ending on the termination date, PBGC would take into account the plan's provisions for determining and applying an average rate of interest in accordance with section 411(b)(5)(B)(vi) of the Code and proposed Treas. Reg. § 1.411(b)(5)-1(e)(2). In addition, the proposed rule sets forth certain default rules that PBGC would apply to the extent that the terms of the plan do not satisfy the plan termination requirements under PPA 2006 or Treasury regulations thereunder, or fail to specify provisions necessary to implement those requirements. Except in the case of certain involuntary plan terminations, PBGC would generally apply its rules to determine the benefits of any participant with an annuity starting date after the plan's termination date or, in the case of a distress termination under ERISA section 4041(c), the plan's proposed termination date. The proposed rule also addresses the interest crediting rules that apply to a plan that terminates during the bankruptcy of the plan sponsor.

In addition, the proposed rule would amend PBGC's regulation on Allocation of Assets in Single-Employer Plans (29 CFR part 4044) to conform the rules for valuing benefits and allocating plan assets to the changes in the benefit determination rules. Under the proposed rule, certain benefits would be calculated differently for valuation purposes than for payment purposes. For example, de minimis benefits would continue to be calculated as annuities for valuation purposes, as under the current regulation, but the method of calculating such benefits for payment purposes would change under the proposed rule. The proposed rule would also amend part 4044 to provide that the priority category 3 benefits of a participant who is eligible but does not retire three years before a plan's termination date (or bankruptcy filing date, if applicable) would be determined based on the participant's account balance and the interest rates under the plan as if the participant had retired three years before the termination date (or bankruptcy filing date, if applicable).

The proposed rule would amend PBGC's regulation on Termination of Single-Employer Plans (29 CFR part 4041) to provide that, for purposes of part 4041, a plan that terminates in a standard termination (or a distress termination where the plan is sufficient for guaranteed benefits) will be deemed to satisfy the plan termination requirements under section 204(b)(5)(B)(vi) of ERISA and section 411(b)(5)(B)(vi) of the Code and Treasury regulations if the plan calculates and pays

---

[4] Under IRS Notice 96-8, plans that use the standard indices to determine their interest crediting rates were permitted to pay the hypothetical account balance, even if this amount was less than the present value of the participant's life annuity payable at normal retirement age determined using the applicable interest rate and the applicable mortality table under section 417(e) of the Code.

[5] In the case of a new plan not in existence on June 29, 2005, these requirements are effective for periods beginning on or after June 29, 2005.

[6] Section 701(e)(4) of PPA 2006 provides that, for a plan maintained under one or more collective bargaining agreements between employee representatives and one or more employers that is ratified on or before August 17, 2006, the interest and three-year vesting requirements will not apply to plan years before -

- The earlier of the date on which the last of the collective bargaining agreements terminates (determined without regard to any extension made on or after August 17, 2006), or January 1, 2008, or

- January 1, 2010.

benefits consistent with the provisions for statutory hybrid plans under part 4022.

A detailed discussion of the proposed rule follows.

Proposed Regulatory Changes

Definition of Statutory Hybrid Plan

Under section 411(a)(13)(C) of the Code,[7] an "applicable defined benefit plan" is a defined benefit plan under which the accrued benefit (or any portion thereof) is calculated as the balance of a hypothetical account maintained for the participant or as an accumulated percentage of the participant's final average compensation; the definition includes any plan that has an effect similar to an applicable defined benefit plan. Treasury's final regulations on Hybrid Retirement Plans use the term "statutory hybrid plan" to describe plans that are subject to the provisions of sections 411(a)(13) and 411(b)(5)(B) of the Code. To maintain a uniform and consistent application of PPA 2006 changes to the rules in this area, PBGC is proposing to amend § 4001.2 to add a definition of a "statutory hybrid plan" that cross-references the definition of a statutory hybrid plan under Treasury regulations.[8]

PBGC Benefit Determinations - In General

PBGC proposes to amend part 4022 to add a new subpart H that would specifically address the determination of benefits payable under a terminating statutory hybrid plan. Subpart H would supplement the general rules in part 4022 for purposes of determining a participant's benefit under the provisions of a statutory hybrid plan and the amount and form of benefits guaranteed or otherwise payable under Title IV of ERISA.

When PBGC trustees a terminated plan (including a statutory hybrid plan), as a first step in determining the benefits payable under Title IV, it determines a participant's benefit in accordance with the terms of the plan on the termination date. As described in proposed new § 4022.121, for statutory hybrid plans, this includes provisions relating to the interest rate(s) and mortality table used by the plan, such as the rate used to determine interest credits and the timing for determining such rate, the frequency at which interest credits are applied, and the interest rate and mortality table (or annuity conversion factor) used to determine the participant's benefit payable in the form of an annuity payable at normal retirement age - provided the plan's provisions satisfy the requirements of section 204(b)(5)(B) of ERISA and section 411(b)(5)(B) of the Code and implementing regulations.

Because statutory hybrid plans use various methods for determining a participant's annuity benefit, PBGC would follow the plan's terms for this purpose. For example, a cash balance plan that defines the accrued benefit as an annuity commencing at normal retirement age, and that - for purposes of sections 411(a)(13) and 411(b)(5) - expresses the accrued benefit as the balance of the participant's hypothetical account, may under its terms determine the participant's annuity by projecting interest credits to the participant's normal retirement date. In that case, PBGC would add interest credits to the participant's hypothetical account balance each interest crediting period beginning after the plan's termination date through the participant's normal retirement date (or the current date, if later) and then use the conversion factors (or the interest rate and the mortality table) specified under the plan as of the termination date to determine the benefit payable as an annuity. Alternatively, if such plan provides for the use of immediate annuity conversion factors, PBGC would add interest credits to the participant's hypothetical account balance through the participant's annuity starting date, then use the conversion factors (or the interest rate and mortality table) specified under the plan as of the termination date to determine the benefit payable as an annuity at the participant's age on the annuity starting date. In the case of a pension equity plan that provides for the use of deferred annuity conversion factors (or an interest rate and mortality table), PBGC would determine the current value of the accumulated percentage of an active participant's final average compensation as of the plan's termination date and apply the conversion factors specified under the plan as of the termination date to determine the benefit payable as an annuity at different future ages to the participant.

If the mortality table specified under the plan as of the termination date used to determine the amount of any benefit payable in the form of an annuity (*i.e.*, the table used to convert a hypothetical account balance to an annuity) is a table that is updated automatically in future years to reflect expected improvements in mortality experience (*e.g.*, the applicable mortality table provided under Code section 417(e)(3)), PBGC would determine benefits payable under the plan based on the mortality table as of the termination date taking into account future adjustments for expected mortality improvements through the annuity starting date.

The provisions of proposed new subpart H would be used to determine the benefits of any participant or beneficiary in a plan covered by the subpart with an annuity starting date after the plan's termination date or, in the case of a distress termination under ERISA section 4041(c), after the proposed termination date. A plan administrator's failure to apply an average interest rate as of the proposed termination date would require benefits to be re-determined using an average rate of interest. The proposed termination date would also be the relevant date if a plan provides a notice of intent to terminate in a distress termination and subsequently terminates under section 4042, and the termination date is the same as the proposed termination date under section 4041(c). If the proposed termination date is moved to a later date in a distress termination case (or in a distress termination that becomes an involuntary termination), benefits determined using an average interest rate between the proposed termination date and the final termination date would be recalculated using the interest rate that would have applied under the plan prior to the plan's final termination date.

Proposed new § 4022.121(a)(3)(ii) provides a special rule for a plan that terminates in an involuntary termination where the termination date is earlier than the date on which PBGC institutes termination proceedings pursuant to section 4042. In that situation, in determining benefits under part 4022, PBGC generally would not change the interest rate(s) (or the mortality table or conversion factor) used by the plan under its provisions to calculate a benefit payable for a participant or beneficiary whose annuity starting date is after the termination date but on or before the date on which PBGC institutes termination proceedings or who submits a completed election for an annuity benefit during that time period. This would protect benefit determinations and participant elections when a plan operates in good faith in accordance with its terms prior to any notice of termination proceedings. PBGC would have discretion not to follow this special rule if warranted under the facts and circumstances, e.g., to avoid abuse.

Variable Rates

Paragraph (c) of proposed new § 4022.121 describes the averaging methodology PBGC would apply upon termination of a plan in the case of a variable rate. In accordance with proposed Treas. Reg. § 1.411(b)(5)-1(e)(2), if the interest crediting rate used to determine a participant's accumulated benefit (or a portion thereof) has been a variable rate during the interest crediting periods in the five-year period ending on the plan's termination date (including a rate that was not the same fixed rate during all such periods), PBGC would determine an average of the interest crediting rates used under the plan during the five-year period. For this purpose, the interest crediting rates used under the plan would include each rate that applied under the terms of the plan during an interest crediting period for which the interest crediting date is within the five-year period ending on the plan's termination date.[9] The average rate would be determined as the arithmetic average of the rates used, expressed as an annual rate.

PBGC would apply the plan's average interest crediting rate to determine the participant's accumulated benefit[10] under the plan beginning after the plan's termination date through the participant's normal retirement date (or annuity starting date, as applicable under the plan). If the plan's termination date occurs in the middle of an interest crediting period, PBGC would credit interest based on the plan's interest crediting rate (on a pro rata basis) for the portion of the interest crediting period ending on the plan's termination date; such rate would not be included in the determination of the average rate. For

---

[7] References to Code provisions used hereinafter should be read to include parallel provisions of ERISA.

[8] Under § 1.411(a)(13)-1(d), a statutory hybrid plan means a defined benefit plan that contains a statutory hybrid benefit formula, which is defined as a benefit formula used to determine all or any part of a participant's accumulated benefit that is either a lump sum-based benefit formula (under which the benefit is expressed as the current balance of a hypothetical account maintained for the participant or as the current value of an accumulated percentage of the participant's final average compensation) or a benefit formula that has an effect similar to a lump sum-based benefit formula.

[9] An interest crediting rate that applied under the terms of the plan only with respect to a date that is distinct from the plan's regular interest crediting date, such as the date of separation from employment or plan termination, would not be included in determining an average of the interest crediting rates that applied under the terms of the plan during the five-year period.

[10] Under Treas. Reg. § 1.411(a)(13)-1(d)(2), a participant's accumulated benefit at any date means the participant's benefit, as expressed under the terms of the plan, accrued to that date. Thus, for example, for a cash balance plan the accumulated benefit is expressed as the current balance of a hypothetical account, and for a pension equity plan the accumulated benefit is expressed as the current value of an accumulated percentage of the participant's final average compensation.

any subsequent partial interest crediting period (*e.g.*, the portion of the interest crediting period following the plan's termination date), PBGC would credit a pro rata amount of the plan's average interest crediting rate. This approach is consistent with the statute and would simplify administration for PBGC.

In the event that the plan used a variable rate during the five-year period ending on the plan's termination date to determine the amount of a participant's benefit payable in the form of an annuity payable at normal retirement age, PBGC would determine the arithmetic average of the interest rates (or tabular adjustment factors) that applied during periods for which the date of each rate (or factor) change was within the five-year period ending on the plan's termination date.

Under Code section 411(b)(5)(B)(vi)(II), the average rate is used to determine the amount of any benefit under the plan payable in the form of an annuity payable at normal retirement age. PBGC would apply an average rate to determine a benefit under the plan that is payable in the form of a life annuity (*i.e.*, an annuity that continues at least as long as the life of the annuitant, such as a straight-life annuity, joint-and-50%-survivor annuity, or 10-year certain and continuous annuity) payable at normal retirement age. In the case of an immediate annuity conversion plan that uses a variable interest rate to determine the amount of a benefit, PBGC would apply an average rate to determine a benefit under the plan payable in the form of a life annuity payable at the annuity starting date. In either case, the averaging requirement would apply only to determine the amount of the benefit in the automatic PBGC form under § 4022.8(b) of PBGC's regulation on Benefits Payable in Terminated Single-Employer Plans, *e.g.*, the form a married participant or an unmarried participant (as applicable) would be entitled to receive from the plan in the absence of an election. If the participant or beneficiary elects an optional PBGC form under § 4022.8(c), PBGC would convert the benefit amount from the automatic PBGC form in accordance with that section.

Paragraph (c) of proposed new § 4022.121 also provides that, consistent with Treasury regulations, if the interest crediting rate in any interest crediting period during the five-year period ending on the termination date is based on a variable rate that is not described in proposed Treas. Reg. § 1.411(b)(5)-1(e)(2)(ii)(B) (*e.g.*, the rate of return on plan assets), PBGC would replace such rate with the third segment rate under Code section 430(h)(2)(C)(iii) for the last calendar month ending before the beginning of the interest crediting period for purposes of determining the average interest crediting rate. In accordance with proposed Treas. Reg. § 1.411(b)(5)-1(e)(2)(ii)(C), PBGC generally would adjust the third segment rate by any maximums or minimums applicable to the interest crediting rate in the period under the plan's terms, but would not adjust the third segment rate to account for any other adjustments under the plan to the interest crediting rate.

Default Rules and Other Rules

Paragraph (d) of proposed new § 4022.121 describes the default rules that PBGC would apply to the extent that plan provisions do not satisfy section 204(b)(5)(B) of ERISA and section 411(b)(5)(B) of the Code and implementing regulations, or that the plan fails to specify provisions necessary to implement applicable statutory and regulatory requirements. In the case of a plan that uses a variable rate but does not provide for the determination of an average rate or an arithmetic averaging methodology to be used upon termination of the plan, PBGC would determine an arithmetic average in the manner described above. If a plan does not specify a mortality table (or otherwise indicate the table or annuity conversion factor to be used), PBGC would use the mortality table provided under section 417(e) of the Code that would apply if the annuity starting date were the plan's termination date (*i.e.*, future adjustments for expected mortality improvements under the mortality table would not be taken into account). If a plan fails to specify an interest crediting rate or annuity conversion interest rate (or otherwise indicate the rate or factor to be used), PBGC would compute an average rate as the arithmetic mean of the 30-year Treasury Constant Maturity rates in effect for the calendar month in which the plan terminates and for the same calendar month in each of the preceding four years.

Under the proposed regulation, PBGC would apply a single average interest crediting rate to determine the benefits of all similarly situated participants under the plan (*i.e.*, the same average interest crediting rate would apply to the extent the same rates applied under the plan to determine all participants' benefits). In the case of a plan that terminates within five years after the effective date of the PPA 2006 termination requirements with respect to the plan, PBGC would determine the average rate by including interest crediting rates used by the plan before the effective date but within the five-year period ending on the termination date. In the case of a plan (or the statutory hybrid benefit formula under a plan) that is in effect for less than five years, PBGC

would determine the average rate based on the interest crediting periods during the time the plan (or the statutory hybrid benefit formula) was in effect.

PPA 2006 Bankruptcy Terminations

Paragraph (e) of proposed new § 4022.121 provides a special rule for determining interest credits in the case of a plan that terminates while the sponsor is in bankruptcy (a PPA 2006 bankruptcy termination, as defined in § 4001.2). PBGC would project the amount of the participant's hypothetical account balance as of the bankruptcy filing date using the following interest rates:

- To credit interest beginning after the bankruptcy filing date and ending on the plan's termination date, the actual interest crediting rate(s) used under the plan during each interest crediting period.

- To credit interest beginning after the plan's termination date and ending on the participant's normal retirement date or, in some cases, annuity starting date, the rate in effect under the plan as of the plan's termination date, including the average interest crediting rate as determined under subpart H if the plan used a variable rate during the five-year period ending on the plan's termination date.

De Minimis Lump Sums

The proposed rule would add a new § 4022.122 to describe how PBGC would make determinations regarding de minimis lump sum payments (currently $5,000 or less under § 4022.7) under a statutory hybrid plan. Consistent with section 411(a)(13)(A) of the Code, if a plan provides for a single sum form of payment equal to the amount expressed as the balance in a hypothetical account, PBGC generally would determine whether the lump sum value of a benefit payable by PBGC is de minimis based on the participant's hypothetical account balance as of the plan's termination date, and, if so, would pay that amount to the participant.

However, regardless of plan provisions, if after August 17, 2006, a plan made lump sum payments based on participants' hypothetical account balances without regard to the present value rules under section 417(e) of the Code, or stated in writing its intent to make lump sum payments on that basis (*e.g.*, through communications to affected participants), PBGC would make de minimis lump sum determinations on that same basis. *I.e.*, PBGC would treat the plan as if it had been amended to reflect plan operation in accordance with section 411(a)(13)(A) of the Code, pursuant to the amendatory period provided under section 1107 of PPA 2006. PBGC would also make de minimis lump sum determinations based on the participants' hypothetical account balances without regard to the section 417(e) rules if there is no single sum form of payment under the plan or no description of the calculation for such a payment.

In the case of a plan that provides for use of section 417(e) of the Code in determining lump sums and that, after August 17, 2006, has *not* made lump sum payments based solely on participants' hypothetical account balances or stated in writing its intent to make lump sum payments on that basis (*e.g.*, through communications to affected participants), PBGC would make de minimis lump sum determinations in accordance with § 4022.7(d) and its operating policy on cash balance plans.

Phase-In of Guarantee of Benefit Increases

The proposed rule would add a new § 4022.123 to PBGC's regulations to describe changes in the terms of a statutory hybrid plan resulting in a benefit increase that would be subject to the phase-in limitations on the PBGC guarantee (*i.e.*, a benefit increase that has been in effect for less than five years on the plan's termination date). Such changes include, but are not limited to, a change in the plan's mortality table, timing or method for crediting interest, or basis for crediting interest or determining the annuity conversion factor (*e.g.*, a change from a fixed rate to a variable rate, or from one variable index to another variable index).

The proposed regulation would clarify that certain adjustments in the interest rate would not be subject to the phase-in limitations. These include: (i) a change in the interest rate under a single variable rate index (*e.g.*, a change in the yield on 5-year Treasury Constant Maturities from one date to another); (ii) a change that is required to comply with the termination requirements of ERISA section 204(b)(5)(B)(vi) and Code section 411(b)(5)(B)(vi) (*e.g.*, a change in the plan's interest rate to an average rate of interest at termination); (iii) a change in the plan's interest crediting rate that is permitted, notwithstanding section 411(d)(6) of the Code, pursuant to Treas. Reg. § 1.411(b)(5)-1(e)(3) (*e.g.*, an amendment to change under certain circumstances to the long-term investment grade corporate bond rate); (iv) a change permitted during the amendatory period under section 1107 of PPA 2006 or any extension of the amendatory period issued by the Treasury Department; and (v) an automatic future update in a mortality table specified under the plan as of the termination date that reflects expected improvements in mortality experience. PBGC believes that excluding such changes from the phase-in rule is warranted. Changes in rate due to the fluctuations of a variable index or to the averaging under the termination requirements would just as likely result in a benefit decrease as a benefit increase. Furthermore, any increase in benefits that might result from the above changes would be moderated by the requirement to average the plan's rates for the five-year period ending on the termination date, and by the substitution of the third segment rate for any variable rate that is not described in proposed Treasury regulation § 1.411(b)(5)-1(e)(2)(ii)(B) (*e.g.*, the rate of return on plan assets) for purposes of determining the average interest crediting rate. Lastly, updates under a mortality table that automatically reflects age improvements are an inherent aspect of the annuity conversion factor used; by contrast, a change to the conversion factor (*e.g.*, from a fixed mortality table to one that updates automatically) by a plan would be subject to phase-in.

Allocation of Assets - Distress and Involuntary Terminations

PBGC proposes to amend part 4044 by adding a new § 4044.52(e) to address the valuation of benefits under a terminating statutory hybrid plan. The proposed regulation provides that benefits should be valued consistent with the general valuation rules of part 4044 and the provisions for the calculation and payment of benefits in subpart H of part 4022.

In two situations, notwithstanding PBGC's calculation of benefits for payment purposes, PBGC would value the benefits under a cash balance plan in the same manner as all other benefits are valued. First, although proposed new § 4022.122 provides for the determination of de minimis lump sums in some cases on the basis of the participant's hypothetical account balance, a benefit payable as a de minimis lump sum would nevertheless be required to be valued, for purposes of part 4044, in the form of a benefit payable as an annuity in the absence of a valid election under the terms of the plan (as is the case under current regulations). Second, despite the special rule in proposed new § 4022.121(a)(3)(ii) that would generally require PBGC to use the plan's interest crediting rate and annuity conversion interest rate to determine benefits commencing or elected during the time period between the plan's termination date and the date on which PBGC institutes termination proceedings, these benefits would be valued, for purposes of part 4044, using the interest rates in effect under the plan (including the five-year average rate, if applicable) as of the plan's termination date.

Proposed new § 4044.52(e)(4) describes the calculation of a priority category 3 benefit under a statutory hybrid plan. Priority category 3 benefits generally are benefits in pay status, or that could have been in pay status, three years before the termination date; priority category 3 benefits come ahead of guaranteed benefits in priority category 4 in the section 4044 asset allocation. In a plan termination that is not a PPA 2006 bankruptcy termination, the priority category 3 benefit for a participant eligible to receive an annuity (taking into account PBGC's rules on the Earliest PBGC Retirement Date under § 4022.10) before the beginning of the threeyear period ending on the termination date but not in pay status as of that date would be determined based on the balance of the participant's hypothetical account and the interest crediting rate and annuity conversion factor under the plan had the participant retired three years before the termination date.[11] In the case of PPA 2006 bankruptcy termination, the bankruptcy filing date would substitute for the termination date in determining whether a participant or beneficiary is eligible for a priority category 3 benefit, and the amount of benefits in priority category 3. A priority category 3 benefit would in no event exceed the benefit amount payable under the terms of the plan as of the plan's termination date (determined by applying the averaging rules under § 4022.121 if the plan uses a variable rate).

Standard and Distress Terminations

The termination requirements under section 411(b)(5)(B)(vi) of the Code, added by PPA 2006, apply to any applicable defined benefit plan upon the termination of the plan. Sections 4041.28(c) and 4041.50 provide that, in general, the plan administrator of a plan that terminates

in a standard termination or a distress termination where the plan is sufficient for guaranteed benefits must close out the plan "in accordance with all applicable requirements under the Code and ERISA." These requirements include the new rules for cash balance plans under section 411(b)(5)(B)(vi) of the Code and implementing Treasury regulations.

The proposed rule would amend § 4041.28(c) to provide that for purposes of part 4041 the plan administrator of a statutory hybrid plan would be deemed to satisfy the applicable Code and ERISA requirements if it calculates and pays benefits consistent with the interest and mortality provisions described in proposed new § 4022.121.

Issues Not Addressed

This proposed rule does not address issues relating to plans in which the interest crediting rate is determined by participant direction, *e.g.*, where the interest crediting rate depends upon choices made by the participant. PBGC will provide further guidance as appropriate.

Applicability

The proposed regulatory changes to implement the plan termination requirements under section 411(b)(5)(B)(vi) of the Code would generally apply to any plan with a termination date in a plan year beginning on or after January 1, 2008. In addition, the proposed changes would apply to any plan that was not in existence on June 29, 2005. Pursuant to sections 701(e)(3) through (e)(5) of PPA 2006, if a plan elected to have these statutory provisions apply for any period after June 29, 2005, and before the plan year beginning on or after January 1, 2008, or if the statutory provisions are first effective for a plan after the first plan year beginning on or after January 1, 2008 (*e.g.*, a collectively bargained plan), these regulatory changes would apply to any plan with a termination date on or after such earlier effective date elected by the plan, or such later effective date provided under PPA 2006. For plans that terminate under part 4041 on or after the effective date of these statutory provisions and pending the issuance of final Treasury regulations, compliance with PPA 2006 would constitute compliance with the new rules for Title IV purposes.[12]

The proposed regulatory changes to implement the lump sum provisions under section 411(a)(13) of the Code would apply to distributions made from a terminated plan with a termination date in a plan year beginning on or after January 1, 2008.

Regulatory Impact Analysis

Regulatory Procedures

Executive Order 12866 "Regulatory Planning and Review" and Executive Order 13563 "Improving Regulation and Regulatory Review"

Executive Orders 12866 and 13563 direct agencies to assess all costs and benefits of available regulatory alternatives and, if regulation is necessary, to select regulatory approaches that maximize net benefits (including potential economic, environmental, public health and safety effects, distributive impacts, and equity). Executive Order 13563 emphasizes the importance of quantifying both costs and benefits, of reducing costs, of harmonizing rules, and of promoting flexibility. Executive Orders 12866 and 13563 require a comprehensive regulatory impact analysis be performed for any economically significant regulatory action, defined as an action that would result in an annual effect of $100 million or more on the national economy or which would have other substantial impacts. In accordance with OMB Circular A-4, the Department has examined the economic and policy implications of this proposed rule and has concluded that the action's benefits justify its costs.

Under Section 3(f)(1) of Executive Order 12866, a proposed rule is economically significant if "it is likely to result in a rule that may . . . [h]ave an annual effect on the economy of $100 million or more or adversely affect in a material way the economy, a sector of the economy, productivity, competition, jobs, the environment, public health or safety, or State, local, or tribal governments or communities." PBGC has determined that this proposed rule does not cross the $100 million threshold for economic significance and is not otherwise economically significant.

The economic effect of the proposed rule is attributable almost entirely to the economic effect of the PPA 2006 changes to terminating

---

[11] Benefits in priority category 3 are limited to the lowest annuity benefit payable under the plan provisions at any time during the five-year period ending on the termination date (or bankruptcy filing date, if applicable). This limitation also affects the benefits of participants who retired between three and five years before the termination date (or bankruptcy filing date, if applicable).

[12] The 2010 final Treasury regulations provide that, for periods after the statutory effective date and before the regulatory effective date, a plan is permitted to rely on the provisions of the 2010 final Treasury regulations, the 2010 proposed Treasury regulations, the 2007 proposed regulations on Hybrid Retirement Plans, 72 FR 73680, 48 (Dec. 28, 2007), and IRS Notice 2007-6 for purposes of satisfying the requirements of sections 411(a)(13) and 411(b)(5) of the Code.

cash balance plans. Accordingly, PBGC is basing its determination on its experience with plans subject to these provisions.

PBGC estimates that, to date, the total economic effects of the PPA 2006 changes - in terms of lower benefits paid to participants and associated savings - is less than $4 million. These effects are primarily due to lower lump sum payments to some participants as a result of the PPA 2006 provisions that allow payment of the hypothetical account balance to participants. Because PBGC generally pays lump sums only when the benefit is de minimis (currently $5,000 or less), and because only a small percentage of participants in cash balance plans trusteed by PBGC receive benefits in lump sum form, the economic effects are relatively small.

PBGC estimates that there will be little if any economic effect from PPA 2006's averaging provisions. As explained in the **Background** section, before the PPA 2006 changes went into effect, if a cash balance plan used a variable interest rate at plan termination to determine accrued benefits, for payment purposes PBGC credited interest to a participant's account using the plan's variable index from the termination date until a participant's normal retirement date or annuity starting date. PPA 2006 requires that a cash balance plan that uses a variable rate for calculating benefits use the average of the rates used under the plan during the five-year period ending on the plan termination date. This change could result in larger benefits payable to some participants and smaller benefits payable to other participants as compared to the pre-PPA 2006 methodology, depending on fluctuations in rates. PBGC believes that these losses and gains in benefits for participants will be largely offsetting.

Although, PBGC cannot predict with certainty which cash balance plans will terminate, the funding level of such plans, or the number of participants that will be paid de minimis lump sum payments, given the relatively low estimate of the effect of the statutory provisions to date, PBGC has determined that the annual effect of the proposed rule will be less than $100 million.

Regulatory Flexibility Act

PBGC certifies under section 605(b) of the Regulatory Flexibility Act (5 U.S.C. 601 et seq.) that the amendments in this proposed rule would not have a significant economic impact on a substantial number of small entities. The amendments implement and in some cases clarify statutory changes made in PPA 2006; they do not impose new burdens on entities of any size. Accordingly, as provided in section 605 of the Regulatory Flexibility Act (5 U.S.C 601 et seq.), sections 603 and 604 do not apply.

Paperwork Reduction Act

The amendments in the proposed rule would change the information requirements approved by the Office of Management and Budget under the Paperwork Reduction Act under OMB control number 1212-0036 (expires December 31, 2013). PBGC is submitting the information requirements relating to these amendments to part 4041 to the Office of Management and Budget for review and approval under the Paperwork Reduction Act. Copies of PBGC's request may be obtained free of charge by contacting the Disclosure Division of the Office of the General Counsel of PBGC, 1200 K Street, NW., Washington, DC 20005, 202-326-4040; the request is also available on www.reginfo.gov.

PBGC estimates that 1,379 plan administrators will be subject to the collection of information requirements under 1212-0036 each year, and that the total annual burden of complying with these requirements is 2,161 hours and $3,098,441. Much of the work associated with terminating a plan is performed for purposes other than meeting these requirements. (Detailed information on these burden estimates is included in PBGC's request.)

Comments on the paperwork provisions under this proposed rule should be sent to the Office of Information and Regulatory Affairs, Office of Management and Budget, Attention: Desk Officer for Pension Benefit Guaranty Corporation, via electronic mail at OIRA_DOCKET@omb.eop.gov or by fax to (202) 395-6974. Although comments may be submitted through [insert date 60 days after date of publication in the Federal Register], the Office of Management and Budget requests that comments be received on or before [insert date 30 days after date of publication in the Federal Register] to ensure their consideration. Comments may address (among other things) -

- Whether the proposed collection of information is needed for the proper performance of PBGC's functions and will have practical utility;
- The accuracy of PBGC's estimate of the burden of the proposed collection of information, including the validity of the methodology and assumptions used;

- Enhancement of the quality, utility, and clarity of the information to be collected; and
- Minimizing the burden of the collection of information on those who are to respond, including through the use of appropriate automated, electronic, mechanical, or other technological collection techniques or other forms of information technology, *e.g.*, permitting electronic submission of responses.

List of Subjects

29 CFR Part 4001

Pensions.

29 CFR Part 4022

Pension insurance, Pensions.

29 CFR 4041

Pension insurance, Pensions, Reporting and recordkeeping requirements.

29 CFR 4044

Pension insurance, Pensions.

For the reasons given above, PBGC proposes to amend 29 CFR parts 4001, 4022, 4041, and 4044 as follows.

PART 4001 - Terminology

1. The authority citation for part 4001 continues to read as follows:

Authority: 29 U.S.C. 1301, 1302(b)(3).

2. In § 4001.2, add a new definition in alphabetical order to read as follows:

§ 4001.2 Definitions

S *tatutory hybrid plan* means a cash balance plan or other statutory hybrid plan under regulations issued by the Department of the Treasury.

PART 4022 - Benefits Payable in Terminated Single-Employer Plans

3. The authority citation for part 4022 continues to read as follows:

Authority: 29 USC 1302, 1322, 1322b, 1341(c)(3)(D), and 1344.

4. In § 4022.2, amend the first paragraph by removing the words "proposed termination date, substantial owner" and adding in their place "proposed termination date, statutory hybrid plan, substantial owner."

5. Add a new subpart H to read as follows:

Subpart H - Calculation of benefits payable under statutory hybrid plans

§ 4022.120 Purpose and scope.

(a) *General.* This subpart H supplements the general rules in part 4022. These rules apply for determining the benefit payable under the provisions of a statutory hybrid plan and the amount of the benefit that PBGC will guarantee or that is payable under title IV of ERISA. To the extent the rules and procedures of this subpart H conflict with the rules and procedures in subparts A through G of part 4022, the provisions of subpart H govern.

(b) *Statutory hybrid plan.* In general, a statutory hybrid plan (defined in § 4001.2 of this chapter) includes a hybrid defined benefit pension plan under the terms of which the accumulated benefit of a participant (or any portion thereof) is expressed as the current balance of a hypothetical account maintained for the participant (a cash balance formula), as the current value of an accumulated percentage of the participant's final average compensation (a pension equity formula), or as a formula with an effect similar to a cash balance or pension equity formula. This subpart H applies with respect to all or any portion of a participant's benefit under a defined benefit plan to the extent such benefit is determined under a statutory hybrid benefit formula.

§ 4022.121 Interest and mortality assumptions and other plan terms.

(a) *In general.* PBGC will determine a participant's benefit based on the terms of the plan, including the interest rate and mortality table otherwise applicable for determining that benefit under the plan, as of the plan's termination date. Special rules apply under paragraph (e) of this section for a PPA 2006 bankruptcy termination.

(1) *Plan terms.* PBGC will determine plan benefits using relevant plan provisions in effect as of the plan's termination date (or, for determining the average rate in the case of a variable rate, within the 5-year period ending on the plan's termination date). All relevant plan provisions (including provisions that become applicable upon plan termination) must be consistent with the requirements under section 204(b)(5)(B) of ERISA and section 411(b)(5)(B) of the Code and regulations thereunder. Relevant plan provisions include, but are not limited to, the following:

(i) The basis and the timing for determining the interest crediting rate used by the plan for each plan year (or portion thereof).

(ii) The periodic frequency at which interest credits are applied (monthly, quarterly, etc.).

(iii) The interest rate and mortality table (or conversion factor) used to determine the amount of any benefit payable in the form of an annuity payable at normal retirement age. If a plan uses a mortality table as of the termination date that is updated automatically to reflect expected improvements in mortality experience (*e.g.,* the applicable mortality table provided under Code section 417(e)(3)), PBGC will take into account future adjustments under that table for expected improvements in mortality experience through each participant's annuity starting date.

(iv) The averaging methodology to be used, if the interest crediting rate or the annuity conversion interest rate under the plan is a variable rate, upon the termination of the plan.

(v) The method for determining a participant's annuity benefit. Examples—

Example 1. Immediate annuity conversion plan. A cash balance plan determines immediate annuity benefits by applying immediate annuity conversion factors to the participant's hypothetical account balance as of the annuity starting date. PBGC will add interest credits to the participant's hypothetical account balance each interest crediting period beginning after the plan's termination date through the participant's annuity starting date and convert the balance to an annuity using the immediate annuity conversion factors (specified under the plan as of the termination date) at the participant's age on the annuity starting date.

Example 2. Deferred annuity conversion plan. A pension equity plan determines annuity benefits by applying deferred annuity conversion factors to the accumulated percentage of the participant's final average compensation at cessation of accruals. PBGC will determine the current value of the accumulated percentage of an active participant's final average compensation as of the plan's termination date and convert this value to an annuity using the deferred annuity conversion factors specified under the plan as of the termination date (followed by an adjustment, if necessary, in the annuity using the plan's early retirement provisions to reflect the participant's age on the annuity starting date) to determine the benefit payable as an annuity at different future ages to the participant.

Example 3. Projected annuity conversion plan. A cash balance plan determines annuity benefits by reference to the accrued benefit, which is determined by projecting the participant's hypothetical account balance with interest credits to the plan's normal retirement age. PBGC will add interest credits to the participant's hypothetical account balance each interest crediting period beginning after the plan's termination date through the participant's normal retirement date (or the current date, if later) and convert the balance to an annuity payable at that age using the immediate conversion factors for that age (or the interest rate and mortality table) specified under the plan as of the termination date (followed by an adjustment, if necessary, in the annuity using the plan's early retirement provisions to reflect the participant's age on the annuity starting date).

(2) *Fixed or variable interest rate and related terms.* If, during the 5-year period ending on the plan's termination date, the plan uses the same fixed interest rate to determine a participant's accumulated benefit or the amount of any benefit under the plan payable in the form of an annuity payable at normal retirement age, PBGC will apply the rules in paragraph (b) of this section. If, during the 5-year period ending on the plan's termination date, the plan uses a variable rate (as defined in paragraph (c)(4)) to determine a participant's accumulated benefit or the amount of any benefit under the plan payable in the form of an annuity payable at normal retirement age, PBGC will apply the rules in paragraph (c) of this section. To the extent that the terms of the plan do not satisfy section 204(b)(5)(B) of ERISA and section 411(b)(5)(B) of the Code and implementing regulations, or that the plan fails to specify provisions necessary to implement applicable statutory and regulatory requirements, PBGC will determine plan benefits using the rules under paragraph (d) of this section. In the case of a PPA 2006

bankruptcy termination, PBGC will apply the interest crediting rules in paragraph (e) of this section.

(3) *Benefits affected.* (i) *General rule.* The provisions of this § 4022.121 apply to determine the benefits of any participant or beneficiary with an annuity starting date after the plan's termination date. If the plan administrator issues a notice of intent to terminate in a distress termination under ERISA section 4041(c), in compliance with § 4041.42 of this chapter, the plan administrator must apply the provisions of this § 4022.121 as of the proposed termination date specified in the notice of intent to terminate under § 4041.43. (If the plan fails to qualify for distress termination, in accordance with § 4041.42(d), benefits determined using an average interest rate must be recalculated using the interest rate otherwise applicable under the plan, disregarding the proposed termination date.)

(ii) *Special rule for involuntary terminations.* Notwithstanding paragraph (a)(3)(i) of this section, if PBGC initiates termination proceedings under ERISA section 4042 and the termination date is earlier than the date on which PBGC institutes such proceedings, PBGC generally will not change the interest rate(s), the mortality table, or other conversion factor used by the plan (in accordance with ongoing plan provisions) to calculate a benefit payable to a participant or beneficiary whose annuity starting date is after the termination date but on or before the date on which PBGC institutes termination proceedings. PBGC also generally will not change the interest rate(s), the mortality table, or other conversion factor used by the plan to calculate the benefit of a participant or beneficiary who submits a completed election for an annuity benefit during the period between the termination date and the date on which PBGC initiates termination proceedings. (This special rule does not apply in the case of a plan that issues a notice of intent to terminate in a distress termination under section 4041(c) and subsequently terminates under section 4042, where the termination date is the same as the proposed termination date under section 4041(c).) PBGC may in its discretion apply the general rule in paragraph (a)(3)(i) instead of the special rule in this paragraph (a)(3)(ii) if warranted under the facts and circumstances (*e.g.,* to avoid abuse).

(b) *Fixed interest rate.* If the interest crediting rate used to determine the participant's accumulated benefit (or a portion thereof) under the plan is the same fixed rate during each interest crediting period for which the interest crediting date is within the 5-year period ending on the plan's termination date, PBGC will use the fixed rate to apply interest credits to a participant's hypothetical account beginning after the termination date and ending on the participant's normal retirement date or annuity starting date, as applicable. If the interest rate (or tabular adjustment factor) used to determine the amount of any benefit under the plan payable in the form of an annuity payable at normal retirement age is the same fixed rate (or factor) for the entire 5-year period ending on the termination date, PBGC will use such fixed rate (or factor) to convert the participant's hypothetical account to an annuity.

(c) *Variable rate.*

(1) *Use of average rate for determining interest credits after termination date.*

(i) If the interest rate used by the plan to determine a participant's accumulated benefit (or a portion thereof) under the plan was a variable rate during the interest crediting periods in the 5-year period ending on the plan's termination date, PBGC will use the average of the interest crediting rates used under the plan during the 5-year period ending on the termination date to apply interest credits to a participant's hypothetical account balance beginning after the termination date and ending on the participant's normal retirement date or annuity starting date, as applicable.

(ii) For purposes of paragraph (c)(1)(i), the average is the arithmetic average, expressed as an annual rate, of the interest crediting rates that applied under the terms of the plan during any interest crediting period for which the interest crediting date is within the 5-year period ending on the termination date (excluding any interest crediting date under the terms of the plan that is distinct from the plan's regular interest crediting date, such as the date of separation from employment or plan termination).

(2) *Use of average rate for determining annuity amount.* If the interest rate (or tabular adjustment factor) used by the plan to determine the amount of any benefit under the plan payable in the form of an annuity payable at normal retirement age is a variable rate during the 5-year period ending on the plan's termination date, PBGC will determine the arithmetic average of the interest rates (or factors) that applied under the terms of the plan during periods for which the date of any rate (or factor) change was within the 5-year period ending on the termination date. The average rate will apply to determine the amount of any

benefit under the plan payable in the form of a life annuity (*i.e.*, an annuity that continues at least as long as the life of the annuitant) payable at normal retirement age, or, in the case of an immediate annuity conversion plan that uses a variable rate to determine the amount of a benefit, to determine the amount of any benefit under the plan payable in the form of a life annuity payable at the annuity starting date. In either case, the averaging requirement will apply only to determine the amount of the benefit in the automatic PBGC form under § 4022.8(b) of PBGC's regulation on Benefits Payable in Terminated Single-Employer Plans, *e.g.*, the form a married participant or an unmarried participant (as applicable) would be entitled to receive from the plan in the absence of an election. If the participant or beneficiary elects an optional PBGC form under § 4022.8(c), PBGC will convert the benefit amount from the automatic PBGC form in accordance with that section.

(3) *Replacement with 3 rd Segment Rate.* If the interest crediting rate in any interest crediting period during the 5-year period ending on the termination date is a variable rate described in § 1.411(b)(5)-1(d)(5) of the Treasury regulations or a variable rate that is impermissible under Treasury regulations, PBGC will replace such rate with the third segment rate under Code section 430(h)(2)(C)(iii) for the last calendar month ending before the beginning of the interest crediting period. Consistent with Treasury regulations, PBGC generally will adjust the third segment rate to account for any maximums or minimums to the interest crediting rate that applied in the period under the plan's terms, but will not adjust the third segment rate with regard to other reductions that applied in the period under the plan.

(4) *Application of average interest rate.* The average interest crediting rate determined under paragraphs (c)(1), (c)(2), and (c)(3) of this section will apply to determine the participant's accumulated benefit beginning after the plan's termination date, and ending on the participant's normal retirement date (or later annuity starting date), or - depending on the terms of the plan - the participant's annuity starting date. If the plan's termination date occurs in the middle of an interest crediting period, the participant's hypothetical account balance will be credited with a pro rata amount of the interest credit the participant would have otherwise received under the terms of the plan for the portion of the interest crediting period ending on the plan's termination date (but this rate will not be included in the average interest crediting rate determined under paragraphs (c)(1), (c)(2), and (c)(3) of this section). For any subsequent partial interest crediting period (*e.g.*, a portion of the interest crediting period following the plan's termination date), the participant's hypothetical account balance will be credited with a pro rata amount of the average interest crediting rate determined under paragraphs (c)(1), (c)(2), and (c)(3).

(5) *Definition of variable rate.* A variable interest rate is a rate of interest that is adjusted at least annually under the plan based on a floating interest rate, yield, or rate of return, and that otherwise satisfies the requirements of section 204(b)(5) of ERISA and section 411(b)(5) of the Code and regulations thereunder. It includes interest credits determined under a plan based on the greater of 2 or more different interest crediting rates (*e.g.*, a fixed rate and a variable rate); a floor applied to certain rates; and a rate that can never be in excess of certain bond-based rates (see Treasury regulations § 1.411(b)(5)-1(d)). Also, for purposes of the averaging rules described in § 4022.121(c), a variable rate includes any rate that was not the same fixed rate on any interest crediting date during the interest crediting periods in the 5-year period ending on the plan's termination date or, in the case of a variable annuity conversion rate (or factor), on the date of any rate (or factor) change within the 5-year period ending on the termination date.

(d) *Default rules for determining benefits.* To the extent that plan provisions do not satisfy section 204(b)(5)(B) of ERISA and section 411(b)(5)(B) of the Code and implementing regulations, or that the plan fails to specify provisions necessary to implement applicable statutory or regulatory requirements (including requirements in paragraph (d)(5) and (d)(6) of this section), PBGC will apply the rules in paragraphs (d)(1) through (d)(6) of this section.

(1) *Averaging requirement or averaging methodology.* If the plan uses a variable rate to determine the participant's accumulated benefit or the amount of any benefit payable as an annuity at normal retirement age, PBGC will determine a participant's benefits using the arithmetic average of the rates of interest used under the plan, as described in paragraph (c).

(2) *Mortality table.* With respect to the mortality table to be used, PBGC will use the mortality table provided under Code section 417(e) that would apply if the annuity starting date were the plan's termination date (*i.e.*, no future projections to the mortality table).

(3) *Interest crediting rate.* Solely with respect to a plan's failure to specify the interest crediting rate to be used, PBGC will compute an

average interest crediting rate as the arithmetic mean of the 30-year Treasury Constant Maturity rates in effect for five calendar months: the calendar month in which the plan terminates, and, for each of the preceding four years, the calendar month that is the same as the calendar month in which the plan terminates. For example, if a plan terminates in July 2009, the relevant months would be July 2009, July 2008, July 2007, July 2006, and July 2005.

(4) *Annuity conversion interest rate.* With respect to an annuity conversion interest rate or conversion factor to be used, PBGC will compute an average annuity conversion interest rate as the arithmetic mean of the 30-year Treasury Constant Maturity rates in effect for five calendar months: the calendar month in which the plan terminates, and, for each of the preceding four years, the calendar month that is the same as the calendar month in which the plan terminates. For example, if a plan terminates in July 2009, the relevant months would be July 2009, July 2008, July 2007, July 2006, and July 2005.

(5) *Five-year period includes plan years before 2008.* PBGC will take into account the interest rates used under the plan prior to the first plan year beginning on or after January 1, 2008 (or the earlier or later effective date described in sections 701(e)(3)-(5) of PPA 2006), if these plan years are part of the 5-year averaging period, for purposes of calculating an average rate of interest. For plans in existence on June 29, 2005, the rates used before the 2008 plan year (or other PPA 2006 effective date for a plan) during the 5-year averaging period are not subject to the requirements of section 204(b)(5)(B) of ERISA and section 411(b)(5)(B) of the Code (except as otherwise provided under Treasury regulations) although PBGC will apply the rules in paragraph (c)(2) of this section to such rates.

(6) *Statutory hybrid benefit formula in effect less than five years.* If the statutory hybrid benefit formula under the plan was in effect for less than five years, PBGC will use the interest rates used under the plan, modified in accordance with this section, during the period the statutory hybrid benefit formula was in effect to calculate the average rate of interest.

(7) *Examples of application of averaging rules.*

Example 1. Projected annuity conversion plan with replacement of 3 rd segment rate. Upon the termination of a cash balance plan, the plan provides a variable index for purposes of determining the interest crediting rate. The plan credits interest annually at the end of each calendar year through the participant's normal retirement date (or the current date, if later). The plan's termination date is June 30, 2015. For the two immediately preceding interest crediting dates within the 5-year period ending on the termination date, December 31, 2014, and December 31, 2013, the plan used the annual rate of return on plan assets as of the end of the preceding plan year as its interest crediting rate. For the three preceding interest crediting dates within the 5-year period, the plan used the rates under a Treasury bond index described in Treas. Reg. § 1.411(b)(5)-1(d)(4) as of the end of the preceding plan year as its interest crediting rate. Based on these rates, the plan used interest crediting rates of 8.00%, -3.00%, 4.50%, 5.50%, and 6.00%, respectively, for the interest crediting periods ending December 31, 2014, December 31, 2013, December 31, 2012, December 31, 2011, and December 31, 2010. When calculating the average rate of interest, PBGC would replace the rate of return on plan assets with the third segment rate for the last calendar month ended before the beginning of each interest crediting period. Assume these third segment rates are 6.40% and 6.70%, respectively. PBGC would replace the 8.00% interest rate with 6.40% and the -3.00% interest rate with 6.70%. PBGC would then calculate the average rate of interest as the arithmetic average of 6.40%, 6.70%, 4.50%, 5.50%, and 6.00%, which equals 5.82% ((6.40 + 6.70 + 4.50 + 5.50 + 6.00)/5). PBGC thus would use a pro rata amount of the annual rate of return on plan assets for the period ending December 31, 2014, to credit a participant's hypothetical account balance for the period from January 1, 2015 through June 30, 2015, and a rate of 5.82% to apply interest credits to a participant's hypothetical account balance each year for the period from July 1, 2015, through the participant's normal retirement date (pro rated for any partial interest crediting period).

Example 2. Immediate annuity conversion plan with fixed tabular conversion factor. The interest crediting rate is the same as in *Example 1*, except that the plan credits interest through the participant's retirement date and provides for immediate annuity conversion factors at any age. Assume a participant has a hypothetical account balance equal to $100,000 as of the plan's termination date on June 30, 2015; this balance includes annual pay credits through December 31, 2014, and a pro rata interest credit through June 30, 2015, based on the plan's interest crediting rate. The participant retires on November 1, 2020, at age 55. PBGC would determine the participant's hypothetical account balance on November 1, 2020, by applying interest credits to the participant's

$100,000 hypothetical account balance at an annual rate of 5.82%, credited on December 31 of each year and pro rated for any partial crediting period. The resulting hypothetical account balance at the participant's retirement is $135,216 ($100,000 x 1.0582 $^{5.33333}$) (this includes pro rata credit for the periods July 1, 2015 through December 31, 2015, and January 1, 2020 through October 31, 2020). PBGC would then determine the amount of the participant's benefit payable as an annuity by converting the hypothetical account balance to an immediate annuity using the plan's immediate annuity conversion factor at age 55. The plan provides for an immediate annuity conversion factor of 14.2 at age 55. Therefore, the resulting monthly annuity benefit for the participant at age 55 is $794 ($135,216 /(14.2 × 12)).

Example 3. Immediate annuity conversion plan with variable conversion interest rate. The facts are the same as in Examples 1 and 2, except that the plan used a variable annuity conversion rate based on the rates under a Treasury bond index described in Treas. Reg. § 1.411(b)(5)-1(d)(4) at the beginning of each plan year. The plan's average annuity conversion rate would include rates on the date of each rate change that occurred within the 5-year period from July 1, 2010 through June 30, 2015. Assume these rates are 5.25%, 4.75%, 5.50%, 4.50%, and 5.50%, respectively, for the date of each rate change on January 1, 2015, January 1, 2014, January 1, 2013, January 1, 2012, and January 1, 2011. PBGC would calculate the arithmetic average of 5.25%, 4.75%, 5.50%, 4.50%, and 5.50%, which equals 5.10% ((5.25 + 4.75 + 5.50 + 4.50 + 5.50)/5). The plan defines the mortality table used to convert account balances to monthly annuity benefits to be GAR94. PBGC would then use 5.10% and mortality table GAR94 to calculate an annuity conversion factor of 14.4198 at age 55. Therefore, the resulting monthly annuity benefit for the participant at age 55 is $781 ($135,216 / (14.4198 × 12)).

(e) *PPA 2006 bankruptcy termination.* In the case of a PPA 2006 bankruptcy termination, PBGC will apply interest credits to a participant's hypothetical account balance determined as of the bankruptcy filing date by using the following interest rates:

(i) The interest rate(s) in effect under the plan for the period beginning after the bankruptcy filing date and ending on the plan's termination date.

(ii) The interest rate as of the plan's termination date - or if the interest rate under the plan is a variable rate as of the termination date, the average rate of interest as determined under paragraphs (c) or (d) of this section - for the period beginning after the termination date and ending on the participant's normal retirement date (or later annuity starting date), or - depending on the terms of the plan -on the participant's annuity starting date.

§ 4022.122 Lump sum payment.

(a) *Lump sum as hypothetical account balance under the plan.* Notwithstanding § 4022.7 of this part, if the plan provides for a single sum payment equal to the balance of the hypothetical account of the participant (or the value of the accumulated percentage of the participant's final average compensation), PBGC will determine whether the benefit is payable as a de minimis lump sum payment and the amount of the lump sum payment based on the participant's hypothetical account balance (or the accumulated percentage of final average compensation) as of the plan's termination date, to the extent payable under title IV of ERISA.

(b) *Lump sum based on section 417(e) under the plan.*

(1) *In general.* If paragraph (a) of this section does not apply (*e.g.,* the plan provides that the present value rules of section 417(e) of the Code apply in calculating the amount of a single sum payment), PBGC will use the methodology in § 4022.7 of this part to determine the lump sum value of the benefit. If either this amount or the participant's hypothetical account balance (or accumulated percentage of final average compensation), as of the termination date, is $5,000 or less, PBGC will pay the greater of the two amounts as a de minimis lump sum payment, except as provided in paragraph (b)(2) of this section.

(2) *Exception.* If, on or after August 18, 2006, the plan has made any lump sum payments based on the hypothetical account balance (or the current value of the accumulated percentage of the participant's final average compensation) without regard to the present value rules of section 417(e) of the Code, or stated in writing its intent to make lump sum payments on that basis, PBGC will calculate the lump sum value of a benefit, to determine whether the benefit is payable as a lump sum and, if so, the amount of the payment, in accordance with paragraph (a) of this section.

(c) *Plan does not describe determination of lump sum amount.* If the plan does not provide for a single sum payment or de minimis lump

sum payment, or does not describe the calculation of such a payment, PBGC will calculate the lump sum value of a benefit, to determine whether the benefit is payable as a lump sum and, if so, the amount of the payment, in accordance with paragraph (a) of this section.

§ 4022.123 Phase-in of guarantee of benefit increases.

(a) *Changes subject to phase-in limitation.* For purposes of applying § 4022.24 and the phase-in limitations on the guarantee under § 4022.25, except as otherwise provided in subsection (b) of this section, a benefit increase as defined under § 4022.2 includes, but is not limited to, a benefit increase that results from a change in the plan's —

(i) Timing or method for crediting interest;

(ii) Fixed mortality table to another fixed mortality table;

(iii) Fixed mortality table to a mortality table that updates automatically in future years to reflect expected improvements in mortality experience (or such updated mortality table to a fixed mortality table), or other change in the basis on which a participant's hypothetical account balance is converted into a benefit payable as an annuity;

(iv) Fixed interest rate to another fixed interest rate; or

(v) Basis for crediting interest to a participant's hypothetical account or for determining the interest factor used to convert a hypothetical account to an annuity. Such a change includes, but is not limited to, a change from a fixed rate basis to a variable rate basis (or vice versa) or a change from one variable index to another variable index.

(b) *Changes not subject to phase-in limitation.* Changes resulting in a benefit increase under a plan that will not be treated as a benefit increase under § 4022.2 include —

(i) A change that is required to comply with the termination requirements of ERISA section 204(b)(5)(B)(vi) and Code section 411(b)(5)(B)(vi) (*e.g.,* a change in the plan's interest rate to an average rate of interest);

(ii) A change in the interest crediting rate that is permitted, notwithstanding section 411(d)(6) of the Code, pursuant to Treasury regulations (*e.g.,* a change that is permitted under Treas. Reg. § 1.411(b)(5)-1(e)(3), including a change under certain circumstances to the longterm investment grade corporate bond rate);

(iii) A change in the interest crediting rate that is permitted during the amendatory period under section 1107 of PPA 2006, or any extension of the amendatory period issued by the Department of the Treasury;

(iv) An adjustment in the interest rate under a specified variable rate index used by the plan; and

(v) An automatic future update in a mortality table specified under the plan as of the termination date that reflects expected improvements in mortality experience (*e.g.,* the applicable mortality table provided under Code section 417(e)(3)).

PART 4041 - TERMINATION OF SINGLE-EMPLOYER PLANS

6. The authority citation for part 4041 continues to read as follows:

Authority: 29 USC 1302(b)(3), 1341, 1344, 1350.

7. In § 4041.2, amend the first paragraph by removing the words "standard termination, termination date" and adding in their place "standard termination, statutory hybrid plan, termination date".

8. In § 4041.28, amend paragraph (c) by redesignating paragraph (4) as paragraph (5), redesignating paragraph (3) as paragraph (4), and adding a new paragraph (3) to read as follows:

§ 4041.28. Closeout of plan.

* * * * *

(c) * * *

* * * * *

(3) *Statutory hybrid plans.* This paragraph (c)(3) applies only for purposes of this part. The plan administrator is deemed to comply with section 204(b)(5)(B)(vi) of ERISA and section 411(b)(5)(B)(vi) of the Code and implementing regulations issued by the Department of the Treasury if the plan administrator distributes plan assets in satisfaction of plan benefits consistent with the provisions in § 4022.121 of this chapter.

9. In § 4041.42, amend paragraph (c) by adding a sentence at the end to read as follows: "The plan administrator of a statutory hybrid plan must do so consistent with the provisions under part 4022, subpart H, of this chapter."

PART 4044 - ALLOCATION OF ASSETS IN SINGLE-EMPLOYER PLANS

10. The authority citation for part 4044 continues to read as follows:

Authority: 29 USC 1301(a), 1302(b)(3), 1341, 1344, 1362.

11. In § 4044.2, amend paragraph (a) by removing the words "single-employer plan, substantial owner" and adding in their place "single-employer plan, statutory hybrid plan, substantial owner".

12. In § 4044.52, add a new paragraph (e) to read as follows:

§ 4044.52 Valuation of Benefits.

* * * * *

(e) *Statutory hybrid plans.*

(1) *In general.* Except as provided in paragraphs (e)(2) through (e)(4) of this section, benefits must be valued under a terminating statutory hybrid plan consistent with the general valuation rules of this subpart B of part 4044, and the provisions for the calculation and payment of benefits described in subpart H of part 4022 of this chapter.

(2) *De minimis lump sum exception.* If a benefit is payable as a de minimis lump sum under § 4022.122, the form to be valued is the benefit payable as an annuity in the absence of a valid election under the terms of the plan, at the expected retirement age, in accordance with §§ 4044.51 through 4044.57 of this part.

(3) *Involuntary termination exception.* If a benefit payment is calculated pursuant to § 4022.121(a)(3)(ii), the benefit will be valued based on the interest crediting rate and the annuity conversion rate in effect under the plan as of the plan's termination date (subject to the rules of §§ 4022.121 through 4022.123, disregarding § 4022.121(a)(3)(ii)), at the expected retirement age, in accordance with §§ 4044.51 through 4044.57 of this part.

(4) *Priority category 3 benefits.* The amount of the priority category 3 benefit under § 4044.13 of this part with respect to a participant who was eligible to receive a priority category 3 benefit will be determined in accordance with paragraphs (e)(4)(i) through (iii) of this section.

(i) In the case of a termination that is not a PPA 2006 bankruptcy termination, the priority category 3 benefit of a participant who is eligible to receive an annuity before the beginning of the 3-year period ending on the termination date, but whose benefit was not in pay status as of that date, will be determined based on the balance of the participant's hypothetical account, the interest crediting rate, and the annuity conversion factor that the plan would have used had the participant retired three years before the termination date (on the same day and month as the termination date). The interest rates as so determined will be used to apply interest credits from such date through the plan's normal retirement age, and to convert the participant's hypothetical account balance to an annuity. (If the plan provides for immediate annuity conversion factors, the amount of the account balance is determined and converted to an annuity as of the date three years before the termination date, based on the rates in effect as of that date.) The benefits in priority category 3 are generally based on the lowest annuity benefit payable under the plan provisions during the 5-year period ending on the termination date.

(ii) In the case of a PPA 2006 bankruptcy termination, the priority category 3 benefit of a participant who is eligible to receive an annuity before the beginning of the 3-year period ending on the bankruptcy filing date, but whose benefit was not in pay status as of that date, will be determined based on the balance of the participant's hypothetical account, the interest crediting rate, and the annuity conversion rate that the plan would have used had the participant retired three years before the bankruptcy filing date (on the same day and month as the bankruptcy filing date). The interest rates as so determined will be used to apply interest credits from such date through the plan's normal retirement age, and to convert the participant's hypothetical account balance to an annuity. (If the plan provides for immediate annuity conversion factors, the amount of the account balance is determined and converted to an annuity as of the date three years before the bankruptcy filing date, based on the rates in effect as of that date.) The benefits in priority category 3 are generally based on the lowest annuity benefit payable under the plan provisions during the 5-year period ending on the bankruptcy filing date.

(iii) In accordance with § 4044.10, the benefit assigned to priority category 3, as determined under paragraphs (e)(4)(i) or (e)(4)(ii), may not exceed the amount of the benefit determined as of the plan's termination date under the plan provisions as of the termination date (including the use of an average rate of interest in the case of a variable rate under § 4022.121).

(5) *Example*: The plan termination is a PPA 2006 bankruptcy termination with a bankruptcy filing date on August 31, 2008. Because Participant A had reached his Earliest PBGC Retirement Date, as defined in § 4022.10, based on plan provisions in effect on August 31, 2005, on the same day and month as the bankruptcy filing date but three years earlier, Participant A has benefits in priority category 3. The plan used the 1-year Treasury Constant Maturity rate of 3.64% for the calendar month prior to the bankruptcy filing date (July 2005) to determine both the interest crediting rate and the annuity conversion rate on August 31, 2005. PBGC would determine Participant A's priority category 3 benefit based on the balance of Participant A's hypothetical account as of August 31, 2005, by using the interest rate used under the plan on August 31, 2005, to apply interest credits from August 31, 2005, through the normal retirement age (as provided under the plan's terms) and convert the participant's hypothetical account balance to an annuity. The participant's priority category 3 benefit would be limited to the amount of the participant's plan benefit as of the termination date, in accordance with § 4044.10, determined by applying interest credits based on the interest rate(s) in effect under the plan for the period from the bankruptcy filing date through the plan's termination date, and the interest rate as of the plan's termination date (including the average of the rates of interest under a variable index used by the plan during the 5-year period ending on the termination date) for the period from the termination date to the normal retirement age).

13. Add new § 4044.76 to subpart B to read as follows:

§ 4044.76 Statutory hybrid plans.

(a) *Valuation.* This section supplements the general rules in part 4044 for the valuation of benefits payable in a terminated statutory hybrid plan.

(b) *Interest and mortality assumptions.* In determining benefits under the plan, the plan administrator must value benefits consistent with the provisions in § 4022.121 of this chapter.

Issued in Washington, D.C., this _24th_ day of _October___, 2011.

Joshua Gotbaum

Director

Pension Benefit Guaranty Corporation

[FR Doc. 2011-28124 Filed 10/28/2011 at 8:45 am; Publication Date: 10/31/2011]

¶ 20,538E

Employee Benefit Security Administration (EBSA): Proposed regulations: Multiple employer welfare arrangements (MEWAs): Patient Protection and Affordable Care Act.— The Employee Benefits Security Administration has issued proposed regulations, pursuant to provisions and authority established under the Patient Protection and Affordable Care Act (P.L. 111-148), that would implement enhanced reporting requirements for MEWAs. Written comments on the proposed regulations are due on or before March 5, 2012.

The proposed regulations, which were published in the Federal Register on December 6, 2011 (76 FR 76222) were reproduced below. The final regulations were published in the Federal Register on March 1, 2013 (78 FR 13781). The preamble to the final regulations is at ¶ 24,314. The final regulations are reproduced at ¶ 14,212, ¶ 14,231A, ¶ 14,247, and ¶ 14,247U.

¶ 20,538F

Employee Benefits Security Administration (EBSA): Proposed regulations: Multiple employer welfare arrangements (MEWAs): Patient Protection and Affordable Care Act.—The Employee Benefits Security Administration has issued proposed regulations, pursuant to provisions and authority established under the Patient Protection and Affordable Care Act (P.L. 111-148), that would allow the Secretary of Labor to issue cease and desist orders when it appears that fraud is taking place or an arrangement is causing immediate danger to the public safety or welfare and would allow the Secretary to seize assets from a MEWA when there is probable cause that the plan is in a financially hazardous condition. The proposed regulations also establish the procedures for use by administrative law judges (ALJs) and the Secretary when a MEWA or other person challenges a temporary cease and desist order. Written comments on the proposed regulations and the proposed form revisions are due by March 5, 2012.

The proposed regulations, which were published in the Federal Register on December 6, 2011 (76 FR 76235), were reproduced below. The final regulations were published in the Federal Register on March 1, 2013 (78 FR 13797). The preamble to the final regulations is at ¶ 24,313. The final regulations are reproduced at ¶ 15,043Q-1, ¶ 15,043Q-2, ¶ 15,043Q-3, ¶ 15,043Q-4, ¶ 15,043Q-50, ¶ 15,043Q-51, ¶ 15,043Q-52, ¶ 15,043Q-53, ¶ 15,043Q-54, ¶ 15,043Q-55, ¶ 15,043Q-56, ¶ 15,043Q-57, ¶ 15,043Q-58, ¶ 15,043Q-59, ¶ 15,043Q-60, ¶ 15,043Q-61, and ¶ 15,043Q-62.

¶ 20,538G

Employee Benefits Security Administration (EBSA): IRS: Group health plans: Health insurance: Wellness programs: Nondiscrimination: Incentives.—The EBSA, IRS, and Department of Health and Human Services have issued proposed regulations, consistent with the Patient Protection and Affordable Care Act (PPACA), concerning nondiscriminatory wellness programs in group health plans. The proposed regulations increase the maximum permissible reward under a health-contingent wellness program offered in connection with a group health plan and any related health insurance coverage from 20% to 30% of the cost of coverage. In addition, the maximum permissible reward would be increased to 50% for wellness programs designed to prevent or reduce tobacco use. Other clarifications regarding the reasonable design of health-contingent wellness programs and the reasonable alternatives they must offer to avoid prohibited discrimination are included in the proposed regulations.

The proposed regulations, which were published in the Federal Register on November 26, 2012 (77 FR 70620), are reproduced at ¶ 20,263H. The final regulations were published in the Federal Register on June 3, 2013 (78 FR 33157). The preamble to the final regulations is at ¶ 23,288. The final regulations are reproduced at ¶ 15,050A-1 and ¶ 15,050R-50H.

¶ 20,538H

Employee Benefits Security Administration (EBSA): Proposed regulations: Abandoned plans: Bankruptcy trustees.—The Employee Benefits Security Administration (EBSA) has issued proposed regulations permitting bankruptcy trustees to use the Labor Department's Abandoned Plan Program to terminate and wind up the plans of sponsors in liquidation under chapter 7 of the U.S. Bankruptcy Code. In conjunction with the proposed regulations, the EBSA has issued a proposed amendment to PT Class Exemption 2006-06, dealing with services provided in connection with the termination of individual account plans (see ¶ 16,715).

The proposed regulations, which were published in the Federal Register on December 12, 2012 (77 FR 74063), are reproduced below.

Employee Benefits Security Administration

29 CFR Parts 2520, 2550, and 2578

RIN 1210-AB47

Amendments to the Abandoned Plan Regulations

AGENCY: Employee Benefits Security Administration, Labor.

ACTION: Proposed regulations.

SUMMARY: This document contains proposed amendments to three regulations previously published under the Employee Retirement Income Security Act of 1974 that facilitate the termination of, and distribution of benefits from, individual account pension plans that have been abandoned by their sponsoring employers. The principal amendments propose to permit bankruptcy trustees to use the Department's Abandoned Plan Program to terminate and wind up the plans of sponsors in liquidation under chapter 7 of the U.S. Bankruptcy Code. In addition, other technical amendments are proposed to improve the operation of the regulations. If adopted, the amendments would affect employee benefit plans, primarily small defined contribution plans, participants and beneficiaries, service providers, and individuals appointed to serve as trustees under chapter 7 of the U.S. Bankruptcy Code.

DATES: Written comments should be received by the Department of Labor on or before February 11, 2013.

ADDRESSES: Written comments may be submitted to the addresses specified below. All comments will be made available to the public. Warning: Do not include any personally identifiable information (such as name, address, or other contact information) or confidential business information that you do not want publicly disclosed. All comments may be posted on the Internet and can be retrieved by most Internet search engines. Comments may be submitted anonymously. Comments may be submitted to the Department of Labor, by one of the following methods:

• *Federal eRulemaking Portal: http://www.regulations.gov.* Follow the instructions for submitting comments.

• *Email: e-ORI@dol.gov.* Include RIN 1210-AB47 in the subject line of the message.

• *Mail:* Office of Regulations and Interpretations, Employee Benefits Security Administration, Room N-5655, U.S. Department of Labor, 200

Constitution Avenue NW., Washington, DC 20210, Attention: Abandoned Plans.

All submissions received must include the agency name and Regulation Identifier Number (RIN) for this rulemaking (RIN 1210-AB47). Comments received will be made available to the public, posted without change to *http://www.regulations.gov* and *http://www.dol.gov/ebsa,* and made available for public inspection at the Public Disclosure Room, N-1513, Employee Benefits Security Administration, 200 Constitution Avenue NW., Washington, DC 20210.

FOR FURTHER INFORMATION CONTACT: Stephanie Ward Cibinic or Melissa R. Dennis, Office of Regulations and Interpretations, Employee Benefits Security Administration, (202) 693-8500. This is not a toll-free number.

SUPPLEMENTARY INFORMATION:

A. Executive Summary

Pursuant to Executive Order 13563, this section of the preamble contains an executive summary of the rulemaking and related prohibited transaction class exemption (published elsewhere in the notice section of today's **Federal Register**) in order to promote public understanding and to ensure an open exchange of information and perspectives. Sections B through G of this preamble, below, contain a more detailed description of the regulatory provisions and need for the rulemaking as well as its costs and benefits.

1. Purpose of Regulatory Action

In 2006, the Department of Labor (the Department) issued regulations establishing a program to facilitate the termination of and distribution of benefits from individual account plans that have been abandoned by their sponsors. In conjunction with the regulations, the Department also issued a class exemption that permits certain transactions associated with these types of terminations and distributions. The regulations and the class exemption (hereinafter referred to collectively as the Abandoned Plan Program or Abandoned Plan Regulations, unless otherwise indicated) currently are not available to plans whose sponsors are in liquidation under chapter 7 of the U.S. Bankruptcy Code (hereinafter referred to as chapter 7 plans). Since the establishment of the Abandoned Plan Program, on-going challenges associated with terminating and winding up chapter 7 plans have persuaded the Department that the Abandoned Plan Program should be expanded. This proposed rulemaking, along with the proposed amendments to the related class exemption, would help abate these challenges by making the Abandoned Plan Program available to bankruptcy trustees who, under the U.S. Bankruptcy Code, may have responsibility for administering such plans. The Secretary of Labor would make these amendments under her authority at section 505 of ERISA to prescribe such regulations as she finds necessary or appropriate to carry out the statute's provisions. The Secretary also has the authority to issue exemptions from ERISA's prohibited transaction rules in accordance with section 408(a) of ERISA and section 4975(c)(2) of the Internal Revenue Code and pursuant to the exemption procedures established in 29 CFR part 2570, subpart B.

2. Summary of Major Provisions

The major provisions of this rulemaking include the proposed amendments contained in paragraph (j) of proposed 29 CFR 2578.1. Pursuant to these proposed amendments, chapter 7 plans would be considered abandoned upon the Bankruptcy Court's entry of an order for relief with respect to the plan sponsor's bankruptcy proceeding. The bankruptcy trustee or a designee would be eligible to terminate and wind up such plans under procedures similar to those provided under the Department's current Abandoned Plan Regulations. If the bankruptcy trustee winds up the plan under the Abandoned Plan Program, the trustee's expenses would have to be consistent with industry rates for similar services ordinarily charged by qualified termination administrators that are not bankruptcy trustees. The proposed amendment to the class exemption would permit bankruptcy trustees, as with qualified termination administrators under the current Abandoned Plan Regulations, to pay themselves from the assets of the plan (a prohibited transaction) for terminating and winding up a chapter 7 plan under an industry rates standard.

3. Summary of Costs and Benefits

The Department estimates that the costs attributable to amending the Abandoned Plan Program to cover chapter 7 plans will be $64,000 annually. The Department believes the benefits of expanding the program will significantly outweigh the costs. Expanding the program will encourage the orderly and efficient termination of chapter 7 plans and distribution of account balances, thereby enhancing the retirement income security of participants and beneficiaries in these plans. Absent the standards and procedures set forth in the amendments, some bankruptcy trustees may lack the necessary guidance to properly update plan records, calculate account balances, select and monitor service providers, distribute benefits, pay fees/expenses, and otherwise efficiently terminate and wind up chapter 7 plans. In addition, significant cost savings would result from the amendments because chapter 7 plans no longer incur costly audit fees required to file the Form 5500 Annual Return/Report. The Department's full cost/benefit analysis is set forth below in Section G of this preamble, entitled "Regulatory Impact Analysis."

B. Background

On April 21, 2006, the Department of Labor (the Department) issued three regulations (the Abandoned Plan Regulations) that collectively facilitate the orderly, efficient termination of, and distribution of benefits from, individual account pension plans that have been abandoned by their sponsoring employers.[1] The first of these regulations, codified at 29 CFR 2578.1, establishes standards for determining when individual account plans may be considered "abandoned" and procedures by which financial institutions (so-called "qualified termination administrators" or "QTAs") holding the assets of such plans may terminate the plans and distribute benefits to participants and beneficiaries, with limited liability under title I of the Employee Retirement Income Security Act of 1974 (ERISA), 29 U.S.C. 1002 et seq. The second regulation, codified at 29 CFR 2550.404a-3, provides a fiduciary safe harbor for qualified termination administrators to make distributions on behalf of participants and beneficiaries who fail to elect a form of benefit distribution (these participants and beneficiaries are sometimes referred to as missing participants or beneficiaries). The third regulation, codified at

29 CFR 2520.103-13, establishes a simplified method for filing a terminal report for abandoned individual account plans. Also on April 21, 2006, the Department granted a prohibited transaction exemption, PTE 2006-06, which facilitates the goal of the Abandoned Plan Regulations by permitting a qualified termination administrator, who meets the conditions in the exemption, to, among other things, select itself or an affiliate to carry out the termination and winding up activities specified in the Abandoned Plan Regulations, and to pay itself or an affiliate fees for those services.[2]

For the reasons set forth in the 2006 preamble, the Abandoned Plan Regulations strictly limit who may be a qualified termination administrator.[3] Specifically, in order to be a qualified termination administrator, an entity, first, must be eligible to serve as a trustee or issuer of an individual retirement plan within the meaning of section 7701(a)(37) of the Internal Revenue Code (Code) and, second, must hold assets of the plan on whose behalf it will serve as the qualified termination administrator.[4] As a result of these conditions, bankruptcy trustees ordinarily do not qualify as qualified termination administrators under the Abandoned Plan Regulations. This fact was acknowledged when the Department published the Abandoned Plan Regulations in 2006.[5]

However, for several reasons, the Department is revisiting its earlier decision to preclude bankruptcy trustees from serving as qualified termination administrators. Pursuant to 11 U.S.C. 704(a)(11), enacted as part of the Bankruptcy Abuse Prevention and Consumer Protection Act of 2005, Public Law 109-8, 119 Stat. 23, when an entity that sponsors an individual account plan is liquidated under chapter 7 of title 11 of the United States Code, the court administering the liquidation proceeding (and/or U.S. Trustee) will appoint a bankruptcy trustee to, among other things, continue to perform the obligations that would otherwise be required of the bankrupt entity with respect to the plan. Therefore, the bankruptcy trustee often is responsible for administering the plan, which may include taking the steps necessary to terminate the plan, wind up the affairs of the plan, and distribute plan benefits.[6] While the U.S. Bankruptcy Code imposes these obligations on bankruptcy trustees, it does not provide guidance or standards for carrying out such activities.

The Department believes that when the sponsor of an individual account plan is in liquidation in a chapter 7 bankruptcy case, the plan should be terminated and wound up in an orderly and efficient manner. However, in bankruptcy cases, as with abandoned plans generally, usually the sponsor is not in a position to carry out this function. Although the trustee of the sponsor's bankruptcy estate has the requisite legal authority, the Department has observed that such trustees may be unaware of their responsibilities and often are unfamiliar with ERISA, or how properly to terminate and wind up a plan. The frequent result is delay in distributing benefits to participants and beneficiaries and excessive cost to the plan.

In the Department's view, a bankruptcy trustee responsible for administering a chapter 7 debtor's employee benefit plan is a fiduciary with respect to the plan for purposes of ERISA. Thus, when taking steps to wind up the affairs of the plan, the trustee must act consistently with ERISA's fiduciary standards. The Department is proposing these regulations (which are in the form of amendments to the Abandoned Plan Regulations), and the accompanying prohibited transaction exemption amendment, in order to provide a process for the bankruptcy trustee to terminate the plan, distribute benefits to participants and beneficiaries, and pay necessary expenses, including to itself, in a manner that helps the bankruptcy trustee meet its fiduciary obligations.

C. Overview of Proposed Rulemaking

In general, this rulemaking proposes to extend the basic framework of the Abandoned Plan Regulations to plans (i.e., chapter 7 plans) whose sponsors are undergoing liquidation under chapter 7 of title 11 of the United States Code.[7] The provisions of the existing Abandoned Plan Regulations would apply to chapter 7 plans in much the same way

---

[1] 71 FR 20820. See also 73 FR 58459 for subsequent amendments with regard to distributions on behalf of a missing non-spouse beneficiary.

[2] 71 FR 20855.

[3] See 71 FR 20821 ("given the authority and control over plans vested in QTAs under the regulation, QTAs must be subject to standards and oversight that will reduce the risk of losses to the plans' participants and beneficiaries").

[4] Section 7701(a)(37) of the Code describes an "individual retirement plan" as an individual retirement account described in section 408(a) of the Code, and an individual retirement annuity described in section 408(b) of the Code. Section 408(a) of the Code describes the term "individual retirement account" as meaning a trust created or organized in the United States for the exclusive benefit of an individual or his beneficiaries, if certain requirements are met. Section 408(b) of the Code describes the term "individual retire-

ment annuity" as meaning an annuity contract, or an endowment contract, which meets certain requirements.

[5] For example, in responding to commenters who argued in favor of conferring qualified termination administrator status on bankruptcy trustees in liquidation cases when the debtor also is the plan administrator, the Department, in the preamble to the Abandoned Plan Regulations, stated its view at that time that such individuals are empowered by virtue of their appointment to take the steps necessary to terminate and wind up the affairs of a plan and, therefore, do not need the authority conferred by the Abandoned Plan Regulations. See 71 FR 20821.

[6] A bankruptcy trustee who undertakes these plan responsibilities is a fiduciary within the meaning of section 3(21) of ERISA.

[7] The proposed extension is limited to plans whose sponsors entered liquidation under chapter 7 of title 11 of the United States Code on the theory that such plans are effectively

they apply now to abandoned plans, except to the extent that they are modified by this proposal to reflect fundamental differences between abandoned plans and chapter 7 plans. In this regard, the most significant amendments to the existing Abandoned Plan Regulations are contained in proposed paragraph (j) of 29 CFR 2578.1. Other less significant or conforming amendments are needed to other parts of § 2578.1 and to the other two regulations (§ 2550.404a-3 and § 2520.103-13) constituting the Abandoned Plan Regulations. Section D of this preamble describes the major proposed changes (the so-called chapter 7 amendments) to the Abandoned Plan Regulations. This rulemaking, however, also proposes to make certain technical changes to the Abandoned Plan Regulations that are unrelated to chapter 7 plans. These amendments are discussed in section E of this preamble. Section F of this preamble discusses the results of the Department's consultation on this proposal with the Internal Revenue Service. Section G contains a detailed Regulatory Impact Analysis. For purposes of readability, the proposed rulemaking republishes the Abandoned Plan Regulations in their entirety, as revised, rather than the specific amendments only.

D. Special Rules for Chapter 7 Plans

1. Discussion of Major Changes to 29 CFR 2578.1—Termination of Abandoned Individual Account Plans

(a) In General

Proposed paragraph (j) of § 2578.1 contains the special rules for chapter 7 plans. This paragraph contains four subparagraphs. Subparagraph (1) sets forth rules for when such plans may be considered abandoned and who may serve as qualified termination administrators. These rules are in lieu of the general rules in paragraphs (b) and (g) of § 2578.1, which do not apply to chapter 7 plans. Subparagraph (2) sets forth the content requirements for the notice of plan abandonment that qualified termination administrators of chapter 7 plans must send to the Department. These content requirements are in lieu of the content requirements in paragraph (c)(3) of § 2578.1, which apply to abandoned plans in general. Subparagraph (3) sets forth special rules for winding up chapter 7 plans. These special rules are in lieu of some, but not all, of the winding up procedures in paragraph (d) of § 2578.1. Subparagraph (4) contains a rule of accountability that is applicable to bankruptcy trustees. The requirements of each of these subparagraphs are described in detail below.

(b) Timing of Abandonment

Proposed paragraph (j)(1)(i) is a timing rule. It provides that a chapter 7 plan shall be considered abandoned upon the entry of an order for relief. No other findings must be made. The bankruptcy trustee then may establish itself or an eligible designee as the qualified termination administrator. Whether to establish itself or an eligible designee as the qualified termination administrator is optional on the part of the bankruptcy trustee. Abandonment status, on the other hand, is not optional; it is achieved by operation of law upon the entry of an order for relief. Proposed paragraph (j)(1)(i) contains a limitation on this status. If at any time before the plan is deemed terminated (plans generally will be deemed to be terminated on the ninetieth (90th) day following the date of the letter from EBSA acknowledging receipt of the notice of plan abandonment), the plan sponsor's chapter 7 proceeding is dismissed or converted to a proceeding under chapter 11 of title 11 of the United States Code, the plan shall not be considered abandoned pursuant to paragraph (j)(1).[8] The Department believes that a plan should not be considered abandoned merely because its sponsor is in reorganization.[9]

(c) Who May Serve as a Qualified Termination Administrator

Proposed paragraph (j)(1)(ii) makes it clear that bankruptcy trustees may serve as qualified termination administrators even if they do not satisfy the rule in paragraph (g) of § 2578.1 that allows only large financial institutions and other asset custodians described in section 7701(a)(37) of the Code to be qualified termination administrators. Except as provided in paragraph (j), a bankruptcy trustee serving as

qualified termination administrator would follow the same termination and winding-up procedures in the Abandoned Plan Regulations as would any other qualified termination administrator. The proposal also allows a bankruptcy trustee the option of designating someone else to serve as the qualified termination administrator. In this regard, however, the proposal strictly limits who the bankruptcy trustee may designate. Proposed paragraph (j)(1)(ii) provides that an "eligible designee" is any person or entity designated by the bankruptcy trustee that is eligible to serve as a trustee or issuer of an individual retirement plan, within the meaning of section 7701(a)(37) of the Code, and that holds assets of the chapter 7 plan. Thus, an eligible designee could be the plan's asset custodian at the time of abandonment or another entity chosen later by the bankruptcy trustee.[10] The bankruptcy trustee would be responsible for the selection and monitoring of any eligible designee in accordance with section 404(a)(1) of ERISA.

(d) Notice of Abandonment

Proposed paragraph (j)(2) provides that, in accordance with the deemed termination provisions in paragraph (c)(1) and (c)(2) of § 2578.1, the qualified termination administrator must furnish to the Department a notice of plan abandonment that meets the content requirements in paragraph (j)(2). This notice essentially is the same as the notice of plan abandonment described in paragraph (c)(3) of § 2578.1 except for modifications that take into account information specific to chapter 7 plans and bankruptcy trustees. A proposed model "Notification of Plan Abandonment and Intent to Serve as Qualified Termination Administrator" reflecting the content requirements of proposed paragraph (j)(2) is being added for chapter 7 plans as Appendix C. Therefore, Appendices C and D have been re-proposed as Appendix D and Appendix E respectively. Paragraph (j)(2)(i) provides that the notice must include the name and contact information of the bankruptcy trustee and, if applicable, the name and contact information of the eligible designee acting as the qualified termination administrator pursuant to proposed paragraph (j)(1). Paragraph (j)(2)(ii) requires information about the chapter 7 plan that the qualified termination administrator is winding up. Paragraph (j)(2)(iii) requires a statement that the plan is considered to be abandoned due to an entry of an order for relief under chapter 7 of the U.S. Bankruptcy Code, and a copy of the notice or order entered in the case reflecting the bankruptcy trustee's appointment to administer the plan sponsor's chapter 7 case. Paragraph (j)(2)(iv)(A) and (B) require the estimated value of the plan's assets as of the entry of an order for relief; the name, employer identification number (EIN), and contact information for the entity holding the plan's assets; and the length of time plan assets have been held by such entity, if held for less than 12 months. Paragraph (j)(2)(iv)(C) and (D) require identification of any assets with respect to which there is no readily ascertainable fair market value, as well as information, if any, concerning the value of such assets, and an identification of known delinquent contributions. Paragraph (j)(2)(v) requires the name and contact information of known service providers to the plan. It also requires an identification of any services considered necessary to wind up the plan, the name of the service provider(s) that is expected to provide such services, and an itemized estimate of expenses for winding up services expected to be paid out of plan assets by the qualified termination administrator. Paragraph (j)(2)(vi) requires a statement indicating that the information provided in the notice is true and complete based on the knowledge of the person electing to be the qualified termination administrator, and that the information is being provided by the qualified termination administrator under penalty of perjury.

(e) Winding-Up Procedures

(i) In General

Paragraph (d) of § 2578.1 sets forth specific steps that a qualified termination administrator must take to wind up an abandoned plan and, with respect to most such steps, the standards applicable to carrying out the particular activity. Under the proposal, paragraph (d) applies to chapter 7 plans except as modified by the provisions in proposed paragraph (j)(3).

(Footnote Continued)

being abandoned by the sponsor as a result of the liquidation. Nonetheless, the Department requests comment on whether there are other similar situations that could or should be covered by the Abandoned Plan Regulations. For example, should the Regulations cover plans whose sponsors are undergoing liquidation under a chapter 11 plan of liquidation? Should the Regulations cover situations when a plan's sponsor enters receivership pursuant to applicable state or federal law (e.g., FDIC receivership)? If the Regulations should be extended to situations beyond the situations covered by the proposed extension, please specifically identify the situation, why the situation should be covered, the costs and benefits of covering the situation, and, if applicable, any state or federal law relevant to the situation.

[8] On the other hand, a plan would not cease to be considered abandoned under proposed paragraph (j)(1) if the sponsor's chapter 7 proceeding is converted to a proceeding under chapter 11 after the plan is deemed terminated. In such circumstances, the qualified termination administrator would be expected to continue winding up the affairs of the plan in accordance with the Abandoned Plan Regulations.

[9] But see note 7.

[10] Any eligible designee should be selected and holding the assets of the chapter 7 plan by the time of the furnishing of the notice of plan abandonment to the Department under paragraph (j)(2) of the proposed amendments.

(ii) Delinquent Contributions

Proposed paragraph (j)(3)(i) contains a conditional requirement to collect delinquent contributions. Specifically, this paragraph provides that the qualified termination administrator of a chapter 7 plan shall, consistent with the duties of a fiduciary under section 404(a)(1) of ERISA, take reasonable and good faith steps to collect known delinquent contributions on behalf of the plan, taking into account the value of the plan assets involved, the likelihood of a successful recovery, and the expenses expected to be incurred in connection with collection. If the bankruptcy trustee designates an eligible designee as defined in proposed paragraph (j)(1)(ii), the bankruptcy trustee shall at the time of such designation notify the eligible designee of any known delinquent contributions. This collection requirement includes both participant contributions withheld from employee paychecks, but not forwarded by the debtor to the plan, as well as delinquent employer contributions owed by the debtor. This collection requirement applies to any qualified termination administrator to a chapter 7 plan whether it is a bankruptcy trustee or an eligible designee.[11]

The Department's present belief is that bankruptcy trustees, by virtue of their knowledge and control of the debtor's estate and of the debtor's ERISA plan, are in the best position both to know of the liquidating sponsor's delinquent contribution debts to the plan and to collect these delinquencies (or to notify the eligible designee so that it can collect them). However, the Department is interested in knowing whether, and under what circumstances, the qualified termination administrator's duty to collect would unavoidably conflict with any duties the bankruptcy trustee may have under the U.S. Bankruptcy Code as the representative of the debtor's estate. Please be specific about when, if ever, such conflicts might arise, whether and why such conflicts are disabling, and the specific provisions of the U.S. Bankruptcy Code that impose the conflicting obligations.

(iii) Reporting Fiduciary Breaches

Proposed paragraph (j)(3)(ii) contains a requirement to report activity to the Department that may be evidence of fiduciary breaches by prior plan fiduciaries. Specifically, the qualified termination administrator of a chapter 7 plan (whether a bankruptcy trustee or eligible designee) must report known delinquent contributions (employer and employee) owed to the plan, and any activity that the qualified termination administrator believes may be evidence of other fiduciary breaches by a prior plan fiduciary that involve plan assets. Thus, for example, evidence of embezzlement by a prior plan fiduciary would be required to be reported. The proposal limits the reporting requirement to evidence of any fiduciary breaches that "involve plan assets" by a prior plan fiduciary. This limitation is intended to prevent a reporting requirement when no plan assets are involved. The Department intends to use this information to pursue and remedy fiduciary breaches where appropriate. Beyond this reporting requirement, a qualified termination administrator to a chapter 7 plan ordinarily will have no further obligations under the Abandoned Plan Regulations with respect to such prior breaches, except with respect to collecting delinquent contributions owed to the plan.[12]

Information concerning fiduciary breaches must be reported in conjunction with the filing of the notice of plan abandonment (paragraph (j)(2)) or the final notice (paragraph (d)(2)(ix)). If the qualified termination administrator uses the model notices, such information may be included in the sections designated for other information. If the bankruptcy trustee designates an eligible designee, the bankruptcy trustee must provide the eligible designee with records under the control of the bankruptcy trustee to enable the eligible designee to carry out its responsibility to report information about fiduciary breaches. In the case of an eligible designee, if after the eligible designee completes the winding up of the plan, the bankruptcy trustee, in administering the debtor's estate, discovers additional information not already reported in the notification required in paragraphs (j)(2) or (d)(2)(ix) that it believes may be evidence of fiduciary breaches that involve plan assets by a prior plan fiduciary, the bankruptcy trustee must report such activity to EBSA in a time and manner specified in instructions developed by EBSA's Office of Enforcement. This supplemental reporting requirement is needed to address circumstances when the bankruptcy trustee

discovers information concerning fiduciary breaches after the eligible designee has completed the termination and winding up process.

(iv) Notification and Distribution Requirements

The notification and distribution requirements applicable to chapter 7 plans under the proposal essentially are the same as the notification and distribution requirements applicable to non-chapter 7 plans under the existing Abandoned Plan Regulations, except as follows. First, proposed paragraph (j)(3)(iii) adds a requirement that participants must be informed that plan termination has occurred as a result of liquidation under the U.S. Bankruptcy Code. Second, proposed paragraph (j)(3)(iv) adds a requirement that the Department must receive certain information about the identity of the bankruptcy trustee and, if applicable, the eligible designee.

Third, proposed paragraph (j)(3)(v) does not grant a bankruptcy trustee the ability to designate itself or an affiliate as the transferee of distribution proceeds. The Abandoned Plan Regulations provide that qualified termination administrators must distribute benefits in accordance with the form of distribution elected by the participant or beneficiary, and when the participant or beneficiary fails to make an election, the qualified termination administrator has the ability to designate itself or an affiliate as the transferee of the distribution proceeds. (See paragraph (d)(2)(vii)(C) of §2578.1.) Typically this would occur where the qualified termination administrator has its own proprietary investment vehicle, such as an individual retirement plan within the meaning of section 7701(a)(37) of the Code. The proposal does not extend this option to bankruptcy trustees based on the Department's understanding that bankruptcy trustees do not maintain proprietary investment vehicles within the meaning of section 7701(a)(37) of the Code.

(v) Payment of Reasonable Fees

Proposed paragraph (j)(3)(vi) addresses fees that a bankruptcy trustee may pay to itself, or others, from the plan's assets in connection with following the termination and winding-up procedures in the proposed amendments. Subparagraph (A) of paragraph (j)(3)(vi) contains the applicable standard in cases where the bankruptcy trustee is the qualified termination administrator. Subparagraph (B) of paragraph (j)(3)(vi) contains the applicable standard in cases when the bankruptcy trustee appoints an eligible designee to serve as the qualified termination administrator.[13] The different standards in these subparagraphs are needed for two reasons: first, expense rates normally charged by bankruptcy trustees for administering estates of chapter 7 debtors may not be appropriate for purposes of carrying out the duties and responsibilities under the proposed amendments with respect to ERISA plans, and second, bankruptcy trustees are not likely to have significant experience in terminating and winding up the affairs of such plans. Finally, subparagraph (C) of paragraph (j)(3)(vi) regulates payments to the bankruptcy trustee by the eligible designee.

Pursuant to proposed paragraph (j)(3)(vi)(A), the qualified termination administrator (i.e., when the bankruptcy trustee is the QTA) is permitted to pay, from plan assets, no more than the reasonable expenses of carrying out his or her authority and responsibility under the proposed amendments. Expenses of plan administration shall be considered reasonable if they are for services necessary to wind up the affairs of the plan and distribute benefits (see §2578.1(d)(2)(v)(B)(*1*)), if they are consistent with industry rates for the same or similar services ordinarily charged by qualified termination administrators who are not bankruptcy trustees (see proposed paragraph (j)(3)(vi)(A)), and if their payment would not constitute a prohibited transaction (see §2578.1(d)(2)(v)(B)(*3*)). This standard is intended to make clear that bankruptcy trustees should look to the rates ordinarily charged by qualified termination administrators who are not bankruptcy trustees, e.g., banks and other asset custodians. Samples of these rates are available to the public in filings made to the Department.[14] These filings may be a helpful source of information for bankruptcy trustees.

The standard in proposed paragraph (j)(3)(vi)(A) (i.e., that expenses must be consistent with industry rates for the same or similar services ordinarily charged by qualified termination administrators who are not

---

[11] Under this provision, an eligible designee's duty to collect delinquent contributions is limited expressly to those delinquent contributions it knows about based on the information provided by the bankruptcy trustee at the time of the designation. Thus, an eligible designee would have no duty to collect delinquent contributions if the bankruptcy trustee failed to disclose them to the eligible designee. Nothing in this section imposes an obligation on the eligible designee to conduct an inquiry or review to determine whether there are delinquent contributions with respect to the plan. See §2578.1(e)(2).

[12] As discussed above, proposed paragraph (j)(3)(i) imposes on a qualified termination administrator to a chapter 7 plan a conditional duty to collect delinquent contributions.

[13] Proposed paragraph (j)(3)(vi)(B) merely confirms that an eligible designee may use the more generally applicable safe harbor at paragraph (d)(2)(v) of §2578.1 without the special modifications contained in proposed paragraph (j)(3)(v)(A) for bankruptcy trustees.

[14] Under §2520.103-13, qualified termination administrators must file the Special Terminal Report for Abandoned Plans (STRAP). STRAPs contain total termination expenses paid by a plan and a separate schedule identifying each service provider and the amount received by that service provider, itemized by expense. STRAPs currently are available on the Department's Web site (see *http://askebsa.dol.gov/AbandonedPlanSearch/UI/QTASearchResults.aspx*).

bankruptcy trustees) is intended to provide clarity and flexibility with respect to decisions regarding fee and expense payments by bankruptcy trustees who elect to be qualified termination administrators. In determining these fees and expenses, bankruptcy trustees still will have to make an inquiry into, and objectively determine, whether any particular fee or expenditure is reasonable using the standard in proposed paragraph (j)(3)(vi)(A). In this regard, the Department specifically requests comments on whether proposed paragraph (j)(3)(vi)(A) provides sufficient clarity as to the type and amount of fees and expenses that may be paid from plan assets in connection with terminating and winding up a plan under this proposal. For example, will bankruptcy trustees have difficulty determining industry rates for termination and winding up services despite the public filings mentioned above? Are these filings searchable in a helpful way to bankruptcy trustees? If proposed paragraph (j)(3)(vi)(A) does not provide sufficient clarity, please explain why not and identify any alternatives that should be considered by the Department.

Proposed paragraph (j)(3)(vi)(C) provides that an eligible designee may pay from plan assets to a bankruptcy trustee the reasonable expenses that the bankruptcy trustee incurs in selecting and monitoring the eligible designee. This provision follows from the requirement in proposed paragraph (j)(1)(ii) that the bankruptcy trustee is responsible for the selection and monitoring of the eligible designee. Whether an expense is "reasonable" ordinarily depends on the facts and circumstances surrounding the particular expense. However, the Department notes that the rates charged to the plan by the bankruptcy trustee for selecting and monitoring the eligible designee are to be judged in relation to the rates charged by a plan fiduciary for similar services, rather than the generally higher fees charged by bankruptcy trustees for legal services provided to the bankruptcy estate. In any event, pursuant to proposed paragraph (j)(3)(vi)(C), the eligible designee would apply the rules in paragraph (d)(2)(v) of §2578.1 in determining whether the payment to the bankruptcy trustee for monitoring services is reasonable. While the Department believes that it would be appropriate for bankruptcy trustees to expect remuneration for providing monitoring services, the Department intends to review closely such remuneration to ensure that arrangements under the proposed amendments are not contrary to the interests of participants and beneficiaries.

(f) Rule of Accountability

Proposed paragraph (j)(4) contains a rule of accountability. The rule provides that a bankruptcy trustee acting as qualified termination administrator, or an eligible designee, shall not, through waiver or otherwise, seek a release from liability under ERISA, or assert a defense of derived judicial immunity (or similar defense) in any action brought against the bankruptcy trustee or eligible designee arising out of its conduct under the proposed amendments. The Department is aware that bankruptcy trustees sometimes request from the bankruptcy court comfort orders seeking relief from ERISA fiduciary liability in their roles as administrators to plans. However, bankruptcy trustees who wind up chapter 7 plans under the Abandoned Plan Regulations benefit from the limited exposure to ERISA liability provided by the regulations. (See paragraph (e) of §2578.1.) The Department believes the regulatory framework, as constructed, serves to minimize to the greatest extent possible the liability and exposure of qualified termination administrators who carry out their responsibilities in accordance with the provisions of the Abandoned Plan Regulations.[15] As a condition to receiving the benefit of the limited liability provided by the Abandoned Plan Regulations, a bankruptcy trustee would not be permitted to seek a release from liability under ERISA. Paragraph (j)(4) does not prevent a bankruptcy trustee from asking a court to resolve an actual dispute involving a plan or to obtain an order required under the U.S. Bankruptcy Code. However, it does bar a trustee from seeking a ruling from a court for approval of its actions, where a trustee has the power to act without judicial approval. For example, a bankruptcy trustee may not seek court approval of the amount to pay a professional from assets of the plan, but must exercise his or her own judgment. In addition, a bankruptcy trustee may not claim it is not subject to suit for breach of fiduciary duty as to the amount of a payment from an ERISA plan because it previously obtained a court order approving the amount of the payment.

2. Discussion of Changes to 29 CFR 2550.404a-3—Safe Harbor for Distributions From Terminated Individual Account Plans

The Abandoned Plan Regulations, in relevant part, provide that, with respect to missing and nonresponsive participants or beneficiaries,[16]

qualified termination administrators shall distribute benefits in the form of direct rollovers to individual retirement plans within the meaning of section 7701(a)(37) of the Code. (See §2578.1(d)(2)(vii)(B).) However, the Abandoned Plan Regulations also contain a special rule for small account balances of $1,000 or less.[17] Under the special rule, a qualified termination administrator may make distributions to certain bank accounts (interest-bearing federally insured bank or savings association accounts) or to State unclaimed property funds. (See 29 CFR 2550.404a-3(d)(1)(iii).) The proposal would add paragraph (d)(iv) to §2550.404a-3 to make clear that the special rule also is available in the case of chapter 7 plans.

3. Discussion of Changes to 29 CFR 2520.103-13—Special Terminal Report for Abandoned Plans

The Abandoned Plan Regulations provide for simplified reporting to the Department for qualified termination administrators that wind up the affairs of abandoned plans. (See 29 CFR 2520.103-13.) The time savings resulting from this abbreviated reporting requirement reduces administrative costs for abandoned plans and preserves account balances, resulting in increased benefits to participants and beneficiaries. The proposed amendments would revise these simplified reporting requirements to make clear that they are available to chapter 7 plans. Specifically, the proposal would revise paragraph (b)(1) of §2520.103-13 to include identification information about the bankruptcy trustee as well as the qualified termination administrator, if the qualified termination administrator is not the bankruptcy trustee.

E. Technical Amendments Unrelated to Chapter 7 Plans

The Abandoned Plan Regulations require qualified termination administrators to state whether they, or any affiliate, are, or in the past 24 months were, the subject of an investigation, examination, or enforcement action by the Department, the Internal Revenue Service, or the Securities and Exchange Commission concerning their conduct as a fiduciary or party in interest with respect to any ERISA covered plan. (See §2578.1(c)(3)(i)(C).) This statement must be included in the notice of plan abandonment furnished to the Department before a plan can be terminated and wound up under the Abandoned Plan Regulations. Although such information does not alone bar a person from serving as a qualified termination administrator, the statement serves as a flagging mechanism to help the Department identify potential arrangements that are not in the best interests of plan participants and beneficiaries. However, the Department is proposing to eliminate this requirement for the following reasons. First, the Department generally can determine from its own records whether a person is, or in the past 24 months was, the subject of an investigation concerning his conduct as a fiduciary or party in interest with respect to any ERISA covered plan. Second, by definition, qualified termination administrators tend to be large financial institutions with many affiliations and, therefore, it may be costly for them to prepare an accurate statement. Third, the requirement appears to deter some qualified persons from serving as qualified termination administrators. In this regard, some individuals have expressed a reluctance to affirm in a notice to the federal government that they or an affiliate are or were under an investigation, examination, or enforcement action by the Department, the Internal Revenue Service, or the Securities and Exchange Commission concerning their conduct as a fiduciary or party in interest with respect to any ERISA covered plan. Because the Department believes that this requirement now is unnecessary and may even discourage the use of the Abandoned Plan Program, it is proposing to remove the requirement from the Abandoned Plan Regulations.

In conjunction with the proposed removal of the investigation statement in §2578.1(c)(3)(i)(C) referenced above, the Department intends to remove a part of the definition of the term "affiliate" in §2578.1(h). In the Abandoned Plan Regulations, the term "affiliate" for general purposes of §2578.1 means any person directly or indirectly controlling, controlled by, or under common control with, the person, or any officer, director, partner or employee of the person. (See §2578.1(h)(1).) However, for the specific purpose of the requirement for qualified termination administrators to state whether they, or any affiliate are, or in the past 24 months were, the subject of an investigation, examination, or enforcement action by the Department, the Internal Revenue Service, or the Securities and Exchange Commission concerning the their conduct as a fiduciary or party in interest with respect to any ERISA covered plan, the Abandoned Plan Regulations contain a narrower definition in §2578.1(h)(2). Given the proposal to eliminate this statement regarding investigations, the Department also

---

[15] 71 FR 20806.

[16] In this context, a missing or nonresponsive participant or beneficiary is a participant or beneficiary who fails to elect a form of distribution within 30 days from the date the notice of plan termination is furnished by the qualified termination administrator.

[17] The justification for the special rule is set forth in the preamble to the Abandoned Plan Regulations. See 71 FR 20828. The conditions related to the special rule are set forth at 29 CFR 2550.404a-3(d)(1)(iii).

is proposing to eliminate the narrower definition of "affiliate." The generally applicable definition of the term "affiliate" would remain in effect. (See modifications in the proposal to paragraph (h) of § 2578.1.)

The Abandoned Plan Regulations generally require the qualified termination administrator to distribute a missing or nonresponsive participant's account balance to an individual retirement plan in the participant's name. (See § 2578.1(d)(2)(vii).) An exception exists for account balances of $1,000 or less, which may be transferred to an interest-bearing, federally-insured bank or savings association account or to the unclaimed property fund of a State, if certain conditions are satisfied. (See § 2550.404a-3(d)(1)(iii).) Sometimes a qualified termination administrator will know that a missing participant whose account balance is greater than $1,000 is deceased and that there is no named beneficiary, or that the named beneficiary also is deceased. In such circumstances, the Abandoned Plan Regulations require the qualified termination administrator to transfer the participant's account balance to an individual retirement plan even if it is unlikely that anyone will ever claim these benefits. The Department has been advised that, in some cases, providers of individual retirement plans will not accept such distributions. The Department is concerned that obstacles like this prevent abandoned plans from being completely terminated and could prevent qualified entities from serving as qualified termination administrators, leaving participants in abandoned plans with no ability to access their retirement benefits. This proposal, therefore, conditionally would permit qualified termination administrators to transfer the account balances of decedents to an appropriate bank account or a state's unclaimed property fund, regardless of the size of the account balance. Such a transfer would be permitted only if the qualified termination administrator reasonably and in good faith finds that the participant and, if applicable, the named beneficiary, are deceased, and includes in the Final Notice to EBSA the identity of the deceased participant and/or beneficiary and the basis for the finding. (See proposed paragraph (d)(1)(v) of § 2550.404a-3.) The Department is soliciting public comments specifically on whether the proposed conditions sufficiently safeguard the rights of participants and beneficiaries. For example, should a qualified termination administrator be prohibited from these transfers if it has actual knowledge that a descendent of the deceased has a claim?

The final step in winding up an abandoned plan under the Abandoned Plan Regulations is filing the Special Terminal Report for Abandoned Plans (STRAP) under § 2520.103-13. As stated in the preamble to the Abandoned Plan Regulations, the purpose of this provision is to provide annual reporting relief relating to abandoned plan filings by qualified termination administrators.[18] The contents of the STRAP include, for example, total assets of the plan as of the deemed termination date, termination expenses paid by the plan, and the total amount of distributions. To file the STRAP, a qualified termination administrator must use the Form 5500 and either the Schedule I or a "Schedule QTA." Instructions for filing the STRAP are not included in the instructions to the Form 5500 Annual Return/Report of Employee Benefit Plan. Specific instructions for completing and filing the STRAP are on EBSA's Web site at *http://www.dol.gov/ebsa/publications/APterminalreport.html*. This proposal would amend paragraph (c)(2) of § 2520.103-13 to clarify and update the specific location of these instructions.

F. Internal Revenue Service

As it did in connection with the existing Abandoned Plan Regulations, the Department conferred with representatives of the Internal Revenue Service regarding the qualification requirements under the Code as applied to plans that are terminated pursuant to 29 CFR 2578.1, as modified by the proposed amendments contained in this document. The Internal Revenue Service advised that it would not challenge the qualified status of any plan terminated under § 2578.1 or take any adverse action against, or seek to assess or impose any penalty on, the qualified termination administrator, the plan, or any participant or beneficiary of the plan (including the qualified status of any chapter 7 plan terminated under these proposed amendments) as a result of such termination, including the distribution of the plan's assets, provided that the qualified termination administrator satisfies three conditions. First, the qualified termination administrator, based on plan records located and updated in accordance with § 2578.1(d)(2)(i), reasonably determines whether, and to what extent, the survivor annuity requirements of sections 401(a)(11) and 417 of the Code apply to any benefit payable under the plan and takes reasonable steps to comply with those requirements (if applicable). Second, each participant and beneficiary has a nonforfeitable right to his or her accrued benefits as of the date of deemed termination under § 2578.1(c)(1), subject to income,

expenses, gains, and losses between that date and the date of distribution. Third, participants and beneficiaries must receive notification of their rights under section 402(f) of the Code. This notification should be included in, or attached to, the notice described in § 2578.1(d)(2)(vi). Notwithstanding the foregoing, as indicated in the preamble to the final Abandoned Plan Regulations (71 FR 20827), the Internal Revenue Service reserves the right to pursue appropriate remedies under the Code against any party who is responsible for the plan, such as the plan sponsor, plan administrator, or owner of the business, even in its capacity as a participant or beneficiary under the plan.[19]

The Internal Revenue Service also advised the Department that chapter 7 bankruptcy trustees using the Abandoned Plan Program would not be expected to use the Employee Plans Compliance Resolution System (EPCRS) as a condition to this relief.

G. Regulatory Impact Analysis

1. Background and Need for Regulatory Action

As stated earlier in this preamble, this document contains proposed amendments to three previously published Abandoned Plan Regulations that facilitate the termination of, and distribution of benefits from, individual account pension plans that have been abandoned by their sponsoring employers. The amendments primarily propose to: (1) Permit bankruptcy trustees to use the Department's Abandoned Plan Regulations to terminate and wind up the plans of sponsors in liquidation under chapter 7 of the U.S. Bankruptcy Code; (2) eliminate the requirement that qualified termination administrators state in a notice to the Department whether they, or any affiliate are, or in the past 24 months were, the subject of an investigation, examination, or enforcement action by the Department, the Internal Revenue Service, or the Securities and Exchange Commission concerning their conduct as a fiduciary or party in interest with respect to any ERISA covered plan; and (3) conditionally permit qualified termination administrators to transfer the account balances of decedents to an appropriate bank account or a state's unclaimed property fund regardless of the size of the account balance. The need for these regulatory changes is explained in detail above in the "Background" section and in the overview sections, C through F, of this preamble.

2. Executive Order 12866 and 13563 Statement

Executive Orders 13563 and 12866 direct agencies to assess all costs and benefits of available regulatory alternatives and, if regulation is necessary, to select regulatory approaches that maximize net benefits (including potential economic, environmental, public health and safety effects, distributive impacts, and equity). Executive Order 13563 emphasizes the importance of quantifying both costs and benefits, of reducing costs, of harmonizing and streamlining rules, and of promoting flexibility. It also requires federal agencies to develop a plan under which the agencies will periodically review their existing significant regulations to make the agencies' regulatory programs more effective or less burdensome in achieving their regulatory objectives. The Department has identified the amendments to the Abandoned Plan Regulations as a retrospective regulatory review project consistent with the principals of Executive Order 13563. The Department believes that the proposed changes to the Abandoned Plan Regulations would improve the overall efficiency of the Abandoned Plan Program, increase its usage, and substantially reduce burdens and costs on bankruptcy trustees terminating the plans of sponsors in chapter 7 liquidation, the plans of bankrupt sponsors, and the participants in these plans.

Under Executive Order 12866, "significant" regulatory actions are subject to the requirements of the executive order and review by the Office of Management and Budget (OMB). Section 3(f) of the executive order defines a "significant regulatory action" as an action that is likely to result in a rule (1) having an annual effect on the economy of $100 million or more, or adversely and materially affecting a sector of the economy, productivity, competition, jobs, the environment, public health or safety, or State, local or tribal governments or communities (also referred to as "economically significant"); (2) creating serious inconsistency or otherwise interfering with an action taken or planned by another agency; (3) materially altering the budgetary impacts of entitlement grants, user fees, or loan programs or the rights and obligations of recipients thereof; or (4) raising novel legal or policy issues arising out of legal mandates, the President's priorities, or the principles set forth in the Executive Order. It has been determined that this proposed rule is not a "significant regulatory action" under section 3(f) of the executive order. Accordingly, OMB has not reviewed this

---

[18] 71 FR 20830.

[19] See 71 FR 20827 (further discussion of the Department's response to commenters on the three IRS conditions).

regulatory action or the Department's assessment of its costs and benefits, which is presented below.

3. Number of Affected Entities

As stated above, the proposed amendments to the Abandoned Plan Regulations would extend the framework of the regulations to chapter 7 plans. In order to estimate the number of entities affected by the Abandoned Plan Regulations as amended by the proposal, the Department must determine the number of abandoned plans that would be eligible to be terminated and wound up under the Abandoned Plan Program. At the inception of the Abandoned Plan Program in 2006, the Department based its estimate of the number of eligible plans upon Form 5500 data. Because the Department has over five years of experience with the Abandoned Plan Program, it now can base its estimate on data from EBSA's Office of Enforcement. These data show that in fiscal year 2007, the Department received 70 applications from potential qualified termination administrators to wind up abandoned plans. The number of applications increased to 331 in fiscal year 2010. Based on the foregoing, the Department estimates that approximately 330 plans covering 1,980 participants (330 plans × 6 participants per plan) would be terminated and wound up under the Abandoned Plan Program each year if the program remains unchanged.

The Department believes that there will be a 50 percent increase in the number of applications to the Abandoned Plan Program if plans of sponsors entering liquidation are permitted to be terminated and wound up under the Abandoned Plan Program. This would increase the total number of applications to 495 plans (330 plans × 1.5), and the number of affected participants to 2,970 (495 plans × 6 participants per plan), assuming that chapter 7 plans have roughly the same number of participants as other eligible plans. The Department welcomes comments regarding these estimates.

4. Costs

The Department estimates that the cost associated with extending the Abandoned Plan Program to chapter 7 plans would total approximately $64,000. These costs only would be imposed on the estimated 165 chapter 7 plans that chose to participate in the program. The Department also has updated its costs and benefits estimate for the entire Abandoned Plan Program to reflect its experience with the program since its inception in 2006. The Department estimates that the 330 abandoned plans participating in the Abandoned Plan Program would incur the following costs: $127,000 in annual costs attributable to abandoned plans' qualified termination administrator filings and notices; $4.48 million attributable to fiduciaries of the approximately 39,000 terminating plans (other than abandoned and chapter 7 plans) continuing to use the Safe Harbor for Distributions from Terminated Individual Account Plans (29 CFR 2550.404a-3), of which $3.52 million is equivalent hour burden cost attributable to in-house clerical staff and benefit managers' time; and $961,000 in mailing cost to distribute the required notices to approximately 3.1 million participants. Overall, the Department estimates that the costs of the regulations and class exemption, as amended by the proposal, would total approximately $4.67 million ($3.52 million in annual equivalent costs and $1.15 million in annual cost burden) but, as stated above, only $64,000 of such costs relate to the proposed amendments. These costs are quantified and discussed in more detail in the Paperwork Reduction Act section, below.

5. Benefits

The proposed amendments provide critical guidance that will encourage the orderly and efficient termination of chapter 7 plans and distribution of account balances, thereby increasing the retirement income security of participants and beneficiaries in such plans. Absent the standards and procedures set forth in the Abandoned Plan Regulations, some bankruptcy trustees may lack the necessary guidance to properly terminate chapter 7 plans and distribute benefits to participants and beneficiaries. Specifically, the Abandoned Plan Regulations clarify the bankruptcy trustee's obligations as qualified termination administrator with respect to updating plan records, calculating account balances, selecting and monitoring service providers, distributing benefits, and paying fees and expenses.

The Department believes that providing this guidance and allowing bankruptcy trustees to serve or designate others to serve as qualified termination administrators will lead to administrative cost savings for trustees that choose to participate in the Abandoned Plan Program. The Department has not quantified these benefits because it does not have sufficient information regarding the characteristics of chapter 7

plans.[20] The Department expects that bankruptcy trustees will decide to participate in the Abandoned Plan Program based on their individual assessment of whether it would be more cost effective to terminate a plan inside or outside of the program.

One of the most significant cost savings that would result from the proposed amendments is that chapter 7 plans no longer would incur costly audit fees that otherwise would diminish plan assets, because bankruptcy trustees will file one streamlined termination report at the end of the winding up process in lieu of the Form 5500 Annual Return/Report.

Other benefits associated with bankruptcy trustees' participation in the Abandoned Plan Program are that the proposed rule would require that a qualified termination administrator of a chapter 7 plan (whether a bankruptcy trustee or eligible designee): (1) Take reasonable and good faith steps to collect known delinquent contributions on behalf of the plan, taking into account the value of plan assets involved, the likelihood of a successful recovery, and the expenses expected to be incurred in connection with the collection of contributions, and (2) report to the Department known delinquent contributions (employer and employee) owed to the plan, and any activity that the qualified termination administrator believes may be evidence of other fiduciary breaches by a prior plan fiduciary that involve plan assets.

With respect to abandoned plans other than chapter 7 plans, the orderly termination of plans will produce quantitative benefits by maximizing account balances payable to participants and beneficiaries because prompt, efficient termination of abandoned plans would eliminate future administrative expenses that would otherwise diminish the plan's assets. In addition, the regulations' specific standards and procedures for terminating abandoned plans will reduce termination costs. Both of these quantitative benefits will reduce the extent to which plan assets are drawn upon to pay plan expenses.

The Department estimates the benefits for such plans by comparing the ongoing administrative costs of maintaining an abandoned plan with the cost of terminating such a plan under the Abandoned Plan Regulations. The magnitude of the costs for a qualified termination administrator to wind up the affairs of an abandoned plan under the Abandoned Plan Regulations is meaningful only when compared to the savings of future administrative expenses that would result from the plan's termination. A comparison of termination costs with administrative savings is complicated by the fact that termination costs will be incurred only once, while the savings in eliminated administrative costs will accrue throughout the years during which the plan would have continued to exist in its abandoned state. In order to assess the balance of costs and benefits, the Department has estimated the present value of future ongoing administrative expenses using a five percent discount rate over a period of three years after termination. The actual duration of abandonment cannot be determined with certainty; however, the Department believes that a period of one to five years provides a reasonable basis to illustrate the potential administrative cost savings that could arise in future years from the termination of abandoned plans.

In order to determine the average costs for winding up abandoned plans under the Abandoned Plan Regulations, the Department examined the Special Terminal Reports for Abandoned Plans STRAPs filed by qualified termination administrators participating in the Abandoned Plan Program since its inception in 2006. These STRAPs indicate that average termination costs were $700 and that 60 percent of the plans incurred termination costs of less than $200. As stated above, the Department estimates that 330 plans would terminate under the Abandoned Plan Program if it remained unchanged, therefore, termination costs would total approximately $231,000 (330 plans × $700 termination costs per plan).

In order to assess the benefits of the proposed amendments, the Department also must estimate the ongoing administrative expenses that would have been incurred by abandoned plans if such plans were not terminated under the Abandoned Plan Program. Since the inception of the Abandoned Plan Program in 2006, the average asset level of plans terminating under the program is $54,000. Data from a recent Investment Company Institute report prepared by Deloitte LLP indicate that 401(k) plans with under $1 million in assets pay approximately 1.41 percent of total net assets in annual administrative fees. Given that over 99 percent of the plans had under $1 million in assets at the time of termination, 1.41 percent would be a reasonable estimate to use to determine administrative expenses that would have been incurred by abandoned plans. Assuming plans that are terminated and wound up under the Abandoned Plan Program pay fees at roughly the same rate

---

[20] The Department invites public comments regarding the characteristics of chapter 7 plans that may participate in the Abandoned Plan Program.

as other small plans, the Department estimates that average ongoing administrative expenses would be approximately $760 per year ($54,000 × .0141).

Based on the foregoing, the present value of administrative expenses that otherwise would have been paid over the three years following termination exceeds the termination cost by approximately $1,470 ($2,170 of ongoing administrative expenses discounted at five percent over three years minus $700 up front termination costs = $1,470) generating expected savings for plan participants and beneficiaries of approximately $490,000 ($1,470 × 330 plans). In subsequent years, the savings resulting from eliminating ongoing administrative expenses that would have been incurred if abandoned plans were not terminated under the proposed amendments would further add to that differential.

Benefits Associated with Amendment to Safe Harbor for Distributions from Terminated Individual Account Plans (29 CFR 2550.404a-3): This section provides a safe harbor under which plan fiduciaries (including qualified termination administrators) of terminated individual account plans can directly transfer a missing or nonresponsive participant's account balance directly to appropriate investment vehicles in the participant's name. An exception exists for account balances of $1,000 or less, which may be transferred to an interest-bearing, federally-insured bank or savings association account or to the unclaimed property fund of a state, if certain conditions are satisfied. As stated above in this preamble, § 2550.404a-3 is being amended to conditionally permit qualified termination administrators to transfer the account balances of decedents to an appropriate bank account or a state's unclaimed property fund, regardless of the size of the account balance. The proposed amendments would remove an obstacle to greater usage of the Abandoned Plan Program by eliminating the need to establish costly individual retirement plans for the account balances of known deceased participants that are over $1,000 when it is unlikely that anyone will claim the funds in such plans.

Benefits Associated with Amendment to Eliminate Statement of Past or Present Investigations: As stated above in this preamble, § 2578.1 is being amended to remove the under investigation statement in the notice of plan abandonment from the qualified termination administrator to the Department (see § 2578.1(c)(3)(i)(C)). The Department believes that, at present, this statement is unnecessary and may even discourage use of the Abandoned Plan Program. The statement is unnecessary because EBSA's Office of Enforcement is able to run searches with only de minimis cost to determine whether potential qualified termination administrators are under investigation by the Department. By encouraging more potential qualified termination administrators to wind up abandoned plans in accordance with the Abandoned Plan Regulations, the Department believes abandoned plan terminations will occur more efficiently, and more participants and beneficiaries of abandoned plans will gain access to their benefits.

6. Paperwork Reduction Act

As part of its continuing effort to reduce paperwork and respondent burden, the Department of Labor conducts a preclearance consultation program to provide the general public and federal agencies with an opportunity to comment on proposed and continuing collections of information in accordance with the Paperwork Reduction Act of 1995 (PRA) (44 U.S.C. 3506(c)(2)(A)). This helps to ensure that requested data can be provided in the desired format, reporting burden (time and financial resources) is minimized, collection instruments are clearly understood, and the impact of collection requirements on respondents can be properly assessed.

Currently, the Department is soliciting comments concerning the information collection request (ICR) included in the proposed rule on the amendments to the Abandoned Plan Regulations. A copy of the ICR may be obtained by contacting the PRA addressee shown below. The Department has submitted a copy of the proposed rule to OMB in accordance with 44 U.S.C. 3507(d) for review of its information collections. The Department and OMB are interested particularly in comments that:

- Evaluate whether the collection of information is necessary for the proper performance of the functions of the agency, including whether the information will have practical utility;

- Evaluate the accuracy of the agency's estimate of the burden of the collection of information, including the validity of the methodology and assumptions used;

- Enhance the quality, utility, and clarity of the information to be collected; and

- Minimize the burden of the collection of information on those who are to respond, including through the use of appropriate automated, electronic, mechanical, or other technological collection techniques or other forms of information technology, e.g., permitting electronic submission of responses.

Comments should be sent to the Office of Information and Regulatory Affairs, Office of Management and Budget, Room 10235, New Executive Office Building, Washington, DC 20503; Attention: Desk Officer for the Employee Benefits Security Administration. OMB requests that comments be received within 30 days of publication of the proposed rule to ensure their consideration.

PRA Addressee: Address requests for copies of the ICR to G. Christopher Cosby, Office of Policy and Research, U.S. Department of Labor, Employee Benefits Security Administration, 200 Constitution Avenue NW., Room N-5718, Washington, DC 20210. Telephone (202) 693-8410; Fax: (202) 219-5333. These are not toll-free numbers. ICRs submitted to OMB also are available at *http://www.RegInfo.gov.*

The Department has assumed that most of the tasks that will be undertaken by qualified termination administrators in connection with abandoned plan terminations are the same as those required in normal plan administration, such as calculating or distributing benefits, and therefore are not accounted for as burden in this analysis because they are either part of the usual business practices of plans or have already been accounted for in ICRs for other statutory and regulatory provisions under title I of ERISA.

The Abandoned Plan Regulations require a qualified termination administrator to send up to five notices in the process of terminating and winding up an abandoned plan. Before winding up an abandoned plan, the qualified termination administrator (other than the qualified termination administrator of a chapter 7 plan) must make reasonable efforts to locate or communicate with the plan sponsor, such as by sending a notice to the last known address of the plan sponsor notifying the sponsor of the intent to terminate and wind up the plan and allowing the sponsor an opportunity to respond. Following the qualified termination administrator's finding of abandonment, or when there is an entry of an order for relief for a chapter 7 plan, the qualified termination administrator must send notice to the Department of its eligibility to serve as qualified termination administrator to wind up the abandoned plan and provide other specified plan information. The qualified termination administrator then sends a notice to the participants and beneficiaries in the plan, written in a manner calculated to by understood by the average plan participant, that their plan is being terminated, what is their account balance and the date on which it was calculated by the qualified termination administrator, a description of the distribution options available under the plan and a request that the participant or beneficiary elect a form of distribution and inform the qualified termination administrator of such election, what will happen to their account if the participant or beneficiary fails to make a distribution election within 30 days of receipt of the notice, and other information regarding their rights under the plan's termination. Upon terminating and distributing the assets of the plan, the qualified termination administrator must send a final notice to the Department stating that the plan has been terminated. The qualified termination administrator attaches to the final notice a STRAP. The Department has estimated the burden as a cost burden to the plan because the qualified termination administrator uses plan assets to pay for these notices and other costs of winding up the plan. These notices are information collection requests (ICRs) subject to the PRA. The hour and cost burden associated with these ICRs are summarized in the following table discussed below.

COST BURDEN OF RULE

	Bankrupt plans Chapter 7 (new to this RIA)	Abandoned plans—non Chapter 7 (in previous RIA)	Terminating plans (in previous RIA)	Total
Notice to Plan Sponsor	$0	$5,500	$0	$5,500
Notice to DOL	8,700	17,300	0	26,000
Bankrupt Plans (Court Order)	3,200	0	0	3,200
Notice to Participants	3,600	7,200	0	10,700
Final Notice	3,300	6,700	0	10,000

	Bankrupt plans Chapter 7 (new to this RIA)	Abandoned plans—non Chapter 7 (in previous RIA)	Terminating plans (in previous RIA)	Total
Bankrupt Plans (Fiduciary Breach)	600	0	600	0
Form 5500 Terminal Report	35,600	71,200	0	106,800
Safe Harbor	0	0	4,480,000	4,480,000
Class Exemption Familiarization	9,400	18,700	0	28,100
Total	64,000	127,000	4,480,000	4,670,000

Notice to Plan Sponsor: This notice requirement only applies to plans that are not chapter 7 plans. The Department estimates that for each of these estimated 330 plans, a qualified termination administrator may utilize 10 minutes of clerical staff time at an hourly labor rate of $28.21 to fill in the needed information on the plan sponsor notice, and five minutes of a financial professional's time at an hourly labor rate of $66.36 to review and sign the notice.[21] This results in approximately 83 hours of clerical staff time with an associated cost burden of $1,600 (55 hours × $28.21 per hour) and 27.5 hours of a financial professional's time with an associated cost burden of $1,800 (27.5 hours × $66.36 per hour).[22]

The rule requires plan sponsor notices to be sent by a method requiring acknowledgement of receipt. Therefore, mailing costs include $6.35 for postage and email receipt of delivery. The mailing costs include paper and print costs of five cents per page for the one page notice. Therefore, the materials and mailing costs are estimated to be $2,100 for the 330 notices. As indicated in the chart above, there are $5,500 in total costs associated with this requirement ($1,600 clerical, $1,800 financial professional and $2,100 in mailing costs) all imposed on plans filing under the Abandoned Plan Program.

Notice of plan abandonment to the Department: The Department estimates that for each of the estimated 495 plans, a qualified termination administrator may utilize 30 minutes of a clerical worker's time at an hourly rate of $28.21 to fill in the needed information on the notice. It also is assumed that 30 minutes of a financial professional's time with an hourly rate of $66.36 will be required to prepare required plan information, and to review and sign the forms. This results in about 248 hours (495 plans × .5 hours) of clerical staff time with an associated cost burden of $7,000 (495 plans × .5 hours × $28.21 per hour), and 248 hours (495 plans × .5 hours) of a financial professional's time with an associated cost burden of $16,400 (495 plans × .5 hours × $66.36 per hour).

The Department assumes that approximately 80 percent of these initial notices to the Department will be sent by mail and that the rest will be submitted electronically (495 plans × .8 fraction by mail = 396 plans send notice by mail). Therefore, mailing costs include $6.35 for postage and email receipt of delivery. The mailing costs include paper and print cost of five cents per page. The model notice is three pages. Therefore, the materials and mailing cost are estimated to be $2,600 (396 plans × ($6.35 + 3 pages × $.05 per page)) for the 396 notices that will be mailed. The total costs of this component are therefore $26,000[23] ($8,700 of which are new costs attributable to the chapter 7 plans, which are ⅓ of the affected plans, and $17,300 of which are cost attributable to ⅔ of the affected plans that are not chapter 7 plans).

Notice of bankruptcy trustee's appointment—Chapter 7 Plans: For the estimated 165 chapter 7 plans, an additional cost would be incurred for the qualified termination administrator to attach a copy of the notice on the case docket or order for relief reflecting the bankruptcy trustee's appointment to administer the plan sponsor's chapter 7 liquidation case as well as identification information regarding the bankruptcy trustee. The Department estimates that it will take 15 minutes of a financial professional's time to prepare the statement and collect required documents and five minutes of clerical time to make required copies. This is expected to impose an additional hour burden of approximately 41 hours (165 plans × .25) on the financial professionals and a cost burden of $2,700 (41 hours × $66.36 per hour) on the financial professionals. For the clerical professionals, the hour burden is estimated at 14 hours (165 plans × .0833 hours) and associated cost burden is $400 (14 hours × $28.21 per hour).

Material requirements are expected to be 10 pages, costing $66 in total ($0.50 per affected plan × .80 fraction of plans that submit initial

notices by paper × 165 plans). The proposed rule requires the notice or order entered in the case reflecting the bankruptcy trustee's appointment to be included with the initial notice. Thus, the total cost of this filing requirement is $3,200 ($2,700 + $400 + $66), all of which is for the 165 Chapter 7 plans.

Notice to Participants and Beneficiaries: The ERISA Advisory Council in the Report of the Working Group on Orphan Plans had indicated most abandoned plans are small plans with 25 or fewer participants and beneficiaries. Thus, initially the Department conservatively estimated that there were 20 participants per plan impacted by the Abandoned Plan Regulations. However, after the inception of the Abandoned Plan Program, updated filings data provided by the Office of Enforcement show that in no year were there on average more than six participants per filing plan. The Department estimates that, using this updated information, approximately 330 plans will apply each year if the Abandoned Plan Regulations remain unchanged. This covers a maximum of 1,980 participants (330 plans × 6 participants per plan). With bankruptcy trustees being permitted to wind up the plans of sponsors in chapter 7 liquidation under the Abandoned Plan Regulations, the Department estimates that there will be a 50 percent increase in applications, bringing the total number of filings up to 495 (330 plans × 1.5). Assuming that chapter 7 plans have roughly the same number of participants as abandoned plans, the total number of participants affected would be 2,970 (495 plans × 6 participants per plan).

The Department estimates that for each of the estimated 495 terminating plans, a QTA may utilize 5 minutes of a financial professional's time to review the notices. Clerical staff will spend on average 30 minutes preparing and mailing the notices (5 minutes per participant × 6 participants). This results in approximately 248 hours (495 plans × 6 participants per plan × .0833 hours per participant) of clerical staff time with an associated cost burden of $7,000 (248 hours × $28.21 per hour) and 41 hours (495 plans × .0833 hours per plan) of a financial professional's time with an associated cost burden of approximately $2,700 (41 hours × $66.36 per hour).

The model notice to participants is two pages. Therefore, the mailing and material costs are estimated to be 55 cents per mailing (2 × $.05 + $0.45). Of the 2,970 participants (495 plans × 6 participants per plan), 38 percent are expected to receive their notices electronically. The Department estimates that 1,840 participants will receive the notice by mail, creating a mailing cost burden of $1,000. In total, the cost burden from the notice to the participants and beneficiaries requirement is approximately $10,700.[24] Because ⅓ of the affected plans are chapter 7 plans, $3,600 of the burden is expected to be for the chapter 7 plans and $7,100 for the ⅔ of affected plans that are abandoned.

Final Notice: The Department estimates that for each of the estimated 495 terminating plans, a qualified termination administrator will utilize 10 minutes of a financial professional's time to review the forms. Clerical staff will spend, on average, 10 minutes per notice preparing and mailing the notices. This results in about 83 hours (495 plans × .167 hours) of clerical staff time with an associated cost burden of $2,300 (83 hours × $28.21 per hour) and 83 hours of a financial professional's time (495 plans × .167 hours) with an associated cost burden of $5,500 (83 hours × $66.36 per hour).

The Department assumes that, as a usual and customary business practice, the final notice to the Department will be sent by a method requiring acknowledgement of receipt. The model final notice is two pages. Therefore, the material costs are estimated to be $.10 per plan and postage of $6.35 per plan. For the 70 percent of plans that are expected to submit their applications by mail, total mailing costs are estimated to be $2,200 for the 495 notices (($6.35 per plan for mailing +$.10 for materials) × 495 plans × .70 fraction of plans submitting by

---

[21] The Department estimates 2012 hourly labor rates to include wages, other benefits, and overhead based on data from the National Occupational Employment Survey (June 2011, Bureau of Labor Statistics) and the Employment Cost Index (September 2011, Bureau of Labor Statistics); the 2010 estimated labor rates are then inflated to 2012 labor rates.

[22] Any discrepancies in calculations in this section and the table above result from rounding. Estimates are rounded to the nearest $10, $100, $1,000, or $10,000. Hour estimates also are rounded in the text.

[23] $26,000 = $7,000 for clerical cost time + $16,400 for financial professional time + $2,600 for mailing.

[24] $7,000 in clerical costs + $2,700 in financial professional costs + $1,000 in mailing costs.

mail). Thus, there is approximately $10,000 in total costs for the final notice. Of that total, approximately $3,300 is dedicated to the ⅓ of affected plans that are chapter 7 plans and $6,700 is attributable to the 330 qualified termination administrator filings for the ⅔ of plans that are abandoned.

Reporting Requirement for Prior Plan Fiduciary Breaches: As discussed earlier in this preamble, the proposed amendments would require qualified termination administrators to chapter 7 plans (whether they are bankruptcy trustees or eligible designees) to report to the Department known delinquent contributions (employer and employee) owed to the plan, and any activity that the qualified termination administrator believes may be evidence of other fiduciary breaches by a prior plan fiduciary that involve plan assets. This information must be reported in conjunction with the filing of the final notice or notice of plan abandonment. If a bankruptcy trustee designates an eligible designee as defined in paragraph (j)(1)(ii) of the proposal, the bankruptcy trustee shall provide the eligible designee with records under the control of the bankruptcy trustee to enable the eligible designee to carry out its responsibilities. If, after the eligible designee completes the winding up of the plan, the bankruptcy trustee, in administering the debtor's estate, discovers additional information that it believes may be evidence of fiduciary breaches by a prior plan fiduciary that involve plan assets, the bankruptcy trustee shall report such activity to the Department.

While the Department has no basis for estimating the percentage of arrangements where the qualified termination administrator must report known delinquent contributions or a past fiduciary breach, the Department assumes for purposes of this analysis that a report will be required in 10 percent of the applications from chapter 7 plans. Thus, given that there are an estimated 165 chapter 7 plans utilizing the exemption, the Department estimates that 17 plans will need to prepare and send this notice. The Department anticipates that one-half hour of a financial professional's time will be required to prepare the notice and five minutes of clerical time will be required to send the notice. The Department therefore estimates that the burden for plans to send the notice to EBSA's Office of Enforcement will be approximately 10 hours (17 plans × (.5 financial professional hours per plan + .0833 clerical hours per plan)) with a cost of $600 for trustees (17 plans × .5 financial professional hours × $66.36/hour + 17 plans × .0833 clerical hours × $28.21/hour) to send the notice. The Department anticipates that most of these notices will be filed with the final notice; therefore, this analysis includes no additional mailing cost. Each notice is expected to cost $0.10 (2 × $0.05). The Department estimates that 70 percent of the plans are expected to submit the final filing by mail, resulting in an additional material cost burden of $1.19 (17 × .7 fraction submitting by mail × $.10). Thus, this new requirement amounts to a cost burden of approximately $600, which is exclusively imposed on chapter 7 plans.

Special Terminal Report for Abandoned Plans (29 CFR 2520.103-13): The Department estimates that it will take small plans 3.25 hours to file the STRAP in accordance with the instructions on the Department's web site. It is assumed that a financial accounting professional will perform this task resulting in an hour burden of 1,600 hours and a cost burden of $66.36 per hour resulting in a cost burden of $106,800 (3.25 hours × $66.36 per hour × 495 plans). For STRAPs submitted electronically, no burden is estimated for paper or mailing costs. For the assumed 70 percent of plans that submit their STRAPs by mail, the additional costs will be approximately $100 (495 plans × 6 pages per terminal report × $.05/page × .70 fraction of plans that submit final notices by mail). Thus, the total cost associated with the report is approximately $106,800 ($106,700 in financial accounting costs and $100 in material costs). Of this total, $35,600 is attributable to the ⅓ of plans that are chapter 7 plans and $71,200 is attributable to the ⅓ of plans that are abandoned. Only the chapter 7 plan costs represent new costs.

Safe Harbor for Distributions from Terminated Individual Account Plans (29 CFR 2550.404a-3): The PRA analysis also includes the burden associated with the notice to participants as required under "The Safe Harbor for Distributions from Terminated Individual Account Plans." To meet the safe harbor, fiduciaries of terminating plans (other than abandoned plans) must furnish a notice to participants and beneficiaries informing them of the plan's termination and the options available for distribution of their account balances. The Department estimates that 3.1 million participants and beneficiaries will receive notices from approximately 39,000 plan sponsors.[25] The Department estimates that clerical professionals will spend, on average, two minutes per notice preparing and distributing the notices. The benefits manager will spend approximately 10 minutes preparing the notice.

This results in an equivalent cost burden of $3.5 million calculated as follows: $2.92 million per year (3.1 million participants × .033 hours per participant × $28.21 per hour) in clerical time, and $607,000 (39,000 plans × .167 hours per plan × $93.31 per hour) in benefit manager costs. In addition, the Department assumes that each participant will receive a one page notice by first class mail resulting in a cost burden of $961,000 (3.1 million notices × ($0.45 for postage + ($0.05 per page × 1 page) × 0.62). Thus, with the updated numbers, total cost burden for terminating plans is $4.48 million. This total includes $3.49 million in equivalent costs from plan clerical time ($2.92 million) and plan benefit manager time ($607,000). There is also $961,000 in cost attributable to mailing the notices. These costs are not attributable to the proposed amendments allowing chapter 7 trustees to participate in the Abandoned Plan Program. They reflect the Department's revised estimates of the entire Abandoned Plans Program and take into account the most recent Form 5500 data.

Abandoned Plan Class Exemption, PTE 2006-06: PTE 2006-06 permits a qualified termination administrator of an individual account plan that has been abandoned by its sponsoring employer to select itself or an affiliate to provide services to the plan in connection with the termination of the plan, and to pay itself or an affiliate fees for these services, provided that such fees are consistent with the conditions of the exemption. The exemption also permits a qualified termination administrator to: designate itself or an affiliate as a provider of an individual retirement plan or other account; select a proprietary investment product as the initial investment for the rollover distribution of benefits for a participant or beneficiary who fails to make an election regarding the disposition of such benefits; and pay itself or its affiliate in connection with the rollover.

Currently, PTE 2006-06 and the accompanying Abandoned Plan Regulations do not cover plans of sponsors involved in chapter 7 bankruptcy proceedings. In this regard, bankruptcy trustees do not meet the definition of qualified termination administrator as set forth in the existing Abandoned Plan Regulations and the class exemption. The proposed amendments expand the definition of qualified termination administrator to include bankruptcy trustees and certain persons designated by them to act as qualified termination administrators in terminating and winding up the affairs of abandoned plans. The Department believes that the proposed amendments to the Abandoned Plan Regulations and PTE 2006-06 will incentivize many bankruptcy trustees to carryout plan terminations consistent with ERISA, which will ultimately benefit participants and beneficiaries of such plans by ensuring abandoned plans are terminated in an orderly and cost-effective manner.

Compliance with the proposed amendments to the Abandoned Plan Regulations is a condition of the proposed amendment to the class exemption; therefore the costs and benefits that would be associated with complying with the proposed amendment to the class exemption have been described and quantified in connection with the economic impact of the proposed regulatory amendments. In its current and proposed amendment form, PTE 2006-06 requires, among other things, that fees and expenses paid to the qualified termination administrator and an affiliate in connection with the termination of an abandoned plan are consistent with industry rates for such or similar services, and are not in excess of rates ordinarily charged by the qualified termination administrator (or affiliate) for the same or similar services provided to customers that are not plans terminated pursuant to the Abandoned Plan Regulations, if the qualified termination administrator (or affiliate) provides the same or similar services to such other customers. The class exemption, in its current and proposed amendment form, also requires that qualified termination administrators ensure that the records necessary to determine whether the conditions of the exemption have been met are maintained for a period of six years, so that they may be available for inspection by any account holder of an individual retirement plan or other account established pursuant to this exemption, or any duly authorized representative of such account holder, the Internal Revenue Service, and the Department. Banks, insurance companies, and other financial institutions that provide services to abandoned plans and their participants and beneficiaries are required to act in accordance with customary business practices, which would include maintaining the records required under the terms of the class exemption, both in its current and proposed amendment form. Accordingly, the recordkeeping burden attributable to the proposed amendment will be handled by the qualified termination administrator and is expected to be small. However, there is an additional cost to directing this process. The Department assumes that a supervisor must devote time to each case in order to study the details of the individual plan, determine whether there have been any violations, and ensure that

[25] These estimates for the number of participants and sponsors are based on 2008 Form 5500 Data filings.

these details are properly incorporated into the notices. Assuming that all qualified termination administrators will take advantage of the proposed exemption, the hour burden attributable to supervisory duties for qualified termination administrators of abandoned plans (including familiarization costs for new qualified termination administrators) is expected to be one half hour for each qualified termination administrator, or 248 hours. Assuming a financial manager's wage rate of $113.39 per hour, this supervisory cost is expected to total $28,100 ($113.39 × 248). Approximately $9,400 of this cost (⅓ of the costs since 165 of the 495 estimated affected plans are chapter 7 plans) is expected to be attributable to financial manager costs dealing with chapter 7 plans and the remaining $18,700 of costs are attributable to financial managers dealing with the ⅔ of abandoned plans.

Also, in certain limited circumstances, both the current exemption and proposed amendment to PTE 2006-06 require qualified termination administrators to provide the Department with a statement under penalty of perjury that services were performed and a copy of the executed contract between the qualified termination administrator and a plan fiduciary or plan sponsor. The Department does not include burden for these requirements as the burden is small, and the statement and contract can be included with other notices sent to the Department.

Type of Review: Proposed Revision of Existing Collection.

Agency: Employee Benefits Security Administration, Department of Labor.

Title: Notices for Terminated Abandoned Individual Account Plans.

OMB Number: 1210-0127

Affected public: Individuals or households; business or other for-profit; not-for-profit institutions.

Respondents: 39,495.

Responses: 3,103,960.

Frequency of Response: One time. *Estimated Total Burden Hours:* 109,833.

Equivalent Costs of Hour Burden: $3,520,000.

Cost Burden: $ 1,150,000.

7. Regulatory Flexibility Act

The Regulatory Flexibility Act (5 U.S.C. 601 et seq.) (RFA) imposes certain requirements with respect to Federal rules that are subject to the notice and comment requirements of section 553(b) of the Administrative Procedure Act (5 U.S.C. 551 et seq.) and which are likely to have a significant economic impact on a substantial number of small entities. Unless an agency determines that a proposed rule is not likely to have a significant economic impact on a substantial number of small entities, section 603 of the RFA requires that the agency present an initial regulatory flexibility analysis at the time of the publication of the notice of proposed rulemaking describing the impact of the rule on small entities and seeking public comment on such impact. Small entities include small businesses, organizations and governmental jurisdictions.

For purposes of analysis under the RFA, EBSA proposes to continue to consider a small entity to be an employee benefit plan with fewer than 100 participants. The basis of this definition is found in section 104(a)(2) of ERISA that permits the Secretary of Labor to prescribe simplified annual reports for pension plans that cover fewer than 100 participants. Under section 104(a)(3), the Secretary may also provide for exemptions or simplified annual reporting and disclosure for welfare benefit plans. Pursuant to the authority of section 104(a)(3), the Department has previously issued at 29 CFR 2520.104-20, 2520.104-21, 2520.104-41, 2520.104-46 and 2520.104b-10 certain simplified reporting provisions and limited exemptions from reporting and disclosure requirements for small plans, including unfunded or insured welfare plans, covering fewer than 100 participants and which satisfy certain other requirements.

Further, while some large employers may have small plans, in general small employers maintain most small plans. Thus, EBSA believes that assessing the impact of these proposed rules on small plans is an appropriate substitute for evaluating the effect on small entities. The definition of small entity considered appropriate for this purpose differs, however, from a definition of small business which is based on size standards promulgated by the Small Business Administration (SBA) (13 CFR 121.201) pursuant to the Small Business Act (15 U.S.C. 631 et seq.). EBSA therefore requests comments on the appropriateness of the size standard used in evaluating the impact of these proposed rules on small entities. EBSA has preliminarily determined that these proposed rules may have a significant beneficial economic impact on a substantial number of small entities. In an effort to provide a sound basis for this conclusion, EBSA has prepared the following initial regulatory flexibility analysis. To the Department's knowledge, there are no federal regulations that might duplicate, overlap, or conflict with the provisions of the proposed amendments to the Abandoned Plan Regulations.

As explained earlier in the preamble, currently, the Abandoned Plan Program does not extend to plans sponsored by employers undergoing liquidation under chapter 7 of title 11 of the United States Code. Over the years, the Department has observed that, on numerous occasions, bankruptcy trustees have not terminated abandoned plans in an orderly and efficient manner. In many instances, such trustees are unaware of their fiduciary obligations under ERISA with respect to terminating plans of debtors and processes through which to wind up such plans.

The Department believes that the participants and beneficiaries would benefit from removing existing impediments that prevent chapter 7 bankruptcy trustees from terminating and winding up abandoned plans. Therefore, the Department is proposing to amend the Abandoned Plan Regulations (the three regulations and the related class exemption) to enable bankruptcy trustees to terminate abandoned plans in a manner consistent with ERISA and current regulations. The amendments would provide bankruptcy trustees with the option to serve as qualified termination administrators or to designate as a qualified termination administrator any person or entity that is eligible to serve as a trustee or issuer of an individual retirement plan and that holds assets of the chapter 7 plan. The Department believes that these amendments will help to preserve the assets of such abandoned plans, thereby maximizing benefits ultimately payable to participants and beneficiaries.

As described earlier in the preamble, the Department estimates that 330 abandoned plans (other than chapter 7 plans) would file under the Abandoned Plan Program. Essentially all abandoned plans are assumed to be small plans. Therefore, the more detailed discussion earlier in the preamble on the costs and benefits of the proposed amendments is applicable to this analysis of costs and benefits under the RFA. In summary, the net benefits of terminating an estimated 330 abandoned plans per year under the proposed amendments is $490,000. Thus, the estimated beneficial impact per plan is approximately $1,500 ($490,000/330 plans) before accounting for fees in individual retirement accounts to which participants and beneficiaries could rollover their distributed account balances. This net benefit analysis is an update of the 2006 estimate, with new information submitted to the Department's Office of Enforcement informing the analysis.

8. Congressional Review Act

This proposed amendment is subject to the Congressional Review Act provisions of the Small Business Regulatory Enforcement Fairness Act of 1996 (5 U.S.C. 801 et seq.) and, if finalized, will be transmitted to the Congress and the Comptroller General for review.

9. Unfunded Mandates Reform Act

For purposes of the Unfunded Mandates Reform Act of 1995 (Pub. L. 104-4), as well as Executive Order 12875, the proposed rule does not include any Federal mandate that will result in expenditures by state, local, or tribal governments in the aggregate of more than $100 million, adjusted for inflation, or increase expenditures by the private sector of more than $100 million, adjusted for inflation.

10. Federalism Statement

Executive Order 13132 (August 4, 1999) outlines fundamental principles of federalism and requires the adherence to specific criteria by Federal agencies in the process of their formulation and implementation of policies that have substantial direct effects on the States, the relationship between the national government and the States, or on the distribution of power and responsibilities among the various levels of government. This proposed rule does not have federalism implications because it has no substantial direct effect on the States, on the relationship between the national government and the States, or on the distribution of power and responsibilities among the various levels of government. Section 514 of ERISA provides, with certain exceptions specifically enumerated, that the provisions of Titles I and IV of ERISA supersede any and all laws of the States as they relate to any employee benefit plan covered under ERISA. The requirements implemented in the proposed rule do not alter the fundamental provisions of the statute with respect to employee benefit plans, and as such would have no implications for the States or the relationship or distribution of power between the national government and the States.

List of Subjects

29 CFR Part 2520

Accounting, Employee benefit plans, Pensions, Reporting and re-cordkeeping requirements.

29 CFR Part 2550

Employee benefit plans, Employee Retirement Income Security Act, Employee stock ownership plans, Exemptions, Fiduciaries, Investments, Investments foreign, Party in interest, Pensions, Pension and Welfare Benefit Programs Office, Prohibited transactions, Real estate, Securities, Surety bonds, Trusts and Trustees.

29 CFR Part 2578

Employee benefit plans, Pensions, Retirement.

For the reasons set forth in the preamble, the Department of Labor proposes to amend 29 CFR chapter XXV as follows:

PART 2520—RULES AND REGULATIONS FOR REPORTING AND DISCLOSURE

1. The authority citation for part 2520 is revised to read as follows:

Authority: 29 U.S.C. 1021-1025, 1027, 1029-31, 1059, 1134 and 1135; and Secretary of Labor's Order 1-2011, 77 FR 1088 (Jan. 9, 2012). Sec. 2520.101-2 also issued under 29 U.S.C. 1132, 1181-1183, 1181 note, 1185, 1185a-b, 1191, and 1191a-c. Sec. 2520.101-4 also issued under 29 U.S.C. 1021(f). Sec. 2520.101-6 also issued under 29 U.S.C. 1021(k) and Pub. L. 109-280, § 502(a)(3), 120 Stat. 780, 940 (2006). Secs. 2520.102-3, 2520.104b-1 and 2520.104b-3 also issued under 29 U.S.C. 1003, 1181-1183, 1181 note, 1185, 1185a-b, 1191, and 1191a-c. Secs. 2520.104b-1 and 2520.107 also issued under 26 U.S.C. 401 note, 111 Stat. 788.

2. Revise § 2520.103-13 to read as follows:

§ 2520.103-13 Special terminal report for abandoned plans.

(a) *General.* The terminal report required to be filed by the qualified termination administrator pursuant to § 2578.1(d)(2)(viii) of this chapter shall consist of the items set forth in paragraph (b) of this section. Such report shall be filed in accordance with the method of filing set forth in paragraph (c) of this section and at the time set forth in paragraph (d) of this section.

(b) *Contents.* The terminal report described in paragraph (a) of this section shall contain:

(1) Identification information concerning the bankruptcy trustee and, if applicable, any eligible designee acting as the qualified termination administrator pursuant to § 2578.1(j)(1)(ii), and the plan being terminated.

(2) The total assets of the plan as of the date the plan was deemed terminated under § 2578.1(c) of this chapter, prior to any reduction for termination expenses and distributions to participants and beneficiaries.

(3) The total termination expenses paid by the plan and a separate schedule identifying each service provider and amount received, itemized by expense.

(4) The total distributions made pursuant to § 2578.1(d)(2)(vii) of this chapter and a statement regarding whether any such distributions were transfers under § 2578.1(d)(2)(vii)(B) of this chapter.

(5) The identification, fair market value and method of valuation of any assets with respect to which there is no readily ascertainable fair market value.

(c) *Method of filing.* The terminal report described in paragraph (a) shall be filed:

(1) On the most recent Form 5500 available as of the date the qualified termination administrator satisfies the requirements in § 2578.1(d)(2)(i) through § 2578.1(d)(2)(vii) of this chapter; and

(2) In accordance with the instructions on EBSA's Web site (*http://www.dol.gov/ebsa/publications/APterminalreport.html*) pertaining to terminal reports of qualified termination administrators.

(d) *When to file.* The qualified termination administrator shall file the terminal report described in paragraph (a) within two months after the end of the month in which the qualified termination administrator satisfies the requirements in § 2578.1(d)(2)(i) through § 2578.1(d)(2)(vii) of this chapter.

(e) *Limitation.* (1) Except as provided in this section, no report shall be required to be filed by the qualified termination administrator under

part 1 of title I of ERISA for a plan being terminated pursuant to § 2578.1 of this chapter.

(2) Filing of a report under this section by the qualified termination administrator shall not relieve any other person from any obligation under part 1 of title I of ERISA.

PART 2550—RULES AND REGULATIONS FOR FIDUCIARY RESPONSIBILITY

3. The authority citation for part 2550 is revised to read as follows:

Authority: 29 U.S.C. 1135, sec. 102, Reorganization Plan No. 4 of 1978, 5 U.S.C. App. 1 and Secretary of Labor's Order No. 1-2011, 77 FR 1088 (Jan. 9, 2012). Sec. 2550.401c-1 also issued under 29 U.S.C. 1101. Sec. 2550.404a-2 also issued under sec. 657, Pub. L. 107-16, 115 Stat. 38. Sections 2550.404c-1 and 2550.404c-5 also issued under 29 U.S.C. 1104. Sec. 2550.408b-1 also issued under 29 U.S.C. 1108(b)(1). Sec. 2550.408b-19 also issued under sec. 611, Pub. L. 109-280, 120 Stat. 780, 972. Sec. 2550.412-1 also issued under 29 U.S.C. 1112.

4. Revise § 2550.404a-3 to read as follows:

§ 2550.404a-3 Safe harbor for distributions from terminated individual account plans.

(a) *General.* (1) This section provides a safe harbor under which a fiduciary (including a qualified termination administrator, within the meaning of § 2578.1(g) or (j)(1)(ii) of this chapter) of a terminated individual account plan, as described in paragraph (a)(2) of this section, will be deemed to have satisfied its duties under section 404(a) of the Employee Retirement Income Security Act of 1974, as amended (the Act)), 29 U.S.C. 1001 et seq., in connection with a distribution described in paragraph (b) of this section.

(2) This section shall apply to an individual account plan only if—

(i) In the case of an individual account plan that is an abandoned plan within the meaning of § 2578.1 of this chapter, such plan was intended to be maintained as a tax-qualified plan in accordance with the requirements of section 401(a), 403(a), or 403(b) of the Internal Revenue Code of 1986 (Code); or

(ii) In the case of any other individual account plan, such plan is maintained in accordance with the requirements of section 401(a), 403(a), or 403(b) of the Code at the time of the distribution.

(3) The standards set forth in this section apply solely for purposes of determining whether a fiduciary meets the requirements of this safe harbor. Such standards are not intended to be the exclusive means by which a fiduciary might satisfy his or her responsibilities under the Act with respect to making distributions described in this section.

(b) *Distributions.* This section shall apply to a distribution from a terminated individual account plan if, in connection with such distribution:

(1) The participant or beneficiary, on whose behalf the distribution will be made, was furnished notice in accordance with paragraph (e) of this section or, in the case of an abandoned plan, § 2578.1(d)(2)(vi) of this chapter, and

(2) The participant or beneficiary failed to elect a form of distribution within 30 days of the furnishing of the notice described in paragraph (b)(1) of this section.

(c) *Safe harbor.* A fiduciary that meets the conditions of paragraph (d) of this section shall, with respect to a distribution described in paragraph (b) of this section, be deemed to have satisfied its duties under section 404(a) of the Act with respect to the distribution of benefits, selection of a transferee entity described in paragraph (d)(1)(i) through (iii) of this section, and the investment of funds in connection with the distribution.

(d) *Conditions.* A fiduciary shall qualify for the safe harbor described in paragraph (c) of this section if:

(1) The distribution described in paragraph (b) of this section is made to any of the following transferee entities—

(i) To an individual retirement plan within the meaning of section 7701(a)(37) of the Code;

(ii) In the case of a distribution on behalf of a designated beneficiary (as defined by section 401(a)(9)(E) of the Code) who is not the surviving spouse of the deceased participant, to an inherited individual retirement plan (within the meaning of section 402(c)(11) of the Code) established to receive the distribution on behalf of the nonspouse beneficiary; or

(iii) In the case of a distribution by a qualified termination administrator (other than a bankruptcy trustee described in § 2578.1(j)(1)(ii)) with respect to which the amount to be distributed is $1,000 or less and that amount is less than the minimum amount required to be invested in an individual retirement plan product offered by the qualified termination administrator to the public at the time of the distribution, to:

(A) An interest-bearing federally insured bank or savings association account in the name of the participant or beneficiary,

(B) The unclaimed property fund of the State in which the participant's or beneficiary's last known address is located, or

(C) An individual retirement plan (described in paragraph (d)(1)(i) or (d)(1)(ii) of this section) offered by a financial institution other than the qualified termination administrator to the public at the time of the distribution.

(iv) In the case of a distribution by a bankruptcy trustee as described in § 2578.1(j)(1)(ii) with respect to which the amount to be distributed is $1,000 or less and the bankruptcy trustee, after reasonable and good faith efforts, is unable to locate an individual retirement plan provider who will accept the distribution, to either distribution option described in paragraph (d)(1)(iii)(A) or (B) of this section.

(v) Notwithstanding paragraphs (d)(1)(iii) and (iv) of this section, the $1,000 threshold may be disregarded in any particular case if the qualified termination administrator reasonably and in good faith finds that the participant and, if applicable, the named beneficiary are deceased; and if the qualified termination administrator also includes in the notice described in § 2578.1(d)(2)(ix)(G) (the Final Notice) the identity of the deceased participant and beneficiary and the basis behind the finding.

(2) Except with respect to distributions to State unclaimed property funds (described in paragraph (d)(1)(iii)(B) of this section), the fiduciary enters into a written agreement with the transferee entity which provides:

(i) The distributed funds shall be invested in an investment product designed to preserve principal and provide a reasonable rate of return, whether or not such return is guaranteed, consistent with liquidity (except that distributions under paragraph (d)(1)(iii)(A) of this section to a bank or savings account are not required to be invested in such a product);

(ii) For purposes of paragraph (d)(2)(i) of this section, the investment product shall—

(A) Seek to maintain, over the term of the investment, the dollar value that is equal to the amount invested in the product by the individual retirement plan (described in paragraph (d)(1)(i) or (d)(1)(ii) of this section), and

(B) Be offered by a State or federally regulated financial institution, which shall be: a bank or savings association, the deposits of which are insured by the Federal Deposit Insurance Corporation; a credit union, the member accounts of which are insured within the meaning of section 101(7) of the Federal Credit Union Act; an insurance company, the products of which are protected by State guaranty associations; or an investment company registered under the Investment Company Act of 1940;

(iii) All fees and expenses attendant to the transferee plan (described in paragraph (d)(1)(i) or (d)(1)(ii) of this section) or account (described in paragraph (d)(1)(iii)(A) of this section), including investments of such plan, (e.g., establishment charges, maintenance fees, investment expenses, termination costs and surrender charges), shall not exceed the fees and expenses charged by the provider of the plan or account for comparable plans or accounts established for reasons other than the receipt of a distribution under this section; and

(iv) The participant or beneficiary on whose behalf the fiduciary makes a distribution shall have the right to enforce the terms of the contractual agreement establishing the plan (described in paragraph (d)(1)(i) or (d)(1)(ii) of this section) or account (described in paragraph (d)(1)(iii)(A) of this section), with regard to his or her transferred account balance, against the plan or account provider.

(3) Both the fiduciary's selection of a transferee plan (described in paragraph (d)(1)(i) or (d)(1)(ii) of this section) or account (described in paragraph (d)(1)(iii)(A) of this section) and the investment of funds would not result in a prohibited transaction under section 406 of the Act, or if so prohibited such actions are exempted from the prohibited transaction provisions by a prohibited transaction exemption issued pursuant to section 408(a) of the Act.

(e) *Notice to participants and beneficiaries.* (1) *Content.* Each participant or beneficiary of the plan shall be furnished a notice written in a manner calculated to be understood by the average plan participant and containing the following:

(i) The name of the plan;

(ii) A statement of the account balance, the date on which the amount was calculated, and, if relevant, an indication that the amount to be distributed may be more or less than the amount stated in the notice, depending on investment gains or losses and the administrative cost of terminating the plan and distributing benefits;

(iii) A description of the distribution options available under the plan and a request that the participant or beneficiary elect a form of distribution and inform the plan administrator (or other fiduciary) identified in paragraph (e)(1)(vii) of this section of that election;

(iv) A statement explaining that, if a participant or beneficiary fails to make an election within 30 days from receipt of the notice, the plan will distribute the account balance of the participant or beneficiary to an individual retirement plan (i.e., individual retirement account or annuity described in paragraph (d)(1)(i) or (d)(1)(ii) of this section) and the account balance will be invested in an investment product designed to preserve principal and provide a reasonable rate of return and liquidity;

(v) A statement explaining what fees, if any, will be paid from the participant or beneficiary's individual retirement plan (described in paragraph (d)(1)(i) or (d)(1)(ii) of this section), if such information is known at the time of the furnishing of this notice;

(vi) The name, address and phone number of the individual retirement plan (described in paragraph (d)(1)(i) or (d)(1)(ii) of this section) provider, if such information is known at the time of the furnishing of this notice; and

(vii) The name, address, and telephone number of the plan administrator (or other fiduciary) from whom a participant or beneficiary may obtain additional information concerning the termination.

(2) *Manner of furnishing notice.* (i) For purposes of paragraph (e)(1) of this section, a notice shall be furnished to each participant or beneficiary in accordance with the requirements of § 2520.104b-1(b)(1) of this chapter to the last known address of the participant or beneficiary; and

(ii) In the case of a notice that is returned to the plan as undeliverable, the plan fiduciary shall, consistent with its duties under section 404(a)(1) of ERISA, take steps to locate the participant or beneficiary and provide notice prior to making the distribution. If, after such steps, the fiduciary is unsuccessful in locating and furnishing notice to a participant or beneficiary, the participant or beneficiary shall be deemed to have been furnished the notice and to have failed to make an election within 30 days for purposes of paragraph (b)(2) of this section.

(f) *Model notice.* The appendix to this section contains a model notice that may be used to discharge the notification requirements under this section. Use of the model notice is not mandatory. However, use of an appropriately completed model notice will be deemed to satisfy the requirements of paragraph (e)(1) of this section.

BILLING CODE **4510-29**-P

APPENDIX TO § 2550A04a-3

NOTICE OF PLAN TERMINATION

[*Date of notice*]

[*Name and last known address of plan participant or beneficiary*]

Re: [*Name of plan*]

Dear [*Name of plan participant or beneficiary*]:

This notice is to inform you that [*name of the plan*] (the Plan) has been terminated and we are in the process of winding it up.

We have determined that you have an interest in the Plan, either as a plan participant or beneficiary. Your account balance in the Plan on [*date*] is/was [*account balance*]. We will be distributing this money as permitted under the terms of the Plan and federal regulations. { *If applicable, insert the following sentence:* The actual amount of your distribution may be more or less than the amount stated in this notice depending on investment gains or losses and the administrative cost of terminating your plan and distributing your benefits.}

Your distribution options under the Plan are { *add a description of the Plan's distribution options* }. It is very important that you elect one of these forms of distribution and inform us of your election. The process for informing us of this election is { *enter a description of the Plan's election process* }.

If you do not make an election within 30 days from your receipt of this notice, your account balance will be transferred directly to an individual retirement plan (inherited individual retirement plan in the case of a

¶20,538H

nonspouse beneficiary). { *If the name of the provider of the individual retirement plan is known, include the following sentence:* The name of the provider of the individual retirement plan is [*name, address and phone number of the individual retirement plan provider*].} Pursuant to federal law, your money in the individual retirement plan would then be invested in an investment product designed to preserve principal and provide a reasonable rate of return and liquidity. { *If fee information is known, include the following sentence:* Should your money be transferred into an individual retirement plan, [*name of the financial institution*]charges the following fees for its services: { *add a statement of fees, if any, that will be paid from the participant or beneficiary's individual retirement plan* }. }

For more information about the termination, your account balance, or distribution options, please contact [*name, address, and telephone number of the plan administrator or other appropriate contact person*].

Sincerely,

[*Name of plan administrator or appropriate designee*]

BILLING CODE 4510-29-C

PART 2578—RULES AND REGULATIONS FOR ABANDONED PLANS

5. The authority citation for part 2578.1 continues to read as follows:

Authority: 29 U.S.C. 1135; 1104(a); 1103(d)(1).

6. Revise § 2578.1 to read as follows:

§ 2578.1 Termination of abandoned individual account plans.

(a) *General.* The purpose of this part is to establish standards for the termination and winding up of an individual account plan (as defined in section 3(34) of the Employee Retirement Income Security Act of 1974 (ERISA or the Act)) with respect to which (1) a qualified termination administrator has determined there is no responsible plan sponsor or plan administrator within the meaning of section 3(16)(B) and (A) of the Act, respectively, to perform such acts, or (2) an order for relief under chapter 7 of title 11 of the United States Code has been entered with respect to the plan sponsor.

(b) *Finding of abandonment.* (1) A qualified termination administrator (as defined in paragraph (g) of this section) may find an individual account plan to be abandoned when:

(i) Either: (A) No contributions to, or distributions from, the plan have been made for a period of at least 12 consecutive months immediately preceding the date on which the determination is being made; or

(B) Other facts and circumstances (such as communications from participants and beneficiaries regarding distributions) known to the qualified termination administrator suggest that the plan is or may become abandoned by the plan sponsor; and

(ii) Following reasonable efforts to locate or communicate with the plan sponsor, the qualified termination administrator determines that the plan sponsor:

(A) No longer exists;

(B) Cannot be located; or

(C) Is unable to maintain the plan.

(2) Notwithstanding paragraph (b)(1) of this section, a qualified termination administrator may not find a plan to be abandoned if, at any time before the plan is deemed terminated pursuant to paragraph (c) of this section, the qualified termination administrator receives an objection from the plan sponsor regarding the finding of abandonment and proposed termination.

(3) A qualified termination administrator shall, for purposes of paragraph (b)(1)(ii) of this section, be deemed to have made a reasonable effort to locate or communicate with the plan sponsor if the qualified termination administrator sends to the last known address of the plan sponsor, and, in the case of a plan sponsor that is a corporation, to the address of the person designated as the corporation's agent for service of legal process, by a method of delivery requiring acknowledgement of receipt, the notice described in paragraph (b)(5) of this section.

(4) If receipt of the notice described in paragraph (b)(5) of this section is not acknowledged pursuant to paragraph (b)(3) of this section, the qualified termination administrator shall be deemed to have made a reasonable effort to locate or communicate with the plan sponsor if the qualified termination administrator contacts known service providers (other than itself) of the plan and requests the current address of the plan sponsor from such service providers and, if such information is provided, the qualified termination administrator sends to each such address, by a method of delivery requiring acknowledge-

ment of receipt, the notice described in paragraph (b)(5) of this section.

(5) The notice referred to in paragraph (b)(3) of this section shall contain the following information:

(i) The name and address of the qualified termination administrator;

(ii) The name of the plan;

(iii) The account number or other identifying information relating to the plan;

(iv) A statement that the plan may be terminated and benefits distributed pursuant to 29 CFR 2578.1 if the plan sponsor fails to contact the qualified termination administrator within 30 days;

(v) The name, address, and telephone number of the person, office, or department that the plan sponsor must contact regarding the plan;

(vi) A statement that if the plan is terminated pursuant to 29 CFR 2578.1, notice of such termination will be furnished to the U.S. Department of Labor's Employee Benefits Security Administration;

(vii) The following statement: "The U.S. Department of Labor requires that you be informed that, as a fiduciary or plan administrator or both, you may be personally liable for costs, civil penalties, excise taxes, etc. as a result of your acts or omissions with respect to this plan. The termination of this plan will not relieve you of your liability for any such costs, penalties, taxes, etc."; and

(viii) A statement that the plan sponsor may contact the U.S. Department of Labor for more information about the federal law governing the termination and winding-up process for abandoned plans and the telephone number of the appropriate Employee Benefits Security Administration contact person.

(c) *Deemed termination.* (1) Except as provided in paragraph (c)(2) of this section, if a qualified termination administrator finds (pursuant to paragraph (b)(1) of this section) that an individual account plan has been abandoned, or if a plan is considered abandoned due to the entry of an order for relief under chapter 7 of title 11 of the United States Code (pursuant to paragraph (j)(1)(i) of this section), the plan shall be deemed to be terminated on the ninetieth (90th) day following the date of the letter from EBSA acknowledging receipt of the notice of plan abandonment, described in paragraph (c)(3) or (j)(2) of this section.

(2) If, prior to the end of the 90-day period described in paragraph (c)(1) of this section, the Department notifies the qualified termination administrator that it—

(i) Objects to the termination of the plan, the plan shall not be deemed terminated under paragraph (c)(1) of this section until the qualified termination administrator is notified that the Department has withdrawn its objection; or

(ii) Waives the 90-day period described in paragraph (c)(1), the plan shall be deemed terminated upon the qualified termination administrator's receipt of such notification.

(3) Following a qualified termination administrator's finding, pursuant to paragraph (b)(1) this section, that an individual account plan has been abandoned, the qualified termination administrator shall furnish to the U.S. Department of Labor a notice of plan abandonment that is signed and dated by the qualified termination administrator and that includes the following information:

(i) *Qualified termination administrator information.* (A) The name, EIN, address, and telephone number of the person electing to be the qualified termination administrator, including the address, email address, and telephone number of the person signing the notice (or other contact person, if different from the person signing the notice);

(B) A statement that the person (identified in paragraph (c)(3)(i)(A) of this section) is a qualified termination administrator within the meaning of paragraph (g) of this section and elects to terminate and wind up the plan (identified in paragraph (c)(3)(ii)(A) of this section) in accordance with the provisions of this section;

(ii) *Plan information.* (A) The name, address, telephone number, account number, EIN, and plan number of the plan with respect to which the person is electing to serve as the qualified termination administrator;

(B) The name and last known address and telephone number of the plan sponsor; and

(C) The estimated number of participants and beneficiaries with accounts in the plan;

(iii) *Findings.* A statement that the person electing to be the qualified termination administrator finds that the plan (identified in paragraph (c)(3)(ii)(A) of this section) is abandoned pursuant to paragraph (b) of this section. This statement shall include an explanation of the basis for such a finding, specifically referring to the provisions in paragraph (b)(1) of this section, a description of the specific steps (set forth in paragraphs (b)(3) and (b)(4) of this section) taken to locate or communicate with the known plan sponsor, and a statement that no objection has been received from the plan sponsor;

(iv) *Plan asset information.* (A) The estimated value of the plan's assets held by the person electing to be the qualified termination administrator;

(B) The length of time plan assets have been held by the person electing to be the qualified termination administrator, if such period of time is less than 12 months;

(C) An identification of any assets with respect to which there is no readily ascertainable fair market value, as well as information, if any, concerning the value of such assets; and

(D) An identification of known delinquent contributions pursuant to paragraph (d)(2)(iii) of this section;

(v) *Service provider information.* (A) The name, address, and telephone number of known service providers (e.g., record keeper, accountant, lawyer, other asset custodian(s)) to the plan; and

(B) An identification of any services considered necessary to carry out the qualified termination administrator's authority and responsibility under this section, the name of the service provider(s) that is expected to provide such services, and an itemized estimate of expenses attendant thereto expected to be paid out of plan assets by the qualified termination administrator; and

(vi) *Perjury statement.* A statement that the information being provided in the notice is true and complete based on the knowledge of the person electing to be the qualified termination administrator, and that the information is being provided by the qualified termination administrator under penalty of perjury.

(d) *Winding up the affairs of the plan.* (1) In any case where an individual account plan is deemed to be terminated pursuant to paragraph (c) of this section, the qualified termination administrator shall take steps as may be necessary or appropriate to wind up the affairs of the plan and distribute benefits to the plan's participants and beneficiaries.

(2) For purposes of paragraph (d)(1) of this section, except as provided pursuant to paragraph (j)(3) of this section (relating to chapter 7 plans), the qualified termination administrator shall:

(i) *Update plan records.* (A) Undertake reasonable and diligent efforts to locate and update plan records necessary to determine the benefits payable under the terms of the plan to each participant and beneficiary.

(B) For purposes of paragraph (d)(2)(i)(A) of this section, a qualified termination administrator shall not have failed to make reasonable and diligent efforts to update plan records merely because the administrator determines in good faith that updating the records is either impossible or involves significant cost to the plan in relation to the total assets of the plan.

(ii) *Calculate benefits.* Use reasonable care in calculating the benefits payable to each participant or beneficiary based on plan records described in paragraph (d)(2)(i) of this section. A qualified termination administrator shall not have failed to use reasonable care in calculating benefits payable solely because the qualified termination administrator—

(A) Treats as forfeited an account balance that, taking into account estimated forfeitures and other assets allocable to the account, is less than the estimated share of plan expenses allocable to that account, and reallocates that account balance to defray plan expenses or to other plan accounts in accordance with (d)(2)(ii)(B) of this section;

(B) Allocates expenses and unallocated assets in accordance with the plan documents, or, if the plan document is not available, is ambiguous, or if compliance with the plan is unfeasible,

(*1*) Allocates unallocated assets (including forfeitures and assets in a suspense account) to participant accounts on a per capita basis (allocated equally to all accounts); and

(*2*) Allocates expenses on a pro rata basis (proportionately in the ratio that each individual account balance bears to the total of all individual account balances) or on a per capita basis (allocated equally to all accounts).

(iii) *Report delinquent contributions.* (A) Notify the Department of any known contributions (either employer or employee) owed to the plan in conjunction with the filing of the notification required in paragraph (c)(3), (j)(2), or (d)(2)(ix) of this section.

(B) Except as provided in paragraph (j)(3)(i) of this section, nothing in paragraph (d)(2)(iii)(A) of this section or any other provision of the Act shall be construed to impose an obligation on the qualified termination administrator to collect delinquent contributions on behalf of the plan, provided that the qualified termination administrator satisfies the requirements of paragraph (d)(2)(iii)(A) of this section.

(iv) *Engage service providers.* Engage, on behalf of the plan, such service providers as are necessary for the qualified termination administrator to wind up the affairs of the plan and distribute benefits to the plan's participants and beneficiaries in accordance with paragraph (d)(1) of this section.

(v) *Pay reasonable expenses.* (A) Pay, from plan assets, the reasonable expenses of carrying out the qualified termination administrator's authority and responsibility under this section.

(B) Expenses of plan administration shall be considered reasonable solely for purposes of paragraph (d)(2)(v)(A) of this section if:

(*1*) Such expenses are for services necessary to wind up the affairs of the plan and distribute benefits to the plan's participants and beneficiaries,

(*2*) Such expenses: (*i*) Are consistent with industry rates for such or similar services, based on the experience of the qualified termination administrator; and

(*ii*) Are not in excess of rates ordinarily charged by the qualified termination administrator (or affiliate) for same or similar services provided to customers that are not plans terminated pursuant to this section, if the qualified termination administrator (or affiliate) provides same or similar services to such other customers, and

(*3*) The payment of such expenses would not constitute a prohibited transaction under the Act or is exempted from such prohibited transaction provisions pursuant to section 408(a) of the Act.

(vi) *Notify participants.* (A) Furnish to each participant or beneficiary of the plan a notice written in a manner calculated to be understood by the average plan participant and containing the following:

(*1*) The name of the plan;

(*2*) A statement that the plan has been determined to be abandoned by the plan sponsor and, therefore, has been terminated pursuant to regulations issued by the U.S. Department of Labor;

(*3*)(*i*) A statement of the participant's or beneficiary's account balance and the date on which it was calculated by the qualified termination administrator, and

(*ii*) The following statement: "The actual amount of your distribution may be more or less than the amount stated in this letter depending on investment gains or losses and the administrative cost of terminating your plan and distributing your benefits.";

(*4*) A description of the distribution options available under the plan and a request that the participant or beneficiary elect a form of distribution and inform the qualified termination administrator (or designee) of that election;

(*5*) A statement explaining that, if a participant or beneficiary fails to make an election within 30 days from receipt of the notice, the qualified termination administrator (or designee) will distribute the account balance of the participant or beneficiary directly:

(*i*) To an individual retirement plan (i.e., individual retirement account or annuity),

(*ii*) To an inherited individual retirement plan described in § 2550.404a-3(d)(1)(ii) of this chapter (in the case of a distribution on behalf of a distributee other than a participant or spouse),

(*iii*) In any case where the amount to be distributed meets the conditions in § 2550.404a-3(d)(1)(iii) or (iv), to an interest-bearing federally insured bank account, the unclaimed property fund of the State of the last known address of the participant or beneficiary, or an individual retirement plan (described in § 2550.404a-3(d)(1)(i) or (d)(1)(ii) of this chapter) or

(*iv*) To an annuity provider in any case where the qualified termination administrator determines that the survivor annuity requirements in sections 401(a)(11) and 417 of the Internal Revenue Code (or section 205 of ERISA) prevent a distribution under paragraph (d)(2)(vii)(B)(*1*) of this section;

(*6*) In the case of a distribution to an individual retirement plan (described in § 2550.404a-3(d)(1)(i) or (d)(1)(ii) of this chapter) a statement explaining that the account balance will be invested in an investment product designed to preserve principal and provide a reasonable rate of return and liquidity;

(*7*) A statement of the fees, if any, that will be paid from the participant or beneficiary's individual retirement plan (described in § 2550.404a-3 (d)(1)(i) or (d)(1)(ii) of this chapter) or other account (described in § 2550.404a-3 (d)(1)(iii)(A) of this chapter), if such information is known at the time of the furnishing of this notice;

(*8*) The name, address and phone number of the provider of the individual retirement plan (described in § 2550.404a-3 (d)(1)(i) or (d)(1)(ii) of this chapter), qualified survivor annuity, or other account (described in § 2550.404a-3 (d)(1)(iii)(A) of this chapter), if such information is known at the time of the furnishing of this notice; and

(*9*) The name, address, and telephone number of the qualified termination administrator and, if different, the name, address and phone number of a contact person (or entity) for additional information concerning the termination and distribution of benefits under this section.

(B)(*1*) For purposes of paragraph (d)(2)(vi)(A) of this section, a notice shall be furnished to each participant or beneficiary in accordance with the requirements of § 2520.104b-1(b)(1) of this chapter to the last known address of the participant or beneficiary; and

(*2*) In the case of a notice that is returned to the qualified termination administrator as undeliverable, the qualified termination administrator shall, consistent with the duties of a fiduciary under section 404(a)(1) of ERISA, take steps to locate and provide notice to the participant or beneficiary prior to making a distribution pursuant to paragraph (d)(2)(vii) of this section. If, after such steps, the qualified termination administrator is unsuccessful in locating and furnishing notice to a participant or beneficiary, the participant or beneficiary shall be deemed to have been furnished the notice and to have failed to make an election within the 30-day period described in paragraph (d)(2)(vii) of this section.

(vii) *Distribute benefits.* (A) Distribute benefits in accordance with the form of distribution elected by each participant or beneficiary with spousal consent, if required.

(B) If the participant or beneficiary fails to make an election within 30 days from the date the notice described in paragraph (d)(2)(vi) of this section is furnished, distribute benefits—

(*1*) In accordance with § 2550.404a-3 of this chapter; or

(*2*) If a qualified termination administrator determines that the survivor annuity requirements in sections 401(a)(11) and 417 of the Internal Revenue Code (or section 205 of ERISA) prevent a distribution under paragraph (d)(2)(vii)(B)(*1*) of this section, in any manner reasonably determined to achieve compliance with those requirements.

(C) For purposes of distributions pursuant to paragraph (d)(2)(vii)(B) of this section, the qualified termination administrator may designate itself (or an affiliate) as the transferee of such proceeds, and invest such proceeds in a product in which it (or an affiliate) has an interest, only if such designation and investment is exempted from the prohibited transaction provisions under the Act pursuant to section 408(a) of the Act.

(viii) *Special Terminal Report for Abandoned Plans.* File the Special Terminal Report for Abandoned Plans in accordance with § 2520.103-13 of this chapter.

(ix) *Final Notice.* No later than two months after the end of the month in which the qualified termination administrator satisfies the requirements in paragraph (d)(2)(i) through (d)(2)(vii) of this section, furnish to the Office of Enforcement, Employee Benefits Security Administration, U.S. Department of Labor, 200 Constitution Avenue NW., Washington, DC 20210, a notice, signed and dated by the qualified termination administrator, containing the following information:

(A) The name, EIN, address, email address, and telephone number of the qualified termination administrator, including the address and telephone number of the person signing the notice (or other contact person, if different from the person signing the notice);

(B) The name, account number, EIN, and plan number of the plan with respect to which the person served as the qualified termination administrator;

(C) A statement that the plan has been terminated and all the plan's assets have been distributed to the plan's participants and beneficiaries on the basis of the best available information;

(D) A statement that plan expenses were paid out of plan assets by the qualified termination administrator in accordance with the requirements of paragraph (d)(2)(v) or (j)(3)(v) of this section;

(E) If fees and expenses paid by the plan exceed by 20 percent or more the estimate required by paragraph (c)(3)(v)(B) or (j)(2)(v)(B)

of this section, a statement that actual fees and expenses exceeded estimated fees and expenses and the reasons for such additional costs;

(F) An identification of known delinquent contributions pursuant to paragraph (d)(2)(iii) of this section (if not already reported under paragraph (c)(3)(iv)(D) or (j)(2)(iv)(D) of this section);

(G) For each distribution in accordance with § 2550.404a-3 (d)(1)(v) (relating to distributions on behalf of deceased participants and beneficiaries), an identification of the deceased participant and, if applicable, the deceased named beneficiary, and the basis behind the finding required by § 2550.404a-3 (d)(1)(v); and

(H) A statement that the information being provided in the notice is true and complete based on the knowledge of the qualified termination administrator, and that the information is being provided by the qualified termination administrator under penalty of perjury.

(3) The terms of the plan shall, for purposes of title I of ERISA, be deemed amended to the extent necessary to allow the qualified termination administrator to wind up the plan in accordance with this section.

(e) *Limited liability.* (1)(i) Except as otherwise provided in paragraph (e)(1)(ii) and (iii) of this section, to the extent that the activities enumerated in paragraphs (d)(2) and (j)(3) of this section involve the exercise of discretionary authority or control that would make the qualified termination administrator a fiduciary within the meaning of section 3(21) of the Act, the qualified termination administrator shall be deemed to satisfy its responsibilities under section 404(a) of the Act with respect to such activities, provided that the qualified termination administrator complies with the requirements of paragraph (d)(2) and (j)(3) of this section as applicable.

(ii) A qualified termination administrator shall be responsible for the selection and monitoring of any service provider (other than monitoring a provider selected pursuant to paragraph (d)(2)(vii)(B) of this section) determined by the qualified termination administrator to be necessary to the winding up of the affairs of the plan, as well as ensuring the reasonableness of the compensation paid for such services. If a qualified termination administrator selects and monitors a service provider in accordance with the requirements of section 404(a)(1) of the Act, the qualified termination administrator shall not be liable for the acts or omissions of the service provider with respect to which the qualified termination administrator does not have knowledge.

(iii) For purposes of a distribution pursuant to paragraph (d)(2)(vii)(B)(*2*) of this section, a qualified termination administrator shall be responsible for the selection of an annuity provider in accordance with section 404 of the Act.

(2) Nothing herein shall be construed to impose an obligation on the qualified termination administrator to conduct an inquiry or review to determine whether or what breaches of fiduciary responsibility may have occurred with respect to a plan prior to becoming the qualified termination administrator for such plan.

(3) If assets of an abandoned plan are held by a person other than the qualified termination administrator, such person shall not be treated as in violation of section 404(a) of the Act solely on the basis that the person cooperated with and followed the directions of the qualified termination administrator in carrying out its responsibilities under this section with respect to such plan, provided that, in advance of any transfer or disposition of any assets at the direction of the qualified termination administrator, such person confirms with the Department of Labor that the person representing to be the qualified termination administrator with respect to the plan is the qualified termination administrator recognized by the Department of Labor.

(f) *Continued liability.* Nothing in this section shall serve to relieve or limit the liability of any person other than the qualified termination administrator due to a violation of ERISA.

(g) *Qualified termination administrator.* A termination administrator is qualified under this section only if:

(1) It is eligible to serve as a trustee or issuer of an individual retirement plan, within the meaning of section 7701(a)(37) of the Internal Revenue Code, and

(2) It holds assets of the plan that is found abandoned pursuant to paragraph (b) of this section.

(h) *Affiliate.* (1) The term affiliate means any person directly or indirectly controlling, controlled by, or under common control with, the person; or any officer, director, partner or employee of the person.

(2) For purposes of paragraph (h)(1) of this section, the term control means the power to exercise a controlling influence over the management or policies of a person other than an individual.

(i) *Model notices.* Appendices to this section contain model notices that are intended to assist qualified termination administrators in discharging the notification requirements under this section. Their use is not mandatory. However, the use of appropriately completed model notices will be deemed to satisfy the requirements of paragraphs (b)(5), (c)(3), (d)(2)(vi), (d)(2)(ix), and (j)(2) of this section.

(j) *Special rules for chapter 7 plans.* (1) Notwithstanding paragraphs (b) and (g) of this section (relating to findings of abandonment and defining the term "qualified termination administrator," respectively), if the sponsor of an individual account plan is in liquidation under chapter 7 of title 11 of the United States Code:

(i) The plan ("chapter 7 plan") shall for purposes of this section be considered abandoned upon the entry of an order for relief. However, the plan shall cease to be considered abandoned pursuant to this paragraph (j)(1) if at any time before the plan is deemed terminated pursuant to paragraph (c) of this section, the plan sponsor's chapter 7 liquidation proceeding is dismissed or converted to a proceeding under chapter 11 of title 11 of the United States Code.

(ii) The bankruptcy trustee, or an eligible designee, may be the qualified termination administrator. An "eligible designee" is any person or entity designated by the bankruptcy trustee that is eligible to serve as a trustee or issuer of an individual retirement plan, within the meaning of section 7701(a)(37) of the Internal Revenue Code, and that holds assets of the chapter 7 plan. The bankruptcy trustee shall be responsible for the selection and monitoring of any eligible designee in accordance with section 404(a)(1) of the Act.

(2) *Notice of Plan Abandonment.* In accordance with paragraph (c) of this section, the qualified termination administrator under this paragraph (j) shall furnish to the U.S. Department of Labor a notice of plan abandonment that is signed and dated by the qualified termination administrator and that includes the following information:

(i) *Qualified termination administrator information.* The name, address (including email address), and telephone number of the bankruptcy trustee and, if applicable, the name, EIN, address (including email address), and telephone number of any eligible designee acting as the qualified termination administrator pursuant to paragraph (j)(1)(ii) of this section;

(ii) *Plan information.* (A) The name, address, telephone number, account number, EIN, and plan number of the plan with respect to which the person is serving as the qualified termination administrator,

(B) The name and last known address and telephone number of the plan sponsor, and

(C) The estimated number of participants and beneficiaries with accounts in the plan;

(iii) *Chapter 7 information.* A statement that, pursuant to paragraph (j)(1) of this section, the plan is considered to be abandoned due to an entry of an order for relief under chapter 7 of the U.S. Bankruptcy Code, and a copy of the notice or order entered in the case reflecting the bankruptcy trustee's appointment to administer the plan sponsor's case;

(iv) *Plan asset information.* (A) The estimated value of the plan's assets as of the date of the entry of an order for relief,

(B) The name, EIN, address (including email address) and telephone number of the entity that is holding these assets, and the length of time plan assets have been held by such entity, if the period of time is less than 12 months,

(C) An identification of any assets with respect to which there is no readily ascertainable fair market value, as well as information, if any, concerning the value of such assets, and

(D) An identification of known delinquent contributions pursuant to paragraph (d)(2)(iii) of this section;

(v) *Service provider information.* (A) The name, address, and telephone number of known service providers (e.g., record keeper, accountant, lawyer, other asset custodian(s)) to the plan, and

(B) An identification of any services considered necessary to carry out the qualified termination administrator's authority and responsibility under this section, the name of the service provider(s) that is expected to provide such services, and an itemized estimate of expenses attendant thereto expected to be paid out of plan assets by the qualified termination administrator; and

(vi) *Perjury statement.* A statement that the information being provided in the notice is true and complete based on the knowledge of the person electing to be the qualified termination administrator, and that the information is being provided by the qualified termination administrator under penalty of perjury.

(3) *Winding up the affairs of the plan.* The qualified termination administrator shall comply with paragraph (d) of this section except as follows:

(i) *Delinquent contributions.* The qualified termination administrator of a plan described in paragraph (j)(1)(i) of this section shall, consistent with the duties of a fiduciary under section 404(a)(1) of ERISA, take reasonable and good faith steps to collect known delinquent contributions on behalf of the plan, taking into account the value of the plan assets involved, the likelihood of a successful recovery, and the expenses expected to be incurred in connection with collection. If the bankruptcy trustee designates an eligible designee as defined in paragraph (j)(1)(ii) of this section, the bankruptcy trustee shall at the time of such designation notify the eligible designee of any known delinquent contributions.

(ii) *Report fiduciary breaches.* The qualified termination administrator of a plan described in paragraph (j)(1)(i) of this section shall report known delinquent contributions (employer and employee) owed to the plan, and any activity that the qualified termination administrator believes may be evidence of other fiduciary breaches that involve plan assets by a prior plan fiduciary. This information must be reported to the Employee Benefits Security Administration in conjunction with the filing of the notification required in paragraph (j)(2) or (d)(2)(ix) of this section. If a bankruptcy trustee designates an eligible designee as defined in paragraph (j)(1)(ii) of this section, the bankruptcy trustee shall provide the eligible designee with records under the control of the bankruptcy trustee to enable the eligible designee to carry out its responsibilities under paragraph (j)(3)(ii) of this section. If, after the eligible designee completes the winding up of the plan, the bankruptcy trustee, in administering the debtor's estate, discovers additional information not already reported in the notification required in paragraphs (j)(2) or (d)(2)(ix) of this section that it believes may be evidence of fiduciary breaches that involve plan assets by a prior plan fiduciary, the bankruptcy trustee shall report such activity to the Employee Benefits Security Administration in a time and manner specified in instructions developed by the Office of Enforcement, Employee Benefits Security Administration, U.S. Department of Labor.

(iii) *Participant notification.* In lieu of the statement required by paragraph (d)(2)(vi)(A)(*2*) of this section, the notice shall include a statement that the plan sponsor is in liquidation under chapter 7 of title 11 of the United States Code and, therefore, the plan has been terminated by the bankruptcy trustee (or its eligible designee).

(iv) *Final notice.* In lieu of the content requirements in paragraph (d)(2)(ix)(A) of this section (relating to the qualified termination administrator), the final notice shall include, the name, address (including email address), and telephone number of the bankruptcy trustee and, if applicable, the name, EIN, address (including email address), and telephone number of the eligible designee.

(v) *Distributions.* Paragraph (d)(2)(vii)(C) of this section (relating to the ability of a qualified termination administrator to designate itself as the transferee of distribution proceeds in accordance with §2550.404a-3) is not applicable in the case of a qualified termination administrator that is the plan sponsor's bankruptcy trustee.

(vi) *Pay reasonable expenses.* (A) If the bankruptcy trustee is the qualified termination administrator, in lieu of the requirements in paragraph (d)(2)(v)(B)(*2*) of this section, expenses shall be consistent with industry rates for such or similar services ordinarily charged by qualified termination administrators defined in paragraph (g) of this section.

(B) If the bankruptcy trustee designates an eligible designee, as defined in paragraph (j)(1)(ii) of this section, to serve as the qualified termination administrator, the requirements in paragraph (d)(2)(v) of this section (as opposed to the requirements in paragraph (j)(3)(vi)(A) of this section) apply to expenses that the eligible designee pays to itself or others.

(C) The eligible designee may pay, from plan assets, the bankruptcy trustee for reasonable expenses incurred in selecting and monitoring the eligible designee.

(4) The bankruptcy trustee or eligible designee shall not, through waiver or otherwise, seek a release from liability under ERISA, or assert a defense of derived judicial immunity (or similar defense) in any action brought against the bankruptcy trustee or eligible designee arising out of its conduct under this regulation.

BILLING CODE 4510-29-P

APPENDIX A TO § 2578.1

NOTICE OF INTENT TO TERMINATE PLAN

[*Date of notice*]

[*Name of plan sponsor*]

[*Last known address of plan sponsor*]

Re: *[Name of plan and account number or other identifying information]*

Dear *[Name of plan sponsor]*:

We are writing to advise you of our concern about the status of the subject plan. Our intention is to terminate the plan and distribute benefits in accordance with federal law if you do not contact us within 30 days of your receipt of this notice. See 29 CFR 2578.1.

Our basis for taking this action is that our records reflect that there have been no contributions to, or distributions from, the plan within the past 12 months. *[If the basis for sending this notice is under § 29 CFR 2578.1(b) (1) (i) (B), complete and include the sentence below rather than the sentence above.* } Our basis for taking this action is *{ provide a description of the facts and circumstances indicating plan abandonment}.*

We are sending this notice to you because our records show that you are the sponsor of the subject plan. The U.S. Department of Labor requires that you be informed that, as a fiduciary or plan administrator or both, you may be personally liable for all costs, civil penalties, excise taxes, etc. as a result of your acts or omissions with respect to this plan. The termination of this plan by us will not relieve you of your liability for any such costs, penalties, taxes, etc. Federal law also requires us to notify the U.S. Department of Labor, Employee Benefits Security Administration, of the termination of any abandoned plan. For information about the federal law governing the termination of abandoned plans, you may contact the U.S. Department of Labor at 1.866.444.EBSA (3272).

Please contact *[name, address, and telephone number of the person, office, or department that the sponsor must contact regarding the plan]* within 30 days in order to prevent this action.

Sincerely,

[Name and address of qualified termination administrator or appropriate designee]

APPENDIX B To § 2578.1 PLANS FOUND ABANDONED PURSUANT TO 29 CFR 2578.1 (b)

NOTIFICATION OF PLAN ABANDONMENT AND INTENT TO SERVE AS QUALIFIED TERMINATION ADMINISTRATOR

[*Date of notice*]

Abandoned Plan Coordinator, Office of Enforcement

Employee Benefits Security Administration

U.S. Department of Labor

200 Constitution Ave., NW, Suite 600

Washington, DC, 20210

Re: Plan Identification

[Plan name and plan number]

[*EIN*]

[*Plan account number*]

[*Address*]

[Telephone number]

Qualified Termination Administrator

[Name]

[Address]

[E-mail address]

[Telephone number]

[EIN]

Abandoned Plan Coordinator:

Pursuant to 29 CFR 2578.1 (b), we have determined that the subject plan is or may become abandoned by its sponsor. We are eligible to serve as a Qualified Termination Administrator for purposes of terminating and winding up the plan in accordance with 29 CFR 2578.1, and hereby elect to do so.

We find that *{check the appropriate box below and provide additional information as necessary}* :

☐ There have been no contributions to, or distributions from, the plan for a period of at least 12 consecutive months immediately preceding the date of this letter. Our records indicate that the date of the last contribution or distribution was *{enter appropriate date}.*

☐ The following facts and circumstances suggest that the plan is or may become abandoned by the plan sponsor *{add description below}:*

We have also determined that the plan sponsor *{check appropriate box below}:*

☐ No longer exists

☐ Cannot be located

☐ Is unable to maintain the plan

We have taken the following steps to locate or communicate with the known plan sponsor and have received no objection *{provide an explanation below}:*

Part I – Plan Information

1. Estimated number of individuals (participants and beneficiaries) with accounts under the plan: [*number*]

2. Plan assets held by Qualified Termination Administrator:
   A.   Estimated value of assets: [*value*]
   B.   Months we have held plan assets, if less than 12:   [*number*]
   C.   Hard to value assets {*select "yes" or "no" to identify any assets with no readily ascertainable fair market value, and include for those identified assets the best known estimate of their value*}:

		Yes	No	
(a)	Partnership/joint venture interests	☐	☐	[*value*]
(b)	Employer real property	☐	☐	[*value*]
(c)	Real estate (other than (b))	☐	☐	[*value*]
(d)	Employer securities	☐	☐	[*value*]
(e)	Participant loans	☐	☐	[*value*]
(f)	Loans (other than (e))	☐	☐	[*value*]
(g)	Tangible personal property	☐	☐	[*value*]

3. Name and last known address and telephone number of plan sponsor:

   _____
   _____
   _____

4. Other:

   _____
   _____
   _____

Part II – Known Service Providers of the Plan

	Name	Address	Telephone
1.			
2.			
3.			

Part III – <u>Services and Related Expenses to be Paid</u>

	Services	Service Provider	Estimated Cost
1.			
2.			
3.			

Part IV – <u>Contact Person</u> *{enter information only if different from signatory}*:

[Name]
[Address]
[E-mail address]
[Telephone number]

Under penalties of perjury, I declare that I have examined this notice and to the best of my knowledge and belief, it is true, correct and complete.

[Signature]
[Title of person signing on behalf the Qualified Termination Administrator]
[Address, e-mail address, and telephone number]

APPENDIX C To § 2578.1 PLANS FOUND ABANDONED PURSUANT TO 29 CFR 2578.1 (j)

NOTIFICATION OF PLAN ABANDONMENT AND INTENT TO SERVE AS QUALIFIED TERMINATION ADMINISTRATOR

[Date of notice]

Abandoned Plan Coordinator, Office of Enforcement

Employee Benefits Security Administration

U.S. Department of Labor

200 Constitution Ave., NW, Suite 600

Washington, DC, 20210

Re: Plan Identification

[Plan name and plan number]

[EIN]

[Plan account number]

[Address]

[Telephone number]

Qualified Termination Administrator

[Name]

[Address]

[E-mail address]

[Telephone number]

[EIN]

[If applicable, include and complete the following pursuant to 29 CFR 2578.1 (j) (2) (i) unless the same as Qualified Termination Administrator information above]:

Bankruptcy Trustee

[Name]

[Address]

[E-mail address]

[Telephone number]

Abandoned Plan Coordinator:

Pursuant to 29 CFR 2578.1 (j)(1), the subject plan is considered abandoned because the sponsor of the plan is in liquidation pursuant to a chapter 7 bankruptcy proceeding.

[Insert as applicable: [I have been appointed to administer the plan sponsor's case under chapter 7 of the U.S. Bankruptcy Code, and attached is a copy of the notice or order entered in the case reflecting my appointment. As the bankruptcy trustee administering this case, I am eligible to serve as Qualified Termination Administrator for purposes of terminating and winding up the plan in accordance with 29 CFR 2578.1, and hereby elect to do so.]

or

[A bankruptcy trustee has been appointed to administer the plan sponsor's case under chapter 7 of the U.S. Bankruptcy Code, and attached is a copy of the notice or order entered in the case reflecting the trustee's appointment. We have been designated by the bankruptcy trustee and are eligible to serve as Qualified Termination Administrator for purposes of terminating and winding up the plan in accordance with 29 CFR 2578.1, and hereby elect to do so.] *]*

Part I – <u>Plan Information</u>

1. Estimated number of individuals (participants and beneficiaries) with accounts
   under the plan: [*number*]

2. Name, EIN, address and email address of the entity holding plan assets (if the entity is
   not the QTA):

   _____

   _____

   _____

   A. Estimated value of plan assets as of the date of the entry of an order for
      relief under chapter 7 of the U.S. Bankruptcy Code: [*value*]
   B. Months entity has held plan assets, if less than 12: [*number*]
   C. Hard to value assets {*select "yes" or "no" to identify any assets with no
      readily ascertainable fair market value, and include for those identified
      assets the best known estimate of their value*}:

		Yes	No	
(a)	Partnership/joint venture interests	☐	☐	[*value*]
(b)	Employer real property	☐	☐	[*value*]
(c)	Real estate (other than (b))	☐	☐	[*value*]
(d)	Employer securities	☐	☐	[*value*]
(e)	Participant loans	☐	☐	[*value*]
(f)	Loans (other than (e))	☐	☐	[*value*]
(g)	Tangible personal property	☐	☐	[*value*]

3. Name and last known address and telephone number of plan sponsor:

   _____

   _____

   _____

4. Other:

   _____

   _____

   _____

Part II – <u>Known Service Providers of the Plan</u>

	Name	Address	Telephone
1.	_____	_____	_____
2.	_____	_____	_____
3.	_____	_____	_____

Part III – <u>Services and Related Expenses to be Paid</u>

	Services	Service Provider	Estimated Cost
1.			
2.			
3.			

Part IV – <u>Contact Person</u> {*enter information only if different from signatory*}:

> [*Name*]
> [*Address*]
> [*E-mail address*]
> [*Telephone number*]

Under penalties of perjury, I declare that I have examined this notice and to the best of my knowledge and belief, it is true, correct and complete.

[*Signature*]
[*Title of person signing on behalf the Qualified Termination Administrator*]
[*Address, e-mail address, and telephone number*]

APPENDIX D TO § 2578.1

NOTICE OF PLAN TERMINATION

[*Date of notice*]

[*Name and last known address of plan participant or beneficiary*]

Re: [*Name of plan*]

Dear [*Name of plan participant or beneficiary*]:

{*Insert as applicable* [We are] *or* [I am]} writing to inform you that the [*name of plan*] (Plan) has been terminated pursuant to regulations issued by the U.S. Department of Labor. The Plan was terminated because it was abandoned by [*name of the plan sponsor*]. {*For plans abandoned pursuant to 29 CFR 2578.1 (j) (1), replace the sentence immediately preceding with the sentence immediately following*}: The Plan was terminated because [name of the plan sponsor] is in bankruptcy and the business is shutting down.

We have determined that you have an interest in the Plan, either as a plan participant or beneficiary. Your account balance on [*date*] is/was [*account balance*]. We will be distributing this money as permitted under the terms of the Plan and federal regulations. The actual amount of your distribution may be more or less than the amount stated in this letter depending on investment gains or losses and the administrative cost of terminating the Plan and distributing your benefits.

Your distribution options under the Plan are {*add a description of the Plan's distribution options*}. It is very important that you elect one of these forms of distribution and inform us of your election. The process for informing us of this election is {*enter a description of the election process established by the qualified termination administrator*}.

{*Select the next paragraph from options 1 through 3, as appropriate.*}
{*Option 1: If this notice is for a participant or beneficiary, complete and include the following paragraph provided the account balance does not meet the conditions of § 2550.404a-3(d) (1) (iii) or (iv).*}

If you do not make an election within 30 days from your receipt of this notice, your account balance will be transferred directly to an individual retirement plan (inherited individual retirement plan in the case of a nonspouse beneficiary) maintained by {*insert the name, address, and*

phone number of the provider if known, otherwise insert the following language* [a bank or insurance company or other similar financial institution]}. Pursuant to federal law, your money in the individual retirement plan would then be invested in an investment product designed to preserve principal and provide a reasonable rate of return and liquidity. {*If fee information is known, include the following sentence:* Should your money be transferred into an individual retirement plan, [*name of the financial institution*] charges the following fees for its services: {*add a statement of fees, if any, that will be paid from the participant or beneficiary's individual retirement plan*}. }

{*Option 2: If this notice is for a participant or beneficiary whose account balance meets the conditions of § 2550.404a-3(d) (1) (iii) or (iv), complete and include the following paragraph.*}

If you do not make an election within 30 days from your receipt of this notice, and your account balance is $1,000 or less, federal law permits us to transfer your balance to an interest-bearing federally insured bank account, to the unclaimed property fund of the State of your last known address, or to an individual retirement plan (inherited individual retirement plan in the case of a nonspouse beneficiary). Pursuant to federal law, your money, if transferred to an individual retirement plan would then be invested in an investment product designed to preserve principal and provide a reasonable rate of return and liquidity. {*If known, include the name, address, and telephone number of the financial institution or State fund into which the individual's account balance will be transferred or deposited. If the individual's account balance is to be transferred to a financial institution and fee information is known, include the following sentence:* Should your money be transferred into a plan or account, [*name of the financial institution*] charges the following fees for its services: {*add a statement of fees, if any, that will be paid from the individual's account*}. }

{*Option 3: If this notice is for a participant or participant's spouse whose distribution is subject to the survivor annuity requirements in sections 401 (a) (ll) and 417 of the Internal Revenue Code (or section 205 of ERISA), complete and include the following paragraph.*}

If you do not make an election within 30 days from your receipt of this notice, your account balance will be distributed in the form of a qualified joint and survivor annuity or qualified preretirement annuity as required by the Internal Revenue Code. {*If the name of the annuity* *provider is known, include the following sentence:* The name of the annuity provider is *[name, address and phone number of the provider].* }

For more information about the termination, your account balance, or distribution options, please contact *[name, address, and telephone number of the qualified termination administrator and, if different, the name, address, and telephone number of the appropriate contact person].*

Sincerely,

[Name of qualified termination administrator or appropriate designee]

APPENDIX E To § 2578.1

FINAL NOTICE

[Date of notice]

Abandoned Plan Coordinator, Office of Enforcement

Employee Benefits Security Administration

U.S. Department of Labor

200 Constitution Ave., NW, Suite 600

Washington, DC, 20210

Re: *Plan Identification*

  [Plan name and plan number]

  [Plan account number]

  [EIN]

  Qualified Termination Administrator

  [Name]

  [Address and e-mail address]

  [Telephone number]

  [EIN]

[If applicable, complete and include the following pursuant to 29 CFR 2578.1 (j) (3) (iv) unless the same as Qualified *Termination Administrator information above]:*

  Bankruptcy Trustee

  [Name]

  [Address]

  [E-mail address]

  [Telephone number]

Abandoned Plan Coordinator:

General Information

The termination and winding-up process of the subject plan has been completed pursuant to 29 CFR 2578.1. Benefits were distributed to participants and beneficiaries on the basis of the best available information pursuant to 29 CFR 2578.1 (d)(2)(i). Plan expenses were paid out of plan assets pursuant to 29 CFR 2578.1 (d)(2)(v) or 29 CFR 2578.1 (j)(3)(vi).

[Include and complete the next section, entitled "Contact Person, " only if the contact person is different from the signatory of this notice. }

Contact Person

  [Name]

  [Address and e-mail address]

  [Telephone number]

[Include and complete the next section, entitled "Expenses Paid" only if fees and expenses paid by the plan exceeded by 20 percent or more the estimate required by 29 CFR 2578.1 (c) (3) (v) (B) or 29 CFR 2578.1 (j) (2) (v) (B).}

Expenses Paid

The actual fees and/or expenses paid in connection with winding up the Plan exceeded by *[insert either:* [20 percent or more] *or [enter the actual percentage]}* the estimate required by 29 CFR 2578.1(c)(3)(v)(B) or 29 CFR 2578.1 (j)(2)(v)(B). The reason or reasons for such additional costs are *[provide an explanation of the additional costs}.*

Other

Under penalties of perjury, I declare that I have examined this notice and to the best of my knowledge and belief, it is true, correct and complete.

[Signature]

[Title of person signing on behalf the Qualified Termination Administrator]

[Address, e-mail address, and telephone number]

Attachment

  Signed at Washington, DC, this 3rd day of December, 2012.

Phyllis C. Borzi,

Assistant Secretary, Employee Benefits Security Administration, Department of Labor.

[FR Doc. 2012-29500 Filed 12-11-12; 8:45 am]

BILLING CODE 4510-29-c

¶ 20,538I

Employee Benefits Security Administration (EBSA): Proposed rules: Group health plans: Preventive health services: Religious employers: Contraceptive services.—The EBSA, the IRS, and the Department of Health and Human Services have issued proposed regulations that clarify the definition of religious employer under the Patient Protection and Affordable Care Act's (PPACA's, P.L. 111-148) no-cost sharing contraceptive coverage requirement for non-exempt, non-grandfathered group health plans. In addition, the proposed rules accommodate nonprofit religious organizations that do not qualify as religious employers by providing their enrollees separate contraceptive coverage, with no copayments, but at no cost to the religious organization.

The proposed regulations, which were published in the Federal Register on February 6, 2013 (78 FR 8456), are reproduced at ¶ 20,263K. The regulations were finalized on July 2, 2013 (78 FR 39869). The preamble to the final regulations is at ¶ 23,289. The final regulations are at ¶ 14,136H, ¶ 15,050R-50PA, and ¶ 15,050R-50PB.

¶ 20,538J

Employee Benefits Security Administration (EBSA): Proposed regulations: IRS: Patient Protection and Affordable Care Act (P.L. 111-148, PPACA): Group health plans: Waiting periods.—The IRS, EBSA, and the Department of Health and Human Services have issued proposed regulations that implement the 90-day waiting period limitation under Sec. 2708 of the Public Health Service Act, as added by the PPACA and incorporated into the Code and ERISA. Sec. 2708 provides that a group health plan and a health insurance issuer offering group health insurance coverage may not apply any waiting period that exceeds 90 days. The proposed regulations would also amend regulations to conform PPACA provisions already in effect and provisions that will become effective in 2014. The proposed regulations would generally apply to plan years beginning on or after January 1, 2014.

The proposed regulations, which were published in the Federal Register on March 21, 2013 (78 FR 17313), are reproduced at ¶ 20,263L. The regulations were finalized on February 24, 2014 (79 FR 10295). The preamble to the final regulations is at ¶ 24,318. The final regulations are at ¶ 15,049I, ¶ 15,049J, ¶ 15,049K, ¶ 15,049L, ¶ 15,049M, ¶ 15,049N, ¶ 15,049O, ¶ 15,050A-1, ¶ 15,050R-50K, ¶ 15,051A-1, and ¶ 15,051B-1.

¶ 20,538K

Pension Benefit Guaranty Corporation (PBGC): Proposed regulations: Reportable events: Waivers.—The Pension Benefit Guaranty Corporation (PBGC) has issued proposed regulations which would amend the reportable events rules. The proposed regulations would create a new reportable event waiver structure that is more closely focused on risk than the current waiver structure. The proposed regulations would also reflect changes made to the funding and premium rules by the Pension Protection Act of 2006 (PPA; P.L. 109-280) and would revise and simplify the descriptions of several reportable events and make some event narrower in order to make compliance less burdensome. Comments on the proposed rules are due by June 3, 2013. A public hearing is schedule for June 18, 2013.

The proposed regulations, which were published in the Federal Register on April 3, 2013 (78 FR 20039), are reproduced below. The regulations were finalized on September 11, 2015 (80 FR 54979). The preamble to the final regulations is at ¶ 24,332. The final regulations are at ¶ 15,302A, ¶ 15,302YY, ¶ 15,315A, ¶ 15,461, ¶ 15,461A, ¶ 15,461B, ¶ 15,461C, ¶ 15,461D, ¶ 15,461E, ¶ 15,461F, ¶ 15,461G, ¶ 15,461H, ¶ 15,461I, ¶ 15,462, ¶ 15,462A, ¶ 15,462B, ¶ 15,462C, ¶ 15,462D, ¶ 15,462E, ¶ 15,462F, ¶ 15,462G, ¶ 15,462H, ¶ 15,462I, ¶ 15,462J, ¶ 15,462K, ¶ 15,462L, ¶ 15,462M, ¶ 15,462N, ¶ 15,462O, ¶ 15,463, ¶ 15,463A, ¶ 15,463B, ¶ 15,463C, ¶ 15,463D, ¶ 15,463E, ¶ 15,463F, ¶ 15,463G, ¶ 15,464, ¶ 15,668C, ¶ 15,670G, ¶ 15,700B, and ¶ 15,700F.

[Billing Code 7709-01-P]

PENSION BENEFIT GUARANTY CORPORATION

29 CFR Parts 4000, 4001, 4043, 4204, 4206, and 4231

RIN 1212-AB06

Reportable Events and Certain Other Notification Requirements

AGENCY: Pension Benefit Guaranty Corporation.

ACTION: Proposed rule.

SUMMARY: Under ERISA, pension plans and the companies that sponsor them are required to report to PBGC a range of corporate and plan events. In 2009, PBGC proposed to increase reporting requirements by eliminating most reporting waivers. Plan sponsors and pension practitioners objected, saying that PBGC would have required reports where the actual risk to plans and PBGC is minimal. On reflection, PBGC agrees. This new proposal exempts most companies and plans from many reports, and targets requirements to the minority of companies and plans that are at substantial risk of default.

PBGC developed a revised proposal under the auspices of Presidential Executive Order 13563, which directs agencies to review and revise existing regulations. Under the new proposal, reporting would be waived for most events currently covered by funding-based waivers if a plan or its sponsor comes within a financial soundness safe harbor based on widely available measures already used in business. Waivers for small plans would be expanded and some other existing waiver provisions would be retained with modifications; other waivers would be eliminated.

In this way, PBGC can reduce unnecessary reporting requirements, while at the same time target its resources to plans that are at risk. The revised proposal will exempt more than 90 percent of plans and sponsors from many reporting requirements. Reporting requirements would also be made simpler and more uniform.

PBGC will also provide for more open and extensive public comment on the proposed rule.

DATES: Comments must be submitted on or before June 3, 2013. A public hearing will be held on June 18, 2013. Outlines of topics to be discussed at the hearing must be submitted on or before June 4, 2013. See **Public Participation** below for more information on the hearing.

ADDRESSES: Comments, identified by Regulation Identifier Number (RIN) 1212-AB06, may be submitted by any of the following methods:

- Federal eRulemaking Portal: http://www.regulations.gov.

  Follow the Web site instructions for submitting comments.

- E-mail: reg.comments@pbgc.gov.

- Fax: 202-326-4224.

- Mail or Hand Delivery: Regulatory Affairs Group, Office of the General Counsel, Pension Benefit Guaranty Corporation, 1200 K Street, NW., Washington, DC 20005-4026.

All submissions must include the Regulation Identifier Number for this rulemaking (RIN 1212-AB06). Comments received, including personal information provided, will be posted to www.pbgc.gov. Copies of comments may also be obtained by writing to Disclosure Division, Office of the General Counsel, Pension Benefit Guaranty Corporation, 1200 K Street NW., Washington DC 20005-4026, or calling 202-326-4040 during normal business hours. (TTY and TDD users may call the Federal relay service toll-free at 1-800-877-8339 and ask to be connected to 202-326-4040.)

Outlines of topics to be discussed at the public hearing on this rule must be submitted by e-mail to regs.comments@pbgc.gov or by mail or courier to Regulatory Affairs Group, Office of the General Counsel, Pension Benefit Guaranty Corporation, 1200 K Street, NW., Washington, DC 20005-4026. See **Public Participation** below for more information on the hearing.

FOR FURTHER INFORMATION CONTACT: Catherine B. Klion, Assistant General Counsel (*Klion.Catherine@PBGC.gov*), Regulatory Affairs Group, Office of the General Counsel, Pension Benefit Guaranty Corporation, 1200 K Street NW., Washington DC 20005-4026; 202-326-4024. (TTY/TDD users may call the Federal relay service toll-free at 1-800-877-8339 and ask to be connected to 202-326-4024.)

SUPPLEMENTARY INFORMATION:

Executive Summary — Purpose of the Regulatory Action

This rule is needed to conform PBGC's reportable events regulation to changes in the law, to avoid unnecessary reporting requirements, to make reporting more efficient and effective, and as a result help preserve retirement plans. It does these things by amending the regulation to track new legal rules, to change the scope of some reportable events, and to replace the existing waiver structure with a new structure including "safe harbors" that relieves reporting burdens on companies and plans where there is little risk to pensions.

PBGC's legal authority for this action comes from section 4002(b)(3) of the Employee Retirement Income Security Act of 1974 (ERISA), which authorizes PBGC to issue regulations to carry out the purposes of title IV of ERISA, and section 4043 of ERISA, which gives PBGC authority to define reportable events and waive reporting.

Executive Summary — Major Provisions of the Regulatory Action

Changing the waiver structure

Under the current waiver structure for reportable events, PBGC often doesn't get reports it needs; at the same time, it gets many reports it *doesn't* need - reports that are unnecessary. This mismatch occurs because the current waiver structure isn't well-tied to the actual risks and causes of plan terminations.

When a reporting waiver keeps PBGC from learning of a reportable event that presents a high level of risk to a plan, its participants, and the pension insurance system, PBGC loses the opportunity to take protective action. That action might include steps such as involuntary plan termination or negotiation with the plan sponsor to improve plan funding.

But when there is no waiver for a low-risk event, the reporting burden of the plan or sponsor involved outweighs the usefulness of the report to PBGC.

In both these cases, the result is to reduce retirement security. In the former case, PBGC is unable to step in to support plan benefits in a timely way, either because a plan may have been terminated that could otherwise have been preserved, or because an involuntary termination occurred after exposure had increased unreasonably. In the latter case, the unnecessary reporting burden may lead some firms to reconsider their decision to sponsor defined-benefit pension plans.

The most significant provision of this rule is to propose a blueprint for a new reportable events waiver structure that is more closely focused on risk than the current waiver structure. Some waivers that poorly identify risky situations — like those based on an apparently modest level of plan underfunding — would be eliminated; at the same time, new "safe harbors" would be established — based on financial soundness — that are better measures of low plan risk.

Conforming to changes in the law

The Pension Protection Act of 2006 (PPA 2006) made changes in the law that affect the test for whether advance reporting of certain reportable events is required. The test is based on the variable-rate premium rules, which PPA 2006 changed. This rule would conform the advance reporting test to the new legal requirements.

Revision of definitions of reportable events

The rule would simplify the descriptions of several reportable events and make some event descriptions narrower so that compliance is easier and less burdensome. One event would be broadened in scope, and clarification of another event would have a similar result. These changes, like the waiver changes, are aimed at tying reporting burden to risk.

Mandatory e-filing

The rule would make electronic filing of reportable events notices mandatory. This would further PBGC's ongoing implementation of the Government Paperwork Elimination Act. E-filing is more efficient for both filers and PBGC and has become the norm for PBGC's regulated community.

Introduction

On January 18, 2011, the President issued Executive Order 13563 on Improving Regulation and Regulatory Review, directing agencies to review and improve their regulatory processes. In the spirit of Executive Order 13563 and in light of the comments received on its 2009 proposal, PBGC reexamined the reportable events regulation and the proposed amendment with several factors in mind:

- Commenters said that under the 2009 proposal, many companies would have been required to report to PBGC on non-pension-focused activities in circumstances where those activities were unlikely to affect their pension plans.[1] To avoid such a result, PBGC has sought ways to establish safe harbors that waive reporting requirements in such circumstances.

- Since the reportable events program was legislated almost four decades ago, a vast quantity of business and financial information has become available through the internet and other means. As a result, PBGC can require less direct reporting from its insured plans and their sponsors.

- When reporting to PBGC is necessary, to the extent practicable PBGC can and should rely on procedures, documents, and performance standards that are already established and accepted. In short, PBGC is trying not to "reinvent the wheel," nor does PBGC want to require insured plans and the companies that sponsor them to do so.

Establishing Financial Soundness Safe Harbors

PBGC proposes to establish safe harbors to enable financially sound businesses and plans to avoid having to report many events, particularly those events that seem to have little chance of threatening pension plans.

- *Establishing Financial Soundness for Companies.* A business would be in the safe harbor if it has adequate capacity to meet its obligations in full and on time, as evidenced by meeting five criteria, including passing a "credit report" test and four other criteria designed to measure various aspects of financial soundness. The credit report test would require that the business have a credit report score from a commercial credit reporting company that is commonly used in the business community and that the score indicate a low likelihood that the company would default on its obligations. (The vast majority of plan sponsors already have credit report scores.) The other criteria would be that the business have: (a) positive net income, (b) no secured debt (with some exceptions, such as purchase-money mortgages and leases), (c) no loan defaults or similar issues, and (d) no missed pension plan contributions (again, with some exceptions). For those in the safe harbor, no post-event reporting would be required for most events to which funding-based waivers currently apply.[2]

- *Establishing Financial Soundness via Plans.* A plan would be in the safe harbor if it were either fully funded on a termination basis or 120 percent funded on a premium basis.[3]

The proposal would also generally provide more small-plan waivers and preserve foreign-entity and *de minimis* waivers but eliminate most other waivers.

In addition, PBGC proposes to simplify reporting rules, to make them more uniform, and where possible to permit submission of information already prepared by plans and companies for other purposes.

Impact of Proposal

Overall, PBGC expects the proposal to exempt or waive more than 90 percent of plans and sponsors from many reporting requirements. The proposal will reduce the burden on the vast majority of companies (estimated at approximately three-fourths) that are financially sound. This reduction may make them less likely to eliminate their defined benefit plans and thereby have a beneficial effect on retirement security generally. In addition, the expansion of small plan waivers could help retention of small plans (which represent about two-thirds of all plans).

Burden on plan sponsors with *de minimis* components in their controlled groups will be reduced because the inclusion of additional *de minimis* waivers for certain events will reduce both reporting and the need to monitor for reportable events to which waivers apply.

Some reportable events present little or no risk to the pension insurance system — where, for example, the plan sponsor is financially sound and the risk of plan termination low. Reports of such events are unnecessary in the sense that PBGC typically reviews but takes no action on them. Based on an analysis of 2011 data, PBGC found that the proportion of such *unnecessary filings would be cut by 88 percent* under the proposed regulation.[4] The total number of filings under the proposed rule would be comparable to those under the present regulation, but they would be much reduced compared to the 2009 proposal, and the proportion of unnecessary reports, and the regulatory burden on financially sound sponsors and plans, would be dramatically reduced. Fewer unnecessary reports means a more efficient reporting system and a greater proportion of filings that present the opportunity for increased plan protection through monitoring and possible intervention in transactions based on risk, leading to better protection for the pension insurance system and retirement security generally.

If PBGC gets a reportable event notice, it can intervene earlier in the process. Using data from 2011, PBGC has estimated the benefit of better targeted reporting under the new proposal in terms of the value of early intervention as a creditor where a reportable event may foreshadow sponsor default. Early intervention as a creditor leads to higher recoveries of plan underfunding. PBGC estimates that the value of early intervention would exceed the dollar equivalent of the increased burden associated with the higher rate of targeted reporting by approximately $3.8 million.

The methodology of these studies is discussed in more detail under *Executive Order 12866 "Regulatory Planning and Review" and Executive Order 13563 "Improving Regulation and Regulatory Review"* at the end of this preamble.

The new proposal is described in more detail below.

Background

The Pension Benefit Guaranty Corporation (PBGC) administers the pension plan termination insurance program under Title IV of the Employee Retirement Income Security Act of 1974 (ERISA). Under section 4007 of ERISA, pension plans covered by Title IV must pay premiums to PBGC. Section 4006 of ERISA establishes the premium rates and includes provisions for determining the variable-rate premium (VRP), which is based on plan funding rules. PBGC's regulations on Premium Rates (29 CFR part 4006) and Payment of Premiums (29 CFR part 4007) implement the premium rules. A number of other provisions of ERISA, and of PBGC's other regulations, refer to funding and premium rules. Thus, any change in the funding and premium rules may require corresponding changes in other PBGC regulations.

---

[1] Among the many comments received on this point: ". . . in many situations in which reporting would be required - the reportable event would not create any meaningful risk that the employer would be unable to meet its plan funding obligations." *ERISA Industry Committee* comment letter, accessible on PBGC's Web site (www.PBGC.gov).

[2] Most reporting requirements under the reportable events regulation call for post-event reports, but in some cases advance reporting is required. The new proposal would conform the advance reporting threshold test to changes in the law and eliminate certain extensions of the time to file (see *Advance-Notice Extensions* below), but would make other changes to

advance-notice provisions only where they refer to post-event notice provisions that would be changed. Except as otherwise noted, this preamble discusses post-event reporting only.

[3] The current regulation provides a waiver in some circumstances based on 80 percent funding on a premium basis. However, in PBGC's experience, that test is inadequate, in that many plans that have undergone distress or involuntary termination nonetheless have been 80 percent funded on a premium basis. See *Financial Soundness Safe Harbor for Plans* below.

[4] To 5 percent under the proposal compared to 42 percent under the present regulation.

Reportable Events

One such regulation is PBGC's regulation on Reportable Events and Certain Other Notification Requirements (29 CFR part 4043), implementing section 4043 of ERISA, which requires that PBGC be notified of the occurrence of certain "reportable events." Reportable events include such plan events as missed contributions, insufficient funds, and large pay-outs and such sponsor events as loan defaults and controlled group changes. Like section 4043, the reportable events regulation generally requires post-event reporting, but also calls for advance reporting for non-public companies where plan underfunding is large. The threshold test for advance reporting measures underfunding by reference to VRP quantities (in particular, the values of assets and vested benefits as determined for VRP purposes).

The Pension Protection Act of 2006 (PPA 2006) changed the plan funding rules in Title I of ERISA and in the Internal Revenue Code of 1986 (Code) and amended the VRP provisions of section 4006 of ERISA to conform to the changes in the funding rules. PBGC amended its premium rates regulation and its premium payment regulation accordingly, effective for plan years beginning after 2007. Since underfunding for purposes of reportable events was measured by reference to the VRP, the thresholds for reportable events also had to be modified. Pending the adoption of conforming amendments to the reportable events regulation, PBGC has issued a series of Technical Updates providing transitional guidance on how the PPA 2006 changes affect compliance with the reportable events requirements.[5]

2009 Proposed Rule

On November 23, 2009 (at 74 FR 61248), PBGC published in the *Federal Register* for notice and comment a proposed rule providing for amendment of PBGC's reportable events regulation to make the advance reporting threshold test consistent with the PPA 2006 funding rules and PBGC's new variable-rate premium rules. The rule also proposed to eliminate most automatic waivers and filing extensions, create two new reportable events based on provisions in PPA 2006, and make other changes to the reportable events regulation. It also provided for amendment of five other PBGC regulations to revise statutory cross-references and otherwise accommodate the statutory and regulatory changes in the premium rules.

PBGC received comments on the proposed rule from eleven commenters — actuaries, pension consultants, and organizations representing employers and pension professionals. In general, the commenters considered the proposal unduly burdensome, primarily because of the elimination of most reportable event waivers. Several commenters urged PBGC to rethink and repropose the rule to address issues raised by the comments.

Executive Order 13563

On January 18, 2011, the President issued Executive Order 13563 on Improving Regulation and Regulatory Review (76 FR 3821, January 21, 2011). Executive Order 13563 encourages identification and use of innovative tools to achieve regulatory ends, calls for streamlining existing regulations, and reemphasizes the goal of balancing regulatory benefits with burdens on the public.

Executive Order 13563 also requires agencies to develop a plan to review existing regulations to identify any that can be made more effective or less burdensome in achieving regulatory objectives. On April 1, 2011 (at 76 FR 18134), PBGC published a request for public comments on developing its preliminary review plan. The five responses to this comment request (all from commenters on the 2009 proposal) included comments on the 2009 proposed rule (largely reflective of those submitted previously) as well as comments on the existing regulation.

New Proposal

PBGC has reconsidered the reportable events regulation and the 2009 proposed amendment in the spirit of Executive Order 13563 and in light of the comments. In addition to conforming the reportable events regulation to PPA 2006's changes to the funding and premium rules, this new proposal includes significant changes to address issues under the regulation in a new way and to reduce burden in areas where

that can be done without unduly compromising the objectives of section 4043.

In particular, the proposal features the introduction of a newly conceived "safe harbor" from reporting in response to comments suggesting that PBGC reduce reporting where risk to the pension insurance system is low. This safe harbor, applicable to five reportable events, would be based on employer financial soundness (*i.e.*, an employer's capacity to meet its financial commitments in full and on time) as determined through credit report scores and the satisfaction of related criteria. A second safe harbor would be available for plans that could meet one of two funding tests that would be more stringent than those currently provided for existing fundingbased waivers. The new proposed rule would also preserve or extend some waivers under the existing regulation that the 2009 proposal would have eliminated.

Under this approach, PBGC would rely more heavily on publicly available sources of information, including information publicly reported to other agencies, to learn about reportable events. As a result, it might take longer for PBGC to learn of some reportable events, but PBGC believes the approach would provide a better balance between the agency's need for information and sponsors' interest in minimizing regulatory burdens on the conduct of their business.

Public comments and regulatory changes (from both the existing regulation and the 2009 proposal) are discussed below in the context of the provisions they relate to.

Reportable Events

PBGC proposes to amend the reportable events regulation to accommodate the changes to the funding and premium rules; to replace many automatic waivers with a new and simpler system of waivers featuring "safe harbors" for five events based on plan sponsors' financial soundness and on high levels of plan funding; and to make other modifications.

Reports required by section 4043 of ERISA tell PBGC about events that may presage distress termination of plans or require PBGC to monitor or involuntarily terminate plans. These important reporting requirements are designed to protect participants and PBGC. When PBGC has timely information about a reportable event, it can take steps to encourage plan continuation — for example, by exploring alternative funding options with the plan sponsor — or, if plan termination is called for, to minimize the plan's potential funding shortfall through involuntary termination and maximize recovery of the shortfall from all possible sources. Without timely information about a reportable event, PBGC typically learns that a plan is in danger only when most opportunities for protecting participants and the pension insurance system may have been lost. But while such information can be critical to the protection of the pension insurance system, the circumstances surrounding some events may make reporting unnecessary. Thus, the regulation includes a system of waivers and extensions to ease reporting burdens in certain cases.

Automatic Waivers and Extensions — Overview

Section 4043.4 of the reportable events regulation provides that PBGC may grant waivers and extensions case by case. In addition, the existing regulation provides automatic waivers and extensions for most of the reportable events. For example, waivers are provided in some cases for small plans, for plans that meet certain funding tests, or for events affecting *de minimis* segments of controlled groups or foreign entities. In cases where it may be impossible to know by the filing due date whether criteria for a particular waiver are met, an extension gives a potential filer an opportunity to determine whether the waiver applies.

PBGC proposes to replace many of these automatic waivers with a new and simpler system, including many of the automatic waivers currently available and featuring new automatic waivers that would apply where a sponsor or plan comes within a financial soundness safe harbor.[6] The proposal would retain the complete waivers provided for certain statutory events — in §§ 4043.21 (disqualification or noncompliance), 4043.22 (amendment decreasing benefits), 4043.24 (termination), and 4043.28 (merger, consolidation, or transfer) — that have been replaced by events defined in the regulation. PBGC also proposes

---

[5] On November 28, 2007, PBGC issued Technical Update 07-2, providing transitional guidance on the applicability of the changes made by PPA 2006, and the corresponding changes proposed for PBGC premium regulations, to the determination of funding-related amounts for purposes of the reportable events regulation. On March 24, 2008, PBGC issued Technical Update 08-2, providing a waiver for reporting of missed quarterly contributions by certain small employers in 2008. On January 9, 2009, PBGC issued Technical Update 09-1, providing interim guidance on compliance with reportable events requirements for plan years beginning in 2009. On April 30, 2009, PBGC issued Technical Update 09-3, providing a waiver or alternative compliance method (depending on plan size) for

reporting of missed quarterly contributions by certain small employers in 2009. On November 23, 2009, PBGC issued Technical Update 09-4, extending the guidance in Technical Updates 09-1 and 09-3 for 2010. On December 3, 2010, PBGC issued Technical Update 10-4, extending the guidance in Technical Update 09-4 for 2011. On December 7, 2011, PBGC issued Technical Update 11-1, extending the guidance in Technical Update 10-4 for 2012. Technical Updates are available on PBGC's Web site, www.pbgc.gov.

[6] See **Summary Chart**, below, for an overview of waivers and safe harbors under the current regulation, the 2009 proposal, and this proposed rule.

to eliminate the automatic extensions under the existing regulation. These extensions are currently needed because many existing waivers are based on facts that may not be known when an event occurs. Since waivers of this kind are being replaced, related extensions are no longer needed.[7]

To give plans and sponsors time to institute any necessary event-monitoring programs and otherwise adjust to changes in the regulation, PBGC is proposing to defer the applicability date of the final rule.

PBGC's experience indicates that many of the automatic waivers and extensions in the existing reportable events regulation are depriving it of early alerts that would enable it to mitigate distress situations. For example, the 2009 proposed rule noted that of the 88 small plans terminated in 2007, 21 involved situations where, but for an automatic waiver, an active participant reduction reportable event notice would have been required an average of three years before termination. Had those notices been filed, the need for some of those terminations might have been avoided, and PBGC might have been able to reduce the impact of other terminations on the pension insurance system.[8] Concerns of this kind led PBGC in 2009 to propose the elimination of most automatic waivers in the reportable events regulation.

The commenters uniformly opposed the proposal to eliminate most waivers. Commenters said that the increase in the public's burden of compliance would outweigh the benefit to the pension insurance system of the additional reporting. They averred that the circumstances in which existing waivers apply pose little risk to PBGC and expressed concern that the proposed changes to the rule would discourage employers from continuing to maintain pension plans covered by Title IV.

In response to the comments, PBGC has attempted to identify circumstances that appear less likely to call for involuntary plan termination and is now proposing a new set of automatic waivers more appropriately tailored to focus on such situations. In particular, PBGC proposes to create safe harbors based on sponsor and plan financial soundness. These safe harbors would apply to post-event reporting requirements for the events of active participant reduction, distribution to a substantial owner, controlled group change, extraordinary dividend, and transfer of benefit liabilities — all the reportable events to which a funding-based waiver applies under the existing regulation, except liquidation and loan default. PBGC feels that the occurrence of one of these latter two events is at odds with the premise of financial soundness underlying the safe harbor and portends likely deterioration in plan funding due to missed contributions. (As discussed below, this consideration would not apply if the event qualified for a foreign-entity or de minimis waiver.)

Financial Soundness Safe Harbor for Plan Sponsors

Many commenters on the 2009 proposal contended that if funding-based waivers were eliminated, plans and plan sponsors would be required to report events posing minimal risk to PBGC and the pension insurance system. To address the issue of risk, PBGC proposes to provide a risk-based "safe harbor." PBGC is open to suggestions from the public to help identify existing, widely accepted standards that could form the basis for such a safe harbor. Pending such suggestions, PBGC is proposing, as discussed below, to base the safe harbor on the adequate capacity of an employer to meet its financial commitments in full and on time based on a combination of five factors, including a standard of financial strength reflected by commercial credit report scores and four confirmatory standards.

The new safe harbor would generally apply if, when a reportable event occurred for a plan, the applicable financial soundness criteria were met by the plan's contributing sponsor[9] or (where the contributing sponsor was a member of a controlled group) by the contributing sponsor's highest U.S. parent in the controlled group (that is, the

highest level U.S. company in the group that was in the contributing sponsor's chain of ownership). For a change in contributing sponsor, the criteria would be applied to the post-transaction sponsor group; for a transfer of benefit liabilities, the criteria would be applied to both the transferor and the surviving transferee plans' sponsor groups. The regulation would refer to an entity that satisfied the applicable criteria as "financially sound."

Focusing on the financial soundness of the plan sponsor (rather than just the funding level of the plan) is consistent with section 4041 of ERISA, which permits distress termination of underfunded pension plans only in situations where plan sponsors are in bankruptcy or severe financial straits. This safe harbor proposal reflects PBGC's experience that the financial soundness of a plan sponsor generally correlates inversely with the risk of an underfunded termination of the sponsor's pension plan. One major component of the risk of underfunded termination is the likelihood that the plan sponsor will, within the near future, fall into one of the "distress" categories in section 4041(c)(2)(B) of ERISA (liquidation, reorganization, or inability to pay debts or support the plan). Another is that the sponsor will go out of business, abandoning the plan and forcing PBGC to terminate it under section 4042 of ERISA. Thus, the risk of underfunded termination of a plan within the near future depends most significantly on the plan sponsor's financial strength.[10]

In particular, PBGC believes the ability of a sponsor to meet its senior unsecured debt obligations reflects the sponsor's ability to meet pension plan funding obligations because of the parity in bankruptcy of senior unsecured debt and pension plan obligations. PBGC's experience with its Early Warning Program[11] suggests that the higher the financial quality of a plan sponsor, the greater is the sponsor's commitment to its pension plan and its ability to meet its pension funding obligations. And analysis of PBGC data indicates that the credit ratings of sponsors of the vast majority of underfunded plans taken over by PBGC were below investment grade for many years before termination.[12]

Typically, sponsors of pension plans that present the greatest exposure for PBGC (large plans that are not fully funded) are rated by one or more large nationally recognized statistical rating organizations (NRSROs) that are registered with the Securities and Exchange Commission. These NRSRO ratings are among the most well-known and widely used measures of financial soundness for such large plan sponsors. But while credit ratings of a plan sponsor or its senior unsecured debt obligations would seem to be a good basis for a financial soundness safe harbor, many plan sponsors (primarily small plan sponsors) do not have such ratings. Furthermore, the Dodd-Frank Wall Street Reform and Consumer Protection Act (Pub.L. 111-203) requires federal agencies to remove references to and requirements of reliance on credit ratings in regulations.[13]

To avoid these drawbacks, PBGC proposes to use, as one of five criteria of financial soundness, credit scores reported by commercial credit reporting companies (CCRCs), which are already issued for the vast majority (over 90 percent) of businesses that sponsor plans covered by Title IV of ERISA. These commercial ratings are substantially different from traditional credit ratings. A CCRC generally assesses the creditworthiness of a business by reference to the ability of the business to pay its trade and other debts rather than by reference to the financial strength of the business reflected in financial statements (as credit rating agencies do). Just as a company's credit score is used by prospective creditors in evaluating the probability that an obligation will be paid, PBGC believes that it can appropriately use such scores as a measure of financial strength, which in turn is an indicator of the level of risk that a company will fail to meet its pension plan funding obligations. CCRCs are not within the purview of the Dodd-Frank Act since the relevant provisions cover credit ratings and credit rating

---

[7] The proposed rule would provide extensions for small plans to determine whether they satisfied the plan financial safe harbor test based on plan funding on a premium basis. There would also be an extension to provide plans time to determine whether the year-end active participant count showed that an active participant reduction event had occurred by attrition at the end of the year.

[8] Examples of the value of early alerts in mitigating distress situations can also be found in other PBGC programs. For example, as part of its Early Warning Program, PBGC negotiated substantial protections from Daimler AG for the pension plans of Daimler's former Chrysler North America division, and the Chrysler plans remain ongoing today. In another case, PBGC negotiated substantial protections under ERISA section 4062(e) for a plan sponsored by Visteon Corporation. When the company filed for Chapter 11 protection in 2009, the company initially contemplated terminating three of its four pension plans, and shifting the obligations to the PBGC's insurance program, which would have caused $100 million in benefit reductions for the company's 22,000 workers and retirees and added

more than $500 million to the PBGC's shortfall. However, due in part to the negotiated protections, all of the company's pension plans remain ongoing today.

[9] For multiple employer plans, all sponsors would have to qualify.

[10] In 2011, 90 percent of reportable events reports from filers that were below investment grade resulted in the opening of case files. For this purpose, "investment grade" means a credit rating of Baa3 or higher by Moody's or BBB- or higher by Standard and Poor's.

[11] See Technical Update 00-3.

[12] See Private Pensions, Recent Experiences of Large Defined Benefit Plans Illustrate Weaknesses in Funding Rules, GAO, May 2005, http://www.gao.gov/new.items/d05294.pdf, p. 30. For this purpose, GAO considered "investment grade" to correspond to a rating of BBB or higher.

[13] See section 939A of the Dodd-Frank Act.

agencies but not credit reporting companies (or, by implication, the credit scores and reports they produce).[14]

To make the credit scores underlying this test for the financial soundness safe harbor as reliable and as uniform as possible, and minimize the burden of obtaining such scores, PBGC proposes to require that a credit score be reported by a CCRC that is commonly used in the business community (*e.g.*, Dun & Bradstreet[15]). To satisfy this criterion for the financial soundness safe harbor, the credit report of a plan sponsor (or highest U.S. parent) by a CCRC that is commonly used in the business community would have to reflect a credit score indicating a low likelihood that the company would default on its obligations.

Scores that satisfy the standard in the regulation may change over time, because of changes in scoring methods or for other reasons. PBGC will provide, and update as necessary, reportable events filing instructions to guide filers in determining whether their credit scores meet the standard. The instructions will include one or more examples of scores by commercial credit reporting companies commonly used in the business community that indicate a low likelihood that a company will default on its obligations. To give an idea of the level of score that PBGC has in mind, a minimum Dun & Bradstreet financial stress score of 1477 would have satisfied the standard in 2011.

PBGC invites commenters to identify CCRCs other than Dun & Bradstreet that are commonly used in the business community now and to suggest ways that PBGC can remain currently informed of the identity of all such CCRCs as usage by the business community changes over time.

This financial strength criterion relies on private-sector commercial credit scores that most plan sponsors (or their U.S. parents) already have and that are used in a wide variety of business contexts. Such scores represent well known, objective, non-governmental assessments of financial soundness. PBGC would not itself evaluate the creditworthiness of plan sponsors as a condition to sponsors' use of the safe harbor. Sponsors would not have to certify or prove creditworthiness to PBGC — or even report a credit score — in order to take advantage of the safe harbor. For a sponsor not currently the subject of credit reporting, PBGC believes it would entail minimal effort and expense to have a CCRC that is commonly used in the business community begin issuing such reports on the sponsor.[16] As discussed below under *Small-Plan Waivers*, small plans would have separate exemptions.

As stated above, a sponsor would come within the financial soundness safe harbor if it passed the "credit report" test and in addition satisfied four further criteria.

One of these further criteria for the sponsor financial soundness safe harbor would be based on whether the sponsor (or its highest-level U.S. parent) has secured indebtedness. A lender's insistence on security reflects a level of concern over whether its loan will be timely repaid, typically because it judges that the borrower's creditworthiness is questionable. Thus, in general, if a company is forced to make use of secured debt, there is the suggestion of risk of loss that must be mitigated by the securing of collateral. If the borrower is a plan sponsor, there is a concomitant risk of underfunded plan termination during that same time frame. Conversely, this implication of risk does not arise where a company is not forced to borrow with security. Thus, an absence of secured indebtedness tends to be associated with a greater degree of financial soundness.

For purposes of this test, PBGC would except indebtedness incurred in connection with the acquisition or improvement of property and secured only by that property — such as mortgages and equipment financing (including capital leases). Secured debt of this kind is not uncommon even for financially sound businesses. But PBGC is aware that there may be other circumstances in which a company capable of borrowing without security might nonetheless choose to offer security to a lender — for example, if doing so would significantly reduce the cost of a loan. PBGC seeks public comment on the extent to which the proposed no-secureddebt test might be failed by plan sponsors whose risk level is in fact as low as that of other sponsors capable of passing

the test. PBGC also seeks suggestions for ways to modify the nosecured-debt test — for example, by carving out a wider class of debt than purchase-money obligations — to make it correspond better with commercial reality.

Another criterion for the sponsor financial soundness safe harbor would be that, for the past two years, the sponsor (or its highest-level U.S. parent) has had positive net income under generally accepted accounting principles (GAAP) or International Financial Reporting Standards (IFRS). This requirement serves to confirm both that the business is successful and that it has been operating for at least two years. (For non-profit entities, "net income" would be measured as the excess of total revenue over total expenses as required to be reported on Internal Revenue Service Form 990.)

In this connection, PBGC seeks public comment on the extent to which there are companies whose financial statements are not prepared using GAAP or IFRS but whose income level is comparable to the standards proposed for this criterion. PBGC seeks suggestions for supplementing the GAAP/IFRS standards with alternative standards to accommodate such companies.

The two remaining criteria are intended similarly to supplement and confirm the general picture of financial soundness painted by the satisfaction of the credit report test. These two requirements would be that the business have no debt service problems and be current with its pension plan contributions. More specifically:

- For the past two years, the business would have to have not met the criteria for an event of default with respect to a loan with an outstanding balance of $10 million or more, regardless of whether the default was cured or if the lender entered into a forbearance agreement or waived the default. Defaults on credit agreements suggest the business may be underperforming and at greater risk of not meeting its debt obligations.

- For the past two years, the business would have to have no missed pension contributions, other than quarterly contributions for which reporting is waived. Like the debt service requirement, this criterion addresses the likelihood that the business will reliably fund its pension plans.

Because of the novelty of the sponsor financial soundness standard and in the spirit of E.O. 13563's call for greater public participation in rulemaking, PBGC specifically invites public comment on the new risk-based financial soundness safe harbor for plan sponsors, as well as suggestions from the public for other tests or combinations of tests on which the sponsor financial soundness safe harbor might be based. PBGC seeks answers to the questions listed under **Public Participation** below and suggestions for alternative approaches to determining financial soundness based on widely-available and accepted financial standards.

Financial Soundness Safe Harbor for Plans

Most of the commenters opposed the elimination from the reportable events regulation of automatic reporting waivers based on plan funding, as proposed in 2009. PBGC now proposes to retain plan funding as a basis for relief from filing requirements for the same five events as the sponsor financial soundness safe harbor discussed above, by providing new "safe harbors" based on plan financial soundness. The standard of financial soundness for these new safe harbors would be a plan's funding status. A special rule would accommodate the needs of small plans in determining funding status.

The safe harbors would be less complex than the current funding-based waivers. The current regulation provides funding-based waivers with several different thresholds — for example, waivers are available where a plan pays no variable-rate premium,[17] has less than $1 million in unfunded vested benefits, or is 80 percent funded for vested benefits. Some waivers are based on a combination of a funding criterion and a non-funding criterion — for example, reporting of a controlled group change event is waived where a plan is 80 percent funded and the plan sponsor is a public company. Different waiver criteria or combinations of criteria apply to different events. PBGC's proposed safe harbors for

---

[14] The Securities Exchange Act of 1934 (the Exchange Act), which is amended by relevant portions of the Dodd-Frank Act, defines a "credit rating" as an assessment of the creditworthiness of an obligor as an entity or with respect to specific securities or money market instruments and a "credit rating agency" as any entity engaged in, among other things, the business of issuing credit ratings. See sections 3(a)(60) and (61) of the Exchange Act. However, the definition of credit rating agency under section 3(a)(61) of the Exchange Act specifically "does not include a commercial credit reporting company."

[15] Dun & Bradstreet provides free credit reports to companies willing to provide certain financial information for analysis and a free alert system to inform companies of changes in their credit scores (to permit inexpensive monitoring) and issues credit reports on at least

90 percent of sponsors of PBGC-covered plans. The United Kingdom's Pension Protection Fund, which performs pension protection functions like PBGC's, uses Dun & Bradstreet analyses to measure the risk of insolvency of sponsoring employers.

[16] A company may have its credit score reported by a CCRC simply by providing relevant data to the CCRC.

[17] In general, the variable-rate premium is based on unfunded vested benefits. However, in some cases no variablerate premium might be owed because of an exemption. For example, before 2008, ERISA provided an exemption from the variable-rate premium for a plan at the "full-funding limit," even if the plan had unfunded vested benefits. The exemption was removed by PPA 2006.

financially sound plans would involve just two alternative tests, which would be the same for all events covered by the safe harbors.

Both tests (like most of the current funding-based waiver tests) would be based on plan funding level, which is a comparison of assets to liabilities. Determining liabilities — calculating a present value for the obligation to pay benefits for years into the future — requires that actuarial assumptions be made about such things as the rate of return on investments, when participants are likely to retire, and how long they are likely to live. The actuarial assumptions used, and thus the present value arrived at, may differ significantly depending on whether the plan is considered "ongoing" — that is, expected to continue in operation indefinitely — or terminating. For example, assumptions about when participants will retire would be different for an ongoing plan than a terminating plan; in a terminating plan, participants generally retire earlier and may receive early retirement subsidies. Liabilities — the present value of future benefits — are typically higher on termination assumptions than on ongoing assumptions, and thus, for a given amount of assets, a plan's termination-basis funding percentage is typically lower than its funding percentage on an ongoing basis.

From PBGC's perspective, it is more appropriate to measure plan funding levels using termination-basis assumptions than ongoing-plan assumptions because termination is what brings a plan under PBGC administration. In the context of the pension insurance system, a plan's funding level on a termination basis provides the better measure of exposure — that is, the magnitude of the financial impact PBGC and participants would suffer if the plan then (or soon thereafter) terminated. But from a plan perspective, funding on an ongoing basis is the more common measure. Variable-rate premiums, required contributions, benefit restrictions, and annual funding notices are all based on ongoing-plan calculations. Unless filing is required under ERISA section 4010 (dealing with annual financial and actuarial information reporting for controlled groups with large underfunding), plans typically do not calculate funding on a termination basis. PBGC considers it desirable to adopt a funding measure that links with calculations that plans already make.

The funding-based waivers in the existing regulation are generally tied to variable-rate premium computations,[18] which use ongoing-plan assumptions. Under the current regulation, plans that are funded for 80 percent of premium liability qualify for reporting waivers for several reportable events. PBGC has found this test to be an inadequate threshold measure, because premium liability is significantly lower than termination liability, so that a plan that is 80 percent funded on a premium basis is likely to be much more significantly underfunded on a termination basis. In developing the revised plan funding safe harbor thresholds, PBGC reviewed plans with at least 100 participants that PBGC trusteed in fiscal years 2009 and 2010 and through April of fiscal year 2011 and compared the funded percentage at the date of plan termination (DOPT) measured on a termination basis to the VRP funded percentage for the plan year before the year in which DOPT occurred.[19] This analysis showed that the average termination funded status at DOPT was 54 percent and the average VRP funded status for the year before DOPT was 84 percent. The analysis also showed great variability of funded status among the plans, and PBGC found no direct correlation between the two funding measures.

If a plan is fully funded on a termination basis, on the other hand, any risk associated with a reportable event can reasonably be ignored because the exposure can reasonably be considered to be zero. PBGC therefore proposes to provide a safe harbor from reporting for most of the events to which funding-based waivers now apply[20] if the plan involved is fully funded on a termination basis on the last day of the plan year preceding the event year. But since funding on a termination basis is not commonly calculated for most plans — and since PBGC wants to provide another way to qualify for the safe harbor that is more accessible and yet provides a reasonably low exposure when compared to a termination-basis measurement — PBGC is also proposing to

extend the safe harbor treatment to any case where the plan involved is 120 percent funded on a premium basis for the plan year preceding the event year.[21]

The 20-percent cushion is needed to help compensate for several differences between the termination-basis funding level and the VRP-basis funding level. First, the VRP funding level is to be measured in general one year earlier than the termination funding level.[22] The lapse of a year raises the risk that funding will deteriorate between the measurement date and the event date. Second, the VRP funded percentage is calculated with ongoing-plan assumptions, which (as discussed above) generally yield higher funding percentages than termination-basis assumptions. Third, premium liability reflects only vested benefits, whereas termination liability is based on all benefits.[23]

As noted above, PBGC data indicate that funded status on a termination basis in the recent past was about 30 percentage points lower than the prior year's VRP funded status. Thus, while a 20-percent VRP cushion will be in some cases more and in others less than enough to reduce exposure to the same near-zero level as full funding on a termination basis, it should overall give an acceptable result for purposes of this safe harbor.

One difficulty with tying the safe harbor to the prior year's premium calculations is that a small plan's premium calculations may be as of a date as late as the last day of the year. For this reason, the premium filing due date for plans with fewer than 100 participants is four months after the end of the premium payment year. To address this situation, PBGC proposes to give a filing extension, in cases where the plan is small, until one month after the prior year's premium filing due date (*i.e.*, five months after the end of the prior year). For a small calendar-year plan, this would mean that for the five reportable events subject to the proposed funding-based safe harbor, the notice date for an event that occurred from January 1st through May 1st would be May 31st.[24]

The corresponding extension under the current reportable events regulation is available only if the plan would have qualified for the funding-based waiver for the preceding year. The proposed rule omits this qualification. Where an event subject to the safe harbor involves a small plan that does not qualify for the safe harbor, therefore, PBGC would get notice of the event as much as three months later than the generally applicable deadline. This delay might significantly impair PBGC's administration of Title IV of ERISA for such plans. On the other hand, an unconditional extension is simpler, and PBGC prefers that the relief provided by this small-plan extension not be diluted with complexity. Considering the lower exposure typically associated with small plans, PBGC is proposing to accept the (probably modest) impairment of its enforcement function in order to make compliance easier for such plans.

Other Safe Harbor Proposals

Alternatively or in addition to the safe harbor proposals described above, PBGC is inviting the public to propose variant safe harbors that build on the same risk-related concepts by altering the mix and/or relative stringency of the constituent tests of the sponsor safe harbor or combining tests from the sponsor and plan safe harbors. Ideally, proposals would reduce reporting burden for plans and sponsors for which reportable events most likely do not pose risks for the pension insurance program and thus focus reporting on higher-risk events. (See **Public Participation** below.)

Small-Plan Waivers

Rather than eliminating the small-plan waiver for active participant reductions (as it proposed in 2009), PBGC now proposes to retain a modified version of the waiver and to make it applicable to more events. Some commenters expressed concern about the adverse effect on small plans of eliminating waivers and extensions for reporting active participant reductions, pointing out that loss of a handful of

---

[18] The sole exception is a waiver for the benefit liability transfer event, which applies if (among other things) the transferor and transferee plans are fully funded using the computation methods for calculating employer liability for terminated plans.

[19] Some 134 plans fall into this category, but 17 were excluded because of incomplete or questionable data.

[20] As discussed above under *Automatic waivers and extensions — overview*, PBGC proposes to exclude the liquidation and loan default events from the funding-based waiver because those two events imply sponsor financial difficulties that may affect plan contributions and lead to a decline in funding level.

[21] Variable-rate premium ("VRP") funding information for a plan year is generally unavailable until the latter part of the year or (for many small plans) the early part of the following year. Thus it is more feasible to base the safe harbor test on premium information for the year before the event year. One of the reasons PBGC chose the ratio of assets to liabilities calculated according to premium rules as the standard for the funding-based

safe harbor, rather than the vested portion of the funding target attainment percentage ("FTAP") defined in section 430(d)(2) of the Internal Revenue Code, is that the FTAP is not reported (and may not be calculated) until a year later than the VRP. Another reason is that the VRP is determined using current market value of assets, whereas the FTAP often reflects an actuarially smoothed assets figure.

[22] For some small plans, premium funding is computed later in the premium payment year and thus nearer (or on) the proposed date for determining termination-basis funding.

[23] PBGC's obligation to pay non-vested benefits is conditioned on the availability of funds from plan assets or recoveries of employer liability for plan underfunding.

[24] No such extension would be needed for plans with 100 or more participants. Such plans calculate premiums as of the first day of the plan year and file premium declarations well before the end of the plan year. Thus, for example, a calendar year plan should know by October 15, 2013, whether it qualified for the premium-based funding safe harbor for events in 2014.

employees as a result of normal turnover in a small company could cross the reporting threshold but be unrelated to financial distress.

As noted in the preamble to the 2009 proposed rule, PBGC data suggest that in nearly a quarter of small-plan terminations, the small-plan reporting waiver has prevented PBGC from learning about problems that might have been resolved through early outreach to plan sponsors, avoiding termination or reducing underfunding. Information from other sources (for example, Form 5500) is typically neither as detailed nor as timely. On the other hand, PBGC can get such information without imposing any additional burden on plans and sponsors. Weighing the disadvantages of relying on these other sources of information against the challenges faced by small plans and their sponsors in reporting active participant reduction events, PBGC is now proposing to provide a waiver for these events like the existing small-plan waiver, except that, for simplicity, small-plan status would be determined in the same way as for purposes of the premium filing rules.

In addition, PBGC proposes to extend the small-plan waiver to three other events: controlled group changes, benefit liability transfers, and extraordinary dividends. Like active participant reductions, these events tend to be less serious than the events for which the safe harbors are unavailable. Furthermore, small plan sponsors typically are not members of controlled groups and generally do not have multiple lines of business. Thus stock or asset spinoffs (which could result in benefit liability transfers) and controlled group changes in general are infrequently experienced by such plans and sponsors. And extraordinary dividend events are relatively unusual for sponsors of plans of any size. In contrast, the burden on small plans and sponsors of monitoring for and reporting these events is relatively significant. Weighing that burden against the number and significance of the resultant reports, PBGC has concluded that small-plan waivers for these events seem appropriate.

Foreign-Entity and De Minimis *Waivers*

The current reportable events regulation provides reporting waivers for several events where the entity or entities involved in the event are foreign entities or represent a *de minimis* percentage of a controlled group.[25] PBGC's 2009 proposal preserved most *de minimis* waivers in the existing regulation but eliminated all foreign-entity waivers, because an increasingly large part of PBGC's insurance supervision and compliance cases deal with foreign controlled group members — a logical consequence of the globalization of the economy. All members of a plan's controlled group, whether domestic or foreign, are liable for plan underfunding. PBGC now proposes to provide both *de minimis* and foreign-entity waivers in tandem for five reportable events.

A number of commenters made the point that it can be difficult for a plan to keep track of events involving foreign controlled group members and argued that events involving foreign entities are too remote to warrant reporting to PBGC. Particular events mentioned in this regard included loan defaults, bankruptcies, controlled group changes, and extraordinary dividends. Commenters also expressed the view that PBGC's processing burden for reports on events involving foreign entities would be disproportionate to the value of the information in the reports, with the implication that requiring such reports would result in a misallocation of PBGC's resources.

PBGC is persuaded that the challenges a plan or sponsor faces in keeping informed about events involving foreign members of the plan's controlled group may prove more burdensome than is currently required to protect the pension insurance system. Furthermore, multinational controlled groups that report publicly tend to be tracked by PBGC's Early Warning Program, which, while it is no substitute for reportable event reports, does give PBGC some idea of the status of such groups. PBGC has concluded that these considerations constitute an appropriate basis for providing relief from reporting, even though that means it must forgo the receipt of useful information that may be important to its monitoring and enforcement activities.

Accordingly, PBGC now proposes to preserve all post-event foreign-entity reporting waivers in the existing regulation. As with all regulatory provisions, PBGC will monitor developments in this area and may revisit this position if experience indicates a need for stronger monitoring mechanisms. In addition, PBGC now proposes to retain all post-event reporting waivers for *de minimis* transactions[26] and to add *de minimis* waivers for two events — loan defaults and non-bankruptcy insolvency[27] — that do not have such waivers under the existing regulation. Thus, this pair of waivers would apply to five events. For liquidation, loan default, and insolvency, the *de minimis* waiver would be available only if the entity involved in the event was not a contributing sponsor. The waiver would use the ten percent *de minimis* standard, even for extraordinary dividends and stock redemptions under § 4043.31, for which the existing *de minimis* waiver is limited to a five percent segment of a controlled group.

Effect of Proposal on Loan Agreements

Some commenters said that, for plan sponsors with loan agreements, the increased reporting resulting from the elimination of waivers could give rise to events of default, a view that PBGC has been unable to substantiate. The commenters, who also said that requiring more reporting could preclude future loans or provide lenders with a pretext for renegotiating loan terms, did not provide any actual loan agreement provisions to support these contentions; to clarify its understanding of the commenters' concerns, PBGC reviewed 25 credit agreements from 20 distressed and/or small public companies.[28] PBGC reasoned that lenders to distressed companies would tend to be particularly sensitive to reportable events and that this heightened sensitivity would be reflected in loan agreement provisions of the kind that commenters expressed concern about. The smaller reporting companies provided a proxy for non-public companies (for which loan agreements are generally not made public).

- An event of default would not be automatically triggered by a reportable event in any of the 25 agreements reviewed, and 17 of the agreements would not have been affected at all by the changes in the 2009 proposed rule. For each of the eight agreements with event-of-default provisions that would have been affected by the 2009 proposal, an event of default would occur only when a reportable event was accompanied by some other significant condition, such as incurring actual liability, creation of grounds for termination, or the occurrence of a material adverse effect.

- Nine of the agreements PBGC reviewed had no requirement that the borrower notify the lender of a reportable event. Six agreements required notice only if some other condition was present (as for events of default). Five defined "reportable event" without regard to whether reporting was waived.

- Fewer than half of the agreements surveyed required representations or warranties about reportable events as a condition to future advances.

The results of examining these loan agreements are consistent with PBGC's experience from reviewing loan documents as part of its direct monitoring of corporate events and transactions of plan sponsors. PBGC has been unable to find a record of any case where the filing of a reportable event notice has resulted in a default under a credit agreement. These observations suggest that the elimination of reporting waivers would not adversely affect most plan sponsors with loan agreements.

Because PBGC's current proposal provides more waivers than the 2009 proposal, commenters' concerns in this area should be lessened. And PBGC's proposed deferral of the applicability date for the final regulation should give plan sponsors time to consult with loan providers about appropriate amendments to loan agreements. However, if this concern is raised in a comment about the current proposal, PBGC requests that the commenter document the basis for the comment by providing copies of relevant loan agreements and information about the

---

[25] Both types of waiver apply to controlled group change, liquidation, and extraordinary dividend; the foreign entity waiver also applies to loan default and bankruptcy. The foreign entity waiver is limited to entities that are not direct or indirect parents of contributing sponsors, and discussion of the foreign-entity waiver in this preamble should be understood to incorporate this limitation.

[26] PBGC proposes to eliminate one of three alternative tests for the annual operating income criterion that must be met for *de minimis* status: that such income not exceed 5 percent of the first $200 million in controlled group net tangible assets. PBGC believes that the other two alternatives provide a sufficient threshold. The change would apply to both post-event and advance notices.

[27] PBGC can obtain bankruptcy filings directly, so a separate PBGC report is unnecessary. For this reason, PBGC proposes to revise the reportable event covering bankruptcy

and similar settlements to limit it to non-bankruptcy events only. See *Bankruptcy and Insolvency* below.

[28] PBGC obtained the loan agreements from the Web site of the Securities and Exchange Commission (*www.sec.gov*). The companies with distressed plans were selected from an online business article titled "40 Companies Sitting on Pension Time Bombs," posted at *http://moneycentral.msn.com/content/P87329.asp*, on August 25, 2004. PBGC found no relationship between the assumed financial straits of the companies' plans and any specific loan agreement provisions that might have reflected lenders' sensitivity to the significance of reportable events. The limited scope of this study reflects the practical difficulty of obtaining and reviewing a statistically significant sample of loan agreements (the vast majority of which are not publicly available) involving sponsors of the more than 27,500 single-employer plans covered by Title IV of ERISA. PBGC nonetheless believes that the loan agreements that were reviewed do offer some insight into loan agreement drafting practices that is relevant to the concerns expressed by commenters.

number and circumstances of plan sponsors that have experienced default or suffered other adverse consequences related to loan agreements as a result of a reportable event.

Advance Reporting Threshold

In general, reportable events must be reported to PBGC within 30 days after they occur. But section 4043(b) of ERISA requires advance reporting by a contributing sponsor for certain reportable events if a "threshold test" is met, unless the contributing sponsor or controlled group member to which an event relates is a public company. The advance reporting threshold test is based on the aggregate funding level of plans maintained by the contributing sponsor and members of the contributing sponsor's controlled group. The funding level criteria are expressed by reference to calculated values that are used to determine VRPs under section 4006 of ERISA. The reportable events regulation ties the statutory threshold test to the related provisions of the premium rates regulation.

The advance reporting threshold test in ERISA section 4043(b)(1) provides that the advance reporting requirements of section 4043(b) are to be applicable to a contributing sponsor if, as of the close of the preceding plan year —

- the aggregate unfunded vested benefits (UVBs) (as determined under ERISA section 4006(a)(3)(E)(iii)) of plans subject to title IV of ERISA which are maintained by such sponsor and members of such sponsor's controlled groups (disregarding plans with no unfunded vested benefits) exceed $50,000,000, and

- the funded vested benefit percentage for such plans is less than 90 percent. For this purpose, the funded vested benefit percentage means the percentage which the aggregate value of the assets of such plans bears to the aggregate vested benefits of such plans (determined in accordance with ERISA section 4006(a)(3)(E)(iii)).

PPA 2006 revised ERISA section 4006(a)(3)(E)(iii) to say that UVBs means, for a plan year, the excess (if any) of the funding target of the plan as determined under ERISA section 303(d) for the plan year by only taking into account vested benefits and by using the interest rate described in ERISA section 4006(a)(3)(E)(iv), over the fair market value of plan assets for the plan year which are held by the plan on the valuation date.

The section 303 of ERISA referred to here is a completely new section added by PPA 2006.[29] Under new ERISA section 303(g)(1), the value of plan assets and the funding target of a plan for a plan year are determined as of the valuation date of the plan for the plan year. Under new ERISA section 303(g)(2), the valuation date for virtually all plans subject to advance reporting under ERISA section 4043 will be the first day of the plan year. Thus, while ERISA section 4043(b)(1) refers to UVBs, assets, and vested benefits "as of the close of the preceding plan year," in nearly all cases these quantities must, with respect to plan years beginning after 2007, be calculated as of the beginning of a plan year. This creates an ambiguity with regard to the date as of which the advance reporting threshold test is to be applied.

This proposed rule, like the prior proposal, would resolve this ambiguity by requiring that the advance reporting threshold test be applied as of the valuation date for "the preceding plan year." That is the same date as of which UVBs, assets, and vested benefits must be determined for premium purposes for the preceding plan year under the premium rates regulation as amended by PBGC's final rule on VRPs under PPA 2006. Measuring these quantities as of that date for purposes of the advanced reporting threshold test will thus be less burdensome than requiring that separate computations be made as of the close of that year. It will also enable a plan to determine before a reportable event occurs (and before an advance report is due) whether it is subject to the advance reporting requirement.

The new proposed rule (like the prior proposal) would make a number of editorial changes to the advance reporting threshold provisions with a view to improving clarity and simplicity as well as accommodating the changes discussed above. It would also provide that the plans whose funding status is taken into account in applying the threshold test are determined as of the due date for the report, and that the "public company" status of a contributing sponsor or controlled group member to which the event relates is also determined as of that date. Although the existing regulation does not explicitly address this issue, PBGC believes it is implicit that these determinations be current. Requiring that they be made as of the due date for the report ensures currency.

Active Participant Reduction

In general, a reportable active participant reduction occurs when the number of active participants is reduced below 80 percent of the number at the beginning of the year or below 75 percent of the number at the beginning of the prior year.

Several commenters remarked that a loss of more than 20 percent of active participants within a year (or more than 25 percent within two years) may result from gradual attrition and that if no waiver is applicable, constant vigilance is required to catch the moment when the threshold for reporting is crossed. Such vigilance could be burdensome for a large plan and might simply not be exercised for a small one. PBGC is sympathetic to this issue and is proposing to modify the definition of the active participant reduction event to address it.

Under the proposed change, a reportable event would occur during the plan year only when the reporting threshold was crossed either within a single 30-day period or as a result of a single cause like the discontinuance of an operation, a natural disaster, a reorganization, a mass layoff, or an early retirement incentive program. Such circumstances should be easy to spot without exercising unusual vigilance. To capture events arising from gradual attrition, the proposed regulation would require that plans measure active participant reductions at the end of each year and report if the threshold has been crossed. Fluctuations within the year would be ignored. If the active participant count at the end of the year were more than 20 percent below the count at the beginning of the year, or more than 25 percent below the count at the beginning of the prior year, reporting would be required. To provide time to count active participants as of the end of the year, the notice date for attrition events would be extended to 120 days after year end, by which time PBGC expects many or most plans to have a final count.[30]

For convenience, if a plan counted participants, for purposes of the following year's premiums, as of a day other than the last day of the year for which active participant loss was being measured (such as where there was a qualifying merger or spinoff), the plan could use the active participant count on that other day as the year-end count for determining whether active participant attrition had exceeded the threshold. However, the reduction in active participants would still be considered to have occurred at the end of the measurement year.

Because this change would render unnecessary the waiver in the 2009 proposed rule for a report within one year of a prior report, that provision is absent from the current proposal. However, the changes now being proposed include the provision from 2009 that dealt with substantial cessations of operations under ERISA section 4062(e) and substantial employer withdrawals under ERISA section 4063(a). Events covered by section 4062(e) or 4063(a) must be reported to PBGC under section 4063(a). With a view to avoiding duplicative reporting, this proposal, like the 2009 proposal, would limit the active participant reduction event by excluding from consideration — in determining whether a reportable active-participant-reduction event has occurred — active participant reductions to the extent that they (1) fall within the provisions of section 4062(e) or 4063(a) and (2) are timely reported to PBGC as required under ERISA section 4063(a).

One commenter expressed satisfaction with this provision; two others raised issues about the interplay of this event and a section 4062(e) event, suggesting, for example, that there was opportunity for confusion between the 30-day notice requirement under section 4043 and the 60-day notice requirement for 4062(e) events. PBGC does not see how this provision would exacerbate any such problems (and indeed believes that it would tend to ameliorate them).[31]

Finally, one commenter requested clarification that participants do not cease to be active if they leave employment with one member of a plan's controlled group to become employed by another controlled group member. PBGC proposes to add a provision to make this point clear.

Missed Contributions

A missed contribution event occurs when a plan sponsor fails to make any required plan contribution by its due date.

PBGC proposes (as it did in 2009) to clarify the language in § 4043.25, dealing with the reportable event of failure to make required contributions. This reportable event does not apply only to contributions required by statute (including quarterly contributions under ERISA section 303(j)(3) and Code section 430(j)(3), liquidity shortfall

---

[29] Section 303 of ERISA corresponds to section 430 of the Code.

[30] In most situations, a rough estimate will be sufficient to determine if the threshold has been crossed.

[31] On August 10, 2010 (at 75 FR 48283), PBGC published a proposed rule to provide guidance on the applicability and enforcement of ERISA section 4062(e). PBGC is currently giving careful consideration to the comments on that proposed rule.

contributions under ERISA section 303(j)(4) and Code section 430(j)(4), and contributions to amortize funding waivers under ERISA section 303(e) and Code section 430(e)). It also applies to contributions required as a condition of a funding waiver that do not fall within the statutory provisions on waiver amortization charges. The proposed revision would make this point clearer.[32]

The 2009 proposed rule called for eliminating all reporting waivers for missed contributions. PBGC now proposes to provide waivers for this event.

Some commenters urged PBGC to retain the grace-period waiver in the current regulation (where payment is made within 30 days after the due date). Commenters pointed out that contributions are sometimes missed through administrative error and that the availability of the grace-period waiver gives sponsors an incentive to make up missed contributions. Commenters also suggested that because new rules require a sponsor to elect to apply a funding balance towards a quarterly installment, a late installment often results from a late election due to administrative error.

PBGC is persuaded that missed contributions that are made up within 30 days do not generally pose excessive risk to the pension insurance system. Form 5500 filings provide another (albeit somewhat later) source of information about late contributions, and there is an independent reporting requirement for large cumulative missed contributions under ERISA section 303(k)(4) and Code section 430(k)(4) (implemented by §4043.81 of the reportable events regulation). Accordingly, the current proposal would restore the grace-period waiver in the existing regulation that the 2009 proposal would have eliminated.

Commenters also urged PBGC to provide small-plan missed-quarterly reporting relief like that which has for years been provided by Technical Update, and PBGC proposes to do so. Commenters said that small plans often forgo or delay quarterly contributions to strategically manage cash flow or until valuations are completed (a practice that does not accord with the law and that PBGC does not condone). Commenters suggested that late quarterly installments often do not signal a plan sponsor's actual financial distress or a plan's imminent termination.

PBGC believes that a small-plan missed-quarterly waiver can strike an effective balance between PBGC's need for information on potentially troubled plans and the reporting challenges faced by small entities. Furthermore, since annual reports on Form 5500 are now filed electronically, PBGC believes that contribution information on Schedule SB to Form 5500 can help round out the information submitted under the reportable events regulation. Thus, PBGC is proposing to add to the regulation a simplified small-plan missed-quarterly waiver to replace the Technical Update waivers. The codified waiver would apply to any failure to make a quarterly contribution to a plan considered small for purposes of the premium filing rules (*i.e.*, having fewer than 100 participants; the waiver under Technical Update 11-1 applies only to plans with fewer than 25 participants). Unlike the grace-period waiver, the small-plan waiver would apply only to quarterly contributions.

Inability to Pay Benefits When Due

In general, a reportable event occurs when a plan fails to make a benefit payment timely or when a plan's liquid assets fall below the level needed for paying benefits for six months.

As in 2009, PBGC proposes to clarify the large-plan waiver of the reporting requirement for inability to pay benefits when due. This waiver provision reflects PBGC's judgment that it need not require reporting of this event by larger plans that are subject to the "liquidity shortfall" rules imposing more stringent contribution requirements where liquid assets are insufficient to cover anticipated disbursement requirements. For these larger plans, (1) if the contributions required by the liquidity shortfall rules are made, the inability to pay benefits when due is resolved, and (2) if the required contributions are not made, that fact is reportable to PBGC as a failure to make required contributions. Accordingly, this provision waives reporting unless the plan is exempt from the liquidity shortfall provisions.

Distribution to Substantial Owner

Distributions to substantial owners must generally be reported if they exceed $10,000 in a year unless the plan is fully funded for nonforfeitable benefits.

One commenter on the 2009 proposal argued that distributions to substantial owners tend to be thought of as routine and may "creep" beyond the $10,000 reporting threshold unremarked and unreported. In response, PBGC proposes to make two changes to the regulation.

First, PBGC proposes to add to the description of this event a provision limiting the event to circumstances where the distributions to one substantial owner exceed one percent of plan assets or the distributions to all substantial owners exceed five percent of plan assets. (The onepercent provision echoes a waiver for this event that is in the existing regulation but that PBGC proposes to eliminate.) In either case, assets would be end-of-year current value of assets as required to be reported on Schedule H or I to Form 5500, and the one percent or five percent threshold would have to be exceeded for each of the two prior years. By requiring notices only for larger distributions that should be noticeable and thus not challenging to detect and report, PBGC believes that it would strike an acceptable balance between the burden of reporting and PBGC's need for timely information about such events.

In addition, PBGC proposes to limit reporting for distributions in the form of annuities to one notice: The first notice required under the normal reporting rules would be the only notice required so long as the annuity did not increase. Once notified that an annuity was being paid to a substantial owner, PBGC would need no further notices that the annuity was continuing to be paid.

Controlled Group Change

A reportable event occurs for a plan when there is a transaction that results, or will result, in one or more persons' ceasing to be members of the plan's controlled group. For this purpose, the term "transaction" includes a written or unwritten legally binding agreement to transfer ownership or an actual transfer or change of ownership. However, a transaction is not reportable if it will result solely in a reorganization involving a mere change in identity, form, or place of organization, however effected.

One commenter asked PBGC to clarify that a reportable event does not occur when there is a reorganization within an employer's controlled group in which a member ceases to exist because it is merged into another member. The example in §4043.29(e)(3) of the current regulation indicates that such a merger is a reportable event because the disappearing member has ceased to be a member of the controlled group. After consideration, PBGC has decided to delete this example from the proposed rule to clarify that such a change solely within a controlled group is not a reportable event for purposes of the regulation.

PBGC has also from time to time received requests to clarify whether an agreement that is not to be effective unless some condition is met, such as the obtaining of some governmental approval or the occurrence of some other event, is nonetheless legally binding within the meaning of the regulation. The proposed rule would provide that whether an agreement is legally binding is to be determined without reference to any conditions in the agreement. PBGC's administration of the pension insurance system may be impaired if reporting is not required until all conditions are met. As for all reportable events, case-by-case waivers may be granted.

Extraordinary Dividends

An extraordinary dividend or stock redemption occurs when a member of a plan's controlled group declares a distribution (a dividend or stock redemption) that alone or in combination with previous distributions exceeds a level specified in the regulation. The current regulation specifies different threshold levels for cash and non-cash distributions and provides a method for aggregating cash and non-cash distributions in order to determine whether in combination they exceed the reporting threshold. Cash distributions must be tested over both a one-year and a four-year period, non-cash distributions only over a one-year period. The cash distribution threshold is 100 percent of net income; the non-cash distribution threshold is ten percent of net assets. Distributions within a controlled group are treated the same as any other distributions.

PBGC proposes to simplify the description of this event. The simplified event would occur when a controlled group member declared a dividend or redeemed its stock and the (cash or non-cash) distribution, alone or together with other cash and non-cash distributions, exceeded 100 percent of net income for the prior fiscal year. Testing would be over a one-year period only. The new formulation would eliminate

---

[32] Such "non-statutory" contributions are not taken into account under ERISA section 303(k) and Code section 430(k), dealing with liens that arise because of large missed contributions, and are therefore disregarded under §4043.81, which implements those provisions. However, violating the conditions of a funding waiver typically means that contributions that were waived become retroactively due and unpaid and are counted for purposes of §4043.81.

much of the computational detail that the existing regulation prescribes for determining whether a reportable event has occurred by providing that the computations be done in accordance with generally accepted accounting principles. Distributions within a controlled group would be disregarded.

Eliminating the four-year test for cash distributions would tend to make more events of this kind reportable. Disregarding intra-group distributions would have the opposite effect. The effect of using only a net income figure as a threshold is harder to assess. But PBGC expects the effects of all of these changes to be modest. And elimination of much of the detail for combining the effects of cash and non-cash distributions should reduce the administrative burden of compliance with the requirement to report such events.

Transfer of Benefit Liabilities

Section 4043(c)(12) of ERISA requires reporting to PBGC when, in any 12-month period, three percent or more of a plan's benefit liabilities are transferred to a person outside the transferor plan's controlled group or to a plan or plans maintained by a person or persons outside the transferor plan's controlled group. Transfers of benefit liabilities are of concern to PBGC because they may reduce the transferor plan's funded percentage and because the transferee may not be as financially healthy as the transferor.

The existing reportable events regulation does not make clear whether the satisfaction of benefit liabilities through the payment of a lump sum or the purchase of an irrevocable commitment to provide an annuity constitutes a transfer of benefit liabilities for purposes of this reporting requirement. PBGC has received inquiries seeking clarification of this point and now proposes (as in 2009) to provide that such cashouts and annuitizations do not constitute transfers of benefit liabilities that must be reported under the regulation.

Section 436 of the Code and section 206(g) of ERISA (as added by PPA 2006) prohibit or limit cashouts and annuitizations by significantly underfunded plans. These provisions thus tend to prevent cashouts and annuitizations that would most seriously reduce a transferor plan's funded percentage. And since cashouts and annuitizations satisfy benefit liabilities (rather than transferring them to another plan), there is no concern about a transferee plan's financial health.

Section 4043.32(a) of the existing reportable events regulation requires post-event reporting not only for a plan that transfers benefit liabilities, but also for every other plan maintained by a member of the transferor plan's controlled group. However, existing § 4043.32(d) provides a waiver that in effect limits the post-event reporting obligation to the transferor plan. Existing § 4043.65 (dealing with advance reporting of benefit liability transfers) does not provide a similar waiver.

PBGC has concluded — as the preamble to the 2009 proposed rule indicated — that it is unnecessary to extend the advance reporting requirement for benefit liability transfers beyond the transferor plan. PBGC thus proposes to revise § 4043.32(a) to narrow the reporting requirement to the transferor plan; to remove § 4043.32(d) (which would be redundant); and to revise § 4043.65(a) to remove the provision requiring that § 4043.32(d) be disregarded. The effect of these changes would be to leave the post-event notice requirement unchanged and to limit the advance notice requirement to the transferor plan.

Loan Default

Under the existing regulation, a loan default reportable event occurs when a loan payment is more than 30 days late (10 days in the case of advance reporting), when the lender accelerates the loan, or when there is a written notice of default based on a drop in cash reserves, an unusual or catastrophic event, or the debtor's persistent failure to meet agreed-on performance levels.

PBGC believes that the significance of loan defaults is so great that reporting should not be restricted to the current list of defaults. Rather, PBGC believes that any default on a loan of $10 million or more — even a default on a loan within a controlled group — should be reported unless a reportable event waiver applies. Accordingly, PBGC proposes to revise the definition of the loan default event so that it covers acceleration by the lender and default of any kind by the debtor.

In addition, PBGC proposes to expand this event to encompass any amendment or waiver by a lender of any loan agreement covenant for the purpose of avoiding a default. PBGC believes that a debtor can often anticipate a default situation, and that when it does, it may typically initiate discussions with its lender with a view to obtaining the lender's waiver of the covenant it expects to breach or an amendment of the loan agreement to obviate the default. In PBGC's view, such actions may reflect financial difficulty and thus, like actual defaults,

pose serious challenges for the pension insurance system. These changes would apply for both postevent notices and advance notices.

PBGC believes that the treatment of loan defaults under the proposed rule is comparable to the treatment that would be experienced with a typical creditor. PBGC seeks the views of the public as to whether that belief is well-founded. PBGC further seeks public comment as to how it might better approximate such a model in its treatment of loan default events, whether there should be a materiality threshold with respect to events of default, and whether there is a category of "technical" defaults that should not be reportable events.

Bankruptcy and Insolvency

The existing regulation defines the bankruptcy reportable event to include bankruptcy under the Bankruptcy Code and any other similar judicial or nonjudicial proceeding. Notice of bankruptcies under the Bankruptcy Code can be (and routinely is) reliably obtained by other means. Accordingly, PBGC proposes to limit the reporting requirement to exclude bankruptcies under the Bankruptcy Code.

Advance-Notice Extensions

The current reportable events regulation provides extensions of the advance-notice filing deadline for three events: funding waiver requests, loan defaults, and bankruptcy/insolvency. The extension for funding waiver requests avoids the need to give one government agency (PBGC) advance notice of a filing with another government agency (IRS). The extensions for notices of loan defaults and bankruptcies or insolvencies accommodate situations where such events occur without the debtors' advance knowledge.

In general, however, a debtor is aware well in advance that a loan default or insolvency event is going to befall it, and indeed is actively engaged in preparation for the event. PBGC thinks it not unreasonable, therefore, that a debtor subject to advance reporting should generally give the advance notice provided for in the statute. Accordingly, PBGC proposes to eliminate reporting extensions for advance notice of loan default and insolvency events, except for events where insolvency proceedings are filed against a debtor by someone outside the plan's controlled group. In such adversarial filing cases, it is reasonable to expect that the debtor is unable to anticipate the event and thus unable to report it in advance.

PBGC is aware that there may be loan defaults that (like adversarial insolvency filings) can come as a surprise to the debtor, making compliance with the advance notice requirement impossible. However, since PBGC believes such loan defaults are very infrequent, the proposed rule does not contain an automatic extension for such situations. If inability to anticipate a loan default event were to make it impossible to comply with the advance notice requirement, the delinquent filer could seek a retroactive filing extension from PBGC based on the facts and circumstances. (An extension may similarly be requested if a filer learns of an impending event such a short time before the advance notice deadline as to make timely filing difficult.) PBGC specifically invites comment on whether this approach represents an adequate solution to any problem of surprise loan defaults that may exist.

Forms and Instructions

PBGC proposes to eliminate some of the documentation that must now be submitted with notices of two reportable events, but to require that filers submit with notices of most events some information not currently called for. Because the additional information to be submitted with notices is now typically requested by PBGC after notices are reviewed, the proposed changes would not significantly impact filers' total administrative burden.

PBGC also proposes, as it did in 2009, to make use of prescribed reportable events forms mandatory and to eliminate from the regulation the lists of information items that must be reported. PBGC anticipates that as it gains experience with the new reporting requirements and engages in further regulatory review, it may find it appropriate to make changes in the information required to be submitted with reportable events notices. In particular, resolution of uncertainties about the operation of PPA 2006 provisions may call for changes in the data submission requirements for failures to make required contributions timely. Forms and instructions can be revised more quickly than regulations can in response to new developments or experience (and both processes are subject to public comment).

PBGC issues three reporting forms for use under the reportable events regulation. Form 10 is for post-event reporting under subpart B of the regulation; Form 10-Advance is for advance reporting under subpart C of the regulation; and Form 200 is for reporting under subpart D of the regulation. Failure to report is subject to penalties under section 4071 of ERISA.

¶20,538K

Under the existing regulation, however, use of PBGC forms for reporting events under subparts B and C of the regulation is optional. The data items in the forms do not correspond exactly with those in the regulation, and the regulation recognizes that filers that use the forms may report different information from those that do not use the forms. PBGC believes that making use of prescribed reportable events forms mandatory would promote greater uniformity in the reporting process and attendant administrative simplicity for PBGC. Eliminating lists of information items from the regulation would mean that the information to be reported would be described in the filing instructions only (rather than in both the filing instructions and the regulation).

Mandatory Electronic Filing

PBGC encourages electronic filing under the existing regulation[33] and now proposes to make it mandatory. This proposal is part of PBGC's ongoing implementation of the Government Paperwork Elimination Act.

Electronic filing has become the norm for PBGC's regulated community. Electronic filing is mandatory for reports under ERISA section 4010 (starting with 2005 information years), PBGC premiums (starting with 2007 plan years for all plans), and Form 5500 (starting with 2009 plan years).

PBGC does not currently have a web-based filing application for reportable events as it does for section 4010 or premium filings. However, it has become common for documents to be created electronically in a variety of digital formats (such as WPD, DOC, and XLS) and easy to create electronic images (for example, in PDF format) of documents that do not exist in electronic form. PBGC proposes that filers be permitted to e-mail filings using any one or more of a variety of electronic formats that PBGC is capable of reading as provided in the instructions on PBGC's Web site. (Forms 10 and 10-Advance do not require signatures, and PBGC already accepts imaged signatures for Form 200 filings.) The current versions of PBGC Form 10, Form 10-Advance, and Form 200 are already available in "fillable" format; in connection with the change to electronic filing, new versions of these forms will be available in "fillable" format to facilitate electronic filing.

PBGC would be able to waive electronic filing for voluminous paper documents to relieve filers of the need to scan them, pursuant to § 4043.4(d) (case-by-case waivers).

PBGC would expect its reportable events e-filing methodology to evolve as internet capabilities and standards change, consistent with resource effectiveness. Such developments would be reflected in PBGC's reportable events e-filing instructions.

PBGC seeks public comment on its proposal to require electronic filing. For example, PBGC would like to know whether there are differences commenters might see between Form 5500 filings and premium filings (which are submitted electronically) and reportable events filings that would make the latter less suited to electronic filing. PBGC would also like to know whether there are particular categories of plans or sponsors that would find electronic filing sufficiently difficult that PBGC should by regulation either exempt them from e-filing (rather than just providing case-by-case exceptions) or defer the applicability of mandatory e-filing to them (*i.e.*, provide for phase-in of the e-filing requirement, and if so, over what period of time). Finally, PBGC seeks comment on e-filing methodology, such as the convenience of submitting documents in the form of data rather than images and the usefulness of pre-filled data fields. Commenters are encouraged to describe actual rather than hypothetical circumstances and to provide comparisons between the burdens that would be associated with e-filing versus paper filing or with one e-filing method versus another. This information will help PBGC evaluate both the appropriateness of e-filing for reportable events in general and the need for special rules to accommodate specific categories of filers.

Other Changes

PBGC's 2009 proposed rule on reportable events would have added two new events to the reportable events regulation. One event would have occurred when a plan's adjusted funding target attainment percentage (AFTAP) was found or presumed to be less than 60 percent. The other event would have occurred when a transfer of $10 million or more was made to a plan's health benefits account under section 420(f) of the Code (as added by PPA 2006) or when plan funding thereafter deteriorated below a prescribed level. Commenters seemed generally accepting of the appropriateness of the former event but questioned the value to PBGC of the latter event. PBGC is not including either event in this proposal. AFTAPs under 60 percent trigger significant restrictions on plans that to some degree provide remediation that serves the same kind of function as the action that PBGC might take upon getting a low AFTAP notice. And PBGC has concluded that its need for health benefit account notices is not great enough to make it clearly appropriate to require them at this time.

PBGC recognizes that the changes made by PPA 2006 in the statutory provisions dealing with missed contributions — which are reportable under §§ 4043.25 and 4043.81 — affect the computation of interest on missed contributions, a circumstance that in turn affects the reporting requirements. This proposed rule includes no amendment to the reportable events regulation dealing with such issues, but PBGC is providing guidance on this subject in the filing instructions. The guidance will be revised if and when necessary to take into account as appropriate any relevant guidance from the Internal Revenue Service.

The proposed rule would clarify that if an event is subject to both post-event and advance notice requirements, the notice filed first satisfies both requirements. (In unusual circumstances, the post-event notice required in connection with a transaction may be due before the advance notice required in connection with the same transaction.)

To conform to the statute, the proposed rule would limit the applicability of the confidentiality provisions in ERISA section 4043(f) to submissions under subparts B and C of the reportable events regulation.

The proposed rule would make a number of editorial and clarifying changes to part 4043 and would add definitional cross-references, change statutory cross-references to track changes made by PPA 2006, and update language to conform to usage in PPA 2006 and regulations and reporting requirements thereunder.[34] Where a defined term is used in only one section of the regulation, the definition would be moved from § 4043.2 to the section where the term is used.

The proposed changes to the reportable events regulation make it unnecessary to define a number of terms at the beginning of the regulation. Accordingly, the definitions of "fair market value of the plan's assets," "Form 5500 due date," "public company," "testing date," "ultimate parent," "unfunded vested benefits," "variable-rate premium," and "vested benefits amount" would be removed from § 4043.2.

Summary Chart

The following table summarizes waiver and safe harbor provisions for reportable events for which post-event reporting is required under the current regulation, the 2009 proposal, and this proposed rule. (As explained in detail above, the current proposal also provides filing relief — like the relief provided by waivers — through changes to the definitions of certain reportable events, including substantial owner distributions and active participant reductions and through the provision of filing extensions such as for active participant reductions that occur by attrition.)

---

[33] The existing regulation contains a "partial electronic filing" provision under which a filing is considered timely made if certain basic information (specified in PBGC's reporting instructions) is submitted on time electronically and followed up within one or two business days (depending on the type of report) with the remaining required information. PBGC's mandatory electronic filing proposal would make the "partial electronic filing" provision anachronistic, and it would be removed.

[34] Section 4043.62(b)(1) of the existing regulation, headed "Small plan," provides a waiver where a plan has 500 or fewer participants. The premium payment regulation keys filing due dates to whether a plan is small (fewer than 100 participants), mid-size (100 or more but fewer than 500 participants), or large (500 or more participants). In the interest of uniformity, PBGC proposes to change § 4043.62(b)(1) to provide a waiver where a plan has fewer than 500 participants and to change the heading to read "Small and mid-size plans."

Events with safe harbors based on company or plan financial soundness[35] or other factors.

Event	Waivers under Current Regulation	Waivers under 2009 Proposal	Revised Proposal – if any of these safe harbors applies, no reporting is required		
			Company Financial Soundness Safe Harbor	Plan Financial Soundness Safe Harbor	Other Safe Harbors
Extraordinary Dividend or Stock Redemption	• Member distributing is de minimis (5%);[36] • Member distributing is non-parent foreign entity (regardless of size); • Member distributing is foreign parent, and distribution is made solely to other controlled group members; • At least 80% funded; • No VRP; or • Less than $1 M in premium underfunding	• Member distributing is de minimis (5%)	Company is financially sound	Plan is financially sound	• Member involved is de minimis (10%); • Member involved is non-parent foreign entity (regardless of size); or • Small plan (fewer than 100 participants)
Change in Contributing Sponsor or Controlled Group	• Member leaving is de minimis (10%); • Member leaving is non-parent foreign entity (regardless of size); • At least 80% funded & public company; • No VRP; or • Less than $1 M in premium underfunding	• Member leaving is de minimis (10%)			
Active Participant Reduction	• Small plan (fewer than 100 participants) • At least 80% funded if not a facility closing; • No VRP; or • Less than $1 M premium underfunding	• Prior event reported within 1 year	Company is financially sound	Plan is financially sound	• Small plan (fewer than 100 participants) Note: filing extension for reductions due to gradual attrition
Transfer of Benefit Liabilities	• IRC 414(l) safe harbor is used for asset transfer; • Plan whose liabilities are all transferred; • Both plans fully funded after transfer using 414(l) assumptions; or • Amount transferred is less than 3% of assets	• None			• Small plan (fewer than 100 participants)
Distribution to Substantial Owner	• At least 80% funded; • No VRP; • Distributions less than IRC 415 limit; or • Distributions less than 1% of assets	• None			• No other safe harbor

[35] Company means the plan sponsor or the U.S. parent company. The proposed financial soundness tests are set forth in § 4043.9 of the proposed regulation and described in the preamble under *Financial Soundness Safe Harbor for Plan Sponsors* and *Financial Soundness Safe Harbor for Plans*.

[36] De minimis is defined in § 4043.2 of both the current regulation and the proposed regulation.

Events with limited or no safe harbors

Event	Waivers under Current Regulation	Waivers under 2009 Proposal	Safe Harbors under Revised Proposal

Bankruptcy/ Insolvency	• Member in bankruptcy is non-parent foreign entity (regardless of size)	• None	• Event revised to exclude Bankruptcy Code cases.
			• Member causing event is -
			  – Not the plan sponsor and is de minimis (10%); or
			  – Non-parent foreign entity (regardless of size)

Liquidation	• Member liquidating is de minimis (10%) and plan survives;
	• Member liquidating is non-parent foreign entity (regardless of size);
	• At least 80% funded & public company and plan survives; or
	• No VRP or less than $1 M in premium underfunding and plan survives
		• None	• Member causing event is -
			  – Not the plan sponsor and is de minimis (10%); or
			  – Non-parent foreign entity (regardless of size)

Loan Default	• Default cured or waived by lender within 30 days or by end of cure period; • Member defaulting is non-parent foreign entity (regardless of size); • At least 80% funded; or • No VRP or less than $1 M in premium underfunding	• Default cured or waived by lender within 30 days or by end of cure period	

Failure to Make Required Contribution	• Missed quarterlies
	  – Plans with fewer than 25 participants if missed quarterly was not due to financial inability; simplified reporting for plans with 25-99 participants if missed quarterly was not due to financial inability (relief provided in Technical Update)
	  – Any sized plan, if made within 30 days of due date
	• Any other missed contribution, if made within 30 days of due date
		• None	• Missed quarterlies of small plans (fewer than 100 participants)
			• Any missed contribution, if made within 30 days of due date

Application for Funding Waiver	• None	• None	• None
Inability to Pay Benefits When Due	• Plan with more than 100 participants (subject to liquidity shortfall rules)	• Plan with more than 100 participants (subject to liquidity shortfall rules)	• Plan with more than 100 participants (subject to liquidity shortfall rules)

Other Regulations

Several other PBGC regulations also refer to plan funding concepts using citations outmoded by PPA 2006: the regulations on Filing, Issuance, Computation of Time, and Record Retention (29 CFR part 4000); Terminology (29 CFR part 4001); Variances for Sale of Assets (29 CFR part 4204); Adjustment of Liability for a Withdrawal Subsequent to a Partial Withdrawal (29 CFR part 4206); and Mergers and Transfers Between Multiemployer Plans (29 CFR part 4231). Thus, these regulations must also be revised to be consistent with ERISA and the Code as amended by PPA 2006 and with the revised premium regulations. This proposed rule would make the necessary conforming revisions.

Applicability

PBGC proposes to make the changes to the reportable events regulation in this proposed rule applicable to post-event reports for reportable events occurring on or after January 1, 2014, and to advance reports due on or after that date. Deferral of the applicability date would provide time for plans and plan sponsors to institute any necessary event monitoring programs to comply with the new rules. PBGC is also giving consideration to making the waiver and safe harbor provisions in the final regulation available (in addition to the waivers in the current regulation) during the period from the effective date of the final rule (30 days after publication in the *Federal Register*) to January 1, 2014.

Public Participation

PBGC welcomes comments from the public on all matters relating to the proposed rule. In particular, PBGC seeks public comments on the following specific questions:

(1) What are the advantages and disadvantages of the proposed safe harbor for financially sound plan sponsors?

(2) What are commenters' experiences with commercial credit reporting companies that might be relevant to developing a reportable events safe harbor? Do credit report scores change when reportable events occur? How often or easily are changes in credit report scores provided to users and the public? Can companies obtain timely updates that allow for an accurate assessment of financial soundness at a particular time?

(3) Does the proposal provide an appropriate way to assess financial soundness of plan sponsors? Is a commercial credit report score an appropriate basis for measuring financial strength for purposes of the safe harbor? Does the secured debt test for financial soundness include and exclude appropriate categories of debt from the test criteria? For example, should receivables financing be excluded from the test? Is the net income test too stringent or too lenient? Do the debt service and plan contribution tests include and exclude appropriate events? Are the proposed standards for the sponsor safe harbor too complex?

(4) Regarding the number and stringency of the criteria for the financially sound company safe harbor:

- Should there be more or fewer criteria than the five proposed in this rule? If more, what should the additional ones be? If fewer, which ones should be eliminated?

- Are the relative stringencies of the criteria appropriate for determining company financial soundness?

- Should alternative combinations of a subset of the five criteria be permissible?

- Should financial soundness criteria for companies and plans be combined?

(5) Are there standard, commonly used metrics that could be applied to determine financial soundness that do not rely on third party commercial credit reporting companies (e.g., based on balance sheet or cash-flow ratios, such as current assets to current liabilities, debt to equity, or some form of debt-service to cash-flow ratio)? Would such metrics be available and appropriate for all plan sponsors? What would be the advantages and disadvantages of using such an approach? Are there other alternatives to determining financial soundness?

(6) Should PBGC adopt other standards of creditworthiness?

(7) For the proposed safe harbor via plans, what alternative funding percentage(s) (on a termination basis or premium basis) should be permitted, and why?

(8) Should PBGC provide other alternative waivers? Should such alternatives be in addition to, or in place of, the proposed financial soundness safe harbors for companies and plans?

(9) How can PBGC implement safe harbors, whether based on financial soundness or other factors, in a consistent, transparent, well-defined, and replicable or verifiable way?

In responding to the above questions, to the extent possible, commenters are requested to provide quantitative as well as qualitative support or analysis where applicable.

A public hearing has been scheduled for June 18, 2013, beginning at 2:00 p.m., in the PBGC Training Institute, Washington, DC, shortly after the close of the comment period. Pursuant to building security procedures, visitors must arrive at 1200 K Street not more than 30 minutes before the hearing starts and present government-issued photo identification to enter the building.

PBGC requests that any person who wishes to present oral comments at the hearing file written comments on this proposed rule (see DATES and ADDRESSES above). Such persons also must submit by June 4, 2013, an outline of topics to be discussed and the amount of time to be devoted to each topic. The outline of topics to be discussed must be submitted by e-mail to regs.comments@pbgc.gov or by mail or courier to Regulatory Affairs Group, Office of the General Counsel, Pension Benefit Guaranty Corporation, 1200 K Street, NW., Washington, DC 20005-4026. An agenda identifying the speakers will be prepared after the deadline for receiving outlines. Copies of the agenda will be available free of charge at the hearing.

Regulatory Procedures

Executive Order 12866 "Regulatory Planning and Review" and Executive Order 13563 "Improving Regulation and Regulatory Review"

PBGC has determined, in consultation with the Office of Management and Budget, that this rule is a "significant regulatory action" under Executive Order 12866. The Office of Management and Budget has therefore reviewed this notice under Executive Order 12866.

Executive Orders 12866 and 13563 direct agencies to assess all costs and benefits of available regulatory alternatives and, if regulation is necessary, to select regulatory approaches that maximize net benefits (including potential economic, environmental, public health and safety effects, distributive impacts, and equity). Executive Order 13563 emphasizes the importance of quantifying both costs and benefits, of reducing costs, of harmonizing rules, and of promoting flexibility. Executive Orders 12866 and 13563 require a comprehensive regulatory impact analysis be performed for any economically significant regulatory action, defined as an action that would result in an annual effect of $100 million or more on the national economy or which would have other substantial impacts. In accordance with OMB Circular A-4, PBGC has examined the economic and policy implications of this proposed rule and has concluded that the action's benefits justify its costs.

As discussed above, some reportable events present little or no risk to the pension insurance system — where, for example, the plan sponsor is financially sound and the risk of plan termination low. Reports of such events are unnecessary in the sense that PBGC typically reviews but takes no action on them. PBGC analyzed 2011 records to determine how many such reports it received for events to which the proposed sponsor safe harbor would apply, then reanalyzed the data to see how many unnecessary reports would have been received if the plan sponsor safe harbor in the proposed rule had been in effect (that is, excluding reports that would have been waived under the plan sponsor safe harbor test).[37] It found that the proportion of unnecessary filings would be much lower under the proposed regulation than under the existing regulation — 5 percent (10 filings) compared to 42 percent (79 filings). Thus, although the total number of filings may be a little higher under the proposed rule, the proportion of unnecessary reports, and the regulatory burden on financially sound sponsors and plans, would be dramatically reduced.

Under Section 3(f)(1) of Executive Order 12866, a regulatory action is economically significant if "it is likely to result in a rule that may . . . [h]ave an annual effect on the economy of $100 million or more or adversely affect in a material way the economy, a sector of the economy, productivity, competition, jobs, the environment, public health or safety, or State, local, or tribal governments or communities." PBGC has determined that this proposed rule does not cross the $100 million threshold for economic significance and is not otherwise economically significant.

This action is associated with retrospective review and analysis in PBGC's Plan for Regulatory Review[38] issued in accordance with Executive Order 13563 on "Improving Regulation and Regulatory Review."

Regulatory Flexibility Act

The Regulatory Flexibility Act imposes certain requirements with respect to rules that are subject to the notice and comment requirements of section 553(b) of the Administrative Procedure Act and that are likely to have a significant economic impact on a substantial number of small entities. Unless an agency determines that a proposed rule is not likely to have a significant economic impact on a substantial number of small entities, section 603 of the Regulatory Flexibility Act requires that the agency present an initial regulatory flexibility analysis at the time of the publication of the proposed rule describing the impact of the rule on small entities and seeking public comment on such impact. Small entities include small businesses, organizations and governmental jurisdictions.

For purposes of the Regulatory Flexibility Act requirements with respect to the proposed amendments to the reportable events regulation, PBGC considers a small entity to be a plan with fewer than 100 participants. This is the same criterion used to determine the availability of the "small plan" waiver under the proposal, and is consistent with certain requirements in Title I of ERISA[39] and the Internal Revenue Code,[40] as well as the definition of a small entity that the Department of Labor (DOL) has used for purposes of the Regulatory Flexibility Act.[41] Using this proposed definition, about 64 percent (16,700 of 26,100) of plans covered by Title IV of ERISA in 2010 were small plans.[42]

Further, while some large employers may have small plans, in general most small plans are maintained by small employers. Thus, PBGC believes that assessing the impact of the proposal on small plans is an appropriate substitute for evaluating the effect on small entities. The definition of small entity considered appropriate for this purpose

---

[37] Filings that involve section 4062(e) events always result in the opening of cases and were excluded from the analysis.

[38] See www.pbgc.gov/documents/plan-for-regulatory-review.pdf.

[39] See, e.g., ERISA section 104(a)(2), which permits the Secretary of Labor to prescribe simplified annual reports for pension plans that cover fewer than 100 participants.

[40] See, e.g., Code section 430(g)(2)(B), which permits plans with 100 or fewer participants to use valuation dates other than the first day of the plan year.

[41] See, e.g., DOL's final rule on Prohibited Transaction Exemption Procedures, 76 Fed. Reg. 66,637, 66,644 (Oct. 27, 2011).

[42] See PBGC 2010 pension insurance data table S-31, http://www.pbgc.gov/Documents/pension-insurance-datatables-2010.pdf.

differs, however, from a definition of small business based on size standards promulgated by the Small Business Administration (13 CFR § 121.201) pursuant to the Small Business Act. PBGC therefore requests comments on the appropriateness of the size standard used in evaluating the impact on small entities of the proposed amendments to the reportable events regulation.

On the basis of its proposed definition of small entity, PBGC certifies under section 605(b) of the Regulatory Flexibility Act (5 U.S.C. 601 *et seq.*) that the amendments in this rule will not have a significant economic impact on a substantial number of small entities. Accordingly, as provided in section 605 of the Regulatory Flexibility Act (5 U.S.C. 601 et seq.), sections 603 and 604 do not apply. This certification is based on the fact that the reportable events regulation requires only the filing of one-time notices on the occurrence of unusual events that affect only certain plans and that the economic impact of filing is not significant. The average burden of submitting a notice — based on the estimates discussed under *Paperwork Reduction Act*, below — is less than 5 ½ hours and $800 (virtually the same as under the current regulation). PBGC invites public comment on this burden estimate.

Paperwork Reduction Act

PBGC is submitting the information requirements under this proposed rule to the Office of Management and Budget for review and approval under the Paperwork Reduction Act. There are two information collections under the reportable events regulation, approved under OMB control number 1212-0013 (covering subparts B and C) and OMB control number 1212-0041 (covering subpart D), both of which expire March 31, 2015. Copies of PBGC's requests may be obtained free of charge by contacting the Disclosure Division of the Office of the General Counsel of PBGC, 1200 K Street, NW., Washington, DC 20005, 202-326-4040.

PBGC is proposing the following changes to these information requirements:

- PBGC's experience is that in order to assess the significance of virtually every post-event filing for a missed contribution, inability to pay benefits, loan default, liquidation, or insolvency, it must obtain from the filer certain actuarial, financial, and controlled group information. Filers are currently required to submit some of this information for some events, but PBGC wants to make its information collection for all these events more uniform. Accordingly, PBGC proposes to require that every post-event filing for one of these events include these items (except that financial information is unnecessary for reports of insolvency because PBGC can typically obtain most of the information from court records). Actuarial information would no longer have to be submitted with postevent notices of other events. (1) The actuarial information required would be a copy of the most recent actuarial valuation report for the plan, a statement of subsequent material changes, and the most recent month-end market value of plan assets. (2) The financial information required would be copies of audited financial statements for the most recent fiscal year. (If audited statements were not immediately available, copies of unaudited financial statements (if available) or tax returns would be required, to be followed up with required financial statements when available.) (3) The controlled group information required would be tailored to the event being reported and would generally include identifying information for each plan maintained by any member of the controlled group, a description of the controlled group with members' names, and the status of members (for example, liquidating or in bankruptcy).

- Similarly, PBGC has found that it needs the same actuarial, financial, and controlled group information for advance-notice filings. For notices of funding waiver requests, the information can typically be gleaned from the copy of the request that accompanies the reportable event notice. And financial information is unnecessary for reports of insolvency because PBGC can typically obtain most of the information from court records. With these exceptions, PBGC proposes to require that every advance notice filing include these items.

- Controlled group changes and benefit liability transfers involve both an "old" controlled group and a "new" controlled group. PBGC already requires submission of controlled group informa-

tion with notices of controlled group changes, and now proposes to do the same for benefit liability transfers.

- Because extraordinary distributions raise questions about controlled group finances, PBGC proposes to require submission of financial information with notices of events of this type.

- Inability to pay benefits and liquidation both raise the specter of imminent sponsor shutdown and plan termination. Accordingly, for notices of these two events (including advance notices of liquidation events), PBGC proposes to require submission of copies of the most recent plan documents and IRS qualification letter, the date or expected date of shutdown, and the identity of the plan actuary if different from the actuary reported on the most recent Form 5500 Schedule SB. Plan documents would no longer be required with notices for other events.

- PBGC proposes to require e-mail addresses for plan administrators, sponsors, and designated contact persons.

- PBGC proposes to require that both post-event and advance report filings state explicitly the date of the event or the actual or anticipated effective date of the event (as applicable). This requirement will avoid the potential for confusion or ambiguity in the description of the event regarding this date.

- PBGC has found that it often does not need the actuarial valuation report that must currently be included with notice of a substantial owner distribution and thus proposes to eliminate that requirement. However, PBGC proposes to add a requirement that notices of this event give the reason for the distribution to help PBGC analyze its significance.

- For both post-event and advance notices of loan defaults, PBGC proposes to require that any cross-defaults or anticipated cross-defaults be described.

- PBGC has found that some filers that should file Form 200 under § 4043.81 of the reportable events regulation (missed contributions totaling over $1 million) file only Form 10 under § 4043.25 (missed contributions of any amount). This has led to delays in enforcing liens under ERISA section 302(f) and Code section 412(n) (corresponding to ERISA section 303(k) and Code section 430(k) as amended by PPA 2006). To address this issue, PBGC proposes that Form 10 filings for missed contributions include the amount and date of all missed contributions since the most recent Schedule SB.

- PBGC proposes to eliminate Form 200 information submission requirements for documents that PBGC typically can now obtain timely on its own and to add new information submission requirements to help it analyze the seriousness of the plan's status and perfect statutory liens triggered by large missed contributions. Documentation to be eliminated would be copies of Form 5500 Schedule SB, SEC filings, and documents connected with insolvency, liquidation, receivership, and similar proceedings. New information to be required would be a statement of material changes in liabilities since the most recent actuarial valuation report, most recent month-end market value of plan assets, description of each controlled group member's status (for example, liquidating or in bankruptcy), information about all controlled group real property, and identity of controlled group head offices.

- PBGC Form 10 currently requires for the bankruptcy/insolvency event that the bankruptcy petition and docket (or similar documents) be submitted. Form 10-Advance requires that all documents filed in the relevant proceeding be submitted. Both forms require that the last date for filing claims be reported if known. PBGC proposes to replace these requirements with a requirement that filers simply identify the court where the insolvency proceeding was filed or will be filed and the docket number of the filing (if known).

PBGC needs the information in reportable events filings under subparts B and C of part 4043 (Forms 10 and 10-Advance) to determine whether it should terminate plans that experience events that indicate plan or contributing sponsor financial problems. PBGC estimates that it will receive such filings from about 1,085 respondents each year and that the total annual burden of the collection of information will be about 5,744 hours and $857,195. This represents a burden comparable to that under the existing regulation, as the following table shows:

Annual burden:	Under existing regulation:	Under proposed rule:
Number of responses	1,026	1,085
Hour burden	5,400 hours	5,744 hours

Annual burden:	Under existing regulation:	Under proposed rule:
Dollar burden	$821,826	$857,195

As discussed above, however, the proposal is designed to reduce burden dramatically on financially sound plans and sponsors (which present a low degree of risk); thus, burden under the proposed rule would be substantially associated with higher-risk events, which are much more likely to deserve PBGC's attention. PBGC separately esti-

mated the average burden changes for low-risk and high-risk entities. The burden for low-risk sponsors would go down from 417 hours and $121,725 to zero. The burden for high-risk sponsors would go up by approximately 760 hours and $157,100.

Low-risk	Volume	Hours	Cost
Current	144	417	$121,725
Proposed	0	0	$0
Change	(144)	(417)	$(121,725)

High-risk	Volume	Hours	Cost
Current	882	4,983	$700,101
Proposed	1,085	5,744	$857,195
Change	203	761	$157,094

PBGC needs the information in missed contribution filings under subpart D of part 4043 (Form 200) to determine the amounts of statutory liens arising under ERISA section 303(k) and Code section 430(k) and to evaluate the funding status of plans with respect to which such liens arise and the financial condition of the persons responsible for their funding. PBGC estimates that it will receive such filings from about 136 respondents each year and that the total annual burden of the collection of information will be about 816 hours and $125,000.[43]

Comments on the paperwork provisions under this proposed rule should be sent to the Office of Information and Regulatory Affairs, Office of Management and Budget, Attention: Desk Officer for Pension Benefit Guaranty Corporation, via electronic mail at OIRA_DOCKET@omb.eop.gov or by fax to (202) 395-6974. Although comments may be submitted through [insert date 60 days after publication in the **Federal Register**], the Office of Management and Budget requests that comments be received on or before [insert date 30 days after publication in the **Federal Register**] to ensure their consideration. Comments may address (among other things) —

- Whether each proposed collection of information is needed for the proper performance of PBGC's functions and will have practical utility;

- The accuracy of PBGC's estimate of the burden of each proposed collection of information, including the validity of the methodology and assumptions used;

- Enhancement of the quality, utility, and clarity of the information to be collected; and

- Minimizing the burden of each collection of information on those who are to respond, including through the use of appropriate automated, electronic, mechanical, or other technological collection techniques or other forms of information technology, *e.g.*, permitting electronic submission of responses.

List of Subjects

29 CFR Part 4000

Employee benefit plans, Pension insurance, Reporting and record-keeping requirements.

29 CFR Part 4001

Employee benefit plans, Pension insurance.

29 CFR Part 4043

Employee benefit plans, Pension insurance, Reporting and record-keeping requirements.

29 CFR Part 4204

Employee benefit plans, Pension insurance, Reporting and record-keeping requirements.

29 CFR Part 4206

Employee benefit plans, Pension insurance.

29 CFR Part 4231

Employee benefit plans, Pension insurance, Reporting and record-keeping requirements.

■ For the reasons given above, PBGC proposes to amend 29 CFR parts 4000, 4001, 4043, 4204, 4206, and 4231 as follows.

PART 4000 — FILING, ISSUANCE, COMPUTATION OF TIME, AND RECORD RETENTION

■ 1. The authority citation for part 4000 is revised to read as follows:

Authority: 29 U.S.C. 1083(k), 1302(b)(3).

■ 2. In § 4000.3, new paragraph (b)(3) is added to read as follows:

§ 4000.3 What methods of filing may I use?

* * * * *

(b) * * *

(3) You must file notices under part 4043 of this chapter electronically in accordance with the instructions on PBGC's Web site, except as otherwise provided by PBGC.

* * * * *

■ 3. In § 4000.53, paragraphs (c) and (d) are amended by removing the words "section 302(f)(4), section 307(e), or" where they occur in each paragraph and adding in their place the words "section 101(f), section 303(k)(4), or".

PART 4001 — TERMINOLOGY

■ 4. The authority citation for part 4001 continues to read as follows:

Authority: 29 U.S.C. 1301, 1302(b)(3).

■ 5. In § 4001.2:

a. The definition of "controlled group" is amended by removing the words "section 412(c)(11)(B) of the Code or section 302(c)(11)(B) of ERISA" and adding in their place the words "section 412(b)(2) of the Code or section 302(b)(2) of ERISA".

b. The definition of "funding standard account" is amended by removing the words "section 302(b) of ERISA or section 412(b) of the Code" and adding in their place the words "section 304(b) of ERISA or section 431(b) of the Code".

c. The definition of "substantial owner" is amended by removing the words "section 4022(b)(5)(A)" and adding in their place the words "section 4021(d)".

■ 6. Part 4043 is revised to read as follows:

---

[43] In comparison, PBGC's most recent annual burden estimate for this information collection was 110 responses, 670 hours, and $102,000.

PART 4043 — REPORTABLE EVENTS AND CERTAIN OTHER NOTIFICATION REQUIREMENTS

Authority: 29 U.S.C. 1082(f), 1302(b)(3), 1343.

Subpart A — General Provisions

§ 4043.1 Purpose and scope.

This part prescribes the requirements for notifying PBGC of a reportable event under section 4043 of ERISA or of a failure to make certain required contributions under section 303(k)(4) of ERISA or section 430(k)(4) of the Code. Subpart A contains definitions and general rules. Subpart B contains rules for post-event notice of a reportable event. Subpart C contains rules for advance notice of a reportable event. Subpart D contains rules for notifying PBGC of a failure to make certain required contributions.

§ 4043.2 Definitions.

The following terms are defined in § 4001.2 of this chapter: benefit liabilities, Code, contributing sponsor, controlled group, ERISA, fair market value, irrevocable commitment, multiemployer plan, PBGC, person, plan, plan administrator, plan year, single-employer plan, and substantial owner.

In addition, for purposes of this part:

De minimis 10-percent segment means, in connection with a plan's controlled group, one or more entities that in the aggregate have for a fiscal year —

(1) Revenue not exceeding 10 percent of the controlled group's revenue;

(2) Annual operating income not exceeding the greater of —

(i) 10 percent of the controlled group's annual operating income; or

(ii) $5 million; and

(3) Net tangible assets at the end of the fiscal year(s) not exceeding the greater of —

(i) 10 percent of the controlled group's net tangible assets at the end of the fiscal year(s); or

(ii) $5 million.

De minimis 5-percent segment has the same meaning as *de minimis* 10-percent segment, except that "5 percent" is substituted for "10 percent" each time it appears.

Event year means the plan year in which a reportable event occurs.

Financially sound has the meaning described in § 4043.9.

Foreign entity means a member of a controlled group that —

(1) Is not a contributing sponsor of a plan;

(2) Is not organized under the laws of (or, if an individual, is not a domiciliary of) any state (as defined in section 3(10) of ERISA); and

(3) For the fiscal year that includes the date the reportable event occurs, meets one of the following tests —

(i) Is not required to file any United States federal income tax form;

(ii) Has no income reportable on any United States federal income tax form other than passive income not exceeding $1,000; or

(iii) Does not own substantial assets in the United States (disregarding stock of a member of the plan's controlled group) and is not required to file any quarterly United States tax returns for employee withholding.

Foreign parent means a foreign entity that is a direct or indirect parent of a person that is a contributing sponsor of a plan.

Notice date means the deadline (including extensions) for filing notice of a reportable event with PBGC.

Participant means a participant as defined in § 4006.2 of this chapter.

U.S. entity means an entity subject to the personal jurisdiction of the U.S. district court.

§ 4043.3 Requirement of notice.

(a) *Obligation to file.*

(1) *In general.* Each person that is required to file a notice under this part, or a duly authorized representative, must submit the information

required under this part by the time specified in §4043.20 (for post-event notice), §4043.61 (for advance notice), or §4043.81 (for Form 200 filings). Any information filed with PBGC in connection with another matter may be incorporated by reference. If an event is subject to both post-event and advance notice requirements, the notice filed first satisfies both filing requirements.

(2) *Multiple plans.* If a reportable event occurs for more than one plan, the filing obligation with respect to each plan is independent of the filing obligation with respect to any other plan.

(3) *Optional consolidated filing.* A filing of a notice with respect to a reportable event by any person required to file will be deemed to be a filing by all persons required to give PBGC notice of the event under this part. If notices are required for two or more events, the notices may be combined in one filing.

(b) *Contents of reportable event notice.* A person required to file a reportable event notice under subpart B or C of this part must file, by the notice date, the form specified by PBGC for that purpose, with the information specified in PBGC's reportable events instructions.

(c) *Reportable event forms and instructions.* PBGC will issue reportable events forms and instructions and make them available on its Web site (www.pbgc.gov).

(d) *Requests for additional information.* PBGC may, in any case, require the submission of additional relevant information not specified in its forms and instructions. Any such information must be submitted for subpart B of this part within 30 days, and for subpart C or D of this part within 7 days, after the date of a written request by PBGC, or within a different time period specified therein. PBGC may in its discretion shorten the time period where it determines that the interests of PBGC or participants may be prejudiced by a delay in receipt of the information.

(e) *Effect of failure to file.* If a notice (or any other information required under this part) is not provided within the specified time limit, PBGC may assess against each person required to provide the notice a separate penalty under section 4071 of ERISA. PBGC may pursue any other equitable or legal remedies available to it under the law.

§4043.4 Waivers and extensions.

(a) *Waivers and extensions — in general.* PBGC may extend any deadline or waive any other requirement under this part where it finds convincing evidence that the waiver or extension is appropriate under the circumstances. Any waiver or extension may be subject to conditions. A request for a waiver or extension must be filed with PBGC in writing (which may be in electronic form) and must state the facts and circumstances on which the request is based.

(b) *Waivers and extensions — specific events.* For some reportable events, automatic waivers from reporting and information requirements and extensions of time are provided in subparts B and C of this part. If an occurrence constitutes two or more reportable events, reporting requirements for each event are determined independently. For example, reporting is automatically waived for an occurrence that constitutes a reportable event under more than one section only if the requirements for an automatic waiver under each section are satisfied.

(c) *Multiemployer plans.* The requirements of section 4043 of ERISA are waived with respect to multiemployer plans.

(d) *Terminating plans.* No notice is required from the plan administrator or contributing sponsor of a plan if the notice date is on or after the date on which —

(1) All of the plan's assets (other than any excess assets) are distributed pursuant to a termination under part 4041 of this chapter; or

(2) A trustee is appointed for the plan under section 4042(c) of ERISA.

§4043.5 How and where to file.

Reportable event notices required under this part must be filed electronically using the forms and in accordance with the instructions promulgated by PBGC, which are posted on PBGC's Web site. Filing guidance is provided by the instructions and by subpart A of part 4000 of this chapter.

§4043.6 Date of filing.

(a) *Post-event notice filings.* PBGC applies the rules in subpart C of part 4000 of this chapter to determine the date that a submission under subpart B of this part was filed with PBGC.

(b) *Advance notice and Form 200 filings.* Information filed under subpart C or D of this part is treated as filed on the date it is received

by PBGC. Subpart C of part 4000 of this chapter provides rules for determining when PBGC receives a submission.

§4043.7 Computation of time.

PBGC applies the rules in subpart D of part 4000 of this chapter to compute any time period under this part.

§4043.8 Confidentiality.

In accordance with section 4043(f) of ERISA and §4901.21(a)(3) of this chapter, any information or documentary material that is not publicly available and is submitted to PBGC pursuant to subpart B or C of this part will not be made public, except as may be relevant to any administrative or judicial action or proceeding or for disclosures to either body of Congress or to any duly authorized committee or subcommittee of the Congress.

§4043.9 Financial soundness.

(a) *In general.* The term "financially sound" is defined in paragraph (b) of this section for an entity that is a plan sponsor or member of a plan sponsor's controlled group and in paragraph (c) of this section for a plan.

(b) *Financially sound sponsor or controlled group member.* For purposes of this part, an entity that is a plan sponsor or member of a plan sponsor's controlled group is "financially sound" as of any date (the determination date) if on the determination date it has adequate capacity to meet its obligations in full and on time as evidenced by its satisfaction of all of the five criteria described in paragraphs (b)(1) through (b)(5) of this section.

(1) The entity is scored by a commercial credit reporting company that is commonly used in the business community, and the score indicates a low likelihood that the entity will default on its obligations.

(2) The entity has no secured debt, disregarding leases or debt incurred to acquire or improve property and secured only by that property.

(3) For the most recent two fiscal years, the entity has positive net income under generally accepted accounting principles (GAAP) or International Financial Reporting Standards (IFRS). For purposes of this provision, net income of a tax-exempt entity is the excess of total revenue over total expenses as required to be reported on Internal Revenue Service Form 990.

(4) For the two-year period ending on the determination date, no event described in §4043.34(a)(1) or (2) (dealing with a default on loan with an outstanding balance of $10 million or more) has occurred with respect to any loan to the entity, regardless of whether reporting was waived under §4043.34(c).

(5) For the two-year period ending on the determination date, the entity has not failed to make when due any contribution described in §4043.25(a)(1) or (2) (dealing with failure to make required minimum funding payments), unless reporting is waived under §4043.25(c) for failure to make the contribution.

(c) *Financially sound plan.* For purposes of this part, "financially sound" means, with respect to a plan for a plan year, that the plan meets the requirements of either paragraph (c)(1) or paragraph (c)(2) of this section.

(1) A plan meets the requirements of this paragraph (c)(1) if, as of the last day of the prior plan year, the plan had no unfunded benefit liabilities (within the meaning of section 4062(b)(1)(A) of ERISA as determined in accordance with §§4044.51 through 4044.57 of this chapter (dealing with valuation of benefits and assets in trusteed terminating plans) and §4010.8(d)(1)(ii) of this chapter.

(2) A plan meets the requirements of this paragraph (c)(2) if for the prior plan year, the ratio of the value of the plan's assets as determined for premium purposes in accordance with part 4006 of this chapter to the amount of the plan's premium funding target as so determined was not less than 120 percent.

Subpart B — Post-Event Notice of Reportable Events

§4043.20 Post-event filing obligation.

(a) *In general.* The plan administrator and each contributing sponsor of a plan for which a reportable event under this subpart has occurred are required to notify PBGC within 30 days after that person knows or has reason to know that the reportable event has occurred, unless a waiver or extension applies. If there is a change in plan administrator or contributing sponsor, the reporting obligation applies to the person who is the plan administrator or contributing sponsor of the plan on the 30th day after the reportable event occurs.

(b) *Extension for certain events.* For the events described in §§ 4043.23, 4043.27, 4043.29, 4043.31, and 4043.32, if the plan's premium due date for the plan year preceding the event year was determined under § 4007.11(a)(1) (dealing with small plans) or § 4007.11(c) (dealing with new and newly covered plans) of this chapter, the notice date is extended until the last day of the seventeenth full calendar month that began on or after the first day of such preceding plan year (the effective date, in the case of a new plan).

§ 4043.21 Tax disqualification and Title I noncompliance.

(a) *Reportable event.* A reportable event occurs when the Secretary of the Treasury issues notice that a plan has ceased to be a plan described in section 4021(a)(2) of ERISA, or when the Secretary of Labor determines that a plan is not in compliance with title I of ERISA.

(b) *Waiver.* Notice is waived for this event.

§ 4043.22 Amendment decreasing benefits payable.

(a) *Reportable event.* A reportable event occurs when an amendment to a plan is adopted under which the retirement benefit payable from employer contributions with respect to any participant may be decreased.

(b) *Waiver.* Notice is waived for this event.

§ 4043.23 Active participant reduction.

(a) *Reportable event.* A reportable event occurs:

(1) *Single-cause event.* When the reductions in the number of active participants under a plan due to a single cause — such as a reorganization, the discontinuance of an operation, a natural disaster, a mass layoff, or an early retirement incentive program — are more than 20 percent of the number of active participants at the beginning of the plan year or more than 25 percent of the number of active participants at the beginning of the previous plan year.

(2) *Short-period event.* When the reductions in the number of active participants under a plan over a short period (disregarding reductions reported under paragraph (a)(1) of this section) are more than 20 percent of the number of active participants at the beginning of the plan year, or more than 25 percent of the number of active participants at the beginning of the previous plan year. For this purpose, a short period is a period of 30 days or less that does not include any part of a prior short period for which an active participant reduction is reported under this section.

(3) *Attrition event.* On the last day of a plan year if the number of active participants under a plan are reduced by more than 20 percent of the number of active participants at the beginning of the plan year, or by more than 25 percent of the number of active participants at the beginning of the previous plan year. The reduction may be measured by using the number of active participants on either the last day of the plan year or the participant count date (as defined in § 4006.2 of this chapter) for the next plan year, but in either case is considered to occur on the last day of the plan year.

(b) *Determination rules.*

(1) *Determination dates.* The number of active participants at the beginning of a plan year may be determined by using the number of active participants at the end of the previous plan year.

(2) *Active participant.* "Active participant" means a participant who —

(i) Is receiving compensation for work performed;

(ii) Is on paid or unpaid leave granted for a reason other than a layoff;

(iii) Is laid off from work for a period of time that has lasted less than 30 days; or

(iv) Is absent from work due to a recurring reduction in employment that occurs at least annually.

(3) *Employment relationship.* The employment relationship referred to in this paragraph (b) is between the participant and all members of the plan's controlled group.

(c) *Reductions due to cessations and withdrawals.* For purposes of paragraphs (a)(1) and (a)(2) of this section, a reduction in the number of active participants is to be disregarded to the extent that it —

(1) Is attributable to an event described in ERISA section 4062(e) or 4063(a), and

(2) Is timely reported to PBGC under ERISA section 4063(a).

(d) *Waivers.*

(1) *Current-year small plan.* Notice under this section is waived if the plan had fewer than 100 participants for whom flat-rate premiums were payable for the plan year preceding the event year.

(2) *Financial soundness.* Notice under this section is waived if —

(i) For each contributing sponsor of the plan, either the sponsor or the sponsor's highest level controlled group parent that is a U.S. entity is financially sound when the event occurs, or

(ii) The plan is financially sound for the plan year in which the event occurs.

(e) *Extension — attrition event.* For an event described in paragraph (a)(3) of this section, the notice date is extended until 120 days after the end of the event year.

§ 4043.24 Termination or partial termination.

(a) *Reportable event.* A reportable event occurs when the Secretary of the Treasury determines that there has been a termination or partial termination of a plan within the meaning of section 411(d)(3) of the Code.

(b) *Waiver.* Notice is waived for this event.

§ 4043.25 Failure to make required minimum funding payment.

(a) *Reportable event.* A reportable event occurs when —

(1) A contribution required under sections 302 and 303 of ERISA or sections 412 and 430 of the Code is not made by the due date for the payment under ERISA section 303(j) or Code section 430(j), or

(2) Any other contribution required as a condition of a funding waiver is not made when due.

(b) *Alternative method of compliance — Form 200 filed.* If, with respect to the same failure, a filing is made in accordance with § 4043.81, that filing satisfies the requirements of this section.

(c) *Waivers.*

(1) *Current-year small plan.* Notice under this section is waived with respect to a failure to make a required quarterly contribution under section 303(j)(3) of ERISA or section 430(j)(3) of the Code if the plan had fewer than 100 participants for whom flat-rate premiums were payable for the plan year preceding the event year.

(2) *30-day grace period.* Notice under this section is waived if the missed contribution is made by the 30th day after its due date.

§ 4043.26 Inability to pay benefits when due.

(a) *Reportable event.* A reportable event occurs when a plan is currently unable or projected to be unable to pay benefits.

(1) *Current inability.* A plan is currently unable to pay benefits if it fails to provide any participant or beneficiary the full benefits to which the person is entitled under the terms of the plan, at the time the benefit is due and in the form in which it is due. A plan is not treated as being currently unable to pay benefits if its failure to pay is caused solely by —

(i) A limitation under section 436 of the Code and section 206(g) of ERISA (dealing with funding-based limits on benefits and benefit accruals under single-employer plans), or

(ii) The need to verify a person's eligibility for benefits; the inability to locate a person; or any other administrative delay if the delay is for less than the shorter of two months or two full benefit payment periods.

(2) *Projected inability.* A plan is projected to be unable to pay benefits when, as of the last day of any quarter of a plan year, the plan's "liquid assets" are less than two times the amount of the "disbursements from the plan" for such quarter. "Liquid assets" and "disbursements from the plan" have the same meaning as under section 303(j)(4)(E) of ERISA and section 430(j)(4)(E) of the Code.

(b) *Waiver — plans subject to liquidity shortfall rules.* Notice under this section is waived unless the reportable event occurs during a plan year for which the plan is exempt from the liquidity shortfall rules in section 303(j)(4) of ERISA and section 430(j)(4) of the Code because it is described in section 303(g)(2)(B) of ERISA and section 430(g)(2)(B) of the Code.

§ 4043.27 Distribution to a substantial owner.

(a) *Reportable event.* A reportable event occurs for a plan when —

(1) There is a distribution to a substantial owner of a contributing sponsor of the plan;

(2) The total of all distributions made to the substantial owner within the one-year period ending with the date of such distribution exceeds $10,000;

(3) The distribution is not made by reason of the substantial owner's death;

(4) Immediately after the distribution, the plan has nonforfeitable benefits (as provided in § 4022.5 of this chapter) that are not funded; and

(5) Either —

(i) The sum of the values of all distributions to any one substantial owner within the oneyear period ending with the date of the distribution is more than one percent of the end-of-year total amount of the plan's assets (as required to be reported on Schedule H or Schedule I to Form 5500) for each of the two plan years immediately preceding the event year, or

(ii) The sum of the values of all distributions to all substantial owners within the oneyear period ending with the date of the distribution is more than five percent of the end-of-year total amount of the plan's assets (as required to be reported on Schedule H or Schedule I to Form 5500) for each of the two plan years immediately preceding the event year.

(b) *Determination rules.*

(1) *Valuation of distribution.* The value of a distribution under this section is the sum of —

(i) The cash amounts actually received by the substantial owner;

(ii) The purchase price of any irrevocable commitment; and

(iii) The fair market value of any other assets distributed, determined as of the date of distribution to the substantial owner.

(2) *Date of substantial owner distribution.* The date of distribution to a substantial owner of a cash distribution is the date it is received by the substantial owner. The date of distribution to a substantial owner of an irrevocable commitment is the date on which the obligation to provide benefits passes from the plan to the insurer. The date of any other distribution to a substantial owner is the date when the plan relinquishes control over the assets transferred directly or indirectly to the substantial owner.

(3) *Determination date.* The determination of whether a participant is (or has been in the preceding 60 months) a substantial owner is made on the date when there has been a distribution that would be reportable under this section if made to a substantial owner.

(c) *Alternative method of compliance — non-increasing annuity.* In the case of a nonincreasing annuity for a substantial owner, a filing that satisfies the requirements of this section with respect to any payment under the annuity and that discloses the period, periodic amount, and duration of the annuity satisfies the requirements of this section with respect to all subsequent payments under the annuity.

(d) *Waivers — financial soundness.* Notice under this section is waived if —

(1) For each contributing sponsor of the plan, either the sponsor or the sponsor's highest level controlled group parent that is a U.S. entity is financially sound when the event occurs, or

(2) The plan is financially sound for the plan year in which the event occurs.

§ 4043.28 Plan merger, consolidation or transfer.

(a) *Reportable event.* A reportable event occurs when a plan merges, consolidates, or transfers its assets or liabilities under section 208 of ERISA or section 414(*l*) of the Code.

(b) *Waiver.* Notice under this section is waived for this event. However, notice may be required under § 4043.29 (for a controlled group change) or § 4043.32 (for a transfer of benefit liabilities).

§ 4043.29 Change in contributing sponsor or controlled group.

(a) *Reportable event.* A reportable event occurs for a plan when there is a transaction that results, or will result, in one or more persons ceasing to be members of the plan's controlled group. For purposes of this section, the term "transaction" includes, but is not limited to, a legally binding agreement, whether or not written, to transfer ownership, an actual transfer of ownership, and an actual change in ownership that occurs as a matter of law or through the exercise or lapse of pre-existing rights. Whether an agreement is legally binding is to be determined without regard to any conditions in the agreement. A transaction is not reportable if it will result solely in a reorganization

involving a mere change in identity, form, or place of organization, however effected.

(b) *Waivers.*

(1) De minimis *10-percent segment.* Notice under this section is waived if the person or persons that will cease to be members of the plan's controlled group represent a *de minimis* 10-percent segment of the plan's old controlled group for the most recent fiscal year(s) ending on or before the date the reportable event occurs.

(2) *Foreign entity.* Notice under this section is waived if each person that will cease to be a member of the plan's controlled group is a foreign entity other than a foreign parent.

(3) *Current-year small plan.* Notice under this section is waived if the plan had fewer than 100 participants for whom flat-rate premiums were payable for the plan year preceding the event year.

(4) *Financial soundness.* Notice under this section is waived if —

(i) For each post-event contributing sponsor of the plan, either the sponsor or the sponsor's highest level controlled group parent that is a U.S. entity is financially sound when the event occurs, or

(ii) The plan is financially sound for the plan year in which the event occurs.

(c) *Examples.* The following examples assume that no waiver applies.

(1) *Controlled group breakup.* Plan A's controlled group consists of Company A (its contributing sponsor), Company B (which maintains Plan B), and Company C. As a result of a transaction, the controlled group will break into two separate controlled groups — one segment consisting of Company A and the other segment consisting of Companies B and C. Both Company A (Plan A's contributing sponsor) and the plan administrator of Plan A are required to report that Companies B and C will leave Plan A's controlled group. Company B (Plan B's contributing sponsor) and the plan administrator of Plan B are required to report that Company A will leave Plan B's controlled group. Company C is not required to report because it is not a contributing sponsor or a plan administrator.

(2) *Change in contributing sponsor.* Plan Q is maintained by Company Q. Company Q enters into a binding contract to sell a portion of its assets and to transfer employees participating in Plan Q, along with Plan Q, to Company R, which is not a member of Company Q's controlled group. There will be no change in the structure of Company Q's controlled group. On the effective date of the sale, Company R will become the contributing sponsor of Plan Q. A reportable event occurs on the date of the transaction (*i.e.,* the binding contract), because as a result of the transaction, Company Q (and any other member of its controlled group) will cease to be a member of Plan Q's controlled group. If, on the 30th day after Company Q and Company R enter into the binding contract, the change in the contributing sponsor has not yet become effective, Company Q has the reporting obligation. If the change in the contributing sponsor has become effective by the 30th day, Company R has the reporting obligation.

§ 4043.30 Liquidation.

(a) *Reportable event.* A reportable event occurs for a plan when a member of the plan's controlled group —

(1) Is involved in any transaction to implement its complete liquidation (including liquidation into another controlled group member);

(2) Institutes or has instituted against it a proceeding to be dissolved or is dissolved, whichever occurs first; or

(3) Liquidates in a case under the Bankruptcy Code, or under any similar law.

(b) *Waivers.*

(1) De minimis *10-percent segment.* Notice under this section is waived if the person or persons that liquidate do not include any contributing sponsor of the plan and represent a *de minimis* 10-percent segment of the plan's controlled group for the most recent fiscal year(s) ending on or before the date the reportable event occurs.

(2) *Foreign entity.* Notice under this section is waived if each person that liquidates is a foreign entity other than a foreign parent.

§ 4043.31 Extraordinary dividend or stock redemption.

(a) *Reportable event.* A reportable event occurs for a plan when any member of the plan's controlled group declares a dividend or redeems its own stock and the amount or net value of the distribution, when combined with other such distributions during the same fiscal year of the person, exceeds the person's net income before after-tax gain or loss on any sale of assets, as determined in accordance with generally accepted accounting principles, for the prior fiscal year. A distribution by a person to a member of its controlled group is disregarded.

(b) *Determination rules.* For purposes of paragraph (a) of this section, the net value of a non-cash distribution is the fair market value of assets transferred by the person making the distribution, reduced by the fair market value of any liabilities assumed or consideration given by the recipient in connection with the distribution. Net value determinations should be based on readily available fair market value(s) or independent appraisal(s) performed within one year before the distribution is made. To the extent that fair market values are not readily available and no such appraisals exist, the fair market value of an asset transferred in connection with a distribution or a liability assumed by a recipient of a distribution is deemed to be equal to 200 percent of the book value of the asset or liability on the books of the person making the distribution. Stock redeemed is deemed to have no value.

(c) *Waivers.*

(1) *Extraordinary dividends and stock redemptions.* Notice under this section of the reportable event described in section 4043(c)(11) of ERISA related to extraordinary dividends and stock redemptions is waived except to the extent reporting is required under this section.

(2) De minimis *10-percent segment.* Notice under this section is waived if the person making the distribution is a *de minimis* 10-percent segment of the plan's controlled group for the most recent fiscal year(s) ending on or before the date the reportable event occurs.

(3) *Foreign entity.* Notice under this section is waived if the person making the distribution is a foreign entity other than a foreign parent.

(4) *Current-year small plan.* Notice under this section is waived if the plan had fewer than 100 participants for whom flat-rate premiums were payable for the plan year preceding the event year.

(5) *Financial soundness.* Notice under this section is waived if —

(i) For each contributing sponsor of the plan, either the sponsor or the sponsor's highest level controlled group parent that is a U.S. entity is financially sound when the event occurs, or

(ii) The plan is financially sound for the plan year in which the event occurs.

§ 4043.32 Transfer of benefit liabilities.

(a) *Reportable event.* A reportable event occurs for a plan when —

(1) The plan makes a transfer of benefit liabilities to a person, or to a plan or plans maintained by a person or persons, that are not members of the transferor plan's controlled group; and

(2) The amount of benefit liabilities transferred, in conjunction with other benefit liabilities transferred during the 12-month period ending on the date of the transfer, is 3 percent or more of the plan's total benefit liabilities. Both the benefit liabilities transferred and the plan's total benefit liabilities are to be valued as of any one date in the plan year in which the transfer occurs, using actuarial assumptions that comply with section 414(l) of the Code.

(b) *Determination rules.*

(1) *Date of transfer.* The date of transfer is to be determined on the basis of the facts and circumstances of the particular situation. For transfers subject to the requirements of section 414(l) of the Code, the date determined in accordance with 26 CFR 1.414(l)-1(b)(11) will be considered the date of transfer.

(2) *Distributions of lump sums and annuities.* For purposes of paragraph (a) of this section, the payment of a lump sum, or purchase of an irrevocable commitment to provide an annuity, in satisfaction of benefit liabilities is not a transfer of benefit liabilities.

(c) *Waivers.*

(1) *Current-year small plan.* Notice under this section is waived if the plan had fewer than 100 participants for whom flat-rate premiums were payable for the plan year preceding the event year.

(2) *Financial soundness.* Notice under this section is waived if, for both the transferor plan (if it survives the transfer) and the transferee plan —

(i) For each contributing sponsor of the plan, either the sponsor or the sponsor's highest level controlled group parent that is a U.S. entity is financially sound when the transfer occurs, or

(ii) The plan is financially sound for the plan year in which the transfer occurs.

§ 4043.33 Application for minimum funding waiver.

A reportable event for a plan occurs when an application for a minimum funding waiver for the plan is submitted under section 302(c) of ERISA or section 412(c) of the Code.

§ 4043.34 Loan default.

(a) *Reportable event.* A reportable event occurs for a plan when, with respect to a loan with an outstanding balance of $10 million or more to a member of the plan's controlled group —

(1) There is an acceleration of payment or a default under the loan agreement, or

(2) The lender waives or agrees to an amendment of any covenant in the loan agreement for the purpose of avoiding a default.

(b) *Notice date.* The notice date is 30 days after the person required to report knows or has reason to know of an acceleration or default under paragraph (a)(1) of this section, without regard to the time of any other conditions required for the acceleration or default to be reportable.

(c) *Waivers.*

(1) De minimis *10-percent segment.* Notice under this section is waived if the debtor is not a contributing sponsor of the plan and represents a *de minimis* 10-percent segment of the plan's controlled group for the most recent fiscal year(s) ending on or before the date the reportable event occurs.

(2) *Foreign entity.* Notice under this section is waived if the debtor is a foreign entity other than a foreign parent.

§ 4043.35 Insolvency or similar settlement.

(a) *Reportable event.* A reportable event occurs for a plan when any member of the plan's controlled group —

(1) Commences or has commenced against it any insolvency proceeding (including, but not limited to, the appointment of a receiver) other than a bankruptcy case under the Bankruptcy Code;

(2) Commences, or has commenced against it, a proceeding to effect a composition, extension, or settlement with creditors;

(3) Executes a general assignment for the benefit of creditors; or

(4) Undertakes to effect any other nonjudicial composition, extension, or settlement with substantially all its creditors.

(b) *Waivers.*

(1) De minimis *10-percent segment.* Notice under this section is waived if the person described in paragraph (a) of this section is not a contributing sponsor of the plan and represents a *de minimis* 10-percent segment of the plan's controlled group for the most recent fiscal year(s) ending on or before the date the reportable event occurs.

(2) *Foreign entity.* Notice under this section is waived if the person described in paragraph (a) of this section is a foreign entity other than a foreign parent.

Subpart C — Advance Notice of Reportable Events

§ 4043.61 Advance reporting filing obligation.

(a) *In general.* Unless a waiver or extension applies with respect to the plan, each contributing sponsor of a plan is required to notify PBGC no later than 30 days before the effective date of a reportable event described in this subpart C if the contributing sponsor is subject to advance reporting for the reportable event. If there is a change in contributing sponsor, the reporting obligation applies to the person who is the contributing sponsor of the plan on the notice date.

(b) *Persons subject to advance reporting.* A contributing sponsor of a plan is subject to the advance reporting requirement under paragraph (a) of this section for a reportable event if —

(1) On the notice date, neither the contributing sponsor nor any member of the plan's controlled group to which the event relates is a person subject to the reporting requirements of section 13 or 15(d) of the Securities Exchange Act of 1934 or a subsidiary (as defined for purposes of the Securities Exchange Act of 1934) of a person subject to such reporting requirements; and

(2) The aggregate unfunded vested benefits, determined in accordance with paragraph (c) of this section, are more than $50 million; and

(3) The aggregate value of plan assets, determined in accordance with paragraph (c) of this section, is less than 90 percent of the aggregate premium funding target, determined in accordance with paragraph (c) of this section.

(c) *Funding determinations.* For purposes of paragraph (b) of this section, the aggregate unfunded vested benefits, aggregate value of plan assets, and aggregate premium funding target are determined by aggregating the unfunded vested benefits, values of plan assets, and premium funding targets (respectively), as determined for premium purposes in accordance with part 4006 of this chapter for the plan year preceding the effective date of the event, of plans maintained (on the notice date) by the contributing sponsor and any members of the contributing sponsor's controlled group, disregarding plans with no unfunded vested benefits (as so determined).

(d) *Shortening of 30-day period.* Pursuant to § 4043.3(d), PBGC may, upon review of an advance notice, shorten the notice period to allow for an earlier effective date.

§ 4043.62 Change in contributing sponsor or controlled group.

(a) *Reportable event.* Advance notice is required for a change in a plan's contributing sponsor or controlled group, as described in § 4043.29(a).

(b) *Waivers.*

(1) *Small and mid-size plans.* Notice under this section is waived with respect to a change of contributing sponsor if the transferred plan has fewer than 500 participants.

(2) *De minimis 5-percent segment.* Notice under this section is waived if the person or persons that will cease to be members of the plan's controlled group represent a *de minimis* 5-percent segment of the plan's old controlled group for the most recent fiscal year(s) ending on or before the effective date of the reportable event.

§ 4043.63 Liquidation.

(a) *Reportable event.* Advance notice is required for a liquidation of a member of a plan's controlled group, as described in § 4043.30.

(b) *Waiver — de minimis 5-percent segment and ongoing plans.* Notice under this section is waived if the person that liquidates is a *de minimis* 5-percent segment of the plan's controlled group for the most recent fiscal year(s) ending on or before the effective date of the reportable event, and each plan that was maintained by the liquidating member is maintained by another member of the plan's controlled group.

§ 4043.64 Extraordinary dividend or stock redemption.

(a) *Reportable event.* Advance notice is required for a distribution by a member of a plan's controlled group, as described in § 4043.31(a).

(b) *Waiver — de minimis 5-percent segment.* Notice under this section is waived if the person making the distribution is a *de minimis* 5-percent segment of the plan's controlled group for the most recent fiscal year(s) ending on or before the effective date of the reportable event.

§ 4043.65 Transfer of benefit liabilities.

(a) *Reportable event.* Advance notice is required for a transfer of benefit liabilities, as described in § 4043.32(a).

(b) *Waivers.*

(1) *Complete plan transfer.* Notice under this section is waived if the transfer is a transfer of all of the transferor plan's benefit liabilities and assets to one other plan.

(2) *Transfer of less than 3 percent of assets.* Notice under this section is waived if the value of the assets being transferred —

(i) Equals the present value of the accrued benefits (whether or not vested) being transferred, using actuarial assumptions that comply with section 414(*l*) of the Code; and

(ii) In conjunction with other assets transferred during the same plan year, is less than 3 percent of the assets of the transferor plan as of at least one day in that year.

(3) *Section 414(l) safe harbor.* Notice under this section is waived if the benefit liabilities of 500 or fewer participants are transferred and the transfer complies with section 414(*l*) of the Code using the actuarial assumptions prescribed for valuing benefits in trusteed plans under § 4044.51-57 of this chapter.

(4) *Fully funded plans.* Notice under this section is waived if the transfer complies with section 414(*l*) of the Code using reasonable actuarial assumptions and, after the transfer, the transferor and transferee plans are fully funded as determined in accordance with §§ 4044.51 through 4044.57 of this chapter (dealing with valuation of benefits and assets in trusteed terminating plans) and § 4010.8(d)(1)(ii) of this chapter.

§ 4043.66 Application for minimum funding waiver.

(a) *Reportable event.* Advance notice is required for an application for a minimum funding waiver, as described in § 4043.33.

(b) *Extension.* The notice date is extended until 10 days after the reportable event has occurred.

§ 4043.67 Loan default.

Advance notice is required for an acceleration of payment, a default, a waiver, or an agreement to an amendment with respect to a loan agreement described in § 4043.34(a).

§ 4043.68 Insolvency or similar settlement.

(a) *Reportable event.* Advance notice is required for an insolvency or similar settlement, as described in § 4043.35.

(b) *Extension.* For a case or proceeding under § 4043.35(a)(1) or (2) that is not commenced by a member of the plan's controlled group, the notice date is extended to 10 days after the commencement of the case or proceeding.

Subpart D — Notice of Failure to Make Required Contributions

§ 4043.81 PBGC Form 200, notice of failure to make required contributions; supplementary information.

(a) *General rules.* To comply with the notification requirement in section 303(k)(4) of ERISA and section 430(k)(4) of the Code, a contributing sponsor of a single-employer plan that is covered under section 4021 of ERISA and, if that contributing sponsor is a member of a parent-subsidiary controlled group, the ultimate parent must complete and submit in accordance with this section a properly certified Form 200 that includes all required documentation and other information, as described in the related filing instructions. Notice is required whenever the unpaid balance of a contribution payment required under sections 302 and 303 of ERISA and sections 412 and 430 of the Code (including interest), when added to the aggregate unpaid balance of all preceding such payments for which payment was not made when due (including interest), exceeds $1 million.

(1) Form 200 must be filed with PBGC no later than 10 days after the due date for any required payment for which payment was not made when due.

(2) If a contributing sponsor or the ultimate parent completes and submits Form 200 in accordance with this section, PBGC will consider the notification requirement in section 303(k)(4) of ERISA and section 430(k)(4) of the Code to be satisfied by all members of a controlled group of which the person who has filed Form 200 is a member.

(b) *Supplementary information.* If, upon review of a Form 200, PBGC concludes that it needs additional information in order to make decisions regarding enforcement of a lien imposed by section 303(k) of ERISA and section 430(k) of the Code, PBGC may require any member of the contributing sponsor's controlled group to supplement the Form 200 in accordance with § 4043.3(d).

(c) *Ultimate parent.* For purposes of this section, the term "ultimate parent" means the parent at the highest level in the chain of corporations and/or other organizations constituting a parent-subsidiary controlled group.

PART 4204 — VARIANCES FOR SALE OF ASSETS

■ 7. The authority citation for part 4204 continues to read as follows:

Authority: 29 U.S.C. 1302(b)(3), 1384(c).

■ 8. Section 4204.12 is amended by removing the figures "412(b)(3)(A)" and adding in their place the figures "431(b)(3)(A)".

PART 4206 — ADJUSTMENT OF LIABILITY FOR A WITHDRAWAL SUBSEQUENT TO A PARTIAL WITHDRAWAL

■ 9. The authority citation for part 4206 continues to read as follows:

Authority: 29 U.S.C. 1302(b)(3) and 1386(b).

■ 10. Section 4206.7 is amended by removing the figures "412(b)(4)" and adding in their place the figures "431(b)(5)".

PART 4231 — MERGERS AND TRANSFERS BETWEEN MULTIEMPLOYER PLANS

■ 11. The authority citation for part 4231 continues to read as follows:

Authority: 29 U.S.C. 1302(b)(3), 1411.

■ 12. In § 4231.2, the definitions of "actuarial valuation" and "fair market value of assets" are amended by removing the words "section

302 of ERISA and section 412 of the Code" where they appear in each definition and adding in their place the words "section 304 of ERISA and section 431 of the Code".

■ 13. In § 4231.6:

a. Paragraph (b)(4)(ii) is amended by removing the figures "412(b)(4)" and adding in their place the figures "431(b)(5)".

b. Paragraph (c)(2) is amended by removing the words "section 412 of the Code (which requires that such assumptions be reasonable in the aggregate)" and adding in their place the words "section 431 of the Code (which requires that each such assumption be reasonable)".

c. Paragraph (c)(5) is amended by removing the figures "412" and adding in their place the figures "431".

Issued in Washington, D.C., this _25 __ day of _March _____, 2013.

Joshua Gotbaum

Director

Pension Benefit Guaranty Corporation

[FR Doc. 2013-07664 Filed 04/02/2013 at 8:45 am; Publication Date: 04/03/2013]

¶ 20,538L

Employee Benefits Security Administration (EBSA): Advance notice of proposed rulemaking: Pension benefit statement: Lifetime income stream.—The Employee Benefits Security Administration (EBSA) has issued an advance notice of proposed rulemaking describing guidance under consideration that would require a participant's accrued benefits to be expressed on the pension benefit statement as estimated lifetime stream of benefits in addition to being presented as an account balance. The advance notice serves as a request for comments on specific language and concepts in advance of the issuance of proposed regulations.

The advance notice of proposed rulemaking, which was published in the Federal Register on May 8, 2013 (78 FR 26727), is reproduced below.

Note: The comment period on the advance notice of proposed rulemaking was extended from July 8, 2013 to August 7, 2013 (78 FR 42027, July 15, 2013).

DEPARTMENT OF LABOR

Employee Benefits Security Administration

29 CFR Part 2520

RIN 1210-AB20

Pension Benefit Statements

AGENCY: Employee Benefits Security Administration, Department of Labor.

ACTION: Advance notice of proposed rulemaking.

SUMMARY: The Department of Labor (Department) is developing proposed regulations regarding the pension benefit statement requirements under section 105 of the Employee Retirement Income Security Act of 1974, as amended (ERISA). This advance notice of proposed rulemaking (ANPRM) describes certain rules the Department is considering as part of the proposed regulations. The rules being considered are limited to the pension benefit statements required of defined contribution plans. First, the Department is considering a rule that would require a participant's accrued benefits to be expressed on his pension benefit statement as an estimated lifetime stream of payments, in addition to being presented as an account balance. Second, the Department also is considering a rule that would require a participant's accrued benefits to be projected to his retirement date and then converted to and expressed as an estimated lifetime stream of payments. This ANPRM serves as a request for comments on specific language and concepts in advance of proposed regulations. The Department intends to consider all reasonable alternatives to direct regulation, including whether there is a way short of a regulatory mandate that will ensure that participants and beneficiaries get constructive and helpful lifetime income illustrations.

DATES: Comments are due on or before [Insert date that is 60 days after publication in the Federal Register].

ADDRESSES: You may submit comments, identified by RIN 1210-AB20, by one of the following methods:

- *Federal eRulemaking Portal: http://www.regulations.gov.* Follow the instructions for submitting comments.

- *E-mail: e-ORI@dol.gov.* Include RIN 1210-AB20 in the subject line of the message.

- *Mail*: Office of Regulations and Interpretations, Employee Benefits Security Administration, Room N-5655, U.S. Department of Labor, 200 Constitution Avenue, NW, Washington, DC 20210, Attention: Pension Benefit Statements Project.

Instructions: All submissions received must include the agency name and Regulation Identifier Number (RIN) for this rulemaking. Comments received will be posted without change to *http://www.regulations.gov* and *http://www.dol.gov/ebsa,* and made available for public inspection at the Public Disclosure Room, N-1513, Employee Benefits Security Administration, 200 Constitution Avenue, NW, Washington, DC 20210, including any personal information provided. Persons submitting comments electronically are encouraged not to submit paper copies.

FOR FURTHER INFORMATION CONTACT: Suzanne Adelman or Tom Hindmarch at (202) 693-8500. This is not a toll free number.

SUPPLEMENTARY INFORMATION:

This ANPRM has two main sections followed by Appendix A. The first section, entitled "Background," contains the relevant statutory language on which the Department is basing the ANPRM and a discussion of the Department's general policy concern underlying the ANPRM. The second section, entitled "Overview of Intended Regulations," presents questions, ideas, and potential language on certain rules the Department is considering as part of proposed regulations under section 105 of ERISA. Each of these sections has multiple subsections. Appendix A contains an example that demonstrates how to calculate a lifetime income illustration, using the regulatory framework in this ANPRM, for a hypothetical male participant, age forty-five, who has a spouse. In conjunction with the publication of this ANPRM, the Department also has made available on its website an interactive calculator that calculates lifetime income streams in accordance with such regulatory framework. This calculator is at *www.dol.gov/ebsa/regs/lifetimeincomecalculator.html.*

I. Background

A. Section 105 of ERISA

Section 105(a) of ERISA, as amended by section 508 of the Pension Protection Act of 2006 (Pub. L. 109-280), requires administrators of defined contribution plans to provide periodic pension benefit statements to participants and certain beneficiaries. 29 U.S.C. 1025(a). Benefit statements must be provided at least annually. If the plan permits participants and beneficiaries to direct their own investments, however, benefit statements must be provided at least quarterly. Section 105(a)(2) of ERISA contains the content requirements for benefit statements. Section 105(a)(2)(A)(i)(I) requires a benefit statement to indicate the participant's or beneficiary's "total benefits accrued." The proposed rules being considered by the Department are pursuant to this section of ERISA, as well as ERISA section 505. Section 505, in relevant part, provides that the Secretary may prescribe such regulations as the Secretary finds necessary or appropriate to carry out the provisions of title I of ERISA. 29 U.S.C. 1135. Collectively, these provisions provide the authority on which the Department is considering a rule that would require a participant's "total benefits accrued" to be expressed as an estimated lifetime income stream of payments, in addition to being presented as an account balance.

B. General Policy Concern Being Addressed by this ANPRM

Workers today face greater responsibility for managing their assets for retirement, both while employed and during their retirement years. This greater responsibility is primarily a result of the trend away from defined benefit plans, where a worker's retirement benefit is typically a specified monthly payment for life, and toward defined contribution plans, where typically contribution, asset allocation, and drawdown decisions are assigned to the participant.[1] Managing finances in order to provide income for life for oneself and one's spouse is a tremendously difficult but important task. The rule under consideration by the Department would provide participants with information that the Department believes will ease the burden of this task.

Research suggests that people want to continue their current lifestyle after they retire and are concerned about having adequate precautionary savings for emergencies or illness.[2] Individuals may not understand, however, what savings, asset allocation, and drawdown decisions are necessary to achieve both of these goals. In particular, participants may have difficulty envisioning the lifetime monthly income that can be generated from an account balance.

In a comment letter to the Department, a national non-profit trade association of investment managers, consultants, recordkeepers, insurance companies, plan sponsors and others stated that "[t]ranslating the amount saved into a future income estimate will serve to remind participants that their DC plan accumulations are needed to generate income throughout retirement. Additionally, when they see that $100,000 may only generate $700 of monthly income for life, the participant may be incented to save more aggressively."[3] The Department believes that expressing a participant's current and projected account balances as lifetime income streams would allow participants to make more informed retirement planning decisions. Recent research supports the hypothesis that providing participants with customized information on the decumulation phase can influence contribution behavior.[4]

In view of the importance of this issue, the Department and the Department of the Treasury, on February 2, 2010, published a request for information, entitled "Request for Information Regarding Lifetime Income Options for Participants and Beneficiaries in Retirement Plans" (RFI). See 75 FR 5253. As stated in the summary to the RFI, the Departments are reviewing the rules under ERISA and the plan qualification rules under the Internal Revenue Code of 1986 (Code) to determine whether, and, if so, how, the Departments could or should enhance, by regulation or otherwise, the retirement security of participants in employersponsored retirement plans and in individual retirement arrangements (IRAs) by facilitating access to, and use of, lifetime income or other arrangements designed to provide a lifetime stream of income after retirement. The RFI contained 39 questions on a wide array of subjects. The Department received in excess of 700 comments in response to the RFI. The Departments subsequently held a joint hearing on lifetime income options for retirement plans on September 14 and 15, 2010, in order to further consider several specific issues. Comments received in response to the RFI, written hearing testimony submitted to the Department, and the Department's official hearing transcripts are available on the Department's Web Site at www.dol.gov/ebsa/regs/cmt-1210-AB33.html.

The RFI contained a section entitled "Disclosing the Income Stream That Can Be Provided From an Account Balance." Within this section, the RFI contained the following questions relevant to this ANPRM:

21. Should an individual benefit statement present the participant's accrued benefits as a lifetime income stream of payments in addition to presenting the benefits as an account balance?

22. If the answer to question 21 is yes, how should a lifetime stream of income payments be expressed on the benefit statement? For example, should payments be expressed as if they are to begin immediately or at specified retirement age? Should benefit amounts be projected to a future retirement age based on the assumption of continued contributions? Should lifetime income payments be expressed in the form of monthly or annual payments? Should lifetime income payments of a married participant be expressed as a single-

life annuity payable to the participant or a joint and survivor-type annuity, or both?

23. If the answer to question 21 is yes, what actuarial or other assumptions (e.g., mortality, interest, etc.) would be needed in order to state accrued benefits as a lifetime stream of payments? If benefit payments are to commence at some date in the future, what interest rates (e.g., deferred insurance annuity rates) and other assumptions should be applied? Should an expense load be reflected? Are there any authoritative tools or sources (online or otherwise) that plans should or could use for conversion purposes, or would the plan need to hire an actuary? Should caveats be required so that participants understand that lifetime income payments are merely estimates for illustrative purposes? Should the assumptions underlying the presentation of accrued benefits as a lifetime income stream of payments be disclosed to participants? Should the assumptions used to convert accounts into a lifetime stream of income payments be dictated by regulation, or should the Department issue assumptions that plan sponsors could rely upon as safe harbors?

After reviewing the responses to these questions, the Department agrees with those commenters who see a need to change the perception of retirement savings from simply a savings account to a vehicle for income replacement during retirement. Showing a participant the monthly retirement income he or she will receive from his or her retirement plan may help change that perception and, perhaps as suggested by many commenters, motivate workers to increase their savings.[5] We also understand from the commenters that, due to the broadening recognition of the importance of improving participants' retirement preparedness, a growing number of plans already provide a lifetime income illustration and often provide access to other lifetime income planning tools or retirement calculators.

Therefore, as part of the proposed regulations under section 105 of ERISA, the Department is considering the following ideas:

- A participant or beneficiary's pension benefit statement would contain that individual's current account balance. In addition, the current account balance would be converted to an estimated lifetime income stream of payments. The conversion illustration would assume the participant or beneficiary had reached normal retirement age under the plan as of the date of the benefit statement, even if he or she is much younger.

- For participants who have not yet reached normal retirement age, the pension benefit statement would show the projected account balance, as well as the lifetime income stream generated by it. A participant or beneficiary's current account balance would be projected to normal retirement age, based on assumed future contribution amounts and investment returns. The projected account balance would be converted to an estimated lifetime income stream of payments, assuming that the person retires at normal retirement age.

- Both lifetime income streams (*i.e.*, the one based on the current account balance and the one based on the projected account balance) would be presented as estimated monthly payments based on the expected mortality of the participant or beneficiary.[6] In addition, if the participant or beneficiary has a spouse, the lifetime income streams would be presented based on the joint lives of the participant or beneficiary and his or her spouse.

- Pension benefit statements would contain an understandable explanation of the assumptions behind the lifetime income stream illustrations. In addition, pension benefit statements would contain a statement that projections and lifetime income stream illustrations are estimates and not guarantees.

---

[1] The number of private defined benefit plans has fallen from just over 103,000 in 1975 to fewer than 48,000 in 2009 (a drop of over 50 percent in the last 34 years). The number of private defined contribution plans has grown from just over 207,000 in 1975 to almost 660,000 in 2009 (an increase of over 200 percent for the same time period). See Employee Benefits Security Administration, U.S. Department of Labor, *Private Pension Plan Bulletin Historical Tables and Graphs* (Mar. 2012), Table E1: Number of Pension Plans by type of Plan, 1975-2009, at http://www.dol.gov/ebsa/pdf/historicaltables.pdf.

[2] Some individuals may also want to leave bequests to their children and other heirs; however, the bequest motive may be less salient in retirement savings and spending decisions than other priorities. See Jonathan Skinner and Stephen P. Zeldes, *The Importance of Bequests and Life-Cycle Saving in Capital Accumulation: A New Answer*, American Economic Review 92(2): 274- 279 (May 2002) and Jeffrey R. Brown, Jeffrey R. Kling, Sendhil Mullainathan and Marian V. Wrobel, *Why Don't People Insure Late Life Consumption? A Framing Explanation of the Under-Annuitization Puzzle*, American Economic Review 98(2): 304-309 (May 2008).

[3] See comment no. 656 in response to the Department's Request for Information Regarding Lifetime Income Options for Participants and Beneficiaries in Retirement Plans.

Comments are available on the Department's Web Site at www.dol.gov/ebsa/regs/cmt-1210-AB33.html.

[4] See Goda, Gopi Shah, Colleen Flaherty Manchester, and Aaron Sojourner, "What Will My Account Really Be Worth? An Experiment on Exponential Growth Bias and Retirement Saving," NBER Working Paper 17927, March 2012. See also ACLI Retirement Choices Study, Greenwald & Associates, April 2010 (Study revealed that 60 percent of respondents say that if the illustration of the participants' lifetime income generated by their retirement plan account would not be enough to meet their retirement needs, they would "start saving more immediately.")

[5] Research also suggests that a small change in information presented on the benefit statement can have a significant impact on savings behavior. See Gopi Shah Goda, Colleen Flaherty Manchester, and Aaron Sojourner, *What Will My Account Really Be Worth? An Experiment on Exponential Growth Bias and Retirement Saving,* NBER Working Paper No. 17927 (March 2012) at http://www.nber.org/papers/w17927.

[6] The term "expected mortality" here refers to the probabilities in a mortality table, as opposed to life expectancy which is a single number that can be calculated from those probabilities.

The Department anticipates that if pension benefit statements were to have these key features, participants and beneficiaries might be in a better position to assess their retirement readiness and to prepare for their retirement.[7] An illustration based on a person's current account balance will provide an immediate baseline to judge their present retirement readiness, i.e., "If I were old enough to retire today, this would be my monthly payment for life." An illustration based on a projected account balance will show, not what the participant has saved to date, but what he or she might realistically expect to have at retirement, i.e., "In twenty years, this could be my monthly payment for life at my current savings rate."

II. Overview of Intended Regulations

This Overview section of the ANPRM presents questions, ideas, and potential language on certain rules the Department is considering as part of proposed regulations under section 105 of ERISA. The goal is to provide an early opportunity for interested stakeholders to provide advice and input into the policy development of future proposed regulations. This Overview section contains multiple subsections pertaining to the major issues raised in response to the RFI. This Overview section is followed by a regulatory framework and Appendix A. Appendix A provides an example of how to use the assumptions in the ANPRM's regulatory framework to calculate a projected account balance and convert the current and projected account balances into lifetime income streams.

A. Current and Projected Account Balances

Among those responding to the RFI, there are competing views as to whether a lifetime income illustration should be based on a participant's or beneficiary's current account balance or a projected account balance. While many commenters believe it is better to provide an illustration based on a current account balance, approximately the same number of commenters believes it is better to provide an illustration based on a projected account balance. A few commenters support both approaches.

Commenters who support using a participant's current account balance generally believe it is better and more helpful to base an illustration on what the participant *actually* has than on what the participant *may* have at some point in the future. They make the following observations. First, participants and beneficiaries will more readily understand illustrations based on actuality than on illustrations based on projections. Second, and related, a person is more likely to take some planning action if he understands the illustration. Third, because projections necessarily will be based on a number of assumptions (e.g., future contributions and future investment returns), such projections are mere guesses and therefore likely to be flawed. Fourth, because lifetime income illustrations are educational in nature, a static number at a point in time should be sufficient to meet that educational purpose. Fifth, illustrations based on current account balances may motivate participants and beneficiaries to save more if the monthly payments are small.

By contrast, those who support the use of projected account balances believe that an illustration based on a projection is actually more relevant and meaningful to a participant than an illustration based on that participant's current account balance, notwithstanding the inherent uncertainty in projecting an account balance. They make the following observations. First, at present it is common practice among financial planners to use projections when providing their clients with financial planning advice. Accordingly, if the Department's goal is to have

pension benefit statements serve as a useful planning tool, then illustrations on benefit statements similarly should be based on projections. Second, projections may be based on assumptions, but not all assumptions are inherently flawed. Several commenters believe that the Department can establish reasonable parameters for assumptions, in order to avoid deception or abuse and increase the accuracy of projections. Third, there is no evidence that participants and beneficiaries necessarily will fail to comprehend a lifetime income illustration, or a projection, merely because it is based on assumptions, particularly where there are sufficient disclosures of the assumptions underlying the projections. Fourth, showing participants and beneficiaries the power of compound earnings may be a significant motivator to increase savings rates. Fifth, an illustration based on current account size simply has no relevance to a participant with decades to retirement age; and, in fact, such incomplete information may very well have the unintended consequence of discouraging savings and participation. Sixth, illustrations based on current balances may be considered flawed because account balances constantly change and, indeed, may change dramatically depending on market fluctuations.

The Department acknowledges the potential merit in both approaches. An illustration based on a participant's or beneficiary's current account balance could serve as an immediate benchmark for that participant because it would show the size of the monthly payment to expect if there were no further savings, gains or losses between now and retirement. It, in effect, shows participants and beneficiaries what they actually have, now, in the form of monthly payments. Although this type of benchmark is simplistic, the commenters may be right that it could motivate participants and beneficiaries to increase their savings rates now, especially if the participant or beneficiary perceives the monthly payment to be small relative to his or her current income needs. An illustration based on a participant or beneficiary's projected account balance, on the other hand, ordinarily will reflect larger monthly payments. The Department also agrees with those commenters who believe this methodology of framing benefits (i.e., showing larger monthly payments than those based on a current account balance) may sufficiently motivate participants and beneficiaries to stay the course or even to increase their savings rates in order to increase their monthly amounts. Although the addition of necessary assumptions under this approach may create some additional uncertainty, this uncertainty can be mitigated somewhat by requiring that only reasonable assumptions be used in the calculations and appropriate cautions be included in the disclosure to participants and beneficiaries.

Accordingly, the Department is considering a proposal that generally would require pension benefit statements for all defined contribution plans to include the following information: (1) the value of the account balance as of the last day of the period covered by the statement (i.e., "current balance"), (2) a projected account balance, and (3) two lifetime income illustrations. The first lifetime illustration would be based on the participant's or beneficiary's current account balance, *i.e.*, the "fair market value of the account balance as of the last day of the period covered by the statement." See ANPRM § 2520.105-1(c)(2)(v). The second lifetime income illustration would be based on a participant's or beneficiary's projected account balance, i.e., "the current dollar value of the projected balance at normal retirement age." See ANPRM § 2520.105(c)(2)(vi). To avoid confusion and unnecessary complication, the second illustration would not be required on any pension benefit statement on behalf of a participant who has reached normal retirement age under the plan as of the date of the benefit statement.

The presentation of this data on a participant's or beneficiary's benefit statement might look something like this:

Current Balance $125,000	Projected Balance $557,534
Monthly Payment $625	Monthly Payment $2,788

This shows both total balances (current and projected) and the monthly payments generated by each. The projected balance ($557,534) and related monthly payment ($2,788) would be discounted by an inflation factor in order to be shown in today's dollars. The reasoning behind this is that by removing inflation from the equation it will be easier for participants and beneficiaries to budget for their retirement years, today. For example, they can compare their projected monthly payments expressed in today's dollars with their current budget needs (i.e., current consumption needs) and see how close they are to covering those needs. If there is an undesirable gap, they might

increase their contributions. The Department invites comments on whether the projected balance and related monthly payment should be discounted for inflation. Many commenters on the RFI believe that projections should be presented in today's dollars in order to put future buying power into a meaningful context.

Many of the sample benefit statements reviewed by the Department show only the projected monthly payment expressed in today's dollars (the $2,788 figure in the example above), and not the discounted projected account balance (the $557,534 figure in the example above).

---

[7] 7 Lena Larsson, Annika Sundén, & Ole Settergren, *Pension Information: The Annual Statement at a Glance*, OECD Journal: General Papers, February 19, 2008 available at: http://www.oecd.org/dataoecd/38/42/44509412.pdf.

The Department welcomes comments on whether it makes more sense to show both the discounted projected account balance ($557,534) and the resulting monthly payments ($2,788), or whether it is enough to show only the resulting monthly payments ($2,788).

All projections and lifetime income illustrations under consideration would be based on the participant's "normal retirement age under the plan." See ANPRM § 2520.105-1(c)(2)(vi), (d)(1), (d)(2)(i) and (e)(4). Section 3(24) defines this as "the earlier of—(A) the time a plan participant attains normal retirement age under the plan, or (B) the later of—(i) the time a plan participant attains age 65, or (ii) the 5th anniversary of the time a plan participant commenced participation in the plan." The Department is considering this date because it already is a significant date for ERISA purposes. However, this date could be a number of years before the participant or beneficiary is actually ready or able to retire from the workforce. A number of commenters suggested using the social security retirement age. Accordingly, the Department specifically welcomes comments on whether the projection and lifetime income illustrations should use a date other than the normal retirement age, as defined in section 3(24) of ERISA, and if so what date and why. For example, comments could address the appropriateness of using age 65, social security retirement age (e.g., currently age 66 or 67 depending upon the participant's birthdate), the minimum required distribution date (e.g., age 71) or some other age.

The mechanics involved in projecting an account balance are discussed below in Section II.B of this document, entitled "Methodology for Projecting an Account Balance." The mechanics involved in converting account balances into lifetime income streams are discussed in Section II.C of this document, entitled "Methodology for Converting an Account Balance into a Lifetime Income Stream."

B. Methodology for Projecting an Account Balance

As explained above, the Department is considering a proposed rule that would require a participant's or beneficiary's current account balance to be projected to his or her normal retirement age under the plan. This section of the ANPRM describes the standards, rules and assumptions being contemplated that plan administrators would have to follow when projecting participant and beneficiary account balances to retirement. In developing these standards, rules and assumptions, the Department believes it is important that: (1) projections be meaningful to participants and beneficiaries, (2) projections not be overly burdensome for plan administrators to perform, and (3) any regulatory framework does not disturb current projection and illustration best practices or stifle innovation in this area.

Based on the RFI comments and the public hearing record, the Department understands the act of calculating a participant's projected account balance ordinarily would require consideration of the following five variables: (1) the participant's current account balance; (2) the number of years until the participant retires; (3) future contributions to the account (both employer and employee); (4) a rate of investment return; and (5) an inflation adjustment to convert the projected amount to today's dollars. The Department specifically requests comments on whether these are the appropriate variables that should be factored into the projections being considered by the Department. If not, why not, and are there other essential variables?

As explained in more detail below, the Department is considering a "reasonableness" standard as a general rule combined with a regulatory "safe harbor." The general rule would permit a broad array of projection "best practices" to continue (which practices we assume meet the "reasonableness" standard), while the safe harbor would offer certainty for those plan administrators who seek that result or who do not currently provide projections. Plan administrators who follow the deterministic conditions of the safe harbor would have the comfort of knowing they have satisfied the primary elements of the general rule (i.e., those elements of the general rule that otherwise would require

discretionary activity of the plan administrator). In this regard, the safe harbor would be an option and not a regulatory requirement.

The general rule being considered by the Department is that "projections shall be based on reasonable assumptions taking into account generally accepted investment theories." See ANPRM § 2520.105-1(d)(1). A projection will not be considered reasonable, however, "unless it is expressed in current dollars and takes into account future contributions and investment returns." Id. Thus, the general rule being considered by the Department does not require any single method or single set of assumptions for projecting an account balance to normal retirement age, although it does require overall reasonableness in light of generally accepted investment theories. Nor does the general rule limit the specific factors that must be considered, although it does require consideration of at least future contributions, investment returns, and inflation.[8]

By contrast, the safe harbor being considered by the Department is narrower and more prescriptive than the general rule under consideration. The contemplated safe harbor would prescribe a specific set of assumptions for contributions, returns, and inflation.[9] The set of assumptions, when used together, would be considered per se reasonable for purposes of the general rule. Thus, by using the safe harbor assumptions together, plan administrators will be deemed to be in compliance with the portion of the general rule that requires them to take into account contributions, returns, and inflation when projecting account balances.

The first assumption is that "contributions continue to normal retirement age at the current annual dollar amount, increased at a rate of three percent (3%) per year."[10] See ANPRM § 2520.105-1 (d)(2)(i). A yearly contribution increase is included in this safe harbor assumption because many workers' contribution elections are expressed as a percentage of wages, and wages tend to increase over a worker's career due to raises, promotions, cost-of-living adjustments, and other factors. The Department is considering a whole number percentage (3%) in order to avoid giving participants and beneficiaries the false impression that account balance projections are exact.

The Department considers a 3% per year increase in wages to be a conservative assumption, and intentionally chooses a conservative assumption in this instance due to the wide variation of wage movement across workers. Some workers, particularly young workers, can expect their wages to rise at a rate higher than 3% per year. However, older workers often see wages increase no faster than the rate of consumer price inflation.[11] The Department believes that more harm would be done by overestimating wage increases for workers whose wages will remain flat than would be done by underestimating wage increases for workers whose wages are likely to rise quickly. The Department welcomes comments on this topic.[12]

The second and third assumptions are investment returns of seven percent (7%) per year (nominal) and a discount rate of three percent (3%) per year for establishing the value of the projected account balance in today's dollars. See ANPRM § 2520.105-1(d)(2)(ii) and (d)(2)(iii). As with the wage increase assumption, the Department is considering whole number percentages (7% and 3%) in order to avoid giving participants and beneficiaries the false impression that account balance projections are exact.

The 3% discount rate is included in the safe harbor to account for consumer price inflation (specifically inflation in the prices of goods that retirees consume). The Department is considering 3% because it reflects both historical inflation and expectations for future inflation. Since 1913, inflation has averaged 3.2 % according to Consumer Price Index data from the Bureau of Labor Statistics. Furthermore, the trustees of the Social Security Trust Fund assume that cost of living adjustments (which are determined by the CPI-W) will average 2.8% between 2019 and 2086. Comments are specifically requested on these

---

[8] The general rule is intended to provide plan administrators with flexibility to preserve current best practices regarding benefit statements and not stifle the development and innovation of technological tools in this area. For example, the general rule would permit plans that have online tools that employ stochastic modeling, such as retirement calculators and similar planning devices, to use the same technology to project account balances on pension benefit statements, provided that the projection methodology meets the reasonableness requirement in the general rule. A stochastic model is a tool for estimating probability distributions of potential outcomes by allowing for random variation in one or more inputs over time usually based on observed historical data for the selected inputs. Probability distributions of potential outcomes are derived from a large number of simulations (stochastic projections) which reflect the random variation in the input(s). The Department specifically welcomes comments on whether the general rule sufficiently facilitates the use of stochastic modeling for pension benefit statements. The Department also welcomes comments on other modeling or projection methods that might be appropriate for benefit statements and whether the general rule facilitates their use.

[9] Two of the five variables (current balance and years to retirement) are information known to the plan at the time the benefit statement is generated and, therefore, the safe harbor would not include assumptions pertaining to those variables.

[10] The assumed dollar amount (not the contribution percentage) would increase by a rate of 3% per year. For example, if contributions for year one were $10,000, the projected contributions would be $10,300 (1.03 × $10,000) for year two, $10,609 (1.03 × 10,300) for year three, and so forth.

[11] There is a large body of literature on age-earnings profiles which shows that workers' wages tend to increase rapidly when young, but at a rate similar to inflation at older ages. See, for example, Murphy, Kevin M. and Finis Welch, "Empirical Age-Earnings Profiles," *Journal of Labor Economics*, Vol. 8, No. 2 (Apr. 1990), pp. 202-229.

[12] See below for a discussion of historical and projected consumer price inflation.

assumptions, taking into account the purpose for which these assumptions are being used.

Why a 7 Percent Rate of Investment Return Assumption?

The 7% safe harbor assumption under consideration is based on historical market returns, actual returns derived by participants in 401(k) plans, and future return forecasts. The 7% rate is a nominal rate of return, which corresponds to an approximate 4% real return assuming 3% inflation in the future.[13] Again a round number is being considered in order to avoid giving participants and beneficiaries the false impression that projected future account balances are exact. The following analysis led the Department to this rate.

From 1996 to 2009, the share of 401(k) assets in equities varied from 56% to 76%.[14] In 2009, this total was approximately 60%. If beginning in 1926, 60% of assets were invested in an equity portfolio that mirrored the S&P 500 and 40% were invested in a bond portfolio and the assets were rebalanced at the beginning of each year without cost to preserve the 60/40 allocation, an investor would have averaged a 5.6% real return through 2010.[15]

However, it is unlikely that average investors would replicate this rate of return and more likely would achieve a lower real rate of return due, in part, to fees and transaction costs. For example, an asset weighted account analysis performed by the Investment Company Institute (ICI) indicates that 401(k) plan expense ratios average approximately 65 basis points.[16] Therefore, expense ratios alone would reduce the average real return to approximately 5%.[17] Average real returns also are reduced by transaction costs, including costs derived from turnover by the fund managers. According to ICI, the average dollar weighted turnover rate of 401(k) mutual fund holders is 43 percent. These transaction costs are not included in expense ratios.[18]

Turnover that occurs due to participants' management of their accounts also reduces average real returns. Some of these transactions represent poor timing of the markets, leading to further underperformance relative to buy-and-hold strategies. Academic literature suggests that participants often mistime their investments by pulling their money out of equities before periods of strong growth and investing more heavily in equities just before a market downturn, with load funds experiencing even worse mistiming.[19]

The measured disparity between the average annual returns that costless buy-and-hold strategies would generate and actual participant returns is consistent with recent Department statistics. Where a dollar invested in a 60/40 balanced fund with no transaction costs would have generated an 8.4% nominal return between 1990-2009, Department of Labor Form 5500 data indicate that large defined contribution plans achieved a nominal return of only 7.1% during the same period.[20]

Moreover, past return information, such as U.S. equity returns between 1926 and 2010, does not provide a sufficient basis for estimating future reasonable expected returns.[21] This was illustrated when the Department solicited peer review comments from economists in 2006 on the application of its Pension Simulation Model to assess the impact of its Qualified Default Investment Alternatives rule (QDIA) on pension savings. The commenters maintained that expected future U.S. equity returns are lower today than historic returns and will remain lower in the future. Based on these comments, the Department revised its initial real equity return assumption used to project future pension savings to approximately 4.9%.[22] Industry groups have reached similar conclusions. For example, as a follow up to a 1997 survey, a 2007 survey asked 400 finance professors to forecast what equity returns would be over the next 30 years; and the estimates were, on average, more than one percent below the 1997 results.[23]

For the reasons discussed above, which take into account historical market returns, actual returns derived by 401(k) plan participants, and future return forecasts, the Department believes that a 7% nominal return assumption (approximately 4% real return and 3% future inflation) is a reasonable rate of return assumption for plan administrators to use when calculating a future account balance at normal retirement age. However, the Department specifically is requesting comments on the appropriateness of this 7% investment return assumption.[24] Are there other valid approaches or data sources EBSA should consider in constructing a prospective safe harbor? Commenters are encouraged to keep in mind the Department's stated objectives (above) behind a projection requirement. Commenters not in favor of this safe harbor assumption are encouraged to provide empirical data supportive of alternative approaches.

Projections and Rules of the Financial Industry Regulatory Authority

National Association of Securities Dealers (NASD) Rule 2210(d)(1)(D), in relevant part, provides that "[c]ommunications with the public may not predict or project performance, imply that past performance will recur or make any exaggerated or unwarranted claim, opinion or forecast."[25] In response to questions regarding the relationship, if any, between the projection requirement under consideration by the Department and NASD Rule 2210(d)(1)(D) of the Financial Industry Regulatory Authority (FINRA), the Department and FINRA staff intend to work together and, if necessary, provide guidance, which may be similar to the guidance provided in connection with the Department's recently finalized participant-level fee disclosure regulation under 29 CFR 2550.404a-5.[26] The Department, therefore, is requesting comments on whether, and to what extent, such guidance is needed and why.

---

[13] To be exact, it would correspond with 3.88% real returns.

[14] These estimates are based on Employee Benefit Research Institute/Investment Company Institute 401(k) plans surveys.

[15] Returns are based on Ibbotson data. The calculations were performed with the bond share of the portfolio being held either all in long-term corporate bonds (40 percent of total funds) or half in intermediate government bonds (20 percent of total funds) and half in long-term corporate bonds (20 percent of the total funds). The relative share made little difference. However, including riskier equities in the portfolio does matter. If 30% of assets were in small cap funds, 30% in an equity portfolio mirroring the S&P 500, and 40% in bonds, the returns would be approximately 1% larger.

[16] Sarah Holden, Michael Halladay, and Shaun Lutz, *The Economics of Providing 401(k) Plans: Services, Fees, and Expenses, 2010,* ICI Research Perspective, Vol. 17, No. 4 (June 2011).

[17] Returns are calculated as a geometric return $g=[(1+r1)(1+r2)\ldots(1+rn)](1/n)$ where rn=returns in the nth year.

[18] Holden, *supra* at footnote 16.

[19] Geoffrey C. Friesen and Travis Sapp, *Mutual Fund Flows and Investor Returns: An Empirical Examination of Fund Investor Timing Ability,* 31 Journal of Banking and Finance, 2796 (2007) available at SSRN: *http://ssrn.com/abstract=957728.* According to the article, the underperformance of investors due to poor timing is over 1.5% compared to what buy-and-hold strategies would have generated. The performance gap with buy and hold strategies due to poor investor timing is twice as large for load funds compared to non-load funds.

[20] The 8.4% returns are based upon Ibbotson data. The hypothetical fund would have 60 percent stocks, 20 percent long term corporate bonds and 20 percent intermediate government bonds. The portfolio would be rebalanced each year at no cost. S *ee* U.S. Department of Labor, Employee Benefits Security Administration, Private Pension Plan Bulletin Historical Tables and Graphs: 1975-2009, Table E21 (March 2012) at http://www.dol.gov/ebsa/publications/form5500dataresearch.html#statisticalsummaries.

[21] Ibbotson data begins in 1926.

[22] *See* http://www.dol.gov/ebsa/regs/peerreview.html#section1. These peer review comments were submitted to help inform the Department's Pension Simulation model that is used to forecast savings outlook for participants. Under the model, a portfolio consisting of 60% equity and 40% long-term government bonds would generate an approximate 7% nominal return.

[23] *See* Ivo Welch, *Views of Financial Economists on the Equity Premium and on Professional Controversies* 73 Journal of Business 501 (2000). *See also* Ivo Welch, *The Consensus Estimate for the Equity Premium by Academic Financial Economists in December 2008,* Social Sciences Research Network Paper No. 1084918, January 18, 2008 (last revised July 22, 2009) at http://ssrn.com/abstract=1084918.

[24] In this regard, one idea the Department intends to explore further is the behavioral effects of this assumption and whether the assumption should be more conservative. As explained in the text above, the 7% expected future investment returns is an average. As such, it is neutral, meaning that individual participants may realize higher or lower returns. In 2010, over 22% of 401(k) participants had fewer than 40% of their 401(k) assets invested in equity, while 40% had over 80% of assets in equity. See Jack Van Derhei, Sarah Holden, Luis Alonso, and Steven Bass, *401(k) Plan Asset Allocation, Account Balances, and Loan Activity in 2010,* EBRI Issue Brief No. 366 (December 2011), Figure 30 at p. 29. Thus, a safe harbor assumption that is aimed at the average 401(k) participant would be out of line with the asset allocation of a majority of 401(k) participants. Participants with conservative asset allocations who, in fact, consistently generate returns lower than the 7% neutral rate assumption will see their projected balance decreasing year after year (even though contributions remain stable). What impact will a declining projected balance have on these participants? At least some literature suggests people dislike declining sequences. See George F. Loewenstein and Drazen Prelec, *Preferences for Sequences of Outcomes,* 100 Psychological Review 91 (1993). Would a more conservative safe harbor assumption (e.g., risk-free return rate, which typically averages about 5% nominal (2% real) returns) have a more positive long-term effect than a neutral assumption on how participants and beneficiaries would view the lifetime income stream illustration and ultimately use it to aid their retirement planning?

[25] In March 2012, the SEC approved new FINRA rules governing communications with the public that will replace NASD Rule 2210. Under the new rules, which took effect in February 2013, a modified version of this provision will be found in FINRA Rule 2210(d)(1)(F). *See* FINRA Regulatory Notice 12-29 (June 2012) (announcing SEC approval of new FINRA communications rules).

[26] *See* FINRA Regulatory Notice 12-02 (January 2012) (providing guidance on application of communications rules to disclosures required by 29 CFR 2550.404a-5). *See also* SEC Staff No Action Letter (October 26, 2011) (agreeing to treat information provided by a plan administrator to participants required by and complying with disclosure requirements of section 404 of ERISA as if it were a communication that satisfies requirements of Rule 482 under the Securities Act of 1933).

C. Methodology for Converting an Account Balance into a Lifetime Income Stream

As explained above, in addition to a participant's or beneficiary's current and projected account balance, the Department is considering a requirement that each balance be expressed as a lifetime stream of income. Thus, each benefit statement ordinarily would contain two monthly estimated payment illustrations, one based on the current balance and a second based on a projected account balance.[27]

The commenters on the RFI identified two methods to convert an account balance to a stream of income in retirement. The first method was described as a "draw down" or "systematic withdrawal" approach. This method assumes the participant will withdraw each year a fixed dollar amount or a fixed percentage (e.g., 4%) of the account until the account is gone. The commenters suggested that three, four or five percent per year might be reliable withdrawal rates for a participant who starts drawing down his account at age 65. The income stream illustrated under this approach would be the fixed dollar amount or fixed percentage, and could be shown as either monthly or annual payments. The second method is the annuitization approach. This approach, for example, expresses the benefit as a lifetime monthly payment to the participant similar in form to a pension payment made from a traditional defined benefit plan. This approach also is the method that insurance companies use to determine payment amounts with their annuity products.

The proposal the Department is considering would use the second method of conversion because, of the two approaches, the second method reflects "lifetime" income whereas the first method reflects an income stream that may or may not be payable for the life of the participant (e.g., in the case of a participant who retires at age 65 and dies at age 94, a 4% draw down, assuming a constant zero rate of return, would exhaust the account in 25 years instead of life). The second method reflects one of the Department's primary goals in encouraging meaningful benefit statements—that plan participants and beneficiaries are informed of their financial readiness for the entirety of their retired lives, not just a portion of it.

According to the RFI commenters and others, there are five relevant factors that must be considered when illustrating or converting an account balance (whether current or projected) to a lifetime income stream. The first is the date the payments would start, often referred to as the "annuity start date" (ASD). The second is the age of the participant or beneficiary at the ASD. The third is the form of payment (e.g., single life annuity). The fourth is the expected mortality of the participant or beneficiary and any spouse. The fifth is the interest rate for the applicable mortality period. The Department specifically requests comments on whether these are the appropriate variables for illustrating an account balance as a lifetime income stream. If not, why not, and are there other essential variables?

Each of the foregoing factors is addressed in ANPRM § 2520.105-1(e). For example, with respect to the form of payment, lifetime income illustrations would be based on level payments for the life of the participant or beneficiary. See ANPRM § 2520.105-1(e)(1)(i). If the participant or beneficiary is married, however, a second illustration would be required. This second illustration would be a level payment for the life of the participant based on the joint lives of the participant/beneficiary and spouse, with a fifty percent survivor's benefit to the surviving spouse. See ANPRM § 2520.105-1(e)(1)(ii). For this purpose, the plan may assume the spouse is the same age as the participant. Id.

The lifetime income illustrations being contemplated would assume that payments begin immediately and that the participant or beneficiary generally is normal retirement age under the plan (e.g., 65 years old) even if the participant or beneficiary is much younger. For example, for a participant age 25 in a plan with a normal retirement age of 65, the

assumed commencement date in a quarterly benefit statement that covered the period October 1, 2015 through December 31, 2015 would be January 1, 2016. See ANPRM § 2520.105-1(e)(4). In addition, the 25-year old participant is assumed to be age 65 (i.e., normal retirement age) on January 1, 2016. However, if the participant is older than normal retirement age, the plan administrator is required to use the participant's actual age.[28]

With respect to mortality and interest rate assumptions, many RFI commenters and others suggested that when a plan offers an annuity form of distribution, the actual mortality and interest rate provisions contained in the plan's annuity contract should be reflected in the lifetime income illustrations.[29] The Department agrees and intends to include this concept as part of the proposed regulation. See ANPRM § 2520.105-1(e)(3). However, for plans that do not offer annuity forms of distribution, the Department is considering a safe harbor approach for mortality and interest rate assumptions (similar to the safe harbor for the projection requirement set forth in ANPRM § 2520.105-1(d)). Specifically, the proposal would start with a general requirement that illustrations must be based on "reasonable" mortality and interest rate assumptions "taking into account generally accepted actuarial principles." See ANPRM § 2520.105-1(e)(2)(i). This standard is intended to be flexible and to preserve current best practices, on the one hand, but protective on the other hand in that it would prohibit the use of assumptions that do not comport with generally accepted actuarial principles. Many commenters on the RFI requested some degree of flexibility in this area in order to match illustrations on benefit statements with illustrations provided through online tools. At the same time, however, other RFI commenters expressed concern with potential ERISA liability in connection with picking mortality and interest rate assumptions for lifetime income illustrations and strongly encouraged the Department to adopt safe harbor assumptions. Accordingly, the Department is considering the following safe harbor assumptions, each of which, when used together, would be deemed reasonable under the general requirements in ANPRM § 2520.105-1(e)(2)(i).

The safe harbor rate of interest under consideration is a "rate of interest equal to the 10-year constant maturity Treasury securities rate, for the first business day of the last month of the period to which the statement relates." See paragraph (e)(2)(ii)(A). One commenter with members representing more than 90% of the assets and premiums in the U.S. life insurance and annuity industry stated that its members believe that the 10-year constant maturity Treasury rate best represents the interest rates that are reflected in actual annuity pricing. In addition, the 10-year constant maturity Treasury rate is published daily to the public and widely recognized.[30] The Department agrees that it may be helpful to participants to use a market rate that approximates what it actually would cost them to buy a lifetime income stream on the open market. In this regard, an illustration based on a current market rate would be especially beneficial for those participants or beneficiaries who are close to retirement, and less so for those farther from normal retirement age.[31]

The Department, however, is specifically requesting comments on whether the 10-year constant maturity Treasury rate assumption is the best interest rate assumption to use in this context, or whether there is a different interest rate or combination of rates that should be used, and why. For example, other RFI commenters mentioned that the Department might give some consideration to using the Pension Benefit Guaranty Corporation (PBGC) select and ultimate rates used to determine liabilities of terminated single-employer plans under section 4044 of ERISA which are published monthly by the PBGC[32] or the "applicable interest rate" under section 417(e)(3)(C) of the Code, although these commenters did not provide reasoning behind their suggestions. The commenter in favor of the 10-year constant maturity Treasury rate is concerned that the PBGC rates may not be sufficiently current for this type of illustration; or that such rates are not appropri-

---

[27] A projected account balance would not be required if the participant has reached normal retirement age under the plan. See ANPRM § 2520.105-1(c)(2)(vi).

[28] If the participant has reached normal retirement age under the plan, the only illustration that would be required for this participant is the illustration based on his or her current account balance. An illustration based on a projected account balance would not be required in these circumstances. See ANPRM § 2520.105-1(c)(2)(vi).

[29] In 2010, 18 percent of private industry workers participated in a defined contribution retirement plan providing an option to take an annuity form of distribution at retirement. See Table 21a of U.S. Department of Labor, Bureau of Labor Statistics, "National Compensation Survey: Health and Retirement Plan Provisions in Private Industry in the United States, 2010," Bulletin 2770, August 2011. Available at: http://www.bls.gov/ncs/ebs/detailedprovisions/2010/ownership/private/table21a.pdf

[30] See www.federalreserve.gov/releases/h15/data.htm.

[31] The Department recognizes that there is no single interest rate assumption that would be perfect for all participants. Those who retire tomorrow and plan to purchase lifetime

income will face pricing that reflects current interest rates. It is clear that for these participants, using an interest rate assumption based on current rates is appropriate. However, participants who are a substantial number of years away from retirement will be faced with annuity pricing that reflects future interest rates that are unknown. An appropriate way to project these future interest rates may be to use a long-term average of historical interest rates, with the belief that interest rates tend to revert to the mean. A third group of participants, those who will retire in a short number of years, are unique still from the other two groups. An example of an appropriate projection of interest rates at the time of retirement for these participants may be some combination of current and historical interest rates. In choosing a safe harbor assumption, the Department must consider all of these groups of participants and how their projections would be affected. For example, if the Department ultimately uses current interest rates as the safe harbor, movement in interest rates would be an additional source of variation in benefits statement projections year over year for participants who are a substantial number of years away from retirement.

[32] See 29 CFR 4044, Appendix B. See also www.pbgc.gov/prac/interest/monthly.html.

ate for pay out annuities. This commenter, in addition, is concerned that the Code section 417(e)(3)(C) rates, which it states are used for converting defined benefit amounts to a lump sum for distribution, do not approximate current annuity prices.

The safe harbor mortality assumption under consideration is "the applicable mortality table under section 417(e)(3)(B) of the Code, in effect for the month that contains the last day of the period to which the statement relates." See ANPRM § 2520.105-1(e)(2)(ii)(B).[33] The section 417(e)(3)(B) applicable mortality table is a unisex table created and published by the Treasury Department.[34] The same commenter that suggested using the 10-year constant maturity Treasury rate also suggested using the section 417(e)(3)(B) applicable mortality table. Other commenters suggested the mortality table used by the PBGC to determine the liabilities of terminated singleemployer plans under section 4044 of ERISA.[35]

The Department selected the section 417(e)(3)(B) applicable mortality table for the following three reasons. First, the Treasury Department periodically updates the mortality table.[36] Second, unlike the PBGC mortality tables, the section 417(e)(3)(B) applicable mortality table is unisex.[37] Third, the table is publicly available and widely known to employee benefit plan service providers. The Department, however, is specifically requesting comments on whether the section 417(e)(3)(B) mortality table is the best mortality assumption to use in this context, or whether there is a different mortality assumption that should be used, and why. For example, one commenter suggested that if the plan did not provide an annuity option, the plan should be permitted to use gender based mortality tables in order to illustrate the dollar amount of a lifetime income stream which the participant or beneficiary could achieve if his or her account was rolled over into an individual retirement account and used to purchase a commercial annuity contract using gender based mortality.[38]

The rules and assumptions for converting current and projected account balances into lifetime income streams, discussed above and set forth in ANPRM § 2520.105-1(e), do not include an "insurance load." In this context, the term "insurance load" is intended to describe the difference between the market price of lifetime income and the price of actuarially fair lifetime income. The insurance load may include insurance company profits, costs of insuring against systemic mortality risk, costs of holding cash reserves, advertising costs, the cost of selection (if not accounted for in the mortality table), and other operating costs. The Department specifically is requesting comments on whether a proposed rule should contain provisions requiring that such loads be factored into lifetime income streams and, if so, how should or could the rules and assumptions in ANPRM § 2520.105-1(e), including the safe harbor assumptions in ANPRM § 2520.105-1(e)(2)(ii), be modified to reflect such a requirement. For example, should the Department consider using a load assumption similar to the one used by the PBGC to determine the value of benefits for a single employer plan that has been involuntarily terminated and placed in trusteeship by the PBGC?[39]

D. Disclosure of Assumptions

Most of the commenters on the RFI indicated that the assumptions underlying any illustration should be disclosed to participants and beneficiaries. The Department agrees that clear disclosure of assumptions is needed for multiple reasons, but primarily in order to make it clear to participants and beneficiaries that projected amounts are not guarantees. The proposal under consideration, therefore, would require disclosure of any assumptions used in the benefit statement with regard to the projected account balance and the illustration of the lifetime income streams. See ANPRM § 2520.105-1(c)(6)(i) and (ii). In addition, the proposal would require that the pension benefit statement include a statement that the lifetime income stream is only an illustra-

tion and that actual periodic payments that may be purchased at retirement will depend on numerous factors and may vary substantially from the lifetime income stream illustration in the benefit statement. See ANPRM § 2520.105-1(c)(6)(iii). The Department is interested in comments on whether it would be helpful to participants and beneficiaries if their benefit statements explained that a consequence of purchasing an annuity outside of their pension plan is that gender-based mortality tables may be used and, if so, men will receive higher monthly payments and woman will receive lower monthly payments.

It is essential that assumption disclosures be written in manner calculated to be understood by the average plan participant. The Department, therefore, is interested in comments and suggestions on how best to achieve this result. For example, is there model language within the financial community or elsewhere that plan administrators could use to plainly explain or describe this information so as to increase its readability and understandability? Are there other formatting or presentation techniques relevant to this inquiry?

E. In-plan Annuities

In addition to traditional distribution annuities, the Department is aware of the marketing and presence of in-plan annuity arrangements as investment options, sometimes generically referred to as "incremental" or "accumulating" annuities. According to the RFI commenters, these are arrangements that permit participants to make ongoing contributions toward the current purchase of a future stream of retirement income payments, which are guaranteed by an insurance company. Thus, conceptually, each contribution buys a small annuity. In this fashion, a participant has the ability to accumulate multiple small annuities over a career which, in the aggregate, could provide significant lifetime income.

More specifically, the RFI commenters explained that under these arrangements, typically, the ongoing participant contributions actually accumulate ownership units, that each such unit has a current market value, and that each unit will pay a fixed amount (usually per month) for the life of the owner commencing at retirement. For example, assume the current purchase price of a unit is $500 and each unit purchased will pay $15 per month, for life, commencing at retirement. A participant who has accumulated 100 units over his career will receive payments of $1,500 per month, for life, commencing at retirement. The RFI commenters further explain that although the current price of a unit ($500 in this example) fluctuates depending on a number of factors, such as the interest rate environment and the employee's age when the unit is purchased, the guaranteed monthly payment of each unit purchased (e.g., $15 in this example) is fixed. RFI commenters also indicate that some products allow the participant to transfer out of the incremental annuity investment option and into another of the plan's designated investment alternatives, such as a mutual fund or other similar plan investment option, prior to normal retirement age or some other date (e.g., the date distributions commence). The price per unit or pay out rate of an in-plan annuity with this transferability feature may differ from one without this feature.

The Department is soliciting comments on how best to factor investments of this type into lifetime income illustrations. For instance, one approach is that the current market value of all in-plan annuity units accumulated by a participant could be added to the rest of that participant's account balance under ANPRM § 2520.105-1(c)(2)(v), before determining the projected account balance under ANPRM § 2520.105-1(c)(2)(vi).[40] A second approach is to add the total guaranteed monthly payment amount derived from all of a participant's in-plan annuity units to the estimated monthly payment amount of the non-annuity portion of the participant's account, if any, determined under ANPRM § 2520.105-1(c)(2)(vii) and (viii).[41] A third approach is to convert the participant's entire account balance, even any part that is

---

[33] The Department welcomes comments on the use of this month to determine the mortality, or whether it would be more appropriate to use the mortality table in effect for the month containing the assumed commencement date as defined in ANPRM § 2520.105-1(e)(4).

[34] Currently, the applicable mortality table is based on the Society of Actuaries, RP 2000 Mortality Tables Report at http://www.soa.org/ccm/content/research-publications/experience-studies-tools/the-rp-2000-mortality-tables, with a fixed blend of 50% of the static male combined mortality rates and 50% of the static female combined mortality rates promulgated under 26 CFR 1.430(h)(3)-1(c). See IRS Notice 2008-85, IRB 2008-42 which published unisex mortality tables for purposes of Code section 417(e)(3)(B) through 2013.

[35] See 29 CFR 4044, Appendix A.

[36] The 417(e)(3)(B) mortality table is derived from the mortality tables prescribed under the funding rules of Code section 430(h)(3)(A) which states that the mortality tables prescribed by the Treasury Department "shall be based on the actual experience of pension plans and projected trends in such experience . . . taking into account results of available independent studies of mortality of individuals covered by pension plans."

[37] To the extent an individual account plan offers an annuity option, the mortality factors have to be the same for males and females to comply with *Arizona Governing Committee v. Norris*, 436 U.S. 1073 (1983).

[38] Since the female mortality tables show a longer life expectancy and the male mortality tables show a shorter life expectancy than a unisex table, the dollar amount of a male participant's monthly payment would be higher and a female participant's monthly payment would be lower in an illustration using gender based tables.

[39] See 29 CFR 4044, Appendix C.

[40] For example, assume a participant has $100,000 invested in certain of the plan's designated investment alternatives. Also assume that in addition to those investments, the participant also has 10 in-plan annuity units and that the current market value of a unit is $500. Under this approach, the participant's total account balance under ANPRM § 2520.105-1(c)(2)(v) would be $105,000, and the lifetime income illustrations would be based on this amount.

[41] For example, assume a participant has accumulated 100 units of an in-plan annuity and that each unit accumulated will pay $15 per month, for life, commencing at retirement. Thus, this participant will receive payments of $1,500 per month, for life, commencing at

not allocated to an inplan annuity option, to a lifetime income stream using the current unit price of the in-plan annuity option.[42]

These three approaches are not necessarily the only options for incorporating the in-plan annuity values in lifetime income illustrations and the Department welcomes suggestions on other approaches. In this regard, commenters are encouraged to address whether, and to what extent, the language in ANPRM § 2520.105-1(e)(3) would need to be modified.[43] In addition, the Department welcomes the submission of actual benefit statements or similar documents showing how plans or insurance companies currently disclose in-plan annuity unit prices and monthly payment guarantees. Finally, given the wide array of ERISA plans and investment products, the Department also is soliciting comments on whether there are any foreseeable product-specific problems for products similar to in-plan annuities.

F. Miscellaneous

Many RFI commenters, hearing witnesses, and others who support lifetime income illustrations believe that the Department should take steps to encourage, rather than require, such illustrations on pension benefit statements. According to these individuals, mandating lifetime income illustrations would be expensive and may expose plan fiduciaries to litigation from plan participants and beneficiaries for a variety of reasons. The most commonly cited reason for potential lawsuits is unmet expectations. For example, if participants and beneficiaries during their working years mistakenly believe that the lifetime income illustrations on their pension benefit statements are promises or guarantees of a specific income stream, the participants and beneficiaries might sue if their actual account balances at retirement do not generate an income stream equal to or greater than the stream depicted in the illustrations in prior pension benefit statements.

The Department believes both concerns may be overstated. As to costs, first, some plans already provide lifetime income illustrations on pension benefit statements.[44] Thus, for these plans, there may be little if any additional cost associated with the ANPRM's regulatory framework. Second, pursuant to section 105 of ERISA, pension benefit statements already are required to include certain participant account information. Thus, for plans not already providing lifetime income illustrations on pension benefit statements, the Department does not believe that adding the lifetime income illustrations described above to these statements should significantly increase the cost of pension benefit statements.

The Department, however, specifically requests comments on the costs (and benefits) of including the illustration described herein in pension benefit statements. In this regard, the Department welcomes ideas on how the cost of the contemplated lifetime income illustrations might be reduced without compromising the anticipated benefits. For example, would there be substantial cost savings if illustrations were required only annually rather than quarterly? If yes, please explain why and quantify if possible. In addition, would there be substantial cost savings if the Department published (and periodically updated) a table of conversion factors based on the safe harbor assumptions contemplated in paragraph (e) of the ANPRM's regulatory framework? Such a table would make it possible to produce projections that satisfy the safe harbor with simple calculations and without the need to reference Treasury rates, mortality tables and other actuarial assumptions.[45] If yes, please explain why and quantify if possible. In addition, would there be substantial cost savings if all benefit statements were required to contain joint and survivor illustrations of the type described in ANPRM § 2520.105-1(e)(1)(ii), as opposed to including such illustrations only in benefit statements of married participants and beneficiaries? In other words, would there be cost savings in not having to track and determine marital status solely for pension benefit statement requirements? If yes, please explain why and quantify if possible.

As to the concern about potential lawsuits based on unrealized expectations, the Department believes this issue might be addressed in two ways. First, benefit statements could include a clear and definitive statement that the lifetime income illustration is an estimate, based on specific assumptions, and not a guarantee. The Department believes this disclosure would serve to put participants and beneficiaries on notice that the illustration is only an estimate and, thereby, minimize the likelihood that they would believe the illustration is a promise or guarantee. The Department specifically requests comments on the extent to which the language in ANPRM § 2520.105-1(c)(6) would accomplish this result. Second, the Department is considering establishing a regulatory safe harbor under section 105 of ERISA for plan administrators to rely on when developing lifetime income illustrations for pension benefit statements. By specifying the precise standards and assumptions a plan administrator would use to make a lifetime income illustration on a pension benefit statement, a regulatory safe harbor would substantially reduce the likelihood of lawsuits against that administrator based on an imprudent or improper calculation of lifetime income. See ANPRM § 2520.105-1(d)(2) and (e)(2)(ii). The Department specifically requests comments on the extent to which the regulatory safe harbor being considered would help address concerns about such potential lawsuits.

Furthermore, the Department has not concluded that the ANPRM's regulatory framework is the only or best approach. The Department intends to consider all reasonable alternatives to direct regulation, including whether there is a way short of a regulatory mandate to get plan administrators voluntarily to provide their participants and beneficiaries with constructive and helpful lifetime income illustrations. In developing the framework, the Department was mindful of the fact that administrators of defined contribution plans have been free to provide lifetime income illustrations to participants and beneficiaries for nearly 40 years since the enactment of ERISA, yet few actually have done so despite the apparent support for them evidenced by the vast majority of responsive RFI commenters and hearing witnesses who supported the concept. This ANPRM, nonetheless, solicits comments on all reasonable ideas, either in lieu of or in conjunction with a direct regulation, to address this very important issue. Commenters are encouraged to be specific with the responses and include data if possible to support their positions. The Department also welcomes the submission of sample benefit statements or similar documents currently being provided to participants and beneficiaries that include lifetime income illustrations.

List of Subjects in 29 CFR Part 2520

Annuity, Defined contribution plans, Disclosure, Employee benefit plans, Employee Retirement Income Security Act, Fiduciaries, Lifetime income, Pensions, Pension benefit statements, Plan administrators, Recordkeepers, Third party administrators For the reasons set forth in the preamble, the Department of Labor proposes to amend 29 CFR part 2520 as follows:

PART 2520—RULES AND REGULATIONS FOR REPORTING AND DISCLOSURE

1. The authority citation for part 2520 is revised to read as follows:

Authority : 29 U.S.C. 1021-1025, 1027, 1029-31, 1059, 1134 and 1135; and Secretary of Labor's Order 1-2011, 77 FR 1088 (Jan. 9, 2012). Sec. 2520.101-2 also issued under 29 U.S.C. 1132, 1181-1183, 1181 note, 1185, 1185a-b, 1191, and 1191a-c. Sec. 2520.101-4 also issued under 29 U.S.C. 1021(f). Sec. 2520.101-6 also issued under 29 U.S.C. 1021(k) and Pub. L.109-280, § 502(a)(3), 120 Stat. 780, 940 (2006). Secs. 2520.102-3, 2520.104b-1 and 2520.104b-3 also issued under 29 U.S.C. 1003,1181-1183, 1181 note, 1185, 1185a-b, 1191, and 1191a-c. Secs. 2520.104b-1 and 2520.107 also issued under 26 U.S.C. 401 note, 111

(Footnote Continued)

retirement based on these 100 units. Also assume this participant has a projected monthly payment of $2,500 based on investments in other designated investment alternatives under the plan (e.g., mutual funds) using the safe harbor assumptions. Under this approach, the guaranteed monthly payment of the inplan annuity ($1,500) could be added to the estimated monthly payment of $2,500, totaling $4,000 per month, for life.

[42] For example, assume a participant had accumulated 100 in-plan annuity units that each pay $15 per month, for life, commencing at retirement (totaling $1,500 per month). Also assume the participant had another $100,000 invested in other designated investment alternatives under the plan (such as mutual funds) and that the purchase price of a unit on the last day of the statement period is $500. Under this approach, the lifetime income illustration could be as if the participant had accumulated an additional 200 units with the $100,000 ($100,000 / $500 = 200), totaling $3,000 per month in retirement income. Thus, the total estimated monthly payment under this approach would be $4,500 ($3,000 + $1,500) per month, for life.

[43] Paragraph (e)(3) provides that "[i]f the plan offers an annuity form of distribution pursuant to a contract with an issuer licensed under applicable state insurance law, the plan

shall substitute actual plan terms for the [safe harbor mortality and interest] assumptions set forth in paragraphs (e)(2)(ii)(A) and (B) of this section."

[44] In one survey of large U.S. plan sponsors, 33% of respondents indicated that they provide retirement income projections to participants on benefit statements. See MetLife, "Retirement Income Practices Study," June 2012 Located at: https://www.metlife.com/retirementincomestudy

[45] For example, such a table would be based on the interest, mortality, and other assumptions selected by the Department and would contain factors for calculating a single life annuity and a joint and 50 percent survivor annuity. The relevant factor multiplied by the number of $1,000 increments comprising the participant's or beneficiary's total account balance would equal the monthly lifetime income stream. Assume, for example, that the participant has an account balance of $100,000 and the factor for single life annuity commencing at age 65 is 5.00 per thousand dollars. The $100,000 account balance would equate to a lifetime income stream of $500 per month ([$100,000 ÷ 1,000] × 5.00).

Stat. 788. Sec. 2520.105-1 also issued under sec. 508(a) of Pub. L. 109-280, 120 Stat. 780.

2. Add § 2520.105-1 to subpart F to read as follows:

§ 2520.105-1 Periodic Pension Benefit Statements—Individual Account Plans

(a) *[Reserved]*

(b) *[Reserved]*

(c) *Content requirements.* A benefit statement furnished under this section shall prominently display the beginning and ending dates of the period covered by the statement and contain the following information, based on the latest information available to the plan:

(1) [Reserved]

(2) *Total benefits accrued.*

(i) - (iv) [Reserved]

(v) The fair market value of the account balance as of the last day of the period covered by the statement;

(vi) If the participant has not reached normal retirement age as defined under the plan, the current dollar value of the projected account balance at normal retirement age determined in accordance with paragraph (d) of this section;

(vii) The amount specified in paragraph (c)(2)(v) of this section expressed as a lifetime income stream in accordance with paragraph (e) of this section; and

(viii) The amount specified in paragraph (c)(2)(vi) of this section expressed as a lifetime income stream in accordance with paragraph (e) of this section.

(3) - (5) [Reserved]

(6) *Explanation of lifetime income stream illustration.*

(i) Disclosure of the assumptions used pursuant to paragraph (d) of this section to establish the present value of the projected account balance required by paragraph (c)(2)(vi);

(ii) Disclosure of the assumptions used pursuant to paragraph (e) of this section to establish the lifetime income stream illustration required by paragraphs (c)(2)(vii) and (c)(2)(viii) of this section; and

(iii) A statement that the lifetime income stream illustrations required under paragraphs (c)(2)(vii) and (c)(2)(viii) of this section are illustrations only and that actual monthly payments that may be received at normal retirement age will depend on numerous factors and may vary from the illustrations in the benefit statement.

(d) *Rules and assumptions for projecting an account balance to normal retirement age.*

(1) *General.* For purposes of paragraph (c)(2)(vi) of this section (which sets forth the requirement to project a current account balance to normal retirement age under the plan), projections shall be based on reasonable assumptions taking into account generally accepted investment theories. A projection is not reasonable unless it is expressed in current dollars and takes into account future contributions and investment returns.

(2) *Safe harbor.* The following set of assumptions, when used together, are deemed reasonable for purposes of paragraph (d)(1) of this section:

(i) Contributions continue to normal retirement age at the current annual dollar amount, increased at a rate of three percent (3%) per year;

(ii) Investment returns are seven percent (7%) per year (nominal); and

(iii) A discount rate of three percent (3%) per year (for establishing the value of the projected account balance in current dollars).

(e) *Rules and assumptions for converting current and projected account balances into lifetime income streams.* For purposes of paragraphs (c)(2)(vii) and (c)(2)(viii) of this section—

(1) *Measuring lives.* A lifetime income stream shall—

(i) Be expressed as a level monthly payment, payable for the life of the participant beginning on the assumed commencement date, as defined in paragraph (e)(4) of this section;

(ii) If the participant is married, also be expressed as a level monthly payment, payable for the life of the participant beginning on the as-

sumed commencement date, as defined in paragraph (e)(4) of this section, with a survivor's benefit, which is equal to fifty percent (50%) of the monthly payment payable to the participant, payable for the life of the surviving spouse. For this purpose, it is permissible to assume the spouse is the same age as the participant; and

(iii) Be based on the assumptions set forth in paragraph (e)(2) of this section subject to the requirements in paragraph (e)(3) of this section.

(2) *Assumptions.*

(i) *General.* The interest and mortality assumptions behind a lifetime income stream shall each be reasonable taking into account generally accepted actuarial principles.

(ii) *Safe harbor.* The following assumptions are deemed reasonable for purposes of paragraph (e)(2)(i) of this section:

(A) A rate of interest equal to the 10-year constant maturity Treasury securities rate, for the first business day of the last month of the period to which the statement relates; and

(B) Mortality as reflected in the applicable mortality table under section 417(e)(3)(B) of the Internal Revenue Code, in effect for the month that contains the last day of the period to which the statement relates.

(3) *Plan terms.* If the plan offers an annuity form of distribution pursuant to a contract with an issuer licensed under applicable state insurance law, the plan shall substitute actual plan terms for the assumptions set forth in paragraphs (e)(2)(ii)(A) and (B) of this section.

(4) *Assumed commencement date.* For purposes of paragraph (e) of this section, the assumed commencement date shall be the first day following the period to which the statement relates, and the participant shall be assumed to be normal retirement age (as defined in section 3(24) of the Act) on this date (unless the participant is older than normal retirement age, in which case the participant's actual age should be used).

(f) [Reserved]

Note: The following appendix will not appear in the Federal Regulations:

APPENDIX A

LIFETIME INCOME ILLUSTRATION

(a) *Purpose.* This Appendix A contains an example that illustrates the application of the safe harbor provisions set forth in ANPRM § 2520.105-1(d) and (e). The example is intended to aid the reader in understanding how the two safe harbors operate, independently and together, when calculating lifetime income streams based on current and projected account balances. The example is not intended as a model format or to provide model content for pension benefit statements, including the explanation for participants and beneficiaries required by ANPRM § 2520.105-1(c)(6).

(b) *Example: Facts.* Plan A is an individual account plan described in section 3(34) of the Act. Since the plan does not provide for the allocation of investment responsibilities to participants and beneficiaries, the plan is required to provide a benefit statement at least once each calendar year. The statement period and the plan year are the 2012 calendar year. Normal retirement age under the Plan is age 65. Participant P is age 45. His birth date is June 30, 1967. He is married. His account balance on December 31, 2012, the last day of the statement period, was $125,000. His contributions (employee and employer) for 2012 were $9,709. His contributions for 2013 are assumed to be $10,000 ($9,709 x 1.03). Contributions are assumed to be made on January 1 each year.

(c) *Safe harbor for projecting an account balance to normal retirement age.* Based on the safe harbor assumptions in ANPRM § 2520.105-1(d)(2) (as reflected in Table 1), the present value of the current balance ($125,000) projected to normal retirement age, as required by ANPRM § 2520.105-1(c)(2)(vi), is $557,534. P's December 31, 2012 account balance of $125,000 is projected to be $467,621 assuming a 7% return, compounded annually. Future contributions increasing at 3%, compounded annually with earnings at 7%, compounded annually, are projected to be $524,575 on June 30, 2032. P's aggregate projected account balance on June 30, 2032 is $992,196 ($467,621 + $524,575). The projected account balance of $992,196 discounted to December 31, 2012 at 3%, compounded annually, is $557,534.

TABLE 1

Normal Retirement Date	June 30, 2032
Number of years in projection	19.5 (January 1, 2013 through June 30, 2032)
Number of contributions	19 ($10,000 per year adjusted by contribution increase rate) + 1 (final contribution of $5,000 in 2032, adjusted by contribution increase rate)
Paragraph (d) (2) (i) safe harbor - contribution increase rate	3% compounded annually
Paragraph (d) (2) (ii) safe harbor - rate of return applied to current account balance of $125,000 and post 2012 projected contributions	7% compounded annually
Paragraph (d) (2) (iii) safe harbor-discount rate used to determine present value of the projected account balance	3% compounded annually

(d) *Safe harbor for converting current and projected account balances into lifetime income streams.* Based on the safe harbor assumptions in ANPRM § 2520.105-1(e) (2) (ii) (as reflected in Table 2), the lifetime income stream illustrations of the current and projected balances required by ANPRM § 2520.105-1(c) (2) (vii) and (c) (2) (viii), respectively, are set forth below. Using the assumptions in Table 2, the factor for converting a single sum into a level monthly payment for the life of P only (Single Life Form) is $5.00 per $1,000 of account balance. The factor for converting a single sum into a level monthly payment for the life of P with a 50% survivor benefit payable to P's spouse following his death (Joint and 50% Survivor Form) is $4.51 per $1,000 of account balance.

TABLE 2

Paragraph (e) (2) (ii) (A) safe harbor -10 year constant maturity Treasury rate on December 3, 2012:	1.63%, compounded annually
Paragraph (e) (2) (ii) (B) safe harbor- Code section 417(e) (3) (B) applicable mortality table:	Unisex mortality table published in IRS Notice 2008-85
Assumed commencement date	January 1, 2013
Assumed Age of P on the assumed commencement date	65
Assumed Age of P's spouse on the assumed commencement date	65 (i.e., same as P)

Applying the factors described above to the December 31, 2012 current and projected account balances, the pension benefit statement would show the following lifetime income streams:

Account Balance On Last Day of Statement Period (12/31/12)	Single Life Form (Monthly Payment for P's Life with No Survivor Benefit)	Joint and 50% Survivor Form	
		Monthly Payment During P's Life	Monthly Payment After P's Death To Surviving Spouse
Current - $125,000	$625	$564	$282
Projected - $557,534	$2,788	$2,514	$1,257

Signed at Washington, D.C., this 17th day of April, 2013.

Phyllis C. Borzi

Assistant Secretary, Employee Benefits Security Administration, Department of Labor.

BILLING CODE 4510-29-P

[FR Doc. 2013-10636 Filed 05/07/2013 at 8:45 am; Publication Date: 05/08/2013]

¶ 20,538M

Pension Benefit Guaranty Corporation (PBGC): Proposed regulations: Premium payments: Due dates.—The Pension Benefit Guaranty Corporation (PBGC) has issued proposed regulations designed to make its premium payment rules more effective and less burdensome. The proposed regulations would, among other things, simplify due dates, coordinate the due date for terminating plans with the termination process, make conforming and clarifying changes to the variable-rate premium rules, and provide for relief from various penalties. The proposed regulations would be effective starting in 2014. Comments on the proposed rules are due by September 23, 2013.

The proposed regulations, which were published in the Federal Register on July 23, 2013 (78 FR 44056), were reproduced below.

A portion of the regulation was finalized on January 3, 2014 (79 FR 347). The preamble is at ¶ 24,317. The final regulation is at ¶ 15,371G and ¶ 15,371J. The regulations were finalized on March 11, 2014 (79 FR 13547). The preamble to the final regulations is at ¶ 24,319. The final regulations are at ¶ 15,302A, ¶ 15,361A, ¶ 15,361B, ¶ 15,361C, ¶ 15,361D, ¶ 15,361F, ¶ 15,371A, ¶ 15,371B, ¶ 15,371G, ¶ 15,371J, ¶ 15,371K, ¶ 15,373, ¶ 15,374, and ¶ 15,501C.

¶ 20,538N

Employee Benefits Security Administration (EBSA): Proposed regulations: IRS: Group health plans: Excepted benefits.—The EBSA, IRS, and Department of Health and Human Services have issued proposed regulations that would amend Code and ERISA regulations regarding excepted benefits, which are generally exempt from the health reform requirements that were added by the Health Insurance Portability and Accountability Act of 1996 (HIPAA, P.L. 104-191) and the Patient Protection and Affordable Care Act (PPACA, P.L. 111-148). The proposed regulations would make amendments concerning dental and vision benefits, limited wraparound coverage, and employee assistance programs. The Departments seek comments on the proposed regulations. Until the regulations are finalized, through at least 2014, for purposes of enforcing the provisions of title XXVII of the Public Health Service Act, part 7 of ERISA, and chapter 100 of the Code, the Departments will consider dental and vision benefits and employee assistance program benefits as meeting the conditions of the proposed regulations to qualify as excepted benefits. To the extent that the final regulations or other guidance concerning vision or dental benefits or employee assistance programs is more restrictive that the proposed regulations, the final regulations or other guidance will not be effective before January 1, 2015.

The proposed regulations, which were published in the Federal Register on December 24, 2013 (78 FR 77632), are reproduced at ¶ 20,263U. All of the final regulations, except the portion pertaining to limited wraparound coverage, were finalized on October 1, 2014 (79 FR 59130). The preamble to the final regulations is at ¶ 23,309. The final regulations are at ¶ 15,051B-1. New proposed regulations on limited wraparound coverage were published in the Federal Register on December 23, 2014. See ¶ 20,538V.

¶ 20,538O

Pension Benefit Guaranty Corporation (PBGC): Proposed regulations: Multiemployer plans: Reporting requirements.—The Pension Benefit Guaranty Corporation (PBGC) has issued proposed amendments to its multiemployer plan regulations designed to make the disclosure of information to the PBGC and to plan participants more efficient and effective and to reduce the administrative burden on plan sponsors. The proposed regulations would reduce the number of actuarial valuations required for certain small terminated but not insolvent plans, shorten the advance notice filing requirements for mergers in situations that do not involve a compliance determination, and remove certain insolvency notice and update requirements. Comments on the proposed rules must be submitted on or before March 31, 2014.

The proposed regulations, which were published in the Federal Register on January 29, 2014 (79 FR 4642), were reproduced below. The regulations were finalized on May 28, 2014 (79 FR 30459). The preamble to the final regulations is at ¶ 24,321. The final regulations are at ¶ 15,449O, ¶ 15,700H, ¶ 15,715R, ¶ 15,715S, ¶ 15,715U, and ¶ 15,715V.

¶ 20,538P

Employee Benefits Security Administration (EBSA): Proposed regulations: IRS: Patient Protection and Affordable Care Act (P.L. 111-148, PPACA): Group health plans: Waiting periods: Employment-based orientation periods.—The EBSA, IRS, and the Department of Health and Human Services have issued proposed regulations that would clarify the maximum allowed length of any reasonable and bona fide employment-based orientation period, consistent with the 90-day waiting period limitation for health insurance coverage as set forth in Sec. 2708 of the Public Health Service (PHS) Act, which was added by the PPACA and incorporated into the Code and ERISA. The proposed regulations would provide that one month is the maximum allowed length of any reasonable and bona fide employment-based orientation period. The Departments will consider compliance with these proposed regulations to constitute compliance with PHS Act Sec. 2708 at least through the end of 2014. To the extent final regulations or other guidance with respect to the application of the 90-day waiting period limitation to orientation periods is more restrictive on plans and issuers, the final regulations or other guidance will not be effective prior to January 1, 2015, and will provide plans and issuers a reasonable time period to comply.

The proposed regulations, which were published in the Federal Register on February 24, 2014 (79 FR 10319), are reproduced at ¶ 20,263W. The regulations were finalized on June 25, 2014 (79 FR 35942). The preamble to the final regulations is at ¶ 23,301. The final regulations are at ¶ 15,050R-50K.

¶ 20,538Q

Employee Benefits Security Administration (EBSA): Proposed regulations: Fiduciaries: Fee disclosure.—EBSA has issued proposed regulations amending the fee disclosure rules issued in February 2012 (¶ 24,307) that would require service providers to furnish plan fiduciaries with a "guide" to required initial disclosures that are contained in multiple or lengthy documents. The guide, which would be provided in a separate document, is intended to enable fiduciaries, especially those responsible for small and medium sized plans, to easily locate and access "all principle data elements required as initial disclosures" in a cost-effective manner.

The proposed regulations, which were published in the Federal Register on March 12, 2014 (79 FR 13949), are reproduced below.

DEPARTMENT OF LABOR

Employee Benefits Security Administration

29 CFR Part 2550

RIN 1210-AB53

Amendment Relating to Reasonable Contract or Arrangement Under Section 408(b)(2) - Fee Disclosure

AGENCY: Employee Benefits Security Administration, Labor.

ACTION: Proposed rule.

SUMMARY: This document contains a proposed amendment to the final regulation under the Employee Retirement Income Security Act of 1974 (ERISA or the Act) requiring that certain service providers to pension plans disclose information about the service providers' compensation and potential conflicts of interest. The amendment would, upon adoption, require covered service providers to furnish a guide to assist plan fiduciaries in reviewing the disclosures required by the final rule if the disclosures are contained in multiple or lengthy documents. This amendment will affect pension plan sponsors and fiduciaries and certain service providers to such plans.

DATES: Written comments on the proposed amendment should be received by the Department on or before [INSERT DATE THAT IS 90 DAYS FOLLOWING FEDERAL REGISTER PUBLICATION].

ADDRESSES: Written comments may be submitted to the addresses specified below. All comments will be made available to the public. *Warning:* Do not include any personally identifiable information (such as name, address, or other contact information) or confidential business information that you do not want publicly disclosed. All comments may be posted on the Internet and can be retrieved by most Internet search engines. Comments may be submitted anonymously. Comments may be submitted to the Department of Labor, identified by RIN 1210-AB08, by one of the following methods:

• *Federal eRulemaking Portal: http://www.regulations.gov.* Follow the instructions for submitting comments.

• *Email: e-ORI@dol.gov.*

• *Mail or Hand Delivery:* Office of Regulations and Interpretations, Employee Benefits Security Administration, Room N-5655, U.S. Department of Labor, 200 Constitution Avenue NW, Washington, DC 20210, *Attention:* RIN 1210-AB08; 408(b)(2) Guide.

Comments received by the Department of Labor may be posted without change to *http://www.regulations.gov* and *http://www.dol.gov/ebsa,* and made available for public inspection at the Public Disclosure Room, N-1513, Employee Benefits Security Administration, 200 Constitution Avenue NW, Washington, DC 20210.

FOR FURTHER INFORMATION CONTACT: Allison Wielobob, Office of Regulations and Interpretations, Employee Benefits Security Administration, (202) 693-8500. This is not a toll-free number.

SUPPLEMENTARY INFORMATION:

A. Background

1. General

On February 3, 2012, the Department published a final rule in the **Federal Register** concerning disclosures that must be furnished before plan fiduciaries enter into, extend or renew contracts or arrangements for services to certain pension plans in order for such a contract or arrangement to be "reasonable," as required by ERISA section

408(b)(2).[1] The final rule was effective for covered plans on July 1, 2012.[2] The final rule was designed to help ensure that pension plan fiduciaries are provided the information they need to assess both the reasonableness of the compensation to be paid for plan services and potential conflicts of interest that may affect the performance of those services. Today, the Department is publishing in the **Federal Register** a proposed amendment to the final rule under which covered service providers would be required to furnish a guide along with the initial disclosures that must be provided to plan fiduciaries in accordance with the final regulation, if the initial disclosures are contained in multiple or lengthy documents.

2. Public Comments on Interim Final Regulation

In the preamble to the interim final rule, the Department requested comment on the format of disclosures required under the rule. Neither the proposal nor the interim final rule required covered service providers to disclose information in any particular format. Further, the preamble to the proposal specifically noted that covered service providers could use different documents from separate sources, as long as all of the documents, collectively, contained the required information. Commenters on the proposal disagreed as to whether this would lead to a cost-effective and meaningful presentation of the required information to responsible plan fiduciaries. In the preamble to the interim final rule, the Department explained that it had not determined whether it was feasible to provide specific and meaningful formatting standards. Accordingly, the Department requested comment on whether to revise the final rule to include a summary disclosure or other formatting requirement.

Commenters on the interim final rule, as on the proposed rule, continued to disagree about the utility of, and feasibility of, requiring a summary of, or otherwise mandating any particular format for the required disclosures. Many commenters argued that the Department should retain the position taken in the proposal and the interim final rule, giving covered service providers flexibility to determine the format of their disclosures. These commenters expressed concern that a "one-size-fits-all" approach could not accommodate the enormous variety of current pension plan service arrangements and likely changes in the future. They also believed that the costs to pension plans, and the participants and beneficiaries of such plans, of such an approach will be significant. Some of these commenters expressed concern that responsible plan fiduciaries would rely solely, and thus improperly, on the summary, rather than reviewing the fuller and more detailed disclosures required by the rule. The commenters also were concerned that requiring the comprehensive disclosures and a summary would result in unnecessarily duplicative disclosures. In addition, if there are discrepancies between the two, commenters argued that questions could arise over which disclosures would govern. These commenters preferred that the Department require covered service providers to furnish an index or "roadmap" to the disclosures. Commenters also suggested that any summary or other formatting requirement the Department may adopt be flexible and not mandate any particular language, formatting, or page limits.

Other commenters, however, supported the addition of a summary disclosure or similar requirement. They argued that plan fiduciaries, especially those for small and medium-sized plans, often are overwhelmed by highly technical disclosures from separate sources, especially concerning plan investments. These commenters suggested placing the burden of organizing this information on covered service providers, who can do so more effectively and at less cost. Further, these commenters believe that associated costs to service providers have been overstated and are likely to be minimal following an initial transition to compliance with any new summary or other formatting requirement. These costs, they argued, would be greatly outweighed by the benefit of increased clarity to responsible plan fiduciaries. One commenter, for example, pointed out that fuller disclosure will not result in increased transparency if the information continues to be obscured in lengthy, technical documents. Some of these commenters suggested information that should be contained in a separate, summary disclosure requirement.

Following review and analysis of these comments, the Department decided to reserve paragraph (c)(1)(iv)(H) of the final rule, published in February 2012. The Department also explained its intention to publish, in a separate proposal, a guide or similar requirement to assist responsible plan fiduciaries' review of the rule's required disclosures. Given the lack of specific suggestions or data on how best to structure such a requirement, and what the real costs of such a requirement would be, the Department was not prepared, at that time, to implement a guide or similar requirement as part of the final rule.

Today, the Department is proposing a regulatory provision requiring that covered service providers furnish a guide along with the initial disclosures required by the rule, if the disclosures are contained in multiple or lengthy documents. The Department believes that plan fiduciaries, especially in the case of small plans, need a tool to effectively make use of the required disclosures. The guide being proposed in this document provides clarity and specificity, while avoiding the uncertainty and burdens that some commenters argued may accompany construction of a "summary" of existing documents. The Department believes that a required summary without some guide to the underlying disclosures themselves, could become the primary document on which some responsible plan fiduciaries rely, which is not the Department's intention.

The Department is proposing a guide requirement in an effort to strike an appropriate balance between the need to facilitate a responsible plan fiduciary's review of information important to a prudent decision-making process and the costs and burdens attendant to the preparation of a new summary disclosure document. The Department believes that covered service providers are best positioned to provide the guide in a cost-effective manner, because they have the specialized knowledge required to determine where the required disclosures are located, and they generally will be able to structure their disclosures so that they need to locate the information only once when preparing guides for large numbers of clients, each of whom otherwise would have to locate the information separately in the underlying disclosures. A guide will assist responsible plan fiduciaries for these plans in finding information that ERISA requires them to assess in evaluating both the reasonableness of the compensation to be paid for plan services and potential conflicts of interest that may affect the performance of those services. A guide will also reduce the costs they otherwise would have incurred searching for such information. Anecdotal evidence suggests that small plan fiduciaries in particular often have difficulty obtaining required information in an understandable format, because such plans lack the bargaining power and specialized expertise possessed by large plan fiduciaries. Therefore, the Department anticipates that the guide requirement will be especially beneficial to fiduciaries of small and medium-sized plans.

To avoid unnecessary cost to covered service providers, the proposal also allows for the fact that, in some cases, covered service providers may already furnish the required disclosures in a concise, single document. If that is the case, then the covered service provider will not be required to provide a separate guide to the disclosures. The Department believes that initial disclosures that are furnished in a concise, single document do not present the same challenges to responsible plan fiduciaries as disclosure that are contained in multiple or lengthy documents.

The Department has not been convinced by commenters that certain required disclosures are more important than others, such that the guide, if required, should include the location of only the most important data. Accordingly, the proposed guide requires that covered service providers disclose the location of all principle data elements required as initial disclosures. Nothing in the proposed amendment, however, would preclude a covered service provider from including additional information with or as part of the guide, as long as such information is not inaccurate or misleading. It is not the Department's goal to limit innovation in how information is effectively communicated to plan fiduciaries. Rather, the Department believes that the required guide to initial disclosures will provide a basic framework for ensuring that responsible plan fiduciaries understand exactly what information is being disclosed to them, and where to find such information.

---

[1] 77 FR 5632 (Feb. 3, 2012); *see also* the interim final rule (75 FR 41600, July 16, 2010) and proposed rule (72 FR 70988, Dec. 13, 2007). The "408(b)(2)" regulation finalized by the Department addresses disclosures that must be furnished before plan fiduciaries enter into, extend or renew contracts or arrangements for services to certain pension plans. The final rule was part of a broader Departmental regulatory initiative to improve transparency of plan fees to plan fiduciaries, the Department, and plan participants and beneficiaries. As part of this initiative, the Department also implemented changes to the information that must be reported concerning service provider compensation as part of the Form 5500 Annual Report. These changes to Schedule C of the Form 5500 complement the final rule

by assuring that plan fiduciaries have the information they need to monitor service providers consistent with their duties under ERISA section 404(a)(1). *See* 72 FR 64731; *see also* frequently asked questions on Schedule C, available on the Department's Web site at http://www.dol.gov/ebsa. Finally, the Department published a final rule in October 2010 requiring the disclosure of specified plan and investment-related information, including fee and expense information, to participants and beneficiaries of participant-directed individual account plans. *See* 75 FR 64910.

[2] *See* 77 FR 5632.

B. Proposed Amendment to Regulations under Section 408(b)(2)

1. Overview of Proposed Amendment

The Department proposes to include, as paragraph (c)(1)(iv)(H) of the final rule, a new requirement that covered service providers furnish a guide along with the initial disclosures required by the rule, if the initial disclosures are contained in multiple or lengthy documents. This guide will assist responsible plan fiduciaries by ensuring that the location of all information required to be disclosed is evident and easy to find among other information that is provided. The Department agrees that covered service providers are in the best position to identify the location of information that otherwise may be difficult for a responsible plan fiduciary to find in multiple, highly technical or lengthy disclosure materials. Specifically, paragraph (c)(1)(iv)(H) provides that, if the information that must be disclosed pursuant to paragraph (c)(1)(iv)(A) through (G) of the final rule (the initial disclosures) is not contained in a single document, or if the document is in excess of a specified number of pages, the covered service provider must furnish to the responsible plan fiduciary a guide that specifically identifies the document and page or other sufficiently specific locator, such as a section, that enables the responsible plan fiduciary to quickly and easily find the specified information, as applicable to the contract or arrangement. The Department has reserved for comment the number of pages that will trigger the guide requirement even if the initial disclosures are furnished in a single document. Commenters should address whether such a page number requirement is an appropriate standard, whether standards must be included to prevent formatting or other manipulation of the page number requirement (e.g., by reducing font size or margins), what number of pages should be included as the standard, and whether any alternative standards exist that would be more beneficial to responsible plan fiduciaries reviewing lengthy documents.

In the Department's view, merely stating, for example, that required information is contained in a separate service contract or prospectus would not be sufficient. This new provision requires a specific locator to find the required information, including not only the identity of the document (to the extent disclosure may be contained in multiple documents) but also where such information is located within the document. In common parlance, a "guide" is a mechanism or tool that serves to direct or indicate information, or that advises or shows the way. Thus, in the context of this proposal, a guide would be helpful to the extent it serves to direct plan fiduciaries to specific relevant information required under the regulation. A document and pagination requirement represents one approach to guide plan fiduciaries by providing them with a direct unambiguous point of reference to the specific place where they could find the information. Alternatively, other locators, for example, direct links to the required information on an Internet/webpage, or section identification within a document may also be helpful but at the same or potentially lower cost. Accordingly, the proposal seeks comments on the use of two alternate locators. Each is equally weighted under the proposal. The first is a document and page requirement. The Department assumes for purposes of this proposal that paginated documents are the norm for employee benefit contracts and other materials subject to disclosure under the regulation. The second choice is a "sufficiently specific" locator, such as a section. This alternative is intended to be more general, but only to the extent still effective. Specifically, in addition to specifying the document or documents where required disclosures are located, the proposal requires that the guide identify the "page or other sufficiently specific locator, such as section, that enables the plan fiduciary to quickly and easily find" the required information. The Department is neutral as between these alternatives because either would satisfy the intended purpose of the guide—to help plan fiduciaries quickly and easily find the required disclosures. The proposal's reference to "section" is meant as an example, however, and not as a safe harbor. Section references, whether by name or number or some other method, would be acceptable locators only if they were sufficiently specific to enable plan fiduciaries to quickly and easily find the relevant information. The proposal allows covered service providers to choose pagination or the more general alternative. Individuals are encouraged to comment on whether a final rule, assuming it were to include a guide requirement, should permit a choice of locators, as proposed, or whether the rule should require only one locator, and why. The Department also welcomes comments on whether page numbers and sections are effective and feasible locators, whether individually or as alternatives, and whether and why other locators may be preferable. The Department also welcomes comment on other mechanisms which could be used in a guide to quickly identify relevant information for fiduciaries and on the benefits and costs of the two options outlined here.

A similar standard applies for information disclosed electronically. A covered service provider may not merely furnish the link to a separate contract or to a prospectus. Either a more specific link directly to the required information must be furnished, or a page or other sufficiently specific locator, such as a section, must be furnished in addition to an electronic hyperlink.

Some interested parties have suggested that a guide requiring inclusion of a specific page or other locator could be difficult and potentially very costly to covered service providers and plans. The Department is particularly interested in comments on this issue. The Department asks that comments specifically identify such challenges and the anticipated cost of addressing them, and explain how currently available technology can or cannot reduce those costs. The Department also is interested in whether web-based approaches, which allow the reader to move readily by hyperlink back and forth between related information in a summary document and the more detailed document or documents from which the summary was derived, could provide an effective alternative for disclosures provided electronically. In offering alternatives, please explain how they would meet the Department's objective in proposing a guide, which is to assist responsible plan fiduciaries by ensuring that the location of all information required to be disclosed is evident and easy to find among other information that is provided.

2. Required Elements; Changes to Guide

If a guide is required, the covered service provider must disclose the location of: (i) the description of services to be provided to the covered plan, as required by paragraph (c)(1)(iv)(A) of the final rule; (ii) the statement concerning services to be provided as a fiduciary and/or as a registered investment adviser, as required by paragraph (c)(1)(iv)(B) of the final rule; (iii) the description of all direct compensation, as required by paragraph (c)(1)(iv)(C)(1) of the final rule; (iv) the description of all indirect compensation, as required by paragraph (c)(1)(iv)(C)(2) of the final rule; (v) the description of any compensation that will be paid among related parties, as required by paragraph (c)(1)(iv)(C)(3) of the final rule; (vi) the description of any compensation for termination of the contract or arrangement, as required by paragraph (c)(1)(iv)(C)(4) of the final rule; (vii) the description of all compensation (and/or a reasonable estimate of the cost to the covered plan) for recordkeeping services, as required by paragraph (c)(1)(iv)(D) of the final rule; and (viii) for covered service providers described in paragraphs (c)(1)(iii)(A)(2) or (c)(1)(iii)(B) of the final rule, the description of any compensation, annual operating expenses, and ongoing expenses (or, if applicable, total annual operating expenses), set forth in paragraph (c)(1)(iv)(E)(1) and (2), as required by paragraphs (c)(1)(iv)(E)(1) and (2) and (c)(1)(iv)(F)(1) of the final rule.

The guide also must identify a person or office, including contact information, that the responsible plan fiduciary may use regarding the disclosures provided pursuant to the final rule. Paragraph (c)(1)(iv)(H)(2). This requirement will further assist responsible plan fiduciaries by clearly identifying an individual or office that the fiduciary may contact to the extent he or she has difficulty locating any information referenced in the guide, or has questions concerning the disclosures themselves. A required guide must be furnished as a separate document. Paragraph (c)(1)(iv)(H)(3). The Department's goal, in requiring that the guide be a separate document, is to ensure that it is brought to the attention of the responsible plan fiduciary and prominently featured so that the fiduciary can use it effectively in his or her review of the required disclosures. The Department solicits comments on whether the separate document requirement, by itself, is likely to ensure that the responsible plan fiduciary adequately understands both the existence and purpose of the guide, or whether other conditions are needed. For instance, in addition to the separate document requirement, would the guide be improved by requiring specific language, such as an introductory statement in the guide as to the purpose of the guide? Further, if the guide is furnished electronically, for example as an attachment to email, would responsible plan fiduciaries benefit from a notice comparable to the notice required pursuant by 29 CFR 2520.104b-1(c)(1)(iii) (requiring the provision of notice to participants at the time a document is furnished electronically that apprises participants of the significance of the document when it is not otherwise reasonably evident as transmitted).

Finally, the proposal includes an amendment to paragraph (c)(1)(v) of the final rule, concerning the disclosure of changes to previously disclosed information. Specifically, the Department proposes to revise paragraph (c)(1)(v)(B)(2) of the rule to require that changes to the information contained in the guide must be disclosed, at least annually to responsible plan fiduciaries. The Department believes that a periodic requirement to disclose any changes to the information contained in the guide will be more beneficial to plan fiduciaries and less burdensome to covered service providers than ongoing and sporadic disclosure each time a change to one component of the guide occurs. The Department solicits comment on whether it would be more effective to require that the entire guide (rather than only changes to information contained in the guide) be disclosed on an annual basis, if changes have occurred during the preceding year.

3. Compliance and Delivery

Several commenters on the interim final rule suggested that if the Department were to adopt a summary or other formatting requirement in the final rule, it should provide an illustration of how a covered service provider may comply with such requirement to encourage consistency and allow for lower cost alternatives. While the Department is not including a model guide as part of this publication, the Department previously posted on its Web site, at *www.dol.gov/ebsa/ pdf/408b2sampleguide.pdf*, a sample guide to initial disclosures that may be useful to plan service providers. The guide was published as an appendix to the final rule as a sample and is an example of what the Department believes guides to initial disclosures may look like in practice.

In addition, commenters on the interim final rule requested guidance on the manner of delivering required information to responsible plan fiduciaries. Nothing in the regulation limits the ability of covered service providers to furnish information required by the regulation to responsible plan fiduciaries via electronic media, for example, on a website.[3] However, unless the information disclosed by a covered service provider on a website is readily accessible to responsible plan fiduciaries, and fiduciaries have clear notification on how to gain such access, the information on the website may not be regarded as furnished within the meaning of the regulation.

C. Request for Comments

As discussed above, the Department believes that the proposed guide requirement strikes an appropriate balance between the need to facilitate responsible plan fiduciaries' review of information and the costs and burdens attendant to preparing such a guide. However, the Department invites comments from interested persons on all aspects of this proposal, including the regulatory alternatives discussed in Section 4 of the Regulatory Impact Analysis, below, that were considered by the Department in developing this proposal.

The Department encourages parties to provide specific suggestions or data concerning the structure of the guide, as proposed, and whether its requirements are feasible and cost-effective. For example, how many (and what types of) products and services will require a guide? Do economies of scale exist such that the guide service providers prepare for one product or service could be used for multiple clients? Can service providers give the Department an estimate of the costs they will incur to create a guide? While aggregate costs of the guide are helpful, commenters are strongly encouraged to break down these costs into their constituent elements when possible. For example, when possible, break down the costs of the guide requirement as applied to each of the specific content requirements in paragraph (c)(1)(iv) of the final rule (i.e., subparagraphs (A) through (G) of the final rule), and as applied to the different types of covered service providers described in paragraph (c)(1)(iii) of the final rule.

The Department also invites comments and suggestions as to alternative tools that would assist plan fiduciaries in reviewing the initial disclosures. Commenters are encouraged to state whether they believe these tools would be more, or less, beneficial to plan fiduciaries, as compared to the proposed guide, taking into account the costs and burdens to covered service providers, and possibly other parties, to prepare such tools.

Further, the Department invites comments on whether the amendment instead should require that covered service providers furnish a summary of specified "key" disclosures? If so, what "key" information warrants inclusion in a summary? How costly would it be to prepare a summary and who would bear its costs? Would these costs decrease significantly after an initial transition period and, if so, how significantly? Which parties, other than covered service providers, might be involved in the preparation of a summary? What liability and other legal issues might arise for covered service providers and others from summarizing "key" information, and how should these issues be managed? How would responsible plan fiduciaries likely use the summarized information and what effect, if any, would it have on their review of the underlying disclosures? Further, what are the likely benefits and

costs of requiring that covered service providers furnish any required tool (whether a guide, a summary, or other tool) in a specified format? Is a guide or other tool likely to increase the probability that responsible plan fiduciaries review the initial disclosures, because the required information is easier to find? What formatting requirements (*e.g.*, a chart, page limits), if any, lend themselves to presentation of the initial disclosures required by the rule? Finally, what innovations in the preparation and delivery of disclosures currently exist in the marketplace, and how might a formatting requirement take advantage of these innovations?

D. Focus Group Testing

Elsewhere in today's *Federal Register*, the Department announced its intention to conduct approximately eight to 10 focus group sessions with approximately 70 to 100 fiduciaries to small pension plans (those with fewer than 100 participants). The purpose of the focus group testing is to explore current practices and effects of EBSA's final regulation. This may provide information about the need for a guide, summary, or similar tool to help responsible plan fiduciaries navigate and understand the required disclosures. The focus group participants will be asked to provide information including the following: (1) their role with respect to their plan; (2) the number of service providers hired by the plan; (3) whether they are aware of and understand the disclosures mandated by the 408(b)(2) final regulation; (4) their experience with receiving the disclosures; (5) whether they were able to find information regarding the services that would be provided and the costs of those services; (6) whether their review of the disclosures impacted their decision-making with regard to hiring, monitoring, or retaining service providers or changing plan investment options; (7) whether their covered service providers furnish a guide or similar organizational tool to help find specific information within the disclosures; and (8) whether a guide to the required disclosures would be beneficial to them, and if so, how much they would be willing to pay to receive a guide. The focus group announcement, published pursuant to the Paperwork Reduction Act of 1995, explains the planned focus group testing in more detail and provides other relevant information, including how and from whom to obtain more information about the planned testing process. The results of the focus group testing will be made available to the public after the testing has been completed. Because this will not occur until after the close of the 90-day comment period for this proposal, the Department may decide to reopen the comment period on this proposal to solicit comments on such results. The Department decided to proceed with both this proposal and the focus group information-gathering techniques simultaneously, rather than consecutively, in order to avoid further, and unnecessary, delay. In making this decision, the Department is mindful of the fact that the ERISA section 408(b)(2) rulemaking, in general, began in 2007[4] and that the final rule was effective on July 1, 2012.[5]

E. Effective Date

The Department proposes that the amendment to the final rule contained in this notice will be effective 12 months after publication of a final amendment in the **Federal Register**. The Department invites comments on whether the amendment, as finalized, should be effective on a different date.

F. Regulatory Impact Analysis

1. Executive Orders 12866 and 13563

Executive Orders 12866 and 13563 direct agencies to assess all costs and benefits of available regulatory alternatives and, if regulation is necessary, to select regulatory approaches that maximize net benefits (including potential economic, environmental, public health and safety effects, distributive impacts, and equity). Executive Order 13563 emphasizes the importance of quantifying both costs and benefits, of reducing costs, of harmonizing rules, and of promoting flexibility. OMB has determined that this action is not "economically significant" within the meaning of 3(f)(1) of the executive order because it is not likely to have an effect on the economy of $100 million or more in any one year. The proposed rule is significant under section 3(f)(4) of the Executive Order, because it raises novel legal or policy issues arising from the President's priorities. Accordingly, the rule has been reviewed by OMB.

2. The Need for Regulatory Action

On February 3, 2012, the Department published a final rule in the **Federal Register** concerning disclosures that must be furnished

---

[3] The Department's regulations at 29 CFR §2520.104b-1 apply solely for purposes of disclosures from plans to participants and beneficiaries and do not extend to disclosures from third parties to plan fiduciaries.

[4] 72 FR 70988 (December 13, 2007).

[5] 77 FR 5632 (February 3, 2012).

before plan fiduciaries enter into, extend or renew contracts or arrangements for services to certain pension plans in order for such a contract or arrangement to be "reasonable," as required by ERISA section 408(b)(2).

In seeking to promote economic efficiency, the final regulation allowed covered service providers to satisfy the disclosure requirements using different documents from various sources as long as the documents, collectively, contained the required disclosures. The Department recognized, however, that allowing the disclosure requirements to be satisfied through multiple documents could make it difficult and time consuming for responsible plan fiduciaries to find and analyze particular disclosures. Moreover, the benefits associated with providing the disclosures could be diluted if the information provided to responsible plan fiduciaries is obscured in long, highly technical documents. Therefore, when publishing the interim final regulation, the Department requested comments regarding whether it should include a summary of or guide to the mandated disclosure requirements. Specifically, the Department requested comments addressing the costs, benefits, and burdens associated with requiring a summary or guide and how it could effectively construct such a requirement to ensure that it is practical and useful.

Based on comments received in response to its request, the Department concluded when it issued the final rule that it lacked specific suggestions or data on how best to structure a guide or similar requirement and what the real costs of such a requirement would be. The Department therefore decided not to include such a requirement in the final rule without providing separately for public review and comment. The Department stated its intent to publish a Notice of Proposed Rulemaking under which covered service providers may be required to furnish a guide or similar tool along with the rule's initial disclosures. The Department believes that a guide will enable the responsible plan fiduciaries to find needed compensation and other information and will reduce the costs they otherwise would incur searching for such information when the required disclosures are contained in multiple or lengthy documents. The Department also believes that covered service providers are best positioned to provide the guide, when required, in a cost-effective manner, because they have the specialized knowledge required to determine where the required disclosures are located, and they generally will need to locate the information only once for a large number of clients, each of whom otherwise would have to locate the information separately. Anecdotal evidence suggests that small plan fiduciaries in particular often have difficulty obtaining required information in an understandable format, because small plans lack the bargaining power and specialized expertise possessed by large plan fiduciaries. Therefore, the Department anticipates that requiring the covered service providers to furnish a guide in circumstances where the required disclosures cannot otherwise be quickly and easily located will especially benefit small plan fiduciaries.

3. *Summary of Impacts*

In accordance with OMB Circular A-4,[6] Table 1 below depicts an accounting statement showing the Department's assessment of the benefits and costs associated with this proposed regulatory action.

Table 1.—*Accounting Table*

Category	Primary Estimate	Low Estimate	High Estimate	Year Dollar	Discount Rate	Period Covered
Benefits						
Annualized Monetized ($millions/year)[7]	40.3	26.9	60.4	2013	7%	2014-2023
	40.3	26.9	60.4	2013	3%	2014-2023
Note: Quantified benefits are from time savings resulting from use of the guide.						
Costs						
Annualized Monetized ($millions/year)	13.4	6.8	22.3	2013	7%	2014-2023
	13.4	6.8	22.3	2013	3%	2014-2023
Note: Quantified costs are for service providers to prepare and deliver a guide.						
Transfers	Not Applicable					

4. *Regulatory Alternatives*

Executive Orders 12866 and 13563 require an economically significant regulation to include an assessment of the costs and benefits of potentially effective and reasonably feasible alternatives to a planned regulation, and an explanation of why the planned regulatory action is preferable to the identified potential alternatives. While this proposed rule is not economically significant, the Department, nevertheless, believes it would be helpful to identify several alternatives considered to enhance the proposed rule's economic efficiency. The major alternatives are discussed below.

Status quo: The Department considered, and rejected, some commenters' views on the interim final rule that the Department should take no further action - *i.e.*, that the Department not adopt a guide or any formatting or similar requirement. These commenters explained that, although they understand the Department's goal in requiring a tool such as a guide, they believe that a "one size fits all" format may not be feasible and that the costs associated with any such tool would be significant. For the reasons discussed at length earlier in this document, the Department continues to believe that furnishing a tool to assist responsible plan fiduciaries' review of the regulation's initial disclosures is essential.

Mandate a summary: As discussed earlier in this preamble, commenters advocating for a summary stressed the need for medium and small plan fiduciaries to have a summary of the required disclosures to help them navigate through and analyze highly technical disclosures that are scattered throughout multiple documents. They argue that service providers could produce summaries more efficiently and at less cost than responsible plan fiduciaries. Other comments raised concerns that mandating the specific format of a summary would hinder innovation and not allow flexibility when dealing with the great variety of pension plan service arrangements. Some commenters raised additional concerns that a summary could unintentionally become the primary document upon which some fiduciaries would rely without thoroughly reviewing all of the required disclosures. Some commenters argued that the benefits of the summary would exceed the cost of preparing it. The Department believes that the costs to provide a summary likely would be higher for many service providers than the cost incurred to provide a guide or roadmap to responsible plan fiduciaries. For this reason, and the other reasons discussed earlier in this document including the concern that fiduciaries could over-rely on the summary, the Department viewed this option as less preferable than a guide requirement. The Department, however, specifically solicits comments on these issues, including ideas on how to overcome the danger that fiduciaries will rely exclusively on the summary, without appropriately considering the more complete disclosures from which the summary was derived.

Conditional exemption: The Department considered mandating a guide, with page number requirement, but exempting covered service providers from this requirement if producing the guide were either impossible or unreasonably burdensome. Since publication of the final rule, some covered service providers have expressed concern to the Department that it would be prohibitively expensive and unreasonably burdensome for them to comply with a guide requirement, especially if such a requirement resembles the sample guide that is available on the Department's website, which includes page number references. Some of these service providers, for example, argue that their service contracts or arrangements and disclosure materials are unique and individualized based on the needs of each of their plan clients, and that this uniqueness makes it unreasonably burdensome, if not practically impossible, in these cases to efficiently produce guides on a group basis. The Department believes, however, that the public record neither supports nor refutes this position, and the Department is not independently aware of any research or studies bearing one way or the other on this issue. As explained earlier in this document, the Department intends to use this proposal as the vehicle to solicit specific comments

[6] Available at *http://www.whitehouse.gov/omb/circulars/a004/a-4.pdf*.

[7] The annualized monetized benefit and cost estimates are the same for the three and seven percent discount rates as the underlying yearly benefits and costs are the same for each year.

and build a robust public record on this issue. The Department generally is skeptical that a guide and page number requirement is unreasonably burdensome in light of advances in technology, such as data tagging, and the standardization of many service agreements and investment and other disclosure documents. Absent credible evidence to the contrary, the Department believes that economies of scale still may be achieved by covered services providers that produce guides for multiple plan clients. Further, a conditional exemption of the type under this alternative also suffers from a degree of inherent ambiguity in that covered service providers and others would need metrics and standards to define the circumstances when the production of a guide was "impossible" or "unreasonably burdensome." This alternative also would treat covered service providers differently in a way that may not be positive and beneficial for plans over the long run. For instance, the Department is concerned that giving an exemption to those covered service providers who cannot currently provide a guide efficiently would effectively reward them for their inefficiency. Also, such an exemption would undercut the policy being advanced by the new 408(b)(2) disclosures.

After analyzing the comments, the Department chose to require covered service providers to provide fiduciaries with a guide to the required disclosures, but to allow the use of page number or a specific locator. The Department believes that the guide requirement strikes an appropriate balance between facilitating a plan fiduciary's evaluation of information critical to a prudent decision-making process and the costs and burdens associated with the preparation of a guide. The guide will provide clarity and specificity, while avoiding the uncertainty and burdens inherent in constructing a summary of the required disclosures. In contrast, a summary could result in unnecessarily duplicative disclosures for at least some service providers to the extent the same information that is disclosed to comply with the initial disclosures is also required to be disclosed on the summary. Further, for some service providers, some information that must be disclosed may be highly technical and may not lend itself to a "simplified" summary. The Department agrees that a summary document may be useful to some fiduciaries, especially in comparing fees and services among competing service providers, but is concerned that a summary may unintentionally become the primary document some responsible plan fiduciaries would rely on, which would be counter to the Department's intention that required disclosures be reviewed and understood by responsible plan fiduciaries.

The Department is making available on its website (http://www.dol.gov/ebsa/pdf/408b2sampleguide.pdf) a sample guide to the initial disclosures to facilitate public comments on this proposal and solicits comments on whether including such a model in the final rule would provide useful guidance and reduce compliance costs for at least some service providers.

5. *Affected Entities and Other Assumptions*

The Department estimates that this proposed rule will affect about 45,000 defined benefit pension plans with over 40.9 million participants and almost 638,000 defined contribution pension plans with approximately 88.7 million participants. The overwhelming majority of the affected businesses sponsoring these plans will be small businesses: out of the affected pension plans, the Department estimates that approximately 35,000 are small defined benefit plans and 563,000 small individual account plans.[8] Most of the defined contribution pension plans, approximately 506,000, are participant-directed individual account plans.

The proposed regulation applies to contracts or arrangements between covered plans and covered service providers. A familiar example is a contract between a recordkeeper and a covered individual account plan under which the recordkeeper will make available a platform of designated investment alternatives consisting of mutual funds, monitor plan and participant and beneficiary transactions, and provide plan administrative services such as maintaining participant accounts, records, and statements.[9] In order to estimate the number of covered service providers and the number of service provider-plan arrange-

ments, the Department used data from Schedule C of the plan year 2011 Form 5500 submissions filed with the Department.

In general, only plans with 100 or more participants that have made payments to a service provider of at least $5,000 are required to file the Form 5500 Schedule C. These plans are also required to report the type of services provided by each service provider. The Department counted the service providers most likely to provide the services described in paragraph (c)(1)(iii) of the final rule, which defines which service providers are "covered" by the rule.[10] In total, there were nearly 12,000 distinct covered service providers reported in the Form 5500 Schedule C data.

The Department acknowledges that this estimate may be imprecise. On the one hand, some of the service providers counted here may not be covered service providers, but the Department is unable to further refine this group due to the limitations of the Schedule C data. On the other hand, because small plans generally do not file Schedule C, the number of covered service providers will be understated if a substantial number of them service only small plans. However, the Department believes that most small plans use the same service providers as large plans; therefore, the estimate based on the Schedule C filings by large plans is reasonable.[11]

Schedule C data was also used to count the number of covered plan-service provider arrangements. On average, defined benefit plans employ more covered service providers per plan than defined contribution plans, and large plans use more covered service providers per plan than small plans. In total, the Department estimates that defined benefit plans have over 136,000 arrangements with covered service providers, while defined contribution plans have over 2 million arrangements. The Department does not have sufficient data to estimate the number of these arrangements that will require a guide because the required disclosures are contained in multiple or lengthy documents. Therefore, for purposes of the analysis, the Department assumes that all of these arrangements will require a guide.

In the interim final and final rule, the Department assumed that 50 percent of disclosures would be delivered electronically. The Department did not receive any comments regarding this assumption; therefore, the Department continues to assume that about 50 percent of disclosures between covered service providers and responsible plan fiduciaries are delivered only in electronic format.

The Department lacks data on the number of service providers that are currently providing a guide or other aid to help responsible plan fiduciaries understand the disclosures provided and find required information. Therefore, the Department has estimated benefits and costs of the rule assuming that currently covered service providers are not providing guides or other aids to their disclosures. To the extent that some covered service providers are already voluntarily providing guides, both benefits and costs will be overestimated.

Similarly, our assumption of 100 percent compliance with the 2012 final rule, if incorrect, would cause our estimate of time savings to be too high. In such a case, however, this proposed rule could have the effect of increasing compliance with the 2012 final rule, which would yield both time costs (associated with review of disclosures) and consumer protection benefits that have not been quantified in this impact analysis.

6. *Benefits*

The final regulation allows covered service providers to make the required disclosures through multiple documents. However, comments on the interim final rule raised concerns that providing many voluminous documents to fiduciaries could overwhelm them and the time and effort needed to find the relevant information still could be substantial. This proposed rule addresses this concern by requiring the covered service provider to provide the responsible plan fiduciary with a guide that specifically identifies the document and page or other specific locator, such as a section, that will allow the responsible plan fiduciary to quickly and easily find the required disclosures if the disclosures are not contained in a single document, or if the document is in excess of

---

[8] Estimates of the number of plans and participants are taken from the EBSA's 2011 Pension Research File, http://www.dol.gov/ebsa/publications/form5500dataresearch.html#planbulletins. Small pension plans are plans with generally less than 100 participants, as specified in the Form 5500 instructions.

[9] In order to be a covered service provider, the regulation also requires that a service provider must reasonably expect $1,000 or more in compensation, direct or indirect, to be received in connection with the services to the plan. 29 CFR 250.408b-2(c)(1)(iii).

[10] In order to provide a reasonable estimate, the Department used Schedule C service codes where it believed a majority of service providers would be covered service providers. The following codes were used: service providers with reported type codes corresponding

to contract administrator, recordkeeping and information management, consulting (pension), custodial (other than securities), custodial (pension), trustee (individual), trustee (bank, trust company, or similar financial institution), insurance agents and brokers, insurance services, trustee (discretionary), trustee (directed), investment advisory (participant), investment advisory (plan), investment management, real estate brokerage, securities brokerage, valuation (appraisals, etc.), copying and duplicating, participant loan processing, participant communications, and foreign entities.

[11] While in general small plans are not required to file a Schedule C, some voluntarily file. Looking at Schedule C filings by small plans, the Department concluded that most small plans reporting data on Schedule C used the same group of service providers as most larger plans.

[RESERVED] number of pages. The positive net benefit of the guide requirement arises from specialization and economies of scale. Covered service providers are most familiar with the documents containing the required disclosures, and will make similar, if not identical, disclosures to many different responsible plan fiduciaries. Therefore, the Department expects that covered service providers will be able to find the information and create a guide, when required, at a lower cost than the responsible plan fiduciary. Some service providers will be able to spread these costs across hundreds, and in some cases, thousands, of arrangements.

The Department estimates that there are 2.2 million covered arrangements between 12,000 covered service providers and nearly 684,000 covered plans for which disclosures are required under the final rule. While some of these arrangements are simple, others are complex and would require much information to be disclosed. The Department is not aware of any information that currently exists that could be used to measure the time savings that would result from the guide in circumstances where a guide would be required.

In order to produce an estimate of possible time savings, the Department conducted an informal study with two groups of staff. One group searched for specified information in plan and investment documents using a guide-like document, while the other group searched for the specified information in the same documents using a list of the documents in which the information could be found. The result of the informal study was that the group that used the guide-like document, on average, saved 30 minutes compared to that group that used the list. While only a subset (a convenience sample) of the information required to be disclosed by the final rule was searched for as part of the informal study, the results provide a basis for a conservative estimate of possible time savings that would result from the guide. Using this time savings as a proxy for the time savings that would be realized by a plan fiduciary, a total annual time savings of 342,000 hours would result (0.5 hours × 684,000 fiduciaries). If the responsible plan fiduciary's time were valued at $118 per hour, the value of the annual time saved would be $40.3 million.[12, 13]

The Department notes that the amount of time savings is uncertain. If the average time savings were only 20 minutes, the total value of the time saving would be $26.9 million, while the value of the time savings would be $60.4 million if the average time savings were 45 minutes. Time savings also will depend on the sophistication and abilities of the individual fiduciary reviewer. For instance, if a reviewing responsible plan fiduciary is sophisticated relative to the informal study's participants, the savings to this fiduciary would be more toward the lower point of this range, and the reverse would be true to the extent the reviewing responsible plan fiduciary is less sophisticated. Time savings might be greater to the extent that responsible plan fiduciaries will have to review changes to previously disclosed information, plans have multiple plan fiduciaries that will experience the time savings, or plans review bids from multiple service providers in response to requests for proposal.

An additional benefit of the guide requirement is that appropriate use of the guide will provide responsible plan fiduciaries with confidence that they have found the relevant information in the covered service provider's disclosures to fulfill their ERISA fiduciary responsibility to determine whether a contract or arrangement is reasonable. This confidence will lead to a further reduction in the time a responsible plan fiduciary spends searching through documents to make certain they have not missed additional relevant information. While the Department was unable to estimate this portion of the time savings, it has the potential to be large.

The guide document used in the informal study included pagination, because page numbers are used in most industry contracts and similar documents that contain the required disclosures, and the Department wanted to obtain an upper-bound estimate of the benefits that would be obtained through the most specific locator, a page number. The Department did not analyze the incremental benefits of providing pagination relative to providing the section or area by name or other identifier, because it does not have the necessary data on the prevalence and characteristics of other identifiers to perform a meaningful analysis. The Department is aware of numerous possible identifiers

other than pagination, for example, by page and line, paragraph, section, chapter, part, and volume. In addition, in the case of electronic media, other identifiers include character, screen, web-page, link, and folder. However, unlike pagination, we have no information on the extent to which these identifiers are used in employee benefit contracts and similar documents. The Department, therefore, solicits comments on the prevalence and characteristics of identifiers other than pagination and their usefulness. The Department also solicits comments on whether there are any relevant federal or state regulatory or similar requirements or standards on effective and not misleading disclosures that should be considered by the Department. Information received will be used to analyze and attempt to quantify the incremental benefits of alternatives to pagination. Our premise is that there is a positive correlation between the precision of the identifier and the ease with which it can be located and the benefits realized, such that more precise and easily located identifiers will result in more time saved, and less precise identifiers will result in less time saved. For instance, if pagination is a more precise identifier than section, identification by section only will result in fewer benefits to plan fiduciaries than identification by pagination. Commenters are encouraged to be specific in identifying and describing the characteristics of identifiers. In addition, please also provide data, if available, on incremental costs of pagination relative to other identifiers.

7. Costs

As stated above, the proposed regulation modifies the requirements of the final rule by requiring covered service providers that provide the required disclosures in multiple or lengthy documents to provide a guide to the disclosures to responsible plan fiduciaries that will enable responsible plan fiduciaries to effectively review the disclosures made under the final regulation. The hour and cost burden associated with the guide requirement result from preparing and distributing the guide. As noted above, the Department estimates that approximately 12,000 covered service providers, 684,000 covered plans, and 2.2 million arrangements with covered plans would be affected by this proposed rule.

Covered service providers are responsible for locating the information and preparing the guide. In the initial year, service providers will have to locate the required information in the disclosures and create the guide. The Department believes that covered service providers will incur lower costs to locate this information than responsible plan fiduciaries, because they are more familiar with the required disclosure documents. Once the covered service provider locates the information in the documents, it can be used to create multiple guides.

While the final rule covers contracts and arrangements, the burden of creating the guide will be proportional to the number of products and services included in the contracts. In order to estimate the total cost associated with the guide requirement, the Department must determine the number of products and services that will require a guide. The Department is uncertain regarding the number of products or services; however, the Department believes that the total number of products offered by financial services firms exceeds the total number of services provided by other service providers. In 2012, there were a total of 16,380 mutual funds, closed-end funds, exchange traded funds, and unit investment trusts.[14] There also were 776 financial service firms that provided investment management services in the U.S. Seventy-six percent of these firms were independent fund advisors and the rest were brokerage firms, banks and thrifts, insurance companies, or non-U.S. fund advisors.

Due to the uncertainty regarding the number of products and services that would be subject to the guide requirement, the Department has created low-range, medium-range, and high-range estimates. The Department calculated these estimates by multiplying the number of products offered by financial service firms (16,380) by three, four and five resulting in a lowrange estimate of 49,140 products and services, a middle-range estimate of 65,520 products and services, and a high-range of 81,900 products and services.

In order to estimate the costs associated with the guide requirement, the Department also must estimate the time required to create a guide for each unique product or service. The Department lacks information

---

[12] EBSA estimates of 2013 labor rates include wages, other benefits, and overhead based on the National Occupational Employment Survey (June 2012, Bureau of Labor Statistics) and the Employment Cost Index (September 2012, Bureau of Labor Statistics). Total labor costs were estimated to average $126.07 per hour over the period for legal professionals, $67.76 for financial professionals, and $29.14 per hour for clerical staff. This estimate uses the average labor rate of a financial manager, $117.88, as a proxy for a plan fiduciary's labor rate.

[13] Many disclosures will stay the same over time, and therefore fiduciaries could experience lesser savings two years after implementation of the rule (and every year

beyond) because they would already have gone through the upfront process of learning which sections of which documents contain the necessary disclosures. On the other hand, plans may put out bids for service providers, for example, once every three to five years, at which time they may review disclosures from multiple service providers and many assets, thereby experiencing abnormally high time savings if they have access to disclosure guides. Given these offsetting effects, the Department assumes that the estimate presented here represents a plausible average across years.

[14] 2013 Investment Company Fact Book, *http://www.icifactbook.org/*, retrieved 11 September 2013.

on the time required by covered service providers to create a guide. The Department believes it is reasonable to assume that it will take a covered service provider no more than one-half hour to locate the required information in its own document. Once the information is found and the appropriate document, page, and (if applicable) section number is noted, the covered service provider can construct the guide. The Department estimates that the relevant information could be found and the guide could be constructed using a total of three hours of a financial professional or similar professional's time with a labor rate of $67.76 per hour, including time to review the document for accuracy.[15] The Department constructs a low-range estimate using two hours, a medium-range estimate using three hours, and a high-range estimate using four hours.

Based on the foregoing, the Department's low-range estimate of the cost covered service providers would incur to create their guides for the products and services is approximately $6.7 million annually (3x16,380 products and services x 2 hours[16] x $67.76), its medium-range estimate is $13.3 million annually (4x16,380 products and services x 3 hours[17] × $67.76), and its high-range estimate is $22.2 million annually (5x16,380 products and services x 4 hours[18] x $67.76).

The Department also conducted a threshold analysis in the Uncertainty section, below, which demonstrates the reasonableness of the assumption that the cost of requiring covered service providers to create a guide is less than the estimated benefit of $40.3 million annually.

The required disclosures, including the guide, can be delivered electronically at minimal costs, because material and mailing costs are not incurred for guides that are delivered electronically. Similar to the final rule, this regulatory impact analysis assumes that about 50 percent of the guides will be sent electronically (1.1 million guides representing 50 percent of the approximately 2.2 million contracts or arrangements) with minimal associated cost. The Department expects guides that are distributed on paper will be one to two pages in length, and that no additional postage will be required, because the guide will be included with the other disclosures being sent to the responsible plan fiduciary. If the guide is two pages, the associated material and printing cost will be $108,000 (1.1 million guides x 2 pages × $0.05 per page).

8. Uncertainty

The Department lacks complete data and empirical evidence to estimate the cost for covered service providers to create the guide. However, the Department believes that the costs to produce the guide will be less than the benefit derived from providing it to responsible plan fiduciaries for several reasons. For example, the burden will be on the covered service provider to provide the location of the required disclosures. This should reduce overall search time, because the covered service provider is more familiar with the documents than the responsible plan fiduciary. In addition, economies of scale will further reduce the costs, since service providers frequently offer multiple products that use similar documents and service multiple clients with the same products. Therefore, a single or very similar guide could be used for many similar products and clients with little or no marginal cost impact. In addition, the Department expects reduced costs to result, because, on average, responsible plan fiduciaries are expected to have higher wages than the financial professional the Department anticipates will construct the guides.

There are several ways covered service providers can develop guides. With respect to guides that include information about investment products (e.g., mutual funds, bank collective funds, or insurance products), the Department believes that over time, the market will evolve such that the issuers of investment products will furnish product-specific investment-related fee and expense information and other material needed to create a guide directly to covered service providers or to a third party electronic data base containing such information, because the issuers can prepare and disseminate the data in the most cost-effective manner. Covered service providers, such as recordkeepers that offer a platform of designated investment alternatives to a covered plan, will receive the fee and expense information and incorporate it into the guides they prepare for responsible plan fiduciaries.

In order to estimate the total cost associated with the guide requirement, the Department must estimate the total number of services and products for which a guide must be prepared. The Department lacks sufficient data to make this estimate. However, the Department believes that the total number of products offered by financial services firms exceeds the total number of services provided by other service providers. In 2012, there were a total of 16,380 mutual funds, closed-end funds, exchange traded funds, and unit investment trusts.[19] There also were 776 financial service firms that provided investment management services in the U.S. Seventy-six percent of these firms were independent fund advisors and the rest were brokerage firms, banks and thrifts, insurance companies, or non-U.S. fund advisors.

In order to create a reasonable upper bound for the total number of products and services that will have to be disclosed in a guide, the Department assumes that five times the number of products offered by financial service firms or 81,900 products and services (16,380 × 5) would require a guide. This estimate accounts for all products and services subject to the guide requirement, and includes circumstances in which the content necessary to create the guide is provided directly to a covered service provider who incorporates it into its own guide for the products and services it provides to the covered plan. For example, recordkeepers often provide a variety of services to plans, including maintaining a platform of designated investment alternatives, as well as administration and monitoring of participant and beneficiary transactions (e.g., enrollment, payroll deductions and contributions, offering designated investment alternatives, and other covered plan investments, loans, withdrawals and distributions). When a recordkeeper enters into a contract or arrangement with a covered plan to provide such services and the designated investment alternatives consist of mutual funds, the recordkeeper may receive investment-related fee and expense data from a mutual fund company, or a third-party electronic database, and the recordkeeper will incorporate this information into the guide for its contract or arrangement with the covered plan.[20]

As stated earlier, the mid-range estimate of the benefits to be derived from creating and providing the guide was $40.3 million. If the Department assumes that an individual with a labor rate of $67.76 per hour creates the guide, then the use of, on average, 7.4 hours[21] to create the guide for each product or service would cause the costs of the proposed rule to equal its estimated benefits. This 7.4-hour total would entail finding all the required information, noting the page and section number, and entering the information on the guide. The Department believes that nearly seven hours is more than adequate time to perform this function and thus the rule's costs are likely to be less than or equal to its benefits.

The Department performed a sensitivity analysis by increasing the estimate of the total number of products. This estimate was obtained by multiplying the number of financial services products (16,380) by seven and ten and then calculating the break-even average number of hours associated with preparing a guide. As the total number of hours to be allocated stayed the same, the associated average hours per product were 5.3 and 3.7 hours respectively as the number of products increases. As implied by the upper bound of four hours for guide creation mentioned in the Cost section, above, the Department believes that 3.7 hours would be more than adequate, on average, to create a guide for a single product or service or to add a product or service to an existing guide, and thus, even using an extremely high assumption regarding the number of affected products per financial services firm, the rule's costs are likely to be less than or equal to its benefits.

The Department's estimates assume that costs to create the guide would remain constant over time. However, the Department expects there will be a downward trend for such costs in future years, because covered service providers (i) already will have guides for most products and services and only would need to update them as appropriate, and (ii) already will have created a template for the guide and will be familiar with how to incorporate information regarding new products and services into the template.

The Department welcomes public comments regarding its estimates of the benefits and costs of the proposed rule. The Department is particularly interested in information and data regarding the potential for time savings to plan fiduciaries, the number of products, services,

---

[15] The Department estimates 2013 hourly labor rates include wages, other benefits, and overhead based on data from the National Occupational Employment Survey (June 2012, Bureau of Labor Statistics) and the Employment Cost Index (September 2012, Bureau of Labor Statistics); the 2012 estimated labor rates are then inflated to 2013 labor rates.

[16] The total associated hour burden is 98,300 hours.

[17] The total associated hour burden is 196,600 hours.

[18] The total associated hour burden is 327,600 hours.

[19] 2013 Investment Company Fact Book, *http://www.icifactbook.org/*, retrieved 11 September 2013.

[20] The estimate also accounts for the situations when covered service providers must include content in the guide regarding indirect compensation received in connection with services described pursuant to paragraph (c)(1)(iv)(A) of the rule.

[21] This number was derived by dividing the $40.3 million mid-range estimate of the cost of the guide by $67.76 per hour and dividing this quotient by the estimated 49,140 products and services that will require a guide.

contracts and arrangements for which a guide would be required, the costs required to create the guide (including costs incurred for system changes and costs related to placing page or section number references in the guide), the potential for economies of scale in constructing the guide, and current best practices in the pension plan service provider industry for providing guides or summaries to clients.

9. *Regulatory Flexibility Analysis*

The Regulatory Flexibility Act (5 U.S.C. 601, et seq.) (RFA) imposes certain requirements with respect to Federal rules that are subject to the notice and comment requirements of section 553(b) of the Administrative Procedure Act (5 U.S.C. 551, et seq.) and which are likely to have a significant economic impact on a substantial number of small entities. Unless an agency determines that a proposal is not likely to have such an impact, section 604 of the RFA requires that the agency present a regulatory flexibility analysis (RFA) describing the rule's impact on small entities and explaining how the agency made its decisions with respect to the application of the rule to small entities. Small entities include small businesses, organizations and governmental jurisdictions.

a. *Need for and Objectives of the Rule*

Service providers to pension plans increasingly have complex compensation arrangements that may present conflicts of interest. Thus, small plan fiduciaries face increasing difficulty in carrying out their duty to assess whether the compensation paid to their service providers is reasonable. This proposed rule is designed to help both large and small plan fiduciaries identify and locate the information they need to negotiate with and select service providers who offer high quality services at reasonable rates and to comply with their fiduciary duties. The Department's requirement for covered service providers to provide a guide to responsible plan fiduciaries will be especially important to small plan fiduciaries as they review and analyze the required disclosures.

b. *Affected Small Entities*

The Department has limited data on the number of small entities affected by the rule. Using the Schedule C data from the Form 5500 the Department estimates that 11,800 service providers listed on the Schedule C have fees reported that total less than $7 million. This estimate of the number of small entities should be viewed as an upper bound as these service providers most likely have other sources of revenue besides pension plans, and fees from the vast majority of small plans are also not captured in this estimate. These service providers generally consist of professional service enterprises that provide a wide range of services to plans, such as investment management or advisory services for plans or plan participants, and accounting, auditing, actuarial, appraisal, banking, consulting, custodial, insurance, legal, recordkeeping, brokerage, third party administration, or valuation services. Many of these service providers have special education, training, and/or formal credentials in fields such as ERISA and benefits administration, employee compensation, taxation, actuarial science, law, accounting, or finance.

c. *Compliance Requirements*

The classes of small service providers subject to the proposed rule include service providers who are ERISA fiduciaries (for example, because they manage plan investments or are fiduciaries to investment vehicles holding plan assets in which the covered plan has a direct entity investment), who provide services as registered investment advisers to plans, who receive indirect compensation (or certain compensation from related parties) in connection with provision of specified services (namely, accounting, auditing, actuarial, appraisal, banking, certain consulting, custodial, insurance, participant investment advisory, legal, recordkeeping, securities or other investment brokerage, third party administration, or valuation services) or who provide recordkeeping or brokerage services involving a platform of investment options for participant-directed individual account plans.

These small covered service providers are required to disclose certain written information to responsible plan fiduciaries in connection with their service contracts or arrangements with covered plans. These proposed regulations require that covered service providers furnish the responsible plan fiduciary with a guide specifically identifying the document, page, and (if applicable) number where the required information is located. Such information includes a description of the services included in the arrangement and what direct and indirect compensation will be received in connection with the arrangement. Service providers whose arrangements include making investment products available to plans additionally must disclose specified investment-related information about such products. The required disclo-sures must be provided to the responsible plan fiduciary reasonably in advance of the parties entering into the contract or arrangement for covered services. Preparing compliant disclosures often will require knowledge of financial products and services and related compensation and revenue sharing arrangements.

As noted earlier in the impact analysis, there are economies of scale in the creation of guides. It would follow that, per product or service, small service providers would experience a cost of guide creation that is higher than the average discussed in section F.7, above.

d. *Agency Steps to Minimize Negative Impacts*

The Department took a number of steps to minimize any negative impact of the proposed rule on small service providers. One of the main reasons the Department chose to require covered service providers to provide a guide to responsible plan fiduciaries, rather than a summary, was that a guide would help small plan fiduciaries locate important information disclosed in multiple, often long and complex documents at a lower compliance cost to covered service providers.

The policy justification for these requirements includes benefits to plan fiduciaries, who will realize savings in the form of reduced search costs more than commensurate to the compliance costs shouldered by covered service providers. Small plan fiduciaries are likely to benefit most. Small covered service providers, while shouldering the cost of providing disclosure, likely will often pass these costs on to their plan clients, who, in turn, are estimated to reap a net benefit, on average, that will more than offset this shifted compliance cost.

10. *Paperwork Reduction Act*

As part of its continuing effort to reduce paperwork and respondent burdens, the Department of Labor conducts a preclearance consultation program to provide the general public and Federal agencies with an opportunity to comment on proposed and continuing collections of information in accordance with the Paperwork Reduction Act of 1995 (PRA 95) (44 U.S.C. 3506(c)(2)(A)). This helps to ensure that requested data can be provided in the desired format, reporting burden (time and financial resources) is minimized, collection instruments are clearly understood, and the impact of collection requirements on respondents can be properly assessed. Currently, the Department is soliciting comments concerning the proposed information collection request (ICR) included in this proposed rule, which would amend OBM Control Number 1210-0133, Contracts or Arrangements under Section 408(b)(2) - Fee Disclosure. A copy of the ICR may be obtained by contacting the individual identified below in this notice. The Department has submitted a copy of the proposed information collection to OMB in accordance with 44 U.S.C. 3507(d) for review of its information collections. The Department and OMB are particularly interested in comments that:

- Evaluate whether the proposed collection of information is necessary for the proper performance of the functions of the agency, including whether the information will have practical utility;

- Evaluate the accuracy of the agency's estimate of the burden of the collection of information, including the validity of the methodology and assumptions used;

- Enhance the quality, utility, and clarity of the information to be collected; and

- Minimize the burden of the collection of information on those who are to respond, including through the use of appropriate automated, electronic, mechanical, or other technological collection techniques or other forms of information technology, e.g., permitting electronic submission of responses.

Comments should be submitted to the addresses listed in the ADDRESSES section at the beginning of this Notice and received by the Department on or before [INSERT DATE THAT IS 90 DAYS FOLLOWING FEDERAL REGISTER PUBLICATION]. Comments also may be submitted to the Office of Management and Budget at the following address: Office of Information and Regulatory Affairs, Attn: OMB Desk Officer for DOL-EBSA, Office of Management and Budget, Room 10235, 725 17th Street, N.W., Washington, DC 20503; by Fax: 202-395-6881 (this is not a toll-free number); or by email: *OIRA_submission@omb.eop.gov*. OMB requests that comments be received within 30 days of publication of the Notice of Proposed Rulemaking to ensure their consideration. A copy of this ICR with applicable supporting documentation; including a description of the likely respondents, proposed frequency of response, and estimated total burden may be obtained free of charge from the RegInfo.gov Web site at *http://www.reginfo.gov/public/do/PRAViewICR?ref_nbr=* [201208-1210-001]or by contacting G. Christopher Cosby, Office of Policy and Research, U.S. Department of Labor, Employee Benefits Security Administration,

200 Constitution Avenue, NW., Room N 5647, Washington, DC 20210. Telephone (202) 219-8410; Fax: (202) 219 4745. These are not toll free numbers.

The information collection requirements of the proposed rule are contained in paragraph (c)(1)(iv)(H), which requires covered service providers to provide responsible plan fiduciaries with a guide specifically identifying the document, page number, and (if applicable) section number where the required data is located within multiple or complex documents.

The Department requested comments regarding a guide requirement when the interim final regulation was published. Although no public comments were received that specifically addressed the paperwork burden analysis of the information collections at the interim final rule stage, the comments that were submitted and described earlier in this preamble, contained information relevant to the costs and administrative burdens attendant to this proposal. The Department took such public comments into account in connection with developing this proposed rule and the paperwork burden analysis summarized below.

Annual Hour Burden

As stated earlier in this preamble, the Department estimated an hour burden range for the guide requirement of: 98,300 hours with an equivalent cost of $6.7 million annually (lowestimate), 196,600 hours with an equivalent cost of $13.4 million annually (medium-estimate), and 327,600 hours with an equivalent cost of $22.2 million annually (high-estimate). The Department's methodology for estimating the hour burden is discussed in detail in the Costs section of the Regulatory Impact Analysis, above.

Annual Cost Burden

As stated earlier in this preamble, the Department estimated that the material and printing cost burden associated with creating the guide would be $108,000 annually. The Department's methodology for estimating the cost burden is discussed in detail in the Costs section of the Regulatory Impact Analysis, above.

These paperwork burden estimates are summarized as follows:

Type of Review: Revision of existing collection.

Agency: Employee Benefits Security Administration, Department of Labor.

Title: Reasonable Contract or Arrangement Under Section 408(b)(2) - Fee Disclosure.

OMB Control Number: 1210-0133.

Affected Public: Business or other for-profit; not-for-profit institutions.

Estimated Number of Respondents: 12,000 annually.

Estimated Number of Responses: 2.2 million.

Frequency of Response: Annually; occasionally.

Estimated Annual Burden Hours: 196,600 hours annually.

Estimated Annual Burden Cost: $108,000 annually.

11. *Congressional Review Act*

The proposed rule is subject to the Congressional Review Act provisions of the Small Business Regulatory Enforcement Fairness Act of 1996 (5 U.S.C. 801 et seq.) and, if finalized, will be transmitted to Congress and the Comptroller General for review. The proposed rule is not a "major rule" as that term is defined in 5 U.S.C. 804, because it is not likely to result in (1) an annual effect on the economy of $100 million or more; (2) a major increase in costs or prices for consumers, individual industries, or Federal, State, or local government agencies, or geographic regions; or (3) significant adverse effects on competition, employment, investment, productivity, innovation, or on the ability of United States-based enterprises to compete with foreign-based enterprises in domestic and export markets.

12. *Unfunded Mandates Reform Act*

For purposes of the Unfunded Mandates Reform Act of 1995 (Pub. L. 104-4), as well as Executive Order 12875, the proposed rule does not include any Federal mandate that may result in expenditures by State, local, or tribal governments in the aggregate of more than $100 million, adjusted for inflation, or increase expenditures by the private sector of more than $100 million, adjusted for inflation.

13. *Federalism Statement*

Executive Order 13132 (August 4, 1999) outlines fundamental principles of federalism, and requires the adherence to specific criteria by

Federal agencies in the process of their formulation and implementation of policies that have substantial direct effects on the States, the relationship between the national government and States, or on the distribution of power and responsibilities among the various levels of government. The proposed rule does not have federalism implications because it has no substantial direct effect on the States, on the relationship between the national government and the States, or on the distribution of power and responsibilities among the various levels of government. Section 514 of ERISA provides, with certain exceptions specifically enumerated, that the provisions of Titles I and IV of ERISA supersede any and all laws of the States as they relate to any employee benefit plan covered under ERISA. The requirements implemented in the proposed rule do not alter the fundamental reporting and disclosure requirements of the statute with respect to employee benefit plans, and, as such, have no implications for the States or the relationship or distribution of power between the national government and the States.

List of Subjects in 29 CFR Part 2550

Employee benefit plans, Exemptions, Fiduciaries, Investments, Pensions, Prohibited transactions, Reporting and recordkeeping requirements, and Securities.

For the reasons set forth in the preamble, the Department of Labor proposes to amend chapter XXV, subchapter F, part 2550 of title 29 of the Code of Federal Regulations as follows:

SUBCHAPTER F - FIDUCIARY RESPONSIBILITY UNDER THE EMPLOYEE RETIREMENT INCOME SECURITY ACT OF 1974

PART 2550—RULES AND REGULATIONS FOR FIDUCIARY RESPONSIBILITY

1. The authority citation for part 2550 is revised to read as follows:

29 U.S.C. 1135 and Secretary of Labor's Order No. 1-2011, 77 FR 1088 (Jan. 9, 2012). Sec. 2550.401c-1 also issued under 29 U.S.C. 1101. Sec. 2550.404a-1 also issued under sec. 657, Pub. L. 107-16, 115 Stat. 38. Sections 2550.404c-1 and 2550.404c-5 also issued under 29 U.S.C.1104. Sec. 2550.408b-1 also issued under 29 U.S.C. 1108(b)(1) and sec. 102, Reorganization Plan No. 4 of 1978, 5 U.S.C. App. 1. Sec. 2550.408b-19 also issued under sec. 611, Pub. L. 109-280, 120 Stat. 780, 972, and sec. 102, Reorganization Plan No. 4 of 1978, 5 U.S.C. App. 1. Sec. 2550.412-1 also issued under 29 U.S.C.1112.

2. Amend 2550.408b-2 by:

a. Adding paragraph (c)(1)(iv)(H):

b. Revising paragraph (c)(1)(v)(B)(2) to read as follows:

§2550.408b-2 General statutory exemption for services or office space.

(c) * * *

(1) * * *

(iv) * * *

(H) Guide to initial disclosures

(1) If the information that must be disclosed pursuant to paragraph (c)(1)(iv)(A) through (G) of this section is not contained in a single document, or if the document is in excess of [RESERVED] pages, the covered service provider shall furnish the responsible plan fiduciary with a guide specifically identifying the document and page or other sufficiently specific locator, such as a section, that enables the responsible plan fiduciary to quickly and easily find the following information, as applicable to the contract or arrangement:

(i) The description of services to be provided to the covered plan, as required by paragraph (c)(1)(iv)(A) of this section;

(ii) The statement concerning services to be provided as a fiduciary and/or as a registered investment adviser, as required by paragraph (c)(1)(iv)(B) of this section;

(iii) The description of all direct compensation, as required by paragraph (c)(1)(iv)(C)(1) of this section;

(iv) The description of all indirect compensation, as required by paragraph (c)(1)(iv)(C)(2) of this section;

(v) The description of any compensation that will be paid among related parties, as required by paragraph (c)(1)(iv)(C)(3) of this section;

(vi) The description of any compensation for termination of the contract or arrangement, as required by paragraph (c)(1)(iv)(C)(4) of this section;

(vii) The description of all compensation (and/or a reasonable estimate of the cost to the covered plan) for recordkeeping services, as required by paragraph (c)(1)(iv)(D) of this section; and

(viii) For covered service providers described in paragraphs (c)(1)(iii)(A)(2) or (c)(1)(iii)(B) of this section, the description of any compensation, annual operating expenses, and ongoing expenses (or, if applicable, total annual operating expenses) set forth in paragraph (c)(1)(iv)(E)(1) and (2), as required by paragraphs (c)(1)(iv)(E)(1) and (2) and (c)(1)(iv)(F)(1) of this section.

(2) The guide described in paragraph (c)(1)(iv)(H)(1) of this section shall identify a person or office, including contact information, that the responsible plan fiduciary may contact regarding the disclosures provided pursuant to this section.

(3) The covered service provider shall furnish the guide described in paragraph (c)(1)(iv)(H)(1) of this section in a separate document.

* * *

(v) * * *

(B) * * *

(2) A covered service provider must, at least annually, disclose any changes to the information required by paragraph (c)(1)(iv)(E), (F), and (H) of this section.

* * *

Signed at Washington, D.C., this 27th day of February, 2014.

Phyllis C. Borzi

Assistant Secretary, Employee Benefits Security Administration, Department of Labor

billing code 4510-29-p

[FR Doc. 2014-04868 Filed 03/11/2014 at 8:45 am; Publication Date: 03/12/2014].

¶ 20,538R

Pension Benefit Guaranty Corporation (PBGC): Proposed regulations: Defined contribution plans: Rollovers: Underfunded defined benefit plan termination: Asset allocation: Maximum benefit guarantee limitation.—The Pension Benefit Guaranty Corporation (PBGC) has issued proposed regulations that would clarify the treatment of benefits rolled over from a defined contribution plan (DC) to a single-employer defined benefit (DB) plan if the DB plan is terminated and trusteed by the PBGC. Under the proposed rule, a benefit resulting from rollover amounts generally would be in the second highest priority of the asset allocation among various classes of benefits and would not be subject to the PBGC's maximum guarantee or phase-in limitations. Comments on the proposed rule are due June 2, 2014.

The proposed regulations were published in the Federal Register on April 2, 2014 (79 FR 18483). The regulations were finalized on November 25, 2014 (79 FR 70090). The preamble to the final regulations is at ¶ 24,325. The final regulations are at ¶ 15,315A, ¶ 15,421A, ¶ 15,421F, ¶ 15,421G, ¶ 15,422A, ¶ 15,422C, and ¶ 15,472B

¶ 20,538S

Employee Benefits Security Administration (EBSA): Proposed regulations: Reporting and disclosure: Group health plans: Health insurance marketplace: COBRA.—EBSA has issued proposed regulations that would amend COBRA notice provisions to better align them with current Patient Protection and Affordable Care Act (P.L. 111-148, PPACA) provisions, as well as future federal law provisions. The proposed regulations would remove the appendices containing the current versions of the model general notice and the model election notice, and change the regulations' language pointing to the model notices in the appendices. EBSA explains that these amendments will allow EBSA to change the model notices as necessary and provide the most current versions of the model notices on the EBSA website. Along with the proposed regulations, EBSA has issued updated model general and election notices that plans may use. The updated model notices are posted on the EBSA website.

The proposed regulations, which were published in the Federal Register on May 7, 2014 (79 FR 26192), are reproduced below.

DEPARTMENT OF LABOR

Employee Benefits Security Administration

29 CFR Part 2590

RIN 1210-AB65

Health Care Continuation Coverage

AGENCIES: Employee Benefits Security Administration, Department of Labor.

ACTION: Proposed rules.

SUMMARY: These proposed regulations contain amendments to notice requirements of the health care continuation coverage (COBRA) provisions of Part 6 of title I of the Employee Retirement Income Security Act of 1974 (ERISA) to better align the provision of guidance under the COBRA notice requirements with the Affordable Care Act provisions already in effect, as well as any provisions of federal law that will become applicable in the future.

DATES: Written comments on this notice of proposed rulemaking are invited and must be received by July 7, 2014.

ADDRESSES: Written comments may be submitted to the Department of Labor as specified below. Any comment that is submitted will be shared with the other Departments and will also be made available to the public. Warning: Do not include any personally identifiable information (such as name, address, or other contact information) or confidential business information that you do not want publicly disclosed. All comments may be posted on the Internet and can be retrieved by most Internet search engines. No deletions, modifications, or redactions will be made to the comments received, as they are public records. Comments may be submitted anonymously.

Comments, identified by "Health Care Continuation Coverage," may be submitted by one of the following methods:

Federal eRulemaking Portal: http://www.regulations.gov. Follow the instructions for submitting comments.

Mail or Hand Delivery: Office of Health Plan Standards and Compliance Assistance, Employee Benefits Security Administration, Room N-5653, U.S. Department of Labor, 200 Constitution Avenue NW., Washington, DC 20210, Attention: Health Care Continuation Coverage.

Comments received will be posted without change to www.regulations.gov and available for public inspection at the Public Disclosure Room, N-1513, Employee Benefits Security Administration, 200 Constitution Avenue NW., Washington, DC 20210, including any personal information provided.

FOR FURTHER INFORMATION CONTACT: Amy Turner or Elizabeth Schumacher, Employee Benefits Security Administration, Department of Labor.

Customer service information: Individuals interested in obtaining information from the Department of Labor concerning employment-based health coverage laws may call the EBSA Toll-Free Hotline at 1-866-444-EBSA (3272) or visit the Department of Labor's Web site (www.dol.gov/ebsa).

SUPPLEMENTARY INFORMATION:

I. Background

The continuation coverage provisions, sections 601 through 608 of title I of the Employee Retirement Income Security Act (ERISA), were enacted as part of the Consolidated Omnibus Budget Reconciliation Act of 1985 (COBRA), which also promulgated parallel provisions of the Internal Revenue Code (the Code) and the Public Health Service Act (the PHS Act).[1] These provisions are commonly referred to as the COBRA provisions, and the continuation coverage that they mandate is commonly referred to as COBRA coverage. COBRA, as enacted, provides that the Secretary of Labor (the Secretary) has the authority under section 608 to carry out the provisions of part 6 of title I of ERISA. The Conference Report that accompanied COBRA divided interpretive authority over the COBRA provisions between the Secretary and the Secretary of the Treasury (the Treasury) by providing that the Secretary has the authority to issue regulations implementing the notice and disclosure requirements of COBRA, while the Treasury is authorized to issue regulations defining the required continuation coverage.[2]

On May 26, 2004, the Department of Labor (Department) issued final regulations implementing various provisions of the COBRA notice requirements and model notices to facilitate compliance with the requirement to provide the general notice of continuation coverage (general notice) as well as COBRA continuation election notice (election notice).[3] The model general notice was issued in an appendix to § 2590.606-1 and the model election notice was issued in an appendix to § 2590.606-4.

In general, under COBRA, group health plans must provide a written notice of COBRA rights to each covered employee and spouse (if any) "at the time of commencement of coverage" under the plan. Generally, the notice must be furnished to each covered employee and to the employee's spouse (if covered under the plan) not later than the earlier of: (1) Either 90 days from the date on which the covered employee or spouse first becomes covered under the plan or, if later, the date on which the plan first becomes subject to the continuation coverage requirements; or (2) the date on which the administrator is required to furnish an election notice to the employee or to his or her spouse or dependent.[4]

In addition to the general notice, group health plans must provide an election notice at the time of certain qualifying events.[5] In general, an individual who was covered by a group health plan on the day before a qualifying event occurred may be able to elect COBRA continuation coverage upon a qualifying event (such as termination of employment or reduction in hours that causes loss of coverage under the plan).[6] Individuals with such a right are called qualified beneficiaries. A group health plan must provide qualified beneficiaries with an election notice, which describes their rights to continuation coverage and how to make an election. The election notice must be provided to the qualified beneficiaries within 14 days after the plan administrator receives the notice of a qualifying event.

On May 8, 2013, the Department issued Technical Release 2013-02 and an updated model election notice with additional information regarding health coverage options that will be available beginning January 1, 2014 under the Patient Protection and Affordable Care Act (Affordable Care Act).[7] The guidance highlighted that some qualified beneficiaries may want to consider and compare health coverage alternatives to COBRA continuation coverage that are available through a new competitive private health insurance market—the Health Insurance Marketplace (Marketplace). The Department also noted that some qualified beneficiaries may also be eligible for a premium tax credit (a tax credit to help pay for some or all of the cost of coverage in plans offered through the Marketplace).

These proposed regulations amend paragraph (g) of § 2590.606-1 and paragraph (g) of § 2590.606-4 and delete the two appendices containing the model notices to better facilitate provision of updated model election notices and solicit comment before promulgation of final regulations.

II. Overview of the Proposed Regulations

These proposed regulations contain amendments to notice requirements of the COBRA provisions of Part 6 of title I of ERISA to better align the provision of guidance under the COBRA notice requirements with the Affordable Care Act provisions already in effect, as well as provide valuable flexibility to respond to provisions of federal law that will become applicable in the future. The proposed amendment will eliminate the current version of the model general notice contained in

the appendix of § 2590.606-1 and the model election notice contained in the appendix of § 2590.606-4 as these model notices are outdated. Additionally, these proposed regulations make technical changes to the instruction language pointing to the model notices in the appendices in paragraph (g) of § 2590.606-1 and paragraph (g) of § 2590.606-4. These changes will permit the Department to amend the model notices as necessary and provide the most current versions of the model notices on the Department's Web site. These changes will also eliminate confusion that may result from multiple versions of the model notices being available in different locations. Contemporaneous with issuance of these proposed regulations, the Department is also issuing updated versions of the model general notice and model election notice, as well as guidance announcing the availability of such updated notices. These updated notices reflect that coverage is now available in the Marketplace and the updated model election notice provides information on special enrollment rights in the Marketplace. The Department invites comment on ways to improve or streamline the model notices, whether the Department's provision of new model notices is sufficient and, if not, whether the Department should expand the underlying content requirements or require use of mandatory language.

The updated model notices are available in modifiable, electronic form on the Department's Web site at *www.dol.gov/ebsa/cobra.html*. As with the earlier models, in order to use these model notices properly, the plan administrator must complete them by filling in the blanks with the appropriate plan information. Until rulemaking is finalized and effective, the Department of Labor will consider use of the model notices available on its Web site, appropriately completed, to be good faith compliance with the notice content requirements of COBRA. The Department notes that the use of the model notices is not required. The model notices are provided solely for the purpose of facilitating compliance with the applicable notice requirements.

III. Economic Impact and Paperwork Burden

A. Executive Orders 12866 and 13563

Executive Orders 12866 and 13563 direct agencies to assess all costs and benefits of available regulatory alternatives and, if regulation is necessary, to select regulatory approaches that maximize net benefits (including potential economic, environmental, public health and safety effects, distributive impacts, and equity). Executive Order 13563 emphasizes the importance of quantifying both costs and benefits, of reducing costs, of harmonizing and streamlining rules, and of promoting flexibility.

Under Executive Order 12866, "significant" regulatory actions are subject to the requirements of the executive order and review by the Office of Management and Budget (OMB). Section 3(f) of Executive Order 12866 defines a "significant regulatory action" as an action that is likely to result in a rule (1) having an annual effect on the economy of $100 million or more, or adversely and materially affecting a sector of the economy, productivity, competition, jobs, the environment, public health or safety, or State, local or tribal governments or communities (also referred to as "economically significant"); (2) creating serious inconsistency or otherwise interfering with an action taken or planned by another agency; (3) materially altering the budgetary impacts of entitlement grants, user fees, or loan programs or the rights and obligations of recipients thereof; or (4) raising novel legal or policy issues arising out of legal mandates, the President's priorities, or the principles set forth in the Executive Order. Pursuant to the terms of the Executive Order, OMB has determined that this action is not "significant" within the meaning of section 3(f) of the Executive Order. Therefore, the proposed rule was reviewed by OMB. However, because the rule merely removes the model notices from the CFR and the model notices themselves remain voluntary, the Department does not expect this rulemaking to result in significant costs or benefits.

B. Regulatory Flexibility Analysis

The Regulatory Flexibility Act (5 U.S.C. 601 et seq.) (RFA) imposes certain requirements with respect to Federal rules that are subject to the notice and comment requirements of section 553(b) of the APA (5 U.S.C. 551 et seq.) and are likely to have a significant economic impact

---

[1] The Code and PHS Act COBRA provisions, although very similar in other ways, are not identical to the COBRA provisions in title I of ERISA in their scope of application. The PHS Act provisions apply only to State and local governmental plans, and the Code provisions grant COBRA rights to individuals who would not be considered participants or beneficiaries under ERISA. *See* PHS Act, 42 U.S.C. 300bb-8; Code section 5000(b)(1).

[2] H.R. Conf. Rep. No. 99-453, 99th Cong., 1st Sess., at 562-63 (1985). The Conference Report further indicates that the Secretary of Health and Human Services, who is to issue regulations implementing the continuation coverage requirements for State and local governments, must conform the actual requirements of those regulations to the regulations issued by the Secretary and the Treasury. *Id.* at 563.

[3] 69 FR 30084 (May, 26, 2004).

[4] See 29 CFR 2590.606-1.

[5] See 29 CFR 2590.606-4.

[6] For more information on COBRA continuation coverage requirements applicable to group health plans, *see* "An Employer's Guide to Group Health Continuation Coverage Under COBRA," available at *www.dol.gov/ebsa/publications/cobraemployer.html*.

[7] See Technical Release 2013-02 available at *http://www.dol.gov/ebsa/newsroom/tr13-02.html*.

on a substantial number of small entities. Unless an agency certifies that such a rule will not have a significant economic impact on a substantial number of small entities, section 603 of the RFA requires the agency to present an initial regulatory flexibility analysis at the time of the publication of the rulemaking describing the impact of the rule on small entities. Small entities include small businesses, organizations and governmental jurisdictions.

As discussed above, the proposed rule would amend the 2004 final regulation by deleting references to the model notices and two appendices containing the model notices to better facilitate provision of updated model election notices and solicit comment before promulgation of final regulations. The proposed rule does not make any material changes to the notices. Therefore, the Department hereby certifies that the proposed rule is not likely to have a significant economic impact on a substantial number of small entities. The Department welcomes public comments regarding its certification.

C. Paperwork Reduction Act

The Office of Management and Budget approved the COBRA model notice information collection request under OMB Control Number 1210-0123, which is scheduled to expire on October 31, 2016. As discussed above, the proposed rule would amend the 2004 final regulation by deleting references to the model notices and two appendices containing the model notices to better facilitate provision of updated model election notices and solicit comment before promulgation of final regulations. The Department does not believe that these minor modifications implement any substantive or material change to the information collection; therefore, no further review is requested of OMB at this time. The Department solicits comment on this understanding.

D. Congressional Review Act

This proposed rule is subject to the Congressional Review Act provisions of the Small Business Regulatory Enforcement Fairness Act of 1996 (5 U.S.C. 801 et seq.) and, if finalized, will be transmitted to Congress and the Comptroller General for review.

E. Unfunded Mandates Reform Act

For purposes of the Unfunded Mandates Reform Act of 1995 (Pub. L. 104-4), as well as Executive Order 12875, this proposed rule does not include any Federal mandate that may result in expenditures by State, local, or tribal governments in the aggregate of more than $100 million, adjusted for inflation, or increase expenditures by the private sector of more than $100 million, adjusted for inflation.

F. Federalism Statement

Executive Order 13132 (Aug. 4, 1999) outlines fundamental principles of federalism and requires the adherence to specific criteria by Federal agencies in the process of their formulation and implementation of policies that have substantial direct effects on the States, the relationship between the national government and the States, or on the distribution of power and responsibilities among the various levels of government. This proposed rule does not have federalism implications because it has no substantial direct effect on the States, on the relationship between the national government and the States, or on the distribution of power and responsibilities among the various levels of government. Section 514 of ERISA provides, with certain exceptions specifically enumerated, that the provisions of titles I and IV of ERISA supersede any and all laws of the States as they relate to any employee benefit plan covered under ERISA. The requirements implemented in this rule do not alter the fundamental provisions of the statute with respect to employee benefit plans, and as such would have no implications for the States or the relationship or distribution of power between the national government and the States.

IV. Statutory Authority

The Department of Labor regulations are adopted pursuant to the authority contained in 29 U.S.C. 1027, 1059, 1135, 1161-1168, 1169, 1181-1183, 1181 note, 1185, 1185a, 1185b, 1185c, 1185d, 1191, 1191a, 1191b, and 1191c; sec. 101(g), Pub. L. 104-191, 110 Stat. 1936; sec. 401(b), Pub. L. 105-200, 112 Stat. 645 (42 U.S.C. 651 note); sec. 512(d), Pub. L. 110-343, 122 Stat. 3881; sec. 1001, 1201, and 1562(e), Pub. L. 111-148, 124 Stat. 119, as amended by Pub. L. 111-152, 124 Stat. 1029; Secretary of Labor's Order 1-2011, 77 FR 1088 (January 9, 2012).

List of Subjects in 29 CFR Part 2590

Continuation coverage, Disclosure, Employee benefit plans, Group health plans, Health care, Health insurance, Medical child support, Reporting and recordkeeping requirements.

For the reasons stated in the preamble, the Department of Labor proposes to amend 29 CFR part 2590 as follows:

PART 2590—RULES AND REGULATIONS FOR GROUP HEALTH PLANS

■ 1. The authority citation for part 2590 continues to read as follows:

Authority: 29 U.S.C. 1027, 1059, 1135, 1161-1168, 1169, 1181-1183, 1181 note, 1185, 1185a, 1185b, 1185c, 1185d, 1191, 1191a, 1191b, and 1191c; sec. 101(g), Pub. L. 104-191, 110 Stat. 1936; sec. 401(b), Pub. L. 105-200, 112 Stat. 645 (42 U.S.C. 651 note); sec. 512(d), Pub. L. 110-343, 122 Stat. 3881; sec. 1001, 1201, and 1562(e), Pub. L. 111-148, 124 Stat. 119, as amended by Pub. L. 111-152, 124 Stat. 1029; Secretary of Labor's Order 1-2011, 77 FR 1088 (January 9, 2012).

■ 2. Section 2590.606-1 is amended by removing the appendix to the section, and revising paragraph (g) to read as follows:

§ 2590.606-1 General notice of continuation coverage.

* * * * *

(g) *Model notice.* The requirements of paragraph (c) of this section are satisfied with respect to a single-employer group health plan if the plan provides a notice in accordance with the model certificate authorized by the Secretary, appropriately modified and supplemented as necessary, consistent with guidance issued by the Secretary. Use of the model notice is not mandatory. The model notice reflects the requirements of this section as they would apply to single-employer group health plans and must be modified if used to provide notice with respect to other types of group health plans, such as multiemployer plans or plans established and maintained by employee organizations for their members. In order to use the model notice, administrators must appropriately add relevant information where indicated in the model notice, select among alternative language, and supplement the model notice to reflect applicable plan provisions. Items of information that are not applicable to a particular plan may be deleted. Use of the model notice, appropriately modified and supplemented, will be deemed to satisfy the notice content requirements of paragraph (c) of this section.

* * * * *

■ 3. Section 2590.606-4 is amended by removing the appendix to the section, and revising paragraph (g) to read as follows:

§ 2590.606-4 Notice requirements for plan administrators.

* * * * *

(g) *Model notice.* The requirements of paragraph (b)(4) of this section are satisfied with respect to a plan administrator if the plan provides a notice in accordance with the model certificate authorized by the Secretary, appropriately modified and supplemented as necessary, consistent with guidance issued by the Secretary. Use of the model notice is not mandatory. The model notice reflects the requirements of this section as they would apply to single-employer group health plans and must be modified if used to provide notice with respect to other types of group health plans, such as multiemployer plans or plans established and maintained by employee organizations for their members. In order to use the model notice, administrators must appropriately add relevant information where indicated in the model notice, select among alternative language, and supplement the model notice to reflect applicable plan provisions. Items of information that are not applicable to a particular plan may be deleted. Use of the model notice, appropriately modified and supplemented, will be deemed to satisfy the notice content requirements of paragraph (b)(4) of this section.

* * * * *

Signed this 1st day of May, 2014.

Phyllis C. Borzi,

Assistant Secretary, Employee Benefits Security Administration, Department of Labor.

[FR Doc. 2014-10416 Filed 5-2-14; 11:15 am]

BILLING CODE 4510-29-P

¶ 20,538T

Employee Benefits Security Administration (EBSA): Proposed rules: IRS: Group health plans: Preventive health services: Religious employers: Contraceptive services.—The EBSA, IRS, and the Department of Health and Human Services have issued proposed regulations that would extend the current religious employer accommodation for nonprofit entities that do not want to provide contraceptive services to certain closely held for-profit entities by changing the definition of an eligible organization that may use the accommodation.

The proposed regulations, which were published in the Federal Register on August 27, 2014 (79 FR 51118), are reproduced at ¶ 20,263X. The proposed regulations were finalized on July 14, 2015 (80 FR 41317). The preamble to the final regulations is at ¶ 23,315. The EBSA final regulations are at ¶ 15,050R-50PB. The IRS final regulations are at ¶ 13,968V-20PB.

¶ 20,538U

Employee Benefits Security Administration (EBSA): Proposed regulations: Top-hat plans: Apprenticeship and Training Plans.—The Employee Benefits Security Administration (EBSA) has issued proposed regulations that would require electronic filing of "top hat" plan statements, and apprenticeship and training plan notices.

The proposed regulations, which were published in the Federal Register on September 30, 2014 (79 FR 58720), are reproduced below.

DEPARTMENT OF LABOR

Employee Benefits Security Administration

29 CFR Part 2520

RIN 1210-AB62

Electronic Filing of Notices for Apprenticeship and Training Plans and Statements for Pension

Plans for Certain Select Employees

AGENCY: Employee Benefits Security Administration, Department of Labor.

ACTION: Proposed rule.

SUMMARY: This document contains proposed regulations that would revise filing procedures for apprenticeship and training plan notices and "top hat" plan statements with the Secretary of Labor to require electronic submission of these notices and statements.

DATES: Comments are due on or before [INSERT DATE 90 DAYS AFTER DATE OF PUBLICATION IN THE FEDERAL REGISTER].

ADDRESSES: You may submit comments, identified by RIN 1210-AB62, by one of the following methods:

- *Federal eRulemaking Portal: http://www.regulations.gov.* Follow the instructions for submitting comments.

- *Email: e-ORI@dol.gov.* Include RIN 1210-AB62 in the subject line of the message.

- *Mail or personal delivery*: Office of Regulations and Interpretations, Employee Benefits Security Administration, Room N-5655, U.S. Department of Labor, 200 Constitution Avenue, NW., Washington, DC 20210.

Instructions: All submissions received must include the agency name and Regulation Identifier Number (RIN) for this rulemaking. Comments received, including any personal information provided, will be posted without change to *http://www.regulations.gov* and *http://www.dol.gov/ebsa,* and made available for public inspection at the Public Disclosure Room, N–1513, Employee Benefits Security Administration, 200 Constitution Avenue, NW., Washington, DC 20210. Persons submitting comments electronically are encouraged not to submit paper copies.

FOR FURTHER INFORMATION CONTACT: Marjorie M. Kress or Eric A. Raps, Office of Regulations and Interpretations, Employee Benefits Security Administration (EBSA), Department of Labor, at (202) 693-8500. This is not a toll-free number.

SUPPLEMENTARY INFORMATION:

Background

Part 1 of Title I of the Employee Retirement Income Security Act of 1974, as amended (ERISA), contains reporting and disclosure requirements applicable to plans covered by ERISA. For instance, sections 103 and 104 of ERISA establish requirements for the publication and filing of annual reports, while sections 102 and 104 of ERISA require plan administrators to furnish summary plan descriptions and summaries of material modifications or changes to participants and beneficiaries.

Section 104(a)(3) of ERISA, however, authorizes the Secretary to exempt any welfare benefit plan from all or part of the reporting and disclosure obligations, or to provide simplified reporting and disclosure, if the Secretary finds that the requirements are inappropriate for these plans. Under this authority, the Secretary, in 1980, issued 29 CFR 2520.104-22, which provides an exemption from the reporting and disclosure provisions of Part 1 of Title I of ERISA for employee welfare benefit plans that provide only apprenticeship or training benefits, or both, if certain conditions are met.[1] Under the regulation, a welfare plan that provides only these benefits is not required to meet the requirements of Part 1 of Title I if the administrator files with the Secretary a notice as described in § 2520.104-22 by mail or personal delivery, takes steps reasonably designed to ensure that the information required to be contained in the notice is disclosed to employees of employers contributing to the plan who may be eligible to enroll, and makes the notice available to these employees upon request.

Similarly, section 110(a) of ERISA permits the Secretary to specify an alternative form of compliance with the reporting and disclosure obligations of Part 1 of Title I for any pension plan or class of pension plans subject to ERISA if certain findings are made. Under the authority of section 110(a), the Department, in 1975, issued regulation 29 CFR 2520.104-23 to provide an alternative method of compliance with the reporting and disclosure requirements of Part 1 of Title I for unfunded or insured pension plans established for a select group of management or highly compensated employees ("top hat" plans).[2] Under the alternative method of compliance, the administrator of a top hat plan will satisfy the requirements for the reporting and disclosure provisions of Part 1 of Title I by filing a statement with the Secretary by mail or personal delivery to the address specified in the regulation, and by providing plan documents, if any, to the Secretary upon request. The statement must include the information listed in the regulation.

Recently, the Department instituted a wholly electronic system (EFAST2) for filing and processing the Form 5500 Annual Return/Report, which is used to report information to the government on certain employee benefit plans and direct filing entities. Form 5500 Annual Return/Reports filed through EFAST2 on or after the 2009 plan years are also available to the general public through the Department's website at *http://www.efast.dol.gov.* The EFAST2 system, however, does not include apprenticeship and training plan notices and top hat statements.[3] Thus, all such notices and statements are filed with the Department on paper though regular mail or personal delivery.

The Department has determined that regular mail or personal delivery are no longer the most efficient or cost-effective ways to file and process these notices and statements. The Department annually receives approximately 120 apprenticeship and training plan notices and approximately 2,000 top hat plan statement filings. To make the information on these notices and statements accessible, the Department converts each paper filing to electronic format. The proposal will eliminate the need for this time-consuming task. Because the internet is widely accessible to persons who file these notices and statements, the Department expects that the regulated community will find electronic filing to be easier and more cost-effective than paper filing.

---

[1] See 40 FR 24647 (June 9, 1975); 40 FR 34529, 34530 (August 15, 1975); and 45 FR 34528, 34529 FN 10 (March 11, 1980).

[2] See 40 FR 24647, 24648 (June 9, 1975) and 40 FR 34530 (August 15, 1975).

[3] The Department also requires that the administrator of a multiple employer welfare arrangement (MEWA) and the administrator of any entity claiming exception (ECE) satisfy Form M-1 reporting obligations by filing electronically. Apprenticeship and training plan notices and top hat statements also are not part of the MEWA and ECE electronic filing process.

Electronic filing should also facilitate the disclosure of the information to participants and beneficiaries, and other interested members of the public since electronically filed documents can be promptly posted on the Department's website. Thus, the Department, filers, and users all stand to benefit from this proposal in ways that are consistent with the goals of the E-Government Act of 2002.[4]

Explanation of Provisions

The proposal would revise the current procedures for filing apprenticeship and training plan notices and "top hat" plan statements with the Secretary of Labor to require electronic submission of these notices and statements. The proposal is not intended to express any view on, and would not change, the current content requirements in the exemption under § 2520.104-22 for apprenticeship and training plans or the alternative method of compliance under § 2520.10423 for top hat plans.[5]

The proposal would revise § 2520.104-22(c) and § 2520.104-23(c) to require internet-based electronic filing of apprenticeship and training plan notices and top hat plan statements with the Secretary through EBSA's website. Once they are filed, these notices and statements would be posted on the Department's website at *http://www.dol.gov/ebsa* and be available to the public. The submission process would be easy to use because the web portal would include instructions for using the electronic filing system and also would assist administrators by ensuring that all of the information required by the regulations would be included in the notice or statement before the filing could be completed through the website. In addition, as previously mentioned, the process would provide an electronic confirmation to the administrator that the filing had been received by EBSA. This assurance would provide a benefit to apprenticeship and training plan administrators and top hat plan administrators that is not available through the existing paper-based filing system. Finally, the design of the electronic filing system will facilitate the requirement that plan administrators of apprenticeship and training plans make notices available to participants upon request.

Dates & Interim Availability of New Electronic Filing System

The Department today is launching its new web-based filing system for the notices described above. See *http://www.dol.gov/ebsa*. Use of this system in lieu of paper-based filing is voluntary pending the adoption of a final rule. The Department encourages administrators of apprenticeship and training plans and administrators of top hat plans to file their plan notices and statements using this new system. Pending issuance of final regulations, the Department will treat administrators who use the new system as having satisfied the requirement to mail the notice or statement to the address listed in §§ 2520.104-22(c) and 2520.104-23(c). The Department is interested in receiving comments on the design and operation of the system and proposes that the final rules would become effective on their date of publication in the *Federal Register* and applicable to all filings made on or after 120 days after that date.[6] After the applicability date, the website filing system would be the exclusive method of filing these notices and statements. Filings with the Secretary by mail and personal delivery would no longer be acceptable.

Regulatory Impact Analysis

1. Executive Orders 12866 and 13563

Executive Orders 12866 and 13563 direct agencies to assess all costs and benefits of available regulatory alternatives and, if regulation is necessary, to select regulatory approaches that maximize net benefits (including potential economic, environmental, public health and safety effects, distributive impacts, and equity). Executive Order 13563 emphasizes the importance of quantifying both costs and benefits, of reducing costs, of harmonizing and streamlining rules, and of promoting flexibility.

Under Executive Order 12866, "significant" regulatory actions are subject to the requirements of the executive order and review by the Office of Management and Budget (OMB). Section 3(f) of Executive Order 12866 defines a "significant regulatory action" as an action that is likely to result in a rule (1) having an annual effect on the economy of $100 million or more, or adversely and materially affecting a sector of the economy, productivity, competition, jobs, the environment, public health or safety, or State, local or tribal governments or communities

(also referred to as "economically significant"); (2) creating serious inconsistency or otherwise interfering with an action taken or planned by another agency; (3) materially altering the budgetary impacts of entitlement grants, user fees, or loan programs or the rights and obligations of recipients thereof; or (4) raising novel legal or policy issues arising out of legal mandates, the President's priorities, or the principles set forth in the Executive Order.

Pursuant to the terms of the Executive Order, OMB has determined that this action is "significant" within the meaning of section 3(f) of the Executive Order. Therefore, the proposed rule was reviewed by OMB. However, because the rule merely would replace the paper-based filing of apprenticeship and training plan notices and top hat plan statements with an electronic filing system, and no substantive change would be made to the notices and statements, the Department does not expect this rulemaking to result in significant costs or benefits. For a further discussion, see the Paperwork Reduction Act section, below.

2. Regulatory Flexibility Analysis

The Regulatory Flexibility Act (5 U.S.C. 601 et seq.) (RFA) imposes certain requirements with respect to Federal rules that are subject to the notice and comment requirements of section 553(b) of the APA (5 U.S.C. 551 et seq.) and that are likely to have a significant economic impact on a substantial number of small entities.

The Department carefully considered the likely impact of this proposed rule on small entities. The proposed rule will implement an electronic submission procedure for administrators of apprenticeship and training plans and top hat plans to file notices and statements described in sections 2520.104-22 and 2520.104-23. The electronic filing system will provide instructions, ensure that plan administrators include all of the required information in their notices and statements, and provide an electronic confirmation that they have been received. The Department expects that an electronic filing system to file apprenticeship notices and top hat statements would be more efficient and cost-effective for small plan administrators than a paper-based filing system, because they no longer will incur material and postage costs associated with delivery by regular mail or personal delivery service. Based on the foregoing, the Department hereby certifies that the proposed rule is not likely to have a significant economic impact on a substantial number of small entities. The Department welcomes public comments regarding its certification.

Section 610 of the RFA requires that an agency review each rule that has or will have a significant economic impact on a substantial number of small entities within ten years of publication of the final rule. EBSA initiates a Section 610 review to determine if the provisions of a rule should be continued without change, rescinded, or amended to minimize adverse economic impact on small entities. In addition to the changes in this proposal, EBSA, under section 610 of RFA, is taking comments on other possible changes or amendments to the two regulations (§§ 2520.104-22(c) and 2520.104-23(c)) that are the subject of the proposed amendments.

3. Paperwork Reduction Act

This Notice of Proposed Rulemaking (NPRM) contains an information collection that is subject to OMB approval under the Paperwork Reduction Act of 1995 (PRA) 44 U.S.C. 3501 et seq. As part of a continuing effort to reduce paperwork and respondent burden, the Department of Labor and OMB conduct a preclearance consultation program to provide the general public and Federal agencies with an opportunity to comment on proposed and continuing collection of information. This helps to ensure that requested data can be provided in the desired format, reporting burden (time and financial resources) is minimized, collection instruments are clearly understood, and the impact of collection requirements on respondents can be properly assessed.

More specifically and as stated earlier in this preamble, section 2520.104-22 provides an exemption to the reporting and disclosure provisions of Part 1 of Title I of ERISA for employee welfare benefit plans that provide only apprenticeship or training benefits, or both, if the plan administrator: (1) Files a notice with the Secretary that provides the name of the plan, the plan sponsor's Employer Identification Number (EIN), the plan administrator's name, and the name and location of an office or person from whom interested individuals can

---

[4] Pub. L. No. 107-347, sec. 2 (Dec. 17, 2002).

[5] We note that the proposed filing system would require the filer to input an email address. Although neither regulation explicitly mentions such an address, we are not viewing this item as a content requirement of the regulations. Rather, the address is needed for system functionality because without it the filer would not receive instantaneous confirmation of the filing.

[6] As noted above, once they are filed, the notices and statements would be posted on the Department's website and available online to the public, One issue we wish to flag for public comment is whether there are any concerns with making any of this information, in particular the email address of the plan administrator, publicly accessible online. Should this address be suppressed for privacy or logistical reasons?

obtain certain information about courses offered by the plan; (2) takes steps reasonably designed to ensure that the information required to be contained in the notice is disclosed to employees of employers contributing to the plan who may be eligible to enroll in any course of study sponsored or established by the plan; and (3) makes the notice available to these employees upon request. The plan administrator must file the notice with the Secretary of Labor by mailing or delivering it to the Department at the address set forth in the regulation.

Section 2520.104-23 provides an alternative method of compliance with the reporting and disclosure provisions of Title I of ERISA for unfunded or insured plans established for a select group of management or highly compensated employees (i.e., top hat plans). In order to satisfy the alternative method of compliance, the plan administrator must: (1) File a statement with the Secretary of Labor that includes the name and address of the employer, the employer EIN, a declaration that the employer maintains a plan or plans primarily for the purpose of providing deferred compensation for a select group of management or highly compensated employees, and a statement of the number of such plans and the employees covered by each; and (2) make plan documents available to the Secretary upon request. Only one statement needs to be filed for each employer maintaining one or more of the plans. The statements may be filed with the Secretary by mail or personal delivery.

The proposed rule would replace the paper-based filing of apprenticeship and training plan notices and top hat plan statements with an electronic filing system. No substantive change would be made to the notices and statements. The Department annually receives approximately 120 apprenticeship and training plan notices and approximately 2,000 top hat plan statement filings. The Department estimates in-house human resource professionals on average will spend 15 minutes preparing each filing at an equivalent cost of $97.69 per hour,[7] and that in-house clerical staff will spend three minutes filing the notices and statements on the Department's electronic filing system, at an equivalent cost of $29.14 per hour, for a total of 36 hours for apprenticeship and training plan notice filings and 600 hours of top hat plan statement filings and an overall total of 636 burden hours. The total equivalent cost for the hour burden is $55,000 ($3,000 for apprenticeship and training plan notices and $52,000 for top hat plan statements). The Department assumes that no other cost burden is associated with this information collection request (ICR), because in-house staff will prepare and file the notices on behalf of each plan.

The Department has submitted an ICR seeking OMB approval for the information collection contained in the proposed rule to OMB. A copy of this ICR with applicable supporting documentation, including a description of the likely respondents, proposed frequency of response, and estimated total burden may be obtained free of charge from the RegInfo.gov Web site at http://www.reginfo.gov/public/do/PRAViewICR?ref_nbr=201407-1210-003 (this link will only become active on the day following publication of this notice); by sending a request by mail or courier to: PRA Clearance Officer, Office of Policy and Research, U.S. Department of Labor, Employee Benefits Security Administration, 200 Constitution Avenue, NW., Room N-5718, Washington, DC 20210; or send an email to *ebsa.opr@dol.gov.*

OMB asks that comments about information collections in this NPRM be submitted by mail or courier to the Office of Information and Regulatory Affairs, Attn: OMB Desk Officer for DOL-EBSA, Office of Management and Budget, Room 10235, 725 17th Street, N.W., Washington, DC 20503; by Fax: 202-395-6881 (this is not a toll-free number); or by email: *OIRA_submission@omb.eop.gov.* Commenters are encouraged, but not required, to send a courtesy copy of any comments to the party identified in the ADDRESSES section of this NPRM. OMB requests that comments be received within 30 days of publication of the proposed rule to ensure their consideration. Comments submitted in response to this request become a matter of public record.

The Department and OMB are particularly interested in comments that:

- Evaluate whether the collection of information is necessary for the proper performance of the functions of the agency, including whether the information will have practical utility;

- Evaluate the accuracy of the agency's estimate of the burden of the collection of information, including the validity of the methodology and assumptions used;

- Enhance the quality, utility, and clarity of the information to be collected; and

- Minimize the burden of the collection of information on those who are to respond, including through the use of appropriate automated, electronic, mechanical, or other technological collection techniques or other forms of information technology, e.g., permitting electronic submission of responses.

These paperwork burden estimates are summarized as follows:

Title: Apprenticeship and Training Plan Notices and Top Hat Plan Statements.

OMB ICR Reference Number: 201407-1210-003.

Affected Public: Private Sector–business or other for-profit and not-for-profit institutions.

Respondents: 2,120 (120 apprenticeship and training plans and 2,000 top hat plans)

Responses: 2,120.

Frequency of Response: Annually.

Estimated Total Annual Burden Hours: 636 (36 for apprenticeship and training plan notices and 600 for top hat plan statements)

Estimated Total Annual Burden Cost: $0.

4. Congressional Review Act

The proposed rule is subject to the Congressional Review Act provisions of the Small Business Regulatory Enforcement Fairness Act of 1996 (5 U.S.C. 801 et seq.) and, if finalized, will be transmitted to Congress and the Comptroller General for review. The proposed rule is not a "major rule" as that term is defined in 5 U.S.C. 804, because it is not likely to result in (1) an annual effect on the economy of $100 million or more; (2) a major increase in costs or prices for consumers, individual industries, or Federal, State, or local government agencies, or geographic regions; or (3) significant adverse effects on competition, employment, investment, productivity, innovation, or on the ability of United States-based enterprises to compete with foreign-based enterprises in domestic and export markets.

5. Unfunded Mandates Reform Act

For purposes of the Unfunded Mandates Reform Act of 1995 (Pub. L. 104–4), as well as Executive Order 12875, this proposed rule does not include any Federal mandate that may result in expenditures by State, local, or tribal governments in the aggregate of more than $100 million, adjusted for inflation, or increase expenditures by the private sector of more than $100 million, adjusted for inflation.

6. Federalism Statement

Executive Order 13132 (August 4, 1999) outlines fundamental principles of federalism, and requires the adherence to specific criteria by Federal agencies in the process of their formulation and implementation of policies that have substantial direct effects on the States, the relationship between the national government and States, or on the distribution of power and responsibilities among the various levels of government. This proposed rule does not have federalism implications because it has no substantial direct effect on the States, on the relationship between the national government and the States, or on the distribution of power and responsibilities among the various levels of government. Section 514 of ERISA provides, with certain exceptions specifically enumerated, that the provisions of Titles I and IV of ERISA supersede any and all laws of the States as they relate to any employee benefit plan covered under ERISA. The electronic filing requirements in this proposed rule do not alter the fundamental reporting and disclosure requirements of the statute with respect to employee benefit plans, and, as such, have no implications for the States or the relationship or distribution of power between the national government and the States.

List of Subjects in 29 CFR Part 2520

Employee benefit plans, Employee Retirement Income Security Act, Pension plans, Pension and welfare plans, Reporting and recordkeeping requirements, Welfare benefit plans.

For the reasons set forth in the preamble, the Department proposes to amend 29 CFR part 2520 as follows:

PART 2520–RULES AND REGULATIONS FOR REPORTING AND DISCLOSURE

1. The authority citation for part 2520 continues to read as follows:

---

[7] The Department estimates 2013 hourly labor rates include wages, other benefits, and overhead based on data from the National Occupational Employment Survey (June 2012, Bureau of Labor Statistics) and the Employment Cost Index (September 2012, Bureau of Labor Statistics); the 2011 estimated labor rates are then inflated to 2013 labor rates.

Authority: 29 U.S.C. 1021-1024, 1027, 1029-31, 1059, 1134 and 1135; Secretary of Labor's Order 1-2011, 77 FR 1088 (January 9, 2012). Sec. 2520.101-2 also issued under 29 U.S.C. 11811183, 1181 note, 1185, 1185a-d, and 1191-1191c. Sec. 2520.103-1 also issued under 26 U.S.C. 6058 note. Sec. 2520.101-6 also issued under 29 U.S.C. 1021(k); Secs. 2520.102-3, 2520.104b-1 and 2520.104b-3 also issued under 29 U.S.C. 1003, 1181-1183, 1181 note, 1185, 1185a-d, 1191, and 1191a-c. Secs. 2520.104b-1 and 2520.107 also issued under 26 U.S.C. 401 note, 111 Stat. 788.

2. Section 2520.104-22 is amended by revising paragraph (c) to read as follows: *§ 2520.104-22 Exemption from reporting and disclosure requirements for apprenticeship and training plans.*

* * * * *

(c) *Electronic filing of notice.* The notice referred to in paragraph (a) of this section shall be filed with the Secretary electronically in accordance with the instructions published by the Department.

3. Section 2520.104-23 is amended by revising paragraph (c) to read as follows: § 2520.104-23 Alternative method of compliance for pension plans for certain selected employees.

* * * * *

(c) *Electronic filing of statement.* Statements referred to in paragraph (b) of this section shall be filed with the Secretary electronically in accordance with the instructions published by the Department.

* * * * *

Signed this 16th day of September, 2014.

———————

Phyllis C. Borzi

Assistant Secretary,

Employee Benefits Security Administration,

U.S. Department of Labor

Billing Code: 4510-29-P

———————

¶ 20,538V

Employee Benefits Security Administration (EBSA): Proposed regulations: IRS: Group health plans: Excepted benefits: Limited wraparound coverage.—The EBSA, IRS, and Department of Health and Human Services have issued proposed regulations that would amend Code and ERISA regulations regarding "excepted benefits," which are generally exempt from the health reform requirements that were added by the Health Insurance Portability and Accountability Act of 1996 (HIPAA, P.L. 104-191) and the Patient Protection and Affordable Care Act (PPACA, P.L. 111-148). The Agencies are seeking public comment on the proposed rules that would amend the definition of excepted benefits to include certain limited wraparound coverage in response to suggestions made on a December 2013 proposed rule (PENSION PLAN GUIDE ¶ 20,263U) from a wide range of stakeholders. The proposed rule proposes a pilot program for wraparound coverage that will sunset.

The proposed regulations, which were published in the Federal Register on December 23, 2014 (79 FR 76931), are reproduced at ¶ 20,264. The regulations were finalized on March 18, 2015 (80 FR 13995). The preamble to the final regulations is at ¶ 24,511. The final regulation is at ¶ 15,051B-1.

———————

¶ 20,538W

Employee Benefits Security Administration (EBSA): IRS: Group health plans: Health insurance coverage: Summary of benefits and coverage: Uniform glossary: Disclosure requirements.—The EBSA, IRS, and Department of Health and Human Services have proposed changes to the regulations that implement the Patient Protection and Affordable Care Act (PPACA, P.L. 111-148) disclosure requirements under section 2715 of the Public Health Service Act to help plans and individuals better understand their health coverage, as well as to gain a better understanding of other coverage options for comparison. It proposes changes to the documents required for compliance with section 2715 of the Public Health Service Act, including a template for the summary of benefits and coverage (SBC), instructions, sample language, a guide for coverage example calculations and the uniform glossary. The proposed regulations, as well as a new set of proposed SBC templates, instructions, an updated uniform glossary, and other materials are being issued to incorporate some of the feedback received and to make some improvements to the template. These modifications clarify when and how a plan or issuer must provide an SBC, and streamline and shorten the SBC template while also adding certain additional elements that will be useful to consumers.

The proposed regulations, which were published in the Federal Register on December 30, 2014 (79 FR 78577), are reproduced at ¶ 20,264A. The regulations were finalized on June 16, 2015 (80 FR 34292). The preamble to the final regulations is at ¶ 23,313. The final regulations are at ¶ 15,050R-50RR.

———————

¶ 20,538X

Employee Benefits Security Administration (EBSA): Proposed rule: Participant-directed individual account plans: 401(k) plans: Participant-level fee disclosure: Annual disclosure deadline.—The EBSA has issued a proposed rule that accompanies a direct final rule (Pension Plan Guide ¶ 24,328) under which EBSA provides a two-month grace period for participant-directed individual account plans—e.g., 401(k) plans—to furnish annual plan and investment-related information (including fee and expense information) to participants. The direct final rule changes the requirement that annual disclosures must be made at least once in any 12-month period to at least once in any 14-month period. The direct final rule is incorporated by reference into the proposed rule. The amended regulation will be effective June 17, 2015, without further action or notice, unless significant adverse comment is received by April 20, 2015. If the Agency receives significant adverse comment during the public comment period, it will withdraw the direct final rule and it will not take effect. EBSA will address those comments in a subsequent final rule based on the proposed rule. There will not be a second comment period.

The proposed regulation document, which was published in the Federal Register on March 19, 2015 (80 FR 14334), is reproduced below.

DEPARTMENT OF LABOR

Employee Benefits Security Administration

29 CFR Part 2550

RIN 1210-AB68

Fiduciary Requirements for Disclosure in Participant-Directed Individual Account Plans—Timing of Annual Disclosure

AGENCY: Employee Benefits Security Administration, Department of Labor.

ACTION: Proposed rule.

SUMMARY: This document proposes to amend the Department of Labor's "participant-level fee disclosure" regulation by making a technical adjustment to an annual timing requirement. In the "Rules and Regulations" section of this issue of the **Federal Register**, we are making this same amendment as a direct final rule. If we receive no significant adverse comment, the direct final rule will go into effect and we will not take further action on this proposed rule. If, however, we receive significant adverse comment, we will withdraw the direct final rule and it will not take effect. In that case, we will address all public comments in a subsequent final rule based on this proposed rule. We will not institute a second comment period on this rule. Any parties interested in commenting must do so during this comment period.

DATES: Comments must be received on or before April 20, 2015.

ADDRESSES: You may submit comments, identified by RIN 1210-AB68 (Fiduciary Requirements for Disclosure in Participant-Directed Individual Account Plans—Timing of Annual Disclosure), by one of the following methods:

• *Federal eRulemaking Portal: http://www.regulations.gov.* Follow the instructions for submitting comments.

• *Email: e-ORI@dol.gov.* Include RIN 1210-AB68 in the subject line of the message.

• *Mail or Hand Delivery:* Office of Regulations and Interpretations, Employee Benefits Security Administration, Room N-5655, U.S. Department of Labor, 200 Constitution Avenue NW., Washington, DC 20210.

Instructions: All submissions received must include the agency name and Regulation Identifier Number (RIN) for this rulemaking. Comments received by the Department of Labor will be posted without change to *http://www.regulations.gov* and *http://www.dol.gov/ebsa,* and made available for public inspection at the Public Disclosure Room, N-1513, Employee Benefits Security Administration, 200 Constitution Avenue NW., Washington, DC 20210, including any personal information provided. *Warning:* Do not include any personally identifiable information (such as name, address, or other contact information) or other confidential business information that you do not want publicly disclosed. All comments may be posted on the Internet and can be retrieved by most Internet search engines. No deletions, modifications, or redactions will be made to the comments received, as they are public records. Comments may be submitted anonymously. Persons submitting comments electronically are encouraged not to submit paper copies.

FOR FURTHER INFORMATION CONTACT: Eric A. Raps, Office of Regulations and Interpretations, Employee Benefits Security Administration, (202) 693-8532. This is not a toll-free number.

SUPPLEMENTARY INFORMATION: In the "Rules and Regulations" section of today's **Federal Register**, the Department of Labor published a direct final rule that amends the definition of the term "at least annually thereafter" contained in 29 CFR 2550.404a-5(h)(1) by substituting the term "14-month period" for the term "12-month period." This **Federal Register** notice incorporates by reference and proposes the same amendment contained in the direct final rule. Please refer to the preamble and the regulatory text of the direct final rule for details, including information and analyses under applicable Executive Orders, the Regulatory Flexibility Act, Paperwork Reduction Act, and Unfunded Mandates Reform Act.

Signed at Washington, DC, this 12th day of March 2015.

Phyllis C. Borzi,

Assistant Secretary, Employee Benefits Security Administration, U.S. Department of Labor.

[FR Doc. 2015-06210 Filed 3-18-15; 8:45 am]

BILLING CODE 4510-29-P

¶ 20,538Y

Pension Benefit Guaranty Corporation (PBGC): Proposed rule: Multiemployer plans: Reporting and disclosure: Plan termination: Plan insolvency: Electronic filing.—The Pension Benefit Guaranty Corporation (PBGC) has issued proposed regulations that would require the electronic filing of certain multiemployer plan notices with the PBGC. Specifically, the proposed regulations would require the following notices to be filed electronically with PBGC: notices of termination under part 4041A, notices of insolvency and of insolvency benefit level under parts 4245 (involving insolvent plans) and 4281 (following mass withdrawal), and applications for financial assistance under part 4281. The PBGC would grant case-by-case exemptions to the electronic filing requirement in appropriate circumstances for filers that demonstrate good cause for exemption. The proposed amendments to the regulations would be applicable for filings made on or after January 1, 2016.

The proposed regulations, which were published in the Federal Register on April 3, 2015 (80 FR 18172), were reproduced below. The regulations were finalized on September 17, 2015 (80 FR 55742). The preamble to the final regulations is at ¶ 24,333. The final regulations are at ¶ 15,302A, ¶ 15,449J, ¶ 15,449P, ¶ 15,715C, ¶ 15,715R, and ¶ 15,715V.

¶ 20,538Z

Employee Benefits Security Administration (EBSA): Proposed regulations: Fiduciary: Employee benefit plans: Individual retirement accounts (IRAs): Investment advice.—EBSA has issued proposed regulations that redefines who is a "fiduciary" of an ERISA employee benefit plan (including an IRA) under Code Sec. 4975)). The proposed regulations would treat persons who provide investment advice or recommendations for a fee or other compensation to a plan, a plan fiduciary, a plan participant or beneficiary, IRA, or IRA owner as fiduciaries in a wider array of advice relationships than existing ERISA and Code regulations. The proposed regulations also withdraws a prior 2010 proposed regulation (PENSION PLAN GUIDE ¶ 20,537Z) concerning the same subject matter. In connection with these proposed regulations, EBSA is also proposing new class prohibited transaction exemptions (PTEs) at (PENSION PLAN GUIDE ¶ 16,718 and ¶ 16,719), and amending existing class PTEs at(PENSION PLAN GUIDE ¶ 16,720, ¶ 16,721, ¶ 16,722, and ¶ 16,723).

The proposed regulations, which were published in the Federal Register on April 20, 2015 (80 FR 21927), are reproduced below.

The time for public comments that was originally scheduled to end July 6, 2015 has been extended to July 21, 2015 (80 FR 34869, June 18, 2015).

The regulations were finalized on April 8, 2016 (81 FR 20945). The preamble to the final regulations is at ¶ 24,338. The final regulations are at ¶ 14,138A and ¶ 14,746C. The final regulations are effective June 7, 2016 and applicable April 10, 2017. In connection with the final regulations, EBSA has also issued final class PTEs and amendments to class PTEs at ¶ 16,650, ¶ 16,650A, ¶ 16,650B, ¶ 16,650C, ¶ 16,650D, and ¶ 16,650E. The PTEs were published in the Federal Register on April 8, 2016, are issued and effective June 7, 2016, and are generally applicable April 10, 2017.

FEDERAL REGISTER

Vol. 80 No. 75

Monday, April 20, 2015

Part III Department of Labor

Employee Benefits Security Administration

29 CFR Parts 2509 and 2510

Definition of the Term "Fiduciary"; Conflict of Interest Rule—Retirement Investment Advice; Proposed Rule

DEPARTMENT OF LABOR

Employee Benefits Security Administration

29 CFR Parts 2509 and 2510

¶20,538Y

RIN 1210-AB32

Definition of the Term "Fiduciary"; Conflict of Interest Rule—Retirement Investment Advice

AGENCY: Employee Benefits Security Administration, Department of Labor.

ACTION: Notice of proposed rulemaking and withdrawal of previous proposed rule.

SUMMARY: This document contains a proposed regulation defining who is a "fiduciary" of an employee benefit plan under the Employee Retirement Income Security Act of 1974 (ERISA) as a result of giving investment advice to a plan or its participants or beneficiaries. The proposal also applies to the definition of a "fiduciary" of a plan (including an individual retirement account (IRA)) under section 4975 of the Internal Revenue Code of 1986 (Code). If adopted, the proposal would treat persons who provide investment advice or recommendations to an employee benefit plan, plan fiduciary, plan participant or beneficiary, IRA, or IRA owner as fiduciaries under ERISA and the Code in a wider array of advice relationships than the existing ERISA and Code regulations, which would be replaced. The proposed rule, and related exemptions, would increase consumer protection for plan sponsors, fiduciaries, participants, beneficiaries and IRA owners. This document also withdraws a prior proposed regulation published in 2010 (2010 Proposal) concerning this same subject matter. In connection with this proposal, elsewhere in this issue of the **Federal Register**, the Department is proposing new exemptions and amendments to existing exemptions from the prohibited transaction rules applicable to fiduciaries under ERISA and the Code that would allow certain broker-dealers, insurance agents and others that act as investment advice fiduciaries to continue to receive a variety of common forms of compensation that otherwise would be prohibited as conflicts of interest.

DATES: As of April 20, 2015, the proposed rule published October 22, 2010 (75 FR 65263) is withdrawn. Submit written comments on the proposed regulation on or before July 6, 2015.

ADDRESSES: To facilitate the receipt and processing of written comment letters on the proposed regulation, EBSA encourages interested persons to submit their comments electronically. You may submit comments, identified by RIN 1210-AB32, by any of the following methods:

Federal eRulemaking Portal: http://www.regulations.gov. Follow instructions for submitting comments.

Email: e-ORI@dol.gov. Include RIN 1210-AB32 in the subject line of the message.

Mail: Office of Regulations and Interpretations, Employee Benefits Security Administration, Attn: Conflict of Interest Rule, Room N-5655, U.S. Department of Labor, 200 Constitution Avenue NW., Washington, DC 20210.

Hand Delivery/Courier: Office of Regulations and Interpretations, Employee Benefits Security Administration, Attn: Conflict of Interest Rule, Room N-5655, U.S. Department of Labor, 200 Constitution Avenue NW., Washington, DC 20210.

Instructions: All comments received must include the agency name and Regulatory Identifier Number (RIN) for this rulemaking (RIN 1210-AB32). Persons submitting comments electronically are encouraged not to submit paper copies. All comments received will be made available to the public, posted without change to http://www.regulations.gov and http://www.dol.gov/ebsa, and made available for public inspection at the Public Disclosure Room, N-1513, Employee Benefits Security Administration, U.S. Department of Labor, 200 Constitution Avenue NW., Washington, DC 20210, including any personal information provided.

FOR FURTHER INFORMATION CONTACT:

For Questions Regarding the Proposed Rule: Contact Luisa Grillo-Chope or Fred Wong, Office of Regulations and Interpretations, Employee Benefits Security Administration (EBSA), (202) 693-8825.

For Questions Regarding the Proposed Prohibited Transaction Exemptions: Contact Karen Lloyd, Office of Exemption Determinations, EBSA, 202-693-8824.

For Questions Regarding the Regulatory Impact Analysis: Contact G. Christopher Cosby, Office of Policy and Research, EBSA, 202-693-8425. (These are not toll-free numbers).

SUPPLEMENTARY INFORMATION:

I. Executive Summary

A. Purpose of the Regulatory Action

Under ERISA and the Code, a person is a fiduciary to a plan or IRA to the extent that he or she engages in specified plan activities, including rendering "investment advice for a fee or other compensation, direct or indirect, with respect to any moneys or other property of such plan . . . " ERISA safeguards plan participants by imposing trust law standards of care and undivided loyalty on plan fiduciaries, and by holding fiduciaries accountable when they breach those obligations. In addition, fiduciaries to plans and IRAs are not permitted to engage in "prohibited transactions," which pose special dangers to the security of

retirement, health, and other benefit plans because of fiduciaries' conflicts of interest with respect to the transactions. Under this regulatory structure, fiduciary status and responsibilities are central to protecting the public interest in the integrity of retirement and other important benefits, many of which are tax-favored.

In 1975, the Department issued regulations that significantly narrowed the breadth of the statutory definition of fiduciary investment advice by creating a five-part test that must, in each instance, be satisfied before a person can be treated as a fiduciary adviser. This regulatory definition applies to both ERISA and the Code. The Department created the test in a very different context, prior to the existence of participant-directed 401(k) plans, widespread investments in IRAs, and the now commonplace rollover of plan assets from fiduciary-protected plans to IRAs. Today, as a result of the five-part test, many investment professionals, consultants, and advisers[1] have no obligation to adhere to ERISA's fiduciary standards or to the prohibited transaction rules, despite the critical role they play in guiding plan and IRA investments. Under ERISA and the Code, if these advisers are not fiduciaries, they may operate with conflicts of interest that they need not disclose and have limited liability under federal pension law for any harms resulting from the advice they provide. Non-fiduciaries may give imprudent and disloyal advice; steer plans and IRA owners to investments based on their own, rather than their customers' financial interests; and act on conflicts of interest in ways that would be prohibited if the same persons were fiduciaries. In light of the breadth and intent of ERISA and the Code's statutory definition, the growth of participant-directed investment arrangements and IRAs, and the need for plans and IRA owners to seek out and rely on sophisticated financial advisers to make critical investment decisions in an increasingly complex financial marketplace, the Department believes it is appropriate to revisit its 1975 regulatory definition as well as the Code's virtually identical regulation. With this regulatory action, the Department proposes to replace the 1975 regulations with a definition of fiduciary investment advice that better reflects the broad scope of the statutory text and its purposes and better protects plans, participants, beneficiaries, and IRA owners from conflicts of interest, imprudence, and disloyalty.

The Department has also sought to preserve beneficial business models for delivery of investment advice by separately proposing new exemptions from ERISA's prohibited transaction rules that would broadly permit firms to continue common fee and compensation practices, as long as they are willing to adhere to basic standards aimed at ensuring that their advice is in the best interest of their customers. Rather than create a highly prescriptive set of transaction-specific exemptions, the Department instead is proposing a set of exemptions that flexibly accommodate a wide range of current business practices, while minimizing the harmful impact of conflicts of interest on the quality of advice.

In particular, the Department is proposing a new exemption (the "Best Interest Contract Exemption") that would provide conditional relief for common compensation, such as commissions and revenue sharing, that an adviser and the adviser's employing firm might receive in connection with investment advice to retail retirement investors.[2] In order to protect the interests of plans, participants and beneficiaries, and IRA owners, the exemption requires the firm and the adviser to contractually acknowledge fiduciary status, commit to adhere to basic standards of impartial conduct, adopt policies and procedures reasonably designed to minimize the harmful impact of conflicts of interest, and disclose basic information on their conflicts of interest and on the cost of their advice. Central to the exemption is the adviser and firm's agreement to meet fundamental obligations of fair dealing and fiduciary conduct—to give advice that is in the customer's best interest; avoid misleading statements; receive no more than reasonable compensation; and comply with applicable federal and state laws governing advice. This principles-based approach aligns the adviser's interests with those of the plan participant or IRA owner, while leaving the adviser and employing firm with the flexibility and discretion necessary to determine how best to satisfy these basic standards in light of the unique attributes of their business. The Department is similarly proposing to amend existing exemptions for a wide range of fiduciary advisers to ensure adherence to these basic standards of fiduciary conduct. In addition, the Department is proposing a new exemption for "principal transactions" in which advisers sell certain debt securities to plans and IRAs out of their own inventory, as well as an amendment to an existing exemption that would permit advisers to receive compensation for extending credit to plans or IRAs to avoid failed securities transactions.

---

[1] By using the term "adviser," the Department does not intend to limit its use to investment advisers registered under the Investment Advisers Act of 1940 or under state law. For example, as used herein, an adviser can be an individual or entity who can be, among other things, a representative of a registered investment adviser, a bank or similar financial institution, an insurance company, or a broker-dealer.

[2] For purposes of the exemption, retail investors include (1) the participants and beneficiaries of participant-directed plans, (2) IRA owners, and (3) the sponsors (including employees, officers, or directors thereof) of non participant-directed plans with fewer than 100 participants to the extent the sponsors (including employees, officers, or directors thereof) act as a fiduciary with respect to plan investment decisions.

In addition to the Best Interest Contract Exemption, the Department is also seeking public comment on whether it should issue a separate streamlined exemption that would allow advisers to receive otherwise prohibited compensation in connection with plan, participant and beneficiary accounts, and IRA investments in certain high-quality low-fee investments, subject to fewer conditions. This is discussed in greater detail in the **Federal Register** notice related to the proposed Best Interest Contract Exemption.

This broad regulatory package aims to enable advisers and their firms to give advice that is in the best interest of their customers, without disrupting common compensation arrangements under conditions designed to ensure the adviser is acting in the best interest of the advice recipient. The proposed new exemptions and amendments to existing exemptions are published elsewhere in today's edition of the **Federal Register**.

B. Summary of the Major Provisions of the Proposed Rule

The proposed rule clarifies and rationalizes the definition of fiduciary investment advice subject to specific carve-outs for particular types of communications that are best understood as non-fiduciary in nature. Under the definition, a person renders investment advice by (1) providing investment or investment management recommendations or appraisals to an employee benefit plan, a plan fiduciary, participant or beneficiary, or an IRA owner or fiduciary, and (2) either (a) acknowledging the fiduciary nature of the advice, or (b) acting pursuant to an agreement, arrangement, or understanding with the advice recipient that the advice is individualized to, or specifically directed to, the recipient for consideration in making investment or management decisions regarding plan assets. When such advice is provided for a fee or other compensation, direct or indirect, the person giving the advice is a fiduciary.

Although the new general definition of investment advice avoids the weaknesses of the current regulation, standing alone it could sweep in some relationships that are not appropriately regarded as fiduciary in nature and that the Department does not believe Congress intended to cover as fiduciary relationships. Accordingly, the proposed regulation includes a number of specific carve-outs to the general definition. For example, the regulation draws an important distinction between fiduciary investment advice and non-fiduciary investment or retirement education. Similarly, under the "seller's carve-out,"[3] the proposal would not treat as fiduciary advice recommendations made to a plan in an arm's length transaction where there is generally no expectation of fiduciary investment advice, provided that the carve-out's specific conditions are met. In addition, the proposal includes specific carve-outs for advice rendered by employees of the plan sponsor, platform providers, and persons who offer or enter into swaps or security-based swaps with plans. All of the rule's carve-outs are subject to conditions designed to draw an appropriate line between fiduciary and non-fiduciary communications, consistent with the text and purpose of the statutory provisions.

Finally, in addition to the new proposal in this Notice, the Department is simultaneously proposing a new Best Interest Contract Exemption, revising other exemptions from the prohibited transaction rules of ERISA and the Code and is exploring through a request for comments the concept of an additional low-fee exemption.

C. Gains to Investors and Compliance Costs

When the Department promulgated the 1975 rule, 401(k) plans did not exist, IRAs had only just been authorized, and the majority of retirement plan assets were managed by professionals, rather than directed by individual investors. Today, individual retirement investors have much greater responsibility for directing their own investments, but they seldom have the training or specialized expertise necessary to prudently manage retirement assets on their own. As a result, they often depend on investment advice for guidance on how to manage their savings to achieve a secure retirement. In the current marketplace for retirement investment advice, however, advisers commonly have direct and substantial conflicts of interest, which encourage investment recommendations that generate higher fees for the advisers at the expense of their customers and often result in lower returns for customers even before fees.

A wide body of economic evidence supports a finding that the impact of these conflicts of interest on retirement investment outcomes is large and, from the perspective of advice recipients, negative. As detailed in the Department's Regulatory Impact Analysis (available at *www.dol.gov/ebsa/pdf/conflictsofinterestria.pdf*), the supporting evidence includes, among other things, statistical analyses of conflicted investment channels, experimental studies, government reports documenting abuse, and basic economic theory on the dangers posed by conflicts of interest and by the asymmetries of information and expertise that characterize interactions between ordinary retirement investors and conflicted advisers. This evidence takes into account existing protections under ERISA as well as other federal and state laws. A review of this data, which consistently points to substantial failures in the market for retirement advice, suggests that IRA holders receiving conflicted investment advice can expect their investments to underperform by an average of 100 basis points per year over the next 20 years. The underperformance associated with conflicts of interest—in the mutual funds segment alone—could cost IRA investors more than $210 billion over the next 10 years and nearly $500 billion over the next 20 years. Some studies suggest that the underperformance of broker-sold mutual funds may be even higher than 100 basis points, possibly due to loads that are taken off the top and/or poor timing of broker sold investments. If the true underperformance of broker-sold funds is 200 basis points, IRA mutual fund holders could suffer from underperformance amounting to $430 billion over 10 years and nearly $1 trillion across the next 20 years. While the estimates based on the mutual fund market are large, the total market impact could be much larger. Insurance products, Exchange Traded Funds (ETFs), individual stocks and bonds, and other products are all sold by agents and brokers with conflicts of interest.

The Department expects the proposal would deliver large gains for retirement investors. Because of data constraints, only some of these gains can be quantified with confidence. Focusing only on how load shares paid to brokers affect the size of loads paid by IRA investors holding load funds and the returns they achieve, the Department estimates the proposal would deliver to IRA investors gains of between $40 billion and $44 billion over 10 years and between $88 billion and $100 billion over 20 years. These estimates assume that the rule would eliminate (rather than just reduce) underperformance associated with the practice of incentivizing broker recommendations through variable front-end-load sharing; if the rule's effectiveness in this area is substantially below 100 percent, these estimates may overstate these particular gains to investors in the front-load mutual fund segment of the IRA market. The Department nonetheless believes that these gains alone would far exceed the proposal's compliance cost. For example, if only 75 percent of anticipated gains were realized, the quantified subset of such gains—specific to the front-load mutual fund segment of the IRA market—would amount to between $30 billion and $33 billion over 10 years. If only 50 percent were realized, this subset of expected gains would total between $20 billion and $22 billion over 10 years, or several times the proposal's estimated compliance cost of $2.4 billion to 5.7 billion over the same 10 years. These gain estimates also exclude additional potential gains to investors resulting from reducing or eliminating the effects of conflicts in financial products other than front-end-load mutual funds. The Department invites input that would make it possible to quantify the magnitude of the rule's effectiveness and of any additional, not-yet-quantified gains for investors.

These estimates account for only a fraction of potential conflicts, associated losses, and affected retirement assets. The total gains to IRA investors attributable to the rule may be much higher than these quantified gains alone for several reasons. The Department expects the proposal to yield large, additional gains for IRA investors, including potential reductions in excessive trading and associated transaction costs and timing errors (such as might be associated with return chasing), improvements in the performance of IRA investments other than front-load mutual funds, and improvements in the performance of defined contribution (DC) plan investments. As noted above, under current rules, adviser conflicts could cost IRA investors as much as $410 billion over 10 years and $1 trillion over 20 years, so the potential additional gains to IRA investors from this proposal could be very large.

The following accounting table summarizes the Department's conclusions:

---

[3] Although referred to herein as the "seller's carve-out," we note that the carve-out provided in paragraph (b)(1)(i) of the proposal is not limited to sales and would apply to incidental advice provided in connection with an arm's length sale, purchase, loan, or bilateral contract between a plan investor with financial expertise and the adviser.

TABLE 1—PARTIAL GAINS TO INVESTORS AND COMPLIANCE COSTS ACCOUNTING TABLE

Category	Primary estimate	Low estimate	High estimate	Year dollar	Discount rate (%)	Period covered
Partial Gains to Investors						
Annualized, Monetized ($millions/year)	$4,243	$3,830	....	2015	7	2017—2026
	$5,170	4,666	....	2015	3	2017—2026

Notes: The proposal is expected to deliver large gains for retirement investors. Because of limitations of the literature and other available evidence, only some of these gains can be quantified. The estimates in this table focus only on how load shares paid to brokers affect the size of loads IRA investors holding load funds pay and the returns they achieve. These estimates assume that the rule will eliminate (rather than just reduce) underperformance associated with the practice of incentivizing broker recommendations through variable front-load sharing. If, however, the rule's effectiveness in reducing underperformance is substantially below 100 percent, these estimates may overstate these particular gains to investors in the front-end-load mutual fund segment of the IRA market. However, these estimates account for only a fraction of potential conflicts, associated losses, and affected retirement assets. The total gains to IRA investors attributable to the rule may be higher than the quantified gains alone for several reasons. For example, the proposal is expected to yield additional gains for IRA investors, including potential reductions in excessive trading and associated transaction costs and timing errors (such as might be associated with return chasing), improvements in the performance of IRA investments other than front-load mutual funds, and improvements in the performance of DC plan investments.
The partial-gains-to-investors estimates include both economic efficiency benefits and transfers from the financial services industry to IRA holders.
The partial gains estimates are discounted to December 31, 2015.

Compliance Costs						
Annualized, Monetized ($millions/year)	$348	....	$706	2015	7	2016-2025
	328	....	664	2015	3	2016-2025

Notes: The compliance costs of the current proposal including the cost of compliance reviews, comprehensive compliance and supervisory system changes, policies and procedures and training programs updates, insurance increases, disclosure preparation and distribution, and some costs of changes in other business practices. Compliance costs incurred by mutual funds or other asset providers have not been estimated.

Insurance Premium Transfers						
Annualized Monetized ($millions/year)	$63	....	....	2015	7	2016-2025
	63	....	....	2015	3	2016-2025
From/To	From: Service providers facing increased insurance premiums due to increased liability risk		To: Plans, participants, beneficiaries, and IRA investors through the payment of recoveries—funded from a portion of the increased insurance premiums			

OMB Circular A-4 requires the presentation of a social welfare accounting table that summarizes a regulation's benefits, costs and transfers (monetized, where possible). A summary of this type would differ from and expand upon Table I in several ways:

• In the language of social welfare economics as reflected in Circular A-4, investor gains comprise two parts: Social welfare "benefits" attributable to improvements in economic efficiency and "transfers" of welfare to retirement investors from the financial services industry. Due to limitations of the literature and other available evidence, the investor gains estimates presented in Table I have not been broken down into benefits and transfer components, but making the distinction between these categories of impacts is key for a social welfare accounting statement.

• The estimates in Table I reflect only a subset of the gains to investors resulting from the rule, but may overstate this subset. As noted in Table I, the Department's estimates of partial gains to investors reflect an assumption that the rule will eliminate, rather than just reduce, underperformance associated with the practice of incentivizing broker recommendations through variable front-end-load sharing. If, however, the rule's effectiveness is substantially below 100 percent, these estimates would overstate these partial gains to investors in the front-load mutual fund segment of the IRA market. The estimates in Table I also exclude additional potential gains to investors resulting from reducing or eliminating the effects of conflicts in financial products other than front-end-load mutual funds in the IRA market, and all potential gains to investors in the plan market. The Department invites input that would make it possible to quantify the magnitude of the rule's effectiveness and of any additional, not-yet-quantified gains for investors.

• Generally, the gains to investors consist of multiple parts: Transfers to IRA investors from advisers and others in the supply chain, benefits to the overall economy from a shift in the allocation of investment dollars to projects that have higher returns, and resource savings associated with, for example, reductions in excessive turnover and wasteful and unsuccessful efforts to outperform the market. Some of these gains are partially quantified in Table I. Also, the estimates in Table I assume the gains to investors arise gradually as the fraction of wealth invested based on conflicted investment advice slowly declines over time based on historical patterns of asset turnover. However, the estimates do not account for potential transition costs associated with a shift of investments to higher-performing vehicles. These transition costs have not been quantified due to lack of granularity in the literature or availability of other evidence on both the portion of investor gains that consists of resource savings, as opposed to transfers, and the amount of transitional cost that would be incurred per unit of resource savings.

• Other categories of costs not yet quantified include compliance costs incurred by mutual funds or other asset providers. Enforcement costs or other costs borne by the government are also not quantified.

The Department requests detailed comment, data, and analysis on all of the issues outlined above for incorporation into the social welfare analysis at the finalization stage of the rulemaking process.

For a detailed discussion of the gains to investors and compliance costs of the current proposal, please see Section J. Regulatory Impact Analysis, below.

II. Overview

A. Rulemaking Background

The market for retirement advice has changed dramatically since the Department first promulgated the 1975 regulation. Individuals, rather than large employers and professional money managers, have become increasingly responsible for managing retirement assets as IRAs and participant-directed plans, such as 401(k) plans, have supplanted defined benefit pensions. At the same time, the variety and complexity of financial products have increased, widening the information gap between advisers and their clients. Plan fiduciaries, plan participants and IRA investors must often rely on experts for advice, but are unable to assess the quality of the expert's advice or effectively guard against the adviser's conflicts of interest. This challenge is especially true of small retail investors who typically do not have financial expertise and can ill-afford lower returns to their retirement savings caused by conflicts. As baby boomers retire, they are increasingly moving money from ERISA-covered plans, where their employer has both the incentive and the fiduciary duty to facilitate sound investment choices, to IRAs where both good and bad investment choices are myriad and advice that is conflicted is commonplace. Such "rollovers" will total more than $2 trillion over the next 5 years. These trends were not apparent when the Department promulgated the 1975 rule. At that time, 401(k) plans did

not yet exist and IRAs had only just been authorized. These changes in the marketplace, as well as the Department's experience with the rule since 1975, support the Department's efforts to reevaluate and revise the rule through a public process of notice and comment rulemaking.

On October 22, 2010, the Department published a proposed rule in the **Federal Register** (75 FR 65263) (2010 Proposal) proposing to amend 29 CFR 2510.3-21(c) (40 FR 50843, Oct. 31, 1975), which defines when a person renders investment advice to an employee benefit plan, and consequently acts as a fiduciary under ERISA section 3(21)(A)(ii) (29 U.S.C. 1002(21)(A)(ii)). In response to this proposal, the Department received over 300 comment letters. A public hearing on the 2010 Proposal was held in Washington, DC on March 1 and 2, 2011, at which 38 speakers testified. The transcript of the hearing was made available for additional public comment and the Department received over 60 additional comment letters. In addition, the Department has held many meetings with interested parties.

A number of commenters urged consideration of other means to attain the objectives of the 2010 Proposal and of additional analysis of the proposal's expected costs and benefits. In light of these comments and because of the significance of this rule, the Department decided to issue a new proposed regulation. On September 19, 2011 the Department announced that it would withdraw the 2010 Proposal and propose a new rule defining the term "fiduciary" for purposes of section 3(21)(A)(ii) of ERISA. This document fulfills that announcement in publishing both a new proposed regulation and withdrawing the 2010 Proposal. Consistent with the President's Executive Orders 12866 and 13563, extending the rulemaking process will give the public a full opportunity to evaluate and comment on the revised proposal and updated economic analysis. In addition, we are simultaneously publishing proposed new and amended exemptions from ERISA and the Code's prohibited transaction rules designed to allow certain broker-dealers, insurance agents and others that act as investment advice fiduciaries to nevertheless continue to receive common forms of compensation that would otherwise be prohibited, subject to appropriate safeguards. The existing class exemptions will otherwise remain in place, affording flexibility to fiduciaries who currently use the exemptions or who wish to use the exemptions in the future. The proposed new regulatory package takes into account robust public comment and input and represents a substantial change from the 2010 Proposal, balancing long overdue consumer protections with flexibility for the industry in order to minimize disruptions to current business models.

In crafting the current regulatory package, the Department has benefitted from the views and perspectives expressed in public comments to the 2010 Proposal. For example, the Department has responded to concerns about the impact of the prohibited transaction rules on the marketplace for retail advice by proposing a broad package of exemptions that are intended to ensure that advisers and their firms make recommendations that are in the best interest of plan participants and IRA owners, without disrupting common fee arrangements. In response to commenters, the Department has also determined not to include, as fiduciary in nature, appraisals or valuations of employer securities provided to ESOPs or to certain collective investment funds holding assets of plan investors. On a more technical point, the Department also followed recommendations that it not automatically assign fiduciary status to investment advisers under the Advisers Act, but instead follow an entirely functional approach to fiduciary status. In light of public comments, the new proposal also makes a number of other changes to the regulatory proposal. For example, the Department has addressed concerns that it could be misread to extend fiduciary status to persons that prepare newsletters, television commentaries, or conference speeches that contain recommendations made to the general public. Similarly, the rule makes clear that fiduciary status does not extend to internal company personnel who give advice on behalf of their plan sponsor as part of their duties, but receive no compensation beyond their salary for the provision of advice. The Department is appreciative of the comments it received to the 2010 Proposal, and more fully discusses a number of the comments that influenced change in the sections that follow. In addition, the Department is eager to receive comments on the new proposal in general, and requests public comment on a number of specific aspects of the package as indicated below.

The following discussion summarizes the 2010 Proposal, describes some of the concerns and issues raised by commenters, and explains the new proposed regulation, which is published with this notice.

B. The Statute and Existing Regulation

ERISA (or the "Act") is a comprehensive statute designed to protect the interests of plan participants and beneficiaries, the integrity of employee benefit plans, and the security of retirement, health, and other critical benefits. The broad public interest in ERISA-covered plans is reflected in the Act's imposition of stringent fiduciary responsibilities on parties engaging in important plan activities, as well as in the tax-favored status of plan assets and investments. One of the chief ways in which ERISA protects employee benefit plans is by requiring that plan fiduciaries comply with fundamental obligations rooted in the law of trusts. In particular, plan fiduciaries must manage plan assets prudently and with undivided loyalty to the plans and their participants and beneficiaries.[4] In addition, they must refrain from engaging in "prohibited transactions," which the Act does not permit because of the dangers to the interests of the plan and IRA posed by the transactions.[5] When fiduciaries violate ERISA's fiduciary duties or the prohibited transaction rules, they may be held personally liable for any losses to the investor resulting from the breach.[6] In addition, violations of the prohibited transaction rules are subject to excise taxes under the Code.

The Code also protects individuals who save for retirement through tax-favored accounts that are not generally covered by ERISA, such as IRAs, through a more limited regulation of fiduciary conduct. Although ERISA's general fiduciary obligations of prudence and loyalty do not govern the fiduciaries of IRAs and other plans not covered by ERISA, these fiduciaries are subject to the prohibited transaction rules of the Code. In this context, however, the sole statutory sanction for engaging in the illegal transactions is the assessment of an excise tax enforced by the Internal Revenue Service (IRS). Thus, unlike participants in plans covered by Title I of ERISA, IRA owners do not have a statutory right to bring suit against fiduciaries under ERISA for violation of the prohibited transaction rules and fiduciaries are not personally liable to IRA owners for the losses caused by their misconduct.

Under this statutory framework, the determination of who is a "fiduciary" is of central importance. Many of ERISA's and the Code's protections, duties, and liabilities hinge on fiduciary status. In relevant part, section 3(21)(A) of ERISA provides that a person is a fiduciary with respect to a plan to the extent he or she (i) exercises any discretionary authority or discretionary control with respect to management of such plan or exercises any authority or control with respect to management or disposition of its assets; (ii) renders investment advice for a fee or other compensation, direct or indirect, with respect to any moneys or other property of such plan, or has any authority or responsibility to do so; or, (iii) has any discretionary authority or discretionary responsibility in the administration of such plan. Section 4975(e)(3) of the IRC identically defines "fiduciary" for purposes of the prohibited transaction rules set forth in Code section 4975.

The statutory definition contained in section 3(21)(A) deliberately casts a wide net in assigning fiduciary responsibility with respect to plan assets. Thus, "any authority or control" over plan assets is sufficient to confer fiduciary status, and any person who renders "investment advice for a fee or other compensation, direct or indirect" is an investment advice fiduciary, regardless of whether they have direct control over the plan's assets, and regardless of their status as an investment adviser and/or broker under the federal securities laws. The statutory definition and associated fiduciary responsibilities were enacted to ensure that plans can depend on persons who provide investment advice for a fee to make recommendations that are prudent, loyal, and untainted by conflicts of interest. In the absence of fiduciary status, persons who provide investment advice would neither be subject to ERISA's fundamental fiduciary standards, nor accountable under ERISA or the Code for imprudent, disloyal, or tainted advice, no matter how egregious the misconduct or how substantial the losses. Plans, individual participants and beneficiaries, and IRA owners often are not financial experts and consequently must rely on professional advice to make critical investment decisions. The statutory definition, prohibitions on conflicts of interest, and core fiduciary obligations of prudence and loyalty, all reflect Congress' recognition in 1974 of the fundamental importance of such advice to protect savers' retirement nest eggs. In the years since then, the significance of financial advice has become still greater with increased reliance on participant-directed plans and self-directed IRAs for the provision of retirement benefits.

In 1975, the Department issued a regulation, at 29 CFR 2510.3-21(c) defining the circumstances under which a person is treated as providing "investment advice" to an employee benefit plan within the meaning of section 3(21)(A)(ii) of ERISA (the "1975 regulation"), and the Department of the Treasury issued a virtually identical regulation under the Code.[7] The regulation narrowed the scope of the statutory definition of fiduciary investment advice by creating a five-part test that

must be satisfied before a person can be treated as rendering investment advice for a fee. Under the regulation, for advice to constitute "investment advice," an adviser who is not a fiduciary under another provision of the statute must—(1) render advice as to the value of securities or other property, or make recommendations as to the advisability of investing in, purchasing or selling securities or other property (2) on a regular basis (3) pursuant to a mutual agreement, arrangement or understanding, with the plan or a plan fiduciary that (4) the advice will serve as a primary basis for investment decisions with respect to plan assets, and that (5) the advice will be individualized based on the particular needs of the plan or IRA. The regulation provides that an adviser is a fiduciary with respect to any particular instance of advice only if he or she meets each and every element of the five-part test with respect to the particular advice recipient or plan at issue.

As the marketplace for financial services has developed in the years since 1975, the five-part test may now undermine, rather than promote, the statutes' text and purposes. The narrowness of the 1975 regulation allows advisers, brokers, consultants and valuation firms to play a central role in shaping plan and IRA investments, without ensuring the accountability that Congress intended for persons having such influence and responsibility. Even when plan sponsors, participants, beneficiaries, and IRA owners clearly rely on paid advisers for impartial guidance, the regulation allows many advisers to avoid fiduciary status and disregard ERISA's fiduciary obligations of care and prohibitions on disloyal and conflicted transactions. As a consequence, these advisers can steer customers to investments based on their own self-interest (e.g., products that generate higher fees for the adviser even if there are identical lower-fee products available), give imprudent advice, and engage in transactions that would otherwise not be permitted by ERISA and the Code without fear of accountability under either ERISA or the Code.

Instead of ensuring that trusted advisers give prudent and unbiased advice in accordance with fiduciary norms, the current regulation erects a multi-part series of technical impediments to fiduciary responsibility. The Department is concerned that the specific elements of the five-part test—which are not found in the text of the Act or Code—now work to frustrate statutory goals and defeat advice recipients' legitimate expectations. In light of the importance of the proper management of plan and IRA assets, it is critical that the regulation defining investment advice draws appropriate distinctions between the sorts of advice relationships that should be treated as fiduciary in nature and those that should not. In practice, the current regulation appears not to do so. Instead, the lines drawn by the five-part test frequently permit evasion of fiduciary status and responsibility in ways that undermine the statutory text and purposes.

One example of the five-part test's shortcomings is the requirement that advice be furnished on a "regular basis." As a result of the requirement, if a small plan hires an investment professional or appraiser on a one-time basis for an investment recommendation or valuation opinion on a large, complex investment, the adviser has no fiduciary obligation to the plan under ERISA. Even if the plan is considering investing all or substantially all of the plan's assets, lacks the specialized expertise necessary to evaluate the complex transaction on its own, and the consultant fully understands the plan's dependence on his professional judgment, the consultant is not a fiduciary because he does not advise the plan on a "regular basis." The plan could be investing hundreds of millions of dollars in plan assets, and it could be the most critical investment decision the plan ever makes, but the adviser would have no fiduciary responsibility under the 1975 regulation. While a consultant who regularly makes less significant investment recommendations to the plan would be a fiduciary if he satisfies the other four prongs of the regulatory test, the onetime consultant on an enormous transaction has no fiduciary responsibility.

In such cases, the "regular basis" requirement, which is not found in the text of ERISA or the Code, fails to draw a sensible line between fiduciary and non-fiduciary conduct, and undermines the law's protective purposes. A specific example is the one-time purchase of a group annuity to cover all of the benefits promised to substantially all of a plan's participants for the rest of their lives when a defined benefit plan terminates or a plan's expenditure of hundreds of millions of dollars on a single real estate transaction with the assistance of a financial adviser hired for purposes of that one transaction. Despite the clear importance

---

[4] ERISA section 404(a).

[5] ERISA section 406. The Act also prohibits certain transactions between a plan and a "party in interest."

[6] ERISA section 409; see also ERISA section 405.

[7] See 26 CFR 54.4975-9(c), which interprets Code section 4975(e)(3). 40 FR 50840 (Oct. 31, 1975). Under section 102 of Reorganization Plan No. 4 of 1978, the authority of the Secretary of the Treasury to interpret section 4975 of the Code has been transferred, with certain exceptions not here relevant, to the Secretary of Labor. References in this document to sections of ERISA should be read to refer also to the corresponding sections of the Code.

of the decisions and the clear reliance on paid advisers, the advisers would not be plan fiduciaries. On a smaller scale that is still immensely important for the affected individual, the "regular basis" requirement also deprives individual participants and IRA owners of statutory protection when they seek specialized advice on a one-time basis, even if the advice concerns the investment of all or substantially all of the assets held in their account (e.g., as in the case of an annuity purchase or a roll-over from a plan to an IRA or from one IRA to another).

Under the five-part test, fiduciary status can also be defeated by arguing that the parties did not have a *mutual* agreement, arrangement, or understanding that the advice would serve as a *primary basis* for investment decisions. Investment professionals in today's marketplace frequently market retirement investment services in ways that clearly suggest the provision of tailored or individualized advice, while at the same time disclaiming in fine print the requisite "mutual" understanding that the advice will be used as a primary basis for investment decisions.

Similarly, there appears to be a widespread belief among broker-dealers that they are not fiduciaries with respect to plans or IRAs because they do not hold themselves out as registered investment advisers, even though they often market their services as financial or retirement planners. The import of such disclaimers—and of the fine legal distinctions between brokers and registered investment advisers—is often completely lost on plan participants and IRA owners who receive investment advice. As shown in a study conducted by the RAND Institute for Civil Justice for the Securities and Exchange Commission (SEC), consumers often do not read the legal documents and do not understand the difference between brokers and registered investment advisers particularly when brokers adopt such titles as "financial adviser" and "financial manager."[8]

Even in the absence of boilerplate fine print disclaimers, however, it is far from evident how the "primary basis" element of the five-part test promotes the statutory text or purposes of ERISA and the Code. If, for example, a plan hires multiple specialized advisers for an especially complex transaction, it should be able to rely upon all of the consultants' advice, regardless of whether one could characterize any particular consultant's advice as primary, secondary, or tertiary. Presumably, paid consultants make recommendations—and retirement investors pay for them—with the hope or expectation that the recommendations could, in fact, be relied upon in making important decisions. When a plan, participant, beneficiary, or IRA owner directly or indirectly pays for advice upon which it can rely, there appears to be little statutory basis for drawing distinctions based on a subjective characterization of the advice as "primary," "secondary," or other.

In other respects, the current regulatory definition could also benefit from clarification. For example, a number of parties have argued that the regulation, as currently drafted, does not encompass advice as to the selection of money managers or mutual funds. Similarly, they have argued that the regulation does not cover advice given to the managers of pooled investment vehicles that hold plan assets contributed by many plans, as opposed to advice given to particular plans. Parties have even argued that advice was insufficiently "individualized" to fall within the scope of the regulation because the advice provider had failed to prudently consider the "particular needs of the plan," notwithstanding the fact that both the advice provider and the plan agreed that individualized advice based on the plan's needs would be provided, and the adviser actually made specific investment recommendations to the plan. Although the Department disagrees with each of these interpretations of the current regulation, the arguments nevertheless suggest that clarifying regulatory text could be helpful.

Changes in the financial marketplace have enlarged the gap between the 1975 regulation's effect and the Congressional intent of the statutory definition. The greatest change is the predominance of individual account plans, many of which require participants to make investment decisions for their own accounts. In 1975, private-sector defined benefit pensions—mostly large, professionally managed funds—covered over 27 million active participants and held assets totaling almost $186 billion. This compared with just 11 million active participants in individual account defined contribution plans with assets of just $74 billion.[9] Moreover, the great majority of defined contribution plans at that time

were professionally managed, not participant-directed. In 1975, 401(k) plans did not yet exist and IRAs had just been authorized as part of ERISA's enactment the prior year. In contrast, by 2012 defined benefit plans covered just under 16 million active participants, while individual account-based defined contribution plans covered over 68 million active participants—including 63 million participants in 401(k)-type plans that are participant-directed.[10]

With this transformation, plan participants, beneficiaries and IRA owners have become major consumers of investment advice that is paid for directly or indirectly. By 2012, 97 percent of 401(k) participants were responsible for directing the investment of all or part of their own account, up from 86 percent as recently as 1999.[11] Also, in 2013, more than 34 million households owned IRAs.[12]

Many of the consultants and advisers who provide investment-related advice and recommendations receive compensation from the financial institutions whose investment products they recommend. This gives the consultants and advisers a strong bias, conscious or unconscious, to favor investments that provide them greater compensation rather than those that may be most appropriate for the participants. Unless they are fiduciaries, however, these consultants and advisers are free under ERISA and the Code, not only to receive such conflicted compensation, but also to act on their conflicts of interest to the detriment of their customers. In addition, plans, participants, beneficiaries, and IRA owners now have a much greater variety of investments to choose from, creating a greater need for expert advice. Consolidation of the financial services industry and innovations in compensation arrangements have multiplied the opportunities for self-dealing and reduced the transparency of fees.

The absence of adequate fiduciary protections and safeguards is especially problematic in light of the growth of participant-directed plans and self-directed IRAs; the gap in expertise and information between advisers and the customers who depend upon them for guidance; and the advisers' significant conflicts of interest.

When Congress enacted ERISA in 1974, it made a judgment that plan advisers should be subject to ERISA's fiduciary regime and that plan participants, beneficiaries and IRA owners should be protected from conflicted transactions by the prohibited transaction rules. More fundamentally, however, the statutory language was designed to cover a much broader category of persons who provide fiduciary investment advice based on their functions and to limit their ability to engage in self-dealing and other conflicts of interest than is currently reflected in the five-part test. While many advisers are committed to providing high-quality advice and always put their customers' best interests first, the 1975 regulation makes it far too easy for advisers in today's marketplace not to do so and to avoid fiduciary responsibility even when they clearly purport to give individualized advice and to act in the client's best interest, rather than their own.

C. The 2010 Proposal

In 2010, the Department proposed a new regulation that would have replaced the five-part test with a new definition of what counted as fiduciary investment advice for a fee. At that time, the Department did not propose any new prohibited transaction exemptions and acknowledged uncertainty regarding whether existing exemptions would be available, but specifically invited comments on whether new or amended exemptions should be proposed. The proposal also provided carve-outs for conduct that would not result in fiduciary status. The general definition included the following types of advice: (1) Appraisals or fairness opinions concerning the value of securities or other property; (2) recommendations as to the advisability of investing in, purchasing, holding or selling securities or other property; and (3) recommendations as to the management of securities or other property. Reflecting the Department's longstanding interpretation of the 1975 regulations, the 2010 Proposal made clear that investment advice under the proposal includes advice provided to plan participants, beneficiaries and IRA owners as well as to plan fiduciaries.

Under the 2010 Proposal, a paid adviser would have been treated as a fiduciary if the adviser provided one of the above types of advice and either: (1) Represented that he or she was acting as an ERISA fiduci-

[8] Angela A. Hung, Noreen Clancy, Jeff Dominitz, Eric Talley, Claude Berrebi, Farrukh Suvankulov, *Investor and Industry Perspectives on Investment Advisers and Broker-Dealers*, RAND Institute for Civil Justice, commissioned by the U.S. Securities and Exchange Commission, 2008, at *http://www.sec.gov/news/press/2008/2008-1_randiabdreport.pdf*

[9] U.S. Department of Labor, *Private Pension Plan Bulletin Historical Tables and Graphs*, (Dec. 2014), at *http://www.dol.gov/ebsa/pdf/historicaltables.pdf*.

[10] U.S. Department of Labor, *Private Pension Plan Bulletin Abstract of 2012 Form 5500 Annual Reports*, (Jan. 2015), at *http://www.dol.gov/ebsa/PDF/2012pensionplanbulletin.PDF*.

[11] U.S. Department of Labor, *Private Pension Plan Bulletin Abstract of 1999 Form 5500 Annual Reports*, Number 12, Summer 2004 (Apr. 2008), at *http://www.dol.gov/ebsa/PDF/1999pensionplanbulletin.PDF*.

[12] Brien, Michael J., and Constantijn W.A. Panis. Analysis of Financial Asset Holdings of Households on the United States: 2013 Update. Advanced Analytic Consulting Group and Deloitte, Report Prepared for the U.S. Department of Labor, 2014.

ary; (2) was already an ERISA fiduciary to the plan by virtue of having control over the management or disposition of plan assets, or by having discretionary authority over the administration of the plan; (3) was already an investment adviser under the Investment Advisers Act of 1940 (Advisers Act); or (4) provided the advice pursuant to an agreement or understanding that the advice may be considered in connection with plan investment or asset management decisions and would be individualized to the needs of the plan, plan participant or beneficiary, or IRA owner. The 2010 Proposal also provided that, for purposes of the fiduciary definition, relevant fees included any direct or indirect fees received by the adviser or an affiliate from any source. Direct fees are payments made by the advice recipient to the adviser including transaction-based fees, such as brokerage, mutual fund or insurance sales commissions. Indirect fees are payments to the adviser from any source other than the advice recipient such as revenue sharing payments from a mutual fund.

The 2010 Proposal included specific carve-outs for the following actions that the Department believed should not result in fiduciary status. In particular, a person would not have become a fiduciary by—

1. Providing recommendations as a seller or purchaser with interests adverse to the plan, its participants, or IRA owners, if the advice recipient reasonably should have known that the adviser was not providing impartial investment advice and the adviser had not acknowledged fiduciary status.

2. Providing investment education information and materials in connection with an individual account plan.

3. Marketing or making available a menu of investment alternatives that a plan fiduciary could choose from, and providing general financial information to assist in selecting and monitoring those investments, if these activities include a written disclosure that the adviser was not providing impartial investment advice.

4. Preparing reports necessary to comply with ERISA, the Code, or regulations or forms issued thereunder, unless the report valued assets that lack a generally recognized market, or served as a basis for making plan distributions. The 2010 Proposal applied to the definition of an "investment advice fiduciary" in section 4975(e)(3)(B) of the Code as well as to the parallel ERISA definition. These provisions apply to both certain ERISA covered plans, and certain non-ERISA plans such as individual retirement accounts.

In the preamble to the 2010 Proposal, the Department also noted that it had previously interpreted the 1975 regulation as providing that a recommendation to a plan participant on how to invest the proceeds of a contemplated plan distribution was not fiduciary investment advice. Advisory Opinion 2005-23A (Dec. 7, 2005). The Department specifically asked for comments as to whether the final rule should include such recommendations as fiduciary advice.

The 2010 Proposal prompted a large number of comments and a vigorous debate. As noted above, the Department made special efforts to encourage the regulated community's participation in this rulemaking. In addition to an extended comment period, the Department held a two-day public hearing. Additional time for comments was allowed following the hearing and publication of the hearing transcript on the Department's Web site and Department representatives held numerous meetings with interested parties. Many of the comments concerned the Department's conclusions regarding the likely economic impact of the proposal, if adopted. A number of commenters urged the Department to undertake additional analysis of expected costs and benefits particularly with regard to the 2010 Proposal's coverage of IRAs. After consideration of these comments and in light of the significance of this rulemaking to the retirement plan service provider industry, plan sponsors and participants, beneficiaries and IRA owners, the Department decided to take more time for review and to issue a new proposed regulation for comment.

D. The New Proposal

The new proposed rule makes many revisions to the 2010 Proposal, although it also retains aspects of that proposal's essential framework. The new proposal broadly updates the definition of fiduciary investment advice, and also provides a series of carve-outs from the fiduciary investment advice definition for communications that should not be viewed as fiduciary in nature. The definition generally covers the following categories of advice: (1) Investment recommendations, (2) investment management recommendations, (3) appraisals of investments, or (4) recommendations of persons to provide investment ad-

vice for a fee or to manage plan assets. Persons who provide such advice fall within the general definition of a fiduciary if they either (a) represent that they are acting as a fiduciary under ERISA or the Code or (b) provide the advice pursuant to an agreement, arrangement, or understanding that the advice is individualized or specifically directed to the recipient for consideration in making investment or investment management decisions regarding plan assets.

The new proposal includes several carve-outs for persons who do not represent that they are acting as ERISA fiduciaries, some of which were included in some form in the 2010 Proposal but many of which were not. Subject to specified conditions, these carve-outs cover—

(1) Statements or recommendations made to a "large plan investor with financial expertise" by a counterparty acting in an arm's length transaction;

(2) offers or recommendations to plan fiduciaries of ERISA plans to enter into a swap or security-based swap that is regulated under the Securities Exchange Act or the Commodity Exchange Act;

(3) statements or recommendations provided to a plan fiduciary of an ERISA plan by an employee of the plan sponsor if the employee receives no fee beyond his or her normal compensation;

(4) marketing or making available a platform of investment alternatives to be selected by a plan fiduciary for an ERISA participant-directed individual account plan;

(5) the identification of investment alternatives that meet objective criteria specified by a plan fiduciary of an ERISA plan or the provision of objective financial data to such fiduciary;

(6) the provision of an appraisal, fairness opinion or a statement of value to an ESOP regarding employer securities, to a collective investment vehicle holding plan assets, or to a plan for meeting reporting and disclosure requirements; and

(7) information and materials that constitute "investment education" or "retirement education."

The new proposal applies the same definition of "investment advice" to the definition of "fiduciary" in section 4975(e)(3) of the Code and thus applies to investment advice rendered to IRAs. "Plan" is defined in the new proposal to mean any employee benefit plan described in section 3(3) of the Act and any plan described in section 4975(e)(1)(A) of the Code. For ease of reference in this proposal, the term "IRA" has been inclusively defined to mean any account described in Code section 4975(e)(1)(B) through (F), such as a true individual retirement account described under Code section 408(a) and a health savings account described in section 223(d) of the Code.[13]

Many of the differences between the new proposal and the 2010 Proposal reflect the input of commenters on the 2010 Proposal as part of the public notice and comment process. For example, some commenters argued that the 2010 Proposal swept too broadly by making investment recommendations fiduciary in nature simply because the adviser was a plan fiduciary for purposes unconnected with the advice or an investment adviser under the Advisers Act. In their view, such status-based criteria were in tension with the Act's functional approach to fiduciary status and would have resulted in unwarranted and unintended compliance issues and costs. Other commenters objected to the lack of a requirement for these status-based categories that the advice be individualized to the needs of the advice recipient. The new proposal incorporates these suggestions: An adviser's status as an investment adviser under the Advisers Act or as an ERISA fiduciary for reasons unrelated to advice are no longer factors in the definition. In addition, unless the adviser represents that he or she is a fiduciary with respect to advice, the advice must be provided pursuant to an agreement, arrangement, or understanding that the advice is individualized or specifically directed to the recipient to be treated as fiduciary advice.

Furthermore, the carve-outs that treat certain conduct as non-fiduciary in nature have been modified, clarified, and expanded in response to comments. For example, the carve-out for certain valuations from the definition of fiduciary investment advice has been modified and expanded. Under the 2010 Proposal, appraisals and valuations for compliance with certain reporting and disclosure requirements were not treated as fiduciary advice. The new proposal additionally provides a carve-out from fiduciary treatment for appraisal and fairness opinions for ESOPs regarding employer securities. Although, the Department remains concerned about valuation advice concerning an ESOP's purchase of employer stock and about a plan's reliance on that advice, the Department has concluded that the concerns regarding valuations

---

[13] As discussed below in Section E. Coverage of IRAs and Other Non-ERISA Plans, in recognition of differences among the various types of non-ERISA plan arrangements described in Code section 4975(e)(1)(B) through (F), the Department solicits comments on whether it is appropriate for the regulation to cover the full range of these arrangements. These non-ERISA plan arrangements are tax favored vehicles under the Code like IRAs, but are not intended for retirement savings.

of closely held employer stock in ESOP transactions raise unique issues that are more appropriately addressed in a separate regulatory initiative. Additionally, the carve-out for valuations conducted for reporting and disclosure purposes has been expanded to include reporting and disclosure obligations outside of ERISA and the Code, and is applicable to both ERISA plans and IRAs. Many other modifications to the other carve-outs from fiduciary status, as well as new carve-outs and prohibited transaction exemptions, are described below in Section IV—"The Provisions of the New Proposal."

III. Coordination With Other Federal Agencies

Many comments to the 2010 rulemaking emphasized the need to harmonize the Department's efforts with rulemaking activities under the Dodd-Frank Wall Street Reform and Consumer Protection Act, Pub. Law No. 111-203, 124 Stat. 1376 (2010), (Dodd-Frank Act), in particular, the Security and Exchange Commission's (SEC) standards of care for providing investment advice and the Commodity Futures Trading Commission's (CFTC) business conduct standards for swap dealers. While the 2010 Proposal discussed statutes over which the SEC and CFTC have jurisdiction, it did not specifically describe interagency coordination efforts. In addition, commenters questioned the adequacy of coordination with other agencies regarding IRA products and services. They argued that subjecting SEC-regulated investment advisers and broker-dealers to a special set of ERISA rules for plans and IRAs could lead to additional costs and complexities for individuals who may have several different types of accounts at the same financial institution some of which may be subject only to the SEC rules, and others of which may be subject to both SEC rules and new regulatory requirements under ERISA.

In the course of developing the new proposal and the related proposed prohibited transaction exemptions, the Department has consulted with staff of the SEC and other regulators on an ongoing basis regarding whether the proposals would subject investment advisers and broker-dealers who provide investment advice to requirements that create an undue compliance burden or conflict with their obligations under other federal laws. As part of this consultative process, SEC staff has provided technical assistance and information with respect to retail investors, the marketplace for investment advice and coordinating, to the extent possible, the agencies' separate regulatory provisions and responsibilities. As the Department moves forward with this project in accordance with the specific provisions of ERISA and the Code, it will continue to consult with staff of the SEC and other regulators on its proposals and their impact on retail investors and other regulatory regimes. One result of these discussions, particularly with staff of the CFTC and SEC, is the new provision at paragraph (b)(1)(ii) of the proposed regulations concerning counterparty transactions with swap dealers, major swap participants, security-based swap dealers, and major security-based swap participants. Under the terms of that paragraph, such persons would not be treated as ERISA fiduciaries merely because, when acting as counterparties to swap or security-based swap transactions, they give information and perform actions required for compliance with the requirements of the business conduct standards of the Dodd-Frank Act and its implementing regulations.

In pursuing these consultations, the Department has aimed to coordinate and minimize conflicting or duplicative provisions between ERISA, the Code and federal securities laws, to the extent possible. However, the governing statutes do not permit the Department to make the obligations of fiduciary investment advisers under ERISA and the Code identical to the duties of advice providers under the securities laws. ERISA and the Code establish consumer protections for some investment advice that does not fall within the ambit of federal securities laws, and vice versa. Even if each of the relevant agencies were to adopt an identical definition of "fiduciary", the legal consequences of the fiduciary designation would vary between agencies because of differences in the specific duties and remedies established by the different federal laws at issue. ERISA and the Code place special emphasis on the elimination or mitigation of conflicts of interest and adherence to substantive standards of conduct, as reflected in the prohibited transaction rules and ERISA's standards of fiduciary conduct. The specific duties imposed on fiduciaries by ERISA and the Code stem from legislative judgments on the best way to protect the public interest in tax-preferred benefit arrangements that are critical to workers' financial and physical health. The Department has taken great care to honor ERISA and the Code's specific text and purposes.

At the same time, the Department has worked hard to understand the impact of the proposed rule on firms subject to the securities laws

and other federal laws, and to take the effects of those laws into account so as to appropriately calibrate the impact of the rule on those firms. The proposed regulation reflects these efforts. In the Department's view, it neither undermines, nor contradicts, the provisions or purposes of the securities laws, but instead works in harmony with them. The Department has coordinated—and will continue to coordinate—its efforts with other federal agencies to ensure that the various legal regimes are harmonized to the fullest extent possible.

The Department has also consulted with the Department of the Treasury and the IRS, particularly on the subject of IRAs. Although the Department has responsibility for issuing regulations and prohibited transaction exemptions under section 4975 of the Code, which applies to IRAs, the IRS maintains general responsibility for enforcing the tax laws. The IRS' responsibilities extend to the imposition of excise taxes on fiduciaries who participate in prohibited transactions.[14] As a result, the Department and the IRS share responsibility for combating self-dealing by fiduciary investment advisers to tax-qualified plans and IRAs. Paragraph (e) of the proposed regulation, in particular, recognizes this jurisdictional intersection.

When the Department announced that it would issue a new proposal, it stated that it would consider proposing new and/or amended prohibited transaction exemptions to address the concerns of commenters about the broader scope of the fiduciary definition and its impact on the fee practices of brokers and other advisers. Commenters had expressed concern about whether longstanding exemptions granted by the Department allowing advisers, despite their fiduciary status under ERISA, to receive commissions in connection with mutual funds, securities and insurance products would remain applicable under the new rule. As explained more fully below, the Department is simultaneously publishing in the notice section of today's **Federal Register** proposed prohibited transaction class exemptions to address these concerns. The Department believes that existing exemptions and these new proposed exemptions would preserve the ability to engage in common fee arrangements, while protecting plan participants, beneficiaries and IRA owners from abusive practices that may result from conflicts of interest.

The terms of these new exemptions are discussed in more detail below and in the preambles to the proposed exemptions. While the exemptions differ in terms and coverage, each imposes a "best interest" standard on fiduciary investment advisers. Thus, for example, the Best Interest Contract Exemption requires the investment advice fiduciary and associated financial institution to expressly agree to provide advice that is in the "best interest" of the advice recipient. As proposed, the best interest standard is intended to mirror the duties of prudence and loyalty, as applied in the context of fiduciary investment advice under sections 404(a)(1)(A) and (B) of ERISA. Thus, the "best interest" standard is rooted in the longstanding trust-law duties of prudence and loyalty adopted in section 404 of ERISA and in the cases interpreting those standards.

Accordingly, the Best Interest Contract Exemption provides:

Investment advice is in the "Best Interest" of the Retirement Investor when the Adviser and Financial Institution providing the advice act with the care, skill, prudence, and diligence under the circumstances then prevailing that a prudent person would exercise based on the investment objectives, risk tolerance, financial circumstances and needs of the Retirement Investor, without regard to the financial or other interests of the Adviser, Financial Institution, any Affiliate, Related Entity, or other party.

This "best interest" standard is not intended to add to or expand the ERISA section 404 standards of prudence and loyalty as they apply to the provision of investment advice to ERISA covered plans. Advisers to ERISA-covered plans are already required to adhere to the fundamental standards of prudence and loyalty, and can be held accountable for violations of the standards. Rather, the primary impact of the "best interest" standard is on the IRA market. Under the Code, advisers to IRAs are subject only to the prohibited transaction rules. Incorporating the best interest standard in the proposed Best Interest Contract Exemption effectively requires advisers to comply with these basic fiduciary standards as a condition of engaging in transactions that would otherwise be prohibited because of the conflicts of interest they create. Additionally, the exemption ensures that IRA owners and investors have a contract-based claim to hold their fiduciary advisers accountable if they violate these basic obligations of prudence and loyalty. As under current law, no private right of action under ERISA is available to IRA owners.

---

[14] Reorganization Plan No. 4 of 1978.

IV. The Provisions of the New Proposal

The new proposal would amend the definition of investment advice in 29 CFR 2510.3-21 (1975) of the regulation to replace the restrictive five-part test with a new definition that better comports with the statutory language in ERISA and the Code.[15] As explained below, the proposal accomplishes this by first describing the kinds of communications and relationships that would generally constitute fiduciary investment advice if the adviser receives a fee or other compensation. Rather than add additional elements that must be met in all instances, as under the current regulation, the proposal describes several specific types of advice or communications that would not be treated as investment advice. In the Department's view, this structure is faithful to the remedial purpose of the statute, but avoids burdening activities that do not implicate relationships of trust and expectations of impartiality.

A. Categories of Advice or Recommendations

Paragraph (a)(1) of the proposal sets forth the following types of advice, which, when provided in exchange for a fee or other compensation, whether directly or indirectly, and given under circumstances described in paragraph (a)(2), would be "investment advice" unless one of the carve-outs in paragraph (b) applies. The listed types of advice are—

(i) A recommendation as to the advisability of acquiring, holding, disposing of or exchanging securities or other property, including a recommendation to take a distribution of benefits or a recommendation as to the investment of securities or other property to be rolled over or otherwise distributed from the plan or IRA;

(ii) A recommendation as to the management of securities or other property, including recommendations as to the management of securities or other property to be rolled over or otherwise distributed from the plan or IRA;

(iii) An appraisal, fairness opinion, or similar statement whether verbal or written concerning the value of securities or other property if provided in connection with a specific transaction or transactions involving the acquisition, disposition, or exchange, of such securities or other property by the plan or IRA; or

(iv) A recommendation of a person who is also going to receive a fee or other compensation to provide any of the types of advice described in paragraphs (i) through (iii) above.

Except for the prong of the definition concerning appraisals and valuations discussed below, the proposal is structured so that communications must constitute a "recommendation" to fall within the scope of fiduciary investment advice. In that regard, as stated earlier in Section III concerning coordination with other Federal Agencies, the Department has consulted with staff of other agencies with rulemaking authority over investment advisers and broker-dealers. FINRA Policy Statement 01-23 sets forth guidelines to assist brokers in evaluating whether a particular communication could be viewed as a recommendation, thereby triggering application of FINRA's Rule 2111 that requires that a firm or associated person have a reasonable basis to believe that a recommended transaction or investment strategy involving a security or securities is suitable for the customer.[16] Although the regulatory context for the FINRA guidance is somewhat different, the Department believes that it provides useful standards and guideposts for distinguishing investment education from investment advice under ERISA. Accordingly, the Department specifically solicits comments on whether it should adopt some or all of the standards developed by FINRA in defining communications that rise to the level of a recommendation for purposes of distinguishing between investment education and investment advice under ERISA.

Additionally, as paragraph (d) of the proposal makes clear, the regulation does not treat the mere execution of a securities transaction at the direction of a plan or IRA owner as fiduciary activity. This paragraph remains unchanged from the 1975 regulation other than to update references to the proposal's structure. The definition's scope remains limited to advice relationships, as delineated in its text and does not impact merely administrative or ministerial activities necessary for a plan or IRA's functioning. It also does not apply to order taking where no advice is provided.

(1) Recommendations To Distribute Plan Assets

Paragraph (a)(1)(i) specifically includes recommendations concerning the investment of securities to be rolled over or otherwise distributed from the plan or IRA. Noting the Department's position in Advisory Opinion 2005-23A that it is not fiduciary advice to make a recommendation as to distribution options even if that is accompanied by a recommendation as to where the distribution would be invested, (Dec. 7, 2005), the 2010 Proposal did not include this type of advice, but the Department requested comments on whether it should be included in a final regulation. Some commenters stated that exclusion of this advice from the final rule would fail to protect participant accounts from conflicted advice in connection with one of the most significant financial decisions that participants make concerning retirement savings. Other commenters argued that including this advice would give rise to prohibited transactions that could disrupt the routine process that occurs when a worker leaves a job, contacts a financial services firm for help rolling over a 401(k) balance, and the firm explains the investments it offers and the benefits of a rollover.

The proposed regulation, if finalized, would supersede Advisory Opinion 2005-23A. Thus, recommendations to take distributions (and thereby withdraw assets from existing plan or IRA investments or roll over into a plan or IRA) or to entrust plan or IRA assets to particular money managers, advisers, or investments would fall within the scope of covered advice. However, as the proposal's text makes clear, one does not act as a fiduciary merely by providing participants with information about plan or IRA distribution options, including the consequences associated with the available types of benefit distributions. In this regard, the new proposal draws an important distinction between fiduciary investment advice and non-fiduciary investment information and educational materials. The Department believes that the proposal's treatment of such non-fiduciary educational and informational materials adequately covers the common types of distribution-related information that participants find useful, including information relating to annuitizations and other forms of lifetime income payment options, but welcomes input on other types of information that would help clarify the line between advice and education in this context.

(2) Recommendations as to the Management of Plan Investments

The preamble to the 2010 Proposal stated that the "management of securities or other property" would include advice and recommendations as to the exercise of rights appurtenant to shares of stock (e.g., voting proxies). 75 FR 65266 (Oct. 22, 2010). The Department has long viewed the exercise of ownership rights as a fiduciary responsibility because of its material effect on plan investment goals. 29 CFR 2509.08-2 (2008). Consequently, individualized or specifically directed advice and recommendations on the exercise of proxy or other ownership rights are appropriately treated as fiduciary in nature. Accordingly, the proposed regulation's provision on advice regarding the management of securities or other property would continue to cover individualized advice or recommendations as to proxy voting and the management of retirement assets in paragraph (a)(1)(ii).

We received comments on the 2010 proposal seeking some clarification regarding its application to certain practices. In this regard, it is the Department's view that guidelines or other information on voting policies for proxies that are provided to a broad class of investors without regard to a client's individual interests or investment policy, and which are not directed or presented as a recommended policy for the plan or IRA to adopt, would not rise to the level of fiduciary investment advice under the proposal. Additionally, a recommendation addressed to all shareholders in a proxy statement would not result in fiduciary status on the part of the issuer of the statement or the person who distributes the proxy statement. These positions are clarified in the proposed regulation.

---

[15] For purposes of readability, this proposed rulemaking republishes 29 CFR 2510.3-21 in its entirety, as revised, rather than only the specific amendments to this section. See 29 CFR 2510.3-21(d)—Execution of securities transactions.

[16] See also FINRA's Regulatory Notice 11-02, 12-25 and 12-55. Regulatory Notice 11-02 includes the following discussion: For instance, a communication's content, context and presentation are important aspects of the inquiry. The determination of whether a "recommendation" has been made, moreover, is an objective rather than subjective inquiry. An important factor in this regard is whether—given its content, context and manner of presentation—a particular communication from a firm or associated person to a customer reasonably would be viewed as a suggestion that the customer take action or refrain from taking action regarding a security or investment strategy. In addition, the more individually tailored the communication is to a particular customer or customers about a specific security or investment strategy, the more likely the communication will be viewed as a recommendation. Furthermore, a series of actions that may not constitute recommendations when viewed individually may amount to a recommendation when considered in the aggregate. It also makes no difference whether the communication was initiated by a person or a computer software program. These guiding principles, together with numerous litigated decisions and the facts and circumstances of any particular case, inform the determination of whether the communication is a recommendation for purposes of FINRA's suitability rule.

(3) Appraisals

The new proposal, like the current regulation which includes "advice as to the value of securities or other property," continues to cover certain appraisals and valuation reports. However, it is considerably more focused than the 2010 Proposal. Responding to comments, the proposal in paragraph (a)(1)(iii) covers only appraisals, fairness opinions, or similar statements that relate to a particular transaction. The Department also expanded the 2010 Proposal's carve-out for general reports or statements of value provided to satisfy required reporting and disclosure rules under ERISA or the Code. The carve-out in the 2010 proposal covered general reports or statements of value that merely reflected the value of an investment of a plan or a participant or beneficiary, and provided for purposes of compliance with the reporting and disclosure requirements of ERISA, the Code, and the regulations, forms and schedules issued thereunder, unless the reports involved assets for which there was not a generally recognized market and served as a basis on which a plan could make distributions to plan participants and beneficiaries. The carve-out was broadened in this proposal to includes valuations provided solely for purposes of compliance with the reporting and disclosure provisions under the Act, the Code, and the regulations, forms and schedules issued thereunder, or any applicable reporting or disclosure requirement under a Federal or state law, or rule or regulation or self-regulatory organization (e.g., FINRA) without regard to the type of asset involved. In this manner, the new proposal focuses on instances where the plan or IRA owner is looking to the appraiser for advice on the market value of an asset that the investor is considering to acquire, dispose, or exchange. In many cases the most important investment advice that an investor receives is advice as to how much it can or should pay for hard-to-value assets. In response to comments, the proposal also contains an entirely new carve-out at paragraph (b)(5)(ii) specifically addressing valuations or appraisals provided to an investment fund (e.g., collective investment fund or pooled separate account) holding assets of various investors in addition to at least one plan or IRA. Also, as mentioned, the Department has decided not to extend fiduciary coverage to valuations or appraisals for ESOPs relating to employer securities at this time because the Department has concluded that its concerns in this space raise unique issues that are more appropriately addressed in a separate regulatory initiative. The proposal's carve-outs do not apply, however, if the provider of the valuation represents or acknowledges that it is acting as a fiduciary with respect to the advice.

Some representatives of the appraisal industry submitted comments on the 2010 Proposal arguing that ERISA's fiduciary duty to act solely in the interest of the plan and its participants and beneficiaries is inconsistent with the duty of appraisers to provide objective, independent value determinations. The Department disagrees. A biased or inaccurate appraisal does not help a plan, a participant or a beneficiary make prudent investment decisions. Like other forms of investment advice, an appraisal is a tool for plan fiduciaries, participants, beneficiaries, and IRA owners to use in deciding what price to pay for assets and whether to accept or decline proposed transactions. An appraiser complies with his or her obligations as an appraiser—and as a loyal fiduciary—by giving plan fiduciaries or participants an impartial and accurate assessment of the value of an asset in accordance with appraisers' professional standard of care. Nothing in ERISA or this regulation should be read as compelling an appraiser to slant valuation opinions to reflect what the plan wishes the asset were worth rather than what it is really worth. As stated in the preamble to the 2010 Proposal, the Department would expect a fiduciary appraiser's determination of value to be unbiased, fair and objective and to be made in good faith based on a prudent investigation under the prevailing circumstances then known to the appraiser. In the Department's view, these fiduciary standards are fully consistent with professional standards, such as the Uniform Standards of Professional Appraisal Practice (USPAP).[17]

4) Recommendations of a Person To Provide Investment Advice or Management Services

The proposal would treat recommendations on the selection of investment managers or advisers as fiduciary investment advice. In the Department's view, the current regulation already covers such advice. The proposal simply revises the regulation's text to remove any possible ambiguity. The Department believes that such advice should be treated as fiduciary in nature if provided under the circumstances in paragraph (a)(1)(iv) and for direct or indirect compensation. Covered advice would include recommendations of persons to perform asset management services or to make investment recommendations. Advice as to the identity of the person entrusted with investment authority over retirement assets is often critical to the proper management and investment of those assets. On the other hand, general advice as to the types of qualitative and quantitative criteria to consider in hiring an investment manager would not rise to the level of a recommendation of a person to manage plan investments nor would a trade journal's endorsement of an investment manager. Similarly, the proposed regulation would not cover recommendations of administrative service providers, property managers, or other service providers who do not provide investment services.

B. The Circumstances Under Which Advice Is Provided

As provided in paragraph (a)(2) of the proposal, unless a carve-out applies, a category of advice listed in the proposal would constitute "investment advice" if the person providing the advice, either directly or indirectly (e.g., through or together with any affiliate)—

(i) Represents or acknowledges that it is acting as a fiduciary within the meaning of the Act or Code with respect to the advice described in paragraph (a)(1); or

(ii) Renders the advice pursuant to a written or verbal agreement, arrangement or understanding that the advice is individualized to, or that such advice is specifically directed to, the advice recipient for consideration in making investment or management decisions with respect to securities or other property of the plan or IRA.

Under paragraph (a)(2)(i), advisers who claim fiduciary status under ERISA or the Code in providing advice would be taken at their word. They may not later argue that the advice was not fiduciary in nature. Nor may they rely upon the carve-outs described in paragraph (b) on the scope of the definition of fiduciary investment advice.

The 2010 Proposal provided that investment recommendations provided by an investment adviser under the Advisers Act would, in the absence of a carve-out, automatically be treated as investment advice. In response to comments, the new proposal drops this provision. Thus, the proposal avoids making such persons fiduciaries based solely on their or an affiliate's status as an investment adviser under the Advisers Act. Instead, their fiduciary status would be determined by reference to the same functional test that applies to all persons under the regulation.

Paragraph (a)(2)(ii) of the proposal avoids treating recommendations made to the general public, or to no one in particular, as investment advice and thus addresses concerns that the general circulation of newsletters, television talk show commentary, or remarks in speeches and presentations at financial industry educational conferences would result in the person being treated as a fiduciary. This paragraph requires an agreement, arrangement, or understanding that advice is directed to, a specific recipient for consideration in making investment decisions. The parties need not have a meeting of the minds on the extent to which the advice recipient will actually rely on the advice, but they must agree or understand that the advice is individualized or specifically directed to the particular advice recipient for consideration in making investment decisions. In this respect, paragraph (a)(2)(ii) differs significantly from its counterpart in the 2010 Proposal. In particular, and in response to comments, the proposal does not require that advice be individualized to the needs of the plan, participant or beneficiary or IRA owner if the advice is specifically directed to such recipient. Under the proposal, advisers could not specifically direct investment recommendations to individual persons, but then deny fiduciary responsibility on the basis that they did not, in fact, consider the advice recipient's individual needs or intend that the recipient base investment decisions on their recommendations. Nor could they continue the practice of advertising advice or counseling that is one-on-one or that a reasonable person would believe would be tailored to their individual needs and then disclaim that the recommendations are fiduciary investment advice in boilerplate language in the advertisement or in the paperwork provided to the client.

Like the 2010 Proposal, and unlike the 1975 regulation, the new proposal does not require that advice be provided on a regular basis. Investment advice that meets the requirements of the proposal, even if provided only once, can be critical to important investment decisions. If the adviser received a direct or indirect fee in connection with its advice, the advice recipients should reasonably expect adherence to fiduciary standards on the same terms as other retirement investors who get recommendations from the adviser on a more routine basis.

---

[17] A number of commenters also pointed to such professional standards as alternatives to fiduciary treatment under ERISA. While the Department believes that such professional standards are fully consistent with the fiduciary duties, the rights, remedies and sanctions under both ERISA and the Code importantly turn on fiduciary status, and advice on the value of an asset is often the most critical investment advice a plan receives. As a result, treating appraisals as fiduciary advice provides an additional layer of protection for consumers without conflicting with the duties of appraisers.

C. Carve-Outs From the General Definition

The Department recognizes that in many circumstances, plan fiduciaries, participants, beneficiaries, and IRA owners may receive recommendations or appraisals that, notwithstanding the general definition set forth in paragraph (a) of the proposal, should not be treated as fiduciary investment advice. Accordingly, paragraph (b) contains a number of specific carve-outs from the scope of the general definition. The carve-out at paragraph (b)(5) of the proposal concerning financial reports and valuations was discussed above in connection with appraisals. The carve-out in paragraph (b)(5)(iii) covers communications to a plan, a plan fiduciary, a plan participant or beneficiary, an IRA or IRA owner solely for purposes of compliance with the reporting and disclosure provisions under the Act, the Code, and the regulations, forms and schedules issued thereunder, or any applicable reporting or disclosure requirement under a Federal or state law, rule or regulation or self-regulatory organization rule or regulation. The carve-out in paragraph (b)(6) covers education. The other carve-outs are limited to communications with plans and plan fiduciaries and do not cover communications to participants, beneficiaries, or IRA owners. These more limited carve-outs are described more fully below. In each instance, the proposed carve-outs are for communications that the Department believes Congress did not intend to cover as fiduciary "investment advice" and that parties would not ordinarily view as communications characterized by a relationship of trust or impartiality. None of the carve-outs apply where the adviser represents or acknowledges that it is acting as a fiduciary under ERISA with respect to the advice.

(1) Seller's and Swap Carve-Outs

(a) The "Seller's Carve-Out"[18]

Paragraph (b)(1)(i) of the proposed regulation provides a carve-out from the general definition for incidental advice provided in connection with an arm's length sale, purchase, loan, or bilateral contract between an expert plan investor and the adviser. It also applies in connection with an offer to enter into such a transaction or when the person providing the advice is acting as a representative, such as an agent, for the plan's counterparty. This carve-out is subject to the following conditions.

First, the person must provide advice to an ERISA plan fiduciary who is independent of such person and who exercises authority or control respecting the management or disposition of the plan's assets, with respect to an arm's length sale, purchase, loan or bilateral contract between the plan and the counterparty, or with respect to a proposal to enter into such a sale, purchase, loan or bilateral contract.

Second, either of two alternative sets of conditions must be met. Under alternative one, prior to providing any recommendation with respect to the transaction, such person:

(1) Obtains a written representation from the plan fiduciary that he/she is a fiduciary who exercises authority or control with respect to the management or disposition of the employee benefit plan's assets (as described in section 3(21)(A)(i) of the Act), that the employee benefit plan has 100 or more participants covered under the plan, and that the fiduciary will not rely on the person to act in the best interests of the plan, to provide impartial investment advice, or to give advice in a fiduciary capacity;

(2) fairly informs the plan fiduciary of the existence and nature of the person's financial interests in the transaction;

(3) does not receive a fee or other compensation directly from the plan, or plan fiduciary, for the provision of investment advice in connection with the transaction (this does not preclude a person from receiving a fee or compensation for other services);

(4) knows or reasonably believes that the independent plan fiduciary has sufficient expertise to evaluate the transaction and to determine whether the transaction is prudent and in the best interest of the plan participants (such person may rely on written representations from the plan or the plan fiduciary to satisfy this condition).

The second alternative applies if the person knows or reasonably believes that the independent plan fiduciary has responsibility for managing at least $100 million in employee benefit plan assets (for purposes of this condition, when dealing with an individual employee benefit plan, a person may rely on the information on the most recent Form 5500 Annual Return/Report filed by the plan to determine the

value of plan assets, and, in the case of an independent fiduciary acting as an asset manager for multiple employee benefit plans, a person may rely on representations from the independent plan fiduciary regarding the value of employee benefit plan assets under management). In that circumstance, the adviser need not obtain written representations from its counterparty to avail itself of the carve-out, but must fairly inform the independent plan fiduciary that the adviser is not undertaking to provide impartial investment advice, or to give advice in a fiduciary capacity; and cannot receive a fee or other compensation directly from the plan, or plan fiduciary, for the provision of investment advice in connection with the transaction. In that circumstance, the adviser must also reasonably believe that the independent plan fiduciary has sufficient expertise to prudently evaluate the transaction.

The overall purpose of this carve-out is to avoid imposing ERISA fiduciary obligations on sales pitches that are part of arm's length transactions where neither side assumes that the counterparty to the plan is acting as an impartial trusted adviser, but the seller is making representations about the value and benefits of proposed deals. Under appropriate circumstances, reflected in the conditions to this carve-out, these counterparties to the plan do not suggest that they are an impartial fiduciary and plans do not expect a relationship of undivided loyalty or trust. Both sides of such transactions understand that they are acting at arm's length, and neither party expects that recommendations will necessarily be based on the buyer's best interests. In such a sales transaction, the buyer understands that it is buying an investment product, not advice about whether it is a good product, from a seller who has opposing financial interests. The seller's invitation to buy the product is understood as a sales pitch, not a recommendation. Also, a representative for the plan's counterparty, such as a broker, in such a transaction, would be able to use the carve-out if the conditions are met.

Although the 2010 Proposal also had a carve-out for sellers and other counterparties, the carve-out in the new proposal is significantly different. The changes are designed to ensure that the carve-out appropriately distinguishes incidental advice as part of an arm's length transactions with no expectation of trust or acting in the customer's best interest, from those instances of advice where customers may be expecting unbiased investment advice that is in their best interest. For example, the seller's carve-out is unavailable to an adviser if the plan directly pays a fee for investment advice. If a plan expressly pays a fee for advice, the essence of the relationship is advisory, and the statute clearly contemplates fiduciary status. Thus, a service provider may not charge the plan a direct fee to act as an adviser, and then disclaim responsibility as a fiduciary adviser by asserting that he or she is merely an arm's length counterparty.

Commenters on the 2010 Proposal differed on whether the carve-out should apply to transactions involving plan participants, beneficiaries or IRA owners. After carefully considering the issue and the public comments, the Department does not believe such a carve-out can or should be crafted to cover recommendations to retail investors, including small plans, IRA owners and plan participants and beneficiaries. As a rule, investment recommendations to such retail customers do not fit the "arm's length" characteristics that the seller's carve-out is designed to preserve. Recommendations to retail investors and small plan providers are routinely presented as advice, consulting, or financial planning services. In the securities markets, brokers' suitability obligations generally require a significant degree of individualization. Research has shown that disclaimers are ineffective in alerting retail investors to the potential costs imposed by conflicts of interest, or the fact that advice is not necessarily in their best interest, and may even exacerbate these costs.[19] Most retail investors and many small plan sponsors are not financial experts, are unaware of the magnitude and impact of conflicts of interest, and are unable effectively to assess the quality of the advice they receive. IRA owners are especially at risk because they lack the protection of having a menu of investment options chosen by a plan fiduciary who is charged to protect the interests of the IRA owner. Similarly, small plan sponsors are typically experts in the day-to-day business of running an operating company, not in managing financial investments for others. In this retail market, a seller's carve-out would run the risk of creating a loophole that would result in the rule failing to improve consumer protections by permitting the same type of boiler-plate disclaimers that some advisers now use to avoid fiduciary status under the current "five-part test" regulation. Persons making investment recommendations should be required to put the interests of the investors they serve ahead of their own. The Department has ad-

---

[18] Although the preamble uses the shorthand expression "seller's carve-out," we note that the carve-out provided in paragraph (b)(1)(i) of the proposal is not limited to sales but rather would apply to incidental advice provided in connection with an arm's length sale, purchase, loan, or bilateral contract between a plan investor with financial expertise and an adviser.

[19] Loewenstein, George, Daylian Cain, Sunita Sah, *The Limits of Transparence: Pitfalls and Potential of Disclosing Conflicts of Interest*, American Economic Review: Papers and Proceedings 101, no. 3 (2011).

dressed legitimate concerns about preserving existing fee practices and minimizing market disruptions through proposed prohibited transaction exemptions detailed below, rather than through a blanket carve-out from fiduciary status.

Moreover, excluding retail investors from the seller's carve-out is consistent with recent congressional action, the Pension Protection Act of 2006 (PPA). Specifically, the PPA created a new statutory exemption that allows fiduciaries giving investment advice to individuals (pension plan participants, beneficiaries and IRA owners) to receive compensation from investment vehicles that they recommend in certain circumstances. 29 U.S.C. 1108(b)(14); 26 U.S.C. 4975(d)(17). Recognizing the risks presented when advisers receive fees from the investments they recommend to individuals, Congress placed important constraints on such advice arrangements that are calculated to limit the potential for abuse and self-dealing, including requirements for fee-leveling or the use of independently certified computer models. The Department has issued regulations implementing this provision at 29 CFR 2550.408g-1 and 408g-2. Including retail investors in the seller's carve-out would undermine the protections for retail investors that Congress required under this PPA provision.

Although the seller's carve-out may not be available in the retail market, the proposal is intended to ensure that small plan fiduciaries, plan participants, beneficiaries and IRA owners would be able to obtain essential information regarding important decisions they make regarding their investments without the providers of that information crossing the line into fiduciary status. Under the platform provider carve-out under paragraph (b)(3), platform providers (i.e., persons that provide access to securities or other property through a platform or similar mechanism) and persons that help plan fiduciaries select or monitor investment alternatives for their plans can perform those services without incurring fiduciary status. Similarly, under the investment education carve-out of paragraph (b)(6), general plan information, financial, investment and retirement information, and information and education regarding asset allocation models would all be available to a plan, plan fiduciary, participant, beneficiary or IRA owner and would not constitute the provision of investment advice, irrespective of who receives that information. The Department invites comments on whether the proposed seller's carve-out should be available for advice given directly to plan participants, beneficiaries, and IRA owners. Further, the Department invites comments on the scope of the seller's carve-out and whether the plan size limitation of 100 plan participants and 100 million dollar asset requirement in the proposal are appropriate conditions or whether other conditions would be more appropriate proxies for identifying persons with sufficient investment-related expertise to be included in a seller's carve-out.[20] The Department is also interested in whether existing and proposed prohibited transaction exemptions eliminate or mitigate the need for any seller's carve-out.

(b) Swap and Security-Based Swap Transactions

Paragraph (b)(1)(ii) of the proposal specifically addresses advice and other communications by counterparties in connection with certain swap or security-based swap transactions under the Commodity Exchange Act or the Securities Exchange Act. This broad class of financial transactions is defined and regulated under amendments to the Commodity Exchange Act and the Securities Exchange Act by the Dodd-Frank Act. Section 4s(h) of the Commodity Exchange Act (7 U.S.C. 6s(h)), and section 15F of the Securities Exchange Act of 1934 (15 U.S.C. 78o-10(h) establishes similar business conduct standards for dealers and major participants in swaps or security-based swaps. Special rules apply for transactions involving "special entities," a term that includes employee benefit plans under ERISA, but not IRAs and other non-ERISA plans.

In outline, paragraph (b)(1)(ii) of the proposal would allow swap dealers, security-based swap dealers, major swap participants and security-based major swap participants who make recommendations to plans to avoid becoming ERISA investment advice fiduciaries when acting as counterparties to a swap or security-based swap transaction. Under the swap carve out, if the person providing recommendations is

a swap dealer or security-based swap dealer, it must not be acting as an adviser to the plan, within the meaning of the applicable business conduct standards regulations of the CFTC or the SEC. In addition, before providing any recommendations with respect to the transaction, the person providing recommendations must obtain a written representation from the independent plan fiduciary, that the fiduciary will not rely on recommendations provided by the person.

Under the Commodity Exchange Act, swap dealers or major swap participants that act as counterparties to ERISA plans, must have a reasonable basis to believe that the plans have independent representatives who are fiduciaries under ERISA. 7 U.S.C. 6s(h)(5). Similar requirements apply for security-based swap transactions. 15 U.S.C 78o-10(h)(4) and (5). The CFTC has issued a final rule to implement these requirements and the SEC has issued a proposed rule that would cover security-based swaps. 17 CFR 23.400 to 23.451 (2012).

Paragraph (b)(1)(ii) reflects the Department's coordination of its efforts with staff of the SEC and CFTC, and is intended to provide a clear road-map for swap counterparties to avoid ERISA fiduciary status in arm's length transactions with plans. The provision addresses commenters' concerns that the conduct required for compliance with the Dodd-Frank Act's business conduct standards could constitute fiduciary investment advice under ERISA even in connection with arm's length transactions with plans that are separately represented by independent fiduciaries who are not looking to their counterparties for disinterested advice. If that were the case, swaps and security-based swaps with plans would often constitute prohibited transactions under ERISA. Commenters also argued that their obligations under the business conduct standards could effectively preclude them from relying on the carve-out for counterparties in the 2010 Proposal. Although the Department does not agree that the carve-out in the 2010 Proposal would have been unavailable to plan's swap counterparty (see letter dated April 28, 2011, to CFTC Chairman Gary Gensler from EBSA's Assistant Secretary Phyllis Borzi), the separate proposed carve-out for swap and security-based swap transactions in the proposal should avoid any uncertainty.[21] The Department will continue to coordinate its efforts with staff of the SEC and CFTC to ensure that any final regulation is consistent with the agencies' work in connection with the Dodd-Frank Act's business conduct standards.

(2) Employees of the Plan Sponsor

The proposal at paragraph (b)(2) provides that employees of a plan sponsor of an ERISA plan would not be treated as investment advice fiduciaries with respect to advice they provide to the fiduciaries of the sponsor's plan as long as they receive no compensation for the advice beyond their normal compensation as employees of the plan sponsor. This carve-out from the scope of the fiduciary investment advice definition recognizes that internal employees, such as members of a company's human resources department, routinely develop reports and recommendations for investment committees and other named fiduciaries of the sponsors' plans, without acting as paid fiduciary advisers. The carve-out responds to and addresses the concerns of commenters who said that these personnel should not be treated as fiduciaries because their advice is largely incidental to their duties on behalf of the plan sponsor and they receive no compensation for these advice-related functions.

(3) Platform Providers/Selection and Monitoring Assistance

The carve-out at paragraph (b)(3) of the proposal is directed to service providers, such as recordkeepers and third party administrators, that offer a "platform" or selection of investment vehicles to participant-directed individual account plans under ERISA. Under the terms of the carve-out, the plan fiduciaries must choose the specific investment alternatives that will be made available to participants for investing their individual accounts. The carve-out merely makes clear that persons would not act as investment advice fiduciaries simply by marketing or making available such investment vehicles, without regard to the individualized needs of the plan or its participants and beneficiaries, as long as they disclose in writing that they are not

---

[20] The proposed thresholds of 100 or more participants and assets of $100 million are consistent with thresholds used for similar purposes under existing rules and practices. For example, administrators of plans with 100 or more participants, unlike smaller plans, generally are required to report to the Department details on the identity, function, and compensation of their services providers; file a schedule of assets held for investments; and submit audit reports to the Department. Smaller plans are not subject to these same filing requirements that are imposed on large plans. The vast majority of plans with fewer than 100 participants have 10 or less participants. They are much more similar to individual retail investors than to large financially sophisticated institutional investors, who employ lawyers and have the time and expertise to scrutinize advice they receive for bias. Similarly, Congress established a $100 million asset threshold in enacting the PPA statutory cross-trading exemption under ERISA section 408(b)(19). In the transactions covered

by 408(b)(19), an investment manager has discretion with respect to separate client accounts that are on opposite sides of the trade. The cross trade can create efficiencies for both clients, but it also gives rise to a prohibited transaction under ERISA § 406(b)(2) because the adviser or manager is "representing" both sides of the transaction and, therefore, has a conflict of interest. The exemption generally allows an investment manager to effect cash purchases and sales of securities for which market quotations are readily available between large sophisticated plans with at least $100 million in assets and another account under management by the investment manager, subject to certain conditions. In this context, the $100 million threshold serves as a proxy for identifying institutional fiduciaries that can be expected to have the expertise to protect their own interests in the conflicted transaction.

[21] http://www.dol.gov/ebsa/pdf/cftc20110428.pdf.

undertaking to provide impartial investment advice or to give advice in a fiduciary capacity.

Similarly, a separate provision at paragraph (b)(4) carves out certain common activities that platform providers may carry out to assist plan fiduciaries in selecting and monitoring the investment alternatives that they make available to plan participants. Under paragraph (b)(4), merely identifying offered investment alternatives meeting objective criteria specified by the plan fiduciary or providing objective financial data regarding available alternatives to the plan fiduciary would not cause a platform provider to be a fiduciary investment adviser. These two carve-outs are clarifying modifications to the corresponding provisions of the 2010 Proposal. They address certain common practices that have developed with the growth of participant-directed individual account plans and recognize circumstances where the platform provider and the plan fiduciary clearly understand that the provider has financial or other relationships with the offered investments and is not purporting to provide impartial investment advice. It also accommodates the fact that platform providers often provide general financial information that falls short of constituting actual investment advice or recommendations, such as information on the historic performance of asset classes and of the investments available through the provider. The carve-outs also reflect the Department's agreement with commenters that a platform provider who merely identifies investment alternatives using objective third-party criteria (*e.g.,* expense ratios, fund size, or asset type specified by the plan fiduciary) to assist in selecting and monitoring investment alternatives should not be considered to be rendering investment advice.

While recognizing the utility of the provisions in paragraphs (b)(3) and (b)(4) for the effective and efficient operation of plans by plan sponsors, plan fiduciaries and plan service providers, the Department reiterates its longstanding view, recently codified in 29 CFR 2550.404a-5(f) and 2550.404c-1(d)(2)(iv) (2010), that a fiduciary is always responsible for prudently selecting and monitoring providers of services to the plan or designated investment alternatives offered under the plan.

Several commenters also asked the Department to clarify that the platform provider carve-out is available in the 403(b) plan marketplace. In the Department's view, a 403(b) plan that is subject to Title I of ERISA would be an individual account plan within the meaning of ERISA section 3(34) of the Act for purposes of the proposed regulation, so the platform provider carve-out would be available with respect to such plans.

Other commenters asked that the platform provider provision be generally extended to apply to IRAs. In the IRA context, however, there typically is no separate independent "plan fiduciary" who interacts with the platform provider to protect the interests of the account owners. As a result, it is much more difficult to conclude that the transaction is truly arm's length or to draw a bright line between fiduciary and non-fiduciary communications on investment options. Consequently, the proposed regulation declines to extend application of this carve-out to IRAs and other non-ERISA plans. As the Department continues its work on this regulatory project, however, it requests specific comment as to the types of platforms and options that may be offered to IRA owners, how they may be similar to or different from platforms offered in connection with participant-directed individual account plans, and whether it would be appropriate for service providers not to be treated as fiduciaries under this carve-out when marketing such platforms to IRA owners. We also invite comments, alternatively, on whether the scope of this carve-out should be limited to large plans, similar to the scope of the "Seller's Carve-out" discussed above.

As a corollary to the proposal's restriction of the applicability of the platform provider carve-out to only ERISA plans, the selection and monitoring assistance carve-out is similarly not available in the IRA and other non-ERISA plans context. Commenters on the platform provider

restriction are encouraged to offer their views on the effect of this restriction in the non-ERISA plan marketplace.

(4) Investment Education

Paragraph (b)(6) of the proposed regulation is similar to a carve-out in the 2010 Proposal for the provision of investment education information and materials within the meaning of an earlier Interpretive Bulletin issued by the Department in 1996. 29 CFR 2509.96-1 (IB 96-1). Paragraph (b)(6) incorporates much of IB 96-1's operative text, but with the important exceptions explained below. Paragraph (b)(6) of the proposed regulation, if finalized, would supersede IB 96-1. Consistent with IB 96-1, paragraph (b)(6) makes clear that furnishing or making available the specified categories of information and materials to a plan, plan fiduciary, participant, beneficiary or IRA owner will not constitute the rendering of investment advice, irrespective of who provides the information (e.g., plan sponsor, fiduciary or service provider), the frequency with which the information is shared, the form in which the information and materials are provided (e.g., on an individual or group basis, in writing or orally, via a call center, or by way of video or computer software), or whether an identified category of information and materials is furnished or made available alone or in combination with other categories of investment or retirement information and materials identified in paragraph (b)(6), or the type of plan or IRA involved. As a departure from IB 96-1, a new condition of the carve-out for investment education is that the information and materials not include advice or recommendations as to specific investment products, specific investment managers, or the value of particular securities or other property. The paragraph reflects the Department's view that the statutory reference to "investment advice" is not meant to encompass general investment information and educational materials, but rather is targeted at more specific recommendations and advice on the investment of plan and IRA assets.

Similar to IB 96-1, paragraph (b)(6) of the proposed regulation divides investment education information and materials into four general categories: (i) Plan information; (ii) general financial, investment and retirement information; (iii) asset allocation models; and (iv) interactive investment materials. The proposed regulation in paragraph (b)(6)(v) also adopts the provision from IB 96-1 stating that there may be other examples of information, materials and educational services which, if furnished, would not constitute investment advice or recommendations within the meaning of the proposed regulation and that no inference should be drawn regarding materials or information which are not specifically included in paragraph (b)(6)(i) through (iv).

Although paragraph (b)(6) incorporates most of the relevant text of IB 96-1, there are important changes. One change from IB 96-1 is that paragraph (b)(6) makes clear that the distinction between non-fiduciary education and fiduciary advice applies equally to information provided to plan fiduciaries as well as information provided to plan participants and beneficiaries and IRA owners, and that it applies equally to participant-directed plans and other plans. In addition, the provision applies without regard to whether the information is provided by a plan sponsor, fiduciary, or service provider.

Based on public input received in connection with its joint examination of lifetime income issues with the Department of the Treasury, the Department is persuaded that additional guidance may help improve retirement security by facilitating the provision of information and education relating to retirement needs that extend beyond a participant's or beneficiary's date of retirement. Accordingly, paragraph (b)(6) of the proposal includes specific language to make clear that the provision of certain general information that helps an individual assess and understand retirement income needs past retirement and associated risks (e.g., longevity and inflation risk), or explains general methods for the individual to manage those risks both within and outside the plan, would not result in fiduciary status under the proposal.[22]

---

[22] Although the proposal would formally remove IB 96-1 from the CFR, the Department notes that paragraph (e) of IB 96-1 provides generalized guidance under section 405 and 404(c) of ERISA with respect to the selection by employers and plan fiduciaries of investment educators and the lack of responsibility of employers and fiduciaries with respect to investment educators selected by participants. Specifically, paragraph (e) states:

As with any designation of a service provider to a plan, the designation of a person to provide investment educational services or investment advice to plan participants and beneficiaries is an exercise of discretionary authority or control with respect to management of the plan; therefore, persons making the designation must act prudently and solely in the interest of the plan participants and beneficiaries, both in making the designation(s) and in continuing such designation(s). See ERISA sections 3(21)(A)(i) and 404(a), 29 U.S.C. 1002 (21)(A)(i) and 1104(a). In addition, the designation of an investment advisor to serve as a fiduciary may give rise to co-fiduciary liability if the person making and continuing such designation in doing so fails to act prudently and solely in the interest of plan participants and beneficiaries; or knowingly participates in, conceals or fails to make reasonable efforts to correct a known breach by the investment advisor. See ERISA section

405(a), 29 U.S.C. 1105(a). The Department notes, however, that, in the context of an ERISA section 404(c) plan, neither the designation of a person to provide education nor the designation of a fiduciary to provide investment advice to participants and beneficiaries would, in itself, give rise to fiduciary liability for loss, or with respect to any breach of part 4 of title I of ERISA, that is the direct and necessary result of a participant's or beneficiary's exercise of independent control. 29 CFR 2550.404c-1(d). The Department also notes that a plan sponsor or fiduciary would have no fiduciary responsibility or liability with respect to the actions of a third party selected by a participant or beneficiary to provide education or investment advice where the plan sponsor or fiduciary neither selects nor endorses the educator or advisor, nor otherwise makes arrangements with the educator or advisor to provide such services.

Unlike the remainder of the IB, this text does not belong in the investment advice regulation. Also, the principles articulated in paragraph (e) are generally understood and accepted such that retaining the paragraph as a stand-alone IB does not appear necessary or appropriate.

As noted, another change is that the Department is not incorporating the provisions at paragraph (d)(3)(iii) and (4)(iv) of IB 96-1. Those provisions of IB 96-1 permit the use of asset allocation models that refer to specific investment products available under the plan or IRA, as long as those references to specific products are accompanied by a statement that other investment alternatives having similar risk and return characteristics may be available. Based on its experience with the IB 96-1 since publication, as well as views expressed by commenters to the 2010 Proposal, the Department now believes that, even when accompanied by a statement as to the availability of other investment alternatives, these types of specific asset allocations that identify specific investment alternatives function as tailored, individualized investment recommendations, and can effectively steer recipients to particular investments, but without adequate protections against potential abuse.[23]

In particular, the Department agrees with those commenters to the 2010 Proposal who argued that cautionary disclosures to participants, beneficiaries, and IRA owners may have limited effectiveness in alerting them to the merit and wisdom of evaluating investment alternatives not used in the model. In practice, asset allocation models concerning hypothetical individuals, and interactive materials which arrive at specific investment products and plan alternatives, can be indistinguishable to the average retirement investor from individualized recommendations, regardless of caveats. Accordingly, paragraphs (b)(6)(iii) and (iv) relating to asset allocation models and interactive investment materials preclude the identification of specific investment alternatives available under the plan or IRA in order for the materials described in those paragraphs to be considered investment education. Thus, for example, we would not treat an asset allocation model as mere education if it called for a certain percentage of the investor's assets to be invested in large cap mutual funds, and accompanied that proposed allocation with the identity of a specific fund or provider. In that circumstance, the adviser has made a specific investment recommendation that should be treated as fiduciary advice and adhere to fiduciary standards. Further, materials that identify specific plan investment alternatives also appear to fall within the definition of "recommendation" in paragraph (f)(1) of the proposal, and could result in fiduciary status on the part of a provider if the other provisions of the proposal are met. The Department believes that effective and useful asset allocation education materials can be prepared and delivered to participants and IRA owners without including specific investment products and alternatives available under the plan. The Department understands that not incorporating the provisions of IB 96-1 at paragraph (d)(3)(iii) and (4)(iv) into the proposal represents a significant change in the information and materials that may constitute investment education. Accordingly, the Department invites comments on whether this change is appropriate.[24]

D. Fee or Other Compensation

A necessary element of fiduciary status under section 3(21)(A)(ii) of ERISA is that the investment advice be for a "fee or other compensation, direct or indirect." Consistent with the statute, paragraph (f)(6) of the proposed regulation defines this phrase to mean any fee or compensation for the advice received by the advice provider (or by an affiliate) from any source and any fee or compensation incident to the transaction in which the investment advice has been rendered or will be rendered. It further provides that the term "fee or compensation" includes, but is not limited to, brokerage fees, mutual fund sales, and insurance sales commissions.

Paragraph (c)(3) of the 2010 Proposal used similar language, but it also provided that the term included fees and compensation based on multiple transactions involving different parties. Commenters found this provision confusing and it does not appear in the new proposal. The provision was intended to confirm the Department's position that fees charged on a so-called "omnibus" basis (e.g., compensation paid based on business placed or retained that includes plan or IRA business) would constitute fees and compensation for purposes of the rule.

Direct or indirect compensation also includes any compensation received by affiliates of the adviser that is connected to the transaction in which the advice was provided. For example, when a fiduciary adviser recommends that a participant or IRA owner invest in a mutual fund, it is not unusual for an affiliated adviser to the mutual fund to receive a fee. The receipt by the affiliate of advisory fees from the mutual fund is indirect compensation in connection with the rendering of investment advice to the participant.

Some commenters additionally suggested that call center employees should not be treated as investment advice fiduciaries where they are not specifically paid to provide investment advice and their compensation does not change based on their communications with participants and beneficiaries. The carve-out from the fiduciary investment advice definition for investment education provides guidelines under which call center staff and other employees providing similar investor assistance services may avoid fiduciary status. However, commenters stated that a specific carve-out for such call centers would provide a greater level of certainty so as not to inhibit mutual funds, insurance companies, broker-dealers, recordkeepers and other financial service providers from continuing to make such assistance available to participants and beneficiaries in 401(k) and similar participant-directed plans. In the Department's view, such a carve-out would be inappropriate. The fiduciary definition is intended to apply broadly to all persons who engage in the activities set forth in the regulation, regardless of job title or position, or whether the advice is rendered in person, in writing or by phone. If, in the performance of their jobs, call center employees make specific investment recommendations to plan participants or IRA owners under the circumstances described in the proposal, it is appropriate to treat them, and possibly their employers, as fiduciaries unless they meet the conditions of one of the carve-outs set forth above.

E. Coverage of IRAs and Other Non-ERISA Plans

Certain provisions of Title I of ERISA, 29 U.S.C. 1001-1108, such as those relating to participation, benefit accrual, and prohibited transactions also appear in the Code. This parallel structure ensures that the relevant provisions apply to all tax-qualified plans, including IRAs. With regard to prohibited transactions, the Title I provisions generally authorize recovery of losses from, and imposition of civil penalties on, the responsible plan fiduciaries, while the Code provisions impose excise taxes on persons engaging in the prohibited transactions. The definition of fiduciary with respect to a plan is the same in section 4975(e)(3)(B) of the IRC as the definition in section 3(21)(A)(ii) of ERISA, 29 U.S.C. 1002(21)(A)(ii), and the Department's 1975 regulation defining fiduciary investment advice is virtually identical to regulations that define the term "fiduciary" under the Code. 26 CFR 54.4975-9(c) (1975).

To rationalize the administration and interpretation of dual provisions under ERISA and the Code, Reorganization Plan No. 4 of 1978 divided the interpretive and rulemaking authority for these provisions between the Secretaries of Labor and of the Treasury, so that, in general, the agency with responsibility for a given provision of Title I of ERISA would also have responsibility for the corresponding provision in the Code. Among the sections transferred to the Department were the prohibited transaction provisions and the definition of a fiduciary in both Title I of ERISA and in the Code. ERISA's prohibited transaction rules, 29 U.S.C. 1106-1108, apply to ERISA-covered plans, and the Code's corresponding prohibited transaction rules, 26 U.S.C. 4975(c), apply both to ERISA-covered pension plans that are tax-qualified pension plans, as well as other tax-advantaged arrangements, such as IRAs, that are not subject to the fiduciary responsibility and prohibited transaction rules in ERISA.[25]

Given this statutory structure, and the dual nature of the 1975 regulation, the proposal would apply to both the definition of "fiduciary" in section 3(21)(A)(ii) of ERISA and the definition's counterpart in section 4975(e)(3)(B) of the Code. As a result, it applies to persons who give investment advice to IRAs. In this respect, the new proposal is the same as the 2010 Proposal.

Many comments on the 2010 Proposal concerned its impact on IRAs and questioned whether the Department had adequately considered possible negative impacts. Some commenters were especially concerned that application of the new rule could disrupt existing broker-

---

[23] When the Department issued IB 96-1, it expressed concern that service providers could effectively steer participants to a specific investment alternative by identifying only one particular fund available under the plan in connection with an asset allocation model. As a result, where it was possible to do so, the Department encouraged service providers to identify other investment alternatives within an asset class as part of a model. Ultimately, however, when asset allocation models and interactive investment materials identified any specific investment alternative available under the plan, the Department required an accompanying statement both indicating that other investment alternatives having similar risk and return characteristics may be available under the plan and identifying where

information on those investment alternatives could be obtained. 61 FR 29586, 29587 (June 11, 1996).

[24] As indicated earlier in this Notice, the Department believes that FINRA's guidance in this area may provide useful standards and guideposts for distinguishing investment education from investment advice under ERISA. The Department specifically solicits comments on the discussion in FINRA's "Frequently Asked Questions, FINRA Rule 2111 (Suitability)" of the term "recommendation" in the context of asset allocation models and general investment strategies.

[25] The Secretary of Labor also was transferred authority to grant administrative exemptions from the prohibited transaction provisions of the Code.

age arrangements that they believe are beneficial to customers. In particular, brokers often receive revenue sharing, 12b-1 fees, and other compensation from the parties whose investment products they recommend. If the brokers were treated as fiduciaries, the receipt of such fees could violate the Code's prohibited transaction rules, unless eligible for a prohibited transaction exemption. According to these commenters, the disruption of such current fee arrangements could result in a reduced level of assistance to investors, higher up-front fees, and less investment advice, particularly to investors with small accounts. In addition, some commenters expressed skepticism that the imposition of fiduciary standards would result in improved advice and questioned the view that current compensation arrangements could cause suboptimal advice. Additionally, commenters stressed the need for coordination between the Department and other regulatory agencies, such as the SEC, CFTC, and Treasury.

As discussed above, to better align the regulatory definition of fiduciary with the statutory provisions and underlying Congressional goals, the Department is proposing a definition of a fiduciary investment advice that would encompass investment recommendations that are individualized or specifically directed to plans, participants, beneficiaries or IRA owners, if the adviser receives a direct or indirect fee. Neither the relevant statutory provisions, nor the current regulation, draw a distinction between brokers and other advisers or carve brokers out of the scope of the fiduciary provisions of ERISA and of the Code. The relevant statutory provisions, and accordingly the proposed regulation, establish a functional test based on the service provider's actions, rather than the provider's title (e.g., broker or registered investment adviser). If one engages in specified activities, such as the provision of investment advice for a direct or indirect fee, the person engaging in those activities is a fiduciary, irrespective of labels. Moreover, the statutory definition of fiduciary advice is identical under both ERISA and the Code. There is no indication that the definition should vary between plans and IRAs.

In light of this statutory framework, the Department does not believe it would be appropriate to carve out a special rule for IRAs, or for brokers or others who make specific investment recommendations to IRA owners or to other participants in non-ERISA plans for direct or indirect fees. When Congress enacted ERISA and the corresponding Code provisions, it chose to impose fiduciary status on persons who provide investment advice to plans, participants, beneficiaries and IRA owners, and to specifically prohibit a wide variety of transactions in which the fiduciary has financial interests that potentially conflict with the fiduciary's obligation to the plan or IRA. It did not provide a special carve-out for brokers or IRAs, and the Department does not believe it would be appropriate to write such a carve-out into the regulation implementing the statutory definition.

Indeed, brokers who give investment advice to IRA owners or plan participants, and who otherwise meet the terms of the current five-part test, are already fiduciaries under the existing fiduciary regulation. If, for example, a broker regularly advises an individual IRA owner on specific investments, the IRA owner routinely follows the recommendations, and both parties understand that the IRA owner relies upon the broker's advice, the broker is almost certainly a fiduciary. In such circumstances, the broker is already subject to the excise tax on prohibited transactions if he or she receives fees from a third party in connection with recommendations to invest IRA assets in the third party's investment products, unless the broker satisfies the conditions of a prohibited transaction exemption that covers the particular fees. Indeed, broker-dealers today can provide fiduciary investment advice by complying with prohibited transaction exemptions that permit the receipt of commission-based compensation for the sale of mutual funds and other securities. Moreover, both ERISA and the Code were amended as part of the PPA to include a new prohibited transaction exemption that applies to investment advice in both the plan and IRA context. The PPA exemption clearly reflects the longstanding concern under ERISA and the Code about the dangers posed by conflicts of interest, and the need for appropriate safeguards in both the plan and IRA markets. Under the terms of the exemption, the investment recommendations must either result from the application of an unbiased and independently certified computer program or the fiduciary's fees must be level (i.e., the fiduciary's compensation cannot vary based on his or her particular investment recommendations).

Moreover, as discussed in the regulatory impact analysis below, there is substantial evidence to support the statutory concern about conflicts of interest. As the analysis reflects, unmitigated conflicts can cause significant harm to investors. The available evidence supports a

finding that the negative impacts are present and often times large. The proposal would curtail the harms to investors from such conflicts and thus deliver significant benefits to plan participants and IRA owners. Plans, plan participants, beneficiaries and IRA owners would all benefit from advice that is impartial and puts their interests first. Moreover, broker-dealer interactions with plan fiduciaries, participants, and IRA owners present some of the most obvious conflict of interest problems in this area. Accordingly, in the Department's view, broker-dealers that provide investment advice should be subject to fiduciary duties to mitigate conflicts of interest and increase investor protections.

Some commenters additionally suggested that the application of special fiduciary rules in the retail investment market to IRA accounts, but not savings outside of tax-preferred retirement accounts, is inappropriate and could lead to confusion among investors and service providers. The distinction between IRAs and other retail accounts, however, is a direct result of a statutory structure that draws a sensible distinction between tax-favored IRAs and other retail investment accounts. The Code itself treats IRAs differently, bestowing uniquely favorable tax treatment on such accounts and prohibiting self-dealing by persons providing investment advice for a fee. In these respects, and in light of the special public interest in retirement security, IRAs are more like plans than like other retail accounts. Indeed, as noted above, the vast majority of IRA assets today are attributable to rollovers from plans.[26] In addition, IRA owners may be at even greater risk from conflicted advice than plan participants. Unlike ERISA plan participants, IRA owners do not have the benefit of an independent plan fiduciary to represent their interests in selecting a menu of investment options or structuring advice arrangements. They cannot sue fiduciary advisers under ERISA for losses arising from fiduciary breaches, nor can the Department sue on their behalf. Compared to participants with ERISA plan accounts, IRA owners often have larger account balances and are more likely to be elderly. Thus, limiting the harms to IRA investors resulting from conflicts of interest of advisers is at least as important as protecting ERISA plans and plan participants from such harms.

The Department believes that it is important to address the concerns of brokers and others providing investment advice to IRA owners about undue disruptions to current fee arrangements, but also believes that such concerns are best resolved within a fiduciary framework, rather than by simply relieving advisers from fiduciary responsibility. As previously discussed, the proposed regulation permits investment professionals to provide important financial information and education, without acting as fiduciaries or being subject to the prohibited transaction rules. Moreover, ERISA and the Code create a flexible process that enables the Department to grant class and individual exemptions from the prohibited transaction rules for fee practices that it determines are beneficial to plan participants and IRA owners. For example, existing prohibited transaction exemptions already allow brokers who provide fiduciary advice to receive commissions generating conflicts of interest for trading the types of securities and funds that make up the large majority of IRA assets today. In addition, simultaneous with the publication of this proposed regulation, the Department is publishing new exemption proposals that would permit common fee practices, while at the same time protecting plan participants, beneficiaries and IRA owners from abuse and conflicts of interest. As noted above, in contrast with many previously adopted PTE exemptions that are transaction-specific, the Best Interest Contract PTE described below reflects a more flexible approach that accommodates a wide range of current business practices while minimizing the impact of conflicts of interest and ensuring that plans and IRAs receive investment recommendations that are in their best interests.

As discussed, the Department received extensive comment on the application of the 2010 Proposal's provisions to IRAs, but comments regarding other non-ERISA plans such as Health Savings Accounts (HSAs), Archer Medical Savings Accounts and Coverdell Education Savings Accounts were less prolific. The Department notes that these accounts are given tax preferences as are IRAs. Further, some of the accounts, such as HSAs, can be used as long term savings accounts for retiree health care expenses. These types of accounts also are expressly defined by Code section 4975(e)(1) as plans that are subject to the Code's prohibited transaction rules. Thus, although they generally may hold fewer assets and may exist for shorter durations than IRAs, the owners of these accounts or the persons for whom these accounts were established are entitled to receive the same protections from conflicted investment advice as IRA owners. Accordingly, these accounts are included in the scope of covered plans in paragraph (f)(2) of the new proposal. However, the Department solicits specific comment

[26] Peter Brady, Sarah Holden, and Erin Shon, *The U.S. Retirement Market, 2009,* Investment Company Institute, Research Fundamentals, Vol. 19, No. 3, May 2010, *at http://www.ici.org/pdf/fm-v19n3.pdf.*

as to whether it is appropriate to cover and treat these plans under the proposed regulation in a manner similar to IRAs as to both coverage and applicable carve-outs.

F. Administrative Prohibited Transaction Exemptions

In addition to the new proposal in this Notice, the Department is also proposing, elsewhere in this edition of the **Federal Register**, certain administrative class exemptions from the prohibited transaction provisions of ERISA (29 U.S.C. 1106), and the Code (26 U.S.C. 4975(c)(1)) as well as proposed amendments to previously adopted exemptions. The proposed exemptions and amendments would allow, subject to appropriate safeguards, certain broker-dealers, insurance agents and others that act as investment advice fiduciaries to nevertheless continue to receive a variety of forms of compensation that would otherwise violate prohibited transaction rules and trigger excise taxes. The proposed exemptions would supplement statutory exemptions at 29 U.S.C. 1108 and 26 U.S.C. 4975(d), and previously adopted class exemptions.

Investment advice fiduciaries to plans and plan participants must meet ERISA's standards of prudence and loyalty to their plan customers. Such fiduciaries also face taxes, remedies and other sanctions for engaging in certain transactions, such as self-dealing with plan assets or receiving payments from third parties in connection with plan transactions, unless the transactions are permitted by an exemption from ERISA's and the Code's prohibited transaction rules. IRA fiduciaries do not have the same general fiduciary obligations of prudence and loyalty under the statute, but they too must adhere to the prohibited transaction rules or they must pay an excise tax. The prohibited transaction rules help ensure that investment advice provided to plan participants and IRA owners is not driven by the adviser's financial self-interest.

Proposed Best Interest Contract Exemption (Best Interest Contract PTE)

The proposed Best Interest Contract PTE would provide broad and flexible relief from the prohibited transaction restrictions on certain compensation received by investment advice fiduciaries as a result of a plan's or IRA's purchase, sale or holding of specifically identified investments. The conditions of the exemption are generally principles-based rather than prescriptive and require, in particular, that advice be provided in the best interest of the plan or IRA. This exemption was developed partly in response to comments received that suggested such an approach. It is a significant departure from existing exemptions, examples of which are discussed below, which are limited to much narrower categories of investments under more prescriptive and less flexible and adaptable conditions.

The proposed Best Interest Contract PTE was developed to promote the provision of investment advice that is in the best interest of retail investors, such as plan participants and beneficiaries, IRA owners, and small plans. The proposed exemption would apply to compensation received by individual investment advice fiduciaries (including individual advisers[27] and firms that employ or otherwise contract with such individuals) as well as their affiliates and related entities, that is provided in connection with the purchase, sale or holding of certain assets by the plans, participants and beneficiaries, and IRAs. In order to protect the interests of these investors, the exemption requires the firm and the adviser to contractually acknowledge fiduciary status, commit to adhere to basic standards of impartial conduct, warrant that they will comply with applicable federal and state laws governing advice and that they have adopted policies and procedures reasonably designed to mitigate any harmful impact of conflicts of interest, and disclose basic information on their conflicts of interest and on the cost of their advice. The standards of impartial conduct to which the adviser and firm must commit are basic obligations of fair dealing and fiduciary conduct to which the Department believes advisers and firms often informally commit—to give advice that is in the customer's best interest; avoid misleading statements; and receive no more than reasonable compensation. This standards-based approach aligns the adviser's interests with those of the plan or IRA customer, while leaving the adviser and employing firm the flexibility and discretion necessary to determine how best to satisfy these basic standards in light of the unique attributes of their business.

As an additional protection for retail investors, the exemption would not apply if the contract contains exculpatory provisions disclaiming or otherwise limiting liability of the adviser or financial institution for violation of the contract's terms. Adopting the approach taken by FINRA, the contract could require the parties to arbitrate individual claims, but it could not limit the rights of the plan, participant, beneficiary, or IRA owner to bring or participate in a class action against the adviser or financial institution.

Additional conditions would apply to firms that limit the products that their advisers can recommend based on the receipt of third party payments or the proprietary nature of the products (*i.e.*, products offered or managed by the firm or its affiliates) or for other reasons. The conditions require, among other things, that such firms provide notice of the limitations to plans, participants and beneficiaries and IRA owners, as well as make a written finding that the limitations do not prevent advisers from providing advice in those investors' best interest.

Finally, certain notice and data collection requirements would apply to all firms relying on the exemption. Specifically, firms would be required to notify the Department in advance of doing so, and they would have to maintain certain data, and make it available to the Department upon request, to help evaluate the effectiveness of the exemption in safeguarding the interests of plan and IRA investors.

The Department's intent in crafting the Best Interest Contract PTE is to permit common compensation structures that create conflicts of interest, while minimizing the costs imposed on investors by such conflicts. The exemption is designed both to impose broad fiduciary standards of conduct on advisers and financial institutions, and to give them sufficient flexibility to accommodate a wide range of business practices and compensation structures that currently exist or that may develop in the future.

The Department is also considering an additional streamlined exemption that would apply to compensation received in connection with investments by plans, participants and beneficiaries, and IRA owners, in certain high-quality, low-fee investments, subject to fewer conditions than in the proposed Best Interest Contract PTE. If properly crafted, the streamlined exemption could achieve important goals of minimizing compliance burdens for advisers and financial institutions when they offer investment products with little potential for material conflicts of interest. The Department is not proposing text for such a streamlined exemption due to the difficulty in operationalizing this concept. However the Department is eager to receive comments on whether such an exemption would be worthwhile and, as part of the notice proposing the Best Interest Contract PTE, is soliciting comments on a number of issues relating to the design of a streamlined exemption.

Proposed Principal Transaction Exemption (Principal Transaction PTE)

Broker-dealers and other advisers commonly sell debt securities out of their own inventory to plans, participants and beneficiaries and IRA owners in a type of transaction known as a "principal transaction." Fiduciaries trigger taxes, remedies and other legal sanctions when they engage in such activities, unless they qualify for an exemption from the prohibited transaction rules. These principal transactions raise issues similar to those addressed in the Best Interest Contract PTE, but also raise unique concerns because the conflicts of interest are particularly acute. In these transactions, the adviser sells the security directly from its own inventory, and may be able to dictate the price that the plan, participant or beneficiary, or IRA owner pays.

Because of the prevalence of the practice in the market for fixed income securities, the Department has proposed a separate Principal Transactions PTE that would permit principal transactions in certain debt securities between a plan or IRA owner and an investment advice fiduciary, under certain circumstances.

The Principal Transaction PTE would include all of the contract requirements of the Best Interest Contract PTE. In addition, however, it would include specific conditions related to the price of the debt security involved in the transaction. The adviser would have to obtain two price quotes from unaffiliated counterparties for the same or a similar security, and the transaction would have to occur at a price at least as favorable to the plan or IRA as the two price quotes. Additionally, the adviser would have to disclose the amount of compensation and profit (sometimes referred to as a "mark up" or "mark down") that it expects to receive on the transaction.

Amendments to Existing PTEs

In addition to the Best Interest Contract PTE and the Principal Transaction PTE, the Department is also proposing elsewhere in the **Federal Register** amendments to certain existing PTEs.

---

[27] By using the term "adviser," the Department does not intend to limit the exemption to investment advisers registered under the Investment Advisers Act of 1940; under the exemption an adviser is individual who can be a representative of a registered investment adviser, a bank or similar financial institution, an insurance company, or a broker-dealer.

Prohibited Transaction Exemption 86-128

Prohibited Transaction Exemption (PTE) 86-128[28] currently allows an investment advice fiduciary to cause the recipient plan or IRA to pay the investment advice fiduciary or its affiliate a fee for effecting or executing securities transactions as agent. To prevent churning, the exemption does not apply if such transactions are excessive in either amount or frequency. The exemption also allows the investment advice fiduciary to act as an agent for both the plan and the other party to the transaction (i.e., the buyer and the seller of securities) and receive a reasonable fee. To use the exemption, the fiduciary cannot be a plan administrator or employer, unless all profits earned by these parties are returned to the plan. The conditions of the exemption require that a plan fiduciary independent of the investment advice fiduciary receive certain disclosures and authorize the transaction. In addition, the independent fiduciary must receive confirmations and an annual "portfolio turnover ratio" demonstrating the amount of turnover in the account during that year. These conditions are not presently applicable to transactions involving IRAs.

The Department is proposing to amend PTE 86-128 to require all fiduciaries relying on the exemption to adhere to the same impartial conduct standards required in the Best Interest Contract PTE. At the same time, the proposed amendment would eliminate relief for investment advice fiduciaries to IRA owners; instead they would be required to rely on the Best Interest Contract PTE for an exemption for such compensation. In the Department's view, the provisions in the Best Interest Contract Exemption better address the interests of IRAs with respect to transactions otherwise covered by PTE 86-128 and, unlike plan participants and beneficiaries, there is no separate plan fiduciary in the IRA market to review and authorize the transaction. Investment advice fiduciaries to plans would remain eligible for relief under the exemption, as would investment managers with full investment discretion over the investments of plans and IRA owners, but they would be required to comply with all the protective conditions, described above. Finally, the Department is proposing that PTE 86-128 extend to a new covered transaction, for fiduciaries who sell mutual fund shares out of their own inventory (i.e., acting as principals, rather than agents) to plans and IRAs and to receive commissions for doing so. This transaction is currently the subject of another exemption, PTE 75-1, Part II(2) (discussed below) that the Department is proposing to revoke.

Several changes are proposed with respect to PTE 75-1, a multi-part exemption for securities transactions involving broker dealers and banks, and plans and IRAs.[29] Part I(b) and (c) currently provide relief for certain non-fiduciary services to plans and IRAs. The Department is proposing to revoke these provisions, and require persons seeking to engage in such transactions to rely instead on the existing statutory exemptions provided in ERISA section 408(b)(2) and Code section 4975(d)(2), and the Department's implementing regulations at 29 CFR 2550.408b-2. The Department believes the conditions of the statutory exemptions are more appropriate for the provision of these services.

PTE 75-1, Part II(2), currently provides relief for fiduciaries selling mutual fund shares to plans and IRAs in a principal transaction to receive commissions. PTE 75-1, Part II(2) currently provides relief for fiduciaries to receive commissions for selling mutual fund shares to plans and IRAs in a principal transaction. As described above, the Department is proposing to provide relief for these types of transactions in PTE 86-128, and so is proposing to revoke PTE 75-1, Part II(2), in its entirety. As discussed in more detail in the notice of proposed amendment/revocation, the Department believes the conditions of PTE 86-128 are more appropriate for these transactions.

PTE 75-1, Part V, currently permits broker-dealers to extend credit to a plan or IRA in connection with the purchase or sale of securities. The exemption does not permit broker-dealers that are fiduciaries to receive compensation when doing so. The Department is proposing to amend PTE 75-1, Part V, to permit investment advice fiduciaries to receive compensation for lending money or otherwise extending credit, but only for the limited purpose of avoiding a failed securities transaction.

Prohibited Transaction Exemption 84-24

PTE 84-24[30] covers transactions involving mutual fund shares, or insurance or annuity contracts, sold to plans or IRA investors by pension consultants, insurance agents, brokers, and mutual fund princi-

pal underwriters who are fiduciaries as a result of advice they give in connection with these transactions. The exemption allows these investment advice fiduciaries to receive a sales commission with respect to products purchased by plans or IRA investors. The exemption is limited to sales commissions that are reasonable under the circumstances. The investment advice fiduciary must provide disclosure of the amount of the commission and other terms of the transaction to an independent fiduciary of the plan or IRA, and obtain approval for the transaction. To use this exemption, the investment advice fiduciary may not have certain roles with respect to the plan or IRA such as trustee, plan administrator, fiduciary with written authorization to manage the plan's assets and employers. However it is available to investment advice fiduciaries regardless of whether they expressly acknowledge their fiduciary status or are simply functional or "inadvertent" fiduciaries that have not expressly agreed to act as fiduciary advisers, provided there is no written authorization granting them discretion to acquire or dispose of the assets of the plan or IRA.

The Department is proposing to amend PTE 84-24 to require all fiduciaries relying on the exemption to adhere to the same impartial conduct standards required in the Best Interest Contract Exemption. At the same time, the proposed amendment would revoke PTE 84-24 in part so that investment advice fiduciaries to IRA owners would not be able to rely on PTE 84-24 with respect to (1) transactions involving variable annuity contracts and other annuity contracts that constitute securities under federal securities laws, and (2) transactions involving the purchase of mutual fund shares. Investment advice fiduciaries to IRA owners would instead be required to rely on the Best Interest Contract Exemption for most common forms of compensation received in connection with these transactions. The Department believes that investment advice transactions involving annuity contracts that are treated as securities and transactions involving the purchase of mutual fund shares should occur under the conditions of the Best Interest Contract Exemption due to the similarity of these investments, including their distribution channels and disclosure obligations, to other investments covered in the Best Interest Contract Exemption. Investment advice fiduciaries to ERISA plans would remain eligible for relief under the exemption with respect to transactions involving all insurance and annuity contracts and mutual fund shares and the receipt of commissions allowable under that exemption. Investment advice fiduciaries to IRAs could still receive commissions for transactions involving non-securities insurance and annuity contracts, but they would be required to comply with all the protective conditions, described above.

Finally, the Department is proposing amendments to certain other existing class exemptions to require adherence to the impartial conduct standards required in the Best Interest Contract PTE. Specifically, PTEs 75-1, Part III, 75-1, Part IV, 77-4, 80-83, and 83-1, would be amended. These existing class exemptions will otherwise remain in place, affording flexibility to fiduciaries who currently use the exemptions or who wish to use the exemptions in the future.

The proposed dates on which the new exemptions and amendments to existing exemptions would be effective are summarized below.

G. The Provision of Professional Services Other Than Investment Advice

Several commenters asserted that it was unclear whether investment advice under the scope of the 2010 Proposal would include the provision of information and plan services that traditionally have been performed in a non-fiduciary capacity. For example, they requested that the proposal be revised to make clear that actuaries, accountants, and attorneys, who have historically not been treated as ERISA fiduciaries for plan clients, would not become fiduciary investment advisers by reason of providing actuarial, accounting and legal services. They said that if individuals providing these services were classified as fiduciaries, the associated costs would almost certainly increase because of the need to account for their new potential fiduciary liability. This was not the intent of the 2010 proposal.

The new proposal clarifies that attorneys, accountants, and actuaries would not be treated as fiduciaries merely because they provide such professional assistance in connection with a particular investment transaction. Only when these professionals act outside their normal roles and recommend specific investments or render valuation opinions in connection with particular investment transactions, would they be subject to the proposed fiduciary definition.

---

[28] Class Exemption for Securities Transactions Involving Employee Benefit Plans and Broker-Dealers, 51 FR 41686 (Nov. 18, 1986), amended at 67 FR 64137 (Oct. 17, 2002).

[29] Exemptions from Prohibitions Respecting Certain Classes of Transactions Involving Employee Benefit Plans and Certain Broker-Dealers, Reporting Dealers and Banks, 40 FR 50845 (Oct. 31, 1975), as amended at 71 FR 5883 (Feb. 3, 2006).

[30] Class Exemption for Certain Transactions Involving Insurance Agents and Brokers, Pension Consultants, Insurance Companies, Investment Companies and Investment Company Principal Underwriters, 49 FR 13208 (Apr. 3, 1984), amended at 71 FR 5887 (Feb. 3, 2006).

Similarly, the new proposal does not alter the principle articulated in ERISA Interpretive Bulletin 75-8, D-2 at 29 CFR 2509.75-8 (1975). Under the bulletin, the plan sponsor's human resources personnel or plan service providers who have no power to make decisions as to plan policy, interpretations, practices or procedures, but who perform purely administrative functions for an employee benefit plan, within a framework of policies, interpretations, rules, practices and procedures made by other persons, are not fiduciaries with respect to the plan.

H. Effective Date; Applicability Date

Final Rule

Commenters on the 2010 Proposal asked the Department to provide sufficient time for orderly and efficient compliance, and to make it clear that the final rule would not apply in connection with advice provided before the effective date of the final rule. Many commenters also expressed concern with the provision in the Department's 2010 Proposal that the final regulation and class exemptions would be effective 90 days after their publication in the **Federal Register**. Some commenters suggested that these effective dates should be extended to as much as 12 months or longer following publication of the new rule to allow service providers sufficient time to make necessary changes in business practices, recordkeeping, communication materials, sales processes, compensation arrangements, and related agreements, as well as the time necessary to obtain and adjust to any additional individual or class exemptions. Several said that applicability of any changes in the 1975 regulation should be no earlier than two years after the promulgation of a final regulation. Other commenters thought that the effective dates in the 2010 proposal were reasonable and asked that the final rules should go into effect promptly in order to reduce ongoing harms to savers.

In response to these concerns, the Department has revised the date by which the final rule would apply. Specifically, the final rule would be effective 60 days after publication in the **Federal Register** and the requirements of the final rule would generally become applicable eight months after publication of a final rule, with the potential exceptions noted below. This modification is intended to balance the concerns raised by commenters about the need for prompt action with concerns raised about the cost and burden associated with transitioning current and future contracts or arrangements to satisfy the requirements of the final rule and any accompanying prohibited transaction exemptions.

Administrative Prohibited Transaction Exemptions

The Department proposes to make the Best Interest Contract Exemption, if granted, available on the final rule's applicability date, *i.e.,* eight months after publication of a final rule. Further, the department proposes that the other new and revised PTEs that it is proposing go into effect as of the final rule's applicability date.[31]

For those fiduciary investment advisers who choose to avail themselves of the Best Interest Contract Exemption, the Department recognizes that compliance with certain requirements of the new exemption may be difficult within the eight-month timeframe. The Department therefore is soliciting comments on whether to delay the application of certain requirements of the Best Interest Contract Exemption for several months (for example, certain data collection requirements), thereby enabling firms and advisers to benefit from the Best Interest Contract Exemption without meeting all the requirements for a limited period of time. Although the Department does not believe that a general delay in the application of the exemption's requirements is warranted, it recognizes that a short-term delay of some requirements may be appropriate and may not compromise the overall protections created by the proposed rule and exemptions. As discussed in more detail in the Notice proposing the Best Interest Contract Exemption published elsewhere in this issue of the **Federal Register**, the Department requests comments on this approach.

I. Public Hearing

The Department plans to hold an administrative hearing within 30 days of the close of the comment period. As with the 2010 Proposal, the Department will ensure ample opportunity for public comment by reopening the record following the hearing and publication of the hearing transcript. Specific information regarding the date, location and submission of requests to testify will be published in a notice in the **Federal Register**.

J. Regulatory Impact Analysis

Under Executive Order 12866, "significant" regulatory actions are subject to the requirements of the Executive Order and review by the Office of Management and Budget (OMB). Section 3(f) of the executive order defines a "significant regulatory action" as an action that is likely to result in a rule (1) having an annual effect on the economy of $100 million or more, or adversely and materially affecting a sector of the economy, productivity, competition, jobs, the environment, public health or safety, or State, local or tribal governments or communities (also referred to as "economically significant"); (2) creating serious inconsistency or otherwise interfering with an action taken or planned by another agency; (3) materially altering the budgetary impacts of entitlement grants, user fees, or loan programs or the rights and obligations of recipients thereof; or (4) raising novel legal or policy issues arising out of legal mandates, the President's priorities, or the principles set forth in the Executive Order. OMB has determined that this proposed rule is economically significant within the meaning of section 3(f)(1) of the Executive Order, because it would be likely to have an effect on the economy of $100 million in at least one year. Accordingly, OMB has reviewed the rule pursuant to the Executive Order.

The Department's complete Regulatory Impact Analysis is available at *www.dol.gov/ebsa/pdf/conflictsofinterestria.pdf.* It is summarized below.

Tax-preferred retirement savings, in the form of private-sector, employer-sponsored retirement plans, such as 401(k) plans ("plans"), and Individual Retirement Accounts ("IRAs"), are critical to the retirement security of most U.S. workers. Investment professionals play a major role in guiding their investment decisions. However, these professional advisers often are compensated in ways that create conflicts of interest, which can bias the investment advice they render and erode plan and IRA investment results. In order to limit or mitigate conflicts of interest and thereby improve retirement security, the Department of Labor ("the Department") is proposing to attach fiduciary status to more of the advice rendered to plan officials, participants, and beneficiaries (plan investors) and IRA investors.

Since the Department issued its 1975 rule, the retirement savings market has changed profoundly. Financial products are increasingly varied and complex. Individuals, rather than large employers, are increasingly responsible for their investment decisions as IRAs and 401(k)-type defined contribution plans have supplanted defined benefit pensions as the primary means of providing retirement security. Plan and IRA investors often lack investment expertise and must rely on experts—but are unable to assess the quality of the expert's advice or police its conflicts of interest. Most have no idea how "advisers" are compensated for selling them products. Many are bewildered by complex choices that require substantial financial literacy and welcome "free" advice. The risks are growing as baby boomers retire and move money from plans, where their employer has both the incentive and the fiduciary duty to facilitate sound investment choices, to IRAs, where both good and bad investment choices are myriad and most advice is conflicted. These "rollovers" are expected to approach $2.5 trillion over the next 5 years.[32] These rollovers, which will be one-time and not "on a regular basis" and thus not covered by the 1975 standard, will be the most important financial decisions that many consumers make in their lifetime. An ERISA plan investor who rolls her retirement savings into an IRA could lose 12 to 24 percent of the value of her savings over 30 years of retirement by accepting advice from a conflicted financial advisor.[33] Timely regulatory action to redress advisers' conflicts is warranted to avert such losses.

In the retail IRA marketplace, growing consumer demand for personalized advice, together with competition from online discount brokerage firms, has pushed brokers to offer more comprehensive guidance services rather than just transaction support. Unfortunately, their traditional compensation sources—such as brokerage commissions, revenue shared by mutual funds and funds' asset managers, and mark-ups on bonds sold from their own inventory—can introduce acute conflicts of interest. Brokers and others advising IRA investors are often able to calibrate their business practices to steer around the narrow 1975 rule

---

[31] See the notices with respect to these proposals, published elsewhere in this issue of the **Federal Register**.

[32] Cerulli Associates, "Retirement Markets 2014: Sizing Opportunities in Private and Public Retirement Plans," 2014.

[33] For example, an ERISA plan investor who rolls $200,000 into an IRA, earns a 6% nominal rate of return with 3% inflation, and aims to spend down her savings in 30 years,

would be able to consume $10,204 per year for the 30 year period. A similar investor whose assets underperform by 1 or 2 percentage points per year would only be able to consume $8,930 or $7,750 per year, respectively, in each of the 30 years. The 1 to 2 percentage point underperformance comes from a careful review of a large and growing body of literature which consistently points to a substantial failure of the market for retirement advice. The literature is discussed in the Department's complete Regulatory Impact Analysis (available at *www.dol.gov/ebsa/pdf/conflictsofinterestria.pdf*).

and thereby avoid fiduciary status and prohibited transactions for accepting conflict-laden compensation. Many brokers market retirement investment services in ways that clearly suggest the provision of tailored or individualized advice, while at the same time relying on the 1975 rule to disclaim any fiduciary responsibility in the fine print of contracts and marketing materials. Thus, at the same time that marketing materials may characterize the financial adviser's relationship with the customer as one-on-one, personalized, and based on the client's best interest, footnotes and legal boilerplate disclaim the requisite mutual agreement, arrangement, or understanding that the advice is individualized or should serve as a primary basis for investment decisions. What is presented to an IRA investor as trusted advice is often paid for by a financial product vendor in the form of a sales commission or shelf-space fee, without adequate counterbalancing consumer protections that are designed to ensure that the advice is in the investor's best interest. In another variant of the same problem, brokers and others provide apparently tailored advice to customers under the guise of general education to avoid triggering fiduciary status and responsibility.

Likewise in the plan market, pension consultants and advisers that plan sponsors rely on to guide their decisions often avoid fiduciary status under the five-part test and are conflicted. For example, if a plan hires an investment professional or appraiser on a one-time basis for an investment recommendation on a large, complex investment, the adviser has no fiduciary obligation to the plan under ERISA. Even if the plan official, who lacks the specialized expertise necessary to evaluate the complex transaction on his or her own, invests all or substantially all of the plan's assets in reliance on the consultant's professional judgment, the consultant is not a fiduciary because he or she does not advise the plan on a "regular basis" and therefore may stand to profit from the plan's investment due to a conflict of interest that could affect the consultant's best judgment. Too much has changed since 1975, and too many investment decisions are made as one-time decisions and not advice on a regular basis for the five-part test to be a meaningful safeguard any longer.

The proposed definition of fiduciary investment advice included in this NPRM generally covers specific recommendations on investments, investment management, the selection of persons to provide investment advice or management, and appraisals in connection with investment decisions. Persons who provide such advice would fall within the proposed regulation's ambit if they either (a) represent that they are acting as an ERISA fiduciary or (b) make investment recommendations pursuant to an agreement, arrangement, or understanding that the advice is individualized or specifically directed to the recipient for consideration in making investment or investment management decisions regarding plan or IRA assets.

The current proposal specifically includes as fiduciary investment advice recommendations concerning the investment of assets that are rolled over or otherwise distributed from a plan. This would supersede guidance the Department provided in a 2005 advisory opinion,[34] which concluded that such recommendations did not constitute fiduciary advice. However, the current proposal provides that an adviser does not act as a fiduciary merely by providing plan investors with information about plan distribution options, including the tax consequences associated with the available types of benefit distributions.

The current proposal adopts what the Department intends to be a balanced approach to prohibited transaction exemptions. The proposal narrows and attaches new protective conditions to some existing PTEs. At the same time it includes some new PTEs with broad but targeted combined scope and strong protective conditions. These elements of the proposal reflect the Department's effort to ensure that advice is impartial while avoiding larger and costlier than necessary disruptions to existing business arrangements or constraints on future innovation.

In developing the current proposal, the Department conducted an in-depth economic assessment of the market for retirement investment advice. As further discussed below, the Department found that conflicted advice is widespread, causing serious harm to plan and IRA investors, and that disclosing conflicts alone would fail to adequately mitigate the conflicts or remedy the harm. By extending fiduciary status to more providers of advice and providing broad but targeted and protective PTEs, the Department believes the current proposal would mitigate conflicts, support consumer choice, and deliver substantial gains for retirement investors and economic benefits that more than justify its costs.

Advisers' conflicts take a variety of forms and can bias their advice in a variety of ways. For example, advisers often are paid more for selling some mutual funds than others, and to execute larger and more frequent trades of mutual fund shares or other securities. Broker-dealers reap price spreads from principal transactions, so advisers may be encouraged to recommend larger and more frequent trades. These and other adviser compensation arrangements introduce direct and serious conflicts of interest between advisers and retirement investors. Advisers often are paid a great deal more if they recommend investments and transactions that are highly profitable to the financial industry, even if they are not in investors' best interests. These financial incentives can and do bias the advisers' recommendations.

Following such biased advice can inflict losses on investors in several ways. They may choose more expensive and/or poorer performing investments. They may trade too much and thereby incur excessive transaction costs, and they may incur more costly timing errors, which are a common consequence of chasing returns.

A wide body of economic evidence, reviewed in the Department's full Regulatory Impact Analysis (available at *www.dol.gov/ebsa/pdf/conflictsofinterestria.pdf*), supports a finding that the impact of these conflicts of interest on investment outcomes is large and negative. The supporting evidence includes, among other things, statistical analyses of conflicted investment channels, experimental studies, government reports documenting abuse, and economic theory on the dangers posed by conflicts of interest and by the asymmetries of information and expertise that characterize interactions between ordinary retirement investors and conflicted advisers. A review of this data, which consistently points to a substantial failure of the market for retirement advice, suggests that IRA holders receiving conflicted investment advice can expect their investments to underperform by an average of 100 basis points per year over the next 20 years. The underperformance associated with conflicts of interest—in the mutual funds segment alone—could cost IRA investors more than $210 billion over the next 10 years and nearly $500 over the next 20 years. Some studies suggest that the underperformance of broker-sold mutual funds may be even higher than 100 basis points. If the true underperformance of broker-sold funds is 200 basis points, IRA mutual fund holders could suffer from underperformance amounting to $430 billion over 10 years and nearly $1 trillion across the next 20 years. While the estimates based on the mutual fund market are large, the total market impact could be much larger. Insurance products, Exchange Traded Funds (ETFs), individual stocks and bonds, and other products are all sold by brokers with conflicts of interest.

Disclosure alone has proven ineffective to mitigate conflicts in advice. Extensive research has demonstrated that most investors have little understanding of their advisers' conflicts, and little awareness of what they are paying via indirect channels for the conflicted advice. Even if they understand the scope of the advisers' conflicts, most consumers generally cannot distinguish good advice, or even good investment results, from bad. The same gap in expertise that makes investment advice necessary frequently also prevents investors from recognizing bad advice or understanding advisers' disclosures. Recent research suggests that even if disclosure about conflicts could be made simple and clear, it would be ineffective—or even harmful.[35]

Excessive fees and substandard investment performance in DC plans or IRAs, which can result when advisers' conflicts bias their advice, erode benefit security. This proposal aims to ensure that advice is impartial, thereby rooting out excessive fees and substandard performance otherwise attributable to advisers' conflicts, producing gains for retirement investors. Delivering these gains would entail compliance costs—namely, the cost incurred by new fiduciary advisers to avoid the prohibited transaction rules and/or satisfy relevant PTE conditions. The Department expects investor gains would be very large relative to compliance costs, and therefore believes this proposal is economically justified and sound.

Because of limitations of the literature and other evidence, only some of these gains can be quantified with confidence. Focusing only on how load shares paid to brokers affect the size of loads IRA investors holding front-end load funds pay and the returns they achieve, we estimate the proposal would deliver to IRA investors gains of between $40 billion and $44 billion over 10 years and between $88 and $100 billion over 20 years. These estimates assume that the rule will eliminate (rather than just reduce) underperformance associated with the practice of incentivizing broker recommendations through variable front-end-load sharing; if the rule's effectiveness in this area is substantially below 100 percent, these estimates may overstate these particular gains to investors in the front-load mutual fund segment of the IRA market. The Department nonetheless believes that these gains alone would far exceed the proposal's compliance cost which are estimated to be between $2.4 billion and $5.7 billion over 10 years, mostly reflecting

---

[34] DOL Advisory Opinion 2005-23A (Dec. 7, 2005).

[35] See Loewenstein *et al.*, (2011) for a summary of some relevant literature.

the cost incurred by new fiduciary advisers to satisfy relevant PTE conditions (these costs are also front-loaded and will be less in subsequent years). For example, if only 75 percent of the potential gains were realized in the subset of the market that was analyzed (the front-load mutual fund segment of the IRA market), the gains would amount to between $30 billion and $33 billion over 10 years. If only 50 percent were realized, the expected gains in this subset of the market would total between $20 billion and $22 billion over 10 years, still several times the proposal's estimated compliance cost

These estimates account for only a fraction of potential conflicts, associated losses, and affected retirement assets. The total gains to IRA investors attributable to the rule may be much higher than these quantified gains alone. The Department expects the proposal to yield large, additional gains for IRA investors, including improvements in the performance of IRA investments other than front-load mutual funds and potential reductions in excessive trading and associated transaction costs and timing errors (such as might be associated with return chasing). As noted above, under current rules, adviser conflicts could cost IRA investors as much as $410 billion over 10 years and $1 trillion over 20 years, so the potential additional gains to IRA investors from this proposal could be very large.

Just as with IRAs, there is evidence that conflicts of interest in the investment advice market also erode plan assets. For example, the U.S. Government Accountability Office (GAO) found that defined benefit pension plans using consultants with undisclosed conflicts of interest earned 1.3 percentage points per year less than other plans.[36] Other GAO reports point out how adviser conflicts may cause plan participants to roll plan assets into IRAs that charge high fees or 401(k) plan officials to include expensive or underperforming funds in investment menus.[37] A number of academic studies find that 401(k) plan investment options underperform the market,[38] and at least one study attributes such underperformance to excessive reliance on funds that are proprietary to plan service providers who may be providing investment advice to plan officials that choose the investment options.[39]

The Department expects the current proposal's positive effects to extend well beyond improved investment results for retirement investors. The IRA and plan markets for fiduciary advice and other services may become more efficient as a result of more transparent pricing and greater certainty about the fiduciary status of advisers and about the impartiality of their advice. There may be benefits from the increased flexibility that the current proposal's PTEs would provide with respect to fiduciary investment advice currently falling within the ambit of the 1975 rule. The current proposal's defined boundaries between fiduciary advice, education, and sales activity directed at large plans, may bring greater clarity to the IRA and plan services markets. Innovation in new advice business models, including technology-driven models, may be accelerated, and nudged away from conflicts and toward transparency, thereby promoting healthy competition in the fiduciary advice market.

A major expected positive effect of the current proposal in the plan advice market is improved compliance and associated improved security of plan assets and benefits. Clarity about advisers' fiduciary status would strengthen EBSA's enforcement activities resulting in fuller and faster correction, and stronger deterrence, of ERISA violations.

In conclusion, the Department believes that the current proposal would mitigate adviser conflicts and thereby improve plan and IRA investment results, while avoiding greater than necessary disruption of existing business practices and would deliver large gains to retirement investors and a variety of other economic benefits, which would more than justify its costs.

K. Initial Regulatory Flexibility Analysis

The Regulatory Flexibility Act (5 U.S.C. 601 *et seq.*) (RFA) imposes certain requirements with respect to Federal rules that are subject to the notice and comment requirements of section 553(b) of the Administrative Procedure Act (5 U.S.C. 551 *et seq.*) and which are likely to have a significant economic impact on a substantial number of small entities. Unless an agency determines that a proposal is not likely to have a significant economic impact on a substantial number of small entities, section 603 of the RFA requires the agency to present an initial regulatory flexibility analysis (IRFA) of the proposed rule. The Department's IRFA of the proposed rule is provided below.

The Department believes that amending the current regulation by broadening the scope of service providers, regardless of size, that would be considered fiduciaries would enhance the Department's ability to redress service provider abuses that currently exist in the plan

service provider market, such as undisclosed fees, misrepresentation of compensation arrangements, and biased appraisals of the value of plan investments.

The Department's complete Initial Regulatory Flexibility Analysis is available at *www.dol.gov/ebsa/pdf/conflictsofinterestria.pdf*. It is summarized below.

The Department believes that the proposal would provide benefits to small plans and their related small employers and IRA holders, and impose costs on small service providers providing investment advice to ERISA plans, ERISA plan participants and IRA holders. Small service providers affected by this rule are defined to include broker-dealers, registered investment advisers, consultants, appraisers, and others providing investment advice to small ERISA plans and IRA that have less than $38.5 million in revenue.

The Department anticipates that broker-dealers would experience the largest impact from the proposed rule and associated proposed exemptions. Registered investment advisers and other ERISA plan service providers would experience less of a burden from the rule. The Department assumes that firms would utilize whichever PTEs would be most cost effective for their business models. Regardless of which PTEs they use, small affected entities would incur costs associated with developing and implementing new compliance policies and procedures to minimize conflicts of interest; creating and distributing new disclosures; maintaining additional compliance records; familiarizing and training staff on new requirements; and obtaining additional liability insurance.

As discussed previously, the Department estimated the costs of implementing new compliance policies and procedures, training staff, and creating disclosures for small broker-dealers. The Department estimates that small broker-dealers could expend on average approximately $53,000 in the first year and $21,000 in subsequent years; small registered investment advisers would spend approximately $5,300 in the first year and $500 in subsequent years; and small service providers would spend approximately $5,300 in the first year and $500 in subsequent years. The estimated cost for small broker-dealers is believed to be an overestimate, especially for the smallest firms as they are believed to have on average simpler arrangements and they may have relationships with larger firms that help with compliance, thus lowering their costs. Additionally, broker-dealers and service providers would incur an expense of about $300 in additional liability insurance premiums for each representative or other individual who would now be considered a fiduciary. Of this expense, $150 is estimated to be paid to the insuring firms and the other $150 is estimated to be paid out as compensation to those harmed, which is counted as a transfer. Any disclosures produced by affected entities would cost, on average, about $1.53 in the first year and about $1.15 in subsequent years. These per-representative and per-disclosure costs are not expected to disproportionately affect small entities.

Although the PTEs allow firms to maintain their existing business models, some small affected entities may determine that it is more cost effective to shift business models. In this scenario, some BDs might incur the costs of switching to becoming RIAs, including training, testing, and licensing costs, at a cost of approximately $5,600 per representative.

Some small service providers may find that the increased costs associated with ERISA fiduciary status outweigh the benefit of continuing to service the ERISA plan market or the IRA market. The Department does not believe that this outcome would be widespread or that it would result in a diminution of the amount or quality of advice available to small or other retirement savers. It is also possible that the economic impact of the rule on small entities would not be as significant as it would be for large entities, because anecdotal evidence indicates that some small entities do not have as many business arrangements that give rise to conflicts of interest. Therefore, they would not be confronted with the same costs to restructure transactions that would be faced by large entities.

L. Paperwork Reduction Act

As part of its continuing effort to reduce paperwork and respondent burden, the Department of Labor conducts a preclearance consultation program to provide the general public and Federal agencies with an opportunity to comment on proposed and continuing collections of information in accordance with the Paperwork Reduction Act of 1995 (PRA) (44 U.S.C. 3506(c)(2)(A)). This helps to ensure that the public understands the Department's collection instructions; respondents can

---

[36] GAO Report, Publication No. GAO-09-503T, 2009.

[37] GAO Report, Publication No. GAO-11-119, 2011.

[38] See *e.g.* Elton *et al.* (2013).

[39] See Pool *et al.* (2014).

provide the requested data in the desired format; reporting burden (time and financial resources) is minimized; collection instruments are clearly understood; and the Department can properly assess the impact of collection requirements on respondents.

Currently, the Department is soliciting comments concerning the proposed information collection requests (ICRs) included in the "carve-outs" section of its proposal to amend its 1975 rule that defines when a person who provides investment advice to an employee benefit plan becomes an ERISA fiduciary. A copy of the ICRs may be obtained by contacting the PRA addressee shown below or at *http://www.RegInfo.gov*.

The Department has submitted a copy of the Conflict of Interest Proposed Rule Carveout Disclosure Requirements to the Office of Management and Budget (OMB) in accordance with 44 U.S.C. 3507(d) for review of its information collections. The Department and OMB are particularly interested in comments that:

• Evaluate whether the collection of information is necessary for the proper performance of the functions of the agency, including whether the information would have practical utility;

• Evaluate the accuracy of the agency's estimate of the burden of the collection of information, including the validity of the methodology and assumptions used;

• Enhance the quality, utility, and clarity of the information to be collected; and

• Minimize the burden of the collection of information on those who are to respond, including through the use of appropriate automated, electronic, mechanical, or other technological collection techniques or other forms of information technology, *e.g.*, permitting electronic submission of responses.

Comments should be sent to the Office of Information and Regulatory Affairs, Office of Management and Budget, Room 10235, New Executive Office Building, Washington, DC 20503; Attention: Desk Officer for the Employee Benefits Security Administration. OMB requests that comments be received within 30 days of publication of the Proposed Investment Advice Initiative to ensure their consideration.

PRA Addressee: Address requests for copies of the ICR to G. Christopher Cosby, Office of Policy and Research, U.S. Department of Labor, Employee Benefits Security Administration, 200 Constitution Avenue NW., Room N-5718, Washington, DC 20210. Telephone (202) 693-8410; Fax: (202) 219-5333. These are not toll-free numbers. ICRs submitted to OMB also are available at *http://www.RegInfo.gov*.

As discussed in detail above, Paragraph (b)(1)(i) of the proposed regulation provides a carve-out to the general definition for advice provided in connection with an arm's length sale, purchase, loan, or bilateral contract between a sophisticated plan investor, which has 100 or more plan participants, and the adviser ("seller's carve-out"). It also applies in connection with an offer to enter into such a transaction or when the person providing the advice is acting as an agent or appraiser for the plan's counterparty. In order to rely on this carve-out, the person must provide advice to a plan fiduciary who is independent of such person and who exercises authority or control respecting the management or disposition of the plan's assets, with respect to an arm's length sale, purchase, loan or bilateral contract between the plan and the counterparty, or with respect to a proposal to enter into such a sale, purchase, loan or bilateral contract.

The seller's carve-out applies if certain conditions are met. Among these conditions are the following: The adviser must obtain a written representation from the plan fiduciary that (1) the plan fiduciary is a fiduciary who exercises authority or control respecting the management or disposition of the employee benefit plan's assets (as described in section 3(21)(A)(i) of the Act), (2) that the employee benefit plan has 100 or more participants covered under the plan, and that (3) the fiduciary will not rely on the person to act in the best interests of the plan, to provide impartial investment advice, or to give advice in a fiduciary capacity.

Paragraph (b)(3) of the proposed regulation provides a carve-out making clear that persons who merely market and make available, securities or other property through a platform or similar mechanism

to an employee benefit plan without regard to the individualized needs of the plan, its participants, or beneficiaries do not act as investment advice fiduciaries. This carve-out applies if the person discloses in writing to the plan fiduciary that the person is not undertaking to provide impartial investment advice or to give advice in a fiduciary capacity.

Paragraph (b)(6) of the proposal makes clear that furnishing and providing certain specified investment educational information and materials (including certain investment allocation models and interactive plan materials) to a plan, plan fiduciary, participant, beneficiary or IRA owner would not constitute the rendering of investment advice if certain conditions are met. One of the conditions is that the asset allocation models or interactive materials must explain all material facts and assumptions on which the models and materials are based and include a statement indicating that, in applying particular asset allocation models to their individual situations, participants, beneficiaries, or IRA owners should consider their other assets, income, and investments in addition to their interests in the plan or IRA to the extent they are not taken into account in the model or estimate.

The seller's carve-out written representation, platform provider carve-out disclosure, and the education carve-out disclosures for asset allocation models and interactive investment materials are information collection requests (ICRs) subject to the Paperwork Reduction Act. The Department has made the following assumptions in order to establish a reasonable estimate of the paperwork burden associated with these ICRs:

• Approximately 43,000 plans would utilize the seller's carve-out;

• Approximately 1,800 service providers would utilize the platform provider carve-out;

• Approximately 2,800 financial institutions would utilize the education carve-out;

• Plans and advisers using the seller's carve-out are entities with financial expertise and would distribute substantially all of the disclosures electronically via means already used in their normal course of business and the costs arising from electronic distribution would be negligible;

• Service providers using the platform provider carve-out already maintain contracts with their customers as a regular and customary business practice and the materials costs arising from inserting the platform provider carve-out into the existing contracts would be negligible;

• Materials costs arising from inserting the required education carve-out disclosure into existing models and interactive materials would be negligible;

• Advisers would use existing in-house resources to prepare the disclosures; and

• The tasks associated with the ICRs would be performed by clerical personnel at an hourly rate of $30.42 and legal professionals at an hourly rate of $129.94.[40]

The Department estimates that each plan would require one hour of legal professional time and 30 minutes of clerical time to produce the seller's carve-out representation. Therefore, the seller's carve-out representation would result in approximately 43,000 hours of legal time at an equivalent cost of approximately $5.6 million. It would also result in approximately 21,000 hours of clerical time at an equivalent cost of approximately $653,000. In total, the burden associated with the seller's carve-out representation is approximately 64,000 hours at an equivalent cost of $6.2 million.

The Department estimates that each service provider using the platform provider carve-out would require ten minutes of legal professional time to draft the needed disclosure. Therefore, the platform provider carve-out disclosure would result in approximately 300 hours of legal time at an equivalent cost of approximately $39,000.

The Department estimates that each financial institution using the education carve-out would require twenty minutes of legal professional time to draft the disclosure. Therefore, this carve-out disclosure would result in approximately 900 hours of legal time at an equivalent cost of approximately $121,000.

---

[40] The Department's estimated 2015 hourly labor rates include wages, other benefits, and overhead are calculated as follows: Mean wage from the 2013 National Occupational Employment Survey (April 2014, Bureau of Labor Statistics *http://www.bls.gov/news.release/pdf/ocwage.pdf*); wages as a percent of total compensation from the Employer Cost for Employee Compensation (June 2014, Bureau of Labor Statistics *http://www.bls.gov/news.release/ecec.t02.htm*); overhead as a multiple of compensation is as-

sumed to be 25 percent of total compensation for paraprofessionals, 20 percent of compensation for clerical, and 35 percent of compensation for professional; annual inflation assumed to be 2.3 percent annual growth of total labor cost since 2013 (Employment Costs Index data for private industry, September 2014 *http://www.bls.gov/news.release/eci.nr0.htm*).

In total, the hour burden for the representation and disclosures required by the carve-outs is approximately 66,000 hours at an equivalent cost of $6.4 million.

Because the Department assumes that all disclosures would be distributed electronically or require small amounts of space to include in existing materials, the Department has not associated any cost burden with these ICRs.

These paperwork burden estimates are summarized as follows:

Type of Review: New collection (Request for new OMB Control Number).

Agency: Employee Benefits Security Administration, Department of Labor.

Title: Conflict of Interest Proposed Rule Carveout Disclosure Requirements.

OMB Control Number: 1210—NEW. *Affected Public:* Business or other for-profit.

Estimated Number of Respondents: 47,532.

Estimated Number of Annual Responses: 47,532.

Frequency of Response: When engaging in excepted transaction.

Estimated Total Annual Burden Hours: 65,631 hours.

Estimated Total Annual Burden Cost: $0.

M. Congressional Review Act

The proposed rule is subject to the Congressional Review Act provisions of the Small Business Regulatory Enforcement Fairness Act of 1996 (5 U.S.C. 801 *et seq.*) and, if finalized, would be transmitted to Congress and the Comptroller General for review. The proposed rule is a "major rule" as that term is defined in 5 U.S.C. 804, because it is likely to result in an annual effect on the economy of $100 million or more.

N. Unfunded Mandates Reform Act

Title II of the Unfunded Mandates Reform Act of 1995 (Pub. L. 104-4) requires each Federal agency to prepare a written statement assessing the effects of any Federal mandate in a proposed or final agency rule that may result in an expenditure of $100 million or more (adjusted annually for inflation with the base year 1995) in any one year by State, local, and tribal governments, in the aggregate, or by the private sector. Such a mandate is deemed to be a "significant regulatory action." The current proposal is expected to have such an impact on the private sector, and the Department therefore hereby provides such an assessment.

The Department is issuing the current proposal under ERISA section 3(21)(A)(ii) (29 U.S.C. 1002(21)(a)(ii)).[41] The Department is charged with interpreting the ERISA and Code provisions that attach fiduciary status to anyone who is paid to provide investment advice to plan or IRA investors. The current proposal would update and supersede the 1975 rule[42] that currently interprets these statutory provisions.

The Department assessed the anticipated benefits and costs of the current proposal pursuant to Executive Order 12866 in the Regulatory Impact Analysis for the current proposal and concluded that its benefits would justify its costs. The Department's complete Regulatory Impact Analysis is available at *www.dol.gov/ebsa/pdf/conflictsofinterestria.pdf*. To summarize, the current proposals' material benefits and costs generally would be confined to the private sector, where plans and IRA investors would, in the Department's estimation, benefit on net, partly at the expense of their fiduciary advisers and upstream financial service and product producers. The Department itself would benefit from increased efficiency in its enforcement activity. The public and overall US economy would benefit from increased compliance with ERISA and the Code and confidence in advisers, as well as from more efficient allocation of investment capital, and gains to investors.

The current proposal is not expected to have any material economic impacts on State, local or tribal governments, or on health, safety, or the natural environment. The North American Securities Administrators Association commented in support of the Department's 2010 proposal.[43]

O. Federalism Statement

Executive Order 13132 (August 4, 1999) outlines fundamental principles of federalism, and requires the adherence to specific criteria by Federal agencies in the process of their formulation and implementation of policies that have substantial direct effects on the States, the relationship between the national government and States, or on the distribution of power and responsibilities among the various levels of government. This proposed rule does not have federalism implications because it has no substantial direct effect on the States, on the relationship between the national government and the States, or on the distribution of power and responsibilities among the various levels of government. Section 514 of ERISA provides, with certain exceptions specifically enumerated, that the provisions of Titles I and IV of ERISA supersede any and all laws of the States as they relate to any employee benefit plan covered under ERISA. The requirements implemented in the proposed rule do not alter the fundamental reporting and disclosure requirements of the statute with respect to employee benefit plans, and as such have no implications for the States or the relationship or distribution of power between the national government and the States.

Statutory Authority

This regulation is proposed pursuant to the authority in section 505 of ERISA (Pub. L. 93-406, 88 Stat. 894; 29 U.S.C. 1135) and section 102 of Plan No. 4 of 1978 (43 FR 47713, October 17, 1978), effective December 31, 1978 (44 FR 1065, January 3, 1979), 3 CFR 1978 Comp. 332, and under Secretary of Labor's Order No. 1-2011, 77 FR 1088 (Jan. 9, 2012).

Withdrawal of Proposed Regulation

Paragraph (c) of the proposed regulation relating to the definition of fiduciary (proposed 29 CFR 2510.3(21)) that was published in the **Federal Register** on October 20, 2010 (75 FR 65263) is hereby withdrawn.

List of Subjects in 29 CFR Parts 2509 and 2510

Employee benefit plans, Employee Retirement Income Security Act, Pensions, Plan assets.

For the reasons set forth in the preamble, the Department is proposing to amend parts 2509 and 2510 of subchapters A and B of Chapter XXV of Title 29 of the Code of Federal Regulations as follows:

SUBCHAPTER A—GENERAL

PART 2509—INTERPRETIVE BULLETINS RELATING TO THE EMPLOYEE RETIREMENT INCOME SECURITY ACT OF 1974

■ 1. The authority citation for part 2509 continues to read as follows:

Authority: 29 U.S.C. 1135. Secretary of Labor's Order 1-2011, 77 FR 1088 (Jan. 9, 2012). Sections 2509.75-10 and 2509.75-2 issued under 29 U.S.C. 1052, 1053, 1054. Sec. 2509.75-5 also issued under 29 U.S.C. 1002. Sec. 2509.95-1 also issued under sec. 625, Pub. L. 109-280, 120 Stat. 780.

§2509.96-1 [Removed]

■ 2. Remove § 2509.96-1.

SUBCHAPTER B—DEFINITIONS AND COVERAGE UNDER THE EMPLOYEE RETIREMENT INCOME SECURITY ACT OF 1974

PART 2510—DEFINITIONS OF TERMS USED IN SUBCHAPTERS C, D, E, F, AND G OF THIS CHAPTER

■ 3. The authority citation for part 2510 is revised to read as follows:

Authority: 29 U.S.C. 1002(2), 1002(21), 1002(37), 1002(38), 1002(40), 1031, and 1135; Secretary of Labor's Order 1-2011, 77 FR 1088; Secs. 2510.3-21, 2510.3-101 and 2510.3-102 also issued under Sec. 102 of Reorganization Plan No. 4 of 1978, 5 U.S.C. App. 237. Section 2510.3-38 also issued under Pub. L. 105-72, Sec. 1(b), 111 Stat. 1457 (1997).

■ 4. Revise § 2510.3-21 to read as follows:

§2510.3-21 Definition of "Fiduciary."

(a) *Investment advice.* For purposes of section 3(21)(A)(ii) of the Employee Retirement Income Security Act of 1974 (Act) and section 4975(e)(3)(B) of the Internal Revenue Code (Code), except as provided in paragraph (b) of this section, a person renders investment advice

---

[41] Under section 102 of the Reorganization Plan No. 4 of 1978, the authority of the Secretary of the Treasury to interpret section 4975 of the Code has been transferred, with exceptions not relevant here, to the Secretary of Labor.

[42] 29 CFR 2510.3-21(c).

[43] Available at *http://www.dol.gov/ebsa/pdf/1210-AB32-PH007.pdf*.

with respect to moneys or other property of a plan or IRA described in paragraph (f)(2) of this section if—

(1) Such person provides, directly to a plan, plan fiduciary, plan participant or beneficiary, IRA, or IRA owner the following types of advice in exchange for a fee or other compensation, whether direct or indirect:

(i) A recommendation as to the advisability of acquiring, holding, disposing or exchanging securities or other property, including a recommendation to take a distribution of benefits or a recommendation as to the investment of securities or other property to be rolled over or otherwise distributed from the plan or IRA;

(ii) A recommendation as to the management of securities or other property, including recommendations as to the management of securities or other property to be rolled over or otherwise distributed from the plan or IRA;

(iii) An appraisal, fairness opinion, or similar statement whether verbal or written concerning the value of securities or other property if provided in connection with a specific transaction or transactions involving the acquisition, disposition, or exchange, of such securities or other property by the plan or IRA;

(iv) A recommendation of a person who is also going to receive a fee or other compensation for providing any of the types of advice described in paragraphs (i) through (iii); and

(2) Such person, either directly or indirectly (*e.g.*, through or together with any affiliate),—

(i) Represents or acknowledges that it is acting as a fiduciary within the meaning of the Act with respect to the advice described in paragraph (a)(1) of this section; or

(ii) Renders the advice pursuant to a written or verbal agreement, arrangement or understanding that the advice is individualized to, or that such advice is specifically directed to, the advice recipient for consideration in making investment or management decisions with respect to securities or other property of the plan or IRA.

(b) *Carve-outs—investment advice.* Except for persons described in paragraph (a)(2)(i) of this section, the rendering of advice or other communications in conformance with a carve-out set forth in paragraph (b)(1) through (6) of this section shall not cause the person who renders the advice to be treated as a fiduciary under paragraph (a) of this section.

(1) *Counterparties to the plan*—(i) *Counterparty transaction with plan fiduciary with financial expertise.* (A) In such person's capacity as a counterparty (or representative of a counterparty) to an employee benefit plan (as described in section 3(3) of the Act), the person provides advice to a plan fiduciary who is independent of such person and who exercises authority or control with respect to the management or disposition of the plan's assets, with respect to an arm's length sale, purchase, loan or bilateral contract between the plan and the counterparty, or with respect to a proposal to enter into such a sale, purchase, loan or bilateral contract, if, prior to providing any recommendation with respect to the transaction, such person satisfies the requirements of either paragraph (b)(1)(i)(B) or (C) of this section.

(B) Such person—

(*1*) Obtains a written representation from the independent plan fiduciary that the independent fiduciary exercises authority or control with respect to the management or disposition of the employee benefit plan's assets (as described in section 3(21)(A)(i) of the Act), that the employee benefit plan has 100 or more participants covered under the plan, and that the independent fiduciary will not rely on the person to act in the best interests of the plan, to provide impartial investment advice, or to give advice in a fiduciary capacity;

(*2*) Fairly informs the independent plan fiduciary of the existence and nature of the person's financial interests in the transaction;

(*3*) Does not receive a fee or other compensation directly from the plan, or plan fiduciary, for the provision of investment advice (as opposed to other services) in connection with the transaction; and

(*4*) Knows or reasonably believes that the independent plan fiduciary has sufficient expertise to evaluate the transaction and to determine whether the transaction is prudent and in the best interest of the plan participants (the person may rely on written representations from the plan or the plan fiduciary to satisfy this subsection (b)(1)(i)(B)(*4*)).

(C) Such person—

(*1*) Knows or reasonably believes that the independent plan fiduciary has responsibility for managing at least $100 million in employee benefit plan assets (for purposes of this paragraph (b)(1)(i)(C), when

dealing with an individual employee benefit plan, a person may rely on the information on the most recent Form 5500 Annual Return/Report filed for the plan to determine the value and, in the case of an independent fiduciary acting as an asset manager for multiple employee benefit plans, a person may rely on representations from the independent plan fiduciary regarding the value of employee benefit plan assets under management);

(*2*) Fairly informs the independent plan fiduciary that the person is not undertaking to provide impartial investment advice, or to give advice in a fiduciary capacity; and

(*3*) Does not receive a fee or other compensation directly from the plan, or plan fiduciary, for the provision of investment advice (as opposed to other services) in connection with the transaction.

(ii) *Swap and security-based swap transactions.* The person is a counterparty to an employee benefit plan (as described in section 3(3) of the Act) in connection with a swap or security-based swap, as defined in section 1(a) of the Commodity Exchange Act (7 U.S.C. 1(a) and section 3(a) of the Securities Exchange Act (15 U.S.C. 78c(a)), if—

(A) The plan is represented by a fiduciary independent of the person;

(B) The person is a swap dealer, security-based swap dealer, major swap participant, or major security-based swap participant;

(C) The person (if a swap dealer or security-based swap dealer), is not acting as an advisor to the plan (within the meaning of section 4s(h) of the Commodity Exchange Act or section 15F(h) of the Securities Exchange Act of 1934) in connection with the transaction; and

(D) In advance of providing any recommendations with respect to the transaction, the person obtains a written representation from the independent plan fiduciary, that the fiduciary will not rely on recommendations provided by the person.

(2) *Employees.* In his or her capacity as an employee of any employer or employee organization sponsoring the employee benefit plan (as described in section 3(3) of the Act), the person provides the advice to a plan fiduciary, and he or she receives no fee or other compensation, direct or indirect, in connection with the advice beyond the employee's normal compensation for work performed for the employer or employee organization.

(3) *Platform providers.* The person merely markets and makes available to an employee benefit plan (as described in section 3(3) of the Act), without regard to the individualized needs of the plan, its participants, or beneficiaries, securities or other property through a platform or similar mechanism from which a plan fiduciary may select or monitor investment alternatives, including qualified default investment alternatives, into which plan participants or beneficiaries may direct the investment of assets held in, or contributed to, their individual accounts, if the person discloses in writing to the plan fiduciary that the person is not undertaking to provide impartial investment advice or to give advice in a fiduciary capacity.

(4) *Selection and monitoring assistance.* In connection with the activities described in paragraph (b)(3) of this section with respect to an employee benefit plan (as described in section 3(3) of the Act), the person—

(i) Merely identifies investment alternatives that meet objective criteria specified by the plan fiduciary (*e.g.*, stated parameters concerning expense ratios, size of fund, type of asset, credit quality); or

(ii) Merely provides objective financial data and comparisons with independent benchmarks to the plan fiduciary.

(5) *Financial reports and valuations.* The person provides an appraisal, fairness opinion, or statement of value to—

(i) An employee stock ownership plan (as defined in section 407(d)(6) of the Act) regarding employer securities (as defined section 407(d)(5) of the Act);

(ii) An investment fund, such as a collective investment fund or pooled separate account, in which more than one unaffiliated plan has an investment, or which holds plan assets of more than one unaffiliated plan under 29 CFR 2510.3-101; or

(iii) A plan, a plan fiduciary, a plan participant or beneficiary, an IRA or IRA owner solely for purposes of compliance with the reporting and disclosure provisions under the Act, the Code, and the regulations, forms and schedules issued thereunder, or any applicable reporting or disclosure requirement under a Federal or state law, rule or regulation or self-regulatory organization rule or regulation.

(6) *Investment education.* The person furnishes or makes available any of the following categories of investment-related information and materials described in paragraphs (b)(6)(i) through

(iv) of this section to a plan, plan fiduciary, participant or beneficiary, IRA or IRA owner irrespective of who provides or makes available the information and materials (*e.g.*, plan sponsor, fiduciary or service provider), the frequency with which the information and materials are provided, the form in which the information and materials are provided (*e.g.*, on an individual or group basis, in writing or orally, or via call center, video or computer software), or whether an identified category of information and materials is furnished or made available alone or in combination with other categories of information and materials identified in paragraphs (b)(6)(i) through (iv), provided that the information and materials do not include (standing alone or in combination with other materials) recommendations with respect to specific investment products or specific plan or IRA alternatives, or recommendations on investment, management, or value of a particular security or securities, or other property.

(i) *Plan information.* Information and materials that, without reference to the appropriateness of any individual investment alternative or any individual benefit distribution option for the plan or IRA, or a particular participant or beneficiary or IRA owner, describe the terms or operation of the plan or IRA, inform a plan fiduciary, participant, beneficiary, or IRA owner about the benefits of plan or IRA participation, the benefits of increasing plan or IRA contributions, the impact of preretirement withdrawals on retirement income, retirement income needs, varying forms of distributions, including rollovers, annuitization and other forms of lifetime income payment options (*e.g.*, immediate annuity, deferred annuity, or incremental purchase of deferred annuity), advantages, disadvantages and risks of different forms of distributions, or describe investment objectives and philosophies, risk and return characteristics, historical return information or related prospectuses of investment alternatives under the plan or IRA.

(ii) *General financial, investment and retirement information.* Information and materials on financial, investment and retirement matters that do not address specific investment products, specific plan or IRA alternatives or distribution options available to the plan or IRA or to participants, beneficiaries and IRA owners, or specific alternatives or services offered outside the plan or IRA, and inform the plan fiduciary, participant or beneficiary, or IRA owner about—

(A) General financial and investment concepts, such as risk and return, diversification, dollar cost averaging, compounded return, and tax deferred investment;

(B) Historic differences in rates of return between different asset classes (*e.g.*, equities, bonds, or cash) based on standard market indices;

(C) Effects of inflation;

(D) Estimating future retirement income needs;

(E) Determining investment time horizons;

(F) Assessing risk tolerance;

(G) Retirement-related risks (*e.g.*, longevity risks, market/interest rates, inflation, health care and other expenses); and

(H) General methods and strategies for managing assets in retirement (*e.g.*, systematic withdrawal payments, annuitization, guaranteed minimum withdrawal benefits), including those offered outside the plan or IRA.

(iii) *Asset allocation models.* Information and materials (*e.g.*, pie charts, graphs, or case studies) that provide a plan fiduciary, participant or beneficiary, or IRA owner with models of asset allocation portfolios of hypothetical individuals with different time horizons (which may extend beyond an individual's retirement date) and risk profiles, where—

(A) Such models are based on generally accepted investments theories that take into account the historic returns of different asset classes (*e.g.*, equities, bonds, or cash) over defined periods of time;

(B) All material facts and assumptions on which such models are based (*e.g.*, retirement ages, life expectancies, income levels, financial resources, replacement income ratios, inflation rates, and rates of return) accompany the models;

(C) Such models do not include or identify any specific investment product or specific alternative available under the plan or IRA; and

(D) The asset allocation models are accompanied by a statement indicating that, in applying particular asset allocation models to their individual situations, participants, beneficiaries, or IRA owners should consider their other assets, income, and investments (*e.g.*, equity in a home, Social Security benefits, individual retirement plan investments, savings accounts and interests in other qualified and non-qualified

plans) in addition to their interests in the plan or IRA, to the extent those items are not taken into account in the model or estimate.

(iv) *Interactive investment materials.* Questionnaires, worksheets, software, and similar materials which provide a plan fiduciary, participant or beneficiary, or IRA owners the means to estimate future retirement income needs and assess the impact of different asset allocations on retirement income; questionnaires, worksheets, software and similar materials which allow a plan fiduciary, participant or beneficiary, or IRA owners to evaluate distribution options, products or vehicles by providing information under paragraphs (b)(6)(i) and (ii) of this section; questionnaires, worksheets, software, and similar materials that provide a plan fiduciary, participant or beneficiary, or IRA owner the means to estimate a retirement income stream that could be generated by an actual or hypothetical account balance, where—

(A) Such materials are based on generally accepted investment theories that take into account the historic returns of different asset classes (*e.g.*, equities, bonds, or cash) over defined periods of time;

(B) There is an objective correlation between the asset allocations generated by the materials and the information and data supplied by the participant, beneficiary or IRA owner;

(C) There is an objective correlation between the income stream generated by the materials and the information and data supplied by the participant, beneficiary or IRA owner;

(D) All material facts and assumptions (*e.g.*, retirement ages, life expectancies, income levels, financial resources, replacement income ratios, inflation rates, rates of return and other features and rates specific to income annuities or systematic withdrawal plan) that may affect a participant's, beneficiary's or IRA owner's assessment of the different asset allocations or different income streams accompany the materials or are specified by the participant, beneficiary or IRA owner;

(E) The materials do not include or identify any specific investment alternative available or distribution option available under the plan or IRA, unless such alternative or option is specified by the participant, beneficiary or IRA owner; and

(F) The materials either take into account other assets, income and investments (*e.g.*, equity in a home, Social Security benefits, individual retirement account/annuity investments, savings accounts, and interests in other qualified and non-qualified plans) or are accompanied by a statement indicating that, in applying particular asset allocations to their individual situations, or in assessing the adequacy of an estimated income stream, participants, beneficiaries or IRA owners should consider their other assets, income, and investments in addition to their interests in the plan or IRA.

(v) The information and materials described in paragraphs (b)(6)(i) through (iv) of this section represent examples of the type of information and materials that may be furnished to participants, beneficiaries and IRA owners without such information and materials constituting investment advice. Determinations as to whether the provision of any information, materials or educational services not described herein constitutes the rendering of investment advice must be made by reference to the criteria set forth in paragraph (a) of this section.

(c) *Scope of fiduciary duty—investment advice.* A person who is a fiduciary with respect to an employee benefit plan or IRA by reason of rendering investment advice (as defined in paragraph (a) of this section) for a fee or other compensation, direct or indirect, with respect to any securities or other property of such plan, or having any authority or responsibility to do so, shall not be deemed to be a fiduciary regarding any assets of the plan or IRA with respect to which such person does not have any discretionary authority, discretionary control or discretionary responsibility, does not exercise any authority or control, does not render investment advice (as defined in paragraph (a)(1) of this section) for a fee or other compensation, and does not have any authority or responsibility to render such investment advice, provided that nothing in this paragraph shall be deemed to:

(1) Exempt such person from the provisions of section 405(a) of the Act concerning liability for fiduciary breaches by other fiduciaries with respect to any assets of the plan; or

(2) Exclude such person from the definition of the term "party in interest" (as set forth in section 3(14)(B) of the Act or "disqualified person" as set forth in section 4975(e)(2) of the Code) with respect to a plan.

(d) *Execution of securities transactions.* (1) A person who is a broker or dealer registered under the Securities Exchange Act of 1934, a reporting dealer who makes primary markets in securities of the United States Government or of an agency of the United States Government and reports daily to the Federal Reserve Bank of New York its positions with respect to such securities and borrowings thereon, or a bank supervised by the United States or a State, shall not be deemed to be a fiduciary, within the meaning of section 3(21)(A) of the Act or section 4975(e)(3)(B) of the Code, with respect to an employee benefit plan or IRA solely because such person executes transactions for the purchase or sale of securities on behalf of such plan in the ordinary course of its business as a broker, dealer, or bank, pursuant to instructions of a fiduciary with respect to such plan or IRA, if:

(i) Neither the fiduciary nor any affiliate of such fiduciary is such broker, dealer, or bank; and

(ii) The instructions specify:

(A) The security to be purchased or sold;

(B) A price range within which such security is to be purchased or sold, or, if such security is issued by an open-end investment company registered under the Investment Company Act of 1940 (15 U.S.C. 80a-1, *et seq.*), a price which is determined in accordance with Rule 22c1 under the Investment Company Act of 1940 (17 CFR270.22c1);

(C) A time span during which such security may be purchased or sold (not to exceed five business days); and

(D) The minimum or maximum quantity of such security which may be purchased or sold within such price range, or, in the case of a security issued by an open-end investment company registered under the Investment Company Act of 1940, the minimum or maximum quantity of such security which may be purchased or sold, or the value of such security in dollar amount which may be purchased or sold, at the price referred to in paragraph (d)(1)(ii)(B) of this section.

(2) A person who is a broker-dealer, reporting dealer, or bank which is a fiduciary with respect to an employee benefit plan or IRA solely by reason of the possession or exercise of discretionary authority or discretionary control in the management of the plan or IRA, or the management or disposition of plan or IRA assets in connection with the execution of a transaction or transactions for the purchase or sale of securities on behalf of such plan or IRA which fails to comply with the provisions of paragraph (d)(1) of this section, shall not be deemed to be a fiduciary regarding any assets of the plan or IRA with respect to which such broker-dealer, reporting dealer or bank does not have any discretionary authority, discretionary control or discretionary responsibility, does not exercise any authority or control, does not render investment advice (as defined in paragraph (a) of this section) for a fee or other compensation, and does not have any authority or responsibility to render such investment advice, provided that nothing in this paragraph shall be deemed to:

(i) Exempt such broker-dealer, reporting dealer, or bank from the provisions of section 405(a) of the Act concerning liability for fiduciary breaches by other fiduciaries with respect to any assets of the plan; or

(ii) Exclude such broker-dealer, reporting dealer, or bank from the definition of the term party in interest (as set forth in section 3(14)(B) of the Act) or disqualified person 4975(e)(2) of the Code with respect to any assets of the plan or IRA.

(e) *Internal Revenue Code.* Section 4975(e)(3) of the Code contains provisions parallel to section 3(21)(A) of the Act which define the term "fiduciary" for purposes of the prohibited transaction provisions in Code section 4975. Effective December 31, 1978, section 102 of the Reorganization Plan No. 4 of 1978, 5 U.S.C. App. 237 transferred the authority of the Secretary of the Treasury to promulgate regulations of the type published herein to the Secretary of Labor. All references herein to section 3(21)(A) of the Act should be read to include reference to the parallel provisions of section 4975(e)(3) of the Code. Furthermore, the provisions of this section shall apply for purposes of the application of Code section 4975 with respect to any plan described in Code section 4975(e)(1).

(f) *Definitions.* For purposes of this section—

(1) "Recommendation" means a communication that, based on its content, context, and presentation, would reasonably be viewed as a suggestion that the advice recipient engage in or refrain from taking a particular course of action.

(2)(i) "Plan" means any employee benefit plan described in section 3(3) of the Act and any plan described in section 4975(e)(1)(A) of the Code, and

(ii) "IRA" means any trust, account or annuity described in Code section 4975(e)(1)(B) through (F), including, for example, an individual retirement account described in section 408(a) of the Code and a health savings account described in section 223(d) of the Code.

(3) "Plan participant" means for a plan described in section 3(3) of the Act, a person described in section 3(7) of the Act.

(4) "IRA owner" means with respect to an IRA either the person who is the owner of the IRA or the person for whose benefit the IRA was established.

(5) "Plan fiduciary" means a person described in section (3)(21) of the Act and 4975(e)(3) of the Code.

(6) "Fee or other compensation, direct or indirect" for purposes of this section and section 3(21)(A)(ii) of the Act, means any fee or compensation for the advice received by the person (or by an affiliate) from any source and any fee or compensation incident to the transaction in which the investment advice has been rendered or will be rendered. The term fee or other compensation includes, for example, brokerage fees, mutual fund and insurance sales commissions.

(7) "Affiliate" includes: Any person directly or indirectly, through one or more intermediaries, controlling, controlled by, or under common control with such person; any officer, director, partner, employee or relative (as defined in section 3(15) of the Act) of such person; and any corporation or partnership of which such person is an officer, director or partner.

(8) "Control" for purposes of paragraph (f)(7) of this section means the power to exercise a controlling influence over the management or policies of a person other than an individual.

Signed at Washington, DC, this 14th day of April, 2015.

Phyllis C. Borzi,

Assistant Secretary, Employee Benefits Security Administration, Department of Labor.

[FR Doc. 2015-08831 Filed 4-15-15; 11:15 am]

BILLING CODE 4510-29-P

¶ 20,539

Pension Benefit Guaranty Corporation (PBGC): Proposed rule: Defined benefit plans: Plan underfunding: Annual financial and actuarial reporting: Waivers.—The PBGC is proposing to amend its regulations on annual financial and actuarial reporting under ERISA §4010 to codify provisions of the Moving Ahead for Progress in the 21st Century Act (P.L. 112-141; MAP-21) and the Highway and Transportation Funding Act of 2014 (HATFA; P.L. 113-159) and related guidance. In addition, the proposed regulations would modify the existing reporting waiver for companies with total underfunding of less than $15 million in all their plans and add two new reporting waivers in order to better balance the burden of reporting with the PBGC's need for information. Also, the proposed regulations make some technical changes. The proposed regulations would be applicable to information years beginning after December 31, 2015.

The proposed regulations, which were published in the Federal Register on July 27, 2015 (80 FR 44312), were reproduced below. The regulations were finalized on March 23, 2016 (81 FR 15432). The preamble to the final regulations is at ¶ 24,337. The final regulations are at ¶ 15,396A, ¶ 15,396C, ¶ 15,396G, and ¶ 15,396J.

¶ 20,539A

Employee Benefits Security Administration (EBSA): Proposed rule: Claims procedures: Disability benefits.—The EBSA has issued proposed regulations that amend claims procedures for employee benefit plans providing disability benefits to revise and strengthen the current rules by adopting new procedural protections and safeguards made applicable to group health plans by the Patient Protection and Affordable Care Act (PPACA, P.L. 111-148). EBSA proposes to better align the processing of claims and appeals for disability benefits with the claims procedure requirements regarding internal claims and appeals for group health plans under regulations implementing the PPACA.

The proposed regulations, which were published in the Federal Register on November 18, 2015 (80 FR 72014), are reproduced below. The regulations were finalized on December 19, 2016 (81 FR 92316). The preamble to the final regulations is at ¶ 24,344. The final regulations are at ¶ 14,931.

DEPARTMENT OF LABOR

Employee Benefits Security Administration

29 CFR Part 2560

RIN 1210-AB39

Claims Procedure for Plans Providing Disability Benefits

AGENCY: Employee Benefits Security Administration, Department of Labor.

ACTION: Notice of proposed rulemaking.

SUMMARY: This document contains proposed amendments to claims procedure regulations for plans providing disability benefits under the Employee Retirement Income Security Act of 1974 (ERISA). The amendments would revise and strengthen the current rules primarily by adopting certain of the new procedural protections and safeguards made applicable to group health plans by the Affordable Care Act. If adopted as final, the proposed regulation would affect plan administrators and participants and beneficiaries of plans providing disability benefits, and others who assist in the provision of these benefits, such as third-party benefits administrators and other service providers that provide benefits to participants and beneficiaries of these plans.

DATES: Written comments should be received by the Department of Labor on or before January 19, 2016.

ADDRESSES: You may submit written comments, identified by RIN 1210-AB39, by one of the following methods:

• *Federal eRulemaking Portal: http://www.regulations.gov.* Follow the instructions for submitting comments.

• *Email: e-ORI@dol.gov.* Include RIN 1210-AB39 in the subject line of the message.

• *Mail:* Office of Regulations and Interpretations, Employee Benefits Security Administration, Room N-5655, U.S. Department of Labor, 200 Constitution Avenue NW., Washington, DC 20210, Attention: Claims Procedure Regulation Amendment for Plans Providing Disability Benefits.

Instructions: All submissions received must include the agency name and Regulatory Identifier Number (RIN) for this rulemaking. All comments will be available to the public, without charge, online at *http://www.regulations.gov* and *http://www.dol.gov/ebsa*, and at the Public Disclosure Room, Employee Benefits Security Administration, Suite N-1513, 200 Constitution Avenue NW, Washington, DC 20210.

Warning: Do not include any personally identifiable or confidential business information that you do not want publicly disclosed. All comments are posted on the Internet exactly as received, and can be retrieved by most internet search engines. No deletions, modifications, or redactions will be made to the comments received, as they are public records.

FOR FURTHER INFORMATION CONTACT: Frances P. Steen, Office of Regulations and Interpretations, Employee Benefits Security Administration, (202) 693-8500. This is not a toll free number.

SUPPLEMENTARY INFORMATION:

A. Executive Summary

In accordance with Executive Order 13563, this section of the preamble contains an executive summary of the proposed rulemaking in order to promote public understanding and to ensure an open exchange of information and perspectives. Sections B through E of this preamble, below, contain a more detailed description of the regulatory provisions and need for the rulemaking, as well as its costs and benefits.

1. Purpose of Regulatory Action

The purpose of this action is to improve the current procedural protections for workers who become disabled and make claims for disability benefits from an employee benefit plan. ERISA requires that plans provide claimants with written notice of benefit denials and an opportunity for a full and fair review of the denial by an appropriate plan fiduciary. The current regulations governing the processing of

claims and appeals were published 15 years ago. Because of the volume and constancy of litigation in this area, and in light of advancements in claims processing technology, the Department recognizes a need to revisit, reexamine, and revise the current regulations in order to ensure that disability benefit claimants receive a fair review of denied claims as provided by law. To this end, the Department has determined to start by proposing to uplift the current standards applicable to the processing of claims and appeals for disability benefits so that they better align with the requirements regarding internal claims and appeals for group health plans under the regulations implementing the requirements of the Affordable Care Act.[1] Inasmuch as disability and lost earnings can be sources of severe hardship for many individuals, the Department thinks that disability benefit claimants deserve protections equally as stringent as those that Congress and the President have put into place for health care claimants under the Affordable Care Act.

2. Summary of Major Provisions

The major provisions in the proposal largely adopt the procedural protections for health care claimants in the Affordable Care Act, including provisions that seek to ensure that: (1) Claims and appeals are adjudicated in manner designed to ensure independence and impartiality of the persons involved in making the decision; (2) benefit denial notices contain a full discussion of why the plan denied the claim and the standards behind the decision; (3) claimants have access to their entire claim file and are allowed to present evidence and testimony during the review process; (4) claimants are notified of and have an opportunity to respond to any new evidence reasonably in advance of an appeal decision; (5) final denials at the appeals stage are not based on new or additional rationales unless claimants first are given notice and a fair opportunity to respond; (6) if plans do not adhere to all claims processing rules, the claimant is deemed to have exhausted the administrative remedies available under the plan, unless the violation was the result of a minor error and other specified conditions are met; (7) certain rescissions of coverage are treated as adverse benefit determinations, thereby triggering the plan's appeals procedures; and (8) notices are written in a culturally and linguistically appropriate manner.

3. Costs and Benefits

The Department expects that these proposed regulations would improve the procedural protections for workers who become disabled and make claims for disability benefits from employee benefit plans. This would cause some participants to receive benefits they might otherwise have been incorrectly denied absent the fuller protections provided by the proposed regulations. In other circumstances, expenditures by plans may be reduced as a fuller and fairer system of disability claims and appeals processing helps facilitate participant acceptance of cost management efforts. Greater certainty and consistency in the handling of disability benefit claims and appeals and improved access to information about the manner in which claims and appeals are adjudicated may lead to efficiency gains in the system, both in terms of the allocation of spending at a macro-economic level as well as operational efficiencies among individual plans.

The Department expects the proposed regulations would impose modest costs on disability benefit plans, because many plans already are familiar with the rules that would apply to disability benefit claims due to their current application to group health plans. As discussed in detail in the cost section below, the Department quantified the costs associated with two provisions of the proposed regulations: the requirement to provide additional information to claimants in the appeals process ($1.9 million annually) and the requirement to provide information in a culturally and linguistically appropriate manner ($1.1 million annually).

B. Background

1. Section 503 of ERISA and the Section 503 Regulations

Section 503 of ERISA requires every employee benefit plan, in accordance with regulations of the Department, to "provide adequate notice in writing to any participant or beneficiary whose claim for benefits under the plan has been denied, setting forth the specific reasons for such denial, written in a manner calculated to be understood by the participant" and to "afford a reasonable opportunity to any participant

---

[1] The Patient Protection and Affordable Care Act, Public Law 111-148, was enacted on March 23, 2010, and the Health Care and Education Reconciliation Act, Public Law 111-152, was enacted on March 30, 2010. (These statutes are collectively known as the "Affordable Care Act.")

whose claim for benefits has been denied for a full and fair review by the appropriate named fiduciary of the decision denying the claim."

In 1977, the Department published a regulation pursuant to section 503, at 29 CFR 2560.503-1, establishing minimum requirements for benefit claims procedures for employee benefit plans covered by title I of ERISA (hereinafter "Section 503 Regulation").[2] The Department revised and updated the Section 503 Regulation in 2000 by improving and strengthening the minimum requirements for employee benefit plan claims procedures under section 503 of ERISA.[3] As revised in 2000, the Section 503 Regulation provided new time frames and enhanced requirements for notices and disclosure with respect to decisions at both the initial claims decision stage and on review. Although the Section 503 Regulation applies to all covered employee benefit plans, including pension plans, group health plans, and plans that provide disability benefits, the more stringent procedural protections apply to group health plans and to claims with respect to disability benefits.[4]

2. The Affordable Care Act Additions to the Section 503 Regulations

Section 715(a)(1) of ERISA, added by the Affordable Care Act, provides that certain provisions of the Public Health Service Act (PHS Act) apply to group health plans and health insurance issuers in connection with providing health insurance coverage as if the provisions were included ERISA. Such provisions include section 2719 of the PHS Act which addresses among other items internal claims and appeals and processes for group health plans and health insurance issuers. Section 2719 of the PHS Act provides that group health plans must have in effect an internal claims and appeals process and that such plans must initially incorporate the claims and appeals processes set forth in the Section 503 Regulation and update such processes in accordance with standards established by the Secretary of Labor.

On July 23, 2010, the Departments of Health and Human Services, Labor, and the Treasury (collectively the Departments) issued interim final regulations implementing PHS Act section 2719 and issued amendments to the IFR on June 24, 2011 (hereinafter "the 2719 IFR").[5] The 2719 IFR updated the Section 503 Regulation to ensure that non-grandfathered group health plans implement an effective internal claims and appeal process, in compliance with the Affordable Care Act.[6]

Elsewhere in today's version of the **Federal Register**, the Departments published final regulations implementing section PHS Act section 2719 (regarding internal claims and appeals and external review processes) and PHS Act 2712 (regarding restrictions on rescissions) (collectively "the 2719 Final Rule"). The 2719 Final Rule implements the requirements regarding internal claims and appeals and external review processes for group health plans and health insurance coverage in the group and individual markets under the Affordable Care Act.

The 2719 Final Rule adopts and clarifies the new requirements in the 2719 IFR that apply to internal claims and appeals processes for non-grandfathered group health plans.

3. Substantial Litigation

Even though fewer private-sector employees participate in disability plans than in other types of plans,[7] disability cases dominate the ERISA litigation landscape today.[8] An aging American workforce may likely be a contributing factor to the significant volume of disability cases. Aging workers initiate more disability claims, as the prevalence of disability increases with age.[9] And as a result, insurers and plans looking to contain disability benefit costs are often motivated to aggressively

dispute disability claims. This aggressive posture coupled with the inherently factual nature of disability claims highlight for the Department the need to review and strengthen the procedural rules governing the adjudication of disability benefit claims.

4. ERISA Advisory Council Recommendations

In 2012, the ERISA Advisory Council undertook a study on issues relating to managing disability in an environment of individual responsibility. The Advisory Council issued a report containing, in relevant part, recommendations for review of the Section 503 Regulation to determine updates and modifications for disability benefit claims, drawing upon analogous processes described in the 2719 IFR where appropriate, to address (1) what is an adequate opportunity to develop the record; and (2) content for denials of such claims.[10]

Based on the foregoing, the Department believes that in order to afford claimants of disability benefits a reasonable opportunity to pursue a full and fair review, as required by ERISA section 503, modifications to the Section 503 Regulation, that align with the updated standards required by the Affordable Care Act and extended to non-grandfathered group health plans in paragraph (b) of the 2719 Final Rule at 29 CFR 2590.715-2719, are necessary.

C. Overview of Proposed Regulation

1. Independence and Impartiality—Avoiding Conflicts of Interest

In order to ensure a full and fair review of claims and appeals, the Section 503 Regulation already contains certain standards of independence for persons making claims decisions, and the proposal would build on these standards by providing new criteria for avoiding conflicts of interest. In alignment with criteria in the 2719 Final Rule, paragraph (b)(7) of the proposal explicitly provides that plans providing disability benefits would have to "ensure that all disability benefit claims and appeals are adjudicated in a manner designed to ensure the independence and impartiality of the persons involved in making the decision." The proposal also would require that decisions regarding hiring, compensation, termination, promotion, or similar matters with respect to any individual (such as a claims adjudicator or medical expert) must not be made based upon the likelihood that the individual will support the denial of disability benefits. For example, a plan would not be permitted to provide bonuses based on the number of denials made by a claims adjudicator. Similarly, a plan would not be permitted to contract with a medical expert based on the expert's reputation for outcomes in contested cases, rather than based on the expert's professional qualifications. These added criteria address practices and behavior which, in the context of disability benefits, the Department finds difficult to reconcile with the "full and fair review" guarantee in section 503 of ERISA and which are questionable under ERISA's basic fiduciary standards.

2. Improvements to Basic Disclosure Requirements

The proposal would amend the current disclosure requirements in three significant respects. First, adverse benefit determinations on disability benefit claims would have to contain a discussion of the decision, including the basis for disagreeing with any disability determination by the Social Security Administration (SSA), by a treating physician, or other third party disability payor, to the extent that the plan did not follow those determinations presented by the claimant. This provision would address the confusion often experienced by claimants when there is little or no explanation provided for their plan's determination and/or their plan's determination is contrary to their doctor's opinion or their SSA award of disability benefits.[11]

---

[2] 42 FR 27426 (May 27, 1977).

[3] 65 FR 70246 (Nov. 21, 2000), amended at 66 FR 35887 (July 9, 2001).

[4] A benefit is a disability benefit, subject to the special rules for disability claims under the Section 503 Regulation, if the plan conditions its availability to the claimant upon a showing of disability. It does not matter how the benefit is characterized by the plan or whether the plan as a whole is a pension plan or a welfare plan. If the claims adjudicator must make a determination of disability in order to decide a claim, the claim must be treated as a disability claim for purposes of the Section 503 Regulation. *See* FAQs About The Benefit Claims Procedure Regulation, A-9 (*http://www.dol.gov/ebsa/faqs/faq_claims_proc_reg.html*).

[5] *See* 75 FR 37188 (June 28, 2010), 75 FR 43330 (July 23, 2010) and 76 FR 37208 (June 24, 2011).

[6] The requirements of the Affordable Care Act and the 2719 IFR do not apply to grandfathered health plans under section 1251 of the Affordable Care Act. The Department in conjunction with the Department of Health and Human Services and the Department of the Treasury published interim final regulations implementing section 1251 of the Affordable Care Act. *See* 75 FR 34538 (June 17, 2010) and 75 FR 70114 (Nov. 17, 2010). Elsewhere in today's version of the **Federal Register**, the Departments published final regulations implementing section 1251 of the Affordable Care Act.

[7] BLS National Compensation Survey, March 2014, at *http://www.bls.gov/ncs/ebs/benefits/2014/ebbl0055.pdf*.

[8] *See* Sean M. Anderson, *ERISA Benefits Litigation: An Empirical Picture*, 28 ABA J. Lab. & Emp. L. 1 (2012).

[9] *See* Francine M. Tishman, Sara Van Looy, & Susanne M. Bruyere, *Employer Strategies for Responding to an Aging Workforce*, NTAR Leadership Center (2012).

[10] The report may be accessed at *http://www.dol.gov/ebsa/publications/2012ACreport2.html*.

[11] *See, e.g., McDonough* v. *Aetna Life Ins. Co.*, 783 F.3d 374, 382 (1st Cir. 2015) (holding that "Aetna's failure to articulate the contours of the own occupation standard, apply that standard in a meaningful way, and reason from that standard to an appropriate conclusion regarding the appellant's putative disability renders its benefits-termination decision arbitrary and capricious."). *See also Montour* v. *Hartford Life and Accident Ins. Co.*, 588 F.3d 623, 637 (9th Cir. 2009) ("Hartford's failure to explain why it reached a different conclusion than the SSA is yet another factor to consider in reviewing the administrator's decision for abuse of discretion, particularly where, as here, a plan administrator operating with a conflict of interest requires a claimant to apply and then benefits financially from the SSA's disability finding.").

Second, adverse benefit determinations would have to contain the internal rules, guidelines, protocols, standards or other similar criteria of the plan that were used in denying the claim (or a statement that these do not exist). Third, a notice of adverse benefit determination at the claim stage would have to contain a statement that the claimant is entitled to receive, upon request, relevant documents. Under the current Section 503 Regulation, such statement is required only in notices of an adverse benefit determination denied on appeal.

These provisions would serve the purpose of ensuring that claimants fully understand why their disability benefit claim was denied so they are able to meaningfully evaluate the merits of pursuing an appeal.[12] As described below, paragraph (p) of the proposal incorporates the provision from the 2719 Final Rule that requires notices to be written in a culturally and linguistically appropriate manner.

3. Right To Review and Respond to New Information Before Final Decision

The proposal would add criteria to ensure a full and fair review of denied disability claims by explicitly providing that claimants have a right to review and respond to new evidence or rationales developed by the plan during the pendency of the appeal, as opposed merely to having a right to such information on request only after the claim has already been denied on appeal, as some courts have held under the Section 503 Regulation. Specifically, the proposal provides that prior to a plan's decision on appeal, a disability benefit claimant must be provided, free of charge, with any new or additional evidence considered, relied upon, or generated by (or at the direction of) the plan in connection with the claim, as well as any new or additional rationale for a denial, and a reasonable opportunity for the claimant to respond to such new or additional evidence or rationale. See paragraph (h)(4)(i)-(iii) of the proposal. Although these important protections are direct imports from the 2719 Final Rule, they would correct procedural problems evidenced in the litigation even predating the ACA.[13] It is the view of the Department that claimants are deprived of a full and fair review, as required by section 503 of ERISA, when they are prevented from responding at the administrative stage level to evidence and rationales.[14] Accordingly, adding these provisions to the Section 503 Regulation would explicitly address this problem and redress the procedural wrongs evidenced in the litigation under the current regulation.

As an example of how these new provisions would work, assume the plan denies a claim at the initial stage based on a medical report generated by the plan administrator. Also assume the claimant appeals the adverse benefit determination and, during the 45-day period the plan has to make its decision on appeal, the plan administrator causes a new medical report to be generated by a medical specialist who was not involved with developing the first medical report. The proposal would require the plan to automatically furnish to the claimant any new evidence in the second report. The plan would have to furnish the new evidence to the claimant before the expiration of the 45-day period. The evidence would have to be furnished as soon as possible and sufficiently in advance of the applicable deadline (including an extension if available) in order to give the claimant a reasonable opportunity to respond to the new evidence. The plan would be required to consider any response from the claimant. If the claimant's response happened to cause the plan to generate a third medical report containing new evidence, the plan would have to automatically furnish to the claimant any new evidence in the third report. The new evidence would have to be furnished as soon as possible and sufficiently in advance of the applicable deadline to allow the claimant a reasonable opportunity to respond to the new evidence in the third report.

The right of disability benefit claimants to review new evidence or new rationales is a less meaningful right standing by itself than if accompanied by a right to respond to the new information. Consequently, the proposal would also grant the claimant a right to respond

to the new information by explicitly providing claimants the right to present evidence and written testimony as part of the claims and appeals process. See paragraph (h)(4)(i) of the proposal.[15]

These new rights (i.e., review and response rights) are being proposed as an overlay to the detailed timing rules already in the Section 503 Regulation. In particular, the Section 503 Regulation already contains timing rules for disability claims that allow plan administrators extensions "for special circumstances" at the appeals stage, with a related tolling provision if the reason for an extension is "due to a claimant's failure to submit information necessary to decide a claim." See 29 CFR 2560.503-1(i)(3)(i) and (i)(4). Comments are requested on whether, and to what extent, modifications to the existing timing rules are needed to ensure that disability benefit claimants and plans will have ample time to engage in the back-and-forth dialog that is contemplated by the new review and response rights.

For instance, is a special tolling rule like the one adopted today for group health plans under the 2719 Final Rule also needed for disability benefit appeals? The 2719 Final Rule, in relevant part, provides "if the new or additional evidence is received so late that it would be impossible to provide it to the claimant in time for the claimant to have a reasonable opportunity to respond, the period for providing a notice of final internal adverse benefit determination is tolled until such time as the claimant has a reasonable opportunity to respond. After the claimant responds, or has a reasonable opportunity to respond but fails to do so, the plan or issuer must notify the claimant of the benefit determination as soon as a plan or issuer acting in a reasonable and prompt fashion can provide the notice, taking into account the medical exigencies." See 29 CFR 2590.715-2719(b)(2)(ii)(C)(2). The proposal does not adopt this tolling provision from the 2719 Final Rule because, as noted above, the existing Section 503 Regulation already permits plans providing disability benefits to take extensions at the appeals stage. This special tolling provision under the 2719 Final Rule was needed for group health plans because the Section 503 Regulation generally does not permit them to take extensions at the appeals stage.

4. Deemed Exhaustion of Claims and Appeals Processes

The proposal would strengthen the deemed exhaustion provision in the Section 503 Regulation in three important respects. First, the more stringent standards in the 2719 Final Rule would replace existing standards for disability benefit claims in cases where the plan fails to adhere to all the requirements of the Section 503 Regulation. Thus, in this respect, the proposal would adopt the 2719 Final Rule's approach, including an exception in paragraph (l)(2)(ii) for errors that are minor and meet certain other specified conditions. Second, in those situations when the minor errors exception does not apply, the proposal clarifies that the reviewing tribunal should not give special deference to the plan's decision, but rather should review the dispute de novo. Third, protection would be given to claimants whose attempts to pursue remedies in court under section 502(a) of ERISA based on deemed exhaustion are rejected by a reviewing tribunal.[16]

The minor errors exception would operate as follows. The proposal would provide that any violation of the procedural rules in the Section 503 Regulation would permit a claimant to seek immediate court action, unless the violation was: (i) de minimis; (ii) non-prejudicial; (iii) attributable to good cause or matters beyond the plan's control; (iv) in the context of an ongoing good-faith exchange of information; and (v) not reflective of a pattern or practice of non-compliance. In addition, the claimant would be entitled upon request, to an explanation of the plan's basis for asserting that it meets this standard, so that claimant could make an informed judgment about whether to seek immediate review.

Too often claimants find themselves without any forum to resolve their disputes if they prematurely pursued their claims in court before exhausting the plan's administrative remedies. To prevent this from happening to disability benefit claimants even more frequently due to

---

[12] See, e.g., Bard v. Boston Shipping Ass'n., 471 F.3d 229, 240 (1st Cir. 2006) ("in relying on the McLaughlin arbitration to reject Bard's claim, the Board relied on a rule, guideline, protocol, or other similar criterion[,][y]et Bard was not notified of even a condensed version of this rule, nor does it appear that he was timely notified that the McLaughlin arbitrator's opinion existed at all.") (internal quotation and citation omitted); Salomaa v. Honda Long Term Disability Plan, 642 F.3d 666, 679 (9th Cir. 2011) ("The review was not 'fair,' as the statute requires, because the plan did not give Salomaa and his attorney and physicians access to the two medical reports of its own physicians upon which it relied, among other reasons. In addition, the plan administrator denied the claim largely on account of absence of objective medical evidence, yet failed to tell Salomaa what medical evidence it wanted.").

[13] See, e.g., Metzger v. Unum Life Ins. Co. of America, 476 F.3d 1161, 1165-67 (10th Cir. 2007) (holding that "subsection (h)(2)(iii) does not require a plan administrator to provide a claimant with access to the medical opinion reports of appeal-level reviewers prior to a final decision on appeal."). Accord Glazer v. Reliance Standard Life Ins. Co., 524 F.3d 1241

(11th Cir. 2008); Midgett v. Washington Group Int'l Long Term Disability Plan, 561 F.3d 887 (8th Cir. 2009).

[14] Brief of the Secretary of Labor, Hilda L. Solis, as Amicus Curiae in Support of Plaintiff-Appellant's Petition for Rehearing, Midgett v. Washington Group Int'l Long Term Disability Plan, 561 F.3d 887 (8th Cir. 2009) (No. 08-2523).

[15] Consistent with paragraph (h)(2)(ii) of the Section 503 Regulation (granting claimants the right to "submit written comments, documents, records, and other information relating to the claim for benefits"), paragraph (h)(4)(i) of the proposal contemplates written evidence and testimony and therefore, in the Department's view, does not entitle the claimant to an oral hearing.

[16] The deemed exhaustion provision in the proposal, if adopted in a final regulation, would supersede any and all prior Departmental guidance with respect to disability benefit claims to the extent such guidance is contrary to the final regulation, including but not limited to FAQ F-2 in Frequently Asked Questions About The Benefit Claims Procedure Regulation (http://www.dol.gov/ebsa/faqs/faq_claims_proc_reg.html).

the interplay between the strict compliance standard and the minor errors exception, the proposal contains a special safeguard for claimants who erroneously concluded their plan's violation of the Section 503 Regulation entitled them to take their claim directly to court. The safeguard provides that if a court rejects the claimant's request for immediate review on the basis that the plan met the standards for the minor errors exception, the claim would be considered as re-filed on appeal upon the plan's receipt of the decision of the court. In addition, within a reasonable time after the receipt of the decision, the plan would be required to provide the claimant with notice of the resubmission. At this point, the claimant would have the right to pursue the claim in accordance with the plan's provisions governing appeals, including the right to present evidence and testimony.

The proposed standards set forth the Department's view of the consequences that ensue when a plan fails to provide procedures for disability benefit claims that meet the requirements of section 503 of ERISA as set forth in regulations. They reflect the Department's view that if the plan fails to provide processes that meet the regulatory minimum standards, and does not otherwise qualify for the minor errors exception, the disability benefit claimant should be free to pursue the remedies available under section 502(a) of ERISA on the basis that the plan has failed to provide a reasonable claims procedure that would yield a decision on the merits of the claim. The Department's intentions in including this provision in the proposal are to clarify that the procedural minimums of the Section 503 Regulation are essential to procedural fairness and that a decision made in the absence of the mandated procedural protections should not be entitled to any judicial deference. In this regard, the proposal provides that if a claimant chooses to pursue remedies under section 502(a) of ERISA under such circumstances, the claim or appeal is deemed denied on review without the exercise of discretion by an appropriate fiduciary. Consequently, rather than giving special deference to the plan, the reviewing court should review the dispute de novo.

5. Coverage Rescissions—Adverse Benefit Determinations

The proposal would add a new provision to address coverage rescissions not already covered under the Section 503 Regulation. For this purpose, a rescission generally is a cancellation or discontinuance of disability coverage that has retroactive effect. The Section 503 Regulation already covers a rescission if the rescission is the basis, in whole or in part, of an adverse benefit determination. For instance, if a plan were to deny a claim based on a conclusion that the claimant is ineligible for benefits due to a rescission of coverage, the claimant would have a right to appeal the adverse benefit determination under the plan's procedures for reviewing denied claims. Other rescissions (those made in the absence of a claim, such as resulting from an internal audit), however, may not be covered by the Section 503 Regulation and, consequently, would not trigger the procedural protections of section 503 of ERISA. Although many rescissions may be proper under the terms of the plan, some rescissions may be improper or erroneous. In the latter case, participants and beneficiaries may face dangerous and unwanted lapses in disability coverage without their knowledge, and without knowing how to challenge the rescission.

Accordingly, the proposed rule would amend the definition of an adverse benefit determination to include, for plans providing disability benefits, a rescission of disability benefit coverage that has a retroactive effect, whether or not, in connection with the rescission, there is an adverse effect on any particular benefit at that time. Thus, for example, a rescission of disability benefit coverage would be an adverse benefit determination even if the affected participant or beneficiary was not receiving disability benefits at the time of the rescission. The specific amendment would expand the scope of the current definition by expressly providing that an "adverse benefit determination" includes a rescission of disability coverage with respect to a participant or beneficiary, and define the term "rescission" to mean "a cancellation or discontinuance of coverage that has retroactive effect, except to the extent it is attributable to a failure to timely pay required premiums or contributions towards the cost of coverage." This new definition is modeled on the definition of rescission in the 2719 Final Rule, but would not be limited to rescissions based upon fraud or intentional misrepresentation of material fact.[17] Consequently, if a plan provides for a rescission of coverage for disability benefits if an individual makes

a misrepresentation of material fact, even if the misrepresentation was not intentional or made knowingly, the rescission would be an adverse benefit determination under this proposal. This proposed change would not prohibit rescissions; rather, it would require plans to treat certain rescissions as adverse benefit determinations, thereby triggering the applicable procedural rights under the Section 503 Regulation.

6. Culturally & Linguistically Appropriate Notices

The proposal contains safeguards for individuals who are not fluent in English. The safeguards would require that adverse benefit determinations with respect to disability benefits be provided in a culturally and linguistically appropriate manner in certain situations. The safeguards include standards that illustrate what would be considered "culturally and linguistically appropriate" in these situations. The safeguards and standards are incorporated directly from the 2719 Final Rule and reflect public comment on that rule. The relevant standards are contained in paragraph (p) of the proposal.

Under the proposed safeguards, if a claimant's address is in a county where 10 percent or more of the population residing in that county, as determined based on American Community Survey (ACS) data published by the United States Census Bureau, are literate only in the same non-English language, notices of adverse benefit determinations to the claimant would have to include a prominent one-sentence statement in the relevant non-English language about the availability of language services.[18] In addition, the plan would be required to provide a customer assistance process (such as a telephone hotline) with oral language services in the non-English language and provide written notices in the non-English language upon request. Oral language services includes answering questions in any applicable non-English language and providing assistance with filing claims and appeals in any applicable non-English language.

Two hundred and fifty-five (255) U.S. counties (78 of which are in Puerto Rico) meet the 10 percent threshold at the time of this proposal. The overwhelming majority of these are Spanish; however, Chinese, Tagalog, and Navajo are present in a few counties, affecting five states (specifically, Alaska, Arizona, California, New Mexico, and Utah). A full list of the affected U.S. counties is available on the Department's Web site and updated annually.[19]

D. Miscellaneous

1. Technical Correction

The Department has determined that a minor technical fix to the Section 503 Regulation is required with respect to disability claims. The Department proposes to clarify that the extended time frames for deciding disability claims, provided by the quarterly meeting rule found in the current regulation at 29 CFR 2560.503-1(i)(1)(ii), are applicable only to multiemployer plans. Accordingly, the proposal would amend paragraph (i)(3) to correctly refer to the appropriate subparagraph in (i)(1) of the Section 503 Regulation.

2. Request for Comments—Statute of Limitations

ERISA does not specify the period after a final adverse benefit determination within which a civil action must be filed under section 502(a)(1)(B) of ERISA. Instead, the federal courts have generally looked to analogous state laws to determine an appropriate limitations period. Analogous state law limitations periods vary, but they generally start with the same event, the plan's final benefit determination. Plan documents and insurance contracts sometimes have limitations periods which may override analogous state laws. These contractual limitations periods are not uniform and the events that trigger their running vary. In addition, claimants may not have read the relevant plan documents or the documents may be difficult for claimants to understand. The Supreme Court recently upheld the use of contractual limitations periods so long as they are reasonable.[20]

A separate issue, not before the Supreme Court in *Heimeshoff* v. *Hartford Life & Accident Ins. Co.*, is whether plans should provide participants with notice with respect to contractual limitations periods in adverse benefit determinations on review. The courts of appeals are currently in disagreement on whether plans should provide such notice under the Section 503 Regulation.[21] Inasmuch as plans are responsible

---

[17] The Affordable Care Act prohibits group health plans from rescinding coverage with respect to an individual once the individual is covered, except in the case of fraud or intentional misrepresentation of material fact. Consequently, the definition of adverse benefit determination in the 2719 Final Rule effectively is limited to these situations. *See* 75 FR 37188 and 75 FR 43330.

[18] The Department provides sample sentences in Model Notices at *www.dol.gov/ebsa/healthreform/regulations/internalclaimsandappeals.html*.

[19] *https://www.cms.gov/CCIIO/Resources/Fact-Sheets-and-FAQs/Downloads/2009-13-CLAS-County-Data.pdf*.

[20] *Heimeshoff* v. *Hartford Life & Accident Ins. Co.*, 134 S.Ct. 604, 611 (2013).

[21] *Compare Moyer* v. *Metropolitan Life Ins. Co.*, 762 F.3d 503, 505 (6th Cir. 2014) ("The claimant's right to bring a civil action is expressly included as a part of those procedures for which applicable time limits must be provided" in the notice of adverse benefit determination on review) *with* Wilson v. *Standard Ins. Co.*, 613 F. App'x 841, 844 n.3 (11th Cir. 2015) (per curiam) ("We are not persuaded by the Sixth Circuit's conclusion that a

for implementing contractual limitations provisions, plans may be in a better position than claimants to understand and to explain what those provisions mean.[22] In addition, it could prove costly to a participant to hire a lawyer to provide an interpretation that should be readily available to the plan at little or no cost. Accordingly, the Department solicits comments on whether the final regulation should require plans to provide claimants with a clear and prominent statement of any applicable contractual limitations period and its expiration date for the claim at issue in the final notice of adverse benefit determination on appeal and with an updated notice of that expiration date if tolling or some other event causes that date to change.

E. Effective Date

The Department proposes to make this regulation effective 60 days after the date of publication of the final rule in the **Federal Register**.

F. Economic Impact and Paperwork Burden

1. Background and Need for Regulatory Action

As discussed in Section B of this preamble, the proposed amendments would revise and strengthen the current rules regarding claims and appeals applicable to ERISA-covered plans providing disability benefits primarily by adopting several of the new procedural protections and safeguards made applicable to ERISA-covered group health plans by the Affordable Care Act. Before the enactment of the Affordable Care Act, group health plan sponsors and sponsors of ERISA-covered plans providing disability benefits were required to implement claims and appeal processes that complied with the Section 503 Regulation. The enactment of the ACA and the issuance of the implementing interim final regulations resulted in disability benefit claimants receiving fewer procedural protections than group health plan participants even though litigation regarding disability benefit claims is prevalent today.

The Department believes this action is necessary to ensure that disability claimants receive the more stringent procedural protections that Congress and the President established for group health care claimants under the Affordable Care Act. This will result in some participants receiving benefits they might otherwise have been incorrectly denied in the absence of the fuller protections provided by the proposed regulation. This will help alleviate the financial and emotional hardship suffered by many individuals when they lose earnings due to their becoming disabled. The proposed rule also should help limit the volume and constancy of disability benefits litigation.

The Department has crafted these proposed regulations to secure the protections of those submitting disability benefit claims. In accordance with OMB Circular A-4, the Department has quantified the costs where possible and provided a qualitative discussion of the benefits that are associated with these proposed regulations.

2. Executive Order 12866 and 13563—Department of Labor

Executive Orders 12866 and 13563 direct agencies to assess all costs and benefits of available regulatory alternatives and, if regulation is necessary, to select regulatory approaches that maximize net benefits (including potential economic, environmental, public health and safety effects; distributive impacts; and equity). Executive Order 13563 emphasizes the importance of quantifying both costs and benefits, of reducing costs, of harmonizing rules, and of promoting flexibility.

Under Executive Order 12866 (58 FR 51735), "significant" regulatory actions are subject to review by the Office of Management and Budget (OMB). Section 3(f) of the Executive Order defines a "significant regulatory action" as an action that is likely to result in a rule (1) having an annual effect on the economy of $100 million or more in any one year, or adversely and materially affecting a sector of the economy, productivity, competition, jobs, the environment, public health or safety, or State, local or tribal governments or communities (also referred to as "economically significant"); (2) creating a serious inconsistency or otherwise interfering with an action taken or planned by another agency; (3) materially altering the budgetary impacts of entitlement grants, user fees, or loan programs or the rights and obligations of recipients thereof; or (4) raising novel legal or policy issues arising out of legal mandates, the President's priorities, or the principles set forth in the Executive Order. It has been determined that this rule is significant within the meaning of section 3(f)(4) of the Executive Order. Therefore, OMB has reviewed these proposed rules pursuant to the Executive Order. The Department provides an assessment of the potential costs and benefits of proposed rule below, as summarized in Table 1, below.

TABLE 1—ACCOUNTING TABLE

Category	Estimate	Year dollar	Discount rate	Period covered
Benefits—Qualitative	The Department expects that these proposed regulations would improve the procedural protections for workers who become disabled and make claims for disability benefits from employee benefit plans. This would cause some participants to receive benefits they might otherwise have been incorrectly denied absent the fuller protections provided by the proposed regulations. In other circumstances, expenditures by plans may be reduced as a fuller and fairer system of disability claims and appeals processing helps facilitate participant acceptance of cost management efforts. Greater certainty and consistency in the handling of disability benefit claims and appeals and improved access to information about the manner in which claims and appeals are adjudicated may lead to efficiency gains in the system, both in terms of the allocation of spending at a macro-economic level as well as operational efficiencies among individual plans.			
Costs				
Annualized	$3,019,000	2015	7%	2016-2025
Monetized	$3,019,000	2015	3%	2016-2025
Qualitative	These requirements would impose modest costs on plan, because many plans already are familiar with the rules that would apply to disability benefit claims due to their current application to group health plans. As discussed in detail in the cost section below, the Department quantified the costs associated with two provisions of the proposed regulations: the requirement to provide additional information to claimants in the appeals process and the requirement to provide information in a culturally and linguistically appropriate manner.			

3. Estimated Number of Affected Entities

The Department does not have complete data on the number of plans providing disability benefits or the total number of participants covered by such plans. All ERISA-covered welfare benefit plans with more than 100 participants are required to file a Form 5500. Only some ERISA-covered welfare benefit plans with less than 100 participants are required to file for various reasons, but this number is very small. Based on current trends in the establishment of pension and health plans, there are many more small plans than large plans, but the majority of participants are covered by the large plans.

Data from the 2013 Form 5500 indicates that there are 34,300 plans covering 52.2 million participants reporting a code indicating they provide temporary disability benefits, and 26,400 plans covering 46.9 million participants reporting a code indicating they provide long-term disability benefits. To put these numbers in perspective, using the CPS and the MEPS-IC, the Department estimates that there are 140,000 large group health plans and 2.2 million small group health plans.

(Footnote Continued)

claims administrator's interpretation of the ambiguous § 2560.503-1(g)(1)(iv) not to require notice in the claim denial letter of the contractual time limit for judicial review necessarily amounts to a failure to comply with § 1133 that renders the contractual limitations provision unenforceable.").

[22] *Cf. Moyer*, 762 F.3d at 507 ("The exclusion of the judicial review time limits from the adverse benefit determination letter was inconsistent with ensuring a fair opportunity for review and rendered the letter not in substantial compliance.")

4. Benefits

In developing these proposed regulations, the Department closely considered their potential economic effects, including both benefits and costs. The Department does not have sufficient data to quantify the benefits associated with these proposed regulations due to data limitations and a lack of effective measures. Therefore, the Department provides a qualitative discussion of the benefits below.

These proposed regulations would implement a more uniform and rigorous system of disability claims and appeals processing that conforms to the rules applicable to group health plans. In general, the Department expects that these proposed regulations would improve the procedural protections for workers who become disabled and make claims for disability benefits from employee benefit plans. This will cause some participants to receive benefits that, absent the fuller protections of the regulation, they might otherwise have been incorrectly denied. In other circumstances, expenditures by plans may be reduced as a fuller and fairer system of claims and appeals processing helps facilitate participant acceptance of cost management efforts. Greater certainty and consistency in the handling of disability benefit claims and appeals and improved access to information about the manner in which claims and appeals are adjudicated may lead to efficiency gains in the system, both in terms of the allocation of spending at a macro-economic level as well as operational efficiencies among individual plans. This certainty and consistency can also be expected to benefit, to varying degrees, all parties within the system and to lead to broader social welfare gains, particularly for participants.

The Department expects that these proposed regulations also will improve the efficiency of plans providing disability benefits by enhancing their transparency and fostering participants' confidence in their fairness. The enhanced disclosure and notice requirements of these proposed regulations would benefit participants and beneficiaries better understand the reasons underlying adverse benefit determinations and their appeal rights.

For example, the proposed regulations would require adverse benefit determinations to contain a discussion of the decision, including the basis for disagreeing with any disability determination by the Social Security Administration (SSA), a treating physician, or other third party disability determinations, to the extent that the plan did not follow those determinations presented by the claimant. This provision would address the confusion often experienced by claimants when there is little or no explanation provided for their plan's determination and/or their plan's determination is contrary to their doctor's opinion or their SSA award of disability benefits.

Under the proposal, adverse benefit determinations would have to contain the internal rules, guidelines, protocols, standards or other similar criteria of the plan that were used in denying the claim (or a statement that these do not exist), and a notice of adverse benefit determination at the claim stage would have to contain a statement that the claimant is entitled to receive, upon request, relevant documents. These provisions would benefit claimants by ensuring that they fully understand why their claim was denied so they are able to meaningfully evaluate the merits of pursuing an appeal.

The proposal also would require adverse benefit determinations for certain participants and beneficiaries that are not fluent in English to be provided in a culturally and linguistically appropriate manner in certain situations. Specifically, if a claimant's address is in a county where 10 percent or more of the population residing in that county, as determined based on American Community Survey (ACS) data published by the United States Census Bureau, are literate only in the same non-English language, notices of adverse benefit determinations to the claimant would have to include a prominent one-sentence statement in the relevant non-English language about the availability of language services. This provision would ensure that certain disability claimants that are not fluent in English understand the notices received from the plan regarding their disability claims and their right to appeal denied claims. The proposal also would provide claimants with the right to review and respond to new evidence or rationales developed by the plan during the pendency of the appeal, as opposed merely to having a right to such information on request only after the claim has already been denied on appeal, as some courts have held under the current regulation. Specifically, the proposal provides that prior to a plan's decision on appeal, a disability benefit claimant must be provided, free of charge, with new or additional evidence considered, relied upon, or generated by (or at the direction of) the plan in connection with the claim, as well as any new or additional rationale for a denial, and a reasonable opportunity for the claimant to respond to such new or additional evidence or rationale. These important protections would benefit participants and beneficiaries by correcting procedural wrongs evidenced in the litigation even predating the ACA.

The voluntary nature of the employment-based benefit system in conjunction with the open and dynamic character of labor markets make explicit as well as implicit negotiations on compensation a key determinant of the prevalence of employee benefits coverage. The prevalence of benefits is therefore largely dependent on the efficacy of this exchange. If workers perceive that there is the potential for inappropriate denial of benefits or handling of appeals, they will discount the value of such benefits to adjust for this risk. This discount drives a wedge in compensation negotiation, limiting its efficiency. With workers unwilling to bear the full cost of the benefit, fewer benefits will be provided. To the extent that workers perceive that these proposed regulations, supported by enforcement authority, reduces the risk of inappropriate denials of disability benefits, the differential between the employers' costs and workers' willingness to accept wage offsets is minimized.

These proposed regulations would reduce the likelihood of inappropriate benefit denials by requiring all disability claims and appeals to be adjudicated by persons that are independent and impartial. Specifically, the proposal would prohibit hiring, compensation, termination, promotion, or other similar decisions with respect to any individual (such as a claims adjudicator or medical expert) to be made based upon the likelihood that the individual will support the plan's benefits denial. This would enhance participants' perception that their disability plan's claims and appeals processes are operated in a fair manner.

The proposal would add criteria to ensure a full and fair review of denied claims by making it explicitly clear that claimants have a right to review and respond to new evidence or rationales developed by the plan during the pendency of the appeal rather than only after the claim has already been denied on appeal, as some courts have held under the current regulation. Specifically, the proposal would require a disability benefit claimant to be provided, free of charge, with new or additional evidence considered, relied upon, or generated by (or at the direction of) the plan in connection with the claim, as well as any new or additional rationale for a denial, and a reasonable opportunity for the claimant to respond to such new or additional evidence or rationale before issuing an adverse benefit determination on review.

Providing a more formally sanctioned framework for adjudicating disability claims and appeals facilitates the adoption of cost containment programs by employers who, in the absence of a regulation providing some guidance, may have opted to pay questionable claims rather than risk alienating participants or being deemed to have breached their fiduciary duty.

In summary, the proposed rules provide more uniform standards for handling disability benefit claims and appeals that are comparable to the rules applicable to group health plans. These rules would reduce the incidence of inappropriate denials, averting serious financial hardship and emotional distress for participants and beneficiaries that are impacted by a disability. They also would enhance participants' confidence in the fairness of their plans' claims and appeals processes. Finally, by improving the transparency and flow of information between plans and claimants, the proposed regulations would enhance the efficiency of labor and insurance markets. The Department therefore concludes that the economic benefits of these proposed regulations will justify their costs.

5. Costs and Transfers

The Department has quantified the primary costs associated with these proposed regulations' requirements to (1) provide the claimant free of charge with any new or additional evidence considered, and (2) to providing notices of adverse benefit determinations in a culturally and linguistically appropriate manger. These requirements and their associated costs are discussed below.

Provision of new or additional evidence or rationale: As stated earlier in this preamble, before a plan providing disability benefits can issue a notice of adverse benefit determination on review on a disability benefit claim, these proposed regulations would require such plans to provide the claimant, free of charge, with any new or additional evidence considered, relied upon, or generated by (or at the direction of) the plan as soon as possible and sufficiently in advance of the date the notice of adverse benefit determination on review is required to be provided and any new or additional rationale sufficiently in advance of the due date of the response to an adverse benefit determination on review. This requirement increases the administrative burden on plans to prepare and deliver the enhanced information to claimants. The Department is not aware of data suggesting how often plans rely on new or additional evidence or rationale during the appeals process or the volume of materials that are received.

For purposes of this regulatory impact analysis, the Department assumes, as an upper bound, that all appealed claims will involve a reliance on additional evidence or rationale. The Department assumes that this requirement will impose an annual aggregate cost of $1.9 million. The Department estimated this cost by assuming that compliance will require medical office staff, or other similar staff in other service setting with a labor rate of $30, five minutes[23] to collect and distribute the additional evidence considered, relied upon, or generated by (or at the direction of) the plan during the appeals process. The Department estimates that on average, material, printing and postage costs will total $2.50 per mailing. The Department further assumes that 75 percent of all mailings will be distributed electronically with no associated material, printing or postage costs.[24]

The Department lacks data on the number of disability claims that are filed or denied. Therefore, the Department estimates the number of short- and long-term disability claims based on the percentage of private sector employees (119 million)[25] that participate in short-and long-term disability programs (approximately 39 and 33 percent respectively).[26] The Department estimates the number of claims per covered

life for long-term disability benefits based on the percentage of covered individuals that file claims under the Social Security Disability Insurance Program (two percent of covered individuals). The Department does not have sufficient data to estimate the percentage of covered individuals that file short-term disability claims. Therefore, for purposes of this analysis, the Department estimates of six percent of covered lives file such claims, because it believes that short-term disability claims rates are higher than long-term disability claim rates.

The Department estimates the number of denied claims that would be covered by the rule in the following manner: For long-term disability, the percent of claims denied is estimated using the percent of denied claims for the Social Security Disability Insurance Program (75 percent). For short-term disability, the estimate of denied claims (three percent) is from the 2012 National Compensation Survey: Employee Benefits in Private Industry in the United States. The estimates are provided in the table below.

---

[23] The Department's estimated 2015 hourly labor rates include wages, other benefits, and overhead are calculated as follows: mean wage from the 2013 National Occupational Employment Survey (April 2014, Bureau of Labor Statistics *http://www.bls.gov/ news.release/archives/ocwage_04012014.pdf*); wages as a percent of total compensation from the Employer Cost for Employee Compensation (June 2014, Bureau of Labor Statistics *http://www.bls.gov/news.release/archives/ecec_09102014.pdf*); overhead as a multiple of compensation is assumed to be 25 percent of total compensation for paraprofessionals, 20 percent of compensation for clerical, and 35 percent of compensation for professional; annual inflation assumed to be 2.3 percent annual growth of total labor cost since 2013

(Employment Costs Index data for private industry, September 2014 *http://www.bls.gov/ news.release/archives/eci_10312014.pdf*).

[24] This estimate is based on the methodology used to analyze the cost burden for the Section 503 Regulation (OMB Control Number 1210-0053).

[25] BLS Employment, Hours, and Earnings from the Current Employment Statistics survey (National) Table B-1.

[26] "Beyond the Numbers: Disability Insurance Plans Trends in Employee Access and Employer Cost," February 2015 Vol. 4 No. 4. *http://www.bls.gov/opub/btn/volume-4/disability-insurance-plans.htm.*

TABLE 2—FAIR AND FULL REVIEW BURDEN

| | Short-Term | | Long-Term | | Total | | |
	Electronic	Paper	Electronic	Paper	Electronic	Paper	All
Denied Claims and lost Appeals with Additional information	63	21	463	154	526	175	701
Mailing cost per event	$0.00	$0.99	$0.00	$0.99	$0.00	$0.99	
Total Mailing Cost	$0.00	$21	$0.00	$153	$0.00	$173	$173
Preparation Cost per event	$2.50	$2.50	$2.50	$2.50	$2.50	$2.50	$2.50
Total Preparation cost	$157	$52	$1,156	$385	$1,313	$438	$1,751
Total	$157	$73	$1,156	$538	$1,313	$611	$1,925

Providing Notices in a Culturally and Linguistically Appropriate Manner: The proposed regulations would require notices of adverse benefit determinations with respect to disability benefits to be provided in a culturally and linguistically appropriate manner in certain situations. This requirement is satisfied if plans provide oral language services including answering questions and providing assistance with filing claims and appeals in any applicable non-English language. These proposed regulations also require each notice sent by a plan to which the requirement applies to include a one-sentence statement in the relevant non-English that translation services are available. Plans also must provide, upon request, a notice in any applicable non-English language.

The Department expects that the largest cost associated with the requirement for culturally and linguistically appropriate notices will be for plans to provide notices in the applicable non-English language upon request. Based on the 2013 ACS data, the Department estimates that there are about 11.4 million individuals living in covered counties that are literate in a non-English Language.[27] To estimate the number of the 11.4 million individuals that might make a request, the Department estimates the number of workers in each state with access to short-term and long-term disability insurance (total population in county* state labor force participation rate* state employment rate).[28] [29] The number of employed workers then was multiplied by an estimate of the share of workers participating in disability benefits, 39 percent for short-term and 33 percent for long term disability.[30]

In discussions with the regulated community, the Department found that experience in California, which has a State law requirement for providing translation services, indicates that requests for translations of written documents averages 0.098 requests per 1,000 members for health claims. While the California law is not identical to these proposed regulations, and the demographics for California do not match other counties, for purposes of this analysis, the Department uses this percentage to estimate of the number of translation service requests that plans could expect to receive. As there are fewer disability claims than health claims, the Department believes that this estimate significantly overstates the cost. Industry experts also told the Department that while the cost of translation services varies, $500 per document is a reasonable approximation of translation cost.

Based on the foregoing, the Department estimates that the cost to provide translation services will be approximately $1.1 million annually (23,206,000 lives * 0.098/1000 * $500).

6. Regulatory Flexibility Act—Department of Labor and Department of Health and Human Services

The Regulatory Flexibility Act (5 U.S.C. 601 *et seq.*) (RFA) imposes certain requirements with respect to Federal rules that are subject to the notice and comment requirements of section 553(b) of the Administrative Procedure Act (5 U.S.C. 551 *et seq.*) and which are likely to have a significant economic impact on a substantial number of small entities. Unless an agency determines that a proposal is not likely to have a significant economic impact on a substantial number of small entities, section 603 of the RFA requires the agency to present an initial regulatory flexibility analysis (IRFA) of the proposed rule. The Department's IRFA of the proposed rule is provided below.

Need for and Objectives of the Rule: As discussed in section B of this preamble, the proposed amendments would revise and strengthen the current rules regarding claims and appeals applicable to ERISA-covered plans providing disability benefits primarily by adopting several of the new procedural protections and safeguards made applicable to ERISA-covered group health plans by the Affordable Care Act. Before the enactment of the Affordable Care Act, group health plan sponsors and sponsors of ERISA-covered plans providing disability benefits were required to implement internal claims and appeal processes that complied with the Section 503 Regulation. The enactment of the Affordable Care Act and the issuance of the implementing interim final regulations resulted in disability plan claimants receiving fewer procedural protections than group health plan participants even though litigation regarding disability benefit claims is prevalent today.

The Department believes this action is necessary to ensure that disability claimants receive the same protections that Congress and the President established for group health care claimants under the Affordable Care Act. This will result in some participants receiving benefits they might otherwise have been incorrectly denied in the absence of the fuller protections provided by the proposed regulation. This will help alleviate the financial and emotional hardship suffered by many individuals when they lose earnings due to their becoming disabled. The proposed rule also should help limit the volume and constancy of disability benefits litigation.

Affected Small Entities: The Department does not have complete data on the number of plans providing disability benefits or the total number of participants covered by such plans. All ERISA-covered welfare benefit plans with more than 100 participants are required to file a Form 5500. Only some ERISA-covered welfare benefit plans with less than 100 participants are required to file for various reasons, but this number is very small. Based on current trends in the establishment of pension and health plans, there are many more small plans than large plans, but the majority of participants are covered by the large plans.

Data from the 2013 Form 5500 indicates that there are 34,300 plans covering 52.2 million participants reporting a code indicating they provide temporary disability benefits, and 26,400 plans covering 46.9 million participants reporting a code indicating they provide long-term disability benefits. To put these numbers in perspective, using the CPS and the MEPS-IC, the Department estimates that there are 140,000 large group health plans and 2.2 million small group health plans.

Impact of the Rule: The Department has quantified the primary costs associated with these proposed regulations' requirements to (1) provide the claimant free of charge with any new or additional evidence considered, and (2) to providing notices of adverse benefit determinations in a culturally and linguistically appropriate manger. These requirements and their associated costs are discussed in the Costs and Transfers section above.

Provision of new or additional evidence or rationale: As stated earlier in this preamble, before a plan can issue a notice of adverse benefit determination on review, these proposed regulations would require plans to provide disability benefit claimants, free of charge, with any new or additional evidence considered, relied upon, or generated by (or at the direction of) the plan as soon as possible and sufficiently in advance of the date the notice of adverse benefit determination on review is required to be provided and any new or additional rationale sufficiently in advance of the due date of the response to an adverse benefit determination on review.

The Department is not aware of data suggesting how often plans rely on new or additional evidence or rationale during the appeals process or the volume of materials that are received. The Department estimated the cost per claim by assuming that compliance will require medical office staff, or other similar staff in other service setting with a labor rate of $30, five minutes[31] to collect and distribute the additional evidence considered, relied upon, or generated by (or at the direction of) the plan during the appeals process. The Department estimates that on average, material, printing and postage costs will total $2.50 per mailing. The Department further assumes that 75 percent of all mailings will be distributed electronically with no associated material, printing or postage costs.

Providing Notices in a Culturally and Linguistically Appropriate Manner: The proposed regulations would require that notices of adverse benefit determinations with respect to disability benefits be provided in a culturally and linguistically appropriate manner in certain situations. This requirement is satisfied if plans provide oral language services including answering questions and providing assistance with filing claims and appeals in any applicable non-English language. These proposed regulations also require such notices of adverse benefit determinations sent by a plan to which the requirement applies to include a one-sentence statement in the relevant non-English language about the availability of language services. Plans also must provide,

---

[27] *http://www.cms.gov/CCIIO/Resources/Fact-Sheets-and-FAQs/ Downloads/2009-13-CLAS-County-Data.pdf.* *http://www.dol.gov/ebsa/pdf/coveragebulle-tin2014.pdf* Table 1C.

[28] Labor force Participation rate: *http://www.bls.gov/lau/staadata.txt* Unemployment rate: *http://www.bls.gov/lau/lastrk14.htm.*

[29] Please note that using state estimates of labor participation rates and unemployment rates could lead to an over estimate as those reporting in the ACS survey that they speak English less than "very well" are less likely to be employed.

[30] "Beyond the Numbers: Disability Insurance Plans Trends in Employee Access and Employer Cost," February 2015 Vol. 4 No. 4. *http://www.bls.gov/opub/btn/volume-4/disability-insurance-plans.htm.*

[31] The Department's estimated 2015 hourly labor rates include wages, other benefits, and overhead are calculated as follows: mean wage from the 2013 National Occupational Employment Survey (April 2014, Bureau of Labor Statistics *http://www.bls.gov/ news.release/archives/ocwage_04012014.pdf*); wages as a percent of total compensation from the Employer Cost for Employee Compensation (June 2014, Bureau of Labor Statistics *http://www.bls.gov/news.release/archives/ecec_09102014.pdf*); overhead as a multiple of compensation is assumed to be 25 percent of total compensation for paraprofessionals, 20 percent of compensation for clerical, and 35 percent of compensation for professional; annual inflation assumed to be 2.3 percent annual growth of total labor cost since 2013 (Employment Costs Index data for private industry, September 2014 *http://www.bls.gov/ news.release/archives/eci_10312014.pdf*).

upon request, such notices of adverse benefit determinations in the applicable non-English language.

The Department expects that the largest cost associated with the requirement for culturally and linguistically appropriate notices will be for plans to provide notices in the applicable non-English language upon request. Industry experts also told the Department that while the cost of translation services varies, $500 per document is a reasonable approximation of translation cost.

In discussions with the regulated community, the Department found that experience in California, which has a State law requirement for providing translation services, indicates that requests for translations of written documents averages 0.098 requests per 1,000 members for health claims. While the California law is not identical to these proposed regulations, and the demographics for California do not match other counties, for purposes of this analysis, the Department used this percentage to estimate of the number of translation service requests plans could expect to receive. Based on the low number of requests per claim, the Department expects that translation costs would be included as part of a package of services offered to a plan, and that the costs of actual requests will be spread across multiple plans.

Duplication, Overlap, and Conflict with Other Rules and Regulations: The Department does not believe that the proposed actions would conflict with any relevant regulations, federal or other.

Based on the foregoing, the Department hereby certifies that these final regulations will not have a significant economic impact on a substantial number of small entities.

7. Paperwork Reduction Act

As part of its continuing effort to reduce paperwork and respondent burden, the Department conducts a preclearance consultation program to provide the general public and Federal agencies with an opportunity to comment on proposed and continuing collections of information in accordance with the Paperwork Reduction Act of 1995 (PRA) (44 U.S.C. 3506(c)(2)(A)). This helps to ensure that the public understands the Department's collection instructions, respondents can provide the requested data in the desired format, reporting burden (time and financial resources) in minimized, collection instructions are clearly understood, and the Department can properly assess the impact of collection requirements on respondents.

As discussed above, these proposed regulations would require plans providing disability benefits to meet additional requirements when complying with the Department's claims procedure regulation. Some of these requirements would require disclosures covered by the PRA. These requirements include disclosing information to ensure a full and fair review of a claim or appeal, and the content of notices of benefit determinations.

Currently, the Department is soliciting 60 days of public comments concerning these disclosures. The Department has submitted a copy of these proposed regulations to OMB in accordance with 44 U.S.C. 3507(d) for review of the information collections. The Department and OMB are particularly interested in comments that:

• Evaluate whether the collection of information is necessary for the proper performance of the functions of the agency, including whether the information will have practical utility;

• Evaluate the accuracy of the agency's estimate of the burden of the collection of information, including the validity of the methodology and assumptions used;

• Enhance the quality, utility, and clarity of the information to be collected; and

• Minimize the burden of the collection of information on those who are to respond, including through the use of appropriate automated, electronic, mechanical, or other technological collection techniques or other forms of information technology, for example, by permitting electronic submission of responses.

Comments should be sent to the Office of Information and Regulatory Affairs, Attention: Desk Officer for the Employee Benefits Security Administration either by fax to (202) 395-7285 or by email to *oira_submission@omb.eop.gov*. A copy of the ICR may be obtained by contacting the PRA addressee: G. Christopher Cosby, Office of Policy and Research, U.S. Department of Labor, Employee Benefits Security Administration, 200 Constitution Avenue NW., Room N-5718, Washington, DC 20210. Telephone: (202) 693-8410; Fax: (202) 219-4745. These are not toll-free numbers. Email: *ebsa.opr@dol.gov*. ICRs submitted to OMB also are available at reginfo.gov (*http://www.reginfo.gov/public/ do/* PRAMain).

ERISA-covered group health plans already are required to comply with the requirements of the Section 503 Regulation. The Section 503 Regulation requires, among other things, plans to provide a claimant who is denied a claim with a written or electronic notice that contains the specific reasons for denial, a reference to the relevant plan provisions on which the denial is based, a description of any additional information necessary to perfect the claim, and a description of steps to be taken if the participant or beneficiary wishes to appeal the denial. The regulation also requires that any adverse decision upon review be in writing (including electronic means) and include specific reasons for the decision, as well as references to relevant plan provisions.

With the implementation of the ACA claims regulations, participants of disability plans receive fewer procedural protections than participants in group health plan participants, while they experience similar if not significantly more issues with the claims review process. These proposed regulations would reduce the inconsistent procedural rules applied to health and disability benefit plan claims and provide similar procedural protections to both groups of plan participants.

The burdens associated with this proposed regulatory requirements are summarized below.

Type of Review: Revised collection.

Agencies: Employee Benefits Security Administration, Department of Labor.

Title: ERISA Claims Procedures.

OMB Number: 1210-0053.

Affected Public: Business or other for-profit; not-for-profit institutions.

Total Respondents: 5,961,000.

Total Responses: 311,867,000.

Frequency of Response: Occasionally.

Estimated Total Annual Burden Hours: 515,000.

Estimated Total Annual Burden Cost: $654,579,000.

8. Congressional Review Act

These proposed regulations are subject to the Congressional Review Act provisions of the Small Business Regulatory Enforcement Fairness Act of 1996 (5 U.S.C. 801 *et seq.*) and, if finalized, would be transmitted to Congress and the Comptroller General for review. The proposed rule is not a "major rule" as that term is defined in 5 U.S.C. 804, because it is not likely to result in an annual effect on the economy of $100 million or more.

9. Unfunded Mandates Reform Act

Title II of the Unfunded Mandates Reform Act of 1995 (Pub. L. 104-4) requires each Federal agency to prepare a written statements assessing the effects of any Federal Mandate in a proposed or final agency rule that may result in annual expenditures of $100 million (as adjusted for inflation) in any one year by State, local and tribal governments, in the aggregate, or the private sector. Such a mandate is deemed to be a "significant regulatory action." These proposed regulations are not a "significant regulatory action." Therefore the Department concludes that these proposed regulations would not impose an unfunded mandate on State, local and tribal governments, in the aggregate, or the private sector.

10. Federalism Statement

Executive Order 13132 outlines fundamental principles of federalism, and requires the adherence to specific criteria by Federal agencies in the process of their formulation and implementation of policies that have "substantial direct effects" on the States, the relationship between the national government and States, or on the distribution of power and responsibilities among the various levels of government. Federal agencies promulgating regulations that have federalism implications must consult with State and local officials and describe the extent of their consultation and the nature of the concerns of State and local officials in the preamble to the final regulation.

In the Departments of Labor's view, these proposed regulations have federalism implications because they would have direct effects on the States, the relationship between the national government and the States, or on the distribution of power and responsibilities among various levels of government to the extent states have enacted laws affecting disability plan claims and appeals that contain similar requirements to the proposal. The Department believes these effects are limited, because although section 514 of ERISA supersedes State laws to the extent they relate to any covered employee benefit plan, it preserves State laws that regulate insurance, banking, or securities. In compliance with the requirement of Executive Order 13132 that agencies examine closely any policies that may have federalism implications or limit the policy making discretion of the States, the Department welcomes input from affected States, including the National Association of Insurance Commissioners and State insurance officials, regarding this assessment.

List of Subjects in 29 CFR Part 2560

Claims, Employee benefit plans, Pensions.

For the reasons stated in the preamble, the Department of Labor proposes to amend 29 CFR part 2560 as set forth below:

PART 2560—RULES AND REGULATIONS FOR ADMINISTRATION AND ENFORCEMENT

■ 1. The authority citation for part 2560 is revised to read as follows:

Authority: 29 U.S.C. 1132, 1135, and Secretary of Labor's Order 1-2011, 77 FR 1088 (Jan. 9, 2012). Section 2560.503-1 also issued under 29 U.S.C. 1133. Section 2560.502c-7 also issued under 29 U.S.C. 1132(c)(7). Section 2560.502c-4 also issued under 29 U.S.C. 1132(c)(4). Section 2560.502c-8 also issued under 29 U.S.C. 1132(c)(8).

■ 2. Section 2560.503-1 is amended by:

■ a. Adding paragraph (b)(7).

■ b. Revising paragraph (g)(1)(v) introductory text.

■ c. Adding paragraphs (g)(1)(vii) and (viii).

■ d. Revising paragraphs (h)(4), (i)(3)(i), and (j)(5) introductory text.

■ e. Adding paragraphs (j)(6) and (7).

■ f. Revising paragraphs (l) and (m)(4).

■ g. Adding paragraphs (m)(9) and (p).

The revisions and additions read as follows:

§2560.503-1 Claims procedure.

* * * * *

(b) * * *

(7) In the case of a plan providing disability benefits, the plan must ensure that all claims and appeals for disability benefits are adjudicated in a manner designed to ensure the independence and impartiality of the persons involved in making the decision. Accordingly, decisions regarding hiring, compensation, termination, promotion, or other similar matters with respect to any individual (such as a claims adjudicator or medical expert) must not be made based upon the likelihood that the individual will support the denial of benefits.

* * * * *

(g) * * * (1) * * *

(v) In the case of an adverse benefit determination by a group health plan—

* * * * *

(vii) In the case of an adverse benefit determination with respect to disability benefits—

(A) A discussion of the decision, including, to the extent that the plan did not follow or agree with the views presented by the claimant to the plan of health care professionals treating a claimant or the decisions presented by the claimant to the plan of other payers of benefits who granted a claimant's similar claims (including disability benefit determinations by the Social Security Administration), the basis for disagreeing with their views or decisions;

(B) Either the specific internal rules, guidelines, protocols, standards or other similar criteria of the plan relied upon in making the adverse determination or, alternatively, a statement that such rules, guidelines, protocols, standards or other similar criteria of the plan do not exist; and

(C) A statement that the claimant is entitled to receive, upon request and free of charge, reasonable access to, and copies of, all documents, records, and other information relevant to the claimant's claim for benefits. Whether a document, record, or other information is relevant to a claim for benefits shall be determined by reference to paragraph (m)(8) of this section.

(viii) In the case of an adverse benefit determination with respect to disability benefits, the notification shall be provided in a culturally and linguistically appropriate manner (as described in paragraph (p) of this section).

* * * * *

(h) * * *

(4) *Plans providing disability benefits.* The claims procedures of a plan providing disability benefits will not, with respect to claims for such benefits, be deemed to provide a claimant with a reasonable opportunity for a full and fair review of a claim and adverse benefit determination unless, in addition to complying with the requirements of paragraphs (h)(2)(ii) through (iv) and (h)(3)(i) through (v) of this section, the claims procedures—

(i) Allow a claimant to review the claim file and to present evidence and testimony as part of the disability benefit claims and appeals process;

(ii) Provide that, before the plan can issue an adverse benefit determination on review on a disability benefit claim, the plan administrator shall provide the claimant, free of charge, with any new or additional evidence considered, relied upon, or generated by the plan (or at the direction of the plan) in connection with the claim; such evidence must be provided as soon as possible and sufficiently in advance of the date on which the notice of adverse benefit determination on review is required to be provided under paragraph (i) of this section to give the claimant a reasonable opportunity to respond prior to that date; and

(iii) Provide that, before the plan can issue an adverse benefit determination on review on a disability benefit claim based on a new or additional rationale, the plan administrator shall provide the claimant, free of charge, with the rationale; the rationale must be provided as soon as possible and sufficiently in advance of the date on which the notice of adverse benefit determination on review is required to be provided under paragraph (i) of this section to give the claimant a reasonable opportunity to respond prior to that date.

* * * * *

(i) * * *

(3) *Disability claims.* (i) Except as provided in paragraph (i)(3)(ii) of this section, claims involving disability benefits (whether the plan provides for one or two appeals) shall be governed by paragraph (i)(1)(i) of this section, except that a period of 45 days shall apply instead of 60 days for purposes of that paragraph.

* * * * *

(j) * * *

(5) In the case of a group health plan—

* * *

(6) In the case of an adverse benefit decision with respect to disability benefits—

(i) A discussion of the decision, including, to the extent that the plan did not follow or agree with the views presented by the claimant to the plan of health care professionals treating a claimant or the decisions presented by the claimant to the plan of other payers of benefits who granted a claimant's similar claims (including disability benefit determinations by the Social Security Administration), the basis for disagreeing with their views or decisions; and

(ii) Either the specific internal rules, guidelines, protocols, standards or other similar criteria of the plan relied upon in making the adverse determination or, alternatively, a statement that such rules, guidelines, protocols, standards or other similar criteria of the plan do not exist.

(7) In the case of an adverse benefit determination on review with respect to a claim for disability benefits, the notification shall be provided in a culturally and linguistically appropriate manner (as described in paragraph (p) of this section).

* * * * *

(l) *Failure to establish and follow reasonable claims procedures.* (1) *In general.* Except as provided in paragraph (l)(2) of this section, in the case of the failure of a plan to establish or follow claims procedures consistent with the requirements of this section, a claimant shall be deemed to have exhausted the administrative remedies available under the plan and shall be entitled to pursue any available remedies under section 502(a) of the Act on the basis that the plan has failed to provide a reasonable claims procedure that would yield a decision on the merits of the claim.

(2) *Plans providing disability benefits.* (i) In the case of a claim for disability benefits, if the plan fails to strictly adhere to all the requirements of this section with respect to a claim, the claimant is deemed to have exhausted the administrative remedies available under the plan, except as provided in paragraph (l)(2)(ii) of this section. Accordingly, the claimant is entitled to pursue any available remedies under section

502(a) of ERISA on the basis that the plan has failed to provide a reasonable claims procedure that would yield a decision on the merits of the claim. If a claimant chooses to pursue remedies under section 502(a) of ERISA under such circumstances, the claim or appeal is deemed denied on review without the exercise of discretion by an appropriate fiduciary.

(ii) Notwithstanding paragraph (l)(2)(i) of this section, the administrative remedies available under a plan with respect to claims for disability benefits will not be deemed exhausted based on *de minimis* violations that do not cause, and are not likely to cause, prejudice or harm to the claimant so long as the plan demonstrates that the violation was for good cause or due to matters beyond the control of the plan and that the violation occurred in the context of an ongoing, good faith exchange of information between the plan and the claimant. This exception is not available if the violation is part of a pattern or practice of violations by the plan. The claimant may request a written explanation of the violation from the plan, and the plan must provide such explanation within 10 days, including a specific description of its bases, if any, for asserting that the violation should not cause the administrative remedies available under the plan to be deemed exhausted. If a court rejects the claimant's request for immediate review under paragraph (l)(2)(i) of this section on the basis that the plan met the standards for the exception under this paragraph (l)(2)(ii), the claim shall be considered as re-filed on appeal upon the plan's receipt of the decision of the court. Within a reasonable time after the receipt of the decision, the plan shall provide the claimant with notice of the resubmission.

* * * * *

(m) * * *

(4) The term "adverse benefit determination" means:

(i) Any of the following: a denial, reduction, or termination of, or a failure to provide or make payment (in whole or in part) for, a benefit, including any such denial, reduction, termination, or failure to provide or make payment that is based on a determination of a participant's or beneficiary's eligibility to participate in a plan, and including, with respect to group health plans, a denial, reduction, or termination of, or a failure to provide or make payment (in whole or in part) for, a benefit resulting from the application of any utilization review, as well as a failure to cover an item or service for which benefits are otherwise provided because it is determined to be experimental or investigational or not medically necessary or appropriate; and

(ii) In the case of a plan providing disability benefits, the term "adverse benefit determination" also means any rescission of disability coverage with respect to a participant or beneficiary (whether or not, in connection with the rescission, there is an adverse effect on any particular benefit at that time). For this purpose, the term "rescission" means a cancellation or discontinuance of coverage that has retroactive effect, except to the extent it is attributable to a failure to timely pay required premiums or contributions towards the cost of coverage.

* * * * *

(9) The term "claim file" means the file or other compilation of relevant information, as described in paragraph (m)(8) of this section, to be considered in the full and fair review of a disability benefit claim.

* * * * *

(p) *Standards for culturally and linguistically appropriate notices.* A plan is considered to provide relevant notices in a "culturally and linguistically appropriate manner" if the plan meets all the requirements of paragraph (p)(1) of this section with respect to the applicable non-English languages described in paragraph (p)(2) of this section.

(1) *Requirements.* (i) The plan must provide oral language services (such as a telephone customer assistance hotline) that include answering questions in any applicable non-English language and providing assistance with filing claims and appeals in any applicable non-English language;

(ii) The plan must provide, upon request, a notice in any applicable non-English language; and

(iii) The plan must include in the English versions of all notices, a statement prominently displayed in any applicable non-English language clearly indicating how to access the language services provided by the plan.

(2) *Applicable non-English language.* With respect to an address in any United States county to which a notice is sent, a non-English language is an applicable non-English language if ten percent or more of the population residing in the county is literate only in the same non-English language, as determined in guidance published by the Secretary.

Signed at Washington, DC, this 6th day of November, 2015.

Phyllis C. Borzi,

Assistant Secretary, Employee Benefits Security Administration, U.S. Department of Labor.

[FR Doc. 2015-29295 Filed 11-13-15; 4:15 pm]

BILLING CODE 4510-29-P

¶ 20,539B

Employee Benefits Security Administration (EBSA): Proposed rule: Safe harbor: State auto-IRA programs: ERISA preemption.— EBSA has issued proposed regulations containing a safe harbor describing circumstances in which a payroll deduction savings program, including one with automatic enrollment, would not create an employee pension benefit plan under ERISA. The goal of the safe harbor is to reduce the risk of state payroll deduction savings programs with automatic enrollment (auto-IRA programs) that conform to the safe harbor being preempted, if they were ever challenged.

The proposed regulations, which were published in the Federal Register on November 18, 2015 (80 FR 72006), were reproduced below. The regulations were finalized on August 30, 2016 (81 FR 59464). The preamble to the final regulations is at ¶ 24,341. The final regulations are at ¶ 14,132.

¶ 20,539C

Pension Benefit Guaranty Corporation (PBGC): Proposed rule: Premiums: Late payment penalties: Reductions: Waivers.—The Pension Benefit Guaranty Corporation (PBGC) has issued proposed regulations that would significantly lower the rate of penalties charged for the late payment of premiums by defined benefit plans and would provide a waiver of most of the penalties for plans with good compliance with premium requirements. The proposed changes would apply to both single-employer and multiemployer plans for late annual (flat- and variable-rate) premium payments for plan years beginning after 2015.

The proposed regulations, which were published in the Federal Register on April 28, 2016 (81 FR 25363), were reproduced below. The regulations were finalized on September 23, 2016 (81 FR 65542). The preamble to the final regulations is at ¶ 24,342. The final regulations are at ¶ 15,371G.

¶ 20,539D

Pension Benefit Guaranty Corporation (PBGC): Proposed rule: Multiemployer defined benefit plans: Critical and declining status: Mergers and transfers: Facilitated mergers: Financial assistance.—The Pension Benefit Guaranty Corporation (PBGC) has released proposed regulations that implement Section 121 of the Multiemployer Pension Reform Act of 2014 (MPRA), which clarified the PBGC's authority to facilitate the merger of two or more multiemployer plans under Title IV of ERISA. Specifically, the proposed regulations would provide guidance on the process of requesting a facilitated merger under ERISA §4231(e), including a request for financial assistance under ERISA §4231(e)(2). In addition, the regulations would reorganize and update the existing regulatory requirements applicable to mergers and transfers between multiemployer plans.

The proposed regulations, which were published in the Federal Register on June 6, 2016 (81 FR 36229), are reproduced below.

PENSION BENEFIT GUARANTY CORPORATION

29 CFR Part 4231

RIN 1212-AB31

Mergers and Transfers Between Multiemployer Plans

AGENCY: Pension Benefit Guaranty Corporation.

ACTION: Proposed rule.

SUMMARY: This proposed rule would amend PBGC's regulation on Mergers and Transfers Between Multiemployer Plans to implement section 121 of the Multiemployer Pension Reform Act of 2014. The proposed rule would also reorganize and update the existing regulation.

DATES: Comments must be submitted on or before August 5, 2016.

ADDRESSES: Comments, identified by Regulation Identifier Number (RIN) 1212-AB31, may be submitted by any of the following methods:

• *Federal eRulemaking Portal: http://www.regulations.gov.* Follow the Web site instructions for submitting comments.

• *Email: reg.comments@pbgc.gov.*

• *Fax:* 202-326-4112.

• *Mail or Hand Delivery:* Regulatory Affairs Group, Office of the General Counsel, Pension Benefit Guaranty Corporation, 1200 K Street NW., Washington, DC 20005-4026. All submissions must include the Regulation Identifier Number for this rulemaking (RIN 1212-AB31). Comments received, including personal information provided, will be posted to *www.pbgc.gov.* Copies of comments may also be obtained by writing to Disclosure Division, Office of the General Counsel, Pension Benefit Guaranty Corporation, 1200 K Street NW., Washington DC 20005-4026, or calling 202-326-4040 during normal business hours. (TTY and TDD users may call the Federal relay service toll-free at 1-800-877-8339 and ask to be connected to 202-326-4040.)

FOR FURTHER INFORMATION CONTACT: Joseph J. Shelton (*shelton.joseph@pbgc.gov*), Assistant General Counsel, Office of the General Counsel, Pension Benefit Guaranty Corporation, 1200 K Street NW., Washington DC 20005-4026; 202-326-4400, ext. 6559; Theresa B. Anderson (*anderson.theresa@pbgc.gov*), Attorney, Office of the General Counsel, 202-326-4400, ext. 6353.

SUPPLEMENTARY INFORMATION:

Executive Summary—Purpose of the Regulatory Action

This rulemaking is needed to implement statutory changes under the Multiemployer Pension Reform Act of 2014 (MPRA) affecting mergers of multiemployer plans under title IV of the Employee Retirement Income Security Act of 1974 (ERISA). The proposed rule also would reorganize and update the existing regulatory requirements applicable to mergers and transfers between multiemployer plans.

PBGC's legal authority for this action is based on section 4002(b)(3) of ERISA, which authorizes PBGC to issue regulations to carry out the purposes of title IV of ERISA, and section 4231 of ERISA, which sets forth the statutory requirements for mergers and transfers between multiemployer plans.

Executive Summary—Major Provisions of the Regulatory Action

Section 121 of MPRA amends the existing rules under section 4231 of ERISA by adding a new section 4231(e), which clarifies PBGC's authority to facilitate the merger of two or more multiemployer plans if certain statutory requirements are met. For purposes of section 4231(e), "facilitation" may include training, technical assistance, mediation, communication with stakeholders, and support with related requests to other government agencies. In addition, subject to the requirements of section 4231(e)(2), PBGC may provide financial assistance (within the meaning of section 4261 of ERISA) to facilitate a merger it determines is necessary to enable one or more of the plans involved to avoid or postpone insolvency.

The proposed rule would provide guidance on the process for requesting a facilitated merger under section 4231(e) of ERISA, including a request for financial assistance under section 4231(e)(2). The proposed rule would also reorganize and update the existing regulation.

Background

PBGC and the Multiemployer Insurance Program

PBGC is a Federal corporation created under title IV of ERISA to guarantee the payment of pension benefits earned by more than 40 million American workers and retirees in over 23,000 private-sector defined benefit pension plans.

PBGC administers two insurance programs—one for single-employer defined benefit pension plans, and a second for multiemployer defined benefit pension plans. This proposed rule would apply only to the multiemployer program.

Multiemployer Mergers and Transfers Under ERISA

Under section 4231(b) of ERISA, mergers of two or more multiemployer plans and transfers of assets and liabilities between multiemployer plans must comply with four requirements:

(1) The plan sponsor must notify PBGC at least 120 days before the effective date of the merger or transfer;

(2) No participant's or beneficiary's accrued benefit may be lower immediately after the effective date of the merger or transfer than the benefit immediately before that date;

(3) The benefits of participants and beneficiaries must not be reasonably expected to be subject to suspension as a result of plan insolvency under section 4245 of ERISA; and

(4) An actuarial valuation of the assets and liabilities of each of the affected plans must have been performed during the plan year preceding the effective date of the merger or transfer, based upon the most recent data available as of the day before the start of that plan year, or as prescribed by PBGC's regulation.

Section 4231(a) of ERISA grants PBGC authority to vary these requirements by regulation. Part 4231 of PBGC's regulations implements and interprets these requirements by providing a procedure under which plan sponsors must notify PBGC of any merger or transfer between multiemployer plans.

MPRA

In December 2014, Congress enacted, and the President signed, the Consolidated and Further Continuing Appropriations Act, 2015,[1] of which MPRA is a part. MPRA contains a number of statutory reforms to assist financially troubled multiemployer plans, and to improve the financial condition of PBGC's multiemployer insurance program.

Section 201 of MPRA amended the rules under section 305 of ERISA to add a new "critical and declining" status for financially troubled multiemployer plans (described below in the discussion of "multiemployer facilitated mergers under MPRA"). Generally, a plan is in critical and declining status if it is in critical status under any subparagraph of section 305(b)(2), and is projected to become insolvent within 15-20 years. Plans in critical and declining status may suspend benefits under section 305(e)(9) of ERISA under certain conditions. The Department of the Treasury (Treasury) has interpretive jurisdiction over the subject matter in section 305.

Sections 121 and 122 of MPRA provide PBGC with new statutory authority to assist critical and declining status plans under certain conditions. Section 121 of MPRA, which is the subject of this rulemaking, authorizes PBGC to facilitate multiemployer plan mergers, including with financial assistance (within the meaning of section 4261) if certain statutory conditions—such as the condition that one or more of the plans involved be in critical and declining status—are met. Section 122 of MPRA amended section 4233 of ERISA to create a new statutory framework for partitions of critical and declining status plans.[2]

Finally, section 131 of MPRA increased the annual premium that multiemployer plans pay to PBGC for 2015 from $13 to $26 per participant. For plan years beginning after 2015, the annual premium increases based on increases in the national average wage index. The annual premium for 2016 is $27 per participant.

Multiemployer Facilitated Mergers—Before MPRA

PBGC provides financial assistance under section 4261 of ERISA to multiemployer plans that are or will be insolvent under section 4245 of ERISA. Generally, a plan is insolvent when it is unable to pay benefits when due during the plan year. PBGC provides financial assistance to

---

[1] Division O of the Consolidated and Further Continuing Appropriations Act, 2015, Public Law 113-235 (128 Stat. 2130 (2014)).

[2] PBGC issued an interim final rule under section 4233 of ERISA on June 19, 2015 (80 FR 35220), and a final rule on December 23, 2015 (80 FR 79687).

an insolvent plan in the form of a loan sufficient to pay its participants' and beneficiaries' guaranteed benefits.

In a few cases before the enactment of MPRA, PBGC provided financial assistance (within the meaning of section 4261 of ERISA) to facilitate the merger of a soon-to-be insolvent multiemployer plan into a larger, more financially secure multiemployer plan. The financial assistance provided was a single payment that covered the cost of guaranteed benefits under the failing plan. In exchange, the larger, more financially secure plan assumed responsibility for paying the full plan benefits of the participants and beneficiaries in the failing plan with which it merged. As a result, the participants and beneficiaries in the failing plan received more than they would have in the absence of a facilitated merger from a financially secure plan that was more likely to remain ongoing. In addition, the financial assistance provided was generally less than PBGC's valuation of the present value of future financial assistance to the failing plan.

For a number of reasons, including the deteriorating financial condition of PBGC's multiemployer insurance program, PBGC was only able to facilitate a few financial assistance mergers before MPRA.

Multiemployer Facilitated Mergers Under MPRA

Section 4231(e)(1) of ERISA provides that upon request by the plan sponsors, PBGC may take such actions as it deems appropriate to promote and facilitate the merger of two or more multiemployer plans. Facilitation may include training, technical assistance, mediation, communication with stakeholders, and support with related requests to other government agencies. The decision to facilitate a merger is within PBGC's discretion. Furthermore, before PBGC may exercise this discretion, it must first determine—in consultation with the Participant and Plan Sponsor Advocate[3]—that the merger is in the interests of the participants and beneficiaries of at least one of the plans, and is not reasonably expected to be adverse to the overall interests of the participants and beneficiaries of any of the plans.

Under section 4231(e)(2), PBGC may also provide financial assistance (within the meaning of section 4261) to facilitate a merger that it determines is necessary to enable one or more of the plans involved to avoid or postpone insolvency, if the following statutory conditions are satisfied:

Critical and declining status. In accordance with section 4231(e)(2)(A) of ERISA, one or more of the plans involved in the merger must be in critical and declining status as defined in section 305(b)(6). A plan is in critical and declining status if the plan is in critical status under any subparagraph of section 305(b)(2), and is projected to become insolvent within the meaning of section 4245 during the current plan year or any of the 14 succeeding plan years (or 19 succeeding plan years if the plan has a ratio of inactive participants to active participants that exceeds two to one, or if the funded percentage of the plan is less than 80 percent). Section 305(b)(3)(A)(i) requires an annual certification from the plan actuary on whether a plan is or will be in critical and declining status for the plan year. Treasury has interpretative jurisdiction over the subject matter in section 305.

Long-term loss and plan solvency. In accordance with section 4231(e)(2)(B), PBGC must reasonably expect that—

• Financial assistance will reduce PBGC's expected long-term loss with respect to the plans involved; and

• Financial assistance is necessary for the merged plan to become or remain solvent.

Certification. In accordance with section 4231(e)(2)(C), PBGC must certify that its ability to meet existing financial assistance obligations to other plans will not be impaired by the financial assistance.

Source of funding. In accordance with section 4231(e)(2)(D), financial assistance must be paid exclusively from the PBGC fund for basic benefits guaranteed for multiemployer plans.

PBGC Notice of Financial Assistance

Section 4231(e)(2) requires that, not later than 14 days after the provision of financial assistance, PBGC provide notice of the financial assistance to the Committee on Education and the Workforce of the House of Representatives; the Committee on Ways and Means of the House of Representatives; the Committee on Finance of the Senate; and the Committee on Health, Education, Labor, and Pensions of the Senate.

PBGC Request for Information

On February 18, 2015, PBGC published in the **Federal Register** (80 FR 8712) a request for information (RFI) to solicit information from interested parties on issues PBGC should consider in implementing sections 4231 and 4233 of ERISA. PBGC received 20 comments in response to the RFI.[4] This proposed rule reflects public input on facilitated mergers stemming from the comments.

In general, commenters expressed strong support for MPRA's changes to the merger rules under section 4231 of ERISA, and urged PBGC to issue timely guidance to the public on the types of information, documents, data, and actuarial projections needed for a request to be complete. Many of these same commenters urged that whenever possible and consistent with statutory requirements, any new regulatory information requirements should be based on information that plans are already required to prepare, or information that plans could easily develop.

A number of commenters also suggested that PBGC provide guidance on the factors and criteria it will use to evaluate proposed facilitated mergers, while another suggested that proposed facilitated mergers should be analyzed individually on a case-by-case basis. In addition, one commenter suggested that PBGC provide guidance on any general limitations it may establish on the amount of financial assistance available for facilitated mergers.

PBGC considered these and other comments and decided it will determine whether to provide further guidance on the evaluation criteria for facilitated mergers, and any limitations PBGC may impose relating to the amount of financial assistance available, based on the experience it gains implementing this proposed rule. While the proposed rule does not impose any additional limitations on the amount of financial assistance available for financial assistance mergers, sections 4231(e)(2) and 4233 of ERISA require PBGC to certify that its ability to meet existing financial obligations to other plans will *not* be impaired by the transaction. Furthermore, because the funds available for financial assistance to insolvent plans under 4261, financial assistance mergers under 4231(e)(2), and partitions under 4233, are derived from the same source—the revolving fund for basic benefits guaranteed under section 4022A (the multiemployer revolving fund)—it is anticipated that the amount of financial assistance available to a critical and declining status plan for a financial assistance merger generally will not exceed the amount available to that plan for a partition (and could be less). Given complexities and uncertainties such as these, the proposed rule includes a provision that would allow a plan sponsor to engage in informal discussions with PBGC before filing a formal request for a facilitated merger.

With respect to the eligibility requirements for a facilitated merger, a few commenters noted that unlike the statutory conditions for a partition under section 4233 of ERISA, which require, among other things, a finding that the plan sponsor has taken all reasonable measures to avoid insolvency, including maximum benefit suspensions, there is no explicit requirement in section 4231(e) to suspend benefits. Given the absence of such a requirement, these commenters urged PBGC *not* to impose one by regulation. Expressing a similar view, another commenter suggested that PBGC guidance under section 4231(e) should *not* result in the automatic imposition of the same requirements, such as benefit suspensions or a certain type of projection, because although each requirement might be appropriate in some cases, it might not be appropriate in all cases.

PBGC agrees with the commenters and consistent with the express terms of the statute, this proposed rule would neither require nor preclude a plan sponsor's application for both benefit suspensions under section 305(e)(9)(G) and a facilitated merger under section 4231(e). PBGC recognizes, however, that although benefit suspensions are *not* required under section 4231(e), some plans may need both benefit suspensions and a financial assistance merger to become or remain solvent. For example, the plan sponsors of two critical and declining status plans that propose a financial assistance merger may need to consider benefit suspensions if the amount of financial assistance available from PBGC is less than the amount necessary for the merged plan to become or remain solvent.

Before considering an integrated transaction involving benefit suspensions and a facilitated merger, however, plan sponsors must carefully consider how the various requirements under sections 305(e)(9) and 4231 would apply to such a transaction. For example, a critical and

---

[3] The Participant and Plan Sponsor Advocate position was created in 2012 by the Moving Ahead for Progress in the 21st Century Act (MAP-21), Public Law 112-141 (126 Stat. 405 (2012)). *See* section 4004 of ERISA for the rules governing this position. PBGC is not defining the Participant and Plan Sponsor Advocate's consultative role in determining how

the merger affects the interests of the participants and beneficiaries of the plans involved, but will let that role evolve based on experience implementing this proposed rule.

[4] The RFI and comments are accessible at *http://www.pbgc.gov/prac/pg/other/guidance/ multiemployer-notices.html.*

declining status plan could merge into a large, well-funded multiemployer plan. In such a case, to the extent any of the benefits previously provided by the critical and declining status plan had been subject to suspension under section 305(e)(9) or become subject to suspension at the same time that the merger occurs, the plan sponsor of the merged plan would become responsible for making the annual determinations necessary for continued benefit suspensions under section 305(e)(9) and the regulations thereunder. Under section 305(e)(9)(C)(ii) of ERISA and the regulations thereunder, benefits may continue to be suspended for a plan year only if the plan sponsor determines, in a written record to be maintained throughout the period of the benefit suspension, that although all reasonable measures to avoid insolvency have been and continue to be taken, the plan is still projected to become insolvent unless benefits are suspended. Absent these determinations, restoration of the suspended benefits would be required.

Finally, one commenter expressed concern that a narrow interpretation of section 4231(e)(2)(B)(ii) would effectively preclude a small, critical and declining status plan from receiving financial assistance to merge into a large, financially healthy multiemployer plan. That section provides, in relevant part, that PBGC must reasonably expect that financial assistance is necessary for the *merged* plan to become or remain solvent.

As explained more fully below in the section-by-section discussion, PBGC does *not* interpret section 4231(e)(2)(B)(ii) to preclude a small, critical and declining status plan from receiving financial assistance to merge into a large, financially healthy multiemployer plan because such an interpretation would be inconsistent with the statute as a whole. Section 4231(e)(2), for example, authorizes PBGC to provide financial assistance to facilitate a merger it determines is necessary to enable *one or more* (but not necessarily all) of the plans involved to avoid or postpone insolvency.

Similarly, section 4231(e)(2)(A) requires only that *one or more* (but not necessarily all) of the plans involved in the merger be in critical and declining status. Given that MPRA neither imposes a requirement that *all* multiemployer plans involved in a financial assistance merger be in critical and declining status, nor requires a finding that the merger is necessary to enable *all* of the plans involved to avoid or postpone insolvency, PBGC does *not* interpret section 4231(e)(2)(B)(ii) to impose any additional eligibility conditions beyond those expressly provided in the statute.

A more detailed discussion of the proposed rule and the RFI comments follows.

Proposed Regulatory Changes

Overview

The proposed rule would amend part 4231 of PBGC's regulations to implement MPRA's changes to section 4231 of ERISA. The proposed rule also would reorganize and update the existing regulation to reflect other changes in law.

Under the proposed rule, part 4231 would provide guidance on: (1) The process for submitting a notice of merger or transfer, and a request for a compliance determination or facilitated merger; (2) the information required in such notices and requests; (3) the notification process for PBGC decisions on requests for facilitated mergers; and (4) the scope of PBGC's jurisdiction over a merged plan that received financial assistance. The proposed rule also would reorganize part 4231 by dividing it into subparts. Subpart A would contain the general merger and transfer rules. Subpart B would provide guidance on procedures and information requirements for facilitated mergers, including those involving financial assistance.

In most instances, implementation of the mergers and transfers addressed in this proposed rule, including facilitated mergers, will involve conduct that is also subject to the fiduciary responsibility standards of part 4 of subtitle B of title I of ERISA. Among other things, these standards require that a fiduciary with respect to a plan act prudently, solely in the interest of the participants and beneficiaries, and for the exclusive purpose of providing benefits to participants and their beneficiaries and defraying reasonable expenses of administering the plan. The fact that a merger or transfer, including a facilitated merger, may satisfy title IV of ERISA and the regulations thereunder is not determinative of whether it satisfies the requirements of part 4 of subtitle B of title I of ERISA (other than section 406(a) and (b)(2), in the event of a compliance determination).

Finally, the proposed rule would be applicable to mergers and transfers for which a notice, and, if applicable, request for a facilitated merger are filed with PBGC on or after the effective date of the final rule. If a plan sponsor chooses to submit an application for a facilitated merger before the issuance of a final rule, then the plan sponsor may need to revise or supplement its request to take into account the requirements under the final rule.

Section-by-Section Discussion

Subpart A—General Provisions

Section 4231.1 of the proposed rule describes the purpose and scope of part 4231, which is to prescribe notice requirements for mergers and transfers of assets or liabilities among multiemployer plans and to interpret other requirements under section 4231 of ERISA.

Section 4231.2 of the proposed rule would amend the current regulation by adding new definitions, and by moving existing definitions defined elsewhere in the current regulation to § 4231.2. For example, the proposed rule would move the existing definition of "effective date" from § 4231.8(a) to § 4231.2.

Under the proposed rule, the term "facilitated merger" would mean a merger of two or more multiemployer plans facilitated by PBGC under section 4231(e) of ERISA, including a merger that is facilitated with financial assistance under section 4231(e)(2).

The term "financial assistance" would mean financial assistance under section 4261, which may be in the form of one or more payments.

The term "financial assistance merger" would mean a facilitated merger for which PBGC provides financial assistance under section 4231(e)(2).

Consistent with the definition of "merged plan" in § 4211.2, the term "merged plan" would mean a plan that is the result of the merger of two or more multiemployer plans.

The proposed rule also would amend the existing definition of "significantly affected plan" in § 4231.2 to include a plan in endangered or critical status, as defined in section 305(b) of ERISA,[5] that engages in a transfer (other than a de minimis transfer). When the regulation was originally published, only plans transferring 15% or more of their assets, or receiving a transfer of unfunded accrued benefits equaling 15% or more of their assets were treated as significantly affected plans.

In PBGC's view, endangered and critical status plans generally present a greater risk of insolvency, and when these plans engage in non-de minimis transfers their risk of insolvency may increase. Consistent with this view, the proposed rule would expand the definition of "significantly affected plan" to include endangered and critical status plans engaging in non-de minimis transfers. Although the proposed rule would apply the stricter plan solvency test under § 4231.6(b) to non-de minimis transfers involving endangered and critical status plans, that test would only apply to *transfers* involving such plans (*not* mergers).

Requirements for Mergers and Transfers

Section 4231.3 of the proposed rule provides guidance on the requirements for mergers and transfers. As under the current regulation, § 4231.3(a) of the proposed rule sets forth the statutory criteria under section 4231(b) of ERISA. The proposed rule also would amend the current regulation to clearly provide that plan sponsors may engage in informal consultations with PBGC to discuss proposed mergers and transfers. As noted above in the discussion of the RFI comments, informal consultation is particularly important in the context of a proposed financial assistance merger because PBGC's ability to provide financial assistance will depend on, among other things, its ability to meet existing financial assistance obligations to other plans.

Section 4231.4 of the current regulation is unchanged under the proposed rule. That section provides guidance on the requirement under section 4231(b)(2) of ERISA that no participant's or beneficiary's accrued benefit may be lower immediately after the effective date of a merger or transfer than the benefit immediately before that date.

Section 4231.5 of the current regulation provides guidance on the actuarial valuation requirement under section 4231(b)(4) of ERISA. For a plan that is not a significantly affected plan, it provides that the actuarial valuation requirement under section 4231(b)(4) is satisfied if an actuarial valuation has been performed for the plan based on the plan's assets and liabilities as of a date not more than three years

---

[5] "Endangered" and "critical" status are plan categories established by the Pension Protection Act of 2006, Public Law 109-280 (120 Stat. 780 (2006)) (PPA).

before the date on which the notice of the merger or transfer is filed. When the regulation was originally published, section 302(c)(9) of ERISA required plans to have an actuarial valuation performed every three years, and PBGC adopted that timeframe for non-significantly affected plans.

Because multiemployer plans are now required under section 304(c)(7) of ERISA[6] to perform actuarial valuations not less frequently than once every year, the proposed rule would amend § 4231.5 to require that each plan involved in a merger or transfer have an actuarial valuation performed for the plan year preceding the proposed effective date of the merger or transfer. The proposed rule further provides that if the valuation is not complete as of the date the plan sponsors file the notice of merger or transfer, the plan sponsors may provide the most recent actuarial valuation performed for the plans with the notice, and the required valuations when complete.

Section 4231.6 of the current regulation provides guidance on "plan solvency" tests that operate as regulatory safe harbors under section 4231(b)(3) of ERISA. Section 4231(b)(3) prohibits a merger or transfer unless "the benefits of participants and beneficiaries are not reasonably expected to be subject to suspension under section 4245." Section 4245, in turn, provides that an insolvent plan must suspend benefits that are above the level guaranteed by PBGC to the extent the plan has insufficient assets to pay such benefits.

For a plan that is not a significantly affected plan, § 4231.6(a) of the current regulation provides that the plan solvency requirement under section 4231(b)(3) of ERISA and § 4231.3(a)(3)(i) is satisfied if one of the following tests are met:

(1) The expected fair market value of plan assets immediately after the merger or transfer equals or exceeds five times the benefit payments for the last plan year ending before the proposed effective date of the merger or transfer, or

(2) In each of the first five plan years beginning on or after the proposed effective date of the merger or transfer, expected plan assets plus expected contributions and investment earnings equal or exceed expected expenses and benefit payments for the plan year.

The proposed rule would amend and reorder these tests in the following manner. First, under § 4231.6(a)(1) of the proposed rule, a plan will satisfy the plan solvency requirement if in each of the first ten plan years beginning on or after the proposed effective date of the merger or transfer, the plan's expected fair market value of assets plus expected contributions and investment earnings equal or exceed expected expenses and benefit payments for the plan year.

Alternatively, under § 4231.6(a)(2) of the proposed rule, a plan will satisfy the plan solvency requirement if the plan's expected fair market value of assets immediately after the merger or transfer equals or exceeds ten times the benefit payments for the last plan year ending before the proposed effective date of the merger or transfer.

Accordingly, in addition to reordering § 4231.6(a)(1) and (2), the proposed rule would change the period of years in § 4231.6(a)(2) of the current regulation from "five plan years" to "ten plan years," and the multiple in § 4231.6(a)(1) from "five times the benefit payments" to "ten times the benefit payments." Based on PBGC's experience under the multiemployer program since the regulation was first published, PBGC believes that the proposed changes will provide a better demonstration that benefits are not reasonably expected to be subject to suspension under section 4245 of ERISA as a result of insolvency. At the same time, PBGC recognizes that the majority of multiemployer plan mergers will broaden the contribution base and stabilize the plans involved. Therefore, as is the case under the current regulation for a plan that cannot satisfy the solvency tests under § 4231.6(a), the proposed rule would continue to allow an enrolled actuary to "otherwise demonstrate" that benefits under the plan are not reasonably expected to be subject to suspension under section 4245 of ERISA as a result of insolvency.

Section 4231.6(b) of the current regulation sets forth a more rigorous solvency test for significantly affected plans. The proposed rule would amend § 4231.6(b)(2) by changing the requirement that assets cover benefit payments for the first "five" years after the proposed effective date to "ten" years. In addition, the proposed rule would amend § 4231.6(b)(4)(i) by changing the amortization period from 25 to 15 years to reflect the amortization period generally applicable to changes in funding of multiemployer plans under PPA.[7] Finally, the proposed rule would amend § 4231.6(c)(1) by requiring withdrawal liability payments to be listed separately from contributions.

Section 4231.7 of the current regulation sets forth special rules for de minimis mergers and transfers. That section would remain unchanged under the proposed rule.

Section 4231.8 of the current regulation sets forth requirements for notices of mergers and transfers, and requests for compliance determinations under section 4231(c). In general, a notice of a merger or transfer must be filed not less than 120 days, or not less than 45 days in the case of a merger for which a compliance determination is not requested, before the effective date of a merger or transfer. Section 4231.8(f) permits PBGC to waive the timing of the notice requirements under certain circumstances.

In the case of a facilitated merger, the proposed rule would amend § 4231.8(a) to require that notice of a proposed facilitated merger be filed not less than 270 days before the proposed effective date of a facilitated merger. As noted above in the discussion of § 4231.2, the proposed rule would also move the definition of "effective date" from § 4231.8(a)(1) to § 4231.2. Finally, the proposed rule would move the information requirements contained in § 4231.8(e) to a new § 4231.9.

Section 4231.9 of the proposed rule would generally retain the existing information requirements in § 4231.8(e) with minor modifications. For example, the de minimis exception contained in § 4231.8(e)(6) would not apply to a request for a financial assistance merger.

Section 4231.10 of the proposed rule (§ 4231.9 of the existing regulation) describes the additional information required for a request for a compliance determination. The proposed rule would amend this section to make clear that a request for a compliance determination must be filed contemporaneously with a notice of merger or transfer. In addition, the proposed rule would delete the "place of filing" provision in § 4231.9(1) as that information is now contained in § 4231.8(e), and would delete certain information requirements as those requirements are now contained in § 4231.9(e).

Section 4231.11 of the proposed rule (§ 4231.10 of the existing regulation) describes the requirements for actuarial calculations and assumptions. The proposed rule would conform the regulation to section 304(c)(3) of ERISA, would specify that calculations must be performed by an enrolled actuary, and would expand the bases upon which PBGC may require updated calculations.

Subpart B—Additional Rules for Facilitated Mergers

Section 4231.12 of the proposed rule provides general guidance on a request for a facilitated merger. A request for a facilitated merger, including a financial assistance merger, must satisfy the requirements of section 4231(b) of ERISA and subpart A of the regulation, in addition to section 4231(e) of ERISA and subpart B. The procedures set forth in the proposed rule would represent the exclusive means by which PBGC will approve a request for a facilitated merger, including a financial assistance merger. Any financial assistance provided by PBGC will be limited by section 4261 of ERISA and with respect to the guaranteed benefits of the plans involved in the merger that are in critical and declining status. In addition, as noted above, because the funds available for financial assistance mergers under section 4231(e), partitions under section 4233, and financial assistance to insolvent plans under 4261, are derived from the same source—the revolving fund for basic benefits guaranteed under section 4022A (the multiemployer revolving fund)—it is anticipated that the amount of financial assistance available to a critical and declining status plan for a financial assistance merger generally will not exceed the amount available to that plan for a partition (and could be less). Finally, while PBGC expects that in most cases the financial assistance it provides in a facilitated merger will be in the form of periodic payments, PBGC agrees with the RFI comment advocating flexibility in the structure of financial assistance (e.g., lump sum or periodic payments), and consistent with past practice will decide the structure of financial assistance on a case-by-case basis.

Section 4231.12 of the proposed rule would also provide guidance on the information required for a request for a facilitated merger. It states that a request must include the information required under §§ 4231.9 (notice of merger or transfer) and 4231.10 (request for compliance determination), as well as a detailed narrative description with supporting documentation demonstrating that the proposed merger is in the interests of participants and beneficiaries of at least one of the plans, and is not reasonably expected to be adverse to the overall interests of the participants and beneficiaries of any of the plans. The narrative description and supporting documentation should reflect, among other

---

[6] Sections 302 and 304 of ERISA were repealed and replaced by PPA. Section 304 of ERISA, as amended by PPA, sets forth the minimum funding standards for multiemployer plans.

[7] See section 304(b) of ERISA.

things, any material efficiencies expected as a result of the merger and the basis for those expectations.

In addition, a request for a financial assistance merger must contain the information described in § 4231.13 (plan information), § 4231.14 (financial assistance merger information), § 4231.15 (actuarial and financial information), and § 4231.16 (participant census data). The proposed rule provides that PBGC may require additional information to determine whether the requirements of section 4231(e) of ERISA are met or to enable it to facilitate the merger. Finally, § 4231.12 of the proposed rule would impose an affirmative obligation on the plan sponsors to promptly notify PBGC in writing if the plan sponsor(s) discovers that any material fact or representation contained in or relating to the request for a facilitated merger, or in any supporting documents, is no longer accurate, or has been omitted.

Information Requirements for Financial Assistance Merger

Section 4231.13 of the proposed rule would provide guidance on the various categories of plan-related information required for a request for a financial assistance merger, such as trust agreements, formal plan documents, summary plan descriptions, summaries of material modifications, and rehabilitation or funding improvement plans. PBGC expects that most, if not all, of the information required under this section should be readily available and accessible by plan sponsors.

Section 4231.14 of the proposed rule sets forth information requirements relating to the proposed structure of a financial assistance merger. The information required includes a detailed description of the financial assistance merger, including any larger integrated transaction of which the proposed merger is a part (including, but not limited to, an application for suspension of benefits under section 305(e)(9)(G) of ERISA), and the estimated total amount of financial assistance the plan sponsors request for each year. It would also require a narrative description of the events that led to the sponsors' decision to request a financial assistance merger, and the significant risks and assumptions relating to the proposed financial assistance merger and the projections provided.

Section 4231.15 of the proposed rule would identify the actuarial and financial information required for a request for a financial assistance merger. The first two information requirements relate to plan actuarial reports and actuarial certifications, which should ordinarily be within the possession of the plan sponsors or plan actuaries. Sections 4231.15(c)-(f) of the regulation would require the submission of certain actuarial and financial information specific to the proposed financial assistance merger, which are necessary for PBGC to evaluate the solvency requirements under section 4231(e)(2) of ERISA.

Under § 4231.15 of the proposed rule, each critical and declining plan must demonstrate that its projected date of insolvency without the merger is sooner than the projected date of insolvency of the merged plan. The plan(s) may take the proposed financial assistance into account in this demonstration.

Section 4231.15 of the proposed rule would also provide guidance on the required demonstration that financial assistance is necessary for the merged plan to become or remain solvent. Under the proposed rule, the type of projection required will depend on whether the merged plan would be in critical status under section 305(b) of ERISA immediately following the merger (without taking the proposed financial assistance into account), as reasonably determined by the actuary. For example, if a critical and declining status plan merges into an endangered status plan, and the actuary anticipates that the merged plan would not meet minimum funding requirements for the coming year without financial assistance, then the merged plan would be in critical status for purposes of the projections. Alternatively, if the actuary anticipates that the merged plan would not be described in section 305(b)(2)(A)-(D) of ERISA immediately after the merger, then the merged plan would not be in critical status for purposes of the projections (even if the merged plan could elect to be in critical status).

Under the proposed rule, the plan's enrolled actuary may use any reasonable estimation for determining the expected funded status of the merged plan. Under an optional approach, the funded status of the merged plan could be determined based on the combined data and projections underlying the status certifications of each of the plans for the plan year immediately preceding the merger (including any selected updates in the data based on the experience of the plans in the immediately preceding plan year). PBGC requests comments on this

issue, including methods to determine whether the merged plan would be in critical status.

Under § 4231.15(f)(1) of the proposed rule, if the merged plan would be in critical status under section 305(b) of ERISA (without taking the proposed financial assistance into account), the plans must demonstrate that financial assistance is necessary for the merged plan to "avoid insolvency" under section 305(e)(9)(D)(iv) of ERISA and the regulations thereunder (excluding stochastic projections). This more rigorous solvency standard is consistent with the "emergence" test under section 305(e)(4)(B) of ERISA, which requires a plan in critical status to show that is not projected to become insolvent for any of the 30 succeeding plan years.

If the merged plan would *not* be in critical status under section 305(b) of ERISA (without taking the proposed financial assistance into account), § 4231.15(f)(2) of the proposed rule provides that the plans must demonstrate that the merged plan is *not* projected to become insolvent during the 20 years beginning after the proposed effective date of the merger with the proposed financial assistance. If such a demonstration can be satisfied without taking the proposed financial assistance into account, or if the amount of financial assistance requested exceeds the amount that satisfies this demonstration, the plan sponsors must demonstrate that financial assistance is necessary to mitigate the adverse effects of the merger on the merged plan's ability to remain solvent.

In summary, under the proposed rule, critical status plans would be subject to a different solvency standard than non-critical status plans. This is consistent with the RFI comments that suggested determining solvency on a case-by-case basis, and maintains flexibility in the solvency demonstration for a merged plan that would *not* be in critical status. To encourage the merger of critical and declining status plans into financially stable plans, the proposed rule provides for a solvency demonstration based on the circumstances and challenges specific to the merged plan (for example, the merger might have an impact on the plan's funding requirements, increase the ratio of inactive to active participants, or decrease the funded percentage of the healthy plan in a manner that can be demonstrated to adversely affect the merged plan's ability to remain solvent long-term). PBGC requests comments on this issue, including alternative approaches or methods to demonstrate plan solvency.

Section 4231.16 of the proposed rule would identify the types of participant census data to include with a request for a financial assistance merger.

Decision on Request for Facilitated Merger

Section 4231.17 of the proposed rule would describe the manner in which PBGC will notify a plan sponsor of PBGC's decision on a request for a facilitated merger. PBGC will approve or deny a request for a facilitated merger in writing and in accordance with the standards set forth in section 4231(e) of ERISA.[8] If PBGC denies a request, PBGC's written decision will state the reason(s) for the denial. If PBGC approves a request for a financial assistance merger, PBGC will provide a financial assistance agreement detailing the total amount and terms of the financial assistance as soon as practicable thereafter. The decision to approve or deny a request for facilitated merger under section 4231(e) of ERISA is within PBGC's discretion, and would be a final agency action not subject to PBGC's rules for reconsideration or administrative appeal.

Jurisdiction Over Financial Assistance Merger

Section 4231.18 of the proposed rule would describe PBGC's jurisdiction over the merged plan resulting from a financial assistance merger. PBGC has determined that maintaining oversight is necessary to ensure compliance with financial assistance agreements, and proper stewardship of PBGC financial assistance. This is also consistent with one of the RFI comments. Based on the foregoing, § 4231.18(a) would provide that PBGC will continue to have jurisdiction over the merged plan resulting from a financial assistance merger to carry out the purposes, terms, and conditions of the financial assistance merger, sections 4231 and 4261 of ERISA, and the regulations thereunder. Section 4231.18(b) would state that PBGC may, upon notice to the plan sponsor, make changes to the financial assistance agreement(s) in response to changed circumstances consistent with sections 4231 and 4261 of ERISA and the regulations thereunder.

---

[8] As noted above, section 4231(e)(1) of ERISA requires a determination by PBGC in consultation with the Participant and Plan Sponsor Advocate to approve a facilitated merger. Section 4231(e)(2) of ERISA sets forth four additional statutory conditions that must be satisfied before PBGC may approve a request for a financial assistance merger.

PBGC will review each request for a facilitated merger, including a financial assistance merger, on a case-by-case basis in accordance with the statutory criteria in section 4231(e) of ERISA.

Request for Comments

In addition to the specific requests for comments identified above, PBGC encourages all interested parties to submit their comments, suggestions, and views concerning the provisions of this proposed rule. In particular, PBGC is interested in any area in which additional guidance may be needed.

Applicability

The amendments to part 4231 would be applicable to mergers and transfers for which a notice, and, if applicable, request are filed with PBGC on or after the effective date of the final rule.

Compliance With Rulemaking Guidelines

Executive Orders 12866 "Regulatory Planning and Review" and 13563 "Improving Regulation and Regulatory Review"

Having determined that this rulemaking is a "significant regulatory action" under Executive Order 12866, the Office of Management and Budget has reviewed this proposed rule under Executive Order 12866.

Executive Orders 12866 and 13563 direct agencies to assess all costs and benefits of available regulatory alternatives and, if regulation is necessary, to select regulatory approaches that maximize net benefits (including potential economic, environmental, public health and safety effects, distributive impacts, and equity). Executive Order 13563 emphasizes the importance of quantifying both costs and benefits, of reducing costs, of harmonizing rules, and of promoting flexibility. Executive Orders 12866 and 13563 require a comprehensive regulatory impact analysis be performed for any economically significant regulatory action, defined as an action that would result in an annual effect of $100 million or more on the national economy or which would have other substantial impacts.

Pursuant to section 1(b)(1) of Executive Order 12866 (as amended by Executive Order 13422), PBGC has determined that regulatory action is required in this area. Principally, this regulatory action is necessary to implement the requirements for a request for a facilitated merger under section 4231 of ERISA, as amended by MPRA.

In accordance with OMB Circular A-4, PBGC also has examined the economic and policy implications of this proposed rule and has concluded that the action's benefits justify its costs. Plan sponsors requesting a facilitated merger should have readily accessible the information needed for a request under this proposed rule. Most of the information requirements pertain to a request for facilitation of a merger with financial assistance. These requirements are largely the same as the information requirements in the interim final rule that PBGC published in the **Federal Register** on June 19, 2015 (80 FR 35220) about partition of a multiemployer plan. Public comments to that interim final rule stated that its information requirements were not overly burdensome.[9] In addition, if the plan sponsors' request for facilitation of a merger with financial assistance is approved, the merged plan benefits by receiving enough financial assistance to remain solvent. The benefits to participants equal or exceed the costs to PBGC. Further, under section 4231(e)(2) of ERISA, PBGC cannot provide financial assistance to facilitate a merger unless its expected long-term loss with respect to the plans is reduced, and PBGC's ability to satisfy existing financial assistance obligations to other plans is not impaired.[10]

Under Section 3(f)(1) of Executive Order 12866, a regulatory action is economically significant if "it is likely to result in a rule that may * * * [h]ave an annual effect on the economy of $100 million or more or adversely affect in a material way the economy, a sector of the economy, productivity, competition, jobs, the environment, public health or safety, or State, local, or tribal governments or communities." OMB has determined that this proposed rule does not cross the $100 million threshold for economic significance and is not otherwise economically significant.

Based on a review of the requirements plans and PBGC must comply with for both partitions and financial assistance mergers, particularly the requirement that PBGC not impair its ability to help other troubled plans, PBGC expects that fewer than 20 plans would be approved for either partition or financial assistance merger over the next three years (about six plans per year), and that the total financial assistance PBGC would provide under both provisions would be less than $60 million per year.

Regulatory Flexibility Act

The Regulatory Flexibility Act imposes certain requirements with respect to rules that are subject to the notice and comment requirements of section 553(b) of the Administrative Procedure Act and that are likely to have a significant economic impact on a substantial number of small entities. Unless an agency determines that a rule is not likely to have a significant economic impact on a substantial number of small entities, section 603 of the Regulatory Flexibility Act requires that the agency present an initial regulatory flexibility analysis at the time of the publication of the proposed rule describing the impact of the rule on small entities and seeking public comment on such impact. Small entities include small businesses, organizations and governmental jurisdictions.

For purposes of the Regulatory Flexibility Act requirements with respect to the proposed amendments to the Annual Financial and Actuarial Information Reporting regulation, PBGC considers a small entity to be a plan with fewer than 100 participants. This is substantially the same criterion PBGC uses in other regulations[11] and is consistent with certain requirements in title I of ERISA[12] and the Internal Revenue Code (Code),[13] as well as the definition of a small entity that the Department of Labor (DOL) has used for purposes of the Regulatory Flexibility Act.[14]

Further, while some large employers may have small plans, in general most small plans are maintained by small employers. Thus, PBGC believes that assessing the impact of the proposed rule on small plans is an appropriate substitute for evaluating the effect on small entities. The definition of small entity considered appropriate for this purpose differs, however, from a definition of small business based on size standards promulgated by the Small Business Administration (13 CFR 121.201) pursuant to the Small Business Act. PBGC therefore requests comments on the appropriateness of the size standard used in evaluating the impact on small entities of the proposed amendments to part 4231.

PBGC certifies under section 605(b) of the Regulatory Flexibility Act that the amendments in this proposed rule would not have a significant economic impact on a substantial number of small entities. In 2014, multiemployer plans with fewer than 250 participants made up just 11% of the total 1,425 multiemployer plans. Accordingly, as provided in section 605 of the Regulatory Flexibility Act (5 U.S.C. 601 *et seq.*), sections 603 and 604 do not apply.

Paperwork Reduction Act

PBGC is submitting the information collection requirements under this proposed rule to the Office of Management and Budget under the Paperwork Reduction Act. An agency may not conduct or sponsor, and a person is not required to respond to, a collection of information unless it displays a currently valid OMB control number.

The collection of information in part 4231 is approved under control number 1212-0022 (expires July 31, 2017). PBGC estimates that there will be 28 respondents each year and that the total annual burden of the collection of information will be about 63.125 hours and $169,995. For purposes of estimating the total annual burden numbers for the collection of information in part 4231, PBGC assumed that it will receive a total of six requests for facilitation of a merger with financial assistance, with a per respondent annual burden of 10 hours and $26,250.

Comments on the information requirements under this proposed rule should be mailed to the Office of Information and Regulatory Affairs, Office of Management and Budget, Attention: Desk Officer for Pension Benefit Guaranty Corporation, via electronic mail at *OIRA_DOCKET@omb.eop.gov* or by fax to (202) 395-6974. Comments may be submitted through August 5, 2016. Comments may address (among other things)—

• Whether the collection of information is needed for the proper performance of PBGC's functions and will have practical utility;

• The accuracy of PBGC's estimate of the burden of the proposed collection of information, including the validity of the methodology and assumptions used;

---

[9] The partition rule and comments are accessible at *http://www.pbgc.gov/prac/pg/other/guidance/final-rules.html.* PBGC published the final rule in the **Federal Register** on December 23, 2015 (80 FR 79687).

[10] *See* sections 4231(e)(2)(B)(i) and 4231(e)(2)(C) of ERISA.

[11] *See, e.g.,* special rules for small plans under part 4007 (Payment of Premiums).

[12] *See, e.g.,* section 104(a)(2) of ERISA, which permits the Secretary of Labor to prescribe simplified annual reports for pension plans that cover fewer than 100 participants.

[13] *See, e.g.,* section 430(g)(2)(B) of the Code, which permits plans with 100 or fewer participants to use valuation dates other than the first day of the plan year.

[14] *See, e.g.,* DOL's final rule on Prohibited Transaction Exemption Procedures, 76 FR 66637, 66644 (Oct. 27, 2011).

• Enhancement of the quality, utility, and clarity of the information to be collected; and

• Minimizing the burden of the collection of information on those who are to respond, including through the use of appropriate automated, electronic, mechanical, or other technological collection techniques or other forms of information technology, *e.g.*, permitting electronic submission of responses.

List of Subjects in 29 CFR Part 4231

Employee benefit plans, Pension insurance, Reporting and recordkeeping requirements.

For the reasons stated in the preamble, PBGC proposes to amend 29 CFR chapter XL by revising part 4231 to read as follows:

PART 4231—MERGERS AND TRANSFERS BETWEEN MULTIEMPLOYER PLANS

Subpart A—General Provisions

Sec.

4231.1 Purpose and scope.

4231.2 Definitions.

4231.3 Requirements for mergers and transfers.

4231.4 Preservation of accrued benefits.

4231.5 Valuation requirement.

4231.6 Plan solvency tests.

4231.7 De minimis mergers and transfers.

4231.8 Filing requirements; timing and method of filing.

4231.9 Notice of merger or transfer.

4231.10 Request for compliance determination.

4231.11 Actuarial calculations and assumptions.

Subpart B—Additional Rules for Facilitated Mergers

4231.12 Request for facilitated merger.

4231.13 Plan information for financial assistance merger.

4231.14 Description of financial assistance merger.

4231.15 Actuarial and financial information for financial assistance merger.

4231.16 Participant census data for financial assistance merger.

4231.17 PBGC action on a request for facilitated merger.

4231.18 Jurisdiction over financial assistance merger.

Authority: 29 U.S.C. 1302(b)(3)

PART 4231—MERGERS AND TRANSFERS BETWEEN MULTIEMPLOYER PLANS

Subpart A—General Provisions

§ 4231.1 Purpose and scope.

(a) *General*—(1) *Purpose.* The purpose of this part is to prescribe notice requirements under section 4231 of ERISA for mergers and transfers of assets or liabilities among multiemployer pension plans. This part also interprets the other requirements of section 4231 of ERISA and prescribes special rules for de minimis mergers and transfers.

(2) *Scope.* This part applies to mergers and transfers among multiemployer plans where all of the plans immediately before and immediately after the transaction are multiemployer plans covered by title IV of ERISA.

(b) *Additional requirements.* Subpart B of this part sets forth the additional requirements for and procedures specific to a request for a facilitated merger.

§ 4231.2 Definitions.

The following terms are defined in § 4001.2 of this chapter: *annuity, Code, EIN, ERISA, fair market value, guaranteed benefit, IRS, multiemployer plan, normal retirement age, PBGC, plan, plan sponsor, plan year,* and *PN.* In addition, the following terms are defined for purposes of this part:

Actuarial valuation means a valuation of assets and liabilities performed by an enrolled actuary using the actuarial assumptions used for

purposes of determining the charges and credits to the funding standard account under section 304 of ERISA and section 431 of the Code.

Advocate means the Participant and Plan Sponsor Advocate under section 4004 of ERISA.

Critical and declining status has the same meaning as the term has under section 305(b)(6) of ERISA and section 432(b)(6) of the Code.

Critical status has the same meaning as the term has under section 305(b)(2) of ERISA and section 432(b)(2) of the Code, and includes "critical and declining status" as defined in section 305(b)(6) of ERISA and section 432(b)(6) of the Code.

De minimis merger is defined in § 4231.7(b).

De minimis transfer is defined in § 4231.7(c).

Effective date means, with respect to a merger or transfer, the earlier of—

(1) The date on which one plan assumes liability for benefits accrued under another plan involved in the transaction; or

(2) The date on which one plan transfers assets to another plan involved in the transaction.

Endangered status has the same meaning as the term has under section 305(b)(1) of ERISA and section 432(b)(1) of the Code, and includes "seriously endangered status" as described in section 305(b)(1) of ERISA and section 432(b)(1) of the Code.

Facilitated merger means a merger of two or more multiemployer plans facilitated by PBGC under section 4231(e) of ERISA, including a merger that is facilitated with financial assistance under section 4231(e)(2) of ERISA.

Fair market value of assets has the same meaning as the term has for minimum funding purposes under section 304 of ERISA and section 431 of the Code.

Financial assistance means periodic or lump sum financial assistance payments from PBGC under section 4261 of ERISA.

Financial assistance merger means a merger facilitated by PBGC for which PBGC provides financial assistance (within the meaning of section 4261 of ERISA) under section 4231(e)(2) of ERISA.

Insolvent has the same meaning as insolvent under section 4245(b) of ERISA.

Merged plan means a plan that is the result of the merger of two or more multiemployer plans.

Merger means the combining of two or more plans into a single plan. For example, a consolidation of two plans into a new plan is a merger.

Significantly affected plan means a plan that—

(1) Transfers assets that equal or exceed 15 percent of its assets before the transfer,

(2) Receives a transfer of unfunded accrued benefits that equal or exceed 15 percent of its assets before the transfer,

(3) Is created by a spinoff from another plan,

(4) Engages in a merger or transfer (other than a de minimis merger or transfer) either—

(i) After such plan has terminated by mass withdrawal under section 4041A(a)(2) of ERISA, or

(ii) With another plan that has so terminated, or

(5) Is in either endangered status or critical status, and engages in a transfer (other than a de minimis transfer).

Transfer and *transfer of assets or liabilities* mean a diminution of assets or liabilities with respect to one plan and the acquisition of these assets or the assumption of these liabilities by another plan or plans (including a plan that did not exist prior to the transfer). However, the shifting of assets or liabilities pursuant to a written reciprocity agreement between two multiemployer plans in which one plan assumes liabilities of another plan is not a transfer of assets or liabilities. In addition, the shifting of assets between several funding media used for a single plan (such as between trusts, between annuity contracts, or between trusts and annuity contracts) is not a transfer of assets or liabilities.

Unfunded accrued benefits means the excess of the present value of a plan's accrued benefits over the plan's fair market value of assets, determined on the basis of the actuarial valuation required under § 4231.5.

§4231.3 Requirements for mergers and transfers.

(a) *General requirements.* A plan sponsor may not cause a multiemployer plan to merge with one or more multiemployer plans or transfer assets or liabilities to or from another multiemployer plan unless the merger or transfer satisfies all of the following requirements:

(1) No participant's or beneficiary's accrued benefit is lower immediately after the effective date of the merger or transfer than the benefit immediately before that date.

(2) Actuarial valuations of the plans that existed before the merger or transfer have been performed in accordance with §4231.5.

(3) For each plan that exists after the transaction, an enrolled actuary—

(i) Determines that the plan meets the applicable plan solvency requirement set forth in §4231.6; or

(ii) Otherwise demonstrates that benefits under the plan are not reasonably expected to be subject to suspension under section 4245 of ERISA.

(4) The plan sponsor notifies PBGC of the merger or transfer in accordance with §§4231.8 and 4231.9.

(b) *Compliance determination.* If a plan sponsor requests a determination that a merger or transfer that may otherwise be prohibited by section 406(a) or (b)(2) of ERISA satisfies the requirements of section 4231 of ERISA, the plan sponsor must submit the information described in §4231.10 in addition to the information required by §4231.9. PBGC may request additional information if necessary to determine whether a merger or transfer complies with the requirements of section 4231 and subpart A of this part. Plan sponsors are not required to request a compliance determination. Under section 4231(c) of ERISA, if PBGC determines that the merger or transfer complies with section 4231 of ERISA and subpart A of this part, the merger or transfer will not constitute a violation of the prohibited transaction provisions of section 406(a) and (b)(2) of ERISA.

(c) *Certified change in bargaining representative.* Transfers of assets and liabilities pursuant to a change of collective bargaining representative certified under the Labor-Management Relations Act of 1947 or the Railway Labor Act, as amended, are governed by section 4235 of ERISA. Plan sponsors involved in such transfers are not required to comply with subpart A of this part. However, under section 4235(f)(1) of ERISA, the plan sponsors of the plans involved in the transfer may agree to a transfer that complies with sections 4231 and 4234 of ERISA. Plan sponsors that elect to comply with sections 4231 and 4234 of ERISA must comply with the rules in subpart A of this part.

(d) *Informal consultation.* Nothing in this part precludes a plan sponsor from contacting PBGC on an informal basis to discuss a potential merger or transfer.

§4231.4 Preservation of accrued benefits.

Section 4231(b)(2) of ERISA and §4231.3(a)(1) require that no participant's or beneficiary's accrued benefit may be lower immediately after the effective date of the merger or transfer than the benefit immediately before the merger or transfer. A plan that assumes an obligation to pay benefits for a group of participants satisfies this requirement only if the plan contains a provision preserving all accrued benefits. The determination of what is an accrued benefit must be made in accordance with section 411 of the Code and the regulations thereunder.

§4231.5 Valuation requirement.

The actuarial valuation requirement under section 4231(b)(4) of ERISA and §4231.3(a)(2) is satisfied if an actuarial valuation has been performed for the plan based on the plan's assets and liabilities as of a date not earlier than the first day of the last plan year ending before the proposed effective date of the transaction. If the actuarial valuation required under this section is not complete when the notice of merger or transfer is filed, the plan sponsor may provide the most recent actuarial valuation for the plan with the notice, and the actuarial valuation required under this section when complete. For a significantly affected plan involved in a transfer, other than a plan that is a significantly affected plan only because the transfer involves a plan that has terminated by mass withdrawal under section 4041A(a)(2) of ERISA, the valuation must separately identify assets, contributions, and liabilities being transferred and must be based on the actuarial assumptions and methods that are expected to be used for the plan for the first plan year beginning after the transfer.

§4231.6 Plan solvency tests.

(a) *General.* For a plan that is not a significantly affected plan, the plan solvency requirement of section 4231(b)(3) of ERISA and §4231.3(a)(3)(i) is satisfied if—

(1) In each of the first ten plan years beginning on or after the proposed effective date of the merger or transfer, the plan's expected fair market value of assets plus expected contributions and investment earnings equal or exceed expected expenses and benefit payments for the plan year; or

(2) The plan's expected fair market value of assets immediately after the merger or transfer equals or exceeds ten times the benefit payments for the last plan year ending before the proposed effective date of the merger or transfer.

(b) *Significantly affected plans.* The plan solvency requirement of section 4231(b)(3) of ERISA and §4231.3(a)(3)(i) is satisfied for a significantly affected plan if all of the following requirements are met:

(1) Expected contributions equal or exceed the estimated amount necessary to satisfy the minimum funding requirement of section 431 of the Code for the ten plan years beginning on or after the proposed effective date of the transaction.

(2) The plan's expected fair market value of assets immediately after the transaction equal or exceed the total amount of expected benefit payments for the first ten plan years beginning on or after the proposed effective date of the transaction.

(3) Expected contributions for the first plan year beginning on or after the proposed effective date of the transaction equal or exceed expected benefit payments for that plan year.

(4) Expected contributions for the amortization period equal or exceed unfunded accrued benefits plus expected normal costs. The actuary may select as the amortization period either—

(i) The first 15 plan years beginning on or after the proposed effective date of the transaction, or

(ii) The amortization period for the resulting base when the combined charge base and the combined credit base are offset under section 431(b)(5) of the Code.

(c) *Rules for determinations.* In determining whether a transaction satisfies the plan solvency requirements set forth in this section, the following rules apply:

(1) Expected contributions after a merger or transfer must be determined by assuming that contributions for each plan year will equal contributions for the last full plan year ending before the date on which the notice of merger or transfer is filed with PBGC. If expected contributions include withdrawal liability payments, such payments must be shown separately. If the withdrawal liability payments are not the assessed amounts, or are not in accordance with the schedule of payments, or include future assessments, include the basis for such differences, with supporting data, calculations, assumptions, and methods. In addition, contributions must be adjusted to reflect—

(i) The merger or transfer;

(ii) Any change in the rate of employer contributions that has been negotiated (whether or not in effect); and

(iii) Any trend of changing contribution base units over the preceding five plan years or other period of time that can be demonstrated to be more appropriate.

(2) Expected normal costs must be determined under the funding method and assumptions expected to be used by the plan actuary for purposes of determining the minimum funding requirement under section 431 of the Code. If the plan uses an aggregate funding method, normal costs must be determined under the entry age normal method.

(3) Expected benefit payments must be determined by assuming that current benefits remain in effect and that all scheduled increases in benefits occur.

(4) The plan's expected fair market value of assets immediately after the merger or transfer must be based on the most recent data available immediately before the date on which the notice is filed.

(5) Expected investment earnings must be determined using the same interest assumption to be used for determining the minimum funding requirement under section 431 of the Code.

(6) Expected expenses must be determined using expenses in the last plan year ending before the notice is filed, adjusted to reflect any anticipated changes.

(7) Expected plan assets for a plan year must be determined by adjusting the most current data on the plan's fair market value of assets to reflect expected contributions, investment earnings, benefit payments and expenses for each plan year between the date of the most current data and the beginning of the plan year for which expected assets are being determined.

§ 4231.7 De minimis mergers and transfers.

(a) *Special plan solvency rule.* The determination of whether a de minimis merger or transfer satisfies the plan solvency requirement in § 4231.6(a) may be made without regard to any other de minimis mergers or transfers that have occurred since the most recent actuarial valuation.

(b) *De minimis merger defined.* A merger is *de minimis* if the present value of accrued benefits (whether or not vested) of one plan is less than 3 percent of the other plan's fair market value of assets.

(c) *De minimis transfer defined.* A transfer of assets or liabilities is *de minimis* if—

(1) The fair market value of assets transferred, if any, is less than 3 percent of the fair market value of assets of all of the transferor plan's assets;

(2) The present value of the accrued benefits transferred (whether or not vested) is less than 3 percent of the fair market value of assets of all of the transferee plan's assets; and

(3) The transferee plan is not a plan that has terminated under section 4041A(a)(2) of ERISA.

(d) *Value of assets and benefits.* For purposes of paragraphs (b) and (c) of this section, the value of plan assets and accrued benefits may be determined as of any date prior to the proposed effective date of the transaction, but not earlier than the date of the most recent actuarial valuation.

(e) *Aggregation required.* In determining whether a merger or transfer is de minimis, the assets and accrued benefits transferred in previous *de minimis* mergers and transfers within the same plan year must be aggregated as described in paragraphs (e)(1) and (2) of this section. For the purposes of those paragraphs, the value of plan assets may be determined as of the date during the plan year on which the total value of the plan's assets is the highest.

(1) A merger is not de minimis if the total present value of accrued benefits merged into a plan, when aggregated with all prior de minimis mergers of and transfers to that plan effective within the same plan year, equals or exceeds 3 percent of the value of the plan's assets.

(2) A transfer is not de minimis if, when aggregated with all previous de minimis mergers and transfers effective within the same plan year—

(i) The value of all assets transferred from a plan equals or exceeds 3 percent of the value of the plan's assets; or

(ii) The present value of all accrued benefits transferred to a plan equals or exceeds 3 percent of the plan's assets.

§ 4231.8 Filing requirements; timing and method of filing.

(a) *When to file.* Except as provided in paragraph (g) of this section, a notice of a proposed merger or transfer, and, if applicable, a request for a compliance determination or facilitated merger (which may be filed separately or combined), must be filed not less than the following number of days before the proposed effective date of the transaction—

(1) 270 days in the case of a facilitated merger under § 4231.12;

(2) 120 days in the case of a merger (other than a facilitated merger) for which a compliance determination under § 4231.10 is requested, or a transfer; or

(3) 45 days in the case of a merger for which a compliance determination under § 4231.10 is not requested.

(b) *Method of filing.* PBGC applies the rules in subpart A of part 4000 of this chapter to determine permissible methods of filing with PBGC under this part.

(c) *Computation of time.* PBGC applies the rules in subpart D of part 4000 of this chapter to compute any time period for filing under this part.

(d) *Who must file.* The plan sponsors of all plans involved in a merger or transfer, or the duly authorized representative(s) acting on behalf of the plan sponsors, must jointly file the notice required by subpart A of this part, and, if applicable, a request for a facilitated merger under § 4231.12.

(e) *Where to file.* See § 4000.4 of this chapter for information on where to file.

(f) *Date of filing.* PBGC applies the rules in subpart C of part 4000 of this chapter to determine the date a submission under this part was filed with PBGC. For purposes of paragraph (a) of this section, the notice, and, if applicable, a request for a compliance determination or facilitated merger, is not considered filed until all of the information required under this part has been submitted.

(g) *Waiver of timing of notice.* PBGC may waive the timing requirements of paragraph (a) of this section and section 4231(b)(1) of ERISA if—

(1) A plan sponsor demonstrates to the satisfaction of PBGC that failure to complete the merger or transfer in less than the applicable notice period set forth in paragraph (a) of this section will cause harm to participants or beneficiaries of the plans involved in the transaction;

(2) PBGC determines that the transaction complies with the requirements of section 4231 of ERISA; or

(3) PBGC completes its review of the transaction.

§ 4231.9 Notice of merger or transfer.

Each notice of proposed merger or transfer required under section 4231(b)(1) of ERISA and this subpart must contain the following information:

(a) For each plan involved in the merger or transfer—

(1) The name of the plan;

(2) The name, address and telephone number of the plan sponsor and of the plan sponsor's duly authorized representative, if any; and

(3) The plan sponsor's EIN and the plan's PN and, if different, the EIN or PN last filed with PBGC. If no EIN or PN has been assigned, the notice must so indicate.

(b) Whether the transaction being reported is a merger or transfer, whether it involves any plan that has terminated under section 4041A(a)(2) of ERISA, whether any significantly affected plan is involved in the transaction (and, if so, identifying each such plan), and whether it is a de minimis transaction as defined in § 4231.7 (and, if so, including an enrolled actuary's certification to that effect).

(c) The proposed effective date of the transaction.

(d) A copy of each plan provision stating that no participant's or beneficiary's accrued benefit will be lower immediately after the effective date of the merger or transfer than the benefit immediately before that date.

(e) For each plan that exists after the transaction, one of the following statements, certified by an enrolled actuary:

(1) A statement that the plan satisfies the applicable plan solvency test set forth in § 4231.6, indicating which is the applicable test, and including the supporting data, calculations, assumptions, and methods.

(2) A statement of the basis on which the actuary has determined under § 4231.3(a)(3)(ii) that benefits under the plan are not reasonably expected to be subject to suspension under section 4245 of ERISA, including the supporting data, calculations, assumptions, and methods.

(f) For each plan that exists before a transaction (unless the transaction is de minimis and does not involve a request for financial assistance, or any plan that has terminated under section 4041A(a)(2) of ERISA), a copy of the most recent actuarial valuation report that satisfies the requirements of § 4231.5.

(g) For each significantly affected plan that exists after the transaction, the following information used in making the plan solvency determination under § 4231.6(b):

(1) The present value of the accrued benefits and plan's fair market value of assets under the valuation required by § 4231.5, allocable to the plan after the transaction.

(2) The fair market value of assets in the plan after the transaction (determined in accordance with § 4231.6(c)(4)).

(3) The expected benefit payments for the plan in the first plan year beginning on or after the proposed effective date of the transaction (determined in accordance with § 4231.6(c)(3)).

(4) The contribution rates in effect for the plan for the first plan year beginning on or after the proposed effective date of the transaction.

(5) The expected contributions for the plan in the first plan year beginning on or after the proposed effective date of the transaction (determined in accordance with § 4231.6(c)(1)).

§4231.10 Request for compliance determination.

(a) *General.* The plan sponsor(s) of one or more plans involved in a merger or transfer, or the duly authorized representative(s) acting on behalf of the plan sponsor(s), may file a request for a determination that the transaction complies with the requirements of section 4231 of ERISA. If the plan sponsor(s) requests a compliance determination, the request must be filed with the notice of merger or transfer under §4231.3(a)(4), and must contain the information described in paragraph (c) of this section, as applicable.

(b) *Single request permitted for all de minimis transactions.* A plan sponsor may submit a single request for a compliance determination covering all de minimis mergers or transfers that occur between one plan valuation and the next. However, the plan sponsor must still notify PBGC of each de minimis merger or transfer separately, in accordance with §§4231.8 and 4231.9. The single request for a compliance determination may be filed concurrently with any one of the notices of a de minimis merger or transfer.

(c) *Contents of request.* A request for a compliance determination concerning a merger or transfer that is not de minimis must contain—

(1) A copy of the merger or transfer agreement; and

(2) For each significantly affected plan, other than a plan that is a significantly affected plan only because the merger or transfer involves a plan that has terminated by mass withdrawal under section 4041A(a)(2) of ERISA, copies of all actuarial valuations performed within the 5 years preceding the date of filing the notice required under §4231.3(a)(4).

§4231.11 Actuarial calculations and assumptions.

(a) *Most recent valuation.* All calculations required by this part must be based on the most recent actuarial valuation as of the date of filing the notice, updated to show any material changes.

(b) *Assumptions.* All calculations required by this part must be performed by an enrolled actuary based on methods and assumptions each of which is reasonable (taking into account the experience of the plan and reasonable expectations), and which, in combination, offer the actuary's best estimate of anticipated experience under the plan.

(c) *Updated calculations.* PBGC may require updated calculations and representations based on the actual effective date of a merger or transfer if that date is more than one year after the notice is filed, based on revised actuarial assumptions, or based on other good cause.

Subpart B—Additional Rules for Facilitated Mergers

§4231.12 Request for facilitated merger.

(a) *General.* (1) The plan sponsors of the plans involved in a proposed merger may request that PBGC facilitate the merger. Facilitation may include training, technical assistance, mediation, communication with stakeholders, and support with related requests to other government agencies. Facilitation may also include financial assistance to the merged plan. PBGC has discretion under section 4231(e) of ERISA to take such actions as it deems appropriate to facilitate the merger of two or more multiemployer plans if it determines, after consultation with the Advocate, that the proposed merger is in the interests of the participants and beneficiaries of at least one of the plans, and is not reasonably expected to be adverse to the overall interests of the participants and beneficiaries of any of the plans involved in the proposed merger. For a facilitated merger, including a financial assistance merger, the requirements of section 4231(b) of ERISA and subpart A of this part must be satisfied in addition to the requirements of section 4231(e) of ERISA and this subpart. The procedures set forth in this subpart represent the exclusive means by which PBGC will approve a request for a facilitated merger under section 4231(e) of ERISA.

(2) *Financial assistance.* Subject to the requirements in section 4231(e) of ERISA and this subpart, in the case of a request for a financial assistance merger, PBGC may in its discretion provide financial assistance (within the meaning of section 4261 of ERISA). Such financial assistance will be with respect to the guaranteed benefits payable under the critical and declining status plan(s) involved in the facilitated merger.

(b) *Information requirements.* (1) A request for a facilitated merger, including a request for a financial assistance merger, must be filed with the notice of merger under §4231.3(a)(4), and must contain the information described in §4231.10, and a detailed narrative description with supporting documentation demonstrating that the proposed merger is in the interests of participants and beneficiaries of at least one of the plans, and is not reasonably expected to be adverse to the overall interests of the participants and beneficiaries of any of the plans. If a

financial assistance merger is requested, the narrative description and supporting documentation may consider the effect of financial assistance in making these demonstrations.

(2) If a financial assistance merger is requested, the request must contain the information required in §§4231.13 through 4231.16 in addition to the information required in paragraph (b)(1) of this section.

(3) *Additional information.* PBGC may require the plan sponsors to submit additional information to determine whether the requirements of section 4231(e) of ERISA are met or to enable it to facilitate the merger.

(c) *Duty to amend and supplement.* During any time in which a request for a facilitated merger, including a request for a financial assistance merger, is pending final action by PBGC, the plan sponsors must promptly notify PBGC in writing of any material fact or representation contained in or relating to the request, or in any supporting documents, that is no longer accurate or was omitted.

§4231.13 Plan information for financial assistance merger.

A request for a financial assistance merger must include the following information for each plan involved in the merger:

(a) The most recent trust agreement, including all amendments adopted since the last restatement.

(b) The most recent plan document, including all amendments adopted since the last restatement.

(c) The most recent summary plan description (SPD), and all summaries of material modification issued since the most recent SPD.

(d) If applicable, the most recent rehabilitation plan (or funding improvement plan), including all subsequent amendments and updates, and the percentage of total contributions received under each schedule of the rehabilitation plan (or funding improvement plan) for the most recent plan year available.

(e) A copy of the plan's most recent IRS determination letter.

(f) A copy of the plan's most recent Form 5500 (Annual Report Form) and all schedules and attachments (including the audited financial statement).

(g) A current listing of employers who have an obligation to contribute to the plan, and the approximate number of participants for whom each employer is currently making contributions.

(h) A schedule of withdrawal liability payments collected in each of the most recent five plan years.

(i) If applicable, a copy of the plan sponsor's application for suspension of benefits under section 305(e)(9)(G) of ERISA (including all attachments and exhibits).

§4231.14 Description of financial assistance merger.

A request for a financial assistance merger must include the following information about the proposed financial assistance merger:

(a) A detailed description of the proposed financial assistance merger, including any larger integrated transaction of which the merger is a part (including, but not limited to, an application for suspension of benefits under section 305(e)(9)(G) of ERISA).

(b) A narrative description of the events that led to the plan sponsors' decision to submit a request for a financial assistance merger.

(c) A narrative description of significant risks and assumptions relating to the proposed financial assistance merger and the projections provided in support of the request.

(d) A detailed description of the estimated total amount of financial assistance the plan sponsors request for each year, including the supporting data, calculations, assumptions, and a description of the methodology used to determine the estimated amounts.

§4231.15 Actuarial and financial information for financial assistance merger.

A request for a financial assistance merger must include the following actuarial and financial information for the plans involved in the merger:

(a) A copy of the actuarial valuation performed for each of the two plan years before the most recent actuarial valuation filed in accordance with §4231.5.

(b) If applicable, a copy of the plan actuary's most recent annual actuarial certification under section 305(b)(3) of ERISA, including a detailed description of the assumptions used in the certification, and the basis under which they were determined. The description must include information about the assumptions used for the projection of future contributions, withdrawal liability payments, and investment returns, and any other assumption that may have a material effect on projections.

(c) A detailed statement certified by an enrolled actuary that the merger is necessary for one or more of the plans involved to avoid or postpone insolvency, including the basis for the conclusion, supporting data, calculations, assumptions, and a description of the methodology. This statement must demonstrate for each critical and declining status plan involved in the merger that the date the plan projects to become insolvent (without reflecting the merger) is earlier than the date the merged plan projects to become insolvent (the merged plan may reflect the proposed financial assistance). Include as an exhibit annual cash flow projections for each critical and declining status plan involved in the merger through the date the plan projects to become insolvent (using an open group valuation and without reflecting the merger). Annual cash flow projections must reflect the following information:

(1) Fair market value of assets as of the beginning of the year.

(2) Contributions and withdrawal liability payments.

(3) Benefit payments organized by participant type (*e.g.*, active, retiree, terminated vested).

(4) Administrative expenses.

(5) Fair market value of assets as of the end of the year.

(d) For each critical and declining status plan involved in the merger, a long-term projection (at least 50 to 90 years) of benefit disbursements by participant type (*e.g.*, active, retiree, terminated vested) (without reflecting the merger) reflecting reduced benefit disbursements at the PBGC-guarantee level beginning with the proposed effective date of the merger (using a closed group valuation and no accruals after the proposed effective date of the merger).

(e) For each critical and declining status plan involved in the merger, a long-term projection (at least 50 to 90 years) of benefit disbursements by participant type (*e.g.*, active, retiree, terminated vested) (without reflecting the merger) reflecting maximum benefit suspensions that would be permissible under section 305(e)(9) of ERISA beginning with the proposed effective date of the merger (using an open group valuation).

(f) A detailed statement certified by an enrolled actuary that financial assistance is necessary for the merged plan to become or remain solvent, including the basis for the conclusion, supporting data, calculations, assumptions, and a description of the methodology. Include as an exhibit annual cash flow projections for the merged plan with the proposed financial assistance (based on the actuarial assumptions and methods that will be used under the merged plan). Annual cash flow projections must reflect the information listed in paragraphs (c)(1) through (5) of this section. In addition, include as an exhibit a statement of whether the merged plan would be in critical status for purposes of paragraph (f)(1) or (2) of this section, including the basis for the conclusion.

(1) If the merged plan would be in critical status immediately following the merger without the proposed financial assistance (as reasonably determined by the enrolled actuary), the enrolled actuary's certified statement must demonstrate that the merged plan will avoid insolvency under section 305(e)(9)(D)(iv) of ERISA and the regulations thereunder (excluding stochastic projections) with the proposed financial assistance.

(2) If the merged plan would not be in critical status immediately following the merger without the proposed financial assistance (as reasonably determined by the enrolled actuary), the enrolled actuary's certified statement must demonstrate that the merged plan is not projected to become insolvent during the 20 plan years beginning after the proposed effective date of the merger with the proposed financial assistance (using the methodologies set forth under section 305(b)(3)(B)(iv) of ERISA and the regulations thereunder). If such a demonstration is possible without the proposed financial assistance, or if the amount of financial assistance requested exceeds the amount needed to satisfy this demonstration, the enrolled actuary's certified statement must demonstrate that financial assistance is necessary to mitigate the adverse effects of the merger on the merged plan's ability to remain solvent.

(g) If applicable, a copy of the plan actuary's certification under section 305(e)(9)(C)(i) of ERISA.

(h) The rules in §4231.6(c) apply to the solvency projections described in §4231.15(c) and (f), unless section 305(e)(9)(D)(iv) of ERISA and the regulations thereunder apply and specify otherwise.

§4231.16 Participant census data for financial assistance merger.

A request for a financial assistance merger must include a copy of the census data used for the projections described in §4231.15(c) and (f), including:

(a) Participant type (retiree, beneficiary, disabled, terminated vested, active, alternate payee).

(b) Gender.

(c) Date of birth.

(d) Credited service for guarantee calculation (*i.e.*, number of years of participation).

(e) Vested accrued monthly benefit.

(f) Monthly benefit guaranteed by PBGC.

(g) Monthly benefit reduced by the maximum benefit suspension permissible under section 305(e)(9) of ERISA.

(h) Benefit commencement date (for participants in pay status and others for which the reported benefit will not be payable at normal retirement age).

(i) For each participant in pay status—

(1) Form of payment, and

(2) Data relevant to the form of payment, including:

(i) For a joint-and-survivor benefit, the beneficiary's benefit amount and the beneficiary's date of birth;

(ii) For a Social Security level income benefit, the date of any change in the benefit amount, and the benefit amount after such change;

(iii) For a 5-year certain or 10-year certain benefit (or similar benefit), the relevant defined period; or

(iv) For a form of payment not otherwise described in this section, the data necessary for the valuation of the form of payment.

(j) If an actuarial increase for postponed retirement applies, or if the form of annuity is a Social Security level income option, the monthly vested benefit payable at normal retirement age in normal form of annuity.

§4231.17 PBGC action on a request for facilitated merger.

(a) *General.* PBGC may approve or deny a request for a facilitated merger, including a request for a financial assistance merger, at its discretion if the requirements of section 4231 of ERISA are satisfied. PBGC will notify the plan sponsor(s) in writing of its decision on a request. If PBGC denies the request, PBGC's written decision will state the reason(s) for the denial. If PBGC approves a request for a financial assistance merger, PBGC will provide a financial assistance agreement detailing the total amount and terms of the financial assistance as soon as practicable thereafter.

(b) *Final agency action.* PBGC's decision to approve or deny a request for a facilitated merger, including a request for a financial assistance merger, is a final agency action for purposes of judicial review under the Administrative Procedure Act (5 U.S.C. 701 *et seq.*).

§4231.18 Jurisdiction over financial assistance merger.

(a) *General.* PBGC will retain jurisdiction over the merged plan resulting from a financial assistance merger to carry out the purposes, terms, and conditions of the financial assistance merger, the financial assistance agreement, sections 4231 and 4261 of ERISA, and the regulations thereunder.

(b) *Financial assistance agreement.* PBGC may, upon providing notice to the plan sponsor, make changes to the financial assistance agreement in response to changed circumstances consistent with sections 4231 and 4261 of ERISA and the regulations thereunder.

Issued in Washington, DC, this 25th day of May, 2016.

W. Thomas Reeder,

Director, Pension Benefit Guaranty Corporation.

[FR Doc. 2016-13083 Filed 6-2-16; 11:15 am]

BILLING CODE 7709-02-P

¶ 20,539E

Employee Benefits Security Administration (EBSA): IRS: Group health plans: Expatriate health plans: Excepted benefits: Reporting and disclosure.—The EBSA, IRS, and Department of Health and Human Services have issued proposed regulations on the rules for expatriate health plans, expatriate health plan issuers, and qualified expatriates under the Expatriate Health Coverage Clarification Act of 2014 (EHCCA), which was enacted as Division M of the Consolidated and Further Continuing Appropriations Act, 2015 (P.L. 113-235). The proposed regulations also provide standards for travel insurance and supplemental health insurance coverage to be considered excepted benefits and require a notice to be furnished in connection with hospital indemnity and other fixed indemnity insurance in the group health insurance market for it to be considered excepted benefits. The regulations are proposed to be applicable for plan years (or, in the individual market, policy years) beginning on or after January 1, 2017. Issuers, employers, administrators, and individuals are permitted to rely on these proposed regulations pending the applicability date of final regulations.

The proposed regulations, which were published in the Federal Register on June 10, 2016 (81 FR 38019), are reproduced at ¶ 20,264J. The regulations concerning short-term, limited duration insurance, standards for travel insurance and supplemental health insurance coverage, and lifetime and annual limits were finalized on October 31, 2016 (81 FR 75316). The Departments intend to address hospital imdemnity or other fixed indemnity insurance, and expatriate health plans in future rulemaking. The preamble to the final regulations is at ¶ 23,328. The EBSA final regulations are at ¶ 15,049J, ¶ 15,050R-50NA, ¶ 15,051B-1, and ¶ 15,051E-1.

¶ 20,539F

Employee Benefits Security Administration (EBSA): Proposed rule: Form 5500 : Annual reporting: Reporting and disclosure.—EBSA has issued proposed regulatory amendments to conform the reporting regulations to DOL, IRS, and PBGC proposed revisions to the Form 5500 (Annual Return/Report of Employee Benefit Plan) and Form 5500-SF (Short Form Annual Return/Report of Small Employee Benefit Plan). The proposed forms revisions (see ¶ 24,019N) and the EBSA implementing regulations are intended to address changes in applicable laws and the employee benefit plan and financial markets, and corresponding shifts in Agency priorities and needs since the last major revision. If the proposed revisions are adopted, the changes generally would apply for plan years beginning on or after January 1, 2019.

The proposed regulations, which were published in the Federal Register on July 21, 2016 (81 FR 47495), are reproduced below.

FEDERAL REGISTER

Vol. 81 No. 140

Thursday, July 21, 2016

Part II Department of Labor

Employee Benefits Security Administration

29 CFR Parts 2520 and 2590

Annual Reporting and Disclosure; Proposed Rule

DEPARTMENT OF LABOR

Employee Benefits Security Administration

29 CFR Parts 2520 and 2590

RIN 1210-AB63

Annual Reporting and Disclosure

AGENCY: Employee Benefits Security Administration, Labor.

ACTION: Proposed rule.

SUMMARY: This document contains proposed amendments to Department of Labor (DOL) regulations relating to annual reporting requirements under Part 1 of Subtitle B of Title I of the Employee Retirement Income Security Act of 1974, as amended (ERISA). The proposed amendments contained in this document would conform the DOL's reporting regulations to proposed revisions to the Form 5500 Annual Return/Report of Employee Benefit Plan and Form 5500-SF Short Form Annual Return/Report of Small Employee Benefit Plan, which are being published concurrently in today's **Federal Register** in a separate Notice of Proposed Forms Revisions (NPFR) prepared jointly by the Department of Labor (DOL), the Internal Revenue Service (IRS), and the Pension Benefit Guaranty Corporation (PBGC) (collectively the Agencies). The proposed regulation, and related forms revisions, would improve employee benefit plan reporting for filers, the public, and the Agencies. The revision is necessary because the annual return/report forms have not kept pace with market developments and changes in the laws covering employee benefit plans, presenting problems with outdated and missing information that negatively impact the Agencies' effective and efficient protection of employee retirement and health benefits. The proposed revisions would affect employee pension and welfare benefit plans, plan sponsors, administrators, and service providers.

DATES: Written comments must be received by the Department of Labor on or before October 4, 2016.

ADDRESSES: To facilitate the receipt and processing of written comment letters on the proposed regulation, EBSA encourages interested persons to submit their comments electronically. You may submit comments, identified by RIN 1210-AB63, by any of the following methods:

Federal eRulemaking Portal: http://www.regulations.gov.

Follow instructions for submitting comments.

Email: e-ORI@dol.gov. Include RIN 1210-AB63 in the subject line of the message.

Mail: Office of Regulations and Interpretations, Employee Benefits Security Administration, Attn: RIN 1210-AB63; Annual Reporting and Disclosure, Room N-5655, U.S. Department of Labor, 200 Constitution Avenue NW., Washington, DC 20210.

Hand Delivery/Courier: Office of Regulations and Interpretations, Employee Benefits Security Administration, Attn: RIN 1210-AB63; Annual Reporting and Disclosure, Room N-5655, U.S. Department of Labor, 200 Constitution Avenue NW., Washington, DC 20210.

Instructions: All comments received must include the agency name and Regulatory Identifier Number (RIN) for this rulemaking (RIN 1210-AB63). Persons submitting comments electronically are encouraged not to submit paper copies. All comments received will be made available to the public, posted without change to *http://www.regulations.gov* and *http://www.dol.gov/ebsa*, and made available for public inspection at the Public Disclosure Room, N-1513, Employee Benefits Security Administration, U.S. Department of Labor, 200 Constitution Avenue NW., Washington, DC 20210, including any personal information provided.

FOR FURTHER INFORMATION CONTACT: Mara S. Blumenthal, Office of Regulations and Interpretations, Employee Benefits Security Administration, U.S. Department of Labor, (202) 693-8523 (not a toll-free number) for all changes other than group health plan information; Suzanne Adelman, EBSA, U.S. Department of Labor, 202-693-8383 (not a toll-free number), for questions relating to the collection of group health plan information.

SUPPLEMENTARY INFORMATION:

I. Executive Summary

A. Purpose of the Regulatory Action

Under Titles I and IV of ERISA and the Internal Revenue Code (Code), pension and other employee benefit plans are generally required to file annual returns/reports concerning, among other things, the financial condition and operations of the plan. Filing a Form 5500 Annual Return/Report of Employee Benefit Plan (Form 5500 Annual Return/Report), or a Form 5500-SF Short Form Annual Return/Report of Small Employee Benefit Plan (Form 5500-SF) (depending on certain plan characteristics), together with any required schedules and attachments (together "the Form 5500 Annual Return/Report"), in accordance with their instructions, generally satisfies these annual reporting requirements. In addition to being an important disclosure document for plan participants and beneficiaries, the Form 5500 Annual Return/Report is a critical enforcement, compliance, and research tool for the DOL, IRS, and the PBGC (together "Agencies"). It is also an important source of information and data for use by other federal agencies,

Congress, and the private sector in assessing employee benefit, tax, and economic trends and policies. In the United States, there are an estimated 2.3 million health plans, a similar number of other welfare plans, and nearly 681,000 private pension plans. These plans cover roughly have 143 million private sector workers, retirees, and dependents, and have estimated assets of $8.7 trillion. The Form 5500 Annual Return/Report is the principal source of information and data concerning the operations, funding, and investments of more than 806,000 of these pension and welfare benefit plans.

Generally, the Agencies have conducted notice and comment rulemaking before making significant changes to the forms and schedules. This proposed revision to the DOL's reporting regulations is needed to implement the forms revisions proposed in the three-agency (DOL, IRS, and the PBGC) Notice of Proposed Forms Revisions (NPFR), which is being published separately in today's **Federal Register**.

As noted above and discussed in detail below, because the Form 5500 Annual Return/Report has not kept pace with market developments and changes in the laws covering employee benefit plans, problems with outdated and missing information negatively impact the Agencies' effective and efficient protection of employee retirement and group health benefits. That fact is reflected in the more than 15 reports that have been issued since the publication of the last major forms revisions from the Government Accountability Office (GAO), the DOL's Office of Inspector General (DOL-OIG), the United States Treasury Inspector General for Tax Administration (the TIGTA), and the ERISA Advisory Council that all call for expanded annual reporting by employee benefit plans and improvements in the Form 5500 Annual Return/Report.[1] In developing these proposed updates to the Form 5500 Annual Return/Report, the DOL, along with IRS and PBGC, carefully considered those reports in determining where changes are needed.

In addition, a significant update being made to the Form 5500 Annual Return/Report is the introduction of basic reporting requirements for all plans that provide group health benefits that have fewer than 100 participants and are covered by Title I of ERISA, most of which are currently exempt from reporting requirements, and the addition of a new schedule (Schedule J) proposed to be required for all group health plans. This reflects a new emphasis on transparency under the Affordable Care Act[2] and a desire to offer plan sponsors the opportunity to satisfy certain Affordable Care Act reporting requirements addressed in this proposal by a more robust Form 5500 Annual Return/Report filing for those group health plans currently required to file and by elimination of the current exemption for plans that provide group health benefits that have fewer than 100 participants that are fully insured, unfunded, or a combination. Once finalized, these proposed changes will result in annual return/report forms that are a more effective policy, enforcement, and research tool, and one that will increase transparency, accountability, and confidence in the employee benefit plan system.

The Agencies' proposed changes to the Form 5500 Annual Return/Report also should be viewed in light of the fact that the last two major revisions of the Form 5500 Annual Return/Report[3] occurred in 1999 and 2009 in connection with a major shift from a paper-based filing system to the current internet-based wholly electronic filing and electronic data processing system (EFAST and now EFAST2), which is operated by a private sector contractor. For the last two major form revision cycles, the Agencies were focused on moving filers to new technologies for filing Form 5500 Annual Return/Report data. In recognition of the burden and challenges that filers would face in migrating to new filing technologies, the Agencies generally deferred proposing major form changes that would add substantial new burdens. In fact, by deferring our current proposals until now, the new EFAST2 capabilities are making more feasible and efficient processing of both the existing and the expanded data we are proposing to collect.

B. Summary of the Major Revisions of the Regulatory Action

The proposed forms revisions and the DOL implementing regulations are intended to address changes in applicable laws and the employee benefit plan and financial markets, and corresponding shifts in agency priorities and needs since the last major revision. The proposed revisions are also expected ultimately to make filing and processing more efficient and accurate and to restore a greater level of transparency in the employee benefit plan market.[4] The proposed forms revisions fall under the following general categories:

1. Modernize Financial and Investment Reporting by Pension Plans

A key component of the proposal would expand and modernize financial and investment information reported by pension plans. Reporting on the financial operations and integrity of U.S. private pension plans (both defined benefit and defined contribution) is critical given the ongoing importance of such plans to the retirement security of America's workforce. Moreover, improved transparency of financial products and investments acquired by plans is critical to the ability of the Agencies to fulfill their statutory oversight role. It is also important for ongoing monitoring of retirement plans by employers, plans, participants and beneficiaries, and policy makers. These proposed changes to financial reporting are specifically designed to improve reporting of alternative investments, hard-to-value assets, and investments through collective investment vehicles and participant-directed brokerage accounts.

An overriding objective of these proposed revisions to the financial information collected as part of the annual return/report is to present plan financial and balance sheet information, including the currently required schedules of assets, in a way that better reflects the investment portfolios and asset management practices of employee benefit plans. The basic objective of ERISA's mandatory financial reporting is to provide information about the reporting entity for the Agencies' enforcement, research, and policy formulation programs; for other federal agencies, Congress, and the private sector to assist them in assessing employee benefit, tax, and economic trends and policies; and for plan participants and beneficiaries and the general public to under-

---

[1] See, e.g., U.S. Gov't Accountability Office, GAO-10-54, Private Pensions: Additional Changes Could Improve Employee Benefit Plan Financial Reporting (2009) (available at www.gao.gov/assets/300/298052.pdf); U.S. Gov't Accountability Office, GAO-14-441, Private Pensions: Targeted Revisions Could Improve Usefulness of Form 5500 Information (2014) (available at www.gao.gov/products/GAO-14-441); 2013 ERISA Advisory Council Report: Private Sector Pension De-risking and Participant Protections, Dep't of Labor, www.dol.gov/ebsa/publications/2013ACreport2.html); Dep't of Labor Office Of Inspector Gen., 05-14-003-12-12, EBSA Could Improve Its Usage of Form 5500 Data (2014) (available at www.oig.dol.gov/public/reports/oa/2014/05-14-003-12-121.pdf); U.S. Gov't Accountability Office, GAO-14-92, Private Pensions: Clarity of Required Reports and Disclosures Could Be Improved (2013) (available at www.gao.gov/assets/660/659211.pdf); U.S. Gov't Accountability Office, GAO-14-92, Private Pensions: Clarity Of Required Reports And Disclosures Could Be Improved, Report to Congressional Requesters (2013) (available at www.gao.gov/assets/660/659211.pdf); U.S. Dep't of Labor Office of Inspector Gen., 09-13-001-12-121, Employee Benefits Security Administration Needs to Provide Additional Guidance And Oversight to ERISA Plans Holding Hard-to-Value Alternative Investments (2013) (available at www.oig.dol.gov/public/reports/oa/2013/09-13-001-12-121.pdf); U.S. Gov't Accountability Office, GAO-12-665, Private Sector Pensions: Federal Agencies Should Collect Data and Coordinate Oversight of Multiple Employer Plans (2012) (available at www.gao.gov/assets/650/648285.pdf); U.S. Dep't of Labor Office Of Inspector Gen., 09-12-002-12-121, Changes Are Still Needed In The ERISA Audit Process To Increase Protections For Employee Benefit Plan Participants (2012) (available at www.oig.dol.gov/public/reports/oa/2012/09-12-002-12-121.pdf); U.S. Gov't Accountability Office, GAO-12-325, 401(K) Plans: Increased Educational Outreach and Broader Oversight May Help Reduce Plan Fees (2012) (available at www.gao.gov/products/GAO-12-325); U.S. Gov't Accountability Office, GAO-08-692, Defined Benefit Plans: Guidance Needed to Better Inform Plans of the Challenges and Risks of Investing in Hedge Funds and Private Equity (2012) (available at www.gao.gov/products/GAO-08-692); Treasury Inspector Gen. for Tax Administration, The Employee Plans Function Should Continue Its Efforts to Obtain Needed Retirement Plan Information (2011) (available at www.treasury.gov/tigta/auditreports/2011reports/201110108fr.pdf); 2011 ERISA Advisory Council Report: Hedge Funds

and Private Equity Investments, Dep't of Labor, www.dol.gov/ebsa/publications/2011ACreport3.html); 2013 ERISA Advisory Council Report: Locating Missing and Lost Participants, Dep't of Labor, www.dol.gov/ebsa/publications/2013ACreport3.html#2; 2010 ERISA Advisory Council Report: Employee Benefit Plan Auditing and Financial Reporting Models, Dep't of Labor, www.dol.gov/ebsa/publications/2010ACreport2.html; 2008 ERISA Advisory Council Report: Working Group on Hard-to-Value Assets and Target Date Funds, Dep't of Labor, www.dol.gov/ebsa/publications/2008ACreport1.html.

[2] The Patient Protection and Affordable Care Act, Public Law 111-148, was enacted on March 23, 2010, and the Health Care and Education Reconciliation Act of 2010, Public Law 111-152, was enacted on March 30, 2010. These statutes generally are collectively known as the "Affordable Care Act."

[3] The Agencies' last tri-agency major revision to the Form 5500 Annual Return/Report series was effective for the 2009 plan year forms. Before that, the last major revision was effective for the 1999 plan year forms and was implemented together with the initial implementation of EFAST. In interim years, the Agencies have made other focused changes, which are set forth annually in the "Changes to Note" section in the instructions.

[4] In addition, this rulemaking and forms revisions are being coordinated generally with a re-bid and updating of the ERISA Filing Acceptance System (EFAST2)—the wholly electronic Form 5500 Annual Return/Report filing and processing system. Unlike the 1999 and 2009 forms revisions, the re-bid of EFAST2 does not involve major changes in the EFAST2 key system requirements, capabilities, and functions. Rather, although there are some changes to the system, the re-bid process is largely being undertaken in response to Federal Acquisition Regulation (FAR) requirements on periodic re-bidding of longer term contracts. Under these circumstances, there may be opportunities to implement various form changes either before or after the re-bid EFAST2 contract is awarded. The timing of the re-bid of EFAST2 and implementation of form changes may also be affected by whether funds necessary for the re-bid or form implementation are appropriated as part of the Agencies' respective budgets. Accordingly, although the overall objective is to implement these proposed form changes as part of a re-bid EFAST2 contract, rulemaking and budget issues may require the Agencies to consider a more staged approach.

stand and monitor better the activities and investments of employee benefit plans. As reflected in the various reports from the GAO, the DOL-OIG, the ERISA Advisory Council, and the TIGTA, the current information collected on the Form 5500 Annual Return/Report and Form 5500-SF is insufficient to satisfy those objectives.

The financial statements contained in the current Schedule H (Large Plan Financial Information) and Schedule I (Small Plan Financial Information) are based on data elements that have remained largely unchanged since the Form 5500 Annual Return/Report was established in 1975. Over the past four decades, the U.S. private pension system has shifted from defined benefit (defined benefit or DB) pension plans toward defined contribution (defined contribution or DC) pension plans, often participant-directed 401(k)-type DC pension plans. The financing of retirement benefits has changed dramatically coincident with the shift from DB to DC pension plans. In 1978, when legislation was enacted authorizing 401(k) plans that allow employees to contribute to their own retirement plan on a pre-tax basis, participants contributed only 29 percent of the contributions to DC pension plans and only 11 percent of total contributions to both DB and DC pension plans. "In the years following 1978, employee contributions to DC pension plans steadily rose to a peak of approximately 60 percent in 1999, where it has remained." *See Dep't of Labor, Private Pension Plan Bulletin Abstract of 2012 Form 5500 Annual Reports*, at 1 (2015). Simultaneously, the number of single-employer DB pension plans has decreased from 92,000 in 1990 to just under 29,000 single-employer pension plans in 2009. *See U.S. Gov't Accountability Office, GAO-09-291, Defined Benefit Pensions: Survey Results of the Nation's Largest Private Defined Benefit Plan Sponsors Highlights* (2009) (available at *http://www.gao.gov/new.items/d09291.pdf*).

The shift from DB pension plans to DC pension plans—and the corresponding increase of participants' own contributions to those plans as opposed to employer contributions—has led to increased responsibility for participants to manage their own retirement savings, which includes having to select among investment options in their retirement plans. *See Private Pension Plan Bulletin Abstract Of 2012 Form 5500 Annual Reports*, at 2 (Of the 516,000 section 401(k)-type plans in 2012, 87.8 percent allowed participants to direct investment of all of their assets, and 3.1 percent allowed participants to direct investment of a portion of their assets.) The need for more relevant and comparable financial information is not limited to 401(k) and other DC pension plans; it also extends to DB pension plans. Reports cited above from GAO, the DOL-OIG, the TIGTA, and the ERISA Advisory Council also have focused on the need for increased transparency and accountability generally in connection with employee benefit plan investments in hard-to-value and alternative assets, as well as assets held through pooled investment vehicles.

Further, the Agencies need better information to effectively oversee and enforce existing rules and regulations. For example, as part of the 1999 and 2009 forms revisions, the Agencies stopped collecting a variety of information regarding ESOPs. ESOPs, however, continue to be a significant enforcement focus and concern for both DOL and the Department of Treasury (Treasury)/IRS. Under the proposal, ESOPs would be required to again report information, on the Schedule E, about their employer stock acquisitions. Plan investment in hard-to-value and other alternative investments, such as derivatives, limited partnerships, hedge funds, private equity, and real estate, was highlighted as an oversight risk by both GAO and the DOL-OIG. Plans invested in derivatives, limited partnerships, hedge funds, private equity, real estate, and other alternative investments would be required under the proposal to identify such investments specifically. Having plans and direct filing entities (DFEs) report this information would be a significant improvement; the Agencies would no longer be limited to identifying issues involving investments in derivatives and other hard-to-value assets by opening investigations on a plan-by-plan basis. For example, regulators would be able to search the data base for particular investments or managers where there were indications that there were problems with such investment or manager for all plans that made such investments. The improved financial transparency in the proposed revisions to the Form 5500 Annual Return/Report data collection in general would better enable public and private data users to identify patterns and trends in plan investments and behavior.

For defined contribution pension plans, especially participant-directed plans, the proposal also would provide better information on employee participation rates in 401(k)-type plans and more relevant information on the types of investment alternatives available in such plans (including information on each designated investment alternative in the plan, information on qualified default investment alternatives, and information on whether the investment alternatives are actively managed or passively managed index funds). As Form 5500 Annual Return/Report information is required by Title I of ERISA to be publicly available, not only would expanded data collection assist in the Agencies' research and policymaking objectives, public access to this information would enable interested private sector and other governmental stakeholders to perform data-based research or help plan sponsors, fiduciaries, and participants and beneficiaries better understand their plan and plan investments. For example, it would be more feasible to compare performance of plans based on types of investments, and get information on how certain plan investment options and structures might correlate to participation, overall performance, or best preparation of workers for retirement.

2. Support Oversight of Group Health Plans and Ongoing Implementation of the Affordable Care Act

The proposed forms revisions and DOL implementing regulations would expand Form 5500 reporting by group health plans[5] by eliminating obsolete exemptions for certain plans from Form 5500 reporting. Specifically, most private employer-sponsored group health plans with fewer than 100 participants that are fully insured, unfunded, or a combination of the two, currently do not file the Form 5500 Annual Return/Report under the terms of the current DOL exemptions. As a result, for policy formulation, research, and regulatory impact analyses, the DOL must rely on surveys, instead of Form 5500 Annual Return/Report data, to generate even basic estimates of the size of the ERISA group health plan universe that is a major part of the nation's health care delivery system. The current lack of information collected on the Form 5500 Annual Return/Report from group health plans impairs the effectiveness of EBSA's ability to develop health care regulations and complicates the DOL's ability to enforce such regulations and educate plan administrators regarding compliance.

In addition, section 1253 of the Affordable Care Act requires the Secretary of Labor to prepare an annual report that includes certain general information on self-insured group health plans using data collected from the Form 5500 Annual Return/Report (the "Self-Insured Health Plan Report"). Current Form 5500 Annual Return/Report data provides the basis only for an incomplete assessment of self-insured plans. For example, information about the amount of outstanding claims for a self-insured plan, a proposed new data element on the Schedule J, would be a critical flag that would identify the need for further inquiry or investigation of a group health plan that may be unable to pay outstanding claims. Early intervention by EBSA could prevent a participant from facing bankruptcy over unpaid medical expenses that otherwise would have been covered had the group health plan been properly funded.

We expect more group health plan filings will help the DOL allocate enforcement resources and streamline enforcement actions. For example, these additional filings will enable the DOL to correlate information reported by different group health plans to help identify widespread noncompliance perpetuated by a common service provider rather than relying on multiple investigations of client plans to detect a pattern of non-compliance by a single service provider. Obtaining a correction by going directly to the service provider makes the correction process more efficient for the service provider and the Department and results in uniform and efficient corrective action for participating plans. EBSA anticipates that Form 5500 Annual Return/Report data may similarly be used in future versions of the biennial Paul Wellstone and Pete Domenici Mental Health Parity and Addiction Equity Act (MHPAEA) Report to Congress on the compliance of group health plans and health insurance coverage offered in connection with such plans with the requirements of MHPAEA. The proposed changes to group health plan reporting thus are important to the government's ability to accomplish oversight obligations under the Affordable Care Act and other federal laws governing group health plans, to more effectively monitor health policy issues as they pertain to ERISA-covered plans, and to provide Congress with accurate information about self-insured plans and whether the plan is complying with the protections of MHPAEA.

---

[5] Under the proposed changes, all "group health plans" that meet the definition in 733(a) of the Act, including plans that claim "grandfathered" status under 29 CFR 2950.715-1251, are required to file some or all of the Form 5500 Annual Return/Report and applicable schedules, including the Schedule J, regardless of whether such plans are exempt from certain market reform requirements under ERISA §732(a) (exemption for certain small group health plans that have less than two participants who are current employees) or ERISA §733(c) (group health plans consisting solely of excepted benefits). Employee welfare benefit plans as defined in ERISA §3(1) that do not meet the definition of "group health plan" under 733 of the Act (*i.e.*, they do not provide benefits for medical care) are not subject to the proposed enhanced reporting requirements applicable to group health plans.

3. Reporting To Satisfy Public Health Service Act Sections 2715A and 2717

Sections 2715A and 2717 of the Public Health Service Act (PHS Act), as added by the Affordable Care Act and incorporated into ERISA section 715,[6] include important new reporting requirements for group health plans and health insurance issuers in the group and individual markets. Specifically, section 2715A of the PHS Act incorporates the transparency provisions of section 1311(e)(3) of the Affordable Care Act to require non-grandfathered group health plans and health insurance issuers offering non-grandfathered group or individual health insurance coverage to make available to the DOL, the Department of Health and Human Services (HHS), Treasury, State insurance commissioner, and the public a host of information on health plan enrollment and claims.[7] This includes: (1) Claims payment policies and practices; (2) periodic financial disclosures; (3) data on enrollment and disenrollment; (4) data on the number of denied claims; (5) data on rating practices; (6) information on cost-sharing and payments with respect to any out-of-network coverage; (7) information on enrollee and participation rights; and (8) other information as determined by the Secretary. Moreover, section 2717 of the PHS Act generally requires non-grandfathered group health plans and health insurance issuers offering non-grandfathered group or individual health insurance coverage to report annually to the DOL, HHS and the Treasury and to enrollees under the plan whether the benefits under the plan: (A) Improve health outcomes through the implementation of activities such as quality reporting, effective case management, care coordination, chronic disease management, and medication and care compliance initiatives, including through the use of the medical homes model as defined for purposes of section 3602 of the Affordable Care Act, for treatment or services under the plan or coverage; (B) implement activities to prevent hospital readmissions through a comprehensive program for hospital discharge that includes patient-centered education and counseling, comprehensive discharge planning, and post discharge reinforcement by an appropriate health care professional; (C) implement activities to improve patient safety and reduce medical errors through the appropriate use of best clinical practices, evidence based medicine, and health information technology under the plan or coverage; and (D) implement wellness and health promotion activities.

These regulations propose conforming amendments in 29 CFR 2590.715-2715A and 29 CFR 2590.715-2717 to clarify that compliance with the reporting requirements in 29 CFR 2520.103-1 (including filing any required schedules to the annual report) by plans subject to ERISA would satisfy the reporting requirements of PHS Act sections 2715A and 2717, incorporated in ERISA through ERISA section 715(a)(1).[8] As explained in FAQs issued August 11, 2015,[9] HHS proposed an information collection for public comment in connection with the transparency provisions of section 1311(e)(3) of the Affordable Care Act. The proposed data collection would collect certain information from Qualified Health Plan (QHP) issuers in Federally-facilitated Exchanges and State-based Exchanges that use the federal eligibility and enrollment platform. The HHS proposal explained that other reporting requirements would be proposed at a later time, through a separate rulemaking with respect to non-Exchange coverage, including those that extend to health insurance issuers offering non-grandfathered group or individual health insurance coverage outside of the Exchanges and non-grandfathered group health plans (including large group and self-insured health plans).[10]

This rulemaking proposes transparency and quality reporting for non-grandfathered group health plans under PHS Act sections 2715A and 2717, as incorporated in ERISA. It takes into account differences in markets and other relevant factors to streamline reporting under multiple reporting provisions and reduce unnecessary duplication. The DOL is proposing to collect and provide high-value data to participants,

beneficiaries, and regulators, such as information about benefits and plan design characteristics, funding, grandfathered plan status, rebates received by the plan (such as medical loss ratio rebates), service provider information (including information regarding any third party administrators, pharmacy benefit managers, mental health benefit managers, and independent review organizations), information on any stop loss insurance, claims processing and payment information (including number of claims filed, paid, appealed and denied), wellness program information, and other compliance information. In addition to improving DOL's oversight and enforcement activities, the collection of high-value data will lead to greater transparency for consumers, which may assist them in making a decision whether to elect the coverage or opt for another plan such as through their spouse's employer, with the caveat that these data will be collected a number of months after the end of the plan year they describe and thus will not be timely for use in concurrent oversight, enforcement, or consumer choice activities. The DOL may propose collecting additional data in the future. The DOL requests comments regarding other plan characteristics that may be helpful for participants to have information on in evaluating their plan. Further, as noted above, this document includes proposed conforming amendments in 29 CFR 2590.715-2715A and 29 CFR 2590.715-2717 to clarify that compliance with the proposed annual reporting requirements by plans subject to ERISA that provide group health benefits would satisfy the ACA reporting requirements under PHS Act sections 2715A and 2717 incorporated in ERISA through ERISA section 715(a)(1). The Department is specifically seeking public comments on those conforming amendments and the proposed annual reporting requirements for plans that provide group health benefits, including the new Schedule J, in light of the Supreme Court's recent decision in *Gobeille* v. *Liberty Mutual Insurance Co.*, 136 S. Ct. 936 (2016).

4. Modernize Data Collection and Usability

This project would standardize and structure the Form 5500 Annual Return/Report to make key retirement and health and welfare benefit data, including information on assets held for investment, more available and usable in the electronic filing and data environment. Modernization is consistent with the Administration's "Smart Disclosure" effort. *Executive Office of the President of the United States, Nat'l Science and Technology Council, Smart Disclosure and Consumer Decision-making: Report of the Task Force on Smart Disclosure* (2013). The proposed changes would enable private sector data users to develop more individualized tools for employers to evaluate both their retirement and welfare plans and for employees to manage their retirement savings and welfare plan choices.

5. Updating and Improving Reporting of Service Provider Fee and Expense Information

The DOL has been engaged in a long term initiative focused on transparency and oversight of service provider and investment fees and expenses. The fee initiative has focused on reporting indirect compensation received by service providers (2009 Form 5500 Annual Return/Report revisions), disclosures about service provider compensation to plan fiduciaries (DOL's regulation, effective in 2012, at 29 CFR 2550.408b-2), and plan disclosures to participants and beneficiaries particularly in 401(k)-type plans (DOL's regulation, effective in 2012, at 29 CFR 2550.404a-5).

The fee disclosure regulations were finalized after the publication of the 2009 forms changes. The 2009 indirect compensation reporting requirements permitted filers to disclose rather than report most indirect compensation. This was in response to commenters concerns about potentially inconsistent requirements in Form 5500 reporting and disclosure under the then proposed disclosure regulations. Accordingly, the 21st Century initiative includes proposed revisions that are designed to harmonize Form 5500 reporting requirements with the

---

[6] Sections 2715A and 2717 of the PHS Act are also incorporated into section 9815(a)(1) of the Code.

[7] Information required under sections 2715A and 2717 of the PHS Act that is provided as part of a Form 5500 Annual Return/Report would be made available to the public and to the plan's participants and beneficiaries. Section 104(b)(4) of ERISA requires the plan administrator, on written request of a participant or beneficiary, to furnish among other documents, a copy of the latest annual report. See also 29 CFR 2520.104b-1(b)(2). The DOL's regulation at 29 CFR 2520.104b-30 provides that the plan administrator of an employee benefit plan may impose a reasonable charge that is not to exceed 25 cents per page to cover the cost of furnishing the latest annual report, but also provides that participants and beneficiaries must be provided at no charge a copy of the statement of the assets and liabilities of the plan and accompanying notes, and the statement of income and expenses of the plan and accompanying notes. See also 29 CFR 2520.104b-10(d)(3) and (4).

[8] The Treasury Department and the IRS intend to publish proposed regulations in 26 CFR 54.9815-2715A and 54.9815-2717 clarifying that group health plans required to file an annual report pursuant to section 104 of ERISA that comply with the reporting requirements in 29 CFR 2520.103-1 (including filing any required schedules to the annual report)

would satisfy the reporting requirements of sections 2715A and 2717 of the PHS Act, as incorporated in the Code. Group health plans that are not required to file an annual report pursuant to section 104 of ERISA but that are subject to sections 2715A and 2717 of the PHS Act as incorporated in the Code, will not be required to do any reporting to comply with sections 2715A and 2717 of the PHS Act, as incorporated in the Code, unless and until the Treasury Department and the IRS issue subsequent further guidance or rulemaking regarding any such reporting by such plans.

[9] *See* FAQs about Affordable Care Act Implementation (Part XXVIII), available at *http://www.dol.gov/ebsa/faqs/faq-aca28.html* and *https://www.cms.gov/CCIIO/Resources/Fact-Sheets-and-FAQs/Downloads/ACA-FAQ-Part-XXVIII-transparency-reporting-final-8-11-15.pdf.*

[10] Nonfederal governmental plans (as defined in PHS Act section 2791(d)(8)(C)) and health insurance issuers (as defined in PHS Act section 2791(b)(2) and ERISA section 733(b)(2)) are not required to file annual reports pursuant to ERISA sections 103 or 104. Accordingly, any reporting required of such plans and issuers to satisfy PHS Act sections 2715A and 2717 will be addressed separately by HHS in future rulemakings and/or guidance.

now final disclosure regulations, especially the ERISA section 408b-2 regulation. The GAO, in particular, recommended that the DOL require plans to report all indirect compensation received by certain of their service providers and to harmonize the ERISA section 408b-2 regulation disclosure and annual reporting requirements. *U.S. Gov't Accountability Office, GAO-14-441, Private Pensions: Targeted Revisions Could Improve Usefulness of Form 5500 Information* (2014) (available at *www.gao.gov/products/GAO-14-441*).

A key purpose of the required fee disclosures in the ERISA section 408b-2 regulation is to help make sure that pension plan fiduciaries can more effectively negotiate service provider fees based on a better understanding of compensation that the service provider expects to receive, including from third-party sources that might represent a conflict of interest. We believe that annually reporting compensation received by a service provider and its sources on the Form 5500 Annual Return/Report will provide a powerful tool and economic basis for improved evaluation of investment, recordkeeping, and administrative service arrangements. We have already seen innovative uses of Form 5500 Annual Return/Report data by private sector companies that have created tools for evaluating and benchmarking employee benefit plans. Further, service provider failures to disclose indirect compensation as required under the ERISA section 408b-2 regulation have resulted in EBSA obtaining corrective monetary recoveries to plans. Comparing disclosures of anticipated compensation under the ERISA section 408b-2 regulation to compensation received as reported on the Form 5500 Annual Return/Report may uncover disparities between anticipated and actual compensation, which may provide the basis for improved targeting of our enforcement actions.

6. Improving Employee Benefit Plan General Compliance With ERISA and the Code

The Form 5500 Annual Return/Report and related financial audit requirements historically have served to establish discipline for plan fiduciaries by requiring an annual examination of the employee benefit plan's financial and administrative operations. The proposed forms revisions and DOL implementing regulations would add selected new questions regarding plan operations, service provider relationships, and financial management of plans. These questions are intended to compel fiduciaries to evaluate plan compliance with important requirements under ERISA and the Code and to provide the Agencies with improved tools to focus oversight and enforcement resources. The proposed regulations would also update the requirements for certifications for limited scope audits under 29 CFR 2520.103-8.

C. Costs and Benefits

The regulatory impact analysis includes a qualitative discussion of the benefits associated with the proposed rules' five primary objectives. Under the current regulations and forms, the Form 5500 Annual Return/Report annually collects data from approximately 816,000 large and small plan filers—pension and all types of welfare plans, including group health—and DFEs with an aggregate annual cost of $488.1 million. The Form 5500 Annual Return/Report is a central part of the Agencies' enforcement programs, but the benefits of an updated Form 5500 Annual Return/Report would extend beyond the value of enhanced enforcement. A modernized Form 5500 Annual Return/Report that is more aligned with current investment practices and reflects the requirements of current law also has benefits for plan sponsors, plan participants, Congress, academics, and others, as explained in more detail below.

As with the current reporting scheme, the proposed revisions are crafted to limit burden increases for small plans, both pension and welfare, including group health plans. The burden increase for small pension plans that are eligible to file the Form 5500-SF is much less than it is for those pension plans filing the Form 5500 Annual Return/Report that have complex portfolios that include alternative and hard-to-value assets or are employee stock ownership plans, which plans are of greater concern with respect to retirement security of their participants. Similarly, the burden increase for fully insured welfare plans that provide group health benefits with fewer than 100 participants, is much less than it is for welfare plans that provide group health benefits and are fully or partially self-insured, which are at greater risk for non-payment of benefit claims. As is discussed in more detail below, the burden increase for small pension plans that are invested in simple,

Form 5500-SF eligible portfolios is very modest, and the changes that apply to those plans (which will mostly apply to all filers) will provide much needed information about the operations, compliance, and asset allocations of such plans. Similarly, welfare plans that provide group health benefits with fewer than 100 participants and that are fully insured, which are currently exempt from filing any Form 5500 Annual Return/Report, would file limited identifying and coverage information. The changes were intentionally limited in order that the burden would be as minimal as possible, while still getting the crucial information about that significant component of the nation's healthcare delivery system and reinforcing for the fiduciaries responsible for many of those plans the need to satisfy important consumer protections required by Title I of ERISA and the Affordable Care Act-related health care benefits. The proposed changes involve only a nominal burden increase for welfare plans other than group health.

Under the proposed regulations and revised forms, the Form 5500 Annual Return/Report would collect data from approximately 2.97 million filers with an aggregate annual cost of $817.0 million. New reporting requirements for the 2.15 million welfare plans that provide group health benefits that we estimate are currently covered under Title I of ERISA, but exempt under current Form 5500 annual reporting rules, represent over 73 percent of the increased burden for the entire proposal. That increase is largely due to the number of new filers and not the per plan cost. Other than the initial filing year burden for learning the new reporting requirements, the burden per plan for even these new filers, almost all of which are fully insured plans with fewer than 100 participants, is very limited because they are only required to provide registration-type and other nominal benefit coverage information.

This expansion in the number of first-time filers that are plans that provide group health benefits that have fewer than 100 participants represents new data on group health care issues that is otherwise unavailable or not gathered in a way that is readily usable for ERISA compliance, policy, and enforcement purposes. From a compliance perspective, requiring reporting will be useful to educate plan sponsors and fiduciaries of their obligations with respect to group health plans. Getting first time information on the full breadth of plans providing health benefits that are subject to ERISA will be key data for policy-making regarding such plans and their participants. From an enforcement perspective, data analysis could lead to detection and intervention in a distressed health plan, which could help minimize financial harm suffered by participants when medical claims are unpaid by such plans. Medical bills contribute to a large and increasing share of personal bankruptcies in the United States.[11] Moreover, the potential burden for new filers is expected to be overcome by satisfying, to some extent, data collections required by Congress in the Affordable Care Act. Sections 2715A and 2717 of the PHS Act, as added by the Affordable Care Act, significantly expand reporting requirements for group health plans subject to ERISA. EBSA is coordinating with HHS on using the Form 5500 Annual Return/Report as an alternative mechanism to satisfy these reporting requirements.[12]

Revisions to the financial schedules (Schedule H and related investment asset reporting changes) and service provider reporting (Schedule C changes) impact predominantly large plans with complex investment portfolios (often involving alternate investments, hard-to-value assets and employer securities). These changes comprise the second and third largest shares of the burden increase, respectively, adding $57.6 million and $12.9 million. Small pension plans that are subject to expanded reporting under these proposed revisions are a small percentage of total small pension plan filers and the additional burdens are generally limited to those plans that choose to invest in alternative and hard-to-value assets, which present more risk and demand more transparency.

Revisions to Schedule D and DFE reporting represent the largest burden reduction within the proposed changes. These changes affect all DFEs and those plans that invest in DFEs and reduce aggregate burden by $10.1 million.

In addition, it is important to note that the total burden associated with the Form 5500 Annual Return/Report has risen from $327.98 million to $488.1 million since the last rulemaking in November 2007 primarily due to the increase in wage rates and the number of plan filers over the last eight years under the current rule. In other words,

---

[11] David U. Himmelstein, M.D., Deborah Thorne, Ph.D., Elizabeth Warren, JD, and Steffie Woolhandler: The American Journal of Medicine, Medical Bankruptcy in the United States, 2007: Results of a National Study. Available online at *http://www.amjmed.com/article/S0002-9343(09)00404-5/abstract?cc=y=*.

[12] Section 2715A of the PHS Act extends the transparency reporting provisions set forth in section 1311(e)(3) of the Affordable Care Act (applicable to issuers of "qualified health

plans" offered on Exchanges) to non-grandfathered group health plans and non-grandfathered group or individual health insurance coverage offered through or outside of Exchanges. As more fully described on pages 13-14 herein, section 2717 of the PHS Act generally requires non-grandfathered group health plans and health insurance issuers offering non-grandfathered group or individual health insurance coverage to submit annual reports to the DOL, HHS and the Treasury regarding quality of care programs offered by the plan.

approximately 90 percent of the $160.1 million increase to the baseline burden since the last RIA was prepared is simply due to changes in the broader economy over the past decade, not this rulemaking.

Estimated Burden Change

Estimated Total Burden Change

	Annual costs (millions)	Annual burden hours [13]
Total for current reporting requirements	$488.1	4.4 million.
Change due to proposed GHP requirements	241.6	2.2 million.
Change due to all other Proposed Requirements	87.2	798,000.
Total for Proposed Reporting Requirements	817.0	7.2 million.
Increase in baseline since 2007 due to update in wage rates . . .	127.0	0.
Increase in baseline since 2007 due to update in number of plans (not including plans subject to new GHP reporting).	16.9	149,000.

[13] The Burden Hours column shows the amount of time necessary to fulfill filing requirements, whether that burden is incurred by the plans themselves or by outside service providers hired by the plans. The Cost column shows the monetized version of those burden hours.

Estimated Burden Change by Type of Filer

Type of filer	Number of filers under current (thousands)	Number of filers under proposed (thousands)	Aggregate annual cost under current requirements (millions)	Aggregate annual cost under proposed requirements (millions)	Aggregate annual cost change (millions)
Form 5500 Large Plans	148.5	148.5	$252.4	$309.3	$56.9
Pension/Large	75.1	75.1	141.2	174.6	33.5
Welfare/Large Health . . .	47.9	47.9	91.7	114.2	22.5
Welfare/Large Non-Health	25.6	25.6	19.6	20.5	1.0
Form 5500 Small Pension and Non-Health Plans	29.7	29.7	14.4	38.3	23.9
Pension ESOP	3.8	3.8	1.8	5.8	4.1
Pension Non-ESOP	22.6	22.6	11.1	29.9	18.8
Welfare/Non-Health . . .	3.3	3.3	1.5	2.5	1.0
Form 5500-SF Small Pension and Non-Health Plans	622.4	622.4	205.8	227.3	21.5
Pension	621.8	621.8	205.6	227.0	21.4
Non-Health Welfare	0.7	0.7	0.2	0.2	0.0
Form 5500 Small Health	6.2	2,158.0	4.1	227.9	223.86
Fully Insured Health . . .	0.0	1,869.0	0.0	69.6	69.6
Other Health	6.2	289.0	4.1	158.2	154.2
DFEs	9.4	8.9	11.4	14.2	2.8
Overall Total	816.3	2,967.5	488.1	817.0	328.8

Note: Some displayed numbers do not sum up to the totals due to rounding.

Large plans—100 participants or more.

Small plans—generally fewer than 100 participants.

Estimated Burden Change by Form Revision

Revisions	Change in annual costs (millions)	Change in annual burden hours (thousands)	Filers under current requirements (thousands)	Filers under proposed requirements (thousands) [14]	Annual cost per affected filer
Changes in Schedule H (Including changes to Schedules of Assets and Reportable Transactions) and Eliminate Schedule I	$57.6	535.4	115.1	114.6	$502
Schedule C	12.9	116.6	82.4	100.2	128
DFE Reporting Changes (Including changes to Schedule D)	-10.1	-94.2	61.1	8.9	-1,137
Schedule E	2.5	22.0	0.0	6.7	374
Completion of lines 1-5 on Form 5500 and lines 1-8 on Schedule J by fully insured GHPs with fewer than 100 participants	69.6	623.0	0.0	1,869	37
Completion of Form 5500 by GHPs with fewer than 100 participants that are unfunded, combination unfunded/fully insured, or funded with a trust and GHPs with 100 or more participants	39.0	349.1	54.1	336.9	116
Completion of Schedule J by GHPs with fewer than 100 participants that are unfunded, combination unfunded/fully insured, or funded with a trust and GHPs with 100 or more participants	133.0	1,179.2	0.0	336.9	395
All Other Revisions	24.4	217.9	1,076.7	1,024.2	24

[14] The elimination of the concept of Master Trust Investment Account reporting and requiring reporting by a master trust instead, whose burden change is accounted for in the DFE Reporting Changes row, results in a reduction in the number of schedules attached. These reductions are reflected in the rows specific to the schedule affected.

II. Discussion of the Proposed Revisions to 29 CFR Part 2520

ERISA section 103 broadly sets out annual financial reporting requirements for employee benefit plans. The Form 5500 Annual Return/Report and the DOL's related regulations generally are promulgated under the ERISA provisions authorizing limited exemptions to these requirements and simplified reporting and disclosure for welfare plans under ERISA section 104(a)(3), simplified annual reports under ERISA section 104(a)(2)(A) for pension plans that cover fewer than 100 participants, and alternative methods of compliance for all pension plans under ERISA section 110. The forms, instructions, and related regulations are also promulgated under the DOL's general regulatory authority in ERISA sections 109 and 505.

The forms, schedules, and instructions, in addition to providing an alternative method of compliance under ERISA section 110 for the mandatory reporting requirements under section 103, also serve to help the DOL carry out its statutory directives under sections 506 and 513 of ERISA. Specifically, section 506(a) of ERISA authorizes the Secretary of Labor to coordinate with other Agencies to avoid unnecessary expense and duplication of functions among Government agencies; the Form 5500 Annual Return/Report is designed to simultaneously satisfy annual reporting requirements for each of the three Agencies and help the Agencies more effectively and efficiently (from both an Agency and a public perspective) enforce the provisions of ERISA and the Code. Section 506(b) gives the DOL responsibility for detecting and investigating civil and criminal violations of Title I of

¶20,539F

ERISA. The Form 5500 Annual Return/Report is one of the important tools the DOL uses to effectuate its responsibility to detect and investigate such violations. Section 513(b)(2) of ERISA specifically directs DOL to undertake research studies relating to pension plans, including but not limited to (A) the effects of this subchapter upon the provisions and costs of pension plans, (B) the role of private pensions in meeting the economic security needs of the Nation, and (C) the operation of private pension plans including types and levels of benefits, degree of reciprocity or portability, and financial and actuarial characteristics and practices, and methods of encouraging the growth of the private pension system. The Form 5500 Annual Return/Report is the most important overall tool DOL has to fulfill this statutory imperative, and the changes in the proposal are essential for required research, as well as enforcement.

The proposed changes to the Form 5500 Annual Return/Report and regulations are designed to: (1) Modernize financial information filed regarding plans; (2) harmonize information on fees and expenses that plans pay to service providers with the information that service providers disclose to plans under 29 CFR 2550.408b-2; (3) enhance mineability of data filed on the Form 5500 Annual Return/Report; (4) require reporting by all plans covered by Title I of ERISA that provide health benefits, including adding a new Schedule J (Group Health Plan Information); and (5) focus filers on compliance with certain ERISA and Code provisions through new questions on plan operations, service provider relationships, and financial management. If adopted, the changes generally would apply for plan years beginning on or after January 1, 2019. See the regulatory impact analysis in this document for a discussion of how the proposed amendments and the proposed form revision address these goals. These revisions are being proposed in conjunction with recompeting the contract for operation of the ERISA Filing and Acceptance System (EFAST2), which is expected to begin processing Plan Year 2019 forms, beginning January 1, 2020. Certain changes may be made earlier, particularly those changes collecting information under the Code or Title IV of ERISA that do not require amendment to DOL regulations to implement (but not those related to group health plans). The Notice of Proposed Forms Revisions published concurrently in today's **Federal Register** sets forth a comprehensive discussion of form and instruction changes that relate to this proposed regulation.

1. Section 2520.103-1

Section 2520.103-1 generally describes the content of the Form 5500 Annual Return/Report as a limited exemption and alternative method of compliance for ERISA-covered employee benefit plans to satisfy annual reporting requirements under Title I. To accommodate the form, schedule, and instruction changes in the Notice of Proposed Forms Revisions, the proposed regulatory amendments in this document would update form and schedule references in § 2520.103-1. The proposal would also require all plans that provide group health benefits, regardless of size, to file the Form 5500 Annual Return/Report in accordance with the instructions. Group health plans, regardless of size, would not be eligible to file the Form 5500-SF.[15] The proposal would also require pension benefit plans with fewer than 100 participants that are required to file the Form 5500 Annual Return/Report to file the Schedule C (Service Provider Information). It would also generally require both large and small employee stock ownership plans to file the Schedule E (ESOP Information). Under the proposal, only DFEs would be required to complete the Schedule D to report participating plan information; plans would no longer be required to file Schedule D because they would be reporting detailed information about the collective investment vehicles in which they invest, including DFEs, on the Schedule of Assets Held for Investment and the Schedule of Assets Disposed of During Plan Year. In order to improve the transparency of reporting for plans that participate in a master trust, the proposal would require that master trusts operate either on a calendar year basis or on the same fiscal year as all the plans that participate in the master trust. In general, a master trust is a trust maintained by a bank or similar institution to hold the assets of more than one plan sponsored by a single employer or by a group of employers under common control.

2. Section 2520.103-2

Section 2520.103-2 describes the content of the Form 5500 Annual Return/Report for a group insurance arrangement (GIA) that files an annual report under § 2520.104-43. The amendments proposed in this document include the requirement to file the proposed new Schedule J.

Group health plans that are part of a GIA would continue to be exempt from filing a Form 5500 Annual Return/Report under 29 CFR 2520.104-43. For plans to be eligible for this exemption, the GIA would have to file a separate Schedule J for each group health plan participating in the GIA.

3. Section 2520.103-3, 2520.103-4, and 2520.103-1(e)

Section 2520.103-3 provides an exemption for employee benefit plans from certain annual reporting requirements for plan assets held in a common collective trust (CCT) maintained by a bank, trust company, or similar institution. Section 2520.103-4 provides a similar exemption for plan assets held in a pooled separate account (PSA) maintained by an insurance carrier. Section 2520.103-1(e) provides for special reporting rules for plans that participate in a master trust. The Notice of Proposed Forms Revisions would alter the annual reporting requirements for plans investing in CCTs, PSAs and master trusts in significant ways to increase the transparency of plan investments in such pooled investment vehicles. The DOL proposes revising language to 29 CFR 2520.103-3, 29 CFR 2520.103-4, and 29 CFR 103-1(e) to reflect those changes.

4. Section 2520.103-6

Section 2520.103-6 sets forth the contents of the Schedule of Reportable Transactions that is part of the Form 5500 Annual Return/Report. The Schedule of Reportable Transactions is required to be filed by plans and DFEs that file their own Form 5500 Annual Return/Report. This schedule is used to report, subject to conditions and exceptions, individual transactions or series of transactions that involve more than five percent of the current value of the assets of the plan or DFE. The existing rules require the schedule to include the name of each party to a "reportable transaction." The form and instructions changes being published concurrently with this document include certain additions and clarifications of the content of the Schedule of Reportable Transactions designed to improve the information regarding parties involved in these significant plan transactions or series of transactions. 29 CFR 2520.103-6(d)(1) sets forth the content requirements for the Schedule of Reportable Transactions. Rather than list all the schedules' content requirements, the proposed amendment to paragraph (d)(1) would simply reference the schedules' contents in the relevant Form 5500 Annual Return/Report instructions.

5. Section 2520.103-8

Section 2520.103-8 implements the limited-scope audit exemption described in ERISA section 103(a)(3)(c). Specifically, this exemption allows a plan to exclude from the examination and report of an independent qualified public accountant (IQPA) any statement or information regarding plan assets held by banks, similar institutions, or insurance carriers if the statement or information is prepared and certified by the bank, similar institution, or insurance carrier. The GAO and the DOL's Inspector General (DOL-OIG) have recommended that the Department revise section 2520.103-8 to improve the information being reported by plan administrators electing a limited scope audit. The DOL agrees that better information is needed by plan administrators in connection with limited scope audits. To address concerns it has observed, as well as to respond to the GAO and the DOL-OIG recommendations,[16] the DOL proposes amending section 2520.103-8. Currently, section 2520.103-8 requires the bank or insurance company to certify the accuracy and completeness of the information being provided by a written declaration which is signed by a person authorized to represent the bank or insurance carrier. The DOL proposes to amend the requirements under section 2520.103-8 to require that the certification:

(1) Appear on a separate document from the list of plan assets covered by the certification;

(2) Identify the bank or insurance company holding those plan assets that are the subject of the certification;

(3) Describe the manner in which the bank or insurance company is holding the assets covered by the certification;

(4) State whether the bank or insurance company is providing current value information regarding the assets covered by the certification, and if so, state that the assets for which current value is being certified are separately identified in the list of assets covered by the certification;

(5) If current value is not being certified for all of the assets covered by the certification, include a caution that the certification is not

---

[15] The details of the limited reporting that would be required for small fully insured group health plans would be set forth in the instructions.

[16] The Agencies discuss various GAO and DOL-OIG recommendations with respect to the Form 5500 Annual Return/Report and the steps the Agencies are taking that are consistent with the recommendations in the Notice of Proposed Forms Revisions published today in the **Federal Register**.

certifying current value information and the asset values provided by the bank or insurance company may not be suitable for use in satisfying the plan's obligation to report current value information on the Form 5500 Annual Return/Report; and

(6) If the certification is being provided by an agent on behalf of the bank or insurance company, a statement certifying that the person providing the certification is an authorized agent acting on behalf of the bank or insurance company and affirming that the bank or insurance company is taking responsibility for the accuracy and completeness of the certification and the underlying records used as a basis for the information being certified.

6. Section 2520.103-10

Section 2520.103-10 identifies the financial schedules that are required to be included as part of the Form 5500 Annual Return/Report, which include the "Schedule of Assets Held for Investment" and "Schedule of Assets Acquired and Disposed within the Plan Year." Paragraph (b)(1)(i) of §2520.103-10 sets forth the content requirements for the Schedule of Assets Held for Investment. The Notice of Proposed Forms Revisions proposes certain additions and clarifications to the content of the Schedule of Assets Held for Investment that are designed to improve the information regarding parties and assets involved in these significant plan investments. Rather than list all the required contents of this schedule, the proposed amendment to paragraph (b)(1)(i) of §2520.103-10 would simply reference the contents of the schedule listed in the relevant Form 5500 Annual Return/Report instructions.

Paragraph (b)(2)(i) of §2520.103-10 sets forth the content requirements for the "Schedule of Assets Acquired and Disposed of During the Plan Year." This proposed amendment reflects the Agencies' proposal to revise and rename the current "Schedule of Assets Acquired and Disposed of Within the Plan Year." Filers would be required to report information on the disposal of certain assets, regardless of when the assets were acquired. The Notice of Proposed Forms Revisions also includes certain proposed additions and clarifications of the content of the Schedule of Assets Disposed of During the Plan Year that are designed to improve the information regarding parties and assets involved in these plan transactions. Rather than list the required contents of the Schedule of Assets Disposed of During the Plan Year, the proposed amendment to paragraph (b)(2)(i) of §2520.103-10 would reference the contents of the schedule listed in the relevant Form 5500 Annual Return/Report instructions.

7. Section 2520.104-20 and 2520.104-26

Section 2520.104-20 provides an exemption from certain annual reporting and disclosure provisions of ERISA for certain welfare plans that cover fewer than 100 participants at the beginning of the plan year and for which benefits are paid exclusively from the general assets of the employer or employee organization sponsoring the plan, exclusively through insurance, or a combination of both. An expansion of the annual reporting of information regarding plans that provide group health benefits is described in detail in the Notice of Proposed Forms Revisions. To implement those changes, the DOL proposes eliminating the existing regulatory exemption for welfare plans that provide group health benefits (the exemption will continue to apply to other small welfare plans). Thus, small plans that provide group health benefits that are unfunded, or a combination of unfunded and fully insured, will be required to file an annual return/report, including the new Schedule J, in accordance with the requirements in the proposed instructions. Under the proposal, small fully insured plans will only be required to answer basic identifying and plan characteristic information on the Form 5500 and limited health plan benefit, insurance, and participant information on the Schedule J. Similarly, the limited exception in §

2520.104-26 for certain unfunded dues-financed welfare plans maintained by employee organizations would be amended to further limit the exemption to those unfunded dues-financed welfare plans that do not provide health benefits.

8. Section 2520.104b-10

Section 104(b)(3) of ERISA provides in part that, each year, administrators must furnish to participants and beneficiaries receiving benefits under a plan materials that fairly summarize the plan's annual report. Section 2520.104b-10 sets forth the requirements for the Summary Annual Report (SAR) and prescribes formats for such reports. The amendments being proposed do not include any change to the SAR requirements. However, in order to facilitate compliance with the SAR requirement, the DOL is updating its cross-reference guide to correspond to the line items of the Form 5500 Annual Return/Report and Form 5500-SF. The cross-reference guide has also been updated to reflect that defined benefit pension plans that furnish an annual funding notice to participants and beneficiaries, pursuant to 29 CFR 2520.101-4, are not required to furnish a SAR. This update reflects statutory changes enacted as part of the Pension Protection Act of 2006 extending the annual funding notice requirements of section 101(f) of ERISA. The cross-reference guide, as before, would continue to be an appendix to 29 CFR 2520.104b-10.

9. Technical and Conforming Changes for Forms and Instructions

Various other technical and conforming changes are being proposed as part of the restructuring of the Form 5500 Annual Return/Report.

III. Regulatory Impact Analysis

Executive Order 12866 and 13563 Statement

Executive Orders 12866 and 13563 direct agencies to assess all costs and benefits of available regulatory alternatives and, if regulation is necessary, to select regulatory approaches that maximize net benefits (including potential economic, environmental, and public health and safety effects; distributive impacts; and equity). Executive Order 13563 emphasizes the importance of quantifying both costs and benefits, reducing costs, harmonizing rules, and promoting flexibility.

Under Executive Order 12866, it must be determined whether a regulatory action is "significant" and therefore subject to the requirements of the Executive Order and review by the Office of Management and Budget (OMB). Section 3(f) of Executive Order 12866 defines a "significant regulatory action" as an action that is likely to result in a rule's (1) having an annual effect on the economy of $100 million or more, or adversely and materially affecting a sector of the economy, productivity, competition, jobs, the environment, public health or safety, or State, local or tribal governments or communities (also referred to as "economically significant"); (2) creating serious inconsistency or otherwise interfering with an action taken or planned by another agency; (3) materially altering the budgetary impacts of entitlement grants, user fees, or loan programs, or the rights and obligations of recipients thereof; or (4) raising novel legal or policy issues arising out of legal mandates, the President's priorities, or the principles set forth in the Executive Order.

Pursuant to the terms of the Executive Order, it has been determined that this regulatory action is likely to have an annual effect on the economy of $100 million or more. Therefore, this action is being treated as "economically significant" and subject to OMB review under section 3(f)(1) of Executive Order 12866. The DOL accordingly has undertaken to assess the costs and benefits of this regulatory action in satisfaction of the applicable requirements of the Executive Order and provides herein a summary discussion of its assessment.

TABLE 1—ACCOUNTING STATEMENT: ESTIMATED COSTS FROM CURRENT REPORTING REQUIREMENTS TO 2019 REPORTING REQUIREMENTS

| Category | Estimates | | | Units | | |
	Primary estimate	Low estimate	High estimate	Year dollar	Discount rate (percent)	Period covered
Benefits:						
Annualized Monetized ($millions/year)	....	....	....	....	....	....
Annualized Quantified	....	....	....	....	....	....
Qualitative	The proposal pursues five main objectives: (1) Improve reliability of reporting and transparency of financial products and investments acquired by plans, especially alternative investments, hard-to-value assets, and investments through collective investment vehicles; foster ongoing monitoring of retirement plans by employers, plans, participants and beneficiaries, and policymakers; and better leverage the ability of the Agencies to fulfill their statutory oversight role. (2) Establish better compliance awareness and education, provide critical data for Agency oversight, collect information needed for Congressionally mandated reports on group health plans, and satisfy certain reporting requirements under sections 2715A and 2717 of the PHS Act as added by the Affordable Care Act and incorporated into ERISA section 715. (3) Standardize and structure the Form 5500 Annual Return/Report to make key retirement and health and welfare benefit data, including information on assets held for investment, more available and usable in the electronic filing and data environment, which, consistent with the Administration's "Smart Disclosure" effort, to enable private sector data users to develop more individualized tools for employers to evaluate their retirement plans and for employees to manage their retirement savings. (4) By harmonizing reporting on Schedule C of the Form 5500 Annual Return/Report with the now final disclosure requirements in DOL's regulation at 29 CFR 2550.408b-2, provide a powerful tool and economic basis for improved evaluation of investment, recordkeeping, and administrative service arrangements, including potential innovative uses of Form 5500 Annual Return/Report data by private sector companies that have created tools for evaluating and benchmarking employee benefit plans, provide tools to benefit participants where failures to disclose indirect compensation received by a service provider have resulted in corrective monetary recoveries to plans, as well as minimize filer confusion with the harmonization of reporting and disclosure requirements. (5) Enhance reporting on plan compliance to improve plan operations, protect participants and beneficiaries and their retirement benefits, and educate and provide annual discipline for plan fiduciaries.					
Costs:						
Annualized Monetized ($millions/year)	372.6	....	....	2016	7	2019 and later.
	366.2	....	....	2016	3	2019 and later.
Annualized Quantified	....	....	....	....	....	....
Qualitative						

Background and Need for Regulatory Action

The Form 5500 Annual Return/Report is the principal source of information and data available to the Agencies concerning the operations, funding, and investments of pension and welfare benefit plans covered by ERISA and the Code. Accordingly, the Form 5500 Annual Return/Report is essential to each Agency's enforcement, research, and policy formulation programs and is a source of information and data for use by other federal agencies, Congress, and the private sector in assessing employee benefit, tax, and economic trends and policies. The Form 5500 Annual Return/Report also serves as the primary means by which the operations of plans can be monitored by plan participants and beneficiaries and the general public.

As discussed in the Notice of Proposed Forms Revisions published concurrently with this document and below, the DOL has received several reports from the GAO, the DOL-OIG, and the ERISA Advisory Council indicating the need for substantive changes to annual reporting forms and regulations. TIGTA has also suggested to the IRS that substantive changes are needed. In response to these reports, the continued shift from DB to DC plans, and legislative and regulatory changes that have been issued since the last major revision to the Form 5500 Annual Return/Report, the DOL has determined that the substantial revisions to the reporting scheme discussed earlier in this preamble and in the Notice of Proposed Forms Revisions, published concurrently, are necessary and appropriate. These changes will ensure that the Agencies, plan participants and beneficiaries and the general public can monitor the operations of employee benefit plans. With their help, the Form 5500 Annual Return/Report will continue to serve its essential functions.

As described earlier in this document, the proposed revisions to the Form 5500 Annual Return/Report reflect priorities of and efforts by the Agencies to improve the quality of the information collected, while limiting wherever possible, especially for small pension plans invested in easy to value assets and plans that provide group health benefits that have fewer than 100 participants that are fully insured, the overall burden of the statutory reporting requirements and the forms. To accomplish this goal, the Agencies have pursued five objectives. The need for regulatory action to achieve these objectives is discussed below.

(1) *Modernizing financial information.*

Modernizing the Schedule H Balance Sheet and Income Statement: The financial statements contained in the current Schedule H (Large Plan Financial Information) and Schedule I (Small Plan Financial Information) are based on data elements that have remained largely unchanged since the Form 5500 Annual Return/Report was established in 1975. Many investments in alternative and hard-to-value assets and those held through collective investment funds that are frequently held by plans and the investment industry today were not as prevalent in 1975. Thus, they do not fit squarely into any of the existing Schedule H reporting categories. Further, some of these investments in alternative and hard-to-value assets, including those held through collective investment funds, are sufficiently complex that plan administrators and plan accountants may not completely understand how they fit into the balance sheet reporting on the Form 5500 Annual Return/Report. This results in inconsistent financial reporting by filers because certain types of investments may arguably fall into one or more categories. For example, a "hedge" fund could potentially be reported as a limited partnership or some other type of collective investment entity, or could be reported in a different reporting category based on the primary assets held through a particular type of collective investment vehicle.

Additionally, many filers simply report investments that do not readily fit into one of the existing categories in "Other." For example, large retirement plans reported having $153 billion in assets that they categorized as "Other" on the Schedule H balance sheet for 2013. DFEs reported an additional approximately $407 billion in assets as "Other" for the 2013 plan year. In order to determine why there is a substantial amount in "Other," the Agencies now have to rely on the current, unstructured Schedule H Line 4i Schedules of Assets, which might not specifically indicate the necessary details, or the Agencies would need to contact the filer for the information. The types of alternative and hard-to-value assets that might be reported in "Other" include: Options, index futures, state and municipal securities, hedge funds, and private equity. Some of these asset types can be fairly complex and merit more

rather than less transparency in order to determine the overall financial health of the plan. The inability to distinguish these types of assets on the Form 5500 Annual Return/Report reduces the form's usefulness for policy analysis and research as well for monitoring plans for enforcement purposes.

A recent GAO report stated, for example, that, "while hedge funds and private equity have very different risk, return, and disclosure considerations from state and municipal securities, all of these investments could be included in the "other plan asset" category."[17] GAO also noted that the plan asset categories on the Schedule H are not representative of current plan investments, and provide little insight into the investments themselves, the level of associated risk, or structures of the investments.[18] The DOL-OIG also recommended that the Agencies revise the Form 5500 Annual Return/Report to improve reporting of hard-to-value assets and alternative investments.[19] Based on their own assessment and experience in research and enforcement and the use of the Form 5500 Annual Return/Report to support these critical agency functions and responsibilities, as well as in response to these recommendations, as discussed in detail earlier in this document, the Agencies are proposing to make changes to the Schedule H balance sheet and income statement.

Modernizing the Schedule H, Line 4i Schedules of Assets: As discussed in detail in the Notice of Proposed Forms Revisions published simultaneously with this document, the Agencies are proposing structural, data element and instruction changes to the current Schedule H, Line 4i(1) Schedule of Assets Held for Investment and Line 4i(2) Schedule of Assets Acquired and Disposed of Within Year. These schedules are filed by plans required to file the Schedule H and by certain DFEs. The Schedules of Assets are a central element of the financial disclosure structure of ERISA. They are the only place on the Form 5500 Annual Return/Report where plans are required to list individual plan investments identified by major characteristics, such as issue, maturity date, interest rate, cost and current value. As such, they are the only part of the Form 5500 Annual Return/Report that can be used to evaluate the year-to-year performance, liquidity, and risk characteristics of a plan's individual investments.

The current reported information, however, suffers from several shortcomings. First, this information is not reported in a data-capturable format. Only an image or picture of the attachments that are currently filed as non-standard attachments to filers' electronic Form 5500 Annual Return/Report filings is available through the EFAST2 public disclosure function. Second, the Line 4i Schedules of Assets are not always found in the same place in each annual return/report. For example, the Line 4i Schedules of Assets are often incorporated in the larger audit report of the plan's IQPA that itself is filed as a nonstandard attachment to the Form 5500 Annual Return/Report. Third, the schedules do not require a standardized method for identifying and describing assets on the Line 4i Schedules. Therefore, under the current reporting rules, the same stock or mutual fund may be identified with various different names or abbreviations.

The creation of more detailed and structured Schedules of Assets is a specific recommendation of the DOL-OIG and the GAO.[20] The proposed changes to the Schedules of Assets are designed to remedy the shortcomings described above. In addition, data capturability of the Line 4i Schedules of Assets will make it much easier and more efficient to monitor plan holdings as computer programs can read and analyze the data much more efficiently. It will allow the Agencies and the interested public to monitor a larger number of pension plans and their asset allocations. The existence of a group of private companies that are transforming the Line 4i Schedule of Assets Held for Investment of the larger pension plans into data-capturable information and using it to compare plan investment menus and investment allocations is a clear indication that plans sponsors and their service providers also are interested in having access to these data. For example, one of these companies sent a letter to DOL stating that they believe that the information on the Form 5500 Annual Return/Report is very useful in "helping the agency understand the performance and design of retirement plans in the market place" and that the data availability fosters "third party data collection and evaluation efforts that in turn help protect retirement plan participants."[21] Plan sponsors can use this information to see how their investment menus compare to similarly situated plans and service providers often use this information to identify plans with underperforming investments in order to attract new

---

[17] GAO, *Private Pensions: Targeted Revisions Could Improve Usefulness of Form 5500 Information*, at 12.

[18] *Id.* at 11-12.

[19] *EBSA Needs to Provide Additional Guidance and Oversight to ERISA Plans Holding Hard-To-Value Alternative Investments*, at 4, 18, and 19.

[20] See *EBSA Needs to Provide Additional Guidance and Oversight to ERISA Plans Holding Hard-to-Value Alternative Investments*, at 17; *Private Pensions: Targeted Revisions Could Improve Usefulness of Form 5500 Information*, at 37.

[21] See August 23, 2010 Comment Letter from Ryan Alfred, President, BrightScope, Inc. Re: Proposed Extension of Information Collection, Form 5500 *http://www.reginfo.gov/public/do/PRAViewDocument?ref_nbr=201009-1210-002).*

business. This can lead to more competition and improved plan performance, which will ultimately benefit participants.

Changes to DFE Reporting: Under the current reporting rules, DFEs are permitted, or in some cases required, to file their own Form 5500 Annual Return/Report. Generally, pension plans that invest in DFEs only are required to report their interest in the DFE but do not have to report detailed information regarding the underlying investments in the DFE. Such plans are required to file a Schedule D on which the plans identify each DFE in which they invest and the year-end values of the plans' interests. Although DFEs file their own Form 5500 Annual Return/Report, only Master Trust Investment Accounts (MTIAs) and entities meeting the conditions of DOL regulation 29 CFR 103-12 (103-12 IEs) are required to include as part of their own Form 5500 Annual Return/Report, detailed asset holdings on the Schedule H, Line 4i Schedules of Assets. Insurance company pooled separate accounts (PSAs) and bank common/collective trusts (CCTs), which together account for 32 percent of large plans' reported DFE holdings, do not report such information, nor are the investing plans required to report it, although the information is required by regulation to be provided by PSAs and CCTs to investing plans on an annual basis.

The Agencies have encountered, and researchers have reported to the DOL,[22] difficulties matching plans' investments in DFEs reported by investing plans and DFEs in which the plans and other DFEs are participating. Some of this stems from incomplete, unreliable, or inconsistent data on Schedule D filings. For example, for 2013, about 57 percent of plans and 17 percent of DFEs that filed a Schedule D and reported non-zero amounts of interest in DFEs on Schedule H have at least one discrepancy in reporting of more than $1,000 between the value of the investment in a DFE on their Schedule D and their Schedule H. There might be some legitimate reasons for these discrepancies, *e.g.* different plan year dates, but these discrepancies make it difficult to verify filing accuracy. Another more troubling issue is that there are more than 7,000 plan filings for 2013 that report investments in DFEs that cannot be directly linked to any applicable DFE filings. This problem primarily involves CCTs and PSAs. Investments in these unlinked DFEs account for more than $382 billion in assets. A serious consequence of not being able to link these plan filings and assets to DFE filings is that the Agencies and participants do not get information on their plan investments and thus are not able to monitor these investments.

GAO has recommended that the Agencies take steps to address the problem of incomplete or inaccurate matching between plan and DFE filings.[23] Therefore, as discussed in detail earlier in this document, the Agencies are proposing to revise the reporting structure of both Schedule H and the Line 4i Schedules of Assets, with corresponding changes to Schedule D, that are intended to ensure that the Agencies, plan fiduciaries, plan service providers, and other users of data have the tools to create a more complete picture of plans' investment in pooled investment vehicles.

Changes to Financial Information Reporting for Small Plans: Small pension plans that are invested in "eligible" plan assets and otherwise meet certain requirements are eligible to file Form 5500-SF, which was established in part to comply with provisions of the PPA requiring a simplified form of reporting for plans with fewer than 25 participants.[24] Currently, the Form 5500-SF does not require filers to breakout assets on the balance sheet into specific categories. Small plans that are not eligible to file the Form 5500-SF because they are invested in hard-to-value and alternative investments currently file Schedule I, but the Schedule I does not require small plan filers to provide detailed plan asset information and does not provide significantly more useful financial information than the Form 5500-SF with respect to alternative and hard-to-value assets.

The lack of specific questions on the investment activity of small pension plans, which comprise over 80 percent of filers, impairs the usefulness of the Form 5500 Annual Return/Report as a tool to obtain a meaningful picture of small plan investments, especially investments in hard-to-value and alternative investments. As the GAO has noted, the limited financial information provided on the Schedule I creates a challenge for participants, beneficiaries, oversight agencies, researchers, and other users of the Form 5500 Annual Return/Report or Form 5500 Annual Return/Report data.[25] Therefore, as discussed in detail in the Notice of Proposed Forms Revisions published today, under the proposal, Form 5500-SF filers would be required to provide a modest

additional breakout of plan investments on the balance sheet. The proposal also would eliminate the Schedule I for small plans that are not eligible to file the Form 5500-SF, predominantly because they are invested in hard-to-value and alternative investments, including employer securities. Under the proposal, such plans instead would be required to complete Schedule H and the Line 4i Schedules of Assets. These changes are designed to ensure that the Agencies are able to collect critical information regarding small plan investments in hard-to-value and alternative investments.

Although the proposed elimination of Schedule I and the addition of basic investment category information to the Form 5500-SF balance sheet would result in additional reporting for those small plans invested in hard-to-value and alternative investments, those small plans with simple investment portfolios would not see a significant increase in their annual reporting burden. In light of changes in the financial environment and increasing concern about investments in hard-to-value assets and alternative investments, however, the Agencies believe that requiring the more detailed financial information regarding hard-to-value investments on the Schedule H is important for regulatory, enforcement, and disclosure purposes for those small plans with more complex portfolios that include hard-to-value or alternative investments. The inherent increased risk posed by hard-to-value or alternative investments affects participants in small plans as well as large plans, but without these proposed revisions, the participants in small plans are left without the protection afforded participants in large plans that comes from the reporting that large plans are already required to do. Although such small plans would be required to complete the Schedule H instead of the Schedule I, including the Schedule H Line 4i(1) and 4i(2) Schedules of Assets, eligible small plans, as under the current rules, would still be eligible for a waiver of the annual examination and report of an IQPA under 29 CFR 2520.104-46, and the number count required to determine eligibility would be changed from the number of participants at the beginning of the plan year to the number of participants with account balances at the beginning of the plan year.

(2) Updating fee and expense information on plan service providers with a focus on harmonizing annual reporting requirements on Schedule C with DOL's final disclosure requirements at 29 CFR 2550.408b-2.

The current rules for reporting indirect compensation on the Schedule C as part of the Form 5500 Annual Return/Report, including the limited reporting option for "eligible indirect compensation," were implemented starting with the 2009 forms.[26] Those changes were part of a three-pronged regulatory initiative that included the DOL's regulations under 29 CFR 2550.408b-2 and participant-level disclosure regulations under 29 CFR 2550.404a-5. At the time the 2009 Schedule C rules were finalized, neither the ERISA section 408b-2 regulation nor the ERISA section 404a-5 regulation had been promulgated. Some elements of the 2009 Schedule C, for example, the eligible indirect compensation provisions, were adopted in light of the fact that it was not certain at the time what the ERISA section 408b-2 final rule would require. Those provisions were also meant to respond to concerns from the regulated community, especially large plan service providers, about having to create two different record-keeping systems to meet the various requirements of the Form 5500 Annual Return/Report and disclosures required under 408b-2 should the later promulgated provisions differ from the Form 5500 reporting requirements on indirect compensation.

Now that EBSA has promulgated the ERISA sections 408b-2 and 404a-5 final regulations, there is a need to harmonize fee reporting under the Schedule C and ERISA section 408b-2 regulations to: (1) Make it easier to understand the disclosure and reporting rules regarding indirect compensation; (2) improve quality of data by minimizing any filer confusion that might result from differences in the two requirements and having all the compensation required to be disclosed to be reported on the Schedule C; (3) reduce burden by synchronizing the record-keeping that would be required for ERISA section 408b-2 regulations before-the-fact disclosure with Schedule C's after-the-fact reporting; and (4) make the information easier to understand for end users of the forms by bringing consistency between the service provider fees disclosed to the plan fiduciaries and the service provider fees reported to the Agencies and made public. In this regard, a recent GAO report stated that some filers advised that there was confusion over what Schedule C requires to be reported, including in comparison to what is required under the ERISA section 408b-2 regulations disclosure scheme.[27] Therefore, as discussed in detail earlier in this document,

---

[22] See "Invisible Pension Investments," Peter J. Wiedenbeck, Rachael K. Hinkle & Andrew D. Martin (*http://sites.lsa.umich.edu/admart/wp-content/uploads/sites/127/2014/08/vatr13.pdf*).

[23] *See*, GAO *Private Pensions: Targeted Revisions Could Improve Usefulness of Form 5500,* at 14-15.

[24] See section 1103(b) of the Pension Protection Act of 1996, Public Law 109-280, 120 Stat. 780 (2006).

[25] GAO *Targeted Revisions Could Improve Usefulness of Form 5500 Information,* at 18.

[26] See 72 FR 74731 (Nov. 16, 2007).

[27] *See* GAO *Targeted Revisions Could Improve Usefulness of Form 5500 Information,* at 22.

the Agencies are proposing various changes to the Schedule C to better harmonize it with the disclosure requirements under the final ERISA section 408b-2 regulation. Among other changes, the Agencies are proposing to eliminate the concept of "eligible indirect compensation" on Schedule C in part because "eligible indirect compensation" was created prior to the finalization of ERISA section 408b-2 rules to address concerns about possible future inconsistencies that are no longer applicable. Instead of being able to rely on the construct of "eligible indirect compensation" to report only the name of the person providing the disclosures to the plan administrator, the proposal would require filers to report all types of compensation for ERISA section 408b-2 "covered" service providers. This change will also help address concerns raised by other data sources on service provider compensation about the completeness of Schedule C compensation data. A recent survey by Deloitte Consulting LLP for the Investment Company Institute reported fees paid by 401(k) plans that greatly exceeded fees reported on the Schedule C at every asset level.[28]

The proposed forms revisions, and implementing DOL regulations, would also require small pension plans that are not eligible to file the Form 5500-SF and welfare plans that are funded with a trust with fewer than 100 participants to file the Schedule C. Currently, only large pension plans and large welfare plans that are not unfunded or insured (e.g., funded using a trust) must file the Schedule C, thus excluding almost 90 percent of current pension plan filers and over 80 percent of current welfare plan filers from having to disclose service provider fees. The DOL recognizes the burdens small plans face in complying with reporting obligations, but must weigh them against the market efficiencies that can be gained through improved transparency and fee disclosure. The DOL therefore proposes to require small pension plans to file Schedule C only if they do not meet the eligibility conditions for filing the Form 5500-SF, which predominantly are those pension plans that are invested in alternative or hard-to-value assets. The DOL proposes to require welfare plans that offer group health benefits with fewer than 100 participants to file Schedule C only if they are not unfunded or insured (e.g., funded with a trust), because those plans are most likely to experience financial difficulties. Defined contribution pension plan Form 5500-SF filers, as well as defined contribution pension plan Form 5500 Annual Return/Report filers required to complete the Schedule H, would also have to attach the comparison chart that is required to be furnished to participants under the DOL's regulation at 29 CFR 2550.404a-5. Although the comparison chart would not be attached in a "structured" format, it would provide, with a minimal burden increase, a picture of the investment earnings and fees for defined contribution pension plans, which constitute the majority of small plan filers.

Requiring those small pension plans that are not eligible to file the Form 5500-SF and welfare plans that include group health benefits with fewer than 100 participants that are not unfunded or insured (e.g., funded with a trust) to complete the Schedule C as part of their Form 5500 Annual Return/Report filing, and requiring Form 5500-SF defined contribution pension plan filers to include the 404a-5 comparison chart should address some of the GAO's concerns that service provider fee information is incomplete because plans with fewer than 100 participants are not currently required to file information about indirect compensation received by the plans' service providers.[29] Both the proposed Schedule C information for small plans not eligible to file the Form 5500-SF and the 404a-5 information would also enable sponsors of small plans to more easily compare fee information between their plans and increase competition for these services. In addition, financial information reporting could be better aligned with recently adopted disclosure rules to ensure that all fees are reported by the plans.[30]

(3) *Enhancing usability of data filed on the annual return/report.*

E-filing, as well as advances in information technology, have changed both the regulated community's and government's ability to use the Form 5500 Annual Return/Report data. The government can now provide the data in a much more timely and comprehensive manner. As a result, the Form 5500 Annual Return/Report data sets are posted on the Internet, updated monthly, and the images of the individual filings and attachments are made available at no cost to the requester.[31] This has allowed the public as well as the Agencies to monitor plan investments and trends more efficiently. Several private companies have

started to build data sets and applications using the Form 5500 Annual Return/Report data to compare plans and service providers and make these services available to plan sponsors and service providers. These developments can lead to better review of plan investments and increased competition, ultimately benefiting plans and participants.

The usefulness of the Form 5500 Annual Return/Report data for comprehensive plan monitoring is dependent on comparable data being available for all or most plans and on the data being available in data-capturable formats. The current financial reporting structures and requirements, however, do not allow the data to be utilized to the fullest extent. As stated above, the Schedule H Line 4i, Schedules of Assets, and the Line 4j, Schedule of Reportable Transactions, as well as other attachments to various schedules (including Schedules MB and SB) are not filed in a standardized electronic format and therefore cannot be searched and analyzed electronically. As a result, the Agencies, other governmental users, including policymakers, and the public have difficulty accessing and making most effective use of key information about pension plan investments.

The proposed requirement for filers to complete a standardized Schedule H Line 4i(1), Schedule of Assets Held for Investment and Line 4i(2) Schedule of Assets Disposed of by End of Plan Year, in a data-capturable format would address some of the critical gaps in available data on pension plan investing, which accounts for over $7.87 trillion of United States savings. The Agencies' proposal to standardize the Schedule H, Line 4i Schedules of Investments also is responsive to the DOL-OIG's recommendation that the Agencies create a searchable reporting format for the Schedule H, Line 4i Schedules of Assets and otherwise increase the accessibility of Form 5500 Annual Return/ Report data, particularly information on hard-to value assets and multiple-employer plans.[32]

In addition, this proposal would enhance the usability of data by replacing some of the attachments to the various schedules (including some attachments to Schedules MB and SB)[33] with text fields and having filers report required information in text fields on the face of the forms and on schedules instead of requiring this information to be filed as non-standard attachments. The Agencies took into account the size and complexity of the attachments in determining which should be text fields and which should continue to be attachments, despite the overarching goal of improving data usability for the complete form. In a few cases, especially for detailed actuarial charts, the Agencies determined that requiring standardized attachments or requiring the information to be provided on the face of the forms and schedules could potentially be overly difficult, costly, and complex, and therefore the costs would outweigh the benefits.

Further improvements would be realized from the proposal's requirement that other currently unstructured data or new elements would also be collected as structured data. These include the lists of employers participating in multiple-employer and controlled group plans required to be attached to the Form 5500 Annual Return/Report or Form 5500-SF; the Schedule H, Line 4a Schedule of Delinquent Contributions, and Schedule H, Line 4j Schedule of Reportable Transactions. Having information on delinquent participant contributions and reportable transactions in a "structured" data format would benefit the Agencies by allowing them to identify common types of violations across plans, more quickly respond to any identified issues, and better determine areas where more enforcement and encouragement of compliance and education is needed. Having this data reported in a structured format would also benefit the Agencies and the general public by identifying the universe of employers that participate in multiple-employer and controlled group plans and allowing them to quickly identify plan sponsors that might be affected by adverse market conditions or financial distress.

In summary, advances and developments in technology allow data users to run increasingly sophisticated analyses using the existing Form 5500 Annual Return/Report data, but this is dependent on the availability of these data in a data-capturable format. In addition to researchers interested in studying trends in the employee benefits industry, some companies have reached out to the DOL to request that Form 5500 Annual Return/Report data be collected in a more standard-

---

[28] Deloitte Consulting LLP (2014, August). *Inside the Structure of Defined Contribution/401(k) Plan Fees, 2013: A Study Assessing the Mechanics of the 'all-in' Fee.* (Available at *https://www.ici.org/pdf/rpt_14_dc_401k_fee_study.pdf*).

[29] See GAO *Targeted Revisions Could Improve Usefulness of Form 5500 Information*, at 25.

[30] *Id.* at 50.

[31] Requests for individual filings and attachments are available at no cost to the requester. Bulk requests are available at a minimal cost to the requester. See Guide to

Submitting Requests Under the Freedom of Information Act, Section VIII (*http://www.dol.gov/dol/foia/guide6.htm*).

[32] See *EBSA Needs to Provide Additional Guidance and Oversight to ERISA Plans Holding Hard-to-Value Alternative Investments*, at 17; see also GAO *Private Pensions: Targeted Revisions Could Improve Usefulness of Form 5500 Information*, at 37; GAO, *Federal Agencies Should Collect Data and Coordinate Oversight of Multiple Employer Plans*, at 30.

[33] The proposed Schedule E, which is based in large part on the Schedule E from 2008 and earlier, would use text fields rather than attachments for some of the previously asked questions.

ized and consistent format.[34] If these data were available in such a format, researchers, businesses and plan professionals could use the data more efficiently to inform employers and participants on plan structures, operations, and finances. Particularly important in a constrained federal budgetary environment, such data will allow EBSA's enforcement staff to monitor many more employee benefit plans in a systematic and efficient way, producing more fruitful investigations and reducing the inefficiencies and disruptions resulting from unnecessary investigations.

(4) *Requiring reporting by all group health plans covered by Title I of ERISA, including adding a new Schedule J (Group Health Plan Information).*

The enactment of the Affordable Care Act expanded DOL's already growing oversight and regulatory responsibilities with respect to the provision of group health benefits to workers in private sector employer-sponsored group health plans. Generally most welfare plans that include group health benefits that have fewer than 100 participants do not currently file the Form 5500 Annual Return/Report. The current regulation exempts small plans from the requirement to file if they are unfunded, fully insured or combination unfunded/fully insured.[35] The current lack of information collected on the Form 5500 Annual Return/Report from group health plans diminishes the effectiveness of EBSA's ability to develop health care regulations and complicates the DOL's ability to enforce such regulations and educate plan administrators regarding compliance. Congress, DOL, other governmental users, private researchers, service providers, and other members of the regulated community currently are not able to confidently estimate even the most basic information regarding group health plans, such as the total number of plans that exist or trends that are occurring in the marketplace.

The Affordable Care Act requires the Secretary of Labor to provide Congress with an annual report containing general information on self-insured employee health benefit plans and financial information regarding employers that sponsor such plans. This "Annual Report on Self-Insured Group Health Plans," by the terms of the statute, must use data from the Form 5500 Annual Return/Report. However, as noted above, those small plans that are self-insured and do not use a trust are not required to file the Form 5500 Annual Return/Report with the DOL and the Form 5500 Annual Return/Report only collects limited information from self-insured plans that do file.[36] Also, as the 2015 Report states, "health benefits may be reported together with certain other benefits, such as disability or life insurance benefits, on a single Form 5500 Annual Return/Report. This makes it difficult to distinguish how the different benefits are financed."[37] To fulfill its responsibility to Congress, the DOL has developed an algorithm to try to infer the funding method for plans that file. This methodology, however, may not accurately identify self-insured plans and can only draw information from the Form 5500 Annual Returns/Reports filed, which are a limited sample, and the methodology may compromise the validity of any conclusions drawn from the report and any resulting policy prescriptions.

In addition, sections 2715A and 2717 of the PHS Act, as added by the Affordable Care Act and incorporated into ERISA section 715, include important new reporting requirements for group health plans subject to ERISA. Specifically, section 2715A of the PHS Act incorporates the transparency provisions of section 1311(e)(3) of the Affordable Care Act to require non-grandfathered group health plans and health insurance issuers offering non-grandfathered group or individual health insurance coverage to make available to the public, and the government a host of information on health plan enrollment and claims, including: (1) Claims payment policies and procedures; (2) periodic financial disclosures; (3) data on enrollment and disenrollment; (4) data on the number of denied claims; (5) data on rating practices; (6) information on cost-sharing and payments with respect to any out-of-network coverage; (7) information on enrollee and participant rights; and (8) other information as determined by the Secretary. Moreover,

section 2717 of the PHS Act generally requires non-grandfathered group health plans and health insurance issuers offering non-grandfathered group or individual health insurance coverage to report annually whether the benefits under the plan: (A) Improve health outcomes through the implementation of activities such as quality reporting, effective case management, care coordination, chronic disease management, and medication and care compliance initiatives, including through the use of the medical homes model as defined for purposes of section 3602 of the Affordable Care Act, for treatment or services under the plan or coverage; (B) implement activities to prevent hospital readmissions through a comprehensive program for hospital discharge that includes patient-centered education and counseling, comprehensive discharge planning, and post discharge reinforcement by an appropriate health care professional; (C) implement activities to improve patient safety and reduce medical errors through the appropriate use of best clinical practices, evidence based medicine, and health information technology under the plan or coverage; and (D) implement wellness and health promotion activities.

These regulations propose conforming amendments in 29 CFR 2590.715-2715A and 29 CFR 2590.715-2717 to clarify that compliance with the reporting requirements in 29 CFR 2520.103-1 (including filing any required schedules to the annual report) by plans subject to ERISA would satisfy the reporting requirements of PHS Act section 2715A and 2717,[38] incorporated in ERISA through ERISA section 715(a)(1).[39] As explained in FAQs issued August 11, 2015,[40] HHS proposed an information collection for public comment in connection with the transparency provisions of section 1311(e)(3) of the Affordable Care Act. The proposed data collection would collect certain information from Qualified Health Plan (QHP) issuers in Federally-facilitated Exchanges and State-based Exchanges using the federal eligibility and enrollment platform. The HHS proposal explained that other reporting requirements would be proposed at a later time, through a separate rulemaking with respect to non-Exchange coverage, including those that extend to health insurance issuers offering non-grandfathered group and individual health insurance coverage outside of Exchanges and non-grandfathered group health plans (including large group and self-insured health plans).

This rulemaking proposes transparency and quality reporting for non-grandfathered group health plans under PHS Act sections 2715A and 2717, as incorporated in ERISA. It takes into account differences in markets and other relevant factors and reduces unnecessary duplication. The DOL is proposing to collect and provide high-value data to participants, beneficiaries, and regulators, such as information about benefits and plan design characteristics, funding, grandfathered plan status, rebates received by the plan (such as medical loss ratio rebates), service provider information (including information regarding any third party administrators, pharmacy benefit managers, mental health benefit managers, and independent review organizations), information on any stop loss insurance, claims processing and payment information (including number of claims filed, paid, appealed and denied), wellness program information, and other compliance information. The collection of high-value data will lead to greater transparency for consumers and assist in their decision-making process.

As discussed in detail in the Notice of Proposed Form Revision, the proposal would make significant changes to group health plan reporting. First, the proposal would add a new Schedule J (Group Health Plan Information). Plans that provide group health benefits that have 100 or more participants, all of which are currently required to file a Form 5500 Annual Return/Report, would have to include the new Schedule J in their annual report, with the remaining reporting requirements generally unchanged, except as proposed to be changed for all filers. Plans that provide group health benefits with fewer than 100 participants that are funded using a trust would generally be required to report the same information as plans that provide group health benefits with 100 or more participants that are funded using a trust; they would no longer be permitted to file the Form 5500-SF. Although this would

---

[34] See August 23, 2010 Comment Letter from BrightScope Re: Proposed Extension of Information Collection, Form 5500 (*http://www.dol.gov/EBSA*).

[35] 29 CFR 2520.104-20.

[36] Only a little over 20,000 self-insured and approximately 4,000 mixed self-insured health plans file annually with the DOL under the current reporting scheme. See "Report to Congress: Annual Report on Self-Insured Group Health Plans," March 2015, page iii (available at *http://www.dol.gov/ebsa/pdf/ACAReportToCongress2015.pdf*).

[37] Id. at v.

[38] The Treasury Department and the IRS intend to publish proposed regulations in 26 CFR 54.9815-2715A and 54.9815-2717 clarifying that group health plans required to file an annual report pursuant to section 104 of ERISA that comply with the reporting requirements in 29 CFR 2520.103-1 (including filing any required schedules to the annual report) would satisfy the reporting requirements of sections 2715A and 2717 of the PHS Act, as

incorporated in the Code. Group health plans that are not required to file an annual report pursuant to section 104 of ERISA but that are subject to sections 2715A and 2717 of the PHS Act as incorporated in the Code, will not be required to do any reporting to comply with sections 2715A and 2717 of the PHS Act, as incorporated in the Code, unless and until the Treasury Department and the IRS issue subsequent further guidance or rulemaking regarding any such reporting by such plans.

[39] Nonfederal governmental plans (as defined in PHS Act section 2791(d)(8)(C)) and health insurance issuers (as defined in PHS Act section 2791(b)(2) and ERISA section 733(b)(2)) are not required to file annual reports pursuant to ERISA section 103. Accordingly, any reporting required of such plans and issuers to satisfy PHS Act sections 2715A and 2717 will be addressed separately by HHS in future rulemakings and/or guidance.

[40] See FAQs about Affordable Care Act Implementation (Part XXVIII), available at *www.dol.gov/ebsa/faqs/faq-aca28.html* and *www.cms.gov/CCIIO/Resources/Fact-Sheets-and-FAQs/Downloads/ACA-FAQ-Part-XXVIII-transparency-reporting-final-8-11-15.pdf*.

require such plans to complete the Schedule C and the Schedule H, for plans with simple investments, there should only be a modest burden increase over completing the Form 5500-SF. Small welfare plans funded with a trust that are invested in assets that are not "eligible plan assets" for purposes of Form 5500-SF filing, are already required to file the Form 5500 Annual Return/Report, along with the Schedule I, and if applicable, Schedule A.

Group health plans that have fewer than 100 participants currently exempt from filing an annual report under 29 CFR 2520.104-20 because they are completely unfunded or combination unfunded/fully insured now would be required to file a Form 5500, a Schedule J, and, if applicable, a Schedule A. Plans that are unfunded pay some or all of their benefits out of the plan sponsors' general assets, which exempts them from state insurance regulation, making the DOL their sole regulatory agency. Because such small plans are not currently required to file the Form 5500 Annual Return/Report, there is no comprehensive and direct source of data about the number and characteristics of these plans. Further, because these plans are small, they are more susceptible to financial difficulties. Because of these concerns, the DOL believes that it is important to have more detailed benefit, financial, and compliance information for "unfunded" plans that are self-insured or partially self-insured than for those small plans that are fully insured. These plans would be required under the proposal to file the complete Form 5500 and Schedule J and, if applicable, Schedule A.

Plans that provide group health benefits that have fewer than 100 participants that are fully insured would be required to answer only limited questions on both the Form 5500 and Schedule J, and would not be required to file any other schedules or attachments. Collecting this limited data on fully insured plans providing group health benefits that have fewer than 100 participants would give the DOL basic information to identify health insurance plans they regulate and allow them to better monitor plan trends and activities, but minimize the reporting burden from more detailed reporting that is more generally required on the Form 5500, Schedule A, Schedule J, and any other applicable schedules that comprise the Form 5500 Annual Return/Report.

(5) *Improving compliance under ERISA and the Code through selected new questions regarding plan operations, service provider relationships, and financial management of the plan.*

In an era of limited financial resources, the Agencies must pursue new and creative ways to maximize the efficacy of their enforcement budgets. Improving compliance under ERISA and the Code reduces the need for costly enforcement actions. Focusing filer compliance through selected new questions regarding plan operations, service provider relationships, and financial management of the plan under ERISA and the Code can also have the effect of allowing the Agencies' enforcement staff to work more efficiently, and therefore better protect plan participants and beneficiaries.

Analysis of Benefits and Costs

The DOL believes that the benefits to be derived from this proposal, including the amendments to the reporting regulations and the forms revisions, would justify their costs. The DOL further believes that these revisions to the existing reporting requirements will enhance protection of ERISA rights by improving the effectiveness of enforcement actions and by improving the quality of data used for research and policymaking purposes. The DOL conducted a detailed assessment of the costs and benefits of these changes.

Benefits

As stated previously, the proposal pursues five main objectives. The various changes to the forms, schedules, instructions, and DOL regulatory exemptions and requirements are together intended to integrate these various objectives, and all of the other goals together are proposed with the intention of supporting the move towards fuller transparency and data mineability overall. Fuller transparency could increase participant trust levels, which could encourage pension plan participants to increase their retirement savings and welfare plan participants to use benefits when needed, resulting in strengthened retirement security and improved public health. The benefits of each of the five main objectives are discussed below.

(1) *Modernizing financial information.*

As stated previously, the financial information, particularly the asset/liability statement, contained in the current Schedule H (Large Plan Financial Information), Schedule I (Small Plan Financial Information), as well as the more recently established Form 5500-SF, is based on data elements that have remained largely unchanged since the Form 5500 Annual Return/Report was established in 1975. Many investments in alternative and hard-to-value assets and held in collective investment funds do not fit squarely into any of the existing reporting categories on Schedule H. As discussed previously, the GAO has expressed concerns that many investments with widely varying risk, return, and disclosure considerations are often reported in the catch-all "other plan asset" category.[41] GAO also noted that the plan asset categories on the Schedule H are not representative of current plan investments, and provide little insight into the investments themselves, the level of associated risk, or structures of the investments.[42] The DOL-OIG also recommended that the Agencies revise the Form 5500 Annual Return/Report to improve reporting of hard-to-value assets and alternative investments.[43]

As part of their overall evaluation of how best to restructure financial reporting to maximize usable data while limiting burden increases, the Agencies also concluded that research and enforcement efforts could be enhanced by updating the asset reporting categories and by standardizing Schedule H Line 4i attachments. Accordingly, the changes the Agencies are proposing to make to the asset breakouts on the balance sheet and income statement components of Schedule H would make the asset reporting more consistent with the current financial marketplace and enable the Agencies, plan sponsors, and participants and beneficiaries to develop a more accurate and detailed picture of the types of assets held by plans, including hard-to-value assets and alternative investments and investment held through collective investment vehicles. The proposed changes take into account many of the sophisticated and complex investments that do not fit neatly into any of the existing program categories, which would lead to consistent reporting by filers and more transparency by limiting the consolidation of many diverse investments into the catch-all "Other" category on the balance sheet on the Schedule H.

The Agencies also opted to revise the Schedule H Line 4i Schedules of Assets attachment into two, distinct structured data attachments. Doing so will produce more consistent data, reduce confusion over the proper format to provide required data, and enable data mineability. Moreover, as discussed in detail earlier in this document and the Notice of Proposed Forms Revisions published simultaneously, the structural, data element and instruction changes to the Schedule H, Line 4i Schedule of Assets Held for Investment the Agencies are proposing will allow the Form 5500 Annual Return/Report to be better used as a tool to evaluate the year-to-year performance of a plan's individual investments. The creation of more detailed and structured Schedule H, Line 4i Schedules of Assets is a specific recommendation of the DOL-OIG and the GAO.[44] The proposed changes to the Schedule H Line 4i Schedules of Assets, in addition to better meeting the needs of the Agencies, other government users, and other end users of the data, should also serve to address the shortcomings identified in these reports.

The proposed changes made to DFE reporting would ensure that the Agencies, plan fiduciaries, plan service providers, and other users of data have the tools to create a more complete picture of plans' investments in pooled investment vehicles. Similarly, the proposed changes to the financial information reported by small plans would improve the utility of the Form 5500 Annual Return/Report as a tool to obtain a meaningful picture of small plan investments in hard-to-value and alternative investments as suggested by GAO and other government oversight and advisory bodies.[45]

Although these changes would result in additional reporting for certain small plans, the Agencies do not expect that small plans with simple investment portfolios would experience a significant increase in their annual reporting burden. Small plans with complex portfolios that include hard-to-value or alternative investments should have more transparent financial statements which may require somewhat more complex financial reporting obligations. In light of changes in the financial environment and increasing concern about investments in hard-to-value assets and alternative investments, the Agencies believe that requiring separate financial information regarding hard-to-value

---

[41] GAO *Targeted Revisions Could Improve Usefulness of Form 5500 Information,* at 12.

[42] *Id.* at 11-12.

[43] *EBSA Needs to Provide Additional Guidance and Oversight to ERISA Plans Holding Hard-To-Value Alternative Investments, Department of Labor Office of Inspector General Report Number: 09-13-001-12-121* at 4, 18, and 19.

[44] *See EBSA Needs to Provide Additional Guidance and Oversight to ERISA Plans Holding Hard-to-Value Alternative Investments,* at 17; *Private Pensions: Targeted Revisions Could Improve Usefulness of Form 5500 Information,* at 37.

[45] Id.

investments is important for regulatory, enforcement, and disclosure purposes.[46]

A major overriding objective of these proposed forms revisions is to modernize the Form 5500 Annual Return/Report information collection so that the presentation of plan trust financial and balance sheet information is a more transparent and detailed reflection of the investment portfolios and asset management practices of employee benefit plans. The basic objective of general financial reporting is to provide information about the reporting entity for the Agencies' enforcement, research, and policy formulation programs, for other federal agencies, Congress, and the private sector in assessing employee benefit, tax, and economic trends and policies; and for plan participants and beneficiaries and the general public in monitoring employee benefit plans. Modernizing the financial reporting instruments will bring greater transparency to plan transactions, which will enhance the efficiency of the Agencies' enforcement efforts. Specifically, the Agencies will be better able to target their enforcement efforts, which will reduce the number of investigations involving plans that are not engaging in problematic activities.

Additionally, ERISA Section 513(a) authorizes and directs the Secretary of Labor and EBSA to conduct a robust research program on employee benefits. The Form 5500 Annual Return/Report is one of the leading sources of data used in this research program. Modernizing the financial information reported on the Form 5500 Annual Return/ Report will improve the quality of the research conducted by internal and external researchers. This improved research will, in turn, improve the quality of policy decisions made by DOL and other governmental policymakers that rely on the Form 5500 Annual Return/Report data.

(2) *Updating fee and expense information on plan service providers with a focus on harmonizing annual reporting requirements on Schedule C with DOL's final disclosure requirements at 29 CFR 2550.408b-2.*

As previously discussed, the proposal would harmonize the Schedule C rules with the DOL's regulations at 29 CFR 2550.408b-2. The Agencies believe that requiring reporting of all indirect compensation (rather than continuing the exemption from reporting for "eligible indirect compensation"), but limiting indirect compensation reporting to the service providers and types of compensation that are required to be disclosed under the ERISA section 408b-2 regulation will provide a particular benefit to plan record keepers. The information required to be reported would be an after the fact reporting of fees that should have been disclosed in advance under the ERISA section 408b-2 regulation. Because the ERISA section 408b-2 regulation requires covered service providers to provide plan administrators the information they need to satisfy their Form 5500 Annual Return/Report obligations with respect to compensation information, the additional burden should be limited to entering the data on the Form 5500 Annual Return/Report.[47]

Currently, given that some significant component of indirect compensation is not reported because it is permitted to be treated as "eligible indirect compensation," and the fact that some filers report formulas instead of dollar amounts, the Agencies and public only have limited information regarding the total compensation that service providers receive and that affects plans' finances and potentially involves conflicts of interests among service providers. Almost 90 percent of 2013 Schedule C filers reported at least one service provider receiving some amount of eligible indirect compensation, and nearly 70 percent of 2013 Schedule C filers reported at least one provider receiving *only* eligible indirect compensation. Filers identifying at least one service provider as receiving some amount of eligible indirect compensation on their Schedules C, according to the overall Form 5500 data, report holding roughly two-thirds of all pension assets. Thus, the limited "eligible indirect compensation" reporting impacts the data relating to service provider fees in connection with the servicing and management of a significant amount of assets. In addition, analysis of these data also indicates that almost 50 percent of Schedule C filers report at least one service provider who provides a formula instead of an explicit or estimated amount of compensation. These filers report holding almost 40 percent of all pension assets. Providing only a formula without an actual or estimated dollar amount of the compensation makes it very hard for plan sponsors or participants to identify the exact amount of compensation.

The proposed rules and the subsequent reported information would make it possible to get a much better understanding on the fees that were transferred between service providers in the form of indirect compensation, therefore allowing plan sponsors and participants to assess the fees that they are incurring. The Agencies anticipate that the increased transparency under the proposal would likely lead to increased competition in the service provider market.

Aligning the Schedule C with ERISA section 408b-2 disclosure should benefit the regulated community by clarifying and streamlining the information reported on the Schedule C, which should reduce filer confusion, and in turn reduce any filer burden caused by the confusion. The updated service provider information will also improve targeting in the Agencies' enforcement efforts, be a resource for independent researchers to identify fee trends, and help policymakers identify opportunities to make regulatory adjustments.

The proposed rule would also require small pension plans that are not eligible to file the Form 5500-SF and welfare plans that provide group health benefits that are not unfunded or insured (*e.g.,* funded using a trust) and have fewer than 100 participants to file Schedule C. Currently, only large plans (for welfare plans, only large plans that are not unfunded or insured) must file a Schedule C, thus a large portion of plans do not disclose service provider compensation, except total administrative expenses, which includes direct compensation to service providers.[48] The Agencies believe that the ideal solution for enforcement, research, policymaking, and participant monitoring purposes would be for all indirect compensation to be required to be reported, but recognize the burdens small plans face in complying with disclosure obligations. The Agencies therefore propose to require small pension plans to file Schedule C only if they do not meet the eligibility conditions for filing the Form 5500-SF, which generally would be those pension plans that are invested in alternative or hard-to-value assets. The Agencies propose to require welfare plans that offer group health benefits with fewer than 100 participants to file Schedule C only if they are funded using a trust. This makes the reporting requirements consistent with those for other welfare plans that are funded using a trust that are required to file the Form 5500. Self-insured plans are more susceptible to experience financial difficulties than fully insured plans. Requiring these small plans to file a Schedule C would address some of the GAO's concerns that not all critical information on indirect compensation is being reported to the Agencies.[49]

(3) *Enhancing mineability of the data filed on the Form 5500 Annual Return/Report.*

As stated previously, a key component of the proposal is to make it easier and more efficient to use the data from the Form 5500 Annual Return/Report for research, policy analysis, and enforcement purposes. The primary way the Agencies propose to enhance the mineability of Form 5500 Annual Return/Report data is by structuring and standardizing the questions on the forms and schedules and structuring certain information currently required to be reported in the form of a nonstandard attachment to the filing. This will improve the integrity of the collected data and allow the Agencies and others to compare, aggregate, and analyze these data.

The Agencies have identified a number of areas where the current method of reporting information impedes data usability and are proposing several changes to facilitate the efficient use of Form 5500 Annual Return/Report data. Data from Schedule H Line 4i (Schedule of Assets), for example, is currently not available in a standardized electronic format and would be very useful for monitoring the performance of plan investments. The proposed rules would require the Schedule H Line 4i, Schedules of Assets, to be filed in a standardized electronic format, which will allow them to be searched and matched to performance data through common software programs. As a result, the Agencies and the public would have much less difficulty accessing key information about the plan's investments. Additional improvements in data mineability and plan monitoring also would be realized from the proposal's requirement that other currently unstructured data or new elements also be collected as structured data under the proposal, including the lists of employers participating in multiple-employer and controlled group plans required to be attached to the Form 5500 Annual Return/Report or Form 5500-SF, the Schedule H, Line 4a

---

[46] Although such small plans would be required to complete the Schedule H instead of the Schedule I, including the Schedule H Line 4i(1) and 4i(2) Schedules of Assets, eligible small plans, as they can under the current rules, would still be eligible for a waiver of the annual examination and report of an IQPA under 29 CFR 2520.104-46.

[47] See 29 CFR 2550.408b-2(c)(iv).

[48] "Direct" compensation is included as an administrative expense item on both the Form 5500-SF and on Schedule H, but it is a total and is not linked to payments to specific

service provider. Because it is not a "balance sheet" item, indirect compensation is not reported as part of the financial statements.

[49] See GAO *Targeted Revisions Could Improve Usefulness of Form 5500 Information* at 25-26 ("Given these various exceptions to fee reporting requirements, Schedule C may not provide participants, the government, or the public with information about a significant portion of plan expenses and limits the ability to identify fees that may be questionable.")

Schedule of Delinquent Contributions, and Schedule H Line 4j Schedule of Reportable Transactions.

Data mineability also would be improved by the proposal's requirement that some data would be reported as text fields instead of as attachments. This would increase the accessibility of data. Similar to the proposed specific data elements for the Schedule H Line 4i Schedules, which replace a suggested format for an unstructured attachment, the Agencies believe, based on their own use of the data to support the research, policy, and oversight efforts of the Agencies, and input from other end users, that data mineability will be enhanced by requiring the use of text fields on the face of the schedules instead of having information filed as non-standard attachments.

Another limitation on data mineability and usability of the current Form 5500 Annual Return/Report is that actuarial information is reported in the form of PDF attachments to the Schedules MB and SB, rather than on the face of the actuarial schedules. Therefore, as discussed above, the proposal would expand data elements on actuarial schedules including information previously reported on unstructured attachments. If questions are directly answered on structured forms and schedules, like the Form 5500 Annual Return/Report and the listed schedules (as opposed to non-standard attachments) the data are "machine-readable" in the 5500 data base, and computer programs can be written to read the data sets created by DOL. This would make more readily searchable and usable actuarial information essential to the Agencies' enforcement efforts and in their ability to target plans with likely compliance issues. Furthermore, the availability of the data would enhance the ability of private-sector auditors using the information to validate a plan actuary's calculations. The data would also provide new opportunities for research. There is no source of system-wide data on defined benefit pension plan participants with age, service, and average benefit levels. The availability of such data would allow for more refined projections of future coverage and benefits adequacy for plan participants and beneficiaries. As more of these data are collected over the years, trends in plan coverages and benefits could more easily be analyzed and identified.

The proposed rules make an additional change to reporting requirements that is expected to make filing some of the plan characteristics easier and more reliable. Instead of having to report all applicable plan characteristic codes under one line item, the proposal would ask for this information grouped by topic. Currently, some filers report an incomplete picture of their plan characteristics. For example, some filers have characteristics that should warrant supplying five or more codes, but instead they only supply two or three. It is expected that the new questions will be easier for filers to respond to and that the data reported will be more accurate.

In summary, these improvements in data mineability will make it more efficient to conduct Form 5500 Annual Return/Report data analysis and to use the data to monitor plans, and identify trends.

(4) *Requiring reporting by all group health plans covered by Title I of ERISA, including adding a new Schedule J (Group Health Plan Information).*

As discussed above, the proposal would eliminate the current exemption from reporting for certain group health plans covered by Title I of ERISA so that all group health plans covered by Title I of ERISA will be required to file a Form 5500 Annual Return/Report. Currently, generally most plans that·provide group health benefits with fewer than 100 participants that meet the conditions of existing regulations are exempt from filing the Form 5500 Annual Return/Report, because they are unfunded, fully insured, or a combination of unfunded/fully insured. Requiring such plans to file would fill an information gap, which would allow the DOL to effectively meet its statutory obligation to enforce the ERISA requirements that apply to group health plans. Currently, the DOL must rely on complaints from plan participants as its primary source to uncover ERISA violations in small plans that are exempt from annual reporting. Eliminating this exemption would provide the DOL with the information necessary to be more proactive and systematic in identifying violations and in providing compliance assistance. The DOL would be able to track total health plan counts and coordinate its enforcement efforts relating to plans providing benefits through common issuers. For example, fully-insured plans using the same insurance provider often contain provisions that are similar. By requiring plans providing group health benefits, that are unfunded, fully insured, or combination unfunded/fully insured and have fewer than 100 participants to identify themselves and the insurance carrier through which they are insured, the DOL should be able to better determine which plans might be affected by noncompliant plan provisions. The DOL also could better coordinate its enforcement efforts with affected service providers and other Federal and State agencies.

This information also would enhance the DOL's ability to develop health care regulations, conduct policy analysis and research with respect to participant trends, and comply with the Affordable Care Act requirement to report to Congress annually regarding self-insured plans.

(5) *Improving compliance under ERISA and the Code through selected new questions regarding plan operations, service provider relationships, and financial management of the plan.*

Improving compliance under ERISA and the Code through selected new questions will bring two main benefits. First, these compliance questions will serve as a form of education for plan administrators and a self-compliance check. The Agencies believe that the new compliance questions under the proposal, as is true of the existing compliance questions, would help plan administrators better understand and monitor required plan behavior and would remind plan administrators to comply with requirements under ERISA and the Code, and thus will improve protections for participants and beneficiaries.

Second, these compliance questions will allow the Agencies, with their limited enforcement budgets, to engage in more sophisticated targeting and compliance assistance. Improvements in data management technology now enable the Agencies to create plan risk profiles to improve the effectiveness of investigations. These compliance questions, including questions on audit and oversight requirements, nondiscrimination, administrative expenses, participant contributions, and automatic enrollment, will improve the risk profiles, which will further enable the Agencies to use their enforcement resources in the most efficient way possible.

Costs

The costs for plans to satisfy their annual reporting obligations would increase under these proposed regulations relative to the current regime.[50] As shown in Table 2 below, the aggregate annual cost of such reporting under the current regulations and forms is estimated to be $488.1 million annually, shared across the 816,000 filers subject to the filing requirement. The DOL estimates that the regulations and forms revisions proposed today will impose an annual burden of $817.0 million on 2.97 million filers, for a total increase of $328.8 million annually.

TABLE 2—SUMMARY OF ANNUAL COSTS: CURRENT REQUIREMENTS VS. PROPOSED REQUIREMENTS

	Total annual costs (millions)	Total annual burden hours (thousands)
Current reporting requirements	$488.1	4,378.5
Change due to Revisions	328.8	2,949.0
Proposed Reporting Requirements	817.0	7,327.5

Because this proposal makes substantial changes to the requirements currently in effect, filers also will experience some one-time transition costs. The DOL estimates that plans will require twice as long to supply the new data elements during the first year, relative to subsequent years, and will therefore encounter one-time transition costs of $328.8 million.

The DOL has analyzed the cost impact of the individual revisions. In doing so, the DOL took account of the fact that various types of plans would be affected by more than one revision and that the sequence of multiple revisions would create an interaction in the cumulative burden on those plans. For example, nearly all pension plans that are required to file the Form 5500 and related schedules, including ESOPs, would be affected by the changes to the Schedule H. ESOPs, however, would

---

[50] The DOL believes that the annual cost burden on filers would be higher still in the absence of the proposed regulations enabling use of the Form 5500 Annual Return/Report in lieu of the statutory requirements. Without the Form 5500 Annual Return/Report, filers would not have the benefits of any regulatory exceptions, simplified reporting, or alternative methods of compliance, and standardized and electronic filing methods.

be affected not only by the proposed Schedule H changes, but also by the proposed restoration of Schedule E. The DOL quantified the individual revisions as described below and shown in Table 3.

(1) *Revised financial reporting on the Schedule H and elimination of the Schedule I.*

Revising the Schedule H, including the revisions to the Schedule H Line 4i Schedules of Assets, and eliminating the Schedule I will increase net costs. The DOL estimates that the net effect of these changes will be to increase the total burden by 535,400 hours. These changes, in conjunction with revisions to the reporting requirements for DFEs, discussed below, will decrease the number of filers reporting on Schedule H and/or Schedule I from 115,100 to 114,600. Applying an hourly labor rate of $114.95 for service providers and $98.25 for plan sponsors, the DOL estimates that this revision will increase the aggregate annual reporting cost by an estimated $57.6 million.[51]

(2) *Required reporting by all group health plans covered by Title I of ERISA, including addition of a new Schedule J (Group Health Plan Information).*

Currently, about 54,000 welfare plans that provide group health benefits file the Form 5500 Annual Return/Report and applicable schedules. Of these 54,000 filers, approximately 48,000 are welfare plans that provide group health benefits with 100 or more participants and the rest are welfare plans that provide group health benefits with fewer than 100 participants. We estimate that this proposed change will increase the number of welfare plan with group health benefit filers to approximately 2.2 million. Of these 2.2 million welfare plans with group health benefits, 1.9 million welfare plans with group health benefits are expected to be fully insured plans with fewer than 100 participants, while 289,000 welfare plans with group health benefits are expected to be unfunded, combination unfunded/fully insured, or funded with a trust with fewer than 100 participants, and approximately 48,000 welfare plans with group health benefits are expected to have 100 or more participants.

The 1.9 million plans that provide group health benefits, have fewer than 100 participants, and are fully insured would be required to complete lines 1-5 on Form 5500 and lines 1-8 on Schedule J. The 289,000 plans that provide group health benefits, have fewer than 100 participants, and are unfunded, combination unfunded/fully insured, or funded with a trust would be required to file a Form 5500, Schedule J, and Schedule A, if applicable, and if they were already required to file a Form 5500 Annual Return/Report (*i.e.*, funded with a trust), they would be required to attach any other applicable schedules. The 48,000 plans that provide group health benefits and have 100 or more participants that already are required to file a Form 5500 Annual Return/Report would be required to attach a Schedule J in addition to any other forms and schedules that they are currently required to submit.

The DOL estimates that requiring plans that provide group health benefits, have fewer than 100 participants, and are fully insured to complete only lines 1-5 of the Form 5500 and lines 1-8 of the Schedule J will increase total burden by 623,000 hours and increase the aggregate annual reporting cost by $69.6 million. Requiring all other plans that provide group health benefits and have fewer than 100 participants (unfunded, combination unfunded/fully insured, or funded with a trust) and all plans that provide group health benefits and have 100 or more participants to file a Form 5500 Annual Return/Report, Schedule J, and any other required schedules and attachments will increase the total burden by 349,100 hours for the Form 5500 Annual Return/Report and 1.2 million hours for the Schedule J. The aggregate annual reporting cost associated with requiring all other group health plans with fewer than 100 participants (unfunded, combination unfunded/fully insured, or funded with a trust) and all group health plans with 100 or more participants to file a Form 5500 Annual Return/Report, Schedule J, and any other required schedules and attachments is $39.0 million for the Form 5500 Annual Return/Report and $133.0 million for the Schedule J.

Based on the foregoing, the DOL estimates that, in total, group health plan annual reporting burden will increase by approximately 2.2 million hours and the aggregate annual reporting cost will increase by $241.6 million.

(3) *Restored Schedule E.*

Approximately 6,700 employee stock ownership plans (ESOPs) will be subject to increased reporting on the restored Schedule E. As discussed above, the Schedule E is intended to provide increased reporting related to areas of concern specific to ESOPs. The DOL estimates that the restored Schedule E will add approximately 22,000 hours of burden and an additional $2.5 million of aggregate annual reporting cost.

(4) *Revised Schedule C.*

As discussed above, Schedule C revisions are intended to harmonize the Schedule C reporting of indirect compensation with the disclosures required under the DOL's final rules on service provider compensation at 29 CFR 2550.408b-2, expand the Schedule C reporting requirement to all pension plans required to file the Form 5500 regardless of size, expand the Schedule C reporting requirement to welfare plans that offer group health benefits with fewer than 100 participants if they are funded with a trust, clarify the indirect compensation reporting requirements, and improve the information plan officials receive regarding amounts received by plan service providers. The expanded reporting requirements are expected to increase the number of Schedule C filers from approximately 82,400 to approximately 100,200. Reporting burden for Schedule C filers is expected to increase by 116,600 hours, *i.e.* roughly an hour per filer, which will produce an additional $12.9 million of annual aggregate reporting cost. Of this $12.9 million increase, $5.3 million is borne by existing filers and is attributable to eliminating the "eligible indirect compensation" reporting relief;[52] $7.2 million is borne by filers newly required to attach a Schedule C;[53] and $0.4 million is borne by existing filers and is attributable to all other changes to the Schedule C.[54]

As indicated in the regulatory impact analysis in the final publication of the regulation at 29 CFR 2550.408b-2, the DOL believes that more transparency of service provider compensation serves to discourage harmful conflicts, reduce information gaps, improve fiduciary decision-making about plan services, enhance value for plan participants, and increase the DOL's ability to redress abuses committed by service providers. 77 FR 5632, 5650 (Feb. 3, 2012). As is true with the improved disclosure required under the DOL's regulation at 29 CFR 2550.404a-5, increased transparency and ability to compare fees (and, on the improved balance sheet and schedules of assets) are expected to reduce participants' time otherwise used for searching for fee and other investment information and to produce substantial additional benefits, in the form of improved investment decisions, although the DOL has not been able to quantify this effect. 75 FR 64910, 64928 (Oct. 20, 2010).

(5) *Changes to reporting requirements and methods for direct filing entities (DFEs), added compliance questions, and all other changes.*

As discussed earlier in the preamble, the rule proposes to make several changes to the DFE filing requirements. For example, the Agencies propose eliminating the concept of Master Trust Investment Accounts (MTIA) reporting and require reporting by a master trust instead. The proposal also would change the filing requirements for a CCT or PSA in which the plan invests by requiring the plan to report the interests in the CCT or PSA on the Schedule H balance sheet (Part I, Line 1b) regardless of whether the PSA or CCT in which the plan invests files a Form 5500 Annual Return/Report as a DFE, changing how assets held through DFEs are reported on the proposed Schedule H Line 4i(1) Schedule of Assets Held for Investment, and eliminate the requirement for plans to file the Schedule D, since the DFE information that had been on Schedule D would now be on plans' Schedule H Line 4i(1) Schedule of Assets Held for Investment. The net effect of these changes to DFE reporting is to reduce the number of Schedule D filers from 61,100 to 8,900, with smaller reductions in the filing of other schedules discussed elsewhere. Reporting burden associated with DFEs is expected to fall by 94,200 hours, which will produce a $10.1 million reduction in aggregate reporting cost.

Additionally, the DOL proposes a series of compliance questions primarily on the Form 5500, Form 5500-SF, and Schedule R. Other miscellaneous changes throughout the forms and schedules include requiring new information on employer matching contributions, employee participation rates and plan design for defined contribution plans, and changes to the reporting on Schedule G.

---

[51] The appropriateness of the labor rates used in the calculations and assumptions are discussed in the Technical Appendix, which can be accessed at the DOL's Web site at *www.dol.gov/ebsa*.

[52] As discussed previously, the DOL is eliminating the limited reporting option for "eligible indirect compensation." The DOL believes that many of the costs associated with gathering and organizing data necessary for expanded service provider reporting, to the extent that the information was not already required to be provided to and kept by the plan administrator for "eligible indirect compensation" that did not have to be reported, have

already been accounted for as part of the RIA for the ERISA section 408b-2 rule. Therefore, these costs reflect only the incremental increase of reporting service provider compensation to the Agencies. Under the proposal, indirect compensation reporting would be limited to the types of service providers and compensation under ERISA section 408b-2, in contrast to all service providers currently having to report on the Schedule C receipt of indirect compensation.

[53] For new filers, this includes the costs of all other changes to the Schedule C.

[54] Costs may not add up to the total due to rounding.

Some of these compliance questions and other miscellaneous changes add burden, while others reduce burden. Together, the DOL estimates that the net effect of these various changes would add approximately 219,300 hours of aggregate reporting burden, which will produce an additional $21.5 million in aggregate reporting cost. In combination with the changes to DFE reporting discussed above, these changes will reduce the aggregate number of forms and schedules filed by 52,500.

Table 3 contains a summary of the changes in costs, expressed both in dollars and in hours, allocated to the changes outlined above and the number of affected filings.

TABLE 3—SUMMARY OF CHANGES TO THE REPORTING REQUIREMENTS

Revisions	Change in costs (millions)	Change in burden hours (thousands)	Number of filers under current requirements (thousands)	Number of filers under proposed requirements (thousands) 55	Δ Cost per affected filer by proposed requirements
Elimination of Schedule I & Change in Schedule H	$57.6	535.4	115.1	114.6	$502
Schedule C	12.9	116.6	82.4	100.2	128
DFE Reporting Changes (Including changes to Schedule D)	-10.1	-94.2	61.1	8.9	-1,137
Schedule E	2.5	22.0	0.0	6.7	374
Completion of lines 1-5 on Form 5500 and lines 1-8 on Schedule J by fully insured GHPs with fewer than 100 participants	69.6	623.0	0.0	1,869	37
Completion of Form 5500 by GHPs with fewer than 100 participants that are unfunded, combination unfunded/fully insured, or funded with a trust and GHPs with 100 or more participants	39.0	349.1	54.1	336.9	116
Completion of Schedule J by GHPs with fewer than 100 participants that are unfunded, combination unfunded/fully insured, or funded with a trust and GHPs with 100 or more participants	133.0	1,179.2	0.0	336.9	395
All Other Revisions 56	24.4	217.9	1,076.7	1,024.2	24
Total (Unique Filers)	328.8	2,949.0	816.3	2,967.5	111

55 The proposed change eliminating the concept of MTIA reporting and requiring reporting by a master trust instead, whose burden change is taken into account in the DFE Reporting Changes row, produces a reduction in the number of schedules included in filings. The change in the number of schedules filed is taken into account in the row specific to the schedule affected.

56 The number of filers in this row exceeds the total number of filers because an individual filer counts more than once when it is affected by more than one revision included in the "All Other Revisions" category.

The proposal does not otherwise alter reporting costs. With the exception of most welfare plans that provide group health benefits, plans currently exempt from annual reporting requirements (such as certain simplified employee pensions (SEPs) and small unfunded, fully insured, or combination unfunded/fully insured welfare plans that do not provide group health benefits) would remain exempt. Also, plans eligible for limited reporting options (such as certain IRA-based pension plans) would continue to be eligible. The revised Form 5500 Annual Return/Report would retain the structure that is familiar to individual and corporate taxpayers—the form would continue to contain basic identifying information, participant counts, and plan characteristics, along with a checklist of the schedules being filed.

Assumptions, Methodology, and Uncertainty

The cost and burden associated with the annual reporting requirement for any given plan will depend upon the specific information that must be provided, given the plan's characteristics, practices, operations, and other factors. For example, a small, single-employer defined contribution pension plan eligible to file the Form 5500-SF should incur far lower costs than a large, multiemployer defined benefit pension plan that holds multiple insurance contracts, engages in reportable transactions, and has many service providers that each received over $5,000 in compensation. The DOL separately considered the cost to different types of plans in arriving at its aggregate cost estimates. The DOL's basis for these estimates is described below.

Assumptions Underlying this Analysis: The DOL's analysis assumes that all benefits and costs will be realized in the first year of the reporting cycle to which the changes apply and within each year thereafter. This assumption is premised on the requirement that each plan will be required to file the Form 5500 Annual Return/Report. The DOL has used a "status quo" baseline for this analysis, assuming that the world absent the proposed regulations will resemble the present.[57]

Methodology: Mathematica Policy Research, Inc. (MPR) developed the underlying cost data, which has been used by the Agencies in estimating burden related to the Form 5500 Annual Return/Report since 1999. *See* 65 FR 21068, 21077-78 (Apr. 19, 2000); Borden, William S., *Estimates of the Burden for Filing Form 5500: The Change in Burden from the 1997 to the 1999 Forms*, Mathematica Policy Research, submitted to DOL May 25, 1999.[58] The cost information was derived from surveys of filers and their service providers, as modified due to comments, which were used to measure the unit cost burden of providing various types of information. The DOL has adjusted these unit costs since 1999 to account for changes to the forms and schedules and increases in the cost of labor and service providers since MPR developed the initial data.

For this forms revision, the DOL used the adjusted MPR unit cost data for pension and non-health welfare plans. The DOL developed the unit cost data for group health plans using the best available data. To develop unit costs for DFEs, the DOL created weighted averages of the unit costs for plans.

To obtain filer counts for pension plans, non-health welfare plans, and DFEs, the DOL used historical counts of Form 5500 Annual Return/Report filers tabulated by type and reported characteristics. For counts of group health plan filers, the DOL used data from the Medical Expenditure Panel Survey, Insurance Component (MEPS-IC) and Census of Business data.

The MEPS-IC is an annual survey of establishments collected by the Agency for Healthcare Research and Quality (AHRQ) about employer sponsored health insurance. AHRQ uses two sources to draw their data: (1) A random sample, from the Census Bureau, of private-sector business establishments with annual payroll greater than zero; and (2) a list of employers or other insurance providers identified by the Medical Expenditure Panel Survey, Household Component respondents who report having private health insurance. In 2013, approximately 39,000 private-sector establishments were surveyed.

In 2003, DOL began using the MEPS-IC as a basis for estimating the number of health plans. The number of plans was based on the share of the total number of establishments that offer health insurance by size. DOL then attempted to correct for establishments that offer multiple health plans by making a reasonable assumption that the share of establishments that reported that they "offer 2 or more plans" offered two distinct plans. Finally, DOL attempted to control for multiple establishments covered by the same plan sponsor by using the Census

of Business ratio of establishment-to-firms and dividing the total number of establishment plans by this ratio to produce an estimate of the number of health "plans" which has been consistently around 2.5 million over the years.

The DOL modeled its approach to calculating burden on the approach used during the 2009 forms revision. Aggregate burden estimates were produced in both revisions by multiplying the unit cost measures by the filer count estimates. The methodology is described in broad terms below.[59]

To estimate aggregate burdens, types of plans with similar reporting requirements were grouped together in various groups and subgroups. As shown in Table 4 below, calculations of aggregate cost were prepared for each of the various subgroups both under requirements in effect prior to this action and under the forms as revised. Table 4 also shows the number of plans within each subgroup affected by the revisions. The universe of filers was divided into four basic types: Defined benefit pension plans, defined contribution pension plans, welfare plans, and DFEs. For the plans, each of these major plan types was further subdivided into multiemployer and single-employer plans.[60] Since the filing requirements differ substantially for small and large plans, the plan types were also divided by plan size. For large plans (100 or more participants), the defined benefit plans were further divided between very large (1,000 or more participants) and other large plans (at least 100 participants, but fewer than 1,000 participants). Small plans (less than 100 participants) were divided similarly, except that they were divided into Form 5500-SF eligible and Form 5500-SF ineligible plans, as applicable. Welfare plans were divided into group health plans and plans that do not provide any group health benefits, while plans that provide group health benefits and have fewer than 100 participants were divided into fully insured group health plans and unfunded, combination unfunded/fully insured plans, or funded with a trust group health plans. DFEs were divided into Master Trusts/MTIAs, CCTs, PSAs, 103-12 IEs, and GIAs. For each of these sets of respondents, burden hours per respondent were estimated for the Form 5500 Annual Return/Report itself and up to seven schedules or the Form 5500-SF (and the Schedule SB, for Form 5500-SF eligible defined benefit pension plans).

We also separately estimated the costs for each of the forms and for each schedule that is part of the Form 5500 Annual Return/Report. When items on a schedule are required by more than one Agency, the estimated burden associated with that schedule is allocated among the Agencies. This allocation is based on how many items are required by each agency. The burden associated with reading the instructions for each item also is tallied and allocated accordingly.

The reporting burden for each type of plan is estimated in light of the circumstances that are known to apply or that are generally expected to apply to such plans, including plan size, funding method, usual investment structures, and the specific items and schedules such plans ordinarily complete. For example, under the proposal, a small, fully insured group health plan would be required to file only basic questions on the Form 5500 and the proposed Schedule J. By contrast, a large single-employer defined benefit pension plan that is intended to be tax-qualified that has insurance products among its investments and whose service providers received compensation above the Schedule C reporting thresholds would be required to submit an annual report completing almost all the line items of the Form 5500, plus Schedule A (Insurance Information), Schedule SB (Single-Employer Defined Benefit Plan Actuarial Information), Schedule C (Service Provider Information), possibly the Schedule G (Financial Transaction Schedules), Schedule H (Financial Information), and Schedule R (Retirement Plan Information), and would be required to submit an IQPA report. In this way, the Agencies intend meaningfully to estimate the relative burdens placed on different categories of filers.

Burden estimates were adjusted for the proposed revisions to each schedule, including items added or deleted in each schedule and items moved from one schedule to another.

The DOL has not attributed a recordkeeping burden to the 5500 Forms in this analysis or in the Paperwork Reduction Act analysis because it believes that plan administrators' practice of keeping financial records necessary to complete the 5500 Forms arises from usual and customary management practices that would be used by any financial entity and does not result from ERISA or Code annual reporting and filing requirements.

---

[57] Further detail can be found in the Technical Appendix, which can be accessed at *www.dol.gov/ebsa*.

[58] The MPR report can be accessed at the DOL's Web site at *www.dol.gov/ebsa*.

[59] Further details about the approach are explained in the Technical Appendix, which can be accessed at the DOL's Web site at *www.dol.gov/ebsa*.

[60] For purposes of this analysis, multiple employer plans were treated as single employer plans.

The aggregate baseline burden is the sum of the burden per form and schedule as filed prior to this action multiplied by the estimated aggregate number of forms and schedules filed.[61] The DOL estimated the burden impact of changes in the numbers of filings and of changes made to the form and the various schedules. The burden estimates use data from the Form 5500 Annual Return/Report for plan year 2013, which is the most recent year for which complete data is available. The Overall Total line in Table 4 shows that the aggregate cost under the current and proposed requirements, respectively, add up to $488.1 million and $817.0 million.

---

[61] Some filers are eligible to file the Form 5500-SF, but choose to file a Form 5500 and attach Schedule I and/or other schedules because they find it less burdensome to do so in their particular situation. In an effort to be conservative in estimating burden, counts of these filings are adjusted to reflect what they would have filed if they had chosen to file the Form 5500-SF.

TABLE 4—NUMBER OF AFFECTED FILERS AND COSTS UNDER PRIOR AND NEW REQUIREMENTS

Type of filer	Number of filers under current requirements (thousands)	Number of filers under proposed requirements (thousands)	Aggregate annual cost under current requirements (millions)	Aggregate annual cost under proposed requirements (millions)
Overall Total	816.3	2,967.5	$488.1	$817.0
Large Plans	148.5	148.5	252.4	309.3
DB/ME/100-1,000 LARGE (Non-ESOP)	0.5	0.5	1.6	1.9
DB/ME/1,000+ LARGE (Non-ESOP)	0.8	0.8	2.8	3.1
DB/SE/100-1,000 LARGE (Non-ESOP)	4.8	4.8	13.0	15.2
DB/SE/1,000+ LARGE (Non-ESOP)	2.8	2.8	8.5	9.6
DC/ME/LARGE (100+ Participants) (Non-ESOP)	1.1	1.1	2.1	2.5
DC/SE/LARGE (100+ Partic.) (ESOP)	2.9	2.9	4.0	6.4
DC/SE/LARGE (100+ Partic.) (Non-ESOP)	62.2	62.2	109.2	135.9
Welfare/LARGE (Health)	47.9	47.9	91.7	114.2
Welfare/ME/LARGE (Non-Health)	0.8	0.8	1.1	1.4
Welfare/SE/LARGE (Non-Health)	24.8	24.8	18.5	19.1
Small Plans Eligible for 5500-SF	622.4	622.4	205.8	227.3
DB/Eligible for 5500-SF/SMALL (Non-ESOP)	41.1	41.1	37.6	39.0
DC/Eligible for 5500-SF/SMALL (Non-ESOP)	580.7	580.7	168.0	188.0
Welfare/Eligible for 5500-SF/SMALL (Non-Health)	0.7	0.7	0.2	0.2
Small Plans Not Eligible for 5500-SF	35.9	2,187.7	18.4	266.1
DB/ME/Not Eligible for 5500-SF/SMALL (Non-ESOP)	0.05	0.05	0.06	0.1
DB/SE/Not Eligible for 5500-SF/SMALL (Non-ESOP)	0.9	0.9	1.0	1.8
DC/ME/Not Eligible for 5500-SF/SMALL (ESOP)	0.001	0.001	0.0004	0.002
DC/ME/Not Eligible for 5500-SF/SMALL (Non-ESOP)	0.1	0.1	0.1	0.2
DC/SE/Not Eligible for 5500-SF/SMALL (ESOP)	3.8	3.8	1.8	5.8
DC/SE/Not Eligible for 5500-SF/SMALL (Non-ESOP)	21.5	21.5	10.0	27.9
Welfare/Not Eligible for 5500-SF/SMALL (Fully Insured Health)	0.0	1,869.0	0.0	69.6
Welfare/Not Eligible for 5500-SF/SMALL (Unfunded, Combination Unfunded/Fully Insured, or Funded with a Trust Health)	6.2	289.0	4.1	158.2
Welfare/ME/Not Eligible for 5500-SF/SMALL (Non-Health)	0.1	0.1	0.1	0.2
Welfare/SE/Not Eligible for 5500-SF/SMALL (Non-Health)	3.2	3.2	1.5	2.4
DFEs	9.4	8.9	11.4	14.2
Master Trust Investment Accounts and Master Trusts	1.6	1.0	2.7	2.2
Common Collective Trusts	4.0	4.0	4.3	6.0
Pooled Separate Accounts	3.2	3.2	3.3	4.7
103-12 Investment Entities	0.5	0.5	0.7	0.9
Group Insurance Arrangements	0.1	0.1	0.4	0.4

Note: Some displayed numbers do not sum up to the totals due to rounding.

DB—defined benefit plans.

DC—defined contribution plans.

SE—single-employer plans.

ME—multiemployer plans.

Large plans—100 participants or more.

Small plans—generally fewer than 100 participants.

Uncertainty Within Estimates: Because the DOL has access to the historical Form 5500 Annual Return/Report filing information, the DOL has good data for the number of pension plans, large welfare plans, including group health plan filers that file the various schedules, and DFEs, and the types of plans those filers represent. However, there is some uncertainty regarding the number of welfare plans that provide group health benefits and have fewer than 100 participants filing. There is also some uncertainty in the unit cost estimates.

There are two main issues with the methodology for counting welfare plans that provide group health benefits. First, MEPS does not differentiate between establishments offering single or multiemployer plans, which implies EBSA over-counts health plans (*i.e.,* a firm offering health insurance is counted as providing benefits to their employees when in fact one multiemployer plan may cover several firms). Second, MEPS-IC respondents that "offer 2 or more plans" are generally referencing plan types (*i.e.* HMO vs PPO) or types of employees (part-time plan vs executive plan) which would likely be included on a single Form 5500 Annual Return/Report with a single plan number on the form, which again would over-count the EBSA estimate.

With regard to the unit cost estimates, the DOL has no direct measure for the unit costs and uses a proxy adapted from the MPR model, which was developed in the late 1990s. In addition, some uncertainty is inherent in any proposed revision to the existing form, and the level of uncertainty increases where the proposal adds a new requirement, such as the proposed new group health plan filing requirements, rather than revising, deleting, or moving existing items from one schedule to another.

Regulatory Alternatives

Executive Order 12866 directs federal agencies promulgating regulations to evaluate regulatory alternatives. The DOL and the other Agencies have done so in the process of developing this proposal. The following summarizes major alternatives considered, but not proposed.

(1) *Alternative approaches for modernizing financial information besides revising the Schedule H and eliminating the Schedule I.*

Most of the changes that are being proposed to modernize the financial information that is reported on the form respond to recommendations from GAO, DOL-OIG, TIGTA, ERISA Advisory Council and other advisory groups. Early in the regulatory process, the Agencies considered revising the Schedule I instead of eliminating it, but the Agencies determined that reporting on alternative and hard-to-value assets, which is not required on the current Schedule I, is just as vital for enforcement purposes for small plans as for large plans. Adding reporting on alternative and hard-to-value assets to the financial statement on Schedule I in a meaningful way would have made Schedule H and Schedule I substantially similar. Therefore, to best effectuate the goal of providing more transparency on plan investments in alternative and hard-to-value assets, which is important for understanding the risks to participants in small plans as well as large, the Agencies concluded that eliminating the Schedule I and requiring small plans with alternative and hard-to-value assets to file the Schedule H was the most appropriate alternative.

(2) *Alternative approaches for group health plan reporting.*

In addition to the proposed annual reporting regime described in detail earlier in this preamble, the DOL considered a variety of other reporting options for group health plans. Among the options considered were (a) using existing IRS data or entering into a data sharing agreement with HHS; (b) requiring all group health plans, including small, fully insured plans to file a complete Form 5500 and Schedule J, along with the other schedules required to be filed currently by group health plans that are not exempt from filing under the existing regulations; and (c) requiring small, fully insured plans to file a Form 5500 and Schedule J every second or third year and requiring those plans to file a registration form in all other years, similar to the Form 5500-C/R structure used prior to 1999.

In an effort to minimize burden and reporting duplication, the DOL reviewed existing IRS health plan data to determine if any of these data would be usable. The DOL concluded that all data collected by the IRS about health plans, such as premium information, minimum essential coverage information, and information on the number of employees covered, is collected specifically to assess Affordable Care Act-related excise taxes and penalties and is subject to a higher threshold for information sharing than most other data collected by federal agencies. Therefore, the DOL concluded that its enforcement, policymaking, and research needs would not rise to the threshold to enable the IRS to share data. The DOL also consulted with HHS to determine whether any of their data might be appropriate; however, HHS does not collect any data on the "plan" level, which is the level of detail needed by the

DOL to inform oversight, Congressional reporting, and policy obligations under Title I of ERISA.

The DOL considered requiring welfare plans that offer group health benefits with fewer than 100 participants that are fully insured to file the complete Form 5500 and Schedule J, as would now be required of welfare plans that offer group health benefits with fewer than 100 participants that are unfunded, combination unfunded/fully insured, or funded with a trust. The DOL also considered requiring welfare plans that offer group health benefits with fewer than 100 participants that are fully insured to attach a Schedule A (in addition to the Form 5500 and Schedule J). The DOL decided against both of these options after weighing the benefits of getting additional data and the likely burdens. DOL also took into account that that the data of most benefit is the proposed new reporting to provide identity, number, and basic funding and benefit structures and types for these plans, which is currently unavailable due to the Form 5500 filing exemption from filing for these plans. More information than that would provide the DOL with somewhat more robust data, but it would not merit the burden of requiring the estimated nearly 2 million small, fully insured plans to report such information, particularly since much of the information is directed towards pension plans and welfare plans that are funded with a trust. For comparison, the DOL estimates that a plan that provides group health benefits with fewer than 100 participants filing a complete Form 5500 Annual Return/Report and a complete Schedule J will incur 5 hours and 14 minutes of burden, while one with fewer than 100 participants answering only limited questions on the Form 5500 and Schedule J will incur only 30 minutes of burden. If the DOL were to require these plans to file a complete Form 5500 and a complete Schedule J, then each of the estimated 2 million welfare plans that offer group health benefits with fewer than 100 participants that are fully insured would incur an additional 4 hours and 44 minutes of burden, at an additional aggregate annual reporting cost of $927.6 million. Attaching a Schedule A requires 2 hours and 45 minutes of burden for welfare plans that offer group health benefits with fewer than 100 participants. If the DOL were to require welfare plans that offer group health benefits with fewer than 100 participants that are fully insured to attach Schedule A, the additional aggregate annual reporting cost would be $583.4 million. The DOL concluded that requiring these fully insured plans to file a complete Form 5500 and Schedule J, as well as potentially Schedule A would grant the DOL slightly more robust data in a significantly more burdensome fashion compared with the chosen option.

The DOL decided, however, that plans that provide group health benefits and have fewer than 100 participants that are not fully insured, *i.e.,* some or all of the funding comes from the general assets of the employer or funded through a trust, would have to complete the full Form 5500 Annual Return/Report and the full Schedule J, as well as the Schedule A, if applicable. The filings for plans that provide group health benefits and have fewer than 100 participants that are unfunded, combination unfunded/fully insured, or funded with a trust would generally be similar to those for plans that provide group health benefits and have 100 or more participants that are funded in the same way. Group health plans that are unfunded, combination unfunded/fully insured, or funded with a trust, by definition, are fully or partially self-insured, and the DOL believes that the additional Schedule J information, in particular, is important for the DOL's role with regard to oversight and to development of the self-insured report.

Relatedly, the DOL also considered not requiring plans that provide group health benefits and have fewer than 100 participants that are funded with a trust to file the more detailed financial and service provider information required of large plans that are funded with a trust, in particular the Schedule C and Schedule H. Small welfare plans that provide group health benefits that are funded with a trust are already filing either the Form 5500-SF or the Form 5500 Annual Return/Report and the Schedule I. If a small welfare plan funded with a trust is required to file a Form M-1 or is invested in alternative or hard-to-value assets, it currently would have to file the Form 5500 with a Schedule I, and, if applicable, Schedule A. As with small pension plans required to file the Form 5500 Annual Return/Report, in general, the proposal would have plans that provide group health benefits and have fewer than 100 participants that are funded using a trust file in the same manner as plans that provide group health benefits that have 100 or more participants that are funded using a trust.

With respect to requiring filing of the Schedule C by plans that provide group health benefits and have fewer than 100 participants that are currently not subject to any filing requirement (*i.e.,* unfunded, fully insured, or combination unfunded/fully insured), the Agencies took into account that the existing 408b-2 regulation only applies to pension plans. Large welfare plans that are funded with a trust are already required to file a Schedule C with service provider compensation information, and the difference in information reporting should not be significant. Moreover, small plans that are funded with a trust would already be required to keep as part of their records information on direct compensation, because direct expenses are reported as administrative expenses of the plan. With respect to indirect compensation, given that the class of service providers for whom indirect compensation must be reported is limited to those identified in 408b-2, a small plan should not have many service providers that would be required to be reported, and so the burden should be minimal. Just as the Agencies believe that it is important to have improved information on small pension plans that invest in alternative and hard-to-value assets, so too, they believe that is important to have the information for small welfare plans that are funded with a trust that invest in such assets. To the extent that small plans funded with a trust are the plans most likely to experience financial difficulties, having this information should help the Agencies and participants and beneficiaries better monitor the financial stability. Additionally, the Form 5500 Annual Return/Report together with the proposed Schedule J would give basic contribution, claims, benefit structure, and group health compliance information. For these reasons, the DOL concluded that the burden of requiring plans that provide group health benefits and have fewer than 100 participants, other than those funded with a trust, to also file the Schedule C and Schedule H would outweigh the benefits of requiring that these schedules be filed; therefore, those plans are not required to do so.

Finally, the DOL considered requiring small, fully insured plans to file a Form 5500 Annual Return/Report and Schedule J every second or third year and requiring those same plans to file a registration form in alternate years. This option was ruled out due to public comments made during the 1999 Form 5500 Annual Return/Report revisions. Prior to the 1999 revisions, some filers were eligible to file the Form 5500-C/R, which included robust reporting during one year and more limited reporting during the second and third years of a three year cycle. Commenters responding to the proposed 1999 revisions were supportive of the DOL's plan to eliminate Form 5500-C/R, and accordingly eliminate the multi-year cycle of reporting, because they felt that it was difficult to keep track of the schedule.[62] In an effort to take those comments into account, the DOL decided not to propose a reporting scheme for small, fully insured group health plans that required filing a registration statement in certain years and more expansive information in other years because DOL thought it would likely be confusing, lead to filer error, and inconsistent reporting. The proposal to have the currently exempt plans that provide group health benefits with fewer than 100 participants complete some or all of the Form 5500 Annual Return/Report and Schedule J was designed to get the minimal amount of information needed for research, policy, and oversight purposes, with the simplest and least amount of reporting.

(3) *Alternative approaches for ESOP-specific reporting.*

In addition to the proposed restoration of the Schedule E, the Agencies also considered whether to add only certain additional ESOP questions to existing schedules, such as the Schedule R, which currently has ESOP questions that were moved to the Schedule R from the Schedule E when the Schedule E was eliminated for 2009 and later filings. As discussed above, before 2009, the Schedule E (ESOP Annual Information) was an IRS-only component of the Form 5500 Annual Return/Report used to collect data on ESOPs. As with other "IRS-only" schedules that were part of the Form 5500 Annual Return/Report, when the DOL mandated electronic filing of the Form 5500 Annual Return/Report as part of EFAST2, the Schedule E was removed from the Form 5500 Annual Return/Report in 2009 due to the statutory limits on the IRS's authority to mandate electronic filing of such information.

The DOL believes that many of the ESOP questions that were eliminated in 2009 because they were "IRS-only" are useful for DOL's enforcement and research programs of DOL, as well as for participants and beneficiaries in ESOPs. In addition, several new questions have been included to provide a more comprehensive view of ESOPs. With the increase in ESOP-specific questions, the use of a single schedule for all ESOP questions would be a more effective and efficient information collection tool for the Agencies than having some questions on the Schedule R and some questions on the Schedule E.

(4) *Alternative approaches for service provider reporting.*

Most of the changes that are being proposed to revise the service provider information that is reported on the form respond to recommendations from GAO, DOL-OIG, TIGTA, and other advisory groups. As discussed previously, the Agencies evaluated whether to require welfare plans that offer group health benefits with fewer than 100 participants to complete the Schedule C. The Agencies also evaluated whether or not to require small pension plans that are required to file the Form 5500 Annual Return/Report to complete the Schedule C, but decided that due to the importance of the information for participants and beneficiaries, plan officials responsible for understanding compensation arrangements, and the Agencies, the benefit outweighed the burden. Because the majority of pension plan filers are small plans that are eligible to file the Form 5500-SF, the Agencies considered whether to add questions to the Form 5500-SF requiring filers to provide indirect compensation information. The Agencies determined that to minimize burden, rather than adding new questions that were a subset or total of those on the Schedule C, they would simply require defined contribution pension plan Form 5500-SF filers to file the comparison chart under the DOL's regulation at 29 CFR 404a-5. This would provide some information (though not in the form of structured data) regarding service provider compensation with only minimal burden.

(5) *Alternative approaches for DFE reporting.*

Most of the changes that are being proposed to revise DFE reporting respond to recommendations from GAO, DOL-OIG, TIGTA, and others. The Agencies considered a variety of alternative ways to improve DFE reporting. Included in those alternatives was expanding Schedule D reporting to require plans to provide the date of the most recent Form 5500 Annual Return/Report filing of the DFEs in which a plan or investing DFE was invested. The Agencies also considered having both plans and CCTs, PSAs, and 103-12 IEs identify on the Schedule H, Line 4i Schedules of Assets the underlying assets of those DFEs. To minimize burden and duplicative reporting, the Agencies instead chose to eliminate the requirement for plans to complete the Schedule D, and have plans and filing DFE's identify on the plan or filing DFEs Line 4i Schedule of Assets underlying assets by category where the DFE has filed a Form 5500 Annual Return/Report. The assets would be broken out by the plan only if a CCT or PSA did not file a Form 5500 Annual Return/Report. The Agencies also considered whether to require plans that file the Form 5500-SF that participate in DFEs to provide more detailed information on those DFEs to help provide a more complete crosswalk between DFE and plan filings. The Agencies determined that the burden would outweigh the benefit in that regard. In addition, the Agencies considered, but decided against, requiring CCTs and PSAs that file the Form 5500 Annual Return/Report and 103-12 IEs to complete both Schedule H, Line 4i Schedules of Assets. The Agencies determined that having such entities complete just the Line 4i(1) Schedule of Assets Held for Investment, and not the Line 4i(2) Schedule of Assets Disposed During Plan Year, would adequately address concerns with quality and usefulness of data, while minimizing burden.

Regulatory Flexibility Act—Initial Regulatory Flexibility Analysis

The Regulatory Flexibility Act (5 U.S.C. 601 *et seq.*) (RFA) imposes certain requirements with respect to Federal rules that are subject to the notice and comment requirements of section 553(b) of the Administrative Procedure Act (5 U.S.C. 551 *et seq.*) and that are likely to have a significant economic impact on a substantial number of small entities. In accordance with section 603 of the RFA, the following reflects EBSA's Initial Regulatory Flexibility Analysis (IRFA) describing the impact of the rule on small entities and seeking public comment on such impact.

For purposes of this IRFA, the DOL continues to consider a small entity to be an employee benefit plan with fewer than 100 participants, as it has in many previous IRFAs measuring the impact of proposed regulatory actions on small employee benefit plans. The definition of small entity considered appropriate for this purpose differs, however, from a definition of small business that is based on size standards promulgated by the Small Business Administration (SBA) (13 CFR 121.201) pursuant to the Small Business Act (15 U.S.C. 631 *et seq.*). The basis of EBSA's definition of a small entity for this IRFA is found in section 104(a)(2) of ERISA, which permits the Secretary to prescribe simplified annual reports for pension plans that cover fewer than 100 participants. While some large employers may have small plans, in general small employers maintain most small plans. The Form 5500 Annual Return/Report impacts any employer in any private sector industry who chooses to sponsor a plan. The DOL is unable to locate any data linking employer revenue to plans to determine the relationship between small plans and small employers in industries whose SBA size standard is revenue-based. For a separate project, the DOL purchased data on ESOPs that file the Form 5500 and on defined contribution pension plans that file the Form 5500-SF from Experian Information Solutions, Inc. The Experian dataset provides the number of employees for the plan sponsor. By merging these data with internal DOL data sources, the DOL determined the relationship between small

---

[62] See 65 FR 5026.

plans and small employers in industries whose SBA size standard is based on a threshold number of employees that varies from 100 to 1,500 employees. Based on these data, the DOL estimates that over 97 percent of small retirement plans and over 80 percent of small health plans are sponsored by employers with less than 100 employees. The DOL estimates that over 99 percent of small retirement plans and over 97 percent of small health plans are sponsored by employers with less than 1,500 employees. Thus, the DOL believes that assessing the impact of these proposed rules on small plans is an appropriate substitute for evaluating the effect on small entities. In previous regulations, the DOL has consulted with the SBA Office of Advocacy concerning use of this participant count standard for RFA purposes, see 13 CFR 121.902(b)(4), and the DOL received no comments suggesting use of a different size standard. The Department solicits public comments on the appropriateness of continuing to use this size standard.

The following subsections address specific components of an IRFA, as required by the RFA.

Need for the rule and its objectives: The DOL is publishing this proposal to amend the regulations relating to the annual reporting and disclosure requirements of section 103 of ERISA simultaneously with the publication of the Notice of Proposed Forms Revisions. The DOL continually strives to tailor reporting requirements to minimize reporting costs, while ensuring that the information necessary to secure ERISA rights is adequately available. The optimal design of reporting requirements in order to satisfy these objectives changes over time. As discussed in the Need for Regulatory Action section above, the Form 5500 and the financial statements contained in the current Schedule H (Large Plan Financial Information) and Schedule I (Small Plan Financial Information) are based on data elements that have remained largely unchanged since the Form 5500 Annual Return/Report was established in 1975. Meanwhile, benefit plan designs and practices have evolved over time in response to market trends in labor, financial, health care, and insurance markets, and markets for various services used by plans. In addition, the technologies available to manage and transmit information continually advance. Therefore, it is incumbent on the Agencies to revise their reporting requirements from time to time to keep pace with such changes. The proposed forms revisions, and associated DOL regulatory amendments in the proposal, are intended to calibrate reporting requirements to take into account certain recent changes in markets, the law (including the Affordable Care Act), and technology, many of which are referred to above in this document.

Description and estimate of number of small entities to which rule will apply: This proposal increases the number of small plans required to comply with annual reporting requirements by requiring approximately 1.9 million welfare plans that provide group health benefits with fewer than 100 participants that previously were exempt from annual reporting to file a Form 5500 Annual Return/Report, completing lines 1-5 on Form 5500 and lines 1-8 on Schedule J. This proposal also requires approximately 289,000 plans that provide group health benefits and have fewer than 100 participants that are unfunded, combination unfunded/fully insured, or funded with a trust to file a Form 5500 Annual Return/Report, where previously roughly 6,000 were required to do so. In total, approximately 2.81 million small pension plans and plans that provide group health benefits covering fewer than 100 participants would be required to comply with annual reporting requirements, where previously approximately 658,000 were required to do so. As described previously, estimates of the number of small pension plans and small welfare plans that do not offer group health benefits are based on 2013 Form 5500 filing data. Estimates of the number of plans that provide group health benefits and have fewer than 100 participants are based on MEPS-IC and Census of Business data.

Description of projected reporting, recordkeeping, and other compliance requirements of the rule: The reporting requirements applicable to small plans are detailed above and in the associated Notice of Proposed Forms Revision. Almost 89 percent of the 2.81 million small plans subject to the proposed annual reporting requirements can satisfy the requirements through streamlined options.

The 1.9 million welfare plans that provide group health benefits with fewer than 100 participants can fulfill the proposed reporting requirements answering lines 1-5 of the Form 5500 and line 1-8 of the Schedule J. For these plans, annual reporting will require the use of a mix of clerical and professional administrative skills.

Over 581,000 small defined contribution pension plans and small welfare plans that do not provide group health benefits can fulfill the proposed reporting requirements with the Form 5500-SF with no schedules required to be attached. All of these plans are eligible for the waiver of audit requirements. For such plans, therefore, satisfaction of the applicable proposed annual reporting requirements is not expected to require the services of an IQPA or auditor, but, like the small, fully insured group health plans, will require the use of a mix of clerical and professional administrative skills. Another 41,000 small defined benefit pension plans and money purchase plans will continue to be eligible to use the streamlined 5500-SF; satisfaction of the proposed reporting requirements will require additional services of an actuary and submission of the Schedule SB or Schedule MB, as applicable, and no other schedules.

The remaining 319,000 small pension and welfare plans will not be eligible to use the Form 5500-SF or any other streamlined reporting option. These plans will be required to file the Form 5500 Annual Return/Report, along with any other schedules required for pension plans or welfare plans that are not fully insured group health plans.[63] Of these plans, approximately 289,000 are welfare plans that provide group health benefits and are unfunded, combination unfunded/fully insured, or funded with a trust, 25,000 are defined contribution pension plans, and over 3,000 are welfare plans that do not provide group health benefits. All will require a mix of clerical and professional administrative skills to satisfy the proposed reporting requirements. Fewer than 1,000 small pension plans that are not eligible to use the Form 5500-SF are defined benefit pension plans that will be required to use an actuary and file Schedule MB or Schedule SB in addition to needing a mix of clerical and professional administrative skills to satisfy the proposed reporting requirements.

Satisfaction of the proposed annual reporting requirements under these regulations is not expected to require any additional recordkeeping that would not otherwise be part of normal business practices.

Table 5 below compares the DOL's estimates of small plans' reporting costs under the requirements in effect prior to this action with those under the new requirements for various classes of affected plans. As shown, costs under the new requirements will be slightly higher for small pension plans and small welfare plans that are eligible to file the Form 5500-SF and significantly higher for small pension and welfare plans that are not eligible to file the Form 5500-SF (including group health plans). As discussed above, the significant increase for group health plans reflects the elimination of prior reporting exemptions for most plans that provide group health benefits and have fewer than 100 participants. The significant increase for small pension plans and small welfare plans that do not offer group health benefits that are not eligible to file the Form 5500-SF results primarily from the changes to financial and service provider reporting. The DOL notes that for the over 90 percent of plans that are eligible for annual reporting under streamlined options, the per-filer cost under the proposed requirements increases by $35-37 annually relative to the current requirements.[64] These estimates take account of the quantity and mix of clerical and professional skills required to satisfy the reporting requirements for various classes of plans.

---

[63] The exact schedules that these plans are required to attach vary based on the plans' specific facts and circumstances.

[64] In the case of the 2.0 million small, fully insured group health plans, the increase in per filer cost is from no cost to $37 per year.

TABLE 5—SMALL PLAN REPORTING COSTS UNDER PRIOR AND NEW REQUIREMENTS

Class of small plan	Number of filers under current requirements (thousands)	Number of filers under proposed requirements (thousands)	Aggregate annual cost under current requirements (millions)	Aggregate annual cost under proposed requirements (millions)	Annual per filer cost under current requirements	Annual per filer cost under proposed requirements
Defined Benefit Pension—Eligible for 5500-SF	41.1	41.1	$37.6	$39.0	$916	$951
Defined Benefit Pension—Not Eligible for 5500-SF	1.0	1.0	1.1	1.9	1,150	1,970
Defined Contribution Pension—Eligible for 5500-SF	580.7	580.7	168.0	188.0	289	324
Defined Contribution Pension—Not Eligible for 5500-SF	25.4	25.4	11.8	33.9	484	1,335
Welfare—Non-Health—Eligible for 5500-SF	0.7	0.7	0.2	0.2	289	324
Welfare—Non-Health—Not Eligible for 5500-SF	3.3	3.3	1.5	2.5	455	758
Welfare—Fully Insured Health	0.0	1,869.0	0.0	69.6	0	37
Welfare—Unfunded, Combination Unfunded/Insured, or Funded with a Trust Health	6.2	289.0	4.1	158.2	654	547
Total for All Small Plans	658.3	2,810.1	224.3	493.4	341	176

In comparison to the costs per filer described in Table 5, the 75,000 large pension plans will incur an average cost of $2,326 under the proposed requirements and the almost 74,000 large welfare plans subject to annual reporting requirements will incur an average cost of $1,833 each year.[65]

Table 6 below compares the DOL's estimates of small plans' reporting costs under the requirements in effect prior to this action with those under the new requirements as a percentage of plan assets for pension plans and welfare plans that do not offer group health benefits and as a percentage of annual health insurance premiums for welfare plans that offer group health benefits to show the impact of the reporting requirement on small plans of differing sizes.[66] As shown, group health plans with five or fewer participants that are unfunded, combination unfunded/fully insured, or funded with a trust incur the highest costs as a result of the proposed reporting requirements, incurring an annual reporting cost of 0.998 percent of their annual health insurance premiums. Non-health welfare plans that are eligible to file Form 5500-SF and have between 6 and 10 participants incur the second highest costs under the proposed reporting requirements. These plans' annual reporting cost is 0.561 percent of their plan assets.

---

[65] Average costs for large plans do not include the costs of obtaining the report of an IQPA or an actuarial report, if such a report is required for the plan's specific situation.

[66] Plan asset data reflects data reported on 2013 Form 5500 filings. Because so few plans that provide group health benefits and have fewer than 100 participants are currently subject to annual reporting requirements and many group health plans do not hold assets in trusts, the DOL concluded that annual health insurance premium data reported by the Kaiser Family Foundation was a more appropriate metric for comparison of group health plans.

TABLE 6—SMALL PLAN REPORTING COSTS UNDER PRIOR AND NEW REQUIREMENTS AS A PERCENTAGE OF PLAN ASSETS OR AGGREGATE ANNUAL HEALTH INSURANCE PREMIUMS

Class of small plan (participants)	Annual per filer cost under current requirements as a percentage of plan assets or aggregate annual health insurance premiums	Annual per filer cost under proposed requirements as a percentage of plan assets or aggregate annual health insurance premiums	Number of plans subject to proposed filing requirements
Defined Benefit Pension—Eligible for 5500-SF:			
5 or Fewer	0.088	0.091	178,694
6-10	0.084	0.087	105,458
11-25	0.067	0.070	139,971
26-50	0.040	0.041	86,936
51-75	0.022	0.023	38,822
76-90	0.018	0.018	14,491
90-99	0.016	0.016	6,341
Defined Benefit Pension—Not Eligible for 5500-SF:			
5 or Fewer	0.002	0.003	566
6-10	0.050	0.086	82
11-25	0.041	0.069	60
26-50	0.016	0.027	40
51-75	0.017	0.028	46
76-90	0.016	0.027	66
90-99	0.020	0.034	90
Defined Contribution Pension—Eligible for 5500-SF:			
5 or Fewer	0.045	0.050	178,694
6-10	0.036	0.040	105,458
11-25	0.024	0.027	139,971
26-50	0.014	0.016	86,936
51-75	0.010	0.011	38,822
76-90	0.008	0.009	14,491
90-99	0.007	0.008	6,341
Defined Contribution Pension—Not Eligible for 5500-SF:			
5 or Fewer	0.011	0.033	15,650
6-10	0.040	0.115	1,856
11-25	0.021	0.062	1,989
26-50	0.012	0.033	1,888
51-75	0.009	0.026	1,362
76-90	0.009	0.026	990
90-99	0.008	0.024	1,086
Welfare—Non-Health—Eligible for 5500-SF:			
5 or Fewer	0.135	0.151	263
6-10	0.501	0.561	61
11-25	0.269	0.301	124
26-50	0.124	0.139	91
51-75	0.036	0.041	58
76-90	0.057	0.064	32
90-99	0.134	0.150	23
Welfare—Non-Health—Not Eligible for 5500-SF:			
5 or Fewer	0.019	0.032	1,917
6-10	0.197	0.328	51
11-25	0.172	0.287	117
26-50	0.038	0.064	218
51-75	0.073	0.123	310
76-90	0.028	0.047	323
90-99	0.150	0.250	404
Welfare—Fully Insured Health:			
5 or Fewer	0.000	0.068	1,869,000
6-10	0.000	0.034	
11-25	0.000	0.014	
26-50	0.000	0.007	

Class of small plan (participants)	Annual per filer cost under current requirements as a percentage of plan assets or aggregate annual health insurance premiums	Annual per filer cost under proposed requirements as a percentage of plan assets or aggregate annual health insurance premiums	Number of plans subject to proposed filing requirements
51-75	0.000	0.005	
76-90	0.000	0.004	
90-99	0.000	0.003	289,000
Welfare—Unfunded, Combination Unfunded/Fully Insured, or Funded with a Trust Health			
5 or Fewer	1.192	0.988	
6-10	0.596	0.496	
11-25	0.238	0.199	
26-50	0.119	0.100	
51-75	0.079	0.066	
76-90	0.066	0.055	
90-99	0.060	0.050	

Note: Due to data constraints, the DOL is unable to break out smaller subgroup plan counts for welfare plans that provide group health benefits with fewer than 100 participants. Instead, the DOL has provided the total number of welfare plans that provide group health benefits with fewer than 100 participants.

The DOL is unaware of any relevant federal rules for small plans that duplicate, overlap, or conflict with these regulations.

Description of steps the DOL has taken to minimize impact on small entities: In developing these regulations and the associated forms revisions, the Agencies considered a number of alternative provisions directed at small plans, many of which are discussed elsewhere in this preamble and in the Notice of Proposed Forms Revision. The DOL believes that the proposed changes to the reporting requirements impose the least amount of burden on small plans, while allowing the DOL to collect sufficient information for it to fulfill its statutory responsibilities. Any efforts to further reduce reporting burden would have had a detrimental impact on the DOL's ability to protect plan participants and beneficiaries.

The new reporting requirements for welfare plans that offer group health benefits with fewer than 100 participants comprise over 83 percent of the increased burden on small plans. The subset of these welfare plans that are fully insured comprises almost 87 percent of welfare plans that offer group health benefits with fewer than 100 participants. As discussed previously, the DOL considered requiring welfare plans that offer fully insured group health benefits with fewer than 100 participants to file a Form 5500 Annual Return/Report and Schedule J annually, or alternatively, on a two or three year cycle. The DOL opted instead to have those plans file only limited information on the Form 5500 Annual Return/Report and Schedule J. Requiring those plans to file a complete Form 5500 Annual Return/Report and Schedule J annually would have added $927.6 million in annual reporting costs relative to the chosen alternative. The DOL also considered requiring welfare plans that offer group health benefits with fewer than 100 participants that are fully insured to attach a Schedule A (in addition to the Form 5500 and Schedule J). If the DOL were to require welfare plans that offer group health benefits with fewer than 100 participants that are fully insured to attach Schedule A, the additional aggregate annual reporting cost would be $583.4 million relative to the option chosen. The DOL rejected both of these options because they added significant cost ($1.5 billion total) with limited additional benefit.

As discussed above, the Schedule I is being eliminated for small plans that are not eligible to file Form 5500-SF because the Schedule I does not require small plans to provide detailed plan asset information. This shortcoming impairs the utility of the Form 5500 Annual Return/ Report as a tool to obtain a meaningful picture of small plan investments in hard-to-value and other assets. As the GAO has noted, the limited financial information provided on the Schedule I creates a challenge for participants, beneficiaries, oversight agencies, researchers, and other users of the Form 5500 Annual Return/Report or its data.[67] Accordingly, under the proposed change, approximately 27,000 small plans that are not eligible to file the Form 5500-SF and currently are required to file the Schedule I would be required to complete the Schedule H and the applicable schedules of assets. Although this would result in additional reporting details for certain small plans, the Agencies do not expect that small plans with simple investment portfolios would see a significant increase in their annual reporting burden. Small plans with complex portfolios that include hard-to-value or alternative investments should have more transparent financial statements which may require somewhat more complex financial reporting obligations. In light of changes in the financial environment and increasing concerns about investments in hard-to-value assets and alternative investments, the Agencies continue to believe that requiring separate financial information regarding hard-to-value investments is important for regulatory, enforcement, and disclosure purposes. The DOL notes that although the proposal would require such small plans to complete the Schedule H instead of the Schedule I, including the Schedule H Line 4i(1) and 4i(2) Schedules of Assets, small plans that are eligible for a waiver of the annual examination and report of an IQPA under current rules would still be eligible for this waiver under the proposal.[68]

The proposed rule would also require approximately 18,200 small plans that are not eligible to file the Form 5500-SF to file Schedule C. Currently, only large plans must file a Schedule C, thus excluding a large portion of plans from having to disclose service provider fees. The Agencies recognize the burdens small plans face in complying with disclosure obligations. The Agencies therefore propose to require small pension plans to file Schedule C only if they do not meet the eligibility conditions for filing the Form 5500-SF, which generally would be those pension plans that are invested in alternative or hard-to-value assets. Small welfare plans that provide group health benefits (which are not eligible to file the Form 5500-SF) would also be required to file the Schedule C if they are not unfunded or insured (*e.g.*, funded using

a trust). This would continue to emphasize sensitivity to reporting burden for small plans with simple investment portfolios, while addressing some of the GAO's concerns that not all critical information on indirect compensations is being reported to the Agencies. See GAO *Targeted Revisions Could Improve Usefulness of Form 5500 Information* at 25-26 ("Given these various exceptions to fee reporting requirements, Schedule C may not provide participants, the government, or the public with information about a significant portion of plan expenses and limits the ability to identify fees that may be questionable.") In addition, the rule would align financial information reporting with recently adopted disclosure rules to ensure that all fees are reported by the plans.[69]

Paperwork Reduction Act Statement

In accordance with the requirements of the Paperwork Reduction Act of 1995 (PRA) (44 U.S.C. 3506(c)(2)), the DOL requests comments on the information collections included in the proposed amendments to the DOL's regulations relating to annual reporting and disclosure requirements under Part 1 of Subtitle B of Title I of ERISA and in the proposed revision of the Form 5500 Annual Return/Report pursuant to Part 1 of Subtitle B of Title I and Title IV of ERISA and the Code. The DOL has submitted an information collection request (ICR) to OMB in accordance with 44 U.S.C. 3507(d), for OMB's review of the DOL's information collections previously approved under OMB Control No. 1210-0110.

A copy of the ICR can be obtained by contacting the U.S. Department of Labor, Employee Benefits Security Administration, Office of Policy and Research, 200 Constitution Avenue NW., Room N-5718, Washington, DC 20210, Telephone: (202) 693-8410; Fax: (202) 219-4745 or at *www.RegInfo.gov*. These are not toll-free numbers.

OMB asks that comments about information collections in this NPRM be submitted by mail or courier to the Office of Information and Regulatory Affairs, Attn: OMB Desk Officer for DOL-EBSA, Office of Management and Budget, Room 10235, 725 17th Street NW., Washington, DC 20503; by Fax: 202-395-6881 (this is not a toll-free number); or by email: *OIRAsubmission@omb.eop.gov*. Commenters are encouraged, but not required, to send a courtesy copy of any comments to the party identified in the **ADDRESSES** section of this NPRM. OMB requests that comments be received within 75 days of publication of the proposed rule to ensure their consideration. Comments submitted in response to this request become a matter of public record. The Department and OMB are particularly interested in comments that:

• Evaluate whether the collection of information is necessary for the proper performance of the functions of the agency, including whether the information will have practical utility;

• Evaluate the accuracy of the DOL's estimate of the burden of the collection of information, including the validity of the methodology and assumptions used;

• Enhance the quality, utility, and clarity of the information to be collected; and

• Minimize the burden of the collection of information on those who are to respond, including through the use of appropriate automated, electronic, mechanical, or other technological collection techniques or other forms of information technology, *e.g.*, permitting electronic submission of responses.

Congressional Review Act

The proposed rules being issued here are subject to the Congressional Review Act provisions of the Small Business Regulatory Enforcement Fairness Act of 1996 (5 U.S.C. 801 *et seq.*) and, if finalized, will be transmitted to the Congress and the Comptroller General for review. The proposed rule is a "major rule" as that term is defined in 5 U.S.C. 804, because it is likely to result in an annual effect on the economy of $100 million or more.

Unfunded Mandates Reform Act Statement and Summary

Title II of the Unfunded Mandates Reform Act of 1995, 2 U.S.C. 1531-1538 requires each Federal agency to prepare a written statement assessing the effects of any Federal mandate in a proposed or final agency rule that may result in an expenditure of $100 million or more (adjusted annually for inflation with the base year 1995) in any one year by State, local, and tribal governments, in the aggregate, or by the private sector. Such a mandate is deemed to be a "significant regulatory action." The current proposal is expected to have such an impact on the private sector, and the DOL therefore hereby provides such an

---

[67] GAO *Targeted Revisions Could Improve Usefulness of Form 5500 Information*, at 18.
[68] 29 CFR 2520.104-46.

[69] Id. at 50.

assessment. The DOL's written statement as required by this act follows:

The DOL is issuing the current proposed regulations and forms revisions under Sections 103, 104, 110 and 505 of ERISA (29 U.S.C. 1023, 1024, 1030, and 1135). Under Titles I and IV of ERISA and the Code, pension and other employee benefit plans are generally required to file annual returns/reports concerning, among other things, the financial condition and operations of the plan. Filing a Form 5500 Annual Return/Report of Employee Benefit Plan or Form 5500-SF Short Form Annual Return/Report of Small Employee Benefit Plan, together with any required schedules and attachments, generally satisfies these annual reporting requirements. The current proposal would amend current reporting regulations and update the existing forms and schedules as explained in the summary information provided above in this document.

The DOL assessed the anticipated benefits and costs of the current proposal pursuant to Executive Order 12866 in the Regulatory Impact Analysis for the current proposal, above, and concluded that its benefits would justify its costs. The current proposal's material benefits and costs generally would be largely confined to the private sector, where plans would incur increased costs from expanded reporting requirements, while participants and beneficiaries and other end-users of the Form 5500 Annual Return/Report data would benefit from improved reporting. The DOL itself, as well as IRS, PBGC, and other governmental users would benefit from increased efficiency in enforcement activity and improved quality in research and policy decisions resulting from reporting data that more accurately reflect the current plan marketplace.

Some employee benefit plans sponsored by tribal governments that are subject to ERISA because they cover employees who are involved in performing commercial activities (whether or not such activities are essential government functions) may be affected by the Federal mandate contained in this rule, if it is adopted as proposed. The DOL does not have sufficient data to estimate the amount of the increase in future compliance costs that would be imposed on tribal governments that sponsor these plans, but it believes such costs would be similar to those imposed on private sector employers that are discussed in the regulatory impact analysis. Such increased costs would not be paid with Federal financial assistance (or otherwise paid for by the government). The DOL is not aware of any available Federal resources to carry out this mandate on tribal governments. The budgetary impact of the mandate will fall on tribal governments that maintain certain employee benefit plans. Apart from this, the DOL does not believe that the mandate will cause any disproportionate budgetary effects on any particular regions of the nation or particular tribal governments, urban, rural or other types of communities, or particular segments of the private sector.

The DOL has not consulted with elected representatives of tribal governments, but will do so after the proposed regulations and forms revisions are published.

In summary, the DOL believes the benefits of this proposed rule are significant, and will result in a modernized annual return/report that has substantially more utility for the agencies, the regulated community, and the public. The proposed rule would also impose increased costs on employee benefit plan sponsors. Tribal governments that sponsor ERISA-covered plans will incur increased costs as will all other sponsors of ERISA-covered plans. The DOL lacks sufficient information to quantify the number of tribal governments impacted by this proposed rule, but believes that the costs imposed on tribal governments will be consistent with the costs imposed on all other sponsors of ERISA-covered plans. Finally, the DOL does not believe that the costs imposed by this proposed rule will have any disproportionate budgetary effects based on any particular regions of the nation or particular tribal governments, urban, rural or other types of communities, or particular segments of the private sector.

Federalism Statement

Executive Order 13132 (August 4, 1999) outlines fundamental principles of federalism and requires adherence to specific criteria by federal agencies in the process of their formulation and implementation of policies that have substantial direct effects on the States, the relationship between the national government and the States, or on the distribution of power and responsibilities among the various levels of government. These proposed rules do not have federalism implications because they would have no substantial direct effect on the States, on the relationship between the national government and the States, or on the distribution of power and responsibilities among the various levels of government. Section 514 of ERISA provides, with certain exceptions specifically enumerated, that the provisions of Titles I and IV of ERISA

supersede any and all laws of the States as they relate to any employee benefit plan covered under ERISA. The requirements implemented in these rules do not alter the fundamental provisions of the statute with respect to employee benefit plans, and as such would have no implications for the States or the relationship or distribution of power between the national government and the States.

List of Subjects

29 CFR Part 2520

Accounting, Employee benefit plans, Pensions, Reporting and recordkeeping requirements.

29 CFR Part 2590

Continuation coverage, Disclosure, Employee benefit plans, Group health plans, Health care, Health insurance, Medical child support, Reporting and recordkeeping requirements.

For the reasons set forth in the preamble, the Department proposes to amend Subchapter C, parts 2520 and 2590 of Title 29 of the Code of Federal Regulations as follows:

PART 2520—RULES AND REGULATIONS FOR REPORTING AND DISCLOSURE

■ 1. The authority section for part 2520 continues to read as follows:

Authority: 29 U.S.C. 1021-1025, 1027, 1029-31, 1059, 1134, and 1135; and Secretary of Labor's Order 1-2011, 77 FR 1088 (Jan. 9, 2012). Sec. 2520.101-2 also issued under 29 U.S.C. 1132, 1181-1183, 1181 note, 1185, 1185a-b, 1191, and 1191a-c. Secs. 2520.102-3, 2520.104b-1, and 2520.104b-3 also issued under 29 U.S.C. 1003, 1181-1183, 1181 note, 1185, 1185a-b, 1191, and 1191a-c. Secs. 2520.104b-1 and 2520.107 also issued under 26 U.S.C. 401 note, 111 Stat. 788.

■ 2. In § 2520.103-1, revise paragraphs (b)(1), (c)(1), (c)(2)(i), (c)(2)(ii)(D), (E), and (e), and add paragraphs (c)(2)(ii)(F) and (c)(2)(iii) to read as follows:

§ 2520.103-1 Contents of the annual report.

* * * * *

(b) * * *

(1) A Form 5500 "Annual Return/Report of Employee Benefit Plan" and any statements or schedules required to be attached to the form, completed in accordance with the instructions for the form, including Schedule A (Insurance Information), Schedule C (Service Provider Information), Schedule E (ESOP Annual Information), Schedule G (Financial Transaction Schedules), Schedule H (Financial Information), Schedule J (Group Health Plan Information), Schedule MB (Multiemployer Defined Benefit Plan and Certain Money Purchase Plan Actuarial Information), Schedule R (Retirement Plan Information), Schedule SB (Single-Employer Defined Benefit Plan Actuarial Information), and other financial schedules described in Sec. 2520.103-10. See the instructions for this form.

* * * * *

(c) * * *

(1) Except as provided in paragraphs (c)(2), (d), (e), and (f) of this section, and in §§ 2520.104-43, 2520.104a-6 and 2520.104-44, the annual report of an employee benefit plan that covers fewer than 100 participants at the beginning of the plan year shall include a Form 5500 "Annual Return/Report of Employee Benefit Plan" and any statements or schedules required to be attached to the form, completed in accordance with the instructions for the form, including Schedule A (Insurance Information), Schedule C (Service Provider Information), Schedule E (ESOP Annual Information), Schedule G (Financial Transactions), Schedule H (Financial Information), Schedule J (Group Health Plan Information), Schedule MB (Multiemployer Defined Benefit Plan and Certain Money Purchase Plan Actuarial Information), Schedule R (Retirement Plan Information), and Schedule SB (Single Employer Defined Benefit Plan Actuarial Information), completed in accordance with the instructions for the form. See the instructions for this form.

(2)(i) The annual report of an employee pension benefit plan or employee welfare benefit plan that does not provide group health benefits and that covers fewer than 100 participants at the beginning of the plan year and that meets the conditions in paragraph (c)(2)(ii) of this section with respect to a plan year may, as an alternative to the requirements of paragraph (c)(1) of this section, meet its annual reporting requirements by filing the Form 5500-SF "Short Form Annual Return/Report of Small Employee Benefit Plan" and any statements or schedules required to be attached to the form, including Schedule SB

(Single Employer Defined Benefit Plan Actuarial Information) and Schedule MB (Multiemployer Defined Benefit Plan and Certain Money Purchase Plan Actuarial Information), completed in accordance with the instructions for the form. See the instructions for this form.

(ii) * * *

(D) Is not a multiemployer plan;

(E) Is not a plan subject to the Form M-1 requirements under § 2520.101-2 (Filing by Multiple-employer Welfare Arrangements and Certain Other Related Entities); and

(F) Is not a group health plan as defined in section 733(a) of the Act.

(iii) The annual report of an employee benefit plan that meets the definition of a group health plan as defined in section 733(a) of the Act that covers fewer than 100 participants at the beginning of the plan year shall include a Form 5500 "Annual Return/Report of Employee Benefit Plan" and any statements or schedules required to be attached to the form, completed in accordance with the instructions for the form, including Schedule A (Insurance Information), Schedule C (Service Provider Information), Schedule H (Financial Information), and Schedule J (Group Health Plan Information). See the instructions for this form.

* * * * *

(e) *Plans that participate in a master trust.* The plan administrator of a plan which participates in a master trust shall file a Form 5500 Annual Return/Report in accordance with the instructions for the form relating to master trusts. For purposes of annual reporting, a master trust is a trust for which a regulated financial institution serves as trustee or custodian (regardless of whether such institution exercises discretionary authority or control respecting the management of assets held in the trust) and in which assets of more than one plan sponsored by a single employer or by a group of employers under common control are held. A master trust must operate either on a calendar year basis or on the same fiscal year as all of the plans that are participating in the master trust. For purpose of this paragraph, a regulated financial institution is a bank, trust company, or similar financial institution regulated, supervised, and subject to periodic examination by a State or Federal agency. Common control is determined on the basis of all relevant facts and circumstances (whether or not such employers are incorporated).

■ 3. In § 2520.103-2, revise paragraph (b)(1) to read as follows:

§ 2520.103-2 Contents of the annual report for group insurance arrangement.

* * * * *

(b) *Contents.* (1) A Form 5500 "Annual Return/Report of Employee Benefit Plan" and any statements or schedules required to be attached to the form, completed in accordance with the instructions for the form, including Schedule A (Insurance Information), Schedule C (Service Provider Information), Schedule D (DFE/Participating Plan Information), Schedule G (Financial Transaction Schedules), Schedule H (Financial Information), a separate Schedule J (Group Health Plan Information) for each participating plan, and the other financial schedules described in § 2520.103-10. See the instructions for this form.

* * * * *

■ 4. In § 2520.103-3, revise paragraph (c) to read as follows:

§ 2520.103-3 Exemption from certain annual reporting requirements for assets held in a common or collective trust.

* * * * *

(c) *Contents.* (1) A plan that meets the requirements of paragraph (b) of this section, and that invests in a common or collective trust that files a Form 5500 report in accordance with § 2520.103-9, shall include in its annual report: information required by the instructions to Schedule H (Financial Information) about the current value of and net investment gain or loss relating to the units of participation in the common or collective trust held by the plan; identifying information in the common or collective trust including its name, employer identification number, and any other information required by the instructions to the Schedule of Assets Held for Investment Purposes and Schedule of Assets Disposed of During Plan Year; and such other information as is required in the separate statements and schedules of the annual report about the value of the plan's units of participation in the common or collective trust and transactions involving the acquisition and disposition by the plan of units of participation in the common or collective trust.

(2) A plan that meets the requirements of paragraph (b) of this section and that invests in a common or collective trust that does not

file a Form 5500 report in accordance with § 2520.103-9, shall include in its annual report: Information required by the instructions to Schedule H (Financial Information) about the current value of and the net investment gain or loss relating to the units of participation in the common or collective trust held by the plan; information required by the accompanying instructions to the "Schedule of Assets Held for Investment" about the current value of the plan's allocable portion of the underlying assets and liabilities of the common or collective trust; identifying information about the common or collective trust including its name, employer identification number, and any other information required by the instructions to the Schedule of Assets Held for Investment Purposes and Schedule of Assets Disposed of During Plan Year; and such other information as is required in the separate statements and schedules of the annual report about the value of the plan's units of participation in the common or collective trust and transactions involving the acquisition and disposition by the plan of units of participation in the common or collective trust.

■ 5. In § 2520.103-4, revise paragraph (c) as follows:

§ 2520.103-4 Exemption from certain annual reporting requirements for assets held in an insurance company pooled separate account.

* * * * *

(c) *Contents.* (1) A plan that meets the requirements of paragraph (b) of this section, and which invests in a pooled separate account that files a Form 5500 report in accordance with § 2520.103-9, shall include in its annual report: Information required by the instructions to Schedule H (Financial Information) about the current value of and net investment gain or loss relating to the units of participation in the pooled separate account held by the plan; identifying information about the pooled separate account including its name, employer identification number, and any other information required by the instructions to the Schedule of Assets Held for Investment Purposes and Schedule of Assets Disposed of During Plan Year; and such other information as is required in the separate statements and schedules of the annual report about the value of the plan's units of participation in the pooled separate account and transactions involving the acquisition and disposition by the plan of units of participation in the pooled separate account.

(2) A plan that meets the requirements of paragraph (b) of this section and which invests in a pooled separate account that does not file a Form 5500 report in accordance with § 2520.103-9, shall include in its annual report: Information required by the instructions to Schedule H (Financial Information) about the current value of and the net investment gain or loss relating to the units of participation in the pooled separate account held by the plan; information required by the accompanying instructions to the "Schedule of Assets Held for Investment" about the current value of the plan's allocable portion of the underlying assets and liabilities of the pooled separate account; identifying information about the pooled separate account including its name, employer identification number, and any other information required by the instructions to the Schedule of Assets Held for Investment Purposes and Schedule of Assets Disposed of During Plan Year; and such other information as is required in the separate statements and schedules of the annual report about the value of the plan's units of participation in the pooled separate account and transactions involving the acquisition and disposition by the plan of units of participation in the pooled separate account.

■ 6. In § 2520.103-6, revise paragraph (d) to read as follows:

§ 2520.103-6 Definition of reportable transaction for annual return/report.

* * * * *

(d) *Contents.* (1) The schedule of reportable transactions shall be filed in the format and include information as described in the instructions for the Form 5500 Annual Return/Report of Employee Benefit Plan.

(2) [Removed]

■ 7. In § 2520.103-8, revise paragraphs (a) and (c) and add new paragraphs (d) and (e) to read as follows:

§ 2520.103-8 Limitation on scope of accountant's examination.

(a) *General.* Under the authority of section 103(a)(3)(C) of the Act, the examination and report of an independent qualified public accountant need not extend to any statement or information prepared and certified by a bank or similar institution or insurance carrier provided the certification meets the requirements of paragraph (d) of this section.

* * * * *

(c) *Excluded information.* Any statements or information certified to by a bank or similar institution or insurance carrier described in paragraph (b) of this section, provided that the statements or information regarding assets so held are prepared and certified to by the bank or insurance carrier in accordance with the requirements of (d) of this section and § 2520.103-5.

(d) *Contents and manner.* The certification described in paragraph (a) of this section shall:

(1) Appear on a separate document from the list of plan assets covered by the certification;

(2) Identify the bank or insurance company holding the plan's assets;

(3) Describe the manner in which the bank or insurance company is holding the assets covered by the certification;

(4) State whether the bank or insurance company is providing current value information regarding the assets covered by the certification in accordance with 2520.103-5, and if so, state that the assets for which current value is being certified are separately identified in the list of assets covered by the certification;

(5) If current value is not being certified for all of the assets covered by the certification, include a caution that the certification is not certifying current value information and the asset values provided by the bank or insurance company may not be suitable for use in satisfying the plan's obligation to report current value information on the Form 5500 Annual Return/Report; and

(6) If the certification is being provided by an agent on behalf of the bank or insurance company, a statement certifying that the person providing the certification is an authorized agent acting on behalf of the bank or insurance company and affirming that the bank or insurance company is taking responsibility for the accuracy and completeness of the certification and the underlying records used as a basis for the information being certified.

(e) The administrator of a plan which meets the requirements of paragraph (b) of this section, and which is not required to have covered by the accountant's examination or report any of the information described in paragraph (c) of this section shall attach to the Form 5500 Annual Return/Report of Employee Benefit Plan the certification of investment information created by certain banks or insurance companies in accordance with the requirements of paragraph (d) of this section to comply with the limited scope audit requirements.

■ 8. In § 2520.103-10, revise paragraphs (b)(1)(i) and (2)(i) to read as follows:

§ 2520.103-10 Annual report financial schedules.

* * * * *

(b) * * *

(1) * * *

(i) A schedule of all assets held for investment purposes at the end of the plan year (see § 2520.103-11) with assets aggregated and identified

as described in the instructions to the Form 5500 Annual Return/ Report of Employee Benefit Plan.

* * * * *

(2) *Assets disposed of during the plan year.* (i) A schedule of all assets disposed of during the plan year (see § 2520.103-11) with assets aggregated and identified as described in the instructions to the Form 5500 Annual Return/Report of Employee Benefit Plan.

* * * * *

■ 9. In § 2520.104-20, revise paragraph (b)(1) to read as follows:

§ 2520.104-20 Limited exemption for certain small welfare plans.

* * * * *

(b) * * *

(1) Which have fewer than 100 participants at the beginning of the plan year, and do not provide benefits consisting of medical care as defined in section 733(a)(2) of the Act;

* * * * *

■ 10. In § 2520.104-26, revise paragraph (b) to read as follows:

§ 2520.104-26 Limited exemption for certain unfunded dues financed welfare plans maintained by employee organizations.

* * * * *

(b) *Application.* This exemption applies only to welfare benefit plans that do not provide benefits consisting of medical care as defined in section 733(a)(2) of the Act that are maintained by an employee organization, as that term is defined in section 3(4) of the Act, paid out of the employee organization's general assets, which are derived wholly or partly from membership dues, and which cover employee organization members and their families.

* * * * *

■ 11. Revise § 2520.104-42 to read as follows:

§ 2520.104-42 Waiver of certain actuarial information in the annual report.

Under the authority of section 104(a)(2)(A) of ERISA, the requirement of section 103(d)(6) of ERISA that the annual report include as part of the actuarial statement (Schedule SB) the present value of all of the plan's liabilities for nonforfeitable pension benefits allocated by termination priority categories, as set forth in section 4044 of title IV of ERISA, and the actuarial assumptions used in these computations, is waived.

■ 12. In § 2520.104b-10, revise the Appendix to § 2520.104b-10 to read as follows:

§ 2520.104b-10 Summary annual report.

* * * * *

APPENDIX TO § 2520.104B-10—THE SUMMARY ANNUAL REPORT (SAR) UNDER ERISA: A CROSS-REFERENCE TO THE ANNUAL REPORT

SAR Item	Form 5500 line items	Form 5500-SF line items
A. Pension Plan (defined contribution pension benefit plans and defined benefit pension plans that do not furnish the annual funding notice under 29 CFR 2520.101-4)		
1. Funding arrangement	Form 5500-10a	Line 13a.
2. Total plan expenses	Sch. H—2j	Line 10h.
3. Administrative expenses	Sch. H—2i(12)(C)	Line 10f.
4. Benefits paid	Sch. H—2e(4)	Line 10d.
5. Other Expenses	Sch. H—Subtract the sum of 2e(4) & 2i(12)(C) from 2j.	Line 10g.
6. Total Participants at end of plan year	Form 5500—7f	Line 7f.
7. Value of plan assets (net):		
a. end of plan year	Sch. H—11 [Col. (b)]	Line 9c [Col. (b)].
b. beginning of plan year	Sch. H—11 [Col. (a)]	Line 9c [Col. (a)].
8. Changes in Net Assets	Sch. H—Subtract 11 [Col. a] from 11 [Col. b]	Line 9c-Subtract [Col. a] from [Col. b].
9 Total Income	Sch. H—2d	Line 10c. Line 10a(1)(A).
a. Employer contributions	Sch. H—2a(1)(A, & 2a(2) if applicable	
b. Employee contributions	Sch. H—2a(1)(B), & 2a(2) if applicable	Line 10a(1)(B).
c. Gains (losses) from sale of assets	Sch. H—2c(4)(C)	Not applicable.
d. Earnings from investments	Sch. H—Subtract the sum of 2a(3) and 2c(4)(C) from 2d.	Line 10b.
10. Name of insurance carriers	Schs. A—1a	Not applicable.
11. Total insurance premiums	Sch. A—5b (total of all contracts)	Not applicable.
12. Unpaid minimum required contribution (S-E plans or Defined contribution plans) or Funding deficiency (ME plans):		

SAR Item	Form 5500 line items	Form 5500-SF line items
a. S-E Defined benefit plans	Sch. SB—43	Same.
b. ME Defined benefit plans	Sch. MB—10	Not applicable.
c. Defined contribution plans	Sch. R—7c, if not zero	Line 16b.

B. Welfare Plan

1. Name of insurance carriers	Schs. A—1a	Not applicable.
2. Total (experience rated and non-experienced rated) insurance premiums.	Schs. A—Sum of 9a(1) and 10a (total of all contracts).	Not applicable.
3. Experience rated premiums	Schs. A—9a(1) (total of all contracts)	Not applicable.
4. Experience rated claims	Schs. A—9b(4) (total of all contracts)	Not applicable.
5. Value of plan assets (net)		
a. end of plan year	Sch. H—11 [Col. (b)]	Line 9c [Col. (b)].
b. beginning of plan year	Sch. H—11 [Col. (a)]	Line 9c [Col. (a)].
6. Changes in Net Assets	Sch. H—Subtract 11 [Col. a] from [Col. b]	Line 9c—Subtract [Col. a] from [Col. b].
7. Total Income	Sch. H—2d	Line 10c.
a. Employer contributions	Sch. H—2a(1)(A) & 2a(2) if applicable	Line 10a(1)(A) if applicable.
b. Employee contributions	Sch. H—2a(1)(B) & 2a(2) if applicable	Line 10a(1)(B) if applicable.
c. Gains (losses) from sale of assets	Sch. H—2c(4)(C)	Not applicable.
d. Earnings from investments	Sch. H—Subtract the sum of 2a(3) and 2c(4)(C) from 2d.	Line 10b.
8. Total plan expenses	Sch. H—2j	Line 10h.
9. Administrative expenses	Sch. H—2i(12)(C)	Line 10f.
10. Benefits paid	Sch. H—2e(4)	Line 10d.
11. Other Expenses	Sch. H—Subtract the sum of 2e(4) & 2i(12)(C) from 2j.	Line 10g.

PART 2590 —RULES AND REGULATIONS FOR GROUP HEALTH PLANS

■ 13. The authority citation for Part 2590 continues to read as follows:

Authority: 29 U.S.C. 1027, 1059, 1135, 1161-1168, 1169, 1181-1183, 1181 note, 1185, 1185a, 1185b, 1191, 1191a, 1191b, and 1191c; sec. 101(g), Pub. L.104-191, 110 Stat. 1936; sec. 401(b), Pub. L. 105-200, 112 Stat. 645 (42 U.S.C. 651 note); sec. 512(d), Pub. L. 110-343, 122 Stat. 3881; sec. 1001, 1201, and 1562(e), Pub. L. 111-148, 124 Stat. 119, as amended by Pub. L. 111-152, 124 Stat. 1029; Secretary of Labor's Order 1-2011, 77 FR 1088 (Jan. 9, 2012).

Subpart C—Other Requirements

■ 14. Add § § 2590.715-2715A and 2590.715-2717 to Subpart C to read as follows:

§2590.715-2715A Provision of additional information.

A group health plan that complies with the requirements of § 2520.103-1 of this Chapter and any implementing guidance (including filing any required schedules to the annual report required by § 2520.103-1) satisfies the requirements of PHS Act section 2715A, as incorporated in ERISA.

§2590.715-2717 Ensuring the quality of care.

A group health plan that complies with the requirements of § 2520.103-1 of this Chapter and any implementing guidance (including filing any required schedules to the annual report required by § 2520.103-1) satisfies the requirements of PHS Act section 2717, as incorporated in ERISA.

Signed at Washington, DC, this 20th day of June 2016.

Phyllis C. Borzi,

Assistant Secretary, Employee Benefits Security Administration, U.S. Department of Labor.

[FR Doc. 2016-14892 Filed 7-11-16; 4:15 pm]

BILLING CODE 4510-29-P

¶ 20,539G

Employee Benefits Security Administration (EBSA): Proposed rule: Safe harbor: State auto-IRA programs: Political subdivisions: ERISA preemption.—The EBSA has issued proposed regulations that will expand a safe harbor from ERISA coverage for state payroll deduction IRA programs beyond states to include a limited number of larger cities and counties. To be qualified, the city or county must have the authority to require employer participation in a payroll deduction savings program. In addition, the city or county must have a population at least equal to that of the least populous state, and may not be in a state that has a state-wide retirement savings program for private-sector employees.

The proposed regulations, which were published in the Federal Register on August 30, 2016 (81 FR 59581), were reproduced below. The regulations were finalized on December 20, 2016 (81 FR 92639). The preamble to the final regulations is at ¶ 24,345. The final regulations are at ¶ 14,132.

¶ 20,539H

Pension Benefit Guaranty Corporation (PBGC): Proposed rule: Missing Participant Program: Plan termination: Single-employer defined benefit plans: Multiemployer defined benefit plans: Defined contribution plans: Pension Protection Act of 2006 (PPA).—The Pension Benefit Guaranty Corporation (PBGC) has issued proposed regulations that expand its existing Missing Participants Program to cover terminated 401(k) and most other defined contribution (DC) plans, multiemployer defined benefit (DB) plans, and certain DB plans that are not currently covered by the program. The proposed regulations will implement the expansion of its Missing Participant Program by establishing rules to handle the benefits of missing participants and beneficiaries under terminated multiemployer plans covered by Title IV similar to the rules for covered single-employer plans, by providing for a similar voluntary program for terminated non-covered plans, and by authorizing the PBGC to prescribe related reporting requirements. The PBGC anticipates the expanded program will be implemented in 2018 (for plans that terminate after 2017), after publication of final regulations.

The proposed regulations, which were published in the Federal Register on September 20, 2016 (81 FR 64699), were reproduced below. The regulations were finalized on December 22, 2017 (82 FR 60800). The preamble to the final regulations is at ¶ 24,355. The final regulations are at ¶ 15,302MM, ¶ 15,312, ¶ 15,315A, ¶ 15,331, ¶ 15,440F-7, ¶ 15,449T, ¶ 15,530P, ¶ 15,530Q, ¶ 15,530R, ¶ 15,530S, ¶ 15,530T, ¶ 15,530U, ¶ 15,530V, ¶ 15,531F, ¶ 15,531G, ¶ 15,531H, ¶ 15,531I, ¶ 15,531J, ¶ 15,531K, ¶ 15,531L, ¶ 15,531W, ¶ 15,531X, ¶ 15,531Y, ¶ 15,531Z, ¶ 15,532, ¶ 15,532A, ¶ 15,532B, ¶ 15,532M, ¶ 15,532N, ¶ 15,532O, ¶ 15,532P, ¶ 15,532Q, ¶ 15,532R, and ¶ 15,532S

¶ 20,539l

Employee Benefits Security Administration (EBSA): Proposed regulations: Fiduciary: Employee benefit plans: Individual retirement accounts (IRAs): Investment advice: Prohibited transaction exemptions (PTEs): Extension of applicability date.—The EBSA has released proposed regulations that would extend for 60 days the applicability date of the fiduciary of conflict of interest rules (Pension Plan Guide ¶ 24,338) as well as the Best Interest Contract Exemption and other related prohibited transactions exemptions (Pension Plan Guide ¶ 16,650, ¶ 16,650A, ¶ 16,650B, ¶ 16,650C, ¶ 16,650D, and ¶ 16,650E). The proposal has been issued in response to a February 3, 2017 Presidential Memorandum that ordered the DOL to undertake an updated economic and legal analysis of the impact of the rules on retiree access to retirement advice and the retirement services industry. Comments (of a very specific nature) are invited on both the proposed 60-day delay and on the rules generally, which have two separate comment periods. If the delay is approved, the applicability date of the final rules and the accompanying prohibited transaction exemptions will be extended from April 10, 2017 to June 9, 2017.

The proposed regulations, which were published in the Federal Register on March 2, 2017 (82 FR 12319), are reproduced below. The regulations were finalized on April 7, 2017 (82 FR 16902). The preamble to the final regulations is at ¶ 24,348. The final regulations are at ¶ 14,138A. Thus, the applicability date of the final rules and the accompanying prohibited transaction exemptions is generally extended from April 10, 2017 to June 9, 2017.

DEPARTMENT OF LABOR

Employee Benefits Security Administration

29 CFR Part 2510

RIN 1210-AB79

Definition of the Term "Fiduciary"; Conflict of Interest Rule—Retirement Investment Advice; Best Interest Contract Exemption (Prohibited Transaction Exemption 2016-01); Class Exemption for Principal Transactions in Certain Assets Between Investment Advice Fiduciaries and Employee Benefit Plans and IRAs (Prohibited Transaction Exemption 2016-02); Prohibited Transaction Exemptions 75-1, 77-4, 80-83, 83-1, 84-24 and 86-128

AGENCY: Employee Benefits Security Administration, Labor.

ACTION: Proposed rule; extension of applicability date.

SUMMARY: This document proposes to extend for 60 days the applicability date defining who is a "fiduciary" under the Employee Retirement Income Security Act (ERISA) and the Internal Revenue Code of 1986 (Code), and the applicability date of related prohibited transaction exemptions including the Best Interest Contract Exemption and amended prohibited transaction exemptions (collectively PTEs) to address questions of law and policy. The final rule, entitled Definition of the Term "Fiduciary;" Conflict of Interest Rule—Retirement Investment Advice, was published in the **Federal Register** on April 8, 2016, became effective on June 7, 2016, and has an applicability date of April 10, 2017. The PTEs also have applicability dates of April 10, 2017. The President by Memorandum to the Secretary of Labor, dated February 3, 2017, directed the Department of Labor to examine whether the final fiduciary rule may adversely affect the ability of Americans to gain access to retirement information and financial advice, and to prepare an updated economic and legal analysis concerning the likely impact of the final rule as part of that examination. This document invites comments on the proposed 60-day delay of the applicability date, on the questions raised in the Presidential Memorandum, and generally on questions of law and policy concerning the final rule and PTEs. The proposed 60-day delay would be effective on the date of publication of a final rule in the **Federal Register**.

DATES: Comments on the proposal to extend the applicability dates for 60 days should be submitted to the Department on or before March 17, 2017. Comments regarding the examination described in the President's Memorandum, generally and with respect to the specific areas described below, should be submitted to the Department on or before April 17, 2017.

FOR FURTHER INFORMATION CONTACT: Luisa Grillo-Chope, Office of Regulations and Interpretations, Employee Benefits Security Administration (EBSA), (202) 693-8825. (Not a toll-free number).

ADDRESSES: You may submit comments, identified by RIN 1210-AB79, by one of the following methods:

Federal eRulemaking Portal: http://www.regulations.gov. Follow the instructions for submitting comments.

Email: EBSA.FiduciaryRuleExamination@dol.gov. Include RIN 1210-AB79 in the subject line of the message.

Mail: Office of Regulations and Interpretations, Employee Benefits Security Administration, Room N-5655, U.S. Department of Labor, 200 Constitution Avenue NW., Washington, DC 20210, Attention: Fiduciary Rule Examination.

Instructions: All submissions must include the agency name and Regulatory Identification Number (RIN) for this rulemaking. Persons submitting comments electronically are encouraged to submit only by one electronic method and not to submit paper copies. Comments will be available to the public, without charge, online at *www.regulations.gov* and *www.dol.gov/ebsa* and at the Public Disclosure Room, Employee Benefits Security Administration, U.S. Department of Labor, Suite N-1513, 200 Constitution Avenue NW., Washington, DC 20210.

Warning: Do not include any personally identifiable or confidential business information that you do not want publicly disclosed. Comments are public records and are posted on the Internet as received, and can be retrieved by most internet search engines.

SUPPLEMENTARY INFORMATION:

A. Background

On April 8, 2016, the Department of Labor (Department) published a final regulation defining who is a "fiduciary" of an employee benefit plan under section 3(21)(A)(ii) of the Employee Retirement Income Security Act of 1974 (ERISA or the Act) as a result of giving investment advice to a plan or its participants or beneficiaries. The final rule also applies to the definition of a "fiduciary" of a plan (including an individual retirement account (IRA)) under section 4975(e)(3)(B) of the Internal Revenue Code of 1986 (Code). The final rule treats persons who provide investment advice or recommendations for a fee or other compensation with respect to assets of a plan or IRA as fiduciaries in a wider array of advice relationships than was true of the prior regulatory definition (the 1975 Regulation).[1]

On this same date, the Department published two new administrative class exemptions from the prohibited transaction provisions of ERISA (29 U.S.C. 1106), and the Code (26 U.S.C. 4975(c)(1)), as well as amendments to previously granted exemptions. The exemptions and amendments (collectively Prohibited Transaction Exemptions or PTEs) would allow, subject to appropriate safeguards, certain broker-dealers, insurance agents and others that act as investment advice fiduciaries, as defined under the final rule, to continue to receive a variety of forms of compensation that would otherwise violate prohibited transaction rules, triggering excise taxes and civil liability.

By Memorandum dated February 3, 2017, the President directed the Department to conduct an examination of the final rule to determine whether the rule may adversely affect the ability of Americans to gain access to retirement information and financial advice. As part of this examination, the Department was directed to prepare an updated economic and legal analysis concerning the likely impact of the final rule, which shall consider, among other things:

- Whether the anticipated applicability of the final rule has harmed or is likely to harm investors due to a reduction of Americans' access to certain retirement savings offerings, retirement product structures, retirement savings information, or related financial advice;

- Whether the anticipated applicability of the final rule has resulted in dislocations or disruptions within the retirement services industry that may adversely affect investors or retirees; and

- Whether the final rule is likely to cause an increase in litigation, and an increase in the prices that investors and retirees must pay to gain access to retirement services.

The President directed that if the Department makes an affirmative determination as to any of the above three considerations or the Department concludes for any other reason after appropriate review that the final rule is inconsistent with the priority of the Administration "to empower Americans to make their own financial decisions, to

---

[1] The 1975 Regulation was published as a final rule at 40 FR 50842 (Oct. 31, 1975).

facilitate their ability to save for retirement and build the individual wealth necessary to afford typical lifetime expenses, such as buying a home and paying for college, and to withstand unexpected financial emergencies," then the Department shall publish for notice and comment a proposed rule rescinding or revising the final rule, as appropriate and as consistent with law. The President's Memorandum was published in the **Federal Register** on February 7, 2017 at 82 FR 9675.

B. Regulatory Impact Analysis

The Department is proposing to delay the applicability date of the final rule and PTEs for 60 days. The Department invites comments on the proposal to extend the applicability date of the final rule and PTEs for 60 days.[2] For this purpose, the comment period will end on March 17, 2017.

There are approximately 45 days until the applicability date of the final rule and the PTEs. The Department believes it may take more time than that to complete the examination mandated by the President's Memorandum. Additionally, absent an extension of the applicability date, if the examination prompts the Department to propose rescinding or revising the rule, affected advisers, retirement investors and other stakeholders might face two major changes in the regulatory environment rather than one. This could unnecessarily disrupt the marketplace, producing frictional costs that are not offset by commensurate benefits. This proposed 60-day extension of the applicability date aims to guard against this risk. The extension would make it possible for the Department to take additional steps (such as completing its examination, implementing any necessary additional extension(s), and proposing and implementing a revocation or revision of the rule) without the rule becoming applicable beforehand. In this way, advisers, investors and other stakeholders would be spared the risk and expenses of facing two major changes in the regulatory environment. The negative consequence of avoiding this risk is the potential for retirement investor losses from delaying the application of fiduciary standards to their advisers.

1. Executive Order 12866 Statement

This proposed extension of the applicability date of the final rule and related exemptions is an economically significant regulatory action within the meaning of section 3(f)(1) of Executive Order 12866, because it would likely have an effect on the economy of $100 million in at least one year. Accordingly, the Department has considered the costs and benefits of the proposed extension, and the Office of Management and Budget (OMB) has reviewed the proposed extension.

The Department's regulatory impact analysis (RIA) of the final rule and related exemptions predicted that resultant gains for retirement investors would justify compliance costs. The analysis estimated a portion of the potential gains for IRA investors at between $33 billion and $36 billion over the first 10 years. It predicted, but did not quantify, additional gains for both IRA and ERISA plan investors. The analysis predicted $16 billion in compliance costs over the first 10 years, $5 billion of which are first-year costs.

By deferring the rules' and related exemptions' applicability for 60 days, this proposal could delay its predicted effects, and give the Department time to make at least a preliminary determination whether it is likely to make significant changes to the rules and exemptions. The nature and magnitude of any such delay of the effects is highly uncertain, as some variation can be expected in the pace at which firms move to comply and mitigate advisory conflicts and at which advisers respond to such mitigation and adjust their recommendations to satisfy impartial conduct standards. Notwithstanding this uncertainty, some delay of the predicted effects seems likely, and seems likely to generate economically significant results. Moreover, the economic effects may be partially dependent on what action the Department ultimately takes, and in the shorter term, what the public anticipates the Department may do. Such delay could lead to losses for retirement investors who follow affected recommendations, and these losses could continue to accrue until affected investors withdraw affected funds or reinvest them pursuant to new recommendations.[3] As an illustration, a 60-day delay in the commencement of the potential investor gains estimated in the RIA published on April 8, 2016, and referenced above, could lead to a reduction in those estimated gains of $147 million in the first year and $890 million over 10 years using a three percent discount rate. The equivalent annualized estimates are $104 million using a three percent discount rate and $87 million using a seven percent discount rate.

The estimates of potential investor losses presented in this illustration are derived in the same way as the estimates of potential investor gains that were presented in the RIA of the final rule and exemptions. Both make use of empirical evidence that front-end-load mutual funds that share more of the load with distributing brokers attract more flows but perform worse.[4]

Relative to the actual impact of the proposed delay on retirement investors, which is unknown, this illustration is uncertain and incomplete. The illustration is uncertain because it assumes that the final rule and exemptions would entirely eliminate the negative effect of load-sharing on mutual fund selection, and that the proposed delay would leave that negative effect undiminished for an additional 60 days. If some of that negative effect would remain under the final rule, and/or if market changes in anticipation of the final rule have already diminished that negative effect, then the impact of the proposed delay would be smaller than illustrated here. The illustration is incomplete because it represents only one negative effect (poor mutual fund selection) of one source of conflict (load sharing), in one market segment (IRA investments in front-load mutual funds). Not included are additional potential negative effects of the proposed delay that would be associated with other sources of potential conflicts, such as revenue sharing, or mark-ups in principal transactions, other effects of conflicts such as excessive or poorly timed trading, and other market segments susceptible to conflicts such as annuity sales to IRA investors and advice rendered to ERISA-covered plan participants or sponsors. The Department invites comments on these points and on the degree to which they may cause the illustration to overstate or understate the potential negative effect of the proposed delay on retirement investors. And if some entities are subject to the current regulation, but might not be subject to the same sort of regulation under a revised proposal, the industry might avoid additional costs now that would otherwise become sunk costs. A 60-day delay could defer or reduce start-up compliance costs, particularly in circumstances where more gradual steps toward preparing for compliance are less expensive. However, due to lack of systematic evidence on the portion of compliance activities that have already been undertaken, thus rendering the associated costs sunk, the Department is unable to quantify the potential change in start-up costs that would result from a delay in the applicability date. The Department requests comment, including data that would contribute to estimation of such impacts. Beyond start-up costs, the delay would likely relieve industry of relevant day-to-day compliance burdens; using the inputs and methods that appear in the April 2016 RIA, the Department estimates associated savings of $42 million during those 60 days. The equivalent annualized values are $8 million using a three percent discount rate and $9 million using a seven percent discount rate.

These savings are substantially derived from foregone on-going compliance requirements related to the transition notice requirements for the Best Interest Contract Exemption, data collection to demonstrate satisfaction of fiduciary requirements, and retention of data to demonstrate the satisfaction of conditions of the exemption during the Transition Period. Estimates are derived from the "Data Collection," "Record Keeping (Data Retention)," and "Supervisory, Compliance, and Legal Oversight" categories discussed in section 5.3.1 of the final RIA and reductions in the number of the transition notices that will be delivered.

The Department also considered the possible impact of a longer extension of the applicability date. Under the RIA published on April 8, 2016, a 180-day delay in the application of the fiduciary standards and conditions set forth in the rule and exemptions would reduce the same portion of potential investor gains from the rule by $441 million in the first year and $2.7 billion over 10 years, while relieving industry of 180 days of day-to-day compliance burdens, worth an estimated $126 million.

The costs and benefits of this proposal are highly uncertain, and may vary widely depending on several variables, including the eventual results of the Department's examination of the final rule and exemptions pursuant to the Presidential Memorandum, and the amount of time that will be required to complete that review and, if appropriate, rescind or revise the rule. The Department invites comments as to whether the benefits of the proposed 60-day delay, including the potential reduction in transition costs should the Department ultimately revise or rescind the final rule, justify its costs, including the potential losses to affected retirement investors. The Department also invites comments on whether it should delay applicability of all, or only part, of

---

[2] The Department would also treat Interpretative Bulletin 96-1 as continuing to apply during any extension of the applicability date of the final rule.

[3] While losses would cease to accrue after the funds are re-advised or withdrawn, afterward the losses would not be recovered, and would continue to compound, as the accumulated losses would have reduced the asset base that is available later for reinvestment or spending.

[4] The methodology is detailed in Appendix B of the RIA.

the final rule's provisions and exemption conditions. For example, under an alternative approach, the Department could delay certain aspects (*e.g.*, notice and disclosure provisions) while permitting others (*e.g.*, the impartial conduct standards set forth in the exemptions) to become applicable on April 10, 2017. The Department also invites comments regarding whether a different delay period would best serve the interests of investors and the industry.

2. Paperwork Reduction Act

The PRA (Pub. L. 104-13) prohibits federal agencies from conducting or sponsoring a collection of information from the public without first obtaining approval from the Office of Management and Budget (OMB). See 44 U.S.C. 3507. Additionally, members of the public are not required to respond to a collection of information, nor be subject to a penalty for failing to respond, unless such collection displays a valid OMB control number. See 44 U.S.C. 3512.

OMB has approved information collections contained in the final fiduciary rule and new and amended PTEs. The Department is not modifying the substance of the information collection requests (ICRs) at this time; therefore, no action under the PRA is required. The information collections will become applicable at the same time the rule and exemptions become applicable. The information collection requirements contained in the final rule and exemptions are discussed below.

Final Rule: The information collections in the final rule are approved under OMB Control Number 1210-0155. Paragraph (b)(2)(i) requires that certain "platform providers" provide disclosure to a plan fiduciary. Paragraph (b)(2)(iv)(C) and (D) require asset allocation models to contain specific information if they furnish and provide certain specified investment educational information. Paragraph (c)(1) requires a disclosure to be provided by a person to an independent plan fiduciary in certain circumstances for them to be deemed not to be an investment advice fiduciary. Finally, paragraph (c)(2) requires certain counterparties, clearing members and clearing organizations to make a representation to certain parties so they will not be deemed to be investment advice fiduciaries regarding certain swap transactions required to be cleared under provisions of the Dodd-Frank Act.

For a more detailed discussion of the information collections and associated burden, see the Department's PRA analysis at 81 FR 20946, 20994.

PTE 2016-01, the Best Interest Contract Exemption: The information collections in PTE 2016-01, the Best Interest Contract Exemption, are approved under OMB Control Number 1210-0156. The exemption requires disclosure of material conflicts of interest and basic information relating to those conflicts and the advisory relationship (Sections II and III), contract disclosures, contracts and written policies and procedures (Section II), pre-transaction (or point of sale) disclosures (Section III(a)), web-based disclosures (Section III(b)), documentation regarding recommendations restricted to proprietary products or products that generate third party payments (Section (IV)), notice to the Department of a Financial Institution's intent to rely on the exemption, and maintenance of records necessary to prove that the conditions of the exemption have been met (Section V). Finally, Section IX provides a transition period under which relief from these prohibitions is available for Financial Institutions and advisers during the period between the applicability date and January 1, 2018 (the "Transition Period"). As a condition of relief during the Transition Period, Financial Institutions must provide a disclosure with a written statement of fiduciary status and certain other information to all retirement investors (in ERISA plans, IRAs, and non-ERISA plans) prior to or at the same time as the execution of recommended transactions. For a more detailed discussion of the information collections and associated burden, see the Department's PRA analysis at 81 FR 21002, 21071.

PTE 2016-02, the Prohibited Transaction Exemption for Principal Transactions in Certain Assets Between Investment Advice Fiduciaries and Employee Benefit Plans and IRAs (Principal Transactions Exemption): The information collections in PTE 2016-02, the Principal Transactions Exemption, are approved under OMB Control Number 1210-0157. The exemption requires Financial Institutions to provide contract disclosures and contracts to Retirement Investors (Section II), adopt written policies and procedures (Section IV), make disclosures to Retirement Investors and on a publicly available Web site (Section IV), maintain records necessary to prove they have met the exemption conditions (Section V), and provide a transition disclosure to Retirement Investors (Section VII).

For a more detailed discussion of the information collections and associated burden, see the Department's PRA analysis at 81 FR 21089, 21129.

Amended PTE 75-1: The information collections in Amended PTE 75-1 are approved under OMB Control Number 1210-0092. Part V, as amended, requires that prior to an extension of credit, the plan must receive from the fiduciary written disclosure of (i) the rate of interest (or other fees) that will apply and (ii) the method of determining the balance upon which interest will be charged in the event that the fiduciary extends credit to avoid a failed purchase or sale of securities, as well as prior written disclosure of any changes to these terms. It also requires broker-dealers engaging in the transactions to maintain records demonstrating compliance with the conditions of the PTE.

For a more detailed discussion of the information collections and associated burden, see the Department's PRA analysis at 81 FR 21139, 21145. The Department concluded that the ICRs contained in the amendments to Part V impose no additional burden on respondents.

Amended PTE 86-128: The information collections in Amended PTE 86-128 are approved under OMB Control Number 1210-0059. As amended, Section III of the exemption requires Financial Institutions to make certain disclosures to plan fiduciaries and owners of managed IRAs in order to receive relief from ERISA's and the Code's prohibited transaction rules for the receipt of commissions and to engage in transactions involving mutual fund shares. Financial Institutions relying on either PTE 86-128 or PTE 75-1, as amended, are required to maintain records necessary to demonstrate that the conditions of these exemptions have been met.

For a more detailed discussion of the information collections and associated burden, see the Department's PRA analysis at 81 FR 21181, 21199.

Amended PTE 84-24: The information collections in Amended PTE 84-24 are approved under OMB Control Number 1210-0158. As amended, Section IV(b) of PTE 84-24 requires Financial Institutions to obtain advance written authorization from an independent plan fiduciary or IRA holder and furnish the independent fiduciary or IRA holder with a written disclosure in order to receive commissions in conjunction with the purchase of Fixed Rate Annuity Contracts and Insurance Contracts. Section IV(c) of PTE 84-24 requires investment company Principal Underwriters to obtain approval from an independent fiduciary and furnish the independent fiduciary with a written disclosure in order to receive commissions in conjunction with the purchase by a plan of securities issued by an investment company Principal Underwriter. Section V of PTE 84-24, as amended, requires Financial Institutions to maintain records necessary to demonstrate that the conditions of the exemption have been met.

For a more detailed discussion of the information collections and associated burden, see the Department's PRA analysis at 81 FR 21147, 21171.

3. Regulatory Flexibility Act

The Regulatory Flexibility Act (5 U.S.C. 601 *et seq.*) (RFA) imposes certain requirements with respect to Federal rules that are subject to the notice and comment requirements of section 553(b) of the Administrative Procedure Act (5 U.S.C. 551 *et seq.*) or any other laws. Unless the head of an agency certifies that a proposed rule is not likely to have a significant economic impact on a substantial number of small entities, section 603 of the RFA requires that the agency present an initial regulatory flexibility analysis (IRFA) describing the rule's impact on small entities and explaining how the agency made its decisions with respect to the application of the rule to small entities. Small entities include small businesses, organizations and governmental jurisdictions.

The Department has determined that this rulemaking will have a significant economic impact on a substantial number of small entities, and hereby provides this IRFA. As noted above, the Department is proposing regulatory action to delay the applicability of the final fiduciary rule and exemptions. The proposed regulation is intended to reduce any unnecessary disruption that could occur in the marketplace if the applicability date of the final rule and exemptions occurs while the Department examines the final rule and exemptions as directed in the Presidential Memorandum.

The Small Business Administration (SBA) defines a small business in the Financial Investments and Related Activities Sector as a business with up to $38.5 million in annual receipts. The Department examined the dataset obtained from SBA which contains data on the number of firms by NAICS codes, including the number of firms in given revenue categories. This dataset allowed the Department to estimate the number of firms with a given NAICS code that falls below the $38.5 million threshold to be considered a small entity by the SBA. However, this dataset alone does not provide a sufficient basis for the Department to estimate the number of small entities affected by the rule. Not all firms within a given NAICS code would be affected by this rule, because being an ERISA fiduciary relies on a functional test and is not based on industry status as defined by a NAICS code. Further, not all firms within a given NAICS code work with ERISA-covered plans and IRAs.

Over 90 percent of broker-dealers (BDs), registered investment advisers (RIAs), insurance companies, agents, and consultants are small businesses according to the SBA size standards (13 CFR 121.201). Applying the ratio of entities that meet the SBA size standards to the number of affected entities, based on the methodology described at greater length in the RIA of the final fiduciary duty rule, the Department estimates that the number of small entities affected by this proposed rule is 2,438 BDs, 16,521 RIAs, 496 insurers, and 3,358 other ERISA service providers. For purposes of the RFA, the Department continues to consider an employee benefit plan with fewer than 100 participants to be a small entity. The 2013 Form 5500 filings show nearly 595,000 ERISA covered retirement plans with less than 100 participants.

Based on the foregoing, the Department estimates that small entities would save approximately $38 million in compliance costs due to the proposed 60-day delay of the applicability date for the final fiduciary rule and exemptions.[5] These cost savings are substantially derived from foregone on-going compliance requirements related to the transition notice requirements for the Best Interest Contract Exemption, data collection to demonstrate satisfaction of fiduciary requirements, and retention of data to demonstrate the satisfaction of conditions of the exemption during the Transition Period. The Department invites comments regarding this assessment.

4. Congressional Review Act

The proposed rule is subject to the Congressional Review Act (CRA) provisions of the Small Business Regulatory Enforcement Fairness Act of 1996 (5 U.S.C. 801 *et seq.*) and, if finalized, would be transmitted to Congress and the Comptroller General for review.

5. Unfunded Mandates Reform Act

Title II of the Unfunded Mandates Reform Act of 1995 (Pub. L. 104-4) requires each Federal agency to prepare a written statement assessing the effects of any Federal mandate in a proposed or final agency rule that may result in an expenditure of $100 million or more (adjusted annually for inflation with the base year 1995) in any one year by State, local, and tribal governments, in the aggregate, or by the private sector. For purposes of the Unfunded Mandates Reform Act, as well as Executive Order 12875, this proposal does not include any federal mandate that we expect would result in such expenditures by state, local, or tribal governments, or the private sector. The Department also does not expect that the proposed rule will have any material economic impacts on State, local or tribal governments, or on health, safety, or the natural environment.

6. Reducing Regulation and Controlling Regulatory Costs

Executive Order 13771, titled Reducing Regulation and Controlling Regulatory Costs, was issued on January 30, 2017. Section 2(a) of Executive Order 13771 requires an agency, unless prohibited by law, to identify at least two existing regulations to be repealed when the agency publicly proposes for notice and comment, or otherwise promulgates, a new regulation. In furtherance of this requirement, section 2(c) of Executive Order 13771 requires that the new incremental costs associated with new regulations shall, to the extent permitted by law, be offset by the elimination of existing costs associated with at least two prior regulations. OMB's interim guidance, issued on February 2, 2017, explains that for Fiscal Year 2017 the above requirements only apply to each new "significant regulatory action that imposes costs." OMB has determined that this proposed rule does not impose costs that would trigger the above requirements of Executive Order 13771.

C. Examination of Fiduciary Rule and Exemptions

As noted above, pursuant to the President's Memorandum, the Department is now examining the fiduciary duty rule to determine whether it may adversely affect the ability of Americans to gain access to retirement information and financial advice. As part of this examination, the Department will prepare an updated economic and legal analysis concerning the likely impacts of the rule.

The Department's April 2016 regulatory impact analysis of the final rule and related exemptions found that conflicted advice was widespread, causing harm to plan and IRA investors, and that disclosing conflicts alone would not adequately mitigate the conflicts or remedy the harm. The analysis concluded that by extending fiduciary protections the new rule would mitigate advisory conflicts and deliver gains for retirement investors.

The analysis cited economic evidence that advisory conflicts erode retirement savings. This evidence included:

- Statistical comparisons finding poorer risk-adjusted investment performance in more conflicted settings;

- experimental and audit studies revealing problematic adviser conduct;

- studies detailing gaps in consumers' financial literacy, errors in their financial decision-making, and the inadequacy of disclosure as a consumer protection;

- federal agency reports documenting abuse and investors' vulnerability;

- a 2015 study by the President's Council of Economic Advisers that attributed annual IRA investor losses of $17 billion to advisory conflicts;

- economic theory that predicts harmful market failures due to the information asymmetries that are present when ordinary investors rely on advisers who are far more expert than them, but highly conflicted; and

- overseas experience with harmful advisory conflicts and responsive reforms.

The analysis estimated that advisers' conflicts arising from load sharing on average cost their IRA customers who invest in front-end-load mutual funds between 0.5 percent and 1.0 percent annually in estimated foregone risk-adjusted returns, which the analysis concluded to be due to poor fund selection. The Department estimated that such underperformance could cost IRA investors between $95 billion and $189 billion over the next 10 years. The analysis further estimated that the final rule and exemptions would potentially reduce these losses by between $33 billion and $36 billion over 10 years. Investors' gains were estimated to grow over time, due both to net inflows and compounding of returns. According to the analysis, these estimates reflect only part of the potential harm from advisers' conflicts and the likely benefits of the new rule and exemptions. The analysis estimated that complying with the new rule would cost $16 billion over ten years, mainly reflecting the cost of consumer protections attached to the exemptions. The Department invites comment on whether the projected investor gains could be offset by a reduction in consumer investment, if consumers have reduced access to retirement savings advice as a result of the final rule, and whether there is any evidence of such reduction in consumer investment to date.

With respect to topics now under examination pursuant to the President's Memorandum, the analysis anticipated that the rule would have large and far-reaching effects on the markets for investment advice and investment products. It examined a variety of potential and anticipated market impacts. Such market impacts would extend beyond direct compliance activities and related costs, and beyond mitigation of existing advisory conflicts and associated changes in affected investment recommendations. It concluded that the final rule and exemptions would move markets toward a more optimal mix of advisory services and financial products. The Department invites comments on whether the final rule and exemptions so far have moved markets or appear likely to move markets in this predicted direction.

The analysis examined the likely impacts of the final rule and exemptions on small investors. It concluded that quality, affordable advisory services would be available to small plans and IRA investors under the final rule and exemptions. Subsection 8.4.5 reviewed ongoing and emerging innovation trends in markets for investment advice and investment products. The analysis indicated that these trends have the potential to deliver affordable, quality advisory services and investment products to all retirement investors, including small investors, and that the final rule and exemptions would foster competition to innovate in consumers' best interest. The Department invites comments on the emerging and expected effects of the final rule and exemptions on retirement investors' access to quality, affordable investment advice services and investment products, including small investors' access.

The Department invites comments that might help inform updates to its legal and economic analysis, including any issues the public believes were inadequately addressed in the RIA and particularly with respect to the issues identified in the President's Memorandum.

---

[5] This estimate includes savings from notice requirements. Savings from notice requirements include savings from all firms because it is difficult to break out cost savings only from small entities as defined by SBA.

For more detailed information, commenters are directed to the final rule and final new and amended PTEs published in the **Federal Register** on April 8, 2016, at 81 FR pages 20946 through 21221, and to the Department's Full Report Regulatory Impact Analysis for Final Rule and Exemptions (RIA), and the additional RIA documents posted on the Department's Web site at *www.dol.gov/agencies/ebsa/laws-and-regu-lations/rules-and-regulations/completed-rulemaking/1210-AB32-2.*

The Department invites comments on market responses to the final rule and the PTEs to date, and on the costs and benefits attached to such responses. Some relevant questions include,

• Do firms anticipate changes in consumer demand for investment advice and investment products? If so, what types of changes are anticipated, and how will firms respond?

• Are firms making changes to their target markets? In particular, are some firms moving to abandon or deemphasize the small IRA investor or small plan market segments? Are some aiming to expand in that segment? What effects will these developments have on different customer segments, especially small IRA investors and small plans?

• Are firms making changes to their line-ups of investment products, and/or to product pricing? What are those changes, what is the motivation behind them, and will the changes advance or undermine firms' abilities to serve their customers' needs?

• Are firms making changes to their advisory services, and/or to the pricing of those services? Are firms changing the means by which customers pay for advisory services, and by which advisers are compensated? For example, are firms moving to increase or reduce their use of commission arrangements, asset-based fee arrangements, or other arrangements? With respect to any such changes, what is the motivation behind them, and will these changes advance or undermine firms' abilities to serve their customers' needs?

• Has implementation or anticipation of the rule led investors to shift investments between asset classes or types, and/or are such changes expected in the future? If so, what mechanisms have led or are expected to lead to these changes? How will the changes affect investors?

• Has implementation or anticipation of the rule led to increases or reductions in commissions, loads, or other fees? Have firms changed their minimum balance requirements for either commission-based or asset-based fee compensation arrangements?

• Has implementation or anticipation of the rule led to changes in the compensation arrangements for advisory services surrounding the sale of insurance products such as fixed-rate, fixed-indexed, and variable annuities?

• For those firms that intend to make use of the Best Interest Contract Exemption, what specific policies and procedures have been considered to mitigate conflicts of interest and ensure impartiality? How costly will those policies and procedures be to maintain?

• What innovations or changes in the delivery of financial advice have occurred that can be at least partially attributable to the rule? Will those innovations or changes make retirement investors better or worse off?

• What changes have been made to investor education both in terms of access and content in response to the rule and PTEs, and to what extent have any changes helped or harmed investors?

• Have market developments and preparation efforts since the final rule and PTEs were published in April 2016 illuminated whether or to what degree the final rule and PTEs are likely to cause an increase in litigation, and how any such increase in litigation might affect the prices that investors and retirees must pay to gain access to retirement services? Have firms taken steps to acquire or increase insurance coverage of liability associated with litigation? Have firms factored into their earnings projections or otherwise taken specific account of such potential liability?

• The Department's examination of the final rule and exemptions pursuant to the Presidential Memorandum, together with possible resultant actions to rescind or amend the rule, could require more time than this proposed 60-day extension would provide. What costs and benefit considerations should the Department consider if the applicability date is further delayed, for 6 months, a year, or more?

• Class action lawsuits may be brought to redress a variety of claims, including claims involving ERISA-covered plans. What can be learned from these class action lawsuits? Have they been particularly prone to abuse? To what extent have class action lawsuits involving ERISA claims led to better or worse outcomes for plan participants? What other impacts have these class action lawsuits had?

• Have market developments and preparation efforts since the final rule and PTEs were published in April 2016 illuminated particular provisions that could be amended to reduce compliance burdens and minimize undue disruptions while still accomplishing the regulatory objective of establishing an enforceable best interest conduct standard for retirement investment advice and empowering Americans to make their own financial decisions, save for retirement and build individual wealth?

• How has the pattern of market developments and preparation efforts occurring since the final rule and exemptions were published in April, 2016, compared with the implementation pattern prior to compliance deadlines in other jurisdictions, such as the United Kingdom, that have instituted new requirements for investment advice? What does a comparison of such patterns indicate about the Department's prospective estimates of the rule's and exemptions' combined impacts?

• Have there been new insights from or into academic literature on contracts or other sources that would aid in the quantification of the rule's and exemptions' effectiveness at ensuring advisers' adherence to a best interest standard? If so, what are the implications for revising the Best Interest Contract Exemption or other regulatory or exemptive provisions to more effectively ensure adherence to a best interest standard?

• To what extent have the rule's and exemptions' costs already been incurred and thus cannot, at this point in time, be lessened by regulatory revisions or delays? Can the portion of costs that are still avoidable be quantified or otherwise characterized? Are the rule's intended effects entirely contingent upon the costs that have not yet been incurred, or will some portion be achieved as a result of compliance actions already taken? How will they be achieved and will they be sustained?

• Have there been changes in the macroeconomy since early 2016 that would have implications for the rule's and exemptions' impacts (for example, a reduction in the unemployment rate, likely indicating lower search costs for workers who seek new employment within or outside of the financial industry)?

• What do market developments and preparation efforts that have occurred since the final rule and exemptions were published in April, 2016—or new insights into other available evidence—indicate regarding the portion of rule-induced gains to investors that consist of benefits to society (most likely, resource savings associated with reduced excessive trading and reduced unsuccessful efforts to outperform the market) and the portion that consists of transfers between entities in society?

• In response to the approaching applicability date of the rule, or other factors, has the affected industry already responded in such a way that if the rule were rescinded, the regulated community, or a subset of it, would continue to abide by the rule's standards? If this is the case, would the rule's predicted benefits to consumers, or a portion thereof, be retained, regardless of whether the rule were rescinded? What could ensure compliance with the standards if they were no longer enforceable legal obligations?

Upon completion of its examination, the Department may decide to allow the final rule and PTEs to become applicable, issue a further extension of the applicability date, propose to withdraw the rule, or propose amendments to the rule and/or the PTEs. In addition to any other comments, the Department specifically requests comments on each of these possible outcomes. The comment period for the broader purpose of examining the final rule and exemptions in response to the President's Memorandum will end on April 17, 2017.

List of Proposed Amendments to Prohibited Transaction Exemptions

For the reasons set forth above, the Department is proposing to amend the Best Interest Contract Exemption (Prohibited Transaction Exemption 2016-01); Class Exemption for Principal Transactions in Certain Assets Between Investment Advice Fiduciaries and Employee Benefit Plans and IRAs (Prohibited Transaction Exemption 2016-02); and Prohibited Transaction Exemptions 75-1, 77-4, 80-83, 83-1, 84-24 and 86-128, as follows:

• The Best Interest Contract Exemption (PTE 2016-01) (81 FR 21002 (April 8, 2016), as corrected at 81 FR 44773 (July 11, 2016)) is amended by removing the date "April 10, 2017" and adding in its place "June 9, 2017" as the *Applicability date* in the introductory **DATES** section and in Section IX of the exemption.

• The Class Exemption for Principal Transactions in Certain Assets Between Investment Advice Fiduciaries and Employee Benefit Plans and IRAs (PTE 2016-02) (81 FR 21089 (April 8, 2016), as corrected at 81 FR 44784 (July 11, 2016)), is amended by removing the date "April 10,

2017" and adding in its place "June 9, 2017" as the *Applicability date* in the introductory **DATES** section and in Section VII of the exemption.

• Prohibited Transaction Exemption 84-24 for Certain Transactions Involving Insurance Agents and Brokers, Pension Consultants, Insurance Companies, and Investment Company Principal Underwriters (49 FR 13208 (April 3, 1984), as corrected 49 FR 24819 (June 15, 1984), as amended 71 FR 5887 (February 3, 2006), and as amended 81 FR 21147 (April 8, 2016)) is amended by removing the date "April 10, 2017" and adding in its place "June 9, 2017" as the *Applicability date* in the introductory **DATES** section.

• Prohibited Transaction Exemption 86-128 for Securities Transactions Involving Employee Benefit Plans and Broker-Dealers (51 FR 41686 (November 18, 1986) as amended at 67 FR 64137 (October 17, 2002) and as amended at 81 FR 21181 (April 8, 2016)) and Prohibited Transaction Exemption 75-1, Exemptions from Prohibitions Respecting Certain Classes of Transactions Involving Employee Benefit Plans and Certain Broker-Dealers, Reporting Dealers and Banks, Parts I and II (40 FR 50845 (October 31, 1975), as amended at 71 FR 5883 (February 3, 2006), and as amended at 81 FR 21181 (April 8, 2016)) are amended by removing the date "April 10 2017" and adding in its place "June 9, 2017" as the *Applicability date* in the introductory **DATES** section.

• Prohibited Transaction Exemption 75-1, Exemptions from Prohibitions Respecting Certain Classes of Transactions Involving Employee Benefit Plans and Certain Broker-Dealers, Reporting Dealers and Banks, Parts III and IV, (40 FR 50845 (October 31, 1975), as amended at 71 FR 5883 (February 3, 2006), and as amended at 81 FR 21208 (April 8, 2016); Prohibited Transaction Exemption 77-4, Class Exemption for Certain Transactions Between Investment Companies and Employee Benefit Plans, 42 FR 18732 (April 8, 1977), as amended at 81 FR 21208 (April 8, 2016); Prohibited Transaction Exemption 80-83, Class Exemption for Certain Transactions Involving Purchase of Securities Where Issuer May Use Proceeds To Reduce or Retire Indebtedness to Parties in Interest, 45 FR 73189 (November 4, 1980), as amended at 67 FR 9483 (March 1, 2002) and as amended at 81 FR 21208 (April 8, 2016); and Prohibited Transaction Exemption 83-1 Class Exemption for Certain Transactions Involving Mortgage Pool Investment Trusts, 48 FR 895 (January 7, 1983), as amended at 67 FR 9483 (March 1, 2002) and as amended at 81 FR 21208 (April 8, 2016) are each amended by removing the date "April 10, 2017" and adding in its place "June 9, 2017" as the *Applicability date* in the introductory **DATES** section.

• Prohibited Transaction Exemption (PTE) 75-1, Exemptions from Prohibitions Respecting Certain Classes of Transactions Involving Employee Benefit Plans and Certain Broker-Dealers, Reporting Dealers and Banks, Part V, 40 FR 50845 (October 31, 1975), as amended at 71 FR 5883 (February 3, 2006) and as amended at 81 FR 21139 (April 8, 2016), is amended by removing the date "April 10, 2017" and adding in its place "June 9, 2017" as the *Applicability Date* in the introductory **DATES** section.

This document serves as a notice of pendency before the Department of proposed amendments to these PTEs.

List of Subjects in 29 CFR Parts 2510 and 2550

Employee benefit plans, Exemptions, Fiduciaries, Investments, Pensions, Prohibited transactions, Reporting and recordkeeping requirements, and Securities.

For the reasons set forth above, the Department proposes to amend part 2510 of subchapter B of Chapter XXV of Title 29 of the Code of Federal Regulations as follows:

Subchapter B—Definitions and Coverage Under the Employee Retirement Income Security Act of 1974

PART 2510—DEFINITIONS OF TERMS USED IN SUBCHAPTERS C, D, E, F, G, AND L OF THIS CHAPTER

■ 1. The authority citation for part 2510 continues to read as follows:

Authority: 29 U.S.C. 1002(2), 1002(21), 1002(37), 1002(38), 1002(40), 1031, and 1135; Secretary of Labor's Order 1-2011, 77 FR 1088; Secs. 2510.3-21, 2510.3-101 and 2510.3-102 also issued under Sec. 102 of Reorganization Plan No. 4 of 1978, 5 U.S.C. App. 237. Section 2510.3-38 also issued under Pub. L. 105-72, Sec. 1(b), 111 Stat. 1457 (1997).

§2510.3-21 [Amended]

■ 2. Section 2510.3-21 is amended by extending the expiration date of paragraph (j) to June 9, 2017, and by removing the date "April 10, 2017" and adding in its place "June 9, 2017" in paragraphs (h)(2), (j)(1) introductory text, and (j)(3).

Signed at Washington, DC, this 27th day of February 2017.

Timothy D. Hauser,

Deputy Assistant Secretary for Program Operations, Employee Benefits Security Administration, Department of Labor.

[FR Doc. 2017-04096 Filed 3-1-17; 8:45 am]

BILLING CODE 4510-29-P

¶ 20,539J

Employee Benefit Security Administration (EBSA): Proposed rule: Claims procedures: Disability benefits.—EBSA has proposed to delay the applicability of final regulations revising the claims procedures for employee benefit plans providing disability benefits, which were published on December 19, 2016 (see ¶ 24,344). The final rules had adopted certain procedural protections and safeguards for disability benefit claims that were already applicable to claims for group health benefits under the Patient Protection and Affordable Care Act (ACA, P.L. 111-148). The final rules were scheduled to apply to claims for disability benefits under ERISA-covered employee benefit plans that are filed on or after January 1, 2018. Under the proposed delay, the rules would be applicable claims filed after April 1, 2018. EBSA is giving the public an opportunity to submit comments concerning the delay of applicability date (by October 27, 2017) and providing relevant information for determining whether to rescind, modify, or retain the final rules (by December 11, 2017).

The proposed regulations, which were published in the Federal Register on October 12, 2017 (82 FR 47409), were reproduced below. EBSA issued final regulations on November 29, 2017 (82 FR 56560). The preamble to the final regulations is at ¶ 24,354. The final regulations are at ¶ 14,931.

Topical Index

References are to paragraph (¶) numbers.

DIS